Guide to Reference Books

Guide to Reference Books

Tenth Edition

Edited by

EUGENE P. SHEEHY

With the assistance of

RITA G. KECKEISSEN

EILEEN McILVAINE

DIANE K. GOON
Columbia University Libraries

JANET SCHNEIDER
University Library
University of Michigan, Dearborn

Science, Technology, and Medicine
compiled by

RICHARD J. DIONNE

ELIZABETH E. FERGUSON
Kline Science Library
Yale University

ROBERT C. MICHAELSON
Seeley G. Mudd Library
for Science & Engineering
Northwestern University

AMERICAN LIBRARY ASSOCIATION

Chicago and London   1986

Composed by Black Dot Graphics
in Times Roman on an
Autologic APS-5 phototypesetting system

Printed on 35-pound Eddy
Vista Opaque, a pH-neutral
stock, and bound in B-grade
Joanna Arrestox linen cloth by
R. R. Donnelley and Sons Company
∞

Library of Congress Cataloging-in-Publication Data

Sheehy, Eugene Paul, 1922–
  Guide to reference books.

  Includes index.
  1. Reference books—Bibliography. I. Title.
Z1035.1.S43 1986   011′.02   85–11208
ISBN 0-8389-0390-8

Contents

❖*This table of contents lists only a few of the subdivisions of some sections.
To locate specific subjects see* Index.

*In general, geographical arrangement within sections follows the pattern:
(1) International; (2) United States; (3) other countries in alphabetical
order. As used below, the note "Arranged by country" is meant to indicate
the foregoing scheme.*

A

General Reference Works

B

The Humanities

C

Social and Behavioral Sciences

D

History and Area Studies

E

Science, Technology, and Medicine

Preface

From its modest beginning in 1902 as Alice Bertha Kroeger's 104-page *Guide to the Study and Use of Reference Books,* through the long periods when it was popularly known as "Mudge" and "Winchell," the *Guide to Reference Books* has grown steadily to its now somewhat unwieldy proportions. Throughout its publishing history, the *Guide* has enjoyed the sponsorship of the American Library Association and, from the time of Isadore Gilbert Mudge's 1911–13 supplement to the second edition, the Reference Department of the Columbia University Libraries has been the work's home base.

This tenth edition of the *Guide* builds firmly on the preceding editions and aims to continue the traditions thereof. Indeed, many of the introductory notes, as well as annotations for certain older materials, are little changed from Constance M. Winchell's last edition, while some of the annotations still bear the stamp of Isadore Mudge. Although there has been less and less emphasis in recent years on the *Guide*'s early function as a study aid for library school students and greater stress on its use by the practicing librarian and research worker, the criterion of *usefulness* which governed Miss Kroeger's first edition remains salient. This is a thorough revision: it represents a review and winnowing of items from the ninth edition and its two supplements, the addition of new (and a few older) materials, and a certain amount of rearrangement and refinement of the classification scheme devised by Miss Winchell for the eighth edition. Inasmuch as the *Guide* has been compiled by librarians at academic institutions, there is a decided emphasis on reference works for scholarly research. The compilers have, however, kept in mind the needs of public and non-specialized libraries, and have endeavored to include representative works intended for the general reader.

It was agreed at the outset that 1984 would be a relatively firm cutoff date for this edition, with selected 1985 imprints admitted when their importance seemed to warrant it. As work progressed, however, the temptation to include 1985 imprints became harder and harder to resist. As a result, those sections completed first (notably the "A" sections) show a minimal number of 1985 publications, whereas 1985 imprints appear with considerable frequency in sections which were completed last. The inclusion of a 1985 publication, therefore, should not be construed as conferring "major" status thereon. Notes on forthcoming revisions of older works, and on 1985 editions received after a section was completed are frequently appended to the annotations.

As in the past, no attempt was made to assign "quotas" for specific subject areas nor to impose strict limits on the number of items to be included in a given section. In the interest of saving space, related items (or works still useful but badly out of date) have often been relegated to a mention in the annotation for another work. What to leave out was often as difficult a decision as what to put in and, for the most part, those decisions were left to the compiler of a particular section; ultimate responsibility for inclusion or exclusion, however, must rest with the principal editor.

Although every effort was made to list the latest edition of each work and to bring the *Guide* as much up to date as possible, the work continues to list a very considerable number of older, out-of-print items. Prices, therefore, have not been given; this conforms to what has become a standard practice of omitting prices from each new edition of the *Guide,* but including them in the intervening supplements (which may be seen as concentrating on recent publications, most of which are likely to be in print at the time a supplement appears). Reprints of older works have again been noted, this information serving as an indication of continued utility as well as probable availability. No concerted effort was made to list all reprints, but they were conscientiously noted whenever encountered in the course of bibliographic verification and reexamination of older titles. As in the ninth edition, Library of Congress classification numbers appear at the end of an entry when available. Users should keep in mind that those numbers come from a variety of sources—LC printed cards, CIP information, and MARC records (sometimes revised) in the RLIN database—and variations may be encountered. In general, class marks are given only for separately classed items, not for individual items within a series which have been classed together. "Locally assigned" classification numbers have not been included in lieu of a Library of Congress record.

A brief section on databases was added to the first supplement to the ninth edition of the *Guide,* but it was quickly apparent that this was an area of such rapid change and expansion that it could not be dealt with adequately in a work of this kind. Neither, of course, could we totally ignore the world of computerized database searching. By way of compromise it was decided to limit our coverage of this vast area to a few standard guides and directories and, rather than attempt to describe precisely the online equivalents of hard-copy bibliographic tools, to provide merely an indication that *some portion* of the published bibliography, index, or other source is available for online searching. Thus, a black bullet (●) following the Library of Congress class mark serves to indicate some online availability, but it does not necessarily mean that the whole file of the publication is searchable online.

The preface to the ninth edition of the *Guide* stated: "With a very few exceptions, entries in this edition have been brought into conformity with those appearing on Library of Congress printed cards or, where such cards were not available, entries as shown in published volumes of the *National Union Catalog.*" Would that life were still so simple! With the implementation of the second edition of the Anglo-American Cataloguing Rules —surely one of the most misguided efforts in library history—and libraries' varying decisions to "close" or "freeze" card catalogs, establish "add-on" units, or move to online catalog access, there could be no easy, generally acceptable solution to the problem posed by corporate entries in a volume such as the *Guide to Reference Books.* Several factors had to be considered: (1) the *National Union Catalog: Pre-1956 Imprints* and similar standard tools for verification/location will, perforce, perpetuate the older forms of entry for years to come; (2) not all libraries will elect to change their old records; (3) the situation was still very much in flux at the time much of the work on this edition of the *Guide* was in progress; and (4) computer tapes from the ninth edition and its supplements were to be utilized as fully as possible in the preparation of the new edition. (The latter point, while mainly a matter of editorial convenience, may also be seen as affecting the price of the *Guide.*) The principal editor, therefore, somewhat arbitrarily decided to continue to use the "pre-A2" forms (e.g., "U.S. Library of Congress") for all older materials, and to adopt "A2" forms (e.g., "University of . . .") only for such bodies as had not figured in the ninth edition and its supplements.

Similarly, in view of recent changes in rules for cataloging of serials, our entries for those publications are not as uniform as might be desired. In the matter of changed titles for current serials the *Guide* reflects both past and current practice: i.e., older cataloging puts the full series under the most recent title; newer cataloging closes the entry and generates a new record for each change of title. Where the latter practice is followed, we have generally made an entry only for the most recent title (or the one current at the time our work of compilation was done), relying on notes preceding or within the annotation to explain the relationship to predecessor publications. In cases where the number and variety of changes are either unusually frequent or relatively insignificant, phrases such as "Title varies" and "Issuing body varies" have been used "to cover a multitude" and, in the interest of saving space, to avoid presenting a welter of similar (and often confusing) variant entries for what is basically a single, ongoing publication. Thus, while the *Guide* may not serve as a norm for citing reference sources, it is hoped that bibliographic verification, location, and the tracing of publishing histories of specific reference works can be effectively pursued on the basis of the entries chosen for listing here. One further anomaly stems from the principal editor's decision to retain "British Museum" as the main entry for older publications of that august institution while entering newer items under "British Library."

Fortunately, all of the contributors to the second supplement to the ninth edition of the *Guide* were willing to continue their work toward this edition. Rita G. Keckeissen (now retired from her position in the Columbia Reference Department) and Eileen McIlvaine again provided much-needed general support and advice on matters of policy, not to mention heroic assistance with the seemingly endless task of proofreading and with the preparation of subject indexing. In addition, the former prepared the Genealogy, Religion, and Applied Arts sections and assisted with the Fine Arts and Music portions, while the latter took responsibility for the History and Area Studies sections. Diane K. Goon again assumed the formidable task of compiling virtually all of the Social and Behavioral Sciences sections; and our colleagues at Yale and Northwestern—Richard J. Dionne, Elizabeth E. Ferguson, and Robert C. Michaelson—again contributed the Science, Technology, and Medicine portions under Dionne's general editorship. A former Columbia associate, Janet Schneider (now with the Reference Department of the University of Michigan, Dearborn) compiled the Government Publications and Education sections. Without the careful work and dedication of these people this edition could not have been completed. All of them have my sincere gratitude.

Each of us, in turn, owes an expression of thanks to a great many people, ranging from our respective library administrators who allowed us time to carry on at least part of the work of compilation during working hours, to the pages who reshelved the many books we were obliged to examine. Friends and colleagues at our own and neighboring institutions have been most helpful in suggesting titles for inclusion and for expediting the availability of various items. Particularly heavy use was made of the Research Libraries of the New York Public Library and of a number of other libraries in the New York metropolitan area. The individual names of those to whom we are indebted would make a very long list and no attempt is made to enumerate them here. Yet, exceptions must always be made: Richard Dionne extends special thanks to Alan M. Hagyard for his valuable contribution toward preparation of the Earth Sciences section; and the undersigned gratefully acknowledges the assistance of Junko Stuveras in preparing the Japanese-language entries for various parts of this compilation.

Thanks are also due many members of the American Library Association's Publishing Division, particularly to Helen Cline, Managing Editor, for her help and guidance throughout the project, and to Mary Huchting,

Editor, who had the arduous task of dealing with the manuscript and seeing it through the press.

Traditionally, the final words of appreciation have been reserved for the loyal and dedicated members of Columbia's Butler Library Reference staff, and in this, my final edition of the *Guide,* it gives particular pleasure to acknowledge their varied contributions, not the least of which was their cooperation in keeping the Reference Department running smoothly during the many months this work was in progress. In addition to the previously mentioned Eileen McIlvaine and Junko Stuveras, they are: Mary Cargill, Anita Lowry, Louise Sherby, and Sarah Spurgin—a list to which must be added the name of our valued colleague in Columbia's Lehman Reference Department, Laura Binkowski. To all of them I am most sincerely grateful.

EUGENE P. SHEEHY

COLUMBIA UNIVERSITY LIBRARIES
JULY 1986

Abbreviations

❖*The following list includes only the principal bibliographical abbreviations used in this book for which some explanation or translation seems needed. Shortened forms of publishers' names and some other abbreviations which are practically self-explanatory, e.g., Assoc., Inst., Soc., etc., have not been included here.*

aarg. (Swed.) aargang: *annual volume*
Abt. (Ger.) Abteilung: *part*
Afd. (Dan.) Afdeling: *part*
afl. (Dutch) aflevering: *part*
A.L.A.: *American Library Association*
ampl. (It.) ampliata: *enlarged*
Aufl. (Ger.) Auflage: *edition*
augm. (Fr.) augmenté: *enlarged*
aum. (Sp.) aumentado: *enlarged*
Ausg. (Ger.) Ausgabe: *printing, edition*
avd. (Nor.) avdeling: *part, volume*

Bd. (Dan.) Bind, (Ger.) Band: *volume*
bd. (Nor.) bind, (Swed.) band: *volume*
bearb. (Ger.) bearbeitet: *compiled, edited*
begr. (Ger.) begründet: *established*
Bull.: *Bulletin*
Burt. (Lettish) Burtricã: *part*

c.: *copyright*
ca.: *circa*
cm.: *centimeters*
col.: *columns, colored*
comp.: *compiled*
compl.: *completed, completely*
Cong.: *Congress*
corr. (Fr.) corrigé, (Sp.) corregido: *corrected*

d. (Ger.) der: *the*
deel (Dutch): *volume, part*
doc.: *document*
dopl. (Czech) doplněné: *enlarged*
druk (Dutch): *printing, copy, edition*

ea.: *each*
ed.: *edition, editor*
éd. (Fr.) édition: *edition*
ed. (It.) edizione, (Sp.) edición: *edition*
Eng.: *English*
erw. (Ger.) erweiterte: *enlarged*
estab. tip. (Sp.) establecimiento tipografico: *publishing company*

f. (Ger.) für: *for*
facsim.: *facsimile*
fasc. (Fr.) fascicule: *fascicle, part, number*

gänzl. (Ger.) gänzlich: *entire, complete*
glav. red. (Russ.) glavnyi redaktor: *chief editor*
GmbH. (Ger.) Gesellschaft mit beschränkter Haftung: *company, limited*
Gos., Gosudarst. (Russ.) Gosudarstvo: *state*
Govt. Prt. Off.: *Government Printing Office*

Hft. (Dan.) Hefte, (Ger.) Heft: *part, number*
hft. (Nor.) hefte: *part, number*
Hlbbd. (Ger.) Halbband: *half binding; half volume*
hrsg. (Ger.) herausgegeben: *published, edited*

il.: *illustrated, illustrations*
impr. (Fr.) imprimé, imprimerie, imprimeur: *printed, printing, printing firm, printer*
impr. (Sp.) imprenta, impresión: *printing office, impression, edition*
Impr. Nat. (Fr.): *Imprimerie Nationale*
incompl.: *incomplete*
Internat.: *International*
Introd.: *Introduction*
Izd., Izdat. (Russ.) izdatel': *publisher*

jaarg. (Dutch) jaargang: *annual volume*
Jahrg. (Ger.) Jahrgang: *annual publication*

l.: *leaves*
Lfg. (Ger.) Lieferung: *number, part*
Lib.: *Library*
livr. (Fr.) livraison: *part, issue*

n. (It.) numero: *number*
Nachtr. (Ger.) Nachtrag: *appendix, supplement*
Nákl. (Czech) náklad, nakladatel: *edition, publisher*
Nakł. (Polish) nakład: *edition, publisher*
n.d.: *no date*
neubearb. (Ger.) neubearbeitet: *revised*
n.F. (Ger.) neue Folge: *new series*

nouv. (Fr.) nouveau, nouvelle: *new*
n.p.: *no publisher, no place*
Nr. (Dan., Ger.) Nummer: *number*
nr. (Nor.) nummer: *number*
n.s.: *new series*
núm. (Sp.) número: *number*
numb.: *numbered*
N.Y.: *New York*

o.a. (Swed.) och andra: *and others*
omarb. (Swed.) omarbetad: *revised*

p.: *page*
pa.: *paper*
Pr.: *Press*
Pref.: *Preface*
prel.: *preliminary*
přepr. (Czech) přepracované: *rewritten*
priv. pr.: *privately printed*
priv. pub.: *privately published*
pt.: *part*
Pub.: *Public*
pub. (Fr.) publié: *published, publication*
Publ.: *Publishers, Publishing*
publ.: *published*
pubn.: *publication*

réd. (Fr.) rédigé: *edited, compiled*
red. (Russ.) redaktor: *editor*
redig. (Swed.) redigerad: *edited*
ref. (Fr.) refondue: *reorganized*
repr.: *reprinted*
rev. (Sp.) revisado: *revised*
revid. (Swed.) reviderad: *revised*
rif. (It.) rifatta: *restored, repaired*
riv. (It.) riveduto: *revised*

sec. (Sp.) sección: *section*
sér. (Fr.) série: *series*
sess.: *session*
Sost. (Russ.) sostavitel': *compiler*

Stat. Off.: *His Majesty's Stationery Office*
subs.: *subscription*
suppl. (Fr.) supplément: *supplement*

t. (Fr.) tome, (Sp.) tomo: *volume*
T., Th. (Ger.) Teil, Theil: *part*
tidskr. (Swed.) tidskrift: *periodical*
tip. (It.) tipografia: *printing firm*
tr.: *translated, translator*
tr. (Fr.) traduit: *translated*
tr. (Swed.) tryckt: *printed*
trad. (Sp.) traducido: *translated*

u. (Ger.) und: *and*
u.A. (Ger.) und Andere: *and others*
übers. (Ger.) übersetzt: *translated*
udarb. (Dan.) udarbeidet: *prepared*
Udg. (Dan.) Udgave: *edition*
uit. (Dutch) uitgaaf: *publication*
uitg. (Dutch) uitgegeven: *published*
ung. (Ger.) ungarische: *Hungarian*
umgearb. (Ger.) umgearbeitete: *revised*
Univ.: *University*
Univ.-Buchdr. (Ger.) Universitäts-Buchdrukerei: *university press*
uppl. (Swed.) upplaga: *edition*
utarb. (Nor.) utarbeidet: *prepared*
utg. (Nor.) utgave: *edition*

v. (It.) volume: *volume*
v. (Ger.) von: *from*
veränd. (Ger.) verändert: *revised*
verb. (Dutch, Ger.) verbeterde, verbesserte: *improved*
verf. (Ger.) verfasst: *written, composed*
verm. (Ger.) vermehrte: *enlarged*
vollst. (Ger.) vollständig: *completely*
vyd. (Czech) vydání: *edition*

Wash.: *Washington, D.C.*
wesentl. (Ger.) wesentlich: *essential, main*

Guide to Reference Books

A

General Reference Works

❖ In Part A are grouped those reference works which are not devoted to special subjects: the universal and national bibliographies, encyclopedias, language dictionaries, periodicals, newspapers, government publications, and dissertations. With these have been included sections on librarianship and library resources, biography, and genealogy. Each section has an introductory note which should be consulted for further information about the types of works included.

Representative works in all these fields will be in most libraries, the number being dependent on the size and type of library. This *Guide* will serve as an aid in the selection of such materials, but should be supplemented by such works as the "Reference books bulletin" section of *Booklist* (AA446) and the guides to reference books published in other countries as listed on p.44–47.

A A

Bibliography

Bibliographies, general and special, are basic materials in a reference collection. In this section of the *Guide* the more general works are treated; subject bibliographies are listed with their subjects where, with few exceptions, they are noted first whether or not the subhead "Bibliography" appears.

General bibliographies fall into several major categories, viz.:

1. Bibliographies of bibliographies, of which outstanding examples are Besterman (AA16) and the *Bibliographic index* (AA17).

2. Library catalogs, particularly those of national libraries, e.g., the Library of Congress (AA123–AA127), the British Museum (now the British Library; AA132), and the

Bibliothèque Nationale in Paris (AA140). These serve not only as comprehensive bibliographies of works in many languages but also, to a large extent, as national bibliographies of their own countries.

3. Specialized bibliographies in the fields of rare books and early manuscripts, of which perhaps the most needed in the general library would be De Ricci's *Census of medieval and Renaissance manuscripts in the United States and Canada* (AA244) and Goff's *Incunabula in American libraries* (AA278).

4. Selective bibliographies, designed to aid librarians and others in the task of book selection, e.g., *The reader's adviser* (AA443); the *Standard catalog* series (AA442, AA469–AA471); as well as such book selection periodicals as *Booklist* (AA446) and *Choice: books for college libraries* (AA455).

5. National bibliographies. These are of prime importance in any but the smallest library, and an extensive collection will be needed in large and academic libraries. American libraries will need the *United States catalog* and the *Cumulative book index* (AA577, AA584); the *Publishers' trade list annual* (AA589) and its complements, *Books in print* (AA590) and *Subject guide to Books in print* (AA591); the *American book publishing record* (AA579); *Publishers' weekly* (AA595) and its companion the *Weekly record* (AA598). Large libraries will, of course, also need the preceding works of Evans (AA557) and Sabin (AA563) and will wish to add the *British national bibliography* (AA827) and whatever other foreign lists are appropriate.

GENERAL WORKS

Guides and manuals

Beaudiquez, Marcelle. Guide de bibliographie générale: méthodique et pratique. München, Saur, 1983. 280p. il.
AA1

Primarily intended for the student preparing for examinations in librarianship, but useful as a basic guide to bibliographic and reference sources. Z1001.A2B4

Bowers, Fredson Thayer. Principles of bibliographical description. Princeton, N.J., Princeton Univ. Pr., 1949. 505p. il. (Repr.: N.Y., Russell & Russell, 1962) **AA2**

A full, detailed treatment of analytical bibliography, as applied to the description of books. Covers the principles of describing incunabula, and English and American books from the 16th to the 20th centuries. Most of the principles would be applicable to printing in other countries.   Z1001.B78

Esdaile, Arundell James Kennedy. Manual of bibliography. [4th] rev. ed. by Roy Stokes. N.Y., Barnes & Noble; London, Allen & Unwin, [1967]. 336p. il. (Library Assoc. series of library manuals, 1)   **AA3**

1st ed. 1931; earlier eds. had title *A student's manual of bibliography.*

A manual treating the nature of bibliography, the history and make-up of the book, illustration, binding, the collation and description of books; with a discussion of some basic bibliographies. In addition to some textual revision and updating of reading lists, there has been considerable rearrangement of the contents in the latest edition.   Z1001.E75

Gaskell, Philip. A new introduction to bibliography. Oxford, Clarendon Pr.; N.Y., Oxford Univ. Pr., 1972. 438p. il.   **AA4**

Intended as a successor to (but not a mere revision of) R. B. McKerrow's *Introduction to bibliography for literary students* (Oxford, Clarendon Pr., 1927), which remains useful for the period up to about 1800. Offers a survey of the mechanical and technical side of book production during both the hand-press period and the machine-press period to 1950. Covers printing type, composition, paper, imposition, press work, warehouse routines, binding, decoration and illustration, printing machines, patterns of production, processes of reproduction, and the book trade in Britain and America. Attention is given to bibliographical description, format of books, meaning of "edition," "impression," etc., dating of editions, variations in copies, cancels, and similar matters. Appendixes include McKerrow's "Note on Elizabethan handwriting"; specimen bibliographical descriptions; examples of transmission of text; and a bibliography. Detailed index.   Z116.A2G27

Harmon, Robert B. Elements of bibliography: a simplified approach. Metuchen, N.J., Scarecrow Pr., 1981. 253p.   **AA5**

A brief guide to the study of bibliography and methods of compilation; combines explanatory text with annotated suggestions for further reading. Indexed.   Z1001.H29

Krummel, Donald William. Bibliographies: their aims and methods. London & N.Y., Mansell, 1984. 192p.   **AA6**

A work for the compiler and for the student of bibliography, with attention given to both theory and practice, characteristics of bibliographies, and their functions. Bibliographies interspersed throughout the volume, plus a bibliography of "Major writings on the compiling of bibliographies 1883–1983," p.161–81. Indexed.   Z1001.K86

Malclès, Louise-Noëlle. Manuel de bibliographie. 3. éd. rev. et mise à jour par Andrée Lhéritier. Paris, Presses Universitaires de France, [1976]. 398p.   **AA7**

1st ed. 1963.

An annotated guide to the study and use of bibliographies. It lists selected general and specialized bibliographies and other reference works in all fields, and thus serves as an abridgment of the author's *Les sources du travail bibliographique* (AA487) for students and those not needing the larger set. International in scope, with emphasis on French materials.   Z1002.M28

Masanov, IUrii Ivanovich. Teoriia i praktika bibliografii; ukazatel' literatury, 1917–1958. Pod red. . . . E. I. Shamurina. Moskva, Izd-vo Vsesoiuznoi Knizhnoi Palaty, 1960. 479p.   **AA8**

A comprehensive guide to the literature in Russian published 1917–58 on the theory and practice of bibliography, including history of the book, publishing, library practice, classification and cataloging, and types of bibliographies. An appendix lists reviews of bibliographies.   Z1002.M45

Mez'er, Avgusta Vladimirovna. Slovarnyi ukazatel' po knigovedeniiu. Moskva, Sotsekgiz, 1931–34. 3v.   **AA9**

1st ed. 1924.

A bibliographical manual and index to the literature, covering such subjects as archive and manuscript lists, bibliographies, dictionaries, reference books, library science, etc. Supplements the 1924 ed. Serves as subject index to many articles related to Russian cultural history.   Z1002.M61

Robinson, Anthony Meredith Lewin. Systematic bibliography; a practical guide to the work of compilation. 4th ed., rev. with an additional chapter by Margaret Lodder. London, Bingley; Munich, etc., K. G. Saur, [1979]. 135p.   **AA10**

A 1963 edition was reproduced from typescript at the School of Librarianship of the University of Cape Town.

Originally intended for students in a bibliography course, the work should also prove useful to the reference librarian called upon to give guidance in methods of compilation and arrangement of a bibliography. In addition to sections on the meaning of bibliography, collection of material and mechanics of compilation, arrangement, and layout, there is a chapter on the application of computers to systematic bibliography.   Z1001.R66

Schneider, Georg. Handbuch der Bibliographie. 4. gänzl. veränd. u. stark verm. Aufl. Leipzig, Hiersemann, 1930. 674p.   **AA11**

A guide to general bibliography, national bibliography, bibliographies of incunabula, newspapers, society publications, etc. Includes lists of biographical dictionaries. Offers comment and annotations. A basic work, though now out of date.

The first three editions (1923–26) contained an introductory theoretical-historical treatment of bibliography, which has been omitted in the 4th ed. An English translation of this portion of the 3d ed. is available under the title *Theory and history of bibliography,* tr. by R. R. Shaw (N.Y., Columbia Univ. Pr., 1934. 306p.). The "5. Aufl." (1969) is an unchanged reprint of the 4th ed.   Z1001.S35

Stein, Henri. Manuel de bibliographie générale. (Bibliotheca bibliographica nova.) Paris, Picard, 1897. 895p. (Repr.: N.Y., Kraus, 1962)   **AA12**

Includes universal bibliographies, national and regional bibliographies, subject bibliographies. Appendixes contain: (1) alphabetical list of places having printing presses before the 19th century, arranged by the modern name, with indication of the Latin name of each place, the date of establishment of its press, and references to sources of information; (2) indexes of periodicals; (3) printed catalogs of libraries.

The main list and appendixes 2 and 3 were continued by the lists of new bibliographies, indexes, and catalogs given in each number of *Le bibliographe moderne,* 1897–1931, edited by Henri Stein.   Z1002.S81

Totok, Wilhelm, Weimann, Karl-Heinz and **Weitzel, Rolf.** Handbuch der bibliographischen Nachschlagewerke. 4., erw., völlig neubearb. Aufl. Frankfurt am Main, V. Klostermann, [1972]. 367p.   **AA13**

1st ed. 1954; 1977 repr. called 5th ed.

A selective bibliography of bibliographies, less extensive than Malclès' *Les sources du travail bibliographique* (AA487) and intended mainly for students' use. Emphasis is on European and American works. This edition revised and updated to include publications through 1971.

A new edition has begun to appear as: Z1002.T68

Totok, Wilhelm. Handbuch der bibliographischen Nachschlagewerke. Hrsg. von Hans-Jürgen und Dagmar Kernchen. 6., erw. völlig neu bearb. Aufl. Frankfurt am Main, Klostermann, [1984]– . v.1– . (In progress)   **AA14**

Contents: Bd.1, Allgemeinbibliographien und allgemeine Nachschlagewerke (472p.).

Represents a thorough revision and updating. v.1 includes chapters on bibliographies of bibliographies, library catalogs, national bibliographies (a major section, p.42–175), periodicals, newspapers, book reviews, theses, official publications, incunabula and rare books, societies and organizations, encyclopedias, and biographical dictionaries. Indexed.　　　　　　　　Z1002.T68

Vitale, Philip H. Bibliography, historical and bibliothecal; a handbook of terms and names. Chicago, Loyola Univ. Pr., [1971]. 251p.　　　　　　　　**AA15**

Intended "to make readily available . . . an identification of those terms and persons that relate significantly to the history of writing, printing, and publishing; to the development of libraries and to the systems of classification which govern the storage of written and printed works in them; and to the concepts of theory and practice which make for the most fruitful use of the works themselves."—*Pref.* Terms and personal names are in separate alphabetical sections.　　　　　　　　Z1006.V5

Bibliography of bibliography

Besterman, Theodore. A world bibliography of bibliographies and of bibliographical catalogues, calendars, abstracts, digests, indexes, and the like. 4th ed., rev. and greatly enl. Lausanne, Societas Bibliographica, [1965–66]. 5v.　　**AA16**

1st ed. 1939–40; 2d ed. 1947–49; 3d ed. 1965–66.

A classified bibliography of separately published bibliographies of books, manuscripts, and patent abridgments. International in scope.

The index volume lists in one alphabet: (1) authors, editors, translators, etc.; (2) titles of serial and anonymous works; (3) libraries and archives, etc.; (4) patents (under "Patents," lists subjects covered by British patent specifications). "Bibliographies which would appear in the index under the same heading as in the text are excluded, unless they appear in the text under more than one heading."—*Pref.*

Although the 3d ed. was to have been the final one, this edition records bibliographies published through 1963, with some later additions. It includes some 117,000 items grouped under about 16,000 headings and subheadings. Supplemented in part by AA30.　　　　　　　　Z1002.B5685

Bibliographic index; a cumulative bibliography of bibliographies, 1937– . N.Y., Wilson, 1938– .　　　　**AA17**

Published in three forms: (1) permanent cumulated volumes, coverage varying; (2) annual volumes to supplement the permanent volumes; (3) current issues published quarterly 1938–June 1951, then semiannually in June and Dec. from Dec. 1951–1969. Beginning 1970, published in April and Aug., with a bound cumulation in Dec.

An alphabetical subject arrangement of separately published bibliographies and bibliographies included in books and periodicals. About 2,600 periodicals, including many in foreign languages, are now examined regularly. An extensive list, useful in itself and as a valuable complement to Besterman (above).　　　　Z1002.B595

Bibliographical services throughout the world, 1950/59, 1960/64, 1965/69, 1970/74, 1975/79. Paris, UNESCO, 1961–84. 5v.　　　　　　　　**AA18**

The 1950/59 volume edited by Robert L. Collison is a cumulative report covering materials derived from the volumes published 1951/59. In two main parts: pt.1, Bibliographical activities in various countries and territories, arranged alphabetically by country and indicating whether or not there is a National Committee of Bibliography, and listing national bibliographies, periodical indexes, current bibliographies of special subjects, etc.; pt.2, Bibliographical activities of international organizations.

The 1960/64 and 1965/69 volumes compiled by Paul Avicenne provide updated information and follow the general plan of the earlier work except that there is no section on international organizations. An introductory survey of the development of bibliographical services during the period precedes the individual countries section.

The 1960/64 volume first appeared in French (Paris, 1967) under the title: *Les services bibliographiques dans le monde.*

Both the 1970/74 and 1975/79 volumes were edited by Marcelle Beaudiquez, the first covering 120 countries, the second 121. Those volumes were also published in French; they follow the general plan

of the series. A 1980 supplement (publ. 1982; 103p.) was also edited by Beaudiquez.　　　　　　　　Z1008.U54

Bibliographische Berichte. Jahrg. 1– , 1959– . Frankfurt a. M., Klostermann, 1959– .　　　　　　　　**AA19**

Frequency varies: quarterly, 1959–62; semiannual, 1963–69; annual, 1970– .

Sponsorship varies: "Im Auftrag des Deutschen Bibliographischen Kuratoriums," 1959–69; "Hrsg. von der Staatsbibliothek Preussischer Kulturbesitz," 1970– .

v.4– , title also in English: *Bibliographical bulletin.*

v.1–3 called "Neue Folge der *Bibliographischen Beihefte* zur *Zeitschrift für Bibliothekswesen und Bibliographie.*"

A classified listing of recent bibliographies—those found in periodicals and books as well as those separately published. Coverage is international with, naturally, a high percentage of German titles; now lists more than 2,000 items per year. "Gesamtregister; Cumulated subject index" covering 1959/63 and 1964/68 publ. 1965–70; no subsequent annual indexes.

An "Ergänzungsband" publ. 1977 is entitled *Geisteswissenschaftliche Fortschrittsberichte; Titelnachweis 1965–1975* (Research progress reports in the humanities; titles registered 1965–1975).

Bohatta, Hanns and **Hodes, Franz.** Internationale Bibliographie der Bibliographien; ein Nachschlagewerk, unter Mitwirkung von Walter Funke. Frankfurt am Main, Klostermann, 1950. T.1, 652p.　　　　　　　　**AA20**

Issued in 7 pts., 1939–50.

A classified bibliography of bibliographies. T.1 covers general and national bibliography and subject bibliography, with author and subject indexes. T.2 was to cover Personalbibliographie.　　　　　　　　Z1002.B682

Collison, Robert Lewis. Bibliographies, subject and national; a guide to their contents, arrangement and use. 3d ed., rev. and enl. London, Crosby Lockwood, [1968]. 203p.　　**AA21**

1st ed. 1951.

A handbook containing 400–500 carefully selected and annotated references to bibliographies. Pt.1 covers subject bibliographies arranged in Dewey Classification order, and pt.2, universal and national bibliographies. Index of subjects and personal names.　　　　　　　　Z1002.C7

Courtney, William Prideaux. A register of national bibliography; with a selection of the chief bibliographical books and articles printed in other countries. London, Constable, 1905–12. 3v.　　　　　　　　**AA22**

v.1–2 list the bibliographies published before 1905; v.3 is a supplement containing about 10,000 additional references, principally to bibliographies published 1905–12.

An old but useful handbook to bibliographies on all subjects, international in scope, though mainly British in origin. Arranged alphabetically by the subjects of the bibliographies listed; refers not only to bibliographies in book form, but also to lists in periodicals and to other analytical materials.　　　　　　　　Z1002.C85

Gray, Richard A. and **Villmow, Dorothy.** Serial bibliographies in the humanities and social sciences. Ann Arbor, Mich., Pierian Pr., 1969. 345p.　　　　　　　　**AA23**

A selective listing arranged by Dewey class numbers with three indexes: title; author, sponsor, publisher; and subject, keyword-in-context. Scope, language, frequency, etc. are indicated by code numbers and letters in lieu of annotations.　　　　Z1002.G814

Harvard University. Library. Bibliography and bibliography periodicals. Cambridge, Publ. by the Harvard Univ. Lib.; distr. by the Harvard Univ. Pr., 1966. 1066p. (Widener Library shelflist, no.7)　　　　　　　　**AA24**

For a note on the series *see* AA145.

19,586 titles. The bibliography classification at Widener is similar to Class Z of the Library of Congress scheme and encompasses "works on the science of bibliography, general bibliographies, library catalogues, catalogues of publishers and booksellers, catalogues of manuscripts, the art of writing, the book arts (printing, binding, etc.), publishing and bookselling, the freedom of the press, copyright, library science, and the history of libraries."—*Note on the classification.* Z1002.H26

Internationale Bibliographie des Buch- und Bibliothekswesens, mit besonderer Berücksichtigung der Bibliographie, 1904–12, 1922–39. Leipzig, Harrassowitz, 1905–40. 13v. and n.F. 1–14. **AA25**

First series, 1904–12, 1922–25, had title *Bibliographie des Bibliotheks- und Buchwesens* and appeared as *Beihefte* to the *Zentralblatt für Bibliothekswesen,* 29, 31–32, 34, 36–37, 39–40, 42, 51, 54, 56, 58. None issued for 1913–21. The new series covers 1926–39.

A comprehensive record of books and periodical articles in different languages on various aspects of bibliography, library science, and library history. Z1002.B61

Internationale Personalbibliographie, 1800–1943. Bearb. von Max Arnim. 2. verb. und stark verm. Aufl. Leipzig, Hiersemann, 1944–52. 2v. **AA26**

A revised edition of a useful bibliography which was first published in 1936, covering the years 1850–1935. This edition has been extended to cover the first half of the 19th century as well as more recent years. It indexes bibliographies contained in books, periodicals, biographical dictionaries, academic annuals, *Festschriften,* etc. In many cases the references lead to biographical as well as to bibliographical information. International in scope with the emphasis on German names, but the first edition should be consulted for many names which were dropped from the second for political reasons. Identification in this edition is simplified by the addition of occupations and, frequently, the date of death. Z8001.A1I57

——— Bd.III, 1944–1959 und Nachträge, von Gerhard Bock und Franz Hodes. Stuttgart, Hiersemann, 1961–63. 659p.

A new edition of this volume is appearing as:

Internationale Personalbibliographie. Begründet von Max Arnim, fortgeführt von Franz Hodes. 2., völlig neubearb. Aufl. von Bd. III (Berichtszeit 1944–1959) in drei bis zum jeweiligen Erscheinungsjahr ergänzten Bänden III–V. Stuttgart, Hiersemann, 1978–84. Lfg.1–18. (In progress) **AA27**

Contents: Lfg.1–18, A–R. (Lfg.18 completes v.4)
Bd.III, A–H, issued in nine Lfg., 1978–81, with the designation "Band III/IV, 1944–75" on the covers, and the edition statement given as "2., überbearb. u. bis zum Berichtsjahr 1975 fortgeführte Aufl. von Band III (1944–1959) mit Nachträgen zur zweiten Aufl. von Band I/II (1800–1943)." The title page issued for that volume carries the edition statement and volume designation as given above.
This new edition of Bd.III was originally planned to extend the period of coverage only through 1975, but from an early stage citations gathered up to time of publication of the individual fascicles have been included. Also incorporates new references for persons included in Bd.I–II of the set (those names being marked with an asterisk). Indexes to the full set are promised. Z8001.A1A72

Northup, Clark Sutherland. Register of bibliographies of the English language and literature, with contributions by Joseph Quincy Adams and Andrew Keogh. New Haven, Conn., Yale Univ. Pr., 1925. 507p. (Cornell studies in English, 9) (Repr.: N.Y., Hafner, 1962) **AA28**

Not so limited as its title indicates; includes also many related bibliographies of other subjects and so serves, to a certain extent, as a general bibliography of bibliography. The English literature sections are superseded by Howard-Hill's *Bibliography of English literary bibliographies* (BD494). Z2011.N87

Ottervik, Gösta. Bibliografier. Kommenterad urvalsförteckning med särskild hänsyn till svenska förhållenden. 3., omarb. och väsentligt utökade uppl. Lund, Bibliotekstjänst, [1966]. 255p. (Sveriges allmänna biblioteksförenings handböcker, 13) **AA29**

1st ed. 1958.
A select bibliography of bibliographies (including certain other reference works of a bibliographic nature, e.g., periodicals, directories, and union lists), with special attention to Swedish publications. Annotated; index. Z1002.O78

Toomey, Alice F. A world bibliography of bibliographies, 1964–1974; a list of works represented by Library of Congress printed catalog cards. A decennial supplement to Theodore Besterman, A world bibliography of bibliographies. Totowa, N.J., Rowman and Littlefield, [1977]. 2v. **AA30**

Compiled as a supplement to the 4th ed. of Besterman (AA16). Limited to separately published bibliographies represented by Library of Congress printed cards, "including, however, some offprints of bibliographies which originally appeared as part of a larger work."—*Note.* Z1002.T67

United States

Jones, Helen Gertrude (Dudenbostel). United States of America national bibliographical services and related activities in 1965–1967. Chicago, Reference Services Div., Amer. Lib. Assoc., 1968. 56p. **AA31**

"This publication represents a combination of three separate reports—one for each of the three years (1965, 1966, and 1967)—prepared in reply to a United Nations Educational, Scientific and Cultural Organization questionnaire" which is sent "to each country annually in order to keep up to date the information in its *Bibliographical Services Throughout the World* [AA18]."—*Pref.* Offers a guide to a variety of publications and bibliographical services; includes a section on interlibrary cooperation. Supplementary articles by M. J. Gibson (bearing the same title) covering the years 1968/69, 1970–78 appeared annually in the Winter issue of the periodical *RQ,* 1970–80. Z1002.J66

Stillwell, Margaret Bingham. Americana: selected bibliographies and bibliographical monographs. (*In her Incunabula and Americana,* p.341–440 [AA268]) **AA32**

An important list of more than 600 bibliographies of Americana before 1800. For full description *see* AA268. Z240.A1S8

Africa

Besterman, Theodore. A world bibliography of African bibliographies. Rev. and brought up to date by J. D. Pearson. Oxford, Blackwell; Totowa, N.J., Rowman and Littlefield, [1975]. 241col. **AA33**

Includes the entries for the various African subjects as found in the 4th ed. of Besterman's *World bibliography of bibliographies* (AA16), plus additional works published through 1972. Arranged by geographical division, with subdivisions by region and subject as pertinent. Indexed. Z3501.A1B47

Garling, Anthea. Bibliography of African bibliographies. Cambridge, [Eng.], African Studies Centre, [1968]. 138p. (Occasional papers, 1) **AA34**

Arranged by region, then by individual country. Z3501.A1G3

Argentina

Geoghegan, Abel Rodolfo. Bibliografía de bibliografías argentinas, 1807–1970. Edición preliminar. Buenos Aires, Casa Pardo, 1970. 164p. (p.131–64 advertisements) **AA35**

A classified listing of the principal Argentinian bibliographies of the period. Brief annotations for most entries. No author index. Z1611.A1G4

Asia

Nunn, Godfrey Raymond. East Asia: a bibliography of bibliographies. [Honolulu], East-West Center Lib., 1967. 92p. (East-West Center. Library. Occasional papers, 7)   **AA36**

A companion to the same author's bibliography of bibliographies for South and Southeast Asia (below). Emphasis is on material in book form rather than periodical materials. Following a section for East Asia in general, there are separate classified listings for China, Japan, and Korea, and a brief section for Mongolia. Indexed.
Z3001.A1N8

———— South and Southeast Asia; a bibliography of bibliographies. [Honolulu], East–West Center Lib., 1966. 59p. (East–West Center. Library. Occasional papers, 4)   **AA37**

Arranged by country, with subdivisions as necessary. Author and subject index. Limited to those bibliographies of major importance to be found in the East West Center and University of Hawaii collections or in the published catalogs of principal libraries.
Z3221.A1N8

Yunesuko Higashi Ajia Bunka Kenkyu Senta, Tokyo. A survey of bibliographies in western languages concerning East and Southeast Asian studies. Tokyo, [1966–69]. 2v. (*Its* Bibliography, no.4–5)   **AA38**

A publication of the Centre for East Asian Cultural Studies, Tokyo. Lists by country or geographical area about 2,200 bibliographies in the social sciences and humanities. v.1 lists bibliographies published in book form; v.2 lists those appearing in periodicals. Each volume has its own index.

Australia

Borchardt, Dietrich Hans. Australian bibliography: a guide to printed sources of information. [3d ed. Rushcutters Bay, N.S.W.], Pergamon, [1976]. 270p.   **AA39**

1st ed. 1963.
A bibliographic survey of printed sources intended for the serious student, much enlarged in this edition. Includes chapters on libraries and library catalogs, encyclopedias and general reference works, general bibliographies, subject bibliographies, sources of biographical information, and government publications. Indexed.
Z4011.B65

Canberra, Australia. National Library. Australian Bibliographical Centre. Australian bibliography and bibliographical services. Canberra, Australian Advisory Council on Bibliographical Services, 1960. 219p.   **AA40**

Subject arrangement with author index. Lists "catalogues and bibliographies in the usual sense, indexes, abstracts, digests, union lists and catalogues, booksellers' lists, calendars of archives and manuscripts, and services designed for bibliographical ends."—*Pref.* Indicates location of copies in Australian libraries.
Z4039.C3

Bolivia

Siles Guevara, Juan. Bibliografía de bibliografías bolivianas. [La Paz], Ministerio de Cultura, Información y Turismo, Impr. del Estado, 1969. 38p.   **AA41**

103 items with annotations.   Z1641.A1S53

Brazil

Basseches, Bruno. A bibliography of Brazilian bibliographies. Uma bibliografia das bibliografias brasileiras. Detroit, Blaine Ethridge, [1978]. 185p.   **AA42**

Introductory matter in English and Portuguese.
An author (or other main entry) listing of nearly 2,500 Brazilian bibliographies published as separates, in periodicals, or as parts of books. Includes works published outside Brazil on Brazilian topics. Index of authors and subjects.   Z1671.B37

Reis, António Simoes dos. Bibliografia das bibliografias brasileiras. Rio de Janeiro, 1942. 186p. il. (Rio de Janeiro. Inst. Nacional do Livro. Coleção B. I. Bibliografia, I)   **AA43**

Lists 712 bibliographies of Brazil arranged chronologically, 1741–1941.   Z1671.A1R4

Bulgaria

Bibliografiia na bulgarskata bibliografiia, 1852–1944. [Sustaviteli Khristo Trenkov et al.] Sofiia, Narodna Biblioteka "Kiril i Metodii," 1981. 311p.   **AA44**

A classed bibliography of nearly 2,600 items. Indexed.
Z2891.A1B52

Petkova, Zornitsa Malcheva. Bibliografiia na bulgarskata bibliografiia, 1944–1969. Sofiia, Narodna Biblioteka "Kiril i Metodii," 1971. 603p.   **AA45**

Although published earlier, this serves as the chronological successor to the above. Classed arrangement; indexed. More than 1,500 items.   Z2891.A1P4

Bibliografiia na bulgarskata bibliografiia. 1963– . Sofiia, Narodna Biblioteka "Kiril i Metodii," 1964– . Annual.   **AA46**

Beginning with the issue for 1973 (publ. 1974) constitutes series 8 of the Bulgarian national bibliography (*Natsionalna bibliografiia na NR Bulgariia;* AA650).

A classed listing with author index. Includes bibliographies published in periodicals as well as in book form; relevant items published outside Bulgaria are also listed.   Z2891.A1B8

Canada

Lochhead, Douglas, comp. Bibliography of Canadian bibliographies. 2d ed., rev. & enl. [Toronto], Publ. in assoc. with the Bibliographical Society of Canada by Univ. of Toronto Pr., [1972]. 312p.   **AA47**

Added title page in French.
1st ed. (1960) comp. by Raymond Tanghe.
This edition lists more than 2,300 bibliographies, each of which has "some Canadian connection, either by subject, compiler, geographical location, etc."—*Introd.* It represents a thorough revision of the earlier edition, incorporating listings from the supplements thereto and new works to mid-1970. Follows an alphabetical author arrangement rather than the earlier classed listing. Index of subjects and compilers. There are some brief annotations in English or French according to the language of the title.   Z1365.A1L6

Caribbean countries

Jordan, Alma and **Comissiong, Barbara.** The English-speaking Caribbean: a bibliography of bibliographies. Boston, G. K. Hall, [1984]. 411p.   **AA48**

A classified listing of "bibliographies produced up to April 1981 about the lands and peoples of the former British Caribbean territories, both island and mainland."—*Pref.* Includes separately published bibliographies and those appearing as parts of books, periodical articles, in conference proceedings, etc.; many are unpublished or issued in mimeographed form. More than 1,400 entries; many brief annotations. Locates copies. Name and subject indexes.
Z1595.J67

Chile

Laval, Ramón Arminio. Bibliografía de bibliografías chilenas. (*In* Santiago de Chile. Bibliografía general de Chile, 1915. v.1, p.i–lxix) **AA49**

———— Suplemento y adiciones, por Herminia Elgueta de Ochsenius. Santiago de Chile, Impr. Cervantes, 1930. 71p.

Lists bibliographies on Chile published either as separates or in periodicals. Z1701.A1L2

China

Tsien, Tsuen-Hsuin. China; an annotated bibliography of bibliographies. Comp. . . . in collaboration with James K. M. Cheng. Boston, G. K. Hall, [1978]. 604p. **AA50**

Lists "a selection of over 2500 bibliographies concerning China, mainly in English, Chinese, and Japanese, with some in French, German, Russian, and other European languages."—*Introd.* Includes separate publications, bibliographies in periodicals and monographs, surveys of the literature of specific fields, etc. In two sections, each with numerous subdivisions: (1) General and special bibliographies; (2) Subject bibliographies (e.g., classics and philosophy, religion, history, geography, literature, etc.). Author, title, and subject indexes. Z3106.T87

Colombia

Giraldo Jaramillo, Gabriel. Bibliografía de bibliografías colombianas. 2. ed. corr. y puesta al día por Rubén Pérez Ortiz. Bogotá, Inst. Caro y Cuervo, 1960. 204p. (Inst. Caro y Cuervo. Publicaciones. Serie bibliográfica, 1) **AA51**

1st ed. 1954.
Lists bibliographies in books and periodicals in classed arrangement with author index. Z1008.C685 no.1

Cuba

Peraza Sarausa, Fermin. Bibliografías cubanas. Wash., [Govt. Prt. Off.], 1945. 58p. (U.S. Library of Congress. [Latin America ser., 7]) **AA52**

At head of title: The Library of Congress. Hispanic Foundation. Introduction in Spanish and English. Annotations in Spanish. A classed bibliography of Cuban bibliographies. Z1511.A1P4

Robaina, Tomás Fernández. Bibliografía de bibliografías cubanas [1859–1972]. [La Habana, Biblioteca Nacional José Martí, 1973] 340p. **AA53**

A classed bibliography of nearly 1,400 items. Includes bibliographies of individuals, periodical indexes, specialized bibliographies, etc. Indexed. Z1511.A1R6

Denmark

Moller, Arne J. Danske Bibliografier, udvalg af Danske bibliografiske Arbejder. København, Levin og Munksgaard, 1929. 28p. **AA54**

A classed listing with index of authors and editors.
Z2561.A1M6

Munch-Petersen, Erland, comp. A guide to Danish bibliography. Copenhagen, Royal School of Librarianship, 1965. 140p. **AA55**

An annotated bibliography of general and subject bibliographies of Danish publications and works relating to Danish topics. Arranged by broad Universal Decimal Classification with author index. Annotations are in English. Z2561.A1M8

Dominican Republic

Florén Lozano, Luis. Bibliografía de la bibliografía dominicana. Ciudad Trujillo, Roques Román, 1948. 66p. **AA56**

A bibliography of bibliographies in all subjects, both those separately published and those included in books and periodicals.
Z1531.F57

Ethiopia

Girma Makonnen. A bibliography of Ethiopian bibliographies, 1932–1972. Addis Ababa, Addis Ababa Univ., University Libraries, 1976. 53p. (Ethiopian bibliographic ser., ser. minor, 2) **AA57**

A classed list with author index. Includes bibliographies appended to books and periodical articles as well as separately published works. 395 items. Z3521.A1G57

Europe, East

Die Bibliographie in den europäischen Ländern der Volksdemokratie; Entwicklung und gegenwärtiger Stand, von Todor Borov [et al.]. Leipzig, Verlag für Buch- und Bibliothekswesen, 1960. 165p. (Bibliothekswissenschaftliche Arbeiten aus der Sowjetunion und den Ländern der Volksdemokratie in deutscher Übersetzung. Reihe B, Bd.3) **AA58**

A guide to the bibliography of Albania, Bulgaria, Poland, Romania, Czechoslovakia, and Hungary. Z2483.B5

Finland

Grönroos, Henrik. Finlands bibliografiska litteratur: kommenterad förteckning. Ekenäs, Ekenäs Tryckeri, 1975. 388p. **AA59**

An annotated bibliography of Finnish bibliographies, both those published in Finland and works published abroad which include sections on Finland. In four main sections: (1) general bibliographies; (2) Finland in foreign literature and foreign countries in Finnish literature; (3) subject bibliographies; (4) author bibliographies. Indexed.

Germany

Leipzig. Deutsche Bücherei. Bibliographie der versteckten Bibliographien. Aus deutschsprachigen Büchern und Zeitschriften der Jahre 1930–1953. Leipzig, Verlag für Buch- und Bibliothekswesen, [1956]. 371p. (Sonderbibliographien der Deutschen Bücherei, 3) **AA60**

Lists bibliographies published 1930–53, as parts of books or in periodicals. Aims to be comprehensive in listing bibliographies consisting of 60 titles or more. Arrangement is alphabetical by subject, with a classified index of subject headings.
Continued by: Z1002.L42

Bibliographie der deutschen Bibliographien; Jahresverzeichnis der selbständig erschienenen und der in deutschsprachigen Büchern und Zeitschriften enthaltenen versteckten Bibliographien. Bearb. von der Deutschen Bücherei. Jahrg.1–12, 1954–65. Leipzig, Verlag für Buch- und Bibliothekswesen, 1957–69. Annual. **AA61**

An annual listing which includes separately published bibliographies as well as those in periodicals and books.
A similar series was published as: Z1002.B58

Bibliographie der deutschen Bibliographien; monatliches Verzeichnis . . . . Jahrg. 1–6. Leipzig, Verlag für Buch- und Bibliothekswesen, 1966–71. Monthly. **AA62**

Superseded *Bulletin wichtiger Literatur-Zusammenstellungen.*
Continued by: Z2221.A1B5

Bibliographie der Bibliographien; monatliches Verzeichnis. Jahrg. 7– . Leipzig, VEB Verlag für Buch- und Bibliothekswesen, 1972– . Monthly. **AA63**

Continues the publication above and assumes its numbering.

Classed arrangement with cumulated annual subject index. Covers both separately published bibliographies and those appearing in books and periodicals, as well as ongoing, annual bibliographies. Includes publications of both East and West Germany, together with selected German-language publications and bibliographies of Germanica published outside Germany.

Widmann, Hans. Bibliographien zum deutschen Schrifttum der Jahre 1939–1950. Tübingen, Niemeyer, 1951. 284p. **AA64**

Because of the breakdown of the well-organized bibliographical system of Germany due to war, this bibliography attempts to list bibliographies of the period dealing with German publications and includes: international bibliographies; bibliographies of books published in Germany; bibliographies of translations into German; regional and personal bibliographies; and bibliographies arranged by subject field.

Greece (Modern)

Phousaras, G. I. Bibliographia tōn Hellēnikōn bibliographiōn, 1791–1947. Athēna, Bibliopōleion tēs "Hestias," 1961. 284p. **AA65**

A classified listing of modern Greek bibliographies—1,614 numbered entries. Indexes by name, subject, date, and place.
Z2281.A1P48

Hungary

A magyar bibliográfiák bibliográfiája, 1956/57– . Budapest, Országos Széchényi Könyvtár, 1960– . Irregular. **AA66**

Added title page in Latin: Bibliographia bibliographiarum hungaricarum.

A detailed listing of bibliographies published in Hungary, including those in books, periodicals, yearbooks, etc., as well as separately published ones. Arranged by Universal Decimal Classification with index of names and subjects. Z1002.M25

India

Kalia, D. R. and **Jain, M. K.** A bibliography of bibliographies on India. Delhi, Concept Pub. Co., [1975]. 204p. **AA67**

A bibliography of bibliographies arranged alphabetically by subject. 1,243 entries; index of authors and subjects. Numerous brief annotations. Z3201.A1K34

Indonesia

Tairas, J. N. B. Indonesia: a bibliography of bibliographies. Daftar karya bibliografi Indonesia. [N.Y., Oleander Pr., 1975] 123p. **AA68**

A revised edition of *Daftar karya bibliografi Indonesia* published in Jakarta, 1973.

Foreword and subject headings in English and Indonesian.

A classified listing of 661 items. Includes: (1) all types of bibliographical works published in Indonesia; (2) bibliographies dealing wholly or partly with Indonesia, published outside Indonesia; (3) important bibliographical listings published as parts of books. Brief descriptive notes in English. Author-title-subject index.
Z3271.A1T313

Ireland

Eager, Alan R. A guide to Irish bibliographical material: a bibliography of Irish bibliographies and sources of information. 2d rev. & enl. ed. London, Lib. Assoc.; Westport, Conn., Greenwood Pr., [1980]. 502p. **AA69**

1st ed. 1964.

A bibliography of bibliographies (including periodical articles and parts of books as well as separately published works) which "aims to serve as a quick reference guide to all who are interested in Irish studies and research work."—*Introd.* Classed arrangement with author and subject indexes. More than 9,500 items in this edition.
Z2031.E16

Italy

Ottino, Giuseppe and **Fumagalli, Giuseppe.** Bibliotheca bibliographica italica. Catalogo degli scritti di bibliologia, bibliografia e biblioteconomia pub. in Italia e di quelli risguardanti l'Italia pub. all'Estero. Roma, Pasqualucci, 1889; Torino, Clausen, 1895–1902. 2v. and 4 suppl.
AA70

Basic volumes, 6,450 entries; supplements—for 1895, 1896, 1896–99, 1900—entries no.6451–8259.

Supplements 1 and 2 by Ottino; supplements 3 and 4 by Emilio Calvi.

The basic bibliography of Italian bibliographies, in classified order covering: history of the book and printing; general, regional, local, personal bibliography; bibliographies of subjects; libraries and library economy.
Continued by: Z2341.A1O8

Fumagalli, Giuseppe. La bibliografia. Roma, Fondazione Leonardo, 1923. lxxxix p., 169p. (Guide bibliografiche)
AA72

P.i–lxxxix contain a survey of Italian bibliography and bibliographers. The rest of the work is a classified bibliography of bibliographies in all fields with an author index. It includes a selection of titles from the Ottino *Bibliotheca* (above) and additional works published from 1901 to 1923. Z2341.A1F9

Istituto Nazionale per le Relazioni Culturali con l'Estero. La bibliografia italiana, a cura di Giannetto Avanzi. 2. ed. interamente rifatta, con tre appendice e una aggiunta. Roma, 1946. 570p. (On cover: Bibliografie italiane)
AA72

Half title: Guida sistematica e analitica degli scritti principali di bibliologia, bibliografia, biblioteconomia pubblicati in Italia dal 1921 al 1946.

The 2d ed. of one of the volumes listed in the series below.

A work of first importance for the record of Italian bibliography. Covers history of the book; general, national, regional, and personal bibliography; libraries, graphic arts, etc. Z1002.I8

——— Bibliografie del ventennio. Roma, 1941. 14v.
AA73

A series of separately published bibliographies listing works published in Italy, 1922–41. Volumes cover: Archeologia, arti figurative, musica. 498p.; La bibliografia italiana. 248p. (*see* AA72 for revised edition); Filologia classica e romanza. 152p.; Geografia e viaggi. 194p.; Letteratura italiana. 238p.; Letterature straniere. 455p.; Medicina. 165p.; Mussolini e il fascismo. 81p.; Scienze economiche e sociali. 167p.; Scienze fisiche, matematiche ed agrarie. 211p.; Scienze naturali. 101p.; Scienze religiose, filosofia, pedagogia. 173p.; Studi storici militari, etnografia popolare. 214p.; Il pensiero giuridico italiano. 5v.

Italia bibliographica 1952–61 . . . 2da ed. migliorata . . . [Firenze], Sansoni, [1953–62]. (Amor di libro) Annual; no more publ.? **AA74**

Ed.: 1952–56, Giuseppe Sergio Martini; 1957–61, Bona Edlmann.

An annual bibliography of bibliographies published in Italy. The first part lists monographs alphabetically by author; the second part lists, by subject, bibliographies appearing in books and periodicals.

Quinquennial indexes: 1952–56, 1956–61. These include indexes by subject and by author.   Z1002.I83

Japan

Amano, Keitaro. Nihon shoshi no shoshi. Tokyo, Gannandō, [1973]– . v.1– . (In progress)   **AA75**

Added title page: *A Japan bibliography of bibliographies.*
Contents: v.1, Generalia (671p.).
v.1 lists bibliographies published up to the end of 1965.
                                                   Z1002.A455

Korea

Koh, Hesung Chun. Korea: an analytical guide to bibliographies. New Haven, Conn., HRAF, 1971. 334p.   **AA76**

For full information *see* DE274.

Latin America

Gropp, Arthur Eric. A bibliography of Latin American bibliographies. Metuchen, N.J., Scarecrow Pr., 1968. 515p.
                                                         AA77

A greatly enlarged and updated version of a work of the same title compiled by Cecil K. Jones, published 1942. Retains about 2,900 items from the earlier work and adds more than 4,000 new references published through 1964. Emphasis is on works of a purely bibliographic nature, with many of the general works listed in Jones excluded here. Arrangement is by subject field rather than by country as in the Jones work. Detailed index.

——— ——— Supplement. Metuchen, N.J., Scarecrow Pr., 1971. 277p.

Adds more than 1,400 references from the 1965–69 period.
                                                   Z1601.A2G76

Cordeiro, Daniel Raposo, ed. A bibliography of Latin American bibliographies: social sciences & humanities. Metuchen, N.J., Scarecrow Pr., 1979. v.1. (272p.)   **AA78**

"Supplementing the original works by Arthur E. Gropp [above]." —*t.p.*

A cumulation, with additional citations to articles gleaned from some 250 periodicals, of the annual working papers prepared for the Subcommittee on the Bibliography of Latin American Bibliographies of the Seminar on the Acquisition of Latin American Library Materials (SALALM) for the years 1969–74. Covers periodical publications 1966–74; monographs of 1969–74. Follows the arrangement of the Gropp compilations; author and subject indexes.
                                                   Z1601.A2G76

A bibliography of Latin American bibliographies, 1975–1979: social sciences and humanities. Haydée Piedracueva, ed. Metuchen, N.J., Scarecrow Pr., 1982. 313p.   **AA79**

"Supplement No.3 to Arthur E. Gropp's *A Bibliography of Latin American Bibliographies.*"—*t.p.*

Like the Cordeiro compilation, consolidates entries from the SALALM *Annual report on bibliographic activities* for the period; covers monographic and periodical publications.   Z1601.A2G76

Gropp, Arthur Eric. A bibliography of Latin American bibliographies published in periodicals. Metuchen, N.J., Scarecrow Pr., 1976. 2v. (1031p.)   **AA79a**

A companion to the same author's *Bibliography of Latin American bibliographies* (AA77).

A classed listing of more than 9,700 items, mainly from the period 1929–65, but including some earlier publications. Lists not only articles which are bibliographic in nature, but also articles which have substantial bibliographies appended. Fully indexed.
                                                   Z1601.A2G76

Seminar on the Acquisition of Latin American Library Materials. Annual report on Latin American and Caribbean bibliographic activities, 1980– . Madison, Univ. of Wisconsin, 1980– . Annual? (SALALM working paper no.A-2, etc.)
                                                         AA80

Editor varies.

Lists recently published bibliographies on Latin American topics, whether published as monographs or as articles in periodicals. Topical arrangement. The annual lists will serve as the basis for further supplements to Gropp's bibliography (*see* AA78).

Watson, Gayle Hudgens. Colombia, Ecuador and Venezuela: an annotated guide to reference materials in the humanities and social sciences. Metuchen, N.J., Scarecrow Pr., 1971. 279p.   **AA81**

Nearly 900 items in subject arrangement.   Z1731.W38

Luxembourg

Hury, Carlo. Luxemburgensia; eine Bibliographie der Bibliographien. 2. Aufl. München, K. G. Saur, 1978. 352p.
                                                         AA82

1st ed. 1964.

A classed, annotated bibliography of bibliographies relating to Luxembourg. Nearly 700 items (books, parts of books, periodical articles). Indexed.

Mexico

Millares Carlo, Augustin and **Mantecón, José Ignacio.** Ensayo de una bibliografía de bibliografías mexicanas. (La imprenta, el libro, las bibliotecas, etc.) México, Biblioteca de la II Feria del Libro y Exposición Nacional del Periodismo, 1943. 224p.   **AA83**

At head of title: Departamento del Distrito Federal. Dirección de Acción Social. Oficina de Bibliotecas.

Arranged by class. 1,777 entries. Includes general bibliographies relating to America that have references to Mexico, and bibliographies relating to Mexico, including general, individual, regional, subject, periodicals, etc.   Z1411.A1M5

Netherlands

U.S. Library of Congress. Netherlands Studies Unit. A guide to Dutch bibliographies. Prep. by Bertus H. Wabeke. Wash., 1951. 193p.   **AA84**

Contents: pt.1, Comprehensive bibliographies: general, Netherlands, overseas territories; pt.2, Subject bibliographies; pt.3, Other bibliographies: academic dissertations, government publications, pamphlets, periodical press, personal bibliographies.

Lists more than 750 bibliographies. If copies are not available in the Library of Congress, an effort has been made to locate at least one copy of every item in a library in the United States.
                                                   Z2416.U6

New Zealand

New Zealand Library Association. A bibliography of New Zealand bibliographies. Prelim. ed. Wellington, 1967. 58p.
                                                         AA85

Limited to those bibliographies "concerned with aspects of New Zealand—its history, government and literature, its economic, industrial and scientific activities."—*Pref.* Index of names.
                                                   Z4101.A1N4

Norway

Sommerfeldt, Wilhelm Preuss. Norsk bibliografisk litteratur, 1919–1943; med tillegg 1944–1946. Oslo, Damm, 1944–46. 47p. (Norsk bibliografisk bibliotek, bd.3, hft.1)   **AA86**

A classified list of Norwegian bibliographies that appeared in books and periodicals during the period indicated.

Peru

Lostaunau Rubio, Gabriel. Fuentes para el estudio del Perú: bibliografía de bibliografías. Lima, [Impr. y Encuadernación Herrera Márquez], 1980. 500p.   **AA87**

A classified, annotated bibliography of bibliographies relating to Peru, including separately published works and those appearing as periodical articles or parts of books. Index of names.
Z1851.A1L67

Philippines

Bernardo, Gabriel Adriano. Bibliography of Philippine bibliographies, 1593–1961. Ed. by Natividad P. Verzosa. Quezon City, Ateneo Univ. Pr., 1968. 192p. (Ateneo de Manila University. Dept. of History. Bibliographical ser., 2)   **AA88**

A chronologically arranged bibliography of bibliographies, library and sales catalogs, and books and pamphlets containing bibliographical information on the Philippines. Many annotations; index.
Z3291.A1B45

Hart, Donn Vorhis. An annotated bibliography of Philippine bibliographies, 1965–1974. [De Kalb], Center for Southeast Asian Studies, Northern Illinois Univ., 1974. 160p. (Northern Ill. Univ. Ctr. for Southeast Asian Studies. Occasional papers, 4)   **AA89**

Intended to supplement Charles O. Houston's *Philippine bibliography* (Manila, 1960) and Shiro Saito's *The Philippines* (1966; DG27). An author listing of 280 items, with index of titles and subjects.
Z3291.A1H37

Poland

Bibliografia bibliografii i nauki o ksiazce. Bibliographia Poloniae bibliographica. 1937/44– . Warszawa, Biblioteka Narodowa, Inst. Bibliograficzny, 1947– . Annual (Irregular).   **AA90**

A classified bibliography of current Polish bibliographies in the fields of bookmaking, librarianship, documentation, etc., including monographs and periodical articles.
Published irregularly as follows: 1937–44 (1965); 1945–46 (1955); 1947 (1947–49. 4 pts.); 1948 (1952); 1949 (1954); 1950–51 (1956); 1952–53 (1957); 1954 (1956); 1955 (1956); 1956 (1958); 1957 (1959); 1958 (1961); 1959 (1961); 1960 (1962); 1961 (1964); 1962 (1966); 1963 (1967); 1966 (1969); 1967, 1968 (1971); 1969 (1973); 1970 (1975); 1971 (1976); 1972 (1979).   Z2521.B54

Czachowska, Jadwiga and **Loth, Roman.** Przewodnik polonisty: bibliografie, słowniki, biblioteki, muzea literackie. Wrocław, Zakład Narodowy Imienia Ossolińskich Wydawnictwo, 1974. 620p.   **AA91**

An extensive guide to Polish dictionaries, general bibliographies, and bibliographies of Polish literature and related fields, plus sections on libraries and museums. Classed arrangement with author and subject indexes.   Z2528.P5C95

Hahn, Wiktor. Bibliografia bibliografij polskich, do 1950 roku. Wyd. 3, uzupełnił Henryk Sawoniak. Wrocław, Zakład Narodowy im. Ossolińskich, 1966. 586p.   **AA92**

1st ed. 1921; 2d ed. 1956.
More than 7,500 bibliographic works published through 1950 are listed. Item numbers from the previous edition are retained, with added items given letter suffixes. Classed arrangement, with author and title indexes.   Z2521.A1H3

Sawoniak, Henryk. Bibliografia bibliografii polskich, 1951–1960. Wrocław, Zakład Narodowy im. Ossolińskich, 1967. 483p.   **AA93**

Added title page and introductory notes in English and Russian.
Extends the period of coverage of W. Hahn's bibliography of the same title (above). Nearly 5,800 items in classed arrangement; author and subject indexes.   Z2521.A1S3

Portugal

Anselmo, António Joaquim. Bibliografia das bibliografias portuguesas. Lisboa, Biblioteca Nacional, 1923. 158p. (Publicações da Biblioteca Nacional. Biblioteca do bibliotecário e do arquivista, 3)   **AA94**

Contents: (1) Bibliografias gerais; (2) Bibliografias especiais e monografias bibliográficas; (3) Publicações periodicas de bibliografia. Author and subject index.   Z2711.A1A6

South Africa

Musiker, Reuben. South African bibliography: a survey of bibliographies and bibliographical work. 2d ed. Cape Town, David Philip, [1980]. 84p.   **AA95**

1st ed. 1970; suppls. 1975 and 1977.
Intended as a companion to Musiker's *South Africa* (DD178) which lists South African reference books. A discursive treatment of South African bibliographical activity, including "national and subject bibliographies, as well as lists of periodicals, newspapers, theses, official publications and manuscripts."—*Pref.* A main entry listing of the 585 items mentioned in the text gives the full bibliographic information. Most of the items are South African publications. Subject index.   Z3601.A1M9

Spain

Foulché-Delbosc, Raymond and **Barrau-Dihigo, Louis.** Manuel de l'hispanisant. N.Y., Putnam, 1920; Hispanic Soc. of America, 1925. 2v. (Repr.: N.Y., Kraus, 1970)   **AA96**

Contents: v.1, Répertoires; v.2, Collections.
A useful manual of Spanish bibliography including material on Portugal as well as on Spain. v.1 lists bibliographies: national, regional, special; biographical works; bibliographies of special subjects; descriptions of public and private archives, libraries, and museums. v.2 gives contents of printed collections and series published 1579–1923.   Z2681.A1F7

Thailand

Hart, Don Vorhis. Thailand: an annotated bibliography of bibliographies. [De Kalb], Center for Southeast Asian Studies, Northern Illinos Univ., distr. by Cellar Book Shop, Detroit, 1977. 96p. (Occasional papers, no.5)   **AA97**

Cites 205 bibliographies relating specifically to Thailand and more than ten pages in length. Arranged alphabetically by author or issuing body, with subject index. Annotations indicate number of entries, arrangement, kinds of indexes, languages of works cited, special features.   DS563.5

Turkey

Başbugoglu, Filiz, Acar, Lâmia and **Ok, Necdet.** 1928–1965 yillari arasinda Türkiye' de basilmuş bibliyografyalarin bibliyografyasi. Ankara, Ayyildiz Matbaasi, 1966. 270p.   **AA98**

A classified, annotated bibliography of Turkish bibliographies. Nearly 500 items. Indexed.   Z2831.A1B3

Union of Soviet Socialist Republics

Bibliografiia sovetskoi bibliografii. 1939, 1946– . Moskva, 1941– . Annual.   **AA99**

Issued by Vsesoiuznaia Knizhnaia Palata. Suspended 1940–45.

A section of the Soviet national bibliography comprising a classified annual index to bibliographies published separately or as parts of books or articles.

Informatsionnyi ukazatel' bibliograficheskikh spiskov i kartotek, sostavlennykh bibliotekami Sovetskogo Soiuza. Moskva, 1957–73. Monthly (frequency varies).   **AA100**

Continues *Vazhneishie bibliograficheskie raboty bibliotek,* issued 1943–48. Ceased publication.

Provides classified lists of currently published bibliographies and card indexes in various fields.

Complemented by: Z2491.A1M63

Moscow. Publichnaia Biblioteka. Svodnyi ukazatel' bibliograficheskikh spiskov i kartotek, sostavlennykh bibliotekami Sovetskogo Soiuza. Obshchestvennye nauki. Khudozhestvennaia literatura. Iskusstvo. 1960–73. Moskva, 1961–74. Annual.   **AA101**

An annual subject cumulation of the information in *Informatsionnyi ukazatel' bibliograficheskikh spiskov i kartotek.* Ceased publication.   Z2491.A1M625

Kirpicheva, Iraida Konstantinova. Bibliografiia v pomoshch' nauchnoi rabote; metodicheskoe i spravochnoe posobie. Pod red. P. N. Berkova. Leningrad, 1958. 480p.   **AA102**

A guide and manual to Russian bibliographies, including a section on bibliographical technique followed by sections on general and subject bibliography.

An abridgment appeared in German translation as: Z1001.K6

——— Handbuch der russischen und sowjetischen Bibliographien: die Allgemeinbibliographien, Fachbibliographien und Nachschlagewerke Russlands und der Sowjetunion. [Tr. from the Russian] Leipzig, Verlag für Buch- und Bibliothekswesen, 1962. 225p. (Bibliothekswissenschaftliche Arbeiten aus der Sowjetunion und den Ländern der Volksdemokratie in deutscher Übersetzung. Reihe B, Bd.5)   **AA103**

Z1001.K615

Leningrad. Publichnaia Biblioteka. Obshchie bibliografii russkikh knig grazhdanskoi pechati, 1708–1955; annotirovannyi ukazatel'. Izd. 2. Leningrad, 1956. 283p. (Bibliografiia russkoi bibliografii)   **AA104**

At head of title: M. V. Sokurova.

1st ed. 1944.

A definitive guide to general bibliographies of Russian books. Gives full description, notes on authors and editors, and citations to pertinent literature and critical reviews. Includes an extensive list of sources, a name index, and chronological chart. The introductory essay on bibliography is by the general editor, P. N. Berkov.

Z2491.A1L43

Mashkova, Mariia Vasil'evna. Istoriia russkoi bibliografii nachala XX veka (do oktiabria 1917 goda). Moskva, Kniga, 1969. 492p.   **AA105**

A history of Russian bibliography of the early 20th century, serving as a continuation of N. V. Zdobnov's work (below). Indexed.   Z2492.5.M36

Zdobnov, Nikolai Vasil'evich. Istoriia russkoi bibliografii do nachala XX veka. Izd. 3. Moskva, Gos. Izd-vo Kul'turnoprosvetitel'noi Lit-ry, 1955. 607p.   **AA106**

1st ed. 1944–47.

Includes bibliographic footnotes.   Z1002.Z42

Uruguay

Musso Ambrosi, Luis Alberto. Bibliografía de bibliografías uruguayas, con aportes a la historia del periodismo en el Uruguay. Montevideo, 1964. 102p.   **AA107**

Lists bibliographies published in or about Uruguay from all periods of that country's history. Classed arrangement; author index.   Z1881.A1M8

Venezuela

Cardozo, Lubio. Bibliografía de bibliografías sobre la literatura venezolana en las bibliotecas de Madrid, Paris y Londres. Maracaibo, Centro de Estudios Literarios de la Univ. del Zulia [y] Centro de Investigaciones Literarias de la Univ. de Los Andes, [1975]. 67p.   **AA108**

An annotated bibliography of about 100 bibliographies.

Z1911.A1C37

Yugoslavia

Bibliografija jugoslovenskih bibliografija, 1945–55, 1956/60. Beograd, Bibliografski Inst. FNRJ, 1958–75. 2v.   **AA109**

Bibliographies on all subjects published in Yugoslavia between 1945 and 1960, in classified arrangement with author and subject indexes. Entries are in Latin characters, with the indication "ćiril" if the work cited is in the Cyrillic alphabet.   Z1002.B5688

UNIVERSAL

Bibliography

See also AA793.

Brunet, Jacques Charles. Manuel du libraire et de l'amateur de livres. 5.éd. originale entièrement refondue et augm. d'un tiers. Paris, Didot, 1860–80. 9v. il.   **AA111**

Facsimile reprint: Berlin, Altmann, 1921–22. 6v.; Paris, Dorbon-Aîné, 1928. 6v.; Copenhagen, Rosenkilde & Bagger, 1966–67. 9v.

v.1–5, Author and title list, A–Z; v.6, Subject index; v.7–8, Supplement, by P. Deschamps and G. Brunet, Author and title list, with subject index in v.8; v.9, Dictionnaire de géographie ancienne et moderne à l'usage du libraire et de l'amateur de livres, par P. Deschamps. 1870.

Brunet's *Manuel* is a general bibliography of rare, important, or noteworthy books not limited to those of any one period or language but especially strong for French and Latin titles and for publications before the 19th century. For each book listed it gives author, full title, place, publisher, date, size, number of volumes, but not generally paging, and, in the case of rare books, bibliographical and critical notes with mention of copies and prices at famous sales, and occasional facsimiles of title pages, printers' marks, etc. The arrangement of the main work (v.1–5) is alphabetical by author and anonymous title, and there are two subject indexes: one in v.6 to the main work and one in v.8 to the supplement. Footnotes throughout v.1–5 refer to titles omitted from the main author list but included in the subject volume (v.6).

Covers much the same ground as Grässe's *Trésor de livres* (AA115) but in general contains a larger portion of French books while Grässe lists more German titles. The two books must often be used together as each lists titles not given in the other.

Z1011.B9M5

Bulletin of bibliography. v.1– , 1897– . Boston, Faxon, 1897– . Quarterly.   **AA112**

Title varies: Apr. 1907–Jan. 1912, *Bulletin of bibliography and magazine subject-index*; Apr. 1912–May/Aug. 1953, *Bulletin of bibliography and dramatic index*; May/Aug. 1956–Oct./Dec. 1978, *Bulletin of bibliography & magazine notes*. Frequency has varied.

Originally devoted to brief bibliographical notes and announcements, reading lists on various topics, and brief bibliographies of interest to librarians, the publication later encompassed indexing features and eventually came to emphasize bibliographies of considerable length on topics in the humanities, social sciences and fine arts; bibliographies of literary figures tended to predominate at various periods. A section of "Births and deaths in the periodical world" (later called "Births, deaths, and magazine notes") quickly became a regular feature and continued through 1978.

A cumulative index to v.1–32 (1897–1975), comp. by Eleanor C. Jones and Margaret L. Pollard, was published in 1977.

Z1007.B94

Enciclopedia de orientación bibliográfica. Director: Tomás Zamarriego. Barcelona, J. Flors, 1964–65. 4v. **AA113**

Contents: v.1, Introducción general; Ciencias religiosas; v.2, Ciencias religiosas; Ciencias humanas; v.3, Ciencias humanas; v.4, Ciencias humanas; Ciencias de la materia y de la vida; Apéndice; Indices.

An annotated subject bibliography with author index; intended as a guide to the best material in all fields. International in scope, but with a heavy concentration of Spanish-language materials and an emphasis on the humanities and religion in particular.

Z1035.7.E5

Georgi, Theophilus. Allgemeines europäisches Bücher-Lexicon. Vor dem Anfange des XVI. seculi bis [1757]. Leipzig, Georgi, 1742–58. 5 pts. and 3 suppl. in 2v. (Repr.: Graz, Akademische Druck- u. Verlagsanstalt, 1966) **AA114**

Pt. 1–4, A–Z; pt.5, French works, A–Z; Suppl. 1–3, 1739–47, 1747–54, 1753–57.

Arranged alphabetically by author, giving, for each work, author, short title, place, publisher, date, price.

Z1012.G35

Grässe, Johann Georg Theodor. Trésor de livres rares et précieux. Dresden, Kuntze, 1859–69. 7v. **AA115**

v.1–6, A–Z; v.7, Supplement.

Facsimile reprints: Paris, Welter, 1900–1901. 8v.; Berlin, Altmann, 1922. 7v.

Based on Brunet (AA111) but contains more entries of German books. Sales prices of books are given.

Z1011.G73

Krieg, Michael O. Mehr nicht erschienen; ein Verzeichnis unvollendet gebliebener Druckwerke. Bad Bocklet, Wien, Walter Krieg Verlag, 1954–58. 2v. (Bibliotheca bibliographica, Bd.II, 1.–2. Teil) **AA116**

A bibliography of works supposed to have been published in several volumes which have never been completed. In the main, the listings are for European publications from the beginning of printing to the early 1930s with emphasis on German works, but some American works are included. In many cases, gives references to bibliographies where the titles are listed.

Z1033.U6K7

Peddie, Robert Alexander. Subject index of books published before 1880. London, Grafton, 1933–48. 4v. **AA117**

1st ser., 1933, 745p.; 2d ser., 1935, 857p.; 3d ser., 1939, 945p.; new ser., 1948, 872p.

Each series furnishes an alphabetical subject list of some 50,000 books in various languages published before 1880 (1881), the date from which the British Museum subject indexes (AA135) continue the record. Includes many small and specific subject entries, e.g., place names, excluding, however, personal names.

The third series includes in its alphabetical arrangement every subject heading used in the three series, with cross references to the first and second series. This record is not continued in the "new series." International in scope, but with a preponderance of English titles.

Z1035.P37

Books in series

Books in series 1876–1949. Original, reprinted, in-print, and out-of-print books, published or distributed in the U.S. in popular, scholarly, and professional series. N.Y., Bowker, [1982]. 3v. (2562p.) **AA118**

Contents: v.1, Series heading index; Subject index to series; Series; v.2, Authors; v.3, Titles.

A chronological predecessor to the ongoing record of series publications cited below. For this compilation the publisher "surveyed all LC cataloging of United States titles back to the inception of LC cataloging, utilizing the resources of Bowker's *American Book Publishing Record 1876–1949* database" (*Pref.*) in order to provide a comprehensive record of publications issued in series. Works are grouped by series title in v.1, with access by authors and titles provided in volumes 2 and 3. An asterisk preceding a series title indicates that the series continues to be listed in the 3d ed. of *Books in series*.

Z1036.B711

Books in series in the United States. [Ed.1–] N.Y., Bowker, [1977–]. Irregular. **AA118a**

1st ed. 1977; 3d ed. 1980 in 3v.

"Original, reprinted, in-print, and out-of-print books, published or distributed in the U.S. in popular, scholarly, and professional series."—*t.p.*

The 1st ed. and its supplement were concerned only with series published 1966 and later. Beginning with the 2d ed., date of publication is no longer a criterion for inclusion. The 3d ed. lists nearly 200,000 titles in over 21,000 series; the contents of that edition are: v.1, Series; v.2, Authors; v.3, Titles.

"In compiling *Books in Series* these sources of series information were reviewed: the Library of Congress *National Union Catalog* and MARC (Machine Readable Cataloging) files; the *Books in Print* Active and Out-of-Print files; series listings included in the *Publishers' Trade List Annual*; publishers' catalogs, brochures or publisher-supplied information; the *American Book Publishing Record 1950–1977* and *1978, 1979, 1980* database, and *Irregular Serials and Annuals*."—*Pref., 3d ed.*

Z1215.B65

Titles in series; a handbook for librarians and students. 3d ed. Metuchen, N.J., Scarecrow Pr., 1978. 4v. **AA119**

Eleanora A. Baer, comp.

1st ed. 1953–60.

Contents: v.1–2, Titles in series; v.3–4, Authors and titles index, Series title index, Directory of publishers.

Lists 69,657 titles appearing in series published throughout the world prior to Jan. 1975. Both numbered and unnumbered series are included. v.1–2 are arranged alphabetically by series title, with series contents listed numerically, chronologically, or alphabetically as appropriate. This edition supersedes earlier editions and their supplements.

AI3.T5

U.S. Library of Congress. Monographic series. Jan./Mar. 1974–82. Wash., Lib. of Congress, 1974–83. 3 qtrly. issues per yr. plus annual cumulation. **AA120**

At head of title: Library of Congress catalogs.

"Compiled and edited by the Catalog Publication Division of the Processing Department, Library of Congress."—*verso of t.p.*

Includes reproductions of Library of Congress printed cards on which a series statement appears in parentheses following the collation. Arrangement is according to series entry which is shown in capital letters preceding the reproduction of the cards for that series. Includes unnumbered as well as numbered series.

Ceased publication with the 1982 cumulation. Superseded by the microform edition of *National union catalog* (AA127).

Z881.U49U54a

Library catalogs

❖Printed catalogs of libraries are useful reference aids to catalogers, reference librarians, and research workers because they supply verification of titles; information about authorship; description of books; editions, contents, or occasional notes which throw light on a reference search; and they often contain analytical or other added entries not given in a particular library's own catalog. They indicate, of course, the location of at least one copy of each title listed. Dictionary and subject catalogs are also useful as subject bibliographies.

The catalogs of the great national libraries, such as the Library of Congress, the British Museum (now the British Library), and the Bibliothèque Nationale, are of particular importance because these libraries are entitled by law to receive copies of all books copyrighted in their respective countries. These catalogs, therefore, are the most comprehensive single records of publications in these countries. National libraries also contain material in many other languages, and their catalogs are often extremely usable records of foreign-language materials.

Numerous printed catalogs of smaller libraries have been issued, only a few of which are listed here. While many of these are old, they may still be useful for bibliographical information and even for locational purposes. A somewhat longer list of American library catalogs is given in Winchell, *Locating books for interlibrary loan*, p.49–55 (AB279), and a more recent listing is Nelson's *Guide to published library catalogs* (AA121). Owing to the high cost of publication, book catalogs were not often produced during the second quarter of this century. With the advance of photo-offset and computer techniques, however, printed catalogs appeared in considerable numbers during the 1960s and 1970s.

Bibliography

Nelson, Bonnie R. A guide to published library catalogs. Metuchen, N.J., Scarecrow Pr., 1982. 342p.   **AA121**

Includes 429 numbered entries for published catalogs in 33 subject sections. Lengthy annotations; subject index and index of libraries.   Z710.N44

Winans, Robert B. A descriptive checklist of book catalogues separately printed in America, 1693–1800. Worcester, American Antiquarian Society, 1981. 207p.   **AA122**

Lists and describes separately published book catalogs "issued in America prior to 1801 by booksellers, publishers, book auctioneers, circulating libraries, social libraries, college libraries, and private libraries."—*Introd.* Chronological arrangement. Lists 278 located items (plus 8 others not known to be extant but for which there is good evidence of publication) and some 393 unnumbered entries for unlocated items, many or most of which "may be bibliographic ghosts." Indexed.   Z1029.W56

National libraries

❖The author catalogs of the Library of Congress–National Union Catalog series represented in the entries AA123–AA127 vary in title, form, and coverage as indicated in the combined annotation. These are complemented by the subject catalog, AA130.

U.S. Library of Congress. A catalog of books represented by Library of Congress printed cards, issued to July 31, 1942. Ann Arbor, Mich., Edwards, 1942–46. 167v. (Repr.: N.Y., Rowman & Littlefield)   **AA123**

———— ———— Supplement: cards issued Aug. 1, 1942–Dec. 31, 1947. Ann Arbor, Mich., Edwards, 1948. 42v. (Repr.: N.Y., Rowman & Littlefield)

Library of Congress author catalog: a cumulative list of works represented by Library of Congress printed cards, 1948–1952. Ann Arbor, Mich., Edwards, 1953. 24v. (Repr.: N.Y., Rowman & Littlefield)   **AA124**

Contents: v.1–23, Authors; v.24, Films.

National union catalog: a cumulative author list representing Library of Congress printed cards and titles reported by other American libraries, 1953–1957. Ann Arbor, Mich., Edwards, 1958. 28v.   **AA125**

Contents: v.1–26, Authors; v.27, Music and phonorecords; v.28, Motion pictures and filmstrips.

———— 1958–1962. N.Y., Rowman & Littlefield, 1963. 54v.

Contents: v.1–50, Authors; v.51–52, Music and phonorecords; v.53–54, Motion pictures and filmstrips.

———— 1963–1967. Ann Arbor, Mich., Edwards, 1969. 72v.

Contents: v.1–59, Authors; v.60–67, Register of additional locations; [v.68–70], Music and phonorecords; [v.71–72], Motion pictures and filmstrips.

———— 1952–1955 imprints: an author list representing Library of Congress printed cards and titles reported by other American libraries. Ann Arbor, Mich., Edwards, 1961. 30v.

Compiled by the Library of Congress under the auspices of the Committee on Resources of American Libraries of the American Library Association.   Z663.7.L512

National union catalog: a cumulative author list. Wash., Lib. of Congress, Card Division. Monthly, with quarterly and annual cumulations.   **AA126**

Because of the immensity of the collections, the excellence of the cataloging, and the full bibliographical descriptions, the *Catalog* of the Library of Congress has been for many years an invaluable work in any library and indispensable in those where research is done. Of first importance in cataloging, acquisition, and reference work, and for the bibliographer and research worker, it is valuable for author bibliography, verification of titles, bibliographical information, historical notes, location of copies, etc.

History: Until 1942, the catalog was produced only on cards, and to make the information available outside of Washington, "depository sets" were placed in various large libraries in different sections of the country. These sets consisted of main entry cards only and were kept up to date by the addition of new cards as printed. To make the catalog even more generally accessible, the Association of Research Libraries, in 1942, sponsored the photographic reproduction of a depository catalog and its publication in book form. The cards were photographed and printed in reduced size. The main catalog includes all cards printed from 1898 to July 31, 1942; the *Supplement,* those issued Aug. 1, 1942–Dec. 31, 1947.

Scope: It is an author and main entry catalog (with cross references but not added entries) of books and other materials for which Library of Congress printed cards were available in: (1) the Library of Congress (as cards had not been printed for all the Library's books, the catalog is not a complete record of the Library's holdings, but does represent a large percentage); (2) many government department libraries; and (3) various libraries throughout the country, as a result of the cooperative cataloging program.

Information given is detailed and represents a high degree of accuracy, usually including, as pertinent: full name of author, dates of birth and death; full title; place, publisher, and date; collation (paging, illustrations, maps, tables, size, etc.); series; edition; notes on contents, history, etc.; tracing for subject headings and added entries; LC class number, sometimes Dewey class number, and LC card number. Frequently a considerable amount of analysis is noted for composite books, sets, periodicals, etc.

1942–1947: It should be noted that the *Supplement* and later cumulations contain cards issued during the periods covered regardless of the imprint date of the book recorded, and revised cards are treated in the same manner as new ones. The *Supplement* also includes some 26,000 title entries for anonymous and pseudonymous works for which the Library of Congress had supplied the authors, the so-called bracketed authors. The title entries were made by crossing out the author's name; the card was then filed under title. For those cards which were printed before Aug. 1942, the author card will be in the main set; for cards printed Aug. 1942–1947, in the *Supplement.*

1948–1952: In this and the following series, besides main entries and cross references for books, pamphlets, maps, music scores, periodicals, and other serials, essential added entries are included. Motion pictures and filmstrips are grouped in v.24.

1953–1957: The great innovation in this period was the move toward a *National union catalog,* by the inclusion of monographs not represented by LC printed cards, reported by some 500 other North American libraries, together with the indication of location of titles by the symbols of libraries. Includes printed cards in all languages written in the Roman, Cyrillic, Greek, Gaelic, or Hebraic alphabets and contains entries for books, pamphlets, maps and atlases, periodicals, and other serials. *Motion pictures and filmstrips* and *Music and phonorecords* are now published separately (*see* BG221, BH91). All serials represented by LC printed cards are included, but holdings of serials not cataloged by the Library of Congress are omitted and listed in *New serial titles* (AE183).

1958–1962: Coverage was expanded to include cards in the Arabic and Indic alphabets and in Chinese, Japanese, and Korean characters. The number of libraries reporting holdings increased to about 750.

(As an aid to faster searching, the four series covering the 1942–62 period have been cumulated and published as: *Library of Congress and national union catalog author lists, 1942–1962: a master cumulation,* comp. by the editorial staff of the Gale Research Company. Detroit, Gale, 1969. 152v.)

1968–1982: Concurrent with, and following the publication of the pre-1956 and the 1956–67 segments of the *NUC* listed below, the catalog continued to appear monthly, with quarterly and annual cumulations. (Quinquennial cumulations were commercially published: 1968–72 by J. W. Edwards, Ann Arbor, Mich.; 1973–77 by Rowman and Littlefield, Totowa, N.J.; no 1978–82 cumulation has yet appeared.) Paper bookform editions ceased with the 1982 issues, and a microfiche edition (AA127) began publication in 1983.

National union catalog, 1952–1955: This series, supplementary to the regular set, and not included in its chronological sequence, lists titles previously included in earlier catalogs with additional locations, as well as newly reported titles, many not represented by LC printed cards. The catalog is not fully edited so that there may be some duplication under variant forms of entry, but cross references are given whenever possible.

Beginning 1983, issued in microform as:

National union catalog. Books [microform]. Jan. 1983– . Wash., Lib. of Congress, 1983– . Monthly. Microfiche.
AA127

Represents entries for works cataloged by the Library of Congress, together with catalog entries prepared by about 1,100 contributing libraries. Supersedes the paper editions of *National union catalog* (AA126), the *Subject catalog* (AA131), the *Chinese cooperative catalog* (AA679), and *Monographic series* (AA120). Includes books, pamphlets, some typescripts, map atlases, monographic microform publications, and monographic government publications. Priority of processing is given to post-1955 publications, but all imprints are included, regardless of date. Entries for nonroman language materials are given in romanized form only. For printed monographs, at least one library location is given.

Utilizes a "register/index" format. Full bibliographic citations (i.e., all information traditionally found on Library of Congress cards) appear in a separate register in a numbered sequence according to the order in which the items were entered. Access to the register is provided by separate indexes for (1) names used as main or added entry; (2) titles; (3) LC series; and (4) LC subjects. Indexes display a shortened form of the record, with reference to the register number for full information; the indexes are cumulative.

For related microform publications of the Library of Congress *see National union catalog. U.S. books* (1983–), *National union catalog. Audiovisual materials* (AA539), *National union catalog. Cartographic materials* (1983–), and *National union catalog. Register of additional locations* (AA129).

National union catalog, pre-1956 imprints. A cumulative author list representing Library of Congress printed cards and titles reported by other American libraries. [London], Mansell, 1968–80. 685v.
AA128

"Comp. and ed. with the cooperation of the Library of Congress

and the National Union Catalog Subcommittee of the Resources and Technical Services Division, American Library Association."— *title page.*

Supersedes the basic Library of Congress *Catalog of books . . .* and its *Supplement,* 1942–47; the *Library of Congress author catalog, 1948–1952;* the *National union catalog, 1952–1955 imprints;* and the *National union catalog . . . 1953–1957.* (The 1953–57 cumulation is fully superseded because, in anticipation of the present compilation, 1956–57 imprints were repeated in the 1958–62 cumulation of the *National union catalog.* However, the volumes for motion pictures, filmstrips, and phonorecords—v.24 of the 1948–52 cumulation; v.27–28 of the 1953–57 set—should not be discarded since these materials are not included in the new catalog.)

In addition to cumulating the entries in the above-mentioned catalogs, this monumental work incorporates entries from the Union Catalog card file at the Library of Congress. Thus it is "a repertory of the cataloged holdings of selected portions of the cataloged collections of the major research libraries of the United States and Canada, plus the more rarely held items in the collections of selected smaller and specialized libraries."—*Introd.* The completed set encompasses some 10 million entries and indicates locations in more than 700 libraries. As the work progressed, pre-1956 imprints reported by participating libraries were added up to about a year before publication of the volume in which the work was entered.

Reference librarians will want to familiarize themselves with the introductory matter relevant to scope, form of entries, etc. In general, the catalog includes entries for books, pamphlets, maps, atlases, and music. Serials are listed if represented by an LC printed card or if separately reported by another library; similarly, individual manuscripts are represented if so reported. Works in Cyrillic, Hebrew, Chinese, Japanese, and other non-Latin alphabets are included only if represented by an LC printed card. *See* and *see also* references are provided; added entries are included in specified circumstances.

v.53–56 (the Bible) did not appear until 1980; *see* BB104 for a note on that sequence. v.609–24 have been reprinted with title: *United States government publications: an author index representing pre-1956 holdings of American libraries . . .* (London, Mansell, 1981. 16v.).

An interesting account of the publishing history of the pre-1956 *NUC* may be found in W. J. Walsh's article, "Last of the monumental book catalogs," in *American libraries* 12:464–68 (Sept. 1981).
Z881.A1U518

Supplementary volumes continue the numbering of the basic set:

—————— Supplement. [London], Mansell, 1980–81. v.686–754.

The supplement is "designed to accommodate the mass of material that has accumulated since the editorial work was begun in 1967. Since then . . . over three million cards have cumulated in those parts of the alphabet previously published."—*Introd.* Entries represent reports from contributing libraries and cards generated by project editors; they comprise (1) new titles; (2) new editions of titles already listed; (3) added entries and cross references supplied by the editorial staff. A separate section at the end of each supplementary volume records additional locations for items already listed (i.e., for items whose initial listings included less than one full line of location symbols). Reports from contributing libraries received to Aug. 1977 and Library of Congress cards received to Aug. 1979 are included.
Z881.A1U518

National union catalog, 1956 through 1967. A cumulative author list representing Library of Congress printed cards and titles reported by other American libraries. Totowa, N.J., Rowman and Littlefield, [1970–72]. 125v.   **AA128a**

"A new and augmented twelve-year catalog being a compilation into one alphabet of the fourth & fifth supplements of the National Union Catalog with a key to additional locations through 1967 and with a unique identifying number allocated to each title. . . . The present compilation is the work of the Cataloging and Editorial staffs of Rowman and Littlefield."—*title page.*

Offers a cumulation of the 1958–62 and 1963–67 quinquennial supplements to the *National union catalog* (AA125). Inasmuch as 1956–57 imprints were repeated in the 1958–62 supplement, this new set serves as a continuation to the *National union catalog, pre-1956 imprints* (AA128). An important feature is the designation of those items for which further locations are given in the *Register of additional locations* (below) as cumulated in the 1963–67 supplement. Added locations are cited in a separate section at the end of each volume of the new set.

National union catalog . . . Register of additional locations. June, 1965–79. Wash., Lib. of Congress, 1965–80. Annual.
AA129

Notes additional locations of titles included in the *National union catalog* (AA125) reported after the annual or quinquennial cumulations have been published. A cumulation of the early volumes of the *Register* was issued as v.60–67 of the 1963–67 quinquennial cumulation of the *National union catalog* and included "additional locations for titles with post-1955 imprints in the 1958–62 and 1963–67 quinquennial cumulations."—*Introd.*

Comprises two lists: one arranged by Library of Congress card number; the other by main entry and representing only those titles for which no card number appears in the *Catalog.*

The 1979 annual was the last to appear in book form. Continued in microform as:

———— ———— Cumulative microform edition, 1968/79– . Wash., Lib. of Congress, 1980– . Annual. Microfiche.

"The cumulative microform edition includes the following: (1) the locations for the 68 to 79 card number series in the 1968–1972 quinquennial, (2) the locations published in the 1973 and later annuals, and (3) the locations currently in process that have been added to the automated file, but not yet published in hard copy."— *1968/79 cum., fiche 1.*

The 1979 annual was the last *RAL* to appear in book form. Using 1968 as the base year, each annual "Cumulative microform edition" provides an update of the complete file.

Library of Congress catalog. Books: subjects, 1950–1954. A cumulative list of works represented by Library of Congress printed cards. Ann Arbor, Mich., Edwards, 1955. 20v.
AA130

———— ———— 1955–1959. Paterson, N.J., Pageant Books, 1960. 22v.; 1960–1964. Ann Arbor, Edwards, 1965. 25v.; 1965–1969. Ann Arbor, Edwards, 1970. 42v.; 1970–1974. Totowa, N.J., Rowman & Littlefield, 1976. 100v.

Quinquennial cumulations of a publication of the same title issued by the Library of Congress on a quarterly basis, cumulating annually. An alphabetical subject arrangement of entries for publications which were cataloged or recataloged during the periods covered, by the Library of Congress and libraries participating in the cooperative cataloging program, and which are represented by LC printed cards. Included are the types of material in the languages indicated for the *National union catalog* (AA126). From 1950 to 1952, maps, motion pictures, and music scores were also included, but from 1953 on, these were issued separately. (*Maps and atlases,* issued separately 1953–55, was discontinued, and those entries are included in the 1955–59 cumulation.) Originally included entries for publications with imprint dates of 1945 or later which had been currently cataloged, but pre-1945 items newly cataloged or recataloged were subsequently added in the annual cumulations.
Continued by: Z881.U49A22

U.S. Library of Congress. Subject catalog. Jan./Mar. 1975–1982. Wash., 1975–84. Quarterly, with annual cumulation.
AA131

At head of title: Library of Congress catalogs.
Represents a change of title for *Library of Congress catalog. Books: subjects* (above) and continues the coverage of that publication. Ceased with the annual cumulation for 1982, being superseded by the microform edition of the *National union catalog* (AA127). No plans have been announced for a cumulation of the 1975–82 volumes.

British Museum. Dept. of Printed Books. General catalogue of printed books. Photolithographic edition to 1955. London, Trustees, 1959–66 [v.1, 1965]. 263v.
AA132

Previous complete edition (entitled *Catalogue of printed books*),

1881–1900. 95v.; Supplement, 1900–1905. 13v. (Photographic reprint: Ann Arbor, Mich., Edwards Bros., 1946–50)

v.1–51, A–Dezw, of a new catalog were published between 1931 and 1954, but mounting costs caused its discontinuance. These volumes included entries cataloged up to the time of the publication of each volume and reflected much recataloging and revision of the previous catalog.

In 1959 the Trustees began to issue, by photo-offset lithography, the Working Catalogue of the Reading Room, covering books cataloged through 1955, without further editing but with the manuscript amendments which were contained in the volumes. Publication began with v.52 and continued through the alphabet, after which v.1–51 were brought up to 1955 to conform to the rest of the set and were reproduced in the same manner.

The catalog is a complete record of the printed books in the Library of the British Museum (now the British Library), which have appeared from the 15th century to the end of 1955, in all languages except the Oriental. The Library is particularly important because of the extent and richness of its collections in all fields and in all languages, and also because its possession of the copyright privilege helps make it the most comprehensive collection of British publications in existence. Its catalog, therefore, is an indispensable bibliographical source for the scholar and librarian. In the main, it is an author catalog only, with catchword title entries, cross references for anonymous books, etc. Subject entries are included to a limited extent, principally for the following: (1) under personal names, biographical works are included; (2) under countries, e.g., England, France, etc., are entered official publications, some works about the country, and many titles in which the name of the country occurs; and (3) under names of sacred books, e.g., Bible, Kur'an, etc., are entered both texts and works about them. Two important reference features are: (1) the large amount of analytical material included (analysis of series, etc.), and (2) the many cross references from names of editors, translators, or other personal names.

The amount of bibliographical information varies; titles taken from the 19th-century catalog usually include only author, title, editor, place, and date, whereas more recent cataloging adds publisher, paging, and size. Some cataloging for early printed books is fairly full.

Special sections to be noted include: Bible (3v. with index); England (5v. with index); Liturgies; London (3v. with index); Periodical publications (3v.). These serve as comprehensive bibliographies of these areas. For Academies *see* CA117. Z921.B87

———— ———— Ten-year supplement, 1956–1965. London, Trustees, 1968. 50v.

———— ———— Five-year supplement, 1966–1970. London, Trustees, 1971–72. 26v.

A series of annual volumes of *Additions* to the *General catalogue* began to appear in 1964, but covered the period 1963–65 only. Entries from those volumes were included in the 10-year supplement, 1956–65.

Although the National Reference Library of Science and Invention (formerly the Patent Office Library) was amalgamated with the British Museum in 1966, its holdings are not recorded in the *General catalogue* nor in the 1966–70 supplement. Attention is called to some arrears in cataloging of United Kingdom materials published 1966–67, and the *BNB* will have to be consulted for those years. Greater conformity with the Anglo-American cataloging rules is evident in the supplements, and recently cataloged periodicals are entered under title instead of the uniform "Periodical publications" heading (although the latter is also employed).

British Library. General catalogue of printed books. Five year supplement. 1971–1975. [London], publ. for the British Library by British Museum Pubns., Ltd., [1978]. 13v.

Nearly 600,000 entries ("About 400,000 main entries with added entries and references"-*Pref.*) for works cataloged 1971–1975. Described as the "Third and last" supplement to the British Museum *General Catalogue*; later information is to be made available through "the products and services derived from the British Library data base" of machine readable-records.

For a cumulation of the main catalog and its supplements through 1975 *see* AA134.
Continued by:

—— General catalogue of printed books, 1976–1982. [Microform] London, British Library, Reference Division, [1982]. 402 microfiches. **AA133**

A continuation of the "BM catalog" (above), this is a "COM" product from MARC records; it provides entries for (1) authors, editors, and corporate bodies; (2) most titles; and (3) persons and publications as subjects. Entries beginning with numbers or symbols appear ahead of the alphabetical sequence. Materials listed are those dated 1976 and later, plus some 1971–75 publications cataloged since preparation of the *General catalogue* supplement covering that period.

—— The British Library general catalogue of printed books to 1975. London, Bingley; London [etc.], K. G. Saur, 1979–84. v. 1–292. (In progress) **AA134**

To be in 360 vol. distr. in the Americas by Gale.

Contents: v.1–292, A–Schle.

"The present printed edition of the *General Catalogue* has been designed to accommodate, in one alphabetic sequence, a complex series of earlier published catalogues: GK1, the first printed catalogue of real substance; GK2, the revision begun in 1931 for the letters A–DEZ; GK3, the photo lithographic cumulated edition begun in 1956 with its three Supplements [*see* above] In addition, the present catalogue will incorporate the many thousands of additions and corrections inserted in the working copies."—*Foreword*

The great advantage of this set is the cumulative aspect which obviates the need to consult supplements as well as the basic volumes, but libraries owning the earlier sets will need to weigh the frequency of use against the very considerable cost of the cumulation. An early review in the *Times Literary Supplememt* (Apr. 4, 1980, p.398) mentions that a "D" prefixed to a shelfmark indicates that the book was destroyed during World War II, although this is not explained in the preface. Z921.L553B74

British Museum. Dept. of Printed Books. Subject index of the modern works added to the library, 1881–1900, ed. by G. K. Fortescue. London, 1902–1903. 3v. **AA135**

Supersedes earlier indexes published for this period. Continued by 5-year supplements as follows:

—— —— 1901–1905, 1906–10, 1911–15, 1916–20, 1921–25, 1926–30, 1931–35 (2v.), 1936–40 (2v.), 1941–45, 1946–50 (4v.), 1951–55 (6v.), 1956–60 (6v). London. 1906–74.

Title varies slightly.

For *Subject index of books published before 1880, see* Peddie (AA117).

An alphabetical subject catalog of the modern works added to the library since 1881. Contains entries for well over 925,000 titles, but is sometimes difficult to use. Subjects are often general rather than specific, with many subheadings, and there is no table of headings used, although there are many cross references. Arrangement under headings is neither alphabetical nor chronological. Bibliographical information usually includes author, brief title, paging, place, and date. Personal names are not included as these are covered in the *General catalogue*.

Various changes were made in the subject heading terminology in the 1956–60 index, many new headings having been added, and some former subheads standing as subject headings in their own right.

Continued by: Z1035.B86

British Library. Dept. of Printed Books. Subject index of modern books acquired, 1961–1970. London, British Library, 1982. 12v. **AA136**

A continuation of the above, adding about 400,000 entries.

Deutscher Gesamtkatalog, hrsg. von der Preussischen Staatsbibliothek. . . . Berlin, Preussische Druckerei- u. Verlags Aktiengesellschaft, 1931–39. v.1–14. **AA137**

v.1–14, A–Beethordnung. No more published.

v.1–8 had title *Gesamtkatalog der preussischen Bibliotheken* and listed books contained in about 18 important libraries. With v.9, 1936, beginning the letter B, the scope was changed to include the contents of some 100 German and Austrian libraries—an ambitious undertaking, unfortunately suspended because of the war. The few volumes published show that, for the letters covered, the work is (1) indispensable for catalogers, reference workers, and bibliographical investigation generally, in the matter of German publications, and (2) useful for non-German subjects, also, as it contains much foreign material in many languages, including English works not listed in the British Museum catalog (AA132) and French works not listed in the catalog of the Bibliothèque Nationale (AA140).

Arranged alphabetically by author and anonymous title; includes books published up to 1930. The cataloging is detailed and exact, and for this reason the volumes issued are still useful. Z929.A1D4

Deutscher Gesamtkatalog. Neue Titel. Berlin, Staatsbibliothek, 1892–1944. **AA138**

Issued weekly (frequency varies slightly), with quarterly and annual cumulations which supplement the *Deutscher Gesamtkatalog* (above).

Title varies. 1910–37 had title *Berliner Titeldrucke*.

Partially cumulated into:

Berlin. Preussische Staatsbibliothek. Berliner Titeldrucke; fünfjahrs Katalog, 1930/34–1935/39. Berlin, Staatsbibliothek, 1935–40. **AA139**

Each cumulation issued in 8v. A–Z, paged continuously.

No more published.

Title varies: 1935/39 called *Deutscher Gesamtkatalog. Neue Titel.*

Lists works published 1930–39 cataloged in more than 100 German libraries, thus supplementing the *Deutscher Gesamtkatalog*.

After World War II the *Berliner Titeldrucke* was continued in part by the following three series: (1) Berliner Titeldrucke. Neue Folge. Zugänge aus der Sowjetunion und den europäischen Ländern der Volksdemokratie. Jahreskatalog, 1954–59 (publ. 1956–62); (2) Berliner Titeldrucke. Neuerwerbungen ausländischer Literatur der wissenschaftlichen Bibliotheken der Deutschen Demokratischen Republik. Reihe, A, B, 1960–63; (3) Berliner Titeldrucke. Neuerwerbungen ausländischer Literatur wissenschaftlicher Bibliotheken der Deutschen Demokratischen Republik. Jahreskatalog, 1964– . Z929.B5N15

Paris. Bibliothèque Nationale. Catalogue général des livres imprimés: Auteurs. Paris, Impr. Nationale, 1900–81. 231v. **AA140**

An important modern catalog, the value of which cannot be overestimated. An alphabetical author catalog, including only entries under names of personal authors, with the necessary cross references; does not include title entries for anonymous books or entries for anonymous classics, periodicals or society transactions or government or corporate authors. The cataloging is excellent; the information given includes author's full name whenever possible, title, place, publisher, date, edition, paging or volumes, format, and occasional notes of contents, original publication in case of reprints from periodicals, etc. An important reference feature, in the case of authors whose works are voluminous, is the detailed alphabetical title index under the author's name, which indicates in what volumes or editions a given work may be found, and also indicates alternative and changed titles. In addition to its comprehensive coverage of French publications, the catalog is particularly strong in other Romance-language and classical materials.

Originally each volume included titles acquired up to the date of publication of that particular volume, so that there is a wide spread in coverage between the first volumes published in 1900 and those issued half a century later. Beginning with v.189, however, no imprints after 1959 have been included, and this policy continues through the end of the alphabet. Z927.P2

Supplemented by:

—— Catalogue général des livres imprimés: auteurs—collectivités-auteurs—anonymes, 1960–1969. Paris, Impr. Nationale, 1972–78. 27v. **AA141**

Contents: Série 1, t.1–23, Caractères latins et caractères grecs; Série 2, t.1, Caractères hébraïques; t.2–3, Caractères cyrilliques; t.4, Caractères arabes.

Supersedes a 1960–64 supplement published 1965–67 in 12v.
Z927.P1957

Rome. Centro Nazionale per il Catalogo Unico delle Biblio-teche Italiane e per le Informazioni Bibliografiche. Primo catalogo collettivo delle biblioteche italiane. Roma, 1962–79. v.1–9. (In progress) **AA143**

Contents: v.1–9, A–Barq.

A first effort toward a national union catalog for Italy. Locates copies in eight collections of the Biblioteche statali in Rome and in the Biblioteche Nazionali in Rome, Florence, Milan, and Naples. Includes works published 1500–1957. A main-entry catalog with entries for anonymous titles, academies, etc.; cross references. Progress on the catalog was seriously delayed as a result of the Florence flood of 1966, and survival of numerous Florentine copies reported in at least the first six volumes is open to question.
Z933.A1R6

Nonnational libraries

United States

Center for Research Libraries. The Center for Research Libraries catalog [microform]. 1st [1982 microfiche] ed. Chicago, CRL, 1982. 229 microfiches. **AA144**

Supersedes the Center's printed catalogs for monographs (published 1969–70; 5v.) and for serials (publ. 1972; 2v.) and includes materials cataloged through July 16, 1982. Approximately 400,000 cards in dictionary arrangement. Annual supplements are planned.
Z881.C512

Harvard University. Library. Widener Library shelflist. Cambridge, Publ. by the Harvard Univ. Lib.; distr. by the Harvard Univ. Pr., 1965–79. no.1–60. **AA145**

This is a series of computer-produced shelflists, each volume of which is devoted to a single classification or a segment of a large class of cataloged materials in the Widener Library. Most numbers are in four parts: (1) a copy of the classification schedule which serves as a key to the second part; (2) a list of the entries in call-number sequence; (3) an alphabetical listing by author or anonymous title; and (4) a chronological listing by date of publication.

Although originally intended primarily for use at the Widener Library, the lists are useful elsewhere as good subject bibliographies, especially so in view of the rich resources of the Harvard collections. In addition, they are being maintained on a current basis so that printouts for supplements or updated editions can be published as desired.

Numbers published are: no.1, Crusades (superseded by no. 32); no.2, Africa (superseded by no.34); no.3, Twentieth century Russian literature (BD1335); no.4, Russian history since 1917 (DC529); no.5–6, Latin America and Latin American periodicals (DB244); no.7, Bibliography and bibliography periodicals (AA24); no.8, Reference collections (superseded by no.33); no.9–13, American history (DB30); no.14, China, Japan, and Korea (DE124); no.15, Periodical classes (AE5); no.16–17, Education and education periodicals (CB14); no.18, Literature: general and comparative (BD8); no.19, Southern Asia (DE88); no.20, Canadian history and literature (BD765); no.21, Latin American literature (BD1194); no.22, Government (CJ19); no.23–24, Economics (CH12); no.25, Celtic literatures; no.26–27, American literature (BD368); no.28–31, Slavic history and literatures (DC46); no.32, General European and world history (DA9); no.33, Reference collections shelved in the Reading Room and Acquisitions Department (AA485; supersedes no.8); no.34, African history and literatures (DD10; supersedes no.2); no. 35–38, English literature (BD500); no.39, Judaica (BB546); no.40, Finnish and Baltic history and literatures (DC125); no.41, Spanish history and literature (DC488); no.42–43, Philosophy and psychology (BA17); no.44, Hungarian history and literature (DC357); no.45–46, Sociology (CC6); no.47–48, French literature (BD960); no. 49–50, German literature (BD816); no.51–52, Italian history and literature (DC394); no. 53–54, British history (DC236); no.55, Ancient history (DA84); no.56, Archaeology (DA85); no.57, Classical studies (BD1377); no.58, Ancient Greek literature (BD1402);

no.59, Latin literature (BD1422); v.60, Geography and anthropology (CL28).

New York. Public Library. Research Libraries. Dictionary catalog of the Research Libraries of the New York Public Library, 1911–1971. [N.Y.], New York Public Library, Astor, Lenox, and Tilden Foundations (distr. by G. K. Hall), [1979–83]. 800v. **AA146**

The 1911 date of the title refers to the opening of the Central Building of the New York Public Library when the newly created card catalog (in preparation for many years) was first available to the public. Thus, this catalog "represents the holdings of book and book-like materials of The Research Libraries . . . as they were developed between 1895 and 1971 [the date after which the book catalog, AA147, was adopted], and includes entries for the holdings of three predecessor collections—those of the Astor Library, Lenox Library, and the library of Samuel Jones Tilden—that became part of the present Library upon their consolidation in 1895."—*p.xxiii.* Includes books, periodicals (together with some indexing of contents of periodicals), and other media in most fields of human knowledge—one of the world's great collections. Reproduces about nine million cards.

"The major part of the collections is represented . . . , including materials for general research, history and the humanities, the social sciences, science and technology, history of the Americas, local history and genealogy, art and architecture, and rare books. It includes entries for parts of the collections of music, dance, theatre, Orientalia, Baltica, Slavonica, and Judaica. It does not include certain forms of material such as manuscripts, maps, prints, etc."—*p.xxiii.*
Z881.N59

——— Dictionary catalog of the Research Libraries; a cumulative list of authors, titles, and subjects representing materials added to the collections beginning January 1, 1972. [N.Y.], Library, [1972–July 1981]. **AA147**

Monthly cumulative supplements, with annual re-cumulations of the full set.

A computer-produced, ongoing record of materials (regardless of publication date) newly added to this important research collection.

Publication was suspended after the July 1981 supplement. "Interim indexes" are issued irregularly for in-house use, but not made generally available.
Z881.N588D5

Great Britain

[Crawford, James Ludovic Lindsay, 26th Earl of]. Bibliotheca Lindesiana . . . Catalogue of the printed books preserved at Haigh Hall, Wigan, co. pal. Lancast. . . . Aberdeen, Univ. Pr., 1910. 4v. **AA148**

The library of a rich general collection which includes many rarities and incunabula.

Additional volumes published with continuing volume numbers: v.5–6, *A bibliography of royal proclamations of the Tudor and Stuart sovereigns and of others published under authority 1485–1714.* Oxford, Clarendon Pr., 1910. 2v.; v.7, *A bibliography . . . of philately.* Aberdeen, Univ. Pr., 1911. 924col. (*see* BF182). Z997.L739

London Library. Catalogue, by C. T. Hagberg Wright and C. J. Purnell. London, 1913–14. 2v. **AA149**

An author catalog of a library of more than 250,000 volumes. This edition incorporates the material of the 1st ed., 1903, and the eight annual supplements to that edition.

——— ——— Supplement, 1913–20, 1920–28, 1928–50. London, 1920–53. 3v.

The 3d supplement adds some 150,000 titles.

——— Subject index of the London Library . . . by C. T. Hagberg Wright. London, 1909–55. v.1–4. **AA150**

v.1, Main subject list; v.2, Additions, 1909–22, by C. T. Hagberg Wright and C. J. Purnell; v.3, Additions, 1923–38; v.4, Additions, 1938–53.
Z921.L6

Oxford. University. Bodleian Library. Catalogus librorum impressorum Bibliothecae Bodleianae in Academia Oxoniensi. . . . Oxford, e Typographeo Academico, 1843–51. 4v.
AA151

An author catalog. v.1–3 included holdings to 1835, with the Gough, Douce, and Oppenheimer collections, academic dissertations, and music excluded. v.4 is a supplementary volume listing accessions of the 1835–47 period.
Z921.O93

Festschriften

See also AA1116–AA1117.

Leistner, Otto. Internationale Bibliographie der Festschriften mit Sachregister. International Bibliography of Festschriften with subject-index. Osnabrück, Biblio Verlag, 1976. 893p.
AA152

The "list of Festschriften arranged by name of the personality or institution honoured" (which provides the citations to the homage volumes) is followed by a subject index to the general content of the works cited. There is no list of the individual essays and their contributors, and therefore no specific subject indexing of the contents. A "list of frequently employed terms in foreign languages with German and English translations," and a section of "general abbreviations" completes the volume.
The first volume of a new edition has appeared as:
Z1033.F4L43

—— Internationale Bibliographie der Festschriften von den Anfängen bis 1979, mit Sachregister. International bibliography of Festschriften from the beginnings until 1979, with subject index. 2d enl. ed. Osnabrück, Biblio-Verlag, 1984– . v.1– .
AA153

To be in 2v.
Kept up-to-date by:

Internationale Jahresbibliographie der Festschriften . . . mit Verzeichnis aller Beiträge, einem Autorenregister und einem Sachregister zu den Festschriften. Jahrg. 1– , 1980– . Osnabrück, Biblio Verlag, 1982– . Annual.
AA154

At head of title: IJBF.
Title (*International annual bibliography of Festschriften*) and preface also in English.
Intended as a continuation of the 2d ed. of Otto Leistner's *Internationale Bibliographie der Festschriften* which covers through 1979. *Festschriften* are listed alphabetically in the first section under the name of the person or institution honored, with full bibliographic information and a list of the contents of each. (A number of volumes are listed without contents, and these are to be analyzed in subsequent issues.) An author index of contributions gives reference to the name of the honoree, as does the subject index (i.e., subject entries refer to the overall content of the *Festschrift*, not to specific contributions). A subject index using English terms gives reference to the corresponding German headings.

New York. Public Library. Research Libraries. Guide to *Festschriften*. Boston, G. K. Hall, 1977. 2v.
AA155

Contents: v.1, The retrospective *Festschriften* collection of the New York Public Library: materials cataloged through 1971; v.2, A dictionary of *Festschriften* in the New York Public Library (1972–1976) and the Library of Congress (1968–1976).
The first volume is a reproduction of the catalog cards for "over 6,000 *Festschriften* collected by NYPL over a fifty-year period, ending in December, 1971" *(Introd.)*, and therefore includes some imprints prior to the 1920s. Unfortunately this is a main-entry arrangement only, with no cross references from names of honorees, editors, etc., and no subject approach. v.2, an infinitely more satisfactory compilation, is a computer-produced dictionary catalog of *Festschriften* added to the NYPL collections 1972–76, plus entries for *Festschriften* available in the Library of Congress MARC data base 1968–76. It offers multiple access: main entry, secondary entries (for editors, persons honored, etc.), and subjects.
Z1033.F4N48

Microforms and reproductions

Dodson, Suzanne Cates. Microform research collections: a guide. 2d ed. Westport, Conn., Microform Review, [1984]. 670p. (Meckler Publishing ser. in library micrographhics management, 9)
AA156

1st ed. 1978.
A title listing of about 375 microform research collections. As far as possible, information given for each includes publisher, date, format, price, reference to published reviews, notes on arrangement and bibliographic control, bibliographies or indexes which serve as keys to the collection, and notes on scope and content of the collection. Index of authors, editors, compilers, and titles (including variant titles) of the microform collections and of the bibliographies, indexes, etc., upon which they are based. A valuable work for the reference librarian, the acquisitions librarian, and the cataloger.
Another volume in the same publisher's series is Ann Niles's *An index to microform collections* (Westport, Conn., Meckler, 1984. 891p.) which provides author and title approaches to 26 microform series "which seem to present the most problems for users, namely those containing monographs."—*Introd.*
Z1033.M5D64

Guide to microforms in print. Author, title. 1978– . Westport, Conn., Microform Review, 1978– . Annual.
AA157
Z1033.M5G8

Guide to microforms in print. Subject. 1978– . Westport, Conn., Microform Review, 1978– . Annual.
AA158

The items above are companion compilations replacing three earlier publications: *Guide to microforms in print* (1961–77), *Subject guide to microforms in print* (1962/63–77) and *International microforms in print* (1974/75). They provide "a cumulative annual listing of microform titles, comprising books, journals, newspapers, government publications, archival material, collections and other projects, etc. [excepting theses and dissertations], which are currently available from micropublishing organizations throughout the world."—*Introd.* Both have introductory matter in English, French, German and Spanish.
The author/title series is an alphabetical main-entry listing; the arrangement of the subject series is based on the Library of Congress classification system. Both include pertinent ordering information.
Beginning 1979, an interim supplement adds new listings in both main-entry and subject arrangements.
Z1033.M5G83

Modern Language Association of America. Reproductions of manuscripts and rare printed books. Short title list. (*In* Modern Language Assoc. of America. Publs. 65:289–338, April 1950)
AA159

"Complete to January 1, 1950."—*p.289.*
"Rotographs or microfilms of the . . . materials listed . . . are now on deposit in the Library of Congress."—*p.289.* These are available for interlibrary loan, or microfilm copies may usually be purchased.
Z1012.M6

National register of microform masters. Comp. by the Library of Congress with the cooperation of the American Library Association and the Association of Research Libraries. Wash., Lib. of Congress, Sept. 1965– . Irregular, then annual.
AA160

Lists and locates microfilm masters (those used only for making copies) from which libraries may acquire prints without the expense of making another master. Originally arranged by LC or NUC card numbers, with a separate section by main entry for those items for which cards are not available; a third section listed serial publications alphabetically by main entry. With the 1970 annual a single, alphabetical listing by main entry was adopted. Includes microform masters of "foreign and domestic books, pamphlets, serials, and foreign doctoral dissertations but excludes technical reports, typescript translations, foreign or domestic archival manuscript collections, U.S. doctoral dissertations, and masters' theses."—*Foreword.* Holdings of commercial microform producers as well as of libraries are represented.
A 1965–75 cumulation, with all reports for the period in a single alphabetical sequence (i.e., with the 1965–69 listings which were

originally arranged by catalog card number integrated into the main-entry listing) was published 1976.   Z1033.M5N3

Philadelphia Bibliographical Center and Union Library Catalogue. Union list of microfilms. Rev., enl., and cumulated ed. Ann Arbor, Mich., J. W. Edwards, 1951. 1961col.   **AA161**

Supersedes the 1942 edition and its 5 supplements. Lists some 25,000 titles held on microfilm by 197 institutions, reported through June 1949. Includes materials of all kinds, the fullness of information depending on what was furnished by the individual library. Arrangement is alphabetical, and each entry gives Library of Congress subject classification, bibliographical information, and the location of negative and positive microfilms and of the originals when available. Newspapers are listed by title, with full information on the years covered and the location of negatives and positives, except when the newspaper was included in *Newspapers on microfilm* (AF10n), in which case reference is given to the latter.

——— ——— 1949–1959. Ann Arbor, 1961. 2v.

A supplement to the basic list, including more than 52,000 entries for all types of materials, reported by 215 libraries during the period July 1, 1949–July 31, 1959. Lists all serials except newspapers, which were listed in *Newspapers on microfilm* (AF10n).

Omits dissertations which are covered by *Dissertation abstracts* (AH19) and various other materials listed in existing bibliographies (*see* Introd.).

No more published.   Z1033.M5P5

U.S. Library of Congress. Processing Dept. British manuscripts project; a checklist of the microfilms prep. in England and Wales for the American Council of Learned Societies, 1941–1945, comp. by Lester K. Born. Wash., 1955. 179p.   **AA162**

Lists the contents of 2,652 reels of microfilm containing reproductions of manuscripts and some rare printed materials found in the libraries in England and Wales. The period covered is from medieval times to the 18th century. Copies of the films may be purchased from the Photoduplication Service of the Library of Congress.   Z6620.G7U5

Reviews

Cumulative microform reviews, 1972–1976. Westport, Conn., Microform Review Inc., [1978]. 619p.   **AA163**

A reprinting, with cumulated title index, of the reviews of micropublications appearing in v.1–5 (1972–76) of the journal *Microform review* (below). Further quinquennial volumes are planned, each to have a cumulative index.

Microform review, v.1, no.1– , Jan. 1972– . Weston, Conn., 1972– . Quarterly.   **AA164**

Allen B. Veaner, ed.

In addition to articles on microform projects and developments of interest to librarians and scholars, a large portion of each issue is devoted to reviews and evaluations of microform series, both current and retrospective.   Z265.M565

Translations

See also Science, Technology, and Medicine, p.1132.

Bibliographia neerlandica. The Hague, Nijhoff, 1962. 598p.   **AA165**

Contents: Pt.1, Books on the Netherlands in foreign languages, 1940–57, comp. by A. M. P. Mollema, p.1–384; pt.2, Translations of Dutch literature, 1900–1957, comp. by P. M. Morel, p.385–491. Indexes, p.493–598.

Title, introductory material, and captions in English, French, German, and Spanish.

E. van Raan's *Het Nederlandse boek in vertaling, 1958–1967; bibliografie van vertalingen van Noord- en Zuidnederlandse werken*

('s-Gravenhage, Staatsuitgeverij, 1974. 233p.) serves as a continuation of the Morel compilation. It, in turn, is continued on an annual basis by:

Het Nederlandse boek in vertaling; bibliografie van vertalingen van Noord- en Zuidnederlandse werken, 1968– . 's-Gravenhage, Staatsuitgeverij, 1969– . Annual with 5-year cumulations.   **AA166**

Issued by Koninklijke Bibliotheek, Hague, and Koninklijke Bibliotheek, Brussel.

Bibliographie der Übersetzungen deutschsprachiger Werke. Verzeichnis der in der Deutschen Bücherei eingegangenen Schriften, bearb. und hrsg. von der Deutschen Bücherei. Leipzig, Verlag für Buch- und Bibliothekswesen, 1954– . Jahrg.1– . Quarterly.   **AA167**

Subtitle varies.

A quarterly bibliography listing translations from German into other languages, published since 1951. Arranged by language, each subdivided by large class groups, with indexes: classified, author, and publisher. Bibliographic information is detailed; the translated title is followed by the original German title in brackets; and prices are included.   Z2234.T7B5

Fromm, Hans. Bibliographie deutscher Übersetzungen aus dem Französischen, 1700–1948 . . . Baden-Baden, Verlag für Kunst und Wissenschaft, 1950–53. 6v.   **AA168**

Title pages and introductory matter in German, French, and English. The main list records books and some periodical articles under author and French title, followed by full bibliographical information of German translations.

v.1–6, Verzeichnis A, Alphabetical list of authors and titles of translations from French, A–Z; Verzeichnis B, Translations of French texts by German authors; Verzeichnis C, Alphabetical list of German collections, series, miscellanies, anthologies, etc., containing only translations from French. Index A, Alphabetical index of translators; Index B, Alphabetical index of German titles arranged in List A under the French titles.   Z2174.T7F7

Index translationum. Répertoire international des traductions. International bibliography of translations. Paris, Internat. Inst. of Intellectual Cooperation, 1932–40. no.1–31; n.s. v.1– , 1948– . Paris, UNESCO, 1949– . Annual.   **AA169**

The first series was quarterly; the new series is annual. Entries are arranged by country, and under country name by the ten major headings of the Universal Decimal Classification. Complete bibliographical information, including the original language and title, are given when available. Both series include indexes of authors, publishers, and translators. The last issue of the first series, published in Jan. 1940, covered 12 countries including the USSR. The new series began with a coverage of 26 countries, which was increased to 75 in 1961, and varies slightly from year to year.   Z6514.T7I42

Cumulative index to English translations, 1948–1968. Boston, G. K. Hall, 1973. 2v.   **AA170**

Cumulates the entries from the annual volumes of the *Index translationum* for those translations published in Australia, Canada, New Zealand, Republic of Eire, Republic of South Africa, United Kingdom, and United States. The overwhelming majority of entries is for translations into English, but a few translations into other languages are included. Entries are reproduced from the original volumes (n.s.v.1–21) of *Index translationum* without reconciliation of variant entries, provision of adequate cross references, or other re-editing.   Z6514.T7C8

Anonyms and pseudonyms

❖Many reference books have been published on the authorship of anonymous and pseudonymous works. They differ considerably in use and authority, their value depending upon their comprehensiveness within their given field, upon the quality of research that has gone into their making, and particularly upon whether or not they give the authority for their attribution of authorship. The last point is of special importance, as the question of authorship is often a matter of dispute and difficult to establish; hence, it is frequently important to be able to check as many sources as possible in order to come to a decision. For a discussion of a selected list of such reference books, *see* the following bibliography:

Bibliography

Taylor, Archer and **Mosher, Fredric J.** The bibliographical history of anonyma and pseudonyma. Chicago, Univ. of Chicago Pr. for the Newberry Lib., 1951. 288p. il.
AA171

Bibliography, p. 207–79.
Preliminary chapters discuss homonyms, Latinized names, pseudepigrapha, anonyma and pseudonyma, confusing titles, and fictitious facts of publication. A classified guide to dictionaries and lists of anonyma and pseudonyma, and an index to the historical chapters are included. Z1041.T3

International

Pseudonyms and nicknames dictionary. Jennifer Mossman, ed. 2d ed. Detroit, Gale, [1982]. 995p. **AA172**

Subtitle: A guide to aliases, appellations, assumed names, code names, cognomens, cover names, epithets, initialisms, nicknames, noms de guerre, noms de plume, pen names, pseudonyms, sobriquets, and stage names of contemporary and historical persons, including the subjects' real names, basic biographical information, and citations for the sources from which the entries were compiled. Covers actors, aristocrats, artists, athletes, authors, clergymen, criminals, entertainers, film stars, journalists, military leaders, monarchs, musicians, playwrights, poets, politicians, popes, rogues, saints, theatrical figures, and other prominent personalities of all nations throughout the ages.
Real names and nicknames are presented in a single alphabetical sequence, with cross reference from the nickname or pseudonym to the real name (where the full information is given). About 90,000 entries.
An "interedition supplement" is published as: CT120.P8

New pseudonyms and nicknames: a guide to new and newly noted epithets, nicknames . . . . Detroit, Gale, 1983– . [v.1]– . **AA173**

v.2 is to be a cumulative supplement. CT120.N39

United States and Great Britain

See also AA311.

Atkinson, Frank. Dictionary of literary pseudonyms; a selection of popular modern writers in English. 3d ed. London, Bingley; Hamden, Conn., Linnet Books, [1982]. 305p.
AA174

1st ed. (1975) had title: *Dictionary of pseudonyms and pennames.*
"This dictionary is limited to writers in English and the selection has been made from those writing in the years 1900 to date."—*Introd.* In two sections: (1) Real names; and (2) Pseudonyms. Sources of information are not indicated, although the preface states that both publishers and the writers themselves were queried in an effort to establish identities. About 9,500 names in this edition.
Z1065.A84

Clarke, Joseph F. Pseudonyms. London, Book Club Associates, [1977]. 252p. **AA175**

Not limited to pen-names, but extends to "anyone well known who changed his or her name. Of the 3400 pseudonyms listed, pennames account for roughly half the collection; stage names a third; the remainder of the entries cover personalities in the various spheres of politics, sport, crime, painting and sculpture, and music."

—*Introd.* Many entries include brief remarks on background and choice of pseudonym. Z1041.C57

Cushing, William. Anonyms; a dictionary of revealed authorship. Cambridge, [Mass.], Cushing, 1889. 829p.
AA176

Includes both English and American works. In two alphabets: (1) anonymous titles followed by name of author; (2) index of authors found only in the *Anonyms.* Does not give authorities.
Z1045.C98A

———— Initials and pseudonyms; a dictionary of literary disguises. N.Y., Crowell, [c1885–88]. 2v. **AA177**

In two series, together including about 18,500 initials and pseudonyms, principally English and American, with a few well-known Continental names. Each series is in two parts: (1) initials followed by real name; (2) real name followed by pseudonym or initials, with short biographical notices. Does not give authorities.
Z1045.C98I

Gaines, Pierce Welch. Political works of concealed authorship relating to the United States, 1789–1810, with attributions. 3d ed., rev. & enl. Hamden, Conn., Shoe String, 1972. 226p. **AA178**

1st ed. (1959) had title: Political works of concealed authorship during the administrations of Washington, Adams and Jefferson, 1789–1809.
941 items chronologically arranged; index of authors and of pseudonyms. Gives sources of the attributions. Z1045.G3

Halkett, Samuel and **Laing, John.** Dictionary of anonymous and pseudonymous English literature. New and enl. ed. by James Kennedy, W. A. Smith and A. F. Johnson. Edinburgh, Oliver and Boyd, 1926–62. 9v. **AA179**

1st ed., Edinburgh, Paterson, 1882–88. 4v.
v.1–6, A–Z. Supplement, v.6, p.273–449; v.7, Index and 2d suppl.; v.8, 1900–50; v.9 (*see* below).
v.8–9 by Dennis E. Rhodes and Anna E. C. Simoni.
A comprehensive list, arranged alphabetically by first word of title not an article, giving for each item listed: title (sometimes shortened), size, paging, place, date, author's name, and (in some cases) the authority for attribution of authorship. The best list for English works, although as most of the authorities cited are general in character, the work is not final authority in cases of disputed authorship.
v.8 aims to give the authorship of as many anonymous and pseudonymous works as possible, published in the English language between 1900 and 1949 inclusive.
From 1950 on, the same kind of information may usually be found in the *British national bibliography* (AA827), for books published in Great Britain, and in the *National union catalog* (AA125).
v.9, originally planned to "consist entirely of additions and corrections to the period before 1900" (*Pref.*), now includes also as many additional items for the 1900–50 period as possible.
A new edition has begun to appear as: Z1065.H17

———— A dictionary of anonymous and pseudonymous publications in the English language. 3d (rev. and enl.) ed. John Horden, ed. [Harlow, Eng.], Longman, [1980]– . [v.1]– . (In progress) **AA180**

At head of title: Halkett and Laing.
Contents: [v.1] 1475–1640.
A thorough revision for which each item in the 2d ed. and its supplements was checked and revised, and the whole cast into a different form: i.e., the new edition is to be presented in three chronological segments (1475–1640, 1641–1700, and 1701–1800), each segment being an alphabetical title listing with indexes. Entries are numbered, and each entry now includes "full documentary evidence for the attribution of authorship made" (*Pref.*); indication is given of erroneous attributions in the 2d ed.; and items not truly anonymous which were entered in the 2d ed. are carried forward with appropriate comment, so that no item from the previous edition is omitted. [v.1] includes an index of writers' names, a list of

pseudonyms (with supposed writer), a table of *STC* numbers, a table of Allison and Rogers numbers, and a table of Greg numbers.

Z1065.H18 1980

Arabic writers

Dāghir, Yūsuf As'ad. Mu'jam al-asmā' al-musta 'ārah wa-aṣḥābihā lā siyyama fī al-adab al-'Arabī al-hadīth. Bayrūt, Maktabat Lubnān, 1982. 291p. **AA181**

A dictionary of pseudonyms of Arabic writers.

Argentina

Cutolo, Vicente Osvaldo. Diccionario de alfónimos y seudónimos de la Argentina (1800–1930). Buenos Aires, Ed. Elche, 1962. 160p. **AA182**

1,100 entries; authority frequently cited. Z1049.A7C8

Australia

Nesbitt, Bruce and **Hadfield, Susan.** Australian literary pseudonyms; an index, with selected New Zealand references. Adelaide, Libraries Board of South Australia, 1972. 134p. **AA183**

Covers a literature that abounds in pseudonyms. Pseudonyms and real names are listed in a single alphabet, the pseudonym being entered as a *see* reference to the original name. Z1107.N47

Belgium

Delecourt, Jules Victor. Dictionnaire des anonymes et pseudonymes, XVᵉ siècle–1900. Mis en ordre et enrichi par G. de LeCourt. Bruxelles, Académie Royale, 1960. v.1. **AA184**

At head of title: Bibliographie nationale.

v.1, 1281p. No more publ.

A reworking and updating of the author's *Essai d'un dictionnaire des ouvrages anonymes et pseudonymes publiés en Belgique au XIVᵉ siècle et principalement depuis 1830* (Bruxelles, 1863. 548p.).

Z1071.D4

Montagne, Victor Alexander de la. Vlaamsche pseudoniemen. Bibliographische opzoekingen. Roeselare, DeSeyn-Verhougstraete, 1884. 132p. **AA185**

Includes some extensive notes, but does not cite sources of attributions. Z1071.M758

Brazil

Barros Paiva, Tancredo de. Achêgas a um diccionario de pseudonymos, iniciaes, abreviaturas e obras anonymas de auctores brasileiros e de estrangeiros, sobre o Brasil ou no mesmo impressas. Rio de Janeiro, J. Leite, 1929. 248p. **AA186**

More than 1,500 entries. Authorities not cited. Z1049.B8B3

Canada

Amtmann, Bernard. Contributions to a dictionary of Canadian pseudonyms and anonymous works relating to Canada. Contributions à un dictionnaire des pseudonymes canadiens et des ouvrages anonymes relatifs au Canada. Montreal, Author, 1973. 144p. **AA187**

Text in English or French.

A listing by pseudonym or anonymous title, without indication of source of the attribution. Addenda, p.137–44. Z1047.A47

Vinet, Bernard. Pseudonymes québécois. Québec, Éditions Garneau, [1974]. 361p. **AA188**

"Édition basée sur l'oeuvre de Audet et Malchelosse intitulée: Pseudonymes canadiens."—*t.p.*

Adds numerous pseudonyms not found in the Audet and Malchelosse work (Montreal, 1936) and cites additional sources.

Z1047.V55

China

Shu, Austin C. W. Modern Chinese authors: a list of pseudonyms. East Lansing, Asian Studies Center, Michigan State Univ., 1969. 108p. (Michigan State Univ. Asian Studies Center. Occasional paper, East Asian ser.) **AA189**

About 2,000 entries. Z1087.C6S56

Colombia

Pérez Ortiz, Rubén. Seudónimos colombianos. Bogotá, 1961. 276p. (Publicaciones del Inst. Caro y Cuervo. Ser. bibliográfica, 2) **AA190**

In two parts: the first is a list by pseudonym, giving real name; the second is a list of Colombian authors indicating any pseudonyms which they have used. Z1731.C6 no.2

Cuba

Figarola-Caneda, Domingo. Diccionario cubano de seudónimos. Habana, Impr. "El siglo XX," 1922. 182p. **AA191**

Authorities not cited. Z1049.C9F4

Czechoslovakia

Dolensky, Antonín. Slovník pseudonymů a kryptonymů v československé literatuře. . . . 3. přepracované vydání. Praha, [Tiskem M. Knappa v Karlíně], 1934. 155p. **AA192**

Authority frequently indicated. Z1066.5.D66

Ormis, Ján Vladimir. Slovník slovenských pseudonymov. Slovenská Národná Knižnica, 1944. 366p. (Knihy Slovenskej národnej knižnice v Turčianskom svätom Martine. Svazok I) **AA193**

Authorities cited. Z1066.5.O7

Dominican Republic

Rodriguez Demorizi, Emilio. Seudónimos dominicanos. Ciudad Trujillo, Ed. Montalvo, 1956. 280p. **AA194**

Authorities sometimes cited. Z1049.D6R6

France

Quérard, Joseph Marie. Les supercheries littéraires dévoilées. . . . 2. éd. Paris, Daffis, 1869–[79]. 7v. (v.1–3, repr.: Paris, Maisonneuve & Larose, 1964) **AA195**

Subtitle: Galerie des écrivains français de toute l'Europe qui se sont déguisés sous des anagrammes, des astéronymes, des cryptonymes, des initialismes, des noms littéraires, des pseudonymes facétieux ou bizarres, etc. 2. éd., considérablement augm., pub. par Gustave Brunet et Pierre Jannet. Suivie 1ᵉ, Du Dictionnaire des ouvrages anonymes, par Ant.–Alex. Barbier. 3. éd., rev. et augm. par Olivier Barbier. . . . 2ᵉ, D'une table générale des noms réels des écrivains anonymes et pseudonymes cités dans les deux ouvrages.

v.1–3, J. M. Quérard. Les supercheries littéraires dévoilées, 2. éd., A–Z; v.4–7, A. A. Barbier. Dictionnaire des ouvrages anonymes. 3. éd., A–Z. Anonymes Latins.

The same edition of Barbier was also issued separately (Paris, Féchoz. 4v.; repr.: Hildesheim, Olms, 1963. 4v.). The *Table générale des noms réels* was never issued.

Gives notes about the books and editions listed, but in general does not give authority for identification of authors. Supplemented by the following: Z1067.Q4S

Brunet, Gustave. Dictionnaire des ouvrages anonymes [de Barbier], suivi des Supercheries littéraires dévoilées [de Quérard]: supplément à la dernière édition de ces deux ouvrages (Edition Daffis). Paris, Féchoz, 1889. 310col., cix p. 122col., xiv p. (Repr.: Paris, Maisonneuve & Larose, 1964)   **AA196**

Contents: Dictionnaire des ouvrages anonymes (Supplément); Essai sur les bibliothèques imaginaires; Les devises des vieux poètes: étude littéraire et bibliographique, par M. Gustave Mouravit; Appel aux bibliophiles, aux érudits et aux curieux ["Désiderata," i.e., une liste d'anonymes et de pseudonymes dont le mystère n'a pas été découvert]; Les supercheries littéraires dévoilées (Supplément); Varia: Pseudonymes étrangers. Traductions supposées. Supercheries typographiques.   Z1067.B92

Germany

Holzmann, Michael and **Bohatta, Hanns.** Deutsches Anonymen-Lexikon. Weimar, Gesellschaft der Bibliophilen, 1902–28. 7v. (Repr.: Hildesheim, Olms, 1961)   **AA197**

v.1–4, 1501–1850; v. 5, supplement, 1851–1908; v.6, 1501–1910, additions and corrections; v.7, 1501–1926, additions and corrections.

Includes, in the four lists, some 83,000 entries. Arranged alphabetically by title, with author's name supplied for each and the authority for the information indicated.   Z1068.H76

—— Deutsches Pseudonymen-Lexikon. Wien, Akademie Verlag, 1906. 323p. (Repr.: Hildesheim, Olms, 1961)   **AA198**

Gives pseudonym, followed by real name, and indicates the authority for the information.   Z1068.H77

Namenschlüssel zu Pseudonymen, Doppelnamen und Namensabwandlungen. 4. Ausg. Hildesheim, Olms, 1965–68. 2v.   **AA199**

Contents: Bd.1, Stand vom 1. Juli 1941; Bd.2, Ergänzungen aus der Zeit vom 1. Juli 1941 bis 31. Dezember 1965.

Bd.1 is a reprint of the 3d ed. of the Preussische Staatsbibliothek's *Namenschlüssel die Verweisungen der Berliner Titeldrucke zu Pseudonymen, Doppelnamen und Namensabwandlungen* (Berlin, 1941); Bd.2 represents additional listings.   Z695.1.P4N34

Greece

Ntelopoulos, Kyriakos. Neoellēnika philologika pseudonyma. Athenai, Kollegion Athenon, 1969. 143p.   **AA200**

More than 1,400 pseudonyms of modern Greek authors. Approach is both from true name of author to pseudonym and from pseudonym to true name. Authority is noted for most entries.   Z1069.N85

Hungary

Gulyás, Pál. Magyar írói álnév lexikon; a magyarországi írók álnevei és egyéb jegyei. Függelék: Néhány száz névtelen munka jegyzéke. Budapest, Akadémiai Kiadó, 1956. 706p.   **AA201**

Added title page in Latin: Lexicon pseudonymorum hungaricum: pseudonyma et alia signa scriptorum regni hungariae.

An alphabetical list of pseudonyms and initials with the author's name supplied for each, and authorities indicated. Includes also a list of anonymous works whose authors were identified.   Z1069.7.G8

India

Chatterjee, Amitabha. Dictionary of Indian pseudonyms. Calcutta, Mukherji Book House, [1977]. 170p.   **AA202**

A dictionary of about 3,500 pseudonyms used by Indian writers in all Indian languages and in English. Gives real name, an identifying phrase, and (when possible) date of birth. Index of real names giving reference to page number only—not to pseudonym. Sources not indicated.   Z1087.I5C43

Virendra Kumar. Dictionary of pseudonmys [sic] in Indian literature. [Delhi], Delhi Library Assoc., 1973. 163p. (Delhi Lib. Assoc. English ser., no.7)   **AA203**

An initial attempt to provide a guide to the real names of pseudonymous Indian authors. Includes writers in various Indian languages. Under the pseudonym is indicated the real name, language, and year of birth of the writer. A second section provides a guide from original name to pseudonym.   Z1087.I5V57

Italy

Melzi, Gaetano, *Conte.* Dizionario di opere anonime e pseudonime di scrittori italiani, o come che sia aventi relazione all'Italia. Milano, Coi Torchi di L. di Giacomo Pirole, 1848–59. 3v. (Repr.: N.Y., Burt Franklin, 1960)   **AA204**

—— —— Supplemento, comp. da Giambattista Passano. Ancona, Morelli, 1887. 517p. (Repr.: N.Y., Burt Franklin, 1960, with Rocco, below)

—— —— Supplemento al Melzi e al Passano di Emmanuele Rocco. Napoli, Chiurazzi, 1888. 16p.

Covers the 16th to the 19th centuries. Many useful bibliographic notes; sources of attribution sometimes indicated.   Z1070.M53

Luxembourg

Hury, Carlo. Dictionnaire de pseudonymes d'auteurs luxembourgeois. Luxembourg, Impr. P. Linden, 1960. 17p. (Bibliographia luxemburgensis, 2)   **AA205**

The list is supplementary to the information on pseudonymous works found in Martin Blum's *Bibliographie luxembourgeoise* (Luxembourg, 1902–32; AA940n).

Mexico

Manrique de Lara, Juana and **Monroy, Guadalupe.** Seudónimos, anagramas e iniciales de escritores mexicanos, antiguos y modernos. 2. ed., corr. y notablemente aumentada. México, [Secretaría de Educación Publica], 1954. 115p.   **AA206**

1st ed. 1943.

A list without sources of attribution.   Z1049.M6M3

Netherlands

Doorninck, Jan Izaak van. Vermomde en naamlooze schrijvers, opgespoord op het gebied der Nederlandsche en Vlaamsche letteren. 2. uitg. der "Bibliotheek van anonymen en pseudonymen." Leiden, Brill, 1883–85. 2 pts. in lv.   **AA207**

Contents: v.1, Pseudonyms and initials. 671col.; v.2, Anonyms. 681col.

Many bibliographical notes and notes on sources are given. Supplemented by: Z1072.D69B2

Kempenaer, A. de. Vermomde Nederlandsche en Vlaamsche schrijvers, vervolg op J. I. van Doorninck's Vermomde en naamlooze schrijvers, opgespoord op het gebiet der Nederlandsche en Vlaamsche letteren. Leiden, Sijthoff, [1928]. 690col. **AA208**

Z1072.D69K

Poland

Bar, Adam. Słownik pseudonimów i kryptonimów pisarzy polskich oraz Polski dotyczących, opracował Adam Bar . . . i Tad. Godłowskiego . . . Kraków, [Nakł. Krakowskiego koła Związku Bibljotekarzy Polskich], 1936–38. 3v. (Prace bibljoteczne Krakowskiego koła Związku Bibljotekarzy Polskich. VII–IX) **AA209**

v.1–2, Alphabetical list of pseudonyms, initials, etc., with full name, title, and source of attribution; v.3, Real name followed by pseudonym.   Z1073.5.B22

Portugal

Fonseca, Martinho Augusto Ferreira da. Subsidios para um diccionario de pseudonymos, iniciaes e obras anonymas de escriptores portuguezes, contribuição para o estudo da litteratura portugueza. Lisboa, Academia Real das Sciencias, 1896. 298p. **AA210**

In three parts: (1) pseudonyms; (2) initials; (3) anonymous works.   Z1078.F67

Romania

Straje, Mihail. Dicționar de pseudonime, alonime [sic], anagrame, asteronime, criptonime ale scriitorilor si publicistilor români. Bucuresti, Editura Minerva, 1973. 810p. **AA211**

A dictionary of Romanian pseudonyms, etc., with references to sources of identification.   Z1080.R6S8

Russia (including the Ukraine)

Dei, Oleksii Ivanovych. Slovnyk ukrains'kykh psevdonimiv ta kriptonimiv (XVI–XX st.). Kyiv, Naukova Dumka, 1969. 557p. **AA212**

A dictionary of about 10,000 pseudonyms; sources are given.   Z1073.D4

Leningrad. Publichnaia Biblioteka. Russkie anonimnye i podpisannye psevdonimami proizvedeniia pechati: 1801–1926: bibliograficheskii ukazatel'. [Sost. G. Z. Guseva i dr.] Leningrad, Gos. Publichnaia Biblioteka, 1977–79. 3v. **AA213**

A title listing of works published anonymously or pseudonymously, with indication of authorship and source of attribution. Does not include material covered in I. F. Masanov's *Slovar' psevdonimov* . . . (below). Index of attributions and pseudonyms in v.3.

Masanov, Ivan Filippovich. Slovar' psevdonimov russkikh pisatelei, uchenykh i obshchestvennykh deiatelei. V chetyrekh tomakh. Podgotovil k pechati IU. I. Masanov. Redaktor B. P. Koz'min. Moskva, 1956–60. 4v. **AA214**

An enlarged edition of Masanov's dictionary of Russian pseudonyms (Moskva, 1941). v.3 completes the Russian alphabet and lists Latin and Greek pseudonyms and other symbols used by Russian authors. v.4 contains a name index and additions to v.1–3.   Z1073.M33

Scandinavia

Andersson, Per. Pseudonymregister. Lund, Bibliotekstjänst, [1967]. 184p. **AA215**

Lists pseudonyms of Swedish writers, giving the true name but no biographical or bibliographical information.   Z1076.A65

Bygdén, Anders Leonard. Svenskt anonym- och pseudonymlexikon. Bibliografisk förteckning öfver uppdagade anonymer och pseudonymer i den svenska litteraturen. Upsala, Berling, 1898–1915. 2v. **AA216**

Includes a supplement, v.2, col.849–1052. Sources of attribution are usually given.   Z1076.B98

Collin, Edvard. Anonymer og Pseudonymer i den danske, norske og islandske Literatur samt i fremmede Literaturer, forsaavidt disse omhandle nordiske Forhold, fra de aeldste Tider indtil Aaret 1860. København, Lund, 1869. 209p. **AA217**

A list of sources is given, but citations thereto are not included with the individual entries for pseudonyms.   Z1074.C69

Ehrencron-Müller, Holger. Anonym- og Pseudonym-Lexikon for Danmark og Island til 1920 og Norge til 1814. København, Hagerup, 1940. 391p. **AA218**

Issued in parts. Sources not cited.   Z1074.E5

Pettersen, Hjalmar Marius. Norsk anonym- og pseudonymlexikon. Kristiania, Steen, 1924. 690col., [34]p. **AA219**

1st ed., 1890, had title: *Anonymer og pseudonymer i den norske literatur 1678–1890.*

Added title page in English: Dictionary of anonyms and pseudonyms in Norwegian literature.

Sources sometimes given.   Z1075.P49

——— ——— Tilføielser og rettelser. (*In* Nordisk tidskrift för bok- och biblioteksväsen 12:118–26. 1925)

Slovak authors

Kormúth, Dezider. Slovník slovenských pseudonymov 1919–1944. Martin, Matica Slovenská, 1974. 594p. (Slovenská národná retrospektívna bibliografia) **AA220**

The first section gives the pseudonym and the corresponding true name. A second section arranged by the Slovak authors' real names gives references to publications in which the pseudonyms were used.   PG5402.K6

Spain

Ponce de León Freyre, Eduardo and **Zamora Lucas, Florentino.** 1.500 seudónimos modernos de la literatura española, (1900–1942). Madrid, Inst. Nacional del Libro Español, 1942. 126p. **AA221**

A brief list without sources.   Z1077.P6

Rodergas i Calmell, Josep. Els pseudònims usats a Catalunya. (Recull de 3.800) Barcelona, Ed. Millà, 1951. 408p. **AA222**

Includes biographical notes, but not sources of attribution.   Z1077.R6

Rogers, Paul Patrick and **Lapuente, Felipe-Antonio.** Diccionario de seudónimos literarios españoles, con algunas iniciales. [Madrid], Gredos, [1977]. 608p. (Biblioteca románica hispánica, 5) **AA223**

Entry is under pseudonym, with index of true names. Entries usually provide citations to one or more publications in which the pseudonym was used. Select bibliography.   Z1077.R63

Spanish America

Medina, José Toribio. Diccionario de anónimos y seudónimos hispanoamericanos. Buenos Aires, Impr. de la Univ., 1925. 2v. in 1. (Buenos Aires, Univ. Nacional. Inst. de Investigaciones Históricas. Publ. 26–27) **AA224**

Many useful notes; sources of attribution sometimes given. Supplemented by: Z1049.A1M4

Victorica, Ricardo. Errores y omisiones del Diccionario de anónimos y seudónimos hispano-americanos de José Toribio Medina. Buenos Aires, Viau & Zona, 1928. 338p.
AA225

An extensive critique by Guillermo Feliú Cruz appeared in *Boletin del Inst. de Investigationes Históricas* 8:254–59; 9:237–80 (abril–junio, oct–dic. 1929) and was reprinted as *Advertencias saludables a un criticastro de mala ley* (Buenos Aires, 1929).
Z1049.A1M41

———— Verdades que levantan roncha. Belitres enfurecidos. *Gaceta del foro,* ano 15, 11 abril 1930, p.273–78.

Has about 16 columns of "Nuevas adiciones al 'Diccionario' de Medina," p.274–78, in alphabetical order.

———— Nueva epanortosis al Diccionario de anónimos y seudónimos de J. T. Medina. Buenos Aires, Rosso, 1929. 207p.   AA226

Entry is by title of the anonymous or pseudonymous work, with cross references from the pseudonym and the true name of the author. Authorities not cited.   Z1049.A1M42

Uruguay

Scarone, Arturo. Diccionario de seudónimos del Uruguay . . . Montevideo, Garcia & Cia., 1942. 632p.   AA227

"Segunda ed. con un Apéndice" of the 3d ed. which was first published under this title in 1941. The first two editions have title: *Apuntes para un diccionario de seudónimos y de publicaciones anónimas.*   Z1049.U8S2

Venezuela

Cardozo, Lubio and **Pintó, Juan.** Seudonimia literaria venezolana (con un apéndice de José E. Machado sobre seudónimos de escritores y políticos venezolanos). Mérida, Univ. de los Andes, Facultad de Humanidades y Educación, Escuela de Letras, 1974. 114p. (Centro de Investigaciones literarias. Serie bibliográfica, 6)   AA228

Offers approach both from pseudonym and from true name of the writer. List of sources consulted, p.17–30.   Z1049.V4C37

Yiddish

Chajes, Saul. Thesaurus pseudonymorum quae in litteratura hebraica et judaeo-germanica inveniuntur. Pseudonymen-Lexikon der hebräischen und jiddischen Literatur. Wien, Glanz, 1933. various pagings.   AA229

Added title page in Yiddish.
In Yiddish, with index in romanized form of name.
Z1069.5.C5

Fictitious imprints

Brunet, Gustave. Imprimeurs imaginaires et libraires supposés; étude bibliographique, suivie de recherches sur quelques ouvrages imprimés avec des indications fictives de lieux ou avec des dates singulières. Paris, Tross, 1866. 290p. (Repr.: N.Y., Burt Franklin, 1963)   AA230

Primarily a bibliography with some notes on variant editions, attributions, etc.   Z1067.B9I

Parenti, Marino. Dizionario dei luoghi di stampa falsi, inventati o supposti in opere di autori e traduttori italiani, con un'appendice sulla data "Italia," e un saggio sui falsi luoghi italiani usati all'estero, o in Italia, da autori stranieri.

Firenze, Sansoni, 1951. 311p. il. (Biblioteca bibliografica italica . . . 1)   AA231

Arranged alphabetically by place, and then chronologically, with an index of actual and pseudonymous authors. Many facsimiles.

Weller, Emil Ottokar. Die falschen und fingirten Druckorte. Repertorium der seit erfindung der Buchdruckerkunst unter falscher Firma erschienenen deutschen, lateinischen und französischen Schriften. 2. verm. und verb. Aufl. Leipzig, W. Engelmann, 1864. 2v. (Repr.: Hildesheim, Olms, 1970. 3v.)   AA232

Chronological arrangement within each volume, v.1 dealing with German and Latin works, 1510–1862; v.2 with French works, 1530–1863; each volume has its own index. v.3 of the reprint edition was originally published 1867 with Weller's *Index pseudonymorum* as "Drittes Supplementheft: Neue Nachträge zu den 'Falschen und fingirten Druckorten,' 2. Aufl. (Leipzig, 1864)." It offers both additional listings and corrections to v.1–2.
Z1041.W43

ANCIENT, MEDIEVAL, AND RENAISSANCE MANUSCRIPTS

❖The field of manuscripts is a very specialized one, rich in guides, bibliographies, and catalogs. Only a few of these dealing with the ancient, medieval, and Renaissance periods are listed here. It should be remembered that one of the main sources for descriptions of manuscripts is the exhibition catalog. Such catalogs, often richly illustrated and with detailed descriptions, are issued by libraries and museums (e.g., the Morgan Library, the Walters Art Gallery in Baltimore, the Huntington Library) to describe particular exhibits. These should be acquired and preserved by libraries as needed.

For American manuscripts in special subject fields, *see* that subject, e.g., History—United States; *see* especially the *National union catalog of manuscript collections* (DB64), the scope of which is much broader than its placement in this guide suggests.

Bibliography

Braswell, Laurel Nichols. Western manuscripts from classical antiquity to the Renaissance: a handbook. N.Y., Garland, 1981. 382p. (Garland reference library of the humanities, v.139)   AA233

An annotated bibliography intended to serve as a guide to the study of early Western manuscripts. Arrangement is meant to proceed from "first steps in identifying a manuscript to its transcription and ultimately its edition."—*Introd.* Includes sections on incipits, paleography, diplomatics and archives, illumination, music, codicology, textual criticism, bibliographies and reference works. Indexed.   Z105.B73

Ker, Neil Ripley. Medieval manuscripts in British libraries. Oxford, Clarendon Pr., 1969–83. v.1–3. (In progress)
AA234

Contents: v.1, London; v.2, Abbotsford–Keele; v.3, Lampeter–Oxford.

Intends to "provide information about manuscripts, other than muniments and binding fragments, written before 1500, in Latin or a Western European language, either by reference to an existing catalogue or by description."—*Pref.*   Z6620.G7K4

Scriptorium; revue international des études relatives aux manuscrits. t.1 (1946/47)– . Anvers, Standaard Boekhandel, [1947–]. plates, facsims. Semiannual.   AA235

Subtitle also in English: International review of manuscript studies. Contributions in English, French, German, and Spanish.

Includes current bibliographies of manuscript studies and facsimile editions.   Z108.S35

Catalogs

Codices latini antiquiores; a palaeographical guide to Latin manuscripts prior to the ninth century. Ed. by E. A. Lowe. Oxford, Clarendon Pr., 1934–71. 11v. and suppl. facsims.
AA236

"Edited under the auspices of the Union Académique Internationale for the American Council of Learned Societies and the Carnegie Institution of Washington."

"A succinct description based upon actual examination of the originals of all known Latin literary manuscripts on papyrus, parchment, or vellum which may be regarded as older than the ninth century, accompanied by a specimen, unreduced, of the script and supplemented by a selected bibliography" [at the end of each volume].

Arranged by present location of manuscripts.

Contents: pt.I, Vatican City; pt.II, Great Britain, Ireland; pt.III–IV, Italy; pt.V, Paris; pt.VI, France; pt.VII, Switzerland; pt.VIII–IX, Germany; pt.X, Austria, Belgium, Czechoslovakia, Denmark, Egypt, and Holland; pt.XI, Hungary, Luxembourg, Poland, Russia, Spain, Sweden, the United States, and Yugoslavia.

Within date and language limits, this is the most comprehensive and detailed catalog of manuscripts ever published. It is far more than a "palaeographical guide" as it includes notes about decoration, content, and history of the manuscripts. Prefaces point out items of particular paleographic or textual importance and discuss characteristics of significant book centers in various regions. The extensive references serve also as a general bibliography of manuscripts.

The supplement "contains newly found representatives from nearly every country" (*Introd.*), includes selected supplementary bibliography for the entire series, and provides an author index to all volumes. The introduction to the supplement notes that "Work is already in progress on a portable volume to contain, as an epilogue to the *C.L.A.* series, the editor's observations and reflections on the material that passed through his hands and along with that epilogue the numerous palaeographical indexes the twelve volumes call for"; however, the death of Lowe in 1969 puts publication of this volume in doubt.

Pt.II, Great Britain and Ireland, was issued in a 2d ed. in 1972, with some corrections and an effort to incorporate the findings of recent scholarship.   Z114.C677

Bibliography

British Library. Dept. of Manuscripts. Catalogue of dated and datable manuscripts, c.700–1600 in the Department of Manuscripts, the British Library. Andrew G. Watson [comp.]. London, British Museum Pubns. [for] the British Library, [1979]. 2v. facsims.   **AA237**

Contents: v.1, The text; v.2, The plates.

953 manuscripts, all but a few from before 1550, in the Cottonian, Arundel, Harley, Sloan, Lansdowne, Burney, King's, Egerton, Stowe, Yates Thompson, and Additional collections are listed alphabetically by collection, then by number. Entry gives collection, number, date and place of origin, author and title, and physical description. Notes cover evidence of date and origin, other manuscripts of the scribe, history of ownership, bibliographical references, and plate number in v.2. List of rejected manuscripts; date index; name index.

British Museum. Dept. of Manuscripts. The catalogues of the manuscript collections [by T. C. Skeat]. Rev. ed. [London], Trustees of the British Museum, 1962. 45p.   **AA238**

First issued in *Journal of documentation* 7:18–60, 1951.

Annotated list of 176 printed and handwritten catalogs of the Museum's various collections of Western manuscripts.

Supplements Kristeller (AA241).   Z6621.B844

British Library. Dept. of Manuscripts. Index of manuscripts in the British Library. Cambridge, Eng., Chadwyck-Healey, 1984– . v.1–4. (In progress; to be in 11v.)   **AA239**

Contents: v.1–4, A–Gren.

An alphabetical personal- and place-name index to manuscript collections acquired by the Library up to 1950. Entries are derived from more than 30 catalogs, both published and unpublished; the finished work (in plan and preparation since 1963) will include more than a million entries. Each entry includes the name of the manuscript item, the collection to which it belongs, its number within the collection, and its folio or article number (which may be used for ordering photocopies). Numerous cross references from variant forms of names.   Z921.L553B74

Kristeller, Paul Oskar. Iter Italicum; a finding list of uncatalogued or incompletely catalogued humanistic manuscripts of the Renaissance in Italian and other libraries. London, Warburg Inst., 1963–83. v.1–3. (In progress)   **AA240**

Contents: v.1, Italy: Agrigento to Novara; v.2, Italy: Orvieto to Volterra; Vatican City; v.3, Alia itinera I: Australia to Germany.

Originally intended to cover only Italian repositories and collections, the work has been expanded to worldwide coverage. It was "conceived primarily as a finding list for certain texts, and the main emphasis is on the textual content of the manuscripts listed."—*Pref.* Geographical arrangement; v.1 and v.2 each has its own index.
Z6611.H8K7

——— Latin manuscript books before 1600; a list of the printed catalogues and unpublished inventories of extant collections. 3d ed. N.Y., Fordham Univ. Pr., [1965]. 284p.
AA241

First published in *Traditio: studies in ancient and medieval history, thought and religion* 6:227–317 (1948) and 9:393–418 (1953). "New ed. rev." publ. 1960.

A valuable guide to public collections in Europe and the United States. Indicates the number of manuscripts included in a list, and analyzes lists covering more than one collection. Excludes archives and most private collections. Includes some lists of Greek and vernacular manuscripts since most collections are not divided according to language. Gives cross references, but no index.

Contents: A, Bibliography and statistics of libraries and their collections of manuscripts; B, Works describing manuscripts of more than one city; C, Printed catalogues and handwritten inventories of individual libraries, by cities.

The 3d ed. reprints the 1960 edition, adding a section of supplementary material (p.233–84) which incorporates the addenda from the previous edition with new listings.   Z6601.A1K7

Paris. Bibliothèque Nationale. Les catalogues imprimés de la Bibliothèque Nationale. Liste établié en 1943 suivie d'un supplément (1944–1952). Paris, 1953. 204p., xxvii p.
AA242

Catalogs of manuscripts: p.4–57, iii–v. Lists some 250 catalogs of manuscripts in various languages, subjects, and collections.

Supplements Kristeller (AA241).   Z927.P196

Richard, Marcel. Répertoire des bibliothèques et des catalogues de manuscrits grecs. 2. éd. Paris, Centre Nationale de la Recherche Scientifique, 1958. 276p. (Inst. de Recherche et d'Histoire des Textes. Pubn. 1)   **AA243**

1st ed. 1948.

Includes lists of manuscripts in periodicals as well as those published separately. Covers collections in Europe, the Middle East, Egypt, and North and South America, indicating size and character. Detailed index.

Contents: 1, Bibliographie; 2, Catalogues spécialisés; 3, Catalogues régionaux; 4, Villes.

"Revues et Actes académiques cités," p.253–60.
Z6601.A1R39

———— ———— Supplément I (1958–1963). Paris, CNRS, 1964. 76p. (Inst. de Recherche et d'Histoire des Textes. Documents, études et répertoires. 9)

Union lists

See also AA234.

Ricci, Seymour de. Census of medieval and Renaissance manuscripts in the United States and Canada, . . . with the assistance of W. J. Wilson. N.Y., Wilson, 1935–40. 3v. (Repr.: N.Y., Kraus, 1961) **AA244**

"Published under the auspices of the American Council of Learned Societies."

Arranged alphabetically by states, cities, and libraries, including private collections. Brief descriptions include: probable date and place of origin, material on which written, size, number of leaves, kind of binding, former owners, and references to printed descriptions.

Contents: v.1, Alabama-Massachusetts; v.2, Michigan-Canada. Errata and addenda; v.3, Indexes: [1], General index of names, titles and headings; [2], Scribes, illuminators and cartographers; [3], *Incipits;* [4], Gregory numbers for Greek and New Testament manuscripts; [5], Present owners; [6], Previous owners.

———— ———— Supplement, originated by C. U. Faye, continued and ed. by W. H. Bond. N.Y., Bibliographical Soc. of America, 1962. 626p.

Gives cross references to the *Census* when additional or corrected information is supplied and for manuscripts whose ownership has changed. Z6620.U5R5

Sinclair, Keith Val. Descriptive catalogue of medieval and Renaissance Western manuscripts in Australia. [Sydney], Sydney Univ. Pr., [1969]. 504p. il. **AA245**

Lists and describes manuscripts to 1550 in public and private libraries throughout Australia. Arranged by state, town, and repository. General index of *incipits*. Z6620.A8S55

Facsimiles

Palaeographical Society, London. Facsimiles of [ancient] manuscripts and inscriptions. 1st–2d ser. London, 1873–1894. 5v. 465pl. (facsims.) **AA246**

Cover title: Facsimiles of ancient manuscripts. . . .

Eds.: E. A. Bond, E. M. Thompson, G. F. Warner.

Issued in parts. 1st ser.: 13 pts. (260pl.); 2d ser.: 10 pts. (205pl.). Each plate with a page of corresponding letterpress giving transcription and description.

Contents: *1st ser.:* v.1, Introduction. Phoenician. Greek. Gothic; v.2, Oscan. Latin and modern languages; v.3, Latin and modern languages. *2d ser.:* v.1, Introduction. Egyptian. Semitic. Greek. Latin and modern languages; v.2, Latin and modern languages.

Lists of manuscripts, etc. in the two series are arranged topographically.

———— ———— Indices to ser. I and II. London, 1901. 63p.

Contents: Chronological; Authors and subjects; Country of origin; Character of handwriting; Ornamentation; Scribes and artists; Materials other than vellum; Present owners; Former owners.

Z113.P15

New Palaeographical Society, London. Facsimiles of ancient manuscripts, etc. 1st–2d ser. London, 1903–30. 4v. 452pl. (facsims.) **AA247**

Eds.: E. M. Thompson, G. F. Warner, F. G. Kenyon, J. P. Gilson, J. A. Herbert, and H. I. Bell.

Issued in parts. 1st ser.: 10 pts. (250pl.); 2d ser.: 13 pts. (202pl.). Each plate with page of corresponding letterpress giving transcription and description.

Contents: *1st ser.:* v.1, Introduction. Greek. Latin and modern languages; v.2, Latin and modern languages; *2d ser.:* v.1, Introduction. Greek. Latin and modern languages; v.2, Latin and modern languages.

———— Indices to 1st ser. London, 1914. 50p.

———— Indices to 2d ser. London, 1932. 43p.

Comp. by F. Wormald.

Contents of both indexes follow the same lines as those in the original series (*see* above).

One of the most comprehensive and useful of the many paleographical sets. Full-page reproductions, with some manuscripts allotted more than one plate. Descriptions include data about the entire volume represented, with information as to its text, history, and miniatures (if any), some of which are also included in the reproductions. References sometimes given. Z113.N489

Société Française de Reproductions de Manuscrits à Peintures, Paris. Bulletin. Année 1–21. Paris, 1911–38. 21v. plates (facsims.). **AA248**

Reproductions and descriptions of important illuminated manuscripts, of both Western and Eastern origin, in the libraries of various countries. Usually, each volume is devoted to manuscripts in a particular library. Descriptions by recognized scholars include bibliographic details, notes on script, provenance, authorship, and text as well as the illumination. ND3345.P16

Bibliography

Paris. Bibliothèque Nationale. Dépt. des Manuscrits. Listes des recueils de fac-similés et des reproductions de manuscrits conservés à la Bibliothèque Nationale, pub. par M. Omont. 3.éd. par Ph. Lauer. [Paris], 1935. 226p. **AA249**

Full entry for each item including analysis of sets. Cross references and comprehensive index.

Contents: I, Recueils de fac-similés classés par ordre alphabétique d'auteurs ou de matières [483 entries]; II, Reproductions de manuscrits: (1) Collections de Leyde, du Vatican, de Paris, de Bruxelles et de Copenhague [90 entries], and (2) Manuscrits classés par ordre alphabétique d'auteurs ou de matières [573 entries]; III, Série orientale, classement par recueils [7 entries] et par ordre alphabétique de langues [17 languages, including Mexican; 128 entries].

This comprehensive list (almost 1,300 entries) is an invaluable aid to manuscript study in many areas. Can be supplemented by the lists published in *Scriptorium* (AA235).

Diplomatics, handwriting and scripts

Boüard, Alain de. Manuel de diplomatique francaise et pontificale. Paris, A. Picard, 1929–52. 2v. plus 3 portfolios of plates. **AA250**

Contents: v.1, Diplomatique générale; v.2, L'acte privé.

CD61.B6

Bresslau, Harry. Handbuch der Urkundenlehre für Deutschland und Italien. 3. Aufl. Berlin, de Gruyter, 1958. 2v. **AA251**

v.2, pt.2, "2.Aufl.," ed. by Hans Walter Klewitz.

———— ———— Register zur 2. und 3. Aufl. zusammengestellt von Hans Schulze. Berlin, de Gruyter, 1960. 116p.

A well-documented manual for the study of German and Italian diplomatics. CD63.B84

Cappelli, Adriano. Lexicon abbreviaturarum. Dizionario di abbreviature latine ed italiane, usate nelle carte e codici specialmente del medio-evo . . . 6.ed. (anastatica) corr. con 9 tavole fuori testo. Milano, Hoepli, 1961. lxxiii p., 531p. facsims. **AA252**

A reprint of the 3d ed., published in 1929.

Main part is an alphabetical list of abbreviations given both in manuscript facsimile and in printed letters followed by the words for which they stand. Supplemental lists include: 1, Conventional signs; 2, Epigraphical abbreviations; 3, Ancient roman and arabic numerals; 4, Signs indicating money, weights, and measures.

Bibliography of works on abbreviations, p.517–31.

An English translation of the introduction has been separately published as: Z111.C24

———— The elements of abbreviation in medieval Latin paleography. Tr. by David Heimann and Richard Kay. Lawrence, Kans., Univ. of Kansas Libraries, 1982. 52p. (Univ. of Kansas pubns. Library ser., 47)   **AA253**

Cappelli's work is supplemented by:

Pelzer, Auguste. Abréviations latines médiévales. Supplément au Dizionario di abbreviature latine ed italiane de Adriano Cappelli. Louvain, Publ. Universitaires; Paris, Béatrice-Nauwelaerts, 1964. 86p.   **AA254**

A "deuxième édition" appeared in 1966 (Paris, Béatrice-Nauwelaerts) with no apparent change except in the prefatory note.
    Z111.C242

Chassant, Alphonse Antoine Louis. Dictionnaire des abréviations latines et françaises usitées dans les inscriptions lapidaires et métalliques, les manuscrits et les chartes du Moyen Âge. 5.éd. Paris, J. Martin, 1884. lii p., 172p. facsims.   **AA255**

1st ed., Evreux, 1846.

"Abréviations latines," p.1–121; "Abréviations françaises," p.123–43.

Gives manuscript form of abbreviations followed by printed words for which they stand. Supplemental lists include: Abbreviations of numerical expressions, conjoined letters or monograms, numbers, dates, and Roman signs used in Christian epitaphs before the seventh century.   Z111.C484

Devreesse, Robert. Introduction à l'étude des manuscrits grecs. Paris, C. Klincksieck, 1954. 347p.   **AA256**

A detailed introduction to the study of Greek manuscripts. In two parts: the first discusses problems such as paper, handwriting, transmission of texts, ancient libraries; the second describes extant Greek manuscripts by topic (Bible, liturgies, medicine, occult sciences, legal, military, etc.).

Frederick William Hall's *A companion to classical texts* (1913) is still useful for its treatment of such matters as: confusions and earlier attempts to remedy them; nomenclature of manuscripts (with names of former possessors); manuscript authorities for the texts of the chief classical authors.   Z4.D4

Hector, Leonard Charles. The handwriting of English documents. [2d ed.] London, Arnold, [1966]. 136p. il.   **AA257**

1st ed. 1958.

"The chief object of this book is to moderate as far as possible the difficulties of reading presented by the hands written in England for administrative, legal or business purposes during the past eight or nine centuries."—*Introd.* In addition to textual discussion of the writers' materials, languages, abbreviations, scribal conventions, etc., there is an extensive set of plates with transcriptions of the passages reproduced thereon.   Z115.E5H4

Martin, Charles Trice. The record interpreter: a collection of abbreviations, Latin words and names used in English historical manuscripts and records. 2d ed. London, Stevens, 1910. 464p. (Repr.: Hildesheim, Olms, 1969)   **AA258**

Contents: (1) Abbreviations of Latin words used in English records; (2) Abbreviations of French words used in English records; (3) Glossary of Latin words found in records and other English manuscripts, but not occurring in classical authors; (4) Latin names of places in Great Britain and Ireland; (5) Latin names of bishoprics in England; (6) Latin names of bishoprics in Scotland; (7) Latin names of bishoprics in Ireland; (8) Latin forms of English surnames; (9) Latin Christian names with their English equivalents.

The 1st ed., published 1892, was an amplification of the appendix to Andrew Wright's *Court-hand restored* (9th ed., 1879).
    Z111.M23

Reynolds, Leighton Durham and **Wilson, Nigel Guy.** Scribes and scholars, a guide to the transmission of Greek and Latin literature. Oxford, Oxford Univ. Pr., 1968. 185p. il.
    AA259

A very readable guide for "beginners in the field of classical studies" describing the history and transcription of texts.
    Z40.R4

Thompson, *Sir* **Edward Maunde.** An introduction to Greek and Latin palaeography. Oxford, Clarendon Pr., 1912. 600p. 250facsims. (Repr.: N.Y., Burt Franklin, 1964)
    AA260

An enlarged edition of the author's *Handbook of Greek and Latin palaeography* (3d ed., 1906).

Gives transcription of each facsimile. Includes chapters on the history of Greek and Roman alphabets, materials and writing implements, forms of books, abbreviations, contractions, and numerals.

Bibliography, p.571–83, includes lists of published facsimiles.
    Z114.T472

Ullman, Berthold Louis. Ancient writing and its influence. N.Y., Longmans, 1932. 234p. 48facsims. on XVIpl.
    AA261

Gives transcription of each facsimile. Devotes three chapters to the origin and development of the Greek alphabet and script, but the major part is given to the Latin scripts of the Middle Ages, including the national hands, Carolingian and Gothic scripts, and the writing of the Italian Renaissance. Includes chapters on abbreviations, ligatures, and numerals.

Bibliography, p.231–34.   Z105.U41

———— The origin and development of humanistic script. Roma, Ed. di Storia e Letteratura, 1960. 146p. 70facsims.
    AA262

A thorough study of the script on which printed roman letters are based. Bibliographical footnotes; index of manuscripts, p.142–44.

Illumination

Oxford. University. Bodleian Library. Illuminated manuscripts in the Bodleian Library, Oxford. Comp. by Otto Pächt and J. J. G. Alexander. Oxford, Clarendon Pr., 1966–73. 3v.   **AA263**

Contents: v.1, German, Dutch, Flemish, French, and Spanish schools; v.2, Italian school; v.3, British, Irish, and Icelandic schools (with addenda to v.1 & 2).

Brief descriptive notes are given, and, for about half the items, small-size illustrations are included. There are indexes of texts and authors, of illuminators and scribes, and of other persons, mainly owners.   ND2897.O9

Scribes and artists

Aeschlimann, Erardo and **Ancona, Paolo d'.** Dictionnaire des miniaturistes du Moyen Âge et de la Renaissance dans les différentes contrées de l'Europe . . . 2.éd. rev. et augm. Milan, Hoepli, 1949. 239p. 155pl. (part col.)   **AA264**

For full information *see* BE332.   N7616.A4

Bradley, John William. A dictionary of miniaturists, illuminators, calligraphers, and copyists, with references to their works, and notices of their patrons, from the establishment of Christianity to the eighteenth century . . . London, Quaritch, 1887–89. 3v. (Repr.: N.Y., Burt Franklin, [1958])
    AA265

For full information *see* BE333.

In addition to these two dictionaries, *see* the lists of scribes and artists in the *Indices* of the Palaeographical Society series (AA246) and the *Indices* of the De Ricci *Census* and *Supplement* (AA244).
    ND2890.B8

EARLY AND RARE BOOKS

Incunabula and early printed books

❖The books listed below are the principal general bibliographies and catalogs of incunabula that should be known by the general librarian. Various important bibliographies of the incunabula of special countries, and catalogs of incunabula in individual libraries, will also be needed for special work. For lists of these *see* Stillwell, *Incunabula and Americana*, p.251–329 (AA268); the list of sources in the *Gesamtkatalog der Wiegendrucke* (AA279); and Goff, *Incunabula in American libraries* (AA278).

For dictionaries of place-names associated with early printing presses, *see* Gazetteers—Ancient and Medieval, p. 946.

Guides

Berkowitz, David Sandler. Bibliotheca bibliographica incunabula; a manual of bibliographical guides to inventories of printing, of holdings, and of reference aids. Waltham, Mass., 1967. 336p. **AA266**

"With an appendix of useful information on place-names and dating, collected and classified for the use of researchers in incunabulistics."—*title page.*

An effort toward providing a bibliographic guide to the study of incunabula. A general section on guides to sources of information on the topic is followed by chapters on registers or catalogs of incunabula. Lacks an index. Z240.A1B4

Haebler, Konrad. Handbuch der Inkunabelkunde. Leipzig, Hiersemann, 1925. 187p. **AA267**

A photographic reprint (Stuttgart, Hiersemann, 1966) of the 1925 edition has been termed "2. Aufl."

A handbook on the literature, history, physical make-up, and printing of incunabula. Z240.H132

Stillwell, Margaret Bingham. Incunabula and Americana, 1450–1800; a key to bibliographical study. N.Y., Columbia Univ. Pr., 1931. (Repr.: N.Y., Cooper Square Pub., 1961) 483p. facsims. **AA268**

Contents: *Incunabula:* 1, Printed books of the 15th century; 2, Identification and collation; 3, Bibliographical reference material; *Americana:* 1, Preliminary survey of sources and methods; 2, Century of maritime discovery, 1492–1600; 3, Two centuries of colonial growth, 1500–1700; 4, Later Americana and the Revolutionary periods; 5, Early printing in America; *Reference sections:* 1, Notes and definitions; 2, Foreign bibliographical terms: French, German, Italian, and Spanish; 3, Latin contractions and abbreviations; 4, Place names of 15th-century printing towns; 5, Incunabula: selected bibliographies and monographs (600 items); 6, 15th-century woodcuts: selected monographs; 7, Americana: selected bibliographies and monographs (more than 600 items).

An indispensable reference work and guide for the collector or librarian. Important both for the text and for the extensive annotated bibliographies. Z240.A1S8

Bibliography

Hain, Ludwig Friedrich Theodor. Repertorium bibliographicum, in quo libri omnes ab arte typographica inventa usque ad annum MD. . . . Stuttgart, Cotta, 1826–38. 2v. in 4. (Repr.: Berlin, Altmann, 1925) **AA269**

A basic list arranged alphabetically, the items numbered serially throughout. The "Hain number" is referred to in many later bibliographies of incunabula. Z240.H15

Copinger, Walter Arthur. Supplement to Hain's Repertorium bibliographicum; or, Collections towards a new edition of that work. London, Sotheran, 1895–1902. 2v. in 3. (Repr.: Leipzig, Lorentz, 1926) **AA270**

Pt.1, nearly 7,000 corrections of and additions to the collation of works described in Hain; pt.2, list of nearly 6,000 volumes not in Hain: v.1, A–O; v.2, P–Z. v.2 also includes "The printers and publishers of the XV century with lists of their works," by Konrad Burger (p.319–670), which is an index to the *Supplement to Hain's Repertorium* and to the works of Campbell, Pellechet, and Proctor. Z240.T15S

Reichling, Dietrich. Appendices ad Hainii-Copingeri Repertorivm bibliographicvm; additiones et emendationes. Monachii, Rosenthal, 1905–11. 7v. (Repr. with suppl.: Milano, Görlich, 1953) **AA271**

Pts.1–6 in two sections each: I, Additions; II, Emendations; pt.[7], Indices fascicvlorvm I–VI.

———— ———— Svpplementvm (maximam partem e bibliothecis Helvetiae collectvm) cvm indice vrbivm et typographorvm. Accedit index avctorvm generalis totivs operis. Monasterii Gvestphalorvm, Theissingianis, 1914. 109p., cxxxv p. Z240.H15S2

Burger, Konrad. Supplement zu Hain und Panzer. Beiträge zur Inkunabelbibliographie, Nummernconcordanz von Panzers lateinischen u. deutschen Annalen u. Ludwig Hain's Repertorium bibliographicum. Leipzig, Hiersemann, 1908. 440p. **AA272** Z240.H151

———— Ludwig Hain's Repertorium bibliographicum. Register. Die Drucker des XV. Jahrhunderts. Leipzig, Harrassowitz, 1891. 428p. (Centralblatt für Bibliothekswesen. Beihefte, Bd.2, Hft.8) (Repr.: Nendeln, Liechtenstein, Kraus, 1968) **AA273** Z671.C39B

Panzer, Georg Wolfgang Franz. Annales typographici ab artis inventae origine ad annum MD. Norimbergae, Zeh, 1793–97. 5v. **AA274**

Arranged by places, then chronologically under place.

———— ———— ab anno MDI ad annum MDXXXVI. Norimbergae, 1798–1803. 6v.

Numbered v.6–11. v.10–11, Indici. Z240.P2

Proctor, Robert. Index to the early printed books in the British Museum; with notes of those in the Bodleian Library. London, K. Paul, 1898–1938. Pts.1–2 in 6v. **AA275**

Pt.1, To 1500: v.1, Germany; v.2, Italy; v.3, Switzerland to Montenegro, including France, Netherlands, Austria-Hungary, Spain, England, Scandinavia, Portugal; v.4, Register. 1898–99. 4v.

A chronological list under each country by names of presses. The index volume contains an alphabetical list of towns, printers, and publishers; a list of books mentioned in Hain and of those not in Hain; authors of books printed in the Low Countries; and books printed in England.

Pt.2, 1501–20: sec.1, Germany, 1903; sec.2, Italy; sec.3, Switzerland and Eastern Europe, by Frank Isaac. London, Quaritch, 1938.

———— ———— Supplements 1898–1902. [London, 1900–1903] 5 pts.

Pts.1–4, Supplements; pt.5, Register. Z240.P96

British Museum. Dept. of Printed Books. Catalogue of books printed in the XVth century now in the British Museum. London, 1908–71. Pts.1–10. facsims. **AA276**

Work supervised by A. W. Pollard.

Pts.1–2, Germany; pt.3, Germany, German-speaking Switzerland and Austria-Hungary; pts.4–7, Italy; pt.8, France, French-speaking Switzerland; pt.9, Holland, Belgium; pt.10, Spain, Portugal.

Arranged under places by printers' names. Gives historical notes about printers, and full title, description, collation, and date of purchase of each book. Pt.3 contains also an introduction by A.W. Pollard, a typographical map, facsimiles, and indexes to pts.1–3 by (1) Hain's numbers, (2) concordance of Proctor's numbers, and (3) printers and towns. Covers the same ground as the first part of Proctor's *Index to the early printed books* (AA275) but with much fuller descriptions. Z240.B85

Index Aureliensis; catalogus librorum sedecimo saeculo impressorum. Aureliae Aquensis, 1962– . v.1– . (Bibliotheca bibliographica Aureliana, 7, 11, 13, 15, etc.) (In progress) **AA277**

Issued in parts 1962– , as "editio princeps" and in bound volumes 1965– , as "editio altera."

Contents: Prima pars—A, v.1–6, A–Carroli; Tertia pars—C, v.1, Indices ad tom. I & II.

An alphabetical main-entry listing of 16th-century imprints, with locations indicated for about 500 libraries throughout the world. The indexes to v.1–2 are by printer, personal name, and place.

Z1014.I5

Union lists

Goff, Frederick Richmond. Incunabula in American libraries; a third census of fifteenth-century books recorded in North American collections. N.Y., Bibliographical Soc. of America, 1964. 798p. **AA278**

First census by the Bibliographical Society, 1919; *Second census* by Margaret Bingham Stillwell, 1940.

A much enlarged edition recording 47,188 copies of 12,599 titles held by 760 owners. Roughly 90 percent of the total registered are held by institutions. The method of listing follows closely that of the *Second census,* and the style is virtually the same. The entries have been renumbered, but the Stillwell number is indicated in a subsidiary position.

Authors are listed alphabetically, in general conforming to Hain, or to the form used in the British Museum *Catalogue of books printed in the XVth century* (AA276), or in the *Gesamtkatalog der Wiegendrucke* (AA279). (Works in Hebrew are listed in a separate section under "Hebraica.") Information under each entry usually includes author (with variant spellings), short title, place, printer, date, size, references to descriptions in printed catalogs, and location of copies.

Additional sections include: Variant author-forms and entries; Index of printers and publishers; Concordances to the numbers used in the *Gesamtkatalog,* Hain, Proctor's *Index,* and the *Second census* if the sequence of numbers has been changed; Deletions from the *Second census;* Addenda.

A reprinting of the 1964 edition (Millwood, N.Y., Kraus Reprint, 1973) is "Reproduced from the annotated copy maintained by Frederick R. Goff, compiler and editor." It includes annotations and corrections in the text, and a new introduction and list of dealers.

Z240.G58

———— ———— A supplement. N.Y., Bibliographical Society of America, 1972. 104p.

Offers additions and corrections to the third census, the additions including 3,560 copies, of which "324 are new titles not previously represented in American ownership."—*Introd.*

Gesamtkatalog der Wiegendrucke, hrsg. von der Kommission für der Gesamtkatalog der Wiegendrucke. Leipzig, Hiersemann, 1925–40. v.1–8¹. **AA279**

Contents: v.1–8¹, A–Federicis. No more published.

As far as published, the most comprehensive record of incunabula yet made, based on information collected during more than 20 years' work by the Kommission. The sections issued record nearly half again as many editions as Hain (AA269), and the information given for each is much fuller, including: (1) author entry, title, date, etc.; (2) collation, types, capitals, and illustrations; (3) transcripts of title, colophon, and other extracts; (4) references to descriptions in Hain and other bibliographies; and (5) location of copies, which includes a complete record of all copies if not more than ten are known and, for commoner books, a selection of copies in representative libraries in different countries, both European and American.

Indispensable in both cataloging and reference work in the scholarly library.

A new edition is appearing as: Z240.G39

———— Hrsg. von der Kommission für den Gesamtkatalog der Wiegendrucke. 2. Aufl., durchgesehener Neudruck der 1. Aufl. Stuttgart, A. Hiersemann; N.Y., Kraus, 1968–81. Bd.1–9¹. (In progress) **AA280**

Contents: Bd.1–9¹, Abano–Friedrich.

The first seven volumes of the new edition are reprints of those published 1925–38. The first part of Bd.8 (publ. 1940) is not reprinted for this edition, and revision and expansion begins with Bd.8, Lfg.1 (publ. 1972). New information is supplied as relevant for materials previously treated in the 1940 fascicule of v.8. The list of locations now includes some 4,000 libraries and collections.

Reviews of new fascicles appear in *The Library,* ser. 5, v.30, p. 339–44 (Dec. 1975; by John L. Flood) and in *TLS,* Aug. 15, 1980, p.922 (by Paul Needham). Z240.A1G47

Accurti, Tommaso. Editiones saeculi XV pleraeque bibliographis ignotae. Annotationes ad opus quod inscribitur "Gesamtkatalog der Wiegendrucke" voll. I–IV. Florentiae, ex "Tipografia Giuntina," 1930. 170p. **AA281**

Z240.A22

———— Aliae editiones saeculi XV pleraeque nondum descriptae. Annotationes ad opus cui titulus "Gesamtkatalog der Wiegendrucke," voll. I–VI. Florentiae, ex "Tipografia Giuntina," 1936. 130p. **AA281a**

Z240.A221

Guarnaschelli, Teresa Maria and **Valenziani, E.** Indice generale degli incunaboli delle biblioteche d'Italia, a cura del Centro Nazionale d'Informazioni Bibliografiche. . . . Roma, Libreria dello Stato, 1943–72. 5v. facsims. il.

AA282

Added title page: Ministero dell' educazione nazionale. Indici e cataloghi. Nuova serie, 1.

A union catalog of incunabula in the libraries of Italy.

Additions and corrections are found in Alfredo Cioni's *Nuovo giunte e correzioni al "Indice genrale degli incunaboli"* (Firenze, Sansoni, 1963. 37p.). Z240.G915

Incunabula in Dutch libraries: a census of fifteenth-century printed books in Dutch public collections. [Gerard van Thienen, ed. in chief] Nieuwkoop, De Graaf, 1983. 2v. (Bibliotheca bibliographica Neerlandica, 17) **AA283**

An alphabetical listing of incunabula in nearly 90 libraries; indexes of printers and places of publication, and a detailed general index.

A review by David McKitterick appears in *TLS* June 8, 1984, p.647.

Ohly, Kurt and **Sack, Vera,** eds. Inkunabelkatalog der Stadt- und Universitätsbibliothek und anderer öffentlicher Sammlungen in Frankfurt am Main. Frankfurt am Main, V. Klostermann, [1966]. 736p. (Kataloge der Stadt- und Universitätsbibliothek, Frankfurt am Main) **AA284**

Issued in 5 Lfg.

An alphabetical main entry listing of more than 3,000 incunabula in libraries and other public collections of Frankfurt am Main, with indexes by printers, owners, and by numbers in Hain and the *Gesamtkatalog der Wiegendrucke.* Z240.O39

Pellechet, Marie Léontine Catherine. Catalogue général des incunables des bibliothèques publiques de France. Paris, Picard, 1897–1909. v.1–3. **AA285**

Contents: v.1–3, A–Gregorius Magnus.

———— ———— Unpublished manuscript by Louis Polain continuing the work from Gregorius to Z. v.4–14 on 11 reels microfilm. **AA286**

Microfilm copy from the original manuscript in the possession of the French government.

Kraus-Thomson has reprinted (Nendeln, Liechtenstein, 1970) the three published volumes from Louis Polain's working copy with his corrections and amendments, together with a photoreproduction (in 23 additional volumes) of the Polain manuscript previously available only on microfilm. Z240.P382

Polain, Louis. Catalogue des livres imprimés au quinzième siècle des bibliothèques de Belgique. Bruxelles, Soc. des Bibliophiles, 1932. 4v. facsims. **AA287**

Contents: v.1–3, A–S; v.4, T–Z; Supplément (no.4070–4109). Additions. Tables: A, Facsimilés; B, Concordance des numéros avec ceux de Campbell, *Gesamtkatalog,* Hain, Pellechet, Voulliéme; C, Imprimeurs; E, Gravures; F, Table générale alphabétique des matières; (D, Table des bibliothèques, announced in the introduction, p.xxi, was not published). Z240.P76

———— ———— Supplément. Bruxelles, Fl. Tulkens pour l'Assoc. des Archivistes et Bibliothécaires de Belgique, 1978. 615p.

Pages 1–286 are devoted to corrections and additions to items in v.1–4. A section of "Nouvelles descriptions" adds items 4110–4804, continuing the item numbering of the basic set. A section of "Tables" provides concordances with standard catalogs of incunabula such as Hain, Goff, Copinger, etc. Z240.C357

Sajó, Géza and **Soltész, Erzsébet,** eds. Catalogus incunabulorum quae in bibliothecis publicis Hungariae asservantur. Budapestini, In aedibus Academiae Scientiarum Hungaricae, 1970. 2v. (1444p.) facsims. **AA288**

Introductory matter in English.
A first effort toward a union catalog of incunabula in Hungary. Lists 7,107 copies of 3,550 editions in 56 libraries and other institutions. Z240.S27

History

Bühler, Curt Ferdinand. The fifteenth-century book: the scribes, the printers, the decorators. Philadelphia, Univ. of Pennsylvania Pr., 1960. 195p. il. **AA289**

Gives an excellent survey of the development of the 15th-century book. Includes bibliographical notes and an index. Z240.B924

Book collecting
Guides and manuals

Benjamin, Mary A. Autographs: a key to collecting. Corr. and rev. ed. N.Y., W. R. Benjamin Autographs, 1963. 313p. 35pl. **AA290**

First publ. 1946.
This edition corrected and revised, with a new preface and a selected list of reference works.
Gives information on terminology, evaluation, facsimiles, reproductions and manuscript copies, care and preservation. Emphasis is on American historical materials. Includes author and subject index. Z41.B4

Bradley, Van Allen. The book collector's handbook of values. [4th rev., enl. ed.] N.Y., Putnam, [1978]. 640p. **AA291**

1st ed. 1972.
Intended not only for the general reader, but for the "serious and sophisticated collector," as well as libraries, scholars, and booksellers. Limited principally to 19th- and 20th-century American and English publications (with a few works published in Europe by English and American authors), having a current retail value of at least $25. Alphabetical author or anonymous title listing. Price range for copies in good condition is indicated, with record of recent auction prices as applicable.
Supersedes the price index in the compiler's *New gold in your attic* (2d ed. N.Y., Fleet Pr., 1968), although the introductory matter in that volume may still prove valuable to the beginning collector. Z1029.B7

Carter, John. ABC for book-collectors. 6th ed. with corrections and additions by Nicolas Barker. London & N.Y., Granada, 1980. 219p. **AA292**

1st ed. 1952.
An alphabetical dictionary of bibliographic and booksellers' terms with definitions as used in Great Britain and the United States. Z1006.C37

Hamilton, Charles. Collecting autographs and manuscripts. Norman, Univ. of Oklahoma Pr., [1961]. 269p. il. **AA293**

Contains information on building a collection, forgeries, evaluation, care and preservation, etc. Includes more than 800 facsimiles of autographs and other reproductions from all countries and periods; a brief, annotated bibliography; and an index of authors, subjects, and titles. Z41.H34

Bibliography

Bennett, Whitman. A practical guide to American book collecting (1663–1940); with all items arranged in sequence as a chronological panorama of American authorship and with each subject considered from bibliographical, biographical and analytical aspects. N.Y., Bennett Book Studios, [1941]. 254p. **AA294**

Lists about 1,000 outstanding American books, with annotations giving bibliographical information about first printing. Z1231.F5B45

British Library. Modern British and American private presses, 1850–1965: holdings of the British Library. [London], Publ. for the British Library by British Museum Pubns., [1976]. 211p. **AA295**

"The present list is based on entries in the General Catalogue of the British Library, arranged (i) alphabetically, by presses; (ii) chronologically within each press; (iii) alphabetically by author or other heading within each year under each press. The entries have been made over a long period, and consequently changes in catalogue practice are reflected by differences in style."—*Pref.* American presses are less fully represented than those of Britain. Indexed. Z1028.B75

Brussel, Isidore Rosenbaum. Anglo-American first editions. . . . London, Constable; N.Y., Bowker, 1935–36. 2v. il. (Half title: Bibliographia; studies in book history . . . no.9–10) **AA296**

Pt.1: East to West, 1826–1900 . . . English authors whose books were published in America before their publication in England. 170p.; pt.2: West to East, 1786–1930 . . . American authors whose books were published in England before their publication in America. 131p.
Gives detailed bibliographical information with descriptive annotations. Z2014.F5B9

Carteret, Léopold. Le trésor du bibliophile romantique et moderne, 1801–75. Paris, Carteret, 1924–28. 3v. and index. il., facsims. **AA297**

v.1–2, Éditions originales, A–Z; v.3, Livres illustrés du XIXᵉ siècle; Index volume, Tables générales, ouvrages cités, illustrateurs et graveurs. Z2161.C32

———— Le trésor du bibliophile: livres illustrés modernes 1875 à 1945, et Souvenirs d'un demi-siècle de bibliophile de 1887 à 1945. Paris, Carteret, 1946–48. 5v. il., facsims. **AA298**

Title varies.
Discussions of various points relating to books and book collecting (editions, illustrations and engravings, etc.), bibliophiles, libraries, manuscripts and autographs, etc. Z2161.C3

Heard, Joseph Norman. Bookman's guide to Americana. 8th ed. Metuchen, N.J., Scarecrow Pr., 1981. 284p. **AA299**

1st ed. 1953.

"The eighth edition, like its predecessors, is an alphabetically arranged compilation of quotations gleaned from recent out-of-print booksellers' catalogs. It is intended to provide the bookseller or book buyer with a record of prices asked for out-of-print titles in the broad field of Americana, including factual or fictional works relating to America or written by Americans."—*Pref.*

Z1207.H43

Howes, Wright. U.S.iana, 1650–1950; a selective bibliography in which are described 11,620 uncommon and significant books relating to the continental portion of the United States. Rev. and enl. [i.e., 2d] ed. N.Y., Bowker, for the Newberry Lib., 1962. 652p.   **AA300**

This list of uncommon books relating to the continental United States, compiled primarily for the use of the average collector, indicates their relative sales value in five categories from $10 to more than $1,000. For the rarer items indication is frequently given of the location of one or more perfect copies in American libraries.

Z1215.H75

Johnson, Merle De Vore. American first editions. 4th ed., rev. and enl. by Jacob Blanck. N.Y., Bowker, 1942. 553p. (Repr.: Cambridge, Mass., Research Classics, 1962)   **AA301**

1st ed., 1929, planned as a continuation of Patrick K. Foley's *American authors, 1795–1895* (Boston, 1897).

Lists the first editions of more than 200 American authors having "collector interest."   Z1231.F5J6

Parenti, Marino. Prime edizioni italiane; manuale di bibliografia pratica ad uso dei bibliofili e dei librai. 2. ed. riv. e ampl. Milano, Libri d'Arte e di Filologia, 1948. 526p.   **AA302**

1st ed. 1935.

An alphabetical list of Italian authors from the 16th to the 19th centuries, with dates of their editions.   Z2354.F5P2

———— Rarità bibliografiche dell' Ottocento; materiali e pretesti per una storia della tipografia italiana nel secolo decimonono. Firenze, Sansoni, 1953–64. v.1–8. il., facsims. (Contributi alla biblioteca bibliografica italica 3, 13, 16, 19, 22, 24, 25, 27)   **AA303**

v.1: 3. ed. rifatta e di molto ampliata.

Contents: v.1–8, A–Erc.

No more published.

Detailed bibliographical information, with descriptive notes and references to sources of rare 19th-century Italian books.

Z2351.P33

Private press books, 1959– . North Harrow, [Eng.], Private Libraries Assoc., 1960– . v.1– . Annual.   **AA304**

Publisher varies.

Ed. by Roderick Cave [and others].

"Attempts to include the work of all private presses printing in English, and the more important of those printing in other languages."—*Note* (v.5, 1963). Alphabetical by name of press, with the titles published during the year covered. A bibliography of "the literature of private printing" appears in each issue. Each year has an index by author and title. The 1970 issue includes a "Cumulative index to private press books 1959–70."   Z1028.P7

Ricci, Seymour de. The book collector's guide; a practical handbook of British and American bibliography. Philadelphia, Rosenbach, 1921. 649p. (Repr.: N.Y., Burt Franklin, 1970)   **AA305**

A guide for the collector and book buyer, covering the period from Chaucer to Swinburne and listing books which because of rarity, market value, etc., were most sought after by collectors, including first editions, illustrated books, 17th-century and 18th-century drama, and standard works. Arranged alphabetically by author, giving bibliographical descriptions, prices at sales, notes, etc.

Z2001.R49

Historical children's books

Bingham, Jane and **Scholt, Grayce.** Fifteen centuries of children's literature: an annotated chronology of British and American works in historical context. Westport, Conn., Greenwood Pr., [1980]. 540p. il.   **AA306**

Aims "to provide a single, annotated chronological listing of significant or representative books written for or used with or appropriated by British and American children from the sixth century to 1945."—*Pref.* For each of six chronological periods there are introductory essays on the historical background, the development of books, and the attitudes toward and treatment of children; these are followed by the annotated chronology for the period. Appendixes include lists of periodicals for children and of facsimiles and reprints of books in the chronology. Indexed.

Z1037.A1B582

Darton, Frederick Joseph Harvey. Children's books in England: five centuries of social life. [2d ed.] Introd. by Kathleen Lines. Cambridge, Univ. Pr., 1958. 367p. facsims.   **AA307**

1st ed. 1932.

A scholarly survey covering the literature from the fables of the Middle Ages to the early 20th century. Devoted to printed works "produced ostensibly to give children spontaneous pleasure, not primarily to teach them. . . ." Thus schoolbooks are omitted.

This edition has corrected a few details in the text and added titles to the chapter bibliographies.   PN1009.A1D35

Muir, Percival Horace. English children's books, 1600 to 1900. London, Batsford; N.Y., Praeger, [1954]. 255p. il.   **AA308**

Supplements Darton's *Children's books in England.* Includes a much broader selection, but treatment is briefer. Excellent bibliographies, with notes and often annotations, accompany each chapter. Profusely illustrated with many reproductions of title pages. Includes index to authors, titles, and illustrations.

A useful work for Australian children's literature is Marcie Muir's *A bibliography of Australian children's books* (London, A. Deutsch, 1970. 1038p.) which includes books relating to Australia regardless of the nationality of the writer or place of publication.

PN1009.A1M8

Gottlieb, Robin. Publishing children's books in America, 1919–1976: an annotated bibliography. N.Y., Children's Book Council, [1978]. 195p.   **AA309**

A classified bibliography of more than 700 items designed "to show the development of American book publishing for children over a fifty-seven-year period: from 1919, when the Macmillan Company established the first separate department for children's books, down to and including 1976."—*Introd.* Items selected deal only with trade books, not textbooks or other educational materials. Includes books, parts of books, and periodical articles. Indexed.

Z472.G67

Gumuchian et Cie., *booksellers, Paris.* Les livres de l'enfance du XVᵉ au XIXᵉ siècle, préface de Paul Gavault. Paris, Gumuchian, [1931?]. 2v. il.   **AA310**

v.1, Text, i.e., Bibliography of 6,251 items, with full bibliographical description of each; v.2, 338 plates, containing a total of 1,080 facsimiles of illustrations from books described in v.1, beautifully reproduced, many of them hand-colored.

Important both for the careful description of rare books and for the wealth of illustration. May be supplemented by two simpler lists issued by the same firm (Catalogues 15 and 18): (1) *100 noteworthy firsts in juvenile literature* (1932. 30p.) and (2) *500 early juveniles* (1933. 39p.).   Z1037.Z9G9

Johnson, Deidre. Stratemeyer pseudonyms and series books: an annotated checklist of Stratemeyer and Stratemeyer Syndicate publications. Westport, Conn., Greenwood Pr., 1982. 343p.   **AA311**

Stratemeyer and his syndicate were responsible for more than 1,300 books, including such popular series as the Nancy Drew, Tom

Swift, Bobbsey twins, and similar works. Recommended for libraries with strong historical children's literature collections.

Z8849.69.J63

Pellowski, Anne. The world of children's literature. N.Y., Bowker, 1968. 538p. il. **AA312**

An international bibliography on the history and development of children's literature. Includes writings on library work with children, reading interests of children, techniques of writing for children, etc. Attention is also given to lists of recommended books, anthologies, and indexes of children's literature, and to biographical materials on children's authors. Most of the nearly 4,500 entries are annotated. Arranged by country; indexed. Z1037.P37

Rahn, Suzanne. Children's literature: an annotated bibliography of the history and criticism. N.Y., Garland, 1981. 451p. (Garland reference library of the humanities, v.263) **AA312a**

In three main sections: (1) historical studies; (2) studies of genres; (3) studies of authors. Concerned with studies in English, mainly of British and American children's literature. Index of names.

PR990.R3

Rosenbach, Abraham Simon Wolf. Early American children's books. With bibliographical descriptions of the books in his private collection. Portland, Me., Southworth Pr., 1933. lix p. 354p. il. **AA313**

Includes: Foreword by A. Edward Newton; Introduction; Early American children's books, p.3–287; Index of authors and titles; Index of printers and publishers; List of printers, publishers, and booksellers; Bibliography.

U.S. Library of Congress. Rare Book Division. Children's books in the Rare Book Division of the Library of Congress. Totowa, N.J., Rowman and Littlefield, 1975. 2v. **AA314**

Contents: v.1, Author; v.2, Chronological.

"As a result of the federal copyright regulations, the Library of Congress has assembled an immense collection of American children's books. For its period—the 19th and 20th centuries—and its country of origin—the United States—this collection outranks any other in the world. From these holdings the Rare Book Division has brought together on its shelves approximately 15,000 volumes of particular interest, maintaining them separately as a special collection, which this publication describes."—*Introd.* Also includes other children's books in the Rare Book Division which are not part of the separate children's book collection. Reproduces the catalog cards describing the books; includes numerous temporary entries for works not found in the *National union catalog.* Z1037.U5U54

Welch, D'Alté Aldridge. A bibliography of American children's books printed prior to 1821. [Worcester, Mass.], American Antiquarian Soc., 1972. 516p. **AA315**

Originally published in the *Proceedings* of the American Antiquarian Society, April 1963–Oct. 1967.

"This bibliography is primarily concerned with narrative books written in English, designed for children under fifteen years of age. They should be the type of book read at leisure for pleasure. The book must have been originally written for children or abridged for them from an adult version."—*p.liii.*

An alphabetical listing by author or other main entry. Locates copies. Index of printers, publishers, and imprints. (A 4-page supplement, "Index to titles listed under author without cross references," was published later for insertion into the book.) A detailed and scholarly work. Z1232.W44

Printers' marks

Delalain, Paul Adolphe. Inventaire des marques d'imprimeurs et de libraires de la collection du Cercle de la Librairie. 2. éd. rev. et augm. Paris, Cercle de la Librairie, 1892. 355p. il. (Bibliothèque technique de la Cercle de la Librairie) **AA316**

Gives names, dates, and addresses of printers with descriptions of

the marks and devices used by them in the various countries of Europe. Z235.P22

McKerrow, Ronald Brunlees. Printers' & publishers' devices in England & Scotland, 1485–1640. London, Bibliographical Soc., 1913. 216p. 69 pl. **AA317**

Contains descriptions and facsimiles of 428 devices, a dictionary of certain printers' names with information about transfers of devices, and five indexes of devices and compartments by: (1) sizes, (2) printers and booksellers, (3) mottoes, (4) initials of designers and engravers, (5) subjects. Z236.G7M2

Polain, Louis. Marques des imprimeurs et libraires en France au XVᵉ siècle. Paris, Droz, 1926. 207p. il. (Documents typographiques du XVᵉ siècle, t.1) **AA318**

Augments and corrects Silvestre's *Marques typographiques* (AA322). Z236.F8P7

Reilly, Elizabeth Carroll. A dictionary of colonial American printers' ornaments and illustrations. Worcester, Amer. Antiquarian Soc., 1975. 515p. il. **AA319**

"The purpose of the dictionary is to aid both bibliographers and historians in their studies of the colonial period. Used judiciously, the listings may facilitate the bibliographer's identification of many books, pamphlets, and broadsides which lack imprints or colophons. The index of printers records the ornaments and illustrations used by each printer and thus provides the means for a study of the changes in his printing stock."—*Introd.* Z208.R43

Renouard, Philippe. Les marques typographiques parisiennes des XVᵉ et XVIᵉ siècles. Paris, Champion, 1926–28. 381p. il. (Revue des bibliothèques, suppl. 14–15) **AA320**

Issued in parts.

Illustrations and descriptions of the marks of Parisian printers. Z236.F8R4

Roberts, William. Printers' marks; a chapter in the history of typography. London & N.Y., Geo. Bell, 1893. 261p. il. **AA321**

A chronological account describing the marks of the early and important printers of Europe. Includes some modern examples, mostly from England. Contains more than 200 illustrations. Z235.R64

Silvestre, Louis Catherine. Marques typographiques. . . . Paris, Jannet, successeur de L. C. Silvestre, 1853; Impr. Renou, 1867. 2v. facsims. **AA322**

Published anonymously in parts.

Subtitle: Recueil des monogrammes, chiffres, enseignes, emblèmes, devises, rébus et fleurons des libraires et imprimeurs qui ont excercé en France, depuis l'introduction de l'imprimerie, en 1470, jusqu'à la fin du seizième siècle: à ces marques sont jointes celles des libraires et imprimeurs qui pendant la même période ont publié, hors de France, des livres en langue française.

Includes more than 1,300 devices. Z236.F8S5

Watermarks

Briquet, Charles Moïse. Les filigranes. Dictionnaire historique des marques du papier dès leur apparition vers 1282 jusqu'en 1600. Facsimile of the 1907 ed. with supplementary material contributed by a number of scholars. Ed. by Allan Stevenson. Amsterdam, Paper Publications Soc., 1968. 4v. il. **AA323**

Originally publ. Paris, Picard, 1907. 4v.

A monumental work with reproductions of more than 16,000 watermarks. For the "New Briquet" Stevenson has contributed a general introduction entitled "How to use 'Les Filigranes'," followed by a group of "Bibliographical and historical illustrations" of use; a selective and annotated bibliography; and, most important, a section of "Addenda and corrigenda." A supplementary index is mainly an index to the new materials, plus some additional references to the original text. In the volumes with plates of watermark reproductions, the use date of each mark has been added in parentheses. Z237.B845

The Briquet album; a miscellany on watermarks, supplementing Dr. Briquet's Les filigranes, by various paper scholars. Hilversum, Holland, Paper Publications Soc., 1952. 158p. il. (Monumenta chartae papyraceae historiam illustrantia, 2) **AA324**

"Indexes to Briquet's *Les filigranes* in German, English and Italian," p.125–54. TS1080.P183

Gravell, Thomas L. and **Miller, George.** A catalogue of American watermarks, 1690–1835. N.Y., Garland, 1979. 230p. il. (Garland reference library of the humanities, v.151) **AA325**

Identifies more than 700 watermarks, giving location of the manuscript, place and date of use, and a reproduction of the watermark. A brief history of each paper mill represented is given in a separate section. Select bibliography, proper name index, and a subject index which provides an approach through the devices used in the watermarks. TS1115.G7

Auction records

American book-prices current, a record of literary properties sold at auction in England, the United States, and in Canada . . . 1894/95– . N.Y., Amer. Book-Prices Current, 1895– . v.1– . Annual. **AA326**

Publisher varies.
Subtitle varies. Before v.64, 1958, included only records of sales held in the United States.
Arrangement and information given vary somewhat but usually include author, title, edition, place and date of publication, size, binding, condition, where sold, date of sale, catalog number of lot, and price. Includes autographs and manuscripts as well as printed materials of all periods and languages. Generally considered the most accurate of the auction record compilations. Z1000.A51

Blogie, Jeanne. Répertoire des catalogues de ventes de livres imprimés. Bruxelles, Fl. Tulkens, 1982– . v.1– . (In progress) **AA327**

Contents: v.1, Catalogues belges appartenant à la Bibliothèque Royale Albert Iᵉʳ.
The series is designed to present an inventory of sales catalogues of printed books found in Belgian libraries.

Book-auction records; a priced and annotated annual record of London [and other] book-auctions, June 1902– . London & N.Y., Henry Stevens, 1903– . v.1– . Quarterly, 1902–40/41; annual, 1941/42– . **AA328**

Publisher varies.
Subtitle varies. From v.12, Edinburgh, Glasgow, and Dublin auctions sometimes included. From 1939/40, also includes principal New York auctions.
Entries are "exact reproductions, abbreviated, of the auctioneers' catalogue-descriptions," and include date of sale, number of lot, price, and name of buyer.
When issued quarterly, each number was arranged alphabetically by author, with an index in each volume. Annual volumes are arranged alphabetically by author.

—— General index, 1902–12, 1912–23, 1924–33, 1934–43, 1944–48, 1948–58, 1958–63, 1963–68. London, Stevens, 1924–71. 8v.

Subtitle: Giving instant clues to the contents . . . and, incidentally, to anonymous authors, autographs, bibliophiles, binders, bindings, distinguished owners, editors, fore-edge paintings, holograph manuscripts, illustrators, notable presses, pseudonyms, translators, etc. Z1000.B65

Book-prices current, Dec. 1886–1956/58. London, Sergeants Pr., 1888–1959. v.1–64. Annual (irregular). **AA329**

Publisher varies.

Subtitle: A record of the prices at which books have been sold at auction.
v.1–27, 1886–1913, arranged by date of sale; v.28–64, 1914–56/58, arranged alphabetically by author and some titles. Useful both as a record of market prices of secondhand books and as a supplement to the various general and national bibliographies for titles and editions not noted in such bibliographies.

—— Index, 1887–96, 1897–1906, 1907–16. London, Stock, 1901–20, 3v.

Z1000.B72

Bookman's price index, v.1– . Detroit, Gale, [1964–]. Annual (slightly irregular). **AA330**

Editor: D. F. McGrath.
A main-entry list. Listings are based on descriptions of books and periodicals which were offered for sale by leading dealers in their catalogs of the period covered. Includes a list of dealers represented. Z1000.B74

Catalogue bibliographique des ventes publiques . . . . 1968/70– . Paris, Éditions Mayer, [1970]– . Irregular. **AA331**

At head of title: O. Matterlin.
Continues Matterlin's *La cote internationale des livres et manuscrits,* 1964/65–1966/68.
Subtitle varies. Volumes usually cover three years, with a year's overlap (e.g., 1978/80, 1980/82).
Provides a record of auction prices for books and manuscripts bringing 500 Francs or more (100F in early volumes). A list of the sales and their dates is followed by an author listing of the works sold with full description, auction at which sold, and price. Coverage is most complete for France, but there is regular coverage of England, Belgium, the United States, plus irregular coverage of Switzerland, Monaco, and Italy.

Jahrbuch der Auktionspreise für Bücher und Autographen. Ergebnisse der Auktionen in Deutschland, Holland, Österreich und der Schweiz. Bd.1– , 1950– . Hamburg, E. Hauswedell, 1951– . Annual. **AA332**

Title varies slightly.
Supersedes *Jahrbuch der Bücherpreise,* Jahrg. 1–34, 1906–39.
Lists the auctions of the year covered, followed by a main-entry listing of the books, manuscripts, and autographs sold, with indication of price realized. Z1000.J235

McKay, George Leslie. American book auction catalogues, 1713–1934; a union list . . . with introd. by Clarence S. Brigham. N.Y., New York Pub. Lib., 1937. 540p. facsims. **AA333**

A "list of some 10,000 auction catalogues . . . issued in what is now the United States, that list books, pamphlets, broadsides, newspapers, manuscripts, autographs and bookplates."—*Pref.* Arranged chronologically. Locates copies.

—— —— Supplement no.1–2. 1946–48. (Repr. from New York Public Library *Bulletin* 50:177–84. 1946; 52:401–12. 1948)

Z999.A1M2

Yearbooks

Rare books: trends, collections, sources, 1983/84– . Alice D. Schreyer, ed. N.Y., Bowker, 1984– . Annual? **AA334**

Intended as an ongoing series providing an overview of activities and developments in the rare book field, together with extensive directory information. The 1983/84 volume (581p.) is in five parts, the first three offering signed essays on trends and developments, the others taking the form of directories of various kinds: (1) Reports from the rare book and manuscript field; (2) Review of bibliographical scholarship and publishing; (3) Issues and programs in the news; (4) Educational opportunities; (5) Directory of collections and sources. Indexed. Z999.R37

PRINTING AND PUBLISHING

General works

Bibliography

Bigmore, Edward Clements and **Wyman, Charles William Henry.** A bibliography of printing, with notes and illustrations. London, Quaritch, 1880–86. 3v. il. (Repr.: N.Y., P. C. Duschnes, 1945. 2v.)   **AA335**

Arranged alphabetically by author, with some subject references and form headings. Biographical, historical, and descriptive annotations.   Z117.B59

Brenni, Vito Joseph. Book printing in Britain and America: a guide to the literature and a directory of printers. Westport, Conn., Greenwood Pr., 1983. 163p.   **AA336**

A selective bibliography with separate sections for Britain and America. Entries are grouped by form (printing manuals, type specimen books, etc.) or as history (subdivided chronologically). Includes sections for music, scientific publishing, writing and calligraphy. The directory of printers, typographers, calligraphers and book designers gives an identifying phrase and dates when known. Indexed.   Z151.B68

Lehmann-Haupt, Hellmut. One hundred books about bookmaking; a guide to the study and appreciation of printing. N.Y., Columbia Univ. Pr., 1949. 87p.   **AA337**

Revised and enlarged edition of the author's *Fifty books about bookmaking* and *Seventy books about bookmaking.*

The titles are largely in English. Classified and annotated.   Z279.L38

McCoy, Ralph Edward. Freedom of the press; an annotated bibliography. Carbondale, Southern Illinois Univ. Pr., [1968]. unpaged.   **AA338**

About 8,000 items—"books, pamphlets, journal articles, films, and other material relating to freedom of the press in English-speaking countries, from the beginning of printing to the present. . . . Subjects include heresy, sedition, blasphemy, obscenity, personal libel, and both positive and negative expressions on freedom of the press."—*Pref.* Author listing; subject index.

———— Freedom of the press: a bibliocyclopedia. Ten-year supplement (1967–1977). Carbondale, Southern Illinois Univ. Pr.; London, Feffer & Simons, [1979]. 557p.

Adds more than half as many publications as in the original volume. Includes some pre-1967 items omitted from the earlier publication (above).   K3255.A12M3

McMurtrie, Douglas Crawford. The invention of printing; a bibliography. Prep. as an activity of the Work Projects Administration (Illinois). Chicago Public Library Omnibus Project . . . section on printing bibliography, co-sponsored by the Chicago Club of Printing House Craftsmen. Chicago, Chicago Club of Printing House Craftsmen, 1942. 413p.   **AA339**

Lists 3,228 titles, of which 2,026 are of separate publications, books, or pamphlets. Copies are located in American and European libraries.

Includes a section of commemorative writings of more than 1,000 items.   Z117.M18

Current

Annual bibliography of the history of the printed book and libraries. 1970– . The Hague, Nijhoff, 1973– . v.1– . Annual.   **AA340**

At head of title: ABHB.

Sponsored by IFLA.

". . . aims at recording all books and articles of scholarly value which relate to the history of the printed book, to the history of the arts, crafts, techniques and equipment, and of the economic, social and cultural environment" as they relate to production, distribution, conservation, and description of books. Writings on modern technical processes are excluded. Relevant doctoral dissertations and book reviews are listed. Classed listing, with name index. Volumes appear well after date of coverage (e.g., v.9 covering 1978 was published 1982).   Z117.A55

Periodicals

Ulrich, Carolyn Farquhar and **Küp, Karl.** Books and printing; a selected list of periodicals, 1800–1942. Woodstock, Vt., Wm. E. Rudge, 1943. 244p.   **AA341**

An annotated and selected bibliography of periodicals classed under such headings as history of printing, printing types, design, layout and typography, illustration, paper, binding, publishing, book trade, collecting, bibliography, libraries, directories, societies, etc.   Z1002.U4

Directories

Adressbuch für den deutschsprachigen Buchhandel, 1977/78– . Frankfurt am Main, Buchhandler-Vereingung GMBH, 1977– . Annual.   **AA342**

Continues *Adressbuch des deutschsprachigen Buchhandels,* publ. 1954–75. With various changes of title (e.g., *Adressbuch des deutschen Buchhandels*), the series goes back to 1839.

Now published in 3v.: (1) Verlage; (2) Buchhandel; (3) Organisationen. Bd.1 carries the subtitle: Buchhandels-Adressbuch für die Bundesrepublik Deutschland; Verzeichnis des Buchhandels der Deutschen Demokratischen Republik; Adressbuch des Österreichischen Buchhandels; Schweizer Buchhandel, Adressbuch; Verzeichnis des Buchhandels anderer Länder. Bd.2–3 omit reference to the German Democratic Republic in the subtitle.

Provides extensive coverage of German, Austrian, and Swiss publishers, book dealers, and related organizations, with selective coverage for other countries. Offers geographical approach, ISBN numbers, etc.   Z317.A26

The African book world & press; a directory. Répertoire du livre et de la presse en Afrique. Hans M. Zell, ed. München, Zell/Saur, 1983. 285p.   **AA343**

Introduction and section headings in English and French; directory information in English or French. A country-by-country listing covering 51 African nations. For each country is given information under as many of the following headings as applicable: (1) University, college, and public libraries; (2) Special libraries; (3) Booksellers; (4) Publishers; (5) Institutional publishers; (6) Periodicals and magazines; (7) Major newspapers; (8) Book industry associations and literary societies; (9) Printers; (10) the government printer of the country. Appendixes include subject index of special libraries; subject index of periodicals; a list of principal dealers in African books in Europe and the U.S.A.

American book trade directory; lists of publishers, booksellers, periodicals, trade organizations, wholesalers, etc. N.Y., Bowker, 1915– . Biennial (formerly triennial).   **AA344**

Title varies: *American book trade manual,* 1915–22; *American booktrade directory,* 1925–49.

Coverage varies. 28th ed. (1982) includes: (1) Retailers & antiquarians in the United States & Canada; (2) Wholesalers of books & magazines in the United States & Canada; (3) Book trade information (auctioneers, appraisers of library collections, dealers in foreign language books, exporters and importers, rental library chains, national and regional associations); (4) Index to retailers & wholesalers in the United States & Canada. The section on United States and Canadian book publishers and the lists of former publishing companies which were a feature of earlier editions were discontinued with the 26th ed. (1980).   Z475.A5

Bowker Editores Argentina. La empresa del libro en América Latina; guía seleccionada de editoriales, distribuidores y librerías de América Latina. [2. ed.] [Buenos Aires], Bowker Editores, [1974]. 307p. **AA345**

1st ed. 1968.

A book-trade directory for the Latin-American nations with listings similar to those found in the *Literary market place* (AA353).

Z490.5.B67

Cassell's Directory of publishing in Great Britain, the Commonwealth and Ireland, 1960/61– . London, Cassell, 1960– . Irregular. **AA346**

Title varies; South Africa and Pakistan included in some issues.

Gives information similar to that provided for the United States in the *Literary market place* (AA353), i.e., lists of British and Commonwealth publishers, agents, associations, book clubs, prizes, etc. Z326.C3

Directory of Indian publishers. Ed.1– . New Delhi, Federation of Publishers & Booksellers Associations in India, [1973]– . **AA347**

Ed.1 is in four sections: (1) Publishers—private sector (arranged by language in which their works are published); (2) Corporate bodies; (3) Book industry adjuncts (e.g., exporters, importers, book review media, book trade journals); (4) Geographical index of publishers. No more published? Z455.D494

Les éditeurs et diffuseurs de langue française, 1983. Répertoire international. [Paris], Cercle de la Librairie, 1982. 374p. **AA348**

Constitutes a 6th ed. of *Répertoire international des éditeurs et diffuseurs de langue française* (3d ed. 1975; earlier eds. appeared 1967 and 1961 under slightly different titles). In two main sections: (1) Table générale des éditeurs, and (2) Table générale des organismes de diffusion, with a classified index for the first and a geographical index for the second. Z282.E35

Gli editori italiani: statistiche e analisi di mercato, dati e indirizzi, leggi e regolamenti. [A cura dell'] Associazione Italiana Editori. 4. ed. Milano, Bibliografica, 1984. 480p. **AA349**

1st ed. 1976. Subtitle has varied.

A directory of Italian publishers which gives, in addition to address and phone number, founding date, areas of specialization, number of titles in print, ISBN prefix, distributors, etc. Includes an introductory survey of Italian publishing, with statistical tables.

Z342.E33

Gorokhoff, Boris I. Publishing in the U.S.S.R. [Bloomington, Ind., 1959] 306p. (Indiana Univ. pubns. Slavic and East European ser., v.19) **AA350**

Surveys the Soviet publishing network for books, magazines, and newspapers, including documentation services and matters of copyright and censorship. Emphasizes science and technology. Extensive statistical appendix.

For a companion volume on Soviet libraries *see* AB98.

Z366.G63

International literary market place, 1965– . N.Y., Bowker, 1965– . Biennial. **AA351**

1965 called "Pilot ed." Annual, 1965–69/70. 1st–5th eds., 1965–69/70, called "European edition"; beginning with the 6th ed. (1971/72, publ. 1971) also includes Africa, Australia, New Zealand, Japan, Israel, and Latin America.

A directory of publishers and book-trade organizations arranged by country; now truly international. Z291.5.I5

Internationales Verlagsadressbuch. Publishers' international directory. Ausgabe 1– . München, Verlag Dokumentation, 1964– . (Handbuch der internationalen Dokumentation und Information, Bd.7) Irregular. **AA352**

Explanatory matter in German and English.

About 154,000 publishers (including a large number of small firms) in the 11th ed. (publ. 1984). An "ISBN register," first introduced with the 6th ed., is published as v.2 of each edition, beginning with the 9th. Z282.I65

Literary market place, 1940– . The business directory of American book publishing. N.Y., Bowker, 1940– . Annual. **AA353**

Subtitle varies.

A useful and usable directory of organizations, periodicals, publishers, etc., which might be helpful in the placing, promotion, and advertising of literary property. Lists officers and key personnel. Classified under such headings as: book publishing, book clubs, associations, book trade events, conferences and contests, agents and agencies, services and suppliers, direct mail promotion, review services, exporters and importers, book manufacturing, magazine and newspaper publishing, radio, television, and motion pictures.

From 1952–71 a supplementary "Names and numbers" volume was published, first as the *Book industry register* (1952/53–59/60), then as the *Book industry telephone directory*. This was an alphabetical listing of the names found in the matching annual volume of *LMP*, giving name, firm, address, telephone, and code number of the section of *LMP* in which the name was listed. Beginning with the 1972/73 edition (publ. 1972) the "Names and numbers" section is included in *LMP* as the final section of the volume. PN161.L5

Microform market place, 1974/75– . Weston, Conn., Microfilm Review, [1974–]. Biennial. **AA354**

Subtitle: An international directory of micropublishing.

Publisher varies.

Contents, 1982/83: Directory of micropublishers; Subject index; Geographic index; Mergers & acquisitions, name changes; Organizations; Bibliography of primary sources; Names & numbers directory.

Micropublishers are listed alphabetically in the first section.

Z286.M5V43

Publishers directory. Ed. 5– , 1984/85– . Detroit, Gale, [1984]– . Irregular. (Ed.5 in 2v.) **AA355**

Subtitle: A guide to more than 9,000 new and established, commercial and nonprofit, private and alternative, corporate and association, government and institution publishing programs and their distributors; includes producers of books, classroom materials, reports, and databases.

Linda S. Hubbard, ed.

Supersedes *Book publishers directory*, eds.1–4, 1977–83.

An alphabetical listing of directory information (address, telephone, ISBN, principal officials, subject specialties, etc.) with indexes of imprints and distributors, subjects, and geographic areas. Excludes vanity presses and publishers covered in *Literary market place*.

Rudkin, Anthony and **Butcher, Irene.** A book world directory of the Arab countries, Turkey and Iran. London, Mansell (distr. in U.S. by Gale), [1981]. 143p. **AA356**

A directory of libraries, booksellers, publishers, institutional publishers, newspapers, and periodicals in the Middle East. Arranged by country, then by type of institution/agency/publication. Numerous classified lists. Z464.A7R64

Sijthoff's Adresboek voor Boekhandel, Uitgeverij, grafische Industrie, Gids voor Dagbladen en Tijdschriften. Leiden, Sijthoff, 1855–1970. v.1–103. Annual (Irregular). **AA357**

Title varies.

A directory of the newspaper and periodical press as well as of the book industry and trade.

Ceased publication. Z352.S58

U.S. book publishing yearbook and directory. 1979/80– . White Plains, N.Y., Knowledge Industry Pubns., [1979]– . Annual. **AA358**

Intended as "an annual record of the important developments and participants in book publishing."—*Pref.* In addition to an overview of the year's events, the yearbook offers a wide range of statistics on the publishing industry (including international statistics), an exhibits and meetings calendar, directories of book publishers and book trade associations, etc. Indexed. Z477.U53

Who distributes what and where; an international directory of publishers, imprints, agents and distributors. 3d ed. N.Y., Bowker, [1983]. 445p. **AA359**

1st ed. 1980.

A directory of publishers and imprints, sales agents, publishers' representatives and distributors throughout the world. Geographic index.

Dictionaries and encyclopedias

Brownstone, David M. and **Franck, Irene M.** The dictionary of publishing. N.Y., Van Nostrand Reinhold, [1982]. 302p. **AA360**

Aims "to provide a modern, concise American dictionary of publishing and allied terms for all those involved in or pursuing work related to the publishing process."—*Pref.* Gives special attention to terms relating to new technologies (computer science, etc.) as they affect publishing. Z282.5.B76

Lexikon des gesamten Buchwesens, hrsg. von Karl Löffler u. Joachim Kirchner unter Mitwirkung von Wilhelm Olbrich. Leipzig, Hiersemann, 1935–37. 3v. **AA361**

An encyclopedia of concise articles, many with bibliographical references, on a great variety of subjects connected with books and the book arts, e.g., printers and printing, publishing, illustration, places of printing, organizations and societies, manuscripts, etc. Contains many biographies. Z118.L67

Lexikon des Buchwesens, hrsg. von Joachim Kirchner. Stuttgart, Hiersemann, 1952–56. 4v. il. **AA362**

Based on the preceding entry, but in somewhat briefer form.

v.1–2 include encyclopedic articles on subjects connected with the book, many with bibliographies. v.3–4 contain plates showing illustrations, facsimiles of title pages, examples of book binding, printing presses, libraries, etc. Z118.L65

Terms

Allen, Edward Monington. Harper's Dictionary of the graphic arts. N.Y., Harper, [1963]. 295p. **AA363**

More than 6,500 basic terms used in the graphic arts industries with definitions and explanations, including descriptions of methods and processes, uses and purposes of tools, etc. Z118.A55

American Paper and Pulp Association. The dictionary of paper, including pulp, paperboard, paper properties, and related papermaking terms. 3d ed. N.Y., 1965. 500p. **AA364**

1st ed. 1940.

Definitions, given in nontechnical language, are full and definite. Terms from the 2d ed. which have been deleted or which have been entered under a different term in the new edition are listed in the appendixes. TS1085.A6

The bookman's glossary. 6th ed., rev. and enl. Ed. by Jean Peters. N.Y., Bowker, 1983. 223p. **AA365**

1st ed. 1925.

Provides "definitions of some 1,800 terms used in book publishing, book manufacturing, bookselling, the antiquarian trade, and librarianship."—*Pref.* Terms from printing, library science, etc., are those which would be likely to be encountered in publishing circumstances, not highly technical terms. Includes brief biographical sketches of "men and women of historic importance in bibliography, the graphic arts, and book publishing." Reflects the increasing use of computers in the book industry. Select reading list; table of proofreader's marks. Z118.B75

Dictionary of the graphic arts industry: in eight languages, English, German, French, Russian, Spanish, Polish, Hungarian, Slovak. Ed. by Wolfgang Müller. Amsterdam & N.Y., Elsevier, 1981. 1020p. **AA366**

Arranged on an English base with equivalent terms from the other

languages in parallel columns; indexes from the other languages. Intended "for interpreters, translators, engineers, technicians, students and scientists—indeed for anyone at all connected with the graphic arts."—*Pref.* Very wide-ranging in coverage. Z118.D523

Dictionnaire à l'usage de la librairie ancienne pour les langues française, anglaise, allemande, suédoise, danoise, italienne, espagnole, hollandaise. Sous la direction de Menno Hertzberger. Paris, International League of Antiquarian Booksellers, 1956. 190p. **AA367**

Title also in English: *Dictionary for the antiquarian booktrade.*

Keyed to the French word, with indexes in each of the other languages. A "Japanese rev. ed." (Tokyo, Antiquarian Booksellers Assoc. of Japan, 1977. 202p.) adds Japanese terms. Z282.D5

Elizarenkova, Tat'iana Petrovna. Russko-Angliiskii slovar' knigovedcheskikh terminov. Pod red. B. P. Kanevskogo. Moskva, "Sovetskaia Entsiklopediia," 1969. 264p. **AA368**

Added title page in English: Russian-English bookman's dictionary.

Lists 9,300 terms relating to bibliography, printing, publishing, the book trade, and librarianship, with English equivalents. Z1006.E555

Elsevier's Dictionary of the printing and allied industries in four languages, English, French, German, Dutch. Comp. and arr. on an English alphabetical base by F. J. M. Wijnekus. Amsterdam [etc.], Elsevier, 1967. 596p. **AA369**

Terms and definitions are given in English, with indexes from the other languages. Z118.E5

Glaister, Geoffrey Ashall. Glaister's Glossary of the book: terms used in papermaking, printing, bookbinding and publishing, with notes on illuminated manuscripts and private presses. 2d ed., completely rev. Berkeley, Univ. of California Pr., [1979]. 551p. il. **AA370**

1960 ed. had title: *Glossary of the book* (American ed. called *An encyclopedia of the book*).

"Of the 3,269 original entries 481 of diminished interest have been omitted. Of the remaining 2,788 most two or three-line entries remain unchanged beyond minor additions, deletions or updating to maintain their usefulness, but 1,050 have been rewritten and extended. . . ."—*Pref.* There are also 1,144 new entries. Alphabeting of entries is now letter by letter rather than word by word. Z118.G55

Isaacs, Alan. The multilingual dictionary of printing and publishing. London, Frederick Muller, [1981]. 289p. **AA371**

Terms from English, German, French, Italian, Spanish and Portuguese are entered in a single alphabet, with the equivalent in the other languages given at each entry. Z118.I86

Kenneison, William Charles and **Spilman, Alan J. B.** Dictionary of printing, papermaking, and bookbinding. London, Newnes, [1963]. 215p. il. **AA372**

Definitions of terms with numerous explanations of practical applications. Z118.K35

Labarre, E. J. Dictionary and encyclopaedia of paper and paper-making, with equivalents of the technical terms in French, German, Dutch, Italian, Spanish and Swedish. 2d ed. rev. and enl. Amsterdam, Swets & Zeitlinger; London, Oxford Univ. Pr., 1952. 488p. il. **AA373**

1st ed. 1937.

A detailed dictionary of technical terms with, in many cases, encyclopedic articles and descriptions, and with foreign-language equivalents. Indexes in each language. TS1085.L3

Móra, Imre. Publisher's practical dictionary in 20 languages. [3d rev. ed.] München, etc., Saur, 1984. 418p. **AA374**

Title also in French (*Dictionnaire pratique de l'édition en 20 langues*) and German (*Wörterbuch des Verlagswesens in 20 Sprachen*); introductory matter in English, French, and German.

The 1st ed. (1974, with title in German and English) was arranged on a German base; this ed. uses an English base with indexes from the other languages. About a thousand terms.   Z1006.M6

Orne, Jerrold. The language of the foreign book trade: abbreviations, terms, phrases. 3d ed. Chicago, Amer. Lib. Assoc., 1976. 333p.   **AA375**

1st ed. 1949.

Includes definitions from 15 languages, arranged by language with English equivalent supplied for each.   Z1006.O7

The Oxford dictionary for writers and editors. Comp. by the Oxford English Dictionary Department. Oxford, Clarendon Pr., 1981. 448p.   **AA376**

"The present work is the successor to eleven editions of the *Authors' and Printers' Dictionary*, first published under the editorship of F. Howard Collins in 1905. The eleventh edition, published in 1973, has been thoroughly revised and extensively rewritten, and a great deal of new material . . . has been incorporated to bring the book up to date in matters of vocabulary and usage and to give it an orientation and purpose that are reflected in its new name."—*Publisher's note*.

A dictionary of proper names, abbreviations, foreign words and phrases, and common words frequently misspelled or misused, with definitions and indication of correct or preferred usage, etc.   PE1628.C54

Schlemminger, Johann. Fachwörterbuch des Buchwesens, Deutsch, Englisch, Französisch; . . . aus Buchhandel, Verlag, Buchgewerbe, Graphik und dem Gesamtgebiet des Buchwesens. 2. wesentlich erw. Aufl. Darmstadt, Stoytscheff, 1954. 367p.   **AA377**

1st ed., 1946, had title: *Buch-Fachwörterbuch; Deutsch, Englisch, Französisch*.

In the first section the German term is given with English and French equivalents in parallel columns. This is followed by an alphabetical list of English terms with German equivalents and a similar list of French terms.   Z1006.S

Schuwer, Philippe. Dictionnaire de l'édition; art, techniques, industrie et commerce du livre. Dictionary of book publishing; creative, technical and commercial terms of the book industry. Paris, Cercle de la Librairie, [1977]. 309p.   **AA378**

French-English and English-French.

Each section lists the words with their equivalents in the other language.   Z118.S53

Stevenson, George A. Graphic arts encyclopedia. 2d ed. N.Y., McGraw-Hill, [1979]. 483p. il.   **AA379**

1st ed. 1968.

Offers definitions of terms, descriptions of processes, etc., in the graphic arts, being concerned with "(1) the products and tools with which an image is formed, (2) the kind of image, and (3) the surface upon which the image is produced."—*Pref*. An index complements the alphabetical arrangement.   Z118.S82

Stiehl, Ulrich. Satzwörterbuch des Buch- und Verlagswesens, Deutsch-Englisch. Dictionary of book publishing; with 12000 sample sentences and phrases, German-English. München, Verlag Dokumentation, 1977. 538p.   **AA380**

Introduction in German and English.

Gives the English equivalent of the German terms, usually followed by one or more examples of English usage. In addition to publishing in general, includes terms relating to editing and copyright, marketing, library science, etc.   Z282.5.S75

Thompson, Anthony. Vocabularium bibliothecarii. English, French, German, Spanish, Russian. Collaborator for Russian, E. I. Shamurin; collaborator for Spanish, Domingo Buonocore. 2d ed. Paris, UNESCO, 1962. 627p.   **AA381**

Classified arrangement with index in English language. Gives equivalents only.

For full information *see* AB42.   Z1006.T47

Handbooks

Balkin, Richard. A writer's guide to book publishing. 2d ed., rev. and expanded. N.Y., Hawthorn/Dutton, [1981]. 239p.   **AA382**

". . . with two chapters by Jared Carter."—*t.p.*

1st ed. 1977.

A common-sense guide to many aspects of book publishing, with good background information, recent statistics, and examples. Chapters include "How to approach a publisher," "How a publisher evaluates a proposal or a manuscript," "How to understand and negotiate a book contract," "How to prepare a final manuscript," "How a manuscript is processed by a publisher," "How a manuscript is turned into a finished book," "How a publisher markets a book." Gives attention to new technology in publishing, small presses, university presses, etc. Indexed.   PN155.B3

Graphic arts manual. Janet N. Field, senior ed. N.Y., Arno Pr., [1980]. 650p. il.   **AA383**

Aims "to provide a comprehensive guide to creating, producing, and purchasing printed materials. Designed to be a practical, wide-ranging, and up-to-date reference book for the graphic arts industry, it contains detailed information on graphic arts technology and processes."—*Pref*. Presented in the form of individual articles written by specialists and grouped under headings such as color, design, manuscript preparation, typography, composition, art preparation, photography, platemaking, inks, binding, etc. Helpful illustrations (photographs, diagrams, line drawings). Detailed index.   Z244.G83

Melcher, Daniel and **Larrick, Nancy.** Printing and promotion handbook; how to plan, produce, and use printing, advertising, and direct mail. 3d ed. N.Y., McGraw-Hill, [1966]. 451p.   **AA384**

1st ed. 1949.

An alphabetically arranged handbook for persons, including beginners, who buy printing and direct-mail services, plan advertising, etc.   Z118.M4

Yearbooks

The book publishing annual. 1984– . N.Y., Bowker, 1984– . Annual.   **AA385**

Prep. by the Book Division, R. R. Bowker Co., in collaboration with the staff of *Publishers weekly*.

Continues *Publishers weekly yearbook* (1983).

A compilation of signed articles which aim "to review in depth and breadth the highlights of the year in book publishing, to analyze and interpret facts and events, to identify trends, to supply new statistical data about the industry, to bring together statistical data that appeared in *Publishers Weekly* during the year . . ."—*Pref*. Provides a useful complement to the *Bowker annual* (AB111).   Z477.P96

History

Berry, William Turner and **Poole, Herbert Edmund.** Annals of printing; a chronological encyclopaedia from the earliest times to 1950. London, Blandford Pr., 1966. 315p. il.   **AA386**

Entries for persons, events, printing devices, and presses are presented chronologically. Index; bibliography.   Z124.B45

Binns, Norman E. An introduction to historical bibliography. 2d ed. rev. and enl. . . . London, Assoc. of Assist. Librarians, 1962. 387p. il.   **AA387**

1st ed. 1953.

A history of bookmaking, from the manuscript book to the printed word, in various countries, with additional chapters on publishing and bookselling, copyright, and development of book-trade bibliography. Bibliographies at the end of each chapter; index.

Z4.B55

Book Subscriptions List Project. Book subscription lists; a revised guide. [Text] by F. J. G. Robinson and P. J. Wallis. Newcastle upon Tyne, H. Hill for The Book Subscriptions List Project, 1975. 120p. **AA388**

Earlier, preliminary lists were issued in duplicated form.

An introductory section provides background and description of subscription lists and points out their potential uses. The "Catalogue of book subscription lists" is chronologically arranged within two main sections: "Lists to 1761" and "Lists 1761–1974." Author index; book trade index; provincial imprint index.

Clair, Colin. A chronology of printing. London, Cassell, 1969. 228p. **AA389**

". . . an attempt to set in their chronological order those matters judged most important in the history of the printed book, its manufacture, design and dissemination."—*Pref.* Z124.C6

Columbia University. Libraries. The history of printing from its beginnings to 1930; the subject catalogue of the American Type Founders Company Library in the Columbia University Libraries. Millwood, N.Y., Kraus, [1980]. 4v. **AA390**

Reproduces the subject cards (with some author and catchword title entries) for this outstanding collection. Nearly 45,000 entries.

Z117.C65

Fumagalli, Giuseppe. Lexicon typographicum Italiae. Dictionnaire géographique d'Italie pour servir à l'histoire de l'imprimerie dans ce pays. . . . Florence, Olschki, 1905. 587p. il. **AA391**

Subtitle: Contenant l^e l'indication de toutes les localités d'Italie géographique et politique, où l'imprimerie a été introduite jusqu'à nos jours, avec la synonymie latine, française, etc., et celle des lieux supposés d'impression; 2e des notices bibliographiques sur les éditions principes de chaque ville, bourg, château, etc., et sur les faits les plus remarquables se rapportant à l'histoire de l'art typographique dans ces localités; 3e des notices biographiques sur les plus célèbres imprimeurs italiens; 4e des notices statistiques sur l'état présent de l'imprimerie en Italie; 5e des renseignements historiques sur les arts auxiliaires de l'imprimerie: lithographie, gravure, papeterie, fabrication des encres, des presses, des caractères, etc.

————— ————— Giunte e correzioni. Additions et corrections. Florence, Olschki, 1939. 84p.

Z155.F97

Hunter, Dard. Papermaking; the history and technique of an ancient craft. 2d ed. rev. and enl. N.Y., Knopf, 1947. 611p. il. **AA392**

1st ed. 1943.

Chronology of papermaking, paper, and the use of paper, 2700 B.C.–A.D. 1945, p.463–584; Bibliography, p.585–602.

TS1090.H816

Lehmann-Haupt, Hellmut [and others]. The book in America; a history of the making and selling of books in the United States. 2d [rev. and enl. American] ed. N.Y., Bowker, 1951. 493p. (Repr.: 1964) **AA393**

1st American ed. 1939. Originally published in Leipzig as: *Das amerikanische Buchwesen*, 1937.

A survey history of book production and distribution in the United States from 1638 to mid-20th century. Bibliography, p.422–66.

Z473.L522

Maxted, Ian. The London book trades, 1775–1800; a preliminary checklist of members. [Folkestone, Kent], Dawson, [1977]. 257p. **AA394**

"The aim of the work is to provide, by approaching a limited selection of wide-ranging sources, a checklist of members of the

book and allied trades in the London area which would be sufficiently comprehensive to serve as a basis for further study and as a much needed stop-gap for the poorly documented period of the late eighteenth century."—*Pref.* Entries for about 4,000 individuals and firms with brief biographical information and notes on publishing and book trade activity (including printing, engraving, binding, music and book selling, etc.). "Key to sources," p.xiv–xvii.

Z152.L8M39

McMurtrie, Douglas Crawford. The book; the story of printing and bookmaking. [3d rev. ed.] N.Y., Oxford Univ. Pr., [1943]. 676p. il. **AA395**

The history of bookmaking, printing, and illustration from early to modern times. Bibliography, p.603–46. Z4.M15

Rouzet, Anne. Dictionnaire des imprimeurs, libraires et éditeurs des XVe et XVIe siècles dans les limites géographiques de la Belgique actuelle. Nieuwkoop, B. de Graaf, 1975. 287p. (Collection du Centre National de l'Archéologie et de l'Histoire du Livre. Publ. 3) **AA396**

Biographical sketches in alphabetical sequence, with tables according to place of activity and addresses by city. Z350.R68

Updike, Daniel Berkeley. Printing types, their history, forms, and use; a study in survivals. [3d ed.] Cambridge, Mass., Belknap Pr., 1962. 2v. il., facsims. **AA397**

1st ed. 1922; 2d ed. 1937.

A richly illustrated historical survey with bibliographical references. Z250.A2U6

Winckler, Paul A. History of books and printing: a guide to information sources. Detroit, Gale, [1979]. 209p. (Books, publishing, and libraries information guide ser., v.2) **AA398**

Sections for general bibliographies and information sources are followed by chapters on materials and techniques used in graphic communication, history of books and printing, nonprint media, periodicals and annuals, associations and societies, libraries and museums, and book dealers. 776 entries, most of them annotated. Indexed. Z117.W54

Biography

Ascarelli, Fernanda. La tipografia cinquecentina italiana. Firenze, Sansoni Antiquariato, 1953. 259p. il. (Contributi alla Biblioteca bibliografica italica, 1) **AA399**

Intended to cover all printers active in Italy up to and including 1600. Arrangement is geographical by region, then alphabetical by city, and chronological by printer. Adequate indexes. Z155.A8

Bibliographical Society, London. [Dictionaries of printers and booksellers in England, Scotland and Ireland]. London, Soc., 1905–32. 5v. (Repr.: 1949–68) **AA400**

Comprises: *Century of the English book trade . . . 1457–1557,* by E. Gordon Duff. 1905. 200p.; *Dictionary of printers and booksellers in England, Scotland and Ireland and of foreign printers of English books, 1557–1640,* by R. B. McKerrow. 1910. 346p.; *Dictionary of the printers who were at work in England, Scotland and Ireland, from 1641 to 1667,* by H. R. Plomer. 1907. 199p.; *Dictionary of the printers and booksellers who were at work in England, Scotland and Ireland from 1668 to 1725,* by H. R. Plomer. 1922. 342p.; *Dictionary of the printers and booksellers who were at work in England, Scotland and Ireland from 1726 to 1775;* those in England by H. R. Plomer, Scotland by G. H. Bushnell, Ireland by E. R. McC. Dix. 1932. 432p.

Good, short biographies, with bibliographies. The different volumes in the series contain indexes as follows: 1457–1557, Index of Christian names, Index of London signs, Chronological index of foreign places, printers and stationers; 1557–1640, Indexes of (1) London signs, (2) London addresses, (3) Places other than London; 1668–1725, Index of printers and places to the two volumes, 1641–1667 and 1668–1725; 1726–1775, Indexes of (1) Places in England, Wales other than London, (2) Places in Scotland other than

Edinburgh, (3) Places in Ireland, (4) Places abroad; Circulating libraries in England and Scotland arranged in order of date.

Geldner, Ferdinand. Die deutschen Inkunabeldrucker; ein Handbuch der deutschen Buchdrucker des XV. Jahrhunderts nach Druckorten. Stuttgart, A. Hiersemann, 1968–70. 2v. il.   **AA401**

Contents: v.1, Das deutschen Sprachgebiet; v.2, Die fremden Sprachgebiete.

Provides notes on the lives and works of German printers of the 15th century. A geographical-chronological arrangement is employed, designed to show the spread of printing from Mainz to other German cities and abroad. Indexed.   Z240.G34

Lepreux, Georges. Gallia typographica; ou, Répertoire biographique et chronologique de tous les imprimeurs de France depuis les origines de l'imprimerie jusqu'à la Révolution. Paris, Champion, 1909–14. 5v. (Revue des bibliothèques. Suppl.)   **AA402**

As originally planned, to consist of 20v. and a general index.

In two series: (1) Série parisienne, and (2) Série départmentale.

Contents: Série parisienne, t.1, Livre d'or des imprimeurs du roi; Série départmentale: t.l, Flandre, Artois, Picardie; t.2, Champagne et Barrois; t.3, Normandie (in 2v.); t.4, Bretagne.

A monumental work, containing full biographies with detailed bibliographical references. Each volume is in two parts: (1) biographies, and (2) documents.   Z144.L59

Muller, Jean. Dictionnaire abrégé des imprimeurs/éditeurs français du seizième siècle. Baden-Baden, Verlag Librairie Heitz, 1970. 150p. (Bibliotheca bibliographica Aureliana, 30)   **AA403**

Arrangement is alphabetical by place; then printers are listed chronologically by dates when they were active in that locality. (For the more important cities such as Paris and Lyons, an alphabetical arrangement of printers' names is used, with a chronological key.) For each printer a reference is given to bibliographical sources concerning his work. Alphabetical index of personal names, and a geographical table of variant place-names.   Z144.M84

Renouard, Philippe. Imprimeurs & libraires parisiens du XVIᵉ siècle; ouvrage publié d'après les manuscrits de Philippe Renouard par le Service des Travaux Historiques de la Ville de Paris. Paris, 1964–79. v.1–3. (In progress)   **AA404**

Contents: v.1–3, Abada–Billon.

First of a series to be devoted to the careers and works of 16th-century Parisian printers and booksellers. Primarily a bio-bibliography, the completed work will also serve as a bibliography of Parisian imprints of the period. Listings for printers predominate, and entries include descriptive notes on their editions; plates at the end of each volume illustrate their typographic traits. Detailed subject index. Useful both as a biographical and as a bibliographical tool.

A special "Fasc. Breyer" was issued in 1982, initiating a new publication pattern: i.e., in addition to the continuing alphabetical sequence (v.4 is reported to be in preparation), information on figures falling outside that sequence will be published as the completed articles become available.   Z305.R4

——— Répertoire des imprimeurs parisiens, libraires, fondeurs de caractères et correcteurs d'imprimerie, depuis l'introduction de l'imprimerie à Paris (1470) jusqu'à la fin du siezième siècle. Paris, M. J. Minard, 1965. 511p.   **AA405**

First published in 1898 under title *Imprimeurs parisiens.* . . . A new edition, with considerable additional material and new references to sources of information, was published in the *Revue des bibliothèques,* v.32–42, 1922–34. The present edition reprints the material for the revised 2d ed. as it appeared in the *Revue des bibliothèques,* with the addition of an index of printers' signs, etc.; an index of streets and landmarks; and a chronological table.

Contents: Libraires, imprimeurs, correcteurs et fondeurs de caractères; Auteurs qui vendaient eux-mêmes leurs ouvrages; Table des adresses classées par rues; Table des enseignes; Liste chronologique; Table des noms personnes.   Z305.R43

Copyright

Chickering, Robert B. and **Hartman, Susan.** How to register a copyright and protect your creative work. N.Y., Scribner's, [1980]. 216p.   **AA406**

Subtitle: A basic guide to the new copyright law and how it affects anyone who wants to protect creative work.

Outlines registration procedures and answers frequently asked questions about copyright. Also treats some special copyright situations.   KF2995.C45

Crawford, Tad. The writer's legal guide. N.Y., Hawthorn Books, [1977]. 271p.   **AA407**

Chapters include: Copyright; Rights of the writer; Contents of written works; Contracts; Marketing literary property; Self-publication and vanity presses; Income taxation; The writer's estate; Public support for writers. Indexed.   KF3084.C7

Hogan, John Charles and **Cohen, Saul.** An author's guide to scholarly publishing and the law. Englewood Cliffs, N.J., Prentice-Hall, [1965]. 167p.   **AA408**

"The problems which this book surveys are those arising out of the scholar's activities as a scholar in connection with research and publication."—*Pref.* Chapters treat of publication agreements, copyright, fair use, photoduplication of copyrighted material, etc. Appendixes include sample forms, suggested readings, and the copyright law of the United States. A clear and useful guide.

Johnston, Donald F. Copyright handbook. 2d ed. N.Y., Bowker, 1982. 381p.   **AA409**

1st ed. 1978.

Aims "to explain the 1976 Copyright Act and to report on legal developments that have taken place since it took effect at the beginning of 1978."—*Pref.* Provides information on kinds of works which are copyrightable, copyright duration, transfer of ownership, copyright notices and registrations, fair use, copyrights and teaching activities, library reproductions, limitations on rights of performance, etc. Appendixes include text of the 1976 Copyright Act, examples of application forms for registration of copyrights, and texts of various guidelines (e.g., for photocopying and interlibrary loan arrangements). Detailed table of contents; index.   KF2994.J63

Miller, Jerome K. Applying the new copyright law: a guide for educators and librarians. Chicago, Amer. Lib. Assoc., 1979. 144p.   **AA410**

An attempt to help librarians and teachers understand and apply the United States copyright law, taking "a middle ground in interpreting the disputed areas such as placing photocopies on reserve, the question of 'spontaneity,' and videotaping television programs." —*Introd.* Appendixes; index.   KF2995.M54

Roberts, Matt. Copyright: a selected bibliography of periodical literature relating to literary property in the United States. Metuchen, N.J., Scarecrow Pr., 1971. 416p.   **AA411**

Cites some 6,200 articles from about 500 periodicals. Classed arrangement without author or detailed subject index.   KF2986.R62

Strong, William S. The copyright book: a practical guide. 2d ed. Cambridge, Mass., MIT Pr., [1984]. 223p.   **AA412**

1st ed. 1981.

Aims "to make available to people whose lives and work are affected by the laws of copyright an understanding of their rights and responsibilities."—*Pref.* Includes chapters on ownership, transfer of copyright, registration of a copyright claim, infringement and fair use (with attention to library copying and home videotaping), etc. Although up-to-date at press time, this deals with a rapidly changing field.   KF2994.S75

United Nations Educational, Scientific and Cultural Organization. Copyright laws and treaties of the world. Wash.,

UNESCO and the Bureau of Nat. Affairs, 1956– . Looseleaf. **AA413**

Kept current by supplements (originally annual, now irregular—e.g., 1979/80 suppl. publ. 1982).

"Comp. by the United Nations Educational, Scientific and Cultural Organization, with the cooperation of the Copyright Office of the United States of America and the Industrial Property Dept. of the Board of Trade of the United Kingdom of Great Britain and Northern Ireland." [varies]

Presents, either in the original English text or in specially prepared English translations, the laws and regulations of some 136 states.

In four parts: I, States, arranged alphabetically; for each state gives: (1) information primarily domestic in scope; (2) information primarily international in scope. II, Territories. III, Multilateral conventions, giving for each convention: the text of the Convention; the status of adherences to the Convention; and the states among which the Convention or portions thereof are applicable. IV, Rome Convention rights in two sections: (1) states, giving an index to national legislation; (2) multilateral conventions, giving the Rome Convention and regional conventions.

Copy preparation

See also Von Ostermann, *Manual of foreign languages,* BC56.

Butcher, Judith. Copy-editing: the Cambridge handbook. 2d ed. Cambridge, Cambridge Univ. Pr., [1981]. 331p. **AA414**

Based on the author's experience at Penguin Books and the Cambridge University Press, but intended as a guide for copy-editors in general. Covers much specialized material as well as general aspects of the work. Detailed index. Appendixes include a glossary and a good "checklist of copy-editing." PN162.B86

Fleischer, Eugene B. A style manual for citing microform and nonprint media. Chicago, Amer. Lib. Assoc., 1978. 66p. **AA415**

Provides rules, with examples, for citing sound recordings, motion pictures, microforms, and other media which are not generally dealt with in style manuals. PN171.F56F57

Lasky, Joseph. Proofreading and copy-preparation; a textbook for the graphic arts industry. [Latest revision] N.Y., Mentor Pr., 1954. 656p. il. **AA416**

1st ed. 1941.

A useful, detailed handbook containing, besides chapters on the practical work of proofreading and preparation of copy, lists of compounds, abbreviations, proper syllabication of words, including Latin, Spanish, and French words, etc. Z253.L35

MacCampbell, Donald. The writing business. N.Y., Crown, [1978]. 120p. **AA417**

A brief, practical guide to the problems and pitfalls of placing manuscripts for publication. Written by an authors' agent. PN151.M27

Miller, Casey and **Swift, Kate.** The handbook of nonsexist writing. N.Y., Lippincott & Crowell, [1980]. 134p. **AA418**

A guide for the "growing number of writers and speakers [who] are trying to free their language from unconscious semantic bias."—*Pref.* Problems and suggested solutions are presented in six sections: (1) *Man* as a false generic; (2) The pronoun problem; (3) Generalizations; (4) Seeing women and girls as people; (5) Parallel treatment; (6) A few more words [discussions of specific terms]. Reference notes; index. PN218.M5

Nicholson, Margaret. A practical style guide for authors and editors. N.Y., Holt, [1967]. 143p. **AA419**

Brief, clear instructions addressed to both the author and the copy editor. Indexed. PN147.N53

Plotnik, Arthur. The elements of editing: a modern guide for editors and journalists. N.Y., Macmillan; London, Collier Macmillan, [1982]. 156p. **AA420**

A book of practical advice for the beginning editorial worker and trainee. Chapters range from "The editorial personality" to "Basic photography for editors" and give attention to processing a manuscript, dealing with authors, copyright, etc. Indexed. PN4778.P59

Seeber, Edward Derbyshire. A style manual for authors, based on the MLA style sheet. Bloomington, Indiana Univ. Pr., [1965]. 96p. **AA421**

Includes sample footnotes and bibliography entries; also notes on foreign-language problems. PN162.S4

Skillin, Marjorie E. [and others]. Words into type. 3d ed., completely rev. Englewood Cliffs, N.J., Prentice-Hall, [1974]. 585p. **AA422**

1st ed. 1948.

A reference source for writers, editors, copy editors, proofreaders, compositors, and printers. Includes sections on preparation of the manuscript, copy and proof, copy-editing style, typographical style, grammar, use of words, typography and illustration. PN160.S52

U.S. Government Printing Office. Style manual. Rev. ed. Wash., Govt. Prt. Off., 1973. 548p. **AA423**

First publ. 1908 under title: *Manual of style.* Frequently revised.

A useful and extensive manual giving the practices of the Government Printing Office on copy preparation, with rules for capitalization, punctuation, abbreviations, etc., and information on foreign languages, including alphabets, with pronunciation, special rules, lists of numbers, etc. Z253.U58

—— Word division; supplement to Government Printing Office style manual. 6th ed. 1962. 190p. **AA424**

This edition includes many new words, particularly scientific and technical words. Gives rules of word division and lists the syllabication of several thousand words. Z253.U58

University of Chicago Press. The Chicago manual of style, for authors, editors, and copywriters. 13th ed., rev. and expanded. Chicago, Univ. of Chicago Pr., [1982]. 737p. **AA425**

1st-12th eds., 1906–69, had title: *A manual of style.*

A standard work, thoroughly revised and updated, which serves as a "how-to" book for authors and editors. In three main sections (Bookmaking; Style; Production and printing), offering practical information and advice on all aspects of manuscript preparation, copyediting, and seeing a work through the press. Glossary of technical terms; bibliography; index. Z253.U69

Bibliography

Howell, John Bruce. Style manuals of the English-speaking world: a guide. Phoenix, Oryx Pr., 1983. 138p. **AA426**

An annotated listing of some 231 style manuals and author's guides, mainly publications of the 1970–83 period. A section of general manuals is followed by a section in which specialized manuals are grouped by subject. Author/title/subject index. Z5165.H68

Bookbinding

Brenni, Vito Joseph. Bookbinding, a guide to the literature. Westport, Conn., Greenwood Pr., 1982. 199p. **AA427**

A topically arranged bibliography with author and subject indexes. Includes sections on technique, materials, tools, decoration, history, etc.; writings on bookplates and book jackets are also listed. Z266.5.B73

Clough, Eric A. Bookbinding for librarians. London, Assoc. of Assist. Librarians, 1957. 204p. **AA428**

A handbook on bookbinding with a glossary and a select bibliography. Z271.C6

Cockerell, Douglas. Bookbinding, and the care of books: a text-book for bookbinders and librarians. 5th ed. London, Pitman, [1953]. 345p. il. **AA429**

1st ed. 1902; various reprintings.
Offers straightforward descriptions of bookbinding methods and procedures, with many line drawings to illustrate the text. Includes a glossary of terms and an index. Z271.C66

Diehl, Edith. Bookbinding, its background and technique. N.Y., Rinehart, 1946. 2v. il. (Repr.: N.Y., Dover, 1980) **AA430**

v.1 gives the history from the Middle Ages to modern times; discusses national styles and specialities, e.g., decoration of book edges, book covers and girdle books, etc.; and includes a bibliography, p.205–19; a glossary, p.223–34; and a section of 91 plates of illustrations of historical bindings. v.2 is devoted to techniques, illustrated with line drawings. A standard work in its field. Z266.D5

Johnson, Pauline. Creative bookbinding. Seattle, Univ. of Washington Pr., [1963]. 263p. il. **AA431**

A practical introduction to bookbinding, including chapters on book design; the parts of a book; materials, tools, and equipment; working procedures; simple constructions and binding procedures; decorated papers; leather; book repair; supply sources; bibliography. Well illustrated. Z266.J6

Library Binding Institute. Library binding handbook. [Boston, 1971] 44p. **AA432**

Called "5th revision"; previous ed. 1963.
". . . represents the best judgment of the industry as to what the minimum requirements are for a volume intended for normal library use."—*Foreword.* Includes recommendations for good binding practices, establishment of a maintenance system within the library, rules to follow for water-damaged books, etc. The text of the LBI "Standard for library binding" is included as an appendix.

Lydenberg, Harry Miller and **Archer, John.** The care and repair of books. Rev. by John Alden. N.Y., Bowker, 1960. 122p. **AA433**

"4th rev. ed."—*verso of title page.*
A practical handbook. Bibliography, p.101–13. Z701.L98

Tauber, Maurice Falcolm, ed. Library binding manual; a handbook of useful procedures for the maintenance of library volumes. Boston, Library Binding Inst., 1972. 185p. il. **AA434**

Revision of the 1951 and 1952 ed. prep. by L. N. Feipel and E. W. Browning.
Chapters include basic considerations in binding, background and development of library binding standards, maintenance of library materials, preparation of materials for the bindery, checklist for examining bindings. Numerous useful appendixes. Z100.T38

Young, Laura S. Bookbinding & conservation by hand: a working guide. N.Y., Bowker, 1981. 273p. il. **AA435**

A practical guide for teachers and students as well as for beginners working on their own. Z271.Y68

Book illustration

See also BE14, BE174.

Bolton, Theodore. American book illustrators; bibliographic check lists of 123 artists. N.Y., Bowker, 1938. 290p. **AA436**

Lists, under the name of the illustrator, the books illustrated by him, and attempts also to note the magazine appearance of the illustrations whenever possible. "Planned as a companion volume to Merle Johnson's *American first editions.*"—*Introd.* Z1023.B71

Brenni, Vito Joseph. Book illustration and decoration: a guide to research. Westport, Conn., Greenwood Pr., 1980. 191p. **AA437**

A classed bibliography of more than 2,100 items (books, pamphlets, parts of books, periodical articles, etc.). Many sections are subdivided chronologically or by country. Indexed. Z5956.I44B7

SELECTION OF BOOKS

❖Book selection in a library must be geared to the interests and needs of the community it serves, whether it be a small town, rural area, industrial center, school, college, university, or business concern. Demands are as varied as the interests of people, and many types of book selection aids are needed.

In special fields, many of the cyclopedias, histories, bibliographies, and manuals contain material of first importance for the right choice of books, either for purchase or for special use. *Living with books,* by Helen E. Haines (2d ed. N.Y., Columbia Univ. Pr., 1950), discusses principles and practices of book selection by libraries and comments on many older guides to selection.

The following list is a selection of general guides which, in purpose of selection, annotation, technical excellence in cataloging and classification, or special indexing, have reference as well as advisory value.

Guides

Books for public libraries. PLA Starter List Comm., Public Lib. Assoc., Amer. Lib. Assoc. 3d ed. Chicago, Amer. Lib. Assoc., 1981. 374p. **AA438**

1st ed. 1971.
Intended "as an alternative book selection tool of representative subject suggestions for planning new public library collections or for assessing library collections being redeveloped."—*Pref.* Lists in-print books arranged according to the 19th ed. of the Dewey Decimal Classification. Includes publisher, date, price, ISBN and LC card numbers as available. Subject and author/title indexes. Z1035.B73

Dickinson, Asa Don. The world's best books, Homer to Hemingway; 3000 books of 3000 years, 1050 B.C. to 1950 A.D. selected on the basis of a consensus of expert opinion. N.Y., Wilson, 1953. 484p. **AA439**

An alphabetical list which is "a unification, a condensation and a revision of, as well as an addition to, its four predecessors." Contains notes about each author and brief description or evaluation of each book. Includes a chronological list and a list classified by subject or literary form.
Earlier works were: *1000 best books; Best books of our time; Best books of the decade 1926–35; Best books of the decade 1936–45.* Z1035.D555

Hackett, Alice Payne and **Burke, James Henry.** 80 years of best sellers, 1895–1975. N.Y., Bowker, 1977. 265p. **AA440**

Earlier editions called *Fifty years of best sellers, 1895–1945; 60 years of best sellers, 1895–1955;* and *70 years of best sellers, 1895–1965.*
Includes dicussions of best sellers, and of best sellers in various subject fields, with lists of best sellers arranged by number of copies sold, by subject, and by year. Z1033.B3H342

Philadelphia. Free Library. Reader Development Program. Reader development bibliography: books recommended for adult new readers. [3d ed.] Annotated and comp. by Melissa

Forinash Buckingham. Syracuse, N.Y., New Readers Pr., [1982]. 86p. **AA441**

1st ed. 1974.

". . . an annotated, graded list of materials for adults who read on an eighth grade reading level or below."—*Introd.* Classed arrangement. Z1039.S55P47

Public library catalog. 8th ed., 1983. Ed. by Gary L. Bogart and John Greenfieldt. N.Y., H. W. Wilson, 1984. 1442p. (Standard catalog ser.) **AA442**

1st–4th eds. (1934–58) publ. under title: *Standard catalog for public libraries.* Editors vary.

A very useful selection guide for the medium-sized public library and the undergraduate college library, this is a carefully selected list of in-print titles with well-chosen descriptive notes drawn from introductory statements and reviews. In three parts: (1) classified catalog, arranged by the abridged Dewey Decimal Classification; (2) author, title, subject, and analytical index; (3) directory of publishers and distributors. 7,777 titles and 12,815 analytical entries in this edition; paperbacks are included when they are the only format available. Does not include fiction; for the *Fiction catalog see* BD234.

Kept up to date by annual supplements. Z1035.P934

The reader's adviser; a layman's guide to literature. 12th ed. N.Y., Bowker, 1974–77. 3v. **AA443**

Contents: v.1, The best in American and British fiction, poetry, essays, literary biography, bibliography, and reference, ed. by Sarah L. Prakken. 808p.; v.2, The best in American and British drama and world literature in English translation, ed. by F. J. Sypher. 774p.; v.3, The best in the reference literature of the world, ed. by Jack A. Clarke. 1034p.

Title of earlier eds. varies: 1921–41, 1958, *Bookman's manual;* 1948–54, *Bessie Graham's Bookman's manual;* 1960, *Reader's adviser and bookman's manual.* Subtitle varies. Compilers: 1921–41, Bessie Graham; 1948–64, Hester R. Hoffman; 1968, Winifred F. Courtney.

Designed primarily for the bookseller and librarian, this is an up-to-date, standard work useful in any library.

"For the first time the work of revising each chapter of the first [two] volume[s] of this edition has been entrusted to a single editor who has special expertise in the area of his chapter."—*Pref.* Those sections are signed with the initials of the contributing editors. v.3 is the work of the general editor of that volume. In addition to expanded coverage, there has been some rearrangement of material within sections and new introductory notes. Brief annotations are provided for many of the items, sometimes including a brief excerpt from a review. v.1 has separate indexes for authors and for titles and subjects; v.2 and 3 have indexes of authors and of titles.

New edition in preparation. Z1035.B7

Regis, *Sister.* The Catholic bookman's guide; a critical evaluation of Catholic literature. Contributors: Vernon J. Bourke [and others]. 1st ed. N.Y., Hawthorn, 1962. 638p. **AA444**

An annotated, classified bibliography covering: sources and evaluation; religion; philosophy and psychology; literature; social sciences. Z7837.R37

Sonnenschein, William Swan. The best books; a readers' guide and literary reference book, being a contribution towards systematic bibliography. 3d ed. (entirely rewritten). London, Routledge, 1910–35. 6v. paged continuously, 3760p. (Repr.: Detroit, Gale, 1969) **AA445**

1st ed. 1887; 2d ed. 1891; suppl. to 2d ed. entitled *Reader's guide,* 1895.

A very comprehensive list, but no longer current.

Pt.1: classes A, Theology; B, Mythology and folklore; C, Philosophy; pt.2: classes D, Society; E, Geography; pt.3: classes F, History and historical biography; G, Archaeology and historical collaterals; pt.4: classes H, Natural science; H*, Medicine and surgery; I, Arts and trades; pt.5: class K, Literature and philology; pt.6: Authors, titles, and subjects index; a synopsis of classification; list of British publishers, learned societies, etc. Z1035.S72

Current

Booklist. 1905– . Chicago, Amer. Lib. Assoc., 1905– . v.1– . Semimonthly (monthly in July and Aug.). **AA446**

The booklist and the *Subscription books bulletin* were combined with v.53, no.1, Sept. 1, 1956, under title *The booklist and subscription books bulletin.* With v.66, no.1, Sept. 1, 1969, the publication reverted to the earlier title and with v.73, no.1, Sept. 1976 the title became simply *Booklist.*

Booklist is a selected, annotated list of recent publications recommended especially for small and medium-sized libraries. Arranged by broad classes, e.g., adult nonfiction and fiction, books for young adults, children's books, and paperback reprints. Beginning with v.66 (1969) audiovisual materials are reviewed regularly. Microcomputer software is also reviewed. Complete bibliographical information is given for each entry, including price. Annotations describe, evaluate, and indicate the kind of library for which the book is recommended. Indexes are now published semi-annually.

The reviews prepared by the ALA Reference and Subscription Books Review Committee (formerly the Subscription Books Committee) now appear in the middle of each issue of *Booklist* under the heading "Reference books bulletin." For cumulations of these reviews *see Subscription books bulletin reviews* (AA501–AA502). Z1035.A9

British book news; a monthly selection of recent books. London, British Council, 1940– . Monthly. **AA447**

Title varies: no.1–14, *A selection of recent books published in Great Britain.* Subtitle varies; publisher varies.

A useful, selective, annotated list of "best books" arranged according to the Dewey Decimal Classification. Each number has an index, and there is a separate cumulation of author and title indexes for the year. Annual issues, 1940–50. Z1035.B838

Bulletin critique du livre français. Paris, Assoc. pour la Diffusion de la Pensée Française, 1945– . v.1– . Monthly. **AA448**

Publisher varies.

A selected list of books in all subject fields published in France, with descriptive annotations. The index of authors cumulates annually. Z2165.B924

Frankfurt am Main. Deutsche Bibliothek. Deutsche Bibliographie; das deutsche Buch; Auswahl wichtiger Neuerscheinungen. 1950– . Frankfurt/M., Buchhändler-Vereinigung, 1950– . Bimonthly. **AA449**

Title varies: 1950–54, no.5, *Das deutsche Buch; Neuerscheinungen der deutschen Verlage.*

Edited by the Deutsche Bibliothek. A selective, classified list, with author index, of new German publications, including annotations. Z2221.D45

Libri e riviste d'Italia; rassegna bibliografica mensile. Roma, Centro di Documentazione, 1950– . Monthly. **AA450**

Title and publisher vary.

A selected list of current Italian publications covering all subject fields, with fairly long reviews. Indexes of subjects and authors cumulate annually.

Also published in English, French, German, and Spanish. English edition: *Italian books and periodicals.* Z2345.L63

Books for college students

Bertalan, Frank J. The junior college library collection. 1970 ed. Newark, N.J., Bro-Dart Foundation, 1970. 503, [129]p. **AA451**

Intends to list "basic, dependable, and useful titles for the libraries of two-year colleges."—*Pref.* Faculty members and librarians from nearly 100 junior colleges throughout the country helped in the selection process for the 1968 edition which has here been revised and expanded by a group of subject specialists. About 21,000 titles. Classified arrangement by Library of Congress class numbers; author index. In general, textbooks and out-of-print items are excluded.   Z1035.B443

Books for college libraries; a core collection of 40,000 titles. A project of the Association of College and Research Libraries. 2d ed. Chicago, Amer. Lib. Assoc., 1975. 6v.   **AA452**

1st ed. 1967.

Contents: v.1, Humanities; v.2, Language and literature; v.3, History; v.4, Social sciences; v.5, Psychology, science, technology; v.6, Index.

A list of monographic titles for college libraries arranged by Library of Congress classification with an author and subject index. Intended as a selection aid for building a well-balanced library collection to support undergraduate courses in all fields. "New aspects include the sharp reduction in number of titles to a minimal 'core collection'; the expansion of individual entries to provide more complete cataloging and classification information; and the use of automated techniques for the production of the list itself."—*Introd.*

A new edition is to be published in 1986.   Z1035.B72

Pirie, James W., comp. Books for junior college libraries; a selected list of approximately 19,700 titles. Chicago, Amer. Lib. Assoc., 1969. 452p.   **AA453**

Intended as a book selection guide for junior and community college libraries supporting liberal arts programs. Compiled with the assistance of 425 consultants and under the sponsorship of the ALA Editorial Committee's Subcommittee on Books for Junior College Libraries. Classed arrangement with author index.   Z1035.P448

Princeton University. Library. Julian Street Library. The Julian Street Library; a preliminary list of titles, comp. by Warren B. Kuhn. N.Y., Bowker, 1966. 789p.   **AA454**

The catalog of an undergraduate dormitory library at Princeton. Not the catalog of an undergraduate instructional library but meant to include "those books most frequently in demand by students for broad supplementary reading and other books in all fields which . . . might open new intellectual avenues for the student."—*Foreword.*

Reproduces Library of Congress cards in classed arrangement. 8,400 titles. Author-subject and title-price indexes.   Z881.P942J8

Current

Choice: books for college libraries. Chicago, Assoc. of College and Research Libraries, 1964– . v.1– . Monthly (except bimonthly, July–Aug.).   **AA455**

A book review journal planned to assist college libraries in the selection of current books. Annotations are written (but not signed) by a large panel of consultants.   Z1035.C5

Books for children and young people

Children's literature abstracts. no.1– , May 1973– . [Birmingham, Eng.], Sub-section on Library Work with Children, International Federation of Library Associations, 1973– . Quarterly.   **AA456**

Includes brief abstracts of books about children's literature and reading as well as notes on books for children.   Z1037.C5446

Cianciolo, Patricia Jean. Picture books for children. 2d ed., rev. and enl. Chicago, Amer. Lib. Assoc., 1981. 237p. il.   **AA457**

1st ed. 1973 prep. by the Picture Book Subcommittee of National Council of Teachers of English, Elementary Booklist Committee.

Intended as "a resource and guide for teachers of children from nursery school through junior high school, for day-care center personnel, for librarians in school and public libraries, for parents, and for any other adult concerned with the selection of well-written, imaginatively illustrated picture books that are of interest to children of all ages and backgrounds."—*Pref.* Brief annotations comment on both text and illustrations. Age group indicated for each title. Author-title-illustrator index.   Z1037.C565

The elementary school library collection: a guide to books and other media. Phases 1–2–3. Lois Winkel, ed., assisted by Mary Virginia Gaver [and others]. 14th ed. Williamsport, Pa., Brodart, 1984. 1055p.   **AA458**

1st ed. 1965.

A frequently revised and updated work "primarily designed to serve as a resource to assist in the continuous maintenance and development of existing collections or for the establishment of new library media centers."—*Introd.* The 14th ed. represents a complete reevaluation of titles from the previous edition and includes new works from the Apr. 1981–Apr. 1983 period. All titles were believed to be in print at press time. Lists 8,906 books, 160 periodicals, 4,248 AV materials. Classed arrangement, with author, title, and subject indexes.   Z1037.E4

Gillespie, John Thomas and **Gilbert, Christine B.** Best books for children, preschool through the middle grades. 2d ed. N.Y., Bowker, 1981. 635p.   **AA459**

1st ed. in this format 1978; earlier volumes publ. 1959–72.

Aims "to provide a list of books, gathered from a number of sources, that are highly recommended to satisfy both a child's recreational reading needs and the demands of a typical school curriculum."—*Pref.* About 10,000 entries, with an additional 3,000 related works mentioned in the brief annotations. Classed arrangement with author/illustrator, title, and subject indexes, plus a list of biographical subjects.   Z1037.G48

Good reading, 1933– . N.Y., Weybright & Talley, 1933– .   **AA460**

New editions published and revised at frequent intervals. Publisher varies. 21st ed. 1978.

Originally issued by Committee on College Reading; sponsored by the College English Association; endorsed by the Adult Education Association of the U.S.A., the American Library Association, and the National Council of Teachers of English; now publ. by Bowker, N.Y.

The 21st ed. is a thorough revision. "More than half of its chapters have been prepared by new editors, and many have new or substantially revised introductions; all its annotated book lists have been updated, and several have been expanded; data about authors, books, editions, and translations are current as of January 1978."—*p.ix.* An annotated list of about 2,500 titles arranged under some 28 subject headings. A very useful and inexpensive compilation.   Z1035.G6

Haviland, Virginia. The best of children's books, 1964–1978. Wash., Lib. of Congress (for sale by Supt. of Docs.), 1980. 90p. il.   **AA461**

Represents a selection of the best works from the Library of Congress Children's Book Section's annual list, *Children's books* (Wash., The Library, 1964–); only in-print items are included. Classed arrangement without index. Gives full bibliographic information, price, annotation, and recommended grade level.

Reprinted with 1979 addenda (N.Y., University Pr. Books, 1981. 126p.)   Z1037.1.H38

—— Children's literature: a guide to reference sources. Wash., Lib. of Congress, 1966. 341p. il.   **AA462**

An annotated bibliography describing "books, articles, and pamphlets selected on the basis of their estimated usefulness to adults concerned with the creation, reading, or study of children's books. Children's literature is here considered to be books for boys and girls up to 14 years of age, or in grades through the eighth."—*Pref.* Indexed.   Z1037.A1H35

—— —— First-second supplement. Wash., Lib. of Congress, 1972–77. 2v.

Covers chiefly publications of the period 1966–74.

Larrick, Nancy. A parent's guide to children's reading. 5th ed., completely rev. Philadelphia, Westminster Pr., 1982. 271p. il.   **AA463**

1st ed. 1958.

An excellent, inexpensive guide in which lists of recommended books on various topics are clearly and concisely presented.
LB1140.5.R4L37

National Association of Independent Schools. Ad Hoc Library Committee. Books for secondary school libraries. 6th ed. N.Y., Bowker, 1981. 844p. **AA464**

1st ed. 1955. Title varies; 3d ed. (1968) called *4000 books for secondary school libraries.*

This edition lists more than 9,000 nonfiction titles and series and is intended "as a comprehensive bibliographic guide and selection aid for librarians, teachers, administrators, and others involved in developing book collections to meet the needs of college-bound students."—*Pref.* Arranged by Dewey Decimal Classification, with author and title indexes; there are separate sections listing professional tools and reference works. Z1035.N2

National Council of Teachers of English. Committee on the Elementary School Booklist. Adventuring with books: a booklist for pre-K–grade 6. Mary Lou White, ed. New ed. Urbana, Ill., The Council, [1981] 472p. **AA465**

Lists and annotates about 2,500 children's books published between the end of 1976 through 1980. Emphasis is on newness and only a few selected older books "have been retained from previous booklists to add balance to the collection."—*Introd.* Criteria for selection included high potential interest for children, literary merit, and (in this edition) equitable treatment of minorities. Topical arrangement with author and title indexes. Z1037.N265

National Council of Teachers of English. Committee on the Senior High School Booklist. Books for you: a booklist for senior high students. Robert C. Small, Jr., chair. New ed. Urbana, Ill., The Council, [1982]. 323p. **AA466**

1st ed. 1945.

An annotated listing of about 1,400 books published or reprinted since 1976 (i.e., since the preparation of the previous edition of *Books for you*), selected "because they are enjoyable to read."—*Introd.* Arranged by categories of reading interest (e.g., Adventure, Animals, Biography, Drama, Ecology, Mystery and crime, etc.). Author and title indexes. Z1037.N343

Perkins, Flossie L. Book and non-book media: annotated guide to selection aids for educational materials. Urbana, Ill., National Council of Teachers of English, [1972]. 298p. **AA467**

A revision of *Book selection media* by Ralph Perkins (rev. ed. 1967).

An alphabetical title listing of selection tools which librarians of public, elementary and high school libraries will find useful. Indicates purpose, scope, special features, publication data, etc. for each title. Includes various guides for specific age and interest groups. Separate indexes list aids for selecting materials for children, for teenagers, for parent-teacher background, and aids for librarians. Z1035.A1.P36

Peterson, Linda Kauffman and **Solt, Marilyn Leathers.** Newbery and Caldecott Medal and Honor books: an annotated bibliography. Boston, G. K. Hall, 1982. 427p. **AA468**

Provides critical annotations of both those books chosen for the Newbery and Caldecott Medals (from 1922 and 1938, respectively) and the "Honor books" considered for the awards through 1981. Chronological arrangement with indexes.

Irene Smith's *A history of the Newbery and Caldecott medals* (N.Y., Viking, 1957. 140p.) provides a narrative account of the awards, together with lists of winners and runners-up. Z1037.P45

Wilson, H. W., *firm, publishers.* Children's catalog . . . Ed.1– . N.Y., Wilson, 1909– . Irregular. **AA469**

14th ed., 1981, ed. by Richard H. Isaacson and Gary L. Bogart, latest publ.

The most comprehensive bibliography in its field (5,901 selected titles in the 14th ed.). Arranged in three parts: pt.1, classified catalog, arranged by Dewey Decimal Classification, giving full

bibliographic information and annotations; pt.2, author, title, subject, and analytical index; pt.3, directory of publishers. Titles especially recommended are starred. A listing by grades, which was a feature of earlier editions, was dropped with the 11th ed. (though grading is still indicated in pt.1). Kept up to date by annual supplements. Z1037.W76

——— Junior high school library catalog. 4th ed. 1980. Ed. by Gary L. Bogart and Richard H. Isaacson. N.Y., Wilson, 1980. 939p. **AA470**

1st ed. 1965. Revised every five years; kept up-to-date by annual supplements.

A relatively recent addition to the "Standard catalog series," assuming part of the coverage of the *Standard catalog for high school libraries* (*see* AA471) and concentrating on books for the 7th through the 9th grades. Follows the plan and arrangement of the publisher's other "Standard catalogs." This edition includes about 4,000 titles and some 9,000 analytical entries. Out-of-print books are not included. Z1037.W765

——— Senior high school library catalog. 12th ed. 1982. Ed. by Gary L. Bogart and Richard H. Isaacson. N.Y., Wilson, 1982. 1299p. **AA471**

1st ed. 1926–28; 2d ed. 1932; now revised every five years. Kept up-to-date by annual supplements.

1st–8th eds. had title: *Standard catalog for high school libraries.* Beginning with the 9th ed., the work was revised for senior high school grades, with grades 7–9 being the province of the *Junior high school library catalog* (AA470).

In three parts: pt.1, classified catalog, arranged according to the Dewey Decimal Classification number with full bibliographical information, suggested subject headings, and annotation; pt.2, author, title, subject, and analytical index, arranged in one alphabet; pt.3, directory of publishers and distributors.

Planned especially for school libraries, but useful also as a guide to selection of books for smaller public libraries. Many adult and young adult books are now included to reflect the more advanced and upgraded curricula now in effect in most high schools. 5,056 titles in this edition, with 15,530 analytical entries. Now limited to in-print items. Z1035.W77

Withrow, Dorothy, Carey, Helen B. and **Hirzel, Bertha M.** Gateways to readable books: an annotated graded list of books in many fields for adolescents who find reading difficult. 5th ed. N.Y., Wilson, 1975. 299p. **AA472**

1st–4th eds., 1944–66, by R. M. Strang and others.

About 1,000 titles arranged by subject, with author and title indexes. Z1039.S5W58

Your reading; a booklist for junior high and middle school students. New ed. Jane Christensen, Chair, and the Committee on the Junior High and Middle School Booklist of the National Council of Teachers of English. Urbana, Ill., The Council, [1983]. 764p. **AA473**

A selected list of some 3,100 works published 1975 and later. Classed arrangement, with author and title indexes. Annotations are meant to appeal to the student reader. For pre-1975 publications reference should be made to the Council's earlier list: *Your reading: a booklist for junior high students,* prep. by Jerry L. Walker, editorial chairman, and the Committee on the Junior High School Booklist (Urbana, Ill., National Council of Teachers of English, 1975. 440p.). Z1037.Y68

Reference books

❖The present edition of this *Guide to reference books* means to give aid on many points in the selection of reference books for different types of libraries. Earlier editions may prove helpful for identifying certain older or more specialized works omitted here. Other lists, prepared in other countries or from different points of view, will contain some titles not included in this book and will help in selection where additional titles are wanted. *See also* AA13–AA14.

American Library Association. Ad Hoc Committee for the Fourth Edition of Reference Sources for Small and Medium-Sized Libraries. Reference sources for small and medium-sized libraries. Co-editors, Jovian P. Lang and Deborah C. Masters. 4th ed. Chicago, The Assoc., 1984. 252p.

AA474

1st–3d eds. (1968–79) had title *Reference books for small and medium-sized libraries;* the title change reflects "the growing number of reference sources available in microform and online formats" (*Pref.*) which are included in this edition along with traditional print materials. Nearly 1,800 items—part of the increased size of this edition accounted for by the inclusion of reference materials for children and young adults (works for those categories of readers being so marked). Intended as a guide for college and large secondary school libraries as well as for public libraries. Items are grouped in subject categories and further subdivided by type of reference source or other suitable subdivision. Sections were prepared by individual compilers or teams of compilers. Good annotations; coverage of various subject fields is unusually even for a work of this kind; index of names and titles. Z1035.1.A47

American Library Association. Subscription Books Committee. Subscription Books Committee manual. [Chicago], Amer. Lib. Assoc., [1969]. 64p. **AA475**

Although prepared by the Committee for the guidance of its members, various sections of the manual will be useful to the librarian and student in evaluating reference materials—particularly Appendix I, "Additional Guidelines for Reviewing Particular Types of Reference Works." Z1035.A1A5

American reference books annual, 1970– . Ed. by Bohdan S. Wynar. Littleton, Colo., Libraries Unlimited, [1970–]. Annual. **AA476**

Each issue covers the reference book output (including reprints) of the previous year (i.e., the 1970 volume covers 1969 publications). Offers descriptive and evaluative notes (many of them signed by contributors), with references to selected reviews. Classed arrangement; author-subject-title index.

Cumulated indexes, v.1–5, 6–10, 11–14 publ. 1975–85 (3v.).
Z1035.1.A55

Beaudiquez, Marcelle and **Béthery, Annie.** Ouvrages de référence pour les bibliothèques publiques: répertoire bibliographique. Nouvelle éd. refondue et augmentée. Paris, Cercle de la Librairie, 1978. 209p. **AA477**

1st ed. 1974 by Beaudiquez and Anne Zundel-Benkhemis.

A selective guide to representative reference works in the broad range of subject fields likely to be of interest to public libraries. Classified arrangement with subdivision by form for encyclopedias, dictionaries, etc. 853 items in this edition (with expanded coverage of science and technology); most entries are briefly annotated. Foreign-language publications are limited mainly to bibliographies of bibliographies; bilingual dictionaries are included. Indexed.
Z1035.1.B43

Bell, Marion Virginia and **Swidan, Eleanor A.** Reference books: a brief guide. 8th ed. Baltimore, Enoch Pratt Free Library, 1978. 179p. **AA478**

1st ed. 1947.

1st–5th eds. comp. by Mary Neill Barton; 6th–7th eds. comp. by Mary Neill Barton and Marion V. Bell.

A standard guide, well selected and with very good annotations. Useful as a selection guide for small and medium-sized libraries and as a handbook for courses in the use of libraries. In two sections: (1) Reference books general in scope; and (2) Reference books in special subjects. 933 titles in this edition; prices are no longer included.

Best reference books, 1970–1980: titles of lasting value selected from American reference books annual. Ed. by Susan Holte and Bohdan S. Wynar. Littleton, Colo., Libraries Unlimited, 1981. 480p. **AA479**

An earlier selection covered 1970–76.

Intended as a selection tool for librarians wishing to improve their collections or those building a new reference collection. Offers a selection of 920 titles, with their annotations as they appeared in the 12v. of *American reference books annual* (AA476).
Z1035.1.B534

Cheney, Frances Neel and **Williams, Wiley J.** Fundamental reference sources. 2d ed. Chicago, Amer. Lib. Assoc., 1980. 351p. **AA480**

1st ed. 1971.

Intended as "an introduction to selected sources of bibliographical, biographical, linguistic, statistical and geographical information," with titles "selected on the basis of their importance in general reference collections in American libraries."—*Pref.* A chapter on "The nature of reference/information service" precedes the chapters devoted to the types of sources just mentioned. The appendix of "Guidelines for particular types of reference works" sets forth the criteria developed by the Reference and Subscription Books Review Committee of the American Library Association. A good introductory manual for the beginning library student as well as for the practicing librarian. Indexed. Z1035.1.C5

Dority, G. Kim. A guide to reference books for small and medium-sized libraries, 1970–1982. Littleton, Colo., Libraries Unlimited, 1984. 410p. **AA481**

Intended as a selection guide for reference collections in small and medium-sized libraries, this is a classified, annotated listing (with references to reviews) of 1,179 titles. Gives full bibliographic information and prices. Annotations often include reference to comparable works or alternate purchase suggestions. Author/title and subject indexes.

Recommended reference books for small and medium-sized libraries and media centers, an annual edited by Bohdan S. Wynar (Boulder, Colo., Libraries Unlimited, 1981–), is a classified listing of items selected from the *American reference books annual* (AA476) of the corresponding year. Z1035.1.D66

Geoghegan, Abel Rodolfo. Obras de referencia de América Latina; repertorio selectivo y anotado de enciclopedias, diccionarios, bibliografías, repertorios biográficos, catálogos, guías, anuarios, índices, etc. [Buenos Aires, Impr. Crisol, 1965] 280p. **AA482**

"Compiled with the assistance of Unesco."—*title page.*

Preface in Spanish, English, and French.

Includes "all types of reference works . . . that refer to Latin America, regardless of subject matter and place of publication" (*Pref.*), thus differing in scope and purpose from Sabor's *Manual* (AA498). Lists 2,694 items arranged by Universal Decimal Classification, with analytical index. Many annotations. Z1601.G4

Guide to New Zealand information sources. [Palmerston North], Massey Univ., 1975–82. v.1–6. (In progress) (Massey University library ser., no.8, 10–11, 13–16) **AA483**

Contents: v.1, Plants and animals (1975); v.2a, Farming, field and horticultural crops (1977); v.2b, Livestock farming, fisheries and forestry (1979); v.3, Education (1978); v.4, Religion (1980); v.5, Official publications (1980); v.6, History (1982).

Undertaken as an effort to compile a new work to replace John Harris' *Guide to New Zealand reference material* (1947; suppls. 1951 and 1957), the decision was later made to publish subject lists a section at a time. Listings are confined to monographic works except when the major source of information for a particular topic is a periodical article. Works included range from the introductory level to the specialized. Annotations are usually evaluative and indicate the level of scholarship. Z4101.B37

A guide to reference materials on India. Comp. and ed. by N. N. Gidwani and K. Navalani. Jaipur, Saraswati Publs., 1974. 2v. (1536p.) **AA484**

A classified guide to the whole range of reference works relating to India. In addition to monographs and multi-volume works, a special effort was made to list reference sources published in series or as parts of books. Aims to be comprehensive rather than selective.

Includes numerous brief annotations, detailed contents of various multi-volume sets, occasional references to reviews, etc. Cutoff date is early 1972. Index of authors, titles and subjects. Z3206.G84

Harvard University. Library. Reference collections shelved in the Reading Room and Acquisitions Department. Classification schedule; classified listing by call number; author and title listing. Cambridge, Harvard Univ. Lib.; distr. by Harvard Univ. Pr., 1970. 130p. (Widener Library shelflist, 33) **AA485**

For a note on the series *see* AA145.

Updates and supersedes no.8 of the shelflist series. Comprises classed lists for the bibliographies and other general reference works shelved in the Widener Reading Room and for those national bibliographies, etc., shelved in the Acquisitions Department. There is a combined alphabetic listing, but no chronological list as in other volumes of the series. Z1035.1.H27

Maichel, Karol. Guide to Russian reference books, ed. by J. S. G. Simmons. Stanford, Calif., Hoover Inst., 1962–67. v.1–2, 5. (Hoover Inst. Bibliographical ser. 10, 18, 32) (No more publ.) **AA486**

Contents: v.1, General bibliographies and reference books. 1962. 92p.; v.2, History, auxiliary historical sciences, ethnography, and geography. 1964. 297p.; v.5, Science, technology, and medicine. 1967. 384p.

The projected 6v. series was expected to list more than 3,500 titles of reference works pertaining to all phases of Russian life. The parts published are classified, annotated guides to materials in Russian and other languages, with broad chronological coverage. Author, title, and subject indexes in each volume. Z2491.M25

Malclès, Louise-Noëlle. Les sources du travail bibliographique. Genève, E. Droz; Lille, Giard, 1950–58. 3v. in 4. **AA487**

Although now considerably out of date, this remains a notable contribution to bibliographical manuals, designed to serve as textbook and guide, with introductions and discussions in each chapter. Not limited to bibliographies; also includes dictionaries, encyclopedias, atlases, texts, important periodicals, collections, and other types of reference and source materials. While basic works of earlier dates are included, emphasis has been put upon publications of the 25-year period preceding compilation, and particularly 1940–50. International in scope, with emphasis on French and European works.

Contents: t.1, General bibliographical survey; bibliographies of bibliographies; universal bibliographies; the book of the 15th and 16th centuries; printed catalogs of libraries; union catalogs; national bibliographies; encyclopedias; biography; periodicals; society publications; periodical indexes; a special section on Slavic and Balkan countries; a section on encyclopedias of the book, and a list of technical dictionaries of publishing and library terms.

t.2, pt.1–2, Bibliographies spécialisées (Sciences humaines), covering prehistory, anthropology, ethnography, sociology; linguistics; history; languages and literatures; religions; geography; archaeology and art; music; political and social sciences; philosophy; and special sections on the language, literature, and history of Slavic and Balkan countries and the Near, Middle, and Far East.

t.3, Bibliographies spécialisées (Sciences exactes et techniques), lists bibliographies, dictionaries, treatises, manuals, yearbooks, periodicals, etc., in the history of science and in the various sciences, including medicine and pharmacy but excluding agriculture.

A full index by author, subject, and title is included in v.1; in v.2, pt.2; and in v.3. Z1002.M4

Musiker, Reuben. Guide to South African reference books. 5th rev. ed. Cape Town, A. A. Balkema, 1971. 136p. **AA488**

1st ed. 1955.

A guide to some 800 works used for reference purposes published, with a few exceptions, in South Africa. Arranged by subject in Dewey Decimal Classification order with author, title, and subject index. For those South African subject areas where standard reference books do not exist, more general sources have been substituted.

———— ———— 4th cumulative supplement, 1970–1976 to 5th rev. ed. Johannesburg, The Library, Univ. of the Witwatersrand, 1977. 112p.

About 100 titles added in this supplement, bringing the total number of supplementary entries to 283.

———— South African reference books and bibliographies of 1979–1980. Johannesburg, Univ. of the Witwatersrand, Lib., 1981. 58p. **AA489**

Serves as a supplement to the compiler's *South Africa* (DD178) and his *South African bibliography* (AA95), listing some 200 items, mainly from the 1979–80 period. Z3601.M82

Neiswender, Rosemary. Guide to Russian reference and language aids. N.Y., Special Libraries Assoc., 1962. 92p. (S.L.A. bibliography, no.4) **AA490**

A listing of 221 titles with evaluative annotations, covering textbooks and readers, dictionaries, encyclopedias, geographical reference works, bibliographies, indexes, translation digests, current biographical sources, etc. Appendixes include a comparative table of seven transliteration systems, a glossary of Russian bibliographic and book-trade terminology, etc. Z2505.N4

Nihon no Sanko Tosho Henshu Iinkai. Guide to Japanese reference books. Chicago, Amer. Lib. Assoc., 1966. 303p. **AA491**

1st Japanese ed. (1962) had title: Nihon no sankō tosho.

A guide to basic Japanese reference works designed for the general reader. Each entry consists of author, title, imprint, collation, and, in most instances, a brief annotation.

The work is divided into four sections: General works, Humanities, Social Sciences, and Science-Technology. Each section is broken down into specific subjects; within each subject, titles are listed according to the following general pattern, as applicable: bibliographies, dictionaries and encyclopedias, handbooks, chronological tables, biographical dictionaries and directories, pictorial works, yearbooks, statistical works, and documents. Included is an alphabetical index to authors, titles, and general subject headings.

This English-language edition provides transliteration of the entries as well as translations of the titles and annotations from the second Japanese edition (Tokyo, 1966), which included materials published up to Sept. 1964; a revised Japanese edition of 1980 includes about 5,500 items published through 1977. The English- and Japanese-language editions were prepared simultaneously. Z3306.N5

———— Supplement. Wash., Lib. of Congress, 1979. 300p.

An English-language edition of the Japanese supplement to this guide, adding about 1,700 items, most of them published from late 1964 through 1970. Includes a cumulated index to the main volume and the supplement. Z1035.8.J3N55

Peterson, Carolyn Sue and **Fenton, Ann D.** Reference books for children. Metuchen, N.J., Scarecrow Pr., 1981. 265p. **AA492**

A revised and updated edition of *Reference books for elementary and junior high school libraries* (2d ed. 1975).

Offers an annotated list of about 900 reference works and selection tools suitable for school and public libraries. Some emphasis on recent publications. Subject arrangement, with author/title and subject indexes. New editions at 5-year intervals are planned. Z1037.1.P4

Printed reference material. Ed. by Gavin Higgens. 2d ed. London, Library Assoc.; Phoenix, Oryx Pr., [1984]. 740p. **AA493**

1st ed. 1980.

A successor to A. D. Roberts' *Introduction to reference books* (3d ed. 1956), intending to provide a practical handbook "for students and researchers; recently appointed reference staff; and practicing librarians, working in small information units, with limited stocks." —*Pref.* Chapters by contributing librarians deal with the reference process and with reference works by type (dictionaries, encyclopedias, biographical dictionaries, newspapers, periodicals, reports and theses, maps and atlases, government publications, statistical sources, etc.). Of British origin. Indexed.   Z1035.1.P74

RSR: reference services review. v.1, no.1– , Jan./Mar. 1973– . Ann Arbor, Mich., Pierian Pr., 1973– . Quarterly.

          AA494

v.1, no.1 preceded by a "pilot issue" dated Nov./Dec. 1972.

Each issue includes a section of reviews of "Recent reference books"; a "Reference book review index"; and a section on "Reference books in print."   Z1035.1.R43

Radford, Wilma. Guide to Australian reference books: humanities. Sydney, Library Assoc. of Australia, 1983. 81p.

          AA495

The first stage of a project intending to provide a published guide to Australian reference sources. Covers works in Dewey classes 100 (Philosophy), 200 (Religion), 400 (Language), 700 (The arts), 800 (Literature). Nearly 400 items with brief annotations; limited to separately published works and Australia volumes within sets.

          Z4001.R33

Reference sources, 1977– . Ann Arbor, Mich., Pierian Pr., 1977– . Annual.   **AA496**

Linda Mark, ed.

Aims to serve as a selection and acquisitions tool in the reference field and as a bibliographic record of the year's book production in that area. Coverage extends to books reviewed in selected library, scholarly, and general interest periodicals (120 journals in v.1, expanded to 270 in v.3) during the preceding year, plus reference books received at the Pierian Press but not yet reviewed. Most of the works are English-language titles and they range from the popular to the scholarly. Listing is by main entry, with cross references from editors, titles, etc., as necessary. Full bibliographic and cataloging information are given, as is price. A descriptive note is provided and review citations are given, often with a brief excerpt from one of the reviews. Reviews appearing in later years are cited in subsequent volumes of the series. General subject index, classified index, and alphabetical subject index.

Serves as a continuation and expansion of the same publisher's *Reference book review index* 1970–72 and 1973–75.

          Z1035.1.R45

Ryder, Dorothy E. Canadian reference sources: a selective guide. 2d ed. [Ottawa], Canadian Lib. Assoc., 1981. 311p.

          AA497

1st ed. 1973; suppl. 1975.

A selective, annotated guide to reference materials relating to Canada and Canadian affairs. Includes works on specific provinces, regions, and cities. In five main sections (General reference works; History and allied subjects; Humanities; Science; Social sciences) with appropriate subdivisions. Lists materials published through Dec. 1980. Good annotations; index. Four appendixes summarize the publishing histories of *Canadiana, Government of Canada publications, Canadian periodical index,* and *Canadian almanac and directory.*   Z1365.R8

Sabor, Josefa Emilia. Manual de fuentes de información; obras de referencia: enciclopedias, diccionarios, bibliografías, biografías, etc. 2. ed. ampliada. Buenos Aires, Editorial Kapelusz, [1967]. 342p.   **AA498**

1st ed. 1957.

A manual and guide designed particularly as a textbook for students but useful in other countries, especially for its information on Latin-American materials. A general introduction on the theory of reference work and the bibliographies pertaining thereto is followed by chapters on encyclopedias, dictionaries, national bibliographies, bibliographies of periodicals and government documents, biographical dictionaries, statistical annuals, and works of general information. Although there is some variation, most sections deal with the works of Spain, Latin America (with special attention to Argentina), France, Italy, Great Britain, Germany, Portugal, the United States, and Russia. The selection is of basic works, the annotations are descriptive and critical, and the whole is a well-planned manual.   Z1035.S14

———— and **Revello, Lydia H.** Bibliografía básica de obras de referencia de artes y letras para la Argentina. Buenos Aires, Fondo Nacional de las Artes, [1968]. 78p. (Bibliografía argentina de artes y letras. Compilatión especial, no.36)

          AA499

An annotated bibliography of 248 reference sources in the fields of Argentine arts and letters. Arranged by Universal Decimal Classification; author-title index.   Z1611.S3

Subscription books bulletin. Chicago, Amer. Lib. Assoc., 1930–56. 27v. Quarterly.   **AA500**

Gives unbiased, critical reviews of encyclopedias, dictionaries, biographical works, atlases, collections, etc. Prepared by a voluntary committee of librarians to help librarians and others in the selection of reference works. The reviews are based on careful examination of the books, and indication is given as to whether or not the work is recommended. (For the criteria and guidelines followed by the Subscription Books Committee *see* AA475.)

Continued in *The booklist* (*see* AA446), Sept. 1, 1956– ; reviews cumulated in: Z1007.S94

Subscription books bulletin reviews, 1956/60–1966/68, prep. by the American Library Association, Subscription Books Committee. Chicago, Amer. Lib. Assoc., 1961–68. 5v.

          AA501

The five volumes contain reprints of the reviews published in *The booklist and subscription books bulletin,* Sept. 1, 1956–Aug. 1968. Each volume is arranged alphabetically by the titles of the works reviewed.

Continued by: Z1035.1.S92

Reference and subscription books reviews, 1968/70– . Chicago, Amer. Lib. Assoc., 1970– . Biennial.   **AA502**

Cumulates the reviews from the "Subscription books" (later "Reference books bulletin") section of *Booklist* (AA446).

Current reviews appear in the "Reference books bulletin" section of *Booklist.* That section, prepared by the American Library Association's Reference Books Bulletin Editorial Board, supersedes the "Reference and subscription books reviews" section published 1969–83. It continues "to provide evaluations of reference works likely to be of use in home, school, public, and/or academic libraries," and includes reference works in any format.

          Z1035.1.S922

Têng, Ssu-yü and **Biggerstaff, Knight.** An annotated bibliography of selected Chinese reference works. 3d ed. Cambridge, Harvard Univ. Pr., 1971. 250p. (Harvard-Yenching Inst. studies, v.2)   **AA503**

1st ed. 1936.

Describes, in English, general and subject bibliographies, encyclopedias, dictionaries, geographical works, biographical works, tables, and yearbooks.   Z1035.T32

U.S. Library of Congress. The Library of Congress main reading room reference collection subject catalog. 2d ed. Comp. and ed. by Katherine Ann Gardner. Wash., Lib. of Congress, 1980. 1236p.   **AA505**

1st ed. 1975.

A computer-produced guide to the Library's Main Reading Room collection of some 17,315 titles (13,385 monographs, 3,930 serials) which constituted the collection on Aug. 15, 1980. Emphasis is on the humanities, social sciences and bibliography. Arranged alphabetically by subject heading, then by main entry.   Z1035.1.U526

Walford, Albert John. Guide to reference material. 3d ed. London, Lib. Assoc., 1973–77. 3v.   **AA506**

1st ed. and suppl. 1959–63.

Contents: v.1, Science & technology; v.2, Social & historical sciences, philosophy & religion; v.3, Generalities, languages, the arts & literature.

Aims "to provide a signpost to reference books and bibliographies published mainly in recent years" (*Introd.*), for the use of librarians, students of librarianship, and research workers. International in scope, but with emphasis on English-language materials. Arrangement is by Universal Decimal Classification, with an entry appearing in more than one place when warranted. Annotations often include critical comment, reference to related works not accorded a separate entry, and citations to reviews. v.3 includes a cumulated subject index to the set and also a cumulated author-title index. A well-edited, standard guide.

A new edition is appearing as: Z1035.W252

Walford's Guide to reference material. 4th ed., ed. by A. J. Walford. [London], Lib. Assoc., [1980–82]. v.1–2. (In progress) **AA507**

Contents: v.1, Science & technology, with the assistance of Anthony P. Harvey and H. Drubba (697p.); v.2, Social & historical sciences, philosophy & religion, with the assistance of Joan M. Harvey and L. J. Taylor (812p.).

This edition, also to be in 3v., is being published over a 6–year period and follows the plan of its predecessor. Once again there is a certain emphasis on English-language materials and on publications of recent years, although an "appreciable amount of older reference material is now available as reprints, and these are represented. As previously, announcements of forthcoming works or volumes are inserted. 'Hidden' bibliographies appearing in periodicals or as parts of books continue to find a place, as do entries for leading reviewing journals."—*Introd.* Each volume has its own index of authors, titles, and subjects (including references to the subsumed entries).

v.1 has entries for about 4,000 titles, with references to about 1,000 more items mentioned in the annotations; v.2 has main entries for some 5,000 items and about 2,000 subsumed entries.

A shortened version has appeared as: Z1035.1.W33

Walford, Albert John. Walford's Concise guide to reference material. London, Lib. Assoc., [1981]. 434p. **AA508**

". . . an updated guide to what are considered by the editor to be the basic items in [v.1 (1979) of the 4th ed. and v.2–3 (1975–77) of the 3d ed. of the larger work], plus more recent material."—*Introd.* Contains about one-sixth of the original entries, with greater emphasis on British and English-language works.

The review in *Library journal* (Jan. 15, 1982, p.154) concludes: "Doubtless British librarians will welcome this abbreviated Walford, but its value for North American librarians is questionable."

Zischka, Gert A. Index lexicorum; Bibliographie der lexikalischen Nachschlagewerke. Wien, Brüder Hollinek; N.Y., Hafner, [1959]. 290p. **AA509**

A bibliography of "encyclopedia-like reference books" rather than a bibliography of dictionaries. International in scope, particularly strong in German works; lists some 7,000 titles grouped in 21 sections, general encyclopedias followed by reference works in various subject fields. No language dictionaries, but in the subject sections are listed such works as specialized dictionaries and encyclopedias, glossaries, handbooks, biographical dictionaries, yearbooks, gazetteers, etc. No subject bibliographies. Annotations limited. Index of personal authors and subject headings, but no title listings, even for anonymous or composite works. Z1035.Z5

Book review indexes

Gray, Richard A. A guide to book review citations; a bibliography of sources. [Columbus], Ohio State Univ. Pr., [1969]. 221p. (Ohio State Univ. Libraries. Publ., no.2) **AA510**

A carefully annotated list of sources of book review citations—both continuing series and separately published works which include such references. Classed arrangement with author, title, and subject indexes. Now somewhat out-of-date. Z1035.A1G7

Bibliographie der Rezensionen, 1900–43. Leipzig, Dietrich, 1901–44. v.1–77. (Internationale Bibliographie der Zeitschriftenliteratur, Abt. C) **AA511**

Ceased publication.

Issues for 1901–10 inclusive (1v. per year) index reviews of books printed in some 3,000 German periodicals. 1911–14, 2v. per year: the first volume of each year indexes reviews in German periodicals, the second volume indexes reviews in about 2,000 periodicals in languages other than German. 1915 has 2v. for German reviews and 1v. for non-German. Volumes for 1916–24 index only German reviews except that v.33 covers non-German publications for 1917–19. 1925–43 are annual volumes alternating German and *fremdsprachigen.* A very comprehensive list, especially useful in American and English research libraries as it indexes many American and English sets not included in the *Book review digest.* Does not give digests or quotations from the reviews listed. The volumes which index reviews in German periodicals cover the same list as the *Bibliographie der deutschen Zeitschriftenliteratur* (AE278) and supplement that work; the volumes indexing non-German periodicals do the same thing for the *Bibliographie der fremdsprachigen Zeitschriftenliteratur* (AE221).

Continued by: AI9.B6

Internationale Bibliographie der Rezensionen wissenschaftlicher Literatur. Jahrg. 1– . Osnabrück, F. Dietrich Verlag, 1971– . Semiannual. **AA512**

Otto Zeller, ed.

Title also in English (International bibliography of book reviews of scholarly literature) and French. Prefatory matter in German, English, and French.

Contents: pt.A, Index of periodicals consulted; pt.B, Classified subject index of book reviews; pt.C, Index of book reviews by reviewed authors; pt.D, Index of book reviews by reviewing authors.

Serves both as a companion to the *Internationale Bibliographie der Zeitschriftenliteratur* (AE222) and as a continuation, after the long hiatus, of the *Bibliographie der Rezensionen* (above). Follows the format of the *IBZ;* full information is given in pts. B, C, and D. Reviews cited in the first volume are mainly of 1968–69 books, but many from earlier in the decade are included. Pt.D, the listing by reviewer, is an unusual feature among ongoing book review indexes. Z5051.I64

Book review digest, 1905– . N.Y., Wilson, 1905– . v.1– . **AA513**

A digest and index of selected book reviews in about 75 English and American periodicals, principally general in character. Arranged alphabetically by author of book reviewed, with subject and title index. "To qualify for inclusion a book must have been published or distributed in the United States. A work of non-fiction must have received two or more reviews and one of fiction four or more reviews in the journals selected."—*Pref. note.* For each book entered, gives a brief descriptive note, quotations from selected reviews with exact reference to periodical in which the review appeared, and references only—without quotation—to other reviews. Indicates length of review in number of words. Compiled mainly from the public library point of view, the reviews indexed being taken principally from the general journals and not to any great extent from the more specialized ones. Published monthly (except Feb. and July), with an annual cumulation in Feb.

Cumulated subject and title indexes for the previous 5-year period are included in the annual volumes for 1921, 1926, 1931, 1936, 1941, 1946, 1951, 1956, and 1961; for the periods 1962–66 and 1967–71, the cumulated index was issued as a separate volume. Z1219.C96

——— Author/title index 1905–1974. Ed. by Leslie Dunmore-Leiber. N.Y., Wilson, 1976. 4v.

For the series which these volumes index *see* above.

Covers nearly 300,000 books. Variant forms of author entries have been reconciled and cross references provided.

Book review index, 1965– . Detroit, Gale, 1965– . v.1– . Bimonthly. **AA514**

Originally published monthly, with quarterly and annual cumulations. Suspended 1969–71, then resumed with three issues covering 1972 and an annual cumulation for 1972 designated as v.8. Beginning 1973, issued bimonthly, with alternate issues cumulating the preceding bimonthly issue, and an annual cumulation. Retrospective indexes covering 1969–71, were published 1974/75 as v.5–7 of the series.

An author listing with abbreviated citations to reviews. Now intends to index all reviews appearing in about 450 publications. Reviews indexed are primarily in the fields of general fiction and nonfiction, humanities, social sciences, librarianship and bibliography, and juvenile and young adult books.   Z1035.A1B6

────── A master cumulation 1969–1979. Ed. by Gary C. Tarbert. Detroit, Gale, [1980]. 7v.

Cumulates the citations for the years indicated. v.6–7 are a title index (the title index was a new feature beginning 1976, but this cumulation includes title indexing for the full period).
Z1011.B63

Canadian book review annual. 1975– . Toronto, Peter Martin Associates, [1976]– . Annual.   **AA515**

Not an index to book reviews, but rather "an evaluative guide to Canadian English-language trade books."—*Pref.* Signed reviews of 200–400 words written for this publication. Classed arrangement; author and title indexes.   F1001.C224

Children's book review index. v.1, no.1– , Jan./Apr. 1975– . Detroit, Gale, 1975– . Annual.   **AA515a**

Citations are derived from the listings in the *Book review index* (AA514)—i.e., citations to reviews of works identified as children's books are repeated in this publication.

A cumulation has appeared as:

────── Master cumulation, 1969–1981. Ed. by Gary C. Tarbert. Detroit, Gale, 1982. 4v.

Combined retrospective index to book reviews in scholarly journals, 1886–1974. Evan Ira Farber, exec. ed. Arlington, Va., Carrollton Pr., 1979–82. 15v.   **AA516**

Contents: v.1–12, Authors; v.13–15, Titles.

Offers "author and title access to more than one million book reviews which appeared in the complete backfiles of 459 scholarly journals in History, Political Science and Sociology."—*Introd.* The author section is arranged alphabetically by author of the book reviewed, giving title of the book and citations to reviews (listed alphabetically by abbreviated journal title, with volume number, date, and initial page of the review); the titles section provides *see* references to the author part. In general, short notices are included as well as full-length reviews. Reviewers' names are not given.

A complementary set has appeared as *Combined retrospective index to book reviews in humanities journals, 1802–1974* (Woodbridge, Conn., Research Pubns., 1982–84. 10v.). It indexes reviews in an additional 150 periodicals in the broad range of the humanities.   Z1035.A1C64

Current book review citations, 1976–82. N.Y., H. W. Wilson, 1976–83. Monthly (except Aug.), with annual cumulation.
AA517

Brings together the book review citations from all the various Wilson periodical indexes. An author (or other main entry) listing gives the full review citation, including the reviewer's name when known; this is followed by a title index. Ceased publication.
Z1035.A1C86

Guía a las reseñas de libros de y sobre Hispanoamérica. 1972– . Detroit, Blaine Ethridge-Books, [1976–]. Annual.   **AA518**

Added title page in English: A guide to reviews of books from and about Hispanic America.

Antonio Matos, comp. and ed.

Introductory matter in Spanish and English; annotations in English or Spanish.

Continues a publication of the same title published in Río Piedras, Puerto Rico, in 1965 covering the years 1960–64, and a second volume (published in Río Piedras in 1973) covering 1965. The intervening years have not yet been covered.

Provides summaries of the reviews as well as citations to reviews. "Hispanic America" as here defined "includes, in addition to Spanish-speaking countries, Brazil, French, Dutch, and English-speaking areas of the Caribbean."—*Pref.* Arranged alphabetically by author, with title index.

Index to Australian book reviews, 1965–81. Adelaide, Libraries Board of South Australia, 1965–81. v.1–17. Quarterly with annual cumulation.   **AA519**

Ceased publication.

Indexes reviews of books by Australian authors (regardless of where published), books published in Australia, and books of Australian interest published abroad. A selected list of about 50 journals (mainly in the fields of literature, social sciences, and humanities) is regularly searched, and selected reviews from a number of other popular magazines are also included. Entry is by author of the book, with indexes by title and by reviewer.

Index to book reviews in the humanities, 1960– . Detroit, Phillip Thomson, 1960– . v.1– . Annual.   **AA520**

Indexes several hundred periodicals, originally all in English, though a number of foreign-language titles were added in the 1970 volume. Several thousand book titles are now included in each issue. v.1 originally had no cumulative index but was issued in cumulated form 1978; in v.2–3, 1961–62, the quarterly issues are cumulated into an annual volume; from 1963– , published annually.

Originally "humanities" was here defined to include history and some aspects of the social sciences, but beginning with v.11 (1970) the term has been restricted to art and architecture; biography, personal narrative and memoirs; drama and dance; folklore; language; literature; music; philosophy; travel and adventure.
Z1035.A1I63

Library journal book review, 1967– . N.Y., Bowker, 1968– . v.1– . Annual.   **AA521**

Reviews appearing in the *Library journal* have been cumulated and reprinted in classed arrangement, with index of authors and titles.   Z1035.A1L48

SELECTION OF PERIODICALS

❖Periodicals form an important part of the reference collections of a library. Current periodicals in many fields are needed to provide up-to-date articles on subjects of contemporary interest, and back files, especially those which are indexed in one or another of the general periodical indexes, are extremely valuable for reference work. However, the acquisition, maintenance, and binding of periodicals becomes an ever expanding item in the library budget, and careful consideration must be given to the selection of titles to be acquired and preserved. Selected and specialized lists will be found in the periodical indexes; e.g., the list in the *Abridged readers' guide* (AE232), which indexes some 25 periodicals, would be useful in the small public or school library, whereas the list of periodicals indexed in the *Readers' guide* (AE231) and the *Social sciences index* (AE236) and *Humanities index* (AE235) would be valuable aids to selection in a larger library; the lists in the subject indexes, e.g., the *Art index* (BE68) and the *Education index* (CB131), would be guides in these fields. It is well to remember that an indexed periodical has far more reference value than one that is not indexed. Some of the book selection guides (*see* p.40–47) include periodicals, and lists such as those by Camp (CB120) and Gerstenberger (BD79) offer information on periodicals in specific subject fields. For other lists of periodicals, *see* the Periodicals section, p.208–39.

Farber, Evan Ira. Classified list of periodicals for the college library . . . with the assistance of Thomas G. Kirk, Jr. and James R. Kennedy, Jr. 5th ed., rev. and enl. Westwood, Mass., Faxon, 1972. 449p. (Useful reference ser., no.99)
AA522

1st ed. 1934; 4th ed. 1957.

A selection aid for the liberal arts college library with a 4-year program and an enrollment of less than 2,000 students. "The purpose of the present edition, like the earlier ones, is to provide an effective aid in selecting journals for: (1) supplying reading collateral to students' courses; (2) keeping the faculty informed of developments in their fields; (3) affording good general and recreational reading; (4) providing in some measure for the research needs of advanced students and faculty."—*Note.* Good annotations; indication of indexing services; title index to the classed list. Only titles which began publication before 1969 are included.   Z6941.F25

Katz, William A. and **Katz, Linda Sternberg.** Magazines for libraries: for the general reader and school, junior college, college, university, and public libraries. 4th ed. N.Y., Bowker, 1982. 958p.   **AA523**

1st ed. 1969.

About 6,500 periodicals are annotated and evaluated in this edition. As before, titles "have been selected to include: (1) some general, nonspecialist periodicals of interest to the layperson; (2) the main English-language research journals sponsored by distinguished societies in the United States, Canada, and Great Britain; and (3) some high-quality commercial publications commonly found in academic/special libraries. Although titles cannot represent the full scope of research publications available for specialized collections, there has been an attempt to provide a balance, by discipline, between specialist versus layperson interests, student versus faculty use, and general science versus research concerns."—*Pref.* Classed arrangement with title and subject index. Names of consultants appear at the beginning of most sections.   Z6941.K2

Marshall, Joan K. Serials for libraries: an annotated guide to continuations, annuals, yearbooks, almanacs, transactions, proceedings, directories, services. N.Y., Neal/Schuman; Santa Barbara, Calif., ABC-Clio, [1979]. 494p.   **AA524**

A classified, annotated selection of about 2,000 irregular serials and annuals, chosen by a panel of librarians to provide guidance for serials selection and to serve as an aid in reference work. Limited largely to English-language publications from the United States. Full bibliographic and order information is given. Includes a "When to buy what" section which indicates the month or season when a given publication is scheduled to appear.   Z1035.1.M27

Richardson, Selma K. Magazines for children: a guide for parents, teachers, and librarians. Chicago, Amer. Lib. Assoc., 1983. 147p.   **AA525**

An alphabetical title listing, with extensive annotations and subject index, of magazines intended primarily for children. "Descriptions and evaluations are intended to allow teachers, librarians, parents, and other interested adults to make judgments about certain titles for purchase, whether for child, classroom, or library." —*Pref.* Includes a section on *Children's magazine guide* (AE259).   PN4878.R5

——— Magazines for young adults: selections for school and public libraries. Chicago, Amer. Lib. Assoc., 1984. 329p.   **AA526**

Together with the same compiler's *Magazines for children* (above), supersedes *Periodicals for school media programs* (1978). Offers annotated listings (with subscription information) of some 600 magazines, including all titles indexed in the *Readers' guide* and a number of other magazines published primarily for adults but widely read by young adults. Also includes a few newspapers and periodical indexes. Title listing with subject index. A useful selection tool.   Z6944.Y68R53

Serials review. v.1, no. 1/2– , Jan./June 1975– . Ann Arbor, Mich., Pierian Pr., 1975– . Quarterly.   **AA527**

Aims "to provide evaluations of periodicals, newspapers, indexes, union lists, periodical bibliographies, other reviewing tools, as well as any literature which is primarily designed to support collection evaluation, development, and preservation."—*verso of t.p.* Also carries articles on periodical selection, problems of serials management and budgeting, etc. Cumulative index of titles reviewed in v.1-5 (1975–79) appears in v.6, no.1 (1980).   PN4832.S47

AUDIOVISUAL MATERIALS

Audio video market place: AVMP. 1984– . N.Y., Bowker, [1984]– . Annual.   **AA528**

Subtitle: A multimedia guide.

Continues *Audiovisual market place*, eds.1–13, 1969–83.

A directory for the AV industry presented along the lines of the *Literary market place* (AA353). The major section, "Producers, distributors & services" is arranged geographically by state, then alphabetically by name of the company, organization, or agency; a classified index to that section is arranged under main headings such as cable programming services, equipment and facilities, libraries, production services, properties, software, unions and guilds (each with numerous subheads). There are also sections for associations, awards and festivals, a calendar, lists of periodicals and reference books, and a "names and numbers" section.

Brown, Lucy Gregor. Core media collection for secondary schools. 2d ed. N.Y., Bowker, 1979. 263p.   **AA529**

1st ed. 1975.

Aims "to provide a qualitative selection guide to nonprint media titles. The majority of the titles . . . are for sound or captioned filmstrips, kits, recordings, and 16mm films; however, 8mm loops, slides, and some video cassettes are also listed. They cover a wide variety of subject and ability levels."—*Pref.* Subject listing with title index; producer/distributor directory.

Core media collection for elementary schools (N.Y., Bowker, 1978. 224p.) is a similar list by the same compiler.   LB1043.Z9B76

Consortium of University Film Centers. Educational film locator of the Consortium of University Film Centers and R. R. Bowker Company. 2d ed. N.Y., Bowker, 1980. 2611p.   **AA529a**

1st ed. 1978.

A "union list" of educational and feature films held by member libraries of the Consortium; the 1980 ed. is a selective compilation of about 40,000 titles held by 52 university film libraries. The "Subject, title and audience level index" lists appropriate film titles; complete bibliographic and descriptive information are given under title in the "Alphabetical list of film descriptions." States lending policies of member libraries, and provides a directory of film producers and distributors.   LB1044.Z9C58

Educational Media Council. Educational media index . . . N.Y., McGraw-Hill, [1964]. 14v.   **AA530**

Contents: v.1, Pre-school and primary, grades K–3; v.2, Intermediate, grades 4–6; v.3, Art and music; v.4, Business education and training; v.5, English language; v.6, Foreign language; v.7, Guidance, psychology, and teacher education; v.8, Health-safety and home economics; v.9, Industrial and agricultural education; v.10, Mathematics; v.11, Science and engineering; v.12, Geography and history; v.13, Economics and political science; v.14, Master title index.

"Guide to the source, content, and cost of non-book materials . . . films, kinescopes and filmstrips . . . slides and transparencies . . . maps, charts, and graphs . . . flat pictures . . . videotapes and phonotapes . . . phonodiscs . . . programmed instructional materials . . . models and mockups . . . cross-media sets."—*Pref.*

Contains bibliographies. Supersedes: *Educational film guide* (N.Y., Wilson, 1936–62. Annual) and *Filmstrip guide* (N.Y., Wilson, 1948–62. Irregular). For critical review *see Subscription books bulletin* 61:1033–38, July 15, 1965.   Z5814.V8E3

Educators guide . . . Randolph, Wis., Educators Progress Service.   **AA531**

This service issues: *Educators guide to free films.* 1941– . Annual; *Educators guide to free filmstrips.* 1949– . Annual; *Educators guide to free audio and video materials.* 1977– . Annual.

These are annotated lists giving source, availability, terms of loan, etc., arranged by subject with subject and title indexes.

The same publisher offers an annual series of guides to free materials in special areas and on special subjects, including: *Educators guide to free guidance materials,* 1962– ; *Educators guide to free science materials,* 1960– ; *Educators guide to free social studies materials,* 1961– ; *Educators guide to free health, physical education and recreation materials,* 1968– ; *Elementary teachers guide to free curriculum materials,* 1944– .

Educators grade guide to free teaching aids, 1955– . Randolph, Wis., Educators Progress Service, 1955– . Annual. Looseleaf.   **AA532**

Annotated lists of free maps, bulletins, pamphlets, exhibits, charts, and books. Arranged by broad subject. Includes title, subject and source indexes.   AG600.E3

The equipment directory of audio-visual, computer and video products. Ed.30– , 1984/85– . Fairfax, Va., NAVA, The International Communications Industries Assoc., [1984]– . il. Annual.   **AA533**

Continues *Audio-visual equipment directory,* eds. 1–29, 1953–83.

Aims "to supply such pertinent facts as could be ascertained from information provided by the manufacturers or their designated agents on items of proven acceptance in the marketplace."—*Foreword.* Includes foreign-made products available in North America; products must be currently on the market; does not include equipment and accessories intended for the amateur photographic, consumer or hi-fi markets. Arranged by equipment category (audio equipment, record players, furniture, learning systems, sound motion picture projectors, video equipment, etc.), then alphabetically by company name. Prices are indicated. Index of trade names; useful charts; directory of ICIA members; index of contributors/manufacturers.

National Audiovisual Center. A reference list of audiovisual materials produced by the United States government, 1978. Wash., D.C., The Center, 1978. 354p., xlvi p.   **AA534**

1974 ed. had title: *A catalog of United States government produced audiovisual materials.*

"This is a list of over 6,000 audiovisual materials selected from over 10,000 programs produced by 175 Federal agencies covering a wide range of subjects. Major subject concentrations in the Center's collection include medicine, dentistry, and allied health; education; science; social studies; industrial/technical training; safety; and the environmental sciences."—*Introd.* A title section provides the full information on a given item, including availability through rental or sale; a subject section serves as an index to the titles. Price list included.

———— ———— Supplement. Wash., The Center, 1980. 54p.

Lists about 600 titles recently added to the Center's collection.

National Information Center for Educational Media. NICEM media indexes. Los Angeles, Nat. Information Center, Univ. of Southern California.   **AA535**

Publisher varies.

The series of indexes issued by the Center covers a wide range of audiovisual materials; most of the volumes in the series are periodically revised. Titles include: *Index to educational audio tapes; Index to educational records; Index to educational videotapes; Index to 8mm motion cartridges; Index to health and safety education (multimedia); Index to educational overhead transparencies; Index to producers and distributors; Index to psychology (multimedia); Index to 16mm educational films; Index to 35mm educational filmstrips; Index to vocational and technical education (multimedia); Index to educational slides; Index to environmental studies (multimedia).*

Rufsvold, Margaret Irene. Guides to educational media: films, filmstrips, multimedia kits, programmed instruction materials, recordings on discs and tapes, slides, transparencies, videotapes. 4th ed. Chicago, Amer. Lib. Assoc., 1977. 159p.   **AA536**

1st ed. 1961. Earlier editions had title: *Guides to newer educational media.*

"This edition identifies and describes 245 educational media catalogs, indexes, and reviewing services; in addition, 35 related publications are mentioned in the annotations."—*Pref.* Offers "a guide to catalogs and lists, services of professional organizations,

and specialized periodicals which systematically provide information on the nonprint educational media."   Z5814.V8R8

Sive, Mary Robinson. Media selection handbook. Littleton, Colo., Libraries Unlimited, 1983. 171p.   **AA537**

Aims to give "detailed directions for the systematic detection of specific needs and for systematic comparison shopping that identifies available, relevant media and assesses their quality in relation to cost and potential usage."—*Pref.* Limited to "nonprint media exclusive of films and to instructional uses at levels from kindergarten through community college." Includes a section on selection tools and sources. Indexed.   LB1043.Z9S58

U.S. Library of Congress. Audiovisual materials. Jan./Mar. 1979–82. Wash., The Library, 1979–83. Quarterly with annual cumulation.   **AA538**

Continues the Library's *Films and other materials for projection* (BG222) which ceased with the 1978 cumulation.

"*Audiovisual Materials* presents motion pictures, filmstrips, sets of transparencies, slide sets, videorecordings, and kits currently cataloged by the Library of Congress, thus serving as an acquisition, reference, and research tool."—*Foreword, 1979.* Aims to list all items in the aforementioned categories "released in the United States or Canada which have educational or instructional value."

Continued by:

NUC. Audiovisual materials [microform]. Jan./Mar. 1983– . [Wash.], Lib. of Congress, [1983?]– . Microfiche.   **AA539**

Includes motion pictures, video recordings, filmstrips, transparency sets, and slide sets released in the United States or Canada, and cataloged by the Library of Congress.

The video source book. Syosset, N.Y., National Video Clearinghouse, 1979– . il. Annual.   **AA540**

The 7th ed. (1985) includes entries for more than 40,000 prerecorded video program titles available on videotape and videodisc, compiled from video and film catalogs and from lists furnished by wholesale distributors. Title listing (giving full information on the programs) with "subject category" index and index of distributors or sources. Includes programs for home, business, and institutional use.   PN1992.95.V52

Wynar, Christine Gehrt. Guide to reference books for school media centers. 2d ed. Boulder, Colo., Libraries Unlimited, 1981. 377p.   **AA541**

1st ed. 1973.

1,936 annotated entries for reference books and selection tools for elementary, junior, and senior high schools. Sections for media sources, media selection, and general reference are followed by subject listings such as: anthropology, biology, crafts, earth sciences, education, environmental studies, fine arts, history, music, political science, etc. Includes references to reviews. Indexed.   Z1037.W98

Reviews

Media review. v.3, no.3– , Nov. 1979– . Pleasantville, N.Y., Media Review, 1979– . Monthly (Sept.–June). Looseleaf.   **AA542**

Continues *Media index* (v.1–3,no.2, Apr. 1978–Oct. 1979).

Subtitle: Professional evaluations of instructional materials.

The looseleaf service includes a newsletter, evaluations, new releases, and a cumulative index.

Media review digest. [v.1]– , 1973/74– . Ann Arbor, Mich., Pierian Pr., 1974– . Annual, with semiannual suppl.   **AA543**

Continues *Multi media reviews index,* 1970–72.

Frequency has varied.

Subtitle: The only complete guide to reviews of non-book media.

Provides citations, with descriptive notes, "to reviews of films and filmstrips; educational and spoken-word records and tapes; slides, transparencies, illustrations, globes, charts, media kits, games and other miscellaneous media forms."—*Introd. 1983.* Separate sections for (1) films and videotapes, (2) filmstrips, (3) records and tapes, and (4) miscellaneous media. Listing is by main entry within each section, with classified and alphabetical subject indexes to the volume as a whole. LB1043.Z9M4

NATIONAL AND TRADE

❖In this section an attempt has been made to list the major retrospective and current national bibliographies from countries throughout the world. No claim to exhaustiveness is made, but special attention has been given to the publishing and book trade records (whether official or commercial) of the developing nations, both as an effort to get these bibliographies on record at an early stage and to encourage their publication and continuation.

Bibliography

Commonwealth Secretariat. Commonwealth national bibliographies: an annotated directory. London, Commonwealth Secretariat, [1977]. 97p. **AA544**

A country-by-country listing, with full descriptions, of national bibliographies (plus some nationally produced serials lists and periodical indexes), published in Commonwealth countries. "Most of the bibliographies appearing in the directory have been produced nationally, but some regional publications have also been included so as to cover those Commonwealth states and dependencies that are too small to warrant their own national bibliographies. In addition, the Accessions Lists produced by Library of Congress Offices for the use of librarians in the U.S.A. have been included so as to supplement inadequate bibliographic coverage in some regions."—*Introd.* Z2000.9.C66

Gorman, G. E. and **Mahoney, M. M.** Guide to current national bibliographies in the Third World. München, H. Zell/K. G. Saur, 1983. 328p. **AA545**

Provides a state-of-the-art report for national bibliographic control in the developing nations, listing "some eighty national bibliographies, complementary compilations or substitute services for sixty developing countries plus ten regional bibliographies for six regions."—*Introd.* Includes only those national bibliographies known to have published at least one volume or issue since 1975 or which began publication by mid-1983. For each country is given a bibliographical citation to the national bibliography or effective substitute, together with its history, scope and content, plus an analysis or critique of the publication and its usefulness. Title index.

Larsen, Knud. National bibliographical services, their creation and operation . . . [Paris], UNESCO, [1953]. 142p. il. (Unesco bibliographical handbooks, 1) **AA546**

A guide to the establishment of national bibliographies, union catalogs, and information services, with information on techniques, administration, etc., and some comment on existing services. Bibliography, p.124–36; index. Z1001.L3

Synoptic tables concerning the current national bibliographies. Comp. by Gerhard Pomassl and a working group of the Deutsche Bücherei. Berlin & Leipzig, 1975. unpaged (25 folded leaves) 36cm. **AA547**

At head of title: Bibliotheksverband der Deutschen Demokratischen Republik; Deutsche Bücherei, Leipzig.

An earlier, mimeographed version was distributed at the IFLA meeting in Grenoble in 1973.

Presents in tabular form information on current national bibliographies published throughout the world. Arranged by continent, then alphabetically by country. As far as available, tables indicate for each country: statistics on book production (1967/68 data), year of legal deposit regulation, editor/compiler (i.e., government agency, national library, institution, or commercial firm) of the national bibliography, title of the bibliography, together with its frequency,

scope, contents, arrangement, indexes, titles listed per year, indication of delays in publication, and comments on special features. Z1002.S89

U.S. Library of Congress. General Reference and Bibliography Division. Current national bibliographies, comp. by Helen F. Conover. Wash., 1955. 132p. (Repr.: N.Y., Greenwood Pr., 1968) **AA548**

An annotated listing of the records of publishing in 67 countries. In addition, the work lists periodical indexes, government publications, and directories of periodicals and newspapers. Dated, but still useful. Z1002.A2U52

Zimmerman, Irene. Current national bibliographies of Latin America; a state of the art study. [Gainesville], Center for Latin American Studies, Univ. of Florida, 1971. 139p. **AA549**

Provides a brief but careful description of the current (i.e., as of 1969) national bibliographical services of the individual countries of South America and the Caribbean. Attention is given to historical aspects and to future plans. Bibliography; index. Dated, but useful for historical information. Z1602.5.Z55

Reprints

Books on demand: author guide; . . . selected books available as on-demand reprints. Ann Arbor, Mich., University Microfilms, 1977– . Irregular. **AA550**

Books on demand: subject guide . . . . Ann Arbor, Mich., University Microfilms, 1977– . Irregular.

Books on demand: title guide . . . . Ann Arbor, Mich., University Microfilms, 1977– . Irregular.

The above three volumes, offering variant approaches to the same 100,000 works, are available separately or as a set. The "on-demand" reprint program makes the works listed in the catalogs available by xerography as full-size bound books or in microfilm. The lists include many early and rare books, but also include books that have only recently gone out of print. Prices of the reprints are indicated.

A review of the 1977 ed. in *Library journal* 103:1384 (July 1978) concludes that the set is "essential for any acquisitions department," but warns that "some of the books listed here are still in *Books in Print* at more reasonable prices."

Guide to reprints, 1967– . Wash., Microcard Eds., [1967–]. Annual. **AA551**

Albert James Diaz, ed.

Originally an "in print" listing for books, journals, and other materials issued in reprint form (i.e., through photographic reproduction of original text, not by re-setting of type) by U.S. publishers; now international in scope, covering reprints from more than 400 publishers throughout the world.

During the period 1964–81 the bimonthly *Bibliographia anastatica* and its successor, the quarterly *Bulletin of reprints,* provided an ongoing record of newly available reprints. Z1000.5.G8

Internationale Bibliographie der Reprints. International bibliography of reprints. Ed. by Christa Gnirss. München, Verlag Dokumentation, 1976–80. 2v. in 4. **AA552**

Contents: Bd.1, Teil 1–2, Bücher und Reihen; Teil 3, Register; Bd.2, Zeitschriften, Zeitungen, Jahrbücher, Konferenzberichte, usw.

Introductory matter in German and English.

"The term 'reprint' is here used to describe all reprinted works produced by photomechanical means in so far as the publisher is not identical with the publisher of the original work."—*Foreword.* Information was initially derived from publishers' catalogs, lists and prospectuses, but additional searching in national bibliographies was done in order to supply full information, including original publication date where possible. Z1033.R4I572

International

International books in print: English language titles published outside the U.S.A. and the United Kingdom. München, etc. K. G. Saur, [1979]– . Irregular. **AA553**

The subtitle explains the scope of this publication. Originally an author-title catalog, but beginning with the 1984 ed. (publ. 1983) it is published in two parts: pt.I, Author-title list (in 2v.) and pt.II, Subject guide (v.1, Classes; v.2, Countries and persons). In the author-title section full information is given under main entry, with cross references from added entries. Lists of participating publishers and central distributors (with addresses) appear in v.2 of each part. The 3d (1984) ed. lists some 140,000 titles from about 4,600 publishers in 95 countries.

United States

Tanselle, George Thomas. Guide to the study of United States imprints. Cambridge, Mass., Belknap Pr. of Harvard Univ. Pr., 1971. 2v. **AA554**

An attempt to record "most of the published research which is relevant to the study of United States imprints."—*Introd.* Bibliographies, checklists, and supplementary studies are listed in nine main categories: (1) Regional lists; (2) Genre lists; (3) Author lists; (4) Copyright records; (5) Catalogues; (6) Book-trade directories; (7) Studies of individual printers and publishers; (8) General studies; and (9) Checklists of secondary material. Indexed.

Z1215.A2T35

Early

See also BD969.

American Antiquarian Society, Worcester, Mass. Library. A dictionary catalog of American books pertaining to the 17th through 19th centuries. Westport, Conn., Greenwood Pr., [1971]. 20v. **AA555**

Reproduction of the catalog cards (author, title, and subject cards in dictionary arrangement) for the Society's collection of American imprints prior to 1821 and first editions of American literary authors through the 19th century.

European Americana: a chronological guide to works printed in Europe relating to the Americas, 1493–1776. N.Y., Readex Books, 1980–82. v.1–2. (In progress) **AA556**

Ed. by John Alden and Dennis C. Landis. At head of title: The John Carter Brown Library.

Contents: v.1, 1493–1600; v.2, 1601–1650.

When completed, the series is to cover the period 1493–1776; it "represents an effort to record in chronological form those works printed in Europe which depict the Americas in verbal terms."—*Pref.* For purposes of the bibliography "The Americas" are defined as "the area from Greenland to the Straits of Magellan, comprising the two Americas, Central America, and geologically related islands in the Caribbean and elsewhere." Bibliographic information for the individual items seeks to provide "a terse and unencumbered presentation of salient American content which at the same time permits identification of the work itself," and bibliographical references to works offering fuller descriptions are often given. Library locations are indicated.

Although "Sabin" (AA563) provided the starting point for compilation, non-Sabin items abound: of the approximately 4,300 entries in v.1, only a fourth appear in Sabin. In addition to an author, title, subject index, each volume offers a "Geographical index of printers and booksellers and their publications" and an "Alphabetical index of printers and booksellers and their geographic locations."

Z1203.E87

Evans, Charles. American bibliography; a chronological dictionary of all books, pamphlets and periodical publica-

tions printed in the United States of America from the genesis of printing in 1639 down to and including the year 1800; with bibliographical and biographical notes. Chicago, pr. for the author, 1903–59. 14v. (Repr.: N.Y., Peter Smith, 1941–67) **AA557**

Publisher varies: v.13–14 published by the American Antiquarian Society, Worcester, Mass.

The most important general list of early American publications, indispensable in the large reference or special library. Includes books, pamphlets, and periodicals, arranged chronologically by dates of publication; gives for each book author's full name with dates of birth and death, full title, place, date, publisher or printer, paging, size, and, whenever possible, location of copies in American libraries. Each volume has three indexes: (1) authors, (2) classified subjects, (3) printers and publishers.

Although Evans had originally hoped to continue to 1820, as indicated on the title pages of v.1–12, 1639–1799 (publ. 1903–34), he finally decided to stop with 1800 and, in fact, carried through the letter M of 1799. v.13 (publ. 1955) starts with the letter N for 1799 and continues through 1800 with author and subject indexes. In this volume, compiled by Clifford K. Shipton, the system used by Evans has been modified somewhat, e.g., titles have been shortened, and cross references are given from the title when anonymous works are listed under author.

v.14 (publ. 1959), edited by Roger Pattrell Bristol, is a cumulated author-title index to the whole work, including pseudonyms, attributed authors, other names appearing on the title page, governmental bodies, etc. Newspapers and almanacs are grouped under these respective headings and are not listed under specific title.

Z1215.E92

Bristol, Roger Pattrell. Supplement to Charles Evans' American bibliography. Charlottesville, publ. for the Bibliographical Society of America and the Bibliographical Society of the University of Virginia by the Univ. Pr. of Virginia, [1970]. 636p. **AA558**

A "checking edition" was issued in parts in 1962. As now published, the supplement adds about 11,200 entries to the Evans listings. Z1215.E92334

——— ——— Index to Supplement . . . Charlottesville, [1971]. 191p.

——— Index of printers, publishers and booksellers indicated by Charles Evans in his American bibliography. Charlottesville, Bibliographical Soc. of the Univ. of Virginia, 1961. 172p. **AA559**

Under each name is indicated—chronologically and then by item number—references to be found in Evans. Z1215.E9233

Shipton, Clifford Kenyon and **Mooney, James E.** National index of American imprints through 1800; the short-title Evans. [Worcester, Mass.], American Antiquarian Soc. and Barre Publs., 1969. 2v. (1028p.) **AA560**

Offers an index to the Readex Microprint edition of *Early American imprints.* It eliminates the need to consult the Evans *American bibliography* (AA557) to obtain the sequence number in the microprint edition, and also incorporates into the single alphabetical listing 10,035 additional items which have turned up since the publication of the Evans work. Most, but not all, of the items in Roger Bristol's supplement to Evans (AA558) are included. Many corrections have been made in the Evans listings. Only one location (i.e., the copy used for the microprint edition) is noted; ghosts and unlocated items are so indicated. An important bibliographic source in its own right. Z1215.S495

Henry E. Huntington Library and Art Gallery, San Marino, Calif. American imprints, 1648–1797, in the Huntington Library, supplementing Evans' American bibliography; comp. by Willard O. Waters. (Repr. from: *Huntington Library Bull.,* no.3, Feb. 1933, p.1–95) **AA561**

Arranged chronologically, with author index. Lists 736 "titles of books, pamphlets, broadsides, maps, etc., supplementary to the Evans bibliography. It comprises, besides items apparently not

listed in that work, a number appearing there but with titles or imprints varying from the copies here described."—[*Prelim. note*].
Z1215.E92

New York. Public Library. Rare Book Division. Checklist of additions to Evans' American bibliography in the Rare Book Division of the New York Public Library, comp. by Lewis M. Stark and Maud D. Cole. N.Y., Lib., 1960. 110p.
AA562

1,289 entries. Lists originals, photostats, and facsimiles, for the latter frequently indicating the location of the original.
Z1215.E95

Sabin, Joseph. Bibliotheca Americana. A dictionary of books relating to America, from its discovery to the present time. Begun by Joseph Sabin, and continued by Wilberforce Eames for the Bibliographical Society of America. N.Y., Sabin, 1868–92; Bibliographical Soc. of America, 1928–36. 29v. (Repr.: Amsterdam, N. Israel, 1961–62)
AA563

An important bibliography of Americana, including books, pamphlets, and periodicals printed in the Western hemisphere, and works about the region printed elsewhere. Comprises 106,413 numbered entries, but the actual number of titles recorded is much greater, as that total does not count the added editions and titles mentioned in the various notes. The arrangement is by author, with some title entries for anonymous works and many entries under names of places. Information given includes full title, place, publisher, date, format, paging, often contents and bibliographical notes with reference to a description or review in some other work, and, in many cases, names of libraries possessing copies.
A list of "Library Location Symbols" is given in v.29, p. 299–305, which is more extensive than the partial list given in v.1.
Z1201.S2

Molnar, John Edgar, comp. Author-title index to Joseph Sabin's Dictionary of books relating to America. Metuchen, N.J., Scarecrow Pr., 1974. 3v. (3196p.)
AA564

Authors and titles in a single sequence; some identification of pseudonyms.
Z1201.S222

Thompson, Lawrence Sidney. The new Sabin: books described by Joseph Sabin and his successors, now described again on the basis of examination of originals, and fully indexed by title, subject, joint authors, and institutions and agencies. Troy, N.Y., Whitston, 1974–83. v.1–9 and indexes. (In progress)
AA565

Represents works from the Sabin period (not all are in Sabin) examined by the compiler either in the original or in microform, with descriptions mainly taken from Library of Congress cards. Items are numbered serially, and each volume is a separate author alphabet. The indexing is seen as a salient feature. A cumulative index to v.1–5 (entries 1–13513) appeared in 1978, and separate indexes have been issued with subsequent volumes. (v.9, publ. 1983, carries entries 21753–23828.)
Z1201.T45

Wing, Donald Goddard. Short-title catalogue of books printed in England, Scotland, Ireland, Wales, and British America . . . 1641–1700. N.Y., Columbia Univ. Pr., 1945–51. 3v.
AA566

For full information and a note on the new edition *see* AA818.
Includes books printed in the American colonies during this period.
Z2002.W5

19th century

Shaw, Ralph Robert and **Shoemaker, Richard H.** American bibliography; a preliminary checklist for 1801–1819. N.Y., Scarecrow Pr., 1958–66. 22v.
AA567

Contents: v.1–19, 1801–1819; [v.20], Addenda; list of sources; library symbols; [v.21], Title index; [v.22], Corrections; author index.
A preliminary checklist "gathered entirely from secondary sources," designed as a first step in filling the gap in American national bibliography between 1800, when Evans stops, and 1820, when

Roorbach starts. The Preface explains purpose and procedure. Each volume covers one year; the Addenda volume lists 1,768 additional items from the full 1801–19 period. Locations of copies are given when they were included in the original citations.
Z1215.S48

Shoemaker, Richard H. Checklist of American imprints for 1820–1829. N.Y., Scarecrow Pr., 1964–71. 10v.
AA568

Vols. for 1826–29 comp. with the assistance of G. Cooper.
Designed as a continuation of Shaw-Shoemaker (above) to provide fuller coverage than Roorbach (AA570). Lists several times as many titles as the latter, with more complete information and location of copies.
Z1215.S5

————— ————— Title index, comp. by M. Frances Cooper. Metuchen, N.J., Scarecrow Pr., 1972. 556p.

Continued by:

A checklist of American imprints for 1830– . Metuchen, N.J., Scarecrow Pr., 1972–82. v.1–5. (In progress)
AA569

Contents: v.1–5, 1830–34.
Various compilers; v.1 comp. by Gayle Cooper.
Z1215.C66

Roorbach, Orville Augustus. Bibliotheca americana, . . .1820–61. N.Y., Roorbach, 1852–61. 4v. (Repr.: N.Y., Peter Smith, 1939)
AA570

v.1, 1820–52, with a list of periodicals published in the United States; v.2, Supplement, Oct. 1852–May 1855; v.3, Addenda, May 1855–March 1858; v.4, March 1858–Jan. 1861.
A trade catalog of American publications, including reprints, arranged alphabetically by author and title, giving publisher, size, price, and, in some cases, date.
Z1215.A5

Kelly, James. The American catalogue of books (original and reprints), published in the United States from Jan. 1861 to Jan. 1871, with date of publication, size, price, and publisher's name. N.Y., Wiley, 1866–71. 2v. (Repr.: N.Y., Peter Smith, 1938. 2v.)
AA571

Continues the record of American bibliography from Roorbach's last volume, giving about the same kind of information. Each volume contains a list of societies and their publications. v.1 also contains a list of pamphlets, sermons, and addresses on the Civil War, 1861–66.
Both Roorbach and Kelly are unsatisfactory, as they are far from complete and often inaccurate, but they must be used as they are the most general lists for the period 1820–70.
Z1215.A5

Stevens, Henry. Catalogue of the American books in the library of the British Museum at Christmas MDCCCLVI. London, Chiswick Pr. for H. Stevens, 1866. 4 pts. in 1v.
AA572

Contents: (1) American books printed in the United States. 628p.; (2) Catalogue of the Canadian and other British North American books. 14p.; (3) Catalogue of the Mexican and other Spanish American and West Indian books. 62p.; (4) Catalogue of the American maps. 17p.
Includes some works not included in Roorbach and gives fuller titles for others that are included there.
Z1207.B862

American catalogue . . . , 1876–1910. N.Y., Publishers' Weekly, 1880–1911. 8v. in 13. (Repr.: N.Y., Peter Smith, 1941)
AA573

Cumulates the *Annual American catalogue,* 1886–1910.
The basic work—1876, Author and title entries of books in print, July 1, 1876; Subject entries. 2v.—is supplemented by volumes covering various periods (e.g., three, five, or eight years) usually with author/title and subject volumes.
The standard American list for the period covered; comprehensive and generally reliable although information given is based upon reports from publishers and not, in most cases, on actual examination of the books themselves. Aims to include, with certain exceptions, all books published in the United States which were for sale to the general public.
Z1215.A5

20th century

American book publishing record cumulative 1876–1949. N.Y., Bowker, 1980. 15v. **AA574**

Contents: v.1–10, Dewey Decimal classes 000–999; v.11, Fiction, Juvenile fiction; v.12, Non-Dewey Decimal classified titles; v.13, Author index; v.14, Title index; v.15, Subject guide.

For the *American book publishing record* and its earlier cumulations *see* AA579.

Entries for this cumulation "were compiled from *A Catalog of Books Represented by Library of Congress Printed Cards* (cards issued from August 1898 through July 1942), *Supplement* (cards issued from August 1942 through December 1947), and *The Library of Congress Author Catalog, 1948–1952*."—*Pref.* About 625,000 entries. Does not include "federal and other governmental publications (with the exception of some city and state government reports), subscription books, dissertations, new printings (as distinct from reprints, re-issues, and revised or new editions), quarterlies, and other periodicals, pamphlets under forty-nine pages, and specialized publications of a transitory nature or intended as advertising."

American book publishing record cumulative 1950–1977. N.Y., Bowker, 1979. 15v. **AA575**

Contents: v.1–10, Dewey Decimal classes 000–999; v.11, Fiction, Juvenile fiction; v.12, Non-Dewey Decimal classified titles; v.13, Author index; v.14, Title index; v.15, Subject guide.

About 900,000 entries. Cumulates entries from the *American book publishing record*, 1960–77, together with "thousands of titles from the *National Union Catalog* for the years 1950 to 1968 and from the Library of Congress MARC tapes for the years 1968 to 1977 that have not appeared in previous cumulations of the *American Book Publishing Record*."—*Pref.*

United States catalog; books in print, Jan. 1, 1928. 4th ed. N.Y., Wilson, 1928. 3164p. **AA576**

1st ed. 1899 (v.1, Author list; v.2, Title index); 2d ed. 1902; 3d ed. Jan. 1, 1912.

Supplements (entitled *Cumulative book index*) for intervening years were published as follows: [cumulation] 1902/1905; annual supplements, 1906–10; [cumulations] 1912/17, 1918/June 1921, June 1921/June 1924; annual supplements, July 1924–Dec.1927.

Z1215.U6

Cumulative book index, a world list of books in the English language, 1928/32– . N.Y., Wilson, 1933– . **AA577**

Often referred to as *CBI*.

Published periodically since 1898 with cumulations to form supplements to the *United States catalog*. Frequency varies. Now published monthly, except Aug. (*see* AA584), cumulating at intervals, with eventual, permanent cumulations.

Cumulations needed to supplement the 4th ed. of the *United States catalog* are: 1928/32 (publ. 1933); 1933/37 (publ. 1938); 1938/42 (publ. 1945); 1943/48 (publ. 1950); 1949/52 (publ. 1953); 1953/56 (publ. 1959); biennial 1957–68; annual since 1969.

The *United States catalog* and the *CBI* constitute a comprehensive record of American publications from 1898 to date that is indispensable for reference work in this field. The most frequently used parts will be the 4th ed. (1928) and its supplements, but the earlier volumes must be used for: (1) books out-of-print by 1928; (2) fuller information, e.g., paging, date, etc., on some titles still in print.

Each volume is a dictionary catalog with entries under author, title, and subject. From Oct. 1982 the work is computer-produced.

The 4th ed. of the *United States catalog* includes publications in the regular book trade; privately printed books; regular importations of American publishers; Canadian books (in English) not also published in the United States; publications of universities, societies, and scientific institutions, e.g., Smithsonian Institution; and a selected list of publications of the national and state governments. For each book, gives: author, short title, edition, publisher, price, and, generally but not always, date, paging, and illustration; gives also Library of Congress card numbers, and, for a book entered in the *Book review digest,* its Dewey Decimal Classification number

and a tracing of the subject headings used for it in the *United States catalog.*

The volumes (1928/32–) have wider scope and include a comprehensive listing of books and pamphlets, in English, issued in the United States and Canada and a selection of publications from other parts of the English-speaking world: Australia, Great Britain, New Zealand, South Africa, etc. Omitted are government documents, maps, sheet music, paperbound editions, and ephemeral material. In proportion to the size of the catalog there are very few inaccuracies, although, as some of the entries have had to be made without examination of the books and are based on publishers' descriptions and lists, the work is not a final authority on bibliographical detail. As a first aid, it is indispensable: (1) in order department work; (2) as an adjunct to the library's own catalog; and (3) as a reference tool for many purposes: verification of titles, authors' names and dates, authorship when only the title or subject of a book is known, lists of books on a given subject, etc. Subject lists of fiction, e.g., ghost stories, sea stories, etc., and the use of the subhead "Fiction" under many subjects make it useful for certain types of questions about fiction.

Each cumulation includes a list of publishers with addresses.

Z1219.M78

Reginald, R. and **Burgess, M. R.** Cumulative paperback index, 1939–1959. Detroit, Gale, [1973]. 362p. **AA578**

Subtitle: A comprehensive bibliographic guide to 14,000 mass-market paperback books of 33 publishers issued under 69 imprints.

Lists paperback publications of the principal American mass-market paperback publishers. Full information is given in the author listing, with index by title. Z1033.P3R4

Current

American book publishing record, 1960– . N.Y., Bowker, 1960– . v.1– . Monthly. **AA579**

At head of title: BPR.

Includes the same information as that given in the weekly lists in *Publishers' weekly* and the successor publication, *Weekly record* (AA598), cumulated monthly and rearranged by subject according to Dewey Decimal numbers. Indexed by author and title. A separate annual index was published for 1962–64 only; since 1965 cumulates into: Z1219.A515

—— BPR annual cumulative, 1965– . N.Y., Bowker, 1966– . Annual. **AA580**

Subtitle: A record of American book production in 1965 [etc.] as cataloged by the Library of Congress and annotated by Publishers' weekly in the monthly issues of the American book publishing record; arranged by subject according to the Dewey Decimal Classification and indexed by author and by title.

Cumulates the monthly listings from *BPR,* including author and title indexes. In turn, cumulates quinquennially as: Z1201.A52

—— BPR cumulative, 1960/64– . N.Y., Bowker, [1968–]. Quinquennial. **AA581**

The early cumulations (1960/64, 1965/69, 1970/74) are superseded by the 1950/77 cumulative set (AA575). Z1201.A52

Children's books in print, 1969– . N.Y., Bowker, 1969– . Annual. **AA582**

Supersedes *Children's books for schools and libraries* (v.1–3, 1966/67–1968/69) and provides expanded coverage for trade books, both paperbound and hard cover. Author, title, and illustrator sections.

Complemented by: Z1037.A1C482

Subject guide to children's books in print, 1970– . N.Y., Bowker, 1970– . Annual. **AA583**

Books are entered in some 7,000 categories, with numerous *see* and *see also* references.

Cumulative book index. N.Y., Wilson, 1898– . Monthly (except Aug.). **AA584**

Often referred to as *CBI*.

Subtitle, 1930– : A world list of books in the English language.

Compiled on the same principles as the cumulated supplements listed in AA577, including, in dictionary catalog form, a record of books published not only in the United States but also in the English language in other parts of the world.

For further information regarding cumulations, etc., *see* AA577.

Z1219.M78●

El-Hi textbooks in print, 1970– . N.Y., Bowker, 1970– . Annual.   **AA585**

Issued 1872–1926 as a number in *Publishers' weekly* under various titles; 1927–55, as the *American educational catalog;* 1956–69, as *Textbooks in print.*

Now a computer-produced bibliography with subject, title, author, and series sections. The 1982 volume is a list of 39,000 elementary, junior and senior high school textbooks and pedagogical books from about 453 publishers.   Z5813.A51

Large type books in print, 1982. [5th ed.] N.Y., Bowker, [1982]. 1023p.   **AA586**

1st ed. (1970) by R. A. Landau and J. S. Nyren; now prep. by R. R. Bowker Company's Data Services Dept.

This edition (produced in 18 point type) lists some 5,000 titles from 50 publishers available in 14 point type or larger. Full publication information (including type size) is given in the subject part which is in two main sections: (1) General reading, and (2) Textbooks, each subdivided topically. There are author and title indexes. A new edition appeared in 1985.   Z5348.L37

Paperbound books in print. N.Y., Bowker, 1955– . Semiannual.   **AA587**

Frequency varies; originally monthly. Now issued in two three-volume sets published in Spring and Fall: v.1, Titles; v.2, Authors; v.3, Subjects and publishers.

Each issue now lists an average of about 200,000 titles of currently available paperbacks.   Z1033.P3P32

Publishers' catalogs annual, 1979– . Westport, Conn., Meckler Publ., 1979– . Annual. Microfiche.   **AA588**

In view of the large number of publishers not represented in *PTLA* (AA589) in recent years, this is an attempt to complete the record by providing microform reproduction of all available catalogs from United States and Canadian publishers. While there is a good deal of overlap between this series and *PTLA,* each includes some catalogs not found in the other. A printed index of publishers accompanies the fiches, giving the address of each publisher and number of the fiche on which the catalog is found; a classified listing of publishers is also included in the accompanying pamphlet.

Publishers' trade list annual, 1873– . N.Y., Bowker, 1873– . Annual.   **AA589**

A collection of publishers' catalogs, arranged alphabetically by publishers' names, and bound up in one, two, three or more large volumes per year. As the catalogs are not compiled on any uniform system, the amount of information given about books varies greatly, ranging from full information and occasional notes in some lists to only short title and price in others; in general, dates of publication are omitted. Lists only books in print. An alphabetical list of the publishers included is given in the first volume. In recent years an increasing number of important publishers have declined, for economic reasons, to have their catalogs included in *PTLA.* This unfortunate trend lessens both the comprehensiveness of *PTLA* and the effectiveness of its companion publication, *Books in print,* as a searching tool.

Except for brief indexes in 1902–1904, no indexes were issued until 1948 when *Books in print* (below) began publication, followed in 1957 by the *Subject guide to Books in print* (AA591).

The volumes for 1903–63 have been published in microform by Meckler Pub., Westport, Conn. (1980; 4100 fiches) with an index compiled by Anthony Abbott which indicates the fiche number (and position on the fiche) of the catalog of a given publisher for a given year.   Z1215.P972

Books in print: an author-title-series index to the Publishers' trade list annual, 1948– . N.Y., Bowker, 1948– . Annual.

AA590

Since 1972 publ. without subtitle.

Each annual includes an author index and a title index (since 1966 authors and titles appear in separate volumes), in each case giving publisher and price. Fuller information may then be found by referring to the pertinent publisher's catalog in the *Publishers' trade list annual.*

A very valuable addition for both acquisitions and reference work in a library. Useful for finding the publisher and price of a book; for finding the author's name if only the title is known; and as an index to the vast amount of material in the *Publishers' trade list annual.*

Beginning 1973 the first of a series of annual mid-year supplements was issued as *Books in print supplement 1972–73,* listing authors, titles, and subjects in separate sections. Issued about six months after the yearly *Books in print* volume, it lists new titles and provides updated information as available.

Now produced from the Bowker Company's BIPS database, a bibliographic file begun in 1948 mainly as a list of titles included in *PTLA.* The database was computerized in the late 1960s and in the following decade was expanded to include information from additional publishers not included in *PTLA;* at present the database is "composed of and compiled from information received on an ongoing basis directly from publishers."—*1982/83.* Inasmuch as there is no evident attempt to reconcile variant forms of an author's name, considerable care must be exercised in searching the author listings.

Beginning Apr. 1982, available in microfiche. The microfiche service provides a fully updated edition of *BIP* four times a year, each quarterly edition including all forthcoming titles six months prior to publication.

Books in print is complemented by: Z1215.P972●

Subject guide to Books in print . . ., 1957– . N.Y., Bowker, 1957– . Annual.   **AA591**

A companion publication to *Books in print,* listing under subject the books to be found there. Conforms to the subject headings and cross references set up by the Library of Congress. Works to which the Library of Congress does not assign subject headings (e.g., fiction, poetry, drama, and Bibles) are not indexed.

A review by ALA's Reference and Subscription Books Review Committee appears in *Booklist* 79: 1294–96 (June 1, 1983).

Z1215.P973

Forthcoming books, now including new books in print; a forecast of books to come . . ., 1966– . N.Y., Bowker, 1966– . v.1– . Bimonthly.   **AA592**

Supersedes the *Publishers' weekly interim index.*

Beginning with v.2, no.6, each issue provides a cumulated list of all books published in the United States since the compilation of the current issue of *Books in print* (AA590) and continues to offer information on titles announced for publication in the next five months. Each issue overlaps and updates the preceding one. Separate author and title sections; publisher, price, and publication date are indicated.   ●

Complemented by:

Subject guide to forthcoming books, 1967– . N.Y., Bowker, 1967– . v.1– . Bimonthly.   **AA593**

A companion to *Forthcoming books* (above), listing the same titles that appear therein according to some 200 subject areas.   ●

Books out-of-print; 1980/83– . N.Y., Bowker, [1983]– . Annual.   **AA594**

Subtitle: Titles which publishers have reported out-of-print or out-of-stock indefinitely in the years [1980/1983]– .

Contents: v.1, Titles; v.2, Authors; publishers.

A reference and book acquisitions tool intended to reduce the expense and time wasted on orders which are unfilled because items have gone out of print or are indefinitely out of stock at the publishers. Publishers were asked to verify the status of "o.p." and "o.s.i." items previously reported to the editors of *Books in print* since 1980, and this compilation is based on those reports. It is important to note that some 35 publishers elected not to participate; their names are listed in the preface.

Publishers' weekly, the book industry journal, 1872– . N.Y., Bowker, 1872– . v.1– . Weekly.   **AA595**

Subtitle varies; publisher varies.

The standard American book-trade journal, containing lists of new publications, lists of books announced for publication, news notes, editorials and articles, advertisements of books wanted, etc. The principal bibliographical list was the weekly list of new publications, for which the amount of information, promptness of listing, and indexing have differed through the years. Beginning Sept. 1974, the *Weekly record* (AA598) is issued as a separate publication and is not bound with *Publishers' weekly.*

Special numbers issued during the year vary but usually include: Spring announcement number in Jan.; Summer announcement number in April; Fall children's book number in July; Fall announcement number in Aug. Z1219.P98

U.S. Copyright Office. Catalog of copyright entries, 1891–1946. Wash., Govt. Prt. Off., 1891–1947. **AA596**

Title varies. Before 1906 issued by the Treasury Dept.; 1906–46, issued by the Copyright Office as *New series.*

Contents: Arrangement differs slightly. Pt.1, *Books,* 1909–27 issued in two groups; 1928–46 in three groups as follows: group 1, v.25–43, *Books* proper (frequency varies; annual index); group 2, v.25–43, *Pamphlets,* etc., including lectures, sermons, maps, etc. (monthly, with annual index); group 3, v.1–19, *Dramatic compositions, motion pictures* (before 1920, motion pictures were included in pt.4; monthly, with annual index). Pt.2, v.1–41, *Periodicals and newspapers,* (quarterly, with annual index). Pt.3, v.1–41, *Musical compositions,* (monthly, with annual index; for full information *see* BH87). Pt.4, v.1–41, *Works of art,* photographs, etc. (quarterly, with annual index).

For 1946 each part was issued as an annual. Z1219.U58C

—— —— Ser.3. Wash., Govt. Prt. Off., 1947–77.

With the third series the arrangement and the format have been changed to make the contents of the set more easily available. The *Catalog* is now subdivided into separate parts following the classification as given in the Copyright Act: pt.1, *Books and pamphlets,* including serials and contributions to periodicals (1947–Jan./June 1953, issued in two sections, pt.1A and pt.1B, which were combined to form the new pt.1 with v.7, no.2, July/Dec. 1953); pt.2, *Periodicals;* pt.3–4, *Dramas and works prepared for oral delivery;* pt.5, *Music* (1947–56, issued in two sections: pt.5A, Published music, and pt.5B, Unpublished music. From 1957, these are combined into pt.5 [*see* BH88]); pt.6, *Maps and atlases;* pt.7–11A, *Works of art,* reproductions, scientific and technical drawings, photographic works, prints, and pictorial illustrations; pt.11B, *Commercial prints and labels;* pts.12–13, *Motion pictures and filmstrips;* pt.14A, *Renewal registrations:* literature, art, film; pt.14B, *Renewal registrations:* music.

Each part was published semiannually and lists the works copyrighted during the period. The *Books* section includes books published in the United States, and, when copyrighted in this country, books in foreign languages published outside the United States, and books in the English language first published abroad.

All types of books are included: literature, fiction, non-fiction, business reports and yearbooks, trade catalogs and directories, manuals, instruction books, research studies in many fields, etc. Z1219.U58C

—— —— 4th ser. Wash., Govt. Prt. Off., 1978– .

Contents: Pt.1, Nondramatic literary works excluding serials and periodicals (quarterly); pt.2, Serials and periodicals (semiannual); pt.3, Performing arts (quarterly); pt.4, Motion pictures and filmstrips (semiannual); pt.5, Visual arts (semiannual); pt.6, Maps (semiannual); pt.7, Sound recordings (semiannual); pt.8, Renewals (semiannual).

This new series coincides with the implementation of the Copyright Act of 1976. Works are entered under title, with an index of authors, claimants, and other names associated with the work in each part; entries include bibliographic description plus information relating to the copyright claim. Entries for published and unpublished materials are interfiled. Although one or two copies must be deposited for registration of copyright, not all works deposited are selected for inclusion in the collections of the Library of Congress.

Issues covering 1978 were the last to be published in paper. The catalog is now published only on microfiche, with some parts available on fiche beginning 1978, other parts beginning 1979. The microfiche is issued in the same eight sections noted above, and each section has been cataloged separately by Library of Congress (e.g., Library of Congress. Copyright Office. *Catalog of copyright entries, fourth series. Part 4, Motion pictures & filmstrips*).

Vertical file index: subject and title index to selected pamphlet material, 1932/34– . N.Y., Wilson, 1935– . Monthly (except Aug.), with annual cumulations. **AA597**

Title varies: v.1–23, 1935–54, *Vertical file service catalog.*

A list of free and inexpensive pamphlets, booklets, leaflets, and similar material considered to be of interest to general libraries. Subjects range from those suitable for school libraries to specialized technical reports. Arranged alphabetically by subject headings (deemed suitable for vertical file use) with title index.

Z1231.P2V48

Weekly record. v.1, no.1– , Sept. 2, 1974– . N.Y., Bowker, 1974– . Weekly. **AA598**

Formerly issued as a section of *Publishers' weekly.*

A main-entry listing based mainly on Library of Congress cataloging and giving full title, imprint, collation, price, Library of Congress and Dewey Decimal classification numbers, subject headings and other tracings. Lists current American books and foreign books distributed in the United States; does not include federal and other government publications, subscription books, dissertations, new printings (as distinct from reprints), pamphlets, ephemera, and most elementary and high school textbooks. Listings for mass market paperbacks, annuals, yearbooks and reprints reflect only those sent to the editorial offices.

Serves as the basis for the *American book publishing record* (AA579). An effort is made to supply any missing prices and to complete the information in C.I.P. entries prior to publication of the *ABPR.* Z1219.W4

Regional

❖The various general publications listed above (AA579–AA598) are reasonably comprehensive for works issued at the main publishing centers, but are less complete for material printed by local presses, especially before 1875. For local publications, regional bibliographies must often be consulted. A good list of such works is given in Stillwell, *Incunabula and Americana,* p.382–408, 423–27 (AA268), and a wide range of bibliographies relating to regional, state, and local publishing may be found through the index to Tanselle's *Guide to the study of United States imprints* (AA554).

A somewhat dated, but still useful list is:

McMurtrie, Douglas Crawford. Locating the printed source materials for United States history; with a bibliography of lists of regional imprints. (*In* Mississippi Valley historical review 31:369–406, Dec. 1944) **AA599**

Lists of regional imprints, arranged alphabetically by state, p.379–403; American imprints checklist, p.403–406.

U.S. Work Projects Administration. Bibliography of research projects reports; check-list of Historical Records Survey publications. Rev. April 1943. Wash., Federal Works Agency, W.P.A., 1943. 110p. (W.P.A. Technical ser. Research and records bibliography, 7) **AA600**

A final record of publications superseding all earlier listings. Lists inventories of federal archives in the states; inventories of county archives; inventories of municipal and town archives; transcriptions of public archives; vital statistics; church archives publications; manuscript publications; American imprints inventory; American portrait inventory; guides to civilian organizations; miscellaneous publications; microfilm records; depositories of unpublished material, etc.

Because of this record, the volumes published in these various series are not listed here, with the exception of the American imprints inventory listed below. Z1223.W85 no.7

Historical Records Survey. American imprints inventory, prep. by the Historical Records Survey, Division of Women's and Professional Projects, Works Progress Administration. Wash., Historical Records Survey, 1937–42. no.1–20, 23–26, 31–32, 36, 38–42, 44–45, 52, and unnumbered issue. **AA601**

no.21–22, 27–30, 33–35, 37, 43, 46–51 had not been published when the work of the *American imprints inventory* ceased.

Contents: no.1, A preliminary check list of *Missouri* imprints, 1808–1850. 1937. 225p.; no.2, M. R. Martin, Check list of *Minnesota* imprints, 1849–1865. 1938. 219p.; no.3, A check list of *Arizona* imprints, 1860–1890. 1938. 81p.; no.4, Check list of *Chicago* ante-fire imprints, 1851–1871. 1938. 727p.; no.5, D. C. McMurtrie, Check list of *Kentucky* imprints, 1787–1810. 1939. 205p.; no.6, D. C. McMurtrie and A. H. Allen, Check list of *Kentucky* imprints, 1811–1820, with notes in supplement to the Check list of 1787–1810 imprints. 1939. 235p.; no.7, A check list of *Nevada* imprints, 1859–1890. 1939. 127p.; no.8, Check list of *Alabama* imprints, 1807–1840. 1939. 159p.; no.9, Lucile M. Morsch, Check list of *New Jersey* imprints, 1784–1800. 1939. 189p.; no.10, Check list of *Kansas* imprints, 1854–1876. 1939. 773p.; no.11, Chicago Historical Society Library, A check list of the Kellogg collection of "patent inside" newspapers of 1876. 1939. 99p.; no.12, D. C. McMurtrie, A check list of the imprints of *Sag Harbor, L.I.,* 1791–1820. 1939. 61p.; no.13, A check list of *Idaho* imprints, 1839–1890. 1940. 74p.; no.14, A check list of *West Virginia* imprints, 1791–1830. 1940. 62p.;

no.15, A check list of *Iowa* imprints, 1838–1860, in supplement to those recorded by Alexander Moffit in the *Iowa journal of history and politics* for Jan. 1938. 1940. 84 (i.e., 85)p.; no.16, List of *Tennessee* imprints, 1793–1840, in Tennessee libraries. 1941. 97p.; no.17, A check list of *Ohio* imprints, 1796–1820. 1941. 202p.; no.18, A check list of *Wyoming* imprints, 1866–1890. 1941. 69 (i.e., 70)p.; no.19, Lucy B. Foote, Bibliography of the official publications of *Louisiana,* 1803–1934. 1942. 579p.; no.20, Check list of *Tennessee* imprints, 1841–1850. 1941. 138p.; no.23–24, 41–42, A check list of *Wisconsin* imprints, 1833–1849, 1850–1854, 1855–1858, 1859–1863. 1942. 4v.; no.25, Check list of *New Mexico* imprints and publications, 1784–1876: imprints, 1834–1876; publications, 1784–1876. 1942. 115p.; no.26, A check list of *Nebraska* non-documentary imprints, 1847–1876. 1942. 132p.;

no.31, A check list of *California* non-documentary imprints, 1833–1855. 1942. 109p.; no. 32, A check list of *Tennessee* imprints, 1793–1840. 1942. 285p.; no.36, A check list of *Utica, N.Y.,* imprints, 1799–1830. 1942. 179p.; no.38 (misnumbered 25), Supplemental check list of *Kentucky* imprints, 1788–1820, including the original printing of the original Kentucky copyright ledger, 1800–1854, and the first account of the run of Baptist minutes in the collection of Mr. Henry S. Robinson, ed. by John Wilson Townsend. 1942. 241p.; no.39, A check list of *Arkansas* imprints, 1821–1876. 1942. 139p.; no.40 and 45, A check list of *Massachusetts* imprints, 1801–1802. 1942. 2v.; no.41–42, *see* no.23–24; no.44, A check list of *Washington* imprints, 1853–1876. 1942. 89p.; no.45, *see* no.40; no.52, Preliminary check list of *Michigan* imprints, 1796–1850. 1942. 224p.; [unnumbered issue] A guide to *Wisconsin* newspapers, Iowa County, 1837–1940. 1942. 142p. Z1215.H67

Africa

The African book publishing record, v.1, no. 1– , Jan. 1975– . [Oxford, Eng., Hans Zell Ltd.], 1975– . v.1– . Quarterly. **AA602**

Now offers subject, author, and country lists of English, French, or African vernacular language books recently published or in press on the African continent. Each issue includes articles on and news of the book trade in Africa, reviews of new magazines or special issues of journals. Beginning with the Apr. 1977 issue, reviews of major publications are included. A directory of publishers is a useful feature. Annual table of contents for the volume, but no index. Z465.7.A35

African books in print; an index by author, title and subject. Ed.1– . London, Mansell, [1975]– . Irregular. **AA603**

Hans M. Zell, ed.

Aims "to provide a systematic, reliable and functional reference tool and buying guide to African published materials currently in print."—*Introd.* Compiled from information supplied by publishers.

The 1st ed. consisted only of pt.1, "English language and African languages," and plans called for a second volume covering publications in French; the two parts were thereafter to be issued in alternate years. That plan was abandoned with the 2d ed. (published 1978), which was issued in two volumes (v.1, Author index; v.2, Subject index, Title index) and carries the title also in French: *Livres africains disponibles.* A 3d ed. was published 1984.

The quarterly journal *African book publishing record* (above) provides an ongoing supplementary and updating service. Z3501.A46

Albania

Legrand, Émile. Bibliographie albanaise; description raisonnée des ouvrages pub. en albanais ou relatifs à l'Albanie du 15. siècle à l'année 1900. Oeuvre posthume, compl. et pub. par Henri Gûys. Paris, Welter, 1912. 228p. **AA604**

Lists books in Albanian and other languages, published in or relating to Albania, 1474–1900. Chronological with author and subject indexes.

Continued by: Z2854.A5L3

Kastrati, Jup. Bibliografi shqipe, 29.XI.1944–31.XII.1958. Tiranë, N. Sh. Botimeve "Naim Frashëri," 1959. 498p. **AA605**

A classified listing of Albanian publications of the period; author index.

Bibliografia kombëtare e Republikës Popullore të Shqipërisë: libri shqip. Bibliographie nationale de la R.P.A.: les livres albanais. Tiranë, Botim i Bibliotekës Kombëtare, 1958– . Quarterly. **AA606**

Title varies slightly.

1959 not published? 1960– called v.1– .

The current national bibliography, listing books, pamphlets, and official publications. Classed listing with author index. Z2854.A5B53

Algeria

Bibliographie de l'Algérie. Année 1, no.1– , Oct. 1963– . Alger, Bibliothèque Nationale, 1964– . Irregular. **AA607**

Title also in Arabic.

The first issue is a classified bibliography of Algerian periodicals published in either French or Arabic. Later numbers offer a classed list of books and theses received on legal deposit at the national library.

Arab nations

The Arab bulletin of publications, 1982– . Prep. in collaboration with Tunisian National Library. Tunis, 1984– . Annual? **AA608**

At head of title: Arab League Educational Cultural and Scientific Organization (ALECSO).

Title page and introductory matter also in Arabic.

An attempt to provide a bibliographic record of all books published in Arabic countries. Separate sections for Arabic and non-Arabic publications; arranged by Dewey Decimal Classification within sections; author and title indexes. The volume for 1982 includes reports from Jordan–United Arab Emirates, Bahrein, Tunisia, Algeria, Syria, Saudi Arabia, Iraq, Oman, Qatar, Kuwait, Libya, Morocco and Lebanon.

Argentina

Anuario bibliográfico de la República Argentina. año [1]–9, 1879–87. Buenos Aires, 1880–88. 9v.　　　**AA609**

Ed. by Alberto Navarro Viola.

A selected, critical annual list, classified by subject; author index.
Z1611.A63

Boletín bibliográfico nacional . . . 1937–1954/56. Publicación oficial. Buenos Aires, 1937–63. no.1–33.　　　**AA610**

Title varies: 1937–49, *Boletín bibliográfico argentino.*
Publisher varies.

An annual (irregular) publication listing books in the original and in translation, translations of foreign books published in Argentina, and foreign books that deal with Argentina. Classified arrangement with author index.　　　Z1615.B69

Gutiérrez, Juan María. Bibliografía de la primera imprenta de Buenos Aires desde su fundación hasta el año 1810 inclusive. . . . Buenos Aires, Impr. de Mayo, 1866. 43p., 34p., 246p.　　　**AA611**

Pt.1, Celebridades argentinas del siglo XVIII; pt.2, Orijenes del arte de imprimir en la America Española; pt.3, Bibliografía de la primera imprenta de Buenos Aires [215 imprints].
Pts.2–3, repr. from *Revista de Buenos Aires,* June 1865–Aug.1866.
Z213.B92G9

Universidad de Buenos Aires. Bibliografía argentina: católogo de materiales argentinos en las bibliotecas de la Universidad de Buenos Aires. Boston, G. K. Hall, 1980. 7v.
AA612

Added title page in English: Argentine bibliography: a union catalogue of Argentinian holdings in the libraries of the University of Buenos Aires.

Photographic reproduction of the cards from the union catalog of Argentinian printed books maintained by the Instituto Bibliotecológico for the 17 central and 56 departmental libraries of the University of Buenos Aires. The purpose of the catalog is to create a national bibliography and it therefore contains author cards for Argentinian books and pamphlets published up to 1979, as well as for works by Argentine authors published abroad.　　　Z1611.U54

Current

Bibliografía argentina de artes y letras. Buenos Aires, Fondo Nacional de las Artes, 1959–72. no.1–49/50. Quarterly (irregular).　　　**AA613**

A selective, classified bibliography, including periodical articles as well as books. Author index in each issue with annual cumulated indexes of names and anonymous titles. Many issues include special bibliographic studies.　　　Z1611.B5

Libros argentinos ISBN. 1982– . [Buenos Aires], Camara Argentina del Libro, [1984]– . Irregular?　　　**AA614**

An in-print list for Argentinian publications arranged by Universal Decimal Classification, with name and subject indexes.

Australia

Canberra, Australia. National Library. Annual catalogue of Australian publications, no.1–25. 1936–60. Canberra, 1937–61.　　　**AA615**

Generally includes books published in Australia, with supplements to previous issues; books of Australian interest published overseas; official publications of the Commonwealth and territories (although these are omitted for 1936 and 1941–44); selected list of

Australian periodicals, annuals, and serial publications; and a directory of Australian publishers.

Superseded by *Australian national bibliography* (AA618).
Z4011.C22

Ferguson, John Alexander. Bibliography of Australia, 1784–1900. Sydney, Angus & Robertson, 1941–69. 7v.　　**AA616**

For complete information *see* DF6.

Foxcroft, Albert Broadbent. Australian catalogue; a reference index to the books and periodicals published and still current in the Commonwealth of Australia. . . . Melbourne, Whitecombe and Tombs, 1911. 118p., 72p.　　　**AA617**

An author and catchword title index to books in print at time of compilation. Includes a list of public documents on sale as of Jan. 1911.　　　Z4011.F69

Current

Australian national bibliography, Jan. 1961– . Canberra, National Library of Australia, 1961– . Semimonthly, with monthly and annual cumulations.　　　**AA618**

Supersedes the *Annual catalogue of Australian publications* (AA615), its monthly supplement *Books published in Australia . . . ,* and the *Monthly list of Australian government publications.*

Frequency and arrangement have varied. Now issued twice monthly (in paper) as a classified list with an author and title index. The second issue of each month is published as a cumulation, with a subject index. Further cumulations are published on microfiche covering Jan.–Apr., Jan.–Aug., and Jan.–Dec.; the annual cumulation is available on microfiche and in paper.

Lists books and pamphlets published in Australia and those published overseas dealing with Australia. Includes government publications, and the first issue of new periodicals, newspapers, etc. Originally a monthly arranged alphabetically by main entry, with comprehensive bibliographic data for each item, prices, Dewey Decimal numbers, and a subject and title index.　　　Z4015.A96

Australian books in print. Melbourne, D. W. Thorpe, 1956– . [Ed.1–] Irregular, then annual.　　　**AA619**

Eds.1–5 called *Australian books in print;* 6th ed. called *Bookseller's reference book;* 7th ed. called *Bookbuyer's reference book.*

In addition to an author-title listing of books in print and a directory of publishers, recent issues include information on library and book trade associations, literary societies, literary awards and prizes.　　　Z4011.A85

Austria

See also Germany, p.71–74.

Langer, Eduard. Bibliographie der österreichischen Drucke des XV. und XVI. Jahrhunderts. Bd.1, Hft.1, Trient-Wien-Schrattenthal, bearb. von Walther Dolch. Wien, Gilhofer & Ranschburg, 1913. 171p.　　　**AA620**

No more published.　　　Z133.L27

Current

Oesterreichische Bibliographie; Verzeichnis der österreichischen Neuerscheinungen. Bearb. von der Österreichischen Nationalbibliothek. 1945– . Wien, 1946– . v.1– .　　　**AA621**

Frequency varies: 1945, annual; 1946, quarterly; 1947–48, monthly; 1949– , semimonthly, with quarterly indexes and annual cumulated indexes.

A listing of trade publications which also includes university and official publications, newspapers, periodicals, and music scores (for

1961–71, included in an annual *Sonderheft* entitled "Praktische Musik"). Classified, with author and subject index.

——— Register 1946–50. Wien, 1951–52. 348p.

——— Verfasser- und Stichwortregister. *See* AA787.

Z2105.O33

Bangladesh

Bangladesh national bibliography, 1972– . Dacca, Directorate of Archives and Libraries, Ministry of Education, 1974– . Annual. **AA622**

"A subject catalogue of new books published in Bangladesh and received under the provision of Copyright Ordinance, 1962; classified with modification according to the Dewey Decimal Classification (16th edition), provided with a full author, title and subject index and a list of Bangladesh publishers whose books have been included in the Bibliography."—*1972 ed., p. 109.*

Title also in Bengali.

In two parts: (1) Bengali; (2) English. Publication runs well behind date of coverage.

Barbados

The national bibliography of Barbados. Jan./Mar. 1975– . Bridgetown, Barbados, Public Library, 1975– . Quarterly, the 4th issue being an annual cumulation. **AA623**

Intends "to list all new works published in Barbados; as well as those works of Barbadians authorship published abroad."—*Pref.* Classed arrangement according to Dewey Decimal Classification, with author/title/series index.

Belgium

Bibliographie nationale. Dictionnaire des écrivains belges et catalogue de leurs publications, 1830–80. Bruxelles, Weissenbruch, 1886–1910. 4v. **AA624**

Aims to furnish a comprehensive record, for the period 1830–80, of works by Belgian authors (either citizens or residents of the country), published either in Belgium or abroad, with record also of earlier works by the same authors and of periodicals with which they were associated as either editors or regular contributors. Includes books, pamphlets, official publications, many reprints from periodicals and newspapers, name (frequently with brief biographical data), title, place, publisher, date, size, paging, illustrations, price. Contents and other notes are frequently included, especially notes of reprints from periodicals. Z2401.B586

Bibliotheca belgica. Bibliographie générale des Pays-Bas, fondée par Ferdinand van der Haeghen. Re-éditée sous la direction de Marie-Thérèse Lenger. Bruxelles, Culture et Civilisation, 1964–75. 7v. **AA625**

Contents: v.1–5, A–Z; v.6, Supplément; v.7, Index général.

Originally published in irregular order in 240 *livraisons,* 1880–1967, now reassembled and published in quarto volumes in alphabetical sequence.

Includes works of the 15th and 16th centuries (with some inclusion of important later works) printed in Belgium and Holland, and books by Belgian and Dutch authors printed elsewhere, giving for each work listed: full title, imprint and collation, location of copies, and often full bibliographical and historical notes with biographical notes about authors and references to sources. The new edition makes this valuable collection of material easily available for the first time, through the rearrangement and the addition of indexes of authors, editors, and printers in v.6, and a detailed general index in v.7. Z2401.B6

Cockx-Indestege, Elly and **Glorieux, Geneviève.** Belgica typographica, 1541–1600; catalogus librorum impressorum ab anno MDXLI ad annum MDC in regionibus quae nunc regni Belgarum partes sunt. Nieuwkoop, B. de Graaf, 1968–80. v.1–2. (Nationaal Centrum voor de Archeologie en de Geschiedenis van het Boek, II) (In progress) **AA626**

A series designed to record all works published in Belgium to 1600. v.1 deals with the collections of the Bibliothèque Royale de Belgique; v.2 describes works of the period in 40 libraries throughout Belgium. Other Belgian and selected foreign libraries are to be surveyed for future volumes. The work is part of a larger project to establish a catalog of all pre-1601 imprints from the Low Countries. Z2402.C6

Coopman, Theophiel and **Broeckaert, Jan.** Bibliographie van den Vlaamschen taalstrijd. Gent, Siffer, 1904–14. 10v. (K. Vlaamsche Academie voor Taal- en Letterkunde) **AA627**

v.1–10, 1787–1886.

A bibliography of Flemish-language materials. Z2424.F5C7

Foppens, Jean François. Bibliotheca belgica, sive Virorum in Belgio vitâ, scriptisque illustrium catalogus, librorumque nomenclatura; continens scriptores à clariss. viris Valerio Andrea, Auberto Miraeo, Francisco Sweetio, aliisque, recensitos, usque ad annum MDCLXXX. Bruxellis, P. Foppens, 1738. 2v. **AA628**

Includes writers of the various Low Countries, arranged alphabetically by Latin form of the name, giving brief biographical notices and lists of their writings. Covers from earliest printing to 1680. Indexes by place and by religious order. Z2410.F69

Vlaamsche bibliographie. Lijst der boeken, vlug- en tijdschriften, muziekwerken, kaarten, platen en tabellen, in België van 1830 tot 1890 verschenen. Uitg. op last der Koninklijke Vlaamsche Academie voor Taal- en Letterkunde, door Fr. de Potter. Gent, Siffer, 1893-[1902]. 894p. **AA629**

Lists the Flemish books published in Belgium. Classified, with author index. Incorporates material included in the various editions of the *Vlaamsche bibliographie,* by F. A. Snellaert (1851–88). Z2424.F5V7

Current

Bibliographie de Belgique; liste mensuelle des publications belges ou relatives à la Belgique, acquises par la Bibliothèque Royale, année 1– , 1875– . Bruxelles, Bibliothèque Royale, 1875– . Monthly. **AA630**

Title (*Belgische bibliografie*) and headings also in Dutch.

This bibliography has undergone many changes in title, scope, plan, editor, and publisher. For the history of these, and for a collation by volumes of the set to 1931, *see* "Histoire des transformations de la Bibliographie de Belgique" by Fernand Remy, in *Bibliographie de Belgique* 57:356–98 (1931). As at present organized, aims to cover books, pamphlets, etc., issued in Belgium; books by Belgian authors published abroad; and books by foreigners relating to Belgium. For 1959–74 these latter were listed in a *Fascicule spécial,* "Liste annuelle des publications d'auteurs belges à l'étranger et des publications étrangères relatives à la Belgique . . ." with separate indexes. Periodicals were included in a separate part through 1926. Beginning with v.108 (1982) the bibliography appears in 12 monthly issues with indexes, all parts cumulating annually, plus three supplements: A, Publications in series (also included in the monthly issues); B, Maps and atlases; C, Music. In 1984 a semimonthly section entitled "Publications annoncées" was added; it provides CIP information on forthcoming publications some three or four months prior to their appearance; after publication, the full bibliographic information is published in the regular issue of the *Bibliographie.*

A classified list with author, title, and subject indexes. Information given for each entry is in full catalog form and includes author's name, full title, place, publisher, date, size, illustrations, and usually price. Z2405.B58

Bénin

Bibliographie du Bénin. Année 1, no.1– , 1976/77– . Porto-Novo, Bibliothèque Nationale, 1978– . Irregular.   **AA631**

At head of title: République Populaire du Bénin. Ministère de la Jeunesse, de la Culture Populaire et des Sports. Direction de la Bibliothèque Nationale.

A classed bibliography of works published in Bénin, together with works about the country published abroad. In four sections: (1) Books; (2) Articles from periodicals; (3) Official publications; (4) Other documents (e.g., maps). Indexed.   Z3686.B52

Bermuda

Bermuda national bibliography. 1983– . [Hamilton], Bermuda Lib., Tech. Serv., [1984]– . Quarterly, with annual cumulation.   **AA632**

The 1983 volume was issued as an annual only; subsequent issues are to appear quarterly.

A classed listing (by Dewey Decimal Classification) with an author/title/series index. Includes "works about Bermuda and Bermudians, published both locally and abroad, works published in Bermuda on other subjects, and works published abroad by Bermudians." There is a separate listing of periodical publications; also lists published and unpublished government reports.

Bolivia

Abecía, Valentín. Adiciones á la Biblioteca boliviana de Gabriel René-Moreno, con un apéndice del editor, 1602–1879. Santiago de Chile, Impr. Barcelona, 1899. 440p.   **AA633**

571 entries, of which no.1–350 are the work of Abecía, and the remainder form part of the appendix by the editor, Enrique Barrenechea. Supplements AA636.   Z1641.B58A

Costa de la Torre, Arturo. Catálogo de la bibliografía boliviana; libros y folletos, 1900–1963. La Paz, [Editorial Universidad Mayor de San Andrés], 1966 [i.e., 1968]–73. v.1–2. (In progress)   **AA634**

Contents: v.1, Prolegomenos [etc.]; pt.1, Escritores bolivianos: libros y folletos, 1908–1963. 1255p; v.2, Adiciones al "Segundo suplemento de la Bibliografía boliviana" de Gabriel René Moreno—1900–1908; Folletos anónimos en general—1908–1963. 1069p.

Continues chronologically René-Moreno's *Biblioteca boliviana* and its supplements (AA636). Additions to the second supplement, 1900–1908, appear in v.2 of the present work—hence the beginning date as indicated in the title. v.1 provides an alphabetical listing of more than 3,000 Bolivian authors with some 8,700 bibliographical entries. An extensive introductory section (p.1–237) provides a comprehensive survey of Bolivian bibliography.

A third volume was to provide a bibliography of foreign authors, 1909–63.   Z1641.C66

Gutiérrez, José Rosendo. Datos para la bibliografía boliviana. 1. sección. La Paz, Arzadum, 1875. 255p.   **AA635**

Lists 2,203 items.

————— ————— 2. suplemento; últimas adiciones y correcciones á la primera sección. La Paz, Impr. de la Union Americana, 1880. 24p., 126p.

Items 2204–3089.
No more published.   Z1641.G9

René-Moreno, Gabriel. Biblioteca boliviana; catálogo de la sección de libros i folletos. Santiago de Chile, Impr. Gutenberg, 1879. 880p. (Readex Microprint)   **AA636**

Arranged alphabetically by title with index of authors, translators,

etc. Full bibliographical information, with annotations; 3,529 entries.

————— ————— 1. suplemento . . . Epítome de un Catálogo de libros y folletos, 1879–99. Santiago de Chile, Impr. Barcelona, 1900. 349p.

Items 3,530–5,176.

————— ————— 2. suplemento, 1900–1908. Santiago de Chile, Impr. Univ., 1908. 349p.

Items 5,177–6,815.
The most important Bolivian bibliography of the period.
  Z1641.B58

Current

Bibliografía boliviana, 1962–74. Cochabamba, Los Amigos del Libro, 1963–75. Annual.   **AA637**

Werner Guttentag Tichauer, ed.

An alphabetical listing of books and pamphlets published in Bolivia, with title and subject indexes and a list of publishers.
Superseded by: Z1641.B5

Bio-bibliografía boliviana, 1975– . La Paz, Los Amigos del Libro, 1976– . Annual.   **AA638**

Werner Guttentag Tichauer, ed.

Supersedes *Bibliografía boliviana* (*above*).

The change of title reflects an increase in the practice of supplying dates and identifying notes for authors whose books are listed. A supplementary list of publications from 1962 to the year preceding the date of coverage appears in each volume.   Z1641.B5

Botswana

National bibliography of Botswana, 1969– . [Gaberones], Botswana Nat. Lib. Service, 1969– . v.1– . 3 nos. per yr.   **AA639**

v.1 had two numbers, the second being cumulative; beginning with v.2, publ. three times a year, the first number covering Jan.–Apr., the second May–Aug., and the third a cumulative issue for the full year.

Listing is by Dewey class numbers, with an alphabetical index of authors, titles, and serials. The list excludes books on Botswana published in other countries, as well as those in the local languages of Botswana published elsewhere. Each issue of a serial appearing less than six times a year is noted, and notices of cessation of serials are included.   Z3559.N38

Brazil

BBB: Boletim bibliográfico brasileiro, Nov./Dez. 1952–Set./Dez. 1967. [Rio de Janeiro, Estante Publicações], 1953–67. Bimonthly (irregular).   **AA640**

Title varies.

Ceased publication.

A classified list, commercially sponsored, claiming to include all Brazilian publications for the period covered and giving full bibliographical information and prices. Does not include serials. Title index in each issue.   Z1671.B6

Bibliografia brasileira, 1938/39–1955, 1963–66. Rio de Janeiro, 1941–67. Irregular.   **AA641**

Publ. by Ministério da Educação e Cultura. Instituto Nacional do Livro (form of name varies).

1938/39 publ. 1941; 1940 publ. 1954; 1941 publ. 1952; 1942/45 publ. 1953 in 2v.; 1946 publ. 1947; 1947/52 publ. 1957; 1953 publ. 1954; 1954 publ. 1956; 1955 publ. 1959; 1956–62 not publ.; 1963/65 publ. 1966; 1966 publ. 1967.

A comprehensive dictionary catalog, arranged by author, title, and subject in one alphabet. Includes trade books only. A list of publishers at the back of each volume.　　　　Z1671.B5

Sacramento Blake, Augusto Victorino Alves do. Diccionario bibliographico brasileiro. Rio de Janeiro, Typ. Nacional, 1883–1902. 7v. (Repr.: Nendeln, Liechtenstein, Kraus, 1969, with *Indice* in v.7)　　　　**AA642**

Arranged alphabetically by *first* names; an author approach by surname is provided by:

———— ———— Indice alphabetico, comp. pelo Jango Fischer. Rio de Janeiro, Impr. Nacional, 1937. 127p.
　　　　Z1681.S12

Current

Rio de Janeiro. Biblioteca Nacional. Boletim bibliográfico. Rio de Janeiro, 1951– . n.s.v.1– . Quarterly.　　**AA643**

Frequency varies.

The new series is much more comprehensive than the old, which began in 1918 and was published irregularly to 1938. Based on legal deposit, it lists Brazilian publications by a simplified decimal classification scheme and includes books, pamphlets, music, official publications, etc. Full bibliographical details are given and, in many cases, prices. Name index including authors and subjects of biographies. The second part of each year includes a classified list of periodicals and a directory of publishers. There has been a considerable time-lag in publication in recent years (e.g., v.16 covering 1966 was distributed in 1971), and 1968–72 will evidently not be published; quarterly issues beginning 1973 are called v.18 and cover current materials.　　　　Z907.R585B

U.S. Library of Congress. Library of Congress Office, Brazil. Accessions list, Brazil. Rio de Janeiro, Lib. of Congress Off., Brazil, 1975– . Bimonthly.　　　　**AA644**

Frequency varies: monthly, Jan. 1975–Oct. 1978.

A main entry listing of commercial, institutional, and government publications published in Brazil and received by the Library of Congress Office. A serials section in each issue has subdivisions for new serials and for additions, changes and deletions. A third section cites special materials (e.g., records, scores, atlases), but does not appear in every issue. An annual author index appears in the last issue of the year.

In 1982 the Office issued a *Cumulative list of serials* covering serials acquisitions of 1975–80. Cumulated supplements are planned.

Supplements the Library's *Catalog of Brazilian acquisitions . . . 1964–1974*, comp. by William V. Jackson (DB307).　　Z1671.U53a

Bulgaria

Pogorelov, Valerij. Opis na starite pechatani Bulgarski knigi (1802–1877g.). Sofija, Narodna Biblioteka, 1923. 795p.
　　　　AA645

A detailed bibliography of publications from the earliest period of Bulgarian printing. Chronological arrangement with author index.

A list of additions compiled by Charles Jelavich from the Library of Congress collections appeared in that Library's *Quarterly journal of current acquisitions* 14:93–94 (1957).　　Z2891.P75

Sofia. Narodna Biblioteka. Bulgarska vuzrozhdenska knizhnina; analitichen repertoar na Bulgarskite knigi i periodichni izdaniia, 1806–1878. Sustavil Man'o Stoianov. Sofia, Nauka i Izkustvo, 1957–59. 2v.　　　　**AA646**

An exhaustive listing of books and periodical articles, with various indexes: chronological, subject, etc. Nearly 30,000 entries.
　　　　Z2898.A4S6

Sofia. Narodna Biblioteka "Kiril i Metodii." Bulgarski knigi, 1878–1944; bibliografski ukazatel. Sofia, Narodna Biblioteka, 1978–83. 6v.　　　　**AA647**

An author listing of Bulgarian imprints.　　Z2891.S64

Teodorov-Balan, Aleksandŭr. Bulgarski knigopis za sto godini, 1806–1905. Sofia, Drzhavna Pechatnitsa, 1909. 1667p.
　　　　AA648

A century of Bulgarian bibliography. More than 15,000 entries; author listing with classified subject index.　　Z2891.T4

Current

Bulgarski knigopis; natsionalna bibliografiia na NR Bulgariia. Sofia, 1897–1973.　　　　**AA649**

Frequency varies: annual, 1897–1944; quarterly, 1945–48; monthly, 1949–68; biweekly, 1969–73.

Title varies; subtitle varies; publisher varies. From 1897 to 1952, issued by the National Library; 1953–63, by the Bulgarian Bibliographical Institute (Bulgarski Bibliografski Institut); 1964–73, by the National Library.

Lists books and new periodicals. Classified arrangement with annual author indexes; beginning 1969 an annual cumulation superseded the biweekly issues. The 1973 annual bears the title of the new series (below).

Continued by:　　　　Z2893.B85

Natsionalna bibliografiia na NR Bulgariia. Sofiia, Narodna Biblioteka "Kiril i Metodii," 1974– .　　　**AA650**

Beginning 1974, the various bibliographic services for Bulgaria are brought together under this general title and issued by the National Library. The following series are included:

Ser.1, *Bulgarski knigopis; knigi, notni, graficheski i kartigrafski izdaniia*. v.78– , 1974– . Bi-weekly with annual cumulation. Subtitle also in English: Books, music, prints, maps. Supersedes, in part, *Bulgarski knigopis* (AA649) and continues its numbering.

Ser.2, *Bulgarski knigopis; sluzhebni izdaniia i disertatsii*. v.78– , 1974– . Monthly with annual index. Subtitle also in English: Official publications and dissertations. Supersedes, in part, *Bulgarski knigopis* (AA649) and continues its volume numbering. The entries for dissertations are also included in:

Bulgarski disertatsii. 1973– （publ. 1974– ）. Annual.

Ser.3, *Bulgarski gramofonni plochi*. 1972– （publ. 1974– ）. Annual.

Ser.4, *Bulgarski periodichen pechat*. 1972– （publ. 1974– ）. Annual. Title also in English: Bulgarian periodicals, newspapers, journals, bulletins and periodical collections. Supersedes a publication of the same title covering 1965–71. Includes all periodical publications listed in the bi-weekly issues of Ser.2 (above) as well as non-official serial publications.

Ser.5, *Letopis na statiite ot bulgarskite spisaniia i sbornitsi*. v.23– . 1974– . Bi-weekly. Title also in English: Articles from Bulgarian journals and collections. Supersedes and continues the volume numbering of a publication of the same title covering 1972–73, which in turn partially superseded *Letopis na periodichnaia pechat* (AE267).

Ser.6, *Letopis na statiite ot bulgarskite vestnitsi*. v.23– , 1974– . Monthly. Title also in English: Articles from Bulgarian newspapers. Supersedes and continues the volume numbering of a publication of the same title covering 1972–73, which in turn partially superseded *Letopis na periodichnaia pechat* (AE267).

Ser.7, *Bulgariia v chuzhdata literatura (Bulgarika)*. 1972– （publ. 1974– ）. Annual. Title also in English: Bulgaria in foreign literature. Continues a publication of the same title covering 1964–71.

Ser.8, *Bibliografiia na bulgarskata bibliografiia*. 1973– （publ. 1974– ）. Annual. Title also in English: Bibliography of Bulgarian bibliographies. Continues a publication of the same title covering 1963–72.

Cameroon

Cameroon imprints. no.1– , Jan./Mar. 1978– . Douala, 1978– . Quarterly.　　　　**AA651**

Subtitle, no.5– : Bulletin du Centre de Diffusion du Livre Camerounais.

Originally an author/anonymous title listing, changing to a classed list with author index when the Cameroon Book Distribution Centre took over the list with no.5 (Jan./Mar. 1979). Annual cumulations for 1978 and 1979 are under consideration.

Canada

Amtmann, Bernard. Contributions to a short-title catalogue of Canadiana. Montreal, 1971–73. 4v.   **AA652**

A main entry listing of books and pamphlets relating to Canada. Auction prices of recent date are indicated.   Z1365.A64

Canada. Public Archives. Catalogue of pamphlets in the Public Archives of Canada, with index, prep. by Magdalen Casey. Ottawa, Acland, 1931–32. 2v. (Publ. of the Public Archives of Canada, no.13)   **AA653**

v.1, 1493–1877; v.2, 1878–1931.

1st ed. 1903; 2d ed., covering period 1611–1867, 1911; 3d ed. 1916. The new edition lists a total of 10,072 items, arranged chronologically, with author and subject indexes in each volume. Includes material published in Canada and pamphlets about Canada published elsewhere.   Z1365.C21

Canadian catalogue of books published in Canada, about Canada, as well as those written by Canadians, with imprint 1921–1949. Consolidated English language reprint edition, with cumulated author index. [Toronto], Toronto Pub. Libraries, 1959. 2v.   **AA654**

v.1, 1921–39; v.2, 1940–49.

Reprints of the English-language sections of the annual lists issued by the Toronto Public Libraries during this period, with a cumulative author index in each of the two volumes.

From 1921 to 1943, included books, pamphlets, and selected government documents; from 1944 to 1949, federal government publications were omitted. Usually each annual number was in two sections: (1) books in English, and (2) books in French. The reprint edition is of the English sections only.

Superseded by *Canadiana* (AA664).   Z1365.C222

Dionne, Narcisse Eutrope. Inventaire chronologique. . . . Québec, 1905–12. 4v. and suppl. (76p.).   **AA655**

Published by the Royal Society of Canada. Also issued in the Society's *Proceedings and transactions,* 2d ser., v.10–12, 14 (1904–1906, 1908), 3d ser., v.5 (1911).

[v.1, pt.1], Inventaire chronologique des livres, brochures, journaux et revues publiés en langue française dans la province de Québec, depuis l'établissement de l'imprimerie au Canada jusqu'à nos jours, 1764–1905; [v.1, pt.2], Tables des noms et des matières; v.2, Québec et Nouvelle France, bibliographie; Inventaire chronologique des ouvrages publiés à l'étranger en diverses langues . . . 1534–1906; v.3, Inventaire chronologique des livres, brochures, journaux et revues publiés en langue anglaise dans la province de Québec . . . 1764–1906; v.4, Inventaire chronologique des cartes, plans, atlas, relatifs à la Nouvelle-France et à la province de Québec, 1508–1908; Inventaire chronologique des livres, brochures, journaux et revues . . . 1. suppl., 1904–12.   Z1392.Q3D5

Gagnon, Philéas. Essai de bibliographie canadienne 1895–1913. Québec, 1895–1913. 2v.   **AA656**

For full information *see* DB183.   Z1365.G2

Haight, Willet Ricketson. Canadian catalogue of books, 1791–1897. Toronto, Haight, 1896–1904. 3v. (Facsimile repr.: Vancouver, Devlin; London, Pordes, 1958)   **AA657**

Basic volume, 1791–1895, pt.1 of a projected list for that period, publ. 1896, 130p.; Supplements 1–2, 1896–97, Annual Canadian catalogue, publ. 1898, 48p. and 1904, 57p.

No more published.   Z1365.H15

Martin, Gérard. Bibliographie sommaire du Canada français, 1854–1954. Québec, Secrétariat de la Province de Québec, 1954. 104p.   **AA658**

A classified list of some 900 items concerning French Canada.   Z1377.F8M3

Morgan, Henry James. Bibliotheca canadensis: or, A manual of Canadian literature. Ottawa, G. E. Desbarats, 1867. 411p.   **AA659**

An alphabetical list of the authors of books, pamphlets, and contributions to the periodical press, with brief biographical notices and lists of their works. The biographical sketches are occasionally of some length and include, in addition to authors whose books are listed, sketches of Canadian journalists for whom no separate publications are noted.   Z1365.M84

Tod, Dorothea D. and **Cordingley, Audrey.** A check list of Canadian imprints, 1900–1925. Prelim. checking ed. Ottawa, Canadian Bibliographic Centre, Public Archives of Canada, 1950. 370p.   **AA660**

Designed to fill the gap in Canadian national bibliography.

An alphabetically arranged checklist of books and pamphlets (of more than 50p.). Government documents and serial publications are not included.   Z1365.T6

Tremaine, Marie. A bibliography of Canadian imprints, 1751–1800. Toronto, Univ. of Toronto Pr., 1952. 705p.   **AA661**

A full record of what is known of the first 50 years of the Provincial press. Books, magazines, pamphlets, newspapers, broadsides, and handbills are included, both those actually issued and those known to have been projected. Full bibliographical information is given for each item, and copies are located in Canadian, American, and foreign libraries. Good descriptive notes make this a guide to the society and thought of the period. A section on printing offices and a good general index to the volume.   Z1365.T7

Current

Canadian books in print: author and title index. 1975– . Toronto, Univ. of Toronto Pr., 1976– . Annual.   **AA662**

Continues an earlier series of the same title covering 1967–74 and which also carried a French title (*Catalogue des livres canadiens en librairie*) through 1972. Now includes only those French-language titles issued by predominantly English-language Canadian publishers (the French-language publications being covered by the irregularly published *Répertoire de l'édition au Québec,* 1972–). Beginning with the 1975 volume the subtitle, "Author and title index," appears on the title page. With the 1983/84 ed. (publ. 1984) the annual hardcover volume is supplemented by complete microfiche editions in April, July, and October of each year.

A companion publication appears as: Z1365.C2196

Canadian books in print: subject index. 1975– . Toronto, Univ. of Toronto Pr., 1976– . Annual.   **AA663**

Continues *Subject guide to Canadian books in print* 1973–74.

Offers a subject arrangement of the materials listed in the preceding item. Includes an alphabetical list of subject headings and a list of publishers with addresses.   Z1365.S9

Canadiana, 1950– . Ottawa, Nat. Lib. of Canada, 1951– . Monthly, with annual cumulations.   **AA664**

Succeeds the *Canadian catalogue of books,* 1921–49 (AA654). For an account of the history of the publication of *Canadiana* and a chronology of the changes in the individual sections *see* Appendix A of Ryder's *Canadian reference sources* (AA497).

Coverage varies considerably. Beginning 1967, arranged in six sections: (1) Fully catalogued and classified material arranged by Dewey classes and including "publications of Canadian origin or interest"; (2) Pamphlet file material; (3) Microforms; (4) Films, filmstrips, etc.; (5) Publications of the Government of Canada; (6) Publications of the Provincial governments of Canada.

Annual volumes cumulate, with minor revisions, the monthly issues with complete indexes; since 1968 a single cumulative index has been published for all six parts.

Automation of the production of *Canadiana* proceeded in stages from 1973 and was completed at the end of 1977, with various changes during the transition period. Beginning 1974, the bibliography appeared in eight parts: (1) Monographs (fully catalogued and classified) [now includes sheet music and scores]; (2) Theses in microform; (3) Serials (fully catalogued and classified) [now includes monographic series]; (4) Pamphlet file material; (5) Sound recordings (fully catalogued and classified); (6) Films, filmstrips and videotapes [not included after the Dec. 1976 issue; thereafter these materials are listed in an annual publication, *Film Canadiana,* prepared by the Canadian Film Institute in cooperation with the National Library]; (7) Publications of the government of Canada; (8) Publications of the provincial governments of Canada. Indexing pattern has varied; in recent years there is an author/title/series index, and separate English and French subject indexes.

Z1365.C23

—— 1968–1976 index. Ottawa, Nat. Lib. of Canada, 1978. 10v.

"This index is the cumulation of Index A information for all of the manually-prepared text of CANADIANA for the years 1968 to 1976; for 1968 to 1973 this included all parts, for 1974 parts III–VIII, and for 1975 and 1976 parts V and VI only. It attempts to provide every type of specific entry under which a publication may be sought. It includes authors (personal and corporate), titles, added entries (i.e. associated names such as editors, joint authors, etc.) and series. It also includes cross-references from headings not used, and where relevant, histories of corporate bodies occurring as authors." —*v.1, [p.1].* Users are cautioned that changes in cataloging rules and filing procedures sometimes mean that separate alphabetical sequences must be searched for publications of a given organization.

Caribbean

Bibliografía actual del Caribe; Current Caribbean bibliography. Hato Rey, P.R., Caribbean Regional Lib., 1951– . v.1– . Annual (irregular) **AA665**

Title varies: early vols. called *Current Caribbean bibliography.* Publisher varies. Vol. covering 1973 (publ. 1976) latest published?

Early issues have subtitle: An alphabetical list of publications issued in the Caribbean countries of France, Great Britain, the Netherlands, and the United States.

Cumulations have been published as follows: 1950–53, publ. 1955; 1954–58, publ. 1961; 1959–61 publ. 1968. Beginning with the 1959–61 cumulative issue, listing is by Universal Decimal Classification with author-title-subject index. Z1595.C8

The CARICOM bibliography, v.1– . Georgetown, Guyana, Caribbean Community Secretariat Library, 1977– . Biennial. **AA666**

Subtitle: A cumulated subject list of current national imprints of the Caribbean Community member countries, arranged according to the Dewey Decimal Classification, 18th ed., and catalogued according to the British text of the Anglo-American rules (1967) and the International Standard Bibliographic Description for Monographs and Serials.

Frequency varies; annual 1977–79.

Aims "to list all material currently published" (*Pref.*) in Antigua, Bahamas, Barbados, Belize, Dominica, Grenada, Guyana, Jamaica, Montserrat, St. Kitts/Nevis/Anguilla, St. Lucia, St. Vincent, Trinidad and Tobago. Full information appears in the classified section; index of authors, titles, series. Excludes periodicals (except first issue, changes of title, and annual reports) and certain types of government publications. v.1 covers mainly 1976 publications, with some of earlier date. Z1501.C35a

Florida. University, Gainesville. Libraries. Technical Processes Dept. Caribbean acquisitions; materials acquired by the University of Florida, 1957/58– . Gainesville, [Univ. of Florida], 1959– . Annual. **AA667**

Lists books, pamphlets, periodicals, newspapers, and microforms "published in or about the Caribbean area, as well as books by authors from the area." Covers the West Indies and Bermuda; Colombia, Venezuela, and the Guianas; Central America and Mexico. Titles in the humanities and social sciences predominate. Classed arrangement with author index. Z1601.F55

Ceylon

See Sri Lanka.

Chile

Briseño, Ramón. Estadística bibliográfica de la literatura chilena. Obra compuesta, en virtud de encargo especial del consejo de la Universidad de Chile. Santiago de Chile, Impr. Chilena, 1862–79. 2v. **AA668**

Contents: t.1, 1812–1859. Impresos chilenos. Obras sobre Chile. Escritores chilenos; t.2, 1860–1876. Prólogo. Prensa chilena por órden alfabético. Prensa chilena por órden cronolójico. Prensa periodística chilena. Bibliografía chilena en el país, desde 1812 hasta 1859. Bibliografía chilena en el extranjero, desde 1860 hasta 1876. Curiosidades bibliográfico-chilenas. Z1701.B85

Medina, José Toribio. Bibliografía de la imprenta en Santiago de Chile desde sus orígenes hasta febrero de 1817. Santiago de Chile, Autor, 1891. 179p. (Readex Microprint) **AA669**

—— —— Adiciones y ampliaciones. Santiago de Chile, Univ. de Chile, 1939. 140p. il.

Z213.S23M4

—— —— Biblioteca hispano-chilena (1523–1817). Santiago de Chile, Autor, 1897–99. 3v. facsims. (Repr.: Amsterdam, N. Israel, 1965) **AA670**

Includes no books printed in Chile, only books printed in Europe or America by Chileans or by Spaniards who wrote in Chile. Lists 876 titles chronologically, with critical and bibliographical notes and references to authorities. Locates copies. Z1701.M48

Montt, Luis. Bibliografía chilena. Santiago de Chile, Impr. Univ., 1904–21. 3v. **AA671**

v.1, 1780–1811 (1918); v.2, 1812–1817 (1904); v.3, 1817–1818 (1921).

Of v.1, 264 pages were printed which the author intended to revise; of v.3, 160 pages were printed; sheets of both of these were destroyed, but in 1918 and 1921, reprints of the pages as originally printed were issued. Z1701.M82

Revista de bibliografía chilena. Publ. por la Biblioteca Nacional, enero 1913–oct. 1918, 1927–29. Santiago de Chile, Impr. Univ., 1913–29. 9v. **AA672**

Quarterly, 1927–29 (1913–18, monthly); 1913–18, have title *Revista de bibliografía chilena y extranjera.* None issued Nov. 1918–26.

No more published.

A valuable contemporary bibliography, which included special bibliographies in addition to the current record. Z1701.R4

Santiago de Chile. Biblioteca Nacional. Impresos chilenos, 1776–1818. Santiago de Chile, 1963. 2v. il., facsims. **AA673**

Contents: v.1, Bibliografía histórica de la imprenta en Santiago de Chile. Impresos chilenos, 1776–1818, textos. Indice cronológico de los impresos que posee la Biblioteca Nacional, 1776–1818; v.2, Descripciones bibliográficas de los impresos chilenos, 1776–1818. Textos manuscritos . . . 1813–14. Indice cronológico de los impresos chilenos, 1776–1818. Indice cronológico de los textos manuscritos. Z1702.S3

—— Bibliografía general de Chile. Por Emilio Vaïsse. Santiago de Chile, Impr. Univ., 1915–[18]. v.1–2. **AA674**

Repr. from *Revista de bibliografía chilena y extranjera.*

1. pt. Diccionario de autores y obras (bio-bibliografía y bibliografía): t.1, Bibliografía de bibliografías chilenas, por R. A. Laval. Diccionario; A–Barros Arana; t.2, Barros Baeza–Bustos.

A bio-bibliographical dictionary, listing writings of Chilean authors. A supplement to t.1 is noted at AA49.

No more published.   Z1701.S3

Williams, Lee H. The Allende years, a union list of Chilean imprints, 1970–1973, in selected North American libraries . . . . Boston, G. K. Hall, 1977. 339p.   **AA675**

For full information *see* DB319.

Current

Anuario de la prensa chilena, 1877–1975. Pub. por la Biblioteca Nacional. Santiago de Chile, 1887–1979. Annual (Irregular).   **AA676**

Annual, 1886–1916. Except for a volume covering 1877–85 (publ. 1952), publication was suspended 1928–62. Resumed with issues covering 5-year periods, though not cumulative: 1917–23, 1922–26, 1927–31 (all publ. 1963); 1932–36 (publ. in 2 pts., 1932–34 and 1935–36), 1937–41, 1942–46, 1947–51, 1952–56 (all publ. 1964); 1957–61 (publ. 1963); annual beginning with the issue for 1962 (publ. 1963).

Catalog of books deposited in the national library under the law of 1872. From 1891, includes books by Chilean authors or relating to Chile published in other countries. An author listing only.

Many volumes contain an appendix of *publicaciones omitidas* from previous volumes. Musical compositions are entered in volumes for 1896–1900.

Servicio bibliográfico chileno, a bookdealer's listing prepared primarily for foreign customers by the firm Zamorano y Caperan, was published monthly (then quarterly) 1940–71. Although it had no indexes or cumulative features, it served as a useful contemporary record during the long period when the *Anuario* was suspended.

Superseded by: Z1705.A58

Bibliografía chilena, 1976/79– . Santiago, Chile, Ediciones de la Dirección de Bibliotecas, Archivos y Museos, 1981– . Annual.   **AA677**

At head of title: Biblioteca Nacional.

The first volume covers 1976–79; annual thereafter, listing materials received on legal deposit during the year of coverage. Annual volumes are arranged by Dewey Decimal Classification, with a general index. Citations include full bibliographic information and show catalog tracings.   Z1701.S23

El libro chileno en venta. 1950/75– . [Santiago de Chile], Servicio de Extensión de Cultura Chilena, [1975]– . Irregular (1979/80 publ. 1982).   **AA678**

An "in print" list for Chile. The first issue is intended as "a cumulative catalog of the bibliographical chilean production between the years 1950–August 1975 . . . available in the chilean book market."—*Foreword.* Subject arrangement by broad Dewey classes, with author and title indexes. Includes prices.

China

Chinese cooperative catalog. Jan. 1975–82. Wash., Lib. of Congress, 1975–82. Monthly, with annual cumulation.   **AA679**

Intended as an aid for libraries acquiring Chinese-language materials, this catalog presents "Library of Congress printed cards, preliminary cards prepared in the Library of Congress at the initial stage of cataloging, and catalog cards submitted by 12 of the larger Chinese collections in the United States. Although most of the entries are monographs, serials are also included."—*Foreword.* Arranged alphabetically by romanized title. Not to be considered a union catalog, since only a single location is usually indicated. 1978–82 issued in microfiche. Merged into *NUC Books* (AA127) in 1983.   Z881.U49C49

Cordier, Henri. L'imprimerie sino-européenne en Chine. Bibliographie des ouvrages publiés en Chine par les Européens au XVIIe et au XVIIIe siècles. Paris, Leroux, 1901.

73p. il. (Publ. de l'École des Langues Orientales Vivantes, 5. sér., t.3)   **AA680**

Lists mainly works written in the Chinese language or translated into Chinese by missionaries.

First published in 1883 as "Essai d'une bibliographie des ouvrages publiés en Chine par les Européens au XVIIe et au XVIIIe siècles" in *Mélanges orientaux* (Publ. de l'École des Langues Orientales Vivantes, 2. sér., t.9).   Z3108.T7C7

Quarterly bulletin of Chinese bibliography [English ed.], v.1–4, 1934–37; n.s. v.1–7, 1940–47. Peiping, Nat. Lib. of Peiping, 1934–47. Irregular.   **AA681**

Includes general articles, book reviews, notes and news, and an annotated, selected list of new books published in China, divided into three sections: (1) Books in Chinese; (2) Books in foreign languages; (3) Government publications. Scope of contents varies.   Z3103.Q23

Colombia

Laverde Amaya, Isidoro. Bibliografía colombiana. Bogotá, M. Rivas, 1895. v.1. 296p.   **AA682**

v.1, A–O; no more published.

Bio-bibliography; includes mainly 19th-century publications, with a few of earlier date.   Z1740.L4

Medina, José Toribio. La imprenta en Bogotá (1739–1821). Notas bibliográficas. Santiago de Chile, Impr. Elzeviriana, 1904. 101p. (Repr.: Amsterdam, N. Israel, 1964)   **AA683**

A chronological listing with descriptive notes.   Z213.B7M4

——— La imprenta en Cartagena de las Indias (1809–1820). Notas bibliográficas. Santiago de Chile, Impr. Elzeviriana, 1904. 70p. (Repr.: Amsterdam, N. Israel, 1964)   **AA684**

Chronological listing with descriptive notes.   Z213.C3M4

Posada, Eduardo, Bibliografía bogotana. Bogotá, Impr. Nacional, 1917–25. 2v. facsim. (Biblioteca de historia nacional, v.16, 36)   **AA685**

Arranged chronologically, 1738–1831, with author and subject indexes both alphabetical and by date.   Z1754.B7P8

Current

Anuario bibliográfico colombiano, 1951– . Bogotá, Inst. Caro y Cuervo, Dept. de Bibliografía, 1952– . Irregular.   **AA686**

Publisher varies.

Lists books, pamphlets, and periodicals published in Colombia, and foreign publications dealing with Colombia. Classified arrangement, with a name index.

The 1951 edition was edited by Pedro R. Carmona; it was incorporated into the next volume, 1951/56, which was edited by Rubén Pérez Ortiz and published 1958. Thereafter, volumes cover one or two years, and publication has been relatively current. José Romero Rojas became editor with the 1963 volume.   Z1731.A58

Bibliografía colombiana, 1961– . Gainesville, Fla., 1961– . v.1– . (Biblioteca del bibliotecario, 61–62, 67–68, etc.) Semiannual.   **AA687**

Title varies; publisher varies.

Fermín Peraza Sarausa, ed., 1961–65.

v.2 (julio–dic. 1961) publ. in a 2d ed., 1972.

An alphabetical main-entry listing with an author-subject index.   Z1731.B5

Costa Rica

Dobles Segreda, Luis. Indice bibliográfico de Costa Rica. San José, Lehmann, 1927–36. v.1–9.   **AA688**

Contents: t.1: sec.1, Agricultura y veterinaria; sec.2, Ciencias físicas y naturales; t.2: sec.3, Filología y gramática; sec.4, Geografía y geología, Lista de mapas de Costa Rica; t.3: sec.5, Matemáticas, ingeniería y finanzas; sec.6, Psicología, filosofía y religión; t.4: sec.7, Novela, cuento y artículo literario; sec.8, Teatro; t.5, sec.9, Historia hasta 1900; t.6, sec.10, Historia desde 1900 hasta 1933; t.7, sec.11, and t.8, sec.11 (cont.), Política y derecho desde 1831 hasta 1935; t.8, sec.12, Milicia; t.9, sec.13, Hígiene y Medicina.

Other volumes were projected to cover *educación, sociología y demografía, poesía,* and an *Indice alfabético de autores (biográfico y bibliográfico),* but have not been published.   Z1451.D63

Lines, Jorge A. Libros y folletos publicados en Costa Rica durante los años 1830–1849. San José, Univ. de Costa Rica, Facultad de Letras y Filosofía, 1944. 151p. il.   **AA689**

Lists 103 titles arranged chronologically with author index.
                                                        Z1451.L5

Current

San José, Costa Rica. Biblioteca Nacional. Boletín bibliográfico; publicaciones nacionales correspondientes al año 1935/38–55. San José, Impr. Nacional, 1939–56. Annual.   **AA690**

Ceased publication.
Superseded by:

Anuario bibliográfico costarricense, 1956– . San José, Impr. Nacional. 1958– . Irregular.   **AA691**

At head of title: Asociación costarricense de bibliotecarios. Comité nacional de bibliografía "Adolfo Bien."

Originally works were listed in two alphabets, one by author, the second classified by subject, with an index of specific subjects and of names not appearing as main entries. Beginning with the issue covering 1959–60, the bibliography became a classified list with author index.

Publication suspended after the 1972/74 volume.   Z1453.A65

Cuba

Anuario bibliográfico cubano: 1937–66. Gainesville, Fla., Anuario Bibliográfico Cubano, 1938–67. 30v.   **AA692**

Through 1959 (publ. 1960) published in Havana.
Ed., Fermín Peraza Sarausa.

An annual with arrangement varying from year to year, but each issue giving excellent coverage. Beginning with the 1953 volume the series appeared with the cover title *Bibliografía cubana,* and that title is used in the prefaces, etc.

The 1956 volume appeared in a 2d ed. in 1966, adding 225 new entries and employing a different arrangement from the earlier edition.   Z1511.A61

–––––– Bibliografía cubana. Complementos: 1937–1961, compilados por Fermín Peraza [Sarausa]. Gainesville, Fla., Univ. of Florida Libraries, 1966. 233p.   **AA693**

Cumulates the addenda sections published in the *Anuario* for the years 1937–59, together with previously unpublished entries for the years 1960–61.

Bachiller y Morales, Antonio. Catálogo de libros y folletos publicados en Cuba desde la introducción de la imprenta hasta 1840. (*In* his *Apuntes para la historia de las letras y de la instrucción publica de la Isla de Cuba.* Habana, P. Mas-

sana, 1861. v.3, p.121–241. Repr. in his *Apuntes . . .* Habana, Cultural, 1936–37. v.3, p.243–457)   **AA694**

Arranged chronologically. No index.

–––––– –––––– Suplementos y adiciones. (Revista de Cuba 7:354–64, 491–98; 8:71–78, 124–35, abril, mayo, julio, agosto 1880)

                                                        F1777.B123

Medina, José Toribio. La imprenta en la Habana (1707–1810): notas bibliográficas. Santiago de Chile, Impr. Elzeviriana, 1904. 199p. (Repr.: Amsterdam, N. Israel, 1964)   **AA695**

Chronological listing with brief descriptive notes.   Z213.H2M4

Revolutionary Cuba: a bibliographical guide, 1966–68. Coral Gables, Fla., Univ. of Miami Pr., 1967–70. Annual.   **AA696**

Fermín Peraza Sarausa, ed., 1966–67. Ceased publication.

Supersedes the *Anuario bibliográfico cubano* (AA692). Scope has been broadened to include materials about, as well as those published in, Cuba since the establishment of the Castro regime. Main entry listing with analytical index.   Z1511.A653

Trelles y Govín, Carlos Manuel. Ensayo de bibliografía cubana de los siglos XVII y XVIII. Seguido de unos apuntes para la bibliografía dominicana y portorriqueña. Matanzas, "El Escritorio," 1907–1908. 228p., and suppl., 76p. (Readex Microprint)   **AA697**

Continued by: Z1511.T85

–––––– Bibliografía cubana del siglo XIX. Matanzas, Quirós y Estrada, 1911–15. 8v. (Readex Microprint)   **AA698**

Contents: t.1, 1800–1825; t.2, 1826–1840. Seguido de una Relación de periódicos publicados en Cuba en el siglo XX, por F. Llaca, y unas Noticias curiosas referentes á escritores de los siglos XVII y XVIII, por M. Perez Beato; t.3–8, 1841–1899. Ensayo de biblioteca cubana del siglo XIX; Indice.   Z1511.T86

–––––– Bibliografía cubana del siglo XX (1900–1916). Matanzas, Quirós y Estrada, 1916–17. 2v. (Readex Microprint)   **AA699**

These two volumes, with those cited in the two preceding entries, make up what is termed the compiler's *Bibliografía cubana.*
                                                        Z1511.T87

–––––– Biblioteca científica cubana. Matanzas, J. F. Oliver, 1918–20. v.1–2. il. (Readex Microprint)   **AA700**

Lists 9,500 titles of books and periodical articles.   Z1511.T872

–––––– Biblioteca geográfica cubana. Matanzas, J. F. Oliver, 1920–25. 340p., and suppl., 64p. (Readex Microprint)   **AA701**

Main work and supplement list 3,900 titles of books and periodical articles.   Z1511.T875

–––––– Biblioteca histórica cubana. Matanzas, J. F. Oliver, 1922–26. 3v. (Readex Microprint)   **AA702**

Lists 17,000 titles of books and periodical articles.   Z1525.T79

Current

Bibliografía cubana. 1917/20– . La Habana, Consejo Nacional de Cultura, 1978– . Annual.   **AA703**

Continues *Bibliografía cubana del siglo XX* by Trelles y Govín (AA699).

Vols. for 1917/20–1963/64 issued by the Departamento Colección Cubana, Biblioteca Nacional José Marti; 1965– by the library. 1917–36 issued in 5v., each covering four years; each volume provides annual main-entry lists of publications from the years of coverage, with a combined index for the full volume. Vols. for 1937–62 not yet published.   Z1511.B5

Czechoslovakia

Bibliografia slovenských kníh, 1919–1938. Martin, Matica Slovenská, 1979. 3v. (Slovenská retrospektívna bibliografia. Séria A. Knihy IIIa)   **AA704**

Slovakian imprints of the period are listed by main entry in v.1–2; v.3 contains indexes. Locates copies.

Bibliografia slovenskej kniznej tvorby. 1939/41–1945/55. Bratislava [etc.], 1948–70. Irregular.   **AA705**

Title varies: 1939/41, *Bibliografický katalog slovenskej kniznej tvorby* (a rev. ed. of *Slovenský bibliografický súpis kníh za roky 1939/41,* publ. 1942).

Vol. for 1942/45 issued as *Slovenská bibliografia.* Ser. B, sv.1; vol. for 1945/55 issued as *Slovenská národná retrospektívná bibliografia.* Ser. A, kn. IV.

A main entry listing of Slovak book production for the period.   Z2124.S56B5

Bibliograficky katalog, roc. 1–7, 1922–28. Red. Lad. J. Zivný. Praha, 1923–28. (Publikace Československého Ústavu Bibliografického v Praze, sv.2–16) Weekly.   **AA706**

Half title in German and French.

Classified, with annual author index. Published by the Institut Bibliographique Tchécoslovaque à Prague.   Z2133.B58

Bibliograficky katalog Československé Republiky; literárni tvorba z roku, 1929–46. V Praze, Nákl. Ministerstva Skolství a Národni Osvěty, 1930–47. 18v. in 21. Annual.   **AA707**

Publisher varies.

A classified, annual catalog of books and pamphlets with indexes of authors and subjects. Does not include periodicals.   Z2133.B582

Caplovic, Ján. Bibliografia tlačí vydaných na Slovensku do roku 1700. Martin, Matica Slovenská, 1972– . Diel 1– . (Slovenská národná retrospektivna bibliografia. Sér. A, Knihy 1a–)   **AA708**

Contents: v.1, Banská Bystrica–Levoča.

A bibliography of Slovak imprints to 1700. Listing is alphabetical by place of publication, then chronological.   Z2137.S6C36

Knihopis českych a slovenskych tisku od doby nejstarsí až do konce XVIII století. Praha, Nákl. Československé Akademie Věd., 1925–67. v.1–2, pts.1–9. (In progress)   **AA709**

Title varies; publisher varies.

Contents: v.1, To 1500, A–Z, and atlas of facsim.; v.2, 1501–1800, pts.1–9, A–Z. (Indexes presumably will follow.)

A bibliography of Czech and Slovakian imprints from early times to the end of the 18th century.

Matica Slovenská, Turčiansky sv. Martin. Knižnica. Katalóg slovákumových kníh Knižnice Matice slovenskeij do roku 1918. [Spracoval a zostavil kolektív pracovníkov Knižnice Matice Slovenskej: Božena Baricová *et al.*] Martin, 1964. 3v.   **AA710**

A main-entry listing of Slovakian imprints and books relating to Slovakia in the library, with chronological and geographical (i.e., place/publisher) indexes in v.3.

Supplemented by: Z926.M35

——— Katalóg slovacikálnych kníh vydaných do roku 1918 v knižnici Matice slovenskej, zost. Anna Podmanická. Martin, Matica Slovenská, 1974. 2v. (1205p.) (Slovenské knižnice, zv. 10–11)   **AA711**

Added title page in Latin: Catalogus librorum slovacicorum usque ad annum 1918 impressorum qui in Bibliotheca 'Matica slovenská' asservantur.

A listing by author or other main entry. Index by place of publication, subdivided by publisher.   Z2137.S6M38

Rizner, L'udovít Vladimir. Bibliografia písomníctva slovenského na sposob slovníka od najstarších čias do konca r.

1900. S pripojenou bibliografiou archeologickou, historickou . . . vydáva matičná sprava. V Turcianskom Sv. Martine, Nákl. Matice Slovenskej, 1929–34. 6v.   **AA712**

An alphabetical catalog of Slovakian literature to 1900. Often gives brief biographical notices of authors.

Supplemented by: Z2137.S6R6

Misianik, Ján. Bibliografia slovenského písomníctva do konca XIX. stor. (Doplnky k Risnerovej bibliografii). Bratislava, Slovenská Akadémia vied a umení, 1946. 300p. il. (Práce z vedeckých ústavov Slovenskej Akadémie vied a umení. Rad.A. Sv.5)   **AA713**

A supplement to Rizner (above).   Z2137.S6M5

Soupis československé literatury za léta 1901–1925. . . . V Praze, Nákl. Svazu Knihkupců a Nakladatelů, 1931–38. 2v. in 3.   **AA714**

Karel Nosovský and Vilém Pražák, eds.

v.1–2, author list, A–Z; v.3, classified subject index.

    Z2131.S72

Current

Bibliograficky katalog Československé Republiky; týdenní sešitové vydání, 1933–59. V Praze, 1933–59. Weekly (irregular).   **AA715**

From 1933 to 1947, published concurrently with the yearly bibliography of the same name (AA707), of which 1946 is the last volume published.

During 1946–50 the weekly was issued in three parts, the titles of which have varied. From 1951 through 1954 the bibliography was designated as *Bibliograficky katalog ČSR* and the three parts were titled: *Česká kniha* (weekly); *Slovenska kniha* (approximately 15 issues per year); *České a slovenské hudebniny* (about 10 issues per year). The first and third of these (Czech books, and Czech and Slovak music) were published by the National Library in Prague, the Slovak books section by the Slovak University in Bratislava; both were legal repositories.

Classified arrangement; annual author and subject indexes for most years; supplements accompany many numbers.

For the period 1955–59 the designations of the first two parts were changed to *České knihy* and *Slovenské knihy.* The third section was superseded by two separate parts: *České hudebniny* and *Slovenské hudebniny.*

Beginning 1960, the overall title of the bibliography became:

Bibliograficky katalog ČSSR, 1960– . Praha, Nákl. Národní Knihovny, 1960– .   **AA716**

The parts making up the bibliography continue to be designated as: *České knihy* (weekly); *Slovenské knihy* (V Martine, Matica Slovenská; monthly, irregular); *České hudebniny* (quarterly); and *Slovenské hudebniny* (V Martine, Matica Slovenská; annual). The Library of Congress has cataloged each part separately.

Beginning 1970 the designation of the Slovak book section was changed to: *Slovenská národná bibliografia. Séria A: knihy* (V Martine, Matica Slovenská; monthly). It continues the volume numbering of the earlier series.

Arrangement of the bibliography remains basically the same within parts throughout the title changes.

Denmark

Early

Nielsen, Lauritz Martin. Dansk Bibliografi, 1482–1550, 1551–1600, med saerligt hensyn til dansk bogtrykkerkunsts Historie. København, Gyldendal, 1919–35. 2v. and Registre (126p.). il.   **AA717**

v.[2] was issued in nine parts, 1931–33.

1482–1550, Author and title list, A–Z, no.1–298. 1919. 247p.; 1551–1600, Author and title list, A–AE, no.299–1672. 1931–33.

677p.; *Registre:* alphabetical author index, alphabetical title index, chronological index, subject index.

Two companion works listing together 1,672 items and giving for each item: title, detailed collation, bibliographical references, and location of copies. Indexes of places and of printers and publishers in each work. Z2562.N67

Bibliotheca danica. Systematisk Fortegnelse over den danske Literatur fra 1482 til 1830, efter Samlingerne i det Store Kongelige Bibliothek i Kjøbenhavn. Udg. Christian Walther Bruun. Kjøbenhavn, Gyldendal, 1877–1931. 4v., suppl., and index. **AA718**

A classified bibliography of Danish materials from 1482 to 1830. v.4 includes a *Supplement* (1914) and a *Register* (1927–31) by Lauritz Nielsen. The index is in three parts: (1) authors; (2) anonymous works; (3) subjects.

A 5v. reprint was issued 1961–63 (Kobenhavn, Rosenkilde og Bagger); in that set v.5 consists of the original supplement, published 1914, and an additional supplement covering 1914–62, by Eric Dal, together with the original indexes and an additional index to the new supplement. Z2561.B58

———— Supplement 1831–1840 til Bibliotheca danica og Dansk Bogfortegnelse, udarb. af H. Ehrencron-Müller. København, Gad, 1943–48. Hft.1–4 (1564col.).

Hft.1, Alfabetisk Fortegnelse, 1943, 422col.; Hft.2, Systematisk Fortegnelse, 1944, col. 425–860; Hft.3–4, Supplement til Bibliotheca danica ... Bibliotheca slesvico-holsatica til 1840; Alfabetisk Fortegnelse, 1945, col.863–1184; Systematisk Fortegnelse, 1948, col.1187–1564.

Hft.1–2 are designed to fill the gap in Danish bibliography between the Bruun *Bibliotheca danica* (AA718), which covers the period to 1830 and the *Dansk Bogfortegnelse* (AA720), which starts with 1841. Hft.3–4 form a catalog of Schleswig-Holstein literature from the earliest times to 1840. Z2561.B58

Mitchell, Phillip Marshall. A bibliography of 17th century German imprints in Denmark and the duchies of Schleswig-Holstein. [Lawrence], Univ. of Kansas Libraries, 1969. 2v. (Univ. of Kansas publs. Lib. ser., 28) **AA719**

"This bibliography records all publications with German title-pages (or titles) known or presumed to have been printed or published within the [17th century] Danish monarchy, including all items which bear an imprint of a printer or bookseller within the monarchy."—*Introd.* Chronological listing with full bibliographical information. Indexes of authors, printers, and titles. Z2562.M55

19th and 20th centuries

Dansk Bogfortegnelse for aarene 1841/58–1973/75. København, Gad, 1861–1977. **AA720**

Cumulates the annual volumes of the same title which began publication in 1851. 19th–century cumulations vary in number of years covered. Quinquennial 1915–69; triennial 1970–75.

From 1915/19 to 1930/34 includes *Islandsk Bogfortegnelse* (AA875).

Covers all material entered for copyright. Alphabetical author and title list, followed by classified list, with a subject index to the latter. Continued by *Dansk Bogfortegnelse* (AA725). Z2561.D19

Ehrencron-Müller, Holger. Stikordsregister til den danske Skønlitteratur. 1841/1908–1909/40. København, Gad, 1918–41. 2v. **AA722**

Vol. for 1909/40 issued in 3 pts. and includes "Stikordsregister til den danske Skønlitteratur indtil 1840" (29p. at end, with special t.p.) which is a title index to books in the field of belles-lettres listed in the *Biblioteca danica* (AA718) and its supplement.

The 1841–1940 volumes provide a title index to books in the fields of belles-lettres which are listed in the *Dansk Bogfortegnelse* through 1940. Z2561.D19

Dania Polyglotta; répertoire bibliographique des ouvrages, études, articles, etc., en langues étrangères parus en Dane-

mark de 1901 à 1944. Copenhague, Bibliothèque Royale, 1947–51. v.1–3. **AA723**

Publié par l'Institut Danois des Échanges Internationaux de Publications Scientifiques et Littéraires sous la rédaction de son directeur K. Schmidt-Phiseldeck avec la collaboration de Henning Einersen.

Contents: v.1, Ouvrages; v.2 Périodiques, études et articles; v.3, Addenda, musique, index.

Includes books and articles published in Denmark in foreign languages by native and foreign scholars. Works in each volume are grouped under language and then arranged by class, with a general author index.

Continued by the annual *Dania Polyglotta*, 1.–24. année, 1945–68. Copenhague, Bibliothèque Royale, 1946–69.

Beginning in 1961 the subtitle of the annual, previously in French, appears in English: Annual bibliography of books, articles, and summaries, etc., in foreign languages printed in Denmark.

With 1969 a new series was begun: Z2574.F6D3

Dania Polyglotta; literature on Denmark in languages other than Danish & books of Danish interest published abroad. n.s.1– , 1969– . Copenhagen, 1970– . Annual. **AA724**

"An annual bibliography compiled by the Danish Department of the Royal Library."—*title page.*

A classified subject listing with author and title index. Z2561.D162

Current

Dansk Bogfortegnelse. Årskatalog. The Danish national bibliography. Books. 1976– . Ballerup, Bibliotekscentralens Forlag, 1977– . Annual. **AA725**

For the earlier series see AA720.

"*The Danish National Bibliography. Books* is compiled by Bibliotekscentralen on the basis of new books and reprints sent in directly from the publishers. The Danish Department of the Royal Library supplements this material with books deposited by printers according to the Act of Legal Deposit."—*verso of t.p.*

The annual volumes constitute a cumulation of materials from several sources, the cumulation pattern and contents varying slightly. The current pattern is as follows: a weekly alphabetical list appears in the periodical *Det danske Bogmarked*. Separately published monthly lists entitled *Dansk Bogfortegnelse* (containing a classified short-title list in addition to the alphabetical section) appear 12 times a year, every third issue constituting a quarterly cumulation. Annual cumulations (the *Årskatalog*) include the alphabetical and classified sections plus a Faroese book list, a Greenlandic book list, and a section of maps. The annuals will continue to cumulate quinquennially. A microfiche edition, cumulated from 1976, is also available, but does not include the special lists.

Dominican Republic

Anuario bibliográfico dominicano, 1946–47. Ciudad Trujillo, 1947–48. 2v. **AA726**

At head of title: Oficina de Canje y Difusion Cultural.

Supersedes the *Boletín bibliográfico dominicano* of which only two numbers were published: no.1, July–Aug. 1945, which covered 1944, and no.2, Sept.–Dec. 1945, which covered 1945.

Z1533.A58

Ecuador

Espinosa Cordero, Nicolás. Bibliografía ecuatoriana, 1534–1809. Cuenca, Impr. del Colegio Nacional "Benigno Malo," 1934. 171p. **AA727**

Issued also as pt.4 of the author's *Estudios literarios y bibliográficos* (Cuenca, 1934. p.93–256).

Includes brief biographical notes of authors. Z1770.E76

Medina, José Toribio. La imprenta en Quito (1760–1818): notas bibliográficas. Santiago de Chile, Impr. Elzeviriana, 1904. 86p. (Repr.: Amsterdam, N. Israel, 1964)   **AA728**

A chronological listing with descriptive notes.   Z213.Q5M4

Current

Anuario bibliográfico ecuatoriano, 1975–   . Quito, Universidad Central del Ecuador, 1976–   . Annual.   **AA729**

At head of title: Universidad Central del Ecuador, Biblioteca General.

The annual volume represents a cumulation of the bimonthly issues of the *Bibliografía ecuatoriana* and includes the sixth number of that series. Ceased publication?

A classed listing in two sections: (1) Bibliografía monográfica, and (2) Bibliografía analítica, the latter providing analytics for collective works and selected periodicals. Indexes of names, titles, and subjects.   Z1761.A68

Ecuador: bibliografía analítica. Ano 1–3, 1979–81. Cuenca, Centro de Investigación y Cultura del Banco Central del Ecuador, 1979–81. 3 nos. per yr.   **AA730**

A new effort toward a current national bibliography. In two sections, each subdivided according to the Universal Decimal Classification: (1) Bibliografía monográfica; (2) Bibliografía analítica (which provides references to periodical articles and collective works). Indexes of names and topical subjects.

Continued on an annual basis by: Z1761.E37

Anuario bibliográfico ecuatoriano. 1982–   . Cuenca, Banco Central del Ecuador, 1984–   . Annual.   **AA731**

England

See Great Britain.

Estonia

Tallinn. Friedrich Reinhold Kreutzwaldi nimeline Eeste NSV Riiklik Raamatukogu. Nõukogude Eesti raamat 1940–1954; koondbibliograafia. Tallinn, Eesti Riiklik Kirjastus, 1956. 513p.   **AA732**

Continued by: Z2533.T26

Kuldkepp, E. and **Toovere, P.** Nõukogude Eesti raamat 1955–1965; koondnimestik. Tallinn, Eesti Raamat, 1972. 1098p.   **AA733**

At head of title: Eesti NSV Ministrite Nõukogu, Riiklik Kirjastuskomittee; Eesti NSV Riiklik Raamatupalat.

Continued by: Z2533.K84

Nõukogude Eesti raamat 1966–1970; koondnimestik. [Koostaja P. Toovere; toimetus M. Sibul, L. Ploompuu ja A. Tann] Tallinn, Eesti Raamat, 1978. 750p.   **AA734**

At head of title: Eesti NSV Ministrite Nõukogu Riiklik Kirjastuste, Polügraafia ja Raamatukaubanduse Komitee Eesti NSV Riiklik Raamatupalat.

Title page also in Russian.

The three items listed above constitute a record of Estonian imprints from 1940 through 1970.   Z2533.N66

Ethiopia

Ethiopian publications: books, pamphlets, annuals and periodical articles published in 1963 and 1964–   . Addis Ababa, Haile Sellassie I Univ., Inst. of Ethiopian Studies, 1965–   . Annual.   **AA735**

"It is intended that subsequent numbers of this publication should appear annually and should become the current Ethiopian National Bibliography."—*Introd. [v.1]* In the early issues, an Ethiopian-language section in alphabetical order is followed by a foreign-language section in classed arrangement with author index. Beginning with the issue covering 1970, both the Ethiopian and the foreign-language sections follow a classed arrangement.

1973 last published?

An official national bibliography of the same title, prepared by the Department of National Library and Archives and reportedly beginning publication in 1980, was not available for examination.   Z3521.E82

Höjer, Christianne. Ethiopian publications. Books, pamphlets, annuals and periodical articles published in Ethiopia in foreign languages from 1942 till 1962. Addis Ababa, Haile Sellassie I Univ., Inst. of Ethiopian Studies, 1974. 146p.   **AA736**

Intends to fill the gap between Stephen G. Wright's *Ethiopian incunabula* (Addis Ababa, 1967) and the annual *Ethiopian publications* (above). A classified list with annual index.   Z3521.H63

Solomon Gebre Christos. A decade of Ethiopian languages publications, 1959–1969. Addis Ababa, Haile Sellassie I Univ. Lib., 1970. 232p.   **AA737**

Title also in Amharic.

Nearly 1,300 items.   Z3521.S65

Finland

Pipping, Fredrik Wilhelm. Luettelo suomeksi präntätyistä kirjoista, kuin myös muutamista muista teoksista, joissa löytyy joku kirjoitus suomen, kielellä, tahi joku johdatus sitä tuntemaan. Helsingfors, Finska Litteratursällsks Tryck, 1856–57. 756p. (Suomalaisen Kirjallisuuden Seuran. Toimituksia. 20)   **AA738**

Lists Finnish imprints in chronological order from 1542 to 1856. Author index.

Suomessa ilmestyneen kirjallisuuden luettelo. Katalog över i Finland utkommen litteratur, 1945–71. Helsinki, Kirjavälitys Oy, 1945–71. Annual.   **AA739**

Title varies; earliest issues called: *Suomessa ilmestyneen kirjallisuuden aineenmukainen uutuusluettelo*. Ceased publication.

Originally a quarterly, classified catalog without index or cumulative features, 1945–48; annual since 1949.

Beginning 1949, lists new Finnish and Swedish books alphabetically in two sections with subject indexes, also divided by language until 1963. Books and parts of series in foreign languages published in Finland are listed as pt.3, but have no subject index until 1963 and subsequent issues, when a single classified index serves for all three parts.

Beginning 1962, title also in German and English.

Current

Suomen kirjallisuus. Finlands litteratur. The Finnish national bibliography. 1544/1877–   . Helsinki, Helsingin Yliopiston Kirjasto [etc.], 1878–   .   **AA740**

1544/1877–1939/43 issued as *Suomalaisen Kirjallisuuden Seuran toimituksia,* 57 osa, 1.–16. lisävihko.

Frequency varies; now issued monthly (some double issues) with annual and quinquennial cumulations.

A basic volume, 1544–1877, by Valfrid Vasenius was followed by five supplements covering 1878–79, 1880–85, 1886–91, 1892–95, 1896–1900. Subsequent cumulative volumes, some of them issued in parts and in irregular order, cover three- or five-year periods, the 1964/66 cumulation being the latest published.

Monthly issues follow a classed subject arrangement, with author/title index; the annual cumulation is a main-entry listing with a classified section giving brief information within UDC classes. Information is furnished by three contributing libraries: the university libraries of Helsinki, Turku, and Jyväskylä.

From 1977, various categories of works previously found in the multi-year cumulations are to be excluded therefrom and published separately: serials, maps, printed music, and literature on Finland published abroad. Z2520.S95

France

Paris. Bibliothèque Nationale. Catalogue général des livres imprimés. Auteurs. Paris, Impr. Nationale, 1900–81. 231v. **AA741**

The Bibliothèque Nationale has received copies of all books published in France since the establishment, by law, of the *dépôt légal* in the reign of Henri II. It has the largest collection of French books in existence, and its printed *Catalogue* is the most important general bibliography of French publications. For full description *see* AA140.

Répertoire de bibliographie française; contenant tous les ouvrages imprimés en France et aux colonies et les ouvrages français publiés à l'étranger, 1501–1930. . . . Paris, Letouzey, 1937–41. Fasc.1–10. **AA742**

v.1 (fasc.1–6), A–Angélique; v.2 (fasc.7–10), Angelis–Arthaud.

An attempt at a comprehensive record of French bibliography, 1501–1930, including, in general, books published in France and books in French published in French colonies and abroad with certain omissions. Unfortunately, no more published.

Z2161.R42

Early

British Museum. Dept. of Printed Books. Short-title catalogue of books printed in France and of French books printed in other countries from 1470 to 1600 now in the British Museum. London, Trustees, 1924. 491p. **AA743**

Books printed in France, p.1–450; Books in French printed elsewhere, p.451–91.

An important record of about 12,000 editions, including many items not found in the printed catalog of the Bibliothèque Nationale. Information given includes: author, brief title, editor, translator, etc., place, publisher, date, size. Z2162.B86

——— A short title catalogue of French books, 1601–1700, in the Library of the British Museum, by V. F. Goldsmith. Folkestone, Dawsons of Pall Mall, 1969–73. 690p. **AA744**

Publ. in 7 fascicles. Contains about 21,000 entries. Includes 17th-century books "written wholly or partly in French, no matter where published" and those "in no matter what language, published or printed at any place which today forms a part of metropolitan France."—*Foreword.* Lists works in the *General catalogue* (AA132), works acquired since 1955, and some earlier accessions not found in the printed catalog. In addition, three extensive collections of "Mazarinades" (pamphlets and satires issued against Cardinal Mazarin) are here fully listed for the first time. Numerous indexes.

For a similar catalog for the 1470–1600 period *see* above.

Z2162.B87

Brunet, Jacques Charles. Manuel du libraire et de l'amateur de livres. 5.éd. augm. Paris, Didot, 1860–80. 9v. **AA745**

For full description *see* AA111.

La Croix du Maine, François Grudé and **Du Verdier, Antoine.** Les bibliothèques françoises de La Croix du Maine et de Du Verdier. Nouv. éd. rev., corr., et augm. . . . par Rigoley de Juvigny. Paris, Sailland & Nyon, 1772–73. 6v. **AA746**

The original edition of La Croix du Maine published Paris, 1584; of Du Verdier, Lyons, 1585. The two works complement each other and form a bio-bibliographical catalog of French publications to about the end of the 16th century. A valuable record although it includes many inaccuracies. Z2162.L145

Le Petit, Jules. Bibliographie des principales éditions originales d'écrivains français du XVe aux XVIIIe siècle. Paris, Quantin, 1888. 583p. il., facsims. (Repr.: Paris, Jeanne et Brulon, 1927) **AA747**

Facsimiles of title pages with long, detailed descriptions of the original editions. Z2174.F5L5

Moreau, Brigitte. Inventaire chronologique des éditions parisiennes du XVIe siècle . . . d'après les manuscrits de Philippe Renouard. Paris, Imprimerie Municipale, 1972–77. v.1–2. (In progress) **AA748**

At head of title: Service des Travaux Historiques de la Ville de Paris.

Contents: v.1, 1501–1510; v.2, 1511–1520.

To be published in ten parts, each part covering a 10-year period. Intended as a short-title catalog of 16th-century books published or sold in Paris, with indication of variant editions and locations of examples. Z305.M67

Répertoire bibliographique des livres imprimés en France au seizième siècle . . . Baden-Baden, Heitz, 1968–80. Fasc.1–30. (Bibliotheca bibliographica Aureliana, 25, 27, 29, etc.) **AA749**

A bibliography of 17th century book publishing throughout France, with the exception of Paris. A cooperative effort of many scholars, the original project was completed in 30 fascicles, the last two of which are devoted to additions and corrections, and indexes. Listing is by place, then by publisher and date. Further additions, published "hors série" but consecutively numbered, are now appearing in the *Bibliotheca bibliographica Aureliana,* v.80– , offering coverage of (1) Strasbourg, (2) miscellaneous provincial towns, (3) Troyes, (4) Douai, and (5) Poitiers; further numbers are planned for Lyon, Caen, and Rouen. Z2162.R4

Tchemerzine, Avenir. Bibliographie d'éditions originales et rares d'auteurs français des XVe, XVIe, XVIIe et XVIIIe siècles contenant environ 6000 fac-similés de titres et de gravures. Paris, Plée, 1927–34. 10v. il. **AA750**

Gives detailed bibliographical descriptions, line-by-line transcriptions, and many reproductions of title pages and engravings.

Z2174.F5T2

18th century

Conlon, Pierre M. Le siècle des lumières: bibliographie chronologique. Genève, Librairie Droz, 1983–84. v.1–3. (Histoire des idées et critique littéraire, v.213) (In progress) **AA751**

Contents: v.1, 1716–1722; v.2, 1723–1729; v.3, 1730–1736.

An attempt to partially fill a gap in 18th century French national bibliography; the completed work is to list French imprints through 1789, together with French writings published outside France. Listing is by year, then by author or anonymous title; author and title indexes are planned. Library locations (including some outside France) are given.

Quérard, Joseph Marie. La France littéraire, ou Dictionnaire bibliographique des savants, historiens et gens de lettres de la France, ainsi que des littérateurs étrangers qui ont écrit en français, plus particulièrement pendant les XVIIIe et XIXe siècles. Paris, Didot, 1827–64. 12v. (Repr.: Paris, Maisonneuve, 1964) **AA752**

v.1–10, A–Z; v.11–12, supplements containing: Corrections, additions; Auteurs, pseudonymes et anonymes; v.11, A–Razy; v.12, Re–Roguet.

Emphasis is on the humanities and pure science.

v.11–12 (publ. 1854–64) list by real name the authors of pseudonymous and anonymous works, giving the pseudonyms under which each has written, with brief biographical information, titles of works, etc. They serve as an index to Quérard's *Supercheries littéraires dévoilées* (AA195). Z2161.Q4

19th and 20th centuries

Biblio, catalogue des ouvrages parus en langue française dans le monde entier, 1934–70. Paris, Service Bibliographique des Messageries Hachette, 1935–71. 37v. Annual.
AA753

Subtitle varies.

Began publication as a monthly (10 issues a year) in Oct. 1933. The first annual cumulation was that for 1934 (publ. 1935).

During its period of publication, the most easily used trade bibliography covering books published in France and French books published in Belgium, Switzerland, Canada, etc. A dictionary catalog, published monthly with annual cumulation, entering each book under author, subject, and title with many cross references. Full information—given under author entry—includes author's name, full title, date, place (if other than Paris), publisher, paging, size, illustrations, series, price.

The monthly issues contained bio-bibliographical sketches, frequently of some length, brief book reviews, etc., which were not carried over into the annual volumes. These bio-bibliographies are indexed in the *Biography index* (AJ10).

Merged with *Bibliographie de la France* in Jan. 1972 to form *Bibliographie de la France—Biblio.* Monthly issues of *Biblio* continued to be published through Dec. 1971, but the annual cumulation for 1971 appears under the merged title, *Les livres de l'année—Biblio,* with the extended coverage of the new series (*see* AA762).
Z2165.B56

Bibliographie de la France; journal général de l'imprimerie et de la librairie. Paris, Cercle de la Librairie, 1811–1971. Année 1–160.
AA754

Arrangement and parts issued vary.

The standard weekly list, recording material received through the *dépôt légal,* including books, pamphlets, official publications, music, prints, and, in addition, a monthly record of gifts to the Bibliothèque Nationale. Beginning 1857, each number consisted of three main parts: (1) *Bibliographie officielle,* (2) *Chronique,* and (3) *Annonces* (to 1919, *Feuilleton*).

1.pt.: The *Bibliographie officielle* contained *Livres,* a classed list of books, pamphlets, etc., recorded with full cataloging information which includes author, full title, place, publisher, date, size, paging, price (if information about price was supplied by publisher), and pressmark of the book in the Bibliothèque Nationale. The following supplements were published at irregular intervals and began at different dates: A, Périodiques; B, Gravures, estampes et photographies; C, Musique; D, Thèses; E, Atlas, cartes et plans; F, Publications officielles gouvernementales et administratives; G, Catalogues des ventes publiques. Special supplements were also issued from time to time. At the end of the year there was a general author and title index to the record of books and gifts, an alphabetical list of new periodicals, an index to musical works, and a table of illustrators. Coverage of these indexes varied somewhat from year to year.

2.pt.: The *Chronique* contained publishing news, postal and copyright information, legal and government notes, occasional historical articles, obituaries, lists of literary prizes, etc.

3.pt.: The *Annonces* section consisted of advertising pages with indexes as follows:

Les livres de la semaine, a classified list, which cumulated into *Les livres du mois,* also classified with indexes of authors and of titles. This, in turn, cumulated into the quarterly and semiannual indexes, *Les livres du trimestre* and *Les livres du semestre,* which were author and title lists rather than classified.

Les livres de l'année, which cumulated these indexes, was in three parts: (1) classified, (2) titles, and (3) authors. It included not only all the works listed in the *Annonces,* but also books listed in the *Bibliographie officielle* which did not appear in the *Annonces.*

Livres et matériel d'enseignement, consisting of publishers' announcements with annual indexes by author and by title under classified headings.

For a full description of the *Bibliographie* and all its parts *see* Malclès, *Les sources du travail bibliographique* 1:122–26 (AA487).

Merged with *Biblio* to form *Bibliographie de la France—Biblio.*
Z2165.B58

Lorenz, Otto Henri. Catalogue général de la librairie française, 1840–1925. Paris, Lorenz, 1867–1945. v.1–34. (Repr.: Nendeln, Liechtenstein, 1966–67)   **AA755**

Publisher varies.

Usually cited as *Lorenz.*

v.1–11, edited by Otto Lorenz; v.12–28, pt.2 by D. Jordell; v.28, pt.3–v.32, by Henri Stein; v.33–34, by the Service Bibliographique Hachette.

The standard French list for the 19th and early 20th centuries. Covers French publications by periods ranging from 3 years to 25 years, the volumes for each period consisting of: (1) a main author and anonymous title list containing full information, i.e., author's full name, full title of book, edition, place (if other than Paris), date, publisher, paging, size, price, and occasional brief notes; and (2) a subject list arranged by broad subjects, with briefer information. Includes books, pamphlets, some theses and annuals, but not periodicals, and lists some Belgian and Swiss publications. Special features are: (1) the inclusion of brief biographical notes about the authors whose works are listed; (2) the linking together of all entries for the same author by cross references from the later volumes to the earlier ones; (3) occasional brief notes which tell whether a book has been crowned by the French Academy; which refer, in case of reissues or later editions, to date of first edition; and which give, in case of books or pamphlets reprinted from periodicals, reference to volume or date of the periodical, etc. The information about original publication in periodicals is often very useful.
Z2161.L86

Quérard, Joseph Marie [and others]. La littérature française contemporaine, 1827–49 . . . Dictionnaire bibliographique . . . accompagné de biographies et de notes historiques et littéraires. Paris, Daguin, 1842–57. 6v. (Repr.: Paris, Maisonneuve, 1965)   **AA756**

A continuation of Quérard's *La France littéraire* (AA752) on the same general plan.

Title varies.
Z2161.Q41

Vicaire, Georges. Manuel de l'amateur de livres du XIXᵉ siècle, 1801–1893. Paris, Rouquette, 1894–1920. 8v.
AA757

v.1–7, A–Z, 1801–1893; v.8, Table des ouvrages cités.

Crowned by the French Academy.

An attempt to do for 19th-century French literature what Brunet's *Manuel* (AA111) does for general literature of an earlier period. Covers some of the same period as Lorenz (AA755), but with a selection of material, listing fewer titles than Lorenz but giving fuller information and annotations for those listed. Gives full titles and bibliographical notes, original price, and, often, prices realized at various auction sales.
Z2161.V62

Current

Bibliographie de la France—Biblio. Paris, Cercle de la Librairie, 1972–Juin 1979. Année 161–68ᴺᴼ·²⁶. Weekly.
AA758

Continued the *Bibliographie de la France* (AA754) and assumed its numbering. Originally the general plan of the publication in three parts continued as outlined above (AA754), but certain changes were effected in the make-up and frequency of portions of Pt.1, *Bibliographie officielle.* The weekly classed lists in the *Livres* section continued to cumulate monthly in a classed arrangement designated as *Les livres du mois.* In July 1979 the weekly *Livres* section was superseded by *Livres-Hebdo* (AA764), while from 1976 other sections had reverted to the earlier title as:

Bibliographie de la France. 1. partie. Bibliographie officielle. Jan. 1976– . Paris, Cercle de la Librairie, 1976– . Année 165– . Semimonthly.
AA759

Frequency has varied (originally weekly); now (1984) the yearly subscription includes 25 semimonthly issues of "Livres," 4 cumulative indexes, and 23 supplementary issues distributed as: I, Publications en série (12 issues and annual index); II, Publications officielles (6 issues and index); III, Musique (4 issues); and IV, Atlas, cartes et plans (1 issue).

The "Livres" section is a classed list according to the Universal Decimal Classification, and full cataloging information, price, and Bibliothèque Nationale shelf mark are given; separate author and title indexes in each issue cumulate quarterly and annually.

Librairie française, catalogue général des ouvrages en vente au 1. jan. 1930. Paris, Cercle de la Librairie, 1931. 3v.
AA760

Continued by compilations in the same form covering 1930–33, 1933–45, 1946–55, 1956–65.

Contents: v.1–2, Répertoire par auteurs; v.3, Répertoire par titres.

Compiled from the annual volumes of *Les livres de l'année* of the *Bibliographie de la France* (AA754). Lists books, new periodicals, publications of corporate bodies, and some documents. Gives for each book listed: author, title, paging, date, publisher, binding, illustration, format, price. Z2161.L69

——— Les livres de l'année, 1933–1938, 1946/48–1970. Annual. **AA761**

Not published 1939–45?

Cumulated the listings in the *Bibliographie de la France* (AA754) and was itself cumulated into the *Librairie française, catalogue général* (above).

Each volume is in three parts: pt.1, Classified by the main divisions of the decimal classification; pt.2, Titles; pt.3, Alphabetical lists of authors, illustrators, publishers, booksellers, etc.

Superseded by: Z2161.L69

Les livres de l'année—Biblio, 1971–79. Paris, Cercle de la Librairie, [1972–80]. Annual. **AA762**

Subtitle: Bibliographie générale des ouvrages parus en langue française.

Cumulates the listings in the *Bibliographie de la France—Biblio* (AA758), using the author-title-subject arrangement in dictionary form as in *Biblio* (AA753).

The volume for 1971 serves as the final cumulation for the monthly issues of *Biblio* as well as the annual cumulation of entries in the *Bibliographie de la France* (AA754). Z2161.L6952

Les livres disponibles, 1977– . [Paris], Cercle de la Librairie, 1977– . Annual. **AA763**

Also called *French books in print.*

Subtitle: La liste exhaustive des ouvrages disponibles publiés en langue française dans le monde. La liste des éditeurs et la liste des collections de langue française.

Originally issued in two parts: (1) Auteurs; (2) Titres; a subject volume arranged by Universal Decimal Classification was added with the 1978 edition.

Supersedes *Le catalogue de l'édition française* (éd. 1–5 publ. 1971–76). Includes books published in French regardless of place of publication. Excludes theses, pamphlets, periodicals, musical scores, and annuals of associations. The lists of publishers and distributors and of publishers' series appear in both volumes.

Tous les livres au format de poche: répertoire (Paris, Cercle de la Librairie, 1981– . Annual; formerly *Répertoire des livres au format de poche*) provides a record of French popular publications available in pocket (paperback) format.

Livres-hebdo. no.1– , Sept.4, 1979– . [Paris, Éditions Professionelles du Livre], 1979– . Weekly. **AA764**

Supersedes the weekly "Chronique" and "Annonces" sections of *Bibliographie de la France—Biblio* (covers originally carried the designation "Bibliographie de la France. Bulletin du livre"). Includes a monthly supplement, *Les livres du mois,* and a quarterly supplement, *Trois mois de nouveautés* (formerly *Les livres du trimestre*), which cumulate the classed lists from the "Livres" sections of the weekly issues and add author and title indexes.

The publication has evolved as a kind of French equivalent of *Publishers' weekly,* with each issue usually in three sections: (1) publishers' announcements and advertisements, and notes on literary prizes and promotions; (2) a magazine section devoted to news notes and articles on the book trade, libraries, etc.; and (3) a classed

list of new publications arranged by Universal Decimal Classification and which cumulates as noted above. Z2165.L8

Un an de nouveautés, 1980– . Paris, Éditions Professionnelles du Livre, 1981– . Annual. (Répertoires livres hebdo) **AA765**

Cumulates the quarterly and semiannual listings in the "Répertoires livres hebdo" series, which in turn supersede the monthly "Livres du mois" supplement to *Livres-hebdo* (above). Serves as a continuation of the annual cumulation of *Bibliographie de la France —Biblio* which covers through 1979. Classified arrangement with author and title indexes.

Regional

❖Many regional bibliographies, for provinces, departments, towns, etc., must often be used for local publications not included in the general bibliographies listed above. Local bibliographies are listed freely in the *Répertoire bibliographique de l'histoire de France* (DC136). For lists of older publications *see* Stein's *Manuel,* p.501–7 (AA12), and the article *"Bibliographie"* in *La grande encyclopédie* 6:637–38 (AC37).

Gambia

National bibliography of the Gambia. v.1, no.1– , Jan./Dec. 1977– . Banjul, National Library of the Gambia, 1978– . Annual. **AA766**

Frequency varies.

Attempts to list all new books and pamphlets published in the Gambia, together with books about the Gambia and Gambians published elsewhere. Also lists first issues of new serials and first issue of a serial under a new title. Arranged by Dewey Decimal Classification, with index of authors, editors, titles, and series.

Germany
Early

Borchling, Conrad and **Claussen, Bruno.** Niederdeutsche Bibliographie; Gesamtverzeichnis der niederdeutschen Drucke bis zum Jahre 1800. . . . Neumünster, Karl Wachholst, 1931–36. 2v. **AA767**

v.1, 1473–1600; v.2, 1601–1800; Nachträge, 1481–1800; Ergänzungen u. Verbesserungen, col.1871–91; Indexes (of places, printers, names, first lines, catchwords, etc.), col.1893–2018; Letze Nachträge u. Verbesserungen, col.2019–20.

Arranged chronologically; lists more than 4,700 items, described in detail with line-by-line transcription and with some location of copies. Z2235.B72

British Museum. Dept. of Printed Books. Short-title catalogue of books printed in the German-speaking countries and German books printed in other countries from 1455 to 1600 now in the British Museum. London, Trustees, 1962. 1224p. **AA768**

One of a series of short-title catalogs, similar in scope and arrangement. Arranged alphabetically by author and anonymous title, with some collective headings, as used in the Museum's *General catalogue of printed books* (AA132), followed by an index of publishers, with titles listed chronologically under publisher. Z2222.B73

Panzer, Georg Wolfgang Franz. Annalen der ältern deutschen Litteratur. . . . Nürnberg, Grattenauer, 1788–1805. 2v. **AA769**

Contents: v.1, to 1520; v.2, 1521–26; Zusätze. . . . Leipzig, Hempel, 1802. 198p. (Suppl. to v.1)

Supplemented by Joseph Heller in *Serapeum*, 4. Jahrg. (1843), p.299–303, 6. Jahrg. (1845), p.312–20, 327–33; and by E. O. Weller's *Repertorium typographicum. Die deutsche Literatur im ersten Viertel des sechzehnten Jahrhunderts.* . . . Nördlingen, 1864 (added title page: George Wolfgang Panzers Annalen der älteren deutschen Literatur, MD–MDXXVI).

Now largely superseded by later compilations of incunabula, e.g., British Museum. *Catalogue of books printed in the XVth century* . . . pts.2–3 (AA276). Z2222.P19

Verzeichnis der im deutschen Sprachbereich erschienenen Drucke des XVI. Jahrhunderts. VD 16. Hrsg. von der Staatsbibliothek in München in Verbindung mit der Herzog August Bibliothek in Wolfenbüttel. Stuttgart, Hiersemann, 1983–84. Abt.I, Bd.1–3. (In progress) **AA770**

Redaktion: Irmgard Bezzel.

Introductory matter in German, English, and French.

Contents: Abt.I, Verfasser, Körperschaften, Anonyma. Bd.1–3, A–Carl.

A catalog of "books printed between 1501 and 1600 in whatever language in the German-speaking areas (Germany, Austria and German-speaking parts of Switzerland and Alsace)."—*Pref.* Reproduces the catalog cards (usually prepared from the book in hand, but sometimes supplied from printed sources or by contributing libraries); library locations are given. To be in some 40 volumes; in addition to the section for authors, corporate bodies and anonyma, there is to be a section for editors, commentators, translators, and literary contributors, and a final section of entries for places of printing, printers, and publishers. Z1014.V47

18th and 19th centuries

❖The 18th and 19th centuries are well covered by series of catalogs published by three German bookdealers: Heinsius, beginning with 1700; Kayser with 1750; and Hinrichs with 1850, thus overlapping each other but together providing a continuous record from 1700 to 1910, when the *Deutsches Bücherverzeichnis* superseded and carried on Kayser and Hinrichs, following the general bibliographical practices of Kayser. A cumulation of these and related bibliographies of the period have been published as *Gesamtverzeichnis des deutschaprachigen Schrifttums* (AA771).

There are subject indexes to Kayser covering 1750–1832 and 1891–1910, and Georg (AA776) provides a subject approach from 1883 to 1912, but there are no cumulated subject indexes for 1700–50 or 1833–82.

Gesamtverzeichnis des deutschsprachigen Schrifttums (GV); 1700–1910. München, K. G. Saur, 1979–85. v.1–130. (In progress) **AA771**

"Bearb. unter der Leitung von Peter Geils und Willi Gorzny; bibliographische und redaktionelle Beratung: Hans Popst und Rainer Schöller."—*t.p.*

Contents: v.1–130, A–Schult.

Forms a chronological predecessor to "GV 1911–1965" (AA777) and is similarly compiled: i.e., entries from existing printed bibliographies and book catalogs have been interfiled and photographically reproduced, not reset. Thus, the main entries from some 178 works published in about 560 volumes are here alphabetically arranged in a single alphabet. Among the better-known sets included are Heinsius (1700–1892; AA772), Kayser (1750–1910; AA773) and Hinrichs (1851–1912; AA774), but numerous dissertation lists and specialized bibliographies are also represented. Z2221.G469

Heinsius, Wilhelm. Allgemeines Bücher-Lexikon, oder vollständiges alphabetisches Verzeichniss der von 1700 bis zu Ende 1892 erschienenen Bücher. . . . Leipzig, Brockhaus, 1812–94. 19v. (Repr.: Graz, Akademische Druck, 1963) **AA772**

No more published. Publisher varies.

Lists books, pamphlets, and periodicals alphabetically by author or catchword title in chronological periods: 1700–1810 in 4v.; thereafter to 1892 in volumes, usually but not always, quinquennial.

Gives author, title, paging, place, publisher, date, and price. Through 1867, prices are given in thalers and neugroschen, after 1867 in marks and pfennigs.

Supplementary lists: 1700–1827, Romane, Schauspiele; 1868–92, Karten und Pläne. Z2221.H47

Kayser, Christian Gottlob. Vollständiges Bücher-Lexikon, 1750–1910. Leipzig, Tauchnitz, 1834–1911. 36v. (Repr.: Graz, Akademische Druck, 1961–62) **AA773**

No more published. Publisher varies.

1750–1832 in 6v. Continued to 1910 by volumes published at irregular intervals.

Lists books, pamphlets, periodicals, etc., in an author list with some title entries, giving, for each book listed, author, title, place, publisher, date, volumes, paging, series, prices of different editions, etc. Entry is generally under the author's name, but works having such titles as Wörterbuch, Lexikon, Jahresverzeichnis, etc., are entered under title rather than compiler, and under that entry are alphabetized by main subject word in title, the alphabetizing word being indicated by a different type or spacing. Before 1870, prices were given in thalers and neugroschen, after that date in marks and pfennigs. Includes some Austrian and Swiss publications.

———— ———— Sachregister. Leipzig, Schumann, 1838. 511p.

Indexes v.1–6, 1750–1832.

———— ———— Sach- und Schlagwortregister, 1891–1910. Leipzig, Tauchnitz, 1896–1912. 5v.

Each index covers two volumes of the main work, as follows: v.27–28, 1891–94; v.29–30, 1895–98; v.31–32, 1899–1902; v.33–34, 1903–1906; v.35–36, 1907–10. Z2221.K23

Hinrichs, *firm, publishers, Leipzig.* Fünfjahrs-Katalog der im deutschen Buchhandel erschienenen Bücher, Zeitschriften, Landkarten, etc.; Titelverzeichnis und Sachregister, 1851–1912. Leipzig, Hinrichs, 1857–1913. 13v. **AA774**

Title varies.

5-year cumulations of *Hinrichs' Halbjahrs-Katalog* (AA779) with additions and corrections. No more published. Z2221.H658

Thelert, Gustav. Supplement zu Heinsius', Hinrichs' und Kaysers Bücher-Lexikon. . . . Grossenhain, Baumert, 1893. 405p. **AA775**

Subtitle: Verzeichniss einer Anzahl Schriften, welche seit der Mitte des neunzehnten Jahrhunderts in Deutschland erschienen, in den gennannten Katalogen aber garnicht oder fehlerhaft aufgeführt sind; mit bibliographischen Bemerkungen. Z2221.T38

Georg, Karl [and others]. Schlagwort-Katalog; Verzeichnis der . . . Bücher und Landkarten in sachlicher Anordnung, 1883–1912. Hannover, 1889–1913. 7v. **AA776**

Subtitle varies; publisher varies.

v.1, 1883–87; v.2, 1888–92; v.3, 1893–97; v.4, 1898–1902; v.5, 1903–1907; v.6, 1908–10; v.7, 1910–12.

Lists, under subject and form headings, works published during these periods. Z2221.G34

20th century

❖Since World War II there have been two bibliographic centers in Germany: the *Deutsche Bücherei* in Leipzig, in East Germany; and the *Deutsche Bibliothek* in Frankfurt am Main, in West Germany. Each publishes a series of bibliographies which follow much the same patterns, i.e., a weekly, a semiannual (or annual), and a quinquennial cumulation. Each attempts to list all books published in both parts of Germany and German books published elsewhere. There is, thus, much duplication, but some entries will be found listed in one work and not in the other.

The *Deutsches Bücherverzeichnis* (AA782), published in Leipzig, continues in the same form the earlier series of the same title which was a continuation of Kayser (AA773).

Gesamtverzeichnis des deutschsprachigen Schrifttums (GV); 1911–1965. Hrsg. von Reinhard Oberschelp; bearb. unter der Leitung von Willi Gorzny, mit einem Geleitwort von Wilhelm Totok. München, Verlag Dokumentation, 1976–81. 150v. **AA777**

Represents a cumulation and integration of the main entries from some fifteen series of German-language national bibliographies and dissertation lists. (Entries from the original publications have been interfiled and photographed, not re-set.) Citations are drawn from the *Deutsches Bücherverzeichnis* (AA782), *Deutsche Bibliographie* (AA786), *Deutsche Nationalbibliographie* (AA778), and from the various German, Austrian, and Swiss dissertation lists. These publications are not, however, fully superseded since the subject indexes are not similarly cumulated and integrated, and all portions of some series are not represented in the new work. Z2221.G47

Current

Leipzig

Deutsche Nationalbibliographie. Reihe A, Reihe B. Leipzig, Börsenverein der Deutschen Buchhändler, 1931– . **AA778**

Subtitle varies.
Continues, with changed title and scope, the *Wöchentliches Verzeichnis*, 1842–1930.
Reihe A, *Neuerscheinungen des Buchhandels* (books in the book trade), weekly; Reihe B, *Neuerscheinungen ausserhalb des Buchhandels* (books outside the book trade, e.g., dissertations, society publications), monthly (formerly semimonthly).
Both sections are classified under broad subject groupings with author, title and catchword index in each issue. Separate quarterly indexes (*Vierteljahrsregister*) for each Reihe. Includes books, periodicals, maps, but not music.
Beginning 1968, "Dissertationen und Habilitationsschriften" are listed in Reihe C. Z2221.H67

———— Ergänzung, 1–2. Leipzig, Börsenverein der Deutschen Buchhändler, 1949. 2v.

Contents: 1, Verzeichnis der Schriften, die 1933–1945 nicht angezeigt werden durften; 2, Verzeichnis der Schriften, die infolge von Kriegseinwirkungen vor dem 8. Mai 1945 nicht angezeigt werden konnten. Z2221.H6712

Halbjahrsverzeichnis der im deutschen Buchhandel erschienenen Bücher, Zeitschriften und Landkarten, mit Voranzeigen von Neuigkeiten, Verlags– und Preisänderungen. Leipzig, Börsenverein der Deutschen Buchhändler, 1798–1944. v.1–292. **AA779**

Title varies. Until 1915 was *Hinrichs' Halbjahrs-Katalog*.
Ceased publication. Continued by: Z2221.H66

Jahresverzeichnis des deutschen Schrifttums, 1945/46–67, bearb. und hrsg. von der Deutschen Bücherei und dem Börsenverein der Deutschen Buchhändler zu Leipzig. Leipzig, Börsenverein, 1948–74. Jahrg.164–70. **AA780**

An annual cumulation of Reihe A and B of the *Deutsche Nationalbibliographie* (AA778).
Each year in two sections: I, *Titelverzeichnis,* listing works by author or catchword title; II, *Stich- und Schlagwortregister,* listing works under catchword title and subject.
Cumulated into the *Deutsches Bücherverzeichnis* (AA782). Superseded by: Z2221.J26

Jahresverzeichnis der Verlagsschriften . . . Jahrg. 171–73. Leipzig, VEB Verlag für Buch- und Bibliothekswesen, 1972–78. **AA781**

Supersedes *Jahresverzeichnis des deutschen Schrifttums* and continues its numbering and pattern of publication. It, in turn, cumulated into the *Deutsches Bücherverzeichnis.*
Full title: Jahresverzeichnis der Verlagsschriften und einer Auswahl der ausserhalb des Buchhandels erschienenen Veröffentlich-

ungen der DDR, der BRD und Westberlins sowie der deutschsprachigen Werke anderer Länder.
Publication was suspended 1971–80 (1981–83 not yet published?); beginning with 1984 coverage, to be superseded by an annual index to Reihe A of the *Deutsche Nationalbibliographie.*
Z2221.J26

Deutsches Bücherverzeichnis; eine Zusammenstellung der im deutschen Buchhandel erschienenen Bücher, Zeitschriften und Landkarten. Nebst Stich- und Schlagwortregister. Bearb. von der Bibliographischen Abteilung des Börsenvereins der Deutschen Buchhändler zu Leipzig, 1911– . Leipzig, VEB Verlag für Buch- und Bibliothekswesen, 1915– . v.1– . **AA782**

Subtitle varies; publisher varies. Issued in parts.
5-year cumulations, claiming to include all titles listed in the *Halbjahrsverzeichnis* and the *Jahresverzeichnis.* Each period is in two sections: (1) *Titelverzeichnis* (listing works by author and anonymous title); (2) *Stich- und Schlagwortregister* (the subject index). The period 1941–50 is covered in one listing and includes works previously omitted because of Nazi proscription or war conditions.
A continuation of Hinrichs and Kayser, compiled on the same general plan as Kayser. Lists German-language publications of the book trade in Germany, Austria, and Switzerland; some works outside the book trade (but not theses or musical texts, as these have bibliographies of their own); the more important official publications; and books in other languages published in Germany. Includes books, periodicals, and maps.
5-year cumulations have appeared through 1966–70 (i.e., through v.58 of the series). No 5-year cumulations will be published for the 1971–80 period. Instead, there will be four cumulations covering 1971–73, 1974–75, 1976–77, and 1978–80. Substantial portions of the 1971–73 and 1974–75 cumulations have been published as of the end of 1984. 5-year cumulations are to resume for the period 1981–85. Z2221.K25

Frankfurt am Main

Deutsche Bibliographie. Wöchentliches Verzeichnis. Frankfurt a. M., Buchhändler-Vereinigung GmbH, 1947– . Weekly. **AA783**

Comp. by the Deutsche Bibliothek, Frankfurt a. M. From 1947 to 1952 was entitled *Bibliographie der deutschen Bibliothek.*
Originally attempted to include a record of all books published in the German language either in Germany or in other countries. Includes prices.
Arrangement has varied slightly; now classified under broad subject groupings, with author, title, subject index.
Beginning with 1965 issues, the bibliography appears in three series: *Reihe A* lists publications available in the book trade (including atlases, but not maps) and is a weekly with indexes cumulating monthly and quarterly (The listings cumulate semiannually in the *Halbjahres-Verzeichnis,* AA785, and quinquennially in the *Deutsche Bibliographie,* AA786.); *Reihe B,* appearing semimonthly with cumulated annual index, lists publications not in the book trade, and selected titles from *Reihe B* appear in the regular semiannual and 5-year lists; *Reihe C,* quarterly, covers maps. Annual indexes for Reihen B and C were published through 1980; beginning 1981, the listings are cumulated in the *Halbjahres-Verzeichnis* and the *Fünfjahres-Verzeichnis.* For information on forthcoming books *see* AA784.
Since Jan. 6, 1966, the bibliography has been produced by a computer-typesetting system with indexes automatically prepared and cumulated on the basis noted above.
Cumulated into AA785. Z2221.F75

Deutsche Bibliographie. Wöchentliches Verzeichnis. Neuerscheinungen Sofortdienst (CIP). Amtsblatt der Deutschen Bibliothek. Frankfurt a. M., Buchhändler-Vereinigung, 1975– . Weekly, with monthly and quarterly cumulations. **AA784**

Began with July 1975.
A supplement to *Reihe A* (but also available on separate subscrip-

tion) giving information on forthcoming books. Weekly issues follow a classed arrangement, the cumulations are main entry listings with *see* references from titles, editors, etc. Entries are based on information supplied for "cataloging-in-publication," thus providing advance listings for persons involved in book selection. Full bibliographic information derived from examination of the book itself is provided in Reihe A of the *Bibliographie* following publication.

Deutsche Bibliographie; Halbjahres-Verzeichnis. Frankfurt a. M., Buchhändler-Vereinigung GmbH, 1951– . Semiannual.   **AA785**

1951–52 had title: *Bibliographie der deutschen Bibliothek; Halbjahres Verzeichnis.*

Subtitle has varied; now reads: Verzeichnis aller im Wöchentlichen Verzeichnis, angezeigten deutschen und im Ausland erscheinen den deutschsprachigen Publikationen.

This semiannual cumulation of the *Wöchentliches Verzeichnis* is in two parts: pt.1, Titelverzeichnis; pt.2, Stich- und Schlagwortregister.
Z2221.F73

Deutsche Bibliographie; Fünfjahres-Verzeichnis. Bücher und Karten. Bibliographie aller in Deutschland erschienenen Veröffentlichungen und der in Österreich und der Schweiz im Buchhandel erschienenen deutschsprachigen Publikationen sowie der deutschsprachigen Veröffentlichungen anderer Länder, 1945/50– . Frankfurt a. M., Buchhändler-Vereinigung, 1952– . Quinquennial.   **AA786**

Represents 5-year cumulations of the various sections of the *Deutsche Bibliographie*. For the 1945–65 period, attempted to list all publications for Germany; German-language trade books published in Austria and Switzerland; and various German-language publications of other countries. Periodicals and annuals were omitted during the 1956–65 period; for the 1966–75 period only a selection of the nontrade publications from Reihe B of the *Deutsche Bibliographie,* and no listings for maps were included. The 1976–80 cumulation includes only the trade publications found in Reihe A. Beginning 1981, the 5-year cumulation is to include all listings from Reihen A, B and C.

For periodicals *see Deutsche Bibliographie: Zeitschriften* (AE75).

Each chronological period is in two parts: T.1, Alphabetisches Titelverzeichnis (alphabetical listing by author and anonymous title); T.2, Stich- und Schlagwortregister (the subject listing).
Z2221.D45

Verfasser- und Stichwortregister zu Deutsche Bibliographie, wöchentliches Verzeichnis; Österreichische Bibliographie; Das schweizer Buch, Ausg. A, Januar 1953–65. Frankfurt a. M., Buchhändler-Vereinigung GmbH, 1953–66. Monthly.   **AA787**

Comp. by the Deutsche Bibliothek, Frankfurt a. M.

From 1953 to June 1960 had title: *Verfasser- und Sachregister.*

An author and catchword-title index to three current national bibliographies—German, Austrian, and Swiss.

Entries are arranged in a single alphabet, with symbols to indicate the Austrian and Swiss items. No cumulations of the monthly issues. Quarterly 1965 only.

Ceased publication.

Verzeichnis lieferbarer Bücher, 1971/72– . Frankfurt am Main, Verlag der Buchhändler-Vereinigung GmbH, 1971– . Biennial.   **AA788**

Ed.5 (1975/76)– have title also in English: *German books in print.* On spine: VLB.

Originally published in two parts per year: "Bücherverzeichnis im Autorenalphabet" and "Titelregister mit Verweisung auf den Autor." Now issued in a single alphabetical sequence with subtitle: Bücherverzeichnis im Autorenalphabet kumuliert mit Titel- und Stichwortregister mit Verweisung auf den Autor. Includes a list of publishers, with addresses. A spring supplement is included in the subscription price, and a separate *ISBN-Register* is also available. Subject approach to the listings is provided by: Z2221.V47

Verzeichnis lieferbarer Bücher: Schlagwort-Verzeichnis. Subject guide to German books in print. 1978/79– . Frankfurt

am Main, Verlag der Buchhändler Vereinigung GmbH, 1979– .   **AA789**

A subject arrangement of the items in the *VLB* (above). A list of headings used now precedes the main text.

WerWasWo? im Taschenbuch; Gesamtverzeichnis aller Taschenbücher (München, Rossipaul, 1981– . Annual) provides an in-print record for German popular publications in pocket format.

Ghana

Ghana national bibliography, 1965– . Accra, Ghana Lib. Board, 1968– . Annual.   **AA790**

Intended as a current national bibliography for the country; includes official publications and, beginning 1966, periodical articles and theses. There is a separate section for publications in the various Ghanian languages (e.g., Fante, Ewe, Twi, Ga). Inasmuch as books about Ghana published elsewhere are also included, the bibliography will serve to supplement A. F. Johnson's *Bibliography of Ghana, 1930–1961* (DD135).   Z3785.G45

Great Britain

British Museum. Dept. of Printed Books. General catalogue of printed books. Photolithographic edition to 1955. London, 1959–66. 263v.   **AA791**

The possession of the copyright privilege helps to make this the most comprehensive collection of British materials in existence, and therefore it serves as an extensive national bibliography. For full information on the *Catalogue* and its supplements *see* AA132.

Lowndes, William Thomas. Bibliographer's manual of English literature, containing an account of rare, curious, and useful books, published in or relating to Great Britain and Ireland, from the invention of printing. . . . New ed. rev., corr., and enl. by H. G. Bohn. London, Bell, 1857–64. 6v. in 11. (Repr.: Detroit, Gale, 1967. 8v.)   **AA792**

Contents: v.1–5 (in 10 pts.), A–Z; v.6, Appendix containing lists of publications of societies and printing clubs, books issued by private presses, lists of series, etc.

Arranged alphabetically by author, with many title and catchword entries. Lists about 50,000 works, giving for each: author, title, place, date, size, with occasional notes as to rarity, value, editions, reprints, etc., and often records of prices at various 19th-century sales. While the prices shown are now only of historical interest, and there are some inaccuracies, the work remains useful for other information. The title and catchword entries are sometimes helpful in verifying citations not easily located in other catalogs.
Z2001.L92

Watt, Robert. Bibliotheca britannica; or, A general index to British and foreign literature. Edinburgh, Constable, 1824. 4v.   **AA793**

v.1–2, Author list, arranged alphabetically, with author's full name and dates, very brief biographical data, and for each book brief information which generally includes title, date, size, number of volumes; v.3–4, An alphabetical subject list, serving as an index to the author volumes, giving for each book its date and brief title, and referring to the section of the author list (indicated by number and letter) where somewhat fuller information can be found. Anonymous titles are listed in this section.

Often useful for material not given in more modern catalogs, but sometimes inaccurate and so must be used with some caution.
Z2001.W34

Corns, Albert Reginald and **Sparke, Archibald.** A bibliography of unfinished books in the English language, with annotations. London, Quaritch, 1915. 255p. (Repr.: Detroit, Gale, 1968)   **AA794**

An alphabetical list of works which began publication but were never finished.   Z1025.C7

Before 1640

Allison, Antony Francis and **Goldsmith, V. F.** Titles of English books (and of foreign books printed in England); an alphabetical finding-list by title of books published under the author's name, pseudonym or initials. [Folkestone, Eng.], Dawson; Hamden, Conn., Archon Books, [1976–77]. 2v. **AA795**

Contents: v.1, 1475–1640; v.2, 1641–1700.

v.1 offers a title approach to Pollard and Redgrave's *Short-title catalogue... 1475–1640* (AA801), including some references to the new edition now in progress. v.2 provides a similar approach to Wing's *Short-title catalogue* (AA818).

A review of v.1 by Paul Morgan (*TLS* 9-24-76, p.1221) expresses reservations about the completeness of the work and the form of entry chosen for many titles. Z2001.A44

Bibliographical Society, London. Hand-lists of books printed by London printers, 1501–1556, by E. G. Duff, W. W. Greg [and others]. London, Soc., 1913. 4 pts. in 1v. il., facsims. **AA796**

Lists of the books printed by 89 printers up to the grant of a charter to the Stationers' Company in 1557. Publication in parts began in 1895 and sections have no continuous paging, thus allowing the completed work to be bound either alphabetically by printers' names or chronologically by their dates. Prepared (and sold only to members of the Society) as a basis for further work in the English bibliography of the period. Z152.L8B5

British Museum. Dept. of Printed Books. Catalogue of books in the library of the British Museum printed in England, Scotland, and Ireland, and of books in English printed abroad to the year 1640. London, Trustees, 1884. 3v. **AA797**

Alphabetically arranged, with index by title, subject, and form, e.g., plays, poems, etc., and an index of printers, booksellers, and stationers. Z2002.B86

Cambridge. University. Library. Early English printed books in the University Library, 1475–1640. Cambridge, Univ. Pr., 1900–1907. 4v. **AA798**

v.1, 1475–1500, Caxton to F. Kingston; v.2, 1501–1640, E. Mattes to R. Marriot and English provincial presses; v.3, Scottish, Irish, and foreign presses, with addenda; v.4, Indexes.

Includes 8,083 titles, arranged by presses, with full indexes of authors and titles, printers and stationers, engravers and painters, towns, portraits, music. Z2002.C17

London. Stationers' Company. A transcript of the registers of the Company of Stationers of London, 1554–1640, ed. by Edward Arber. London, priv. pr., 1875–77; Birmingham, 1894. 5v. **AA799**

In chronological order with no indexes, these are transcripts of the manuscript registers. Difficult to use and sometimes inaccurate. For the most part superseded by Pollard and Redgrave, *Short-title catalogue* (AA801). Z2002.S79

Greg, *Sir* **Walter Wilson,** ed. A companion to Arber. Oxford, Clarendon Pr., 1967. 451p. **AA800**

Subtitle: Being a calendar of documents in Edward Arber's *Transcript of the registers of the Company of Stationers of London, 1554–1640;* with text and calendar of supplementary documents.

A chronological calendar of the documents and illustrative matter interpolated into Arber's *Transcript* (AA799), plus additional, similar documents not in Arber. Indexed. Z151.3.G68

Pollard, Alfred William and **Redgrave, G. R.** A short-title catalogue of books printed in England, Scotland and Ireland, and of English books printed abroad, 1475–1640; comp. ... with the help of G. F. Barwick ... and others. London, Bibliographical Soc., 1926. 609p. (Repr.: Oxford, Univ. Pr., 1946) **AA801**

Frequently cited as *STC.*

The most comprehensive record of English books for this period including about 26,500 editions (26,143 numbers, with several hundred items inserted with subnumbers). Arranged alphabetically by author and other main entries; gives, for each item, author, brief title, size, printer, date, reference to entry of the book in the Stationers' registers, and indication of libraries possessing copies. This last important feature aims to record all known copies of very rare items and, in the case of commoner books, a selection in representative British and American libraries and collections. The total number of libraries referred to is 148 (133 British, 15 American).

A new edition has begun to appear as: Z2002.P77

——— ——— 2d ed., rev. & enl., begun by W. A. Jackson & F. S. Ferguson, completed by Katharine F. Pantzer. London, Bibliographical Society, 1976– . v.2– . (In progress) **AA802**

Contents: v.2, I–Z.

The first published part of the new edition of this important catalog. "The earlier completion of volume 2 is the result of Miss Pantzer's taking over the work of final revision on the death of William A. Jackson in 1964 at the letter R. The later letters of the alphabet represented a later stage in Jackson's own revision, and Miss Pantzer has felt that this, and the fact that she has personally overseen all these parts of the work, enable her and the Society to lay this volume before the public as having reached as definitive a stage as is possible in a work of this nature."—*Pref.*

v.1, A–H, was announced for publication in early 1986, with a third volume containing an index of printers and booksellers, as well as additions and corrections, to follow. Z2002.P77

Bishop, William Warner. A checklist of American copies of "Short-title catalogue" books. 2d ed. Ann Arbor, Univ. of Michigan Pr., 1950. 203p. **AA803**

Compiled as a convenient guide to the location of *STC* titles in American libraries, this is a record of *STC* numbers with indication of holdings in some 110 libraries and collections. The 2d ed. includes corrections and additions to the list in the first edition, published 1944, and records the holdings of about ten more libraries. Z2002.P772B5

Henry E. Huntington Library and Art Gallery, San Marino, Calif. Huntington Library supplement to the record of its books in the Short title catalogue ... comp. by C. K. Edmonds. Cambridge, Harvard Univ. Pr., 1933. 152p. (Huntington Library Bull. Oct. 1933, p.1–152) **AA804**

Contains two lists: (1) short-title list of books included in the *STC* of which the Huntington copies are either unrecorded or recorded incorrectly, and (2) a list, with full cataloging information, of books or editions within the period not recorded in the *STC.* Z733.S24B4

Morrison, Paul Guerrant. Index of printers, publishers, and booksellers in A. W. Pollard and G. R. Redgrave, A short-title catalogue. ... Charlottesville, Bibliographical Soc. of the Univ. of Virginia, 1950. 82p. **AA805**

Z2002.P77

Newberry Library, Chicago. English books and books printed in England before 1641 in the Newberry Library; a supplement to the record in the Short title catalogue, comp. by Gertrude L. Woodward. Chicago, 1939. 118p. **AA806**

Z2012.N531

Ramage, David. A finding-list of English books to 1640 in libraries in the British Isles (excluding the national libraries and the libraries of Oxford and Cambridge). Based on the numbers in Pollard and Redgrave's Short-title catalogue. ... Durham, Eng., Council of the Durham Colleges, 1958. 101p. **AA807**

"A project of the Standing Conference of National and University Libraries."—*title page.*

Gives additional locations for some 14,000 *STC* items, arranged by *STC* number, plus a supplementary list of titles not in *STC.* Z2002.P772R3

Shaaber, Matthias Adam. Check-list of works of British authors printed abroad, in languages other than English, to 1641. N.Y., Bibliographical Soc. of America, 1975. 168p. **AA808**

"British authors" are here defined as "(1) all writers born in the British Isles, including those who spent most of their lives abroad, (2) all writers born elsewhere who spent considerable parts of their mature lives in the British Isles."—*Pref.* Anonymous works are included if there is "direct evidence" or a consensus of opinion that they are of British origin." Locates copies. Z1012.S49

17th and 18th centuries

Arber, Edward. Term catalogues, 1668–1709 A.D. with a number for Easter term, 1711 A.D. London, Arber; N.Y., Dodd, 1903–1906. 3v. (Repr.: N.Y., Johnson, 1965) **AA809**

Subtitle: A contemporary bibliography of English literature in the reigns of Charles II, James II, William and Mary, and Anne; edited from the very rare quarterly lists of new books . . . issued by the booksellers of London.

Copies of contemporary records arranged chronologically, with indexes by titles, names, and subjects in each volume. Z2002.A31

Bibliotheca annua: or, The annual catalogue for the year, 1699– [March 25, 1704]. London, J. Nutt, 1700–1703. no.1–4. (Repr.: London, Gregg, 1964) **AA810**

Subtitle [varies slightly]: Being an exact catalogue of all English and Latin books, printed in England from January, 169 ⁸₉, to [March 25, 1704]. To which is added the titles of French books imported within the said time; as also most of the prizes [*sic*] that they are generally sold for.

Classified annual catalogs, with indexes for some years, and for these years the work is easier to use than the *Term catalogues* (AA809). Titles are quite full, and include edition, publisher, and price.

British Museum. Dept. of Printed Books. Thomason Collection. Catalogue of the pamphlets, books, newspapers, and manuscripts relating to the Civil War, the Commonwealth, and Restoration, collected by George Thomason, 1640–1661. London, Trustees, 1908. 2v. **AA811**

Running title: The Thomason tracts.

A very rich collection for this period, arranged chronologically with author, anonymous title, and subject index. Newspapers, 1641–43, listed in v.2, p.371–440. Z2018.B85

Cameron, William James and **Carroll, Diana J.** Short title catalogue of books printed in the British Isles, the British Colonies and the United States of America and of English books printed elsewhere, 1701–1800, held in the libraries of the Australian Capital Territory. Canberra, Nat. Lib. of Australia, 1966–70. 3v. **AA812**

A union list of 18th-century books in Australian libraries. v.3 is a supplement edited by Ivan Page. Z2002.C23

Clough, Eric A. A short-title catalogue arranged geographically of books printed and distributed by printers, publishers and booksellers in the English provincial towns and in Scotland and Ireland up to and including the year 1700. London, Lib. Assoc., 1969. 119p. **AA813**

Arranged by city. Based on Pollard and Redgrave's *Short-title catalogue . . . 1475–1640* (AA801) and Wing's *Short-title catalogue, 1641–1700* (AA818). Designed to complement H. G. Aldis's *List of books printed in Scotland before 1700* (AA1068), E. R. McC. Dix's *Catalogue of early Dublin-printed books, 1601–1700* (AA893), and Falconer Madan's *Oxford books* (Oxford, 1895–1931); it therefore omits items appearing in those lists. Z2002.C62

Eighteenth-century British books: an author union catalogue extracted from the British Museum general catalogue of printed books, the catalogues of the Bodleian Library, and

of the University Library, Cambridge. By F. J. G. Robinson [et al.]. Folkestone, Eng., Dawson, 1981. 5v. **AA814**

It is generally agreed that this compilation was a seriously misguided effort (*see* reviews in *The book collector*, Autumn 1981, p.413; the *TLS*, Dec. 11, 1981, p.1450; and *The library*, Dec. 1982, p.453); it is mentioned here to avoid possible confusion with the ongoing Eighteenth Century Short Title Catalogue project, records of which are currently available online through the RLIN network and which should eventually become available in paper or microform. Full texts of the books represented in the latter file are being reproduced on microfilm in a series entitled *The eighteenth century* [a microfilm collection based on the Eighteenth century short title catalog (ESTC)] (Woodbridge, Conn., Research Pubns., 1983–). Z1016.E36

London. Guildhall Library. A list of books printed in the British Isles and of English books printed abroad before 1701 in Guildhall Library. [London], Corporation of London, 1966–67. 2 pts. **AA815**

Contents: pt.1, A–K; pt.2, L–Z, with addenda and concordance.

More than 6,500 items. pt.2 includes a table of *Short-title catalogue* and Wing numbers with the corresponding Guildhall Library entry number. Z2002.L62

London catalogue of books. . . . **AA816**

Bibliographies with this title, published first by Bent and later by Hodgson, were issued covering, with considerable duplication of years, books published in Great Britain from 1700 to 1855. The 19th-century volumes formed one of the sources from which the 1801–36 and 1835–63 volumes of the *English catalogue* (AA825) were compiled and for ordinary purposes are therefore not often needed; but a library having the 18th-century volumes will still use them for material not included in Watt (AA793) or Lowndes (AA792).

For a record of editions published *see* Adolf Growoll, *Three centuries of English booktrade bibliography*. N.Y., Dibdin Club, 1903. 195p. Z2001.E5

London. Stationers' Company. Transcript of the registers of the worshipful Company of Stationers; from 1640–1708 A.D. London, priv. pr., 1913–14. 3v. **AA817**

Ed. by G. E. Briscoe Eyre. Entries transcribed by H. R. Plomer. Z2002.L653

Wing, Donald Goddard. Short-title catalogue of books printed in England, Scotland, Ireland, Wales, and British America and of English books printed in other countries, 1641–1700. N.Y., pr. for the Index Society by the Columbia Univ. Pr., 1945–51. 3v. **AA818**

Published as a continuation of Pollard and Redgrave's *Short-title catalogue . . . 1475–1640* (AA801). Items are located in more than 200 libraries; relatively common books are given five locations in Great Britain and five in the United States in as varied geographical areas as possible in order to provide convenient locations for scholars in various parts of the country. It is not a census of copies, and "it is only when less than five copies are located in either British or American libraries that any deduction can be drawn that copies mentioned are all that the editor has found."—*Pref.* Location symbols are not those used by the *STC* (AA801) or the *National union catalog* (AA128), but follow a system devised by Wing.

The scope and method of selection and entry are described in the preface, which should be carefully read before the book is used in order not to misinterpret or misunderstand the information given. Z2002.W5

——— ——— 2d ed., rev. & enl. N.Y., Index Committee of the Modern Language Assoc. of America, 1972–82. v.1–2. (In progress) **AA819**

Contents: v.1, entries A1–E2926; v.2, entries E2927–O1000.

This revised and enlarged edition adds new information acquired since publication of the original work. Scope and method remain the same, except that the number of libraries represented has been increased to more than 300. "Unfortunately, about seven or eight percent of the numbers in the revised first volume were shifted one or two numbers to fill gaps caused by moving entries elsewhere.

Confusingly, some new entries appeared with numbers assigned to an entirely different work in the first edition. A complete list of these number changes, giving a correlation of old and new numbers and providing references for those items moved to places in the second and third volumes, is published [in v.2]."—*Pref., v.2.* Users of v.2 "may be assured that no number has been reassigned in this volume, except those designated 'entry cancelled' in the first edition and thus never allocated in print for a specific book."

D. F. McKenzie's review of v.2 in the *TLS* of Dec. 17, 1982, p.1403, points out certain shortcomings of the work.

Z2002.W52

Oxford. University. Christ Church Library. The Christ Church holdings in Wing's Short-title catalogue, 1641–1700, of books of which less than 5 copies are recorded in the United Kingdom. Comp. by Walter G. Hiscock. [Oxford], Christ Church, 1956. 165p. **AA820**

—— The Christ Church supplement to Wing's Short-title catalogue, 1641–1700, by W. G. Hiscock. Oxford, pr. for Christ Church at the Holywell Pr., 1956. 47p. **AA821**

A list of works in Christ Church not listed by Wing, with a section of errata in Wing. Z2002.W5O9

Morrison, Paul Guerrant. Index of printers, publishers, and booksellers in Donald Wing's Short-title catalogue. . . . Charlottesville, Univ. of Virginia Pr. for the Bibliographical Society of the Univ. of Virginia, 1955. 217p. **AA822**

Similar to the compiler's index to Pollard and Redgrave.

Philadelphia. Library Company. A check-list of the books in the Library Company of Philadelphia in and supplementary to Wing's Short-title catalogue, 1641–1700, by Edwin Wolf. Philadelphia, 1959. 106p. **AA823**

Nearly 4,000 titles, listed by Wing number.

University Microfilms International. Accessing Early English books, 1641–1700: a cumulative index to units 1–32 of the microfilm collection. Ann Arbor, Mich., Univ. Microfilms Internat., 1981–82. 4v. **AA824**

Contents: v.1, Author index and cross index; v.2, Title index; v.3, Subject index; v.4, Reel/position to Wing number index.

Provides indexes to the first 32 units (about 25,000 titles) of the microform series *Early English books . . .,* the project designed to microfilm all available items listed in Wing's *Short title catalogue* (AA818). Subject indexing is by Library of Congress headings. Through a programming error, Wing numbers were omitted from citations in v.1–3; a cross index from reel/position number to Wing number has therefore been furnished in v.4. Z2002.U586

19th and 20th centuries

English catalogue of books . . . issued . . . in Great Britain and Ireland . . . 1801–1965. London, S. Low, 1864–1901; Publishers' Circular, 1906–66. **AA825**

Volume covering 1801–36, published in 1914 and unnumbered, includes authors and catchword titles in one alphabet. [v.1] covers 1835–63. Later 19th-century volumes were published at irregular intervals; 1901–35 volumes cover 5-year periods; 1936–41; 1942–47; 1948–52; 1952–55; 1956–59; 1960–62; 1963–65. Ceased publication.

The standard English trade list during its period of publication. Reasonably comprehensive for books and pamphlets issued at main publishing centers, but less complete for the provincial presses. Arrangement is alphabetical by author with title and catchword subject entries, except that from 1837 to 1889 the subject entries are in separate index volumes (*see* below). Information given varies, but usually includes author, title, publisher, date, size, and price.

With the 1960–62 volume, arrangement is changed: (1) paperback section, authors and titles in one alphabet; (2) author section, giving the full bibliographical information; (3) title section, including inverted titles; (4) maps and atlases; (5) list of publishers.

Cumulated the annual *English catalogue of books,* 1835–1965 (the 1966–68 volumes remain uncumulated).

Over the years, the information for the compilation was derived mainly from the weekly *Publishers' circular . . .* (1837–1959). During the period 1959–66, this was incorporated into a monthly, *British books,* which continued the volume numbering of the earlier publication and offered articles, announcements, etc., as well as the listings of new books which served as the basis for the *English catalogue.* (In 1967, *British books* was absorbed by *The publisher,* which assumed the volume numbering of the former and, in turn, ceased with the issue of Dec. 1970.) Z2001.E52

—— Index to the English catalogue of books, 1837–1889. London, S. Low, 1858–93. 4v.

Forms a subject index to v.1–4 of the author catalog. No more published, as from v.5 on, the *English catalogue* includes authors and catchword subjects in one alphabet.

Nineteenth century short title catalogue. Series I, Phase I, 1801–1815. [Newcastle-upon-Tyne, Eng.], Avero, [1984]– . v.1–2. (In progress) **AA826**

". . . extracted from the catalogues of the Bodleian Library, the British Library, the Library of Trinity College, Dublin, the National Library of Scotland, and the University Libraries of Cambridge and Newcastle."—*t.p.*

Pref. signed J. W. Jolliffe.

Contents: v.1–2, A–H.

These volumes represent the first phase of a massive project designed to provide a comprehensive bibliographic record of "British books" published during the 19th century. "British books are taken to include all books published in Britain, its colonies and the United States of America; all books in English wherever published; and all translations from English."—*Introd.* A second series will cover the period 1816–70, and a third series 1871–1918.

This segment was compiled from the in-house and published catalogs of the six libraries named above. As far as possible, entries from those catalogs have been adapted to the form and order of the British Museum *General catalogue* (AA132), with cross references from alternative entries; thus the listing is basically by author or anonymous title (although the latter often takes the form of keyword entry). Each entry carries a reference number and, as applicable, includes an author statement (with epithet or life span dates), short title, as many as three Dewey classification numbers, the edition statement (which gives date, place of publication other than London, number of parts, and the names of editors, translators, etc.), and library locations. Each volume has an imprint index (i.e., by place of publication) and a subject index according to the broad Dewey class numbers assigned to the items.

Introductory and explanatory matter is disappointingly brief (e.g., there is no sample entry to illustrate the various components of a typical citation). The review by Robin Alston in *TLS* (April 6, 1984, p.381) supplies a good deal of useful information on both the background of the catalog and the content of the entries.

British national bibliography, 1950– . London, Council of the British Nat. Bibliography, British Museum, 1950– . **AA827**

Published weekly (except at Easter and Christmas) with cumulations at intervals which have varied (currently Jan.–Apr. and May–Aug.), and an annual volume. (For 3- to 5-year cumulations, *see* below.) Now printed "from computer-controlled typesetting."

Beginning 1976, the annual cumulation is issued in 2v.: v.1, Subject catalogue (arranged by Dewey class numbers); v.2, Indexes (offering separate author/title and alphabetical subject approaches).

An excellently planned and executed national bibliography, prepared at the British Library and based upon the books deposited at the Copyright Office. It aims to list and describe every new work published in Great Britain with certain specific exceptions: periodicals (except the first issue of a new periodical or a periodical under a new title); music; maps; certain government publications; cheap novelettes, etc.

The main section in each issue is classified by the Dewey Decimal Classification. Each weekly issue has an author and title index, and the last issue for each month now has a cumulated author/title index and a cumulated subject index for the month. Each cumulation is now in three sections: (1) Classified subject section; (2) Author and title section; and (3) Subject index. The author/title section includes entries for editors, translators, and series.

Full cataloging detail is given in the classified section, including: author, title, place, publisher, date, paging, illustrations, centimeter size, series, and price. The author/title section provides briefer information, adequate for many purposes, giving author, title, publisher, price, and classification number (the latter serving as an index number for finding the more detailed information in the classified section). The subject index is an alphabetical subject approach to the classification numbers used during the period covered by the cumulation.

Annual volumes for the 1951–70 period are superseded by the *Cumulated subject catalogue* and the *Cumulated index* noted below. A *Cumulated author & title index, 1971–1973* (publ. 1977) provides a single alphabetical sequence of author and title entries from the annual indexes for the period, but the annual volumes are not superseded.

Beginning in 1977 the *BNB* carries advance cataloging information in the form of CIP (cataloging in publication) records in the weekly lists, thus increasing the bibliography's usefulness as a current selection tool since the entries appear as much as two months in advance of publication of the books themselves. Such entries are identified in the annotations as "CIP entry." As titles are published and deposited in the Copyright Receipt Office the corresponding entries are expanded to include full cataloging information and the full form appears in subsequent interim cumulations and in the annual volume identified as "CIP rev."   Z2001.B75

—————— Cumulated subject catalogue, 1951/54–1968/70. London, 1958–73.

1951–54, 2v.; 1955–59, 3v.; 1960–64, 3v.; 1965–67, 3v.; 1968–70, 2v.

Cumulations of the material appearing in the classified sections of the annual volumes, originally made by cutting and arranging the entries in classified sequence and reproducing by photo-offset printing; beginning with 1960–64 cumulation, rephotographing has been done by Fotolist camera. Information, therefore, is that current at the time of the annual volumes. (Material from the 1950 volume was omitted from the first cumulation due to difference in format, and that volume is not superseded.)   Z2001.B752

—————— Cumulated index, 1950/54–1968/70. London, 1955–73.

Quinquennial 1950–64; triennial, 1965–70.

Each volume is a cumulation in one alphabetical sequence of the author, title, and subject sections of the annual volumes. These indexes serve as keys to the *Cumulated subject catalogue* and thus together they provide a comprehensive record of British publications for the period, superseding the annual volumes.

Whitaker's Five-year cumulative book list, 1939/43– ; the complete list of all books published in the United Kingdom, . . . giving details as to author, title, sub-title, size, number of pages, price, date, classification and publisher of every book. London, Whitaker, 1945– . v.1– .   **AA828**

Title varies; some volumes are 4-year cumulations; 1973–75 is a 3-year cumulation.

1939/43, authors and titles in one alphabet; 1944/47–1948/52, authors and titles in separate alphabets; 1953/57– , authors, titles, and some subjects in one alphabet.   Z2005.W58

Whitaker's Cumulative book list . . . , 1924– . London, Whitaker, [1924–]. v.1– .   **AA829**

Issued quarterly, cumulating throughout the year; since 1939, cumulating into larger volumes as listed above.

Subtitle varies, 1982: The complete list of all books published in the United Kingdom during the period, giving details as to author, title, subtitle, size, number of pages, price, date, classification, Standard Book Number and publisher of every book, in one alphabetical arrangement under author, title and subject, where this forms part of the title.

Arrangement has varied; now a dictionary arrangement of authors, titles, and some subjects. Kept up-to-date by weekly lists in *The bookseller* (AA831).   Z2005.W57

Whitaker's Books of the month and books to come, Jan. 1970– . London, J. Whitaker, 1970– . Monthly.   **AA830**

A service designed "to provide a record of the past month's books, together with those announced for publication in the next two months."—*Introd.* Replaces the monthly cumulated list of "Publications of the month" previously appearing in *The bookseller* (below) and incorporates listings for forthcoming books. ("Publications of the week" remains a feature of *The bookseller,* and *Whitaker's Cumulative book list* [above] provides the quarterly and annual cumulations.)   Z2005.W56

The bookseller: the organ of the book trade, 1858– . London, Whitaker, 1858– .   **AA831**

Subtitle varies.

Monthly, 1858–1908; weekly, 1909– .

Includes weekly alphabetical lists of new publications and reissues. Through 1969 the weekly lists cumulated monthly in the last issue of the month and these, in turn, cumulated into *Whitaker's Cumulative book list.* Beginning Jan. 1970, the monthly cumulative feature was incorporated into *Whitaker's Books of the month . . .* (above).   Z2005.B72

British books in print; the reference catalogue of current literature . . . 1874– . London, Whitaker, 1874– . Irregular.   **AA832**

Title and subtitle vary: 1874–1961, *The reference catalogue of current literature.*

Subtitle, 1982: The national inclusive book-reference index of books in print and on sale in the United Kingdom with details as to author, title, editor, translator, reviser, year of publication or year of latest edition, number of edition, size, number of pages, illustrations, series, binding—where not cloth—price, whether net or nonnet, publisher's name, and standard book number.

1874–1932, a collection of publishers' catalogs bound together alphabetically by name of firm, with a detailed index in a separate volume. Published about every fourth year during that period. Thereafter, published at irregular intervals and consolidated into two lists, author and title, including information as given in subtitle. Beginning 1971, a computer-produced annual with authors, titles, and catchwords in a single alphabetical sequence.

    Z2001.R33

Paperbacks in print: a reference catalogue of . . . paperbacks in print and on sale in Great Britain. London, Whitaker, 1960–81. Annual.   **AA833**

Title and subtitle vary. Semiannual (irregular), eds.1–18; annual, ed.19–28.

Arrangement has varied.

Superseded by: Z1033.P3P28

British paperbacks in print. 1982– . London, Whitaker, 1982– . Annual.   **AA834**

Subtitle, 1982 ed.: A reference catalogue of over 50,000 paperbacks in print and on sale in the United Kingdom; arranged in one alphabetical author, title and subject list.

Scope is limited "to books of 96 pages or more which are reprints of original hardback books, simultaneous publications, or originals, issued by firms recognised by the book trade as paperback publishers."—*Pref.* Includes English-language paperbacks published abroad but "available in the United Kingdom through a sole stockholding agent." Computer produced. Forms a companion to *British books in print* (AA832), with similar format and arrangement.

Privately printed

Dobell, Bertram. Catalogue of books printed for private circulation, collected by Bertram Dobell and now described and annotated by him. London, Dobell, 1906. 238p. (Repr.: Detroit, Gale, 1966)   **AA835**

An author list, with full descriptions, including author's name, title, size, paging, date, price, size of edition when known, and bibliographical and historical notes with occasional quotations from the books themselves. Includes some, but not all, of the books listed by Martin (below).

Some 939 titles from this list are now in the Library of Congress, having been acquired in the Dobell collection of privately printed books purchased in 1914.   Z1028.D63

Martin, John. Bibliographical catalogue of privately printed books. 2d ed. London, publ. for the author by J. Van Voort, 1854. 593p. il. (Repr.: N.Y., Johnson Reprint, 1968)
AA836

The 1st ed., 1834, was in two parts: (1) List of books, omitting pamphlets, arranged chronologically 1672–1833, giving author's name, title, place and printer when known, date, size and paging, with many bibliographical and historical notes and occasional references to authorities and copies; (2) List of books printed at private presses and for distribution among members of literary clubs, arranged by presses. General index of authors and titles. The list by presses contains some material not found in the appendix volume of Lowndes (AA792). The 2d ed. is a revision of the first part only, correcting some errors, adding previously omitted titles, and extending the list to 1853, but omitting the section of private presses.   Z1028.M38

Regional

❖The general works listed above are reasonably comprehensive for books issued at the main publishing centers, but are less inclusive for material of local interest issued by provincial printers. For works of this latter type, local bibliographies of towns and counties must be consulted; particularly for the period prior to the commencement of the *British national bibliography* (AA827). A list of some of these was given in the *Guide to reference books,* 7th ed., p.38–39, and is not repeated here. They vary greatly in character but, taken as a whole, they serve three main purposes: (1) as lists of local imprints; (2) as bibliographies of local history; (3) as regional biographical dictionaries, since some of them include biographical sketches of local writers, etc. As they sometimes include considerable analysis of material in periodicals, and even newspapers, they supplement, to that extent, the indexes to periodicals.

Greece

Gkinēs, Dēmētrios S. and **Mēxa, Balērios G.** Hellēnikē bibliographia, 1800–1863. Anagraphē tōn kata tēn chronikēn tautēn periodon opou dēpote Hellēnisti ekdothentōn bibliōn kai entypōn en genei. . . . Brabeutheisa hypo tes Akadēmias Athenōn. En Athenais, Grapheion Demosieumatōn Akadēmias Athenōn, 1939–57. 3v. (Pragmateiai tes Akadēmias Athenōn, Tomos 11)   **AA837**

Contents: T.I, 1800–1839; T.II, 1840–1855; T.III, 1856–1863, and supplement, 1800–1855.
Intended as a continuation of the Legrand bibliographies (below).

Ladas, Geōrgios G. and **Chatzēdēmos, Athanasios D.** Hellēnikē bibliographia; symbole sto dekato ogdoo aiōna. Athēna, 1964–76. 2v. (Prosthekes, diorthōseis kai symplērōseis sten Hellenike bibliographia tōn Émile Legrand, Louis Petit kai Hubert Pernot)   **AA838**

A listing of 18th-century publications. Serves as a supplement to Legrand's bibliography for the same period (AA844).   Z2292.L25

———— Hellēnikē vivliographia tōn etōn 1791–1795. Athēna, 1970. 431p.   **AA839**

A continuation of the compilers' earlier compilation (above).
Z2292.L25

———— Hellēnikē vivliographia tōn etōn 1796–1799. Athēna, 1973. 415p.   **AA840**

Designated as v.2 of the compilers' 1970 volume covering 1791–95 (above).
Supplemented by: Z2292.L25

———— Hellēnike vivliographia tōn etōn 1791–1799. Prosthēkeis kai symplērōseis. Seira protē. Athēna, 1976. 32p.
AA841

Legrand, Emile Louis Jean. Bibliographie hellénique, ou, Description raisonnée des ouvrages publiés en grec par des Grecs aux XVᵉ et XVIᵉ siècles. Paris, Leroux, 1885–1906. 4v. il. (Repr.: Paris, Maisonneuve, 1963. 4v.)   **AA842**

Publisher varies. Title varies.
Covers the period 1476–1600 as follows: v.1–2, Works published in Greek by the Greeks, 1476–1599; v.3, Works published in Latin by the Greeks, 1469–1550; v.4, Works published in Greek and other languages, 1551–1600.   Z2292.L51

———— Bibliographie hellénique, ou, Description raisonnée des ouvrages publiés par des Grecs au dix-septième siècle. Paris, Picard, 1894–96; Maisonneuve, 1903. 5v.   **AA843**

Contents: v.1, 1601–1644; v.2, 1645–1690; v.3, 1691–1700, Notices biographiques; v.4–5, Notices biographiques [cont'd.].
Broader in scope than the author's volumes for the 15th and 16th centuries, including *tout ouvrage ayant un Grec pour auteur ou éditeur, tout ouvrage auquel le nom d'un Grec est attaché d'une façon quelconque.*   Z2292.L52

———— Bibliographie hellénique, ou, Description raisonnée des ouvrages publiés par des Grecs au dix-huitième siècle; oeuvre posthume, complétée et pub. par Louis Petit et Hubert Pernot. Paris, Garnier, 1918–28. 2v. il.   **AA844**

Covers 1701–90.
Listings supplementary to the three Legrand bibliographies cited above appear in: Manousakas, M. I. "Prosthekai kai symplerōseis eis ten Helleniken bibliographian tou E. Legrand (Symbole prōte)." *In:* Akademia Athenōn. Mesaiōnikon Archeion. *Epeteris* 7:34–83 (1957).   Z2292.L53

———— Bibliographie ionienne; description raisonnée des ouvrages publiés par les Grecs des Sept-Îles ou concernant ces îles du 15. siècle à l'année 1900. Oeuvre posthume complétée et pub. par Hubert Pernot. Paris, Leroux, 1910. 2v.   **AA845**

Contents: v.1, 1494–1854; v.2, 1855–1900.   Z2304.I7L4

Ntelopoulos, Kyriakos. Hellenika vivlia. Greek books. 1975– . Athenai, "Manoutios," 1976– . Annual.
AA846

Added title page in English. Preface in Greek and English.
Only 2v. publ.?
"A contribution to the Greek bibliography."—*t.p.*
Lists books published in Greece in the Greek language during the year of coverage and available in the book trade. Arranged according to a modified Dewey Decimal Classification. Indexes of names and of series (Greek names and foreign names in separate alphabets). Does not include Greek publications in foreign languages, nor publications in Greek published abroad. Entries are derived mainly from the quarterly issues of *Nea vivlia—New books,* the bibliographic bulletin of the Hestia bookstore, with some augmentation from other sources. Volumes for 1976– include a supplement for the preceding year.   Z2281.N75

Politēs, Nicolaos G. Hellēnikē bibliographia: katalogos tōn en Helladi ē hupo Hellēnōn allachou ekdothentōn bibliōn apo tou etous. v.p., 1907–32. 3v.   **AA847**

Imprint varies: v.1–2, Athens, P. D. Sakellarios; v.3, pt.1, Athens, Spendone; v.3, pt.2, Thessalonika, M. Triantspullos.
v.1–2 repr. from: *Athens. Ethnikon kai kapodistriakon panepistēmion. Epistēmonikē epetēris* 3:393–540, 1906–1907 (publ. 1909); 6:139–612, 1909–10 (publ. 1911); v.3, issued in 2pts., 1927–32.
v.1–2 cover years 1907–10 (with some additions going back to 1906 in v.2); v.3, 1911–20. Includes books published in Greece and books by Greeks published elsewhere.   Z2281.P77

Current

Bulletin analytique de bibliographie hellénique, 1945–73. Athènes, Inst. Français d'Athènes, 1947–80. Annual.

AA848

1945 (v.6), fasc.1, was published 1947; 1946 (v.7) appeared in 3 fasc. in 1947; 1947 was published in 1948 in three issues (fasc. 1/2, 3/4, and 5); 1948– , annual. The earlier volumes (v.1–5 for 1940–44, and v.6, fasc.2–3) and v.24–27 (covering 1963–66) are not yet published.

In two sections: (1) books and pamphlets; (2) periodicals. Classified arrangement with author index. Full bibliographical detail, followed by abstracts or reviews.

Continued by: Z2285.A75

Bulletin signalétique de bibliographie hellénique. v.35– , 1974– . Athènes, Inst. Français d'Athènes, 1981– . Annual.

AA849

Supersedes the *Bulletin analytique . . .* (above) and assumes its numbering.

With the change of title, coverage is limited to books, pamphlets, and theses. Retains the classed arrangement with name index. Annotations follow some entries.

Greek bibliography. Athens, Nat. Prt. Off., 1960– . v.1– . Quarterly.

AA850

At head of title: Ministry to the Prime Minister's Office. General Direction of Press, Research and Cultural Relations Division.

A preliminary issue, designated no.1, was issued in Feb. 1959. The publication is an English-language edition of a new Greek national bibliography, *Deltion hellēnikēs bibliographias,* same date, same numbering. Arrangement is classified, with indexes scheduled for the fourth quarterly issue of each year. An edition in French is also published, but content of the three editions is not identical. Publication has fallen well behind the goal of "current" (e.g., no.19 [v.5, no.4], covering 1964 was published 1969, and nothing later has appeared).

Guatemala

[Bibliografía guatemalteca] Collección bibliográfica del tercer centenario de la fundación de la primera imprenta en Centro América. Guatemala, Tipografía Nacional, 1960–63. v.1–10.

AA851

An attempt to provide a record of printing in Guatemala from 1660 to the present by combining older works covering the early periods with new compilations for more recent times.

Contents: v.1, Juan Enrique O'Ryan. Bibliografía guatemalteca de los siglos XVII y XVIII. 2. ed. [1660–1800]. (Text is a reprint of *Bibliografía de la imprenta en Guatemala en los siglos XVII y XVIII.* Santiago de Chile, 1897.)

v.2, José Toribio Medina. La imprenta en Guatemala, 1660–1821. 2. ed. 1960. 2v. (Originally published in Santiago de Chile, 1910.) Includes two supplements of *Algunas adiciones,* one by Gilberto Valenzuela, v.2, p.637–72, published originally in *La imprenta en Guatemala* (1933. 72p.), and the other by Arturo Taracena Flores, v.2, p.673–92.

v.3–5, Gilberto Valenzuela. Bibliografía guatemalteca, y catálogo general de libros, folletos, periódicos, revistas, etc. (v.3, 1821–1830, 2. ed. [1. ed. 1933]; v.4, 1831–1840; v.5, 1841–1860.)

v.6–10, Gilberto Valenzuela Reyna. Bibliografía guatemalteca, y catálogo general de libros, folletos, periódicos, revistas, etc. (v.6, 1861–1900; v.7, 1901–1930; v.8, 1931–1940; v.9, 1941–50; v.10, 1951–60).

These volumes give detailed bibliographical information with annotations about books, pamphlets, etc., and in many cases the texts of decrees, official notices, etc. No more published.

José Luis Reyes Monroy's *Bibliografía de la imprenta en Guatemala (Adiciones de 1769 a 1900)* (Guatemala, Editorial "José de Pineda Ibarra," 1969. 143p.) supplements the early volumes of the series.

Guatemala. Tipografía Nacional. Catálogo general de libros, folletos y revistas editados en la Tipografía Nacional de Guatemala desde 1892 hasta 1943. Guatemala, [Tipografía Nacional], 1944. 352p.

AA852

Alphabetical by year; no index.   Z1465.G8

Índice bibliográfico guatemalteco, 1951–52, 1958–59/60. Guatemala, Inst. Guatemalteco-Americano, 1952–61. Annual (irregular).

AA853

At head of title: Cooperación Interbibliotecaria.

Gonzálo Dardon Córdova, ed.

Volumes covering 1953–57 not published? Volume for 1959/60 published 1961. Ceased publication?

An author and subject catalog of books, periodical articles, and pamphlets published in Guatemala, together with some works about Guatemala published abroad.   Z1461.I5

Villacorta Calderon, José Antonio. Bibliografía guatemalteca; exposiciones abiertas en el Salón de historia y bellas artes del Museo Nacional, en los meses de noviembre de 1939, 40, 41 y 42. Guatemala, Tipografía Nacional, 1944. 638p. il.

AA854

Based on the exhibit on the history of printing in Guatemala held at the Museo Nacional. Covers the period from the introduction of printing in 1660 to 1942, with extensive bibliographies, location of copies, facsimiles of title pages, etc.   Z1461.V5

Guyana

Guyanese national bibliography. 1973– . Georgetown, Guyana, National Library, [1974–]. Quarterly with annual cumulation [i.e., the 4th issue of the year is the annual cumulation].

AA855

"A subject list of new books printed in the Republic of Guyana, based on the books deposited at the National Library, classified according to the Dewey Decimal Classification 16th edition, catalogued according to the British Text of the Anglo-American Cataloguing Rules, 1967 and provided with a full author, title and subject index and a List of Guyanese Publishers."—*t.p., 1973.*

Beginning 1975, includes nonbook materials; classification follows the 18th edition of Dewey; subject entries are omitted from the index; and a "List of single bills, acts, subsidiary legislation and parliamentary debates" forms an appendix to each issue.

Z1791.G88

Haiti

Bissainthe, Max. Dictionnaire de bibliographie haïtienne. Wash., Scarecrow Pr., 1951. 1052p.

AA856

Includes three main bibliographic lists, each arranged alphabetically and covering: (1) works published in Haiti, or by Haitians abroad, Jan. 1804–Dec. 1949; (2) works published in Hispaniola and Santo Domingo, or concerning them, from the beginning to 1949; (3) newspapers and periodicals from Santo Domingo and Haiti, 1764–1949, and an index of journalists working on them. Title and subject indexes. Many entries have brief annotations—both bio- and bibliographical—and library locations are given. Complements Duvivier (below).   Z1531.B5

————— ————— Supplement. Metuchen, N.J., Scarecrow Pr., 1973. 269p.

Covers publications of the 1950–70 period, plus some older works.

Max Manigat's *Haitiana 1971–1975 (Bibliographie haïtienne)* (LaSalle, Que., Can., Collectif Paroles, 1980. 83p.) provides a year-by-year listing of publications by Haitians and others on Haiti, Santo Domingo, Hispaniola, and related subjects, plus an appendix of works not listed in the supplement to Bissainthe's bibliography. *Haitian publications: an acquisitions guide and bibliography* by Lygia Maria F. C. Ballantyne (Wash., Lib. of Congress, Processing Serv., Hispanic Acquisitions Project, 1979. 53p.), in addition to supplying information on the book trade and non-commercial publishing, includes as appendixes directories of bookstores and publishers in Haiti, an annotated list of current serial titles, and a checklist of Haitian monographs, 1970–79.

Duvivier, Ulrick. Bibliographie générale et méthodique d'Haïti. . . . Port-au-Prince, Haïti, Impr. de l'État, 1941. 2v. **AA857**

Covers material published in Haiti from the earliest period to date of publication. Classed arrangement; no index. Z1531.D88

Honduras

Durón, Jorge Fidel. Índice de la bibliografía hondureña. Tegucigalpa, Impr. Calderón, 1946. 211p. **AA858**

Attempts to list all works published in Honduras (alphabetized by first letter only). For these it largely supersedes the *Repertorio* listed below. However, the *Repertorio* includes some items not included in the *Índice*. Z1471.D77

—— Repertorio bibliográfico hondureño. Tegucigalpa, Impr. Calderón, 1943. 68p. **AA859**

At head of title: Instituto Hondureño de Cultura Interamericana.
The first tentative edition of a national bibliography covering all periods. Books exhibited at the Primera Exposición y Feria del Libro Hondureño y Americano are listed in the first three sections: (1) Repertorio bibliográfico hondureño; (2) Libros de autores norte-americanos; (3) Libros de autores chilenos. Sec.4 is a list of books published in Honduras, and sec.5, an "Índice de nombres." All sections and index are alphabetized by first letter only. Index is a list of names only, without page references. Z1471.D8

García, Miguel Angel. Bibliografía hondureña. [Tegucigalpa], Banco Central de Honduras, [1971–72]. 2v. **AA860**

Contents: v.1, 1620–1930; v.2, 1931–1960.
A chronological listing without indexes. Locates copies.
Z1471.G37

—— Anuario bibliográfico hondureño, 1961–1971. [Tegucigalpa], Banco Central de Honduras, [1973?]. 512p. **AA861**

Books are listed in classed arrangement, year by year, and there are separate lists of periodical publications interspersed. Confusingly arranged, with no general index or table of contents.
Z1471.G36

Current

Anuario bibliográfico hondureño, 1980– . [Tegucigalpa], Ciudad Universitaria, 1982– . Annual. **AA862**

At head of title: Universidad Nacional Autónoma de Honduras. Sistema Bibliotecario.
Aims to list Honduran publications on a year-by-year basis. Books are listed first by main entry, then by subject category; a section of government publications follows a similar arrangement. A separate section lists periodicals by title.

Hungary

Magyar Tudományos Akadémia, Budapest. Régi magyarországi nyomtatványok, 1473–1600. Budapest, Akadémiai Kiadó, 1971. 928p. **AA863**

Added title page in Latin: Res litteraria Hungariae vetus operum impressorum, 1473–1600.
Borsa Gedeon, ed.
Augments and expands much of the data in Károly Szabó's *Régi magyar könyvtár* (below). Lists, describes, and locates copies of "the publications issued prior to the year 1601 in Hungary in any language or abroad completely or partly in Hungarian."—*Guide to*

the work. References to citations in earlier bibliographies and to published descriptions or discussions of the works are given. Photo-reproductions of title pages and selected pages from the volumes listed provide an additional aid to identification. Indexes of printers, places of publication, titles, subjects, etc. Z2142.M34

Szabó, Károly. Régi magyar könyvtár. Budapest, A Magyar Tudományos Akadémia Könyvkiadó Hivatala, 1879–98. 3v. in 4. **AA864**

v.1, Books in Hungarian, 1531–1711; v.2, Non-Hungarian books published in Hungary, 1473–1711; v.3, Hungarian authors, non-Hungarian books published outside Hungary: pt.1, 1480–1670; pt.2, suppl., 1671–1711 and author index.
Supplemented by: Z2142.S98

—— —— Adalékok Szabó Károly Régi magyar könyvtár c. munkájának I–II kötetéhez. Pótlások és igazitások 1472–1711, egybeállitotta Sztripszky Hiador. [Az 1912. évi kiad. uj kiadása]. Budapest, [Országos Széchényi Könyvtár], 1967. 621p. **AA865**

An extensive supplement to Szabó was prepared by Hiador Sztripszky and published in multigraphed form; it includes an index by town (then by printer) to the first two volumes of Szabó's bibliography. Sztripszky's work (*Appendix ad I–II tomos. . . .* Budapest, 1912. 710p.) has been retyped and is published here together with a reproduction of previously unpublished proof sheets of Lajos Dézsi's supplement of Szabó's work. Z2142.S98

Magyar könyvészet, 1712/1860–1911/20. Budapest, Magyar Könyvkereskedök Országos Egyesülete, 1885–1971. 13v. (Repr.: Budapest, Országos Széchényi Könyvtár, 1969) **AA866**

Title varies; publisher varies.
Many volumes have added title page: Bibliographia Hungariae.
Contents: [ser.1], 1712–1860, by Géza Petrik. 4v. publ. 1888–92; Suppl. to v.1–4 publ. 1971 (561p.); [ser.2], 1860–75, by Géza Petrik. 467p. publ. 1885; [ser.3], 1876–85, by Sándor Kiszlingstein. 556p. publ. 1890; [ser.4], 1886–1900, by Géza Petrik. 2v. publ. 1908–13; [ser.5], 1901–10, by Géza Petrik and Imre Barcza. 2v. publ. 1917–28; [ser.6], 1911–20, by Sándor Kozocsa. 2v. publ. 1942.
Arranged alphabetically by author and anonymous title.
Z2141.M23

Magyar könyvészet, 1921–1944: a Magyarországon nyomtatott könyvek szakosított jegyzéke. Közreadja az Országos Széchényi Könyvtár. Budapest, [Országos Széchényi Könyvtár, 1980–83]. v.1, 6–7. (In progress) **AA867**

Contents: v.1, Általános müvek—Filozófia—Vallás (publ. 1983); v.6, Nyelvészet—Irodalom (publ. 1981); v.7, Magyar irodalom (publ. 1980).
A classified (by Universal Decimal Classification) bibliography designed to fill the gap between Géza Petrik's compilation for 1712–1920 (AA866) and that for 1945–60 listed below (AA868). To be complete in 8v., the final volume to be an alphabetical index to the set.
The work will supersede "the bibliographical attempts broken off during the period between the two World Wars, combining into a unified whole the incomplete bibliographical fragments (1921–1935), the annual alphabetical bibliographies of the National Library (1936–1941) and the bibliographical quarterlies of the Hungarian Sociological Institute (1942–March 1944)."—*Pref., v.1.* A retrospective bibliography for the 1961–75 period is also in preparation.
Z2141.M256

Magyar könyvészet, 1945–60; a Magyarországon nyomtatott könyvek szakositott jegyzeke. Közreadja az Országos Széchényi Könyvtár. Budapest, 1964–68. 5v. **AA868**

Added title page in Latin: Bibliographia Hungarica, 1945–60. Catalogus systematicus librorum in Hungaria editorum.
Contents: v.1, Opera universalia, philosophia, theologia, sociologia, linguistica; v.2, Scientia naturales, medicina, agronomia; v.3, Technica; v.4, Artes, litteratura, geographia, historia; v.5, Index alphabeticus ad tomos 1–4; Additamenta ad tomos 1–4.
Represents a cumulation of *Magyar nemzeti bibliográfia* (AA870),

with the addition of coverage for 1945. Arranged by Universal Decimal Classification, with author and anonymous-title index.

Z925.M29

――― A magyarországi könyvek, zenemüvek és térképek cimjegyzéke. 1961/62– . Budapest, Országos Széchényi Könyvtár, 1963– .   **AA869**

Subtitle varies.

Annual cumulation (with variations) of material in *Magyar nemzeti bibliográfia* (AA870) with an author index.

Current

Magyar nemzeti bibliográfia. Bibliographia Hungarica. Kiadja az Országos Széchényi Könyvtár. 1 füzet, január-március 1946–77. Budapest, 1946–77. Monthly.   **AA870**

A classed listing with headings in Hungarian, Russian, English, and French. 1946, quarterly; 1947–77, monthly. Monthly and annual indexes until 1960. Thereafter, only monthly indexes, as it was cumulated in *Magyar könyvészet* (AA869).

Cumulation of issues from the early years was published as AA868.

Continued by: Z2143.M32

Magyar nemzeti bibliográfia könyvek bibliográfiája. évf.32^{16}– , Aug. 31, 1977– . Budapest, Országos Széchényi Könyvtár, 1977– . Semimonthly.   **AA871**

Represents a change of title for *Magyar nemzeti bibliográfia. Bibliographica Hungarica* (above), and continues its volume numbering. Classed arrangement (with index) remains the same, and the issues will continue to be cumulated in *Magyar könyvészet* (AA869).

Iceland

Cornell University. Library. Catalogue of the Icelandic collection bequeathed by Willard Fiske. Comp. by Halldór Hermannsson. Ithaca, N.Y., 1914. 755p.   **AA872**

"When this catalogue went to press the collection numbered about 10,200 volumes. . . . The catalogue, however, does not comprise all of these, since the Runic portion containing some 500 volumes, and a few other books, have not been recorded . . . some few titles are included which are to be found in the University library outside of the collection."—*Pref.*

Contents: Author catalog; Supplement, Subject-index.

――― ――― Additions, 1913–26, comp. by Halldór Hermannsson. Ithaca, N.Y.; London, Milford, 1927. 284p.

――― ――― Additions, 1927–42, comp. by Halldór Hermannsson. Ithaca, N.Y., Cornell Univ. Pr., 1943. 295p.

Some 5,000 items are included in this supplement, making a total in the collection of 21,830. This supplement also includes various titles to be found in the library outside the collection.   Z2556.C6

――― Catalogue of Runic literature, forming a part of the Icelandic collection bequeathed by Willard Fiske. Comp. by Halldór Hermannsson. London & N.Y., Oxford Univ. Pr., 1918. 105p.   **AA873**

Z2556.A2C8

Islandica; an annual relating to Iceland and the Fiske Icelandic collection in Cornell University Library. Ithaca, N.Y., Cornell Univ. Lib., 1908– .   **AA874**

The bibliographical volumes of this set by Halldór Hermannsson include: v.1, Bibliography of the Icelandic sagas and minor tales. 1908. 126p. (*see also* v.24); v.2, The Northmen in America. 1909. 94p.; v.3, Bibliography of the sagas of the kings of Norway and related sagas and tales. 1910. 75p. (*see also* v.26); v.4, The ancient laws of Norway and Iceland. 1911. 83p.; v.5, Bibliography of the mythical-heroic sagas. 1912. 73p. (*see also* v.26); v.6, Icelandic authors of today, with an appendix giving a list of works dealing with modern Icelandic literature. 1913. 63p.; v.9, Icelandic books of the

16th century (1534–1600). 1916. 72p. (*see also* v.29); v.11, The periodical literature of Iceland down to the year 1874; an historic sketch. 1918. 100p.; v.13, Bibliography of the Eddas. 1920. 95p. (*see also* v.37); v.14, Icelandic books of the 17th century (1601–1700). 1922. 121p. (*see also* v.29); v.19, Icelandic manuscripts. 1929. 80p.; v.23, Old Icelandic literature; a bibliographical essay. 1933. 50p.; v.24, The sagas of Icelanders; a supplement [to v.1]. 1935. 113p.; v.26, The sagas of the kings and the mythical-heroic sagas; two bibliographical supplements [to v.3 and v.5]. 1937. 84p.; v.29, Bibliographical notes [including] Additions to the bibliographies of Icelandic books of the 16th and 17th centuries [v.9 and v.14]. 1942. 91p.; v.37, Jóhann S. Hannesson. Bibliography of the Eddas. A supplement to v.13. 1955. 110p.; v.38, Jóhann S. Hannesson. The sagas of Icelanders (Íslendinga sögur). 1957. 123p.; v.40, Phillip M. Mitchell and Kenneth H. Ober. Bibliography of modern Icelandic literature in translation, including works written by Icelanders in other languages. 1975. 317p.   PT7108.I7

Islandsk Bogfortegnelse, 1899–1910, 1912–1920, af Bogi T. J. Melsted. København, 1899–1922. Annual (irregular).   **AA875**

Supplement to *Dansk Bogfortegnelse* (AA720) and bound with it as follows: 1899–1910 with volume for 1899–1910; 1912 with 1914; 1913–14 with 1915; 1915 with 1917; 1916–18 with 1918; 1919 with 1921; 1920 with 1922.   Z2561.D19

――― 1915/19–1930/34. [*In* Dansk Bogfortegnelse, 1915/19–1930/34 (AA720)]

5-year cumulations.

Kiel. Universität. Bibliothek. Islandkatalog der Universitätsbibliothek Kiel und der Universitäts- und Stadtbibliothek Köln, bearb. von Olaf Klose. Kiel, Universitätsbibliothek, 1931. 423p. (Kataloge der Universitätsbibliothek Kiel, hrsg. von Christoph Weber, 1)   **AA876**

Lists more than 7,900 titles, in classified arrangement with author and title index.

Current

Íslenzk bókaskrá. The Icelandic national bibliography. 1974– . Reykjavík, Landsbókasafn Íslands, 1975– . Annual.   **AA877**

Prefatory matter in Icelandic and English.

"The Icelandic National Bibliography is a continuation of two older bibliographies, the 'Íslenzk rit' which appeared in 'Arbok Landsbókasafns Íslands' (Year Book of the National Library) 1945–75, and 'Bókaskrá Bóksalafélags Íslands' (Bookseller's Association List) 1937–73. These two works had different functions, the first being a bibliographic source for Icelandic publications and the second a practical aid for booksellers; the new bibliography is intended to combine the two functions."—*Pref. 1974.*

An alphabetical author/main entry listing, with a classified section; separate sections for new serial titles, maps and charts and sound recordings (the latter now listed in a separately paged annual supplement); plus a statistical summary of the year's publishing output. Entries in the alphabetical section appear under an author's given name, not the surname.

"A preliminary edition appears in *Íslenzk bókatidindi*, published by the Society of Icelandic Publishers."—*Pref.*   Z2590.A3I84

India

Index translationum indicarum: a cumulation of entries for India in "Index translationum," UNESCO, Paris, v.2–11. Cumulation by D. L. Banerjee. Calcutta, Nat. Lib., 1963. 450p.   **AA878**

A cumulation of some 2,800 translations published in India, 1947–58, and listed in *Index translationum* (AA169). Arranged by Indian language and then alphabetically by author. Gives author of original, title of translation, name of translator, place, publisher, date, pages, illustrations, price, and language and title of the original. Z3201.I58

National bibliography of Indian literature, 1901–1953. Gen. eds.: B. S. Kesavan and V. Y. Kulkarni. New Delhi, Sahitya Akademi, 1962–74. 4v. **AA879**

Contents: v.1, Assamese, Bengali, English, Gujarati; v.2, Hindi, Kannada, Kashmiri, Malayalam; v.3, Marathi, Oriya, Panjabi, Sanskrit. v.4, Sindhi, Tamil, Telugu, Urdu.

Covering 1901 through 1953, this work aims to include "books of literary merit, and important and significant books" in the following categories: general works, philosophy and religion, social sciences, linguistics, arts, literature, history, biography and travel, and miscellaneous. In Roman script with annotations in English. Z3201.N3

Current

Indian book industry; book production and distribution journal. v.1, no.1– , Oct. 1969– . Delhi, Sterling Pub., 1969– . Monthly. **AA880**

Patterned after *Publishers' weekly*. Includes a monthly listing of current Indian publications in English—an alphabetical author listing with Dewey Decimal class numbers indicated. Z457.I48

Indian books, 1969– . Varanasi, India, Indian Bibliographic Centre, 1970– . Annual. **AA881**

Subtitle: A bibliography of Indian books published or reprinted . . . in the English language.

In view of the very considerable time lag in the appearance of the *Indian national bibliography* (AA884), this series is intended as a current record of Indian publications in English. Author, title, and subject sections, plus a directory of publishers.

Three other attempts to provide a current record for Indian publications have been abandoned: *Impex reference catalogue of Indian books* (New Delhi, Indian Book Export and Import Co.), an "in-print" listing of Indian books in English, appeared in 1960 with a 1960–62 supplement published 1962; *Books of India, a reference catalogue* . . . (Bombay, Publisher's World), appeared in 1964 with a volume covering 1963 only; and *Indian Books* (Delhi, Researchco Reprints), another annual listing of Indian books in English, was published 1972–76, offering coverage for 1971–74/75.

In effect, superseded by: Z3201.I65

BEPI: a bibliography of English publications in India, 1976– . Delhi, D. K. F. Trust, 1977– . Annual. **AA882**

"An integrated author-title-subject index to scholarly and significant publications of the year."—*t.p.*

The 1976 volume includes a considerable number of earlier imprints. Separate author, title, and subject sections. Z3201.B18

Indian books in print, 1955/67– . Delhi, Indian Bibliographies Bureau, [1969]– . Irregular. **AA883**

Sher Singh, comp. & ed.

Subtitle: A bibliography of Indian books published . . . in English language.

Beginning with 1972/73, issued in 3v.: (1) Authors; (2) Titles; (3) Subject guide (i.e., a classified listing according to Dewey Decimal Classification system). The 1981 ed. lists nearly 80,000 English-language books from Indian publishers.

Indian national bibliography. Gen. ed., B. S. Kesavan. Calcutta, Central Reference Lib., 1958– . v.1– . Quarterly, with annual cumulation, 1958–63; monthly, with annual cumulation, 1964– . **AA884**

A 5-year cumulation called "Cumulated index, 1958–1962" appeared in 1970. Monthly issues not published 1968–70; the annual volumes for those years are to be published.

A national bibliography which attempts to list all new publications appearing in the 15 major languages of the country, including first issues of new periodicals but excluding musical scores, maps, and several categories of ephemera.

Vernacular scripts have been transliterated into the Roman alphabet, and the text is in English. Each issue is in two parts: pt.1, General publications; pt.2, Government publications. In each sec-

tion the entries are classified by Dewey Decimal Classification with a detailed index of authors, titles, and subjects.

There is a very considerable time lag in publication of the annual cumulations. Z3201.A2I5

Indonesia

Catalogus dari buku-buku jang diterbitkan di Indonesia, 1870/1937–1954. Bandung, etc., Gedung Buku Nasional, [etc., 1940]–55. 6v. in 7. **AA885**

Title varies slightly (also in Dutch: *Catalogus van boeken en tijdschriften uit. in Ned. Oost-Indië*). Publisher varies.

G. Ockeloen, ed.

1870–1937 issued in 2v. (i.e., separate listings for Dutch and Indonesian publications); the Dutch listings for 1938–41 were published 1942, but the Indonesian listings were destroyed by war action; 1942–44 not published (although very few books were issued during the war and almost no bibliographic data on them exist); 1945–49 issued in 2 pts., the first covering Indonesian and Western language books, the second being a re-compilation from original cards of the listings of Indonesian books for the 1937–41 period; further volumes cover 1950–51, 1952–53, and 1955.

Superseded by *Berita bibliografi* (AA887). Z3278.A5C3

Projek Perpustakaan Nasional. Bibliografi nasional Indonesia: kumulasi 1945–1963. Djakarta, Balai Pustaka, 1965. 2v. **AA886**

A main entry listing with subject and title indexes. Intends to include all works (excepting government documents) published in Indonesia during the period specified. The word "kumulasi" (cumulation) of the subtitle is meant to indicate that the work is based on three earlier bibliographies: G. Ockeloen's *Catalogus dari buku-buku jang diterbitkan di Indonesia* (above); the *Berita bibliografi* of the Indonesian publishing house Gunung Agung (AA887); and the *Berita bulanan* of the Kantor Bibliografi Nasional (AA889). Z3261.P76

Current

Berita bibliografi, 1955–75. Djakarta, Gunung Agung, 1955–75. Monthly, with annual cumulations. **AA887**

A commercially sponsored national bibliography. Lists books, pamphlets, periodicals, and newspapers published in Indonesia, as well as Indonesian books published overseas. In dictionary arrangement: author, title, and subject in one alphabet.

Continued by: Z3273.B44

Berita Idayu bibliografi. 1976– . [Jakarta, Yayasan Idayu], 1976– . Monthly. **AA888**

Each issue usually includes one or more articles relating to the Indonesian book trade, Indonesian authors, etc., but a section called "Berita bibliografi" which serves as a continuation of the earlier series of that title (above) makes up the bulk of the publication; it is a classed listing with an author/title index which cumulates annually (beginning 1977, authors and titles cumulate separately) in the final issue of the year.

Indonesia. Kantor Bibliografi Nasional. Bibliografi nasional Indonesia, 1963– . [Djakarta], 1963– . no.1, Th.XI– . Quarterly (irregular). **AA889**

A continuation of the Office's *Berita bulanan*, v.1–10, 1953–62, monthly.

Not published Oct.–Dec. 1964 (no.4, Th.XII) and Apr.–Dec. 1965 (no.2–5, Th.XIII); a cumulated issue called "Kumulasi 1964–1965" was published to fill the gap. Volumes for 1966–69 not yet published? Resumed with no.1, Th.XVII, April 1970, the next issue for that year being no.2, Th.XVII, Sept.–Dec. 1970.

A classified list by Dewey Decimal Classification, with author index. Produced by the Office of National Bibliography; serves as the official list, but because it depends on the deposit of books (which is not required by law) it is not so comprehensive as the commercial list noted above (AA887). Z3261.A36

Iran

Ketābhā-ye Īrān. v.1– , 1333– sh. [1954/55–]. Tehrān, An-joman-e Ketàb, 1334– sh. [1955–]. Annual. **AA890**

Title varies.
In Persian. Ed. by Iraj Afshar.
No.3– have added title page in English: Bibliography of Persia; national bibliography, pub. by the Book Society of Persia. 1969 latest published?

Teheran. Kitābkhānah-i Millī. Kitābshināsī-i milli. Intishār-āt-i Iran, 1963– . Teheran, 1963– . no.1– . Quarterly. **AA891**

Added title page: National bibliography, Iranian publications (varies: Iranian national bibliography).
Frequency varies: originally annual.
A classified subject listing. Z3366.T4

Iraq

Maktabah al-Watanīyah (Iraq). Qism al-Biblūghrāfiyā wa-al-Ihsā'. Intāj al-fikrī al-'Irāqī li-'ām 1975– . [Baghdad], 1977– . Annual? (Silisat al-ma'ājim wa-al-fahāris, 15 [etc.]) **AA892**

Added title page: *Bibliography of Iraqi publications.*
In English, French, or Arabic. Z3036.M34

Ireland

Dix, Ernest Reginald McClintock. Catalogue of early Dub-lin-printed books, 1601 to 1700, with an historical introduc-tion and bibliographical notes by C. Winston Dugan. Dub-lin, [O'Donoghue; London, Dobell], 1898–1905. 4v. and suppl., all paged continuously, 386p. **AA893**

———— ———— Supplement of additions to pts.I–IV. Dub-lin, 1912. p.325–86.

Z2032.D61

Dublin. National Library of Ireland. List of publications deposited under the terms of the Industrial and Commercial Property (Protection) Act, 1927. no.1–5, Aug. 1927/Dec. 1929–1935/36. Dublin, Stat. Off., [1930–37]. Annual. **AA894**

Contents: (1) Books and pamphlets; (2) Annuals; (3) Periodicals and publications of societies; (4) Official publications issued by the Stationery Office; (5) Newspapers; (6) Music; (7) Maps.

Z921.D82

Current

Irish publishing record, 1967– . Dublin, School of Librarian-ship, University College Dublin, 1968– . Annual. **AA895**

Publisher varies.
Originally undertaken as a bibliographical project by students in the School of Librarianship at University College, Dublin. Begin-ning with the 1970 issue (publ. 1972), comp. by the School of Librarianship on behalf of the Irish Association for Documentation and Information Services.
A classified list with indexes of names and of titles. Covers publications of both the Republic of Ireland and Northern Ireland, and includes books, pamphlets, the first number of new periodicals, yearbooks, musical scores and works on music, and government publications of general interest. Z2034.I87

Israel

Halevy, Shoshana Dyamont. Ha-Sefarim ha-ivriyim she-nidpesu bi-Yerushalayim . . . 1841–1891. [Jerusalem, Kir-yath Sepher, 1963] 202p. il. **AA896**

On verso of title page: The printed Hebrew books in Jerusalem during the first half century (1841–1891). Z3478.J4H3

Current

Israel book news. no.1– , Wint. 1983– . Tel Aviv, Israel Export Inst., Book and Printing Center, 1983– . Quarterly. **AA897**

At head of title: IBN.
In English.
Includes articles on publishing and the book world, plus notes on a brief selection of new publications.
During the period Aug. 1970–Jan. 1980 the Center published the quarterly *Israel book world* which offered similar information. The Center also publishes *Books from Israel* (1964?–), an annual catalog of selected Israeli publications of interest to libraries and the book trade. Z449.7.I83

Kirjath sepher; quarterly bibliographical review. Jerusalem, Jewish Nat. and Univ. Lib., 1924– . Quarterly. **AA898**

Each issue carries a classified listing of new publications. The list is now arranged in three sections: (1) Israel publications; (2) Hebraica and Judaica; and (3) Periodicals. Annual index.

Z6367.K57

Italy

Bibliografia italiana; bollettino delle pubblicazioni italiane ricevute per diritto di stampa dalla Biblioteca Nazionale Centrale di Firenze. Anno 1–67, 1867–1933. Milano, etc., 1868–1933. Monthly (varies slightly). **AA899**

Anno 1–37 (1867–1903) had subtitle: Giornale dell' Associazione tipografico-libraria italiana . . . .
From 1886 to 1900 the *Bibliografia*, compiled at the Biblioteca Nazionale Centrale di Firenze, was also issued by the library under title *Bollettino delle pubblicazioni italiane ricevute per diritto di stampa* (AA901).
Published in two parts, 1867–69: I, Bibliografia; II, Avvisi. Published in three parts, 1870–87: 1, Catalogo delle pubblicazioni italiane; 2, Cronaca; 3, Avvisi. Beginning wth 1888, the *Cronaca* and *Avvisi* were discontinued in that form, being superseded by the *Giornale della libreria* (AA909). Z2345.B58

British Museum. Dept. of Printed Books. Short-title cata-logue of books printed in Italy and of Italian books printed in other countries from 1465 to 1600 now in the British Museum. London, Trustees, 1958. 992p. **AA900**

An author catalog, giving shortened title, place, publisher, date, and size, similar in scope and arrangement to the Museum's other catalogs in this series. Appended is a lengthy list of printers and publishers, with titles printed by each, arranged chronologically.

Z2342.B7

Florence. Biblioteca Nazionale Centrale. Bollettino delle pubblicazioni italiane ricevute per diritto di stampa, 1866–1957. Firenze, Biblioteca, 1886–1957. 72v. Monthly. **AA901**

Classified, with annual indexes. During its span, the most com-plete current record of Italian publications, based on copyright deposit.
Ceased publication. Continued by *Bibliografia nazionale italiana* (AA907).
A cumulation into one alphabet was published as: Z2345.F63

———— Catalogo cumulativo 1886–1957 del Bollettino delle pubblicazioni italiane ricevute per diritto di stampa dalla

Biblioteca Nazionale Centrale di Firenze. Nendeln, Liechtenstein, Kraus Reprint, 1968–69. 41v. **AA902**

At head of title: Centro Nazionale per il Catalogo Unico delle Biblioteche Italiane e per le Informazioni Bibliografiche, Roma.

v.1–39 are a cumulated author listing, A–Z; v.40–41 comprise "Indice degli autori secondari" and "Aggiunte."

Computer-produced, this set represents a cumulation of the nearly 640,000 entries from the *Bollettino* and provides an important bibliographical tool for Italian publications. Pagliaini (AA905) remains, of course, indispensable in the large reference collection. Z2345.F65

Michel, Suzanne P. and **Michel, Paul-Henri.** Répertoire des ouvrages imprimés en langue italienne au XVIIe siècle. Firenze, Olschki, 1970–79. v.1–2. (Biblioteca di bibliografia italiana, 59–) (In progress) **AA903**

Contents: v.1–2, A–B.

More comprehensive than the same editors' bibliography of 17th-century Italian imprints in French libraries (below), but does not locate copies. Z2342.M52

—— Répertoire des ouvrages imprimés en langue italienne au XVIIe siècle conservés dans les bibliothèques de France. Paris, Éditions du Centre National de la Recherche Scientifique, 1967–80. v.1–7. (In progress) **AA904**

Contents: v.1–7, A–S.

Indicates locations in French libraries. Z2342.M5

Pagliaini, Attilio. Catalogo generale della libreria italiana, 1847–99. Milano, Assoc. Tip.-Libr. Ital., 1901–22. 6v. **AA905**

Author and title list, 3v., 1901–1905; Subject index, 3v., 1910–22.

—— —— 1.–4. supplemento. Milano, Assoc. Tip.-Libr. Ital., 1912–58. 11v.

1st suppl., 1900–10, Authors and titles. 2v. 1912–14; 2d suppl., 1911–20, Authors and titles. 2v. 1925–28; Subject index to 1st–2d suppl., 1900–20. 4v. 1933–40; 3d suppl., 1921–30, Authors and titles. 2v. 1932–38; 4th suppl., 1931–40, Authors and titles. 2v. 1956–58.

Subject indexes have not been published for the 3d and 4th supplements.

The standard Italian list, covering a period of 53 years in its basic volume and continued by decennial supplements. The 1847–99 volumes include more than 200,000 titles, comprising the principal books and pamphlets of the period but omitting minor pamphlets, periodicals, separates, and government and society publications. Consists of: (1) Main author and title list, giving fairly full information, i.e., author's name, title (somewhat abridged), place, publisher, date, paging, size, illustrations, original price when obtainable; (2) Subject index to the author list. Based upon the catalogs of the large Italian libraries, catalogs of book dealers and publishers, and about 200 Italian bibliographies.

The supplements follow the arrangement, coverage, and format of the original set. Z2341.A85

Short-title catalog of books printed in Italy and of books in Italian printed abroad, 1501–1600, held in selected North American libraries. Boston, G. K. Hall, 1970. 3v. **AA906**

Contributing libraries checked their holdings against the British Museum's *Short-title catalogue of books printed in Italy* (AA900), adding citations for items not listed therein. About 40 American libraries are represented, as is the Gennadius Library of the American School of Classical Studies in Athens. Z2342.S56

Current

Bibliografia nazionale italiana; nuova serie del Bollettino delle pubblicazioni italiane ricevute per diritto di stampa. Gennaio, 1958– . Firenze, 1958– . Anno 1– . Monthly. **AA907**

—— Catalogo alfabetico annuale, 1958– . Firenze, Biblioteca Nazionale Centrale, 1961– . v.1– . Annual.

At head of title of each series: Centro Nazionale per il Catalogo Unico delle Biblioteche Italiane e per le Informazioni Bibliografiche.

A national bibliography in two forms. The monthly series is a successor to the *Bollettino* (AA901), being a current record of books and pamphlets received by legal deposit. Entries are presented in catalog card form; arrangement is by Dewey Decimal Classification; bibliographical information is complete, usually including prices; and tracings for subject and added entries are indicated. Author-title index in each issue, but no cumulated index.

This series is complemented, but not superseded, by the annual volumes into which the monthly entries are cumulated into an alphabetical main entry catalog, including all information from the monthly listings except the tracings and the classification numbers. Without the latter, the annual series cannot be said to serve as an author index to the monthly classified sections, although it does include an index of subjects and one of secondary names. v.1, 1958, also contains separate alphabets for musical scores, serials and *numeri unici*, and maps.

Publication was disrupted following the Nov. 1966 flood disaster in Florence, and monthly issues were irregular for a time. An issue designated as "Supplementi, 1" was published 1971 and included additional entries for the period 1958–69. Z2341.B5

Catalogo dei libri in commercio, 1970– . Milano, Associazione Italiana Editori, 1970– . Irregular. **AA908**

1970 vol. had title: *Catalogo dei libri italiani in commercio.*

Eds. for 1970–75 each issued in 1v.; eds. for 1976– issued in 3v. each: Autori, Soggetti, Titoli.

An "in print" listing for Italian publications. The 1970 volume listed about 52,000 works from some 340 publishing houses; by 1981 numbers had increased to some 164,000 titles from 1,371 publishers.

Giornale della libreria; pubblicazione settimanale, 1888– . Milano, Assoc. Italiana Editori, 1888– . v.1– . Monthly. **AA909**

Publisher and frequency vary.

Superseded the *Cronaca* and *Avvisi,* published until 1887 as pts.2 and 3 of the *Bibliografia italiana* (AA899).

Contains classified lists of recent publications and announcements of forthcoming publications. As it appears more promptly than the *Bibliografia nazionale italiana,* it is useful for current information. Z2345.G49

Italy. Ufficio della Proprietà Letteraria, Artistica e Scientifica. Bollettino. n.s. v.1– . Roma, 1945– . Monthly (Irregular). **AA910**

Issued by the Presidenza del Consiglio dei Ministri, Servizi Informazioni e Proprietà Intellettuale (varies slightly).

Like the *Bollettino* of the Biblioteca Nazionale Centrale in Florence (AA901) and the *Bibliografia nazionale italiana* (AA907), this is a copyright depository listing; its book section, however, arranged by subject areas and with cumulated annual author indexes, is said to be not so complete as the Florence listings. Includes lists of phonograph records and moving pictures.

Libri e riviste d'Italia; rassegna bibliografica mensile. Anno 1, no.1– , Marzo 1950– . Roma, Capriotti, 1950– . Monthly. **AA911**

On cover (varies): Edito sotto gli auspicii del Centro di documentazione della Presidenza del Consiglio dei Ministri. . . .

Subtitle varies.

Each issue in three sections: (1) "Libri," consisting of reviews of new books listed by class; (2) "Riviste," giving annotated contents of journals arranged alphabetically by titles of the journals under broad classifications; (3) "Rassegna bibliografica," a classified listing of new titles published in Italy, giving complete bibliographical information, including price. Z2345.L63

Ivory Coast

Bibliographie de la Côte d'Ivoire. [1969]– . Abidjan, Bibliothèque Nationale, 1970– . v.[1]– . Annual. **AA912**

A national bibliography with separate sections for books, periodicals, periodical articles (including selected articles in periodicals published outside the country), official publications, and a miscellaneous section for pamphlets, theses, etc. Classed arrangement within each section. Indexed.   Z3689.B5

Jamaica

Institute of Jamaica, Kingston. The Jamaican national bibliography, 1964–1974. Millwood, N.Y., Kraus International, [1981]. 439p.   **AA913**

"This bibliography represents a cumulation of the entries in the 1964–1970 *Jamaican National Bibliography,* which was published in 1973, and the titles of those Jamaican publications acquired and cataloged by the West India Reference Library, Institute of Jamaica, between 1971 and 1974."—*Pref.* In addition, works published in Jamaica in 1963 have been included, as have works by Jamaicans published outside Jamaica, and works about Jamaica published elsewhere. Arrangement is by broad subject categories, with an index of authors, editors, corporate bodies, and titles. Separate list of Jamaican periodicals and newspapers.   Z1541.I54

Jamaican national bibliography, 1968– . Kingston, Inst. of Jamaica, 1969– . Annual.   **AA914**

Supersedes *Jamaican accessions* (1965–67) and, like that publication, is based on the accessions of the West India Reference Library, with additional entries (beginning 1967) from the Jamaica Library Service and the Library of the University of the West Indies. Lists books and pamphlets, periodicals, maps, and newspapers. Includes both Jamaican publications and materials about Jamaica published elsewhere.

Japan

Samura, Hachiro. Kokusho kaidai. [Rev. and enl. ed.] Tokyo, Rikugōkan, 1926. 2v. (Repr.: Kyoto, Rinsen Shoten, 1968)   **AA915**

An annotated bibliography of some 25,000 Japanese books published up to 1867.

Kokuritsu Kokkai Toshokan, Tokyo. Kokuritsu Kokkai Toshokan zōsho mokuroko, . . . Tokyo, 1960– . Ser.1– . (In progress?)   **AA916**

English title: National Diet Library. Catalog: a catalog of publications acquired. . . .

Ser.1 covers 1948–58 (5v.); ser.2, 1959–68 (10v.).

A catalog of Japanese and Chinese publications acquired by the National Diet Library. In classed arrangement: pt.1, General works, philosophy and religion, history and geography; pt.2, Social sciences; pt.3, Science, technology, industry; pt.4, Arts, languages, literature; Subject and author indexes; pt.5, Title index.   Z955.T6414

Meiji zenki shomoku shūsei. Tokyo, Meiji Bunken Shiryo Kankokai, 1971–75. 20v.   **AA917**

Reprints various copyright records and lists of trade publications from the 1876–99 period.

Kokusho sōmokuroku. Tokyo, Iwanami Shoten, 1963–76. 9v.   **AA918**

A very comprehensive listing of books written, edited, or translated by Japanese to 1867. About 500,000 titles which were checked against the holdings of 426 libraries in Japan. v.9 is an author index.   Z3301.K8

Current

Zen-Nihon shuppanbutsu sōmokuroku [Japanese national bibliography]. 1948– . Tokyo, Kokuritsu Kokkai Toshokan, 1951– . Annual.   **AA919**

An annual cumulation of the National Diet Library's weekly list

of current acquisitions, *Nōhon shūhō,* which began publication on an irregular basis in 1948. Volume covering 1976 is the latest published. Superseded in effect by the annual index to *Nihon zenkoku shoshi* (AA921).

A subject listing, including books, periodicals, newspapers, films, records, maps, etc.; government publications are under issuing agency. Title index. With v.12, 1959, issued in two parts: pt.1, Government publications; pt.2, Non-governmental publications. 1948–69 suppl. publ. 1975.

Nihon zenkoku shoshi shūkanban. Japanese national bibliography, weekly list. Tokyo, Kokuritsu Kokkai Toshokan, 1981– . Weekly.   **AA920**

Supersedes *Nōhon shūhō* (1948–80).

The current national bibliography, listing government publications by agency and non-government publications according to the Japanese decimal classification; includes separate sections for juvenile literature, braille and large-print books, technical reports, foreign-language publications, etc. Suppl. A, Pamphlets, is issued quarterly; Suppl. B, Periodicals, monthly. Quarterly author and title indexes.

An annual index is provided by:

Nihon zenkoku shoshi shomei choshamei sakuin. Tokyo, Nihon Toshokan Kyokai, 1982– . Annual.   **AA921**

Title varies; 1982 ed. called *Japan/MARC shomei choshamei sakuin.*

An index to the weekly list with relatively full bibliographic information for each entry.

Nihon shoseki sōmokuroku. Tokyo, Nihon Shoseki Shuppan Kyokai, 1977– . Annual.   **AA922**

A list of books currently available in the trade; similar to *Books in print.* The 1985 issue lists more than 359,000 items in title arrangement, with index volume offering author and series approaches, plus a directory of publishers and an appendix of pertinent statistical information.   Z3301.N53

Shuppan nenkan, [1950]– . Tokyo Shuppan Nyūsusha, 1951– . Annual.   **AA923**

Includes information (with statistics) on publishing for the previous year; a classified listing of books published; new periodicals; lists of publishers, organizations, etc.; and laws and ordinances governing publication; excludes government publications. Title index.

This title supersedes *Nihon shuppan nenkan,* which appeared in 2v. (1943–44/46 and 1947/48; no volume was issued for 1949), and was preceded by *Shuppan nenkan* (1930–41) and *Shoseki nenkan* (1942). A separate annual dealing with periodicals, *Zasshi nenkan,* was published from 1939 to 1942, when it merged with *Nihon shuppan nenkan.*

Jordan

Bibliyūghrāfiyā al-watanīyah al Urdunīyah, 1979– . Amman, Jordan Lib. Assoc., 1980– . Annual.   **AA925**

Added title page in English: *The Jordanian national bibliography.* Prefatory matter in Arabic and English.

Aims to list "all types of published materials produced in Jordan by individuals, private and official organisations excluding school text books and audio-visual aids."—*Pref.* Classified arrangement according to the Dewey Decimal Classification, with author-title and subject indexes. Separate section for English-language publications.   Z3471.B52

Kenya

Kenya national bibliography, 1980– . Nairobi, Kenya Nat. Lib. Serv., Nat. Reference & Bibliographic Dept., [1983]– . Annual.   **AA926**

Subtitle: A classified subject bibliography of current publications produced in Kenya & foreign materials of interest to Kenya and/or written by Kenyans, arranged according to the Dewey Decimal Classification and catalogued according to the Anglo-American Cataloguing Rules, with a full author & title index.

Lists books, research reports, conference proceedings, pamphlets, maps, first issues of new serials (and subsequent title changes), selected audiovisual and non-print materials published in Kenya. Foreign publications of interest to Kenya and works by Kenyans published abroad are marked with an asterisk. Based on publications received at the National Library under the legal deposit act and on materials acquired by the Library through purchase, gift, and exchange.

A retrospective bibliography for pre-1980 imprints is planned.

Latin America

British Museum. Dept. of Printed Books. Short-title catalogues of Portuguese books and of Spanish-American books printed before 1601, now in the British Museum, by H. Thomas. London, Quaritch, 1926. 55p.　　**AA927**

The Portuguese section was issued in an enlarged edition (AA1033), but as no significant additions had been made to the Spanish-American section up to 1940, this part was not revised. A 19p. volume of Spanish-American books was published 1944. *See also* AA1091–AA1092.　　Z2712.B86

Historia y bibliografía de las primeras imprentas rioplatenses, 1700–1850; misiones del Paraguay, Argentina, Uruguay, por Guillermo Fúrlong [and others]. Buenos Aires, Ed. Guaranía, 1953–75. v.1–4. il. (In progress?)　**AA928**

Contents: t.1, La imprenta en las reducciones del Paraguay, 1700–27. La imprenta en Córdoba, 1765–67. La imprenta en Buenos Aires, 1780–84; t.2, La imprenta en Buenos Aires, 1785–1807; t.3, La imprenta en Buenos Aires, 1808–1810. La imprenta en Montevideo, 1807–1810; v.4, La imprenta en Buenos Aires, 1810–1815.

Designed to furnish a complete record of printing in Argentina, Paraguay, and Uruguay from 1700 to 1850. A history of early printing in the area is followed by the bibliography. Information about each item is detailed, including transcript of title page or colophon, collation, location, contents, description of type, etc. Biographical notes on author and printer are often given, and references to other bibliographical sources.　　Z213.A69H5

Medina, José Toribio. Biblioteca hispano-americana (1493–1810). Santiago de Chile, Impreso y grabado en casa del autor, 1898–1907. 7v. il. (Repr.: Amsterdam, N. Israel, 1958–62; also Readex Microprint)　　**AA929**

Contents: t.1–5, 1493–1810; t.6, Prólogo. Sin fecha determinada, siglo XVII–XIX. Adiciones. Ampliaciones. Dudosos. Manuscritos; t.7, Algo más de Léon Pinelo. Nuevas adiciones. Sin fecha determinada. Ultimas adiciones. Ampliaciones. Notas biográficas. Índice alfabético.　　Z1601.M49

———— Historia y bibliografía de la imprenta en el antiguo vireinato del Río de la Plata. La Plata, Taller de Publicaciones del Museo, 1892. 4 pts. in lv. il. (Historia y bibliografía de la imprenta en la América Española . . . [pt.2])　　**AA930**

Publisher varies.

Added half-title: Anales del Museo de la Plata. Materiales para la historia física y moral del continente sud-americano. Publicados bajo la dirección de Francisco P. Moreno . . . Sección de historia americana. III.

Contents: pt.1, Historia y bibliografía de la imprenta en el Paraguay (1705–1727); pt.2, En Córdoba del Tucumán (1766); pt.3, En Buenos Aires (1780–1810); pt.4, En Montevideo (1807–1810). Índice alfabético.　　Z212.M49

———— Notas bibliográficas referentes á las primeras producciones de la imprenta en algunas ciudades de la América Española (Ambato, Angostura, Curazao, Guayaquil, Maracaibo, Neuva Orleans, Nueva Valencia, Panamá, Popayán, Puerto España, Puerto Rico, Querétaro, Santa Marta, Santiago de Cuba, Santo Domingo, Tunja y otros lugares),

(1754–1823). Santiago de Chile, Impr. Elzeviriana, 1904. 116p.　　**AA931**

　　Z212.M53

Pan American book shelf. Wash., Pan Amer. Union, Columbus Memorial Lib., 1938–48. 11v. Monthly.　　**AA932**

A useful monthly bibliography with annual author index. Listed books currently received in the Columbus Memorial Library—usually, but not always, recent material.

Ceased publication with the Dec. 1948 issue. Succeeded by *LEA; librarians, editors, authors; libros, editores, autores* (Wash., 1949–50. no.1–12) which in turn was superseded by *Revista interamericana de bibliografía* (AA934) in Jan. 1951.　　Z881.W3255

Current

Fichero bibliográfico hispanoamericano. N.Y. & Buenos Aires, Bowker, 1961– . v.1– . Quarterly; monthly, Oct. 1964– .　　**AA933**

Attempts to list all new books published in the Americas in the Spanish language in all subjects and by all publishers. Arranged by Dewey Decimal Classification with an index by authors and titles, followed by a list of publishers.　　Z1201.F5

Inter-American review of bibliography; Revista interamericana de bibliografía. v.1– . Wash., Dept. of Cultural Affairs, Pan Amer. Union, 1951– . il. Quarterly (frequency varies).　　**AA934**

Includes lists of recent books, bibliographies, and reviews. Annual index.　　Z1007.R4317

Libros en venta en Hispanoamérica y España; por autor, por título, por materia. Servicio informativo preparado por el equipo de Bowker Editores baja la dirección de Mary C. Turner. 2. ed. Buenos Aires, Bowker, 1974. 2v. (2185p.)　　**AA935**

1st ed. 1964; suppls. 1–4 covered 1964/66–71.

An "in print" record for books in the Spanish languages, listing more than 87,000 titles published in Spain, the United States, and the Latin-American countries: Argentina, Bolivia, Colombia, Costa Rica, Cuba, Chile, Dominican Republic, Ecuador, El Salvador, Guatemala, Honduras, Mexico, Nicaragua, Panama, Paraguay, Peru, Puerto Rico, Uruguay, and Venezuela.

This edition includes listings for some 120,000 books. About 1,300 publishers and distributors are represented. Separate author, title, and subject listings.

Suplemento 1975 (304p.) was published 1977; *Suplemento 1976/1977* (539p.) appeared 1978; *Suplemento 1978* (304p.) was published 1978; *Suplemento 1979/80* (283p.) in 1981; and *Suplemento 1981* (187p.) in 1982. A 3d ed. (with a subject guide) was scheduled for publication in 1985 in 3v.　　Z1601.L593

United Nations Educational, Scientific and Cultural Organization. Centro Regional para el Fomento del Libro en América Latina. Boletín bibliográfico CERLAL. Año 1, no.1– , Julio 1974– . Bogotá, UNESCO, Centro Regional para el Fomento del Libro en América Latina, 1974– . Quarterly.　　**AA936**

A regional current bibliography covering Spanish and Portuguese publications of Bolivia, Colombia, Chile, Ecuador, Peru and Venezuela. Classed listing with author and title indexes. No cumulations to date.　　Z1601.U5a

Latvia

Jēgers, Benjamins. Latviešu trimdas izdevumu bibliografija, 1940–1960. [Stockholm], Daugava, [1968–72]. 2v.　　**AA937**

Added title page in English: Bibliography of Latvian publications published outside Latvia, 1940–1960.

Contents: v.1, Books and pamphlets; v.2, Serials, music, maps, programmes & catalogues. v.2 includes indexes.

An alphabetical author listing of Latvian publications in exile.   Z2535.J4

———— ———— 1961–1970. [Stockholm], Daugava, [1977]. 460p.   **AA938**

Added title page in English: Bibliography of Latvian publications published outside Latvia, 1961–1970.

Continues the listings from the earlier compilation covering 1940–60 (above), with items numbered consecutive to the entries in the first two volumes. This volume covers books and pamphlets, serials, music, maps, etc., in separate listings. Indexes of subjects, places of publication, publishers, persons, and titles.

Liechtenstein

Liechtensteinische Bibliographie. Jahrg.1– , 1974– . Vaduz, Liechtensteinische Landesbibliothek, 1975– . Annual.   **AA939**

At head of title: Liechtensteinische Landesbibliothek, Vaduz.

A classed bibliography with author/anonymous title and subject indexes. Includes serials.   Z2124.L53L53

Luxembourg

Bibliographie luxembourgeoise, 1944/45– . Luxembourg, Bibliothèque Nationale, 1946– . Annual.   **AA940**

Pierre Frieden, comp., 1944–53.

The first issue covered Sept. 10, 1944–Dec. 31, 1945; subsequent issues cover the calendar year.

The national bibliography, listing all materials published in Luxembourg, including official publications, new periodicals, and newspapers. Coverage varies. Since 1958, includes outstanding articles in periodicals. Arrangement is classified and, since 1958, has author and subject indexes.

An earlier work by Martin Blum, *Bibliographie luxembourgeoise ou Catalogue de tous les ouvrages ou travaux littéraires publiés par des Luxembourgeois ou dans le Grand-Duché de Luxembourg* (Luxembourg, 1902–32. 2v.) partially covered the period 1902–32.   Z2461.B5

Madagascar

Fontvieille, Jean Roger. Bibliographie nationale de Madagascar, 1956–1963. [Tananarive], Univ. de Madagascar, [1971]. 511p.   **AA941**

Fills the gap between G. Grandidier's *Bibliographie de Madagascar* (DD153) and the *Bibliographie annuelle de Madagascar* (below). Classed arrangement with author-title index.   Z3701.F66

Bibliographie annuelle de Madagascar, 1964–69. Tananarive, Bibliothèque Universitaire et Bibliothèque Nationale, [1966–73]. Annual.   **AA942**

At head of title: Université de Madagascar.

A national bibliography which lists Madagascar imprints, new Madagascar periodicals, maps, etc., and also indexes Madagascar periodicals. In addition, books and periodical articles relating to Madagascar but published elsewhere are included. Classed arrangement with author index. Continues the listings in G. Grandidier's *Bibliographie de Madagascar* (DD153) which covered 1500–1955, and J. Fontvieille's *Bibliographie nationale de Madagascar, 1956–1963* (above).

Continued by: Z3701.B5

Bibliographie nationale de Madagascar. 1970/71– . Antanarivo, Bibliothèque Universitaire et Bibliothèque Nationale, [1979]– .   **AA943**

At head of title: Université de Madagascar.

Represents a change of title for the *Bibliographie annuelle de Madagascar* (above), which ceased with the issue for 1969. Retains the classed arrangement with author index.   Z3701.B5

Malawi

National Archives of Malawi. Malawi national bibliography. Ed.1– , 1967– . Zomba, National Archives, 1968– . Annual (irregular).   **AA944**

Continues the National Archives' *List of publications deposited in the Library of the National Archives, 1965–66.*

Lists books, pamphlets, and first issues of new serials as deposited with the National Archives in accordance with the "Printed Publications Ordinance." Employs the Dewey Decimal Classification. Author/title index beginning 1975. Titles in African languages are followed by an English translation.   Z3577.N37a

Malaysia

Bibliografi negara Malaysia. Malaysian national bibliography. 1967– . Kuala Lumpur, Perkhidmatan Perpustakaan Negara, Arkib Negara Malaysia, 1969– . Quarterly.   **AA945**

Issued annually 1967–74; 1975– , quarterly, the fourth issue being an annual cumulation.

Lists "materials published in Malaysia which are deposited in the National Library of Malaysia under the provisions of the *Preservation of Books Act, 1966,* and includes books, pamphlets, Government publications, new serial titles, maps and posters. However, it excludes popular magazines, comics, commemorative and travel brochures, souvenir programmes and trade catalogues."—*Pref., 1975 annual.*

In two sections: (1) a classified section according to Dewey Decimal Classification in which the full bibliographic information is given; and (2) an alphabetical author/title/series index. An alphabetical subject index to the Dewey class numbers is added in the annual cumulation.   Z3261.B5

Mallorca

Bassa, Ramon, Bover, Jaume and **Carlos, Pere.** Llibres editats a Mallorca (1939–1972). [Palma de Mallorca, Ed. J. Mascaró Pasarius, 1972] 322p.   **AA946**

A classified listing of Mallorcan imprints, with author and title indexes.   Z2704.M23B3

Mexico

Andrade, Vicente de Paula. Ensayo bibliográfico mexicana del siglo XVII. 2.ed. México, Impr. del Museo Nacional, 1899 [1900]. 803p. (Readex Microprint)   **AA947**

Reprinted in part from the *Memorias de la Sociedad Científica Antonio Alzate,* 1894.

Lists 1,228 titles, transcribed line for line. Arranged chronologically and followed by alphabetical indexes of authors and of anonymous works.   Z1412.A55

Anuario bibliográfico mexicano, 1931–33, 1940–1941/42. México, Secretaría de Relaciones Exteriores, 1932–34, 1942–44.   **AA948**

1931–33 comp. by Felipe Teixidor; 1940–1941/42 by Julián Amo. 1934–39 not published.

The 1931–33 issues are alphabetical author listings based on the copyright accessions of the National Library; those for 1940–1941/42 are classified lists, with a combined author index for 1941–42.   Z1411.A62

Beristain de Souza, José Mariano. Biblioteca hispano americana septentrional; o, Catálogo y noticias de los literatos que o nacidos o educados, o florecientes en la América Septentrional Española, han dado a luz algún escrito, o lo han dejado prep. para la prensa, 1521–1850. [3. ed.] México, Ed. Fuente Cultural, [1947]. 5v. in 2. il., facsims. **AA949**

1st ed. 1816–21; 2d ed. 1883. 3v.
v.1–5, A–Z. Also includes *Suplemento especial* to v.5 (called v.6?) and lists of anonyms, bio-bibliographical notes, and indexes. Based upon the 2d ed., this is a reissue, with additions and corrections. Arrangement is confusing and must be studied with care.

——— ——— Suplemento especial II–III. México, Ed. Fuente Cultural, 1951. 2v. il., facsims.

Also numbered as v.7–8 of the main work. Z1412.B53

Berroa, Josefina. México bibliográfico, 1957–1960; catálogo general de libros impresos en México. México, J. Berroa, 1961. 189p. **AA950**

An author list of approximately 4,000 titles, followed by a subject index. Gives full information, including prices. Z1411.B4

García Icazbalceta, Joaquín. Bibliografía mexicana del siglo XVI. Catálogo razonado de libros impresos en México de 1539 á 1600, con biografías de autores y otras ilustraciones . . . Nueva edición por Augustín Millares Carlo. México, Fondo de Cultura Económica, 1954. 581p. il., facsims. (Biblioteca americana, proyectada y publicada por Pedro Henríquez Ureña y publicada en memoria suya; Serie de literatura moderna: historia y biografía [27]) **AA951**

1st ed. 1886.
This edition uses the text of the original which listed 116 titles, transcribed line for line, without change of wording, but with additions and emendations resulting from later investigation. Additional titles are included, with an appendix, and an analytical index. Quotations and very full bibliographical and historical notes are given, with references to sources and, in many cases, location of copies. Z1412.G2

González de Cossio, Francisco. La imprenta en México, 1594–1820; cien adiciones a la obra de Don José Toribio Medina. México, Antigua Librería Robredo, 1947. 205p. facsims. **AA952**

Z1411.G6

——— La imprenta en México, 1553–1820. 510 adiciones a la obra de José Toribio Medina en homenaje al primer centenario de su nacimiento. México, Univ. Nacional de México, 1952. 354p. facsims. **AA953**

The second work continues the first and does not duplicate the entries given there. Both volumes include full bibliographical information and line-by-line transcriptions. Z1411.G65

León, Nicolás. Bibliografía mexicana del siglo XVIII. México, Francisco Díaz de León, 1902–08. v.1^{1-6a}. facsims. **AA954**

Publication first begun in *Anales del Museo Michoacano,* 1890. Planned to be issued in two parallel sections: one purely bibliographical (including reprints in whole or in part of the rarer works); the other (which remains unpublished) biographical, historical, and critical. Line-by-line transcription. Each part A–Z (pt.6a, incomplete, A–N).

——— ——— Índice[s] . . . arreglado por Roberto Valles. México, Ed. Vargas Rea, 1945–46. 3v. (Biblioteca Aportación Histórica)

Índice de nombres, 1945. 61p.; Índice de impresos, 1946. 29p.; Índice de anónimos, 1946. 44p. Z1416.M45

Medina, José Toribio. La imprenta en México (1539–1821). Santiago de Chile, Autor, 1908–12. [v.1, 1912] 8v. il. (Repr.: Amsterdam, N. Israel, 1965; also Readex Microprint) **AA955**

12,412 entries. Z1411.M49

——— La imprenta en Guadalajara de México (1793–1821); notas bibliográficas. Santiago de Chile, Impr. Elzeviriana, 1904. 104p. (Repr.: Amsterdam, N. Israel, 1964) **AA956**

Z211.G9M4

——— La imprenta en la Puebla de Los Angeles (1640–1821). Santiago de Chile, Cervantes, 1908. 823p. il. (Repr.: Amsterdam, N. Israel, 1964) **AA957**

Z211.P9M4

——— La imprenta en Mérida de Yucatán (1813–21): notas bibliográficas. Santiago de Chile, Impr. Elzeviriana, 1904. 32p. (Repr.: Amsterdam, N. Israel, 1964; also Readex Microprint) (Ed. commemorativa del centenario de nacimiento del autor, con un prólogo y dos apéndices por Victor M. Suárez. Mérida, Ed. Suárez, 1956. 102p.) **AA958**

Z211.M4M4

——— La imprenta en Oaxaca (1720–1820): notas bibliográficas. Santiago de Chile, Impr. Elzeviriana, 1904. 29p. (Repr.: Amsterdam, N. Israel, 1964.) **AA959**

Z211.O2M4

——— La Imprenta en Veracruz (1794–1821): notas bibliográficas. Santiago de Chile, Impr. Elzeviriana, 1904. 34p. (Repr.: Amsterdam, N. Israel, 1964) **AA960**

Z211.V4M4

Valton, Emilio. Impresos mexicanos del siglo XVI (incunables americanos) en la Biblioteca Nacional de México, el Museo Nacional y el Archivo General de la Nación. Estudio bibliográfico precidido de una introducción sobre los orígenes de la imprenta en América. México, Impr. Universitaria, 1935. 244p. il., facsims. **AA961**

Detailed bibliographical descriptions of 16th-century Mexican imprints. Z1412.V21

Current

Bibliografía mexicana, no.1– , Enero–Feb. 1967– . [México], Biblioteca Nacional, 1967– . Bimonthly. **AA962**

At head of title: Universidad Nacional Autonoma de México.
A classed bibliography with author-title-subject index in each issue. No cumulations to date.
Publication suspended after 1980.

Boletín bibliográfico mexicano; reseña bimestral de libros y folletos, impresos en los E. U. Mexicanos, Oct. 1939– . México, 1939– . Monthly to 1947; bimonthly 1947– . **AA963**

Subtitle varies.
A classified listing. Z1415.B65

México. Biblioteca Nacional. Anuario bibliográfico, 1958–69. México, Biblioteca Nacional, 1967–76?. Annual. **AA964**

At head of title: Universidad Nacional Autonoma de México.
The first official Mexican national bibliography to appear since the *Anuario bibliográfico mexicano* (AA948) which covered through 1941/42. (1958 was chosen as the beginning date for the new annual since that is the point at which the law regarding legal deposit was made generally effective.) Classed arrangement with author-title-subject index.
Absorbed by *Bibliografía mexicana* (AA962). Z1411.M5

Namibia

Strohmeyer, Eckhard. NNB: Namibische National-Bibliographie. Namibian national bibliography, 1971/75– . Basel, Basler Afrika Bibliographien, 1978– . [v.1]– . (Mitteil-

ungen der Basler Afrika Bibliographien, v.20, 21, 24–)
Biennial? **AA965**

Contents: [v.1] 1971–75; [v.2] 1976–77; [v.3] 1978–79.

These volumes represent an attempt by an individual compiler to provide a Namibian national bibliography in lieu of a governmental or institutional effort. Aims to include "all written materials of Namibian concern, no matter whether they are published inside the country or elsewhere."—*Foreword*. Materials in both European and African languages are listed; only items actually examined by the compiler are included. Classed arrangement with author/title index; some annotations. A considerable portion of the entries deals with natural sciences and related subjects. At least one library location is given for each item. Z3771.S77

Netherlands

Early

British Museum. Dept. of Printed Books. Short-title catalogue of books printed in the Netherlands and Belgium and of Dutch and Flemish books printed in other countries from 1470 to 1600 now in the British Museum. London, Trustees, 1965. 274p. **AA966**

Comp. by A. F. Johnson and V. Scholderer.

"The series of short-title catalogues of books in the British Museum printed before 1601 now covers . . . all those countries of the European continent where there was a considerable output of early printing . . . , and in addition Spanish America."—*Pref.*

An author catalog with index of printers and publishers.

Z2402.B7

Nijhoff, Wouter and **Kronenberg, M. E.** Nederlandsche bibliographie van 1500 tot 1540. 'sGravenhage, Nijhoff, 1923. 1002p. **AA967**

A comprehensive record of the imprints of this period, giving full titles and collation, with bibliographical references and location of copies.

————— ————— 1.–4. aanvulling. 1925–34. 328p.

————— ————— 2. deel, door M. E. Kronenberg. 1936–40. 1158p.

Titles are numbered in continuation of the basic work.

————— ————— Inleiding tot een derde deel. Winst en verlies. 1942. 175p.

————— ————— 3. deel, door M. E. Kronenberg. 1951–71. 5 pts.

Pt.3 of this 3d series includes various indexes: of printers, names, etc.; pts.4–5 offer supplementary listings, bringing to 4,532 the total number of entries. Z2402.N692

Peeters-Fontainas, Jean F. Bibliographie des impressions espagnoles des Pays-Bas Méridionaux. Nieuwkoop, B. De Graaf, 1965. 2v. (Centre National de l'Archéologie et de l'Histoire du Livre. Publ., 1) **AA968**

Prefatory matter in French and Spanish.

A 1933 ed. had title: *Bibliographie des impressions des Pays-Bas.*

Lists works by Spanish authors which were produced in the presses of the Spanish Netherlands from 1520 to 1785. Arranged alphabetically by author or anonymous title, with a chronological table at the end of v.2. There is also an appendix showing illustrations of printers' marks. Bibliographical details are complete; locations are indicated. Z2402.P44

17th–19th centuries

Abkoude, Johannes van. Naamregister van de bekendste en meest in gebruik zynde Nederduitsche boeken, welke sedert het jaar 1600 tot het jaar 1761 zyn uitgekomen. . . . Nu overzien, verb. en tot het jaar 1787 verm. door Reinier Arrenberg. 2. druk. Rotterdam, Arrenberg, 1788. 598p. **AA969**

First published 1743–56; revised and reissued by Arrenberg, 1773.

————— Alphabetische naamlijst van boeken, welke . . . 1790–1832, in Noord-Nederland zijn uitgekomen. 'sGravenhage, van Cleef, 1835. 755p., 159p. **AA970**

By J. de Jong.

Continued by: C. L. Brinkman, *Alphabetische naamlijst . . . 1833–1849* (AA972).

————— Alphabetische naamlijst van fonds-artikelen, voorkomende in het naamregister van Nederlandsche boeken, alsmede in de Alphabetische naamlijst van boeken, achtervolgens uitg. bij R. Arrenberg en de Gebroeders van Cleef, en waarvan het regt van eigendom aan anderen is overgegaan. 'sGravenhage, van Cleef, 1839. 122p. **AA971**

Z2431.A28

Brinkman, Carel Leonhard. Alphabetische naamlijst van boeken, plaat- en kaartwerken, die . . . 1833–1849 in Nederland uitg. of herdrukt zijn. Amsterdam, Brinkman, 1858. 792p. **AA972**

————— Alphabetische naamlijst van boeken, plaat- en kaartwerken . . . 1850–1862. Amsterdam, Brinkman, 1868. 1010p.

————— Alphabetische naamlijst van boeken, plaat- en kaartwerken . . . 1863–1875. Amsterdam, Brinkman, 1878. 1249p.

————— Alphabetische naamlijst van boeken, plaat- en kaartwerken. . . . Wetenschappelijk register . . . 1850–1875. Met alphabetische opgave der onderwerpen. Bewerkt door R. van der Meulen. Amsterdam, Brinkman, 1878. 464p.

Superseded and continued by *Brinkman's Catalogus van boeken* (AA975). Z2431.A29

Pamphlets

Hague. Koninklijke Bibliotheek. Catalogus van de pamfletten-verzameling berustende in de Koninklijke Bibliotheek. Bewerkt, met aanteekeningen en een register der schrijvers voorzien, door W. P. C. Knuttel. 'sGravenhage, Algemeene Landsdrukkerij, 1889–1920. 9v. **AA973**

v.1–7, Chronological, 1486–1853; v.8, Supplement; v.9, Alphabetical subject index, 1486–1795. Z2444.P18H2

Muller, Frederik. Bibliotheek van Nederlandsche pamfletten. Naar tijdsorde gerangschikt en beschreven door P. A. Tiele. Amsterdam, Frederik Muller, 1858–61. 3v. **AA974**

Chronological list, 1482–1702 (9,668 entries). Z2444.P18M9

19th and 20th centuries

Brinkman's Catalogus van boeken en tijdschriften. 1850/82– . Amsterdam, Brinkman, 1883–93; Leiden, Sijthoff, 1903– . **AA975**

Title varies slightly.

1850–82, 1437p.; 1882–91, 2v.; 1891–1900, 2v.; 1901–10, 2v.; 1911/15– , published in 5-year cumulations, each in several sections with separate title pages.

Supersedes the annual volumes of *Brinkman's Cumulatieve catalogus* (AA978).

Each issue, except that for 1850–82 which has only the *Catalogus,* is in two main parts, separately paged: (1) *Catalogus,* or main author and title list, giving full information including author, title, editor or translator (if any), illustration, size, paging, publisher, date, price; (2) *Repertorium,* or subject index to the *Catalogus,* giving brief information only and referring to the word under which full information is found in the *Catalogus.* From 1891–1900 on, each *Repertorium* contains a *Titel-catalogus,* supplementary to *Brinkman's Titel-catalogus* (AA976). In the issue for 1926–30, the scope of the work was enlarged to include: (1) separate lists of periodicals and (2) Dutch works published in Belgium. (In the 1926–30 volume this is a separate list; in later volumes such titles are incorporated into the main alphabet.)

Beginning 1984, *Nederlandse bibliografie, B-lijst* (Alphen aan den Rijn, Samsom Uitg.) serves as a supplement to *Brinkman's,* listing publications of government agencies, scientific institutes, university reports and papers, and privately-published academic dissertations not generally distributed through the usual commercial channels.

Z2431.A3

Brinkman's Titel-catalogus van de sedert het begin dezer eeuw tot 1888 in Nederland verschenen werken op het gebied der nieuwe letterkunde (romans, novellen, gedichten, tooneelstukken en kinder-boeken) . . . Bewerkt onder toezicht en met voorbericht van R. van der Meulen. Amsterdam, Brinkman, [1888–89]. 232p. **AA976**

A title index—for works of fiction, poetry, drama, music, juvenile literature, etc.—to *Brinkman's Catalogus* (AA975). Gives brief title, date, and author's name, the latter supplying the cross reference to the fuller description in *Brinkman's Catalogus.* Continued by supplements included in *Brinkman's Catalogus.* Z2431.A297

Bibliotheca belgica. Bibliographie générale des Pays-Bas. Bruxelles, 1964–70. 6v. **AA977**

For full record *see* AA625.

Current

Brinkman's Cumulatieve catalogus van boeken, . . . in Nederland en Vlaanderen zijn uitg. of herdrukt, benevens aanvullingen over voorafgaande jaren in een alfabet gerangschikt volgens auteur, titel en onderwerp. Leiden, Sijthoff, 1846– . v.1– . Monthly, with annual cumulations. **AA978**

Publisher varies; before 1881, Amsterdam, Brinkman. Title varies: before 1930, had title *Brinkman's Alphabetische lijst.*

Before 1930, an annual list on the same plan as the main author list in *Brinkman's Catalogus* (AA975) with brief subject index to the author list. From 1930 on, published at varying intervals with cumulations, the last number of the year covering 12 months and forming an annual volume.

Superseded by the quinquennial volumes (AA975).

Z2431.A46

New Zealand

Bagnall, Austin Graham, ed. New Zealand national bibliography to the year 1960. Wellington, Govt. Printer, 1969–80. v.1–4 in 5v. (In progress; to be in 5v.) **AA979**

Contents: v.1, To 1889; v.2–4, 1890–1960.

"The bibliography is primarily a catalogue of printed books and pamphlets; periodicals and annual reports are omitted."—*Introd.,v.2.* Principles of inclusion and exclusion are carefully detailed in the introduction; it should be noted, in particular, that books published outside New Zealand are included if they contain some significant reference to the country, or if the author was a resident (as opposed to an expatriate) New Zealander; also excluded are New Zealand reprintings of books first published outside the country and with no New Zealand bibliographical association.

Publication of v.1 (1980, in 2 pts.) was delayed until work was completed on the later period, both to take advantage of experience acquired in compilation of the other volumes and because of the reasonably adequate coverage of T. M. Hocken's *Bibliography of the literature relating to New Zealand* (Wellington, 1909) and James Collier's *The literature relating to New Zealand* (Wellington, 1889). A wider range of materials is included in v.1 than in the rest of the set (e.g., more Maori language items); annotations have been supplied for many items; but it does not include periodical articles as do Hocken and Collier. 6,229 entries in v.1; about 32,000 in the

complete work. v.1 has its own index; an index to v.2–4 is to appear in v.5, along with corrections and some 2,000 additional items located since publication of the main text. Z4101.B28

New Zealand. General Assembly. Library. Copyright publications, 1933/34–66. Wellington, Govt. Printer, [193?]–66. **AA980**

Ceased publication; superseded by *New Zealand national bibliography* (AA982).

An annual list, supplemented by monthly lists in mimeographed form, of material received under the provisions of the Copyright Act. Full bibliographical information is given, including prices. There are sections listing government publications, overseas publications of New Zealand interest, maps, new periodicals, and periodicals that have ceased publication. Z975.W42

Current

Current national bibliography of New Zealand books and pamphlets published in 1950–65. (*In* Index to New Zealand periodicals, 1950–65, AE297) **AA981**

An alphabetical author, title, and subject list of all books and pamphlets published in New Zealand, and those published elsewhere by New Zealanders or having reference to New Zealand.

Superseded by:

New Zealand national bibliography, Feb. 1967– . Wellington, Nat. Lib. of New Zealand, 1967– . Monthly, with annual cumulation. **AA982**

Replaces the *Current national bibliography of New Zealand books* (above) and *Copyright publications* (AA980). The first annual cumulation covers 1966 and was compiled from the records of the two earlier publications.

Each issue in three sections: (1) Books and pamphlets (including government publications as well as works published overseas dealing with New Zealand or by New Zealand authors); (2) Maps; (3) New periodicals (including notices of cessation). Main, added, subject, and title entries are all interfiled in the first section; tracings, price, and Dewey class number are given with most main entries.

Beginning 1983, the bibliography is available only on microfiche, and from 1984 is issued monthly in four sections (Register; Author/title; Subjects; and Non-books plus addresses) with annual cumulation. Z4101.N57

New Zealand books in print, 1957– . Wellington, New Zealand Book Publishers Assoc., 1957– . Irregular. **AA983**

5th ed. 1970.

Title varies (1957, 1961 issues called *A list of New Zealand books in print*); publisher varies.

Beginning with the 4th ed. (1968), sponsored by the New Zealand Book Publishers Association.

Originally a classified listing. Beginning 1968, the arrangement is alphabetical by main entry, with title and classified indexes.

Nicaragua

Managua. Biblioteca Americana de Nicaragua. Bibliografía de libros y folletos publicados en Nicaragua (en 1942, o antes según fecha de publicación), que se encuentran en algunas bibliotecas particulares de Nicaragua. A bibliography of books and pamphlets published in Nicaragua (with 1942 or earlier as date of publication) to be found in certain private libraries of Nicaragua. Managua, Ed. Nuevos Horizontes, [1945]. 157p. (*Its* Serie bibliográfica, no.4, pt.1, enero 1945) **AA984**

Continued by:

—— Bibliografía de trabajos publicados en Nicaragua . . . A bibliography of works published in Nicaragua. 1943–45/47. [Managua, Ed. Nuevos Horizontes], 1944–48. v.1–3.

(*Its* Serie bibliográfica, no. 1, 6, 7–9, julio 1944, mayo 1945, mayo 1948) **AA985**

Ed., 1943–44, Graciela González.
Ceased publication. Z1481.M3

Nigeria

Nigerian publications; current national bibliography, 1950/52–72. Ibadan, Ibadan Univ. Pr., 1953–73. Annual. **AA986**

Early volumes carried subtitle: A list of works received under the Publications Ordinance by the Library, University College, Ibadan.

Lists books and pamphlets published in Nigeria, or about Nigeria or by Nigerians published abroad. Includes official publications and first issues of periodicals.

Superseded by: Z3553.N5N5

The national bibliography of Nigeria, 1973– . Lagos, National Library of Nigeria, 1974– . Annual. **AA987**

Covers "books and pamphlets published in Nigeria and received under the legal deposit provisions . . . as well as those about Nigeria or by Nigerians published abroad. In addition, it includes a section on Nigerian periodicals and newspapers."—*Pref. 1974.* Originally arranged by author or other main entry within five sections: (1) works in English; (2) government publications; (3) works in vernacular (i.e., Nigerian languages); (4) Nigeriana published outside the country; (5) Nigerian periodicals and newspapers. Beginning with the issue covering 1976 a single classified sequence (with index) is used for types 1–4, and there is a separate listing of new Nigerian periodicals and newspapers. Z3597.N37

Northern Nigerian publications, 1966–72; books and pamphlets received . . . under the Publications Law, . . . Zaria, Kashim Ibrahim Lib., Ahmadu Bello Univ., 1967–73. Annual. **AA988**

An alphabetical author listing.
Ceased publication. Z3553.N5N63

University of Ibadan. Library. Nigerian publications, 1950–1970. Comp. in the Ibadan University Library. [Ibadan], Ibadan Univ. Pr., 1977. 430p. **AA989**

Constitutes a partial cumulation of the annual issues of *Nigerian publications* (AA986) for the 1950–70 period; the 1971–72 issues of that series are not superseded, nor are the earlier volumes fully superseded since the lists of "Nigeriana published outside the country" are not cumulated. Arranged by main entry within three sections: (1) Nonofficial publications in English; (2) Official publications; (3) Publications in Nigerian languages (grouped by language).

A prefatory note states: "Throughout the period, 1950–1970, no single library could lay claim to having a comprehensive collection of all works produced in Nigeria. This twenty-year cumulation of works deposited at Ibadan University Library, should therefore be used along with two other annual lists, to obtain a complete picture of publications produced in Nigeria. They are: *Northern Nigeria Publications* (Zaria, Kashim Ibrahim Library, Ahmadu Bello University) 1965– and *A list of publications acquired under the Western Nigeria Publications Law no. 177 of 1957* (Ibadan, Western Regional Library) May 1959– ."

Periodicals and newspapers are excluded, having been covered in *Nigerian periodicals and newspapers, 1950–70* (AE131). Z3597.U54

Norway

Early

Bibliotheca norvegica. Christiania, Cammeyer, 1899–1924. 4v. **AA990**

Each volume has added title page in English. Individual volumes issued in parts.

Hjalmar Pettersen, ed.

Contents: v.1, Norsk boglexikon, 1643–1813 (English title page: Descriptive catalogue of books printed in Norway, 1643–1813). 1899–1908. 621p.; v.2, Norge og nordmaend i udlandets literatur (Norway and the Norwegians in foreign literature; descriptive catalogue of books and papers relating to Norway). 1908–17. 843p.; v.3, Norske forfattere før 1814 (Norwegian authors before 1814; descriptive catalogue of their works). 1911–18. 595p.; v.4, Norske forfattere efter 1814. 1. samling med suppl. til Bibliotheca norvegica I–III (Norwegian authors; descriptive catalogue of their works printed in foreign countries). 1913–24. 798p. Z2591.P49

19th and 20th centuries

Hauff, Nils Selmer. Stikords-katalog over norsk literatur, 1883–1907. Kristiania, Cappelen, [1908–1909]. 93p. **AA991**

Issued in six parts.
A catchword-title index to Norwegian materials for this period. Z2591.H23

Norsk bokfortegnelse, 1814/47–1966/70. Kristiania, 1848–1921; Oslo, Norske Bokhandlerforening, 1928–76. (In progress) **AA992**

Title varies; publisher varies.

Now compiled by the University Library, Oslo. Cumulates the issues of the *Årskatalog* (AA995).

19th-century cumulations vary in number of years covered. Decennial, 1891–1920; quinquennial, 1921– . The 1971/75 cumulation was published 1984 in 2v.

Includes books, pamphlets, periodicals, official publications, theses, and maps. Arranged alphabetically by author and title, giving full bibliographical description, followed by a classified section. Z2591.N865

Universitetsforlaget. Norwegian scholarly books, 1825–1967; complete alphabetical list. Oslo [etc.], Universitetsforlaget, [1968]. 339p. **AA993**

Inasmuch as the Universitetsforlaget publishes nearly all Norwegian scholarly books and journals, this volume represents most of the scholarly output of the country for the long period indicated. Author-title listing. Z2593.U53

Current

Bok og samfunn. Jan. 20, 1977– . Oslo, Norske Bokhandlerforening, 1977– . il. 36 issues per yr. **AA994**

Continues *Norsk bokhandlertidende* (1880–1976).

Frequency varies. Originally issued in two parts, A–utgave and B–utgave.

Offers news of the book trade, with a brief list of new books in each issue.

Norsk bokfortegnelse. The Norwegian national bibliography. Årskatalog, 1952– . Utarb. ved Universitetsbiblioteket i Oslo, Norske Avdeling. Oslo, Norske Bokhandlerforening, 1953– . Annual. **AA995**

Supersedes the *Åarskatalog over norsk litteratur,* 1893–1951. Quarterly issues cumulate into annual volumes, then into the quinquennial publications (*see* AA992).

Arrangement is alphabetical by author and title; there are also series entries with contents. Maps are listed separately, and there is a classified index.

Pakistan

National Book Centre of Pakistan. Books from Pakistan published during the decade of reforms, 1958–1968. [2d ed.] Karachi, [1968]. 159p. **AA996**

1st ed. published 1967 under title: English language publications from Pakistan.

A classified list without author index.

Continued by: Z3191.N29

Books from Pakistan. 1969– . Karachi, Nat. Book Centre of Pakistan, 1970– . Annual. **AA997**

On cover: A bibliography of English language publications.

1969–70 called "annual supplement"; 1971– called "annual publication."

A classed listing with author and title indexes. Z3191.N292

The Pakistan national bibliography. 1947/61– . Karachi, Govt. of Pakistan, Directorate of Archives & Libraries, Nat. Bibliographical Unit, 1967– . Annual. **AA998**

1963/64 publ. 1973 in lv.; 1965–67, 1970–71 not yet publ.

Two fascicles (1, General works to Islam, 001 to 297; 2, Social sciences to Languages, 300 to 492) of a retrospective bibliography covering publications of 1947–61 (i.e., from the time Pakistan became an independent nation to 1962 when coverage of the annual volumes of the national bibliography begins) were compiled by the Pakistan Bibliographical Working Group and published by the National Book Centre of Pakistan 1973–75. Five additional fascicles were planned for that series.

In accordance with the copyright ordinance of 1962, an attempt is being made to provide national bibliographic coverage from that date forward. Following publication of the 1962 annual in 1967 an effort was made to put the bibliography on a more current basis; thus, the 1968 volume was published 1970 and, apart from a 1970/71 hiatus, annual volumes have been appearing about two years after date of coverage. Simultaneously, some work has gone forward toward filling the 1963–67 gap.

Includes books and first issues of periodicals deposited according to the copy ordinance. Arranged by Dewey Decimal Classification, with author, title, subject index. Z3191.P33

Panama

Herrera, Carmen D. de. Bibliografía de libros y folletos, 1958–1960. Panama, Grupo Bibliografico Nacional de Panama, 1960. 44l. **AA999**

Arranged by year, then by main entry, with books and pamphlets in separate alphabets.

Panama (City). Biblioteca Nacional. Bibliografía panameña. Panama, 1953. 66p. **AA1000**

At head of title: Ministerio de Educación, Comité Nacional Pro-bibliotecas, Biblioteca Nacional.

An alphabetical listing, in preliminary form, of books, pamphlets, and documents printed in Panama in the 20th century, with a few titles on Panama published elsewhere.

Papua New Guinea

Papua New Guinea national bibliography. Mar. 1981– . Waigani, National Library Service of Papua New Guinea, 1981– . Quarterly with annual cumulation. **AA1001**

Continues in part the *New Guinea bibliography* publ. by University of Papua New Guinea, 1967–80. Material from Irian Jaya and the Solomon Islands (included in the earlier series) is now excluded.

Arranged by Dewey Decimal Classification with author/title/series and subject indexes. Lists monographs, first issues of serials (as well as subsequent name changes), maps, and audiovisual materials published in Papua New Guinea. Overseas publications dealing with Papua New Guinea or by Papua New Guineans are also included. Z4811.N48

Paraguay

Asunción. Biblioteca Nacional. Bibliografía paraguaya: catálogo de la biblioteca paraguaya "Solano López." Asunción, Talleres Nacionales de H. Kraus, 1906. 984p. **AA1002**

Rich in material relating to the early history of Paraguay.

Z907.A86

Bibliografía nacional paraguaya. Obras publicados entre los años 1971–1977. Edición preliminar. Asunción, Univ. Nacional de Asunción, Escuela de Bibliotecologia, 1978. 42p. **AA1003**

A first attempt to provide retrospective coverage of works published in and about Paraguay. 523 items in an alphabetical subject arrangement.

Fernández-Caballero, Carlos F. S. The Paraguayan bibliography. A retrospective and enumerative bibliography of printed works of Paraguayan authors. Asunción & Washington, Paraguay Arandú Books, 1970–75. 2v. (In progress?) **AA1004**

At head of title, v.1: Aranduká ha kuatiañeé paraguai rembiapocué; v.2, Paraguái tai hűme, tove Paraguái arandu talsarambi ko yvy apére.

v.2 publ. by the Seminar on the Acquisition of Latin American Library Materials as its *Bibliography,* no.3.

v.1 is an author listing of some 1,423 items; v.2, with some 2,363 entries, extends many of the author bibliographies in v.1 and lists additional works by Paraguayans and works on Paraguay published from the 18th century to 1974; in addition to having its own subject index, v.2 provides a separate subject index to v.1. Z1821.F45

Peru

Biblioteca peruana. Apuntes para un catálogo de impresos. Santiago de Chile, Biblioteca del Inst. Nacional, 1896. 2v. **AA1005**

Ed. by Gabriel René-Moreno.

Contents: v.1, pts.1–2, Libros y folletos peruanos de la Biblioteca del Instituto Nacional; v.2, pts.1–2, Libros y folletos peruanos de la Biblioteca Nacional y notas bibliográficas.

A basic work, fully annotated. Z1851.B58

Medina, José Toribio. La imprenta en Lima (1584–1824). Santiago de Chile, Autor, 1904–07. 4v. (Repr.: Amsterdam, N. Israel, 1965; also Readex Microprint) **AA1006**

Z213.L5M4

——— La imprenta en Arequipa, el Cuzco, Trujillo y otros pueblos del Perú durante las campañas de la independencia (1820–1825); notas bibliográficas. Santiago de Chile, Impr. Elzeviriana, 1904. 71p. (Repr.: Amsterdam, N. Israel, 1964; also Readex Microprint) **AA1007**

Z213.P4M4

Peru. Biblioteca Nacional, Lima. Bibliografía nacional. Enero/marzo 1978– . Lima, Biblioteca Nacional, Instituto Nacional de Cultura, 1978– . Monthly (irregular). **AA1008**

On cover: Libros, artículos de revistas y periódicos.

A combined national bibliography and periodical index. Employs a classed arrangement, with separate sections for books and pamphlets and for periodical articles. Contents notes or brief annotations are provided for most entries. Index of names and broad subjects. No cumulative indexes to date.

Vargas Ugarte, Rubén. Impresos peruanos. Lima, [Ed. San Marcos], 1949–57. 7v. in 6. (*His* Biblioteca peruana, t.6–12) **AA1009**

Contents: v.1, Impresos peruanos publicados en el extranjero 1546–1825; v.2–7, Impresos peruanos 1584–1825.

Aims to include all books and pamphlets published in Peru;

arranged chronologically, with author index in each volume. Line-by-line transcription, with detailed bibliographical description. Locates copies. v.1 is concerned with publications appearing outside Peru. Z1866.V3

Current

Anuario bibliográfico peruano, 1943- . Lima, 1945- . v.1- . (Ediciones de la Biblioteca Nacional, 1-) **AA1010**

Frequency varies: annual 1943–48; biennial 1949/50–1953/54; triennial 1955/57- . (1970/72 publ. 1978)

A national bibliography which attempts to record books, pamphlets, and all other publications printed in Peru, as well as works of Peruvian authors and works relating to Peru printed abroad. Classified, with indexes of periodicals, authors, etc.

Each volume includes a section of periodicals and newspapers, and a separate bio-bibliographical section of Peruvian authors who died during the years covered. These bibliographies are extensive and are indexed separately. Z1851.A5

Lima. Universidad de San Marcos. Biblioteca. Boletin bibliográfico, v.1–39, 1923–66. Lima, 1923–66. Quarterly (irregular). **AA1011**

Suspended 1930–Oct. 1934 and 1967–72; a cumulative issue for the latter period was planned for 1973 publication. Ceased publication.

Usually each year includes a list of books and pamphlets published in Peru, with full bibliographical information, and a list of articles from Peruvian periodicals. Z782.L77B

Peru. Biblioteca Nacional, Lima. Catalogo de autores de la colección peruana. . . . Boston, G. K. Hall, 1979. 6v. **AA1012**

Added title page: Author catalog of the Peruvian Collection, National Library of Peru.

Contents: v.1–5, Libros y folletos; v.6, Publicaciones periódicas; Mapas y planos.

An author listing of some 94,000 books, pamphlets, periodicals, and maps, published 1553–1977; includes works by Peruvian authors and works about Peru. Z1879.P47

Philippines

Bernardo, Gabriel Adriano. Philippine retrospective national bibliography: 1523–1699. [Manila], Nat. Lib. of the Philippines, [1974]. 160p. il. (Occasional papers of the Dept. of History, Ateneo de Manila bibliographical ser., no.3) **AA1013**

Includes three categories of foreign and Philippine imprints: "(1) those which deal in whole or in part with the Philippines and were printed abroad, (2) all those printed in the Philippines of any nature, and (3) those written by Filipinos."—*Introd.* Chronological listing in two main sections, (1) Foreign imprints; (2) Philippine imprints. Author/subject index. 760 items. Z3298.A35B47

Medina, José Toribio. Bibliografía española de las Islas Filipinas (1523–1810). Santiago de Chile, Impr. Cervantes, 1897–[98]. 556p. **AA1014**

Reprinted from *Anales de la Universidad de Chile,* 1897–98.

A list of 667 titles arranged chronologically, with author index. Z3291.M40

—— La imprenta en Manila desde sus orígenes hasta 1810. Santiago de Chile, Autor, 1896. 280p. facsim. (Repr.: Amsterdam, N. Israel, 1964, with the *Adiciones*) **AA1015**

—— —— Adiciones y ampliaciones. Santiago de Chile, Autor, 1904. 203p.

Z3291.M40

Pérez, Angel and **Güemes, Cecilio.** Adiciones y continuación de "La imprenta en Manila" de d. J. T. Medina; ó rarezas curiosidades bibliográficas filipinas de las bibliotecas de esta capital. Manila, Santos y Bernal, 1904. 620p. (Readex Microprint) **AA1016**

Z186.P5M6

Retana y Gamboa, Wenceslao Emilio. La imprenta en Filipinas; adiciones y observaciones á la Imprenta en Manila de d. J. T. Medina. Madrid, Minuesa de los Ríos, 1897. 276cols. (Readex Microprint) **AA1017**

Z3291.M497

—— Aparato bibliográfico de la historia general de Filipinas. Madrid, Minuesa de los Ríos, 1906. 3v. **AA1018**

v.1, 1524–1800; v.2, 1801–86; v.3, 1887–1905.

Includes: (1) Philippine imprints regardless of subject; (2) Books about the Philippines regardless of what language written in or where published; (3) Publications of Filipinos wherever printed.

Arranged by years with the following indexes in v.1: (1) Anónimos y principales materias, refundidos; (2) Publicaciones periódicas; (3) Biblioteca idiomática oriental; (4) Lugares geográficos; (5) Nombres propios de personas. Z3291.R4

—— Tablas cronológica y alfabética de imprentas e impresores de Filipinas (1593–1898). Madrid, Victoriano Suárez, 1908. 114p. (Readex Microprint) **AA1019**

Z186.P5M52

Current

Philippine bibliography, 1963/64–1970/72. Diliman, [Quezon], Univ. of the Philippines Lib., 1965–73. 5v. **AA1020**

An effort toward establishing a national bibliography for the Philippines. Includes items published in the Philippines, works by Filipinos published elsewhere, and works by foreign authors treating solely, or in large part, Philippine subjects. Entries comprise books, pamphlets, government publications, and first issues of new periodicals. Non-government and government publications are listed in separate alphabetical sequences. Title and subject index.

Superseded by: Z3291.P48

Philippine union catalog. Jan./Mar. 1974- . Quezon City, Univ. of the Philippines Library, 1974- . 3 quarterly issues per yr. plus annual cumulation. **AA1021**

Supersedes *Philippine bibliography* 1963–1972 (above).

"An author list of Filipiniana materials currently acquired by the University of the Philippines Library and other libraries."—*t.p.*

Gives full catalog entries for "Filipiniana materials including books, theses, music scores, phonodiscs, tapes, microfilms, new serial titles and other materials, or reproductions of any of these forms. It also includes government documents and publications except individual acts, bills and ordinances. Pamphlets of less than five pages, unless of research value, are excluded."—*Introd.* Includes both current materials and older works recently acquired by participating libraries. Author listing with title and subject indexes.

Philippine national bibliography. Jan./Feb. 1974- . Manila, National Library of the Philippines, 1974- . Bimonthly with annual cumulations. **AA1022**

1974 annual publ. 1976.

Aims to list "new works published or printed in the Philippines, by Filipino authors, or about the Philippines, including unpublished materials."—*Pref., 1974.* Includes books, pamphlets, government publications, first issues of newspapers and periodicals, theses and dissertations. The "Book list or main sequence" is arranged by type of publication (e.g., books and pamphlets; periodicals, newspapers, annuals), then alphabetically by main entry. Author/title/series index and subject index. Z3296.P53

Poland

Wierzbowski, Teodor. Bibliographia polonica XV ac XVI ss. . . . Varsoviae, Kowalewski, 1889–94. 3v. (Repr.: Nieuwkoop, B. DeGraaf, 1961) **AA1023**

v.1 contains titles of works in the Warsaw University Library (destroyed by fire); v.2–3, works found in other libraries, Polish and foreign, with indication of location. Arranged chronologically with indexes of authors, subjects, persons, and places. Z2522.W65

Estreicher, Karol J. T. Bibliografia polska. Kraków, Czionkami Drukarni Universytetu Jagiellońskiego, 1870–1939; 1951. 34v. **AA1024**

In three series: ser.1, an alphabetical list covering 1800–70. 7v. (v.1–5, A–Z; v.6–7, Supplement, A–Z); ser.2, chronological lists, 1455–1880. 4v. (v.8–9, 1455–1799; v.10, 1800–1870; v.11, 1871–1889); ser.3, alphabetical list, 15th–18th centuries, v.1–23 (whole no. v.12–34), A–Zał.

The exhaustive bibliography of Polish imprints from 1455 to 1880.

Continued to 1900 by: Z2521.E82

———— Bibliografia polska XIX. stulecia; lata 1881–1900. Kraków, Spólki Ksiegarzy Polskich, 1906–16. 4v.

Z2521.E84

———— Bibliografia polska XIX. stulecia. Wyd. 2. Kraków, [Państwowe Wydawn. Naukowe, Oddział w Krakowie], 1959–79. v.1–12. (Polska Akademia Nauk. Bibliografia polska Karola Estreichera, cz.1, t.1–12) (In progress) **AA1025**

Added title page in French.
Contents: v.1–12, A–J.
A 2d ed. of this important 19th-century bibliography.

Z2521.E85

20th century

Dąbrowska, Wanda, Czarnecka, J. and **Słomczewska, J.** 555 książek wydanych w okresie powojennym. Warszawa, Ludowy Inst. Oświaty i Kultury, 1946. 80p. **AA1026**

Lists 555 books published in Poland, July 1944–May 1, 1946. Classified, with author and title index and subject index.

Z2526.D3

Przewodnik bibljograficzny. ser.1, v.1–37, no.6, 1878–June 1914; ser.2, v.1–9, 1920–28; ser.3, v.1–5, 1929–33. Kraków, Zaklad Narodowy Imienia Ossolinskich, 1878–1933.

AA1027

July 1914–19 not numbered in series; called *Bibliografia polska,* v.1–6.
Continued by AA1029. Z2523.P92

London. Polish Library. Bibliography of books in Polish or relating to Poland published outside Poland since Sept. 1st, 1939. London, 1954–66. 3v. **AA1028**

Janina Zabielska, comp.
Contents: v.1, 1939–1951; v.2, 1952–1957 and supplements to 1939–1951; v.3, 1958–1963 and supplement to 1939–1957.
Each volume arranged chronologically. Z2528.A5P6

Current

Przewodnik bibliograficzny; urzedowy wykaz druków wydanych w Rzeczypospolitej Polskiej. . . . R.1 (13), nr.1/3– . Warszawa, Biblioteka Narodowa, 1946– . Weekly (frequency varies). **AA1029**

Superseded *Urzedowy wykaz druków, 1928–39,* and continues its numbering in parentheses. v.1 (publ. 1955) is a retrospective volume for 1944–45. Includes Polish imprints, books, pamphlets, new periodicals, and many government publications, and also foreign publications dealing with Poland which are in the National Library. Arrangement is classified, with an annual alphabetical index. Some volumes also have subject indexes. Z2523.P93

Portugal
Early

Academia das Sciencias de Lisboa. Bibliografia geral portuguesa. Lisboa, Impr. Nacional, 1941–42. v.1–2. il. **AA1030**

Date on cover of v.2: 1944.
Contents: v.1–2, Século XV.
Detailed bibliographical descriptions with introduction and notes, facsimiles, and the following indexes in each volume: Matérias, Gravuras, Impressores, Bibliotecas e arquivos, Toponímico, and Geral. Z2711.A3

Anselmo, António Joaquim. Bibliografia das obras impressas em Portugal no século XVI. Lisboa, Oficinas Gráficas da Biblioteca Nacional, 1926. 367p. il. (Publicações da Biblioteca Nacional) **AA1031**

Reprinted from *Anais das bibliotecas e arquivos,* sér.2, v.2–6, 1921–25.
Detailed bibliographical descriptions. Z2712.A61

Barbosa Machado, Diogo. Bibliotheca lusitana historica, critica, e cronologica. Na qual se comprehende a noticia dos authores portuguezes, e das obras, que compuseraõ desde o tempo da promulgaçaõ da ley da graça até o tempo prezente. Lisboa, 1741–59. 4v. (Repr.: Coimbra, Atlântida Editora, 1965–67; also Readex Microprint) **AA1032**

A bio-bibliographical work arranged by given names, providing much information not available in later works. Covers from early times to mid-18th century.

An abridgment by B. J. de Sousa-Farinha, entitled *Summario da Bibliotheca lusitana,* was published in Lisbon, 1786–87. 3v.

Z2722.B23

British Museum. Dept. of Printed Books. Short-title catalogue of Portuguese books printed before 1601, now in the British Museum, by Henry Thomas. London, Trustees, 1940. 43p. **AA1033**

A revised and enlarged edition of the Portuguese section of an earlier catalog (AA927).

Manuel II, King of Portugal. Livros antigos portuguezes, 1489–1600, da bibliotheca de Sua Majestade Fidelissima, descriptos por S. M. el-rei D. Manuel . . . Cambridge, Univ. Pr., 1929–35. 3v. il. **AA1034**

Contents: v.1, 1489–1539; v.2, 1540–1569; v.3, 1570–1600 e Supplemento 1500–1597. Z2712.M29

General

Coimbra, Carlos. Dicionario de bibliografia portuguesa . . . Edição de A. Gusmão Navarro. Lisboa, Torres, 1933–37. v.1. **AA1035**

Issued in parts, looseleaf. No more published. Covers "A–Barros" (with a few sheets giving entries for various other parts of the alphabet). An attempt to list Portuguese books of all periods.

Z2720.C68

Silva, Innocencio Francisco da. Dicionário bibliografico portuguêz. Estudos aplicaveis a Portugal e ao Brasil. Lisboa, Impr. Nacional, 1858–1923. v.1–22. il. **AA1036**

Contents: v.1–7, A–Z; v.8–22 (also called suppl. 1–15), A–Z, A–Au.
v.10–22 "continuados e ampliados por Brito Aranha."
A bio-bibliography arranged alphabetically by *first* names of authors. Includes books published from the 15th to the 19th centuries. Z2720.S58

——— ——— Indice alfabético, [por] José Soares de Souza. [São Paulo?], Dept. de Cultura, Divisião de Bibliotécas, 1938. 264p.

Current

Boletim de bibliografia portuguesa, v.1–46, 1935–80. Lisboa, Biblioteca Nacional, 1937–80. Annual, 1935–51; monthly, 1955–80. **AA1037**

Not published 1940–42; 1952–54.

The national bibliography for Portugal, listing books, pamphlets, some periodical articles, and government publications. The annual volumes were arranged alphabetically by author. Beginning in 1955, published monthly and arranged by Universal Decimal Classification.

Continued by:

Boletim de bibliografia portuguesa. Monografias. v.47– , Jan./Jun. 1981– . Lisboa, Biblioteca Nacional, 1982– . Quarterly. **AA1038**

Continues in part *Boletim de bibliografia portuguesa* (above) and assumes its numbering. (1981 issued in 3 fasc.: no.1/2, 3/4 and indexes.)

Also referred to as *BBP. Monografias.*

Arranged by Universal Decimal Classification, with author, title, and systematic indexes. Companion publications are the *Boletim de bibliografia portuguesa. Publicações em série* (1981–) and *Boletim de bibliografia portuguesa. Documentos não textuais* (1981–).

Livros de Portugal; mensário bibliográfico, no.60– , Maio 1952– . Lisboa, Grémio Nacional dos Editores e Livreiros, 1952– . Monthly, then quarterly. **AA1039**

Began publication in Nov. 1940 (no.1–58?, 1940–46); suspended publication. Resumed with no.60, maio 1952.

Contains notes, advertisements, etc., and a list of recent books. Only issues called "Suplemento" have appeared in recent years.

Z2715.L783

Puerto Rico

Anuario bibliográfico puertorriqueño; índice alfabético de libros, folletos, revistas y periódicos publicados en Puerto Rico durante 1948– , comp. por Gonzálo Velazquez. Río Piedras, Estado Libre Asociado de Puerto Rico, Dept. de Instrucción Pública, 1950– . v.1– . Annual. **AA1040**

Publisher varies.

An author, subject, and title listing of books, pamphlets, and periodicals. An excellent catalog, but slow in appearing (e.g., 1973/74 publ. 1982).

Z1551.A6

Rhodesia

See also Zimbabwe.

Hartridge, Anne, comp. Rhodesia national bibliography, 1890 to 1930. Salisbury, National Archives, 1977. 50p. (National Archives of Rhodesia. Bibliographical ser., no.2) **AA1041**

A first step toward providing coverage from 1890 (the date of "commencement of administration and modern commerce within Rhodesia"—*Foreword*) to 1961, the beginning date for annual bibliographic records for the area (*see* below).

Classed arrangement according to the Dewey Decimal Classification, with index of authors, editors, etc. and titles. Lists books, pamphlets, maps, serials (including newspapers), and government publications published in Rhodesia.

Rhodesia national bibliography, 1967–78. Salisbury, Rhodesia Nat. Archives, 1968–79. Annual. **AA1042**

Subtitle: List of publications deposited in the Library of the National Archives.

Supersedes the National Archives of Rhodesia's *List of publications deposited in the library,* which covered 1961–66 (publ. 1963–67). The 1961 volume included the Federation of Rhodesia and Nyasaland; subsequent volumes are limited to items published in what was then Rhodesia (previously Southern Rhodesia, now Zimbabwe) and excludes those published in Northern Rhodesia and Nyasaland. Includes books, pamphlets, and first issues of new serials; official government publications and annual reports of local authorities are also listed. Classed arrangement (with index, beginning 1970).

Continued by *Zimbabwe national bibliography* (AA1155).

Z3573.R5R54

Romania

Adamescu, Gheorghe. Contribuţiune la bibliografia române-asca. Bucureşti, Cartea Româneasca, 1921–28. 3pts. **AA1043**

For annotation *see* BD1317.

Bianu, Ioan, Hodos, Nerva and **Simonescu, Dan.** Bibliografia româneasca veche 1508–1830. Ed. Academiei Române. Bucureşti, Atelierele Socec & Co., 1903–43. 4v. il. **AA1044**

Issued in parts: v.1, 1508–1716; v.2, 1716–1808; v.3, 1809–1830; v.4, Additions et corrections (1943) by Ioan Bianu and Dan Simonescu.

An exhaustive bibliography, arranged chronologically, with index of names and titles. Z2921.B58

Veress, Endre. Bibliografia româna-ungara. Bucureşti, Cartea Româneasca, 1931–35. 3v. il. **AA1045**

Contents: v.1, Românii in literatura ungara şi Ungurii in literatura româna (1473–1780); v.2, 1781–1838; v.3, 1839–78.

Records some 2,377 titles in chronological order with full description and location of copies. Each volume has added title page and preface in French. Z2928.R4V5

Current

Bucharest. Biblioteca Centrala de Stat. Anuarul cărţii din Republica Populara Romīna, 1952–1954. Bucureşti, Ed. Stiinţifica, 1957. 410p. **AA1046**

Classed arrangement, with alphabetic index of authors and titles. No more published. Z2921.B8

——— Bibliografia Republicii Populare Romîne: cărţi, albume, hărţi, note muzicale. [Bucureşti], 1951–67. Anul 1–16. Semimonthly. **AA1047**

Title varies. v.1–5 issued by the Romanian Ministerul Culturii under title: *Buletinul bibliografic al cărţii.*

The national bibliography. Lists books, maps, and some government publications in classified order, with indexes of names and titles in each issue. (Early volumes had quarterly cumulations of the indexes, but these were abandoned after 1964.)

Superseded by: Z2923.B82

Bibliografia Republicii Socialiste România: Cărţi, albume, hărţi. 1968– . [Bucureşti], Biblioteca Centrala de Stat a Republicii Socialiste România, 1968– . Anul 17– . Semimonthly. **AA1048**

Together with *Bibliografia Republicii Socialiste România: Note muzicale, discrui,* supersedes the 1951–67 series (above) and assumes its numbering. Z2923.B5

Russia and the U.S.S.R.

General

U.S. Library of Congress. Cyrillic union catalog. N.Y., Readex Microprint Corp., 1963. 1244 cards in 7 boxes. (Micro-opaque) **AA1049**

Contents: pt.I, Authors and added entries; p.II, Titles, with complete listing of library locations; pt.III, Subjects.

A union catalog of more than 700,000 cards, representing 178,226 titles in Russian, Belorussian, Bulgarian, Serbian, and Ukrainian. Substantially complete for monographic holdings of the Library of Congress as of March 1956. Reported holdings of 185 other American libraries are also included, with the most complete information on locations in pt.II. "The title catalog is a useful finding aid for the reader who knows the title of a given book but not its author. It is also useful to the reader unversed in the intricate rules of cataloging corporate authors."—*Introd.* Library of Congress card numbers, where available, appear in parentheses following title. English translations of titles, other than belles-lettres, are given for all post-1917 publications. Subject catalog contains form headings for fiction, drama, poetry. The microform set is accompanied by a booklet: *Cyrillic union catalog of the Library of Congress; description and guide to the Microprint edition* (N.Y., 1964. 12p.).

Pt. I is, in effect, superseded by:

—— **Catalog Publication Division.** The Slavic Cyrillic union catalog of pre-1956 imprints. Totowa, N.J., Rowman & Littlefield, 1980. Microfiche (174 sheets, 48x). **AA1050**

A successor to the *Cyrillic union catalog* (above), considerably expanded in scope. Reproduces the catalog cards from the Slavic Union Catalog at the Library of Congress for books, pamphlets, maps, atlases, periodicals, and other serials published before 1956 in the Cyrillic alphabet and in seven languages: Russian, Church Slavic, Belorussian, Ukrainian, Bulgarian, Serbian, and Macedonian. It represents more than 350,000 entries (main and added entries and cross references) as cataloged by the Library of Congress and participating libraries, and held by 220 libraries in the United States and Canada. Arranged by main entry, with essential added entries and cross references (although the main entry must be consulted for locations). No attempt was made to edit contributed copy for conformity with LC practice, and the searcher should be aware that inconsistencies in form of entry are to be expected. Most entries use the Cyrillic alphabet rather than transliteration as in the *Cyrillic union catalog*. The latter catalog, of course, remains useful for subject and title approaches.

16th and 17th centuries

Zernova, Antonina S. Knigi kirillovskoi pechati, izdannye v Moskve v XVI-XVII vekakh; svodnyi katalog. Pod. red. N. P. Kiseleva. Moskva, 1958. 150p. **AA1051**

At head of title: Ministerstvo kultura RSFSR. Gosudarstvennaia ordena Lenina Biblioteka SSSR im. V. I. Lenina. Otdel redkikh knig.

A union catalog of 16th- and 17th-century Moscow imprints in *kirillitsa* printing type, the alphabet for Russian prior to reform under Peter I and continued for ecclesiastical printing. Describes copies in six of the largest libraries of Moscow and Leningrad.

Z7044.C4Z4

18th century

Akademiia Nauk URSR, Kiev. Biblioteka. Knigi grazhdanskoi pechati XVIII veka; katalog knig, khraniashchiksia v Gosudarstvennoi Publichnoi Biblioteke Ukrainskoi SSR. Sost.: S. O. Petrov. Kiev, 1956. 300p. **AA1052**

Catalog of the books and journals, printed between 1708 and 1800 in Russian, which are preserved in the State Library in Kiev. Arrangement is by author, or title of anonymous work, with indexes

for translators, places of publication and publishers' names, and broad subject fields. Continued by AA1059. Z2501.A4

Bykova, Tat'iana Aleksandrovna and **Gurevich, Miron M.** Opisanie izdanii, napechatannykh pri Petre I. Svodnyi katalog. . . . Red. i vstup. stat'ia P. N. Berkova. Moskva, Izd-vo Akademii Nauk SSSR, 1955–58. 2v. il. **AA1053**

At head of title: Gosudarstvennaia Publichnaia Biblioteka imeni M. E. Saltykova-Shchedrina i Biblioteka Akademii Nauk SSSR.

Each volume also has special title page.

Contents: v.1, Opisanie izdanii grazhdanskoi pechati. 1708–ianvar' 1725g. 625p.; v.2, Opisanie izdanii napechatannykh kirillitsei 1689-ianvar' 1725g. 402p.

v.1 is a descriptive bibliography with extensive annotations of works published in the Russian "civic" type introduced under Peter I. Locational symbols are given for libraries in Moscow and Leningrad. Appendixes list books in foreign languages published in Russia. v.2 is a detailed, descriptive bibliography of Russian books printed in the pre-reform alphabet, *kirillitsa*, between 1689 and 1725; appendixes include foreign books pertaining to Russia.

These two volumes of a Russian union catalog are continued, chronologically, by *Svodnyi katalog russkoi knigi . . . XVIII veka, 1725–1800* (AA1056).

Supplemented by: Z2492.B94

—— —— Dopolneniia i prilozheniia. Leningrad, 1972. 272p. **AA1054**

At head of title: Biblioteka Akademii Nauk SSSR. Gosudarstvennaia Publichnaia Biblioteka imeni M. E. Saltykova-Shchedrina. Leningradskoe Otdelenie Instituta Istorii SSSR. Akademii Nauk SSSR.

A supplement to the above. Scope has been extended to cover through December 1727, and information from sources not searched for compilation of the basic volumes is included here.

Sopikov, Vasilii Stephanovich. Opyt rossiiskoi bibliografii. [Izd. 2] Red., V. N. Rogozhin. St. Petersburg, 1904–06. 5v. **AA1055**

Originally published 1813–21.

v.1 is a classed arrangement of books under the heading "Church Slavic." v.2–5 list other books in Russian to 1813.

Subject index in P. O. Morozov, *Alfavitnyi ukazatel' imen . . .* 1876. 47p.; various indexes in V. N. Rogoshin, *Ukazatel' . . .* 1908. 253p.

Although largely replaced by more recent bibliographies for the 18th century, the Sopikov number is often cited as part of the bibliographic description in later works. Z2491.S71

Svodnyi katalog russkoi knigi grazhdanskoi pechati XVIII veka, 1725–1800. Red. kollegia: I. P. Kondakov i dr. Moskva, Izd. Gos. Biblioteki SSSR im. Lenina, 1962–67. 5v. **AA1056**

Forms a chronological section of a union catalog of Russian books from 1708 to the present. Includes works of five pages or more published in Russia or abroad. Entries are annotated, refer to entry numbers in earlier standard bibliographies, and give locational symbols for copies in the major libraries of Leningrad and Moscow.

For the bibliography of the first quarter of the 18th century, *see* AA1053. Z2492.S85

—— Dopolneniia, razyskivaemye izdanniia utochneniia. [Redaktsionnaia kollegiia: N. M. Sikorskii] Moskva, Kniga, 1975. 189p.

Lists acquisitions of participating libraries from 1967; corrections to v.1–4; citations to reviews and indexes. Includes a list of unlocated books.

A complementary publication is:

Svodnyi katalog knig na inostrannykh iazykakh, izdannykh v Rossii v XVIII veke, 1701–1800. [Red. kollegia: V. A. Filov i dr.] Leningrad, "Nauka," Leningradskoe Otd-nie, 1984– . v.1– . (In progress) **AA1057**

Contents: v.1, A–G.

Lists foreign-language books published in Russia during the period. Z2491.S9

U.S. Library of Congress. Eighteenth century Russian publications in the Library of Congress: a catalog. Prep. by Tatiana Fessenko. Wash., Slavic and Central European Division, Reference Dept., Lib. of Congress, 1961. 157p. **AA1058**

More than 1,300 fully cataloged works with identification "in almost 100 instances . . . [of] the foreign authors of Russian translations which up to now have been listed as anonymous in Russian bibliographies."—*Pref.* Appendixes for other tentative identifications and for itemized holdings of incomplete works. Title index. Z2502.U5

19th and 20th centuries

Akademiia Nauk URSR, Kiev. Biblioteka. Knigi pervoi chetverti XIX veka; katalog knig, khraniashchikhsia v Gosudarstvennoi Publichnoi Biblioteke Ukrainskoi SSR. Sost.: S. O. Petrov. Kiev, 1961. 398p. **AA1059**

Continues the Library's catalog of 18th-century books (AA1052) with 2,800 works published in the first quarter of the 19th century, primarily St. Petersburg and Moscow imprints. Arranged by author or anonymous title, with indexes for translators and editors, cities and publishers, and broad subject. Annotations include references to 19th-century bibliographic listings. Z2503.A5

U.S. Library of Congress. Processing Dept. Monthly index of Russian accessions. Wash., Govt. Prt. Off., 1948–69. v.1–22[1-5]. Monthly. **AA1060**

Title varies: 1948–57, *Monthly list of Russian accessions.*
Ceased publication with v.22, no.5, May 1969.

A union list of Russian-language monographs and periodicals issued in and outside the Soviet Union, received by the Library of Congress and a group of cooperating libraries. Whenever possible, publications printed in other languages in the Soviet Union are also included. Each issue is in three parts: pt.A, Monographs; pt.B, Periodicals, with their tables of contents translated into English; pt.C, Alphabetical subject index to A and B under English subject headings. Pts.A and B are classified in 17 main subject groups. Beginning v.21, no.1 (April 1968) the subject headings previously used in pt.C were replaced by classes based on the Universal Decimal Classification.

All titles are given first in English, followed by the Russian title in transliteration. Beginning with v.5, an author index to monographs and a periodical location index are included annually as appendixes to the first two issues of the following volume (varies slightly). These are preceded by a cumulative index to v.1–3, April 1948–March 1951, issued in one volume (1953), and a cumulative index to v.4, April 1951–March 1952 (1957). In each issue pt.C included a list of Russian periodicals available in English translation from cover to cover.

The Library's Processing Department also issued, in similar format, a monthly *East European accessions index* (1951–61. 10v.) which covered monographs published after 1944, and periodicals after 1950, received by the Library of Congress and certain other American libraries, published in ten East European countries (except Russia) or elsewhere in their languages. Z2495.U6

U.S. Library of Congress. Reference Dept. Russia: a check list preliminary to a basic bibliography of materials in the Russian language. Wash., 1944–46. pts.1–10. **AA1061**

Contents: pt.1, Belles lettres; pt.2, Economic conditions and social history prior to 1918; pt.3, Fine arts; pt.4, Law and institutions prior to 1918; pt.5, Folklore, linguistics and literary forms; pt.6, Church and education prior to 1918; pt.7, History, including auxiliary sciences, prior to 1918; pt.8, Theatre and music prior to 1918; pt.9, Soviet Union; pt.10, Reference books.

Each section is arranged alphabetically. Titles are given in transliteration according to Library of Congress rules. In general, superseded by the Library's *Cyrillic union catalog* (AA1049). Z663.28.R8

Current

Ezhegodnik knigi SSSR; sistematicheskii ukazatel', 1941– . Moskva, Izd-vo Vsesoiuznoi Knizhnoi Palaty, 1946– . Annual. **AA1062**

Continues *Ezhegodnik knigi* issued by RSFSR, Gosudarstvennaia Tsentral'naia Knizhnaia Palata, annually for the years 1925–29 (Moskva, 1927–31); and *Ezhegodnik knigi*, 1935 (Moskva, 1936). Semiannual 1946–56. Issued in 2v., 1959– , of which v.1 covers social sciences and humanities and v.2, science and technology.

The book annual of the Soviet national bibliography. Cumulates, in classified arrangement, a selection from the weekly *Knizhnaia letopis'* (below). Indexes for names, titles, languages other than Russian, translations from foreign languages, and subjects. Z2401.E9

Knizhnaia letopis' . . . v.1– , 1907– . Moskva, 1907– . Weekly. **AA1063**

Issued by Vsesoiuznaia Knizhnaia Palata.
1907– , available on microfilm from Library of Congress. Repr.: N.Y., Kraus, 1965.
For a detailed history of the title with a list of indexes and bibliography, *see* Sokurova, *Obshchie bibliografii russkikh knig grazhdanskoi pechati, 1708–1955,* p.179–222 (AA104), and Gracheva and Frantskevich, *Gosudarstvennaia bibliografiia SSSR,* p.13–25 (AA1065).

As the principal organ of Soviet national bibliography, this work currently lists, in Russian, books and pamphlets published in the USSR in all languages. Each issue contains a language index to non-Russian publications.

Arranged in 31 classes. Each entry includes a classification number based on a variant of the Universal Decimal Classification. Quarterly indexes: name, geographical, and subject. *Ukazatel' seriinykh izdanii* is an annual index to publishers' series. An annual cumulation of a selection of titles from the weekly appears as *Ezhegodnik knigi SSSR* (AA1062). Z2491.K5

Complemented by a monthly supplement:

———— Dopolnitel'nyi vypusk, 1961– . Moskva, 1961– . Monthly. **AA1064**

Issued by Vsesoiuznaia Knizhnaia Palata.
A monthly supplement to the main organ of Soviet national bibliography, *Knizhnaia letopis'* (above). Includes certain types of publications formerly registered in the weekly, but categories transferred have varied. In general, lists small editions if printed in 101 copies or more and over five pages in length, and unpriced materials not intended for the book trade. List of dissertations, included in 1961, was omitted in 1962 and 1963, and resumed in 1964. Quarterly indexes (name, subject, and geographical) and annual index to publishers' series.

For an account of the publications which make up the current Soviet national bibliographies *see:*

Gracheva, Iia Borisovna and **Frantskevich, Valentina N.,** eds. Gosudarstvennaia bibliografiia SSSR. Spravochnik. Izd.2, perer. i dop. Moskva, "Kniga," 1967. 111p. **AA1065**

At head of title: Vsesoiuznaia Knizhnaia Palata.
1st ed. 1952 had title *Gosudarstvennaia registratsionnouchetnaia bibliografiia SSSR;* comp. by IU. I. Masanov.
Describes in detail the various publications forming the current national bibliographies of Russia and the republics of the Soviet Union. Z2492.5.G7

Whitby, Thomas Joseph and **Lorkovic, Tanja.** Introduction to Soviet national bibliography. Littleton, Colo., Libraries Unlimited, 1979. 229p. **AA1066**

An introductory section, which traces the development of Soviet national bibliography from tsarist times to the present and describes the current activities of the All-Union Book Chamber, is followed by a translation of *Gosudarstvennaia bibliografiia SSSR. Spravochnik* (above) under the title "Guide to the organs of national bibliography in the USSR." Appendixes include a glossary of terms (i.e., English equivalents of Russian terms) and a bibliography, p.211–24. Indexed. Z2492.5.W47

Rwanda

Lévesque, Albert. Contribution to the national bibliography of Rwanda, 1965–1970. Contribution à la bibliographie nationale du Rwanda. [2d ed.] Boston, G. K. Hall, [1979]. 542p. **AA1067**

Prefatory matter in English and French; subject headings in French.

A 1st ed. (1974) had limited circulation.

Offered as "a contribution to the future Bibliographie Nationale Rwandaise" (*Introd.*) as well as a supplement to J. R. A. M. Clément's *Essai de bibliographie Ruanda-Urundi* (Usumbura, 1959) and to the bibliographies of Heyse (DD197) and Walraet (DD168). Aims to list all works published in Rwanda during the period, together with writings about Rwanda published abroad. The compiler admits failure to achieve exhaustiveness in either category owing to lack of a copyright law, the size of the task, and the difficulty of locating ephemeral materials. Lists some 4,500 items in classed arrangement, with author/subject and title indexes.   Z3721.L48

Scotland

See also Great Britain, p.74–79.

Aldis, Harry Gidney. List of books printed in Scotland before 1700, including those printed furth of the realm for Scottish booksellers, with brief notes on the printers and stationers. [Edinburgh], Edinburgh Bibliographical Soc., 1904. 153p. **AA1068**

A preliminary hand list of 3,919 titles, arranged chronologically with an alphabetical index, and an index of printers, booksellers, and stationers.   Z2051.A55

Ferguson, Mary and **Matheson, Ann.** Scottish Gaelic union catalogue: a list of books printed in Scottish Gaelic from 1567 to 1973. Edinburgh, National Library of Scotland, 1984. 200p. **AA1069**

Intended as a finding list rather than a full bibliography: "Since not all copies of works were individually examined, the Catalogue cannot be regarded as a totally reliable bibliographical tool" (*Introd.*), and information found in Donald Maclean's *Typographia Scoto-Gadelica* (Edinburgh, Grant, 1915. 372p.), for example, is not fully superseded. More than 3,000 entries for items in Scottish and British libraries; plans call for a supplement of foreign library holdings.   Z2039.G3F47

Current

Bibliography of Scotland, 1976/77– . Edinburgh, H.M.S.O., 1978– . Annual. **AA1070**

Subtitle: A catalogue of books published in Scotland and of books published elsewhere of Scottish relevance, prepared from accessions received by the National Library of Scotland.

At head of title: National Library of Scotland.

The first volume lists items published after 1975 and processed by the National Library in 1976–77; subsequent annual volumes continue to list post-1975 items processed during the year of coverage. In addition to books as specified in the subtitle, selected periodical articles on Scottish topics acquired by the National Library, and music are included. First issues of new periodicals and changes of title are recorded. In two sections: (1) Topographical; (2) Subject. Name index.   Z2069.B52

Singapore

Singapore national bibliography, 1967– . Singapore, Nat. Lib., [1969–]. Annual. **AA1071**

Quarterly lists of deposit publications were previously published only in the Singapore *Government gazette*.

Aims to list all works published in the Republic of Singapore; based on materials received at the National Library. Arrangement is by Dewey Decimal Classification, with author, title, and subject index.   Z3248.S5A3

South Africa

Nienaber, Petrus Johannes. Bibliografie van Afrikaanse boeke. 2. druk, met'n aanvullende lijs. Johannesburg, 1954– . Deel 1– . Irregular. **AA1072**

1st ed. 1943–54 in 3v.; Deel 3– not designated as "2. druk."

Contents: Deel 1, 6 Apr. 1861–6 Apr. 1943 (1952); Deel 2, Apr. 1943–Okt. 1948 (1958); Deel 3, Nov. 1948–Okt. 1953 (1954); Deel 4, Nov. 1953–Junie 1958 (1958); Deel 5, Julie 1958–Feb. 1963 (1963); Deel 6, Maart 1963–Des. 1966 (1967); Deel 7, Jan 1967–Des. 1970 (1971); Deel 8, Jan. 1971–Des. 1974 (1977); Deel 9, Jan. 1975–Des. 1977 (1981).

A comprehensive bibliography. Each volume is in three main sections: (1) Author list; (2) Title list; (3) Classified list.   Z3601.N512

S. A. Katalogus/Catalogue; 5th complete ed., 1900–1954, and list of publishers in South Africa. Johannesburg, Technical Books & Careers, 1956. v.1, A–K. **AA1073**

4th ed. 1900–50.

Title varies: earlier editions called *South African catalogue of books; Suid-Afrikaanse katalogus.*

An author-title listing of books published in South Africa since 1900. The cumulated editions do not always include all previously listed titles, and therefore earlier editions should be preserved.   Z3601.S8

Current

Africana nova. Sept. 1958–1969. Capetown, South African Pub. Lib., 1958–69. Quarterly. **AA1074**

Subtitle: A quarterly bibliography of books currently published in and about the Republic of South Africa. Based on the accessions to the Africana Department, South African Public Library, including material received by Legal Deposit.

Ceased publication.

In English and Afrikaans. Arranged by Dewey Decimal Classification, with author index in each issue, and annual index. Preceded by lists of current publications published in the *Quarterly bulletin* of the South African Public Library, Sept. 1946–June 1958.   Z3603.A65

South African national bibliography; Suid-Afrikaanse nasionale bibliografie, 1959– . Pretoria, State Lib., 1960– . Quarterly, with annual cumulation. **AA1075**

At head of title: SANB.

Replaces the State Library's monthly copyright list, *Publications received . . . ,* issued since 1938 in mimeographed form, unclassified and noncumulating. This new series, based on legal deposit, is arranged by Dewey Decimal Classification with a name and title index.

A cumulation for the period 1968–71 was published 1973 in 2v.   Z3603.P7

Spain

General

Aguiló y Fustér, Mariano. Catálogo de obras en lengua catalana impresas desde 1474 hasta 1860. Madrid, Rivadeneyra, 1923. 1077p. il. **AA1076**

A classified catalog of books in the Catalan language, with a general index and an index of printers.   Z2704.C35A27

Boston. Public Library. Ticknor Collection. Catalogue of the Spanish library and of the Portuguese books bequeathed by George Ticknor. Boston, 1879. 476p.   **AA1077**

A dictionary catalog of an important 19th-century collection. Includes also the collection of Spanish and Portuguese literature in the general library.

A 1970 reprint (Boston, G. K. Hall) includes an appendix, p.477–550, listing material acquired since publication of the original catalog.   Z2691.B74

California. University. Library. Spain and Spanish America in the libraries of the University of California; a catalogue of books. Berkeley, 1928–30. 2v.   **AA1078**

Contents: v.1, General and departmental libraries; v.2, The Bancroft Library.

A catalog of very rich collections. Each volume is arranged alphabetically with a subject index.   Z2709.C16

Heredia y Livermore, Ricardo, *Conde de Benahavis.* Catalogue de la bibliothèque de M. Ricardo Heredia. Paris, E. Paul, 1891–94. 4v. il.   **AA1079**

A sales catalog of this famous collection of Spanish and other rare works. For index *see* AA1082.   Z2709.H54

Hidalgo, Dionisio. Diccionario general de bibliografía española. Madrid, Impr. de las Escuelas Pias, 1862–81. 7v.   **AA1080**

A general list of works published in Spain, arranged alphabetically by title, with author and classed indexes.   Z2681.H63

Llordén, Andrés. La imprenta en Málaga; ensayo para una tipobibliografía malagueña. Málaga, Caja de Ahorros Provincial, [1973]. 2v.   **AA1081**

Arranged by printer or press; an historical note is followed by a bibliography of the works published by each.   Z174.M22L55

Molina Navarro, Gabriel. Índice para facilitar el manejo y consulta de los catálogos de Salvá y Heredia. Madrid, Molina, 1913. 162p.   **AA1082**

A combined index to the catalogs of Salvá (AA1086) and Heredia (AA1079).   Z997.H54

Palau y Dulcet, Antonio. Manual del librero hispano-americano; bibliografía general española e hispano-americana desde la invención de la imprenta hasta nuestros tiempos, con el valor comercial de los impresos descritos. 2. ed. corr. y aum. por el autor. Barcelona, Librería Palau, 1948–77. 28v.   **AA1083**

1st ed. 1923–27. 7v.

A very useful, comprehensive, alphabetical record, listing material under author, or under title for anonymous works. Covers material published in Spain and Spanish America from the beginning of printing to mid-20 century.

An index to the set has begun to appear as: Z2681.P16

Palau Claveras, Agustin. Indice alfabetico de titulos- materias, correcciones, conexiones y adiciones del Manual del librero hispano-americano de Antonio Palau y Dulcet. Empuries, Palacete Palau Dulcet; Oxford, Dolphin, 1981–84. v.1–4. (In progress)   **AA1084**

Contents: v.1–4, A–Millà.

Ribelles Comín, José. Bibliografía de la lengua valenciana. . . . Madrid, "Rev. de Arch., Bibl. y Museos," 1915–31. 3v. facsim.   **AA1085**

Subtitle: O sea catálogo razonada por orden alfabético de autores de los libros, folletos, obras dramáticas, periódicos, coloquios, coplas, chistes, discursos, romances, alocuciones, cantares, gozos, etc., que escritos en lengua valenciana y bilingüe, han visto la luz pública desde el establecimiento de la imprenta en España hasta nuestros días.

v.1, siglo XV (i.e., descriptions and notes of printed editions to 1918 of works in the Valencian dialect composed before the end of the 15th century); v.2, siglo XVI; v.3, siglo XVII.

No more published.   Z2704.V1R4

Salvá y Pérez, Vicente. Catálogo de la biblioteca de Salvá, escrito por Pedro Salvá y Mallen, y enriquecido con la descripción de otras muchas obras, de sus ediciones, etc. Valencia, Impr. de Ferrer de Orga, 1872. 2v. il. (Repr.: Barcelona, Porter-Libros, 1963)   **AA1086**

A classified catalog, with indexes, giving detailed descriptions of works published from the 16th to the mid-19th centuries.

See AA1082 for index.   Z2709.S25

Simón Díaz, José. Impresos del siglo XVII; bibliografía selectiva por materias de 3.500 ediciones príncipes en lengua castellana. Madrid, Consejo Superior de Investigaciones Científicas, 1972. 926p.   **AA1087**

Classed arrangement modeled on the Dewey Decimal system. Author and detailed subject indexes.   Z2682.S543

Vaganay, Hugues. Bibliographie hispanique extra-péninsulaire; 16e et 17e siècles. (*In* Revue hispanique 42:1–304. 1918)   **AA1088**

A listing of 1,198 works of authors from the Hispanic peninsula, which were printed outside Spain from 1502 to 1700. Arranged chronologically.

Early

Antonio, Nicolás. Bibliotheca hispana vetus; sive, Hispani scriptores qui ab Octaviani Augusti aevo ad annum Christi MD. floruerunt. Matriti, J. Ibarra, 1788. 2v. facsims.   **AA1089**

Z2681.A632

—— Bibliotheca hispana nova; sive, Hispanorum scriptorum qui ab anno MD. ad MDCLXXXIV, floruere notitia. Matriti, J. de Ibarra, 1783–88. 2v.   **AA1090**

The date 1783 on the title page of v.1 is a misprint for 1788.

2d ed., edited by T. A. Sánchez, J. A. Pellicer, and R. Casalbón; 1st ed. published 1672 as *Bibliotheca hispana.*

Together the two works provide an indispensable record of the writings of persons born in the Spanish peninsula regardless of the language in which they wrote. The volumes covering to 1500 are in narrative form; those covering 1500–1684 are arranged as a bibliographical dictionary.   Z2681.A633

British Museum. Dept. of Printed Books. Short-title catalogue of books printed in Spain and of Spanish books printed elsewhere in Europe before 1601 now in the British Museum, by Henry Thomas. London, 1921. 101p.   **AA1091**

Reprinted as a section of the Museum's *Short-title catalogues of Spanish, Spanish-American and Portuguese books printed before 1601* (below).   Z2682.B86

—— Short-title catalogues of Spanish, Spanish-American and Portuguese books printed before 1601 in the British Museum, by Henry Thomas. Photolithographic reprint in 1v. London, British Museum, [1966]. 169p.   **AA1092**

Reprints the 1921 volume for books printed in Spain, the 1944 volume for Spanish-American books (AA927n), and the 1940 volume for Portuguese books (AA1033).   Z2682.B87

Goldsmith, Valentine Fernande. A short title catalogue of Spanish and Portuguese books, 1601–1700, in the Library of the British Museum (The British Library—Reference Division). Folkestone, Dawsons of Pall Mall, 1974. 250p.   **AA1093**

Includes "1. Books written wholly or partly in Spanish or Portuguese, no matter where published; 2. Books, in no matter what language, published or printed at any place which today forms part of Spain or Portugal."—*Definitions.* Books lost or destroyed during World War II are listed whether or not the library has replaced them. Continues chronologically the Museum's *Short-title catalogue of books printed in Spain and of Spanish books printed elsewhere in Europe before 1601* (AA1091).

Errors and shortcomings of the work are pointed out in D. W. Cruickshank's review in *The library,* ser. 5, 29:463–67 (Dec. 1974).
Z2686.G64

Haebler, Konrad. Bibliografía ibérica del siglo XV. Enumeración de todos los libros impresos en España y Portugal hasta el año de 1500 con notas críticas. La Haya, Nijhoff; Leipzig, Hiersemann, 1903–17. 2v. **AA1094**

Each volume alphabetically arranged with detailed bibliographical information and annotations. Indexes of printers, etc.
Z240.H1

Hispanic Society of America. Printed books, 1468–1700, in the Hispanic Society of America; a listing by Clara Louisa Penney. N.Y., 1965. 614p. (Hispanic notes and monographs. Catalogue series) **AA1095**

Two previous listings of the Society's early books were prepared by the same compiler: *List of books printed before 1601 in the Library of the Hispanic Society of America* (N.Y., 1929; Offset reissue, with additions, N.Y., 1955) and *List of books printed 1601–1700, in the Library* (N.Y., 1938).

This catalog combines the listings in the two earlier bibliographies and adds some 2,000 pamphlets and other additions to the Library since 1938. Alphabetical arrangement by main entry, with short title and usually a reference to another published source for additional information or a more complete description. Omits the "Check list of Hispanic printing sites and printers, 1468?–1700," which appeared as Appendix II of the 1938 publication. It should be noted that most of the pre-1701 items are not represented in the catalog of the Library published by G. K. Hall (Boston, 1962). Z1012.H58

Madrid. Biblioteca Nacional. Catálogo colectivo de obras impresas en los siglos XVI al XVIII existentes en las bibliotecas españolas. Ed. provisional. Madrid, [Instituto Bibliografico Hispanico], 1972–78. Sección I,[v.1–12]. (In progress) **AA1096**

Contents: Sección I, Siglo XVI, Letra A–R.

A main-entry catalog reproducing the catalog cards for the relevant items and indicating library locations. Z1012.M22

Vindel, Francisco. Manual gráfico-descriptivo del bibliófilo hispano-americano (1475–1850), con un prólogo de Pedro Sáinz Rodríguez. Madrid, [Impr. Góngora], 1930–34. 12v. in 13. il. **AA1097**

Contents: v.1–10, A–Z; v.11, Tasación e índices; v.12, Suplemento, siglo XV.

An author list of 3,442 books, mainly early. Information for each includes: author's name, title, place, publisher or printer, date, size, generally paging. A special feature is that for each item a reproduction of some page of the work, usually title page or colophon, is given. Z2681.V77

20th century

Catálogo general de la librería española e hispanoamericana, 1901–30. Autores. Madrid, Inst. Nacional del Libro Español, 1932–51. 5v. **AA1098**

Publisher varies.

A comprehensive list giving full name of author, title, edition, place, publisher, date, paging, size, price. Z2681.C35

Catálogo general de la librería española, 1931–1950. Madrid, Inst. Nacional del Libro Español, 1957–65. 4v. **AA1099**

This series follows the same plan as the preceding one, but does not include Spanish-American imprints. Z2681.C34

Bibliografía española; revista general de la imprenta, de la librería y de las industrias que concurren á la fabricación del libro. Madrid, Asociación de la Librería, 1901–22. 22v. Semimonthly, then monthly. **AA1100**

Subtitle varies.
Continued by: Z2685.B58

Bibliografía general española e hispanoamericana, 1923–marzo/abril 1942. Madrid-Barcelona, 1923–42. 16v. **AA1101**

Monthly, 1923–36; bimonthly, 1941–42. Publication suspended July 1936–Jan. 1941. 1923–36 in three parts: (1) *Bibliografía,* a list of new publications, giving for each item author's name, title, place, date, publisher, paging, size, and price; (2) *Crónica;* (3) *Anuncios.* v.1–9 have a general author index to the books listed in the monthly *Bibliografía;* v.10 has, instead, a cumulated author list of the entries in v.9–10.
Continued by: Z2685.B59

Bibliografía hispánica, año 1–16, mayo/junio 1942–dic. 1957. Madrid, Inst. Nacional de Libro Español, 1942–57. Monthly. **AA1102**

Ceased publication.

Each monthly issue in two sections: (1) articles on the book trade, bibliographies, book reviews, etc.; (2) *Repertorio bibliográfico,* which is a classed list of books published, with an annual index of authors and titles. This section is usually paged separately and continuously, with a special title page, so that it may be bound separately. Variations are: v.1, 1942, *Repertorio* paged separately in each issue but not continuously; v.2–3, 1943, *Repertorio* is not separately paged; v.8, 1948, *Bibliografía* published three times per year, *Repertorio* published separately monthly; v.9, 1949–57, monthly issues containing both sections, paged separately.
Continued by *El libro español* (AA1106). Z2685.B6

Bibliotheca hispana; revista de información y orientación bibliográficas. v.1–31. Madrid, Consejo Superior de Investigaciones Científicas, Inst. Nicolás Antonio, 1943–73. Quarterly. **AA1103**

Ceased publication.

Originally issued in three sections; beginning with v.13, issued in two sections, each of which had four issues per year and its own annual index. The sections contain the following subject materials: sec.1, Letras: Obras generales, bibliografía, religión, filosofía, pedagogía, estadística y demografía, sociología y política, economía, derecho, filología, literatura, geografía, historia, arte (ceased with v.30, no. 2/3); sec.2, Ciencias: Ciencia en general, matemáticas, astronomía, física, química, ciencias naturales, medicina, ingeniería y construcción, ciencia y arte militares, agricultura y ganadería, industria, comercio, economía doméstica (ceased with v.31, no.1). Entries are annotated, and periodical articles are also included.
Z2685.B597

Current

Anuario español e hispano-americano del libro y de las artes gráficas con el Catálogo mundial del libro impreso en lengua española dirigido por Javier Lasso de la Vega Jimenez-Placer. Madrid, Ed. del Anuario Maritimo Español, 1945–59. 10v. Biennial (early volumes irregular). **AA1104**

v.1–2 had title *Catálogo de los libros publicados en España en 1944 [en 1945];* publ. 1945–46.
v.1–10 cover 1944–57. Ceased publication.
Arranged by decimal classification with author indexes. v.5 and 9 include *Relación de las tesis doctorales manuscritas existentes en la biblioteca de la Universidad de Madrid;* v.10 includes *Las tesis doctorales leídas en la Universidad de Chile.* Some volumes have cumulated indexes. Z2681.A64

Bibliografía española, 1958– . Madrid, 1959– . Annual (varies). **AA1105**

At head of title: Ministerio de Educación Nacional. Dirección General de Archivos y Bibliotecas, Servicio Nacional de Información Bibliográfica.
Frequency varies: monthly 1969–75.
A national bibliography based on copyright receipts in the national library. Arranged by Universal Decimal Classification, with index of authors, titles, and subjects, and with supplementary lists of publishers, series, and periodicals.
1964–66 not yet published. Z2685.B583

El libro español; revista mensual . . . , t.1, núm.1– , Enero 1958– . Madrid, Inst. Nacional del Libro Español, 1958– . Monthly; biweekly. **AA1106**

The merger of the Institute's two former titles: *Bibliografía hispánica* and the more popular *Novedades editoriales españolas* with its supplement *Libros del mes.* The new title is much like the former *Bibliografía,* the first half consisting of articles of interest to the book trade, bibliographic studies, etc.; and the other half being the list of new books, the *Repertorio bibliográfico clasificado por materias.* Annual author, title, and subject indexes are issued for the *Repertorio.* Z2685.L5

———— Indices de la producción editorial española, 1968–1972: autores y obras anónimas, títulos y conceptos, editores. [Madrid], Instituto, 1972. 636p.

Provides cumulative indexes to v.11–15 (1968–72) of *El libro español.*

Libros españoles en venta ISBN, 1983/84– . Madrid, Agencia Española del ISBN, [1984]– . 3v. Biennial? **AA1107**

Also called *Spanish books in print.*
Continues *Libros españoles ISBN,* which in turn continued *Libros españoles: catalogo ISBN.*
1983/84 issued in 3v.: Titulos, Autores, Materias.

Sri Lanka

Ceylon national bibliography, 1963– . Nuwara Eliya, Ceylon, Nat. Bibliography Branch, Dept. of the Govt. Archivist, 1964–71. v.1–9. Monthly (some combined issues). **AA1108**

In Sinhalese, Tamil, and English.
A current record of material deposited with the Registrar of Books and Newspapers. Each language division is in two parts (varies slightly): (1) Alphabetical author, title, and subject index; (2) Classified by Dewey Decimal Classification system. No cumulated indexes.
Two preliminary numbers were issued (in English only), no.1–2, Nov. and Dec. 1962, but they apparently are not counted in the subsequent voluming.
Continued by:

Sri Lanka jatika grantha namavaliya. Ilankait teciya nurpattiyal. Sri Lanka national bibliography. v.10– . Colombo, Dept. of Nat. Archives, 1972– . **AA1109**

Continues the *Ceylon national bibliography* (above) and assumes its numbering.
In Sinhalese, Tamil, and English.

Swaziland

Swaziland national bibliography . . . with current information. 1973/76– . Kwaluseni, Univ. of Botswana and Swaziland, Univ. College of Swaziland, 1977– . Irregular. **AA1110**

The first volume covers 1973–76, 1977 was separately published, and 1978/82 appeared in 1v. in 1984. Lists "all known publications issued in Swaziland . . . with the exception of certain ephemeral items and those items which are regarded as confidential or restricted. In addition, all publications in Siswati, including those published outside Swaziland, are included in the bibliography."—*Pref.*
Arranged by Dewey Decimal Classification with author/title index. Appendixes include a list of foreign publications on Swaziland, Swaziland legislation and law reports, and forthcoming books and works in progress.
Serves in part to supplement *Swaziland official publications, 1880–1972* (see AG183). Z3560.S93

Sweden

Early

Sveriges bibliografi intill år 1600, av Isak Collijn. Uppsala, Svenska Litteratursällskapet, 1927–38. 3v. il. (Svenska litteratursällskapet. Skrifter, 10:5–18) **AA1111**

Published in parts.
Contents: Bd.1, 1478–1530 (publ. 1934–38); bd.2, 1530–82 (publ. 1927–31); bd.3, 1583–99 (publ. 1932–33); Alfabetiskt register till bd.1, bd.2–3; Typografiska tabeller, 1483–1525, 1526–99.
v.1 is a revision of *Sveriges bibliografi, 1481–1600,* by G. E. Klemming and Aksel Anderson (Uppsala, 1927. 216p.).
Arranged chronologically, with alphabetical indexes. Gives full descriptions, with bibliographical references and location of copies.
Continued by: Z2622.S962

Sveriges bibliografi, 1600—talet. Bidrag till en bibliografisk förteckning, av Isak Collijn. Uppsala, Almqvist, 1942–46. 2v. (Svenska litteratursällskapet. Skrifter 10:19–23) **AA1112**

Arranged alphabetically with no chronological approach. Gives brief biographical facts of authors, full description, and location of copies. Covers 17th century. Z2621.S955

Swedish imprints, 1731–1833; a retrospective national bibliography, prep. at the Center for Bibliographical Studies, Uppsala (CBSU). Uppsala, Dahlia Books, 1977–83. Introd. & pt.1–19. (In progress) **AA1113**

Rolf E. DuRietz, gen. ed.
An effort toward a comprehensive retrospective bibliography of works printed and/or published in the area constituting the sovereign territory of Sweden during the 1731–1833 period. The bibliography is being published in parts, each part having its own index; cumulated indexes are published at intervals. Within each part arrangement is chronological-alphabetical. Supplementary entries in later parts correct and augment information appearing in the first entry for a given work. Z2621.S975

19th and 20th centuries

Linnström, Hjalmar. Svenskt boklexikon, 1830–65. Stockholm, Linnström, 1883–84. 2v. **AA1114**

Alphabetical arrangement. Includes brief biographical data for most authors.
Continued by: Z2621.S95

Svensk bok-katalog för aren 1866/75–1966/70. Stockholm, Tidningsaktiebolaget Svensk Bokhandel, 1878–1983. (In progress) **AA1115**

Publisher varies.
Beginning with the volumes for 1941/50, issued by the Bibliographical Institute of the Royal Library in Stockholm, and also called *The Swedish national bibliography.*
1866/75, 1876/85, 1886/95 published as 10-year volumes. Thereafter, published as 5-year cumulations except for 1941/50.
Includes books, pamphlets, periodicals, government publications, and theses. Each cumulation is in two parts: (1) alphabetical author and title list; (2) classed list. Z2621.S95

Taube, Gurli Elisa (Westgren). Svensk festskriftsbibliografi, åren 1891–1925. Uppsala, Appelbergs Boktr., 1954. 168p. (Svenska bibliotekariesamfundets skriftserie, 2) **AA1116**

Festschriften are listed by name of honoree, with full contents notes for each volume. A second section groups the individual contributions by subject field. Index of contributors.
Continued by:

Malmström, Rosa. Svensk festskriftsbibliografi 1936–1960. Bibliography of Swedish homage volumes 1936–1960. Göteborg, Universitetsbiblioteket, 1967. 390p. (Acta Bibliothecae Universitatis Gothoburgensis, 10) **AA1117**

Follows the plan of the earlier volume, with a somewhat more refined breakdown in the subject section. The 1926–35 period remains to be covered.   Z2649.M3

Current

Svensk bokförteckning. The Swedish national bibliography, ed. by the Bibliographical Institute of the Royal Library, Stockholm. 1953– . Stockholm, Svensk Bokhandel, 1953– .
                                                        AA1118

Supersedes an earlier monthly publication with the same title, issued 1913–52, and *Aarskatalog för svenska bokhandeln,* 1861–1952.

Frequency varies; beginning 1977, published six times a year at intervals of one to three months, with an annual cumulation. The monthly issues are main-entry lists only; the cumulations include a classified section. Cumulates into the *Svensk bok-katalog* (AA1115).
                                                        Z2625.S952

Svensk bokhandel. arg.1– , Jan. 4, 1952– . Stockholm, 1952– . il. Weekly.   **AA1119**

Official organ of Svenska Bokförläggareföreningen and Svenska Bokhandlareföreningen.

Frequency varies; now 32 issues per yr.

Formed by the union of *Bokhandlaren* and *Svensk bokhandelstidning.*

Offers news and announcements concerning the book trade, with a "Svensk bokförteckning" section which cumulates into the monthly publication of that title.   Z407.S84

Switzerland

Bern. Schweizerische Landesbibliothek. Catalogue . . . Liste alphabétique des imprimés parus jusqu'en 1900. . . . Bern, Francke, 1910.   **AA1120**

Added title page in German. Preface in German and French.
Contents: Abt. A: Histoire et géographie. 2v.
No more published.   Z949.B54

—— Katalog . . . Systematisches Verzeichnis der schweizerischen oder die Schweiz betreffenden Veröffentlichungen, 1901–20, 1921–30, 1931–40, 1941–47. Bern, Huber, [1927]–54.   **AA1121**

Added title page: *Catalogue de la Bibliothèque Nationale Suisse. Répertoire méthodique des publications suisses ou relatives à la Suisse.* Contents and preface in German and French.

The catalog for each period is in two volumes: v.1, Classed list, arranged by the Decimal Classification; v.2, Biographical and topographical catalog, each arranged alphabetically.

A subject list which serves both as a short-title catalog of the works listed and as an index to the fuller descriptions in the *Bibliographisches Bulletin* (*Bulletin bibliographique*) (AA1129) for the same years. Gives author, brief title, date of publication, and also the year of the *Bulletin,* if that differs from publication date, in which full description is given.

Ceased publication. Continued by AA1123.   Z949.B552

Lonchamp, Frédéric Charles. Bibliographie générale des ouvrages publiés ou illustrés en Suisse et à l'étranger de 1475 à 1914 par des écrivains et des artistes suisses. . . . Paris et Lausanne, Librairie des Bibliophiles, 1922. 500p. il.
                                                        AA1122

A list of 3,376 items giving for each: author, title, date, printer or publisher, size, paging, and note of illustrations, with name of artist. Indexes of titles and of artists.   Z1023.L835

Schweizer Bücherverzeichnis. Répertoire du livre suisse. Elenco del libro svizzero. Katalog der schweizerischen Landesbibliothek. 1948/50– . Zürich, Schweizerischer Buchhändler- und Verlegerverein, 1951– . Quinquennial (since 1951).   **AA1123**

Cumulates the titles listed in *Das schweizer Buch* (AA1129), and

supersedes the *Systematisches Verzeichnis* (AA1121). Beginning with 1951/55, forms pt.1 of the *Schweizerische Nationalbibliographie.*

In two parts: (1) Author catalog (including anonymous titles) with index of catchwords, editors, translators, etc.; (2) Subject catalog in German with an index from the French forms.   Z949.B56

Das schweizerische Buch; Le livre en Suisse. 1896–1914. Bern, Kollektivausstellung Schweizer. Verleger, 1914. 287p.
                                                        AA1124

Classed arrangement with author index.
Continued by: Z2771.S42

Schweizerischer Buchhändlerverein. Das schweizerischer Buch, 1914–1930. Zürich, Orell Füssli, 1931. 282p.
                                                        AA1125

                                                        Z2771.S42

—— Livres suisses; Das Buch der Schweiz, 1931–1938. Zürich, Schweizerische Landesausstellung, 1939. 232p.
                                                        AA1126

Both of the above are classified listings with author indexes. They are complemented by: Z2771.S42

Société des Libraires et Éditeurs de la Suisse Romande, Geneva. Catalogue des éditions de la Suisse romande, rédigé par Alex. Jullien. . . . Genève, Jullien, 1902–12; Société, 1929. 3v. and suppl.   **AA1127**

A record of books published in French Switzerland. Alphabetical listing by author or other main entry.

Basic volume listing books in print in 1900, publ. 1902. 280p.; Supplements, 1901–1909 publ. 1912. 181p.; 1910–27 publ. 1929. 404p.; Supplément, corrections . . . comprenant en particulier les éditions Edwin Frankfurter à Lausanne, publ. 1929. 16p.
Continued by: Z2771.S75

—— Catalogue des ouvrages de langue française publiés en Suisse, 1928–1945, red. par Alexandre Jullien. Neuchâtel, Impr. Delachaux et Niestle, 1948. 377p.   **AA1128**

An alphabetical main-entry listing.

Current

Das schweizer Buch; Bibliographisches Bulletin der schweizerischen Landesbibliothek, Bern. Le livre suisse . . . Il libro svizzero, 1901– . Bern-Bümpliz, Benteli, 1901– . v.1– .
                                                        AA1129

Frequency varies. Title varies: 1901–42, *Bibliographisches Bulletin der Schweiz.* Publisher varies.

1943–75, issued in 2 ser.: Série A, semimonthly, listing publications in the book trade; Série B, bimonthly, listing publications outside the book trade, e.g., theses, institutional publications, etc. Each issue is in classified arrangement with author, title, and subject index.

Beginning 1976, a single combined list is published semimonthly and covers all types of publications. The classified arrangement with author/title/subject index is retained. Indexes cumulate semi-annually and annually. Issue no. 16 is a special issue devoted to music.

Cumulates into the 5-year *Schweizer Bücherverzeichnis* (AA1123).
                                                        Z2775.S35

—— Série A . . . Verfasser- und Stichwortregister. *See* AA787.

Tanzania

Printed in Tanzania, 1969–73. [Dar es Salaam], Tanganyika Lib. Services Board, 1970–76. Annual.   **AA1130**

On cover, 1969: A list of publications printed in mainland Tanzania during 1969 and deposited with the Tanganyika Library Service and the Library of the University of Dar es Salaam, together with some publications published in Tanzania but printed elsewhere.

The 1969 issue represents a first attempt to produce a cumulative national bibliography, items received on legal deposit having previously been listed only in the *Bulletin* of the University of Dar es Salaam Library. Arrangement is by Dewey Decimal Classification, with a full index. Plans call for a retrospective cumulative volume covering 1964–68.

Continued by: Z3753.T3P74

Tanzania national bibliography, 1974/75– . Dar es Salaam, Tanzania Library Service, 1977– . Annual (varies). **AA1131**

Continues *Printed in Tanzania* (above). Employs the same classified arrangement, but has separate author and title indexes. Now includes various mimeographed materials, conference papers, and annual reports. Became a monthly publication in 1983, although some of the intervening annuals are not yet published.

Z3588.P74

Trinidad and Tobago

Trinidad and Tobago national bibliography. v.1– , Jan./June 1975– . [Port of Spain], Central Library of Trinidad and Tobago, 1975– . Quarterly, with annual cumulation.

AA1132

"A subject list of material published and printed in Trinidad and Tobago, classified according to the Dewey Decimal Classification, 18th edition, cataloged according to the British Text of the Anglo-American Cataloguing Rules, 1967 and the International Standard Bibliographic Description for Monographs and Serials. It is provided with a full author, title and series index and a list of Trinidad and Tobago publishers."—*t.p., v.1.*

Aims to list all works published and printed in Trinidad and Tobago, omitting only certain government publications (e.g., acts, bills, gazettes). Z1561.T7T74

Tunisia

Bibliographie nationale de la Tunisie, publications non officielles. 1956/68–1976. Tunis, Service Documentaire, 1974–77. 5v. **AA1133**

Issued by the Bibliothèque Nationale of Tunisia.

Title varies slightly. Title also in Arabic.

An issue published 1970 as "Série II, Année 1, 1969" was superseded by retrospective compilations covering 1956/68 (publ. 1974) and 1969/73 (publ. 1975), and annual volumes for 1974–76. Each volume is a classed listing according to the Universal Decimal Classification system, with separate sections for Western language and Arabic publications.

Continued by: Z3681.B529

Bibliographie nationale de Tunisie, 1977– . Tunis, Service du Dépôt Légal et des Publications, 1977– . Annual.

AA1134

At head of title: Ministère des Affaires Culturelles. Bibliothèque Nationale.

Frequency varies: originally bimonthly, then quarterly.

Added title page in Arabic.

Supersedes the earlier series of similar title (above). Now includes both official and nonofficial publications; separate sections for Arabic and Western language materials, with classified arrangement within sections.

Turkey

Türkiye bibliyografyasi, 1934– . Ankara [etc.], Türk Tarih Kurumu Basimevi, 1935– . **AA1135**

Annual, 1934; semiannual, 1935–38; quarterly, 1939–43; monthly, 1944–48; quarterly, 1949– . Publisher varies.

A classified catalog with author and title indexes in each issue 1934–43; annual indexes 1944– . Records books, pamphlets, and government publications in Turkish and other languages. Includes a separate section of new periodicals and newspapers.

Cumulations have been published as: Z2835.T93

―――― 1928/1938, 1939/1948. Istanbul, Devlet Basimevi, 1939; 1957–64. (Türkiye cümhuriyeti maarif vekilligi [1939/48–maarif vekaleti]. Basma yazi ve resimleri derleme müdürlügü) **AA1136**

Cumulative decennial volumes superseding the annuals (above).

1928/1938 in 2v.: v.1, Official publications; v.2, Non-official publications, arranged by Universal Decimal Classification.

1939/1948 in 3v.: v.1, arranged by Universal Decimal Classification, covering general, philosophy, religion, social sciences, and philology, publ. 1957; v.2, covering abstract science, applied science, literature, history, geography, and biography, publ. 1962; v.3, alphabetical index, publ. 1964.

Yeni yayinlar; aylik bibliyografya dergisi. Cilt: 1– . Tem. 1956– . Ankara, 1956– . Monthly. **AA1137**

Includes a classified list of recent publications. Z2835.Y4

Union of Soviet Socialist Republics

See Russia and the U.S.S.R.

Uruguay

Estrada, Dardo. Historia y bibliografía de la imprenta en Montevideo, 1810–1865. Montevideo, Librería Cervantes, 1912. 318p. (Readex Microprint) **AA1138**

Chronological arrangement. Supplemented by: Z213.M7E8

Arredondo, Horacio. Bibliografía uruguaya; contribución. Montevideo, El Siglo Ilustrado, 1929. 182p. il. (Readex Microprint) **AA1139**

"Apartado de la Revista del Instituto Histórico y Geográfico del Uruguay, t.6, no.2."—*title page.*

Arranged chronologically, 1559–1865. Line-by-line transcription. Locates copies.

Current

Anuario bibliográfico uruguayo, 1946–49, 1968– . Montevideo, Biblioteca Nacional, 1947–51, 1969– . Annual. **AA1140**

Volumes covering 1950–67 not published.

Lists books and pamphlets in classed arrangement with author index. Beginning with the volume covering 1968 a section for periodicals was added, with listings by title and subject classes. Z1881.A5

Bibliografía uruguaya. Montevideo, Biblioteca del Poder Legislativo, 1962– . Irregular. **AA1141**

Began publication as a quarterly in 1962; annual volumes were issued for 1963–64, and an addenda for 1963 was published 1966. These issues are superseded by a cumulative volume covering 1962–68 published 1971 in 2v. 1969/72 published 1977 in 2v.; 1973/77 published in 1983 in 2v.

An alphabetical author listing with title and systematic indexes. Z1881.M76

Venezuela

Medina, José Toribio. La imprenta en Caracas (1808–1821); notas bibliográficas. Santiago de Chile, Impr. Elzeviriana, 1904. 29p. (Readex Microprint) **AA1142**

Z213.C2M4

Villasana, Angel Raúl. Ensayo de un repertorio bibliográfico venezolano. Caracas, 1969–79. 6v. (Banco Central de Venezuela. Colección cuatricentenario de Caracas, 8) **AA1143**

On cover: (Años 1808–1950).

A new bibliography for the period 1808–1950. Includes books and pamphlets by Venezuelans published both at home and abroad, and works by foreigners published in Venezuela. Works appearing in anthologies and collections are also noted. Concerned with works of literature, history and general culture; scientific and technical works are excluded. Many descriptive and explanatory notes.

Z1921.V5

Current

Anuario bibliográfico venezolano, 1942–54, 1967/68– . Caracas, Tipografía Americana, 1944– . Irregular. **AA1144**

At head of title: República de Venezuela. Biblioteca Nacional, Caracas.

Publisher varies.

Preceded by volume called Año 1, 1916.

Published irregularly: 1942–45, annual; 1947/48, publ. 1950; 1949/54, publ. 1960 in 2v.; 1967/68 publ. 1977; 1969/74, v.1 (A–G) publ. 1979; 1975 publ. 1977; 1976 publ. 1980; 1977 publ. 1982.

Lists books, pamphlets, government publications, etc., and periodical articles. The second volume of the 1949/54 issue was devoted to material about Venezuela published abroad. A well-arranged, classed list with author, subject, and title index, and an index of printers.

Publication was suspended 1961–76, but good progress has been made toward filling the gap between this series and the *Bibliografía venezolano* (below).

Bibliografía venezolana. Año 1, no.1– , Enero/Marzo 1970– . Caracas, Biblioteca Nacional, Centro Bibliográfico Venezolano, 1970– . Quarterly. **AA1145**

On cover: BV; Bibliografía venezolana.

A new current national bibliography for Venezuela. Classed arrangement. The first issue lists publications of the final months of 1969. If plans are successful for the resumption of the *Anuario bibliográfico venezolano* (above) on a current basis, that publication will serve as the annual cumulation of the quarterly issues of the new *Bibliografía.*

Wales

See also Great Britain, p.74–79.

Bibliotheca celtica, a register of publications relating to Wales and the Celtic peoples and languages for the years 1909–1927/28. Aberystwyth, Nat. Lib. of Wales, 1910–34. 9v. **AA1146**

Includes works written in one of the Celtic languages or relating to any of the Celtic peoples, and works written in English on non-Celtic subjects by Welshmen.

—— n.s. Aberystwyth, 1939–62. (In progress)

Contents: v.1, 1929/33 (publ. 1939); v.2, 1934/38 (publ. 1952); v.3, 1939/43 (publ. 1961); v.4, 1944/48 (publ. 1962).

This series follows the same general plan as the first series, but

omits works written by Welshmen in English on non-Celtic subjects. Two more volumes are planned to cover 1949–52.

—— 3d ser., 1953– . Aberystwyth, 1954– . Annual.

This annual series continues the earlier set and increases its coverage by adding periodical articles on Celtic subjects.

Z2071.B56

Cardiff, Wales. Free Libraries. Catalogue of printed literature in the Welsh Department, by John Ballinger and J. I. Jones. Cardiff, Free Lib. Committee; London, Sotheran, 1898. 559p. **AA1147**

An author and subject catalog, in one alphabet, of Welsh materials.

Z2089.C26

Rowlands, William. Cambrian bibliography: containing an account of the books printed in the Welsh language, or relating to Wales, from the year 1546 to the end of the eighteenth century; with biographical notices. Ed. and enl. by D. Silvan Evans. Llanidloes, J. Pryse, 1869. 762p. **AA1148**

Annotations, etc., in Welsh; English preface. Z2071.R88

Yugoslavia

Kukuljevic-Sakcinski, Ivan. Bibliografia hrvatska. 1. Tiskane knjige. Zagreb, Brzotiskom, D. Albrechta, 1860. 233p. **AA1149**

Added title page: Bibliografia jugoslavenska. Kn. I.

Z2124.C7K9

—— —— Dodatak k prvomu dielu. Tiskane knije. Zagreb, 1863. 31p.

No more published.

The main volume and supplement list Croatian books from early times to 1860.

Novakovic, Stojan. Srpska biblijografija za noviju književnost. Beogradu, Drzhavnoj Shtampariji, 1869. 644p. **AA1150**

Covers the period 1741–1867.

Arranged chronologically with author and subject indexes.

Z2931.N89

Simonic, Franc. Slovenska bibliografija. I. del.: Knjige, 1550-1900. Ljubljana, Natisnila J. Blasnikova Tikarna, 1903–05. 627p. **AA1151**

Alphabetical arrangement of books in Slovenian or by Slovenian authors. Additions were published annually in the periodical *Slovenska matica v Ljubljani, Zbornik,* v.3–9, 1901–1906. Z7041.S59

Current

Bibliografija Jugoslavije: knjige, brošure i muzikalije, 1950– . Beograd, Bibliografski Inst. FNRJ, 1950– . Monthly. 1950–52; semimonthly, 1953– . **AA1152**

Caption title also in Serbian, English, and French.

Lists books, pamphlets, sheet music, and government publications in Serbian, Croatian, and other languages. Classified by Universal Decimal Classification with author/title and subject indexes.

The 1945–49 period is covered by *Jugoslovenska bibliografija* (Beograd, Direkcija za Informacije Vlade FNRJ, 1949–50. 5v.).

For a companion section of the current Yugoslav national bibliography *see* AE314, which covers periodical articles. Z2951.B37

Slovenska bibliografija, 1945/1947– . Časopisje in knjige, članki in leposlovni prispevki v časopisju in zbornikih izdala in založila narodna in univerzitetna knjiznica v

Ljubljani. Ljubljana, Drzavna Založba Slovenije, 1948– .
Annual.   **AA1153**

A bibliography of Slovenian books and periodicals. Classified by
Universal Decimal Classification with author indexes.
                                                Z2957.S6S55

Zambia

The national bibliography of Zambia. 1970/71– . Lusaka,
National Archives of Zambia, [1972]– . Annual (beginning
with the issue covering 1972).   **AA1154**

Attempts to list "all work published in Zambia and received by
National Archives of Zambia under the Printed Publication Act"
during the period covered. Includes "books, pamphlets, first issues
of new serials, publications of statutory bodies and government
publications, excluding Acts, Bills, Parliamentary debates and Gazettes."—*Introd.* Arranged by Dewey Decimal Classification, with
author and title index.   Z3573.Z3N37

Zimbabwe

Zimbabwe national bibliography. 1979– . Salisbury, National Archives, 1980– . Annual.   **AA1155**

Represents a change of title for the *Rhodesia national bibliography,* (AA1042), of which the last volume covered 1978. The bibliography continues to list "books, pamphlets, maps and the first issues
of new serials (periodicals, newspapers, etc.) published in Rhodesia
and Zimbabwe Rhodesia."—*Introd.* Arranged by Dewey Decimal
Classification with author/title/series index. Also notes serial cessations in a separate section.   Z3573.R5R54

A B

Librarianship and Library Resources

❖Reference materials pertaining to libraries include works
used primarily by librarians as well as those needed by
readers. The former concern library techniques and methodology; the latter are mainly directories of libraries: libraries of specific countries, special libraries, or collections in
particular fields. Many of these directories, both of the
United States and of other countries, will help scholars to
locate libraries which house special collections or which are
strong in specified subjects. In some cases specialties are
described in considerable detail; in others, a mere listing of
outstanding collections is given. For the most part, directories of library and archival resources in specific subject fields
are listed with their respective subjects in this *Guide.*

Readers may occasionally wish to consult the library's
manuals and codes, such as the list of subject headings or
the classification scheme, and the librarian should, if possible, make these available to persons interested.

GENERAL WORKS

Bibliography

Barr, Larry J., McMullen, Haynes and **Leach, Steven G.**
Libraries in American periodicals before 1876: a bibliography with abstracts and an index. Jefferson, N.C., McFarland, 1983. 426p.   **AB1**

Serves as a chronological predecessor to Cannons' bibliography
(below), extending coverage "back to the beginning, as far as
periodicals published in the United States are concerned."—*Introd.*
Geographical arrangement, with "world" and intercontinental topics first, then the United States (subdivided for states, cities, etc.),
then foreign countries. 1,473 items with abstracts. Indexed.
                                                Z666.B33

Cannons, Harry George Turner. Bibliography of library
economy; a classified index to the professional periodical
literature in the English language relating to library economy, printing, methods of publishing, copyright, bibliography, etc. from 1876 to 1920. Chicago, Amer. Lib. Assoc.,
1927. 680p. (Repr.: N.Y., B. Franklin, 1970)   **AB2**

1st ed. 1910.
Includes an alphabetical index to the classified lists, but no author
index.
Continued by *Library literature* (AB14).   Z666.C21

Columbia University. Libraries. Library Service Library.
Dictionary catalog of the Library of the School of Library
Service, Columbia University. Boston, G. K. Hall, 1962. 7v.
                                                AB3

—————— 1st supplement. Boston, G. K. Hall, 1976.
4v.

Reproduction of the catalog cards for an outstanding collection on
libraries and librarianship. About 127,000 cards in the main set,
with another 62,000 in the supplement. Includes entries for a
historical collection of children's literature now housed in Columbia's Rare Book and Manuscript Library.   Z881.N6295

Danton, Joseph Periam. Index to Festschriften in librarianship. With the assistance of Ottilia C. Anderson. N.Y.,
Bowker, 1970. 461p.   **AB4**

An index to approximately 3,300 articles in 283 *Festschriften*
published 1864–1966. Authors, editors, subjects, and cross references appear in a single alphabet.   Z666.D35

—————— and **Pulis, Jane F.** Index to Festschriften in librarianship, 1967–1975. München & N.Y., K. G. Saur, 1979.
354p.   **AB5**

A continuation of Danton's 1970 volume (above). "This volume
covers approximately 1,500 articles in 143 works, 104 published
from 1967 to 1975 inclusive" (*Introd.*), the remainder being from
the earlier period. Follows the dictionary arrangement of the previous volume.   Z666.D36

Gropp, Arthur E. Bibliografía sobre las bibliotecas
nacionales de los países latinoamericanos y sus
publicaciones. Wash., Pan Amer. Union, 1960. 58p. (Pan
American Union. Columbus Memorial Library. Bibliographic ser., no.50)   **AB6**

A total of nearly 1,200 items (books and articles) on national
libraries and library systems in Latin America. Arrangement is by
country, with an author index.   Z738.G75

**Handbuch der internationalen Dokumentation und Informa-
tion.** Bd.1– . München, Verlag Dokumentationen der Technik, 1956– . Irregular.   **AB7**

Title varies: 1956–72, *Handbuch der technischen Dokumentation
und Bibliographie.*
1956–60 issued in looseleaf format.
Now constitutes 17 volumes, each with a distinctive title in both
German and English, and most of them issued in new editions at
varying intervals: Bd.1, International scientific documentation and

information; Bd.2, International bibliography of the book trade and librarianship; Bd.3, International bibliography of bibliographies in technology science and economics; Bd.4, International bibliography of specialized dictionaries; Bd.5, International bibliography of directories; Bd.6, World guide to periodicals; Bd.7, Publishers' international directory; Bd.8, World guide to libraries; Bd.9, International dictionary of abbreviations of organizations; Bd.10, World guide to universities; Bd.11, International bibliography of translations; Bd.12, World guide to trade associations; Bd.13, World guide to scientific associations; Bd.14, Anglo-American and German abbreviations; Bd.15, International directory of booksellers; Bd.16, Museums of the world; Bd.17, World guide to special libraries.

Harris, Michael H. A guide to research in American library history. 2d ed. Metuchen, N.J., Scarecrow Pr., 1974. 275p. **AB8**

1st ed. 1968.
Sections on "state of the art," philosophy and methodology for research in American library history, and basic sources are followed by "An annotated bibliography of graduate research in American library history," p.41–253. Indexed. Z731.H3

Internationale Bibliographie des Buch- u. Bibliothekswesens, 1904–12, 1922–39. Leipzig, Harrassowitz, 1905–40. 13v. and n.F.1–14. **AB9**

Each issue contains a section giving material about libraries.
For full description *see* AA25. Z1002.B61

Knoop-Busch, Hedda. Beiträge aus deutschen Festschriften auf dem Gebiet des Buch- und Bibliothekswesens 1947–1965. Göttingen, Evan. Bibliothekar-Lehrinst., 1970. 67*l.* (Arbeiten aus dem Evangelischen Bibliothekar-Lehrinstitut Göttingen, 3) **AB10**

Some 58 commemorative volumes are listed and their contents analyzed in a classified arrangement. Author index. Contributions are mainly in German.
Supplemented by: Z666.K58

Preuss, Erika. Beiträge aus deutschen Festschriften auf dem Gebiet des Buch- und Bibliothekswesens 1966–1970. Göttingen, Evang. Bibliothekar-Lehrinst., 1973. 63*l.* (Arbeiten aus dem Evangelischen Bibliothekar-Lehrinstitut Göttingen, 5) **AB11**

Z666.P888

Linares, Emma. Bibliografía bibliotecológica. Wash., Pan Amer. Union, 1960. 233p. (Pan American Union. Columbus Memorial Library. Bibliographic ser., no.49) **AB12**

A classified list of 3,000 items on library organization and operation. Includes books, parts of books, articles, and documents, mostly in Spanish or English. Author index.

Current

Information science abstracts. v.1– , Mar. 1966– . [Wash.], 1966– . Bimonthly. **AB13**

Title varies: 1966–67, *Documentation abstracts;* 1968, *Documentation abstracts and information science abstracts.*
Frequency varies.
Sponsoring bodies vary; originally issued by the American Documentation Institute and the Division of Chemical Literature of the American Chemical Society.
Lists and provides abstracts of books, journals, conference proceedings, reports, and patents in the fields of information science, documentation, and related areas. Classed arrangement; now has author and subject indexes in each issue, the indexes cumulating annually. Currently offers abstracts of relevant articles from nearly 700 journals. Z699.A1I575●

Library literature, 1921/32– . N.Y., Wilson, 1934– . Bimonthly, with annual cumulation. **AB14**

Subtitle and publisher vary.
Frequency varies; formerly quarterly, with annual and triennial cumulations.

An index to current books, pamphlets, periodical literature, films, microforms, and theses relating to librarianship, arranged alphabetically by author and subject. Some 200 journals are now covered. Includes foreign material. Abstracts and digests appearing in earlier issues were discontinued after 1958.
Prior to 1978 book review citations were listed under the book's main entry in the body of the index; thereafter they appear in a separate section. Reviews of audiovisual materials and periodicals are cited only in the body of the index. Z666.L69●

Library science abstracts, 1950–68. London, Lib. Assoc., 1950–68. Quarterly. **AB15**

Classified abstracts taken from some 200 periodicals, books, pamphlets, reports, etc. Annual indexes by author and by name and subject. International in scope.
Ceased publication; superseded by: Z671.L617

Library & information science abstracts, no.1– , Jan./Feb. 1969– . London, Library Assoc., 1969– . Monthly. **AB16**

Frequency varies.
Represents a change of title for *Library science abstracts* (above), with expanded scope. Coverage is international; all abstracts appear in English; classified arrangement. Monthly name and subject indexes cumulate annually. Now publishes more than 6,000 abstracts per year. Z671.L6●

Year's work in librarianship, 1928–50. London, Lib. Assoc., 1929–54. v.1–17. **AB17**

v.1–11 (1929–38); v.12 (1939–45); v.13–17 (1946–50).
Running comment, each chapter by a specialist, on the principal publications of the year in various fields of librarianship and bibliography. Gives full bibliographical references in footnotes, and includes both books and periodical articles.
Ceased publication; superseded by: Z666.Y39

Five years' work in librarianship, 1951/55–1961/65. London, Lib. Assoc., 1958–68. Quinquennial. **AB18**

Supersedes *Year's work in librarianship* (above) and follows the same plan. "Primarily a report and assessment of developments in Britain . . . of international bodies and significant developments in other countries particularly in the Commonwealth."—*Introd.*
Ceased with the volume for 1961/65; superseded by: Z666.F5

British librarianship and information science, 1966/70– . London, Lib. Assoc., 1972– . Quinquennial. **AB19**

Aims to "present a *picture* of what . . . happened during the five-year period" (*Introd.*), not a comprehensive review of the literature of each topic treated. Confined to British librarianship and information science, with concentration on main trends and developments.
Z666.B7

Dissertations

Library and information studies in the United Kingdom and Ireland, 1950–1974: an index to theses. Ed. by Peter J. Taylor. [London], Aslib, [1976]. 69p. **AB20**

A bibliography of theses in librarianship and information work which "seeks to bring together in one list all of those theses accepted in full or partial requirement for [higher] degrees, either in library schools or other departments of the universities."—*Introd.* Chronological listing with author and detailed subject indexes. Theses accepted after 1974 are listed in the Library Association's *RADIALS bulletin.* Z666.L374

Library Association. Library. FLA theses: abstracts of all theses accepted for the fellowship of the Library Association from 1964. Comp. by L. J. Taylor. London, British Lib., Lib. Assoc. Lib., [1979]. 90p. **AB21**

A subject listing, with abstracts. 297 entries; author and detailed subject indexes. Complements *Library and information studies* (above), which does not include FLA theses. Z666.L39

Magnotti, Shirley. Master's theses in library science, 1960–1969. Troy, N.Y., Whitston, 1975. 366p. **AB22**

—— —— 1970–1974. Troy, N.Y., Whitston, 1976. 198p.

The basic volume lists about 2,500 master's theses from 31 accredited library schools; the supplement adds some 700 titles from 24 schools (plus a few titles from the earlier period). The 1960–69 volume is an author listing with subject index; the 1970–74 supplement repeats the full citation in the subject section.

Z666.M27

—— Library science research, 1974–1979. Troy, N.Y., Whitston, 1982. 179p. **AB23**

Serves as a continuation of the above. The change of title reflects the inclusion of "final research reports" accepted by many schools in lieu of the master's thesis. About 750 items. Z669.7.M3

Schlachter, Gail A. and **Thomison, Dennis.** Library science dissertations, 1925–1972; an annotated bibliography. Littleton, Colo., Libraries Unlimited, 1974. 293p. (Research studies in library science, no. 12) **AB24**

A chronological listing, with author and subject indexes. Drawing their citations from the standard American dissertation lists, the compilers have listed "those doctoral studies which were either accepted by library schools or concerned with areas bearing a close relationship to the field of librarianship (e.g., communications, information services, education, etc.)."—*Introd.* As far as possible, each entry is annotated as to purpose, procedure, and findings.

Supersedes an earlier list by Nathan M. Cohen *et al.*, *Library science dissertations, 1925–60* (Wash., G.P.O., 1963). Z674.R4

—— —— 1973–1981: an annotated bibliography. Littleton, Colo., Libraries Unlimited, 1982. 414p. (Research studies in library science, no.18)

A supplement to the above, adding about a thousand dissertations from the 1973–81 period.

Periodicals

Janzing, Grażyna. Library, documentation, and archives serials. Ed. by K. R. Brown. 4th ed. The Hague, Internat. Federation for Documentation, 1975. 203p. (FID publ. 532) **AB25**

1st ed. 1956 had title: *Library and documentation periodicals.*

About 950 serials listed in this edition, with subscription information. A section for publications of international organizations is followed by a country listing, a section for abstracting, indexing and current awareness services, and a list of ceased titles. Title index and selected list of titles arranged by subject specialty. Information was drawn mainly from responses to questionnaires. Z666.I55

Handbooks of usage

Baker, Robert K. Doing library research: an introduction for community college students. Boulder, Colo., Westview Pr., 1981. 283p. **AB26**

Aims to take into consideration the disparate backgrounds of community college students and the diverse curricular offerings available to them. Z675.J8B34

Cook, Margaret Gerry. The new library key. 3d ed. N.Y., Wilson, 1975. 264p. il. **AB27**

1st ed. 1956. Based on Zaidee Brown's *The library key* (7th ed. rev. N.Y., Wilson, 1949).

Intended mainly for college students and adults. Discusses the preparation of a term paper; the make-up and use of a book; the card catalog; library classification systems; periodicals and periodical indexes; and general and special reference books. Indexed.

Z711.2.C75

Downs, Robert Bingham and **Keller, Clara D.** How to do library research. 2d ed. Urbana, Univ. of Illinois Pr., [1975]. 298p. **AB28**

1st ed. 1966.

Sections on "America's libraries," library catalogs, and "Practical use of reference books" are followed by what are essentially annotated bibliographies of various types of reference works, plus a section on non-book materials. Z1035.1.D68

Gates, Jean Key. Guide to the use of libraries and information sources. 5th ed. N.Y., McGraw-Hill, [1983]. 338p. **AB29**

1st ed. 1962.

Aims "to provide a brief but comprehensive treatment of libraries, with emphasis upon the many kinds of library materials, their organization and arrangement, and their usefulness for specific purposes. . . . Particular attention is paid to academic libraries and to ways of using them most effectively."—*Pref.* Z710.G27

Katz, William A. Your library: a reference guide. 2d ed. N.Y., Holt, Rinehart and Winston, [1984]. 242p. il. **AB30**

1st ed. 1979.

A guide for students and others unfamiliar with the use of libraries. In three sections (the first two of which are meant to be read throughout): (1) How to use the library (including a section on the research paper); (2) Basic reference works; (3) Subject reference sources. Index of subjects and titles. Z710.K38

Shapiro, Lillian L. Teaching yourself in libraries: a guide to the high school media center and other libraries. N.Y., Wilson, 1978. 180p. il. **AB31**

Aims to suggest ways in which the individual can learn to solve problems at his own pace and in his own way: "Each chapter, instead of constituting a visit to [the] library, is a gathering together of related ideas and titles on a subject of interest and importance to many people."—*Introd.* Indexed. Z665.5.S52

Encyclopedias and dictionaries

ALA world encyclopedia of library and information services. Robert Wedgeworth, ed. Chicago, Amer. Lib. Assoc., 1980. 601p. il. **AB32**

Intended for students, practitioners, and the general public, the encyclopedia "seeks to explain fundamental ideas, record historical events and activities, and portray those personalities, living and dead, who have shaped the field."—*Pref.* Truly international in scope, with articles on status and condition of libraries in 162 countries. Includes information on library organizations, associations, and agencies, education for librarianship, etc. Dictionary arrangement; signed articles; bibliographies. A "parallel index" places index entries in the margin parallel to the text.

A review by J. C. Swan in *Library journal* 106:1051–52 (May 15, 1981) finds much to commend in the volume, but points to an "uncertainty of purpose" and laments the lack of a "real index."

Z1006.A18

Encyclopedia of library and information science. Allen Kent and Harold Lancour, eds. N.Y., Dekker, [1968–84]. v.1–37. (In progress) **AB33**

Contents: v.1–33, A–Z; v.34–35, Author and subject indexes; v.36–37, Supplements 1–2.

International in scope. Signed articles in dictionary arrangement, most of them of considerable length and carrying bibliographies. Articles on all aspects of library work and related aspects of the book world, together with survey articles on libraries and library service in individual countries and major cities. Includes biographies of deceased persons in the field of librarianship.

Supplements are designed to update existing articles, treat new topics, add biographies of important figures recently deceased, and to cover certain topics omitted from the main set because not submitted on time. Each supplementary volume is arranged in a separate alphabet.

A critical appraisal of the first 29 volumes (A–Systems analysis) by K. F. Kister appears in *Library journal* 106:1051 (May 15, 1981).

Z1006.E57

Landau, Thomas, ed. Encyclopaedia of librarianship. 3d rev. ed. London, Bowes & Bowes; N.Y., Hafner, [1966]. 484p. **AB34**

1st ed. 1958.

An alphabetical work covering all aspects of librarianship, with entries varying in length from a few words to signed articles of several pages. Usage covered is almost entirely British. Some articles include bibliographies. Z1006.L3

Lexikon des Bibliothekswesens. Hrsg. von Horst Kunze und Gotthard Rückl. 2., neubearb. Aufl. Leipzig, Bibliographisches Inst., 1974–75. 2v. **AB35**

1st ed. 1969.

Brief articles on aspects of library science, library terms, and closely related matters. Articles are signed with the initials of contributors and usually include bibliographical references. v.2 includes a *Registerteil* which gives equivalents of the German terms in Russian, English, French, and Spanish, plus lists of terms in those languages, with German equivalents. Z1006.L46

Milkau, Fritz, ed. Handbuch der Bibliothekswissenschaft. Begründet von Fritz Milkau, 2. verm. und verb. Aufl. hrsg. von Georg Leyh. Wiesbaden, Harrassowitz, 1950–65. 3v. in 4, and Registerband. **AB36**

1st ed. 1931–42 (3v. and index).

Issued in parts.

Contents: v.1, Schrift und Buch; v.2, Bibliotheksverwaltung; v.3, Geschichte der Bibliotheken (2 Hälfte); Registerband, bearb. von Renate Bellmann.

A scholarly work on the history of books, libraries, and librarianship with emphasis on German and Western European aspects of the subject. Long, signed articles with many bibliographical footnotes. Z670.M642

The state of the library art, ed. by Ralph R. Shaw. New Brunswick, N.J., Graduate School of Lib. Service, Rutgers Univ., 1960–61. 5v. **AB37**

Contents: v.1, pts.1–2, in 1v.: Cataloging and classification, by Maurice F. Tauber. Subject headings, by Carlyle J. Frarey; pts. 3–5, in 1v.: Classification systems, by Maurice F. Tauber and Edith Wise. Gifts, by Donald E. Thompson. Exchanges, by Donald E. Thompson; v.2, pts.1–2, in 1v.: Training laymen in use of the library, by George S. Bonn. Bibliographies, abstracts, and indexes, by Margaret S. Bryant; pt.3, Charging systems, by Leila H. Kirkwood; pt.4, pts.1–3, in 1v.: Buildings by Ralph E. Ellsworth. Shelving, by Louis Kaplan. Storage warehouses, by Jerrold Orne; v.4, pts.1–5, in 1v.: Notched cards, by Felix Reichmann. Feature cards (peek-a-boo cards), by Lawrence S. Thompson. Punched cards, by Ralph Blasingame, Jr. Electronic searching, by Gerald Jahoda. Coding in yes-no form, by Doralyn J. Hickey; v.5, pt.1, Production and use of microforms, by Reginald Hawkins; pt.2, Reading devices for microimages, by Jean Stewart and others; pt.3, Full-size photocopying, by William R. Hawken.

A series of handbooks with articles by specialists, reviewing and summarizing the literature. Each part includes an extensive bibliography. Most sections now considerably dated.

Terms

The ALA glossary of library and information science. Heartsill Young, ed. Chicago, Amer. Lib. Assoc., 1983. 245p. **AB38**

Successor to a 1943 publication prep. by Elizabeth H. Thompson and entitled *A.L.A. glossary of library terms.* Compiled with the assistance of specialists in various areas, this edition is seen as "a contribution toward the development of standard terminology, or a set of terms, which will enable librarians and other information scientists better to communicate with each other and with specialists in related fields."—*Foreword.* In addition to library and information science, terms are drawn from printing and publishing, graphic arts, computer science, telecommunications, reprography, educational technology, administrative science, and archives administration. Z1006.A48

Harrod, Leonard Montague. Harrod's Librarians' glossary of terms used in librarianship, documentation and the book crafts, and reference book. 5th ed., rev. and updated by Ray Prytherch. Aldershot, Hants., Gower, [1984]. 861p. **AB39**

1st ed. 1939.

Includes "standard librarianship terms, printing and publishing terms, archive terms and terms used in related fields" *(Pref.)* with additions to this edition being "principally in the areas of information technology, telecommunications, and computer applications" relevant to the library profession. A work of British origin, but with attention given to American institutions, organizations, etc., and to differences between British and American terminology.

Z1006.H32

Pipics, Zoltán. Dictionarium bibliothecarii practicum. Ad usum internationalem in XXII linguis. Wörterbuch des Bibliothekars in zweiundzwanzig Sprachen. The librarian's practical dictionary in twenty-two languages. 7. correcta et aucta editio. Budapest, Akadémiai Kiadó, 1977. 385p. **AB40**

6th ed. (München, 1974) also 385p.

Based on the author's *A könyvtáros gyakorlati szótára* (Budapest, 1963), using German rather than Hungarian as the base language. Presents library terms in 22 languages. Z1006.P67

Rosenberg, Kenyon C. Dictionary of library and educational technology. 2d ed., rev. and expanded. With the assistance of Paul T. Feinstein. Littleton, Colo., Libraries Unlimited, 1983. 185p. **AB41**

A rev. ed. of *Media equipment: a guide and dictionary* by Rosenberg and J. S. Doskey (1976).

A work for the librarian and teacher responsible for the selection, use, and care of audiovisual equipment. A section on criteria for equipment selection precedes the dictionary. Terms relating to reprography, micrographics, communications, and computers are included in this edition along with those dealing with other media equipment. Selected bibliography. TS2301.A7R66

Thompson, Anthony. Vocabularium bibliothecarii: English, French, German, Spanish, Russian. Collaborator for Russian, E. I. Shamurin; collaborator for Spanish, Domingo Bonocore. 2d ed. Paris, UNESCO, 1962. 627p. **AB42**

1st ed. 1953; suppl. 1958.

About 2,800 terms are included; definitions are given only where a word has two meanings, or where there is no equivalent in one of the languages. Terms are arranged in columns by Universal Decimal Classification number, and translation is from English into the other languages, with indexes by each language to classification number.

Mu'jam al-mustalaḥāt al-maktabīyah (1965; 692p.) is a photo-offset reproduction of this edition with an introduction and index in Arabic, and with the Arabic vocabulary inserted in the right-hand column of the pages of the glossary. Z1006.T47

——— ——— Supplementum Hungaricum, szerk. Pipics Zoltán. Budapest, Akadémiai Kiadó, 1971. 251p.

Vaillancourt, Pauline M. International directory of acronyms in library, information, and computer sciences. N.Y., Bowker, 1980. 518p. **AB43**

About 5,500 entries, both "true" acronyms and initialisms. "Nine categories of acronyms are represented: associations, societies and organizations in the library, information and computer sciences; commonly used terms from these fields; meetings, conferences and workshops of a continuing nature; publications, including books, journals, and data tapes; libraries and information centers; information-related government agencies; commercial firms; consortia, networks and systems; and research or experimental projects and services."—*Pref.* Not only supplies the names or terms for which the initials stand, but also gives additional identifying information such as address of an organization, function, etc. For the comprehensive collection only. Z1006.V33

❖Additional bilingual and multilingual glossaries include: *Russian-English glossary of library terms,* by A. Dmitrieff

(N.Y., Telberg, 1966. 158p.); *Library terms . . . Englisch-deutsch und deutsch-englisch,* by Otti Gross (Hamburg, Eberhard Stichnote, 1952. 163p.); *A complete dictionary of library terms; technical terms used in libraries, bibliographies and by printing and binding trades in English, German, French, Chinese and Japanese languages,* by Fujio Mamiya (Rev. and enl. ed. Tokyo, Japan Lib. Bureau, 1952. 615p.); *Rječnik bibliotekarskih stručnih izraza; Vocabularium bibliothecarii . . . English-Croatian-Serbian,* by Anthony Thompson (Prema 2. Zagreb, 1965. 184p.); *Podręczny słownik bibliotekarza,* by Helena Więckowska and Hanna Pliszczyńska (Warszawa, Panstwowe Wydawnictwo Naukowe, 1955. 309p.); *Bibliotekstermer: svenska, engelska, franska, tyska* (2. uppl. Lund, Biblioteksjänst, 1965. 70p.); *Dizionario tecnico di biblioteconomia italiano, spagnolo, inglese,* by Beatriz Massa Gil (México, Editorial Trillas, 1971. 242p.); *An English-Italian dictionary of library science,* by Joseph N. Failli (Prelim. ed. Firenze, 1979. 382p.).

Directories
International

See also AB7.

Esdaile, Arundell J. K. National libraries of the world: their history, administration and public services. 2d ed. compl. rev. by F. J. Hill. London, Lib. Assoc., 1957. 413p.
AB44

1st ed. 1934.
Describes the national libraries of 32 countries. Each library is treated in a separate chapter giving history, description of buildings, catalogs, departments, staff, finances, etc., and a brief bibliography.
Z721.E74

Fang, Josephine Riss and **Songe, Alice H.** International guide to library, archival, and information science associations. 2d ed. N.Y., Bowker, 1980. 448p.
AB45

1st ed. 1976.
Offers information on 59 international and 450 national library associations—i.e., "nonprofit associations related to librarianship, documentation, information science, and archives, including associations of institutions, staff (both professional and nonprofessional), and associations for professional education."—*Introd.* Entries are based on information supplied by the association, supplemented by research of the literature. Includes a general bibliography, 1975–80, and a list of official journals and selected newsletters. Indexes of official names of the associations, chief officers, subjects, and countries.
Z673.A1F33

Internationales Bibliotheks-Handbuch. World guide to libraries. Comp. by Klaus G. Saur. Ed.1– . N.Y., Bowker; München, Verlag Dokumentation, 1966– . Irregular (6th ed. 1983)
AB46

1st ed. had title *Internationales Bibliotheksadressbuch.*
Issued as Bd.8 of *Handbuch der internationalen Dokumentation und Information* (AB7).
Now gives addresses and indicates subject specialties of more than 42,700 public, academic, and special libraries in over 167 countries.
Z721.I63

Lewanski, Richard Casimir, comp. European library directory; a geographical and bibliographical guide. [Firenze], Olschki, 1968. 774p.
AB47

Title also in French, German, Italian, Russian, and Spanish. Preface in English, French, and German.
A companion to the compiler's *Subject collections in European libraries* (AB114).
Z789.L39

Minerva-Handbücher. Ergänzungen zu "Minerva," Jahrbuch der gelehrten Welt. Berlin, de Gruyter, 1927– .
AB48

Contents: 1.Abt. *Die Bibliotheken:* Bd.1, Deutsches Reich. 1929; Bd.2, Österreich. 1932; Bd. 3, Schweiz. 1934.
2. Abt. *Die Archive:* Bd.1, Deutsches Reich, Dänemark, Estland, Finnland, Lettland, Litauen, Luxemburg, Niederlande, Norwegen, Österreich, Schweden, Schweiz. 1932.
3. Abt. *Die deutschen Museen:* Bd.1, Die Museen in Bayern. 1939; Bd.2, Die Museen in Nordwest-Deutschland. 1942.
4. Abt. *Die gelehrten Gesellschaften:* Bd.1, Die deutschen Kommissionen und Vereine für Geschichte und Altertumskunde. 1940.
AS2.M615

United Nations Educational, Scientific and Cultural Organization. Guide to national bibliographical information centres. Guide des centres nationaux d'information bibliographique. 3d ed. rev. and enl. [Paris], UNESCO, [1970]. 195p.
AB49

1st ed. 1953.
Lists 186 centers in 77 countries. Scientific and technical centers were more fully covered in the *World guide to science information and documentation services* (1965) and the *World guide to technical information and documentation services* (1969).
For information relating to the international exchange of publications *see* AB196.
Z674.5.A2U52

World guide to library schools and training courses in documentation. Guide mondial des écoles de bibliothécaires et documentalistes. 2d ed. London, Bingley; Paris, Unesco, [1981]. 549p.
AB50

1st ed. 1972.
Provides brief information on library schools and other institutions in some 86 countries. Listing is by country, then by name of institution. Information is given in English or French.
Z668.W85

United States

American Library Association. ALA handbook of organization and membership directory. 1980/81– . Chicago, Amer. Lib. Assoc., 1980– . Annual.
AB51

Formed by the union of *A.L.A. handbook of organization* (publ. 1971–) and *A.L.A. membership directory* (publ. 1949–79). The handbook portion is also published separately.
The directory includes institutional as well as personal memberships.
Z673.A5H37

American library directory; a classified list of libraries in the United States and Canada with personnel and statistical data. N.Y., Bowker, 1923– . Annual.
AB52

Frequency varies (1951– called Ed.19–); subtitle varies; compiler varies. Earlier lists were a feature of the *American library annual* publ. 1912–18.
Libraries are arranged alphabetically by state and then by city. Gives name, librarian (and usually names of department heads), number of volumes, circulation, income, budget, special collections. For large libraries information is more detailed. Statistical information regarding public libraries precedes each state, region and province division. Additional lists include (38th ed., 1985): networks, consortia and other cooperative library organizations; library schools and training courses; library systems; libraries for the blind and physically handicapped; libraries serving the deaf and hearing impaired; state and provincial public library agencies; state school library agencies; national and model interlibrary loan codes; United States Armed Forces libraries overseas; United State Information Agency centers. Indexed.
Z731.A53

Directory of special libraries and information centers. Ed.1– . Detroit, Gale, [1963–].
AB53

Subtitle, ed.2– , 1968– : A guide to special libraries, research libraries, information centers, archives, and data centers maintained by government agencies, business, industry, newspapers, educational institutions, nonprofit organizations, and societies in the field of science, technology, medicine, law, art, religion, history, social sciences and humanistic studies.
9th ed. (1985) in 3v.
About 17,500 listings in the 9th ed. United States and Canadian

libraries are now listed by name, sponsoring body, or institution in a single alphabetical sequence, with a subject index in v.1; appendixes list networks and consortia, libraries for the blind and physically handicapped, patent depository libraries, federal information centers, federal job information centers, and United Nations depository libraries. v.2 offers geographic and personnel indexes.

v.1 is kept up to date between editions by: Z731.D56

New special libraries; a periodic supplement to the . . . Directory of special libraries and information centers. Detroit, Gale, [1971]– .   **AB54**

Lists new or previously overlooked libraries. Two issues appear between editions of the directory, with a cumulated index in the second issue.

Medical Library Association. Directory. Chicago, 1950– . Irregular.   **AB55**

Publisher varies; content varies.
Lists personal and institutional members.

North American film and video directory: a guide to media collections and services. Comp. by Olga S. Weber. N.Y., Bowker, 1976. 284p.   **AB56**

Represents "both a revision and extension of the pioneer *Directory of film libraries in North America,* published by the Film Library Information Council in 1971, in that in addition to updating data on film and other media services, information has been expanded to include institutions offering video services and/or maintaining video tape collections."—*Pref.*   Z675.M4M43

Special Libraries Association. Directory of members. N.Y., Assoc., 1937– . Irregular.   **AB57**

Title varies; 1st ed. called *List of members.*
Now provides chapter and division lists as well as the alphabetical directory of members.   Z673.S81D5

Subject directory of special libraries and information centers. Ed. 1– . Detroit, Gale, 1975– . Irregular.   **AB58**

Ed. by Margaret L. Young [and others].
Issued in 5v.
"A subject classified edition of material taken from *Directory of special libraries and information centers* covering special libraries." —*t.p.*
Contents: v.1, Business and law libraries; v.2, Education and information science libraries; v.3, Health sciences libraries; v.4, Social sciences and humanities libraries; v.5, Science and technology libraries.
A re-arrangement of the entries from the *Directory of special libraries. . . .* (AB53).   Z675.A2S83

Africa

Directory of documentation, libraries and archives services in Africa. Répertoire des services de documentation, de bibliothèque et d'archives d'Afrique. 2. éd. by Dominique Zidouemba, rev. and enl. by Éric de Grolier. Paris, Unesco, 1977. 311p. (Documentation, libraries and archives: Bibliographies and reference works, 5)   **AB59**

"Replaces and supersedes the Directory of archives, libraries and schools of librarianship in Africa, published in 1965 . . . prepared by E. W. Dadzie and J. T. Strickland."
Information in English or French.
A directory of libraries, archives, and information centers in 40 countries. A section of general references and notes on international cooperative arrangements and associations precedes the country listings. Indexes in English and French.   Z857.A1D57

Argentina

Deransart, Pierre. Bibliothèques et systèmes documentaires en Argentine et au Brésil. LeChasnay, Inst. de Recherche d'Informatique et d'Automatique, [1977?]. 145p.   **AB60**

Limited to the principal libraries and documentation centers of the two countries. For each library, provides a considerable amount of directory information according to a fixed scheme. Text in French; separate sections for Argentina and for Brazil.   Z769.A1D47

Australia

National Library of Australia. Guide to the National Union Catalogue of Australia. 4th ed. Canberra, Nat. Lib. of Austral., 1978. 198p.   **AB61**

While the basic purpose of this guide is to provide information for libraries contributing to the National Union Catalog and using its related services, a substantial part of the book is an alphabetical listing of more than 850 libraries with their addresses.   Z975.A1C3

Austria

See also AB74.

Vereinigung Österreichischer Bibliothekare. Handbuch österreichischer Bibliotheken. [1. ed.–] Wien, Österreichische Nationalbibliothek, 1953– . (Biblos-Schriften, Bd.1, 14, 30–31, 34, 47, 62, 71–)   **AB62**

Issued in parts, the parts being separately revised at irregular intervals. The 1971/72 edition is in 2v.: (1) Bibliotheksverzeichnis (a directory of Austrian libraries and archives) and (2) Statistik und Personalverzeichnis (a section of biographical sketches followed by tables of statistics for Austrian libraries).   Z793.V43

Belgium

Beirens, Gerard. Bibliotheekgids van Belgie. Bruxelles, Archives et Bibliothèques de Belgique, 1974–75. 9v. (Gidsen —Archief- en Bibliotheekwezen in België, 1)   **AB63**

Geographical arrangement. Information for each library follows a set pattern, giving name, address, type of library, times of opening, classification system, size of collection, etc.   Z813.A1B35

Brazil

See also AB60.

Fundação Instituto Brasileiro de Geografia e Estatística. Guia das bibliotecas brasileiras 1976. Rio de Janeiro, The Institute, 1976. 1017p.   **AB64**

Earlier volumes with the same title were published 1941–69 by the Instituto Nacional do Livro, Rio de Janeiro.   Z769.A1G83

Canada

See also AB52.

Directory of Canadian archives. Annuaire des dépôts d'archives canadiens. [Ottawa], Bureau of Canadian Archivists, [1981]. 130p.   **AB65**

Ed. by Judith Beattie [et al.].
A joint project of the Association of Canadian Archivists and the Association des Archivistes du Québec. Represents a revised and updated edition of the 1977 *Directory of Canadian records and manuscript repositories.*
Gives address, hours of opening, etc., and brief notes on holdings. Federal repositories are listed first, with others listed by province or territory. Indexed.

Directory of library associations in Canada. Ed.1–5. Ottawa, Library Documentation Centre, Nat. Lib. of Canada, 1974–79.   **AB66**

Provides information regarding founding date, objectives, meetings, publications, officers, etc.

Ceased publication.   Z673.A1D57

National Library of Canada. Canadian library directory. Ottawa, 1974–76. 2v.   **AB67**

B. Anderson, comp.

Contents: v.1, Federal government libraries (with text in English and French); v.2, University, college and special libraries (English and French texts published in separate volumes).

Provides information on subject strengths and special collections, as well as address, telephone, name of librarian, etc.

Z675.G7N39

China

Directory of Chinese libraries. Ed. by Wang Enguang, Wu Renyong, Xie Wanruo. Pei-ching, Chung-kuo Hsueh Shu Chu Pan She (distr. in U.S.A. by Gale, Detroit), 1982. 428p. il. (World books reference guide, no.3)   **AB68**

Title also in Chinese; text in Chinese and English.

In two main sections: (1) a selected list of about 500 libraries with foreign-language holdings (with indication of subject fields) and (2) list of about 2,700 libraries (public, academic, and special) with addresses. All entries appear in both Chinese and English.

Z845.C5C493

Cuba

Directorio de bibliotecas de Cuba, 1943– . La Habana, Anuario Bibliográfico Cubano, 1943– . (Biblioteca del bibliotecario, 2) Irregular.   **AB69**

Fermín Peraza y Sarausa, comp.

Publisher varies.

1968 last published?   Z753.D5

Denmark

Faellesrepraesentationen for den danske Bibliotekarstand. Dansk Biblioteksfører, ved Henning Einersen og Mogens Iversen. 3. udg. København, Dansk Bibliografisk Kontor, 1955. 137p.   **AB70**

1st ed. 1915.

A directory of scholarly, technical, and public libraries. Includes indexes by name of library and by subject.   Z823.F3

Finland

Liinamaa, Matti and **Heikkilä, Marjatta.** Suomen tieteellisten Kirjastojen opas. 6. uusittu ja täydennetty painos. Helsinki, Suomen Tieteellinen Kirjastoseura, 1981. 175p.   **AB71**

Title also in English: *Guide to research libraries and information services in Finland.*

In English, Finnish, and Swedish.

1st ed. 1950 by Eino Nivanka.   Z829.A1L54

France

Paris. Bibliothèque Nationale. Répertoire des bibliothèques et organismes de documentation. Paris, 1971. 733p.   **AB72**

At head of title: Direction des Bibliothèques et de la Lecture Publique.

Previous edition (1963) issued by Direction des Bibliothèques de France under title: Répertoire des bibliothèques d'étude et organismes de documentation.

A directory and survey of 3,210 libraries and documentation

centers of France. In two sections ("Région parisienne" and "Departements") plus index. In addition to name and address, information usually includes information on hours of opening, regulations of use, catalogs and classification system, resources, history, publications, etc.   Z797.A1P35

———— ———— Supplement. Paris, 1973. 265p.

Serrurier, Cornelia. Bibliothèques de France; description de leurs fonds et historique de leur formation. La Haye, Nijhoff, 1946. 346p.   **AB73**

Describes about 70 important French libraries, mainly municipal, giving for each a historical sketch, indication of content, brief listing of important holdings, and bibliographical references.   Z797.S53

Germany

Handbuch der Bibliotheken Bundesrepublik Deutschland, Österreich, Schweiz. [Hrsg. von Helga Lengenfelder] München, K. G. Saur, 1984. 329p.   **AB74**

Listing is by type of library within separate sections for Germany, Austria, and Switzerland. Subject index.   Z801.A1H35

Jahrbuch der Bibliotheken, Archive und Informationsstellen der Deutschen Demokratischen Republik. Jahrg. 1– , 1959– . Berlin, 1961– . Irregular.   **AB75**

Title varies.

A directory of libraries, archives, and documentation centers, giving detailed information including statistics. Contains a list of union catalogs and a directory of persons employed.   Z801.J15

Jahrbuch der deutschen Bibliotheken, hrsg. vom Verein deutscher Bibliothekare. Leipzig, Harrassowitz, 1902– . v.1– . Annual (Irregular).   **AB76**

Imprint varies; frequency varies.

Principal contents of v.49, 1981: (1) List of libraries arranged alphabetically by towns; (2) List of librarians with brief biographical data. Some volumes include a section of statistics. Now concerned with the Bundesrepublik Deutschland and West Berlin.   Z801.J2

Great Britain

Aslib. Aslib directory. Ed. by Ellen M. Codlin. 4th ed. London, Aslib, 1977–80. 2v.   **AB77**

1st ed. 1928.

Contents: v.1, Information sources in science, technology and commerce; v.2, Information sources in the social sciences, medicine and the humanities.

In this edition "the main consideration for inclusion was the propensity of an organisation to make information available, whether freely, by subscription, as consultants, or by publications, even if, in some cases, they had no formal information services."—*Introd.* Organizations included range from large to small and include commercial, scientific and technical, academic, and governmental libraries, together with producers of abstracts, statistics, and similar data. The earlier geographic arrangement of the directory has been abandoned in favor of an alphabetical listing by name of organization; size of collection is no longer indicated. Each volume has its own subject index.   Z791.A1A82

Directory of London public libraries. Ed.1– . London, Association of Metropolitan Chief Librarians, 1956– . Irregular.   **AB78**

1st ed. 1956.

Gives information regarding officers, addresses, services, hours, etc., of the central and branch libraries of the London boroughs.

Z791.D5

Libraries in the United Kingdom and the Republic of Ireland. 11th ed. London, Library Assoc., 1985. 171p.   **AB79**

1st–4th eds. had title *Address list of public library authorities.*

Gives address, telephone number, and name of librarian for public, university and college, polytechnic, and selected national, government and special libraries. Includes a section for schools of librarianship. Indexed.

Libraries, museums and art galleries year book, 1897– . London, Clark, 1897– . Irregular.   **AB80**

Principal contents, 1978/79 ed. (publ. 1981): (1) The British Library; (2) Public libraries of the United Kingdom; (3) Special libraries (academic, commercial, industrial, society, etc.) of the United Kingdom; (4) Museums, art galleries, and stately homes of the United Kingdom; (5) Republic of Ireland (public libraries, special libraries, museums, art galleries, and stately homes). Indexed.   Z791.L7

Library Association. The Library Association year book. London, Assoc., [1891]– . Annual since 1964.   **AB81**

None published 1896–98, 1906, 1908, 1910–13.
Includes officers and council, committees, royal charter and by-laws, election regulations, and list of members.   Z673.L7Y

Library Association. Medical Section. Directory of medical libraries in the British Isles. 4th ed. London, Assoc., 1976. 199p.   **AB82**

Lists medical, dental, pharmaceutical, and veterinary libraries, giving address, date of founding, description of collections, hours, etc. Includes index of establishments, index of personnel, and an index of special collections.   Z675.M4L5

Munby, Alan Noel Latimer. Cambridge college libraries; aids for research students. 2d ed. Cambridge, Eng., W. Heffer, 1962. 56p.   **AB83**

1st ed. 1960.
Descriptions of the research facilities of 22 college libraries plus the Fitzwilliam Museum and the University Archives. Devotes itself to the rare and early collections, not the "working libraries."   Z792.M86

Taylor, L. J. and **Taylor, E. A.** Library resources in London and South East England. 2d ed. London, Library Assoc., Reference, Special and Information Section, 1979. 275p.   **AB84**

1st ed. (1969) ed. by S. Eagle.
A directory for the area, with a subject index to the special strengths of the various collections. One of a series of directories published by the Reference, Special and Information Section of the Library Association; other volumes deal with library resources of the East Midlands (1979), the North East (1977), North West England (1980), South West England and the Channel Isles (1978), Wales (1975), West Midlands (1977), and Yorkshire and Humberside (1980).   Z791.L6E2

India

Directory of booksellers, publishers, libraries & librarians in India. Ed.1– , 1968/69– . New Delhi, Premier, 1968– . Irregular.   **AB85**

2d ed. 1973 last published?
Includes lists of special, state and public libraries, plus a who's who of librarians.   Z455.D49

Indian Association of Special Libraries and Information Centres. Directory of special and research libraries in India. Calcutta, Oxford Book & Stationery Co., 1962. 282p.   **AB86**

Lists 123 libraries, including academic and public with special research collections. In columnar form gives information as to size, administration, personnel, resources, etc. Arranged alphabetically by name of library with indexes to name, place, subject, and nature of management.
A more recent listing is Niharkanti Chatterjee's *Directory of research and special libraries in India and Sri Lanka* (Calcutta, Information Research Academy, 1979–80. 2v.).   Z955.I45

Italy

Annuario delle biblioteche italiane. Roma, Palombi, 1969–81. 5v.   **AB87**

Publ. under the direction of the Direzione Generale delle Accademie e Biblioteche e per la Diffusione della Cultura.
Earlier editions with the same title were publ. 1949–54 (3v. plus suppl.) and 1956–59 (3v.).
University, public, and other libraries are arranged alphabetically under towns, and described with considerable detail, including historical information. Contains bibliographic references.

Japan

Libraries in Japan. Ed. by J.L.A. International Exchange Committee. New ed. Tokyo, Japan Library Assoc., 1980. 48p. il.   **AB88**

An English-language guide to representative libraries in Japan, intended for foreign visitors. Selected from all types of libraries in all parts of Japan, the 26 entries include a high school library, a number of municipal and prefectural libraries, university and research libraries, the National Diet Library, and several special libraries. Also included are a brief history of Japanese libraries, the text of the 1950 library law, a list of library-related associations, and statistics on Japanese libraries (as of 1979).   Z845.J4L52

Senmon jōhō kikan sōran [1982]: tsuketari, senmon jōhō kikan tōkei. Directory of special libraries, Japan. [Henshū Senmon Toshokan Kyōgikai Chōsa Tōkei Iinkai] Tōkyō, Senmon Toshokan Kyōgikai, [1982]. 491p.   **AB89**

1st ed. 1969.
Lists both public and private libraries, giving directory information, size of holdings, subject strengths, services offered, and relevant publications. Indexes by subject field and by prefecture.   Z845.J4S44

Shoshi Kenkyū Konwakai. Zenkoku toshokan annai: fu Chihōshi shuyō bunken mokuroku, Chihō shishi shuyō mokuroku ichiran, Zenkoku chihō shuppansha, Semmon koshoten narabi ni shuyō shuppanbutsu ichiran. Tokyo, San'ichi Shobō, 1979. 2v.   **AB90**

A directory of Japanese libraries of all types, geographically arranged by prefecture, then by name of library. Includes a select bibliography of local history sources, a list of local history journals, a directory of publishers, and a directory of antiquarian bookstores.   Z854.J4S54

Mexico

Directorio de bibliotecas de la República Mexicana. Secretária de Educación Pública, Dirección General de Publicaciones y Bibliotecas. 6a ed. México, Dirección General de Publicaciones y Bibliotecas, 1979. 3v.   **AB91**

1st ed. 1962.
Geographical arrangement with indexes of institutions, personal names, subjects, etc. v.3 is a supplement.   Z739.A1M44

Netherlands

Bibliotheek- en documentatiegids voor Nederland, samengesteld onder auspiciën van de Centrale Vereniging voor Openbare Leeszalen en Bibliotheken, Nederlandse Vereniging van Bibliothecarissen en het Nederlands Instituut voor Documentatie en Registratuur. 'sGravenhage, 1957. 246p.   **AB92**

A directory of 1,125 libraries and documentation centers, arranged by town, giving name of library, address, hours of opening, size of collection, etc. Includes name and subject index. Revises data in two earlier works: *Nederlandse bibliotheekgids* (4th ed. 1949) and *N.I.D.E.R. documentatiegids voor Nederland* (1937).   Z815.B5

Pakistan

Pakistan Bibliographical Working Group. A guide to Pakistan libraries, learned and scientific societies and educational institutions, biographies of librarians in Pakistan. Rev. ed. Karachi, 1960. 166p. (*Its* Publ. no.3)   **AB93**

Contents: sec.1, Libraries; sec.2, Educational institutions; sec.3, Museums and art galleries; sec.4, Learned and scientific societies and institutions; sec. 5, Biographies of librarians; Index.
AS569.P23A6

Puerto Rico

Alamo de Torres, Daisy. Directorio de bibliotecas de Puerto Rico. Rio Piedras, P.R., Asociación Estudiantes Graduados de Bibliotecología, Univ. de Puerto Rico, 1979. 100p.
AB94

Libraries are grouped by type (academic, special, etc.), then by place.   Z753.P9A4

Spain

Spain. Dirección General de Archivos y Bibliotecas. Guía de las bibliotecas de Madrid. Madrid, Servicio de Publicaciones del Ministerio de Educación Nacional, 1953. 556p. (*Its* Guías de archivos y bibliotecas)   **AB95**

Publicaciones de educación nacional, obra no.8.

Covers the national library and the university, college, research, scientific, government, and special libraries in Madrid. Gives history, description of collections, publications, information as to administration, regulations of use, etc.   Z832.M168

Switzerland

See also AB74.

Schweizerische Vereinigung für Dokumentation. Archive, Bibliotheken und Dokumentationsstellen der Schweiz . . . 4. Aufl. des "Führer durch die schweizerische Dokumentation." Bern, Amt für Wissenschaft und Forschung 1976. 805p.   **AB96**

Title also in French and Italian.

Arranged geographically; lists and describes the libraries and documentation centers (academic, public, commercial, etc.) of Switzerland. Indexes of institutions, of catchwords and personal names, and of subject specialties.   Z837.S44

Union of Soviet Socialist Republics

Biblioteki SSSR. Spravochnik. Moskva, "Kniga," 1973–74. 2v.   **AB97**

Contents: v.1, Biblioteki RSFSR; v.2, Biblioteki soiuznykh respublik.

Libraries are classed according to type (general, scientific and technical, medical, etc.). Gives information on holdings as well as address, telephone, etc. Each volume has its own index.
Z819.A1B5

Horecky, Paul L. Libraries and bibliographic centers in the Soviet Union. [Bloomington, Ind., 1959]. 287p. (Indiana Univ. publ. Slavic and East European ser., v.16)   **AB98**

Surveys library networks and collections, catalogs and cataloging,

buildings and equipment, and the library profession. Bibliography, p.259–75.

For a companion volume on Soviet publishing see AA350.
Z819.H6

Venezuela

Marín, Olivia. Directorio de bibliotecas venezolanas. Caracas, Univ. Central de Venezuela, [1974]. 99p.   **AB99**

Libraries are grouped by type (special, military, national, public, etc.). Indexed.   Z785.M37

Biography

A biographical directory of librarians in the United States and Canada. 5th ed. Chicago, Amer. Lib. Assoc., 1970. 1250p.   **AB100**

1st ed. 1933; 2d ed. 1943; 3d ed. 1955; 4th ed. 1966.
1st–4th eds. had title: *Who's who in library service.*
Lee Ash, ed.
"Sponsored by the Council of National Library Associations"—*reverse of half-title.*
About 20,000 biographies of professional librarians in the 5th ed.
Z720.A4W47

Who's who in library and information services. Joel M. Lee, ed. in chief. Chicago, Amer. Lib. Assoc., 1982. 559p.
AB101

Forms a successor to *A biographical directory of librarians in the United States and Canada* (above) and its predecessor, *Who's who in library service.*

Although requirements for inclusion were somewhat more stringent than was the case for the earlier series, scope for this volume extends to "librarians and information scientists; archivists; library school faculty and other educators; scholars in subject specialties associated with libraries or library education programs; publishers, editors, and journalists whose primary activity is in librarianship and information fields; trustees; others who have made notable contributions to library and information services."—*p.IX.*
Z720.A4W45

Dictionary of American library biography. Editorial board: George S. Bobinski, Jesse Hauk Shera, Bohdan S. Wynar. Littleton, Colo., Libraries Unlimited, 1978. 596p.   **AB102**

A collection of biographical sketches (about 1,000 to 6,000 words each) of 302 outstanding men and women of the library field. Emphasis is on "figures of national importance, based on the following criteria: contributions of national significance to library development; writings that influenced library trends and activities; positions of national importance . . . ; major achievements in special fields of librarianship; significant scholarly, philanthropic, legislative, or governmental support or activity that affected American libraries. To ensure proper historical perspective, only those people deceased as of June 30, 1976, were considered for inclusion." —*p.xxxi.* Articles are signed and include bibliographies. Supplementary sketches appear irregularly in the *Journal of library history* beginning with v.15, no.1 (1980).   Z720.A4D5

Frati, Carlo. Dizionario bio-bibliografico dei bibliotecari e bibliofili italiani dal sec. XIV al XIX. Firenze, Olschki, 1933. 705p. il.   **AB103**

———— ———— Aggiunte de Marino Parenti. Firenze, Sansoni Antiquariato, 1952–60. 3v.

A biographical dictionary of Italian librarians and bibliophiles with detailed lists of works by and about each of them. Includes index by place of libraries mentioned and author index to the works cited.   Z720.A4I8

Kósa, Géza Attila. Biographical dictionary of Australian librarians (formerly Who's who in Australian libraries). 2d ed. Melbourne, Burwood State College, 1979. 201p.
AB104

1st ed. 1968 had title *Who's who in Australian libraries.*
1,492 biographical sketches in this edition. Information was gathered by questionnaires distributed by the Library Association of Australia. The directory of libraries and the membership directories found in the earlier edition have been omitted. Z720.A46A85

New York State Library School Association. New York State library school register, 1887–1926. James I. Wyer memorial ed. [i.e., 6th ed.]. N.Y., Assoc., 1959. 175p. il. **AB105**

A biographical register of the faculty and graduates of the New York State Library School during the period of its existence. Important because so many outstanding members of the library profession graduated from this famous school.

————— ————— Supplement. 1963. 16p.

Z669.N6185

Ruiz Cabriada, Agustín. Bio-bibliografía del Cuerpo Facultativo de Archiveros, Bibliotecarios y Arqueólogos, 1858–1958. Madrid, 1958. 1342p. (Junta Técnica de Archivos, Bibliotecas y Museos. Ediciones conmemorativas del centenario del Cuerpo Facultativo, 1858–1958. no.7) **AB106**

Alphabetical by author; an extensive listing of the publications in a variety of fields by several hundred scholars connected with the Cuerpo. A brief biographical sketch precedes the listings for each. Combined index of authors, titles, subjects. Z5055.S48R8

Sabzwari, Ghaniul Akram and **Usmani, M. Wasil.** Who's who in librarianship in Pakistan. Karachi, Lib. Promotion Bureau, [1969]. 273p. il. **AB107**

Includes a brief "who was who" section and a geographical listing of libraries in addition to the current biographical sketches.
Z720.A46P36

Who's who in librarianship and information science, ed. by Thomas Landau. 2d ed. London, Abelard-Schuman, [1972]. 311p. **AB108**

1st ed. (1954) had title: *Who's who in librarianship.*
More than 2,000 biographical sketches; standards for inclusion are not indicated in this edition. Z720.A46G75

Who's who in New Zealand libraries, 1951– . Wellington, New Zealand Lib. Assoc., 1951– . Irregular. **AB109**

Includes an index by institutions. Z720.A4N4

Yearbooks

American Library Association. ALA yearbook. 1976– . Chicago, Amer. Lib. Assoc., 1976– . il. Annual. **AB110**

Subtitle: A review of library events 1975– .
An annual record of the events, activities, topics of current interest, etc., which reflect the varied concerns of the Association and its members. Includes obituary notices, state reports, etc. Indexed. Z673.A5A14

The Bowker annual of library and book trade information. Ed.1– , 1956– . Sponsored by the Council of National Library Associations. N.Y., Bowker, 1956– . Annual.
AB111

Title varies: 1956–58, *American library annual* [new series]; 1959–60, *American library and book trade annual.*
A compendium of miscellaneous information. Principal contents of 28th ed. (1983): Reports from the field (on copyright law, federal agencies, national associations, etc.); Legislation, funding, and grants; Library education, placement, and salaries; Research and statistics; International reports and statistics; Reference information; Directory of organizations. Indexed. Z731.A47

LIBRARY RESOURCES

International

Annuaire international des archives. International directory of archives (à jour en janvier 1975/ as of January, 1975). Paris, Presses Universitaires de France, 1975. 480p. (Archivum, v.22/23, 1972/73) **AB112**

1955 ed. (with 1959 suppl.) had title *International directory of archive services.*
Introductory matter in French, English, Spanish, and German.
Provides directory information on "those archive repositories open to the public and having materials of value for historical research."—*Foreword.*
Fuller information on the principal repositories was provided in v.15 (1965) of *Archivum* which is entitled "Les grandes dépots d'archives du monde: notices sur les archives les plus importantes pour la recherche historique internationale." CD1.A18 v.22/23

Lewanski, Richard C. Eastern Europe and Russia/Soviet Union: a handbook of West European archival and library resources. N.Y. [etc.], K. G. Saur, 1980. 317p. (American Council of Learned Societies/Social Science Research Council. Joint Committee on Eastern Europe. Publ.ser. 3)
AB113

Intended as "an inventory in directory format of the principal research resources, facilities, and services available in some 1,000 repositories—institutions of higher learning and research, libraries, archives, and museums—in various European countries."—*Pref.*
Arranged by country, then by city and repository; broad subject index. For each repository usually indicates scope of collection or subject profile, notes on special collections, number of volumes, type of catalog or catalogs, restrictions, availability of interlibrary loan, etc. Z2483.L48

————— Subject collections in European libraries. 2d ed. London & N.Y., Bowker, [1978]. 495p. **AB114**

1st ed. 1965.
Designed as a companion to Ash's guide to subject collections in the United States and Canada (AB115), this directory concentrates chiefly on libraries of northwestern Europe. Entries are arranged by Dewey class numbers, with an alphabetical subject index to the classification. Within classes the arrangement is alphabetical by country. Indicates size and character of collection, restrictions, photocopy facilities, etc. Z789.L4

United States

Ash, Lee, comp. Subject collections. 5th ed., rev. & enl. N.Y., Bowker, 1978. 1184p. **AB115**

Subtitle: A guide to special book collections and subject emphases as reported by university, college, public, and special libraries and museums in the United States and Canada.
1st ed. 1958.
Arranged alphabetically by subject, then geographically. Information is based on questionnaires completed by holding libraries, resulting in some unevenness.
A 6th ed. was published 1985 in 2v. Z731.A78

Directory of Jewish archival institutions. Ed. by Philip P. Mason. Detroit, pub. for the National Foundation for Jewish Culture by Wayne State Univ. Pr., 1975. 76p. il.
AB116

A brief guide to the major archival collections in the American Jewish Archives, American Jewish Historical Society, Leo Baeck Institute, Bund Archives of the Jewish Labor Movement, Dropsie University, Hebrew Union College–Jewish Institute of Religion Manuscript Library, Library of the Jewish Theological Seminary of America, and YIVO Institute for Jewish Research.
Briefer, but broader in scope, is Josef Fraenkel's *Guide to the Jewish libraries of the world.* (London, 1959. 64p.). Z6366.D57

Downs, Robert Bingham. American library resources; a bibliographical guide. Chicago, Amer. Lib. Assoc., 1951. 428p.   **AB117**

A bibliography of bibliographies rather than a description of resources, since it indicates holdings of libraries only insofar as there are bibliographies listing them. Bibliographies, union lists, surveys, checklists, and catalogs of particular libraries and special collections from all parts of the country are included, whether published in periodicals or separately as books or pamphlets. In a few cases unpublished bibliographies are also listed. In general, the arrangement follows the Dewey Decimal Classification. A full index by author, subject, and library helps in locating individual titles as well as special collections on particular subjects. However, it must be borne in mind that other libraries may have collections of equal or greater importance for which no lists are available.

———— ———— Supplement 1950–1961. 1962. 226p.

———— ———— Supplement 1961–1970. 1972. 244p.

———— ———— Supplement 1971–1980. 1981. 209p.

A cumulative index for 1870–1970 has appeared as: Z1002.D6

Keller, Clara D. American library resources cumulative index, 1870–1970. Chicago, Amer. Lib. Assoc., 1981. 89p.

An author/subject index.

East Central and Southeast Europe: a handbook of library and archival resources in North America. Paul Horecky, chief ed., David H. Kraus, assoc. ed. Santa Barbara, Calif., Clio Pr., [1976]. 467p. (Joint Committee on Eastern Europe. Publ. ser., 3)   **AB118**

Intends "to provide scholars, librarians, students, and researchers with a basic reference tool for the study of the essential collections available in major libraries, archives, and research institutions in the United States and Canada, by outlining the profiles of these collections and offering broad guidance to their subject and area contents. The focus is on the humanities and the socioeconomic and political sciences."—*Foreword.* Covers material on Albania, Bulgaria, Czechoslovakia, East Germany, Greece, Hungary, Poland, Romania, and Yugoslavia. Collections of some forty libraries, archives, and research institutions are described, with major surveys of up to 5,000 words in length. Descriptions are signed by contributors and include bibliographic citations. Institutions are arranged alphabetically. An "Area and subject guide" serves as an index.   Z2483.E2

Grant, Steven A. and **Brown, John H.** The Russian Empire and Soviet Union: a guide to manuscripts and archival materials in the United States. Boston, G. K. Hall, 1982. 632p.   **AB118a**

"Kennan Institute for Advanced Russian Studies, The Wilson Center."—*t.p.*

Lists and briefly describes "materials in U.S. archives and manuscript repositories that relate to the Russian Empire, Soviet Union, and the many distinct nationalities therein."—*Introd.* Covers the "broadest possible range of subjects" and includes collections found in public and private institutions, libraries, museums, ethnic organizations, church and business archives, historical societies, and some private collections. Arranged by state, then by city and repository, with detailed subject index. References are given to published descriptions and finding aids for individual collections.
                                                              Z2491.G66

Hilton, Ronald, ed. Handbook of Hispanic source materials and research organizations in the United States. 2d ed. Stanford, Calif., Stanford Univ. Pr., 1956. 448p.   **AB119**

1st ed. 1942.

Covers libraries, museums, art galleries, etc. having collections or doing research in the Hispanic field. Deals mainly with the fine arts, humanities, and the social sciences, with some exceptional collections in the natural sciences included. Arranged by state, city, and library, with descriptions of collections; in some cases lists rare items. "Hispanic" comprises Spain, Portugal, and Hispanic America of the pre- and post-Columbian periods, Florida, Texas, the Southwest, and California until annexation by the United States.

A "versión y adaptación española de Lino Gómez Canedo" was published in Madrid in 1957.   F1408.3.H65

Jackson, William Vernon. Resources of research libraries; a selected bibliography. Pittsburgh, Univ. of Pittsburgh Book Center, 1969. 65p.   **AB120**

Intended as a select list of references for those interested in the overall subject of library resources rather than in collections relating to a specific subject field. Includes sections for general studies, spatial and financial aspects, description and evaluation of library resources, cooperative agreements for library development, union catalogs and bibliographical centers, etc.   Z675.R45J3

Meckler, Alan M. and **McMullin, Ruth.** Oral history collections. N.Y., Bowker, 1975. 344p.   **AB121**

For full information *see* DB63.

Manfred J. Waserman's *Bibliography on oral history* (Rev. ed. N.Y., Oral History Assoc., 1975. 53p.) lists about 300 items on oral history published through 1974.

National inventory of documentary sources in the United States. Teaneck, N.J., Chadwyck-Healey, [1983–85]. pt.1–3. microfiche. (In progress)   **AB121a**

Contents: pt.1, Federal records; pt.2, Manuscript Division, Library of Congress; pt.3, State archives, libraries and historical societies.

Consists of microform reproductions of published and unpublished finding aids, registers, indexes and collection guides available for collections of manuscripts and documentary sources in the various participating repositories. The inventory is being published in four parts, each covering a different type of archive (or single repository, in the case of pt.2) as noted above; a fourth part is to cover academic libraries and other repositories. The "Federal records" section includes the U.S. National Archives, Smithsonian Institution archives, and presidential libraries. Printed indexes accompany pts.1 and 2; computer-produced microfiche indexes are promised for pts.3–4. Parts may be purchased separately.

Ruggles, Melville J. and **Mostecky, Vaclav.** Russian and East European publications in the libraries of the United States. N.Y., Columbia Univ. Pr., 1960. 396p. (Columbia University studies in library service, no.11)   **AB122**

Surveys problems of selection, acquisition, finance, cataloging, and bibliographic control, and provides extensive quantitative data on existing collections.   Z2483.R82

Special collections in children's literature. Ed. by Carolyn W. Field. Chicago, Amer. Lib. Assoc., 1982. 257p. il.   **AB123**

Represents a revised and updated edition of Field's *Subject collections in children's literature* (N.Y., Bowker, 1969).

Comp. in consultation with the National Planning for Special Collections Committee, Association for Library Service to Children.

Provides a subject approach to special collections of children's books at 267 institutions in the United States and Canada. Within the alphabetical subject arrangement, repositories are listed and an indication is given of the type and extent of holdings. A directory of collections lists the repositories by state; appendix of references to descriptive articles, catalogs of the collections, etc. Indexed.
                                                              Z688.C47S63

Special Libraries Association. Special library resources. N.Y., Assoc., [1941–47]. 4v.   **AB124**

Contents: v.1, United States and Canada; v.2, Alabama–Montana; v.3, Nebraska–Wyoming, Canada; v.4, Indexes. v.1–2 ed. by Rose L. Vormelker; v.3–4 by Isabel L. Towner.

Covers research library collections in the special library field and in public and university libraries. Arranged alphabetically by state, city, and library. Usually gives name, address, number of books, pamphlets, periodicals, etc. For the most part v.2–3 include additional libraries not covered in v.1; v.4 includes an organization index and a subject index.   Z675.A2S65

U.S. Library of Congress. Special collections in the Library of Congress: a selective guide. Comp. by Annette Melville. Wash., Lib. of Congress, 1980. 464p. il.   **AB125**

Describes about 300 collections—"thematically related groups of material maintained as separate units within the general holdings of the Library of Congress."—*Introd.* Provides references to published descriptions of the collections. Indexed.   Z733.U58U54

U.S. National Archives and Records Service. Guide to the National Archives of the United States. Wash., for sale by Supt. of Docs., 1974. 884p.   **AB126**

For full information *see* DB70.

Williams, Sam P., comp. Guide to research collections of the New York Public Library. Chicago, Amer. Lib. Assoc., 1975. 336p.   **AB127**

Supersedes Karl Brown's *Guide to the reference collections of the New York Public Library* (N.Y., 1941).

A guide to the principal resources and special collections in this vast library system. In four main sections, each with numerous subdivisions: (1) General materials; (2) The humanities; (3) The social sciences; (4) The pure and applied sciences. Index of subjects and collections.   Z733.N6W54

Wynar, Lubomyr Roman. Slavic ethnic libraries, museums and archives in the United States: a guide and directory. Chicago, [Amer. Lib. Assoc.], 1980. 164p.   **AB128**

At head of title: Association of College and Research Libraries, American Library Association and Center for the Study of Ethnic Publications, School of Library Science, Kent State University.

Arranged by ethnic group (Bulgarian-American through Yugoslavian-American). Gives information on size and scope of the collections, staff, access, publications, etc. Includes societies, associations, fraternal organizations, etc., which maintain libraries or archival collections.   Z1361.S5W9

❖ Directories of special library associations are also available, e.g., the Music Library Association, Medical Library Association, American Association of Law Libraries, etc., as are various local and regional directories of libraries, e.g., *Directory of special libraries in Boston and vicinity (9th ed. 1983); Directory of libraries and information sources in Philadelphia and vicinity* (14th ed. 1977); *Special libraries directory of greater New York* (14th ed. 1977); *Library and reference facilities in the area of the District of Columbia* (11th ed. 1983).

Australia and New Zealand

Downs, Robert Bingham. Australian and New Zealand library resources. London, Mansell; Melbourne, Thorpe, 1979. 164p.   **AB129**

Records the results of a survey of Australian and New Zealand libraries. Arrangement is by general subjects and types of material, with brief descriptions of those collections having significant resources for advanced study and research. References are given to published bibliographies, descriptions of collections, etc. Bibliography, p.121–45. Indexed.

Canada

See also AB65, AB115.

National Library of Canada. Research collections in Canadian libraries. [Ottawa, Information Canada, 1972–82]. [pt.] I$^{1-6}$; [pt.] II$^{4-8}$. (In progress)   **AB131**

Contents: [pt.] I, Universities: 1, Prairie provinces; 2, Atlantic provinces; 3, British Columbia; 4, Ontario; 5, Quebec; 6, Canada; [pt.] II, Special studies: 4, Slavic and East European resources in Canadian academic and research libraries; 5, Collections of official publications; 6, Fine arts library resources in Canada (2v.); 7, Music resources in Canadian collections; 8, Dance resources in Canadian libraries.

Comprises results of a survey undertaken by the National Library of Canada. Reports take different forms, offering descriptive and/or statistical information by subject.   Z735.A1O88

France

Chauleur, André. Bibliothèques et archives: comment se documenter? 2ème éd. Paris, Economica, [1980]. 334p.   **AB132**

"Guide pratique à l'usage des étudiants, des professeurs, des documentalistes et archivistes, des chercheurs . . ."—*t.p.*

"Publié pour l'Institut National de Recherche Pédagogique."—*t.p.*

1st ed. 1978.

A guide for students and research workers in the libraries and archives of France. An "Introduction bibliographique" has been provided in this edition; it is followed by separate sections for libraries and for archives, each section providing directory information for the repositories (which are grouped by type). There are extensive sections on the Bibliothèque Nationale and the Archives Nationales. Indexed.   Z797.A1C47

Welsch, Erwin K. Libraries and archives in France: a handbook. Rev. ed. N.Y., Council for European Studies, 1979. 147p.   **AB133**

1st ed. 1973.

Intended as "a compact and portable source of basic information of the kind most frequently needed by students and scholars working in France for the first time."—*Introd.* Emphasis is on resources for modern French history and the social sciences. In three sections: (1) Libraries in the Paris region; (2) Archives in the Paris region; (3) Departmental archives and libraries. Gives address, hours of opening, size of collections, terms of access, etc., and references to published descriptions of the collections.

Z797.A1W44

Germany

Archive. Archive im deutschsprachigen Raum. 2. Aufl. Berlin, W. de Gruyter, 1974. 2v. (1418p.)   **AB134**

At head of title: Minerva-Handbücher.

Aufl. 1, 1932, published as *Minerva-Handbücher: 2. Abt. Die Archive,* Bd.1 (AB48).

Offers information on about 8,000 archives in Germany (both East and West Germany), Austria, Switzerland, Luxembourg and Lichtenstein, together with a few archives in Czechoslovakia and Poland. Indexes by type of archive, by country, and by city. Includes private as well as public archives.   CD1000.A72

Gebhardt, Walther. Spezialbestände in deutschen Bibliotheken: Bundesrepublik Deutschland einschl. Berlin (West). Im Auftrag der Deutschen Forschungsgemeinschaft. Berlin, W. de Gruyter, 1977. 739p.   **AB135**

Added title page: Special collections in German libraries: Federal Republic of Germany incl. Berlin (West).

Preface in English and German.

"The special collections in this catalogue are to be understood as products of the printing press (including printed graphics) as well as phototechnical or other methods of reproduction, collected because of their subject matter or because of their external form or by reason of their . . . origin, e.g., scholars' personal libraries, monastic libraries, church and school libraries. They must also be of a certain size and be useful as source material for the researcher."—*Pref.* Arranged by city, with a subject index.   Z801.A1G4

Welsch, Erwin K. Libraries and archives in Germany. Pittsburgh, Council for European Studies, [1975]. 275p.

AB136

Intended as "a practical and portable guide primarily for those scholars planning a first research trip abroad."—*Introd.* In addition to information on the collections, facilities, etc. of individual libraries and archives, there is a section on regional catalogs and union lists, and separate sections on "Library bibliography" and "Archive bibliography."   Z675.R45W45

Great Britain

British Museum. The British Museum, a guide to its public services. London, Trustees, 1962. 72p. il.   **AB137**

Offers brief descriptions of individual departments and their varied collections, with notes on the catalogs and other facilities for readers.

The 1976 *British Museum guide* (295p.) is concerned with the rich collections of antiquities, prints and drawings, etc., not the book and manuscript collections.   AM101.B85

Burkett, Jack. Special library and information services in the United Kingdom. 3d ed. rev. London, Lib. Assoc., 1972–74. 2v.   **AB138**

1st ed. 1961.

Contents: v.1, Industrial and related library information services in the United Kingdom. 263p.; v.2, Government and related library and information services in the United Kingdom. 217p.

A survey of specific types of library and information services rather than a directory. v.1 "is concerned with industry and commerce both in the private and public sectors, and with other organizations whose activities are closely related."—*Pref.* v.2 "traces the evolution of government as reflected in its libraries and demonstrates the significant effect that changes in government policy have had on the departments that carry out this policy."   Z791.A1B86

Downs, Robert Bingham. British and Irish library resources: a bibliographical guide. London, Mansell, 1981. 427p.   **AB139**

"A rev. and updated ed. of *British library resources,* first published in 1973."—*t.p.*

Intends to "record all published library catalogs—general and special; all checklists of specialized collections in libraries; calendars of manuscripts and archives; exhibition catalogs; articles descriptive of library collections; guides to individual libraries and their holdings; directories of libraries—both general and in specialized fields; union lists of periodicals, newspapers, and other serials; and any other records, descriptive, analytical, or critical, that may guide the scholar, research worker, or advanced student in finding significant materials to meet his needs."—*Introd.* Includes libraries of the United Kingdom and Eire. Classed arrangement with index.

Z791.A1D68

Esdaile, Arundell. The British Museum Library, a short history and survey. London, Allen and Unwin, 1946. 388p.   **AB140**

Contents: pt.1, Historical survey; pt.2, The collections and their catalogues.   Z792.B863E8

Foster, Janet and **Sheppard, Julia.** British archives: a guide to archive resources in the United Kingdom. Detroit, Gale, [1982]. 533p.   **AB141**

Attempts to provide directory information on as many places as the compilers could learn of "where archives, in the widest sense of the word, are held and are made relatively accessible."—*Introd.* Information was collected mainly by questionnaire and, as far as possible, the following information is given for each repository: address, telephone, person to whom to address inquiries, opening times, terms of access, historical background notes, collecting policy, major collections (with significant names and dates), nonmanuscript material, finding aids, facilities for use and reproduction, publications (i.e., guides or descriptions of collections). General index to collections (mainly personal and institutional names) and a "Key subject word" index.   CD1040.F67

Irwin, Raymond. The libraries of London. 2d ed. rev. London, Lib. Assoc., 1961. 332p.   **AB142**

1st ed. 1949.

Based on a series of lectures by specialists; describes in some detail the history, purpose, collections, etc., of the great national libraries, the libraries of the University of London, libraries of various learned societies, and a selected group of special libraries. References throughout the text.   Z791.L852

Ker, Neil Ripley. Medieval libraries of Great Britain; a list of surviving books. 2d ed. London, Offices of the Royal Historical Soc., 1964. 424p. (Royal Hist. Soc. Guides and handbooks, no.3)   **AB143**

1st ed. 1941.

"Intended as a guide to medieval books and book-catalogues and to the modern catalogues in which they are described."—*Pref.*

Z723.K47

Roberts, Stephen Andrew, Cooper, Alan and **Gilder, Lesley.** Research libraries and collections in the United Kingdom: a selective inventory and guide. London, Bingley; Hamden, Conn., Linnet Books, [1978]. 285p.   **AB144**

Aims to present "a general package of information about research libraries and collections in the United Kingdom, which can be used as a point of departure for more detailed information."—*Pref.* Entries are grouped as (1) National libraries, specialist libraries and public libraries; (2) University libraries; (3) Polytechnic libraries (England and Wales); (4) Scottish central institutions.

A review by the A.L.A. Subscription Books Committee concludes that "selectivity allied to indexing by what the reporting library considers important in its own collection means that this volume will be useful but will have to be handled with careful interpretation and alongside other works such as the *ASLIB Directory.*"—*Booklist* 76:1003.   Z791.A1R6

Standing Conference on Library Materials on Africa. The SCOLMA directory of libraries and special collections on Africa. 4th rev. and expanded ed. Ed. by Harry Hannam. München, Saur, 1983. 183p.   **AB145**

For full information *see* DD45.

Walker, Gregory, ed. Directory of libraries and special collections on Eastern Europe and the U.S.S.R. London, Crosby Lockwood; Hamden, Conn., Archon Books, [1971]. 159p.   **AB146**

At head of title: SCONUL Slavonic and East European Group.

". . . deals with material in the British Isles on any subject relating to, published in, or in a language of, the territory at present occupied by Albania, Bulgaria, Czechoslovakia, the D.D.R. (only since 1945), Greece (only since 1821), Hungary, Jugoslavia, Poland, Romania and the U.S.S.R. (in Asia as well as in Europe)."—*Introd.*

Z2483.W35

Italy

Guida generale degli archivi di Stato italiani. Direttori: Piero D'Angiolini, Claudio Pavone. Roma, 1981– . v.1– . (In progress)   **AB147**

At head of title: Ministero per i Beni Culturali e Ambientali. Ufficio Centrale per i Beni Archivistici.

Supersedes an earlier guide, *Gli archivi di Stato italiani* (Bologna, 1944).

A section on the Archivio Centrale dello Stato (v.1, p. 33–295) is followed by descriptions of state archives arranged alphabetically by city. Sections on the individual city archives are usually subdivided by historical period, then by office or agency, with notes on the principal collections.   CD1424.G84

Lewanski, Rudolf J. Guide to Italian libraries and archives. N.Y., Council for European Studies, [1979]. 101p.

AB148

A directory of major archives and libraries, arranged by city and furnishing brief information on holdings, special collections, hours of opening, etc., together with references to published descriptions, catalogs, and finding aids. A section entitled "Subject collections" lists the repositories by subject field.   Z809.A1L48

Japan

Kokuritsu Kokkai Toshokan, Tokyo. Sankō Shoshibu. Zenkoku tokushu korekushon yōran. Tōkyō, Dō Toshokan, 1977. 15p., 217p., 46p.   **AB149**

In colophon: Directory of special collections in Japanese libraries. 1st ed. 1956.

This edition lists 2,291 collections in 669 repositories. Geographic arrangement, with name and subject indexes. Gives brief description of subject coverage and holdings, together with information about access, availability of printed catalogs, etc.   Z845.J4K57

Latin America

Nauman, Ann Keith. A handbook of Latin American & Caribbean national archives. Guía de los archivos nacionales de America Latina y el Caribe. Detroit, Blaine Ethridge–Books, [1983]. 127p.   **AB150**

Intended for "the potential first-time user of archival collections in Mexico, Central and South America, the Outer Islands and nations of the Caribbean. It is designed to provide pertinent data relative to what the user may expect to encounter in the way of materials and services, and what, if any, requirements and restrictions apply."—*Introd.* Information for most countries was derived from questionnaires completed at the respective national archives; text appears in English and Spanish in separate sections.   CD3680.N38

Naylor, Bernard, Hallewell, Laurence and **Steele, Colin.** Directory of libraries and special collections on Latin America and the West Indies. [London], Athlone Pr., 1975. 161p. (London. Univ. Inst. of Latin American Studies. Monographs, no.5)   **AB151**

For full information *see* DB265.

Poland

Lewanski, Richard Casimir, comp. Guide to Polish libraries and archives. Boulder, Colo., East European Quarterly (distr. by Columbia Univ. Pr.), 1974. 209p. (East European monographs, no.6)   **AB152**

Aims "to provide American and other English-reading scholars and researchers a comprehensive guide to materials in Polish repositories of manuscript and printed records."—*Introd.* Emphasis is on resources for study of Polish history, civilization, and society. Listing is by city, then by repository. A "subject profile" for each library is usually supplemented by a listing of special collections or unique features. Published catalogs and descriptions of the libraries or special collections are noted. Subject index.   Z817.A1L48

Sweden

Ottervik, Gösta and **Möhlenbrock, Sigurd.** Bibliotek i Sverige; vägledning för besökare, lantagare, biblioteksaspiranter. Stockholm, Almqvist & Wiksell, [1964]. 209p. il.   **AB153**

Offers historical surveys of the various types of libraries (academic, public, national, regional, special, etc.) in Sweden, with notes on the principal libraries, their collections and publications. Indexed.

Much of the historical and descriptive information appears in English in the authors' earlier *Libraries and archives in Sweden* (Stockholm, 1954).   Z827.A1O7

Union of Soviet Socialist Republics

Grimsted, Patricia Kennedy. Archives and manuscript repositories in the USSR: Estonia, Latvia, Lithuania, and Belorussia. Princeton, N.J., Princeton Univ. Pr., [1981]. 929p.   **AB155**

Constitutes a companion to the compiler's earlier volume for Moscow and Leningrad (below). Aims "to serve as a starting point for the foreign scholar planning research in the Baltic republics and Belorussia" *(Pref.)* by providing descriptions of archival and manuscript collections and providing references to additional published descriptions, finding aids, and guides to those collections. Each of the four republics is treated separately, and there is an introductory historical survey and general bibliography for each section. Author/title and subject indexes.   CD1735.B34G74

—— Archives and manuscript repositories in the USSR: Moscow and Leningrad. Princeton, Princeton Univ. Pr., [1972]. 436p.   **AB156**

Intended "first to serve as a starting point for the foreigner planning research in the Soviet Union" *(Pref.)*, but also as a guide for scholars, librarians, and others who need information about holdings and published finding aids of the various collections.

For each repository there is information on contents (usually with an historical note), working conditions, and published descriptions and inventories. An historical survey of Russian archives, a chapter on procedural information, and a bibliography of general Russian archival and research aids are followed by sections treating the individual repositories grouped as: (1) Central state archives; (2) Archives and manuscript collections of the Academy of Sciences; (3) Special archives; (4) Manuscript divisions of libraries and museums in Moscow; (5) Manuscript divisions of libraries and museums in Leningrad; (6) Republic and local state archives in Moscow and Leningrad.   CD1711.G7

—— —— Supplement 1: Bibliographical addenda. Zug, Switzerland, InterDocumentation Co., [1976]. 203p. (Bibliotheca Slavica, 9)

A bibliographical supplement listing publications appearing through the end of 1973 (and including numerous pre-1970 publications which were omitted from the original volume) plus a few 1974 imprints. Items in the supplement which are available in the publisher's (i.e., IDC) microfiche series are so noted, and a "microfiche correlation table" for items in the main volume is provided.

Yugoslavia

Jovanovič, Slobodan and **Rojnič, Matko.** A guide to Yugoslav libraries and archives. Paul L. Horecky, chief ed.; Elizabeth Beyerly, tr. and assoc. ed. [Columbus, Ohio, Am. Assoc. for the Advancement of Slavic Studies, 1975] 113 p. (Joint Committee on Eastern Europe publ. ser., 2)   **AB157**

Offers historical notes on the libraries, descriptions of book and manuscript collections, and references to published writings on the libraries.   Z841.A1J68

LIBRARY AND INFORMATION SCIENCE

Guides and bibliography

Dyer, Esther R. and **Berger, Pam.** Public, school, and academic media centers: a guide to information sources. Detroit, Gale, [1981]. 237p. (Books, publishing, and libraries information guide ser., 3)   **AB158**

A selected, annotated bibliography. A section on general works is followed by sections on periodicals and annuals, management, services and access to information, collection development, facilities and equipment, and trends in the field. Author, title, and subject indexes.   Z675.S3D94

Lilley, Dorothy B. and **Badough, Rose Marie.** Library and information science: a guide to information sources. Detroit, Gale, [1982]. 151p. (Books, publishing, and libraries information guide ser., 5)   **AB159**

A selective guide in four main sections: (1) Recent changes that affect the literature search; (2) Search strategy models; (3) Information sources by form of material; (4) Types of information sources. Indexed.   Z687.L54

Magrill, Rose Mary and **Rinehart, Constance.** Library technical services: a selected, annotated bibliography. Westport, Conn., Greenwood Pr., 1977. 238p.   **AB160**

In seven main sections: (1) Organization of technical services; (2) Acquisition of materials; (3) Organization of materials; (4) Maintenance of materials; (5) Circulation of materials; (6) Serials; (7) Special materials (e.g., non-book materials, government publications, maps, microforms). Brief annotations; name and subject indexes. More than 1,200 items, with emphasis on recent publications.   Z688.5.M25

Mount, Ellis. Scientific and technical libraries in the seventies: a guide to information sources. Detroit, Gale, [1981]. 157p. (Books, publishing, and libraries information guide ser., 4)   **AB161**

Aims to bring together "a collection of abstracts which the compiler feels is representative of the most useful publications of the 1970s on the operation, management, and collections of all types of sci-tech libraries and information centers."—*Pref.* Arranged by broad subject categories with numerous subdivisions. Author and subject indexes.   Z675.T3M755

Purcell, Gary R. and **Schlachter, Gail Ann.** Reference sources in library and information services: a guide to the literature. Santa Barbara, Calif., ABC-Clio, [1984]. 359p.   **AB162**

A comprehensive guide to the literature of library and information science and services, intended for the librarian, the library school student, the library educator, and others interested in library issues and services. In two main sections, with detailed subdivisions: (1) General reference works, listing about 700 sources with annotations; (2) Subject-related reference works, listing and annotating about "500 reference works that concentrate on one or more library-related issues, developments, processes, institutions, or techniques" *(Introd.),* arranged alphabetically by subject area. Author, title, and geographic indexes.   Z666.P96

Sable, Martin Howard. The protection of the library and archive: an international bibliography. N.Y., Haworth Pr., [1984]. 183p.   **AB163**

Originally published as a special issue of *Library & archival security,* v.5, nos.2/3 (Summer/Fall 1983).

Nearly 1,100 items are listed chronologically within topical sections (e.g., fire, flood and water damage, theft and loss, vandalism). Author index.   Z679.6.S26

Handbooks

Art library manual; a guide to resources and practice. Philip Pacey, ed. London & N.Y., Bowker in assoc. with the Art Libraries Assoc., [1977]. 423p.   **AB164

A manual for art librarians; chapters by specialists are concerned with "problems of acquisition, organization, accomodation, exploitation and conservation."—*Introd.* Materials discussed include general art bibliographies, quick reference sources, art books, photographs and reproductions, slides and filmstrips, loan collections of original works of art, etc.   Z675.A85A79

Daniel, Evelyn H. and **Notowitz, Carol I.** Media and microcomputers in the library: a selected, annotated resource guide. [Phoenix, Ariz.], Oryx Pr., 1984. 157p.   **AB165**

Intended for "those who have professional responsibility for multimedia collections, particularly school library media specialists, community college librarians, and media librarians in public and academic libraries."—*Introd.* Lists books and periodical materials in three main sections: (1) General information; (2) Types of media; (3) Functional activities for all media. There is also a brief section on "special issues" (e.g., copyright). Indexed.
                                                    Z688.N6D36

Guidelines for newspaper libraries. Written by members of the Newspaper Division of Special Libraries Association. [2d ed.] Reston, Va., American Newspaper Publishers Assoc. Foundation, [1983]. 134p. il. (looseleaf)   **AB166**

1st ed. 1974.

Intended as a practical guide to the daily operation of a newspaper library. Includes sections on starting the library, administration, equipment, public service, indexing and filing systems, clipping collections, automation, etc. Glossary; bibliographic references.
                                                    Z675.N4G84

Handbook of special librarianship and information work. 5th ed. L. J. Anthony, ed. London, Aslib, 1982. 416p.
                                                        AB167

1st–3d eds. (1955–67) by Wilfred Ashworth; 4th ed. (1975) by W. E. Batten.

Chapters by contributing librarians deal with the organization and administration of special libraries, with attention given to computer-based and online retrieval systems, audiovisual and non-book media, and information networks. Reflects English practice. Includes bibliographic references; indexed.   Z675.A2A75

Harleston, Rebekah M. and **Stoffle, Carla J.** Administration of government documents collections. Littleton, Colo., Libraries Unlimited, 1974. 178p.   **AB168**

". . . a manual of the procedures involved in processing government documents, in libraries with either separate or integrated collections of federal documents."—*Introd.* Concerned with United States government documents. Bibliography; index.

                                                    Z7164.G7H37

Hospital library management. Jana Bradley, ed. Chicago, Medical Lib. Assoc., 1983. 412p. il.   **AB169**

Designed "as a comprehensive guide to providing library service in hospitals" and "planned as a sequel to the extremely influential *Library Practice in Hospitals: A Basic Guide* [1972], edited by Harold Bloomquist, and is intended to be especially useful for the librarian newly entering the profession or transferring from another library specialty."—*Pref.* In four main sections, each made up of chapters by contributing librarians: (1) Selecting, acquiring, and organizing library materials; (2) Providing library services; (3) Managing library services; (4) Providing special services. Indexed.
                                                    Z675.H7H69

How to start an audiovisual collection. Myra Nadler, ed. Metuchen, N.J., Scarecrow Pr., 1978. 157p.   **AB170**

A manual for the inexperienced librarian or administrator who needs to start an audiovisual collection or services. Chapters were contributed by librarians and consultants with practical experience in the field. "Definitions and glossary," p.106–51.   Z717.H68

Irvine, Betty Jo. Slide libraries: a guide for academic institutions, museums, and special collections. 2d ed. Littleton, Colo., Libraries Unlimited, 1979. 321p.   **AB171**

1st ed. 1974.

Nine chapters offer background of the field and outline "standard administrative practices, classification systems, production methods, physical facilities, and supplies and equipment, indicating basic guidelines for the efficient organization and administration of these visual resource collections."—*Pref.* Selected bibliography, p.241–81; directory of distributors and manufacturers of equipment and supplies; directory of slide sources; and directory of slide libraries. Indexed.   Z692.S65I7

Jones, Frances M. Defusing censorship: the librarian's guide to handling censorship conflicts. Phoenix, Ariz., Oryx Pr., 1983. 229p.   **AB172**

Offers "practical advice, guidelines, and tools for managing censorship conflicts" *(Foreword),* using recent censorship cases in school and public libraries as background. Includes problems relating to exhibits, programs, and use of library meeting rooms, as well as printed and audiovisual materials. Sample policy statements; recommended reading; index. Z675.S3J727

Jones, Malcolm. Music librarianship. London, Bingley; N.Y., K. G. Saur, 1979. 130p. (Outlines of modern librarianship, 5) **AB173**

A general overview of music libraries and librarianship, the literature of music, and music library organization and routines. Reflects British practice. ML111.J65

Larsgaard, Mary. Map librarianship; an introduction. Littleton, Colo., Libraries Unlimited, 1978. 330p. **AB174**

"The focus . . . is on the actual techniques of map librarianship, from the selection and acquisition of individual maps . . . to the administration of an entire map library."—*Introd.* Chapters cover: (1) Selection and acquisition of maps; (2) Map classification; (3) Map cataloging and computer applications; (4) Care, storage, and repair of maps; (5) Public relations and reference services; (6) Administration; (7) Map librarianship: a brief overview. Numerous appendixes list publishers, reference works, review sources, suppliers of maps and map library equipment, etc. Bibliography and supplemental readings. Indexed. A 2d ed. was scheduled for 1985 publication.

Harold Nichols' *Map librarianship* (2d ed. London, Bingley, 1982. 272p.) covers subject areas similar to those in the Larsgaard book, but with a British emphasis; it is intended for the practicing map librarian or curator and has less of a textbook approach. Z692.M3L37

Law librarianship: a handbook. Ed. by Heinz Peter Mueller and Patrick E. Kehoe. Littleton, Colo., publ. for the Amer. Assoc. of Law Libraries by F. B. Rothman, 1983. 2v. (896p.) (AALL publications ser., no.19) **AB175**

Intended "as a practical manual reflecting accepted current methods for organizing and providing service to all types of law libraries —large, small, academic, state, county, court, and private. The volume is designed for use by almost anyone working in the field."—*Introd.* Chapters by individuals or teams of contributors cover such topics as the history and development of the modern law library, administration of specific types of law libraries, library planning, reference, circulation, acquisitions, cataloging and classification, government documents, microforms and audiovisuals, preservation, rare materials, and automation. There are separate chapters on the Law Library of the Library of Congress, United Kingdom law libraries, and libraries in Canada. Selected bibliographies; index. Z675.L2L3835

Library data collection handbook. Mary Jo Lynch, ed. Chicago, Amer. Lib. Assoc., 1981. 228p. il. **AB176**

Outlines the types of data useful in describing library resources and library programs, and defines the terms involved. Aims to provide "library managers, boards of trustees, and other library decision makers with guidance in identifying factual and comparative data useful in developing policies and making decisions."—*Introd.* Z670.L717

Manual of business library practice. Malcolm J. Campbell, ed. 2d ed. London, Clive Bingley [1984]. 238p. **AB177**

A text concentrating on British experience in business and commercial libraries. Chapters by librarians and information specialists on the pattern of business information, organization and administration of libraries, and information sources. Z675.B8M35

Manual of law librarianship: the use and organization of legal literature. Ed. by Elizabeth M. Moys. Boulder, Colo., publ. for the British and Irish Assoc. of Law Librarians [by] Westview Pr.; London, André Deutsch, 1976. 733p. **AB178**

A thorough manual of law librarianship in the British Isles, with chapters contributed by specialists. Bibliographies at the end of each chapter; "Index of works cited," p.663–715. Z675.L2M27

Medical Library Association. Handbook of medical library practice. 4th ed. Louise Darling, ed. Chicago, Medical Lib. Assoc., 1982–83. 2v. **AB179**

For full information *see* EK4.

Mount, Ellis. University science and engineering libraries, their operation, collections, and facilities. Westport, Conn., Greenwood Pr., [1975]. 214p. (Contributions in librarianship and information science, no. 15) **AB180**

Discusses the major aspects of science-engineering library service. "The plan of the book is to proceed from broad topics, such as the general nature of the libraries involved and their organization, to more specific points, e.g., staffing, collection development, reference services, uses of computers, and the planning of library facilities."— *Pref.* Bibliographic notes; index. 2d ed. announced for 1985 publication. Z675.U5M68

Music Library Association. Manual of music librarianship. Carol June Bradley, ed. [Ann Arbor, Music Lib. Assoc., 1966] 140p. **AB181**

Chapters on the various aspects of music librarianship have been contributed by specialists in the field.

A new edition of Eric T. Bryant's 1959 guide, *Music librarianship,* was announced for 1985 publication by Scarecrow Pr., Metuchen, N.J. ML111.B78

Osborn, Andrew Delbridge. Serial publications: their place and treatment in libraries. 3d ed. Chicago, Amer. Lib. Assoc., 1980. 486p. il. **AB182**

Describes the principles of serials organization, their selection, acquisition, checking, cataloging, housing, reference use and circulation, binding, microreproduction, abstracting and indexing, union lists, etc.; has a brief section on the publications of the League of Nations, United Nations, and Organization of the American States, and a "Postscript" on the future of library work with serials. Indexed. Z692.S5O8

Picture librarianship. Ed. by Helen P. Harrison. [Phoenix, Ariz.], Oryx Pr., 1981. 542p. il. **AB183**

Aims "to provide a manual of techniques and practices in libraries . . . [and] a source to which the librarian can turn when faced with a new collection or situation, or when problems arise."— *Introd.* Chapters on techniques and organization are followed by a series of case studies and surveys of picture libraries; all are by contributing librarians or other specialists. Bibliography; index. Z717.P52

Public Library Association. Audiovisual Committee. Guidelines for audiovisual materials and services for large public libraries. Chicago, ALA, 1975. 35p. **AB184**

A revised edition of *Guidelines for audiovisual materials and services for public libraries* (Chicago, 1970).

Intended "as a yardstick for large public libraries and library systems serving populations of 150,000 or more that wish to establish audiovisual services or to strengthen their existing collections and services."—*Introd.*

The Committee has also published *Recommendations for audiovisual materials and services for small and medium-sized public libraries* (Chicago, 1975). Similarly, the Audio-Visual Committee of the Association of College and Research Libraries has published *Guidelines for audio-visual services in academic libraries* (Chicago, 1968). Z717.P82

Wilson, Louis Round and **Tauber, Maurice F.** The university library: the organization, administration, and functions of academic libraries. 2d ed. N.Y., Columbia Univ. Pr., 1956. 641p. (Columbia Univ. studies in library service, no.8) **AB185**

1st ed. 1944.

A standard work, now out of date in various areas. Aims to reevaluate the service of academic libraries in terms of books, personnel, and quarters, and to formulate policies as to their organization, function, and administration. Each chapter is followed by a bibliography. Z675.U5W745

Wright, Keith C. Library and information services for handicapped individuals. Littleton, Colo., Libraries Unlimited, 1979. 196p. **AB186**

Intends "to provide an overview of the major handicapping conditions and identify the kinds of library services needed by handicapped individuals."—*Introd.* Chapters on the legal situation, blind and visually impaired persons, deaf and hearing impaired persons, mentally handicapped individuals, and the aged. Bibliographic references; list of selected organizations providing services to the handicapped; and a directory of sources for materials and information. Z711.92.H3W74

Acquisitions work, collection development, and maintenance

See also Preservation work.

American Library Association. Collection Development Committee. Guidelines for collection development. David L. Perkins, ed. Chicago, The Association, [1979]. 78p. **AB187**

Offers guidelines for the formulation of collection development policies, for the evaluation of the effectiveness of library collections, for the review of library collections, and for the allocation of library materials budgets. Z687.A518

Bonk, Wallace John and **Magrill, Rose Mary.** Building library collections. 5th ed. Metuchen, N.J., Scarecrow Pr., 1979. 380p. **AB188**

1st ed. 1959.
Essentially a textbook for library school students which aims to "introduce common principles, accepted procedures, unresolved questions, and current selection and acquisition tools for a general collection development course."—*Pref.* In three main sections: (1) Selection; (2) Acquisitions; (3) Maintenance. Numerous appendixes. Indexed. Z687.B66

Buckeye, Nancy Melin. International subscription agents: an annotated directory. 4th ed. Chicago, Amer. Lib. Assoc., 1978. 112p. **AB189**

1st ed. 1963. Compiler varies.
This edition reports on 250 agents. Business data were eliminated because fluctuating money markets rendered the information of little value to libraries. A 5th ed. by W. R. Perryman was published 1985. Z282.B82

Hubbard, William J. Stack management: a practical guide to shelving and maintaining library collections. Chicago, Amer. Lib. Assoc., 1981. 102p. il. **AB190**

A revision of William Jesse's *Shelf work in libraries* (1952).
Offers guidance for the librarian in charge of physical maintenance of book collections. Includes sections on moving and shifting books; weeding, storing, and paging; care of books; shelflist, missing books, and inventory. Indexed. Z703.5.J4

Katz, Bill and **Gellatly, Peter.** Guide to magazine and serial agents. N.Y., Bowker, 1975. 239p. **AB191**

Not simply a directory of serials agents as such, but a work designed to give "enough background information concerning serials and their management to provide an understanding of the agent-library relationship" (*Pref.*) together with "facts, details, and descriptions of the major and selected smaller domestic and foreign serials subscription agents." Directory of subscription agents, p.199–239. Z689.K33

Kim, Ung Chon. Policies of publishers: a handbook for order librarians. 1982 [i.e., 3d] ed. Metuchen, N.J., Scarecrow Pr., 1982. 161p. **AB192**

1st ed. 1975.
Indicates policies of about 400 publishers in regard to matters such as prepayment, discounts, returns, shipping and billing, back

orders, standing orders, and approval plans. Information was gathered mainly by questionnaire. Z475.K55

Lane, Alfred H. Gifts and exchange manual. Westport, Conn., Greenwood Pr., [1980]. 121p. **AB193**

A manual of practical procedures for maintaining a gift and exchange program in a library. Includes a special chapter on exchange work in academic libraries. Sample forms and letters; index. Z690.L36

Magrill, Rose Mary and **Hickey, Doralyn J.** Acquisitions management and collection development in libraries. Chicago, Amer. Lib. Assoc., 1984. 229p. **AB194**

A successor to Stephen Ford's *The acquisition of library materials* (1973), "intended primarily as an overview of the way in which library acquisitions plans are managed—what they try to accomplish and what methodologies are often used—and the processes through which the collection is designed, developed, and evaluated."—*Introd.* Includes chapters on bibliographic searching, purchasing individual items, vendor-controlled order plans, acquisition of serials, gifts and exchanges, etc. Bibliography; index.
George Lowy's *A searcher's manual* (Hamden, Conn., Shoe String Pr., 1965. 104p.) describes "actual and desirable practice" in the area of bibliographic searching. Z689.M19

Slote, Stanley J. Weeding library collections—II. 2d rev. ed. Littleton, Colo., Libraries Unlimited, 1982. 198p. il. **AB195**

1st ed. 1975.
In two parts: (1) "Background and introduction to weeding" summarizes opinion and research regarding library weeding; (2) "The weeding process" is a step-by-step guide to preferred methods of weeding. Bibliography; index. Z703.6.S55

United Nations Educational, Scientific and Cultural Organization. Handbook on the international exchange of publications. Ed. by Frans Vanwijngaerden. 4th ed. Paris, Unesco, 1978. 165p. (Documentation, libraries, and archives: Bibliographies and reference works, 4) **AB196**

1st ed. 1950.
Aims to provide: "(a) a guide on the methodology, organization and management of the international exchange of publications . . . (b) a detailed up-to-date directory of exchange centres with a national responsibility, providing practical information on their activities and services. . . ."—*Pref.* Z690.U454

Wynar, Bohdan S. Library acquisitions; a classified bibliographic guide to the literature and reference tools. 2d ed. Littleton, Colo., Libraries Unlimited, 1971. 239p. **AB197**

1st ed. 1968.
Includes book and periodical materials. Numerous annotations. Z689.W9

Administration

See also AB161, AB167, AB169, AB175.

Kohl, David F. Administration, personnel, buildings and equipment: a handbook for library management. Santa Barbara, Calif., ABC-Clio, [1985]. 304p. (Handbooks for library management [1]) **AB198**

First in a planned series of six "Handbooks for library management" (called "Library administrator's handbook series" in the introduction) which, "rather than abstracting complete studies or providing only citations to research, instead presents summaries of individual research findings grouped by subject."—*Introd.* Within the three categories mentioned in the title, topics are arranged alphabetically; there is a detailed table of contents, but no subject index. Covers studies from the period 1960–83. A "Bibliography of articles," p.239–94, gives full citations and references from the text are by number; index of authors of articles.
Library management by Robert D. Stueart and John T. Eastlick (2d ed. Littleton, Colo., Libraries Unlimited, 1981. 292p.) is intend-

ed both as a textbook for the student and a guide for the practicing librarian. Z678.K63

White, Herbert S. Managing the special library: strategies for success within the larger organization. White Plains, N.Y., Knowledge Industry Pubns., [1984]. 152p. **AB199**

In effect, supersedes *Special libraries: a guide for management* (2d ed., 1981) by Janet Ahrensfeld, Elin Christianson and David King.

A management guide for the practicing special librarian and for the library school student at the master's level. Select bibliography; index. Z675.A2W45

Archives

Association des Archivistes Français. Manuel d'archivistique; théorie et pratique des archives publiques en France. Paris, S.E.V.P.E.N., 1970. 807p. **AB200**

At head of title: Ministère des Affaires Culturelles. Direction des Archives de France.

Detailed discussions of theory and practice governing all aspects of the administration and management of archives. A collaborative effort, with signed contributions. CD1191.A8

Basic international bibliography of archive administration. Bibliographie internationale fondamentale d'archivistique. Comp. by Michel Duchein, N.Y., K. G. Saur, 1978. 250p. (Archivum, v.25) **AB201**

Introductory matter and explanatory notes in English and French.

Aims to include "only works or articles, general in interest and permanent in nature."—*Pref.* International in scope and intended for the professional archivist. Emphasizes "the problems of collecting, sorting, arranging, listing, making accessible and preserving, looked at from the archivist's point of view." Classed arrangement with author and subject indexes. CD1.A18 v.25

Dictionary of archival terminology. Dictionnaire de terminologie archivistique: English and French, with equivalents in Dutch, German, Italian, Russian and Spanish. Peter Walne, ed. München, K. G. Saur, 1984. 226p. (ICA handbooks ser., 3) **AB202**

Supersedes the *Lexicon of archival terminology* (1964).

About 500 terms "in common use throughout the archival profession" *(Introd.)* are arranged in alphabetical order by English form of the word, with the corresponding French terms in parallel columns; definitions are given in both English and French; Dutch, German, Italian, Russian and Spanish equivalent terms appear after the definitions. Indexes from all languages other than English. CD945.D3

Evans, Frank Bernard. The history of archives administration: a select bibliography. Paris, Unesco, 1979. 255p. (Documentation, libraries and archives: Bibliographies and reference works, 6) **AB203**

A select bibliography of writings on archives "as they document the accomplishments and the needs of national communities throughout the world. It is intended to assist in the development of training courses and studies in which the past as recorded in archives is used to serve the needs of the present and the future."—*Pref.* In three main sections: (1) Introduction to archives administration; (2) Evolution of archives administration; and (3) Survey of archival agencies and programs (arranged by country or region). Subject and author indexes. Z5140.E865

——— Modern archives and manuscripts: a select bibliography. [Wash.] Soc. of Amer. Archivists, 1975. 209p. **AB204**

"This publication is confined almost exclusively to writings in the English language and its emphasis is upon archival theory and practice in the United States. It is intended only as an introduction to the subject, and does not eliminate the need for more comprehensive or annotated bibliographies on selected subjects."—*Introd.* Classed arrangement within four main sections: (1) Introduction to archives administration; (2) Survey of archival functions; (3) Ameri-

can archival agencies and archives: an overview; (4) International archival developments. Subject and author indexes. Z5140.E87

Iredale, David. Enjoying archives: what they are; where to find them; how to use them. Newton Abbot, [Eng.], David & Charles, [1973]. 264p. **AB205**

A guide to work with British documents and archives, primarily for the amateur and beginning researcher. Includes chapters on research methods, types of archives (e.g., national archives, family muniment room, cathedral, parish, municipal, etc.), paleography, and handwriting. Brief bibliography; index. CD1041.I73

Schellenberg, Theodore R. The management of archives. N.Y., Columbia Univ. Pr., 1965. 383p. (Columbia Univ. studies in library science, 14) **AB206**

Defines and discusses the principles and techniques of arranging and describing documentary material. Bibliography; index. While some of the same ground is covered in the author's *Modern archives, principles and techniques* (Chicago, 1956), that volume is not wholly superseded. CD950.S29

Society of American Archivists. Basic manual series. Chicago, The Society, 1977– . Irregular. **AB207**

Contents: Appraisal & accessioning, by M. J. Brichford (1977); Arrangement & description, by D. B. Gracy II (1977); Reference & access, by S. E. Holbert (1977); Security, by T. Walch (1977); Surveys, by J. A. Fleckner (1977); Exhibits, by G. F. Casterline (1980); An introduction to automated access, by H. T. Hickerson (1981); Public programs, by A. E. Pederson (1982); Maps and architectural drawings, by R. E. Ehrenberg (1982); Reprography, by C. H. Sung (1982); Conservation, by M. L. Ritzenthaler (1983).

Each manual deals briefly with a specific archival function.

Cataloging

Manuals

Mann, Margaret. Introduction to cataloging and the classification of books. 2d ed. Chicago, Amer. Lib. Assoc., 1943. 276p. il. **AB208**

The standard text prior to adoption of AACR2. Z695.M27

Shera, Jesse Hauk and **Egan, Margaret Elizabeth.** The classified catalog: basic principles and practices. With a code for the construction and maintenance of the classified catalog by Jeannette M. Lynn and Zola Hilton. Chicago, Amer. Lib. Assoc., 1956. 130p. il. **AB209**

Includes bibliography, p.122–27. Z695.S535

Wynar, Bohdan S. Introduction to cataloging and classification. With the assistance of Arlene Taylor Dowell and Jeanne Osborn. 6th ed. Littleton, Colo., Libraries Unlimited, 1980. 657p. il. **AB210**

1st ed. 1964 (called "Preliminary ed.").

A widely used text which now incorporates basic rules from AACR2. A 7th ed. was scheduled for publication in 1985.

Another recent text is Lois Mai Chan's *Cataloging and classification: an introduction* (N.Y., McGraw-Hill, 1981. 397p.). Z693.W94

MARC formats

U.S. Library of Congress. Automated Systems Office. MARC formats for bibliographic data. [By Elaine W. Woods under contract to the Automated Systems Office] Wash., The Office, 1980. ca.1000p. in various pagings. (Looseleaf; quarterly updates) **AB211**

"This document was produced from an online data base and represents the culmination of a cooperative project between the Library of Congress and the Research Libraries Information Network (RLIN)."—*Foreword.*

Presents the formats with descriptions.

Walt Crawford's *MARC for library use: understanding the USMARC formats* (White Plains, N.Y., Knowledge Industry Pubns., 1984. 222p.) aims "to show what MARC is, how it works and how it is changing."—*Introd.*

The Ohio College Library Center's *On-line cataloging* (Columbus, Ohio State Univ. Libs., 1973; looseleaf for updating) is "an instructional manual for libraries employing the on-line cataloging system of the Ohio College Library Center" *(Pref.)* which explains tagging and coding of bibliographic data to conform with the MARC format.   Z699.4.M2U48

Special subjects

Boggs, Samuel Whittemore and **Lewis, Dorothy Cronwell.** The classification and cataloging of maps and atlases. N.Y., Special Libraries Assoc., 1945. 175p. il.   **AB212**

A manual of practice, intended primarily for separate map collections.   Z695.6.B6

Daily, Jay Elwood. Cataloging phonorecordings: problems and possibilities. N.Y., M. Dekker, [1975]. 172p.   **AB213**

The volume "is not meant to advocate a method of cataloging . . . [but] is offered as a means of understanding what the possibilities are."—*Pref.*   ML111.5.D34

Dunkin, Paul Shaner. How to catalog a rare book. 2d ed., rev. Chicago, Amer. Lib. Assoc., 1973. 105p. il.   **AB214**

1st ed. 1951.
Treats cataloging problems peculiar to rare books, with special attention to title transcription and collation.   Z695.74.D8

Fleischer, Eugene B. and **Goodman, Helen C.** Cataloging audiovisual materials: a manual based on the Anglo-American Cataloguing Rules II. N.Y., Neal-Schuman, [1980]. 388p.   **AB215**

A manual for the cataloging of nonprint materials, with sections on cartographic materials, sound recordings, motion pictures and videorecordings, graphic materials, 3-dimensional materials, and kits.   Z695.66.F57

Redfern, Brian L. Organising music in libraries. [Rev. and rewritten ed.] London, Bingley; Hamden, Conn., Linnet Books, 1978–79. 2v.   **AB216**

1st ed. 1966.
Contents: v.1, Arrangement and classification; v.2, Cataloguing.
Provides a thorough introduction to cataloging codes and international standards, with comparisons of different systems.
                  ML111.R4

Reichmann, Felix and **Tharpe, Josephine M.** Bibliographic control of microforms. Westport, Conn., Greenwood Pr., [1972]. 256p.   **AB217**

"Sponsored by the Association of Research Libraries under contract with the Office of Education."—*t.p.*
Of special interest to the reference librarian is Appendix 4, "A microform bibliography," which has sections for (1) catalogs and lists, (2) collections and series, (3) manuscript and archival collections, and (4) reference books. All of these sections include helpful annotations, and there is an index to the microform bibliography.
                  Z1033.M5R43

Weihs, Jean Riddle, Lewis, Shirley and **Macdonald, Janet.** Nonbook materials; the organization of integrated collections. 2d ed. [Ottawa], Canadian Lib. Assoc., 1979. 134p.
                  AB218

A preliminary edition appeared in 1970; 1st ed. 1973.
Offers recommendations for cataloging of a wide range of nonbook materials, incorporating interpretation and explication of principles and rules set out in AACR2. It was "written for all types of libraries and media centres which wish to have an all-media catalogue, i.e., one in which the entries for all materials, both book and nonbook, are interfiled."—*Introd.*   Z695.66.W44

Codes

United States

Anglo-American cataloguing rules, prep. by the American Library Association . . . [et al.]; ed. by Michael Gorman and Paul W. Winkler. 2d ed. Chicago, Amer. Lib. Assoc.; Ottawa, Canadian Lib. Assoc., 1978. 620p.   **AB219**

1st ed. 1967. A 2d printing, with corrections appeared 1979.
Aims to reconcile in a single text the North American and British texts of 1967 and to incorporate into a single text the amendments and changes already agreed upon. The need to pay particular attention to developments in machine processing of bibliographic records is seen to have been largely achieved through the "integrated and standard framework for the systematic description of all library materials" *(Pref.)* as presented in Pt.I, "Descriptions," of this edition. Pt.II is devoted to "Headings, uniform titles, and references." Guidelines for applying the rules are further set forth in Margaret Maxwell's *Handbook for AACR2: explaining and illustrating the Anglo-American cataloguing rules, second edition* (Chicago, Amer. Lib. Assoc., 1980. 463p.).   Z694.A5

———— Revisions 1983. Joint Steering Committee for Revision of AACR. Chicago Amer. Lib. Assoc., 1984. 99p.

AACR2 decisions and rule interpretations. Comp. by C. Donald Cook with the assistance of Glenna E. Stevens. 2d ed. Ottawa, Canadian Lib. Assoc., 1982. 680p. in various foliations.   **AB220**

Subtitle: A consolidation of the decisions and rule interpretations for the Anglo-American cataloguing rules, second edition, made by the Library of Congress, the National Library of Canada, the British Library and the National Library of Australia, including official revisions of AACR2 approved by the Joint Committee for Revision of AACR.   Z694.A34

Gorman, Michael. The concise AACR2: being a rewritten and simplified version of Anglo-American cataloguing rules, second edition. Chicago, Amer. Lib. Assoc., 1981. 164p.
                  AB221

An abridgment, reorganization and rewording of the basic rules.
                  Z694.G64

France

Association Française de Normalisation. Direction des Bibliothèques. Code de catalogage des imprimés communs. Dictionnaire des cas. [Paris, 1945] 256p., 125p.   **AB222**
                  Z695.A927

Paris. Bibliothèque Nationale. Département des Imprimés. Usages suivis dans la rédaction du Catalogue général des livres imprimés de la Bibliothèque Nationale, recueillis et coordonnés par E. G. Ledos. Nouvelle éd. entièrement refondue par Armand Rastoul. Paris, Bibliothèque Nationale, 1940. 70p.   **AB223**
                  Z695.P231P2

Germany

Instruktionen für die alphabetischen Kataloge der preussischen Bibliotheken vom 10. Mai 1899. 2.Ausg. in der Fassung vom 10. August 1908. Berlin, Behrend, 1909. 179p. (Repr. 1944)   **AB224**
                  Z695.P97

———— The Prussian instructions; rules for the alphabetical catalogs of the Prussian libraries, tr. from the 2d ed., authorized Aug. 10, 1908, with an introd. and notes, by Andrew D. Osborn. Ann Arbor, Univ. of Michigan Pr., 1938. 192p. (Univ. of Michigan general library publ. no.4)
                  AB225
                  Z695.P973

Fuchs, Hermann. Kommentar zu den Instruktionen für die alphabetischen Kataloge der preussischen Bibliotheken. 3. erneut durchgesehene Aufl. Wiesbaden, O. Harrassowitz, 1962. 302p. il. **AB226**

1st ed. 1955.   Z695.I54F8

Great Britain

See also AB219.

British Museum. Dept. of Printed Books. Rules for compiling the catalogues of printed books, maps and music in the British Museum. Rev. ed. London, Trustees, 1936. 67p. **AB227**

Z695.B86

Vatican

Vatican. Biblioteca Vaticana. Norme per il catalogo degli stampati. 3. ed. Città del Vaticano, Biblioteca, 1949. 396p. **AB228**

1st ed. 1931; 2d ed. 1939.   Z695.V34

——— Rules for the Catalog of printed books, tr. from the 2d Italian ed. by Thomas J. Shanahan [and others]; ed. by Wyllis E. Wright. Chicago, Amer. Lib. Assoc., 1948. 426p.

One of the most comprehensive codes. Spanish translation published as *Normas para catalogación de impresos* (Edición española. Ciudad del Vaticano, Biblioteca Apostólica Vaticana, 1940. 472p.); French translation published as *Règles pour le catalogue des imprimés* (Edition française. Cité du Vaticano, Bibliothèque Apostolique Vaticane, 1950. 402p.). Z695.V342

Classification

Manuals

Herdman, Margaret May. Classification: an introductory manual. 3d ed., rev. by Jeanne Osborn. Chicago, Amer. Lib. Assoc., 1978. 44p. **AB229**

1st ed. 1934.
A brief introduction with selected bibliography. Z696.A4H47

Bibliography

Case Western Reserve University. Bibliographic Systems Center. Selected materials in classification; a bibliography, comp. by Barbara Denison. N.Y., Special Libs. Assoc., [1968]. 142p. **AB230**

Supersedes the Special Libraries Association's *Guide to the SLA loan collection of classification schemes . . .* (1961; first publ. 1945 under title *Classification schemes and subject headings lists*).
Lists about 1,500 titles in the loan collection of the Center.
Z696.C3

Dahlberg, Ingetraut. Classification systems and thesauri, 1950–1982. Frankfurt, Indeks Verlag, 1982. 143p. (FID publ. 610) **AB231**

Lists more than 2,200 items (classification schedules, subject outlines, thesauri, and subject heading lists) in classified arrangement. Further volumes are planned, with an expected total of 16,000 items to be covered.

Schedules

U.S. Library of Congress. Subject Cataloging Division. Classification: Classes A–Z. Wash., Govt. Prt. Off., 1917–81. **AB232**

Contents: *Outline of the Library of Congress classification.* 2d ed. 1970. 21p.; Class A: *General works.* 4th ed. 1973. 40p.; Class B, subclasses B–BJ: *Philosophy, psychology.* 3d ed. 1979. 250p.; Class B, [subclasses] BL–BX: *Religion.* 2d ed. 1962. 639p.; Class C: *Auxiliary sciences of history.* 3d ed. 1975. 126*l.;* Class D: *History: General and Old World.* 2d ed. 1959, repr. with suppl. pages 1966. 747p., 55p.; Class E–F: *History: America.* 3d ed. 1958, repr. with suppl. pages 1965. 607p. 23p.; Class G: *Geography, maps, anthropology, recreation.* 4th ed. 1976. 435p.; Class H, subclasses H–HJ: *Social sciences, economics.* 4th ed. 1981. 400p.; Class H, subclasses HM–HX: *Social sciences, sociology.* 4th ed. 1980. 400p.; Class K, subclass K: *Law (general).* 1977. 68*l.,* 69–92p.; Class K, subclass KD: *Law of the United Kingdom and Ireland.* 1973. 114*l.,* 115–63p.; Class K, subclass KE: *Law of Canada.* 1976. 134*l.,* 135–81p.; Class K, subclass KF: *Law of the United States.* 1969. 333p.; Class L: *Education.* 3d ed. 1951, repr. with suppl. pages 1966. 200p., 69p.; Class M: *Music and books on music.* 3d ed. 1978. 228*l.;*

Class N: *Fine arts.* 4th ed. 1970. 280*l.;* Class P, P–PA: *Philology, linguistics, classical philology, classical literature.* 1928, repr. with suppl. pages 1968. 16p., 447p., 47p., 24p.; Class P, subclass PG: *Russian literature.* 1948, repr. with suppl. pages 1965. 256p., 15p.; Class P, subclass PQ, pt.1: *French literature.* 1936, repr. with suppl. pages 1966. 185p., 17p.; Class P, subclass PQ, pt.2: *Italian, Spanish, and Portuguese literatures.* 1937, repr. with suppl. pages 1965. 223p., 29p.; Class P, subclass PT, pt.1: *German literature.* 1938, repr. with suppl. pages, 1966. 312p., 17p.; Class P, subclass PT, pt.2: *Dutch and Scandinavian literatures.* 1942, repr. with suppl. pages 1965. 102p., 27p.; Class P, subclasses P–PM supplement: *Index to languages and dialects.* 2d ed. 1957, repr. with suppl. pages 1965. 71p., 5p.; Class P, subclasses PB–PH: *Modern European languages.* 1933, repr. with suppl. pages 1966. 226p., 51p.; Class P, subclasses PJ–PM: *Languages and literatures of Asia, Africa, Oceania, America, mixed languages, artificial languages.* 1935, repr. with suppl. pages 1965. 246p., 191p.; Class P, subclasses PN, PR, PS, PZ: *General literature, English and American literature, fiction in English, juvenile belles lettres.* 2d ed. 1978. 277*l.,* 279–351p.;

Class Q: *Science.* 6th ed. 1973. 282*l.,* 283–415p.; Class R: *Medicine.* 4th ed. 1980. 363p.; Class S: *Agriculture, plant and animal industry, fish culture and fisheries, hunting sports.* 3d ed. 1952, repr. with suppl. pages 1965. 101p., 63p.; Class T: *Technology.* 5th ed. 1971. 266*l.,* 267–370p.; Class U: *Military science.* 4th ed. 1974. 59*l.,* 61–75p.; Class V: *Naval science.* 3d ed. 1974. 91p.; Class Z: *Bibliography and library science.* 5th ed. 1980. 354p.

Immroth, John Phillip. Immroth's Guide to the Library of Congress classification. 3d ed. [by] Lois Mai Chan. Littleton, Colo., Libraries Unlimited, 1980. 402p. il. **AB233**

1st ed. 1968.
Intended as a simple introduction to the use of the Library of Congress classification, its characteristics, format of schedules and tables, etc. This edition revised and updated to reflect current policies and practices. A new chapter on classification of special types of library materials has been added. Z696.U4I5

Dewey, Melvil. Dewey Decimal Classification and relative index. Ed. 19. Lake Placid Club, N.Y., Forest Pr., 1979. 3v. **AB234**

Contents: v.1, Tables; v.2, Schedules; v.3, Index.
First published anonymously in 1876 under title *A classification and subject index;* 2d–14th eds. published under title *Decimal classification and relativ index.*
Responsibility for editorial policy rests with the Decimal Classification Editorial Policy Committee, a joint committee of the Lake Placid Club Education Foundation, the American Library Association, and the Library of Congress. Z696.D519

——— ——— 10th abridged ed. Lake Placid Club, N.Y., Forest Pr., 1971. 529p.

Lake Placid Club Education Foundation. Guide to the use of Dewey Decimal Classification, based on the practice of the Decimal Classification Office at the Library of Congress. Lake Placid Club, N.Y., Forest Pr., 1962. 133p. **AB235**

A practical guide designed to help the classifier by providing instructions and directions for the use of the Decimal Classification schedules.

A more recent guide is C.D. Batty's *An introduction to the nineteenth edition of the Dewey decimal classification* (London, Bingley, 1981. 168p.). Z696.D5199

Bliss, Henry Evelyn. A bibliographic classification, extended by systematic auxiliary schedules for composite specification and notation. N.Y., Wilson, 1940–53. 4v. in 3.
AB236

The first two volumes of a 2d ed. appeared in 1952 (N.Y., Wilson. 2v. in 1), covering: Introduction; Anterior tables and systematic schedules, Classes A–K: the sciences. Additional volumes of the new edition have been issued by Butterworths, London, 1977–81: Class H, Anthropology, Human biology, Health sciences; Class I, Psychology, Psychiatry; Class J, Education; Class P, Religion; Class Q, Social welfare; Introduction and auxiliary schedules.

For description of this classification, *see* M. F. Tauber, "Classification systems," in *The state of the library art*, v.1, pt.3 (AB37).
Z696.B635

International Federation for Documentation, Brussels. Classification décimale universelle. Tables de classification pour les bibliographies, bibliothèques, archives, administrations, publications, brevets, musées et ensembles d'objets pour toutes les espèces de documentation en général et pour les collections de toute nature. Édition complète, publiée avec le concours de la Commission Internationale de la Classification Décimale et du Nederlandsch Instituut voor Documentatie en Registratuur (La Haye). . . . [Bruxelles], 1927–33. 4v. and index. il. (*Its* Publ. 151) **AB237**

———— ———— 5. ed. internationale. Bruxelles, 1939– . (In progress)
Z696.D6

British Standards Institution. Universal Decimal Classification. 2d English full ed. London, The Institution, 1977– . (BS: 1000) (FID publ. no. 483) **AB238**

The first "English full edition" was published 1943–75(?) and could scarcely be called complete, some parts being more than 25 years old. 22 parts of the new edition have appeared through 1983. An earlier abridgment was published as: Z696.U862

International Federation for Documentation, Brussels. Universal Decimal Classification. Abridged English ed. 3d ed. rev. London, British Standards Inst., 1961. 254p. (*Its* Publ. 289 rev.)

A complementary work is: Z696.D6I5625

British Standards Institution. Guide to the Universal Decimal Classification (UDC). London, [1963]. 128p. (FID publ. no. 345) **AB239**

Two other works on the classification system and its status are: *The Universal Decimal Classification; the history, present status and future prospects of a large general classification scheme,* by Anthony C. Foskett (London, Linnet Books, 1973. 171p.) and *Towards a theory for U.D.C.: essays aimed at structural understanding and operational improvement,* edited by Jean Michel Perreault (London, Bingley, 1969. 241p.). Z696.D6B7

Ranganathan, Shiyali R. Colon classification; basic classification. [6th ed., repr. with amendments] Bombay, N.Y., Asia Pub. House, [1963]. 3 pts. in 1v. (Madras Lib. Assoc. Publ. ser. 26) **AB240**

Contents: pt.1, Rules; pt.2, Schedules of classification; pt.3, Schedules of classics and sacred books with special names.

For description of this classification *see* M. F. Tauber, "Classification systems," in *The state of the library art*, v.1, pt.3 (AB37).
Z696.R193

U.S. National Library of Medicine. Classification. 3d ed. [rev.] Bethesda, Md., [1969]. 286p., 16p. (Public Health Service publ. no.1108) **AB241**

Subtitle: A scheme for the shelf arrangement of books in the field of medicine and its related sciences.

1st ed. entitled *Classification: medicine.* 1951.

The notation was developed from the block of letters, QS–QZ and

W, unused by the Library of Congress and assigned to the National Library of Medicine. Z697.M4U5

Harvard University. Graduate School of Business Administration. Baker Library. A classification of business literature. [Rev. ed.] Hamden, Conn., Shoe String, 1960. 256p.
AB242

1st ed. 1937.

Substantially a reissue of the 1st ed. with major changes only in the B schedule for *Business and economic theory,* and minor changes to reflect new techniques and concepts. Designed primarily to serve a large collection of business materials. Z697.B9H32

National League for Nursing. The Bellevue classification system for nursing school libraries. N.Y., Nat. League for Nursing, 1965. 58*l.* **AB243**

Reprinted from the League's *Library handbook for schools of nursing* (2d ed. N.Y., The League, 1953. 265p.). Z696.B45N35

New York. Union Theological Seminary. Library. Classification of the Library of Union Theological Seminary . . . prep. by Julia Pettee. Rev. and enl. ed. With additions and corrections, 1939–December 1966, ed. by Ruth C. Eisenhart. N.Y., Union Theological Seminary, 1967. 793p.
AB244

Z697.T5N5

Subject headings
Manuals

Chan, Lois Mai. Library of Congress subject headings: principles and application. Littleton, Colo., Libraries Unlimited, 1978. 347p. (Research studies in library science, no.15) **AB245**

In many respects a successor to Haykin's work (below). "This book attempts to re-examine the underlying principles of *Library of Congress Subject Headings* in light of recent developments and some of the recent theories and to describe current subject cataloging practice as carried out by the Library of Congress."—*Pref.*
Z674.R4 no.15

Haykin, David Judson. Subject headings; a practical guide. Wash., Govt. Prt. Off., 1951. 140p. (Repr.: N.Y., Gordon Pr., 1978) **AB246**

A manual of rules and practices used in the choice and use of subject headings, with examples. Based mainly on the procedure followed at the Library of Congress. Z695.H36

Schedules

Atkins, Thomas V., ed. Cross-reference index; a subject heading guide. N.Y., Bowker, 1974. 255p. **AB247**

An alphabetical listing of subject headings used in the Library of Congress list (AB254), the Sears list (AB252), the *Readers' guide,* the *New York Times index, PAIS,* and the *Business periodicals index,* showing which terms are used in each index, alternate headings, and *see also* references. A 2d ed. was scheduled for 1985 publication.
Z695.A954

Ball, Miriam Ogden, comp. Subject headings for the information file. 8th ed. N.Y., Wilson, 1956. 179p. **AB248**

1st ed. 1917. Compiler varies.

Designed for use by public libraries; this edition has been revised to include additional scientific and technical terms. Based on headings in use in the Public Library of Newark, N.J. Z695.B24

Kapsner, Oliver Leonard. Catholic subject headings. [6th ed.] Contributing eds., Mary Consuelo O'Connell, [and others]; gen. eds., Catherine M. Pilley, Matthew R. Wilt. Haverford, Pa., Catholic Lib. Assoc., [1981]. 240p.
AB249

1st ed. 1942; 5th ed. 1963.

"Based on the 5th edition . . . , this modification is updated with current usage reflecting the changes in terminology since Vatican II and supplemented by *The Catholic periodical and literature index* and the 9th edition of the *Library of Congress subject headings*."— *t.p.*   Z695.1.T3K29

Muench, Eugene V. Biomedical subject headings; a reconciliation of National Library of Medicine (MeSH) and Library of Congress subject headings. 2d ed. [Hamden, Conn.], Shoe String, 1979. 774p.   **AB250**

1st ed. 1971.

National Library of Medicine subject headings are given in alphabetical sequence, with the corresponding Library of Congress headings in parallel columns. "The purpose of this comparative listing of these two controlled vocabularies is to state precisely where they are alike and where they are different and to enable librarians to convert this information from one system to the other to suit the objectives of the local library."—*Introd.*

Z695.1.M48M8

Pettee, Julia. List of theological subject headings and corporate church names based upon the headings in the catalogue of the Library of Union Theological Seminary, New York City. 2d ed. Chicago, Amer. Lib. Assoc., 1947. 653p.

AB251

Incorporates the Library of Congress subject headings in theology. Appendix gives historical and descriptive information on all the church bodies in the list.   Z695.1.T3P4

Sears, Minnie Earle. List of subject headings. 12th ed., ed. by Barbara M. Westby. N.Y., Wilson, 1982. 624p.

AB252

1st ed. 1923. 1st–3d eds. by Minnie Earle Sears; 4th–5th eds. by Isabel S. Monro; 6th–8th eds. by Bertha Margaret Frick; 9th–12th eds. by Barbara M. Westby. 1st–5th eds. had title *List of subject headings for small libraries.*

Uses the Library of Congress form of headings, abridged and simplified to meet the needs of smaller libraries, though modifications of Library of Congress headings have been kept to a minimum. Dewey Decimal Classification numbers, which were a feature of earlier editions, were dropped from the 9th and 10th eds., but have now been restored.   Z695.S43

Subject headings for the literature of law and international law, and index to LC K schedules. Comp. by Tillie Krieger. 3d ed. Littleton, Colo., Publ. for the American Assoc. of Law Libraries by F. B. Rothman, 1982. 356p. (AALL publ. ser., no.16)   **AB253**

1st–2d eds., 1963–69, ed. by Werner B. Ellinger.

Takes "the needs of a law school library as its primary focus" *(Pref.)* in the hope that the volume will also meet the needs of other law libraries. In this edition the Library of Congress call numbers are indicated for the subject classes.   Z695.1.L3S9

U.S. Library of Congress. Subject Cataloging Division. Library of Congress subject headings. 9th ed. Wash., Lib. of Congress, 1980. 2v. (2591p.)   **AB254**

1st–7th eds. had title: *Subject headings used in the dictionary catalogs of the Library of Congress.*

A cumulated edition of the subject headings established and applied by the Library from 1897 through Dec. 1978. "Two major changes were made by computer program to the contents of this edition. First, the previously announced adoption of indirect local subdivision has been implemented with the substitution of the instruction *(Indirect)* for *(Direct)*. . . . Second, many free-floating form and topical subdivisions were removed from the list under specific subjects if no cross-references to the subdivisions were involved. 'Free-floating subdivisions' are those that catalogers may use as appropriate without the usage being specifically authorized in the list."—*Introd.*

Various "nonprint" headings omitted from the 8th ed. have been restored, but it should be noted that "Only those headings established for works being cataloged currently are included; no effort is made to include retroactively those headings previously established,

unless an existing older heading is involved in the reference structure of a new heading. As a result, a remarkable unevenness of coverage will be apparent in the list, with uncommon names printed while well-known but previously established names are not included." A list of "Categories of former nonprint headings now included" is provided, together with one of categories still omitted. Certain other useful lists (e.g., "Most commonly used subdivisions") found in the 8th ed. are omitted here.

Kept up to date by weekly lists and quarterly cumulative supplements.   Z695.U4749

———— Music subject headings used on printed catalog cards of the Library of Congress. Wash., 1952. 133p.

AB255

ML111.U75

Filing and indexing

American Library Association. Filing Committee. ALA filing rules. Chicago, Amer. Lib. Assoc., 1980. 50p.   **AB256**

This publication is the "successor to *A.L.A. Rules for Filing Catalog Cards* (1942) and *ALA Rules for Filing Catalog Cards*, second edition (1968)."—*Introd.* It is to be considered a new work rather than a new edition "since the new rules are applicable to bibliographic displays in other than card formats." Glossary; index.

Z695.95.A52

Collison, Robert Lewis. Indexes and indexing; a guide to the indexing of books, and collections of books, periodicals, music, recordings, films and other material, with a reference section and suggestions for further reading. 4th rev. ed. London, Benn; N.Y., DeGraff, 1972. 232p.   **AB257**

1st ed. 1953.

A standard guide to indexing practices. In three sections: (1) The indexing of books; (2) Wider indexing (including indexing of music and recordings, films, periodicals; compiling and arranging a bibliography, etc.); (3) Reference section (proof reading; basic rules; annotated list of works for the indexer's library). Indexed.

Z695.9.C63

Knight, Gilfred Norman. Indexing, the art of: a guide to the indexing of books and periodicals. London, Allen & Unwin, [1979]. 218p.   **AB258**

An introduction to the mechanics of indexing, with attention to headings and subheadings, subject headings, proper names, cross references, alphabetizing, etc. Chapters on periodical and newspaper indexing, cumulative indexing, editing, and proof correcting. Indexed.   Z695.9.K58

Rather, John Carson and **Biebel, Susan C.** Library of Congress filing rules. Wash., Lib. of Congress, 1980. 111p.

AB259

A provisional version was publ. 1971 under title: *Filing arrangement in the Library of Congress catalogs.*

Supersedes *Filing rules for the dictionary catalogs in the Library of Congress* (1956).

Sets forth the rules applied in 1981 along with the adoption of AACR 2. Thus, "these filing rules were written to arrange headings formulated under various cataloging rules and practices. In those situations in which AACR 2 and pre-AACR 2 headings have contradictory characteristics, the filing rules were written to accommodate the new [i.e., "Add-on"] catalog, which will include only AACR 2 and AACR 2-compatible headings."—*Introd.* The rules apply to the Library's computer-produced bibliographic products.

Z695.95.R37

Wellisch, Hans H. Indexing and abstracting: an international bibliography. Santa Barbara, Calif., ABC-Clio, [1980]. 308p.   **AB260**

"Publ. in cooperation with the American Society of Indexers and the Society of Indexers (U.K.)"—*t.p.*

A topically arranged bibliography of nearly 2,400 items, most of them annotated. Nearly all items published before 1950 were included, but a more selective policy was followed for later publications. Author and subject indexes.   Z695.9.W44

———— Indexing and abstracting, 1977–1981: an international bibliography. Santa Barbara, Calif., ABC-Clio., 1984. 276p.

A continuation of the above, adding more than 1,400 items, including some publications from the earlier period.

Z695.9.W438

Wheeler, Martha Thorne. Indexing; principles, rules and examples. 5th ed. Albany, Univ. of the State of New York, 1957. 78p. (N.Y. [State] Univ. Bull. no.1445)   **AB261**

1st ed. 1905.
An excellent manual.   Z695.9.N53

Information storage and retrieval

Automated library systems

Automation in libraries: a LITA bibliography, 1978–1982. Comp. by Anne G. Adler [and others]. [Ann Arbor, Mich.], Pierian Pr., 1983. 177p. (Library hi tech ser., no.1)
AB262

A classified bibliography of more than 2,500 citations. Name index.

Earlier coverage is provided by Maxine MacCafferty's *An annotated bibliography of automation in libraries and information systems, 1972–1975* (London, Aslib, 1976. 147p.) which was intended as a continuation of *An annotated bibliography of library automation 1968–1972,* compiled by Lynne Tinker (London, Aslib, 1973).

Z678.9.A2A96

Boss, Richard W. The library manager's guide to automation. 2d ed. White Plains, N.Y., Knowledge Industry Pubns., [1984]. 169p.   **AB263**

1st ed. 1979.
A brief guide to planning, selecting and implementing automated systems for a variety of library applications.

Ian Lovecy's *Automating library procedures: a survivor's handbook* (London, Library Assoc.; Phoenix, Oryx Pr., 1984. 247p.) is the work of a British librarian and is intended as a practical guide for the non-specialist faced with responsibility for introducing automation into the day-to-day operations of a library; it gives attention to issues which automation raises and suggests possible solutions to some of the problems.

In Sheila S. Intner's *Access to media: a guide to integrating and computerizing catalogs* (N.Y., Neal-Schuman, 1984. 301p.) the emphasis is on the treatment of "media," particularly nonprint materials, and the desirability of integrating bibliographic records for print and nonprint collections. It offers a plan of action "for change from manual, nonintegrated bibliographic systems to integrated and automated systems as an ultimate goal."—*Pref.*

Z678.9.B66

Byerly, Greg. Online searching: a dictionary and bibliographic guide. Littleton, Colo., Libraries Unlimited, 1983. 288p.   **AB264**

A dictionary of online searching terminology is followed by a classified, annotated bibliography of the literature of the subject. Author and subject indexes.   Z699.2.B9

Encyclopedia of information systems and services. Ed. by John Schmittroth, Jr. 6th ed. Detroit, Gale, [1985]. 2v.
AB265

For full information *see* EJ253.

Hawkins, Donald T. Online information retrieval bibliography, 1964–1982. Medford, N.J., Learned Information, [1983]. 311p.   **AB266**

A reprinting of the compiler's bibliography which was published as a supplement to the first issue of *Online review* (Mar. 1977) and the six annual updates which also appeared in that journal. A

seventh update was published in the June and Aug. 1984 issues of *Online review;* an eighth update as a supplement to the Aug. 1985 issue of that journal.   Z699.2.H39

Matthews, Joseph R. Choosing an automated library system: a planning guide. Chicago, Amer. Lib. Assoc., 1980. 119p. il.   **AB267**

Intended for medium and small libraries. Offers a plan of action for selecting and implementing an automated system. Includes chapters on "Needs analysis," "Considering alternatives," "Selection process," "The contract," "Installing the computer" and "Implementing the system." Bibliographic notes; glossary; select bibliography; index.

Matthews is also the editor of *A reader on choosing an automated library system* (Chicago, Amer. Lib. Assoc., 1983. 390p.).

Z678.9.M37

Saffady, William. Introduction to automation for librarians. Chicago, Amer. Lib. Assoc., 1983. 304p. il.   **AB268**

In two parts: (1) The fundamentals (offering chapters on computer hardware; computer software; data processing concepts; automated office systems) and (2) Library applications (computerized circulation control systems; automated cataloging; automated reference service; automated acquisitions and serials control). Indexed.

Z678.9.S25

Database directories

Computer-readable databases: a directory and data sourcebook. Martha E. Williams, ed. in chief. Chicago, Amer. Lib. Assoc., 1985. 2v.   **AB269**

Contents: v.[1], Science, technology, medicine; v.[2], Business, law, humanities, social sciences.

1st ed. 1976 had title *Computer-readable bibliographic data bases;* title, co-editors, and publisher have varied in subsequent editions.

Provides information on more than 5,300 databases, "both word-oriented (e.g., bibliographic, full-text, and directory information) and numeric (e.g., properties, time series, and statistical information) databases."—*Pref.* In general, data was obtained directly from the database producers; entries include, as applicable: basic information (name, producer, frequency of update, size, language, etc.); notes on subject matter and scope; indexing/coding/classification; data elements; user aids. Name, subject, producer, and processor indexes for the full set are included in both volumes.

Z699.22.C66

Data base directory. 1984/85– . White Plains, N.Y., Knowledge Industry Pubns. in cooperation with the American Soc. for Information Science, [1984]– . Annual.   **AB270**

An alphabetical listing of databases available online in North America, with subject and producer indexes. For each database indicates subject, provides a summary of content, and gives information on corresponding printed source (if any), subject access, producer services, time coverage of data file, vendor and price information, original data sources, language, restrictions, and search aids available.   QA76.9.D3D295

Datapro directory of on-line services. Delran, N.J., Datapro Research Corp., [1985]– . 2v. (looseleaf)   **AB271**

A looseleaf news and reporting service designed to provide up-to-date information about, and evaluation of, developments in the online industry. v.1 is concerned with "material on the information retrieval services segment of the on-line industry. It contains detailed reports on the major database providers . . . , hundreds of profiles on companies offering and maintaining public databases, and nearly 2,000 abstracts of publicly accessible databases."— *User's guide.* v.2 offers detailed reports on about 100 major remote computing service vendors (and brief notes on many others). "These reports highlight each company's processing resources, application/industry-specific services, and the networking services that connect you to the time-sharing service."

Directory of online databases. v.1, no.1– , Fall 1979– . Santa Monica, Calif., Cuadra Associates, [1979]– . Quarterly. **AB272**

". . . designed to help subscribers keep abreast of the vast amount of information contained in online databases . . . available for interactive access by users from remote computer terminals. These databases contain numeric, textual, or combinations of numeric and textual information, in a wide range of subject access. . . ."—*Introd.* Also intended "to help subscribers identify databases of particular interest and provide a direct link to the suppliers of those online database services." An alphabetical listing of databases indicates type, subject, producer, online service, conditions of access, content, coverage, and updating. Also lists databases by subject and by producer. Directory of addresses of producers.

Interlibrary loan

Borchardt, D. H. and **Thawley, J. D.** Guide to the availability of theses. München & N.Y., K. G. Saur, 1981. 443p. (IFLA publications, 17) **AB273**

"Comp. for the section of university libraries and other general research libraries."—*t.p.*

Provides information on the availability—through interlibrary loan, photocopying, etc.—of theses and dissertations at 698 individual institutions in 85 countries. Includes reference to each country's "national thesis bibliography," if any. Z5053.B67

Boucher, Virginia. Interlibrary loan practices handbook. Chicago, Amer. Lib. Assoc., 1984. 195p. il. **AB274**

Serves as a successor to S. K. Thomson's *Interlibrary loan procedures* manual (1970). Intended "for those without interlibrary loan experience who seek advice on how to proceed" and describes "the procedures outlined in interlibrary loan codes."—*Pref.* Includes chapters on both borrowing and lending, reproduction and copyright concerns, dissertations and masters' theses, international interlibrary loan, and managing the interlibrary loan operation. Appendixes of codes, forms, policy statements, etc. Bibliography of verification sources; index. Z713.B7

Canadian Library Association. Information Services Section. Interlibrary loan procedures manual. [Ottawa, 1971] 25p. **AB275**

The Association has also issued an *Interlibrary loan telex manual* (rev. ed., 1982). Z713.5.C3C335

International Federation of Library Associations and Institutions. Office for International Lending. A brief guide to centres of international lending and photocopying. 2d ed. Boston Spa., Eng., IFLA Office for Internat. Lending, British Lib. Lending Div., 1979. 21, [164] p. **AB276**

1st ed. 1975.

A country-by-country directory, indicating whether there is a national union catalogue, a central national lending service, and procedures to be followed in placing requests for loan or photocopy. Based on information supplied by 106 institutions in 74 countries. Z713.I67

International Federation of Library Associations and Institutions. Section on Interlending. International loan services and union catalogues: a manual . . . ed. by Valentin Wehefritz. 2d completely rev. ed. Frankfurt am Main, Klostermann, 1980. 294p. (Zeitschrift für Bibliothekswesen und Bibliographie. Sonderheft, 17) **AB277**

1st ed. 1974. An earlier (1961) publication by L. Brummel and E. Egger had title: *Guide to union catalogues and international loan centers.*

Introductory matter in French, English, German and Russian; entries are in the language of the country, with notes in two of the languages just mentioned.

A section on principles and guidelines for international lending precedes the main part of the work which is arranged by country according to the French form of the country names, listing for each the national bibliography, union catalogs (printed and unprinted),

international loan centers (if any), and principal special collections. Index of names of countries. Z695.83.I59

Morris, Leslie R. and **Brautigam, Patsy Fowler.** Interlibrary loan policies directory. 2d ed. Chicago, Amer. Lib. Assoc., 1984. 448p. **AB278**

1st ed. 1975 by Sarah K. Thomson.

Sets forth the interlibrary lending policies of more than 800 U.S. libraries regarding books, periodicals, microforms, government publications, dissertations and theses, audiovisual materials, and computer software. Also indicates availability of, and charges for, photocopying services. Information based on responses to a questionnaire. Arranged by state, then by library name; index of library names. Z713.5.U6M67

Winchell, Constance Mabel. Locating books for interlibrary loan, with a bibliography of printed aids which show location of books in American libraries. N.Y., Wilson, 1930. 170p. **AB279**

Pt.1, Locating books for interlibrary loan, a discussion of the standards to be met and the reference methods to be followed in finding books not in the home library; pt.2, Some 800 printed aids which show location of books in American libraries. An older work, still valuable for the principles set forth. Z1002.W75

Library instruction

Beaubien, Anne K., Hogan, Sharon A. and **George, Mary W.** Learning the library: concepts and methods for effective bibliographic instruction. N.Y., Bowker, 1982. 269p. **AB280**

A guide for developing and implementing an academic bibliographic instruction program. Intended as a companion volume to *Theories of bibliographic education: designs for teaching* by Cerise Oberman and Katina Strauch (N.Y., Bowker, 1982). Z710.B37

Breivik, Patricia Senn. Planning the library instruction program. Chicago, Am. Lib. Assoc., 1982. 146p. **AB281**

A work for the librarian involved in library instruction. Aims to provide "a clear understanding of the educational and political milieu in which library user-education programs must exist, as well as an understanding of the practical steps involved in planning and implementing them."—*Introd.* Indexed. Z711.2.B75

Lockwood, Deborah L. Library instruction: a bibliography. Westport, Conn., Greenwood Pr., 1979. 166p. **AB282**

Intended as a bibliographic aid to the librarian developing an instructional program. Arranged in three main sections (with appropriate subdivisions): (1) General philosophy; (2) Types of libraries; (3) Teaching methods and formats. Name index. Z710.L62

Renford, Beverly and **Hendrickson, Linnea.** Bibliographic instruction: a handbook. N.Y., Neal-Schuman, [1980]. 192p. **AB283**

Intended "as a practical guide for those involved in developing or improving library-user education programs and activities."—*Pref.* Chapters treat general orientation; printed guides, handouts, and bibliographies; course-related instruction; credit instruction; computer-assisted instruction; audiovisual aids and equipment. Indexed. Z711.2.R38

Preservation work

Banks, Paul Noble. A selective bibliography on the conservation of research library materials. Chicago, Newberry Lib., 1981. 198p. **AB284**

A classed listing with author index. The primary aim of the selection is "to provide the information available in English that is most useful to librarians and archivists concerned with conservation, and to conservators of bibliothecal and archival materials."—*Pref.* Z701.B26

Cunha, George Daniel Martin and **Cunha, Dorothy Grant.** Conservation of library materials; a manual and bibliography on the care, repair, and restoration of library materials. 2d ed. Metuchen, N.J., Scarecrow Pr., 1971–72. 2v.　**AB285**

1st ed. 1967.

A manual of practical guidance, together with a bibliography on books and their preservation.

———— Library and archives conservation: the 1980s and beyond. Metuchen, N.J., Scarecrow Pr., 1983. 2v. il.　**AB286**

Intended to be used in conjunction with the compilers' earlier work (above), emphasis here being on developments during the ten years following preparation of that work. v.1 offers chapters on the care, restoration and repair of library materials; v.2 is a bibliography of 4,882 items. Each volume has its own index.　Z701.C784

Darling, Pamela W. and **Webster, Duane E.** Preservation planning. Wash., Assoc. of Research Libraries, Office of Management Studies, 1982. 2v.　**AB287**

Contents: v.1, An assisted self-study manual for libraries (117p.); v.2, Resource notebook (626p.).

The "manual" is designed to help a library analyze its collection in preparation for a planning study; the "notebook" offers background and technical readings for planning and implementing a preservation program.

The *Preservation education directory; educational opportunities in the preservation of library materials, 1981,* ed. by Susan G. Swartzburg and Susan B. White for the Preservation of Library Materials Section, Education Committee, Resources and Technical Services Division, American Library Association (Chicago, 1981. 30p.), lists preservation programs and courses available at accredited library schools, together with workshops and related educational opportunities in other institutions.

Harrison, Alice W., Collister, Edward A. and **Willis, R. Ellen.** The conservation of archival and library materials: a resource guide to audiovisual aids. Metuchen, N.J., Scarecrow Pr., 1982. 190p.　**AB288**

Lists and describes a selection of audiovisual aids relating to the conservation of archival and library materials. Indexed.　Z701.H28

Kyle, Hedi. Library materials preservation manual: practical methods for preserving books, pamphlets, and other printed materials. Bronxville, N.Y., N. T. Smith, [1983]. 160p. il.　**AB289**

An introduction to the techniques of preservation "geared to the needs of the aspiring preservation librarian or layman."—*Introd.* Describes basic treatments for many commonly encountered preservation problems, combining explanatory text and illustrations. List of supply sources; selected bibliography; index.　Z701.K94

Morrow, Carolyn Clark and **Schoenly, Steven B.** A conservation bibliography for librarians, archivists, and administrators. Troy, N.Y., Whitston, 1979. 271p.　**AB290**

In two main parts, the first being a selected, annotated bibliography arranged under such headings as: Conservation administration, Environmental protection, Conservation techniques. Pt.II is meant to be a comprehensive bibliography of the literature since 1966 (and repeats the citations found in Pt.I). Subject index.　Z701.M54

Morrow, Carolyn Clark and **Walker, Gay.** The preservation challenge: a guide to conserving library materials. White Plains, N.Y., Knowledge Industry Pubns., [1983]. 231p. il.　**AB291**

A work which "reviews the physical causes of deterioration, summarizes what has been learned thus far about controlling or even reversing the process, [and] describes procedural and organizational strategies for prolonging the life of record materials."—*Introd.* Includes chapters on developing preservation programs in libraries, case studies of preservation programs, and technological solutions to preservation problems. Select bibliography; index.

Morrow's *Conservation treatment procedures: a manual of step-by-step procedures for the maintenance and repair of library materials* (Littleton, Colo., Libraries Unlimited, 1982. 191p.) offers a combination of brief text and photographs illustrating the basic techniques for repair and maintenance of books, pamphlets, etc.　Z701.M547

National preservation report. v.1, no.1–3, Apr.–Dec. 1979. Wash., Lib. of Congress, 1979.　**AB292**

Supersedes *Newspaper and gazette report* (AF6), which ceased with v.6, no.3, Dec. 1978.

Provides reports "on national and international developments in the preservation, bibliographic control, and location of endangered and deteriorating library materials, such as books, periodicals, news-papers, pamphlets, manuscripts, maps, government documents, etc., held by U.S., Canadian and selected foreign libraries and producers of microforms."—*verso of t.p.* Includes notices of materials newly available in microform and a section of "Intentions to microfilm," listing specific newspaper titles which individual institutions have proposed to film. Ceased publication; superseded in effect by *National preservation news* (Wash., Lib. of Congress, July, 1985–).　Z265.N365

Roberts, Matt T. and **Etherington, Don.** Bookbinding and the conservation of books: a dictionary of descriptive terminology. Wash., Lib. of Congress, 1982. 296p. il.　**AB293**

"Although this dictionary is intended first and foremost for those actively involved in one or more aspects of the overall field of bookbinding and book conservation, including bookbinders, conservators of library and archival materials, and the like, it is perhaps no less intended for those working in related fields, such as bibliography and librarianship, where the many terms and expressions relating to the overall field may be less familiar and even more confusing."—*Pref.* Clear, concise definitions; helpful line drawings and other illustrations; cross references. References to item numbers in the bibliography (p. 289–96) are given at the end of most entries.　Z266.7.R62

Swartzburg, Susan G. Preserving library materials: a manual. Metuchen, N.J., Scarecrow Pr., 1980. 282p. il.　**AB294**

Not a "how to" manual for repair or restoration, but a series of chapters discussing "collection maintenance, ranging from good housekeeping to the installation of environmental controls" and offering guidelines and principles "to help librarians analyze their own situations and to prepare programs to meet the particular needs of their libraries."—*Introd.* Covers the various media found in library collections—books, microforms, records, slides, films, tapes, etc. Selected readings; useful appendixes; index.

Also edited by Swartzburg, *Conservation in the library: a handbook of use and care of traditional and nontraditional materials* (Westport, Greenwood Pr., 1983. 234p.), offers chapters by conservators and preservation specialists on care and preservation of such materials as manuscripts and documents, bookbindings, photographs, slides, microforms, motion picture films, videotapes, sound recordings, and videodiscs.　Z701.S92

Reference work

Beaudiquez, Marcelle. Guide de bibliographie générale: méthodologie et pratique. München [etc.], K. G. Saur, 1983. 280p. il.　**AB295**

Intended primarily as a guide for students of librarianship, but useful to the practicing librarian for its annotations and comments concerning various standard reference sources and bibliographies (e.g., an extensive description of the *Bibliographie de la France*).

Hede, Agnes Ann. Reference readiness: a manual for librarians and students. 3d ed., rev. and updated. Hamden, Conn., Library Professional Pubns., 1984. 187p.　**AB296**

1st ed. 1971.

A work "for the student librarian, the practicing librarian, and the researcher" *(Introd.)* intended to be used in conjunction with examination of the reference books themselves: i.e., offers an annotation of the reference source, followed by a list of features to be examined or noted, and suggested comparison with similar works. Sources are grouped by type, and there is a section on computer sources and services. Indexed. Z1035.1.H4

Hutchins, Margaret. Introduction to reference work. Chicago, Amer. Lib. Assoc., 1944. 214p. **AB297**

An older publication which is still a good general introduction to reference work. Includes sections on: (1) The scope of reference work; (2) Reference questions; (3) Selection of reference materials; (4) Organization of reference materials; (5) Organization and administration of reference service; (6) The less common functions of a reference librarian; and (7) Evaluating and reporting reference work. Z711.H985

Katz, William A. Introduction to reference work. 4th ed. N.Y., McGraw-Hill, [1982]. 2v. **AB298**

1st ed. 1969.

Contents: v.1, Basic information sources; v.2, Reference services and reference processes.

A revised and updated edition of this now standard work. The 2v. set serves as a basic text for the study of reference work. v.1 alone may serve as a guide for student, layman, or librarian; basic sources are grouped therein by type, and many are treated at some length. v.2 is concerned with principles and practices of reference service. Z711.K32

Murfin, Marjorie E. and **Wynar, Lubomyr R.** Reference service: an annotated bibliographic guide. Littleton, Colo., Libraries Unlimited, 1977. 294p. **AB299**

A bibliographic guide to the literature of reference service, covering publications on all aspects of library reference work appearing during the period 1876–1975. Topically arranged in 14 chapters, with author and title indexes. Z711.M86

Reference and online services handbook: guidelines, policies, and procedures for libraries. Ed. by Bill Katz and Anne Clifford. N.Y., Neal-Schuman, [1982]. 581p. **AB300**

Primarily a collection of reference services policy statements encompassing "the essential guidelines, procedures, and policies necessary in the day-to-day operations of an effective reference operation in the academic, public, and, to a lesser extent, special library."—*Introd.* An overview of policy statements (with sections by contributing librarians) is followed by policy statements from academic and public libraries, and a further section of online policy statements from academic, public, and special libraries. Indexed. Z711.K33

Stevens, Rolland Elwell and **Walton, Joan M.** Reference work in the public library. Littleton, Colo., Libraries Unlimited, 1983. 269p. **AB301**

Intended as "an aid to librarians with varying levels of training and experience" *(Pref.),* whether at the professional or paraprofessional level, and addressing the types of questions most often asked in "the average public library." Arranged according to the frequency with which questions are likely to arise, beginning with general reference sources (encyclopedias, dictionaries, etc.) and ready reference tools (almanacs, telephone numbers and addresses, etc.), and continuing through various subject fields and areas of special interest. Introductory notes for each section, with annotated lists of reference sources. Author/title and subject indexes. Z711.S797

Reprography

Association for Information and Image Management. Buying guide: registry of equipment, supplies, and services. Silver Spring, Md., The Association, 1984– . Annual. **AB302**

Subtitle varies.

Continues the *Registry of micrographics equipment, supplies, and services* (1983) which in turn continued the *Buyer's guide to micro-*

graphic equipment products and services (1975–80), both issued under the Association's earlier name, National Micrographics Association. Those publications superseded the earlier *Buyer's guide to microfilm equipment* (1971–74) issued under the Association's original name, National Microfilm Association.

Lists various types of equipment, supplies, and services, with specifications, features, prices, etc., often set out in tabular form for easy comparison.

A *Guide to micrographic equipment,* last issued in 1979 under the Association's earlier name, is no longer published.

Directory of library reprographic services. 8th ed., comp. and ed. by Joseph Z. Nitecki. [Westport, Conn.], Publ. for the Reproduction of Library Materials Section, RTSD-Amer. Lib. Assoc., by Meckler Publishing, [1982]. 540p. **AB303**

1st ed. 1959.

Title of earlier editions varies: 4th ed. called *Directory of institutional photocopying services.* Compiler varies.

Provides information on copying and duplicating services available in 428 United States and 92 non-U.S. libraries. Information (presented in tabular form and showing photoduplication services offered by each library, address, charges, etc.) is based on responses to questionnaires. Geographical arrangement. Z265.N56

Folcarelli, Ralph J., Tannenbaum, Arthur C. and **Ferragamo, Ralph C.** The microform connection: a basic guide for libraries. N.Y., Bowker, 1982. 210p. il. **AB304**

Aims "to present important information that librarians might need when they are confronted with the fact that they must administer a collection, or when they are asked their opinions about starting one."—*Pref.* Includes information on microform software and hardware, selecting and acquiring microforms, organizing and maintaining the collection, etc. Glossary; bibliography; index.

Microforms in libraries: a reader, ed. by Albert James Diaz (Weston, Conn., Microform Review, 1975. 428p.) is a collection of articles on various aspects of microform collections and micropublishing in relation to libraries. Z692.M5F44

Gabriel, Michael. Micrographics, 1900–1977: a bibliography. Mankato, Minnesota, Scholarly Pr., [1978] 266p. (plus index) **AB305**

Aims to bring together "all known English references to monographic, periodical, and technical report literature for the years 1900–1977."—*Introd.* Citations are grouped in categories such as "Microforms and libraries," "Cataloging and classification," "Computer-output-microform (COM) in libraries," "Business micrographs," "Microphotography," "Micrographics equipment," "User studies." Author index. Z265.A1G32

Hawken, William R. Copying methods manual. Chicago, Amer. Lib. Assoc., [1966]. 375p. il. **AB306**

Describes and discusses photocopy methods, techniques, and problems in four main sections: (1) Factors affecting the characteristics of copies; (2) Physical characteristics of research materials; (3) Processes; and (4) Methods and techniques. Indexed. Z48.H32

International micrographics source book. 1980/81– . New Rochelle, N.Y., Microfilm Pub. Co., [1980]– . Biennial. **AB307**

Continues *International microfilm source book* (1976/77–78/79).

A directory to sources, services and associations in the field of micrographics. Includes an index to products and an index to sources, guides to micrographic dealers and consultants, microfilm and COM service bureaus, micropublishers, and associations. Also features a calendar and a bibliography in each issue. TR835.I53

Kish, Joseph L. Micrographics: a user's manual. N.Y., Wiley, [1980]. 196p. il. **AB308**

A work for the office manager as well as for the information systems technician, written in non-specialist language, and aiming to provide "a clear, concise, understanding of micrographics and an appreciation of how this technology can be used . . . to reduce operating costs while improving information creation, dissemination, storage, and retrieval."—*Pref.* Glossary; index. Z265.K53

LaHood, Charles George and **Sullivan, Robert C.** Reprographic services in libraries: organization and administration. Chicago, Library Technology Program, Amer. Lib. Assoc., 1975. 74p. (LTP pubns., no.19) **AB309**

Intends to provide guidelines "for those libraries attempting to establish reprographic services departments for the first time, and specifically for the personnel responsible for organizing, managing, or administering these departments."—*Pref.* Emphasis is on "planning, organization, and administration . . . , rather than on technical processes or laboratory procedures." Z681.L34

The micrographics index. 1974– . Silver Spring, Md., Nat. Micrographics Assoc., 1974– . Irregular. **AB310**

An index to the collection of books, journal articles, manuscripts, and pamphlets at the NMA Resource Center of the National Micrographics Association. The 1977 index (406p.) combines the entries from the original 1974 volume and its 1976 supplement with new materials added to the collection for a total of 2,227 entries. Register format with indexes of journals, keywords, authors, and subjects. TR835.M499

National Micrographics Association. Glossary of micrographics. Silver Spring, Md., The Association, [1980]. 33p. **AB311**

A rev. ed. of the work of the same title issued under the Association's earlier name, National Microfilm Association (5th ed. 1971).

Aims "to standardize the use of and meaning of terms associated with micrographics and to provide an accurate, understandable guide for both the beginner and expert."—*Foreword.* TR835.N28

Veaner, Allen B. The evaluation of micropublications; a handbook for librarians. Chicago, Lib. Technology Program, Amer. Lib. Assoc., [1971]. 59p. (LTP publ. no.17) **AB312**

A straightforward review of technical aspects of micropublications—format, film types, generations, polarity, photoreproduction, etc.—is followed by a step-by-step procedure of evaluation, both bibliographic and physical. Includes a useful checklist of considerations to be applied to micropublications, which is used as a guide for contributors to *Microform review* (AA64). Bibliography. Z265.V4

A C

Encyclopedias

❖A good encyclopedia, or collection of encyclopedias, forms the backbone of much of the reference work in any library. Such books should be selected with care and used intelligently, with full understanding on the part of reference librarians of the relative merits and defects of the different works. The making of an authoritative encyclopedia is a very expensive undertaking, calling for heavy outlay for experienced writers, good editorial planning and oversight, and accurate printing and proofreading. Such work cannot be done cheaply, and reputable publishers recognize this fact and spend what is necessary to produce an authoritative, well-edited work. However, inferior publications of questionable authority often appear on the market and prospective purchasers should learn to discriminate between good and poor quality encyclopedias, and to weigh their individual needs and requirements before making a choice.

Continuous revision. Most of the good, general encyclopedias, including the juvenile encyclopedias, are now following the "continuous revision" policy, which means that instead of publishing thoroughly revised numbered editions at spaced intervals, editorial staffs are kept constantly at work surveying subjects and planning revision, so that with each annual printing changes are made to bring some articles up to date. Many of the encyclopedias try to revise all articles in a given subject field at the same time, but in some cases topics may be changed in one part of the work and left unchanged in others. Even with careful editing this method results in inconsistencies and some unevenness, as the editors themselves admit. A large portion of the material is stable and may be left untouched for several years; other parts are revised as deemed necessary, frequently in rotation over a period of years. Some subjects are changed with almost every printing, dates and statistics are altered frequently, and new facts and developments added. Sometimes whole articles are entirely rewritten, either by the original contributor or by someone else; material may be cut from one part of an article to make room to insert something new in another part; and in some cases short articles may be omitted entirely. In some years a greater amount of revision may be made than in others.

Purchasing an encyclopedia. An encyclopedia should never be purchased without a full knowledge of its character and an examination of the work itself. If the librarian does not have the requisite knowledge or the opportunity to make a careful comparison, purchase should be deferred until the book has been examined and reviewed by experts.

Over the years the "Reference books bulletin" (AA502) and its predecessor publications have provided helpful reviews of new encyclopedias and reevaluations of established sets (the latter at about five-year intervals), together with general surveys of currently available encyclopedias. For example, "Encyclopedias: a survey and buying guide," a 5-part article prepared by the American Library Association's Reference and Subscription Books Review Committee, appeared in *Booklist* 75:632–41, 708–15, 767–72, 830–33, 882–91 (Dec. 1, 1978–Feb. 1, 1979). Following a discussion of suggested criteria for evaluating an encyclopedia, the article offers a survey of 20 general encyclopedias; it has been reprinted in the 1978/79 cumulation of *Reference and subscription books reviews* (p.152–89) under the title "Purchasing an encyclopedia: 12 points to consider" and also as a separate pamphlet using the latter title (Chicago, Amer. Lib. Assoc., 1979. 38p.). The same committee's "Six multi-volume adult encyclopedias" in *Booklist* 79:515–32 (Dec. 1, 1982) provides assessments of the *Academic American, Collier's,* the *Americana, Funk & Wagnalls,* the *Britannica,* and *World book.* Beginning with the Dec. 15, 1984 issue of the "Reference books bulletin," the Reference Books Bulletin Editorial Board provides an annual feature on encyclopedias as an update to its general surveys and quinquennial reevaluations. Many of the annotations for English and American encyclopedias listed below reflect the opinions expressed in those reviews and surveys.

Kister's *Encyclopedia buying guide* (AC11) also offers useful evaluations for both the librarian and the general public. In addition, it provides an overview of encyclopedia publishing, information on sales methods, comparison shopping, and an "Encyclopedia evaluation checklist."

For encyclopedias using continuous revision, librarians will need to develop a buying policy and to decide on how often sets should be replaced. It is frequently better to depend on current publications and yearbooks for recent information and events and to use encyclopedias for the articles of basic and lasting importance.

If a library cannot afford the latest edition of a good expensive encyclopedia, it is better to buy a secondhand copy of a recent printing of a thoroughly good work than a cheap new encyclopedia of the hack-work or purely commercial type. An encyclopedia that was once good is never entirely superseded, and this fact should be taken into account if the publisher of a new work or a new edition offers a discount on the new edition for the return of the old. The small library may be justified in giving up its old edition, but the large library which does much reference work should keep one copy of each of such older works. These are useful in supplying: (1) information as to the condition or view of a given subject, art, or science at the date when the book was compiled, and (2) minor biographical and other articles omitted from the later edition to make space for new material.

Testing an encyclopedia. Read the preface carefully to ascertain the purpose and scope of the encyclopedia. What do the editors intend to do? For whom is the work prepared? For children? If designed for schools or colleges, are the contents geared to curriculum needs and to the indicated age levels? What is the scope? How were the topics to be treated chosen? How much revision is noted?

Having read the preface, check the volumes to see how well the promises have been carried out. If the set is a new work, compare it with other works of the same general size and type. If it is a revised edition, compare it with the preceding edition and sometimes with even earlier editions to test the amount and kind of revision. Check certain sections in each, comparing articles for changes in wording, dates, omissions, additions, etc. Is the article signed by the same writer as in the previous editions or has it been written by another? Have the bibliographies been revised and new titles added? Read articles on subjects with which you are familiar and check them for accuracy, adequacy, and up-to-dateness.

In general, test the work for authority, bibliographies, arrangement, and physical make-up as follows:

I. Authority
  A. Editor—is he capable and experienced and has he really edited the book himself or merely allowed the use of his name?
  B. Contributors—are the articles signed? Are the writers outstanding in their fields?
  C. Publisher—is the firm well known, reputable, and experienced?
  D. Plan—is there a definite plan followed consistently throughout and showing editorial supervision?
    1. Are articles full and adequate or too brief?
    2. Do the articles show balance in selection and treatment? Longer articles for important subjects, briefer ones for less important topics?
    3. Does the work maintain a high standard throughout?
  E. Accuracy and up-to-dateness
    1. Is it an entirely new work?
    2. Is it based on an earlier work?
      a) Has it been completely revised and reset?
      b) Does it use the continuous revision policy?
      c) Have old plates been used with only slight alterations?
      d) Has revision been made consistently throughout?
    3. Are articles dated?

      a) Is information dated for such frequently changing figures as population, statistics, election figures, crop reports, wages, etc.?
      b) Are maps dated?
  F. Viewpoint—does it show signs of national, political, religious, or other point of view which influences the slant or shows bias or prejudice?
II. Bibliographies
  A. Purpose
    1. Are they to serve as sources for the authority of the article and for additional information?
    2. Are they reading lists on given subjects?
  B. Arrangement
    1. Are they appended to the articles?
    2. Are they grouped together in a single volume?
  C. Adequacy
    1. Is the bibliographical information adequate and given in good form? (Minimum requirements: author's name, with initials, title, place, date.)
    2. Are titles of recent date included?
    3. If it is a revised work, have the bibliographies been revised and new works added?
    4. Are they arranged so as to be easily usable?
    5. Are books in foreign languages included?
III. Arrangement
  A. Alphabetical
    1. Are there long articles covering large fields or many short articles on small subjects?
    2. Is the arrangement "letter by letter" or "word by word"?
    3. Is there a comprehensive index which leads to small subjects within long articles?
  B. Topical
    1. Are there tables of contents showing the arrangement?
    2. Is there an alphabetical index?
IV. Format and physical make-up
  A. General appearance
    1. Paper, typography
      a) Is the paper of good quality? Will it withstand heavy usage?
      b) Is the typography clear, of good size, and well spaced?
      c) Are the headings clear, simple, and easy to use?
    2. Illustrations, plates, diagrams, maps, etc.
      a) Are these of good quality and well reproduced?
      b) Do they amplify and explain points in the articles they accompany or are they merely used to add to the general attractiveness of the book? Are they adjacent to the text they illustrate?
    3. Binding
      a) Is it substantial and suited for hard wear?
      b) Are the volumes numbered clearly on the spines?
      c) If arrangement is alphabetical, is there clear indication of coverage on the spines, i.e., are there sufficient letters given so that it is obvious where one volume ends and the next begins?
      d) If arrangement is topical, are contents noted on spines?
  B. Special features
    1. Does the set include supplementary lists or appendixes?
    2. Are there errata lists?

3. Does it include special lists of abbreviations used?

4. Does it indicate pronunciation?

5. How are cross references given?

   a) In the body of the work?

   b) In the index?

   c) Are they accurate and usable or are there "blind" references?

V. Method of keeping the work up to date

  A. Supplements

    1. If there are supplements, how often are they issued?

    2. Are they arranged in the same manner as the basic set?

    3. Are articles in the basic set brought up to date in the supplement?

    4. Are there cross references to the main work?

    5. Do the new articles maintain the standard of the original?

  B. Annuals

    1. Is the standard of authority maintained? Are articles signed?

    2. Is there any connection maintained with the basic work, by means of cross references or other device?

    3. How promptly are volumes issued?

    4. Does the date given in the title refer to the year covered or the year published?

    5. Is there any cumulated index to preceding volumes?

AMERICAN AND ENGLISH

(The *Britannica* excepted, encyclopedias using the continuous revision policy are entered without dates.)

Academic American encyclopedia. Princeton, N.J., Aretê Publ. Co. 21v. il.   **AC1**

First published in 1980, this is a relatively new work intended "for students in junior high school, high school, or college and for the inquisitive adult."—*Pref.* Coverage is meant to be comprehensive throughout the various fields of knowledge and international in viewpoint. Articles average about 500 words or less. "The list of entries (and their lengths) reflects the curriculum of American schools and universities," although treatment of individual topics is by no means meant to be exhaustive; the work falls somewhere between the *World book* and the *Britannica* in scope and depth of treatment. According to the preface, about 90 percent of the articles were contributed by scholars not part of the encyclopedia staff; 75 percent of the articles are signed; and 35 percent are biographical entries (although those articles constitute a much smaller percentage of the total text; living persons are included). Bibliographies of English-language books accompany many of the articles, emphasis here being on recent and in-print materials within the understanding of the intended audience. *See* and *see also* references are employed, together with the use of small capitals within articles to signal related articles. Pronunciation is indicated for difficult personal and place names and for foreign words used as article headings. Uses a 2-column page with numerous illustrations (mainly in color), maps, charts, and tables inset in the article or placed in close proximity thereto. v.21 is an index of some 250,000 entries; illustrations and map locations are included in the index references. Continuous revision policy.

Although its earlier reviews had expressed a need for more *see also* references and greater consistency in cross-referencing, together with a concern about uneven writing (e.g., failure to explain or define various terms and concepts), A.L.A.'s Reference Books Bulletin Editorial Board in its "1984 annual encyclopedia roundup" (*Booklist* 81:566, Dec. 15, 1984) concludes that the *Academic*

American "continues to present a broad spectrum of up-to-date information that adults and high school students need—and presents it accurately, objectively and concisely."

The full text of the encyclopedia has been made available for online computer searching through commercial vendors, and a report of an 8-month analysis of that service appears in the "Reference books bulletin" section of *Booklist* 80:1164–68 (Apr. 15, 1984). It states that "In many library situations, the online version will probably not be necessary alternatives to the current printed edition. However, in libraries and homes where the *AAE* is frequently used for ready-reference purposes, the semiannual update feature of the online version is a useful supplement to an older print version."

Grolier academic encyclopedia is the title used for marketing this work outside the United States and Canada.   AE5.A23●

Encyclopedia Americana. N.Y., Chicago, Encyclopedia Americana. 30v. il.   **AC2**

History: 1st ed. 1903–1904, 16v. unpaged; several partial revisions, especially an edition in 22v., published 1912 under the title *The Americana,* which included some new articles and changes in others. The 1918–20 edition was a complete revision, reset throughout, with much new material; it is the basis of succeeding editions. Now uses the continuous revision policy (*see* p.132).

A good, comprehensive encyclopedia for general use. Important articles are signed with full name and title of the contributor; some have bibliographies. Illustrations are numerous, maps are included with articles, and references to them are included in the index. Alphabeting is word by word. Pronunciation is frequently indicated. For the most part, articles are short, and on very specific subjects, but many articles of some length and on broad topics are included.

The *Americana* has always been particularly strong in its information about American towns and cities; and there is an abundance of biographical sketches (including numerous ones of living persons). Other special features are the evaluations of particular books, operas, musical compositions, works of art, etc.

Since 1943 the index volume (v.30) has been an alphabetical index arranged in dictionary form, instead of the classed index of previous editions. It is kept to date with each printing and should always be consulted in order that pertinent material treated in various parts of the work will not be overlooked.

In its "1984 annual encyclopedia roundup" (*Booklist* 81:570, Dec. 15, 1984) ALA's Reference Books Bulletin Editorial Board reaffirmed its earlier assessment that the *Americana* is "Highly recommended for homes and libraries, for all readers from upper elementary grades upwards and for any readership which needs an up-to-date, general purpose, high-quality American encyclopedia."
  AE5.E333

Encyclopaedia Britannica. A new survey of universal knowledge. 1st–14th eds. Chicago [etc.], Encyclopaedia Britannica, 1768–1973.   **AC3**

History: 1st ed. 1768–71. 3v.; 9th ed. 1875–89. 25v.; 10th ed., a supplement to the 9th ed., with a combined index to the main work and the supplement, 1902–1903. 10v.; 11th ed. 1911. 29v.; 12th ed. 1922. 3v. and 13th ed. 1926. 3v., not revisions of the whole work but supplements to the 11th ed.; 14th ed. 1929. 24v. From 1929, used the continuous revision policy (*see* p.132), and did not number editions. For the 15th ed. *see* below.

The most famous encyclopedia in English, and for some purposes the best. Until modified in the 20th-century editions, it differed from most European and American encyclopedias in its fundamental plan, which called for a collection of important monographs on large subjects by specialists, often very scholarly and of lasting importance, with good bibliographies, excellent illustrations, but no separate treatment of small topics and no biographical sketches of living persons. Narrow or very specific topics were treated only as parts of broader subjects and could be found only through the index. This plan, which was seen most typically in the 9th ed., was modified somewhat in the supplementary 10th ed. and still more, to meet modern demands, in the 11th ed. With the 14th ed. the traditional monographic policy was largely abandoned in favor of shorter articles under more specific headings.

Although the library fortunate enough to have sets of all editions of the *Britannica* will still make occasional use of the early editions for older subjects or points of view, biographies, etc., the 1st–8th eds. are now mainly of only historical interest. The 9th and 11th eds. and their supplements, however, still will be used. The 9th ed., under the able editorship of William Robertson Smith, was the high watermark of the *Britannica,* and its scholarly articles may be used profitably for subjects where recent information is not essential. The 11th ed., although more popular in style than the great 9th, is scholarly and carefully edited, and should still keep its place on the shelves of the reference room.

Recent editions: The 14th ed., first published in 1929, was revised, reset, and reorganized to include short articles on small subjects as well as many long articles. Some of the latter have been carried over from the 9th and 11th eds., sometimes revised and abridged but still carrying the signature of the original author. Although now essentially an American work, the set still reflects traces of its British origins, e.g., in spelling, in some headings, and in the relative length of treatment of many British topics. As noted above, the continuous revision policy was followed from 1929, and editions were not numbered until publication of the new 15th ed. (below).

A useful and generally well-made encyclopedia, with long, detailed articles on many subjects. Articles are signed with initials, the list of contributors being given in the index volume. Alphabeting is letter by letter; pronunciation is not indicated. Maps are included in the index volume, with a separate index. Bibliographies appended to some articles include titles in various languages, and give place of publication and date. Frequently, even if the article has been rewritten, the bibliographies have not been brought up to date. In recent years the tendency has been to shorten the bibliographies and to omit scholarly works in favor of those easily available. v.24 includes a comprehensive, detailed index which must always be used in order that all pertinent material may be found.

Because the 15th ed., appearing under the title *The new Encyclopaedia Britannica,* represents a radical departure from its predecessors in makeup and treatment, it is considered in a separate entry in this guide (*see* below). Most libraries having a relatively recent printing of the 14th ed. will probably want to keep that set on the reference shelves along with the new edition for some years to come.

AE5.E363

The new Encyclopaedia Britannica. 15th ed. Chicago, Encyclopaedia Britannica. 30v. il. **AC4**

Contents: Propaedia (Outline of knowledge), 1v.; Micropaedia (Ready reference and index), 10v.; Macropaedia (Knowledge in depth), 19v. (The Micropaedia and Macropaedia are numbered by the publisher as v.1–10 and v.1–19 respectively.)

Reduced to its simplest terms, the changed structure of this edition which first appeared in 1974 means that the long, monographic articles of the type which distinguished the 11th ed. have been brought together in the *Macropaedia,* while brief factual information best imparted through the more fragmented, direct-entry approach of the 14th ed. is presented in the *Micropaedia.* Until the 1985 printing, the conventional index was dispensed with, and the index function incorporated into the *Micropaedia.* (For a note on the 1985 revision with index, *see* below; the following remarks relate mainly to the set as issued through 1984 without index.)

The 10-volume *Micropaedia,* then, was intended as both the index to the *Macropaedia* and an independent ready reference source offering some 102,200 articles ranging from a few lines up to 750 words in length. The 19-volume *Macropaedia* comprises about 4,200 "in depth" articles, none of which is less than 1,000 words in length. These are signed articles by a world-wide roster of authorities, and include selective, briefly annotated bibliographies.

Topics in the *Micropaedia* which are given fuller treatment under an identical heading in the *Macropaedia* are signalled by a volume and page reference immediately following the bold-face entry; references to related articles in the *Macropaedia* are supplied at the end of many entries in the *Micropaedia,* and cross references are used freely throughout the 10-volume set. Users of the work should begin always with the *Micropaedia* entries: salient facts and dates presented there may suffice, but more importantly, time will usually be saved because topical headings in the *Macropaedia* show considerable variation from those of the 14th ed. and the direct-entry approach of many other encyclopedias. And, while biographies abound in the *Micropaedia,* relatively few figures have been accorded the fuller treatment of the *Macropaedia.* In general, biographical

coverage is uneven; there is very selective inclusion of living persons.

Most articles are newly written (those in the *Macropaedia* are usually by a scholar other than the contributor of the corresponding article in the 14th ed.); maps are scattered throughout the set rather than collected in an atlas section; professional jargon has been eliminated as far as possible; and the language and style are such that "at least some portion of the article should be readable to the layman to whom, at a minimum, the significance and general bearings of the subject must be made comprehensible." However, this is truly an adult encyclopedia with much of the material at the college level.

The *Propaedia* (a single volume, unnumbered in the set) resulted from an attempt by the editors to construct a "workable and defensible" outline of human knowledge which would "set forth in some orderly way the major topical rubrics that must ultimately be dealt with in a general encyclopedia." Its disciplinary overviews can be useful to the beginner in a given subject field, and its references to the *Macropaedia* can serve as a guide for independent study. A "Library guide" first issued in 1981 as a separate purchase was intended to compensate in part for lack of an index.

Updating continues to be effected through the yearbook (AC15), and a continuous revision policy, but the extent of the latter has been disappointingly slight to date, with the *Micropaedia* being generally more up-to-date than the *Macropedia.*

An extensive review by ALA's Reference and Subscription Books Review Committee appears in *The booklist* 71:1021–28 (June 1, 1975). A re-appraisal in *Booklist* 79:524–28 (Dec. 1, 1982) points out that "In many cases, the indexing/cross-referencing system in the Micropaedia has not been adequately executed"; that "the quality of some of the Micropaedia references is questionable"; and that "the arrangement of *NEB* will discourage some users from finding all of the information provided on topics and/or possibly prevent others from finding *any* information." Widespread dissatisfaction with the arrangement, and often-voiced lament over lack of a conventional index has persuaded the publisher to correct the latter fault.

The 1985 *New Encyclopaedia Britannica* may be said to constitute a "revised 15th edition," with the following contents: v.1–12, Micropaedia (Ready reference); v.13–29, Macropaedia (Knowledge in depth); [v.30] Propaedia (Outline of knowledge and Guide to the Britannica); [v.31–32] Index [to v.1–29]. Thus, the *Micropaedia* has been expanded from 10 to 12 volumes; the *Macropaedia* reduced from 19 to 17, with the number of articles in the latter cut to 681. Some articles in the *Micropaedia* now exceed the previous limit of 750 words. The most significant change, however, is the inclusion of a 2-volume index of about 400,000 references, the publisher conceding in the prefatory matter that the *Britannica* "is so vast a work that it cannot be used to greatest advantage without first consulting the INDEX." Indexing is to volume number and quarter of the page; illustrations are noted; and there are cross references from variant forms and spellings. Index rules and abbreviations are given at the front of each index volume; reminders concerning various conventions observed in the index appear at the bottom of each page and as italic inserts scattered through the index columns.

While the re-instatement of a conventional index is a tremendous improvement, the other changes in this latest revision have yet to be fully assessed. Still and all, the *Britannica* remains the most scholarly English-language encyclopedia available. AE5.E363

Chambers's Encyclopaedia. New rev. ed. Oxford and New York, Pergamon, [1967]. 15v. il. **AC5**

History: 1st ed., ed. by Andrew Findlater, 1850–68; new ed., recast by David Patrick, 1888–92; 1923–27 rev. and reset; new ed. 1950. A "new rev. ed.," 1973, shows limited revisions.

A new edition of this well-known British encyclopedia with a new format, new selection of articles, and a reapportionment of space was published in 1950. Later editions are revisions of this, with very limited changes, and the whole is now much in need of reworking. The work "addresses itself to the educated layman who has some general grounding in a variety of subjects from which he can proceed to more exact and detailed information in a special field."—*Pref.*

Includes many short articles on small or very specific topics. Most articles are signed with initials. Contributors include outstanding scholars, primarily British. Population figures are dated; illustrations are good but not distinguished; pronunciation is not indicated. Not all articles have bibliographies, but when given they usually include the standard works on the topic as well as recent publications.

v.15, Maps and indexes, includes: maps by John Bartholomew and Sons, with a section of historical maps; an index to the maps which gives very brief gazetteer information; a list of contributors with titles of principal articles contributed by each; a classified list of articles; and a general subject index to the whole work with many cross references. AE5.C443

Collier's Encyclopedia. N.Y., Collier. 24v. il., maps. **AC6**

1st ed. 1949–51. 20v.

v.24, Bibliography and index.

Uses the continuous revision policy (*see* p.132).

A usable, readable encyclopedia for the student and layman. Aimed at the high school and junior college level; is more advanced than the juvenile encyclopedias in its treatment and choice of subjects, but its coverage is not so great and information is not usually so detailed as in the *Britannica* (AC3) or the *Americana* (AC2). However, there has been somewhat greater emphasis on scholarly quality over the years. The style is popular, clear, and concise. Many articles are long and well developed, others are short under very specific headings, but broad entries predominate. A high percentage of articles is signed with full names of contributors. Alphabeting is letter by letter. Pronunciation is indicated by the international phonetic alphabet. Illustrations, both in color and black-and-white, are pertinent and well reproduced; maps are prepared by Rand McNally.

Bibliographies are not given at the ends of articles but are grouped together in the last volume, where they serve as reading lists in the various subject fields; they are updated at regular intervals. Arranged under broad subjects with subdivisions. Insofar as possible, within each subdivision, general and elementary subjects are treated first, followed by more advanced and specialized works. Titles, starting at high school level and progressing through college level and beyond, are selected with a view to their availability, and therefore most are of a recent date; all are in the English language. In recent printings, lists of "Further readings" have been appended to some articles, especially those of very current interest.

The consolidated index indexes text, illustrations, maps, and bibliography.

In its "1984 annual encyclopedia roundup" ALA's Reference Books Bulletin Editorial Board enumerates *Collier's* strengths as "a readable and authoritative text geared to nonspecialists, a high level of excellence for accuracy and objectivity, relatively up-to-date coverage of topics (although improvement here is always possible), an excellent Index with more than 400,000 entries (particularly necessary because of the number of omnibus articles), and an attractive, readable format." AE5.C683

Funk & Wagnalls new encyclopedia. Joseph Laffan Morse, ed. in chief. N.Y., Funk & Wagnalls. 27v. il., maps. **AC7**

Editions prior to 1971 had title: *The new Funk & Wagnalls encyclopedia.*

A general encyclopedia for junior high school through adult audiences, designed to be sold in supermarkets throughout the United States and Canada. Kept up to date by a continuous revision policy. Articles range from a few lines of brief identification to several pages; some articles are signed. Index in v.26–27; classified bibliography in v.27.

The 1984 re-assessment in "Reference books bulletin" (*Booklist* 81:570, Dec. 15, 1984) terms the set "a good, straightforward provider of facts on people, places, and things" and, while not as scholarly or detailed as various larger works, "offers excellent value for its price." A useful, inexpensive choice for the home library. AE5.F83

Lincoln library of essential information. Buffalo, N.Y., Frontier Pr. il. **AC8**

First published 1924 and selectively updated from printing to printing, some editions issued in more than one volume.

A serviceable compendium of factual information topically rather than alphabetically presented. Numerous graphs, charts, and tables;

alphabetical index. With the 39th ed. (1978) the title was changed to *The new Lincoln library encyclopedia* and the work was issued in 3v.; it has now reverted to the original title, and the 1985 printing [43d ed.] appears in 2v. Unfortunately, updating has often been minimal and currency of information not a strong point. AG105.L55

The new Columbia encyclopedia. Ed. by William H. Harris and Judith S. Levey. 4th ed. N.Y., Columbia Univ. Pr., 1975. 3052p. il., maps. **AC9**

Eds.1–3 (1935–63) had title: *The Columbia encyclopedia.*

A compact, reputable work for home, office, or library. This is a fully revised and updated edition of some 50,000 articles; maps and line drawings are now interspersed with the text; and the work was computer set, allowing presentation of more information per page. Strong in place names and biography, it follows the tradition of earlier editions as a work of ready reference, offering articles "on the arts and literature, geography, the life and physical sciences, and the social sciences."—*Pref.* As far as possible, information was current as of the end of 1974; population figures were the most recent available at time of writing; and "coverage of Africa, Asia, and South America has been greatly expanded. In keeping with the increased knowledge and sophistication of readers, the science entries in this edition include more advanced and detailed technical information than those in previous editions." All articles in the 3d ed. were reviewed and revised or replaced as necessary. Cross references are generously provided; pronunciation is indicated for unfamiliar or difficult names and terms; brief, selected bibliographies appear at the end of many articles. The volume remains an excellent reference source for quick reference.

The concise Columbia encyclopedia, edited by Judith S. Levey and Agnes Greenhall (N.Y., Columbia Univ. Pr., 1983. 943p.), a work of about 15,000 entries, is based on the *New Columbia encyclopedia,* but includes much updated information as well as condensed or rewritten material from the larger work. The concise version is also available as *The concise Columbia encyclopedia in large print* (N.Y., Columbia Univ. Pr., 1984. 8v.). AG5.C725

The Random House encyclopedia. James Michell, ed. in chief. New rev. ed. N.Y., Random House, [1983]. 2918p. il., maps. **AC10**

1st ed. 1977.

A single-volume work, planned as a family encyclopedia and with no one particular level of readership in mind. In two main sections: (1) Colorpedia and (2) Alphapedia. "The function of the *Colorpedia* section is to provide general knowledge [i.e., through lengthy articles with color illustrations on topics arranged in sections on the universe, the earth, life on earth, man, history and culture, man and science, man and machines]; the function of the *Alphapedia* section is to provide brief answers to factual questions [i.e., through concise entries on very specific topics, alphabetically arranged]."—*p.12.* Cross references are provided from the "Alphapedia" to the longer articles in the other section, and "every important person, place, or thing mentioned on a *Colorpedia* page has an *Alphapedia* entry." Articles are unsigned, but each "Colorpedia" section has an introduction by an outstanding scholar, and there is a list of major contributors and consultants. Bibliography p.2759–68; atlas section p.2780–2918.

The Reference Books Bulletin Editorial Board withheld recommendation of the new edition because the editors failed to revise the page numbers of the atlas index, thus rendering that feature of the encyclopedia fairly useless (*Booklist,* July 1984, p.1536). The publisher has since issued an errata slip advising the user to "add 62 to the page number given" in order to obtain the correct page reference in the atlas section. AG5.R25

Guides

Encyclopedia buying guide, 1975/76– . N.Y., Bowker, 1976– . Irregular. **AC11**

Kenneth F. Kister, ed.

Subtitle: A consumer guide to general encyclopedias in print.

Serves as a continuation of Walsh's *General encyclopedias in print* (1963–74). The 3d ed. (1981) "reviews all general English-language encyclopedias published or distributed in the United States and

Canada as of early 1981."—*Pref.* Compares and evaluates at some length 36 in-print encyclopedias; includes both adult and children's encyclopedias in both multi-volume and single-volume format. An appendix provides information on discontinued sets.

Z1035.W267

Bibliography

Walsh, James Patrick. Anglo-American general encyclopedias; a historical bibliography, 1703–1967, by S. Padraig Walsh. N.Y., Bowker, 1968. 270p.   **AC12**

More than 400 English-language general encyclopedias are included, with notes on the publishing history of each and indication of relationships to earlier or later sets. Evaluative statements are given for most titles; *Subscription books bulletin* reviews are cited as applicable. There is an index of originators, compilers, editors, etc.; a chronology; and a general bibliography, but not the full bibliographical detail and footnote references to be expected in a work of this kind.   Z5849.E5W3

Encyclopedia annuals

❖For a recent survey *see* the article "Encyclopedia annuals, supplements, and yearbooks: a 1985 overview" in the "Reference books bulletin" section of *Booklist* 82:36–43 (Sept. 1, 1985).

Americana annual, an encyclopedia of events, 1923– . N.Y., Americana Corp., 1923– . v.1– . il.   **AC13**

The date in the title is the date of publication; the record of events is for the previous year. Serves both as an annual supplement to the *Encyclopedia Americana* (AC2) and as an annual record of progress and events. Contains many biographies and has a necrology list at the end of each volume (position varies). Survey articles are signed with full names and titles of contributors.   AE5.A55

Appleton's Annual cyclopaedia and register of important events . . . v.[1]–15, 1861–75; v.16–35 (n.s., v.1–20), 1876–95; v.36–42 (3d ser., v.1–7), 1896–1902. N.Y., Appleton, 1862–1903. 42v. il.   **AC14**

Index for 1861–75 (v.1–15), 1876. 442p.; Index for 1876–87 (v.16–28; n.s., v.1–12), 1888. 144p. Other indexes included in the set are: Index to n.s., v.1–20, 1876–95, in n.s. v.20, p.769–866; Index to 3d ser. v.1–7, 1896–1902, in 3d ser. v.7, p.845–66.

Published as an annual supplement to the *American cyclopaedia.* Of little use now as a supplement, but still useful for: (1) record of the events of a given year, especially the political, governmental, economic, and military events, which are given with greater detail in this year-by-year record than in later general accounts; volumes covering the Civil War and Reconstruction periods are useful to students of American history; (2) many minor articles, particularly obituaries and biographies, which are either omitted from later encyclopedias or given briefer treatment than in the annual volume for the year when the person was of especial interest.   AE5.A7

Britannica book of the year, 1938– . Chicago, Encyclopaedia Britannica, 1938– . il. Annual.   **AC15**

Annual volumes to serve as yearly surveys and as supplements to the *Encyclopaedia Britannica* (AC3–AC4). The date in the title is the date of publication; the record of events is for the previous year. Includes many signed survey articles as well as short articles under specific headings. Some biography is included. A necrology list is included under "Obituaries."   AE5.E364

New international year book, a compendium of the world's progress, 1907–65. N.Y., Dodd, 1908–31; Funk & Wagnalls, 1932–66. il.   **AC16**

Ceased publication. Subtitle varies slightly.

An authoritative annual intended as a supplement to the *New international encyclopaedia* and as an annual record of the progress and events in any subject during the year prior to publication of the

volume. Plan and arrangement vary. Latest volumes published include signed survey articles and brief biographical sketches. An obituary list is at the back of each volume.   AE5.I64

Year book (Macmillan Educational Company). 1982– . N.Y., Macmillan; London, Collier, [1981]– . Annual. il.   **AC17**

Successor to a publication which began 1939 (covering events of 1938) as *National yearbook;* volumes covering 1941–73 called (with numerous slight variations) *Collier's Yearbook,* then *Year book covering the year . . .* 1974–81 (publ. 1973–80).

Usually referred to as *Collier's Yearbook,* this work serves as a supplement both to *Collier's Encyclopedia* (AC6) and to *Merit students encyclopedia* (AC20), though it is basically an annual survey, alphabetically arranged, without cross references to either set.

Juvenile

Britannica junior, prep. under the supervision of the editors of the Encyclopaedia Britannica. . . . Chicago, Encyclopaedia Britannica. 15v. il.   **AC18**

"Published with the editorial advice of the faculties of the University of Chicago and the University Laboratory Schools."

Planned for elementary and junior high school levels. First published in 1934 as a reissue, with some alterations, of *Weedon's Modern encyclopedia.* Has since been much revised and now uses the continuous revision policy (*see* p.132).

Articles are written as simply as possible on the subjects in which children are most likely to be interested. They are not signed, but a list of contributors is given in v.1, with the titles of the articles for which each is responsible. v.1 is a "Ready reference index" which serves as a full index to the set and also includes brief explanatory or descriptive statements on many topics. Alphabeting is letter by letter. Pronunciation is indicated. Typeface is large and clear; illustrations, in color and in black-and-white, are good but not distinguished. v.15 includes an atlas section with its own index.

AG5.B8

Compton's Pictured encyclopedia and fact-index. Chicago, Compton. 24v. (varies) il.   **AC19**

Subtitle: To inspire ambition, to stimulate the imagination, to provide the inquiring mind with accurate information told in an interesting style, and thus lead into broader fields of knowledge, such is the purpose of this work.

Issued annually since 1922. Uses the continuous revision policy (*see* p.132).

A good juvenile encyclopedia and one of the leading American works in this field. Planned especially for upper elementary and high school use; attempts to keep in close touch with school needs, but is useful for the adult who needs a somewhat simpler article than that given in the standard encyclopedias for adults.

General policy is to use long articles on large subjects, with smaller subjects analyzed or treated in the "Fact-index" (*see* below). Has a clear, direct style and pays especial attention to illustration, charts and maps. Indicates pronunciation of unusual words. Alphabeting is letter by letter. For some of the longer articles reference outlines for organized study are given, and certain articles include brief bibliographies, sometimes divided into lists of books for younger readers and books for advanced students and teachers.

Instead of a general index volume, a "Fact-index" at the end of each volume serves as a guide to all volumes for subjects beginning with the letter or letters covered in that volume. The "Fact-index" is not only an analytical index to all text and illustrative material in the main work, but also includes dictionary-type information, brief biographical sketches, etc., on subjects not treated elsewhere.

Supplemented by the *Compton yearbook: an illustrated factual record of outstanding events.*   AG5.C73

Merit students encyclopedia. [N.Y.], Macmillan Educational Corp. 20v. il.   **AC20**

First published 1967.

Intended for the use of students from the 5th grade through high school. Emphasis is placed on the encyclopedia's "curriculum orientation," with individual articles written to be understood at the grade level at which the subject is taught. Material for younger readers is placed at the beginning of an article and more advanced information incorporated as the article is developed. Signed articles; only the longer ones include a bibliography or suggestions for further reading. Pronunciation is indicated. v.20 includes an index.

The *Yearbook* (AC17) issued by Macmillan Educational Co. serves to update both this set and *Collier's Encyclopedia.*

AE5.M38

The new book of knowledge; the children's encyclopedia. N.Y., Grolier. 21v. il., maps.   **AC21**

First published 1912 under title *The book of knowledge;* printings through 1965 had that title.

Intended to interest a wide range of readers from those in early childhood to students nearly ready to use an adult encyclopedia; thus, articles are written at various levels of understanding, with the main emphasis being for children in grades three to six. Longer articles are signed by contributors or consultants. Suggested activities or projects are incorporated into some articles to further the educational value. Alphabetical arrangement with *see* and *see also* references, plus a "dictionary index" at the back of each volume (i.e., with the index section corresponding to the portion of the alphabet dealt with in that particular volume) providing factual information as well as references to pertinent information in other volumes of the set. This fragmented arrangement of the index is not particularly effective, and a combined index has been added as v.21 of recent editions. Bibliographies do not appear in the main set, but a bibliography keyed to topics in the encyclopedia (and with reading levels indicated) makes up the first part of a paperbound supplement entitled "Home and school reading and study guides." Continuous revision policy.   AG5.B64

World book encyclopedia. . . . Chicago, Field Enterprises Educ. Corp. 22v. (varies) il.   **AC22**

Issued annually. Uses the continuous revision policy (*see* p.132).

A good juvenile encyclopedia, one of the leading American works in the field; approximates the form and treatment of the standard works for adults and so is especially good for the older child who is nearly ready to use adult material.

Alphabeting is word by word. For the most part the work has short articles on narrow topics, although some long articles are also included. Articles are signed. There are many cross references to related subjects. Pronunciation is indicated for unusual names and words. Bibliographies are brief but well chosen, sometimes with short annotations. Illustrations and graphs, in color and black-and-white, are clear and pertinent.

The final volume is now termed a "Research guide/index." It is a general index with some 200 reading and study guides on important topics interspersed through the alphabetical sequence.

Supplemented by the *World book year book, an annual supplement.*

The work has been reproduced as a voice recording (1980) on cassette tapes, with indexes in braille and large type.

A review of the 1983 edition in the "Reference books bulletin" section of *Booklist* 80:791–94 (Feb. 1, 1984) concludes that the encyclopedia "is especially designed to serve the reference needs of students in grades 4–12 and to serve also as a general adult reference source. . . . Recommended to homes and all types of libraries for its eminently accessible and up-to-date, well-illustrated coverage of topics on which a broad spectrum of persons need information."

AE5.W55

FOREIGN LANGUAGE

❖While a good encyclopedia in English must always be the basis of encyclopedia reference work in a library used by English-speaking readers, foreign encyclopedias offer much that cannot be found in English works: the *Enciclopedia italiana* (AC58), for example, far surpasses any other ency-

clopedia in the quality and number of its illustrations and contains some articles superior to anything found elsewhere; *Enciclopedia universal (Espasa)* (AC79) is rich in Spanish and Spanish-American subjects, especially biography; *La grande encyclopédie* (AC37) contains articles on topics in European history and literature not available in the same quality in other encyclopedias, while the various editions of *Larousse* (AC38–AC41) have a wealth of articles on small topics—minor biography, individual works of literature, plays, theaters, and songs—not easily found in other encyclopedias.

In general, library use of such works will be for three main types of questions: (1) to find an article in a foreign language for a reader who does not use English readily; (2) to find a foreign article that is better than the corresponding article in English; or (3) to find something on topics omitted altogether in English encyclopedias—usually topics in biography, topography, history, or literature of the country of origin of the encyclopedia. It is for this third type of question that the foreign encyclopedia is most frequently used in American libraries.

Thus, the user of reference books will often need to make use of the great foreign encyclopedias, but to use them adequately requires a somewhat different technique from that required to use an encyclopedia in English. Theoretically the library assistant should know the language of the encyclopedia, but much can be done with a very slight knowledge of the language if the user has an intelligent "dictionary habit" and will keep certain basic points in mind. Often one does not need to read the article, but merely to find it for a reader who will use it. Without the correct technique, however, one may actually miss an article, even though it is in its proper alphabetical place. Two of the points which the library assistant with a limited knowledge of foreign languages needs to keep in mind are: (1) the alphabet of the language being used, and (2) variations in the forms of names: proper, personal, geographical, etc. The alphabet must be kept in mind because even languages using Latin alphabet have variations in letters which *must be known* if an article is to be found in its correct alphabetical place. In Spanish, for example, there are two-letter sounds not found in English, Ch and Ll, and a word or name beginning Ch follows Cz; in Norwegian the letters Ø and Å come after Z; Czech has 41 letters; and other languages show other variations.

Variations in form of proper names must also be kept in mind, especially when the initial letter is affected. The reference assistant looking for an Italian article on Hannibal, for example, will find it under Anibale; if looking for articles on St. Stephen, one must look under Étienne in a French encyclopedia, Esteban in a Spanish, Stefano in an Italian. When looking for an Italian article on John Adams, one must be prepared to recognize Giovanni Adams; when looking for a medieval personage named John, one must search under John, Jean, Jehan, Johann, Johannes, Jan, Giovanni, or other variations according to the language of the reference work used. Surnames do not show so great a variation, but their alphabetizing must be watched, e.g., in a Swedish encyclopedia the biography of the German writer Görres will alphabetize at the end of the letter G, many pages after Gy, instead of with Go, as it does in German and English. Geographical names, of course, vary in form also: an Italian article on Florence must be looked for under the Italian Firenze. Keeping in mind these points about alphabets and forms of names will help even an inexperienced reference assistant to use foreign encyclopedias intelligently.

A selection of *general* encyclopedias in foreign languages are entered below. For encyclopedias *about* a particular country or with a strong national emphasis, *see* that country under History and Area Studies (p.973).

Brazilian and Portuguese

Enciclopédia Barsa. Elaborado sob a supervisão dos editôres da Encyclopaedia Britannica. William Benton, ed. Rio de Janeiro, Encyclopaedia Britannica Editôres, [1965]. 16v. il., maps.   **AC23**

A general encyclopedia for the student and the general reader. Not a translation or adaptation of the *Encyclopaedia Britannica*, but follows its plan of organization. Some signed articles and bibliographies. v.14 includes an atlas; v.15 is an index; v.16 offers "Planos de estudio" with outlines of major fields of study, bibliographies, and references to relevant articles in the encyclopedia.   AE37.E5

Encyclopedia e diccionario internacional, organizado e redigido com a collaboração de distinctos homens de sciencia e de lettras brasileiros e portuguezes. W. M. Jackson, ed. Lisboa, Rio de Janeiro, [1919]. 20v. il.   **AC24**

A good popular encyclopedia in Portuguese, general in scope but with special emphasis upon Brazilian names and topics. Contains a large amount of Brazilian biography.   AE37.E5

Czech

Masarykův slovník naučný; lidová encyklopedie všeobecných vědomostí. . . . V Praze, Nákl. "Československého Kompasu," 1925–33. 7v. il.   **AC25**

Contains little bibliography but has many biographies, including those of persons still living at time of compilation.   AE51.M3

Ottův slovník naučný. Illustrovaná encyklopaedie obecných vědomostí. V Praze, Otto, 1888–1909. 28v. il.   **AC26**

Contents: v.1–27, A–Z; v.28, Supplement.

The standard Czech encyclopedia. Signed articles, many biographies, some bibliography (including works in many languages). Maps, many folded; town plans; illustrations include plates and line drawings in text.

Supplemented by: AE51.O8

Ottův slovník naučný nové doby; dodatky k velikému Ottovu slovníku naučnému. Redakci vede B. Němec. V Praze, "Novina," 1930–43. 6v. il.   **AC27**

Publisher varies.   AE51.O84

Danish

Hagerups Illustrerede Konversations Leksikon. 4. gennemsete og forøgede Udg. redigeret af P. Engelstoft. København, Hagerup, 1948–53. 10v. il.   **AC28**

1st ed. 1892–1900; 3d ed. 1921–25.

A general encyclopedia with short articles, most of them signed. Little or no bibliography.   AE41.H3

Salmonsens Konversationsleksikon. 2. Udg. København, Schultz, 1915–30. 26v. il.   **AC29**

1st ed. had title: *Salmonsens Store illustrerede Konversationsleksikon.* 1893–1911. 19v.

Contents: v.1–25, A–Ø; v.26, Supplement.

The standard Danish encyclopedia, with signed articles, bibliographies, maps, town plans, and illustrations. Marks pronunciation of proper names.

Supplemented by the *Salmonsen Leksikon Tidsskrift* (København, Schultz, 1941–57. Aarg. 1–15) which was monthly with biennial indexes. (No index for 1956–57; 10-year index, 1941–50, publ. 1951.)   AE41.S2

Dutch

Eerste Nederlandse systematisch ingerichte encyclopaedie . . . Samengesteld onder leiding van H. J. Pos, J. M. Romem [and others]. Amsterdam, E.N.S.I.E., [1946–60]. 12v. il.   **AC30**

A classed encyclopedia, each article written by a specialist. Includes bibliographies.

v.10, Lexicon en register; v.11, Supplement; v.12, Lexicon en register, beknopt overzicht der wereldgeschiedenis in synchronistische tabellen.

v.10 includes, in the same alphabet with the index, much encyclopedic information not covered in the main set: e.g., biographical sketches, gazetteer information about places, definitions of historical terms; v.12 is an index to v.11 (the supplement) and also a lexicon adding new entries and bringing up to date material in v.10. Includes much gazetteer information.   AE19.E3

Grote Winkler Prins encyclopedie in 25 delen. Achtste geheel nieuwe druk. Amsterdam, Elsevier, [1979–84]. 25v. and suppl. il., maps.   **AC31**

Hoofdredactie: Prof. Dr. R. C. van Caenegem [et al.].

1st ed. 1870–82; 5th ed., 1932–38, had title *Winkler Prins' Algemeene encyclopaedie;* 6th ed. 1947–54 called *Winkler Prins Encyclopedie.*

The standard Dutch work, originally based on Brockhaus (*see* AC42), with well-balanced articles, some of them signed; some include bibliographies listing works in various languages. Illustrations and maps are good. Biographies include living persons.

This is a revised and updated edition, completely reset and employing a new format (three columns of text on a somewhat larger page). There are many new articles (although some from the previous edition are omitted) and virtually all of those carried over show at least minor changes. An impressive list of contributors appears in v.1. Bibliographies have been updated but, generally speaking, there appear to be fewer bibliographic references than in the previous edition. Most illustrations are new; they are more numerous, and mainly in color. Greater use is made of charts and diagrams. v.25 includes a general index and a separate index to the maps. The supplementary volume (designated "Encyclopedisch Supplement 1984") is an alphabetical arrangement of new and complementary articles covering the 1976–83 period, plus a necrology.   AE19.W5262

Finnish

Uusi tietosanakirja. Päätoimittaja: Veli Valpola. [4. painos] Helsinki, Tietosanakirja, [1960–66]. 24v. il.   **AC32**

1st ed., 1931–39, had title *Iso tietosanakirja.*

Largest of the Finnish encyclopedias (more than 250,000 entries). A good general work, well printed and with numerous maps and illustrations. Signed articles; includes biographies of living persons. Final volume is an index.

A recent work designed for the home market is *Kodin Suuri tietosanakirja* (Espoo, Weilin & Göös, 1975–80. 15v.).   AE21.I72

French

Encyclopaedia universalis. Paris, Encyclopaedia Universalis France, Editeur, 1968–74. 20v. il.   **AC33**

Contents: v.1–16, A–Z; v.17, Organum; v.18–20, Thesaurus.

A major encyclopedia. v.1–16 make up the encyclopedia proper; v.18–20 are a "Thesaurus" or analytical index which includes many brief biographical sketches and articles entered under very specific terms. v.17, the "Organum," is intended as a kind of summary or overview of human knowledge, and is in two main sections: (1) a series of signed essays on "L'homme et son savoir," and (2) a group of articles (fairly extensive, and including bibliographies) on very specific "Thèmes et problèmes" (e.g., acupuncture; femmes et féminisme; otages); these are followed by "Tableaux de relations" and "Les prévisions et les nombres (années 1960–2000)."

The tendency is to long, comprehensive articles under fairly broad headings, rather than the briefer, more specific entries generally found in recent English-language encyclopedias. Biographical sketches are included for major figures in v.1–16. Articles are signed with the initials of the contributor, bibliographies are appended, and references to related articles are given. Legible typeface; a well-spaced, 3-column format; and numerous illustrations, maps, and charts are among the favorable features of the work. A new edition began publication in 1984.

Kept up to date by: AE25.E3

Universalia, 1974– . Les événements, les hommes, les problèmes en 1973– . Paris, Encylopaedia Universalis, 1974– . Annual. **AC34**

At head of title: Encyclopaedia universalis.

A series of yearbooks supplementing the *Encyclopaedia universalis* (above). Each volume in five sections: (1) La marche du temps (a brief summary of the year's events chronologically presented); (2) Points d'histoire (essays on contemporary events and problems); (3) Thèmes et problèmes (alphabetically arranged articles on events, countries, personalities, and special topics); (4) Vies et portraits (obituary notes on figures who died during the year covered); (5) Statistiques pour l'année (graphs, tables, and explanatory texts).

Encyclopédie, ou Dictionnaire raisonné des sciences, des arts et des métiers, par une société des gens de lettres. Mis en ordre & publié par m. Diderot; & quant à la partie mathématique, par m. d'Alembert. Paris, Briasson, [etc.], 1751–65. 17v. (Repr.: Stuttgart, F. Frommann Verlag, 1969. 35v. incl. suppl. and indexes noted below) **AC35**

——— Supplément à l'Encyclopédie . . . Amsterdam, M. M. Rey, 1776–77. 4v.

——— Recueil de planches, sur les sciences, les arts libéraux, et les arts méchaniques, avec leur explication . . . Paris, Briasson, 1762–72. 11v.

——— Suite du Recueil des planches . . . Paris, Panckoucke, 1777. 22p.

——— Table analytique et raisonnée des matieres contenues dans les XXXIII volumes in-folio du Dictionnaire . . . et dans son supplément . . . Paris, Panckoucke, 1780. 2v.

Published in various editions (e.g., Lausanne & Berne, Sociétés Typographiques, 1780–82. 36v.).

Often cited as *Diderot*.

The famous work by the 18th-century French encyclopedists, with emphasis on the arts, sciences, and mechanical trades, reflecting the philosophical concepts of the time. AE25.E53

Encyclopédie française. . . . Paris, Comité de l'Encyclopédie Française, [1935–66]. 21v. il. Looseleaf. **AC36**

Contents: v.1, L'outillage mental: pensée, langage, mathématique. 1937. Nouv. éd. 1957; v.2, La physique. 1955; v.3, Le ciel et la terre. 1956; v.4, La vie. 1937. Nouv. éd. 1960; v.5, Les êtres vivants. 1937; v.6, L'être humain. 1936–54; v.7, L'espèce humaine. 1936; v.8, La vie mentale. 1938–56; v.9, L'univers économique et social. 1960; v.10, L'état moderne. 1938–56. Nouv. éd. 1964; v.11, La vie internationale: divisions et unité du monde actuel. 1957; v.12. Chimie: science et industries. 1958; v.13, Industrie, agriculture. 1962; v.14, La civilisation quotidienne. 1954; v.15, Éducation et instruction. 1939; v.16–17, Arts et littératures. 1935–36; v.18, La civilisation écrite. 1939; v.19, Philosophie, religion. 1957; v.20, Le monde en devenir (Histoire, évolution, prospective). 1959; v.21, Répertoire général.

A non-alphabetical encyclopedia containing monographic articles grouped by large classes, and with alphabetical index to each volume to serve until the general index was published. Illustrations, though good, are not numerous, and there is comparatively little bibliography. (The announced plan of publication called for a volume of bibliography, which was not published.) The index volume includes a summary outline of the individual volumes, and the following separate indexes: Index alphabétique des collaborateurs; Index alphabétique des noms propres; Index des notions importantes; Index alphabétique géographique.

Some of the first volumes to be published have been replaced by new editions which are, in reality, wholly new volumes, in some cases written from a different viewpoint, e.g., v.10, *L'état moderne.* The 1st ed. of that volume was written in the day of fascism, nazism, etc., and the new edition presents quite a different concept.

AE25.E47

La grande encyclopédie, inventaire raisonné des sciences, des lettres et des arts, par une société de savants et de gens de lettres; sous la direction de Berthelot, Derenbourg, [etc.]. Paris, Lamirault, [1886–1902]. 31v. il. **AC37**

Secrétaire général: v.1–18, F. Camille Dreyfus; v.19–31, André Berthelot.

v.23–31 published by Société Anonyme de La Grande Encyclopédie.

The most important 19th-century French encyclopedia, with authoritative signed articles, excellent bibliographies, and many entries under small subjects. Out-of-date now for sciences, etc., but an excellent authority in many other fields, especially for medieval and Renaissance subjects, and for literature, history, etc., of continental Europe. Very good for French and other continental biographical and gazetteer information. The bibliographies are especially important. Has fewer illustrations and plates than recent English and American encyclopedias. AE25.G72

La grande encyclopédie. Paris, Larousse, [1971–78]. 21v. il. **AC38**

A wholly new work comprising about 8,000 entries with admitted emphasis on technology and technological advances, the physical and social sciences, and political and social economy. Articles are signed with initials of contributors. Many up-to-date bibliographies; numerous illustrations (most of them in color), charts, and tables. v.21 is an index. AE25.G69

——— Supplément. Paris, Larousse, 1981. 673p.

Covers events of 1971–76.

Larousse, Pierre. Grand dictionnaire universel du XIXe siècle. . . . Paris, Larousse, [1865–90?]. 17v. **AC39**

Contents: v.1–15, A–Z; v.16, Suppl. A–Z; v.17, Suppl. A–Z.

A famous encyclopedia, well edited and well written—one of first importance and still useful in many cases. Combines the features of dictionary and encyclopedia, and as an encyclopedia is an extreme example of entry under small subject, including many articles on individual works of literature (e.g., poems, plays, novels, romances, newspapers, periodicals, songs, etc., entered under their titles), and a very large amount of minor biography not included in other general encyclopedias. Gives words and music (melody only) of about 600 songs. Good for questions relating to European literature, biography, and history. AE25.L32

Larousse mensuel illustré, revue encyclopédique universelle, pub. sous la direction de Claude Augé et Paul Augé, 1907–57. Paris, Larousse, 1907–57. v.1–14 and index to v.1–7. il. **AC40**

v.1, 1907–10; v.2–12, 3 years to a volume; v.13, 1952–55; v.14, 1956–57 (v.11, 1938–mai 1940 and v.11, no.400, 1938–47). Ceased publication.

An excellent monthly encyclopedia designed as a supplement to the *Nouveau Larousse illustré* (1898–1907. 8v.). Each monthly number is alphabetical, with a final alphabetical index for each volume; and for v.1–7 (1907–28), a cumulated index in a separate volume. A good source for contemporary French biography, obituaries, portraits, etc. Contains many reviews of plays, novels, and other literary works. The issues for 1914–18 include many articles on World War I; and no.400, 1938–47, entitled *La seconde guerre mondiale* (522p.), includes a chronology and its own index.

AE25.L4

Grand Larousse encyclopédique en dix volumes. Paris, Larousse, [1960–64]. 10v. il. **AC41**

Essentially a new work although based on the series of earlier Larousse encyclopedias. The general plan remains the same, i.e., a dictionary as well as an encyclopedia, articles are brief, and entries specific. Some articles are based on those in older sets, but many are new or rewritten, information is brought up-to-date, and there are new illustrations and plates, which in general are superior to those previously used. Bibliographies, arranged by encyclopedia entry, are grouped at the back of the volume with *see* references at the ends of the appropriate articles; titles are almost entirely in French.

Largely supersedes the *Nouveau Larousse illustré* (1898–1907. 8v.) and the *Larousse du XXe siècle* (1958. 6v.). AE25.G64

―――― Supplément. Paris, Larousse, [1968]. 918, cvi p. il.

Intends to provide information on recent political, social, and cultural events, together with biographical sketches of contemporary figures, many of whom have achieved prominence in recent years or were omitted from the main set. In general, updating does not extend beyond mid-1967, though some 1968 events are recorded. A bibliography of about 100 pages appears at the end of the volume; it is arranged by encyclopedia entry, as in the main set, and includes publications through 1967.

―――― 2e supplément. Paris, Larousse, [1975]. 1v., unpaged.

This supplement covers events, personalities, etc., of the 1968–75 period.

German

Der Grosse Brockhaus. 16. völlig neubearb. Aufl. Wiesbaden, Brockhaus, 1952–63. 14v. il. **AC42**

1st ed. 1796–1808; frequently revised; 15th ed. 1928–35, in 21v. Earlier editions called *Brockhaus' Konversations-Lexikon.*

Contents: v.1–12, A–Z; v.13, Ergänzungsband; v.14, Zweiter Ergänzungsband. (Atlas volume also issued in uniform format; for annotation *see* CL308.)

The most recent complete edition (*see* below for 17th edition) of a standard German encyclopedia, earlier editions of which influenced encyclopedia-making in many countries.

This edition is a revision and complete resetting; it is more condensed, having 12v. instead of 21. Characterized by short articles on very specific subjects; profusely illustrated, including many small illustrations in text. Articles are unsigned, many have bibliographies which are sometimes quite extensive. Illustrations include good maps, black-and-white and colored plates, many portraits, coats of arms of cities, etc. Includes biographies of living persons.

Briefer encyclopedic works issued by the Brockhaus firm include *Der neue Brockhaus* (6. völlig neubearb. Aufl. 1978–80. 6v.; a 7th ed. began to appear 1984) and *Der Brockhaus* (Völlig neu bearb. Aufl. 1984. 2v.). AE27.G67

Brockhaus Enzyklopädie in zwanzig Bänden. 17. völlig neubearb. Aufl. des Grossen Brockhaus. Wiesbaden, Brockhaus, 1966–81. 25v. il. **AC43**

See above for 16th and earlier editions.

Contents: v.1–20, A–Z; v.21, Karten; v.22–23, Ergänzungen; v.24, Bildwörterbuch der deutschen Sprache; v.25, Ergänzungen.

This edition, completely revised and reset, is comparable in coverage to the 15th ed. Character of the work remains the same: predominantly short articles on a wide range of topics; numerous illustrations and maps; inclusion of biographies of living persons, etc. Many short articles are carried over from the 16th ed.; some are augmented; and many new entries have been added. Bibliographies have been revised and emphasize recent publications. Good paper and clear reproduction of illustrations make for good appearance.

AE27.G672

Der Grosse Herder; Nachschlagewerk für Wissen und Leben. 5. neubearb. Aufl. von Herders Konversationslexikon. Freiburg, Herder, 1953–56. 10v. **AC44**

1st ed. 1854–57; 4th ed. 1931–35 in 12v.

Contents: v.1–9, A–Z; v.10, Der Mensch in seiner Welt.

A well-illustrated, well-made general encyclopedia with short articles and little bibliography, written from the Catholic viewpoint.
AE27.H5

―――― Ergänzungsband. 1962. 2v.

Each of these two volumes includes material supplementary to the main work, and has additional sections on *Die Welt in unserer Zeit:* T.1, Natur und Technik; T.2, Geist und Kultur.

Der neue Herder; neu in sechs Bänden mit einem Grossatlas. Freiburg, Herder, [1965–68]. 6v. il. **AC45**

Since this work is in only 6v. (plus atlas), articles are briefer and coverage is less comprehensive than in *Der grosse Herder* (above) on which it is based. Information has been updated, however; new articles have been introduced (e.g., many new biographical notes); and most plates and illustrations are new. Bibliographies are not included at the ends of articles. For the atlas *see* CL310.

AG27.N393

Meyers enzyklopädisches Lexikon ... 9., völlig neu bearb. Aufl. Mit 100 signierten Sonderbeiträgen. Mannheim, Bibliographisches Institut, 1971–81. 29v. il., maps. **AC46**

1st ed. 1840–55.

Contents: Bd.1–25, A–Z; Bd.26, Nachträge; Bd.27, Weltatlas; Bd.28, Personenregister; Bd.29, Bildwörterbuch, Deutsch-Englisch-Französich.

This is the latest edition in a long line of encyclopedias bearing the name of Meyer and originally published in Leipzig. The 1st–8th eds. (1840/55–1936/42) carried the title (with slight variations) *Meyers Konversations-Lexikon.* (The 8th ed. was incomplete, only 9v. having been published, and was strongly influenced by Nazi ideology.) The Meyer firm was liquidated in 1945, and the first post-war "Meyers" appeared as *Meyers neues Lexikon* (1961–64 in 8v., with a 1969 suppl.); a new edition of that title was published 1978–81 (8v. and atlas).

This edition marks a return to the quality and standards of the 6th and 7th eds. of the Meyer encyclopedias. While brief entries still abound, important topics receive very full treatment, and bibliographies are often extensive and generally up-to-date. Maps and charts accompany country articles, and there are thousands of diagrams and illustrations (both in color and in black-and-white), most of them small, but of high quality. Biographical sketches include living persons. Atlas and index volumes are promised, but are optional purchases.

A *Jahrbuch* series began publication 1974 with a "Berichtszeitraum 1973." The 1978 *Jahrbuch* includes a cumulated index 1974–78. AE27.M6

❖Of the older German encyclopedias, these two are outstanding and, in the research library, are frequently useful for topics not treated in modern encyclopedias:

Allgemeine Encyclopädie der Wissenschaften und Künste von genannten Schriftstellern bearb. und hrsg. von J. S. Ersch und J. G. Gruber. Leipzig, Brockhaus, 1818–89. 167v. il. **AC47**

Contents: 1st sec., A–G. 99v.; 2d sec., H–Lig. 43v.; 3d sec., O–Phyx. 25v.

Unfinished. Editors vary, but set is usually referred to as *Ersch und Gruber Encyclopädie.*

A scholarly work particularly useful for biography, bibliography, and geographical information.

Grosses vollständiges Universal-Lexikon aller Wissenschaften und Künste. ... Halle, J. H. Zedler, 1732–50. 64v. ports. **AC48**

One of the great encyclopedias. Particularly useful for biography and bibliography of the 16th and 17th centuries. AE27.G7

―――― Nöthige Supplemente. ... Leipzig, 1751–54. v.1–4.

Contents: v.1–4, A–Caq. No more of the supplement published.

Greek

Megalē hellēnikē enkyklopaideia. Ekdosis 2., enēmerōmenē dia symplērōmatōn. Athēnai, Ekdotikos Organismos "Ho Phoinix," [1959–64?]. 24v. and suppl. v.1–4.   **AC49**

Ed. by Paulos Drandakēs.
1st ed. 1926–34. 24v.
A general encyclopedia in modern Greek. Many articles are of some length and have bibliographies. Illustrations are poor. A supplement in 4v. appeared 1959–63(?), and a complete revision of v.10 (on Greece) was published 1964(?).   AE29.M42

Neōteron enkyklopaidikon lexikon; methodikē kai systēmatikē sympyknōsis kai eklaikeusis holōn tōn andrōpinōn gnōseōn. [2d ed.] Athēnai, Ekdosis tēs Enkyklopaidikēs Epithēōreseōs "Hēlios," [1957–59]. 18v. il.   **AC50**

A general encyclopedia in modern Greek, including many long articles as well as short ones, some of them signed. Includes very little bibliography. The poor quality of the paper results in poor reproduction of illustrations.   AE29.N4

Hebrew

ha-Entsiklopedyah ha-'ivrit. [Encyclopaedia hebraica] [Jerusalem, 1949–81] 32v. il.   **AC51**

Text in Hebrew. A general encyclopedia with articles contributed and signed by outstanding Jewish and non-Jewish scholars. Bibliographies include titles in many languages. Illustrated in black-and-white with occasional color plates.
A supplement (1092 col.) to v.1–16 was publ. 1966.   AE30.E5

Hungarian

Révai nagy lexikona; az ismeretek enciklopédiája. Budapest, Révai Testvérek, 1911–27. 20v.; v.21, 1935. il.   **AC52**

Unsigned articles, the longer ones with bibliographies of some length. Includes biographies of living persons. Illustrations in black-and-white, plus some good color plates; maps. v.19; p.769–863, and v.20–21 are supplements.   AE31.R4

Uj magyar lexikon. [Szerkesztette az Akadémiai Kiadó lexikonszerkesztösége. Szerkesztö bizottság: Berei Andor et al.] Budapest, Akadémiai Kiadó, [1959–72]. 7v.   **AC53**

A relatively new work, in dictionary arrangement, with generally brief articles. Strong in geographical and personal names, the latter including contemporaries. Point of view is stated in the preface as Marxist-Leninist. No bibliographies. Useful for current information, but does not replace older works. v.7 is a supplement.   AE31.U44

Italian

Dizionario enciclopedico italiano. Roma, Istit. della Enciclopedia Italiana, [1955–61]. 12v. il.   **AC54**

An encyclopedic dictionary, giving meanings of words with etymologies and examples of usage, and concise encyclopedic articles. These latter are not signed and have no bibliographies, but include a large number of biographies, characters of fiction, titles of individual works of literature, gazetteer information, detailed discrimination of word meanings, etc. Includes abbreviations. Illustrations are excellent, some in color, and more numerous than in many encyclopedias. Excellent maps.   AE35.D516

Enciclopedia. [Direzione Ruggiero Romano] Torino, G. Einaudi, 1977–84. 16v. il.   **AC55**

Half title: Enciclopedia Einaudi.
Offers long, signed articles on fairly broad topics; bibliographies include works in many languages. Following each article is a note on related articles with indication of how they elaborate or supplement the information which precedes. Charts and graphs are included in the articles, but other illustrations are concentrated in sections of plates. v.16 is an index with extensive charts and graphs showing interrelationships of topics as well as a conventional alphabetical index.   AE35.E45

Enciclopedia europea. [Milano], Garzanti, [1976–84]. 12v. il. maps.   **AC56**

Contents: v.1–11, A–Z; v.12, Bibliografia, Repertorio, Statistiche.
A new general encyclopedia. Brief articles under specific headings predominate, but there are numerous long, signed articles. Many illustrations, small but clearly reproduced and presented in close proximity to the articles concerned. Occasional bibliographic references within articles, but bibliographies are not appended. The final volume includes a classified bibliography.

Enciclopedia del novecento. Roma, Istituto della Enciclopedia Italiana, [1975–84]. v.1–7. il. (In progress)   **AC57**

Contents: v.1–7, Acidi nucleari-Vitamine.
Serves as a complement to the *Enciclopedia italiana* (AC58), offering long, signed articles by an international roster of scholars surveying 20th-century developments on relatively broad topics and issues (e.g., anarchismo, armamenti, arte, astronomia e astrofisica, cattolicesimo, chemioterapia, cinema, consumi, criminalità). Bibliographies; charts and graphs; numerous illustrations, some in color.

Enciclopedia italiana di scienze, lettere ed arti. [Roma], Istit. della Enciclopedia Italiana, fondata da Giovanni Treccani, 1929–37. 35v. il.   **AC58**

An important encyclopedia with excellent long articles, many bibliographies, and a wealth of illustrations of all types, i.e., excellent maps and colored plates, dark sepia plates of unusual quality, and innumerable text illustrations, some of which are almost equal to plates. Some articles have a fascist viewpoint. All articles, even very short ones, are signed. Includes many biographical articles, genealogical articles containing additional biographies, and biographies of living persons. While all subjects are illustrated, the illustrations for localities and landmarks, and particularly for art subjects are most notable; many portraits.   AE35.E5

———— v.36, Indici. 1939.

A detailed index to the set, including Appendice I.

———— Appendice I. 1938. 1147p. il.

Includes new articles, and additions and corrections to the main set. Four parts of an appendix were published 1934–36, covering the letters A–Pavia. Material in these is not entirely taken over in Appendice I, and therefore the earlier parts should be preserved by libraries which received them.

———— Appendice II, 1938–1948. 1948–49. 2v. il.; Appendice III, 1949–1960. 1961. 2v. il.; Appendice IV, 1961–78. 1979–81. 3v. il.

Supplements are on the same basic plan as the main work, i.e., an alphabetical arrangement of articles signed by authorities, with bibliographies. Well illustrated, though the illustrations are not so plentiful or so beautifully reproduced as in the main work. Cross references are used liberally when additions and corrections are made to articles in previous volumes. The final volume in each set includes an analytical index.

Grande dizionario enciclopedico UTET, fondato da Pietro Fedele. 3. ed. interamente riv. e accresciuta. [Torino], Unione Tipografico-Editrice Torinese, [1966–79]. 20v. and Appendice.   **AC59**

1st ed. 1933–40.
Contents: v.1–19, A–Z; v.20, Indici; Atlanti.
A fully revised and expanded edition. A good general encyclopedia with many short articles and an abundance of good quality illustrations, both black-and-white and in color. A high percentage of articles is signed. Some of the longer entries carry quite extensive bibliographies, and even the brief ones often cite one or more works on the subject. Many biographical sketches, including some living persons. The appendix covers events and developments to 1978. A

Cronologia universale (1273p.) was published 1979 in the same format as the encyclopedia, but is not numbered as a part of the set.

AE35.G7

Japanese

See also DE266.

Ban'yu hyakka dai-jiten. Tokyo, Shôgakukan, 1972–76. 24v. il. **AC60**

A topically arranged general encyclopedia with entries arranged by Japanese phonetic alphabet within subject fields. Articles are generally on specific topics; some have brief bibliographies. v.21 is an index of some 400,000 entries plus a chronological table; v.22–24 offer atlases of the world, Japan, and human anatomy.

AE35.2.B35

Dai-Nihon hyakka jiten. Tokyo, Shôgakukan, [c.1967–72]. 23v. il. **AC61**

Popularly known as "Japonica."

A richly illustrated general encyclopedia with brief entries for topical subjects, proper names, titles of literary works, etc.; functions also as a dictionary. Includes bibliographies. There are two atlases, a dictionary of art treasures of Japan and the world (v.20–21), and an index (v.19) which is, in effect, a single-volume encyclopedia.

Kodansha's *Daijiten desuku* (Encyclopedia of contemporary knowledge; Tokyo, 1983. 1832p.) is a one-volume work offering brief articles with color illustrations and good maps. AE35.2.D3

Heibonsha dai-hyakka jiten. Encyclopedia Heibonsha. Tokyo, Heibonsha, 1984–85. 16v. il. **AC62**

A successor to the same publisher's *Sekai dai-hyakka jiten* first published 1955–59 and most recently issued 1981 in 37v. plus a supplement, and with yearbooks through 1984.

Consists mainly of short articles, signed but usually without bibliographic references. Entries for about 7,000 topics and terms. Black-and-white illustrations.

Dai-hyakka jiten (Tokyo, Heibonsha, 1931–34. 26v., with suppls. publ. 1934–50 in 4v., and an index publ. 1935) is a comprehensive general encyclopedia of pre-World War II Japan still of interest to historians.

Bibliography

Sogô, Masaki and **Asakura, Haruhiko.** Jisho kaidai jiten. Tokyo, Tokyodo, 1977. 538p. **AC63**

A guide to encyclopedias and dictionaries in all subject fields, arranged by title according to Japanese phonetic alphabet, but lacking a subject index.

Issued irregularly, *Jiten jiten sôgo mokuroku* (Tokyo, Shuppan nyûsusha) provides a comprehensive, in-print list of dictionaries and encyclopedias published or distributed in Japan; the 1985 volume lists works in print as of June 1984. Z5849.J3S64

Norwegian

Aschehougs konversasjonsleksikon. 5. utg. Red. Arthur Holmesland [and others]. Oslo, Aschehoug, 1968–73. 20v. il. **AC64**

1st ed. published as *Illustreret norsk konversations-leksikon,* 1907–13. 6v.; 4th ed. 1954–61. 18v.

A complete revision of this standard work, adhering to the principles of the previous editions: i.e., short, popularly written articles, all but the briefest of them signed; numerous illustrations (some in color); maps; many biographies, including persons still living; very little bibliography. Particularly strong in contemporary Norwegian biography. v.20 is an index. AE43.I34

Norsk allkunnebok. Redaktør: A. Sudman [and others]. Oslo, Gonna, [1948–66]. 10v. and atlas. il. **AC65**

The first encyclopedia to be written entirely in the *nynorsk* (*landsmal*) language. Short articles, most of them signed.

AE43.N6

Polish

Orgelbrand, Samuel. S. Orgelbranda Encyklopedja powszechna z ilustracjami i mapami. Warszawa, Orgelbrand, 1898–1912. 18v. il. **AC66**

Contents: v.1–16, A–Z (supplement included in v.16); v.17–18, Supplement.

Short, popularly written articles; many biographies. AE53.O6

Wielka encyklopedia powszechna PWN. [Komitet redakcyjny; przewodniczacy: Bogdan Suchodolski] Warszawa, Państwowe Wydawn. Naukowe, [1962–70]. 13v. il. **AC67**

A general encyclopedia of about 82,000 entries; mainly brief articles. Longer articles are signed; many include selective bibliographies. v.13 is an index.

The part of v.9 dealing exclusively with Poland has been issued separately as *Polska* (Warszawa, 1967. 230p.). AE53.W44

Russian

Bol'shaia sovetskaia entsiklopediia; redaktsiei N. I. Bukharina, V. V. Kuibysheva [and others]. Moskva, "Sovetskaia Entsiklopediia," 1926–47. 65v. il. **AC68**

The most extensive of the Russian encyclopedias, Soviet in treatment, international in scope. Signed articles; extensive bibliographies. AE55.B6

———— Soiuz sovetskikh sotsialisticheskikh respublik. 1947. 1946 col., lxxx p. il.

A historical supplement on the USSR. Classed arrangement, with no index and therefore difficult to use. Does not include government and politics. Chronology, p.i–xl; bibliography, p.xli–lxxx.

Translated into German as *Enzyklopädie der Union der Sozialistischen Sowjetrepubliken,* hrsg. von S. I. Wawilor [u.A.] (Berlin, Verlag Kultur und Fortschritt, 1950. 2v. il.). This includes a personal name index.

———— 2. izd. Moskva [1949]–58. 51v. il. **AC69**

A new edition of the Soviet encyclopedia, revised and reset, with most of the articles new or rewritten; articles in the 1st ed. are signed, in the 2d they are not; etymological derivations are given much more freely in the 1st ed.; bibliographies are quite extensive and for the most part contain only Russian titles, although for articles on foreign subjects some titles in other languages are occasionally included. Illustrations and maps are more numerous and of better quality in the newer work, and the general make-up of the volume is more attractive.

The main alphabet ends with v.49; v.50 is devoted to the USSR, corresponding to the supplement to the first edition; v.51 supplements the 2d ed. as a whole, with some 950 articles, many of which are biographical, and it contains tables of weights and measures, currencies, and foreign words and phrases.

v.50 has been translated into German as *Die UdSSR; Enzyklopädie der Union der Sozialistischen Sowjetrepubliken,* hrsg.: W. Fickenscher unter Mitwirkung von H. Becker [et al.] (Leipzig, Verlag Enzyklopädie, 1959. 1104p. il.).

———— Alfavitnyi ukazatel' ko vtoromu izdaniiu. [Leningrad, 1960] 2v.

An alphabetical index to subjects and authors. AE55.B62

———— 3. izd. Glav. Red. A. M. Prokhorov. Moskva, Izd. Sovetskaia Entsiklopediia, 1970–78. 30v. in 31. il. **AC70**

A complete revision, use of a smaller typeface and more stringent editing resulting in the lesser number of volumes in this edition.

Quality of the work remains at the previous level, and the total number of entries (about 100,000) much the same. As to be expected, emphasis is on achievements in Communist-dominated areas and on those subjects (e.g., philosophy, economics, political science, sociology) which support the Soviet ideology. Articles are signed by contributing scholars; bibliographies accompany many articles. v.30 includes a supplement, p.574–631.

An English translation has appeared as: AE55.B623

Great Soviet encyclopedia; a translation of the third edition. N.Y., Macmillan; London, Collier Macmillan, [1973–83]. 31v. and index.   **AC71**

A translation of the 3d ed. of the *Bol'shaia sovetskaia entsiklopediia* (above), "unannotated and as true as possible to the content and meaning intended by the editors of the original edition in Russian."—*Publisher's foreword.* Means "to convey the scope and point of view of the Great Soviet Encyclopedia and to bring to scholars and others with a serious professional interest in Soviet affairs a primary source through which they can gain a richer knowledge and understanding of the contemporary Soviet Union."

The work was translated on a volume-for-volume basis (only "certain articles that can be classified simply as dictionary or gazetteer entries" were omitted) and articles are arranged within each translated volume according to the English form of the entry or transliterated form of the personal and place names. Thus, while the preponderance of entries in v.1 begins with the letter A, terms such as "Diamond," "Highway," and "Zulu War" are also found therein because the Russian term begins with "A". (The index noted below makes the latter articles readily findable.) The advantage of this arrangement was that the English translation became available relatively soon after publication of the Russian original. Even so, some updating was deemed necessary, and articles which were substantially changed in this respect are marked as "updated." A complete list (in transliteration) of all articles in the Russian equivalent volume is given, with an asterisk preceding those entries for which the articles are not translated. Bibliographies are carried over into the translation, with Western-language citations given in the original language; Russian citations in transliteration.

v.31 is a translation of the long country article on the U.S.S.R. contained in v.24² of the 3d ed. of the *Bol'shaia . . .*; additional, up-to-date information has been supplied with the translation.

An extensive review article by Patricia K. Grimsted appears in *Wilson Library bulletin* 49:728–40 (June 1975).   AE5.B5813

Entsiklopedicheskii slovar', T-va "Br. A. i I. Granat' i Ko." 7. sovershevno/perer. izd. Moskva, Br. A. i I. Granat' [1910–48]. v.1–55, 57–58 and suppl. (publ. 1936).   **AC72**

v.56 not published.

For notes on publication schedule and content of specific volumes *see* Kaufman (AC76), p.72–78; Maichel (AA486), p.68–69; and Simmons (DC541), p.61–62.

Uneven in treatment, but occasionally useful for material not included in the other encyclopedias.

Malaia sovetskaia entsiklopediia. Glav. red. B. A. Vvedenskii. 3. izd. [Moskva], "Bol'shaia Sovetskaia Entsiklopediia," [1958–60]. 10v. il.   **AC73**

1st ed. 1928–31. 10v.

A 3d ed. of the shorter Soviet encyclopedia, containing some 50,000 articles as compared with 31,000 in the 2d ed. (1933–47) of 11v. A general encyclopedia with some emphasis on terms of non-Russian origin.

——— Alfavitnyi predmetno-imennoi ukazatel'. [Index] 3. izd. [Moskva, 1961] 600p.

AE55.M34

Novyi entsiklopedicheskii slovar'. Izdateli F. A. Brokgauz (Leiptsig), I. A. Efron (S.-Petersburg). S.-Petersburg, Brokgauz-Efron, [1912–17?]. v.1–29. il.   **AC74**

Contents: v.1–29, A–Otto. No more published.

A revised edition, showing considerable change, of the great Russian *Brockhaus* (publ. 1890–1907 in 41v. and 2 suppl.). Valuable for historical subjects.   AE55.E62

Annual

Bol'shaia sovetskaia entsiklopediia. Ezhegodnik, 1957– . Moskva, 1957– . il. Annual.   **AC75**

Records events, chiefly of the preceding year, by country (the USSR and constituent republics, and other countries of the world) and under such headings as international organizations, science and technology, and international cultural events. Each volume contains a biographical directory of persons of various nationalities. A detailed table of contents, but no index.   AE55.B64

Bibliography

Kaufman, Isaak Mikhailovich. Russkie entsiklopedii. Moskva, 1960. v.1.   **AC76**

At head of title: Ministerstvo kul'tury RSFSR. Gosudarstvennaia ordena Lenina Biblioteka SSSR im. V. I. Lenina.

Contents: v.1, Obshchie entsiklopedii, bibliografiia i kratkie ocherki. No more publ.

Provides detailed bibliographic descriptions, with notes and commentary, for Russian encyclopedias. v.1 describes 22 general encyclopedias of the pre-Revolutionary and Soviet periods, indicating the publishing date for each volume of each edition.

Z2505.D55K3

Spanish

Diccionario enciclopédico abreviado, versiones de la mayoría de las voces en francés, inglés, italiano y alemán y sus etimologías. 6. ed. Madrid, Espasa-Calpe, 1954–55. 7v. il.   **AC77**

1st ed. 1940.

A general encyclopedia with, for the most part, brief articles and no bibliography. For many words gives equivalents in French, English, Italian, and German, plus etymologies. Illustrations not clearly reproduced.   AE61.D45

——— Apéndice. Madrid, Espasa-Calpe, 1965. 1575p.

Includes many new entries in addition to updating articles from the main set through 1964. A special section at the end supplies information on new developments as late as Sept. 1965.

Diccionario enciclopédico Salvat. 11. ed. Barcelona, Salvat Editores, [1964]. 12v. il.   **AC78**

1st ed. publ. under title *Diccionario Salvat.*

A medium-sized, general encyclopedia. Articles are usually brief, but some are lengthy; they are unsigned, and include little or no bibliography. Illustrations and maps are good.   AE61.D62

Enciclopedia universal ilustrada europeo-americana. Barcelona, Espasa, [1907?–33]. 80v. in 81. il.   **AC79**

Contents: v.1–70 in 71v., A–Z; Apéndice, v.1–10, A–Z.

Often cited as *Espasa.*

A useful encyclopedia for the large reference or special library. It has long articles, bibliographies, good illustrations and maps, and includes short articles on small subjects; especially strong in biography and in gazetteer information. Special features are the many maps: geographical, geological, historical, and statistical; the numerous plans of even small cities; colored plates of uniforms, flags, coins, etc. of each country; and the reproductions of paintings and other works of art (usually given under title, or sometimes under the artist's name). Useful for its large amount of Spanish and Spanish-American biography.

Etymologies are included, and equivalents of words are given in French, Italian, English, German, Portuguese, Catalan, and Esperanto.   AE61.E6

——— Suplemento anual, 1934– . Barcelona, Espasa-Calpe, 1935– .

Arrangement of supplementary volumes is different from that of the basic work, i.e., instead of a straight alphabetical arrangement of all material, articles are arranged alphabetically by large classes, e.g., Agricultura, Biografía, Geografía, Química, etc., with small topics in an alphabetical arrangement under some of these large classes, and a general alphabetical index to all classes and topics at the end of the volume.

Volumes cover 1934, 1935, 1936–39 (2v.), 1940–41, 1942–44, 1945–48, 1949–52, 1953–54, 1955–56, 1957–58, 1959–60, 1961–62, 1963–64, 1965–66, 1967–68, 1969–70, 1971–72, 1973–74, 1975–76, 1977–78, 1979–80.

Gran enciclopedia Rialp, G E R. Madrid, Ediciones Rialp, 1971–76. 24v. il. **AC80**

Contents: v.1–23, A–Z; v.24, Index.

A work featuring signed articles with bibliographies. Most articles are of considerable length; few run to less than half a column. Bibliographies emphasize Spanish-language materials. List of contributors and advisory editors (with indication of qualifications) in v.1. Elaborately illustrated with black-and-white and color photos; charts, maps, diagrams. AE61.G75

Swedish

Bonniers Folklexikon. Stockholm, Nordiska Uppslagsböcker, 1951–55. 5v. il. **AC81**

Short, unsigned articles with some bibliographical notes. Includes small, generally clear illustrations with some colored plates and maps. Strong in biographical and gazetteer information. A short, useful encyclopedia for the library which does not need the more extensive *Svensk uppslagsbok.*

Focus, uppslagsbok; Almqvist & Wiksells stora illustrerade bildnings- och uppslagsverk. Stockholm, Almqvist & Wiksell, [1958–60]. 5v. il. **AC82**

A general encyclopedia with many short articles and small illustrations. v.5 is an index with a section of synonyms and one of tables of statistics and miscellaneous information. AG45.F6

Svensk uppslagsbok. 2. omarb. och utvidg. upplagan. Malmö, Förlagshuset Norden, 1947–55. 32v. il. **AC83**

1st ed. 1929–37. 30v. and suppl.

An excellent modern encyclopedia edited by a board of specialists; well printed and beautifully bound. Many articles are signed. Bibliographies are scant. Profusely illustrated with pertinent maps, city plans, portraits, and many fine photographs. Contains numerous biographical sketches, including living persons. AE45.S82

Turkish

Türk ansiklopedisi. Ankara, Millî Egitim Basimevi, 1946–84. 33v. il., maps. **AC84**

v.1–4 had title *Inönü ansiklopedisi;* title changed with *fasikül* 34. v.1–16 issued in parts.

Published under the auspices of the Turkish government. International and general in scope, with emphasis on Turkish and Islamic materials. Contains a large amount of biography, including living persons. Articles are usually short, unsigned, and without much bibliography. Illustrations and maps are plentiful.

FACT BOOKS AND COMPENDIUMS

An almanack; 1869– . London, Whitaker, 1869– . v.1– . Annual. **AC85**

Generally known as *Whitaker's almanac.*

Subtitle (varies): Containing an account of the astronomical and other phenomena and a vast amount of information respecting the government, finances, population, commerce, and general statistics of the various nations of the world.

Particularly strong in statistics of the British Commonwealth, with brief statistics for other countries. Index at front.

AY754.W5

Information please almanac, atlas and yearbook, 1947– . Planned and supervised by Dan Golenpaul Associates. N.Y., Simon & Schuster, 1947– . Annual. **AC86**

Publisher varies. Title varies.

An almanac of miscellaneous information, with a general topical arrangement and a subject index. Includes extensive statistical and historical information on the United States; chronology of the year's events; statistical and historical descriptions of the various countries of the world; sports records; motion picture, theatrical, and literary awards, etc.; and many kinds of general information. Sources for many of the tables and special articles are noted. A "People" section lists many celebrated persons, giving profession, place and date of birth, and death date if deceased. Names in this section are not indexed individually in the general index. AY64.I55

World almanac and book of facts, 1868– . N.Y., World-Telegram, 1868– . v.1– . Annual. **AC87**

Title varies; publisher varies.

The most comprehensive and most frequently useful of the American almanacs of miscellaneous information. Contains statistics on social, industrial, political, financial, religious, educational, and other subjects; political organizations; societies; historical lists of famous events, etc. Well up-to-date and, in general, reliable; sources for many of the statistics are given. A useful handbook, and one with which the reference worker should familiarize himself thoroughly. Alphabetical index at the front of each volume. Each issue before 1915 had also a short index of notable articles in preceding volumes. AY67.N5W7

Guinness book of world records. N.Y., Sterling, 1956– . il. Annual. **AC88**

Also issued in a British ed. with title: *The Guinness book of records;* 1st American ed. had title *Guinness book of superlatives.*

Publisher varies.

Editors and compilers, Norris McWhirter and Ross McWhirter.

A compendium of information concerning the longest, shortest, tallest, deepest, fastest, etc., in relation to natural features, man-made structures, people, events and achievements (in sports, politics, arts and entertainment), etc., grouped in topical sections (e.g., The human being; The animal and plant kingdoms; The scientific world; The business world). Indexed. AG243.G87

Kane, Joseph Nathan. Famous first facts: a record of first happenings, discoveries, and inventions in American history. 4th ed., expanded and rev. N.Y., Wilson, 1981. 1350p. **AC89**

1st ed. 1933.

Aims to establish the earliest date of various occurrences, achievements, inventions, etc. Dictionary arrangement with many cross references. Gives brief description or explanation together with the date; some references to sources. This edition "includes more than 9,000 firsts in American history. These pertain to Americans and to events that have occurred in the United States."—*Pref.* Indexes by years, by days of the month, by personal name, and by geographical location. AG5.K315

The people's almanac. Ed. by David Wallechinsky and Irving Wallace. N.Y., Doubleday, 1975. 1478p. il. **AC90**

In endeavoring to produce "a reference book to be read for pleasure," the editors admit to sacrificing "a small degree of comprehensiveness for detail."—*p.xv.* A general almanac with a good deal of unusual and out-of-the-way information. Contributions are signed (some material is reprinted from indicated sources); suggestions for further reading are sometimes given. Indexed. AG106.P46

The people's almanac #2. By David Wallechinsky and Irving Wallace. N.Y., Morrow, 1978. 1416p. il. **AC91**

Designed to be consulted alongside the earlier volume (above), and so carries new information, articles, etc.; some headings and subject sections remain constant.

There have also been "spin-offs" from the original volume: *The book of lists* (1977) and *The people's almanac presents The book of predictions* (1980).

Further supplementary information and updating is provided by: AG106.P465

The people's almanac #3. By David Wallechinsky and Irving Wallace. N.Y., Morrow, 1981. 722p. il.   **AC92**

AB106.P466

A D

Language Dictionaries

❖For a general survey of the whole field of language dictionaries consult the article "Dictionary" in *Encyclopaedia Britannica,* 11th edition. This is valuable for its historical information and includes an extensive bibliography of dictionaries in many languages, though many of these, now, of course, are considerably out of date.

Dictionaries are the main sources for information about words: their spelling, pronunciation, meaning, derivation, etc. Theoretically the dictionary is concerned only with the word, not with the thing represented by the word, differing in this respect from the encyclopedia which gives information primarily about the thing. Practically, however, the large modern dictionary is very often encyclopedic and gives information about the thing as well as the word, thus combining the features of the two types of reference books. As the large English dictionary is the most familiar "family reference book," this encyclopedic feature has been continually strengthened by the addition of many special lists and excellent illustrations, until the best modern works of this sort can now be used for many more purposes than information about words. Dictionaries which contain many illustrative quotations can often be used to find or identify a quotation, thus supplementing the special dictionaries of quotations. The student of reference books should familiarize himself with the special features and supplementary lists of each of the great dictionaries if he wishes to make each of these books serve all the purposes that it can be made to serve.

Dictionaries should be purchased cautiously. Because they are expensive undertakings, unscrupulous publishers sometimes offer a reprint of an old work with little or no revision, but with a change of title. The prospective purchaser, therefore, should use the same care in examining a dictionary before purchase as is recommended in the case of encyclopedias.

In studying a dictionary the student should follow the general directions for examining reference books and, keeping in mind the purpose of the dictionary, should also note carefully the following points:
1. Period of the language covered
2. Vocabulary
   a) Extent and how counted—is the count by main words only or does it include all derived and compound forms, etc.?

   b) Special elements included, e.g., slang, dialect, obsolete forms, scientific or technical terms, etc.
3. Treatment of each word, with reference to:
   a) Spelling, including plurals, verb tenses, participles
   b) Syllabication and hyphenization
   c) Pronunciation—how marked; is the system accurate and intelligible?
   d) Etymology
   e) History—are changes in meaning, usage, etc., marked and dated?
   f) Definition—is it clear, correct, adequate?
   g) Illustrative quotations—are they given freely, with exact reference, and in chronological order and dated so that the history can be traced?
   h) Standard and usage—is a word indicated as obsolete, colloquial, etc.?
   i) Encyclopedic information
   j) Synonyms and antonyms
4. Illustrations
5. Abbreviations—to what extent included, and how, i.e., in separate list or in main alphabet?
6. Special types of words included in addition to the ordinary vocabulary, i.e., Christian names, foreign phrases, biographical lists, geographical names, etc. To what extent are these included, and where: in main alphabet or in appended lists?
7. Special features

ENGLISH LANGUAGE

❖Dictionaries of the English language have been divided rather arbitrarily, according to their place of compilation and publication, into American and English dictionaries. Of course, both types cover the same field—the English language as a whole—and conform, in the main, to the same standards, but there are certain minor differences. In cases where there are known differences in spelling, pronunciation, meaning, etc., each dictionary will generally give both usages, but the English work will prefer the English usage or form, while the American work will prefer the American. An American dictionary generally includes more Americanisms; an English dictionary, more local English terms, colonial words, etc.

Bibliography

Collison, Robert Lewis. Dictionaries of English and foreign languages; a bibliographical guide to both general and technical dictionaries with historical and explanatory notes and references. 2d ed. [N.Y.], Hafner, 1971. 303p.   **AD1**

1st ed. (1955) had title: *Dictionaries of foreign languages.*
The earlier edition provided historical and critical notes on the general, special, and bilingual dictionaries of the languages of Europe, Asia, and Africa, together with special lists of French, German, Italian, Spanish, Russian, and Scandinavian dialect dictionaries, and an appendix listing technical dictionaries in various languages arranged by subject. The new edition, much revised and updated, adds new chapters on early and modern English-language dictionaries, the Celtic languages, and comparative philology.
Z7004.D5C6

Kister, Kenneth F. Dictionary buying guide: a consumer guide to general English-language wordbooks in print. N.Y., Bowker, 1977. 358p.   **AD2**

A successor to S. P. Walsh's *English language dictionaries in print* first published by Bowker in 1965 and issued as part of *Home reference books in print* in 1969.

Intended for the consumer who is contemplating purchase of a dictionary, and "especially designed to assist individuals—parents, students, educators, word buffs, gift givers, secretaries, professional people of all kinds—who want authoritative information about the numerous and sometimes indistinguishable dictionaries currently available from American publishers and distributors."—*Pref.* Reviews at some length (giving full bibliographic citation plus information on purpose and scope, authority, vocabulary treatment, encyclopedic features, graphics, a summary of strong and weak points, and references to other critical opinions) 58 general adult English-language dictionaries; evaluates more briefly some sixty school and children's dictionaries; and offers concise coverage of about 225 "special-purpose dictionaries and wordbooks" (dictionaries of etymology, slang, synonyms, idioms and usage; style manuals; secretary's handbooks, etc.). Author-title-subject index.

Z2015.D6K57

Mathews, Mitford McLeod. A survey of English dictionaries. Oxford, Univ. Pr.; London, Milford, 1933. 123p. il. (Repr.: N.Y., Russell & Russell, 1966)   **AD3**

A historical survey of English dictionaries from earliest times to the 19th century. Also includes chapters on "The historical principle in lexicography," "Review of lexicographic methods," and "Chief features of some modern dictionaries."   Z2015.D6M4

Murray, *Sir* **James A. H.** Evolution of English lexicography. Oxford, Univ. Pr., 1900. 51p. (Repr.: College Park, Md., McGrath, 1970)   **AD4**

An interesting and authoritative survey of the history and development of the English dictionary.   PE1611.M9

Starnes, DeWitt Talmage and **Noyes, Gertrude Elizabeth.** The English dictionary from Cawdrey to Johnson, 1604–1755. Chapel Hill, Univ. of North Carolina Pr., 1946. 299p. il.   **AD5**

Includes a bibliography and census of copies in American libraries of all known editions, p.228–41.   PE1611.S68

American

Century dictionary and cyclopedia, with a new atlas of the world. [Rev. and enl. ed.] N.Y., Century, [c1911]. 12v. il.   **AD6**

1st ed. 1889–91, 6v., with two supplementary volumes, *Cyclopedia of names,* 1894, and *Atlas,* 1897; partially revised from time to time and plates altered, but never entirely revised and reset. Revisions to note especially are: (1) 1901 edition, 10v., v.1–8, Dictionary, v.9, Names, v.10, Atlas; (2) two supplementary volumes published 1909, numbered v.11–12 to continue the 1901 edition and containing about 100,000 new words, senses, and phrases and a 92p. supplement to the *Cyclopedia of names;* (3) the 1911 edition, 12v.

Contents: v.1–10, Dictionary; v.11, Cyclopedia of names; v.12, Atlas.

Printed from the same plates as the earlier editions, but with alterations in the plates to include a considerable amount of new material. In addition, there is bound at the end of each volume the corresponding portion of the alphabet from the two supplementary volumes published 1909, making two alphabets in each volume linked together by cross references.

The most comprehensive and detailed American dictionary and the best example of the encyclopedia type, including detailed etymologies and thousands of illustrative quotations, with exact reference to source. Now out-of-date for current usage but still useful for many types of questions.

v.11, *Cyclopedia of names,* includes personal and geographical names, famous works of literature and art, monuments, etc. Pronunciation is indicated. To a large extent, but not entirely, superseded by the *New Century cyclopedia of names* (AJ37).

PE1625.C4 1911

New Century dictionary of the English language, based on matter selected from the original Century dictionary and entirely rewritten, with the addition of a great amount of new material. . . . ed. by H. G. Emery and K. G. Brewster; revision ed., Catherine B. Avery. N.Y., Appleton-Century-Crofts, [1953]. 2v. (2820p.)   **AD7**

1st ed.1927.

Supplements: Synonyms and antonyms, Abbreviations, Business terms, Foreign words and phrases, Proper names exclusive of biography and geography, Biographical names, Geographical names.

Not a revision of the *Century dictionary* (above), but a much smaller work including a smaller vocabulary selected from the *Century* with new definitions and a different selection of quotations. More than 160,000 entries with more than 12,000 illustrative quotations.   PE1625.C4

Funk & Wagnalls new Standard dictionary of the English language, prep. by more than 380 specialists and other scholars under the supervision of Isaac K. Funk, Calvin Thomas, F. H. Vizetelly. N.Y., Funk & Wagnalls, 1964. 2816p. il.   **AD8**

1st ed., 1893, had title *Standard dictionary;* the *New Standard,* first published in 1913, is a thorough revision of the 1893 edition, reset and printed from new plates throughout. Later issues or reprints of this edition show changes in the plates, insertion of new words, etc.; e.g., the issues published since World War II include some new words inserted in their proper alphabetical place by cutting out or compressing old material, and late editions include a supplement of new words.

Contents: (1) Dictionary, including in one alphabet all ordinary dictionary words and also the various proper names, i.e., biographical, geographical, mythological, biblical, etc.; Supplement of new words and additional meanings, p.xxxvi–lxix; (2) Appendix: Disputed pronunciations, Rules for simplified spelling, Foreign words and phrases, Statistics of population.   PE1625.S7 1963

Random House dictionary of the English language. Jess Stein, ed. in chief. N.Y., Random House, [1966]. 2059p. il., maps.   **AD9**

Various printings.

A new work, but bearing many of the characteristics of the same publisher's *American college dictionary* (AD12). From the standpoint of physical size, it is more comparable to the single-volume edition of the *Shorter Oxford dictionary* (i.e., the *Oxford universal dictionary,* 3d ed., 1955. 2515p.; AD29n) than to the standard unabridged dictionaries. More than 260,000 entries. Relative up-to-dateness is its chief attraction for libraries; encyclopedic scope of entries (i.e., the inclusion of personal and place-names in the main alphabetic sequence), plus the inclusion of several foreign word lists, an atlas section, a list of reference books, etc., and the fairly moderate price give it appeal for home purchase.   PE1625.R3

Webster's New international dictionary of the English language. 2d ed., unabridged . . . a Merriam-Webster. William Allan Neilson, ed. in chief; Thomas A. Knott, gen. ed.; Paul W. Carhart, managing ed. Springfield, Mass., Merriam, 1961. cxxxvi p., 3194p. il.   **AD10**

1st ed. of *Webster's Dictionary,* 1828; the *New international,* 1909; 2d ed. of *New international,* 1934, revised throughout and reset. Later printings show some changes and corrections in plates, mainly in spelling, punctuation, or pronunciation, but in some cases adding new information or revising the treatment. In 1939 a "New words" section was added at the front of the book, p.xcvii–civ; in 1961, this section was called "Addenda section," p.xcvii–cxxxv. It includes several thousand new words or words used with new or different meanings, including scientific and technical terms, slang, abbreviations, etc.

Contents: (1) Dictionary, including in the same list both the usual dictionary words and also foreign phrases, abbreviations, proverbs, noted names of fiction, and all proper names except those in the biographical and geographical lists; (2) Appendix: (a) Abbreviations, (b) Arbitrary signs and symbols, (c) Forms of address, (d) Pronouncing gazetteer, (e) Pronouncing biographical dictionary. In addition to the foregoing, the "Reference history" edition contains a separately paged supplement "Reference history of the world" by A. B. Hart, c1934.

The oldest and most famous American dictionary, well rounded, with no marked specialization or bias, ably edited, reliable, and noted particularly for the clearness of its definitions. For many years the most used and, for general purposes, the most useful of the 1-volume dictionaries. A special feature introduced in the 1909 edition and continued in the 2d ed. (1934) is the divided page, containing in the upper part the main words of the language and in the lower part, in finer print, various minor words, e.g., different kinds of cross references, reformed spellings, such biblical proper names as are entered only to show pronunciation, a few obsolete words and a few extremely rare words, and foreign-language quotations, proverbs, and longer phrases. Other special points to remember in using the work are: definitions given in historical sequence; pronunciation indicated by Webster phonetic alphabet (not by the International phonetic system); hyphenization indicated by single hyphen, division of syllables by either accent or centered period. Vocabulary claimed is "600,000 vocabulary entries."

PE1625.W3

Webster's Third new international dictionary of the English language, unabridged. A Merriam-Webster. Ed. in chief: Philip Babcock Gove and the Merriam-Webster editorial staff. Springfield, Mass., Merriam, 1961. 2662p. il. **AD11**

". . . a completely new work, redesigned, restyled and reset."—*Pref.* Not only new, but vastly different from the 2d ed. (above); it was probably the most controversial reference book of the generation, both attacked and defended in the newspaper and periodical press. Because of its departures from accepted Webster practices, thorough familiarity with the introduction is essential to efficient use of the text. A few of the major points to be observed are:

Usage: This edition presents the language as currently *used,* with a new concept of acceptability of usage, construction, pronunciation, etc.; therefore, much is included, often without qualification, which (particularly at the time of the work's original publication) was regarded by many as colloquial, vulgar, or incorrect.

Scope: Some 100,000 new entries appear, with new scientific and technical terms especially well represented, but the total has been reduced from 600,000 to 450,000, meaning that many obsolete and rare words have been dropped; the divided page system has been abandoned; abbreviations are included in the main alphabet; the gazetteer and the biographical dictionary have been dropped; all proper nouns have been excluded, although proper adjectives remain, all in lower case. An 8-page "Addenda" section of new words was added to the 1966 printing; that section was increased to 16 pages in 1971, to 32 pages in 1976, and to 48 pages in 1981.

Treatment of words: Individual definitions, in the Webster tradition, are generally clear and to the point; meanings are given as before, chronologically, with early usage first; etymologies have been expanded; pronunciations are given as used in "general cultivated conversational usage as well as in formal platform speech"; regional pronunciations are also frequently shown; indication of pronunciation is given by a newly devised system with the key only in the introduction, not on each page; the devices to indicate word division, stress, and hyphenization have been revised and are explained and illustrated in the introduction; punctuation and indentation are at a minimum.

Quotations: Illustrative quotations are abundant, undated, and almost exclusively from recent sources, many of them popular. Citations are to author only.

Regardless of varying opinions of editorial judgment, this edition will be essential in American libraries, though the 2d ed. will be wisely retained as well. PE1625.W36

Desk dictionaries

❖Good desk dictionaries are needed both in libraries and in homes, and librarians should know the main features and merits of the various works available. Those listed below are planned for much the same kind of use and include comparable vocabularies. All have been issued in recent editions and include new words and meanings; all are authoritative;

all give clear, concise definitions, etymologies, synonyms, antonyms, etc.; and most have small line drawings.

General arrangement in each differs, as does the arrangement under individual entry, and systems of indicating pronunciation vary. Some of the particular features and special points of each are noted below.

The publisher also issues other editions and/or abridgments of these dictionaries; *see* publishers' catalogs for their announcements.

"Desk dictionaries: a consumer's guide" in *Reference books bulletin (see* AA502), Dec. 1, 1983, p.538–44, offers thirteen points for consideration when purchasing a desk dictionary and provides critical commentary on *The American Heritage dictionary,* the *Oxford American dictionary,* the *Random House college dictionary, Webster's New world dictionary of the American language, Webster's Ninth new collegiate dictionary,* and *The World Book dictionary,* plus briefer comment on a few additional titles.

American college dictionary. Clarence L. Barnhart, ed. in chief; Jess Stein, managing ed.; assisted and advised by 355 authorities and specialists. N.Y., Random, 1962. 1444p. il. **AD12**

1st ed. 1947; 1965 printing called "Newly revised" on dust jacket, but pagination unchanged.

A modern, desk-size dictionary designed to provide an accurate guide to current usage. All entries are in one alphabet, including proper names of persons and places, abbreviations, foreign phrases, inflected forms of words in which the stem is changed, etc. Pronunciation is indicated by the "traditional textbook key," given on the endpapers and in abbreviated form at the bottom of every other page. Definitions are given in reverse chronological order, modern usage first. Etymologies follow. Typography is particularly good.

PE1628.A55

The American Heritage dictionary. 2d college ed. William Morris, ed. Boston, Houghton Mifflin, [1982]. 1568p. il. **AD13**

The American Heritage dictionary of the English language, ed. by William Morris, was first published 1969 in a "larger format edition," then reprinted in smaller size designated as "New college edition" (1976). This 2d college edition "represents the first complete revision" of the 1969 work.

Offers about 200,000 definitions, covering "the vocabulary ranging from the language of Shakespeare to the idiom of the present day."—*Introd.* Aims "to present the most prevalent, contemporary sense or meaning of a word first, with the other shades of meaning following." Emphasis has been placed on offering guidance to good usage, both through the employment of usage-context indicators (e.g., slang, regional) and the addition of "usage notes" which reflect the opinions of a usage panel in regard to controversial or dubious locutions. Etymologies are given (though less fully than in the 1969 ed.); pronunciation symbols appear at the bottom of each double-page spread. There are separate biographical and geographical sections at the end of the volume; names of mythological and legendary figures and certain other proper nouns appear in the main sequence.

Connie Eble's review in *American speech* 59:72–84 (Spr. 1984) compares the first and second editions and expresses disappointment with the latter. PE1625.A54

Oxford American dictionary. N.Y., Oxford Univ. Pr., 1980. 816p. **AD14**

Ed. by Eugene Ehrlich and others.

A new work based on the *Oxford paperback dictionary,* but using American lexicographers and editors. "It has been compiled for everyday use in home, school, office, and library. It emphasizes concise and precise definitions presented in a straightforward way. It does not use synonyms to define words unless they help distinguish shades of meaning. It supplies the most common current meanings, spellings, and pronunciations. All spellings and pronunciations are American unless otherwise labeled."—*p.xvi.*

Hunter B. Smeaton's review in *Library journal,* Nov. 1, 1980, p.

2318, notes that the dictionary's "appended matter is scant, etymologies are few, and its treatment of pronunciation leaves much to be desired. It is the body of the work which is important to most readers, however, and in this major respect it is highly recommended."

The work has been issued in paperback by Avon Books, New York.
PE2835.O9

The Random House college dictionary. Rev. ed. [N.Y., Random House, 1975] 1568p. il. **AD15**

"Based on The Random House dictionary of the English language, the unabridged edition. Jess Stein, editor in chief."—*t.p.*

1st ed., 1968, had title *The Random House dictionary of the English language, College edition.* Various reprintings.

A desk dictionary following the style of the parent work (AD9). Includes synonyms, etymologies, etc.; proper names and abbreviations appear in the main alphabet. Appendixes include signs and symbols, directories of United States and Canadian universities and colleges, English given names, and a brief manual of style.
PE1625.R34

Webster's Ninth new collegiate dictionary. Springfield, Mass., Merriam-Webster, [1983]. 1563p. il. **AD16**

1st ed. 1898; 8th ed. 1973; frequently reprinted.

The 9th ed. has nearly 160,000 entries and some 200,000 definitions, including many new words and new meanings. Based on *Webster's Third* (AD11), it reflects the concepts and policies of that dictionary, with emphasis on "standard language"; slang and colloquialisms are well represented, but are frequently not designated as such. Trademarks and service marks are so labeled, as are regional, dialectal, archaic and obsolete terms; selected abbreviations are included in the main alphabet.

Pronunciation is indicated by diacritics and a phonetic transcription, a brief table of which is given at the bottom of each right-hand page. Etymologies are full and are given at the beginning of the entry; definitions follow in chronological order, the most recent sense or meaning coming last. A new feature in this edition is the placing of a date before the first sense of each entry word, indicating "when the earliest example known to us of the use of that sense was written or printed."—*Pref.* Notes on synonyms discriminate from one another words of closely associated meaning. Illustrative quotations occur frequently, and usage notes are occasionally given at the end of an entry.

Appendixes: Foreign words and phrases; Biographical names; Geographical names; Colleges and universities; Signs and symbols; Handbook of style.

Thomas L. Clark's review in *American speech* 59:70–72 (Spr. 1984) calls this "the best *Collegiate* to date." PE1628.W5638

Webster's New World dictionary of the American language. 2d college ed. David B. Guralnik, ed. in chief. N.Y., World, [1970]. 1692p. il. and phonodisc. **AD17**

1st ed. 1953; various reprintings.

A fully revised and updated edition. Format and arrangement of the earlier edition are retained: proper names, place-names, abbreviations, foreign phrases, etc., are all included in one alphabet; pronunciation and etymologies are given; definitions are given in chronological order, earliest meanings first. Usage labels continue to be used, and Americanisms are indicated by a star. Appendixes include a directory of colleges and universities of the United States; tables of weights and measures; special signs and symbols; and a "Guide to punctuation, mechanics, and manuscript form."

The accompanying phonodisc is an "audio supplement" to the pronunciation guide and phonemic symbols.

Also issued (without phonodisc) in an edition bound with C. G. Laird's *Webster's New World thesaurus* (1971). PE1625.W33

Juvenile dictionaries

❖A number of dictionaries have been published especially adapted to the use of school children of various age levels. For the most part, these are based on recorded usage of words found in the textbooks and other reading materials in use in the schools. The *Reference books bulletin* (*see* AA502) should be consulted for more detailed reviews of these dictionaries. Appropriate volumes of the "Standard catalog" series (AA469–AA471) will also be helpful in their selection, as will the reviews in item AD26.

American Heritage school dictionary. Boston, Houghton Mifflin, [1977]. 992p. il. **AD18**

Intended for use in grades six through nine.

The same publisher has issued Stephen Krensky's *My first dictionary* (1980. 340p.) for use in the primary grades. PE1628.A626

Macmillan dictionary for children. William D. Halsey, editorial director. Rev. ed. N.Y., Macmillan; London, Collier Macmillan, [1982]. 756p. il. **AD19**

1st ed. 1975.

About 30,000 entries. Intended for the beginning reader through the middle grades. PE1628.5.M27

Macmillan dictionary for students. Judith S. Levey, exec. ed.; William D. Halsey, ed. N.Y., Macmillan, [1984]. 1190p. il. **AD20**

Earlier eds. entitled *Macmillan contemporary dictionary* (1979) and *Macmillan dictionary* (text ed., 1981).

More than 100,000 definitions. A *Reference books bulletin* review (June 1, 1985, p.1383) terms this a good choice "for students who lack extensive experience in using dictionaries since it offers them remedial assistance through its clear, step-by-step introductory explanation of how to use the dictionary and interpret its entries."

Scott, Foresman beginning dictionary. By E. L. Thorndike, Clarence L. Barnhart. Glenview, Ill., Scott, Foresman, [1979]. 718p. il. **AD21**
PE1628.T64

Scott, Foresman intermediate dictionary. By E. L. Thorndike, Clarence L. Barnhart. Glenview, Ill., Scott, Foresman, [1983]. 1066p. il. **AD22**
PE1628.5.S36

Scott, Foresman advanced dictionary. By E. L. Thorndike, Clarence L. Barnhart. Glenview, Ill., Scott, Foresman, [1979]. 1186p. il. **AD23**

All three of the above items are available in "Doubleday editions" with the Doubleday, Garden City, N.Y., imprint, and each is a revision of the well-known Thorndike-Barnhart dictionaries of similar title which date from the 1940s and 1950s.
PE1628.5.T49

Webster's New World dictionary for young readers. David B. Guralnik, ed. in chief. New rev. ed. [Cleveland], W. Collins, [1979]. 880p. il. **AD24**

1st ed. 1976 was a new ed. of the "elementary ed." of *Webster's New World* dictionary (1961–71). Various printings.

Intended for grades four through eight. More than 44,000 entries. PE1628.W563

The World book dictionary. Ed. by Clarence L. Barnhart, Robert K. Barnhart. Prep. in cooperation with World Book, Inc. Chicago, World Book, Inc., [1983]. 2v. (124, 2430p.) il. **AD25**

1st ed. 1963; frequently revised (latest major revision 1976).

Designed as a companion to the *World book encyclopedia* (AC20) and meant to be "useful to all members of the family and to students of various ages."—*p.4.* About 225,000 terms and some 3,000 illustrations; definitions are clear and easy to understand, with careful consideration for younger readers; most common meanings are presented first. Examples of usage are frequently given. Pronunciation is indicated; a brief pronunciation key appears at the bottom of each right-hand page. Various educational materials, charts and lists occupy a separately paged section preceding the dictionary proper. PE1625.W73

Reviews

Dictionaries for children and young adults: reviews. Prep. by the Reference Books Bulletin Editorial Board, American Library Association. Chicago, Amer. Lib. Assoc., 1983. 38p. **AD26**

Contains evaluations of nine dictionaries *(Macmillan very first dictionary; The rainbow dictionary; My first dictionary; Children's dictionary; Macmillan dictionary for children; Scott, Foresman beginning dictionary; Webster's Elementary dictionary; Webster's New world dictionary for young readers; The American Heritage school dictionary).* Designed to assist parents, teachers, and librarians in making the appropriate choice for an individual child or appropriate age group. PE1611.D52

English

Murray, *Sir* **James Augustus Henry.** New English dictionary on historical principles; founded mainly on the materials collected by the Philological Society. Oxford, Clarendon Pr., 1888–1933. 10v. and suppl. **AD27**

Contents: v.1–10, A–Z; Supplementary volume: Historical introduction, p.vii–xxvi; Supplement A–K, 542p.; L–Z, 325p.; List of spurious words, p.327–30; Bibliography, i.e., list of books most commonly quoted in the Dictionary, 91p.

Known variously as *Murray's Dictionary,* the *New English dictionary,* and the *Oxford dictionary.* Often cited as *NED,* or *OED.* For history of the work *see* its Supplementary volume, p.vii–xxvi.

The great dictionary of the language, compiled on a different plan from any of the other standard English dictionaries and serving a different purpose. It is based upon the application of the historical method to the life and use of words, and its purpose is to show the history of every word included from the date of its introduction into the language, giving differences in meaning, spelling, pronunciation, usage, etc., at different periods of the last 800 years, and supporting such information by numerous quotations from the works of more than 5,000 authors of all periods, including all writers before the 16th century and as many as possible of the important writers since then. The vocabulary is very full, and is intended to include all words now in use or known to have been in use since 1150, excluding only words which had become obsolete by 1150. Within these chronological limits, aims to include: (1) all common words of speech and literature, and all words that approach these in character, the limits being extended further into science and philosophy than into slang and cant; (2) in scientific and technical terminology, all words English in form except those of which an explanation would be intelligible only to a specialist, and such words not English in form as are in general use or belong to the more familiar language of science; and (3) dialectal words before 1500, omitting dialectal words after that date except when they continue the history of a word once in general use, illustrate the history of a literary word, or have a literary currency.

Words included are classified as: (1) main words, (2) subordinate words, and (3) combinations; information for all main words is entered under the current modern or most usual spelling, or, if obsolete, under most typical later spelling, with cross references from all other forms. Information given about each main word is very full and includes: (1) identification, with (a) usual or typical spelling, (b) pronunciation, indicated by respelling in an amplified alphabet or, in case of obsolete words, by marking of stress only, (c) grammatical designation, (d) specification, e.g., musical term, etc., (e) status, if peculiar, e.g., obsolete, archaic, etc., (f) earlier spelling, (g) inflexions; (2) morphology, including derivation, subsequent form history, etc.; (3) signification, arranged in groups and historically, with marking of obsolete senses, erroneous uses, etc.; (4) quotations, arranged chronologically to illustrate each sense of a word, about one quotation for each century, given with exact reference. The complete work has a total vocabulary of 414,825 words and includes 1,827,306 quotations.

The most important use of this dictionary is for historical information about a word, but it has many other secondary uses, e.g., while not intentionally encyclopedic, it has a good deal of encyclopedic information including some not given in other dictio-

naries, and while not specializing in slang, it does include many colloquial and slang words, Americanisms, etc. Where such words are included, the information is often better than in the special slang dictionaries.

The supplementary volume is a partial, not a complete, supplement, in that it does not comprise all supplementary material collected since the publication of the first parts of the original work but is limited in the main to new words and senses of the 50 years preceding publication, with inclusion also of: (1) other items of modern origin and currency omitted in the main work; (2) earlier evidence of American uses; and (3) some correction or amplification of previous definitions to bring the work into line with more recent research. Recent words added include scientific and technical terms, colloquialisms, and slang—American, British, and colonial—and a larger proportion of proper names than in the original work. This volume is, of course, being superseded by the multi-volume supplement noted below, which began to appear in 1972.

The *New English dictionary,* large and comprehensive though it is, is necessarily selective, and could not include all words for the whole period covered or even all material collected during the compilation of the work. Since the completion of the dictionary in 1928, four period and regional dictionaries, on the same extensive plan, either have been published or are in course of publication to supplement the *New English dictionary* by including words, uses, illustrations, etc. which could not be included in that dictionary. These are:

Middle English dictionary, begun under the editorship of Prof. Clark S. Northup at Cornell University, continued under Prof. Samuel Moore, Dr. Thomas A. Knott, and Prof. Hans Kurath at the University of Michigan, and later edited there by Sherman M. Kuhn, John Reidy, and Robert E. Lewis (AD140).

Dictionary of American English, under the editorship of Sir William Alexander Craigie and James R. Hulbert (Univ. of Chicago Pr., 1936–44. 4v.) (AD113).

Dictionary of the older Scottish tongue, begun under the editorship of Sir William Alexander Craigie and now being edited by A. J. Aitken (AD129).

Scottish national dictionary, under the editorship of William Grant and David Murison (AD133).

For the new supplement to the *Oxford English dictionary see* below. PE1625.M7

———— Oxford English dictionary, being a corrected reissue, with an introduction, supplement and bibliography, of A New English dictionary on historical principles; founded mainly on the materials collected by the Philological Society and ed. by James A. H. Murray, Henry Bradley, W. A. Craigie, C. T. Onions. . . . Oxford, Clarendon Pr., 1933. 12v. and suppl. **AD28**

A reprint, on thinner paper and with somewhat smaller margins, from the plates of the original edition with the correction of such typographical errors as had been discovered.

In 1895 "a new name for the Dictionary was introduced, though no change was made on the title-page. On the cover of the section containing *Deceit* to *Deject* . . . above the title, appeared for the first time the designation 'The Oxford English Dictionary,' which was repeated on every section and part issued after 1 July of that year. The new name, being more distinctive than the old, has steadily come more and more into use, and the abbreviation O.E.D. tends to supplant N.E.D., although the latter is still frequently employed."— *Historical introd., p.xx.* PE1625.M7

———— ———— A supplement to the Oxford English dictionary. Ed. by R. W. Burchfield. Oxford, Clarendon Pr., 1972–82. v.1–3. (In progress)

Contents: v.1–3, A–Scz.

To be in 4v., superseding the 1933 supplement. The final volume will include a bibliography of works cited.

"The vocabulary treated is that which came into use during the publication of the successive sections of the main Dictionary—that is, between 1884, when the first fascicle of the letter A was published, and 1928, when the final section of the Dictionary appeared—together with accessions to the English language in Britain and abroad from 1928 to the present day."—*Pref.* Includes additional uses, earlier and later examples, etc., of words appearing in the main set, together with corrections as in the earlier supplement. The completed supplement will contain an estimated 50,000 main words. v.4 (with bibliography of sources) was scheduled for publication in early 1986.

———— The shorter Oxford English dictionary on historical principles; prep. by William Little, H. W. Fowler and Jessie Coulson. Rev. and ed. by C. T. Onions. 3d ed. compl. reset with etymologies by G. W. S. Friedrichsen and with revised addenda. Oxford, Clarendon Pr., [1973]. 2672p. **AD29**

1st ed. 1933; 3d ed. 1944, repr. with rev. addenda, 1956; frequently repr. with revisions. Also publ. in 1v. as the *Oxford universal dictionary* (1955. 2515p.).

An authorized abridgment of the *New English dictionary,* which, while in the main an abridgment, also includes some additional material, especially new words too recent to have been included in the original work, or older words omitted there, with some later illustrative quotations. Important, therefore, in the library which already has the larger work, as well as in the small library which has not been able to afford the complete *Oxford English dictionary.*

"The aim of this Dictionary is to present in miniature all the features of the principal work. It is designed to embrace not only the literary and colloquial English of the present day together with such technical and scientific terms as are most frequently met with . . . but also a considerable proportion of obsolete, archaic and dialectal words and uses."—*Pref.*

The reset version of 1973 is notable for two features: (1) Etymologies of the words have been revised; and (2) there is a new "Addenda" section "drawn chiefly from the material assembled for the new Supplement to the *O.E.D.* . . . , and presenting notable accessions to the English language in the period since the *O.E.D.* appeared."—*Publisher's note.* PE1625.L53

Early modern English, additions and antedatings to the record of English vocabulary, 1475–1700. Richard W. Bailey, ed. Hildesheim, Olms, 1978. 367p. **AD30**

Concerned with "words and senses . . . overlooked or omitted by the editors of the *Oxford English Dictionary*" (*Pref.*), thus serving as a supplement to that work for the early modern period. For each word an excerpt illustrating usage is given, together with citation to the source. There is an appendix of "Early modern English texts cited" and another of "Secondary sources consulted."

The listings here "form an addition to the citations already published as part of *Michigan early modern English materials* [Ann Arbor, Xerox University Microfilms, 1975. 2v.] and generally follow the editorial conventions of that work."—*Introd.* PE891.E3

-Ologies & -isms: a thematic dictionary. 2d ed. Laurence Urdang, ed. in chief. Detroit, Gale, [1981]. 365p. **AD31**

1st ed. 1978.

Concerned primarily with words ending in *ology, ity, ism,* and *ic* and their forms in various parts of speech. Words are arranged in thematic categories; definitions, variant spellings, and related forms are given. An index enables the user to locate a specific word within a category.

A Reference and Subscription Books Review Committee evaluation in *Booklist* 78:1555 (Aug. 1982) points out deficiencies in the selection of terms and inadequate cross-referencing in the index; it concludes that "As a reference tool in a school, public, or college library, it may disappoint as often as it satisfies."

A similar work, comp. by Mary Walton and the staff of the Free Public Libraries and Museum, Sheffield, Eng., is *'Isms; a dictionary of words ending in -ism, -ology, and -phobia* (Sheffield, Corp. of Sheffield and EP Publ. Ltd., 1968. 100p. 2d ed., repr. 1972). PE1680.O4

Desk dictionaries

The concise Oxford dictionary of current English; based on the Oxford English dictionary and its supplements. 7th ed., ed. by J. B. Sykes. Oxford, Clarendon Pr., 1982. 1264p. (Repr. with corrections 1983) **AD32**

1st ed. 1911 ed. by H. W. Fowler and F. G. Fowler.

An excellent, small desk dictionary based on the work done for the *Oxford English dictionary* (AD28). Aims to include words in

current speech, scientific and technical terms, many colloquial and slang expressions, etc. The 6th ed. (1976) was a thorough revision drawing on the files built up for the supplements to the *O.E.D.,* eliminating a good deal of material no longer regarded as current, and increasing the number of terms and usages from outside the British Isles. Revisions are less extensive in the 7th ed.; files for the *O.E.D.* supplements continued to be utilized. About 40,000 headwords. PE1628.F78C7

Garmonsway, George Norman and **Simpson, Jacqueline,** comps. The Penguin dictionary of English. Baltimore, Penguin, [1965]. 799p. **AD33**

Aims "to capture and record *Modern* English and to present a selection of its vocabulary—i.e., the vocabulary in actual written and spoken use in the mid twentieth century."—*Pref.* Americanisms are liberally represented, as are slang and colloquialisms. Pronunciation is indicated, but it should be remembered that this is British rather than American. No etymologies. PE1625.G3

Oxford illustrated dictionary. Text ed. by J. Coulson [and others]. Illustrations ed. by Helen Mary Petter. 2d ed. Oxford, Clarendon Pr., 1975. 998p. il. **AD34**

An illustrated dictionary including much encyclopedic material in addition to the usual dictionary information, and various explanatory illustrations usually in the form of line drawings.

Vocabulary is "based on that of the *Concise Oxford dictionary,* and the definitions retain its historical ordering" (*Pref.*), but there is less full treatment of the more familiar words in order to give a wider scope to the treatment of things, often by means of illustration. All terms are in one alphabet, including proper nouns, abbreviations, foreign phrases, etc. As far as possible, pronunciation is shown without respelling, by placing symbols over the letters; when respelling is necessary, a phonetic system is used. Little or no etymology.

A useful dictionary, from the English viewpoint. PE1628.O9

Abbreviations

❖Lists of abbreviations are important in most libraries. Some of the separately compiled lists follow. Abbreviations are also included freely in the *Century dictionary* (AD6), *Funk & Wagnalls new Standard* (AD8), and *Webster's Third new international* (AD11). The desk dictionaries also usually include abbreviations. The lists in *Who's who* (AJ236) and *Who's who in America* (AJ84) are useful for the abbreviations of societies, academies, degrees, etc. For abbreviations of the names of organizations, societies, and international associations, *see* AD35, CK429–CK430; for abbreviations of periodical titles *see* AE13–AE15.

Acronyms, initialisms & abbreviations dictionary. Ed. 5– . Detroit, Gale, 1976– . Irregular. **AD35**

1st ed. (1960) had title: *Acronyms dictionary;* 2d–4th eds., *Acronyms and initialisms dictionary.* Now issued in three volumes, each volume separately titled: v.1, Acronyms, initialisms & abbreviations dictionary; v.2, New acronyms, initialisms & abbreviations; v.3, Reverse acronyms, initialisms & abbreviations dictionary. Each part may be purchased separately. v.1 of each ed. is kept up to date by a periodic supplement designated as v.2 (i.e., *New acronyms.* . . .).

Subtitle, v.1, 9th ed. (1984): A guide to over 300,000 acronyms, initialisms, abbreviations, contractions, alphabetic symbols, and similar condensed appellations. Covering: aerospace, associations, biochemistry, business and trade, domestic and international affairs, education, electronics, genetics, government, labor, medicine, military, pharmacy, physiology, politics, religion, science, societies, sports, technical drawings and specifications, transportation, and other fields. P365.A28

DeSola, Ralph. Abbreviations dictionary. Expanded international 6th ed. N.Y., Elsevier, [1981]. 966p. **AD36**

"Abbreviations; acronyms; anonyms; appellations; computer terminology; contractions; criminalistic and data-processing terms;

eponyms; geographical equivalents; government agencies; historical, musical and mythological characters; initialisms; medical and military terms; nations of the world; nicknames; parts of the world; short forms; shortcuts; signs and symbols; slang; superlatives; winds of the world; zip coding; zodiacal signs."—*t.p.*

1st ed. 1958.

Anonyms, contractions, eponyms, geographical name equivalents, nicknames and short forms are interfiled with the abbreviations and acronyms. Numerous special lists (e.g., airlines of the world; astronomical constellations, stars and symbols; birthstones; diacritical and punctuation marks; numbered abbreviations) are appended.

PE1693.D4

Paxton, John. Everyman's dictionary of abbreviations. Repr. with rev. suppl. London, Dent, [1983]. 393p. **AD37**

1st ed. 1974 had title: *Dictionary of abbreviations* (repr. with revisions and suppl. 1981).

Aims "to provide a representative selection of the old and the new . . . to serve the purposes of the student and scholar, the administrator, the business man, the exporter and the community of the general reader at home and at work."—*Pref.* P365.P3

Bibliography

Abbreviations, acronyms, ciphers & signs. Annie M. Brewer, ed. Detroit, Gale, [1981]. 323p. **AD38**

Reproduces the Library of Congress catalog cards for some 900 items whose titles include any one of the words "abbreviations, acronyms, ciphers, signs" or whose L.C. subject tracings use one or more of those words. Arranged by L.C. classification, with keyword index. Includes materials in all languages. Z7004.A33A22

Basic English

Ogden, Charles Kay. The general Basic English dictionary, giving more than 40,000 senses of over 20,000 words, in Basic English. . . . N.Y., Norton, [1942]. 441p. il. **AD39**

Originally published in London, Evans Bros., 1940 (repr. 1964). The American edition adds, p.439–41, lists of Basic English words by form, such as Operations, 100; Things: 400 General, 200 Pictorial; Qualities: 100 General, 50 Opposites.

"For the use of learners of English. . . . Using only the 850 words of Basic . . . and fifty international words, which go with them, it gives a knowledge of over 20,000 English words, covering at least 40,000 separate senses and special word-groups. . . . Great care has been given to idioms."—*Note.* PE1073.5.O372

Etymology

❖For the etymology of the English language the best authority is Murray's *New English dictionary* (AD27). Smaller and specialized works include:

Eponyms dictionaries index. Ed. by James A. Ruffner. Detroit, Gale, [1977]. 730p. **AD40**

"A reference guide to persons, both real and imaginary, and the terms derived from their names, providing basic biographical identification and citing dictionaries, encyclopedias, word books, journal articles, and other sources for additional information: includes acts, analyses, awards, axioms, bills, cases, circles, codes, coefficients, collections, commissions, complexes, costumes, diseases, dynasties, effects, equations, expeditions, experiments, forces, formulas, functions, laws, maneuvers, medals, methods, mixtures, organs, paradoxes, phenomena, presses, prizes, processes, ratios, reactions, rebellions, rules, schemes, societies, solutions, styles, syndromes, systems, techniques, tests, theories, trophies, unity, and wars."—*t.p.* PE1596.E6

—— 1st ed. suppl., no.1– , Mar. 1984– . Detroit, Gale, 1984– . Irregular.

Ed. by Jennifer Mossman and James A. Ruffner.

Offers supplemental listings, following the plan of the main work.

Hendrickson, Robert. Human words; the compleat unexpurgated, uncomputerized human wordbook. Philadelphia, Chilton, [1972]. 342p. **AD41**

"Containing herein the true unadulterated stories of more than 3,500 unique and remarkably eponymous personalities: saints and sinners, losers and winners, lovers and hatemongers, murderers and masochists, scalawags and saviors . . . that have given their names to the language."—*title page.* PE1596.H4

Klein, Ernest. A comprehensive etymological dictionary of the English language, dealing with the origin of words and their sense development, thus illustrating the history of civilization and culture. Amsterdam, [etc.], Elsevier, 1966–67. 2v. **AD42**

The work of a Czech scholar and linguist. Contains substantially more entries than the *Oxford dictionary of English etymology* (AD44), including origins of mythological and given names and assigning some etymologies not found in the Oxford work. The *Oxford dictionary . . .* , however, will prove adequate in all but the largest collections, and its dating of meanings by century offers a distinct advantage. PE1580.K47

Morris, William and **Morris, Mary.** Morris dictionary of word and phrase origins. N.Y., Harper & Row, [1977]. 654p. **AD43**

Incorporates new material with that previously published in the three volumes of the same authors' *Dictionary of word and phrase origins* (N.Y., 1962–71). There has been some revision and shortening of the earlier material, and an index has been provided in lieu of the *see* references previously employed in the body of the work. Popular treatment, with very little scholarly apparatus. PE1580.M6

Oxford dictionary of English etymology. Ed. by C. T. Onions with the assistance of G. W. S. Friedrichsen and R. W. Burchfield. Oxford, Clarendon Pr., 1966. 1025p. (Repr. with corrections 1969) **AD44**

The first really comprehensive etymological dictionary of the English language since Skeat (AD49), and sure to be the standard for years ahead. About 24,000 entries. For each entry, pronunciation is given, followed by a selection of meanings or senses in chronological sequence to show the general trend of development; the century in which the word or meaning is first recorded is indicated by a roman numeral. A thoroughly scholarly work, and, despite many space-saving symbols and abbreviations, very easy to use. Offers less information on various individual terms than does Partridge's *Origins* (AD46), but breadth of coverage is much greater. PE1580.O5

Partridge, Eric. Name into word: proper names that have become common property. A discursive dictionary. London, Secker & Warburg, 1949; N.Y., Macmillan, 1950. 644p. **AD45**

Common words derived from personal, geographical, and other names, with "discursive" explanations. PE1583.P35

—— Origins: a short etymological dictionary of modern English. 4th ed. London, Routledge & Paul, [1966]. 972p. **AD46**

1st ed. 1958.

An etymological dictionary of the most common words in modern English. Omits dialect and slang, except in a few instances, and does not include many scientific and technical terms. PE1580.P3

Schröer, Michael Martin Arnold. Englisches Handwörterbuch in genetischer Darstellung auf Grund der Etymologien und Bedeutungsentwicklungen, mit phonetischer Aussprachebezeichnung und Berücksichtigung des Amerikanischen und der Eigennamen, mitbearbeitet und hrsg. von P. L. Jaeger. Heidelberg, Carl Winter, 1937–70. 3v. **AD47**

Issued in parts.

A scholarly dictionary in German on the etymology of English words, with many examples of usage, etc. PF3640.S53

Shipley, Joseph Twadell. The origins of English words; a discursive dictionary of Indo-European roots. Baltimore, Johns Hopkins Univ. Pr., [1984]. 636p. **AD48**

Arranged by Indo-European root, with an index of English words (and foreign phrases used in English) derived therefrom. As the subtitle indicates, definitions are presented in a discursive manner, with numerous sidelights and examples of usage of the English forms. Notes on "Frequent word forms and transformations," and a brief bibliography precede the main text. PE1571.S46

Skeat, Walter William. An etymological dictionary of the English language. New ed., rev. and enl. [4th ed.] Oxford, Clarendon Pr., 1910. 780p. **AD49**

A standard scholarly work giving full histories of more than 14,000 words, with references to sources.

Contents: (1) Dictionary; (2) Appendix: Lists of Prefixes, Suffixes, Homonyms, Doublets, Indogermanic roots; Distribution of words according to languages from which they are derived. PE1580.S5

——— A concise etymological dictionary of the English language. New and corr. imp. Oxford, Clarendon Pr., 1911. 663p. (Repr. 1958) **AD50**

Explanations, etymologies, histories, and quotations are much abbreviated. PE1580.S52

Weekley, Ernest. Etymological dictionary of modern English. London, Murray; N.Y., Dutton, 1921. 1659col. (Repr.: N.Y., Dover, 1967) **AD51**

A popular work, for the general reader rather than for the specialist, giving the histories of the literary and colloquial vocabulary, omitting most scientific terms. PE1580.W5

——— A concise etymological dictionary of modern English. . . . Rev. ed. London, Secker & Warburg; N.Y., Dutton, 1952. 480p. **AD52**

An abridged version of the above, which it does not supersede. References to "remote languages" and illustrative quotations are omitted; some new words are added and others dropped.
PE1580.W53

Idioms and usage

Britannica book of English usage. Ed. by Christine Timmons and Frank Gibney. Garden City, N.Y., Doubleday/Britannica Books, 1980. 655p. **AD53**

Made up in part by excerpts from articles in the *Encyclopaedia Britannica* and partly by new contributions. In three main sections: (1) English today and how it evolved; (2) The basic tools [with subsections on grammar, spelling, pronunciation, words and dictionaries, the library, and abbreviations]; (3) Writing and speaking effectively. Bibliography; index. PE25.B7

Bryant, Margaret M., ed. Current American usage. N.Y., Funk & Wagnalls, [1962]. 290p. **AD54**

A handbook which "attempts to bring together the most recent information about frequently debated points of usage in English speech and writing."—*Introd.* Debated points in current usage are discussed with citations to dictionaries, linguistic treatments, and articles in current periodicals, as well as to special investigations made especially for use in this book. PE2835.B67

Copperud, Roy H. American usage and style: the consensus. N.Y., Van Nostrand Reinhold, [1980]. 433p. **AD55**

"This book revises, brings up to date, and consolidates two earlier ones: *A Dictionary of Usage and Style* and *American Usage: the Consensus* [1970]."—*Pref.* Compares the judgments of various current dictionaries on disputed points and offers the compiler's own views on those points. PE1460.C648

Evans, Bergen and **Evans, Cornelia.** A dictionary of contemporary American usage. N.Y., Random House, 1957. 567p. **AD56**

An informally written, scholarly, and sometimes witty dictionary of contemporary American usage, reflecting the personal opinions of the authors. Arranged alphabetically, with explanations of grammar and rhetoric, word usage, literary concepts, clichés, phrases, idioms, figures of speech, etc. Informative and provocative. PE2835.E84

Follett, Wilson. Modern American usage; a guide. Ed. and completed by Jacques Barzun [and others]. N.Y., Hill & Wang, [1966]. 436p. **AD57**

While this work deals with many of the same terms as Nicholson's *Dictionary of American-English usage* (AD61) and Fowler's *Dictionary of modern English usage* (AD58), and although it includes a smaller number of entries, the individual style and the length of many of the discussions make it a worthwhile companion to those works. An extensive appendix on the use of *shall* and *will,* and another on punctuation. PE2835.F6

Fowler, Henry Watson. Dictionary of modern English usage. 2d ed., rev. by Sir Ernest Gowers. Oxford, Clarendon Pr., 1965. 725p. **AD58**

1st ed. 1926.

Alphabetically arranged; definitions of terms—sometimes with disputed spellings and spelling of plurals, pronunciation, etc.—are interspersed with brief essays on the use and misuse of words and expressions, parts of speech, etc. Reflects the author's personal opinions, and comments are often astringent and witty. The revision by Sir Ernest Gowers aims to bring the work up-to-date without sacrificing the "Fowleresque flavour." It adds a classified guide to enable the reader to find items given by Fowler under enigmatic titles. PE1628.F65

Horwill, Herbert William. Dictionary of modern American usage. 2d ed. Oxford, Clarendon Pr., 1944. 360p. **AD59**

1st ed. 1935. Frequently reprinted.

Not a dictionary of standard American usage, but a handbook, by an English writer, intended primarily to assist English visitors in America or English readers of American books and magazines by explaining words or phrases which have a meaning or use in the United States different from that in England. Includes about 1,300 main words. PE2835.H6

Morris, William and **Morris, Mary.** Harper dictionary of contemporary usage. N.Y., Harper & Row, [1975]. 650p. **AD60**

"With the assistance of a panel of 136 distinguished consultants on usage."—*t.p.*

". . . treats of virtually every aspect of today's language—idioms, slang, vogue words, and regionalisms, as well as all the vast range of words used in formal speech and writing."—*Introd.* Opinions of the "usage panel" are reported in the form of percentages of approval and disapproval and in quotations from opinions of individual panel members. PE1680.M59

Nicholson, Margaret. A dictionary of American-English usage, based on Fowler's Modern English usage. N.Y., Oxford Univ. Pr., 1957. 671p. **AD61**

For Fowler's *Dictionary of modern English usage, see* AD58.

". . . an adaptation of MEU, not a replacement. AEU is a simplified MEU, with American variations, retaining as much of the original as space allowed."—*Pref.* Some of the articles were shortened, some omitted, and new entries and illustrations added. Fowler's own mannerisms have been retained. PE2835.N5

Oxford dictionary of current idiomatic English. Comp. by A.P. Cowie and R. Mackin. London, Oxford Univ. Pr., 1975–83. 2v. **AD62**

Contents: v.1, Verbs with prepositions & particles; v.2, Phrases, clauses and sentence idioms.

Intends to provide a specialized dictionary of idiomatic usage "which is sufficiently broad in scope to answer the various practical requirements of the learner."—*Gen. Introd.* Idiomatic phrases are defined in "concise and readily intelligible statements . . . which do not assume an understanding of . . . expressions given elsewhere in the dictionary." Examples of usage from contemporary speech and writing are given; caveats against wrong usage or wrong constructions are frequently included. A valuable work for the foreign-language speaker learning English. PE1689.O94

Picturesque expressions: a thematic dictionary. Laurence Urdang, editorial director; Nancy LaRoche, ed. in chief. Detroit, Gale, [1980]. 408p. **AD63**

Includes both old and new figurative expressions grouped in thematic categories. Phrases are defined, their origins explained, and the approximate date of appearance in the written language is indicated when possible. Examples of use are sometimes given. PE1689.P5

Schur, Norman W. English English. [Essex, Conn.], Verbatim, [1980]. 332p. **AD64**

An earlier ed. (1973) had title: *British self-taught.*

A revised and expanded edition of a work giving American equivalents of British terms and expressions, together with explanatory notes for many of the entries. PE1460.S45

Weiner, E. S. C. The Oxford guide to English usage. Oxford, Clarendon Pr., [1983]. 238p. **AD65**

Reprinted with corrections 1984.

A work "intended for anyone who needs simple and direct guidance about the formation and use of English words—about spelling, pronunciation, meanings, and grammar—and who cannot claim any specialist training in these subjects."—*Pref.* Concerned with "correct and acceptable standard British English" with American variants noted, particularly in the section on pronunciation. Word index. PE1091.W44

Wood, Frederick Thomas. Current English usage; a concise dictionary. London, Macmillan; N.Y., St. Martin's, 1962. 273p. **AD66**

A concise handbook of British origin, indicating the correct and incorrect use of words and expressions. PE1460.W66

———— English prepositional idioms. London, Macmillan; N.Y., St. Martin's, 1967. 562p. **AD67**

The alphabetical listing of prepositions and their various uses (with examples of usage) is followed by a section dealing with idiomatic phrases introduced by a preposition and with the idiomatic use of prepositions after verbs, adjectives, verbal nouns, etc., these phrases being arranged by key word and including many examples. A useful work for the native speaker as well as for the foreign student of English. PE1335.W6

Indexes

Idioms and phrases index. Laurence Urdang, ed. in chief. Detroit, Gale, [1983]. 3v. (1691p.) **AD68**

Subtitle: An unrivaled collection of idioms, phrases, expressions, and collocations of two or more words which are part of the English lexicon and for which the meaning of the whole is not transparent from the sum of the meanings of the constituent parts, also including nominal, verbal, and other phrases which exhibit syntactic and semantic character peculiar to the English language, the entries gathered from more than thirty sources, each described in the bibliography provided, with all items arranged alphabetically both by first word and any significant words.

An index to the sources where definitions or discussions of the idioms may be found, not a dictionary of the terms. Source books range from compilations such as *Brewer's Dictionary of phrase and fable* (BD89) through various dictionaries of slang and idioms, and including *Words and phrases index* (AD117). PE1689.I3

New words

The Barnhart dictionary companion; a quarterly to update "the" dictionary. v.1, no.1– , Jan. 1982– . Cold Spring, N.Y., Barnhart, 1982– . Quarterly. **AD69**

Newsletter format; the bulk of each issue is devoted to new words and meanings not found in current dictionaries. Cumulated index in issues 2–4 of each volume.

The Barnhart dictionary of new English since 1963. [Ed. by] Clarence L. Barnhart, Sol Steinmetz [and] Robert K. Barnhart. Bronxville, N.Y., Barnhart/Harper & Row, [1973]. 512p. **AD70**

"By 'New English' we mean those terms and meanings which have come into the common or working vocabulary of the English-speaking world during the period from 1963 to 1972."—*Pref.* Includes old words in new applications, idiomatic phrases, figurative and transferred meanings of names, and scientific and technical terms which are not necessarily new but which have recently become part of the common vocabulary.

Pronunciation is indicated for hard or unfamiliar words; area labels (U.S., British, Canadian) are given for regional terms; usage labels (other than "slang") are not used. Illustrative examples of usage attempt to place the term in full context, and a complete citation to the source follows each quotation. PE1630.B3

The second Barnhart dictionary of new English. [Ed. by] Clarence L. Barnhart, Sol Steinmetz, and Robert K. Barnhart. Bronxville, N.Y., Barnhart/Harper & Row, [1980]. 520p. **AD71**

A continuation of the above, following the basic editorial principles and practices of that work. In general, usage notes are fuller than in the earlier volume, and a date for "our earliest available evidence for use of a word or meaning" *(Pref.)* is supplied in brackets. The two volumes cover some 10,000 "words and meanings not entered or inadequately explained in standard dictionaries." PE1630.B3

9,000 words; a supplement to Webster's Third new international dictionary. Springfield, Mass., Merriam-Webster, [1983]. 218p. **AD72**

This is "essentially the most recent Addenda section of Webster's Third New International Dictionary [*see* AD11]; it contains most of the entries of its predecessor, 6,000 Words [publ. 1976], and the new material for 1981."—*Pref.* Includes some new terms not found in the "Addenda section" and many illustrative quotations not included therein. (Author of a quotation is cited, but not the specific work in which it appears.) PE1630.A16

Obsolete

❖Smaller dictionaries of unusual, obsolete, and provincial words are often useful for additional instances and quotations and for incidental information about local customs, observances, etc., even though most or all of the words in such dictionaries are now included in the large works of Murray (AD27) and Wright (AD118). The following are the best-known dictionaries of this type.

Halliwell-Philips, James Orchard. Dictionary of archaic and provincial words, obsolete phrases, proverbs, and ancient customs from the 14th century. 13th ed. London, Routledge, 1889. 2v. **AD73**

1st ed. 1847. Frequently reprinted without change.

Defines archaic and provincial words and gives many illustrative quotations showing their use.

Supplemented by: PE1667.H3

Davies, Thomas Lewis Owen. Supplementary English glossary. London, Bell, 1881. 736p. **AD74**

PE1630.D3

Nares, Robert. Glossary of words, phrases, names, and allusions in the works of English authors, particularly of Shakespeare and his contemporaries. New ed., with considerable additions both of words and examples, by J. O. Halliwell and Thomas Wright. London, Routledge, 1905. 981p. **AD75**

1st ed. 1822; 1st Halliwell and Wright ed. 1857. Frequently reprinted.

Rich in quotations. PE1667.N3

Skeat, Walter William. Glossary of Tudor and Stuart words, especially from the dramatists. Ed., with additions, by A. L. Mayhew. Oxford, Clarendon Pr., 1914. 461p. (Repr.: N.Y., B. Franklin, 1968) **AD76**

PE1667.S5

Pronunciation

BBC pronouncing dictionary of British names. 2d ed., ed. and transcribed by G. E. Pointon. Oxford, Oxford Univ. Pr., 1983. 274p. **AD77**

1st ed. 1971, ed. by G. M. Miller.

Indicates pronunciation (by both International Spelling Association symbols and English modified spelling) of "titles, family names (i.e., surnames), certain Christian names (or personal first names), place names, those of institutions and societies, and adjectival forms of proper names, drawn from England, Wales, Scotland, Northern Ireland, the Isle of Man, and the Channel Islands."—*Introd.*

PE1660.B3

Ehrlich, Eugene H. and **Hand, Raymond.** NBC handbook of pronunciation. 4th ed., rev. and updated. N.Y., Harper & Row, [1984]. 539p. **AD78**

1st ed. 1943 by James F. Bender; 3d ed. 1964 rev. by Thomas L. Crowell, Jr.

Now a standard guide to "General American" speech, this edition includes more than 21,000 "commonly used words and proper names as well as perennially difficult names from history and the arts."—*Pref.* Employs a "readily understandable respelling system to indicate pronunciation"; primary and secondary stresses are also indicated; there is a brief pronunciation key at the bottom of facing pages. PE1137.E52

Greet, William Cabell. World words, recommended pronunciations. 2d ed. rev. and enl. N.Y., Columbia Univ. Pr., 1948. 608p. **AD79**

A revised and much enlarged revision of *War words,* published in 1943, and of *World words,* published 1944. Gives pronunciation of some 25,000 names and words including battlefields, places made familiar by the war, names of persons in the news, and difficult words. Pronunciation is given "by a simplified Websterian alphabet . . . and by a phonetic respelling."—*p.lii.* Compiled especially for radio broadcasters of the Columbia Broadcasting System. Includes the pronunciation of many names not easily found elsewhere.

PE1660.G7

Jones, Daniel. Everyman's English pronouncing dictionary, containing 58,000 words in international phonetic transcription. 12th ed. [rev.] N.Y., Dutton, [1963]. 539p. **AD80**

Earlier editions had title *An English pronouncing dictionary.*

Words, including some proper names, are listed, followed by pronunciation in the phonetic alphabet. No definitions.

PE1137.J55

Kenyon, John Samuel and **Knott, Thomas Albert.** A pronouncing dictionary of American English. [2d ed.] Springfield, Mass., Merriam, [1953]. 484p. il. **AD81**

1st ed. 1944.

A dictionary giving the pronunciation, by the phonetic alphabet, of the colloquial speech of cultivated Americans, recording the variant pronunciations in different parts of the country, as East, West, South, North. Besides the common words, includes proper names, especially for America; some British personal and place-names; a few foreign names of general interest; and names in literature and history likely to be encountered by college students in their reading. No definitions. PE1137.K37

Lass, Abraham Harold and **Lass, Betty.** Dictionary of pronunciation. N.Y., Quadrangle, [1976]. 334p. **AD82**

A guide to pronunciation of 8,000 English-language words which are frequently mispronounced or have one or more acceptable variant pronunciations. Pronunciations are given phonetically (and a "pronunciation key" appears on every right-hand page of the book) for each variant accepted by four standard desk dictionaries; a small numeral beside each pronunciation serves to indicate consensus of preference. PE1137.L38

Noory, Samuel. Dictionary of pronunciation: guide to English spelling and speech. 4th ed. N.Y., Cornwall Books, [1981]. 517p. **AD83**

1st ed. 1965.

Pronunciation is indicated according to a simplified system developed by the compiler. Syllabication and part of speech are also indicated. Separate section for personal and place names. About 45,000 words in the main section.

The Reference and Subscription Books Review Committee's review in *Booklist* 79:581 (Dec. 15, 1982) concludes: "Since Noory's word list has not changed since 1965, it seems appropriate to compare his book with the *NBC Handbook of Pronunciation* (3d ed., 1964). *NBC* lists only about 20,000 words, including proper nouns, but it has a more thoroughly developed set of pronunciation symbols, and this makes it preferable. Libraries lacking an older edition of *Noory* should acquire this edition, but any library with an earlier edition still usable will want to give *Noory* a low priority." (Note also, that the *NBC handbook* is now available in a new edition [AD78].) PE1137.N65

Ross, Alan Strode Campbell. How to pronounce it. London, Hamish Hamilton, [1970]. 177p. **AD84**

The author is "here only concerned with the spoken English of the British Isles" and aims "to distinguish between U or educated pronunciation on the one hand, and non-U or uneducated pronunciation on the other."—*Introd.* In many instances the correct pronunciation is followed by a wrong one to explain or illustrate the difference. International phonetic alphabet is used to indicate pronunciation. PE1137.R63

Punctuation

Partridge, Eric. You have a point there; a guide to punctuation and its allies. With a chapter on American practice by John W. Clark. London, Hamish Hamilton, 1953. 230p. (Repr. 1964) **AD85**

PE1450.P3

Shaw, Harry. Punctuate it right! N.Y., Barnes & Noble, [1963]. 176p. **AD86**

A useful, well-arranged handbook explaining current practices of American punctuation. Includes many examples. PE1450.S45

Rhymes

Holofcener, Lawrence. A practical dictionary of rhymes, based on new principles for songwriters and other versifiers. N.Y., Crown, 1960. 211p. **AD87**

A lengthy introduction on some of the techniques of song writing precedes the list of rhymes. PE1519.H6

Johnson, Burges. New rhyming dictionary and poets' handbook. Rev. ed. N.Y., Harper, 1957. 464p. **AD88**

1st ed. 1931.

Contents: Forms of English versification with examples; Rhyming dictionary, one-syllable rhymes, two-syllable rhymes, three-syllable rhymes.   PE1519.J6

[Lathrop, Lorin Andrews] Rhymers' lexicon, comp. and ed. by Andrew Loring [pseud.] . . . introd. by George Saintsbury. 2d ed. rev. London, Routledge; N.Y., Dutton, 1905. 879p. (Repr.: Detroit, Gale, 1971)   **AD89**

Contents: pt.1, monosyllables and words accented on the last syllable; pt.2, words accented on the penult; pt.3, words accented on the antepenult.   PE1519.L3

Stillman, Frances. The poet's manual and rhyming dictionary. Based on The improved rhyming dictionary by Jane Shaw Whitfield. N.Y., Crowell, [1965]. 387p.   **AD90**

In two sections: (1) "the poet's manual," which includes chapters on rhythm and meter, verse forms, etc.; and (2) the dictionary proper.   PE1505.S8

Wood, Clement. Wood's Unabridged rhyming dictionary, introd. by Ted Robinson. . . . Cleveland, N.Y., World, 1943. 1040p. (Repr.: N.Y., Simon and Schuster, 1981)   **AD91**

Gives rhyming sounds for single, double, and triple rhymes grouped according to consonantal opening. Rhymes are based on sound, not spelling, and pronunciation is given. Also includes sections on: The vocabulary of poetry, Complete formbook for poets, Fixed forms, Mechanics of rhyme, Versification self-taught, and Advanced versification.   PE1519.W62

Slang

Burke, William Jeremiah. The literature of slang . . . with an introductory note by Eric Partridge. N.Y., N.Y. Pub. Lib., 1939. 180p. (Repr. from the New York Pub. Lib. Bull. 1936–38) (Repr.: N.Y., N.Y. Pub. Lib.; Detroit, Gale, 1965)   **AD92**

An annotated, classified bibliography of books, articles, and miscellanea, with author index. Covers the literature of various types of cant, jargon, and slang.   Z2015.S6B9

Barrère, Albert and **Leland, C. G.** Dictionary of slang, jargon & cant; embracing English, American and Anglo-Indian slang, pidgin English, gypsies' jargon and other irregular phraseology. London, Bell, 1897. 2v.   **AD93**

PE3721.B3

Berrey, Lester V. and **Van den Bark, Melvin.** American thesaurus of slang; a complete reference book of colloquial speech. 2d ed. N.Y., Crowell, 1953. 1272p.   **AD94**

1st ed. 1942.

Arranged in two parts: (1) general slang and colloquialisms subdivided into categories arranged according to dominant idea; and (2) special slang of particular classes and occupations including such sections as underworld, trades and occupations, sports, military, western, etc. Includes an alphabetical word index. In the 2d ed. new words have been added and outmoded terms omitted, so that the new edition does not entirely supersede the earlier one.

PE3729.A5B4

Farmer, John Stephen and **Henley, W. E.** Slang and its analogues, past and present; a dictionary, historical and comparative of the heterodox speech of all classes of society for more than three hundred years, with synonyms in English, French, German, Italian, etc. London, Routledge, 1890–1904. 7v. (Repr.: N.Y., Kraus, 1965. 7v. in 3)   **AD95**

An older and still useful slang dictionary, listing about 100,000 words. Gives explanation, derivation, kind of usage, illustrative quotations with references to sources, and synonyms in French, German, Italian, and Spanish.

An abridged edition was published 1905 (533p.)

A "revised edition" with the title *Dictionary of slang and its analogues* was announced for publication in 8v. by University Books, New Hyde Park, N.Y., but only volumes 1 and 8 appeared

(1966); v.1 of that edition is a reprint (with the addition of two extensive introductory essays) of the only published volume of a revised edition, and v.8 contains Farmer's *Vocabula amatoria* (1896), on the erotic slang of the French language.   PE3721.F4

Landy, Eugene E. The underground dictionary. N.Y., Simon and Schuster, [1971]. 206p.   **AD96**

Brief definitions of words drawn from the underground language of various subcultures.   PE3721.L3

Major, Clarence. Dictionary of Afro-American slang. N.Y., International Publ., [1970]. 127p.   **AD97**

". . . a book of the words and phrases used by black people irrespective of their origin."—*Introd.* Dates are frequently inserted to indicate the period at which a word or phrase was most popular.

PE3727.N4M3

Maurer, David W. Language of the underworld. Collected and ed. by Allan W. Futrell & Charles B. Wordell. [Lexington], Univ. Pr. of Kentucky, [1981]. 417p.   **AD98**

Essentially a reprinting of some twenty of Maurer's articles (with glossaries) which appeared in a variety of scholarly publications, each article dealing with the argot of a specific subcultural group. A key word index enables the user to locate terms in the individual glossaries.   HV6085.M38

Partridge, Eric. A dictionary of slang and unconventional English, colloquialisms and catch phrases, fossilised jokes and puns, general nicknames, vulgarisms and such Americanisms as have been naturalized. Ed. by Paul Beale. London, Routledge & Kegan Paul, [1984]. 1400p.   **AD99**

Previous editions of this work had reprinted the original 1937 publication and added a cumulated supplement of new terms. The present edition incorporates the supplementary entries into the main alphabet along with many new entries, modifications, and corrections, a high percentage of which had been collected by Partridge prior to his death in 1979; post-1978 entries contributed by Beale carry the latter's initials. An appendix of "items too unwieldy to fit comfortably into the main text" (e.g., Australian underworld terms, bird-watchers' slang) have been added in an appendix.

Partridge is also the author of several specialized slang dictionaries: *A dictionary of Forces' slang, 1939–1945* (London, Secker & Warburg; N.Y., Saunders, 1948. 212p.); *Slang, today and yesterday, with a short historical sketch and vocabularies of English, American and Australian slang* (London, Routledge, 1933. 476p.); and *A dictionary of the underworld, British and American* (3d ed. London, Routledge, 1968. 886p.).   PE3721.P322

Spears, Richard A. Slang and euphemism: a dictionary of oaths, curses, insults, sexual slang and metaphor, racial slurs, drug talk, homosexual lingo, and related matters. Middle Village, N.Y., David Publishers, [1981]. 448p.   **AD100**

Intended as "a record of the usage of prohibited words and subjects among speakers of English" (*Introd.*) since the beginnings of the English language. Entries include variant forms, definition, often a statement concerning origin or derivation, location of use and/or period of use as applicable. Source for the entry word is sometimes given. Cross references.   PE3721.S67

Wentworth, Harold and **Flexner, Stuart Berg.** Dictionary of American slang. 2d supplemented ed. N.Y., Thomas Y. Crowell, [1975]. 766p.   **AD101**

The original (1960) edition was reprinted in 1967 and a 48-page supplement was added. In this latest edition the main section again remains unchanged, but the new supplement includes "all of the material that appeared in the first supplement of 1967 plus about 1,500 new slang terms and definitions that have become current since then."—*Pref. to the Suppl.*

A very full listing, including many previously "taboo" expressions, with considerable explanation of usage, and a high percentage of references to source and date. The appendix includes various classified lists and an extensive bibliography. The best of the American slang dictionaries.   PE2846.W4

Synonyms and antonyms

Bernstein, Theodore Menline. Bernstein's Reverse dictionary. With the collaboration of Jane Wagner. [N.Y.], Quadrangle, [1975]. 277p. **AD102**

Not a "reverse dictionary" in the usual sense of the term. The intent here is to enable the user to work from a definition to the term; functions also as a dictionary of synonyms. PE1591.B45

Crabb, George. Crabb's English synonyms. Rev. and enl. by the addition of modern terms and definitions arranged alphabetically, with complete cross references throughout, with introd. by John H. Finley. N.Y., Harper, 1945. 717p. **AD103**

1st ed. 1817; several times revised or reprinted. A spot check of the 1945 printing shows no change from the 1917 centennial edition.

An alphabetical list arranged by the first word of a group of synonymous words, with explanation and differentiation of the use and meaning of the words in the group; cross references from each of the words. PE1591.C7

The Doubleday Roget's Thesaurus in dictionary form. Sidney I. Landau, ed. in chief. Garden City, N.Y., Doubleday, 1977. 804p. **AD104**

A dictionary of synonyms rather than a thesaurus in the sense of Roget's classified arrangement. A list of antonyms is given for many of the words. PE1591.D6

Hayakawa, Samuel Ichiyé [et al.]. Funk & Wagnalls modern guide to synonyms and related words. N.Y., Funk & Wagnalls, [1968]. 726p. **AD105**

A new dictionary of synonyms, with terms defined, compared, and contrasted in textual essays that are precise and highly readable. Cross references (mainly intended to show relationships rather than synonymy) and antonyms are given as appropriate. Index.
PE1591.F8

March, Francis Andrew. March's Thesaurus and dictionary of the English language. Introd. by Clarence L. Barnhart. Under the editorial supervision of Norman Cousins; with a new suppl. by R. A. Goodwin and Stuart Flexner. N.Y., Abbeville Pr., [1980]. 1312p. **AD106**

1st ed., 1902, had title *A thesaurus dictionary of the English language*. This is a reprint of the 1958 edition which appeared as *March's Thesaurus-dictionary*, plus a new supplement.

A standard work, giving for each word a definition and cross references to key words under which will be found groups of words of related significance. The supplement (p.1191–1312) has been considerably expanded and updated. PE1625.M3

Rodale, Jerome Irving. The synonym finder. Completely rev. by Laurence Urdang and Nancy La Roche. Emmaus, Pa., Rodale Pr., [1978]. 1361p. **AD107**

Although it is not expressly stated, this is a thorough revision of Rodale's *The word finder* (1947) which, in turn, derived from three earlier publications: *The verb-finder, The adjective-finder,* and *The adverb-finder*. Follows a dictionary arrangement, with entries arranged alphabetically, and all relevant parts of speech listed under a single headword. Usage (i.e., slang, informal) and technical labels are provided as appropriate; "gist information" is often supplied in parentheses to help the user avoid inappropriate choices. About 1,500,000 words.

A review in *Library journal* (Mar. 1, 1979, p.619) notes that, although it lists fewer words, *Webster's New dictionary of synonyms* (AD111) "is to be preferred because it differentiates between connotative and denotative meanings." PE1591.R64

Roget's Thesaurus of English words and phrases. New ed. prep. by Susan M. Lloyd. [London], Longman, [1982]. 1247p. **AD108**

1st ed. 1852 by Peter Mark Roget; frequently revised; latest previous revision by Robert A. Dutch, 1962.

A grouping of words according to ideas within a classification

scheme devised by Roget. Whereas a synonym dictionary "provides alternatives for a given word . . . a thesaurus offers a variety of ways to express a given idea."—*Pref.* Within six main sections (abstract relations; space; matter; intellect; volition; emotion, religion and morality) terms are grouped under 990 "heads" (reduced from 1,000 for Dutch's 1962 ed.) or ideas which the words express. An index facilitates use. PE1591.R7

Roget's II: the new thesaurus. By the editors of the American Heritage dictionary. Boston, Houghton Mifflin, [1980]. 1072p. **AD109**

Represents a departure from traditional thesaurus presentation, employing a dictionary arrangement and two-column format. "In the left-hand column . . . all entries are arranged in alphabetical order and are classified by part of speech. Every word is accurately defined, as is each sense of a word for which more than one meaning has been included. Sentences and phrases using the entry words in context provide guidance in usage. In the right-hand column synonyms and idioms are listed alphabetically within groups and are presented adjacent to each defined meaning of each discrete sense."
—*Pref.* PE1591.R737

Webster's Collegiate thesaurus. Springfield, Mass., G. & C. Merriam, [1976]. 944p. **AD110**

". . . a wholly new book resulting from long study and planning and differing from existent thesauruses in a number of significant respects."—*Pref.* Employs a conventional dictionary arrangement, and gives synonyms, related terms, idiomatic equivalents, antonyms, and contrasted words as applicable. Cross references are indicated by placing relevant words in small capitals. Less full than the following item. PE1591.W38

Webster's New dictionary of synonyms; a dictionary of discriminated synonyms, with antonyms and analogous and contrasted words. [2d ed.] Springfield, Mass., Merriam, [1968]. 909p. **AD111**

First published 1942; previous editions had title *Webster's Dictionary of synonyms.*

A comprehensive dictionary of synonyms, including also antonyms and lists of analogous words and their opposites. Words of like meaning are distinguished from one another by careful discrimination and illustrations from classical and contemporary writers. Includes an introduction on the history of English synonymy. This edition revised, updated, and reset. For many purposes the most useful of the dictionaries of synonyms.

Webster's New world dictionary of synonyms, prep. by Ruth Kimball Kent (N.Y., Simon and Schuster, 1984. 255p.), is intended as "a handy guide to distinguishing the subtle differences that exist" among groups of words "that have nearly the same meaning."—*Foreword.* It is based on material in *Webster's New world dictionary. . . ,* 2d college ed. (AD17). PE1591.W4

Regional and dialect

American

❖There are three important dictionaries of American English: Craigie's *Dictionary of American English on historical principles* (AD113), Mathews's *Dictionary of Americanisms on historical principles* (AD114), and Thornton's *American glossary* (AD115), which together give a fairly comprehensive coverage. Mencken's *American language* (BC81), while not technically a dictionary, is useful for its historical treatment and the large number of words included. Additional lists and articles on special, historical, and current usage may be found in *American speech,* 1925– ; *Dialect notes,* published by the American Dialect Society, 1890–1939; and the Society's monographic *Publications,* 1944– . Wall and Przebienda's *Words and phrases index* (AD117) provides indexing of words treated in these and similar publications.

While the above are the most generally useful dictionaries, some older works are still occasionally helpful for historical purposes, e.g., J. R. Bartlett, *Dictionary of Americanisms* (1877); Sylva Clapin, *New dictionary of Americanisms* (1902); James Maitland, *American slang dictionary* (1891). Some of the more recent slang dictionaries should be used for contemporary speech.

Adams, Ramon Frederick. Western words; a dictionary of the American West. New ed., rev. and enl. Norman, Univ. of Oklahoma Pr., [1968]. 355p.   **AD112**

1st ed. 1944.

Coverage has been extended beyond the "cowman's language" of the earlier edition to include the vocabulary of "the sheepman, the freighter and packer, the trapper, the buffalo hunter, the stagecoach driver, the western-river boatman, the logger, the sawmill worker, the miner, the western gambler—and the Indian."—*Introd.*

PE2970.W4A3

Craigie, *Sir* **William Alexander** and **Hulbert, James R.** Dictionary of American English on historical principles. Chicago, Univ. of Chicago Pr.; London, Oxford Univ. Pr., 1936–44. 4v.   **AD113**

The bibliography (v.4, p.2529–52) gives "a record of the bulk of the reading done for the Dictionary," and expands into completeness the short-title references used in citations.

Compiled on historical principles, with explanations of meaning or use dated when period is clearly determined, and with illustrative quotations dated and arranged chronologically. Symbols indicate: a word or sense found in English before 1600; a word or sense originating within the present limits of the United States; a term or sense known only from the passage cited.

Does not attempt to present a complete historical dictionary of every word which has been current since the settlement of the first English colonists but, instead, to show "those features by which the English of the American colonies and the United States is distinguished from that of England and the rest of the English-speaking world," including for that purpose "not only words or phrases which are clearly or apparently of American origin, or have greater currency here than elsewhere, but also every word denoting something which has a real connection with the development of the country and the history of its people."—cf. *Pref., p.v.*

The period covered is to the end of the 19th century, with later information for some words established before that date. Types of words included are: names of plants, trees, and animals; names of natural or artificial products; and special terms, e.g., topographical, medical, legal, military, naval, business, educational, etc. Colloquialisms are included, but slang and dialect words are restricted to those of early date or special prominence.   PE2835.C72

Mathews, Mitford McLeod. A dictionary of Americanisms on historical principles. Chicago, Univ. of Chicago Pr., [1951]. 2v. (1946p.)   **AD114**

Bibliography, p.1913–46.

More limited in scope than Craigie's *Dictionary of American English* (above); deals with *Americanisms,* meaning "a word or expression that originated in the United States," including (1) outright coinages; (2) foreign words which first became English in the United States; and (3) words used in senses first given them in American usage (cf. *Pref.*). Compiled from sources up to time of publication, excluding manuscript material. Many of the quotations are the same as in Craigie, although the bibliographies vary widely. Definitions and illustrative quotations are given chronologically; usually only one pronunciation is indicated. Some variant spellings are given.

A selection of entries from this work has been published as *Americanisms* (Chicago, Univ. of Chicago Pr., 1966. 304p.); it may prove useful in the small library unable to afford the 2v. set.

PE2835.D5

Thornton, Richard H. An American glossary, being an attempt to illustrate certain Americanisms upon historical principles. London, Francis; Philadelphia, Lippincott, 1912; New Haven, Conn., Amer. Dialect Soc., 1931–39. 3v. (v.3 *in Dialect notes,* 1931–39) (Repr.: With an introduction by Margaret M. Bryant. N.Y., Ungar, 1962. 3v.)   **AD115**

Contents: v.1–2, A–Z; v.3, Supplement A–Z.

Includes: (1) forms of speech now obsolete or provincial in England which survive in the United States; (2) words and phrases of American origin; (3) nouns indicating quadrupeds, birds, trees, etc., that are distinctly American; (4) names of persons, of classes of people, and of places; (5) words that have assumed a new meaning; (6) words and phrases of which there are earlier examples in American than in English writers.

The list of words is largely historical and includes little modern slang. For each word a definition and explanation are given as well as illustrative quotations with exact references to sources, chronologically arranged. These quotations are numerous, some 14,000 in the first two volumes, and are taken from books, pamphlets, newspapers, and periodicals published in various parts of the country.

The Supplement, edited by Louise Hanley, is based on material collected by Thornton after the publication of his *Glossary* and later turned over by him to the American Dialect Society. Examples and illustrative quotations are from a wide general reading, but especially full for the *Congressional globe* and *Congressional record,* 1860–1900, with indication, for words taken from this source, of both the name of the speaker and the part of the country from which he came. This third volume, though first published in *Dialect notes,* is separately paged and has its own title page, so that it can be bound to stand with v.1–2.   PE2835.T6

Wentworth, Harold. American dialect dictionary. N.Y., Crowell, 1944. 747p.   **AD116**

"American printed sources quoted," p.737–47.

Includes more than 10,000 terms with 60,000 quotations showing usage. "Deals mainly with dialect in the sense of localisms, regionalisms, and provincialisms; folk speech, urban as well as rustic New England and Southern United States dialects viewed in their deviations from General Northern or Western. . . ."—*Pref.*

PE2835.W4

Indexes

Wall, C. Edward and **Przebienda, Edward.** Words and phrases index. Ann Arbor, Mich., Pierian Pr., 1969–70. 4v.   **AD117**

Subtitle: A guide to antedatings, new words, new compounds, new meanings, and other published scholarship supplementing the Oxford English Dictionary, Dictionary of Americanisms, Dictionary of American English and other major dictionaries of the English language.

v.1 lists unusual words, compound words, and phrases, with citations to pertinent articles or notes appearing in *American notes and queries* (1962–67), *American speech* (1925–66), *Britannica book of the year* (1945–67), and *Notes and queries* (1925–66); v.2 indexes materials from the same publications, but in a different arrangement —by keyword nouns, verbs, adjectives, and adverbs; v.3 includes about 50,000 references to *American notes and queries* (1941–49), *College English* (1939–68), *Dialect notes* (1890–1939), and the *Publications* of the American Dialect Society (1944–47); v.4 includes material from the same sources as v.3, again in different arrangement, plus new entries from *California folklore quarterly* (1942–47) and *Western folklore* (1948–67).   PE1689.W3

British

Wright, Joseph. English dialect dictionary; being the complete vocabulary of all dialect words still in use, or known to have been in use during the last 200 years; founded on the publications of the English Dialect Society. . . . London, Frowde, 1898–1905. 6v. (Repr.: N.Y., Hacker, 1962)   **AD118**

Contents: v.1–6, A–Z; Supplement, Bibliography, Grammar.

Aims to cover the complete vocabulary of all English dialect words still in use, or known to have been in use from 1700 on, in England, Ireland, Scotland, and Wales, including words occurring in both the literary language and the spoken dialect. Gives for each word: (1) exact geographical area over which it extends; (2) pronunciation; and (3) etymology. Includes American and colonial words still in use in Great Britain or contained in early books and glossaries. Gives many illustrative quotations and, incidentally, considerable information about popular games, customs, and superstitions, with bibliographical references to sources of fuller information. PE1766.W8

Commonwealth

Baker, Sidney John. New Zealand slang; a dictionary of colloquialisms, the first comprehensive survey yet made of indigenous English speech in this country—from the argot of whaling days to children's slang in the twentieth century. Christchurch, N.Z., Whitcombe and Tombs, [1941]. 114p. **AD119**

PE3729.N4B3

Beeton, Douglas Ridley and **Dorner, Helen.** A dictionary of English usage in Southern Africa. Capetown & N.Y., Oxford Univ. Pr., 1975. 196p. **AD120**

Preliminary work for the *Dictionary* was carried out through the journal *English usage in Southern Africa*. Aims to provide a glossary of local vocabulary and idiom; to indicate mistakes and problems which are characteristically South African, as well as those common to speakers of English in general; and to list departures from standard English encountered in South African speech.

PE3451.B36D5

Branford, Jean. A dictionary of South African English. New enl. ed. Cape Town, Oxford Univ. Pr., 1980. 361p. **AD121**

1st ed. 1978.
Offers a wide-ranging, but carefully selected vocabulary intended for the South African with an interest in dialect, its background and usage, for the tourist or immigrant, and for the overseas student of South African literature. In general, an entry gives pronunciation (for non-English terms), grammatical designation, definition, etymology, and illustrative quotations (usually drawn from fairly recent sources).
"This new edition contains roughly 450 complete new entries and a further 300 improved upon or otherwise expanded, where new material or new meanings have come to light."—*Pref.*

PE3451.B7

Cassidy, Frederic Gomes and **Le Page, R. B.** Dictionary of Jamaican English. 2d ed. Cambridge, Cambridge Univ. Pr., [1980]. 509p. **AD122**

A reprinting of the 1967 edition with the addition of a supplement, p.491–509.
A "historical, descriptive dictionary of the English language in all forms it has taken in Jamaica since 1655."—*Gen. introd.*

PE3313.Z5C3

Dictionary of Canadianisms on historical principles. Produced . . . by the Lexicographical Centre for Canadian English, Univ. of Victoria . . . Walter S. Avis, ed. in chief. Toronto, W. J. Gage, 1967. 926p. il. **AD123**

An important work designed "to provide a historical record of words and expressions characteristic of the various spheres of Canadian life during the almost four centuries that English has been used in Canada."—*Introd.* Gives meanings and, where relevant, etymologies and pronunciation (in International Phonetic Alphabet), together with dated examples from printed sources. Extensive bibliography, p.882–926. PE3243.D5

Dictionary of Newfoundland English. Ed. by G. M. Story, W. J. Kirwin, J. D. A. Widdowson. Toronto, Univ. of Toronto Pr., [1982]. 625p. **AD124**

A regional lexicon of Newfoundland and coastal Labrador English. The editors' "guiding principles . . . have been to look for words which appear to have entered the language in Newfoundland or to have been recorded first, or solely, in books about Newfoundland; words which are characteristically Newfoundland by having continued in use here after they died out or declined elsewhere, or

by having a different form or developed a different meaning, or by having a distinctly higher or more general degree of use."—*Introd.*

PE3245.N4D53

Johnston, Grahame. The Australian pocket Oxford dictionary. Melbourne, Oxford Univ. Pr., [1976]. 975p. **AD125**

"Based on *The pocket Oxford dictionary of current English,* first edited by F. G. and H. W. Fowler [1924]."—*t.p.*
"The distinctive feature of this book is its attempt to cover as informatively and comprehensively as possible within limited space the vocabulary, idioms, and pronunciation of Australian English." —*p.xx.* PE3601.Z5J6

Pettman, Charles. Africanderisms; a glossary of South African colloquial words and phrases, and of place and other names. London & N.Y., Longmans, 1913. 579p. **AD126**

Good definitions. Illustrative quotations are given with date and exact page reference. PE3401.P4

Wilkes, Gerald Alfred. A dictionary of Australian colloquialisms. Sydney, Sydney Univ. Pr.; London, Routledge & Paul, [1978]. 370p. **AD127**

"This dictionary is planned, in a modest way, 'on historical principles.' It seeks to record the history of each word, through examples of usage."—*Introd.* Examples are dated, and citations to sources are given.
An older work, *Austral English* by Edward Ellis Morris (London, Macmillan, 1898. 525p.), includes words, phrases and usages from Australasia in general. PE3601.Z5W5

Yule, *Sir* Henry and **Burnell, A. C.** Hobson-Jobson; a glossary of colloquial Anglo-Indian words and phrases, and of kindred terms, etymological, historical, geographical and discursive. New ed., by William Crooke. London, Murray, 1903. 1021p. **AD128**

A standard work still not superseded. PE3501.Y8

Scottish

Craigie, *Sir* William Alexander. Dictionary of the older Scottish tongue from the 12th century to the end of the 17th. Chicago, Univ. of Chicago Pr.; London, Oxford Univ. Pr., 1932–83. Pts.1–31. (In progress) **AD129**

Contents: pts.1–31, A–Pn.
Beginning with pt.17, ed. by A. J. Aitken and others.
"Intended to exhibit the whole range of the Older Scottish vocabulary, as preserved in literature and documentary records, and to continue the history of the language to 1700, so far as it does not coincide with the ordinary English usage of that century."—*Pref. note.* PE2116.C7

Jamieson, John. Etymological dictionary of the Scottish language . . . to which is prefixed a dissertation on the origin of the Scottish language. New ed., carefully rev. and collated, with the entire supplement incorporated, by John Longmuir and David Donaldson. Paisley, Gardner, 1879–82. 4v. and suppl., 1887. **AD130**

1st ed., 2v., 1808; suppl. by Jamieson, 2v., 1827; an edition incorporating the words of the supplement but omitting its quotations, ed. by J. Johnstone, 1840–41; the rev. ed. by Longmuir and Donaldson, as above.
A comprehensive work, now out-of-date for etymologies, but still useful for the number of words included, the definitions, and the large amount of incidental information on local usages, customs, etc. PE2106.J3

———— Jamieson's Dictionary of the Scottish language abridged by J. Johnstone and rev. and enl. by Dr. Longmuir, with suppl. . . . by W. M. Metcalfe. Paisley, Gardner, 1910. 2v. in 1. **AD131**

1st ed. of the Johnstone abridgment of Jamieson, 1840; ed. rev. by Longmuir, 2v., 1867.

Contents: v.1, The Johnstone-Longmuir abridgment. 635p.; v.2, Supplementary dictionary, by W. M. Metcalfe. 263p.

PE2106.J36

Jarvie, James Nicol. Lallans; a selection of Scots words arranged as an English-Scottish dictionary, with pronunciation and examples. London, Wren Books, 1947. 159p.

AD132

English-Scottish. Includes Scots proverbs and quotations.

PE2106.J38

Scottish national dictionary, designed partly on regional lines and partly on historical principles, and containing all the Scottish words known to be in use or to have been in use since *c.* 1700; ed. by William Grant and David Murison. Edinburgh, Scottish Nat. Dictionary Assoc., 1931–76. 10v.

AD133

Scope: "The *Scottish National Dictionary* deals with (1) Scottish words in existence since *c.* 1700: (a) in Scottish literature, (b) in public records, (c) in glossaries and in dictionaries, (d) in private collections, (e) in special dialect treatises, and (2) Scottish words gathered from the mouth of dialect speakers by competent observers. The general vocabulary will include (1) Scottish words that do not occur in Standard English except as acknowledged loan words; (2) Scottish words the cognates of which occur in St. Eng.; (3) words which have the same form in Scots and St. Eng. but have a different meaning in Sc., *i.e.,* so-called Scotticisms; (4) legal, theological or ecclesiastical terms which within our period have been current in Scottish speech . . . (5) words borrowed since *c.* 1700 (from other dialects or languages) which have become current in General Scots, or in any of its dialects, especially Gaelic words in counties on or near the Sc. Western limit and Gypsy words in the Border counties." —*Introd., p.xlv.*

Treatment: for each word gives variant spellings, grammatical function, status (e.g., obsolete, colloquial, etc.), pronunciation, illustrative quotations with exact references to sources, and origin of word, if known.

v.10 includes a "Miscellanea" section giving lists of personal names, place-names, fairs and markets, Scottish currency, weights and measures; a supplement; a "List of works quoted in the Dictionary"; and "A list of scientific terms with Scottish connections."

PE2106.S4

Anglo-Norman

Modern Humanities Research Assoc. Anglo-Norman dictionary. Under the general editorship of Louise W. Stone and William Rothwell. London, Modern Humanities Research Assoc., 1977–83. Fasc.1–3. (In progress)   **AD134**

At head of title: The Modern Humanities Research Association in conjunction with the Anglo-Norman Text Society.

Contents: Fasc.1–3, A–L.

"The purpose of this Dictionary is to facilitate the reading and understanding of a wide variety of texts written in the French used in the British Isles between the time of the Norman Conquest and the late fifteenth century. To this end, each separate sense of each word listed is illustrated by a quotation, chosen on semantic rather than on historical grounds."—*Introd.*

PC2946.M6

Anglo-Saxon

Bessinger, Jess Balsor. A short dictionary of Anglo-Saxon poetry, in a normalized early West-Saxon orthography. Toronto, Univ. of Toronto Pr., 1960. 87p.   **AD135**

"A gloss to the crucial 40 per cent of the poetic vocabulary—some 3000 parent words."—*Pref.*

PE279.B4

Borden, Arthur R. A comprehensive Old-English dictionary. [Wash.], University Pr. of America, [1982]. 1606p.

AD136

Aims to provide as complete a list of Old-English words as possible, including all those found in earlier dictionaries and those

in glosses of standard texts and readers. Indicates part of speech and meaning.

PE279.B48

Bosworth, Joseph. Anglo-Saxon dictionary based on the manuscript collections of the late Joseph Bosworth, ed. and enl. by T. Northcote Toller. Oxford, Clarendon Pr., 1882–98. 1302p. (Repr. 1972)   **AD137**

—— —— Supplement, by T. Northcote Toller. Oxford, Clarendon Pr., 1908–21. 768p. (Repr. 1972, with enl. addenda and corrigenda, below)

—— —— —— Enlarged addenda and corrigenda by Alistair Campbell to the supplement by T. Northcote Toller. Oxford, Clarendon Pr., 1972. 68p.

1st ed. 1838.

Still the standard work, with many illustrative quotations and exact references to sources. The letters A–G are extensively revised and enlarged in the Supplement.

PE279.B52

Hall, John Richard Clark. Concise Anglo-Saxon dictionary. 4th ed., with a supplement by Herbert D. Meritt. Cambridge, Univ. Pr., 1960. 432p., [20p.].   **AD138**

1st ed. 1894; 3d ed., rev. and enl., 1931.

References are given to the headings in the *New English dictionary* (AD27) under which quotations are cited from the Anglo-Saxon texts, thus making it serve as an index to the large amount of valuable information on Old English words included in the *NED* but often overlooked because it is found under the headings of words now obsolete.

PE279.H3

Jember, Gregory K. English-Old English, Old English-English dictionary. Boulder, Colo., Westview Pr., [1975]. 178p.

AD139

In two parts: (1) English-Old English; (2) Old English-English. Each section provides equivalents for about 5,000 of the most common words. Intended as an aid to the student in writing Old English.

PE279.J4

Middle English

Middle English dictionary. Hans Kurath, ed.; Sherman M. Kuhn, assoc. ed. Ann Arbor, Univ. of Michigan Pr., 1952–85. Pts. A–R$^{1-3}$. (In progress)   **AD140**

Editor varies. Hans Kurath, 1946–61; Sherman M. Kuhn, 1961–83; Robert E. Lewis [and others], 1984– .

This important dictionary, a research project of the University of Michigan, is based on a large collection of Middle English quotations, which includes all those assembled for the *New English dictionary* (AD27), both published and unpublished, in addition to hundreds of thousands gathered for this work. It is to be completed in some 65 parts and will include about 10,000 pages. The bibliography and a full description of the editing plan appeared as a separate part in 1954 with the title *Plan and bibliography* (105p.).

To cover the language from 1100 to 1475; gives the history of a word, with many illustrative quotations arranged chronologically. Many cross references.

PE679.M54

Stratmann, Franz Heinrich. Middle-English dictionary, containing words used by English writers from the 12th to the 15th century; new ed. rearranged, rev., and enl. by Henry Bradley. Oxford, Clarendon Pr., 1891. 708p. (Repr. 1963)

AD141

This standard work will still be useful until the *Middle English dictionary* (above) is completed. Gives etymologies and references to sources.

PE679.S7

Foreign words and phrases

Bliss, Alan Joseph. A dictionary of foreign words and phrases in current English. N.Y., Dutton; London, Routledge, 1966. 389p.   **AD142**

Indicates language of origin (but not pronunciation), definition,

and date (i.e., century) introduced into English. Literal meaning of the term is given if it differs substantially from that of the definition.
PE1670.B55

Guinagh, Kevin. Dictionary of foreign phrases and abbreviations. 3d ed. N.Y., Wilson, 1983. 261p.   **AD143**

1st ed. 1965.

Lists, in a single alphabet, foreign phrases, proverbs, abbreviations, etc., frequently used in written and spoken English. Translations and, where necessary, brief explanatory notes are given; also a list of phrases arranged by language.   PE1670.G8

Pei, Mario Andrew and **Ramondino, Salvatore.** Dictionary of foreign terms. N.Y., Delacorte Pr., [1974]. 366p.   **AD144**

Indicates the language from which the word or phrase derives, pronunciation, and meaning of "useful, interesting and timely" foreign terms frequently encountered in the English-speaking world.
PE1670.P44

FOREIGN LANGUAGES

❖Foreign-language dictionaries are important in any library, though their use will vary greatly according to the size and type of the library and the character of the library clientele. The needs of the small library used by English-speaking readers may be met by a modest equipment of French, German, Spanish, Italian, and Latin dictionaries, while the small or branch library in a locality which has a considerable foreign population will need also the dictionaries of the languages represented in the community. Large public libraries, and especially university libraries, need the best dictionaries of all principal languages and many minor languages.

Two main types of dictionaries are represented in the following list: (1) the standard monolingual dictionary, such as Grimm (AD361), and (2) the bilingual dictionary, such as the various French-English and German-English dictionaries. The first type is the more complete and must be consulted when the fullest vocabulary or detailed and historical information is needed, but it can be used only by someone fairly familiar with the language and is not generally needed in the smaller library. The second type, which is the kind most used in the average library, is planned for people who are learning a language, is much less complete in vocabulary, and usually contains no historical information, as its main purpose is not detailed definition but the explanation of a foreign word by its equivalent in another language. Emphasis in this listing has naturally been placed on the foreign-language-into-English dictionary, although in some cases others are included, e.g., Greek-German. While all of the major and a good many of the lesser-known languages are represented here, listings for the latter—e.g., the numerous Indian and African languages—are highly selective.

The ordinary bilingual dictionary is generally satisfactory for most words of the literary language but is often weak in scientific terms and technical expressions. For these, scientific and technical dictionaries should be consulted.

Bilingual dictionaries also differ according to the users for whom they are compiled. In a French-English dictionary, prepared for the use of English-speaking students learning French, the French-English section is the more important, and this will be developed carefully, while the English-French section may be given briefer treatment. The reverse is true of a dictionary prepared for French students learning English. A library which can afford to have several dictionaries of a language should take this difference into account and represent both points of view.

As so large a proportion of the use of foreign dictionaries in an American library is for the purpose of finding the English meaning of a foreign word, the many other possible uses of such books are sometimes overlooked. The larger dictionaries frequently contain some encyclopedic information; those that include many quotations may often be used to supplement the dictionaries of foreign quotations; and the larger historical or dialectal dictionaries which include obsolete words, local usages, etc., may be used for information on small points of local history, manners and customs, folklore, etc.

See name of subject for scientific, technical, and other special dictionaries, e.g., Chemistry—Dictionaries, etc.

For more extensive lists of dictionaries, consult the bibliographies, AD145–AD156.

Bibliography

See also Collison, AD1.

Bibliographie der Wörterbücher, erschienenen in der Deutschen Demokratischen Republik, Rumänischen Volksrepublik, Tschechoslowakischen Sozialistischen Republik, Ungarischen Volksrepublik, Union der Sozialistischen Sowjetrepubliken, Volksrepublik Bulgarien, Volksrepublik China, Volksrepublik Polen. . . . 1945/61– . Warszawa, Wydawnictwa Naukowo-Techniczne, [1965]– . [v.1]– . Biennial. (v.9, 1977/78 publ. 1981)   **AD145**

Frequency varies. Title varies slightly. Editors vary.

Title also in Polish and English. English title: Bibliography of dictionaries published in Bulgarian People's Republic, Chinese People's Republic, Czechoslovak Socialist Republic, German Democratic Republic, Hungarian People's Republic, Polish People's Republic, Rumanian People's Republic, Union of Soviet Socialist Republics. (China was dropped after v.3, 1965/66)

Each volume lists dictionaries in all fields, published in the countries named in the title during the period of coverage. Titles are translated into German and/or Russian as applicable. Indexes of authors, titles, languages, and subjects.   Z7004.D5B55

Brewer, Annie M. Dictionaries, encyclopedias, and other word-related books. Ed. . . .with the assistance of Marie Browne. 3d ed. Detroit, Gale, [1982]. 3v. plus suppl. (1983. 236p.)   **AD146**

Subtitle: A classed guide to dictionaries, encyclopedias, and similar works, based on Library of Congress catalog cards, and arranged according to the Library of Congress classification system. Including compilations of acronyms, Americanism, colloquialisms, etymologies, glossaries, idioms and expressions, orthography, provincialisms, slang, terms and phrases, and vocabularies in English and all other languages.

1st ed. 1975.

Contents: v.1, English books; v.2, Multiple languages (with English as one language); v.3, Non-English books.

This edition "includes all of the entries from the first and second editions, plus L.C. cards issued from 1979 to October 1981 and additional entries gathered by reading *The Library of Congress Shelflist,* microfiche edition."—*Introd.* The supplement includes L.C. cards issued from Nov. 1981 to Aug. 1983.

A note on the 2d ed. in *Booklist* 76:1079 terms the work expensive and difficult to use.   Z5848.B73

Calcutta. National Library. A bibliography of dictionaries and encyclopaedias in Indian languages. Calcutta, 1964. 165p.   **AD147**

Lists nearly 2,200 items in modern Indian languages. Includes scientific, technical, and other subject encyclopedias and dictionaries, and also biographical dictionaries. Works are grouped by language, with author-subject-title index.

Haugen, Eva Lund. A bibliography of Scandinavian dictionaries. White Plains, N.Y., Kraus Internat., [1984]. 387p. **AD148**

". . . lists dictionaries published between 1510 and 1980 that are entirely in one of the Scandinavian languages (Danish, Faroese, Icelandic, Norwegian, or Swedish) or that translate one of the Scandinavian languages into one or more other languages."—*p.xvii.* Sections for monolingual, bilingual, and multilingual dictionaries are subdivided by subject matter or language, as appropriate. More than 2,500 items. Author and subject indexes. Z2555.H39

Hendrix, Melvin K. An international bibliography of African lexicons. Metuchen, N.J., Scarecrow Pr., 1982. 348p. **AD149**

More than 2,600 entries relating to some 600 languages and about 200 dialects. As used here, "lexicon" refers to "any stock of words or word elements compiled for an African language in order to present materials of diverse linguistic interest."—*Introd.* Thus, semantic and etymological studies are included as well as dictionaries, vocabularies, word lists, conversation and phrase books, glossaries, etc. Z7106.H45

International bibliography of specialized dictionaries. Fachwörterbücher und Lexika; ein internationales Verzeichnis. 6th ed. München, K. G. Saur, 1979. 470p. (Handbook of international documentation and information, v.4) **AD150**

1st ed. 1960 had title *Technik und Wirtschaft in fremden Sprachen.* Helga Lengenfelder, ed.
Lists some 5,700 mono- and multi-lingual dictionaries published since 1970. Z7004.D5I57

Lewanski, Richard Casimir, comp. A bibliography of Slavic dictionaries. Bologna, Ist. Informatico Italiano, 1972–73. 4v. (v.3, 1972) **AD151**

v.1 first issued 1959 as *A bibliography of Polish dictionaries;* 1959–63 edition issued by New York Public Library in 3v.
Contents: v.1, Polish; v.2, Belorussian, Bulgarian, Czech, Kashubian, Lusatian, Old Church Slavic, Macedonian, Polabian, Serbocroatian, Slovak, Slovenian, Ukrainian; v.3, Russian; v.4, Supplement [covering Belorussian, Bulgarian, Czech, Kashubian, Lusatian, Macedonian, Old Church Slavic, Polabian, Russian, Serbocroatian, Slovak, Slovenian, Ukrainian; author, language, and subject indexes].
A comprehensive bibliography of Slavic dictionaries, not only dictionaries of language, but of abbreviations, biography, orthography, quotations, philosophy, science, etc. Z7041.L58

U.S. Library of Congress. General Reference and Bibliography Division. Foreign language-English dictionaries. Wash., 1955. 2v. **AD152**

Contents: v.1, Special subject dictionaries, 1,524 items, with emphasis on science and technology; v.2, General language dictionaries, 1,465 items.
A revised edition of the Library's *Foreign language-English dictionaries,* comp. by Grace Hadley Fuller (1942–44). Z7004.D5U52

Wajid, Mohammad. Oriental dictionaries: a select bibliography. Karachi, Lib. Promotion Bureau, 1967. 54p. (Lib. Promotion Bureau publ. no.2) **AD153**

Lists 345 dictionaries of the Arabic, Balochi, Bengali, Gujarati, Hindi, Hindustani, Kashmiri, Persian, Punjabi, Pushto, Sanskrit, Sinhi, Turkish, and Urdu languages. Some brief annotations. Z7004.D5W3

Walford, Albert John and **Screen, John Ernest Oliver.** A guide to foreign language courses and dictionaries. 3d ed., rev. and enl. London, Library Assoc., 1977. 343p. **AD154**

1st–2d ed. (1964–67) by A. J. Walford had title: *A guide to foreign language grammars and dictionaries.*
A complete revision, considerably expanded as to the number of languages covered. The work now "provides a running commentary on selected courses, audio-visual aids and dictionaries in most of the main European languages, plus Arabic, Chinese and Japanese. It is intended for teachers, students, graduates taking up a particular language for the first time, scientists (for acquiring a reading knowledge of a language on a minimum of grammar), tourists, business men and librarians (for book-selection and stock revision)."—*Introd.* Information is presented in sections according to type and level of user. Z5818.L35

World dictionaries in print 1983: a guide to general and subject dictionaries in world languages. N.Y., Bowker, [1983]. 579p. **AD155**

Based on the entries in Bowker's *Books in print* and *Associations' publications in print* databases, augmented by information solicited by questionnaire from publishers throughout the world. Lists more than 13,000 publications in some 238 language categories from publishers in about 100 countries. Full information appears in both the subject and title indexes; the author/editor/compiler index supplies titles; the language index lists titles within language categories. Includes technical and subject dictionaries (both monolingual and multilingual) as well as language dictionaries *per se.*

Zaunmüller, Wolfram. Bibliographisches Handbuch der Sprachwörterbücher: ein internationales Verzeichnis von 5600 Wörterbüchern der Jahre 1460–1958 für mehr als 500 Sprachen und Dialekte. Stuttgart, Hiersemann, 1958. 496col. **AD156**

A very useful, annotated bibliography of language dictionaries attempting to be complete for those published during the 100 years prior to preparation of this work, with a selection of those published between 1460 and 1850. The first and the last editions are noted. The most important items are starred. Arranged alphabetically under language names with subdivisions for the large language groups. These subdivisions usually include as pertinent: (1) General (monolingual) dictionaries since 1850; (2) Bilingual or polylingual dictionaries; (3) Orthography, pronunciation, dictionaries of names; (4) Synonyms, style, usage, rhymes, etc.; (5) Slang, foreign words; (6) Dialect dictionaries; (7) Etymological dictionaries; (8) Dictionaries of old speech; (9) General dictionaries before 1850. Includes an index of names and one of the languages under each continent. Z7004.D5Z3

Afrikaans

Bosman, Daniël Brink, Merwe, I. W. van der and **Hiemstra, L. W.** Tweetalige woordebook: Afrikaans-Engels, Engels-Afrikaans. 7., verb. uitg. Kaapstad, Tafelberg-Uitgewers, 1981. 1901p. **AD157**

1st ed. 1931–36 in 2v. by Bosman and Merwe.
The word list for the English-Afrikaans section is based on the *Concise Oxford dictionary;* the Afrikaans list was developed for this publication. PF862.B617

Kritzinger, Matthys Stefanus Benjamin. Groot woordebook: Afrikaans-Engels, Engels-Afrikaans. 12. uitg. Pretoria, Van Schaik, 1981. 1623p. **AD158**

Prior to 1937 published as *Woordeboek Afrikaans-Engels, Engels-Afrikaans.*
Kritzinger's *Handige woordebook: Afrikaans-Engels; Handy dictionary: English-Afrikaans* (Pretoria, Van Schaik, 1976. 750p.) is a shorter work including "most of the words which the intelligent reader uses and needs" *(Foreword),* but omitting proverbs, expressions, abbreviations, and some vocabulary found in the larger version. PF862.K7

Schoonees, Pieter Cornelis, ed. Woordeboek van die Afrikaanse taal. Pretoria, Die Staatsdrukker, 1950–84. v.1–7. il. (In progress) **AD159**

Editors vary.
Contents: v.1–7, A–Kor.
Planned as the standard Afrikaans dictionary and sponsored by the government, the Suid-Afrikaanse Akademie vir Wetenskap en

Kuns, and the University of Stellenbosch; the work of scholars from all over the Union. No etymologies or historical developments are given; pronunciation is indicated only in doubtful cases.

PF862.S35

Terblanche, Hendrik Josephus. Nuwe praktiese woordeboek. New practical dictionary. 5th improved and enl. ed. Johannesburg, Afrikaanse Pers-Boekhandel, 1966. 883p. **AD160**

1st ed. 1949.

English-Afrikaans; Afrikaans-English.

Intends to represent the spoken and written language of everyday life, with emphasis on current idiom and general practice.

PF862.T43

Albanian

Drizari, Nelo. Albanian-English and English-Albanian dictionary. 2d enl. ed., with a suppl. of new words. N.Y., Ungar, 1957. 320p. **AD161**

1st ed., 1934, had title *Fjalór Shqip-Inglisht dhe Inglisht-Shqip*.

PG9591.D7

Fjalor i gjuhës së sotme shqipe (me rreth 41,000 fjalë). [Hartuar nën drejtimin e Androkli Kostallarit (kryeredaktor)] Tirane, 1980. 2273p. **AD162**

At head of title: Akademia e Shkencave e RPS të Shqipërise. Instituti i Gjuhësisë dhe i Letërsise.

Kici, Gasper and **Aliko, Hysni.** English-Albanian dictionary. [Roma, Tip. Editrice Romana, 1969] 627p. **AD163**

Added title-page in Albanian: Fjalor anglisht-shqip.

Intended primarily for the Albanian immigrant to North America.

PG9591.K5

Mann, Stuart Edward. An historical Albanian-English dictionary. London, Longmans, 1948. 601p. **AD164**

A standard work concerned primarily with linguistics but useful as a bilingual dictionary.

PG9591.M32

—— An English-Albanian dictionary. Cambridge, Univ. Pr., 1957. 434p. **AD165**

". . . in some degree the counterpart of my *Historical Albanian-English dictionary*. . . . It is an attempt to express the essential vocabulary of the English literary language in modern literary Albanian."—*Pref.* PG9591.M28

Amharic

Baeteman, Joseph. Dictionnaire amarigna-français, suivi d'un vocabulaire français-amarigna. Dire-Daoua (Ethiopie), Impr. Saint Lazare, 1929. 1262col., 426col. **AD166**

PJ9237.F8B3

Leslau, Wolf. English-Amharic context dictionary. Wiesbaden, Harrassowitz, 1973. 1503p. **AD167**

The first modern English-Amharic dictionary in many years. The English term is followed by the Amharic equivalent, plus an English sentence using the word and an Amharic translation thereof.

PJ9237.E7L43

—— Concise Amharic dictionary: Amharic-English, English-Amharic. Wiesbaden, Harrassowitz, 1976. 538p. **AD168**

Intends to provide an up-to-date reference work for the student of Amharic. PJ9237.E7L424

Arabic

Badger, George Percy. English-Arabic lexicon, in which the equivalents for English words and idiomatic sentences are rendered into literary and colloquial Arabic. London, Paul, 1881. 1244p. **AD169**

A famous 19th-century work. PJ6640.B3

Blachère, Régis, Chouémi, Moustafa and **Denizeau, Claude.** Dictionnaire arabe-français-anglais. (Langue classique et moderne) Arabic/French/English dictionary. Paris, Maisonneuve et Larose, 1964–84. v.1–4[7] (fasc. 1–43). (In progress) **AD170**

Beginning with fasc.37, editorship was assumed by Moustafa Chouémi and Charles Pellat.

Intends "to comprise all the vocabulary that constitutes . . . 'literary' Arabic."—*Foreword*. Meanings are given in French, then in English. PJ6645.F6B6

Deutsche Morgenländische Gesellschaft. Wörterbuch der klassischen arabischen Sprache . . . hrsg. durch die Deutsche Morgenländische Gesellschaft. Wiesbaden, Harrassowitz, 1957–84. v.1–2[1-12]. (In progress) **AD171**

"Auf Grund der Sammlungen von August Fischer, Theodor Nöldeke, Hermann Reckendorf, und anderer Quellen."—*title page*.

A scholarly work of classical Arabic with extensive references to the literature. The main words are translated into both German and English.

Elias, Elias Antoon and **Elias, Edward E.** Elias' Modern dictionary, English-Arabic. 16th ed. [Cairo, Elias], 1969. 816p. **AD172**

Frequently reprinted.

About 68,000 words. PJ6640.E6

—— Elias' Modern dictionary, Arabic-English. 9th ed., with several additions and alterations. Cairo, Elias, 1962. 870p. il. **AD173**

"Containing about 64,500 words."—*verso of title page*.

PJ6640.E6

Lane, Edward William. Arabic-English lexicon, derived from the best and the most copious eastern sources. In two books: the first containing all the classical words and significations commonly known to the learned among the Arabs; the second, those that are of rare occurrence and not commonly known. Book I. London, Williams & Norgate, 1863–93. 1v. in 8 pts., paged continuously. (Repr.: Cambridge, Islamic Text Soc., 1984. 2v.) **AD174**

Book II never published.

Includes references to the literature.

A review by Robert Irwin of the 1984 reprint appears in *TLS* 4–26–85, p.474. PJ6640.L3

The Oxford English-Arabic dictionary of current usage, ed. by N. S. Doniach. Oxford, Clarendon Pr., 1972. 1392p. **AD175**

Intended both for English-speaking students of Arabic and for Arabic-speaking students of English. Includes formal literary English, colloquial, and slang usage, with the closest Arabic equivalent at the same level of usage.

The Concise Oxford English-Arabic dictionary of current usage (London, Oxford Univ. Pr., 1982. 461p.) is a condensed and updated version. PJ6640.O93

Spiro, Socrates, *Bey.* Arabic-English and English-Arabic vocabulary of the modern and colloquial Arabic of Egypt. 2d–3d ed. rev. Cairo, Elias, 1923–29. 2v. **AD176**

Arabic-English. 2d ed. 1923. 518p.; English-Arabic. 3d ed. 1929. 325p.

A dictionary of the colloquial Arabic of Egypt. PJ6767.S6

Theodory, Constantine. A dictionary of modern technical terms. Arabic-English. Beirut, Dar-al-Kutub Pr., 1959. 464p.   **AD177**

Added title page in Arabic.

Includes much more than scientific and technical terms, e.g., proverbs and aphoristic phrases, literary expressions, political and diplomatic phrases, military terms and expressions, psychological and educational terms, etc. Grouped into chapters by general topic.

Wehr, Hans. A dictionary of modern written Arabic (Arabic-English). ed. by J. Milton Cowan. 4th ed., considerably enl. and amended. Wiesbaden, Harrassowitz, 1979. 1301p.
                                                         AD178

The 1961 ed. was a translated, edited, and enlarged version of the author's *Arabisches Wörterbuch für die Schriftsprache der Gegenwart* (Leipzig, Harrassowitz, 1952. 2v.; Supplement, 1958).

This edition incorporates new words and usages as well as some older material not previously included. "The number of new entries, including lemmata as well as compounds, idiomatic phrases and new definitions of head words, runs to approximately 13,000" (*Pref.*), and in some 3,000 instances "smaller additions (new transcriptions, plural forms, prepositional government of verbs, cross-references, etc.) have been inserted, errors corrected, obsolete entries eliminated." Additions and deletions were accomplished by "cutting and pasting" rather than resetting, with some resulting inconsistencies in presentation and arrangement.   PJ6640.W43

Woodhead, D. R. and **Beene, Wayne,** eds. A dictionary of Iraqi Arabic: Arabic-English. Wash., Georgetown Univ. Pr., [1967]. 509p. (Georgetown Univ., Inst. of Languages and Linguistics. Arabic ser., 10)   **AD179**

A dictionary of the colloquial Arabic spoken in Baghdad; "designed to allow Americans to understand Iraqi Arabic."—*Introd.*

Wortabet, John and **Porter, Harvey.** English-Arabic and Arabic-English dictionary; with a supplement of modern words and new meanings by John L. Mish. [Enl. ed.] N.Y., Ungar, 1954. 455p., 423p.   **AD180**

The reprint of a basic dictionary, with a supplement containing modern words and expressions.   PJ6640.W57

Wortabet, William Thomson. Wortabet's Arabic-English dictionary. 4th ed. Beirut, Librairie du Liban, [1968]. 802p.
                                                         AD181

"With the collaboration of Rev. John Wortabet . . . and Professor Harvey Porter."—*t.p.*

Added title page in Arabic.

A reprint of the 3d ed. published in Beirut, 1913, under title: *Arabic-English dictionary* (1st ed. 1888).   PJ6640.W6

Armenian

Aukerian, Haroutiun. Dictionary, English and Armenian. 2d ed. Venice, Armenian Academy of St. Lazarus, 1868. 815p.
                                                         AD182

Added title page in Armenian.

1821–25 ed. in 2v. by Aukerian and John Brand.   PK8091.A8

Froundjian, Dirair. Armenisch-deutsches Wörterbuch. München, R. Oldenbourg, 1952. 505p.   **AD183**

Added title page in Armenian.

A useful dictionary of modern Armenian, including many technical terms.   PK8093.F7

Kouyoumdjian, Mesrob G. A comprehensive dictionary, Armenian-English. Cairo, Sahag-Mesrob Pr., [1950]. 1158p. (Repr.: Watertown, Mass., Baikar Armenian Daily, 1970)
                                                         AD184

A dictionary of modern Armenian, giving equivalents in English.

Kouyoumdjian is also the compiler of *A Comprehensive dictionary of idioms, English-Armenian* (Cairo, Vozguedar, 1969. 668p.).
                                                         PK8091.K6

Aryan

See also AD48.

Buck, Carl Darling. A dictionary of selected synonyms in the principal Indo-European languages; a contribution to the history of ideas. Chicago, Univ. of Chicago Pr., 1949. 1515p. (Repr. 1965)   **AD185**

Arranged by semantic groupings. Under each term the equivalent word is given in about 30 of the major Indo-European languages, followed by a description of its etymology and semantic history.
                                                         P765.B8

Carnoy, Albert Joseph. Dictionnaire étymologique du proto-indo-européen. Louvain, Publications Universitaires, 1955. 223p. (Bibliothèque du Muséon, v.39)   **AD186**

At head of title: Université de Louvain. Institut Orientaliste.
                                                         P725.C3

Pokorny, Julius. Indogermanisches etymologisches Wörterbuch. Berne, A. Francke, 1948–69. 2v. (1183p., 495p.)
                                                         AD187

Issued in parts.

A standard etymological dictionary of the various Indogermanic languages. More than a revision of the Walde-Pokorny *Vergleichendes Wörterbuch der indogermanischen Sprachen* (Berlin, de Gruyter, 1927–32), which was based on materials published only through 1923. This uses sources through 1947, and is arranged according to the European, rather than the Indian, alphabet. v.2 contains indexes.   P725.P63

Turner, *Sir* **Ralph Lilley.** A comparative dictionary of the Indo-Aryan languages. London, Oxford Univ. Pr., 1962–66. 841p.   **AD188**

Published in 11 pts.

A comparative dictionary of more than 50 of the related languages of India, descended from that of the Aryan invaders, with English translations. Frequently gives references to the literature. Words are given in transliteration into the roman alphabet.   PK175.T8

—— —— Indexes, comp. by Dorothy Rivers Turner. London, Oxford Univ. Pr., 1969. 357p.

The indexes list all the 140,000 words quoted in the *Dictionary* for purposes of comparison, arranged by language or language-group.

—— —— Phonetic analysis, by R. L. Turner and D. R. Turner. London, Oxford Univ. Pr., 1971. 231p.

Assyro-Babylonian

Bezold, Carl. Babylonisch-assyrisches Glossar; nach dem Tode des Verfassers unter Mitwirkung von Adele Bezold zum Druck gebracht von Albrecht Götze. Heidelberg, Winter, 1926. 343p.   **AD189**
                                                         PJ3540.B4

Chicago. University. Oriental Institute. The Assyrian dictionary. Editorial Board: Ignace J. Gelb [and others]. Chicago, Oriental Inst., 1956–80. v.1–11, 16, 21. (In progress)
                                                         AD190

Editors vary.

Cited as *CAD*, i.e., *Chicago Assyrian dictionary.*

Contents: v.1¹⁻², A; v.2, B; v.3, D; v.4, E; v.5, G; v.6, H; v.7, I–J; v.8, K; v.9, L; v.10¹⁻², M; v.11¹⁻², N; v.16, S; v.21, Z.

A scholarly Assyrian-English dictionary, giving meanings in English with examples and citations to literature. Of first importance.
                                                         PJ3525.C5

Deimel, Anton. Šumerisches Lexikon. Rome, Sumptibus Pontificii Inst. Biblici, 1927–50. 4v. (Scripta Pontificii Inst. Biblici)   **AD191**

Contents: T.1, Lautwerte der Keilschriftzeichen in šumerischen, akkadischen und hethitischen Texten; T.2, Vollständige Ideogram-

Sammlung. 4v.; T.3, Bd.1, Šumerisch-akkadisches Glossar. Bd.2, Akkadisch-šumerisches Glossar; T.4, Bd.1, Pantheon babylonicum. Bd.2, Planetarium babylonicum, von P. Gössman.   PJ4037.D35

Muss-Arnolt, William. Concise dictionary of the Assyrian language. Berlin, Reuther; N.Y., Lemcke, 1905. 1202p.   **AD192**

Assyrian, English, and German.   PJ3525.M7

Soden, Wolfram von. Akkadisches Handwörterbuch unter Benutzung des lexikalischen Nachlasses von Bruno Meissner (1868–1947). Wiesbaden, Harrassowitz, 1959–81. 3v.   **AD193**

Issued in parts.

A scholarly work, somewhat less comprehensive than the *Assyrian dictionary* (AD190). A detailed review of early parts appears in *Bibliotheca orientalis* 17:166–68 (1960).   PJ3540

Basque

Griera y Gaja, Antonio. Vocabolario vasco (ensayo de una interpretación de la lengua vasca). [Barcelona], Instituto Internacional de Cultura Románica, 1960. 2v. (Biblioteca filologica-historica, 2–7)   **AD194**

Gives Spanish equivalent and derivation of the Basque term.   PH5177.S7G7

Lhande, Pierre. Dictionnaire basque-français et français-basque (dialectes labourdin, bas-navarrais et souletin) d'après le Dictionnaire basque-espagnol-français de l'abbé R. M. de Askué [i.e., Azkué] et les dictionnaires manuscrits des abbés M. Harriet, M. Hiribarren et Pierre Foix. Paris, G. Beauchesne, 1926–38. v.1.   **AD195**

v.1, Basque-français (1117p.), published in 9 pts.
The standard work.   PH5177.F8L5

Bengali

Dev, Ashu Tosh. Students' favourite dictionary: English-to-Bengali & English. 20th ed. [new thoroughly rev.] Calcutta, S. C. Mazumder, 1964. 1630p.   **AD196**

Subtitle: Etymological, explanatory, with pronunciation, compound words, phrases, current technical terms, . . . foreign words and phrases, historical, mythological and classical allusions, proverbs, etc.   PK1687.D45

Sen, Sukumar. An etymological dictionary of Bengali: c.1000–1800 A.D. Calcutta, Eastern Publishers, [1971]. 2v. (968p.)   **AD197**

Bengali-English. (Bengali in roman script.)
About 15,000 entries.   PK1681.S4

Breton

Ernault, Émile. Dictionnaire étymologique du breton moyen. (*In* his Le mystère de Sainte Barbe. Nantes, Soc. des Bibliophiles Bretons, 1885–87. p.189–400)   **AD198**

An etymological dictionary of medieval Breton.   DC611.B842A6

——— Glossaire moyen-breton. 2. éd. corr. et augm. Paris, Bouillon, 1895–96. 833p.   **AD199**

Supplement to the above.
Forms v.2 of Henry d'Arbois de Jubainville and Émile Ernault's *Études grammaticales sur les langues celtiques* (Paris, 1881–96).

Includes words found in manuscripts and texts of the 12th to the 16th centuries inclusive, together with an etymological treatment of some modern terms.

Hemon, Roparz. Geriadur istorel ar brezhoneg. Dictionnaire historique du breton. Paris, Preder, 1958–79. 3232p.   **AD200**

Published in parts. Abbreviations of works cited, p.3219–30.

Hemon is also the compiler of *Dictionnaire français breton* (Nouv. éd. Brest, al Liamm, 1974. 420p.) and *Nouveau dictionnaire breton* (4ᵉ éd. Brest, al Liamm, 1970. 849p.).

Vallée, François. Grand dictionnaire français-breton, avec le concours de É. Ernault et R. Le Roux. Rennes, Éd. de l'Impr. Commerciale de Bretagne, 1931 [i.e. 1934]. 814p.   **AD201**

——— ———Supplément. La Baule, Skridou Breizh, 1948. 176p.

    PB2837.V3

Bulgarian

Angliisko-bulgarski rechnik. [Red. Marko Minkov] S'staviteli: T. Athanassova [et al.]. Sofia, Izd. Bulgarskata Akad. na Naukite, 1973. 2v.   **AD202**

Added title page in English: English-Bulgarian dictionary.
    PG979.A48

Bulgarski etimologichen rechnik. Sustavili V. I. Georgiev [et al.]. Sofiia, BAN, 1962–82. t.1–3³. (In progress)   **AD203**

At head of title: Bulgarska Akademiia na Naukite. Institut Bulgarski Ezik.

Contents: t.1–3³, A–Lastun.

An extensive etymological dictionary. Bibliography of sources cited, v.1, p.XII–XCV.

Issued in fascicules; title page of t.1 bears the date 1971.
    PG963.B8

Chakalov, Gocho G. Bulgarsko-angliiski rechnik. Sofia, Nauka i Izkustvo, 1961. 982p.   **AD204**

A standard reference dictionary.   PG979.C53

Mladenov, Stefan and **Balan, Alexsandar Teodorov.** Bulgarski tulkoven rechnik. Sofia, "Decho Stefanov," 1951. v.1.   **AD205**

Contents: t.1, A–K. 1126p.
A scholarly dictionary, still unfinished.   PG975.M57

Rechnik na bulgarskiia ezik. [Glav. red. Kristalina Cholakova] Sofiia, Izd-vo na Bulgarskata Akademiia na Naukite, 1977–81. v.1–3. (In progress)   **AD206**

Contents: v.1–3, A–Deiatel.

An extensive new work with emphasis on examples of usage (and providing citations to sources of the examples). Includes many technical and specialized terms.

The Academy's *Rechnik na suvremennaia bulgarski ezik* (Sofia, Bulgarska Akad. Naukite, 1955–59. 3v.) remains useful while this new work is in progress.   PG975.R39

Abbreviations

U.S. Library of Congress. Slavic and Central European Division. Bulgarian abbreviations: a selective list, prep. by Konstantin Z. Furness. Wash., Govt. Prt. Off., 1961. 326p.   **AD207**

A listing of abbreviations culled from Bulgarian texts with the emphasis on governmental and other organizational titles, and some general terms. Each entry gives the Bulgarian abbreviation with its transliteration, and the expansion in Bulgarian and in English translation.   PG984.U5

Burmese

Judson, Adoniram. The Judson Burmese-English dictionary. Rev. and enl. by Robert C. Stevenson; ed. by F. H. Eveleth. Rangoon, Amer. Baptist Mission Pr., 1921. 1123p. (Repr.: Rangoon, Baptist Board of Publ., 1953)   **AD208**

                                 PL3957.J834

—— English and Burmese dictionary. 8th ed. Rangoon, Amer. Baptist Mission Pr., 1922. 928p.   **AD209**

     Also published in London by Kegan Paul.   PL3957.J82

Stewart, John Alexander and **Dunn, C. W.,** comps. Burmese-English dictionary. London, Luzac, 1940–69. Pts.1–5. (In progress)   **AD210**

     Imprint varies. Published under the auspices of the University of Rangoon until 1950 when it was transferred to the School of Oriental and African Studies, London University.

     Vocabulary is drawn from Burmese literature from its beginning in the 15th century A.D. to the present; comprehensive bibliographies of sources are included. Although not strictly an etymological dictionary, etymological notes are given. An important scholarly work which will presumably supersede Judson (AD208).

                                 PL3957.S8

Catalan

Aguiló y Fúster, Mariano. "Diccionari Aguiló"; materials lexicogràfics aplegats. Rev. i publ. sota la cura de Pompeu Fabra i Manuel de Montoliu. Barcelona, Inst. d'Estudis Catalans, 1914–34. 8v. (Biblioteca filològica de l'Inst. de la Llengua Catalana, III, VIII)   **AD211**

     A scholarly work with illustrative quotations and references to the literature.   PC3889.A4

Alcover Sureda, Antonio Maria. Diccionari català-valencià-balear; inventari lexical y etimològich de la llengua que parlen Catalunya espanyola y Catalunya francesa, el regne de València, les illes Balears y la ciutat d'Alguer de Sardenya, en totes ses formes literàries y dialectals, antigues y modernes. Palma de Mallorca, Alcover, 1930–62. 10v.   **AD212**

     A dictionary of the literary and spoken language as found in the various parts of Spain and the islands where Catalan is used. Gives etymologies and regional variations.   PC3889.A5

Corominas, Joan. Diccionari etimològic i complementari de la llengua Catalana. Barcelona, Curial Edicions Catalanes, 1980–82. v.1–3. (In progress)   **AD213**

     Contents: v.1–3, A–Fi.

     Gives etymologies, with references to earlier dictionaries, grammars, linguistic studies, collections of documents, etc.

                               PC3883.5.C6

Diccionari enciclopèdic de la llengua catalana amb la correspondència castellana. Nova ed., redactada segons les normes de l' "Institut d'Estudis Catalans," la qual conté tots els vocables, modismes i aforismes, mots tècnics de ciències, arts i indústries, biografies de personatges cèlebres, antics i moderns, nom i descripció de poblacions, rius i muntanyes de les comarques on és parlat et català en qualsevol de les seves variants. Barcelona, Salvat, 1930–35. 4v. il.   **AD214**

     Previously published under title *Diccionari de la llengua catalana ab la correspondència castellana* (1888–89. 2v.).   PC3889.D5

Fabra, Pompeu. Diccionari manual de la llengua catalana. Barcelona, Editorial EDHASA, [1983]. 1331p.   **AD215**

     Based on Fabra's *Diccionari general de la llengua catalana* (1st ed. 1932).   PC3889.D49

Celtic

Holder, Alfred. Alt-celtischer Sprachschatz. Leipzig, Teubner, 1896–1913. 3v.   **AD216**

     v.3 includes a *Nachträge* (incomplete) to v.1.   PB1089.H6RR

Chinese

Tz'u hai. [Ed. by] Tz'u hai pien chi wei yüan hui. [Rev. and enl. ed.] Taipei, Chung Hua shu chu, [1979]. 3v. (4915p.) il.   **AD217**

     A standard encyclopedic dictionary published in various formats and frequently reprinted.   PL1420.T86

Wieger, Leon. Chinese characters, their origin, etymology, history, classification and signification. Tr. into English by Leo Davrout. 2d ed., enl. and rev. according to the 4th French ed. N.Y., Paragon Book Repr. Corp., 1965. 820p. il.   **AD218**

     "Unabridged and unaltered republication of the 2d ed. . . . 1927."—*verso of title page.*   PL1171.W6

Bilingual

Chen, Janey. A practical English-Chinese pronouncing dictionary. English, Chinese characters, Romanized Mandarin and Cantonese. Rutland, Vt., Tuttle, 1972. 601p.   **AD219**

                                   PL1455.C579

Chi, Wen-shun. Chinese-English dictionary of contemporary usage. Berkeley, Univ. of California Pr., [1977]. 484p.   **AD220**

     A dictionary of some 1,200 entries for new words and words with new definitions resulting from the institutional and ideological changes of the last forty years.   PL1455.C59.

Cowles, Roy T. The Cantonese speaker's dictionary. [Hong Kong], Hong Kong Univ. Pr., 1965. 1318p., 232p.   **AD221**

     "In Romanized Cantonese, being handled entirely from the standpoint of the speech and for the benefit of the foreign student." —*Foreword.* About 133,000 entries, with English equivalents. The romanized form is keyed to a "character code book" (which makes up the second part of the volume) to designate the Chinese characters.   PL1736.C6

Fenn, Courtenay Hughes. The five thousand dictionary, a Chinese-English pocket dictionary and index to the character cards of the College of Chinese Studies, California College in China, originally comp. by Courtenay H. Fenn . . . with the assistance of Mr. Chin Hsien Tseng. 5th ed. with add. and rev. by George D. Wilder . . . and Mr. Chin Hsien Tseng. . . . Peking, [printed at the Union Pr.], 1940. 696p.   **AD222**

     Repr. as: Rev. Amer. ed. (Cambridge, Harvard Univ. Pr., 1942. 694p.). Various later reprintings.   PL1455.F4

Giles, Herbert Allen. Chinese-English dictionary. 2d ed. rev. and enl. Shanghai, Kelly; London, Quaritch, [1909]–12. 3v. (Repr.: N.Y., Paragon Repr. Corp., 1964. 2v.)   **AD223**

                                   PL1455.G6

Huang, Po-fei. Cantonese dictionary: Cantonese-English: English-Cantonese. By Parker Po-fei Huang. New Haven, Conn., Yale Univ. Pr., 1970. 489p.   **AD224**

     About 20,000 entries in the English-Cantonese section. The primary object of the work is "to help the English-speaking student understand and communicate in the oral-aural mode of Cantonese." —*Pref.*   PL1736.H8

Mathews, Robert Henry. Mathews' Chinese-English dictionary. Rev. Amer. ed., publ. for the Harvard-Yenching Institute. Cambridge, Harvard Univ. Pr., 1943. 1226p. **AD225**

Originally published in 1931; various reprintings.

"Within the necessary limitations of a photographic edition, and as far as interstices of the original edition allow, errors have been corrected, pronunciations and definitions revised, and new entries inserted—in all amounting to some 15,000 items. A whole introduction on pronunciation has been added, and a list of the syllabic headings is included for quick reference. . . . An additional feature of the new edition is that all cases of the neutral, i.e., unstressed, tone are indicated."—*Foreword* to American edition.

PL1455.M34

—— A Chinese-English dictionary, comp. for the China Inland Mission. Rev. English index. Publ. for the Harvard-Yenching Institute. Cambridge, Harvard Univ. Pr., 1944. 186p. **AD226**

PL1455.M34

The Pinyin Chinese-English dictionary. Ed. in chief, Wu Jinrong. Beijing [etc.], Commercial Pr.; San Francisco, Pitman, [1979]. 976p. **AD227**

A desk dictionary compiled by an editorial committee of the Beijing Foreign Languages Institute and representing contributions of some 50 people. "There are over 6,000 single-character entries, including a small number of characters with variant tones. There are over 50,000 compound-character entries and over 70,000 compound words, set phrases and examples. Apart from everyday words and expressions, a number of common classical Chinese words, dialect words, four-character idioms, proverbs and common scientific expressions from both the natural and social sciences have been included."—*Foreword.* PL1455.P55

Tsui hsin hsiang chieh Ying Hua ta tz'ŭ tien. A new English-Chinese dictionary. 2d rev. ed. Beijing & Hongkong, Commercial Pr.; N.Y., John Wiley, [1984]. 1613p. **AD228**

"First ed. [1953] by Zheng Yi Li and Cao Cheng Xiu. 2d rev. ed. ed. by Zheng Yi Li [and others]."—*t.p.* PL1455.C583

Williams, Samuel Wells. A syllabic dictionary of the Chinese language; arranged according to the Wu-Fang Yuen Yin, with the pronunciation of the characters as heard in Peking, Canton, Amoy and Shanghai. Shanghai, Amer. Presbyterian Mission Pr., 1903. 1254p. **AD229**

A reprint of the 1874 edition, with four pages of "Errata and corrections." PL1455.W65

Yale University. Institute of Far Eastern Languages. Dictionary of spoken Chinese. New Haven, Yale Univ., Pr., 1966. 1071p. (Yale linguistic ser., 8) **AD230**

"A revision of War Department Technical manual TM 30-933, *Dictionary of spoken Chinese,* published . . . 1945."—*Acknowledgments.*

Chinese-English and English-Chinese. Intended for the student of colloquial Mandarin. Yale romanization used throughout.

PL1455.Y295

Bibliography

Chinese dictionaries: an extensive bibliography of dictionaries in Chinese and other languages, comp. and ed. by the Chinese-English Translation Assistance Group, James Mathias, managing ed. Westport, Conn., Greenwood Pr., [1982]. 446p. **AD231**

An earlier listing, *A compilation of Chinese dictionaries,* comp. and ed. by S. Hixson and J. Mathias, was published under CETA sponsorship by Yale University Pr., 1975.

Aims "to identify as many Chinese monolingual, bilingual, and polyglot dictionaries as possible."—*Pref.* A section of general dictionaries (p.3–90) is followed by specialized dictionaries listed accord-

ing to subject areas. Title and language indexes. (An appendix of additional titles has its own index.) More than 2,700 entries.

Z3108.L5C483

U.S. Library of Congress. Chinese-English and English-Chinese dictionaries in the Library of Congress: an annotated bibliography. Comp. by Robert Dunn. Wash., Lib. of Congress, 1977. 140p. **AD232**

In two main sections: (1) special subject dictionaries listed alphabetically by subject field; (2) general language dictionaries. Indexes of authors and titles, plus a Chinese-character author and title list. 569 items with annotations. Z3109.U53

Coptic

Cerny, Jaroslav. Coptic etymological dictionary. Cambridge & N.Y., Cambridge Univ. Pr., [1976]. 384p. **AD233**

"My guiding principle in compiling this dictionary has been to adopt only etymologies which I considered certain, probable or at least possible."—*Pref.* Serves as a complement to W. E. Crum's *Coptic dictionary* (below) which omits etymologies, and offers references to Crum's work. Gives bibliographic references to sources for the etymologies.

For a review of this "great work of scholarship" see the appraisal by H. S. Smith in the *Bulletin* of the School of Oriental and African Studies 41:358–62 (1978). PJ2163.C4

Crum, Walter Ewing. Coptic dictionary. Oxford, Clarendon Pr., 1939. 953p. **AD234**

Issued in 6 pts., 1929–39.

Coptic-English.

Includes illustrative quotations with references to sources. Indexes in English, Greek, and Arabic.

A Concise Coptic-English lexicon comp. by Richard Smith (Grand Rapids, Mich., Eerdmans, 1983. 81p.) is a useful work for the beginning student. PJ2181.C7

Cornish

Nance, Robert Morton. An English-Cornish dictionary. Marazion, pr. for the Federation of Old Cornwall Societies by Worden, 1952. 200p. **AD235**

1st ed., 1934, by R. M. Nance and A. S. D. Smith.

PB2537.E5N3

—— A new Cornish-English dictionary. St. Ives, pr. for the Federation of Old Cornwall Societies by James Lanham, 1938. 209p. **AD236**

PB2537.E5N33

Williams, Robert. Lexicon Cornu-Britannicum; a dictionary of the ancient Celtic language of Cornwall, in which the words are elucidated by copious examples from the Cornish works now remaining; with translations into English. Llandovery, Roderic, 1865. 398p. **AD237**

"The synonyms are also given in the cognate dialects of Welsh, Armoric, Irish, Gaelic, and Manx."—*title page.* PB2537.E5W6

Loth, Joseph. Remarques et corrections au Lexicon Cornu-Britannicum de Williams. Paris, Bouillon, 1902. 70p. **AD238**

Czech

Česká Akademie Věd a Uměni. Třída 3. Příruční slovník jazyka českého. Vydává Československá Akademie Věd. V Praze, Státní Pedagogické Nakl., 1935–57. 8v. in 9. **AD239**

The authoritative dictionary of the Czech language, with illustrative examples from standard authors. Issued by the Czech Academy.
PG4625.C4

Československá Akademie Věd. Ústav pro Jazyk Český. Slovník spisovného jazyka českého. Praha, Akademia Nakl. Československé Akademie Věd, 1971. 4v.　**AD240**

Contents: v.1-3, A-U; v.4, V-Ž, Doplňky a opravy.
Originally issued in parts, 1958-71. Also issued with title in Czech and English (*Dictionary of the Czech literary language*) by Univ. of Alabama Pr. (University, Ala., 1966-71. 4v.)
A smaller work based on the preceding Academy dictionary, but including more up-to-date words.　PG4625.C45

Trávníček, František. Slovník jazyka českého. 4. přepr. a dopl. vyd. Praha, Slovanské Nakl., 1952. 1081p.　**AD241**

Earlier editions were by Pavel Vása and F. Trávníček: *Slovník jazyka českého* (Prague, Borový, 1935-36; 3d ed. 1946).
A standard work.　PG4625.T7

Bilingual

Anglicko-český a česko-anglický slovník; autorský kolektiv vedený Ivanem Poldaufem; členové kolektivu Jan Caha, Alena Kopecká a Jiří Krámský. 5 vyd. Praha, Státni Pedagogické Nakl., 1982. 1223p.　**AD242**

1st ed. 1971.
A useful two-way dictionary.　PG4640.A484

Česko-anglický slovník středního rozsahu. Zprac. Ivan Poldauf. 4. vyd. Praha, Státní Pedagogické Nákl., [1972]. 1214p.　**AD243**

Added title page in English: Czech-English dictionary; medium.
1st ed. 1959.　PG4640.C43

Procházka, Jindrich. Slovník anglicko-český a česko-anglický . . . English–Czech and Czech–English dictionary. 16th rev. and enl. ed. Prague, Orbis, 1959. 423p., 589p.　**AD244**

Subtitle: Giving pronunciation of all English words, with special regard to idiomatic phrases and phraseology of commercial correspondence.
Frequently reprinted; editors vary.　PG4640.P73

Abbreviations

U.S. Library of Congress. Slavic and Central European Division. Czech and Slovak abbreviations: a selective list, ed. by Paul L. Horecky. Wash., 1956. 164p.　**AD245**

"Entries for the most part denote governmental, political, economic, cultural, and social bodies" (*Pref.*) with some general terms that are commonly abbreviated.　Z663.47.C9

Etymology

Holub, Josef and **Lyer, Stanislav.** Stručny etymologický slovník jazyka českého se zvláštním zřetelem k slovům kulturním a cizím. [2. vydání připravil Ivan Lutterer] Praha, SPN, [1978]. 527p.　**AD246**

1st ed. 1967.
A brief etymological dictionary.　PG4580.H63

Machek, Václav. Etymologický slovník jazyka českého. 2. opr. a dopln. vyd. Praha, Academia, 1968. 866p.　**AD247**

1st ed., 1957, had title *Etymologický slovník jazyka českého a slovenského*.
An etymological dictionary of the Czech and Slovak languages.
PG4580.M3

Danish

Danske Sprog- og Litteraturselskab, Copenhagen. Ordbog over det danske Sprog, grundlagt af Verner Dahlerup; med Understøttelse af Undervisningsministeriet og Carlsbergfondet . . . København, Gyldendal, 1919-1954. 27v.
AD248

———— Liste over Forkortelser med en Lydskrifttavle og en Efterskrift. København, 1956. 113p.

The scholarly dictionary of the Danish language since 1700, giving etymologies, illustrative quotations, etc.　PD3625.D28

Bilingual

Brynildsen, John. Dictionary of the English and Dano-Norwegian languages. Danisms supervised by Johannes Magnussen, English pronunciation by Otto Jespersen. Copenhagen, Gyldendal, 1902-07. 2v.　**AD249**

Added title page: Engelsk-dansk-norsk Ordbog.
Issued in 40 pts., 1900-1907.
Still one of the best English-Dano-Norwegian dictionaries.
PD3640.B8

Kjaerulff Nielsen, Bernhard. Engelsk-dansk ordbog. Anden udgave. [København], Gyldendal, [1981]. 1273p.　**AD250**

1st ed. 1964.
An excellent work giving grammatical details, pronunciation, variant meanings, and examples of usage.　PD3640.K4

Magnussen, Johannes Julius Claudi [and others]. Danish-English [and English-Danish] dictionary. Copenhagen, Gyldendal; London, Allen & Unwin, 1947-54. 2v.　**AD251**

v.1, 5th ed., by Hermann Vinterberg and Knud Herløv (412p.); v.2, 6th ed., by Hermann Vinterberg and Bodil Ladgaard (476p.).
Also publ. N.Y., McKay, 1954 as *McKay's Modern Danish-English, English-Danish dictionary*.　PD3640.M32

Nudansk ordbog. [Redaktion, Lis Jacobsen *et al.*] 11. revid. og förgede udg. ved Erik Oxenvad. Copenhagen, Politiken, 1982. 2v. (1100p.)　**AD252**

1st ed. 1953.
Concise definitions; derivation and part of speech indicated. About 50,000 terms.　PD3625.N8

Vinterberg, Hermann and **Bodelsen, Carl Adolf.** Dansk-engelsk Ordbog . . . 2d rev. og udvid. København, Gyldendal, Nordisk Forlag, 1966. 2v.　**AD253**

1st ed. 1954-56; various reprintings.　PD3640.V5

Etymology

Falk, Hjalmar Sejersted and **Torp, Alf.** Norwegisch-dänisches etymologisches Wörterbuch. Auf Grund der Übersetzung von H. Davidsen neu bearb. deutsche Ausg., mit Literaturnachweisen strittiger Etymologien sowie deutschem und alt-nordischem Wörterverzeichnis. Heidelberg, Winter, 1910-11. 2v.　**AD254**

Translated from *Etymologisk ordbog over det norske og det danske sprog* (Kristiania, 1903-1906).　PD2683.F33

Kalkar, Otto. Ordbog til det aeldre danske Sprog. 1300-1700. København, Thiele, 1881-1907. 4v.　**AD255**

———— ———— Nachträge, 1908-1918.

———— ———— Kilde-fortegnelse og Forkortelses-liste til 1.-5. bd. 1925. xxviii p.

The standard work for Old Danish, preceding in time that covered by the *Ordbog over det danske Sprog* (AD248).　PD3625.K4

Dravidian

Burrow, Thomas and **Emeneau, Murray Barnson.** A Dravidian etymological dictionary. 2d ed. Oxford, Clarendon Pr., 1984. 853p. **AD256**

1st ed. 1961; suppl. 1968.

The Dravidian languages are spoken in southeastern India and northern Ceylon. This dictionary gives etymologies of all known Dravidian languages with English equivalents. Treats the four major literary languages and many non-literary ones. Bibliography and list of sources, p. xxi–xxxiv.

The 2d ed. incorporates material from the earlier edition and its supplement with results of new scholarship and information published elsewhere. PL4609.B8

Dutch

Dale, Johan Hendrik van. Groot woordenboek der Nederlandse taal, door C. Kruyskamp. 10e, geheel opnieuw bewerkte en zeer verm. druk. 'sGravenhage, M. Nijhoff, 1976. 2v. (3230p.) **AD257**

1st ed. 1864.

At head of title: Van Dale.

An excellent, well-established dictionary. Words from the supplement to the previous edition are now incorporated into the body of the work. PF625.D3

——— Van Dale's Nieuw Handwoordenboek der Nederlandse taal. 7. geheel nieuwe uitg. 'sGravenhage, Nijhoff, 1956. 1097p. **AD258**

A concise edition of the preceding.

Verschueren, Joseph. Modern woordenboek. 6. herziene druk, met medewerking van W. Pée en A. Seeldraeyers. Turnhout, Brepols, [1956]. 2v. il. **AD259**

Subtitle: Geheel in de nieuwe spelling steeds bijgewerkt in het kumulatief bijvoegsel.

An encyclopedic dictionary somewhat on the style of the *Petit Larousse,* including both dictionary information and encyclopedic articles on persons, places, and subjects.

Woordenboek der Nederlandsche taal. 'sGravenhage, Nijhoff, 1882–1985. v.1–19, [20–23]. (In progress) **AD260**

Ed. by M. de Vries and others.

Contents: v.1–19, A-Verhypotheken; v.20$^{1-11}$, Veriabel-Vermelden; v.21 [complete], Ves-Vluwe; v.22$^{1-10}$, Vo-Voor; v.23$^{1-7}$, Vr-Vroegtijdig.

——— Supplement, 1942–56. v.1.

——— Bronnenlijst, bewerkt door C. H. A. Kruyskamp. 1943. 144p.

——— ——— 1.–2. Aanvulling (1953–66). 2v.

The standard dictionary compiled on historical principles, with etymologies, references to sources, synonyms, etc. PF625.W6

Early

Verdam, Jacob. Middelnederlandsch handwoordenboek. 2. uitg. 'sGravenhage, Nijhoff, 1932. 811p. (Repr. 1979) **AD261**

Enlarged from the 1st ed., 1911, with revision of section Sterne-Z by C. H. Ebbinge Wubben.

Supplemented by: PF776.V3

Voort van der Kleij, J. J. van der. Middelnederlandsch handwoordenboek. Supplement. Leiden, Nijhoff, 1983. 354p. **AD261a**

PF776.V66

Verwijs, Eelco and **Verdam, Jacob.** Middelnederlandsch woordenboek. 'sGravenhage, Nijhoff, 1885–1953. 11v. **AD262**

Contents: deel 1–9, A–Z; deel 10^1, Tekstcritiek van J. Verdam, en Bouwstoffen, eerste gedeelte (A–F) door Willem de Vreese; deel 10^2, Bouwstoffen, tweede gedeelte (G–Z) door G. I. Lieftinck; deel 11, afl.1–5, Aanvullingen en verbeteringen op het gebied van dijken waterschapsrecht, bodem en water, aardrijkskunde, enz. door A. A. Beekman (A–Z).

A comprehensive dictionary of the older language. v.10 includes an extensive bibliography of sources; v.11, additions and corrections in the fields of water rights, geography, etc. PF776.V3

Bilingual

Bruggencate, Karel ten. Engels woordenboek. 19. druk bewerkt door J. Gerritsen en N. E. Osselton. Groningen, Wolters, [1981–82]. 2v. **AD263**

1st ed. 1895–96.

Contents: v.1, Engels-Nederlands; v.2, Nederlands-Engels. (v.2 is a 5th printing of the 18th ed.)

A practical desk dictionary, reflecting current usage.

PF640.B8

Cassell's English-Dutch, Dutch-English dictionary: Engels-Nederlands, Nederlands-Engels woordenboek. Completely rev. by J. A. Jockin-La Bastide and G. van Kooten. London, Cassell; N.Y., Macmillan, [1981]. 602p., 729p. **AD264**

Earlier editions of *Cassell's Dutch-English, English-Dutch dictionary* (first publ. 1951; last revision 1965) were edited by F. P. H. Prick van Wely. The 1978 edition of the present title by Jockin-La Bastide and Kooten corresponded to their 36th ed. of *Kramers' Engels woordenboek* (AD265); it was revised and reset in 1980. A practical, up-to-date work for the student, business person, or general reader. PF640.C375

Kramers, Jacob. Kramers' Engels woordenboek. 36. geheel herziene en vermeerderde druk, bewerkt door J. A. Jockin-La Bastide en G. van Kooten. Amsterdam, Van Goor, [1978]. 2v. **AD265**

1st ed. 1917–19?

Contents: v.1, Engels-Nederlands (602p.); v.2, Nederlands-Engels (729p.).

A standard bilingual dictionary. Pronunciation is indicated in the English-Dutch part. PF640.K7

Etymology

Franck, Johannes. Franck's Etymologisch woordenboek der Nederlandsche taal. 2. druk door Dr. N. van Wijk. Met registers der Nieuwhoogduitsche woorden, enz. 'sGravenhage, Nijhoff, 1912. 897p. (Repr. with Suppl., Nijhoff, 1949) **AD266**

Issued in 14 pts., 1910–12.

——— ——— Supplement door C. B. van Haeringen. 'sGravenhage, Nijhoff, 1936. 235p.

PF580.F82

Bibliography

Claes, Frans M. A bibliography of Netherlandic dictionaries: Dutch-Flemish. München, Kraus International, [1980]. 314p. (World bibliography of dictionaries) **AD267**

Aims to list "all monolingual, bilingual and polyglot dictionaries with a Netherlandic text, specialized . . . as well as general works, including dictionaries, vocabularies and glossaries of abbreviations, synonyms and homonyms, foreign words, individual authors, proverbs and quotations as well as etymological, orthographical, geographical, onomastic, rhyming, reverse, dialectical and slang lexicographic works."—*Introd.* In three main sections: (1) Monolingual (in classed arrangement); (2) Bilingual (arranged by language); and (3) Polyglot. Indexed.   Z2445.D6C49

Meertens, Pieter Jacobus and **Wander, B.** Bibliografie der dialecten van Nederland, 1800–1950. In opdracht van de Dialectencommissie der Koninklijke Nederlandse Akademie van Wetenschappen. Amsterdam, Noord-Hollandsche Uitg. Mij., 1958. 400p.   **AD268**

An extensive bibliography arranged by province and then by city, preceded by a section of general materials.   Z2445.D5M4

Egyptian

Budge, Ernest Alfred Thompson Wallis. An Egyptian hieroglyphic dictionary. With an index of English words, king list and geographical list, with indexes, list of hieroglyphic characters, Coptic and Semitic alphabets, etc. London, Murray, 1920. 1356p.   **AD269**

PJ1425.B8

A dictionary of Late Egyptian. Leonard H. Lesko, ed.; Barbara Switalski Lesko, collaborating ed. Berkeley, Calif., B.C. Scribe Pubns., [1982–84]. v.1–2. (In progress)

AD270

A computer-generated work (with hieroglyphs) based on selected texts in readily available editions and translations. ". . . for our *lexicographical* purposes we have generally restricted our period as the Nineteenth through the end of the Twenty-first Dynasties and we have included literary, some historical and almost no religious literature."—*Pref.* To be in 3v., with a volume of names projected as a later undertaking.   PJ1425.D53

Erman, Adolf and **Grapow, Hermann.** Wörterbuch der aegyptischen Sprache; im Auftrage der Deutschen Akademien. Leipzig, Hinrichs, 1926–63. 7v. (Repr.: Berlin, Akademie Verlag, 1971)   **AD271**

PJ1430.E65

————— ————— Die Belegstellen, bearb. von H. Grapow und W. Erichsen. Leipzig, Hinrichs, 1935–53. v.1–5.

An authoritative work in German, covering both the hieratic and the hieroglyphic vocabularies.   PJ1430.E66

Faulkner, Raymond O. A concise dictionary of Middle Egyptian. Oxford, Printed for the Griffith Inst. at the Univ. Pr., 1962. 327p.   **AD272**

Estonian

Nurm, E., Raiet, E. and **Kindlam, M.** Õigekeelsuse sõnaraamat. Tallinn, Eesti Riiklik Kirjastus, 1960. 871p.   **AD273**

At head of title: Eesti NSV Teaduste Akadeemia, Keele ja Kirjanduse Instituut.   PH623.N8

Saareste, Andrus Kustas. Eesti keele mõisteline sõnaraamat. Dictionnaire analogique de la langue estonienne. Avec un index pourvu des traductions en français. Stockholm, Kirjastus Vaba Eesti, 1958–[68?]. 4v. (Eesti Teadusiliku Seltsi Rootsis väljaane, 3)   **AD274**

Issued in parts.

An analogical dictionary of the Estonian language containing "the entire subject matter of Wiedemann's Dictionary [AD276]; new words now commonly used . . . ; dialectal words . . . ; examples to make clear all nuances of meaning and style, taken from colloquial or standard Estonian; proverbs; and pictures of objects which cannot be described adequately or which are comparatively rare. At the end of the Dictionary there will be an alphabetical index in Estonian and French of all words to be found in it."—[*Descriptive statement*] Addenda in v.4.   PH623.S2

Bilingual

Saagpakk, Paul Friidrih. Eesti-inglise sõnaraamat. Estonian-English dictionary. New Haven, Yale Univ. Pr., [1982]. 1180p.   **AD275**

Prefatory matter in Estonian and English.

The work "has two main objects: first to enable Estonians to find the British and American words and idioms most closely corresponding to those in Estonian; and second, to provide world philologists and students of language with a means of learning Estonian thoroughly, whether for purposes of philological research or with a view to reading Estonian literature."—*Pref.* Includes an introduction with "A grammatical survey of the Estonian language" by Johannes Aavik, p.xxxvii–lxxxvii.   PH625.S325

Wiedemann, Ferdinand Johann. Eesti-saksa sõnaraamat . . . Estnisch-deutsches Wörterbuch. 3. unveränderter Druck . . . von Jakob Hurt redigierten Aufl. Mit einer Einleitung versehen von Albert Saareste. Dorpat, Estnische Literaturgesellschaft, 1923. Tartu, Eesti Kirjanduse Seltsi Kirjastus, 1923. 1406col., cix p. map.   **AD276**

1st ed., St. Petersburg, 1869.

The Estonian and German titles are printed side by side. Introduction in Estonian and German.   PH625.W5

Etymology

Mägiste, Julius. Estnisches etymologisches Wörterbuch. [Helsinki, Helsingin Yliopiston Monistuspalvelu, 1983] 12v. (4106p.)   **AD277**

On cover: Finnisch-Ugrische Gesellschaft.

Ethiopian

Dillmann, August. Lexicon linguae Aethiopicae cum indice Latino. Lipsae, T. O. Weigel, 1865. 1522col. (3v.) (Repr.: N.Y., Ungar, 1955)   **AD278**

PJ9093.D5

Grébaut, Sylvain. Supplément au Lexicon linguae Aethiopicae . . . (1865) et édition du lexique de Juste d'Urbin (1850–1855). Paris, Impr. Nationale, 1952. 520p.   **AD279**

PJ9093.G7

Aklilu, Amsalu. Etymologischer Beitrag zu Dillmanns Lexicon . . . 1962. 74p.   **AD280**

Thesis, Tübingen.

Fijian

Capell, Arthur. A new Fijian dictionary, comp. for the government of Fiji. [3d ed.] Suva, Fiji, Government Printer, 1968. 407p.   **AD281**

First published 1941; 2d ed. 1957.
Fijian-English; English-Fijian.   PL6235.Z5C3

Finnish

Suomalaisen Kirjallisuuden Seura. Nykysuomen sanakirja. Valtion toimeksiannosta teettänyt Suomalaisen Kirjallisuuden Seura. [Päätoimittaja: Matti Sadeniemi] 2. painos. Porvoo, Söderström, 1957–62. 6v.   **AD282**

An authoritative dictionary of contemporary Finnish.

PH275.S8

Bilingual

Alanne, Vieno Severi. Suomalais-englantilainen suursana-kirja; Finnish-English general dictionary. [3d ed.] [Porvoo], W. Söderström, 1968. 1111p. **AD283**

1st ed. 1919.
Earlier printings had title: Suomalais-englantilainen sanakirja. This is a reprint of the 3d ed., 1956. PH279.A6

Hart, Kingsley A. and **Lahtinen, Aarne T. K.** Englantilais-suomalainen idiomisanakirja; English-Finnish dictionary of idioms. Helsinki, Otava, [1965]. pt.1. (In progress?) **AD284**

Contents: pt.1, Verbal idioms. 340p.
Gives an unidiomatic explanation of the term, one or more examples of English usage, and Finnish equivalents of the English examples. A "Finnish-English cross-reference index" offers an approach from Finnish to English. PH279.H35

Hurme, Raija and **Pesonen, Maritta.** Englantilais-suomalainen suursanakirja. English-Finnish general dictionary. 2. tark. ja korj. p. [Porvoo], Söderström, 1978. 1182p. **AD285**

1st ed. 1973.
"The editors have primarily had in mind a general dictionary to meet the needs of Finnish readers. ... Throughout the work, however, we have taken pains not to forget foreign users with their special problems."—*Foreword.* Gives pronunciation and examples of usage. PH279.H8

Tuomikoski, Aune and **Slöör, Anna.** Englantilais-suomalainen sanakirja. 6. painos. Helsinki, Suomalaisen Kirjallisuuden Seura, 1973. 1100p. (Suomalaisen Kirjallisuuden Seuran Toimituksia 212. osa) **AD286**

Added title page: English-Finnish dictionary.
Definitions given with examples and variant meanings.
PH279.T8

Vuolle, Aino. Suomalais-englantilainen sanakirja. [11. painos] Porvoo, Söderström, [1974]. 484p. **AD287**

1st ed. 1940.
Added title page: Finnish-English dictionary. PH279.V8

———— Englantilais-suomalainen koulusanakirja. 13., painos. Porvoo, Helsinki, Söderström, 1973. 535p. **AD288**

Useful concise dictionaries, frequently reprinted. PH279.V78

Finno-Ugric

Collinder, Bjorn. Fenno-Ugric vocabulary; an etymological dictionary of the Uralic languages. Stockholm, Almqvist & Wiksell, [1955]. 211p. **AD289**

French

Académie Française, Paris. Dictionnaire de l'Académie Française. 8. éd. Paris, Hachette, 1931–35. 2v. **AD290**

Issued in 7 pts. 1931–35.
1st ed. 1694.
The standard conservative dictionary of the French language for spelling and usage. Does not include etymologies or show historical development. Primarily for the literary language; includes very few scientific and technical terms. PC2625.A3

Davau, Maurice, Cohen, Marcel and **Lallemand, Maurice.** Dictionnaire du français vivant. Nouv. éd., entièrement rev. et augm. [Paris], Bordas, [1979]. 1344p. **AD291**

1st ed. 1972.
A desk dictionary for the student and general reader. Gives pronunciation (in International Phonetic Alphabet), etymology, definitions, and examples of usage. Emphasis is on contemporary vocabulary and use. About 34,000 words. PC2625.D3

Dictionnaire du français contemporain illustré. [Direction: Jean Dubois] Paris, Larousse, [1980]. 1263p. il. **AD292**

Follows the plan and principles of the *Nouveau dictionnaire du contemporain* (1st ed. 1967) which defined terms and gave examples of contemporary usage, and of which Dubois was also editor. Incorporates various new terms and meanings, with greater attention to the sciences. About 33,000 terms. PC2625.D46

Grand Larousse de la langue française . . . [Sous la direction de Louis Guilbert, René Lagane et Georges Niobey] Paris, Larousse, [1971–78]. 7v. **AD293**

Comparable in physical size to Robert's *Dictionnaire alphabétique* (AD301), but less comprehensive than that work. In addition to definition and transcription in International Phonetic Alphabet, each entry includes: etymology, examples of usage, indication of level of usage, synonyms and antonyms. Limited to words in use in the 19th and 20th centuries, including a generous number of current technical terms.
v.7 includes a "Bibliographie des matériaux utilisés pour la partie historique du dictionnaire," p.6634–6730. PC2625.G7

Hatzfeld, Adolphe and **Darmesteter, Arsène.** Dictionnaire général de la langue française du commencement du XVIIe siècle jusqu'à nos jours. 9. éd. Paris, Delagrave, 1932. 2v. (Repr. 1964) **AD294**

1st ed. published in parts, 1890–1900.
Gives etymologies, examples showing first usage, changes in meaning, etc. PC2625.H4

Imbs, Paul. Trésor de la langue Française; dictionnaire de la langue du XIXe et du XXe siècle (1789–1960). Paris. Éditions du Centre National de la Recherche Scientifique, 1971–83. v.1–10. (In progress) **AD295**

Contents: v.1–10, A–Losangique.
Originally planned as a comprehensive historical dictionary—a "French O.E.D."—for the 19th and 20th centuries and eventually covering all the earlier period as well. v.1 includes definitions, illustrations from fully identified texts, history, etymology with sources, pronunciation in International Phonetic Alphabet, citations to books and articles for further information, frequency of occurrence in texts cited, and detailed indications of usage and syntax. Some compressions, notably in the number of textual examples, were made in v.2. Beginning with v.3, the scope was reduced drastically to permit completion in about 15 volumes rather than the 60 the original design would have demanded.
An early review, with remarks on the changed scope of the work appears in *TLS*, Aug. 3, 1973, p.909. PC2625.I4

Larousse, Pierre. Nouveau Larousse classique: dictionnaire encyclopédique. Paris, Larousse, 1957. 1284p. il., maps. **AD296**

Previous editions published with title *Larousse classique illustré.*
Designed for students, the vocabulary of this desk-size dictionary has been adapted to their needs, including such technical and scientific words as they will find in the course of their work. Includes personal and geographical names, and gives other encyclopedic information. AG25.L23

———— Nouveau petit Larousse; dictionnaire encyclopédique pour tous. [Direction de l'ouvrage: Étienne Gillon, et al.] [Ed.] 1968. Paris, Librairie Larousse, [1967, c1968]. 1789p. il. **AD297**

A popular desk dictionary which has gone through various editions entitled *Nouveau petit Larousse illustré* and *Petit Larousse.*
"70,500 articles, 5535 illus. en noir, 56p. en couleurs dont 26 hors-texte cartographiques, et un atlas en couleurs à la fin de l'ouvrage."—*title page.*
Pt.1 gives definitions of words, pronunciation in International Phonetic Alphabet, and usage, and is followed by a short section of foreign phrases. Many new words from science and the social sciences are included in this edition. Pt.2 is an encyclopedia of *arts, lettres, sciences,* mainly biographical. AG25.L25

Larousse de la langue française: Lexis. Paris, Larousse, [1979]. 2109p. **AD298**

1st ed. 1975.

A work for the general reader and the student. About 76,000 terms, with emphasis on thorough coverage of current vocabulary, but with attention to science and technology, literary language, idioms and locutions, etc. PC2625.L344

Littré, Émile. Dictionnaire de la langue française. Éd. intégrale. Paris, J. Pauvert, 1956–58. 7v. **AD299**

Éd. intégrale: la seule complète des étymologies et des différents suppléments et additifs reclassés dans le texte selon les intentions de l'auteur.

A reprint of the famous Littré (1873–78; 4v. and suppl.) in modern format, in which the material in the supplement of the early work has been incorporated into the main alphabet. An older work still important for the history, etymology, and grammar of the French language. Includes many quotations from literature with exact references to sources.

An abridgment was published as: PC2625.L3

—— Dictionnaire de la langue française. Abrégé du dictionnaire de É. Littré par A. Beaujean. 12. éd. conforme pour l'orthographe à la dernière éd. du Dictionnaire de l'Académie Française. Paris, Hachette, 1914. 1295p., 123p. (Repr.: Paris, Éds. Universitaires, 1950. 1294p.) **AD300**

Robert, Paul. Dictionnaire alphabétique et analogique de la langue française; les mots et les associations d'idées. . . . Paris, Société du Nouveau Littré, 1970. 6v. **AD301**

Originally issued in 56 pts., 1951–64.

A historical dictionary of the French language, giving for each entry: etymology, definitions, synonyms, antonyms, and cross references to words with related meaning, with extensive quotations from French writers, selected to clarify usage and trace historical changes in meaning. Sponsored by the Académie Française.
PC2625.R552

—— —— Supplément. Rédaction dirigée par Alain Rey et Josette Rey-Debove. Paris, Société du Nouveau Littré, 1970. 514p.

—— Le petit Robert 1: dictionnaire alphabétique et analogique de la langue française. Rédaction dirigée par A. Ray et J. Rey-Debove. Nouvelle éd. revue, corr. et mise à jour 1984. Paris, Le Robert, [1984]. 2171p. **AD302**

1st ed. 1967.

Individuals and smaller libraries unable to afford the 6v. parent work (above) may well want to acquire this excellent, up-to-date dictionary. Includes International Phonetic Association transcription, but omits biographical and geographical entries such as are found in the *Petit Larousse* (AD297). PC2625.R553

Bilingual

Collins-Robert French-English, English-French dictionary. By Beryl T. Atkins [and others]. London, Collins, [1978]. 717p., 781p. **AD303**

Added title page in French: *Robert-Collins dictionnaire français-anglais, anglais-français,* avec la collaboration du comité du Robert sous la présidence de Paul Robert.

Represents a collaborative effort of the Collins staff with Paul Robert and the Société du Nouveau Littré. Aims to "meet the needs of a wide range of users, from those with an academic or professional commitment—teachers at all levels, translators, students of French or English, as the case may be—through business people whose affairs demand an ability to conduct discussion or correspondence in both languages, to the large numbers of people of each nationality who are interested in the language, literature and culture of the other."—*Pref.* Includes about 100,000 headwords and compounds, and approximately the same number of phrases and idioms in current usage. PC2640.C69

The concise Oxford French dictionary. French-English ed. by H. Ferrar; English-French ed. by J. A. Hutchinson and J.-D. Biard. 2d ed. Oxford, Clarendon Pr.; N.Y., Oxford Univ. Pr., 1980. 596p., 267p. **AD304**

1st ed. 1934–40 (2v.) ed. by Abel Chevalley, M. Chevalley and G. W. F. R. Goodridge.

About 40,000 head words in the French-English section and about 30,000 in the English-French. The former ranges from classical to contemporary vocabulary; the latter relies heavily on the 6th ed. of the *Concise Oxford dictionary* (AD32) for choice of vocabulary.
PC2640.C54

Deak, Étienne and **Deak, Simone.** Grand dictionnaire d'américanismes, contenant les principaux termes américains avec leur équivalent exact en français. 5. éd. augm. Paris, Éditions du Dauphin, 1973. 823p. **AD305**

1st ed., 1956, by Étienne Deak had title *Dictionnaire d'américanismes.*

Provides French equivalents of American slang terms, popular phrases, and idiomatic expressions. PC2640.D4

Guiraud, Jules. Dictionnaire anglais-français [et français-anglais] à l'usage des professeurs, des littérateurs, des traducteurs, des commerçants, des industriels, des élèves, des facultés, des grandes écoles et des classes supérieures des lycées et collèges . . . 3. éd. Paris, Belin, 1947. 2v. **AD306**

Anglais-français, 2187p.; Français-anglais, 1127p.

Includes general, literary, and scientific terms, proper names, etc. Indicates differences in meanings and is rich in examples showing usage. PC2640.G8

Harrap's Modern college French and English dictionary, by J. E. Mansion. French-English, English-French, complete in one volume. Completely rev. & enl. ed., rev. by M. Ferlin and P. Forbes. Ed. by D. M. Ledésert and R. P. L. Ledésert. N.Y., Scribner's, [1972, c1967]. lv., various pagings. **AD307**

First published 1940–44 in 2v.; rev. and reset ed. 1967 in lv. Earlier printings and editions had title: *Harrap's Shorter French and English dictionary* and *Harrap's New shorter French and English dictionary.*

An abridgment of *Harrap's Standard French and English dictionary* (1947–48; *see* note for entry below), incorporating many terms from the supplements to that work and adding a considerable amount of other new material. PC2640.H32

Harrap's New standard French and English dictionary, ed. by J. E. Mansion. Completely rev. and enl. ed.; rev. and ed. by R. P. L. Ledésert and Margaret Ledésert. London, Harrap; N.Y., Scribner's, [1971–80]. 4v. **AD308**

1st ed. of the French-English part 1934; rev. ed. 1940, with suppls. 1950, 1955, and 1961. Published 1947–48 under title *Harrap's Standard French and English dictionary.* The English-French part originally appeared in 1939; there were numerous reprintings, plus three separately published supplements 1950–61; an American edition was published as *Heath's Standard French and English dictionary* (Boston, Heath, 1962).

Contents: [v.1–2 (originally designated as "pt.1")] French-English; v.3–4, English-French.

A new edition of an important dictionary which, although designed for the general reader, includes a great number of technical terms.

A thorough revision which aims at producing "a work of manageable dimensions and of wide scope."—*Pref.* Particular attention was given to the vocabulary of modern technical, scientific, and industrial development; colloquial and idiomatic expressions are freely included (with appropriate marking of slang, vulgarisms, etc.). Phonetic symbols used are those of the International Phonetic Association as revised by Gimson.

While commending the new layout and generous addition of technical terms in the first part, the reviewer in *TLS* (Apr. 6, 1973) expresses reservations about the overall quality of the revision, noting failure to sufficiently update older materials. Peter Rickard's review in *TLS* May 9, 1980, p.532, terms v.3–4 "an exceptionally thorough, reliable and accurate English-French dictionary which will be indispensable to student and specialist alike for a very long time."

A "condensed version" has appeared as *Harrap's Shorter French and English dictionary,* ed. by Peter Collin and others (London, Harrap, 1982. 798p.); it incorporates "a certain number of modifications and additions to bring the text fully up to date."—*Pref.*

PC2640.H32

Larousse modern French-English [English-French] dictionary by Marguerite-Marie Dubois [and others]. N.Y., McGraw-Hill, [1960]. 2v. in 1. (768p., 752p.) il. **AD309**

Various later printings.

A desk dictionary, the work of several French, British, and American collaborators. Colloquial and slang expressions are included. PC2640.L3

New Cassell's French dictionary: French-English, English-French. Compl. rev. by Denis Girard [and others]. N.Y., Funk & Wagnalls, [1962]. 762p., 655p. **AD310**

First published 1920 with title *Cassell's French-English, English-French dictionary.* Frequently reprinted.

A familiar and useful desk dictionary which has gone through five editions and many reprintings. This is a thoroughly revised work by different editors: many new words have been added, as well as new meanings; obsolete terms have been omitted; and errors have been rectified. Includes translations of phrases and expressions. Gives pronunciation. PC2640.C3

The Oxford-Duden pictorial French-English dictionary. Oxford, Clarendon Pr., 1983. 1v., various paging. il. **AD311**

Like the German "Oxford-Duden" (AD379), this is based on the German *Bildwörterbuch* "published as Volume 3 of the ten-volume *Duden* series of monolingual German dictionaries."—*Foreword.* On the principle that certain kinds of information can better be conveyed by pictures than by description or explanation, the work employs a series of 384 plates in subject arrangement; each object illustrated is numbered, and the corresponding French terms and their English equivalents are given on the same or facing page. Indexes from both languages. PC2680.O93

Abbreviations

Dubois, Michel. French and international acronyms & initialisms dictionary. 2d ed., rev. & augm. N.Y., Marlin Publrs. Internat., [1977]. 404p. **AD312**

A revised and expanded edition of *Sigles nationaux & internationaux,* first published 1973.

"... deciphers over 25,000 acronyms and other abbreviated forms derived primarily from French business and industry, economic and social activities, politics and government" *(Pref.),* together with similar abbreviations from the international scene.

AS8.D7813

Etymology

Bloch, Oscar and **Wartburg, Walther von.** Dictionnaire étymologique de la langue française. 6. éd. Paris, Presses Universitaires de France, 1975. 682p. **AD313**

1. éd. 1932.

An etymological dictionary of contemporary French, giving date of earliest appearance, derivatives, etc. PC2580.B55

Dauzat, Albert, Dubois, Jean and **Mitterand, Henri.** Nouveau dictionnaire étymologique et historique. 3e éd. rev. et corr. Paris, Larousse, [1974]. 804p. **AD314**

1st ed., 1938, by Albert Dauzat. Earlier eds. entitled *Dictionnaire étymologique de la langue française.*

A work for the general reader and the student, giving brief etymological information, date of earliest usage, definition, derivatives, etc. PC2580.D35

Gamillscheg, Ernst. Etymologisches Wörterbuch der französischen Sprache. 2. vollst. neu bearb. Aufl. Heidelberg, Winter, 1966–69. 1326p. [Sammlung romanischer Elementar- und Handbücher. Reihe 3. Wörterbücher, Bd.5] **AD315**

Issued in 17 Lfg.

1st ed. 1928.

A scholarly dictionary in German with references to sources. Not as comprehensive as Wartburg (AD317), but a useful one-volume work. PC2580.G32

Picoche, Jacqueline. Dictionnaire étymologique du français. [Nouv. éd.] Paris, Robert, [1983]. 827p. **AD316**

1st ed. 1979.

In addition to etymologies and dates of usage, for many words there are lists of variants and derived forms grouped as popular or learned (sometimes further subdivided for terms derived from the Latin and from the Greek). PC2580.P48

Wartburg, Walther von. Französisches etymologisches Wörterbuch; eine Darstellung des galloromanischen Sprachschatzes. Bonn, Klopp; Basel, Helbing und Lichtenhahn, 1928–82. [v.1–25, incomplete; *see* below] (In progress) (Repr.: Tübingen, J. C. B. Mohr, 1948–) **AD317**

Imprint varies.

The great German dictionary of French etymology, giving the historical development of the meanings of the words with dates. Includes dialectal forms.

Published in *Lieferungen* numbered consecutively as issued but forming parts of different volumes. Lfg. 1–138 published to 1984; volumes completed are: v.1–14, A–Z; v.15–17, Germanische Elemente; v.18, Anglizismen; v.19, Orientalia; v.20, Entlehnungen aus den übrigen Sprachen; v.21, Materialen unbekannten oder unsicheren Ursprungs, Teil 1. Partially completed volumes are: v.22$^{1-2}$, Materialen unbekannten oder unsicheren Ursprungs; v.23$^{1-3}$, Materialen unbekannten oder unsicheren Ursprungs; v.24$^{1-6}$, Gänzlich neubearbeitete Ausgabe von Band 1 (Teil 1), A-anhelare; v.25^1, Gänzlich neubearbeitete Ausgabe von Band 1 (Teil 2), apaideutos-architectus.

The *Dictionnaire étymologique de l'ancien français (DEAF),* an ambitious new work based on Wartburg but restricted to the vocabulary of the mid-9th to mid-14th centuries, was begun under the editorship of Kurt Baldinger (Québec, Presses de l'Université Laval, 1971–74), starting with the letter G. Unfortunately the project had to be abandoned after publication of the "Complément bibliographique," fascicles G1–G3 (G–genoil) and an index to those fascicles. One of the objectives of the work was to correct inaccuracies found in Godefroy (AD341). PC2580.W3

Slang

Esnault, Gaston. Dictionnaire historique des argots français. Paris, Larousse, [1965]. 644p. **AD318**

More substantial than many French slang dictionaries. Indicates etymology in most instances, and cites examples of early usage. PC3741.E8

Hérail, René James and **Lovatt, Edwin A.** Dictionary of modern colloquial French. London & Boston, Routledge & K. Paul, [1984]. 327p. **AD319**

Intends to bridge the gap between the kind of French learned in colleges and universities and that encountered in everyday French conversation. About 8,000 headwords. For each French term there is given, whenever possible, three English equivalents in decreasing levels of colloquiality. PC2640.H47

Leitner, Moses Jonathan and **Lanen, J. R.,** eds. Dictionary of French and American slang. N.Y., Crown, [1965]; London, Harrap, [1966]. 272p. **AD320**

Introductory matter in English and French.

An American-French and French-American dictionary. For each term or idiom the meaning is given in correct terminology of the other language, followed by equivalent idiomatic or slang expressions. PC3741.L58

Marks, Georgette A. and **Johnson, Charles B.** Harrap's English-French dictionary of slang and colloquialisms. London, Harrap, [1974]. 299p. **AD321**

American edition published with title *The new English-French dictionary of slang and colloquialisms* (N.Y., Dutton, 1975).

For the non-specialist. Intends to enable French-speaking people "to cope with the English slang and colloquialisms they are likely to come across [in travel or in reading], and also to help English speakers to find the French equivalents of current words and expressions in non-standard English."—*Foreword.*

A companion to Joseph Marks's *French-English dictionary of slang and colloquialisms* (below). The two works have been issued together in a single volume as *Harrap's French and English dictionary of slang and colloquialisms* by Georgette A. Marks and Charles B. Johnson (London, Harrap, 1980. 299p., 255p.) and published in France as *Harrap's Dictionnaire argot/Slang dictionary* using the Harrap imprint. PE3721.M28

Marks, Joseph. Harrap's French-English dictionary of slang and colloquialisms. Rev. and completed by Georgette A. Marks and Albert J. Farmer. London, Harrap, [1970]. 255p. **AD322**

American edition published with title *French-English dictionary of slang* (N.Y., Dutton, 1971).

Attempts to present "a judicious selection of popular words and phrases with appropriate English renderings" (*Foreword*), striking a balance between expressions of long standing and "very recent slang which may well turn out to be ephemeral." A companion to the above. PC3741.M33

Rheims, Maurice. Dictionnaire des mots sauvages (écrivains des XIXᵉ et XXᵉ siècles). Paris, Larousse, 1969. 605p. **AD323**

Includes words coined, obsolete terms revived, and provincialisms borrowed by French writers of the 19th and 20th centuries. Literary context of each term is shown, followed by a note on usage. PC2460.R5

Sandry, Géo and **Carrère, Marcel.** Dictionnaire de l'argot moderne. 11. éd. rev., augm. et mise à jour. Paris, Éd. du Dauphin, [1980]. 489p. **AD324**

A general section is followed by special lists in various categories, e.g., business, racing, prison, etc., which are not duplicated in the main list. PC3741.S35

Synonyms

Bailly, René. Dictionnaire des synonymes de la langue française; sous la direction de Michel de Toro. Paris, Larousse, [1946]. 626p. **AD325**

A convenient, usable, alphabetically arranged dictionary giving definitions, discriminations in meanings, and examples of usage. PC2591.B3

Bénac, Henri. Dictionnaire des synonymes, conforme au dictionnaire de l'Académie française. Paris, Hachette, [1983]. 1026p. **AD326**

First publ. 1956.

A dictionary of synonyms with explanation and examples showing discriminations in meaning. PC2591.B4

Bertaud du Chazaud, Henri. Dictionnaire des synonymes. [Nouv. éd.] Paris, Robert, [1983]. 516p. **AD327**

1971 ed. had title: *Nouveau dictionnaire des synonymes.* About 20,000 entry words. PC2591.B44

Lafaye, Pierre Benjamin. Dictionnaire des synonymes de la langue française avec une introduction sur la théorie des synonymes. 11. éd. suivie d'un supplément. Paris, Hachette, 1929. 1106p., 336p. **AD328**

1st ed. 1858; 3d ed., 1865–69, was the first edition to include the supplement.

A standard older work giving definitions, explanations, and examples. PC2591.L2

Idioms and usage

Brueckner, John H. Brueckner's French contextuary. Englewood Cliffs, N.J., Prentice-Hall, [1975]. 613p. **AD329**

Aims "to provide full contextual illustrations of over 11,500 basic English words used in combination and translated into idiomatic French. . . . It also provides the native French speaker with a clear analysis of English meanings and many of the common uses of the same basic words."-*Gen.Introd.* In four main sections: (1) adjectives, (2) nouns, (3) verbs, (4) adverbs and other parts of speech. English and French parallel columns. PC2460.B78

Colin, Jean Paul. Dictionnaire des difficultés du français. Paris, Robert, [1978]. 857p. **AD330**

1971 ed. had title *Nouveau dictionnaire des difficultés du français.*

Concerned with words which pose problems in regard to pronunciation, conjugation, orthography, form, gender, usage (including word order and idiomatic phrases), and meaning. In addition to clarification of one or more of the foregoing points, distinctions are often made between similar or related terms which are likely to be confused with the word under consideration. PC2460.C58

Dournon, Jean-Yves. Dictionnaire d'orthographe et des difficultés du français. Paris, Hachette, [1974]. 648p. **AD331**

About 38,000 entries, with indication of part of speech, gender, etc., as applicable. Some 8,000 terms are marked with a dot and an explanation of the point of difficulty is provided. PC2460.D65

Dupré, P. Encyclopédie du bon français dans l'usage contemporain: difficultés, subtilités, complexités, singularités. Paris, Éditions de Trévise, [1972]. 3v. **AD332**

A guide to good usage of about 10,000 terms. Words are treated at some length, with definitions from standard dictionaries quoted, Academy strictures cited, and illustrations of usage given from published sources. PC2460.D88

Gerber, Barbara L. and **Storzer, Gerald H.** Dictionary of modern French idioms. N.Y., Garland, 1976. 2v. (1228p.) **AD333**

Intended "to serve both as a dictionary of expressions and as a handbook for colloquial usage."—*Pref.* In pt.1 the idioms are presented topically (e.g., travel and transportation, dining, stores, apartments, schools), with sentences to illustrate meaning in context, and review exercises at the end of each section. Pt.2 is the dictionary proper, taking the form of French and English indexes to the idioms. PC2460.G46

Hanse, Joseph. Nouveau dictionnaire des difficultés du français moderne. [Paris], Duculot, [1983]. 1014p. **AD334**

Not merely a revised and updated edition of Hanse's *Dictionnaire des difficultés grammaticales et lexicologiques* (Paris, Baude, 1949), but a greatly expanded work based on new research and taking advantage of recent linguistic studies and new dictionaries published since 1949 (and often cited in the text). PC2630.H33

Levieux, Michel and **Levieux, Eleanor.** Beyond the dictionary in French. N.Y., Funk & Wagnalls; London, Cassell, [1967]. 156p. **AD335**

Explains the form of usage and places in context selected terms which are likely to cause difficulties for the student despite a thorough grounding in French. PC2680.L4

Rey, Alain and **Chantreau, Sophie.** Dictionnaire des expressions et locutions. Nouvelle éd. revue et augmentée. Paris, Robert, [1982]. 1035p. **AD336**

1st ed. 1979.

Offers definitions of terms and phrases, giving examples of usage and datings. Entry is under keyword within the phrase or expression, and there is an index by first substantive word in the expression. PC2460.R43

New words

Gilbert, Pierre. Dictionnaire des mots contemporains. Paris, Robert, [1980]. 739p. **AD337**

A 1971 work by Gilbert was entitled *Dictionnaire des mots nouveaux.*

A dictionary of new words (including words used in new senses and phrases) with dated examples and references to sources—mainly publications since 1960. PC2630.G54

Old–17th century

Cayrou, Gaston. Le français classique, lexique de la langue du dix-septième siècle expliquant d'après les dictionnaires du temps et les remarques des grammairiens, le sens et l'usage des mots aujourd'hui vieillis ou différemment employés. 6. éd. rev. et corr. Paris, Didier, [1948]. 884p. il. **AD338**

1st ed. 1923.
A dictionary of 17th-century French, with many quotations from the literature and exact references to sources. Includes some 2,200 words. PC2650.C3

De Gorog, Ralph Paul. Lexique français moderne-ancien français. [Athens], Univ. of Georgia Pr., [1973]. 481p. **AD339**

An index in modern French to all the words in the abridged Godefroy *Lexique de l'ancien français* (1901; AD342). Brings together the various old equivalents of modern words. Shares the limitation of the original by not showing the usage in Old French of words which have persisted. PC2889.D4

Dubois, Jean, Lagane, René and **Lerond, Alain.** Dictionnaire du français classique. [3 éd.] Paris, Larousse, [1971]. 564p. **AD340**

2d ed. (1965) by Dubois and Lagane.
A dictionary of the language of the great classical texts of the 17th century, providing definitions of words which have changed their meaning or have become obsolete; provides citations to writers of the period. PC2650.D83

Godefroy, Frédéric Eugène. Dictionnaire de l'ancienne langue française, et de tous ses dialectes, du IXe au XVe siècle, composé d'après le dépouillement de tous les plus importants documents, manuscrits ou imprimés, qui se trouvent dans les grandes bibliothèques de la France et de l'Europe, et dans les principales archives départementales, municipales, hospitalières ou privées. Pub. sous les auspices du Ministère de l'instruction publique. Paris, Bouillon, 1891–1902. 10v. (Repr.: N.Y., Kraus, 1961) **AD341**

Issued in parts. Imprint varies.
Contents: v.1–7, A–Traioir; v.8, Traire–Z; Complément, A–Carrefour; v.9–10, Complément, Carrel–Z.
The standard dictionary of old French, with a wealth of illustrative quotations. PC2889.G6

—— Lexique de l'ancien français, pub. par les soins de J. Bonnard et Am. Salmon. Paris, Welter, 1901. 544p. **AD342**

An abridgment of the larger work (above), omitting the quotations and many of the words, but including some additional words. PC2889.G7

Grandsaignes d'Hauterive, Robert. Dictionnaire d'ancien français, moyen âge et renaissance. Paris, Larousse, 1947. 591p. **AD343**

Gives spelling variations, meaning, modern approximation, etymology, time when current, etc. PC2889.G74

Huguet, Edmond Eugène Auguste. Dictionnaire de la langue française du seizième siècle. Paris, Champion; Didier, 1925–67. 7v. **AD344**

Published in parts, 1925–67.
A scholarly dictionary of 16th-century French, including words no longer in use and those whose meanings have changed. Rich in illustrative examples, with exact references to source.
Wilhelm Kesselring's *Dictionnaire chronologique du vocabulaire français: le XVIe siècle* (Heidelberg, C. Winter, 1981. 758p.) lists words year-by-year according to first appearance in a French text, 1501–1600, and includes a bibliography of sources cited. PC2650.H7

Tobler, Adolf. Tobler-Lommatzsch, Altfranzösisches Wörterbuch; Adolf Toblers nachgelassene Materialien bearb. und . . . hrsg. von Erhard Lommatzsch . . . Wiesbaden, Steiner, 1925–76. v.1–10. (In progress) **AD345**

Imprint varies.
Contents: v.1–10, A–T.
"Von der 25. Lieferung an mit Unterstützung der Akademie der Wissenschaften und der Literatur (Mainz)."—*title page.*
An outstanding German work, which attempts to include all words of the 12th to the 14th centuries, being particularly strong in the literary language. Gives etymologies of each word with examples of usage and references to other treatments. PC2893.T6

Vandaele, Hilaire. Petit dictionnaire de l'ancien français. Paris, Garnier, [1940]. 536p. **AD346**

Compiled to furnish students with a compact, convenient dictionary to Old French. Not a substitute for Godefroy (AD341), but useful as a small dictionary. PC2889.V3

Bibliography

See also Collison (AD1); Zaunmüller (AD156); *Guide to reference books,* 7th ed., p.234–35, for additional regional and dialect bibliographies.

Baldinger, Kurt. Introduction aux dictionnaires les plus importants pour l'histoire du français; recueil d'études. [Paris], Klincksieck, 1974. 184p. (Bibliothèque française et romane. Série D: Initiation, textes et documents, 8) **AD347**

A collection of essays (one by Baldinger, the remainder by his seminar students) on the purpose, scope, strengths and weaknesses of the important etymological and historical French dictionaries from Wartburg (AD317) to DEAF (AD317*n*). PC2571.B3

Klaar, R. M. French dictionaries. [London, Centre for Information on Language Teaching and Research], 1976. 71p. **AD348**

At head of title: Specialised bibliography.
An annotated list of French monolingual, French-English and English-French dictionaries available in Dec. 1975. Includes dictionaries of etymology, phonetics, place names, proper names, and slang. Z2175.D6K58

Levy, Raphael. Répertoire des lexiques du vieux français. N.Y., Modern Language Assoc. of America, 1937. 64p. **AD349**

Gives the titles of all printed alphabetical lists of words of Old French, with various indexes. The period studied covers from the 11th through the 15th centuries. Z2175.D6L6

Wartburg, Walther von. Bibliographie des dictionnaires patois. Paris, Droz, 1934. 146p. map. (Société de Publications Romanes et Françaises, v.8) **AD350**

A comprehensive listing of regional and dialect dictionaries from all parts of France, and from other French-speaking countries. A review, with some additions and corrections by Raphael Levy, appeared in *Modern language notes* 50:128 (1935).
Location of copies of the dictionaries listed is indicated in George S. C. Adams, *Census of French and Provençal dialect dictionaries in American libraries* (Lancaster, Pa., Lancaster Pr., 1937. [Linguistic

Soc. of America special publ.]), which also indicates some additional titles. Z2175.D5W3

—— —— Supplément, publié par Hans-Erich Keller, avec la collaboration de Jean Renson. Genève, Droz, 1955. 56p. (Société de Publications Romanes et Françaises, v.52)

The supplement lists dictionaries published from 1934–55, and in some cases corrects errors found in the main volume.

Friesian

Dijkstra, Waling [and others]. Friesch woordenboek (Lexicon frisicum), met medewerking van anderen, benevens lijst van Friesche eigennamen, bewerkt door Johan Winkler . . . Uitg. ingevolge besluit der Staten van Friesland, onder toezicht van de door Gedeputeerde staten benoemde commissie . . . Leeuwarden, Meijer, [1896–1911]. 4v. **AD351**

v.4 has title: Friesche naamlijst (Onomasticon frisicum) door Johan Winkler (1898). This includes both personal and geographical names. PF1493.D33

Frysk wurdboek. [Utjefte fan de Fryske Akademy] Bolswert, A. J. Osinga, 1952–56. 2v. (v.1, 1956) **AD352**

v.1, Frysk-Nederlânsk; v.2, Nederlânsk-Frysk.
v.1 replaces the earlier *Lyts Frysk wirdboek* (1944). PF1493.F7

Gaelic

Dwelly, Edward. The illustrated Gaelic-English dictionary, containing every Gaelic word and meaning given in all previously published dictionaries, and a great number never in print before, to which is prefixed a concise Gaelic grammar. [7th ed.] Glasgow, Cairm Publs., 1971. 1034p. 675 il. **AD353**

1st ed. 1901–11.
"The first edition . . . appeared in parts under the title of *Faclair gàidhlig le dealbhan,* and the nom-de-plume of 'Ewen Mac-Donald.' "—*Pref.*
Appendix: Proper names, and persons and places mentioned in old Gaelic folktales and poetry from Armstrong's *Gaelic dictionary.* PB1591.D8

Maclennan, Malcolm. A pronouncing and etymological dictionary of the Gaelic language; Gaelic-English, English-Gaelic. Edinburgh, Grant, 1925. 613p. (Repr.: Aberdeen, Aberdeen Univ. Pr., 1979) **AD354**

PB1591.M29

MacLeod, Norman and **Dewar, Daniel.** Dictionary of the Gaelic language: I. Gaelic and English; II. English and Gaelic. Edinburgh, Grant, 1909. 1005p. **AD355**

First published 1845. PB1591.M3

Ganda

Murphy, John D. Luganda-English dictionary. Wash., Consortium Pr., Catholic Univ. of Amer. Pr., 1972. 651p. (Publications in the languages of Africa, 2) **AD356**

". . . intended primarily, but not exclusively, for English-speaking students of Luganda, particularly those who wish to read the Luganda-language press and other literature in the language."—*Pref.* PL8201.4.M87

Snoxall, R. A. Luganda-English dictionary. Oxford, Clarendon Pr., 1967. 357p. **AD357**

Intended for the speaker of English. Some 8,000 entries. Words are arranged alphabetically, but many words (especially nouns

derived from verbs) appear also under the verb stem. Illustrative sentences given. PL8201.S6

Georgian

Akademiia Nauk Gruzinskoi, SSR, Tiflis. Tolkovyi slovar' gruzinskogo iazyka. Glav. red. G. Akhvlediani [i dr.]. Pod obshchei red. Arn. Chikobava. Tbilisi, 1950–64. 8v. **AD358**

Added title page in Georgian: Khartuli enis ganmartebithi lekhsikoni. Text in Georgian. PK9125.A47

Cherkesi, E. Georgian-English dictionary. [Oxford], pr. for the Trustees of the Marjory Wardrop Fund, Univ. of Oxford, 1950. 257p. **AD359**

An excellent dictionary, based on a textual comparison of the English and Georgian versions of the books of the Old and New Testaments and other sources. The *Russian-Georgian dictionary* of D. Chubinashvili (1886) and the works of early Georgian scholars were used as reference. Ancient as well as modern Georgian terms are included. PK9125.C47

Gvardzhaladze, Tamara and **Gvardzhaladze, Isidore.** English-Georgian dictionary by Thamar and Isidore Gvarjaladze. 2d ed. 8000 words. Tbilissi, State Publ. House, 1955. 450p. **AD360**

Added title page in Georgian. PK9125.G9

German

Grimm, Jakob Ludwig Karl and **Grimm, Wilhelm.** Deutsches Wörterbuch. Leipzig, Hirzel, 1854–1960. 16v. **AD361**

On cover (varies): Im Auftrage des Deutschen Reiches und Preussens mit Unterstützung des Reichministeriums des Innern, des Preussischen Ministeriums für Wissenschaft, Kunst und Volksbildung, und der Preussischen Akademie der Wissenschaften.

The great dictionary of the German language, completed in 1960 after more than 100 years in preparation. Since it was issued in *Lieferungen,* not in alphabetical sequence, but in various parts of the alphabet simultaneously, the volumes show wide divergence in dates of publication, as well as in scope and method of presentation.

Compiled on historical principles. The design of the Brothers Grimm "was to give an exhaustive account of the words of the literary language (New High German) from about the end of the 15th century, including their earlier etymological and later history, with references to important dialectal words and forms; and to illustrate their use and history abundantly by quotations. . . ."—*Encyclopaedia Britannica,* 11th ed., 8:189.

As the dictionary uses small letters throughout instead of capitals for common nouns, it is the main German authority for noncapitalization of nouns in German. PF3625.G7

—— —— Quellenverzeichnis, bearb. . . . von A. Huber [et al.]. Leipzig, Hirzel, 1971. 1094p.

Issued in 7 Lfg., 1966–71.
A new edition of *Grimm* has begun to appear as:

—— Deutsches Wörterbuch. Hrsg. von der Deutschen Akademie der Wissenschaften zu Berlin in Zusammenarbeit mit der Akademie der Wissenschaften zu Göttingen. Neubearbeitungen. Leipzig, Hirzel, 1965–83. Bd.1$^{1-10}$, 6$^{1-11}$. (In progress) **AD362**

1st ed. 1854–1960 (above).
Contents: Hinweise; Bd.1, Lfg.1–10, A–Affrikata; Bd.6, Lfg. 1–11, D–Durchstreichen.
A revised and expanded edition of this important dictionary, incorporating results of new research and carrying on the thorough and scholarly traditions of the earlier work. PF3625.G72

Karg-Gasterstädt, Elisabeth and **Frings, Theodor.** Althochdeutsches Wörterbuch; auf Grund der von Elias von Stein-meyer hinterlassenen Sammlungen im Auftrag der Sächsischen Akademie der Wissenschaften zu Leipzig. . . . Bearbeiter: Siegfried Blum [et al.]. Berlin, Akademie-Verlag, 1952–84. Bd.1 (in 21 Lfg.), 2$^{1-3/4}$, 3$^{1-14/15}$. (In progress) **AD363**

Contents: Bd.1, A–B; Bd.2$^{1-3/4}$, C–thar ubari; Bd.3$^{1-14/15}$, E–fortenĭgî.
A scholarly dictionary of Old High German, with many examples and exact references to the literature. PF3975.K35

Lexer, Matthias von. Matthias Lexers Mittelhochdeutsches Taschenwörterbuch. (Mit neubearb. u. erw. Nachträgen) 37. Aufl. Stuttgart, Hirzel, 1983. 504p. **AD364**

1st ed. 1879; various reprintings.
A standard small dictionary of Middle High German. A larger work is the author's *Mittelhochdeutsches Handwörterbuch* (Leipzig, 1872–78. 3v. and Nachträge).
The first section is a reprint of earlier editions. The Nachträge section was prepared by Ulrich Pretzel. PF4327.L42

Paul, Hermann. Deutsches Wörterbuch. 7. durchges. Aufl. bearb. von Werner Betz. Tübingen, Max Niemeyer, 1976. 841p. **AD365**

1st ed. 1897.
A standard work, strong in the historical development of words.
PF3625.P4

Schulz, Hans. Deutsches Fremdwörterbuch. Strassburg, Trübner; Berlin, de Gruyter, 1913–42. 2v. **AD366**

Forms v.2 of the series "Wörterbücher der Deutschen Akademie."
An authoritative work dealing with words of foreign origin, with examples and dated references to sources. PF3670.S4

Der Sprach-Brockhaus; deutsches Bildwörterbuch. 8., völlig neubearb. und erw. Aufl. Wiesbaden, Brockhaus, 1972. 835p. il. **AD367**

1st ed. 1935.
A practical desk-sized dictionary, which includes geographical names, technical terms, colloquialisms, etc. Small line drawings are used to illustrate the text. PF3629.S65

Trübners deutsches Wörterbuch; im Auftrag der Arbeitsgemeinschaft für deutsche Wortforschung, hrsg. von Alfred Götze. Berlin, de Gruyter, 1936–57. 8v. **AD368**

Issued in parts.
An excellent dictionary, strong in etymologies and word histories, with many references to sources. PF3580.T7

Wahrig, Gerhard. Deutsches Wörterbuch: mit einem "Lexikon der deutschen Sprachlehre." Hrsg. in Zusammenarbeit mit zahlreichen Wissenschaftlern und anderen Fachleuten. Völlig überarbeitete Neuausg. [München], Mosaik, [1980]. 4358 col. **AD369**

"Die Neuausgabe . . . wurde bearbeitet von Ursula Hermann."—*verso of t.p.*
The 1975 publication with this title represented a revised and updated edition of Wahrig's *Das grosse deutsche Wörterbuch* (1966).
A large (about 220,000 words and idioms) "desk dictionary," easy to use despite the three-column format and relatively small type. As applicable, conjugation or declension is indicated by number keyed to tables at the front of the volume. Includes a fairly detailed dictionary of grammatical terms by Walter Ludewig, columns 49–236.
PF3625.W2

——— **Krämer, Hildegard** and **Zimmermann, Harald.** Brockhaus Wahrig: deutsches Wörterbuch. Wiesbaden, Brockhaus; Stuttgart, Deutsche Verlags-Anstalt, 1980–84. 6v. **AD370**

An extensive new work which includes some 220,000 keywords and 550,000 definitions. Examples of usage are given; field of use is indicated for the many scientific and technical terms included.
PF3625.B7

Wörterbuch der deutschen Gegenwartssprache. Hrsg. von Ruth Klappenbach und Wolfgang Steinitz. Bearbeiter: R.

Klappenbach und H. Malige-Klappenbach. Berlin, Akademie-Verlag, 1961–76. 6v. **AD371**

At head of title: Akademie der Wissenschaften zu Berlin. Institut für deutsche Sprache und Literatur.
Issued in parts.
A dictionary of the present-day language, with examples from and references to modern writers. The final volume contains an "Alphabetisches Verzeichnis der Quellen." PF3625.W62

Bilingual

Betteridge, Harold T. Cassell's German-English, English-German dictionary; Deutsch-englisches, englisch-deutsches Wörterbuch. Completely revised. London, Cassell; N.Y., Macmillan, [1978]. 1580p. **AD372**

Betteridge's first edition of this work, entitled *The new Cassell's German dictionary* (1958) was an almost completely rewritten edition of the work edited for many years by Karl Breul. This "first Macmillan revision" is an expanded edition, completely revised and reset, incorporating many new words and usages. Gives phonetic transcriptions of head words. One of the most useful bilingual dictionaries. PF3640.B453

Flügel, Johann Gottfried. Allgemeines englisch-deutsches und deutsch-englisches Wörterbuch von Felix Flügel. 3. verb. u. verm. Abdruck der 4. gänzlich umgearb. Aufl. von J. G. Flügel's Vollständigem Wörterbuch. . . . Braunschweig, G. Westermann, 1908. 2v. in 3. **AD373**

Added title page in English: A universal English-German and German-English dictionary.
T.1, Bd.1–2, Englisch-deutsch; T.2, Deutsch-englisch.
An older dictionary rich in quotations with exact references to sources. PF3640.F55

Harrap's Standard German and English dictionary. Ed. by Trevor Jones. London, Harrap, [1963–74]. pt.1 [v.1–3]. (In progress) **AD374**

Contents: pt.1, [v.1–3], German-English, A–R (in 3v.).
A scholarly dictionary intended for general use. Each word is treated separately instead of under groupings. Scientific terms are included. Gives examples of usage. PF3640.H3

Harrap's Concise German and English dictionary: English-German/German-English in one volume. Ed. by Robin Sawers. London, Harrap; [Lincolnwood, Ill.], National Textbook Co., [1982]. 499p., 627p. **AD375**

Aims "to provide a dictionary slightly smaller than the existing medium-sized volumes, omitting obscure or literary usage, but with more generous treatment of the entries—full grammatical information and pronunciation and plenty of examples."—*Pref.* Introductory matter in English and German. Includes a list of common abbreviations for each language. PF3640.H29

Langenscheidt's New Muret-Sanders encyclopedic dictionary of the English and German languages. Compl. rev. 1962. Ed. by Otto Springer. London, Methuen; N.Y., Barnes & Noble, 1962–75. 2pts. in 4v. **AD376**

Added title page: Der neue Muret-Sanders, Langenscheidts enzyklopädisches Wörterbuch der englischen und deutschen Sprache.
German edition has title: Langenscheidts enzyklopädisches Wörterbuch der englischen und deutschen Sprache.
Contents: pt.1, English-German; pt.2, German-English.
The *Muret-Sanders Enzyklopädisches englisch-deutsches und deutsch-englisches Wörterbuch* (Grosse Ausg. Berlin-Schöneberg, Langenscheidt, 1908. 2v. in 4) has long been an outstanding bilingual dictionary.
The 1962 edition is, in effect, a new work although based on the old. Printed in roman type, each word has received new treatment, and thousands of new words have been added to make the work representative of 20th-century usage. "In pronunciation, spelling, and vocabulary, American English is treated with the same degree of completeness and accuracy as British English . . ." (*Pref.*), but some reviewers feel that American usage has been emphasized. Includes

scientific and technical terms; for biological terms, the Latin names are given following the German equivalent. Pronunciation is indicated; idiomatic phrases and colloquialisms are given.

PF3640.L257

Langenscheidt's Condensed Muret-Sanders German dictionary: German-English. Heinz Messinger, ed. Berlin, Langenscheidt, [1982]. 1296p.   **AD377**

Based on the German-English part of the 4v. ed. (above), but "it is by no means simply the result of a systematic halving of the larger dictionary" (*Pref.*); rather, it involved "a word-for-word scrutiny and careful sifting of the original material." About 14,000 entry words.   PF3640.L25732

Messinger, Heinz. Langenscheidts Grosswörterbuch, Englisch-Deutsch. Berlin, Langenscheidt, [1972]. 1104p.

AD378

An "in between" size dictionary which "aims to take the middle course between Langenscheidt's encyclopedic 'New Muret-Sanders' and the 'Concise English-German Dictionary' [Langenscheidts Handwörterbuch, Englisch], profiting from the merits of both works."—*Pref.* About 120,000 entries.   PF3640.M54

The Oxford-Duden pictorial German-English dictionary. Ed. by the Dudenredaktion and the German Section of the Oxford University Press Dictionary Department. Oxford, Clarendon Pr., 1980. 677p., 87p., 96p. il.   **AD379**

A cooperative effort of two highly reputable publishers, the dictionary is "based on the third, completely revised edition of the German *Bildwörterbuch* published as Volume 3 of the ten-volume *Duden* series of monolingual German dictionaries. The English text represents a direct translation of the German original and follows the original layout as closely as possible."—*Foreword.*

The intention is to help the reader visualize the object denoted by a given word or term. Terms are grouped by subject and illustrated in some 384 plates (chiefly line drawings), with the German terms and English equivalents given on the same or facing page. German and English indexes allow the dictionary to be used as either German-English or English-German. Covers a wide range of technical and everyday vocabulary.   PF3629.O9

Spalding, Keith. An historical dictionary of German figurative usage. Oxford, Blackwell, 1952–84. Fasc.1–39. (In progress)   **AD380**

Contents: Fasc.1–39, A–Pflug.

Records figurative expressions, proverbs, quotations, and other established phrases appearing in German literature since approximately 1750, with explanations in English; the annotations illustrating use and change of meaning are often drawn from sources preceding this date. Equivalent English phrases or expressions are given for each entry. A complete list of sources is planned for the conclusion of the work.   PF3440.S7

Wildhagen, Karl and **Héraucourt, Will.** The new Wildhagen German dictionary; German-English, English-German. [Eds.: Eva Ruetz and Richard Wiezell] Chicago, Follett, 1965. 1296p., 1061p.   **AD381**

Subtitle: An encyclopedic and strictly scientific representation of the vocabulary of the modern and present-day languages, with special regard to syntax, style, and idiomatic usage.

Previous ed. in 2v., 1962; the English-German part was first published 1938, the German-English part, 1953/54.

This is a single-volume edition of the 1962 publication in 2v. It shows only minor changes in the German-English part, but there has been significant expansion (about 30 percent) in the English-German section. A well-edited desk dictionary.   PF3640.W546

Bibliography

Kühn, Peter. Deutsche Wörterbücher: eine systematische Bibliographie. Tübingen, Niemeyer, 1978. 266p. (Reihe germanistische Linguistik, 15)   **AD382**

A classified bibliography of general and specialized German-language dictionaries and various other types of "word books"

(including dictionaries of names, quotation books, concordances, etc.). Includes bilingual and multilingual dictionaries. About 2,700 items. Author index.   Z2235.D6K83

Lemmer, Manfred. Deutscher Wortschatz; Bibliographie zur deutschen Lexikologie. Halle, Niemeyer, 1967. 123p.

AD383

A bibliography of German-language dictionaries and of works on German lexicography. Some brief annotations.   Z2235.L4

Abbreviations

Koblischke, Heinz. Grosses Abkürzungsbuch: Abkürzungen, Kurzwörter, Zeichen, Symbole. 3., durchgesehene Aufl. Leipzig, VEB Bibliographisches Institut, 1983. 504p.

AD384

1st ed. 1969 had title: *Abkürzungsbuch.*

International coverage; gives German translation of foreign-language terms.   PF3693.K6

Etymology

See also AD361.

Kluge, Friedrich. Etymologisches Wörterbuch der deutschen Sprache. 21. Aufl. . . . bearb. von Walther Mitzka. Berlin, de Gruyter, 1975. 915p.   **AD385**

A standard work frequently reprinted with varying amounts of revision.

Especially strong in word development with dated examples of usage. Includes a *Sachverzeichnis* of words grouped into categories, and a bibliography of sources, p.xi–xvi.   PF3580.K5

Slang

Küpper, Heinz. Illustriertes Lexikon der deutschen Umgangssprache. [Stuttgart], Klett, [1982–84]. 8v. il.   **AD386**

An extensive slang dictionary with indication of dates of origin or usage, derivation, etc. Heavily illustrated (mainly in color) with pictures drawn from a wide range of sources including contemporary advertising and newsphotos as well as various examples of world art.   PF3815.K87

——— Wörterbuch der deutschen Umgangssprache. 3. neubearb. und erw. Aufl. [Hamburg], Claassen Verlag, 1963–70. 6v.   **AD387**

1st ed. 1955.

Contents: Bd.1, Erklärendes Wörterbuch; Bd.2, 10,000 neue Ausdrücke von A–Z; Bd.3, Hochdeutsch–Umgangsdeutsch; Gesamtstichwortverzeichnis; Ergänzungen . . . ; Bd.4, Berufsschelten und Verwandtes; Bd.5, 10,000 neue Ausdrücke von A–Z (Sachschelten); Bd.6, Jugenddeutsch von A bis Z.

A dictionary of German slang and colloquial expressions.

PF3625.K8

Wolf, Siegmund A. Wörterbuch des Rotwelschen; Deutsche Gaunersprache. Mannheim, Bibliographisches Inst., [1956]. 430p.   **AD388**

A historical dictionary of underworld slang, with dated references to the literature.

Synonyms

Dornseiff, Franz. Der deutsche Wortschatz nach Sachgruppen. 7. Aufl. mit alphabetischem Generalregister. Berlin, de Gruyter, 1970. 166p., 922p.   **AD389**

1st ed. 1933–34.

This edition considerably expanded, especially in supplementary material and index. The main part is arranged as a thesaurus in 20 main categories with many subdivisions. A detailed index refers to the appropriate sections. PF3591.D6

Eberhard, Johann August. Synonymisches Handwörterbuch der deutschen Sprache. 17. Aufl. durchgängig umbearb., verm. und verb. von Otto Lyon. Mit Übersetzung der Wörter in die englische, französische, italienische, und russische Sprache. Leipzig, Grieben, 1910. 1201p. **AD390**

A treatment of some 1,600 German words giving synonyms and showing discrimination in meanings. Equivalents are given in English, French, Italian, and Russian. PF3591.E3

Farrell, Ralph Barstow. Dictionary of German synonyms. 3d ed. Cambridge, University Pr., 1977. 412p. **AD391**

1st ed. 1953.

Arranged by English word with German equivalents and definitions; differences in meaning are discussed and examples of German usage are given. Particularly useful for the student.

This edition "introduces no innovation except an appendix comprising a list of difficult German words—difficult because their meaning is not readily perceived or because they have no exact equivalent in English."—*Pref.* Some examples and explanations have been improved so long as extensive resetting of type was not involved. PF3591.F37

Görner, Herbert and **Kempcke, Günter.** Synonymwörterbuch; sinnverwandte Ausdrucke der deutschen Sprache. Aufl. 3. Leipzig, VEB Bibliographisches Institut, 1975. 643p. **AD392**

1st ed. 1973.

A dictionary of synonyms and synonymous expressions. PF3591.G6

Wehrle, Hugo and **Eggers, Hans.** Deutscher Wortschatz: ein Wegweiser zum treffenden Ausdruck. 12. Aufl. Stuttgart, Ernst Klett, 1961. 821p. **AD393**

12th ed. of Anton Schlessing's *Deutscher Wortschatz* (1st ed. 1880–81), an outstanding work for many years.

This edition has been much enlarged, completely revised, and rearranged. The first part is arranged systematically by idea, in much the manner of Roget's *Thesaurus* (AD108). The second part is an alphabetical list of words referring to the paragraph sections of the first part. PF3591.W39

New words

Heberth, Alfred. Neue Wörter: Neologismen in der deutschen Sprache seit 1945. Wien, Verband der Wissenschaftlichen Gesellschaften Österreichs, 1977. 240p. **AD394**

A dictionary of new words which have achieved currency in German speech since World War II. Indicates derivation of terms, country of origin for loan-words, etc.

Supplemented by: PF3445.H4

—— Neue Wörter 2: Neologismen in der deutschen Sprache seit 1945. Wien, Verband der Wissenschaftlichen Gesellschaften Österreichs, 1982. 75p.

Usage

Anderson, Beatrix and **North, Maurice.** Cassell's Colloquial German: a handbook of idiomatic usage. Completely rev. London, Cassell; N.Y., Macmillan, [1980]. 176p. **AD395**

1st ed. 1968 had title: *Beyond the dictionary in German.*

Aims to help guard against misinterpretations and to supply information on current usage. PF3680.A5

Mackensen, Lutz, ed. Neues deutsches Wörterbuch. Rechtschreibung, Grammatik, Stil, Worterklärung, Fremdwörterbuch. Laupheim (Wttbg.), Pfahl, 1952. 837p. **AD396**

A modern dictionary of some 128,000 words, indicating correct usage.

Regional and dialect

For regional and dialect dictionaries *see* Collison (AD1); Zaunmüller (AD156); *Guide to reference books,* 7th ed., p.237–38.

Grebo

Innes, Gordon. A Grebo-English dictionary. London, Cambridge Univ. Pr., 1967. 131p. (West African language monographs, no.6) **AD397**

The first Grebo dictionary in a century. Based on the speech of an informant and incorporates all the identifiable words of J. L. Wilson's *Dictionary of the Grebo language* (1839). Intended for the speaker of English. PL8821.I49

Greek

Estienne, Henri. Thesaurus graecae linguae, ab Henrico Stephano constructus. Post editionem anglicam novis additamentis auctum, ordineque alphabetico digestum tertio ediderunt Carolus Benedictus Hase . . . Guilielmus Dindorfius et Ludovicus Dindorfius. Paris, Didot, 1831–65. 8v. in 9. **AD398**

1st ed. 1572.

An authoritative dictionary from its first publication, reedited by outstanding scholars in the 19th century. Still of first importance. PA442.E8

Snell, Bruno and **Fleischer, Ulrich.** Lexikon des frühgriechischen Epos. Mit Unterstützung der Unesco, der Deutschen Forschungsgemeinschaft und der Joachim-Jungius-Gesellschaft, Hamburg, vorbereitet und hrsg. vom Thesaurus Linguae Graecae . . . Göttingen, Vandenhoeck und Ruprecht, 1955–84. v.1–2$^{1-2}$. (In progress) **AD399**

Editors vary.

Contents: v.1–2$^{1-2}$ (Lfg.1–11), α – 'επαμίντωρ.

A new *Thesaurus linguae graecae,* attempting to list all words in the texts of the earliest literary works up to, but not including, the works of Antimachos; covers Homer, Hesiod, and others. As planned, the Greek *Thesaurus* will consist of a series of dictionaries, each covering a different literary period.

Bilingual

Liddell, Henry George and **Scott, Robert.** Greek-English lexicon. . . . A new ed. rev. and augm. throughout by Henry Stuart Jones . . . with the assistance of Roderick McKenzie . . . and with the cooperation of many scholars. . . . [9th ed.] Oxford, Clarendon Pr., 1925–40. 2111p. **AD400**

1st ed. 1843. This new 9th ed. is revised throughout and enlarged by the addition of many words including scientific and technical terms.

Issued in 10 pts., 1925–40. Frequently reprinted. (A 1968 printing [2042p., 153p.] is available with the 1968 supplement [below] bound in.) Preliminary leaves include: List of authors and works, p.xvi–xli; Epigraphical publications, p.xli–xliii; Papyrological publications, p.xliii–xlv; Periodicals, p.xlv–xlvi; General list of abbreviations, p.xlvi–xlviii. Addenda and corrigenda, p.2043–2111.

The standard Greek and English lexicon, covering the language to about 600 A.D., omitting Patristic and Byzantine Greek. Omits place-names for which Passow's dictionary (AD401) must be used. PA445.E5L6

—— —— A supplement, ed. by E. A. Barber. Oxford, Clarendon Pr., 1968. 153p.

Incorporates the "Addenda et corrigenda" section from the 9th ed., adds new words, and amends earlier articles.

———— ———— Abridged. 26th ed. rev. and enl. Chicago, Follett, 1941. 835p.

PA445.E5L7

Passow, Franz. Handwörterbuch der griechischen Sprache. Neubearb. und zeitgemäss umgestaltet von Val. Chr. Fr. Rost und Friedrich Palm. Des ursprunglichen Werkes 5. Aufl. Leipzig, Vogel, 1841–57. 2v. in 4.　　**AD401**

The standard Greek and German lexicon, useful to the English reader also because it includes geographical names omitted from Liddell and Scott (AD400). A new, much enlarged edition by Wilhelm Crönert was started, but only pts.1–3 (A–An) were issued (Göttingen, Vandenhoeck, 1912–13).　　PA445.G3P3

Preisigke, Friedrich. Wörterbuch der griechischen Papyrus-urkunden mit Einschluss der griechischen Inschriften, Aufschriften, Ostraka, Mumienschilder usw. aus Ägypten, . . . hrsg. von Emil Kiessling. Heidelberg, Selbstverlag des Erben, 1925–71. v.1–4¹⁻⁴. (In progress)　　**AD402**

Imprint varies.
Contents: Bd.1–2, A–Ω; Bd.3, Besondere Wörterliste; Bd.4, Lfg.1–4, α – 'επικόπτω.
A Greek-German dictionary of words found in the papyrus documents, inscriptions, etc.　　PA3369.P75

———— ———— Supplement, hrsg. von Emil Kiessling. Amsterdam, Hakkert, 1969–71. 450p.

Contents: Suppl.1 (1940–66), issued in 3 Lfg.

Woodhouse, Sidney Chawner. English-Greek dictionary; a vocabulary of the Attic language. London, Routledge, 1910. 1029p.　　**AD403**

Frequently reprinted.　　PA445.E5W6

Yonge, Charles Duke. English-Greek lexicon; ed. by Henry Drisler. N.Y., Amer. Book Co., 1890 [c.1870]. 663p., cxv p.　　**AD404**

Includes *Greek synonyms from the French of Alex. Pillon,* edited with notes by T. K. Arnold (cxv p.); and an appendix of Greek proper names.
Now largely superseded, except for dialect words.

PA445.E5Y5

Etymology

Boisacq, Émile. Dictionnaire étymologique de la langue grecque, étudiée dans ses rapports avec les autres langues indo-européennes. 4. éd., augm. d'un index par Helmut Rix. Heidelberg, Winter, 1950. 1256p.　　**AD405**

1st ed. 1907–16.
This edition includes a useful index which lists the words in all languages cited in the text.　　PA421.B6

Chantraine, Pierre. Dictionnaire étymologique de la langue grecque; histoire des mots. Paris, Klincksieck, [1968–80]. 4v.　　**AD406**

"Ouvrage publié avec le concours du Centre National de la Recherche Scientifique."—*title page.*
Emphasizes the history of *use* of the vocabulary. Etymologies follow those of Frisk's *Griechisches etymologisches Wörterbuch* (below) for the most part, except when new evidence or recent scholarship indicates otherwise.　　PA422.C5

Frisk, Hjalmar. Griechisches etymologisches Wörterbuch. Heidelberg, Winter, 1954–72. 3v. (Indogermanische Bibliothek. II.Reihe-Wörterbücher)　　**AD407**

Issued in parts. A "2. unveränderte Aufl." appeared 1972–73.
An authoritative work tracing the etymologies of classical Greek with references to sources, etc.
v.3 is "Nachträge, Wortregister, Corrigenda und Nachwort."

PA422.F7

Hofmann, Johann Baptist. Etymologisches Wörterbuch des Griechischen. München, Oldenbourg, 1950. 433p.

AD408

A small, dependable work, more up-to-date than Boisacq (AD405).　　PA445.G3H6

Pronunciation

Allen, William Sidney. Vox Graeca; a guide to the pronunciation of classical Greek. 2d ed. Cambridge, Univ. Pr., 1974. 174p.　　**AD409**

A companion to the same author's *Vox latina* (AD562) and, like that volume, a guide to the principles of pronunciation rather than a pronouncing dictionary.　　PA267.A4

Christian and medieval

Bauer, Walter. A Greek-English lexicon of the New Testament and other early Christian literature: a translation and adaptation of the fourth revised and augmented edition of Walter Bauer's Griechisch-deutsches Wörterbuch zu den Schriften des Neuen Testaments und der übrigen urchristlichen Literatur, [by] William F. Arndt and F. Wilbur Gingrich. 2d ed., rev. & aug. by F. Wilbur Gingrich and Frederick W. Danker from Walter Bauer's 5th ed., 1958. Chicago, Univ. of Chicago Pr., [1979]. 900p.　　**AD410**

1st ed. 1957.
This edition "contains Bauer's additions as well as a number of changes and additions" (*Foreword*) by the editors of the translation.
A list of corrections in spellings, oversights in accents, etc., is included in the generally favorable review by D. J. Georgacas in *Classical philology* 76:153–59 (Apr. 1981).　　PA881.B38

Alsop, John R. An index to the revised Bauer-Arndt-Gingrich Greek lexicon, second edition, by F. Wilbur Gingrich and Frederick W. Danker. Grand Rapids, Mich., Zondervan, [1981]. 525p.　　**AD411**

Entries are listed "in the order in which they appear in the New Testament, beginning with chapter one of Matthew, and proceeding verse by verse to the end of Revelation."—*Pref.* Reference to page number is provided, together with an English gloss.

PA881.A72A45

Du Cange, Charles Du Fresne. Glossarium ad scriptores mediae & infimae graecitatis . . . réimp. du Collège de France. Paris, Geuthner, 1943. 2v. in 1 (2426col.). (Repr.: Graz, 1958)　　**AD412**

1st ed. 1688.
In spite of its age, still the authoritative dictionary of medieval Greek, including many quotations with exact reference to sources.

PA1125.D8

Gingrich, Felix Wilbur. Shorter lexicon of the Greek New Testament. 2d ed., rev. by Frederick W. Danker. Chicago, Univ. of Chicago Pr., 1983. 221p.　　**AD413**

1st ed. 1965.
A greatly condensed version, with some revision, of the translation and adaptation of Walter Bauer's *Griechisch-deutsches Wörterbuch zu den Schriften des Neuen Testaments* by William F. Arndt and F. W. Gingrich, first published in 1957 under the title *A Greek-English lexicon of the New Testament and other early Christian literature* (AD410). "Emphasis is placed on the bare meanings of words; for more information the user must consult BAGD or other works. However, . . . the student will find here fresh information or modification of conclusions reached in the larger lexicon."—*Pref.*

PA881.G5

Lampe, Geoffrey William Hugo. A patristic Greek lexicon. Oxford, Clarendon Pr., 1961–68. 1568p.　　**AD414**

Published in 5 pts.
"The object of this work is primarily to interpret the theological and ecclesiastical vocabulary of the Greek Christian authors from

Clement of Rome to Theodore of Studium."—*Pref.* It is complementary to Liddell-Scott-Jones in that common meanings of words noted there are not repeated in the Lampe work, though unusual usages may be. Biblical words and usages to be found in the Septuagint and the New Testament are also omitted. List of authors and works, p.xi–xlv.

Moulton, James Hope and **Milligan, George.** Vocabulary of the Greek Testament, illustrated from the papyri and other non-literary sources. London, Hodder, 1914–29. [pref. 1929] 835p. **AD415**

Originally published in 8 pts., 1914–29, 835p.; reprintings (1930, etc.) have 705p. PA881.M7

Sophocles, Evangelinus Apostolides. Greek lexicon of the Roman and Byzantine periods (from B.C. 146 to A.D. 1100). Memorial ed., ed. by J. H. Thayer. N.Y., Scribner, 1887. 1188p. (Repr.: N.Y., Ungar, 1957. 2v.) **AD416**

1st ed. 1870. Various reprintings.
A dictionary of the later classical Greek of the Roman and Byzantine periods. Useful for the Church Fathers. PA1125.S7

Modern Greek

Akadēmia Athēnōn, Athens. Lexikon tēs hellēnikēs glōssēs. Historikon lexikon tēs neas hellēnikēs tēs te koinōs homiloumenēs kai tōn idiōmatōn. Athēnai, Typographeion "Hestia," 1933–53. v.1–4¹. **AD417**

Contents: v.1–4¹, a–gargaros. No more published.

Dēmētrakos, Dēmētrios B. Mega lexikon tēs Hellēnikēs glōssēs. Athens, Demetrákou, 1936–50. 9v. **AD418**

Ed. by Iōannēs S. Zerbos.
Covers all periods from ancient times to mid-20th century.
PA441.D4

Kykkōtēs, Hierotheos. English-modern Greek and modern Greek-English dictionary including English and Greek grammar, geographical and proper names, and abbreviations. [3d ed.] London, P. Lund, [1957]. 2v. in 1 (644p.). **AD419**

1st ed. 1942.
A useful small dictionary with appendixes of abbreviations, proper names, grammatical rules, etc. PA1139.E5K85

Kyriakidēs, Achilleus. Modern Greek-English dictionary with a Cypriote vocabulary. 2d ed. (rev. throughout). Athens, Constantinides, 1909. 908p. **AD420**

1st ed. 1892.
A standard dictionary of modern Greek, giving examples of usage, etc. PA1139.E5K89

Mega anglo-hellēnikon lexikon; syntachthen hypo epiteleiou epistēmonōn, technikōn kai logotechnōn. Athēnai, Ekdoseis "Odysseus," [1962?]. 4v. **AD421**

An English-Modern Greek dictionary, giving many examples of usage, colloquial phrases, etc. Pronunciation of English words is shown by the phonetic alphabet.

Penguin-Hellenews anglo-hellēnikon lexikon. Vasismeno eiz ten ekdosin. The Penguin English dictionary, by G. N. Garmonsway. [Athena], Hellenews-Paideia, 1975. 926p. **AD422**

English-Greek only. The vocabulary is based on the *Penguin dictionary of English* (AD33).
B. Hunter Smeaton's review in *Library journal* 103:1497 (Aug. 1978) concludes that "For sheer scope, modernity, and inclusion of living illustrative phrases, it is unrivaled among smaller-format English-Greek dictionaries now available. Unfortunately, it is designed for users who already know Greek, and can sift out the new from the old." PA1139.E5P34

Pring, Julian Talbot. The Oxford dictionary of modern Greek. English-Greek. Oxford, Clarendon Pr.; N.Y., Oxford Univ. Pr., 1982. 370p. **AD423**

Aims "to give Greek equivalents of English words and phrases with illustrations of their idiomatic usage. In principle the renderings are into colloquial language of everyday use, varying from subtle to commonplace, from the polite or profound to the trivial and unbuttoned."—*Pref.* PA1139.E5P77

——— The Oxford dictionary of modern Greek (Greek-English). Oxford, Clarendon Pr., 1965. 219p. **AD423a**

Intended both for general reference and for the language student; covers "the vocabulary of everyday affairs and general literature."—*Pref.* PA1139.E5P76

"Proias" lexikon tēs Neas Hellēnikēs glōssēs: orthographikon kai hermēneutikon; syntachthen hypo epitropēs philologōn kai epistēmonōn epimeleia Geōrgiou Zeugōlē. Ekd. 2. epēuxēmenē. Athēnai, Ekdot. Oikos S.P. Dēmētrakou, [196–?]. 2v. **AD424**

Previously publ. under title *Lexikon Neas Hellēnikēs glōssēs* (195–?) and *Lexikon tēs Hellēnikēs glōssēs* (1933). PA1131.L42

Swanson, Donald Carl Eugene. Vocabulary of modern spoken Greek. English-Greek and Greek-English . . . with the assistance of Sophia P. Djaferis. Minneapolis, Univ. of Minnesota Pr., 1959. 408p. **AD425**

PA1139.E5S9

Gujarati

Deshpande, Pandurang Ganesh. A modern English-Gujarati dictionary. Bombay, Oxford Univ. Pr., 1982. 809p. **AD426**

Title also in Gujarati.
About 35,000 headwords and derivatives. PK1846.D428

Hausa

Abraham, Roy Clive. Dictionary of the Hausa language. 2d ed. London, Univ. of London Pr., [1962]. 992p. **AD427**

1st ed. 1949.
A comprehensive Hausa-English dictionary intended for the speaker of English. Tones are marked by diacritics; part of speech is indicated; illustrative phrases and sentences are included.
PL8233.A7

Hawaiian

Judd, Henry, Pukui, Mary Kawena and **Stokes, John F. G.** Introduction to the Hawaiian language (an English-Hawaiian vocabulary) . . . with a complementary Hawaiian-English vocabulary. Honolulu, Tongg Pub. Co., 1945. 314p. **AD428**

Subtitle: Comprising five thousand of the commonest and most useful English words and their equivalents, in modern Hawaiian speech, correctly pronounced. PL6446.J8

Pukui, Mary Kawena and **Elbert, Samuel H.** Hawaiian dictionary: Hawaiian-English, English-Hawaiian. Honolulu, Univ. of Hawaii Pr., 1971. 402p., 188p. **AD429**

Originally published in two volumes, the Hawaiian-English part first appearing in 1957 (3d ed. 1965; suppl. 1966) and the English-Hawaiian part in 1964. Based to some extent on the Lorrin Andrews *Dictionary of the Hawaiian language* revised by Henry H. Parker (Honolulu, 1922), the Hawaiian-English part comprises about 26,000 entries and is the most comprehensive and up-to-date dictionary for the language. Unfortunately this edition was not fully reset, and a supplement of "New entries and meanings" should be kept in mind. Other supplements include a glossary of Hawaiian gods and their specializations. The English-Hawaiian part supplies Hawaiian equivalents for about 12,500 English terms.

PL6446.P795

Hebrew

Ben-Yehudah, Eliezer. Thesaurus totius Hebraitatis et veteris et recentioris, auctore Elieser Ben Iehuda. Berlin-Schöneberg, Langenscheidt; Jerusalem, Ben-Yehudah Hozaa-la'Or, [1908]–59. 16v. **AD430**

Added title pages in Hebrew, German, French, and English. Equivalents are given in these languages, but all explanations are in Hebrew. v.8–16 edited by Morris [i.e., Moses] Hirsch Segal.

English title: *A complete dictionary of ancient and modern Hebrew.*

PJ4830.B36

Grasowsky, Judah. Millon 'ivri. 9th ed. [Tel Aviv], [1957]. 1113p. **AD431**

Includes both Biblical and modern Hebrew.   PJ4830.G82

Bilingual

Alcalay, Reuben. The complete English-Hebrew dictionary. Tel Aviv, Massadah Pub. Co., 1959–61. 4v. (4270 col.) **AD432**

Various reprintings, including 1v. ed. (2884 col.).
Title page and introduction in Hebrew. Added title page in English. Vocabulary is extensive; gives equivalents only.
Romanized title: Milon angli 'ivri shalem.   PJ4833.A4

——— The complete Hebrew-English dictionary. Bridgeport, Conn., publ. for Media Judaica by Prayer Book Pr., [1965]. 2884col. **AD433**

Added title page in Hebrew: Milon 'ivri-angli shalem.
A companion to the compiler's *Complete English-Hebrew dictionary.* PJ4833.A42

Avinoam, Reuben and **Sachs, H.** Compendious Hebrew-English dictionary comprising a complete vocabulary of Biblical, Mishnaïc, medieval and modern Hebrew, comp. by Reuben Avinoam (Grossman) in collaboration with H. Sachs, rev. & ed. by M. H. Segal. Tel Aviv, Dvir, [1965?]. 423p. **AD434**

Added title page in Hebrew: Milon 'ivri-angli shalem.
PJ4833.A9

Gesenius, Friedrich Heinrich Wilhelm. Hebräisches und aramäisches Handwörterbuch über das Alte Testament . . . 17. Aufl. Leipzig, Vogel, 1921. 1013p. **AD435**

Hebrew-German with German-Hebrew index.
Gives etymologies and references to sources.   PJ4835.G5G45

——— Hebrew and English lexicon of the Old Testament, with an appendix containing the Biblical Aramaic. . . . Boston, Houghton, 1907. 1127p. (Corr. impression. Oxford, Clarendon Pr., 1952. 1126p.) **AD436**

Subtitle: Based on the lexicon of William Gesenius as translated by Edward Robinson. Edited, with constant reference to the Thesaurus of Gesenius as completed by E. Rödiger, and with authorized use of the latest German editions of Gesenius' Handwörterbuch über das Alte Testament, by Francis Brown with the coöperation of S. R. Driver and Charles A. Briggs.
The best Hebrew-English dictionary of biblical Hebrew.
PJ4833.G4

Goldberg, Nathan. New functional Hebrew-English, English-Hebrew dictionary, with illustrative sentences and derivative words and expressions. N.Y., Ktav Pub. House, 1958. 355p. **AD437**

Title also in Hebrew: ha-Milon ha-shimushi he-hadash.
PJ4833.G6

Jastrow, Marcus. Dictionary of the Targumim, the Talmud Babli and Yerushalmi, and the Midrashic literature. With an index of Scriptural quotations. London, Luzac; N.Y., Putnam, 1903. 2v. (Repr.: Brooklyn, Traditional Pr., 1975) **AD438**

A photographic reprint was issued by Shapiro, Vallentine (London, 1926).
A standard English dictionary of Talmudic Hebrew.
PJ5205.J3

Kaufman, Judah. English-Hebrew dictionary by Israel Efros, Judah Ibn-Shmuel Kaufman, Benjamin Silk, ed. by Judah Kaufman. Tel Aviv, Dvir, [1929]. 751p. **AD439**

Frequently reprinted.
Title also in Hebrew: Milon angli-'ivri.   PJ4833.K2

Koehler, Ludwig Hugo and **Baumgartner, Walter.** Lexicon in Veteris Testamenti libros. Wörterbuch zum hebräischen Alten Testament in deutscher und englischer Sprache. A dictionary of the Hebrew Old Testament in English and German, ed. by Ludwig Koehler; Wörterbuch zum aramäischen Teil des Alten Testaments in deutscher und englischer Sprache. A dictionary of the Aramaic parts of the Old Testament in English and German, ed. by Walter Baumgartner. Leiden, Brill, 1948–53. 1138p. **AD440**

Preface and introduction in German and English. Equivalents of terms also given in German and English. Includes quotations with exact references to sources.

——— ——— Supplementum. Leiden, Brill, 1958. 227p.

Includes tables of scripts and transcriptions; abbreviations and signs; a German word list with Hebrew and Aramaic equivalents; additions and corrections.
A new edition is in progress as: PJ4833.K6

——— Hebräisches und aramäisches Lexikon zum Alten Testament. 3. Aufl. neu bearb. von Walter Baumgartner. Unter Mitarbeit von Benedikt Hartmann und E. Y. Kutscher. Leiden, Brill, 1967–83. Lfg.1–3. (In progress) **AD441**

Editors vary.
Earlier editions (*see* above) had title: Lexicon in Veteris Testamenti libros.
Completely revised and reset, with materials from the supplement incorporated.
A related work is: PJ4835.G5K58

Holladay, William Lee. A concise Hebrew and Aramaic lexicon of the Old Testament. Based upon the lexical work of Ludwig Koehler and Walter Baumgartner. Leiden, Brill, 1971. 425p. **AD442**

Inasmuch as the 3d ed. of the Koehler-Baumgartner lexicon (above) omits renderings in English, this is an effort to provide an English edition of that work in abridged format. It uses material from the 3d ed. of Koehler-Baumgartner so far as available, and depends on the earlier editions for the remainder of the alphabet.
PJ4833.H6

Segal, Moses Hirsch. A concise Hebrew-English dictionary comprising the Hebrew of all ages. Tel Aviv, Dvir, 1955. 260p. **AD443**

Bound with *A concise English-Hebrew dictionary with the English pronunciation in Hebrew transliteration* (4th ed. by H. Danby and M. H. Segal. Tel Aviv, 1947. 461p.). Various printings.
PJ4833.S4

Sivan, Reuben and **Levenston, Edward A.** The new Bantam-Megiddo Hebrew & English dictionary. N.Y., Schocken Books, [1977]. 399p., 294p. **AD444**

First published N.Y., Bantam Books, 1975.
Added title page in Hebrew.
Hebrew-English and English-Hebrew. Based on *The Megiddo modern dictionary* (Hebrew-English by R. Sivan; English-Hebrew by E. A. Levenston and R. Sivan. Tel-Aviv, Megiddo, 1965–66. 2v.).
"The Hebrew column in both parts of the dictionary is given in

the *plene* spelling, in accordance with the latest rules of the Hebrew Language Academy."—*Pref.* PJ4833.S56

Hindi, Hindustani, Panjabi, Urdu

(These languages have very close affiliations.)

Craven, Thomas. New royal dictionary; English into Hindustani and Hindustani into English, comp. originally by Rev. Thomas Craven . . . and in subsequent editions rev. and enl.; 1932 ed. rev. by Bishop J. R. Chitambar. Lucknow, Methodist Pub. House, 1932. 328p., 372p. **AD445**

Contents: pt.1, English-Hindustani; pt.2, Hindustani-English.
Printed in the roman alphabet. PK1986.C8

Fallon, S. W. New Hindustani-English dictionary, with illustrations from Hindustani literature and folk-lore. Banāras, Medical Hall Pr.; London, Trübner, 1879. 1216p. (Repr.: Lahore, Central Urdu Board, 1976) **AD446**

PK1986.F3

———— New English-Hindustani dictionary, with illustrations from English literature and colloquial English, tr. into Hindustani. . . . Lahore, Gulab Singh, [1905]. 703p. il. (Repr. 1941) **AD447**

PK1986.F28

Pathak, Ram Chandra. Bhargava's Standard illustrated dictionary of the English language (Anglo-Hindi ed.). 12th ed., thoroughly rev. & enl. Varanasi, Bhargava, [1973]. 1432p. il. **AD448**

PK1936.P3

———— Bhargava's Standard illustrated dictionary of the Hindi language (Hindi-English ed.). Rev. and enl. Varanasi, Bhargava, [1964]. 1280p. il. **AD449**

Both of the above works frequently reprinted. PK1936.P3

Raghu Vira. A comprehensive English-Hindi dictionary of governmental and educational words and phrases. Nagpur, Lokesh Chandra, Internat. Academy of Indian Culture, 1955. 189p., 1579p. il. (Sarasvati-Vihara ser. v.35) **AD450**

". . . the most comprehensive dictionary of the modern Hindi language yet published."—J. A. Mish, N.Y. Pub. Lib., in *Library journal* 81:2694 (Nov. 15, 1956).
Particularly strong in all aspects of governmental administration, law and political science, and the sciences. PK1937.R3

Satya Prakash. Mānaka Angrezī-Hindī kośa. Standard English-Hindi dictionary. 1971. 49p., 1573p. **AD451**

English-Hindi only. PK1936.S35

Singh, Maya. The Panjábí dictionary. [2d ed.] Patiala, Language Dept., 1961. 1221p. **AD452**

"Reproduced from the 1st ed. (Lahore, Munshi Gulab Singh, 1895)."—*verso of title page.*
Panjabi-English.

Ferozsons English-Urdu dictionary. English words with their equivalents in Urdu. 4th ed. Comp. by a Board of Eds. Lahore, Ferozsons, 1961. 910p. **AD453**

PK1976.F4

Ferozsons Urdu-English dictionary; Urdu words, phrases & idioms with English meanings and synonyms. 4th ed. Lahore, Ferozsons, [1964]. 831p. **AD454**

1st ed. 1960. PK1976.F42

Platts, John Thompson. Dictionary of Urdū, classical Hindī and English. London, Oxford Univ. Pr., 1960. 1259p. **AD455**

"Reprinted . . . from sheets of the 5th (1930) impression."—*verso of title page.*
First published 1884. PK1986.P4

Hittite

Chicago. University. Oriental Institute. The Hittite dictionary of the Oriental Institute of the University of Chicago. Ed. by Hans G. Güterbock and Harry A. Hoffner. Chicago, The Institute, 1980– . v.3, fasc.1– . (In progress) **AD456**

Contents: v.3, fasc.1, L – -ma.
A new Hittite-English dictionary intended for English-speaking scholars and students and to be of intermediate length. Publication was begun "with the letter 'L' to avoid immediate overlap with Annelies Kammenhuber's Hittite-German work [*Hethitisches Wörterbuch.* 2. Aufl. Heidelberg, Winter, 1975–]."—*Foreword.* Aims "to give complete coverage of the representative occurrences of each Hittite word" (*Pref.*), but does not seek to be exhaustive. Attempts to "give the user a maximum of usable information, allowing him to see not only our conclusions but the basis for them. The CHD does not attempt to determine the Proto-Indo-European origins of Hittite words. In that sense it is not an etymological dictionary. Words borrowed into Hittite from some identifiable foreign source will be noted as such." P945.Z8

Puhvel, Jaan. Hittite etymological dictionary. Berlin, etc., Mouton, [1984]– . v.1– . (Trends in linguistics. Documentation, 1) (In progress) **AD457**

Contents: v.1–2 in 1v., Words beginning with A; Words beginning with E and I.
A pioneering effort in which as many entries as possible are presented as "self-contained micro-essays of a format best suited to the item at hand. When no etymology is rated certain, the discussion often proceeds from the less likely possibilities and ends up with the most probable. When the preferred etymology is featured as virtually certain, it is usually stated and discussed first, and discarded alternatives, to the extent that they are deemed historically interesting, are mentioned in a coda."—*Pref.* P945.Z8

Hungarian

Magyar értelmezö kéziszótár. Szerk. Juhász József [et al.]. 2. valtozatlan kiad. Budapest, Akademiai Kiadó, 1975. 1550p. il. **AD458**

1st ed. 1972.
About 70,000 entry words. PH2625.M27

Magyar Tudományos Akadémia, Budapest. Nyelvtudományi Intézet. A magyar nyelv értelmezö szótára. Budapest, 1959–62. 7v. **AD459**

Géza Bárczi and Laśzló Országh, eds.
A thorough and carefully edited dictionary of standard modern Hungarian. Usage is illustrated by copious quotations, with sources indicated. PH2625.M3

Szarvas, Gábor and **Simonyi, Zsigmond.** Magyar-nyelvtörténeti szótár a legrégibb nyelvemlékektöl a nyelvújításig. Budapest, V. Hornyánszky, 1890–93. 3v. **AD460**

Added title page in Latin: Lexicon linguae hungaricae aevi antiquioris, auspiciis Academiae Scientiarum Hungaricae.
A dictionary of the early Hungarian language compiled on historical principles. PH2625.S8

Bilingual

Országh, László. Angol-magyar szótár. English-Hungarian dictionary. 4 kiad. Budapest, Akadémiai Kiadó, 1974. 2v. **AD461**

PH2640.O715

—— Magyar-angol szótár. Hungarian-English dictionary. 3d ed. with addenda. Budapest. Akadémiai Kiadó. 1969. 2v. (2159p.)   **AD462**

2d ed. 1963 in 1v. (2144p.).
The text is unchanged but for the addition of an "Addenda and corrigenda" section, p.2147–59.   PH2640.O73

—— Angol-magyar kéziszótár. A concise English-Hungarian dictionary. 8. kiad. Budapest, Akadémiai Kiadó, 1975. 1091p.   **AD463**

PH2640.O67

—— Magyar-angol kéziszótár. A concise Hungarian-English dictionary. 6 kiad. Budapest, Akadémiai Kiadó, 1973. 1179p.   **AD464**

PH2640.O725

Abbreviations

U.S. Library of Congress. Slavic and Central European Division. Hungarian abbreviations: a selective list, comp. by Elemer Bako. Wash., Govt. Prt. Off., 1961. 146p.   **AD465**

Approximately 2,500 abbreviations, followed by the full word or words in Hungarian and the English equivalent. Emphasis is on governmental and other organizational names; but terms frequently found in Hungarian publications are also included.   PH2693.U5

Etymology

Bárczi, Géza. Magyar szófejtö szótár. Budapest, Egyetemi Nyomda, 1941. 348p.   **AD466**

Bibliography, p.xix–xxiii.   PH2580.B3

Gombocz, Zoltán and **Melich, János.** Magyar etymologiai szótár. Lexicon critico-etymologicum linguae Hungaricae. A Magyar Tudományos Akadémia megbizásábol . . . Budapest, Magyar Tudományos Akadémia, 1914/30–44. Pt.1–17.   **AD467**

Contents: pt.1–10, A–érdĕm. 1599col.; pt.11–17, erdö-gaz. 1160col.
No more published.   PH2580.G6

A magyar nyelv történeti-etimológiai szótára. Budapest, Akadémiai Kiadó, 1967–76. 3v.   **AD468**

Föszerkesztö: Benkö Loránd [et al.].
Introductory remarks also in German.
An important new etymological dictionary. Gives derivation, earliest known date of occurrence, and examples of usage, plus bibliographical references to philological discussions and research.
PH2580.M3

Bibliography

Halasz de Beky, I. L. Bibliography of Hungarian dictionaries, 1410–1963. Toronto, Univ. of Toronto Pr., [1966]. 148p.   **AD469**

1,025 entries in two main sections: language dictionaries, and subject dictionaries. Only the latest edition is cited in most instances. English translations of Hungarian titles are provided except where the title gives no information beyond the languages included.
Z2148.L5H3

Ibo

Welmers, Beatrice F. and **Welmers, William E.** Igbo: a learner's dictionary. Los Angeles, [African Studies Center, Univ. of Calif.], 1968. 396p.   **AD470**

"This dictionary has been prepared primarily for speakers of English who have acquired at least a minimum of competence in speaking Igbo, and who are aware of the major structural patterns of Igbo."—*Introd.* English-Igbo and Igbo-English. About 2,000 entries in each section. Represents colloquial speech.   PL8261.Z5W4

Icelandic

Arngrímur Sigurdsson. Islenzk-ensk ordabók. Reykjavík, Prents-midjan Leiftur, [1970]. 925p.   **AD471**

Offers English equivalents only, without indication of parts of speech or examples of usage.   PD2437.A7

Blöndal, Sigfús. Islandsk-dansk ordbog. Hoved-medarbejdere: Björg Thorláksson Blöndal, Jon Ófeigsson, Holger Wiehe. Reykjavík, Thorláksson, 1920–24. 1052p.   **AD472**

Old Icelandic, including dialect and colloquial words.
PD2437.B5

—— —— Supplement. Redaktører Halldór Halldórsson [et al.]. Reykjavík, Islandsk-Dansk Ordbogsfond, 1963. 200p.

Cleasby, Richard. An Icelandic-English dictionary, initiated by Richard Cleasby. Subsequently rev., enl., and compl. by Gudbrand Vigfusson. 2d ed. with a suppl. by Sir William A. Craigie containing many additional words and references. Oxford, Clarendon Pr., 1957. 833p.   **AD473**

The original edition, first published in 1874, was started by Cleasby and completed by Vigfusson. This is a lithographic reprint with the addition of a 52p. supplement. The introduction and biographical sketch of Cleasby included in the first edition are omitted, but the section on grammar is reprinted.   PD2379.C5

Fritzner, Johan. Ordbog over det gamle norsk sprog. Omar., forøget og forbedret udg. . . . Kristiania, Den Norske Forlagsforening; Chicago, Relling, 1886–96. 3v. (Repr.: Oslo, Møller, 1954–55)   **AD474**

—— —— Tillegg . . . ved Didrik Arup Seip og Trygve Knudsen. Oslo, Møller, 1955. 155p.

1st ed. 1867.
Includes many references, quotations, variations in meaning, etc.
PD2381.F7

Íslenzk ordabók, handa skólum og almenningi. [Redaktører] Árni Bödvarsson. Reykjavík, Bókaútgáfa Menningarsjóds, 1963. 852p.   **AD475**

A scholarly work which includes both old and new Icelandic, and which covers literary and written language as well as that of colloquial speech.   PD2437.I83

Zoëga, Geir Tómasson. Íslenzk-ensk ordabók. [2d–3d ed.] Reykjavík, Kristjánsson, 1922–32. 2v.   **AD476**

Added title page in English.
Contents: Icelandic-English, 1922. 631p.; English-Icelandic, 1932. 712p.
Frequently reprinted.   PD2437.Z7

Etymology

Jóhannesson, Alexander. Isländisches etymologisches Wörterbuch. Bern, A. Francke, 1951–56. 1406p.   **AD477**

Issued in parts.
Contains some 20,000 words, including so-called poetic words and mythological names but omitting personal and place-names. Arrangement is by Indo-germanic roots, with an index of Icelandic words. Linguistic literature through 1950 has been drawn upon.
PD2431.J6

Vries, Jan de. Altnordisches etymologisches Wörterbuch. Leiden, Brill, 1957–61. 689p.   **AD478**

Issued in 9 pts.

Old Icelandic and Old Norwegian. Gives equivalents in other Scandinavian languages, references to sources, etc.   PD1805.V7

Indo-European

See Aryan.

Indonesian

Echols, John M. and **Shadily, Hassan.** An Indonesian-English dictionary. 2d ed. Ithaca, N.Y., Cornell Univ. Pr., [1963]. 431p.   **AD479**

1st ed. 1961.

Indonesian-English only. "Intended to be a practical, comprehensive dictionary of modern Indonesian ... A large number of technical terms have been included, but no attempt has been made to be exhaustive."—*Pref.* Includes illustrative phrases and sentences.   PL5076.E25

—— An English-Indonesian dictionary. Ithaca, N.Y., Cornell Univ. Pr., [1975]. 660p.   **AD480**

Includes "the most common words and phrases in American English ... with the Indonesian equivalent."—*Pref.* Intended primarily for the use of Indonesians.   PL5076.E23

Van Goor's Kamus Inggeris ketjil. Inggeris-Bahasa Indonesia; Bahasa Indonesia-Inggeris, oleh A. L. N. Kramer. 4. druk. Den Haag, G. B. Van Goor, 1959. 600p.   **AD481**

Added title page in Dutch.   PL5125.K73

Van Goor's Concise Indonesian dictionary; English-Indonesian, Indonesian-English. A. L. N. Kramer, ed. The Hague, Van Goor, 1952. 359p. (Repr.: Rutland, Vt., Tuttle, 1966)   **AD482**

Title page also in Indonesian.

A concise dictionary prepared primarily for schools and elementary usage.   PL5125.V29

Irish

Royal Irish Academy, Dublin. Contributions to a Dictionary of the Irish language. ... Dublin, Academy, [1939]–76.   **AD483**

Parts published irregularly as completed.

Published parts include: A, arr. by Anne O'Sullivan and E. G. Quin (1964–67. 2 fasc., 484col.); B, arr. by Maura Carney and Máirín O Daly (1975. 246col.); C, arr. by Próinséas Ní Chatháin, Máirín O Daly, P. Ó Fiannachta and others (1968–74. 3 fasc., 640col.); degra–duus, arr. by Mary E. Byrne and Maud Joynt (1959–60. 2 fasc., 460col.); G, arr. by Mary E. Byrne (1955. 178col.); H, arr. by Maura Carney (1976. 2col.); I, arr. by Máirín O Daly and Anne O'Sullivan (1952. 2 fasc., 234col.); L, arr. by Máirín O Daly and P. Ó Fiannachta (1966. 252col.); M, arr. by Maud Joynt (1939. 208col.); N-O-P, arr. by Maud Joynt (1940. 212col.); R, arr. by Maud Joynt (1944. 124col.); S, arr. by Máirín O Daly, Anne O'Sullivan, and E. G. Quin (1953. 434col.); T, arr. by David Greene and E. G. Quin (1943–48. 2 fasc., 394col.); U, arr. by Teresa Condon (1942. 98col.).

"The object of the present publication is to make immediately available ... the mass of collected material ... in the Royal Irish Academy pending publication of the ... Dictionary as planned. This and the following fasciculi are then to be regarded merely as 'Contributions' towards a dictionary, not as installments of the final work."—*Note* in fasc.M.   PB1291.R6

—— Dictionary of the Irish language based mainly on Old and Middle Irish materials; general ed., Osborn Bergin. Dublin, Academy, 1913–57. Fasc.1–4.   **AD484**

Contents: fasc.1, D–Degóir, ed. by Carl J. S. Marstrander, 1913; fasc.2, E–Extais, ed. by Maud Joynt and Eleanor Knott, 1932; fasc.3, F–fochraic, ed. by Maud Joynt and Eleanor Knott, 1957; fasc.4, fochratal–futhu, ed. by Maud Joynt and Eleanor Knott, 1957.

The authoritative dictionary of the Irish language, based on materials collected for many years by the Academy from printed books, manuscripts, and the spoken language. Arranged on historical principles, with many quotations illustrating the development both of meanings of words and of their grammatical inflections. Begins with the letter D, leaving A–C to be published last, because the letters A–Dn were covered in Kuno Meyer's *Contributions to Irish lexicography* (Halle, Niemeyer; London, Nutt, 1906. 670p.), of which the Academy's dictionary is a continuation.

Work on the *Dictionary* fascicles was abandoned after publication of the letter F in 1957, but earlier and later parts of the alphabet continued to be published as *Contributions* (above). In some libraries the fascicles of the *Dictionary* and those of the *Contributions* have been bound together and cataloged as a 4-volume set with title page (issued by the Academy) bearing the dates 1913–76 and carrying the title *Dictionary of the Irish language. ...* This combined edition constitutes the full work and no further work on either series is planned.

The Academy has issued a *Dictionary of the Irish language ... Compact edition* (Dublin, 1983. 632p.) which reproduces in a single alphabetical sequence the fascicles of both the *Contributions* and the *Dictionary.* Type size is greatly reduced in this photographic reproduction, four pages of the original fascicles appearing on each page of the "Compact edition." The "Historical note" by E. G. Quin, originally published 1976, serves as an overall introduction, and the "Additions and corrections" for the letters A, B, C and F are reproduced at the end of the volume.   PB1291.R7

Bilingual

De Bhaldraithe, Tomás. English-Irish dictionary. Baile Átha Cliath, Oifig an tSoláthair, 1959. 864p.   **AD485**

"Made and printed for the Stationery Office by Hely's Ltd., Printers, Dublin."

"The aim of this dictionary is the practical one of providing Irish equivalents for English words and phrases in common use. It is not then to be regarded as an exhaustive word-store of modern literary Irish or of the current spoken language."—*Pref.*   PB1291.D4

Dinneen, Patrick Stephen. Irish-English dictionary; being a thesaurus of the words, phrases and idioms of the modern Irish language. New ed. rev. and greatly enl. Dublin, publ. for the Irish Texts Society by the Educ. Co. of Ireland, 1927. 1340p.   **AD486**

1st ed. 1904; various printings.   PB1291.D5

McKenna, Lambert Andrew Joseph. English-Irish dictionary. Dublin, Govt. Publs., 1935. 1546p.   **AD487**

Title also in Irish. Planned as a complement to Dinneen (above).   PB1291.M15

Etymology

Vendryes, Joseph. Lexique étymologique de l'irlandais ancien. Dublin, Dublin Inst. for Advanced Studies; Paris, Centre National de la Recherche Scientifique, 1959–78. [Fasc.1]–4. (In progress)   **AD489**

Contents: [fasc.1], A; fasc.2–4, M–U.

Following each Irish word is a brief equivalent in French. The etymology is then presented in detail with exact references to sources.

Since the death of Vendryes in 1960, the work has been carried on by other hands.   PB1288.V4

Italian

Accademia della Crusca, Florence. Vocabolario degli Accademici della Crusca. 5. impressione. Firenze, Tip. Galileiana di M. Cellini ecc., 1863–1923. v.1–11. **AD490**

1st ed. 1612.

Contents: v.1–11, A–O.

The great dictionary of the Academy, published in various editions. The 5th ed. was never completed; it was planned to replace it by: PC1625.A32

Accademia d'Italia. Vocabolario della lingua italiana. Milano, Soc. Anonima per la Pubblicazione del Vocabolario, 1941– . v.1. **AD491**

Contents: v.1, A–C. No more published.

A scholarly work with quotations showing usage. PC1625.A2

Battaglia, Salvatore. Grande dizionario della lingua italiana. [Redazione, direttore: Giorgio Bárberi Squarotti] Torino, Unione Tipografico-Editrice Torinese, 1961–81. v.1–11. (In progress) **AD492**

———— ———— Indice degli autori citati nei volumi 1–8. 1973. 121p.

Contents: v.1–11, A–Orac.

Designed to replace, as a new work—not a revision, the century-old standard *Dizionario della lingua italiana* of Nicolò Tommaseo and Bernardo Bellini (Torino, Unione Tip.-Ed., 1861–79. 4v. in 8).

A scholarly work, with the collaboration of many specialists; planned on historical principles, giving full definitions and examples of meanings and usages in chronological order. Numerous citations to sources both early and modern, which are listed in the separate *Indice*. PC1625.B3

Devoto, Giacomo and **Oli, Gian Carlo.** Vocabolario illustrato della lingua italiana. N.Y., Funk & Wagnalls, [1968]. 2v. il. **AD493**

An illustrated dictionary (produced in Italy although published by an American firm) and an unusually fine work from the point of view of both format and content: good type, paper, and illustrations, as well as extensive, up-to-date vocabulary. PC1625.D4

Palazzi, Fernando. Novissimo dizionario della lingua italiana. [Ed. riv. e aggiornata] a cura di Gianfranco Folena. Milano, Fratelli Fabbri, [1974]. 1624p. il. **AD494**

1st ed. 1939.

About 74,000 entries in this edition. Derivation of words is indicated. PC1625.P17

Panzini, Alfredo. Dizionario moderno delle parole che non si trovano nei dizionari comuni. 10. ed., ristampa dell' ottava edizione curata . . . da Alfredo Schiaffini e Bruno Migliorini. Con un proemio di A. Schiaffini e con un appendice di dodicimila voci nuovamente compilata da B. Migliorini. Milano, Hoepli, 1963. 1093p. **AD495**

1st ed. 1905.

A dictionary reflecting the opinions of the author who attempted to list and define words in many categories—political, scientific, and general—not found in the standard dictionaries. PC1625.P2

Bilingual

Cassell's Italian-English, English-Italian dictionary, prep. by Piero Rebora, with the assistance of Francis M. Guercio and Arthur L. Hayward. 7th ed. London, Cassell, 1969. 1096p. **AD496**

First published 1958.

A general dictionary of the Italian language as written and spoken today. PC1640.C33

Dizionario delle lingue italiana e inglese. Vladimiro Macchi, ed. Firenze, Sansoni, [1970–75]. 2v. in 4. **AD497**

Contents: v.1, Italiano-Inglese. 2v.; v.2, Inglese-Italiano. 2v.

Added title page in English; introductory matter in Italian and English.

A new work published by Harrap in London (with title *Sansoni-Harrap standard Italian-English, English-Italian dictionary*) as well as by Sansoni in Florence. About 100,000 entries are included in the Italian-English part. Personal and place names appear in the main alphabetical sequence. PC1640.D47

Dizionario inglese/italiano, italiano-inglese. Torino, Società Editrice Internazionale, [1981]. 1894p. **AD498**

"Adattamento e ristrutturazione dell' originale 'Advanced Learner's Dictionary of Current English' [publ. 1963] della Oxford University Press."—*t.p.*

Intended as an up-to-date bilingual dictionary based on a practical, functional vocabulary. Pronunciation is indicated in the English-Italian section; examples of usage are given; and British and American forms are indicated where usage differs between those countries.

A review by B. H. Smeaton in *Library journal* 4-15-82, p.800, calls this a "superb bilingual dictionary" for speakers of Italian who want access to English, but not the other way around: "Those who don't know Italian will be better served by another dictionary, such as the *Concise Cambridge Italian Dictionary* or the *Cambridge Italian Dictionary*." PC1640.D54

Hazon, Mario. Garzanti comprehensive Italian-English, English-Italian dictionary. N.Y., McGraw-Hill, 1963. 2099p. **AD499**

Published 1961 under title *Dizionario inglese-italiano, italiano-inglese*. Various Italian printings with title *Grande dizionario* (e.g., 27 ed. Milano, Garzanti, 1981. 2099p.).

A well-edited and useful work. Coverage is excellent, including many technical and colloquial words. Includes proper names, personal and geographical. PC1640.H35

Lysle, A. de R. and **Gualtieri, Lora Lamia.** Nuovo dizionario moderno delle lingue italiana e inglese. Ed. riv. e aggiornata, con aggiunta di un supplemento commerciale. Torino, Casanova, 1950–51. 2v. **AD500**

Contents: v.1, Inglese-italiano; v.2, Italiano-inglese.

Earlier editions published under title *Nuovo dizionario moderno-razionale-pratico inglese-italiano*.

A modern dictionary including words in common use, colloquial and slang expressions, scientific and technical words, etc. PC1640.L8

Pekelis, Carla. A dictionary of colorful Italian idioms. N.Y., Braziller, [1965]. 226p. **AD501**

Subtitle: A treasury of expressions most commonly found in Italian speech and writing today, with their American equivalents. PC1640.P4

Ragazzini, Giuseppe. The Follett Zanichelli Italian dictionary; English-Italian, Italian-English. With the collaboration of Adele Biagi and Camilla Roatta. Chicago, Follett, [1968]. 1864p. **AD502**

First published 1967 with title *Dizionario inglese-italiano, italiano-inglese*.

A new work of about 250,000 terms. Numerous examples of usage, including many colloquialisms. PC1640.R26

Reynolds, Barbara. The Cambridge Italian dictionary. Cambridge, Univ. Pr., 1962–81. 2v. **AD503**

Contents: v.1, Italian-English. 899p.; v.2, English-Italian. 843p.

"First, and underlying all its criteria, is the fact that [the *Dictionary*] has been compiled, selected, and arranged from the point of view of the English-speaking user."—*Introd.*

Emphasis is on inclusiveness and elucidation of vocabulary for both the literary scholar and the student of the spoken language. Thus, many little-used and obsolete words are included, together with numerous terms from specialized vocabularies; the editors have relied on subject specialists for the selection of these terms and for their definitions. Etymological derivation is not usually given, but etymologically related words are often grouped together, with cross references from the alphabetical listings of the individual terms.

Although Hoare's *Italian dictionary* (2d ed. 1925) is an acknowledged predecessor of v.1, the present work is not to be considered a mere revision. The word list for v.2 reflects British usage, including Americanisms only if current in Britain. The vocabulary of specialties—such as economics, sociology, political science, philosophy—are well represented. PC1640.R4

──── The concise Cambridge Italian dictionary. [London], Cambridge Univ. Pr., [1975]. 792p. **AD504**

"The Italian-English section is based on *The Cambridge Italian Dictionary* [above], which it follows closely in style and conventions. The English-Italian section represents a selection of material compiled in preparation for the English-Italian volume of that publication."—*Introd.* PC1640.R44

Etymology

Battisti, Carlo and **Alessio, Giovanni.** Dizionario etimologico italiano. Firenze, G. Barbèra, 1950–57. 5v. **AD505**

Sponsored by the Istituto di Glottologia of the Università di Firenze.

The first extensive etymological dictionary in Italian, giving derivations, similar words in other languages, definitions, etc. Coverage is comprehensive including archaic and modern terms, scientific and technical words, and some dialectal forms. PC1580.B3

Cortelazzo, Manlio and **Zolli, Paolo.** Dizionario etimologico della lingua italiana. [Bologna], Zanichelli, [1979–83]. v.1–3. (In progress) **AD506**

Contents: v.1–3, A–N.

In addition to etymology of the term, gives definitions and examples of usage (with date and author of illustrative quotation). PC1580.C67

Pfister, Max. Lessico etimologico italiano: LEI. Wiesbaden, Reichert, [1979–84]. v.1, fasc.1–8. (In progress) **AD507**

Contents: v.1, fasc.1–8, Ab–Alburnus (completes v.1).

An ambitious and scholarly work on the etymology of the Italian language and its dialects (but excluding those areas covered by W. von Wartburg's *Französisches etymologisches Wörterbuch* [AD317] and M. L Wagner's *Dizionario etimologico sardo* [Heidelberg, 1960–64]). Not only provides sources and datings of usage, but cites other dictionaries, linguistic atlases, etc., and provides references to linguistic studies. A "Supplemento bibliografico" (publ. 1979) contains a key to the abbreviations used in the first fascicle and bibliographic citations to the primary and secondary sources referred to therein. PC1580.P38

Synonyms

Cinti, Decio. Dizionario dei sinònimi e dei contrari. 13. ed. Novara, Ist. Geografico De Agostini, [1965]. 653p. **AD508**

1st ed. 1947.

A small, useful dictionary of synonyms and antonyms. PC1591.C5

Tommaseo, Niccolò. Dizionario dei sinonimi della lingua italiana. Nuovissima ed., accuratemente corr. Milano, Bietti, [1935]. 1330p. **AD509**

1st ed. 1904.

A thesaurus arranged by category, with definitions showing discrimination of meaning. PC1591.T65

Usage

Gabrielli, Aldo. Dizionario linguistico moderno; guida pratica per scrivere e parlar bene. 4. ed. riveduta. [Verona], Mondadori, [1965, c1956]. 1187p. **AD510**

A practical manual of modern Italian for writers and speakers. In two parts: pt.1 is an alphabetically arranged dictionary of usage giving grammatical and stylistic rules, with examples of idiomatic construction, foreign words and phrases, etc.; pt.2 is an alphabetical list of words giving gender, transitive and intransitive verbs, some proper nouns, etc.

Japanese

Daijiten. Tokyo, Heibonsha, 1974. 2v. **AD511**

1st ed. 1934–36 in 26v.; reduced-size repr. 1953–54 in 13v.

More than 700,000 words; arranged in phonetic alphabet order *(gojū-on)* and indexed by ideograms. AG35.2.D3

Gakken kokugo daijiten. Tokyo, Gakushū Kenkyūsha, 1978. 2270p. **AD512**

14th printing 1985.

Kindaichi Haruhiko and Ikeda Yasaburō, eds.

A dictionary of current usage with examples taken from works by 250 contemporary writers. Includes synonyms. PL675.G27

Kōjirin. [6th ed.] Tokyo, Sanseido, 1983. 2111p., 46p., 48p. **AD513**

1st ed. 1925 was a revised and enlarged ed. of *Jirin* by Kanazawa Shōzaburo (first publ. 1907); successive editions updated to reflect current usage.

Includes a section on grammar, a pronunciation guide to difficult-to-read ideograms, and a dictionary of abbreviations in roman alphabet which are currently used in Japanese. PL675.K595

Nihon kokugo daijiten. Tokyo, Shōgakukan, 1972–76. 20v. **AD514**

A standard dictionary which includes both historical and contemporary usage, with some emphasis on the latter. v.1 includes a 16-page supplement listing sources. PL675.N46

Ōtsuki, Fumihiko. Dai-genkai. Tokyo, Fuzambo, 1932– 37. 5v. **AD515**

A revised and enlarged edition of *Genkai* (1890). A revised edition of v.1–4 (i.e., without v.5, the index), *Shintei genkai,* was published 1956.

Basically a dictionary of classical Japanese. Words are arranged in phonetic alphabet order. Gives pronunciation, etymology, examples of usage (with sources), as well as definitions. The indexes in v.5 include a separate index for foreign words. PL675.O79

Shinmura, Izuru. Kōjien. [3d ed.] Tokyo, Iwanami Shoten, 1983. 2667p. **AD516**

1st ed. 1935 had title: *Jien.*

A standard single-volume work. PL675.S49

Bilingual

Koine, Yoshio, ed. Kenkyūsha's New English-Japanese dictionary. Rev. and enl. 5th ed. Tokyo, Kenkyūsha, 1980. 2477p. **AD517**

1st ed. 1927.

More than 140,000 words. Indicates American and British pronunciation; gives etymology. Includes a thesaurus of synonyms and a foreign phrase list. A standard English-Japanese dictionary. PL679.K39

Masuda, Koh. Kenkyūsha's New Japanese-English dictionary; Kenkyūsha shin Wa-Ei daijiten. Revised 4th ed. Tokyo, Kenkyūsha, 1974. 2110p. **AD518**

1st ed. 1918. Various printings.

About 80,000 words, with 160,000 derivatives. Numerous examples of usage. Arranged according to roman alphabet; transliteration is by Hepburn system. Numerous appendixes. PL697.K4

Nakajima, Fumio, ed. Iwanami Ei-Wa daijiten; Iwanami's Comprehensive English-Japanese dictionary. Tokyo, Iwanami Shoten, 1970. 2124p. **AD519**

More than 110,000 words. Includes pronunciation (British and American), etymology, idiomatic phrases. Supplement includes geographic and personal names, abbreviations and symbols. One of the standard works. PL697.I83

Shōgakukan-Random House English-Japanese dictionary. Tokyo, Shōgakukan, 1973. 4v. and suppl. **AD520**

A joint project of the Japanese and American publishing houses. The supplement includes a history of the English language and a comparative study of British and American pronunciation.
PL679.S64

Pronunciation of names

O'Neill, Patrick Geoffrey. Japanese names; a comprehensive index by characters and readings. N.Y. & Tokyo, Weatherhill, 1972. 359p. **AD521**

Title also in Japanese: *Nihon jinmei chimei jiten.*
A pronouncing dictionary for Japanese proper names in two parts: (1) From characters to readings (with ideograms arranged by number of strokes); (2) From readings to characters.
A similar guide by Araki Ryōzō is *Nanori jiten* (Tokyo, Tokyōdō, 1959. 306p.; repr. 1981). PL683.O5

Early–17th century

Iwanami kogo jiten. Tokyo, Iwanami Shoten, 1982. 1488p. **AD522**

Ed. by Ono Susumu, Satake Akihiro and Maeda Kingoro.
First published 1974.
Over 40,000 words, covering from ancient times through the first half of the Edo period. Rich in examples of usage. Includes a guide to historical grammar, old calendar, etc. PL675.O63

Kadokawa kogo dai jiten. Tokyo, Kadokawa Shoten, 1982– . v.1–2. (In progress) **AD523**

Ed. by Nakamura Yukihiko, Okami Masao and Sakakura Atsuyoshi.
Contents: v.1–2, a–sa.
To be in 4v. A historical dictionary designed to aid in the understanding of classical texts from the ancient to early modern period. Examples of usage. PL682.K32

Kogo dai jiten. Tokyo, Shōgakukan, 1978. 1936p. **AD524**

Ed. by Nakada Norio, Wada Toshimasa and Kitahara Yasuo.
Covers vocabulary from ancient to early modern times. Arranged in phonetic alphabet order. Gives examples of usage, with sources.
PL682.K78

Nippo jisho. Vocabulario da lingoa de Iapam. Tokyo, Iwanami Shoten, 1960. 822p. **AD525**

A scholarly edition of a 16th-century Japanese-Portuguese dictionary compiled by Jesuit missionaries; useful for the study of early modern Japanese. PL681.P6V6

Kazakh

Shnitnikov, Boris Nikolayevich. Kazakh-English dictionary. The Hague, Mouton, 1966. 301p. (Indiana Univ. pubn. Uralic and Altaic ser., v.28) **AD526**

Kazakh to English only. PL65.K44S4

Khmer

Cambodian-English dictionary. [Ed. by] Robert K. Headley, Jr. [et al.]. Wash., Catholic Univ. of Amer. Pr., 1977. 2v. (1495p.) il. (Publications in the languages of Asia, 3) **AD527**

Intended as a "reasonably comprehensive, accurate, and, above all, usable" (*Pref.*) compilation including "not only current literary and standard spoken forms of Khmer, but also archaic, obsolete, obsolescent, dialectal, and argot forms." Gives etymologies "for almost all known or suspected Indo-European loan words as well as for most of the Chinese, Thai, and Vietnamese borrowings."
PL4326.C3

Huffman, Franklin E. and **Proum, Im.** English-Khmer dictionary. New Haven, Yale Univ. Pr., 1978. 690p. **AD528**

"The primary objective of this dictionary is to provide a corpus of basic words and phrases which it would be useful for Western students of Khmer to know how to say (or write) in standard Khmer. The dictionary contains some 40,000 English entries and subentries."—*Introd.* Also intends to offer complete coverage of basic American English vocabulary for Khmer students learning English.
PL4326.H85

Jacob, Judith M. A concise Cambodian-English dictionary. London & N.Y., Oxford Univ. Pr., 1974. 242p. **AD529**

Aims "to provide a handy reference book of basic modern Khmer vocabulary for the English-speaking reader. Every effort has been made to cover the recurrent vocabulary of 20th-century prose publications—newspapers, novels, articles, etc.—as well as that of the spoken language."—*Introd.* PL4326.J3

Korean

Gale, James Scarth. Unabridged Korean-English dictionary. 3d ed., ed. by Alexander A. Pieters. Seoul, Christian Literature Soc., 1931. 1781p. **AD530**

First published in 1897 as *A Korean-English dictionary.*
Contains some 82,000 definitions; includes names of persons and places. PL937.G3

Martin, Samuel Elmo, Lee, Yang Ha and **Chang, Sung-Un.** A Korean-English dictionary. New Haven, Yale Univ. Pr., 1967. 1902p. **AD531**

An important work attempting "to give a full and accurate portrayal of the basic native Korean vocabulary."—*Introd.*
PL937.E5M3

New English-Korean dictionary. Editorial adviser, Kwang Man Kauh; general eds., Sung Shik Cho, Byung Jo Chung, Pong Shik Kang. Rev. ed. [Seoul], Omungak, [1973]. 2453p. il. **AD532**

1st ed. 1964.
A less comprehensive, but useful recent work is the *Standard English-Korean dictionary for foreigners: romanized,* ed. by B. J. Jones (Elizabeth, N.J., Hollym Internat. Corp., 1982. 386p.).
PL937.E5N4

Underwood, Horace Grant. A concise dictionary of the Korean language in two parts, Korean-English & English-Korean. Yokohama, Kelly & Walsh; N.Y., Randolph, 1890. 196p., 292p. **AD533**

PL937.U57

Underwood, Joan V. Concise English-Korean dictionary, romanized. Rutland, Vt., Tokyo, Charles E. Tuttle Co., 1954. 320p. **AD534**

Subtitle: The 8,000 most useful English words and phrases with Korean equivalents in both roman and Korean letters.
A small pocket dictionary. Various printings. PL937.U6

Yu, Hyong-gi. New Life Korean-English dictionary. Hyung-ki J. Lew, ed. Amer. ed. Wash., Educ. Services, 1952. 866p. **AD535**

PL937.E5Y82

Kurdish

McCarus, Ernest Nasseph. A Kurdish-English dictionary, dialect of Sulaimania, Iraq. Ann Arbor, Univ. of Michigan Pr., [1967]. 194p. **AD536**

The language of this work "is strictly that of Sulaimania, Iraq, predominantly literary, but including spoken language as well."—*Introd.* PK6906.M3

Wahby, Taufiq and **Edmonds, Cecil John.** A Kurdish-English dictionary. Oxford, Clarendon Pr., 1966. 179p. **AD537**

"The Kurdish of this Dictionary is the standard language of belles-lettres, journalism, official and private correspondence, and formal speech as it has developed, on the basis of the Southern-Kirmanj dialect of Sulamani in Iraq, since 1918."—*Introd.* Kurdish words are given in roman transliteration. PK6906.W3

Lao

Kerr, Allen D. Lao-English dictionary. Wash., Consortium Pr., Catholic Univ. of Amer. Pr., 1972. 2v. (Publications in the languages of Asia, 2) **AD538**

Vocabulary was drawn from earlier dictionaries and from current vernacular publications. PL4251.L34K4

Lappish

Nielsen, Konrad. Lappisk ordbok, grunnet på dialektene i Polmak, Karasjok og Kautokeino. Oslo, Aschehoug; Cambridge, Harvard Univ. Pr.; London, Williams, 1932–56. 4v. (Inst. for Sammenlignende Kulturforskning. [Publikasjoner] ser. B: Skrifter, 17) **AD539**

English title: Lapp dictionary, based on the dialects of Polmak, Karasjok and Kautokeino.

Lappish, English, and Norwegian. Preliminary matter in Norwegian and English in parallel columns.

v.1–3 publ. 1932–38. v.4, the vocabulary classified according to the meanings of the words, with many illustrations of Lappish life and customs, publ. 1956. PH725.N5

Latin

Thesaurus linguae latinae, editus auctoritate et consilio academiarum quinque germanicarum Berolinensis, Gottingensis, Lipsiensis, Monacensis, Vindobonensis. Lipsiae, Teubner, 1900–83. (In progress) **AD540**

Contents: v.1–8, A–M; v.9², O; v.10¹¹, p–palpebra; v.10²¹⁻³, porta-praecipuus.

The great dictionary of the language, in Latin; indispensable in the university or large reference library. Plans to record, with representative quotations from each author, every word in the text of each Latin author down to the Antonines, with a selection of important passages from the works of all writers to the seventh century. In the section A–B, proper names are included in the main alphabet, but from C on they are given in the following supplement:

——— Supplementum: Nomina propria [Onomasticon]. Lipsiae, Teubner, 1907–23. v.2–3¹⁻².

Contents: v.2–3¹⁻², C–Don.

——— Index librorum scriptorum inscriptionum ex quibus exempla adferuntur. Lipsiae, Teubner, 1904. 109p.

——— ——— Supplementum. 1958. 13p.

PA2361.T4

Bacci, Antonio. . . . Lexicon vocabulorum quae difficilius latine redduntur. Ed. 4. Rome, Soc. Libraria "Studium," [1963]. 846p. (v.1 of his Varia latinitatis scripta) **AD541**

A dictionary giving Latin translations for the Italian forms of modern words and terms, such as atom bomb, diploma, countess, hypodermic injection, professional; also includes geographical names and divisions (e.g., Korea, Colombia, etc.). PA2824.B32

Bilingual

Andrews, Ethan Allen, ed. Harper's Latin dictionary. A new Latin dictionary founded on the translation of Freund's Latin-German lexicon. Rev., enl., and in great part rewritten by Charlton T. Lewis and Charles Short. N.Y., Cincinnati, Amer. Book Co., 1907. 2019p. **AD542**

1st ed. 1879. 1955 reprint (Oxford, Clarendon Pr.) entitled *A Latin dictionary.*

The most generally useful of the Latin-English dictionaries. Frequently reprinted. PA2365.E5A7

Cassell's New Latin-English, English-Latin dictionary, by D. P. Simpson. London, Cassell, [1959]. 883p. **AD543**

American edition has title *Cassell's New Latin dictionary; Latin-English, English-Latin* (N.Y., Funk & Wagnalls, 1960).

A thoroughly revised edition of this long-popular desk dictionary. Issued with various printing dates. PA2365.L3C3

Levine, Edwin B., Beach, Goodwin B. and **Bocchetta, Vittore E.** Follett world-wide Latin dictionary; Latin-English, English-Latin (American English). Chicago, Follett, 1967. 767p. **AD544**

About 40,000 entries. Offers Latin equivalents for many modern terms and idioms. A useful work for the student. PA2365.E5L65

Lewis, Charlton T. Latin dictionary for schools. N.Y., Cincinnati, Amer. Book Co., 1916. 1191p. (Repr.: Oxford, Clarendon Pr., 1953) **AD545**

Various reprintings.

Not a complete Latin dictionary but a work designed to include and explain "every word or phrase in Latin books commonly read in schools."—*Pref.* A very usable dictionary for the student. PA2365.E5L7

Smith, *Sir* William and **Hall, Theophilus D.** Copious and critical English-Latin dictionary. N.Y., Amer. Book Co., 1871. 754p. **AD546**

Includes a dictionary of proper names. PA2365.E5S6

Smith, *Sir* William. Smaller Latin-English dictionary [3d ed.] rev. by J. F. Lockwood. London, Murray, 1933. 823p. (Repr.: N.Y., Barnes & Noble, 1960) **AD547**

1st ed. 1855; 2d ed. 1881. Frequently reprinted.

Includes tables of the Roman calendar, measures, weights, and monetary units. PA2365.E5S6

Etymology

Ernout, Alfred and **Meillet, Antoine.** Dictionnaire étymologique de la langue latine, histoire des mots. 4. éd., 2ᵉ tirage augm. de corr. nouv. Paris, Klincksieck, 1967. 828p. **AD548**

Ouvrage publié avec le concours du Centre National de la Recherche Scientifique.

1st ed. 1932. 4th ed. first published 1959–60. Various printings.
One of the best of the modern etymological dictionaries. PA2342.E7

Walde, Alois. Lateinisches etymologisches Wörterbuch. 3. neubearb. Aufl. von J. B. Hofmann. Heidelberg, Winter, 1938–54. 2v. (Indogermanische Bibliothek. II. Reihe, Wörterbücher) **AD549**

───── ───── Register zusammengestellt von Elsbeth Berger. 1956. 287p.

A scholarly etymological dictionary which indicates the first appearance of each Latin word with references to documents and usage. PA2342.W2

Early Christian era

Blaise, Albert. Dictionnaire latin-français des auteurs chrétiens. Revu spécialement pour le vocabulaire théologique par Henri Chirat. Turnhout, Éd. Brepols, 1967. 914p. **AD550**

Reprint of the Strasbourg, 1954, edition with the addition of "Addenda et corrigenda."

Covers from Tertullian to the end of the Merovingian period, i.e., from the end of the first to the seventh century, and includes new terms and classical terms with new meanings. Many quotations with exact reference to sources. Bibliography of works cited, p.9–29. PA2308.B6

Oxford Latin dictionary. Ed. by P. G. W. Glare. Combined ed. Oxford, Clarendon Pr.; N.Y., Oxford Univ. Pr., 1982. 2126p. **AD551**

Originally issued in parts, 1968–82.

An important scholarly work, long in plan and preparation. Treats classical Latin from its beginnings to the end of the second century A.D. and includes words from both literary and nonliterary sources. Etymological notes are brief; quotations illustrating usage are arranged in chronological order. PA2365.E5O9

Sleumer, Albert. Kirchenlateinisches Wörterbuch . . . 2. sehr verm. Aufl. des "Liturgischen Lexikons" unter umfassendster Mitarbeit von . . . Joseph Schmid, hrsg. von . . . Albert Sleumer. . . . Limburg a.d. Lahn, Steffen, 1926. 840p. **AD552**

Subtitle: Ausführliches Wörterverzeichnis zum Römischen Missale, Breviarium, Rituale, Graduale, Pontificale, Caeremoniale, Martyrologium, sowie zur Vulgata und zum Codex juris canonici; desgleichen zu den Proprien der Bistümer Deutschlands, Österreichs, Ungarns, Luxemburgs, der Schweiz und zahlreicher kirchlicher Orden und Kongregationen. BX1970.S55

Souter, Alexander. Glossary of later Latin to 600 A.D. Oxford, Clarendon Pr., 1949. 454p. **AD553**

Later reprintings "from corrected sheets of first ed."—*verso of title page.*

Covers the Christian literature from 180 A.D. to 600 A.D., and thus was planned to supplement the *Oxford Latin dictionary* which treats classical Latin, omitting Christian Latin authors. PA2308.S6

Medieval

Arnaldi, Francesco. Latinitas italicae medii aevi inde ab a. CDLXXVI usque ad a. MXXII lexicon imperfectum cura et studio. . . . Bruxelles, 1936–67. 4 pts. (*In* Bulletin Du Cange, [v.10–34]) **AD554**

───── ───── Addenda, fasc.1–5. (*In* Bulletin Du Cange, v.35–36, 38, 40, 42; 1967–82) (In progress)

Contents: Addenda, fasc.1–5, A–Gyrus.

Published in the *Bulletin Du Cange* without separate paging.

Du Cange, Charles Du Fresne, *Sieur.* Glossarium mediae et infimae latinitatis conditum a Carolo Du Fresne, domino Du Cange; auctum a monachis Ordinis S. Benedicti, cum supplementis integris D. P. Carpenterii, Adelungii, aliorum, suisque digessit G. A. L. Henschel; sequuntur Glossarium gallicum, Tabulae, Indices auctorum et rerum, Disserta-

tiones. Ed. nova, aucta pluribus verbis aliorum scriptorum a Léopold Favre. Niort, L. Favre, 1883–87. 10v. il. (Repr.: Paris, Librairie des Sciences et des Arts, 1937–38; Graz, Akademische Druck- & Verlagsanstalt, 1954. 10v. in 5) **AD555**

Contents: v.1–8, A–Z; v.9, Glossaire français; v.10, Indices.

The great dictionary of medieval Latin, originally published 1678 and several times revised. This is the latest edition but is very little changed from the edition of 1840–57, 8v., which is still usable and as good for general purposes as the later edition.

───── ───── Petit supplément au Dictionnaire de Du Cange par Charles Schmidt. Strasbourg, Heitz, 1906. 71p. PA2289.D8

Latham, Ronald Edward. Dictionary of medieval Latin from British sources. Prep. . . . under the direction of a committee appointed by the British Academy. London, Publ. for the British Academy by Oxford Univ. Pr., 1975–81. fasc.1–2. (In progress) **AD556**

Contents: fasc.1–2, A–C.

"This dictionary is designed to present a comprehensive picture of the Latin language current in Britain from the sixth century to the sixteenth. . . . Sources later than 1550 are normally excluded, though some use has been made of Latin records in the Medieval tradition as late as the seventeenth century."—*Pref.* Three categories of material are distinguished, with varying fullness of treatment: "(a) The use by British authors of CL words in approximately their basic classical meanings" is afforded fairly brief treatment; "(b) Words and usages that belong to the post-classical development of Latin as a whole are dealt with more fully"; and (c) "The fullest treatment is reserved for what is distinctively British, either because of its links with Anglo-Saxon, Anglo-Norman, or some other vernacular . . . , or because it reflects the growth of institutions with specifically British features." Etymology is indicated where not self-evident. Quotations are dated in boldface type. Bibliography of sources cited in fasc.1, p.xvi–xlv; bibliography supplement in fasc.2. PA2891.L28

───── Revised Medieval Latin word-list from British and Irish sources. London, publ. for the British Academy by Oxford Univ. Pr., 1965. 524p. **AD557**

A revision and enlargement of Baxter and Johnson's *Medieval Latin word-list* (Oxford, 1934). A word list rather than a formal dictionary. Gives brief information, i.e., Latin word, date, and equivalent English word or phrase. PA2891.L3

Maigne d'Arnis, W. H. Lexicon manuale ad scriptores mediae et infimae latinitatis, ex glossariis Caroli Dufresne, D. Ducangii, D. P. Carpentarii, Adelungii et aliorum, in compendium accuratissime redactum; ou, Recueil de mots de la basse latinité. Paris, Migne, 1866. 2336col. **AD558**

Gives definitions in Latin and in French. PA2889.M3

Mittellateinisches Wörterbuch bis zum Ausgehenden 13. Jahrhundert. . . . München, C. H. Beck, 1959–76. Bd.1–2¹⁻⁷. (In progress) **AD559**

In Gemeinschaft mit den Akademien der Wissenschaften zu Göttingen, Heidelberg, Leipzig, Mainz, Wien, und der Schweizerischen Geisteswissenschaftlichen Gesellschaft, hrsg. von der Bayerischen Akademie der Wissenschaften und der Deutschen Akademie der Wissenschaften zu Berlin.

Contents: Abkürzungs- und Quellenverzeichnisse. 94p.; Bd.1–2⁷, A–comprovincialis.

A number of German-speaking Latinists are collaborating to produce another scholarly dictionary of medieval Latin. Designed to extend the scope of the standard *Thesaurus,* i.e., to cover the centuries from the decline of classical Latin to the end of the 13th century, it follows generally the plan of the *Thesaurus* in its treatment of individual words. Among many sources drawn upon for vocabulary, the extensive series *Monumenta germaniae historica* is particularly heavily utilized.

Niermeyer, Jan Frederik. Mediae latinitatis lexicon minus: lexique latin médiéval—français/anglais; a medieval Latin-

French/English dictionary. Composuit J. F. Niermeyer, perficiendum curavit C. van de Kieft. Leiden, Brill, 1976. 2v.   **AD560**

Originally issued in parts, 1954–76. v.2 entitled "Abbreviationes et index fontium."

A scholarly dictionary designed to be less bulky than Du Cange but more extensive than the word lists. Explanations of meanings are given both in French and in English, and there are numerous quotations showing the history and usage of words. The majority of the quotations come from sources between A.D. 550 and 1150.   PA2364.N5

Novum glossarium mediae latinitatis ab anno DCCC usque ad annum MCC; ed. curavit Consilium Academiarum Consociatarum. [Hafniae], Ejnar Munksgaard, 1957–80. (In progress)   **AD561**

Issued in parts.

Contents: L–Nysus, ed. by Franz Blatt; O, ed. by Franz Blatt and Yves Lefèvre.

Designed to cover the "general" language of authors from the 9th to the 13th centuries. Word treatment is primarily lexicographic rather than historical or encyclopedic. Supplements but does not replace Du Cange.   PA2893.F7N65

——— Index scriptorum novus mediae latinitatis ab anno DCCC usque ad annum MCC qui afferuntur in Novo glossario ab Academiis Consociatis iuris publici facto. Hafniae, Munksgaard, 1973. 246p. Fasc. unnumbered.

An earlier list was published 1957.

A long list of periodicals and collections precedes the index of abbreviations (with full citations to sources). Useful not only in connection with the dictionary, but for identifying medieval texts generally.

Pronunciation

Allen, William Sidney. Vox latina, a guide to the pronunciation of classical Latin. 2d ed. Cambridge, Univ. Pr., 1978. 132p.   **AD562**

1st ed. 1965.

An explanation of the rules and principles of classical pronunciation, not a pronouncing dictionary.   PA2117.A5

Bibliography

Starnes, DeWitt Talmage. Renaissance dictionaries, English-Latin and Latin-English. Austin, Univ. of Texas Pr., 1954. 427p. il.   **AD563**

A history of English-Latin and Latin-English lexicography down to the 18th century, particularly of the period 1500–1660. Includes a bibliography of references pertaining to the history of Latin-English lexicography, p.393–94, and a short-title list of Latin-English and English-Latin dictionaries (1500–*ca.*1800) in American libraries with location of copies.   PA2353.S7

Lettish

Anglu-latviešu vārdnīca: sastādijis autoru kolektivs M. Stradinas redakcijā. Riga, Latvijas Valsts Izdevniecība, 1957. 916p.   **AD564**

More comprehensive, with more meanings and phrases, than the dictionary by Dravnieks (below). Gives pronunciation of English words by phonetic alphabet.   PG8979.A5

Dravnieks, Jēkabs. English-Latvian dictionary (Angliski-latviska vārdnīca). [N.Y.], Grāmatu Draugs, [195–?]. 606p.   **AD565**

1st ed., Riga, 1933.   PG8979.D7

Mühlenbach, K. K. Mülenbacha Latviešu valodas vārdnīca. Redigējis, papildinājis, turpinājis J. Endzelīns . . . K. Mühlenbachs Lettisch-deutsches Wörterbuch. Red., ergänzt und fortgesetzt von J. Endzelin. Riga, 1923–32. 4v.   **AD566**

Repr.: Cikāgā, Cikāgās Baltu Filologu Kopa, 1953–56. 6v. (v.5–6 by J. Endzelin and E. Housenberg, *see* supplement below)

Lettish-German. A scholarly work, including etymologies.   PG8981.M8

——— ——— Papildinājumi un labojumi. Ergänzungen und Berichtigungen [von] J. Endzelin und E. Hausenberg. 2. unv. Aufl. Chicago, Der Gruppe der Lettischen Balto-Filologen in Chicago, 1956. 2v.

Issued in parts, 1934–56.

An A–Z supplement, published as v.5–6 of the main set.

Turkina, Eizenija. Latviešu-anglu vārdnīca. M. Andersones redakcijā. 3., atkārtotais izdevums. Rīgā, Latvijas Valsts I zdevniecība, 1963; [København], Imanta, 1964. 775p.   **AD567**

Added title page in English: Latvian-English dictionary.
Approx. 31,000 entries.   PG8979.T83

Lithuanian

Lietuvos TSR Mokslų Akademija, Vilna. Lietuvių Kalbos ir Literatūros Institutas. Dabartinés lietuvių kalbos žodynas. Apie 60,000 žodžių. II papildytas leidimas. Red. kolegija: J. Kruopas (at sak redaktorius). Vilnius, "Mintis," 1972. 974p.   **AD568**

1st ed. 1954.   PG8675.L5

Bilingual

Anglų-lietuvių kalbų žodynas. 2., pataisytas ir papildytas leidimas. Apie 30,000 žodžiu ir posakių. Redagavo A. Laučka ir A. Dantaitė. Vilnius, Valstybinė politinės ir mokslinės literatūros leidykla, 1961. 595p.   **AD569**

At head of title: V. Baravykas.
1st ed. 1958.
English-Lithuanian.   PG8679.A57

Lalis, Anthony. Lietuviškos ir angliškos kalbu žodynas. Sutaisē Antanas Lalis . . . 3., isnaujo taisytas ir gausiai papildytas, spaudimas. Chicago, Ill., Turtu ir spauda "Lietuvos," 1915. 2 pts. in 1v.   **AD570**

Added title page in English: Dictionary of the Lithuanian and English languages. 3d rev. and enl. ed.   PG8679.L33

Niedermann, Max, Senn, Alfred and **Salys, Anton.** Wörterbuch der litauischen Schriftsprache, litauisch-deutsch. Heidelberg, C. Winter, 1926–68. 5v. (Indogermanische Bibliothek. II. Reihe, Wörterbücher)   **AD571**

Published in parts. Editors vary.

A dictionary of the modern literary language, giving examples of usage.   PG8681.N6

Peteraitis, Vilius. Lietuviškai angliškas žodynas; Lithuanian-English dictionary. 2. laida. [Chicago], Letuviskos Knygos Klubas, 1960. 586p.   **AD572**

1st ed. 1948.

Prepared for the use of Lithuanians in English-speaking countries.   PG8679.P38

Piesarskas, Bronius and **Svecevičius, B.** Lietuvių-anglų kalbų žodynas: apie 50,000 žodžių. Vilnius, "Mokslas," 1979. 911p.   **AD573**

Added title page in English: *Lithuanian-English dictionary: about 50,000 words.*

Gives English equivalents, with frequent examples of usage.   PG8679.P5

Etymology

Fraenkel, Ernst. Litauisches etymologisches Wörterbuch. Heidelberg, C. Winter, 1962–65. 2v. (1560p.) (Indogermanische Bibliothek. II. Reihe, Wörterbücher)　**AD574**

Issued in parts 1955–65. Bd.1, A–prive, appeared in 8 pts., 1955–58; a new title page and preliminary matter issued 1962.
An extensive etymological dictionary.　PG8663.F7

Malay

Wilkinson, Richard James. Malay-English dictionary (romanised). Mitylene, Greece, Printed by Salavopoulos and Kinderlis; Singapore, Kelly and Walsh, 1932. 2v. (Repr.: London, Macmillan, 1957. 2v. in 1)　**AD575**

PL5125.W62

——— An abridged Malay-English dictionary (romanised). 8th ed., rev. and enl. by A. E. Coope and Mohd. Ali bin Mohamed. London, Macmillan; N.Y., St. Martin's, 1961. 307p.　**AD576**

A dictionary and grammar of the Malayan language by William Marsden (Oxford, etc., Oxford Univ. Pr., 1984. 2v.) is a reprinting of Marsden's *Dictionary of the Malayan language in two parts, Malayan and English and English and Malayan* (London, 1812) and his *Grammar of the Malayan language* (London, 1812).

PL5125.W58

Winstedt, *Sir* **Richard Olof.** An unabridged Malay-English dictionary. 6th ed., enl. Kuala Lumpur, Malaysia, Marican, [1965]. 390p.　**AD577**

PL5125.W7

——— A practical modern English-Malay dictionary. 6th ed. with an appendix. Kuala Lumpur, Marican, [1963]. 421p.　**AD577a**

PL5125.W69

Maori

Biggs, Bruce. The complete English-Maori dictionary. [Auckland], Auckland Univ. Pr./Oxford Univ. Pr., [1981]. 227p.　**AD578**

"The scope of this Dictionary does not include examples of the use of the Maori words. [William L.] Williams's Maori to English dictionary [6th ed., 1957] remains an indispensable source for such information."—*Introd.*　PL6465.Z5B5

Mende

Innes, Gordon. A Mende-English dictionary. London, Cambridge Univ. Pr., 1969. 155p.　**AD578a**

Intended for the speaker of English. Based on the Eastern dialect (of Sierra Leone). Approximately 6,500 entries with tones indicated by letters.　PL8511.Z5I5

Mongolian

Boberg, Folke. Mongolian-English dictionary. Stockholm, Förlaget, Filadelfia, [1954–55]. 3v.　**AD579**

Contents: v.1–2, Mongolian-English, A–Vivangkhirit; v.3, English-Mongolian, A–Zodiac and Index to v.1–2.
The first Mongolian dictionary "published to a Western language since 1849."—*Pref.*　PL406.B6

Hangin, John G. A concise English-Mongolian dictionary. Bloomington, Indiana Univ. Pr., 1970. 287p. (Indiana Univ. publs. Uralic and Altaic ser., 89)　**AD580**

"About 10,000 words in English together with their equivalents in modern Mongolian."—*Foreword.* Examples of usage are given for frequently occurring verbs, prepositions, and common expressions.
PL406.H34

Lessing, Ferdinand D., ed. Mongolian-English dictionary. Comp. by Mattai Haltod [and others]. Berkeley, Univ. of California Pr., 1960. 1217p.　**AD581**

"Excluding the strictly archaic language, the dictionary contains the vocabulary of all periods from 1940 on, including the modern terminology developed since sovietization ... strictly technical Buddhist terms and expressions are presented in a special Supplement."—*Introd.*

Selected bibliography of dictionaries and grammars, p.xiv.
PL406.L4

Norse, Old

See Icelandic.

Norwegian

See also AD249.

Knudsen, Trygve and **Sommerfelt, Alf.** Norsk riksmålsordbok. Oslo, Aschehoug, 1930–57. 2v. in 3.　**AD582**

Issued in parts, 1930–57.
The standard Norwegian dictionary of the "literary" language—the language of the educated class—with many illustrative quotations showing usage, primarily since 1870.　PD2688.K6

Norsk ordbok; ordbok over det norske folkemalet og det Nynorske skriftmalet. Utg. av Det Norske samlaget; Alf Hellevik, hovudredaktør. Oslo, Det Norske Samlaget, 1966–[77]. v.1–2⁴. (In progress)　**AD583**

Contents: v.1–2⁴, A–fir-kant.

Bilingual

Bjerke, Lucie and **Soraas, Haakon.** English-Norwegian dictionary. London, Harrap, 1964. 562p.　**AD584**

"First published in Norway 1963 by H. Aschehoug & Co. (W. Nygaard) Oslo."—*verso of t.p.*　PD2691.B48

Cappelens store engelsk-norsk ordbok. Redaktører: Bjarne Berulfsen, Herbert Svenkerud. Oslo, Cappelen, [1968].　**AD585**

"Utarbeidet på grunnlag av B. Kjaerulff-Nielsen. Engelsk-dansk ordbog. Copenhagen, 1964."—*verso of t.p.*
English-Norwegian only. Many examples of usage; pronunciation of English entry words given in phonetic spelling.　PD2691.C3

Gleditsch, Th. [and others]. English-Norwegian dictionary. London, Allen & Unwin, [1950]. 855p.　**AD586**

From the 2d Norwegian ed. (Oslo, 1948).
A dictionary of modern written and spoken English for the general reader.　PD2691.G53

Jorgenson, Theodore and **Galdal, Peter.** Norwegian-English school dictionary. Rev. ed. [Northfield, Minn.], St. Olaf College Pr., 1955. 448p.　**AD587**

1st ed. 1943.

Uses the new orthography made obligatory by the language reform of 1938, but also gives many parallel forms and may be used in reading older literature. Shows articles, plural endings, principal parts, forms of the adjectives. etc. PD2691.J6

Norwegian English dictionary; a pronouncing and translating dictionary of modern Norwegian [Bokmål and Nynorsk] with a historical and grammatical introduction. Einar Haugen, ed. in chief. Oslo, Universitetsforlaget; Madison, Univ. of Wisconsin Pr., 1965. 500p. **AD588**

Added title page in Norwegian.

Primarily intended "as a tool for the learning of Norwegian by American students."—*Pref.* Includes both Dano-Norwegian (Bokmål) and New Norwegian (Nynorsk). PD2691.N6

Etymology

Torp, Alf. Nynorsk etymologisk ordbog. Kristiania, Aschehoug, 1919. 886p. **AD589**

Treats Nynorsk or Landsmål, the language of the "country people." PD2683.T6

Nubian

Armbruster, Carl Hubert. Dongolese Nubian, a lexicon: Nubian-English, English-Nubian. Cambridge, Univ. Pr., 1965. 268p. **AD590**

Intended for the English speaker. In the Nubian-English section, words are arranged under main word; the English-Nubian section is alphabetical. Part of speech, etymology, and illustrative sentences are given. PL8573.A7

Pali

Buddhadatta, Ambalangoda Polvatté. English-Pali dictionary. [Colombo, Ceylon], Pali Text Society, [1955]. 588p. **AD591**

PK1091.B8

—— Concise Pali-English dictionary. [2d ed.] Colombo, Colombo Apothecaries Co., 1968. 294p. **AD592**

Pali Text Society, London. Pali-English dictionary, ed. by T. W. Rhys Davids and William Stede. Chipstead (Surrey), Soc., 1921–25. 4v. (Repr.: London, Luzac, 1947–49 and 1959) **AD593**

Issued in 8 pts.

A standard dictionary with references to sources. PK1091.P33

Trenckner, Vilhelm. A critical Pali dictionary, begun by V. Trenckner; rev., cont. and ed. by Dines Andersen, Helmer Smith and Hans Hendricksen. Copenhagen, [publ. for the Royal Danish Academy by] Munksgaard, 1924/48–82. v.1–2$^{1-12}$. (In progress) **AD594**

Editor varies; publisher varies.

Contents: v.1–2^{12}, A–U]umpa. Epilegomena to v.1, by Helmer Smith, publ. 1948 (97p.), containing abbreviations, bibliography, concordances, devices of transliteration.

v.1 and Epilegomena published 1924–48; publication resumed in 1960, again from the beginning of the alphabet, but not duplicating the work previously published.

A scholarly critical dictionary with English definitions and many references to sources. PK1091.T7

Panjabi

See Hindi, Hindustani, Panjabi, Urdu.

Persian

Āryānpūr Kāshānī, 'Abbās. The new unabridged English-Persian dictionary, by Abbas Aryanpur (Kashani), with the collaboration of Jahan Shah Saleh and numerous consultants, translators, etc. [Tehran, Amir-Kabir Pub. & Prt. Inst., 1963–64] 5v. **AD595**

"This book is based on Webster's International Dictionary, and The Shorter Oxford Dictionary, attempting to give Persian equivalents of all the words of Oxford and all the key-words of Webster."— *Introd.* PK6379.A7

Hayyīm, Sulaymān. The larger English-Persian dictionary, designed to give the Persian meanings of 80,000 words, idioms, phrases and proverbs in the English language, as well as the transliteration of difficult Persian words. Téhéran, Bēroukhim, 1941–43. 2v. **AD596**

Added title page in Persian.

Various reprintings.

Each volume has Addenda, including some words omitted from the text, important proper names, foreign words and phrases, a few colloquial and slang expressions, abbreviations used in English literature, and Persian abbreviations. PK6379.H26

—— New Persian-English dictionary, complete and modern, designed to give the English meanings of over 50,000 words, terms, idioms, and proverbs in the Persian language as well as the transliteration of the words in English characters. Together with a sufficient treatment of all the grammatical features of the Persian language. Téhéran, Bēroukhim, 1960–62. 2v. **AD597**

First published 1934–36. PK6379.H3

—— The shorter Persian-English dictionary treating 30,000 words and idioms used in modern Persian. 3d ed. rev. and enl. Téhéran, Bēroukhim, 1963. 814p. **AD598**

1st ed. 1954. PK6379.H34

Palmer, Edward H. A concise dictionary of the Persian language. London, Routledge & Paul, 1949. 726col. **AD599**

English-Persian and Persian-English. PK6379.P3

Razi, F. D. The modern Persian dictionary (Persian-Urdu-English), comp. by F. D. Razi, assisted by M. Rasheed Ahmed. Lahore, Ripon Printing Pr., 1952. 240p. **AD600**

Title also in Persian. PK6379.R3

Wollaston, *Sir* **Arthur Naylor.** A complete English-Persian dictionary, comp. from original sources. London, Murray, 1904. 1491p. **AD601**

1st impression: London, Low, 1894. PK6379.W7

Pidgin English

Mihalic, Francis. The Jacaranda dictionary and grammar of Melanesian Pidgin. [Milton, Q.], Jacaranda, [1971]. 375p. **AD602**

A 1957 version had title: *Grammar and dictionary of Neo-Melanesian.* This is a revised and expanded edition, taking into account new developments in the language.

Includes Melanesian Pidgin to English and English to Melanesian Pidgin. Select bibliography, p.52–54. PM7891.Z5M5

Polish

Polska Akademia Nauk. Słownik staropolski. [Komitet redakcyjny: Kazimierz Nitsch, et al.] Warszawa, 1953–84. v.1–9¹⁻². (In progress) **AD603**

Contents: v.1–9¹⁻², A–Tłoka.
A scholarly dictionary of Old Polish. PG6729.P6

Skorupka, Stanisław. Słownik frazeologiczny języka polskiego. Wyd. 2. Warszawa, Wiedza Powszechna, 1974. 2v. **AD604**

1st ed. 1967–68.
A dictionary of terms with examples to illustrate variant meanings, figurative usage, etc. PG6689.S5

———— **Auderska, Halina** and **Łempicka, Zofia.** Maly słownik języka polskiego. Warszawa, Państwowe Wydawnictwo Naukowe, 1968. 1033p. **AD605**

About 35,000 terms. PG6625.S83

Słownik języka polskiego. Redaktor naczelny Witold Doroszewski. Warszawa, Wieda Powszechna, 1958–69. 11v. **AD606**

———— Indeks a tergo do Słownika języka polskiego pod. red. Witolda Doroszewskiego. [Opracował zespół pod kierunkiem Renaty Grzegorczykowej i Jadwigi Puzininy] Warszawa, Państwowe Wydawn. Naukowe, 1973. 558p.

A major scholarly dictionary of the Polish language, with many references to the literature. v.11 is a supplement. PG6625.S48

Słownik języka polskiego. [Wyd. 2. Red. nauk. Mieczysław Szymczak] Warszawa, Państwowe Wydawn., Nauk., 1982–83. 3v. **AD607**

1st ed. 1978–81.
About 80,000 entries. PG6625.S523

Bilingual

Kościuszko Foundation dictionary: English-Polish, Polish-English. The Hague, Mouton, 1959–61. 2v. (Poland's Millennium series of the Kościuszko Foundation) **AD608**

Contents: v.1, English-Polish, by K. Bulas and F. J. Whitfield; v.2, Polish-English, by K. Bulas, L. L. Thomas and F. J. Whitfield.
The second volume emphasizes "twentieth century standard Polish"; the first volume includes some English dialect and slang. Examples of usage are given. A substantial bilingual dictionary. PG6640.K65

Lilien, Ernest. Dictionary. Słownik. Buffalo, Drukiem Dziennika dla wszystkich [1944]–51. fasc.1–19 (960p.). il. **AD609**

Contents: pt.1, English-Polish, A–hellbent.
Ceased publication.
An extensive and well-executed dictionary of current Polish, including many technical and scientific terms. Unfortunately, never completed. PG6640.L5

Stanisławski, Jan. Wielki słownik angielsko-polski. Red. naukowy, Wiktor Jassem. Warszawa, Wiedza Powszechna, 1964. 1175p. **AD610**

Added title page: The great English-Polish dictionary.
"Comprises over 100,000 words, phrases and expressions commonly used in the English language of the 19th and 20th centuries." —*Pref.* Includes also terms in technology, medicine and science, colloquialisms, Americanisms, etc. PG6640.S3

———— Wielki słownik polsko-angielski: z suplementem. Redaktor naukowy: Wiktor Jassem. Wyd.5, supl.3. Warszawa, Państwowe Wydawnictwo Wiedza Powszechna, 1980. 2v. **AD611**

Added title page: The great Polish-English dictionary, supplemented.

1st ed. 1969; suppl. 1977.
A reprinting of the 1969 ed. with the corresponding portions of the 1977 supplement reprinted at the end of each volume. About 180,000 entries in the basic work, plus about 10,000 in the supplement. A companion to the compiler's English-Polish dictionary (above). PG6640.S843

Abbreviations

U.S. Library of Congress. Slavic and Central European Division. Polish abbreviations: a selective list, comp. by Janina Wojcicka. 2d ed. rev. and enl. Wash., 1957. 164p. **AD612**

1st ed. 1955.
Lists some 2,600 abbreviations which have gained currency in Poland since 1945—particularly names of government agencies, societies, companies, and institutions—but with some general abbreviations as well. Z663.47.P6

Etymology

Brückner, Alexander. Słownik etymologiczny języka polskiego. [2.wyd.] Warszawa, Wiedza Powszechna, 1957. 805p. (Repr. 1970) **AD613**

A reprint, with new introduction, of a work published: Kraków, Nakład i Własność Krakowskiej Spółki Wydawniczej, 1927. PG6580.B7

Sławski, Franciszek. Słownik etymologiczny języka polskiego. Kraków, Nakł. Tow. Milośników. Języka Polskiego, 1952–82. v.1–5⁵. (In progress) **AD614**

Contents: v.1–5⁵, A–łżywy.
Redaktorzy: Kazimierz Nitsch i Andrzej Siudut. PG6580.S5

Pronunciation

Słownik wymowy polskiej PWN. The dictionary of Polish pronunciation. . . . Redakcja naukowa Mieczyslaw Karas, Marla Madejowa. [Warszawa], Państwowe Wydawnictwo Naukowe, 1977. 564p. **AD615**

Title also in French, German, and Russian; preface in Polish, English, French, German, and Russian.
Aims to show the pronunciation of "Standard Polish . . . the common medium of expression among Poles."—*p.XL.* Uses the International Phonetic Alphabet. PG6137.S6

Bibliography

Grzegorczyk, Piotr. Index lexicorum Poloniae: bibliografia słowników polskich. Warszawa, Państwowe Wydawn. Naukowe, 1967. 286p. **AD616**

A bibliography of Polish dictionaries, including dictionaries of specific subjects, and of general encyclopedias. Author, title, and subject indexes. Z2528.L5G7

Polyglot

Britannica world language dictionary, comp. under the direction of the editorial staff of Encyclopaedia Britannica. [Chicago, 1955] [1529]–2065p. **AD617**

First published 1954 in *Funk & Wagnalls new practical standard dictionary of the English language,* v.2, p. [1529]–1944.
Gives, in parallel columns, the most common English words and their translations into six other languages; this is followed by sections for French, German, Italian, Spanish, Swedish, and Yiddish, each section giving the most common words of that language,

with pronunciation and English equivalent. Also includes brief grammatical rules, useful expressions, etc. P361.B7

Dony, Yvonne P. de. Léxico del lenguaje figurado, comparado, en cuatro idiomas: castellano, français, English, deutsch. 27,846 locuciones distribuídas en 4071 grupos. Buenos Aires, Ed. Desclée, De Brouwer, 1951. 804p. **AD618**

A dictionary of expressions, proverbs, idioms, etc., arranged in groups under the main Spanish word with equivalents in French, English and German. Indexes in each of the languages.

PB331.D6

Duden pictorial encyclopedia in five languages: English, French, German, Italian, Spanish. 2d enl. ed. Over 30,000 key words explained in pictures. . . . N.Y., F. Ungar, [1958]. 2v. il. **AD619**

"Based on the widely used Duden picture vocabularies, which originally were produced in Germany, in the late 1930's."—*Pref.* 1st ed. 1943.

Covers science and arts, state and community, man, family and home, trades and vocations, trade and transport, physical culture and recreation, etc., with drawings, keyed to expressions in the various languages. Indexes in the five languages. P361.D8

Portuguese

Dicionário contemporâneo da língua portuguesa Caldas Aulete. 3.a ed. brasileira. . . . [Lisboa], Editora Delta, 1974. 5v. il. **AD620**

Subtitle: Novamente rev., atualizada e aumentada pela introd. de termos da tecnologia recente, pelo registro dos vocábulos usados no Brasil e pela extensão dos apêndices por Hamílcar de Garcia; com estudos sobre a origem e evolução da língua portuguesa, sua expansão no Brasil, e uma exposição da pronúncia normal brasileira por Antenor Nascentes.

Various printings.

Based on Caldas Aulete's *Diccionario contemporâneo da língua portugueza,* first published 1881. PC5327.D515

Ferreira, Aurélio Buarque de Holanda. Novo dicionário da língua portuguesa. Rio de Janeiro, Editora Nova Fronteira, [1975]. 1517p. **AD621**

Emphasis is on Brazilian Portuguese. PC5327.F44

Figueiredo, Cândido de. Dicionário da língua portuguêsa. 14. ed. actualizada segundo as regras do Acordo Ortográfico . . . e em perfeita harmonia com o "Vocabulário resumido" de 1947 da Academia das Ciências. Lisbon, Bertrand, 1956. 2v. **AD622**

Earlier eds. had title: *Novo dicionario de língua portuguesa.* Includes etymologies.

Freire, Laudelino de Oliveira. Grande e novíssimo dicionário da língua portuguesa . . . com a colaboraçao técnica do professor J. L. de Campos. . . . Rio de Janeiro, A. Noite, [1939–44]. 5v. **AD623**

A large dictionary including some 208,000 entries, giving etymologies, examples of usage, etc. Paged continuously. PC5327.F7

Lima, Hildebrando de and **Barroso, Gustavo.** Pequeno dicionário brasileiro da língua portuguêsa. 11. ed. 4. impr., supervisionada e consideràvelmente aum. por Aurélio Buarque de Hollanda Ferreira com a assistência de José Baptista da Luz, e revista e aumentada por inúmeros especialistas. Rio de Janeiro, Civilizaçao Brasileira, 1969. 1301p. il **AD624**

1st ed. edited by Hildebrando de Lima and revised by various editors through the years.

A standard and practical dictionary of Brazilian Portuguese.

PC5327.L5

Mesquita de Carvalho, José. Dicionário prático da língua nacional. 19. ed. Sao Paulo, Editore Egeria, [1969, c1966]. 1185p. **AD625**

1st ed. 1945. Frequently reprinted.

Brazilian Portuguese. Gives derivations, cognates, etc.

PC5327.M45

Moraes Silva, António de. Grande dicionário da língua portuguesa. 10. ed. rev., corrigida, muito aumentada e actualizada segunda as regras do Acordo Ortográfico Luso-Brasileiro de 10 de agosto de 1945, por Augusto Moreno, Cardoso Júnior e José Pedro Machado. [Lisboa], Ed. Confluéncia, 1949–59. 12v. **AD626**

Earlier editions published under title *Diccionário da lingua portugueza.*

v.1–11, A–Z. v.12 consists of a number of special sections: an epitome of Portuguese grammar; a statement of the Acordo Ortografia and its decisions; and various word lists: foreign words and phrases, place-names, irregular verbs, root words, abbreviations, addenda, etc.

A famous dictionary, first published in 1789. Of first importance and generally considered to be the best Portuguese dictionary. Includes quotations from the literature in chronological order and showing usage.

This edition takes into account the Portuguese-Brazilian *Acordo Ortográfico* of 1945, which aimed at instituting a uniform system of orthography for the Portuguese language. PC5327.M733

Nascentes, Antenor. Dicionário da língua portuguêsa, elaborado por Antenor Nascentes a fim de ser submetido à Academia para as devidas alteraçoes. [Rio de Janeiro], Academia Brasileira de Letras, 1961–67. 4v. **AD627**

A preliminary publication intended to serve as the basis for the development of an official Academy dictionary. After revisions, deletions, etc., it was expected that the dictionary would appear as a single-volume work. PC5327.N3

Soares, Antonio Joaquim de Macedo. Dicionário brasileiro da língua portuguêsa; elucidário etimológico crítico das palavras e frases que, originárias do Brasil, ou aqui populares, se não encontram nos dicionários da língua portuguêsa, ou nêles vêm com forma ou significação differente 1875–1888. Coligido, revisto e completado por Julião Rangel de Macedo Soares. Rio de Janeiro, Ministerio da Educaçao e Cultura, Instituto Nacional do Livro, 1954–55. 2v.

AD628

PC5446.S6

Bilingual

Ferreira, Julio Albino. Dicionário inglês-português. Nova ed. Rev. e melhorada pelo Dr. Armando de Morais. Porto, Barreira, [1952–54]. 2v. in 1. **AD629**

v.2 has title *Dicionário português-inglês.*
One of the better bilingual dictionaries. PC5333.F

Houaiss, Antônio and **Avery, Catherine B.** The new Appleton dictionary of the English and Portuguese languages. Assoc. ed.: José E. A. do Prado . . . N.Y., Appleton, 1964. 636p., 665p. **AD630**

Added title page in Portuguese. Various printings.

Contents: pt.1, English-Portuguese; pt.2, Portuguese-English.

Each part contains approximately 60,000 words and expressions. Particular emphasis is on Portuguese as it is spoken and written in Brazil. Equivalents are given or, when necessary, explanations or definitions. Includes a large general vocabulary as well as a wide selection of words from specialized fields. Pronunciation is indicated by the phonetic system. PC5333.H6

Michaelis, Henriette. Novo Michaelis; dicionário ilustrado. Baseado em material selecionado do antigo dicionário Michaelis e inteiramente remodelado, revisto e aumentado pela Seção Lexicográfica das Edições Melhoramentos, sob a orientação de Fritz Pietzschke. São Paulo, Ed. Melhoramentos; Wiesbaden, Brockhaus, [1958–61]. 2v. il. **AD631**

Added title page in English.
On spine: Brockhaus picture dictionary.

Contents: v.1, English-Portuguese; v.2, Portuguese-English.

English subtitle: Comprehensive modern vocabulary; idiomatic phrases, pronunciation key, numerous plates with more than 4,000 conceptions, based on matter selected from the original Michaelis dictionary and completely reorganized, revised, and enlarged.

Based on the *Novo dicionário da língua portugueza e ingleza* by Henriette Michaelis ([8.ed.] Leipzig, Brockhaus, 1945), frequently reprinted and long a standard work of current Portuguese. Includes technical terms used in commerce and industry, the arts and sciences, etc. PC5333.M582

Taylor, James Lumpkin. A Portuguese-English dictionary. Rev., with corrections and additions by the author and Priscilla Clark Martin. Stanford, Calif., Stanford Univ. Pr., 1970. 655p. (Repr.: Rio de Janeiro, Record, 1982) **AD632**

1st ed. 1958 (655p.); this edition shows limited revisions.

Contains some 60,000 entries, including Brazilian Portuguese. Planned "to provide an everyday working tool for as large a number of persons as possible."—*Introd.* Gives not only English equivalents, but often one or more synonyms and, in some cases, examples of usage. Includes many technical and scientific terms, particularly the names of Brazilian fauna and flora. PC5333.T3

Etymology

Dicionário etimológico da língua portuguesa, com a mais antigua documentação escrita e conhecida de muitos dos vocábulos estudados [por] José Pedro Machado. 2. ed. [Lisboa], Editorial Confluência, [1967-73]. 3v. **AD633**

Issued in fascicules. PC5305.D52

Nascentes, Antenor. Dicionário etimológico da língua portuguesa. . . . com prefácio de W. Meyer Lübke. Rio de Janeiro, F. Alves, 1932-52. 2v. **AD634**

v.2 is devoted to proper names. PC5305.N3

Silva Bastos, J. T. da. Diccionário etymológico, prosódico e orthográphico da lingua Portugueza. Contendo grande cópia de novos termos e accepções e um supplemento . . . 2ª ed. Lisboa, Parceria António Maria Pereira, 1928. 1434p. **AD635**

PC5327.S5

Synonyms

Costa, Agenor. Dicionário de sinônimos e locuções da língua portuguêsa. [3. ed. Rio de Janeiro], Editôra Fundo de Cultura, [1967]. 5v. (2370p.) il. **AD636**

2d ed. 1960, in 2v. PC5315.C6

Nascentes, Antenor. Dicionário de sinónimos. 3a. ed. rev. por Olavo Anibal Nascentes. Rio de Janeiro, Editora Nova Fronteira, 1981. 485p. **AD637**

1st ed. 1957.

There is an index of entry words and synonyms rather than cross references within the text. PC5315.N3

Bibliography

Almeida, Horácio de. Catálogo de dicionários portugueses e brasileiros. [Rio de Janeiro, Companhia Brasileira de Artes Gráficas], 1983. 132p. **AD638**

A main-entry listing of general and specialized dictionaries. No index.

Provençal

Alibert, Louis. Dictionnaire occitan-français d'après les parlers languedociens. Nouv. éd. Toulouse, Institut d'Etudes Occitanes, [1977]. 699p. **AD639**

This is a corrected reprint of the 1966 edition. PC3376.A4

Barthe, Roger. Lexique français-occitan. Nouv. éd., rev. et augmentée. Paris, [Association des Amis de la Langue d'Oc], 1973. 238p. **AD640**

1st ed. 1970.

A companion work is: PC3376.B3

——— Lexique occitan-français. Paris, [Association des Amis de la Langue d'Oc], 1980. 238p. **AD641**

Originally issued 1972. PC3376.B34

Levy, Emil. Petit dictionnaire provençal-français. 4 ed. Heidelberg, Winter; N.Y., Adler's Foreign Books, 1966. 387p. **AD642**

1st. ed. 1909.

Romanian

Academia Română, Bucharest. Dicționarul limbii române intocmit și publicat după îndemnul și cu cheltuiala Maiestătii Sale Regelui Carol I . . . București, Librariile Socec & comp. si C. Sfetea, 1913-40. v.[1-2]. **AD643**

Contents: v.1[1], A–B; v.1[2], C–Cojoaică; v.2[1], F–I; v.2[1-3], J–Lojniță.

A scholarly dictionary compiled on historical principles, including literary, obsolete, and regional terms; etymologies; and examples of usage. Definitions and explanations are in Romanian, but an equivalent word in French is also given.

Resumed publication in a new series as:

Dicționarul limbii române (DLR). Serie nouă. București, Editura Academiei Republicii Populare Române, 1965-80. T.VI, VII[1-2], VIII[1-4], IX, XI. (In progress) **AD644**

At head of title: Academia Republicii Populare Române.

Contents: t.VI, M; t.VII[1-2], N–O; t.VIII[1-4], P–Presimțire; t.IX, R; t.XI, S. (T.VI issued in fascicules; VII–VIII issued in bound volumes)

A continuation, in a slightly changed format, of the preceding item. French equivalents are no longer given as they were in the A–L parts. PC775.D48

Breban, Vasile. Dicționar al limbii române contemporane: de uz curent. București, Editura Științifică, 1980. 680p. **AD645**

Emphasis is on contemporary vocabulary. PC775.B7

Dicționarul explicativ al limbii române. [Conducătorii lucrării: Ion Coteanu, Luiza Seche, Mircea Seche] [București], Editura Academiei Republicii Socialiste România, 1975. 1049p. il. **AD646**

At head of title: Academia Republicii Socialiste România. Institutul de Lingvistică din București.

About 60,000 entries. PC775.D46

Dicționarul limbii romîne literare contemporane. [București], Editura Academiei Republicii Populare Romîne, 1955-57. 4v. **AD647**

Includes examples of 20th-century usage, with references to the literature. List of sources in v.4. PC775.D5

Dicționarul limbii romîne moderne. [București], Ed. Academiei Republicii Populare Romîne, 1958. 961p. il **AD648**

At head of title: Academia Republicii Populare Romîne. Institutul de Lingvistica din București.

An abridged dictionary, based on the preceding item. PC775.D52

Bilingual

Dicţionar englez-român. [Bucureşti], Editura Academiei Republicii Socialiste România, 1974. 825p. **AD649**

At head of title: Academia Republicii Socialiste România. Institutul de Lingvistică Bucureşti.

A comprehensive English-Romanian dictionary (about 120,000 entries); gives pronunciation of the English entry word in phonetic transcription. PC779.D485

Leviţchi, Leon. Dicţionar român-englez. Ediţia a 3-a revizuită de autori şi de Andrei Bantaş. Bucureşti, Editura Ştiinţifică, 1973. 1088p. **AD650**

1st ed. 1960.
A companion volume for English-Romanian is: PC779.L4

——— and **Bantaş, Andrei.** Dicţionar englez-român. Bucureşti, Editura Ştiinţifică, 1971. 1068p. **AD651**

Gives pronunciation of the English entry words in phonetic transcription.

Bantaş is also the compiler of *Dicţionar de buzunar englez-român, român-englez* (Ediţia a 2-a. Bucureşti, Editura Ştiinţifică, 1973. 1133p.). PC779.L39

Romansh

Società Retoromantscha. Dicziunari rumantsch grischun, publichà de la Società Retorumantsha cul agüd de la Confederaziun, dal Chantum grischun e da la Lia rumantscha. Fundà da Robert de Planta e Florian Melcher. Redacziun: Chasper Pult [et al.]. Cuoira, Bischofberger, 1939–84. v.1–7[17]. (In progress) **AD652**

Publisher varies.
Contents: v.1–7[17], A–Güstamaint.
A scholarly work giving etymologies, references to sources, and explanations in German. PC937.G5S6

Velleman, Antoine. Dicziunari scurznieu da la lingua ladina . . . Ladinisches Notwörterbuch mit deutscher, französischer und englischer Übersetzung. . . . Abridged dictionary of the Ladin (or Romansh) language, with German, French and English translation and numerous indications referring to topography and population. Samaden, Engadin Pr., 1929. 928p. **AD653**

Romansh-German-French-English dictionary. PC937.A1V4

Russian

Akademiia Nauk SSSR. Institut IAzykoznaniia. Slovar' russkogo iazyka. Moskva, Gos. Izd-vo Inostrannykh i Natsional'nykh Slovarei, 1957–61. 4v. **AD654**

v.2–4 issued by the Academy's Institut Russkogo IAzyka.
A general dictionary of the Russian language. Emphasis is on current usage with examples quoted from Russian literature of the 19th and 20th centuries. Intended for more general use than the larger, specialized lexicon *Slovar' sovremennogo russkogo literaturnogo iazyka* (below). PG2625.A4

Akademiia Nauk SSSR. Institut Russkogo IAzyka. Slovar' sovremennogo russkogo literaturnogo iazyka. Moskva, Izd-vo Akad. Nauk SSSR, 1950–65. 17v. **AD655**

Issuing body varies.
The major dictionary for modern literary Russian, based on the vocabulary used in literary, artistic, social, political, and general scientific works of the 19th and 20th centuries. Entries include the field in which the word is used, variant meanings, some variant forms, derivations, references to other dictionaries, and—in most cases—extensive illustrative quotations with their sources. Loan words from other languages are numerous. PG2625.A533

——— **Slovarnyi Sektor.** Slovar' russkikh narodnykh govorov. Sostavil F. P. Filin. Leningrad, Nauka [Leningradskoe Otd-nie], 1965–83. v.1–19. (In progress) **AD656**

Contents: v.1–19, A–Nakuchit'.
A dictionary of 19th- and 20th-century vocabulary of Russian dialects. Attempts to include all Russian dialects, even those spoken in foreign-language areas. PG2735.A48

Dal', Vladimir Ivanovich. Tolkovyi slovar' zhivogo velikorusskago iazyka. Pod red. I. A. Boduena-de-Kurtene. S. Peterburg, Izd. T-va. M. O. Vol'f, [1904–12?] 4v. **AD657**

Edition note varies: v.1–3: 4th ed., stereotype; v.4: 3d ed. Various reprintings.
The standard pre-Revolutionary dictionary for Russian and dialect vocabulary, including slang. The 3d and 4th eds. include revisions made by J. Baudouin de Courtenay. PG2625.D316

Daum, Edmund and **Schenk, Werner.** A dictionary of Russian verbs: bases of inflection; aspects; regimen; stressing; meanings. Leipzig, VEB Verlag; N.Y. Hippocrene Books [1974]. 750p. **AD658**

"With an essay on the syntax and semantics of the verb in present-day Russian by Professor Rudolf Ruzicka.—*t.p.*
A translation of *Die russischen Verben* (München, 1963).
About 20,000 verbs in alphabetical order, with inflected forms, etc. PG2271.D313

Lunt, Horace Gray. Kratkii slovar' drevnerusskogo iazyka (XI–XVII vekov). München, W. Fink, 1970. 85p. **AD659**

Added title page, cover title (Concise dictionary of Old Russian) and prefatory matter in English.
". . . intended for the student who is ready to read extensively in medieval Russian cultural works."—*Pref.* The equivalent term or definition is given in modern Russian. PG2743.L8

Ozhegov, Sergei Ivanovich. Slovar' russkogo iazyka. Okolo 57000 slov. Pod red. . . . N. IU. Shvedovoi. Izd. 10e, stereotip. Moskva, Sov. Entsiklopediia, 1973. 847p. **AD660**

1st ed. 1949. PG2625.O9

Tolkovyi slovar' russkogo iazyka. Sostavili: G. O. Vinokur [i dr.], pod red. D. N. Ushakova. Moskva, Gos. Izd-vo Inostrannykh i Natsional'nykh Slovarei, 1935–40. 4v. (Repr.: Moscow, 1948; Ann Arbor, 1948) **AD661**

Editors vary. Publisher varies.
This general dictionary, published earlier than the Academy's 4v. work (AD654), retains value for the inclusion of words and definitions of contemporary political significance. PG2625.T6

Bilingual

Gal'perin, Il'ia Romanovich. Bolshoi anglo-russkii slovar'. Moskva, "Sovetskaia Entsiklopediia," 1972. 2v. **AD662**

Added title page: *New English-Russian dictionary.*
Though intended primarily for Russians reading English-language texts, numerous features recommend it for use by English-speaking students of Russian: prefatory material appears in both languages; stress is marked for Russian words; many compound and idiomatic expressions are allotted separate entries; and emphasis is on the modern language. About 150,000 entries. PG2640.G3

Katzner, Kenneth. English-Russian, Russian-English dictionary. N.Y., Wiley, [1984]. 904p. **AD663**

"This dictionary constitutes a first in many respects. It is the first full-size English-Russian or Russian-English dictionary to be compiled and published in the United States. It is the first to be based on American, rather than British, English. And it is the first full-size dictionary published anywhere, including the Soviet Union, to contain English-Russian and Russian-English sections in the same volume."—*Pref.* For English words having more than one meaning, a synonym or "label" is given in parentheses to indicate which meaning is being rendered into Russian.　　　PG2640.K34

Langenscheidt's Russian-English, English-Russian dictionary, with special emphasis on American English. Berlin, Langenscheidt; London, Methuen, 1964. 505p.　　**AD664**

Pt.I by E. Wedel; pt.II by A. Romanov.

General vocabulary has approximately 35,000 entries, with references to declension and conjugation tables for Russian. Americanisms are "followed by their respective British semantic (or orthographic) equivalents."—*Pref.*　　　PG2640.L3

Müller, Vladimir Karlovich. English-Russian dictionary. 7th ed., new rev. ed. completely reset. N.Y., Dutton, [1965]. 1192p.　　**AD665**

1st American ed. 1944.

The English-Russian part of the earlier Müller dictionaries, re-edited by the Moscow State Pedagogical Institute of Foreign Languages. This edition runs to 70,000 words, and incorporates extensive revisions and additions. Corresponds to the 11th ed. published in Moscow in 1965 (912p.; various reprintings).

For the Russian-English companion volume *see* Smirnitskii (AD667).　　　PG2640.M813

Russko-angliiskii slovar'. Okolo 34000 slov. Sostavili: A. M. Taube [i dr.]. Pod red. R. K. Daglisha. Izd. 3., stereotipnoe. Moskva, Sovetskaia Entsiklopediia, 1970. 1052p.　**AD666**

Added title page in English: Russian-English dictionary.

1st ed. 1965.

A work for students, with a certain emphasis on literary language.　　　PG2640.R84

Smirnitskii, Aleksandr Ivanovich. Russian-English dictionary; 50,000 words approx. Comp. by O. S. Akhmanova [and others] under the general direction of A. I. Smirnitsky. 7th ed. N.Y., Dutton, [1966]. 766p.　　**AD667**

Added title page in Russian: *Russko-angliiski slovar'.*

The 3d ed., 1959, was an American printing of the 3d Russian ed. first published 1952. This represents the first resetting since the 3d ed.

Although certain features favor the Russian-speaking user, this is a useful up-to-date general dictionary.

The 1973 printing (N.Y., Dutton. 766p.) is called "9th ed." as published by "Sovetskaia Entsiklopediia," Moscow, 1971.　　　PG2640.S5

Transliterated dictionary of the Russian language. Eugene Garfield, ed. Philadelphia, ISI Pr., 1979. 382p.　**AD668**

"An abridged dictionary consisting of Russian-to-English and English-to-Russian sections."—*t.p.*

An unorthodox dictionary which gives the Russian word in transliteration rather than in the Cyrillic alphabet, and with the entries arranged according to the Roman alphabet in both the Russian and English sections. Gives equivalent terms and indicates part of speech for the Russian terms. About 17,000 entries in the Russian-to-English section. Transliteration system used is that of the British Standards Institute.　　　PG2640.T7

Wheeler, Marcus. The Oxford Russian-English dictionary. 2d ed. Oxford & N.Y., Oxford Univ. Pr., 1984. 930p.　　**AD669**

1st ed. 1972.

"This work is intended as a general-purpose dictionary of Russian as it is written and spoken. It is designed primarily, though not exclusively, for the use of those whose native language is English."—*Introd.* About 50,000 entries. To a large extent this is a reprinting, with corrections, of the 1972 ed., but some new entries and additional meanings have been inserted; an "Index of supplementary material" has been supplied to signal those additions. An appendix of Russian geographical names with English equivalents has also been added.

A companion work is:　　　PG2640.W5

The Oxford English-Russian dictionary. Ed. by P. S. Falla. Oxford, Clarendon Pr.; N.Y., Oxford Univ. Pr., 1984. 1052p.　　**AD670**

Includes "over 90,000 words, vocabulary items and illustrative phrases" *(Pref.),* the English vocabulary being based mainly on the most recent editions of the *Concise Oxford dictionary* and the *Oxford advanced learner's dictionary.*　　　PG2640.O9

Wilson, Elizabeth A. M. The modern Russian dictionary for English speakers: English-Russian. Oxford, Pergamon; Moskva, Izd. "Russkii IAzyk," [1982]. 715p.　　**AD671**

Intended as a practical dictionary "for the student whose approach to the Russian language will be through English. . . . The vocabulary comprises the words which the average educated man might want to use in speaking or writing Russian, including the simple technical terms in common use."—*Introd.*　PG2640.W54

Abbreviations

Alekseev, Dmitrii Ivanovich, Gosman, I. G. and **Sakharov, G. V.** Slovar' sokrashchenii russkogo iazyka; 15,000 sokrashchenii. 2-e izd., ispr. i dop., Moskva, Russkii IAzyk, 1977. 415p.　　**AD672**

1st ed. 1963.

In addition to full expansion of the term, shows pronunciation, stress, and, for those abbreviations and acronyms used substantively, grammatical gender. The more important journals are included, as well as Russian forms of abbreviations for international and foreign organizations.　　　PG2693.A4

Crowe, Barry. Concise dictionary of Soviet terminology, institutions, and abbreviations. Oxford, N.Y., Pergamon, [1969]. 182p.　　**AD673**

"The purpose of this dictionary is to provide a glossary of 'Sovietisms,' by which is meant the host of abbreviations, neologisms, portmanteau words and references to institutions which readers of Soviet literature constantly come across."—*Pref.*　　　PG2693.C7

Kramer, Alex A. Sokrashcheniia v sovetskikh izdaniiakh. Abbreviations in soviet publications. [Trenton, Scientific Russian Translating Service, 1965] 396p.　　**AD674**

Some 19,500 Russian abbreviations with expansion and English translation are given. There is an added section for signs and symbols.　　　PG2693.K72

U.S. Library of Congress. Aerospace Technology Division. Glossary of Russian abbreviations and acronyms. Wash., Lib. of Congress, 1967. 806p.　　**AD675**

23,600 entries. Abbreviations and their meanings are given in Cyrillic alphabet, and transliteration and translation are provided in parallel columns.　　　PG2693.U47

Etymology

Preobrazhenskii, Aleksandr Grigor'evich. Etymological dictionary of the Russian language. N.Y., Columbia Univ. Pr., 1951. 674p., 416p., 144p. (Columbia Slavic studies)　　**AD676**

The republication, in one volume, of a dictionary of value for the study of the history of the Russian language, literature, and civilization and of Indo-European comparative linguistics. v.1–2 (A–Suleia) appeared first, 1910–16; v.3 was published in 1949. The reprint follows the original except for alteration to modern orthography.

Also reprinted, Moscow, 1958, as *Etimologicheskii slovar' russkogo iazyka.*　　　PG2580.P7

Vasmer, Max. Etimologicheskii slovar' russkogo iazyka. Perevod s nemetskogo i dopolneniia O. N. Trubacheva. Pod red. i s predisl. B. A. Larina. Moskva, Progress, 1964–73. 4v.　　**AD677**

Added title page: *Russisches etymologisches Wörterbuch.*

A Russian translation of the Heidelberg edition (below) with additions and corrections (by the Russian editors) indicated.　　　PG2580.V316

———— Russisches etymologisches Wörterbuch. Heidelberg, C. Winter, [1950–58]. 3v. (Indogermanische Bibliothek. II Reihe, Wörterbücher) **AD678**

Issued in parts.

A dictionary of importance for the etymology of the Russian language, its dialects, and foreign words used in Russian. Bibliography of sources, v.1, p.xi–xliii. PG2580.V3

Synonyms

Aleksandrova, Zinaida Evgen'evna. Slovar' sinonimov russkogo iazyka. Pod red. L. A. Chesko. 3-e stereotip. Moskva, Izd. Sovetskaia Entsiklopediia, 1971. 600p. **AD679**

1st ed. 1968.
About 9,000 terms. PG2591.A43

Slovar' sinonimov russkogo iazyka. V 2-kh t.[Avt. vved. i glav. red. A. P. Evgen'eva]. Leningrad, Nauka, 1970–71. 2v. **AD680**

At head of title: Akademiia Nauk SSSR. Institut Russkogo Iazyka. PG2591.S6

Slovar' sinonimov; spravochnoe posobie. Leningrad, Izdatel'stvo "Nauka," 1975. 648p. **AD681**

At head of title: Akademiia Nauk SSSR. Institut Russkogo IAzyka.

Editor, A. P. Evgen'eva.

Evgen'eva is also the editor of the more comprehensive *Slovar' sinonimov russkogo iazyka* (above). PG2591.S58

Usage

Jaszczun, Wasyl and **Krynski, Szymon.** A dictionary of Russian idioms and colloquialisms; 2,200 expressions with examples. [Pittsburgh], Univ. of Pittsburgh Pr., [1967]. 102p. **AD682**

Russian idioms with English definitions. PG2460.J3

Kunin, Aleksandr Vladimirovich. Anglo-russkii frazeologicheskii slovar'. Izd. 4-e, pererab. i dop. Moskva, Russkii Iazyk, 1984. 942p. **AD683**

Added t.p. in English: *English-Russian phraseological dictionary.*
1st ed. 1955.

About 20,000 English idioms with Russian equivalents. Examples from English sources are given with Russian translation to illustrate usage in context. PE1129.S4K8

Bibliography

Aav, Yrjö. Russian dictionaries: dictionaries and glossaries printed in Russia, 1627–1917. Zug, Switz., Inter Documentation, [1977]. 196p. **AD684**

Lists "general dictionaries and vocabularies published separately or printed in Russian newspapers, periodicals and series in Russia before the year 1918."—*Pref.* Technical and specialized dictionaries are not included. Z2505.D6A18

Akademiia Nauk SSSR. Institut Russkogo IAzyka. Slovari, izdannye v SSSR; bibliograficheskii ukazatel', 1918–1962. [Sostaviteli: M. G. Izhevskaia i dr. Redaktory: V. V. Veselitskii, N. P. Debets] Moskva, Nauka, 1966. 231p. **AD685**

A bibliography of Russian dictionaries and bilingual dictionaries of which one language is Russian. Classed arrangement within language groupings. Author and language indexes.
Z7004.D5A55

Kaufman, Isaak Mikhailovich. Terminologicheskie slovari; bibliografiia. Moskva, Sovetskaia Rossiia, 1961. 419p. **AD686**

An annotated bibliography of glossaries and subject dictionaries, primarily Russian, published from the 18th century through 1961.

Classified arrangement, with alphabetical indexes for authors and titles, and subjects. The 1,755 entries include lists of specialized terminology in periodical literature, as well as separately published dictionaries. Z7004.D5K3

Zalewski, Wojciech. Russian-English dictionaries with aids for translators; a selected bibliography. [2d ed.] N.Y., Russica, 1981. 101p. ("Russica" bibliography ser., 1) **AD687**

1st ed. 1976.

Attempts to include "all significant Russian-English dictionaries published after World War II. A rigorous selection has been applied to general bilingual dictionaries, while subject bilingual dictionaries have been emphasized."—*Introd.* Brief descriptive annotations for most items. Z2505.D6Z34

Samoan

Milner, George Bertram. Samoan dictionary: Samoan-English, English-Samoan. London, N.Y., Oxford Univ. Pr., 1966. 464p. **AD688**

A new work intended to "serve as an up-to-date standard work of reference in matters of spelling and translation."—*Pref.*
PL6501.Z5M5

Sanskrit

Apte, Vaman Shivaram. The practical Sanskrit-English dictionary. Eds.-in-chief: P. K. Gode and C. G. Karve. Rev. and enl. ed. Poona, Prasad Prakashan, 1957–59. 3v. **AD689**

1st ed. 1890.

A revision of the earlier text with the addition of new words, changes of meaning, and more quotations. PK933.A65

Böhtlingk, Otto von and **Roth, Rudolph.** Sanskrit-Wörterbuch hrsg. von der Kaiserlichen Akademie der Wissenschaften. St. Petersburg, Buchdr. der K. Akademie der Wissenschaften, 1855–75. 7v. **AD690**

"Verbesserungen und Nachträge zu Theil 1–5," Bd.5, col. 941–1678; "Verbesserungen und Nachträge zum ganzen Werke," Bd.7, col.[1685]–1822. PK935.G5B7

Böhtlingk, Otto von. Sanskrit-Wörterbuch in kürzerer Fassung. St. Petersburg, Buchdr. von der K. Akademie der Wissenschaften, 1879–89. 7v. in 1. **AD691**

———— ———— Nachträge . . . bearb. von Richard Schmidt. Leipzig, Harrassowitz, 1928. 398p. (Repr.: Graz, Akademische Druck- u. Verlagsanstalt, 1959. 7v. in 3)

PK935.G5B73

An encyclopaedic dictionary of Sanskrit on historical principles. Gen. ed., A. M. Ghatage. Poona, Deccan College Postgraduate and Research Institute, 1976–82. v.1–3¹. (In progress) **AD692**

v.1–2 issued in 3 pts. each.
Contents: v.1–3¹, A–Adhim.

A work (in progress since 1948) "based on an entirely new reading of the original texts and a fresh extraction of the material without relying on the earlier lexicons."—*Pref.*

A review by J. C. Wright of the first two published parts in the *Bulletin* of the London University School of Oriental and African Studies calls this "a monumental glossary which offers fuller concordances of Vedic and classical Sanskrit than have been available heretofore, together with a massive and long overdue attack upon the medieval literature, including epigraphy and traditional grammar, both fairly fully exploited for the first time."—*v.41, p.388 (1978).* PK933.E5

Mayrhofer, Manfred. Kurzgefasstes etymologisches Wörterbuch des Altindischen. A concise etymological Sanskrit dictionary. Heidelberg, C. Winter, 1953–80. 4v. (Indogermanische Bibliothek. II. Reihe, Wörterbücher)   **AD693**

Issued in parts.

A Sanskrit-German etymological dictionary. The basic language is German, but all Sanskrit catchwords are translated also into English, the substance of the introduction is summarized in English, and the list of abbreviations is in German and English. v.4 contains indexes in various languages.

Monier-Williams, *Sir* **Monier.** A dictionary, English and Sanskrit. Lucknow, Akhila Bharatiya Sanskrit Parishad, 1957. 859p.   **AD694**

"1st ed. 1851; reprinted lithographically in India from sheets of the 1st ed. by Bureau of Agricultural Information, Uttar Pradesh, Lucknow, 1957."—*verso of title page.*   PK933.M5

—— A Sanskrit-English dictionary etymologically and philologically arranged with special reference to cognate Indo-European languages . . . New ed., greatly enl. and improved, with the collaboration of Prof. E. Leumann . . . Prof. C. Cappeller, and other scholars. Oxford, Clarendon Pr., 1899. 1333p.   **AD695**

Various reprintings.

Sanskrit-English, with etymologies and references to the literature.   PK933.M6

Serbo-Croatian

Jugoslavenska Akademija Znanosti i Umjetnosti. Rječnik hrvatskoga ili srpskoga jezika. Obraduje D. Daničić. U Zagrebu, U Knížarnici L. Hartmana, 1880–1976. 23v.   **AD696**

Issued in parts.

Editors vary; publisher varies.

The standard dictionary of the Yugoslavian Academy. Includes specialized usage, e.g., law, and includes extensive references to dictionaries and other sources.   PG1374.R5

Bilingual

Benson, Morton. An English-SerboCroatian dictionary. [Philadelphia], Univ. of Pennsylvania Pr., 1979. 669p.   **AD697**

Basic vocabulary is standard, contemporary English, including important scientific and technical terms. Aims to present "the American variant of English as reflected in the speech of educated Americans and in the press."—*Introd.* Forms a companion to Benson's *SerboCroatian-English dictionary* (below).   PG1376.B38

—— SerboCroatian-English dictionary. [Philadelphia], Univ. of Pennsylvania Pr., 1971. 807p.   **AD698**

Added title-page in Serbo-Croatian: Srpskohrvatsko-Engleski rečnik.

About 60,000 entries. "An attempt has been made to limit the scope . . . to the vocabulary used in the speech of educated Yugoslavs and in the daily press. Important scientific and technical terms are included."—*Introd.* A careful and scholarly work.   PG1376.B4

Bogadek, Francis Aloysius. New English-Croatian and Croatian-English dictionary. 3d ed. enl. and corr. N.Y., Hafner, [1944]. 2v. in 1. (Repr. 1949, 1957)   **AD699**

1st ed. 1926.   PG1377.B72

Drvọdelić, Milan. Englesko-hrvatṣki ili srpski rječnik. Preradio Željko Bujas. 5. izd. Zagreb, Školska Knjiga, 1978. 880p.   **AD700**

Added title page: English-Croatian or Serbian dictionary.

1st ed. 1954 had title: *Englesko-hrvatski rječnik;* 2d–3d eds. (1962–70), *Englesko-hrvatskosrpski rječnik.*

A companion work is: PG1377.D77

—— Hrvatsko ili srpsko engleski rječnik. Preradio Željko Bujas. 4. izd. Zagreb, Školska Knjiga, 1978. 847p.   **AD701**

Added title page: Croatian or Serbian-English dictionary.

1st ed. 1953 had title: *Hrvatsko-engleski rječnik.*

Petrovic, Ilija M. Praktičan englesko-srpski rečnik sa označenim izgovorom i akcentom engleskih reči i dodatim spiskom ličnik i geografskih imena. 2. izd. Beograd, Prosveta, 1951. 770p.   **AD704**

Added title page in English: A practical dictionary of the English and Serbian languages.

English subtitle: Designed to give the pronunciation and accent of English words, containing also an appendix of personal and geographical names.

1st ed. 1933.   PG1376.P4

Abbreviations

Plamenatz, Ilija P. Yugoslav abbreviations; a selective list. 2d enl. ed. Wash., Slavic and Central European Div., Reference Dept., Lib. of Congress, 1962. 198p.   **AD705**

1st ed.1959.

"Intended . . . to include the more common abbreviations which have come into use since World War II, especially names of government institutions and official bodies, industrial and trade establishments and the more important newspapers and periodicals. . . ."—*Introd.*

The main list contains nearly 3,000 abbreviations; the 2d ed. adds some 200 newly identified abbreviations in an appendix.

PG1386.P55

Shona

Hannan, M. Standard Shona dictionary. 2d ed. [Salisbury, Rhodesia Literature Bureau, 1974] 996p.   **AD706**

1st ed. 1959.

"Comp. for the Rhodesia Literature Bureau."—*t.p.*

A Shona-English dictionary with an English index of words that appear in the definitions.   PL8681.4.H3

Slovak

Slovenská Akadémia Vied. Ústav Slovenského Jazyka. Slovník slovenského jazyka. [Vedecký redaktor: Štefan Peciar] Bratislava, Vydavatel'stvo Slovenskej Akadémie Vied, 1959–65. 5v.   **AD707**

A Slovakian dictionary compiled by the Academy.

PG5375.S55

Bilingual

Hrobak, Philip Anthony. Hrobak's English-Slovak dictionary; unabridged. [Rev. 2d ed.] N.Y., R. Speller, [1965]. 702p.   **AD708**

Previous ed. 1944.

A reprint with only a few pages of additions.   PG5379.H7

Simko, Ján. Anglicko-slovenský slovník. 3. vyd. Bratislava, SPN, 1971. 1443p.   **AD709**

1st ed. 1967.   PG5379.S5

Vilikovská, Julia and **Vilikovský, Pavol.** Slovensko-anglický slovník. 4. vyd. Bratislava, SPN, 1984. 524p.   **AD710**

Added title page: Slovak-English dictionary.
1st ed. 1959.   PG5379.S63

Slovenian

Bezlaj, France. Etimološki slovar slovenskega jezika. Ljubljana, Slovenska Akademija Znanosti in Umetnosti, Institut za Slovenski Jezik, 1976–82. v.1–2. (In progress)   **AD711**

Contents: v.1–2, A–O.
A scholarly work with citations to sources. Bibliography of works cited, v.1, p.ix–xxvi.   PG1883.B4

Slovenska Akademija Znanosti in Umetnosti, Ljubljana. Slovenski pravopis. [Sest. Anton Bajec et al. Nova izdaja] Ljubljana, Državna Založba Slovenije, 1962. 1054p.   **AD712**

The standard Slovenian dictionary, superseding the 1950 edition. Contains some 100,000 words, two thirds more than the earlier work.   PG1888.S5

——— **Inštitut za Slovenski Jezik.** Slovar slovenskega knjižnega jezika. [Glavni uredniški odbor: Anton Bajec i dr.] Ljubljana, Slovenska Akademija Znanosti in Umetnosti, Inštitut za Slovenski Jezik; Državna Založba Slovenije, 1970–79. v.1–3. (In progress)   **AD713**

Contents: v.1–3, A–Pren.
A new and scholarly work.   PG1888.S5

Bilingual

Grad, Anton, Škerlj, Ružena and **Vitorovič, Nada.** Veliki angleško-slovenski slovar. Ljubljana, Državna Založba Slovenije, 1984. 1377p.   **AD714**

Added t.p. in English: The great English-Slovene dictionary.
Various printings.
Includes pronunciation of the English words.
A small, "two way," dictionary is Daša Komac's *Angleško-slovenski in slovensko-angleški slovar; English-Slovene and Slovene-English dictionary* (Ljubljana, Cankarjeva Založba, 1981. 787p.).
                                               PG1891.G73

Kotnik, Janko. Slovensko-angleški slovar. 8. izd. Ljubljana, Državna Založba Slovenije, 1978. 831p.   **AD715**

Added title page: Slovene-English dictionary.
1st ed. 1945 had title: *Slovenian-English dictionary.*
                                               PG1891.K6

Somali

Abraham, Roy Clive. English-Somali dictionary. London, Univ. of London Pr., [1967]. 208p.   **AD716**

English vocabulary in alphabetic order, but for compactness, cross references used liberally, with Somali equivalents given under the related word to which reader is directed. Standard orthography used.   PJ2533.A18

——— Somali-English dictionary. [London], Univ. of London Pr., [1966]. 332p.   **AD717**

Approximately 8,000 entries, in transcription, with tone indicated by numbers. Intended for the English-language speaker. Illustrative sentences. A grammatical outline is included.   PJ2533.A2

Spanish

Academia Española, Madrid. Diccionario histórico de la lengua española. Seminario de Lexicografía: Director, Julio Casares . . . Madrid, 1960–83. v.1–2⁵. (In progress)
                                               AD718

Contents: pts.1–2⁵, A–Alzo.
A new attempt at a major historical dictionary of the language to replace the earlier unfinished work with the same title (Madrid, Hernando, 1933–36. v.1–2, A–Cevilla).
Each word is treated in scholarly detail, with variations in meaning illustrated by numerous quotations, chronologically listed. Citations are given to exact source. Extensive list of works consulted.

——— Diccionario manual e ilustrado de la lengua española. [2.ed.] Madrid, Ed. Espasa-Calpe, 1950. 1572p. il.
                                               AD719

First published 1927; various printings.   PC4625.A34

Alonso Pedraz, Martin. Enciclopedia del idioma; diccionario histórico y moderno de la lengua española (siglos xii al xx), etimológico, tecnológico, regional e hispano-americano. Madrid, Aguilar, 1958. 3v.   **AD720**

Intended to be more comprehensive in number of words listed but less detailed in treatment of individual words than the Academia Española's *Diccionario histórico* (AD718). For many words, treatment is full, giving etymology, morphology, definitions with citations of usage, examples of phrasal combinations, and dates of appearances in early dictionaries. For other words for which there are no new or specialized meanings, the standard definitions from the Academia's *Diccionario* are often used almost verbatim.
                                               PC4667.A4

Diccionario de la lengua española. Real Academia Española. 20a ed. Madrid, La Academia, 1984. 2v. (1416p.)
                                               AD721

1st ed. 1726–39 had title: Diccionario de la lengua castellana.
A standard work which includes etymologies. This edition revised and reset; words from the supplement to the 19th ed. (1970) have been incorporated into the alphabetical sequence.   PC4625.A3

Vox; diccionario general ilustrado de la lengua española. Prólogos de Ramón Menéndez Pidal y Samuel Gili Gaya; revisión por Samuel Gili Gaya. 6. reimpresión. Barcelona, Bibliograf, 1980. 1711p. il.   **AD722**

1st ed. 1945.
A good general dictionary which includes etymologies, synonyms, etc.   PC4625.V6

Bilingual

Cassell's Spanish-English English-Spanish dictionary. Diccionario Español-Inglés Inglés-Español. Completely rev. by Anthony Gooch [and] Angel García de Paredes. London, Cassell; N.Y., Macmillan, [1978]. 1109p.   **AD723**

1st ed. 1959.
A fairly thorough revision of this desk dictionary. A review by Roger Wright in *Bulletin of Hispanic studies* (56:325) notes that the English-Spanish section is greatly revised and much improved, demonstrating "a care for accuracy and concern to be useful." The Spanish-English part (which was the superior section in the 1st ed.) shows less revision. He concludes that the revision represents a great improvement but contends that the approach used in the *Collins* dictionary (AD730) is "more practical" and that it remains the first choice of the two.   PC4640.C35

Cuyás, Arturo. Appleton's New Cuyás English-Spanish and Spanish-English dictionary. Rev. and enl. by Lewis E. Brett (part 1) and Helen S. Eaton (part 2) with the assistance of Walter Beveraggi-Allende. Revision ed., Catherine B. Avery. 5th ed. rev. N.Y., Appleton-Century-Crofts, 1972. 698p., 589p.   **AD724**

Added title-page in Spanish.
1st ed. 1928.
A standard desk dictionary. In this latest revision the compilers have "added new words from all fields of interest; dropped those words that are no longer of frequent use; and modified those that have acquired new meanings of more precise equivalents in Spanish or in English."—*Pref.*   PC4640.C8

García-Pelayo y Gross, Ramón and **Durand, Micheline.** Gran diccionario moderno: español/inglés [y English/Spanish] Larousse. México, D.F. [etc.], Ediciones Larousse, [1984]. 1542p. **AD725**

Introductory matter in Spanish and English.

An extensive new work in the Larousse tradition. Its principal aim "is to gather together all the words, classic and *modern,* which go to make up the rich Anglo-Hispanic cultural heritage. Special care has been taken with the new technical and scientific terms progress brings, and which appear in our newspapers and periodicals and on radio and television every day. Equally, attention has been devoted to neologisms and foreign words in common use and to more recent colloquialisms."—*Foreword.* Pronunciation is indicated in the English-Spanish part. Numerous examples of usage are given. Americanisms appear frequently in both parts: "Amer." designates Latin American words or phrases, "U.S." precedes North American ones.

A shorter version has been published as *Diccionario general español-inglés [y English-Spanish],* ed. by Ramón García-Pelayo y Gross (Paris, etc., Ediciones Larousse, 1984. 431p., 499p.).

Martínez Amador, Emilio M. Standard English-Spanish and Spanish-English dictionary . . . 3. ed. Boston, Heath; Barcelona, Ed. Ramón Sopena, [1958]. 2139p. **AD726**

Added title page in Spanish (with Barcelona imprint).

1st ed. 1946.

Subtitle: Each part contains over 60,000 entries including thousands of modern colloquialisms, idioms, Americanisms, and technical terms; full lists of geographical terms, proper names, common abbreviations, and tables of weights and measures in both languages, together with introductions on pronunciation for both English and Spanish.

Raventós, Margaret Hambleton. A modern Spanish dictionary. London, English Universities Pr., [1953]. 1v., various pagings. **AD727**

Includes many new terms; does not generally include Latin-American variations of words. Special lists of geographical names with different spellings in the two languages, proper names, abbreviations, weights and measures, and currency. PC4640.R3

Simon and Schuster's International dictionary. Diccionario internacional Simon and Schuster. English/Spanish, Spanish/English. Tana de Gámez, ed. in chief. N.Y., Simon and Schuster, [1973]. 1605p. **AD728**

Prefatory matter in Spanish and English.

A new desk dictionary with more than 200,000 entries. Includes scientific and technical terms, vulgarisms, loan words. Extensive use of illustrative phrases to indicate usage and idioms. Numerous proper and place-names and abbreviations are listed in the main alphabetical sequences. Pronunciation of English entry words is indicated according to International Phonetic Alphabet, with distinction made where American and British pronunciation differs; distinction is also made between American and British usage.

PC4640.S48

Simon and Schuster's Concise international dictionary: English/Spanish, Spanish/English. Tana de Gámez, ed. in chief. N.Y., Simon and Schuster, [1975]. 1379p. **AD729**

Added title page in Spanish: *Diccionario conciso internacional Simon and Schuster.*

Introductory matter in English and Spanish.

An abridgment of the 1973 *Simon and Schuster's International dictionary* (above), with the addition of some new material.

PC4640.S48

Smith, Colin. Collins Spanish-English, English-Spanish dictionary. London, Collins, [1971]. 602p., 640p. **AD730**

Added title page in Spanish: Collins diccionario Español-Inglés, Inglés-Español.

Aims to "embrace no more than the typical *parole* or personal language of the average educated English speaker of 1970, and that of the corresponding speaker of Spanish."—*Introd.* A superior work in the desk-size field. PC4640.S595

The University of Chicago Spanish dictionary. 3d rev. and enl. ed. Comp. by Carlos Castillo and Otto F. Bond. Rev. by D. Lincoln Canfield. Chicago, Univ. of Chicago Pr., [1977]. 488p. **AD731**

Added title page in Spanish.

Subtitle: A new concise Spanish-English and English-Spanish dictionary of words and phrases basic to the written and spoken languages of today, plus a list of 1000 idioms and sayings, with variants and English equivalents.

1st ed. 1948.

Intended for "the American learner of Spanish and the Spanish-speaking learner of English, with special reference to New World usages as found in the United States and in Spanish America."—*Foreword.* PC4640.U5

Velázquez de la Cadena, Mariano. New revised Velázquez Spanish and English dictionary. Comp. . . . with Edward Gray and Juan L. Iribas; newly revised by Ida Navarro Hinojosa, Manuel Blanco-González and R. J. Nelson. New rev. 1985 ed. Piscataway, N.J., New Century, [1985]. 698p., 34p., 788p. **AD732**

First published 1852 under title *A pronouncing dictionary of the Spanish and English languages;* frequently reprinted with revisions. 1973 ed. had title *New pronouncing dictionary of the Spanish and English languages.*

A useful and authoritative Spanish-English dictionary for general purposes. This edition includes a "1985 supplement" to the Spanish-English part comprising "Contemporary additions of scientific, technological, commercial, and colloquial terms to maintain the authority of this work for accurate modern Spanish as used in Latin America and Spain."—*Suppl., p.1.* PC4640.V55

Vox: new college Spanish and English dictionary. English-Spanish/Spanish-English. Comp. by Carlos F. MacHale and the editors of Biblograf, S.A. North American ed. prep. by the editors of National Textbook Co. Lincolnwood, Ill., Nat. Textbook Co., [1984]. 1456p. maps. **AD733**

1st ed. 1966.

Various grammatical explanations and rules are inserted in boxes placed within the alphabetical sequence of both the English-Spanish and Spanish-English sections. Many examples of usage; numerous appendixes. PC4640.V68

Etymology

Coromimas, Juan. Diccionario crítico etimológico de la lengua castellana. Madrid, Gredos, [1954–57]. 4v. (Biblioteca románica hispánica. 5. Diccionarios etimológicos) (Repr.: Berne, Francke, 1970) **AD734**

A comprehensive etymological dictionary giving dates of origin of words, with quotations showing usages and derivations. Covers the languages of both Spain and Spanish America and includes the ancient languages, such as pre-Roman Iberian and vulgar Arabic, as well as dialects and Latin-American influences.

v.4 includes *Adiciones y rectificaciones,* p.897–1092, and *Indices,* p.1093–1224.

Coromimas has also compiled the *Breve diccionario etimológico de la lengua castellana* (3. ed. Madrid, Grados, 1973. 627p.)

PC4580.C59

Garcia de Diego, Vicente. Diccionario etimológico español e hispánico. Madrid, Ed. S.A.E.T.A., [1954]. 1069p. **AD735**

PC4580.G33

Synonyms

Benot y Rodríguez, Eduardo. Diccionario de ideas afines y elementos de tecnología. Con un prólogo especial para la edición argentina, de Alfonso López Miranda, y un apéndice con las 3000 voces nuevas incluídas en la última edición del Diccionario de la Academia española. Buenos Aires, Ed. Anaconda, [1940]. 1515p. **AD736**

A classified dictionary of synonyms modeled on Roget's *Thesaurus* (AD108).

———— ———— 2. ed. popular. 1942. 1417p.

PC4591.B4

Casares y Sánchez, Julio. Diccionario ideológico de la lengua española; desde la idea a la palabra, desde la palabra a la idea. 2. ed., corr., aumentada y puesta al día. Barcelona, Ed. G. Gili, 1959. 1xxv p., 482p., 887p. **AD737**

First published 1942. Frequently reprinted (3. tirada 1966).
Contents: pt.1, Parte sinóptica; pt.2, Parte analógica; pt.3, Parte alfabética.
Pt.2 consists of lists of words grouped by association of ideas; pt.3 is an alphabetical dictionary defining these words. PC4625.C3

Usage

Gerrard, Arthur Bryson. Cassell's Beyond the dictionary in Spanish; a handbook of everyday usage. 2d ed., rev. and enl. N.Y., Funk & Wagnalls, [1972]. 226p. **AD738**

1st ed. 1953. A "4th ed." (London, Cassell, 1967. 160p.) by Gerrard and José de Heras Heras had subtitle "a handbook of colloquial usage."
Intended as an aid toward bridging the gap between literary and spoken language. Similar to the Levieux volume for French idiomatic usage (AD335). PC4445.G4

Moliner, María. Diccionario de uso del español. Madrid, Editorial Gredos, [1966–67]. 2v. (Biblioteca románica hispánica. 5. Diccionarios [5]) **AD739**

Various printings.
Synonyms and related terms are given; derivation is indicated for many words. PC4625.M6

Medieval–18th century

Boggs, Ralph Steele [and others]. Tentative dictionary of medieval Spanish. Chapel Hill, N.C., 1946. 2v. (537p.) **AD740**

A preliminary work, issued in multigraph form, sponsored by the Old Spanish Group of the Modern Language Association. Useful until a complete dictionary for this period is published.

Gili y Gaya, Samuel. Tesoro lexicográfico (1492–1726). Madrid, Consejo Superior de Investigaciones Científicas, Patronato "Menendez Pelayo" Instituto "Antonio de Nebrija," 1947–[57]. Fasc.1–4. **AD741**

Contents: fasc.1–4, A–E. No more published.
The completed work was to have included the combined entries from all available dictionaries of the Spanish language, both published and in manuscript, which appeared between 1492 and 1726. All definitions and translations for each word are listed chronologically by first appearance. PC4620.G5

Bibliography

Espinosa Elerick, María Luz. Annotated bibliography of technical and specialized dictionaries in Spanish-Spanish and Spanish-English, with commentary. Troy, N.Y., Whitston, 1982. 100p. **AD742**

Title also in Spanish.
An alphabetical listing of 86 Spanish and bilingual and polyglot technical dictionaries of which one of the languages is Spanish. Full descriptions and annotations appear in both Spanish and English in parallel columns. Index of descriptors. Z2695.D6E43

Fabbri, Maurizio. A bibliography of Hispanic dictionaries: Catalan, Galician, Spanish, Spanish in Latin America and

the Philippines. Imola, Galeati, 1979. 381p. (Collana bibliografica, 1) **AD743**

Lists some 3,500 "dictionaries, vocabularies, glossaries and word-lists of a general character—synonyms, etymologies, homonyms, foreign words, dialects, slangs, proverbs, verbs, etc.—as well as of texts dealing with technical and scientific micro-languages and the highly specialized terminology of these fields."—*Pref.* Separate sections for monolingual (subdivided for dialects, etymology, etc.), bilingual, and polyglot dictionaries. Arranged by author within sections. Appendix: "A bibliography of Basque dictionaries." Author, language, and subject indexes. Z2695.D6F32

Indexes

Romera-Navarro, Miguel. Registro de lexicografía hispánica. Madrid, Consejo Superior de Investigaciones Científicas, 1951. 1013p. **AD744**

Supplement to *Revista de filología española* (Anejo LIV).
An alphabetical index of 50,000 Spanish words, with 80,000 references to etymologies, linguistic studies, etc., in monographs, treatises, and scholarly journals. PC4580.R75

Regional and dialect

For regional dictionaries consult Collison (AD1); *Guide to reference books,* 7th ed., p.249–50.

Galván, Roberto A. and **Teschner, Richard V.** El diccionario del español chicano. The dictionary of Chicano Spanish. Rev. ed. Silver Spring, Md., Inst. of Modern Languages, Inc., [1977]. 144p. **AD745**

1st ed. (1975) had title *El diccionario del español de Tejas.*
Contains almost 8,000 words and phrases, some with citations, from conversational Spanish of Texas, California, Arizona, New Mexico, Colorado, and Florida, which are "not included, as yet, in the more readily available reference lexicons."—*Pref.* Not intended as a complete dictionary, but as a supplement to standard dictionaries of Spanish. PC4829.T4G3

Sumerian

See Assyro-Babylonian.

Swahili

Inter-Territorial Language (Swahili) Committee to the East African Dependencies. A standard English-Swahili [Swahili-English] dictionary (founded on Madan's English-Swahili dictionary), [prep.] under the direction of the late Frederick Johnson. London, Oxford Univ. Pr., H. Milford, 1939. 2v. **AD746**

Various reprintings. The two parts are also published separately (i.e., Swahili-English, 548p.; English-Swahili, 635p.).
A revision of the dictionaries by Arthur C. Madan and Bp. Edward Steere.
Ludwig Krapf's *Dictionary of the Swahili language,* first published 1882, has also been reprinted at intervals (e.g., N.Y., Negro Universities Pr., 1969. 433p.).

Kamusi ya Kiswahili sanifu. Imetungwa na kuhaririwa katika Sehemu ya Kamusi ya Taasisi ya Uchunguzi wa Kiswahili, Chuo Kikuu cha Dar es Salaam. Wanajopo, Hamisi Akida [et al.]. Dar es Salaam, Oxford Univ. Pr., 1981. 325p. **AD746a**

"A standard Swahili-Swahili dictionary."—*verso of t.p.*

PL8703.K34

Rechenbach, Charles William. Swahili-English dictionary. Wash., Catholic Univ. of Amer. Pr., 1967. 641p. **AD747**

A comprehensive dictionary intended for speakers of English. Built on the *Standard Swahili-English* (AD746), bringing the vocabulary up-to-date and including extensive developments since World War II. Includes loan words and lists of derivative words.

PL8703.R4

Snoxall, R. A. A concise English-Swahili dictionary. Kamusi ya Kiingereza-Kiswahili. [Repr., rev.] London, Oxford Univ. Pr., [1961]. 325p. il.   **AD748**

Intended for speakers of Swahili. About 8,000 entries and illustrations. Phonetic transcription, part of speech, level of style and equivalent Swahili word or sentence given.   PL8703.S6

Swedish

Illustrerad svensk ordbok. Redaktör: Bertil Molde. Medarbetare: Daniel Andreae [et al.]. 3. revid. uppl. Stockholm, Natur och Kultur, [1964]. 1917p. il.   **AD749**

1st ed. 1955. Various printings.
A modern Swedish dictionary with line drawings.   PD5625.I4

Östergren, Olof. Nusvensk ordbok. Stockholm, Wahlström & Widstrand, 1919–72. 10v.   **AD750**

Issued in 127pts., 1915–72.
An important dictionary of modern Swedish.   PD5625.O4

Söderwall, Knut Fredrik. Ordbok öfver svenska medeltidsspråket. Lund, Berlingska Boktryckeri, 1884–1918. 2v. in 3. (Samlingar utgifna af Svenska Fornskrift-Sällskapet)
AD751

Issued in 24 pts.

——— ——— Supplement. 1925–73. Hft.1–35. 1149p.

A dictionary of the Swedish of medieval times.   PD5876.S6

Svenska Akademien. Ordbok öfver svenska språket. Lund, Lindstedt, 1898–1983. v.1–29¹. (In progress)   **AD752**

Contents: v.1–29¹, A–Spelman.
The great Academy dictionary of modern Swedish, giving etymologies, references to the literature with dates, etc.

——— ——— Supplement 1–2. 1899–1975.

The supplements offer bibliographies of sources cited in the dictionary.   PD5625.S8

Bilingual

Kärre, Karl. Engelsk-svensk ordbok: skolupplaga. Under medverkan av Grenville Grove. 3. omarb. uppl. Nacka, Esselte Studium, 1978. 973p.   **AD753**

1st ed. 1935.
A standard work.   PD5640.K3

Prisma's Modern Swedish-English and English-Swedish dictionary. [1st American ed.] Minneapolis, Univ. of Minnesota Pr.; Stockholm, Bokförlaget Prisma, [1984]. 542p., 394p.
AD754

Swedish-English part, 1st ed. 1970; English-Swedish part, 1st ed. 1964. Swedish ed. had title: *Modern engelsk-svensk och svensk-engelsk ordbok.*
Indicates pronunciation and stress. Emphasis on modern vocabulary, with inclusion of terms from science and technology, business, etc. About 52,000 entry words in the Swedish-English part.
PD5640.M564

Svensk-engelsk ordbok. Leksikonred. chef: Rudolf Santesson. Nacka, Esselte Studium, 1980. 979p.   **AD755**

First published 1968.
A companion work is:

Stora engelsk-svenska ordboken. A comprehensive English-Swedish dictionary. [Red., Rudolf Santesson, et al.] [Nacka], Esselte Studium, 1980. 1071p.   **AD756**

PD5640.S8

Etymology

Hellquist, Elof. Svensk etymologisk ordbok. Ny omarb. ach utv. uppl. Lund, C. W. K. Gleerup, [1939]. 2v.   **AD757**

Issued in 18 pts., 1935–39. A reprint of this edition with minor changes and corrections was published as a 3d ed., 1948. (Repr. 1957, 1970)
A standard work including place- and personal names, with etymologies and cognate words in various western European languages.   PD5580.H42

Synonyms

Dalin, Anders Fredrik. Svenska språkets synonymer. 7. uppl. Granskad av Ingrid Schöier. Föregående uppl. granskad av N. Gösta Bergman. Stockholm, Beckman, 1971. 432p.
AD758

1st ed. 1870.
Words are arranged in groups by association, with definitions showing discrimination in meanings.   PD5591.D3

Wessén, Elias. Vara ord, deras uttal och ursprung. Kortfattad etymologisk ordbok. Stockholm, Svenska Bokförlaget, Norstedts, 1961. 502p. (Nämnden för svensk språkvåd)
AD759

A revised and enlarged edition of Lars Levander and E. Wessén's *Vara ord* (Stockholm, Bonnier, 1932).
An alphabetically arranged dictionary of synonyms.

Syriac

Brockelmann, Carl. Lexicon Syriacum. Ed. 2, aucta et emendata. Halis Saxonum, Niemeyer, 1928. 930p.   **AD760**

Issued in parts, 1923–28.
1st ed. 1895.   PJ5493.B7

Goshen-Gottstein, Moshe Henry. A Syriac-English glossary. With etymological notes. Based on Brockelmann's Syriac chrestomathy. Wiesbaden, Harrassowitz, 1970. 95p.
AD761

Intended for students of Semitics who do not know Latin or German.   PJ5491.G6

Oraham, Alexander Joseph. Oraham's Dictionary of the stabilized and enriched Assyrian language and English. [Chicago, Consolidated Pr. (Assyrian Pr. of America), 1943] 576p.   **AD762**

Added title page and preface in Syriac.
Not a dictionary of classical Assyrian but of that language sometimes called by scholars "Nestorian Syriac"; includes "the ancient, medieval and the modern literary phases of this language." —*Foreword.*   PJ5491.O7

Payne Smith, Robert, ed. Thesaurus syriacus, collegerunt Stephanus M. Quatremere, Georgius Henricus Bernstein [et al.]. Oxford, e Typ. Clarendoniano, 1879–1901. 2v. (Repr.: Hildsheim, Olms, 1981. 2v., plus suppl.)   **AD763**

——— ——— Supplement . . . collected and arranged by his daughter, J. P. Margoliouth. Oxford, Clarendon Pr., 1927. 345p.

PJ5493.P3

——— Compendious Syriac dictionary, founded upon the Thesaurus syriacus of R. Payne Smith, ed. by J. Payne Smith (Mrs. Margoliouth). Oxford, Clarendon Pr., 1903. 626p. **AD764**

Syriac-English.
An abridgment of the *Thesaurus* (above). PJ5491.P3

Tagalog

Ramos, Teresita V. Tagalog dictionary. Honolulu, Univ. of Hawaii Pr., 1971. 330p. **AD765**

Tagalog-English only. About 4,000 entries, representing "the high frequency words that are necessary for a non-Tagalog speaker to be able to communicate effectively in day-by-day conversational situations."—*Introd.* PL6056.R3

Santos, Vito C. Pilipino-English dictionary, with an introduction by Teodoro A. Agoncillo. Rev. ed. Metro Manila, Philippines, National Book Store, 1983. 2675p. **AD766**

1st ed. 1978.
About 68,000 entries, including terms from local dialects and loan-words from Spanish, English, Malay, etc. Syllabication is indicated, as are accents and parts of speech; synonyms are frequently given. PL6056.S34

Tamil

Gnana Prakasar, S. An etymological and comparative lexicon of the Tamil language . . . with indexes of words quoted from Indo-European languages. [Ceylon], Thirumakal Pr., 1938–46. v.1[1-6]. **AD767**

Tamil-English-Tamil.
Etymological and philological treatment of Tamil and other Dravidian dialects. PL4759.G58

English-Tamil dictionary. Chief ed.: A. Chidambaranatha Chettiar. With a foreword by A. Lakshmanaswami Mudaliar. [Madras], Univ. of Madras, 1963–65. 3v. **AD768**
PL4756.E55

Madras. University. Tamil lexicon, published under the authority of the University of Madras. [Madras], Univ. of Madras, 1924–36. 6v. **AD769**

Issued in 24 pts., with various imprints, 1924–36.
Gives transliterations and English translations for more than 100,000 Tamil words. All previous dictionaries in the language were drawn upon, and many outstanding scholars collaborated in the compilation. Terminology of special fields—e.g., law, architecture, medicine—is included. The outstanding dictionary of the language. Does not include etymologies. PL4756.M3

——— ——— Supplement. 1938–39. 2v.

Thai

Haas, Mary Rosamond. Thai-English student's dictionary . . . with the assistance of George V. Grekoff [and others]. Stanford, Calif., Stanford Univ. Pr., 1964. 638p. **AD770**
PL4156.H3

McFarland, George Bradley. Thai-English dictionary. . . . Stanford, Calif., Stanford Univ. Pr.; London, Milford, Oxford Univ. Pr., [1944]. 1019p., 39p. (Repr. 1982) **AD771**

A photolithographic reprint of the first edition originally published in Bangkok in 1941.
Based on earlier dictionaries, this is a new work reflecting modern usage. Gives Thai script, transliteration, and definition in English.

Includes scientific terms. In the addenda the scientific Latin names of flora, birds, fishes, shells, and snakes are translated into Thai. PL4187.M18

Plang Phloyphrom and **Golden, Robert Dorne.** Pru's Standard Thai-English dictionary . . . with the cooperation of Brother Urbain-Gabriel. [Bangkok], Āthōn Banpraditt; agent: Pricha Co., 1955. 1774p. **AD772**

Gives Thai script, transliteration, and equivalent word in English. PL4187.P5

So Sethaputra. New model English-Thai dictionary. [4th] Library ed. Bangkok, Thai Watana Panich, [1979]. 2v. **AD773**

1st ed. 1940. Publ. in various eds.
Aims to illustrate rather than define; gives illustrative phrases and sentences rather than equivalents and definitions. PL4187.S4

Tibetan

Bell, *Sir* Charles Alfred. English-Tibetan colloquial dictionary. 2d ed. Calcutta, Bengal Secretariat Book Depot, 1920. 562p. (Repr.: Calcutta, Firma KLM Private, 1977) **AD774**

Originally published as the second part of Bell's *Manual of colloquial Tibetan,* 1905.
Tibetan words in Tibetan and also in romanized type. PL3637.B4

Buck, Stuart H. Tibetan-English dictionary, with supplement. Wash., Catholic Univ. of America Pr., 1969. 833p. (Publications in the languages of Asia, 1) **AD775**

"The primary purpose of the present dictionary is to provide full and accurate definitions of the vocabulary used in current publications in the Tibetan language, especially those appearing in Communist China."—*Introd.* PL3637.B8

Das, Sarat Chandra. A Tibetan-English dictionary with Sanskrit synonyms. Rev. and ed. under the orders of the government of Bengal, by Graham Sandberg . . . and A. William Heyde . . . Calcutta, Bengal Secretariat Book Depot, 1902. 1353p. **AD776**

Added title page in Tibetan. Various printings.
With Sanskrit equivalents of the respective Tibetan words, selected by native Indian scholars of medieval and later days, in collaboration with Tibetan lotsawas or translators, and supplemented by Pandit Satis Chandra Acharya Vidyabhusan.—cf. *Revisors' pref.* PL3637.D3

Goldstein, Melvyn C. English-Tibetan dictionary of modern Tibetan. Comp. with Ngawangthondup Narkyid. Berkeley, Univ. of California Pr., [1984]. 485p. **AD777**

Since it was assumed "that this dictionary will be used primarily by teachers, students, and scholars, we have included not only 'basic' English lexical items . . . but also terms that might be useful in research or scholarly communication."—*Introd.* Emphasis is on spoken rather than literary language. PL3637.T52G65

——— Tibetan-English dictionary of modern Tibetan. [2d ed.] Kathmandu, Ratna Pustak Bhandar, 1978. 1234p. (Bibliotheca Himalayica, ser. 2, v.9) **AD778**

1st ed. 1975.
About 40,000 entries. Vocabulary was drawn mainly from modern textual sources, with heavy emphasis on that used in newspapers and magazines.

Jäschke, Heinrich August. Tibetan-English dictionary, with special reference to the prevailing dialects, to which is added an English-Tibetan vocabulary. Prep. and publ. at the charge of the Secretary of State for India in Council. London, Kegan Paul, 1949. 671p. (Repr.: London, Kegan Paul, 1965) **AD779**

First printed 1881. Several times reprinted. PL3637.J2

Tsonga

Cuenod, René. Tsonga-English dictionary. Johannesburg, Swiss Mission in South Africa, 1967. 286p. **AD780**

Limited to the Tsonga spoken in the Transvaal.

The Mission has also issued an *English-Tsonga, Tsonga-English* pocket dictionary (6th ed. Johannesburg, The Mission, 1974. 214p.).
PL8731.4.C8

Turkish

Ağakay, Mehmet Ali. Türkçe sözlük. Gözden geçirilmiş 6. baski. Ankara, Türk Tarih Kurumu Basimevi, 1974. 893p. **AD781**

2d ed. 1955. PL189.A4

Demiray, Kemal. Temel türkce sözlük. Istanbul, Inkilâp ve Aka Kitabeuleri, [1982]. 1133p. il. **AD782**

Includes a biographical/geographical section, p.1047–1133.

Tuglaci, Pars. Okyanus ansiklopedik sözlük. [4. bask] [Istanbul], Cem Yayinevi, 1980. 10v. il. **AD783**

1st ed. publ. 1971–74 under title: *Okyanus; 20. yüzyil ansiklopedik Türkçe sözlük.*

An encyclopedic dictionary including place names, etc. English and French equivalents are given for many terms, sometimes with examples of usage. v.10 is a supplement. PL189.T87

Bilingual

Alderson, Anthony Dolphin and **İz, Fahir,** eds. The concise Oxford Turkish dictionary. Oxford, Clarendon Pr., 1959. 807p. **AD784**

Abridged edition of *A Turkish-English dictionary* by H. C. Hony (1957) and *An English-Turkish dictionary* by F. İz (1952). Suitable for student use.

Reduces the original volumes to about one-third of their length. Omits close synonyms, geographical and scientific terms easily recognizable and "those Arabic and Persian forms now commonly replaced by Turkish ones."—*Pref.* PL137.A4

Hony, H. C. and **İz, Fahir.** The Oxford Turkish-English dictionary. 3d ed. [by] A. D. Alderson and Fahir İz. Oxford, Clarendon Pr., 1984. 526p. **AD785**

Added title page in Turkish.

1st–2d eds. (1947–57) by H. C. Hony had title: *A Turkish-English dictionary.*

A modern work with emphasis on common terms and idioms. In this edition "a great deal of the obsolete Arabic-Persian heritage has been omitted; this has been balanced by the incorporation of a large portion of the Turkish neologisms and of the European loanwords."—*Pref.* Idiomatic phrases now appear under first word (rather than "least common" word) of the phrase according to modern Turkish practice. Spellings conform to the 1977 recommendations of the Turkish Language Institute. PL191.H6

İz, Fahir and **Hony, H. C.** The Oxford English-Turkish dictionary. 2d ed. [by] A. D. Alderson and Fahir İz. Oxford & N.Y., Oxford Univ. Pr., 1978. 619p. **AD786**

Title page also in Turkish.

1st ed. 1952.

Like the earlier edition, this was "compiled mainly with a view to the needs of the Turkish student," (*Pref.*) and all guidance material is given in Turkish. PL191.I93

Redhouse, *Sir* James William. Turkish and English lexicon, shewing in English the significations of the Turkish terms.

Constantinople, pr. for the Amer. Mission by A. H. Boyajian, 1890. 2224p. (Repr.: Beirut, Librairie du Liban, 1974) **AD787**

PL191.R52

İngilizce-Türkçe Redhouse sözlügü. Redhouse English-Turkish dictionary. Istanbul, Redhouse Yayinevi, [1977]. 1152p. **AD788**

Based on the *Revised Redhouse dictionary, English-Turkish* (1950).

"The dictionary reflects the American point of view of its editors; however British usages in vocabulary, meanings, spelling and pronunciation have usually been noted."—*Pref.* PL191.I49

Redhouse cağdaş Türkçe-İngilizce Sözlügü. Contemporary Turkish-English dictionary. İstanbul, Redhouse, [1983]. 455p. **AD789**

Intended as "a basic vocabulary of Turkish as it is used today in the Republic of Turkey."—*Notes.* Gives English equivalents (usually in American English) of the Turkish words and phrases.

Redhouse yeni Türkçe-İngilizce sözlük. New Redhouse Turkish-English dictionary. [1. baski yaninevi. İstanbul, Redhouse, 1968] 1292p. **AD790**

"A new dictionary based largely on the Turkish-English Lexicon prepared by Sir James Redhouse and published in 1890 by the Publication Department of the American Board."—*half-title page.*

"The intention has been to include every word, and as nearly as possible every set phrase or locution, that has been used in standard Turkish as it has been spoken within the geographical area now called Turkey in the last two hundred years."—*Pref.* PL191.R55

Twi

Christaller, Johann Gottlieb. Dictionary of the Asante and Fante language, called Tshi (Twi) . . . [Ed. by J. Schweizer] 2d ed., rev. and enl. Basel, pr. for the Basel Evangelical Missionary Society, 1933. 607p. **AD791**

First published 1881.

"Based on the Akuapem dialect which was reduced to writing about 1838, and became afterwards the literary form."—*Pref.* This edition adds new words, meanings, and phrases in addition to the contents of the earlier edition. PL8751.Z5C5

Ukrainian

Akademiia Nauk URSR, Kiev. Instytut movoznavstva. Ukrainsko-russkii slovar'. Glav. redaktor I. M. Kyrychenko. Kiev, Izd-vo Akademii Nauk Ukr. SSR, 1953–63. 6v. **AD792**

Added title page in Ukrainian.

A major Ukrainian-Russian dictionary, giving examples of usage in Ukrainian from literary and other sources. PG3893.R8A54

Andrusyshen, C. H. and **Krett, J. N.** Ukrains'ko-anhliis'kyi slovnyk. Ukrainian-English dictionary. Toronto, publ. for the Univ. of Saskatchewan by Univ. of Toronto Pr., 1957. 1163p. **AD793**

First published by the Univ. of Saskatchewan, 1955.

Approximately "95,000 words with full definitions plus about 35,000 . . . phrases."—*Foreword.* The orthography, based on a system of 1928, "does not differ radically" from the system accepted officially in the Ukrainian SSR in 1946.

Podvez'ko, M. L. Ukrains'ko-angliisky slovnyk. Bliziko 60,000 sliv. Izd. 2. Kiev, Radianskaia Shkola, 1957. 1018p. **AD794**

1st ed. 1952.

Also publ. as *Ukrainian-English dictionary* (2d ed. rev. N.Y., Saphrograph Co., 1963). PG3891.P62

——— and **Balla, M. I.** Anhlo-ukraïns'kyi slovnyk; bliz'ko 65000 sliv. Kiiv, "Radyans'ka shkola," 1974. 663p.
AD795

Added title page in English: English-Ukrainian dictionary; about 65,000 words. PG3891.P6

Rudnyts'kyi, IAroslav Bohdan. An etymological dictionary of the Ukrainian language. 2d rev. ed. Winnipeg, Ukrainian Free Academy of Sciences, 1966–72. pts.1–10. **AD796**

Contents: pts. 1–5, A–Voro (issued in 1v., 1966); pts.6–10, voroplian–G. (Completes v.1) No more published?

1st ed. 1962–66. This is a reprinting with revisions.

An introductory section (0/11) published 1972 precedes the revised issue of pts.1–5. Pts. 6–10 were similarly to be revised and reprinted, and this plan followed until completion. Pt.10 includes corrigenda, bibliography, and bibliographical abbreviations used in v.1. PG3883.R812

Slovnyk ukraïns'koi movy. [Red. kolehiia: I. K. Bilodid (holova), ta inshi] Kyiv, Nauk. Dumka, 1970–80. 11v.
AD797

The first general language academy dictionary for spoken and literary Ukrainian. Includes specialized terms from science, law, linguistics, journalism, etc. Extensive illustrations of usage from end of the 18th century to the present. Includes a long list of sources, with full bibliographical information. v.11 includes a supplement. PG3888.S6

Urdu

See Hindi, Hindustani, Panjabi, Urdu.

Uzbek

Waterson, Natalie. Uzbek-English dictionary. [Oxford], Oxford Univ. Pr., 1980. 190p. **AD798**

"This dictionary was planned primarily for English users but with Uzbek learners also in mind. . . . The aim was to cover the essential vocabulary of modern spoken Uzbek."—*Introd.* Gives examples of usage as well as meanings of the words. PL55.U84W3

Vietnamese

Le-Van-Hung, *Mrs.* and **Le-Van-Hung,** *Dr.* Vietnamese-English dictionary, with the international phonetic system and more than 30,000 words and idiomatic expressions. Paris, Éd. Europe-Asie, 1955. 820p. **AD799**
PL4376.L55

Nǵuyên, Dình-Hòa. Essential English-Vietnamese dictionary. With the assistance of Patricia Nguyen Thi My-Huong. Rutland, Vt., C. E. Tuttle, [1983]. 316p. **AD800**

Title also in Vietnamese.

English terms with indication of parts of speech and the Vietnamese equivalents. Compiled with the needs of students of English-as-a-second-language in mind. PL3476.N34

——— Vietnamese-English student dictionary. Rev. and enl. ed. Saigon, Vietnamese-American Assoc., [1967]; Carbondale, Southern Illinois Univ. Pr., [1971]. 675p.
AD801

1st ed. 1959 had title *Vietnamese-English dictionary.*
PL4376.N355

U.S. Armed Forces Security Agency School, Wash., D.C. Vietnamese-English etymological glossary. [Wash.], 1952. 367p. **AD802**

"The contents are confined especially to political and military terminology . . . therefore the glossary does not pretend to be an exhaustive or even a comprehensive dictionary."—*Introd.*
PL4376.U5

Welsh

Evans, Daniel Silvan. Dictionary of the Welsh language. Carmarthen, Spurrell, 1887–1906. Pts.1–5. **AD803**

Contents: pts.1–5, A–Eiddig. 1892p. No more published.

Welsh-English. Includes many quotations, with references to sources. PB2191.E68

Evans, H. Meurig and **Thomas, W. O.** Y geiriadur mawr: the complete Welsh-English, English-Welsh dictionary. 11th ed. Llandybie, C. Davies, 1983. 492p., 367p. **AD804**

1st ed. 1958.

Based on the compilers' *New Welsh dictionary* (1953), but greatly enlarged and improved. Includes new technical terms along with a great many obsolete words. PB2191.E685

Geiriadur Prifysgol Cymru. A dictionary of the Welsh language. Golygydd: R. J. Thomas. Cyhoeddwyd ar ran Bwrdd Gwybodau Celtaidd, Prifysgol Cymru. Caerdydd, Gwasg Prifysgol Cymru, 1967–84. Pts. 1–33. (In progress)
AD805

Contents: pts.1–33, A–Lledneisgamp. Pts.1–21 make up v.1 and are available in a single bound volume from Lawrence Verry, Inc., Mystic, Conn.

A scholarly historical Welsh-English dictionary which follows the same general pattern as the *Oxford English dictionary* (AD28). Each entry gives etymology, definition in Welsh, English equivalent, and date of earliest use of the word. Most entries also give illustrative quotations drawn from an extensive bibliography of sources. PB2189.G4

Spurrell, William. Geiriadur saesneg a chymraeg; Spurrell's English-Welsh dictionary, ed. by J. Bodvan Anwyl, aided by the late Sir Edward Anwyl. Foreword by the Right Hon. David Lloyd George . . . 11th ed. rev. and enl. Carmarthen, W. Spurrell, 1937, 2v. in 1. **AD806**

In two parts: pt.1, English-Welsh; pt.2, Welsh-English.

v.2 has special title page: Geiriadur cymraeg a saesneg. Spurrell's Welsh-English dictionary . . . 13th ed. thoroughly rev.
PB2191.S75

Yiddish

Groyser verterbukh fun der Yidisher shprakh. Great dictionary of the Yiddish language. Editors in chief: Judah A. Joffe [and] Yudel Mark. N.Y., Yiddish Dictionary Committee, 1961–80. v.1–3. il. (In progress) **AD807**

Main title page and text in Yiddish.

A scholarly all-inclusive Yiddish-Yiddish dictionary covering the language from the earliest extant records to the living Yiddish of today and in all countries where Yiddish was or is spoken. Includes scholarly and dialectic words, and slang. To be in 12v.
PJ5117.G7

Bilingual

Abelson, Paul, ed. English-Yiddish encyclopedic dictionary: a complete lexicon and work of reference in all departments of knowledge. N.Y., Jewish Pr. Publ. Co., 1915. 1749p. il.
AD808

Added title page in Yiddish. PJ5117.A2

Harkavy, Alexander. English-Yiddish [Yiddish-English] dictionary. 22d ed. rev. and enl. N.Y., Hebrew Pub. Co., [195–?]. 2v. in 1. **AD809**

1st ed. 1898–1900?
Frequently reprinted. PJ5117.H5

Kogos, Fred. A dictionary of Yiddish slang and idioms. N.Y., Citadel, [1968]. 167p. **AD810**

Yiddish-English and English-Yiddish. Yiddish words are given phonetically in roman characters. PJ5117.K58

Weinreich, Uriel. Modern English-Yiddish, Yiddish-English dictionary. N.Y., YIVO Institute for Jewish Research, 1968. 789p. **AD811**

"The Dictionary is designed in the main for persons who have a firm grounding in English and at least a rudimentary command of Yiddish. . . . Accordingly, the Yiddish rather than the English material has been phonetically and grammatically analyzed, and English glosses have been used, wherever appropriate, to specify semantic detail."—*Author's pref.* A scholarly and useful work.
PJ5117.W4

Yoruba

Abraham, Roy Clive. Dictionary of modern Yoruba. London, Univ. of London Pr., [1958]. 776p. il. **AD812**

A comprehensive Yoruba-English dictionary intended for speakers of English. Includes idioms, current phrases, proverbs, riddles, descriptions of flora and fauna with illustrations. Historical, religious and ethnological background facts of the vocabulary are explained and extensively cross referenced. PL8823.A2

Delano, Isaac O. A dictionary of Yoruba monosyllabic verbs. [Ile-Ife, Nigeria], Institute of African Studies, Univ. of Ife, 1969. 2v. **AD813**

A preliminary edition produced in 1965 was entitled *A modern dictionary of Yoruba usage.*
". . . intended for those who already have a fair knowledge of Yoruba but need help in speaking it correctly and writing it with taste and accuracy."—*Introd.* PL8822.D45

Yugoslavian

See Serbo-Croatian.

Zulu

Doke, Clement Martyn, Malcolm, D. McK. and **Sikakana, J. M. A.,** comps. English-Zulu dictionary. Johannesburg, Witwatersrand Univ. Pr., 1958. 572p. **AD814**

A companion to Doke's *Zulu-English vocabulary* (below); the two works were published in a single volume in 1958 (572p., 342p. 2d impr. 1971).
Emphasis is on current usage, with considerable inclusion of slang, colloquialisms, and idioms. PL8843.D6

———— and **Vilakazi, Benedict Wallet.** Zulu-English dictionary. 2d ed. rev. with addendum. Johannesburg, Witwatersrand Univ. Pr., 1958. 918p. **AD815**

1st ed. 1948; 2d ed. (rev.) 1953, reprinted 1958 (3d impr. 1972).
Based on earlier works, this is a dictionary of current usage, including idiomatic forms, some scientific and technical words, etc.
PL8843.D65

Doke, Clement Martyn. Zulu-English vocabulary. Johannesburg, Witwatersrand Univ. Pr., 1958. 342p. (Repr. 1971) **AD816**

An abridgment of the dictionary of Doke and Vilakazi (above), made by deleting derivative forms, etymologies, illustrative phrases and sentences, rarer words and meanings, etc. PL8843.D65

McLaren, James. A new concise Xhosa-English dictionary. First rev. by W. G. Bennie and put into standard orthography by J. R. R. Jolobe. [New ed. in standard orthography. Cape Town], Longmans, [1963]. 194p. (Repr. 1975) **AD817**

First published under title *A concise Kaffir-English dictionary.*
PL8323.M35

A E

Periodicals

❖Periodicals form a very important element in reference work in any library, supplementing the book collections in several important ways. They are especially useful for supplying:

1. Latest information available in print (particularly important in the sciences, in technology, and in political, economic, and industrial questions of current interest).
2. Information on which the library has no books or about which no books are written (as in the case of very new, small, or obscure subjects, or subjects of purely local or temporary interest).
3. Contemporary opinion on a given subject, person, book, etc. (Periodicals, newspapers, and contemporary memoirs are the three main sources for such information, and, of these three, periodical files are the most easily used and the most serviceable in the average library.)
4. Current bibliographies (particularly annual or periodic bibliographies in a given subject field).

To make the best use of periodical literature and to answer the ordinary questions about periodicals, the reference worker needs, in addition to the catalog of his or her own library, three types of reference aids. These are:

1. The *bibliography* or *catalog* of periodicals, which is a list of the periodicals themselves (but not an index to the contents), and furnishes information about the periodicals listed, their correct titles, history, character, editors, prices, publishers, etc.
2. The *union list* of periodicals, which supplies information as to where sets of the periodicals included in the list may be found. Such lists are usually national, regional, or local. They may be general, e.g., the *Union list of serials in libraries of the United States and Canada* (AE182), or by subject field or special type of publication, e.g., *Union list of little magazines* (AE187).
3. The *index* to periodicals, which furnishes a guide to the contents of files of periodicals, serving the same purpose

for articles in periodicals that the library catalog does for books in the library.

BIBLIOGRAPHY

See also AE199.

British Museum. Dept. of Printed Books. Catalogue of printed books: periodical publications. 2d ed. London, Museum, 1899–1900. 2v. 1716col., 508col. **AE1**

Repr. as v.41 of the Edwards reprint of the British Museum *Catalogue of printed books.*

Arranged alphabetically by place of publication with an index of titles. Gives brief information about each title, i.e., title, dates, place, and note of changed titles. For the verification of titles this is an important general list for the period before 1900 because of (1) the great number of periodicals included, and (2) the convenient double arrangement by place and by title. Z6945.B86

——— General catalogue of printed books. Photolithographic ed. to 1955. London, 1963. v.184–86 (Periodical publications). **AE2**

Arranged alphabetically by place of publication. v.185 is devoted to London. No title index. This new catalog includes 20th-century publications, but it loses some of its value because of the lack of the title index.

Deutsche Forschungsgemeinschaft. Verzeichnis ausgewählter wissenschaftlicher Zeitschriften des Auslandes, VAZ. Wiesbaden, Franz Steiner Verlag, 1957. 749p. (*Its* Veröffentlichungen) **AE3**

——— ——— Register. Wiesbaden, 1957. 333p. (*Its* Veröffentlichungen)

An attempt to present a critical selection of the most important titles of the world's periodical literature. Those considered fundamental for a given field are designated "A," and those serving more specialized research purposes "B." Classed arrangement with alphabetical index by title. Z6945.D39

Duprat, Gabrielle, Liutova, Ksenia and **Bossuat, Marie-Louise.** Bibliographie des répertoires nationaux de périodiques en cours. London and Paris, Fédération Internationale des Associations de Bibliothécaires and UNESCO, 1969. 141p. (Manuels bibliographiques de l'UNESCO, 12; IFLA/FIAB manuels internationaux, 3) **AE4**

Identifies and describes on a country-by-country basis the directories and bibliographies of current periodicals available at the end of 1966. Now useful mainly as a research source concerning older materials. AS4.U8A154

Harvard University. Library. Periodical classes; classified listing by call number, alphabetical listing by title. Cambridge, Harvard Univ. Lib.; distr. by Harvard Univ. Pr., 1968. 758p. **AE5**

For a note on the series *see* AA145.
Nearly 26,000 titles. Z6945.H34

International directory of little magazines & small presses. Ed. 9– , 1973/74– . Paradise, Calif., Dustbooks, 1973– . Annual. **AE6**

Supersedes *Directory of little magazines* (eds. 1–8, publ. 1965–72 with slightly varying titles) and continues its numbering.

Ed. by Len Fulton and others.

Entries for little magazines and for small presses appear in a single alphabetical listing. In addition to the expected directory information, listings usually include comments by the editors regarding policies and types of material published, and lists of recent contributors. Z6944.L5D5

Irregular serials and annuals; an international directory. Ed.1– . N.Y., Bowker, 1967– . Biennial (beginning 1972). **AE7**

Kept up to date between editions by *Ulrich's Quarterly.*

A companion to *Ulrich's International periodicals directory* (AE10), following the general format and classified arrangement of that work and attempting the same international coverage. The two publications are now issued in alternate years. The 9th ed. (publ. 1984) provides publication information on some 34,000 serials issued annually, less frequently than once a year, or irregularly. Lists a wide range of foreign and domestic yearbooks, transactions, proceedings, etc., including the many "advances" and "progress in" series in the pure and applied sciences.

Content has varied. Now includes a list of cessations and suspensions since the last edition, an index of serial publications of international organizations, and an index by ISSN numbers (in addition to the expected title index). Z6941.I78●

Kressel, Getzel. Guide to the Hebrew press. Zug, Switz., Inter Documentation, [1979]. 151p. **AE8**

Offers descriptive notes and publication information on nearly 140 periodicals and newspapers selected for inclusion in the publisher's "Jewish Studies Microform Project." PN5650.K69

Sources of serials. Ed. 1– . N.Y., Bowker, [1977–]. **AE9**

"International serials publishers and their titles, with copyright and copy availability information."—*t.p., 2d ed. 1981.*

Based on a name authority file developed by Bowker in connection with publication of *Ulrich's International periodicals directory, Irregular serials and annuals,* and *Ulrich's Quarterly.* The 2d edition "includes 65,000 publishers and corporate authors arranged under 180 countries, listing 96,600 current serial titles they publish or sponsor."—*Pref.* Entry is by name of publisher or sponsoring body and includes address, co-publisher information if any, distributor information, and lists of titles of serials with indication of frequency and ISSN designation; copyright information is indicated by symbols. Publisher imprints and subsidiaries of publishing houses are interfiled as entries for publishers. Cross references; index of publishers and corporate authors. Z6941.S74●

Ulrich's International periodicals directory; a classified guide to current periodicals, foreign and domestic. Ed.1– . N.Y., Bowker, 1932– . Biennial. **AE10**

Title varies: 1932–38, *Periodicals directory;* 1943–63, *Ulrich's Periodicals directory.*

Frequency varies; beginning with 13th ed. (1969/70; publ. 1969), biennial. A companion publication, *Irregular serials and annuals* (AE7), is now issued in alternate years, and updating of both works is provided by *Ulrich's Quarterly* (below).

A very useful classified list of periodicals from many countries (about 64,800 titles in the 22d ed., publ. 1983). Coverage has varied in the different editions. Titles are grouped in subject classifications arranged alphabetically. Entries usually include, as pertinent: title, subtitle, sponsoring group, date of origin, frequency, price, editors, publisher, place of publication, annual and cumulative indexes. International Standard Serial Number (ISSN) and Dewey Decimal Classification number are now also included with the entry, as is information on: bibliographies, book reviews, film reviews, music and record reviews, illustrations, maps, charts, advertisements, statistics, circulation, etc. An especially useful feature is the indication of the indexing and abstracting services in which titles are included. Includes a list of periodicals which have ceased since the previous edition of the directory; index of titles and subjects. Recent editions include an "Index to publications of international organizations."

With the 11th ed. (publ. 1965–66) "International" was added to the title to emphasize "the broad scope of its coverage which limits the selection of entries only to those in the Roman alphabet or with subtitles and abstracts in English."—*Pref., 11th ed.* Both the 11th and 12th eds. had separate volumes (published in alternate years) for science and technology and for the humanities and social sciences. In the 13th ed. the directory reverted to the earlier plan of a single alphabetical arrangement for all subject classes.

Earlier issues continue to be useful, both for the listing of periodicals which have ceased publication and for special lists included, e.g.: *A list of clandestine periodicals of World War II,* by Adrienne Florence Muzzy, in the 5th ed. 1947. Z6941.U5●

Ulrich's Quarterly; a supplement to Ulrich's International periodicals directory and Irregular serials and annuals. v.1, no.1– , Spr. 1977– . N.Y., Bowker, 1977– . Quarterly.

AE11

Supersedes *Bowker serials bibliography supplement* (1972–76).

Provides a record of new serial titles, title changes, and cessations between issues of the biennial publications (above) mentioned in the subtitle. Indexes of titles, title changes and cessations cumulate in each issue of a given volume.   ●

Union of International Associations. Directory of periodicals published by international organizations. Répertoire des périodiques publiés par les organisations internationales. 3d ed. Brussels, The Union, [1969]. 240p. (FID publ., no.449)

AE12

1st ed. 1953.

"The present edition describes 1734 periodicals: 1475 published by 1071 non-governmental organizations and 259 published by 125 intergovernmental organizations."—*Introd.*   AS8.U38

Abbreviations

For abbreviations of scientific and technical periodical titles *see* p.1137.

Alkire, Leland G. Periodical title abbreviations. 4th ed. Detroit, Gale, [1983]. 2v.   **AE13**

1st ed. 1969, by C. E. Wall. Beginning with the 3d ed. (1981), published in three parts which may be purchased separately.

Subtitle: Covering periodical title abbreviations in science, the social sciences, the humanities, law, medicine, religion, library science, engineering, education, business, art, and many other fields.

Contents: v.1, Periodical title abbreviations: by abbreviation; v.2, Periodical title abbreviations: by title. A third section, designated by the publisher as v.3 (but usually cataloged as a separate serial publication), consists of two "interedition" supplements entitled *New periodical title abbreviations.*

v.1 of the 4th ed. includes more than 55,000 abbreviations. International coverage.   Z6945.A2W34

Leistner, Otto. ITA, Internationale Titelabkürzungen von Zeitschriften, Zeitungen, wichtigen Handbüchern, Wörterbüchern, Gesetzen usw. 3. erw. Aufl. Osnabrück, Biblio Verlag, 1981. 2v. (1265p.)   **AE14**

Title also in English: International title abbreviations of periodicals, newspapers, important handbooks, dictionaries, laws, etc.

1st ed. 1967–70.

A very useful guide to the full form of thousands of abbreviations for periodicals, newspapers, and related works published throughout the world and in all subject fields.   Z6945.A2L4

Rust, Werner. Verzeichnis von unklaren Titelkürzungen deutscher und ausländischer Zeitschriften. Leipzig, Harrassowitz, 1927. 142p.   **AE15**

A world list of initial abbreviations, arranged alphabetically. Gives full name of periodical and alternate abbreviation.   Z6945.A2R

Translations

See also EA36–EA42.

Gremling, Richard C. English language equivalent editions of foreign language serials. [2d ed.] Bound Brook, N.J., Literature Service Associates, [1966]. various paging.

AE16

1st ed. 1959.

Lists periodicals by original title and gives title and beginning date of cover-to-cover translations or other English-language equivalent edition. An English title index enables the user to relate the translated title to its foreign-language source.   Z1007.G7

Journals in translation. 3d ed. Boston Spa, Wetherby, W. Yorkshire, U.K., British Library Lending Division; Delft, The Netherlands, International Translations Centre, [1982]. 183p.   **AE17**

1st ed. 1976 publ. by the British Library Lending Division; the 1978 rev. ed., publ. jointly by the BLLD and the International Translations Centre, replaced both the earlier edition and the Centre's *Translations journals* (1970–1974/75).

Provides bibliographic information on cover-to-cover translation journals and those offering selected articles in translation; most are translations into English. Title listing with keyword index. Indicates those titles held by the BLLD and sources (such as NTIS) from which copies may be ordered.   Z6944.T7J68

Guides for authors

See also BD79.

Birkos, Alexander S. and **Tambs, Lewis A.** Academic writer's guide to periodicals. [Kent, Ohio], Kent State Univ. Pr., [1971–75]. v.1–3. (In progress?)   **AE18**

Publisher varies.

Contents: v.1, Latin American studies; v.2, East European and Slavic studies; v.3, African and black American studies.

Projected as a 7-volume series of guides covering Latin America, Eastern Europe and Russia/USSR, Africa, Middle East, Asia and the Pacific area, Western Europe and Scandinavia, and the United States.

Each volume is intended as a guide for the academic author desiring to place an article for journal publication. Lists and provides directory information on periodicals and monograph series which publish at least part of their articles in English or accept manuscripts in English.

Directory of publishing opportunities in journals and periodicals. Ed.4– , 1979– . Chicago, Marquis Academic Media, [1979]– . Irregular.   **AE19**

Continues: *Directory of publishing opportunities* (ed.1–3, 1971–75; title varies).

The 5th ed. (1981) "includes more than 3,900 specialized and professional journals, over 450 of which appear for the first time with this edition."—*Pref.* Entries are arranged alphabetically within 73 subject fields. Gives address, beginning date, changes of title, subscription data, editorial description, and information for submitting manuscripts for each journal. Indexes of (1) periodicals; (2) subjects; (3) sponsoring organizations; (4) editorial staff.   Z6944.S3D57

United States

Bibliography and history

Children's periodicals of the United States. Ed. by R. Gordon Kelly. Westport, Conn., Greenwood, [1984]. 591p.

AE20

Intends "to provide brief, authoritative descriptions of a broad sample of American periodicals for children" (*Pref.*) and thereby supplement the brief accounts found in Mott's *History* (AE28). Signed articles on individual magazines discuss history and content, and are followed by notes on sources of additional information and details of publication history. Appendixes: selected bibliography of American children's periodicals; chronological and geographical listings of magazines. Indexed.   PN4878.C48

Devers, Charlotte M., Katz, Doris B. and **Regan, Mary Margaret,** eds. Guide to special issues and indexes of periodicals. 2d ed. N.Y., Special Libraries Assoc., 1976. 289p.   **AE21**

1st ed. 1962.

Provides information on, "in alphabetical sequence, 1,256 periodicals which publish one or more of the following: *Specials* (features, supplementary issues and/or sections appearing on a continuing annual/semi-annual/quarterly basis); an *Editorial Index* (other than a table of contents); and an *Advertiser Index* (a page locator of the advertisers appearing in the issue)."—*Introd.* Subject index.

A 3d ed. under the editorship of Miriam Uhlan was scheduled for publication in mid-1985.   Z6951.S755

Edgar, Neal L. A history and bibliography of American magazines, 1810–1820. Metuchen, N.J., Scarecrow Pr., 1975. 379p.   **AE22**

The major portion of the work is an annotated bibliography of American magazines (p.85–257), giving very full information about more than 200 periodicals of the period. Appendixes include a list of exclusions, a chronological list, a register of printers, and a selected bibliography. Indexed.   PN4877.E3

Goldwater, Walter. Radical periodicals in America, 1890–1950; a bibliography with brief notes. With a genealogical chart and a concise lexicon of the parties and groups which issued them. New Haven, Conn., Yale Univ. Lib., 1964. 51p.   **AE24**

A list of 321 titles with information on volumes and dates, and with brief annotations.   Z7164.S67G57

Hoffman, Frederick John, Allen, Charles and **Ulrich, Carolyn F.** The little magazine; a history and a bibliography. Princeton, N.J., Princeton Univ. Pr., 1946. 440p. il.   **AE25**

"A little magazine is a magazine designed to print artistic work which for reasons of commercial expediency is not acceptable to the money-minded periodicals or presses."—*Introd.*

In two sections: (1) History, p.1–230; (2) Bibliography, p.233–398, followed by a detailed index to titles, change of titles, editors, contributors, etc. The history gives a general survey of little magazines from about 1910, with discussion of the more important ones, many of which included the first works of writers who later achieved prominence, and thus have a definite place in the literary history of the period. The annotated bibliography gives, in chronological order, detailed information about a long, selected list of these little magazines which will be of particular use to libraries in determining titles, number of issues published, outstanding contributors, etc.

A "Second printing" of the work (Princeton, 1947. 450p.) incorporates a few corrections, but changes "consist primarily of additional titles of magazines either started since May, 1945, or discovered by the authors since that date."—*p.ix.* The index was also revised to reflect the changes in this printing.   PN4836.H6

Hoornstra, Jean and **Heath, Trudy.** American periodicals, 1741–1900; an index to the microfilm collections: American periodicals, 18th century; American periodicals, 1800–1850; American periodicals, 1850–1900, Civil War and Reconstruction. Ann Arbor, Mich., University Microfilms Internat., 1979. 341p.   **AE26**

Offers cumulative title, editor, subject and reel number indexes to the three microfilm collections mentioned in the subtitle. The title index (with cross references for title changes, etc.) provides full bibliographic information and notes on character and content. The subject index lists relevant periodical titles under the Library of Congress subject headings assigned during cataloging.   Z6951.H65

The little magazine in America: a modern documentary history. Ed. by Elliott Anderson and Mary Kinzie. [Yonkers, N.Y.], Pushcart, [1978]. 770p. il.   **AE27**

Intended as a companion to Hoffman, Allen, and Ulrich's *The little magazine* (above). "Rather than a historical overview, or even a collaboration between historians," this volume offers "a large collection of essay-memoirs by prominent and representative little magazine editors, publishers, and contributors, including a generous selection of photo-documents and an annotated bibliography of 84 important magazines of the period."—*Pref.* Indexed.
                                                                    PN4878.3.L5

Mott, Frank Luther. A history of American magazines. Cambridge, Harvard Univ. Pr., 1938–68. 5v. il.   **AE28**

Contents: v.1, 1741–1850; v.2, 1850–65; v.3, 1865–85; v.4, 1885–1905; v.5, Sketches of 21 magazines, 1905–30, with a cumulative index to the 5v.

A comprehensive history with many bibliographical footnotes throughout and a chronological list of the magazines at the end of v.1–3. Because of these and the detailed indexes, the publication is of great value in reference work.

Left unfinished at the author's death, v.5 appeared without the projected general discussion of magazine publication for the period, which Mott had proposed to include. Nonetheless, the sketches included in the final volume and the overall index make a valuable addition to the set.   PN4877.M63

White, Cynthia L. Women's magazines, 1693–1968. London, Michael Joseph, [1970]. 348p.   **AE29**

Primarily a survey of the history, growth, and character of British and American women's magazines, but includes useful lists of women's magazines and a bibliography.

Women's periodicals and newspapers from the 18th century to 1981, compiled by Maureen E. Hady and others in association with the State Historical Society of Wisconsin (Boston, G. K. Hall, 1982. 376p.), is a union list of holdings of libraries in Madison, Wis.
                                                                    PN5124.W6W5

Wisconsin. University–Madison. Library. Catalog of little magazines: a collection in the Rare Book Room, Memorial Library, University of Wisconsin–Madison. Comp. and ed. by Robert F. Roeming. [Madison], Univ. of Wisconsin Pr., [1979]. 137p.   **AE30**

A catalog of "one of the largest and most complete collections of little magazines in the United States" (*Foreword*)—about 3,650 titles. Arrangement is by title with cross references from variant titles. Addenda list of titles added Nov. 1977–June 1979.
                                                                    Z6944.L5W57

Directories

Ayer directory of publications. Philadelphia, Ayer, 1880–1982. v.1–114. maps. Annual.   **AE31**

Title varies: 1930–69, *N. W. Ayer and Son's Directory of newspapers and periodicals;* 1970–71, *Ayer directory: newspapers, magazines . . . .*

Absorbed Rowell's *American newspaper directory* (1869–1908. 40v.) in 1910.

Long the standard American list; comprehensive, listing newspapers and periodicals, but not claiming completeness, as it intentionally omits certain classes of papers, e.g., publications of schools and smaller colleges, local church papers, and most house organs issued merely to exploit goods of their firms. The main list gives: (1) some descriptive and statistical matter about each state; a list of its counties (originally marking those which have no newspapers); and considerable gazetteer information about each city, i.e., its distance and direction from some important place, its railroads, leading manufactures, products, and institutions, and (2) detailed information about each paper or periodical listed, including its name, frequency, character or political character, date of foundation, size of column and page, subscription price, circulation figures, names of editors and publishers. Has many good maps, at least one for each state.

Continued by: Z6951.A97

The IMS . . . Ayer directory of publications, 1983– . Fort Washington, Pa., IMS Pr., 1980– . Ed.115– . Annual.
                                                                    AE32

Supersedes the *Ayer directory of publications* (above) and continues its numbering.

Subtitle 1984: The professional's reference of print media published in the United States, Canada, Puerto Rico, Virgin Islands, Bahamas, Bermuda and the Republic of the Philippines.

Arrangement and content of the directory continues to be much the same. Principal contents 1984: (1) General information; (2) Maps; (3) Catalog of publications (United States publications arranged by state or territory and city; Canada arranged by province and city; Bermuda, Philippines, and Bahamas); (4) Cross reference sections (providing an alphabetical index to subject classifications; newspaper feature editors listed by state and city; lists of agricultural, college, foreign-language, Jewish, fraternal, black, and religious publications; newsletters; general circulation magazines grouped by classification; trade and technical publications grouped by classification; lists of daily newspapers, daily periodicals, and weekly, semiweekly and tri-weekly newspapers); (5) Title index, with place of publication for each title. Z6951.A97

Editor and publisher. International yearbook, 1920/21– . N.Y., Editor and Publisher, 1921– . Annual. **AE33**

Issued annually by the weekly *Editor and publisher* staff. Contains a large amount of useful statistical and directory information in the field of American and foreign journalism.

Intends to be a complete listing of all United States daily newspapers, with circulation, rates, executive personnel, departmental managers, and editors; weekly newspapers; printing equipment and its suppliers; syndicated services; organizations; schools of journalism; foreign correspondents, etc.; as well as listings of daily newspapers of Canada and of countries throughout the world. PN4700.E4

MIMP. Magazine industry market place: the directory of American periodical publishing, 1980– . N.Y., Bowker, [1979–]. **AE34**

Intends to provide for the magazine industry the type of directory information which the *Literary market place* (AA353) supplies for the book publishing world. The first part of the work is an alphabetical title listing of periodical publications with full directory information given therein. Periodical titles are then classified by type of publication (e.g., Business, Consumer, Farm, Literary, News, Professional, Religious) and again by subject matter (e.g., Advertising, Agriculture, Art, Current events, Education, Law, Military, Poetry, Women). There are numerous additional lists of specialized publishers (micropublishers, newsletters and reference books for the trade, etc.), magazine organizations and associations, agents and agencies, special services (consultants, market research, translators, photographers, mailing lists, subscription agents, distributors, publication printers, back-date periodical dealers). A "Names and numbers" section on colored paper completes the volume. Z475.M18

Muller, Robert H., Spahn, Theodore Jurgen and **Spahn, Janet M.** From radical left to extreme right. 2d ed., rev. and enl. Ann Arbor, Mich., Campus Publishers; Metuchen, N.J., Scarecrow Pr., [1970]–76. 3v. **AE35**

Subtitle: A bibliography of current periodicals of protest, controversy, advocacy, or dissent, with dispassionate content-summaries to guide librarians and other educators through the polemic fringe. 1st ed. 1967.

A greatly expanded edition, v.3 being a supplement. Periodicals are grouped under such headings as: Radical left, Marxist-Socialist left, Underground, Anarchist, Libertarian, Utopian, Liberal, Civil rights, Sex, Peace, Conservative, Anti-Communist. In addition to directory-type information, a summary of content and editorial policy (based on examination of at least three issues) is included for each periodical. v.3 includes a title index to the full set. Z7165.U5M82

Murphy, Dennis D. Directory of conservative and libertarian serials, publishers, and freelance markets. 2d ed. [Tucson, Author], 1979. 64p. **AE36**

1st ed. 1977.

Gives directory information and policies of "organizations which publish or distribute, and some bookstores and book clubs which specialize in libertarian or conservative works."—*Introd.* Entries for serials predominate. Z475.M87

Standard periodical directory. Ed.1– , 1964/65– . N.Y., Oxbridge, 1964– . Irregular. **AE37**

Subtitle, 9th ed. (1985): The largest authoritative guide to United States & Canadian periodicals . . . information on more than 65,000 publications.

Alphabetical subject arrangement with index of titles and subjects. Information given includes name and address of publisher,

editorial content and scope, year founded, frequency, subscription rate, total circulation, advertising rate, etc. Z6951.S78

Working press of the nation. Ed. 1– . N.Y., Farrell Pub., 1945– . Biennial; annual since 1959. **AE38**

First issue was entitled *Working press of New York City.*

Content has varied; now issued in 5v. per year. Contents of the 1984 ed.: v.1, *Newspaper directory* (listing daily and weekly newspapers of the United States, feature syndicates, news and photo services, with index of editorial personnel by subject, index of Sunday supplements, etc.); v.2, *Magazine directory* (listing some 5,000 magazines grouped by subject area, with title index); v.3, *TV and radio directory* (listing about 9,500 radio and television stations, plus some 25,700 local programs by subject); v.4, *Feature writer and photographer directory* (giving home addresses and fields of interest of about 2,000 writers and photographers); v.5, *Internal publications directory* (giving information on publications of more than 3,500 U.S. companies, government agencies, etc.; for the 1952–74 period this information appeared in the *Gebbie Press house directory*). Z6951.W6

Africa

See also AE157.

Thomassery, Marguerite. Catalogue des périodiques d'Afrique noire francophone (1858–1962) conservés à l'IFAN. Dakar, Institut Français d'Afrique Noire, 1965. 117p. (Institut Français d'Afrique Noire. Catalogues et documents, 19) **AE39**

Includes official serial publications as well as periodicals of general interest. Z3503.T48

Argentina

Ferreira Sobral, Eduardo F. Publicaciones periódicas argentinas, 1781–1969. Buenos Aires, Ministerio de Agricultura y Ganadería de la Nación, 1971– . v.1– . (In progress?) **AE40**

v.1 is an alphabetical list of Argentinian periodicals for the long period indicated. v.2 is to provide chronological and geographical lists and statistical summaries.

Publicaciones periódicas argentinas; registradas para el sistema internacional de datos sobre publicaciones seriadas (ISDS). Buenos Aires, Centro Argentino de Información Científica y Tecnológica del CONICET, 1981. 217p. **AE41**

Lists some 1,457 Argentinian periodicals registered for the ISDS by late 1980, a considerable number of which are no longer current. Listing is by ISSN, with a title index.

A 58p. supplement was published 1983. Z6954.A6P93

Australia and New Zealand

Australian serials in print, 1981– . Melbourne, D. W. Thorpe, [1981]– . Annual. **AE42**

Replaces *Current Australian serials* published by the National Library of Australia, 1963–75.

Aims to list any serial publication "that is produced in Australia, no matter how frequently or infrequently, regularly or irregularly, under the same name, and available to the public."—*Introd.* An alphabetical title listing which includes newspapers, magazines, directories, yearbooks, newsletters, society proceedings, etc. Z6961.C8

Press, radio & TV guide: Australia, New Zealand and the Pacific Islands. Ed.1– . Sydney, Country Pr. Ltd., 1914– . Irregular. **AE43**

Publisher varies; frequency varies.

Title varies: 1914–68, *The press directory of Australia and New Zealand.*

A listing of newspapers, periodicals, and radio and television stations arranged geographically. Gives directory information, including considerable statistical and gazetteer information about places. Alphabetical index.

Austria

Handbuch Österreichs Presse, Werbung, Graphik. Wien, Verband Österreichischer Zeitungsherausgeber, 1953– . Annual.   **AE44**

Gives statistical and directory information on Austrian newspapers and periodicals. Classified with title index.

Belgium

Annuaire officiel de la presse belge. Officieel Jaarboek van de belgische Pers. Éd. par l'Association Générale de la Presse Belge. [Bruxelles, Impr. "IMIFI," 1950– .] Irregular.   **AE45**

In addition to directory information on Belgian newspapers and periodicals, there are extensive sections devoted to journalists, professional associations, specialist groups, and much miscellaneous information useful to the Belgian journalist.   PN4709.A48

Catalogus van Belgische en Luxemburgse periodieken. 4de uitg. Brussel, Nederlandse Kamer van Koophandel voor België en Luxemburg, 1981. 308p.   **AE46**

1st ed. 1962.

In two parts: (1) a classified section which lists the periodical titles under 114 subject headings, and (2) an alphabetical title list giving full information about each periodical.

Hove, Julien van. Répertoire des périodiques paraissant en Belgique. Bruxelles, Librairie Encyclopédique, 1951. 358p.   **AE47**

Added title page: Repertorium van de België verschijnende tijdschriften.

Alphabetical listing of more than 2,000 periodicals currently appearing in Belgium, with full bibliographical data. Indexes by subject, editorial bodies, and place of publication.

———— ———— Supplément 1–4. 1955–72. 304p., 215p., 222p., 328p.

The supplements list new periodicals published through 1968, as well as omissions from the previous volumes, changes in title, and cessations.   Z6956.B4H6

Marechal, Yvon. Répertoire pratique des périodiques [belges] édités en langue française. 3ᵉ éd. Bruxelles, Les Auteurs Réunis, 1982. 267p.   **AE48**

1st ed. 1970.

A classed listing of current serials, with addresses and indication of periodicity. Title index.   Z6956.B4M27

Brazil

Rio de Janeiro. Instituto Brasileiro de Bibliografia e Documentação. Periódicos brasileiros de cultura. Rio de Janeiro, 1968. 280p.   **AE49**

A preliminary edition appeared in 1956.

More than 2,000 periodicals are listed according to Universal Decimal Classification, with subject and title indexes. Supplementary lists have appeared periodically in the Institute's *Noticias* beginning with the issue of Set./Dez. 1968.   Z6954.B8R55

Bulgaria

Bulgarski periodichen pechat 1844–1944; anotiran bibliografski ukazatel. Sofiia, Nauka i Izkustvo, 1962–69. 3v.   **AE50**

Added title page in German: Bulgarische periodika 1844–1944; annotiertes bibliographisches Verzeichnis.

Comp. by Dimitur P. Ivanchev.

v.1–2 are an exhaustive alphabetical listing of Bulgarian periodicals, with notes on the history, editors, etc., of each. v.3 lists foreign-language periodicals published in Bulgaria, includes a section of additions and corrections, and provides full indexing for the set.

Continued by: Z6956.B9B88

Spasova, Mariia Vladimirova. Bulgarski periodichen pechat, 1944–1969: bibliografski ukazatel. Sofiia, Narodna Biblioteka "Kiril i Metodii," 1975. 3v.   **AE51**

At head of title: Narodna Biblioteka "Kiril i Metodii."

Added title page in German: Bulgarische Periodika.

Continues the bibliographic record of Bulgarian periodicals begun with the three-volume work above.

v.3 comprises indexes and tables.   Z6956.B9S76

Bulgarski periodichen pechat. 1972– . Sofiia, Narodna Biblioteka "Kiril i Metodii," 1974– . Annual. (Natsionalna bibliografiia na NR Bulgariia, ser.4)   **AE52**

An earlier series of the same title covered 1965–71 (*see* AA650).

Provides an annual record of periodical publications with indication of numbers or issues actually published, new titles, etc.

Canada

Beaulieu, André and Hamelin, Jean. Les journaux de Québec de 1764 à 1964. Québec, Presses de l'Université Laval; Paris, A. Colin, 1965. 329p. (Les cahiers de l'Institut d'Histoire, 6)   **AE53**

Lists, by place of publication, magazines and newspapers published in the province of Quebec. Gives beginning and closing dates, frequency, founder when known, locations in Quebec libraries if any, and, often, notes on the publication's history. Chronological and alphabetical title indexes.   Z6954.C21Q33

Canadian serials directory. Répertoire des publications sériées canadiennes. Toronto, Univ. of Toronto Pr., 1972– . Irregular (2d ed. publ. 1977).   **AE54**

Text in English and French.

An alphabetical listing of serials (magazines, annuals, yearbooks, proceedings and transactions of societies, special-interest newspapers) published in Canada. Subject index and index of publishers and sponsoring bodies. Indicates type of publication, frequency, format, price, circulation, etc.   Z6954.C2C23

The IMS . . . Ayer directory of publications. Fort Washington, Pa., Ayer, 1980– . Annual.   **AE55**

For full information *see* AE32.

With its predecessor publication (AE31), provides a convenient record of Canadian newspapers and periodicals. *McKim's Directory of Canadian publications* (1892–1942) gave full particulars of newspapers and periodicals as well as gazetteer information on places of publication.

China

Tung, Julia. Bibliography of Chinese academic serials, pre-1949: material in Hoover Institution on War, Revolution, and Peace. Stanford, Calif., East Asian Collection, Hoover Inst., Stanford Univ., [1982]. 107p.   **AE56**

Titles are listed alphabetically by romanized title (Wade-Giles system) followed by Chinese title and bibliographic details in

Chinese characters; Hoover Institution call numbers and holdings are indicated. Index of Chinese titles.   Z6944.S3T86

U.S. Library of Congress. Chinese periodicals in the Library of Congress. Comp. by Han Chu Huang. Wash., Lib. of Congress, 1978. 521p.   **AE57**

A title listing of some 6,400 titles of Chinese periodicals in all subject fields, "excluding only Chinese legal serials in the custody of the Far Eastern Law Division of the Law Library of the Library of Congress."—*Foreword.* Includes all Chinese-language serials from the period 1868 to 1975 in the Chinese collection of the Chinese and Korean Section of the Library of Congress Orientalia Division. Entries are arranged according to the Wade-Giles system of romanization, with the Chinese characters also given. "When a title in Pinyin romanization or in a western language appears in the original publication, it is included in the entry, followed by a cross-reference."—*Notes.*   Z6958.C5U53

Colombia

Bogotá. Biblioteca Nacional. Catálogo de todos los periódicos que existen desde su fundación hasta el año de 1935, inclusive. Ed. oficial. Bogotá, El Gráfico, 1936. 2v.   **AE58**

Contents: t.1, Periódicos nacionales, A–P; t.2, Periódicos nacionales, R–Z. Periódicos extranjeros, A–Z.

A listing of the issues of periodicals in the National Library. Does not give bibliographical information beyond title, name, and numbers and dates of issues held.   Z6954.C7B6

Instituto Colombiano para el Fomento de la Educación Superior. División de Documentación y Fomento Bibliotecario. Directorio de publicaciones periódicas colombianas. Bogotá, La División, 1975. 199*l.*   **AE59**

A title listing of Colombian periodicals, giving (as far as available) issuing body, place and beginning date of publication. Intended as a preliminary list until such time as a detailed catalog can be prepared.   Z6954.C7I57

Congo

Berlage, Jean. Répertoire de la presse du Congo Belge (1884–1954) et du Ruanda-Urundi (1920–1954) . . . Bruxelles, Commission Belge de Bibliographie, 1955. 64p. (Bibliographia belgica, 10)   **AE60**

Title also in Flemish.

365 titles in alphabetical arrangement with four indexes: (1) chronological, (2) place-names, (3) broad classification, and (4) publisher (persons and organizations).   Z2407.B5 no.10

Cuba

Directorio de revistas y periódicos de Cuba, 1942–68. La Habana, Anuario Bibliográfico Cubano, 1942–53; Gainesville, Fla., 1963–68. Annual. (Biblioteca del bibliotecaria)   **AE61**

Ed., Fermín Peraza y Sarausa.
Publication suspended, 1954–62.
The 1965 edition lists more than 200 titles of periodicals published in Cuba, with a special section of more than 100 titles of Cuban periodicals published outside Cuba.   Z6954.C9D5

Pittsburgh. University. Library. Cuban periodicals in the University of Pittsburgh libraries. By Eduardo Lozano. 3d ed. Pittsburgh, Univ. of Pittsburgh Libs., 1981. 87p.   **AE62**

An alphabetical title listing of 340 publications, both currently received and inactive. Detailed holdings notes; subject index.   Z6954.C9P5

Czechoslovakia

Malec, Karel. Soupis bibliografí novin a časopisů, vydávaných na území Československé republiky. Praha, Orbis, 1959. 216p.   **AE63**

Bibliography of bibliographies of Czechoslovak periodicals and newspapers from the 18th century through 1958.   Z2131.A1M3

Denmark

See also AE156.

Nielson, Torben. Current Danish periodicals; a select list. Copenhagen, Royal Library, 1965. 45p.   **AE64**

A classed list of those Danish periodicals "considered the most important from an international point of view."—*Pref.* Title index.   Z6956.D4N5

East Europe

U.S. Library of Congress. Slavic and Central European Division. The USSR and Eastern Europe; periodicals in Western languages. 3d ed., rev. and enl. Comp. by Paul L. Horecky and Robert G. Carlton. Wash., Lib. of Congress, 1967. 89p.   **AE65**

1st ed. 1958.
Covers current periodicals concerned with Albania, the Baltic countries, Bulgaria, Czechoslovakia, Hungary, Poland, Romania, the Soviet Union, and Yugoslavia. A select list of defunct periodicals considered of continuing research value to students of these areas is also included.   Z2483.U5

France

Arbour, Roméo. Les revues littéraires éphémères paraissant à Paris entre 1900 et 1914. Répertoire descriptif. Paris, Librairie José Corti, 1956. 93p.   **AE66**

Lists 154 "little magazines" published in Paris which lived less than four years, with locations in Parisian libraries. Gives full bibliographical description, with names of editors, etc., as well as the names of the principal contributors. Index of personal names and an appendix of 31 titles not found in the libraries of Paris.

Caron, Pierre and **Jaryc, Marc.** Répertoire des périodiques de langue française, philosophiques, historiques, philologiques et juridiques. Publié par la Fédération des Sociétés Françaises de Sciences Philosophiques, Historiques, Philologiques et Juridiques. Paris, Maison du Livre Français, 1935. 351p.   **AE67**

Alphabetical list, p.1–278, no.1–1421; Supplément, p.279–92, no.1421–76; IIᵉ supplément, no.1477–96.

———— ———— 1. supplément, no.1477–1686. 1937. 68p.

Incorporates, in regular alphabetical order and numbering, the titles (no.1477–96) of the original IIᵉ supplément.

———— ———— 2. supplément, no.1687–1900. 1939. 62p.

The basic work with its supplements forms an important list of French periodicals existing in the 1930s, giving exact title, date of founding, names and addresses of chief editors, periodicity, average number of pages per volume, size, price, etc. Indexes of persons, places, and subjects.   Z6956.F8C3

Hatin, Louis Eugène. Bibliographie historique et critique de la presse périodique française. . . . Paris, Firmin-Didot, 1866. cxviip., 660p. il. (Repr.: Hildesheim, Olms, 1965)   **AE68**

Subtitle: Catalogue systématique et raisonné de tous les écrits périodiques de quelque valeur publiés ou ayant circulé en France depuis l'origine du journal jusqu'à nos jours, avec extraits, notes historiques, critiques, et morales, indication des prix que les principaux journaux ont atteints dans les ventes publiques, etc.

A retrospective bibliography with detailed bibliographical and historical notes about each periodical listed. Covers 1631–1865. Useful for historical information, though not complete.

Z6956.F8H36

Paris. Bibliothèque Nationale. Catalogue des périodiques clandestins diffusés en France de 1939 à 1945, suivi d'un catalogue des périodiques clandestins diffusés à l'étranger. Paris, Bibliothèque Nationale, 1954. 282p.   **AE69**

Preparé et redigé successivement par Renée Roux-Fouillet et Paul Roux-Fouillet.

Lists clandestine periodicals to be found in the Bibliothèque Nationale, either in the original or in photostatic copies.

In three sections: (1) Periodicals distributed in France (about 1015 titles); (2) Periodicals distributed in other countries (about 71 titles); (3) Supplement. Index.

——— **Département des Périodiques.** Bibliographie de la presse française politique et d'information générale, 1865–1944. Paris, Bibliothèque Nationale, 1964– . (In progress) **AE70**

Chronologically, a successor to Hatin (AE68). Limited to journals (mainly dailies and weeklies) of political or general news nature. 89 fascicules, each covering a *département* (and numbered alphabetically by name thereof), are being issued as they are completed; the finished work is to comprise 4v., with a general preface and a title index. Each fascicule includes a preface or historical note, an alphabetical listing with bibliographical details of the periodicals, and a chronological table of titles.   Z6956.F8P32

——— Répertoire de la presse et des publications périodiques françaises, 1977/1978. 6ᵉ éd. Paris, Bibliothèque Nationale, 1981. 2v. (1599p.)   **AE71**

"Préparée par le Service français du Département des Périodiques."—*t.p.*

Contents: v.1, Répertoire systématique des périodiques vivants; v.2, Index alphabétique des titres, Index alphabétique des collectivités, Liste des périodiques disparue entre le 1ᵉʳ octobre 1965 et 31 décembre 1976.

1st–5th eds. covered 1956/57, 1957/60, 1960/63, 1963/66, 1966/71. The 5th ed. departed from the policy of earlier ones (which listed periodicals which began publication during the period of coverage) in that it combined the listings from the 4th ed. with new titles of the 1966–71 period. v.1 of the 6th ed. is a comprehensive, classified list of periodicals (with full details of publication) which were current during the period Jan. 1977–Mar. 1978; all titles from the previous edition which ceased publication during the period Oct. 1, 1965–Dec. 31, 1976 are relegated to an alphabetical title list at the end of v.2, and the date and number of the last issue is indicated for each periodical. An alphabetical title index to the classified section is also provided in v.2. About 20,400 titles in this edition; earlier editions remain useful, of course, for reference purposes.

——— Répertoire national des annuaires français, 1958–1968, et supplément signalant les annuaires reçus en 1969. Par Monique Lambert. Paris, Bibliothèque Nationale, 1970. 311p.   **AE72**

A classed list with alphabetical title index.   Z2174.Y4P29

Place, Jean-Michel and **Vasseur, André.** Bibliographie des revues et journaux littéraires des XIXᵉ et XXᵉ siècles. Paris, Chronique des Lettres Françaises, 1973–77. v.1–3. (In progress)   **AE73**

Gives detailed descriptions of French literary journals of the period, contents of each issue published, and illustrative extracts. Chronologically arranged by starting date of publication, with some overlap of v.1–2 (covering 1840–99); v.3 is designated as covering 1915–30 and includes an index of names cited. About 15 titles in each volume.   PQ2.P5

Current

Annuaire de la presse française et de la publicité, 1880– . Paris, Administration et Rédaction, 1880– . v.1– . il. Annual.   **AE74**

Title varies. Continues E. Mermet's *La publicité en France,* 1878–80.

Publisher varies.

An important and useful bibliography and annual, containing not only full information about French journals and the French press but also a considerable amount of directory, gazetteer, political, and governmental information needed by French journalists. Contains many illustrations. Scope and contents of volumes before 1914 differ somewhat from the volumes issued since 1914.

Principal contents, 1983: names of French government officials; press associations with names of officers and members; list of journalists with indication of publication with which associated; suppliers; advertising agencies; lists of papers and periodicals published in (1) Paris, arranged alphabetically by classes, (2) *départements,* arranged alphabetically by *départements* and towns, (3) cities abroad. Indexes of French newspapers and periodicals, foreign newspapers, names, advertising agencies, etc.   Z6956.F8A6

Germany

Deutsche Bibliographie: Zeitschriften-Verzeichnis, 1945–1952, 1953–1957, 1958–1970, 1971–1976, 1977–1980. Bibliographie der in Deutschland erscheinenden periodischen Veröffentlichungen sowie der deutschsprachigen Periodica Österreichs, der Schweiz und anderer Länder. Bearb. von der Deutschen Bibliothek, Frankfurt a. M. Frankfurt a. M., GmbH, 1954– . v.1– . (In progress)   **AE75**

Title varies slightly; subtitle varies.

Volume for each period issued in parts.

A comprehensive list of German-language publications appearing in Germany and other countries. For each title usually gives: editor, publisher, size, price, frequency, irregularities in publication, and changes in title.

Each period dealt with in two parts: (1) a classified section, and (2) an index section. The latter includes indexes by title, editor, publisher, society or sponsoring organization, and subject.

Z6956.G3F67

Diesch, Carl Hermann. Bibliographie der germanistischen Zeitschriften. Leipzig, Hiersemann, 1927. 441p. (Modern Language Assoc. of America. Germanic Sec. Bibliographical publ. v.1)   **AE76**

A chronological, classed arrangement covering from the 18th to the 20th centuries. Lists more than 4,600 titles with information on full title, editor, volumes and years published, place, publisher, etc. Title and name indexes.   Z7037.A1D5

Kirchner, Joachim. Bibliographie der Zeitschriften des deutschen Sprachgebietes bis 1900. Stuttgart, Hiersemann, 1966–77. 3v.   **AE77**

Contents: Bd.1, Von den Anfängen bis 1830; Bd.2, 1831–1870; Bd.3, 1871–1900.

Published in parts.

A bibliography of periodicals from German-speaking regions for the period to 1900. Arrangement is by subject field, then chronological within subjects. Editors and changes of title are noted; files are located.

Bd.1 was originally meant to include periodicals to 1870, and the final volume was to be an index. As published, Bd.1 covers only through 1830; each volume has its own detailed index.

Z6956.G3K53

Maas, Lieselotte. Handbuch der deutschen Exilpresse 1933–1945. Handbook of the German exile press 1933–1945. Hrsg. von Eberhard Lämmert. München, C. Hanser, 1976–81. 3v. (Sonderveröffentlichungen der Deutschen Bibliothek, 2,3,9)   **AE78**

A very full record of German periodicals published outside Germany during the Nazi regime. In addition to bibliographic details of more than 400 serials, provides lists of contributors and locations of files of the publications. Indexes of names and pseudonyms, organizations, countries and places of publication.

Z6956.G3M27

Current

Stamm Leitfaden durch Presse und Werbung. Ausgabe 29– . [Essen, Stamm Verlag], 1976– . Annual.   **AE79**

Title also in English *(Annual directory through press and advertising)* and French. Introduction and index in German, English, and French.

At head of title: Presse- und Medien-Handbuch.

Continues *Stamm-Leitfaden für Presse und Werbung* (ed. 25–28, 1972–75), which in turn superseded *Die Leitfaden für Presse und Werbung* (ed. 1–24, 1947–71), and assumes its numbering.

Arrangement and coverage has varied slightly, but content has been fairly consistent throughout the changes of title. Principal contents of Ausg. 36, 1983: pts.1–2, German newspapers (alphabetical and geographical lists); pts.3–4, German magazines and annuals (alphabetical and classified lists); pt.5, German newspapers and periodicals published in non-German-speaking countries; selected newspapers and periodicals published outside Germany; pt.6, Television, radio, and film advertising; pts.7–9, Poster and miscellaneous advertising; advertising agencies; pt. 10, Suppliers directory. Includes both the Federal Republic of Germany and the German Democratic Republic.

Great Britain

See also AE29.

Before 1800

Couper, William James. The Edinburgh periodical press; being a bibliographical account of the newspapers, journals, and magazines issued in Edinburgh from the earliest times to 1800. Stirling, Mackay, 1908. 2v. facsims.   **AE80**

Contents: v.1, 1642–1711; v.2, 1711–1800.
Full bibliographical information with historical sketches.

PN5139.E39C7

Crane, Ronald Salmon and **Kaye, F. B.** Census of British newspapers and periodicals, 1620–1800. Chapel Hill, Univ. of North Carolina Pr.; London, Cambridge Univ. Pr., 1927. 205p. (Repr.: London, Holland, 1966)   **AE81**

Lists 970 papers and periodicals, with indication of the holdings in 62 American libraries.

Contents: (1) British periodicals, 1620–1800, accessible in American libraries; (2) British periodicals, 1620–1800, not found in American libraries; (3) Chronological index; (4) Geographical index of periodicals published outside of London.   Z6956.E5C8

Oxford. University. Bodleian Library. Catalogue of English newspapers and periodicals in the Bodleian Library, 1622–1800. By R. T. Milford and D. M. Sutherland. Oxford, Bibliographical Soc., 1936. p.167–346. (Oxford Bibliographical Soc. Proceedings and papers, v.4, pt.2)   **AE82**

An alphabetical title catalog, p.171–344; index to editors, authors, and contributors, p.345–46.   Z1008.O98

Ward, William Smith. British periodicals & newspapers, 1789–1832; a bibliography of secondary sources. [Lexington], Univ. Pr. of Kentucky, [1972]. 386p.   **AE83**

A companion to Ward's *Index and finding list of serials published in the British Isles, 1789–1832* (Lexington, 1953), offering a bibliography of writings about the magazines and newspapers listed in that work, including writings on their editors, publishers, and readership. Topical arrangement with author index.   Z6956.G6W37

Weed, Katherine Kirtley and **Bond, Richmond Pugh.** Studies of British newspapers and periodicals from their beginning to 1800; a bibliography. Chapel Hill, Univ. of North Carolina Pr., 1946. 233p. (Studies in philology, extra ser., no.2)   **AE84**

Contents: Bibliographies and bibliographical studies; Beginnings of the newspaper; General studies; Individual newspapers and periodicals; Editors, authors, and publishers; Towns and counties; Special subjects; Newspapers and periodicals in Europe and in America.

Lists some 2,100 books and periodical articles printed mainly 1800–1940, listed by subject with author index.   P25.S82 no.2

19th century and after

Madden, Lionel and **Dixon, Diana.** The nineteenth-century periodical press in Britain; a bibliography of modern studies, 1901–1971. N.Y., Garland, 1976. 280p. (Garland reference library of the humanities, v.53)   **AE85**

A relatively brief section on "Bibliographies, finding lists and reports on bibliographical projects" is followed by a fairly long one on "General history of periodicals and newspapers"; both are arranged chronologically by date of publication. The bulk of the volume is devoted to section C, "Studies of individual periodicals and newspapers," and section D, "Studies and memoirs of proprietors, editors, journalists and contributors," each arranged alphabetically by title/name, then chronologically by date of the study. Author index only; some brief annotations. About 2,600 items.

Z6956.G6M3

Noyce, John L. The directory of British alternative periodicals, 1965–1974. Hassocks, [Eng.], Harvester Pr.; Atlantic Highlands, N.J., Humanities Pr., [1979]. 359p.   **AE86**

A title listing of British underground and alternative periodicals of the period indicated, giving publication information, description (including many historical notes), format, library locations when available, and references to directory listings, reviews, notices, etc. In general, excludes "poetry and traditional politics—though entries have been included for those titles which were an important part of the underground and alternative press. In the absence of any other listing, and in view of their importance in the counter-culture of the time," anarchist and libertarian periodicals have been included. Indexed.   Z6956.G6N69

Spiers, John. The underground and alternative press in Britain; a bibliographical guide with historical notes. [Brighton, Eng.], Harvester Pr., 1974. 77p.   **AE87**

"Published with a title and chronological index as a companion to the Underground/Alternative Press collection prepared for microfilm publication by Ann Sexsmith and Alastair Everitt."—*t.p.*

Offers bibliographic and historical notes on sixty-odd British underground and alternative press periodicals included in the publisher's basic microform set for the 1961–73 period. The microform series has been continued on an annual basis with printed guides for the individual years edited by divers hands.   Z6944.U5S64

Victorian periodicals: a guide to research. Ed. by J. Don Vann and Rosemary T. Van Arsdel. N.Y., Modern Language Assoc. of Amer., 1978. 188p.   **AE88**

Presents chapters by specialists on resources for research and special problems encountered in work with Victorian periodicals, giving attention to bibliographic control, finding lists, biographical sources, histories of the periodical press, and identification of authors. Includes a separate chapter on circulation and the stamp tax. Identifies areas where further research and bibliographic work are needed. Indexed.   PN5124.P4V5

The Waterloo directory of Victorian periodicals, 1824–1900. Phase I. [Montreal], publ. for the Univ. of Waterloo by Wilfrid Laurier Univ. Pr., [1976]. 1187p.   **AE89**

"Sponsored by the Research Society for Victorian Periodicals and Waterloo Computing in the Humanities."—*t.p.*

Editors: Michael Wolff, John S. North, Dorothy Deering.

An attempt to make "conveniently available in one alphabetical listing the newspaper and periodical titles published in England, Ireland, Scotland, and Wales at any time between 1824 and 1900." —*Pref.* Includes some 29,000 entries (about 4,400 of them cross references), covering all fields of publication: government, church, trade, the professions, the sciences and humanities. Titles were gleaned chiefly from the *British union-catalogue of periodicals* (AE196), the *Union list of serials* (AE182), the British Museum's catalog of newspapers for 1801–1900 (AF42*n*), and the Times's *Tercentenary handlist of English and Welsh newspapers, magazines and reviews* (AF44). Information available on many titles is admittedly sketchy, but the following points are covered as far as possible: subtitle, numbering, publication dates, editor, place of publication, publisher, printer, price, size, frequency, illustrations, circulation, sponsoring body, indexing, mergers, alternate titles, and descriptive or explanatory notes. Discrepancies between earlier listings are also noted.

"Phase II" of the project is planned to result in "a comprehensive directory . . . based on the alphabetical listing of Phase I, augmented and corrected by actual shelf-checks" (*Pref.*) and supplying additional categories of information. A subject guide to the present volume is promised.   Z6956.G6W63

Current

Benn's Press directory. Ed. 126– , 1978– . Tonbridge, Eng., Benn's Pubns. Ltd., 1978– . Annual.   **AE90**

Continues *Newspaper press directory,* ed.1–125, originally published by C. Mitchell, then by Benn, 1846–1977.

Issued in two parts, now designated as *Benn's Press directory: United Kingdom* and *Benn's Press directory: international.*

Contains particulars of newspapers, periodicals, house organs, etc., published in the United Kingdom, with less full information on the press and periodical publications of other countries throughout the world. The U.K. section includes information on radio and television broadcasting.   Z6956.E5M6

Current British journals. Ed. by David P. Woodworth. 3d ed. Boston Spa, [Eng.], Publ. by the British Library Lending Div. in assoc. with the UK Serials Group, 1982. 312p.   **AE91**

1st–2d eds. (1970–73) had title: *Guide to current British journals.*

Arranged by Universal Decimal Classification, with an alphabetical index of titles and a subject index to the UDC numbers. Entries include title, date of first issue, publisher's name and address, indication of main subject content, frequency, where indexed or abstracted, title changes, availability in microform, ISSN. Prices are omitted in this edition. Entries are based mainly on information supplied by individual publishers.   Z6956.G6G84

Willing's Press guide, 1874– . London, Willing, 1874– . v.1– . Annual.   **AE92**

A useful, standard list for Great Britain, with some international coverage and some variation in content over the years.

Principal contents of 110th ed., 1984: Alphabetical list of newspapers and periodicals published in the United Kingdom, including the year of establishment, when published, price and publisher's name and address; Overseas section (listing newspaper and periodicals by region, then by country); Classified index to publications; Newspaper index (listing U.K. newspapers grouped as National and Greater London, England, Wales, Scotland, Channel Islands, Isle of Man, Northern Ireland, Republic of Ireland, and referring to the alphabetical list for full details); and a directory of services and supplies.   Z6956.E5W5

Hungary

Dezsényi, Béla. A magyar hirlapirodalom elsö százada (1705–1805). Budapest, Magyar Nemzeti Múzeum Orszá-

gos Széchényi Könyvtara, 1941. 66p. (Magyarország idöszaki sajtójának könyvészete, 1)   **AE94**

Lists, with location, periodicals and newspapers published in Hungary from 1705 to 1805.   PN5168.H8D4

Kemény, György. Magyarország idöszaki sajtója, 1911–töl 1920–ig. Budapest, Magyar Nemzeti Múzeum Országos Széchényi Könyvtára, 1942. 474p. (Magyarország idöszaki sajtójának könyvészete, 4)   **AE95**

An alphabetical list of periodicals and newspapers published in Hungary from 1911 to 1920.

Budapest. Országos Széchényi Könyvtár. A magyar sajtó bibliográfiája, 1945–1954. Dezsényi Béla, Falvy Zoltán [és] Fejér Judit. Budapest, "Müvelt Nép," 1956. 159p. (Az Országos Széchényi Könyvtár kiadványai, 36)   **AE96**

Alphabetical listing of periodicals and newspapers published in Hungary between 1945 and 1954.   Z6956.H8D4

Magyar nemzeti bibliográfia. Idószaki kiadványok bibliográfiája. 1981– . Budapest, Országos Széchényi Könyvtár, 1983– . Annual.   **AE97**

Continues: *Kurrens idószaki kiadványok,* 1976–80.

Introductory matter in Hungarian, English, and Russian.

A comprehensive record of current periodicals (including yearbooks and directories, professional and local publications, etc.) and newspapers. Title listing with index of corporate bodies.

India

Gandhi, H. N. D., Lal, Jagdish and **Agrawal, Suren.** Indian periodicals in print, 1973. Delhi, Vidya Mandal, [1973]. 2v.   **AE98**

An alphabetical title list of periodicals (including newspapers) which indicates language, title changes, beginning date, frequency, sponsoring body and address, and price. Sponsor and subject indexes. Serves as an extensive bibliography, though out of date as an in-print list.   Z6958.I4G35

Gidwani, N. N. and **Navalani, K.** Current Indian periodicals in English: an annotated guide. 2d rev. enl. ed. Jaipur, Saraswati Publs., 1978. 403p.   **AE99**

1st ed. (1969) had title: *Indian periodicals.*

A classified listing of about 5,000 English-language periodicals published in India. Index of titles and subject headings. Brief annotations (indicating scope, indexing, etc.) accompany many of the entries.   Z6958.I4G5

Indonesia

Reid, Anthony, Jubb, Annemarie and **Jahmin, J.** Indonesian serials, 1942–1950, in Yogyakarta libraries, with a list of government publications in the Perpustakaan Negara, Yogyakarta. Canberra, Australian Univ. Pr. in assoc. with the Faculty of Asian Studies, Australian Nat. Univ., 1974. 133p. (Oriental monograph ser., 15)   **AE100**

Includes newspapers as well as periodicals. Listing is by place of publication. Indexed.   Z3275.R44

Thung, Yvonne and **Echols, John M.** A guide to Indonesian serials (1945–1965) in the Cornell University Library. Ithaca, N.Y., Dept. of Asian Studies, Cornell Univ., 1966. 151p. (Cornell Univ. Modern Indonesia Project. Bibliography ser.)   **AE101**

Supersedes an earlier publication by Benedict R. Anderson, *Bibliography of Indonesian publications . . . 1945–1958* (Ithaca, N.Y., 1959).   Z6958.I45T5

Iran

A directory of Iranian periodicals. 1969–76/77. Tehran, Tehran Book Processing Centre, 1969–77. Irregular. **AE102**

Poori Soltani, comp.

Publisher varies. Also published in Persian.

Each issue is a listing of periodicals (i.e., magazines appearing at least twice a year) currently published during the period covered. Alphabetical title listing, with subject and name indexes.

Israel

Tronik, Ruth. Israeli periodicals & serials in English & other European languages: a classified bibliography. Metuchen, N.J., Scarecrow Pr., 1974. 193p. **AE103**

"Broadly speaking, this bibliography records materials emanating from scientific institutions, institutions of higher learning and learned societies to the scientific world at large."—*Introd.* Includes both current and defunct publications. Z6985.I8T76

Italy

Italy. Consiglio Nazionale delle Ricerche. Periodici italiani scientifici, tecnici e di cultura generale. 5.ed. interamente rinnovata, 1939. Roma, Arti Grafiche Trinacria, 1939. 3v. **AE104**

Gives detailed information about Italian periodicals current in the 1930s. Z7403.I88

Majolo Molinari, Olga. La stampa periodica romana dell' Ottocento. Roma, Istituto di Studi Romani, 1963. 2v. **AE105**

A comprehensive bibliography of some 1,700 Italian 19th-century periodicals with bibliographical details and descriptive annotations. Arranged alphabetically with indexes: chronological, subject, and name. Bibliography, v.2, p.1143–88. Z6956.I8M3

Periodici italiani 1886–1957. Roma, Istituto Centrale per il Catalogo Unico delle Biblioteche Italiane e per le Informazione Bibliografiche, 1980. 940p. **AE106**

A list of Italian periodicals extracted from the *Catalogo cumulativo 1886–1957 del Bollettino delle pubblicazioni italiane* (AA902) of the Biblioteca Nazionale Centrale, Florence.

Continued by:

Periodici italiani 1968–1981. Roma, Istituto Centrale per il Catalogo Unico delle Biblioteche Italiane e per le Informazione Bibliografiche, 1983. 612p. **AE107**

A title listing with indexes of title changes, supplements, editors, and corporate bodies.

Current

Annuario della stampa italiana, a cura della Federazione Nazionale della Stampa Italiana, 1954/55–59/60. Milano/Roma, Fratelli, Bocca, 1954–59. Irregular. **AE108**

A continuation of the annual of the same title publ. 1916–42.

Includes texts of laws of the press, professional organizations, material on journalism in Italy, and lists of periodicals and newspapers, Italian journalists, associations, etc. Z6956.I8A6

Catalogo dei periodici italiani 1981– . Roberto Maini [ed.]. [Milano], Editrice Bibliografica, [1980]– . Irregular? **AE109**

2d ed. 1983.

A directory of currently published Italian periodicals in three sections: title, subject, place of publication. Full information (address, frequency, price, etc.) appears in both the author and subject sections. Z6956.I8C18

Repertorio analitico della stampa italiana: quotidiani e periodici, 1964–69. Milano, Messaggerie Italiane, 1963–69. **AE110**

Lists periodicals in a simplified Dewey Decimal Classification with title index. The main list gives title, frequency, and city of publication; the title index indicates subscription prices.

An *Indirizzi* volume was published 1965 and 1966, listing the periodicals in alphabetical order with addresses. Z6956.I8R4

Japan

Nihon shimbun zasshi benran. Tokyo, Shimbun Zasshi Chō-saki, 1962– . Annual. **AE111**

A handbook of Japanese magazines and newspapers. A section covering United Nations resolutions and other relevant public documents is followed by a directory of trade organizations and a classified directory of newspaper and periodical publishers. Index of publishing companies and their officials.

Nihon zasshi sōran. Tokyo, Shuppan Nyūsu-sha, 1963– . Irregular. **AE112**

The 1984 ed. provides directory information on 21,001 titles published in Japan and current as of Dec. 1983. Periodicals are grouped in six categories: general; scholarly journals; government publications; association publications; literary society publications; and publicity or corporate in-house publications. Arrangement varies within categories. Title index; publishers' directory. Z6958.J3N56

Zasshi shimbun sōkatarogu. Periodicals in print. Tokyo, Media Research Center, 1979– . Annual. **AE113**

The 5th ed. covers 14,796 titles current as of Dec. 1983 (11,224 Japanese magazines; 3,431 newspapers and newsletters; and 141 foreign publications). Classified arrangement with indexes of titles and classification codes.

While not as complete as *Nihon zasshi sōran* (above) for periodicals or *Nihon shimbun nenkan* (AF50) for newspapers, this has the advantage of annual updating as well as covering both types of publication in a single volume. Z6958.J3Z37

Korea

Yi, Pyong-mok. Han'guk ǔi taehak chŏnggi kanhaengmul. [Bibliography of university periodicals of Korea, 1945–1964, with directory of institutions of higher education, by Byung Mock Rhee.] Seoul, Dept. of Lib. Science, Yonsei Univ., 1964. 265p. (Library Science ser. of Yonsei Univ., no.15) **AE114**

Added title page and abstract in English.

A listing of "all known periodicals which have ever been or are currently published by the higher learning institutions . . ."—*Abstract.* Z6958.K6Y5

Latin America

See also AA145.

Committee on Latin America. Literature with language, art and music. Ed. by L. Hallewell. London, Committee on Latin America, 1977. 253p. (Latin American serials, v.3) **AE115**

A listing by country of publication of Latin American periodicals on linguistics, literature, art and music held in British libraries. Z5961.L3C65

La Plata. Universidad Nacional. Biblioteca. Catálogo de periódicos sudamericanos existentes en la Biblioteca Pública de la Universidad (1791–1861). La Plata, 1934. 231p.
AE116

Detailed bibliographical information concerning Latin-American periodicals published 1791–1861. Z6954.A6L25

Levi, Nadia [et al.], comp. Guía de publicaciones periódicas de universidades latinoamericanas. México, Universidad Nacional Autónoma de México, 1967. 406p. **AE117**

At head of title: Unión de Universidades de América Latina. Hemeroteca Universitaria Latinoamericana.

A title listing within country divisions is followed by a classified index by faculty or subject field and a university index. Z6944.S3L4

Maison des Sciences de l'Homme. Service d'Échange d'Informations Scientifiques. Liste mondiale des périodiques spécialisés: Amérique Latine. World list of specialized periodicals: Latin America. Paris, Mouton, [1974]. 186p. (*Its* Publications, série C. Catalogues et inventaires, 5). **AE118**

Provides directory and brief descriptive information on 381 periodicals devoted to Latin America (regardless of where published) and limited to the "social and human sciences" (i.e., social and cultural anthropology, sociology, political science, economics, demography, linguistics, social psychology). Arranged by country of publication. Subject and title indexes. Z1605.M33

Pan American Union. Repertorio de publicaciones periódicas actuales latinoamericanas. Directory of current Latin American periodicals. Répertoire des périodiques en cours publiés en Amerique latine. [Paris], UNESCO, [1958]. 266p. (UNESCO bibliographical handbooks [8]) **AE119**

Lists 3,375 titles, arranged by Universal Decimal Classification, with geographical index and subject indexes in Spanish, English, and French. No title index. Z6954.S8P3

Zimmerman, Irene. A guide to current Latin American periodicals: humanities and social sciences. Gainesville, Fla., Kallman Pub. Co., 1961. 357p. **AE120**

"Primarily an annotated, evaluative bibliography . . ."—*Introd.* Lists 668 active periodicals and 117 on a "casualty list." Includes periodicals published in South and Central America, Mexico, and the West Indies, together with those published in the United States by Latin Americans and those dealing with Latin-American languages and literatures, etc.

Main arrangement is alphabetical by country, followed by a classified section and a chronological listing. The annotations, given in the first section, are full in descriptive and evaluative information. The "casualty list" records those periodicals from which the author had not been able to elicit recent information. Z6954.S8Z5

Latvia

Latviešu periodika: bibliogrāfisks rādītājs. Riga, "Zinātne," 1976–77. 2v. **AE121**

At head of title: Latvijas PSR Zinātņu Akadēmija. Fundamentālā Bibliotēka.

Contents: v.1, 1768–1919; v.2, 1920–1940.

A 1966 ed. covered 1768–1919 only.

A bibliography of Latvian periodicals, with full publication details, editors' names, etc. Numerous tables and indexes. Z6956.L36L35

Latvijas PSR periodiskie izdevumi. Riga, Latvijas PSR Valsts Grāmatu Palāta, 1982– . v.1– . (In progress) **AE122**

Added title page in Russian: Periodicheskie izdaniia.

Contents: v.1, 1940–1960.

A bibliography of Latvian periodicals with full bibliographical description and detailed record of all issues published.

Malaysia

Harris, L. J. Guide to current Malaysian serials. Kuala Lumpur, Univ. of Malaya Lib., 1967. 73p. **AE123**

Classified list with title and subject index. Descriptive and bibliographical notes. Z6958.M3H3

Roff, William R. Bibliography of Malay and Arabic periodicals published in the Straits Settlements and peninsular Malay states 1876–1941; with an annotated union list of holdings in Malaysia, Singapore and the United Kingdom. London, Oxford Univ. Pr., 1972. 74p. (London oriental bibliographies, 3) **AE124**

A revision and expansion of the same compiler's *Guide to Malay periodicals, 1876–1941* (Singapore, 1961). In addition to new and updated information on holdings, locations, and availability of microfilms, some new titles have been added, U.K. locations supplied, and historical or explanatory notes appended for most entries. A chronological listing with indexes of titles and of proper names. Z6958.M3R64

Mexico

Directorio de publicaciones periódicas mexicanas: 1981. Guanajuato, Gto., [1982]. 200p. **AE125**

At head of title: Universidad de Guanajuato. Dirección General de Bibliotecas. Departamento de Investigaciones Bibliotecológicas.

A title listing with subject and geographic indexes. Gives beginning date, address, frequency, subscription price, and circulation.

Mendoza López, Margarita. Catálogo de publicaciones periódicas mexicanas. México, 1959. 262p. **AE126**

At head of title: Centro Mexicano de Escritores.

Listing is by place of publication, then alphabetical by title. Detailed directory-type information is given, with auxiliary lists of titles for which full information was not available. Z6954.M6M4

Near and Middle East

Ahmed-Bioud, Abdelghani. 3200 revues et journaux arabes de 1800 à 1965; titres arabes et titres translittérés. Répertoire établi par Ahmed-Bioud. Paris, Bibliothèque Nationale, 1969. 252p. **AE127**

At head of title: Maison des Sciences de l'Homme.

Locates files of the periodicals listed in libraries throughout the world (e.g., Harvard and Princeton locations are noted). Alphabetical title listing, with index by transliterated form. Includes a supplement of "230 revues et journaux tunisiens." Z6957.A34

Aman, Mohammed M. Arab periodicals and serials: a subject bibliography. N.Y., Garland, 1979. 252p. (Garland reference library of social science, v.57). **AE128**

A subject listing of "serials and periodicals in Arabic, English, French and other European languages published in the Arab countries or in the Western hemisphere."—*Introd.* Includes current publications and some which have ceased; daily and weekly newspapers, irregular serials, and annuals are included along with monthly and quarterly magazines and government-sponsored series. Subject categories (such as Agriculture, Biological sciences, Business and industry, Children and youth, Economics, General periodicals, Middle East studies, Public administration) are in alphabetical order, with titles arranged alphabetically therein. About 2,700 items. No index. Z3013.5.A42

Bloss, Ingeborg and **Schmidt-Dumont, Marianne.** Zeitschriftenverzeichnis Moderner Orient, Stand 1979. Union list of Middle East periodicals (up to 1979). Hamburg, Deutsches Orient-Institut, Dokumentations-Leitstelle Moderner Orient, 1980. 657p. (Dokumentationsdienst Moderner Orient, B, 1) **AE129**

Prefatory matter in German and English.

A union list of Middle East periodicals in the libraries of the Federal Republic of Germany and West Berlin. Limited to those periodicals which were current in 1918 or which have begun publication since that date. Titles in non-Roman alphabets are given in transliteration.   Z3015.B57

Netherlands

Handboek van de Nederlandse pers en publiciteit. Uitg. 42– , Sept. 1974– . Semiannual.   **AE130**

Continues *Handboek van de Nederlandse pers* (1964–74) which, in turn, continued a looseleaf ed. of the same title publ. 1956–63.

The main part of each volume is now an alphabetical list of periodicals and newspapers with directory information. Includes a classified list of titles, plus special lists of new publications, title changes, cessations, etc.   Z6956.N45H352

New Zealand

See Australia and New Zealand.

Nigeria

Ibadan, Nigeria. University. Library. Nigerian periodicals and newspapers, 1950–1970. [Ibadan], Ibadan Univ. Lib., 1971. 122p.   **AE131**

Subtitle: A list of those [periodicals and newspapers] received by Ibadan University Library under the country's various deposit legislations from April 1950 to June 1970.

Supersedes the edition covering 1950–55 (publ. 1956). Includes periodicals which were already being published in 1950 when deposit legislation went into effect.   Z6960.N5I2

National Library of Nigeria. Serials in print in Nigeria, 1967– . Lagos, 1967– . Irregular. (National Library publs. 5, 15, etc.)   **AE132**

Includes newsletters, annuals, and government serials as well as magazines and newspapers.

Pakistan

Moid, A. and **Siddiqui, Akhtar H.** A guide to periodical publications and newspapers of Pakistan. Karachi, Pakistan Bibliographical Working Group, Karachi Univ. Lib., [1953]. 60p. (*Its* Publ. no.2)   **AE133**

A classified arrangement with very brief information: title, address, frequency, and price.   Z3193.M6

Philippines

Golay, Frank H. and **Hauswedell, Marianne H.** An annotated guide to Philippine serials. Ithaca, N.Y., Southeast Asia Program, Dept. of Asian Studies, Cornell Univ., 1976. 131p. (Data paper, 101).   **AE134**

Based on the holdings of the Cornell University Library. Arranged as two lists, each with its own index: (1) non-governmental serials; (2) government serials.   Z6958.P5G64

Poland

Bibliografia czasopism i wydawnictw zbiorowych, 1958– . Warszawa, Biblioteka Narodowa, Inst. Bibliograficzny, 1960– . Annual.   **AE135**

Also has title *Bibliography of Polish serials.*

An alphabetical listing of periodicals with three indexes: (1) classified; (2) by organization or institution; (3) by editor.

Issue for 1971 (publ. 1974) last published?   Z6956.P7B5

Kowalik, Jan. Bibliografia czasopism polskich wydanych poza granicami Kraju od wrzesnia 1939 roku. Lublin, Katolicki Uniwersytet Lubelski, 1976. 4v.   **AE136**

Added title page in English: *World index of Polish periodicals published outside of Poland since September 1939.* Introductory matter in Polish and English.

" . . . provides information about more than 3000 Polish periodicals published around the world in some sixty countries from September 1939 through September 1972."—*Introd.* Arranged by title, with indexes by subject, editor, and place of publication. Locates copies.   Z6956.P7K59

Krakow. Uniwersytet Jageillonska. Biblioteka. Katalog czasopism polskich Biblioteki Jagiellonskiej. [Pod red. Stanisława Grzeszczuka] Wyd. 2. Krakow, Nakładem Uniwersytetu Jagiellonskiego, 1974–82. v.1–5, 6²–8. (Varia, zesz. 94, 116, 131, 139, 144, 153, 162, 174) (In progress)   **AE137**

Contents: v.1–5, A–N; v.6², Praca szkolna–Q; v.7–8, R–Wiadomsci zeglarskie.

A main-entry catalog of Polish periodicals in the library, with an issue-specific record of holdings.   Z6956.P7K72

London. Polish Library. Catalogue of periodicals in Polish or relating to Poland and other Slavonic countries published outside Poland since September 1st, 1939. 2d ed. Comp. by Maria Danilewicz and Barbara Jabłońska. London, 1971. 126p.   **AE138**

Added title page and preface in Polish.

1st ed. 1964.

Lists more than 1,000 titles in alphabetical sequence.

     Z6956.P7L6

Polska Akademia Nauk. Pracownia Historii Czasopiśmiennictwa Polskiego XIX–XX Wieku. Bibliografia prasy polskiej, 1944–1948. Prasa krajowa. Warszawa, Państwowe Wydawnictwo Naukowe, [1966]. 323p. (*Its* Materiały i studia do historii prasy i czasopiśmiennictwa polskiego, zesz. 1)   **AE139**

A chronological bibliography of the Polish press, with indexes by journal title, editor, and place of publication.   Z6956.P7P62

Portugal

Boletim de bibliografia portuguesa. Publicações em série. 1982– . Lisboa, Biblioteca Nacional, [1983]– . Annual.   **AE140**

A companion publication to the *Boletim de bibliografia portuguesa. Monografias* (AA1038).

An alphabetical title listing of new serial publications, with full bibliographical information; indexes by issuing/sponsoring bodies, by subjects, and by places of publication.

Romania

Newspapers and periodicals from Romania. Journaux et périodiques de Roumanie. Zeitungen und Zeitschriften aus Rumänien. 1958– . [Bucharest], Cartimex, 1958– . Irregular.   **AE141**

Text in English, French, and German.

A classified listing with alphabetical index. 1970 latest published? Z6956.R8N48

Publicaţiunile periodice româneşti (ziare, gazete, reviste). Bucureşti, Socec, 1913–69. 2v. **AE142**

v.2 issued by the Biblioteca of the Academia Republicii Socialiste România with title *Publicaţiile periodice româneşti.*

Contents: v.1, Catalog alfabetic, 1820–1906, descriere bibliografica de Nerva Hodoş şi Al.-Sadi Ionescu; v.2, Catalog alfabetic, 1907–1918, Supplement, 1790–1906, descriere bibliografica de George Baiculescu, Georgeta Radvica şi Neonila Onofrei.

A title listing with full bibliographical information, notes on title changes, editors, supplements issued, etc. Z2923.P9

Russia and the U.S.S.R.

Dement'ev, Aleksandr Grigor'evich, ed. Russkaia periodicheskaia pechat' (1702–1894); spravochnik. Moskva, Gospolitizdat, 1959. 835p. **AE143**

Z6956.R9D4

Cherepakhov, Matvei Samoilovich and **Fingerit, E. M.,** eds. Russkaia periodicheskaia pechat' (1895–Oktiabr' 1917); spravochnik. Moskva, Gospolitizdat, 1957. 351p. **AE144**

The two items above are companion publications. They are chronologically arranged and well-indexed handbooks giving extensive factual information, with political commentary, on the major social and literary periodicals (journals, almanacs, and newspapers) published in and outside Russia between 1702 and 1917. Included are editors' names, major contributors, special features, and references to supplements and indexes. PN5274.C43

Knyzhkova Palata Ukraïns'koi RSR. Periodychni vydannia URSR, 1918–1950: zhurnaly. Bibliohrafichnyi dovidnyk. Kharkiv, 1956. 461p. **AE145**

A bibliography of Ukrainian periodicals of the period.

Z6956.U4K5

Lisovskii, Nikolai Mikhailovich. Russkaia periodicheskaia pechat' 1703–1900 gg., bibliografiia i graficheskiia tablitsy. Petrograd, Shumakhore, 1915. 267p. tables. **AE146**

The standard bibliography for 18th- and 19th-century Russian journals and newspapers. Chronologically arranged, with indexes.

Z6956.R9L39

—— Bibliografiia russkoi periodicheskoi pechati 1703–1900 gg. (Materialy dlia istorii russkoi zhurnalistiki). Petrograd, 1915. 1067p. **AE147**

A separate printing of the previous title, in smaller format and without tables.
See also the handbook *Russkaia periodicheskaia pechat', 1702–1894* (AE143). Z6956.R964

Leningrad. Publichnaia Biblioteka. Bibliografiia periodicheskikh izdanii Rossii 1901–1916. Pod obshchei red. V. M. Barashenkova [i dr.]. Leningrad, 1958–61. 4v. **AE148**

Title also in English, German, French.
At head of title: L. N. Beliaeva, M. K. Zinov'eva, M. M. Nikiforov.

Full bibliographic description of periodicals, other than illegal publications, published within the territory of pre-1917 Russia. Includes newspapers; excludes annuals and almanacs. Entries are arranged alphabetically, with numerous indexes in v.4.

Supersedes the checking edition, *Predvaritel'nyi spisok periodicheskikh izdanii Rossii, 1901–1916* (Leningrad, 1949).

Z6956.R9L353

Vsesoiuznaia Knizhnaia Palata. Periodicheskaia pechat' SSSR, 1917–1949; bibliograficheskii ukazatel'. Moskva, 1955–63. 10v. in 11. **AE149**

[v.1¹⁻²], Zhurnaly, trudy i biulleteni po obshchestvenno-politicheskim i sotsial'no-ekonomicheskim voprosam. 1958. 317p., 267p.
[v.2] —— po estestvennym naukam i matematike. 1956. 219p.

[v.3] —— po tekhnike i promyshlennosti. 1955. 315p.
[v.4] —— po transporty, sviazy i kommunal'nomu delu. 1955. 124p.
[v.5] —— po sel'skomu khoziaistvu. 1955. 230p.
[v.6] —— po kul'turnomy stroitel'stvu, narodnomu obrazovaniiu i prosveshcheniiu. 1956. 198p.
[v.7] —— po zdravookhraneniiu, meditzine, fizicheskoi kul'ture i sportu. 1956. 170p.
[v.8] —— po iazykoznaniiu, literaturovedeniiu, khudozhestvennoi literature i iskusstvu. 1958. 218p.
[v.9] —— po voprosam pechati, bibliotechnogo dela i bibliografii. 1959. 191p.
[v.10], Svodnye ukazateli. 1963. 863p.

The major retrospective bibliography of periodicals, other than newspapers, published in the USSR in all languages from Nov. 1917 through 1949. Includes numbered series appearing irregularly. Gives full bibliographic information as to periodicity, numbering, title changes, etc. Each volume contains alphabetical index of titles, index of journals in languages other than Russian, index by place of publication, and index of publishers and issuing organizations; master indexes in the last volume.

Continued chronologically by the quinquennial cumulations of *Letopis' periodicheskikh izdanii SSSR* (AE152). Z6956.R9V8

Schatoff, Michael. Half a century of Russian serials, 1917–1968; cumulative index of serials published outside the USSR. Ed. by N. A. Hale. N.Y., Russian Book Chamber Abroad, 1970–72. 4pts. **AE150**

Contents: pts.1–3, 1917–1956, A–Z; pt.4, 1957–1968, A–Z.

Lists newspapers and magazines published in Russian outside the USSR. Indicates place and dates of publication, and editor if known.

Pt. 1 (1917–56, A–M) appeared in a 2d ed., rev., 1972.

Z6956.R9S35

Smits, Rudolf. Half a century of Soviet serials, 1917–1968; a bibliography and union list of serials published in the USSR. Wash., Lib. of Congress, 1968. 2v. **AE151**

Supersedes Smits's earlier compilation, *Serial publications of the Soviet Union, 1939–1957* (Wash., 1958). Scope is herein extended to include "all known serial publications appearing in the Soviet Union at regular or irregular intervals since 1917, in all except oriental languages such as Armenian, Georgian, Kirghiz, etc."— *Pref.* More than 29,700 entries; symbols for U.S. and Canadian libraries are given whenever a title is known to be represented in a collection (but, as in the earlier compilation, an exact record of individual holdings is not attempted). Z6956.R9S58

Current

Letopis' periodicheskikh izdanii SSSR. 1933–70. Moskva, Izd-vo Vsesoiuznoi Knizhnoi Palaty, 1933–75. Annual. **AE152**

Suspended 1940–45.

Quinquennial cumulations have been published for 1950/54, 1955/60 (in 2v.), 1961/65 (2 pts. in 3v.), 1966/70 (in 2v.).

Lists all Soviet periodical publications. Pt.1 includes journals, proceedings, bulletins, and those annuals and collections which appear with continuous numbering. Pt.2 lists newspapers geographically, with alphabetical and subject indexes. The 1966/70 cumulation supersedes only the *Novye* parts.

Supplements, for continuing titles and for new and changed titles, appeared as: Z6956.R9L36

—— Trudy, uchennye zapiski, sborniki i drugie prodolzhaiushchiesia izdaniia. 1961–1970. Moskva, 1963–72. Annual.

—— Novye, pereimenovannye i prekrativshiesia zhurnaly i gazety. S. IAnvaria 1961 g. po–1970. Moskva, 1963–72. Cumulative.

The annual volumes of the main work are continued in part by:

Letopis' periodicheskikh i prodolzhaiushchikhsia izdanii. Sborniki, 1971– . Moskva, Kniga, 1976– . Annual.

AE153

Issued by: Gosudarstvennyi Komitet SSSR po Delam Izdatelstv, Poligrafii i Knizhnoi Torgovli [i] Vsesoiuznaia Knizhnaia Palata.

A comprehensive listing of periodical publications; newspapers are listed in a biennial *Biulleteni* section (AF64). A separate *Novye* section is issued annually, beginning with an issue covering Jan. 1976–Mar. 1977 (publ. 1977).

Cumulates quinquennially in: Z6956.S65L474

Letopis' periodicheskikh i prodolzhaiushchikhsia izdanii. 1971/75– . Moskva, Kniga, 1977– . Quinquennial.

AE154

Issued in two parts: v.1, Zhurnaly; v.2, Gazety. (1971/75 publ. 1977–81 in 2v.; 1976/80, chast 1, publ. 1983; in progress).

Z6956.S65L47

Bibliography

Leningrad. Publichnaia Biblioteka. Obshchie bibliografii russkikh periodicheskikh izdanii, 1703–1954, i materialy po statistike russkoi periodicheskoi pechati; annotirovannyi ukazatel'. Pod red. P. N. Berkova. Leningrad, 1956. 139p. (Bibliografiia russkoi bibliografii)   AE155

At head of title: M. V. Mashkova i M. V. Sokurova.

General bibliographies, annotated, of the Russian periodical press, together with statistical material. Supplements the bibliography of book bibliographies by Sokurova (AA104).   Z2491.A1L44

Scandinavia

Media Scandinavia. [Ed.1–] København, Danske Reklamebureauers Brancheforening, 19?– . Annual.   AE156

Title varies: 19?–59, Eberlins Bladliste; 1960–61, Bladlisten; 1962–70, Media.

"Media Scandinavia contains—in Danish and English—information on advertising media in Denmark, Norway, Sweden, Finland, Iceland and the Faroe Islands."—*t.p., Ed.33, 1984.*

Lists daily newspapers, weeklies, trade papers, annuals, and other advertising media, associations, etc. Arranged by country, with fullest coverage for Denmark.

South Africa

Advertising & press annual of Southern Africa. 1977–80. Cape Town, National Pub. Co., 1977–80. Annual.

AE157

Supersedes *Advertising & press annual of Africa* (1966–76).

Concerned only with Southern Africa. 1977 ed. in three main sections: (1) Press guide (to newspapers and periodicals of Southern Africa); (2) Radio, TV, cinema and outdoor advertising; (3) Mail advertising and postal information. Brief "who's who in advertising and publishing."

Superseded by:

Promadata: promotion, marketing & advertising data. 1981– . Johannesburg, Clarion Communications Media (PTY) Ltd., [1981]– . Annual.   AE158

The "Press guide" section includes magazines, yearbooks, etc., as well as newspapers. Has sections for radio and television advertising, advertising agencies, marketing services, etc.   Z6959.A65

Saul, C. Daphne. South African periodical publications, 1800–1875; a bibliography. Capetown, Univ. School of Librarianship, 1949. 45p.   AE159

Lists periodicals, almanacs, directories, and yearbooks; excludes newspapers, government publications, and annual reports of socie-

ties. Gives the usual bibliographical information and locates copies in South African libraries.   Z6960.S6S33

Southeast Asia

U.S. Library of Congress. Southeast Asia: Western-language periodicals in the Library of Congress. Comp. by A. Kohar Rony. Wash., Lib. of Congress, 1979. 201p.   AE160

A main-entry listing of nearly 2,300 periodicals in the Library of Congress collections which contain "information on Southeast Asia, including Brunei, Burma, Cambodia, Indochina, Indonesia, Laos, Malaysia, the Philippines, Portuguese Timor, Singapore, Thailand, and Vietnam, and on Melanesia and Polynesia."—*Pref.* Includes Western-language publications both from and outside those areas, and some which only occasionally deal with the region. Indicates holdings. Index by geographical area.   Z3221.U524

Spain

Bibliografía española. Suplemento de publicaciones periódicas. 1979– . Madrid, Dirección General del Libro y Bibliotecas, Instituto Bibliográfico Hispánico, [1980]– . Annual.

AE161

A classed listing of new periodical publications, giving full bibliographic information, frequency, etc.   Z2685.B572

Givanel Mas, Juan. Bibliografía catalana: premsa. Barcelona, [Impr. Altés], 1931–37. 3v. il.   AE162

Gives detailed bibliographical information about periodicals published in Catalonia, 1792–1925, arranged chronologically under cities. v.3 is an alphabetical index with historical notes and many facsimiles.   Z6956.S7G4

Instituto Bibliográfico Hispánico, Madrid. Revistas españolas, 1973–1978: repertorio bibliográfico. Madrid, El Instituto, 1978–79. 2v.   AE163

At head of title: Ministerio de Cultura, Dirección General del Libro y Bibliotecas, Subdirección General de Bibliotecas.

Contents: [v.1] 1973–77; [v.2] 1977–78.

An alphabetical title listing of Spanish periodicals being published during the periods indicated, plus listing by place of publication.

Z6956.S7I56

Madrid. Biblioteca Nacional. Publicaciones periódicas existentes en la Biblioteca Nacional; catálogo redactado y ordenado por Florentino Zamora Lucas y María Casado Jorge. Madrid, Dirección General de Archivos y Bibliotecas, Servicio de Publicaciones del Ministerio de Educación Nacional, 1952. 718p. il.   AE164

A classed list of almost 9,000 titles with alphabetical index of titles. Indicates place of publication, holdings of the library, and (sometimes) frequency.   Z6945.M14

—— **Hemeroteca Municipal.** Catálogo de las publicaciones periódicas madrileñas existentes en la Hemeroteca Municipal de Madrid, 1661–1930. Madrid, Artes Gráficas Municipales, 1933. 360p.   AE165

Arranged chronologically; alphabetical and chronological indexes.

Z6956.S7M16

Spain. Instituto de Cultura Hispánica. Departamento de Información. Catálogo de revistas españolas. Madrid, Ed. Cultura Hispánica, 1948. 216p.   AE166

A classified list of periodicals, omitting those of very limited interest. Gives detailed information for each, including editors, publishers, contributors, size, frequency, etc., but not dates. Subject and title indexes.   Z6956.S7S67

Current

Anuario de la prensa española, v.1– . Madrid, Editora Nacional, 1943– . Irregular. **AE167**

Some editions published in 2v.: pt.1, newspapers; pt.2, periodicals.

Edited for the Ministerio de Información y Turismo, Dirección General de Prensa.

v.1, 1943; v.2, 1945/46, v.3–5, 1953–62; vols. for 1965 and 1970[1] issued without *año* number.

Gives detailed information, including address, personnel, format, size, number of copies printed, etc. Z6956.S7S65

Sweden

See also AE156.

Lundstedt, Bernhard Wilhelm. Sveriges periodiska litteratur. Bibliografi. Stockholm, Iduns Tryckeri, 1895–1902. 3v. **AE168**

v.1, 1645–1812; v.2, Stockholm, 1813–94; v.3, Landsorten, 1813–99.

Gives detailed bibliographical information about Swedish periodicals and newspapers of the period. Each volume has its own title index; v.3 includes a systematic index for the set. Z6956.S9L9

Svensk tidskriftsförteckning. Current Swedish periodicals. 1967/68– . Stockholm, Tidningsaktiebolaget Svensk Bokhandel, 1968– . Triennial. **AE169**

"Redigerad av Bibliografiska Institutet vid Kungl. Biblioteket i Stockholm."—*t.p.*

In English and Swedish.

An alphabetical listing giving full bibliographic information on current periodicals, followed by a classed listing of the titles. Kept up to date by information in *Svensk bokförteckning.*

Switzerland

Bern. Schweizerische Landesbibliothek. Verzeichnis der laufenden schweizerischen Zeitschriften. Catalogue des périodiques suisses, revues, journaux, annuaires, almanachs, collections, etc., reçus par la Bibliothèque Nationale à Berne. 2. éd. refondue et considérablement augm., publ. par la direction de la Bibliothèque. Bern-Bümpliz, Benteli, [1925]. 217p. **AE170**

———— ———— Nachtrag, 1926–30. Bern-Bümpliz, Benteli, 1926–31. 5v.

A classified list with title index. Z6956.S92B3

Schweizerischer Zeitschriften- und Zeitungskatalog. Catalogue des revues et journaux suisses. Olten, Schweizerisches Vereinssortiment, [1945]. 239p. **AE171**

Classed list with title index of periodicals currently published in Switzerland and information on complete title, publisher, address, beginning date, frequency, size, general coverage, etc. Z6956.S92S35

Schweizer Zeitschriftenverzeichnis; Répertoire des périodiques suisses; Repertorio dei periodici svizzeri, 1951/55– . Zürich, Schweizerisches Buchhändler- und Verleger-Vereins, 1956– . Quinquennial. **AE172**

Forms pt.2 of the *Schweizerische Nationalbibliographie* (AA1123).

Gives quite complete bibliographical information for periodicals published in Switzerland. Except for newspapers, lists many kinds of serial publications appearing at least once a year—i.e., periodicals, annuals, almanacs, etc.—though certain categories are omitted (e.g., annual reports, religious tracts, business bulletins).

Classified arrangement with title index. Z6956.S92S33

Current

Katalog der Schweizer Presse: Zeitschriften, Fachblätter. Catalogue de la presse suisse: périodiques, journaux professionnels. [Zürich, Verband Schweizerischer Werbegesellschaften, 1969–] Annual. **AE173**

Subtitle varies.

Supersedes *Zeitungskatalog der Schweiz,* publ. 1950–68.

Introductory matter in German and French. Information is presented in tabular form. HF6023.K36

Taiwan

Annotated guide to Taiwan periodical literature, 1966– . Taipei, Prep. and distr. by Chinese Materials and Research Aids Service Center, 1966– . v.1– . **AE174**

Robert L. Irick, ed.

v.1 (102p.) provides directory information on more than 500 periodicals registered with the Ministry of the Interior, Republic of China, in 1964–65. Classed arrangement. No more published? Z6958.F6A75

Tunisia

Abdeljaoued, Mohamed. Répertoire de la presse et des publications périodiques tunisiennes. Tunis, École Normale Supérieure, 1979. 78p. **AE175**

A classed listing, with title index, of periodicals (including annual and irregular publications as well as those appearing more frequently) published in Tunisia. Indicates beginning date, address, frequency, etc. Includes both French and Arabic publications. Some periodicals known or thought to have ceased between 1975 and 1979 are still included with a note on cessation.

Yugoslavia

Bibliografija Jugoslavije: serijske publikacije. jan./mart 1975– . Beograd, Jugoslovenski Bibliografski Institut, 1975– . Quarterly with annual index. **AE176**

Title page in Croat, Serbian, and Macedonian.

Continues *Bibliografija jugoslovenske periodike* publ. 1956–74.

A current listing of periodicals and newspapers. Z6956.Y9B48

Jugoslovenski casopisi (izbor). Ed.[1]–2. Beograd, Jugoslovenski Centar za Tehničku i Naučnu Dokumentaciju, 1953–55. **AE177**

Title also in English (*Yugoslav periodicals: selection*), French, and German.

A classified list with title index. All headings are given in the four languages: Yugoslavian, English, French, German. Titles are also translated into the four languages. Gives publisher, address, beginning date, frequency, price, language of text, etc. Z6956.Y9J8

UNION LISTS

❖In general, union lists are entered under the name of the country or region where the holding libraries are located; thus, *Lithuanian periodicals in American libraries* is listed under "United States."

International

See also AE129, AE210–AE211.

Bakunina, Tatiana A. L'émigration russe en Europe; catalogue collectif des périodiques en langue russe, établi par Tatiana Ossorguine-Bakounine. Paris, Institut d'Études Slaves, 1976–77. 2v. (Institut d'Études Slaves. Bibliothèque russe, t.40¹) **AE178**

Contents: [v.1] 1885–1940 (340p.); [v.2] 1940–1970, établi par Anne-Marie Volkoff (139p).

Lists and locates files of Russian émigré publications published in the Russian language in European countries other than Russia. v.1 is in two parts: 1855–Feb. 1917, and Mar. 1917–1939, each being an alphabetical title listing. Entries are given in Cyrillic characters, with notes on holdings, etc., in French. Indexes of transliterated titles and of names cited. About 1,900 entries. Z6956.R9B25

The bibliography of South Asian periodicals: a union-list of periodicals in South Asian languages. Comp. by Graham W. Shaw, Salim Quraishi. [Brighton] Sussex, Harvester Pr.; [Totowa, N.J., Barnes & Noble, 1982]. 135p. **AE179**

A union catalog for six British libraries. South Asia is defined as encompassing India, Pakistan, Bangladesh, Nepal, Bhutan, Sikkim, Sri Lanka and Afghanistan. Aims to record all serials written wholly or partly in a South Asian language and published anywhere in the world which can be found in the cooperating libraries. Listing is by language. Z6958.S57B5

Nunn, Godfrey Raymond. Japanese periodicals and newspapers in Western languages: an international union list. London, Mansell, 1979. 235p. **AE180**

An international list of some 3,500 periodicals and newspapers held by libraries in Great Britain, Canada, the United States, and Japan. Z6958.J3N86

United States

Bibliography

U.S. Library of Congress. General Reference and Bibliography Division. Union lists of serials; a bibliography. Comp. by Ruth S. Freitag. Wash., 1964. 150p. **AE181**

Updates the bibliography compiled by D. C. Haskell and Karl Brown which appeared in the 2d ed. of the *Union list of serials in libraries of the United States and Canada* (N.Y., 1943. p.3053–65). Lists more than 1,200 union lists, arranged geographically by region and country. Includes both separately published works and lists published in journals or as parts of books. Z6945.U5U53

Lists

Union list of serials in libraries of the United States and Canada. 3d ed., ed. by Edna Brown Titus. N.Y., Wilson, 1965. 5v. (4649p.) **AE182**

History: 1st ed. 1927 (Supplements, Jan. 1925–Dec. 1932. 2v.); 2d ed. 1943 (Supplements, Jan. 1941–Dec.1949. 2v.), ed. by Winifred Gregory. (For a history of the *Union list* and its predecessors, *see* Preface by Howard Rovelstad.)

The 1st ed. contained entries for some 75,000 serial titles with location of holdings in 225 libraries in the United States and Canada. The 2d ed. was enlarged to some 115,000 titles with locations in 650 libraries. The two supplements brought this record up to Dec. 1949 with additional titles. These two editions proved that this comprehensive union list was indispensable in American libraries doing research and reference work with periodicals. Therefore, under the sponsorship of the Joint Committee on the Union List of Serials, with the cooperation of the Library of Congress, and funded by a grant from the Council on Library Resources, Inc., a 3d ed. was prepared.

The 3d ed. follows closely the pattern of the 2d, listing the entries

in the 2d ed., plus those in the two supplements, with the addition of almost 12,000 new titles which began publication before 1950, thus listing more than 156,000 titles, with holdings in 956 cooperating libraries. For the titles acquired by cooperating libraries since the 2d ed. and its supplements, additional locations are reported for "significant titles only—titles not commonly held. Additional locations were not to be listed whenever ten or more locations had already been listed in the second edition and supplements unless considered both desirable and necessary—e.g., geographical considerations."—*Introd.*

Each entry gives catalog description of title (under *latest* form of name), a statement of what constitutes a complete set, and indicates changes of title and exact holdings in reporting libraries, with cross references from all changed titles and alternate entries. Includes all types of serial publications except: government publications (other than periodicals and monograph series issued by governments); United Nations publications; administrative reports of societies, universities, corporations, etc.; almanacs; gift books; American newspapers; English and other foreign newspapers after 1820; law reports and digests; publications of agricultural and other experiment stations; local religious, labor, and fraternal organizations; boards of trade; chambers of commerce; national and international conferences and congresses, etc.; house organs (unless of technical and scientific value); alumni, undergraduate, and intercollegiate fraternal publications; trench papers; and in general all titles having a highly limited or ephemeral value.—cf. *Introd.* It was found to be impractical to incorporate entries for titles in the Far Eastern languages.

This edition, covering to Dec. 1949, will be the last in this form. Continued for periodicals begun after 1950 by *New serial titles* (below) Z6945.U45

New serial titles; a union list of serials commencing publication after Dec. 31, 1949. Wash., Lib. of Congress, Jan. 1953– . **AE183**

Monthly with annual cumulations (beginning 1969, in 8 monthly issues, 4 quarterly issues, and annual cumulation), which are self-cumulative through periods of three or more years. As of 1984 a set of cumulations includes 1950–70 in 4v.; 1971–75 in 2v.; 1976–80 in 2v.; 1981–83 in 3v.

Prepared under the sponsorship of the Joint Committee on the Union List of Serials; serves as a continuation of the *Union list* (above).

Lists periodicals which began publication in 1950 and later, giving place of publication and statement of beginning date (and closing date if pertinent) with record of holdings in about 700 United States and Canadian libraries. Additional locations are published in each cumulation. Through 1980, a section at the back of each cumulation listed "Changes in serials" and noted changes for all serials regardless of their beginning date. "These changes include title changes, changes in the name or catalog entry of corporate authors, cessations, suspensions, resumptions and the like."

See below for the 1950–70 cumulation.

In 1981, *NST* became a product of the CONSER (CONversion of SERials) Project, an online cooperative database, with coverage including reports of all serials contributed to the CONSER file, regardless of beginning date of publication. Information is now presented in traditional "card catalog" format, with the fullness of the record depending on the amount of data available in the CONSER record. Catalog "tracings" are included along with bibliographic information and library locations. Generally speaking, records appear as "open" entries; there is no indication of holdings of individual libraries. The "Changes in serials" feature last appeared in the 1976–80 cumulation. Z6945.U5S42

——— 1950–1970 cumulative. Wash., Lib. of Congress; N.Y., Bowker, 1973. 4v.

Represents considerably more than a mere cumulation of the information in the earlier volumes (above). The complete *NST* file has been converted to a computer data base, thousands of revisions have been incorporated, thousands of additional library locations supplied, and International Standard Serial Numbers (ISSN) added. The supplementary "Changes in serials" section appears at the end of v.4. Although the cumulation was edited by the Bowker Company, utilizing that firm's computer-produced publication system, further *NST* quarterly and annual cumulations continue to be published by Library of Congress.

Special care must be taken in searching corporate entries in this cumulation owing to irregularities in the filing (e.g., "Mauritania. Journal officiel" files between "Mauritania. Gouverneur. Discours . . ." and "Mauritania. Laws, statutes, etc. Recueil des lois. . . .").

—————— 1950–1970, subject guide. N.Y., Bowker, 1975. 2v. (3692p.) **AE183a**

"Based on the *New Serial Titles 1950–1970* published by Library of Congress and R. R. Bowker Company."—*t.p.*

Offers a subject approach, according to the Dewey Decimal Classification, of the titles appearing in the 1950–70 cumulation of *New serial titles* (above). Information from the cumulation was edited and refined to provide greater consistency and utility. A list of subject headings in alphabetical sequence (with Dewey class number indicated) and an index to the subject headings serve as guides for the user. There is also a list of the subject headings in numerical sequence, and a correlation table indicating the range of Dewey numbers included in the subject heading numbers employed in the guide. Z6945.N42

Balys, John P. Lithuanian periodicals in American libraries: a union list. Wash., Lib. of Congress, 1982. 125p. **AE184**

Lists and locates files of "newspapers, periodicals, and serial publications in the Lithuanian language published anytime and anywhere; periodicals on Lithuanian matters in other languages; and periodicals published in the territory of Lithuania in any language and at any time."—*Introd.* Only titles found in United States and Canadian libraries are included. Z6956.S65B34

Danky, James Philip. Undergrounds: a union list of alternative periodicals in libraries of the United States and Canada. Madison, State Historical Soc. of Wis., 1974. 206p. **AE185**

"The purpose of this list is to bring a heterogeneous group of often little-known periodicals to the attention of North American researchers and librarians."—*Introd.*

An alphabetical listing, with geographic index. Gives title, place of publication, and library location, but no indication of holdings or dates of publication. Indicates availability on microfilm, indexing in *Alternative press index* (AE240), and citations in other lists or directories. Z6944.U5D3

Indiana University. Libraries. Current Japanese serials in the humanities and social sciences received in American libraries. Bloomington, Indiana Univ. Lib., East Asian Collection, 1980. 337p. **AE186**

"Sponsored by the Japan-U.S. Friendship Commission."—*t.p.*

"The primary purpose of this listing . . . is to provide a tool for making judgments on curtailing and adding Japanese subscriptions."—*Pref.* A romanized title listing of nearly 4,400 serials. Symbols for holding libraries are given without indication of actual holdings. Z6958.J3I5

—————— Union list of little magazines . . . Chicago, Midwest Inter-Lib. Center, 1956. 98p. **AE187**

Subtitle: Showing holdings of 1037 little magazines in the libraries of Indiana University, Northwestern University, Ohio State University, State University of Iowa, University of Chicago, University of Illinois.

Willging, Eugene Paul and **Hatzfeld, Herta.** Catholic serials of the nineteenth century in the United States; a descriptive bibliography and union list. First series. Wash., Catholic Univ. of America Pr., 1968. 2v. **AE188**

First published as a series of 15 articles in the *Records* of the American Catholic Historical Society, Philadelphia, from 1954 to 1963. Information was revised and updated for this publication.

Covers 29 states in alphabetical order. For each state there is given: historical background, description of publications with library locations, special bibliography, alphabetical and chronological tables, etc.

States having longer histories and more extensive lists of Catholic publications are covered in the second series:

—————— —————— Second series. Wash., Catholic Univ. of America Pr., 1959–68. 15 pts.

Contents: pt.1, Minnesota, North Dakota and South Dakota; pt.2, Wisconsin; pt.3, Illinois; pt.4, Indiana; pt.5, Pennsylvania; pt.6, Iowa; pt.7, Michigan; pt.8, California; pt.9, Missouri; pt.10, Massachusetts; pt.11, Maryland and District of Columbia; pt.12, Kentucky and Ohio; pt.13, Louisiana, Mississippi, Texas; pt.14, v.1, New York City; pt.14, v.2, New York State; pt.15, Statistical analysis of 1st ser., pts.1–2 and 2d ser., pts.1–14.

The second series follows the arrangement of the first.
Z6951.W5

Belgium

Brussels. Bibliothèque Royale de Belgique. Catalogue collectif belge et luxembourgeois des périodiques étrangers en cours de publication, rédigé sous la direction de A. Cockx. Bruxelles, Culture et Civilisation, 1965. 2v. (1982p.) **AE189**

Title and introductory matter in Flemish and French.

Provides a finding list in libraries of Belgium and Luxembourg of periodicals currently published outside those areas. Some 400 libraries reported holdings, and the list of these forms a useful directory indicating accessibility, hours, and special services.
Z6945.B907

Canada

See also AE182–AE183.

Ottawa. National Library. Periodicals in the social sciences and humanities currently received by Canadian libraries. Inventaire des périodiques de sciences sociales et d'humanités possèdent les bibliothèques canadiennes. Ottawa, 1968. 2v. **AE190**

Preface and explanatory matter in French and English.

Offered as an "interim publication" pending publication of a proposed full-scale union list for Canadian libraries. Lists about 12,000 titles held by 179 libraries. Z6945.O895

France

Inventaire des périodiques étrangers et des publications en série étrangères reçus en France par les bibliothèques et les organismes de documentation en 1965. [4. éd.] Paris, Bibliothèque Nationale, 1969. 1207p. **AE191**

At head of title: Direction des Bibliothèques et de la Lecture Publique. Inventaire Permanent des Périodiques Étrangers en Cours (I.P.P.E.C.).

1st ed. 1956; 3d ed. 1962. Earlier editions had title: *Inventaire des périodiques étrangers reçus en France.*

Lists about 43,000 publications received in some 2,300 participating libraries and other repositories. Covers all subject fields. Gives title, subtitle, place of publication, and locations of files, but not dates of publication.

Paris. Bibliothèque Nationale. Département des Périodiques. Catalogue collectif des périodiques du début du XVIIe siècle à 1939, conservés dans les bibliothèques de Paris et dans les bibliothèques universitaires des départements. Paris, 1967–81. 5v. **AE192**

Contents: v.1–4, A–Z; v.5, Additions et corrections; Tables des collectivités citées.

An important union list of periodicals held by some 73 libraries in France. Unfortunately, coverage has been limited to serials which began publication before 1940. Excluded are: daily papers after 1849; almanacs; annual directories; administrative publications of limited interest (e.g., local church bulletins, alumni magazines).

Slavic periodicals in the Cyrillic alphabet are also excluded since these are listed in a separate catalog (AE193).

Entry is under first word of the title not an article. Thus, there are a great number of entries under "Proceedings," "Bulletin," etc., but the "Tables des collectivités citées" in v.5 enables the user to identify the publications of specific societies, organizations, and similar issuing bodies. Entries include dates of publication, notes on title changes, issuing body, supplements, cumulative indexes, and library locations with indication of exact holdings.   Z6945.P236

―――― Périodiques slaves en caractères cyrilliques; état des collections en 1950. Paris, 1956. 2v. (*Its* Catalogue collectif des périodiques conservés dans les bibliothèques de Paris et dans les bibliothèques universitaires de France)   **AE193**

―――― ―――― Supplément, 1951–1960. Paris, 1963. 495p.

―――― ―――― Addenda et errata, état général des collections en 1960. Paris, 1965. 222p.

A union list of periodical holdings of 46 libraries of Paris and of French universities. Russian, Ukrainian, Belorussian, Bulgarian, and Serbian titles are listed in one alphabet. Newspapers are excluded. Slavic periodicals in Latin characters are listed in the general section of the Bibliothèque Nationale's *Catalogue collectif des périodiques* (above).   Z6945.P24

Germany

Bruhn, Peter. Gesamtverzeichnis russischer und sowjetischer Periodika und Serienwerke; hrsg. von Werner Philipp. Wiesbaden, in Kommission bei O. Harrassowitz, [1960–76]. 4v. (Berlin. Freie Universität. Osteuropa Inst. Bibliographische Mitteilungen, 3)   **AE194**

Locates files of Russian and Soviet periodicals in libraries of the Federal Republic of Germany and West Berlin. Notable for its broad chronological, linguistic, and geographical coverage. Includes newspapers, yearbooks, almanacs, and numbered series; also publications of official and semiofficial Russian and Soviet groups abroad. Title listing, with a "Nachtrag" in v.3; v.4 is an index.

Gesamtverzeichnis ausländischer Zeitschriften und Serien 1939–1958 (GAZS). Bearb. und hrsg. von der Staatsbibliothek der Stiftung Preussischer Kulturbesitz. Wiesbaden, Harrassowitz, 1959–68. 5v.   **AE195**

Sponsoring body varies. Issued in parts.

An earlier series, *Gesamtverzeichnis der ausländischen Zeitschriften (GAZ) 1914–1924*, was issued by the Prussian Auskunftsbureau der deutschen Bibliotheken (Berlin, 1927–29).

An extensive list of non-German periodicals, with holdings in German libraries indicated in detail. Unfortunately, there is no key to the symbols used to indicate libraries; for this, reference must be made to Wolfgang Voigt's *Sigelverzeichnis für die Bibliotheken der Bundesrepublik Deutschland* (Wiesbaden, Harrassowitz, 1960).

―――― Nachträge. Marburg an der Lahn, Staatsbibliothek der Stiftung Preussische Kulturbesitz, 1966–76. 29 pts.

Great Britain

See also AE179, AE210.

British union-catalogue of periodicals; a record of the periodicals of the world, from the seventeenth century to the present day, in British libraries. Ed. for the Council of the British Union-Catalogue of Periodicals by James D. Stewart, with Muriel E. Hammond and Erwin Saenger. N.Y., Academic Pr.; London, Butterworths Scientific Publs., 1955–58. 4v.   **AE196**

Lists more than 140,000 titles contained in about 440 libraries with indication of holdings; an important addition to any library's collection of union lists. Includes many periodicals not in the *Union*

list of serials (AE182), and the difference in form of entry makes possible a different approach in identifying titles.

Periodicals are listed under the first word of the title, not an article, except that periodicals issued by an organization are entered under the name of the organization unless the title is specific in itself. All periodicals are entered under their *earliest* known names, followed by particulars of all changes of name in chronological sequence. References are given from all later names to the original name. Similarly all academies, societies, and other organizations are entered under their *original* names, with particulars of alternate names, and all changes of organization. References from all variants are given to the original name.

Alphabetization is by the words printed in heavy type; all minor words, articles, prepositions, conjunctions, etc., are printed but ignored in filing. Variant spellings such as "Bollettino" and "Bullettino" are amalgamated. Other details are explained at the beginning of v.1.

All locations for commonly held periodicals are not necessarily given, but in the case of rare periodicals all reported holdings, fragmentary or otherwise, have been included.

Supersedes for most purposes the *Union catalogue of the periodical publications in the university libraries of the British Isles* (London, Nat. Central Lib., 1937. 712p.).

―――― Supplement to 1960. Ed. for the Council of the British Union-Catalogue of Periodicals by James D. Stewart with Muriel E. Hammond and Erwin Saenger. London, Butterworths, 1962. 991p.

Includes entries for new periodicals reported as first appearing since publication of the main volumes, some expanded or amended entries, and some entries for earlier periodicals not previously reported.   Z6945.B87

British union-catalogue of periodicals, incorporating World list of scientific periodicals. New periodical titles. 1960/68–80. London, Butterworths, 1964–81. Quarterly; annual cumulations.   **AE197**

Ed. for the National Central Library by Kenneth I. Porter.

A cumulative issue for 1960–68, ed. by Kenneth I. Porter and C. J. Koster, was published 1970.

Aims to list periodicals and serials which began in or after 1960, changed title, began a new series, or ceased publication. Serves as a continuing supplement to both the *British union-catalogue* and the *World list* (EA53). Lists library holdings in British libraries.

Continued by: Z6945.B874

Serials in the British Library, together with locations and holdings of other British and Irish libraries. no.1– , June 1981– . [London], The British Library, 1981– . Quarterly printed issues; annual cumulation on microfiche.   **AE198**

Supersedes in part the quarterly *British union-catalogue of periodicals* which ceased with 1980 (AE197). Lists serial titles newly acquired by the British Library, together with locations, holdings, and additional titles reported by a small number of other libraries "selected on account of their geographical location or the significance of their collections."—*Pref.* (Some 21 libraries are covered, including various divisions of the British Library.) Full cataloging information is given. Main entry listing with many cross references.

Travis, Carole and **Alman, Miriam.** Periodicals from Africa: a bibliography and union list of periodicals published in Africa. Boston, G. K. Hall, [1977]. 619p.   **AE199**

At head of title: Standing Conference on Library Materials on Africa.

Aims to present "as comprehensive a list as possible of periodicals published in Africa, and at the same time, to give locations for those titles held in libraries in the United Kingdom."—*Introd.* (Egypt is excluded, and only those South African periodicals held in U.K. libraries are listed.) Arrangement is alphabetical by country of publication, then by title; comprehensive title index. Holdings of "some 60 university, national, government and private libraries, representing the major African collections in the United Kingdom" are recorded, but bibliographic information on many titles not located in those libraries is also given.   Z3503.T73

———— ———— First supplement. Comp. and ed. by David Blake and Carole Travis. Boston, G. K. Hall, [1984]. 217p.

Adds about 7,000 titles.

Italy

Catalogo dei periodici esistenti in biblioteche di Roma. Roma, 1975. 986p. **AE200**

At head of title: Unione Internazionale degli Istituti de Archeologia, Storia e Storia dell'Arte in Roma.

A union list of periodical holdings of some 35 libraries in Rome. Z6945.C343

Pinto, Olga. Elenco dei periodici correnti di scienze umane posseduti dalle biblioteche di Roma al 1 gennaio 1964. Roma, Società Liber, [1967]. 527p. **AE201**

Locates files of 8,770 current periodicals covering the humanities and social sciences in 155 libraries of Rome. Z6945.P57

Vatican. Biblioteca Vaticana. Catalogo delle pubblicazioni periodiche esistenti in varie biblioteche di Roma e Firenze. Città del Vaticano, 1955. 495p. **AE202**

Pubblicato con la collaborazione dell' Unione Internazionale degli Istituti di Archeologia, Storia e Storia dell' Arte in Roma.

A union list of some 9,000 periodicals to be found in 27 libraries of Rome and Florence, indicating holdings. Z6945.V3

Mexico

Velásquez Gallardo, Pablo and **Nadurille, Ramon.** Catálogo colectivo de publicaciones periódicas existentes en bibliotecas de la República Mexicana. México, Instituto Nacional de Investigaciones Agrícolas, 1968. 2v. **AE203**

A union list of the periodical holdings of about 130 cooperating libraries. Z6945.V4

Netherlands

Koninklijke Bibliotheek (Netherlands). Centrale catalogus van periodieken en seriewerken in Nederlandse bibliotheken (CCP). 3. uitg. 'sGravenhage, De Bibliotheek, 1983. 14v. **AE204**

1st ed. 1971–73.
"Abridged introduction" in English.
A union list of periodicals and serial publications in libraries of the Netherlands. Main entry listing; about 200,000 titles; holdings are specific. Z6945.H16

New Zealand

Union list of serials in New Zealand libraries. 3d ed. Wellington, Nat. Lib. of New Zealand, 1969–70. 6v. **AE205**

1st ed. 1953; 2d ed. 1964–68. Section 2, "Conferences, symposia, etc." (Wellington, 1968. 244p.) of the 2d ed. is not superseded by the new edition.

Updated by means of a monthly card service which lists new serials and significant additional holdings of those previously cited. Z6945.N285

Philippines

Quezon, Philippines. University of the Philippines. Inter-Departmental Reference Service. Union list of serials of government agency libraries of the Philippines. Comp. by Maxima M. Ferrer [et al.]. Rev. and enl. ed. Manila, 1960. 911p. **AE206**

Includes nearly 8,000 entries of foreign and domestic periodicals, representing the holdings of 79 libraries in the Philippines.

The alphabetical list, which gives full information, is followed by a classified list of the serials included. Z6945.Q4

Portugal

Centro de Documentação Científica, Lisbon. Publicações periódicas estrangeiras, inventariadas nas bibliotecas portuguesas. Lisboa, Inst. Para a Alta Cultura, 1948–59. 6v. **AE207**

Contents: [v.1] Ciências médicas. 1948; [v.2] Etnologia, ciências naturais, agro-pecuária. 1953; [v.3] Matemática, astronomia, física, química, engenharia, indústria. 1955; [v.4] Ciências sociais. 1956; v.5, Filosofia, religião, pedagogia, filologia, literatura, belas-artes, geografia, história. 1958. v.6, Generalidades. 1959.

Gives title, place of publication, beginning date, changes of title, etc., with holdings of Portuguese libraries. Z6945.C4

———— ———— Aditamento ao 1.º volume (1948); ciências médicas. Lisboa, 1960. 286p.

South Africa

Catalogue of Union periodicals, ed. for the National Research Council and National Research Board. Percy Freer, ed. Johannesburg, 1943–52. 2v. and suppls. **AE208**

Contents: v.1, Science and technology; 1st suppl., 1949; 2d suppl., 1953; v.2, Humanities.

A union list of periodicals in some 82 libraries of the Union of South Africa. Gives title, place of publication, date of founding, and symbols showing location. Z6945.A1C3

Periodicals in South African libraries. Tydskrifte in Suid-Afrikaanse biblioteke. 2d ed. [comp. for] South African Council for Scientific and Industrial Research and Human Sciences Research Council. Pretoria, 1972–73. **AE209**

Issued in parts.
1st ed., 1961, published in looseleaf format.
A union list for South African libraries. Z6945.P452

South and Southeast Asia

Moon, Brenda Elizabeth. Periodicals for South-East Asian studies: a union catalogue of holdings in British and selected European libraries. London, Mansell, 1979. 610p. **AE210**

At head of title: South-East Asia Library Group.

Originally undertaken as a union catalog of British library holdings of Southeast Asian periodicals, the published checklist extends to periodicals for which no holdings were reported and includes not only British resources, but also those of a number of libraries in France, Germany, and the Netherlands. Attempts "to include all periodicals, both current and extinct, of Asian or East Asian interest if they are considered to be of substantial value for South-East Asian studies, whether published in South-East Asia or outside these areas."—*p.ix.* Serves as a useful complement to G. R. Nunn's *Southeast Asian periodicals* (AE211).

Arrangement is by title (or issuing body in the case of bulletins, etc.); publications in non-Roman scripts are entered in romanized form. Periodicals of all frequencies are included, but those appearing irregularly or less than annually are not comprehensively covered. Z3221.M59

Nunn, Godfrey Raymond. Southeast Asian periodicals: an international union list. [London], Mansell, [1977]. 456p. **AE211**

A union list of "some 26,000 periodicals published since the beginning of the nineteenth century."—*Introd.* Arrangement is by country (Burma; Cambodia; Indonesia; Laos; Malaysia, Singapore and Brunei; Philippines; Thailand; Timor; Vietnam), then by title or other main entry. In addition to locations in libraries of the countries covered, selected libraries in Australia, Canada, France, India, Great Britain, Netherlands, Portugal, Spain, and the United States are represented. Z6958.S6N85

Ranganathan, Shiyali Ramamrita [and others]. Union catalogue of learned periodical publications in South Asia. Publ. with the assistance of UNESCO. Delhi, Indian Lib. Assoc.; London, G. Blunt, 1953. v.1. (Indian Lib. Assoc. English ser., 7) **AE212**

Contents: v.1, Physical and biological sciences. 390p. No more published.

Lists holdings in libraries of Indonesia, Malaya, Thailand, Burma, Ceylon, and India. Z6945.R15

Spain

Spain. Dirección General de Archivos y Bibliotecas. Catálogo colectivo de publicaciones periódicas en bibliotecas españolas. [Madrid, 1971–76]. v.1–5[1]. **AE213**

Contents: v.1, Derecho y administración [pública]; v.2, Medicina; v3, Agricultura y veterinaria; v.4, Ciencias de la educación; v.5, Humanidades, tomo I: Ciencias historicas.

A union list of serials in Spanish libraries as of 1969. Within each volume periodicals are listed alphabetically by title with library location and indication of holdings. At the end of the volume, titles are grouped by subclasses (e.g., in v.1, under headings for canon law, civil law, military law, etc.; in v.2, anatomy, pathology, internal medicine, etc.). Libraries in more than 50 cities are represented. Z6945.S694

Switzerland

Vereinigung Schweizerischer Bibliothekare. Verzeichnis ausländischer Zeitschriften und Serien in schweizerischen Bibliotheken. Répertoire des périodiques étrangers reçus par les bibliothèques suisses. 6. Aufl. Bern, Vereinigung Schweizerischer Bibliothekare, 1981. 1355p. **AE214**

1st ed. 1904.

A union list of foreign periodicals in Swiss libraries. The 4th ed. (1955) listed some 34,000 titles. This edition is concerned with serials published after World War II (i.e., those which began publication after Dec. 31, 1945 and older series which continued or resumed publication after that date); for titles which ceased before 1946, the user is referred to the 4th ed. The list of cooperating libraries precedes the main-entry listing; holdings information is precise. Z6945.V8

INDEXES

Bibliography

Abstracting and indexing services directory. Ed.1, issue no.1– , July 1982– . Detroit, Gale, 1982– . Irregular. **AE215**

Subtitle: A descriptive guide to abstracting journals, indexes, digests, serial bibliographies, catalogs, title announcement bulletins, and similar information access and alerting publications in all areas of science, technology, medicine, business, law, social sciences, education, and humanities.

John Schmittroth, Jr., ed.

Ed.1 publ. in three issues, July 1982–Dec. 1983; cumulative index

of publications, publishers, and keywords in issue no.3. The keyword index is not an adequate substitute for subject indexing. Z695.93.A27

Covington, Paula Hattox. Indexed journals: a guide to Latin American serials. [Madison, Wis., SALALM Secretariat, Memorial Lib., Univ. of Wis., 1983] 458p. (Seminar on the Acquisition of Latin American Library Materials. Bibliography ser., 8) **AE216**

Both an aid for determining where articles in a given journal are indexed or abstracted and an evaluative guide to the indexing and abstracting services. More than 100 indexes are listed by subject discipline with an indication of their coverage and relevance to Latin American research interests. Journals are listed by title, then by subject, then by country of publication; in each list the abbreviations for the pertinent indexing/abstracting services follow the individual titles. Journals relating wholly to Latin America or published in Central or South America or the Caribbean (except those concerned with pure and applied sciences) are included.

Elena Ardissone has compiled a *Bibliografía de índices de publicaciones periódicas argentinas* (Buenos Aires, Univ. de Buenos Aires, Inst. Bibliotecologico, 1984. 52p.) listing more than 150 indexes, mainly for individual periodicals.

Kujoth, Jean Spealman. Subject guide to periodical indexes and review indexes. Metuchen, N.J., Scarecrow Pr., 1969. 129p. **AE217**

Offers a subject approach to lists of periodical indexes and reviewing media. Z6293.K84

Marconi, Joseph V. Indexed periodicals; a guide to 170 years of coverage in 33 indexing services. Ann Arbor, Mich., Pierian Pr., 1976. 416p. **AE218**

". . . an alphabetically arranged listing of those periodical and serial titles identified as being indexed in some 33 (counting title changes) American, British and Canadian periodical indexes, showing the indexes in which they were covered and the dates indexed. . . . The overall scope of this volume ranges from 1802 into mid-1973, consisting of approximately 11,000 periodical and serial titles, title changes, and cross references."—*Introd.*

New York. Public Library. A check list of cumulative indexes to individual periodicals in the New York Public Library, comp. by Daniel C. Haskell. N.Y., Library, 1942. 370p. **AE219**

An alphabetical list of thousands of cumulative indexes to periodicals in various languages, mainly of the 19th and 20th centuries, which are available in the New York Public Library, with the addition of a few not available there.

"A cumulative index is to be understood as one which indexes at least 3 volumes . . . and makes at least a slight attempt at the classification of the periodical's contents, either an arrangement by authors or by subjects."—*Pref.* Z6293.N45

International

Arts & humanities citation index. 1976– . Philadelphia, Inst. for Scientific Information, 1978– . **AE220**

Publ. in two softbound issues (Jan./Apr. and May/Aug.) and a hardbound cumulative issue (covering Jan./Dec.) each year. Each issue in two physical parts: (1) Guide and journal lists; Citation index; "Permuterm" subject index; (2) Source index; Corporate index.

Patterned on the *Science citation index* and *Social sciences citation index,* and using the same general format and approach to indexing. This is "a multidisciplinary index to the journal literature of the arts and humanities. It covers every substantive item in each journal issue indexed: articles, letters, editorials, notes, meeting abstracts, discussions, corrections, errata; poems, short stories, excerpts from books, plays, music scores; chronologies, bibliographies, discographies, filmographies, etc.; and reviews of books, films, records, art exhibits, TV and radio programs, and dance, music, and theatrical performances."—*Introd.* About 1,300 journals are now covered. To overcome the problem of articles with non-descriptive titles an "enrichment policy" was inaugurated, and such articles are indexed as though the titles contained the name of an artist, work of art or literary work which the article concerns; illustrations of works of art, musical scores, etc., are also indicated.   AI3.A63●

Bibliographie der fremdsprachigen Zeitschriftenliteratur; Répertoire bibliographique international des revues; International index to periodicals, 1911–25, 1925/26–62/64. Gautszch b. Leipzig, Dietrich, 1911–64. v.1–22, n.F.v.1–51. (Internationale Bibliographie der Zeitschriftenliteratur, Abt. B) (Repr.: N.Y., Kraus Reprint, 1961)   **AE221**

An important index, similar in general plan and arrangement to the *Bibliographie der deutschen Zeitschriftenliteratur* (AE278). Indexes about 1,400 periodicals and general works in the principal non-German languages. The first series is a subject index only; the second series includes, in addition, author indexes. Beginning with n.F.v.4, some supplementary indexing of material earlier than the covering date of the volume is included.

With its wide coverage, this index is very useful for finding materials in American and English periodicals, as well as in French, Italian, and other European publications. Because of the lack of French periodical indexes, it is particularly important for French articles.

N.F.v.26–29 (1944–48) not published. Merged into *Internationale Bibliographie der Zeitschriftenliteratur* (below).   AI9.B7

Internationale Bibliographie der Zeitschriftenliteratur aus allen Gebieten des Wissens, hrsg. von Otto Zeller. Jahrg.1– , 1963/64– . Osnabrück, Felix Dietrich, 1965– . 12v. per yr.   **AE222**

Title also in English and French: *International bibliography of periodical literature covering all fields of knowledge. Bibliographie internationale de la littérature périodique dans tous les domaines de la connaissance.* Often referred to as "IBZ."

Frequency has varied.

A continuation in combined form of the *Bibliographie der deutschen Zeitschriftenliteratur* (AE278) and the *Bibliographie der fremdsprachigen Zeitschriftenliteratur* (AE221).

A subject index to world periodical literature. The subject headings are in German with cross references from English and French forms. Author index.

An index of key-words used in this and its predecessor series has been published as: AI9.I5

——— Register der Schlagwörter 1896–1974. Hrsg. von Otto Zeller. Osnabrück, F. Dietrich, 1975. 2v.

Title also in English (Index of key-words 1896–1974) and French.

Indicates whether a given index term has ever been used in the long series, but references to specific volumes are given only for the 1965–74 period.   AI9.I53

United States and Great Britain

❖A comparison of the coverage and content of eight periodical indexes with the *Readers' guide* (AE231) may be found in the article "Indexing of popular periodicals: the state of the art," by Brian Aveney and Rod Slade, *Library journal* 103:1915–23 (Oct. 1, 1978).

Access; the supplementary index to periodicals. Jan./Apr. 1975– . Syracuse, N.Y., Gaylord Professional Pubs., 1975– . 3 times a yr., the 3d issue being an annual cumulation.   **AE223**

John Gordon Burke and Ned Kehde, eds.

Intends to complement rather than duplicate the efforts of other general periodical indexes. (As a general principle, titles picked up by *Readers' guide* will be dropped from *Access.*) Now indexes about 140 titles representing "regional and city magazines as well as a balanced subject-oriented list of general and special interest periodicals."—*Introd.* Author and subject entries in separate sections.   AI3.A23

The American humanities index. v.1, no.1/2– , Spr./Sum. 1975– . Troy, N.Y., Whitston, 1975– . Quarterly with annual cumulation.   **AE224**

Stephen Goode, ed.

An author and subject index to scholarly and critical magazines, plus a number of little magazines. Designed to complement rather than duplicate other indexing services. 96 periodicals indexed in the first issue, with list now expanded to about 225 titles.   AI3.A278

Magazine index. 1976– . Los Altos, Calif., Information Access Corp., 1976– . Microfilm. Monthly.   **AE225**

Indexes about 435 popular magazines, with each monthly microfilm issue being a full cumulation. Filing is in two parts: (1) Alphabetical listings from A to Z; (2) Numerical listings from 1 to one million. The alphabetical section has two groups of data: (1) Subject headings, titles of reviewed materials, and product names; (2) Names of persons in the news and authors' names. Most recently published articles appear first. Reviews are indexed under title of the work reviewed, by names of persons featured in the review, and by author of the review; reviews are graded. Information on how to use the index and the list of magazines indexed appears at each end of the microfilm reel. Full title of the magazine is given in the citation, not an abbreviation. After five years, citations are dropped from the microfilm and the items dropped cumulate on microfiche.

A review in the Library of Congress *Information bulletin* 38:370 (Sept. 7, 1979) points out that "A significant weakness . . . is its lack of name authority control."

Two printed looseleaf services are included in the subscription: (1) *Hot topics* lists recent articles on subjects of current topical interest; (2) *Product evaluations* lists recent product reviews as found in the microform index.   ●

The new periodicals index. v.1, no.1– , Jan./June 1977– . Boulder, Colo., Mediaworks Ltd., 1977– . Semiannual.   **AE226**

". . . indexes all articles from a list of alternative and new age magazines, journals, newspapers and newsletters. The purpose of the index is to provide access to the wealth of important new information these periodicals offer on the New Culture, the still-evolving manifestation of the recent wave of change in technology, spiritual life, lifestyles, energy, ecology, health, diet, feminism, community, art, music, politics and the media."—*Introd., v.1, no.1.* Initially indexed 62 titles. A subject-author index (author entries being provided for "major" articles). No cumulations. v.4 (1980) publ. 1983.

Poole's Index to periodical literature, 1802–81. Rev. ed. Boston, Houghton, 1891 [pref. 1891, c.1882]. 2v. (Repr.: N.Y., P. Smith, 1938; Gloucester, Mass., P. Smith, 1963)   **AE227**

——— Supplements, Jan. 1882–Jan.1, 1907. Boston, Houghton, [c.1887–1908]. 5v.

Originally ed. by William Frederick Poole, continued by him and W. I. Fletcher, with the cooperation of members of the American Library Association.

Contents: v.1, 1802–81; 1st suppl., 1882–86; 2d suppl., 1887–91; 3d suppl., 1892–96; 4th suppl., 1897–1901; 5th suppl., 1902–1906.

The pioneer index and, though long discontinued, still an important index to American and English periodicals, since it covers the longest period (105 years) and indexes the large total of about 590,000 articles in 12,241 volumes of 479 American and English periodicals. A subject index only; includes *no author entries.* Authors' names appear frequently as entries, but only as subject entries for biographical or critical articles about them. To make intelligent use of the index the user should remember the following four points: (1) no author entries; (2) all articles having a distinct subject are entered under that subject; (3) articles having no subject, i.e., fiction, poems, plays, are entered under first word of the title not an article; (4) book reviews are entered in two ways: (a) reviews of a book which has a definite subject are entered under subject of the book; (b) reviews of a book which does not have a distinct subject, i.e., a novel, poetry, a drama, are entered under the name of the author reviewed. Approximately complete for the periodicals covered, except in the following respects: (1) very brief articles, notes, etc. are generally omitted; (2) minor book reviews are not included; and (3) some English periodicals noted in v.1 are incompletely indexed because of failure in collaboration between English and American indexers. Information given about each article includes its title, author's name in parentheses when it was known or could be ascertained, abbreviated title of periodical, and volume and page reference. Neither inclusive paging nor date is given, but the date (year only) can be ascertained from the "Chronological Conspectus" in each volume. Indexes principally periodicals of a general nature, but a few selected periodicals on special subjects are included. In general, the work of both indexing and printing is very accurate, with comparatively few typographical errors. For list of errata *see Bulletin of bibliography* 2:24–25, 40–41, 56–58, 75–76, 133–34; 3:25; 4:11–12, 72 (Jan. 1900–Oct. 1905).   AI3.P7

———— Cumulative author index for Poole's index to periodical literature, 1802–1906. Comp. and ed. by C. Edward Wall. Ann Arbor, Mich., Pierian Pr., 1971. 488p.   **AE228**

Lists alphabetically the names that appear in parentheses in *Poole's,* with citation to volume, page and column of the *Poole's* citation.

Inasmuch as many of the author identifications in *Poole's* are questionable, this work should be used with caution.

Poole's Index, date and volume key. By Marion V. Bell and Jean C. Bacon. Chicago, Assoc. of College and Research Libraries, 1957. 61p. (ACRL monograph 19)   **AE229**

In this "key the 479 periodical titles indexed in the various volumes of *Poole's Index* are thrown into one alphabet" (p.19) and the date is shown, in tabular form, for each volume number, thus obviating the necessity for checking a title in the "Chronological conspectus" in each volume of *Poole's.*

A similar aid is Vinton A. Dearing's *Transfer vectors for Poole's Index to periodical literature* (no.1, Titles, volumes, and dates; Los Angeles, Pison Pr., 1967. 95p.) which lists the periodicals alphabetically by abbreviation, with full title, dates indexed, and the volume number of *Poole's* in which a given date appears.

Nineteenth century readers' guide to periodical literature, 1890–1899, with supplementary indexing, 1900–1922, ed. by Helen Grant Cushing and Adah V. Morris. . . . N.Y., Wilson, 1944. 2v.   **AE230**

An author, subject, and illustrator index to the material in 51 periodicals (1,003 volumes) mainly in the period from 1890 to 1899. Some indexing has been done for volumes published after 1899 "in order to make the indexing of each title complete from the year 1890 to the time when it was added to the list of one of the Wilson indexes. Fourteen of the 51 titles included have been indexed beyond 1899, some as far as 1922."—*Pref.*

Periodicals indexed are mainly general and literary, but some are included from special fields. Book reviews are listed under author entry only. More than 13,000 poems are listed under "Poems" by title. Full entry is under author's name. Poems on particular persons, events, etc., are also under subject.

In some 19th-century periodicals the editorial practice was to publish articles anonymously, e.g., in the *Edinburgh review* and the *Quarterly review.* For many of these articles the authors' names have been ascertained from the publishers' records and are indicated in this index.

These two volumes were planned as part of a larger project to cover the whole 19th century by a modern periodical index in dictionary form, but no further volumes have been published. *See* AE260 for a related effort.   AI3.R496

Readers' guide to periodical literature [cumulated], 1900– . N.Y., Wilson, 1905– . v.1– .   **AE231**

A cumulative index made up of three forms or sections: (1) cumulated volumes covering two to five years (i.e., 1935–Feb. 1965, two years to a volume; previous volumes covered from three to five

years); (2) annual cumulations (beginning with v.25, Mar. 1965–Feb. 1966, these are final cumulations); and (3) issues published semimonthly, Sept. to June; monthly, July–Aug., cumulating at intervals until the last number of each current volume which covers 12 months and forms a new annual volume.

The *Readers' guide* began in 1901 as an index for the small library, covering at first only 15 of the more popular periodicals, and gradually extended until in 1903 it absorbed the *Cumulative index* (1896–1903) and in 1911 took over the work of the *Annual library index* (AE242). List of periodicals indexed varies from volume to volume. Beginning with v.19, 1953, the *Readers' guide:* (a) indexes U.S. periodicals of broad, general, and popular character, and (b) aims to provide a well-balanced selection of U.S. popular, nontechnical magazines representing all the important scientific and humanistic subject fields. About 174 periodicals of general interest are now included.

This is a modern index of the best type. Its special features are: (1) full dictionary cataloging of all articles, i.e., their entry under author, subject, and (when necessary) title; (2) uniformity of entries, due to the fact that the work is done by a few professional indexers rather than by many voluntary collaborators; (3) use of catalog subject headings instead of catchword subject; (4) full information in the references, i.e., exact date and inclusive paging, illustrations, portraits, etc.; (5) cumulative features which keep the index up to date without multiplying alphabets to be consulted; (6) indexing of all book reviews, through 1904, under author reviewed; after 1905, reviews are generally omitted because included in the *Book review digest* (AA513); (7) indexing, in the second and third cumulated volumes, of some 597 composite books, thus forming an unofficial continuation of the *A.L.A. index . . . to general literature* (BD227). This book indexing was abandoned after 1914.   AI3.R48●

Abridged readers' guide to periodical literature, July 1935– . Author and subject index to a selected list of periodicals. N.Y., Wilson, 1936– . v.1– .   **AE232**

An index to 24–58 periodicals, designed especially for school and small public libraries unable to afford the regular *Readers' guide* (above). For the public library which is growing and can possibly afford the greater expense, the unabridged Guide is the better investment.

Monthly except June–Aug., cumulating annually. Biennial cumulations were publ. through v.14.   AI3.R493

Popular periodical index. no 1– , Jan./June 1973– . Camden, N.J., 1973– . Semiannual.   **AE233**

A subject index (with some author entries) now indexing some 39 popular periodicals not covered in the standard periodical indexes. Book reviews are grouped under "Book reviews." No cumulations.   AI3.P76

Social sciences and humanities index: formerly International index, 1907/15–74. N.Y., Wilson, 1916–74. v.1–61.   **AE234**

Title varies: v.1–2, *Readers' guide to periodical literature supplement;* v.3–52, *International index to periodicals* (with various subtitles); v.53, no.1, June 1965–Mar. 1974, *Social sciences and humanities index.* (Volume numbering of the cumulations differs from that of the quarterly issues; e.g., v.3–18 of the cumulated set called *International index.*)

A cumulative index made up of three forms: (1) permanent cumulated volumes covering four, three, or two years; (2) annual volumes; and (3) current numbers issued quarterly, June, Sept., Dec., and March (frequency varies).

An important index for the large or scholarly library. An author and subject index of the same plan as the *Readers' guide* (AE231) but covering periodicals of a different type, i.e., the more scholarly journals in the humanities and social sciences. Coverage varies, with the transfer of titles to new Wilson subject indexes, etc., and the addition of new titles. Before World War II a number of foreign titles were included, e.g., in v.8, 1937–40, 221 titles were indexed: 125 American, 39 English, 3 Canadian, 25 French, 20 German, 4 Oriental, 2 Italian, 1 each Dutch, Irish, and Spanish. Since the war, foreign titles have been dropped, as have psychological and scientific periodicals. In 1973, indexed about 200 American and English periodicals.

Superseded by the *Humanities index* (AE235) and the *Social sciences index* (AE236).   AI3.R49

Humanities index. v.1, no.1– , June 1974– . N.Y., Wilson, 1974– . v.1– . Quarterly with annual cumulations.   **AE235**

Supersedes in part the *Social sciences and humanities index* (above).

"Subject fields indexed include archaeology and classical studies, area studies, folklore, history, language and literature, literary and political criticism, performing arts, philosophy, religion and theology, and related subjects."—*Prefatory note, v.1.* Originally indexed 117 of the titles from the *Social sciences and humanities index,* plus 143 new titles as elected by subscribers to the index; now indexes nearly 300 English-language titles. Author and subject entries; a separate book review section has been added, with entry under author of the book reviewed.   AI3.H85●

Social sciences index. v.1, no.1– , June 1974– . N.Y., Wilson, 1974– . Quarterly, with annual cumulations.   **AE236**

Continues in part the *Social sciences and humanities index* (AE234).

Comprises an author and subject index to "periodicals in the fields of anthropology, area studies, economics, environmental science, geography, law and criminology, medical sciences, political science, psychology, public administration, sociology and related subjects."—*Prefatory note, v.2.* As in the *Humanities index* (above), a separate section of book reviews appears at the end of each issue. Originally included 77 periodical titles indexed in the discontinued *Social sciences and humanities index* plus 186 titles newly selected by the subscribers to the index; now indexes some 307 English-language periodicals.   AI3.S62●

Subject index to periodicals, 1915–61. London, Lib. Assoc., 1919–62. Annual (quarterly, 1954–61, with annual cumulations).   **AE237**

Ceased publication.

An English index, begun in 1915 under the title *Athenaeum subject index;* title changed in 1919 to *Subject index.* The 1915–16 volume has an author-subject arrangement cumulated from preliminary class lists. Continued by class lists 1917–19, in one set, with a general author index, and 1920–22, one volume per year, with no author index.

1923–25 not published.

The form was changed in 1926, becoming an alphabetical subject list (with no author index) to articles on definite subjects. Magazine fiction, poetry, and essays not on definite subjects were omitted. Until the time of World War II (approximately 1940), it indexed more than 500 periodicals, principally British and American but including a number of foreign titles. Though duplicating much of the indexing in the *Readers' guide* (AE231) and the then *International index* (AE234), it indexed many periodicals not covered by those indexes, including British local-history periodicals, antiquarian society proceedings, etc.

During World War II, the indexing of foreign titles was discontinued, and with the 1947 volume (publ. 1949), the indexing of American periodicals was also dropped. Later volumes indexed more than 300 titles, entirely British.

Regional lists, including entries of local interest, were collected and issued annually by county, with Scotland as a separate issue.

Ceased publication in this form with the 1961 volume. Continued by indexes covering special subjects: *British humanities index* (below) and *British technology index* (EJ8n).   AI3.A72

British humanities index, 1962– . London, Lib. Assoc., 1963– . Quarterly, with annual cumulations.   **AE238**

A continuation in part of the *Subject index to periodicals* (above). This section to cover "all material relating to the arts and politics." Quarterly issues are by subject only; annuals are in two parts—a subject section and an author section—each giving full indexing information. Now indexes about 380 British periodicals including many in local history.   AI3.B7

❖Among the more specialized periodical indexes the following are frequently useful:

Abstracts of popular culture. v.1–3^{A-B}. Bowling Green, Ohio, Bowling Green Univ. Popular Pr., 1976–82. Biannual.   **AE239**

Subtitle: A bi-annual publication of international popular phenomena.

Frequency has varied. Ceased publication.

"By 'Popular Culture' we mean all aspects of life which are not academic or creative in the narrowest and most esoteric sense of the words. . . . Important topics such as film, television, radio, popular literature, fairs, parades, theater, amusements, music, circuses, carnivals, urban and rural life, the counter culture, ethnic and women's studies, folklore, the family sports, leisure and work, humor, and all other aspects of the 'New Humanities' " (*Introd., v.1A*) are included.

Indexes relevant articles from a wide range of periodicals; abstracts are very brief. Full citations appear in an author listing, and there is a subject index. Also aims to provide information on unpublished papers on popular culture and to serve as a clearinghouse for copies of such papers.   Z7164.S66A27

Alternative press index, v.1, no.1/2– , July/Dec. 1969– . [Northfield, Minn.], Radical Research Center, [1970–]. Quarterly (irregular).   **AE240**

Publisher varies.

"An index to the publications which amplify the cry for social change and social justice."—*title page, v.1.*

Provides a subject index to more than 200 liberal, radical, and "underground" periodicals, most of them not indexed elsewhere.   AI3.A27

Annual literary index, 1892–1904. Including periodicals, American and English; essays, book-chapters, etc. N.Y., Publishers' Weekly, 1893–1905. 13v.   **AE241**

AI3.A5

Annual library index, 1905–1910. Including periodicals, American and English; essays, book-chapters, etc. N.Y., Publishers' Weekly, 1906–11. 6v.   **AE242**

These two indexes, although differing slightly in arrangement, served as a continuation of *Poole's* (AE227), forming the basis for the 5-year supplements. However, they added author indexing never incorporated in *Poole's*. Except for this indexing, they were largely superseded by *Poole's* and the *A.L.A. index . . . to general literature* (BD227).   AI3.A5

Annual magazine subject index, 1907–49; a subject index to a selected list of American and English periodicals and society publications. Boston, Faxon, 1908–52. 43v.   **AE243**

Ceased publication.

v.1 had title *Magazine subject index* and is a basic volume indexing 79 periodicals (44 from their first issues to Dec. 31, 1907, and 35 for the year 1907).

An index of subjects only, not of authors or titles, except that fiction when included is indexed under author's name. Indexes material with exact references and indication of illustrations, maps, etc. Intended as a supplement to other indexes and so aims to include no periodicals indexed in established indexes. While the list of periodicals is general in character, about half of the titles relate to history, especially local history; the index specializes also in travel, mountaineering, exploration, outdoor life, and fine arts. Indexes all important articles in the periodicals covered but omits short articles, poetry, and most fiction, though continued stories and short stories by notable writers are included.

Includes many local-history titles, especially transactions of local-history societies indexed in Griffin, *Bibliography of American historical societies* (DB143). As these are often indexed back to the date when Griffin stopped, the index constitutes an informal continuation of Griffin. The only exception to the rule not to index material included elsewhere is in the case of these history periodicals.

The entries in the 43v. are cumulated into one alphabet in: AI3.M26

Cumulated magazine subject index, 1907–1949; a cumulation of the F. W. Faxon Company's *Annual magazine* subject index . . . Cumulated by G. K. Hall & Co. Boston, G. K. Hall, 1964. 2v. **AE244**

A photographic reproduction of the actual entries originally printed in the *Annual magazine subject index,* clipped and rearranged in one alphabetical sequence. For coverage *see* AE243.

AI3.C76

Bloomfield, Barry Cambray. An author index to selected British 'little magazines,' 1930–1939. [London], Mansell, 1976. 153p. **AE245**

Indexes 73 periodicals of the period, less than a dozen of which are included in the *Comprehensive index to English-language little magazines* (AE257). With the exception of *Caravel* (published in Majorca, but containing "a considerable amount of poetry by young British writers"—*Pref.*) all were published in the United Kingdom. With a few exceptions noted in the preface, all magazines are fully indexed. This is an author index only, although the form heading "Films reviewed" provides cross references to film reviews, and cross references to book reviews are provided under the name of the author of the book reviewed. AI3.B56

Catholic periodical index; a cumulative author and subject index to a selected list of Catholic periodicals, 1930–66. N.Y., Catholic Lib. Assoc., 1939–67. Quarterly, with biennial cumulations. v.1–13. **AE246**

1930–33 forms the first permanent volume in a series of 4-year cumulations to June 1948; thereafter biennial.

Indexes, by author and subject, 50 to more than 200 periodicals published mainly in the United States, Canada, England, and Ireland.

Continued as: AI3.C32

Catholic periodical and literature index, v.14– , 1967/68– . Haverford, Pa., Catholic Lib. Assoc., [1968-]. Bimonthly, with biennial cumulations. **AE247**

Subtitle (varies): A cumulative author-subject index to a selective list of Catholic periodicals and an author-title-subject bibliography of adult books by Catholics, with a selection of Catholic-interest books by other authors.

Beginning July 1968, the *Catholic periodical index* (above) and *The guide to Catholic literature* (BB417) were combined in a single publication under this new title, which continues the volume numbering of the Index. Coverage of both the earlier publications is maintained. Regularly indexes about 135 periodicals; about 2,500 books are listed each year. Through v.20 (1979/80) book review citations appear in a separate section at the end of the cumulated volumes. AI3.C32

Chicano periodical index: a cumulative index to selected Chicano periodicals between 1967 and 1978. Boston, G. K. Hall, 1981. 972p. **AE248**

For full information *see* CC490.

Index to little magazines. Denver, Alan Swallow, 1949–70. **AE249**

Publisher varies; compilers vary.

Frequency varies: began publication with volume for 1948 (publ. 1949). Annual, 1948–52; 1953/55 publ. in 1v., 1957; biennial, 1956/57–66/67. Retrospective volumes have been issued covering 1900–19 and 1920–39 (publ. 1969–74 with title *Index to American little magazines*), 1940–42 (publ. 1967) and 1943–47 (publ. 1965). The 1966/67 volume (publ. 1970) was the last to appear.

Indexes a selective list of from 31 to more than 50 titles. Periodicals are mainly literary; indexing is by author and subject (many of the subjects being quite broad). Coverage varies from volume to volume, as does treatment of book reviews. AI3.I54

Index to Commonwealth little magazines. [v.1–],1964/65– . N.Y., Johnson Reprint Corp., 1966- . Biennial (irregular). **AE250**

Stephen H. Goode, ed.

An author-subject index comparable to the American *Index to little magazines* (above). Retrospective, as well as continuing, volumes are planned.

To date volumes have appeared covering 1964/65, 1966/67, 1968/69, 1970/73, 1974/75 and 1976/79 (2v., ed. by Sarah V. Gray). AI3.I48

Index to selected periodicals received in the Hallie Q. Brown Library. Decennial cumulation, 1950–59. Ed., Charlotte W. Lytle. Boston, G. K. Hall, 1961. 501p. **AE251**

Title varies; uncumulated volumes called *Index to selected Negro periodicals.*

Covers Negro periodicals not indexed elsewhere. An author-subject index. Book reviews are listed under that heading. Supersedes annual volumes for the period. Continued by quarterly and annual issues compiled jointly by the staffs of the Hallie Q. Brown Library and the Schomburg Collection, New York Public Library.

A second cumulative volume appeared as:

Index to periodical articles by and about Negroes. Cumulated 1960–1970. Boston, G. K. Hall, 1971. 606p. **AE252**

Continued by annual volumes for 1971/72. Superseded by:

AI3.O4

Index to periodical articles by and about blacks. 1973– . Boston, G. K. Hall, 1977- . Annual. **AE253**

Represents a change of title for *Index to periodical articles by and about Negroes* (above).

Now indexes 25 periodicals of interest for Afro-American studies. Beginning 1980, authors and subjects are in separate sections. AI3.O4

Index to U.S. government periodicals. 1972– . Chicago, Infordata Intl. Inc., 1974- . Quarterly, the 4th issue being an annual cumulation. **AE254**

". . . published quarterly in May, August, November and March. Indexing for the fourth quarter is included in the annual cumulative issue published in March."—*verso of t.p.*

Began publication with the quarterly issues for 1974; retrospective annual volumes for 1972 and 1973 were subsequently published.

"A computer-generated guide to 156 selected titles by author and subject."—*t.p., 1976.* The number of periodicals indexed varies from year to year. Includes various periodicals not sent to Depository Libraries, and many which are distributed directly by department or issuing agency rather than through the Government Printing Office.

Reviewing the 1981 cumulative volume (*Booklist* 79:402–03, Nov. 1, 1982), the ALA Reference and Subscription Books Review Committee concludes that "the eclectic nature of this index needs no justification, since in many libraries the body of journals it indexes is treated separately from other journals. Diversity makes this, then, a general index, similar to *Readers' Guide* in breadth but not in depth. Its greatest utility will probably be in depository libraries, especially regional depositories." The publication also serves as an index to *Current U.S. government periodicals on microfiche* published by Microfilming Corporation of America. Z1223.Z9I5

Library Association. Wales and Monmouthshire Branch. Subject index to Welsh periodicals. 1931–1946/55. Swansea, 1934–64. 7v. **AE255**

Indexes periodicals (excluding newspapers and some denominational publications) published in Wales, in both Welsh and English, and periodicals published elsewhere which include material of Welsh and general Celtic interest. AI9.W4L5

Review of reviews. Index to the periodicals of 1890–1902. [v.1]–13. London, N.Y., Review of Reviews, 1891–1903. 13v. Annual. **AE256**

Title varies: v.1, *Annual index of periodicals and photographs for 1890;* v.2–4, *Index to the periodical literature of the world.*

Primarily a subject index, but contains a fair number of author entries also, especially in the later volumes. Indexes material under broad subjects and gives full bibliographical information with reference to the volume, month, and page of the *Review of reviews* where a summary or other notice of the article is to be found. Indicates maps and illustrations. Number of periodicals indexed varies from 117 in 1890 to 195 in 1902. Principally useful because it covers many English periodicals (about 100 in the later volumes) not indexed in *Poole's* (AE227). AI3.R5

Sader, Marion, ed. Comprehensive index to English-language little magazines, 1890–1970. Series one. Millwood, N.Y., Kraus-Thomson, 1976. 8v. **AE257**

An index to 100 English-language little magazines of the period indicated, 59 of which are "partly or totally American."—*Pref.* It aims to index complete files of defunct publications; magazines which were still current are completely indexed through 1970, with some 1971 issues included. Selection of titles for this first series—it is indicated that work has begun on a second series—was made by Felix Pollak, formerly of the University of Wisconsin Libraries, with the advice of Charles Allen, well-known authority on the American little magazine. Indexing is by personal name only, with designation of "Works by" and/or "Works about" under each name. Book reviews are entered under both the author of the book and the name of the reviewer, with an additional subject entry if the book is a biography or a critical work devoted to an individual writer or artist, etc. In addition to the expected details of pagination, date, etc., each contribution has been categorized as to type (article, poem, excerpt, illus., etc.). Z6944.L5S23

Subject index to children's magazines. Madison, Wis., 1948–81. v.1–33. Monthly (except June and July); semiannual cumulations in Feb. and Aug. **AE258**

Editors vary.

Indexes by subject some 40–50 magazines useful to elementary and junior high school libraries.

Continued by: Z6944.C5W5

Children's magazine guide. v.34, no.1– , Sept. 1981– . Madison, Wis., Rowland, 1981– . Monthly Aug.–Mar., bimonthly Apr.–May. **AE259**

Feb. and Aug. issues are semi-annual cumulations.

Continues the *Subject index to children's magazines* (above) and assumes its numbering. It continues to be a subject index.

Wellesley index to Victorian periodicals, 1824–1900. Walter E. Houghton, ed. [Toronto], Univ. of Toronto Pr.; [London], Routledge & Paul, [1966–79]. v.1–3. (In progress) **AE260**

Subtitle: Tables of contents and identification of contributors with bibliographies of their articles and stories.

Planned as a "multi-volumed work that would provide students of the age with a new and better subject index, a book review index, and an author index" (*Introd.*) to magazines of the period. The completed project will offer more detailed coverage than *Poole's Index* (AE227) and the *Nineteenth century readers' guide* (AE230), and will index some journals omitted from those works. Work was begun with the author part as the most badly needed. The first volume deals with 8 major journals; the second, with another 12 of the principal monthlies and quarterlies of the period. v.3 covers an additional 15 periodicals, the most important of which is the *Westminster review.* The whole promises to be a model of careful research and editing.

In each volume, Part A offers issue-by-issue tables of contents of the magazines, with identification of the contributors and references to the evidence for attribution. Poetry is omitted. Part B, "Bibliographies of contributors," furnishes an author approach, listing the articles of each contributor and referring to item number in Part A for the full citation. An index of initials and pseudonyms is included; v.2 and v.3 have appendixes of corrections and additions. Z2005.H6

Albania

Bibliografia kombëtare e Republikës Popullore të Shqipërisë: artikujt e periodikut shqip. Bibliographie nationale de la R.P.A.: articles de la presse albanaise. Tiranë, Botim i Bibliotekës Kombëtare, 1961– . v.1– . Monthly. **AE261**

Frequency varies; title varies slightly.

An index to periodical articles; classed arrangement with author index. Z6956.A5B53

Australia

New South Wales. Public Library, Sydney. Mitchell Library. Australian periodical index, 1944/49–60/63. Sydney, Trustees, 1950-64. **AE262**

Title varies: 1944/49–52/55 called *Index to periodicals.*

A preliminary issue covering 1944–49 was published in 1950 as *The Mitchell Library index to periodicals.* Subsequent volumes cover varying periods, and from 1956 represent annual cumulations of monthly indexes issued as part of the *NSW Library bulletin.*

A subject index only. Z4011.N4

Belgium

Bibliographie de Belgique: 2ème partie, Sommaire des périodiques, 1897–1914. Bruxelles, Van Oest, 1897–1914. **AE263**

Title and frequency vary. 1899–1911 issued as third part of *Bibliographie de Belgique* with title *Bulletin des sommaires;* 1912–13 issued as second part, with title *Sommaire des périodiques;* 1899–1911 issued at irregular intervals, usually monthly (sometimes bimonthly or quarterly) with annual author index; 1912–14, semiannual with annual author and subject indexes. Each number is a classed subject index arranged by the Universal Decimal Classification numbers. Indexes a large number of periodicals, giving fairly full information for each article. A cumbersome but usable index supplying material not easily found in any other way.

Discontinued 1915 because of World War I. Continued by:

―――― 2ème partie, Bulletin mensuel des articles de fond parus dans les revues belges. Janv., 1921–25. Bruxelles, Service de la Bibliographie de Belgique, 1921–25. n.s.v.47–51. Monthly.

No more published.

Roemans, Robert. Bibliographie van de moderne Vlaamsche literatuur, 1893–1930. 1. deel. Kortrijk, Steenlandt, 1930–34. Afl. 1–10. **AE264**

No more published.

1. deel: De Vlaamsche tijdschriften.

An index to the literary articles in Flemish periodicals, indexed periodical by periodical, with cumulated author indexes to poetry, prose, and critical articles.

Continued by: Z2424.F5R7

―――― and **Assche, Hilda van.** Bibliografie van de Vlaamse tijdschriften. Hasselt, Heideland, 1960–71. Reeks I–III. **AE265**

Contents: Reeks I, Vlaamse literaire tijdschriften van 1930 tot en met 1965; Reeks II, Vlaamse niet-literaire tijdschriften van 1886 tot en met 1961; Reeks III, Vlaamse literaire tijdschriften vanaf 1969.

Reeks I indexes literary periodicals, poetry, prose, theater, and critical articles; some issues are devoted to a single periodical, while others index several. Reeks II indexes periodicals in the fields of linguistics, philology, folklore, history, etc. Reeks III indexes literary journals.

Reeks III is continued by: AI5.R6

Bibliografie van de literaire tijdschriften in Vlaanderen en Nederland; de tijdschriften verschenen 1972– . Antwerp, Roemans, 1974– . Annual. **AE266**

Continues *Bibliografie van de Vlaamse tijdschriften,* Reeks III (above).

Journals are listed individually in separate sections for Flemish and Dutch periodicals. Gives full information for each journal, including names of editors, number of issues published, etc., followed by lists of authors and their contributions grouped as poetry, prose, criticism, etc. Author and subject indexes. Coverage is somewhat broader than literature, many of the journals encompassing areas such as art, music, or photography.

Bulgaria

Letopis na periodichniia pechat; mesecher bibliografski biuletin na statii ot spisaniia, vestnitsi i sbornitsi. god. 1–20, ian. 1952–71. Sofia, 1952–71. Monthly.   **AE267**

Monthly issues are arranged by a classified scheme, with author indexes. Annual cumulated author index.

Beginning 1972, continued in two sections: *Letopis na statiite ot bulgarskite spisaniia i sbronitsi* (god. 21, 1972– ; biweekly), which indexes periodicals, and *Letopis na statiite ot bulgarskite vestnitsi* (god. 21, 1972– ; monthly), which indexes newspapers. Both assume the volume numbering of the earlier series, and both are issued by the Narodna Biblioteka.   AI15.L37

Letopis na statiite ot bŭlgarskite spisaniia i sbornitsi. g.21– . Sofiia, Narodna Biblioteka Kiril i Metodii, 1972– . Biweekly.   **AE268**

Continues in part: *Letopis na periodichniia pechat* (above), and assumes its numbering.

Issued as "Seriia 5" of the *Natsionalna bibliografiia na NR Bŭlgariia* (AA650).

Follows the plan of the earlier series.   AI15.L375

Canada

Canadian periodical index, 1928–47. Toronto, Pub. Libraries Branch, Ontario Dept. of Educ., 1928–47.   **AE269**

Publisher varies.

Frequency varies. Set consists of: quarterly issues, 1928–30; annual cumulation, 1931 (publ. 1932); quarterly issues, 1932; not published 1933–37; annual volumes (being cumulations of the quarterly indexes published in the *Ontario library review*), 1938–47.

An author and subject index to Canadian periodicals, most of which are not indexed in other periodical indexes. Covers a varying number of titles, usually between 30 and 40.

Continued by: AI3.C262

Canadian index to periodicals and documentary films; an author and subject index, Jan. 1948–Dec. 1959. Ed. by Margaret E. Wodehouse [and] Ruth Mulholland. Ottawa, Canadian Lib. Assoc., 1962. 1180p.   **AE270**

Added title page in French: *Index de périodiques et de films documentaires canadiens.*

Cumulation, which supersedes annual volumes published as *Canadian index; a guide to Canadian periodicals and films.*

A bilingual index by author and subject to some 60 to 80 Canadian periodicals. Subject headings are in English, but French cross references are given to the English headings. Includes documentary films. Book reviews are listed under the form heading "Book reviews."

Kept up to date by monthly and annual volumes, 1960–63 (v.13–16); title change with v.17 as follows: AI3.C242

Canadian periodical index. Index de périodiques canadiens. v.17– . Ottawa, Canadian Lib. Assoc., 1964– . Monthly, with annual cumulations.   **AE271**

An author and subject index to Canadian periodicals, following the plan of the *Canadian index to periodicals* (above). The listing of films in the earlier index has been taken over by the National Library and appears in *Canadiana.* Now indexes about 135 periodicals.   AI3.C242

Czechoslovakia

Články v českých časopisech. roč. 1– , 1953– . V Praze, Národní Knihovna, [1953–]. Monthly.   **AE272**

Title varies.

Constitutes a part of the *Bibliograficky katalog ČSSR* (AA716). A classified index with annual cumulative indexes for some years.   AI15.C55

Denmark

Dansk Tidsskrift-Index, v.1–64, 1915–78, udg. af Statens Bibliotekstilsyn. København, Dansk Bibliografisk Kontor, 1916–79. 64v.   **AE273**

Publisher varies.

A classified subject index. Later volumes include subject and author indexes. Number of periodicals indexed varies: v.1, 165; about 300 in the 1970 issue.

Each volume contains a section of *Personalhistorie* listing biographical articles.

Merged with *Avis kronik indeks* (AF87) to form: AI13.D3

Dansk artikelindeks; aviser og tidsskrifter. 1979– . Udarbejdet af Bibliotekscentralen. Ballerup, Bibliotekscentralens Forlag, 1981– . Monthly with annual cumulations.   **AE274**

Added title page in English: *The Danish national bibliography: articles; newspapers and journals.*

Introductory matter in Danish and English.

Serves as a continuation of both the *Dansk tidsskrift index* (above) and the *Avis kronik index* (AF87), providing indexing of substantive articles from 25 newspapers and about 550 periodicals published in Denmark (including the Faroe Islands). Full citations are given in a classified section according to the Danish Decimal Classification; author and subject indexes refer to the classified section. Book reviews are excluded.

The annual cumulation may be purchased without the monthly issues.

Thomsen, Svend. Danske blandede Tidsskrifter, 1855–1912; inholdsoversigt til 27 danske Tidsskrifter, udarb. af Ellen Bruun [and others]. København, Bianco Lunos, 1928–29. 2v.   **AE275**

At head of title: Københavns Kommunebiblioteker.

A classified subject index of articles contained in 27 general periodicals, arranged by a decimal classification, with author and alphabetical subject indexes to the classified part. Useful as supplying indexing of some material earlier than that covered by the more comprehensive *Dansk Tidsskrift-Index,* 1915– (AE273). Later indexing of 5 of the 27 periodicals covered is given in the *Dansk Tidsskrift-Index.*   AI13.T4

Finland

Suomen aikakauslehti-indeksi. Index to Finnish periodicals, 1959– . Turku, Turun Yliopiston Kirjasto, 1961– . Annual.   **AE276**

Leena Nuotio, ed.

A classified listing with name index.

A retrospective volume of the same title by Maija Palperi covering 1803–63 was published 1974 (211p.).   AI19.F5N8

France

France. Centre National de la Recherche Scientifique. Bulletin signalétique. Paris, C.N.R.S., 1940– .   **AE277**

Since 1940 the Centre National de la Recherche Scientifique has published a *Bulletin signalétique* (originally its *Bulletin analytique*), an indexing service with a long and complicated bibliographic history. The *Bulletin* was first published in two sections covering the pure and applied sciences, with a section for philosophy and the humanities being added in 1947. Over the years, each of those sections has been superseded by a number of separate indexes, each carrying the title *Bulletin signalétique* plus a number and subtitle designating the specific subject field covered by that section; frequency varies from section to section, indexes in the humanities usually appearing quarterly and those in the sciences appearing monthly. Literally thousands of French and foreign language journals are now indexed annually, and the bibliographic information is stored in a computerized database. A number of the separate sections of the *Bulletin signalétique* are listed in this *Guide* in the relevant subject sections. •

French periodical index, 1973/74– . Westwood, Mass., Faxon, 1976– . Annual. **AE277a**

Comp. by Jean-Pierre Ponchie.

Preface and table of contents in English and French.

Intended as a guide to "up-to-date information concerning contemporary France."—*Pref.* The 1973/74 volume indexes seven periodicals; in the 1976 volume this number had been increased to ten. Publication is running well behind schedule. Indexing is under broad subject headings (arranged alphabetically according to the French form of the heading) roughly corresponding to the categories used in weekly news magazines (e.g., business and economy, food, art, entertainment, environment, armed forces, medicine and health, religion, sports). Within categories the listing is chronological (except that the "people" section is alphabetical by name); titles are usually given as they appear in the original publication. Articles of at least a column or more are indexed. Further refinement of subject categories would greatly increase facility of use. AI7.F7

Germany

Bibliographie der deutschen Zeitschriftenliteratur, mit Einschluss von Sammelwerken. . . . 1896–1964. Gautzsch b. Leipzig, 1897–1964. v.1–128. Semiannual. (Internationale Bibliographie der Zeitschriftenliteratur, Abt. A) **AE278**

Title varies.

A comprehensive index valuable because of the large number of important German periodicals, transactions, yearbooks, and other composite works indexed. Semiannual volumes with no cumulation necessitate the consultation of many alphabets. Except in the case of v.34–35, 40, 40a–41, and 43–46, for which combined author indexes in three separate volumes have been published, each volume consists of: (1) a subject index arranged alphabetically by rather broad subjects, giving for each article indexed its title, author's name in parentheses when known, reference to periodical by key number (instead of title), page, and sometimes volume; and (2) an author index to the subject part (omitted in some volumes). The number of periodicals indexed is large, ranging from 275 in the first volume to some 4,500 in later volumes. The retrospective indexing of the *Ergänzungsbände* carries the work back to 1861. Important in university work and in large libraries which have many German periodicals, but not generally recommended for other libraries. Often especially useful for biography because it indexes many yearbooks of learned societies containing obituary notices.

In 1965 merged into *Internationale Bibliographie der Zeitschriftenliteratur* (AE222). AI9.B512

———— Gesamt-register der Schlagworte aus Bd.66–75, 76–85. Leipzig, Dietrich, 1940–43. 2v.

———— Gesamt-register der Schlagworte zu Abt. A. *Bibliographie der deutschen Zeitschriftenliteratur.* Bd.97–113, und Abt. B. *Bibliographie der fremdsprachigen Zeitschriftenliteratur,* n.F., Bd.30–39. Osnabrück, Dietrich, 1957. 533p.

———— Ergänzungsband 1–20. Gautzsch b. Leipzig, Dietrich, 1908–42. v.1–20.

Numbered in set as v.22A, 24A, 28A, 30A, 32A, 33A, 35A, 35B, 36B, 37A, 39B, 41A, 42A, 72A, 78A, 80A, 82A.

Contents: Ergbd.1, 1896–98; 2, 1896–1908; 3, 1893–95; 4, 1891–92; 5, 1889–90; 6, 1911–13; 7, 1887–88; 8, 1913–14; 9, 1885–86; 10, 1914–15; 11, 1883–84; 12, 1881–82; 13, 1915–17; 14, 1879–81; 15, 1876–78; 16, 1873–75; 17, 1870–73; 18, 1868–70; v.19, 1865–67; v.20, 1861–67.

Gesamtinhaltsverzeichnis der wissenschaftlichen Zeitschriften der Universitäten und Hochschulen der Deutschen Demokratischen Republik. 1951/52– . Berlin, 1959– . Irregular. **AE279**

Frequency varies: quinquennial issues cover 1951/56–1957/61; annual 1962–65; biennial 1966–69; annual 1970–74; biennial 1975/76– .

Indexes the periodicals issued by selected universities and Hochschulen of Eastern Germany. Classified arrangement with author index.

Hocks, Paul and **Schmidt, Peter.** Index zu deutschen Zeitschriften der Jahre 1773–1830. Nendeln, Liechtenstein, KTO Pr., 1979– . Abt.I– . (In progress?) **AE280**

Contents: Abt.I, Bd.1–3, Zeitschriften der Berliner Spätaufklärung.

Abt.I indexes 14 journals published during the late years of the "Berlin enlightenment" (i.e., journals ranging in dates from 1783 to 1811). Bd.1 provides an issue-by-issue listing of the contents of each journal; Bd.2 offers indexes of names (*Namenregister*) and of specific types of contributions or titles with recurring phrases (*Gattungsregister*); and Bd.3 is a *Stichwortregister* or catchword index.

AI9.H54

Hungary

Magyar folyóiratok repertóriuma. Repertorium bibliographicum periodicorum Hungaricorum. Kiadja az Országos Széchényi Könyvtár. 1946–77. Budapest, 1946–77. Semimonthly. **AE281**

A supplement to *Magyar nemzeti bibliográfia* (AA870). Originally appeared quarterly, then monthly, then semimonthly.

A classified index to Hungarian literary and scientific periodicals, with semimonthly and annual author indexes.

Continued by: AI19.H8M27

Magyar nemzeti bibliográfia időszaki kiadványok repertóriuma. Évf. 32^{15}– , Aug. 15, 1977– . Budapest, Országos Széchényi Könyvtár, 1977– . Semimonthly. **AE282**

Represents a change of title for the *Magyar folyóiratok repertóriuma* (above), which closed with évf. 32, füzet 14 (July 13, 1977), and continues its volume numbering. Coverage and arrangement remain the same. Forms a companion publication to *Magyar nemzeti bibliográfia könyvek bibliográfiája* (AA871). AI19.H8M27

India

Guide to Indian periodical literature (social sciences and humanities). v.1– , 1964– . Gurgaon, Prabhu Book Service, [1968–]. Quarterly. **AE283**

Originally appearing as a monthly, publication was suspended after eight issues. With the issue for Jan.-Mar. 1967 (v.4, no.1), publication was resumed on a quarterly basis with annual cumulations. A cumulated volume covering 1964 has since been published, and annual volumes were issued to fill the 1965–66 gap. Now indexes about 400 Indian journals. Author and subject entries in dictionary arrangement. Z6958.I4G8

Index India, v.1, no.1– , Jan./Mar. 1967– . Jaipur, Rajasthan Univ. Lib., 1967– . Quarterly. **AE284**

N. N. Gidwani, ed.

Subtitle: A quarterly documentation list of selected articles, editorials, notes and letters, etc., from periodicals and newspapers published in English language all over the world.

Classified arrangement with alphabetical subject and author indexes. Beginning with v.2, no.1, essays and studies in collections of works by diverse hands are also indexed. Concerned wholly with material relating to India.

India (Republic). Parliament. House of the People. Abstracts and index of articles, v.1–12, 1958–62. New Delhi, Lok Sabha Secretariat, 1958–62. Monthly. **AE285**

Incorporates the "Abstracting service" and the "Monthly list of selected articles" which were previously issued as separate periodicals.

In two parts: pt.1, Abstracts, giving "digests of important articles on political, economic, social, legal, parliamentary, and other subjects"; pt.2, an index to the contents of periodicals and newspapers received in the Parliament Library.

Ceased publication and merged with its *Abstracts of reports* to form its *Abstracts of books, reports and articles* (AG147). AI3.I7

Israel

Mafteah le-khitve-'et be-'Ivrit. 1977– . Yerushalayim, Yotse le-or 'avur Universi'tat 'Hefah, 1978– . Annual. **AE286**

Added title page in English: *Index to Hebrew periodicals.*
At head of title: University of Haifa. Library.
Ed. by Elhanan Adler and others.

An index of authors (or other main entry) and subjects, with a separate section for book reviews. Beginning 1982, also available on microfiche. PN5650.M28

Italy

Italy. Parlamento. Camera dei Deputati. Biblioteca. Catalogo metodico degli scritti contenuti nelle pubblicazioni periodiche italiane e straniere. Parte 1. Scritti biografici e critici. Roma, 1885–1935. 10v. and index. **AE287**

For full information *see* AJ17.

Italy. Provveditorato Generale dello Stato. Pubblicazioni edite dallo stato o col suo concorso: Spoglio dei periodici e delle opere collettive 1901–40. Roma, Libreria dello Stato, 1926–42. **AE288**

Basic work, 1901–25, 2v. (publ. 1926); 1926–30, 2v. (publ. 1931); 1931–35, 2v. (publ. 1937); 1936–40, 2v. (publ. 1942).

A subject index to more than 200 Italian periodicals and collected works which are either government publications or issued under government auspices or aid. Each volume in two parts: (1) Index to biographical and critical articles arranged alphabetically by name of person written about, and (2) Subject index, arranged by large classes, e.g., agriculture, archaeology, etc., with subdivisions under each, and an alphabetical index of small topics referring to the large classes. Entries in the biographical section are repeated in the classed section. Information given about each article is full, including author and title of article, and title, volume, inclusive paging, and date of the volume in which it appears. AI11.I82

Japan

Zasshi kiji sakuin. Japanese periodicals index. Tokyo, Nichigai Asoshiëtsu, 1948– . Quarterly. **AE289**

Subtitle varies; sponsoring body varies; frequency varies.

Now published quarterly in three parts: *Jimbun shakai hen* (Humanities and social science, 1948–); *Kagaku gijutsu hen* (Science and technology, 1950–); *Igaku yakugaku hen* (Medical sciences and pharmacology, 1978–). The humanities and social sciences section currently indexes 1,815 periodicals. Articles in that section are classified in eleven categories; an annual supplement provides an author index, personal and corporate name index, schedule of classification, and the list of periodicals indexed.

Following automation of the index in 1975 a number of cumulations have been published, e.g., cumulative volumes for each of the eleven subject categories of the humanities and social sciences section for the periods 1948–54, 1955–64, 1965–69 and 1970–74. General indexes by author and by subject keyword have also been published for 1948–64 (publ. 1981) and 1965–74 (publ. 1977).

A number of subject bibliographies are "spin-offs" from the index: e.g., *Kokusai kankei ni kansuru jūnenkan no zasshi bunken mokuroku* [Bibliography of journal articles on international relations] (Tokyo, Nichigai Associates, 1981. 265p.) and *Seijigaku ni kansuru 17-nenkan no zasshi bunken mokuroku* [Bibliography of periodical articles on political science] (Tokyo, Nichigai Associates, 1981. 2v.). AI19.J3Z38

Latin America

Columbus Memorial Library, Washington, D.C. Index to Latin American periodical literature, 1929–1960. Boston, G. K. Hall, 1962. 8v. **AE290**

Photoreproduced from catalog cards, this set is compiled from index cards prepared at the Library of the Pan American Union and includes "approximately 250,000 entries of authors, subjects and other secondary entries. Until 1951 . . . only entries by subject were made, except for well-known authors and authors of articles having literary value."—*Pref.* Indexing is on a broad, selective basis from an estimated 3,000 different titles mainly of Latin-American origin. Z1601.P16

———— ———— 1st suppl., 1961–1965. Boston, G. K. Hall, 1968. 2v.

Materials indexed in the *Índice general de publicaciones periódicas latino-americanas* (AE293) are not included in this supplement.

———— ———— [2d suppl.] 1966–70. Boston, G. K. Hall, 1980. 2v.

Adds about 51,000 entries.

HAPI-Hispanic American periodicals index, 1970/74– . Los Angeles, UCLA Latin American Center Publs., Univ. of California, [1977–]. Annual. **AE291**

Barbara G. Cox, ed.

Began publication on an annual basis with the 1975 volume (publ. 1977); a set of three retrospective volumes covering 1970/74 was published 1984 (v.1–2, Subjects; v.3, Authors), bridging the gap between the cessation of the *Index to Latin American periodical literature* (AE290) and the first published volume of *HAPI*.

A subject and author index to articles of interest to Latin Americanists appearing in some 200 journals published in South and Central America, the United States, Europe, and the Caribbean. "The journals were selected with the assistance of the SALALM Committee on Bibliography and an international panel of indexers for their scholarly value and representative coverage of editorial viewpoint, subject matter, and geographical area. Included are leading journals in all major disciplines of the social sciences and the humanities: archaeology and anthropology; art; economics; development, and finance; folklore; film; geography; history; language and linguistics; literature; music; philosophy; political science; sociology; and others."—*Introd.* Journals published in Latin America are indexed in full; those published elsewhere are selectively indexed for items relevant to Latin America. Author and subject listings in separate sections; full bibliographic citations are furnished in both sections. Book reviews are listed in the subject section under author of the book.

Hispanic American periodicals index: articles in English 1976–1980 (Westwood, Mass., Faxon, 1984. 403p.) is a "spin-off" from the annual volumes of *HAPI;* it has the advantage of offering a cumulation of the English-language articles indexed and simplifies the search process for the person who reads only English. Z1605.H16

Índice de artículos de publicaciones periódicas en el área de ciencias sociales y humanidades: acumulado 1974–1979. Bogotá, Instituto Colombiano para el Fomento de la Educación Superior, 1983. 2v. **AE292**

Also called v.5, no.1, 1983.

Cumulates the issues of the index of the same title which appeared irregularly beginning July 1975 and which, in turn, continued the *Índice latinoamericano de ciencias sociales y humanidades,* 1970–73.

A subject arrangement of citations to articles appearing in more than 150 Latin American periodicals, with author index. Coverage of Colombian periodicals is particularly strong. List of periodicals indexed specifies the issues covered. **AI17.I48**

Índice general de publicaciones periódicas latino-americanas. Humanidades y ciencias sociales. Index to Latin American periodicals. Humanities and social sciences. v.1–10, no.2, 1961–Abr./Jun. 1970. Boston, G. K. Hall, 1962–71. Quarterly, with annual cumulations. **AE293**

Prep. by the Columbus Memorial Library of the Organization of American States. Jorge Grossmann, ed.

"A guide to articles appearing in selected Latin American periodicals in the humanities and social sciences."—*Introd.* Originally an author and subject index; arrangement was changed with v.3 to an alphabetical listing by subject. Entries are under the Spanish form of the subject heading, with an auxiliary list of corresponding English terms. The annual volume for 1963 is a single alphabetical subject listing with author and title indexes. Annual volumes for 1964–69 (v.4–9) reprint the quarterly subject listings without interfiling of entries, but add a cumulated author index.

Ceased with v.10, no.2, and no cumulation of v.10 was published. **Z1605.I55**

Leavitt, Sturgis Elleno. Revistas hispanoamericanas: índice bibliográfico, 1843–1935. Recopilado . . . con la colaboración de Madaline W. Nichols y Jefferson Rea Spell. Santiago de Chile, Fondo Histórico y Bibliográfico José Toribio Medina, 1960. 589p. **AE294**

"Homenaje al Sesquicentenario de la independencia nacional, 1810–1960."—*title page.*

A classified index to the material in 56 Spanish-American periodicals, primarily in literature, linguistics, and folklore. Name index. An appendix lists those libraries in the United States holding complete sets of the periodicals indexed.

A list of "Errata" compiled by Leavitt appeared as: Kentucky. University. Library. Occasional contribution, no.123. 6p. **AI17.L4**

Malaysia

Indeks majalah Malaysia. Malaysian periodicals index. 1973– . Kuala Lumpur, Perpustakaan Negara Malaysia, 1974– . **AE295**

Frequency varies; from 1980 issued semiannually with two parts to each issue (pt.1, Classified section with subject index; pt.2, Author/title section).

Supersedes in part: *Indeks majallah kini Malaysia Singapura dan Brunei* (Index to current Malaysian, Singapore and Brunei periodicals) publ. 1969–71 and covering 1967–68.

Introductory matter in Malay and English.

Now indexes about 180 periodicals in Malay, English, Chinese and Tamil. The subject section is arranged by Dewey Decimal Classification with subject indexing in English. Also indexes working papers from conferences held in the area. **AI3.I26**

Netherlands

Nijhoff's Index op de Nederlandse en Vlaamse periodieken, Sept. 1909–70. 'sGravenhage, Nijhoff, 1910–73. v.1–60. Monthly. **AE296**

Title varies.

A monthly index to general periodicals, including a few newspapers. Each number contains authors and subjects in one alphabet with a separate list of book reviews at the end. No cumulations, but beginning with the volume for 1925, there is an annual author index and a catchword subject index. The number of periodicals indexed varies from 19 in the earlier volumes to more than 60.

Ceased publication. **AI5.N4**

New Zealand

Index to New Zealand periodicals, 1940– . Wellington, New Zealand Lib. Assoc., 1940– . **AE297**

Title varies: 1950–65, *Index to New Zealand periodicals & Current national bibliography of New Zealand books & pamphlets.*

Imprint varies; coverage varies.

Frequency varies: 1940 issue, prep. by the Otago Branch of the Library Association as a preliminary index to 12 periodicals; v.1–2, 1941–42, issued quarterly, cumulated annually; v.3, no.1, Jan.–June 1943; publication suspended July 1943–Dec. 1946; 1941–46 cumulation published 1949; 1947–49 published semiannually with annual cumulation; annual volumes have appeared since 1957, with irregular cumulations as noted below. From 1979, publ. 3 times a year with annual cumulation.

Volumes for 1950–65 include the *Current national bibliography.* The periodical index sections for 1958–60 inclusive were cumulated into one volume (publ. 1961) with the *Current national bibliography* for 1960, but the national bibliography sections were not cumulated. 1961–62 also cumulated into one volume.

This is a subject index with cross references from author entries to the subject listing. Now indexes about 220 New Zealand periodicals on a selective basis, plus some articles on New Zealand published elsewhere. **Z6962.N5I5**

Nigeria

Index to Nigeriana in selected periodicals, 1965– . Lagos, Nat. Lib. of Nigeria, 1967– . Annual. (National Library publ. 6, 11, 18, etc.) **AE298**

Issue for 1965 had title: *Index to selected Nigerian periodicals.*

An author (or anonymous title) and subject index to articles of Nigerian interest appearing in a selection of periodicals, most of them published in Nigeria. 28 journals are indexed in the 1967 issue (publ. 1970). **Z965.N38**

Norway

Deichmanske Bibliotek, Oslo. Register til en del norske tidsskrifter. Kristiania, Arnesens Bog & Accidenstrykkeri, 1908–11. 2v. **AE299**

Contents: v.1, Topografi; v.2, Norsk biografi.

Arranged by subject, each volume indexes one topic. v.1 (1908) indexes the topographical articles in 75 periodicals of varying dates from about the beginning of the 19th century to 1907; v.2 indexes nearly 15,000 biographical articles in more than 700 periodicals of the 19th and the first part of the 20th century, giving not only references to periodicals, but also dates of birth and death and very brief characterization for each name indexed. The list of periodicals included in v.2 furnishes a nearly complete bibliography of Norwegian periodicals for the 19th and early 20th centuries.

Z2595.D32

Norsk tidsskriftindex, 1918–65, systematisk fortegnelse over indholdet av norske periodiske skrifter. Oslo, Steenske Forlag, 1919–71. v.1–46. Annual. **AE300**

Subtitle varies; publisher varies.

A classified subject index with an alphabetical subject index to some 250 Norwegian periodicals.

Issued in annual volumes, with a general title page, list of abbreviations and periodicals indexed, and alphabetical subject index to the classed lists for v.1–3 (1918–20), v.4–8 (1921–25), v.9–13 (1926–30), v.14–18 (1931–35), v.19–23 (1936–40), v.24–25 (1941–42), v.26–28 (1943–45), v.29–33 (1946–50); thereafter, only annual issues were published. Superseded by the annual *Norske tidsskriftartikler* which began publication 1981 with a volume covering 1980.

Beginning with v.18 (1935), the publisher changed and the index became a part of the bibliographical series *Norsk bibliografisk bibliotek,* v.18 being numbered as bd.1, hft.5 in that series (with retrospective numbering of v.14–17 as bd.1, hft.1–4), and v.19–23 as bd.4. The detailed indexing of articles of individual biography, formerly a feature of the index under the heading "Personalhistorie," is omitted from 1931 and included, instead, in a separate series, the first volume of which is *Biografiske artikler i norske tidsskrifter 1931–35,* numbered as bd.2, hft.3 of the *Norsk bibliografisk bibliotek.*   AI13.N6

Papua New Guinea

New Guinea periodical index. v.1– , 1968– . Boroko, Papua New Guinea, Univ. of Papua New Guinea Library, 1968– . Quarterly with annual cumulation.   **AE301**

Frequency varies.

Aims to bring together references to "all major articles published anywhere in the world about any aspect of New Guinea."—*Introd.* Based on the periodical acquisitions of the New Guinea Collection in the University of Papua New Guinea Library (and includes some non-current and photocopied material from journals not in that library). Originally an author/subject arrangement; beginning 1981, a topical listing with author and people/places indexes.

Suspended after v.15, no.2 (Apr./June 1983).   Z4811.U54a

Philippines

Index to Philippine periodicals, Oct. 1955/Sept. 1956– . Manila, Inter-Departmental Reference Service, Inst. of Public Administration, Univ. of the Philippines, 1956– . v.1– . Annual.   **AE302**

Frequency varies. Originally a quarterly, later semiannual with annual cumulations. v.14, covering 1968–69, publ. 1972.

Now indexes about 130 periodicals by author and subject in one alphabet.   AI3.I63

Selected Philippine periodical index, June 1969– . Dumaguete City, Silliman Univ., 1969– . Semiannual (irregular).   **AE303**

Now issued irregularly as a supplement to the *Silliman journal,* the index was a regular feature of that quarterly publication from Jan. 1956 to 1969. An author-subject index to about 40 Philippine periodicals. Some years not covered.   AI3.S45

Romania

Lupu, Ioan [et al.]. Bibliografia analitică a periodicelor românești. București, Editura Academiei Republicii Socialiste România, 1966–70. v.1–2. (In progress?)   **AE304**

Contents: v.1, pts.1–3, 1790–1850; v.2, pts. 1–3, 1851–58.

An annotated bibliography of Romanian periodical articles relating to political, economic, and cultural matters. Arranged by Universal Decimal Classification.   Z2929.L86

Singapore

Singapore periodicals index, 1969/70– . Singapore, Nat. Lib., [1973–]. Annual.   **AE305**

Supersedes in part *Index to current Malaysian, Singapore and Brunei periodicals* 1967–68, publ. 1969–71.

Classed arrangement with author and subject indexes. Separate author index of Chinese entries. Now indexes about 110 periodicals.   AI3.S57

South Africa

Index to South African periodicals. v.1– , 1940– . Johannesburg, Johannesburg Public Lib., 1941– . Annual.   **AE306**

Added title page in Afrikaans.

Cumulations have been issued for the periods 1940–49 (4v.), 1950–59 (3v.), 1960–69 (microfiche), 1970–74 (microfiche).

1940–42 issued by the South African Library Association.

The 1940/49 cumulation is in three sections: v.1–2, Subject list of English articles; v.3, Subject list of Afrikaans articles; v.4, Author section. Later volumes are arranged in a single alphabetical sequence combining author and subject entries. Now indexes about 500 South African periodicals—the scholarly and scientific quite fully, others selectively.   AI3.I65

Spain

Colección de índices de publicaciones periódicas, dirigida por Joaquín de Entrambasaguas. Madrid, Inst. "Nicolás Antonio" del Consejo Superior de Investigaciones Científicas, 1946–53. v.1–16.   **AE307**

Each volume is an index to an individual periodical, usually from the 19th century. In some cases extracts from articles or annotations are included. Usually gives: name, place, subject, title, first-line index, and a selection of plates or illustrations.

Indice español de humanidades. v.1– , enero/jun. 1978– . Madrid, Instituto de Información y Documentación en Ciencias Sociales y Humanidades, Centro Nacional de Informatión y Documentación, C.S.I.C., 1978– . Semiannual.   **AE308**

Reproduces the tables of contents of the journals indexed and provides author and keyword subject indexing. About 170 periodicals indexed in the first issue.   AS1.I5

Tortajada, A. and **Amaniel, C. de.** Materiales de investigación: índice de artículos de revistas (1939–1949). Madrid, Consejo Superior de Investigaciones Científicas, Biblioteca General, 1952. 2v.   **AE309**

Arranged alphabetically by author and subject. Indexes some 125 periodicals in both the humanities and the sciences.   AI17.T6

Switzerland

Studer, Maja. Analytische Bibliographie der Gesamtregister schweizerischer Zeitschriften; Bibliographie analytique des tables générales des périodiques suisses. Bern, Schweizerische Landesbibliothek, 1974. 125p.   **AE310**

A classed listing of Swiss periodicals having one or more cumulative indexes, with indication of type of index and period covered. Alphabetical title index.   Z6293.S87

Turkey

Türkiye makaleler bibliyoğrafyasï. Bibliographie des articles parus dans les périodiques turcs. Mart 1952– . Ankara, Türk Tarih Kurumu Basimevi, 1952– . (Millî Kütüphane Bibliyoğrafya Enstitüsü. Yayinlari; Bibliothèque Nationale, Inst. de Bibliographie. Publ.) Quarterly. **AE311**

Place, publisher, series and frequency vary.

Indexes articles in periodicals, annuals, and society publications appearing in Turkey. Arrangement is classified, with annual author index. All titles are given in both Turkish and French, and very brief annotations are given in some cases.

Union of Soviet Socialist Republics

Letopis zhurnal'nykh statei. T.1– , 1926– . Moskva, 1926– . Weekly. **AE312**

Frequency varies.

Title varies: 1926–37, *Zhurnal'naia letopis'*.

A weekly index of wide scope covering more than 1,700 journals, series, and continuing publications of academies, universities and research institutes in humanities, science, and the social sciences. Excluded are popular magazines, children's literature, and government publications. Entries, averaging some 3,500 an issue, are arranged in the 31 sections of the Soviet classification scheme. Each issue identifies the specific journal numbers indexed; the annual *Spisok zhurnalov* . . . cumulates this information. Indexes of names and localities were published quarterly 1956–77; starting 1978, indexes are issued bi-monthly. **AI15.L4**

Masanov, IUrii Ivanovich, Nitkina, N. V. and **Titova, Z. D.** Ukazateli soderzhaniia russkikh zhurnalov i prodolzhaiushchikhsia izdanii 1755–1970 gg. Moskva, "Kniga." 1975. 437p. **AE313**

At head of title: Gosudarstvennaia publichnaia biblioteka im. M. E. Saltykova-Shchedrina.

A bibliography of indexes to individual Russian journals. Arranged alphabetically by title of the journal. Indexed.
Z6956.R9M37

Yugoslavia

Bibliografija Jugoslavije: članci i prilozi u časopisima i listovima. Jan./Mart, 1950– . Beograd, Bibliografski Inst. FNRJ, [1950–]. **AE314**

Subtitle varies; frequency varies.

A classified index to Yugoslav periodicals in all fields. Beginning with the first issue of 1952, it appears in sections, of which Series A covers social sciences; Series B, natural and applied sciences; Series C, philology, art, sport, literature, music. Semiannual indexes.

Bibliografija rasprava, članaka i književnih radova u časopisima Narodne Republike Hrvatske, 1945/46–52. Zagreb, Jugoslovenska Akademija Znanosti i Umjetnosti, 1948–56. Annual. **AE315**

Index to Croatian periodicals; classified, with alphabetical indexes by author and subject. The first volume covers the years 1945–46; subsequent issues are annual. **AI15.B5**

Zagreb. Jugoslavenski Leksikografski Zavod. Bibliografija rasprava, članaka i knjizevnih radova. [Glavni redaktor: Mate Ujević] Zagreb, Leksikografski Zavod, 1956–77. v.1–5 in 12v. (In progress) **AE316**

Beginning with v.4, pt.1, volumes have title: *Bibliografija rasprava i članaka,* with Slavko Batušić as editor.

A retrospective periodical index, planned to be in 25v., to form a comprehensive record of articles published in Yugoslavia since 1800 in magazines, newspapers, yearbooks, and collections. Arrangement is by large classifications, with indexes. The first 4v. (in 7 pts.) are devoted to various categories of literature; v.4 (in 4 pts.) is concerned with history; v.5 with the plastic arts. Z2951.Z3

A F

Newspapers

❖Newspapers are very important in certain aspects of reference work. Current issues are helpful on questions of the day, events, policies, opinion, politics, personalities, and many others. Back volumes serve the same purpose for the contemporary history of an earlier period, and often record details of a situation, or information local in its application, that are not found in general reference books. Bound files of newspapers have always been valuable additions to the reference equipment of a library that could afford them. However, they created many problems because of the difficulties and expense of binding, shelving, and preserving them, particularly because of the rapid deterioration of newsprint. In recent years files of many newspapers have been microfilmed, and in this form are available for purchase or interlibrary loan. For a record of newspapers available in microform, *see* the volumes of *Newspapers in microform* listed below (AF10, AF25).

To make intelligent use of newspapers the reference worker needs the same type of reference aids that are needed for periodicals, i.e.: (1) indexes, (2) bibliographies, and (3) lists of holdings of other libraries. These differ in some ways from the corresponding aids for periodicals. For example, no general index to newspapers similar to the *Readers' guide* (AE231) is available, and the various online databases provide indexing of only a limited number of titles. Considerations of cost and practicability aside, a comprehensive newspaper index is not so necessary as an index to a wide range of periodicals. Since most metropolitan newspapers publish reports of important events at approximately the same time, the date of an event is the clue needed, and an index of dates, or an index of one newspaper, will furnish a workable index to most newspapers for subjects of general interest—but not, of course, to purely local or special articles, editorials, and many obituaries.

The most used printed newspaper indexes in American libraries are the *New York times index* (AF77) and the *Times* (London) *index* (AF93).

Generally speaking, the bibliographies and union lists included in this section are concerned mainly with newspapers. It should be kept in mind, however, that many of the bibliographies and directories in the preceding section on periodicals will contain information about newspapers.

BIBLIOGRAPHIES AND UNION LISTS

International

See also AF18.

Arndt, Karl John Richard and **Olson, May E.** The German language press of the Americas. München, Verlag Dokumentation, [1973–80]. 3v. **AF1**

Added title page in German: *Die deutschsprachige Presse der Amerikas.*

Publisher varies.

Contents: v.1, History and bibliography, 1732–1968: United States of America (3d rev. ed. enl. by an appendix, publ. 1976); v.2, History and bibliography, 1732–1968: Argentina, Bolivia, Brazil, Canada, Chile, Colombia, Costa Rica, Cuba, Dominican Republic, Ecuador, Guatemala, Guyana, Mexico, Paraguay, Peru, USA (addenda), Uruguay, Venezuela (publ. 1973); v.3, German-American press research from the American Revolution to the Bicentennial (publ. 1980).

v.1 was first published 1965 with title *German-American newspapers and periodicals, 1732–1955;* it was reprinted 1965 with an appendix added.

The United States section is arranged by state, then by city; other sections are by country, then by city. As far as possible, gives changes of title, names of editors and publishers, frequency, circulation, etc., for the individual German-American newspapers and periodicals. Locates files in American and European libraries.

v.3 is a selection of essays in German or English, chiefly reprints, relating to the history and influence of the German-language press in America. Z6956.G3A75

Feuereisen, Fritz and **Schmacke, Ernst.** Die Presse in Afrika; ein Handbuch für Wirtschaft and Werbung. The press in Africa; a handbook for economics and advertising. 2. Aufl. Pullach/München, Verlag Dokumentation, 1973. 280p. **AF2**

1st ed. 1968. Z6959.F47

—— Die Presse in Asien und Ozeanien; ein Handbuch für Wirtschaft und Werbung. The press in Asia and Oceania; a handbook for economics and advertising. 2. Aufl. Pullach/München, Verlag Dokumentation, 1973. 376p. **AF3**

1st ed. 1968. Z6957.F48

—— Die Presse in Lateinamerika; ein Handbuch für Wirtschaft und Werbung. The press in Latin America; a handbook for economics and advertising. 2. Aufl. Pullach/München, Verlag Dokumentation, 1973. 268p. **AF4**

1st ed. 1968.

The three items above are companion volumes. Each has text in German and English; format and organization are the same for each, with information on the press of individual nations presented in tabular form. Within country sections newspapers are listed by title, with information as to address, frequency, circulation, type of readership, and advertising. Alphabetical title and geographical indexes in each volume. Z6954.A1F4

Foreign newspaper report. 1973–75. [Wash.], Lib. of Congress, 1973–75. **AF5**

Newsletter of the Foreign Newspaper Microfilming Coordinator's office. Intended to provide "current data about various foreign newspaper acquisition and microfilming programs, announcements of newly available titles and cooperative microfilming projects, information about bibliographic and technical standards in newspaper microfilming, and other news of interest to the research community."—*no.1, 1973.* It carried information previously included in the ARL Foreign Newspaper Microfilm Project *Circular letter,* which ceased publication with no.21 (Feb. 1971).

Superseded by: Z663.2F66

Newspaper and gazette report. 1976–78. Wash., Lib. of Congress, 1976–78. 3 nos. per yr. **AF6**

"The title change . . . marks the expansion of the current program and enables us to include information on both foreign and domestic newspapers."—*no.1, 1976.* Beginning 1977, the December issue contained an annual index; a cumulative index covering 1973–76 was published 1978.

Continued in part by the *National preservation report* (AB292).

Fraenkel, Josef. The Jewish press of the world. 7th ed. London, Cultural Dept. of the World Jewish Congress, [1972]. 128p. **AF7**

1st ed. 1953.

Offers directory information on more than 950 Jewish newspapers and periodicals published throughout the world. Includes a statistical summary indicating linguistic and geographic distribution of the papers. Z6367.F7

Iben, Icko. The Germanic press of Europe; an aid to research. Münster [Westf.], Fahle, 1965. 146p. (Studien zur Publizistik. Bremer Reihe, Bd.5) **AF8**

An attempt to list and locate files of the "most significant" newspapers of the Benelux countries (Belgium, Netherlands, and Luxembourg) and Scandinavia for the guidance of researchers. Also includes selected pre-1949 newspapers from the Dutch East Indies (Indonesia), and selected newspapers from the Netherlands West Indies. Arranged by country. Indexes of names and titles.

PN5110.I2

Merrill, John C., Bryan, Carter R. and **Alisky, Marvin.** The foreign press; a survey of the world's journalism. Baton Rouge, Louisiana State Univ. Pr., [1970]. 365p. **AF9**

Previous ed. 1964; Merrill's original *Handbook of the foreign press* was published in 1959.

Offers a country-by-country survey of the press, with statistics, information about leading newspapers, etc. The 1970 edition includes a new overview of the United States press and expansion of the African section. PN4736.M39

U.S. Library of Congress. Catalog Publication Division. Newspapers in microform: foreign countries, 1948–1972. Wash., Lib. of Congress, 1973. 269p. **AF10**

At head of title: Library of Congress catalogs.

With its companion volume, *Newspapers in microform: United States* (AF25), supersedes the 6th ed. of *Newspapers on microfilm* (Wash., 1967). Includes reports through Summer 1972. Lists 8,620 titles in 1,935 localities as reported by about 550 domestic and foreign libraries and commercial firms. Arranged by country, then by city of publication. Title index. Z6945.U515

—— Newspapers in microform: foreign countries, 1973–1977. Wash., Lib. of Congress, 1978. 449p. **AF11**

"This publication cumulates the Foreign Countries sections of the annual issues [below] for 1973 through 1976 and the reports contributed in 1977 to form a quinquennial supplement to the previous cumulation" (*Pref.*) covering 1948–72 (above). For the volume dealing with United States newspapers *see* AF26.

Both of the above items are superseded by *Newspapers in microform: foreign countries, 1948–1983* (Wash., Lib. of Congress, 1984. 504p.) which cumulates the 1948–72 and 1973–77 volumes and incorporates reports from the annual volumes published through 1982 along with reports received through 1983. Z6945.U515

—— Newspapers in microform. 1973– . Wash., Lib. of Congress, 1975– . Annual. **AF12**

Serves as a supplement to both *Newspapers in microform: foreign countries, 1948–1972* (AF10) and *Newspapers in microform: United States, 1948–1972* (AF25), listing reports for foreign and domestic newspapers in separate sections, with a combined title index. No 1983 volume was published in anticipation of the 1948–83 cumulation noted above.

U.S. Library of Congress. Periodical Division. A check list of foreign newspapers in the Library. . . . newly comp. under the direction of Henry S. Parsons. Wash., Govt. Prt. Off., 1929. 209p. **AF13**

1st ed. 1904.

Arranged geographically by country of publication, and under each city alphabetically by title of newspaper. Gives for each paper exact statement of Library of Congress files. Includes almost 2,700 titles, published in 79 countries in 21 languages. Title index.

Z881.U5

U.S. Library of Congress. Serial Division. Newspapers received currently in the Library of Congress. Ed. 3– . Wash., Lib. of Congress, 1972– . **AF14**

Supersedes *Newspapers currently received & permanently retained* last published 1968.

The 8th ed. (1982) "lists 349 United States and 1,090 foreign newspapers which are received and retained on a permanent basis and an additional 187 United States and 49 foreign newspapers retained on a current basis only."—*Pref.*　　Z6945.U5N42

—— Postwar foreign newspapers; a union list. Wash., 1953. 231p.　　**AF15**

Includes Russian but not Latin-American newspapers. (For Latin-American newspapers *see* AF51.) Arrangement is alphabetical by country, then by city, with a title index. Frequency and date of establishment are given where known. Reports the holdings of 76 libraries in the United States.　　Z6945.U5N44

U.S. Library of Congress. Slavic and Central European Division. Newspapers of east central and southeastern Europe in the Library of Congress. Robert G. Carlton, ed. Wash., 1965. 204p.　　**AF16**

Detailed holdings of post-World War I newspapers (both newsprint and microfilm files) are given in alphabetical arrangement by country, then by city of publication. Newspapers for the Baltic countries—Estonia, Latvia, and Lithuania—published from 1917 to the date of initial occupation by the Soviet Union in the summer of 1940 are included. Indexes by language and by title, plus a guide to places of publication.　　Z6955.U52

Webber, Rosemary. World list of national newspapers: a union list of national newspapers in libraries in the British Isles. London, Butterworths, [1976]. 95p.　　**AF17**

Comp. under the auspices of the Standing Conference of National and University Libraries in contract with the Social Science Research Council.

A title listing with index by country. For British and Irish newspapers, "all newspapers having national circulation have been listed" (*Introd.*), as have regional newspapers which regularly carry a significant amount of national news; all foreign newspaper holdings are reported. Holdings of the British Library's Newspaper Library at Colindale have *not* been included.　　Z6945.W385

United States

See also IMS Ayer directory (AE32); *Editor and publisher* (AE33); *Working press of the nation* (AE38).

American newspapers, 1821–1936; a union list of files available in the United States and Canada, ed. by Winifred Gregory under the auspices of the Bibliographical Society of America. N.Y., Wilson, 1937. 791p. (Repr.: N.Y., Kraus, 1967)　　**AF18**

A union list of first importance which lists the exact holdings of newspapers in nearly 5,700 depositories, such as libraries, county courthouses, newspaper offices, and private collections. In addition to the main union list, contains (p.787–89) "A bibliography of union lists of newspapers," compiled by Karl Brown and Daniel C. Haskell.　　Z6945.A53

Brigham, Clarence S. History and bibliography of American newspapers, 1690–1820. Worcester, Mass., Amer. Antiquarian Soc., 1947. 2v. (Repr.: Hamden, Conn., Archon, 1962. 2v. [incl.] Additions and corrections)　　**AF19**

Originally published in the *Proceedings* of the American Antiquarian Society, 1913–27. This cumulated edition, a work of the first importance, includes corrections, additions, and more detailed listings. Arranged alphabetically by state and town, it lists 2,120 newspapers published between 1690 and 1820 with indication of location of files in all parts of the country. Historical notes for each paper give title, date of establishment, exact dates of changes of titles, names of editors and publishers, frequency, etc.

The bibliography is followed by lists of libraries and private owners, an index of titles, and an index of printers.

With *American newspapers,* 1821–1936 (AF18), this forms a comprehensive record of American newspaper files from 1690–1936.　　Z6951.B86

—— —— Additions and corrections. 1961. 50p. (Repr. from the *Proceedings* of the American Antiquarian Society, April 1961)

Brigham's work is complemented by:

Lathem, Edward Connery, comp. Chronological tables of American newspapers, 1690–1820; being a tabular guide to holdings of newspapers published in America through the year 1820. Barre, Mass., Amer. Antiquarian Soc. and Barre Pub., [1972]. 131p.　　**AF20**

A companion to Brigham (above), intended to serve as an aid "in approaching, on a chronological basis, available issues of American newspapers for the period through 1820."—*Introd.*　　Z6951.L3

Campbell, Georgetta Merritt. Extant collections of early black newspapers: a research guide to the black press, 1880–1915; with an index to the Boston *Guardian,* 1902–1904. Troy, N.Y., Whitston, 1981. 401p.　　**AF21**

Consolidates publication and locational information from a number of earlier sources, and adds various new titles and locations. Arranged by place of publication (state, city, title of newspaper). Holdings information is specific; microfilm availability is indicated. The *Guardian* index occupies p.231–384.　　Z6944.N39C35

Hebrew Union College—Jewish Institute of Religion. American Jewish Periodical Center. Jewish newspapers and periodicals on microfilm, available at the American Jewish Periodical Center. Cincinnati, 1957. 56p.　　**AF22**

The Center is attempting to microfilm every Jewish newspaper and periodical in any language, published in the United States up to 1925, with a selected number after that date. The films are available on interlibrary loan. Geographical arrangement by state and then by city, with language divisions within city listings. Brief bibliographic and contents notes; names and titles index.

—— —— Supplement 1, by H. C. Zafren. Cincinnati, 1960. 28p. (Repr. from *Studies in bibliography and booklore,* 4, no.2, Dec. 1959)

Indicates locations of original files used for filming and lists missing issues.　　Z6944.J4H4

Iowa Pilot Project. A bibliography of Iowa newspapers, 1836–1976. Comp. by the Iowa Pilot Project of the Organization of American Historians—Library of Congress United States Newspaper Project. Alan Schroder, director. [Des Moines], Iowa State Historical Dept./Div. of the State Historical Soc., 1979. 371p.　　**AF23**

Important not merely as a bibliography and union list of a single state's newspapers, but as a pilot project for a proposed successor to Gregory's *American newspapers* (AF18).

A similar list, unrelated to the O.A.H./L.C. project is Carol K. Kolar's *Union list of North Dakota newspapers, 1864–1976* (Fargo, North Dakota Inst. for Regional Studies, 1981. 448p.).

Z6952.I6I67

North, Simon Newton Dexter. History and present condition of the newspaper and periodical press of the United States, with a catalogue of the publications of the census year. Wash., Govt. Prt. Off., 1884. 446p. maps. (*In* U.S. Census Office. 10th Census, v.8)　　**AF24**

A history of the newspaper and periodical press 1639–1880, with maps and statistical tables; a catalog of periodical publications issued during the census year June 1, 1879–May 31, 1880; and a chronological history.

Appendix D, "Bound files of American newspapers in the possession of the American Antiquarian Society, Worcester, Mass."

PN4855.N6

U.S. Library of Congress. Catalog Publication Division. Newspapers in microform: United States 1948–1972. Wash., 1973. 1056p.　　**AF25**

With its companion volume, *Newspapers in microform: foreign countries* (AF10), supersedes *Newspapers on microfilm* (1st–6th ed., 1948–67).

A union list which offers "a cumulation of all reports contained in the United States section of *Newspapers on Microfilm* (1948–67), together with reports received through the summer of 1972."—*Introd.* Includes various microfiche and micro-opaque forms as well as negative and positive microfilm copies. Lists 34,289 titles reported by 843 libraries and 48 commercial firms. Arrangement is by state, then by city of publication, with a title index. Indicates dates of publication, changes of title, mergers, etc.; holdings notes show inclusive dates held and type of microform (e.g., microfilm master, microfilm service copy, microfiche master).

Z6951.U469

——— Newspapers in microform: United States, 1973–1977. Wash., Lib. of Congress, 1978. 642p.   **AF26**

"This publication cumulates the United States sections of the annual issues [*see* AF12] for 1973 through 1976 and the reports contributed in 1977 to form a quinquennial supplement to the previous cumulation" (*Pref.*) covering 1948–72 (AF25). For the volume dealing with foreign newspapers *see* AF11.

Both of the above items are superseded by *Newspapers in microform: United States, 1948–1983* (Wash., Lib. of Congress, 1984. 2v.) which cumulates the 1948–72 and 1973–77 volumes and incorporates reports from the annual volumes published through 1982 along with reports received through 1983.   Z6951.U469

U.S. Library of Congress. Periodical Division. Check list of American 18th century newspapers in the Library of Congress, originally comp. by John Van Ness Ingram. New ed. rev. and enl. under the direction of Henry S. Parsons. Wash., Govt. Prt. Off., 1936. 401p.   **AF27**

1st ed. 1912.

Arranged alphabetically by state, subdivided by town. Gives for each newspaper: date of establishment; changes in title; names of printers, publishers, and editors; and a statement of the Library of Congress file. Title index, and index to printers, publishers, and editors.   Z6951.U47

University of Notre Dame. Library. Directory of Roman Catholic newspapers on microfilm: United States. Notre Dame, Ind., Memorial Lib., Univ. of Notre Dame, 1982. 69p.   **AF28**

A catalog of the Notre Dame Library's holdings—"one of the finest collections of Roman Catholic newspapers in the United States."—*Pref.*   Z7837.5.U54

Wynar, Lubomyr Roman and **Wynar, Anna T.** Encyclopedic directory of ethnic newspapers and periodicals in the United States. 2d ed. Littleton, Colo., Libraries Unlimited, 1976. 248p.   **AF29**

1st ed. 1972.

Arrangement is alphabetical under ethnic press (e.g., Albanian press, Arabic press, etc.). Includes both English- and foreign-language publications.   Z6953.5.A1W94

❖Numerous state checklists and regional union lists of newspapers have been compiled for specific areas of the United States. Examples of publications of this kind include: *A bibliography of newspapers in fourteen New York counties,* ed. by Sylvia G. Faibisoff and Wendell Tripp (Cooperstown & Ithaca, 1978. 316p.); *Guide to Ohio newspapers 1793–1973; union bibliography of Ohio newspapers available in Ohio libraries,* ed. by Stephen Gutgesell (Columbus, 1974. 412p.); *Indiana newspaper bibliography; historical accounts of all Indiana newspapers published from 1804 to 1980 and locational information for all available copies,* by John W. Miller (Indianapolis, 1982. 538p.); *Louisiana newspapers, 1794–1961: a union list of Louisiana newspaper files available in public, college and university libraries in Louisiana,* ed. by T. N. McMullan for the Louisiana State University and Agricultural and Mechanical College Library (Baton Rouge, 1965. 281p.); *Newspaper resources of Southeast Texas,* comp. by Virginia B. Murphy, Daisy Ashford, and Pamela B. Covington (Houston, 1971. 63p.); *Guide to North Carolina newspapers on microfilm,* by Roger C. Jones (Raleigh, 1982. 92p.); *Tennessee newspapers; a cumulative list of microfilmed Tennessee newspapers in the Tennessee State Library,* a progress report of the Tennessee State Library and Archives (Nashville, 1969. 127p.); *A union list of newspapers in the libraries of the Fort Worth-Dallas major resource centers,* ed. by Mary Oleta Wittenmyer for the Texas Christian University Library (Fort Worth, 1969. 144p.); and *Newspaper resources of metropolitan Detroit libraries; a union list,* comp. by Howard A. Sullivan and Thelma Friedes for the Wayne State University Libraries (Detroit, 1965. 46p.).

Newsletters

National directory of newsletters and reporting services. Ed.1– . Detroit, Gale, 1966– . Irregular.   **AF30**

Subtitle (varies): A reference guide to national, international, and selected foreign newsletters, information services, financial services, association bulletins, training and educational services.

Lists and briefly describes publications (other than house organs) which "confine their content to treatment of a particular subject or activity," and present "material which has a time value—such as reports of specific events or developments in the field, or announcements of future happenings."—*Introd.* Classed arrangement with title, publisher, and subject indexes.

There is considerable overlap with the *Standard periodical directory* (AE37).   Z6941.N3

Africa

See also AF2.

U.S. Library of Congress. Serial Division. African newspapers in selected American libraries. Ed.1– . Wash., 1956– .   **AF31**

The 3d ed., 1965, records current and retrospective holdings in 33 selected libraries. It lists 708 titles, in positive microfilm and hard copy. Country/city arrangement; title index.

Maidel K. Cason's *African newspapers currently received by American libraries* (Evanston, Herskovits Lib. of African Studies, Northwestern Univ. Lib., 1983. 18p.) lists titles currently received, without indication of holdings.   Z6959.Z9U5

Australia

Newpapers in Australian libraries; a union list. 3d ed. Canberra, Nat. Lib. of Australia, 1973–75. 2v.   **AF32**

1st ed. (1959; suppl.1–3, 1960–64) had title *Union list of newspapers in Australian libraries.*

Contents: pt.1, Overseas newspapers; pt.2, Australian newspapers.

This edition lists and locates about 2,300 overseas newspapers and some 4,000 Australian papers. Geographical arrangement, with title index for each section. Includes microfilm and original files.   Z6945.C1792

Belgium

Bertelson, Lionel. La presse d'information: tableau chronologique des journaux belges. [Bruxelles, 1974] 287p.   **AF33**

At head of title: Institut pour Journalistes de Belgique.

In two main sections: (1) Les journaux disparus (subdivided by period); (2) Les journaux actuels (subdivided as "quotidiens" and "hebdomadaires"). Within subsections, the newspapers are listed by beginning date of publication. Index of titles.   Z6956.B4B43

Canada

National Library of Canada. Newspaper Section. Union list of Canadian newspapers held by Canadian libraries. Liste collective des journaux canadiens disponibles dans les bibliothèques canadiennes. Ottawa, The Library, 1977. 483p. **AF34**

Text in English and French.

Reflects the Canadian newspaper holdings of more than 125 Canadian libraries; both original and microfilm files are represented. Arranged by province, then by city, with an alphabetical listing of titles under city; title index. Includes titles for which bibliographical information was available but no location reported.

A *Union list of non-Canadian newspapers held by Canadian libraries* was issued by the Reference Branch of the National Library in 1968 (69p.). Z6954.C2N36

China Coast

King, Frank H. H. and **Clarke, Prescott.** A research guide to China-Coast newspapers, 1822–1911. [Cambridge], East Asian Research Center, Harvard Univ., 1965. 235p. (Harvard East Asian monographs, 18) **AF35**

Includes notes on the history, development, character, and use of China-Coast newspapers; an annotated list of the newspapers; biographies of China-Coast editors and publishers; a finding list of extant copies of the papers; a bibliography; and an index.
Z6958.C5K5

Czechoslovakia

Potemra, Michal. Bibliografia slovenských novín a časopisov do roku 1918. V Martine, Matica Slovenská, 1958. 145p. (Slovenská národná bibliografia. Séria B. Periódiká, zväzok la) **AF36**

At head of title: Štátna vedecká knižnica v Košiciach.

Bibliography of Slovak newspapers and journals up to 1918, including those of the resistance movement abroad and handwritten publications, with locations in libraries. Geographical, name, and chronological indexes; summaries in Russian, French, English, and German.

A similar survey and bibliography of foreign newspapers and journals of Slovakia up to 1918 is provided by:

—— Bibliografia inorečových novín a časopisov na Slovensku do roku 1918. V Martine, Matica Slovenska, 1963. 818p. (Slovenská národná bibliografia. Séria B. Periódiká, zväzok 1b) **AF36a**
Z6956.S63S5

Finland

Kaarna, Väinö and **Winter, Kaarina.** Suomen sanomalehdistön bibliografia, 1771–1963. Bibliografi över Finlands tidnings-press, 1771–1963. Bibliography of the Finnish newspapers, 1771–1963. Helsinki, Helsingin Yliopisto Kirjasto, 1965. 130p. (Helsingin Yliopiston Kirjaston julkaisuja, 31) **AF37**

About 1,250 Finnish newspapers are listed alphabetically by title. Places and dates of publication, names of editors, party affiliations, etc., are indicated. There is a chronological index to the listings, an index by place of publication, and an index of personal names.
Z6956.F5K2

France

Paris. Bibliothèque Nationale. Département des Périodiques. Bibliographie de la presse française politique et d'information générale, 1865–1944. Paris, 1964– . (In progress) **AF38**

For full information *see* AE70.

—— Répertoire collectif des quotidiens et hebdomadaires publiés dans les départements de la France métropolitaine de 1944 à 1956 et conservés dans les archives et bibliothèques de France. Paris, Univ. de Paris, Inst. Français de Presse, 1958. 153p. **AF39**

Cover title: Journaux français, 1944–1956.

Gives title, place of publication, date of first issue, and location of files.

Continued by: Z6956.F8P34

—— Catalogue collectif des journaux quotidiens d'information générale publiés en France métropolitaine de 1957 à 1961. Paris, 1962. 129p. **AF40**

Germany

Hagelweide, Gert. Deutsche Zeitungsbestände in Bibliotheken und Archiven. Düsseldorf, Droste Verlag, [1974]. 372p. (Bibliographien zur Geschichte des Parlamentarismus und der politischen Parteien. Heft 6) **AF41**

Added title page in English: German newspapers in libraries and archives; a survey.

Introductory matter in German and English.

"Hrsg. von der Kommission für Geschichte des Parlamentarismus und der politischen Parteien und dem Verein Deutscher Bibliothekare e. V."—*t.p.*

An effort to provide reasonably up-to-date information on files of German newspapers. "For the period from 1700 to 1969 (with several supplements up to 1972), it covers a total of 2,018 German newspapers with an overall number of 4,411 titles arranged according to 222 German places of publication, within the German frontiers of 1939, which have been and are of special historic interest as far as the press is concerned."—*Publishers' pref.* Title index.
Z6956.G3H33

Great Britain

See also AF17.

British Library. Newspaper Library, Colindale. Catalogue of the Newspaper Library, Colindale. London, Publ. for the British Library Board by British Museum Publs. Ltd., 1975. 8v. **AF42**

Contents: v.1, London; v.2, England and Wales, Scotland, Ireland; v.3–4, Overseas countries; v.5–8, Alphabetical title catalogue.

"The Newspaper Library at Colindale (formerly the British Museum Newspaper Library) contains about half a million volumes and parcels of daily and weekly newspapers and periodicals, including London newspapers and journals from 1801 onward, English provincial, Scottish and Irish newspapers from about 1700 onward, and large collections of Commonwealth and foreign newspapers. It contains no London newspapers published before 1801 (which are in the Burney Collection at Bloomsbury), no newspapers in oriental languages (which are in the Department of Oriental Manuscripts and Printed Books at Bloomsbury), and very few periodicals which appear monthly or less frequently."—*Introd.*

Effectively supersedes the 1905 supplement to the British Museum's *Catalogue of printed books* entitled *Newspapers published in Great Britain and Ireland, 1801–1900* (London, Clowes, 1905. 532 col.).

Hewitt, Arthur Reginald. Union list of Commonwealth newspapers in London, Oxford and Cambridge. [London], publ. for the Inst. of Commonwealth Studies by the Athlone Pr., Univ. of London, 1960. 101p.　　　**AF43**

Based on the holdings of the British Museum; indicates files—in 62 libraries and newspaper offices—of newspapers published in the Commonwealth nations. (Irish Free State newspapers are not included; newspapers published in Anglo-Egyptian Sudan pre-1955 are included, though this was never part of the Commonwealth.) Arrangement is alphabetical by country and territory of origin. Title index.　　　Z6945.H55

Times, London. Tercentenary handlist of English & Welsh newspapers, magazines & reviews. London, Times, 1920. 324p.　　　**AF44**

Comp. by J. G. Muddlman.

Contents: Sec.I: London and suburban press, arranged chronologically, 1620–1919. Separate list, periodicals in Armenian, Hebrew, Yiddish, Russian, and Turkish. Title index to Sec.I; Sec.II: The provincial press, arranged chronologically by date of the first known issue, 1801–1919. Title index to Sec.II.

A chronological bibliography of English periodicals from 1620 to 1919, which attempts to include all types of periodicals except: (1) official periodicals issued during the war; (2) annuals and yearbooks; (3) publications of societies classed as academies in the British Museum; and (4) local church periodicals. While avowedly incomplete for the difficult period of the 18th century, claims to be nearly exhaustive for the 17th and 19th centuries. Based upon the collections of the British Museum. Each title is listed under the date of the earliest copy which has been found for examination, and the information given for it includes: number and date of the earliest issue; date of discontinuance, if known; and in some cases name of printer, editor, distributor, and a reference to the library or collection if it is other than the British Museum's general collection.

Useful as a means of identifying titles, and as showing, by its chronological arrangement, what periodicals are available for a given date.

Additions and corrections by Rowland Austin appeared in *Notes and queries,* 12th ser., v.8 (1921) and v.10 (1922).　　　Z6956.E5T5

India

India (Republic). Office of the Registrar of Newspapers. Press in India. Annual report of the Registrar of Newspapers for India. 1st– . New Delhi, 1956– .　　　**AF45**

Title varies: 1956–64, *Report.*

Pt.1 is a statistical survey of the newspaper and periodical press. Pt.2 is a geographically arranged directory of newspapers and periodicals, giving publisher's name and address, editor, price, circulation figures, field of interest, etc. Title index.

　　　Z6958.I4A25

Ireland

See also AF42.

Munter, Robert LaVerne. A handlist of Irish newspapers, 1685–1750. London, Bowes & Bowes, 1960. 35p. (Cambridge Bibliographical Society. Monograph no.4)　　**AF46**

Listing is by place of publication, then chronological. Locates files of the papers in Irish and English libraries. Indexes of printers and altered titles.

Munter has also published *History of the Irish newspaper, 1685–1760* (1967).　　　Z6956.I7M8

Israel

Israel. Lishkat ha-'itonut. Newspapers and periodicals appearing in Israel. 1966– . [Tel-Aviv?], Govt. Press Office, 1966– . Irregular.　　　**AF47**

Includes a list by frequency (i.e., daily newspapers, weeklies,

quarterlies, etc.), a list of government serial publications, and a classified list. Title index.　　　Z6958.I8A32

Japan

Japanese press. 1949– . [Tokyo], Japan Newspaper Publishers' and Editors' Assoc., 1949– . Annual (irregular).

　　　AF48

Title varies.

Articles surveying the current state of the Japanese press are followed by a directory of newspapers, news agencies, broadcasting stations, television newsreel agencies, and overseas correspondents.

　　　PN5401.J36

Kokuritsu Kokkai Toshokan. Shimbun mokuroku. Tokyo, K.K.T., 1981. 248p.　　　**AF49**

On verso of title page: National Diet Library. List of newspapers.

Lists titles and holdings of all newspapers available at the National Diet Library, including foreign papers.

Nihon shimbun nenkan. Tokyo, Nihon Shimbun Kyōkai, 1947– . Annual.　　　**AF50**

In addition to directory information on individual newspapers and broadcasting companies, includes texts of codes relating to the press and radio; a general survey of the press; lists of awards, newspaper directories, university courses in journalism; and a who's who of the press.　　　PN4709.N52

Latin America

See also AF1, AF4.

Charno, Steven M. Latin American newspapers in United States libraries; a union list comp. in the Serial Division, Library of Congress. Austin, publ. for the Conference on Latin American History by the Univ. of Texas Pr., [1969]. 619p. (Conference on Latin American History. Publ. no.2)

　　　AF51

Lists about 5,500 Latin American newspapers held by 70 reporting libraries. Arrangement is by place of publication, first by country, then by city. A detailed record of holdings is provided; both original and microfilm copies are recorded. Includes official gazettes before 1900; excludes specialized papers whose nature is evident from the title. Covers Puerto Rico and the 20 Latin American republics.

An earlier list by Arthur E. Gropp, *Union list of Latin American newspapers in libraries in the United States* (Wash., Pan American Union, 1953) listed about 5,000 titles held by 56 libraries.

　　　Z6947.C5

Near and Middle East

Auchterlonie, James Paul Crawford and **Safadi, Yasin H.** Union catalogue of Arabic serials and newspapers in British libraries. London, Mansell, 1977. 146p.　　　**AF52**

Added title page in Arabic.

Covers all British "national and university libraries with substantial holdings of Arabic serials with the exception of Leeds and Glasgow which were unable to participate."—*Introd.* Entry is under transliterated form of title (or other main entry), with indexes in both transliteration and in Arabic.　　　Z6958.A6A93

Pourhadi, Ibrahim Vaqfi. Persian and Afghan newspapers in the Library of Congress, 1871–1978. Wash., Lib. of Congress, 1979. 101p.　　　**AF53**

An alphabetical title listing of 326 newspapers from Iran and Afghanistan which are in the Library of Congress collections. Gives publication dates, place of publication, frequency, publisher or owner of license, LC holdings, and a brief annotation indicating the character of the publication. Titles are given in transliteration and in English translation. Indexed.   Z6958.I65P875

U.S. Library of Congress. Arab-world newspapers in the Library of Congress. Prep. by George Dimitri Selim. Wash., Lib. of Congress, 1980. 85p.   **AF54**

Lists both those newspapers held by the Library of Congress "that are published in the Arab countries in either Arabic or Latin scripts and those published outside the Arab countries in Arabic script."— *Pref.* Separate sections for Arabic, English, French, German, Italian, and Spanish language newspapers. Listing is by country and city of publication, then by title. Indexed.

Netherlands

Handboek van de Nederlandse pers en publiciteit. Uitg. 42– , Sept. 1974– . Semiannual.   **AF55**

For full information *see* AE130.

New Zealand

New Zealand. General Assembly. Library. A union catalogue of New Zealand newspapers preserved in public libraries, newspaper offices, etc. G. H. Scholefield, Chief Librarian. Wellington, E. V. Paul, Govt. Pr., 1938. 38p.   **AF56**

"Essentially a finding list" of New Zealand newspapers, and of Australian and British newspapers useful to the study of New Zealand history, in New Zealand libraries and important research libraries in Australia and Great Britain. Arranged by city; gives title, dates of beginning and termination, frequency, and physical size. Title index.   Z6962.N5N5

———— A checklist of newspapers in New Zealand libraries, 1938–1959; a provisional supplement to the Union catalogue of New Zealand newspapers, 1938. Wellington, 1959. 28p.

Norway

Oslo. Universitet. Bibliotek. Norske aviser, 1763–1969; en bibliografi. Oslo, 1973–74. 2v.   **AF57**

Contents: v.1, Alfabetisk fortegnelse, v.2, Registerband.
A bibliography of Norwegian newspapers of the period. Gives beginning and closing dates, frequency, editors, etc.
                                                        Z6956.N8O82

Pakistan

Pakistan. Press Information Dept. General list of newspapers and periodicals published in Pakistan. Karachi, Manager, Govt. of Pakistan Pr., 1956– . Semiannual. (*Its* Reference ser. no.1)   **AF58**

Title varies; frequency varies.
"A general list of the newspapers published in Pakistan and known to have been in existence in the last six months: giving periodicity, place of publication and name of the editor. . . ." —*Note.*
1960 last published?   Z6958.P2A3

Philippines

Saito, Shiro and **Mak, Alice W.** Philippine newspapers: an international union list. Honolulu, Philippine Studies Pro-

gram, Center for Asian and Pacific Studies, Univ. of Hawaii, 1984. 273p. (Philippine Studies occasional paper, 7)
                                                        AF59

Constitutes a revised, enlarged and updated edition of Saito's *Philippine newspapers in selected American libraries* (1966). This edition includes newspapers published in the Philippines and held by libraries in Australia, Canada, England, the Philippines, and the United States. In two parts: (1) listing by place of publication (with title index) and (2) listing by repository.

Poland

"Prasa," Robotnicza Spółdzielnia Wydawnicza, Warsaw. Zakład Badań Prasoznawczych. Materiały do bibliografii dziennikarstwa i prasy w Polsce, w latach 1944–1954; wybór. [Opracował Zespół Biblioteki Stowarzyszenia Dziennikarzy Polskich: Maria Bzowska (et al.). Pod redakcja Jana Halperna] Warszawa, Państwowe Wydawnictwo Naukowe, 1957. 788p.   **AF60**

An extensive bibliography of more than 10,000 titles on the history and organization of journalism and the press in Poland.
                                                        Z6956.P7P7

Russia and the U.S.S.R.

Knyzhkova Palata Ukraïns'koi RSR. Periodychni vydannia URSR, 1917–1960: hazety. Bibliohrafichnyi dovidnyk. Kharkiv, Redaktsiino-vydavnychyi viddil Knyzhkovoi palaty URSR, 1965. 575p.   **AF61**

A detailed bibliography of the Ukrainian newspapers of the period.   Z6956.U4K52

Kuznetsov, Ivan Vasil'evich and **Fingerit, Efim Markovich.** Gazetnyi mir Sovetskogo Soiuza. 1917–1970 gg. Moskva, Izd-vo Mosk. Un-ta, 1972–76. 2v. il.   **AF62**

Contents: v.1, Tsentral'nye gazety; v.2, Respublikanskie, kraevye, oblastnye i okruzhnye gazety.
A listing of Russian newspapers of the period, with extensive notes on the publishing history of each. In v.1 newspapers are arranged in chronological sections; v.2 is arranged by individual Soviet republics, then by title. Volumes are separately indexed.
                                                        PN5274.K8

Leningrad. Publichnaia Biblioteka. Gazetnyi Otdel'. Alfavitnyi sluzhebnyi katalog russkikh dorevoliutsionnykh gazet, 1703–1916. Leningrad, 1958. 279p.   **AF63**

The Leningrad Public Library's holdings of Russian newspapers published between 1703 and 1916, listed alphabetically, with a geographical-chronological index. Omitted are illegal publications included in the Library's *Volnaia russkaia pechat'* (Peterburg, 1920), and newspapers published abroad in Russian, except those published in Harbin and Port Arthur.   Z6956.R9L357

Letopis' periodicheskikh i prodolzhaiushchikhsia izdanii. Biulleteni, 1971/72– . Moskva, Kniga, 1978– . Biennial.
                                                        AF64

Issued by: Gosudarstvennyi Komitet SSSR po Delam Izdatelstv, Poligrafii i Knizhnoi Torgovli [i] Vsesoiuznaia Knizhnaia Palata.
Continues in part: *Letopis' periodicheskikh izdanii SSSR* (AE152).
A comprehensive listing of Russian newspapers and similar publications. For cumulative listings of newspapers *see* AE154.
                                                        Z6956.S65L473

Stanford University. Hoover Institution on War, Revolution, and Peace. Soviet and Russian newspapers at the Hoover Institution, a catalog. Comp. by Karol Maichel. [Stanford, Calif.], 1966. 235p. (Hoover Inst. bibliographical ser., no.24)   **AF65**

1,108 entries in alphabetical title arrangement. Includes émigré papers. In addition to Hoover holdings, reference is made to files of the newspapers in the Library of Congress and the Columbia University Libraries.   Z6945.S7983

U.S. Library of Congress. Newspapers of the Soviet Union in the Library of Congress (Slavic 1954–1960; non-Slavic, 1917–1960). Prep by Paul L. Horecky [and others]. Wash., Slavic and Central European Div., Reference Dept., 1962. 73p.   **AF66**

Includes some pre-1954 titles added to the Library's collection since 1954, and therefore not included in *Russian, Ukrainian, and Belorussian newspapers* (below). Also lists Baltic newspapers from 1940 to 1960. Arranged alphabetically by place of publication; title index. Includes microfilm files.   Z6956.R9U55

————— **Slavic and Central European Division.** Russian, Ukrainian, and Belorussian newspapers, 1917–1953; a union list. Comp. by Paul L. Horecky. Wash., 1953. 218p.   **AF67**

An expansion of a working paper issued by the Division in 1952 under title: *Preliminary checklist of Russian, Ukrainian, and Belorussian newspapers published since January 1, 1917 . . . preserved in United States libraries.*

Holdings as of May 1953 are given for 39 participating U.S. libraries. Arranged by place of publication, with title index and a guide to places of publication by Union Republics. Degree of completeness of holdings is indicated as poor, moderate, substantial, or extensive, without listing of actual issues held. Microfilm files are included.   Z6956.R9U66

South Africa

A list of South African newspapers, 1800–1982, with library holdings. Pretoria, State Library, 1983. 253p.   **AF68**

Includes holdings of a number of libraries outside South Africa. Indicates microfilm files in the reporting libraries and a given library's intention to film at a future date. Title listing, with index by place of publication.   PN5471.L57

Pretoria. State Library. South African newspapers available on microfilm. Pretoria, State Lib., 1975. 118p.   **AF69**

A title listing of all South African newspapers known to have been microfilmed, indicating dates available on film, years still to be filmed, holder of negatives, number of reels, and price at date of reporting. In addition, there is a historical summary for each newspaper (all summaries appearing in English, with the summary repeated in the language of the newspaper if it is other than English).   Z6960.S6P73

Switzer, Les and **Switzer, Donna.** The black press in South Africa and Lesotho: a descriptive bibliographic guide to African, coloured, and Indian newspapers, newsletters, and magazines, 1836–1976. Boston, G. K. Hall, [1979]. 307p.   **AF70**

"Black press" is defined in terms of readership, and the work focuses on publications "directed primarily at, or intended for, an African, Indian and Coloured audience."—*Introd.* Publications are grouped according to the orientation of the sponsoring bodies or special interest groups they are designed to serve. Bibliography of secondary sources, p.279–90. Indexed.   Z6960.S6S94

Switzerland

Blaser, Fritz. Bibliographie der schweizer Presse, mit Einschluss der Fürstentums Liechtenstein. Bibliographie de la presse suisse. Bibliografia della stampa svizzera. Basel, Birkhäuser Verlag, 1956–58. lv. in 2 (1441p.). (Quellen der Schweizer Geschichte, n.F. 4.Abt.: Handbücher, Bd.7)   **AF71**

An extensive listing of the Swiss and Liechtenstein press, which attempts to include all dailies and periodicals published before 1803 and all political papers and periodicals after 1803; omits scientific and literary periodicals. Gives detailed information about each title. Arranged alphabetically with chronological and geographical indexes.

Title and introductory material in German, French, and Italian, with the annotation in the language of the publication.

INDEXES

United States

[Bell & Howell newspaper indexes] Wooster, Ohio, Bell & Howell, 1972– .   **AF72**

In 1972 Bell & Howell instituted a monthly "4-in-1" *Newspaper index* covering the *Chicago tribune,* the *Los Angeles times,* the *New Orleans times-picayune* and the *Washington post,* with a separate annual cumulation for each paper. That combination was abandoned after 1974 and each index was issued separately thereafter. Indexing of the *Chicago tribune* and the *Washington post* continued through 1981 (with coverage of the latter newspaper spanning 1971–81; for subsequent indexing of the *Washington post see* AF83, below); that of the other two papers still continues on a current basis.

Meanwhile, Bell & Howell's indexing service has been extended to a number of other newspapers: *The Boston globe* (1983–); *Chicago sun-times* (1979–82); *The Denver post* (1976–); *The Detroit news* (1976–); *The Houston post* (1976–); *National observer* (1962–77); *St. Louis post-dispatch* (1975–); and *San Francisco chronicle* (1976–). Subscriptions to those indexes currently published include 8 monthly issues, 4 quarterly cumulations, and a bound annual cumulation. Cumulations for the 1972–75 period are also available for a number of the titles.

In addition to the above, Bell & Howell has issued an index on microfilm to the *New York tribune,* 1841–1924, and publishes on a current basis *The index to black newspapers,* 1977– . The latter is issued quarterly with an annual cumulation; it indexes ten newspapers from throughout the United States, including the *Amsterdam news* (N.Y.), *Atlanta daily world, Chicago defender,* and *Michigan chronicle* (Detroit).

Christian Science monitor. Index to the Christian Science monitor. 1960–78. Boston, Christian Science Pub. Soc., 1960–79. Monthly, with semiannual and annual cumulations.   **AF73**

Title varies: *Cumulated index of the Christian Science monitor; Subject index of the Christian Science monitor.*

Coverage of regional editions of the newspaper has varied over the years; format of all editions was made uniform as of Apr. 1, 1975 so that page positions are thereafter identical for all, but references to special regional sections are identified in the index.

Continued by: AI21.C46

Bell and Howell Company. Indexing Center. Bell & Howell's Index to the Christian Science monitor. Jan. 1979– . Wooster, Ohio, Bell & Howell, 1979– . Monthly with annual cumulations.   **AF74**

A computer-produced index in two sections: (1) Subject index (of general and specific topics) and (2) Personal name index (of persons who figured in the news).

National newspaper index, 1979– . Los Altos, Calif., Information Access Corp., 1979– . Microfilm. Monthly.   **AF75**

An index to the *Christian Science monitor,* the *New York times,* and the *Wall Street journal* (with the *Los Angeles times* and the *Washington post* added in 1982), produced independently of the printed indexes to those newspapers (AF74, AF77, AF82) and, like the same publisher's *Magazine index* (AE225), published only on microfilm and updated monthly; each monthly microfilm issue is a full cumulation. Indexing is cover-to-cover except for weather charts, stock market tables, crossword puzzles and horoscopes, all of which are excluded. Subscription price is scaled according to the subscribing library's book budget.

The current month's indexing for both this index and the *Maga-*

zine index is updated daily and available for online searching as the *Newsearch* database. At mid-month, newspaper index data and magazine index data for the preceding month are transferred to their respective indexes for microfilm distribution and online searching as *National newspaper index, Legal resource index* and *Magazine index.* ●

New York daily tribune index, 1875–1906. N.Y., Tribune Assoc., 1876–1907. 31v. **AF76**

Annual; no more published.

A much briefer index than the *New York times index* (below), but useful for the period covered. *See also* AF72. AI21.N5

New York times index. v.1– , 1913– . N.Y., Times, 1913– . v.1– . Semimonthly, with annual cumulation. **AF77**

Frequency varies; 1913–29, quarterly with no cumulations, the four quarterly parts constituting a volume; 1930, monthly with quarterly cumulations and an annual cumulated volume; 1931–47, monthly with annual cumulations; 1948– , semimonthly with annual cumulations.

A carefully made subject index giving exact reference to date, page, and column, and plentiful cross references to names and related topics. The brief synopses of articles answer some questions without need to refer to the paper itself. Indexes the Late City edition of the *New York times,* the edition that is microfilmed and used for bound files, but also serves as an independent index to dates and even as a guide to the reporting of current happenings in other newspapers (and thereby justifies the subtitle, "Master-key to the news").

Users of the *Index* should be aware that in recent years the weekday editions of the newspaper have special feature sections ("Sports Monday," "Living," etc.) with parts designated by the letters A, B, C and D, but these are represented in the *Index* by the Roman numerals I, II, III and IV, respectively.

Beginning 1978, quarterly cumulations of the *Index* are issued for the first three quarters of the year, with the annual volume "serving, in effect, as the fourth quarterly cumulation covering the entire year."

Before publication of the "Prior series" (*see* below), an "in-house" index covering 1851–58, 1860, 1863–June 1905 had been made available on microfilm. AI21.N44

———— Prior series. N.Y., Bowker, [1966–76]. 15v. **AF78**

Publisher varies.

Contents: v.1, Sept. 1851–Dec.1862; v.2, 1863–1874; v.3, 1875–1879; v.4, 1880–1885; v.5, 1886–1889; v.6, 1890–1893; v.7, 1894–1898; v.8, 1899–June 1905; v.9, July 1905–Dec. 1906; v.10–15, 1907–1912.

The "Prior series" is designed to provide index coverage in book form from 1851 to 1912. Some volumes represent new indexing, others are reprintings of existing indexes originally prepared for staff use; i.e., the handwritten index for Sept. 1851–Aug. 1858 is reproduced in facsimile; the index for the remainder of 1858 through 1862 and the volumes for July 1905–1912 are newly prepared (though they are presented year by year rather than in cumulated form); the other volumes are reprinted from indexes previously printed for staff use. When the older indexes cover only 3- or 6-month periods they have not been cumulated, and users of the index must be careful to check a number of alphabets within a given volume.

Falk, Byron A. and **Falk, Valerie R.** Personal name index to "The New York times index," 1851–1974. Succasunna, N.J., Roxbury Data Interface, [1976–83]. 22v. **AF79**

An index to the volumes of the *New York times index* (above) rather than to the newspaper itself; i.e., references are to the date and page of the *Index* volumes. Brings together in a single alphabetical sequence names found throughout the *Index* volumes, including names appearing in index categories such as "Book reviews," "Concerts," "Deaths," "Disappearances," etc. Z5301.F28

———— ———— 1975–79 supplement. Verdi, Nev., Roxbury Data Interface, [1984]– . v.23– . (In progress)

To be in 3v., numbered consecutively with the basic set.

Besides indexing personal names appearing in the 1975–79 volumes, "Additional names and all errata entries from 1851–1974 Times Indexes are also included."—*Introd.* That is, names missed or not yet published in *New York times* indexes when the basic set began publication are picked up in this supplement.

Morse, Grant W. Guide to the incomparable New York times index. N.Y., Fleet Academic Editions, [1980]. 72p. il. **AF80**

A guide to use of the *Index,* with attention to filing rules, headings and subheadings, cross references, and special features. Calls attention to some of the changes which the *Index* has undergone over the years. AI21.N453M67

NewsBank index. Jan. 1982– . [New Canaan, Conn.], NewsBank, 1982– . Monthly, with quarterly and annual cumulations. **AF81**

Continues *NewsBank urban affairs library* issued in various sections 1970–81.

A current awareness service issued in conjunction with, and serving as an index to, microfiche of the articles indexed (known as *NewsBank*). Articles are selected from more than 100 newspapers from throughout the United States and are of broad interest in socio-economic, political, international and scientific areas. (Separate NewsBank services, *Review of the arts* and *Names in the news,* cover articles on film and television, fine arts, performing arts and literature, and material on individuals and specific groups, respectively.) Indexing is by fairly broad subject headings (with some entries for individuals and organizations, plus numerous cross references) with geographical subdivisions; index references (which do not include dates) are to the microfiche, which is arranged in fourteen broad subject categories.

Not a newspaper index *per se* since it is tied to the microfiche service, but useful for its regional approach to news events and its countrywide coverage.

Wall Street journal. Index. 1958– . [N.Y.], Dow Jones, 1959– . Monthly, with annual cumulations. **AF82**

Based on the final Eastern edition of the paper. In two parts: (1) corporate news (indexed by company name); (2) general news. Special sections for book reviews, personalities, deaths, theater reviews.

Indexes for the 1955–57 period have been published by Bell & Howell, Wooster, Ohio. HG1.W26●

The official Washington post index. v.1, no.1– , Jan. 1979– . Woodbridge, Conn., Research Pubns., 1979– . Monthly, with annual cumulation. **AF83**

Annual cumulation for 1981 has title: *The Washington post index.*

For the period 1972–81 an index to the *Washington post* was issued by Bell & Howell, Wooster, Ohio (*see* AF72).

Guides

See also AF112.

Milner, Anita Cheek. Newspaper indexes: a location and subject guide for researchers. Metuchen, N.J., Scarecrow Pr., 1977–82. 3v. **AF84**

Information relates mainly to card files and unpublished indexes, and was gathered by questionnaires sent to libraries, newspapers, historical and genealogical societies. The first part of v.1 is a listing by state and county of the various newspapers indexed, with indication of dates and special topics covered, together with location of the index; the second part is a listing of indexes by repository, with notes on type of indexes maintained. v.2–3 offer data on newspaper indexes of various kinds in repositories not covered in v.1, plus some updating of earlier entries.

A somewhat similar publication, originally intended as a looseleaf service to be updated annually, the *Lathrop report on newspaper indexes: an illustrated guide to published and unpublished newspaper indexes in the United States & Canada,* comp. by Norman M. and Mary Lou Lathrop (Wooster, Ohio, Lathrop Enterprises, 1979. 1v.), appeared only in a 1979/80 edition. It provides information on the scope, method of compilation, availability, etc., of a wide range of newspaper indexes as indicated in the subtitle.   Z6951.M635

Bulgaria

Natsionalna bibliografiia na NR Bŭlgariia. Seriia 6: Letopis na statiite ot bŭlgarskite vestnitsi. g.23– . Sofiia, Narodna Biblioteka Kiril I Metodii, 1974– . Monthly.   **AF85**

Other title: Bulgarian national bibliography. Series 6: Articles from Bulgarian newspapers.

Continues *Letopis na statiite ot bŭlgarskite vestnitsi* (1972–73) which, in turn, continued in part *Letopis na periodichniia pechat* (AE267).   AI15.L377

Canada

Canadian news index. v.1– , 1977– . Toronto, Micromedia Ltd., 1977– . Monthly, with annual cumulation.   **AF86**

Title varies: 1977–79, *Canadian newspaper index.*
Publisher varies.
Originally covered the *Montreal star, Toronto globe and mail, Toronto star, Vancouver sun, Winnipeg free press;* now provides a guide to the contents of about thirty Canadian newspapers and magazines with news content. Separate sections for topical subjects and personal names.

Denmark

Avis-Kronik-Index, udgivet af Folkebibliotekernes bibliografiske Kontor med Støtte af Undervisningsministeriet og Pressen. København, Munksgaard, 1940–78. Aarg.1–39. Monthly.   **AF87**

A monthly, classified index of the main contents of 35–50 Danish daily newspapers. Especially valuable for biographical material and literary reviews. Annual indexes of authors, artists, plays, films, book reviews, and biographical articles.

Joined with the *Dansk tidsskrift-index* in 1979 to form *Dansk artikelindeks* (AE274).   AI13.A9

France

Le monde, Paris. Index analytique. 1965– . [Paris, Le Monde, 1967–]. Annual.   **AF88**

An alphabetical subject index giving reference to date of issue only. Boldface capitals are used within entries to call attention to names of persons, many of whom are not given separate entries within the main alphabetical sequence although the names do appear in a "List of names cited" at the end of each letter of the alphabet. Obituaries, reviews of books, films, etc., are grouped under appropriate headings. An important addition for the large research library.

An English-language *Index of "Le monde"* was published monthly by the U.S. Joint Publications Research Service for the period 1958–72. This was a broad subject approach without cumulations. Indexing was also included in the computer-based *France-actualité* (Québec, Microfor Inc.) during its brief period of publication (1978–80).

Retrospective indexing of *Le monde* has been undertaken in a separate series:

———— Index analytique, 1944/45–49. [Paris, Le Monde, 1969–80]. (In progress)   **AF89**

Represents an effort to index the newspaper for the period 1944–64. Follows the arrangement of the "annual" series above.   AI21.M58

Le temps. Tables du journal Le temps. Paris, Éditions du Centre National de la Recherche Scientifique, 1966–83. v.1–10. (In progress)   **AF90**

Contents: v.1, 1861–1865; v.2, 1866–1870; v.3, 1871–1875; v.4, 1876–1880; v.5, 1881–1885; v.6, 1886–1888; v.7, 1889–1891; v.8, 1892–1894; v.9, 1895–1897; v.10, 1898–1900.

At head of title: Institut Français de Presse. Section d'Histoire.

When completed, this indexing project will cover the long run of *Le temps* from 1861 through 1942. Like the index to *Le monde* (above), this will become an important tool for research in French history, literature, and related subjects. Each volume is in the form of a series of annual indexes (arranged topically within broad geographical sections) plus 5-year cumulative proper-name and subject indexes. Articles giving accounts of great events and appearing contemporaneously with those events are not indexed since it is assumed that they can easily be located through the date.   AI21.T375

Germany

Monatliches Verzeichnis von Aufsätzen aus deutschen Zeitungen in sachlich-alphabetischer Anordnung, mit Jahres-Gesamt-Sach-und-Verfasser-Register. 1909–44. Gautzsch bei Leipzig, Dietrich, 1909–44. v.1–31. (Bibliographie d. deutschen Zeitschriftenliteratur, Abt. A. Beilage Bde.)   **AF91**

Ceased publication.
Weekly, 1928–29; fortnightly, 1909–22, 1930–33; monthly, 1934–44. An index to the principal articles in German and some Austrian papers. The issues for one year form a volume, with a subject and an author index to the volume. Not published 1923–27; during that period indexing of the same papers was included in the *Bibliographie der deutschen Zeitschriftenliteratur* (AE278).   AI9.B513

Zeitungs-Index. Jahrg. 1, nr.1– , Jan./März 1974– . Pullach bei München, Verlag Dokumentation, 1974– . Quarterly.   **AF92**

"Verzeichnis wichtiger Aufsätze aus deutschsprachigen Zeitungen."—*t.p.*
Willi Gorzny, ed.
A subject index to 19 German-language newspapers (mainly weeklies), including two Zürich publications and one from Vienna. Listing is chronological under topical heading. Entry includes author's name (for the high percentage of signed articles), title of article, newspaper abbreviation, volume number, date, and page. The index itself does not cumulate, but an annual "Register" issue includes a "Verfasser-register," a "Systematisches Register," and a "Geographisches Register."   AI9.Z44

Great Britain

Times, London. Index to the Times. 1906–72. London, Times, 1907–73.   **AF93**

Title varies: 1906–13, *The annual index;* 1914–Jan./Feb. 1957, *The official index.*

Frequency varies: 1906–June 1914, monthly with annual cumulations for 1906–13 and semiannual cumulation Jan.–June 1914; July 1914–56, quarterly; 1957–72, bimonthly. No cumulations.

Detailed alphabetical index referring to date, page, and column. Indexes the Final edition of the *Times,* as well as matter appearing in earlier editions but not in the final issue. Indexes book reviews both under author's name and under heading "Books reviewed." Indexed the *Times literary supplement* from 1906 to 1921. A good and very useful index.

Superseded by *The Times index* (AF95).   AI21.T35

———— Palmer's Index to the Times newspaper, 1790–June 1941. London, Palmer, 1868–1943. (Repr.: N.Y., Kraus, 1965)   **AF94**

Quarterly, beginning with the index covering Oct.–Dec. 1867, published in 1868. The indexes for preceding volumes have been issued in the reverse order, beginning with the one covering July–Sept. 1867, published in 1875.

Much briefer than *The official index* noted above, but useful because of the importance of the newspaper and the long period covered by the index. Indexing of obituary, death, and funeral notices under the heading "Deaths," in each volume, frequently supplies biographical material difficult to find elsewhere.

AI21.T5

The Times index. Jan./Mar. 1973– . Reading, Eng., Newspaper Archive Developments, 1973– . Monthly, with annual cumulation beginning 1977. **AF95**

Published quarterly 1973–76. Also called *London Times index*. Supersedes *Index to the Times* (AF93).

Now indexes *The Times, The Sunday Times, The Times literary supplement, The Times educational supplement, The Times educational supplement Scotland,* and *The Times higher education supplement.* Indexing practices of the preceding series are continued (e.g., book reviews are listed under the name of the author of the book as well as under "Books reviewed and noticed"; obituaries under name of the deceased; theater reviews under "Theatrical productions," and motion picture reviews under "Films"). AI21.T46

The Times, London. The Times index. 1785–90. Reading, Eng., Newspaper Archive Developments Ltd., [1978–84]. **AF96**

Forms a predecessor to *Palmer's Index* (AF94), providing indexing for the first six years (1785–90) of the London *Times* (and the *Daily universal register,* as it was titled until 1787). Represents new indexing, but some issues of the newspaper were unobtainable and had to be omitted.

India

Indian news index; a quarterly subject guide to selected English newspapers of India. v.1–7, 1965–71. Ludhiana, Panjab Univ. Extension Lib., 1965–71. **AF97**

Frequency varies; v.2–5 not publ.

Indexes materials deemed as "of permanent interest and research value" (*Introd.*) in six to eight Indian newspapers, including the *Times of India* and *Hindustan times.* When the same news appears in various papers, indexing is to the one which presents it in the best form. Subject subdivisions under country are used to bring together all items relating to a given country or state. A separate name index provides access to contributions of individual writers.

An index for the *Times of India* was published 1973–78 by Microfilm and Index Service, Bombay. AI3.I73

Indian press index. v.1, no.1– , Apr. 1968– . Delhi, Delhi Lib. Assoc., 1968– . Monthly, with cumulated alphabetical subject and author indexes, and a quarterly book review supplement. **AF98**

A pilot fascicule was issued Sept. 1968, covering newspapers published in March 1968.

The first regular number indexed the contents of 18 English-language papers published in India; by 1972 the number of papers indexed was increased to 26. AI3.I75

Pakistan

Pakistan press index; a monthly index to newspapers of Pakistan. v.1– , Apr. 1966– . Karachi, Documentation and Information Bureau, 1966– . Monthly. **AF99**

Supersedes *Dawn index* publ. June 1965–Mar. 1966.

An alphabetical subject index to *Dawn, Morning news, Pakistan observer,* and *Pakistan times.* Since April 1968 has included a "News and views digest" which condenses selected articles from the papers indexed. No cumulations. Ceased after July 1969? AI3.P3

Union of Soviet Socialist Republics

Current digest of the Soviet press. v.1– , Feb. 1, 1949– . N.Y., Joint Committee on Slavic Studies, 1949– . Weekly. **AF100**

Imprint varies: founded by the American Council of Learned Societies and the Social Science Research Council and first publ. by those organizations; later publ. by the American Association for the Advancement of Slavic Studies and now as an independent non-profit corporation affiliated with AAASS and ACLS.

Each issue includes in English translation, without comment, articles taken from Soviet newspapers and periodicals, in full or abridged. Each item is documented, giving: the source with date of issue and paging, number of words, and indication noting complete translation or condensation. Arranged by subject with quarterly indexes. Through v.25 (1973) each issue included a complete index to the contents of the two leading Soviet dailies, *Pravda* and *Izvestiia;* for a continuation of that feature *see* below (AF102).

Beginning with v.28, 1976, annual indexes are issued separately. D839.C87

Letopis' gazetnykh statei. Moskva, 1936– . Monthly. **AF101**

Frequency varies; originally weekly.

Issued by Vsesoiuznaia Knizhnaia Palata.

Indexes the most important articles from numerous metropolitan, regional, and subject newspapers. Classified subject arrangement. Personal and geographical name indexes in each issue. Annual indexes were published 1948–55. AI15.L35

Pravda. Index to Pravda. 1975–77. [Columbus, Ohio], Amer. Assoc. for the Advancement of Slavic Studies, 1975–78. Monthly with annual cumulation. **AF102**

Supersedes in part *Index to Pravda and Izvestia* (Jan. 1974) which, in turn, superseded the weekly index to those newspapers appearing in the *Current digest of the Soviet press* (AF100).

A computer-produced index compiled from the newspaper's national edition. In two parts: subjects and personal names.

Ceased publication. AI21.P73152

JOURNALISM

Bibliography

Price, Warren C. The literature of journalism, an annotated bibliography. Minneapolis, Univ. of Minnesota Pr., [1959]. 489p. **AF103**

Lists more than 3,000 items (in English), most of them annotated. "The base of the work is frankly historical and biographical, with more than two-fifths of all the titles in these two categories" (*Foreword*), but sections are included for selected works on press management, public opinion, radio and television, foreign press, etc. Classified arrangement with author, subject, and anonymous title index. Z6940.P7

———— and **Pickett, Calder M.** An annotated journalism bibliography, 1958–1968. Minneapolis, Univ. of Minnesota Pr., [1970]. 285p. **AF104**

Forms a supplement to Price's *The literature of journalism* (above), adding nearly 2,200 items (a few of them from the earlier period). Alphabetically arranged by author or other main entry, with a detailed subject index. Z6940.P69

Swindler, William F. A bibliography of law on journalism. N.Y., Columbia Univ. Pr., 1947. 191p. **AF105**

Annotated bibliography of books and articles on U.S. and international law relating to freedom of the press, censorship, access to public records, libel, privacy, copyright, etc. Classed, with author and subject indexes.　　　　Z661.A1S8

Wolseley, Roland Edgar. The journalist's bookshelf; an annotated and selected bibliography of United States journalism. 7th ed. Philadelphia, Chilton, 1961. 225p.　**AF106**

1st ed. 1939.

Originally intended to supplement Carl L. Cannon's *Journalism: a bibliography* (N.Y., N.Y. Pub. Lib., 1924. 360p.). In view of the publication of Price's bibliography (AF103), the 7th ed. aims to present a selected, annotated bibliography of United States journalism, including new titles not in Price and some categories (e.g., high school journalism, fiction relating to journalism) not covered by Price. Classed arrangement, with indexes of authors and titles.　　　　Z6940.J6

Dissertations

Journalism abstracts. v.1– , 1963– . Minneapolis, Assoc. for Education in Journalism, 1963– . Annual.　**AF107**

Imprint varies.

On cover: M.A., M.S., and Ph.D. theses in journalism and mass communication.

Master's and doctoral theses are listed in separate alphabets by author. Subject index.

Annual listings of dissertations in journalism have also appeared in *Journalism quarterly*, v.27–48 (1950–71). Title and coverage of these reports have varied from year to year: some are reports of research in progress by staff members and graduate students in American schools of journalism; others are limited to reports of doctoral dissertations completed.　　　　PN4725.J67

Dictionaries and encyclopedias

Kent, Ruth K. The language of journalism. [Kent, Ohio], Kent State Univ. Pr., [1971]. 186p.　**AF108**

Covers journalistic jargon, technical terms, graphic arts terms, and abbreviations most commonly used by the journalist. Lists sources of reference; partially annotated bibliography.　　　　PN4728.K4

Koszyk, Kurt and **Pruys, Karl H.** Wörterbuch zur Publizistik. München-Pullach, Verlag Dokumentation, 1970. 539p.　**AF109**

A dictionary of terms, many of the entries including extensive background information and bibliographic references. Indexes of names, subjects, and newspapers and periodicals mentioned in the text. Classed bibliography, p.435–539.　　　　PN4728.K67

Paneth, Donald. The encyclopedia of American journalism. N.Y., Facts on File, [1983]. 548p. il.　**AF110**

Attempts to cover all aspects of the field—history of journalism, types of media, the news gathering process, people, styles, technology—with emphasis on "the idea and the ideal of freedom of the press."—*Introd.* Cross references; bibliographic references. A subject index groups entry words in broad subject categories.　　　　PN4755.P26

World press encyclopedia. Ed. by George Thomas Kurian. N.Y., Facts on File, [1982]. 2v. (1202p.) graphs.　**AF111**

Aims to present "a definitive survey of the state of the press in 180 countries."—*Pref.* In four sections: International press; World's developed press systems; Smaller and developing press systems; Minimal and underdeveloped press systems. Essays consider a country's press on the economic, political, professional, and philosophic levels. For each country treats such topics as the economic framework, press laws, censorship, news agencies, education and training. Bibliographies.　　　　PN4735.W6

Directories

Directory of newspaper libraries in the U.S. and Canada. Grace D. Parch, ed. N.Y., Special Libraries Assoc., 1976. 319p.　**AF112**

"Project of the Newpaper Division, Special Libraries Association."—*t.p.*

A directory of libraries maintained by newspaper publishers. Aims "to provide convenient, complete, accurate and up-to-date information on newspaper libraries including their collections, services and personnel."—*Pref.* Geographical arrangement, with personnel and place-name indexes. Notes on library resources include availability of indexes (published and unpublished) and of microfilm files of the newspaper, and indication of services available to outsiders.　　　　Z675.N4D57

Weiner, Richard. News bureaus in the U.S. 7th ed. [N.Y., Author, 1984] 182p.　**AF113**

1st ed. 1969.

An aid for publicists, journalists, etc. Arranged by state, with major publications listed according to the city in which its editorial headquarters is located. Gives address, telephone number, and name of person in charge, plus helpful notes on many of the larger publications. Indexed.　　　　Z6951.W4

—— Syndicated columnists. 3d ed. [N.Y.], Weiner, [1979]. 295p.　**AF114**

1st ed. 1975; 2d ed. 1977.

The major section of the book (pp.13–194) is devoted to chapters surveying the history and current status of newspaper syndicates and syndicated columnists. "A principal feature of this book is to provide the addresses of major syndicated columnists" (*p.8*); they are listed alphabetically within various subject categories. Entries provide name, office or home address, telephone number, name of column, and distributing syndicate. Bibliography; index.

A new edition was announced for publication in 1985.　　　　PN4888.S9W4

Editorials

Editorials on file. v.1– , Jan. 1970– . N.Y., Facts on File, 1970– . Looseleaf. Semimonthly.　**AF115**

Brief introductory information on editorial subjects (drawn from the weekly *Facts on file* news service) is followed by a selection of approximately 15–25 editorials reprinted in their entirety from U.S. and Canadian newspapers of the preceding half-month. Monthly subject indexes cumulate quarterly and annually.　　　　D839.E3

History

Fischer, Heinz Dietrich. Deutsche Zeitungen des 17. bis 20. Jahrhunderts. Pullach, Verlag Dokumentation, 1972. 415p. (Publizistik-historische Beiträge, Bd.7)　**AF116**

Comprises chapters by individual contributors on some 25 leading German newspapers, summarizing the history of each. Bibliographic footnotes; index of names.

Fischer is also the author of *Deutsche Zeitschriften des 17. bis 20. Jahrhunderts* (Pullach, Verlag Dokumentation, 1973. 445p.) and *Deutsche Publizisten des 15. bis 20. Jahrhunderts* (Pullach, Verlag Dokumentation, 1971. 419p.)　　　　PN5204.F48

Geschichte der deutschen Presse. Berlin, Colloquium Verlag, 1966–72. 3v. (Abhandlungen und Materialen zur Publizistik, Bd.5–7)　**AF117**

Contents: v.1, Deutsche Presse bis 1815, von Margot Lindemann; v.2, Deutsche Presse im 19. Jahrhundert, von Kurt Koszyk; v.3, Deutsche Presse 1914–1945, von Kurt Koszyk.

Each volume includes an extensive bibliography, and each has its own index.　　　　PN5204.L5

Histoire générale de la presse française. Publiée sous la direction de Claude Bellanger [et al.]. Paris, Presses Universitaire de France, 1969–76. 5v. il. **AF118**

A comprehensive history of the French newspaper and periodical press from its origins to the present. Attention is given to provincial and specialist publications as well as to those at the national level, and there are notes on the history, scope, and influence of numerous individual newspapers and periodicals. Each volume has its own indexes and there are bibliographies in v.1–3 and 5, following a chapter-by-chapter arrangement; bibliography for v.4, which covers 1940–58, is included in v.5. PN5174.H5

Lee, Alan J. The origins of the popular press in England, 1855–1914. London, Croom Helm; Totowa, N.J., Rowman and Littlefield, [1976]. 310p. maps. **AF119**

Without purporting to be a full-scale history, "this study examines both the objective changes in society at large and in the industry itself in the half-century after the repeal of the newspaper stamp, and the ways in which the older liberal vision of the press was affected by those changes."—*Introd.* Bibliographic footnotes; select bibliography; tables; maps showing newspaper distribution; index.

In Brian Lake's *British newspapers: a history and guide for collectors* (London, Sheppard Pr., 1984. 213p.) the historical information is brief, and emphasis is squarely on collecting. PN5117.L4

Mott, Frank Luther. American journalism; a history, 1690–1960. 3d ed. N.Y., Macmillan, [1962]. 901p. il. **AF120**

1st ed. 1941; 2d ed. 1950.

A detailed history with bibliographical notes. The 3d ed. includes a section on electronic media and the growth of the "mass audience" as it relates to U.S. journalism. PN4855.M63

Merrill, John Calhoun and **Fisher, Harold A.** The world's great dailies: profiles of fifty newspapers. N.Y., Hastings House, [1980]. 399p. il. **AF121**

Offers profiles—historical notes, discussions of policies, strengths and weaknesses—of those newspapers which the editors believe "represent the very best in the world's journalism, regardless of how differently this journalism may manifest itself in different cultures and ideological contexts."—*Pref.* Bibliographical footnotes; selected bibliography; index. PN4731.M446

Biography

American newspaper journalists, 1873–1900. Ed. by Perry J. Ashley. Detroit, Gale, 1983. 392p. il. (Dictionary of literary biography, v.23) **AF122**

PN4871.A49

American newspaper journalists, 1901–1925. Ed. by Perry J. Ashley. Detroit, Gale, [1984]. 385p. il. (Dictionary of literary biography, v.25) **AF123**

Like other volumes in the series (BD416), the two volumes above offer signed biographical sketches of some length with bibliographies of works by and about the journalists. Also locates collections of papers in many instances. PN4871.A5

Journalist biographies master index. Alan E. Abrams, ed. Detroit, Gale, [1979]. 380p. (Gale biographical index ser., no. 4). **AF124**

Subtitle: A guide to 90,000 references to historical and contemporary journalists in 200 biographical directories and other sources.

In addition to the standard biographical sources referred to in the subtitle, "indexes textual references to individuals which appear in about 15 historical studies of the field of journalism."—*Introd.*

A review by the Reference and Subscription Books Review Committee in *Booklist* 88:1209–11 (May 1, 1981) notes "flaws in coverage"—e.g., spotty coverage of journalists listed in *Biography index.* Z6940.J58

Who was who in journalism, 1925–1928. Detroit, Gale, [1978]. 664p. (Gale composite biographical dictionary ser., no.4) **AF125**

"A consolidation of all material appearing in the 1928 edition of *Who's who in journalism,* with unduplicated biographical entries from the 1925 edition of *Who's who in journalism,* originally compiled by M. N. Ask (1925 and 1928 editions) and S. Gershanek (1925 edition)."—*t.p.*

The 1928 edition is reprinted as the main portion of the book; biographical sketches from the 1925 edition which were not updated or repeated in the 1928 edition are brought together in a separate alphabetical section printed on colored paper at the back of the volume. PN4871.W65

A G

Government Publications

❖Much important reference material is to be found in the reports, bulletins, and other publications issued by the various national, state, and municipal governments. These publications, generally known as "government publications" or "public documents," cover topics in nearly the whole field of knowledge, but are most important for subjects in the fields of social and political science, economics, finance, labor, industry, statistics, education, history, etc., and in certain sciences such as agriculture, ethnology, geology, meteorology, aeronautics, and related technologies, to the study and promotion of which certain government bureaus or commissions are devoted. No extended reference work can be done in questions of labor conditions in America, for example, without the use of some of the publications of the U.S. Department of Labor, or in American geology without those of the U.S. Geological Survey.

Public documents are popularly supposed to be difficult to use and understand, and because this difficulty is overrated, reference workers often fail to make the best use of such material. The documents are published in complicated forms and sets, and must be located through the printed catalogs, bibliographies, and indexes provided for the purpose, but for the periods covered by modern indexes, they are no harder to find than periodical literature which has to be located through periodical indexes. Morehead's guide (AG21) is the most up-to-date source for explanations of the use of United States government publications and their indexes. For the *Index to U.S. government periodicals see* AE254.

For indexes and bibliographies relating to special subjects, *see* those subjects. Listed below are some of the most important general guides and indexes for the United States and Great Britain, and also a few bibliographies for other countries. Palic's *Government publications* (AG10) is useful for identifying publications of foreign governments.

There is no satisfactory guide or comprehensive index to city and county government publications. Some of the more important of these documents are indexed in the Public Affairs Information Service *Bulletin* (CA35), and a selection of publications of municipalities, urban counties, and special districts are listed in the *Index to current urban documents* (AG81).

INTERNATIONAL

Guides

The bibliographic control of official publications. Ed. by John E. Pemberton. Oxford, Pergamon, 1982. 172p. il. (Guides to official publications, v.11) **AG1**

A collection of contributed essays by librarians from Australia, Canada, Ireland, the United States, and the United Kingdom describing the systems developed in specific libraries for bibliographic control of official publications (from international organizations as well as individual countries). The aim is to stimulate work toward a system which would be universally applicable.

Z1001.B5146

Brown, Everett Somerville. Manual of government publications: United States and foreign. N.Y., Appleton, [1950]. 121p. (Repr.: N.Y., Johnson, 1964) **AG2**

A brief manual which discusses the government publications of the various countries of the world. Out-of-date, but still useful for its list of principal government publications of foreign countries.

Z7164.G7B85

Cherns, J. J. Official publishing: an overview. An international survey and review of the role, organisation and principles of official publishing. Oxford, Pergamon, [1979]. 527p. (Guides to official publications, v.3) **AG3**

Examines official publishing of 22 countries, the United Nations and its principal agencies, and a few other international bodies. Provides introductory information on the scope and importance of official publishing, a survey by country and international organization, and reviews the growth and control of publishing. Indexed.

Z286.G69C47

A guide to official gazettes and their contents. Comp. by John E. Roberts. Wash., Lib. of Congress, Law Lib., 1985. unpaged. **AG4**

On cover: Revised ed.

Aims "to create a reference tool to assist researchers unfamiliar with the legal publications of foreign jurisdictions in identifying and using official gazettes."—*Introd.* Includes entries for all sovereign nations and some semi-dependent entities. Gives current data only, not changes of title or references to earlier titles. Arranged alphabetically by country name, giving title of the gazette, commonly used abbreviation, frequency, language(s) of publication, list of gazette contents (with indication of whether or not international agreements and court decisions are included), frequency and arrangement of indexes, if any. K520.R63

Bibliography

See also AG188.

International Committee for Social Sciences Documentation. Étude des bibliographies courantes des publications officielles nationales: guide sommaire et inventaire. A study of current bibliographies of national official publications; short guide and inventory. Comp. by Jean Meyriat. [Paris], UNESCO, [1958]. 260p. (UNESCO bibliographical handbooks, 7) **AG5**

Introductory matter in French and English. Annotations sometimes in one language, sometimes in the other.

Lists national bibliographies, official journals, document bibliographies, legislative publications, etc., of all independent states.

Z7164.G715

National official gazettes available in microform. Wash., Lib. of Congress, 1978. (*In* Newspaper and gazette report, v.6, no.2, Aug. 1978, p.33–102) **AG6**

"This compilation of the national official gazettes of the world available in microform supersedes all other lists published previously in the *Newspaper and Gazette Report* [*see* AF6] and its predecessors. Listed are all titles reduced to microform through the cooperative foreign official gazette microfilming program of the New York Public Library and the Library of Congress. In addition to these two institutions, which have been engaged in this preservation program since 1973, thirty-four other foreign and domestic institutions, known to hold in microform a significant portion of a nation's gazette, are also included."—*p.33.*

Supersedes the New York Public Library, National and Local Gazettes Microfilming Program's 1961 *Cumulative list* and its 1962 supplement.

New York. Public Library. Research Libraries. Catalog of government publications in the Research Libraries. Boston, G. K. Hall, 1972. 40v. **AG7**

Photoreproduction of the catalog cards for more than a million volumes of government publications or public documents. Arranged by political jurisdiction. Serials and monographs are separated under each agency; serials are arranged alphabetically, monographs according to date of publication. Census material is arranged by numbered censuses, serial publications, and monographs. No subject entries.

—— Dictionary catalog of government publications: supplement 1974. Boston, G. K. Hall, [1976]. 2v. **AG8**

A supplement to the above. Continued by two separate annual series, one for United States publications (AG34), the other for foreign publications (below). Z7164.G7N54

—— Bibliographic guide to government publications—foreign. 1975– . Boston, G. K. Hall, 1976– . Annual. **AG9**

Serves as a partial supplement to the Library's *Catalog of government publications . . .*, listing relevant publications cataloged by the Research Libraries during the year of coverage, plus additional entries from the Library of Congress MARC tapes. A dictionary catalog employing the format of the *Dictionary catalog of the Research Libraries* (AA146).

For United States government publications *see* AG34.

Z7164.G7N54

Palic, Vladimir M. Government publications; a guide to bibliographic tools. 4th ed. Wash., Lib. of Congress, 1975. 441p. **AG10**

3d ed., 1942, by James B. Childs, had title: *Government document bibliography in the United States and elsewhere.*

"This guide outlines bibliographic aids in the field of official publications issued by the United States, foreign countries, and international government organizations. It is intended to be a practical guide directing the researcher, the student, and, last but not least, the reference librarian to bibliographic tools which may help him to identify or locate the materials needed."—*Pref.* In three main sections: (1) United States of America; (2) International governmental organizations; (3) Foreign countries. Indexed.

Z7164.G7C5

United Nations. Dag Hammarskjöld Library. Government gazettes; an annotated list of gazettes held in the Dag Hammarskjöld Library. N.Y., 1964. 50p. **AG11**

An alphabetical list, by country, of gazettes held as of Sept. 1964. Entries include title, place of publication, frequency, and a brief description of content. JX1977.A2

United Nations. Library, Geneva. Répertoire des données publiées régulièrement dans les journaux officiels. Analysis of material published regularly in official gazettes. Genève, 1958. 39p. (*Its* Listes bibliographiques, nouv. sér., no.1) **AG12**

Revised and expanded edition of an earlier list published by the League of Nations Library in 1935.

In three sections: (1) analysis by country; (2) subject index; (3) inventory of the entire collection of official gazettes.

Z7164.G7U5

Union lists

List of the serial publications of foreign governments, 1815–1931, ed. by Winifred Gregory, for the American Council of Learned Societies, American Library Association, National Research Council. N.Y., Wilson, 1932. 720p. (Repr.: N.Y., Kraus, 1966) **AG13**

A union list, on the same general plan as the *Union list of serials* (AE182), for a type of serial publication excluded from that list, i.e., government serials, including only genuine government serials and omitting publications of universities, societies, etc., which are subsidized by a government. Arranged alphabetically by country name (except that Russia is in a separate list at the end), with subarrangement by government departments, bureaus, etc., and with indication of holdings of the various publications in some 85 American libraries. Z7164.G7L7

Library resources

Directory of government document collections & librarians. 4th ed. Barbara Kile and Audrey Taylor, eds. Bethesda, Md., Congressional Information Service, [1984]. 690p. **AG14**

Sponsored by the Government Documents Round Table, American Library Association.

1st ed. 1974.

Aims to provide a variety of information about government document collections and the institutions, organizations, agencies, and individuals concerned with documents librarianship. Covers all libraries in the United States and its territories and possessions that have been identified as having collections of documents. Foreign and international documents collections are included, as well as United States federal, state and local documents. Geographical arrangement of the repositories, with subject and name indexes.

Z7164.G7D57

UNITED STATES

Guides

See also AB168.

Boyd, Anne Morris. United States government publications. 3d ed. rev. by Rae Elizabeth Rips. N.Y., Wilson, 1949. 627p. **AG15**

1st ed. 1931; 2d ed. 1940. Though now out-of-date on some points, this remains a useful guide for various historical matters.

After a discussion of the nature, printing, and distribution of catalogs and indexes of United States government publications, the arrangement of material then follows that of the organization of the government, i.e., the legislative, judicial, and executive branches, each subdivided by major divisions: Congress; the courts; the ten Departments; and independent agencies and institutions.

Lists and describes the important and typical publications of each, but does not attempt to be complete. Includes the many changes in government departments and agencies made during the second World War and postwar years to July 1948. Z1223.Z7B7

Downey, James A. U.S. federal official publications: the international dimension. Oxford, Pergamon, [1978]. 352p. (Guides to official publications, v.2) **AG16**

1975 ed. had title: *U.S. federal government publications.*

"This account of United States Federal Government publications is written with the foreign user in mind. . . . it is concerned with . . .

what is being published and how, especially for the foreigner, to acquire it."—*Pref.* Pt.I discusses bibliographic control and acquisitions through agencies, commercial firms, NTIS, etc. Pt.II lists the major government agencies, some of their publications of particular international interest, and acquisitions methods. Indexed.

Z1223.Z7D68

Garner, Diane L. and **Smith, Diane H.** The complete guide to citing government documents; a manual for writers and librarians. Comp. for the Government Documents Round Table, American Library Association. Bethesda, Md., Congressional Information Service, [1984]. 142p. **AG17**

Intended as a supplement to standard citation manuals, this useful guide provides explanations and examples of citation forms for United States government documents, state, local and regional documents, and international documents. Indexed.

Z7164.G7G37

Herman, Edward. Locating United States government information: a guide to sources. Buffalo, N.Y., William S. Hein, 1983. 250p. **AG18**

A guide to locating U.S. government publications, presented in workbook format, with questions, answers, and bibliography at the end of each chapter. In addition to congressional publications, deals with federal statistics sources, census information, technical reports, maps, etc. Indexed. Z1223.Z7H46

Leidy, William Philip. A popular guide to government publications. 4th ed. N.Y., Columbia Univ. Pr., 1976. 440p. **AG19**

The 1st ed. (1953) covered some 2,500 titles published 1940–50; the 2d ed. (1963), about 2,300 titles published 1951–62; and the 3d ed. (1968), about 3,000 titles published mainly 1961–66. This edition lists mainly publications of the 1967–75 period. Arrangement is by broad subject, with a detailed subject index. Complete bibliographic information is given, and some items are annotated.

Z1223.Z7L4

McIlvaine, Betsy. A consumers', researchers', and students' guide to government publications. N.Y., Wilson, 1983. 115p. **AG20**

Designed to encourage the use of government documents. In three sections: (1) an overview of the various types of publications and their uses; (2) detailed descriptions of the major government document indexes; (3) examples of use. Bibliography; index.

Z1223.Z7M27

Morehead, Joe. Introduction to United States public documents. 3d ed. Littleton, Colo., Libraries Unlimited, 1983. 309p. il. **AG21**

1st ed. 1975.

A guide for the librarian and the student; intends "to set forth an introductory account of the basic sources of information that comprise the bibliographic structure of federal government publications."—*Pref.* Sections on public documents, the Government Printing Office, the Superintendent of Documents, the depository library system, technical report literature, selected information sources for federal government publications, legislative branch materials, publications of the Presidency, selected categories of executive branch and independent agency publications, legal sources of information. Appendixes. Indexed. Z1223.Z7M67

Nakata, Yuri. From press to people: collecting and using U.S. government publications. Chicago, Amer. Lib. Assoc., 1979. 212p. **AG22**

". . . designed as a handbook for the beginning documents librarian and for others interested in promoting the use of government publications."—*Introd.* Chapters treat government printing, the federal depository library program, organization and arrangement of documents, collection development, the *Monthly catalog*, cataloging and classification, technical reports, data base services, reference work with government documents, routines and record-keeping in the documents library. Appendixes; index.

Nakata has collaborated with Susan J. Smith and William B.

Ernst, Jr., on a manual entitled *Organizing a local government documents collection* (Chicago, Amer. Lib. Assoc., 1979. 61p.).

Z688.G6N34

Newsome, Walter L. New guide to popular government publications for libraries and home reference. Littleton, Colo., Libraries Unlimited, 1978. 370p. **AG23**

A revised and updated edition of Linda C. Pohle's *Guide to popular government publications . . .* (1972). Offers an annotated list (arranged alphabetically by topic) of "the more interesting and useful publications available at reasonable prices from the U.S. Government Printing Office, or in many cases, free from issuing agencies or the Consumer Information Center."—*Introd.* Includes a section on acquiring government publications, and appendixes giving information on government audiovisual materials, selected agency publication catalogs, and commercially available reprints of popular government publications. Indexed. "Currency or long-term popular interest has been the primary selection criterion for the approximately 2,500 titles in this edition." Z1223.Z7P63

Schmeckebier, Laurence Frederick and **Eastin, Roy B.** Government publications and their use. 2d rev. ed. Wash., Brookings Inst., [1969]. 502p. **AG24**

1st ed. 1936; rev. ed. 1961.

Although now considerably out of date, this remains a useful guide to government publications with descriptions, including classification and distribution, of catalogs and indexes, bibliographies, Congressional publications, constitutions (federal and state), laws (federal and state), court decisions, administrative regulations, presidential papers, foreign affairs, reports, organization and personnel, maps, etc. Includes list of government periodicals, and microfacsimile editions of government publications. Answers many questions as to what was published, when, by whom, in what form, etc. Z1223.Z7S3

Wynkoop, Sally. Subject guide to government reference books. Littleton, Colo., Libraries Unlimited, 1972. 276p.
AG25

An introductory guide to reference works published by the U.S. Government Printing Office and government agencies. Classed arrangement; annotations; index. *Government reference books* (AG28) serves as a continuing supplement. Z1223.Z7W95

Bibliography

Body, Alexander C. Annotated bibliography of bibliographies on selected government publications and supplementary guides to the Superintendent of Documents classification system. [Kalamazoo], Western Michigan Univ., 1967. 181p. **AG26**

A bibliography of bibliographies arranged by Superintendent of Documents classification. Subject index in addition to guides to the classification system.

—— —— Supplement. 1st–3d. [Kalamazoo], 1968–72.

Continued by: Z1223.Z7B65

Kovacs, Gabor. Annotated bibliography of bibliographies on selected government publications and supplementary guides to the Superintendent of Documents classification system. Supplement. 5th– . [Greeley, Colo., Univ. of Northern Colorado], 1977– . Irregular. **AG27**

Includes cumulative microfiche index to the previous volumes.

Government reference books. Ed.1– , 1968/69– . [Littleton, Colo.], Libraries Unlimited, 1970– . Biennial. **AG28**

Compiler varies.

An annotated listing of bibliographies, directories, dictionaries, statistical works, handbooks, almanacs, and similar reference sources published by the United States government. Classed arrangement

with author-title-subject index. Includes Superintendent of Documents classification numbers. Z1223.Z7G68

Gray, Constance Staten. U.S. government directories, 1970–1981; a selected, annotated bibliography. Littleton, Colo., Libraries Unlimited, 1984. 260p. **AG29**

"This bibliography is an annotated list of directories published by departments and agencies of the United States federal government between January 1970 and December 1981."—*Introd.* The 575 titles are arranged by broad subject category. Appendixes and title and subject indexes. Complements Larson's guide (AG33)

Z7164.A2G685

Guide to U.S. government serials & periodicals, 1959–72. McLean, Va., Documents Index, 1959–72. **AG30**

Comp. by John L. Andriot.

Frequency varies; coverage varies. Some issues have supplements offering updated information. 1959 called "pilot ed.," with title: *U.S. government serials & periodicals.*

Contents of 1972 edition (issued in 1v.): v.1, Current government agencies; v.2, Non-current government agencies, Discontinued SuDocs class numbers.

Offers an annotated listing of "important current Government publications issued on a recurring basis."—*Foreword, 1972 ed.*

Superseded by: Z1223.Z7A574

Guide to U.S. government publications. 1973– . McLean, Va., Documents Index, 1973– . **AG31**

Imprint and format vary. 1973–76 issued as looseleaf publication with quarterly updates; 1976–78 publ. in 4v.; 1978/79 issued in 3v.; beginning 1980, issued in 2v., v.1 being an annual and v.2 an irregular publication.

"We inaugurated a plan in 1980 whereby the *Guide* was published in two hardback volumes. Volume 1 contained the SuDocs classes for all agencies in existence on January 1, 1980 plus those agencies which had been abolished between January 1, 1975 through December 31, 1979. Volume 2 contained the SuDocs classes for those agencies abolished prior to January 1, 1975."—*Foreword.* A new edition of v.2 is planned for 1985. Provides annotations of important government series and periodicals currently being published, and a complete list of Superintendent of Documents classification numbers.

Korman, Richard I. Checklist of government directories, lists, and rosters. Westport, Conn., Meckler; Cambridge, Eng., Chadwyck-Healey, [1982]. 51p. **AG32**

Lists 300 titles from the Library of Congress collections which provide "a working knowledge of the organization, administrative scope and personnel of 78 nations."—*Pref.* Some annotations.

Z7164.A2K67

Larson, Donna Rae. Guide to U.S. government directories, 1970–1980. Phoenix, Ariz., Oryx Pr., 1981–85. 2v.

AG33

"Directories are defined . . . as information sources for the names of people, groups, or places, government or private, that include some location identification or contact codes."—*Introd.* Lists and annotates directories published by the U.S. government. Arranged by Supt. of Docs. classification number, with subject index.

The 1981 publication (191p.) carries no volume designation; "v.2: 1980–84" (214p.) is a supplement listing publications of 1979/80–84. Z1223.A12L37

New York. Public Library. Research Libraries. Bibliographic guide to government publications—U.S. 1975– . Boston, G. K. Hall, 1976– . Annual. **AG34**

Serves as a partial supplement to the Library's *Catalog of government publications . . .* (AG7), listing relevant publications cataloged by the Research Libraries during the year of coverage, plus additional entries from the Library of Congress MARC tapes. A dictionary catalog employing the format of the *Dictionary catalog of the Research Libraries* (AA146).

For foreign government publications *see* AG9. Z7164.G7N54

Scull, Roberta A. A bibliography of United States government bibliographies, 1968–1973. Ann Arbor, Mich., Pierian Pr., 1975. 353p. **AG35**

Z1223.A12S37

———— ———— 1974–1976. Ann Arbor, Mich., Pierian Pr., 1979. 310p. **AG36**

The 1968–73 volume lists more than 1,200 items in classed subject arrangement with index of subjects and distinctive titles. Most entries are annotated. Aims to include all bibliographies listed in the *Monthly catalog* (AG51) for the period, plus selected listings from other sources.

The 1974–76 volume follows the plan of the earlier work, listing some 2,500 bibliographies. Special features of this volume are the inclusion of several hundred Tennessee Valley Authority bibliographies (not found in the *Monthly catalog*) and about 300 Government Printing Office "Subject bibliographies," *see* AG56.

Z1223.A12S372

Van Zant, Nancy Patton. Selected U.S. government series; a guide for public and academic libraries. Chicago, Amer. Lib. Assoc., 1978. 172p. **AG37**

Designed as a selection aid for small and medium-sized public and academic libraries. Lists about 600 items in broad topical arrangement. Annotations include a brief statement about the issuing agency, the range of topics covered (with a few examples), and a statement of recommendation. Indexed. Z1223.Z7V36

Zink, Steven D. United States government publications catalogs. N.Y., Special Libraries Assoc., [1982]. 111p. (SLA bibliography, no.8) **AG38**

Lists more than 200 titles of current catalogs published by various government agencies. Annotated entries are arranged by issuing agency and include complete title and Superintendent of Documents classification number. Subject index. Z1223.A12Z56

Catalogs and indexes

The Serial set

❖The collected edition of United States government publications is known as the *Congressional edition* or *Serial set*. It includes Senate and House journals (through the 82d Congress, 1952), Senate and House documents, and Senate and House reports. The documents include a large variety of reports from executive departments and independent bodies which are printed in the set by order of Congress. (For further description of this set, *see* Morehead [AG21].)

For purposes of easy arrangement, each bound volume is given a serial number. (A volume may include from one to several individual items.) Volumes are numbered consecutively beginning with the 15th Congress (1817). In many libraries documents are arranged on the shelves by these serial numbers, and the number must be ascertained in order to find a particular document. These serial numbers are included in many of the lists and indexes noted below, sometimes in numerical lists and sometimes under specific entries. A complete record, with some overlapping, can be found in the following: 15th–60th Congress (1817–1909) in the *Checklist* (AG48); 54th–76th Congress (1895–1940) in the *Document catalog* (AG50) under "Congressional documents" list; 73d–96th Congress (1933/34–80) in the *Numerical lists* (AG55); 97th Congress (1981/82–) in the *Monthly catalog U.S. serial set supplement* (AG53).

The *American state papers,* which contain reprints of the documents of the first 14 Congresses (1789–1817), grouped by class into 38v., have been assigned special serial numbers from 01–038. These numbers can be found in the *Checklist* (AG48).

Congressional Information Service. CIS U.S. serial set index. Wash., Congressional Information Service, [1975–79]. Pt.1–12. 3v. per pt. **AG39**

Contents: Pt.1, American state papers and the 15th–34th Congresses, 1789–1857 (1977); Pt. 2, 35th–45th Congresses, 1857–1879 (1977); Pt.3, 46th–50th Congresses, 1879–1889 (1978); Pt.4, 51st–54th Congresses, 1889–1897 (1978); Pt.5, 55th–57th Congresses, 1897–1903 (1978); Pt.6, 58th-60th Congresses, 1903–1909 (1979); Pt.7, 61st–63d Congresses, 1909–1915 (1979); Pt.8, 64th–68th Congresses, 1915–1925 (1979); Pt. 9, 69th–73d Congresses, 1925–1934 (1975); Pt. 10, 74th–79th Congresses, 1935–1946 (1976); Pt. 11, 80th–85th Congresses, 1947–1958 (1976); Pt.12, 86th–91st Congress, 1st session, 1959–1969 (1976). Each part consists of a 2v. "Index of subjects and keywords" and a volume of "Finding lists" (i.e., "Private relief and related actions—Index of names of individuals and organizations"; "Numerical list of reports and documents"; "Schedule of serial volumes").

Aims to provide an index to the complete "U.S. Serial set" for the period 1789–1969. (It also serves as point of access to the CIS full text collection of the "Serial set" on microfiche.) Titles and reference numbers of "Serial set" documents were converted to machine-readable form, "making extensive use of existing secondary sources of this information such as the Government Printing Office's *Numerical Lists and Schedule of Volumes* and its predecessor, the *Document Index*."—*User guide.* Accuracy was verified through cross-checking with the "Serial set" volumes themselves, and a subject and keyword index was computer-generated. Editorial effort was focused "on careful review and revision of the subject-keyword index, to increase its ease of use, to structure extensive listings into meaningful breakdown, to reduce distracting redundancy, to eliminate meaningless terms, and to improve the thoroughness of the coverage."

The "Private relief and related actions" section of each part is "a separate index for documents concerned with . . . actions of Congress affecting specified individuals in specific circumstances. Such separate coverage provides access to reports on specific legislation, and at the same time allows exclusion of voluminous listings from the Index of Subjects and Keywords."—*User guide.* It is an alphabetical index to names of persons and organizations cited as recipients of proposed relief or related action. It is important to remember that the distinction between public actions (which are covered in the "Subject and keywords index") and private actions cannot always be clearly made, and both indexes should be consulted for thorough research.

Although the enriched keyword and subject indexing of this compilation should obviate the use of Poore (AG45), Ames (AG46), the *Document catalog* (AG50), and the *Monthly catalog* (AG51) for locating "Serial set" documents of the relevant periods, those earlier indexes are not superseded for listings of the many other publications not included in the "Serial set." Moreover, because of variations in indexing practice between the earlier publications and the CIS set, the former may sometimes provide a more satisfactory approach to a given topic (i.e., despite the "enrichment," subject indexing appears to be mainly keyword-in-title). Z1223.Z9C65

Early period to 1893

Greely, Adolphus Washington. Public documents of the first fourteen Congresses, 1789–1817. Papers relating to early Congressional documents. Wash., Govt. Prt. Off., 1900. 903p. (56th Cong., 1st sess. Senate doc. 428) (Repr.: London, Johnson, 1963) **AG40**

A chronological listing by Congress number, then by type (e.g., Senate documents, Senate reports, etc.), with index of names.

———— ———— Supplement. Wash., Govt. Prt. Off., 1904.

Reprinted from the *Annual report* of the American Historical Association, 1903, 1:343–406. Z1223.A 1900

Kanely, Edna A. Cumulative index to Hickcox's monthly catalog of United States government publications, 1885–1894. Arlington, Va., Carrollton Pr., [1981]. 3v. (2292p.) **AG41**

"Now, with the completion of this index set, cumulative subject and author access is at last provided to the ten annual catalogs of U.S. Government publications which were compiled and published privately by John H. Hickcox."—*Foreword.* For Hickcox's catalog *see* AG49.   Z1233.A1823

——— Cumulative subject index to the Monthly catalog of United States government publications, 1895–1899. Wash., Carrollton Pr., 1977. 2v.   **AG42**

Provides a single-alphabet subject index to the *Monthly catalog* (AG51) issues from 1885–99, including new indexing for the previously unindexed issues of Jan. 1895–Nov. 1897. Entries were coordinated with those from Dec.1897–Dec. 1899.

Z1223.A1K36

Lester, Daniel W. and **Lester, Marilyn A.** Checklist of United States public documents 1789–1976. Arlington, Va., U.S. Historical Documents Inst., [1978]. 5v.   **AG43**

"A dual media edition of the U.S. Superintendent of Documents' public documents library shelflists with accompanying indexes."—*t.p.*

Contents: v.1, pt.1, Supt. of Docs. classification number index; pt.2, Table of contents of microfilm reels; v.2, U.S. government author-organization index; v.3, Department keyword indexes to U.S. government author-organizations; v.4, U.S. government serial titles (comp. by the staff of the U.S. Hist. Docs. Inst.); v.5, Master keyword index to the publication issuing offices of the U.S. Government, 1789–1970, and Supplemental master keyword index, 1971–76.   Z1223.Z7L46

——— **Faull, Sandra K.** and **Lester, Lorraine E.,** comps. Cumulative title index to United States public documents, 1789–1976. Arlington, Va., United States Historical Documents Institute, 1979–82. 16v.   **AG44**

Provides a listing of the titles contained in the Public Documents Library of the Government Printing Office. "Indexed titles include all items classified and cataloged in the Superintendent of Documents Classification System since it was created in 1895, through June of 1976, plus all earlier materials in the collection."—*Introd.* Entries include title, publication date, Superintendent of Documents number and microfilm reel code.   Z1223.Z7L47

Poore, Benjamin Perley. A descriptive catalogue of the government publications of the United States, Sept. 5, 1774–March 4, 1881, comp. by order of Congress. Wash., Govt. Prt. Off., 1885. 1392p. (48th Cong., 2d sess. Senate Misc. doc. 67) (Repr.: Ann Arbor, Mich., Edwards, 1953)
AG45

Arranged chronologically, with general index. For each document gives full title, author, date, and a brief abstract of contents. Exact reference is given to the series in which each document appears. Contains much valuable material, but is difficult to use for quick reference because the index is not sufficiently complete, detailed, or specific.   Z1223.A 1885

U.S. Dept. of the Interior. Division of Documents. Comprehensive index to the publications of the United States government, 1881–1893, by John G. Ames. Wash., Govt. Prt. Off., 1905. 2v. (58th Cong., 2d sess. House doc. 754) (Repr.: Ann Arbor, Mich., Edwards, 1953; N.Y., Johnson, 1970)   **AG46**

The *Comprehensive index,* 1889–93, by J. G. Ames, published in 1894, is superseded by this work.

Bridges the gap between Poore's *Descriptive catalogue* (AG45) and the first volume of the *Document catalog* (AG50).

Arranged in three columns. In the first is given the author of the document or the department by which it was issued; in the second, a list of the documents arranged alphabetically by the key word in the title; in the third, if the document is in the serial set, reference is made to the Congress, session, and volume of the series in which each is embraced, and the number of the document. Personal name index.

Although not entirely complete, a good usable index, but less minute and detailed than the *Document catalog.* Indicates the

different editions in which a document was issued and gives serial numbers in a table under the heading "Congressional documents."
Z1223.A 1905

U.S. Superintendent of Documents. Tables of and annotated index to the Congressional series of United States public documents. Wash., Govt. Prt. Off., 1902. 769p.   **AG47**

In two parts: (1) tables of the American state papers and the documents of the 15th through the 52d Congress, arranged by serial number; and (2) minute alphabetical subject index to these documents. The first part is now superseded by the third edition of the *Checklist* noted below, but the subject index is still useful as a key to the Congressional set before 1893.   Z1223.A 1902

——— Checklist of United States public documents, 1789–1909. 3d ed. rev. and enl. Wash., Govt. Prt. Off., 1911. v.1, 1707p. (Repr.: N.Y., Kraus, 1962. v.1)   **AG48**

v.1 Lists of Congressional and departmental publications; v.2 was to have been an index, but was never issued.

A checklist, not a catalog, covering Congressional documents through the 60th Congress, and department and bureau publications to the end of 1909. Lists (1) American state papers, with serial numbers; (2) Congressional documents, 15th–60th Congresses, with serial numbers; (3) Department publications arranged alphabetically by government author; (4) Proceedings of Congress; (5) Miscellaneous publications of Congress, committee reports, etc.; (6) Papers of Revolutionary period and first 14 Congresses. The list of departmental publications gives, for periodical publications, a statement of the volumes and dates which constitute a complete set, and the serial numbers if the publication is contained also in the serial set; for separate publications the full title and date are given, and the serial number if the document appears also in the serial set. The preface contains a list and description of previous indexes and catalogs of the United States documents. This edition replaces the 2d ed. of the *Checklist* and the tables of the *Tables and index* (AG47), but not its index section.

A brief errata list is printed in the *Monthly catalog,* May, 1912, p. 720–21 (AG51).   Z1223.A113

United States government publications: a monthly catalogue, 1885–1894, by John H. Hickcox with Superintendent of Documents classification numbers added by Mary Elizabeth Poole. Repr. ed. Arlington, Va., Carrollton Pr., [1978]. 10v. in 6.   **AG49**

Reprint of the edition published in Washington, D.C., by J. H. Hickcox, 1885–89; W. H. Lowdermilk Co., 1889–94.

This catalog was privately published and includes both congressional and executive department publications. Arrangement is by author and subject in one alphabet, with numerous cross references. Indexed. The reprint edition is enhanced by the addition of Superintendent of Documents classification numbers.   Z1223.Z7U523

1893 to date

U.S. Superintendent of Documents. Catalog of the public documents of Congress and of other departments of the government of the United States for the period March 4, 1893–Dec. 31, 1940. Wash., Govt. Prt. Off., 1896–1945. v.1–25.   **AG50**

The "comprehensive index" provided for by the act approved Jan. 12, 1895. Publication terminated with v.25.

This index, which is generally referred to by its binder's title as the *Document catalog,* forms for the years 1893 to 1940 the permanent and complete catalog of all government publications both Congressional and departmental. It is a dictionary catalog in form, listing all documents under author (governmental or personal), subject, and, when necessary, title; gives full catalog information for each book or pamphlet included. Includes a large amount of analysis; refers to all editions in which a document has appeared; and gives serial numbers for documents in the serial set, as follows: in v.1–4, serial numbers are given only in the table under the entry "Congressional documents"; beginning with v.5, serial numbers are *also* given throughout the list under the main (i.e., author) entry for each document, but not under the analytical entries. Z1223.A13

—— Monthly catalog of United States government publications, 1895– . Wash., Govt. Prt. Off., 1895– . Monthly.
AG51

Title varies: 1895–June 1907, *Catalogue of the United States public documents;* July 1907–1939, *Monthly catalog, United States public documents;* 1940–50, *United States government publications: monthly catalog.*

A current bibliography of publications issued by all branches of the government, including both the Congressional and the department and bureau publications. Each issue contains general instructions for ordering documents, and a list of documents published arranged by the department and bureau until 1976. An annual subject and agency index appeared in each volume and, beginning with July 1945, a monthly index in each issue until 1974 when separate personal author and title indexes were added.

Beginning with the issue for July 1976, the catalog was converted to MARC format, with full cataloging according to Anglo-American cataloging rules provided for each item. "The *Monthly Catalog* utilizes AACR and Library of Congress main entries. Subjects are derived from *Library of Congress Subject Headings* 8th edition and its supplements. The catalog consists of text and four indexes—author, title, subject, and series/report number."—*Pref., July 1976.* Up-to-date information regarding sales status ("in stock," "out of print," etc.) is provided by the *GPO sales publications reference file* (Wash., Govt. Prt. Off., Feb. 1977– ; monthly; microfiche).

A reprint edition for the period 1895–1940, with Superintendent of Documents classification numbers added, was published by Carrollton Press, Wash., D.C., 1975–78 (40v. in 58).

A directory of United States government periodicals and subscription publications (title varies) was published semiannually 1951–60 (usually Feb. and Aug.); annually 1961–76 (in Feb. issue). It was replaced by an annual *Serials supplement,* 1977–84 which was in turn seperseded by the *Periodicals supplement* (*see* AG52).
Z1223.A18●

—— —— Supplements: 1941–1942, 1943–1944, 1945–1946. Wash., Govt. Prt. Off., 1947–48. 3v.

These supplements include publications received by the Public Documents Division Library, not listed previously in any Superintendent of Documents catalog. No further supplements published, as, beginning in April 1947, all documents are listed in the *Monthly catalog* as received, regardless of publication date.

—— —— Periodicals supplement. 1985– . Wash., Govt. Prt. Off., 1985– . Annual. **AG52**

Also available in microform.

Continues the annual *Serials supplement* published 1977–84, which replaced the *Directory of United States government periodicals and subscription publications* published semiannually, 1951–60 (usually Feb. and Aug.), and annually 1961–76 (Feb. issue).

—— —— United States congressional serial set supplement. 97th Congress– , 1981/82– . Wash., Govt. Prt. Off., 1985– . **AG53**

Also issued in microform.

Provides access to the *Serial set,* replacing the *Numerical list.* Arranged according to type of publication: Senate documents, Senate treaty documents, Senate reports, Senate executive reports, House documents and House reports. Gives complete bibliographic citations. Author, title, subject, series/report, bill number, stock number, and title keyword indexes.

—— —— Decennial cumulative index, 1941–1950 . . . Wash., Govt. Prt. Off., 1953. 1848p.

"Index to the monthly issues from January 1941 to December 1950 and the Supplements for 1941–42, 1943–44, and 1945–46."—*title page.*

—— —— —— 1951–1960. Wash., Govt. Prt. Off., 1968. 2v.

"Index to the monthly issues from January 1951 to December 1960."—*title page.*

—— —— Decennial cumulative personal author index, 1941–1950, 1951–1960. Ed. by Edward Przebienda. Ann Arbor, Mich., Pierian Pr., 1971. 2v.

—— —— Quinquennial cumulative personal author index, 1961–1965, 1966–1970, 1971–75. Ed. by Edward Przebienda. Ann Arbor, Mich., Pierian Pr., 1972–79. 3v.

Cumulative subject index to the Monthly catalog of United States government publications, 1900–1971. Comp. by William W. Buchanan and Edna M. Kanely. Wash., Carrollton Pr., 1973–75. 15v. **AG54**

Merges the numerous annual indexes of the *Monthly catalog* (AG51) with the two decennial and one 6-month index (July–Dec. 1934), plus new indexing for the previously unindexed issues of June 1906–Dec. 1908, thus providing a subject approach in one alphabet to over 800,000 government publications from a 72-year period. Cross references have been included, but variant subject entries and spellings were considered too numerous to be integrated. Therefore, the user must consult both "aeroplanes" and "airplanes" as well as "aircraft," etc. Chronological and numerical subheadings are used when deemed more appropriate than an alphabetical arrangement within large topics. "Major segments" such as states, larger U.S. government organizations, and other extensive, self-contained subject areas such as "Bibliographies" are set off from surrounding entries by special half-title pages; later reprinting of these segments is planned.

Citation is to year of the *Monthly catalog* and page (prior to Sept. 1947) or item number. Unfortunately, libraries holding only the biennial *Document catalog* (AG50) from 1895 to 1940 will not be able to turn directly from the index to the appropriate page. Although the large number of entries under the broader headings will still necessitate considerable searching in the cited issues of the *Monthly catalog,* librarians and researchers working in a documents collection arranged according to the Superintendent of Documents classification and relying on the *Monthly catalog* as their main approach to this collection will find the *Cumulative subject index* a useful tool.

U.S. Superintendent of Documents. Numerical lists and schedule of volumes of the reports and documents of the 73d Congress, 1933/34–80. Wash., Govt. Prt. Off., 1934–82. **AG55**

Usually a separate volume appeared for each session of Congress.

Prior to 1941, the set is superseded by the "Congressional documents" tables in the *Document catalog* (AG50). From the 77th Congress, 1st sess., Jan. 3, 1941 through the 96th Congress, 1980, it must be used to obtain serial numbers for the Congressional reports and documents which were listed only in the *Monthly catalog* (AG51), and without serial number.

Ceased publication. Beginning with volumes for the 97th Congress, 1981/82– , the *Serial set* numbers will be found in the *United States congressional serial set supplement* to the *Monthly catalog* (*see* AG53). Z1223.A15

—— [Subject bibliographies] Wash., Govt. Prt. Off., 1975– . Irregular. **AG56**

Supersedes the *Price lists* that were published irregularly 1898–1975.

"There are over 21,000 different publications, periodicals, and subscription services for sale by the Superintendent of Documents. Topics range from accidents and accident prevention to zoology and touch on nearly every facet of human life. Since an average of 3,000 new titles enters the sales inventory each year, and a similar number of titles become outdated or superseded by revised editions, it is impractical to issue a single catalog listing all of the titles sold.

"Instead, we have created over 250 Subject Bibliographies which list publications on a single subject or field of interest."—*Index, Mar. 15, 1982.*

Most entries in the bibliographies are briefly annotated and include order information. Each bibliography carries an "SB" number and the subject indexing refers to those numbers. A subject index is issued periodically.

It should be noted that *Price list* 36, "Government periodicals and subscription services," continues to be revised and issued quarterly. It lists more than 500 subscription services published by more than

450 federal agencies and available from the Superintendent of Documents. It also lists new subscription services, discontinued subscriptions, title changes, and latest prices.

U.S. Library of Congress. Serial and Government Publications Division. Popular names of U.S. government reports. 4th ed. Comp. by Bernard A. Bernier, Jr. and Karen A. Wood. Wash., Lib. of Congress, 1984. 272p. **AG57**

1st ed. 1966. Compilers vary.

Provides bibliographic records for 1,555 reports of U.S. executive, legislative, and judicial bodies. Arrangement is under popular name by which reports are generally known; a corporate author and subject index is included. Z1223.A199U54

United States government publications (non-depository). Jan. 1953– . N.Y., Readex Microprint, 1953– . Monthly. **AG58**

Consists of all nondepository items, reproduced in full in microprint, on cards measuring 6 by 9 inches, for use in a Readex Microprint reader (published on microfiche beginning with 1981 coverage). Arrangement is by *Monthly catalog* entry number (AG51). A companion series, *United States government depository publications,* is also available in a Readex Microprint edition beginning 1956.

Bibliography-index to current U.S. JPRS translations: JPRS *see* U.S. Joint Publications Research Service, East Europe; Albania, Bulgaria, Czechoslovakia, East Germany, Hungary, Poland, Rumania, Yugoslavia. v.1–8, July/Sept. 1962– July 1969/June 1970. [N.Y.], R & M Pubs., CCM Info Corp., [1962–70]. Monthly. **AG59**

Title varies.
Superseded by: Z2483.B52

Transdex; bibliography and index to the United States Joint Publications Research Service (JPRS) translations. v.9–12, 1970/71–74. N.Y., CCM Info Corp., 1971–74. Monthly with semiannual cumulations. **AG60**

Supersedes the *Bibliography-index* (above) and assumes its numbering.
Superseded by: AS36.U574

Transdex index. 1975– . Wooster, Ohio, Micro Photo Div., Bell and Howell Co., 1975– . Monthly paper issues with annual cumulation on microfiche. **AG61**

Lists and indexes all JPRS translations. Arranged in four major divisions: Series and *ad hoc* title section; Bibliographic section; Keyword section; Personal names section.

Readex Microprint Corporation. Index to Readex microprint edition of JPRS reports (Joint Publications Research Service), [1958/63–]. N.Y., Corporation, [1964–]. **AG62**

1958/63 index prep. by Mary Elizabeth Poole.

The JPRS reports, which are mainly translations of a wide variety of articles and technical writings from Communist-bloc countries, are listed in the *Monthly catalog* (AG51) and thus are reproduced in the microprint edition of nondepository publications. The 1958/63 index is a correlation of the JPRS numbers and the *Monthly catalog* numbers under which they are arranged in the microprint edition. Its use will obviate the necessity of checking a report under author or subject in the *Monthly catalog* when the JPRS number is known.

JPRS reports are also available in a Readex Microprint edition from 1958, with a subject index provided on a semiannual basis since Jan. 1966.

U.S. Library of Congress. Exchange and Gift Division. Non-GPO imprints received in the Library of Congress; a selective checklist, 1967/69–75. Wash., Lib. of Cong., 1970–76. Annual. **AG63**

Attempts to list U.S. government publications not published by the Government Printing Office which fall outside the scope of the *Monthly catalog* or other principal bibliographies of government publications. Main entry listing with subject index. Discontinued because of expanded coverage by the *Monthly catalog* (AG51). Z1223.A12A5

Legislative branch

Congressional Information Service. Index to publications of the United States Congress. v.1, no.1– , Jan. 1970– . Wash., 1970– . Monthly with quarterly index cumulations and final clothbound cumulation in 2v. per yr. **AG64**

At head of title: *CIS index.* Annual volumes designated as *CIS/Annual.*

An ambitious service offering brief abstracts of the following types of Congressional publications: committee hearings, committee prints, House and Senate documents, House and Senate reports, House and Senate special publications, Senate executive reports, Senate treaty documents. Detailed index of subjects and names (including names of witnesses at hearings, etc.), plus an index of bill, report, and document numbers, and one of committee and subcommittee chairmen. KF49.C62●

—— CIS/Annual, 1970– . Wash., 1971– . Annual. 2v. per yr. **AG65**

Contents: pt.1, Abstracts of Congressional publications and legislative histories; pt.2, Index to Congressional publications and public laws.

Cumulates the abstracts of hearings, reports, committee prints, and other Congressional papers from the monthly issues of the *CIS index* (above), and offers a cumulative index to them. In addition, the annual provides brief descriptions and legislative histories of public laws enacted during the period covered.

Two further cumulations have appeared as: KF49.C62●

—— CIS/Five-year cumulative index, 1970–1974. Wash., 1975. 2v.

—— CIS/Four-year cumulative index, 1975–1978. Wash., [1979]. 3v.

These volumes revise and supersede the *CIS annual* index volumes for the years indicated and are designed to be used with the annual abstract volumes. The subject index includes topical subjects and names; the supplementary indexes cover titles; bill, report, and document numbers; and committee and subcommittee chairmen. KF49.C2●

Congressional committee prints and hearings

Congressional Information Service, Inc. CIS US congressional committee hearings index. Wash., C.I.S., [1981–84]. (In progress) **AG66**

Contents: pt.I, Earliest hearings through 64th Congress (not yet publ.); pt.II, 65th–68th Congresses (1984. 5v.); pt. III, 69th–73d Congresses (1984. 5v.); pt.IV, 74th–78th Congresses (1983. 6v.); pt.V, 79th–82d Congresses (1983. 6v.); pt.VI, 83d–85th Congresses (1982. 5v.); pt.VII, 86th–88th Congresses (1982. 5v.); pt.VIII, 89th–91st Congresses (1981. 5v.).

Parts are being published in reverse order. Each part contains the following sections: (1) Reference bibliography (giving full bibliographic data on hearings from the period covered, notes on subject content, subject descriptors, names of witnesses, etc.); (2) Index by subjects and organizations; (3) Index by personal names; (4) Supplementary indexes (e.g., bill number, Supt. of Docs. classification number). KF40.C56

—— CIS US congressional committee prints index from the earliest publications through 1969. Wash., Congressional Information Service, [1980]. 5v. **AG67**

Contents: [v.1–2] Reference bibliography; [v.3–4] Index by subjects and names; [v.5] Finding aids.

Serves as a guide to the publisher's *U.S. congressional committee prints on microfiche* series and as an independent bibliography and index of committee prints through 1969. (Committee prints are included in the *CIS/Index to publications of the U.S. Congress* [AG64] beginning 1970.) The "Reference bibliography" volumes provide bibliographic data on some 15,000 committee prints, virtually all of which are included in the microfiche series. In addition to the 2-volume index of subjects and names, the "Finding aids" volume includes indexes by title, by Congress and Committee, by bill number, and by Superintendent of Documents number.

Z1223.Z7C66

U.S. Congress. Senate. Library. Index of Congressional committee hearings (not confidential in character) prior to Jan. 3, 1935, in the United States Senate Library. Wash., Govt. Prt. Off., 1935. 1056p. **AG68**

Z1223.A

—— Cumulative index of Congressional committee hearings (not confidential in character) from 74th Congress (Jan. 3, 1935) through 85th Congress (Jan. 3, 1959) in the United States Senate Library. Indexed and comp. under the direction of Felton M. Johnston, secretary of the Senate, by Richard D. Hupman, librarian [and others]. Wash., Govt. Prt. Off., 1959. 823p.

Z1223.A3

—— —— Supplement 1–7. Wash., Govt. Prt. Off., 1963–84. 7v.

Quadrennial cumulations cover 1959/63, 1963/67, 1967/71, 1971/74; biennial cumulations cover 1975/76, 1977/78, and 1979/80.

Legislative debates

U.S. Congress. Congressional record: containing the proceedings and debates of the 43d Congress– , March 4, 1873– . Wash., Govt. Prt. Off., 1873– . v.1– . **AG69**

Issued daily while Congress is in session; revised and issued in bound form at the end of the session. The issue for each session is numbered as one volume and paged continuously though bound in several parts. There are frequent indexes during the session and a final index to the whole volume, this index sometimes bound separately, sometimes included in the last bound part.

Contains the Presidents' messages, Congressional speeches and debates in full, and record of votes. Does not include text of bills. Each index is in two parts: (1) Alphabetical index of names and subjects, giving (under subject) bills and bill number, and (2) History of bills and resolutions, arranged by number. This second index is the one to use for full information about a bill, as it gives page references to all material in the *Record* about the bill, from its introduction to its final passage and signing. Beginning with the 80th Congress, March 17, 1947, a section called "Daily digest" is included.

For material before 1873 the following earlier compilations should be consulted: (1) *Debates and proceedings* (generally known by its binder's title, *Annals of Congress*), 1st–18th Congress, 1789–1824. 42v. (Publ. 1834–56); (2) *Register of debates,* 18th Congress, 2d sess.–25th Congress, 1st sess., 1824–37. 14v. in 29 (publ. 1825–37); and (3) *Congressional globe,* 23d–42d Congress, 1833–73. 46v. in 108 (publ. 1834–73).

For further information concerning the *Congressional record, see* Morehead's guide (AG21).

It seems worth noting that the "Appendix" to the *Record* (containing material not germane to the proceedings of Congress, and which has often been published elsewhere) was not included in the bound volumes for the 83d Congress, 2d session, through the 90th Congress, 1st session (although the appendix from the daily issues was available on microfilm and continued to be indexed in the indexes to the bound set). Beginning with the 90th Congress, 2d session, this type of material again appears in the bound volumes in a section entitled "Extension of remarks"; this section is regularly indexed and, since pagination is continuous, "A" numbers are no longer used. JR11.R5●

Executive branch

Cumulated indexes to the Public papers of the Presidents of the United States. Millwood, N.Y., KTO Pr., 1977–83. [v.1–8] (In progress) **AG70**

Contents: Herbert C. Hoover, 1929–1933 (1980); Harry S. Truman, 1945–1953 (1979); Dwight D. Eisenhower, 1953–1961 (1978); John F. Kennedy, 1961–1963 (1977); Lyndon B. Johnson, 1963–1969 (1978); Richard M. Nixon, 1969–1974 (1978); Gerald R. Ford, 1974–1977 (1980); Jimmy Carter, 1977–1981 (1983).

For each of the Presidents, combines and integrates into one volume the separate indexes appearing in the annual volumes of the *Public papers* series (AG74).

U.S. Congress. Senate. Library. Presidential vetoes, 1789–1976. Wash., Govt. Prt. Off., 1978. 533p. **AG71**

Previous ed. 1969.

Arranged chronologically by Congresses and the administrations in which the vetoes occurred. Index of names and subjects. Includes a statistical summary. KF42.2

U.S. President. Codification of presidential proclamations and executive orders, 1961/77– . [Wash.], Off. of the Federal Register, [1979]– . Irregular. **AG72**

Vol. covering Jan. 20, 1961–Jan. 20, 1981 publ. 1981 (980p.).

"Provide[s] in one convenient reference source proclamations and Executive orders with general applicability and continuing effect."—*Foreword.* Arranged in 50 chapters according to the title designations of the *Code of federal regulations* and the *United States code.* Contains text and all amendments in effect. Disposition tables and subject index. KF70.A473

—— A compilation of the messages and papers of the Presidents . . . (with additions and encyclopedic index by private enterprise). N.Y., Bureau of Nat. Literature, [1917?]. 20v. **AG73**

Originally published: Wash., Govt. Prt. Off., 1896–99. 10v. (House misc. doc. 210, 53d Cong., 2d sess.), covering 1789–1897. Published by authority of Congress by James D. Richardson.

Additional volumes bring the record through the terms of Calvin Coolidge, 1929. These were commercially published in various editions with varying volume numbers, usually without publication dates. (For record *see* Schmeckebier, p.330–39 [AG24].)

Commercially published Presidential messages cover the administrations of Herbert Hoover, 1929–33, and Franklin D. Roosevelt, 1933–45.

Continued officially by: J81.B96g

—— Public papers of the Presidents of the United States, containing the public messages, speeches, and statements of the President. Wash., 1958– . Annual. **AG74**

Contents: Harry S. Truman, 1945–53. 8v. (publ. 1961–66); Dwight D. Eisenhower, 1953–61. 8v. (publ. 1958–61); John F. Kennedy, 1961–63. 3v. (publ. 1962–64); Lyndon B. Johnson, 1963–69. 7v. (publ. 1964–70); Richard M. Nixon, 1969–74. 6v. (publ. 1971–75); Gerald R. Ford, 1974–76/77. 6v. (publ. 1975–79); Jimmy Carter, 1977–81. 9v. (publ. 1977–82); Ronald Reagan, 1981–83. 4v. (publ. 1982–84; in progress).

Published by the Office of the Federal Register, National Archives and Records Service, General Services Administration.

A series designed to include the public messages and statements of the Presidents. Beginning with the Carter administration, coverage was expanded to include materials published in the *Weekly compilation* noted below. Annual volumes are published soon after the close of each calendar year.

A supplementary, up-to-date record is: J80.A283

Weekly compilation of presidential documents. Aug. 2, 1965– . [Wash., Office of the Federal Register; distr. by Govt. Prt. Off.], 1965– . v.1– . Weekly. **AG75**

Publishes "transcripts of the President's news conferences, messages to Congress, public speeches, and statements, and other Presidential materials released by the White House up to 5 p.m. on each Friday."—*v.1, no.1, p.2.* Annual index. J80.A284

O'Hara, Frederic J. A guide to publications of the Executive branch. Ann Arbor, Mich., Pierian Pr., 1979. 287p.
AG76

Attempts to provide an understanding of the function and operation of the government agencies. Arranged by department; includes an essay about each agency, SuDocs classification numbers, and descriptions of useful publications such as agency catalogs, bibliographies, career literature, dictionaries, statistical compilations, and directories. Agency, personal name, title, and subject indexes.
Z1223.Z7O48

Tollefson, Alan M. and **Chang, Henry C.,** comps. A bibliography of presidential commissions, committees, councils, panels, and task forces, 1961–1972. Minneapolis, Govt. Publs. Div., Univ. of Minnesota Libraries, 1973. 30p.
AG77

Lists 243 reports selected from the *Monthly catalog* (AG51) and *Popular names of U.S. government reports* (AG57). Arranged alphabetically by main entry, with indexes by personal name, title, and subject-keyword.
Z1223.Z7T66

State publications

Guides

Lane, Margaret T. State publications and depository libraries: a reference handbook. Westport, Conn., Greenwood Pr., [1981]. 573p.
AG78

Intended mainly for "administrators of state document distribution programs and librarians attempting to establish depository library programs."—*Pref.* Pt.I, "Characteristics of depository library legislation," provides an overview and comparative study of the situation; pt.II, "State publications—the literature," offers a bibliography and survey of the literature; pt.III, "The states," cites pertinent legislation (current as of mid-1980) for each state, followed by commentary and bibliography. Indexed.
Z688.G6L36

———— State publications; depository distribution and bibliographical programs. Comp. for the State and Local Documents Task Force, Government Documents Round Table, American Library Association. [Austin], Texas State Publications Clearinghouse, Texas State Library, 1980. 178p. (*Its* Documents monograph ser., no.2)
AG78a

———— ———— Supplement. 1981. 49p. (*Its* Documents monograph ser., no.2A)

Attempts to survey the distribution and bibliographical control of state documents. Information, supplied by the individual states, includes name of agency, legal authority, place of agency within state and parent organization, depository libraries (if any), document distribution, dissemination of cataloging data, availability of microforms, checklists and other publications available, and budget. The supplement contains reports from states not included in the basic volume, plus reports from the Center for Research Libraries and the Library of Congress.
Z1223.5.T35 no.2

Bibliography

See also CJ185.

Parish, David W. State government reference publications: an annotated bibliography. 2d ed. Littleton, Colo., Libraries Unlimited, 1981. 355p.
AG79

1st ed. 1974.
1,756 annotated entries arranged according to the following bibliographic classifications: official state bibliographies; blue books; legislative manuals and related references; state government finances; statistical abstracts and other data sources; directories; tourist guides; audiovisual guides, atlases and maps; bibliographies and general references. Indexed by title and personal authors, and by subject.
Z1223.5.A1P37

U.S. Library of Congress. Exchange and Gift Division. Monthly checklist of state publications. v.1– , 1910– . Wash., Govt. Prt. Off., 1910– . Monthly.
AG80

Title varies: 1910–21, *Monthly list of state publications.*
Sponsoring division at Library of Congress varies.
A current bibliography, arranged alphabetically by states' names, of the publications of the states, territories, and insular possessions of the United States. Though limited to the publications received by the Library of Congress, it is approximately complete, as the Library aims to acquire all such material issued. Each title is given with full cataloging information, including contents in the case of composite reports. Since the annual index refers to the contents notes as well as to the main titles, the list can be made to serve as a subject index as well as a bibliography. Beginning in 1963, periodicals are listed semiannually in the June and Dec. issues, with the Dec. list cumulative for the year.
Z1223.5.A1U5

Municipal publications

Index to current urban documents. v.1– . July/Oct. 1972– . Westport, Conn., Greenwood Pr., 1972– . Quarterly with annual cumulation.
AG81

Originally indexed federal, state, and local documents. With v.2, federal and state documents are omitted and the index is concerned with county documents and documents of "the largest cities in all the fifty states and territories and Canada." Emphasis is on documents "concerned with public affairs, i.e., social, political, economic and public administration matters." A geographic listing (alphabetical by city or county) is followed by a subject index.
Z7165.U5I654

Municipal government reference sources: publications and collections. Ed. for the American Library Association Government Documents Round Table by Peter Hernon [and others]. N.Y., Bowker, 1978. 341p.
AG82

"This source guide is a cooperative, pioneering effort to identify municipal reference sources on a large scale. Under the auspices of the Task Force on Local Documents of the American Library Association's Government Documents Round Table, information was gathered by over one hundred volunteer workers under the direction of the project's editors. Concentration is on large urban areas. The arrangement is by state and, within state, by municipality. When pertinent, an overview of a given city is provided, describing special characteristics of that municipality's publishing program or distinctive features of its government—its history or structure."—*Pref.* Subject index.
Z1223.6.A1M85

AFRICA

See also under names of individual countries.

Balima, Mildred Grimes. Botswana, Lesotho, and Swaziland; a guide to official publications, 1868–1968. Wash., General Reference and Bibliography Div., Lib. of Congress (distr. by Supt. of Docs.), 1971. 84p.
AG83

"This bibliography includes citations to documents of the former High Commission Territories during British protection and since independence, together with reports prepared by agencies or individuals with official authorization and funds. . . . To increase the usefulness . . . , a number of relevant British official papers have been included, some of which pertain to Bechuanaland (Botswana) and Swaziland before the establishment of British protectorates."—*Pref.*
Z3559.B3

Boston University. Libraries. Catalog of African government documents. 3d ed., rev. & enl. Boston, G. K. Hall, 1976. 679p.
AG84

1st–2d eds., 1960–64, had title: *Catalog of African government documents and African area index.*
Reproduces the catalog cards in classed arrangement (based on

the Library of Congress schedule J700–881). This edition lists more than 13,000 titles, many of them serials. A classed catalog with country index; listing under country is by main entry only. The "African area index" does not appear in this edition.
Z3507.5.B67

Gibson, Mary Jane. Portuguese Africa; a guide to official publications. Wash., General Reference and Bibliography Div., Reference Dept., Lib. of Congress, 1967. 217p. **AG85**

Covers documents from 1850 to 1964, listing "publications of the governments of Angola, the Cape Verde Islands, Mozambique, Portuguese Guinea, and the São Thomé e Principe Islands and also of Portugal pertaining to its African possessions."—*Pref.* Arranged by geographical area; index of subjects and individual authors. American library location indicated for many items. Z3871.G5

Howell, John Bruce. East African community: subject guide to official publications. Wash., Lib. of Congress, 1976. 272p. **AG86**

"This is a subject guide to official publications of the East African Community and its predecessors for the period 1926 to 1974, and of the East African region (including Kenya, Tanzania, and Uganda) for the period 1859 to 1974 issued by Great Britain or one of the three partner states."—*Pref.* Subject arrangement similar to that used in *Africa South of the Sahara* (DD86). Indexed. Z3582.H69

Rishworth, Susan Knoke. Spanish-speaking Africa; a guide to official publications. Wash., General Reference and Bibliography Div., Lib. of Congress, 1973. 66p. **AG87**

Includes "Equatorial Guinea, Spanish Sahara, Ifni, and that part of northern Morocco known as the Spanish Zone until it was united with the rest of the country when Morocco became independent from France in 1956."—*Pref.* Lists published official records of those areas and publications of the Spanish government issued on behalf of its African territories. Z2689.R57

U.S. Library of Congress. African Section. Madagascar and adjacent islands; a guide to official publications. Comp. by Julian W. Witherell. Wash., General Reference and Bibliography Div., Reference Dept., Lib. of Congress, 1965. 58p. **AG88**

Includes "materials dating from the establishments of French administrations in Madagascar, the Comoro Islands, and Réunion, and the British administrations in Mauritius and Seychelles."—*Pref.* Z3702.U5

—— Official publications of British East Africa, comp. by Helen F. Conover and Audrey A. Walker. Wash., 1960–63. 4v. **AG89**

Contents: pt.1, The East Africa High Commission and other regional documents. 67p.; pt.2, Tanganyika. 134p.; pt.3, Kenya and Zanzibar. 162p.; pt.4, Uganda. 100p. Z3582.U5

—— Official publications of French Equatorial Africa, French Cameroons, and Togo, 1946–1958, comp. by Julian W. Witherell. Wash., 1964. 78p. **AG90**

A list of publications of the various governments concerned with AEF (Afrique Equatoriale Française)—Chad, Gabon, Middle Congo, Ubangi-Shari, French Cameroons, Togo, France, French Union —and United Nations publications bearing directly on French Cameroons and Togo. Largely superseded by the two following publications: Z3961.U5

Witherell, Julian W., comp. French-speaking central Africa: a guide to official publications in American libraries. Wash., General Reference and Bibliography Div., Lib. of Congress, 1973. 314p. **AG91**

Includes "documents of former Belgian and French possessions from the beginning of colonial rule to the time of independence as well as publications of national governments and regional and provincial administrations from independence to 1970. Also included are League of Nations and United Nations documents on Ruanda-Urundi and Cameroon, selections of Belgian and French official publications pertaining to their former territories, and

material published by government-sponsored organizations."— *Pref.* Arranged by country; index of personal names and subjects. Z3692.W5

—— French-speaking West Africa; a guide to official publications. Wash., General Reference and Bibliography Div., African Section, Lib. of Congress, 1967. 201p. **AG92**

Lists as comprehensively as possible the published government records from the mid-19th century to date of compilation, including "publications of the federation of French West Africa, its eight component colonies (later territories), the French administration in the mandated territory (later trust territory) of Togo, and documents of the autonomous and national governments of each state."—*Pref.*

An earlier guide, *Official publications of French West Africa, 1946–1958,* was compiled by Helen F. Conover and issued by the General Reference and Bibliography Division, Library of Congress (Wash., 1960). Z3672.W5

AUSTRALIA

Australian official publications. Ed. by D. H. Borchardt. [Melbourne], Longman Cheshire, [1979]. 365p. **AG93**

A series of essays by specialists presents an overview of the government of Australia on three levels—national, state, and municipal/shire/county—and of their current publications. Parliamentary and judicial publications are each treated separately, followed by topical sections on statistics, environment, and conservation. Distribution, bibliographic control, and access to government publications are treated in a final section. Indexed. Z4019.A97

Canberra, Australia. National Library. Australian government publications, 1961– . Canberra, Commonwealth Govt. Pr., 1962– . Quarterly with annual cumulation.
AG94

Frequency varies: 1961–70, annual.
Supersedes the Library's *Monthly list of Australian government publications,* 1952–60, and the annual cumulation in its *Annual catalogue of Australian publications.* Z4019.C33

Coxon, Howard. Australian official publications. Oxford, Pergamon, [1981]. 211p. il. (Guides to official pubns., v.5) **AG95**

A guide to the types of publications issued by official organizations and agencies. An introductory essay on the framework of the Australian government is followed by sections for (1) the Commonwealth Parliament; (2) Commonwealth departments and statutory authorities; (3) distribution and availability of publications; (4) the states of Australia; (5) the internal territories. Brief bibliography of Australian official publications; index. Z4019.C69

Zalums, Elmar. Western Australian government publications, 1829–1959; a bibliography. 2d ed. Canberra, Nat. Lib. of Australia, 1971. 95p. **AG96**

Preliminary ed. 1968.
An alphabetical listing under corporate entry of publications by or on behalf of the state (colonial, prior to 1901) government and its agencies. Brief history of each department or agency is given. Index by subject, distinctive title, and personal name. Parliamentary papers have been excluded. Z4435.Z34

BRAZIL

Lombardi, Mary. Brazilian serial documents: a selective and annotated guide. Bloomington, Indiana Univ. Pr., 1974. 445p. **AG97**

Listing is by issuing agency, with index of titles and agencies. A detailed table of contents serves as an outline of government structure. About 1,400 entries with full bibliographical details and notes on the agencies.   Z1679.L65

CANADA
Guides

Bishop, Olga Bernice. Canadian official publications. Oxford, Pergamon, [1981]. 297p. il. (Guides to official pubns., v.9)   **AG98**

Aims "to introduce the student to the various types of publications issued by both Parliament and the departments and agencies of the federal government as well as the types of information which may be found in the various documents."—*Pref.* Chapters deal with specific types of publications, cite examples, and provide background information. Indexed.   Z1373.3.B48

Higgins, Marion Villiers. Canadian government publications; a manual for librarians. Chicago, Amer. Lib. Assoc., 1935. 582p. il.   **AG99**

Beginning with the French regime, 1608–1760, lists Canadian government publications to 1935, including a historical summary of issuing bodies. Arrangement is by department with subject and author index.   Z1373.C2H6

Bibliography

Government of Canada publications. Publications du gouvernement du Canada. Quarterly catalogue trimestriel, v.27– , Jan./Mar. 1979– . Ottawa, 1979– . Quarterly, with annual index.   **AG100**

Continues *Catalogue of official publications of the Parliament and government of Canada,* 1928–48; *Canadian government publications: catalogue,* v.1–17, 1953–69. Earlier volumes of the present series (with slight variations in the subtitle) were published by different agencies: 1954–70 by Dept. of Public Printing and Stationery; 1971–75 by Information Canada; 1976–78 by Dept. of Supply and Services; beginning 1979 issued by the Canadian Government Publishing Centre.

In three parts: pt.1, Parliamentary publications; pt.2, Departmental publications; pt.3, Index. Pts.1 and 2 are in two sections: English and French; the index is bilingual.

Henderson, George Fletcher. Federal royal commissions in Canada, 1867–1966; a checklist. [Toronto], Univ. of Toronto Pr., [1967]. 212p.   **AG101**

A chronological listing of nearly 400 Canadian federal royal commissions, with notes on the appointment of the commission and indication of whether or not the report was printed; if so, in what form; and whether or not the report has been located. Index of subjects, names of commissioners, and authors and titles of special studies.   Z1373.H4

Provincial publications

Pross, Catherine A. Guide to the identification and acquisition of Canadian government publications: provinces and territories. 2d ed. Halifax, N.S., Dalhousie Univ., Univ. Libs., School of Lib. Serv., 1983. 103p. (Dalhousie Univ. Libs. and School of Lib. Serv. Occasional paper 16, rev.)   **AG102**

1st ed. 1977.
Arranged by province or territory. In addition to providing information about publication activity and how to purchase the documents, indicates collection strengths of various libraries in order to facilitate interlibrary borrowing.   Z1373.3.P7

❖Records of Canadian provincial publications are provided

by: *Publications of the government of British Columbia, 1871–1947,* by Marjorie C. Holmes (Victoria, 1950. 254p.); *Publications of the government of the Province of Canada, 1841–1867,* by Olga B. Bishop (Ottawa, Nat. Lib., 1963. 351p.); *Publications of the governments of the Northwest Territories, 1876–1905 and of the Province of Saskatchewan, 1905–1952,* by Christine MacDonald (Regina, Legislative Lib., 1952. 109p.); *Publications of the governments of Nova Scotia, Prince Edward Island, New Brunswick, 1758–1952,* by Olga B. Bishop (Ottawa, Nat. Lib., 1957. 237p.); *Publications of the government of Ontario, 1867–1900,* by Olga B. Bishop (Toronto, Ministry of Govt. Services, 1976. 409p.); *Publications of the government of Ontario, 1901–1955,* by Hazel I. MacTaggart (Toronto, Univ. of Toronto Pr., 1964. 303p.); *Publications of the government of Ontario, 1956–1971,* by Hazel I. MacTaggart (Toronto, Ministry of Govt. Services, 1975. 410p.); *Ontario royal commissions and commissions of inquiry, 1867–1978,* by Susan Waintman and Ana Tampold (Toronto, Legislative Lib., 1980. 74p.); and *Répertoire des publications gouvernementales du Québec de 1867 à 1964,* by André Beaulieu, Jean-Charles Bonenfant and Jean Hamelin (Québec, Impr. de la Reine, 1968. 554p.; *Supplément, 1965–68,* 1970. 388p.). Mohan Bhatia's *Canadian provincial government publications* (Rev. & enl. ed. Saskatoon, Univ. of Saskatchewan Lib., 1971. 19p.) is a bibliography of relevant bibliographies.

DENMARK

Bibliografi over Danmarks offentlige Publikationer. Årg. 1– , 1948– . København, Dansk Bibliografisk Kontor, 1949– . Annual.   **AG103**

At head of title: Impressa publica Regni Danici 1948– .
Title varies: 1948–59, *Bibliografisk, Fortegnelse over statens Tryksager og statsunderstøttede Publikationer.*
An index of government publications arranged under issuing office, with indexes by subject and person.   Z2569.A25

FINLAND

Finland. Eduskunta. Kirjasto. Valtion virallisjulkaisut. Statens officiella publikationer. Government publications in Finland. 1961– . Helsinki, 1962– . Annual.   **AG104**

An index of government publications arranged by Finnish names of agencies with cross references from the Swedish names. Name index and separate subject indexes for publications in Finnish, in Swedish, and in other languages (the latter index being in English).   Z2520.A3F25

Finland. Valtion Painatuskeskus. Luettelo. Helsinki, [1967]– . Irregular.   **AG104a**

A classified general catalog of Finnish official publications issued at irregular intervals, with supplementary volumes (*Lisäluettelo*) between editions.
1973 last published?   Z2520.A3F34

FRANCE

Bibliographie de la France. Supplément II, Publications officielles; notices établies par la Bibliothèque Nationale. 1977– . [Paris, Cercle de la Librairie], 1977– . 6 nos. per yr.   **AG105**

Continues the "Publications officielles" section of the *Bibliogra-*

phie de la France designated as "Supplément F" during the 1950–71 period and continued as a supplementary publication during the time the national bibliography was entitled *Bibliographie de la France-Biblio* (*see* AA758).

Lists publications from the national to the local level; entries are now classed in nine sections: (1) Budgets, lois et traités; (2) Assemblées constitutionnelles; (3) Cours et jurisdictions; (4) Administration centrale; (5) Administration locale; (6) Administration outremer; (7) Établissements publics; (8) États étrangers; (9) Organizations intergouvernementales. Index in each issue, cumulating annually.

Commission de Coordination de la Documentation Administrative. Répertoire des publications périodiques et de série de l'administration française. [Paris, Documentation Française, 1973] 368p. **AG106**

Lists and describes about 850 serial publications (periodicals, annuals, series of various kinds) issued by French official agencies. Listing is by ministry or other sponsoring body, with title and subject indexes. Information was current as of 1972. Z2169.C64

Dampierre, Jacques de. Les publications officielles des pouvoirs publics: étude critique et administrative. Paris, Picard, 1942. 628p. **AG107**

Contains a detailed historical description of the official publications of France. Those of a few of the major countries of the world—e.g., United States, Great Britain, the Netherlands, Italy, and Germany—are briefly noted. Z7164.G7D3

France. Journal officiel de la République Française. Ed. complete. 1870– . **AG108**

Preceded by: *Gazette nationale, ou Moniteur universel*, 1789–1810; *Moniteur universel, journal officiel*, 1811–68; *Journal officiel de l'Empire Français*, 1869–4 Sept. 1870.

From 1881, in several parts, the main ones being: (1) Lois et décrets; (2) Débats parlementaires: (a) Sénat, and (b) Assemblée Nationale; (3) Documents administratifs; (4) Impressions; (5) Avis et rapports du Conseil Economique et Social.

Designations vary.

Appears daily except Mondays and holidays; contains texts of national laws and decrees, important administrative orders and proclamations, and parliamentary debates and committee reports.

Indexes (Tables) published annually.

For more complete information, *see* Westfall's guide (below).

Westfall, Gloria. French official publications. Oxford, etc. Pergamon Pr., [1980]. 209p. il. (Guides to official pubns., v.6) **AG109**

Offers a survey of French official publishing, with discussion of official publications and their issuing bodies and the problems of bibliographic control, dissemination, and acquisition of French government documents. Attention is given to the publishing history of various series and to available guides, indexes and bibliographies. Devotes a separate chapter to the *Journal officiel*. Indexed.

Z2169.W47

GAMBIA

See Sierra Leone and Gambia.

GERMANY

Childs, James Bennett. German Federal Republic official publications, 1949–1957, with inclusion of preceding zonal official publications; a survey. Wash., Lib. of Congress, Reference Dept., Serial Div., 1958. 2v. in 1 (887p.). **AG110**

Contents: v.1, Bundespräsident—Bundesministerium der Justiz; v.2, Bundesministerium für das Post- und Fernmeldewesen—Zonal period.

Describes the agencies of the Federal Republic and of the zonal organization with lists of their publications. Those of the member states are not included. Both serial and monographic publications are listed with indication of Library of Congress holdings as of Oct. 1957. Z663.44.G4

Deutsche Bibliographie: Verzeichnis amtlicher Druckschriften, 1957/58– . Frankfurt a. M., Buchhändler-Vereinigung, 1962– . Biennial. **AG111**

Lists official publications of the government—legislative bodies and institutions—as well as publications of semiofficial institutions of the German Federal Republic and West Berlin. Z2229.D48

Leipzig. Deutsche Bücherei. Monatliches Verzeichnis der reichsdeutschen amtlichen Druckschriften . . . v.1–17, no.6, 1928–1944. Berlin, Reichs- und Staatsverlag GmbH., 1928–44. 17v. **AG112**

Z2229.A15

GHANA

Witherell, Julian W. and **Lockwood, Sharon B.** Ghana; a guide to official publications, 1872–1968. Wash., General Reference and Bibliography Div., Reference Dept., Lib. of Congress, 1969. 110p. **AG113**

Includes "publications of the Gold Coast (1872–1957) and Ghana (1957–68) and a selection of British Government documents relating specifically to the Gold Coast, Ghana, and British Togoland. Also included are League of Nations and United Nations publications on British Togoland. The emphasis of the guide is on official documents held by the Library of Congress and other American libraries represented in the National Union Catalog."—*Pref.*

Z3785.W5

GREAT BRITAIN

Guides

Bond, Maurice F. Guide to the records of Parliament. London, H.M.S.O., 1971. 352p. **AG114**

". . . describes the complete range of records preserved within the Palace of Westminster: the records of both Houses of Parliament; all documents which have been presented to the two Houses or purchased by them; and the papers which have accumulated in the various Parliamentary and non-Parliamentary offices of the Palace." —*Pref.* Deals with both manuscript and printed records. Includes historical notes pertinent to the various types of records. Indexed.

CD1063.B63

Butcher, David. Official publications in Britain. London, Bingley, [1983]. 161p. **AG115**

Aims to provide "a concise and up-to-date introduction to the full range of current official publishing" (*Pref.*), including official publishing activity of government departments, national bodies, and local authorities as well as H.M.S.O. Includes a chapter on bibliographic control of government publications and one on the selection, acquisition, and exploitation of official publications in libraries. Bibliographic references; index. Z2009.B93

British Library. Official Publications Library. Check list of British official serial publications. Ed. 7– . [London], The British Lib., [1975–]. Irregular. (11th ed., 1980) **AG116**

1st–6th eds. (1967–72) issued by the British Museum State Paper Room.

A listing of serial publications of the British government. Listing is by title, except in cases where the issuing body is considered an essential part of the title—e.g., annual reports, bulletins, etc.—and is entered first. Indicates issuing body, availability, frequency, latest part received in the British Library. Z2009.B87

Ford, Percy and **Ford, Grace.** A guide to parliamentary papers: what they are; how to find them; how to use them. 3d ed. Shannon, Ire., Irish Univ. Pr., 1972. 87p.   **AG117**

1st ed. 1955.

A useful introductory guide, giving a brief history and description of the contents of the papers and indexes. The appendix includes notes on collections of papers, and lists of indexes, catalogs, and official guides to sources.   Z2009.A1F6

Ollé, James G. An introduction to British government publications. 2d ed., rev. and enl. London, Assoc. of Asst. Librarians, 1973. 175p.   **AG118**

1st ed. 1965.

Informative chapters dealing with the government publishers, parliamentary and non-parliamentary publications, examples of government publications, methods of tracing and acquiring these publications, the publications of Northern Ireland, and government publications in libraries.   Z2009.O4

Pemberton, John E. British official publications. 2d rev. ed. Oxford, Pergamon, [1973]. 328p.   **AG119**

1st ed. 1971.

A detailed description and explanation of the various categories of British government publications, including a chapter on non-HMSO official publications. Specimen pages from the more important items are reproduced. Includes numerous useful tables: Concordance of command papers, 1833–1972; Alphabetical list of royal commissions, 1900–72; Table of regnal years; Select alphabetical list of departmental committees, working parties, tribunals of inquiry, etc., 1900–72.   Z2009.P45

Richard, Stephen. Directory of British official publications: a guide to sources. 2d ed. London, Mansell, [1984]. 431p.   **AG120**

1st ed. 1981.

". . . attempts to solve problems facing librarians, members of the public and booksellers who find considerable difficulty not only in hearing of official publications that are of interest . . . but in obtaining copies of known publications."—*Introd.* Not a bibliography of official publications, but a directory of the organizations which issue and distribute them. Organizations are grouped geographically (i.e., United Kingdom, Great Britain, England and Wales; Northern Ireland; Scotland, etc.) then by type (central government; libraries, museums, galleries; research council establishments, etc.). Entries provide information on the types of publications issued, the subjects covered, and availability of the publications. Indexed.   Z2009.R533

Rodgers, Frank. A guide to British government publications. N.Y., H. W. Wilson, 1980. 750p.   **AG121**

A guide to British parliamentary and other government publications, giving an indication of the types of publications issued by each department or agency and some background information on the issuing body itself. In three main sections—General; Parliamentary; Executive agencies—with the publishing activities of the various government departments serving as the organizational framework. "While the main focus is on central departments, a fairly liberal interpretation has been made of the status of other official and quasi-official bodies, so as to include many of the committees, boards, councils and other agencies active as publishers."—*Introd.* The author's 1967 *Guide to British parliamentary papers* served as the basis of some of the early chapters. Well indexed.

A very useful work surveying a vast range of publications in relatively brief space.   Z2009.R62

Bibliography

Rodgers, Frank. Serial publications in the British parliamentary papers, 1900–1968; a bibliography. Chicago, Amer. Lib. Assoc., 1971. 146p.   **AG122**

Lists some 1,300 serial publications which have appeared in the House of Commons Sessional Papers since 1900. Arranged by issuing agency, with useful historical notes on the principal agencies.   Z2009.R63

Catalogs and indexes
18th century

Gt.Brit. Parliament. House of Commons. Catalogue of parliamentary reports and a breviate of their contents, arranged under heads according to the subjects, 1696–1834. [London, 1836]. 220p. (Repr.: Oxford, Blackwell, 1953)   **AG123**

Indexes the "1st series" of parliamentary reports (15v.), the reports in the *Journals,* and those in the *Sessional papers,* 1801–34.

The reprint (entitled *Hansard's Catalogue and breviate . . .*) includes a "Select list of House of Lords papers not in this breviate" by P. Ford and G. Ford.   J301.K62

——— Catalogue of papers printed by order of the House of Commons from the year 1731 to 1800, in the custody of the Clerk of the Journals. [London], 1807. [v.p., i.e., 101p.] (Repr.: London, HMSO, 1953)   **AG124**

Consists of three chronological lists, each with its own subject index: (1) Bills; (2) Reports; and (3) Accounts and Papers.   J301.A2

——— House of Commons sessional papers of the eighteenth century. Ed. by Sheila Lambert. Wilmington, Del., Scholarly Resources, Inc., [1975]. 2v.   **AG125**

A session-by-session list; within each session entries are grouped as bills, reports, or accounts and papers. An index in v.2 (p. 425–83) provides a subject approach. The papers have been reproduced on microfilm by Scholarly Resources, Inc.   J301.K625

19th and 20th centuries

Catalogue of British official publications not published by HMSO. 1980– . Cambridge, Eng., Chadwyck-Healey, 1981– . Bimonthly, with annual cumulations.   **AG126**

"The majority of the publications listed in the Catalogue are available on microfiche from Chadwyck-Healey."—*t.p.*

A listing of the publications of some 350 organizations "financed or controlled completely or partially by the British Government, which are *not* published by Her Majesty's Stationery Office (HMSO)."—*Scope.* Includes periodicals, pamphlets, technical reports, memoranda, publicity material, audiovisual aids, etc. Entry is by issuing agency; subject index.

Gt.Brit. Parliament. House of Commons. General alphabetical index to the bills, reports, estimates, accounts and papers printed by order of the House of Commons and to the papers presented by command, 1801–1948/49. London, Stat. Off., 1853–1960. 4v.   **AG127**

Consists of the following four unnumbered volumes: (1) General index to the accounts and papers, reports of the commissioners, estimates, etc., 1801–1852; (2) Indexes to bills and reports, 1801–1852, in two sections: General index to the bills, and General index to the reports of select committees; (3) General index, 1852–1899; and (4) General index, 1900–1948/49.

An index to the documents included in the parliamentary papers of the House of Commons, not including the papers of the House of Lords except insofar as these are duplicated in the Commons papers, and not including the publications of the bureaus and departments. Arranged alphabetically by rather large subjects; does not include many analytical entries. Gives fairly full information about each paper, including its full title, date, and bill, document, or command number, and a reference to the year and volume of the sessional papers in which it is to be found, and the paging as made up for the House of Commons set.

For most purposes these indexes supersede the decennial and annual indexes for the periods covered, although the latter may still be useful for analyses of comprehensive series and for the numerical lists of command papers.

——— General alphabetical index to the bills, reports, estimates, accounts and papers printed by order of the House of Commons and to the papers presented by command, 1950–1958/59– . London, Stat. Off., 1963– .

Decennial cumulation of the annual indexes. Does not include the numerical lists. A continuation of the decennial indexes, 1870–1949, now superseded by the 50-year indexes.

——— List of the bills, reports, estimates, and accounts and papers printed by order of the House of Commons and of the papers presented by command ... with a general alphabetical index thereto, 1801– . London, Stat. Off., 1802– . Annual. **AG128**

Issued annually as the final volume for each session of the *Sessional papers* of the House of Commons.

From 1828, contains not only an index, but also a list of bills and papers in their numerical order; in 1834, a list of command papers is added, and, in 1867, a preliminary list showing the make-up of the set for each session.

The index section is superseded through 1958/59 by the 50-year and 10-year indexes described above, but the numerical lists are still the only ones available for the period prior to 1833. Command papers of the 1833–1961/62 period, asked for by number only, can be identified through Di Roma and Rosenthal's list (below).

Di Roma, Edward and **Rosenthal, Joseph A.**, comps. A numerical finding list of British command papers published 1833–1961/62. [N.Y.], New York Pub. Lib., 1967. 148p. **AG129**

Eliminates the need to consult the annual numerical lists (above) in order to find the appropriate volume in the collected series of British sessional papers. Z2009.D5

Gt.Brit. Parliament. House of Lords. General index to sessional papers printed by order of the House of Lords or presented by special command. London, Eyre, 1860–86. 3v. **AG130**

Publisher varies. v.1 repr.: London, Stat. Off., 1938.
Contents: v.1, 1801–59; v.2, 1859–70; v.3, 1871–85.
From 1886 to 1920, annual indexes were published. Subsequently the only lists printed are unnumbered annual lists of titles. J301.J6

Gt. Brit. Stationery Office. Catalogues and indexes of British government publications, 1920–1970. Bishops Stortford, Chadwyck-Healey, 1974. 5v. **AG131**

Reprint of the catalogs published by H.M.S.O., London.
Contents: v.1, Consolidated indexes to British government publications, 1936–1970; v.2, Annual catalogues of British government publications, 1920–1935; v.3, Annual catalogues of British government publications, 1936–1950; v.4, Annual catalogues of British government publications, 1951–1960; v.5, Annual catalogues of British government publications, 1961–1970. Z2009.G85

——— Cumulative index to the annual catalogues of Her Majesty's Stationery Office publications, 1922–1972. Comp. by Ruth Matteson Blackmore. Wash., D.C., Carrollton Pr., 1976. 2v. **AG132**

Represents "a merger of twenty-three separate annual and quinquennial indexes" *(User's guide)* into a single alphabet, giving references to entries in the original catalogs (AG133, AG134). Variant forms of subject headings used at different periods have not been reconciled and cross references from such forms are not always provided. Basic purpose of the cumulation was to provide an index to the microfilm edition of documents for the period published by United States Historical Documents Institute. Z2009.G85

——— Government publications, 1922– . London, Stat. Off., 1923– . Annual. **AG133**

Title varies: *Consolidated list of parliamentary and Stationery Office publications,* 1922; *Consolidated list of government publications,* 1923–50; *Government publications: consolidated list,* 1951–

53; *Government publications: catalogue,* 1954–55; *Catalogue of government publications,* 1956–71.

Continues the *Quarterly list . . . of official publications* (London, Stat. Off., 1897–1922).

——— Consolidated index to government publications, 1936/40– . London, Stat. Off., 1952– . Quinquennial. **AG134**

Five of these 5-year indexes have now appeared and consolidate the indexing of the annual lists, which are consecutively paged in anticipation of the publication of the indexes. Z2009.G822

——— Government publications monthly list. London, Stat. Off. Monthly. **AG135**

Intended primarily as sales catalogs, these are superseded by *Government publications* (AG133).

——— The sale catalogues of British government publications, 1836–1921. Dobbs Ferry, N.Y., Oceana, 1977. 4v. **AG136**

Reprint of the catalogs published by H.M.S.O., London, 1836–1921.
Contents: v.1, 1836–1889; v.2, 1890–1900; v.3, 1901–1911; v.4, 1912–1921. Z2009.G85

Irish University Press. Checklist of British parliamentary papers in the Irish University Press 1000-volume series, 1801–1899. Shannon, Ire., Irish Univ. Pr., [1972]. 218p. **AG137**

Offers chronological and subject approaches to the contents of the selected papers reprinted in the IUP subject sets. Z2019.I73

Irish University Press series of British parliamentary papers. [General] index. Shannon, Irish Univ. Pr., [1968]. 8v. **AG138**

Title on spine: British parliamentary papers. Reprint edition.
Contents: v.1, 1696–1834, Hansard's Catalogue; v.2, 1801–1852, Reports of select committees; v.3, 1801–1852, Accounts and papers; v.4, 1852–1869, Bills, reports, estimates, accounts, and papers; v.5, 1801–1852, Bills, printed by order of the House of Commons; v.6, 1870–1879, Bills, reports, estimates, accounts, and papers; v.7, 1880–1889, Bills, reports, estimates, accounts, and papers; v.8, 1890–1899, Bills, reports, estimates, accounts, and papers.

A reprint of existing indexes (e.g., those noted in AG123, AG127), not new indexing prepared specifically for the Irish University Press "1000-volume series." On each index page there is "an overprinted heading at the top of the outside margin" *(verso of t.p.)* so that keying to the I.U.P. set can be added by hand or by pasting in slips supplied "from time to time" by the publisher. Z2019.I74

Select lists

Ford, Percy and **Ford, Grace.** Select list of British parliamentary papers, 1833–1899. Oxford, Blackwell, 1953. 165p. (Rev. repr.: Shannon, Irish Univ. Pr., 1969) **AG139**

Arranged by subject, with an alphabetical index. Includes the "reports and all other material issued by committees and commissions or similar bodies of investigation into economic, social and constitutional questions, and matters of law and administration."— *Introd.* Supplements the *Catalogue of parliamentary reports . . .* 1696–1834 (AG123). J301.M3

——— A breviate of parliamentary papers 1900–1916; the foundation of the welfare state. Oxford, Blackwell, 1957. 470p. (Rev. repr.: Shannon, Irish Univ. Pr., 1969) **AG140**

A guide, with abstracts, to 1,048 reports of British royal commissions and other committees of inquiry, in the fields of constitutional, economic, financial, and social policy and of legal administration. Arrangement is by broad subject field, with an outline of the subject classification, a detailed subject list of individual documents, and an index. The abstracts will be a useful supplement to small collections of parliamentary papers, as well as a guide to more complete sets. JN549.F59

—— A breviate of parliamentary papers, 1917–1939. Oxford, Blackwell, 1951; N.Y., Macmillan, 1952. 571p. (Rev. repr.: Shannon, Irish Univ. Pr., 1969) **AG141**

A guide to 1,200 reports selected and arranged as the one above. JN549.F6

—— A breviate of parliamentary papers, 1940–1954; war and reconstruction. Oxford, Blackwell, 1961. 515p. **AG142**

"Follows the same general pattern as the two previous breviates." —*Introd.* JN549.F62

—— and **Marshallsay, Diana.** Select list of British parliamentary papers, 1955–1964. Shannon, Irish Univ. Pr., [1970]. 117p. **AG143**

Follows the broad subject arrangement of the Fords' *Select list . . .* 1833–1899 (AG139) and the three breviates (above) to which it is the chronological successor.

Ford, Percy. Ford list of British parliamentary papers 1965–1974, together with specialist commentaries, ed. by Diana Marshallsay and J. H. Smith. Nendeln, Liechtenstein, KTO Pr., 1979. 452p. **AG144**

Chronological successor to the Fords' *Select list* (AG139), the three breviates, and Ford and Marshallsay's *Select list* (AG143). Broad subject arrangement; subject/title index and chairman/author index. Z2009.A1F59

Richard, Stephen. British government publications; an index to chairmen and authors. London, Lib. Assoc., 1974–[82]. 3v. **AG145**

Contents: v.1, 1800–1899; [v.2], 1900–1940; v.3, 1941–1978.

v.1 (publ. 1982) has subtitle: An index to chairmen of committees and commissions of inquiry. v.3 (also publ. 1982) is a cumulation of A. M. Morgan's index covering 1941–66 (2d ed. 1973) and A. M. Morgan and L. R. Stephen's index for 1967–71 (publ. 1976), plus additional indexing through 1978.

Provides access to the many British government reports popularly referred to by name of the chairman of the individual committee. In each volume listing is by name of chairman or author, with full citation to the report (including command number or reference to House of Lords papers as relevant). v.2 includes an "Alphabetical list of Royal Commissions and distinctive titles of committees, 1900–1940," with the name of the chairman indicated. Z2009.R53

Parliamentary debates

Gt. Brit. Parliament. Parliamentary debates, v.1–41 (1803–20); n.s. v.1–25 (1820–30); 3d ser. v.1–356 (1830–90/91); 4th ser. v.1–199 (1892–1908); 5th ser.: Commons, v.1– (1909–); Lords, v.1– (1909–). London, 1804– . **AG146**

Generally cited as *Hansard.* Publisher varies.

There is a general index to the 66v. of the 1st–2d series (London, Baldwin, 1834. 2v.); for series 3–5 the sessional indexes—sometimes in separate volumes, sometimes included in the last volume of debates of the session—must be used.

The 5th series is official and contains complete and verbatim reports of debates, and all division lists. The 1st–4th series were unofficial; their reports of debates are neither complete nor verbatim, and not all division lists are given in full. For an interesting account of parliamentary debates of the 19th to the 20th century *see* H. D. Jordan, "Reports of parliamentary debates 1803–1908," in *Economica* 11:437–49, Nov. 1931.

The period before 1803 is covered by Cobbett's *Parliamentary history of England from the earliest period to the year 1803* (London, Hansard, 1806–20. 36v.), which is, of course, a retrospective compilation rather than a current record. For an account of sources upon which it is based, or which are available for the early period, *see* "General collections of reports of parliamentary debates for the period since 1660," in: London. University. *Bulletin of the Institute of Historical Research* 10:171–77, Feb. 1933. J301.H22

INDIA

India. Parliament. Library. Abstracts of books, reports and articles. v.13– , Jan./Mar. 1975– . New Delhi, Parliament Lib., 1975– . Quarterly. **AG147**

Supersedes *Abstracts and index of reports and articles* (1963–Jan. 1975) which was formed by the merger of the *Abstracts of reports* (1955–62) and *Abstracts and index of articles* (1958–62), both of which were issued by the Indian Parliament's House of the People.

Abstracts are presented in a classed arrangement with subject and author indexes in each issue; no cumulation of the indexes. AS472.I44A27

Macdonald, Teresa. Union catalogue of the serial publications of the Indian government, 1858–1947, held in libraries in Britain. [London], Mansell, 1973. 154p. **AG148**

At head of title: Centre of South Asian Studies, University of Cambridge.

"The scope of the catalogue is limited to English-language material published in India, by the Central or Provincial Governments, and the Governments of the major Princely states, and appearing within the period 1858 to 1947."—*Introd.* Arrangement is by subject within sections for Central government, Provinces, etc. Z3205.M15

Singh, Mohinder. Government publications of India; a survey of their nature, bibliographical control and distribution systems (including over 1500 titles). Delhi, Metropolitan Book Co., [1967]. 270p. **AG149**

Chapters are devoted to the individual ministries and the major departments and agencies issuing publications. Z3205.S63

IRELAND

Maltby, Arthur and **McKenna, Brian.** Irish official publications: a guide to Republic of Ireland papers, with a breviate of reports 1922–1972. Oxford, etc., Pergamon, [1980]. 377p. (Guides to official pubns., v.7) **AG150**

A companion to Maltby's *Government of Northern Ireland* (AG151) and *Ireland in the nineteenth century* (1979). The "guide" section (p.1–22) precedes the "breviate" which is topically arranged. Name and subject indexes. Z2035.M345

IRELAND, NORTHERN

Maltby, Arthur. The government of Northern Ireland, 1922–72; a catalogue and breviate of Parliamentary papers. Dublin, Irish Univ. Pr.; N.Y., Barnes & Noble, 1974. 235p. **AG151**

Patterned after the Ford breviates for British Parliamentary papers (AG139–AG144). Aims "to catalogue and summarize the principal Northern Ireland papers for the fifty-year span from March 1922, the date of the first command paper, to the time of the prorogation of Stormont in March 1972."—*Introd.* Entries are grouped in categories such as: Machinery of government, National finance, Agriculture and food supply, Transport, Labour, Social security, Housing, Social problems. Indexed. Z2035.M34

ISRAEL

Israel. Ganzakh ha medina veha-sifriyah. Israel government publications, 1952– . Jerusalem, Govt. Printer, 1952– . Frequency varies. **AG152**

Title also in Hebrew.

Volumes for 1952–56 comp. by the State Archives and Library and publ. under title *List of government publications.*

Separate sections for European-language publications and for Hebrew publications. Z3477.A56

JAPAN

Kokuritsu Kokkai Toshokan, Tokyo. Shibu Toshokanbu. List of Japanese government publications in European languages, 1945–1958. Rev. and enl. ed. Tokyo, 1959. 82p. **AG153**

Titles and abstracts are in European languages.

Includes publications of all government agencies, as well as those of the Japan Monopoly Corporation, the Japanese National Railways, the Nippon Telegraph and Telephone Public Corporation, and the Bank of Japan; also a list of SCAP (Supreme Commander for the Allied Powers) publications, 1946–52, owned by the American Embassy Library and the National Diet Library.

Kuroki, Tsutomu. An introduction to Japanese government publications. Tr. by Masako Kishi. Oxford, Pergamon, [1981]. 204p. (Guides to official pubns., v.10) **AG154**

A guide to the contents and characteristics of Japanese government publications. Pt.I describes the structure of government publications; pt.II discusses publication and distribution; pt.III explains retrieval of government documents; pt.IV contains an annotated bibliography of government publications. Indexed. Z3305.K8713

U.S. Library of Congress. Japanese national government publications in the Library of Congress: a bibliography. Thaddeus Y. Ohta, comp. Wash., Govt. Prt. Off., 1981. 402p. **AG155**

A guide to the extensive collection of Japanese government publications in the Library of Congress. 3,376 title entries arranged in four main sections: (1) legislative branch; (2) executive branch; (3) judicial branch; and (4) public corporations and research institutes. A high percentage of entries is for serial publications; some 350 bilingual or English-language publications are included. Index of romanized Japanese titles and one of non-Japanese titles. Z3305.U54

KENYA

Howell, John Bruce. Kenya: subject guide to official publications. Wash., Lib. of Congress, 1978. 423p. **AG156**

A subject guide to official publications of Kenya from the period 1886 to 1975. Included are citations to documents by the Republic of Kenya (1963–75), the Kenya Colony and Protectorate, (1920–1963), and the East Africa Protectorate (1895–1920), Great Britain (1886–1975), and the East African Community and its predecessors (1926–75). Subject arrangement follows that of *Africa south of the Sahara; index to periodical literature* (1971; DD86). Indexed. Locates copies. Z3587.H68

LATIN AMERICA

See also under names of individual countries.

Latin American serial documents: a holdings list. Comp. by Rosa Quintero Mesa. Ann Arbor, Mich., Univ. Microfilms, Xerox Education Group, 1968–77. 12v. **AG157**

Contents: v.1, Colombia; v.2, Brazil; v.3, Cuba; v.4, Mexico; v.5, Argentina; v.6, Bolivia; v.7, Chile; v.8, Ecuador; v.9, Paraguay; v.10, Peru; v.11, Uruguay; v.12, Venezuela.

Each volume provides a bibliography with locations for as many serial documents as could be identified for each country from the time of its formation or date of independence. Lists are based on the holdings of the University of Florida Library, but each has been checked in those libraries which once had Farmington Plan assignments for the area in question. In addition, individual lists have been checked in other libraries having special collections or special interest in a given country.

U.S. Library of Congress. A guide to the official publications of the other American republics. Wash., Govt. Prt. Off., 1945–49. v.1–19. (Latin Amer. ser.) (Repr.: N.Y., Johnson, 1964) **AG158**

James B. Childs, gen. ed. 1945; Henry V. Besso, gen. ed. 1946–49. Contents: v.1, Argentina. 1945. 124p.; v.2, Bolivia. 1945. 66p.; v.3, Brazil, comp. by John De Noia. 1948 (1949). 223p.; v.4, Chile, comp. by Otto Neuburger. 1947. 94p.; v.5, Colombia, [comp. by] James B. Childs. 1948. 89p.; v.6, Costa Rica, comp. by Henry V. Besso. 1947. 92p.; v.7, Cuba. 1945. 40p.; v.8, Dominican Republic, comp. by John De Noia. 1947. 40p.; v.9, Ecuador, comp. by John De Noia. 1947. 56p.; v.10, El Salvador, comp. by John De Noia. 1947. 64p.; v.11, Guatemala, comp. by Henry V. Besso. 1947. 88p.; v.12, Haiti. 1947. 25p.; v.13, Honduras. 1947. 31p.; v.14, Nicaragua, comp. by John De Noia. 1947. 33p.; v.15, Panama, comp. by John De Noia. 1947. 34p.; v.16, Paraguay, [comp. by] James B. Childs. 1947. 61p.; v.17, Peru, comp. by John De Noia. 1948 (1949). 90p.; v.18, Uruguay, comp. by John De Noia and Glenda Crevenna. 1948 (1949). 91p.; v.19, Venezuela, comp. by Otto Neuburger. 1948 (1949). 59p.

A series of guides, each of which gives information about general publications, including official gazettes, session laws, codes, constitution, etc., followed by the publications of the legislative, executive, and judicial branches. Z1605.U64

MALAYSIA

Malaysia. Jabatan Cetak Kerajaan (Sabah). Senarai penerbitan-penerbitan lengkap. Kota Kinabalu, Sabah, Jabatan, 1982?– . Annual. **AG159**

In Malay and English.

Preceded by a quarterly *Current list of publications* (Kuala Lumpur, Govt. Prt. Dept., 1955?–66); an annual *Senarai penerbitan lengkap: Current list of publications* (Kuala Lumpur, Jabatan Chetak Kerajaan, 1965–75); and an annual *Senarai penerbitan: List of publications* (Kuala Lumpur, Jabatan Cetak Kerajaan, 1976?–81?). A classified list. Z3247.M356a

MAURITIUS

Deerpalsingh, S. A bibliography of Mauritian government publications, 1955–1978. Moka, Mauritius, Mahatma Gandhi Institute Library, 1979. 61p. **AG160**

Covers government publications of the pre-independence period (1955–68) as well as those published after independence (1968–78). In two sections: (1) serials; (2) non-serial publications. Indexed.

MEXICO

Fernández de Zamora, Rosa María. Las publicaciones oficiales de México; guía de publicaciones periódicas y seriadas, 1937–1970. México, Universidad Nacional Autónoma de México, Instituto de Investigaciones Sociales, 1977. 238p. (Univ. Nacional Autónoma de México. Inst. de Investigaciones Bibliográficas. Ser. guías, 5) **AG161**

Continues *Mexican government publications* by A. M. Ker (Wash., 1940).

Introductory chapters on official publications, their production and distribution, are followed by detailed listings of official serial publications for the period indicated. The lists are arranged by issuing agency and include contents notes for many of the series. Index of subjects and titles.   Z1419.F4

NETHERLANDS

Bibliografie van in Nederland verschenen officiële en semi-officiële uitgaven. v.1–48 (1929–76). 'sGravenhage, Koninklijke Bibliotheek, 1929–76. 48v. Annual.   **AG162**

Title varies.

Lists government publications by agency. Includes provincial publications. Personal name and subject index.

Continued by: Z2439.H14

Bibliografie van in Nederland verschenen officiële uitgaven bij rijksoverheid en provinciale besturen. v.49– (1977–). 's-Gravenhage, Koninklijke Bibliotheek, 1978– . Annual.   **AG163**

NEW ZEALAND

Guide to New Zealand information sources. Pt.V: Official publications, comp. by C. L. Carpenter. Palmerston North, N.Z., Massey Univ. Lib., 1980. 41p. (Massey Univ. Lib. ser. 15)   **AG164**

In addition to dealing with current official publications and early provincial papers, there are sections on British and Australian parliamentary papers relating to New Zealand and on New Zealand statistical publications.

NIGERIA

Stanley, Janet. Nigerian government publications, 1966–1973; a bibliography. Ile-Ife, Nigeria, Univ. of Ife Pr., [1975]. 193p.   **AG165**

Aims "to include all publications of the federal government of Nigeria, the four regional governments (January 1966 to May 1967) and the twelve state governments (June 1967 to December 1973)." —*Introd.* Serves as a continuation of S. B. Lockwood's *Nigeria: a guide to official publications* (below).   Z3597.S73

U.S. Library of Congress. African Section. Nigeria; a guide to official publications. [Rev. ed.] Comp. by Sharon Burdge Lockwood. Wash., Lib. of Congress, 1966. 166p.   **AG166**

A revision of the guide comp. by Helen F. Conover and publ. 1959 under title: *Nigerian official publications, 1869–1959.* This edition covers publications of Nigerian governments 1861–1965.   Z3553.N5U48

NORWAY

Oslo. Universitet. Bibliotek. Bibliografi over Norges offentlige publikasjoner, 1956– . Oslo, Universitetsforlaget, 1957– . v.[1]– . Annual.   **AG167**

"Comprises both government publications and publications edited with grants from government."—*Note.*   Z2599.O8

PAKISTAN

Pakistan. Catalogue of the government of Pakistan publications. 1947?– . Karachi, Manager of Publ., 1947?– . Irregular.   **AG168**

Arranged by departments; lists publications available for sale. Includes a separate list of periodicals.

1962 (with supplement corrected up to 5-7-66) last published? An unofficial cumulation is provided by: Z3195.A22

Moreland, George B. and **Siddiqui, Akhtar H.** Publications of the government of Pakistan, 1947–1957. [Karachi], Inst. of Public and Business Admin., Univ. of Karachi, 1958. 187p.   **AG169**

Cumulates and indexes the irregularly published issues of the *Catalogue of government of Pakistan publications* (above), adding some additional listings.   Z3195.M6

Siddiqui, Akhtar H. Pakistan government publications: their nature, content, production, and distribution. [Lahore], Vanguard Books, [1981]. 97p.   **AG170**

Describes types of government publications, their bibliographic control, acquisition, production and distribution; includes brief descriptions of the various agencies and the nature and content of their publications. Also lists government periodical publications.   Z3195.S5

PAPUA NEW GUINEA

Government publications of Papua and New Guinea, no.1/2– , Jan./June 1968– . Port Moresby, New Guinea, Administrative College, 1968– . Quarterly.   **AG171**

Subtitle: A quarterly list of titles received by the Library of the Administrative College of Papua and New Guinea.

A listing by issuing agency. 1971 last published?   Z4812.G66

PHILIPPINES

Philippine Library and Museum, Manila. Legislative Reference Division. Checklist of publications of the government of the Philippine Islands, Sept. 1, 1900 to Dec. 31, 1917, comp. by Emma O. Elmer. Manila, 1918. 288p.   **AG172**

Continued by:

Bibliographical Society of the Philippines. Checklist of Philippine government documents, 1917–1949, comp. by Consolacion B. Rebadavia . . . Quezon City, Univ. of the Philippines Lib., 1960. 817p.   **AG173**

A retrospective bibliography of more than 6,000 items.   Z3295.B52

———— Checklist of Philippine government documents, 1950. Wash., Lib. of Congress, 1953. 62p.

755 numbered items.   Z3295.B5

Philippines (Republic). Bureau of Public Libraries. Philippine government publications. v.1, no.1, Jan. 1958–59.   **AG174**

Frequency varies: monthly or bimonthly.

The first current record of the government publications of the Republic of the Philippines.

Superseded by:

Checklist of Philippine government publications. 1961–72/73. [Manila], 1962–74. Annual.   **AG175**

At head of title: Republic of the Philippines, Department of

Education, National Library, Public Documents, Exchange and Gifts Division.

Listing is by issuing agency. Not indexed. 1962–63 included only items available for exchange.

Continued in part by:

Checklist of exchange materials. The National Library. 1974/75– . Manila, Public Documents, Exchange and Gifts Division, 1975– . Annual. **AG176**

A main-entry listing of government publications available on exchange. No index.

Quezon, Philippines. University of the Philippines. Institute of Public Administration. Library. List of Philippine government publications, 1945–1958, comp. by Andrea C. Ponce and Jacinta C. Yatco. Manila, 1959–60. 2v. **AG177**

Contents: pt.1, Publications of agencies under the Dept. of Agriculture and Natural Resources, Dept. of Commerce and Industry, Dept. of Education, and Dept. of Labor; pt.2, Publications of agencies under the Depts. of Finance, Foreign Affairs, Health, and Justice, comp. by Jacenta y Ingles and Ursula G. Picachi.

Z3295.Q5

THE RHODESIAS AND NYASALAND

U.S. Library of Congress. African Section. The Rhodesias and Nyasaland; a guide to official publications. Comp. by Audrey A. Walker. Wash., General Reference and Bibliography Div., Reference Dept., Lib. of Congress, 1965. 285p. **AG178**

Covers "as comprehensively as possible, the published records of administration in the former Federation of Rhodesia and Nyasaland and in the three territorial governments of Northern Rhodesia, Southern Rhodesia, and Nyasaland from 1889 to 1963."—*Pref.*

Z3573.R5U5

Willson, Francis Michael Glenn and **Passmore, Gloria C.** Catalogue of the parliamentary papers of Southern Rhodesia, 1899–1953. Salisbury, S. Rhodesia, Dept. of Government, Univ. College of Rhodesia and Nyasaland, 1965. 484p. **AG179**

"A catalogue of most of the papers [i.e., reports and papers, other than legislative documents] laid before the Legislative Council and Legislative Assembly of Southern Rhodesia during the years from the first meeting of the Legislative Council in 1899 until the creation of the Federation of Rhodesia and Nyasaland in 1953."—*p.v.*

Continued by: JQ2921.A23

Wilding, Norman W. Catalogue of the parliamentary papers of Southern Rhodesia and Rhodesia, 1954–1970, and the Federation of Rhodesia and Nyasaland, 1954–1963. Salisbury, University College of Rhodesia, 1970. 161p. (Univ. College of Rhodesia. Source book, no.6) **AG180**

In two sections: (1) Southern Rhodesia and Rhodesia; (2) Federation of Rhodesia and Nyasaland. Within each section, numbered series, series of select and standing committees, and petitions are first listed in chronological order, followed by a classified listing of those items plus additional papers not belonging to the preceding categories. Indexed. Z3573.R5

SIERRA LEONE AND GAMBIA

U.S. Library of Congress. African Section. Official publications of Sierra Leone and Gambia, comp. by Audrey A. Walker. Wash., General Reference and Bibliography Div., Reference Dept., Lib. of Congress, 1963. 92p. **AG181**

A listing of some 700 titles, 500 having to do with Sierra Leone and 200 with Gambia. Historical notes accompany each section.

Z3533.S5U5

SOMALILAND

U.S. Library of Congress. General Reference and Bibliography Division. Official publications of Somaliland, 1941–1959; a guide, comp. by Helen F. Conover. Wash., 1960. 41p. **AG182**

Has separate sections for Somaliland under Italian administration, British Somaliland, and French Somaliland. Subject index. Lists about 170 titles, including a bibliography of chief sources.

Z3516.U5

SWAZILAND

Pretoria. State Library. Swaziland official publications, 1880–1972; a bibliography of the original and microfiche edition. Pretoria, State Lib., 1975. 190p. (*Its* Bibliographies, no.18) **AG183**

A classed bibliography, with the first four sections "arranged in a sort of logical development-of-the-Territory order: historical background, concessions, constitutional development and parliament." —*Notes.* Includes both official and semi-official publications. Indexed.

SWEDEN

Sweden. Riksdagen. Bibliotek. Årsbibliografi över Sveriges offentliga publikationer, utg. av Riksdagsbiblioteket. 1931/33– . Stockholm, Beckmans, 1934– . Annual. **AG184**

A listing by department or issuing agency, with personal name and subject indexes. Z2629.S94

SWITZERLAND

Bern. Schweizerische Landesbibliothek. Bibliographie der schweizerischen Amtsdruckschriften. Bibliographie des publications officielles suisses. Bd.1– , 1946– . Bern, 1947– . **AG185**

Frequency varies; recent issues cover two years.

Originally this listing of official publications was drawn from *Das schweizer Buch* (AA1129). Beginning with Bd. 22/23 (1967/68) the list attempts to be as comprehensive as possible in its coverage of monographic publications of the cantons and municipalities of Switzerland as well as of federal government publications regularly listed in the national bibliography. Z2779.B4

TUNIS

Tunis. Dar al-Kutub al-Qawmiyah. Récapitulation des périodiques officiels parus en Tunisie de 1881 à 1955, par Hélène Pilipenko et Jean Rousset de Pina. Tunis, 1956. 108p. **AG186**

At head of title: Royaume de Tunis, Ministère de l'Éducation Nationale, Bibliothèque Nationale de Tunisie.

A detailed listing of official periodical publications arranged by issuing agency, with title, name, and agency indexes.

Z6960.T8T8

UGANDA

Gray, Beverly Ann. Uganda: subject guide to official publications. Wash., Lib. of Congress, 1977. 271p.   **AG187**

Comp. in the African Section, General Reference and Bibliography Division, Library of Congress.

A topical listing of "official publications of Uganda for the period 1893 to 1974. Every attempt was made to include documents issued by Uganda, Great Britain, and the East African Common Services Organization and its predecessors before October 1962, and by Uganda, the East African Common Services Organization, and the East African Community after independence. Included also are publications prepared by organizations and individuals on behalf of the Uganda government."—*Pref.* Indexed.   Z3586.G7

UNION OF SOVIET SOCIALIST REPUBLICS

Official publications of the Soviet Union and Eastern Europe, 1945–1980; a select annotated bibliography. Ed. by Gregory Walker. [London], Mansell, [1982]. 620p.   **AG188**

Covers Albania, Bulgaria, Czechoslovakia, German Democratic Republic, Hungary, Yugoslavia, Poland, Romania, and the U.S.S.R., each country being dealt with by an individual contributor. Each chapter has an introduction outlining postwar political and administrative developments and the state of official publishing. "Official publications" has been interpreted broadly and contributors "were asked to include what they regarded as the most important material within the general guidelines for coverage . . ., and to give details of any existing bibliographies which offered useful data on official publications."—*Pref.* Within country sections publications are grouped topically under such headings as: Constitutional documents, General party documents, General statistics, Military affairs, Economic affairs. "Where documents are available in Western published sources, these are stated."—*Introd.* The lists of bibliographies and general reference works are not limited to official publications of the country concerned. The U.S.S.R. is accorded much fuller treatment than the other countries. Indexed.   Z2483.W34

URUGUAY

Musso Ambrosi, Luis Alberto. Bibliografía del Poder Legislativo desde sus comienzos hasta el ano 1965. Montevideo, [Centro de Estudios del Pasado Uruguayo], 1967. 236p.   **AG189**

A bibliography of the official publications of Uruguay's National Congress from 1830 through 1965, plus some earlier publications of provincial bodies for 1825–30.

VENEZUELA

Instituto Autónomo Biblioteca Nacional. Sección de Publicaciones Oficiales. Catálogo de publicaciones oficiales 1840–1977. Por Beatriz Martínez de Cartay. Mérida, Imprenta Oficial del Estado Mérida, 1978. 445p.   **AG190**

A listing by ministry or other issuing body of Venezuelan official publications on file at the Biblioteca Nacional. Full bibliographical citations are given; indexed.   Z1919.I55

A H

Dissertations

❖Dissertations for the doctorate form a special class of publications, and catalogs or bibliographies of these dissertations, both American and foreign, assume definite importance in university, reference, or special libraries where much use is made of thesis material. As the doctor's degree is usually given only for original work, and as each doctoral dissertation should deal with some aspect of a subject not previously treated, the value of a dissertation to the reader interested in the subject is obvious.

While some dissertations are issued by commercial publishers, and some are privately printed, many are available only in typewritten form or on microfilm. Only those issued by commercial publishers appear in the trade bibliographies; the others are listed in special bibliographies of dissertations, of which there are various types:

I. National
  A. Completed
    1. General—covering the dissertations of all the universities of a given country
      a) Cumulative—covering a number of years
      b) Annual
    2. Subject—covering the theses of all universities in a given country in a particular subject field
  B. In progress

II. Individual university
  A. Lists
  B. Abstracts

In addition, there are a few subject lists which attempt international coverage for a given field.

These bibliographies are of primary importance in research libraries: (1) to show the student trying to select a thesis subject whether that subject has already been treated or is being worked on; (2) to show at what university a particular dissertation was written; (3) to show the acquisitions department whether a publication not listed in the trade lists is a dissertation; (4) to show the research worker what material has been written on very special subjects; (5) to provide biographical data about the authors of dissertations, since this information is included in some of the lists.

The general practice used to be to distribute printed dissertations to university libraries and to special libraries interested in particular subjects. Now most dissertations are submitted in manuscript and are available, on interlibrary loan or for purchase, either on microfilm or in Xerox print (*see Dissertation abstracts international,* AH19). Many of these may be purchased from University Microfilms International, Ann Arbor, Mich., but in some cases it is necessary to write directly to the university where the dissertation was written.

Publication of the *Comprehensive dissertation index* (AH15) has greatly simplified the bibliographic search for dissertations, and that set obviates the need to check some of the older bibliographies listed in this section. However, because *CDI* is still likely to be found only in the larger academic and research libraries, the older works will continue to be useful.

For current work, especially in university libraries where it is essential to keep informed of research being done, the various lists of "dissertations in progress" are very useful.

In the following lists only the national bibliographies of completed dissertations are included, except (1) in a few cases, e.g., Germany, where extensive lists of individual universities precede the years covered by the national lists; and (2) in the case of small countries, e.g., Norway, where there is no national list, and therefore the list of the main university serves as such. Borchardt and Thawley's *Guide to the availability of theses* (AB273) emphasizes the availability of theses and dissertations through interlibrary loan, photocopying, on-site use, etc., at institutions in some 85 countries, but includes reference to each country's "national thesis bibliography," if any.

Abstracts and lists from individual universities will at times provide information not found in the general bibliographies. Reynold's *Guide to theses and dissertations* (AH11) provides an international listing of bibliographies of dissertations. An old, but occasionally useful list of bibliographies from American universities is Thomas R. Palfrey and Henry E. Coleman's *Guide to bibliographies of theses, United States and Canada* (2d ed. Chicago, Amer. Lib. Assoc., 1940); a supplement by Ralph P. Rosenberg appeared in *Bulletin of bibliography* 18:181–82, 201–203 (Sept./Dec. 1945–Jan./Apr. 1946).

For lists of dissertations—both completed and in progress—in particular subjects, *see* under subject.

GUIDES AND MANUALS

❖This section includes a number of aids for writers of undergraduate research papers as well as guides and manuals relating to doctoral research and preparation of the dissertation.

Allen, George R. The graduate students' guide to theses and dissertations; a practical manual for writing and research. San Francisco, Jossey-Bass, 1973. 108p. **AH1**

Using a question-and-answer format, the author considers seven steps in the research process: selecting a research topic, getting a research committee, preparing a research proposal, collecting data, analyzing data, writing the final report, and defending the research effort. Generalized answers are given, but consideration is given to practices which vary from school to school, etc. A useful and informative guide. LB2369.A595

Campbell, William Giles, Ballou, Stephen Vaughan and **Slade, Carole.** Form and style: theses, reports, term papers. 6th ed. Boston, Houghton Mifflin, [1982]. 210p. **AH2**

1st ed., 1939, had title *A form book for thesis writing.*
A guide for the writer and the typist, with sample pages illustrating style and placement of footnotes, bibliographic citations, etc., according to both the MLA and University of Chicago style manuals. Indexed. LB2369.C3

Dugdale, Kathleen. A manual of form for theses and term reports. 5th rev. ed. Bloomington, Ind., 1972. 59p. **AH3**

1st ed. 1950.
Designed primarily for students, but also useful to "those preparing manuscripts for publication and for those writing research reports concerning governmental, industrial, or scientific research."—*Foreword.* Includes many sample pages. LB2369.D8

Hurt, Peyton. Bibliography and footnotes; a style manual for students and writers. 3d ed. rev. and enl. by Mary L. Hurt Richmond. Berkeley, Univ. of California Pr., 1968. 163p. **AH4**

1st ed. 1936.
Very useful for form of footnotes, etc., with a good section on citations to government documents and publications of international organizations. Z1001.H95

Madsen, David. Successful dissertations and theses. San Francisco, Jossey-Bass, 1983. 174p. **AH5**

"A guide to graduate student research from proposal to completion."—*verso of t.p.*
Offers practical information on the dissertation process; includes a sample proposal, sample pages, etc. LB2369.M32

Meyer, Michael. The Little, Brown guide to writing research papers. Boston, Little, Brown, [1982]. 241p. **AH6**

Intended "for both freshman English courses and upper division students who must write research papers for courses in a variety of disciplines."—*Pref.* Chapters include "Shaping the topic," "Researching the topic," "Using the sources," "Writing the drafts," etc. Gives attention to use of the library, note-taking, footnoting, bibliography. LB2369.M42

Modern Language Association of America. MLA handbook for writers of research papers. 2d ed. [by] Joseph Gibaldi, Walter S. Achtert. N.Y., The Association, 1984. 221p. **AH7**

1st ed. 1977.
Intended both as a classroom text and a reference tool, the handbook "describes a set of conventions governing the written presentation of research. The recommendations on the mechanics and format of the research paper reflect the practices recommended by the Modern Language Association . . . and required by college teachers throughout the United States and Canada."—*Pref.* This edition incorporates recent revisions in MLA style and has the undergraduate student as its primary audience. (The *MLA style sheet* [rev. 1970] is meant for literary and linguistic scholars who publish in learned journals.) Numerous examples; index. PE1478.M57

Turabian, Kate L. A manual for writers of term papers, theses, and dissertations. 4th ed. Chicago, Univ. of Chicago Pr., [1973]. 216p. **AH8**

1st ed. 1937.
A well-organized and widely used manual, primarily for the graduate student. LB2369.T8

——— Student's guide for writing college papers. 2d ed., rev. Chicago, Univ. of Chicago Pr., [1969]. 205p. **AH9**

1st ed. 1963.
Intended primarily for undergraduate use. LB2369.T82

Weidenborner, Stephen and **Caruso, Domenick.** Writing research papers; a guide to the process. N.Y., St. Martin's Pr., [1982]. 198p. il. **AH10**

Intended specifically for college freshmen; emphasis is on the process of producing a research paper and the steps that students find most difficult. Chapters conclude with review questions and exercises; two sample research papers are included. Indexed. LB1047.3.W44

BIBLIOGRAPHY

Bibliography of bibliography

Reynolds, Michael M. A guide to theses and dissertations; an annotated, international bibliography of bibliographies. Detroit, Gale, [1975]. 599p. **AH11**

"This bibliography is a retrospective international listing of bibliographies of theses and dissertations produced through 1973, which appear as separate listings."—*Introd.* Includes both serial and one-time publications. Subject arrangement, with indexes of institutions, of names and titles, and of specific subjects. A new edition was scheduled for 1985 publication by Oryx Pr., Phoenix.

Z5053.R49

International

See also AH19.

Dissertation abstracts international [Section] C: European abstracts. v.37, no.1– , Autumn 1976– . [Ann Arbor, Mich.], University Microfilms International, 1976– . 4 issues per yr.   **AH12**

Forms a third section of *Dissertation abstracts international* (AH19) and carries its numbering.

Subtitle: Abstracts of dissertations submitted for doctoral and post-doctoral degrees at European institutions.

Each issue follows the subject arrangement of sections A and B of *DAI,* with author and subject indexes. (Only the author index cumulates annually.) A full bibliographic citation to the dissertation is followed by an indication of the language of the work (if other than English), and a brief abstract; University Microfilms order number is given when the full text is available on demand from U.M.I.; for those not available on film a reference copy is usually located. Western European universities contribute the bulk of the listings (and the representation from some countries is disappointingly small). There is an ongoing effort to expand coverage and to increase the availability of the dissertations in microform.

LB2369.D47●

Oxford. University. Bodleian Library. Catalogus dissertationum academicarum quibus nuper aucta est Bibliotheca Bodleiana MDCCCXXXII. Oxford, Typ. Acad., 1834. 448p., 63p.   **AH13**

A listing of dissertations from various universities in the Bodleian Library in 1832.   Z921.O95D5

Paris. Bibliothèque Nationale. Dépt. des Imprimés. Catalogue des dissertations et écrits académiques provenant des échanges avec les universités étrangères et reçus par la Bibliothèque Nationale, 1882–1924. Paris, Klincksieck, 1884–1925. t.1–43.   **AH14**

Dissertations received by the Bibliothèque Nationale from European universities, arranged by university.   Z5053.P22

United States

Comprehensive dissertation index, 1861–1972. Ann Arbor, Mich., Xerox Univ. Microfilms, 1973. 37v.   **AH15**

Contents: v.1–4, Chemistry; v.5, Mathematics and statistics; v.6–7, Astronomy and physics; v.8–10, Engineering; v.11–13, Biological sciences; v.14, Health and environmental sciences; v.15, Agriculture; v.16, Geography and geology; v.17, Social sciences; v.18–19, Psychology; v.20–24, Education; v.25–26, Business and economics; v.27, Law and political science; v.28, History; v.29–30, Language and literature; v.31, Communication and the arts; v.32, Philosophy and religion; v.33–37, Author index.

A computer-generated index, by key words and authors, which attempts to list all dissertations accepted at universities of the United States during the long period indicated. (Numerous Canadian and other foreign universities are among the schools included, but no claim for completeness of listing is made for universities outside the United States.)

In effect supersedes the Library of Congress lists of American doctoral dissertations (AH16), the Wilson lists (AH17), and the various indexes to *Dissertation abstracts* (AH19). Also includes some dissertations not found in those lists because the data base embraces many published and unpublished lists provided by the

individual universities. (The editors note some conflicts and discrepancies resulting from reliance on these varied sources, but some errors and omissions have been corrected in the supplements; e.g., the 1978 supplement incorporated the entries for Harvard University dissertations from the 1927–33 period inadvertently omitted from the basic set.)

Within each subject volume the listing is alphabetical by keyword. Full citations appear in both the author and subject listings: these include complete title, author's full name if known, date, university, pagination when available, citation to *Dissertation abstracts* or other printed list, and University Microfilms publication number for dissertations which are available on microfilm from that agency.

Kept up-to-date by annual supplements which follow the arrangement of the basic set: Z5053.C64●

———— Supplement. 1973– . Ann Arbor, Mich., Univ. Microfilms Internat., 1974– . Annual.

A 5-year cumulation covering 1973–77 has been superseded by a 10-year cumulation (publ. 1984 in 38v.) covering 1973–82.

U.S. Library of Congress. Catalog Division. List of American doctoral dissertations printed in 1912–38. Wash., Govt. Prt. Off., 1913–39. 27v.   **AH16**

Contents of each volume: (1) Alphabetical list of theses printed during the year; (2) Classified list, arranged under the broad classes of the Library of Congress scheme; (3) Index of subjects; (4) Doctors whose theses have been printed during the year, arranged by institutions.

Lists 1 and 2 give full catalog information and, in case of reprints, indicate the periodical or other publication in which the thesis was first printed. Includes the *printed* theses of about 45 colleges and universities. No more published.   Z881.U5

Doctoral dissertations accepted by American universities, 1933/34–1954/55. Comp. for the Assoc. of Research Libraries. N.Y., Wilson, 1934–56. no.1–22.   **AH17**

Ceased publication.

A list of dissertations (United States and Canada) arranged by subject and then by university, giving for each dissertation its author, title, and—in the case of those printed—bibliographical data as to separate publication or inclusion in some periodical or collection. Alphabetical author index.

Continued by: Z5055.U49D6

American doctoral dissertations, 1955/56– . Comp. for the Assoc. of Research Libraries. Ann Arbor, Mich., Univ. Microfilms, 1957– . Annual.   **AH18**

Title varies: 1955/56–1963/64 called *Index to American doctoral dissertations.*

Through 1964/65 issued annually as no.13 of *Dissertation abstracts* (later *Dissertation abstracts international*). It consolidates into one list the dissertations for which doctoral degrees were granted in the United States and Canada during the academic year covered, as well as those available on microfilm from University Microfilms.

Arranged by subject classification with author indexes. The subject classification must be used with care, as there are not sufficient subject breakdowns to make it easy to discover what has been done in a particular field (though additional sections and subsections have been added to the subject lists in recent issues). Preliminary tables give information on the publication and lending of dissertations, and the distribution of doctorates by university and subject field.

Z5055.U49A62

Dissertation abstracts international. Ann Arbor, Mich., Univ. Microfilms, 1938– . v.1– . Monthly.   **AH19**

Title varies: v.1–11, 1938–51, issued as *Microfilm abstracts* (with a cumulative author index); v.12–29, 1952–June 1969, called *Dissertation abstracts.*

Subtitle varies; coverage varies.

A compilation of abstracts of doctoral dissertations submitted to University Microfilms International, by a varying number of cooperating universities (about 370 in 1984). The dissertations themselves are microfilmed and are available for purchase from University Microfilms. For each, an abstract is included in *Dissertation abstracts* or reference is given to an individual university's series of abstracts. The main list is arranged alphabetically by subject field and then by university; each listing includes title, order number, author's name, university, date, name of supervisor, abstract, and number of pages. Each issue includes a subject index and an author index. Pt.2 of issue no.12 (June) of each year since 1961/62 is a cumulated subject and author index for the year. This includes *only* the dissertations abstracted and not all those in *American doctoral dissertations* (above).

Beginning with v.27, appears in two separate sections monthly: (A) The humanities and social sciences; (B) The sciences and engineering. Author and subject indexes for both parts originally appeared in each section, with page references distinguished as *A* or *B*. Pt.2 of issue no.12 of each year continues to be the cumulative index for the volume and includes both sections. Beginning with v.30, the indexes are mechanized "keyword title indexes," and the cumulations for parts A and B are separately published. Subscriptions are accepted for one or both sections.

A "Retrospective index to v.1–29" (Ann Arbor, Univ. Microfilms, 1970. 9v. in 11) provided author and subject indexes to the first 29v.; it was effectively superseded by the *Comprehensive dissertation index*.

The title change from *Dissertation abstracts* to *Dissertation abstracts international* was made with v.30, no.1 (July 1969), with a view to including foreign dissertations, and a number of European institutions are now represented among the cooperating institutions. (*see* AH12) Z5053.D57●

Master's theses

Black, Dorothy M., comp. Guide to lists of master's theses. Chicago, Amer. Lib. Assoc., 1965. 144p. **AH20**

In two main sections: (1) lists of master's theses in special fields; and (2) lists of master's theses of specific institutions. There are also a few general lists and a list of sources. Descriptive annotations are provided, and information on lists published in series, etc., is unusually detailed. Deals only with printed sources. Useful for interlibrary loan work as well as being an aid to research at the graduate level. Z5055.U49B55

Masters abstracts: abstracts of selected masters theses on microfilm. Ann Arbor, Mich., Univ. Microfilms, 1962– . v.1– . Quarterly. **AH21**

v.1, 1962/63, semiannual.

Published abstracts of a selected list of master's essays, from various universities, available on microfilm. Classified arrangement.

Cumulative subject and author indexes for v.1–5 and v.6–10 were distributed as part of the regular subscription; a cumulative index to v.1–15 has been made available for separate purchase. Z5055.U49M3

Master's theses in the arts and social sciences, no.1– , 1976– . Cedar Falls, Ia., Research Pubns., [1977–]. Annual. **AH22**

H. M. Silvey, ed.

A classed listing (under about three dozen subject categories) of master's theses in the arts and social sciences (excluding pure and applied sciences and the field of education) reported by graduate schools in the United States and Canada during the year of coverage. Author and institutional indexes. Z5055.U5M465

Argentina

Buenos Aires. Universidad. Instituto Bibliotecológico. Tesis presentadas a la Universidad de Buenos Aires, 1961/62– . Buenos Aires, 1965– . Biennial (varies). **AH23**

Listing is by faculty, with author index. Z5055.A69B947

Australia

Union list of higher degree theses in Australian university libraries. Cumulative ed. to 1965, ed. by Enid Wylie. Hobart, Univ. of Tasmania Lib., 1967. 568p. **AH24**

Supersedes the edition by M. J. Marshall (Hobart, 1959) and its supplements, and extends the period of coverage.

A union list from ten university libraries. Includes both master's and doctoral theses in classified arrangement with author and subject indexes. Z5055.A698U5

——— Supplement: 1966–1968, 1969–1971, 1972–1973. Hobart, Univ. of Tasmania Lib., 1971–76. 3v.

Continued on an annual basis as:

Union list of higher degree theses in Australian libraries. Suppl., 1974– . Hobart, Univ. of Tasmania Lib., 1976– . Annual. **AH25**

Arranged by subject field, with author and keyword indexes.

Austria

Vienna. Universität. Philosophische Fakultät. Verzeichnis über die seit dem Jahre 1872 an der Philosophischen Fakultät der Universität in Wien eingereichten und approbierten Dissertationen. Wien, 1935–36. 3v. **AH26**

Arranged by large subjects, with a catchword subject index at end of each group and an author index at end of each volume. Z5055.A9V6

——— ——— Bd.4, Nachtrag: Verzeichnis der 1934 bis 1937 an der Philosophischen Fakultät der Universität in Wien u. der 1872 bis 1937 an der Philosophischen Fakultät der Universität in Innsbruck eingereichten und approbierten Dissertationen. . . . Wien, [1937]. 292p.

v.4 of the basic set listed above; providing a 1934–37 supplement to the Vienna list and a basic list for Innsbruck.

Verzeichnis der an der Universität Wien approbierten Dissertationen, 1937/1944–64/65. Wien, Kerry, 1954–69. 5v. **AH27**

Lisl Alker and H. Alker, eds.
Classified, with combined author and subject index. Z5055.A9V56

Gesamtverzeichnis österreichischer Dissertationen. v.1– , 1966– . Wien, Verlag Notring der Wissenschaftlichen Verbände Österreichs, 1967– . Annual. **AH28**

A combined list of doctoral dissertations submitted at Austrian universities. Listing is by university, then by faculty. Author and subject indexes.

Belgium

Répertoire des thèses de doctorat. Repertorium van doctorale proefschriften. 1971/72– . [Bruxelles, Ministère des Affaires Étrangères, 1973– . Annual. **AH29**

An alphabetical author listing followed by a KWIC index. Includes dissertations submitted at universities of Brussels, Ghent, Liège, and Louvain. Z5055.B5R45

Bolivia

Guía nacional de tesis. La Paz, SYFNID, 1981–82. 2v. **AH30**

At head of title: Ministerio de Planeamiento y Coordinación, Sistema y Fondo Nacional de Información para el Desarrollo

(SYFNID); Centro Internacional de Investigaciones para el Desarrollo (CIID–Canada).

Contents: v.1, 1960–77; v.2, 1978–82.

The first volume lists theses from nine Bolivian universities, the second from ten. Listing is by university, then by faculty, with author and subject indexes. Z7409.G84

Bulgaria

Bulgarski disertatsii. 1973– . Sofiia, Narodna Biblioteka "Kiril i Metodii," 1974– . Annual. **AH31**

Constitutes annual cumulations of dissertation citations appearing monthly in *Bulgarski knigopis. Ser.2: Sluzhebni izdaniia disertatsii* (AA650).

Lazarov, Mikhail and **Dancheva, Iota.** Disertatsii, zashtiteni v chuzhbina ot bŭlgari 1878–1968; bibliografski ukazatel. Sofía, 1975. 333p. **AH32**

At head of title: Narodna Biblioteka "Kiril i Metodii."

An international list of dissertations submitted by Bulgarians at universities throughout the world. Classed arrangement with indexes by author, language, and university. Z5053.L39

Stanisheva, Lazarina and **Shopova, S.** Bibliografiia na disertatsiite, zashtiteni v Bŭlgariia, 1929–1964. Sofiia, 1969. 586p. **AH33**

At head of title: Universitetska Biblioteka, Sofiia.

Title also in English: Bibliography of dissertations, defended in Bulgaria, 1929–1964. Preface and table of contents in Bulgarian, Russian and English.

Includes dissertations from the time that the doctorate was first conferred in Bulgaria. Classed listings, with author and subject indexes. Publication information is indicated for printed dissertations. Z5055.B87S73

Canada

See also AH17–AH19.

Ottawa. Canadian Bibliographic Centre. Canadian graduate theses in the humanities and social sciences, 1921–1946. Ottawa, E. Cloutier, Printer to the King, 1951. 194p. **AH34**

3,043 theses, arranged by subject and then by institution, with an author index and English and French subject indexes. Information given usually includes: author, title, pagination, degree, date, professor in charge, and a very brief note on scope and content. Tables at the end give distribution of theses by subject, etc., and library practice with regard to loan of theses. Z5055.C2O88

Canadian theses. Thèses canadiennes, 1960/61– . Ottawa, Nat. Lib. of Canada, 1962– . Annual. **AH35**

A previous list was issued for 1952 in 1953; none published for 1953–59.

Arranged by broad classification based on the Dewey Decimal Classification, then by university. Author index.

Denmark

Copenhagen. Universitet. Bibliotek. Danish theses for the doctorate and commemorative publications of the University of Copenhagen, 1836–1926, a bio-bibliography. Copenhagen, Levin and Munksgaard, 1929. 395p. **AH36**

In two parts: (1) classed list, arranged by the main classes of the Decimal Classification; (2) alphabetical author list, which gives brief biographies of the authors with references to fuller biographies elsewhere, and also serves as an author index to the classed list. Bibliographical detail given for each thesis includes: author's name, title, English translation of a Danish title (sometimes with brief

abstract in English), date, paging, illustrations, date of oral defense. Subject index.

Continued by: Z5055.D3C8

——— Danish theses for the doctorate, 1927–1958; a bibliography . . . Copenhagen, Univ. Lib., 1962. 249p.

Arranged alphabetically by author with subject index.

Finland

See also AH88–AH90.

Hjelt, Otto Edvard August. Det Finska universitetets disputations- och program-litteratur under åren 1828–1908 systematiskt ordnad. Dissertationes academicae et programmata Universitatis litterarum Fennorum Helsingforsiae annis 1828–1908 edita. Helsingsfors, Helsingfors Centraltryckeri, 1909. 162p. **AH37**

Z5055.F5H7

Kärmeniemi, Kaija. Opinnäytteiden bibliografia; luettelo Helsingin Yliopistossa, Turun Yliopistossa ja Yhteiskunnallisessa Korkeakoulussa vuoteen 1956 mennessä humanististen tieteiden aloilta laadituista tutkielmista. Helsinki, Suomalaisen Kirjallisuuden Seura, 1959. 164p. (Tietolipas no.15) **AH38**

Lists Finnish dissertations up to 1956.

Vallinkoski, J. Turun Akatemian väitöskirjat, 1642–1828. Die dissertationen der alten Universität Turku (Academia Aboënsis) 1642–1828. Helsinki, 1962–69. 2v. (Helsingin Yliopiston kirjaston julkaisuja, 30; Publications of the University Library at Helsinki, 30) **AH39**

Issued in parts.

A listing of dissertations written at the old Finnish university at Turku (Abo). Z5055.F55V3

France

Bibliographie analytique des thèses (1899–1965). Association internationale des docteurs (lettres) de l'Université de Paris. [Paris], L'Association, 1967. 213p. **AH40**

Continued by:

Bibliographie analytique des thèses de doctorat des universités de France (1966–1974). Avec la collaboration de Françoise Grivot [et al.]. Paris, AIDLUPA; Sherbrooke, Québec, Éditions Naaman, [1977]. 98p. **AH41**

At head of title: Association Internationale des Docteurs (Lettres et Sciences Humaines) de l'Université de Paris et des Autres Universités de France.

Listing is by year, then by university, with an author index. There are also cumulative indexes by personal name as subject, by topical subject, and by geographic terms figuring in the titles for the two volumes (i.e., 1899–1965 and 1966–74) of the bibliography.

Z5055.F79B5

Maire, Albert. Répertoire alphabétique des thèses de doctorat ès lettres des universités françaises, 1810–1900. Paris, Picard, 1903. 226p. **AH42**

A list of 2,182 theses, arranged alphabetically by author. Gives for each: author, title, place, publisher, date, paging, university, and whether published in any other form. Marks rejected theses. Includes a chronological list by universities and a subject index.

Z5055.F79M22

Mourier, Athénaïs and **Deltour, F.** Notice sur le doctorat ès lettres, suivie du Catalogue et de l'analyse des thèses françaises et latines admises par les facultés des lettres depuis

1810. 4. éd., corr. et considérablement augm. Paris, Delalain, [1880]. 442p.   **AH43**

Continued by: Z5055.F79M8

Recueil Mourier-Deltour. Catalogue et analyse des thèses latines et françaises . . . Année scolaire 1880/81–[1901/02]. Paris, Delalain, [1882–1902]. 22v.   **AH44**

The main list and the annuals, together covering 1810–1902, include practically the same theses as Maire's *Répertoire* (AH42), but arrange them by years and universities instead of alphabetically, and give, in addition to title and pagination, full contents of each thesis and very brief biographical data. Main use is for contents. Indexes: (1) subjects, and (2) authors.   Z5055.F79M9

France. Direction des Bibliothèques de France. Catalogue des thèses de doctorat soutenues devant les universités françaises, 1884/85–1972. Paris, [etc.], 1885–1973.   **AH45**

Issuing agency varies.

Title varies: 1884–1959, *Catalogue des thèses et écrits académiques.*

Issued annually, five annuals forming a volume. The official French list. Each annual issue, 1885–1913, is arranged alphabetically by university, with subarrangement by *faculté;* beginning with 1914, the arrangement is by *faculté,* with author indexes since 1957. Gives for each thesis: author's name, full title, place, publisher, and since 1930/31, date, size, and paging. Of great value in the university library, as the French theses are among the most important published.

Continued by: Z5055.F78

France. Service des Bibliothèques. Catalogue des thèses de doctorat soutenues devant les universités françaises. Nouv. sér. 1973– . Paris, 1974– .   **AH46**

This series is to cease with the volume covering 1977/80 (originally scheduled for publication in 1984).

Superseded by: Z5055.F78

Inventaire des thèses de doctorat soutenues devant les universités françaises. 1981– . [Paris], Univ. de Paris I, Bibliothèque de la Sorbonne, Direction des Bibliothèques, des Musées et de l'Information Scientifique et Technique, 1982– . Annual.   **AH47**

At head of title: Ministère de l'Éducation Nationale. Direction Générale des Enseignements Supérieurs et de la Recherche.

Issued in three sections per year: (1) Droit, sciences économiques, sciences de gestion; Lettres, sciences humaines, théologies; (2) Médecine, médecine vétérinaire, odontostomatologie, pharmacie; (3) Sciences.

Within each discipline theses are listed by university, then alphabetically by author; author index for each section, plus an "index des spécialités" in sections (1) and (3).

Germany

Berlin. Universität. Bibliothek. Verzeichnis der Berliner Universitätsschriften, 1810–85. Berlin, Weber, 1899. 848p.   **AH48**

Arranged by faculty with author index.   Z5055.G4B5

Milkau, Fritz. Verzeichniss der Bonner Universitätsschriften, 1818–1885. Bonn, Cohen, 1897. 440p.   **AH49**

A chronological listing of dissertations and other university publications.   Z5055.G4B7

Pretzsch, Karl. Verzeichnis der Breslauer Universitätsschriften, 1811–1885. Breslau, Korn, 1905. 387p.   **AH50**

Dissertations are listed by faculty, then chronologically. Includes sections for other university publications.   Z5055.G4B8

Mundt, Hermann. Bio-bibliographisches Verzeichnis von Universitäts- u. Hochschuldrucken (Dissertationen) vom

Ausgang des 16. bis Ende des 19. Jahrhunderts. Leipzig, Carlsohn, 1934–80. 4v.   **AH51**

Publisher varies.

Contents: Bd.1, A–Kühn (appeared as Lfg. 1–9, 1934–36); [Bd.2], Kühn–Ritter (appeared as Lfg. 10–13, 1937–42); Bd.3, Ritter–Zz (publ. 1977) and Bd.4, Personenregister, by Konrad Wickert.

A list of theses containing brief biographical data about the various persons connected with them, arranged alphabetically by respondent. Chiefly German, with some Dutch and Scandinavian dissertations.   Z5053.M89

Klussmann, Rudolf. Systematisches Verzeichnis der Abhandlungen welche in den Schulschriften sämtlicher an dem Programmtausche teilnehmenden Lehranstalten erschienen sind. Leipzig, Teubner, 1889–1916. 5v.   **AH52**

Classified, with index of places and index of authors. Covers 1876–1910.   Z5055.G29K6

Pennsylvania. University. Library. Catalog of the Programmschriften collection. Boston, G. K. Hall, 1961. 117p., 260p.   **AH53**

Approximately 5,000 scholarly pamphlets, largely in the humanities, selected from a much larger collection. A subject index is the key to the reproduced typed cards, arranged by author.

Z881.P41

Annuals

Bibliographischer Monatsbericht über neu erschienene Schul- , Universitäts- und Hochschulschriften, 1889/90–1942/43. Leipzig, Fock, 1890–1943. Jahr. 1–54.   **AH54**

Ceased publication with v.54, no.1/2, June 1943.

Classified arrangement, with annual author index and, from v.4 on, an annual *Sachregister.* Superseded for most purposes by the *Jahresverzeichnis der deutschen Hochschulschriften* (AH58).

Z5055.G39B6

Deutsche Bibliographie. Hochschulschriften-Verzeichnis. Frankfurt a. M., Buchhändler-Vereinigung, 1972– . Monthly with annual cumulative index.   **AH55**

Forms part of the *Deutsche Bibliographie* (AA783).

Lists German academic theses from 1971 on. Classed arrangement with author, title, subject index in each issue, the index cumulating annually.   Z5055.G29D47

Deutsche Nationalbibliographie . . . Reihe C, Dissertationen und Habilitationsschriften. Leipzig, VEB Verlag für Buchund Bibliothekswesen, 1968– . Monthly.   **AH56**

A classed listing of academic theses from German universities, together with some dissertations written in German but submitted in other countries (mainly Switzerland). Includes published and unpublished works. Index of authors and subjects in each issue, but no cumulative index.

Jahresverzeichnis der an den deutschen Schulanstalten erschienenen Abhandlungen, 1889–1930. Berlin, de Gruyter, 1890–1931. v.1–28.   **AH57**

Publisher varies.

v.1–27 cover one year each, 1889–1915; v.28 covers 15 years, 1916–30. Arranged alphabetically by author with subject indexes.

Z5055.G39G49

Jahresverzeichnis der deutschen Hochschulschriften, 1885–1969. Bearb. von der Deutschen Bücherei. Leipzig, VEB Verlag für Buch- und Bibliothekswesen, 1887–1973. Jahrg. 1–85.   **AH58**

Publisher varies.

Title varies: 1924–35, *Jahresverzeichnis der an den deutschen Universitäten und Hochschulen erschienen Schriften.*

The standard official German list including the theses of all the German universities from 1885, the theses of the Technische Hochschulen from 1913, and the theses of the Hochschulen der Länder from 1924. Arranged by university, with an author index in each volume, a separate subject index for Bd.1–5, and a subject index in each volume, Bd.6–85. Gives for each thesis: author's full name, title of thesis, date, publisher, paging, size, and whether reprinted from some scientific journal, report, etc.

Continued by: Z5055.G39B5

Jahresverzeichnis der Hochschulschriften. Jahrg. 88– , 1972– . Leipzig, VEB Verlag für Buch- und Bibliothekswesen, 1975– . Annual.   **AH59**

Continues the *Jahresverzeichnis der Hochschulschriften der DDR, der BRD und Westberlins* (Jahrg. 86–87, covering 1970–71) which in turn superseded the *Jahresverzeichnis der deutschen Hochschulschriften* (AH58) which ceased with Jahrg. 85 covering 1969; *Jahrgang* numbering has been continuous throughout the periods of title variation, and arrangement and coverage remain the same. Title continues to vary.

Ghana

Dua-Agyemang, H. Legon theses: a checklist of theses and dissertations accepted for higher degrees by the University of Ghana, Legon, 1964–1977. Legon, Balme Lib., Univ. of Ghana, 1978. 35p.   **AH60**

A subject listing with author index. Includes master's theses as well as doctoral dissertations.

Great Britain

Aslib. Index to theses accepted for higher degrees in the universities of Great Britain and Ireland. . . . v.1– , 1950/51– . London, Aslib, 1953– . v.1– . Annual.   **AH61**

Title varies.
Classified arrangement, and alphabetically by university within subject categories. Subject and author indexes.   Z5055.G69A84

Cambridge. University. Abstracts of dissertations approved for the Ph.D., M.Sc., and M.Litt. degrees in the University of Cambridge . . . 1925/26–1956/57. Cambridge, Univ. Pr., 1927–59.   **AH62**

Ceased publication. Continued by: AS122.C3

——— Titles of dissertations approved for the Ph.D., M.Sc., and M.Litt. degrees in the University of Cambridge, 1957/58– . Cambridge, Univ. Pr., 1958– . v.1– . Annual.
                                                         AH63

                                                    Z5055.G7C3

Oxford. University. Committee for Advanced Studies. Abstracts of dissertations for the degree of doctor of philosophy, v.1–13, 1925/28–1940. Oxford, Univ. Pr., 1928–47. 13v.   **AH64**

                                                    AS122.O9

——— Successful candidates for the degree of D.Phil., B.Litt., and B.Sc., with titles of their theses, v.1– , 1940/49– . Oxford, 1950– . Annual   **AH65**

Name of Committee varies slightly; committee name omitted 1974/75– . Title varies.   Z5055.G7O9D

Retrospective index to theses of Great Britain and Ireland, 1716–1950. Roger R. Bilboul, ed. Santa Barbara, Calif., American Bibliographical Center–Clio Pr., [1975–77]. 5v.
                                                         AH66

Contents: v.1, Social sciences and humanities; v.2, Applied sciences and technology; v.3, Life sciences; v.4, Physical sciences; v.5, Chemical sciences.

"The aim of this publication is to provide information for scholars on the existence of theses completed for higher degrees in Great Britain and Ireland up to 1950 when Aslib began the annual publication of its lists [AH61]."—*Foreword.* Concentrates on theses in manuscript or typescript and "does not attempt to list the earlier

printed theses whether they are full texts of theses by individuals or the broadsheets announcing the propositions to be disputed and the names of the candidates." Intended as a checklist only, and does not pretend to strict bibliographical accuracy.

Each volume is in two parts: (1) an alphabetical subject arrangement under index headings based on those used in the *British humanities index;* and (2) an author index; both parts give the full citation. Subject indexing was done manually, mainly on the basis of titles (although this is not a keyword-in-title index as such).

Hungary

Budapest. Müszaki Egyetem. Központi Könyvtar. A Magyar müszaki egyetemeken elfogadott doktori disszertációk jegyzéke. 1958/63– . Budapest, 1964– .   **AH67**

Title also in German, Russian, and English (*Guide to theses accepted by Hungarian technical universities for doctors' degrees*). Titles of dissertations given in Hungarian, English, German, and Russian; abstracts in Hungarian.

1958–63 publ. in 1v.; biennial 1964/65–1970/71; annual 1972–'.
Arranged by faculty, with author and subject indexes.

Magyar Tudományos Akadémia, Budapest. Könyvtár. Kandidátusi és doktori disszertációk katalógusa, 1952/61–68/70. Budapest, 1962–72. v.1–5.   **AH68**

Title and prefatory matter also in Russian and English (*Catalogue of dissertations for master and doctor degrees*).

A catalog of the unpublished theses to be found in the Academy's library. Classed arrangement with author index.

Absorbed by: Magyar Tudományos Akadémia, Budapest. Könyvtár. *A Magyar Tudományos Akadémia Könyvtára Kézirattárának katalógusai,* of which v.10 is:

Kállay, István. Kandidátusi és doktori disszertációk (1953–1975. januar 31). Budapest, 1978. 358p.   **AH69**

                                                    Z6621.M25125 v.10

India

Inter-university Board of India and Ceylon. A bibliography of doctoral dissertations accepted by Indian universities, 1857–1970. New Delhi, 1972–75. [v.1–24]   **AH70**

Contents: [v.1] Education, library science, journalism; [v.2] Psychology; [v.3] Political science, law, public administration; [v.4] Sociology; [v.5] Economics, commerce, management; [v.6] Mathematics, astronomy, statistics; [v.7] English, Chinese, French, German; [v.8] Geography; [v.9] Physics; [v.10] Hindi; [v.11] Kannada, Malayalam, Tamil, Telugu; [v.12] Assamese, Bengali, Gujarati, Marathi, Oriya, Punjabi; [v.13] Earth sciences; [v.14] History, fine arts; [v.15] Engineering, technology; [v.16] Pali, Prakrit, Sanskrit; [v.17] Botany; [v.18] Chemistry; [v.19] Philosophy, religion; [v.20] Urdu, Persian, Arabic; [v.21] Agriculture, animal husbandry; [v.22] Zoology; [v.23] Palaeontology, anthropology, biology; [v.24] Medical sciences.

Supersedes the Board's *Bibliography of doctorate theses in science and arts accepted by Indian universities,* published irregularly since 1935.

Classed arrangement within volumes, with author index.
Continued in part by: Z5055.I57I56

Bibliography of doctoral dissertations, 1970–75: social sciences & humanities. New Delhi, Assoc. of Indian Universities, 1979. 688p.   **AH71**

Forms a supplement to the above. Subject arrangement according to Dewey Decimal classes. Author index.

A series entitled *Indian dissertation abstracts* began publication on a quarterly basis in 1973. Sponsored by the Indian Council of Social Science Research Associations of Indian Universities, it is devoted to summaries of doctoral dissertations in the social sciences. Publication is running well behind schedule.

                                                    Z5055.I57A84

Netherlands

Catalogus van academische geschriften in Nederland verschenen, jaarg. 1–29/30, 1924–52/53; Nieuwe reeks, jaarg. 1–15, 1962–76. Utrecht, Nederlandsche Vereeniging van Bibliothecarissen, 1925–79. **AH72**

Issuing body varies. Title varies; through 1945, included Nederlands Indie. 1954/61 not publ.

Arranged by university. Combined author and subject index for jaarg.1–5, 1924–28, which form v.1; later volumes have author index only.

Ceased publication; continued by:

Bibliografie van Nederlandse proefschriften. Dutch theses. [Jaarg.] 1– , 1977– . Utrecht, Bibliotheek der Rijksuniversiteit, 1980– . Annual. **AH73**

Supersedes *Catalogus van academische geschriften in Nederland verschenen* (above).

Theses are listed under the faculty in which completed. Author index, but no detailed subject approach.

The Bibliotheek Vrije Universiteit (Amsterdam) has issued a chronological and alphabetical arrangement of its dissertations: *Dissertaties 1880–1968* (Amsterdam, 1969. 137p.).

New Zealand

Jenkins, David Lloyd. Union list of theses of the University of New Zealand, 1910–1954. Wellington, New Zealand Lib. Assoc., 1956. unpaged. **AH74**

Arranged by subject field, then chronologically. Author index.
Z5055.N72N484

Jamieson, Donald Graham. Union list of theses of the universities of New Zealand; supplement 1955–1962, with some additions and corrections to the 1910–1954 list. Wellington, New Zealand Lib. Assoc., 1963. 86p. **AH75**

Swift, Catherine G. Union list of higher degree theses of the universities of New Zealand; supplement 1963–1967. Wellington, New Zealand Lib. Assoc., 1969. 137p. **AH76**

—— Union list of higher degree theses in New Zealand libraries; supplement 1968–1971. Wellington, New Zealand Lib. Assoc., 1972. 90p. **AH77**

The Jamieson and Swift compilations supplement the basic list by Jenkins. In the 1963–67 and 1968–71 supplements the arrangement within subject categories is alphabetical by author rather than chronological as was previously the case. Z5055.N7S84

Norway

Andresen, Gunnar W. Doctores kreert ved Universitetet i Oslo, 1817–1961; en bibliografi . . . med en historisk innledning; om doktorgraden ved vårt universitet av Leiv Amundsen. Oslo, Universitetsforlaget, 1962. 100p. **AH78**

Doctoral dissertations from the University of Oslo arranged by faculty, with author index.

Norwegian dissertations are regularly listed in the *Norsk bokfortegnelse* (AA992), but are not segregated therein.
Z5055.N92O852

Peru

Lima. Universidad Nacional Mayor de San Marcos. Repertorio de tesis, 1972– . Lima, Dirección Universitaria de Biblioteca y Publicaciones, 1978– . Annual. **AH79**

Elba Muñoz de Linares and Luisa Manrique de Cuadra, comps.

Although limited to the theses (bachelor's and doctor's) of the Universidad Nacional Mayor de San Marcos, this series is seen as a first step toward listing Peruvian theses on a national and international basis. Author listing with subject index and an index by academic program.
Z5055.P454L5544

Philippines

Nemenzo, Catalina A. Graduate theses in Philippine universities and colleges, 1908–1969; an annotated bibliography. [Quezon City], Philippine Center for Advanced Studies, University of the Philippines, 1974. 4v. (P.C.A.S. Bibliography ser., 1974, no.1) **AH80**

Contents: Pt.1, Agriculture-Education (Curriculum); pt.2, Education (Educational institutions)–English (Language); pt.3, English (Literature)–Psychology; pt.4, Public administration–Zoology.

A classified listing of nearly 8,400 theses written for the master's and doctor's degree; more than 4,900 of the entries include descriptive annotations. Author and subject indexes. An estimated 90 to 95 percent of the theses deals with problems relating to the Philippines.

Philippines. National Science Development Board. Compilation of graduate theses prepared in the Philippines, 1913–1962 [i.e., 1960]. Manila, [1964?]. 437p. **AH81**

Listing is by subject field; no author index. Includes both master's and doctoral theses.

—— —— 1961–1965. Manila, [1970?] 320p.

An author index is provided in the supplement.
Z5055.P47C65

Poland

Katalog rozpraw doktorskich i habilitacyjnych. 1959/61– . Warszawa, Państwowe Wydawn. Naukowe, 1962– . Annual. **AH82**

Issued by Ministerstwo Nauki Szkolnictwa Wyzszego Techniki (varies).

A classified listing with brief abstracts; author index.

Romania

Teze de doctorat, 1948–1970: lucrări susținute în țară de autori români și străini și lucrări susținute în străinătate de autori români. București, 1973. 627p. **AH83**

At head of title: Biblioteca Centrală Universitară București.

A classed listing with indexes of authors, names mentioned in titles of the theses, and directors of the theses. Z5055.R64B878

South Africa

Robinson, Anthony Meredith Lewin. Catalogue of theses and dissertations accepted for degrees by the South African universities; Katalogus van proefskrifte en verhandelinge vir grade deur die Suid-Afrikaanse universiteite goedgekeur, 1918–1941. . . . (Publ. with the assistance of the National Research Board). . . . Cape Town, 1943. 155p. **AH84**

1,757 items. Classified, with subject and author indexes. Continued by:
Z5055.S45R6

Malan, Stephanus I. Gesamentlike katalogus van proefskrifte en verhandelinge van die Suid-Afrikaanse universiteite. Union catalogue of theses and dissertations of the South African universities, 1942–1958. Potchefstroom, Univ. for Christian Higher Education, 1959. 216p. **AH85**

Title page and introductory materials in Afrikaans and English. A classified list with author index. Z5055.S45M3

———— ———— Aanvulling. Supplement, no.1– , 1959– . Potchefstroom, 1960– . Annual.

A cumulated catalog (*Gesamentlike katalogus van proefskrifte . . .*) covering the years 1918–84 has been made available on microfiche by the Potchefstroom University Library.

Spain

Madrid. Universidad. Catálogo de las tesis doctorales manuscritas existentes en la Universidad de Madrid. Madrid, González, 1952. 36p. **AH86**

Entries cover the total holdings of manuscript doctoral theses, and are arranged alphabetically under broad subject. No author or subject index. Z5055.S5M57

———— Tesis doctorales leidas en la Universidad de Madrid. (*In* Madrid. Universidad. Revista [later Rivista de la Universidad Complutense de Madrid]. v.3– , 1954–) Annual. **AH87**

Title varies; some issues publ. in more than 1v. An annual listing of completed dissertations, with abstracts. Z5055.S5M667

Sweden

Marklin, Gabriel. Catalogus disputationum in academiis Scandinaviae et Finlandiae Lidenianus continuatus a Gabr. Marklin. Upsaliae, Reg. Academiae Typ., 1820. 3 pts. **AH88**

Contents: (1) Disputationes upsalienses; (2) Disputationes lundenses. Disputationes christianienses; (3) Disputationes aboënses. Covers 1778–1819. Z5055.S79M3

———— ———— Ad Catalogum disputationum in academiis Sveciae Lidenianum supplementa addidit Gabr. Marklin. Upsaliae, Reg. Academiae Typ., 1820. 117p.

———— Catalogus disputationum in academiis Sveciae et Fenniae . . . a Gabr. Marklin. . . . Stockholm, 1874. 3v. in 1. **AH89**

First issued Upsaliae, 1856. Contents: (1) Disputationes upsalienses; (2) Disputationes lundenses; (3) Disputationes fennorum. Covers 1820–55. Z5055.S79M31

Josephson, Aksel Gustav Salomon. Avhandlingar ock program, utg. vid svenska ock finska akademier ock skolor, 1855–1890. Uppsala, [1891–1897]. 2v. **AH90**

Author list with classified index. Continued by: Z5055.S79J8

Nelson, Axel Herman. Akademiska afhandlingar vid Sveriges universitet och högskolor läsåren 1890/91–1909/10 jämte förteckning öfver svenskars akademiska afhandlingar vid utländska universitet under samma tid. Uppsala, Akademiska Bokhandeln, [1911–12]. 149p. **AH91**

An author list with classified index. Continued by: Z5055.S79N4

Tuneld, John. Akademiska avhandlingar vid Sveriges universitet och högskolor, läsåren 1910/11–1939/40; bibliografi. Lund, [Ohlsson], 1945. 336p. **AH92**

An author list with classified index.

Switzerland

Jahresverzeichnis der schweizerischen Hochschulschriften, 1897– ; Catalogue des écrits académiques suisses, 1897– . Basel, Verlag der Universitätsbibliothek, 1898– . Bd.1– . Annual. **AH93**

Publisher varies; title varies. Arranged by university. Each issue has an author index (1925, Personen-Register) and, 1926– , a catchword subject index.

———— Verfasser-Register zu den Jahrgängen 1897/98–1922/23. Basel, Univ.-Bibliothek, 1927. 87p.

Z5055.S89J21

Union of Soviet Socialist Republics

See also AA1064.

Moscow. Publichnaia Biblioteka. Katalog kandidatskikh i doktorskikh dissertatsii, postupivshikh v Biblioteku imeni V. I. Lenina i Gosudarstvennuiu Tsentral'nuiu Nauchnuiu Meditsinskuiu Biblioteku. 1957, 2-oe polugodie– . Moskva, 1958– . Monthly (varies). **AH94**

The principal current bibliography for the texts of Soviet dissertations in all fields, as deposited with the Lenin Library and the Central State Library of Medicine.

Current bibliographic listing of the authors' printed summaries of 15–50 pages in length is provided by: "Avtoreferaty dissertatsii," in *Knizhnaia letopis'; dopolnitel'nyi vypusk* (AA1064) for the years 1961, 1964– .

For a history of these titles and related lists, *see* Eleanor Buist, "Soviet dissertation lists since 1934," in *Library quarterly* 33:192–207 (Apr. 1963). Z5055.R89M63

West Indies

Mona, Jamaica. University of the West Indies. Library. Theses accepted for higher degrees, August 1963/July 1974– . Prep. by the Univ. of the West Indies Lib. Mona, Jamaica, The University, [1976]– . Annual beginning with 1974/75 academic yr. **AH95**

Lists all theses accepted, plus an abstract of each doctoral dissertation. Arranged by faculty, with author and subject indexes. Z5055.J29M655

Yugoslavia

Belgrad. Univerzitet. Biblioteka. Spisak prinova rukopisnih doktorskih disertacija. 1963– . Beograd, [1964]– . Annual (slightly irregular). **AH96**

Title varies slightly. A classed listing with author index. Includes dissertations from universities throughout Yugoslavia.

Retrospective coverage for the University of Belgrade is provided by: Belgrad. Univerzitet. *Bibliografija doktorskih disertacija, 1951–1963,* comp. by Milica Dodiç (Belgrad, 1964. 109p.), an English translation of which appeared under title *Bibliography of the thesis* [*sic*], *1951–1963* (Beograd, 1964?). Z5055.Y79B44a

online search process; making vast collections of biographical dictionaries available in microform sets (e.g., the *British biographical archive,* AJ224); or offering online retrieval of full texts of biographical articles.

A J

Biography

❖Dictionaries of biography are among the most used reference books in any collection, and even a small library will need several works in this class. There are three main types of biographical dictionaries: (1) general; (2) national or regional; and (3) professional or occupational. Each of these may be subdivided into (1) general or retrospective, and (2) contemporary.

In this section are listed general biographical works, both retrospective and current, from various countries. For biographical dictionaries in specialized fields, *see* those subjects, e.g., Education, Medical Sciences, etc.

The basic works needed in almost any American library would include: the *Dictionary of American biography* (AJ63); the latest, or at least a recent, edition of *Who's who in America* (AJ84); *Current biography* (AJ52); and *Webster's Biographical dictionary* (AJ46). To these would probably be added the appropriate regional who's who and, where possible, the *Biography index* (AJ10). Many libraries will need professional and occupational works such as *American men and women of science* (EA221); the *Directory of American scholars* (AJ90); Baker's *Biographical dictionary of musicians* (BH187), etc.; and the large library will want many of the works from other countries.

In examining biographical dictionaries, they should be tested for the points enumerated in the general instructions for examining reference books, and, in addition, any evidence of lack of objectivity in the selection of names. Unscrupulous publishers will sometimes include articles on comparatively unknown persons, with the expectation, or on condition, that these persons will pay for inclusion or will subscribe for the book. The inclusion of such articles puts the book in the commercial or "vanity" class and casts doubt upon the authority of all articles. Such books are not necessarily to be rejected if they happen to be the only ones in their field, but they must always be used with caution.

"Biographical reference sources: a selective checklist" in the "Reference books bulletin" section of *Booklist* 80:1314–27 (May 15, 1984) and 80:1447–61 (June 15, 1984) provides a survey of some 200 titles of relevant works available from publishers in mid-1983. Descriptive information is presented mainly in tabular form; inclusion is not meant to constitute a recommendation. The list is intended as an aid to librarians in identifying useful biographical sources of various types.

Technological advances are having a pronounced effect on the search for biographical information, often simplifying that search through the production of "master indexes" to works of collective biography (e.g., *Biography and genealogy master index,* AJ8, and the Marquis Company's *Index to all books,* AJ19); providing access to those indexes via the

GENERAL WORKS

Bibliography

Biographical books, 1876–1949. N.Y., Bowker, [1983]. 1768p. **AJ1**

A companion to the previously published volume for 1950–80 (below). Entries were derived from the database used to produce the *American book publishing record cumulative, 1876–1949* (AA574). A "vocation index" which lists the names of the biographees by vocation or areas of interest (with cross references) precedes the "name/subject index" in which topical subject headings and entries for names of the biographees are interfiled, and which provides the full Library of Congress cataloging information; author and title indexes follow. More than 40,000 titles are included. Z5301.B48

Biographical books, 1950–1980: vocation index; name/subject index; author index; title index; biographical books in print index. N.Y., Bowker, [1980]. 1557p. **AJ2**

Derived from the database used to produce the *American book publishing record* (AA579) and its various cumulations, the work "was produced from records stored on magnetic tape, edited by computer programs, and set in type by computer-controlled photocomposition."—*Pref.* The "name/subject" index reproduces the full cataloging information as found in *ABPR* for all works in that database which are of a biographical nature (biographies, autobiographies, collective biographies, letters, diaries, journals, biographical dictionaries, and directories) published or distributed in the United States since 1950. Includes reprints, paperbacks, and juvenile literature. Approach in the name/subject section is mainly by name of biographee, but form headings such as "Poets, American" are interfiled with personal names. The vocation index lists names by field or profession; author and title indexes refer to page numbers in the name/subject section. The "in print" index is an unnecessary frill, since the letters "BIP" follow citations for in-print items in the name/subject section. Seriously flawed by the great number of duplicate entries and other evidence of careless editing.

Z5301.B68

Farrell, Mary A. Who's whos: an international guide to sources of current biographical information. N.Y., New York Metropolitan Reference and Research Library Agency, 1979. 102p. (METRO misc. pubn. no. 22) **AJ3**

An annotated listing of "the most current and comprehensive sources of biographical information on living persons in all countries and territories of the world, with the exception of Canada, Great Britain and the United States" (*Introd.*), most of them published between 1970 and 1980. A section of regional works precedes the alphabetical listing by country. Includes some sources which are not strictly biographical dictionaries, but which include some current biographical information. Z5301.F37

Jarboe, Betty M. Obituaries: a guide to sources. Boston, G. K. Hall, 1982. 370p. **AJ4**

A bibliography of books, periodical articles, scrapbooks, clipping files, and some manuscript sources which include obituary notices or provide indexing to such notices. In three sections: (1) International sources;·(2) United States sources (subdivided by state); (3) Foreign sources. Appendix of obituary card files. Many annotations; detailed subject index. Z5305.U5J37

Slocum, Robert B. Biographical dictionaries and related works. Detroit, Gale, [1967]. 1056p. **AJ5**

Subtitle: An international bibliography of collective biographies, bio-bibliographies, collections of epitaphs, selected genealogical works, dictionaries of anonyms and pseudonyms, historical and specialized dictionaries, biographical materials in government manuals, bibliographies of biography, biographical indexes, and selected portrait catalogs.

Devoted principally to biographical dictionaries. About 4,800 entries grouped as universal, national, and vocational biography, with appropriate subdivisions. Author, title, and subject indexes. Aims to represent all languages and cultures.   Z5301.S55

—— —— Supplement. Detroit, Gale, [1972]. 852p; 2d supplement. Detroit, Gale, [1978]. 922p.

The first supplement contains approximately 3,400 additional entries; the second about 3,800.

U.S. Library of Congress. General Reference and Bibliography Division. Biographical sources for foreign countries. Wash., 1944–45. no.1–4.   **AJ6**

Contents: pt.1, General, comp. by Helen D. Jones; pt.2, Germany and Austria, comp. by Nelson R. Burr; pt.3, The Philippines, comp. by Helen D. Jones; pt.4, The Japanese Empire, comp. by Nelson R. Burr.

Annotated bibliographies "designed to present a record of sources for biographical information on living persons in foreign countries. . . . In general . . . restricted to publications issued within the past twenty years."—*Foreword, pt.1.*

In addition to general dictionaries of biography, includes a wide variety of sources, e.g., monographs, registers of national and local governments, official gazettes, city directories, yearbooks and membership lists of professional and technical associations, proceedings of conventions and congresses, periodicals, school directories, etc. Classed arrangement with author and subject indexes.   Z5301.U5

Indexes

See also AJ39–AJ41.

Biography almanac. Annie Brewer, ed. Detroit, Gale, [1981]. 1164p.   **AJ7**

Subtitle: A comprehensive reference guide to more than 20,000 famous and infamous newsmakers from biblical times to the present as found in over 300 readily available biographical sources.

Gives brief identification, date and place of birth (and death) as available, and reference to sources where further information may be found. Emphasis is on names which occur in the popular news media.   Z5301.B49

Biography and genealogy master index. 2d ed. Ed. by Miranda C. Herbert and Barbara McNeil. Detroit, Gale, 1980. 8v. (Gale biographical index ser., 1)   **AJ8**

Subtitle: A consolidated index to more than 3,200,000 biographical sketches in over 350 current and retrospective biographical dictionaries.

1st ed. (1975) had title *Biographical dictionaries master index.*

Provides citations to biographical sketches in some 350 works of collective biography and related sources; multiple citations are given for many names.

The review by the A.L.A. Reference and Subscription Books Review Committee in *Booklist* 78:978–79 (Mar. 15, 1982) recommends this edition "for very large public and academic libraries and for the central collections of cooperative reference service systems."   Z3505.U5B56●

—— Supplement, 1981/82– . Detroit, Gale, 1982– . Irregular.

Supplements covering 1981/82 (3v.), 1983 (2v.) and 1984 (1v.) were published 1982–84, adding about two million citations. A cumulative supplement covering 1981/85 was announced for publication in mid-1985 in 6v.

The basic set and its supplements are available on microfiche as:

Bio-base: a periodic cumulative master index on microfiche to sketches found in about 500 current and historical biographical dictionaries. 1984 master cumulation. Detroit, Gale, 1984. Microfiche.   **AJ9**

Includes a separate booklet, "Introduction and bibliographic

key," which describes the set and gives full citations for the volumes included in the index.

Biography index; a cumulative index to biographical material in books and magazines. N.Y., Wilson, 1947– . v.1– .   **AJ10**

A quarterly index to biographical material, published in Nov., Feb., May, and Aug. with annual and 3-year cumulations. "It includes current books in the English language wherever published; biographical material from the 1,500 periodicals [in 1984, some 2,600 periodicals] now regularly indexed in the Wilson indexes, plus a selected list of professional journals in the fields of law and medicine; obituaries of national and international interest from the *New York Times.* All types of biographical material are covered: pure biography, critical material of biographical significance, autobiography, letters, diaries, memoirs, journals, genealogies, fiction, drama, poetry, bibliographies, obituaries, pictorial works and juvenile literature. Works of collective biography are fully analyzed. Incidental biographical material such as prefaces and chapters in otherwise non-biographical books is included. Portraits are indicated when they appear in conjunction with indexed material. . . ."—*Pref., v.1.*

In two sections: (1) Name alphabet, giving for each biographee, insofar as possible, full name, dates, nationality, and occupation or profession with index references; (2) Index by profession and occupation. Large categories such as authors are divided by nationality.

The first volume indexes publications back to Jan. 1, 1946.   Z5301.B5●

Chevalier, Cyr Ulysse Joseph. Répertoire des sources historiques du Moyen Âge; bio-bibliographie. Nouv. éd. refondue, corr. et considérablement augm. Paris, Picard, 1903– 1907. 2v. (Repr.: N.Y., Kraus, 1960)   **AJ11**

The most complete and important work for the medieval period, arranged alphabetically, giving under the French form of each name: (1) brief biographical data, i.e., characterizing phrase and dates of birth and death, and (2) references to books, periodicals, society transactions, etc., where some account of the personage may be found. Very useful for out-of-the-way names, or for complete lists of references on more familiar names; less useful for quick reference work on more familiar names because too much material is given for the ordinary reader. For the large and university library.

For complete set *see* DA146.   Z6203.C53

Codman, Ogden. Index of obituaries in Boston newspapers, 1704–1800. Boston, G. K. Hall, 1968. 3v.   **AJ12**

Contents: v.1, Deaths within Boston; v.2–3, Deaths outside Boston.

Photoreproduction of the indexes compiled for Codman and bequeathed by him to the Boston Athenaeum. Indexes obituaries in seven newspapers, some of them selectively and for varying lengths of time.   F73.25.C6

Essay and general literature index. N.Y., Wilson, 1934– .   **AJ13**

Contains a large amount of analytical material for biography and criticism of individuals and thus often serves as an index of biography. For full description *see* BD228.

Hyamson, Albert Montefiore. A dictionary of universal biography of all ages and of all peoples. 2d ed. entirely rewritten. N.Y., Dutton, 1951. 679p.   **AJ14**

1st ed. 1916.

Not a biographical dictionary in the general sense of the term, but an index to the persons appearing in 24 standard biographical dictionaries of various countries. Most of the entries consist of a single line, giving name, dates, nationality, profession, and symbol for source.   CT103.H9

Internationale Personalbibliographie, 1800–1943. Bearb. von Max Arnim. 2. verb. und stark verm. Aufl. Leipzig, Hiersemann, 1944–52. 2v.   **AJ15**

Primarily an index to bibliographies of individuals, but as many of the bibliographies indexed have accompanying biographical data, the work serves also as an index to biographical articles. For full description *see* AA26. Z8001.A1A72

Ireland, Norma Olin. Index to women of the world from ancient to modern times: biographies and portraits. Westwood, Mass., Faxon, 1970. 573p. (Useful reference ser., no.97) **AJ16**

A companion to the compiler's *Index to scientists* (1962). Provides references to biographical sketches of about 13,000 women which appear in 945 collective biographies and a few series, such as *Current biography*. Includes indication of portraits.

Z7963.B6I73

Italy. Parlamento. Camera dei Deputati. Biblioteca. Catalogo metodico degli scritti contenuti nelle pubblicazioni periodiche italiane e straniere. Parte 1. Scritti biografici e critici. Roma, Tip. della Camera dei Deputati, 1885–1935. 10v. and index. **AJ17**

Contents: v.1, to 1883; suppl.1, 1884–87 and earlier; suppl. 2, 1887–88 and earlier; suppl.3, 1889–94; suppl.4, 1895–1900; suppl.5, 1901–06; n.s. v.1, 1907–12; n.s. v.2, 1913–18; n.s. v.3, 1919–24; n.s. v.4, 1925–30. Indice generale, a tutto l'anno 1906 (publ. 1909. 117p.).

Not a general index but a subject catalog of biographical articles in the sets of periodicals (19,785 volumes) contained in the library of the Italian Chamber of Deputies. Each volume has: (1) a main subject list, arranged by name of biographee, which gives for each article indexed the title, author, and the title and volume or year of the periodical in which it is to be found, and (2) a brief author index referring to the subject list. The supplements index the volumes added during the period covered and earlier material omitted from the first volume. The *Indice generale* refers to all names included in the subject lists of the first volume and supplements 1–5. Sets indexed include the principal Italian periodicals and society transactions and also many important English, French, German, and Spanish titles. AI11.I8

Lobies, Jean-Pierre. IBN: Index bio-bibliographicus notorum hominum. Osnabrück, Biblio Verlag, 1972– . (In progress) **AJ18**

Originally issued in fascicules (later in bound volumes), the total work is expected to take more than 15 years to complete. Designed as an index to bio-bibliographical information in 2,000 collective works covering all periods and countries, it will also serve as a bibliography of such works.

To be in five parts: (A) General introduction; (B) List of the evaluated bio-bibliographical works; (C) Corpus alphabeticum; (D) Supplement; (E) General index of references. In pt.B, universal biographical works are listed first, followed by listings according to geographical, historical, or linguistic principles. Each source listed in pt.B is assigned an identifying number; in the alphabetical list of biographees in pt.C reference is made to these numbers as means of locating the bio-bibliographical information.

"Pars C," *Corpus alphabeticum*: I, "Sectio generalis," has been published through v.31 (covering through "Carafa, G.G."); supplementary listings through "Azzoni" appear in vols. 10–12. The first two volumes of subsection VI of the *Corpus alphabeticum*, "Sectio sinica cum supplemento coreano," appeared 1976–79 and cover "A–Bo Zong;" a volume of subsection III, "Sectio armeniaca," covering A–D, was published 1982. Z5301.L7

Marquis Who's Who Publications: Index to all books. 1974– . Chicago, Marquis, [1975–]. Biennial. **AJ19**

An index to the names of all persons whose biographical sketches appear in current editions of eleven Marquis biographical directories, with reference to the work in which the biography appears.

Z5311.M37a

The New York times obituaries index, 1858–1968. N.Y., Times, 1970. 1136p. **AJ20**

A very useful work which "brings together, in a single alphabetical listing, all the names entered under the heading 'Deaths' in the issues of The New York Times Index from September 1858 through December 1968, . . . a total of over 353,000 names."—*Introd.* It must be kept in mind that indexing policies regarding accidental deaths, suicides, etc., have varied over the years and that the names of certain prominent persons do not, therefore, appear in this index.

CT213.N47

The New York times obituaries index, 1969–1978. N.Y., New York Times, 1980. 131p. il. **AJ21**

Designated in the introduction as *Obituaries index II.*

Forms a 10-year supplement to the 1858–1968 index (above). Adds references to *New York times* obituaries of some 36,000 persons. Unlike the earlier volume, this one includes "certain well known persons whose deaths are listed in the 'Murders' and 'Suicides' sections of *The New York Times Indexes* for the years covered."—*Introd.* In addition, full-text reprints of *New York times* obituaries of 50 notable figures precede the index section. There is also a section of addenda and errata for the first volume of the series.

CT213.N47

Nicholsen, Margaret E. People in books: a selective guide to biographical literature arranged by vocations and other fields of reader interest. N.Y., Wilson, 1969. 498p. **AJ22**

"The purpose . . . is to identify by vocation or field of activity, by country, and by century, the subjects of biographies and other biographical writings which are recommended for libraries serving children, young adults, and adults."—*Pref.* Index of biographees.

Z5301.N53

————— ————— 1st supplement. N.Y., H. W. Wilson, 1977. 792p.

"The present volume indexes lists published from 1967 through 1971. Since these include such basic and comprehensive lists as the *Public Library Catalog,* the *Senior High School Library Catalog,* and the *Children's Catalog,* as well as the *Booklist,* the new volume is an independent tool, though it includes many of the major books of continuing interest that were in the 1969 [volume]."—*Pref.*

Z5301.N53

Oettinger, Eduard Maria. Bibliographie biographique universelle. Dictionnaire des ouvrages relatifs à l'histoire de la vie publique et privée des personnages célèbres de tous les temps et de toutes les nations, depuis le commencement du monde jusqu'à nos jours . . . enrichi du répertoire des bio-bibliographies générales, nationales et spéciales. Bruxelles, Stienon, 1854. 2v. (Repr.: Paris, Lacroix, 1866) **AJ23**

Arranged alphabetically by biographee with dates and brief identifying phrase, this work lists, in chronological order, separately published works about a large number of eminent persons of all times and of all countries. v.2 includes lists of general, national and local, and subject biographical dictionaries. Z5301.O3

O'Neill, Edward Hayes. Biography by Americans, 1658–1936; a subject bibliography. Philadelphia, Univ. of Pennsylvania Pr.; London, Milford, 1939. 465p. **AJ24**

Attempts to record all known biographies written by Americans, except that in the case of particularly famous men only the more important books are listed. The main section, arranged alphabetically by the subject of the biography, lists separately published works and analyzes the 707 collective biographies listed in the second part. Z5301.O58

Phillips, Lawrence Barnett. Dictionary of biographical reference; containing over 100,000 names; together with a classed index of the biographical literature of Europe and America. New ed. rev., corr., and augm. with supplement to date, by Frank Weitenkampf. [3d ed.] London, Low; Philadelphia, Gebbie, 1889. 1038p. (Repr.: Graz, Akademische Druk- u. Verlagsanstalt, 1966) **AJ25**

1st ed. 1871. 1020p.; 2d ed., under title *Great index of biographical reference,* 1881. 1036p.

International in scope and covering all periods. Gives full name, identifying phrase, dates, and reference to collections where biographical material can be found. Indexes some 40 biographical collections and other works. CT108.P56

Riches, Phyllis M. Analytical bibliography of universal collected biography, comprising books published in the

English tongue in Great Britain and Ireland, America and the British dominions . . . London, Lib. Assoc., 1934. 709p.   **AJ26**

An index to biographies of persons of various periods and nationalities in collected works in the English language. In four sections: (1) analytical index, arranged alphabetically by biographee; (2) a bibliography of the works analyzed; (3) a chronological list of the biographees; and (4) a list arranged by profession or trade.   Z5301.R53

Spradling, Mary Mace. In black and white: a guide to magazine articles and books concerning more than 15,000 black individuals and groups. 3d ed. Detroit, Gale, [1980]. 2v.   **AJ27**

1st ed. 1971.

This edition provides references to biographical information about some 15,000 individuals and groups throughout the world. Includes many citations to newspaper articles (including papers from Chicago, Detroit, St. Louis, San Francisco, New York, Boston, Toronto, etc.). Index of occupations and bibliography of books, magazines, and newspapers cited.   Z1361.N39S655

Ungherini, Aglauro. Manuel de bibliographie biographique et d'iconographie des femmes célèbres . . . Turin, Roux; Paris, Nilsson, 1892–1905. 3v., [i.e. main work, 896col.; 1st suppl., 634col.; 2d suppl., 758col.]   **AJ28**

A useful index to material about women of all countries and all periods. Gives an identifying phrase with dates of birth and death, lists monographic biographies in various languages, and cites portraits, autographs, etc. A cumulated index in the second supplement.   Z7963.B6U5

INTERNATIONAL

Biographie universelle (Michaud) ancienne et moderne. Nouv. éd., publiée sous la direction de M. Michaud, rev., corr. et considérablement augm. d'articles omis ou nouveaux; ouvrage rédigé par une société de gens de lettres et de savants. Paris, Mme. C. Desplaces, 1843–65. 45v.   **AJ29**

Usually cited as *Michaud.*

The 1st ed., in 84v. including supplements, was published 1811–57. Issue of the new edition, revised and enlarged, was begun in 1843. Its publication was interrupted in 1852 by a law suit undertaken by Mme. Desplaces, its publisher, against the firm of Didot Frères, which had started a rival dictionary, the *Nouvelle biographie universelle ancienne et moderne,* edited by Hoefer (AJ38), and had incorporated many articles taken in whole or in part from *Michaud.* After various decisions and reversals, the suit was finally won by Mme. Desplaces in 1855, Didot was forbidden to copy any more of the biographical sketches, and the publication of *Michaud* was resumed. The Didot dictionary, under a changed title and without the pirated articles, was also continued. For an interesting account of this famous suit, by R. C. Christie, *see Quarterly review* 157:204–26 (repr. in his *Selected essays and papers.* London, Longmans, 1902).

The most important of the large dictionaries of universal biography, still very useful. While *Michaud* and the rival work by Hoefer cover much the same ground, there are definite and well-recognized differences. In spite of various inaccuracies, *Michaud* is more carefully edited; its articles, signed with initials, are longer and often better than those in *Hoefer;* its bibliographies (except in one respect, as noted below) are better; and it contains more names in the second half of the alphabet, N–Z. *Hoefer* contains more names, especially minor ones, in the part A–M; has some articles which are better than the corresponding articles in *Michaud;* and in the bibliographies gives titles in the original language, whereas *Michaud* translates into French.   CT143.M5

Biographisches Lexikon zur Geschichte Südosteuropas. München, Oldenbourg, 1970–81. 4v.   **AJ30**

v.1 issued in parts.

Covers figures from Hungary, Romania, Yugoslavia, Bulgaria,

Albania, Greece, Turkey, and areas of the Ottoman Empire. Signed articles with bibliographic references on persons from all periods prior to 1945. "Personenregister" in v.4.   DR33.B56

Chambers's Biographical dictionary. Ed. by J. O. Thorne. Rev. ed. N.Y., St. Martin's, [1969]. 1432p.   **AJ31**

Previous ed. 1961.

A good small dictionary covering the great of all nations and of all times. First published in 1897 and reprinted several times with changes. In this edition new biographies have been inserted and sketches of contemporary figures updated, but usually at the expense of shortening other entries; a few sketches have been deleted altogether.   CT103.C4

Dictionary of Scandinavian biography. Ernest Kay, gen. ed. London, Melrose Pr., [1972]. 467p.   **AJ32**

3,600 biographical sketches of prominent men and women of Denmark, Finland, Iceland, Norway, and Sweden.   CT1243.D53

Heinzel, Erwin. Lexikon historischer Ereignisse und Personen in Kunst, Literatur und Musik. Wien, Hollinek. [1956]. 782p. il.   **AJ33**

Confines its listings to those historically important persons and events of many countries that have subsequently received substantial treatment in literature, music, or art. For each person or event, gives a statement of biographical or historical background and a summary of the extent and nature of the treatment the subject has received in the arts. These are followed by a list of the literary, musical, and artistic works concerning the subject (e.g., poems, novels, dramas, operas, symphonies, portraits, busts, etc.).   D9.H48

The international dictionary of women's biography. Comp. and ed., Jennifer S. Uglow. N.Y., Continuum, [1982]. 534p. il.   **AJ34**

Intended as a quick reference source for biographical information on women in many fields. Includes women "whose role in history, or their contribution to society or use of talent would be remarkable regardless of their sex" (*Foreword*), those whose life or work directly affected the position of women, and those who have become legendary or caught the public imagination. A "subject index" lists the biographees according to various categories.   CT3202.I57

Jöcher, Christian Gottlieb. Allgemeines Gelehrten-Lexikon, darinne die Gelehrten aller Stände sowohl männ- als weiblichen Geschlechts, welche vom Anfange der Welt bis auf ietzige Zeit gelebt, und sich der gelehrten Welt bekannt gemacht, nach ihrer Geburt, Leben, merckwürdigen Geschichten, Absterben und Schriften aus en glaubwurdigsten Scribenten in alphabetischer Ordnung beschrieben werden. Leipzig, Gleditsch, 1750–51. 4v.   **AJ35**

Contents: v.1–4, A–Z.

—— —— Fortsetzung und Ergänzungen. . . . Leipzig, Gleditsch, 1784–87; Delmenhorst, Jöntzen, 1810; Bremen, Heyse, 1813–19; Leipzig, Selbstverlag der Deutschen Gesellschaft, 1897. v.1–7. (Repr.: Hildesheim, Georg Olms Verlagsbuchhandlung, 1961)

Contents: v.1–7, A–Romuleus (no more published).

v.1–2 by J. C. Adelung; v.3–6 by H. W. Rotermund; v.7 by Otto Günther.

A comprehensive and still very useful compilation of biographical sketches of persons of many nationalities and periods but particularly strong for the Middle Ages. The original work includes those persons living before 1750; the supplement adds more from that period, as well as others of a slightly later date. References are given to sources, and bibliographies, especially in the supplement, are quite full.   Z1010.J63

Levy, Felice D., comp. Obituaries on file. N.Y., Facts on File, [1979]. 2v.   **AJ36**

Brings together the brief obituary notices which appeared in *Facts on file* (DA193) from its beginning in late 1940 through 1978. The alphabetical arrangement of obituaries is followed by a day-by-day chronological listing indicating who died on a given date, and a subject index designed to enable the user "to locate the name of a person through a country or job classification, company affiliation or work of art."—*Pref.* CT120.L43

New Century cyclopedia of names, ed. by Clarence L. Barnhart with the assistance of William D. Halsey [and others]. N.Y., Appleton, 1954. 3v. **AJ37**

A complete modernization and revision of the *Century cyclopedia of names* originally issued as v.11 of the *Century dictionary and cyclopedia* (AD6).

More than twice as large as the previous work, this edition contains entries for more than 100,000 proper names: "persons, places, historical events, plays and operas, works of fiction, literary characters, works of art, mythological and legendary persons and places and any other class of proper names of interest or importance today."—*Pref.* Pronunciation is indicated; articles vary in length from two lines to more than half a page. Numerous appendixes, including a chronological table of world history, lists of rulers, genealogical charts, and a list of prenames with pronunciations. PE1625.C43

Nouvelle biographie générale depuis les temps plus reculés jusqu'à nos jours, avec les renseignements bibliographiques et l'indication des sources à consulter; publiée par MM. Firmin Didot Frères, sous la direction de M. le Dr. Hoefer. Paris, Firmin Didot, 1853–66. 46v. (Repr.: Copenhague, Rosenkilde & Bagger, 1963–69) **AJ38**

Usually cited as *Hoefer.*

Begun in 1852 under the title *Nouvelle biographie universelle;* title later changed to *Nouvelle biographie générale.* There are three editions of v.1–2: (1) edition with the title *Nouvelle biographie universelle ancienne et moderne,* containing the 405 pirated articles from *Michaud* (*see* AJ29); (2) edition with title *Nouvelle biographie universelle depuis les temps les plus reculés,* with those articles omitted; (3) edition with title *Nouvelle biographie générale.* This last is the one usually found in libraries.

Planned to be more concise and more comprehensive than *Michaud,* to include names of people then living, and to list many minor names omitted from *Michaud.* It does include more names in the first part of the alphabet. For other points of comparison *see Biographie universelle* (AJ29). CT143.H5

Obituaries from the Times 1951–1960, including an index to all obituaries and tributes appearing in the Times during the years 1951–1960. [Reading, Eng.], Newspaper Archive Developments Ltd.; Westport, Conn., Meckler Books, [1979]. 896p. **AJ39**

Frank C. Roberts, comp.

Although the third volume published, this is chronologically the first of the series (*see* below) providing full text of selected obituaries from the *Times* of London plus an index to all obituaries and tributes appearing in that newspaper during the period covered.

"In this volume there are 1,450 entries. There is of course some overlap with the relevant volume of the *Dictionary of National Biography.* . . . , but twenty-eight per cent of the notices refer to British subjects who do not appear in the *Dictionary of National Biography* and twenty-nine per cent are foreign subjects."—*Pref.* CT120.O16

—— **1961-1970;** including an index to all obituaries and tributes appearing in the Times during the years 1961–1970. Reading, Eng., Newspaper Archive Developments Ltd., [1975]. 952p. **AJ40**

Frank C. Roberts, comp.

In two parts: "The second contains an index of all entries appearing in the obituary columns of the *Times* between January 1, 1961 and December 31, 1970. The first part reprints in full an alphabetically-arranged selection of about 1,500 obituary notices of the period. The selection has been made with regard to the public importance of the subject of the obituary, the intrinsic interest of what was written about him, and the need to reflect the wide range of nationalities and walks of life which the *Times* obituary columns encompass."—*Pref.* CT120.O15

—— **1971-1975;** including an index to all obituaries and tributes appearing in the Times during the years 1971–1975.

[Reading, Eng.], Newspaper Archive Developments Ltd.; [Westport, Conn.], Meckler Books, [1978]. 647p. **AJ41**

The first of a promised series of 5-year supplements to the volume covering 1961–70 (above). Reprints a selection of about 1,000 obituaries from the 1971–75 period, and provides an index to all obituaries and tributes appearing in the *Times* during those years.

Oettinger, Eduard Maria. Moniteur des dates. Biographisch-genealogisch-historisches Welt-Register enthaltend die Personal-Akten der Menschheit . . . von mehr als 100,000 geschichtlichen Persönlichkeiten aller Zeiten und Nationen von Erschaffung der Welt bis auf den heutigen Tag. . . . Leipzig, Denicke, 1869–73; Hermann, 1873–82. 9v. **AJ42**

Contents: v.1–6, A–Z; v.7–9, Supplément.

v.1–6 edited by Oettinger and published in parts, 1866–68, with title *Moniteur des dates, contenant un million de renseignements biographiques, généalogiques et historiques;* v.7–9 have title *Moniteur des dates . . . Supplément;* commencé par Edouard-Marie Oettinger, considérablement augm. . . . réd. et éd. par Hugo Schramm.

Articles are very brief, usually three or four lines, but the work is very comprehensive and includes some names not easily found elsewhere. CT154.O3

Robert, Paul. Dictionnaire universel des noms propres, alphabétique et analogique. Rédaction générale: Alain Rey et Josette Rey-Debove. Paris, Société du Nouveau Littérature, 1974. 4v. il. **AJ43**

A dictionary of personal and place names, fictional and mythological characters, titles (using the French form) of literary works, motion pictures, etc. Information is often surprisingly full (e.g., country articles are sometimes several pages in length); illustrations are excellent and copious. AG25.R6

Thomas, Joseph. Universal pronouncing dictionary of biography and mythology. 5th ed. Philadelphia, London, Lippincott, [1930]. 2550p. **AJ44**

Usually cited as *Lippincott's Biographical dictionary.*
1st ed. 1870; 3d ed. 1901.

A useful general biographical dictionary in English. Includes men and women of all nations and periods, and names from the Greek, Roman, Teutonic, Sanskrit, and other mythologies. Articles in general are brief, though a few are long; particular attention is given to pronunciation; and there is some bibliography, though this is a minor feature. Appendixes: (1) Vocabulary of Christian (or first) names, with pronunciation, and equivalents in the principal foreign languages; (2) Disputed or doubtful pronunciations. CT103.L7

Vapereau, Gustave. Dictionnaire universel des contemporains contenant toutes les personnes notables de la France et des pays étrangers . . . Ouvrage rédigé et tenu à jour avec le concours d'écrivains de tous les pays. 6. éd. entièrement refondue et considérablement augm. Paris, Hachette, 1893. 1629p. **AJ45**

—— —— Supplément. Paris, Hachette, 1895. 103p.

A dictionary of notable persons of the latter half of the 19th century, of Europe and the Americas. CT148.V3

Webster's Biographical dictionary; a dictionary of names of noteworthy persons, with pronunciations and concise biographies. Springfield, Mass., Merriam, [1972]. 1697p. **AJ46**

1st ed. 1943; frequently reprinted with minor changes and updatings.

A pronouncing biographical dictionary of "upwards of 40,000" names, not restricted by period, nationality, race, religion, or occupation. Includes living persons. Gives brief, condensed biographical sketches and makes a particular point of showing syllabic division and pronunciation of all names. While piecemeal updating and insertion of new names from printing to printing have kept the work reasonably current, it would benefit from a thorough revision and resetting. CT103.W4

Who's who in central and east Europe. 1933/34, 1935/36, ed. by Stephen Taylor. Zurich, Central European Times Pub. Co., [1935–37]. 2v. **AJ47**

Subtitle: A biographical dictionary containing . . . biographies of prominent people from Albania, Austria, Bulgaria, Czechoslovakia, Danzig, Estonia, Finland, Greece, Hungary, Latvia, Liechtenstein, Lithuania, Poland, Rumania, Switzerland, Turkey and Yugoslavia.

Now much out of date and partially replaced by some of the publisher's other works covering specific countries, but still useful for names of the period not easily found elsewhere. D412.A1W5

Contemporary

Contemporary authors; a bio-bibliographical guide to current authors and their works. Detroit, Gale, 1962– . v.1– . Annual. **AJ48**

Frequency varies. Indexes cumulate at frequent intervals.

Published to give an up-to-date source of biographical information on current authors in many fields—humanities, social sciences, and sciences—and from many countries. Sketches attempt to give, as pertinent: personal facts (including names of parents, children, etc.), career, writings (as complete a bibliography as possible), work in progress, sidelights, and occasional biographical sources.

Revised and updated biographies from this series have appeared in: Z1224.C6

——— 1st revision. Detroit, Gale, [1967–79]. v.1–44 in 11v. **AJ49**

These volumes represent both an updating and a cumulation of the corresponding volumes of the original series; none of the earlier sketches has been omitted.

Continued as:

——— New revision series. Detroit, Gale, [1981]– . v.1– . Irregular. **AJ50**

Subtitle: A bio-bibliographical guide to current writers in fiction, general nonfiction, poetry, journalism, drama, motion pictures, television, and other fields.

Ann Evory, ed.

This new series represents a major change from the method of preparation and policy for inclusion of the "1st revision" series (above). "No longer will all of the sketches in a given *Contemporary Authors* volume be updated and published together as a revision volume. Instead, sketches from a number of volumes will be assessed, and only those sketches requiring *significant change* will be revised and published" (*Pref.*) in the "New revision series" volumes. Updated sketches from previous revisions will also be included. The latest *Contemporary authors* cumulative index also serves as the index to the "New revision series." Z1224.C665

——— Permanent series. A bio-bibliographical guide to current authors and their works. Detroit, Gale, [1975]– . v.1– . Irregular. **AJ51**

Clare D. Kinsman, ed.

"The *Permanent Series* will consist of biographical sketches which formerly appeared in regular volumes of *Contemporary Authors* [AJ48]. Sketches . . . have been removed from regular volumes at the time of revision for one of two reasons: (1) The subject of the sketch is now deceased; (2) The subject of the sketch is approaching or has passed normal retirement age and has not reported a recently published book or a new book in progress."—*Pref.* Some revision and updating is done prior to publication of a sketch in this series. The cumulative index to the current series of *Contemporary authors* includes references to sketches in the "permanent series." Z1010.C65

Current biography. v.1– , 1940– . N.Y., Wilson, 1940– . il. Monthly (except Dec.). **AJ52**

Published monthly, with a bound annual cumulation, *Current biography yearbook,* which includes all biographical sketches and obituary notices revised and brought up to date. Each monthly issue carries a cumulative index for all issues of the current year, and each yearbook includes a cumulated index to all preceding volumes for 10-year periods.

Now includes about 150 biographies annually of persons of various nationalities, professions, and occupations, who are currently prominent in their particular fields. Information given generally includes: full name, dates of birth and death, occupation and reason for newsworthiness, address, a biographical sketch of about 2,500 words, with portrait and references to sources for further information. Each cumulation contains a classified list by occupations. CT100.C8

——— Cumulated index, 1940–1970. N.Y., Wilson, [1973]. 113p.

International who's who, 1935– . London, Europa Publs. and Allen & Unwin, 1935– . Annual (slightly irregular). **AJ53**

Offers brief biographical data on prominent persons throughout the world. CT120.I5

Labande, Edmond-René and **Leplant, Bernadette.** Répertoire international des médiévistes. Poitiers, Centre d'Études Supérieures de Civilisation Médiévale, Univ. de Poitiers, 1971. 2v. (Publications du Centre d'Études Supérieures de Civilisation Médiévale, 5) **AJ54**

An earlier directory with the same title, edited by P. Gallais and others, appeared in 1965. Two similar works concerned only with European medievalists were edited by Marie-Thérèse d'Alverny in 1953 and 1960.

Offers biographical data on about 4,800 medievalists throughout the world. Includes lists of published works and works in progress. Four indexes in v.2: (1) residences; (2) spécialisations; (3) revues et collections; and (3) médiévistes décédés depuis 1964. D116.5.L32

France. Institut de Recherche et d'Histoire des Textes. Répertoire international des médiévistes. International directory of medievalists. 5ème éd. Paris, München, etc., K. G. Saur, 1979. 2v. **AJ55**

Prefatory matter in French, English, and German.

A continuation of the 1971 publication of the same title by Labande and Leplant (above). It offers bio-bibliographies of some 6,000 medievalists in 43 countries and lists their publications which have appeared since 1969. Geographical and specialty indexes are not provided in this edition. D116.5.L32

Lewytzkyj, Borys and **Stroynowski, Juliusz.** Who's who in the Socialist countries: a biographical encyclopedia of 10,000 leading personalities in 16 communist countries. N.Y., K.G. Saur; München, Verlag Dokumentation, 1978. 736p. **AJ56**

Offers biographical sketches of contemporary figures (a few recently deceased persons are included) in socialist countries, compiled mainly from information in the editors' personal archives. In addition to political leaders, figures from the fields of economics, the arts and sciences, the military, and religion are included. The prefatory matter does not specify countries covered, but the list includes Albania, Bulgaria, China, Cuba, Czechoslovakia, East Germany, Estonia, Hungary, Laos, Latvia, Lithuania, Poland, Romania, U.S.S.R., Vietnam, and Yugoslavia; country representation and depth of coverage varies widely. CT120.L44

New York times biographical service; a compilation of current biographical information of general interest. v.1, no.1– , Jan. 7, 1970– . N.Y., Times, 1970– . Looseleaf. Monthly. **AJ57**

Title varies: v.1–6 called *New York times biographical edition.*

Frequency varies; originally weekly.

Offers photomechanical reproduction of major biographical articles (both obituaries and special, news-oriented biographical sketches) which have appeared in issues of the *New York times.* Index of names cumulates annually. CT120.N45

Who's who in the world. Ed.1– , 1971/72– . Chicago, Marquis, [1970–]. Biennial.   **AJ58**

About 25,000 biographies in the first edition, representing some 150 countries; the number of entries has increased significantly in later editions. The principal factors in selection were: "(1) The position of responsibility held and (2) the level of achievement attained by the individual."—*p.viii.* Invites comparison with the *International who's who* (AJ53) and includes many of the same names, though each work includes some that the other does not.

CT120.W5

Who's who in world Jewry. 1955– . N.Y., Pitman, 1955– .
AJ59

Frequency varies; publisher varies.

The fourth edition (1978) includes about 12,000 sketches of prominent Jews in various parts of the world, with a high percentage from the United States and Israel. Inclusion is based on influence, position, and achievement. Jews living in the Soviet Union are included for the first time in the fourth edition.   DS125.3.A2W5

UNITED STATES

American women, 1935–1940: a composite biographical dictionary. Ed. by Durwood Howes. Detroit, Gale, [1981]. 2v. (Gale composite biographical dictionary ser., 6)   **AJ60**

"A consolidation of all material appearing in the 1939–40 edition of *American women,* with a supplement of unduplicated biographical entries from the 1935–1936 and 1937–1938 editions."—*t.p.*

Constitutes a reprint (complete with all prefatory matter) of the 1939–40 edition (Los Angeles, 1939), with the unduplicated sketches from the two earlier volumes reproduced in a single sequence printed on yellow paper at the back of v.2.   CT3260.A473

Appleton's Cyclopaedia of American biography, ed. by J. G. Wilson and John Fiske. N.Y., Appleton, 1894–1900. 7v. il. (Repr.: Detroit, Gale, 1968)   **AJ61**

Contents: v.1–6, A–Z, suppl. A–Z, analytical index; v.7, suppl. A–Z; Pen names, nicknames, sobriquets; Lists of deaths in v.1–6; Signers of the Declaration of Independence, presidents of the Continental Congress, presidents, vice-presidents, unsuccessful candidates for those offices, cabinets, 1789–1897; analytical index to v.7.

Includes names of native and adopted citizens of the United States (including persons living at time of compilation) from time of earliest settlement; eminent citizens of Canada, Mexico, and other countries of North and South America; and names of men of foreign birth closely identified with American history.

Contains fairly long articles; little bibliography; many portraits, principally small insets in the text; and many fascimiles of autographs. A peculiarity of arrangement to be remembered is that under each family name arrangement is not alphabetical but by seniority in the family. The analytical index is useful for subjects and for names not treated separately. Practically superseded by the *Dictionary of American biography* (AJ63), but still useful for names and certain types of information not given there. Not entirely accurate; for interesting accounts of some curious fictitious biographies *see:* (1) J. H. Barnhart. "Some fictitious botanists," *Journal of the N.Y. Botanical Garden* 20:171–81, Sept. 1919; (2) Margaret Castle Schindler. "Fictitious biography," *American historical review* 42:680–90, July 1937; and (3) "84 phonies," *Letters* 3, no.19: 1–2, Sept. 14, 1936.

An edition entitled *Cyclopedia of American biography* (N.Y., Press Assoc. Compilers, 1915. 6v.), a new enlarged edition of *Appleton's Cyclopaedia of American biography,* is printed from the same plates as the original edition, with the omission of some of the older articles, the inclusion of some new ones, and the addition of a supplementary list at the end of each volume. Six supplementary (nonalphabetical) volumes to this edition, numbered as volumes 7–12, 1918–31, were sold separately.

No cumulated index for the set.   E176.A659

Biographical directory of the governors of the United States, 1789–1978. Ed. by Robert Sobel and John Raimo. Westport, Conn., Meckler Books, [1978]. 4v.   **AJ62**

Offers short biographies, a page or less in length, incorporating such basic information as dates of birth and death, ancestry, family, religion, political affiliation, electoral results, and political and private careers. Arranged alphabetically by state, then in chronological order of the governorship. Short bibliographies included. Contributors are identified, but biographical sketches are not signed. An index of names of biographees in the full set appears in each volume.

A review by Sally Linden in *Library journal* 103:1968 (Oct.1, 1978) points out certain factual errors.

A supplementary volume edited by J. W. Raimo offers biographies of 87 individuals who held office between Jan. 1978 and Jan. 1983 (Westport, Conn., Meckler, 1985. 352p.).

See also CJ178.   E176.B573

Dictionary of American biography. Publ. under the auspices of the American Council of Learned Societies. N.Y., Scribner; London, Milford, 1928–37. 20v. and Index. (Repr.: N.Y., Scribner, 1943. 21v.; 1946, 11v. on thin paper)
AJ63

The scholarly American biographical dictionary designed on the lines of the English *Dictionary of national biography* (AJ217) with signed articles and bibliographies. Planned to include noteworthy persons of all periods who lived in the territory now known as the United States, excluding British officers serving in America after the colonies declared their independence. More than 13,600 biographies in the basic set. Does not include living persons.

As compared with the other principal dictionaries in this field the *DAB* is narrower in scope than *Appleton's* (AJ61), which includes Canadian and Latin-American names, and less inclusive than the *National cyclopaedia* (AJ68), which includes many more minor names. However, it has articles of more distinction than either of those works and much more bibliography. In most cases, the articles are excellent, but there are occasional inaccuracies in both articles and bibliographies.

The reprint edition listed above has a list of errata, v.1, p.xiii–xxxi, with this note: "In making this reprinting of the *Dictionary of American biography,* such corrections as have so far come to the attention of the editors have been made either in the plates or in the following list."

Editors: v.1–3, Allen Johnson; v.4–7, Allen Johnson and Dumas Malone; v.8–20, Dumas Malone; Suppl. 1, Harris E. Starr; Suppl. 2, Robert L. Schuyler and Edward T. James; Suppl. 3, Edward T. James; Suppl. 4, John A. Garraty and Edward T. James; Suppl. 5–7, John A. Garraty.

———— Supplements 1–7. N.Y., Scribner, 1944–81.

v.1, to Dec. 31, 1935; v.2, 1936–40; v.3, 1941–45; v.4, 1946–50; v.5, 1951–55; v.6, 1956–60; v.7, 1961–65.

The first supplement includes 652 memoirs of persons who died prior to the end of 1935; the second adds 585 sketches of figures who died 1936–40; the third contains biographies of 573 persons who died during the 1941–45 period; the fourth adds 561 biographies of persons who died 1946–50; the fifth adds biographies of 556 persons who died 1951–55; the sixth adds sketches of 524 persons who died 1956–60; the seventh adds 572 sketches of those who died during the 1961–65 period, and includes a consolidated list of biographies in all seven supplements.

Beginning with Suppl. 5, the preface states that "certain 'standard' facts not necessarily important for the individual . . . [which were included in earlier supplements] for the benefit of sociologists and other scholars interested in collective biography" are generally omitted from the supplements. Such information, however, was gathered on data sheets which will be on file with the *DAB* papers in the Library of Congress.

———— Index. N.Y., Scribner, 1937. 613p.

Contains six separate indexes: (1) Names of subjects of biographies, with authors; (2) Contributors, with subjects of their articles; (3) Birthplaces, arranged alphabetically by (a) states, and (b) foreign countries; (4) Schools and colleges attended by persons included in the dictionary; (5) Occupations; (6) Topics.

Prepared by the publishers, not by the editors, of the dictionary.

E176.D56

Concise dictionary of American biography. 3d ed. complete to 1960. N.Y., Scribner, [1980]. 1333p. **AJ64**

1st ed. 1964.

Presents the essential facts of every article in the *Dictionary of American biography* (above) and its first six supplements in summary form. This edition is actually a reprint of the 2d ed., 1977, with the addition of a supplementary section, p.1233–1333, for the 1951–60 period. As in the parent volumes, no subject who died later than 1960 is included, but in a few cases where recent scholarship has revealed new information, some revisions of the original text have been made. Outstanding titles by authors are listed, but bibliographical sources are omitted. About 17,000 entries in this edition.

A more selective single-volume work (about 1,000 entries) is the *Encyclopedia of American biography* edited by John A. Garraty and Jerome L. Sternstein (N.Y., Harper & Row, 1974. 1241p.) which includes brief interpretive essays along with factual accounts of the subjects' lives. *Webster's American biographies* by Charles L. Van Doren and Robert McHenry (Springfield, Mass., Merriam, 1975. 1233p.) offers brief sketches (averaging 350 words) of some 3,000 persons. E176.D564

Dockstader, Frederick J. Great North American Indians: profiles in life and leadership. N.Y., Van Nostrand Reinhold, [1977]. 386p. il. **AJ65**

Offers biographical sketches of about 300 notable native Americans. List of books for further reading, pp.355–69. Tribal listing, chronology, and an "Index of names" which includes names of all people mentioned in the text, together with variants of the Indian names. Many portraits. E89.D55

Herman, Kali. Women in particular: an index to American women. Phoenix, Oryx Pr., 1984. 740p. il. **AJ66**

An index to biographical articles on women to be found in some 54 works of collective biography. In five sections offering a variety of approaches to the information: (1) Field and career index; (2) Religious affiliation index; (3) Ethnic and racial index; (4) Geographical index; and (5) Alphabetical index. Biographees are entered in as many of the first four sections (and subsections) as are applicable, with full information (name, dates, occupation or field of activity, places of residence, religion, ethnicity, and references to biographical sources) repeated at each entry. The alphabetical index refers to section and entry numbers in the earlier parts.

HQ1412.H47

Logan, Rayford W. and **Winston, Michael R.** Dictionary of American Negro biography. N.Y., Norton, [1982]. 680p.

AJ67

Intended to meet the need for a comprehensive biographical dictionary of American Negroes based on scholarly research. Includes only persons who died prior to Jan. 1, 1970. Signed articles with notes on sources. "Historical significance," rather than eminence or achievement per se, was the principal criterion and numerous figures of regional or local importance are included "as illustrations of the broad participation of Negroes in the development of the United States."—*Introd.* E185.96L6

National cyclopaedia of American biography. N.Y., White, 1892–1984. v.1–63. il. (In progress?) Some volumes issued in rev. ed. **AJ68**

The most comprehensive American work, less limited and selective than the *Dictionary of American biography* (AJ63), and more up to date than *Appleton's* (AJ61). Articles are unsigned, in general being written by members of an editorial force from questionnaires and other information supplied by families of the biographees. No bibliographies. The special reference use of the *National cyclopaedia* is in its comprehensiveness. Not alphabetically arranged, so must be used through the general indexes. Each volume is also separately indexed.

The volume issued in 1984 is designated "N–63" and includes biographies of both deceased and living persons (the latter having been treated theretofore only in the "Current" or "lettered" vol-

umes noted below), "because it is likely to be the final volume. . .issued under the auspices of the present publisher."—*Pref.*

E176.N27

—— Current volumes, A–M. N.Y., White, 1930–78. il. (In progress?) **AJ69**

Includes only persons living at the time of compilation, the biographies given being considerably longer than those in *Who's who in America.* Each volume is separately indexed, and all are cumulatively indexed in the general index as noted below. *See* above concerning v.N–63.

—— Index. Clifton, N.J., T. White Co., 1984. 576p.

Supersedes the earlier indexes issued in looseleaf form and the bound volumes published 1971 and 1979. Covers the entire set as published 1891–1984: i.e., the permanent series, v.1–62; the current series, v.A–M; and v."N–63" which includes both living and deceased persons. Indexes not only the main biographical articles, but also names, institutions, events, and other subjects mentioned in the articles.

Notable names in American history: a tabulated register. 3d ed. of White's Conspectus of American biography. [Clifton, N.J.], James T. White & Co., 1973. 725p. **AJ70**

An expanded and updated edition of the work which first appeared as the "Conspectus" part of the "Conspectus and index" volume (1906) of the *National cyclopaedia of American biography* (AJ68). 2d ed. publ. 1937 as *White's Conspectus of American biography.*

Includes many chronological lists of officeholders of various kinds—e.g., presidents, cabinet members, Congressmen, judges, governors of the states, leaders of the Confederacy, foreign service representatives, mayors of selected cities, presidents of universities and colleges, church dignitaries, business executives, recipients of awards, prizes, etc. An index of names is provided in this edition, but references to volume and page in the *National cyclopaedia* are not included. Inasmuch as a number of lists (e.g., "Americans in fiction, poetry, and the drama," "Pseudonyms and sobriquets," "Anniversary calendar") have been dropped, libraries having the 2d ed. will want to retain it on the reference shelf. E176.N89

Notable American women, 1607–1950; a biographical dictionary. Cambridge, Mass., Belknap Pr. of Harvard Univ. Pr., 1971. 3v. **AJ71**

Edward T. James, ed.; Janet Wilson James, assoc. ed.
Prep. under the auspices of Radcliffe College.

Biographical sketches of more than 1,350 women, the majority of whom are not included in the *DAB.* "Only one group of women, the wives of the presidents of the United States, were admitted . . . on their husbands' credentials. For the others the criterion was distinction in their own right of more than local significance. The subjects chosen were necessarily women whose work in some way took them before the public."—*Pref.* Length of article depends on importance of the biographee, complexity of career, and availability of material. Includes some women who were not citizens of the United States, but spent a number of years in this country and engaged in important activity during those years. A scholarly work with bibliographies; all but a very few of the articles are signed. Serves as a valuable supplement to the *DAB.* CT3260.N57

Notable American women: the modern period. A biographical dictionary. Ed. by Barbara Sicherman [and others]. Cambridge, Belknap Pr. of Harvard Univ. Pr., 1980. 773p.

AJ72

Forms a supplement to the above, adding biographies of 442 women who died during the 1951–75 period. Basic selection criteria included: "the individual's influence on her time or field; the importance and significance of her achievement; the pioneering or innovative quality of her work; and the relevance of her career for the history of women."—*Pref.* Signed articles; bibliographies; classified list of biographies. CT3260.N573

Sabine, Lorenzo. Biographical sketches of loyalists of the American Revolution, with an historical essay. Boston, Little, 1864. 2v. (Repr.: Port Washington, N.Y., Kennikat, 1966) **AJ73**

Offers sketches of the Tories, varying in length from a few lines to two or three pages. Frequently gives genealogical information.
Supplemented by: E277.S12

Palmer, Gregory. Biographical sketches of Loyalists of the American Revolution. Westport, Conn., Meckler, [1984]. 959p. **AJ74**

A supplement to Sabine (above), not a revised edition. New and expanded information was derived from the Loyalist Claims Commission records in the Public Record Office, London. Each entry is marked to indicate whether Palmer's information is supplementary to Sabine's main text, to his supplementary fragments, or altogether new. Lacks cross references from variant forms of names as found in Sabine. E277.P24

Wakelyn, Jon L. Biographical dictionary of the Confederacy. Westport, Conn., Greenwood Pr., 1977. 601p. **AJ74a**

Provides biographical information on "the political, business, and intellectual figures of Rebel society" *(Pref.)* as well as the military leaders. Five appendixes offer lists and tables showing: (1) Geographical mobility before and after the Civil War; (2) Principal occupations; (3) Religious affiliation; (4) Education; (5) Prewar and postwar political party affiliation. Bibliography; index. E467.W2

Warner, Ezra J. Generals in blue; lives of the Union commanders. [Baton Rouge], Louisiana State Univ. Pr., [1964]. 679p. il. **AJ75**

A companion to the volume for Confederate Army officers (below), this one presenting biographical sketches of the 583 general officers of the Union Army. E467.W29

———— Generals in gray; lives of the Confederate commanders. [Baton Rouge], Louisiana State Univ. Pr., [1959]. 420p. il. **AJ76**

Includes biographical sketches of the 425 general officers of the Confederate Army, with emphasis on military careers during the Civil War. E467.W3

Who was who in America: Historical volume, 1607–1896. A component volume of Who's who in American history. Chicago, Marquis, 1963. 670p. **AJ77**

Subtitle: A compilation of sketches of individuals, both of the United States of America and other countries, who have made contribution to, or whose activity was in some manner related to the history of the United States, from the founding of the Jamestown Colony to the year of continuation by volume 1 of *Who was who.*

Includes tables of presidents and vice-presidents of the United States, cabinet officers, justices of the Supreme Court, first governors and years of admission of the several states, some major events in United States history, etc.

A revised edition (1967. 689p.) includes about 200 additional sketches. E176.W64

Who was who in America; a companion biographical reference work to Who's who in America. Chicago, Marquis, 1942–81. v.1–7. (In progress) **AJ78**

Contents: v.1, 1897–1942; v.2, 1943–50; v.3, 1951–60; v.4, 1961–68; v.5, 1969–73; v.6, 1974–76; v.7, 1977–81.

Includes sketches removed from *Who's who in America* because of death of the biographee; date of death and, often, interment location is added.

With the *Historical volume* (above), these volumes form a series entitled *Who's who in American history.* v.6 includes a cumulated index to the series. E176.W64

Willard, Frances Elizabeth and **Livermore, Mary A.** A woman of the century; 1470 biographical sketches accompanied by portraits of leading American women in all walks of life. Buffalo, N.Y., Charles Wells Moulton, 1893. 812p. il. (Repr.: Detroit, Gale, 1967) **AJ79**

Useful for biographies of American women of the 19th century, many of whom do not appear in other biographical reference works. E176.W691

College graduates

❖ A library doing much reference work in American biography will do well to build up as comprehensive a collection as possible of biographical registers of American schools and colleges. While many alumni directories include only names and addresses, the biographical and historical registers frequently include more detailed information than can readily be found elsewhere. Outstanding examples of these registers are listed below:

Dexter, Franklin Bowditch. Biographical sketches of the graduates of Yale college. N.Y., Holt, 1885–1912. 6v. **AJ80**

Covers 1701–1815. Good biographies with full bibliographies of works by biographees and references to authorities. LD6323.D5

Yale University. Obituary record of graduates . . . 1859–1951. New Haven, Conn., 1860–1952. no.1–110. Annual. **AJ81**

Ceased publication. Supplemented retroactively by: LD6324

———— Biographical notices of graduates of Yale college, including those who graduated in classes later than 1815, who are not commemorated in the annual obituary records. Issued as a supplement to the Obituary Record. By Franklin Bowditch Dexter. New Haven, Conn., 1913. 411p. **AJ82**

Covers the years 1815–84.

Sibley, John Langdon. Biographical sketches of those who attended Harvard College with bibliographical and other notes. Boston, Mass. Historical Soc., 1873–1975. v.1–17. il. (In progress) **AJ83**

v.1–3 have title: *Biographical sketches of graduates of Harvard University.* Also called *Sibley's Harvard graduates.*
v.4–16 ed. By C. K. Shipton.
v.1–17 cover 1642–1771. LD2139.S5

Contemporary

❖*Who's who in America* (AJ84) is the best-known and generally the most useful of the current biographical works for information about persons of national prominence. For persons not listed there or for whom additional information is desired, other compilations of various kinds are available, only a few of which can be listed here. Most of these fall into one of the following categories:

1. *National.* Other national works are of varying degrees of worth and usefulness. Some of them include longer, more discursive biographies than *Who's who in America,* such as those in *Current biography* (AJ52). Others of the commercial or "vanity" type must be used with caution.
2. *Local.* These include both sectional and state works. The A. N. Marquis Company publishes a series of sectional compilations including *Who's who in the East* (AJ85); *Who's who in the Midwest* (AJ86); *Who's who in the South and Southwest* (AJ87); and *Who's who in the West* (AJ88). These are listed below. Various state publications are also available, e.g., *Who's who in New York* (1960); *Who's who in North Dakota* (1984).
3. *Professional or business,* e.g., *Who's who in finance and industry* (CH284); *American men and women of science* (EA221). These will be found under their proper subject in this book.
4. *Foreign-American,* e.g., *Italian-American who's who* (1935–66). These should be acquired by libraries according to local need.
5. *Religious or racial,* e.g., *American Catholic who's who* (AJ89); *Who's who in American Jewry* (AJ92); *Who's who*

in colored America (AJ93); and various denominational works listed under Religion, p.340.

Who's who in America, a biographical dictionary of notable living men and women. Chicago, Marquis, 1899– . v.1– . Biennial.   **AJ84**

The standard dictionary of contemporary biography, containing concise biographical data, prepared according to established practices, with addresses and, in the case of authors, lists of works. Issued biennially and constantly expanded since 1899. The standards of admission are high, aiming to include the "best-known men and women in all lines of useful and reputable achievement," including (1) those selected on account of special prominence in creditable lines of effort, and (2) those included as a matter of policy on account of official position.

The 43d ed. (1984/85) lists more than 75,000 persons, and has a section of "Biographies in Marquis who's who regional editions" providing reference to names in those volumes. Includes the names of leading government officials of Canada and Mexico, and recipients of major national and international awards. Inclusion of non-Americans has varied over the years. Each edition is thoroughly revised, new biographies added, and others dropped. For names of persons dropped because of death, *see Who was who* (AJ78); for those dropped for other reasons, *see* "Non-current listings" in *Indices and necrology* (below). A "Retiree index" now lists names deleted because the biographee retired from active work; it gives reference to the last sketch published in this set. Beginning with the 39th, each edition includes a "Necrology" listing.

A separately published volume designated "Geographic index; professional area index" was made available beginning with the 42d ed. (1982/83).

During the period Dec. 1939–Aug. 1959 a *Monthly supplement and international who's who* was published as a supplementary service, giving sketches concerned with "who's who in world news—and why." A cumulated index to v.1–10 (1939–49) of this series was published separately and also in *Who was who* 2:605–54.

E176.W642●

———— Indices and necrology. [v.1], 1952; [v.2], 1954; [v.3], 1958.

Contents: Non-current listings from v.1–22, 23–26 (1899–1950/51) in [v.1]; from v.27–30 (1952/53–1958/59) in [v.3].

Vocational-geographical index to v.26 (1950/51) in [v.1]; to v.28 (1954/55) in [v.2]; to v.30 (1958/59) in [v.3].

Necrology, v.28 (1954/55) in [v.2]; v.29 (1956/57) in [v.3].

❖The Marquis sectional who's whos are designed to supplement *Who's who in America* (AJ84) and to give representative coverage of a region. Each volume now averages some 20,000 names, selected on the same principles of "reference usefulness" used for the national work; a few of these, deemed especially newsworthy, are duplicated in *Who's who in America* and in the regional volume. Each regional volume includes a list indicating names from the area to be found in *Who's who in America*.

Who's who in the East; a biographical dictionary of leading men and women of the eastern United States. v.1– , 1942/43– . Chicago, Marquis, 1943– . v.1– . Biennial (slightly irregular).   **AJ85**

Publisher varies; subtitle varies; coverage varies. 1964/65 called 9th ed. and scope broadened to include eastern Canada.

Now covers Connecticut, Delaware, the District of Columbia, Maine, Maryland, Massachusetts, New Hampshire, New Jersey, New York, Pennsylvania, Rhode Island, Vermont, and the Canadian provinces of New Brunswick, Nova Scotia, Prince Edward Island, Quebec, and the eastern half of Ontario.   E747.W643

Who's who in the Midwest; a biographical dictionary of noteworthy men and women of the central and midwestern states. Ed.1– , 1949– . Chicago, Marquis, 1949– . Biennial (slightly irregular).   **AJ86**

Subtitle varies; coverage varies. With the 9th ed. (1965/66) coverage was extended to include central Canada.

Now covers Illinois, Indiana, Iowa, Kansas, Michigan, Minnesota, Missouri, Nebraska, North Dakota, Ohio, South Dakota, and Wisconsin, and the Canadian provinces of Manitoba and western Ontario.   E747.W644

Who's who in the South and Southwest; a biographical dictionary of noteworthy men and women of the southern and southwestern states. Chicago, Marquis, [1950–]. Biennial (slightly irregular).   **AJ87**

Subtitle varies; coverage varies.

Issue for 1950 called 2d ed., but is first under Marquis editorship. An earlier volume of the same title was published 1947 by Larkin, Roosevelt & Larkin of Chicago.

Now covers Alabama, Arkansas, Florida, Georgia, Kentucky, Louisiana, Mississippi, North Carolina, Oklahoma, South Carolina, Tennessee, Texas, Virginia, West Virginia, Puerto Rico, and the Virgin Islands, together with some figures from Mexico. ("Notables of Mexico" were first included in the 11th ed., 1969/70.)

E747.W645

Who's who in the West; a biographical dictionary of noteworthy men and women of the Pacific coastal and western states. Chicago, Marquis, [1949–]. Biennial (slightly irregular).   **AJ88**

Title varies: *Who's who on the Pacific coast, Who's who in the Far West.* Subtitle varies; coverage varies. Beginning with the 9th ed. (1965/66) coverage extended to include western Canada.

Now covers Alaska, Arizona, California, Colorado, Hawaii, Idaho, Montana, Nevada, New Mexico, Oregon, Utah, Washington, and Wyoming, and the Canadian provinces of Alberta, British Columbia, and Saskatchewan.   E747.W646

American Catholic who's who, 1934/35–80/81. Detroit, Walter Romig, [1934]–80. Biennial.   **AJ89**

Ceased publication.

An earlier edition, edited by G. P. Curtis, was published in 1911 by B. Herder in St. Louis.   E184.C3A6

Directory of American scholars; a biographical directory. Ed.[1]– . N.Y., Bowker, 1942– . Irregular.   **AJ90**

Publisher varies.

2d ed. 1951; 3d ed. 1957; 4th ed. 1963–64; 5th ed. 1969; 6th ed. 1974; 7th ed. 1978; 8th ed. 1982.

Contents, 8th ed.: v.1, History; v.2, English, speech and drama; v.3, Foreign languages, linguistics and philology; v.4, Philosophy, religion and law.

About 37,500 biographies of currently active United States and Canadian scholars in the 8th ed. Achievement in research, publication of scholarly works, and attainment of position of substantial responsibility are among the chief criteria for inclusion. Scholars in fields that cross the discipline groupings are given a full entry in only one volume, with cross references in others, as necessary. Geographic index in each volume and a name index to the full set in v.4. Early editions continue to be important biographical sources in large academic libraries.   LA2311.C32

Polner, Murray. American Jewish biographies. N.Y., Facts on File, [1982]. 493p.   **AJ91**

Offers biographical sketches by editorial staff writers, ranging in length from a single column to a page or more, "of men and women who have distinguished themselves either in American life or American Jewish life. . . .The criteria used are that they are alive, are citizens of the United States and consider themselves Jewish."—*Pref.* Occasional bibliographic references.   E184.J5P625

Who's who in American Jewry. 1980 ed. Los Angeles, Standard Who's Who, [1980]. 726p.   **AJ92**

"Incorporating The directory of American Jewish institutions."—*t.p.*

An earlier series with the same title appeared 1926–38 in 3v.

Offers biographical sketches of some 6,000 "Jewish men and women who have achieved distinction in a particular field of human endeavour or who hold leadership positions in the Jewish or national community."—*Pref.*

The directory section lists about 10,000 "American Jewish organizations, synagogues, educational institutions, youth groups, libraries, periodicals, hospitals and camps in the United States and Canada," giving address, telephone, and executive officer.

E184.J5W62

Who's who in colored America; a biographical dictionary of notable living persons of Negro descent in America. Ed.1–7, 1927–50. Yonkers, N.Y., Burckell, [1927–50]. **AJ93**

Publ. at irregular intervals.
Publisher and subtitle vary.
Biographical sketches of Negroes outstanding in all fields and professions. Includes a geographical listing and a vocational listing.
A similar, more recent publication is: E185.96.W54

Who's who among black Americans. Ed.1– , 1975/76– . Northbrook, Ill., Who's Who Among Black Americans, Inc., 1976– . Irregular. **AJ94**

"Reference value" is cited as the prime basis of selection. "Individuals became eligible for listing by virtue of positions achieved through election or appointment to office and by distinguished achievement in meritorious careers."—*Pref.* As far as possible, information was collected by questionnaires to the biographees. About 10,000 entries in the first edition; this was increased to about 16,000 in the third (1981). E185.96.W52

Who's who of American women: a biographical dictionary of notable living American women. Ed.1– , 1958/59– . Chicago, Marquis, 1958– . Biennial. **AJ95**

13th ed. 1983/84.
Subtitle varies. 7th ed. and later publ. without subtitle. Coverage varies; some eds. include Canadian women and "world notables."
Selection is based on individual achievement and general reference interest, conforming to the pattern and standards of other Marquis publications.
An earlier work, by a different publisher, entitled *American women* was published in three editions (Los Angeles, American Publ., 1935–39). Unduplicated entries from those volumes were reprinted as *American women, 1935–1940* (AJ60). E176.W647

Bibliography

See also BD471–BD474.

Kaplan, Louis. A bibliography of American autobiographies . . . in association with James Tyler Cook, Clinton E. Colby, Jr., Daniel C. Haskell. Madison, Univ. of Wisconsin Pr., 1961. 372p. **AJ96**

6,377 numbered entries arranged alphabetically by author. The subject index indicates occupation, locale, and important historical events, as well as some other categories. Many of the headings are subdivided by period, e.g., Doctors: to 1800, 1800–1850, 1850–1900, 1900–1945.
Continued by: Z1224.K3

Briscoe, Mary Louise, ed. American autobiography, 1945–1980: a bibliography. [Madison], Univ. of Wis. Pr., [1982]. 365p. **AJ97**

A companion to the Kaplan work (above). Lists more than 5,000 autobiographies published in book form during 1945–80; some pre-1945 items not cited in Kaplan have been included. Main-entry listing; annotations; subject index. Z5305.U5A47

AFGHANISTAN

Adamec, Ludwig W. Historical and political who's who of Afghanistan. Graz, Akademische Druck- u. Verlagsanstalt, 1975. 385p. **AJ98**

Offers concise biographical information on about 1,500 persons. In four parts: Who is who, 1945–1974; Who was who, 1747–1945;

Afghan government positions, 1901–1974; Genealogies of important Afghan families in 92 tables. DS355.A3

—— Who's who of Afghanistan (Democratic Republic of Afghanistan). 1st supplement. Graz, Akademische Druck- u. Verlagsanstalt, 1979. 53p. **AJ99**

The who's who section is followed by a diplomatic list, corrections to the first edition, addenda, and a list of "Afghan government positions, 1978–1979." DS355.A3

AFRICA

See also under individual countries and regions.

Africa who's who. [Ed.1] [London], Publ. by Africa Journal Ltd. for Africa Books Ltd., [1981]. 1169p. **AJ100**

On spine: *Know Africa.*
A companion to the same publisher's *Makers of modern Africa* (a retrospective collection of some 500 biographies of deceased Africans; London, 1981. 591p.) and *Africa today* (a reference work dealing with 54 African countries; London, 1981. 1506p.). Offers biographical sketches on about 7,000 Africans from all nations and professions.
An earlier effort under the auspices of *Africa journal* was the *Africa yearbook and who's who* (1977) which included a biographical section.

Dictionary of African biography. Ed.1–2. London, Melrose Pr., 1970–71. **AJ101**

v.1 is called "1970"; v.2, "1971–2." No more publ.
Presents biographical sketches of "persons of achievement in all the nations in membership with the Organization of African Unity." —*Foreword.* Omits references to persons of the Republic of South Africa, Southern Rhodesia, and the Portuguese colonies in Africa. CT1920.D52

Dictionary of African biography. N.Y., Reference Publs. Inc., [1977–79]. v.1–2. il. (In progress) **AJ102**

At head of title: The encyclopaedia Africana.
Contents: v.1, Ethiopia, Ghana; v.2, Sierra Leone, Zaïre.
To be in 20v. The idea for the dictionary originated with W. E. B. DuBois and has been carried forward as a cooperative effort of the African states. Articles deal with "the personalities of the past who . . . influenced the history and development of their various countries."—*Introd.* Living persons are excluded. Each country section is preceded by a historical introduction. Articles are signed by the contributors (including some European and American, as well as African, scholars) and carry bibliographies. DT18.D55

Les élites africaines. Ed. 1–5, 1970/71–79. Paris, Ediafric, 1971–79. **AJ103**

Issued as "Numéro spécial du Bulletin de l'Afrique noire."
On cover, éd.3: Cameroun, RCA, Congo, Côte d'Ivoire, Dahomey, Gabon, Haute-Volta, Mali, Mauritanie, Niger, Sénégal, Tchad, Togo.
A who's who of government officials for the countries named above. DT533.A2E4

Lipschutz, Mark R. and **Rasmussen, R. Kent.** Dictionary of African historical biography. London, Heinemann; Chicago, Aldine, [1978]. 292p. **AJ104**

" . . . designed as a handbook for the field of sub-Saharan, or black, African history as it is generally taught in high-school and college-level courses. The material included . . . is drawn from the best available specialized sources, but as a whole it reflects the biases and omissions found in regional histories and general survey texts, that is, those books typically read in introductory courses."—*Introd.* About 800 entries, mainly biographical sketches, but including lists of rulers (e.g., "Gold Coast, Governors of"), explanations of titles, and similar related matters. Bibliography, pp. 259–80. Subject index. DT352.6.L56

Segal, Ronald. Political Africa; a who's who of personalities and parties. London, Stevens & Sons, 1961. 475p.

AJ105

For full description *see* CJ243. DT18.S4

Who's who in East Africa, 1963/64–67/68. Nairobi, Marco Surveys, 1964–68. 3v. **AJ106**

Covers Kenya, Tanzania, and Uganda, with separate alphabetical sequence for each country. DT433.A2W5

ARGENTINA

Cutolo, Vicente Osvaldo. Nuevo diccionario biográfico argentino (1750–1930). Buenos Aires, Editorial Elche, 1968–83. v.1–5. (In progress) **AJ107**

Contents: v.1–5, A–Sa.
Intended as a dictionary of national biography for the period indicated. Entries range in length from a few lines to several columns; many include brief bibliographies. CT653.C87

Muzzio, Julio A. Diccionario histórico y biográfico de la República Argentina. Buenos Aires, Roldan, 1920. 2v. (445p.) il. **AJ108**

Primarily a biographical work; covers all periods. F2805.M99

Sosa de Newton, Lily. Diccionario biográfico de mujeres argentinas. Buenos Aires, [Author], 1972. 414p. **AJ109**

Brief biographical sketches of outstanding Argentinian women, including living persons. CT3290.S67

Udaondo, Enrique. Diccionario biográfico argentino. . . .Buenos Aires, Casa Ed. "Coni," 1938. 1151p.

AJ110

At head of title: Institución Mitre.
Contains some 3,300 biographies in the period 1800–1920. Little or no bibliography. F2805.U36

—— Diccionario biográfico colonial argentino. Obra prologada por Gregorio Araoz Alfaro. . . . Buenos Aires, Ed. Huarpes, 1945. 980p. il. **AJ111**

At head of title: Institución Mitre.
Covers the colonial period of Argentina from the discovery and conquest of the Rio de la Plata to 1810. A companion volume to the preceding item. F2805.U37

Yaben, Jacinto R. Biografías argentinas y sudamericanas; introducción del Juan B. Terán. . . . Buenos Aires, Ed. "Metrópolis," 1938–40. 5v. il. **AJ112**

v.1, 2, and 4 contain lists of works used in compilation. v.5 includes a supplement containing new biographies and additional material on biographies previously published. A large proportion of the work is devoted to biographies of military and naval men.
F2805.Y23

Contemporary

Quién es quién en la Argentina; biografías contemporáneas. [Ed.1]– , 1939– . Buenos Aires, Kraft, [1939–]. Irregular. **AJ113**

9th ed. 1968 latest published? F2805.Q55

Quién es quién en América del Sur. Diccionario biográfico argentino. Ed.1– , 1982/83– . [Buenos Aires], Publicaciones Referenciales Latinoamericanas, [1982]– . Biennial? **AJ114**

A who's who of contemporary Argentinians in the broad range of academic and professional life, arts and communication, government, religion, politics, etc. CT652.Q53

❖For additional works on Argentine biography *see* Sabor, *Manual de fuentes de información* (AA498), p.252–58.

AUSTRALIA

Australian dictionary of biography. [Melbourne], Melbourne Univ. Pr., 1966–83. v.1–9. (In progress) **AJ115**

Contents: v.1–2, 1788–1850; v.3–6, 1851–1890; v.7–9, 1891–1939, A–Las.
General ed., Douglas Pike and others.
Publication has been supported in a variety of ways on a national basis, and the dictionary is planned as a scholarly work with the "burden of writing . . . shared almost equally by university historians and by members of Historical and Genealogical Societies and other specialists."—*Pref.* Most articles are signed, but there are some unsigned entries prepared by the Dictionary staff. Citations to published and manuscript sources are given.
A chronological division has been established: there are 2v. for the 1788–1850 period; 4v. for the 1851–1890 period; and there will be 6v. for 1891–1939. "The placing of each individual's name in the appropriate section has been generally determined by when he did his most important work. . . . For articles that overlap the chronological division, preference has usually been given to the earlier period."—*Pref.* While most entries are of obvious significance, some names in the early period were chosen merely as examples of the "Australian experience." Some 7,000 articles are to be included. A provisional list of names for the next period was inserted in the final volume of each of the first two sections to serve as a guide until a complete index is published. DU82.A9

Serle, Percival. Dictionary of Australian biography. Sydney, Angus and Robertson, [1949]. 2v. **AJ116**

Patterned on the *Dictionary of national biography* (AJ217), this work contains "1030 biographies of Australians, or men who were closely connected with Australia, who died before the end of 1942." The sketches average two to three columns in length and include bibliographies of source material at the end of each. DU82.S47

Contemporary

Who's who in Australia. Ed.[1]– . Melbourne, Herald and Weekly Times, 1922– . Triennial (slightly irregular).

AJ117

Title varies slightly. Publisher varies.
Incorporates John's *Notable Australians,* which was first published in 1906.
Subtitle: An Australian biographical dictionary and register of titled persons. DU82.W5

AUSTRIA

Wurzbach, Constantin, *Ritter von Tannenburg.* Biographisches Lexikon des Kaiserthums Oesterreich, enthaltend die Lebensskizzen der denkwürdigen Personen, welche seit 1750 in den österreichischen Kronländern geboren wurden oder darin gelebt und gewirkt haben. Wien, Zamarski, 1856–91. 60v. **AJ118**

Subtitle and imprint vary.
The standard Austrian work covering the period from 1750. Contains 24,254 biographies of inhabitants of the various lands included in the former Austrian Empire. Gives biographies of some length, with bibliographies.

—— —— Register zu den Nachträgen in Wurzbachs 'Biographischen Lexikon d. Kaiserthums Österreich' . . . Wien, Gilhofer, 1923. 16p.

An index to the supplements included in v.9, 11, 14, 22, 23, 24, 26 and 28. CT903.W8

Neue österreichische Biographie ab 1815. Wien, Amalthea-Verlag, 1923–82. Abt.1,Bd.1–21; Abt.2,Bd.1. (In progress)
AJ119

Bd.1–8 had title *Neue österreichische Biographie, 1815–1918.* Bd.10–21 have subtitle *Grosse Österreicher* (varies slightly).
Long, signed articles with bibliographies—and in many cases, portraits—of 19th- and 20th-century Austrians. Not alphabetically arranged, but with a cumulated index at the back of each volume beginning with v.8.
Abt.2, Bd.1 is a bibliography listing biographical dictionaries and collective biography in two parts: (1) by subject or specialty; and (2) by geographical division. CT912.N4

Österreichisches biographisches Lexikon, 1815–1950. Hrsg. von der Österreichischen Akademie der Wissenschaften. Nach Vorarbeiten von Anton Bettelheim und Oswald Redlich unter Mitwirkung bewährter Sachkenner und der Leitung von Leo Santifaller, bearb. von Eva Obermayer-Marnach. Graz-Köln, Böhlaus, [1954–83]. Lfg.1–40. (In progress) **AJ120**

Contents: Bd.1–8 (Lfg.1–40), A–Ražun.
Designed to continue Wurzbach, *Biographisches Lexikon* (AJ118) and *Neue österreichische Biographie* (AJ119). Includes sketches of prominent persons of the former Austro-Hungarian Empire and the succeeding state of Austria who were active in the arts, sciences, and politics, and who died prior to 1951. Sketches are brief and unsigned, but include bibliographies of works both by and about the subject. CT903.O4

"Wer ist wer"; Lexikon österreichischer Zeitgenossen. Wien, Selbst-Verlag "Wer ist wer," 1937. 420p. **AJ121**

Contains about 1,500 biographies of personalities prominent before World War II, with a subject index by professions, specialties, etc. DB98.A1W4

Contemporary

Österreicher der Gegenwart; Lexikon schöpferischer und schaffender Zeitgenossen. Wien, Österreichische Staatsdruckerei, 1951. 419p. **AJ122**

Edited at the Österreich-Institut.
Bio-bibliographical data on about 2,650 Austrians living at time of compilation; vocational index.

Who's who in Austria; a biographical dictionary . . . of prominent personalities from and in Austria. Ed.[1]– . [Montreal], Intercontinental Book and Pub. Co., 1954– . Biennial. **AJ123**

Subtitle varies slightly. Imprint varies.
10th ed. 1982/83.
In English. Each volume in two parts: (1) Who's who section; and (2) Directory of organizations, institutes, associations, and enterprises. DB36.W45

BELGIUM

Académie Royale des Sciences, des Lettres, et des Beaux-arts de Belgique. Biographie nationale. Bruxelles, Bruyland-Christophe, 1866–1944. 28v.; v.29– , 1956– . (In progress) **AJ124**

Publisher varies.
Contents: v.1–27, A–Z; v.28, Table générale; v.29–42, Supplément (v.1–15¹), publ. 1956–83.
Long, signed articles by specialists, with bibliographies. Includes no living persons and, as names were not selected for inclusion until a person had been dead ten years, the earlier volumes contain mainly persons who died before 1850. The supplement includes

both early names and names of the 19th and 20th centuries. For names of more recent date this dictionary may be supplemented usefully by the long, signed obituaries, with detailed bibliographies, in the *Annuaire* of the Académie Royale. For these obituaries published to 1914, the following general index is helpful: CT1163.A2

—— **Annuaire:** Table des notices biographiques publiées dans l'Annuaire (1835–1914). Bruxelles, Hayez, 1919. 55p. **AJ125**

Also published in the issue of the *Annuaire* for 81ᵉ–85ᵉ années, 1915–1919, p.113–67. Complément, 1915–1926, in *Annuaire* for 92ᵉ année, 1926, p.129–33.

—— Notices biographiques et bibliographiques concernant les membres, les correspondants et les associés. 1.–5. éd., 1854–1909. Bruxelles, Hayez, 1855–1909. 5v. **AJ126**

Brief biographical sketches with long bibliographies. Each edition includes some names from the previous edition, but also omits and adds other names. Z5055.B4A2

Académie Royale des Sciences d'Outre-Mer, Biographie coloniale belge. Belgische koloniale biografie. Bruxelles, Académie, 1948–68. 6v. il. (In progress?) **AJ127**

Publisher varies.
v.6 has title: *Biographie belge d'outre-mer.*
Devoted to persons, mostly but not exclusively Belgians, who contributed to the history and development of the Belgian Congo. No name is chosen for inclusion until at least ten years after the person's death. Sketches vary in length, but all are signed and dated, and many include bibliographies. Each volume is a separate alphabetical listing, with a cumulative index to the preceding volumes. DT663.A2A6

Nationaal biografisch woordenboek. Brussels, Paleis der Academiën, 1964–81. v.1–9. (In progress) **AJ128**

At head of title: Koninklijke Vlaamse Academiën van Belgie.
A Flemish biographical dictionary which includes sketches of numerous persons who were omitted from the Belgian *Biographie nationale* (AJ124). Each volume is an alphabetical A–Z listing with a cumulative index in each successive volume. Bibliographical references are appended to each article. CT1163.N37

Seyn, Eugène de. Dictionnaire biographique des sciences, des lettres et des arts en Belgique. Bruxelles, Éd. l'Avenir, 1935–36. 2v. il. **AJ129**

Covers all periods, and includes living persons. Articles are brief, with many portraits but little or no bibliography *about* the names included, although, in the case of writers, lists of works are given. Many of the biographies of authors are adapted from the articles in the compiler's *Dictionnaire des écrivains belges* (BD945). CT1163.S4

Contemporary

Who's who in Belgium and Grand Duchy of Luxembourg. [Ed.1–2]. Brussels, Intercontinental Book and Pub. Co., 1959–62. 2v. **AJ130**

Title varies: 1st ed., 1957/58, had title *Who's who in Belgium, including the Belgian Congo.*
Subtitle: A biographical dictionary containing about 7,000 biographies of prominent people in and of Belgium and the Grand Duchy of Luxembourg. DH513.W45

Wie is wie in Vlaanderen. Ed.1– , 1980– . [Brussels], Cegos Makrotest, [1980]– . **AJ131**

Rik Decan, ed.
The 1st ed. offers biographical sketches of about 12,000 contemporary figures.
Complemented by:

Qui est qui en Belgique francophone. Ed.1– , 1981/85– . [Bruxelles], Editions BRD, [1981]– . **AJ132**

Rik Decan, ed.
Intended as a companion to *Wie is wie in Vlaanderen* (above). The 1st ed. offers brief biographies of about 10,000 French-speaking Belgians.

Bibliography

Dhondt, Jan and **Vervaeck, Solange.** Instruments biographiques pour l'histoire contemporaine de la Belgique. 2.éd. Louvain, Éd. Nauwelaerts, 1964. 88p. (Centre Inter-universitaire d'Histoire Contemporaine. Cahiers, 13)   **AJ133**

1st ed. 1960.
A bibliography of general and specialized sources for Belgian biography.

BOLIVIA

Arze, José Roberto. Figuras bolivianas en las ciencias sociales; diccionario biográfico boliviano. La Paz, Ed. Los Amigos del Libro, 1984. 185p.   **AJ134**

Although highly selective, coverage is broader than the title suggests. Useful bibliography of relevant biographical sources, pp. 1163–72.

Quién es quién en Bolivia. [La Paz], Ed. Quién es Quién en Bolivia, 1942– . Irregular.   **AJ135**

1959 latest published?   F3305.Q5

BRAZIL

Brazil. Ministerio da Viação e Obras Públicas. Serviço de Documentação. Dados biográficos dos ministros, 1861–1961. [Rio de Janeiro, 1962.] 164p.   **AJ136**

Offers biographical sketches of a number of Brazilian cabinet members.   F2505.A45

Segadas Machado-Guimarães, Argeu de. Diccionario bio-bibliographico brasileiro, de diplomacia, politica externa e direito internacional. Rio de Janeiro, Autor, 1938. 482p.   **AJ137**

A biographical dictionary of Brazilian statesmen and a bibliography of Brazilian foreign relations, all in one alphabetical arrangement. Primarily 19th and 20th centuries but includes some earlier material.   Z1680.S4

Velho Sobrinho, João Francisco. Dicionário bio-bibliográfico brasileiro. Rio de Janeiro, [Ministério da Educação e Saude], 1937–40. v.1–2. il.   **AJ138**

Contents: v.1–2, A–Buxton. No more published.
Fairly long sketches with bibliographies.   Z1680.V43

Contemporary

Coutinho, Afrânio. Brasil e Brasileiros de hoje. Rio de Janeiro, Ed. Sul Americana, 1961. 2v.   **AJ139**

About 7,000 who's who-type sketches of contemporary Brazilians.   F2505.C6

Quem é quem no Brasil; biografias contemporaneas. Ed.1– . São Paulo, Soc. Brasileira de Expansão Commercial, 1948– . Irregular.   **AJ140**

10th ed. 1972 last published?
Biographies are grouped according to profession or subject field, with an alphabetical index of names.   F2505.Q4

Who's who in Brazil. Ed.1–6, 1968/69–76/77. São Paulo, [1968–76?]. Biennial.   **AJ141**

Biographies appear in English and Portuguese (Ed.6 in Portuguese only).
Continued by: CT683.W5

The international registry of who's who. Ed.7– , 1978/79– . São Paulo, Intercontinental de Promoções, [1978?]– . Irregular.   **AJ142**

Ed. for 1978/79 issued in 3v. with sketches in English and Portuguese; an "Ed. especial" (publ. 1980? in 2v.) is in Portuguese only.   CT683.W5

CANADA

Dictionary of Canadian biography. Toronto, Univ. of Toronto Pr., [1966–83]. v.1–5, 9–11. (In progress)   **AJ143**

General ed., George W. Brown.
Also published in French under title *Dictionnaire biographique du Canada,* by Les Presses de l'Université Laval, Quebec.
Contents: v.1, 1000–1700; v.2, 1701–1740; v.3, 1741–1770; v.4, 1771–1800; v.5, 1801–1820; v.9, 1861–1870; v.10, 1871–1880; v.11, 1881–1890.
These are the volumes published to date of a work, established in 1959, designed to "supply full, accurate and concise biographies of all noteworthy inhabitants of the Dominion of Canada (exclusive of living persons)."—*Introd.* A scholarly reference work with signed articles and bibliographic references for each biography, it differs from the *DNB,* etc., in being organized by periods rather than in a basic alphabetical sequence with supplements by period. Articles range from a minimum of 200 words to a maximum of 10,000, with the majority expected to fall within the 300–1,000 range, the lower figure permitting inclusion of notes on more minor figures than is usual in a work of this kind. Articles were submitted in English or French, according to the preference of the contributor, then translated for the alternate edition.
The completed set will be a truly outstanding reference source. In addition to the biographical entries in v.1, there is a series of brief introductory essays serving to place the biographies in a historical framework, plus a general bibliography of the sources most frequently cited in the articles. Each volume includes an index of names of persons mentioned in the articles (excepting those who had no connection with Canada). Numerous cross references, both from alternate forms of names and to related articles.   F1005.D49

Allaire, Jean Baptiste Arthur. Dictionnaire biographique du clergé canadien-français. St.-Hyacinthe, [Québec], Impr. de "La Tribune," 1908–20. 4v. il.   **AJ144**

Contents: v.1, Les anciens; v.2, Les contemporains; v.3, Suppléments, 1–6; v.4, Le clergé canadien-français, revue mensuelle; Table générale des quatre volumes.
Consists of two main volumes—six supplements forming one volume—and 24 monthly numbers. The general index at the end of v.4 links together these 32 alphabets. Short articles; many small portraits.   F1005.A41

The Macmillan dictionary of Canadian biography. Ed. by W. Stewart Wallace. 4th ed. rev., enl. and updated by W. A. McKay. Toronto, Macmillan, [1978]. 914p.   **AJ145**

"Canadians who died before 1976."—*verso of t.p.*
1st ed. 1926; earlier eds. had title: *The dictionary of Canadian biography.*
Until the *Dictionary of Canadian biography* (AJ143) is completed, this remains the best general dictionary of Canadian biography of all periods and classes, exclusive of living persons. Contains concise biographical sketches with bibliographies.   CT283.D52

Morice, Adrien Gabriel. Dictionnaire historique des Canadiens et des Métis français de l'Ouest. Québec, Garneau, 1908. 329p.   **AJ146**

A historical biographical dictionary of the French explorers of the Canadian Northwest.   Z1060.3.M85

Standard dictionary of Canadian biography; the Canadian who was who. Eds., Charles G. D. Roberts and Arthur L. Tunnell. Toronto, Trans-Canada Pr., 1934–38. 2v. **AJ147**

Contains fairly long biographies, with bibliographies, of Canadians who died 1875–1937. Articles are signed with initials. Each volume is arranged alphabetically, with a list in v.2 of the sketches in v.1.   F1005.S82

Contemporary

See also AJ85, AJ86, AJ88.

Les biographies françaises d'Amérique. 2. éd. [Montréal], Journalistes Associés, 1950. 913p. il.   **AJ148**

1st ed. 1942.

Nonalphabetical; biographies are grouped by profession or occupation, with index. Lists living persons of the French ethnic groups.   F1027.B582

Canadian who's who. v.1– , 1910, 1938/39– . Toronto, Trans-Canada Pr., [1910–]. v.1– . Irregular; annual.

AJ149

Subtitle: With which is incorporated 'Canadian men and women of the time.' A biographical dictionary of notable living men and women.

Publisher varies; beginning with v.15 (1980), published by Univ. of Toronto Pr. on an annual basis.

Alphabetical arrangement with a classified index. Includes biographies of some persons in *Who's who in Canada* (AJ151), but each work includes names not in the other.   F1033.C23

Creative Canada; a biographical dictionary of twentieth-century creative and performing artists. [Toronto], Univ. of Toronto Pr., [1971–72]. 2v.   **AJ150**

"Comp. by Reference Division, McPherson Library, University of Victoria, B.C. Publ. in assoc. with McPherson Library . . . by University of Toronto Press."—*title page.*

Presents biographical information on "those creative and performing artists who have contributed as individuals to the culture of Canada in the twentieth century, and who have had this individual contribution recognized in print."—*Pref., v.1.* Includes deceased as well as living artists of this century; non-Canadians are included if their work in Canada has had significant national influence.

v.2 (publ. 1972) includes a cumulated index for v.1–2.

NX513.A1C7

Who's who in Canada. An illustrated biographical record of men and women of the time. Ed. 16– . Toronto, Internat. Pr., 1922– . il. Biennial.   **AJ151**

Subtitle varies.

Continues, with same volume numbering, *Who's who and why;* 1921 called 15th year of issue.

Originally nonalphabetical with an alphabetical index; now alphabetical with a corporate index listing officers of major businesses.

F1033.W62

CARIBBEAN COUNTRIES

British Caribbean who, what, why. 1st ed. Ed. and pub., Lloyd Sydney Smith. Glasgow, Scot., Bell and Bain, 1956. 1v.   **AJ152**

v.1, 1955/56. No more published.

Covers: Jamaica, Trinidad, Barbados, British Guiana, British Honduras; (Windward Islands) Grenada, St. Lucia, St. Vincent, Dominica; (Leeward Islands) Antiqua, St. Kitts-Nevis, Montserrat, and British Virgin Islands.

In five sections: (1) General material on government, organizations, and geography; (2) Who's who, arranged by country and subdivided by profession or business; (3) Colonial affairs; (4) Directory of business firms; (5) Overseas business organizations trading with the British Caribbean. A detailed table of contents and a name index are included.   F2131.B85

Personalities Caribbean. Ed.1– , 1962– . Kingston, Jamaica, Personalities Ltd., 1962– . Biennial.   **AJ153**

Subtitle: The international guide to who's who in the West Indies, Bahamas and Bermuda.

Ed.1 had title: *Personalities in the Caribbean.*

Has separate sections for individual countries, islands, etc.

F2175.P4

CHILE

Figueroa, Pedro Pablo. Diccionario biográfico de Chile. 4. ed. Santiago, Impr. y Encuadernación Barcelona, 1897–1902. 3v. il.   **AJ154**

1st ed. 1887; 2d ed. 1888; 3d ed. 1891.

Earlier editions include names dropped from later editions, and the later editions add new names and incorporate corrections and additional information for sketches previously included. Primarily 19th century with a few earlier names.   F3055.F48

——— Diccionario biográfico de estranjeros en Chile. Santiago, Impr. Moderna, 1900. 258p.   **AJ155**

Biographies of foreigners who lived in Chile.   F3055.F49

Figueroa, Virgilio. Diccionario histórico, biográfico y bibliográfico de Chile, por Virgilio Figueroa (Virgilio Talquino), 1800–1930. Santiago, "Balcells and Co.," 1925–31. 5v. in 4. il.   **AJ156**

Title varies: v.1 has title *Diccionario histórico y biográfico de Chile, 1800–1925.*

Arranged alphabetically by family name and then by seniority in the family rather than alphabetically. Most articles conclude with bibliographies of source materials.   F3055.F56

Medina, José Toribio. Diccionario biográfico colonial de Chile. Santiago, Impr. Elzeviriana, 1906. 1004p. il.

AJ157

A biographical dictionary covering from the age of discovery through the 18th century. Corrections are supplied by:

F3055.M49

Prieto del Rio, Luis Francisco. Muestras de errores y defectos del "Diccionario biográfico colonial de Chile por José Toribio Medina." Santiago, Impr. y Encuadernación Chile, 1907. 124p.   **AJ158**

F3055.M495

Contemporary

Diccionario biográfico de Chile. 1936– . Santiago, Empresa Periodistica Chile, 1936– . Triennial (irregular). **AJ159**

The current biographical dictionary for Chile.   F3055.D45

CHINA

❖Biographical sections are frequently included in the yearbooks listed under Statistics, e.g., *China year book* (CG177).

The following list includes selected works on Chinese biography in languages other than Chinese:

Association for Asian Studies. Ming Biographical History Project Committee. Dictionary of Ming biography, 1368–1644. L. Carrington Goodrich, ed. N.Y., Columbia Univ. Pr., 1976. 2v. (1751p.) il.   **AJ160**

Signed biographies (with bibliographies) of important persons from the 300 years of the Ming dynasty. Indexes of names, titles of books, and detailed subjects.　　　DS753.5.A84

Bartke, Wolfgang. Chinaköpfe. Kurzbiographien der Partei- und Staatsfunktionäre der Volksrepublik China. Hannover, Verlag für Literatur und Zeitgeschehen, [1966]. 454p. (Schriftenreihe des Forschungsinstituts der Friedrich-Ebert-Stiftung. B. Historisch-politische Schriften)　　　**AJ161**

In addition to the biographical sketches of political personalities, there are sections on the organization of the Chinese Communist party and the government agencies of the Chinese People's Republic, together with a list of the various party and government officials as of Oct. 1966.　　　DS778.A1B3

────── Who's who in the People's Republic of China. Armonk, N.Y., M. E. Sharpe, [1981]. 729p. il.　　**AJ162**

"A publication of the Institute of Asian Affairs in Hamburg."—*t.p.*

Intended as a guide to the currently active leaders of China; information was drawn "primarily from the daily Chinese press. . . and reports from the Summary of World Broadcasts of the BBC."—*Pref.* Includes government and mass organization officials at levels specified in the standards for inclusion. Names are entered according to the Pinyin system of transliteration; Chinese characters and Wade-Giles romanization are also given. Details concerning date and place of birth, education, etc., were often not available and numerous entries consist only of positions held and a chronology of appointments and official activities. Many entries include a photograph. An extensive appendix offers background tables, lists of party, government, and mass organization officials, etc.　　　DS778.A1B33

Biographical dictionary of Republican China. Howard L. Boorman, ed. N.Y., Columbia Univ. Pr., 1967–79. 5v.　　　**AJ163**

Intended as a supplement to A. W. Hummel's *Eminent Chinese of the Ch'ing period* (AJ167) and concentrating on figures of the period 1911–49. Includes both living and deceased persons; about 600 biographies in the complete set. The final volume includes an extensive bibliography which lists the writings by the subject of each article in the dictionary, together with the sources (books, periodicals, manuscripts) used in preparing the article. v.5 is a personal name index. A substantial and scholarly work.　　　DS778.A1B5

Giles, Herbert Allen. A Chinese biographical dictionary. London, Quaritch; Shanghai, Kelly and Walsh, 1898. 1022p.　　　**AJ164**

A standard dictionary in English, not completely superseded by the Library of Congress volumes listed below. May be supplemented and corrected on certain points by the use of the following: E. von Zach. "Einige Verbesserungen zu Giles' Chinese biographical dictionary." *Asia major* 3:545–68. 1926; Paul Pelliot. "A propos du 'Chinese biographical dictionary' de M. H. Giles. *Ibid.* 4:377–89. 1927; Paul Pelliot. "Les Yi nien lou." *T'oung pao* 25:65–81. 1927.　　　DS734.G46

Gillis, Irvin Van Gorder and **Yü, Ping-yüeh.** Supplementary index to Giles' "Chinese biographical dictionary." Peiping, 1936. 88p.　　　**AJ165**

Perleberg, Max. Who's who in modern China (from the beginning of the Chinese Republic to the end of 1953). . . . Hong Kong, Ye Olde Printerie, 1954. 428p. il.　　　**AJ166**

Subtitle: Over two thousand detailed biographies of the most important men who took part in the great struggle for China, including detailed histories of the political parties, government organizations, a glossary of new terms used in contemporary Chinese together with a double index in Chinese and English and two charts.

Includes persons both living and dead. Now much out-of-date, but may be useful for the period covered. Entries are of the usual who's who type, with much additional information on government structure and personnel for both Nationalist and Communist China. The indexes cover only the biographical sections. Text is in English.　　　DS734.P4

U.S. Library of Congress. Orientalia Division. Eminent Chinese of the Ch'ing period (1644–1912). Ed. by Arthur W. Hummel. Wash., Govt. Prt. Off., 1943–44. 2v.　　**AJ167**

Designed to include some 800 sketches of eminent Chinese of the last 300 years, primarily of the epoch ruled by the Ch'ing dynasty (1644–1912). A very useful reference work, with detailed, authoritative, signed articles and references to sources. "No independent sketches are included for persons who died after 1912; but it was found possible to incorporate information, sometimes in considerable detail, of many men who lived after that date, and of not a few who are still living."—*Editor's note.*　　　DS734.U65

Contemporary

See also AJ56.

Who's who in China; biographies of Chinese leaders. Shanghai, China Weekly Review, 1918–50. v.1–6. il.　　　**AJ168**

Publisher varies; subtitle varies.

1st ed. 1918; 2d ed. 1920; 3d ed. 1925; 3d ed. Suppl. [1928?]; 4th ed. 1932; 4th ed. Suppl. 1933; 5th ed. 1936; 5th ed. Suppl. 1940; 6th ed. 1950.

The 5th ed. is the first in the series to include biographies of women.　　　DS734.W5

Who's who in Communist China. Ed.[1]– . [Kowloon], Hong Kong, Union Research Institute, [1966–].　　　**AJ169**

Ed.[2] published 1969–70 in 2v.

Biographies of major personalities in contemporary political, diplomatic, military, cultural, and scientific affairs. Information was drawn from the biographical files of the Union Research Institute and from major Chinese Communist and foreign publications. Text is in English, with Chinese characters added for personal and place-names. About 1,600 biographies in the 2d ed., earlier sketches having been reviewed and updated as necessary; biographies of some recently deceased persons were retained because of continuing influence.　　　DS778.A1W45

Bibliography

Wu, Eugene Wen-chin. Leaders of twentieth-century China; an annotated bibliography of selected Chinese biographical works in the Hoover Library. Stanford, Calif., Stanford Univ. Pr., 1956. 106p. (Hoover Institute and Library. Bibliographical ser.4)　　　**AJ170**

Approximately 500 items, including collections, dictionaries, and serials, as well as individual biographies. Names are listed in roman type, followed by Chinese characters.　　　Z3106.W8

COLOMBIA

Ospina, Joaquín. Diccionario biográfico y bibliográfico de Colombia. . . . Bogotá, Ed. de Cromos, 1927–39. 3v. il.　　　**AJ171**

Imprint varies.

Covers from the Spanish conquest to the 20th century. Includes persons of many professions who contributed to the development of the country.　　　F2255.O84

Quién es quién en Colombia, 1978. Biografías contemporáneas. Bogotá, Temis, 1978. 400p. il.　　　**AJ172**

An earlier series with the same title appeared in four editions (Bogotá, Oliverio Perry, 1944–70).

The first edition of a new who's who series for contemporary Colombians. A "Clasificación por profesiones" (p.387–400) groups the names of the biographees by occupation.　　　CT706.Q53

CONGO

See also AJ127, AJ130.

Artigue, Pierre. Qui sont les leaders congolais? Bruxelles, Éd. Europe-Afrique, [1961]. 375p. **AJ173**

1st ed. 1960.
The 2d ed. is more political than the first and includes more than 800 biographical sketches of senators, deputies, ministers, and other officials, business leaders, journalists, etc. DT663.A2A7

COSTA RICA

Who's who in Costa Rica, 1979/80– . [San José, Costa Rica, Lubeck S.A., 1979]– . il. Irregular? **AJ174**

"Professions—commerce—government. Bilingual edition—English Spanish."—*t.p., 1979/80.*
Each biographical sketch is given in both English and Spanish. The biographical section is followed by a "Business & government institutions section," again with information in both English and Spanish. CT586.W47

CUBA

See also AJ56.

Peraza Sarausa, Fermín. Diccionario biográfico cubano. Habana, Ed. Anuario Bibliográfico Cubano, 1951–68. v.1–14. **AJ175**

Imprint varies; v.12–14 publ. in Gainesville, Fla.
Contents: v.1–7, Abad–Z; v.8–11, A–Iz; v.12–14 *see* below.
Volumes 1–11 were a re-issue (1951–60), in mimeographed form, of a collection of Cuban biographies which originally appeared in *El mundo* (Havana). Only persons no longer living are included.
Because information files for the project were destroyed after the Communist takeover in Cuba, the original scheme of the publication had to be abandoned. v.12 offers a new series of biographies in alphabetical sequence, A–L, plus a general index to v.1–12; v.13–14 each presents new biographies in a complete alphabet, and each volume carries an index to sketches in the full series. F1755.P4

———— Personalidades cubanas. Habana, Ed. Anuario Bio-bibliográfico Cubana, 1957–68. v.1–8. **AJ176**

Imprint varies.
v.1–7 cover 1957–59; v.8–10 have subtitle *Cuba en el exilio.*
A companion work to the preceding; gives brief sketches of living persons. v.10 includes a general alphabetical index to the series. F1755.P45

CZECHOSLOVAKIA

See also AJ56.

Biographisches Lexikon zur Geschichte der böhmischen Länder. Hrsg. im Auftrag des Collegium Carolinum von Heribert Sturm. Wien, Oldenbourg, 1974–83. Bd.1–2⁸. (In progress) **AJ177**

Contents: Bd.1, A–H; Bd.2, Lfg.1–8, I–Me.
The completed work is expected to include about 10,000 brief biographical sketches. References to other biographical sources are given at the end of the articles. CT933.B56

Kdo je kdo v Československu. Biografie žijících osob se stálým bydlištěm v ČSSR. Vyd.1. Praha, Československá Tisková Kancelář, 1969. 1v. **AJ178**

Contents: v.1, A–J. No more published.
A who's who for Czechoslovakia. CT930.K37

Kuhn, Heinrich and **Böss, Otto.** Biographisches Handbuch der Tschechoslowakei. München, R. Lerche, 1961. 640p. (Veröffentlichungen des Collegium Carolinum) **AJ179**

In German. Preliminary sections, giving personnel of party and state organizations, societies, institutions, universities, etc., are followed by the biographical section which offers sketches of the who's who type. CT930.K8

DENMARK

See also AJ32.

Dansk biografisk Haandleksikon, redig. af Svend Dahl og P. Engelstoft. Kjøbenhavn, Gyldendal, 1920–26. 3v. il. **AJ180**

Less comprehensive than Bricka (below), this work includes some 6,000 rather brief biographical sketches, signed, with bibliographies and small illustrations. Covers from early to modern times. CT1263.D3

Dansk biografisk Leksikon, grundlagt af C. F. Bricka, redig. af Povl Engelstoft under Medvirkning af Svend Dahl; udg. med Støtte af Carlsbergfondet. København, Schultz, 1933–44. 27v. **AJ181**

Contents: v.1–26, A–Østrup; v.27, Supplement.
Signed articles with bibliographies, covering from early times to period of publication, and including names of living persons. A revised, much enlarged edition of Bricka's *Dansk biografisk Lexikon* (1887–1905. 19v.), although some names recorded there were not taken over into the new edition.
A 3d ed. is in progress: CT1263.D33

———— 3. udg. Red., Sv. Cedergreen Bech. [København], Gyldendal, [1979]–83. v.1–14. (In progress) **AJ181a**

"Grundlagt 1887 af C. F. Bricka og videreført 1933–44 af Povl Engelstoft under medvirken af Svend Dahl."—*t.p.*
Contents: v.1–14, Abbestée-Trepka.
A revised and expanded edition of this standard work. Some names have not been carried over from the previous edition, but many new entries (representing some early figures as well as persons deceased since preparation of the previous edition) have been added. Articles are signed; bibliographies are included. An asterisk after the contributor's name indicates that the article was carried over from the 2d ed. without substantial change. CT1263.D33

Marquard, Emil. Danske gesandter og gesandtskabspersonale indtil 1914. Udg. af Rigsarkivet. København, I Kommission hos Eijnar Munksgaards Forlag, 1952. 493p. **AJ182**

A biographical dictionary of Danish diplomats, in two parts: (1) up to 1648, and (2) 1648–1914. Each section is arranged by the country to which the diplomats were assigned. Name index. JX1811.A2M3

Contemporary

Kraks blaa bog; nulevende danske maends og kvinders levnedsløb. København, Krak, 1910– . v.1– . Annual. **AJ183**

The standard Danish who's who. 1979 has a general index to the names included in v.1–70, 1910–78. DL144.K7

Bibliography

Erichsen, Balder and **Krarup, Alfred.** Dansk personalhistorisk Bibliografi; systematisk Fortegnelse over Bidrag til

Danmarks Personalhistorie (i Tilslutning til Bibliotheca danica). København, Gads, 1917. 806p. (Dansk historisk Bibliografi. 3. Bd.) **AJ184**

Includes books and analytical material, indexing many articles in periodicals. Lists more than 15,000 references. As it usually gives dates of birth or death and some characterizing phrase, it can be used for such direct biographical information, as well as for its bibliographical references.

Continued informally by the indexing of biographical articles, also with dates and characterizing phrases, given in the *Dansk Tidsskrift-Index* under the heading *Personalhistorie*; for description *see* AE273. Z2576.E68

ECUADOR

Aguilar Paredes, Jaime. Grandes personalidades de la patria ecuatoriana: galería biográfica. 2. ed. Ambata, Ed. Pio XII, 1979. 376p. **AJ185**

1st ed. 1973.
About 40 biographical sketches in non-alphabetical sequence. Bibliography of biographical works, pp.369–74. F3705.A48

Pérez Marchant, Braulio. Diccionario biográfico del Ecuador. Quito, Escuela de Artes y Oficios, 1928. 515p. il. **AJ186**

Covers all periods, but is mainly 19th century. F3705.P43

ETHIOPIA

See also AJ102.

The dictionary of Ethiopian biography. [Addis Ababa, Institute of Ethiopian Studies, 1975–] v.1– . (In progress) **AJ187**

Editors: Belaynesh Michael, S. Chojnacki, Richard Pankhurst.
Contents: v.1, From early times to the end of the Zagwe dynasty c.1270 A.D.
"Because of the limited historical sources available for the early period covered [in v.1] . . . the majority of entries are devoted to kings, religious leaders, warriors and other personalities who appear on coins, inscriptions and in manuscripts."—*Pref.* Includes persons "irrespective of nationality who, for good or ill, played a significant rôle in the area." Signed articles; bibliographies. CT2153.D53

FINLAND

See also AJ32.

Finsk biografisk handbok, under medvärken af fackmän utg. af Tor Capelan. Helsingfors, Edlunds Förlag, 1903. 2v. **AJ188**

Issued in parts, 1895–1903.
Signed biographical sketches, but little bibliography. CT1220.F5

Heikinheimo, Ilmari, ed. Suomen elämäkerrasto. Helsinki, Werner Söderström, [1955]. 855p. il. **AJ189**

Fairly brief sketches of personalities of all periods, with many portraits. Particularly strong for the 18th and 19th centuries. DK448.H4

Kuka kukin oli. Who was who in Finland. Henkilötietoja 1900-luvulla kuolleista julkisuuden suomalaisista. Helsingissä, Otava, [1961]. 593p. **AJ190**

Covers 1900–61.

Contemporary

Kuka kukin on (Aikalaiskirja). Who's who in Finland. Henkilötietoja nykypolven suomalaisista, 1920– . Helsingissä, Kustannusosakeyhtiö Otava, [1920]– . Irregular. **AJ191**

Title varies: 1920–41, *Aikalaiskirja*.
1982 latest published. CT1220.K8

Vem och vad? Biografisk handbok, 1920– . Helsingfors, H. Schildt, 1920– . Irregular. **AJ192**

Published quinquennially through 1941, but because of the war the volume due in 1946 was not published until 1948; irregular thereafter. CT1220.V4

FRANCE

❖The principal 19th-century dictionaries of French biography are the international works: *Biographie universelle* (Michaud) (AJ29) and *Nouvelle biographie générale* (Hoefer) (AJ38). *See also* Paris. Bibliothèque Nationale. *Répertoire de l'histoire de la Révolution Française,* v.1, Personnes (DC150).

Académie des Sciences (France). Index biographique de l'Académie des Sciences du 22 décembre 1666 au 1^{ier} octobre 1978. [4.éd.] Paris, Gauthier-Villars, 1979. 513p. **AJ193**

Earlier eds. appeared 1939, 1954 and 1968.
Lists, with brief biographical information, all persons who have been members or *correspondants* of the Academy since its origin in 1666. Q46.A163

Dictionnaire de biographie française. Paris, Letouzey, 1933–83. v.1–16^2. (In progress) **AJ194**

Issued in parts, 1929– . Editors vary.
Contents: v.1–16, fasc.2, A–Goislard.
An important dictionary of national biography; planned to be a much more extensive work than the corresponding dictionaries of English and American biography. Articles, which in the main are shorter than those in the *Dictionary of national biography* (AJ217), are signed with the writers' names, and nearly all have bibliographies, some of which are very extensive. CT143.D5

Haag, Eugène and **Haag, Émile.** La France protestante; ou, Vies des protestants français qui se sont fait un nom dans l'histoire depuis les premiers temps de la Réformation jusqu'à la reconnaissance du principe de la liberté des cultes par l'Assemblée Nationale. Paris, Genève, Cherbuliez, 1846–59. 10v. **AJ195**

There is a later edition of which only v.1–6 (A–Gasparen) were published (Paris, Sandoz, 1877–88).
Sketches vary in length from a few lines to several pages. Bibliographies are composed largely of material by, rather than about, the biographee, but these are extensive. v.10 consists of *Pièces justificatives,* and includes the texts of edicts, laws, and other source materials relating to Protestantism in France. BX4843.H32

Hommes et destins (Dictionnaire biographique d'outremer). Paris, Académie des Sciences d'Outre-Mer, [1975]–81. 4v. (Académie des Sciences d'Outre-Mer. Publications. Travaux et mémoires, n.s., no.2, 5, 9) **AJ196**

A biographical series concerned with outstanding figures in French colonial territories, including citizens of the new nations, explorers, administrators, missionaries, doctors, anthropologists, engineers, etc., who made significant contributions in those areas. Includes about 500 signed biographies, mainly of 20th century figures. Bibliographies include writings by and about the individual. v.3 comprises some 250 sketches of deceased persons of prominence in Madagascar; the 35 sketches of Madagascar personalities included in v.1–2 are not repeated, but are listed in the front matter of v.3.

The final volume adds 264 sketches from various territories and includes a name index for v.1–4. CT1014.H65

Kuscinski, August. Dictionnaire des conventionnels. Paris, Au Siège de la Société, 1916–19. 615p. (Société de l'Histoire de la Révolution Française) **AJ197**

Issued in parts.

Biographical sketches of the members of the National Convention, 1792–95.

Robert, Adolphe, Bourloton, Edgar and **Cougny, Gaston.** Dictionnaire des parlementaires français, comprenant tous les membres des assemblées et tous les ministres français depuis le Ier mai 1789 jusqu'au Ier mai 1889. Paris, Bourloton, 1891. 5v. il. **AJ198**

Offers biographical sketches of French parliamentarians and ministers.

Continued by the *Dictionnaire des parlementaires français* under the editorship of Jean Jolly (CJ297).

For complete citation *see* CJ298. JN2771.R7

Contemporary

Dictionnaire biographique français contemporain. 2.éd., 1954–55. Paris, Pharos, Agence Internat. de Documentation Contemporaine, 1954. 708p. il. **AJ199**

1st ed. 1950.

A dictionary of contemporary French biography, with an index by profession, society membership, etc. Bibliographies are usually given of works by a writer, but only occasionally are works about a person listed.

——— Supplements 1–2, 1955–56.

Each includes a few new sketches and brief notes bringing to date some of the biographies in the main work. DC406.D5

Nouveau dictionnaire national des contemporains, 1961/62–68. Paris, Éd. du Nouveau Dictionnaire National des Contemporains, 1962–68. 5v. **AJ200**

An illustrated biographical dictionary of contemporary personalities with fairly long sketches in the general style and format of the *Dictionnaire national des contemporains* dirigé par Nath Imbert (Paris, Lajeunesse, 1936–39. 3v. il.), which included more than 3,000 names of persons prominent in the 1930s. DC412.N58

Who's who in France; dictionnaire biographique. Ed.1– , 1953/54– . Paris, Lafitte, 1953– . Biennial. **AJ201**

1st ed., 1953/54, had title *Who's who in France: Paris,* and was restricted to persons living in Paris.

Later editions cover all of France, as well as French persons overseas and French-speaking peoples in African nations, etc. Sketches are of the usual who's who type. In spite of the English title, sketches and explanatory text are in French. In addition to the biographical sketches, there is a section listing government officials, information about large business firms, etc.

An earlier, similar publication, *Qui êtes-vous?* (Paris, Delagrave), appeared in three editions: 1908, 1909, 1924. DC705.A1W46

Regional

❖Many dictionaries of local biography have been published. Titles of some of these may be found in Schneider's *Handbuch der Bibliographie,* p.502–503 (AA11).

GERMANY

Allgemeine deutsche Biographie; hrsg. durch die Historische Commission bei der K. Akademie der Wissenschaften. Leipzig, Duncker, 1875–1912. 56v. **AJ202**

Contents: v.1–45, A–Z; v.46–55, Nachträge bis 1899, Andr–Z (A–Ad included in v.45); v.56, General Register.

The outstanding German biographical dictionary, containing long, signed articles, with bibliographies, on persons from early times to the end of the 19th century. Does not include living persons. As there are supplementary sections in many volumes, it is essential that the index be used to find the complete record.

For biographies of persons deceased since the compilation of this work, the following may be used as informal supplements: CT1053.A5

Biographisches Jahrbuch und deutscher Nekrolog, 1896–1913; hrsg. von Anton Bettelheim. Berlin, Reimer, 1897–1917. v.1–18 and separate index volume. Annual. **AJ203**

Each volume contains: (1) section of long, signed articles, with bibliographies, on prominent Germans who died during the year; (2) a necrology of briefer notices; and (3) index. The index volume is a combined index to v.1–10 (1896–1905).

Continued by: CT1050.B5

Deutsches biographisches Jahrbuch, hrsg. vom Verbande der Deutschen Akademien, 1914–23, 1928–29. Berlin, Deutsche Verlagsanstalt, 1925–32. v.1–5, 10–11. **AJ204**

Contents: v.1, 1914–16; v.2, 1917–20; v.3, 1921; v.4, 1922; v.5, 1923; v.10, 1928; v.11, 1929.

Contains long, signed articles, many with bibliographies, and a necrology list of briefer notices. No cumulated index. CT1050.D4

Deutsches biographisches Archiv: eine Kumulation aus 254 der wichtigsten biographischen Nachschlagswerke für den deutschen Bereich bis zum Ausgang des neunzehnten Jahrhunderts. Hrsg. von Bernhard Fabian. München, K. G. Saur, 1982. 1421 microfiches accompanied by descriptive pamphlet. **AJ205**

Advertised under title: *German biographical archive.*

Like the same publisher's *British biographical archive* (AJ224), cumulates into a single alphabet the biographical sketches from a wide range of biographical dictionaries, both single and multi-volume works; about 250,000 entries in all.

Die grossen Deutschen: deutsche Biographie, hrsg. von Hermann Heimpel, Theodor Heuss, Benno Reifenberg. Berlin, Propyläen-Verlag, 1957–58. (v.1–2, 1958) 5v. il. **AJ206**

Nonalphabetical; gives in chronological order signed biographies, several pages in length, of 234 figures outstanding in German cultural, religious, military and political history, etc., from 672 to recent times.

The original edition was edited by Willy Andreas and Wilhelm von Scholz (1935–37). The new edition is greatly rewritten, many articles are by different authors, and the illustrations—some in color, some facsimiles—have been changed. v.5 is a supplementary volume with a cumulated index to the set. CT1054.G72

Neue deutsche Biographie. Hrsg. von der Historischen Kommission bei der Bayerischen Akademie der Wissenschaften . . . Berlin, Duncker und Humblot, 1953–82. Bd.1–13 (In progress) **AJ207**

Contents: Bd.1–13, Aachen-Laven.

A newly compiled work, not intended to supersede the *Allgemeine deutsche Biographie* (AJ202), although many of the same names appear in it along with persons who have died since the older work was published and some additional names from earlier periods. Articles are signed, and bibliographies, including materials by and about biographees, are given at the end of each article. References to portraits are sometimes noted. An index in each volume, covering the part of the alphabet contained therein, includes references to all entries in the *Allgemeine deutsche Biographie,* thus calling attention to articles omitted from the newer work.

Rössler, Hellmuth and **Franz, Günther.** Biographisches Wörterbuch zur deutschen Geschichte. 2., völlig neubearb. und stark erw. Aufl. bearb. von Karl Bosl, Günther Franz, Hanns Hubert Hofmann. München, Francke Verlag, [1973–75]. 3v. **AJ208**

1st ed. 1952 included some 2,000 individual biographies, in all fields and from Roman times to 1933, mainly of Germans but also of some foreigners important in the history of Germany.

This is a new and enlarged edition, with numerous articles added and bibliographies updated. The work now covers down to the present, and about four-fifths of the material is either new or rewritten. Name index in v.3.

Reviews in *Erasmus* 27:426–30 (1975) and 30:630 (1978), while recognizing the importance of the work, point to "weaknesses in conception and execution" as well as certain factual errors in the text.　　　　　　　　　　　　　　　　　　　DD85.R572

Contemporary

Biographisches Handbuch der deutschsprachigen Emigration nach 1933. München, K. G. Saur, 1980–83. 3v. in 4.
　　　　　　　　　　　　　　　　　　　　　　　　AJ209

"International biographical dictionary of Central European emigrés 1933–1945, sponsored by Research Foundation for Jewish Immigration, Inc., New York, and Institut für Zeitgeschichte München, directed by Herbert A. Strauss and Werner Röder."—*half-t.p.*

v.1 has title in German; v.2 has title in English.

Contents: v.1, Politik, Wirtschaft, Öffentliches Leben; v.2, The arts, sciences, and literature (in 2v.); v.3, Gesamtregister; Index.

Offers some 8,700 biographical sketches of persons (living and deceased) who emigrated from Central European areas during the period of the Third Reich. v.3 offers indexes by names, pseudonyms, cover names and name changes, by countries of intermediate emigration and final settlement, by occupations, plus selected references to parties, associations, and institutions mentioned in the text.
　　　　　　　　　　　　　　　　　　　　　　　　DD68.B52

Kürschners deutscher Gelehrten-Kalender . . . 1925– . Berlin, W. de Gruyter, 1925– .　　　　　　　　　　**AJ210**

2d ed. 1926; 3d ed. 1928; 4th ed. 1931; 5th ed. 1935; 6th ed. 1940/41; 7th ed. 1950; 8th ed. 1954; 9th ed. 1961; 10th ed. 1966; 11th ed. 1970; 12th ed. 1976; 13th ed. 1980; 14th ed. 1984.

A biographical dictionary of German scholars in non-literary fields, an offshoot of *Kürschners deutscher Literatur-Kalender* (BD853). The editions vary considerably in size and content, both as to names included and as to supplementary information. The 1983 edition is in 3v., treating about 41,500 personalities. Extensive bibliographical listings.　　　　　　　　　　Z2280.K96

Wer ist wer? Das deutsche who's who. [Ausg.1]– . Hrsg. von Walter Habel. Berlin, Arani, [1905]– .　　　　　**AJ211**

Title varies: v.1–9 (1905–28), *Wer ist's?;* v.10 (1935), *Degener's Wer ist's?* Frequency varies; 22d ed. publ. 1983.

v.1–10 ed. by H. A. L. Degener.

The standard German who's who, offering sketches of personalities in all fields. 14th ed. (publ. 1962–65), issued in 2v., the first covering "Bundesrepublik Deutschland und West Berlin," the second, the German Democratic Republic. Later eds. are concerned with personalities of the German Federal Republic and West Berlin, with some Swiss and Austrian figures included in recent volumes. About 40,000 entries in the 22d ed.　　　　　　DD85.W3

Who's who in Germany: a biographical dictionary . . . 1956– . Munich, Oldenbourg, 1955– . Irregular.　**AJ212**

Publisher varies; subtitle varies.

Another in the English-language series of who's whos of European countries. Includes biographical sketches and a directory of organizations, associations, and institutions in the Federal Republic of Germany. The 8th ed. (1982/83) includes about 17,000 biographies of prominent persons.　　　　　　　　　　DD85.W45

Who's who in the arts and literature. Ed.1– . Ottobrunn nr. Munich, Who's Who-Book & Pub., 1975– . Irregular.
　　　　　　　　　　　　　　　　　　　　　　　　AJ213

Title varies; originally entitled *Who's who in the arts,* the work omitted literature and concerned itself only with figures from the Federal Republic of Germany. The 3d ed. (1982) includes "20,000 prominent artists and authors from the Federal Republic of Germa-

ny, Austria and Switzerland."—*t.p.* That edition is in 4v.: v.1–2, Fine arts; v.3, Literature; v.4, Applied arts and music.

Regional

❖Many dictionaries and collections of local biography often contain names or information not given in the general dictionaries of German biography. A useful list of these regional works is given in Schneider's *Handbuch der Bibliographie,* p.485–97 (AA11).

GERMANY, EAST

See also AJ56.

Buch, Günther. Namen und Daten wichtiger Personen der DDR. 3., überarb. u. erw. Aufl. [Berlin], Dietz, [1982]. 384p.
　　　　　　　　　　　　　　　　　　　　　　　　AJ214

1st ed. 1973.

Provides biographical information on prominent persons of the German Democratic Republic. "Nekrolog," p.363–84.
　　　　　　　　　　　　　　　　　　　　　　　CT1099.2.B82

SBZ-Biographie; ein biographisches Nachschlagebuch über die Sowjetische Besatzungszone Deutschlands. Hrsg. von Bundesministerium für gesamtdeutsche Fragen. Bonn, Deutscher Bundes-Verlag, 1958– .　　　　　　　**AJ215**

Title varies: 1958, *Wer ist wer in der SBZ?*

1964 last published?

Biographical sketches of persons in East Germany.

GHANA

See also AJ102.

Ghana who's who. 1972/73– . Accra, Bartels, 1972– . Irregular.　　　　　　　　　　　　　　　　　　　　　**AJ216**

Subtitle: A . . . biographical dictionary of prominent men and women in the country, including an encyclopaedia of useful information.　　　　　　　　　　　　　　　　DT510.6.A1G45

GREAT BRITAIN

Dictionary of national biography, ed. by Sir Leslie Stephen and Sir Sidney Lee. [Reissue.] London, Smith, Elder, 1908–09. 22v. (Repr. 1938.)　　　　　　　　　　　**AJ217**

Contents: v.1–21, A–Z; v.22, 1st suppl., Additional names, 1901.

—— 2d–8th supplements. Oxford, Univ. Pr., 1912–81. 7v.

2d suppl., 1901–11, ed. by Sir Sidney Lee. 1912; 3d suppl., 1912–21, ed. by H. W. C. Davis and J. R. H. Weaver. 1927; 4th suppl., 1922–30, ed. by J. R. H. Weaver. 1937; 5th suppl., 1931–40; ed. by L. G. Wickham Legg. 1949; 6th suppl., 1941–50, ed. by L. G. Wickham Legg and E. T. Williams. 1959; 7th suppl., 1951–60, ed. by E. T. Williams and Helen M. Palmer. 1971; 8th suppl., 1961–70, ed. by E. T. Williams and C. S. Nichols.

—— Index and epitome, ed. by Sir Sidney Lee. London, Smith, Elder, 1903–13. 2v.

Contents: Index and epitome to main set and 1st suppl. (22v.) 2d ed. 1906. 1456p.; Index . . . to 2d suppl. 1913. 129p.

History: Founded by George Smith of the London firm of Smith, Elder and Co., and originally published by that firm as follows: Main work and 1st suppl. 63v. 1885–1901; Index and epitome to v.1–63,

1903. 1456p.; Errata for v.1–63. 1904. 299p.; 2d suppl. 3v. 1912; Index and epitome to 2d suppl. 1913. 129p.; Reissue of 63v. ed., on thinner paper, with the incorporation in the text of the material in the Errata volume. 22v. 1908–1909. Presented, 1917, by the heirs of George Smith, to the Oxford University Press, to be continued by that institution. In 1920 the Press reissued the 2d supplement, on thin paper, in 1v. and has continued the work by publishing the 3d–8th supplements and *The concise dictionary.* Though the original work has not been revised by the present publisher, an informal revision of many articles is to be found in the Errata notes published in the *Bulletin* of the Institute of Historical Research of London University; a cumulation of those notes for the 1923–63 period was published by G. K. Hall in 1966 (*see* below).

Constitutes the most important reference work for English biography, containing signed articles by specialists, and excellent bibliographies; important names are treated at great length, minor names more briefly, and all are generally reliable and scholarly. Scope includes all noteworthy inhabitants of the British Isles and the Colonies, exclusive of living persons; also noteworthy Americans of the colonial period. The supplements bring the record down to 1970. Each supplement includes a cumulative index covering all entries from 1901 in one alphabetical sequence.　　DA28.D45

————— The concise dictionary. London, Oxford Univ. Pr., [1953–61]. 2v.　　**AJ218**

A reprinting of the *Index and epitome* (above) with corrections and additions extending coverage through 1950.

Contents: pt.1, From the beginning to 1900; being an epitome of the main work and its supplement. 1503p. [The reprint lists, on p.1457–1503, corrections and additions.]; pt.2, 1901–1950; being an epitome of the twentieth century *D.N.B.* down to the end of 1950. 528p. [Includes a "Select subject index," p.485–528.]

The concise dictionary serves a double purpose, i.e., it is both an index and also an independent biographical dictionary (since it gives abstracts, each about one-fourteenth of the length of the original article).　　DA28.D56

v.2 is superseded by:

————— The concise dictionary. Part II, 1901–1970. Oxford, Oxford Univ. Pr., 1982. 747p.

Supersedes the "Part II, 1901–1950" volume published 1961. Adds epitomes through 1970, but omits the "Select subject index" found in the earlier volume.

————— Corrections and additions to the Dictionary of national biography, cumulated from the Bulletin of the Institute of Historical Research, University of London, covering the years 1923–1963. Boston, G. K. Hall, 1966. 212p.　　**AJ219**

At head of title: Institute of Historical Research, London.

Assembles the "Corrections and additions" from the *Bulletin* in alphabetical sequence, providing a convenient and essential supplement to the *DNB.*　　DA28.L65

Bellamy, Joyce M. and **Saville, John.** Dictionary of labour biography. [London], Macmillan; [Clifton, N.J.], A. M. Kelley, [1972–84]. v.1–7. (In progress)　　**AJ220**

An ambitious biographical dictionary which intends to include "not only the national personalities of the British labour movement but also the activists at regional and local level."—*Introd.* Indeed, "everyone who made a contribution, however modest, to any organisation or movement, provided that certain basic details of their career can be established," is to be included. The period of coverage is from 1790 to the present, but excluding living persons. It is expected that 15 to 20 volumes will be required to treat figures down to 1914. Each volume is alphabetically arranged and includes biographies without regard to date of the biographee's activity, and a consolidated index appears in each successive volume; a system of cross references is also provided, referring to both earlier and later volumes. v.6 includes a list of additions and corrections for v.1–5.　　HD8393.A1B44

Biographical dictionary of modern British radicals. Ed. by Joseph O. Baylen and Norbert J. Gossman. [Hassocks, Sussex], Harvester Pr.; [Atlantic Highlands, N.J.], Humanities Pr., [1979]–83. 3v.　　**AJ221**

Contents: v.1, 1770–1830; v.2, 1830–70; v.3, 1870–1914.

"For the purpose of this biographical dictionary, the term 'Radical' has been interpreted to include those persons whose programmes and work involved something more than a moderate adjustment of policy or minor change in the operation of political, social and economic institutions. More specifically, our primary interest is in two categories of Radicals: (1) those who hoped to change in some fundamental way the old order in which Britain was dominated by the landed aristocracy and the established Church; and (2) those who sought to alter the social and economic structure of society through positive state action, to achieve a more equitable distribution of wealth and social welfare legislation."—*Introd.*

Supplements the *Dictionary of national biography* (AJ217), including many persons not found therein and correcting sketches in the *DNB* as necessary. Complements the *Dictionary of labour biography* (above) and provides cross references to sketches of individuals which also appear in that work. Articles are of substantial length, are signed with the names of contributing scholars, and include bibliographic references.　　HN400.R3B56

Boase, Frederic. Modern English biography, containing many thousand concise memoirs of persons who have died since 1850, with an index of the most interesting matter. Truro, Netherton, 1892–1921. 6v. (Repr.: London, Frank Cass, 1964.)　　**AJ222**

Contents: v.1–3, A–Z, Index; v.4–6 (Suppl. v.1–3), A–Z.

A useful work, particularly for minor 19th-century names not included in the *Dictionary of national biography* (AJ217). Good subject index, including lists of pseudonyms, fancy names, class lists, etc.　　CT773.B6

British and Irish biographies, 1840–1940. David Lewis Jones, ed. Microfiche ed. Teaneck, N.J., Chadwyck-Healey Inc., 1984– . Pt.1– . (In progress)　　**AJ223**

To be issued in six parts over a 3-year period, this is a reproduction on microfiche of some 272 biographical dictionaries (totalling about 1,200 volumes). The biographical works, many of them multivolume sets, annuals, etc., are reproduced in full as published and a computer-produced index of names is provided; i.e., the biographical sketches are not cumulated into a single alphabet as in the *British biographical archive* (below).

British biographical archive. . . Microfiche ed. Laureen Baillie, managing ed. München, K. G. Saur, 1984– . (In progress. To be on 1200 microfiches.)　　**AJ224**

Subtitle [from fiche pocket]: A one-alphabet cumulation of 310 of the most important English-language biographical reference works originally published between 1601 and 1929.

Reproduces on microfiche the biographical sketches contained in works of collective biography as noted in the subtitle. Range of coverage is very broad, including both single and multi-volume works and works of local and specialized interest as well as general biographical dictionaries. Includes multiple sketches of more famous figures; source of the sketch is given at the end of each entry.

Catholic who's who, 1908–52. London, Burns, 1908–52. Annual (slightly irregular).　　**AJ225**

Title varies; until 1935, *Catholic who's who and yearbook.*
Suspended 1943–51. Ceased publication.　　DA28.8C3C33

The Europa biographical dictionary of British women; over 1000 notable women from Britain's past. Ed. by Anne Crawford [et al.]. [London], Europa; Detroit, Gale, [1983]. 436p.　　**AJ226**

The work of a team of six editors and eighty contributors. Only deceased women are included; articles are signed; bibliographical references are usually appended. Representation is broad, covering from earliest to recent times, and including those involved in public affairs; those active in feminist movements, social reform, philanthropy, and religious life; those "who influenced the course of events in a more informal way" (e.g., wives of kings and politicians); and those who "pursued traditional female occupations: actresses, singers, entertainers and writers and artists."—*Introd.*　　CT3320.E94

Gillow, Joseph. A literary and biographical history; or, Bibliographical dictionary of the English Catholics from the breach with Rome, in 1534, to the present time. London, Burns; N.Y., Catholic Pub. Soc., [1885–1902]. 5v. (Repr.: N.Y., Burt Franklin, 1961)   **AJ227**

Gives some 2,000 biographies. Useful for names not included in the *Dictionary of national biography* and for more information about some names which are there. Especially useful for the bibliographies which are very full.

May be supplemented by: Z2010.G483

Kirk, John. Biographies of English Catholics in the eighteenth century, by the Rev. John Kirk, being part of his projected continuation of Dodd's Church history, ed. by J. H. Pollen and Edwin Burton. London, Burns, 1909. 293p.   **AJ228**

    BX4676.K5

Thorpe, Arthur Winton, ed. Burke's Handbook to the most excellent Order of the British Empire; containing biographies, a full list of persons appointed to the Order . . . London, Burke, 1921. 703p. il.   **AJ229**

This order was established by Letters Patent on June 4, 1917, its members to be those who in either civil or military capacities rendered important services to the Empire. Therefore, this is a volume devoted primarily to the outstanding persons of the First World War.   CR4821.T5

Valentine, Alan Chester. The British establishment, 1760–1784; an eighteenth-century biographical dictionary. Norman, Univ. of Oklahoma Pr., [1970]. 2v.   **AJ230**

About 3,000 entries, nearly half of which do not appear in the *Dictionary of national biography.* "Though these skeleton biographies profess a reasonably thorough coverage only of the period from 1760 to 1784, their usefulness extends beyond that period. The biographical data about many of the individuals go back to 1700 or forward into the nineteenth century."—*Foreword.*   CT781.V3

Ward, Thomas Humphry. Men of the reign; a biographical dictionary of eminent persons of British and colonial birth who have died during the reign of Queen Victoria. London, Routledge, 1885. 1020p. (Repr.: Graz, Akad. Druck- u. Verlagsanstalt, 1968)   **AJ231**

A concise biographical dictionary of 19th-century personalities, containing some names included in neither the *Dictionary of national biography* (AJ217) nor Boase, *Modern English biography* (AJ222).   DA581.1.W2

Wedgwood, Josiah Clement. History of Parliament, 1439–1509. v.1, Biographies of the members of the Commons House. London, Stat. Off., 1936. v.1 (984p.). col. coats of arms.   **AJ232**

A list of 2,600 men, out of a possible total of 3,800 known to have been elected members of 29 Parliaments, 1439–1509, with biographical data about each and many bibliographical footnotes referring to sources. As only 60 of the 2,600 names are included in the *Dictionary of national biography,* this work is important for British biography as well as for Parliamentary history.

For description of set *see* CJ357.   JN505.W4

Who was who, 1897–1915, 1916–1928, 1929–1940, 1941–1950, 1951–1960, 1961–1970, 1971–1980; a companion to Who's who; containing the biographies of those who died during the period. London, Black, 1929–81. 7v.   **AJ233**

1897–1915 has been published in four editions: 1st ed. June 1920; 2d ed., with addenda and corrigenda, 1929; 3d ed., with rev. corrigenda, 1935; 4th ed., with rev. addenda and corrigenda, 1953.

For the most part the original sketches as they last appeared in *Who's who* (AJ236) are reprinted with the date of death added, but in a few instances additional information has been incorporated.   DA28.W65

———— A cumulated index, 1897–1980. London, Black; N.Y., St. Martin's Pr., [1981]. 746p.   **AJ234**

Provides an index to v.1–7 of the series. Death dates which did not appear in *Who was who* have been added in the index whenever available.

Contemporary

Kelly's Handbook to the titled, landed, and official classes, 1880–1977. London, Kelly Directories, 1880–1977. v.1–101. Annual.   **AJ235**

Brief biographical sketches of those who have hereditary or honorary titles; members of Parliament; government officials; landed proprietors; distinguished members of the dramatic, literary, and artistic worlds; and leaders in commerce and industry.

    CS419.K5

Who's who, an annual biographical dictionary, with which is incorporated "Men and women of the time." London, Black; N.Y., St. Martin's, 1849– . v.1– . Annual.   **AJ236**

The pioneer work of the who's who type and still one of the most important. Until 1897, it was a handbook of titled and official classes and included lists of names rather than biographical sketches. With 1897, called "First year of new issue," it changed its character and became a biographical dictionary of prominent persons in many fields. It has been developed and enlarged along these lines ever since. It is principally British, but a few prominent names of other nationalities are included. Biographies are reliable and fairly detailed; they give main facts, addresses, and, in case of authors, lists of works.

For a compilation of biographies of deceased persons selected from the volumes 1897–1980, see *Who was who* (AJ233).

    DA28.W6

Bibliography

Hart, Hester E. R. and **Johnston, Marjorie.** Bibliography of the registers (printed) of the universities, inns of court, colleges and schools of Great Britain and Ireland. (*In* London. University. Inst. of Historical Research. *Bull.,* 9:19–30, 65–83, 154–70, June, Nov. 1931, Feb. 1932; 10:109–13, Nov. 1932)   **AJ237**

A bibliography of registers, most of which include some biographical material. Pt.1, Universities, inns of court, colleges, and other similar institutions; pt.2, Schools; Addenda and corrigenda.

Hepworth, Philip, ed. Select biographical sources: the Library Association manuscripts survey. London, Lib. Assoc., 1971. 154p. (Lib. Assoc. Research Publ., 5)   **AJ238**

A preliminary effort to indicate location of manuscripts of biographical interest in British repositories. Similar to *American literary manuscripts* (BD389), but not limited by nationality (e.g., some Americans are included).   Z6616.A2H4

Matthews, William. British autobiographies; an annotated bibliography of British autobiographies published or written before 1951. Berkeley, Univ. of California Pr., 1955. 376p.   **AJ239**

Information given includes full name of author, abbreviated title, and date of publication with brief and pithy annotations. Arranged alphabetically by author with an index under headings indicating professions and occupations, places and regions, reminiscences, wars, and general topics.   Z2027.A9M3

Royal Commonwealth Society. Library. Biography catalogue, by Donald H. Simpson. London, Soc., 1961. 511p.

    AJ240

An index of biographical materials contained in the Society's library about persons in the Empire and the Commonwealth, and those in the United Kingdom and elsewhere connected with British imperial affairs. Books and periodical articles are both included. There is an extensive listing and index, by country, of works of collective biography, and an index of authors.   Z5301.R6

Stauffer, Donald Alfred. The art of biography in 18th century England: Bibliographical supplement. Princeton, N.J., Princeton Univ. Pr., 1941. 293p.   **AJ241**

A subject and author index of biographies and autobiographies written or translated in England 1700–1800, with a "chronological table of the most important biographical works in England, 1700–1800." A supplement to the author's *The art of biography in 18th century England* (Princeton, 1941).

Preceded by the author's *English biography before 1700* (Cambridge, Harvard Univ. Pr., 1930), which included a bibliography of early biographies published before 1700, p.289–372.

CT34.G7S67

Indexes

Index Society, London. An index to the biographical and obituary notices in the Gentleman's magazine, 1731–1780. London, British Record Soc., 1886–91. 677p. (Publ. of the British Record Soc. . . . Index Soc., v.15)   **AJ242**

Issued in parts.
A brief identifying phrase usually appears with the name.
Continued by: AI3.I4

Nangle, Benjamin Christie. The Gentleman's magazine biographical and obituary notices, 1781–1819: an index. N.Y., Garland, 1980. 422p. (Garland reference library of the humanities, v.212)   **AJ243**

A continuation of the Index Society compilation (above). As in the earlier publication, an identifying word or phrase is given with most names.   AP4.G312N36

Musgrave, *Sir* **William.** Obituary prior to 1800 (as far as relates to England, Scotland, and Ireland) comp. by Sir William Musgrave . . . and entitled by him "A general nomenclator and obituary, with reference to the books where the persons are mentioned, and where some account of their character is to be found." Ed. by Sir George J. Armytage. London, 1899–1901. 6v. (Publ. of the Harleian Soc., v.44–49)   **AJ244**

An alphabetical index to a large number of obituaries and biographies found in some 85 works. Gives name, date of death, sometimes a characterizing word or phrase, and reference to the book or other publication where a biography or obituary notice may be found. Very useful, especially for names not included in the *Dictionary of national biography* (AJ217).

GREECE

Viographiko lexiko prosōpikotētōn: who's who 1979. Athena, Ekdotikos Organismos Viographiko Lexiko Prosōpikotētōn, Who's Who, 1979. 768p. il.   **AJ245**

About 2,500 short biographies of contemporary figures in all fields.

HONG KONG

Hong Kong who's who: an almanac of personalities and their history. 1958/1960– . Hong Kong, [1959?]– .   **AJ246**

[2d ed.] 1970/73 publ. 1970.
Includes biographical sketches of prominent personalities, both oriental and occidental.   DS796.H7H68

HUNGARY

Jásznigi, Alexander and **Parlagi, Imre.** Das geistige Ungarn, biographisches Lexikon, hrsg. von Oskar von Krücken [pseud.] u. Imre Parlagi. Wien, Braumüller, [1918]. 2v.   **AJ247**

Includes principally writers, artists, and men in public life.
CT950.J3

Magyar életrajzi lexikon. Föszerkesztö Kenyeres Ágnes. Budapest, Akadémiai Kiadó, 1967–81. 3v. il.   **AJ248**

Brief biographical sketches of Hungarians of all periods (excluding living persons). Includes some bibliographical references; many small portraits. v.3 is a supplement.   DB922.M25

Szinnyei, József. Magyar írók; élete és munkái a Magyar Tudományos Akadémia megbizásából. Budapest, Hornyánszky V., 1891–1914. 14v.   **AJ249**

Continued by the following: Z2141.S9

Gulyás, Pál. Magyar írók; élete és munkái. Új sorozat. Budapest, Magyar Könyvtárosok és Levéltárosok Egyesülete, 1939–1944. v .1–6.   **AJ250**

Contents: v.1–6, A–Dzurányi. Ceased publication.
Based on principles of the *DNB*, this work includes biographies of notable Hungarians of all periods. More comprehensive than Jásznigi (AJ247) for the portion of the alphabet covered.
See also Wurzbach's *Biographisches Lexikon der Kaiserthums Oesterreich* (AJ118), which includes biographies of 3,344 Hungarians.   PH3028.G8

Contemporary

See also AJ56.

Fekete, Márton. Prominent Hungarians, home and abroad. 3d ed. London, Szepsi Csombor Literary Circle, 1979. 548p.   **AJ251**

1st ed. 1966.
Includes a list of persons deceased since the previous edition (1973).   CT963.F44

Szy, Tibor, ed. Hungarians in America; a biographical directory of professionals of Hungarian origin in the Americas. [2d ed.] N.Y., Kossuth Foundation, [1966]. 488 p. (East European biographies and studies, v.2)   **AJ252**

1st ed. 1963.   E184.H95S9

ICELAND

See also AJ32.

Ólason, Páll Eggert. Íslenzkar æviskrár frá landnámstímum til ársloka 1940. Reykjavík, Íslenzka Bókmenntafélags, 1948–52. 5v.   **AJ253**

A national biographical dictionary covering all periods up to 1940. Living persons are not included. Entries are brief but include bibliography. Biographees are entered under first name according to Icelandic usage.   CT1280.O55

INDIA

Buckland, Charles Edward. Dictionary of Indian biography. London, Sonnenschein, 1906. 494p. (Repr.: N.Y., Greenwood, 1969)   **AJ254**

Contains about 2,600 concise biographies of persons—English, Indian, or foreign—noteworthy in the history, service, literature, or science of India since 1750.   DS434.B8

Hayavadana Rao, Conjeeveram. Indian biographical dictionary, 1915. Madras, Pillar, [1915?]. 472p., 31p.   **AJ255**

Brief biographies, of the who's who type, of both natives and Europeans. Supplements give warrant of precedence, New Year's and Birthday honors, list of clubs, etc.

Sen, Siba Pada, ed. Dictionary of national biography. Calcutta, Inst. of Historical Studies, 1972–74. 4v.   **AJ256**

Limited to the period 1800 to 1947, but including personalities from the whole of pre-1947 India; some living persons are included. Aims to deal with "people from all walks of life—politics, religious and social reforms, education, journalism, literature, science, law, business and industry, etc.—who made some tangible contribution to national life from the beginning of the 19th century to the achievement of independence."—*Pref.* Figures at the local as well as the national level are included, but the individual must not only have "achieved some reputation in his own sphere of work or profession but must also have made some contribution, either directly or indirectly, to the growth of national consciousness or development of society." In general, figures in the performing arts and athletics are omitted, but were to be included in supplementary volumes. Articles are signed; bibliographies are appended. About 1,400 entries.   CT1502.S46

Who's who in India, containing lives and portraits of ruling chiefs, nobles, titled personages and other eminent Indians. Popular ed. Lucknow, Newul Kishore Pr., 1911–14. 1610p. and 2 suppl. il.   **AJ257**

Contains eight separate biographical lists, classified by states and provinces, each list arranged in general order of precedence, not alphabetically. General alphabetical index at end. Many portraits. Only native Indians included.   DS434.W5

Contemporary

India who's who, 1969– . New Delhi, INFA Publs., [1969–]. Annual.   **AJ258**

Subtitle: Leaders—listed professionwise. (Varies)
Biographical sketches of prominent Indians are presented under professional categories. Index of biographees.   CT1506.I53

Who's who in India, Burma and Ceylon. [Ed.1]–9. Poona, Sun Pub. House, 1911–38. Irregular.   **AJ259**

Title varies: *Who's who in India.* Imprint varies.
Contents of 9th ed. 1938: The royal family and provincial governors, p.1–34; Indian princes and chiefs, p.37–122; General, p.125–818; Who's who in Indian industries and commerce, p.1–48; Index, p.i–xxiii.
Other volumes bearing the title *Who's who in India* were published 1967 by Guide Publs., New Delhi, and in 1973 by Kothari Publs., Calcutta.   DS434.W43

IRAN

See also AJ309.

Iran who's who. Ed.1– , 1972– . Tehran, Echo of Iran, 1972– .   **AJ260**

Only one ed. publ.?
Biographical sketches, in English, of "important Iranian personalities in political, social, administrative, cultural, scientific, art, literature and sports fields."—*Introd.*   CT1886.I7

IRELAND

Boylan, Henry. A dictionary of Irish biography. [Dublin], Gill & Macmillan, [1978]. 385p.   **AJ261**

Intended as a successor to J. S. Crone's *Concise dictionary of Irish biography* (below), aiming to steer a middle course between the brevity of that work and the diffuseness of A. J. Webb's *Compendium of Irish biography* (1878) by "giving the important facts and events of the subject's career in chronological order and including, where possible, a sentence or quotation 'to give the flavour of the

man'."—*Introd.* Birth in Ireland was the first criterion for inclusion, but this was "modified to admit those who, though born abroad, had an Irish parent, or were of Irish descent, lived and worked in Ireland or made a considerable contribution to Irish affairs." Only deceased persons are included. Select bibliography, p.379–85.   CT862.B69

Crone, John Smyth. A concise dictionary of Irish biography. Rev. and enl. ed. Dublin, Talbot Pr.; N.Y., Longmans, 1937. 290p.   **AJ262**

1st ed. 1928.
Brief biographical sketches of "notable Irish men and women in every sphere of activity," from the early days to the 20th century. Does not include living persons. Appendix, p.271–90.
   DA916.C7

Ryan, Richard. Biographia hibernica. A biographical dictionary of the worthies of Ireland, from the earliest periods to the present time. London, Ryan, 1819–21. 2v.   **AJ263**

Long, discursive sketches.   DA916.A1R9

Who's who, what's what and where in Ireland. London, G. Chapman, 1973. 735p. il.   **AJ264**

Primarily a biographical directory, with separate sections for the Republic of Ireland and Northern Ireland. Includes numerous statistical tables, directories of government agencies, professional organizations, etc., as well as biographical sketches of individuals.
   CT793.W48

ISRAEL

Who's who: Israel, 1945/46–68. Tel Aviv, Who's Who in the State of Israel Pub. House, 1945–68. il. Biennial.   **AJ265**

Title varies: 1945/46, Palestine and Transjordan who's who; 1947, Palestine personalia; 1949, Who's who in the State of Israel.
Continued by: DS125.3.A2W53

Who's who in Israel and in the work for Israel abroad. Ed.14– , 1969/70– . Tel Aviv, Bronfman & Cohen, [1969]– . Biennial.   **AJ266**

In addition to the biographical sketches there are lists of government officials and a section on public and private organizations, etc.
   DS125.3.A2W54

ITALY

Dizionario biografico degli italiani. [Redazione, direttore: Alberto M. Ghisalberti] Roma, Istit. della Enciclopedia Italiana, 1960–83. v.1–29. (In progress)   **AJ267**

Contents: v.1–29, Aaron–Corvo.
A scholarly dictionary of national biography with signed biographies of Italians from the 5th century to the present, exclusive of living persons. A bibliography of source material is included for each sketch. The plan is to publish about two volumes a year, the completed set to comprise some 40,000 biographies.
   CT1123.D5

Enciclopedia biografica e bibliografica "Italiana." . . . Milano, Istit. Ed. Italiano, Bernardo Carlo Tosi, 1936–44. ser.4–50. il. (Incomplete)   **AJ268**

Announced for publication in 48 series, each devoted to a special class, e.g., writers, soldiers, scientists, actors, etc. Includes biographies of medium length, unsigned, but supplied with bibliographies and with illustrations taken from contemporary sources. Planned on a large scale but never carried to completion. Series were published in irregular order, and many were never issued.   CT1123.E6

Il movimento operaio italiano: dizionario biografico, 1853–1943. [A cura di] Franco Andreucci, Tommaso Detti. [Roma], Editori Riuniti, [1975–79]. 6v. il.   **AJ269**

Offers signed articles of substantial length, with bibliographies, on persons active in the Italian workers' movement.

v.6 is an index and includes a general bibliography, p. 159–308.

HD8483.A1M68

Savino, Edoardo. La nazione operante; albo d'oro del fascismo profili et figure . . . 3. ed. riv. e amp. Novara, Istit. Geografico de Agostini, 1937. 784p. il. **AJ270**

Contains some 2,150 biographies of prominent Fascists in all fields. DG574.S3

Contemporary

Chi è? Dizionario degli Italiani d'oggi. Ed.1–7. Roma, Scarano, 1928–61. **AJ271**

Issued irregularly: Suppl. 1929; 2. ed. 1931; 3. ed. 1936; 4. ed. 1940; 5. ed. 1948; 6. ed. 1957; 7. ed. 1961.

Another work with the same title was issued in 1908 by Guido Biagi.

A who's who of contemporary Italian personalities.

DG463.C62

Personaggipiu'. Ed. 1– . Milano, Who's Who in Italy, [1982]– . Irregular? **AJ272**

Subtitle, ed.1: Enciclopedia biografica contenente oltre 4.400 biografie dei personaggi più rappresentativi della vita italiana in campo economico, politico, letterario, scientifico, artistico, religioso, sportivo, ecc.

Vaccaro, Gennaro. Panorama biografico degli italiani d'oggi. Roma, Armando Curcio Editore, [1956]. 2v. (1648p.) **AJ273**

Contains some 25,000 biographical sketches of living Italians.

CT1133.V3

Who's who in Italy. [Ed.1–] 1957/1958– . Milano, Intercontinental Book and Pub., 1958– . Irregular. **AJ274**

Publisher varies.

The biographical section is followed by an appendix which offers various lists of government officials and diplomatic representatives, together with classified lists (with addresses) of cultural institutions, religious and industrial organizations, etc. About 8,000 biographies in the 4th ed. (1983). DG578.W5

Bibliography

Manzoni, Cesare. Biografia italica; saggio bibliografico di opere italiane a stampa per servire alla biografia italiani. Osnabrück, Biblio Verlag, 1981. 592p. **AJ275**

Introductory matter in Italian, English and German.

A bibliography of reference works containing biographical sketches of well known or famous Italians. Includes general biographical dictionaries and works of collective biography, volumes of local and regional biography, etc. Works are grouped by type, subdivided geographically as appropriate. Index of authors, editors, and anonymous titles.

Pizzi, Francesco. Italica gens; repertori a stampa di biografia generale italiana. Cremona, Moschetti, 1934. 131p.

AJ276

A bibliography of 1,238 biographical works in three parts: (1) general; (2) arranged by locality; and (3) arranged by subject. Author index.

JAMAICA

Who's who, Jamaica, British West Indies. An illustrated biographical record of outstanding Jamaicans and others connected with the island. Ed.1– , 1934/35– . Kingston, Who's Who (Jamaica), 1935– . Irregular. **AJ277**

Title varies: 1934/35–1939/40, *Who's who and why in Jamaica.* Subtitle varies. F1865.W63

JAPAN

❖The following entries represent some of the major Japanese biographical dictionaries, plus a number of English-language sources.

Dai-Nihon hakushi roku. Who's who in "Hakushi" in great Japan. Kuro Iseki, ed. Tokyo, Hattensha, [1921–30]. v.1–5. il. **AJ278**

Title varies slightly.

A dictionary of contemporary biography of Japanese who are *Hakushi,* or holders of the doctor's degree in various fields. Articles are in Japanese and English. Arranged by subjects: v.1, Law, Pharmacology; v.2–4, Medicine; v.5, Engineering.

Supplemented for the period 1888–1955 by *Nihon hakushi roku* (Tokyo, Kyoiku Gyosei Kenkyu-jo, 1956–64. 8v.), with annual supplements through 1962. A 4v. work of the same title (Tokyo, Teikoku Chiho Gyoseigakkai, 1967) lists recipients of the doctorate during the period 1957–65. CT1836.I8

Dai-Nihon jinmei jiten. Tokyo, Heibonsha, 1953–55. 10v.

AJ279

A Japanese equivalent of the *Dictionary of national biography* (AJ217). v.1–6 offer biographies of about 50,000 persons from antiquity to the 20th century; v.7–8 are devoted to non-Japanese figures; v.9 includes some 8,000 persons still living in 1955; v.10 contains indexes.

The set is supplemented by *Nihon jinmei daijiten: gendai* (Tokyo, Heibonsha, 1979) which adds about 6,000 biographies of persons who died before 1978.

Kinsei jinmei roku shûsei. Mori Senzô and Nakajima Masatoshi, eds. Tokyo, Benseisha, 1976–78. 5v. **AJ280**

A photographic reproduction of 64 biographical dictionaries from the Edo period. Literary figures predominate. v.1–2 represent regional compilations; v.3–4 are biographical dictionaries by specialty; v.5 is an index. DS872.A1K55

Meiji ishin jinmei jiten. [Ed. by] Nihon Rekishi Gakkai [Japanese Historical Assoc.]. Tokyo, Yoshikawa Kôbunkan, 1981. 1096p. **AJ281**

An authoritative biographical dictionary of 4,295 men and women from the Meiji Restoration era (c.1853–1871). Articles are unsigned, but there were more than 180 contributors. Bibliographies; index of variant names. DS881.5.A1M43

Contemporary

Japan biographical encyclopedia and who's who. [1st ed.]– . Tokyo, Japan Biographical Research Dept., Rengo Pr., 1958– . **AJ282**

2d ed. 1961; 3d ed. 1964/65. No more published?

Gives, in English, concise biographical sketches of notables in all fields, of all periods, living and dead, with names of religious, mythical, and legendary beings and a very few foreigners. Appendixes list: additional names, members of Japanese diets and cabinets, emperors, diplomatic representatives to and from other countries, a chronology of Japanese history, etc. DS834.J7

Jinji koshin roku. [Ed.1–] Tokyo, Jinji Koshinsha, 1903– . Irregular. **AJ283**

A who's who of Japan. Ed.31 (1981, in 2v.) included some 110,000 Japanese and foreign residents of Japan. DS885.5.A1J5

Nenkan jimbutsu joho jiten, 1981– . Tokyo, Nichigai Associates, 1981– . Annual. **AJ284**

A yearbook of biographical data. The 1984 ed. (in 3v.) covers about 10,500 people (including selected non-Japanese figures) who were the subjects of some 30,000 articles appearing in 13 major newspapers and 42 periodicals during the year 1983. Entries are grouped by broad field (v.1, politics, economics, business and industry; v.2, arts, sciences, literature, and society; v.3, entertainment, sports, and miscellaneous) and give brief biographical information together with citations to the magazine and newspaper articles. CT203.J3N45

Who's who in Japan, 1912–40/41. Tokyo, Who's Who in Japan Pub. Off., [1911–40]. v.1–21. Annual (slightly irregular). **AJ285**

No more published.

In English, on the general plan of the English *Who's who.* Includes a section on Europeans in Japan. DS834.A1W5

A new series of the same title has begun publication:

———— 1984/85– . Hong Kong and N.Y., International Culture Inst., 1984– . **AJ286**

About 42,000 entries in the 1984/85 ed.; information is given in English.

Indexes

Jinbutsu referensu jiten. Tokyo, Nichigai Associates, 1983. 7v. **AJ287**

A master index to 37 biographical sources (in 110v.); includes some 180,000 Japanese names. In four parts: (1) Antiquity to 1603; (2) Modern period, 1603 to 1868; (3) Contemporary period, since 1868; (4) Indexes. CT203.J3J45

KENYA

See also AJ106.

Who is who in Kenya. 1982/83– . Nairobi, Africa Book Services, [1982]– . il. Irregular? **AJ288**

A biographical dictionary of contemporary figures arranged by occupational or professional categories. Many entries provide only an address, not a biographical sketch.

LATIN AMERICA

Quién es quién en Venezuela, Panamá, Ecuador, Colombia. [Bogotá], Oliverio Perry, [1952]. 1074p. il. **AJ289**

Each country is separately treated, with (in all) some 5,000 biographical sketches of the who's who type alphabetically arranged; many of the entries are accompanied by small portraits of varying quality. Includes lists of pseudonyms and of biographees by occupation, and an index—all divided by country and then arranged alphabetically. F2205.Q54

Who's who in Latin America; a biographical dictionary of notable living men and women of Latin America. Founded in 1935 by Percy Alvin Martin. (3d ed. rev. and enl.) . . . ed. by Ronald Hilton. . . . Stanford, Calif., Stanford Univ. Pr.; Chicago, Marquis, [c1945–51]. 7v. **AJ290**

Contents: pt.1, Mexico; pt.2, Central America and Panama; pt.3, Colombia, Ecuador, and Venezuela; pt.4, Bolivia, Chile, and Peru; pt.5, Argentina, Paraguay, and Uruguay; pt.6, Brazil; pt.7, Cuba, Dominican Republic, and Haiti.

The first two editions, 1935 and 1940, 1v. each, were edited by P. A. Martin. This edition, revised and reorganized, includes some 8,000 biographies, whereas the 2d ed. included only slightly over

1,500. However, as each country is treated separately, the great disadvantage of this edition is the number of alphabets which must be checked if the nationality of the person searched for is not known. F1407.W55

Bibliography and indexes

Mundo Lo, Sara de. Index to Spanish American collective biography. Boston, G. K. Hall, [1981]– . v.1– . (In progress) **AJ291**

Contents: v.1, The Andean countries.

Essentially a bibliography of works of collective biography (including encyclopedias, anthologies, general and specialized histories, as well as biographical dictionaries and "who's who" type publications), with annotations and detailed contents notes, followed by an index of persons mentioned in the notes. (In general, works containing information on less than 300 people are fully analyzed; more comprehensive works are not analyzed.) v.1 includes sections for Bolivia, Colombia, Chile, Ecuador, Peru, and Venezuela, with appropriate topical subdivisions. Locates copies in United States and Canadian libraries. Z1609.B6M86

Toro, Josefina del. A bibliography of the collective biography of Spanish America. . . . Río Piedras, P.R., Univ., 1938. 140p. (University of Puerto Rico. Bull., ser. IX, no.1, Sept. 1938) **AJ292**

A very useful annotated list of 488 works of collective biography, arranged by country with author index. Z1609.B6T6

LEBANON

See also AJ309.

Who's who in Lebanon. Ed.1– , 1963/64– . Beyrouth, Éditions Publitec, [1964–]. Biennial (slightly irregular). **AJ293**

Eds. 1–5 have text in French; later eds. in English. DS80.75.W5

LITHUANIA

See also AJ56.

Biržiška, Vaclovas. Aleksandrynas: biographies, bibliographies, and bio-bibliographies of old Lithuanian authors to 1865. Chicago, Lithuanian-Amer. Cultural Fund, 1960–65. 3v. **AJ294**

Added title page and text in Lithuanian.

Contents: v.1, 16th–17th centuries, with a preface in English. 431p.; v.2, 18th–19th centuries. 497p.; v.3, 19th century. 454p. PG8703.B53

LUXEMBOURG

Biographie nationale du pays de Luxembourg depuis ses origines jusqu'à nos jours; collection présentée par Jules Mersch. Luxembourg, Impr. de la Cour Victor Buck, 1947–75. 11v. il. **AJ295**

Nonalphabetical. Each fascicule includes some six to nine long articles on persons or families of various periods in the history of Luxembourg, often with bibliographies and many illustrations. Two fascicules form a volume, continuously paged and including an index to the names appearing in the articles in each volume.

Fasc.1 was published in a revised and corrected edition, 1957.

The final fascicule is a "Table des principaux personnages traités dans les volumes 1 à 11" which indicates birth and death dates and an identifying note as well as giving reference to volume and page for the biographical sketch. DH904.B5

Who's who in Belgium and Grand Duchy of Luxembourg. [Ed. 1–2] Brussels, Intercontinental Book and Pub. Co., 1959–62. **AJ296**

For full record *see* AJ130.

MADAGASCAR

Hommes et destins (Dictionnaire biographique d'outre-mer). Paris, Académie des Sciences d'Outre-Mer, [1979]. v.3. **AJ297**

For full information *see* AJ196.

MALAYSIA

Who's who in Malaysia & Singapore. [Ed.1–], 1956– . Kuala Lumpur, Economy Printers, 1956– . il. Biennial (irregular). **AJ298**

Publisher varies. Title varies: 1956–1959/60, *Leaders of Malaya and who's who;* 1963–67, *The who's who in Malaysia;* 1969–71/72, *The who's who—Malaysia and Singapore;* 1973/74–77/78, *Who's who in Malaysia and guide to Singapore;* 1978/79, *Who's who in Malaysia, Singapore & Brunei;* 1979/80, *Who's who in Malaysia & Singapore;* 1982, *Who's who in Malaysia & profiles of Singapore.*

15th ed. (1983/84) in 2v. (i.e., separate volumes for Malaysia and for Singapore).

Includes sections on rulers and government officials and a section of obituary notices in addition to the regular who's who portions. DS595.5.L4

MEXICO

Beristain de Souza, José Mariano. Biblioteca hispano americana septentrional. [3d ed.] México, Ed. Fuente Cultural, 1947. 5v. in 2. il. **AJ299**

For full record *see* AA949.
Includes bio-bibliographical information about authors. Z1412.B53

Mestre Ghigliazza, Manuel. Efemérides biográficas (defunciones-nacimientos). México, Antigua Librería Robredo, J. Porrúa, 1945. 347p. **AJ300**

A chronological arrangement, by year of death, of outstanding Mexicans who died between 1822 and 1945. Gives field of activity or title, place and date of birth and death. Alphabetical index. F1205.M37

Peral, Miguel Angel. Diccionario biográfico mexicano. México, Ed. P.A.C., [1944]. 2v. and Apéndice. **AJ301**

v.1–2 paged continuously, 894p.; Apéndice, 465p.
Covers 544 to 1944, and gathers much material in one place, but with certain shortcomings, e.g., date of birth and death are frequently omitted and no bibliographical data or references to sources are given. F1205.P42

Sosa, Francisco. Biografías de Mexicanos distinguidos. Ed. de la Secretaría de Fomento. México, Oficina Tipográfica de la Secretaría de Fomento, 1884. 1115p. **AJ302**

Fairly long sketches. Covers all periods. No bibliography. F1205.S71

Valverde Tellez, Emeterio. Bio-bibliografía eclesiástica mexicana (1821–1943). México, Ed. Jus, 1949. 3v. **AJ303**

Contents: v.1–2, Obispos; v.3, Sacerdotes.
Biographical sketches with long bibliographies of the bishops and other clergy of the Catholic Church in Mexico. Z7778.M4V3

Contemporary

See also AJ87.

Camp, Roderic Ai. Mexican political biographies, 1935–1981. 2d ed., rev. and exp. Tucson, Univ. of Arizona Pr., [1982]. 447p. **AJ304**

For full information *see* CJ397.

Who's notable in Mexico. v.1– . México, D. F., Who's Who in Mexico, [1972–]. **AJ305**

Lucien F. Lajoie, ed.
An English-language biographical directory. CT556.W48

Bibliography

Iguíniz, Juan Bautista. Bibliografía biográfica mexicana. México, Universidad Nacional Autónoma de México, Instituto de Investigaciones Históricas, 1969. 431p. (Instituto de Investigaciones Históricas. Serie bibliográfica, 5) **AJ306**

A 1930 edition was designated "t.1, Repertorios biográficos"; a second part devoted to "Monografías bibliográficas" was never published. The present work represents an updating and expansion of the previously published part, bringing the number of analyzed collective biographical works to more than 1,300. Z5305.M6I22

NEAR AND MIDDLE EAST

The international who's who of the Arab world. [Ed.1–] 1978/79– . London, Internat. Who's Who of the Arab World Ltd., [1978–]. Irregular. **AJ307**

2d ed. 1984.
Aims to present up-to-date information on "leading personalities of the Arab World in all walks of life" (*Pref.*), including "prominent Arabs living outside their countries of birth." A "Directory" at the end of the volume lists the biographees by country, then by occupation or field of activity. CT1860.I57

Who's who in the Arab world. Ed.1– , 1965/66– . Beirut, Éditions Publitec, [1965–]. Irregular. **AJ308**

". . . constitutes a comprehensive survey of 15 Arab Countries with details of their economic and social structure, their government and investment possibilities within the framework of the Economic and Social Development Plans now under way in these countries. The book also contains a biographical dictionary listing more than 3,000 leading personalities in the Arab World."—*title page, 3d ed. (1971/72).* The survey covers 20 countries in the 7th ed. (1984/85).

A companion volume to *Who's who in Lebanon* (AJ293). D198.3.W5

Who's who in U.A.R. and the Near East: the greatest biographical work in the Middle and Near East. Ed.1–24. Cairo, [19?–59]. Annual. **AJ309**

Ceased publication.
Title varies: 19?–47, *Le mondain égyptien, The Egyptian who's who;* 1948–51, *Who's who in Egypt and the Middle East;* 1952–1957/58, *Who's who in Egypt and the Near East.* (Title also in Arabic and in French: *Le mondain égyptien et du Proche-Orient.*)

1959 called 24th ed. Includes UAR, Sudan, Iran, Libya, Cyprus, Lebanon, Jordan, Iraq, Saudi-Arabia, India, Pakistan, Ceylon, Indonesia, Ethiopia, and Aden.

The first section is arranged by country, giving brief descriptive information with names of governmental officials, diplomatic representatives, and business firms, followed by an alphabetical listing of persons with addresses and brief biographical information.

DT44.W47

NEPAL

Who is who—Nepal. 1972/74– . Kathmandu, Kathmandu School of Journalism, [1974–].   **AJ310**

Subtitle: A biographical dictionary of the distinguished Nepali personalities.

The first work of its kind for this country. 2d ed. (1975/77) last publ.?   CT1529.W48

NETHERLANDS

Aa, Abraham Jacobus van der. Biographisch woordenboek der Nederlanden. Nieuwe uitg. Haarlem, Brederode, 1852–78. 12v. il.   **AJ311**

A valuable work including sketches on persons from medieval times to mid-19th century. The length of articles varies from a few lines to two or three columns. Includes considerable bibliography both by and about the biographees.

Molhuysen, Philip Christiaan, Blok, P. J. and **Kossmann, F. K. H.,** eds. Nieuw Nederlandsch biografisch woordenboek. Leiden, Sijthoff, 1911–37. 10v.   **AJ312**

Each volume is arranged alphabetically and has a cumulated index to all previous volumes. v.10 has an index to the set. Adequate, signed articles; bibliographies.   CT1143.M7

Biografisch woordenboek van Nederland. Onder eindredactie van Dr. J. Charité. 'sGravenhage, Nijhoff, 1979– . v.1– . (In progress)   **AJ313**

Publ. under the auspices of the Bureau der Rijkscommissie voor Vaderlandse Geschiedenis, 'sGravenhage.

A chronological successor to the *Nieuw Nederlandsch biografisch woordenboek* (above), providing biographical sketches of persons deceased since 1910. Signed articles; bibliographies of writings by and about the biographee, and indication of collections of papers and archival materials. No schedule of further volumes has been set, but each will presumably be a full alphabetical sequence of articles with cumulative indexes in successive volumes.   CT1143.B56

Persoonlijkheden in het koninkrijk der Nederlanden in woord en beeld; Nederlanders en hun werk met een inleiding van H. Brugmans; mede bevattende de biografieen van de leden van het koninklijk huis door N. Japikse. Amsterdam, Van Holkema & Warendorf, 1938. 1748p. il.

AJ314

Includes some 5,000 biographies of living persons, with portraits.

Contemporary

Wie is dat? Biografische gegevens van Nederlanders die een vooraanstaande plaats in het maatschappelijk leven innemen met vermelding van adressen. [Ed.1–6] 'sGravenhage, Nijhoff, 1931–56.   **AJ315**

2d ed. 1932; 3d ed. 1935; 4th ed. 1938; 5th ed. 1948. An earlier volume with different subtitle appeared in 1902.

No more published?

Subtitle varies.
The Netherlands who's who.   DJ103.W62

NEW ZEALAND

Scholefield, Guy Hardy. A dictionary of New Zealand biography. Wellington, Dept. of Internal Affairs, 1940. 2v.

AJ316

A national biographical dictionary, modeled on the *DNB* (AJ217), of persons who have distinguished themselves in the history of New Zealand since organized European migration began. "Bibliography," v.1, p.xviii–xxix.   CT2886.S35

Who's who in New Zealand. (Established 1908) Wellington, Reed, 1924– .   **AJ317**

Subtitle varies. Imprint varies.
11th ed. 1978.

Contains preliminary directory material, including lists of officials of government, church, and education, and diplomatic representatives; election returns; titles and dignities, etc. Biographies are of the usual who's who type.   DU402.W5

NIGERIA

Orimoloye, S. A. Biographia Nigeriana: a biographical dictionary of eminent Nigerians. Boston, G. K. Hall, [1977]. 368p.   **AJ318**

An attempt to provide a who's who of contemporary Nigerians and other prominent figures living and working in Nigeria. Information was gathered from questionnaires; there is some emphasis on academic figures.   CT2526.O74

Who's who in Nigeria; a biographical dictionary. [Ed.1–] A "Daily Times" publication. Lagos, Nigerian Printing and Pub. Co., [1956–]. Irregular.   **AJ319**

3d ed. (1978) latest publ.?

A current biographical dictionary for prominent people of the country; includes some Europeans as well as native Nigerians.

DT515.6.A1W5

NORWAY

See also AJ32.

Norsk biografisk leksikon. Redaktion: Edv. Bull, Anders Krogvig, Gerhard Gran. Oslo, Aschehoug, 1923–83. v.1–19[1–3] (hft.1–93). (In progress)   **AJ320**

Contents: v.1–19[1–3] (hft.1–93), A–Wolff.
Imprint and editors vary.

Long articles signed by specialists; bibliographies. Covers from the earliest times to the present and includes living persons.

CT1293.N6

Contemporary

Hvem er hvem? [1912]– . Oslo, Aschehoug, 1912– .

AJ321

2d ed. 1930; 3d ed. 1934; 4th ed. 1938; 5th ed. 1948; 6th ed. 1950; 7th ed. 1955; 8th ed. 1959; 9th ed. 1964; 10th ed. 1968; 11th ed. 1973; 12th ed. 1979; 13th ed. 1984.

The Norwegian who's who. The 13th ed. includes 4,300 biographical sketches.   DL444.H8

Bibliography

Andresen, Harald. Norsk biografisk oppslagsliteratur; katalog utarb. for Norsk Slektshistorisk Forening. [Oslo], Cammermeyer, [1945]. 218p. **AJ322**

A bibliography of Norwegian sources for biographical materials, arranged by fields of specialization.

Deichmanske Bibliothek, Oslo. Register til norske tidsskrifter: v.2, Norsk biografi (til 31/12/1909). Kristiania, Cammermeyer, 1911. 599p. **AJ323**

Lists nearly 15,000 names, giving for each: dates of birth or death, some characterizing phrase, and references to biographical articles in Norwegian periodicals. Because of the dates and characterizing phrases the work can be used for some direct biographical information as well as for its indexing.

Continued informally by similar indexing, also with dates and characterizing phrases, in the *Norsk tidsskriftindex,* 1921–30 (AE300), under the heading *Personalhistorie;* from 1931–40 in: Z2595.D32

Biografiske artikler i norske tidsskrifter, 1931–1935, 1936–1940. Oslo, Fabritius, 1936–47. 2v. (Norsk bibliografisk bibliotek, bd.2, hft.3; bd.7) **AJ324**

Editors: 1931/35, W. P. Sommerfeldt; 1936/40, Vilhelm Haffner.

PAKISTAN

Biographical encyclopedia of Pakistan. Ed.1– , 1955/56– . Lahore, Biographical Research Inst., Pakistan, for Internat. Pub., [1956?–]. **AJ326**

Chief ed., Khan Tahawar Ali Khan.

5th ed., 1971/72 (erroneously called "4th edition" in Preface) latest publ.?

Biographical data on important contemporary figures in Pakistan. Arranged in broad occupational groups with alphabetical index. DS381.B5

PARAGUAY

Quién es quién en el Paraguay? Buenos Aires, Ed. F. Monte Domecq, 1941– . v.1– . il. Irregular. **AJ327**

Ed. 8 publ. 1980.

Successive volumes omit names included in earlier ones and add new names, making it necessary to consult all volumes. Includes government and commercial directory information. F2665.Q5

PERU

Beltroy, Manuel, ed. Peruanos notables de hoy; biografías de peruanos representativos contemporáneos. 1.ed. Lima, Sanmarti, [1957]. 202p. **AJ328**

Who's who type of sketches on outstanding personalities. Includes a classified list. F3405.B33

Diccionario biográfico del Perú . . . Raúl Garbin Díaz, Raúl Garbin Jr., Julio Cárdenas Ramírez. 1. ed. 1943–44. . . . [Lima, "Escuelas Americanas," 1944] 977p. il. **AJ329**

A combination who's who, commercial directory, and government roster. F3405.D5

Mendiburu, Manuel de. Diccionario histórico-biográfico del Perú. 2.ed. con adiciones y notas bibliográficas publicada por Evaristo San Cristóval. . . . Lima, "Enrique Palacios," 1931–35. 11v. il. **AJ330**

"Catálogo de las obras y manuscritos que deben consultarse para la historia de la América latina y particularmente del Perú."—*v.1, p.15–52.*

Historical and biographical articles in one alphabet, with a subject index in each volume and a general index at the end. Includes fairly long articles with references to sources.

—— —— Apéndice. Lima, Gil, 1935–36. v.1–3, A–N.

A new edition has begun to appear as: F3405.M54

—— —— 3.ed. Lima, Editorial Arica, [1976]– . v.1– . (Colección Perú historia: serie verde, El Virreinato, 1) (In progress) **AJ331**

Contents: v.1, Abad–Amat.

Paz-Soldán, Juan Pedro. Diccionario biográfico de peruanos contemporáneos. [Nueva ed. corr. y aum.] Lima, Lib. e Impr. Gil, 1921. 449p. il. **AJ332**

1st ed. 1917.

Biographical sketches with bibliographies of writings by, but not about, biographees. F3405.P28

PHILIPPINES

Manuel, E. Arsenio. Dictionary of Philippine biography. Quezon City, Filipiniana Publ., 1955– . v.1– . il. (In progress?) **AJ333**

The first volume of a proposed series planned to include nonliving individuals who have contributed significantly to Philippine history and culture. v.1 contains, in A–Z arrangement, biographical sketches not limited to any particular period and varying in length from half a page to about 30 pages. Fairly extensive bibliographies of works by and about the persons. DS653.7.M3

POLAND

See also AJ56.

Akademja Umiejętności, Kraków. Polski słownik biograficzny. Kraków, Nakł. Polskiej Akademji Umiejętności, 1935–83. v.1–27, (In progress) **AJ334**

Publisher varies.

Contents: v.1–27, A–Potocki.

A scholarly dictionary with signed articles and full bibliographies; only deceased persons are included. CT1230.P65

Who's who in Poland. Ed.1– , 1982– . Ed. by Interpress Publishers, Warsaw. Zurich, Who's Who Verlag GmbH, 1982– . Irregular? **AJ335**

Subtitle: A biographical directory comprising about 4.000 entries on leading personalities in Poland and information on major state, political, diplomatic, scientific and artistic institutions, and organizations.

Following the section of biographical sketches is an "index" which gives directory information on some 800 institutions, organizations, associations, foreign embassies, etc.

Wisniewski, Joseph. Who's who in Poland. [Toronto, Professional Translators and Publishers, 1981] 243p. **AJ336**

Offers brief biographical sketches (sometimes no more than occupational identification or organizational affiliation) of contemporary figures, with emphasis on government and party officials and opposition activists. Lists of government organizations and office holders are appended.

PORTUGAL

Quem é alguém (Who's who in Portugal). Dicionário biográfico das personalidades em destaque do nosso tempo, 1947– . Lisboa, Portugália Editora, [1947]– .   **AJ337**

Only one issue published?
A who's who of contemporary Portuguese personalities.
CT1363.Q3

❖As there is no national biographical dictionary for Portugal, Portuguese encyclopedias should be consulted for biographical articles. *See also* I. F. de Silva, *Dicionario bibliográphico portuguez* (AA1036) for the biographical notes given for authors.

PUERTO RICO

Quién es quién en Puerto Rico; diccionario biográfico de record personal. Dir. y ed., Conrado Asenjo. Ed.1–4, 1933/34–1948/49. San Juan, Impr. Real Hermanos, [1933–48].   **AJ338**

Publisher varies.
No more published.   F1955.Q85

Rosa-Nieves, Cesáreo and **Melón, Esther M.** Biografías puertorriqueñas: perfil histórico de un pueblo. Sharon, Conn., Troutman Pr., [1970?]. 487p.   **AJ339**

Biographees are mainly contemporary and early 20th-century figures.   F1955.R6

RHODESIA

See also AJ347, AJ400.

Prominent African personalities of Rhodesia. [Salisbury, Rhodesia], Cover Publicity Services, [1977?]. 196p. il.   **AJ340**

A who's who type of directory. Principles of selection are not indicated.   CT1976.P76

SALVADOR

García, Miguel Angel. Diccionario histórico-enciclopédico de la República de El Salvador. San Salvador, Tip. "La Luz," 1927–51. v.1–13. (In progress?)   **AJ341**

Contents: v.1–13, A–Col.
Includes biography. For full description *see* DB397.
F1483.G21

SAUDI ARABIA

See also AJ309.

Who's who in Saudi Arabia, 1976/77– . Jeddah, Saudi Arabia, Tihama, [1977]– . [Ed.1]– .   **AJ342**

3d ed. 1983/84.
An English-language who's who for Saudi Arabia.
CT1890.W47

SCOTLAND

Anderson, William. The Scottish nation; or, The surnames, families, literature, honours and biographical history of the people of Scotland. Edinburgh, Fullarton, 1878–80. 3v. il.
AJ343

First published 1859–63.
Fairly long articles giving the histories of families and biographies of individuals, illustrated by woodcuts and steel engravings and often with facsimiles of autographs.   CT813.A6

Watt, Donald Elmslie Robertson. A biographical dictionary of Scottish graduates to A.D. 1410. Oxford, Clarendon Pr., 1977. 607p.   **AJ344**

"The intention has been to be as thorough as possible in collecting information on all Scots who had university training" *(Introd.)* from about 1150 to 1410 when St. Andrew's University was founded. As far as possible, biographies are uniformly presented, with references to sources of information provided.

SIERRA LEONE

See also AJ102.

Who's who in Sierra Leone. [Ed.1]– . [Freetown, Lyns Publicity Inc., 1980]– . Irregular?   **AJ345**

Mallyveen Roy Johnson, comp.
A first effort toward a current biographical record for the country.
CT2446.W48

SOUTH AFRICA

Dictionary of South African biography. W. J. de Kock, ed. in chief. [Pretoria], Nasionale Boekhandel Bpk. for National Council for Social Research, Dept. of Higher Education, [1968–81]. v.1–4. (In progress)   **AJ346**

Also published in Afrikaans. Publisher varies; editor varies.
A scholarly work designed to present biographies "of all those who have since the earliest European contact with the southern extremity of Africa made a contribution of importance to the course of South African history."—*Introd.* There is no overall alphabetical or chronological sequence: arrangement is alphabetical within each volume, and each volume includes whatever sketches were available at the time it was readied for press. There is a cumulated index to v.1–4 in v.4. Persons who have had a significant influence on South African affairs and events are included even though they may never have visited South Africa. Articles are signed with the initials of contributors; bibliographies are appended; and there are usually notes on iconography.
v.1–4 include about 3,400 biographies and cover "all the important figures who lived before the twentieth century."—*Pref., v.4.* Although the original plan was to include only those who died before 1950, that date was extended through 1959 for v.2, through 1965 for v.3, and through 1970 for v.4. There will presumably be additional volumes for successive decades.   CT1924.D53

Rosenthal, Eric, comp. Southern African dictionary of national biography. London, Warne, [1966]. 430p.   **AJ347**

The work of a single compiler rather than a cooperative effort. About 2,000 brief biographical sketches of deceased persons who figure in the history of the Republic of South Africa, South West Africa, Rhodesia, Zambia, Malawi, Mozambique, Swaziland, Bechuanaland, and Basutoland. A classified list of entries by profession or occupation precedes the dictionary proper. No bibliographies.   CT1923.R6

Contemporary

The black who's who of Southern Africa today. Ed.1– , 1979– . Johannesburg, African Business Pubns., 1979– . il. Irregular? **AJ348**

A general reference section (lists of government officials, etc.) and a list of universities and their staffs precede the biographical section.

Who's who of southern Africa (incorporating South African who's who and the Central African who's who). 1907– . Johannesburg, Wootton & Gibson, 1907– . Annual. **AJ349**

Imprint varies; subtitle varies.

Subtitle, 1984: An illustrated biographical record of prominent personalities in the Republic of South Africa, SWA/Namibia, Zimbabwe, the neighboring countries and Mauritius. DT752.S5

SOUTH PACIFIC

O'Reilly, Patrick. Calédoniens; répertoire bio-bibliographique de la Nouvelle-Calédonie. 2ᵉ éd. Paris, Musée de l'Homme, 1980. 416p. il. **AJ350**

Includes persons living and deceased who have contributed to the growth and prosperity of the colony: administrators, scientists, engineers, travelers, missionaries, etc., and also the principal Caledonian chiefs. Gives titles of works by authors, and occasional references to sources. DU720.O74

———— Hébridais; répertoire bio-bibliographique des Nouvelles-Hébrides. Paris, Musée de l'Homme, 1957. 289p. il. (Publications de la Société des Océanistes, no.6) **AJ351**

Several hundred biographical sketches of people of all periods connected with the life of the New Hebrides, European as well as native. Gives titles of works by authors, but no references to sources. Includes an index by professions. DU760.O7

———— and **Teissier, Raoul.** Tahitiens; répertoire bio-bibliographique de la Polynésie française. Paris, Musée de l'Homme, 1962. 534p. (Publications de la Société des Océanistes, no.10) **AJ352**

Includes fairly long articles on people of all periods connected with Tahiti, native and European, and an index by professions. DU870.O6

———— ———— Supplement. Paris, Musée de l'Homme, 1966. 103p. il. (Publications de la Société des Océanistes, no.17)

Who's who in Oceania 1980–1981. Comp. by Robert D. Craig and Russell T. Clement. Laie, Hawaii, Brigham Young Univ., Inst. for Polynesian Studies, [1980]. 219p. **AJ353**

"The majority of entries . . . deal with personalities in the fields of government, education, science, and religion. Admission was based on subjective decisions regarding the position of responsibility held and the level of achievement attained by the individual."—*Pref.* In most cases, information was supplied by the biographee.

Serves as a successor to the "who's who" section which appeared in the *Pacific Islands yearbook* through 1968. CT2775.W48

SPAIN

❖No general modern dictionary of national biography is available for Spain. The large Spanish encyclopedias, and especially the *Espasa* (AC79), include many biographies of Spaniards and Spanish-Americans. For names and information not found there, works of collective biography and the numerous regional and special biographical dictionaries

should be consulted. A useful bibliography of older regional and special works is given in the following:

Foulché-Delbosc, Raymond and **Barrau-Dihigo, Louis.** Manuel de l'hispanisant. N.Y., Putnam, 1920–25. 2v. **AJ354**

v.1 includes: list of general biographies, p.41–60; regional biographies, arranged by place, p.60–81; list of biographical works on special classes, e.g., artists, etc., p.81–119.

For full description *see* AA96. Z2681.A1F7

Couceiro Freijomil, Antonio. Diccionario bio-bibliográfico de escritores. Santiago de Compostela, Ed. de los Bibliófilos Gallegos, 1951–54. 3v. (Enciclopedia gallega, 1) **AJ355**

Brief biographical sketches of authors of Galicia in various subject fields, with extensive bibliographies. Covers all periods down to the present. Z2690.C6

Diccionari biogràfic. Barcelona, Alberti, 1966–70. 4v. **AJ356**

A biographical dictionary for Catalonia. Mainly brief sketches of figures from all periods, including some living persons. No principal editor or editorial board is indicated; articles are unsigned and without bibliographies. "Apèndix" in v.4, p.523–83. DP302.C58D5

Esperabé Arteaga, Enrique. Diccionario enciclopédico ilustrado y crítico de los hombres de España. [Nueva ed., reformada, ampliada y completada] Madrid, Artes Gráficas Ibarra, [1957?]. 530p. **AJ357**

Brief biographical sketches of Spaniards of various periods including living persons. Illustrations are poor; no bibliographies. DP58.E82

Contemporary

Figuras de hoy; enciclopedia biográfico nacional ilustrada de las personalidades de la actualidad. Madrid, Ed. Ciencia y Cultura, [1951]. 744p. **AJ358**

Cover title: *Enciclopedia figuras de hoy.*

Brief sketches of contemporary persons. DP271.A2F5

Who's who in Spain. Ed.1– . Barcelona, Intercontinental Book and Pub. Co., 1963– . **AJ359**

Subtitle, 1963: A biographical dictionary containing about 6,000 biographies of prominent people in and of Spain and 1,400 organizations.

Text in English. No more published? DP271.A2W5

SUDAN

Hill, Richard Leslie. A biographical dictionary of the Sudan. 2d ed. [London], Frank Cass, 1967. 409p. **AJ360**

1st ed., 1951, had title: *A biographical dictionary of the Anglo-Egyptian Sudan.* It included short notices of some 1,900 people who died before 1948. This volume reprints the earlier edition, adding a section of "Notes and corrections," p.392–409. An asterisk added to a name in the main body of the work signals a reference to the additions and corrections section. DT108.05.A2H5

SWEDEN

See also AJ32.

Svenska män och kvinnor; biografisk uppslagsbok. Stockholm, Bonnier, [1942–55]. 8v. il. **AJ361**

Nils A. E. Bohman, ed.

Covers from the earliest times to the present and includes living persons. Articles are brief but are signed. Almost no bibliography except for the titles of books written by persons included. Differs from the *Svenskt biografiskt lexikon* (below) in the brevity of its sketches and its lack of bibliography. Should be useful in libraries which do not need the extensive information given in the larger work, and in all libraries until that set is completed.   CT1313.S58

Svenskt biografiskt lexikon. Redaktionskommitté: J. A. Almquist [o.a.]. Redaktör: Bertil Boëthius. Stockholm, Bonnier, 1917–84. v.1–24. il. (In progress)   **AJ362**

Contents: v.1–24, A–Malmros. Chronological index to v.1–10 is included in v.10, p.769–94.

An excellent work with long, signed articles, bibliographies, and many portraits. Includes persons of all periods but no longer covers living persons, although these were considered in v.1–10.

Contemporary

Vem är det. Svensk biografisk handbok, 1912– . Stockholm, Norstedt, [1912]– . v.1– . Biennial (3 yrs. between 1920–23).   **AJ363**

Subtitle varies.

The standard Swedish who's who. About 10,000 sketches in v.36, 1983.   DL644.V4

Bibliography

Ågren, Sven. Svensk biografisk uppslagslitteratur; biografisk förteckning. Uppsala, Almqvist & Wiksell, 1929. 423p.   **AJ364**

Added title page: Svenska bibliotekariesamfundets skriftserie. I.

Classified, with author and subject index. Includes material dealing with Swedish Finland (to 1809) and other Swedish possessions, as well as with Swedes in foreign countries. Lists more than 2,000 biographical dictionaries, registers, collective biographies, etc., which include Swedish biography.   Z5305.S9A2

SWITZERLAND

Dictionnaire historique et biographique de la Suisse. . . . Neuchâtel, Admin. du Dictionnaire, 1921–34. 7v. and suppl. il.   **AJ365**

Contains a large amount of genealogy and biography, including information on persons still living at time of compilation. For full description *see* DC503.   DQ51.D5

Keller, Willy. Schweizer biographisches Archiv. Zürich, Verlag Internat. Publikationen, 1952–58. 6v. il.   **AJ366**

A dictionary of contemporary Swiss biography. Each volume is arranged alphabetically from A to Z, distribution of biographies among the volumes being arbitrary. Sketches of the usual who's who type are presented in that one of the four official languages used by the biographee; good photographs of most of the biographees appear in a separate section of plates at the end of each volume. v.6 includes a cumulated index to the set.   CT1383.K4

Neue schweizer Biographie; nouvelle biographie suisse; nuova biografia svizzera. Chefredaktion, A. Bruckner. Basel, Buchdruckerei zum Basler Berichthaus, 1938. 612p. il.   **AJ367**

Contains about 5,000 biographies of contemporary native Swiss,

the majority with pictures. Sketches are in the language of the subject—German, French, or Italian.   CT1383.N4

———— Nachtrag. 1941/42. Basel, [1942]. 111p. il.

Schweizer Schriftsteller der Gegenwart; Écrivains suisses d'aujourd'hui; Scrittori svizzeri d'oggi; Scriptuors svizzers da noss dis. Bern, Francke Verlag, [1962]. 200p.   **AJ368**

Gives who's who type of information, including lists of the authors' works. Sketches are, as far as possible, in the language of the individual author.   PT3874.S3

Schweizerisches Zeitgenossen-Lexikon. Lexique suisse des contemporains. Lessico svizzero dei contemporanei. Begründet und redigiert von Hermann Aellen. 2. Ausg. Bern und Leipzig, Gotthelf-Verlag, [1932]. 1023p.   **AJ369**

1st ed. 1921; Suppl. 1923–26.

Language of each sketch is that used by the biographee: German, French, or Italian. Who's who type of information.   CT1383.S3

Contemporary

Who's who in Switzerland, including the Principality of Liechtenstein, 1950/51– . Geneva, Nagel, [1952]– . Irregular.   **AJ370**

In English. The 1984/85 ed. includes about 3,500 biographies. Beginning with the 1962/63 edition, includes only a "who's who" section, omitting the directory of organizations found in earlier volumes.   DQ52.W5

Bibliography

Barth, Hans. Bibliographie der schweizer Geschichte. Basel, Basler Buch- und Antiquariatshandlung, 1914–15. 3v.   **AJ371**

A very full bibliography of separately published biographies is given in v.2, p.116–404. For full description *see* DC499.

Bern. Schweizerische Landesbibliothek. Katalog . . . Personenkatalog, 1901–1920, 1921–1930, 1931–1940, 1941–1947. Bern, Huber, 1929–51. 4v. (*In its* Systematisches Verzeichnis der schweizerischen oder die Schweiz betreffenden Veröffentlichungen)   **AJ372**

Lists of biographical works published in Switzerland during the period are arranged alphabetically by the name of the biographee.

For description of the complete work *see* AA1121.

Bibliographie der Schweizergeschichte, Jahrg. 1913– . Zurich, Leemann, 1914– . Annual.   **AJ373**

This current bibliography of Swiss history has a section entitled "Personengeschichte" which, particularly in its earlier volumes, is very complete in its indexing of biographical and obituary articles on natives and residents of Switzerland.

For full description *see* DC500.   Z2786.B58

Brandstetter, Josef Leopold. Repertorium über die in Zeit- und Sammelschriften der Jahre 1812–1890, 1891–1900, enthaltenen Aufsätze und Mitteilungen schweizergeschichtlichen Inhaltes. Basel, Basler Buch- und Antiquariatshandlung, 1892–1906. 2v.   **AJ374**

v.2 by Hans Barth.

Each volume contains a list of biographical articles and obituaries in more than 300 periodicals and other collective works, which—because the entry gives dates of birth and death and, in many cases, a brief characterizing phrase—furnishes some direct information as well as the references to the articles indexed. For full description *see* DC501.   Z2786.B81

TURKEY

Contemporary

Türkiye' de kim kimdir. Istanbul, Tanitim Yayinlari, 1977. 324p. il.   **AJ375**

An earlier work of the same title (Istanbul, 1961-62) was published in English translation as *Who's who in Turkey* (Wash., 1963).

Who's who in Turkey, 1958- . Comp. and ed. by Afşin Oktay, Ankara, Oktay, 1958- .   **AJ376**

2d ed. 1960. No more published?
In English. Includes sketches of persons prominent in contemporary affairs of Turkey.   DR592.A1W5

UNION OF SOVIET SOCIALIST REPUBLICS

(Including retrospective Russian works)

Akademiia Nauk, SSSR. Materialy dlia biograficheskago slovaria dieistvitel'nykh chlenov Imperatorskoi Akademii Nauk. Petrograd, 1915-17. 2v. (Imperatorskaia Akademiia Nauk, 1889-1914. v.3)   **AJ377**

Extensive biographical sketches of academicians, with detailed bibliographies.

Deiateli revoliutsionnogo dvizheniia v Rossii; bio-bibliograficheskii slovar'. Ot predshestvennikov dekabristov do padeniia tsarizma. Pod red. V. Vilenskogo-Sibiriakova i dr. Moskva, 1927-34. v.1-2, 3$^{1-2}$, 5$^{1-2}$. il.   **AJ378**

v.4 not published? v.3 and v.5 incomplete?
At head of title: Vsesoiuznoe obshchestvo politicheskikh katorzhan i ssyl'no-poselentsev.
A biographical dictionary of the Revolutionary movement.   DK188.3.D45

Institut zur Erforschung der UdSSR. Who was who in the USSR; a biographic directory containing 5,015 biographies of prominent Soviet historical personalities. Metuchen, N.J., Scarecrow Pr., 1972. 677p.   **AJ379**

Ed. by Heinrich E. Schulz, Paul K. Urban, Andrew I. Lebed.
Concerned with deceased persons active in the period 1917-67 and including "a certain number of biographies of people who actively campaigned against the Soviet regime or were later exiled or put to death by the Soviet authorities."—*Pref.*   CT1212.I57

Koch, Hans, ed. 5000 Sowjetköpfe; Gliederung und Gesicht eines Führungskollektivs. Köln, Deutsche Industrie-Verlag, [1959]. 862p.   **AJ380**

Biographical sketches, compiled at the Osteuropa Institut, Munich, representing an expansion of the *"Sowjetköpfe"* section of the Institute's *Sowjetbuch.* Contains a directory of organizations with the names of leading personnel.   DK275.A1K6

Russkii biograficheskii slovar' . . . izdan pod nabliudeniem predsiedatelia I. Russkago Istoricheskago Obshchestva A. A. Polovtsova. S.-Peterburg, "Kadima," 1896-1918. 25v.   **AJ381**

Publisher varies.
Arranged alphabetically but not published in that order, some volumes in the last of the alphabet appearing before earlier letters; parts of the alphabet not yet covered when work was discontinued are the letters V, Gog-Gia, E, M, Nik-Nia, Tk-Tia, U; volumes after v.2 are not numbered. Contains signed articles of some length with bibliographies; especially strong for material about the upper and ecclesiastical classes of pre-Revolutionary Russia.
A preliminary list with additional names and brief identification appeared in Russkoe Istoricheskoe Obshchestvo, *Sbornik,* v.60-62.   CT1203.R7

See also AJ56.

Biographical dictionary of dissidents in the Soviet Union, 1956-1975. Comp. and ed. by S. P. de Boer, E. J. Driessen and H. L. Verhaar. The Hague, Nijhoff, 1982. 679p.   **AJ382**

Outgrowth of a project initiated at the Institute of Eastern European Studies, Univ. of Amsterdam.
Provides biographical sketches of dissidents active during the period of coverage; supplements are planned for dissidents who became active after 1975. Criteria for inclusion and method of presenting the biographical data are carefully spelled out in the introduction. Glossary; select bibliography.   DK275.A1B56

Portraits of prominent USSR personalities. [New series] v.1-4. Jan. 1968-Oct. 1971. Metuchen, N.J., Scarecrow Pr., 1968-71. Quarterly.   **AJ383**

Comp. by the Institute for the Study of the USSR, Munich, Germany.
This series "is a quarterly supplement to the biographical directory *Prominent Personalities in the USSR* (formerly *Who's Who in the USSR*) which enables the interested reader to keep pace with the changes among the Soviet élite in the intervals between the publication of the parent volume."—*[Editors' note].*
Supersedes an earlier publication of the same title published in Munich, 1966-67, in 180 issues.   DK37.P6

Porträts der UdSSR-Prominenz. München, Inst. zur Erforschung der UdSSR, 1960-61. Nr.1-24. Looseleaf.   **AJ384**

Approximately 500 biographies of prominent persons of the Soviet Union, with references to printed sources. Similar to the English-language series (above).

Prominent personalities in the USSR. Comp. by the Institute for the Study of the USSR, Munich, Germany. Metuchen, N.J., Scarecrow Pr., 1968. 792p.   **AJ385**

Subtitle: A biographic directory containing 6,015 biographies of prominent personalities in the Soviet Union.
Supplemented on a quarterly basis by *Portraits of prominent USSR personalities* (AJ383).   DK275.A1W534

Simmonds, George W., ed. Soviet leaders. N.Y., Crowell, [1967]. 405p.   **AJ386**

Biographical sketches signed by scholars, and with selected bibliographies of 42 of the "most influential figures in contemporary Soviet society."—*Introd.* Includes leaders in the arts and sciences as well as in political, diplomatic, and military services.

DK275.A1S5

Who's who in the Soviet Union: a biographical encyclopedia of 5,000 leading personalities in the Soviet Union. Ed. by Borys Lewytzkyj. München, Saur, 1984. 428p.   **AJ387**

Updates the information about Soviet figures found in the same editor's *Who's who in the socialist countries* (1978; AJ56) and, like that work, is based on information in the editor's private archives. "All changes in the biographies of Party, State, Komsomol, and Trade Union leaders and functionaries between the end of 1976 and 1982 are full noted. Less completely noted are changes in the biographies of authors, artists, and other groups. . . ."—*Foreword.* Extensive indexes list party, government, and military leaders (including officials of the individual republics), plus lists of authors, scientists, artists, etc. There are also lists of persons who died and who were relieved or dismissed since publication of the earlier volume.   DK37.W48

Who's who in the USSR, 1961/62-1965/66. Montreal, Intercontinental Book and Pub. Co., 1962-66. 2v.   **AJ388**

Subtitle, 1965/66: A biographical directory containing about 5,000 biographies of prominent personalities in the Soviet Union, compiled by the Institute for the Study of the USSR, Munich, Germany.
Publisher varies.

In English. Names and titles of works are transliterated.

The Institute's earlier compilation, not entirely superseded because of different coverage, appeared as *Biographic directory of the USSR* (N.Y., Scarecrow Pr., 1958. 782p.).   DK275.A1W53

Bibliography

Kaufman, Isaak Mikhailovich. Russkie biograficheskie i bio-bibliograficheskie slovari. Moskva, Gos. Izd-vo Kul'turno-Prosvet. Lit-ry, 1955. 751p.   **AJ389**

1st ed. 1950.

A valuable guide to Russian biography and bio-bibliography from the 18th century through 1954.   Z5305.R9K32

URUGUAY

Fernández Saldaña, José María. Diccionario uruguayo de biografías, 1810–1940. Montevideo, Editorial Amerindia, 1945. 1366p.   **AJ390**

Sketches range in length from a single column to several pages and include figures from many fields—diplomats, military men, writers, artists, etc. Few references to sources.   F2705.F38

Quién es quién en el Uruguay. [Montevideo], Central de Publicaciones S.R.L., [1979?]. 688p. il.   **AJ391**

On cover: Arte, banca, ciencias, comercio, industria, profesiones. Personas, empresas e instituciones, 1979–1980.

A "Perfil del Uruguay" precedes the biographical section; a classified section of "Empresas e instituciones" provides information on major corporations and industrial enterprises.   CT742.Q53

Scarone, Arturo. Uruguayos contemporáneos; nuevo diccionario de datos biográficos y bibliográficos. Montevideo, Barreiro y Ramos, 1937. 610p.   **AJ392**

1st ed. 1918. This edition completely revised and rewritten. Includes more than 1,200 names in the main alphabet. The 71 names in the appendix are of persons who have died since the publication of the earlier edition.   F2705.S282

VENEZUELA

Diccionario biográfico de Venezuela. Eds.: Garrido Mezquita y Compania, pub. bajo la dirección técnica de Julio Cárdenas Ramírez. 1.ed. Madrid, Bláss, 1953. 1558p. il., maps.   **AJ393**

Besides biographical sketches, contains much statistical and gazetteer information interspersed with the who's who. Persons, associations, and states are arranged in a single alphabet, with a commercial and industrial directory by trade, and indexes by profession to the biographical section. Lists mainly living persons, but has some full-page articles on Venezuelans of historic importance. In spite of the confusing arrangement, this is useful for the great amount of information included.   F2305.D5

Venezolanos eminentes (Primera serie). [Caracas], Fundación Eugenio Mendoza, [1983]. 445p. il.   **AJ394**

This first series offers long, signed articles on twenty eminent Venezuelans from the 16th to the 19th centuries. Chronological arrangement, with index. Bibliographies.

The foundation has also published *Venezolanos del siglo XX* (Caracas, 1982. 3v. il.), which follows a similar plan.   CT753.V46

VIETNAM

See also AJ56.

Who's who in Vietnam. [Ed.1–] Saigon, Vietnam Pr., 1967– . Irregular.   **AJ395**

3d ed. 1974 latest publ.?

Persons selected for inclusion are "those who are holding elected positions, high-ranking government posts, and those who have scored outstanding achievements in social, cultural and economic domains."—*3d ed.*   DS557.A5A555

WALES

Y Bywgraffiadur Cymreig hyd 1940; paratowyd dan nawdd Anrhydeddus Gymdeithas y Cymmrodorion. Llundain, 1953. 1110p.   **AJ396**

A biographical dictionary in Welsh planned on the lines of the *DNB* and covering A.D. 400–1940, but not including living persons. Articles are written by specialists; are signed; and include references to sources and, for writers, extensive bibliographies.

Largely supersedes earlier works, but, if needed, the list of abbreviations, p.xxx–lii, serves as a bibliography of these.

An English translation with additions and corrections appeared as: DA710.A1B9

Dictionary of Welsh biography down to 1940, under the auspices of the Honourable Society of Cymmrodorion. Oxford, Blackwell, 1959. 1157p.   **AJ397**

"The present English edition is not a mere translation of the Welsh volume. The intervening years have enabled the Editors to pick up the fruits of later research and to make many corrections."
—*Pref.*   DA710.A1B913

YUGOSLAVIA

See also AJ56.

Ko je ko u Jugoslaviji. Beograd, Hronometar, 1970. 1208p.   **AJ398**

At head of title: Jugoslovenski savremenici.

The Yugoslav "who's who." An early work of the same title was published 1928. The first postwar edition appeared in 1957, and a new edition by a different publisher was published 1968.   DR316.K63

Slovenski biografski leksikon . . . Ljubljana, [Slovenska Akademija Znanosti in Umetnosti], 1925–82. v.1–4$^{1-2}$. (In progress)   **AJ399**

Issued in fascicules. Publisher varies.

Contents: v.1, A–Luzar. 1925–32; v.2, Maas–Qualle. 1933–52; v.3, Raab–Svikarsic. 1960–71; v.4$^{1-2}$, Táborská–Vodaine.

Long, signed articles, many with bibliographies.

ZIMBABWE

See also AJ340.

Mitchell, Diana. Who's who, 1981–82: nationalist leaders in Zimbabwe. Causeway, Zimbabwe, D. Mitchell, [1982]. 170p. il.   **AJ400**

At head of title: Makers of history.

Label on cover states: Contains updated 1982–83 supplement, 24 pages including Cabinet reshuffle and 80 new entries.

Constitutes a rev. ed. of *African nationalist leaders in Rhodesia who's who* by Robert Cary and Diana Mitchell (1977). Biographies are presented in narrative form, often in the words of the biographee.   DT962.6.M57

A K

Genealogy

❖Genealogy is the study of family history and as such may require special techniques and the searching of records of many kinds. Guides, such as Doane and Bell's *Searching for your ancestors* (AK6), Greenwood's *Researcher's guide to American genealogy* (AK10), and Stevenson's *Search and research* (AK19), may be helpful, but the average library will not find it possible to have available the materials necessary for detailed genealogical research, including the genealogies of individual families, local histories, parish registers, etc. A bibliographic guide to many such sources is Filby's *American and British genealogy and heraldry* (AK24). Some large libraries have extensive genealogical collections, notably the Library of Congress, the New York Public Library, the Newberry Library in Chicago, the Los Angeles Public Library, and the Allen County Public Library in Fort Wayne, Ind., and some special libraries are also devoted to this work, such as the Genealogical Library of the Church of Jesus Christ of Latter-Day Saints in Salt Lake City. Local libraries often collect material relating to their own community or area, and may have sources not available in larger collections. When a library cannot supply a reader with genealogical material, he should be referred to one or more of the specialized libraries. Lists will be found in the library directories, e.g., *Subject collections* by Lee Ash (AB115).

This section includes some of the guides, bibliographies and other sources useful in American and English genealogy; a selection of peerages and other compilations of European nobility; and reference works on heraldry, orders and decorations, flags, and personal names. The increased interest of Americans in genealogy in recent years in reflected in the newer guides (e.g., AK2, AK17) which, though describing sources in foreign countries, are written for Americans interested in tracing the antecedents of immigrant ancestors.

UNITED STATES

Guides

Andereck, Paul A. and **Pence, Richard A.** Computer genealogy: a guide to research through high technology. Salt Lake City, Ancestry, 1985. 280p. il.   **AK1**

Presents "a plain-language non-technical guide" (*Foreword*) for applying computer technology to genealogical research. Chapters on hardware, software and its variations, and suggestions on help in getting started. Glossary; index.   CS14.A52

Baxter, Angus. In search of your European roots; a complete guide to tracing ancestors in every country in Europe. Baltimore, Genealogical Pub. Co., 1985. 289p.   **AK2**

Describes genealogical resources in 30 European countries, giving information on archival repositories from the national to the municipal level, and on the historical and political background that has affected or created the records. Includes a chapter on the Mormon records (i.e., those microfilmed in Europe) in Salt Lake City, and another on Jewish record repositories.

Similar, but more specialized titles by Baxter are his *In search of your roots; a guide for Canadians . . .* (Toronto, Macmillan, 1978. 293p.), with coverage for Canada and briefer attention to some foreign countries; and his *In search of your British & Irish roots* (N.Y., Morrow, 1982. 304p.) which describes English, Welsh, Scottish and Irish sources.

A work intended more for background than for the actual search is Noel Currer-Briggs' *Worldwide family history* (London, Routledge & Kegan Paul, 1982. 230p.) which gives brief descriptions of the types of records to be found in European and Islamic countries, China and Japan, together with chapters on migration from many countries to the United States and other English-speaking countries.   CS403.B39

Beard, Timothy Field and **Demong, Denise.** How to find your family roots. N.Y., McGraw-Hill, [1977]. 1007p.   **AK3**

In four sections: (1) How to find your ancestors; (2) Books to help you search; (3) Tracing your family's history in America; (4) Tracing your family's history abroad. The first section offers essays on methods and sources; the remainder is principally long lists of published sources and directory information on archives and societies relevant to genealogical research.   CS16.B35

Blockson, Charles L. with **Fry, Ron.** Black genealogy. Englewood Cliffs, N.J., Prentice-Hall, [1977]. 232p.   **AK4**

Includes chapters on the use of family and public documents, slave records, and other sources useful in tracing Afro-American genealogy. Two appendixes: A "directory of research resources" listing names and addresses of record and information centers in the United States and abroad; a list of newspapers important in black genealogical searching. Index; bibliography.   CS21.B55

Cerny, Johni and **Eakle, Arlene.** Ancestry's Guide to research: case studies in American genealogy. Salt Lake City, Ancestry, 1985. 364p. il.   **AK5**

A companion volume to the authors' *The source* (AK55). Offers "research instruction through applying the basics in case studies," with emphasis on "familiarizing the novice researcher with primary and original sources" (*Introd.*) necessary for tracing American ancestors. One short chapter on two ethnic groups (Cherokee and slave) and another on immigrant ancestors. Indexed.   CS49.C46

Doane, Gilbert Harry and **Bell, James B.** Searching for your ancestors: the how and why of genealogy. [5th ed.] Minneapolis, Univ. of Minnesota Pr., [1980], 270p.   **AK6**

1st ed. 1937.

In two parts: (1) a manual and guide to genealogical searching, with chapters on such subjects as the finding and use of family papers, town records, cemeteries, church records; how to arrange a genealogy; (2) chapters on ethnic origins and research in some 20 foreign countries. Includes a useful bibliography of the most used guides and materials.   CS16.D6

Ethnic genealogy: a research guide. Ed. by Jessie Carney Smith. Westport, Conn., Greenwood Pr., [1983]. 440p. il.   **AK7**

In three main sections: (1) General information on sources, procedures, and genealogical research; (2) Utilizing major repositories for genealogical research; (3) Sources available to specific ethnic groups. Each section has chapters by contributing scholars discussing methods and procedures, and listing pertinent bibliographic sources, repositories, etc. Numerous illustrative forms and sample records. Indexed.   CS49.E83

Genealogical guide to German ancestors from East Germany and Eastern Europe (AGoFF-Wegweiser—English ed.). Ed. by Arbeitsgemeinschaft ostdeutscher Familienforscher e.V., Herne, Germany. Tr. by Joachim O. R. Nuthack and Adalbert Goertz. Neustadt/Aisch, Degener, 1984. 158p. maps.
                                                             AK8

Tr. of the 2d ed. (1982) of *Wegweiser für die Forschung nach Vorfahren aus den ostdeutschen und sudetendeutschen Gebieten sowie aus den deutschen Siedlungsbebieten in Ost- und Südosteuropa.*

A section of "Supraregional information" lists family research societies, vital statistics sources, relevant archives and libraries, and various other research aids, together with suggestions for working with certain types of records or in particular localities. A "Regional information" section (with helpful maps) offers similar listings of aids and resources for genealogical research in former German territories and German settlements in Central, Eastern and Southeastern Europe. Indexed.   CS684.W4413

Genealogical research: methods and sources. Ed., Milton Rubincam. Rev. ed. Wash., Amer. Soc. of Genealogists, 1980–83. 2v.   **AK9**

1st ed. 1960–71.

v.1 offers chapters by various authors on methods, interpretation, rules of evidence, materials for research (original sources, public and institutional records, secondary materials), regional genealogy of Eastern U.S. and of Canada, pre-American ancestry and special subjects (heraldry, law, names). v.2 covers regional genealogy of states to the Mississippi, Florida, and special subjects (Ontario, Huguenots, Jewish migrations, black genealogy).   CS16.G43

Greenwood, Val D. The researcher's guide to American genealogy. Baltimore, Genealogical Pub. Co., 1973. 535p. il.
                                                            AK10

Aims "to provide a meaningful and comprehensive guide to the records used in American genealogical research."—*Pref.* Pt.1, "Background to research," deals with various aspects, problems, and tools of research; pt.2, "Records and their use," treats specific types of records, such as birth and death records, census reports, wills, deeds, land records, court records, church records, military records, etc. There is a final chapter on Canadian research. Indexed.
                                                         CS47.G73

Kurzweil, Arthur. From generation to generation: how to trace your Jewish genealogy and personal history. N.Y., Morrow, 1980. 353p. (Repr.: N.Y., Schocken, 1982)
                                                            AK11

In two parts: pt.I gives a lively account of the author's investigation of his own family history; pt.II identifies and describes sources for Jewish genealogy, with instructions on methods and procedures. Bibliographical references throughout; index.   CS21.K87

Parker, J. Carlyle. Library service for genealogists. Detroit, Gale, [1981]. 362p. (Gale genealogy and local history ser., 15)   **AK12**

Aims to provide guidance to the librarian in administration, collection development and reference work in the many aspects of genealogy. Bibliography with full information in each chapter. Indexed.

The Summer 1983 issue of *Library trends* (v.32, no.1, ed. by Diane Foxhill Carothers) dealt with the subject "Genealogy and libraries" in a collection of articles "meant to inform librarians of what is happening today in genealogy."—*Introd.*

A British counterpart of the Parker work is Richard Harvey's *Genealogy for librarians* (London, Bingley, 1983. 166p.) which describes sources for English, and to a lesser extent, Welsh, Scottish and Irish, genealogical sources.   Z5313.U5P37

Pine, Leslie Gilbert. American origins. Garden City, N.Y., Doubleday, 1960. 357p. (Repr.: Baltimore, Genealogical Pub. Co., 1980)   **AK13**

A handbook of European genealogical sources intended for the American inquirer who has ascertained his first immigrant ancestor

and wishes to trace that ancestor in Europe. Chapters are devoted to genealogical research in individual countries, with accounts of the types of records and sources available.   CS16.P55

Platt, Lyman De. Genealogical historical guide to Latin America. Detroit, Gale, [1978], 273p. (Gale genealogy and local history ser., v.4)   **AK14**

Aims to provide basic information for Latin American genealogical research. Covers the 20 countries of Central and South America and the Caribbean once under Spanish or Portuguese dominion. Ten chapters on common problems (research standards, ecclesiastical organization and records, paleography, research aids, etc.) are followed by chapters on the history, records and archives of the individual countries. Some countries' records are covered in greater detail than others. Indexed.   CS95.P58

Rose, James and **Eichholz, Alice.** Black genesis. Detroit, Gale, [1978]. 326p. (Gale genealogy and local history ser., v.1)   **AK15**

A guide for research in black genealogy. Background chapters concerning general references, oral history, national archives and federal records, war records, migratory patterns, and slavery are followed by a survey of source materials in the United States, West Indies, and Canada. Indexed.   CS21.R57

Rottenberg, Dan. Finding our fathers; a guidebook to Jewish genealogy. N.Y., Random House, [1977]. 401p.   **AK16**

An introductory guide to research in Jewish genealogy, with emphasis on "American Jews of European ancestry, and especially East European ancestry."—*Pref.* Chapters on methods, archives and general sources are followed by "A source guide to Jewish family genealogies" (p.141–375), an alphabetical listing of family names (including cross references from variant and related forms) with references to sources of information. Bibliography, p.376–401.
                                                         CS21.R58

Ryskamp, George R. Tracing your Hispanic heritage. Riverside, Calif., Hispanic Family History Research, 1984. 954p. il.   **AK17**

Includes sections for: (1) Techniques and principles: organizing and evaluating information, language, handwriting, names, etc.; (2) Record types (church, civil, census, military, etc.); (3) Spain (geography, archives, reference works on Spain). Glossary; data forms; abbreviations; index. Concerns genealogy research chiefly in Spain, but includes examples and descriptions for many Hispanic countries. Numerous bibliographical references.

Smith, Clifford Neal and **Smith, Anna Piszczan-Czaja.** American genealogical resources in German archives (AGRIGA): a handbook. München, Verlag Dokumentation; N.Y., Bowker, 1977. 336p.   **AK18**

An English-language handbook "devoted to the primary source materials of German-American genealogical interest to be found in the archives of [West] Germany" and West Berlin, focusing on the "direct documentary links between the old and new worlds."—*Pref.* Drawn from *Americana in deutscher Sammlungen*, an inventory of German archival materials which bear on America, compiled by the Deutsche Gesellschaft für Amerikastudien at the University of Cologne (1967), but not widely distributed. Arranged as geographic, subject, and name indexes.   E184.G3S659

Stevenson, Noel C. Search & research. Salt Lake City, Deseret Book Co., 1977. 216p.   **AK19**

1st ed. 1951.

A general introduction to methodology in genealogical research, records and sources is followed by a state-by-state listing of pertinent libraries, historical societies and archives, special reference books; military rosters, rolls and records; official records; federal census records; and individual state census records. Also gives sources for Canada, England and Wales, Scotland, Northern Ireland, and Eire. Brief index.   Z5313.U5S8

Wright, Norman Edgar. Preserving your American heritage: a guide to family and local history. Provo, Utah, Brigham Young Univ. Pr., [1981]. 285p.   **AK20**

1974 ed. had title: *Building an American pedigree.*

A basic guide to genealogy and family history, with detailed descriptions of important sources and repositories. Bibliography; index.   CS47.W68

Bibliography and indexes

American genealogical index; Fremont Rider, ed. . . . publ. by a committee representing the cooperating subscribing libraries. . . . Middletown, Conn., 1942–52. 48v.   **AK21**

Begun in 1936 as a surname index printed on cards; now issued in book form giving full name entries.—cf. *Pref.* v.1–48 are in A–Z arrangement.

Will be superseded by: CS44.A6

American genealogical-biographical index to American genealogical, biographical and local history materials. . . . Publ. . . . by the Godfrey Memorial Library. Fremont Rider, ed. Middletown, Conn., 1952–85. v.1–136. (In progress)   **AK22**

Constitutes series 2 of the item above.
Contents: v.1–136, A–Pierce.   Z5313.Z15A55

Cappon, Lester Jesse. American genealogical periodicals: a bibliography with a chronological finding-list. [2d printing with additions] N.Y., New York Pub. Lib., 1964. 32p.   **AK23**

1st printing 1962.
Detailed bibliographical descriptions of national and local genealogical periodicals. The 2d printing adds a geographical finding list by state.   Z5313.U5C3

Filby, P. William. American & British genealogy & heraldry: a selected list of books. 3d ed. Boston, New England Historic Genealogical Soc., 1983. 736p.   **AK24**

1st ed. 1970.
Aims "to present to American and Canadian libraries a comprehensive bibliography through Fall 1981."—*Introd.* Within sections for the United States, Latin America, Canada, England, Ireland, Scotland, Wales, British dominions and former dominions, and World, works are grouped by type/topic (e.g., bibliographies; records, guides, indexes; biographies; manuals and aids; immigration; religions) or by individual country; there are separate subsections for the individual states and provinces of the U.S. and Canada. Heraldry and chivalry are accorded separate sections. Many items are briefly annotated, and relationships between publications are noted. 9,773 entries, all but a few in English; detailed index.
                                                              Z5311.F55

———— Passenger and immigration lists bibliography, 1538–1900: being a guide to published lists of arrivals in the United States and Canada. Detroit, Gale, [1981]. 195p.
                                                                AK25

Revises and greatly expands the 3d ed. of Harold Lancour's *A bibliography of ship passenger lists, 1538–1825* as revised by Richard J. Wolfe (1963). Cites more than 1,200 published lists, with annotations specifying contents. Fully indexed. Designed for use with the editor's *Passenger and immigration lists index* (AK35).
                                                            Z5313.U5F54

———— ———— Supplement with combined index to basic volume and supplement. Detroit, Gale, [1984]. 132p.

Adds more than 600 new sources published 1981–84 or which were omitted from the original list.

Genealogical periodical annual index, 1962– . Catherine M. Mayhew, comp. Laird C. Towle, ed. Bowie, Md., Heritage Books, 1963– . (1981 vol. publ. 1985)   **AK26**

Editor varies; publisher varies.
Aims to index the contents of genealogical periodicals with some inclusion of articles of like interest from other periodicals.
                                                              CS42.G467

Index to American genealogies; and to genealogical material contained in all works such as town histories, county histories, local histories, historical society publications, biographies, historical periodicals, and kindred works, alphabetically arranged. 5th ed. rev., improved, and enl. Albany, N.Y., Munsell, 1900. 352p. and suppl. 1908. 107p. (Repr.: Detroit, Gale, 1966)   **AK27**

Cover title: *Munsell's genealogical index.*
The basic volume (1900) indexes about 50,000 references; the supplement continues indexing for 1900–1908.   Z5313.U515

Jacobus, Donald Lines. Index to genealogical periodicals [1931–52]. Rev. ed., by Carl Boyer. Newhall, Calif., C. Boyer, 1983. 373p.   **AK28**

1st ed. 1932–53.
This revision cumulates the six indexes of the original work. Arranged in three sections: name index, place index, topic index. The "Key to genealogical periodicals" adds useful notes on various periodical indexes of a genealogical nature.   Z5313.U5J22

Kaminkow, Marion J. A complement to Genealogies in the Library of Congress: a bibliography. Baltimore, Magna Carta Book Co., 1981. 1118p.   **AK29**

"Identifies genealogies on individual families, produced up until the end of 1976 that are *not* listed" *(Introd.)* among the Library of Congress holdings, and locates copies in 24 American libraries. About 20,000 entries. Index of secondary names. Complements AK38.   Z5319.K35

National Genealogical Society. Index of Revolutionary War pension applications in the National Archives. Bicentennial ed., rev. & enl. Wash., 1976. 658p. (Special publication, Nat. Genealogical Soc., no.40)   **AK30**

1st ed. 1966; originally published in parts as supplements to the Society's *Quarterly,* 1943–62.
An alphabetical name index incorporating the "many cross-references, corrections and additions, and changes of order" made "when the National Archives microfilmed the Revolutionary War Pension and Bounty Land Warrant applications and the items related to them" *(Introd.)* from its Record Group 15.   CS42.N43

New York. Public Library. Local History and Genealogy Division. Dictionary catalog of the Local History and Genealogy Division. Boston, G. K. Hall, 1974. 20v.   **AK31**

Contents: v.1–18, Dictionary catalog of the Local History and Genealogy Division; Supplement, v.1–2, United States local history catalog.
Reproduction of the catalog cards for this extensive collection covering local history, genealogy, nomenclature (forenames and surnames), heraldry, and vexillology. Represents some 100,000 volumes. "Contains entries for materials cataloged for the collection through December 1971. Beginning in January 1972, all additions to the collection of the Local History and Genealogy Division have been included in the Dictionary catalog of the Research Libraries [AA147]."—*Foreword.*
The two-volume supplement is subtitled "A modified shelf list arranged alphabetically by state, and alphabetically by locality within each state"; it represents the Library's collection of county, city, town, and village histories of all areas of the United States. The publisher's *Bibliographic guide to North American history,* 1977– , serves as an ongoing supplement to this section.   Z881.N59

Newberry Library, Chicago. Genealogical index. Boston, G. K. Hall, 1960. 4v. (3915p.)   **AK32**

A photographic reproduction of a valuable index containing more than 400,000 surnames with references to sources in which the name appears, e.g., town and county histories, vital records, printed genealogies, etc.   CS44.N42

Obal, Thaddeus J. A bibliography for genealogical research involving Polish ancestry. [Hillsdale, N.J.], Obal, 1978. 83p. in various pagings.   **AK33**

". . . attempts to incorporate all aspects of Polish genealogical research."—*Introd.* Lists more than 500 books and articles on Polish genealogy, research methodology, geographical materials, selected histories, etc. A library location is frequently indicated. Supersedes "working drafts" of 1975 and 1976.   Z1361.6O2

Parker, J. Carlyle. City, county, town and township index to the 1850 federal census schedules. Detroit, Gale, [1979], 215p. (Gale genealogy and local history ser., v.6)   **AK34**

An aid for genealogists. Indicates the county in which a city, town or township is located, and supplies "the National Archives microfilm order numbers and the microfilm call numbers used by the Genealogical Department Library of the Church of Jesus Christ of Latter-day Saints in Salt Lake City, Utah."—*Introd.*   CS65.P37

Passenger and immigration lists index; a guide. Ed. by P. William Filby with Mary K. Meyer. Detroit, Gale, [1981]. 3v. (2339p.)   **AK35**

"A guide to published arrival records of about 500,000 passengers who came to the United States and Canada in the seventeenth, eighteenth and nineteenth centuries."—*t.p.*

A "preliminary edition" was published 1980.

This work "brings together in one alphabet citations to information about passengers . . . whose names appear in a broad collection of published passenger lists or naturalization records."—*Introd.* Some 500,000 names from about 300 sources, with many duplications (since a name may appear in more than one record). Entry usually gives name, age, place and year of arrival or of naturalization record.   CS68.F537

——— Supplement 1982, 1983, 1984. Ed. by P. William Filby with Mary K. Meyer. Detroit, Gale, 1983–[85]. 3v. (950p., 982p., 616p.)

The 1982 supplement adds 200,000 citations from more than 360 published passenger and naturalization lists; that for 1983 adds another 200,000 names from 185 additional lists; and that for 1984 an additional 125,000 citations from 115 lists. The full work now includes more than a million entries.

Sperry, Kip. Index to genealogical periodical literature, 1960–1977. Detroit, Gale, [1979]. 166p. (Gale genealogy and local history ser., v.9)   **AK36**

A selective list of major "periodical articles describing research techniques and procedures, genealogical and historical sources and collections, as well as international genealogical subjects."—*Pref.* Pt.I is the subject index (a list of subject headings with citations to sources, but without authors and titles). Pt.II lists alphabetically by author the articles indexed in the first part.   Z5313.U5S64

——— A survey of American genealogical periodicals and periodical indexes. Detroit, Gale, [1978]. 199p. (Gale genealogy and local history ser., v.3)   **AK37**

Introductory chapters on basic genealogical research sources and procedures, American genealogical periodical literature (value, types, and limitations), and access to the periodical literature are followed by individual indexes or groups of indexes. Appendixes offer a list of additional indexes (with brief annotations) and a select list of periodicals. Indexed.   Z5313.U5S65

U.S. Library of Congress. Genealogies in the Library of Congress; a bibliography. Ed. by Marion J. Kaminkow. Baltimore, Magna Carta Book Co., 1972. 2v.   **AK38**

Updates and expands the Library's *American and English genealogies in the Library of Congress* (2d ed., 1919). "This new edition can . . . be considered as three tools in one: a guide to genealogical monographs which may be found in the Library of Congress and in other libraries; the Library's own particular index [i.e., the "Family Name Index," a card file in the Local History and Genealogy Room] to genealogies in sources not primarily genealogical in nature; and a guide to the unique collection of nonprinted genealogies held by the Library, other than those in its Manuscript Division."—*Editor's note.* About 20,000 entries. Complemented by AK29.

     Z5319.U53

——— ——— Supplement 1972–1976. Baltimore, Magna Carta, 1977. 285p.

Includes some older works as well as publications of the 1972–76 period.

U.S. National Archives and Records Service. Guide to genealogical research in the National Archives. Wash., Nat. Archives Trust Fund Board, [1983]. 304p. il.   **AK39**

Supersedes *Guide to genealogical records in the National Archives* by M. B. Colket and F. E. Bridgers (1964).

A brief introduction stresses the value and limitations of federal records for genealogical research and offers remarks about "the organization of records in general, finding aids, microfilm, and research facilities and special programs at the National Archives Building and the Federal Archives and Records Centers."—*Introd.* Individual chapters (grouped by broad subject areas such as population and immigration, military records, etc.) deal with specific groups of records, their extent, general content, and finding aids. Indexed.   Z5313.U5U54

Yantis, Netti Schreiner. Genealogical and local history books in print. 4th ed. [Springfield, Va.], Genealogical Books in Print, 1985. 2v. (1722p.)   **AK40**

1st ed. 1975 had title *Genealogical books in print.*

A classified list with prices and sources of more than "30,000 books and microforms valuable to those tracing their ancestry."—*Cover.* The "Family genealogies" section is indexed.

     Z5313.U5Y35

Zubatsky, David S. and **Berent, Irwin M.** Jewish genealogy; a sourcebook of family histories and genealogies. N.Y., Garland, 1984. 422p. (Garland reference library of social science, 214)   **AK41**

Aims to provide a comprehensive listing of sources, published and unpublished, for Jewish genealogies, family histories, and individual family names. A bibliography of general works is followed by an alphabetical listing of family names with citations to genealogies, family histories, family trees, etc.; includes many references to papers in foreign archives (mainly English and Israeli), but not to private collections. Numerous cross references.   Z6374.B5B47

Dictionaries and compendiums

Burke's Distinguished families of America; the lineages of 1600 families of British origin now resident in the United States of America. London, Burke's Peerage, 1948. p.2529–3021. col. coats of arms.   **AK42**

Originally published as the American section of Burke's *Genealogical and heraldic history of the landed gentry,* 16th ed., 1939. (Repr. as *Prominent families in America with British ancestry.* N.Y. & London, House & Maxwell, 1971.)   CS45.B8

Burke's Presidential families of the United States of America. 2d ed. London, Burke's Peerage, 1981, 597p. 94p. il.   **AK43**

Hugh Montgomery-Massingberd, ed.

A chapter is devoted to each of the 39 presidents, Washington through Reagan, each chapter divided into sections for: (1) biography; (2) portraits; (3) chronology; (4) writings; (5) lineage; (6) descendants; (7) brothers and sisters; and (8) notes. Indexed.

     CS69.B82

Coldham, Peter Wilson. Bonded passengers to America. Baltimore, Genealogical Pub. Co., 1983. 9v. in 3. il.

     AK44

v.2–3 originally publ. with title *English convicts in Colonial America* (1974–76. 2v.).

Contents: v.1, History of transportation, 1615–1775; v.2, Middlesex, 1617–1775; v.3, London, 1656–1775; v.4, Home counties, 1655–1775; v.5, Western Circuit, 1664–1775; v.6, Oxford Circuit, 1663–1775; v.7, Norfolk Circuit, 1663–1775; v.8, Northern Circuit, 1665–1775; v.9, Midland Circuit, 1671–1775.

"Intended as a key to sources from which further information may be obtained."—*Introd., v.2.* v.2–9 list names alphabetically with reference to specific British court records.   CS61.C62

Dobson, David. Directory of Scottish settlers in North America, 1625–1825. Baltimore, Genealogical Pub. Co., 1984–85. v.1–4. (In progress) **AK45**

Drawing on archival sources and such contemporary publications as government documents and Scottish newspapers, this compilation "brings together . . . the names of all Scots emigrants appearing in ships' passenger lists before 1825."—*Introd.* Alphabetical by name, with (typically) age, occupation, names and ages of family members, port of embarkation, destination, date and source of data.

Dobson has published a similar work for a shorter period: *Directory of Scots banished to the American plantations, 1650–1775* (Baltimore, Genealogical Pub. Co., 1983. 239p.). E184.S3D63

The famine immigrants: lists of Irish immigrants arriving at the port of New York, 1846–1851. Ira A. Glazier, ed. Baltimore, Genealogical Pub. Co., 1983–85. v.1–5. (In progress) **AK46**

Contents: v.1–5, Jan. 1846–May 1850.

Transcribes names of Irish passengers as recorded in ship manifests. Arranged chronologically by ship list. Data includes name, age, sex, occupation, ship's name, port of origin and date of arrival. Name index. E184.I6F25

Hotten, John Camden. The original lists of persons of quality, emigrants, religious exiles, political rebels . . . and others who went from Great Britain to the American plantations. N.Y., Bouton; London, Chatto, 1874. 580p. (Repr.: Baltimore, Genealogical Pub. Co., 1983) **AK47**

Supplemented by: E187.5.H795

Omitted chapters from Hotten's original lists of persons of quality and others who went from Great Britain to the American plantations, 1600–1700: census returns, parish registers, and militia rolls from the Barbados census of 1679/80. Ed. by James C. Brandow. Baltimore, Genealogical Pub. Co., 1982. 245p. **AK48**

Supplements the earlier work by listing the Barbados registers omitted by Hotten, and by transcribing the militia rolls and other lists in the Public Record Office. CS69.O45

Kaminkow, Marion J. and **Kaminkow, Jack.** Mariners of the American Revolution; with an appendix of American ships captured by the British during the Revolutionary War. Baltimore, Magna Carta Book Co., 1967. 248p. **AK49**

Provides notes on American seamen captured by the British, with references to published diaries and to unpublished British official records. E203.K33

—— Original lists of emigrants in bondage from London to the American colonies, 1719–1744. Baltimore, Magna Carta Book Co., 1967. 211p. (Repr. 1981) **AK50**

Lists the names of 7,283 persons transported for criminal acts and misdemeanors. Compiled from the Treasury Money Books in the Public Record Office, London.

John Wareing's *Emigrants to America: indentured servants recruited in London 1718–1733* (Baltimore, Genealogical Pub. Co., 1985. 111p.) adds 1,544 previously unpublished names drawn from archival documents in the City of London Record Office. Gives person's name, agent's name, destination, date, and page number in the register from which transcribed. E187.5.K33

Meyer, Mary Keysor and **Filby, P. William.** Who's who in genealogy & heraldry, [1981]– . Detroit, Gale, [1981]– . v.1– . (In progress) **AK51**

Presents in "who's who" format information (personal, career, publications, special interests) on about 900 genealogists, chiefly American. A second volume is planned.

Meyer is both editor and publisher of *Meyer's Directory of genealogical societies in the U.S.A. and Canada: with an appended list of independent periodicals endorsed by the Federation of Genealogical Societies* (5th ed. Mt. Airy, Md., 1983. 93p.) which lists about 1,500 societies. CS.M49

Olsson, Nils William. Swedish passenger arrivals in New York, 1820–1850. Stockholm, Kungl. Bibl.; Chicago, Swed-

ish Pioneer Historical Soc., 1967. 391p. il. (Acta Bibliothecae Regiae Stockholmiensis, 6) **AK52**

E184.S23O43

—— Swedish passenger arrivals in U.S. ports 1820–1850 (except New York): with additions and corrections to Swedish passenger arrivals in New York 1820–1850. Stockholm, Kungl. Bibl., 1979. 139p. (Acta Bibliothecae Regiae Stockholmiensis, 32) **AK52a**

Both volumes transcribe passengers' names, with age, sex and occupation, from ship manifests for the period. Many names are annotated with further information culled from archival sources in Sweden and the United States. For each ship are given name, date of arrival and port of origin. Place and name indexes.

Olsson is also the author of the instructional guide addressed to Americans: *Tracing your Swedish ancestry* (Rev.ed. Stockholm, Ministry for Foreign Affairs, 1974. 27p.; repr. 1977).

E184.S23O43

Savage, James. A genealogical dictionary of the first settlers of New England, showing three generations of those who came before May, 1692, on the basis of the Farmer's Register. Boston, Little, 1860–62. 4v (Repr.: Baltimore, Genealogical Pub. Co., 1965) **AK53**

v.4 of the reprint includes also: F3.S2

—— Genealogical notes and errata to Savage's Genealogical dictionary . . . by C. H. Dall. Lowell, Mass., Elliott, 1881. 8p.

—— A genealogical cross index of . . . the Genealogical dictionary of James Savage, by O. P. Dexter. N.Y., Dexter, 1884. 38p.

Smith, Clifford Neal and **Smith, Anna Piszczan-Czaja.** Encyclopedia of German-American genealogical research. N.Y., Bowker, 1976. 273p. **AK54**

Attempts to "survey the material available to the genealogist seeking to link American lineages with their origins in German-speaking Europe"—*(Pref.)* through bibliographical essays. Includes some background material on German customs, sociological stratification and governmental organization useful to the genealogist. Indexed. E184.G3S66

The source: a guidebook of American genealogy. Ed. by Arlene Eakle and Johni Cerny. Salt Lake City, Ancestry, 1984. 786p. il. **AK55**

Aims to provide "a solid introduction to the major American record types from their beginnings to 1910."—*Introd.* Following a general introduction to records and techniques, 23 chapters (each by an expert) describe in some detail: (1) Major record sources (e.g., censuses; church, court, and business records, etc.); (2) Published sources (city directories, newspapers, reference books); and (3) Special resources (for immigrant origins, records of various ethnic groups; use of databases). Appendixes of sources of genealogical information, societies, and publishers; glossary; bibliographic index and subject index. Numerous illustrations of typical documents and records. Valuable to the historian as well as the genealogist.

CS49.S65

Stern, Malcolm H. First American Jewish families: 600 genealogies, 1654–1977. Cincinnati, Amer. Jewish Archives, 1978. 419p. **AK56**

A revision and expansion of the author's *Americans of Jewish Descent* (1960), offering genealogies of Jewish families established in the United States by 1840. Schematic charts for each family show names, dates and places of birth, marriage and death, military service in America's wars, and interrelationships. Almost 40,000 individuals are included. Sources of data indicated for each genealogy. Name index; bibliography of sources. CS59.S76

Swierenga, Robert P. Dutch emigrants to the United States, South Africa, South America, and Southeast Asia, 1835–1880: an alphabetical listing by household heads and independent persons. Wilmington, Del., Scholarly Resources, [1983]. 346p. **AK57**

Offers coded information from emigration lists in Dutch archives, including name, occupation, sex, age, religion, presumed reason for emigrating, economic status, tax assessment class, number of women, children and servants in household, destination, year of departure, province and municipality of origin. 21,800 names.

CS827.A1S89

——— Dutch immigrants in U.S. ship passenger manifests, 1820–1880: an alphabetical listing by household heads and independent persons. Wilmington, Del., Scholarly Resources, [1983]. 2v. **AK57a**

Coded information includes person's name, sex, age, occupation, place of origin, ship's name, port of origin, port and date of arrival. Indication of specific source of citation enables searcher to locate the record readily. E184.D9S95

U.S. Bureau of the Census. Heads of families at the first census, 1790. Wash., Govt. Prt. Off., 1907–09. 12v. (Various reprintings) **AK58**

Contents: Maine, New Hampshire, Vermont, Massachusetts, Rhode Island, Connecticut, New York, Pennsylvania, Maryland, Virginia, North Carolina, South Carolina. The statistics for Virginia are from the state census of 1782–85; those for all other states, from the federal census of 1790. Of great value for genealogical reference work, in that it shows in what towns families of any given surname were living in the year 1790, and so indicates what local records should be examined for further information. E302.5.U57

Whyte, Donald. A dictionary of Scottish emigrants to the U.S.A. Baltimore, Magna Carta Book Co., 1972. 504p. (Repr. 1981) **AK59**

A listing of Scottish emigrants prior to 1855. Gives birth and death dates as available and brief notes of genealogical interest.

E184.S3W49

CANADA

See also AK2n.

Godbout, Archange. Nos ancêtres au XVIIᵉ siècle: dictionnaire généalogique et bio-bibliographique des familles canadiennes. Livr. 1–[6]. (Extrait du Rapport de l'Archiviste de la Province de Québec, 1951/53–1965) **AK60**

Contents: Livr. 1–[6], A–Brassard. No more publ.

A re-edited edition of v.1 of Tanguay (AK63) on a different plan, designed to give the genealogical origins of those Canadian families founded before 1700 which have present-day descendants.

Jetté, René. Dictionnaire généalogique des familles du Québec . . . avec la collaboration du programme de recherche en démographie historique de l'Université de Montréal. Montréal, Presses de l'Univ. de Montréal, 1983. 1176p. **AK61**

A thorough reworking and expansion of Tanguay's work (AK63), compiled with the aim of reconstructing the history of early Quebec families. Data drawn chiefly from parish registers of baptism, marriage and burial. When complete, the work will supersede Tanguay and supplements to or revisions of that work (e.g., Godbout, above). This volume covers 1621 to 1730, and no schedule of publication for further parts is mentioned although the compiler refers to the work as "la première partie."

Alphabetically arranged by family name. Indexes of persons about whom little is known, and of variant names. CS88.Q4J47

Roy, Antoine. Bibliographie de généalogies et histoires de familles. (Extrait du Rapport de l'Archiviste de la Province de Québec, 1940/41, p.95–332) **AK62**

An index to Quebec genealogies in books and periodical articles. In two sections, the first arranged by author; the second by family name.

Tanguay, Cyprien. Dictionnaire généalogique des familles canadiennes, depuis la fondation de la colonie jusqu'à nos jours. Montréal, E. Senécal, 1871–90. 7v. (Repr.: N.Y., AMS Pr., 1969) **AK63**

1st ser., v.1, 1608–1700; 2d ser., v.2–7, 1701–1763.

The 2d series includes some entries later than 1763 (belonging to a projected 3d series). CS81.T3

——— Complément au Dictionnaire généalogique Tanguay [par] J.-Arthur Leboeuf. Montréal, Société Généalogique Canadienne-Française, 1957–77. 2v. in 1.

1st ed. 1957–64.

Contents: v.1, Première série (1957); v.2, Nouvelle deuxième série (1977).

Additions and corrections to Tanguay.

EUROPE

Almanach de Gotha, annuaire généalogique, diplomatique et statistique, 1763–1944, 1959 incomplete. Gotha, Perthes, 1763–1959. Annual. **AK64**

For full description *see* CJ224.

The first section was very useful for the genealogies of the royal and princely houses of Europe up to 1940; this is now, for the most part, continued in the *Genealogisches Handbuch des Adels* (AK68). Ceased publication. CS27.A2

❖Many other annuals of the nobility of the various countries of Europe have been published, most of which were suspended or discontinued before World War II. Some of the most important were the various series of the *Gothaisches genealogisches Taschenbuch* (Gotha, Justus Perthes), issued to cover various periods from 1765–1944. They included series on the Fürstliche Häuser, Adelige Häuser, Freiherrliche Häuser, Gräfliche Häuser, etc.

Others include: *Annuaire de la noblesse de France* (Paris & London, 1843– ; title varies; publisher varies); *Noblesse belge* (Bruxelles, 1847–1941; title varies); *Annuario della nobilità italiana* (Bari, 1879–1905); *Nederlands adelsboek* ('sGravenhage, 1903–); *Sveriges ridderskap och adels kalender* (Stockholm, 1854–); *Danmarks adels Aarbog* (Kjøbenhavn, 1884–); *Anuario de la nobleza de España* (Madrid, 1908–14).

Burke's Royal families of the world. London, Burke's Peerage, 1977–80, v.1–2. (In progress; to be in 3v.) **AK65**

Contents: v.1, Europe and Latin America; v.2, Africa and the Middle East.

A work on royal genealogy. Scope is restricted to "families which have reigned, at one time or another, since the middle of the nineteenth century."—*Pref.* Entries are alphabetical by country, with a historical sketch of the monarchy and of each royal family, followed by the genealogy of that family. Bibliography and index in each volume.

v.3 will cover Asia and Oceania.

Coutant de Saisseval, Guy. Les maisons impériales et royales d'Europe. Paris, Éditions du Palais-Royal, [1966]. 587p. **AK66**

Notes on the royal houses, their arms, titles, rules of succession, and living members. D412.7.C65

Europäische Stammtafeln. Stammtafeln zur Geschichte der europäischen Staaten. Neue Folge. Hrsg. von Detlev Schwennicke. Marburg, Stargardt, 1978–85. v.1–4, 6–8 (in 9v.; v.1 publ. 1980) (In progress) **AK67**

1st ed. 1936 by Wilhelm Karl Prinz von Isenburg.

Contents: Bd.1, Die deutschen Staaten (160 tables); Bd.2, Die ausserdeutschen Staaten (206 tables); Bd.3, T1.1, Herzogs- und Gräfenhäuser des Heiligen Römischen Reiches, andere europäische Fürstenhäuser (tables 1–200); Bd.3, T1.2, Nichtstandesgemässe und illegitime Nachkommen der regierenden Häuser Europas (tables

201–400); Bd.3, T1.3, Andere grosse europäische Familien illegitime Nachkommen spanischer und portugiesischer Königshäuser (tables 401–600); Bd.4, Standesherrliche Häuser I (168 tables); Bd.6–7, Familien des Alten Lotharingien I–II (160, 168 tables); Bd.8, West- Mittel- und Nordeuropäische Familien (163 tables).

Offers genealogical tables, with sources indicated, of kings, rulers and noble houses of Europe. This *Neue Folge* expands and supersedes earlier editions by Wilhelm Karl Prinz von Isenburg and Frank Baron Freytag von Loringhoven.

Genealogisches Handbuch des Adels, bearb. unter Aufsicht des Ausschusses für adelsrechtliche Fragen der deutschen Adelsverbände in Gemeinschaft mit dem Deutschen Adelsarchiv, Limburg a.d. Lahn, C. A. Starke, 1951–85. v.1–86. il. (In progress) **AK68**

Issued in five series: the first treats the reigning houses of Europe, the others include German families only. Information is detailed, and lineage is indicated from the earliest dates.

Contents: Fürstliche Häuser (Royal houses), v.1–12, 1951–84 (the reigning houses of Europe); Adelslexikon, v.1–5, 1972–84, A–I; Adelige Häuser (Nobility): A, v.1–17, 1953–83; B, v.1–16, 1954–85; Freiherrliche Häuser (Barons): A, v.1–13, 1952–82; B, v.1–8, 1954–82; Gräfliche Häuser (Counts): A, v.1–7, 1952–73; B, v.1–4, 1953–73; v.8–11. 1976–83.

Each volume has an index of all names in that volume; most have also an index of families in previously published volumes of their series. CS617.G45

International register of nobility. Bruxelles, Internat. Off. of Publicity, 1955–61. v.1–2. **AK69**

Publisher varies.

v.1, 1955, 223p.; v.2, 1959–1960. 1604p.

v.2 bears the subtitle: Dictionnaire généalogique de la noblesse européenne, and is in four parts: (1) Maisons souveraines; (2) Maisons ex-souveraines; (3) Noblesse européenne; (4) Ordres de chevalerie.

Text in French.

Ruvigny and Raineval, Melville Amadeus Henry Douglas Heddle de la Caillemotte de Massue de Ruvigny, *9th Marquis of.* Titled nobility of Europe. An international peerage, or "Who's who," of the sovereigns, princes and nobles of Europe. London, Harrison, 1914. 1598p. il. (coats of arms). (Repr., London, Burke's Peerage, 1980) **AK70**

Contains fairly full accounts of existing titles of nobility and biographies of living members (in 1914) of each family included in one international list, arranged alphabetically under the chief title borne by the head of the house. With a full index to surnames, variant spellings, merged titles, and titled members of a family whose names differ from that of the head of the house. Claims to be fairly complete for all British, Spanish, Belgian, and Portuguese titles; for French ducal titles; and for Austrian, German, Hungarian, Swedish, Dutch, Danish, and Finnish titles above the rank of baron. CS404.R8

FRANCE

Arnaud, Etienne. Répertoire de généalogies françaises imprimées. [Paris], Berger-Levrault, [1978–82]. 3v. **AK71**

Provides about 150,000 references from 50,000 French family names to genealogical accounts in published genealogical sources. More than 1,400 genealogical works are cited, with references to them given in abbreviated form under the individual family names.

v.3, p.73–181 is the *Supplément aux tomes 1 et 2* (i.e., A–M). Z5305.F7A75

Dictionnaire des dynasties bourgeoises et du monde des affaires, publié sous la direction de Henry Coston. Paris, Éditions A. Moreau, [1975]. 599p. **AK72**

Aims to provide historical background information on the leading families of France not of the nobility. Gives information on their origin; financial, industrial, and commercial enterprises which they direct; political affiliations, etc. HC272.5A2D5

La Chesnaye-Desbois, François Alexandre Aubert de. Dictionnaire de la noblesse . . . de la France. . . . 3. éd. Paris, Schlesinger, 1863–76. 19v. (Repr.: Nendeln, Kraus, 1969) **AK73**

Subtitle: Contenant les généalogies, l'histoire & la chronologie des familles nobles de la France, l'explication de leurs armes et l'état des grandes terres du royaume. . . . On a joint à ce dictionnaire le tableau généalogique et historique des maisons souveraines de l'Europe et une notice des familles étrangères, les plus anciennes, les plus nobles et les plus illustrés. 3.éd. entièrement refondue . . . & augm. d'une table générale de tous les noms de familles, de terres, de fiefs, d'alliances cités dans le cours de l'ouvrage. . . .

v.1–19 in A–Z arrangement. Lorenz (6:58; AA755) states that the work was to extend to 22v., with an armorial; v.20–22 and the armorial were, however, never published.

Saffroy, Gaston. Bibliographie des almanachs et annuaires administratifs, ecclésiastiques et militaires français de l'ancien régime; et des almanachs et annuaires généalogiques et nobiliaires du XVIe siècle à nos jours. Paris, Librairie G. Saffroy, 1959. 109p. **AK74**

806 numbered entries, most of them annotated. Useful for the historian as well as for the specialist in genealogy. Gives detailed accounts of the *Almanach de Gotha* (AK64) and other genealogical almanacs.

—— Bibliographie généalogique, héraldique et nobiliaire de la France, des origines à nos jours, imprimés et manuscrits. Paris, G. Saffroy, 1968–79. 4v. il. **AK75**

Contents: v.1, Généralités (nos.1–16008); v.2, Provinces et colonies françaises, orient latin, réfugiés (nos.16009–33963); v.3, Recueils généalogiques généraux, monographies familiales et études particulières (nos.33964–52222); v.4, Table générale: auteurs, titres anonymes, matières.

A comprehensive classed bibliography of published and manuscript writings relating to French genealogy. Z5305.F7S22

Sereville, Etienne de and **Saint Simon, François de.** Dictionnaire de la noblesse française. Paris. Soc. Française au XXe siècle, [1976?]. 1214p. plates, il. **AK76**

The main portion of the work is an alphabetical listing of "Notices sur les familles nobles," giving place of origin, description of arms, and a historical note on the family, documenting its elevation to noble status. Includes statistics on the French nobility in 1975; a bibliography, p.65–89; a glossary; and an "Index des noms de terre." Supplemented by: CS587.S47

Saint-Simon, F. de. Dictionnaire de la noblesse française: supplément. Paris, Éditions Contrepoint, [1977], 668p. **AK77**

Offers additions and corrections to the basic volume and two new sections, "La noblesse pontificale" and "La noblesse étrangère" (i.e., titles held by French families, but originating abroad). CS587.S23

Woelmont, Henri de. Notices généalogiques. 1–8. sér. Paris, Champion, 1923–35. v.1–8 and suppl. **AK78**

The eight series contain notices of 1,200 noble French families, some still in existence and some extinct, giving for each: description of the arms, bibliography, brief history of the family, and the genealogy. Each volume is arranged alphabetically by family names. Each volume has its own index to all names mentioned in articles as well as those used for headings; index of family names for the set in série 8. The supplementary volume contains additions and corrections to ser. 1–4. CS583.W62

GERMANY

Familiengeschichtliche Bibliographie, hrsg. unter dem Schutze der Arbeitsgemeinschaft der deutschen familien-

und wappenkundlichen Vereine, 1900– . . . . Leipzig, Zentralstelle für Deutschen Personen u. Familiengeschichte, 1932–79. v.1–7, 11$^{1-3}$, 16^1. (In progress) (Repr.: v.1–6, Wiesbaden, Sändig, 1969) **AK79**

v.1, 1900–20, by Friedrich Wecken, is a basic volume for that period and contains 13,912 entries. v.2, 1921–26, by Friedrich Wecken, comprises annual lists, the six lists totalling 8,033 entries. v.3, 1927–30, by Johannes Hohlfeld, is also made up of annual lists. v.4, 1931/32, 1933, 1934, by Johannes Hohlfeld. Register. v.5, pt.1, Bibliographie, 1935, by Johannes Hohlfeld; pt.2, Bibliographie, 1897–99, by Gunther Preuss-Tantzen; pt.3, Heraldischer Bibliographie, by Egon *Freiherr* von Berchem. v.6, pt.1–2, Bibliographie, 1936/37, by Johannes Hohlfeld; pt.3, Gesamtregister zur familiengeschichtlichen Bibliographie 1897–1937 und zur Heraldischen Bibliographie, Bd.1, by Johannes Hohlfeld und Fritz Ranitzsch. v.7, pts.1–7, 1938–45, by Johannes Hohlfeld. v.11, pts.1–3, 1960–62, by Heinz F. Friedrichs. v.8–15 not yet published. v.16, pt.1, 1975–77, Bücher und Broschüren, by Heinz F. Friedrichs, 1979. CS610.F3

Kneschke, Ernst Heinrich. Neues allgemeines deutsches Adels-Lexicon im Vereine mit mehreren Historikern. Leipzig, Voigt, 1859–70. 9v. (Repr.: Hildesheim, Olms, 1973) **AK80**

An older biographical dictionary of the German nobility with bibliographies. Alphabetically arranged. CS617.K6

GREAT BRITAIN

Guides and bibliography

See also AK24.

Gardner, David E. and **Smith, Frank.** Genealogical research in England and Wales. Salt Lake City, Utah, Bookcraft Pub., [1956–64]. 3v. **AK81**

Individual volumes have appeared in various editions: v.1, 7th ed., 1967; v.2, 4th ed., 1970; v.3, 2d ed. 1966.

Notes on the principal genealogical sources for England and Wales (but excluding Scotland and Ireland) for the period 1538 to the present are followed by chapters on birth, marriage, and death records; parish records; records of religious groups; military records; county records; apprenticeship records; poll books; etc. v.3 is concerned with paleography and the reading of ancient documents. CS414.G3

Gibson, Jeremy Sumner Wycherly. Wills and where to find them. [Chichester, Eng.], Phillimore, publ. for the British Record Soc.; Baltimore, Genealogical Pub. Co., [1974]. 210p. **AK82**

Concerned with records in England and Wales. Brief sections on Ireland and Scotland. CD1068.A2G5

Hamilton-Edwards, Gerald Kenneth Savery. In search of British ancestry. 4th ed. Baltimore, Genealogical Pub. Co., 1983. 212p. **AK83**

Published in Britain with title *In search of ancestry* (1983). 1st ed. 1966.

A step-by-step guide to genealogical research, indicating the usefulness of, and approaches to, various types of published and unpublished records. Covers English, Scottish and Welsh sources. Bibliography; index. CS414.H35

Humphery-Smith, Cecil R. A genealogist's bibliography. London [etc.], Phillimore, 1976. 93p. **AK84**

This revision of H. G. Harrison's *Select bibliography of English genealogy* (1937) is "intended primarily for students of genealogy and family history," concentrating "on those works which will assist students" . . . before General Registration [1837] and national Censuses."—*p.1.* General sections and special topics precede an arrangement by counties. Glossary of terms; no index.

Z5305.G7H85

Kaminkow, Marion J. Genealogical manuscripts in British libraries; a descriptive guide. Baltimore, Magna Carta Book Co., 1967. 140p. **AK85**

A listing of 279 libraries with indication of whether or not they hold genealogical manuscripts. Brief notes are provided on the types of manuscripts held, and reference is made to any published guides or descriptions of the collections. Indexes of family names, of places, and of authors and subjects. Z5305.G7K3

——— A new bibliography of British genealogy, with notes. Baltimore, Magna Carta Book Co., 1965. 170p. **AK86**

Aims "to list books that have not been listed elsewhere, and to indicate where to look for a list of those that have."—*Introd.* Classed arrangement with author and partial subject index.

Z5313.G69K3

Marshall, George William. The genealogist's guide. Reprinted from the last ed. of 1903 [i.e., 4th] with a new introduction by Anthony J. Camp. Baltimore, Genealogical Pub. Co., 1967. 880p. (Repr. 1980) **AK87**

1st ed. 1879.

A standard work which provides an alphabetical index to pedigrees "contained in every important genealogical and topographical work, as well as those in many of minor importance."—*Pref.*

Z5313.G69M42

Whitmore, John Beach. A genealogical guide; an index to British pedigrees, in continuation of Marshall's "Genealogist's guide (1903)." London, Walford, 1953. 658p. **AK88**

Originally publ. in parts in Harleian Society *Publications* 99, 101–102, 104 (1947–53).

Continued by: Z5313.G69W45

Barrow, Geoffrey Battiscombe. The genealogist's guide: an index to printed British pedigrees and family histories, 1950–1975. London, Research Pub. Co.; Chicago, Amer. Lib. Assoc., 1977. 205p. **AK89**

Supplements G. W. Marshall's *Genealogist's guide* (1903; AK87) and J. B. Whitmore's *Genealogical guide* (1953; AK88) both by updating and by including books and articles omitted in those earlier volumes. Cites surname and abbreviated title of source of information. Z5313.G69B36

Pine, Leslie Gilbert. The genealogist's encyclopedia. Newton Abbot, David & Charles; N.Y., Weybright and Talley, [1969]. 360p. **AK90**

Arranged by chapters intended more or less for consecutive reading, but the use of subheads within chapters and the addition of an index facilitates reference use. Glossaries of general and heraldic terms, p.321–49. CS9.P48

Thomson, Theodore Radford. A catalogue of British family histories. [3d ed. with addenda] London, Research Pub. Co., [1980]; Rutland, Vt., Tuttle, 1981. 229p. **AK91**

1st ed. 1928.

"This book purports to be a complete list of British Family Histories, that is, books written as histories of families generally acknowledged to be English, Scots, Welsh or Irish."—*Pref.* Does not include reprints from periodicals, collections of pedigrees, biographies, histories of businesses, books dealing with more than one family, or books published in America. The 1980 reprint (of 3d ed. 1976) adds some 400 recent or previously omitted titles, with date (but rarely place) of publication. Z5315.G69T4

Dictionaries and compendiums

Burke, *Sir* **John Bernard.** Burke's Genealogical and heraldic history of the peerage, baronetage, and knightage. London, Burke, 1826– . il. (coats of arms). Annual, 1851–1940; quadrennial since 1949 (slightly irregular). **AK92**

Title, publisher, and frequency vary.

Contents vary; 1970: Special articles; Royal family; Peerage and baronetage, arranged alphabetically by title, giving brief account of present holder of title, names of wife, children, heir, lineage, date of creation, arms (both illustration and description), residence; Archbishops and bishops; Knightage; Peerages in order of precedence, Extinct titles, etc.

The only modern peerage which gives full lineage.

The 2d impression of this edition (1975; with abridged supplement, elimination of some special articles, but otherwise unchanged) announced that future editions are to be issued "once every generation (i.e., every fifteen to twenty years)."—*Pref.*

CS420.B85

—— Genealogical and heraldic history of the colonial gentry. London, Harrison, 1891–95. 2v. il. (Repr.: Baltimore, Genealogical Pub. Co.; London, Heraldry Today, 1970) **AK93**

Gives pedigrees and coats of arms of leading families in British Colonies. Indexed. CS425.B7

—— Burke's Genealogical and heraldic history of the landed gentry, founded by John Burke and Sir Bernard Burke. 18th ed., ed. by Peter Townend. London, Burke's Peerage, 1965–72. 3v. il. (coats of arms). **AK94**

History: 1st ed., *Burke's Commoners of Great Britain and Ireland,* 1833–35. 3v. After the 9th edition, 1898, Irish families were omitted and transferred, instead, to a separate work, *Landed gentry of Ireland,* now *Burke's Irish family records* (AK106).

While the avowed purpose of the work is for genealogical and heraldic information, it is often very useful for biographical data or facts about names omitted from the biographical dictionaries. Gives brief sketch of present head of family, names of wife and children, lineage, arms (both illustration and description), and seat. Cumulative index in v.3. CS425.B8

—— Genealogical history of the dormant, abeyant, forfeited, and extinct peerages of the British Empire. New ed. London, Harrison, 1883. 642p. coats of arms. (Repr.: London, Wm. Clowes for Burke's Peerage, 1969) **AK95**

1st ed. 1831. CS422.B88

Burke's Family index. London, Burke's Peerage Ltd. (distr. in U.S.A. by Arco Publ. Co., N.Y.), 1976. 171p. il. **AK96**

". . . provides a guide to the most complete and up-to-date version of a family's narrative pedigree in a Burke's publication since 1826."—*p.xxxi.* Includes "A bibliography of Burke's, 1826–1976," by Rosemary Pinches, p.xii–xxx. Z5305.G7B87

Cokayne, George Edward. Complete baronetage. Exeter, Pollard, 1900–1909. 5v. and index volume. (Repr.: Gloucester, A. Sutton, 1983. 6v. in 1) **AK97**

v.1, English baronetcies, 1611–25, and Irish, 1619–25; v.2, English, Irish and Scottish, 1625–49; v.3, English, Irish and Scottish, 1649–64; v.4, English, Irish and Scottish, 1665–1707; v.5, Great Britain and Ireland, 1707–1800, and Jacobite, 1688–1788. Index volume: Index and appendix. CS424.C68

—— The complete peerage; or, A history of the House of Lords and all its members from the earliest times . . . rev. and much enl. London, St. Catherine Pr., 1910–59. 13v. in 14. (Compact repr.: N.Y., St. Martin's Pr., 1984. 13v. in 6) **AK98**

Title and editors vary.

v.1–5 had title *Complete peerage of England, Scotland, Ireland, Great Britain, and the United Kingdom, extant, extinct, or dormant.*

Contents: v.1–12, 14, A–Z; v.13 (1940), *Peerage creations and promotions from 22 Jan. 1901 to 31 Dec. 1938.*

The most complete record of the British peerage, giving full accounts, with bibliographical references to sources of information and many biographical details. Important as a supplement to biographical dictionaries as well as for genealogical information. CS421.C71

Debrett's Peerage, baronetage, knightage and companionage, with Her Majesty's Royal warrant holders. London, Kelly's Directories, 1713–1974. il. Annual. **AK99**

Title varies slightly. Editors and publishers vary.

Subtitle, 1973/74: Comprises information concerning the peerage, Privy Counsellors, baronets, knights, knights' widows, and companions of orders.

Gives biographical data, arms (illustration and description), living children, living collateral branches, predecessors, etc.

CS420.D32

Debrett's Peerage and baronetage, with Her Majesty's royal warrant holders. 1976– . Kingston upon Thames, Kelly's Directories, Ltd., 1976– . Irregular. **AK100**

Publisher varies.

Supersedes in part *Debrett's Peerage, baronetage, knightage, and companionage* (above) which ceased with the volume for 1973/74.

"Comprises information concerning the royal family, the peerage, privy counsellors, Scottish Lords of Session, baronets, and chiefs of names and clans in Scotland."—*t.p., 1976.*

"In future, Debrett will be published at longer intervals than previously."—*p.14, 1976.* Users are referred to *Kelly's handbook* (AJ235) for information on the knightage and companionage.

Doyle, James William Edmund. Official baronage of England, showing the succession, dignities, and offices of every peer from 1066 to 1885. London, Longmans, 1886. 3v. il. **AK101**

CS421.D75

Haydn, Joseph Timothy. The book of dignities . . . 3d ed. London, W. H. Allen, 1894. xxiii p., 1170p. (Repr.: Baltimore, Genealogical Pub. Co., 1970) **AK102**

1st ed. 1851.

Subtitle: Containing lists of the official personages of the British Empire, civil, diplomatic, heraldic, judicial, ecclesiastical, municipal, naval and military . . . with the sovereigns and rulers of the world from the foundation of their respective states; the orders of knighthood of the United Kingdom and India, etc. etc. DA34.H3

Pine, Leslie Gilbert. The new extinct peerage, 1884–1971, containing extinct, abeyant, dormant & suspended peerages, with genealogies and arms. Baltimore, Genealogical Pub. Co., 1973. 313p. il. **AK103**

In addition to providing information on peerages which have become extinct, dormant or abeyant during the 1884–1971 period, the work includes some peerages extinct before 1884, but which were omitted from Burke's *Extinct peerages* (AK95). CS422.P56

Smith, Frank. A genealogical gazetteer of England. Baltimore, Genealogical Pub. Co., 1968. 599p. (Repr.: 1982) **AK104**

Subtitle: An alphabetical dictionary of places, with their location, ecclesiastical jurisdiction, population, and the date of the earliest entry in the registers of every ancient parish in England.

Effectively supersedes older works of similar content, e.g., A. M. Burke's *Key to the ancient parish registers of England and Wales* (1908). DA640.S6

Steel, D. J., Steel, A. E. F. and **Field, C. W.** National index of parish registers. London, Soc. of Genealogists, 1966–84; v.1–6¹, 7, 11¹, 12. (In progress) **AK105**

Subtitle: A guide to Anglican, Roman Catholic and nonconformist registers before 1837, together with information on marriage licences, bishop's transcripts, and modern copies.

Editors vary.

Contents: v.1, Sources of births, marriages and deaths before 1837, pt.1 (1967); v.2, Sources for nonconformist genealogy and family history (1973); v.3, Sources for Roman Catholic and Jewish genealogy and family history, index v.1–3 (1974); v.4, South East England: Kent, Surrey and Sussex (1980); v.5, South Midlands and Welsh Border, comprising the counties of Gloucestershire, Herefordshire, Oxfordshire, Shropshire, Warwickshire, and Worcestershire (1976); v.6, North Midlands, pt.1: Staffordshire (1982); v.7, East Anglia, Cambridgeshire, Norfolk and Suffolk (1983); v.11, North East England, pt.1: Durham and Northumberland (1979; 2d ed. 1984); v.12, Sources for Scottish genealogy and family history (1970). CD1068.A2S8

IRELAND

Burke's Irish family records. Ed., Hugh Montgomery-Massingberd. [5th ed.] London, Burke's Peerage; N.Y., distr. by Arco Pub. Co., 1976. 1237p.   **AK106**

1st ed. 1899.

Represents a change of title for *Burke's Landed gentry of Ireland* issued in four editions, 1899–1958.

Contains "genealogical histories of 514 Irish families from their earliest recorded male ancestor down to the present day, set out in narrative style, with biographical entries for each member of the family."—*Contents.* Does not supersede earlier editions since not every family appearing in preceding editions is contained herein.

    CS482.B87

MacLysaght, Edward. Irish families; their names, arms, and origins. Dublin, H. Figgis, 1957. 366p. il   **AK107**

    CS498.M3

—— More Irish families. [Rev. and enl. ed.] Blackrock, Co. Dublin, Irish Academic Pr., 1982. 254p.   **AK108**

"In effect an enlarged second volume" of *Irish families* (above), consisting of the author's *More Irish families* (1960) and *Supplement to Irish families* (1964) "carefully revised and in many cases added to, all the entries [now] integrated in the text."—*Pref.* An essay on the Irish chieftainries and additions to the first volume are included. Indexed.   CS498.M32

ITALY

Spreti, Vittorio, *Marchese.* Enciclopedia storico-nobiliare italiana; famiglie nobili e titolate viventi riconosciute dal R. governo d'Italia compresi: città, communità, mense vescovili, abazie, parrocchie ed enti nobili e titolati riconosciuti. Milano, Ed. Encic. Stor.–Nob. Ital., 1928–35. 6v. and Appendix, v.1–2. il. (coats of arms). (Repr.: Bologna, Forni, 1981)   **AK109**

A historical, biographical encyclopedia of titled Italian families.

    CS757.S7

—— and **Azzi Vitelleschi, Giustiniano degli.** Saggio di bibliografia araldica italiana. Supplemento a l'Enciclopedia storico-nobiliare italiana. Milano, Ed. Encic. Stor.–Nob. Ital., 1936. 230p. (Repr.: Bologna, Forni, 1974)   **AK110**

A bibliography of Italian heraldry and nobility.

SCOTLAND

Ferguson, Joan P. S. Scottish family histories held in Scottish libraries. Edinburgh, Scottish Central Lib., 1960. 194p.   **AK111**

Locates copies of published works and a few manuscripts. Arranged by family name.   Z5313.S4F4

Hamilton-Edwards, Gerald Kenneth Savery. In search of Scottish ancestry. 2d ed. Chichester, Sussex, Phillimore, 1983; Baltimore, Genealogical Pub. Co., 1984. 252p.   **AK112**

A guide to the sources of Scottish genealogical information, prefaced by "An outline of Scottish history." Changes in this edition include information on new calendars, indexes, etc., and on the transfer of documents to various repositories.   CS463.H35

Stuart, Margaret. Scottish family history, a guide to works of reference on the history and genealogy of Scottish families. Edinburgh, Oliver & Boyd, 1930. 386p. (Repr.: Baltimore, Genealogical Pub. Co., 1978)   **AK113**

Includes books, pamphlets, and a large amount of analysis of periodicals, composite books, collections, etc.   Z5313.S4S9

Clans and tartans

Adam, Frank. The clans, septs, and regiments of the Scottish Highlands, rev. by Sir Thomas Innes of Learney. 8th ed. Edinburgh, London, Johnston and Bacon; Baltimore, Genealogical Pub. Co., 1970. 624p. il. (Repr. 1975)   **AK114**

Includes colored plates of tartans.

Covers the history and structure of the clan system, Celtic culture, the Highland regiments, clan insignia and heraldry, clan lists and statistics, etc.   DA880.H6A6

Innes, *Sir* **Thomas.** The tartans of the clans and families of Scotland. 8th ed. Edinburgh, Johnston & Bacon, [1971]. 300p. il. (116 col. plates of tartans).   **AK115**

1st ed. 1938.

Introductory chapters discuss the clan system, order of succession, etc., followed by clans arranged alphabetically, with one-page histories, and colored plates of the tartans.   DA880.H76I5

SPAIN

Instituto Internacional de Genealogía y Heráldica. Índice nobiliario español. Recop. y redac. por Vicente de Cardenas y Vicent [et al.]. Madrid, Ed. Hidalguía, 1955. 754p. (Guía nobiliaria universal. Sección española)   **AK116**

Brief listings of the Spanish nobility indicating titles, etc., and a section on military orders, societies of nobles, etc.

—— —— Suplemento 1957–1960. Recop. y redac. por el Barón de Cobos de Belchite. Madrid, Ed. Hidalguía, 1960. 87p. (Guía nobiliaria universal)

    CS947.I5

HERALDRY

Bolton, Charles Knowles. Bolton's American armory; a record of coats of arms which have been in use within the present bounds of the United States. Boston, Faxon, 1927. 223p. (Useful reference ser.) (Repr.: Baltimore, Heraldic Book Co., 1964)   **AK117**

    CR1209.B6

Boutell, Charles. Boutell's Heraldry. Rev. by J. P. Brooke-Little. [Rev. ed.] London, N.Y., Warne, [1983]. 368p. il.   **AK118**

Based on Boutell's *Manual of heraldry* (1863) and *English heraldry* (1867).

A standard work covering all aspects of the subject. Minor revisions and updating in this edition. A new chapter, "How to use arms," one on recent trends, and a revised critical bibliography are included.   CR21.B7

Briggs, Geoffrey. Civic & corporate heraldry; a dictionary of impersonal arms of England, Wales & N. Ireland. London, Heraldry Today; Detroit, Gale, [1971]. 432p. il.   **AK119**

Concerned with current arms borne "by lawful authority," but including "some few unauthorised coats which are so well known that their omission would cause surprise."—*Pref.* Arranged by name of corporate body.   CR492.B75

Burke, *Sir* **John Bernard.** The general armory of England, Scotland, Ireland, and Wales, comprising a registry of armorial bearings from the earliest to the present time. With a supplement. London, Harrison, 1884. 1185p. il. (Repr.:

London, Wm. Clowes for Burke's Peerage, 1961; Baltimore, Genealogical Pub. Co., 1976) **AK120**

An enlarged edition (first publ. 1842) of *Encyclopaedia of heraldry; or, General armory of England, Scotland and Ireland,* published in many editions.
Supplemented by: CR1619.B73

Humphery-Smith, Cecil R. General armory two: Alfred Morant's additions and corrections to Burke's General armory. Ed. and augmented . . . . London, Tabard Pr., 1973; Baltimore, Genealogical Pub. Co., 1974. 230p. il. **AK121**

Contains all the "extra material and corrections" *(Introd.)* that Morant made to the original work and an appendix of names and information on coats of arms drawn from sources later than Burke and Morant. CR1619.H86

Child, Heather. Heraldic design; a handbook for students. London, G. Bell, [1965]. 180p. il. (Repr.: Baltimore, Genealogical Pub. Co., 1982) **AK122**

Aims "to give the student of design sufficient information about the structure and detail of heraldic insignia to enable him to produce well balanced designs of coats of arms."—*Introd.* Indexed.
CR31.C5

Fairbairn, James. Book of crests of the families of Great Britain and Ireland. 4th ed. rev. and enl. by A. C. Fox-Davies. Edinburgh, Jack, 1905. 2v. il. (Various printings: e.g., London, Heraldry Today, 1983) **AK123**

1st ed. 1859. Rev. ed. 1860. 2v. (American ed.: N.Y., 1911 had title *Fairbairn's Crests . . .*).
A volume of plates with an index to crests arranged by surnames; a glossary; and a section of mottoes. CR57.G7F2

Fox-Davies, Arthur Charles. Armorial families, a directory of gentlemen of coat-armour. 7th ed. London, Hurst and Blackett, 1929. 2v. il. (Repr.: Rutland Vt., Tuttle, 1970; Newton Abbot, David & Charles, 1970) **AK124**

Arranged by families with descriptions of coats of arms, mottoes, etc. CR1618.F6

—— The book of public arms: a complete encyclopaedia of all royal, territorial, municipal, corporate, official and impersonal arms. New ed., containing over 1300 drawings. London & Edinburgh, Jack, 1915. 876p. il. **AK125**

CR492.F7

—— A complete guide to heraldry. [New ed.] Rev. and annotated by J. P. Brooke-Little. London, Nelson, 1969. 513p. il. **AK126**

Founded upon the author's *Art of heraldry* (1904; repr. London, Orbis, 1985). First published 1909. Later reprintings with revisions by C. A. H. Franklyn.
An annotated edition rather than a revision of Fox-Davies's original text. The editor has tried, "by detailing twentieth-century official heraldic practice, to make the book as valuable to the student of heraldry today as when it was first published," with the added advantage that "the reader will be able to see exactly how heraldry and heraldic thought has evolved during the past half century."—*Pref.* Only obvious anachronisms in the text have been changed.
CR21.F73

Henning, Eckart and **Jochums, Gabriele.** Bibliographie zur Heraldik: Schrifttum Deutschlands und Österreichs bis 1980. Köln, Böhlau, 1984. (Bibliographie der historischen Hilfswissenschaften, Bd.1) **AK127**

Presents an extensive systematic bibliography of books and articles on the basis, history and law of heraldry and on the arms of Germany and Austria, their provinces, counties, cities, towns, and families. Author, subject, and name indexes.

Innes, Thomas. Scots heraldry, a practical handbook on the historical principles and modern application of the art and science . . . [2d ed. rev. and enl.] Edinburgh, Oliver and

Boyd, 1956. 258p. il. (Repr.: Baltimore, Genealogical Pub. Co., 1971) **AK128**

1st ed. 1934. CR1652.I5

Jougla de Morenas, Henri. . . . Grand armorial de France; catalogue général des armoiries des familles nobles de France. Paris, Éd. Héraldiques, 1934–49. 6v. il. **AK129**

—— —— Supplément. Paris, Soc. du Grand Armorial de France, 1952. 447p. il.

CR1801.J6

New England Historic Genealogical Society. Committee on Heraldry. A roll of arms. Boston, 1928–80. Pts.1–9. coats of arms. (In progress) **AK130**

Pts.1–2 reprinted from the *New England historical and genealogical register,* Apr. 1928 and July 1932, with a corrected re-issue 1950.
Of first importance. Names of American families having registered arms, with descriptions and line drawings. Arranged by registration number, with an alphabetical index of surnames in each part. CR1209.N45

Rietstap, Johannes Baptist. Armorial général; precédé d'un Dictionnaire des termes du blason. 2. éd., refondue et augm. Gouda, van Goor, [1884]–87. 2v. il. (Repr.: N.Y., Barnes & Noble, 1965) **AK131**

Publisher varies.
A general work on European arms, dealing with more than 100,000 families entitled to hereditary honors. CR1179.R52

—— —— Supplément par V. [and] H. Rolland. La Haye, Nijhoff, 1926–54. 7v. in 8. il.

v.1–2 issued in 36 pts., 1904–26. v.2 bound in 2v.

CR1179.R52

—— —— —— Table du supplément, par Henri Rolland. Lyon, Soc. de Sauvegarde Historique, 1951. 1v. (unpaged)

Indexes v.1–6 of the *Supplément.* These 6v. (bound in 7) are called v.1–7 in the index.
The supplements include both illustrations and blazons.
CR1179.R52

—— —— Armoiries des familles contenues dans l'Armorial général. Paris, Inst. Héraldique Universel, 1903–26. 6v. il.

Plates of coats of arms (blazons) described in the *Armorial général,* arranged in alphabetical order. v.2–6 have title *Planches de l'Armorial général,* par H. and V. Rolland. v.5–6 have imprint: La Haye, Nijhoff, 1921–26. CR1179.R55

—— —— General illustrated armorial, by V. and H. Rolland. [3d ed.] Lyon, Soc. de Sauvegarde Historique, [1953?]. 6v. (Repr. as: V. & H. V. Rolland's illustrations to the Armorial général. Baltimore, Heraldic Book Co., 1967)

A 3d ed. of the above, published with the text material in English.
CR1179.R653

Roll of Scottish arms. Ed. by Lt. Col. Gayre of Gayre and Nigg and Reinold Gayre of Gayre and Nigg the Younger. Edinburgh, the Armorial, 1964 [i.e. 1965]–69. pt.I, v.1–2. (In progress) **AK132**

Contents: pt.I, v.1–2, A–Z.
"A complete roll of Scottish armorial bearings arranged alphabetically, giving the names, ranks, titles, designations and blazons as they appear in the original manuscript."—*Introd.* CR1659.R6

Terminology

Brooke-Little, John Philip. An heraldic alphabet. New and rev. ed. London, Macdonald and Jane's, [1975]. 226p. il.
AK133

Definitions prefaced by an essay on heraldry as "seen through the eyes of a herald rather than purely historically or academically."— *Foreword*. Recommended as an inexpensive substitute for libraries unable to afford Franklyn and Tanner's *Encyclopaedic dictionary of heraldry* (below). This edition includes corrections, additions, and some new illustrations.   CR13.B76

Franklyn, Julian and **Tanner, John.** An encyclopaedic dictionary of heraldry. Oxford & N.Y., Pergamon, [1970]. 367p. il.   **AK134**

Provides definitions of terms employed in heraldry, usually with some indication of usage. Major terms used in foreign heraldry are also included.   CR13.F7

Parker, James. A glossary of terms used in heraldry. New ed. Rutland, Vt., Tuttle, [1970]. 659p. il.   **AK135**

"Originally published in 1894 and based on H. Gough's A glossary of terms used in British heraldry, which was published in 1847."—*L.C. card*.
Still one of the more useful glossaries.   CR1618.G6

Stalins, Gaston Ferdinand Laurent, *Baron*. Vocabulaire-atlas héraldique en six langues: français-English-deutsch-español-italiano-Nederlandsch, par le baron Stalins avec la collaboration de René le Juge de Segrais [et al.]. Paris, Soc. du Grand Armorial de France, 1952. 119p. il.   **AK136**

At head of title: Académie Internationale d'héraldique.
Pt.1 (p.10–39) gives the principal terms used in heraldry, in six languages, in table form and numbered; the numbers correspond to the illustrations in the plates. Pt.2 (p.42–71) gives an alphabetical listing of terms for each of the six languages, with the number of its representation in the plates. Pt.3 (p.75–119) consists of 23 black-and-white plates, each containing several small but clear figures representing the heraldic terms in pts.1–2. A clear, concise guide to heraldic terminology.   CR13.S8

ORDERS AND DECORATIONS

❖Information on orders and decorations is given in many genealogical annuals, such as the *Almanach de Gotha* (AK64), Burke's *Peerage* (AK92), etc., and in many older official registers, such as the French *Almanach national* (CJ301), the Belgian *Almanach royal officiel* (CJ258), etc.

American Numismatic Society. Numismatic notes and monographs. N.Y., Society.   **AK137**

From 1922 to 1945, the American Numismatic Society devoted several numbers of its *Numismatic notes and monographs* series to the orders and decorations of various countries.

Burke, *Sir* **John Bernard,** ed. The book of orders of knighthood and decorations of honour of all nations, comprising an historical account of each order, military, naval, and civil, from the earliest to the present time, with lists of the knights and companions of each British order. London, Hurst and Blackett, 1858. 411p. 100 col.pl.   **AK138**
    CR4653.B8

Hieronymussen, Poul Ohm. Orders, medals and decorations of Britain and Europe in colour. . . . translated [from the Danish] by Christine Crowley. 2d ed. London, Blandford, 1970. 256p. il. (Repr. 1975)   **AK139**

Originally published as *Europaeiske ordner i farver* (Copenhagen, 1966). 1st English ed. 1967.
Illustrates and describes present-day international European orders.   CR4515.H513

Jocelyn, Arthur. Awards of honour; the orders, decorations, medals and awards of Great Britain & the Commonwealth from Edward III to Elizabeth II. London, A. & C. Black, 1956. 276p. il. col.pl.   **AK140**

Contains description of the orders, decorations, etc., with colored plates.   CR4529.G7J6

Nicolas, *Sir* **Nicholas Harris.** History of the orders of knighthood of the British Empire; of the Order of the Guelphs of Hanover; and of the medals, clasps, and crosses, conferred for naval and military services. London, Hunter, 1842. 4v. il.   **AK141**
    CR4801.N5

Rosignoli, Guido. Ribbons of orders, decorations and medals. Poole, Blandford Pr., 1976; N.Y., Arco, [1977]. 165p. il.   **AK142**

"This book deals mainly with service ribbons, worn on their own on the breast, although general information on the decorations and medals they represent is also included in the text."—*Introd*. Country-by-country arrangement. Color illustrations.   CR4661.R67

Werlich, Robert. Orders and decorations of all nations: ancient and modern, civil and military. 2d ed. [Wash., Quaker Pr., 1974] 476p. il.   **AK143**

1st ed. 1965.
Illustrates and describes the major awards of all countries. Arranged by country; general index.   CR4509.W4

Wyllie, Robert E. Orders, decorations and insignia, military and civil; with the history and romance of their origin and a full description of each . . . with 367 illustrations (over 200 in colour). N.Y., London, Putnam, [1921]. 269p. il.   **AK144**

Contains historical and descriptive information, with many excellent illustrations of the medals, ribbons, badges, etc., of the United States, Great Britain, Belgium, China, Cuba, Czechoslovakia, France, Greece, Hawaii, Italy, Japan, Monaco, Montenegro, Panama, Poland, Portugal, Rumania, Russia, and Serbia. Includes also information on shoulder insignia, insignia of rank, and insignia and colors of arms of service of the World War I period.   CR4509.W9

FLAGS

Campbell, Gordon and **Evans, Idrisyn Oliver.** The book of flags. 7th ed. London, Oxford Univ. Pr., 1974. 124p. il.   **AK145**

1st ed. 1950.
Emphasis is on flags of Britain, with separate sections for the British Isles and for the United States; other countries are listed within geographic regions.   CR101.C3

Flags of the world. Ed. by E. M. C. Barraclough and W. G. Crampton. 2d ed. [of 1978 ed.] with revisions and supplement. [London & N.Y.], F. Warne, [1981]. 262p. il.   **AK146**

Based on *The flags of the world; their history, blazonry, and associations*, by F. Edward Hulme, publ. 1897. Editions by H. G. Carr published 1953 and 1961. First published under Barraclough's editorship 1965.
Offers histories and descriptions of the flags and standards of the various countries of the world, with special emphasis on British flags. In this edition new material (1978–81) appears in the supplement, p.241–52, and is cross-referenced to the main text.
    CR109.F554

Furlong, William Rea and **McCandless, Byron.** So proudly we hail: the history of the United States flag. Wash., Smithsonian Inst. Pr., 1981. 260p. il.   **AK147**

Treats flags of exploration and discovery and various other predecessors of the U.S. flag as well as the "Stars and Stripes" and its evolution. Numerous appendixes, including the history of the pledge of allegiance, flag etiquette, etc. Bibliography; index.
    CR113.F93

Gt.Brit. Admiralty. Flags of all nations. [Rev. ed.] London, H. M. Stat. Off., 1955–58. v.1–2. il. Looseleaf.   **AK148**

v.1 repr. 1965, incorporating amendments and changes.

Previous edition entitled *Drawings of the flags of all nations* (1930).

Contents: v.1, National flags and ensigns; v.2, Standards of rulers, sovereigns and heads of state; Flags of heads of ministries, and of naval, military and air force officers.

Consists of colored plates, little or no text. Announced to be in 3v.; v.3 not published? V300.G72

Pedersen, Christian Fogd. Alverdens flag i farver: Politikens flaglexikon. 3. udgave . . . illustrationer, Thor Axelsen Drejer, Verner Hancke, Niels Jønsson. [København], Politiken, 1979. 279p. il. **AK149**

1st ed. 1970. The 1970 ed. was also published in English translation with title *The international flag book in color* (N.Y., Morrow, 1971).

Illustrations and descriptions of about 900 flags of nations, states, colonies, naval and mercantile flags, official flags of Heads of State. Includes coats of arms of about 180 states throughout the world. Glossary and index. CR109.P413

Quaife, Milo M., Weig, Melvin J. and **Appleman, Roy E.** The history of the United States flag from the Revolution to the present, including a guide to its use and display. Publ. in co-operation with the Eastern National Park and Monument Assoc. N.Y., Harper, [1964? c1961]. 190p. il. **AK150**

"Second edition . . . which incorporates the story and an illustration of the Hawaiian flag."

Gives the history of the flag and other United States symbols, e.g., the seal; use and display, etc. CR113.Q32

Shankle, George Earlie. State names, flags, seals, songs, birds, flowers and other symbols. Rev. ed. N.Y., Wilson, 1941 [i.e., 1951, c1938]. 524p. il. (Repr.: Westport, Conn., Greenwood, 1970) **AK151**

1st ed. 1938.

Subtitle: A study based on historical documents giving the origin and significance of the state names, nicknames, mottoes, seals, flags, flowers, birds, songs, and descriptive comments on the capitol buildings and on some of the leading state histories, with facsimiles of the state flags and seals. E155.S43

Smith, Whitney. The flag book of the United States. N.Y., Morrow, [1970]. 306p. il. **AK152**

Offers historical and explanatory material together with illustrations of flags, seals, and coats of arms of the United States and of the individual states and territories. JC346.Z3S63

———— Flags and arms across the world. N.Y., McGraw-Hill, [1980]. 256p. il. **AK153**

"A field guide to the flags of the 174 nations of the world. National flags, coats of arms, state and provincial flags, presidential and ministerial banners—nearly 1,000 full-color illustrations, with maps, history, and thorough documentation."—*verso of t.p.*

Revises and updates the international section of the author's *Flags through the ages* (below). Indexed. JC345.S56

———— Flags through the ages and across the world. N.Y., McGraw-Hill, [1975]. 357p. col. il. **AK154**

In three main sections: (1) Flags through the ages (History of flags; Flags that made history; Customs and etiquette; National flag histories); (2) Flags across the world (Flags of the world's 157 nations and their subdivisions; International flags; Ethnic minority flags); (3) Symbols. A good deal of background information and explanatory text accompanies the illustrations. Glossary of terms; index. JC345.S57

Talocci, Mauro. Guide to the flags of the world. Rev. and updated by Whitney Smith. Tr. from the Italian by Ronald Strom. N.Y., Morrow, 1982. 271p. il. **AK155**

1977 Italian ed. had title: *Guida alle bandiere di tutto il mondo.*

Arranged by continent, then by country, with an added section for international flags. Flags and coats of arms are illustrated in color, with brief notes on historical background and symbols depicted. Glossary; index. CR101.T3413

NAMES

Bibliography

Singerman, Robert. Jewish and Hebrew onomastics, a bibliography. N.Y., Garland, 1977. 132p. **AK156**

Presents "the first attempt at bringing under bibliographic control all significant literature on the etymology, history and folklore of Jewish and Hebrew personal names."—*Introd.* Lists books, parts of books and articles concerning biblical, ancient, and modern names of many countries. 1,195 entries. Indexed. Z6824.S5

Smith, Elsdon Coles. Personal names, a bibliography. N.Y., New York Pub. Lib., 1952. 226p. (Repr.: Detroit, Gale, 1965) **AK157**

Reprinted from the *Bulletin* of the New York Public Library, 1950–51.

A classified bibliography of 3,415 monographs and periodical articles on names, with brief, critical annotations. Library locations are given. Alphabetical index. Z6824.S55

Personal names

See also AK195.

Audebert, Antoine. Dictionnaire analytique des prénoms. Paris, Calmann-Lévy, [1956]. 229p. **AK158**

Gives origin and meaning of French forenames.

CS2375.F8A85

Bahlow, Hans. Unsere Vornamen im Wandel der Jahrhunderte. Limburg a.d. Lahn, Starke, 1965. 113p. (Grundriss der Genealogie, 4) **AK159**

Indicates derivation and changes in form of given names; cross references are provided from variant forms. CS2375.G3B26

Chuks-orji, Ogonna. Names from Africa; their origin, meaning, and pronunciation. Ed. and with a commentary by Keith E. Baird. Chicago, Johnson, 1972. 89p. **AK160**

A dictionary of given names, indicating pronunciation, meaning, language and country of origin. CS2375.A33C48

Dunkling, Leslie and **Gosling, William.** Everyman's Dictionary of first names. London, Dent, [1983]. 304p. **AK161**

Publ. in U.S. as *The Facts on File dictionary of first names* (N.Y., 1984).

In addition to explaining where various first names come from, the dictionary indicates "when they have been most used, and if possible, why they were most used at that particular time."—*Introd.* Includes references to other name dictionaries, to literary uses, popularity of a name occasioned by film stars and other prominent personalities, diminutive forms, cross references, etc. Information on popularity and continued use of specific names was derived from numerous surveys and sources cited in the introduction. "Since this dictionary has some 4,500 entries, dealing with more than 10,000 names, we feel justified in claiming that the first names borne by at least 95% of the English-speaking population are in this book." CS2367.D837

Egger, Carl. Lexicon nominum virorum et mulierum. 2. ed. Romae, Studium, [1963]. 263p. **AK162**

A dictionary of personal names, each given in Italian, French, Spanish, English and German, with their Latin equivalents and etymologies. P769.E3

Kolatch, Alfred J. Complete dictionary of English and Hebrew first names. Middle Village, N.Y., Jonathan David, [1984]. 488p. **AK163**

1st ed. 1948 had title: *These are the names*; rev. ed. 1967 entitled *The name dictionary.*

Masculine and feminine names are given in separate alphabets. Hebrew characters are included for the Hebrew names.

CS2367.K63

—— The Jonathan David dictionary of first names. Middle Village, N.Y., Jonathan David, [1980]. **AK164**

A more comprehensive list than the author's *Complete dictionary* . . . (above); i.e., not restricted to Hebrew names. Gives meaning and etymology, variant forms, contemporary examples, etc. Masculine and feminine names in separate alphabets. CS2367.K64

Loughead, Flora Haines Apponyi. Dictionary of given names, with origins and meanings. 2d ed. rev. and corr. Glendale, Calif., A. H. Clark, 1958 [c1933]. 248p. **AK165**

1st ed. 1933. CS2367.L

Puckett, Newbell Niles. Black names in America: origins and usage. Ed. by Murray Heller. Boston, G. K. Hall, [1975]. 561p. **AK166**

At head of title: Newbell Niles Puckett Memorial gift, John G. White Department, Cleveland Public Library.

Chapters 1–4 offer background material, chronological and regional lists of names, and various types of statistics. Chapter 5 is a "Dictionary of African origins." There is also an "Index of unusual names" and a bibliography of principal sources. E185.89.N3P82

Stewart, George Rippey. American given names; their origin and history in the context of the English language. N.Y., Oxford Univ. Pr., 1979. 264p. **AK167**

A historical sketch of the use, frequency, etc., of given names in America is followed by a dictionary arrangement (p.43–258) of selected names, indicating whether each is usually applied to male or female, the language from which derived, meaning, and (in most cases) a "history" of the name as it occurs in United States usage, with indication of popularity, etc.

A review by ALA's Reference and Subscription Books Review Committee concludes that this is "the best available reference book on American personal nomenclature."—*Booklist* 76:997–98.

CS2375.U6S74

Wells, Evelyn. What to name the baby (a treasury of names). 15,000 names to choose from. Garden City, N.Y., Doubleday, [1953]. 326p. **AK168**

1st ed., 1946, had title *A treasury of names.*

A useful guide for quick reference to foreign equivalents of American forenames.

Another dictionary of this type, addressed "to the general, rather than to the learned, public" *(Author's note),* is Eric Partridge's *Name this child* (3d ed., rev. & much enl. London, H. Hamilton, 1951. 296p.); it is a dictionary of British and American given or Christian names. CS2367.W43

Withycombe, Elizabeth Gidley. The Oxford dictionary of English Christian names. 3d ed. Oxford & N.Y., Clarendon Pr., [1977]. 310p. **AK169**

1st ed. 1945.

"The present edition contains about forty names not included in the previous editions, as well as a number of new cross-references. The main work of revision, as before, consists of many small corrections, emendations, and additions to existing articles, many of which reflect the changes in usage, frequency, and status of names. . . . "—*Pref.* Gives sources for earliest usage. CS2375.G7W5

Woods, Richard D. Hispanic first names; a comprehensive dictionary of 250 years of Mexican-American usage. Westport, Conn., Greenwood, [1984]. 224p. (Bibliographies and indexes in anthropology, 1) **AK170**

For each name or variant the appropriate parent form was determined and under this form (or "main entry") is given the full information: phonetic transcription, gender, English equivalent (if any), derivation or meaning, diminutives and variants. *See* references are provided from all variant forms. CS2375.U6W66

Yonge, Charlotte Mary. History of Christian names. New ed. rev. London, Macmillan, 1884. 476p. (Repr.: Detroit, Gale, 1966) **AK171**

1st ed. 1863.

Contains a glossary of Christian names (Preface, p.19–144) which gives the meaning and refers to the body of the book where a full description will be found with derivations, forms in various languages, etc. CS2367.Y6

Nicknames

Sifakis, Carl. The dictionary of historic nicknames; a treasury of more than 7,500 famous and infamous nicknames from world history. N.Y., Facts on File, [1984]. 566p. **AK172**

Nicknames and real names are interfiled in a single alphabet, the nickname providing a *see* reference to the real name (where full information regarding origin of the nickname is given). An index groups the names by occupation or other identifying category.

CT108.S53

Twentieth century American nicknames. Ed. by Laurence Urdang; comp.by Walter C. Kidney and George C. Kohn. N.Y., Wilson, 1979. 398p. **AK173**

Nicknames and the formal names of persons, places, etc., are entered in a single alphabet; variant nicknames are given with the entry. CT108.T83

Surnames

British and American

See also AK166.

Cottle, Basil. The Penguin dictionary of surnames. 2d ed. [London], Allen Lane, [1978]. 444p. **AK174**

1st ed. 1967.

Concerned with surnames of the British Isles and those of British ethnic stock in the Commonwealth and the United States. This edition enlarged from about 8,000 to about 12,000 names.

CS2505.C67

Fransson, Gustave. Middle English surnames of occupation, 1100–1350, with an excursus on toponymical surnames. Lund, Gleerup; London, Williams & Norgate, 1935. 217p. (Lund studies in English, no.3) (Repr.: Nendeln, Liechtenstein, Kraus, 1967) **AK175**

CS2505.F7

Hassall, William Owen. History through surnames. Oxford, N.Y., Pergamon, [1967]. 224p. il. **AK176**

Attempts to show "how each surname is itself a product of, and a monument of, the past, and how surnames not only each have their own histories but themselves reflect and illustrate the past."—*Pref.* Indexed. CS2385.H3

Reaney, Percy Hide. A dictionary of British surnames. 2d ed. with corrections and additions by R. M. Wilson. London, Routledge and K. Paul, 1976. 398p. **AK177**

1st ed. 1958.

Gives etymologies, origins, different forms, and references to sources. Now includes about 10,700 entries. To some extent supersedes Charles W. Bardsley, *Dictionary of English and Welsh surnames* (London, Frowde, 1901. 837p.), although this may still be useful. CS2385.R4

—— The origin of English surnames. London, Routledge & K. Paul; N.Y., Barnes & Noble, [1967]. 415p. (Repr. 1980) **AK178**

Aims "to give a general account of the development of English surnames, their classification, changes in pronunciation and spelling, and the gradual growth of hereditary family names."—*Pref.* Based largely on the author's *Dictionary of British surnames* (above), but with the addition of some new material. CS2505.R4

Smith, Elsdon Coles. New dictionary of American family names. N.Y., Harper & Row, [1972]. 570p. **AK179**

An earlier edition (1956) had title: *Dictionary of American family names.* The new edition is greatly enlarged and, in addition to the most common American surnames, includes many less common but interesting names. Indicates national origin and meaning of the name without attempt to provide etymological origins and bibliographic references.

The same author's *American surnames* (Philadelphia, Chilton, 1969) offers a running account of the origins of the most common American family names, with special attention to social conditions and customs surrounding the adoption of surnames in England and in Europe. CS2481.S55

Woods, Richard Donovon and **Alvarez-Altman, Grace.** Spanish surnames in the Southwestern United States: a dictionary. Boston, G. K. Hall, [1978]. 154p. **AK180**

Gives information on origin and meaning of the more common Spanish surnames found in the Southwest. Sources of information are cited. CS2745.W66

African

See also AK160, AK166.

Madubuike, Ihechukwu. A handbook of African names. Wash., Three Continents Pr., [1976]. 233p. **AK181**

The author acknowledges that "the work in its present form and content is tentative."—*Pref.* Sections are devoted to specific ethnic groups, and a brief discussion of naming conventions and practices for each is followed by a selected list of typical names and their meanings. There is an "Alphabetical list of some African names," p.181–227. CS375.A33M3

Canadian

Dionne, Narcisse Eutrope. Les Canadiens-français. Origine des familles émigrées de France, d'Espagne, de Suisse, etc., pour venir se fixer au Canada, depuis la fondation de Québec jusqu'à ces derniers temps et signification de leurs noms. Québec, Garneau; Montréal, Granger, 1914. 611p. **AK182**

CS2700.D5

French

Chapuy, Paul. Origine des noms patronymiques français (donnant l'étymologie de 10,000 noms de famille) suivi d'une étude sur les noms de famille basques. Paris, Dorbon-Ainé, [1934]. 350p. **AK183**

CS2695.C5

Dauzat, Albert. Dictionnaire étymologique des noms de famille et prénoms de France. Ed., rev. et augm. par Marie-Thérèse Morlet. Paris, Larousse, [1980]. 624p. **AK184**

Reprint of the 1951 ed. with a new supplement, p. 605–[26.] CS2691.D3

Le petit Robert 2. Sous la direction de Paul Robert. [3. éd. rev., corr. et mis à jour] Paris, SNL–Le Robert, 1977. 1992p. il. **AK185**

At head of title: Dictionnaire universel des noms propres alphabétique et analogique.

First published 1974. Frequently reprinted; 1983 called 8th ed.

An abridgment of Robert's *Dictionnaire universel des noms propres* (AJ43), forming a companion volume to the language dictionary commonly known as *Le petit Robert* (AD302). AG25.P45

German

Bach, Adolf. Deutsche Namenkunde. 2. stark erw. Aufl. Heidelberg, Winter, 1952–56. 3v. in 5. (Repr. 1974–81) **AK186**

Contents: Bd.1, Die deutschen Personennamen. 2. stark erw.; Bd.2, Die deutschen Ortsnamen; [Bd.] 3, Registerband, bearb. von D. Berger.

1st ed. of Bd.1 appeared in 1943 as v.18 of Paul's *Grundriss der germanischen Philologie* (BC102).

For Bd.2, Die deutschen Ortsnamen, *see* CL221. PF3576.B33

Bahlow, Hans. Deutsches Namenlexikon: Familien- und Vornamen nach Ursprung und Sinn erklärt. [Neu bearb.] Bayreuth, Gondrom, [1980]. 576p. **AK187**

Includes family names, forenames, and some place-names. 15,000 entries.

Frequently reprinted, showing minor changes in text and updated bibliography. 1984 (Frankfurt, Suhrkamp. 598p.) called 7th ed. CS2541.B3

Brechenmacher, Josef Karlmann. Etymologisches Wörterbuch der deutschen Familiennamen. 2., von Grund auf neubearb. Aufl. der "Deutschen Sippennamen." Limburg/ Lahn, Starke, 1957–63. 2v. (Sippenbücherei, Bd. 5–9) **AK188**

Also issued in 21 parts, 1957–63.

The most comprehensive dictionary of German family names, including more than 28,500 names. CS2545.B73

Gottschald, Max. Deutsche Namenkunde. Unsere Familiennamen nach ihrer Entstehung und Bedeutung. 4. Aufl. Mit e. Nachw. u. e. bibliograph. Nachtr. von Rudolf Schützeichel. (Nachdr. d. 3, verm. Aufl. besorgt von Eduard Brodführer.) Berlin, de Gruyter, 1971. 646p. **AK189**

1st ed. 1932.

Gives origins and meanings of German surnames. CS2545.G6

Irish

MacLysaght, Edward. Surnames of Ireland. 6th ed. [Dublin], Irish Academic Pr., [1985]. 312p. map. **AK190**

1st ed. 1964 had title *Guide to Irish surnames.*

Presents "an epitome of essential facts" *(Pref.)* contained in the *Irish families* series (AK107–AK108). Brief entries give origin, meaning and principal locality of name, often with reference to longer treatment in *Irish families*. There has been little change from edition to edition. CS2411.M25

Italian

Bongioanni, Angelo. Nomi e cognomi; saggio di ricerche etimologiche e storiche. Torino, Bocca, 1928. 268p. (Piccola biblioteca di scienze moderne, no.367) **AK191**

Short entries for names of saints, of religious significance, names from Frankish and Longobard civilizations, from medieval literature, etc.

De Felice, Emidio. Dizionario dei cognomi italiani. Milano, Mondadori, 1978. 351p. (Gli Oscar studio, 59) **AK192**

Lists surnames with variants, totaling more than 14,000 names, and giving derivation, geographic origin, and distribution. Indexed. CS2715.F44

Fucilla, Joseph Guerin. Our Italian surnames. Evanston, Ill., Chandler's, 1949. 299p. **AK193**

Includes bibliographies. CS2715.F8

Jewish

Kaganoff, Benzion C. A dictionary of Jewish names and their history. N.Y., Schocken Books, [1977]. 250p. **AK194**

The "history," p.1–115, is concerned with both first names and family names; the "Dictionary of selected Jewish names," p. 117–211, gives brief information on the origin and meaning of family names. Indexes of names and of subjects. CS3010.K28

Portuguese

Guérios, Rosário Farâni Mansur. Dicionário etimológico de nomes e sobrenomes. 2. ed., rev. e ampl. São Paulo, Editora Ave Maria, 1973. 231p. **AK195**

1st ed. 1949.
An introductory essay on names (p.13–43) precedes the dictionary section. Includes both given names and surnames. CS2761.G8

Russian

Benson, Morton. Dictionary of Russian personal names, with a guide to stress and morphology. [2d ed., rev.] Philadelphia, Univ. of Pennsylvania Pr., [1967]. 175p. (Univ. of Pennsylvania studies in East European languages and literatures) **AK196**

1st ed. 1964.
A chapter on the stress and declension of surnames is followed by a list of surnames with accents; a chapter on Russian given names with lists and explanations of diminutives; and a brief bibliography. Only minor changes and corrections in this edition. CS2811.B4

Unbegaun, Boris Ottokar. Russian surnames. Oxford, Clarendon Pr., 1972. 529p. **AK197**

Aims "to discuss the modern system of Russian surnames in both its morphological and its semantic aspects."—*Pref.* Historical data are included "whenever they throw useful light on the modern system," but the work is not a history of Russian surnames. More than 10,000 surnames are cited. Bibliography; indexes of all quoted surnames and of surname-terminations. PG2576.U5

Scottish

Black, George Fraser. The surnames of Scotland; their origin, meaning, and history. N.Y., New York Pub. Lib., 1962. 838p. (Repr. from the New York Public Library. Bull. Aug. 1943–Sept. 1946) **AK198**

Revision of the 1946 ed., with new amendments and additions, p.831–34, by Mary Elder Black.
A monumental work giving origin, meaning, and history of Scottish surnames from the earliest times, with references to sources.

South African

Rosenthal, Eric. South African surnames. Cape Town, H. Timmins, 1965. 262p. **AK199**

In addition to a list of about 2,500 surnames and their meanings, there is a section dealing at length with some 50 of the most popular names and the people who bore those names. CS3080.S6R6

Spanish

See also AK180.

Gosnell, Charles Francis. Spanish personal names; principles governing their formation and use which may be presented as a help for catalogers and bibliographers. N.Y., Wilson, 1938. 112p. (Inter-American bibliographical and library association. Publ., ser.I, v.3) (Repr.: Detroit, Ethridge-Books, 1971) **AK200**

Originally written as a master's thesis at the School of Library Service, Columbia University.
Bibliography, p.89–101. Z695.G67

B

The Humanities

❖The meaning of the term "the humanities" has changed and developed over the years. In the nineteenth century it meant primarily the Greek and Roman classics, with the inclusion at times of rhetoric, grammar, and belles-lettres. As recently as 1934, the second edition of Webster's *New international dictionary* (AD10) defined it as "the branches of polite learning regarded as primarily conducive to culture; esp., the ancient classics and belles-lettres. . . ." The term now seems to include those branches of learning having a cultural character as distinguished from the social and physical sciences. The interpretation used in this *Guide* is that developed in many subject-arranged libraries and embraces the following: philosophy, religion, linguistics and philology, literature, the fine arts, theater arts, and music.

In most of these categories there are guides to the literature—e.g., De George's *The philosopher's guide to sources . . .* (BA2); Wilson and Slavens' *Research guide to religious studies* (BB3); Arntzen and Rainwater's *Guide to the literature of art history* (BE1); Duckles' *Music reference and research materials* (BH2)—which should be consulted for titles not listed in the present work. In the field of comparative literature, Baldensperger and Friederich's *Bibliography of comparative literature* (BD2) will be useful, as will Thompson's *Key sources in comparative and world literature* (BD20). Under specific literatures are listed such useful guides as Gohdes and Marovitz's *Bibliographical guide to the study of the literature of the U.S.A.* (BD358), Patterson's *Literary research guide* (BD360) and Altick and Wright's *Selective bibliography for the study of English and American literature* (BD489); Hansel's *Bücherkunde für Germanisten* (BD804); Osburn's *Research and reference guide to French studies* (BD954); and Palfrey, Fucilla and Holbrook's *A bibliographical guide to the Romance languages and literatures* (BD929). A. Robert Rogers' *The humanities: a selective guide to information sources* (2d. ed., Littleton, Colo., Libraries Unlimited, 1979. 355p.) is a library school text covering books and other information sources in philosophy, religion, the visual and performing arts, language and literature.

B A

Philosophy

GUIDES

❖Reference works in philosophy are largely bibliographical, with some encyclopedias and dictionaries; therefore, general histories and textbooks are especially needed as supplementary materials. The relatively recent *Encyclopedia of philosophy* (BA75) and the *Dictionary of the history of ideas* (BA70) are important publications in this field, and Baldwin's *Dictionary of philosophy and psychology* (BA66) continues to be a useful reference work. The bibliographical guides by De George (BA2) and Koren (BA3) will be particularly helpful to the graduate student and the beginning research worker.

Rand's *Bibliography of philosophy, psychology, and cognate subjects* (BA26) is now much out-of-date but is still useful for material up to the end of the nineteenth century. The *Journal of philosophy* published an annual bibliography from 1933 to 1936 (BA11), when the record was taken over by the *Bibliographie de la philosophie* (BA31, BA32), published by the Institut International de Philosophie. The *Philosopher's index* (BA35) and its retrospective supplements offer international coverage of books and periodical articles from 1940 to date. Together these give a fairly comprehensive record for the last half-century. Several bibliographies published in various European countries will also be useful in large or more specialized libraries.

Bertman, Martin A. Research guide in philosophy. Morristown, N.J., General Learning Pr., [1974]. 252p.　　**BA1**

A research guide for the undergraduate, with information on research methods, use of the library, selective bibliography, glossary of terms, etc.　　B52.B43

De George, Richard T. The philosopher's guide to sources, research tools, professional life and related fields. Lawrence, Regents Pr. of Kansas, [1980]. 261p.　　**BA2**

Represents a reworking, updating, and expansion of the author's *Guide to philosophical bibliography and research* (1971). Now in three main sections: (1) Philosophy; (2) General research tools; and (3) Related fields (Religion; Humanities; Fine arts; Social sciences; Physical sciences, mathematics, and engineering; Professions). The first section (p.1–166) has major subdivisions for (a) general works, (b) sources for the history of philosophy (further subdivided by period and with sections for individual philosophers), (c) branches, movements and regions of systematic philosophy, and (d) serials, publishing, and professional life. Many entries are annotated. Index of authors, subjects, and most titles.　　Z7125.D445

Koren, Henry J. Research in philosophy; a bibliographical introduction to philosophy and a few suggestions for dissertations. Pittsburgh, Duquesne Univ. Pr., [1966]. 203p.　　**BA3**

A research guide for the beginning graduate student, with special attention to bibliographical aids and reference works in the field.　　Z7125.K65

Matczak, Sebastian A. Philosophy: its nature, methods and basic sources. N.Y., Learned Pubns., 1975. 280p. (Philosophical questions ser., 4)　　**BA4**

Aims "to introduce the student to the basic sources of research in philosophy and to its problems taken as a whole."—*Introd.* Classed arrangement of the sources; indexed.　　Z7125.M285

Tice, Terrence N. and **Slavens, Thomas P.** Research guide to philosophy. Chicago, Amer. Lib. Assoc., 1983. 608p. (Sources of information in the humanities, no.3)　　**BA5**

In three main sections: (1) The history of philosophy (offering bibliographic essays on specific chronological periods, with subsections for individual philosophers); (2) Areas of philosophy (with similar essays on epistemology, logic, metaphysics, philosophy of history, etc.); and (3) Reference works (p.503–15; listing reference works by type, with annotations). Indexed.　　B52.T5

Vasoli, Cesare. Il pensiero medievale. Orientamenti bibliografici. Bari, Laterza, [1971]. 301p.　　**BA6**

A useful bibliographic guide for the student. Cites both selected editions and critical studies of major and many minor writers of the period.　　Z7125.V32

BIBLIOGRAPHY

Bibliography of bibliography

Guerry, Herbert. A bibliography of philosophical bibliographies. Westport, Conn., Greenwood Pr., [1977]. 332p.　　**BA7**

In two parts: (1) Bibliographies of individual philosophers (alphabetical by philosopher); (2) Subject bibliographies (alphabetical by subject). 2,353 items, with selective, brief annotations. In general, includes "only bibliographies that have been published separately or appeared as contributions to journals," but lists "a few significant bibliographies which were published as appendixes to monographs or as parts of larger bibliographies."—*Introd.* Author index.　　Z7125.A1G83

International

Albert, Ethel M., Kluckhohn, Clyde [and others]. A selected bibliography on values, ethics, and esthetics in the behavioral sciences and philosophy, 1920–1958. Glencoe, Ill., Free Pr., 1959. 342p.　　**BA8**

At head of title: Harvard University, Laboratory of Social Relations, Cambridge, Mass. and Center for Advanced Study in the Behavioral Sciences, Stanford, Calif.

A listing of some 2,000 titles of books and periodical articles published during the period covered.　　Z7128.W6A4

Baker, John Arthur. A select bibliography of moral philosophy. Oxford, J. Hannon & Co., 1977. 144p. (Oxford. Univ. Sub-faculty of Philosophy. Study aids, v.9)　　**BA9**

A selective, classed bibliography "of current moral philosophy in the analytical tradition, making no attempt to cover other traditions or historical schools, except where reference to them is useful in order to supplement the modern reading."—*Foreword.* Detailed table of contents, but no index.　　Z5873.B2

Bibliographische Einführungen in das Studium der Philosophie, hrsg. von I. M. Bochenski. Bern, Francke, 1948–53. no.1–23.　　**BA10**

Contents: (1), I. M. Bochenski and F. Monteleone. Allgemeine philosophische Bibliographie. 42p.; (2) Ralph B. Winn. Amerikanische Philosophie. 32p.; (3) E. W. Beth. Symbolische Logik und Grundlegung der exakten Wissenschaften. 28p.; (4) Régis Jolivet. Kierkegaard. 33p.; (5) Olaf Gigon. Antike Philosophie. 52p.; (6) P. J. de Menasce. Arabische Philosophie. 49p.; (7) M. F. Sciacca. Italienische Philosophie der Gegenwart. 36p.; (8) M. D. Phillippe. Aristoteles. 48p.; (9) Régis Jolivet. Französische Existenzphilosophie. 36p.; (10) M. F. Sciacca. Augustinus. 32p.; (11) Karl Dürr. Der logische Positivismus. 24p.; (12) Olaf Gigon. Platon. 30p.; (13/14) Paul Wyser. Thomas von Aquin. 78p.; (15/16) Paul Wyser. Der Thomismus. 120p.; (17) F. van Steenberghen. Philosophie des Mittelalters. 52p.; (18) Othmar Perler. Patristische Philosophie. 44p.; (19) Georges Vajda. Jüdische Philosophie. 40p.; (20/21) C. Régamey. Buddhistische Philosophie. 86p.; (22) Odulf Schäfer. Johannes Duns Scotus. 34p.; (23) Otto Friedrich Bollnow. Deutsche Existenzphilosophie. 40p.

A series of brief bibliographies on various aspects of philosophy; includes 20th-century materials for the most part.

Bibliography of philosophy, 1933–36. N.Y., Journal of Philosophy, 1934–37. v.1–4.　　**BA11**

Reprinted from *Journal of philosophy.*

Annual classified lists with alphabetical name indexes. Intended to include all the scholarly philosophical literature published during the year in English, French, German, and Italian, with some items in other languages.

No more published.　　Z7125.B58

Blackwell, Richard J. A bibliography of the philosophy of science, 1945–1981. Westport, Conn., Greenwood Pr., [1983]. 585p.　　**BA12**

Sections for bibliographies and general works are followed by topically subdivided sections on aspects of scientific method, philosophical issues concerning science, special topics in the philosophy of the physical sciences, and special topics in the philosophy of the biological sciences. Lists books and periodical articles. Index of personal names.　　Z7405.P74B57

Brie, G. A. de, ed. Bibliographia philosophica, 1934–1945. Bruxellis, Ed. Spectrum, 1950–54. 2v.　　**BA13**

Contents: v.1, Bibliographia historiae philosophiae. 664p.; v.2, Bibliographia philosophiae. 798p.

A comprehensive bibliography which aims to list all philosophical literature (books, periodicals, and many book reviews) published from 1934 to 1945, in Danish, Dutch, English, French, German, Italian, Norwegian, Portuguese, Spanish, and Swedish.

v.1 (no.1–23057) is arranged chronologically according to the lives of the philosophers of different historical periods and schools.

v.2 (no.23058–48178) lists publications treating philosophy in its doctrinal aspects, in a classified arrangement. Combined name index to both volumes. Z7125.B7

Buenos Aires. Universidad Nacional. Instituto Bibliotecológi-co. Bibliografía filosófica del siglo XX; catálogo de la Exposición Bibliográfica Internacional de la Filosofía del Siglo XX. Buenos Aires, Ed. Peuser, [1952]. 465p. **BA14**

A classified list of some 4,000 20th-century philosophical writings in various languages, showing location of copies in six Argentinian libraries. No annotations. Z7130.B95

Geldsetzer, Lutz. Bibliography of the International Congresses of Philosophy. Bibliographie der Internationalen Philosophie Kongresse. Proceedings/Beiträge, 1900–1978. München, K. G. Saur, 1981. 207p. **BA15**

Cites the publications of the first 16 meetings of the World Congress of Philosophy, listing individual papers (with pagination), and providing author and subject indexes thereto. Z7125.G4513

Gothie, Daniel L. A selected bibliography of applied ethics in the professions, 1950–1970; a working sourcebook with annotations and indexes. Charlottesville, Univ. Pr. of Virginia, [1973]. 176p. **BA16**

Entries are grouped in categories such as Business and management, Engineering, Government and politics, Health sciences, Law, etc., with some further subdivision. Author and subject indexes. Z5873.G68

Harvard University. Library. Philosophy and psychology. Cambridge, Mass., Harvard Univ. Lib., distr. by Harvard Univ. Pr., 1973. 2v. (Widener Library shelflist, 42–43) **BA17**

For a note on the series see AA145.
Contents: v.1, Classification schedule; Classified listing by call number; Chronological listing; v.2, Author and title listing.
Lists materials in "the *Phil* classification, which contains nearly 59,000 books, periodicals, and pamphlets concerning metaphysics in general, cosmology, ontology, epistemology, logic, aesthetics, and psychology."—*Pref.* Z7130.H3

Hoffmans, Jean. La philosophie et les philosophes: ouvrages généraux. Bruxelles, Van Oest, 1920. 395p. **BA18**

Contents: Dictionaries; treatises and manuals; histories—general, by periods, by countries, by systems, etc.; editions and translations of philosophical works, periodicals, bibliographies.
Lists works on philosophical subjects published in Western languages from about the 17th to the early 20th centuries. Z7125.H69

Jordak, Francis Elliott. A bibliographical survey for a foundation in philosophy. [Wash.], Univ. Pr. of America, [1978]. 435p. **BA19**

An annotated bibliography "designed for small and medium sized libraries . . . , as well as for the people who use these libraries in order to obtain a firm foundation in philosophy."—*Introd.* Classed arrangement; indexed.

McLean, George F. An annotated bibliography of philosophy in Catholic thought, 1900–1964. N.Y., Ungar, [1967]. 371p. **BA20**

For full information see BB419.

———— A bibliography of Christian philosophy and contemporary issues. N.Y., Ungar, [1967]. 312p. **BA21**

For full information see BB223.

Matczak, Sebastian A. Philosophy: a select, classified bibliography of ethics, economics, law, politics, sociology. Louvain, Nauwelaerts, 1970. 308p. (Philosophical questions ser., 3) **BA22**

A select bibliography in the field of philosophy and related disciplines. Classed arrangement with author index. Z5873.M3

The philosopher's index; a retrospective index to U.S. publications from 1940. Bowling Green, Ohio, Philosophy Documentation Ctr., Bowling Green State Univ., [1978]. 3v. **BA23**

Contents: v.1–2, Subject index; v.3, Author index.
An index to "approximately 15,000 articles from U.S. journals published during the 27 year period, 1940–1966, and approximately 6,000 books published during the 37 year period, 1940–1976."—*p.vii.* It thus offers retrospective indexing for journal articles published prior to the beginning of the quarterly *Philosopher's index* (BA35), and complementary coverage for book publications from the longer period. Z7127.P474●

The philosopher's index: a retrospective index to non-U.S. English language publications from 1940. Bowling Green, Ohio, Philosophy Documentation Center, Bowling Green State Univ., [1980]. 3v. **BA24**

A companion to the volumes for United States publications from 1940 (above).
Provides author and subject approaches to "original philosophy books published outside of the United States in English between 1940 and 1978, and articles published in philosophy journals outside of the United States in English between 1940 and 1966."—*Pref.* Includes about 12,000 articles and some 5,000 books. Z7127.P473B72●

Philosophic abstracts. N.Y., Philosophic Abstracts, 1939–54. v.1–16. (Index v.1–12) **BA25**

No more published.
An abstract journal giving abstracts in English of philosophical works published in various countries. B1.P46

Rand, Benjamin. Bibliography of philosophy, psychology, and cognate subjects. N.Y., Macmillan, 1905. 2v. (Repr.: N.Y., Peter Smith, 1949) **BA26**

Forms v.3 of Baldwin's *Dictionary of philosophy* (BA66); also sold separately. An important bibliography of the subject in English, though now out-of-date.
Contents: I, General; II, History of philosophy. Bibliographies of individual philosophers of all periods (arranged alphabetically); III, Systematic philosophy, logic, aesthetics, philosophy of religion, ethics, psychology. B41.B3 v.3

Tobey, Jeremy L. The history of ideas: a bibliographical introduction. Santa Barbara, Calif., Clio Books, [1975–76]. 2v. **BA27**

Contents: v.1, Classical antiquity; v.2, Medieval and early modern Europe.
v.1 offers a series of bibliographic essays on "the important research and reference tools and scholarly works on the history of ideas and its related fields of philosophy, science, aesthetics, and religion in antiquity."—*Postscript.* A similar plan is followed in v.2. Z7125.T58

Totok, Wilhelm. Handbuch der Geschichte der Philosophie. Frankfurt am Main, V. Klostermann, [1964–81]. v.1–4. (In progress) **BA28**

Contents: v.1, Altertum. Indische, chinesische, griechisch-römische Philosophie. Helmut Schröer, ed.; v.2, Die Philosophie des Mittelalters, unter Mitarbeit von Hiltraut Helderich und Helmut Schröer; v.3, Renaissance, unter Mitarbeit von Erwin Schadel [et al.]; v.4, Frühe Neuzeit, 17. Jahrhundert, unter Mitarbeit von Erwin Schadel [et al.].
An extensive bibliographic listing, international in scope. v.1 lists publications for the years 1920–60 in subject arrangement with author index; v.2 includes materials published 1920–66; v.3, 1920–75; v.4, 1920–78. B82.T6

Varet, Gilbert. Manuel de bibliographie philosophique. Paris, Presses Universitaires de France, 1956. 2v. (Logos: introduction aux etudes philosophiques) **BA29**

Contents: v.1, Les philosophies classiques. 494p.; v.2, Les sciences philosophiques. p.496–1058.
A useful manual comprising a comprehensive selection of materi-

als in various languages, listing books and periodical articles. Covers ancient, medieval, and modern philosophy. Annotated.

Z7125.V3

Wainwright, William J. Philosophy of religion: an annotated bibliography of twentieth-century writings in English. N.Y., Garland, 1978. 776p. (Garland reference library of the humanities, v.111) **BA30**

". . . addressed to professional philosophers and graduate students who work in the analytic tradition and who are primarily interested in the solution of philosophical problems rather than in the investigation of the systems of individual philosophers or the history of philosophical movements."—*Introd.* More than 1,100 items grouped in categories such as "The divine attributes," "Arguments for the existence of God," "The problem of evil," "Mysticism and religious experience," etc. Index of authors, editors, and reviewers. Z7821.W34

Current

Bibliographie de la philosophie . . . [année] 1–10. 1937–52/53. Paris, Vrin, 1937–58. 10v. **BA31**

At head of title: Institut International de Philosophie.

Publication suspended, juil. 1939–déc. 1945; resumed with v.4, 1946.

An international bibliography of books, periodical articles, and doctoral dissertations.

Superseded by:

———— Bulletin trimestriel. Bibliography of philosophy, a quarterly bulletin. Paris, Vrin, 1954– . v.1– . Quarterly.
BA32

Published for the International Federation of Philosophical Societies under the auspices of the International Council of Philosophy and Humanistic Studies with the aid of Unesco and of the French National Centre for Scientific Research.

Title page and preliminary matter in French and English.

Now an abstract journal dealing with books only. The abstracts are usually in the language of the original work, but with translations into either English or French. Z7127.B5

Bibliographie Philosophie. Jahrg. 1– . Berlin, Zentralstelle für die Philosophische Information und Dokumentation, Institut für Gesellschaftswissenschaften, 1967– . Quarterly.
BA33

Arrangement has varied; now a classed bibliography with noncumulative author and subject (name and keyword) indexes. Includes citations to monographs, periodical articles, reviews, and theses; a German library location is indicated for each monograph. Runs heavily to publications from Germany and East European Communist nations. Z7127.B62

Bulletin signalétique 519: Philosophie. Paris, Centre de Documentation du C.N.R.S., 1947– . v.1– . Quarterly.
BA34

For fuller information on *Bulletin signalétique, see* AE277 and EA76.

Title varies: v.1–9, *Bulletin analytique: Philosophie;* v.10–14, *Bulletin signalétique: Philosophie. Sciences humaines;* v.15–22, *Sciences humaines: Philosophie;* v.23, *Philosophie, sciences religieuses.*

An exhaustive classified index to periodicals from countries throughout the world. Brief abstracts are given in French. Author and subject indexes cumulate annually. Z7127.F7118●

The philosopher's index; an international index to philosophical periodicals and books. v.1, no.1– , Spring, 1967– . Bowling Green, Ohio, Bowling Green Univ., 1967– . Quarterly, with annual cumulations. **BA35**

Title varies.

Originally an index to "major American and British philosophical periodicals, selected journals in other languages, and related interdisciplinary publications," with separate author and subject listings.

With the volume covering 1969, abstracts (usually written by the authors of the articles indexed) are included as available, and entries in the separate subject and author indexes refer (by means of a special reference code) to the "Bibliographic data and abstracts" section where the full citations are found. A biennial cumulation for 1967–68 was published 1969 and includes some additional indexing for the period. Beginning 1980, books as well as periodicals are included: monographs, translations, bibliographies, biographies, text books, dissertations, dictionaries, and anthologies. With v.18 (1984), non-English language books are indexed and abstracted.

Z7127.P47●

Répertoire bibliographique de la philosophie, t.1– , fév. 1949– . Louvain, Éd. de l'Inst. Supérieur de Philosophie, 1949– . Quarterly. **BA36**

At head of title: Société Philosophique de Louvain.

Publié sous les auspices de l'Institut International de Philosophie avec le patronage de l'UNESCO.

Continues the *Répertoire bibliographique* which appeared quarterly as a supplement to *Revue philosophique de Louvain,* 1934–48.

A comprehensive bibliography of books and articles on philosophy appearing in various countries. Classified lists with annual author indexes. A list of book reviews appears annually in the Nov. issue.

Koren's guide (BA3) includes a useful discussion of the organization of the *Répertoire,* its coverage and use. Z7127.R42

Dissertations

See also BA49.

Bechtle, Thomas C. and **Riley, Mary F.** Dissertations in philosophy accepted at American universities, 1861–1975. N.Y., Garland, 1978. 537p. (Garland reference library of the humanities, v.112) **BA37**

An author listing of more than 7,500 doctoral dissertations accepted at 120 United States and Canadian universities. "As a rule, only those authors have been included whose dissertations are primarily concerned with philosophy and whose degrees have been earned in a department of philosophy."—*Pref.* There were, however, numerous variant situations wherein content of the dissertation (i.e., whether or not it was "essentially concerned with philosophical concepts") determined its inclusion or exclusion. Detailed subject index. Z7125.B38

Flasche, Hans and **Wawrzinek, Utta.** Materialen zur Begriffsgeschichte; eine Bibliographie deutscher Hochschulschriften von 1900–1955. Bonn, Bouvier, 1960. 718p. (Archiv für Begriffsgeschichte, Bd.5) **BA38**

A bibliography of nearly 9,500 academic dissertations in philosophy and religion from universities throughout Germany. Follows an alphabetical arrangement of topical subjects with indexes of authors treated in the theses, and of authors of the theses.

Marti, Hanspeter. Philosophische Dissertationen deutscher Universitäten 1660–1750: eine Auswahlbibliographie. München, K. G. Saur, 1982. 705p. **BA39**

Arranged by name of the *Präses,* then by name of *Respondent* (i.e., author of the dissertation). Indexes of place names, authors, and subjects. Locates copies. Z7126.M37

Periodicals

See also BA56.

Hogrebe, Wolfram, Kamp, Rudolf and **König, Gert.** Periodica philosophica; eine internationale Bibliographie philosophischer Zeitschriften von den Anfängen bis zur Gegenwart. Düsseldorf, Philosophia Verlag, [1972]. 728col. (Kleine philosophische Bibliographien aus dem Philosophischen Inst. der Univ. Düsseldorf, 2) **BA40**

An international listing, by title, of periodicals in the field of philosophy. Gives country and place of publication, publisher, frequency, dates of publication with corresponding volume number for each year, changes of title, and special field of interest.

Z7127.H65

Philosophie. Liste mondiale des périodiques spécialisés. Philosophy. World list of specialized periodicals. 'sGravenhage, Mouton, 1967. 124p. (Maison des Sciences de l'Homme. Service d'Échange d'Informations Scientifiques. Publications. Sér. C. Catalogues et inventaires, 1) **BA41**

"Only periodicals of a scientific nature have been selected, i.e., those publishing original studies and articles by university or other specialists."—*Pref.* Z7127.P52

U.S. Library of Congress. General Reference and Bibliography Division. Philosophical periodicals, an annotated world list by David Baumgardt. Wash., 1952. 89p. **BA42**

Lists periodicals from 71 political areas, with brief annotations. Frequency, date of inception, editor, and publisher (with complete address) are given for each title. Alphabetical index of titles.

Z7127.U5

Belgium

Gerlo, Aloïs and **Vervliet, Hendrik D. L.** Bibliographie de l'humanisme des anciens Pays-Bas, avec un répertoire bibliographique des humanistes et poètes néo-latins. Bruxelles, Presses Universitaires de Bruxelles, 1972. 546p. (Instrumenta humanistica, 3) **BA43**

Based on an earlier bibliography by A. Gerlo and E. Lauf, *Bibliographie de l'humanisme belge* (Bruxelles, 1965), but omitting the lengthy "Bibliographie générale concernant l'humanisme européen" which constituted nearly a third of that work.

A selective, classed bibliography of about 5,700 items. Index of names. The *Bibliographie internationale de l'humanisme et de la Renaissance* (DA158) serves to keep the work up-to-date.

Z7128.H9G42

China

Chan, Wing-tsit. Chinese philosophy, 1949–1963; an annotated bibliography of Mainland China publications. Honolulu, East-West Center Pr., [1967]. 290p. **BA44**

Nearly 1,000 books and periodical articles in classed arrangement with an index of names. Most entries are annotated.

Z7129.C5C48

—————— An outline and an annotated bibliography of Chinese philosophy. [Rev. ed.] New Haven, Conn., Yale Univ., Far Eastern Publs., 1969. 220p. (Sinological ser., no.4) **BA45**

Previous ed. 1961; supplement 1965.
Chronological arrangement by philosophical periods.

Z7129.C5C5

Fu, Charles Wei-Hsün and **Chan, Wing-tsit.** Guide to Chinese philosophy. Boston, G. K. Hall, [1978]. 262p. **BA46**

". . . prepared as part of the Asian Philosophies and Religions Project of the Council for Intercultural Studies and Programs, undertaken by the Foreign Area Materials Center, University of New York/State Education Department."—*Pref.*

Intended primarily for college instructors and students; limited mainly to English-language sources, with some important French and German material included. Topical arrangement; author and title index. Z7129.C5F8

Colombia

Herrera Restrepo, Daniel. La filosofía en Colombia: bibliografía 1627–1973. Cali, Universidad del Valle, División de Humanidades, [1974?]. 247p. **BA47**

In two parts: (1) Parte historica; (2) Parte sistematica. Lists writings of Colombian scholars on all aspects of philosophy and all periods. Z7129.C6H47

France

Miller, Joan M. French structuralism: a multidisciplinary bibliography with a checklist of sources for Louis Althusser, Roland Barthes, Jacques Derrida, Michel Foucault, Lucien Goldmann, Jacques Lacan, and an update of works on Claude Lévi-Strauss. N.Y., Garland, 1981. 553p. (Garland reference library of the humanities, v.160) **BA48**

In three parts: general and introductory works; works by and about individuals named in the subtitle (including reviews); structuralism as applied to various subjects, from aesthetics to social sciences. Period covered is mainly 1968–78 since this work complements J. V. Harari's *Structuralists and structuralism, a selected bibliography of French contemporary thought* (Ithaca, Diacritics, 1971) and François and Claire Lapointe's *Claude Lévi-Strauss and his critics* (CE18). Includes 5,300 citations, some with contents notes. Author and subject indexes. Z7128.S7M54

Germany

Gabel, Gernot U. Bibliographie österreichischer und schweizerischer Dissertationen zur deutschen Philosophie 1885–1975. Köln, Gemini, 1982. 89p. (Bibliographie zur Philosophie, 5) **BA49**

An author listing of 1,082 items with subject index. Serves as a supplement to Flasche and Wawrzinek (BA38) for dissertations on German philosophy.

Gabel is also the compiler of *Canadian theses on German philosophy, 1925–1975: a bibliography* (2d rev. ed., Köln, Edition Gemini, 1984. 47p.; Bibliographien zur Philosophie, 6). Z7129.G3G33

Greece

Voumvlinopoulos, Georges E. Bibliographie critique de la philosophie grecque depuis la chute de Constantinople à nos jours, 1453–1953. [Athènes, Presses de l'Institut Français d'Athènes, 1966] 236p. **BA50**

A bibliography of writings by and about Greek philosophers for the long period indicated. Z7129.G7V6

India

Dr. C. P. Ramaswami Aiyar Research Endowment Committee. A bibliography of Indian philosophy. Madras, 1963–68. Pt.1–2. **BA51**

Intended as a bibliography for research in Sanskrit and philosophical studies. Pt.1 is a bibliography "of source-books in Sanskrit and, where available, of their translations in English, relating to the Upanishads, the Bhagavad Gita, the Nyaya, the Vaiseshika, the Sankhya, the Yoga, the Mimamsa and the Vedanta systems comprising Advaita, Visishtadvaita and Dvaita."—*Pref.* Pt. 2 lists works relating to Navya Nyaya, Jainism, Buddhism, Saiva, Siddhanta, the Vedas, the Dharma Sutras, Sakta Tantra and works on Bhakti.

Z7129.I5D63

Encyclopedia of Indian philosophies: bibliography. Comp. by Karl H. Potter. [Rev. ed.] Princeton, Princeton Univ. Pr., [1983]. 1023p.   **BA52**

A revised and expanded edition of the 1970 *Bibliography of Indian philosophies* (designated as v.1 of the *Encyclopedia of Indian philosophies,* BA74), incorporating the supplementary lists published irregularly in the *Journal of Indian philosophy* and much new material. In four main sections: (1) Sanskrit texts and authors whose dates are known; (2) Sanskrit texts, authors' dates unknown; (3) Sanskrit texts, authors and dates unknown; (4) Secondary literature (subdivided by philosophical school; omits material in non-Western languages). About 13,700 entries. Indexes of names of persons, of titles of texts, and topical index to books and articles.

Z7129.I5E52

Italy

Istituto di Studi Filosofici. Bibliografia filosofica italiana, 1850–1900. Roma, ABETE, [1969]. 644p.   **BA53**

Follows the plan of the Istituto's earlier bibliography (below).

Z7125.I79

———— Bibliografia filosofica italiana dal 1900 al 1950 . . . Roma, Ed. Delfino, 1950–56. 4v.   **BA54**

"A cura dell' Istituto di Studi Filosofici e del Centro Nazionale di Informazioni Bibliografiche, con la collaborazione del Centro di Studi Filosofici Cristiani di Gallarate."—*title page.*

Covers books and periodical articles published in Italy between Jan. 1900 and Dec. 1949; arrangement is alphabetical by author, with writings *on* an author following those *by* him. v.4 includes: Additions and corrections; Anonyms and pseudonyms; and *Bibliografia ragionata delle riviste filosofiche italiane dal 1900 al 1955* a cura di Enrico Zampetti. This last is also published separately; *see* BA56.

Continued by: Z7125.I8

Bibliografia filosofica italiana, anno 1949– . Milano, Carlo Marzorati, 1951– . Annual.   **BA55**

Sponsored by the Centro di Studi Filosofici Cristiani di Gallarate.

Annual bibliography of Italian writings in the field, including periodical articles as well as monographs. Classed arrangement with name index.   Z7125.B55

Zampetti, Enrico. Bibliografia ragionata delle riviste filosofiche italiane dal 1900 al 1955. Roma, Università, 1956. 136p.   **BA56**

Reprinted from v.4 of the *Bibliografia filosofica italiana dal 1900 al 1950* (BA54).

Gives detailed descriptions of Italian philosophical periodicals of the period covered.   Z7129.I8I8

Mexico

Bibliografía filosófica mexicana, 1968– . [México, D.F.], Universidad Nacional Autónoma de México, 1970– . no.1– . Annual.   **BA57**

A classed bibliography with name index.   Z7125.B554

Netherlands

See also BA43.

Poortman, Johannes Jacobus. Repertorium der Nederlandse wijsbegeerte. Amsterdam, Wereldbibliotheek, 1948–68. 3v.   **BA58**

A bibliography of philosophical works printed in Dutch in the Netherlands regardless of the nationality of the author, and of works by Netherlanders wherever printed. In two parts: (a) alphabetical by subject; and (b) alphabetical by philosopher. [v.2] publ. as a supple-

ment (1958) covers material appearing 1947–57; v.3 covers publications of 1958–67.   Z7129.D8P6

Poland

Polska Akademia Nauk. Komitet Filozoficzny. Bibliografia filozofii polskiej. . . . [Opracowała Alicja Kadler] Wyd. 1. Warszawa, Państwowe Wydawnictwo Naukowe, 1955–71. [v.1–3]   **BA59**

Contents: 1750–1830; 1831–1864; 1865–1895.

Editors vary.

Each volume is arranged alphabetically by philosopher, listing writings both by and about.

At head of title, v.2–3: Polska Akademia Nauk. Instytut Filozofii i Socjologii.   Z7125.P6

Spain

Díaz Díaz, Gonzalo and **Santos Escudero, Ceferino.** Bibliografía filosófica hispánica (1901–1970). Madrid, Consejo Superior de Investigaciones Científicas, Instituto de Filosofía "Luis Vives," Departamento de Filosofía Española, 1982. 1371p.   **BA60**

A bibliography of more than 35,700 items in classed arrangement, with author index. Detailed table of contents and many *see also* references, but no subject index. Includes books and periodical articles.   Z7129.S8D5

Martínez Gómez, Luis. Bibliografía filosófica española e hispanoamericana (1940–1958). Barcelona, Juan Flors, 1961. 500p. (Libros "Pensamiento." Serie: Difusión, no.1)   **BA61**

A classified listing of more than 10,000 items—books and articles—primarily a cumulation of the bibliographic sections of the Spanish philosophical journal *Pensamiento.* Name index.

Z7129.S8M3

Switzerland

See also BA49.

Schweizerische Philosophische Gesellschaft. Bibliographie der philosophischen, psychologischen und pädagogischen Literatur in der deutschsprachigen Schweiz, 1900–1940, hrsg. von E. Heuss, [u.A.]. Basel, Verlag für Recht und Gesellschaft, 1944. 207p. (*Its* Jahrbuch . . . Beiheft II)   **BA62**

———— [Supplement], 1941–1944, von Hans Zantop, 1945. p.218–78. (*Its* Jahrbuch, v.5, Separatum)

Lists alphabetically, by author, books and periodical articles on philosophy, psychology, and education published in German-speaking Switzerland. The main part of the work includes German works only; the supplement covers German, French, and Italian.

Union of Soviet Socialist Republics

Bibliographie der sowjetischen Philosophie. Freiburg/Schweiz, Ost-Europa Inst., [1959–68]. v.1–7. (Sovietica; Veröffentlichungen des Ost-Europa Instituts, Universität Freiburg/Schweiz, 1–2, 6, etc.)   **BA63**

Vorwort signed I. M. Bochenski.

Contents: v.1, Die "Voprosy Filosofii," 1947–56; v.2, Bücher, 1947–56. Bücher und Aufsätze, 1957–58; v.3, Bücher und Aufsätze, 1959–60; v.4, Ergänzungen, 1947–60; v.5, Register, 1947–60; v.6, Bücher und Aufsätze, 1961–63; v.7, Bücher und Aufsätze, 1964–66.

Lists major books and articles in philosophy published in the Soviet Union from 1947. Author and subject indexes.

Z7129.R9B5

DICTIONARIES AND ENCYCLOPEDIAS

Angeles, Peter A. Dictionary of philosophy. N.Y., Barnes & Noble, [1981]. 326p. **BA64**

A quick-reference source for students, laypersons, and teachers. Offers "informal and understandable definitions for important philosophic terms," especially those "most commonly covered in beginning philosophy courses."—*Pref.* B41.A53

Austeda, Franz. Lexikon der Philosophie. [5., völlig neu bearb. Aufl.] Wien, Hollinek, [1979]. 340p. **BA65**

1st ed. 1954; previous editions entitled *Wörterbuch der Philosophie.*

In two parts: (1) Philosophen (Daten, Standpunkte, Leistungen, Werke); (2) Philosophien (Disziplinen, Probleme, Richtungen, Begriffe). The biographical section includes philosophers from earliest times to the present. B43.A86

Baldwin, James Mark. Dictionary of philosophy and psychology, including many of the principal conceptions of ethics, logic, aesthetics, philosophy of religion, mental pathology, anthropology, biology, neurology, physiology, economics, political and social philosophy, philology, physical science and education, and giving a terminology in English, French, German and Italian. N.Y., Macmillan, 1901–05. 3v. in 4. il. (Repr.: Gloucester, Mass., Peter Smith, 1960)
BA66

Contents: v.1–2, A–Z. Indexes: (1) Greek terms, (2) Latin terms, (3) German terms, (4) French terms, (5) Italian terms; v.3, Bibliography of philosophy (*see* Rand, BA26).

The first encyclopedia of the subject in English, excellent and authoritative when issued and still useful for many topics though now out-of-date for modern developments. Concise rather than exhaustive in treatment, with signed articles by specialists and many bibliographies. Covers the whole field but is fuller for modern than for earlier aspects of the subject and does not attempt to cover the whole of Greek and scholastic philosophy. Includes very brief biographies of men no longer living. Special features are the inclusion of French, German, and Italian equivalents of English terms used as entries, and the indexes of foreign terms used in the articles.

A new edition, 1910, differed from the original only in the correction of a few typographical errors. B41.B3

Blanc, Elie. Dictionnaire de philosophie ancienne, moderne et contemporaine. Paris, Lethielleux, 1906. 1248 col. (Repr. with suppls.: N.Y., B. Franklin, 1972) **BA67**

—— —— Supplément . . . années 1906, 1907, 1908. Paris, 1908. 154 col.

Offers explanations of philosophical terms and schools, and brief biographical sketches of philosophers of all periods. B42.B55

Brugger, Walter, ed. Philosophisches Wörterbuch. . . . 14. neu bearb. Aufl. Freiburg, etc., Herder, 1976. 592p.
BA68

1st ed. 1945; various reprintings.

Explanations of philosophical terms, with bibliographies. Includes an outline of the history of philosophy from ancient times to the present day, citing works and developments. B43.B69

—— and **Baker, Kenneth.** Philosophical dictionary. Spokane, Gonzaga Univ. Pr., [1972]. 460p. **BA69**

A translation and adaptation of Brugger's *Philosophisches Wörterbuch* (13th ed. Freiburg, 1967). Bibliographies have been omitted, as have some articles "that are of particular concern to Germans" (*Pref.*); the latter have been replaced by "new articles dealing with contemporary Anglo-American concerns." B43.B713

Dictionary of the history of ideas: studies of selected pivotal ideas. Philip P. Wiener, ed. in chief. N.Y., Scribner's, [1973–74]. 4v. and index. **BA70**

Articles of substantial length, covering a wide range of topics in intellectual history have been contributed by an international roster of scholars. There is an emphasis on interdisciplinary, cross-cultural relations, with a view to helping to "establish some sense of unity of human thought and its cultural manifestation in a world of ever-increasing specialization and alienation."—*Pref.*

As set forth in the "Analytical table of contents," the areas forming the basic framework for the selected topics are: (1) the history of ideas about the external order of nature studied by the physical and biological sciences, ideas also present in common usage, imaginative literature, myths about nature, metaphysical speculation; (2) the history of ideas about human nature in anthropology, psychology, religion, and philosophy as well as in literature and common sense; (3) the history of ideas in literature and the arts in aesthetic theory and literary criticism; (4) the history of ideas about or attitudes to history, historiography, and historical criticism; (5) the historical development of economic, legal, and political ideas and institutions, ideologies, and movements; (6) the history of religious and philosophical ideas; and (7) the history of formal mathematical, logical, linguistic, and methodological ideas.

Articles appear in alphabetical sequence; bibliographies are included; and a series of "see also" references at the end of each article serves to link related topics. A separate index volume (published after the appearance of the main set) greatly facilitates use of the work. CB5.D52

Eisler, Rudolf. Handwörterbuch der Philosophie. 2. Aufl. neuhrsg. von Richard Müller-Freienfels. Berlin, Mittler, [1922]. 785p. (Repr.: Düsseldorf, Mikrobuch- und Film Gesellschaft, 1949) **BA71**

1st ed. 1913.

A condensation of the author's *Wörterbuch der philosophischen Begriffe* (below), utilizing also some material from his *Philosophen-Lexikon* (1912). An excellent small work—useful where short, concise articles are wanted, but not a substitute in a research library for the two larger works. Includes bibliographies. B43.E32

—— Wörterbuch der philosophischen Begriffe, historischquellenmässig. 4. völlig neubearb. Aufl. hrsg. unter Mitwirkung der Kantgesellschaft. Berlin, Mittler, 1927–30. 3v. **BA72**

1st ed. 1889. 1v.; 2d ed. 1904. 2v.; 3d ed. 1910. 3v.

Scholarly articles with bibliographies, on philosophical concepts and terms, tracing their use, meanings, and treatment through the writings of the philosophers, and giving many references to sources. For the specialist rather than the general reader. Of first importance in advanced work.

Literatur–Verzeichnis, v.3, p.695–906.

For the first parts of a new edition *see* BA85. B43.E4

Enciclopedia filosofica. 2. ed. interamente rielaborata. [Firenze], Sansoni, [1968–69]. 6v. il. **BA73**

At head of title: Centro di Studi Filosofici di Gallarate.
1st ed. 1957 in 4v.

A scholarly encyclopedia with signed articles and bibliographies. Treats philosophical concepts and schools and relevant matters in literature, science, law, etc. Includes many biographical articles. The 2d ed. is a complete revision: bibliographies have been updated, numerous new entries appear, and many entries have been revised or expanded. v.6 includes three main indexes: (1) classified by theoretical concept; (2) classified by historical development; and (3) an analytical index of terms and personal names referred to in the text but not used as entries. B44.E52

The encyclopedia of Indian philosophies [by] Sibajiban Bhattacharya [and others]. Delhi, Publ. for Amer. Inst. of Indian Studies by Motilal Banarsidass, 1970–81. v.1–3. (In progress) **BA74**

Publisher varies.

Contents: v.1, Bibliography of Indian philosophies, comp. by Karl H. Potter (*see* BA52); [v.2] Indian metaphysics and epistemology: the tradition of Nyaya-Vaisesika up to Gangesa, ed. by Karl H.

Potter; v.3, Advaita Vedānta up to Samkara and his pupils, ed. by Karl H. Potter.

The encyclopedia draws on an international team of scholars in an "attempt to provide a definitive account of current knowledge about each of the systems of classical Indian philosophy."—*Pref., v.1.*

B131.E5

Encyclopedia of philosophy. Paul Edwards, ed. in chief. N.Y., Macmillan, [1967]. 8v.   **BA75**

An important work, broader in scope than Baldwin's *Dictionary of philosophy and psychology* (BA66) and with articles of generally more substantial length. Designed "to cover the whole of philosophy as well as many of the points of contact between philosophy and other disciplines. The *Encyclopedia* treats Eastern and Western philosophy; it deals with ancient, medieval, and modern philosophy; and it discusses the theories of mathematicians, physicists, biologists, sociologists, psychologists, moral reformers, and religious thinkers where these have had an impact on philosophy."—*Introd.* Nearly 1,500 signed articles—about 900 of them on individual philosophers—were contributed by an international group of some 500 scholars. The final volume includes an index.   B41.E5

Enzyklopädie Philosophie und Wissenschaftstheorie. Unter ständiger Mitwirkung von Siegfried Blasche [et al.] in Verbindung mit Gereon Wolters hrsg. von Jürgen Mittelstrass. Mannheim, Bibliographisches Institut, 1980– . Bd.1– . il. (In progress; to be in 3v.)   **BA76**

Contents: Bd.1, A–G.

Offers signed articles, with bibliographies, on terms and persons important to the fields of philosophy, scientific knowledge, and the history and philosophy of science. Equivalent terms in English, Greek, Latin, etc., are frequently given with the entry word.

B43.E59

Ferrater Mora, José. Diccionario de filosofía. 6. ed. Madrid, Alianza, 1979. 4v.   **BA77**

1st ed. 1941. Reprintings of the 6th ed. also carry ed. numbers in an "Alianza diccionarios" series.

A useful general encyclopedia with many biographical sketches (including living persons), and articles on philosophical schools, concepts, etc. Not limited by country or period. Extensive bibliographies.

A "Cuadro synoptico" and a "Cuadro cronológico" in v.4 list topical entries by subject categories and biographical entries chronologically.   B45.F4

Foulquié, Paul. Dictionnaire de la langue philosophique. 4ᵉ éd. Paris, Presses Universitaires de France, 1982. 778p.   **BA78**

1st ed. 1962. The 1969 ed. is designated as a 4th ed. in its 1982 reprinting.

Lists words in groups under main root word, with cross references from derivative forms. Each entry gives etymology and definitions, indicating various areas of usage; synonyms; and illustrative quotations from the literature, with brief references to sources. (Unfortunately, no full bibliography of these sources is included, and the quotations are not dated.)   B42.F6

Hoffmeister, Johannes. Wörterbuch der philosophischen Begriffe. 2. Aufl. Hamburg, Felix Meiner, 1955. 687p. (Die philosophische Bibliothek, Bd.225)   **BA79**

1st ed. 1944.

Based on the work originally edited by Friedrich Kirchner and Carl Michaelis (6th ed. 1911).

Concise articles on philosophical terms and concepts with some bibliography. Does not include biography.   B43.H6

Lacey, Alan Robert. A dictionary of philosophy. London, Routledge & Kegan Paul, [1976]. 239p.   **BA80**

A work for "the layman or intending student" which aims "to take some of the commonest terms and notions in current English-speaking philosophy and to give the reader some idea of what they mean to the philosopher and what sort of problems he finds associated with them."—*Pref.* Cross references; some bibliographies.   B41.L32

Lalande, André. Vocabulaire technique et critique de la philosophie. 13ᵉ éd. Paris, Presses Universitaires, 1980. 1323p.   **BA81**

1st ed. 1926.

A standard work which first appeared in parts in the *Bulletin* of the Société Française de Philosophie, 1902–23. In addition to definitions of terms, examples of use by philosophers, and bibliographic notes, etymologies are usually given, as are equivalents in German, English, and Italian.   B42.L3

Peters, Francis Edwards. Greek philosophical terms; a historical lexicon. N.Y., New York Univ. Pr.; London, Univ. of London Pr., 1967. 234p.   **BA82**

Intended for the "intermediate student" of Greek philosophy rather than for the beginner or the advanced scholar. Cross references are liberally used throughout, as are textual citations to the philosophers. English-Greek index.   B49.P4

La philosophie. Les idées, les oeuvres, les hommes. [Paris, Centre d'Étude et de Promotion de la Lecture, 1969] 544p.   **BA83**

A dictionary of contemporary philosophy. Includes nine long, signed articles on key topics (such as Marxism, existentialism, psychoanalysis, epistemology, structuralism) and briefer treatment of 400 terms and philosophers. Index of English terms with their French equivalents.   B42.P48

Reese, William L. Dictionary of philosophy and religion: Eastern and Western thought. [Atlantic Highlands], N.J., Humanities Pr.; [Hassocks], Sussex, Harvester Pr., [1980]. 644p.   **BA84**

Although primarily a dictionary of terms, the work includes numerous articles on the thought and work of major philosophers and religious leaders.   B41.R43

Ritter, Joachim, ed. Historisches Wörterbuch der Philosophie. Völlig neubearb. Ausg. Basel, Schwabe; Darmstadt, Wissenschaftliche Buchgesellschaft, [1971–81]. Bd.1–5. (In progress)   **BA85**

Contents: v.1–5, A–Mn.

A complete revision of Rudolf Eisler's *Wörterbuch der philosophischen Begriffe* (BA72). Some entries in the older work—those dealing with psychology, for example—have been dropped, some have been expanded, and much new material has been added. A scholarly and up-to-date compilation with contributions by more than 700 scholars.   B43.R58

Rozental', Mark Moiseevich and **IUdin, Pavel Fedorovich.** A dictionary of philosophy. Tr. from the Russian; ed. by Richard R. Dixon and Murad Saifulin. Moscow, Progress Publishers, 1967. 494p.   **BA86**

An English translation of *Filosofskii slovar'* (Moscow, 1963).

B48.R9R713

Urmson, James Opie, ed. The concise encyclopedia of Western philosophy and philosophers. [2d ed. rev. in new format] London, Hutchinson, [1975]. 319p.   **BA87**

1st ed. 1960.

A work for the non-specialist, with signed articles of a "minimum length compatible with accuracy and intelligibility."—*Introd.* Principles of selection included "a fairly narrow interpretation of what constitutes philosophy"; emphasis on the needs of the non-specialist, with a minimum of attention to "very technical problems and the philosophers who specialized in them"; and English-language orientation (i.e., "philosophers whose works are not available in translation into English have been omitted or given treatment shorter perhaps than their merits").   B41.U7

World philosophy: essay-reviews of 225 major works. Ed. by Frank N. Magill; assoc. ed., Ian P. McGreal. Englewood Cliffs, N.J., Salem Pr., [1982]. 5v.   **BA88**

". . . an enlargement and elaboration of the two-volume *Masterpieces of World Philosophy in Summary Form,* first published in 1961."—*Pref.*

The 225 major works are presented in chronological arrangement, from sixth century B.C. to the middle of the present century. A signed review essay on each major work is followed by a section of "pertinent literature" which offers notes on at least two critical studies of the work in question; a selected list of additional readings, briefly annotated, is also given for each major work. Indexes of major authors, of authors of the "pertinent literature," and of authors of the additional recommended readings in v.5; glossary of philosophical terms in v.1.　　　　　　　B29.W68

Wuellner, Bernard. A dictionary of scholastic philosophy. 2d ed. Milwaukee, Bruce, [1966]. 339p.　　　**BA89**

1st ed. 1956.

A dictionary giving explanations and definitions of terms, with some references to sources. Includes charts and diagrams.

B50.S35W8

HISTORY

Bréhier, Émile. Histoire de la philosophie . . . 9ᵉ éd. rev. et bibliographie mise à jour par Pierre-Maxime Schuhl. Paris, Presses Universitaires de France, 1967– .　　**BA90**

Originally published 1926–32 (2v. in 7) with the following contents: t.1, L'antiquité et le moyen âge: I. Période hellénique. II. Période hellénistique et romaine. III. Moyen âge et renaissance; t.2, La philosophie moderne: I. Le dix-septième siècle. II. Le dix-huitième siècle. III. Le XIXᵉ siècle—Période des systèmes (1800–1850); IV. Le XIXᵉ siècle après 1850. Le XXᵉ siècle; Fascicule supplémentaire (Paris, Alcan, 1938–49. 2v.).

The 9th ed. remains incomplete. An "Éd. revue et mise à jour" by P.-M. Schuhl and Maurice de Candillac, *et al.* was publ. in 3v. with the following contents: v.1, Antiquité et Moyen-âge (11th ed., 1983. 712p.); v.2, 17ᵉ–18ᵉ siècles (8th ed., 1981. 520p.); v.3, 19ᵉ–20ᵉ siècles (6th ed., 1981. 568p.).

A standard history with selective bibliographies.

An English translation has appeared as:　　　B77.B7212

―――― The history of philosophy. Tr. by Joseph Thomas. Chicago, Univ. of Chicago Pr., [1963–69]. 7v.　　**BA91**

Handbook of world philosophy: contemporary developments since 1945. Ed. by John R. Burr. Westport, Conn., Greenwood Pr., [1980]. 641p.　　　**BA92**

". . . the comprehensive object of this book is to provide an internationally representative sample since 1945 of the characters, directions, wealth, and varieties of the reflections and activities called 'philosophic' as described, interpreted, and evaluated by philosophers particularly knowledgeable about the region or country being discussed; to exhibit the increasingly international development of philosophy; and to point to future possibilities."—*Introd.* Twenty-eight essays by contributing scholars treat developments in an individual country, pair of countries, or broad geographic area. Essays are grouped in six sections (Western Europe, Australia, and Israel; Eastern Europe; The Americas; Africa and the Republic of South Africa; Islamic countries; Asia); each ends with a select bibliography of books and articles, and a list of journals. Appendixes: (1) Directory of philosophical associations; (2) Congresses and meetings. Indexed.　　　　　B804.A1H36

Ueberweg, Friedrich. Grundriss der Geschichte der Philosophie. 11.–12. Aufl. hrsg. von Karl Praechter. Berlin, Mittler, 1923–28. 5v. (Repr.: Basel, B. Schwabe, 1957)　　**BA93**

Each volume also has special title page.

1st ed. 1862–66 in 3v.

Contents: v.1, Die Philosophie des Altertums. 12. Aufl., hrsg. von Karl Praechter; v.2, Die patristische und scholastische Philosophie. 11. Aufl., hrsg. von Bernhard Geyer; v.3, Die Philosophie der Neuzeit bis zum Ende des 18. Jahrhunderts. 12. Aufl., hrsg. von Max Frischeisen-Köhler und Willy Moog; v.4, Die deutsche Philosophie des neunzehnten Jahrhunderts und der Gegenwart. 12. Aufl., hrsg. von Traugott K. Oesterreich; v.5, Die Philosophie des Auslands vom Beginn des 19. Jahrhunderts bis auf die Gegenwart. 12. Aufl., hrsg. von Traugott K. Oesterreich.

An important reference history, particularly useful for its full bibliographies (up to about 1920) and its biographical information. Covers ancient; patristic and scholastic; and modern philosophy.

The English translation, *History of philosophy* (N.Y., Scribner's, 1892. 2v.) is from the 4th German edition and does not include the bibliographic apparatus.

A new edition has begun to appear as:　　　B82.U19

Grundriss der Geschichte der Philosophie. Begründet von Friedrich Ueberweg. Völlig neubearbeite Ausgabe. Basel, Schwabe, 1983– . (In progress)　　　**BA94**

Contents: Die Philosophie der Antike. Bd.3, Ältere Akademie, Aristoteles, Peripatos, hrsg. von Hellmut Flashar (Die ältere Akademie, von H. J. Krämer; Aristoteles, von H. Flashar; Der Peripatos, von F. Wehrli).

BIOGRAPHY

Philosophen-Lexikon; Handwörterbuch der Philosophie nach Personen, verf. und hrsg. von Werner Ziegenfuss und Gertrud Jung. Berlin, W. de Gruyter, 1949–50. 2v.

BA95

A biographical dictionary of philosophers of all periods and all countries, but with the emphasis on philosophy since Hegel. Planned to take the place of the earlier *Philosophen-Lexikon* by Rudolf Eisler (Berlin, Mittler, 1912. 889p.) and on the same general plan as that work, but with longer articles, inclusion of additional names, and considerable additional material on names included by Eisler. Nearly all articles, even the short ones, have bibliographies.

The first six parts, A–Juvalta, were published in 1937, but further publication was prohibited on political grounds. The present text of both volumes remains almost unaltered except for the addition of some later death dates and of bibliographical data—to 1945 for German publications, to 1939 for other countries.　　B43.P5

Riedl, John Orth. Catalogue of Renaissance philosophers (1300–1650), comp. by Robert A. Baker [and others] under the direction of John O. Riedl. Milwaukee, Marquette Univ. Pr., 1940. 179p.　　　　　　　**BA96**

Arranged by schools with alphabetical author index. Gives biographical notes and bibliographies of writings.　　Z7125.R54

DIRECTORIES

Directory of American philosophers. Ed.1– , 1962/63– . Bowling Green, Ohio, Philosophy Documentation Center, Bowling Green Univ., 1962– . Biennial.　　　**BA97**

Publisher varies.

United States and Canadian universities appear in separate sections. Listing is alphabetical by state or province, then by institution, with a listing of philosophy faculty members at each institution. Also includes sections for societies, institutes, publishers, and journals in the field. Indexes of philosophers, institutions, publishers, etc.　　　　　　　　　B935.D5

International directory of philosophy and philosophers. Ed. 1– , 1966– . Bowling Green, Ohio, Philosophy Documentation Center, Bowling Green Univ., 1966– . Irregular.

BA98

Publisher varies.

1st ed. published under the auspices of the International Institute of Philosophy with the aid of Unesco; it had an added title page in French, introductory matter in English and French, and text in English or French. Beginning with 2d ed. (1972/73) issued as a companion volume to *Directory of American philosophers* (above).

Pt.1 is a list of international philosophical organizations; pt.2, arranged by country or territory, lists colleges and universities (with names of members of the philosophy staffs), institutes and research centers, philosophical associations and societies, philosophy journals, and publishers who specialize to some degree in philosophical works. Indexed. B35.I55

INDIVIDUAL PHILOSOPHERS

❖This selective listing of bibliographies, concordances, dictionaries, etc., for individual philosophers indicates the range of reference works which can be located with relative ease through library catalogs, the *Bibliographic index,* etc. Among the many similar works which might be mentioned are: *Concordance of Boethius,* by Lane Cooper (Cambridge, Mass., Mediaeval Academy of America, 1928. 467p.); *John Dewey; a centennial bibliography,* by Milton Halsey Thomas (Chicago, Univ. of Chicago Pr., 1962. 370p.); *Martin Heidegger: bibliography and glossary,* by Hans-Martin Sass (Bowling Green, Ohio, Philosophy Documentation Center, 1982. 513p.); *Søren Kierkegaard; international bibliografi,* by Jens Himmelstrup (København, Nyt Nordisk Forlag, 1962. 216p.); *Søren Kierkegaard-litteratur, 1961–1970,* by Aage Jørgensen (Aarhus, Akademisk Boghandel, 1971. 99p.); *80 years of Locke scholarship; a bibliographical guide,* by Roland Hall and Roger Woolhouse (Edinburgh, University Pr., 1983. 215p.); and *Pierre Teilhard de Chardin: a comprehensive bibliography,* by Joseph M. McCarthy (N.Y., Garland Pr., 1981. 438p.)

For the early philosophers, *see also* the bibliographies of classical literature, p.514–20.

Aristotle

See also BA10.

Aristoteles. Aristotle dictionary, ed. by Thomas P. Kiernan. N.Y., Philosophical Lib., 1962. 524p. **BA99**

Introduction by Theodore E. James, p. 7–163.
"References are made to the appropriate *loci* of the quotations . . . in the Bekker edition of the Greek published in 1831."—*p.162.*
Arranged by subject word in English, with exact references to sources. PA3926.Z8K53

Barnes, Jonathan, Schofield, Malcolm and **Sorabji, Richard.** Aristotle: a selective bibliography. [Oxford, Sub-faculty of Philosophy, Univ. of Oxford, 1977] 88 [i.e. 111] p. (Study aids, v.7) **BA100**

A select bibliography for the student. Z8044.B37

Bonitz, Hermann. Index Aristotelicus. Berlin, Reimer, 1870. 878p. (Repr.: Graz, Akademische Druck- und Verlagsanstalt, 1955) **BA101**

Forms part of v.5 of the Bekker edition of Aristotle (Berlin, 1831–70). PA3926.Z8B6

Organ, Troy Wilson. An index to Aristotle in English translation. Princeton, N.J., Princeton Univ. Pr., 1949. 181p. (Repr.: N.Y., Gordian Pr., 1966) **BA102**

Based on the translation by W. D. Ross and J. A. Smith. (Oxford, Univ. Pr., 1908–31. 11v.). Does not include the *Fragments* or the *Constitution of Athens.* B401.O7

Augustine

See also BA10.

Andresen, Carl. Bibliographia Augustiniana. [2., völlig neubearb. Aufl.] Darmstadt, Wissenschaftliche Buchgesellschaft, 1973. 317p. **BA103**

Preface in German and Latin. Includes material by and about St. Augustine. Classified arrangement; indexed. Z8047.7.A53

Bavel, Tarsicius J. van. Répertoire bibliographique de Saint Augustin, 1950–1960. Steenbrugis, In Abbatia Sancti Petri, 1963. 991p. (Instrumenta patristica, 3) **BA104**

About 5,500 entries, with annotations. Z8047.7.B35

Institut des Études Augustiniennes. Fichier augustinien. Boston, G. K. Hall, 1972. [2 pts. in] 4v. **BA105**

Added title page in English; preface in French and English.
Contents: [pt.I] v.1–2, Fichier-auteurs; [pt.II] v.1–2, Fichiermatières.
Aims to list both primary works and "all published studies on Augustine and related subjects."—*Pref.* In the author section writings by Augustine are followed by an alphabetically arranged author list of works about him. Studies include books, parts of books, and articles. In the subject section the secondary works are rearranged in a topical scheme; here the table of contents showing the detailed breakdown must serve as an index. Covers through 1970.

———— ———— Supplement 1. Boston, G. K. Hall, 1981. 516p.

Extends the coverage through 1978, adding some older works, corrections and improvements.
Terry L. Miethe's *Augustinian bibliography, 1970–1980; with essays on the fundamentals of Augustinian scholarship* (Westport, Conn., Greenwood Pr., 1982. 218p.) lists earlier bibliographies, works on the life of Augustine, and (in classed arrangement) Augustinian studies. Z8047.7.I57

Croce

Cione, Edmondo. Bibliografia crociana. [Roma], Bocca, [1956]. 481p. (Biblioteca di scienze moderne. 155) **BA106**

Lists works by and about Croce.

Descartes

Sebba, Gregor. Bibliographia Cartesiana: a critical guide to the Descartes literature, 1800–1960. The Hague, Nijhoff, 1964. 510p. (Archives internationales d'histoire des idées. International archives of the history of ideas, 5) **BA107**

Contents: pt.1, Introduction to Descartes studies; pt.2, Alphabetical bibliography, 1800–1960; pt.3, Indices: systematic and analytical.

Lists books and periodical articles in many languages. Supersedes the author's *Descartes and his philosophy: a bibliographical guide . . . 1800–1958* (Athens, Ga., 1959. v.1; no more published). Z8227.7.S38

Duns Scotus

See also BA10.

Schäfer, Odulf. Bibliographia de vita, operibus et doctrina Iohannis Duns Scoti, doctoris subtilis ac Mariani, saec. XIX–XX. Romae, Orbis Catholicus-Herder, 1955. 223p. **BA108**

An alphabetical listing of 4,506 numbered entries—including books and periodical articles—about Duns Scotus. Name and analytical indexes. Z8248.4.S3

Epictetus

Oldfather, William Abbott. Contributions toward a bibliography of Epictetus; appendix: Jacob Schenk's Translation of the Encheiridion, Basel 1534, facsimile reproduction from the copy in the British Museum. [Urbana], Univ. of Illinois, 1927. 201p.   **BA109**

———— ———— A supplement, ed. by Marian Harman, with a preliminary list of Epictetus manuscripts by W. H. Friedrich and C. U. Faye. Urbana, Univ. of Illinois, 1952. 177p.

The main work lists more than 1,175 entries of works and translations. Locates copies. The supplement follows the arrangement of the earlier volume, and adds information found in the examination of volumes in European libraries and elsewhere.
Z8267.O44

Erasmus

Haeghen, Ferdinand van der. Bibliotheca Érasmiana: répertoire des oeuvres d'Érasme. Nieuwkoop, B. de Graaf, 1961. 3 pts. in lv. (Repr. of the Gand, 1893 ed.)   **BA110**

Contents: 1.sér., Liste sommaire et provisoire des diverses éditions de ses oeuvres; 2.sér., Auteurs publiés, traduits ou annotés par Érasme. Liste sommaire et provisoire; 3. sér., Sources. Biographies d'Érasme et écrits le concernant; ouvrages qui contiennent des notes d'Érasme, des extraits de ses oeuvres, etc.   Z8268.H16

Margolin, Jean Claude. Quatorze années de bibliographie érasmienne, 1936–1949. Paris, Vrin, 1969. 431p. (De Pétrarque à Descartes, 21)   **BA111**

Nearly 1,200 entries, with annotations. Chronological arrangement, with author index.   Z8268.M33

———— Douze années de bibliographie érasmienne, 1950–1961. Paris, Vrin, 1963. 204p. (De Pétrarque à Descartes, 6)   **BA112**

About 500 items in chronological arrangement, with author index. Annotated. Continued by: Z8268.M3

———— Neuf années de bibliographie érasmienne (1962–1970). Paris, Vrin; Toronto, Univ. of Toronto Pr., 1977. 850p. (De Pétrarque à Descartes, 33)   **BA113**

Z8268.M32

Hegel

Gabel, Gernot U. Hegel: eine Bibliographie der Dissertationen aus sieben westeuropäischen Ländern, 1885–1975. Hamburg, Gemini, 1980. 50p. (Bibliographien zur Philosophie, 2)   **BA114**

An author listing of dissertations from Belgium, Germany, France, Great Britain, Netherlands, Austria and Switzerland; period of coverage varies for the individual countries. Subject index.
Z8394.6.G3

Steinhauer, Kurt. Hegel bibliography; background material on the international reception of Hegel within the context of the history of philosophy. München, K. G. Saur, 1980. 894p.   **BA115**

Title also in German. Introductory and explanatory matter in English and German.

A bibliography of Hegel's own works is followed by a chronological listing of secondary works from the period 1802–1975. Keyword index.

A *Hegel-Lexikon* by Hermann Glockner (2. verb. Aufl. Stuttgart, F. Frommann, 1957. 2v.) was published as part of Glockner's edition of Hegel's *Sämtliche Werke*.   Z8394.6.S83

Hume

Hall, Roland. Fifty years of Hume scholarship: a bibliographical guide. Edinburgh, Univ. Pr., [1978]. 150p.   **BA116**

Supersedes an earlier Hume bibliography by Hall (1971).

Lists Hume literature from 1925 to 1976, together with a list of the principal writings on Hume for the 1900–1924 period. Chronological arrangement with author, language, and subject indexes.
Z8427.3.H34

Jessop, Thomas Edmund. A bibliography of David Hume and of Scottish philosophy from Francis Hutcheson to Lord Balfour. London, A. Brown, 1938. 201p. (Repr.: N.Y., Russell and Russell, 1966)   **BA117**

Lists works by and about Hume, p.5–71; other Scottish philosophers, p.75–189.   Z8427.3.J58

Kant

Eisler, Rudolf. Kant-Lexikon; Nachschlagewerk zu Kants sämtlichen Schriften, Briefen und handschriftlichen Nachlass; hrsg. unter Mitwirkung der Kantgesellschaft. Berlin, Mittler, 1930. 642p.   **BA118**

Arranged by German word with explanations and exact references to sources.   B2751.E4

Walker, Ralph Charles Sutherland. A selective bibliography on Kant. 2d ed. Oxford, Sub-faculty of Philosophy, Univ. of Oxford, 1978. 68p. (Study aids, v.5)   **BA119**

1st ed. 1975.

A guide for the student, offering a useful selection from the vast quantity of available material.

Gernot U. Gabel's *Immanuel Kant: eine Bibliographie der Dissertationen aus den deutschsprachigen Ländern 1900–1975* (Hamburg, Gemini, 1980. 62p.; Bibliographien zur Philosophie, 3) offers a chronological listing of 659 dissertations, with author and subject indexes.   Z8460.W24

Leibniz

Leibniz-Bibliographie: die Literatur über Leibniz bis 1980. Begründet von Kurt Müller, hrsg. von Albert Heinekamp. 2. neu bearb. Aufl. Frankfurt am Main, Vittorio Klostermann GmbH, 1984. 742p. (Veröffentlichungen des Leibniz-Archivs, 10)   **BA120**

1st ed. 1967.

A comprehensive bibliography of writings about Leibniz. The writings of Leibniz are listed in Emile Ravier's *Bibliographie des oeuvres de Leibniz* (Paris, Alcan, 1937. 703p.; repr., Hildesheim, Olms, 1966). Dissertations are listed in Gernot U. Gabel's *Leibniz: eine Bibliographie europäischer und nordamerikanischer Hochschulschriften 1875–1975* (Köln, Gemini, 1983. 46p.; Bibliographien zur Philosophie, 7).   Z8496.18.H44

Nietzsche

Gabel, Gernot U. Friedrich Nietzsche: Leben und Werk im Spiegel westeuropäischer Hochschulschriften, 1900–1975; eine Bibliographie. 2d ed. Hamburg, Edition Gemini, [1978]. 36p.   **BA121**

A chronological listing of 342 items with author and subject indexes.   Z8628.85.G3

Reichert, Herbert William and **Schlechta, Karl.** International Nietzsche bibliography. Rev. and expanded. Chapel Hill, Univ. of North Carolina Pr., 1968. 162p. (Univ. of North Carolina. Studies in comparative literature, 45)   **BA122**

1st ed. 1960.

Lists more than 4,500 items—books and periodical articles—about Nietzsche. Arranged by language, then alphabetically by author within each language group. New listings since the 1960 edition are grouped mainly in a separate sequence (again by language) of the article) at the end, items 4001–4566. A subject index has been added.   Z8628.N5R4

Plato

See also BA10.

Ast, Friedrich. Lexicon Platonicum; sive, Vocum Platonicarum index. Lipsiae, Weidmann, 1835–38. 3v. (Repr.: N.Y., B. Franklin, 1969)   **BA123**

Josef Zürcher's *Lexicon academicum* (Paderborn, Verlag F. Schöningh, 1954. 36p.) serves as a supplementary dictionary of Greek proper names.   B351.A72

McKirahan, Richard D. Plato and Socrates: a comprehensive bibliography, 1958–1973. N.Y., Garland, 1978. 592p. (Garland reference library of the humanities, v.78)   **BA124**

Supplements the bibliography "Plato (1950–1957)" by H. F. Cherniss which appeared in *Lustrum,* v.4–5 (1959–60). Separate sections for Plato and Socrates, each topically subdivided. Author index. About 4,600 items.   Z8696.M34

Martinez, Julio A. A bibliography of writings on Plato, 1900–1967. [San Diego], San Diego State Univ. Lib., [1978]. 94p.   **BA125**

A selected list of books and periodical articles, useful to undergraduate and graduate students alike. In two sections: (1) general works on Plato; (2) works on the individual dialogues. No index.   Z8696.M37

Yale University. Library. The Plato manuscripts; a new index. Prep. by the Plato Microfilm Project of the Yale University Library under the direction of Robert S. Brumbaugh and Rulon Wells. New Haven, Yale Univ. Pr., 1968. 163p.   **BA126**

"This *Index,* based on a new cataloguing from microfilm of the extant pre-1500 manuscripts containing Plato's works in whole or part, is a necessary first step toward the complete reediting of a new edition of Plato's works."—*Introd.* Manuscripts are listed by library and by dialogue.   Z6616.P57Y35

Thomas Aquinas

See also BA10.

Deferrari, Roy Joseph and **Barry,** *Sister* M. Inviolata. A lexicon of St. Thomas Aquinas based on the Summa theologica and selected passages of his other works. . . . With the technical collaboration of Ignatius McGuiness. [Wash., Catholic Univ. of America Pr., 1948–53] 1185p.   **BA127**

Issued in 5 fascicles.

Arranged by Latin words, with their different English meanings and with Latin quotations from the *Summa theologica* and indications of exact sources.   B765.T54D38

—————— A complete index of the Summa theologica of St. Thomas Aquinas. [Baltimore? 1956] 386p.   **BA128**

An *index verborum,* prepared in conjunction with the authors' *Lexicon of St. Thomas Aquinas* (above).   BX1749.T6D4

Index Thomisticus: Sancti Thomae Aquinatis operum omnium indices et concordantiae in quibus verborum omnium et singulorum formae et lemmata cum suis frequentiis et

contextibus variis modis referuntur quaeque auspice Paulo VI Summo Pontifice consociata plurium opera atque electronico IBM automato usus digessit Robertus Busa. Stuttgart-Bad Cannstatt, Frommann-Holzboog, 1974–80. 49v. and 7v. suppl.   **BA129**

Provides for the scholar a sophisticated computer-produced linguistic analysis of 118 writings of St. Thomas Aquinas and of 61 other works associated with the *corpus thomisticum,* documenting the vocabulary and usage of 179 Latin works from the 9th to the 16th century. Introductory matter in Latin. Supplement contains the text of all works analyzed. Main set in three parts: Sectio I, Indices (i.e., tables of all works included, with specifying codes), 10v.; Sectio II, Concordantiae operum Thomisticorum, 31v.; Sectio III, Concordantiae operum aliorum auctorum, 8v.

A further example of computer applications in the field of philosophy and religion is provided by *A concordance to the works of St. Anselm,* ed. by G. R. Evans (Millwood, N.Y., Kraus Internat. Pubns., 1984. 4v.).   B765.T53Z85

Mandonnet, Pierre Félix and **Destrez, J.** Bibliographie thomiste. 2. éd. rev. et completée par M. D. Chenu. Paris, J. Vrin, 1960. 119p. (Bibliothèque thomiste, 1)   **BA130**

1st ed. 1921.

A classified bibliography of 2,283 books and articles published before 1921, the appendix to this edition adding only earlier works omitted from the original edition. Includes materials on the life, works, philosophy, theology and influence of Aquinas. Indexed.

Supplemented by: Z8870.M27

Bourke, Vernon Joseph. Thomistic bibliography, 1920–1940. . . . The modern schoolman, supplement to v.21. St. Louis, 1945. 312p.   **BA131**

Lists more than 6,660 books and periodical articles in various languages. Classified arrangement with indexes.   Z8870.B67

Miethe, Terry L. and **Bourke, Vernon J.** Thomistic bibliography, 1940–1978. Westport, Conn., Greenwood Pr., [1980]. 318p.   **BA132**

Continues the Bourke compilation (above). Lists nearly 4,100 items in classed arrangement, with personal name index. Detailed table of contents, but no subject index.   Z8870.M53

B B

Religion

❖In the field of religion, both Christian and non-Christian, reference materials are very extensive. They include encyclopedias, dictionaries, directories, and manuals in English and in other languages, which should be acquired by libraries according to need.

A basic working collection of materials in English might include: *Encyclopaedia of religion and ethics* (BB51); the *New Catholic encyclopedia* (BB439); *Encyclopaedia Judaica* (BB580); one or more editions of the Bible and concordances to them (*see* p.347–48, 352–54); *The interpreter's dictionary of the Bible* (BB167); Stevenson, *Home book of Bible quotations* (BB147); Julian, *Dictionary of hymnology* (BB341); *World Christian encyclopedia* (BB250); *Yearbook* of *American and Canadian churches* (BB347); and whatever denominational yearbooks are needed.

Large libraries, and libraries specializing in religious materials, will need to add many of the more specialized works, including some of those in foreign languages.

GENERAL WORKS

Guides

Adams, Charles Joseph, ed. A reader's guide to the great religions. 2d ed. N.Y., Free Pr., [1977]. 521p.   **BB1**

1st ed. 1965.

A bibliographic guide to the history and traditions of the world's principal religions. Chapters by specialists on primitive religion, the ancient world, Mexico, Central and South America, Hinduism, Buddhism, Sikhs, Jainas, religions of China and Japan, Judaism, Christianity, Islam. Appendix: "The history of the history of religions," by C. H. Long. Author and subject indexes.   Z7833.A35

Kennedy, James R. Library research guide to religion and theology: illustrated search strategy and sources. Ann Arbor, Mich., Pierian Pr., 1974. 53p. il. (Library research guides ser., no.1)   **BB2**

A manual, principally for the undergraduate, on methods of searching topics in religion and theology and on writing term papers. Includes information on use of the card catalog, basic reference tools, choosing a research topic, evaluating sources.
BL41.K45

Wilson, John F. and **Slavens, Thomas P.** Research guide to religious studies. Chicago, Amer. Lib. Assoc., 1982. 192p. (Sources of information in the humanities, 1)   **BB3**

In two parts: (1) Introduction to religious scholarship (a series of bibliographic essays on various aspects of the study of religion) and (2) Reference works (with general works grouped by type, followed by works on particular religions subdivided by type; all entries are annotated). Indexed.   BL41.W5

Bibliography

Barrow, John Graves. A bibliography of bibliographies in religion. [Ann Arbor, Mich., Edwards Bros., 1955] 489p.
BB4

Based on the author's doctoral dissertation, Yale University, 1930.

A comprehensive work attempting "to bring together all separately published bibliographies in the field of religion" (*Pref.*), from the 15th century to the present, and in many languages. Primarily Christian, but with a brief section on non-Christian religions. Brief annotations. Chronological listing under subject fields, with author index. Locates copies in numerous American and European libraries.   Z7751.B33

Beit-Hallahmi, Benjamin. Psychoanalysis and religion: a bibliography. Norwood, Pa., Norwood Eds., 1978. 182p.
BB5

"This work covers those writers that follow psychoanalysis as formulated by Freud and his recognized disciples. . . . Works inspired by the theories of Jung and Adler were not included."—*Introd.* Emphasis is on works which have religion as their main topic, and "most works included are attempts to relate religion and psychoanalysis in a meaningful way." Items are first listed in a classed arrangement, then citations are repeated in full in a so-called "Alphabetical listing and index."   Z7204.P8B43

Berkowitz, Morris I. and **Johnson, J. Edmund.** Social scientific studies of religion: a bibliography. [Pittsburgh], Univ. of Pittsburgh Pr., [1967]. 258p.   **BB6**

A classified bibliography of some 6,000 items. Emphasis is on English-language studies which relate religion to other social-behavioral variables. Covers through 1965. Author index.   Z7751.B47

Bibliographie zur alteuropäischen Religionsgeschichte. Berlin, W. de Gruyter, 1967–74. 2v. (Arbeiten zur Frühmittelalterforschung, Bd. 2, 5)   **BB7**

Contents: v.1, 1954–64, ed. by Peter Buchholz (subtitle: Literatur zu den antiken Rand- und Nachfolgekulturen im aussermediterranen Europa unter besonderer Berücksichtigung der nichtchristlichen Religionen); v.2, 1965–69, ed. by Jürgen Ahrendts (subtitle: Eine interdisziplinäre Auswahl von Literatur zu den Rand- und Nachfolgekulturen der Antike in Europa unter besonderer Berücksichtigung der nichtchristlichen Religionen).

5,298 items in v.1; 7,628 items in v.2. Classed arrangement within geographical divisions. Author and subject indexes.   Z7757.F9B5

Bowman, Mary Ann. Western mysticism: a guide to the basic works. Chicago, Amer. Lib. Assoc., 1978. 113p.   **BB8**

A selective bibliography "designed as a guide to the literature for reference librarians in academic, public, and church-related libraries; undergraduate students; and general readers."—*Pref.* Classed arrangement. Author-title and subject indexes.   Z7819.B68

Capps, Donald, Rambo, Lewis and **Ransohoff, Paul.** Psychology of religion: a guide to information sources. Detroit, Gale, [1976]. 352p. (Philosophy and religion information guide ser., v.1)   **BB9**

A section of general works in psychology of religion is followed by sections for each of the six "dimensions" of religion: the mythological, ritual, experiential, dispositional, social, and directional. Each section has four to eight subsections, and there are author, title, and subject indexes. Materials are largely limited to publications from the period 1950–74, with fuller coverage for 1960–74 inasmuch as W. W. Meissner's *Annotated bibliography in religion and psychology* (BB17) is very comprehensive for the earlier years. Books and articles of special merit are annotated.   Z7204.R4C36

Diehl, Katharine Smith. Religions, mythologies, folklores: an annotated bibliography. 2d ed. N.Y., Scarecrow Pr., 1962. 573p.   **BB10**

1st ed. 1956.

An annotated bibliography covering the "literature of faith and practice in all cultures. It includes books of general and specific reference, literatures, literary and historical guides, various scriptures and commentaries, records of institutional accomplishment, and biographies."—*Pref.* Classified arrangement with author and title index.   Z7751.D54

Earhart, H. Byron. The new religions of Japan: a bibliography of western-language materials. 2d ed. Ann Arbor, Center for Japanese Studies, Univ. of Mich., 1983. 213p. (Michigan papers in Japanese studies, 9)   **BB11**

1st ed. 1970.

Expands the earlier edition to include about 1,450 books, articles and dissertations on nineteenth- and twentieth-century religions of Japan. Classified arrangement; author and subject indexes.
Z7834.J3E2

Gorman, G. E. and **Gorman, Lyn.** Theological and religious reference materials: general resources and biblical studies. Westport, Conn., Greenwood, [1984]– . [v.1]– . (Bibliographies and indexes in religious studies, 1) (In progress; to be in 4v.)   **BB12**

Aims to introduce "students to the full range of reference materials likely to be required in theological or religious studies" (*Pref.*) but is addressed also to scholars and clergy. An "international and interdenominational" selection of 2,200 annotated entries representing many points of view. Includes general reference books, general theological materials and biblical resources arranged alphabetically by author in broad categories, subdivided by form. Length of sections makes for awkward browsing (e.g., more than 100 Bible dictionaries). Author, title and subject indexes.

v.2–4 are to cover systematic and moral theology and church history; practical theology and related subjects in the social sciences; comparative and non-Christian religions. Z7770.G66

International bibliography of the history of religions. Bibliographie internationale de l'histoire des religions . . . 1952– . . . . Leiden, Brill, 1954–79. 20v. **BB13**

Under the supervision of C. J. Bleeker. Published in connection with the periodical *Numen,* with the support of Unesco and under the auspices of the International Council for Philosophy and Humanistic Studies, by the International Association for the History of Religions.

Lists books and articles published during the year on the history of the various religions of the world. Classified arrangement. No author indexes until 1958/59.

Continued by: Z7833.I53

Science of religion: abstracts and index of recent articles. v.5– , 1980– . Amsterdam, Institute for the Study of Religion, Free University [and] Dept. of Theology and Religious Studies, Univ. of Leeds, 1980– . v.5– . Quarterly. **BB14**

v.1–4, 1976–79 publ. under title: *Science of religion bulletin: abstracts and index of recent articles.*

Publ. under the auspices of the International Association for the History of Religions on the recommendation of the International Council for Philosophy and Humanistic Studies with the financial support of Unesco.

A "systematic bibliography of articles contributing to the academic study of religions" *(Scope statement),* covering religions of both East and West, ancient and modern. Analyzes about 250 journals. Quarterly author and subject indexes cumulate in the final issue of each volume; cumulated author and subject indexes for 1976–80 publ. in v.5, no.4.

Jones, Charles Edwin. A guide to the study of the Pentecostal movement. Metuchen, N.J., Scarecrow Pr. & Amer. Theological Lib. Assoc., 1983. 2v. (ATLA bibliography ser., no.6) **BB15**

An extensive English language bibliography on Pentecostalism in many parts of the world and according to many traditions and churches. In four parts: pt.1 lists literature of the movement without reference to doctrinal tradition; pt.2 classifies materials by doctrinal emphasis, divided and subdivided by church or group, with each subsection preceded by a historical sketch; pt.3 is a list of Bible schools, colleges, seminaries (with directory information); pt.4, "Biography," identifies persons in the movement, citing sources of information about them. Z7845.P4J66

Karpinski, Leszek M. The religious life of man: guide to basic literature. Metuchen, N.J., Scarecrow Pr., 1978. 399p. **BB16**

Offers the undergraduate an annotated bibliography of 2,032 entries. In six parts: religions of mankind (general); religions of the past; Judaism, Christianity, Islam; Asian religions; beliefs of native peoples; the occult. Indexed. Z7751.K36

Meissner, William W. Annotated bibliography in religion and psychology. N.Y., Academy of Religion and Mental Health, 1961. 235p. **BB17**

Aims to be "of value to psychologists and to psychiatrists in relating knowledge and activity of their scientific disciplines to the concerns and demands of religious workers" *(Pref.)* and to religious workers in understanding better "the purposes and techniques of the psychological sciences." 2,905 entries, chiefly articles, in classified arrangement. Author index.

Mitchell, Robert Cameron and **Turner, Harold W.** A comprehensive bibliography of modern African religious movements. [Evanston, Ill., Northwestern Univ. Pr., 1966] 132p. **BB18**

Lists references in all languages on non-Islamic modern African religious movements. 1,313 items, many with annotations; index.

Two supplements appeared in *Journal of religion in Africa,* 1968 and 1970. Z7757.A2M5

Mitros, Joseph F. Religions; a select, classified bibliography. N.Y., Learned Publs.; Louvain, Nauwelaerts, 1973. 435p. (Philosophical questions ser., 8) **BB19**

A classified bibliography intended for the student preparing a research paper. Includes a section on methods of research and one on reference sources. Covers all major denominations and the history, philosophy, and development of religion in all periods. Titles are mainly in English, but some foreign-language works are included. Annotations for items considered of first importance. Index of names. Z7751.M57

Morris, Raymond P. A theological book list. Produced by the Theological Education Fund of the International Missionary Council for theological seminaries and colleges in Africa, Asia, Latin America and the Southwest Pacific. Oxford, Blackwell; Naperville, Ill., Allenson's, distr., [1960]. 242p. **BB20**

Continued by: Z7751.M6

Ward, Arthur Marcus [and others]. A theological book list . . . produced by the Theological Education Fund, for theological seminaries and colleges in Africa, Asia, Latin America and the Southwest Pacific. [Oxford, Blackwell; Naperville, Ill., Allenson's], 1963. 1v., various pagings. **BB21**

Contents: Works in English, comp. by A. Marcus Ward; French, comp. by Frank Michaeli; German, comp. by Hans Werner Gensichen; Portuguese, comp. by Aharon Sapsezian; Spanish, comp. by Carlos Gattinoni.

Continued by:

A theological book list, 1968; in four sections: English [by] A. Marcus Ward, French [by] J.-J. von Allmen, Portuguese [by] Aharon Sapsezian, Spanish [by] Emilio Castro. [London], Theological Education Fund [distr. by Allenson's, Naperville, Ill., 1968]. 1v., various pagings. **BB22**

A theological book list, 1971; in five sections: English [by] A. Marcus Ward, French [by] J.-J. von Allmen, German [by] Hans Chr. Deppe, Portuguese [by] Aharon Sapsezian, Spanish [by] Emilio Castro. [London], Theological Education Fund, 1971. 5 pts., in 1v.

These volumes list publications of 1966–70. The English section includes a list of reprints of books in the *Theological book list,* 1960, and its two supplements. Z7751.T43

New York. Union Theological Seminary. Library. Alphabetical arrangement of main entries from the shelf list. Boston, G. K. Hall, 1960 [i.e., 1965]. 10v. **BB23**

The catalog cards previously reproduced (1960) in shelflist sequence are here rearranged by main entry. (The volumes in shelflist arrangement can be used for subject searching, following the classification scheme outlined in item AB244.)

O'Brien, Betty A. and **O'Brien, Elmer J.** Religion index two, Festschriften 1960–1969. [Philadelphia], American Theological Library Assoc., [1980]. 741p. **BB24**

Includes 821 volumes of *Festschriften* with subject and author indexing on the pattern of other *Religion index two* (BB42) volumes. Z7751.O23

Ofori, Patrick E. Black African traditional religions and philosophy; a select bibliographic survey of the sources from the earliest times to 1974. Nendeln, Liechtenstein, KTO Pr., 1975. 421p. **BB25**

"This bibliography covers all the major ethnic groups of black Africa. Black Africa, as used in the context of this bibliography, means Africa south of the Sahara, and it includes all the major ethnic groups drawn roughly from Senegal in the West, along the southern boundary of the Sahara desert, through Central Ethiopia to Somalia in the East, through west, central, eastern and Southern Africa, including Madagascar."—*Introd.* Arranged by geographic area (Africa in general, West Africa, Central Africa, East Africa, Southern Africa), then by country and by ethnic groups within country sections. Some of the larger ethnic sections are subdivided according to such categories as "Religious beliefs and conceptions," "Birth, initiation and funeral rites," "Festivals," "Myths, superstitions, taboos," etc. Author and ethnic indexes.   Z834.A3O34

Phillips University, Enid, Okla. Graduate Seminary. Library. An index of *Festschriften* in religion in the Graduate Seminary Library of Phillips University. John L. Sayre and Roberta Hamburger, comps. Enid, Okla., Haymaker Pr., 1970. 121p.   **BB26**

Provides an author and subject approach to the contents of 84 volumes of *Festschriften,* most of them not included in Metzger's *Index of articles on the New Testament and early church published in Festschriften* (BB103).   Z7751.S38

—————— —————— New titles, 1971–1973. Enid, Okla., Seminary Pr., 1973. 136p.

Religion and society in North America: an annotated bibliography. Robert deV. Brunkow, ed. Santa Barbara, Calif., ABC-Clio, [1983]. 515p. (Clio bibliography ser., 12)   **BB27**

4,304 entries, with abstracts, for periodical articles relating to "the history of religion in the United States and Canada since the seventeenth century."—*Pref.* Items were drawn from v.11–18 of *America: history and life* (DB47). Classed arrangement; indexed by author and subject.   Z7831.R44

Religious books, 1876–1982. N.Y., Bowker, [1983]. 4v. (4389p.)   **BB28**

Contents: v.1–3 Subject index; v.4, Author and title indexes.

Provides a subject approach, with author and title indexes, to more than "one hundred years of Library of Congress cataloging on religious titles published or distributed in the United States."—*Pref.* Lists about 130,000 items in core religious subjects and peripheral areas selected from the *American book publishing record* database which contains all U.S. *National union catalog* and MARC tape monographs, plus titles cataloged at Bowker. Cataloging information is complete, including L.C. and Dewey class marks, tracings, notes, etc., but variations reflect changes in Library of Congress cataloging practice; similarly, L.C. subject headings no longer in current use are included in the "Subject index" section.   Z7751.R385

Religious books and serials in print, 1978/1979– . N.Y., Bowker, 1978– . Biennial. (3d ed., 1982/83)   **BB29**

Aims to be "a subject oriented bibliography covering all the world's religions from Anglicanism to Zen."—*Pref.* Information was drawn from the publisher's records for *Books in print, Forthcoming books,* Ulrich's periodicals directory and its supplementary quarterly, and *Irregular serials and annuals.* In addition, more than a hundred publishers whose materials have previously not appeared in those publications are represented. Thus serves as an in-print list for United States publications on religion and related subjects. In two main sections: (1) Books, listed by subject, by author, and by title, plus a "Sacred works index" which lists in-print editions of the Bible and the sacred books of many religions; (2) Serials, using a classified arrangement with full information (as in *Ulrich's*), with a title index.   Z7751.R387

Sandeen, Ernest Robert and **Hale, Frederick.** American religion and philosophy: a guide to information sources. Detroit, Gale, [1978]. 377p. (American studies information guide ser., v.5)   **BB30**

Intends "to provide students and scholars of religion and philosophy in the United States with a general introduction to recent secondary sources and key primary documents."—*Pref.* Serves in part as a supplement to Burr's *Critical bibliography of religion in America* (BB220), being designed especially to survey the literature which has appeared since that work was published in 1961. Classed arrangement with author, title, and subject indexes.   Z7757.U5S25

Shupe, Anson D., Bromley, David G. and **Oliver, Donna L.** The anti-cult movement in America; a bibliography and

historical survey. N.Y., Garland, 1984. 169p. (Garland reference library of social science, v.130)   **BB31**

Lists 1,001 items on religious counter-movements and opposition to religious cults in America. Presented in seven topical chapters, each with an introductory essay. Author index.   Z7835.C86S55

Thompson, Laurence G. Studies of Chinese religion: a comprehensive and classified bibliography of publications in English, French, and German through 1970. Encino, Calif., Dickenson Pub. Co., [1976]. 190p.   **BB32**

" . . . deals solely with Chinese *religion,* and includes items pertaining to the so-called Classics and philosophy only when these address themselves to religious matters."—*Pref.* In three main sections: (1) Bibliography and general studies; (2) Chinese religion exclusive of Buddhism; and (3) Chinese Buddhism; pts.2 and 3 are topically subdivided. Index of authors, editors, compilers, etc. Includes books and periodical articles.   Z7757.C6T56

Turner, Harold W. Bibliography of new religious movements in primal societies. Boston, G. K. Hall, [1977–78]. v.1–2. (In progress?)   **BB33**

Contents: v.1, Black Africa; v.2, North America.

To be in 4v. "The religious movements with which this bibliographic series are concerned are defined as those which arise in the interaction of a primal society with another society where there is great disparity of power or sophistication."—*Introd.* Later volumes are to deal with Latin America and the Caribbean, and Asia and Oceania.

v.1 is designed to "correct, cumulate and update" Turner and Mitchell's *Comprehensive bibliography of modern African religious movements* (BB18) and its two supplements which appeared in the *Journal of religion in Africa* (1968 and 1970). While the new work adds material through mid-1976, it is more selective and omits some material from the earlier lists. Some Islamic movements are now included. Geographical arrangement with "Index of authors and sources." About 1,900 items. Brief annotations (mainly descriptive) for most items.

v.2 is devoted to the United States, subdivided by Indian tribe, cult or group; shorter sections for Canada, Alaska, Greenland, and Northern Mexico. Indexes of (1) authors and sources, (2) films, records and tapes, and (3) main movements and Indian individuals.   Z7833.T87

Vande Kemp, Hendrika and **Malony, H. Newton.** Psychology and theology in Western thought, 1672–1965: a historical and annotated bibliography. Millwood, N.Y., Kraus Internat. Pubns., [1984]. 367p.   **BB34**

A historical bibliography on the integration of psychology and theology, listing book-length publications, monographs, and pamphlets (but not periodical articles) providing "information on earlier, less accessible sources."—*Pref.* 1,047 entries. Name, institution, title, and subject indexes.   Z7204.R4V36

Wainwright, William J. Philosophy of religion: an annotated bibliography of twentieth-century writings in English. N.Y., Garland, 1978. 776p. (Garland reference library of the humanities, v.111)   **BB35**

For full information *see* BA30.

Women religious history sources: a guide to repositories in the United States. Ed. by Evangeline Thomas, CSJ. N.Y., Bowker, 1983. 329p.   **BB37**

"The all-inclusive term *women religious* in the title refers to women called *sisters* in the active orders and *nuns* in the contemplative orders of the Catholic, Orthodox, and Episcopal churches and to those called *deaconesses* in the Lutheran, Methodist, and Mennonite churches."—*Pref.* Repositories are listed by state, then city, and notes on background and holdings are given. Bibliography, p.143–68. A "Table of U.S. founding dates" (chronological rather than by name of order) and a "Biographical register of foundresses and major superiors" (giving personal dates, order, and entry number for the repository) are useful appendixes. Indexed. Makes a useful companion to Hinding's *Women's history sources* (CC554).   Z7839.W65

Dissertations

Council on Graduate Studies in Religion. Doctoral dissertations in the field of religion, 1940–1952: their titles, location, fields, and short précis of contents. [N.Y.], Columbia Univ. Pr. for the Council, [1954]. 194p. **BB38**

Published as a supplement to the *Review of religion*, v.18.

———— ———— Supplement. 1952–77. Annual.

Title varies; 1964–77 called *Dissertation title index.*

The main work is an alphabetical list by author of 425 dissertations with brief abstracts. The supplements are annual author lists only; most include a list of dissertations in progress. Classified lists now appear in the Council's quarterly, *Religious studies review.*

Z7751.C7

Little, Lawrence Calvin. Researches in personality, character and religious education: a bibliography of American doctoral dissertations, 1885 to 1959. With an index prep. by Helen-Jean Moore. [Pittsburgh], Univ. of Pittsburgh Pr., 1962. 215p. **BB39**

Cover title: Bibliography of American doctoral dissertations in religious education, 1885 to 1959.

A listing of more than 6,300 doctoral dissertations arranged alphabetically by author with subject index. Z7849.L54

Indexes and abstract journals

Christian periodical index (a selected list). 1958– . Prep. by Librarians of the Association of Christian Librarians. [Buffalo], The Association, 1958– . v.1– . Quarterly, with annual and triennial cumulations. **BB40**

Subtitle varies: 1983– , An index to subjects and authors and to book and media reviews.

Frequency has varied; originally an annual with 5-year cumulations.

An index by authors and subjects to about 60 evangelical and fundamentalist periodicals, chiefly from the United States. Reviews are listed in a separate section. Z7753.C5

Religion index one: periodicals. 1949– . Chicago, American Theological Lib. Assoc., 1953– . Semiannual, with biennial cumulation. **BB41**

Subtitle: A subject index to periodical literature, including an author index with abstracts and a book review index.

Title varies: 1949–75/76 called *Index to religious periodical literature;* v.1–4, 1949–59, issued in a single volume, revised and expanded, in 1985, under the current title.

Cumulated volumes: v.1, 1949–52; v.2, 1953–54; v.3, 1955–56; v.4, 1957–59; v.5, 1960–62; biennial thereafter.

Indexes religious and archaeological periodicals from the United States, Canada, England, France, Germany, Japan, Scotland, and other countries. Coverage and number of periodicals indexed vary. Now includes 380 titles. Each volume includes a listing of book reviews. Protestant in viewpoint, but indexes a number of Catholic and Jewish periodicals. Employs the three-part arrangement introduced in 1975: (1) Subject index; (2) Author index with abstracts; and (3) Book review index. The revised v.1–4 lacks the separate book review section.

Religion index two: multi-author works (below) is a companion publication. Z7753.A5●

Religion index two: multi-author works, 1976– . [Chicago], American Theological Lib. Assoc., 1978– . [v.1–] Annual. **BB42**

A companion to *Religion index one: periodicals* (above), this new series indexes, by subject and author, composite works by various authors published during the year covered. "Each volume will appear about a year after the end of the imprint year of the majority of books indexed."—*Pref., 1976.* Includes Western-language publications which are collections by more than one author, which are intended to be scholarly, and which have a religious or theological subject focus. 340 books are indexed in the 1983 volume. Subjects and authors in separate sections. Z7751.R35●

Religious and theological abstracts. v.1– , Mar. 1958– . Myerstown, Pa., Theological Pub., 1958– . v.1– . Quarterly. **BB43**

A nonsectarian abstracting service, giving brief abstracts in English of articles appearing in a selected list of religious periodicals—including Christian, Jewish, and Muslim journals—in various languages. Author, subject, and biblical indexes for each volume.

BR1.R286

Richardson, Ernest Cushing. An alphabetical subject index and index encyclopaedia to periodical articles on religion, 1890–1899. N.Y., Scribner, 1907–11. 2v. **BB44**

Title varies.

Subject volume, 1907. 1168p.; author volume (called *Periodical articles on religion*), 1911. 876p.

An index to 58,000 articles by 21,000 writers, in more than 600 periodicals and transactions in English and the principal foreign languages, on the religions of the world. The subject volume, arranged alphabetically, has a special feature not ordinarily found in indexes, i.e., each heading used is briefly defined, or a person or place is identified and followed by a reference to some encyclopedia article. The author volume indexes the same articles as the subject volume. Z7753.R55

❖In addition to those noted above, there are a number of other indexes in this field which may prove useful in the very large or specialized collection: *Guide to social science and religion in periodical literature* (Flint, Mich., National Periodical Library, 1964–); *Mosher periodical index* (formerly *Subject index to select periodical literature;* Dallas, Mosher Library, Dallas Theological Seminary, 1969–); *Book reviews of the month: an index to reviews appearing in selected theological journals* (Fort Worth, Tex., Roberts Library, Southwestern Baptist Seminary, 1962–); *Répertoire bibliographique des institutions chrétiennes* (Strasbourg, 1967–); and the "Elenchus bibliographicus" section of the journal *Ephemerides theologicae lovanienses.*

Bibliography

Regazzi, John J. and **Hines, Theodore C.** A guide to indexed periodicals in religion. Metuchen, N.J., Scarecrow Pr., 1975. 314p. **BB45**

An alphabetical listing of some 2,700 periodicals with indication of which of 17 abstracting and indexing services includes each title. An "inverted title listing" which lists the journals under each important word in the title is intended as an aid for locating garbled or partially remembered titles. Z7753.R34

Schwertner, Siegfried. Internationales Abkürzungsverzeichnis für Theologie und Grenzgebiete: Zeitschriften, Serien, Lexika, Quellenwerke mit bibliographischen Angaben. International glossary of abbreviations for theology and related subjects. Berlin & N.Y., W. de Gruyter, 1974. 348p. **BB46**

Title also in French; introduction in English, French and German.

"Intended as a contribution toward the standardization of the title abbreviation" *(Introd.)* of theological works, listing abbreviations for about 7,500 periodicals, serials, dictionaries, and other source works. In two sections: (1) by proposed abbreviation, with full title; (2) by full title with abbreviation and bibliographical notes. An expanded version reprinted in *Theologische Realenzyklopädie* (BB66) adds about 800 titles in a supplement. Z6945.A2S35

Walsh, Michael J. Religious bibliographies in serial literature: a guide . . . , on behalf of the Assoc. of British Theological and Philosophical Libraries. Westport, Conn., Greenwood Pr., 1981. 216p.　　　　**BB47**

Lists in alphabetical order 178 bibliographical tools, mainly periodical indexes and journals, devoted entirely to, or including entries for, topics in religion. Excellent full descriptions of bibliographical information, arrangement, and coverage; critical comment included. Subject and title indexes.　　　Z7753.W34

Dictionaries and encyclopedias

Abingdon dictionary of living religions. Keith Crim, gen. ed. Nashville, Abingdon, [1981]. 830p. il.　　　　**BB48**

Intended as a guide to the historical development, beliefs, and observances of religions which are being practiced today. Each major religious tradition has an extensive article devoted to it, and there are briefer articles on more specific topics and aspects of each, including entries for regional developments in religions which have spread to various geographical locations. Signed articles; bibliographies; cross references.　　　BL31.A24

Dictionary of comparative religion. S. G. F. Brandon, gen. ed. London, Weidenfeld & Nicolson; N.Y., Scribner, [1970]. 704p.　　　　**BB49**

Brief, signed articles intended "to treat the various religions proportionately to their significance in the history of human culture."—*Pref.* Bibliographies follow most articles. Scholar specialists served as sectional editors for articles dealing with aspects of Buddhism, Hinduism, Islam, and the religions of China and the Far East. There is both a general index and a synoptic index which lists articles relating to a specific religion or an individual country.　　　BL31.D54

Dictionnaire des religions. Directeur de la publication, Paul Poupard. Comité de redaction, Jacques Vidal [et al.]. Paris, Presses Universitaires de France, [1984]. 1830p.　　　**BB50**

Designed to cover the whole phenomenon of religion. Offers an alphabetical arrangement of topics selected from five categories: the science of religion; ancient religions; the Bible and Judaism; Christianity and its history; present day religions of Africa, Asia and Oceania. Entries for concepts, beliefs, names, places, gods, feasts, religious and intellectual movements, and sacred texts were drawn from the religions which have left their mark on the intellectual and spiritual development of mankind. Signed articles range in length from a paragraph to many pages; cross references; brief, up-to-date bibliographies. Many biographical entries for persons, past and present, notable in theology, spirituality, ecumenism, philosophy, psychology, and the history or science of religion.　　　BL31.D55

Encyclopaedia of religion and ethics; ed. by James Hastings, with the assistance of John A. Selbie and Louis H. Gray. Edinburgh, Clark; N.Y., Scribner, 1908–27. 12v. and index. il.　　　　**BB51**

Low-priced edition on thinner paper, 7v.

The most comprehensive work in this class in English, including: articles on all religions; ethical systems and movements; religious beliefs and customs; philosophical ideas; moral practices; related subjects in anthropology, mythology, folklore, biology, psychology, economics, and sociology; and names of persons and places connected with any of these subjects. Signed articles; full bibliographies.　　　BL31.E4

Encyclopedic dictionary of religion. Ed. by Paul Kevin Meagher, Thomas C. O'Brien, Sister Consuelo Maria Aherne. Wash., Corpus Pubns. [for] Sisters of St. Joseph of Philadelphia, [1979]. 3v.　　　　**BB52**

Compiled under Catholic auspices (and stemming from an effort to keep together and further utilize the expertise developed for the *New Catholic encyclopedia*, BB439) but ecumenical in its coverage. Signed articles, usually including bibliographic references. Many

biographical entries and entries for institutions, religious orders, etc. Entries relate chiefly to Christianity; viewpoint is Roman Catholic.　　　BR95.E494

Ferguson, John. An illustrated encyclopaedia of mysticism and the mystery religions. London, Thames and Hudson, 1976; N.Y., Seabury, 1977. 228p. il.　　　　**BB53**

Brief articles on names, terms, and movements relating to various forms of mysticism. Demonology, magic, and witchcraft are excluded. "Bibliography of secondary sources," p.217–27.　　BL625.F44

Herzog, Johann Jakob. Realencyklopädie für protestantische Theologie und Kirche, begründet von J. J. Herzog; in 3. verb. und verm. Aufl. . . . hrsg. von Albert Hauck. Leipzig, Hinrichs, 1896–1913. 24v.　　　　**BB54**

Contents: v.1–21, A–Z; v.22, Index; v.23–24, Suppl., A–Z.

Long, signed articles by specialists, and full bibliographies. The most extended German work—and one of the most important in any language from the Protestant point of view. Formed the basis for the *New Schaff-Herzog* (BB63). Still of value in the theological, university, or large reference library.　　　BR95.H4

Lexikon für Theologie und Kirche; begründet von Michael Buchberger. 2. völlig neubearb. Aufl. . . . hrsg. von Josef Höfer und Karl Rahner. Freiburg, Herder, 1957–65. 10v. and Register.　　　　**BB55**

1st ed. 1930–38 in 10v.

Signed articles, some of considerable length, with bibliographies, covering various religions, practices, faiths, and rituals. Includes biography. From the Roman Catholic point of view.　　BR95.L48

―――― Das Zweite Vatikanische Konzil; Dokumente und Kommentare. Hrsg. von Heinrich Suso Brechter [et al.]. Freiburg, Herder, 1966–68. 3v.

Documents in Latin and German; commentary in German.　　　BR95.L48

Mead, Frank Spencer. Handbook of denominations in the United States. New 8th ed. Rev. by Samuel S. Hill. Nashville, Abingdon, [1985]. 320p.　　　　**BB56**

1st ed. 1951.

Provides brief sketches incorporating background, beliefs, governance, membership, etc., of more than 200 religious groups. Interpretive essay on religion in America today, p.262–73. Bibliography; index.　　　BR516.5.M38

Melton, J. Gordon. The encyclopedia of American religions. Wilmington, N.C., McGrath, [1978]. 2v.　　　　**BB57**

A survey of some 1,200 churches, denominations, sects, and cults known to have been established in the United States by 1976, with information on groups formed up to 1978. (Religions of North American Indians and gypsies are excluded.) Religions are grouped into 17 "families" whose members are related historically, theologically, or geographically. A general essay covering the heritage, theology, and life style introduces each "family"; descriptions of member groups follow, and usually include history, important names, principal location, related institutions, and statistics. Bibliographical footnotes. Each volume separately indexed.　　　BL2530.U6M443

Nordisk teologisk uppslagsbok för kyrka och skola. Redaktion: Ragnar Askmark [et al.]. Lund, Gleerup; København, Munksgaard, [1952–57]. 3v. il.　　　　**BB58**

Published in Denmark and Norway with the title *Nordisk teologisk leksikon.*

A general religious encyclopedia with signed articles and fairly extensive bibliographies listing works in various languages. Includes biographies. Index.　　　BR95.N62

Parrinder, Edward Geoffrey. Dictionary of non-Christian religions. 2d ed. [i.e., rev. repr.] [Amersham, Bucks], Hulton, 1981. 320p. il.　　　　**BB59**

1st ed. 1971.

"Covers the whole field of the religions of the world, with the exception of Christianity and the Bible."—*Introd.* Brief entries for gods, heroes, cults, beliefs, places, etc., especially for Hinduism, Buddhism and Islam. No bibliography; short reading list appended.

BL31.P36

The Penguin dictionary of religions. Ed. by John R. Hinnells. [London], Allen Lane, [1984]. 550p. il., maps. **BB60**

Publ. in the United States as *Facts on File dictionary of religions.*

The work of an international team of 29 scholars from a variety of academic disciplines. Emphasis is on "living religions," but ancient religions, astrology, magic, and the occult are also treated. Basically a dictionary of terms, but entries go well beyond brief definitions. Includes an extensive classed bibliography (p.381–446), a synoptic index (which lists all articles relating to a given religion or group of religions), and a general index. BL31.P38

Die Religion in Geschichte und Gegenwart; Handwörterbuch für Theologie und Religionswissenschaft. 3. völlig neubearb. Aufl. . . . hrsg. von Kurt Galling. Tübingen, Mohr, 1957–65. 7v. il. **BB61**

1st ed. 1909–13.

Cited as *RGG.* An authoritative work containing long, signed articles by specialists. From an advanced Protestant point of view but includes articles on Catholic doctrines. Full bibliographies. Many biographical sketches, including articles on living persons. v.7 is the *Registerband.* BL31.R42

Rice, Edward. Eastern definitions. Garden City, N.Y., Doubleday, 1978. 433p. il. **BB62**

Subtitle: A short encyclopedia of religions of the Orient; a guide to common, ordinary, and rare philosophical, mystical, religious, and psychological terms from Hinduism, Buddhism, Sufism, Islam, Zen, Taoism, the Sikhs, Zoroastrianism, and other major and minor Eastern religions.

"The terms encountered in this work are in most cases those most likely to be met by the average curious reader of both popular and scholarly works written in or translated into English."—*Foreword.* Articles range in length from a few lines to several pages. Cross references; no bibliography. BL31.R52

Schaff-Herzog encyclopedia. New Schaff-Herzog encyclopedia of religious knowledge, embracing biblical, historical, doctrinal and practical theology and biblical, theological and ecclesiastical biography, from the earliest times to the present day; based on the 3d ed. of the Realencyklopädie founded by J. J. Herzog and ed. by Albert Hauck. S. M. Jackson, ed. in chief. N.Y., Funk & Wagnalls, 1908–12. 12v. and index. (Repr.: Grand Rapids, Mich., Baker Book House, 1949–50. 13v.) **BB63**

One of the most important reference books on its subject in English. Based upon the 3d ed. of the Herzog-Hauck *Realencyklopädie* (BB54), and thus Protestant in tone, it is not a mere translation of the German work since much of the material has been condensed, fresh material added, and the bibliographies extended and improved. Not limited to the Christian religion but includes articles on other religions and religious leaders. Covers the whole field of biblical and historical theology, including separate articles of all sects, denominations and churches, organizations and societies, missions, doctrines, controversies, etc. Biographical notices include those of men living at the time the work was published. The bibliography is in three forms: (1) general bibliographical survey, with critical comment, in the preface (p.xii–xiv); (2) bibliographical appendix at the beginning of each volume, listing recent (at time of publication) literature; and (3) bibliographies appended to each article.

Supplemented by: BR95.S43

Twentieth century encyclopedia of religious knowledge: an extension of the New Schaff-Herzog encyclopedia of religious knowledge. Ed. in chief, Lefferts A. Loetscher. Grand Rapids, Mich., Baker Book House, 1955. 2v. (1205p.) **BB64**

These volumes may be used either with the preceding set or independently. They include biographical sketches of persons both living and dead; articles on newer subjects; and articles which update subjects previously treated. Articles are signed and usually include bibliographies. BR95.S435s

Shulman, Albert M. The religious heritage of America. N.Y., A. S. Barnes; London, Tantivy Pr., [1981]. 527p. **BB65**

Aims to present "the salient facts about the many religions, cults, and sects in America in simple language and concise form."—*Introd.* The bulk of the book comprises entries for individual religions, sects, etc.; in general, information is presented in a uniform pattern: chronological profile, origin, name, structure and polity, doctrine and belief. Indexed. BL2530.U6S5

Theologische Realenzyklopädie. In Gemeinschaft mit Horst Robert Balz [et al.], hrsg. von Gerhard Krause und Gerhard Müller. Berlin & N.Y., W. de Gruyter, 1976–85. Bd.1–13; Abkürzungsverzeichnis. (In progress) **BB66**

Contents: Bd.1–13, A–Gottesbeweise; indexes.

To be in 30 volumes of about 800 pages (five *Lieferungen*) each; publishing schedule calls for publication of six *Lieferungen* per year.

In some respects a successor to the *Realencyklopädie für protestantische Theologie und Kirche* (BB54), but a new work employing a broader interpretation of "theology" and less concerned with the strictly Protestant point of view. Long, scholarly articles (most of them many pages in length) signed by the contributors, and including extensive bibliographies. Each volume has its own index, and a general index is promised as the final volume of the set.

BR95.T47

Directories

Butler, Francis J. and **Farrell, Catherine E.** Foundation guide for religious grant seekers. 2d ed. Chico, Calif., Scholars Pr., [1984]. 139p. **BB67**

1st ed. 1979.

A handbook whose "basic function is to guide the reader to the right sources of information" and "to help answer the question: Is a foundation grant really what is needed or wanted?"—*Introd.* Directory information on more than 300 foundations known to have funded religious organizations in the past, and short chapters on printed and other sources of information, the grant-seeking process, religious philanthropy, and building constituency support.

BV774.5.B87

The directory of religious organizations in the United States. 2d ed. Falls Church, Va., McGrath, [1982]. 518p. **BB68**

1st ed. 1977.

An alphabetical title listing of more than 1,600 general organizations (exclusive of religious orders) which have a religious purpose—departments of national churches, professional associations, volunteer groups, government agencies, businesses, and fraternal societies. Indicates religious affiliation, principal officer, address, statement of purpose, type of activities, founding date, membership, publications, etc. An index to types of activity would have been useful. BL2530.U6D57

Graduate studies in religion. Waterloo, Ont., Pub. for the Council on Graduate Studies in Religion by the Council on the Study of Religion, [1982]. 63p. **BB69**

"Offers basic information on graduate programs" (*User's guide*), and to a lesser extent on undergraduate studies, at the 28 member institutions in the United States and Canada that constitute the Council on the Study of Religion.

World Council of Churches. Handbook, member churches. Ed. by Ans J. van der Bent. Geneva, Switz., The Council, [1982]. 281p. **BB70**

Lists "statistical information, brief historical surveys and notes on the present concerns, programmes and activities of the churches" (*Introd.*) which constitute the Council. An introductory section covers national and regional councils and conferences to which member churches belong. Arranged by continent, then by country.

BR157.W68

Sacred books

Collections

The Bible of the world; ed. by Robert O. Ballou in collaboration with Friedrich Spiegelberg . . . N.Y., Viking, 1939. 1415p. **BB71**

Brings together "the scriptural essence of eight great living source religions."—*Introd.* Notes; bibliography. BL70.B5

Champion, Selwyn Gurney. The eleven religions and their proverbial lore, a comparative study. . . . Foreword to the American ed., by Rufus M. Jones. . . . A reference book to the eleven surviving major religions of the world, with introductions by thirteen leading authorities. N.Y., Dutton, 1945. 340p. **BB72**

A book of quotations arranged under religion by keyword, with subject-matter index and alternative chief-word index. Bibliography, p.336–60. BL80.C337

Hume, Robert Ernest. Treasure house of the living religions; selections from their sacred scriptures. N.Y., Scribner, 1932. 493p. **BB73**

A classified anthology of 3,074 selected quotations from the sacred books of the 11 great historical religions—Buddhism, Christianity, Confucianism, Hinduism, Islam, Jainism, Judaism, Shinto, Sikhism, Taoism, and Zoroastrianism—with exact indication of source of each quotation; a full "Bibliography showing the canonical order of constituent documents of the several sacred scriptures together with the English translations of each document," p. 405–43; and an alphabetical topical index. A work of wide and precise scholarship, useful to the general reader for the interest of the selections and to the specialist for both selections and bibliographical materials. BL70.H8

Sacred books of the Buddhists, translated by various Oriental scholars . . . London, H. Frowde, Oxford Univ. Pr., 1895–1978. 33v. **BB74**

Title pages vary. Publisher varies.
Begun under the editorship of F. M. Müller, and similar in plan to the *Sacred books of the East* series (below).

Sacred books of the East, tr. by various oriental scholars and ed. by F. Max Müller. Oxford, Clarendon Pr., 1879–1910. 50v. (Repr.: N.Y., Dover, 1963–69) **BB75**

Contents: v.1, 15, The Upanishads, tr. by F. Max Müller; v.2, 14, The sacred laws of the Âryas, tr. by Georg Bühler; v.3, 16, 27, 28, The sacred books of China, the texts of Confucianism, tr. by James Legge; v.4, 23, 31, The Zend-Avesta, tr. by James Darmesteter and L. H. Mills; v.5, 18, 24, 37, 47, Pahlavi texts, tr. by E. W. West; v.6, 9, The Qur'ân, tr. by E. Palmer; v.7, The Institutes of Vishnu, tr. by Julius Jolly; v.8, The Bhagavadgîtâ, with the Sanatsugâtîya and the Anugîtâ, tr. by Kâshinâth Trimbak Telang; v.10, The Dhammapada, tr. from Pâli by F. M. Müller; The Sutta-nipâta, tr. from Pâli by V. Fausböll; v.11, Buddhist suttas, tr. from Pâli by T. W. Rhys Davids; v.12, 26, 41, 43, 44, The Satapathabrâhmana, tr. by Julius Eggeling; v.13, 17, 20, Vinaya texts, tr. from the Pâli by T. W. Rhys Davids and Hermann Oldenberg;
v.19, The Fo-sho-hing-tsan-king by Asvaghosha, tr. by Samuel Bael; v.21, The Saddharma-pundarika, tr. by H. Kern; v.22, 45, Gaina sûtras, tr. from Prâkit by Herman Jacobi; v.25, The laws of Manu, tr. by G. Bühler; v.29, 30, The Grihya-sûtras, tr. by Hermann Oldenberg; v.32, 46, Vedic hymns, tr. by F. M. Müller and H. Oldenberg; v.33, The minor law books, pt.1, tr. by Julius Jolly; v.34, 38, 48, The Vedânta sûtras, tr. by George Thibaut; v.35, 36, The questions of King Milinda, tr. by T. W. Rhys Davids; v.39, 40, The sacred books of China, the texts of Tâoism, tr. by James Legge; v.42, Hymns of the Atharva-veda, tr. by Maurice Bloomfield; v.49, Buddhist Mâhâyana texts, tr. by E. B. Cowell; v.50, General index, by M. Winternitz.
Includes all the most important works of the seven non-Christian religions that have influenced the civilization of Asia: the Vedic-Brahmanic system, Buddhism, Jainism, Islam, Confucianism, Taoism, and the Parsi religion. The excellent and detailed general index

can be used for both large and small topics, beliefs, myths, names of deities, etc. Index also issued separately, as follows:

Winternitz, Moriz. Concise dictionary of Eastern religion, being the index volume to the Sacred books of the East. Oxford, Clarendon Pr., 1910. 683p. **BB76**

Published also under the title: *A general index to the names and subject matter of the Sacred books of the East.* BL1010.S32

Sacred texts of the world: a universal anthology. Ed. by Ninian Smart and Richard D. Hecht. N.Y., Crossroad, 1982. 408p. **BB77**

Selections are drawn from the scriptures and oral traditions of religions from all parts of the world and from earliest times to the twentieth century. "Both religious traditions which have passed out of existence and the latest religions" *(Introd.),* including "secular worldviews" are represented. Little bibliography. BL70.S247

Textual sources for the study of Zoroastrianism. Ed. and tr. by Mary Boyce. Totowa, N.J., Barnes & Noble; Manchester, Univ. Pr., 1984. 166p. il. **BB78**

Presents a selection of "ancient texts . . . retranslated for this anthology" *(Foreword),* together with some modern texts which bear on Zoroastrianism. Includes an introductory background chapter, bibliography, and glossarial index. A companion to the editor's *Zoroastrians* (BB607). BL1571.T44

The Bible

❖While the Bible is not a reference book in the ordinary sense of the term, at least one copy should be in even the small reference collection, and others should be acquired as needed. In recent years, many new translations and versions have been made directly from the original Hebrew and Greek manuscripts, and take into account modern archaeological discoveries. For a bibliography of English Bibles, *see* Margaret T. Hills, *The English Bible in America* (BB94).

Bible. Various versions.

The principal versions in English at present are:

1. *King James* or *Authorized Version* (1611), still the most used Bible among Protestants. The *New King James Version* (1982) introduces "present-day vocabulary, punctuation, and syntax" where necessary, but strives to preserve "the legacy of the original translators."—*Introd.*
2. *American Revised Version* or *American Standard Version* (1901), which differs on some points from the *English Revised Version* (1885). Revised to provide "a more current English idiom" *(Pref.)* and published as the *New American Standard Bible* (1971), it is more literal than other modern translations.
3. *Revised Standard Version* (N.Y., Nelson, 1952). The New Testament appeared first, in 1946. Translated into modern English by a group of American scholars under the general editorship of Luther A. Weigle. *The Oxford annotated Bible, with the Apocrypha,* ed. by Herbert G. May and Bruce M. Metzger (N.Y., Oxford Univ. Pr., 1965. 1544p., 298p.) uses the text of the *Revised Standard Version.*
4. *New English Bible* (N.Y., Oxford Univ. Pr. and Cambridge Univ. Pr., 1970. 3v.; the New Testament volume is 2d ed.). Undertaken to provide a faithful rendering of the best available texts into contemporary English idiom, the work was "planned and directed by representatives of the Baptist Union of Great Britain and Ireland, the Church of England, the Church of Scotland, the Congregational Church in England and Wales, the Council of

Churches for Wales, the Irish Council of Churches, the London Yearly Meeting of the Society of Friends, the Methodist Church of Great Britain, the Presbyterian Church of England, the British and Foreign Bible Society, the National Bible Society of Scotland."—*p.ii.*

The Oxford study edition of the *NEB,* with Samuel Sandmal as general editor, M. Jack Suggs, New Testament editor, and Arnold J. Tkacik, Apocrypha editor (N.Y., Oxford Univ. Pr., 1976. 1036p., 257p., 333p. [100p.] maps) includes introductions to individual books and groups of books as well as general background articles on Scripture; there are also annotations throughout "dealing with literary, historical, theological, geographical, and archaeological aspects of the text, and . . . cross-references" (*Pref.*) to related passages. An index of people, places and themes in the Bible is provided, as well as maps with index.

5. *Douay Bible,* the 16th-century Roman Catholic translation of the Latin Vulgate. It differs from the Protestant Bible in the number and order of the books, and in the fact that the Apocryphal books are accepted as canonical and are interspersed with the other books. Also known as *Douay-Rheims Bible.*

6. *New American Bible,* "translated from the original languages with critical use of all the ancient sources by members of the Catholic Biblical Association of America; sponsored by the Bishops' Committee of the Confraternity of Christian Doctrine."—*Pref.* (N.Y., Kenedy; London, Collier-Macmillan, 1970) A new translation intended for contemporary American readers; it incorporates (with certain revisions) those portions of the Old Testament published in the "Confraternity edition" (Paterson, N.J., St. Anthony Guild Pr., 1952–69). A new edition is in preparation.

7. *Jerusalem Bible* (Garden City, N.Y., Doubleday, 1966). Derives from the French version edited at the Dominican École Biblique de Jerusalem and known as *La Bible de Jerusalem* (Paris, Éditions du Cerf, 1956, etc.). The introductions and notes are "a direct translation from the French, though revised and brought up to date in some places" (*Foreword*), but translation of the Biblical text goes back to the original languages. A new edition entitled *New Jerusalem Bible* was published 1985.

8. *Jewish version.* Good reference editions of the English translation of the Old Testament, first published in 1917, then 1955, are available. The new translation by leading contemporary Jewish scholars was published by the Jewish Publication Society, Philadelphia (1962–82 in 3v.): *The Torah* (1962; 2d ed., 1967), *The Prophets* (1978), and *The Writings* (1982).

A convenient collection of various English translations of the New Testament is the *New Testament octapla,* ed. by Luther A. Weigle (N.Y., Nelson, 1962). Versions represented are: Tyndale, Great Bible, Geneva Bible, Bishops' Bible, Rheims, King James, American Standard, Revised Standard.

Among other good modern translations of the Bible the following are notable: *Moffatt Bible* (N.Y., Harper, 1925); *Complete Bible, an American Translation:* the Old Testament, tr. by J. M. Powis Smith; the Apocrypha and New Testament, tr. by Edgar J. Goodspeed (Chicago, Univ. of Chicago Pr., 1939); *New Testament in modern English,* tr. by J. B. Phillips (N.Y., Macmillan, 1958; rev. ed., 1972); the translation from the Latin Vulgate, by Ronald A. Knox (N.Y., Sheed & Ward, 1954); and the *New International Version:* the New Testament (Grand Rapids, Mich., Zondervan, 1973), published under the sponsorship of the New

York Bible Society International. (The last named version was completed in 1978 with the publication of The Old Testament.)

Herbert Dennett's *A guide to modern versions of the New Testament: how to understand and use them* (Chicago, Moody Pr., 1966) provides historical and descriptive notes on the various versions, together with some assessment of the quality of each. Similarly, for the Bible as a whole, *The word of God: a guide to English versions of the Bible,* ed. by Lloyd R. Bailey (Atlanta, J. Knox Pr., 1982) presents essays by biblical scholars on English translations to help the reader choose a Bible for himself. Another book with the same purpose is Jack Pearl Lewis' *The English Bible, from KJV to NIV: a history and evaluation* (Grand Rapids, Mich., Baker, 1981) which examines the strengths and weaknesses of twelve major translations.

In the larger library bilingual or polyglot editions are sometimes needed. Three recent publications of this type are: (1) the *NIV interlinear Hebrew-English Old Testament,* ed. by John R. Kohlenberger (Grand Rapids, Mich., Zondervan, 1979– ; to be in 4v.), which interlines Hebrew and English, with the text of the *New International Version* in the right-hand margin; three volumes covering Genesis to the Song of Songs were issued 1979–82 and the final volume is scheduled for 1985 publication; (2) the *NIV triglot Old Testament* (Grand Rapids, Mich., Zondervan, 1981. 1v., unpaged) which presents in parallel columns "the two most important ancient texts of the Old Testament—the Hebrew according to the Masoretic Text and the Greek according to the Septuagint—together with the modern English of the New International Version."—*Introd.*; and (3) the *NASB interlinear Greek-English New Testament,* ed. by Alfred Marshall (Grand Rapids, Mich., Regency Reference Library, 1984. 1027p.) which offers an interlinear arrangement of the *Novum Testamentum Graece* text (Nestle, 21st ed.), and a literal English translation by the editor, the English equivalent appearing directly beneath the Greek original, thus "illustrating an essential stage" (*Foreword*) in translation; the *NASB* text appears in a narrow left-hand column.

The Apocrypha.

Among the various editions and versions of the Apocrypha are:

1. *Apocrypha and pseudepigrapha of the Old Testament in English,* with introductions and critical and explanatory notes to the several books. Ed. by R. H. Charles. Oxford, Clarendon Pr., 1913. 2v. Repr. 1963.

2. *The Old Testament pseudepigrapha,* ed. by James H. Charlesworth. Garden City, N.Y., Doubleday, 1983– . v.1– . (In progress) Contents: v.1, Apocalyptic literature and testaments. "Designed for the scholar and for the interested non- specialist."—*Pref.* A wider selection than that of Charles (above, v.2), with some texts translated into English for the first time. Each work is preceded by an introduction covering text, manuscripts, provenance, significance and select bibliography. When completed, this edition will supersede that of R. H. Charles.

3. *The Apocryphal Old Testament,* ed. by H. F. D. Sparks. Oxford, Clarendon Pr., 1984. 990p. Presents new (or revised) translations of the more important non-canonical Old Testament books, the selection corresponding roughly to R. H. Charles' *Apocrypha and Pseudepigrapha of the Old* Testament, v.2 (1913), and intended for general rather than strictly academic use.

4. *Apocrypha,* according to the Authorized Version, ed. by Robert H. Pfeiffer. N.Y., Harper, 1953. 295p.

5. *Apocrypha of the Old Testament.* Revised Standard Version. N.Y., Nelson, 1957. 250p. *The Oxford annotated Apocrypha* (N.Y., Oxford Univ. Pr., 1965. 298p.) uses the Revised Standard Version; the volume has been reprinted as part of the *Oxford annotated Bible* (*see* "Versions," no.3, above).

6. *New Testament Apocrypha,* by Edgar Hennecke, ed. by William Schneemelcher. English translation by A. J. B. Higgins [and others], ed. by R. McL. Wilson. Philadelphia, Westminster, 1963–65. 2v. v.1, Gospels and related writings; v.2, Writings relating to the Apostles, apocalypses, and related subjects; tr. from the completely revised 3d German edition.

7. *The apocryphal New Testament,* being the apocryphal acts, epistles, and apocalypses, with other narratives and fragments. Trans. by M. R. James. Oxford, Clarendon Pr., 1924. 584p. Intended for the general reader.

Bibliography

See also BB12.

A bibliographical guide to New Testament research. [3d ed.] R. T. France, ed. [Sheffield, Eng.], JSOT Pr., [1979]. 56p. (Repr. 1983) **BB79**

1st ed. 1968.
A guide for the student, listing sources (with some annotations) for research in numerous areas of New Testament research. Topical arrangement; no index.

British and Foreign Bible Society. Library. Historical catalogue of the printed editions of Holy Scripture in the library of the . . . Society. Comp. by T. H. Darlow and H. F. Moule. London, Bible House, 1903–11. 2v. in 4. (Repr.: N.Y., Kraus, 1963) **BB80**

Contents: v.1, English; v.2, Polyglots and languages other than English: pt.1, Polyglots. Acawoio–Grebo; pt.2, Greek–Opa; pt.3, Ora–Zulu. Indexes.
An indispensable catalog of editions of the Bible, arranged chronologically under each language; annotated. Five indexes: (1) Languages and dialects (more than 600); (2) Translators, revisers, editors, etc.; (3) Printers, publishers, etc; (4) Places of printing; and (5) General subjects (names of Bibles, etc.).
For a revision of v.1, *see* Herbert (BB93); of the African sections, *see* Coldham (BB86). Z7770.B73

British Museum. Dept. of Printed Books. General catalogue of printed books. Photolithographic ed. to 1955. v.17–19: Bible. London, Museum, 1965. 3v. **BB81**

An extensive collection of the Bible: (1) Complete editions by language, chronologically under language; (2) Selections; (3) Old Testament, followed by sections and individual books; (4) Books of the Apocrypha; (5) New Testament, sections, individual books, N.T., Apocrypha; (6) Appendix; (7) Index by language; (8) Select index of titles. Recent additions are listed in the B.M *Catalogue supplements:* 1956–65, v.4–5; 1966–70, v.3; 1971–75, v.2; 1976–82 (in microfiche), fiches 34–35. Z921.B8702

Burchard, Christoph. Bibliographie zu den Handschriften vom Toten Meer. Berlin, Alfred Töpelmann, 1957–65. 2v. (Beihefte zur Zeitschrift für die alttestamentliche Wissenschaft, 76, 89) **BB82**

A bibliography of books and periodical articles on the Dead Sea Scrolls, in various languages. Z6371.D4B8

Chambers, Bettye Thomas. Bibliography of French Bibles: fifteenth- and sixteenth-century French-language editions of the scriptures. Genève, Droz, 1983. 548p. il. (Travaux d'humanisme et renaissance, no.192) **BB83**

Aims to "present . . . a standardized, comprehensive bibliographical description of 'ideal copy' of every French-language edition of the Bible and New Testament published in the fifteenth and sixteenth centuries."—*Introd.* Lists in chronological order 554 entries, with full bibliographical description and notes, together with library locations. Z7771.F8C48

Childs, Brevard S. Old Testament books for pastor and teacher. Philadelphia, Westminster Pr., [1977]. 120p. **BB84**
Z7772.A1C48

Martin, Ralph P. New Testament books for pastor and teacher. Philadelphia, Westminster Pr., [1984]. 152p. **BB85**

The above are companion volumes which offer guidance in the selection and use of books for understanding and studying the Bible. Each evaluates a selection of introductions, encyclopedias, commentaries, etc. Indexed. Z7772.L1M3

Coldham, Geraldine Elizabeth, comp. A bibliography of Scriptures in African languages. London, British and Foreign Bible Soc., 1966. 2v. **BB86**

Contents: v.1, Polyglot; Acholi–Mousgoum; v.2, Mpama–Zulu; Indexes.
"A revision of the African sections of the Darlow and Moule 'Historical Catalogue of the Printed Editions of Holy Scripture' [BB80], with additions to 1964."—*title page.* Z7771.A4C6

———— ———— Supplement, 1964–1974. London, British and Foreign Bible Soc., 1975. 198p.

Intended for use with the 1966 volume, which it supplements, and not as a separate work. Includes Scriptures published 1964–74 and editions of earlier years omitted from the basic work. Long lists of "Language name corrections" and "Geographical name corrections" help to update a rapidly changing nomenclature.
Z7771.A4C6

Cully, Iris V. and **Cully, Kendig Brubaker.** A guide to biblical resources. Wilton, Conn., Morehouse-Barlow, [1981]. 153p. **BB87**

Aims "to offer . . . guidance into the rich resources of meaning, scholarship, and interpretation which biblical study entails."—*Pref.* Presents chapters, with English-language bibliographies, on background materials, reference books, translations, versions, adults' and children's courses, and the Bible in worship, in literature and the arts. Popular in tone; addressed to the general reader.
BS600.2.C796

Fee, Gordon D. New Testament exegesis: a handbook for students and pastors. Philadelphia, Westminster Pr., [1983]. 154p. **BB88**

Offers a guide and textbook "primarily concerned with the exegetical process itself" and includes "suggestions for moving 'from text to sermon.'"—*Introd.* Methods and procedures described, with bibliographical notes on the necessary materials throughout. Author index.
A companion volume is: BS476.F38

Stuart, Douglas K. Old Testament exegesis: a primer for students and pastors. 2d ed., rev. and enl. Philadelphia, Westminster Pr., [1984]. 142p. **BB89**

1st ed. 1980.
Offers a "step-by-step guide to OT exegesis" intended as "nontechnical and simple without being simplistic."—*Pref.* Addressed to seminary students and pastors. Includes annotated list of aids and resources. Author and subject indexes. BS476.S83

Fitzmyer, Joseph A. The Dead Sea Scrolls; major publications and tools for study. With an addendum (January 1977). [Missoula, Mont.], Scholars Pr. for the Society of Biblical Literature, [1977]. 171,[5]p. (Sources for biblical study, 8) **BB90**

1st ed. 1975.
This handbook, originating in a course taught by the author, aims to explain the sigla of the Scrolls; indicate place of publication of texts; explain contents of texts; and introduce the student to tools of

study. Also notes major secondary publications: bibliographies, surveys, concordances, dictionaries, translations, and materials on selected topics. Index of modern authors and of biblical passages.
     Z6371.D4F58

───── An introductory bibliography for the study of Scripture. Rev. ed. Rome, Biblical Institute Pr., 1981. 154p. (Subsidia Biblica, 3)   **BB91**

1st ed., 1961, by G. S. Glanzman and J. A. Fitzmyer.
Aims to guide the "student who is beginning theology or the study of Scripture in a serious way" *(Pref.)* to basic titles and the most important secondary works. Classified arrangement. Evaluative annotations; book reviews noted; index of modern authors.

Gottcent, John H. The Bible as literature: a selective bibliography. Boston, G. K. Hall, [1979]. 170p.   **BB92**

A classed bibliography, with sections for editions and translations, general reference works, the Bible as a whole, the Old and New Testaments, the individual books of the Bible, and the Apocrypha. Brief annotations; index. "Though it should be useful to both biblical scholars and literary critics, it is aimed primarily at those trained in secular literary studies."—*Introd.*   Z7770.G68

Herbert, Arthur Sumner. Historical catalogue of printed editions of the English Bible: 1525–1961; rev. and expanded from the edition of T. H. Darlow and H. F. Moule, 1903. London, British and Foreign Bible Soc.; N.Y., Amer. Bible Soc., [1968]. 549p.   **BB93**

A revision and expansion of v.1 of the Darlow and Moule work (BB80). This edition is not based solely on the collection in the British and Foreign Bible Society Library, but draws on the holdings of other outstanding collections in both Britain and the United States and indicates locations therein.   Z7771.E5H47

Hills, Margaret Thorndike, ed. The English Bible in America: a bibliography of editions of the Bible & the New Testament published in America, 1777–1957. N.Y., Amer. Bible Soc. and the New York Pub. Lib., 1961. 477p.
     BB94

A chronological, annotated listing of Bibles in the English language published in the United States and Canada, with indication of locations of copies. Six indexes: (1) geographical of publishers and printers; (2) alphabetical of publishers and printers; (3) translations, translators, and revisers; (4) editors and commentators; (5) edition titles; and (6) general index.   Z7771.A5H5

Hort, Erasmus. The Bible book: resources for reading the New Testament. N.Y., Crossroad, 1983. 209p.   **BB95**

Offers the general reader, beginner or advanced, a helpful introduction to New Testament study and understanding. In ten chapters, covering versions, commentaries, concordances, New Testament Greek, atlases, encyclopedias, etc. Lists older titles "of proven usefulness" and also "the best of what is currently available."—*Pref.* Critical annotations concerning contents, special features and level. Author index.   Z7772.L1H4

Humphrey, Hugh. A bibliography for the Gospel of Mark, 1954–1980. N.Y., E. Mellen Pr., [1981]. 163p. (Studies in the Bible and early Christianity, 1)   **BB96**

Offers a classified list of books, essays in collections and journal articles compiled from *Elenchus bibliographicus biblicus* (BB115), 1954–78, expanded by listings from *New Testament abstracts* (BB117) and the bibliographical section of *Ephemerides theologicae lovanienses* for more recent publications. 1,599 entries. Author index.   Z7772.M1H85

Hurd, John Coolidge. A bibliography of New Testament bibliographies. N.Y., Seabury, 1966. 75p.   **BB97**

Intended as an aid to historical-critical study of the New Testament. Lists bibliographies appearing in both books and periodicals, and is concerned with New Testament literature rather than editions of the New Testament. Some annotations; subject arrangement; no author index.   Z7772.L1H8

Jerusalem. École Biblique et Archéologique Française. Bibliothèque. Catalogue de la Bibliothèque. . . . Catalog of the

Library of the French Biblical and Archeological School, Jerusalem, Israel. Boston, G. K. Hall, 1975. 13v.   **BB98**

The catalog of an important collection strong in scripture studies, archaeology, papyrology, linguistics, etc. Includes both books and articles in a single alphabet of authors and subjects. Subject headings in French.   Z7770.J36

Langevin, Paul Émile. Bibliographie biblique. Biblical bibliography. Biblische Bibliographie. Bibliografia biblica. Bibliografía bíblica. 1930–1975. Québec, Presses de l'Université Laval, 1972–78. 2v.   **BB99**

v.1 gives citations to Biblical studies gleaned from 70 Roman Catholic periodicals, and a selection of Catholic books. In five main sections (Introduction to the Bible; Old Testament; New Testament; Jesus Christ; Biblical Themes) with numerous subdivisions. Author index and index of subject headings.
v.2 continues coverage of the 70 journals dealt with in v.1 for the years 1971–75 and adds indexing of 50 others for 1930–75. Includes references to some 800 books analyzed chapter by chapter. The additional titles are not limited to journals of Catholic origin.
     Z7770.L35

La Sor, William Sanford. Bibliography of the Dead Sea Scrolls, 1948–1957. Pasadena, Calif., Library, Fuller Theological Seminary, 1958. 92p. (Fuller Library Theological Seminary bibliographical ser., 2; Fuller Library bulletin 31)
     BB100

A classed bibliography of almost 3,000 entries. In three sections: General works; Texts of Qumran; Interpretation of the Qumran literature. Author index. Supplemented by Bastiaan Jongeling's *A classified bibliography of the finds in the desert of Judah* (Leiden, Brill, 1971) and by the bibliographies in each quarterly issue of *Revue de Qumran.*   Z6371.D4L3

Marrow, Stanley B. Basic tools of biblical exegesis; a student's manual. A reprint of the 1976 ed. with addenda et corrigenda. Rome, Biblical Inst. Pr., 1978. 75p. (Subsidia biblica, 2)   **BB101**

First publ. 1971 under title: *Biblical methodology, a student's manual of basic tools.*
Works are grouped as: Bibliographical sources, Texts and versions, Grammars, Lexica, Dictionaries, Concordances, Apocrypha and pseudepigrapha, Subsidiary material. 215 items; many annotations. Index.   Z7770.M3

Metzger, Bruce Manning, ed. Index to periodical literature on Christ and the Gospels. Leiden, Brill, 1966. 602p. (New Testament tools and studies, v.6)   **BB102**

Indexes pertinent articles from 160 periodicals in 16 languages, each periodical being indexed from beginning date through 1961. Classed arrangement; author index.
Another bibliography in the same series is Andrew J. Mattill and Mary B. Mattill's *A classified bibliography of literature on the Acts of the Apostles* (Leiden, Brill, 1966. 513p.).   Z7772.M1M4

───── Index of articles on the New Testament and the early church published in *Festschriften.* Philadelphia, Soc. of Biblical Literature, 1951. 182p. (Journal of Biblical literature. Monograph ser., v.5)   **BB103**

An index to some 2,350 articles to be found in 640 collections of *Festschriften* published up to the end of 1950 in various languages. From these collections only articles pertinent to the subject have been included.

───── ───── Supplement. Philadelphia, Soc., 1955. 20p.

     Z7772.L1M4

National Union Catalog, pre-1956 Imprints. Volumes 53–56. The Bible; texts and translations of the Bible and the Apocrypha and their books from The national union catalog, pre-1956 imprints. [London, Mansell, 1980] 5v.
     BB104

A reprinting, with an "index," of the Bible volumes of the *National union catalog (see* AA128), forming an important bibliography of manuscripts, "texts and translations of the Bible and its component parts."—*Introd.* About 63,000 entries representing some 700 languages. The index is an alphabet of 18,000 entries—editors, translators, titles of selections, etc.—supplying "all the non-Bible' approaches to the material . . . together with some references from variant names used in the Index itself."—*Introd.* Index references are to the main card for the work.

NUC supplements 1956–67, v.12; 1968–72, v.10; 1973–77, v.12, and subsequent annual cumulations record recently cataloged texts.
Z881.A1U5182

North, Eric McCoy. The book of a thousand tongues; being some account of the translation and publication of all or part of the Holy Scriptures into more than a thousand languages and dialects with over 1100 examples from the text. Publ. for the American Bible Society. N.Y., Harper, 1938. 386p. il. (Repr.: Detroit, Gale, 1971)   **BB105**

Descriptive notes and facsimiles of extracts from printed Bibles in more than a thousand languages. Useful for identifying Bibles in varying tongues, including many versions in English. Includes chronological lists of the languages in which the Bible has been published in whole or in part.   P352.A2N6

Pope, Hugh. English versions of the Bible. Rev. and ampl. by Sebastian Bullough. St. Louis, Herder, 1952. 787p. (Repr.: Westport, Conn., Greenwood Pr., 1972)   **BB106**

A history of both Catholic and Protestant versions, with a bibliography of books about the Bible. Bibliography, p.686–718.
BS455.P74

Rumball-Petre, Edwin A. R. America's first Bibles, with a census of 555 extant Bibles. Portland, Me., Southworth-Athoensen Pr., 1940. 184p.   **BB107**

Descriptions of America's first Bibles, with a census showing locations of copies.   Z7770.R85

———Rare Bibles: an introduction for collectors and a descriptive check list. [2d ed., rev.] N.Y., Philip Duschnes, 1954. 53p. (Repr. 1963)   **BB108**

1st ed. 1938.
An annotated bibliography of rare copies of the Bible in various languages.   Z7770.R89

San Francisco Theological Seminary, San Anselmo, Calif. Dept. of New Testament Literature. Graduate Seminar in New Testament. Bibliography of New Testament literature, 1900–1950. Prep. by the Graduate Seminar in New Testament (1952–1953), under the direction of John Wick Bowman . . . Ed. by Tadashi Akaishi. San Anselmo, San Francisco Theological Seminary, 1953. 312p.   **BB109**

A classified, annotated bibliography of nearly 2,400 books and some periodical articles in the English language.   Z7772.L1S3

Society for Old Testament Study. Eleven years of Bible bibliography; the book lists of the Society for Old Testament Study, 1946–56. Ed. by H. H. Rowley. Indian Hills, Colo., Falcon's Wing Pr., 1957. 804p.   **BB110**

Reprints of the annual classified, annotated book lists on the Old Testament and related subjects, published by the Society for Old Testament Study, with a cumulated author index. The annual lists comprise books published in various languages, with notes written by contributing scholars.
Continued by: Z7770.S6

——— A decade of Bible bibliography; the book lists of the Society for Old Testament Study, 1957–1966. G. W. Anderson, ed. Oxford, Blackwell, 1967. 706p.   **BB111**

Z7772.A1S66

——— Bible bibliography, 1967–1973, Old Testament. Ed. by Peter R. Ackroyd. Oxford, Blackwell, 1974. 505p.   **BB112**

The two items above represent compilations of book lists for the periods mentioned in the titles. They are continued by the Society's *Book list* (Durham, Eng., Soc., 1974–).   Z7772.A1S64

Stegmüller, Friedrich. Repertorium biblicum medii aevi. Madrid, Consejo Superior de Investigaciones Científicas, Inst. Francisco Suárez, 1940 [i.e., 1950]–61. 7v.   **BB113**

Contents: v.1, Initia biblica. Apocrypha. Prologi; v.2–5, Commentaria: Auctores; v.6–7, Commentaria: Anonyma (arranged alphabetically by place of publication).

v.1 contains a long treatment of apocryphal writings (p.25–250) and a list of prefaces to the Bible (p.253–306). v.2–7 list patristic and medieval commentaries on the Bible, with *incipits* and *explicits,* editions, manuscripts, and bibliography.   Z7770.S835

Wagner, Günter. An exegetical bibliography of the New Testament: Matthew and Mark. Macon, Ga., Mercer Univ. Pr., [1983]. 667p.   **BB114**

Provides references to book and periodical materials relating to New Testament studies, "ranging from Old Testament background to the theology of the Early Church."—*Pref.* Listing is by chapter and verse (with separate sections for the gospels of Matthew and Mark); citation is to specific pages within a book or article.
Z7772.M1W33

Indexes and abstract journals

Elenchus bibliographicus biblicus. v.49– , 1968– . Rome, Biblical Institute Pr., 1968– . Annual (1980 v. publ. 1983).   **BB115**

Prior to v.49, appeared as part of the journal *Biblica.*
An extensive, international bibliography; classed arrangement with author and detailed subject index. Cites book reviews.
Z7770.E63

Internationale Zeitschriftenschau für Bibelwissenschaft und Grenzgebiete; International review of Biblical studies; Revue internationale des études bibliques, 1951/52– . Stuttgart, Verlag Katholisches Bibelwerk, 1952– . Bd.1– . Annual.   **BB116**

An international bibliography and abstract journal of Biblical studies. Classed arrangement with author indexes. Most of the abstracts are in German.   Z7770.I57

New Testament abstracts. v.1– , 1956– . Cambridge, Mass., Weston School of Theology, 1956– . v.1– . 3 times a year.   **BB117**

Imprint varies.
Presents abstracts in English of articles on the New Testament which have appeared in Catholic, Protestant, and Jewish periodicals in many languages.
Each volume includes an index of Scripture texts and an index of authors, plus a separate list of book reviews.   BS410.N35

Old Testament abstracts. v.1, no.1– , Feb. 1978– . Wash., Catholic Biblical Assoc. of Amer., 1978– . 3 nos. per yr.   **BB118**

Subtitle: A thrice-yearly bibliography of literature relating to the Old Testament.
Covers (1983) about 300 journals offering annually some 900 abstracts of articles on all phases of Old Testament scholarship. Separate book review section in each issue. Annual indexes (of authors, scripture texts, and words in Hebrew and other ancient languages) in the third issue of each volume.   BS410.O42

St. John's University, Collegeville, Minn. Library index to biblical journals. 5th ed. Ed. by Thomas Peter Wahl. Collegeville, St. John's Univ. Pr., 1971. 1v. (unpaged)   **BB119**

4th ed. (1969) had title *Computer scripture bibliography.*
A computer-produced cumulated index to 22 important scripture journals, arranged in classed order, with author index. Twelve of the titles have been analyzed from first date of publication to 1970 (or last volume published); the others are indexed for varying periods.
Z7770.S33

History

Cambridge history of the Bible. Cambridge, Univ. Pr., 1963–70. 3v.   **BB120**

Contents: v.1, From the beginnings to Jerome, ed. by P. R. Ackroyd and C. F. Evans; v.2, The West, from the Fathers to the Reformation, ed. by G. W. H. Lampe; v.3, The West, from the Reformation to the present day, ed. by S. L. Greenslade.

v.3, treating the most recent period, was the first to appear. The Ackroyd-Evans volume "represents the logical extension back into the beginnings of the biblical literature and sets out to trace the essential features of the process by which the Bible as we know it came into being, and how it came to be canonised and interpreted under Judaism and in the early years of the Christian Church."—*Pref.* The Lampe volume is primarily concerned with the history of the Bible in medieval western Europe; that by Greenslade (published 1963) carries the history forward to mid-20th century, treating translations of the Bible into Western languages, and its various versions. The Greenslade volume was designated as v.3 after publication of the other volumes in 1970.

A one-volume history of English Bibles, covering translations from Anglo-Saxon times to the 1970s is F. F. Bruce's *History of the Bible in English* (3d ed., N.Y., Oxford Univ. Pr., 1978. 274p.; 1961 and 1970 eds. had title *The English Bible*).   BS445.C26

Concordances

The complete concordance to the Bible: New King James version. Nashville, Nelson, [1983]. 1083p.   **BB121**

A list of 363 words not indexed follows the preface.

BS425.C65

A concordance to the Apocrypha/Deuterocanonical books of the Revised Standard Version. Derived from the Bible Data Bank of the Centre Informatique et Bible (Abbey of Maredsous). [Grand Rapids, Mich.], Eerdmans; [London], Collins, 1983. 479p.   **BB122**

Inasmuch as the Apocrypha were omitted from the Revised Standard Version of 1952, they are not included in Ellison's concordance to the RSV (BB124). This volume includes "an entry for every word that appears in the 1977 edition of the RSV Apocrypha/Deuterocanonicals."—*Introd.*   BS1700.C66

Cruden, Alexander. Complete concordance to the Old and New Testament . . . with . . . a concordance to the Apocrypha. . . . London, Warne, [Pref. 1737]. 719p.   **BB123**

1st ed. 1737. Frequently reprinted by various publishers.
Contents: (1) Common words; (2) Proper names; (3) Apocryphal books.
A well-known older concordance, issued in many editions by various publishers. Not complete, and now superseded, as far as the canonical books are concerned, by the later concordances noted below, but still useful for its concordance to the Apocrypha. Some modern reprints omit the Apocrypha section.   BS425.C8

Ellison, John William. Nelson's Complete concordance of the Revised Standard Version Bible, comp. under the supervision of John W. Ellison. N.Y., Nelson, [1957]. 2157p.   **BB124**

Prepared with the help of a computer, the concordance is exhaustive, listing the context and location of each word, except for some 150 frequently used words which would seldom, if ever, be the keywords in a passage.
Nelson's Concise concordance (1961) lists only the principal words.   BS425.E4

Gant, William John. The Moffatt Bible concordance; a complete concordance to: The Bible, a new translation by James Moffatt. N.Y., Harper, [1950]. 550p.   **BB125**

Also published in London by Hodder and Stoughton with title *Concordance of the Bible in the Moffatt translation.*   BS425.G3

Goodrick, Edward W. and **Kohlenberger, John R.** The NIV complete concordance: the complete English concordance to the New International Version. Grand Rapids, Mich., Zondervan, [1981]. 1044p.   **BB126**

A concordance to the "New International Version" of the Bible (p.348).
". . . this is a complete, not an exhaustive, concordance. While every reference is given for every word indexed, not every NIV word is indexed. Every *key* word in the NIV is indexed, and only those that would have a very limited value in a concordance are omitted."—*Pref.*   BS425.G6

Hazard, Marshall Custiss. A complete concordance to the American Standard Version of the Holy Bible. N.Y., Nelson, [c1922]. 1234p.   **BB127**

Subtitle: Contains about 300,000 references, arranged under 16,000 headings and subheadings; includes the alternative marginal readings; gives the pronunciation and meaning of all proper names and places, with biographical and geographical information which make it serve as a Bible dictionary as well as a concordance.
BS425.H3

Joy, Charles Rhind. Harper's Topical concordance. Rev. and enl. ed. N.Y., Harper, 1962. 628p.   **BB128**

1st ed. 1940.
Some 25,000 texts arranged under more than 2,100 topics, with cross references. Designed for the person looking for texts or quotations on a given subject. Uses the King James text.
BS432.J63

Metzger, Bruce Manning and **Metzger, Isobel M.** The Oxford concise concordance to the Revised Standard Version of the Holy Bible. N.Y., Oxford Univ. Pr., 1962. 158p.   **BB129**

Prepared for the general reader; selection of words and passages was planned to include the most significant and noteworthy. Proper names are included in the main alphabet, and brief digests of biographical or geographical facts are often given.   BS425.M4

Modern concordance to the New Testament. Ed. and rev. following all current English translations of the New Testament by Michael Darton. Garden City, N.Y., Doubleday; London, Darton Longman & Todd, [1976]. 786p.   **BB130**

"Based on the French *Concordance de la Bible, Nouveau Testament* produced under the aegis of the Association de la Concordance française de la Bible."—*t.p.*
A thematic and verbal concordance in English and Greek designed to serve as a guide to the themes, subjects, and ideas of the New Testament as well as to specific words occurring therein. Its underlying purpose is to lead the student to the Greek text on which modern English translations are founded. "The presentation is by subject matter: 341 themes subdivided under their Greek roots according to sense."—*p.xii.* Headings are in English, with the Greek words given at the beginning of each subsection and with English and Greek indexes.   BS2305.M6

Morrison, Clinton. An analytical concordance to the Revised Standard Version of the New Testament. Philadelphia, Westminster Pr., [1979]. 770p. maps.   **BB131**

". . . makes accessible [by relating the English term to the Greek original] relevant material that otherwise would be unknown. The present work is an analytical concordance to the Revised Standard Version of the New Testament, second edition, which is an English translation from the original Greek."—*p.xi.* In two parts: (1) the concordance proper, arranged according to English words in alphabetical order; (2) the "index-lexicon," arranged according to transliterated Greek words in alphabetical order, and giving the English forms used to translate them in the *RSV.*   BS2305.M67

Nelson's Complete concordance of the New American Bible. Stephen J. Hartdegen, gen. ed. Nashville, Thomas Nelson, [1977]. 1274p.   **BB132**

A computer-generated verbal concordance to the text of the *New American Bible* (p.348). Employs small, but very legible type on a three-column page, with keywords set in boldface capitals to make for ease of use.   BS425.N36

New American Standard exhaustive concordance of the Bible. Hebrew-Aramaic and Greek dictionaries. Robert L. Thomas, gen. ed. Nashville, Tenn., Holman, [1981]. 1695p. **BB133**

A concordance using the text of the *New American Standard Bible* (p.347). Not only indicates the verse in which a word is to be found, but "also notes the original Hebrew, Aramaic or Greek word from which the English word was translated."—*Pref.* The latter is accomplished by keying the English words in the body of the concordance to numbered entries in the abridged dictionaries of the original languages at the back of the volume. BS425.N385

Strong, James. Exhaustive concordance of the Bible. London, Hodder; N.Y., Hunt, 1894 [c1890]. 1340p., 262p., 126p., 79p. **BB134**

Frequently reprinted (e.g., N.Y., Abingdon, 1980).

The most complete concordance, giving every word of the text of the King James Version and a comparative concordance of the Authorized and Revised versions; also includes brief dictionaries of the Hebrew and Greek words of the original, with references to the English words. 47 very common words are cited in the appendix by reference only and are not given in the main concordance. BS425.S8

Thompson, Newton Wayland and **Stock, Raymond.** Complete concordance to the Bible (Douay version). St. Louis, London, Herder, 1945. 1914p. **BB135**

First published in 1942 under title *Concordance to the Bible (Douay version).*

This edition is much enlarged, with many additional words and additional references to words included in the first edition. BS425.T45

Young, Robert. Analytical concordance to the Bible . . . about 311,000 references, subdivided under the Hebrew and Greek originals with the literal meaning and pronunciation of each . . . Also index lexicons to the Old and New Testaments . . . and a complete list of Scripture proper names. 22d American ed. rev. by W. B. Stevenson. N.Y., Funk & Wagnalls, [1955]. 1090p., 93p., 23p., 51p. **BB136**

1st ed. 1879; rev. ed., rev. by W. B. Stevenson, 1902; editions of later date (by various publishers) are reprints of this, with some slight revision, and include varying supplementary material, such as "Recent discoveries in Bible lands," by William F. Albright. BS425.Y7

❖The following concordances to the Latin, Greek, and Hebrew texts are useful in the large reference library:

The computer Bible. Editors: J. Arthur Baird [and] David Noel Freedman. [Wooster, Ohio], Biblical Research Associates, [1971]–82. v.1–5, 7–25. (In progress) **BB137**

Contents: v.1, A critical concordance to the synoptic Gospels, by J. Arthur Baird (rev.ed., 1971); v.2, An analytical linguistic concordance to the Book of Isaiah, by Jehuda Radday; v.3, The Johannine Epistles, by A. Q. Morton and S. Michaelson; v.4, An analytical linguistic key-word-in-context concordance to the Books of Haggai, Zechariah and Malachi, by Yehuda T. Radday; v.5, A critical concordance to the Gospel of John, ed. by A. Q. Morton and S. Michaelson; v.7, A critical concordance to the Acts of the Apostles, ed. by A. Q. Morton and S. Michaelson; v.8, A critical word book of Leviticus, Numbers, Deuteronomy, by Peter M. K. Morris and Edward James; v.9, A linguistic concordance of Ruth and Jonah: Hebrew vocabulary and idiom, by Francis I. Andersen and A. Dean Forbes; v. 10, Eight minor prophets: a linguistic concordance, by Francis I. Anderen and A. Dean Forbes; v.[11], An analytical linguistic key-word-in-context concordance to the Book of Judges, by Yehuda T. Radday; v.12, Syntactical and critical concordance to the Greek text of Baruch and the Epistle of Jeremiah, by R. A. Martin; v.13, A critical concordance to the Letter of Paul to the Romans, by A. Q. Morton, S. Michaelson, J. David Thompson; v.14–14A, A linguistic concordance of Jeremiah: Hebrew vocabulary and idiom; Common nouns, by Francis I. Andersen and A. Dean Forbes; v.15, Synoptic abstract, by Joseph B. Tyson and

Thomas R. W. Longstaff; v.16, An analytical linguistic key-word-in-context concordance to Esther, Ruth, Canticles, Ecclesiastes, Lamentations, by Yehuda T. Radday and G. M. Leb; v.17, A critical word book of the Pentateuch, by Peter M. K. Morris and Edward B. James; v.18, An analytical linguistic key-word-in-context concordance to the Book of Genesis, by Yehuda T. Radday; v.19, A critical concordance to I and II Corinthians, by A. Q. Morton, S. Michaelson, J. David Thompson; v.20, Linguistic density plots in Zechariah, by H. Van Dyke Parunak; v. 21, A critical concordance to the Letter of Paul to the Galatians, by A. Q. Morton, S. Michaelson, J. David Thompson; v.22, A critical concordance to the Letter of Paul to the Ephesians, by A. Q. Morton, S. Michaelson, J. David Thompson; v.23, A critical concordance to the Letter of Paul to the Philippians, by A. Q. Morton, S. Michaelson, J. David Thompson; v.24, A critical concordance to the Letter of Paul to the Colossians, by A. Q. Morton, J. Michaelson, J. David Thompson; v.25, A critical concordance to the pastoral epistles I, II Timothy, Titus, Philemon, by A. Q. Morton, S. Michaelson, J. David Thompson.

". . . a long range project consisting of a series of indexes and concordances of a new type. These will be studies of all portions of the Bible, using computers to index, arrange, and cross-correlate exhaustive masses of data for critical research. These will be done by an international team of scholars working with every type of critical discipline, and will be published as they are completed."—*Gen. Introd.* BS421.C64

Computer Konkordanz zum Novum Testamentum Graece von Nestle-Aland, 26. Auflage, und zum Greek New Testament, 3d edition, hrsg. vom Institut für Neutestamentliche Textforschung und vom Rechenzentrum der Universität Münster, unter besonderer Mitwirkung von H. Bachmann und W. A. Slaby. Berlin, W. de Gruyter, 1980. 1963, 64 cols. **BB138**

A computer-produced concordance to the two texts of the *Vollständige Konkordanz* (BB145), without citation to variants as provided in that work. An interim work covering only part of the alphabet was published 1977.

Dutripon, François Pascal. Concordantiae Bibliorum Sacrorum Vulgatae editionis ad recognitionem jussu Sixti V Pontif. Max. . . . 8e éd. Parisiis, Bloud et Barral, 1880. 1484p. **BB139**

1st ed. 1838.

An older standard concordance to the Vulgate. BS423.D8

Hatch, Edwin and **Redpath, Henry A.** A concordance to the Septuagint and the other Greek versions of the Old Testament (including the Apocryphal books). Oxford, Clarendon Pr., 1897–1906. 2v. and suppl. (Repr.: Graz, Akademische Druck- und Verlagsanstalt, 1954. 2v., with a Supplement by Henry A. Redpath. 272p.) **BB140**

BS1122.H3

Lisowsky, Gerhard. Konkordanz zum hebräischen Alten Testament, nach dem von Paul Kahle in der Biblia hebraica edidit R. Kittel, besorgten masoretischen Text unter verantwortlicher Mitwirkung von Leonhard Rost. Stuttgart, Privilegierte Württembergische Bibelanstalt, [1958]. 1672p. **BB141**

Published in 12 Lfg. 1955–57. Follows the Masoretic text.

In Hebrew, with translation of many words into German, Latin, and English. Prefatory matter in German, Latin, and English. BS1121.L55

Mandelkern, Salomon. Veteris Testamenti concordantiae hebraicae atque chaldaicae, quibus continentur cuncta quae in prioribus concordantiis reperiuntur vocabula, lacunis omnibus expletis, emendatis cuiusquemodi vitiis, locis ubique denuo excerptis atque in meliorem formam redactis, vocalibus interdum adscriptis, particulae omnes adhuc nondum collatae, pronomina omnia hic primum congesta atque enarrata, nomina propria omnia separatim commemorata, servato textu masoretico librorumque sacrorum ordine. Editio altera locupletissime aucta et emendata. Berlin, Margolin, 1937. 1532p., 16p. (Repr.: Jerusalem, Tel Aviv, Margolin; Graz, Akademische Druck- und Verlagsanstalt, 1955. 2v.)   **BB142**

1st published 1896. In Hebrew and Latin.

Added title page (1955): Concordance on the Bible. New ed., rev., corr., and completed by Chaim Mordecai Brecher, with supplementary corrections and notes by Abraham Avrunin. With an English introduction by Harry Freedman and incorporating *Otzar halexicografia haivrit* by A. R. Malachi.   BS1121.M3

Moulton, William Fiddian and **Geden, A. S.** A concordance to the Greek Testament, according to the texts of Westcott and Hort, Tischendorf and the English revisers. 5th ed., rev. by H. K. Moulton. Edinburgh, Clark, 1978. 1110p.
          BB143

1st ed. 1897.

A supplement (p.1035–1110) gives complete citations to seven words cited in previous editions only by chapter and verse. For this addition the Greek text of the United Bible Societies' 3d ed. (1975) is used. Another feature is the use of the numbers from *Strong's Exhaustive concordance* which have been placed at the head of each word.   BS2302.M8

Novae concordantiae Bibliorum sacrorum iuxta Vulgatam versionem critice editam quas digessit Bonifatius Fischer OSB. [Stuttgart-Bad Cannstatt], Frommann-Holzboog [1977]. 5v.   **BB144**

A computer-produced concordance to the *Biblia sacra iuxta Vulgatam versionem adiuvantibus Bonifatio Fischer* (Stuttgart, Württembergische Bibelanstalt, 1975. 2v.), the new text based on the important manuscripts and two modern critical editions.
          BS423.F57

Vollständige Konkordanz zum griechischen Neuen Testament; unter Zugrundelegung aller modernen kritischen Text-ausgaben und des Textus receptus in Verbindung mit H. Riesenfeld, H.-U. Rosenbaum, Chr. Hannick, neu zusammengestellt unter der Leitung von K. Aland. Berlin & N.Y., De Gruyter, 1975–83. 2v. (Arbeiten zur neutestamentlichen Textforschung, Bd.4)   **BB145**

Issued in parts.

A new concordance which takes into account modern New Testament scholarship and includes variants from all important sources.   BS2302.V64

Quotations

Bible. English. Selections. Biblical quotations. Ed. by Jennifer Speake. London, Hamlyn, 1982; N.Y., Facts on File, 1983. 203p.   **BB146**

Arranged by book of the Bible, from Genesis to Revelation, with index of key words and thematic headings. Text used is that of the Authorized Version.   BS391.2.S63

Stevenson, Burton Egbert. The home book of Bible quotations. N.Y., Harper, [1949]. 645p.   **BB147**

Quotations are arranged under subject with many cross references; there is a word concordance index to the whole. Based on the King James Version, with a few references to variations in the Revised Version. Includes the Apocrypha of both the Old and the New Testaments. Exact citation is given to book, chapter, and verse.
          BS432.S667

Dictionaries and handbooks

❖While some glossaries are included here, standard dictionaries of Hebrew, of biblical Greek, and of Latin are listed with foreign language dictionaries in section AD.

Allmen, Jean Jacques von. A companion to the Bible. N.Y., Oxford Univ. Pr., 1958. 479p.   **BB148**

A translation of the author's *Vocabulaire biblique* (2. éd. Neuchâtel, Delachaux, 1956. 318p.). Prepared as a "popular manual of Biblical theology the principal ideas of which are classified alphabet-

ically."—*Pref.* Articles are written and signed by a group of French and Swiss Protestant scholars. Scripture quotations are from the Revised Standard Version of the Bible.   BS440.A473

Armstrong, Terry A., Busby, Douglas L. and **Carr, Cyril F.** A reader's Hebrew-English lexicon of the Old Testament. Grand Rapids, Mich., Zondervan, [1980]– . v.1– . (In progress)   **BB149**

Contents: v.1, Genesis-Deuteronomy.

Lists Old Testament Hebrew terms used fifty times or less, giving English translation, frequency and page reference to the Brown, Driver and Briggs *Hebrew and English lexicon of the Old Testament* (AD436). The work is addressed to the "student and pastor . . . as a means to a more rapid reading of the Hebrew text" *(Pref.)* and is not meant as a replacement for a standard lexicon.   PJ4833.A69

The Bible almanac. Ed. by James I. Packer, Merrill C. Tenney, William White, Jr. Nashville, Thomas Nelson, [1980]. 765p. il.   **BB150**

Aims "to present in plain terms the information that is most helpful in interpreting the Bible accurately" *(Pref.)*—i.e., information on the "coinage, weights and measures, foods, means of travel, animal and vegetable life, chronology, social manners and customs, languages and literary forms, and many other aspects of human life" in biblical times. Information is presented in 46 sections, with illustrations, maps, and tables to elucidate the text. References to Scripture appear throughout; occasional bibliographic citations; index.   BS635.2.B48

Blair, Edward P. Abingdon Bible handbook. Nashville, Abingdon Pr., [1975]. 511p. il.   **BB151**

For the intelligent layman. Intended as a companion to serious Bible study, not as a commentary on each book of the Bible. In three sections: "The Bible today"; "The Bible in history" (with sections on the Old Testament, the Apocrypha, the New Testament, and the background of the Bible); and "The Bible and faith and life." Indexed.   BS475.2.B5

Botterweck, G. Johannes and **Ringgren, Helmer.** Theologisches Wörterbuch zum Alten Testament. Stuttgart, Kohlhammer, 1973–84. Bd.1–5¹/². (In progress)   **BB152**

Issued in *Lieferungen* beginning 1970; title page of Bd.1 is dated 1973. To be in about 8v.

Contents: Bd.1–5¹/², 'āb-nādah.

An English translation is appearing as: BS440.B57

—— Theological dictionary of the Old Testament. John T. Willis, translator. Grand Rapids, Mich., Wm. B. Eerdmans, [1974–80]. v.1–4. (In progress)   **BB153**

A translation of the *Theologisches Wörterbuch zum Alten Testament* (above).

Contents: v.1–4, 'abh-hms.

A presentation of "the fundamental concepts intended by the respective words and terms" *(Introd.)* of the Old Testament. Arranged alphabetically according to the Hebrew term.
          BS440.B5713

Bridges, Ronald and **Weigle, Luther A.** The Bible word book concerning obsolete or archaic words in the King James version of the Bible. N.Y., Nelson, [1960]. 422p.   **BB154**

Prepared for the general reader; has articles on 827 obsolete or archaic words used in the King James version, the meanings of which have changed. Explains the original meaning and shows what words have been used to replace them in the Revised Standard Version; with an index to the words and phrases from the Revised Version.   BS186.B7

Catholic biblical encyclopedia, by John E. Steinmueller and Kathryn Sullivan. N.Y., J. F. Wagner, [1956]. 2v. in 1. il.
          BB155

Contents: Old Testament, introd. by Athanasius Miller (1956. 1163p.); New Testament, introd. by the late James M. Vosté (c1950. 679p.).

The second part was originally published separately. Intended "for the great majority of educated people" rather than for the biblical specialist. Articles vary in length from a few lines to several pages, and include biographical, geographical, archaeological, and dogmatic subjects. Pronunciation is indicated. A special chapter on Mariology is appended to the volume. BS440.C36

Cheyne, Thomas Kelly and **Black, J. S.** Encyclopaedia biblica; a critical dictionary of the literary, political, and religious history, the archaeology, geography, and natural history of the Bible. N.Y., Macmillan, 1899–1903. 4v. il. **BB156**

Reprinted in 1v. on India paper, with rectification of some typographical errors, 1914.

Signed articles by specialists, with bibliographies. Prepared with the cooperation of many foreign scholars, primarily for the scholar and professional Bible student. Standpoint is that of advanced higher criticism. BS440.C5

Dheilly, Joseph. Dictionnaire biblique. [Tournai], Desclée, [1964]. 1260p. maps. **BB157**

Deals with biblical themes, people, and institutions, and the history and geography of biblical places, with references to archaeological research. Articles range in length from a single line to several pages. BS440.D45

Encyclopedia of biblical theology: the complete Sacramentum verbi. Ed. by Johannes B. Bauer. N.Y., Crossroad, 1981. 1141p. **BB158**

Translated from the 3d enl. and rev. ed. (1967) of Bauer's *Bibeltheologisches Wörterbuch*. Publ. 1970 as *Sacramentum verbi* and repr. 1976 as *Bauer Encyclopedia of biblical theology.*

A work of Roman Catholic biblical scholarship, representing contributions of German, Austrian, Swiss, and French scholars. BS440.B46713

Encyclopedic dictionary of the Bible, tr. by Louis F. Hartman. N.Y., McGraw-Hill, 1963. 2634col. il. **BB159**

Subtitle: A translation and adaptation of A. van den Born's *Bijbels woordenboek.* 2d rev. ed. 1954–1957.

A Catholic Bible dictionary exhibiting modern scholarship. BS440.B523

Exegetisches Wörterbuch zum Neuen Testament. Hrsg. von Horst Balz u. Gerhard Schneider. Stuttgart, Kohlhammer, 1980–83. 3v. **BB160**

Issued in parts, 1978–83.

A dictionary, by Catholic and Lutheran scholars from the German-speaking world, of the Greek vocabulary of the New Testament with German translation and exegetical articles. Signed entries; bibliographies; index of German equivalents. Less detailed than Kittel (BB169). BS2312.E9

Gehman, Henry Snyder. The new Westminster dictionary of the Bible. Philadelphia, Westminster Pr., [1970]. 1027p. il. **BB161**

A thorough reworking, in the light of new biblical scholarship and research, of the *Westminster dictionary of the Bible,* originally edited by John D. Davis and later revised and rewritten by Gehman (Philadelphia, Westminster Pr., 1944). BS440.G4

Hastings, James. Dictionary of the Bible, dealing with its language, literature and contents, including the biblical theology. Edinburgh, Clark; N.Y., Scribner, 1898–1904. 5v. il. **BB162**

v.5 is an "extra" volume, containing indexes, maps, and some articles not alphabetically arranged.

A standard older work with signed articles and bibliographies. From a less advanced point of view than Cheyne (BB156), and intended for use by the general reader as well as by the Bible student.

—— Dictionary of the Bible. Rev. ed. by Frederick C. Grant and H. H. Rowley. N.Y., Scribner, [1963]. 1059p. il. **BB163**

1st ed. 1909. Frequently reprinted. An independent work, not a condensation of Hastings's larger work above.

This edition has been thoroughly revised in the light of modern discoveries and scholarship. References are to the Revised Standard Version of the Bible with cross references from the Authorized Version and the Revised Version. BS440.H5

—— Dictionary of Christ and the Gospels. N.Y., Scribner; Edinburgh, Clark, 1906–08. 2v. il. **BB164**

Complementary to Hastings's *Dictionary of the Bible* (BB162). Purpose is to give an account of (1) everything relating to the person, life, work, and teaching of Christ, whether found in the Gospels or elsewhere, and (2) everything contained in the Gospels. Planned especially for preachers; most of the articles are written by men who were or had been preachers. Signed articles; bibliographies. BS440.H3

—— Dictionary of the Apostolic church. N.Y., Scribner; Edinburgh, Clark, 1916–22. 2v. **BB165**

A continuation of the above, doing for the rest of the New Testament what that work did for the Gospels.

The two items above have been reprinted as *Dictionary of the New Testament* (Grand Rapids, Baker Book House, 1973. 4v.). BS440.H4

The international standard Bible encyclopedia. Geoffrey W. Bromiley, gen. ed. Rev. ed. Grand Rapids, Mich., Eerdmans, [1979–82]. v.1–2. (In progress) **BB166**

Contents: v.1–2, A–J.

1st ed. 1915; rev. 1930.

"Although some of the most durable of the original material" has been retained, this new edition, thoroughly updated in "both matter and format" is "to all intents and purposes a new, or at least a completely reconstructed encyclopedia."—*Pref.* Addressed to teachers, students, pastors, and the interested layperson; contains an alphabetical arrangement of articles which define, identify, and explain terms and topics in the Bible and biblical studies. Included are all personal and geographical names in the Bible, together with entries for subjects that bear on transmission of texts, interpretation, biblical theology, etc. "Great care has been taken to maintain what the preface of the first edition described as the attitude of 'a reasonable conservatism'." Entries range in length from a line or two to several pages; all except the shortest are signed, and most have bibliographies. BS440.I6

The interpreter's dictionary of the Bible; an illustrated encyclopedia identifying and explaining all proper names and significant terms and subjects in the Holy Scriptures, including the Apocrypha, with attention to archaeological discoveries and researches into the life and faith of ancient times. N.Y., Abingdon, [1962]. 4v. il. **BB167**

George Arthur Buttrick, ed.

A scholarly encyclopedic dictionary designed for the preacher, scholar, student, teacher, and general reader, based on recent discoveries and referring to both the King James Version and the Revised Standard Version, to the Apocrypha, the Pseudepigrapha, the Dead Sea Scrolls, and other ancient manuscripts. Articles have been contributed by scholars from many countries, are signed, and usually include bibliographies. The illustrations, both in color and in black-and-white, are good and pertinent, and there is a section of colored maps, as well as outline maps inserted in the text. Indispensable for modern biblical study.

—— Supplementary volume. Keith Crim, gen. ed. Nashville, Abingdon, [1976]. 998p.

Updates articles in the 1962 publication and adds new articles on topics not previously treated. Provides cross references to earlier articles where appropriate. BS440.I63

Jenni, Ernst. Theologisches Handwörterbuch zum Alten Testament . . . unter Mitarbeit von Claus Westermann. München, C. Kaiser, 1971–76. 2v. **BB168**

Treats theologically relevant words of the Old Testament, with regard to history, meaning, and use. Signed entries with many bibliographic references, as well as the biblical citations. Hebrew, Aramaic, German word indexes, and name index in v.2.

BS440.J43

Kittel, Gerhard, ed. Theological dictionary of the New Testament. Tr. and ed. by Geoffrey W. Bromiley. Grand Rapids, Mich., Eerdmans, [1964–76]. 10v. **BB169**

v.5–9, ed. by Gerhard Friedrich; v.10 by R. E. Pitkin.

Translated from *Theologisches Wörterbuch zum Neuen Testament* (Stuttgart, 1932–72. 9v.).

A scholarly work of great importance, treating every word of religious or theological significance in the New Testament. The work of many German Bible scholars. Signed contributions. v.10 contains indexes of English keywords, Greek keywords, and biblical references. Also includes a list of contributors with their contributions and an essay on biblical scholarship, "Pre-history of the *Theological dictionary of the New Testament.*" PA881.K513

Léon-Dufour, Xavier, ed. Dictionary of biblical theology . . . tr. under the direction of P. Joseph Cahill. 2d ed. rev. and enl. Revisions and new articles tr. by E. M. Stewart. N.Y., Seabury Pr., [1973]. 711p. **BB170**

Translation of *Vocabulaire de théologie biblique* (1st ed. 1962; 2d ed. 1970); 1st ed. in English translation, 1967.

Major theological themes of the Bible are presented in signed articles contributed by outstanding biblical scholars and exegetes. In the new edition some 40 articles have been added, and there are additional cross references. Intended for the laity as well as for the clergy. BS543.A1L413

—— Dictionary of the New Testament. Tr. from 2d French ed. by Terrence Prendergast. N.Y., Harper & Row, [1980]. 458p. il., maps. **BB171**

An alphabetical arrangement of more than 1,000 entries of theological, historical, literary significance. Explanations include original Greek term (often with its Hebrew antecedent) and citations to scriptural use. Many cross references. A lengthy introduction supplies the context of the New Testament, covering the land and its people, culture, politics and law, domestic life, the faith of Israel, the Scriptures, worship and morality. BS2312.L4513

McKenzie, John L. Dictionary of the Bible. Milwaukee, Bruce, [1965]. 954p. il. **BB172**

The work of a Jesuit priest; intended for the general reader. Mainly brief entries, although some articles run to several pages. Etymology of many terms is indicated. General bibliography, but none for individual articles. BS440.M36

Miller, Madeleine Sweeny and **Miller, J. Lane.** Harper's Bible dictionary. Rev. by eminent authorities. [8th ed.] N.Y., Harper & Row, [1973]. 853p. il. **BB173**

1st ed. 1952.

An encyclopedic dictionary which treats the archaeology, geography and chronology of the Bible, including names of persons and places, ideas, books of the Bible, phrases, objects, etc. Pronunciation is often indicated. This edition thoroughly revised in the light of new archaeological and biblical research. Photographs, line drawings, and maps are used as illustrations. BS440.M52

New Bible dictionary. 2d ed. Organizing ed., J. D. Douglas; revision ed., N. Hillyer. Leicester, Eng., Inter-Varsity Pr.; Wheaton, Ill., Tyndale House, [1982]. 1326p. il., maps. **BB174**

1st ed. 1962.

A complete revision of a now standard work. Offers signed articles by contributing scholars (predominantly British and Commonwealth); some brief bibliographies. Bible references are to the Revised Standard Version. The text is that of the same publisher's *Illustrated Bible dictionary* (1980. 3v.); maps and illustrations are drawn from that edition. Indexed.

The new international dictionary of New Testament theology. [German text] Lothar Coenen, Erich Beyreuther and Hans Bietenhard, eds.; trans., with additions and revisions, from the German . . . , ed. by Colin Brown. Exeter, Paternoster Pr., 1975–[82]. 3v. and Addenda. **BB175**

A translation, with additions and revisions, of *Theologisches Begriffslexikon zum Neuen Testament* (Wuppertal, Brockhaus, 1970–71. 3v.).

Treats New Testament terminology of theological importance. Material from the original is rearranged in this translation so as to group related New Testament Greek terms under concepts arranged alphabetically by English word. Greek terms are treated in their classical, Old Testament and New Testament meanings. Each volume indexed. v.3 includes indexes (of Hebrew and Aramaic words, of Greek words; of subjects) to all 3v. The Addenda (1982. 20p.) updates the bibliographies of the set.

Intended as a companion volume to *The new international dictionary of the Christian church* (BB240). BS2397.N48

Odelain, O. and **Séguineau, R.** Dictionary of proper names and places in the Bible. Tr. and adapted by Matthew J. O'Connell. Garden City, N.Y., Doubleday, 1981. 479p. maps. **BB176**

Translated and adapted from *Dictionnaire des noms propres de la Bible* (Paris, Cerf et Desclée de Brouwer, 1978).

Intended as a companion to the *Jerusalem Bible* (p.348). Identifies all proper names and places in both the Old and New Testaments, with reference to Bible chapter and verse. BS435.O3313

Osterloh, Edo and **Engelland, Hans.** Biblisch-theologisches Handwörterbuch zur Lutherbibel und zu neueren Übersetzungen. Mit einem Querregister. 2. durchg. und erg. Aufl. Göttingen, Vandenhoeck & Ruprecht, 1959. 752p. **BB177**

1st ed. published in parts 1950–54.

More than 30 persons from all branches of the Evangelical church in Germany collaborated in the compilation of this dictionary, based on the terminology of the Luther Bible. Many cross references are given from terms used in other German Bibles, and there is also a cross index of words from *Das Neue Testament deutsch,* the *Menge-Bibel,* and the *Zürcher-Bibel.* Exact references are given for Bible citations, but there is little bibliography.

A "3. Aufl." (Göttingen, Vandenhoeck & Ruprecht, 1964 [c1954]. 752p.) was not available for examination. BS440.O8

Reicke, Bo Ivar and **Rost, Leonhard.** Biblisch-historisches Handwörterbuch; Landeskunde, Geschichte, Religion, Kultur, Literatur. Göttingen, Vandenhoeck & Ruprecht, [1962–79]. 4v. il. maps. **BB178**

A scholarly encyclopedia with signed articles and bibliographies. Emphasis is on understanding biblical and related terms, including personal and place-names in their historical context and in the light of recent scholarship and archaeological research. Plates, line drawings, and maps illustrate the text. Register und Historisch-archäologische Karte Palästinas in v.4. BS440.R44

Richardson, Alan. A theological word book of the Bible. London, SCM Pr., 1950; N.Y., Macmillan, [1951]. 290p. (Repr. 1962) **BB179**

Aims "to elucidate the distinctive meanings of the keywords of the Bible" (*Pref.*) from the theological point of view. Articles are written by specialists, mainly British, and are signed. BS440.R53

Soulen, Richard N. Handbook of biblical criticism. 2d ed. (rev. and augm.). Atlanta, John Knox Pr., [1981]. 239p. **BB180**

1st ed. 1976.

For the beginning student and non-specialist. Described as a "pocket reference . . . to be used whenever a name, a term, or an abbreviation is met for the first time unidentified, unexplained, or without a clarifying illustration; or, when its meaning is simply forgotten."—*Introd.* Includes entries for methodologies, technical terms and phrases, research tools and texts, names (chiefly deceased biblical scholars), theological terms, and abbreviations.

BS511.2.S68

Theological wordbook of the Old Testament. R. Laird Harris, ed. Chicago, Moody Pr., [1980]. 2v. **BB181**

A work for the "busy pastor or earnest Christian worker who has neither the time nor background for detailed technical study" (*Introd.*) but who needs "a tool for the study of the significant words of the Hebrew Bible." Essays on the words selected for extensive treatment were contributed by 46 scholars of various denominations and are signed with the contributors' initials. Vocables not chosen for essay treatment are given one-line definitions. Arrangement is according to the consonants of the Hebrew alphabet; related words are presented with the root from which they derive. Bibliographies accompany many of the articles. BS440.T49

Turner, Nicholas. Handbook for biblical studies. Philadelphia, Westminster; Oxford, Blackwell, [1982]. 145p. **BB182**

Offers a glossary of technical terms peculiar to biblical studies (including foreign words usually left untranslated), brief summaries of the books of the Bible, sources, authors, and manuscripts commonly referred to in biblical scholarship. Aims to enable the reader "to become sufficiently familiar with the terminology of scholarly argument to learn from it and to participate in it."—*Final word.* Tables of chronologies, alphabets, and a "Theological who's who" of the Fathers and modern scholars. BS417.T78

Vigouroux, Fulcran Grégoire and **Pirot, Louis.** Dictionnaire de la Bible, contenant tous les noms de personnes, de lieux, de plantes, d'animaux mentionnés dans les Saintes Écritures, les questions théologiques, archéologiques, scientifiques relatives à l'Ancien et au Nouveau Testament et des notices sur les commentateurs anciens et modernes. Paris, Letouzey, 1907–83. 5v. and suppl. v.1–10⁴ (fasc.1–57). il. (In progress) **BB183**

Contents: v.1–5, A–Z (publ. 1907–12); Supplément, ed. by Louis Pirot [and others], v.1–10⁴ (fasc.1–57), A–Routes.

The standard Bible dictionary from the French Catholic point of view, containing long, signed articles by Catholic scholars, good bibliographies, and excellent illustrations. Differs from Hastings' *Dictionary of the Bible* (BB162) and Cheyne's *Encyclopaedia biblica* (BB156) on several points, notably in the inclusion of separate biographical articles, with bibliographies, on the various commentators on the Bible, ancient, modern, Catholic, Protestant, and Jewish. BS440.V7

The Wycliffe Bible encyclopedia. Charles F. Pfeiffer, Howard F. Vos and John Rea, eds. Chicago, Moody Pr., [1975]. 2v. (1851p.) il. **BB184**

The work is comprehensive in its coverage, including every personal and place name mentioned in the Bible, important doctrines, and theological terms. "Doctrinal articles . . . adhere to Christian orthodoxy, the fundamentals of the faith generally accepted by believers of conservative, evangelical persuasion."—*Pref.* BS440.W92

Ziefle, Helmut W. Dictionary of modern theological German. Grand Rapids, Mich., Baker Book House, [1982]. 199p. **BB185**

Offered as an aid in the study of theological German. A basic theological vocabulary of about 10,000 German entries with English equivalents "for reading the Bible and German theological texts."—*Pref.* Includes Scripture references to Luther's translation of the Bible. BR95.Z53

❖There are available a number of smaller dictionaries, generally popular in tone, concerning specific aspects of the Bible. Among these are: *Who's who in the Bible* (N.Y., Bonanza, 1980. 448p., 448p.), originally published in 2v.: *Who's who in the Old Testament* by Joan Comay (1971) and *Who's who in the New Testament* by Robert Brownrigg (1971); *All of the women of the Bible* by Edith Deen (N.Y., Harper, 1955. 410p.); *Encyclopedia of Bible creatures* by Vilhelm Møller-Christensen and Karl Eduard Jordt Jørgensen, tr. from the Danish by Arne Unhjem (Philadelphia, Fortress Pr., 1965. 302p.); *Plants of the Bible* by Michael Zohary (Cambridge, Cambridge Univ. Pr., 1982. 223p.), which identifies and describes biblical plants and includes

excellent illustrations; and an "All series" by Herbert Lockyer which includes among its dozen or more titles *All the men of the Bible* (Grand Rapids, Mich., Zondervan, 1958. 381p.) and *All the trades and occupations of the Bible* (Grand Rapids, Mich., Zondervan, 1969. 327p.).

Archaeological handbooks

Corswant, Willy. Dictionnaire d'archéologie biblique. Revu et illustré par Édouard Urech. Neuchâtel, Paris, Delachaux et Niestlé, [1956]. 324p. il. **BB186**

Planned especially as an aid to teachers of the Bible; is concerned with the private, civil, and religious life of the Jews and early Christians, and with the flora, fauna, and minerals of Israel. Written in nontechnical language, illustrated with line drawings. At the end of each article, references are given to the biblical texts.

An English translation was published as *A dictionary of life in Bible times* (N.Y., Oxford Univ. Pr., 1960. 308p.).

Encyclopedia of archaeological excavations in the Holy Land. Ed., English ed., Michael Avi-Yonah. Englewood Cliffs, N.J., Prentice-Hall, 1975–78; London, Oxford Univ. Pr., 1976–78. 4v. il., maps, tables. **BB187**

A revised translation of *Entsiklopedyah la-ḥafirot arke'ologiyot be-Erets Yisrael.*

The Hebrew edition (Jerusalem, 1970. 2v.) is updated to the end of 1971. Presents a comprehensive summary of excavated sites in Palestinian archaeology. Selected bibliography at the end of each entry. v.4 includes indexes of names and of places. DS111.A2E5

Negev, Avraham, ed. Archaeological encyclopedia of the Holy Land. N.Y., Putnam's, [1972]. 354p. il. (Repr.: Englewood, SBS Pub., 1980) **BB188**

Brief articles concerned chiefly with "the geographical names mentioned in the Bible, both places in the Holy Land and countries and cities in other parts of the Middle East, identifying them as far as possible, describing the excavations that have been carried out at or near them, and analysing the importance of the finds they have yielded."—*Pref.* Includes entries on artifacts, ancient customs, etc. References to specific Bible passages and to early writers such as Josephus and Strabo are made, but there is no bibliography of modern sources. DS111.A2N38

The new international dictionary of biblical archaeology. Edward M. Blaiklock, R. K. Harrison, gen. eds. Grand Rapids, Mich., Regency Reference Lib., Zondervan, [1983]. 485p. il., maps. **BB189**

Offers entries for personal and place names, deities, terms, texts, etc., important in biblical archaeology. Except for some brief definitions, all articles are signed with the initials of the contributors; bibliographic references follow most articles; numerous cross references. A section of 33 colored maps (on unnumbered pages) has its own index. Intended for a broad readership: "Our object has not been primarily polemical or evidential. We have sought, within prescribed limits, to present basic facts. Those who use the book must, for the most part, draw their own theological conclusions."—*Pref.* BS622.N48

Pfeiffer, Charles F., ed. The Biblical world; a dictionary of Biblical archaeology. Grand Rapids, Mich., Baker Book House, [1966]. 612p. il. **BB190**

Articles on biblical topics as related to archaeological studies and research. More than 40 contributors are listed, but articles are unsigned. Bibliographies accompany many entries. BS622.P4

Commentaries

Anchor Bible. Garden City, N.Y., Doubleday, 1964– . v.1– . (In progress) **BB191**

Contents: v.1, Genesis (1964); v.6, Joshua (1982); [v.6a] Judges (1975); v.7, Ruth (1975); [v.7a] Lamentations (1972); [v.7b] Esther (1971); [v.7c] Song of Songs (1977); v.8, I Samuel (1980); v.9, II Samuel (1984); [v.12] I Chronicles (1965); [v.13] II Chronicles (1965); [v.14] Ezra. Nehemiah (1965); [v.15] Job (1965); [v.16] Psalms I (1–50) (1966); [v.17] Psalms II (51–100) (1968); [v.17a] Psalms III (101–150) (1970); [v.18] Proverbs. Ecclesiastes (1965); v.20, Second Isaiah (1968); [v.21] Jeremiah (1965); v.22, Ezekiel 1–20 (1983); v.23, Daniel (1978); v.24, Hosea (1980); [v.26] Matthew (1971); v.28, Luke (I–IX) (1981); [v.29] The Gospel according to John (I–XII) (1966); [v.29a] The Gospel according to John (XIII–XXI) (1970); v.30, The Epistles of John (1982); [v.31] Acts of the Apostles (1967); [v.32] I Corinthians (1976); [v.34] Ephesians, 1–3 (1974); [v.34a] Ephesians, 4–6 (1974); [v.36] To the Hebrews (1972); [v.37] Epistles of James, Peter and Jude (1964); [v.38] Revelation (1975); [v.41] I Maccabees (1976); v.41a, II Maccabees (1983); [v.42] I and II Esdras (1974); v.43, Wisdom of Solomon (1979); [v.44] Daniel, Esther and Jeremiah: the additions (1977).

A project of Protestant, Catholic, and Jewish scholars. Offers new translations of the books of the Bible with extensive commentary.

BS1922.A1 1964.G3

Black, Matthew, ed. Peake's Commentary on the Bible. Old Testament ed., H. H. Rowley. London, N.Y., Nelson, 1962. 1126p. maps.   **BB192**

1st ed. by Arthur Samuel Peake, 1919; Supplement, 1936.

This edition is brought up-to-date in the light of modern discoveries and scholarship and is based on the Revised Standard Version. Contributions are by specialists from the British Commonwealth and the United States.   BS491.B57

The Broadman Bible commentary. Gen. ed. Clifton J. Allen. Nashville, Broadman Pr., [1969–72]. 12v.   **BB193**

v.1 revised 1973.

A new and up-to-date commentary using the text of the Revised Standard Version. The work of an international group of Baptist scholars.   BS491.2.B67

Brown, Raymond Edward, Fitzmyer, Joseph A. and **Murphy, Roland Edmund,** comps. The Jerome biblical commentary. Englewood Cliffs, N.J., Prentice-Hall, [1968]. 2v. in 1. (637p., 889p.) il.   **BB194**

Contents: v.1, The Old Testament, ed. by R. E. Murphy; v.2, The New Testament and topical articles, ed. by J. A. Fitzmyer and R. E. Brown.

An important work offering "a compact commentary on the whole Bible written by Roman Catholic scholars."—*Editor's pref.* Includes bibliographies, many cross references, and a general index.

BS491.2.B7

Guthrie, Donald and **Motyer, J. A.** eds. The new Bible commentary, revised. [3d ed., completely rev. and reset] Grand Rapids, Mich., Eerdmans, [1970]. 1310p.   **BB195**

1st ed. 1953, ed. by Francis Davidson.

Based on the text of the Revised Standard Version. This revision includes five new general articles as well as a number of new commentaries on the individual books of the Bible.   BS491.2.G8

Harvey, Anthony Ernest. The new English Bible: companion to the New Testament. [Cambridge, Eng.], Cambridge Univ. Pr., Oxford Univ. Pr., 1970. 850p.   **BB196**

Designed to be read, section by section, along with the New Testament itself (following the text of the 2d ed. of the New English Bible). The work is "concerned with questions which anyone may be expected to ask who approaches the New Testament in general . . . without any previous introduction."—*Pref.* Indexed.

BS2341.2.H37

International critical commentary on the Holy Scriptures, under the editorship of the Rev. Samuel Rolles Driver, the Rev. Alfred Plummer and the Rev. Charles Augustus Briggs. Edinburgh, Clark; N.Y., Scribner, 1896–1937. v.1–45.   **BB197**

Various reprintings.

Commentaries on individual books of the Bible, each by an authority.

Interpreter's Bible: The Holy Scriptures in the King James and Revised Standard versions with general articles and introduction, exegesis, exposition for each book of the Bible. N.Y., Nashville, Abingdon, [1951–57]. 12v.   **BB198**

A guide and commentary to the Bible by some 125 scholars, prepared for the general reader, the teacher, and the preacher. Includes long introductions with bibliographies to the whole Bible, to each Testament, and to each book. Each is written and signed by an individual scholar. Includes the text of both versions, exegesis and exposition.   BS491.2.I55

Interpreter's one-volume commentary on the Bible; introd. and commentary for each book of the Bible including the Apocrypha, with general articles. Ed. by Charles M. Laymon. Nashville, Abingdon Pr., [1971]. 1386p. il., maps.   **BB199**

Includes contributions by American, British and Canadian scholars. Intended for "ministers, lay and nonprofessional persons engaged in studying or teaching in the church school, college students, and those who are unequipped to follow the more specialized discussions of biblical matters, but who desire a thoroughly valid and perceptive guide in interpreting the Bible."—*Pref.* General articles include the geographical and historical setting, the languages of the Bible, measures and money, and a chronology. Subject index.

BS491.2.I57

The layman's Bible commentaries. London, SCM Pr., [1960–65]. 25v.   **BB200**

Imprint varies.

Prepared by Protestant scholars; presents clearly written commentaries for the layman on each book of the Bible.

Moffatt New Testament commentary, based on the new translation by James Moffatt. N.Y., Harper, 1927–50. 17v.   **BB201**

Various reprintings.

Scholarly commentaries, in readable style, on each book of the New Testament. Each includes the Moffatt text.

Neil, William. Harper's Bible commentary. N.Y., Harper & Row, [1962]. 544p. (Repr.: 1975)   **BB202**

A companion work to *Harper's Bible dictionary* (BB173). Designed to be read with either the Revised Standard Version or the King James Version. An excellent concise commentary, first published in England with title *One volume Bible commentary* (London, Hodder, 1962).   BS491.2.N4

A new Catholic commentary on Holy Scripture. Reginald Cuthbert Fuller, gen. ed. [Rev. ed.] [London], Nelson, [1969]. 1377p.   **BB203**

Serves as a new and updated edition of the *Catholic commentary* edited by Bernard Orchard (London, Nelson, 1953). This is a thorough revision, with only about a fifth of the material from the earlier volume being retained. Bibliographies include citations as late as 1968. Numbering of chapters and verses now follows that of the Revised Standard Version. Includes general introductory articles to the whole work, to the Old Testament, and to the New Testament, each signed by a scholar; the commentaries are also signed.

BS491.2.N48

The new layman's Bible commentary in one volume. Eds., G. C. D. Howley, F. F. Bruce, H. L. Ellison. Grand Rapids, Mich., Zondervan, [1979]. 1712p.   **BB204**

Publ. in England as *The Bible commentary for today* (London, Pickering & Inglis, 1979. 1712p.).

The New Testament section (p.[1059]–1712) was first published as *A New Testament commentary* (London, Pickering & Inglis, 1969). References in the Old Testament section of the 1979 1-volume edition to *A New Testament commentary* refer to the 1969 edition; the number 1046 must therefore be added to the page number to obtain the relevant page in the 1-volume edition.

Based on the Revised Standard Version of the Bible. Intended "to appeal to the non-expert in theology as well as those with a fuller training and insight in that field of study."—*Pref.*   BS491.2.N49

Hebrew interpretation

Bible. O.T. Pentateuch. The Pentateuch and Haftorahs; Hebrew text, English translation and commentary. Ed. by J. H. Hertz. 2d ed. London, Soncino Pr., 1960. 1067p.   **BB205**

1st ed. 1929–36; frequently reprinted.
Added title page in Hebrew.
Presents the Hebrew text with the Jewish Publication Society's English translation; commentary aims for "exposition . . . of the 'plain sense' of the Sacred Text; and . . . of its religious message as affecting everyday problems of human existence."—*Pref.*

Encyclopaedia biblica [Entsiklopediyah mikra'it]; thesaurus rerum biblicarum alphabetico ordine. Digestus . . . Hierosolymis, Sumptibus Inst. Bialik, [1950–82]. 8v. il.   **BB206**

The product of modern Hebrew scholarship, published under the auspices of the Jewish Agency of Palestine and the Museum of Jewish Antiquities of the Hebrew University in Jerusalem. The contributors are, for the most part, Israeli scholars and are authorities in their fields. The articles, written entirely in modern literary Hebrew, are signed with initials, and usually are accompanied by bibliographies which list books both in Hebrew and in western European languages.   BS440.E5

Kasher, Menachem Mendel. Encyclopedia of Biblical interpretation, a millenial anthology. Tr. under the editorship of Rabbi Dr. Harry Freedman. N.Y., Amer. Biblical Encyclopedia Soc., [1953–79]. v.1–9. (In progress)   **BB207**

Contents: v.1–6, Genesis; v.7–9, Exodus, 1–20:23.
A monumental collection of Jewish interpretations of the Bible, based on the author's *Humash Torah Shelemath,* giving the text of the Pentateuch and an anthology of passages drawn from the Talmudic-Midrashic literature pertaining to each verse of the Bible, with indication of sources, and a commentary containing exegetical passages from ancient and modern sources with notes, bibliographies and subject indexes.   BS1225.K363

Plaut, W. Gunther. The Torah: a modern commentary. N.Y., Union of American Hebrew Congregations, [1981]. 1787p.   **BB208**

Contents: Commentaries on Genesis, Exodus, Numbers, Deuteronomy, by W. G. Plaut; commentary on Leviticus, by B. J. Bamberger; essays on Near Eastern literature (preceding each commentary), by W. W. Hallo. Also includes original Hebrew text and the Jewish Publication Society's English translation of the Pentateuch and of the Haftaroth.
A modern commentary reflecting the liberal point of view.   BS1225.3.P55

Atlases

Aharoni, Yohanan and **Avi-Yonah, Michael.** The Macmillan Bible atlas. Rev. ed. N.Y., Macmillan; London, Collier-Macmillan. [1977]. 184p. il. maps. 30cm.   **BB209**

264 maps of various sizes, with explanatory text. Aims "to show, as far as possible through maps of each event, the changes and historical processes in the lands of the Bible."—*Pref.* This edition incorporates recent archaeological information, especially on Jerusalem. Indexed.   G2230.A2

Grollenberg, Luc H. Atlas of the Bible. Tr. and ed. by Joyce M. H. Reid and H. H. Rowley. [London], N.Y., Nelson, 1956. 165p. il., maps. 36cm.   **BB210**

A translation of the 2d Dutch edition, *Atlas van de Bijbel* (Amsterdam, Elsevier, 1954), published with Catholic imprimatur. A scholarly work, with a wealth of illustrations and a text summarizing biblical history, geography, and archaeology, including a discus-

sion of the Dead Sea Scrolls. 35 maps, well conceived and executed. A gazetteer index contains the names of geographical features, towns, and peoples, and the names of individuals who played especially important roles in biblical history.   BS620.G752

Kraeling, Emil Gottlieb Heinrich. Rand McNally Bible atlas. [2d ed.] Chicago, Rand McNally, [1962]. 487p. il., maps. 27cm.   **BB211**

1st ed. 1956. 487p.
For the general reader. The extensive text is primarily a historical discussion of geographical references in the Bible, told in the sequence of the books of the Bible with archaeological and historical background. Many illustrations in black-and-white and a section of 22 maps in the center of the volume, with a geographical index to the place-names appearing on the maps and in the text.   BS630.K7

—— Rand McNally historical atlas of the Holy Land. Chicago, 1959. 88p. il., maps. 26cm.   **BB212**

An abridged version of the 1956 ed. of the above.   G2230.K72

Oxford Bible atlas. Ed. by Herbert G. May, with the assistance of G. N. S. Hunt. 3d ed. rev. by John Day. N.Y., Oxford Univ. Pr., 1984. 144p. il. 26cm.   **BB213**

1st ed. 1962.
A well-illustrated work with attractive maps, textual explanations, etc. Text is not so extensive as in the Rand McNally, Westminster, or Grollenberg atlases, but it is a useful, inexpensive atlas. This edition revised to incorporate new biblical research and recent archaeological data.   BS630.O96

Smith, George Adam. Atlas of the historical geography of the Holy Land. London, Hodder, 1915. 60p., 12p. 57 col. maps. 38cm.   **BB214**

A standard, older atlas, still useful for its excellent maps although not abreast of modern scholarship.

Wright, George Ernest and **Filson, Floyd Vivian.** The Westminster historical atlas to the Bible. Rev. ed. Philadelphia, Westminster, [1956]. 130p. il., maps. 37cm.   **BB215**

1st ed. 1945.
A scholarly atlas, with much archaeological information (though now somewhat out-of-date), historical discussion, and illustrations. The maps are clear and well drawn. Three indexes: (1) to the text; (2) to the maps, including a topographical concordance to the Bible; and (3) to Arabic names identified with biblical places in Syria and Palestine.   BS630.W7

Koran

Koran; tr. from the Arabic by J. M. Rodwell. 2d rev. and amended ed. London, Quaritch, 1876. 562p.   **BB216**

Frequently reprinted in Everyman's library, with introd. by G. Margoliouth (London, Dent; N.Y., Dutton, 1953. 506p.).   BP109.R

Koran. The Koran interpreted, by Arthur J. Arberry. London, Allen & Unwin; N.Y., Macmillan, [1955]. 2v.   **BB217**

Frequently reprinted, e.g., Oxford, 1964.
Contents: v.1, Suras I–XX; v.2, Suras XXI–CXIV.
A translation which seeks "to imitate, however imperfectly, those rhetorical and rhythmical patterns which are the glory and the sublimity of the Koran."—*Pref.*   BP109.A7

Kassis, Hanna E. A concordance of the Qur'an. Berkeley, Univ. of Calif. Pr., [1983]. 1444p.   **BB218**

Utilizes the English text of A. J. Arberry's *The Koran interpreted* (Oxford, 1964). Arranged alphabetically by transliterated form of the Arabic term, with indexes of English words.   BP133.K37

CHRISTIANITY

General works

Bibliography

Bollier, John A. The literature of theology: a guide for students and pastors. Philadelphia, Westminster Pr., [1979]. 208p. **BB219**

Intended "to help the reader become independent in finding the books, the journal articles, or the information needed in the pursuit of either academic study or professional ministry."—*Pref.* Concentrates on reference works—bibliographies, encyclopedias, dictionaries, indexes, abstracts, handbooks, guides, manuals, commentaries, etc.—with considerable attention given to English-language Bible versions. 543 entries, topically arranged, with descriptive and evaluative annotations. Author/title index.   Z7751.B67

Burr, Nelson Rollin. A critical bibliography of religion in America. Princeton, N.J., Princeton Univ. Pr., 1961. 2v. (Princeton studies in American civilization, no.5) **BB220**

The final volume (bound in 2v.) of a series of 4v., *Religion in American life*, by James Ward Smith and A. Leland Jamison. A very comprehensive bibliography in classified arrangement with running commentary. Main divisions: pt.1, Bibliographical guides, general surveys and histories; pt.2, Evolution of American religion; pt.3, Religion and society; pt.4, Religion in the arts and literature; pt.5, Intellectual history, theology, philosophy, and science. Tables of contents, and an author index, but no subject index.

The author's *Religion in American life* (N.Y., Appleton-Century-Crofts, 1971. 171p.) is a selective bibliography intended "for graduate and advanced undergraduate students" *(Pref.)* of American civilization. Emphasis is on 20th century research and on the sociology of religion.

Eisen, Sydney and **Lightman, Bernard V.** Victorian science and religion: a bibliography with emphasis on evolution, belief, and unbelief, comprised of works published from c.1900–1975. [Hamden, Conn.], Archon Books, 1984. 696p. **BB221**

Lists in classified arrangement 6,267 books, articles and dissertations "dealing with ideas and institutions in Victorian science and religion" and concentrates "on the period from about 1830 to 1900."—*Introd.* In three parts: (A) Main currents; (B) Natural theology, geology and evolution; (C) Religion—ideas and institutions. Many subdivisions for leading Victorian philosophers, theologians and scientists. Author and subject indexes. A supplement of more recent materials is planned.   Z5320.E57

Kepple, Robert J. Reference works for theological research: an annotated selective bibliographical guide. 2d ed. Wash., D.C., University Pr. of America, [1981]. 283p.   **BB222**

1st ed. 1978.

A guide for the student, teacher, and librarian. Works are grouped by type; annotations indicate coverage, arrangement, special features, etc. In view of the existence of James McCabe's *Critical guide to Catholic reference books* (BB418), "works about the Roman Catholic church or produced under its auspices" *(Introd.)* are included on a very selective basis.   Z7751.K46

——— ——— Supplement 1981/82 ed. Chestnut Hill, Philadelphia, Westminster Theological Seminary, 1982. 14p.

Supplements the above, listing new editions, additional works, together with updated annotations and revised entries. Annual supplements are planned until a new edition of the basic work is published.

McLean, George F. A bibliography of Christian philosophy and contemporary issues. N.Y., Ungar, [1967]. 312p. (Philosophy in the 20th century: Catholic and Christian, v.2) **BB223**

A selective, classified listing of books and periodical articles of the

past 30 years. An appendix lists the philosophy dissertations presented in the Catholic universities of the United States and Canada. Indexed.   Z7821.M26

New York. Union Theological Seminary. Library. Catalogue of the McAlpin collection of British history and theology; comp. and ed. by Charles Ripley Gillett. N.Y., 1927–30. 5v. **BB224**

Contents: v.1–4, 1500–1700; v.5, Index.

A rich collection of material including many pamphlets on British theology and history. Chronologically arranged.   Z7757.E5N5

——— ——— Acquisitions 1924–1978. Boston, G. K. Hall, 1979. 427p.

This supplement reproduces the catalog cards for materials added during the 1924–78 period. In two sections, the first a dictionary arrangement of author, title, and subject entries; the second a chronological arrangement of the main entry cards by date of publication.

O'Brien, Elmer, ed. Theology in transition; a bibliographical evaluation of the "decisive decade," 1954–1964. [N.Y.], Herder and Herder, [1965]. 282p.   **BB225**

A bibliographic survey, by a group of Catholic theologians, of recent publications in the field of theology.

A briefer, annotated guide to the literature is Urban J. Steiner's *Contemporary theology; a reading guide* (Collegeville, Minn., Liturgical Pr., [1965]. 111p.).   BT28.O2

Ofori, Patrick E. Christianity in tropical Africa: a selective annotated bibliography. Nendeln, [Liechtenstein], KTO Pr., 1977. 461p.   **BB226**

Brings together in a classified arrangement books, articles, pamphlets, theses and unpublished mimeographed materials in many languages and "from numerous scattered sources from 1841–1974" *(Introd.)* to provide a basic guide to African Christianity. Arranged by broad region, then alphabetically by country. 2,859 entries. Author index.   Z7757.A24O36

Recent homiletical thought; a bibliography. Nashville, Tenn., Abingdon Pr., [1967–83]. 2v.   **BB227**

Subtitle varies; publisher varies.

Contents: v.1, 1935–65, ed. by William Toohey and William W. Robinson; v.2, 1966–79, ed. by A. Duane Litfin and Haddon W. Robinson.

A topical listing of books, articles, and theses on various aspects of preaching and on Protestant and Catholic homiletical theory and practice. Brief annotations for most items; expanded coverage of journals in v.2; author index.   Z7826.R4

The study of liturgy. Ed. by Cheslyn Jones, Geoffrey Wainwright, Edward Yarnold. London, SPCK; N.Y., Oxford Univ. Pr., [1978]. 547p. il.   **BB228**

Serves as an introduction to the study of Christian liturgy and a guide to more advanced study of the subject. Chapters were contributed by specialists and include bibliographies. In three main sections: (1) A theology of worship; (2) The development of the liturgy (general introduction; initiation; the Eucharist; ordination; the Divine Office; the calendar; the setting of the liturgy); (3) Pastoral orientation. Indexed.   BV176.S76

Theologischer Jahresbericht, 1881–1913. Tübingen, Mohr, 1882–1916. v.1–33.   **BB229**

An important serial bibliography of books and periodical material; for the university, theological, or large reference library. Discontinued after the outbreak of World War I.

Theologische Literaturzeitung. v.1– , 1876– . Leipzig, Hinrichs, 1876– . Biweekly.   **BB230**

——— Bibliographisches Beiblatt. Die theologische Literatur des Jahres 1922–42. Leipzig, Hinrichs, 1922–43. Biweekly, 1922–24; semiannual, 1925–35; annual, 1936–42.

A comprehensive survey of book and periodical material in many languages.   Z7753.T392

Vaterunser Bibliographie. Hrsg. v. Monica Dorneich. Jubiläumsgabe der Stiftung Oratio Dominica. Freiburg im Breisgau, Herder, 1982. 240p. **BB231**

Title page also in English.

In two parts: (1) 1,800 books, parts of books and articles arranged alphabetically by author on the Our Father (in many languages, though German predominates, and with fullest coverage for 1945–75 but including some earlier and later material); (2) a music bibliography, in classed order, of vocal and instrumental settings and of recordings of the Lord's Prayer, 1945–78. Z7825.5.V37

Williams, Ethel L. and **Brown, Clifton F.** The Howard University bibliography of African and Afro-American religious studies; with locations in American libraries. Wilmington, Del., Scholarly Resources, [1977]. 525p. **BB232**

Some 13,000 entries (books, periodical articles, parts of books) in five main sections: (1) African heritage; (2) Christianity and slavery in the New World; (3) The black man and his religious life in the Americas; (4) Civil rights movement; (5) The contemporary religious scene. Appendix I is a selected listing of manuscripts; Appendix II is an "Autobiographical and biographical index" which includes references to biographical material in periodical articles and parts of books. Indexed. No standards for inclusion are mentioned, and works listed range from scholarly works to popular accounts appearing in national weeklies. Z1361.N39W555

Dictionaries and encyclopedias

❖For many questions asked by English-speaking readers, the *Encyclopaedia of religion and ethics* (BB51) and the *New Schaff-Herzog* (BB63) will be adequate. In the large reference library it will often be necessary to use some of the foreign works, especially for topics in foreign church history, foreign religious biography, etc. The most extended modern work of reference in the field of theology is the great French series now in course of publication under the general title *Encyclopédie des sciences religieuses,* composed of the following separate works: *Dictionnaire d'archéologie chrétienne* by Cabrol (BB251); *Dictionnaire d'histoire et de géographie ecclésiastiques* by Baudrillart (BB234); *Dictionnaire de théologie catholique* by Vacant and Mangenot (BB440); *Dictionnaire de la Bible* by Vigouroux (BB183); and *Dictionnaire de droit canonique* (CK280). These are listed separately under their subjects. Parts of this series contain the finest material on the subject published in any language, and the work as a whole represents the highest level of French Catholic scholarship. The price of the sets puts them beyond the reach of the small or medium-sized library, and the work is too specialized to be of much use except in a theological library, a large general reference library, or a library specializing in medieval and ecclesiastical history and literature.

Baker's Dictionary of Christian ethics. Carl F. H. Henry, ed. Grand Rapids, Baker Book House, [1973]. 726p. **BB233**

"While this dictonary aims to be authentically evangelical, it does not impose upon readers a partisan view that obscures all differences between, for example, Calvinist and Arminian or pacifist and non-pacifist traditions. In some instances . . . contributors were deliberately chosen for their differing perspectives."—*Pref.* Signed articles, many with bibliographic references appended.

BJ1199.B34

Baudrillart, Alfred. Dictionnaire d'histoire et de géographie ecclésiastiques, commencé sous la direction de Mgr. Alfred Baudrillart, continué par A. de Meyer et Ét. van Cauwenbergh, avec le concours d'un grand nombre de collaborateurs. Paris, Letouzey, 1912–[83]. v.1–20³. il. (In progress) **BB234**

Issued in parts, beginning 1909; title page of v.1 dated 1912.
Editors vary; since v.16 "sous la direction de R. Aubert."

Contents: v.1–20³ (fasc. 117/118), A–Giffoni.

Scope of the work covers all subjects in the history of the Roman Catholic church, and other churches as they affect the Roman church, from the beginning of Christianity to the present time. The geographical material includes separate articles on towns and other small divisions, past and present, indicating the connection of the place with ecclesiastical history, its present ecclesiastical status, a list of its religious institutions, and (in case it is or has been an episcopal see) a list of the bishops, etc. Includes biographical articles on: all important and some minor names in the Roman Catholic church; members of other churches who have had any effect on the Roman church; ecclesiastical and theological writers; saints in the Russian and other churches; ecclesiastical musicians, artists, etc. Signed articles; good bibliographies. BR95.B3

The concise Oxford dictionary of the Christian church. Ed. by Elizabeth A. Livingstone. 2d ed. abr. Oxford and N.Y., Oxford Univ. Pr., 1977. 570p. **BB235**

An abridgment of the 2d ed. of *The Oxford dictionary of the Christian church* (1974; BB248). Answers "the questions who and what" and refers the reader "to the corresponding article in the parent volume" (*Pref.*) for fuller information and bibliography. BR95.O82

Corpus dictionary of Western churches. Thomas C. O'Brien, ed. Wash., Corpus Publs., [1970]. 820p. **BB236**

Concerned with "the Churches that have developed throughout the history of Western Christianity" (*Pref.*), with special attention to North American churches in the Western tradition. In addition to entries for the various denominations, there are subsidiary articles on events and personalities in church history, doctrines, documents, practices, etc. About 2,300 concise, unsigned articles representing the contributions of more than 100 scholars and specialists of many faiths. Compiled under Roman Catholic auspices, but ecumenical in intent. BR95.C67

Davies, John Gordon, ed. A dictionary of liturgy and worship. N.Y., Macmillan, [1972]. 385p. il. **BB237**

Intends "to provide background knowledge about worship for those who are regularly involved in it or would learn something about it. It seeks to concentrate upon the information that Christians need in order to participate with understanding in the worship of the traditions to which they belong."—*Pref.* While emphasis is on Christian churches, some attention is given to other major world religions. Signed articles by liturgical experts of various faiths. Some bibliographic references. (Repr. as *Westminster dictionary of worship.* Philadelphia, Westminster Pr., 1979.) BV173.D28

A dictionary of Christian spirituality. Ed. by Gordon S. Wakefield. [London], SCM Pr., [1983]. 400p. **BB238**

Also publ. as *The Westminster dictionary of Christian spirituality* (Philadelphia, 1983).

Offers signed articles, most of them with bibliography, on terms, persons, movements, etc., including aspects of non-Christian religions as they relate to Christian spirituality. BV4488.W47

Dictionnaire de spiritualité, ascétique et mystique, doctrine et histoire, fondé par Marcel Viller, F. Cavallera et J. de Guibert, . . . avec le concours d'un grand nombre de collaborateurs. Paris, Beauchesne, 1932–84. Fasc.1–78/79. (In progress) **BB239**

Contents: v.1–12¹ (fasc. 1–78/79), A–Photius.
Editors vary.

Offers long, signed articles with bibliographies and references to sources; includes many bibliographies. BX841.D67

Douglas, James Dixon. The new international dictionary of the Christian church. Rev. ed. Exeter, [Eng.], Paternoster Pr.; Grand Rapids, Mich., Zondervan, [1978]. 1074p. **BB240**

1st ed. 1974.

An international group of about 180 scholars has contributed signed articles on a wide range of topics relating to the history, development, and practices relating to the Christian church. Many biographical sketches. Some articles include bibliographical references. Cross referencing is effected both through conventional *see* references and use of an asterisk following a name or term in the text of an article. Strong in American church history and evangelical movements. Minor revisions in this edition. BR95.D68

Encyclopedia of theology: the concise *Sacramentum mundi.* Ed. by Karl Rahner. N.Y., Seabury Pr., [1975]. 1841p. **BB241**

"This volume contains revised versions of the major articles on theology, biblical science and related topics from *Sacramentum Mundi* [BB443], together with a large number of articles from the major German works *Lexikon für Theologie und Kirche* [BB55] and *Theologisches Taschenlexikon,* and entirely new articles on topics of major importance written for the occasion by Professor Rahner and others."—*Pref. Note.* BR95.E48

Evangelisches Kirchenlexikon; kirchlich-theologisches Handwörterbuch . . . hrsg. von Heinz Brunotte u. Otto Weber. Göttingen, Vandenhoeck & Ruprecht, [1955–61]. 4v. **BB242**

A German Protestant encyclopedia designed as a modern supplement to older works of reference on Christian theology and church affairs, emphasizing recent literature. Entries include theological concepts, clerical terms, national and geographical areas—with emphasis on their religious history—and biographies. Long articles are signed and include bibliographies.

v.4, the *Register,* contains a list of the several hundred contributors to the set, a subject index, and an extensive *Biographischer Anhang.* The last gives brief biographical information on nearly 15,000 persons connected with Christianity through the ages, with references to citations in the main set.

A "2. unveränderte Aufl." was issued 1961–62. BR95.E9

Macquarrie, John. Dictionary of Christian ethics. Philadelphia, Westminster, [1967]. 366p. **BB243**

Signed articles by 80 scholars and theologians on basic ethical concepts, ethical systems, non-Christian ethics, traditional biblical and theological ethics, and ethical problems of the modern world—all presented solely from the point of view of their ethical content or influence. BJ63.M3

Malloch, James M. A practical church dictionary, ed. by Kay Smallzried. N.Y., Morehouse-Barlow, [1964]. 520p. **BB244**

A dictionary prepared from the viewpoint of the Episcopal church but with an ecumenical approach that includes other Protestant, Roman Catholic, and Eastern Orthodox churches. Definitions were written by Malloch. No bibliography with the articles; "Books for further reference," p.517–20. BR95.M37

Metford, J. C. J. Dictionary of Christian lore and legend. [London], Thames and Hudson, [1983]. 272p. il. **BB245**

Aims "to provide, in convenient and concise form, a guide to the essentials of [the] Christian tradition in the arts, music and literature."—*Foreword.* Entries for saints, biblical figures and events, liturgical terms, etc. For the non-specialist. BR95.M396

A new dictionary of Christian theology. Ed. by Alan Richardson and John Bowden. [London], SCM Pr., [1983]. 614p. **BB246**

Publ. in the United States as *Westminster dictionary of Christian theology.*

Based on Richardson's *Dictionary of Christian theology* (1969).

Relatively brief, signed articles (with bibliographies) on contemporary theological issues, terms, etc. Focus "is on theological thinking against a historical background rather than on historical events or figures."—*Pref.*

Ökumene Lexikon: Kirchen. Religionen. Bewegungen, hrsg. in Verbindung mit Athanasios Basdekis . . . [et al.] von Hanfried Krüger, Werner Löser und Walter Müller-Romheld. Frankfurt am Main, Lembeck, Knecht, [1983]. 1326p. il. **BB247**

Offers signed articles by 300 Lutheran, Catholic and Orthodox contributors on concepts, doctrines, churches, persons, places and events. Entries vary from a paragraph to several pages; most have bibliographies. Where interpretation of a term or doctrine differs among confessions, each view is presented in a separate article. BR95.O38

The Oxford dictionary of the Christian church. 2d ed., ed. by F. L. Cross and E. A. Livingstone. London, Oxford Univ. Pr., 1974. 1518p. **BB248**

1st ed., 1957, by F. L. Cross; repr., with corrections 1961 and 1966.

A revised, updated, and expanded edition of this useful work containing more than 6,000 articles, some of considerable length. Although about half the entries were written by contributing scholars, in the interests of uniformity none is signed. Bibliographies are appended to most articles. Coverage is broad, including historical and doctrinal development, many biographies, definitions of ecclesiastical terms and customs, etc. BR95.O8

Westminster dictionary of church history. Ed.: Jerald C. Brauer. Philadelphia, Westminster Pr., [1971]. 887p. **BB249**

Offers definitions and explanations "concerning the major men, events, facts and movements in the history of Christianity," alphabetically arranged. BR95.W496

World Christian encyclopedia: a comparative study of churches and religions in the modern world, AD 1900–2000. Ed. by David B. Barrett. Oxford, Oxford Univ. Pr., 1982. 1010p. il., maps. **BB250**

A topical and comparative encyclopedia of many aspects of Christianity as found in about 20,800 denominations "spread among some 8,990 peoples speaking 7,010 languages in the modern world."—*Pref.* Offers country-by-country surveys, numerous statistical tables, chronologies, directory information, etc.; information is based on the research efforts of an international network of collaborators, contributors and local editors. The work "includes information on all the types and activities of organized Christianity, gives the data in an interdenominational or ecumenical presentation, and sets the whole in the context of all other religions including new religions and atheism."—*Introd.* Select bibliography; atlas section; dictionary of terms. Indexes.

Embodies various characteristics of the *World Christian handbook* (London, 1949–68) and the *Bilan du monde* (Tournai, 1958–64).

A highly favorable review appears in *Booklist* 79:692 (Jan. 15, 1983). BR157.W67

Christian antiquities

Cabrol, Fernand and **Leclerq, Henri.** Dictionnaire d'archéologie chrétienne et de liturgie, publié sous la direction de Henri Marrou. Paris, Letouzey, 1907–53. 15v. il. **BB251**

Issued in parts.

Excellent signed articles, with full bibliographies, on institutions, manners, and customs of primitive Christianity, and on the architecture, Christian art, iconography, symbols, epigraphy, paleography, numismatics, liturgy, rites, and ceremonies of the early church to the time of Charlemagne. Covers much of the same ground as Smith's *Dictionary of Christian antiquities* (BB253) but with fuller and more up-to-date treatment. BR95.C2

Reallexikon für Antike und Christentum; Sachwörterbuch zur Auseinandersetzung des Christentums mit der antiken Welt. In Verbindung mit Franz Joseph Dölger, Hans Lietzmann, [and others], hrsg. von Theodor Klauser. Stuttgart, Hiersemann, 1950–84. v.1–13[1]. (In progress) **BB252**

Editors vary.

Contents: Bd.1–13[1] (Lfg. 1–98), A–Hagel.

Presents long, signed articles by many scholars dealing with the relationship of the ancient world to Christianity up to the sixth century A.D. BR131.R4

Smith, *Sir* **William** and **Cheetham, Samuel.** Dictionary of Christian antiquities, being a continuation of the "Dictionary of the Bible." London, Murray; Boston, Little, 1875–80. 2v. il. (Repr.: N.Y., Kraus, 1968) **BB253**

Treats subjects connected with the organization of the church: its officers, legislation, discipline, and revenues; social life; ceremonials, church music, vestments, instruments, and insignia; ecclesiastical architecture and art and their symbolism; sacred days, burial places, etc. Omits literature, sects, doctrines, heresies, etc., as such subjects are covered in the companion work *Dictionary of Christian biography* (BB254). Covers period to the age of Charlemagne. Long, signed articles; exact references to many sources; bibliographies. Not abreast of modern scholarship but still useful on many points.

BR95.S6

Smith, *Sir* **William** and **Wace, Henry.** Dictionary of Christian biography, literature, sects and doctrines. London, Murray; Boston, Little, 1877–87. 4v. (Repr.: N.Y., AMS Pr., 1967) **BB254**

A companion work to the entry above.

Aims to supply an adequate account, based upon original authorities, of all persons connected with the church—down to the age of Charlemagne—about whom anything is known, of all literature connected with them, and of the controversies about doctrine and discipline in which they were engaged. Pays special attention to subjects and names in English, Scottish, and Irish church history. Signed articles; bibliographies. BR95.S65

Wace, Henry and **Piercy, William C.** Dictionary of Christian biography and literature to the end of the sixth century, A.D., with an account of the principal sects and heresies. London, Murray; Boston, Little, 1911. 1028p. **BB255**

A revised and abridged edition of Smith's *Dictionary of Christian biography* (BB254). Adds later references but does not supersede Smith, which is still useful for its long articles, for minor names, and for subjects of the seventh and eighth centuries (this edition covering only the first six centuries). BR95.W3

Terms

Harvey, Van Austin. A handbook of theological terms. N.Y., Macmillan, [1964]. 253p. **BB256**

"My aim has not been to provide definitions of obscure theological terms but to indicate how such terms, ancient and modern, have been variously used in differing circumstances and what is at issue in these various uses."—*Pref.* BR95.H32

Purvis, John Stanley. Dictionary of ecclesiastical terms. London, Nelson, [1962]. 204p. **BB257**

Gives definitions of ecclesiastical terms, primarily as used in England, including those used in the Church of England and in the Roman Catholic and Eastern Orthodox churches. BR95.P8

White, Richard Clark. The vocabulary of the church: a pronunciation guide. N.Y., Macmillan, 1960. 178p. **BB258**

Emphasis is on proper nouns and biblical words; gives word and pronunciation only. "The standard pronunciation is American religious usage."—*Introd.* BR95.W53

Biography

❖Most of the encyclopedias listed above include biographies, in some cases of considerable reference importance. In some instances the yearbooks (e.g., BB355, BB457) include contemporary biography. The following entries are limited to biography and include many names not given in the more general works.

Biographisch-bibliographisches Kirchenlexikon. Bearb. u. hrsg. von Friedrich Wilhelm Bautz. Hamm (Westf.), Verlag Traugott Bautz, [1975]–78. v.1–2⁵ (Lfg.1–15). (In progress) **BB259**

Issued in fascicles.
Contents: v.1–2⁵, Aalders–Heusser-Schweizer.
Biographical sketches are followed by lists of works by and about the individuals. Biographees include saints, popes, bishops, clergymen, theologians, church historians, hymn writers and composers of church music, literary authors of religious significance, etc.

Bowden, Henry Warner. Dictionary of American religious biography. Edwin S. Gaustad, advisory ed. Westport, Conn., Greenwood Pr., 1977. 572p. **BB260**

With a view to correlating "historical materials related to American religious figures" (*Pref.*), the volume presents biographical sketches of 425 persons from "all denominations that played a significant role in our nation's past." For each biographee, available details of vital statistics, education, and career are briefly noted preceding a discussion of the life work and influence of the figure. Bibliographies at the end of the articles cite works both by and about a person. BL72.B68

Haag, Eugène and **Haag, Émile.** La France protestante; ou, Vies des protestants français qui se sont fait un nom dans l'histoire . . . Paris, Cherbuliez, 1846–59. 10v. **BB261**

For description *see* AJ195.

Moyer, Elgin Sylvester. Wycliffe biographical dictionary of the church. Rev. and enl. by Earle E. Cairns. Chicago, Moody Pr., [1982]. 449p. **BB262**

Represents a revision of Moyer's *Who was who in church history* (rev. ed. 1968).

Offers "brief biographies of over two thousand men and women of all races, from all parts of the world, who have made major contributions to the cause of Christ."—*Pref.* BR1700.2.M66

Sprague, William Buell. Annals of the American pulpit; or, Commemorative notices of distinguished American clergymen of various denominations, from the early settlement of the country to the close of the year 1855. With historical introductions. N.Y., R. Carter, 1857–[69]. 9v. il. (Repr.: N.Y., Arno Pr., 1969) **BB263**

Contents: v.1–2, Trinitarian Congregational; v.3–4, Presbyterian; v.5, Episcopalian; v.6, Baptist; v.7, Methodist; v.8, Unitarian Congregational; v.9, Lutheran; Reformed Dutch; Associate; Associate Reformed; Reformed Presbyterian.

A useful work of sketches, averaging two or three pages in length, with extensive bibliographies of the publications by the biographee. Has an alphabetical index for each denomination but no general index.

Another useful series for biographical information on early American clergy comprises the following works by Frederick Lewis Weis: *The colonial clergy of the Middle Colonies: New York, New Jersey, and Pennsylvania, 1628–1776* (Worcester, Mass., Amer. Antiquarian Soc., 1957); *The colonial clergy of Maryland, Delaware and Georgia* (Lancaster, Mass., 1950); *The colonial clergy of Virginia, North Carolina, and South Carolina* (Boston, 1955); and *The colonial clergy and the colonial churches of New England* (Lancaster, Mass., 1936). These lists give only brief biographical information.

BR569.S7

Who's who in religion. Ed.1–2, 1975/76–77. Chicago, Marquis, [1975–77] **BB264**

The 1st ed. contained about 16,000 biographies; this figure was increased to about 18,000 in the 2d ed. (publ. 1977). Names of persons included were drawn from the following general categories: (1) church officials (both lay and clergy); (2) clergy, selected for outstanding contributions to activities of their respective faiths; (3) religious educators in the field of higher education; (4) lay leaders. Information was supplied by the biographees; a few sketches compiled by Marquis editors are marked with an asterisk.

BL2530.U6W48

Williams, Ethel L. Biographical directory of Negro ministers. 3d ed. Boston, G. K. Hall, 1975. 584p. **BB265**

1st ed. 1965.
Furnishes biographical data on living Negro ministers active and influential in local or national affairs. Geographical index. This edition includes 1,442 biographical sketches of the "who's who" type. BR563.N4W5

Saints

Attwater, Donald. The Penguin dictionary of saints. 2d ed. rev. and updated by Catherine Rachel John. Harmondsworth, Eng. and N.Y., Penguin, 1983. 352 p. **BB266**

1st ed. 1965.

A good brief dictionary. Includes a short glossary of terms preceding the alphabetical listing of more than 750 saints. The saint's symbol in art is frequently indicated. BX4655.8.A8

Baring-Gould, Sabine. The lives of the saints, with introduction and additional lives of English martyrs, Cornish, Scottish, and Welsh saints, and a full index to the entire work. New and rev. ed. illustrated by 473 engravings. Edinburgh, Grant, 1914. 16v. il. **BB267**

Contents: v.1–15, Jan.–Dec. (July, Oct., and Nov. in 2v. each); v.16, Appendix; indexes.

A standard work on the lives of the saints arranged day by day throughout the year. BX4655.B3

Bibliotheca sanctorum. [Roma], Istituto Giovanni XXIII nella Pontificia Università Laterense, [1961?–70]. 12v. and index. il. **BB268**

Offers signed articles, with bibliographies, on figures of the Old and New Testaments, angels, saints, persons declared blessed or venerable or whose cause for canonization has been introduced. Four indexes: general name index, feast days, patronage, names of contributors. BX4655.8.B5

Book of saints; a dictionary of servants of God canonized by the Catholic Church. Comp. by the Benedictine monks of St. Augustine's Abbey, Ramsgate. 5th ed., entirely rev. and reset. London, A. & C. Black; N.Y., Crowell, [1966]. 740p. **BB269**

1st ed. 1921. The 4th ed. (1947) was a complete reworking and expansion; this is a corrected edition with some revisions and additions.

A concise handbook which includes all saints in the Roman martyrology and some others, particularly those who have given place-names to towns and villages in the British Isles. BX4655.B6

Butler, Alban. Lives of the saints. New ed. rev. and copiously supplemented by Herbert Thurston. London, Burns; N.Y., Kenedy, 1926–38. 12v. **BB270**

BX4654.B8

—— —— Complete ed., rev. and supplemented by Herbert Thurston and Donald Attwater. N.Y., Kenedy, [1956]. 4v. (Repr.: Westminster, Md., Christian Classics, 1981) **BB271**

The 12v. edition was thoroughly revised by Thurston. In the 4v. edition, revised by Attwater, many sketches have been included without alteration, some brief ones have been omitted, and a few sketches of recently canonized saints added. The homilies originally included have been omitted.

A brief version was published as *Butler's Lives of the saints* (Concise ed., ed. by Michael Walsh. San Francisco, Harper & Row, 1985. 466p.).

—— A dictionary of saints; based on Butler's Lives of the saints, complete ed. Comp. by Donald Attwater. N.Y., Kenedy, [1958]. 280p. **BB272**

2,500 brief entries, each with reference to the fuller treatment in Butler's *Lives* (1956). BX4654.B8

Delaney, John J. Dictionary of saints. Garden City, N.Y., Doubleday, 1980. 647p. **BB273**

Offers brief entries on some 5,000 "saints and *beati* about whom . . . the modern reader would be most likely to seek information."— *Introd.* Intended for the general reader "seeking a concise resume of the pertinent facts in particular saints' lives." Includes lists of saints

as patrons and intercessors, patrons of countries and places, and their symbols in art; a chronological chart of popes and world rulers; and calendars of the Roman and Byzantine rites. No bibliography. BX4655.8.D44

Farmer, David Hugh. The Oxford dictionary of saints. Oxford, Clarendon Pr., 1978. 435p. **BB274**

Offers brief accounts of about 1,000 saints of English origin, saints of foreign origin who died in England, and those who were known and venerated there. Select bibliographies give citations to official sources, the best hagiographical studies, and sometimes to popular works. BX4659.G7F37

The saints: a concise biographical dictionary, ed. by John Coulson. London, Burns; N.Y., Hawthorn, [1958]. 496p. il. **BB275**

Contains brief biographies of more than 2,200 saints. Many of the articles, although not signed, are contributed by authorities in the field. Profusely illustrated with colored and black-and-white plates. BX4655.S28

❖The foregoing are popular works, useful for ordinary purposes. For research use, however, the indispensable works are the *Acta sanctorum* and other publications of the Bollandists described below. For an account of the *Acta sanctorum, see* the *Catholic encyclopedia* 2:630–39.

Acta sanctorum quotquot toto orbe coluntur, vel a catholicis scriptoribus celebrantur, quae ex Latinis et Graecis, aliarumque gentium antiquis monumentis collegit, digessit, notis illustravit Joannes Bollandus . . . operam et studium contulit Godefridus Henschenius. . . . Editio novissima curante Joanne Carnandet. Parisiis, Palmé, 1863–1940. Jan.–Dec. 67v. **BB276**

Contents: Jan.–Apr., 3v. each; May, 7v. and Propylaeum; June–July, 7v. each; Aug., 6v.; Sept. 8v.; Oct. 13v. in 14; Nov., v.1–4 and Propylaeum; Dec., Propylaeum. BX4655.A2

—— Ad Acta sanctorum . . . supplementum, volumen complectens Auctaria Octobris et Tabulas generales. Scilicet ephemerides et indicem alphabeticum decem priorum mensium . . . cura et opera L. M. Rigollot. Parisiis, 1875. 2v. **BB277**

—— Supplément aux Acta sanctorum pour des vies de saints de l'époque mérovingienne par M. l'Abbé C. Narbey. . . . Paris, Le Soudier, 1899–1900. v.1–2. **BB278**

Supplemented by:

Analecta bollandiana, v.1– . Bruxelles, Soc. des Bollandistes; Paris, Picard, 1882– . Semiannual. **BB279**

Frequency varies.

Subtitle: Révue critique d'hagiographie.

Gives the current bibliography of the subject, with critical reviews of new publications, and supplements the *Acta sanctorum* (above) by printing texts, commentaries, etc., not included in the *Acta*. BX4655.A3

—— Indices in tomos I–XX (1882–1901), XXI–XL (1902–1922), XLI–LX (1923–1942). Bruxelles, Soc. des Bollandistes, 1904–45. 3v.

—— Table générale des articles publiés en 80 ans, 1882–1961. Bruxelles, 1962. 33p.

Bibliotheca hagiographica graeca. 3. éd. mise à jour et considérablement augmentée par François Halkin. Bruxelles, Soc. des Bollandistes, 1957. 3v. (Subsidia hagiographica, no.8a) **BB280**

Contents: t.1–2, A–Z; t.3, Supplément, appendices, et tables.

1st ed. 1895; 2d ed. 1909.

This revision brings up-to-date the listing of Greek hagiographical manuscripts and documents, and includes numerous items and early editions not previously listed. Z7844.B53

———— Auctarium, par François Halkin. Bruxelles, Société des Bollandistes, 1969. 386p. (Subsidia hagiographica, no.47)

Offers corrections and additions to the 3d ed. Z7844.B53

Bibliotheca hagiographica latina antiquae et mediae aetatis. Ed. Socii Bollandiani. Bruxellis, 1898–1901. 2v. (1304p.) (Subsidia hagiographica, no.6) (Repr.: Bruxelles, Soc. des Bollandistes, 1949) **BB281**

———— Supplementi. Ed. altera auctior. 1911. 355p. (Subsidia hagiographica, no.12)

Z7844.B55

Bibliotheca hagiographica orientalis. Ed. Socii Bollandiani. Bruxellis, apud editores [Beyrouth, (Syrie), Impr. Catholique], 1910. 287p. (Studia hagiographica, 10) (Repr.: Bruxelles, Soc. des Bollandistes, 1954) **BB282**

Z7844.B57

Creeds

Schaff, Philip. Bibliotheca symbolica ecclesiae universalis. The creeds of Christendom, with a history and critical notes. N.Y. & London, Harper, [1919]. 3v. **BB283**

1st ed. 1877. Various reprintings and revisions of individual volumes.

Contents: v.1, History of creeds (church by church, with many bibliographical references) v.2, Creeds of the Greek and Latin churches (giving for each the full Greek or Latin text and an English translation in parallel columns, with an index of subjects) v.3, Creeds of the Evangelical Protestant churches (in language of original with parallel English translation); index of subjects.

BT990.S4

Costume

Norris, Herbert. Church vestments: their origin & development. London, Dent, 1949. 190p. il. **BB284**

Illustrated with plates and line drawings. Based on the author's *Costume and fashion,* it treats the history and development of the classical garments used in the church. BV167.N67

Church history and expansion

History

American church history series, consisting of a series of denominational histories published under the auspices of the American Society of Church History. Gen. eds.: Philip Schaff, H. C. Potter, S. M. Jackson. N.Y., Christian Literature Co. (Scribner), 1893–97. 13v. (v.13 repr. 1901; set publ. in microfiche: Chicago, Lib. Resources, 1970) **BB285**

Now much out-of-date but still occasionally useful. Consists of separate histories of major denominations by various authors. Includes a bibliography of American church history, 1820–93, in v.12. BR515.A5

Berkhout, Carl T. and **Russell, Jeffrey B.** Medieval heresies: a bibliography, 1960–1979. Toronto, Pontifical Inst. of Mediaeval Studies, 1981. 201p. (Subsidia mediaevalia, 11) **BB286**

Lists books (with references to reviews) and periodical articles in a classed arrangement, with author, subject, and manuscript indexes. More than 2,000 items. Z7779.H3B52

Internationale ökumenische Bibliographie. International ecumenical bibliography. Bibliographie oecuménique internationale. v.1/2– , 1962/63– . Mainz, Matthias-Grünewald; München, Kaiser, [1967]– . Irregular. **BB287**

v.1/2, 1962/63 (publ. 1967); v.3/4, 1964/65 (publ. 1970); v.5, 1966 (publ. 1972); v.6, 1967 (publ. 1973); continued on an annual basis through v.9, 1970 (publ. 1976); irregular thereafter (v.15/16 covering 1976/77, publ. 1983). Publication to end with volume covering 1979.

An important international bibliography listing writings (books and periodical articles) dealing with the ecumenical movement or church life, and theological publications concerned with ecumenical or controversial theology. Classed arrangement; author index.

Z7845.1.I5

Jedin, Hubert and **Dolan, John,** eds. Handbook of church history. N.Y., Herder & Herder, etc., [1965–81]. 10v. **BB288**

Title varies: later vols. entitled *History of the church.*

Contents: v.1, From the apostolic community to Constantine, by Karl Baus; v.2, The imperial church from Constantine to the early Middle Ages, by Karl Baus [et al.]; v.3, The church in the age of feudalism, by Friedrich Kempf [et al.]; v.4, From the High Middle Ages to the eve of the Reformation, by Hans-Georg Beck [et al.]; v.5, Reformation and Counter Reformation, by Erwin Iserloh [et al.]; v.6, The church in the age of absolutism and enlightenment, by Wolfgang Müller; v.7, The church between Revolution and Restoration, by Roger Aubert [et al.]; v.8, The church in the age of liberalism, by Roger Aubert [et al.]; v.9, The church in the Industrial Age, by Roger Aubert [et al.]; v.10, The church in the modern age, by Gabriel Adriányi [et al.].

Tr. from Jedin's *Handbuch der Kirchengeschichte,* 3d ed. (1962–79. 7v. in 10).

A scholarly history which "examines not only the Church's external career in the world but also her inner life, the development of her doctrine and preaching, her ritual and devotion."—*Pref.* Bibliographies for each chapter indicate sources, general literature, and special studies. BR145.2.J413

Oxford history of the Christian church. Oxford, Clarendon Pr.; N.Y., Oxford Univ. Pr., 1976– . (In progress) **BB289**

A monograph series (only the first volume carries a series number) with useful bibliographies, to be in about 20v. Volumes published to date are: A history of the churches in the United States and Canada, by Robert T. Handy (1976. 471p.); The Popes and European revolution, by Owen Chadwick (1981. 646p.); The Frankish church, by John Michael Wallace-Hadrill (1983. 463p.).

Pfaff, Richard W. Medieval Latin liturgy: a select bibliography. Toronto, Univ. of Toronto Pr., [1982]. 129p. (Toronto medieval bibliographies, 9) **BB290**

A selection of approximately a thousand studies concerned with "the history of the medieval Latin liturgy from the late fourth century . . . to the sixteenth-century Reformation."—*Pref.* Following sections for general and background materials there are sections for the Mass, the Daily Office, occasional Offices, the liturgical year and observances, and various special liturgies. Author index.

Z7813.P42

Piepkorn, Arthur Carl. Profiles in belief: the religious bodies of the United States and Canada. N.Y., Harper & Row, 1977–79. v.1–4 (in 3v.). (In progress?) **BB291**

Contents: v.1, Roman Catholic, Old Catholic, Eastern Orthodox; v.2, Protestant denominations; v.3–4 (in 1v.), Evangelical, fundamentalist, and other Christian bodies.

Arranged by "families" of churches with an introductory essay which carries notes and bibliography. Articles on individual religious bodies include history, basic beliefs, practices, statistics, and address of the group's headquarters. Each volume is indexed.

BL2530.U6P53

Rouse, Ruth and **Neill, Stephen Charles,** eds. A history of the ecumenical movement. 2d ed. with rev. bibliography. Philadelphia, Westminster Pr., 1967–[70]. 2v. **BB292**

v.1 first published 1954; v.2, first published in this edition, appears without edition statement, and is edited by Harold E. Fey. Contents: v.1, 1517–1948; v.2, 1948–1968.

A survey history from the period of the Reformation to 1968, each section written by a specialist. v.1 has a classed bibliography, p.745–801; the bibliography in v.2, p.447–508, is arranged in chapters corresponding to the chapters of the text.

Two earlier bibliographies of the ecumenical movement are *The ecumenical movement in bibliographical outline* by Paul A. Crow (N.Y., Dept. of Faith and Order, Nat. Council of the Churches of Christ, 1965. 80p.) and *Critical bibliography of ecumenical literature* by Josephus F. Lescrauwaet (Nijmegen, Bestel Centrale V.S.K.B., 1965. 93p.).   BX6.5.R62

Schaff, Philip. History of the Christian church. New ed., thoroughly rev. and enl. N.Y., Scribner, 1882–1910. 7v. in 8. il.   **BB293**

1st ed. 1867; various reprintings.
A detailed, documented history.   BR145.S3

Sweet, William Warren. Religion on the American frontier. A collection of source material. Chicago, Univ. of Chicago Pr., 1931–46. v.1–4. il.   **BB294**

Publisher varies. No more published.
Contents: [v.1], The Baptists, 1783–1830 (1931); v.2, The Presbyterians, 1783–1840 (1936); v.3, The Congregationalists, 1783–1850 (1939); v.4, The Methodists, 1783–1840 (1946).
Each volume includes bibliography.

Vekene, Emil van der. Bibliotheca bibliographica historiae sanctae inquisitionis. Bibliographisches Verzeichnis der gedruckten Schrifttums zur Geschichte und Literatur der Inquisition. Vaduz, Topos Verlag, [1982–83]. 2v.   **BB295**

Constitutes a revised and expanded edition of the compiler's *Bibliografía de la Inquisición* (1963).
Foreword and explanatory notes in Spanish, German, and English.
Publications relating to the Inquisition are listed chronologically within topical and geographical sections. Index of authors and anonymous publications and index to periodicals and *Festschriften.* 4,808 entries.   Z7805.V43

World Council of Churches. Library. Classified catalog of the ecumenical movement. Boston, G. K. Hall, 1972. 2v.
                                                      BB296

Reproduction of the catalog cards for a collection of about 11,000 items, mainly in English, but international in scope.
                                                      Z7845.1.W63

——— ——— 1st supplement. Boston, G. K. Hall, 1981. 517p.

Adds materials from 1973–80, as well as publications of earlier years accessioned since publication of the basic set.

Source books

Ayer, Joseph Cullen. A source book for ancient church history, from the apostolic age to the close of the conciliar period. N.Y., Scribner, 1913. 707p. (Repr.: N.Y., AMS Pr., 1970)   **BB297**

A standard work.

Documents on Christian unity. George K. A. Bell, ed. London and N.Y., Oxford Univ. Pr., 1929–58. Ser.1–4 in 4v.
                                                      BB298

Ser.1, 1920–24; ser.2, 1924–30; ser. 3, 1930–48; ser. 4, 1948–57.
A collection of documents designed to illustrate the growth of the ecumenical movement throughout the world. A selection of the documents from the 1st and 2d series, 1920–30, was republished in 1955.   BX8.A1D6

Gee, Henry and **Hardy, William John.** Documents illustrative of English church history, comp. from original sources. London and N.Y., Macmillan, 1896. 670p. (Repr.: N.Y., Kraus, 1966)   **BB299**

Covers A.D. 314–1700.   BR741.G3

Kidd, Beresford James. Documents illustrative of the history of the church. London, Soc. for Promoting Christian Knowledge; N.Y., Macmillan, 1920–41. v.1–3.   **BB300**

Contents: v.1, to A.D. 313; v.2, 313–461; v.3, *ca.* 500–1500.
Partially superseded by James Stevenson's *A new Eusebius; documents illustrative of the history of the church to A.D.337. Based upon the collection ed. by B. J. Kidd* (London, S.P.C.K., 1957. 427p.).
Kidd also edited *Documents illustrative of the continental Reformation* (Oxford, Clarendon Pr., 1911).   BR45.T66K5

Patrology

❖For certain kinds of reference work—especially in large reference libraries, theological libraries, and in college and university work in medieval history, literature, and philosophy—the writings of the Fathers of the Church, either in the original Latin or Greek, or in English translation, are often wanted. The following are important collections for such needs:

Texts

Migne, Jacques Paul. Patrologiae cursus completus, sive Bibliotheca universalis . . . omnium SS. patrum, doctorum, scriptorumque ecclesiasticorum. . . . Series latina . . . a Tertulliano ad Innocentium III. Parisiis, Migne, 1844–64. 221v.   **BB301**

Contents: v.1–217, Texts; v.218–221, Indexes.

——— ——— Supplementum, accurante Adalberto Hamman. Paris, Garnier, 1958–71. v.1–4.

                                                      BR60.M412

——— ——— Series graeca . . . a S. Barnaba ad Photium. Parisiis, Migne, 1857–66. 161v. in 166.

——— ——— ——— Indices digessit Ferdinandus Cavallera. Parisiis, Garnier, 1912. 218p.

                                                      BR60.M5

——— ——— ——— Index locupletissimus [by] Theodorus Hopfner. Paris, Guethner, 1928–45. 2v.

                                                      BR60.M52

Monumental sets, useful both for the large amount of material included and for the indexes, especially the full subject indexes of many kinds included in v.218–21 of the *Series latina,* and the place index to the *Series graeca.* Texts included are all reprints; those in the *Series graeca* are given both in Latin and in Greek, in parallel columns. (Both series repr.: N.Y., Adlers, 1965–71)
This series is being superseded by sections of:

Corpus Christianorum. Series Latina. Turnholti, Typographi Brepols, 1953– . v.1– . (In progress)   **BB302**

To comprise about 250v.
v.1 published 1954; volumes are not issued in numerical sequence. More than 125v. have been published to date, as well as 2v. of *Initia* (1971–79).
"Designed to supplant Migne's Patrologia Latina with new critical texts or the best of those currently extant; the series follows the critical catalog or prospectus of E. Dekkers, Clavis Patrum Latinorum, published in 1951 [2d ed. 1961; BB309] as v.3 of Sacris eruditi, St. Peter's Abbey, Steenbrugge, Belgium."—*LC card.*
                                                      BR60.C49

——— Continuatio Mediaevalis, 1966– . (In progress)

To be composed of texts of the 8th to the 12th centuries, in about 75 volumes; more than 50v. publ. to date.

——— Series Graeca, 1977– . (In progress)

Chiefly post-Nicene Fathers. 11v. publ. to date.

——— Series Apocryphorum, 1983– . (In progress)

2v. publ. to date.

——— Instrumenta lexicologica latina, 1982– . (In progress)

Series A, *Formae,* provides concordances, etc., for certain texts. 15v. publ. to date.

Ante-Nicene Fathers; translations of the writings of the Fathers down to A.D. 325. Alexander Roberts and James Donaldson, eds. American repr. of the Edinburgh ed., rev. and chronologically arranged with brief prefaces and occasional notes by A. C. Coxe. Buffalo, N.Y., Christian Literature Co., 1885–96. 10v. (Repr.: Grand Rapids, Mich., Eerdmans, 1956) **BB303**

The Edinburgh edition, with title *Ante-Nicene Christian library,* was published by Clark, 1867–72, in 24v.

A collection of the writings of the Apostolic Fathers down to 325 A.D., in English translation. Contents of American edition: v.1–8, Text; v.10, Additional volume, containing early Christian works . . . and selections from the commentaries of Origen, etc.; v.9, Bibliographical synopsis, by E. C. Richardson. General index to v.1–8, by Bernard Pick. BR60.A5

Select library of Nicene and post-Nicene Fathers of the Christian church, ed. by Philip Schaff. 1st–2d ser. tr. into English. N.Y., Christian Literature Co., 1886–1900. 28v. (Repr.: Grand Rapids, Mich., Eerdmans, 1961) **BB304**

English translations of the "most important works of Greek Fathers from Eusebius to Photius, and of the Latin Fathers from Ambrose to Gregory the Great."—*Pref.* BR60.S4

Bibliography and indexes

Biblia patristica; index des citations et allusions Bibliques dans la littérature patristique. Paris, Éditions du Centre National de la Recherche Scientifique, 1975–82. v.1–3 and suppl. (In progress) **BB305**

At head of title: Centre d'Analyse et de Documentation Patristique [Strasbourg]. Equipe de Recherche Associée au Centre National de la Recherche Scientifique: J. Allenbach [et al.].

Contents: v.1, Des origines à Clément d'Alexandrie et Tertullien; v.2, Le troisième siècle (Origène excepté); v.3, Origène; Suppl., Philon d'Alexandre.

A computer-produced index offering correspondence tables arranged according to books of the Old Testament and listing (in abbreviated form): biblical book, chapter and verse, together with relevant patristic author, work, book chapter, paragraph, page and line. BR66.5.U53

Bibliographia patristica: Internationale patristische Bibliographie. 1956– . Berlin, W. de Gruyter, 1959– . v.1– . Biennial. (v.24/25, 1979–80, publ. 1984) **BB306**

A committee of patristic scholars of various confessions contributes to this listing of studies about the early Christian Fathers and related historical and theological topics. Each volume contains more than 1,000 entries from some 900 journals and series. Includes book reviews. Z7791.B5

———— Supplementum 1– . Berlin, W. de Gruyter, 1980– . Irregular.

Contents: Suppl. 1, Voces: eine Bibliographie zu Wörtern und Begriffen aus der Patristik (1918–1978) [von] H. J. Sieben. 461p.

This supplementary volume is in two sections, Greek and Latin, each an alphabetical list of words and concepts in the writings of the Church Fathers, with citations to books, parts of books, journal articles, *Festschriften* and encyclopedia contributions. Indexed. Z7791.S6

Stewardson, Jerry L. A bibliography of bibliographies on Patristics. Evanston, Ill., Garrett Theological Seminary Lib., 1967. 52p. **BB307**

Lists almost 200 bibliographies published as books, parts of books, journal articles, in encyclopedias, etc. Most entries are annotated and reviews are often noted. Armenian, Ethiopian, Georgian and Arabic literature are excluded; Syriac literature was not searched exhaustively.

Manuals and dictionaries

Altaner, Berthold and **Stuiber, Alfred.** Patrologie: Leben, Schriften u. Lehre d. Kirchenväter. 8., durchges. u. erw. Aufl. Freiburg, etc., Herder, 1978. 672p. **BB308**

1st ed., 1938, by Altaner.

An extensive bibliographical work with comments on the lives, writings, and teachings of the Church Fathers. Translated into French, Spanish, and Italian; and into English (based on the 5th German ed.) as *Patrology,* tr. by Hilda C. Graef (2d ed. N.Y., Herder, 1961. 659p.).

In this edition, the text of the 7th ed. (1966) is reprinted, unchanged, with additional bibliography (to 1977) placed in the *Anhang,* p.535–662, and keyed to original entries. A 1980 printing is called "9. Aufl." BR67.A37

Dekkers, Eligius. Clavis patrum latinorum, qua in novum Corpus Christianorum edendum optimas quasque scriptorum recensiones a Tertulliano ad Bedam; commode recludit Eligius Dekkers; opera usus qua rem praeparavit et iuvit Aemilius Gaar, Vindobonensis. Ed. altera, aucta et emendata. Steenbrugis, In abbatia Sancti Petri, [1961]. 640p. (Sacris erudiri; jaarboek voor godsdienstwetenschappen. 3, 1961) **BB309**

1st ed. 1951.

A key to the Latin writings of the Church Fathers that have appeared in collections and periodicals. Three indexes: (1) Index nominum et operum; (2) Index systematicus; (3) Initia.

Dizionario patristico e di antichità cristiane. Diretto da Angelo Di Berardino. [Casale Monferrato], Marietti, [1983]– . v.1– . (In progress; to be in 3v.) **BB310**

At head of title: Institutum Patristicum Augustinianum, Roma.

Contents: v.1, A–F.

Designed as a reference source on specific topics in early Christianity; coverage ends with the eighth century. Signed articles with bibliographies deal with persons, doctrines, sects, and topics in art and archaeology, geography, history, liturgy, philosophy, spirituality, and theology. v.3 is to contain charts and indexes. BR66.5.D58

Geerard, Maurice. Clavis Patrum Graecorum. Turnhout, Brepols, 1974–83. v.1–4. (In progress) **BB311**

Added t.p.: Clavis Patrum Graecorum: qua optimas quaeque scriptorum Patrum Graecorum recensiones a primaevis saeculis usque ad Octavum commode recluduntur.

Contents: v.1 (1983), Patres antenicaeni; v.2, Ab Athanasio ad Chrysostomum; v.3, A Cyrillo Alexandrino ad Iohannem Damascenum; v.4, Concilia. Catenae.

A key to the writings of the Greek Fathers and to related works. Primary bibliography (editions, ms. sources, versions) and critical materials. A fifth volume will contain indexes. Z7791.G43

Quasten, Johannes. Patrology. Utrecht, Spectrum, Westminster, Md., Newman, 1950–60. 3v. **BB312**

Contents: v.1, The beginnings of patristic literature; v.2, The Ante-Nicene literature after Irenaeus; v.3, The golden age of Greek Patristic literature: from the Council of Nicaea to the Council of Chalcedon.

" . . . a new Patrology that strives to place at the disposal of the English-reading public a solid introduction to Early Christian literature."—*Pref.* Extensive bibliographies list critical editions, translations into modern languages, and articles and monographic studies of the writings discussed.

Continued by: BR67.Q32

Patrologia. Ed. by Angelo Di Berardino. v.3, Dal Concilio di Nicea (325) al Concilio di Calcedonia (451): i Padri latini. [Casale Monferrato], Marietti, 1978. 602p. **BB313**

At head of title: Institutum Patristicum Augustinianum, Roma.

A continuation of Quasten (above) which, in its Italian translation, was published in two volumes. Covers the Latin Fathers from Nicea to Chalcedon. Each chapter by a scholar from the Istituto Patristico Augustinianum di Roma. Incorporates scholarly research through the late 1970s.

Steidle, Basilius. Patrologia, seu historia antiquae litteraturae ecclesiasticae, usui scholarum. Friburgi Brisgoviae, Herder, 1937. 294p. **BB314**

Serves as a key to the works of both Greek and Latin Fathers and to other early writings in hagiography, liturgy, etc. Lists editions, translations and secondary materials. Preface and section introductions in Latin. Indexed. Z7791.S83

Missions

❖No single comprehensive bibliography of Protestant missions is available comparable to Streit's *Bibliotheca missionum* (BB323) which treats Catholic missions. For a listing of various bibliographies, largely specialized, *see* John G. Barrow, *A bibliography of bibliographies in religion*, p.286—301 (BB4).

Amistad Research Center. Author and added entry catalog of the American Missionary Association Archives, with references to schools and mission stations. Westport, Conn., Greenwood Pr., [1970]. 3v. **BB315**

A catalog of about 105,000 items, mainly letters, from the extensive American Missionary Association collections (approximately 350,000 manuscript pieces). In addition to providing materials for a detailed history of the Association and its evangelistic and reform activities in America, concern with "the Negro problem" has resulted in accumulations of valuable materials relating to abolition, the Underground Railroad, the education of Negro freedmen, etc. The Amistad Research Center is in Nashville, Tenn. Z7817.A45

Bibliografia missionaria, anno 1– . Comp. dal Giovanni Rommerskirchen [and others]. Roma, Pontificia Universitaria di Propaganda Fide, 1935– . v.1– . Annual. **BB316**

Publisher varies; editors vary.

v.1 covers Jan.1, 1933–June 30, 1934; v. 2, July 1, 1934–Dec. 31, 1935; v. 10, 1943–46. Other volumes are annual, with 4-year cumulated indexes; since v.37 (1973), annual indexes.

A bibliography of Catholic missions. Classified arrangement with author and subject indexes. Since 1961, includes an appendix of *Documenti e problemi missionari.* Z7838.M6B5

Harvard University. Library. Chinese-Japanese Library. Catalog of Protestant missionary works in Chinese: Harvard-Yenching Library, Harvard University. Comp. by John Yung-Hsiang Lai. Boston, G. K. Hall, 1980. 339p.
BB317

The dictionary catalog of a unique Chinese-language collection which includes "many versions and editions of the Bible and its separate books, as well as catechisms; commentaries; hymnbooks; prayer books; text books; and serials and small tracts, both religious and secular."—*Introd.* Languages represented are literary Chinese, spoken Mandarin, and various dialects. The nucleus of the collection, that of the American Board of Commissioners of Foreign Missions, was expanded to include related materials; publication dates range from 1810 to about 1927. Wade-Giles romanization is used for Chinese author and title headings, with other information in the original script.

A preliminary (microfilm) edition, "A catalog of the TA collection in the Harvard-Yenching Library," appeared in 1977.
Z7757.C6H37

Latourette, Kenneth Scott. A history of the expansion of Christianity. N.Y., Harper, 1937–45. 7v. maps. **BB318**

A comprehensive survey of missions from the earliest times to the 1940s, with an extensive bibliography in each volume.
BR145.L3

Laures, John. Kirishitan bunko; a manual of books and documents on the early Christian missions in Japan . . . 3d rev. and enl. ed. Tokyo, Sophia Univ., 1957. 536p. il. (Monumenta nipponica monographs, no.5) **BB319**

Subtitle: With special reference to the principal libraries in Japan,

and more particularly to the collection at Sophia University, Tokyo; with an appendix of ancient maps of the Far East, especially Japan. 1st ed. 1940.

A bibliography of documents (books, articles, manuscripts) relating to the Christian missions from their beginnings in the 16th century to the first years after the reopening of Japan to relations with the West. Catholic viewpoint.

Mission handbook: North American Protestant ministries overseas. Ed. by Samuel Wilson. 12th ed. [Monrovia, Calif.], Missions Advanced Research and Communication Center, 1980. 714p. **BB320**

1st ed., 1953, had title: *Check list of foreign missionary agencies in the United States.* Title of later editions varies.

Provides directory information, both descriptive and statistical (on finances and personnel) for about 900 Protestant agencies engaged in, or supporting, ministries outside North America.

Neill, Stephen Charles, Anderson, Gerald H. and **Goodwin, John.** Concise dictionary of the Christian world mission. London, Lutterworth; Nashville, Abingdon Pr., [1971]. 682p. **BB321**

Brief, signed articles on the spread of Christianity in various countries of the world, biographies of missionary leaders, and topics and problems relating to missionary work. Bibliographic references accompany most entries. BV2040.N44

New York. Missionary Research Library. Dictionary catalog. Boston, G. K. Hall, 1968. 17v. **BB322**

Approximately 273,000 entries by author, title, and subject. Many entries for periodical articles by important authors are included. Missionary journals held by the Library are listed in v.17.
Z817.N54

Streit, Robert. Bibliotheca missionum, begonnen von P. Robert Streit, fortgeführt von P. Johannes Dindinger. Freiburg, Herder, 1916–74. v.1–30. (Veröffentlichungen des Internationalen Inst. für Missionswissenschaftliche Forschung) **BB323**

Imprint varies; editors vary.

Contents: v.1, Grundlegender und allgemeiner Teil; v.2–3, Amerikanische Missionsliteratur, 1493–1699, 1700–1909; v.4–5, Asiatische Missionsliteratur, 1245–1599, 1600–1699; v.6, Missionsliteratur Indiens, der Philippinen, Japans und Indochinas, 1700–1799; v.7, Chinesische Missionsliteratur, 1700–1799; v.8, Missionsliteratur Indiens und Indonesiens, 1800–1909; v.9, Missionsliteratur der Philippinen, 1800–1909; v.10, Missionsliteratur Japans und Koreas, 1800–1909; v.11, Missionsliteratur Indochinas, 1800–1909; v.12–14, Chinesische Missionsliteratur, 1800–1884, 1885–1909, 1910–1950; v.15–20, Afrikanische Missionsliteratur, 1053–1599, 1600–1699, 1700–1879, 1880–1909, 1910–1940; v.21, Missionsliteratur von Australien und Ozeanien, 1525–1950; v.22, Grundlegender und allgemeiner Teil, 1910–1935, und Nachtrag zu Bd.1; v.23, Grundlegender und allgemeiner Teil, 1936–1960; v.24–26, Amerikanische Missionsliteratur, 1910–24, 1925–44, 1945–60; v.27, Missionsliteratur Indiens, 1910–1946, und Nachtrag zu B.M. IV bis VIII; v.28, Missionsliteratur Südasiens (Indien, Pakistan, Birma, Ceylon), 1947–68; v.29, Missionsliteratur Südostasiens, 1910–1970; v.30, Missionsliteratur Japans und Koreas, 1910–1970 und Nachtrag zu B.M. IV, V, VI, X.

The great Catholic bibliography of missions. Includes voyages, relations, official documents, etc. Gives full bibliographical details, critical estimates, annotations, references to sources, and (in many cases) location of copies in European libraries. Z7838.M6S9

Statistics

See also BB250.

Churches and church membership in the United States, 1980: an enumeration by region, state and county, based on data reported by 111 church bodies. [Ed. by] Bernard Quinn [and others]. Atlanta, Glenmary Research Ctr., [1982]. 321p. maps. **BB324**

"This report contains statistics for 111 Judaeo-Christian church bodies, providing information [as of 1980] on the number of their churches and members for regions, states and counties of the United States."—*Pref.* Tables providing national, regional, and state summaries are followed by tables showing number of churches and church membership by county and denomination. BR526.C48

Johnson, Douglas W., Picard, Paul R. and **Quinn, Bernard.** Churches & church membership in the United States: an enumeration by region, state, and county; 1971. Wash., D.C., Glenmary Research Ctr., [1974]. 237p. maps. **BB325**

"This report contains statistics by region, state and county on Christian churches and church membership for 1971. Fifty-three denominations are included, representing an estimated 80.8 percent of church membership in the United States."—*Pref.*

Offers tables for (1) churches and church membership by denomination; (2) churches and church membership by region, state and denomination; and (3) churches and church membership by state, county and denomination. BR526.J64

National Council of the Churches of Christ in the U.S.A. Bureau of Research and Survey. Churches and church membership in the United States; an enumeration and analysis by counties, states and regions. N.Y., Council, 1956–58. Ser.A–ser.E. **BB326**

Contents: ser.A, no.1–4, Major faiths by regions, divisions, and states; ser. B, no.1–8, Denominational statistics by regions, divisions, and states; ser.C, no.1–59, Denominational statistics by states and counties; ser.D, no.1–6, Denominational statistics by metropolitan areas; ser.E, no.1–3, Socio-economic characteristics. BR526.N3

U.S. Bureau of the Census. Religious bodies: 1936. Wash., Govt. Prt. Off., 1941. 3v. **BB327**

Contents: v.1, Summary and detailed tables; v.2–3, Separate denominations: statistics, history, doctrine, organization, and work.

Statistics given are, as nearly as possible, those for the year 1936, and cover, for the continental United States: membership, church edifices and parsonages, value of church property and debt on same, expenditures, and Sunday schools. Previous full reports for this century covered 1906, 1916, and 1926.

Since 1936, full reports have not been made by the Bureau of the Census, although very abbreviated statistics are given in its *Current population reports: Population characteristics,* Ser.P-20, no.79 (1957). More detailed figures are included in the *Yearbook of American and Canadian churches* (BB347). HA201.1936.A32

Atlases

Anderson, Charles S. Augsburg historical atlas of Christianity in the Middle Ages and Reformation. Minneapolis, Augsburg, [1967]. 61p. il. 29cm. **BB328**

Maps with accompanying text; intended as a study aid for church history. G1796.E4A5

Atlas zur Kirchengeschichte; die christlichen Kirchen in Geschichte und Gegenwart. Hrsg. von Hubert Jedin, Kenneth Scott Latourette und Jochen Martin. Freiburg, Herder, [1970]. various pagings. 35cm. **BB329**

152 pages of maps and charts are accompanied by nearly 80 pages of commentary; bibliographical references follow each section of commentary. Detailed index. G1046.E4A8

Emmerich, Heinrich. Atlas hierarchicus. Descriptio geographica et statistica Ecclesiae Catholicae tum Occidentis tum Orientis. Mödling, St. Gabriel-Verlag, 1968. 76p. col. maps. 45cm. **BB330**

A new edition of Karl Streit's *Atlas hierarchicus* (2. Aufl., 1929). Supplements [1–5]: Historical introduction and explanation of maps inserted. Text in English, French, German, Italian, and Spanish, giving descriptive and historical information.
G1046.E4E4

Freitag, Anton [and others]. Atlas du monde chrétien; l'expansion du christianisme à travers les siècles. Paris, Bruxelles, Elsevier, 1959. 215p. il. 35cm. **BB331**

The historical maps (in color) are far outnumbered by the pages of photographs (of people, places, works of art) and explanatory text. Index of proper names.

A revision and translation was published as: BV2100.F7

———— The twentieth century atlas of the Christian world; the expansion of Christianity through the centuries. N.Y., Hawthorn, [1963, i.e., 1964]. 199p. il. maps. 35cm. **BB332**

A pictorial atlas, from the Catholic point of view.
BV2100.F713

Gaustad, Edwin Scott. Historical atlas of religion in America. Rev. ed. N.Y., Harper & Row, [1976]. 189p. il., maps. 32cm. **BB333**

1st ed. 1962.

A work which—by maps, charts, tables, and text—shows the expansion and development of the churches and membership of the various denominations from 1650 to 1970.

In the new edition, "The generally unrevealing state maps of the earlier edition have now been replaced with county maps for the mid-twentieth century. . . . New maps have been added . . . along with several new charts and updated line graphs. A new fold-out color map reflects denominational distribution in 1970, while an additional map indicates the Protestant-Catholic dominance county-by-county."—*Pref.* G1201.E4G3

Halvorson, Peter L. and **Newman, William M.** Atlas of religious change in America, 1952–1971. Cartography by Mark C. Nielsen. Wash., Glenmary Research Center, [1978]. 95p. maps. **BB334**

"In the early 1950's the National Council of Churches sponsored a unique county level census-type study of religious adherence [*see* BB326]. Nearly twenty years later, a similar study was jointly sponsored by the Glenmary Research Center, the National Council of Churches, and the Lutheran Church-Missouri Synod [*see* BB325]. This *Atlas* presents time-series data from these two landmark and several supplemental data sources."—*Introd.* 35 religious denominations are represented; for each is given a summary statement and four maps showing changes by county, 1952–71. G1201.E4H3

Meer, Frederik van der and **Mohrmann, Christine.** Atlas of the early Christian world; tr. and ed. by Mary F. Hedlund and H. H. Rowley. [London], Nelson, 1958. 215p. incl. 42 maps. il. 36cm. **BB335**

A translation of the work originally published as *Atlas van de oudchristelijke wereld* (Amsterdam, Elsevier, 1958). Includes 620 plates illustrating the history of Christianity for the first six centuries, covering sculpture, architecture, mosaics, Christian cities, etc. The 42 maps are the work of Van der Meer and show in great detail the various parts of the Roman Empire, with plans of important cities and regions, churches, monuments, dioceses, etc. The text comments on the historical and geographical background and describes the illustrations. Indexed. G1046.E4M6

Hymnology

Analecta hymnica medii aevi, hrsg. von Guido Maria Dreves und Clemens Blume. Leipzig, Reisland, 1886–1922. v.1–55. (Repr.: N.Y., Johnson Reprint Corp., 1961; also available in microform from Microcard Eds., Wash., D.C.) **BB336**

A very comprehensive collection, giving texts of hymns and detailed historical and bibliographical notes.

———— Register, in Zusarb. mit Dorothea Baumann [et al.] hrsg. von Max Lütolf. Bern, Francke, 1978. 3v. in 2.

Contents: v.1 (in 2v.), Verzeichnis der Textanfängen; v.2, Gattungen, Liturgische Bestimmungen, Verfasser.

Indexes in v.2 refer to entry numbers in the first-line index in v.1, which in turn gives volume and page in the set. BV468.A622A5

Chevalier, Cyr Ulysse Joseph. Repertorium hymnologicum. Catalogue des chants, hymnes, proses, séquences, tropes en usage dans l'église latine depuis les origines jusqu'à nos jours. Louvain, Bruxelles, Soc. des Bollandistes, 1892–1920. 6v. (Repr.: Louvain, Lefever, 1959?) **BB337**

Published in parts as a separately paged supplement to the *Analecta bollandiana,* 1889–1920 (BB279).

For each hymn gives *incipit,* saint or feast of the church to which the hymn belongs and its place in the office, number of strophes, author's name, date of composition if known, and reference to manuscripts or printed sources in which the hymn is found.
Z7838.L7C5

Dictionary of American hymnology: first line index. A project of the Hymn Society of America. Leonard Ellinwood, ed. N.Y., University Music Editions, 1984. 179 reels microfilm with looseleaf guide. **BB338**

Microfilm reproduction of more than a million alphabetically arranged data cards of the first-line hymn index compiled by the Hymn Society. Indexes 4,634 American hymnals and general gospel songbooks from 1640 to the present. Gives data for source hymnal, first line, title, author. Hymnals are listed in numerical code sequence on Reel 001; the alphabetical list is contained in:

Bibliography of American hymnals; comp. from the files of the Dictionary of American hymnology, a project of the Hymn Society of America. Leonard Ellinwood, ed. N.Y., University Music Editions, [1983]. 27 microfiches. **BB339**

Lists the hymnals indexed in the *Dictionary* (above), plus others for a total of 7,500 works.

Diehl, Katharine Smith. Hymns and tunes: an index. N.Y., Scarecrow Pr., 1966. 1185p. **BB340**

Indexes the hymns from 78 hymnals by first lines, variant first lines, and authors. The hymn tunes are indexed by names and variants, by composers, and by a systematic index to the melodies.
BV305.D5

Julian, John. A dictionary of hymnology setting forth the origin and history of Christian hymns of all ages and nations. Rev. ed. with new supplement. London, Murray; N.Y., Scribner, 1907. 1768p. (Repr.: Grand Rapids, Mich., Kregel, 1985. 2v.) **BB341**

1st ed. 1892; the revised edition corrects some typographical errors and adds a supplement of 131 pages to cover later information, and new indexes.

Contents: (1) Dictionary; (2) Cross reference index to first lines in English, French, German, Latin, etc.; (3) Index of authors, translators, etc.; (4) Appendix, A–Z, late articles; (5) Appendix, A–Z, additions and corrections to articles in main part; (6) New supplement; (7) Indexes to appendixes and supplement.

Deals with Christian hymns of all ages and nations, with special reference to those in the hymnbooks of English-speaking countries. Articles on subjects in hymnology, hymn writers, and separate hymns—all in one alphabet; important subjects are treated at considerable length. Signed articles; bibliographies. BV305.J8

McCutchan, Robert Guy. Hymn tune names: their sources and significance. N.Y., Nashville, Abingdon, [1957]. 206p. **BB342**

An alphabetical list of the names of hymn tunes, indicating melody and time, and giving the origin and history of the name.
ML3186.M22

McDormand, Thomas Bruce and **Crossman, Frederic S.** Judson concordance to hymns. Valley Forge, Pa., Judson Pr., [1965]. 375p. **BB343**

Provides a subject approach to hymns as well as a kind of concordance. Lines from hymns are arranged by keyword with reference to the table of first lines. 2,342 hymns are included.
BV305.M3

Parks, Edna D. Early English Hymns: an index. Metuchen, N.J., Scarecrow Pr., 1972. 168p. **BB344**

Hymns are listed alphabetically by first line, with indication of meter, number of stanzas or lines, author's name, publication date and page reference in a collection, and indication of composer's name and the tune when available. Includes numerous items not in Julian (BB341). Publication dates are mainly 17th century. Bibliography; indexes of authors and of composers. BV305.P37

Perry, David W. Hymns and tunes indexed by first lines, tune names, and metres, compiled from current English hymnbooks. Croydon, Hymn Society of Great Britain & Ireland and the Royal School of Church Music, 1980. 310p. **BB345**

Locates hymns in 37 British hymnbooks "in wide current use for adult congregational worship."—*Introd.* BV305.P47

Protestant denominations

General works

Yearbooks

Annuaire protestant, 1880– ; La France protestante et les églises de langue française. Paris, Fischbacher, 1880–. v.1– . Annual. (Année 96, 1984) **BB346**

Title varies; subtitle varies.

Directory and institutional information for France and overseas French-speaking regions; no biography.

Yearbook of American and Canadian churches, 1916– . Publ. by the National Council of the Churches of Christ in the U.S.A. N.Y., 1916– . Annual. (v.51, 1983) **BB347**

Title, publisher, and frequency vary. v.1–2, *Federal Council year book;* v.3–8, *Year book of the churches;* v.9 (1927) *Handbook of the churches;* 1933–72, *Yearbook of American churches.*

Now covers the organizations and activities of all faiths. Some issues contain a biographical section. BR513.Y4

❖Many denominations publish annuals and/or directories; only a few of the larger denominations are listed here, and many of these have been formed by mergers of various bodies. For information about other denominations *see* the *Yearbook of American and Canadian churches* (BB347), and the annual reports or yearbooks of individual denominations; the latter are useful for denominational facts and figures, lists of ministers, etc.

Baptist

Encyclopedia of Southern Baptists. Nashville, Broadman, 1958–82. 4v. and index. il. **BB348**

Offers signed articles with bibliographies; includes many biographical sketches. Covers the history, methods, and work of Southern Baptists, including organizations, institutions, colleges, newspapers, etc., as well as articles on their viewpoint on religious beliefs and practices. Vols. 3 and 4 update and expand the first two volumes, covering developments of 1956–70 and 1970–80, respectively; a system of cross references to the earlier volumes is provided. The 36-page "Index to volumes I–IV" lists articles in the full set.
BX6211.E5

Starr, Edward Caryl. A Baptist bibliography, being a register of printed material by and about Baptists, including works written against the Baptists. Rochester, N.Y., Amer. Baptist Historical Soc., 1947–76. 25v. **BB349**

Imprint varies.

Arranged alphabetically by author, with an index in each volume to joint authors, translators, Baptist publishers, distinctive titles, and subjects. Locates copies. Z7845.B2S8

Whitley, William Thomas. A Baptist bibliography; being a register of the chief materials for Baptist history, whether in manuscript or in print, preserved in Great Britain, Ireland, and the Colonies . . . comp. for the Baptist Union of Great Britain and Ireland. London, Kingsgate Pr., 1916–22. 2v. (Repr.: Hildesheim, Olms, 1984. 2v. in 1) **BB350**

Contents: v.1, 1526–1776; v.2, 1777–1837. Addenda, 1613–53. Indexes: (1) Anonymous pamphlets, (2) Authors, (3) Places, (4) Subjects.

Locates copies in 31 libraries, mainly British. Z7845.B2W6

Yearbooks

American Baptist Churches in the U.S.A. Yearbook, 1973– . Valley Forge, Pa., 1973– . il. Annual. **BB351**

Continues the *Yearbook* of the American Baptist Convention, 1950–72. Issued 1908–49 as *Yearbook* of the Northern Baptist Convention, which absorbed the *American Baptist yearbook* in 1941. (Issuing agency changed name to American Baptist Convention in 1950; to American Baptist Churches in the U.S.A. in 1973.)

Includes records of the biennial meeting of the association and reports of activities of the national boards.

Beginning 1973, directory and statistical information is separately published in: BX6207.A3

———— Directory. . . . Valley Forge, Pa., 1971– . Annual. **BB352**

BX6207.A316

Southern Baptist Convention. Executive Committee. Annual. Nashville, Tenn., 1847?– . Annual (biennial until 1866). **BB353**

Includes proceedings, reports, statistics, directory information, etc.

Brethren churches

The Brethren encyclopedia. Philadelphia, Brethren Encyclopedia, Inc., 1983–84. 3v. (2126p.) il. **BB354**

Offers signed articles, with bibliographies, on the "life, belief, practice and heritage" of "those religious bodies that trace their origin to the Brethren movement."—*Introd.* Included are the Brethren Church, the Church of the Brethren, the Dunkard Brethren, the Fellowship of Grace Brethren Churches, and the Old German Baptist Brethren. Strong in biography. v.3, "Lists—maps," contains statistical data, a list of ministers and elders, 1708–1980, extensive bibliography, chronology, maps, and corrections and additions to v.1–2. BX7821.2B74

Church of England

Yearbooks

Church of England. Year book. 80th– , 1963– . London, Church Information Office, 1963– . il. Annual. **BB355**

Title varies. Vols. for 1963–70 issued as *Official year book* of its National Assembly; 1971/72– as the *Official year book* of its General Synod.

Continues: Church of England. National Assembly. *Official year book,* 1883–1962.

Provides general directory information and gives brief biographies of members of the General Synod, of bishops, deans, provosts, archdeacons, and Lambeth Palace staff. BX5015.C45

Crockford's Clerical directory, 1858– . Oxford, Univ. Pr., 1858– . v.1– . il. (88th issue, 1980–82) **BB356**

Frequency varies; now triennial.

Subtitle varies. For 1980–82: A reference book of the clergy of the provinces of Canterbury and York and of other Anglican provinces and dioceses.

Includes biographical sketches for Church of England clergy in the British Isles and overseas, as well as statistical and directory information.

History

LeNeve, John. Fasti ecclesiae anglicanae; or, A calendar of the principal ecclesiastical dignitaries in England and Wales, and of the chief officers in the universities of Oxford and Cambridge, from the earliest time to the year MDCCXV . . . corrected and continued to the present time by T. Duffus Hardy. Oxford, Univ. Pr., 1854. 3v. **BB357**

Lists of ecclesiastical dignitaries, bishops, archdeacons, prebendaries, etc., arranged by diocese, with alphabetical indexes of names. Some biographical information.

LeNeve's work first appeared in 1716 in 1v. The LeNeve-Hardy compilation is being revised and expanded in three series:
BX5197.L5

———— Fasti ecclesiae anglicanae, 1066–1300. London, Institute of Historical Research; Athlone Pr., 1968–77. v.1–3. (In progress) **BB358**

Contents: v.1, St. Paul's, London, comp. by D. E. Greenway; v.2, Monastic cathedrals (Northern and Southern provinces), comp. by D. E. Greenway; v.3, Lincoln, comp. by D. E. Greenway.
BR754.A1L44

———— Fasti ecclesiae anglicanae, 1300–1541. [London], Univ. of London, Inst. of Historical Research; Athlone Pr., 1962–67. 12v. **BB359**

v.12 is "Introduction, errata and index," comp. by Joyce M. Horn.

———— Fasti ecclesiae anglicanae, 1541–1857. [London], Univ. of London, Inst. of Historical Research; Athlone Pr., 1969–79. v.1–5. (In progress) **BB360**

Contents: v.1, St. Paul's, London, comp. by J. M. Horn; v.2, Chichester Diocese, comp. by J. M. Horn; v.3, Canterbury, Rochester and Winchester Dioceses, comp. by J. M. Horn; v.4, York Diocese, comp. by J. M. Horn and D. M. Smith; v.5, Bath and Wells Diocese, comp. by J. M. Horn and D. S. Bailey. BR754.A1L443

Ollard, Sidney Leslie, Crosse, Gordon and **Bond, M. F.** Dictionary of English church history. [3d ed. rev.] London, Mowbray; N.Y., Morehouse, [1948]. 698p. **BB361**

1st ed. 1912; 2d ed. 1919.

Scope of this work is strictly that of the English church, i.e., the provinces of Canterbury and York, and does not include discussion of the church in Ireland, Scotland, or America. Good signed articles with brief bibliographies (usually undated) on history, beliefs, controversies, architecture, costume, music, etc., of the church. Many biographies of persons deceased. A special feature is the list of bishops under the name of each see. High Church point of view.
BX5007.O5

Service books

Church of England. Book of Common Prayer. The Book of common prayer and administration of the sacraments, and other rites and ceremonies of the church according to the use of the Church of England. . . . Oxford, Univ. Pr.
BB362

For editions *see* current issues of the *Oxford Bible catalogue* of the Oxford University Press.

———— Annotated Book of common prayer, being an historical, ritual and theological commentary on the devotional system of the Church of England by John Henry Blunt. New impression, 1899; reissue, with additions, and corrections. London, Longmans; N.Y., Dutton, 1903 [pref. 1883]. 732p.
BB363

BX5145.B6

———— The Alternative Service book of 1980: services authorized for use in the Church of England in conjunction with the Book of Common Prayer, together with the Liturgical Psalter. London, Clowes, 1980. 1292p. **BB364**

The service book of revised liturgical forms. "Intended to supplement the Book of Common Prayer, not to supersede it."—*Pref.*

Bibliography

Benton, Josiah Henry. The Book of common prayer and books connected with its origin and growth; catalogue of the collection of Josiah Henry Benton. . . . 2d ed. prep. by William Muss-Arnolt. Boston, priv. pr., 1914. 142p.   **BB365**

1st ed. 1910.
A collection of books of common prayer of the Churches of England, Ireland, and Scotland; the Protestant Episcopal church of the United States; and others.   Z7813.B41

Muss-Arnolt, William. The Book of common prayer among the nations of the world; . . . a study based mainly on the collection of Josiah Henry Benton. London, Soc. for Promoting Christian Knowledge, 1914. 473p.   **BB366**

Subtitle: . . . a history of translations of the prayer book of the Church of England and of the Protestant Episcopal church of America.   BX5145.M8

Dictionaries

The Prayer book dictionary. Eds., George Harford, Morley Stevenson. London, Pitman, 1912. 832p. il.   **BB367**

Treats principally the English prayer book, with slight information about the prayer book of the Protestant Episcopal church. An alphabetical dictionary dealing with the "origins, history, use and teaching of the several authorized editions of the Book of Common Prayer . . . all accompanying ceremonies and supplementary rites . . . ."—*Introd.*

Church of Ireland

Phillips, Walter Alison. History of the Church of Ireland, from the earliest times to the present day. London, Oxford Univ. Pr., 1933–34. 3v.   **BB368**

Bibliography in each volume.   BX5500.P5

Church of Scotland

Macgregor, Malcolm B. The sources and literature of Scottish church history. Glasgow, McCallum, 1934. 260p. (Repr.: N.Y., Octagon, 1972)   **BB369**

An annotated bibliography of sources and secondary materials. Includes biographical sketches of outstanding persons in Scottish religious history from the earliest times.   Z7778.S3M2

Scott, Hew. Fasti ecclesiae scoticanae; the succession of ministers in the Church of Scotland from the Reformation. New ed., rev. and continued to the present time under the superintendence of a committee appointed by the General Assembly. Edinburgh, Oliver and Boyd, 1915–28. 7v.; v.8–10, 1950–81.   **BB370**

1st ed. 1866–71, 3v. in 6.
Publisher varies.
v.1–7 cover from 1560–1914. A brief historical sketch of each minister is given, with a list of his writings and bibliographical references where such are available. Each volume has a bibliography of local and parish histories. Number of biographies is more than 15,000.
v.8 is a supplementary volume covering 1914–28, with addenda and corrigenda, 1560–1949; v.9, ed. by J. A. Lamb, covers 1929–54; v.10, ed. by D. M. Macdonald, covers 1955–75.   BX9099.S4

Watt, Donald Elmslie Robertson. Fasti ecclesiae scoticanae medii aevi ad annum 1638. 2d draft. Edinburgh, Printed for the Scottish Record Society by Smith & Ritchie Ltd., 1969. 411p. (Scottish Record Soc. New ser., 1)   **BB371**

A draft "was circulated in duplicated typescript in 1959."–*Pref.*
The lists attempt to provide a record "of the succession in the principal offices of the dioceses, cathedrals and collegiate foundations of the medieval Scottish church. They concentrate on the evidence for the dates of appointment and death or resignation, and when these are unknown references are provided for the earliest and latest dates of occurrences which connect a holder with an office."—*Introd.*

Congregational

See United Church of Christ.

Disciples of Christ

See United Church of Christ.

Friends, Society of

Quaker records; being an index to "The annual monitor," 1813–92, containing over 20,000 obituary notices of members of the Society of Friends, alphabetically and chronologically arranged. Ed. by Joseph J. Green. London, Hicks, 1894. 458p. il.   **BB372**

Gives name, residence, year of death, age at death, and reference to the obituary in *The annual monitor.*

Smith, Joseph. Descriptive catalogue of Friends' books, or books written by members of the Society of Friends . . . from their first rise to the present time . . . with critical remarks and occasional biographical notices. London, J. Smith, 1867. 2v. (Repr.: N.Y., Kraus, 1970)   **BB373**

———— ———— Supplement. London, Hicks, 1893. 364p. (Repr.: N.Y., Kraus, 1970)

An alphabetical catalog of books about Quakers, or written by Quakers, including "all writings by authors before joining, and by those after having left the society."—*title page.* Full entries, sometimes with annotations. Many biographical notes.   Z7845.F8S7

———— Bibliotheca anti-Quakeriana; or, A catalogue of books adverse to the Society of Friends, alphabetically arranged, with biographical notices of the authors, together with the answers which have been given to some of them. . . . London, J. Smith, 1873. 474p. (Repr. with *Bibliotheca Quakeristica* [below]: N.Y., Kraus, 1968)   **BB374**

Includes the definitive "Muggletonian" bibliography (on Ludowick Muggleton, an English sectarian and critic of Quakerism).   Z7845.F8S6

———— Bibliotheca Quakeristica, a bibliography of miscellaneous literature relating to the Friends (Quakers), chiefly written by persons not members of their society; also of publications by authors in some way connected; and biographical notices. London, J. Smith, 1883. 32p.   **BB375**
                    Z7845.F8S6

Swarthmore College. Friends Historical Library. Catalog of the book and serials collections of the Friends Historical Library of Swarthmore College. Boston, G. K. Hall, 1982. 6v.   **BB376**

Photographic reproduction of the catalog cards for a notable Quaker collection (more than 40,000 volumes) which includes imprints from the 17th century to the present. Arrangement is a single alphabet of authors, titles and subjects. v.6 contains lists of serials, broadsides, and tracts.

Lutheran

American Lutheran Church. Yearbook. 1961– . Minneapolis, Augsburg Pub. House, 1960– . Annual. **BB377**

Statistical and directory information.
Corporate body organized in 1960, combined the American Lutheran Church, the Evangelical Lutheran Church, and the United Evangelical Lutheran Church. BX8009.A54

Lutheran Church in America. Yearbook. 1963– . Philadelphia, Board of Publication, Lutheran Church in America, 1962– . Annual. **BB378**

Statistical and directory information. BX8048.2.A35

Lutheran Church—Missouri Synod. Statistical yearbook. 1884– . St. Louis, Mo., Concordia Pub. House, 1884– . Annual. **BB379**

Title varies. Published in German, 1884–1917.
Detailed statistics plus directory information.
BX8061.M7A32

Lutheran book of worship, prep. by the churches participating in the Inter-Lutheran Commission on Worship: Lutheran Church in America, the American Lutheran Church, the Evangelical Lutheran Church of Canada, the Lutheran Church-Missouri Synod. Minneapolis, Augsburg Pub. House; Philadelphia, Board of Pubns., Lutheran Church in America, [1978]. 960p. music. **BB380**

A hymnal for congregational use that includes the major services, complete with musical settings. Other editions are the "Ministers ed.," with supplementary materials for leaders of worship; and the "Accompaniment ed.," with keyboard settings for the music of the liturgy. A commentary is Philip Pfatteicher and Carlos R. Messerli's *Manual on the liturgy: Lutheran book of worship* (Minneapolis, Augsburg Pub. House, 1979. 421p.), which is "designed to assist the various leaders of corporate worship to understand, plan, and carry out their several tasks."—*Pref.* BX8067.A3L76

Bodensieck, Julius, ed. The encyclopedia of the Lutheran church. Ed. for the Lutheran World Federation. Minneapolis, Augsburg Pub. House, [1965]. 3v. (2575p.) **BB381**

Signed articles, generally scholarly in tone, treating of Lutheran doctrine, history, and activity, together with brief descriptions of other religions and beliefs as related to Lutheranism. Some articles include bibliographies. BX8007.B6

Lutheran cyclopedia. Erwin L. Lueker, ed. Rev. ed. St. Louis, Concordia, [1975]. 845p. **BB382**

1st ed. 1954.
The previous edition was prepared under the auspices of the General Literature Board of the Lutheran Church, and drew upon materials from an earlier (1927) *Concordia cyclopedia.* This edition does not mention official church sponsorship, but the cooperation of various affiliates is noted.
Offers brief articles on important aspects of the history, thought, and teachings of the Lutheran church and various related matters. For the revised edition, the number of entries has been substantially increased, various articles have been reworked, new bibliographic references supplied, and special efforts made "to improve objectivity."—*Pref.* Although biographies of persons of various denominations and periods are included, it is understandably strong for Lutherans; for the most part, living persons are omitted.
BX8007.L8

Mennonite

Bender, Harold Stauffer. Two centuries of American Mennonite literature, a bibliography of Mennonitica Americana, 1727–1928. Goshen, Ind., Mennonite Historical Soc., Goshen College, 1929. 181p. facsims. (Studies in Anabaptist and Mennonite history, 1) **BB383**

Chronologically arranged by date of publication under distinct groups of Mennonites, with author and title indexes.
Z7845.M4B4

The Mennonite encyclopedia; a comprehensive reference work on the Anabaptist-Mennonite movement. Hillsboro, Kan., Mennonite Brethern Pub. House, 1955–59. 4v. il. **BB384**

Index of titles issued in lithographed form, 1960 (132p.).
Treats historical and contemporary topics relating to the Anabaptist-Mennonite movement from its beginning in the 16th century to the present time. Covers theology, ethics, history, and biography with special emphasis on existing and extinct congregations and institutions. Articles vary in length from a few lines to several columns, are signed, and include bibliographies. BX8106.M37

Mennonitisches Lexikon, hrsg. von Christian Hege und Christian Neff. Frankfurt am Main, Authors, 1913–67. 4v. il. **BB385**

Issued in parts.
Signed articles with bibliographies. BX8106.M4

Springer, Nelson P. and **Klassen, A. J.** Mennonite bibliography, 1631–1961. Scottdale, Pa., Herald Pr., 1977. 2v. **BB386**

Contents: v.1, International, Europe, Latin America, Asia, Africa; v.2, North America, Indices.
Comp. under the direction of the Institute of Mennonite Studies.
Serves as a continuation of Hans J. Hillerbrand's *Bibliography of Anabaptism, 1520–1630* (Elkhart, Ind., Inst. of Mennonite Studies, 1962). Aims "to report published materials of Mennonite authorship and statements about Mennonites by non-Mennonites. These include periodicals, books, pamphlets, dissertations, festschrifts, symposia, and encyclopedia and periodical articles."—*Pref.* Topical arrangement within geographical divisions; indexes of authors, subjects, and books reviewed. More than 28,000 items.
Z7845.M4S67

Methodist

The encyclopedia of world Methodism. Nolan B. Harmon, gen. ed. Prep. and ed. under the supervision of The World Methodist Council and The Commission on Archives and History. [Nashville, Tenn.], United Methodist Publ. House, [1974]. 2v. (2814p.) il. **BB387**

Aims "to give helpful information regarding the history, doctrines, institutions, and important personages, past and present, of World Methodism."—*Pref.* Inasmuch as expenses of the project were underwritten by the United Methodist Church in America, and because that "is the largest organized body among Methodist Churches of the world," a proportionately greater part of the work is devoted to that church. Articles are signed; many include bibliographies. Very strong in biography. BX8211.E5

Rowe, Kenneth E. Methodist union catalog, pre–1976 imprints. Metuchen, N.J., Scarecrow Pr., 1975–81. v.1–5. (In progress) **BB388**

Contents: v.1–5, A–Hazzard.
A preliminary edition, ed. by Brooks Little, appeared in 1967.
Represents holdings relating to Methodism of some 200 libraries "that have been reported to the editor or recorded in printed catalogs."—*Introd.* Main entry listing with locations. Includes variant editions. Some British and European libraries are represented.
Z7845.M5R69

Sourcebook of American Methodism. Ed. by Frederick A. Norwood. Nashville, Abingdon, [1982]. 683p. **BB389**

"Aims to present representative source readings" covering 200 years of American Methodism "useful . . . with a textbook . . . or [in] independent study."—*Introd.* Chronologically arranged; sources are cited. No index. A companion to the editor's *Story of American Methodism* (Nashville, Abingdon, 1974. 448p.).
BX8235.S68

United Methodist Church (United States). General minutes of the annual conferences . . . Evanston, Ill., Section of Records and Statistics, 1968– . Annual.   **BB390**

Supersedes *General minutes of the annual conferences* issued by the Dept. of Research and Statistics of the Methodist Church, 1940?–67.   BX8382.2.A1U57b

United Methodist studies: basic bibliographies, comp. and ed. by Kenneth E. Rowe. Nashville, Tenn., Abingdon, [1982]. 40p.   **BB391**

Provides "a selected list of the most important basic resources for persons responsible for teaching seminary-level courses in United Methodist history, doctrine, and polity."—*Purpose.* A classified list of standard texts and modern critical interpretations.

Z7845.M5U54

Who's who in the Methodist church. [2d ed.] Nashville, Tenn., Abingdon Pr., [1966]. 1489p.   **BB392**

"Comp. by the Editors of Who's who in America and the A. N. Marquis Co., Inc., with the cooperation of the Council of Secretaries of the Methodist Church."—*title page.*

1st ed., 1952, entitled *Who's who in Methodism.*

About 25,000 biographies of officials, etc., of the church and its related organizations and of Methodists prominent in all fields of activity.   BX8213.W52

Mormon

Bitton, Davis. Guide to Mormon diaries & autobiographies. Provo, Utah, Brigham Young Univ. Pr., [1977]. 417p.   **BB393**

An author list of 2,894 diaries, journals, memoirs, etc., of the 19th and 20th centuries; descriptive notes range from a paragraph to a column of text. Indexed.   Z7845.M8B58

Brigham Young Univ., Provo, Utah. College of Religious Instruction. A catalogue of theses and dissertations concerning the Church of Jesus Christ of Latter-Day Saints, Mormonism and Utah. Provo, Brigham Young Univ. Printing Service, [1971]. 742p.   **BB394**

Includes master's theses and doctoral dissertations from institutions throughout the United States through 1969. Classed arrangement with detailed subject index.

Clement, Russell T. Mormons in the Pacific: a bibliography. Laie, Hawaii, Inst. for Polynesian Studies, [1981]. 239p.   **BB395**

Sub-title: Holdings at the Brigham Young University-Hawaii Campus, Brigham Young University-Utah Campus and the Church Historical Department.

Offers "a concentrated attempt to list all books, pamphlets, periodicals, personal diaries, journals, mission histories, ephemera, and selected periodical articles concerning Mormons and the Mormon experience" *(Introd.)* in Polynesia, Micronesia and Melanesia. Author listing with name and geographic/subject indexes. 2,873 entries; annotations.

Biographical information on Mormons in the western and southwestern United States and southwestern Canada, 1820–1981, is indexed in Marvin E. Wiggins' *Mormons and their neighbors* (Provo, Harold B. Lee Lib., Brigham Young Univ., 1984. 2v.) which analyzes 194 published volumes containing 75,000 biographical sketches.

Flake, Chad J. A Mormon bibliography, 1830–1930; books, pamphlets, periodicals, and broadsides relating to the first century of Mormonism. Salt Lake City, Univ. of Utah Pr., 1978. 825p. il., facsims.   **BB396**

A main entry listing of more than 10,000 items pertaining wholly or partly to the first century of Mormonism: "books, periodicals, Mormon newspapers or predominantly Mormon newspapers . . . , pamphlets, and broadsides."—*Pref.* Not intended as a complete union catalog of Mormonism, but aims "to include adequate locations where an item could be found." Principles of inclusion and exclusion, form of entry, etc., are carefully stated in the preface. Chronological index.   Z7845.M8F55

Utah. University. Library. Widtsoe Collection. Holdings of the University of Utah on Utah and the Church of Jesus Christ of Latter-day Saints. L. H. Kirkpatrick, ed. Salt Lake City, 1954. 285p.   **BB397**

Entries for Mormonism and for Utah are in separate sections. Most of the Mormon entries are briefly annotated.   Z7845.M8U8

Presbyterian

Prince, Harold B. A Presbyterian bibliography: the published writings of ministers who served in the Presbyterian Church in the United States during its first hundred years, 1861–1961, and their locations in eight significant theological collections in the U.S.A. Metuchen, N.J., Scarecrow Pr.; [Philadelphia], Amer. Theological Lib. Assoc., 1983. 452p. (ATLA bibliography ser., no.8)   **BB398**

A union list of published materials by and about Presbyterian ministers. 4,187 entries arranged alphabetically by author. Indexed.   Z7845.P9P83

United Presbyterian Church in the U.S.A. General Assembly. Minutes of the General Assembly. Philadelphia, 1967– . Ser. 7, v.1– . Annual.   **BB399**

[Ser. 1]–6, 1870–1966.

Imprint varies. Corporate body united (1958) the Presbyterian Church in the U.S.A. and the United Presbyterian Church of North America.

Contents vary: Ser. 7, 1967–72, in three parts: (1) Journal; (2) Annual reports; (3) Statistics; 1973– in two parts: (1) Journal (containing proceedings and reports of agencies and councils); (2) Statistical tables and Presbytery rolls.   BX8951.A4

Protestant Episcopal

Yearbooks

Clerical directory of the Protestant Episcopal church in the United States of America. N.Y., Church Hymnal Corp., 1898–1968.   **BB400**

Previous titles: *Lloyd's Clerical directory* and *Stowe's Clerical directory.*

Contains biographical sketches of the clergymen of the Protestant Episcopal church throughout the world; issued approximately every third year (none issued between 1941 and 1947). Ceased 1968; information now included in: BX5830.S8

Episcopal clerical directory. Ed.25– , 1975– . N.Y., Church Hymnal Corp., 1975– . Biennial.   **BB401**

Continues the *Episcopal clergy directory* (ed.24, 1972) and its predecessor, *Clerical directory of the Protestant Episcopal Church,* and continues their numbering.

Offers who's who type "biographical data for all Episcopal clergy in good standing, both active and retired."—*Foreword, 1983.*

The Episcopal church annual. 1830– . N.Y., Morehouse-Gorham, 1830– . Annual.   **BB402**

Established in 1830 as *The churchman's almanac;* 1882–1952, *The living church annual.* Title varies somewhat through the years. In 1953 assumed the present title.

General directory and institutional information, with clergy list.   BX5830.L5

Book of Common Prayer

❖The *Book of common prayer* of the Protestant Episcopal Church of the United States was adopted after the Revolution and put into use in 1790. There have been three revisions: in 1892, 1928 and 1979. The 1928 revision made numerous changes in arrangement of material, the addition of new prayers, and the rewriting of others. In 1934 a standardized paging was approved for the main part of the book, i.e., from Morning Prayer to the end of the Articles of Religion. In 1943, additional material was added to the prefatory paging, which uses roman numerals. The *Index* noted below (BB404) is based on these revisions. In 1977 a revised "proposed" text was published for a trial period and was adopted in 1979.

Episcopal Church. The Book of Common Prayer and administration of the sacraments and other rites and ceremonies of the church: together with the Psalter or Psalms of David according to the use of the Episcopal Church. N.Y., Church Hymnal Corp.; [Greenwich, Conn., Seabury Pr., 1979]. 1001p. **BB403**

The most recent revision, now in use in the United States. A detailed commentary on this edition is Marion Hatchett's *Commentary on the American prayer book* (N.Y., Seabury Pr., 1980. 670p.); the prayer book text is not included, but page references to it are provided.

For the previous edition and commentary see BB405–BB406.
BX5943.A1

Pepper, George Wharton. An analytical index to the Book of common prayer; and a brief account of its evolution. Together with a revision of Gladstone's Concordance to the Psalter. Philadelphia, Winston, [1948]. 251p. **BB404**

Based on the 1928 revision, with the prefatory matter paged according to the resolution of 1943 and the remainder upon the pagination provided for by the resolution of 1934. Includes a table showing the principal changes in the Psalter made in the revision of 1928, and a concordance to the Psalter. The computer-produced *Concordance to the American Book of Common Prayer,* ed. by Milton Huggett (N.Y., Church Hymnal Corp., 1970. 470p.) provides a general context concordance to the text. BX5945.P43

Protestant Episcopal Church in the U.S.A. Book of Common Prayer. Book of common prayer and administration of the sacraments and other rites and ceremonies of the church, according to the use of the Protestant Episcopal church in the United States of America, together with the Psalter or Psalms of David. N.Y., Oxford Univ. Pr., 1944. 611p. **BB405**

The 1928 revision is paged according to the Standard prayer book. Available in numerous editions. A modern printing with commentary is kept in print as:

——— The Oxford American prayer book commentary, by Massey Hamilton Shepherd, Jr. N.Y., Oxford Univ. Pr., 1950. 1v., various pagings. **BB406**

This is a facsimile reproduction of the Oxford, 1944, edition of the *Book of common prayer,* with commentary on facing pages. BX5945.S5

Dictionaries

Harper, Howard V. The Episcopalian's dictionary: church beliefs, terms, customs, and traditions explained in layman's language. N.Y., Seabury Pr., [1975]. 183p. **BB407**

Definitions intended for the layman. BX5007.H37

Reformed

Reformed Church in America. Commission on History. Historical directory of the Reformed Church in America, 1628–1978. Peter N. VandenBerge, ed. 2d ed. Grand Rapids, Eerdmans, [1978]. 385p. (Historical ser. of the Reformed Church in Amer., no.6) **BB408**

1st ed. 1966. A successor to Charles E. Corwin's *Manual of the Reformed Church in America* (5th ed. 1922; suppl. 1933).
Offered as "the best single source of essential information about the Reformed Church's ministers, missionaries, congregations, institutions, and judicatories."—*Foreword.* 8,000 individual entries for Ministers of the Word and for other ministries. Includes a list of churches and a number of chronological lists. BX9507.A55

Shaker

Richmond, Mary L. Hurt., comp. Shaker literature: a bibliography. Hancock, Mass., Shaker Community; distr. by University Pr. of New England, 1977. 2v. **BB409**

Contents: v.1, By the Shakers; v.2, About the Shakers.
About 4,000 entries. Each volume in two main parts: (1) Books, pamphlets, broadsides; (2) Periodical articles; each part is arranged by author or other main entry. Index of titles and joint authors in v.2. Z7845.S5R52

United Church of Christ

Dexter, Henry Martyn. The Congregationalism of the last 300 years, as seen in its literature . . . with a bibliographical appendix. N.Y., Harper, 1880. 716p., 326p. **BB410**

Includes *Collections toward a bibliography of Congregationalism,* 326p., 7,250 entries.
The bibliography is still the most extensive one on Congregationalism. BX7131.D4

On the trail of the UCC: a historical atlas of the United Church of Christ. Comp. and ed. by Carolyn E. Goddard. N.Y., United Church Pr., [1981]. 127p. maps. **BB411**

Intended "to help readers become acquainted with" the various "branches that have come together to form the United Church of Christ."—*Introd.* Offers a map for each of the 39 Conferences of the UCC showing locations of churches (about 6,000 in all) with brief historical notes. BX9884.O6

Peel, Albert. The Congregational two hundred, 1530–1948. London, Independent Pr., [1948]. 288p. **BB412**

Incorporates *A hundred eminent Congregationalists,* 1927.
Biographical sketches of 200 outstanding Congregationalists in England and America. BX7259.P4

Spencer, Claude Elbert. An author catalog of Disciples of Christ and related religious groups. Canton, Mo., Disciples of Christ Historical Soc., 1946. 367p. **BB413**

A catalog of works on many subjects by members of the Disciples of Christ. Gives dates and places of birth and death of the authors, when known. Z7845.D6S67

——— Theses concerning the Disciples of Christ and related religious groups. [2d ed.] Nashville, Tenn., Disciples of Christ Historical Soc., 1964. 94p. **BB414**

1st ed. 1941.

United Church of Christ. Yearbook. 1962– . Philadelphia, 1962– . Annual. **BB415**

Imprint varies. 1983 edition carries statistics for 1982.
Offers statistical and directory information.
Corporate body united, in 1957, the Congregational Christian churches with the Evangelical and Reformed Church. Continues the *Yearbook* of the Congregational Christian churches, which had been a continuation of the *Congregational yearbook* and the *Christian annual.* BX9884.A1U55

Roman Catholic church

Bibliography

Ellis, John Tracy and **Trisco, Robert.** A guide to American Catholic history. 2d ed., rev. and enl. Santa Barbara, ABC-Clio, [1982]. 265p. **BB416**

1st ed. 1959.

About 1,250 annotated entries in classed arrangement, with author/title/subject index. Covers through 1979. Omits the section on manuscript repositories found in the first edition.

Z7778.U6E38

Guide to Catholic literature, 1888–1940. Detroit, Romig, 1940. 1240p. **BB417**

Issued in 5 pts., A–Z.

Subtitle: An author-subject-title index in one straight alphabet of books and booklets, in all languages, on all subjects by Catholics or of particular Catholic interest, published or reprinted during the fifty-two years, January 1, 1888 to January 1, 1940, with more than a quarter of a million biographical, descriptive, and critical notes, each with complete reference to its authoritative source for further reference, reading, and study.

Under the author entry, material is entered in this order: (1) biography of the author, (2) books by him, (3) books and appreciable parts of books about him and his works, and (4) magazine articles about him and his works. Critical annotations and brief extracts from reviews, with exact citations, are included. Subject and title entries are cross references to the author entry.

———— v. 2–8, 1940–67, . . . ed. by Walter Romig. Detroit, Romig, [1945–68].

Issued as annual volumes cumulating into quadrennial supplements: 1940–44, 1944–48, 1948–51, 1952–55, 1956–59, 1960–63, 1964–67.

On the same plan as the basic volume.

Merged with *Catholic periodical index* to form *Catholic periodical and literature index* (AE247). Z7837.G9

McCabe, James Patrick. Critical guide to Catholic reference books. 2d ed. Littleton, Colo., Libraries Unlimited, 1980. 282p. (Research studies in library science, no.2) **BB418**

1st ed. 1971.

Concerned with reference works "whose contents or point of view relate in some way to Catholicism."—*Introd.* Classed arrangement within five broad chapters: (1) General works; (2) Theology; (3) The humanities; (4) Social sciences; (5) History. About 1,100 carefully selected items, with emphasis on English-language materials. Good annotations; author/title/subject index. Z674.R4 no.2

McLean, George F. An annotated bibliography of philosophy in Catholic thought, 1900–1964. N.Y., Ungar, [1967]. 371p. (Philosophy in the 20th century: Catholic and Christian, v.1) **BB419**

Includes book and periodical materials. Classed arrangement; index. Z7821.M25

Parsons, Wilfrid. Early Catholic Americana; a list of books and other works by Catholic authors in the United States, 1729–1830. . . . N.Y., Macmillan, 1939. 282p. **BB420**

Includes 1,187 numbered entries, in chronological arrangement, with author index. Locates copies.

Supersedes, except for the notes and comment, the *Bibliotheca Catholica Americana* of J. M. Finotti (1872). Z7837.P24

Bowe, Forrest. List of additions and corrections to Early Catholic Americana. Contribution of French translations (1724–1820). N.Y., Franco-Americana, 1952. 101p. il. **BB421**

A supplement of French translations not found in Parsons (above).

Vollmar, Edward R. The Catholic church in America: an historical bibliography. 2d ed. N.Y., Scarecrow Pr., 1963. 399p. **BB422**

1st ed. 1956.

Lists, alphabetically by author, books and periodical articles covering the period 1850–1961, including master's essays and doctoral dissertations dealing with the history of the Catholic church in America. Only theses from the regular degree-granting Catholic colleges have been included. Subject index.

Z7778.U6V6

Liturgy and ritual

See also BB452.

❖The history of liturgical texts in the Church (through the mid-1960s) is briefly described in the article "Liturgical books of Roman rite" in the *New Catholic encyclopedia,* 8:890–92. (A much earlier, but more detailed description of the subject is the article "Liturgical books" in the *Catholic encyclopedia,* 9:296–302.) The more important of these texts, used virtually unchanged for four hundred years, are retained in this edition of the *Guide* (*see* BB423, BB425).

The new liturgical books, published in accordance with the directives of the Second Vatican Council, and now in the vernacular, are cited in the article "Liturgical books of the Roman rite" in the *New Catholic* encyclopedia, 17:352–54, and are described in that volume under individual entries (e.g., "Sacramentary," "Lectionaries"). The more important of these books, in the English translation used in the United States, are listed below (*see* BB429–BB432).

Recent developments are noted in the *Catholic almanac,* 1984, "Liturgical developments," p.22–26.

For fuller description of the books mentioned *see* the above-cited articles in the Catholic encyclopedias (BB438 and BB439).

The "Catholic Church. Liturgy and ritual" section of v.99 of the *National union catalog—pre-1956 imprints* (AA128) constitutes an excellent bibliography of these works as published prior to the recent reforms. The items noted below, although not covering the whole rite of the church, will be adequate for many questions of a general or historical nature.

Catholic Church. Liturgy and Ritual. Breviary. Breviarium Romanum ex decreto Sacrosancti Concilii Tridentini restitutum S. Pii V Pontificis Maximi jussu editum aliorumque pontificum cura recognitum Pii Papae X, auctoritate reformatum. Editio vigesima juxta typicam. Rome, Paris, Desclée & Socii, [1948–49]. 4v. **BB423**

Issued in four unnumbered volumes covering the four seasons, i.e., *Pars verna* (spring); *Pars aestiva* (summer); *Pars autumnalis* (autumn); *Pars hiemalis* (winter). BX2000.A2

———— Roman breviary in English, restored by the Sacred Council of Trent . . . Ed. by Joseph A. Nelson. N.Y., Benziger, [1950–51]. 4v. **BB424**

BX2000.A4

Catholic Church. Liturgy and Ritual. Ritual. Rituale Romanum Pauli V Pontificis Maximi jussu editum, aliorumque pontificum cura recognitum, atque auctoritate Ssmi D. N. Pii Papae XI ad normam codicis juris canonici accommodatum; cui accedit benedictionum et instructionum appendix. Editio quinta post typicam. Turonibus, Typ. A. Mame; N.Y., Benziger, 1928. 710p., 29p. **BB425**

Gives the complete Latin text.

———— The Roman ritual, in Latin and English . . . tr. and ed. . . . by Philip T. Weller. Milwaukee, Bruce, [1947–52]. 3v. **BB426**

Contents: v.1, The sacraments and processions; v.2, Christian burial, exorcism, reserved blessings, etc.; v.3, The blessings.

BX2035.A2

Catholic Church. Liturgy and Ritual. Missal, English. Saint Andrew Bible missal. [Wash.], Ctr. for Pastoral Liturgy, Catholic Univ. of Amer.; Brepols, Hirten, 1982. 1015p. **BB427**

Translated and adapted from *Missel Dominical de l'Assemblée,* prep. by the Benedictines of Saint-André d'Ottignies, Brepols, 1981. Readings are from the *New American Bible.* BX2130.S34

Catholic Church. Liturgy and Ritual. Martyrology, English. The Roman martyrology, in which are to be found the eulogies of the saints and blessed approved by the Sacred Congregation of Rites up to 1961. An English tr. from the 4th edition after the typical edition (1956) approved by Pope Benedict XV (1922). Ed. by J. B. O'Connell. London, Burns & Oates; Westminster, Md., Newman Pr., [1962]. 412p. **BB428**

BX2014.A403

Catholic Church. Liturgy and Ritual. Lectionary for Mass; English translation [i.e., version] approved by the National Conference of Catholic Bishops and confirmed by the Apostolic See; with the New American version of Sacred Scripture . . . . N.Y., Catholic Book Pub. Co., 1970. 1122p. **BB429**

At head of title: The Roman missal, revised by decree of the Second Vatican Council and published by authority of Pope Paul VI.

Contains the three-year cycle of scripture readings for the eucharistic liturgy for Sundays and solemn feasts; the two-year cycle for weekdays; the one-year cycle for saints' feasts; responsorial psalms; gospel or alleluia verses; and readings for a wide variety of other Masses. Indexed.

The edition published by Liturgical Press (Collegeville, Minn., 1970) uses the *RSV Catholic edition* of Scripture, and that by Benziger (N.Y., 1970), the *Jerusalem Bible* text.   BX2003.A4

—— The liturgy of the hours, according to the Roman rite. N.Y., Catholic Book Pub. Co., 1975–76. 4v.   **BB430**

At head of title: The Divine Office revised by decree of the Second Vatican Ecumenical Council and published by authority of Pope Paul VI.

English translation prep. by the International Commission on English in the Liturgy.

Contents: v.1, Advent season. Christmas season; v.2, Lenten season. Easter season; v.3, Ordinary time, weeks 1–17; v.4, Ordinary time, weeks 18–34.

The new breviary revised according to modern liturgical norms. Biblical readings are from the *New American Bible.*   BX2000.A4

—— The rites of the Catholic Church as revised by decree of the Second Vatican Ecumenical Council and published by authority of Pope Paul VI. N.Y., Pueblo Pub. Co., [1976–80]. 2v.   **BB431**

English translation prep. by the International Commission on English in the Liturgy.

Selected sections of the new Rituale Romanum and Pontificale Romanum.

Brings together in one compilation the revised texts of administration of the sacraments and other rites which were published individually starting in 1969. Includes pertinent excerpts from the Constitution on the Sacred Liturgy for each section.   BX2033.A4

—— The sacramentary: approved for use in the dioceses of the United States of America by the National Conference of Catholic Bishops and confirmed by the Apostolic See. N.Y., Catholic Book Pub. Co., 1974. 83p., 1099p. il. **BB432**

At head of title: The Roman missal, revised by decree of the Second Vatican Council and published by authority of Pope Paul VI.

Translation by the International Commission on English in the Liturgy, with additions and adaptations for the U.S. by Bishops' Committee on the Liturgy, of the sacramentary first published in Rome in 1970 under title *Missale Romanum.*

Contains all the texts proper to the priest for the celebration of the Eucharist and other sacraments or rites celebrated at Mass. Together with the *Lectionary* (BB429), replaces the Roman missal.

BX2037.A4

Bohatta, Hanns. Bibliographie der Breviere, 1501–1850. Leipzig, Hiersemann, 1937. 349p.   **BB433**

A bibliography of breviaries, including Roman breviaries and those of the various orders. Indexes by title, date, printer or publisher, and place of publication.   Z7838.L7B55

—— Bibliographie der Livres d'Heures (Horae B.M.V.), officia, hortuli animae, coronae B.M.V., rosaria und cursus B.M.V., des XV. und XVI. Jahrhunderts. 2. verm. Aufl. Wien, Gilhofer & Ranschburg, 1924. 92p.   **BB434**

1st ed. 1909.

An annotated, classified list of Books of Hours of the 15th and 16th centuries.   Z7838.H6B8

Britt, Matthew. A dictionary of the Psalter, containing the vocabulary of the Psalms, hymns, canticles and miscellaneous prayers of the breviary Psalter. N.Y., Benziger, 1928. 299p.   **BB435**

A dictionary of the Latin words, with English equivalents, and quotations given in each language. Concerned primarily with the Vulgate text, but translations of the Hebrew text are given when they throw light on obscure terms in the Vulgate text.   BX2033.B7

Weale, William Henry James. Bibliographia liturgica; catalogus missalium, ritus latini ab anno MCCCCLXXIV impressorum, iterum edidit H. Bohatta. London, Quaritch, 1928. 380p.   **BB436**

1st ed. 1886.

A listing of Latin missals by: pt.1, place-name; pt.2, order. Chronological and typographical indexes.   Z7838.L7W3

History

See also BB416.

Ellis, John Tracy. Documents of American Catholic history. [Rev. ed.] Chicago, Regnery, [1967]. 2v. (702p.)   **BB437**

1st ed. 1959.

Contents: v.1, The church in the Spanish colonies to the Second Plenary Council at Baltimore in 1866; v.2, From the Second Plenary Council . . . to the present.

Offers a collection of texts from 1493 to 1966. "Document" is "broadly interpreted to include any written record that would illustrate an event from a contemporary point of view."—*Pref.* Includes papal documents, laws, charters and also private writings, printed letters, etc. Source is cited in introductory note to each section. Indexed.   BX860.C37

Encyclopedias

Catholic encyclopedia; an international work of reference on the constitution, doctrine, discipline and history of the Catholic church. N.Y., Encyclopedia Pr., [c1907–22]. 17v. il.   **BB438**

Contents: v.1–15, A–Z. Errata; v.16, Additional articles. Index; v.17, Supplement.

Authoritative work with long, signed articles by specialists, and good bibliographies and illustrations. Very useful for many questions on subjects in medieval literature, history, philosophy, art, etc., as well as for questions of Catholic doctrine, history, biography. Long a standard work in English, but in some respects not so complete as the great French Catholic works, and is now somewhat out-of-date.

In 1936, v.1 of a revised and enlarged edition was published by the Gilmary Society in New York, but no further volumes appeared in that edition. Despite the appearance of the *New Catholic encyclopedia* (BB439), the set continues to be useful and should be retained in the reference collection.

—— Supplement II. Ed. by Vincent C. Hopkins. N.Y., Gilmary Soc., [1950–58]. 2v. Looseleaf.

Also called v.18.

A record of events since the original publication in 1913 and the first Supplement in 1922. Consists of signed articles by scholars from many countries, dealing with events arranged by country. Other articles treat dogmas, orders, persons, etc. Bibliographies.

BX841.C25

New Catholic encyclopedia. Prep. by an editorial staff at the Catholic University of America. N.Y., McGraw-Hill, [1967–79]. 17v. il. (Repr.: Palatine, Ill., Publishers Guild, 1981) **BB439**

Subtitle: An international work of reference on the teachings, history, organization, and activities of the Catholic Church, and on all institutions, religions, philosophies, and scientific and cultural developments affecting the Catholic Church from its beginnings to the present.

Ed. in chief, William J. McDonald.

Not merely a revision of the *Catholic encyclopedia* (BB438), but a new work intended to be "abreast of the state of knowledge and reflecting the outlook and interests of the second half of the 20th century."—*Pref.* About 17,000 signed articles contributed by some 4,800 scholars, both Catholic and non-Catholic. Emphasis is on the Catholic church in the United States and the English-speaking world, but scope is international (e.g., special attention has been given to the church in Latin America). Biographies of living persons are excluded, although works of outstanding living figures are often discussed in pertinent survey articles. Good-quality illustrations and maps are numerous; bibliographies accompany most of the articles. v.15 is an index. v.16, "Supplement" (publ. 1974) covers developments of 1967–74. v.17, "Supplement: Change in the Church" (publ. 1979) is an alphabetical arrangement of articles which are self-contained, but also designed to reflect the "impact of post conciliar thought and life" on entries in the basic set. Scope is outlined in the preface, and topics are listed therein. Bibliographies for most articles. The earlier set will continue to be useful on various counts: more extensive treatment of certain topics, some entries do not appear in the new work, different bibliographic citations are given, etc.

A Subscription Books Committee review may be found in *The booklist* 68:161. BX841.N44

Dictionnaire de théologie catholique contenant l'esposé des doctrines de la théologie catholique, leurs preuves et leur histoire, commencé sous la direction de A. Vacant et E. Mangenot continué sous celle de É. Amann. . . . Paris, Letouzey, 1909–50. 15v. il. **BB440**

Authoritative; long, signed articles and excellent bibliographies. More exhaustive in treatment than the English-language Catholic encyclopedias. Good for topics and names in scholastic and medieval philosophy. More recent information on topics treated in earlier volumes is frequently given under allied subjects in later volumes.

BX841.D68

———— Tables générales, par Bernard Loth et Albert Michel. Paris, Letouzey, 1951–72. 3pts.

Issued in 18 fascicles.

A synthesis of materials in the encyclopedia brought together under specific headings arranged alphabetically. In some cases new material, principally bio-bibliographical, has been inserted in the index in order to bring the matter in earlier volumes up-to-date.

BX841.D6822

Enciclopedia cattolica. Città del Vaticano, Enciclopedia Cattolica, [1949–54]. 12v. il. **BB441**

A work of major importance. Written in Italian and mainly by Italian scholars, it deals with all matters pertaining to the Catholic church, historical and contemporary. Articles vary in length from a few lines to several pages, are signed, and include long bibliographies which give dates and exact references. Profusely illustrated.

v.12 includes an *Indice sistematico*, col.1840–2134.

BX841.E47

Migne, Jacques Paul. Encyclopédie théologique. 1.–3. sér. Dictionnaires sur toutes les parties de la science religieuse. Paris, Migne, 1845–66. 168v. in 170. **BB442**

The various dictionaries in this set are unequal in value—some of them were uncritical even when new—and many of them are now

entirely superseded by later and more scholarly works. They cover a wide field, however; include some subjects for which there are no comprehensive modern dictionaries (e.g., the *Dictionnaire des mystères*); and some of them contain a large amount of minor biography. Such dictionaries may still be useful even though they do not give the latest critical information. For complete contents *see* Paris. Bibliothèque Nationale. *Catalogue général des livres imprimés,* v.114, col. 948–62 (AA140), Lorenz, *Catalogue général,* v.3 and 6 (AA755), or *National union catalog: pre–1956 imprints* (AA128), v.383, p.118–19. BL31.M5

Sacramentum mundi; an encyclopedia of theology. [N.Y., etc.], Herder & Herder; London, Burns & Oates, [1968–70]. 6v. **BB443**

Ed. by Karl Rahner et al.

Also published in Dutch, French, German, Italian, and Spanish.

The work of an international roster of Catholic theologians which attempts "to formulate present-day developments of the understanding of the faith, basing itself on modern theological investigations of the key themes of the theological disciplines."—*Gen. Pref.* Includes signed articles of substantial length, bibliographies, and cross references. General index in v.6. BR95.S23

Wetzer, Heinrich Joseph. Wetzer und Welte's Kirchenlexikon, oder Encyklopädie der katholischen Theologie und ihrer Hülfswissenschaften. 2. Aufl. in neuer Bearb. unter Mitwirkung vieler katholischen Gelehrten begonnen von Joseph, cardinal Hergenröther, fortgesetzt von Franz Kaulen. Freiburg im Breisgau, Herder, 1882–1901. 12v. and index. **BB444**

An older standard German Catholic encyclopedia, with signed articles.

Namen- und Sachregister. 1903. 604p. BX841.W4

Dictionaries

Addis, William E. and **Arnold, Thomas.** A Catholic dictionary, containing some account of the doctrine, discipline, rites, ceremonies, councils, and religious orders of the Catholic church. [16th ed.] Rev. by T. B. Scannell [and others]. London, Routledge and Paul, 1957. 860p. **BB445**

1st ed. 1883.

A dictionary of Catholic doctrines prepared by British scholars.

BX841.A3

Bouyer, Louis. Dictionary of theology. Tr. by Charles Underhill Quinn. [N.Y., Desclée, 1965]. 470p. **BB446**

Originally published in French under the title *Dictionnaire théologique* (Tournai, 1963).

Articles range from a few lines to several pages, and seek to "give precise definitions of theological terms, and at the same time to provide a concise synthesis of Catholic doctrine in terms equally understandable to the layman and the specialist."—*Foreword.*

BR95.B6413

A Catholic dictionary (The Catholic encyclopaedic dictionary). Ed. by Donald Attwater. 3d ed. N.Y., Macmillan, 1958. 552p. **BB447**

Originally published in 1931 under the title *The Catholic encyclopaedic dictionary.*

Includes definitions and meanings of terms, names, and phrases in the philosophy, theology, canon law, liturgy, institutions, etc., of the Catholic church. Omits biography except for the saints in the general calendar of the Roman church. BX841.C35

The Catholic encyclopedia dictionary; containing 8,500 articles on the beliefs, devotions, rites, symbolism, tradition and history of the church; her laws, organizations, dioceses, missions, institutions, religious orders, saints; her part in promoting art, science, education and social welfare. Comp.

and ed. under the direction of the editors of the Catholic encyclopedia. N.Y., Gilmary Soc., [1941]. 1095p. il.

BB448

A reissue, with no revision, of the *New Catholic dictionary,* published in 1929 by the Universal Knowledge Foundation.

Concise articles, many of them signed, on all phases of Catholic life. Includes biography.　　　　　BX841.N4

Hardon, John A. Modern Catholic dictionary. Garden City, N.Y., Doubleday, 1980. 635p.　　　　**BB449**

". . . the main focus of the dictionary and the bulk of its contents are definably, even exclusively, Roman Catholic. An effort was made to include every significant concept of the Church's doctrine in faith and morals, ritual and devotion, canon law and liturgy, mysticism and spirituality, ecclesiastical history and organization."—*Introd.* Special attention was given to the 2d Vatican Council. Terms from the social sciences, when included, are defined or described from the Catholic point of view.　　　　　BX841.H36

Maryknoll Catholic dictionary. Comp. and ed. by Albert J. Nevins. [Wilkes-Barre, Pa.], Dimension Books, [1965]. 710p.　　　　**BB450**

Offers definitions of standard Catholic words and terms, and attempts to reflect movements and changes in liturgy and Catholic thinking since the second Vatican Council. Intends to give "clear and accurate explanations rather than strict definitions" (*Introd.*) and should, therefore, be especially useful to lay people, including non-Catholics. Includes some biographical data on deceased Catholics of the United States and Canada.　　　　BX841.M36

O'Carroll, Michael. Theotokos: a theological encyclopedia of the Blessed Virgin Mary. Rev. ed. with suppl. Wilmington, Del., M. Glazier, 1983. 390p.　　　**BB451**

1st publ. 1982.

Offers a dictionary arrangement of names, doctrines, devotions and biblical references that bear on Marian theology. A large proportion of entries are names of theologians, past and present, whose writings on Mary are outlined in brief. Bibliography for each article.

Podhradsky, Gerhard. New dictionary of the liturgy. English ed., ed. by Lancelot Sheppard. Staten Island, N.Y., Alba House, [1967]. 208p. il.　　　　**BB452**

A translation, with the addition of new material, of the author's *Lexikon der Liturgie* (Innsbruck, 1962).　　　BV173.P613

Rahner, Karl and **Vorgrimler, Herbert.** Dictionary of theology. 2d ed. Tr. by Richard Strachan [and others]. N.Y., Crossroad, 1981. 541p.　　　　**BB453**

1st ed. (1965) had title *Theological dictionary.*

A translation of the authors' *Kleines theologisches Wörterbuch* (10th ed., 1976). 2d English ed. has title *Concise theological dictionary* (London, Burns & Oates, 1983. 541p.).

Intends "to provide brief explanations, in alphabetical order, of the most important concepts of modern Catholic dogmatic theology for readers who are prepared to make a certain intellectual effort." —*Pref.*　　　　　BR95.R313

Biography

Delaney, John J. Dictionary of American Catholic biography. Garden City, N.Y., Doubleday, 1984. 621p.　**BB454**

Aims "to provide in straightforward fashion factual information about the lives and activities of those Catholic men and women in the United States from the times of the explorers to the present time."—*Introd.* Presents brief information without bibliographies of sources. About 1,500 entries; no living persons included.

BX4670.D45

—— and **Tobin, James Edward.** Dictionary of Catholic biography. Garden City, N.Y., Doubleday, [1961]. 1245p.

BB455

Includes biographical sketches of some 15,000 persons who have

contributed to the development of the Catholic church from the beginning to 1961, but does not include living persons.

BX4651.2.D4

American Catholic who's who, 1934/35– . *See* AJ89.

Catholic who's who, 1908– . London. *See* AJ225.

Yearbooks and directories

Annuario pontificio, 1716– . Roma, Tipografia Poliglotta Vaticana, 1716– . il. Annual.　　　　**BB456**

Contains list of popes from St. Peter on; Roman Catholic hierarchy at Rome and throughout the world, with brief biographical notes; institutions and offices at Rome; list of religious orders with dates of founding and name of present head; Latin names of sees according to the Roman Curia, with classical Latin and vernacular names; Latin names of religious orders; index of personal names, etc.　　　　　BX845.A75

Catholic almanac. Huntington, Ind., Our Sunday Visitor, Inc., 1969– . Annual.　　　　**BB457**

Publisher varies.

Represents a change of title for the *National Catholic almanac* (previously *St. Anthony's almanac* and *Franciscan almanac*), 1904–68.

Includes much miscellaneous information, e.g., annual survey of news, ecclesiastical calendar, glossary of terms in Catholic use, the Catholic church in various countries of the world, statistics, directory of information, etc.　　　　　AY81.R6N3

The Catholic directory of England and Wales. 1973– . Liverpool, Publ. for the Hierarchy by The Universe, 1973– . Annual.　　　　**BB458**

Imprint varies.

Continues: *Catholic directory,* 1838–1970. 1971–72 not publ.

Gives directory information on churches, clergy, institutions, schools, etc.　　　　　BX1491.A1C25

Official Catholic directory, 1886– . N.Y., Kenedy, 1886– . il. Annual.　　　　**BB459**

Title varies; imprint varies.

Useful annual, containing a large amount of detailed directory, institutional, and statistical information about the organization, clergy, churches, missions, schools, religious orders, etc., of the Catholic church in the United States and its possessions. Coverage varies.　　　　　BX845.C5

Popes, cardinals, bishops

See also BB330.

Eubel, Conrad. Hierarchia catholica medii et recentioris aevi; sive, Summorum pontificum S.R.E. cardinalium, ecclesiarum antistitum series, e documentis tabularii praesertim Vaticani collecta, digesta, edita. Monasterii, Sumptibus et Typis Librariae Regensbergianae; Patavia, "Il Messaggero di S. Antonio," 1913–78. v.1–8. (In progress)　**BB460**

Editors vary.

v.1–3 have title *Hierarchia catholica medii aevi* and were first issued 1898–1910; reissued in an "Editio altera," 1913–23.

Contents: v.1–8, 1198–1903.

Chronological lists of the popes and cardinals, and of the bishops in all countries, arranged alphabetically by the Latin name of the diocese. Index by modern name.　　　　BX4651.E8

Gams, Pius Bonifacius. Series episcoporum ecclesiae Catholicae, quotquot innotuerunt a Beato Petro Apostolo. Ratisbonae, G. J. Manz, 1873–86. 963p., 108p. and suppl., 148p. (Repr.: Leipzig, Hiersemann, 1931; Graz, Akad. Verlagsanstalt, 1957)　　　　**BB461**

Historical list of the bishops of each see from the beginning. Useful in the large or research library. Supplement covers 1870–85.

BX4666.G3

Mann, Horace Kinder. The lives of the popes in the early Middle Ages.... London, Kegan Paul, 1925–32. 18v. in 19. (Repr.: Vaduz, Kraus, 1964–69) **BB462**

A documented history covering the years 590–1305.

v.1–12 are 2d ed.; v.6–18 have title *Lives of the popes in the Middle Ages.*   BX1070.M3

Pastor, Ludwig, *Freiherr von.* History of the popes, from the close of the Middle Ages. Drawn from the secret archives of the Vatican and other original sources. From the German. Tr. and ed. by F. I. Antrobus, E. F. Peeler [and others]. London, Hodges, 1891–1953. 40v.   **BB463**

Imprint varies.

English translation of the author's *Geschichte der Päpste.*

Covers from 1305 to 1799.   BX955.P35

Papal and conciliar documents

Carlen, Mary Claudia, *Sister.* Dictionary of papal pronouncements: Leo XIII to Pius XII, 1878–1957. N.Y., Kenedy, [1958]. 216p.   **BB464**

Includes all encyclicals from 1878 through 1957 and a selection of documents in other categories. Arranged alphabetically by title; gives the first few words of the original text, followed by the type of document, date, occasion or group addressed, and a statement of content. Index of subjects and personal and corporate names.

BX873.7.C3

Catholic Church. Pope. The papal encyclicals. Comp. by Claudia Carlen. [Wilmington, N.C.], McGrath, 1981. 5v.

BB465

Aims "to provide a collection to which students and scholars can turn ... for a specific text or ... the entire corpus of papal teaching."—*Introd.* 280 papal encyclicals in English translation, chronologically arranged, from Benedict XIV to John Paul II (i.e., 1740–1981), each with citation to Latin text and with source of translation. Index of titles and subjects.   BX860.C37

———— The papal encyclicals in their historical context, by Anne Fremantle. [N.Y.], New American Library, [1963]. 448p.   **BB466**

Earlier ed. 1956.

Includes excerpts in English from important encyclicals from earliest times to 1963, and includes a complete chronological list since 1740.   BX860.A36

Deretz, Jacques and **Nocent, A.** Dictionary of the Council. Wash. & Cleveland, Corpus Books, [1968]. 506p.   **BB467**

An abridged translation of *Synopse des textes conciliaires* (1966).

Quotes salient paragraphs of Council documents with citations to source. Arranged alphabetically by topics such as freedom, holiness, human dignity, peace, salvation. Useful where full text is not needed.   BX830 1962.A48D43

Dizionario del Concilio ecumenico Vaticano secundo. In collaborazione. Direttore Salvatore Garofalo, redattore capo Tommaso Federici. Roma, UNEDI, 1969. 2034cols.

BB468

"Testi del Concilio Vaticano II," cols.74–574.

A chronology of the second Vatican Council is followed by the official texts of Council documents (in Italian). The dictionary is an alphabetical arrangement of articles on topics, tenets, etc. (e.g., Aborto, Arte sacra, Ateismo, Chiesa, Ecumenismo, Maria, Penitenza) dealt with by the Council.   BX830 1962.A48D58

Vatican Council (2d, 1962–1965). Documents of Vatican II; the conciliar and postconciliar documents. Austin P. Flannery, ed. Grand Rapids, Mich., Eerdmans, 1975–82. 2v.

BB469

v.2 has subtitle: More postconciliar documents.

v.1 offers English translations of the sixteen Vatican Council II documents, together with 49 subsequent "Roman documents which amplify, elucidate or apply the major themes" *(Pref.)* of the Council's work. v.2 adds 58 more postconciliar constitutions, directives, etc., on liturgy, ecumenism, religious life, ministry, current problems, education, from 1966–82. Cites Latin sources. Indexed.

BX830 1962.A3F55

Religious orders

❖For a comprehensive listing of bibliographies and bio-bibliographies of religious orders of all periods, *see* John G. Barrow, *A bibliography of bibliographies in religion,* p.236–56 (BB4).

Cottineau, L. H. Répertoire topo-bibliographique des abbayes et prieurés. Mâcon, Protat, 1935–70. 3v.   **BB470**

v.1–2 issued in parts, 1935–38; v.3, Tables, published 1970.

Arranged by the place where the religious house is situated; gives variant forms of name, location with reference to larger places, order to which religious house belongs, sometimes brief history of the house, and references to sources of information.   Z7839.C84

Cowan, Ian Borthwick and **Easson, David E.** Medieval religious houses, Scotland: with an appendix on the houses in the Isle of Man. 2d ed. London, Longman, [1976]. 246p.

BB471

1st ed. 1957 by D. E. Easson.

A revision and expansion, adding new information based on recent research. Serves as a companion to the Knowles and Hadcock (BB476) and the Gwynn (BB473) volumes.   BX2597.E2

Dizionario degli istituti di perfezione, diretto da Guerrino Pelliccia e da Giancarlo Rocca. [Roma], Edizione Paoline, [1974–83]. v.1–7. (In progress)   **BB472**

To be in 9v.

Contents: v.1–7, A–Rzadka.

Offers signed articles ranging from a paragraph to many pages on the history and structure of about 4,000 Catholic religious orders, societies, etc., of the past and present, on monasticism of the East and West, and on religious life and institutions other than Roman Catholic. Many biographical articles on founders of religious orders, and entries on related material such as terminology of religious life, monastic architecture, etc. All but the shortest essays have bibliographies. Contributors are identified and their credentials listed. Indexes are planned.   BX2420.D58

Gwynn, Aubrey Osborn and **Hadcock, Richard Neville.** Medieval religious houses: Ireland; with an appendix to early sites. [London], Longmans, [1970]. 479p.   **BB473**

A companion to Knowles and Hadcock's volume on the religious houses of England and Wales (BB476) and I. B. Cowan's volume for Scotland (BB471). "The first section deals with Early Irish Monasteries which appear to have existed from the fifth century or later until the eleventh century or later; this is followed by a section on the cathedrals, and the third and main section deals with the religious orders, as in the volumes on England and Wales, and Scotland."—*Pref.* Index of places and of alternate names or spellings.   BX2600.G9

Hélyot, Pierre. Dictionnaire des ordres religieux. Paris, Migne, 1859–63. 4v. il. (1ᵉʳᵉ encyclopédie théologique, publ. par M. l'Abbé Migne, t.20–23)   **BB474**

Subtitle: Histoire des ordres monastiques, religieux et militaires, et des congrégations séculières de l'un et de l'autre sexe, qui ont été établies jusqu'à présent.... Mise par ordre alphabétique, corr. et augm. ... d'un supplément où l'on trouve l'histoire des congrégations omises par Hélyot, et l'histoire des sociétés religieuses établies depuis que cet auteur a publié son ouvrage, par Marie-Léandre Badiche.

An older work, useful in the absence of a later dictionary of the subject.   BX2460.H5

Kapsner, Oliver Leonard. Catholic religious orders; listing conventional and full names in English, foreign language, and Latin, also abbreviations, date and country of origin and founders, comp. . . . with the sponsorship of the Catholic Library Association; 2d ed. enl. Collegeville, Minn., St. John's Abbey Pr., 1957. 594p.   **BB475**

1st ed. 1948.

A listing of names of orders primarily for the use of library catalogers, but with its many cross references from the variant forms it may also serve as a handy guide for others. Information under the main entry includes variant forms of name, abbreviation, founder, date, and country of founding.   BX2420.K3

Knowles, David and **Hadcock, Richard Neville.** Medieval religious houses, England and Wales. [Rev. ed.] N.Y., St. Martin's Pr., [1972]. 565p. maps.   **BB476**

A revised, expanded and corrected edition of the 1953 work of the same title which, in turn, was based on Knowles's *Religious houses of medieval England* (London, 1940).

Houses are grouped by religious order, with information given on history, wealth, numerical strength of the resident community, architectural remains, etc. Extensive documentation, index, tables, maps.   BX2592.K56

Molette, Charles. Guide des sources de l'histoire des congrégations féminines françaises de vie active. Paris, Éditions de Paris, 1974. 475p.   **BB477**

"Ouvrage publié avec le concours du Centre National de Recherche Scientifique."—*t.p.*

In two main sections: (1) Introduction historique; (2) Sources et bibliographie (p.107–379). The latter part lists nearly 400 religious congregations alphabetically by name of the order and indicates address, founding date, etc., information on the order's archives, publications, and bibliographical references to writings about an order and its members. Indexes of names, of places, and of groups (societies, congregations, etc.).

❖Bibliographies and bio-bibliographies for the individual religious orders have great usefulness in the large research library. Among the numerous works of this type are: *Bibliographia Augustiniana* by David Aurelio Perini (Firenze, 1929–37. 4v.); *A Benedictine bibliography,* by Oliver L. Kapsner (2d ed. Collegeville, Minn., 1962–82. 2v. and Suppl.); *Bibliotheca Carmelitana,* ed. by Gabriel Wessels (Rome, 1927. 2v. in 1); *Bio-bibliographia Franciscana Neerlandica,* by Benjamin de Troeyer (Nieuwkoop, 1969–70. 2v.) and his *Bio-bibliographia franciscana neerlandica ante saeculum XVI* (Nieuwkoop, 1974. 3v.); *Bibliothèque de la Compagnie de Jésus* (Bruxelles, 1890–1932. 12v.) and *Bibliothèque des écrivains de la Compagnie de Jésus* (Liège, 1869–76. 3v.), both by Augustin de Backer; *Bibliographie sur l'histoire de la Compagnie de Jésus, 1901–1980,* by László Polgár (Roma, Institutum Historicum S.I., 1981–83. 2v. publ. to date; to be in 7v.).

Eastern churches

Atiya, Aziz Suryal. A history of eastern Christianity. Enl. and updated . . . with . . . supplement to part 1 [and] supplementary bibliography. Millwood, N.Y., Kraus, [1980]. 492p. il., maps.   **BB478**

1st ed. 1968.

Surveys the "Coptic and Ethiopic, Jacobite, Nestorian, Armenian, Indian, and Maronite [churches] and the vanished churches of Nubia and North Africa."—*Pref.* This edition adds a chapter on "Copts abroad" and supplementary bibliography.   BX103.2.A8

Attwater, Donald. The Christian churches of the East. [New ed.] Leominster, [Eng.], Thomas More Books, 1961–62. 2v.   **BB479**

Contents: v.1, Churches in communion with Rome; v.2, Churches not in communion with Rome.

A revision of the author's *The Catholic Eastern churches* (1935) and *The dissident Eastern churches* (1937). Includes bibliographies.   BX230.A78

Eastern Christianity: a bibliography selected from the ATLA religion database. Ed. by Paul D. Petersen. Rev. ed. Chicago, Amer. Theol. Lib. Assoc., 1984. 781p.   **BB480**

1st ed. 1982.

A computer-produced bibliography including journal articles 1949–59 and 1975 to mid-1983; chapters in multi-author works since 1970; *Festschriften* articles 1960–69 and articles from *Research in ministry* since 1981. Classed arrangement with author/editor and book review indexes.

Fortescue, Adrian. The lesser Eastern churches. London, Catholic Truth Soc., 1913. 468p. il. (Repr.: N.Y., AMS, 1972)   **BB481**

Treats the various churches of the Nestorians; the Copts; the Abyssinians, Jacobites, and Malabar Christians; and the Armenians.

A continuation of the author's *Orthodox Eastern church* (below).   BX106.F67

——— The Orthodox Eastern church. 3d ed. London, Catholic Truth Soc., 1911. 451p. il.   **BB482**

Frequently reprinted.   BX320.F6

——— The Uniate Eastern churches; the Byzantine rite in Italy, Sicily, Syria, and Egypt, ed. by George D. Smith. London, Burns Oates & Washbourne; N.Y., Benziger, 1923. 244p. (Repr.: N.Y., Ungar, 1957)   **BB483**

"List of books," p.xi–xxi.   BX4713.F6

Dictionaries

Langford-James, Richard Lloyd. A dictionary of the Eastern Orthodox church. London, Faith Pr., [1923]. 144p. (Repr.: N.Y., B. Franklin, 1976)   **BB484**

An alphabetical dictionary of the rites, customs, and ceremonies of the Eastern Orthodox church.   BX230.L3

Liturgy and ritual

Orthodox Eastern Church. Liturgy and Ritual. Service book of the Holy Orthodox-Catholic Apostolic church, comp., tr. and arr. from the Old Church-Slavonic service books of the Russian church, and collated with the service books of the Greek church, by Isabel Florence Hapgood. Rev. ed., with endorsement by Patriarch Tikhon. 5th ed. Englewood, N.J., Antiochian Orthodox Christian Archdiocese of New York and all North America, 1975. 615p.   **BB485**

BX350.A5H3

King, Archdale Arthur. The rites of Eastern Christendom. Rome, Catholic Book Agency, 1947–48. 2v.   **BB486**

A history and description of the development of the Eastern liturgies.   BX4710.K5

BUDDHISM

See also BB74.

Bibliography

Beautrix, Pierre. Bibliographie du bouddhisme. Bruxelles, Institut Belge des Hautes Études Bouddhiques, [1970]– .

v.1– . (In progress?) (Institut Belge des Hautes Études Bouddhiques. Sér. bibliographies, 2)   **BB487**

Contents: v.1, Éditions de textes.

In addition to the bibliography of published editions of Buddhist texts, there is a section listing pertinent manuscript catalogs. A further volume, "Traductions de textes," is promised.

Z7860.3.I5

—— Bibliographie du bouddhisme Zen. Bruxelles, Institut Belge des Hautes Études Bouddhiques, [1969]. 114*l.* (Institut Belge des Hautes Études Bouddhiques. Sér. bibliographies, 1)   **BB488**

More than 700 entries grouped as: (1) Généralités; (2) Textes et commentaires; (3) Doctrine et philosophie; (4) Histoire et biographie; (5) Art; (6) Littérature; (7) Études comparatives. Author index.

Z7864.Z4

—— —— Premier supplément. Bruxelles, Institut Belge des Hautes Études Bouddhiques, [1975]. 119*l.* (Institut Belge des Hautes Études Bouddhiques. Sér. bibliographies, 4)

836 additional entries, following the classed order of the basic volume. Author index.

A bibliography on Japanese Buddhism, ed. by Bandō Shōjun [and others]. Tokyo, CIIB Pr., 1958. 180p.   **BB489**

A classified bibliography listing books and periodical articles (1,660 numbered items) written mainly in European languages up to July 1958. Locates copies in Japanese libraries.   Z7835.B9B63

Bussho kaisetsu daijiten. Comp. by Ono Gemmyō. Tokyo, Daitō Shuppansha, [1964–78]. 14v.   **BB490**

1st ed. 1933–36. 12v.

A comprehensive annotated list of books and manuscripts on Buddhism in Japanese and Chinese. More than 72,000 entries. The 1st ed. listed publications up to 1932. This ed. reprints those volumes with two supplements (v.12–13) which add materials of 1932–65. v.14 is a revision of v.12 of the earlier ed., a discussion of sources.   Z7860.B87

Conze, Edward. Buddhist scriptures: a bibliography. Ed. and rev. by Lewis Lancaster. N.Y., Garland, 1982. 161p. (Garland reference library of the humanities, v.113)   **BB491**

A bibliographic guide to the editions, translations, and studies of the Buddhist scriptures.   Z7862.C66

Grönbold, Günter. Der buddhistische Kanon: eine Bibliographie. Wiesbaden, Harrassowitz, 1984. 70p.   **BB492**

A bibliography of the history of the Buddhist canon. Lists editions of the Pali, Sanskrit, Chinese, Japanese, Korean, Tibetan, Mongolian, Manchurian, and Tangut canons; ancient and modern canon catalogs, secondary works on Buddhist literature publications. Indexed.

Hanayama, Shinsho. Bibliography on Buddhism; ed. by the Commemoration Committee for Prof. Shinsho Hanayama's sixty-first birthday. Tokyo, Hokuseido Pr., 1961. 869p.   **BB493**

An extensive bibliography of 15,073 numbered entries, arranged alphabetically with subject index. Lists books and articles in Western languages primarily of the 19th and 20th centuries—prior to 1928 when the *Bibliographie bouddhique* (BB499) was started.   Z7835.B9H3

Reynolds, Frank E. Guide to Buddhist religion . . .; with John Holt and John Strong; arts section by Bardwell Smith . . . . Boston, G. K. Hall, [1981]. 415p.   **BB494**

One of a series of guides prep. by the Project on Asian Philosophies and Religions. Although undertaken as a guide for teachers of religion at the undergraduate level, the work is also meant to be useful to those engaged in Buddhological research and as a means of pointing out "older materials which are presently inaccessible and need to be made more available, as well as areas in which new scholarly work needs to be done."—*Pref.* Classed arrangement; annotations; author/title and subject indexes. Includes both books

and periodical articles. Materials are mainly in English, but some French items of first importance are listed; includes publications through the early 1970s only.   Z7860.R48

Satyaprakash. Buddhism: a select bibliography. Gurgaon/New Delhi, Indian Documentation Service, [1976]. 172p. (Subject bibliography ser., 1)   **BB495**

"This bibliography . . . indexes 2,565 articles, research papers, notes, news and book reviews, from 84 journals and the daily *Times of India,* published through the fifteen-year period from 1962 to mid-1976."—*Pref.* Includes 450 books. Chiefly Indian publications. Arranged in a single alphabet of authors and subjects.   Z7860.S28

Vessie, Patricia Armstrong. Zen Buddhism: a bibliography of books and articles in English, 1892–1975. [Ann Arbor, Mich.], University Microfilms International, 1976. 81*l.*   **BB496**

"Publ. under the aegis of the East Asia Library, University of Washington."—*t.p.*

Some 760 items in classed arrangement. Lacks an index.   Z7864.Z4V47

Yoo, Yushin. Buddhism: a subject index to periodical articles in English, 1728–1971. Metuchen, N.J., Scarecrow Pr., 1973. 162p.   **BB497**

Broad subject arrangement, with author/subject and title indexes.   Z7860.Y65

—— Books on Buddhism: an annotated subject guide. Metuchen, N.J., Scarecrow Pr., 1976. 251p.   **BB498**

A classed listing of some 1,300 items, with author and title indexes.   Z7860.Y64

Current

Bibliographie bouddhique, 1928/29–1954/58. Paris, Librairie d'Amérique et d'Orient, 1930–67. Fasc.1–32.   **BB499**

Publisher varies.

Indexes: fasc.1–6, 1928–34, in fasc.6; fasc.7–23, 1934–50, in fasc.23 bis; fasc.24–31, 1951–58, in fasc.32.

An important annotated bibliography which includes both books and the indexing of some 200 periodicals in many languages. Some issues include special retrospective author bibliographies.

Dictionaries and encyclopedias

A dictionary of Buddhism. Introd. by T. O. Ling. N.Y., Scribner's, [1972]. 277p.   **BB500**

Entries on Buddhism have been extracted from S. G. F. Brandon's *Dictionary of comparative religion* (BB49).   BQ130.D5

Encyclopaedia of Buddhism, ed. by G. P. Malalasekera. Colombo, Govt. Pr., 1961–79. v.1–4¹. il. (In progress)   **BB501**

Contents: v.1–4¹, A–Cittavisuddhi.

Designed as a scholarly and definitive work and produced under the aegis of the government of Ceylon.

Arrangement is in dictionary form with articles on all aspects of Buddhist thought, history, and civilization, including personal and place-names, literary works, and, especially, religious and moral concepts. Articles vary in length; many of the longer ones are signed, others have initials only. For some, bibliographies are appended, but in many others, references are cited only within the text.   BL1403.E5

Hackmann, Heinrich Friedrich. Erklärendes Wörterbuch zum chinesischen Buddhismus; Chinesisch-Sanskrit-Deutsch. Nach seinem handschriftlichen Nachlass überarb. von Johannes Nobel. Leiden, Brill, 1951–54. Lfg.1–6. (In progress?)   **BB502**

Contents: Lfg.1–6, A–Ni.

The first issues of a Buddhist encyclopedia intended to be complete in 12 fascicles.

Humphreys, Christmas. A popular dictionary of Buddhism. 2d. ed. London, Curzon Pr.; Totowa, N.J., Rowman and Littlefield, 1976. 223p. **BB503**

1st ed. 1962.

Originally based on *A brief glossary of Buddhist terms* by Arthur Charles March (London, Buddhist Lodge, 1937), later expanded for inclusion in *A Buddhist student's manual* (1956).

Designed for the English-speaking student of Buddhism who is not a trained scholar. Includes those terms of special meaning found in books on Buddhism. This edition incorporates corrections, minor additions and improved cross referencing. BQ130.H85

Soothill, William Edward and **Hodous, Lewis.** A dictionary of Chinese Buddhist terms, with Sanskrit and English equivalents and a Sanskrit-Pali index. London, Kegan Paul, 1937. 510p. (Repr.: Taipei, Ch'eng-Wen, 1968.) **BB504**

Definitions in English. BL1403.S6

HINDUISM

See also BB75.

Bibliography

Dandekar, Ramchandra Narayan. Vedic bibliography. Bombay, Karnatak Pub. House; Poona, Univ. of Poona, 1946–73. v.1–3. (In progress) **BB505**

v.3 publ. by Bhandarkar Oriental Research Inst., Poona.

Subtitle of v.1: An up-to-date, comprehensive, and analytically arranged register of all important work done since 1930 in the field of the Veda and allied antiquities including Indus Valley civilisation.

v.2–3 continue the record, 1946 to mid-1972, listing about 12,000 books and periodical articles. The work may be regarded as a continuation of Renou's *Bibliographie védique* (BB509). Z7090.D3

Dell, David [and others]. Guide to Hindu religion. Boston, G. K. Hall, [1981]. 461p. **BB506**

A classified, annotated bibliography intended for "undergraduate teachers of Hinduism and others who may wish to pursue Hinduism's study on their own."—*Pref.* Mainly books, but includes some significant periodical articles. Section 12 is devoted to research aids. Author index. Z7835.B8D44

Holland, Barron. Popular Hinduism and Hindu mythology: an annotated bibliography. Westport, Conn., Greenwood Pr., [1979]. 394p. **BB507**

A classed bibliography intended for "anyone interested in aspects of popular Hinduism, both general and specific, whether students, research scholars, teachers, devotees, or merely interested persons." —*Pref.* Nearly 3,500 items—books, articles, and dissertations. Limited to English and other European languages; "does not include works on Hinduism beyond the confines of peninsular India." Many brief, descriptive annotations. Indexed. Z7835.B8H64

Kapoor, Jagdish Chander. Bhagavad-Gītā, an international bibliography of 1785–1979 imprints . . . with an introduction by George Hendrick. N.Y., Garland, 1983. 371p. (Garland reference library of the humanities, v.306) **BB508**

"Includes all translations, commentaries, commentaries on commentaries, and books on or about the Bhagavad-Gītā" *(Foreword)* for the period specified and notes locations in libraries in many parts of the world. Arranged by language, then by date of publication. Fifty languages are represented. Indexes of translators, of authors, of titles and subjects. Z7835.B8K36

Renou, Louis. Bibliographie védique. Paris, Adrien-Maisonneuve, 1931. 339p. **BB509**

A classed bibliography listing materials in many languages on the Vedas and the history of Hinduism, primarily of the 19th and 20th centuries. Z7090.R41

Concordances and indexes

Bloomfield, Maurice. A Vedic concordance, . . . Cambridge, Harvard Univ. Pr., 1906. 1078p. (Harvard oriental ser., v.10) (Repr.: Delhi, Motilal Banarsidass, 1964) **BB510**

Subtitle: Being an alphabetic index to every line of every stanza of the published Vedic literature and to the liturgical formulas thereof, that is, an index to the Vedic mantras; together with an account of their variations in the different Vedic books. PK3009.B6

Macdonnell, Arthur Anthony and **Keith, Arthur B.** Vedic index of names and subjects. London, Murray, publ. for the Govt. of India, 1912. 2v. (Repr.: Delhi, Motilal Banarsidass, 1967) **BB511**

An index by proper name and subject to Vedic literature from its earliest forms (*ca.* 1200 B.C.) to the rise of Buddhism (*ca.* 500 B.C.). Includes personal and geographical names and subjects, e.g., agriculture, caste, economic conditions, customs, law, position of women, and many others. PK3009.M3

Dictionaries and encyclopedias

Dowson, John. A classical dictionary of Hindu mythology and religion, geography, history, and literature. 12th ed. London, Routledge and Paul, 1972. 411p. (Trübner's oriental ser.) **BB512**

1st ed. 1879. Frequently reprinted with very little change.

Includes names of gods, personal and geographical names, and subjects. BL1105.D6

Stutley, Margaret and **Stutley, James.** A dictionary of Hinduism, its mythology, folklore and development 1500 B.C.– A.D. 1500. London, Routledge & Kegan Paul, [1977]. 372p. **BB513**

Publ. in U.S.A. as *Harper's Dictionary of Hinduism.*

Designed to "meet the requirements of the modern student and general reader."—*Pref.* Most entries are brief, although some run to several columns. References to texts and sources are often given; bibliography, p.353–68. BL1105.S78

Walker, George Benjamin. Hindu world; an encyclopedic survey of Hinduism. London, Allen & Unwin; N.Y., Praeger, [1968]. 2v. **BB514**

Information "is derived largely from standard works of recognized authorities, supplemented by material drawn from traditional Indian sources."—*Pref.* Dictionary arrangement, plus a subject index. Bibliographies are appended to many articles. BL1105.W34

ISLAM

See also BB216–BB218.

Bibliography

Gabrieli, Giuseppe. Manuale di bibliografia musulmana. Parte 1. Bibliografia generale. Roma, Tipografia dell' Unione Editrice, 1916. 491p. **BB515**

A comprehensive bibliography of books and periodical materials,

in many languages, on all phases of Moslem life and culture. Includes comparative tables of Mussulman and Christian calendars.
Z7046.G22

Geddes, Charles L. An analytical guide to the bibliographies on Islam, Muhammad, and the Qur'an. [Denver], American Institute of Islamic Studies, [1973]. 102p. (Amer. Inst. of Islamic Studies. Bibliographic series, no.3)   **BB516**

An annotated bibliography of more than 200 bibliographies.
Z7835.M6A54

Guide to Islam. [By] David Ede [and others]. Boston, G. K. Hall, [1983]. 261p.   **BB517**

A bibliography of nearly 3,000 items (books and periodical articles) which aims "to introduce the English-language reader to significant publications on Islam as a religion and a civilization."—*Pref.* Intended mainly for the undergraduate and graduate student; a few basic works in French and German have been included. Classed arrangement; detailed table of contents; author and subject indexes. Most entries are briefly annotated. Cut-off date, unfortunately, is 1976.   Z7835.M6G84

London. University. School of Oriental and African Studies. Library. Index Islamicus, 1906–1955: a catalogue of articles on Islamic subjects in periodicals and other collective publications, comp. by J. D. Pearson, with the assistance of Julia F. Ashton. Cambridge, Eng., W. Heffer, [1958]. 897p. (Repr.: London, Mansell, 1972)   **BB518**

Indexes more than 26,000 articles appearing in periodicals, *Festschriften,* and other collected works, published 1906–55. Periodicals devoted to the field of Islam are indexed completely; other periodicals in many languages are indexed for articles on Islamic subjects. Articles are arranged by a detailed classification system with an author index.

———— ———— Supplement, 1956–1960. 1962. 316p.

Nearly 7,300 additional citations.

———— ———— 2d Suppl., 1961–1965. 1967. 342p.

Adds more than 8,100 new entries, including citations from many new periodicals.

———— ———— 3d Supplement, 1966–1970. Comp. by J. D. Pearson and Ann Walsh. London, Mansell, [1972]. 384p.

About 8,000 entries.

———— ———— 4th supplement, 1971–75. London, Mansell, 1977. 429p.

Represents a cumulation of the five annual issues for the period, plus some additions noted after those parts were published. About 10,000 entries.

———— ———— [5th supplement] 1976–1980. London, Mansell, 1983. 2v.

Contents: pt.1, Articles, comp. by J. D. Pearson; pt.2, Monographs, comp. by J. D. Pearson and Wolfgang Behn.

Cumulates the contents of issues 1–20 (v.1–5) of the *Quarterly Index Islamicus* (below). Each volume in classed order with author index. 14,187 articles; 7,908 monographs.

Beginning 1977, issued quarterly as: Z7835.M6L6

The quarterly Index Islamicus. v.1, no.1– , Jan. 1977– . London, Mansell, 1977– . Quarterly, with 5-yr. cumulations. (Also available on microfiche)   **BB519**

J. D. Pearson, ed.

Subtitle: Current books, articles and papers on Islamic subjects.

Includes citations to books as well as to periodical articles. Analyzes more than 1,300 periodicals, *Festschriften* and other collections. Personal name and subject indexes in each issue. With v.7, no.4 (Nov. 1983) the classification scheme was revised to reflect expanded interest in social sciences of the Middle East and Islam.

The 5-year cumulations form supplements to *Index Islamicus* (above).   Z3013.Q34

Ofori, Patrick E. Islam in Africa south of the Sahara: a select bibliographic guide. Nendeln, [Liechtenstein], KTO Pr., 1977. 223p.   **BB520**

The third of the compiler's guides to religions in Africa (*see* BB25, BB226). Lists 1,170 books, pamphlets, articles, and theses, chiefly in European languages, arranged by broad geographic region, then by country. No Arabic-language material included. Some entries are annotated. Author index.   Z7835.M6O36

Pfannmüller, Gustav. Handbuch der Islam-Literatur. Berlin, W. de Gruyter, 1923. 436p.   **BB521**

A comprehensive, critical manual with bibliographies listing materials in various languages on Islamic religious literature.
Z7835.M6P5

Sauvaget, Jean. Introduction to the history of the Muslim East: a bibliographical guide. Based on the 2d ed. as recast by Claude Cahen. Berkeley, Univ. of California Pr., 1965. 252p. (Repr.: Westport, Conn., Greenwood Pr., 1982)   **BB522**

For full information *see* DE28.

Shinar, Pessah. Essai de bibliographie sélective et annotée sur l'Islam maghrébin contemporain: Maroc, Algérie, Tunisie, Libye (1830–1978). Paris, Éditions du Centre National de la Recherche Scientifique, 1983. 506p.   **BB523**

At head of title: Centre de Recherches et d'Études sur les Sociétés Méditerranéennes.

An annotated bibliography of Islam in the countries of Northwest Africa mentioned in the subtitle. Islam is here considered as a "total phenomenon," so that social, cultural, ethical, educational, etc., aspects are included along with religious matters. Classed arrangement within geographical sections. Indexes of authors, subjects, and places. About 2,000 entries in French, English, Arabic, Spanish, Italian, and German.   Z7835.M6S5

Dictionaries and encyclopedias

Encyclopaedia of Islam. New ed. . . . ed. by H. A. R. Gibb, J. H. Kramers, E. Lévi-Provençal, J. Schacht . . . under the patronage of the International Union of Academies, Leiden, Brill; London, Luzac, 1954–83. v.1–5[8] (fasc.93/94), Suppl. 1/2–5/6, Index to v.1–3. (In progress)   **BB524**

1st ed. 1911–38 in 4v. and suppl.

Contents: v.1–5[8], A–Madjarra; Suppl., fasc. 1/2–5/6, al-'Abbās–al-'Irākī.

A completely new edition of the most important reference work in English on Islamic subjects.

A work of high scholarship and authority, containing signed articles, with bibliographies, on subjects in biography, history, geography, religious beliefs, institutions, manners and customs, tribes, industries, sciences, and terms of different sorts; with special emphasis in the new edition on economic and social topics and on artistic production. Geographical material includes separate articles on towns and larger political divisions in the Ottoman Empire, and in foreign countries in which Islam is of importance. More cross references in English and French have been introduced to facilitate usage by non-Orientalists.

The index to v.1–3, comp. by H. Pearson and J. D. Pearson, is chiefly of names of persons, places, institutions, and notions. A second, inclusive index is planned when v.5 is complete.

Until this edition is completed, it will be necessary to continue use of the 1st ed.   DS37.E523

Handwörterbuch des Islam, im Auftrag der K. Akademie van Wetenschappen, Amsterdam, hrsg. von A. J. Wensinck und J. H. Kramers. Leiden, Brill, 1941. 833p. il.   **BB525**

A scholarly work with long, signed articles and extensive bibliographies.   BP40.H3

Shorter Encyclopaedia of Islam, ed. on behalf of the Royal Netherlands Academy by H. A. R. Gibb and J. H. Kramers. Leiden, Brill; London, Luzac, 1953. 671p. il.   **BB526**

Consists mainly of articles on the religion and law of Islam taken from the first edition of the *Encyclopaedia of Islam* (1911–38; 4v. and suppl.), with the addition of some new entries and the revision of some of the older material. Bibliographies have often been brought up-to-date, and there is a useful "Register of subjects" which indexes the entries under English-language headings.

DS37.E52

JAINISM

See also BB75.

Guérinot, Armand Albert. Essai de bibliographie Jaina, répertoire analytique et méthodique des travaux relatifs au Jainisme. Paris, Leroux, 1906. 568p. il. (Ministère de l'Instruction Publique. Annales Musée Guimet. Bibliothèque d'études, t.22) **BB527**

A classed bibliography of 852 works on Jainism.

Supplemented by *Notes de bibliographie jaina* in *Journal asiatique*, 10. sér., 10:47–148 (1909). Z7835.J2G9

Jain, Chhotelal. . . . Jaina bibliography, ed., rearranged, rev. and aug. . . . by Satya Ranjan Banerjee. 2d rev. ed. New Delhi, Vir Sewa Mandir, 1982– . v.1–2. (In progress) **BB528**

1st ed. 1945.

Covers the entire field of Jainism, listing books, parts of books, reports, censuses, journal articles published from about 1800 to 1960, in English and European languages. About 3,000 entries in classed arrangement on art, history, biography, religion, philosophy, language and literature, etc. Annotations often summarize the work cited. An index is to be published as v.3. Z7835.J2J33

JUDAISM

See also Bible, p.348.

Bibliography

Benjacob, Isaac. Ozar Ha-Sepharim (Bücherschatz). Bibliographie der gesammten hebraeischen Literatur mit Einschluss der Handschriften (bis 1863). Wilna, Benjacob, 1880. 678p. **BB529**

Title pages in Hebrew, Russian, German, and Latin. Text in Hebrew. Arranged alphabetically. Includes entries for 17,000 Hebrew books and manuscripts published up to 1863. Z7070.B33

Berlin, Charles. Index to Festschriften in Jewish studies. Cambridge, Mass., Harvard College Lib.; N.Y., Ktav Publ. House, 1971. 319p. **BB530**

Indexes 243 volumes of *Festschriften* dealing with Jewish studies and published since the appearance of Marcus and Bilgray's *Index to Jewish Festschriften* (BB553). Articles are first listed in an alphabetical author section, then by subject under specific topical headings. Z6366.B45

Bibliographical essays in medieval Jewish studies. [N.Y.], Anti-Defamation League of B'nai B'rith, [1976]. 392p. (The study of Judaism, v.2) **BB531**

Six bibliographic essays by specialists, addressed primarily to the non-specialist. Brief contents: The Jews in Western Europe; The church and the Jews; The Jews under Islam; Medieval Jewish religious philosophy; Medieval Jewish mysticism; Minor Midrashim. Z6368.B53

Blumenkranz, Bernhard. Bibliographie des Juifs en France. En collaboration avec Monique Lévy. [Toulouse], Privat, [1974]. 349p. **BB532**

Offers wide coverage (more than 4,000 entries), covering history, law, economics, social history, religion, culture. Classified arrangement. Author and subject indexes.

An earlier publication by the same author and with the same title was published 1961 (Paris, Centre d'Études Juives. 188p.).

Z6373.F7B5

Braham, Randolph L. The Hungarian Jewish catastrophe: a selected and annotated bibliography. 2d ed., rev. and enl. [N.Y.], Social Science Monographs and Institute for Holocaust Studies, City Univ. of N.Y. (distr. by Columbia Univ. Pr.), 1984. 501p. (East European monographs, no.162) **BB533**

1st ed. 1962.

"Aims . . . to bring under one cover all the important references" to both separately published and periodical literature on the subject for "scholars, researchers and officials, as well as interested laymen." —*Introd.* About 2,500 entries in many languages; classified arrangement. Includes general reference works, background studies on Jews in Hungary, the Holocaust in that country, and events of the postwar era. Author, name, geographic, and subject indexes.

Z6373.H8B7

Brickman, William W. The Jewish community in America; an annotated and classified bibliographical guide. N.Y., B. Franklin, [1977]. 396p. (Burt Franklin ethnic bibliographical guides, 2) **BB534**

Aims "to present to scholars, teachers, and other interested persons a descriptively and, in part, critically annotated collection of over 800 basic and specialized writings in English, Hebrew, Yiddish, Ladino, German, French, Hungarian, Polish, and Russian" which "throw light on the Jewish experience in America from the Colonial period to the present."—*Pref.* Classified arrangement with main entry index. Appendix of reprints of documents and relevant articles. Z6373.U5B75

Brisman, Shimeon. A history and guide to Judaic bibliography. Cincinnati, Hebrew Union College Pr.; N.Y., Ktav Publ. House, 1977. 325p. (*His* Jewish research literature, v.1; Bibliographica Judaica, 7) **BB535**

Concerned only with works devoted wholly to Jewish bibliography. In eight chapters: (1) General Hebraica bibliographies; (2) Catalogs of Hebraica book collections; (3) Bio-bibliographical works; (4) Subject bibliographies of Hebraica literature; (5) Judaica bibliographies; (6) Bibliographical periodicals; (7) Index to Jewish periodicals and monographs; (8) Miscellaneous Jewish bibliographical works. Indexed. Z6366.B8

Celnik, Max and **Celnik, Isaac.** A bibliography on Judaism and Jewish-Christian relations; a selected, annotated listing of works on Jewish faith and life, and the Jewish-Christian encounter. N.Y., Anti-Defamation League of B'nai B'rith, 1965. 68p. **BB536**

Lists about 300 "currently obtainable" items in classed arrangement. Z6370.Z9C4

Cohen, Yitshak Yosef. Jewish publications in the Soviet Union, 1917–1960. Bibliographies comp. and arr. by Y. Y. Cohen with the assistance of M. Piekarz . . . ed. by Kh. Shmeruk. Jerusalem, Historical Soc. of Israel, 1961. 502p. **BB537**

In Hebrew; added title page, preface, and table of contents in English.

Lists Hebrew and Yiddish publications of the Soviet Union for the period indicated.

Supplemented by: Z7070.C68

Pinkus, B. and **Greenbaum, A. A.** Russian publications on Jews and Judaism in the Soviet Union, 1917–1967; a bibliography. Ed. by Mordechai Altshuler. Jerusalem, Soc. for Research on Jewish Communities, 1970. 273p., 113p. **BB538**

Z6373.R9P5

Cutter, Charles and **Oppenheim, Micha Falk.** Jewish reference sources: a selective, annotated bibliographic guide.

N.Y., Garland, 1982. 180p. (Garland reference library of social science, v.126) **BB539**

An annotated listing of reference works by type (e.g., bibliographies, encyclopedias, directories, etc.) or by subject. 371 entries. Author and title indexes. Z6366.C87

Eichstädt, Volkmar. Bibliographie zur Geschichte der Judenfrage. Bd.1, 1750–1848. Hamburg, Hanseatische Verlagsanstalt, 1938. 267p. (Schriften des Reichsinstitutes für Geschichte des Neuen Deutschlands) **BB540**

No more published.

A classified bibliography of more than 3,000 books and articles, primarily in German, published from 1750 to 1848 on the Jewish question. Z6372.E34

Fluk, Louise R. Jews in the Soviet Union: an annotated bibliography. N.Y., Amer-Jewish Committee, [1975]. 44p. **BB541**

Lists "significant and accessible" writings on Soviet Jewry appearing in English between Jan. 1967 and Sept. 1974. Z6373.R9F58

Frankfurt am Main. Stadtbibliothek. Katalog der Judaica und Hebraica. Frankfurt am Main, M. Lehrberger, 1932. v.1 (646p.). **BB542**

No more published.

v.1, Judaica, ed. by A. Freimann, is an extensive classified catalog of materials on Jews and Judaism. Z6375.F83

Friedberg, Bernhard. Bet eked sepharim; bibliographical lexicon of the whole Hebrew and Jewish-German literature, inclusive of the Arab, Greek, French-Provençal, Italian, Latin, Persian, Samaritan, Spanish-Portuguese and Tartarian works, printed in the years 1474–1950 with Hebrew letters. 2d ed., enl., improved and rev. [Tel-Aviv, 1951–56] 4v. **BB543**

1st ed. 1928–31.

Title pages in Hebrew and English. Citations in Hebrew. Indexes in v.4. Z7070.F755

Gurock, Jeffrey S. American Jewish history; a bibliographical guide. [N.Y.], Anti-Defamation League of B'nai B'rith, [1983]. 195p. **BB544**

Aims "to identify which are the most useful volumes extant for studying and exploring the major issues in American Jewish history."—p.1. Comprises a series of bibliographic essays (e.g., "The era of German migration," "The era of East European migration") with bibliography and suggestions for further research. Indexed. Z6373.U5G87

Harvard University. Library. Catalogue of Hebrew books. Cambridge, distr. by Harvard Univ. Pr., 1968. 6v. **BB545**

Contents: v.1–4, Authors and subjects; v.5–6, Titles.

Photoreproduction of the catalog cards for the Harvard Judaica collection numbering approximately 100,000 volumes, of which 40,000 are in Hebrew, 10,000 in Yiddish, and the balance in other languages.

—— —— Supplement 1. Cambridge, 1972. 3v.

Contents: v.1, Classified listing. Appendix: Judaica in the Houghton Library; v.2, Authors and selected subjects; v.3, Titles. Z7070.H27

—— Judaica: classification schedule, classified listing by call number, chronological listing, author and title listing. Cambridge, Mass., publ. by Harvard Univ. Lib., distr. by Harvard Univ. Pr., 1971. 302p. (Widener Library Shelflist, 39) **BB546**

Lists about 9,000 titles in the *Jud* and *PJud* classes. An additional 1,725 items of rare Judaica from the Houghton Library are included in the chronological and alphabetical listings.

For a note on the series see AA145. Z6375.H36

Hebrew Union College—Jewish Institute of Religion. American Jewish Archives. Guide to the holdings of the American

Jewish Archives, by James W. Clasper and M. Carolyn Dellenbach. [Cincinnati], Amer. Jewish Archives, [1979], 211p. (American Jewish Archives. Pubns., no.11) **BB547**

The *Manuscript catalog of the American Jewish Archives* was published 1971 (Boston, G. K. Hall. 4v.) with a 1978 supplement (1v.), reproducing the catalog cards for the collection. This volume provides a brief descriptive guide to the collection. In four sections: (1) Manuscript collections; (2) Microfilms from other repositories; (3) Theses, dissertations, and essays; and (4) Special files. Detailed index. Z6373.U5H43

Hebrew Union College—Jewish Institute of Religion. Library. Dictionary catalog of the Klau Library, Cincinnati. Boston, G. K. Hall, 1964. 32v. **BB548**

Reproduces the catalog cards for this outstanding collection (about 200,000 items) of Judaica. The first 27v. represent the dictionary catalog of the collection; v.28–32 offer a Hebrew-title catalog of all books and periodicals printed in Hebrew characters. Z6375.H4

—— Jewish Americana . . . A supplement to A. S. W. Rosenbach: An American Jewish bibliography. [Cincinnati], Amer. Jewish Archives, 1954. 115p. facsims. (Monographs of the American Jewish archives, no.1) **BB549**

Subtitle: A catalogue of books and articles by Jews or relating to them printed in the United States from the earliest days to 1850 and found in the Library of the Hebrew Union College—Jewish Institute of Religion in Cincinnati.

For the Rosenbach work see BB559.

Continued by: Z6366.R812

Levine, Allan E. An American Jewish bibliography. Cincinnati, Amer. Jewish Archives, 1959. 100p. (Monographs of the American Jewish archives, no.11) **BB550**

Subtitle: A list of books and pamphlets by Jews or relating to them printed in the United States from 1851 to 1875, which are in the possession of the Hebrew Union College—Jewish Institute of Religion Library in Cincinnati. Z6366.L48

Lehmann, Ruth Pauline. Anglo-Jewish bibliography, 1937–1970. London, Jewish Historical Society of England, 1973. 364p. **BB551**

A classified bibliography of writings on Jews in Great Britain and the Commonwealth. Follows the basic arrangement of Roth's *Magna bibliotheca . . .* (BB561), with the addition of some new sections and subsections. Intended as a guide to "facilitate and stimulate research" rather than as an exhaustive bibliography. Predominantly periodical articles. Detailed table of contents and author/subject index.

The same compiler's *Nova bibliotheca anglo-judaica. . . . 1937–1960* (London, 1960. 232p.) was an updating of pt.1 of Cecil Roth's *Magna bibliotheca. . . .* This volume extends the period of coverage, but does not include all items in the *Nova.* Z6373.G7L39

Lubetski, Edith and **Lubetski, Meir.** Building a Judaica library collection: a resource guide. Littleton, Colo., Libraries Unlimited, 1983. 185p. **BB552**

Intends "to provide a resource tool for the acquisition librarian." —*Introd.* In two parts: (1) a classified list of well annotated selection aids for current and retrospective Judaic materials in many formats (including general tools wherever specialized sources are meager); (2) an international directory of publishers, bookdealers, antiquarian bookdealers and media publishers and distributors. Z688.J48L82

Marcus, Jacob Rader and **Bilgray, Albert.** An index to Jewish *Festschriften.* Cincinnati, Hebrew Union College, 1937. 154p. (Repr.: N.Y., Kraus, 1970) **BB553**

Indexes the contents of 53 *Festschriften,* published before 1936, by author, title, and subject.

Marcus, Jacob Rader, ed. An index to scientific articles on American Jewish history. Cincinnati, Amer. Jewish Archives, 1971. 240p. (American Jewish Archives. Pubns., 7) **BB554**

An author-title-subject index to "the important articles in the scholarly Jewish periodicals dealing with the life, culture, and history of the American Jew."—*Pref.* Includes references to 13 periodicals from various periods ranging from 1892–1968.

Z6372.M35

Milano, Attilio. Bibliotheca historica italo-judaica. Firenze, Sansoni Antiquariato, 1954. 209p. (Contributi alla Biblioteca bibliografica italica, 6)   **BB555**

A bibliography of books and periodical articles on the Jew in Italy. Indexes by locality, by subject, and by author.

—— —— Supplemento 1954–1963. Firenze, Sansoni, 1964. 82p. (Contributi alla Biblioteca bibliografica italica, 26)

Z6373.I8M5

New York. Public Library. Reference Dept. Dictionary catalog of the Jewish collection. Boston, G. K. Hall, 1960. 14v.

BB556

A photographic reproduction of the card catalog of one of the great Jewish collections of the world. Contains some 250,000 entries for books, periodicals, and analytics. Lists works in Hebrew and Yiddish, and in European languages, on the history and tradition of the Jewish people of all times and in all countries.   Z6375.N6

—— —— Supplement 1. Boston, G. K. Hall, 1975. 8v.

Adds materials cataloged through 1971, but with many omissions.

New York. Public Library. Research Libraries. Hebrew-character title catalog of the Jewish collection. Boston, G. K. Hall, 1981. 4v.   **BB557**

Lists the contents of the Hebrew-character volumes of the 1960 *Dictionary catalog* (v.12–14) and its 1975 supplement (v.7–8; above), integrating them into one title list according to the Hebrew alphabet. Represents more than 52,000 volumes (published through 1971) in Hebrew, Yiddish, Ladino-Arabic and Judeo-Persian. To be used in preference to the earlier *Dictionary catalog* volumes because hundreds of Hebrew-character titles were omitted in photographing cards for the 1975 supplement.

Romano, Giorgio. Bibliografia italo-ebraica (1848–1977). Firenze, Olschki, 1979. 208p. (Biblioteca di bibliografia italiana, 88)   **BB558**

Lists works written in Italian and works translated into Italian. Classified index and index of authors, editors, and translators.

Z6366.R65

Rosenbach, Abraham Simon Wolf. An American Jewish bibliography; being a list of books and pamphlets by Jews or relating to them printed in the United States from the establishment of the press in the colonies until 1850. [Baltimore, Lord Baltimore Pr., 1926] 486p. facsims. (American Jewish Historical Soc. Pubn. no.30)   **BB559**

A detailed bibliography of almost 700 items, arranged chronologically, with author index. Locates copies.
Continued by BB549.   Z6366.R81

Rosenberg, Louise Renée. Jews in the Soviet Union; an annotated bibliography, 1967–1971. N.Y., Amer. Jewish Committee, [1971]. 59p.   **BB560**

Nearly 300 items; limited to English-language publications. Index of names and places.
For a bibliography of Russian materials on this topic, *see* BB538.

Z6373.R9R58

Roth, Cecil. Magna bibliotheca anglo-judaica; a bibliographical guide to Anglo-Jewish history. New ed. rev. and enl. London, Jewish Historical Soc. of England, Univ. College, 5698 (1937). 464p.   **BB561**

A revised edition of *Bibliotheca anglo-judaica,* comp. by Joseph Jacobs and Lucien Wolf (London, 1888). In two parts: pt.1, "Histories," consisting largely of secondary works; pt.2, "Historical material," listing primary sources usually up to the year 1837, though

material on the reform movement is extended to 1842 and on Jewish emancipation to 1858. Classified arrangement.
Continued by Lehmann, *Anglo-Jewish bibliography* (BB551).

Z6373.G7R4

Rothenberg, Joshua. Judaica reference materials; a selective annotated bibliography. Waltham, Mass., Brandeis Univ. Lib., 1971. 87p.   **BB562**

"Preliminary ed."
A classed bibliography based on reference holdings in the Brandeis University Library.   Z6366.R84

Sable, Martin H. Latin American Jewry: a research guide. Cincinnati, Hebrew Union College Pr.; N.Y., Ktav, 1978. 633p. (Bibliographica Judaica, no.6)   **BB563**

A classed bibliography offering "a broad selection of scholarly and popular materials . . . , covering almost all aspects of the impact of Jewry in and on Latin America and its individual nations, regions and places from 1492 to 1974."—*Pref.* 5,375 entries; author and subject indexes.   Z6373.L3S22

Schwab, Moïse. Index of articles relative to Jewish history and literature published in periodicals, from 1665 to 1900. Augm. ed. with an introd. and edited list of abbreviations by Zosa Szajkowski. N.Y., Ktav, [1972]. 539p., 409–613p.

BB564

A reprinting with additions, of Schwab's *Répertoire des articles relatifs à l'histoire et à la littérature juives, parus dans les périodiques, de 1665 à 1900* (Paris, 1914–23), an extensive bibliography of articles in many languages arranged alphabetically by author. In addition to new introductory material, this edition includes a reproduction of the handwritten index of subjects and Hebrew words which appeared in a lithographed edition of 1900, but which was omitted from the later, printed volume. An errata list has also been added.   Z6366.S413

Shunami, Shlomo. Bibliography of Jewish bibliographies. 2d ed., enl. Jerusalem, Magnes Pr., Hebrew Univ., 1965. 992p. (Repr. with corrections, 1969)   **BB565**

Added title page in Hebrew; prefatory matter in English and Hebrew.
1st ed. 1936.
Combines the listings from the earlier edition and its supplements with new and previously omitted materials. Now includes more than 4,700 entries for bibliographies on editions of the Bible and its parts, commentaries, versions, etc.; history and religion of Israel; Jewish literature, etc.   Z7070.A1S5

—— —— Suppl. to 2d ed. enl. Jerusalem, Magnes Pr., 1975. 464p., 16p.

Added title page in Hebrew.
About 2,000 entries, mainly publications from the 10-year period following appearance of the main volume.

Singerman, Robert. Antisemitic propaganda: an annotated bibliography and research guide. N.Y., Garland, 1982. 448p. (Garland reference library of social science, v.112)

BB566

The main portion of the work is an annotated list of antisemitic writings arranged by date of publication. A "Research guide" (p.331–76) lists "hard-to-locate research material about individual propagandists and movements" *(Introd.)* in a classed arrangement. Indexed.   Z6372.S54

—— The Jews in Spain and Portugal: a bibliography. N.Y., Garland, 1975. 364p.   **BB567**

Lists "published materials pertaining to the Jewish presence in Spain and Portugal from antiquity to the present day" *(Introd.),* with emphasis on Jewish history and culture. More than 5,000 entries in classified arrangement.   Z6373.S7S55

Spector, Sheila. Jewish mysticism: an annotated bibliography on the Kabbalah in English. N.Y., Garland, 1984. 399p. (Garland library of social science, v.210)   **BB568**

"Provides access to the sources available to English readers from the seventeenth century on" (*Introd.*) and to secondary materials of both Jewish and Christian authorship. Classified arrangement; chapters are subdivided for primary and secondary works, then chronologically by publication date. Includes books and articles. Indexes of primary sources, of authors, of subjects. 1,500 entries.

Z6371.C2S67

The study of Judaism; bibliographical essays. [N.Y., Ktav for] Anti-Defamation League of B'nai B'rith, [1972]. 229p.
BB569

Contents: Judaism in New Testament times, by Richard Bavier; Rabbinic sources, by John T. Townsend; Judaism on Christianity: Christianity on Judaism, by Frank Talmage; Modern Jewish thought, by Fritz Rothschild and Seymour Siegel; The contemporary Jewish community, by Lloyd Gartner; The holocaust: anti-Semitism and the Jewish catastrophe, by Henry Friedlander. Z6370.S8

Szajkowski, Zosa. Franco-Judaica; an analytical bibliography of books, pamphlets, decrees, briefs and other printed documents pertaining to the Jews in France, 1500–1788. N.Y., Amer. Academy for Jewish Research, 1962. 160p.
BB570

An annotated bibliography of more than 1,700 entries.

Z6373.F7S9

2000 books and more; an annotated and selected bibliography of Jewish history and thought. Ed. by Jonathan Kaplan. Jerusalem, Magnes Pr., Hebrew Univ., [1983]. 483p.
BB571

At head of title: Rothberg School for Overseas Students, The Hebrew University; Dor Hemschech Institutes, The World Zionist Organization.

Aims "to furnish the educator, the student and the librarian with a basic list of books that are of major importance for the study of Jewish History and the History of Jewish Thought, and to assist them in the selection of books best suited to their respective needs and interests."—*Introd.* Includes works in Hebrew, English, German, Spanish, Portuguese and French. Arranged by historical period (subdivided topically), with a separate section on Jewish communities. Index of names.

Introductory matter and section headings in English and Hebrew.

Z6366.K33

Wiener Library, London. German Jewry; its history, life and culture. [Ed. by Ilse R. Wolff] London, Vallentine, Mitchell, 1958. 279p. (Wiener Library. Catalogue ser., no.3) (Repr.: Westport, Conn., Greenwood Pr., 1975) **BB572**

A classified catalog of materials relating to the history and life of the German-speaking Jews of Central Europe. Although some earlier works are included, most of the titles have been published since World War I. Z6375.W5

Yad Washem Martyrs' and Heroes Memorial Authority, Jerusalem [and] Yivo Institute for Jewish Research, N.Y. Joint documentary projects. Bibliographical series. N.Y., [Yivo Inst.], 1960–74. v.1–14. (In progress?) **BB573**

Contents: v.1, Guide to Jewish history under Nazi impact, by Jacob Robinson and Philip Friedman (1960. 425p.); v.2, Bibliography of books in Hebrew on the Jewish catastrophe and heroism in Europe, ed. by Philip Friedman (1960. 433p. In Hebrew); v.3, Bibliography of Yiddish books on the catastrophe and heroism, by Philip Friedman and Joseph Gar (1962. 330p. In Yiddish); v.4, The Hungarian Jewish catastrophe: a selected and annotated bibliography, by Randolph L. Braham (1962. 86p.; for rev. ed. *see* BB533); v.5–8, The Jewish holocaust and heroism through the eyes of the Hebrew press; a bibliography, ed. by Mendel Piekarz (1966. 4v. In Hebrew); v.9–10, Bibliography of articles on the catastrophe and heroism in Yiddish periodicals, by Joseph Gar (1966–69. 2v. In Yiddish); v.11, Bibliography of Yiddish books on the catastrophe and heroism, ed. by David Bass [additions for 1960–70, to v.3, above] (1970. 54p. In Yiddish).; v.12, The holocaust and after: sources and literature in English, by Jacob Robinson, assisted by Mrs. Philip Friedman (1973. 353p.); v.13–14, The holocaust and its aftermath; Hebrew books published in the years 1933–1972 (1974. 2v. In Hebrew).

A series of bibliographies essential for the study of the Holocaust. Most volumes are in Hebrew, but all include English title page and front matter.

Dissertations

Bihl, Wolfdieter. Bibliographie der Dissertationen über Judentum und jüdische Persönlichkeiten, die 1872–1962 an österreichischen Hochschulen (Wien, Graz, Innsbruck) approbiert wurden. Wien, Notring der Wissenschaftlichen Verbände Österreichs, 1965. 51p. **BB574**

About 500 items; author index. Z6366.B5

Kisch, Guido and **Roepke, Kurt.** Schriften zur Geschichte der Juden, eine Bibliographie der in Deutschland und der Schweiz 1922–1955 erschienenen Dissertationen. Tubingen, Mohr, 1959. 49p. (Schriftenreihe wissenschaftlicher Abhandlungen des Leo Baeck Inst. of Jews from Germany, 4) **BB575**

Z6366.K55

Kisch, Guido Judaistische Bibliographie. Ein Verzeichnis der in Deutschland und der Schweiz von 1956–1970 erschienenen Dissertationen und Habilitationsschriften. Basel, Stuttgart, Helbing & Lichtenhahn, 1972. 104p.
BB576

Classified lists with author and subject indexes. Z6366.K54

Indexes

Index to Jewish periodicals. v.1– , June 1963– . Cleveland, 1963– . Semiannual. **BB577**

Subtitle: An author and subject index to selected English language journals of general and scholarly interest. •

Numbered as a quarterly, but issues are double numbers, 1/2 covering July–Dec., 3/4 covering Jan.–June. Cumulated volume covers June 1963–May 1964; no further cumulations published.

Now indexes about 40 periodicals. Includes book reviews.

Z6367.I5

Dictionaries and encyclopedias

Ausubel, Nathan. The book of Jewish knowledge: an encyclopedia of Judaism and the Jewish people, covering all elements of Jewish life from biblical times to the present. N.Y., Crown, [1964]. 560p. il. **BB578**

An alphabetical encyclopedia dealing with the history, culture, and ethics of the Jews from biblical to modern times. BM50.A8

Encyclopaedia Judaica; das Judentum in Geschichte und Gegenwart. Berlin, Verlag Eschkol, [1928–34]. v.1–10. il.
BB579

Contents: v.1–10, Aach–Lyra. No more published.

v.1–2, only, issued also in an edition in Hebrew.

A scientific work of high scholarship, with signed articles and valuable bibliographies, covering all aspects of Jewish life, thought, literature, religion, customs, history, etc., especially full in biography. DS102.8.E5

Encyclopaedia Judaica. [Jerusalem], Encyclopaedia Judaica; N.Y., Macmillan, [1972]. 16v. il. **BB580**

An important work stemming from the unification of efforts to complete the old *Encyclopaedia Judaica* (above) and to produce a new Jewish encyclopedia in English. Offers a comprehensive and up-to-date view of world Jewry in about 25,000 articles by an international list of contributors. Most articles are signed with initials; those contributed by internal editors are so designated. All but the briefest entries carry bibliographies (with preference given to English-language materials when quality studies are available in English). Living persons are included among the many biographees.

Index of about 200,000 entries. A special section of supplementary entries incorporating new and updated information appears in v.16. Corrigenda section also in v.16.

The American Library Association's Subscription Books Committee has indicated certain reservations about the work in its review in *The booklist* 69:209–12. DS102.8.E496

—— Decennial book, 1973–1982: events of 1972–1981. Jerusalem, Encyclopaedia Judaica, [1982]. 684p. il. **BB581**

Covers the ten-year period subsequent to the publication of the *Encyclopaedia*, "incorporating the material of the *Year Books* along with a great deal of new material."—*Introd.* Includes feature articles; new and updating articles, the latter with cross references to the basic set; diary of events, 1973–81; necrology. Indexed. DS102.8.E495

—— Year book. 1973– . Jerusalem, Encyclopaedia Judaica, [1973]– . il. Frequency varies. **BB582**

1973 volume covers events of 1972, etc. Recent volumes cover two years.

In each volume a section of feature articles is followed by an alphabetically arranged section of "New facts, new entries," which offers supplementary information on matters treated in the basic work, as well as wholly new entries. The feature articles are lengthy essays by specialists on a wide range of topics, many of which are of special interest at time of publication. Indexed. DS102.8E498

Encyclopedia of Zionism and Israel. Raphael Patai, ed. N.Y., Herzl Pr., 1971. 2v. il. **BB583**

Concerned with the history and development of the Zionist movement and its constituent organizations throughout the world. With the exception of a general historical survey article, the material on Israel concentrates on the modern period (i.e., beginning with the latter half of the 19th century). There are brief entries for places in Israel. Biographies are limited mainly to Zionist leaders and Israeli statesmen and public officials; articles on persons who achieved fame in other areas deal primarily with their Zionist activities. About 3,000 articles; most of the longer ones are signed. Selective bibliography at the end of v.2. DS149.E597

Encyclopedia Talmudica; a digest of halachic literature and Jewish law from the Tannaitic period to the present time, alphabetically arr. . . . Ed., Shlomo Josef Zevin. English tr. ed. by Isidore Epstein and Harry Freedman. Jerusalem, Talmudic Encyclopedia Inst., [1969–74]. v.1–2. (In progress) **BB584**

Contents: v.1–2, 'Aleph–'Erez ha'Amin.
A translation of *Entsiklopedyah talmudit.*
Intended as a "comprehensive presentation . . . of all Halakhic subjects dealt with in the Talmud and in post-Talmudic Rabbinic literature" (*Introd.*), with indication of sources, reasonings, and variations of opinion relevant to each subject. Arrangement is according to the Hebrew alphabet of the original work, but an English table of contents is supplied. BM500.5.E613

Encyclopédie de la mystique juive. Paris, Berg International, [1977]. 1528col. il. **BB585**

"Ouvrage réalisé sous la direction de Armand Abécassis et Georges Nataf."—*t.p.*
Offers articles on various aspects of Jewish mysticism. French translations of relevant texts accompany the articles and bibliographies are appended. BM723.E58

Everyman's Judaica: an encyclopedic dictionary. Ed. by Geoffrey Wigoder. Jerusalem, Keter Publ. House; London, W. H. Allen, [1975]. 673p. il. **BB586**

Intended as a complement to the multi-volume *Encyclopaedia Judaica* (BB580); i.e., "designed as a handy reference work giving basic facts and figures."—*Introd.* Very brief entries. Numerous charts and tables; profusely illustrated. Strong in biographical entries. DS102.8.E68

Jewish encyclopedia; a descriptive record of the history, religion, literature, and customs of the Jewish people from the earliest times to the present day; prep. under the

direction of Cyrus Adler [and others] . . . Isidore Singer, managing ed. N.Y., Funk & Wagnalls, 1901–06. 12v. il. (Repr.: N.Y., Ktav, 1964?) **BB587**

A standard encyclopedia in English, with signed articles by specialists and with bibliographies. Now out-of-date, but still useful for its biographies and other historical information. DS102.8.J6

Jüdisches Lexikon; ein enzyklopädisches Handbuch des jüdischen Wissens . . . hrsg. von Georg Herlitz und Bruno Kirschner. Berlin, Jüdischer Verlag, [1927–30]. 4v. in 5. il. (Repr.: Königstein, Athenäum, 1982) **BB588**

More popular in character than the *Encyclopaedia Judaica* (BB579), with brief signed articles and some bibliography. Many illustrations. DS102.8.J8

Lexikon des Judentums. Chefredakteur, John F. Oppenheimer. [Gütersloh, Ger.], Bertelsmann, [1967]. 928col. il. **BB589**

Brief articles on a wide range of topics pertaining to Judaism, including biographical notes on both living and deceased persons. DS102.8.L44

The new standard Jewish encyclopedia. New rev. ed., ed. by Geoffrey Wigoder. 5th ed. Garden City, N.Y., Doubleday, 1977. 2028col. il. **BB590**

4th ed. 1970 by Cecil Roth and Geoffrey Wigoder; prior to 1970 published under title *The standard Jewish encyclopedia* (1st ed. 1959).
A compilation of concise factual and biographical information, intended primarily as a work of contempoary reference, placing special emphasis on recent developments in Jewish history, and on the American community and the State of Israel, but also "covering every phase of Jewish life, literature, and thought from their beginning."—*Pref.* Biographical sketches include living persons. DS102.8.S73

Shulman, Albert M. Gateway to Judaism: encyclopedia home reference. South Brunswick, N.J., T. Yoseloff, [1971]. 2v. (1056p.) **BB591**

A topical encyclopedia for the student and layman. Sections on the literature of the Jewish people, doctrine and beliefs, Jewish calendar and holidays, etc. Detailed index in v.2. BM570.S57

Universal Jewish encyclopedia . . . an authoritative and popular presentation of Jews and Judaism since the earliest times; ed. by Isaac Landman . . . N.Y., Universal Jewish Encyclopedia, Inc., [1939–44]. 10v. and reading guide and index (78p.). il. **BB592**

A useful encyclopedia, more popular in treatment than the scholarly *Jewish encyclopedia* (BB587), but somewhat more up-to-date than that work. Especially strong in its treatment of American subjects and of pre-World War II matters. Many biographies, including living persons. Some articles are signed and some have bibliographies. Now largely superseded by the *Encyclopaedia Judaica* (BB580). DS102.8.U5

Werblowsky, Raphael Jehuda Zwi and **Wigoder, Geoffrey,** eds. The encyclopedia of the Jewish religion. Jerusalem, Massada-P.E.C. Pr.; N.Y., Holt, 1966. 415p. il. **BB593**

Concentrates on religion (i.e., "belief and practices, religious movements and doctrines, as well as the names and concepts that have played a rôle in Jewish religious history"—*Pref.*) without trying to embrace all aspects of Jewish life, culture, and history. Less comprehensive, therefore, than the 2v. *New standard Jewish encyclopedia* (and without the biographies of prominent contemporary Jews, for example), but a useful work for the layman. BM50.W45

Biography

Rosenbloom, Joseph R. A biographical dictionary of early American Jews: colonial times through 1800. [Lexington], Univ. of Kentucky Pr., [1960]. 175p. **BB594**

Attempts to list all persons identifiable as Jews in America before

1800, with such biographical facts as can be found in manuscript and printed sources.   E184.J5R63

Wininger, Salomon. Grosse jüdische National-Biographie, mit mehr als 12,000 Lebensbeschreibungen namhafter jüdischer Männer und Frauen aller Zeiten und Länder. Ein Nachschlagewerk für das jüdische Volk und dessen Freunde. Cernauti, "Arta," [1925–37?]. v.1–7¹⁻⁷.   **BB595**

Issued in parts.

Contents: v.1–5, A–St; v.6, St–Z, Nachträge, A–Geldern; v.7 (incomplete), Geiler–Z, 2.Nachträge, A–Fink. No more published.

An international biographical dictionary of Jews primarily from the Middle Ages to the 20th century, with a few of earlier date. The number of sketches noted in the title varies from 8,000 to 12,000.   DS115.W5

Who's who in American Jewry, see AJ92.

Who's who in world Jewry, see AJ59.

History

Baron, Salo Wittmayer. A social and religious history of the Jews. 2d ed. rev. and enl. N.Y., Columbia Univ. Pr., 1952–83. v.1–18 and index to v.1–8. (In progress)   **BB596**

1st ed. 1937. 3v.

Contents: v.1–2, Ancient times; v.3–8, High Middle Ages, 500–1200; v.3, Heirs of Rome and Persia; v.4, Meeting of East and West; v.5, Religious controls and discussions; v.6, Laws, homilies, and the Bible; v.7, Hebrew language and letters; v.8, Philosophy and science; v.9–18, Late Middle Ages and era of European expansion: v.9, Under Church and Empire; v.10, On the Empire's periphery; v.11, Citizen or alien conjurer; v.12, Economic catalyst; v.13, Inquisition, Renaissance, and Reformation; v.14, Catholic restoration and wars of religion; v.15, Resettlement and exploration; v.16, Poland-Lithuania 1500–1650; v.17, Byzantines, Mamelukes, and Maghribians; v.18, The Ottoman Empire, Persia, Ethiopia, India, and China.

Covers from ancient times to 1650. Studies the history of the Jews in the various countries and societies in which they have lived. Each volume includes "Notes" (explanations, descriptions, and references to sources).   DS112.B315

The Cambridge history of Judaism. Ed. by Louis W. D. Davies, Louis Finkelstein. Cambridge & N.Y., Cambridge Univ. Pr., [1984]– . v.1– . (In progress; to be in 4v.)   **BB597**

Contents: v.1, Introduction (The geography of Palestine and the Levant . . .; Numismatics; Calendars and chronology); The Persian period.

Presents a scholarly history incorporating the "new data provided by archeology, new knowledge of the Apocryphal, Pseudepigraphical, Qumranic and Gnostic writings, and recent critical work on the Rabbinic sources" in chapters by scholars chosen "from various religious and non-religious backgrounds, and from various countries, so that the work may be truly ecumenical and international." —*Pref.* To cover from the Babylonian exile to the codification of the Mishnah, and to include extensive background on the context in which Judaism developed. Footnotes appear with the text; chapter bibliographies are at the back of the book. Index; chronological tables.

Succeeding volumes are to cover the Hellenistic age, the Roman period to CE 70, and CE 70 to CE 235.   BM155.2.C35

Handbooks

Birnbaum, Philip. A book of Jewish concepts. Rev. ed. N.Y., Hebrew Pub. Co., [1975]. 722p.   **BB598**

1st ed. 1964.

Aims "to provide in a single handy volume the essential teachings of Judaism."—*Introd.* Articles range in length from a brief paragraph to two or more pages. Arrangement is alphabetical according to the Hebrew form of the term, with an English translation or transliteration provided for each term; Hebrew and English indexes. Intended for rabbis, teachers, students and laymen.   BM50.B55

Klein, Isaac. A guide to Jewish religious practice. N.Y., Jewish Theological Seminary of America (distr. by Ktav Publ. House), 1979. 588p. (Moreshet ser., 6)   **BB599**

A guide to Conservative Jewish practice. Includes "all the rules and regulations that observant Jews regard as norms, and on which they usually seek guidance from their rabbis."—*Pref.* Bibliography; index.   BM700.K54

Trepp, Leo. The complete book of Jewish observance. N.Y., Summit Books, [1980]. 370p. il.   **BB600**

Intended as an aid to Jews in studying their heritage and in performing the commandments, practices, ceremonies, and rituals of Judaism. In two main sections, the first following the Jewish year, the second the cycle of life. Individual festivals, rites, and ceremonies are discussed in their historical context and attention is given to modern developments. Indexed.   BM690.T73

Yearbooks

American Jewish year book, 5660– , Sept. 5, 1899– . N.Y., Jewish Pub. Soc., 1899– . v.1– . Annual. (v.83, 1983)   **BB601**

Imprint varies.

Contains important directory and statistical information, and a review of the year's events relating to Jewish matters in America and other countries. Each volume contains special articles, biographies, necrologies, and bibliographies. Many of these from earlier issues continue to have reference value. v.40 includes a subject index to special articles in v.1–40, and v.83 a similar index for v.51–82.   E184.J5A6

Jewish year book; an annual record of matters Jewish. 5657– . (1896–). London, "Jewish Chronicle," 1896– . v.1– .   **BB602**

Contains statistical and institutional information for the British Commonwealth, bibliographies, and a who's who.   DS135.E5A3

Zionist yearbook. 1951/52– . London, Zionist Federation of Great Britain and Ireland, 1951– . Annual.   **BB603**

Includes directory information about Zionist organizations in Great Britain and abroad; governmental information about Israel; biographical notices.   DS149.A3843

SHINTOISM

Herbert, Jean. Bibliographie du Shintô et des sectes shintôistes. Leiden, Brill, 1968. 73p.   **BB604**

An author listing of more than 1,100 books and pamphlets; subject index.   Z7835.S5H4

Holtom, Daniel Clarence. The national faith of Japan; a study in modern Shinto. London, Kegan Paul; N.Y., Dutton, 1938. 329p. (Repr.: N.Y., Paragon, 1965)   **BB605**

A good historical survey; bibliographical footnotes.   BL2220.H58

Kato, Genchi, Reitz, Karl and **Schiffer, Wilhelm.** A bibliography of Shinto in Western languages, from the oldest times till 1952. Tokyo, Meiji Jingu Shamusho, 1953. 58p.   **BB606**

Alphabetical arrangement. Index; no annotations. Appendix, prep. by Rev. Wilhelm Schiffer, lists books and articles on Shinto published 1941–52.   Z7835.S5K3

ZOROASTRIANISM

See also BB78.

Boyce, Mary. Zoroastrians, their religious beliefs and practices. London & Boston, Routledge & Kegan Paul, 1979. 252p. **BB607**

Presents the history of Zoroastrianism from its beginnings to the 20th century. Offered as an introduction to the subject for university religion students. Short bibliography, chiefly of English-language sources. Indexed.

A more detailed work by the same author, to be in several volumes, has begun publication as *A history of Zoroastrianism* (Leiden, Brill, 1975– . v.1–). BL1525.B695

Dhalla, Maneckji N. History of Zoroastrianism. London, N.Y., Oxford Univ. Pr., 1938. 525p. **BB608**

A documented history of Zoroastrianism and its literature and beliefs from earliest to modern times. The bibliography lists translations of the sacred texts into Western languages as well as works about Zoroastrianism. BL1570.D5

Oxtoby, Willard Gurdon. Ancient Iran and Zoroastrianism in Festschriften: an index. Waterloo, Ont., Council on the Study of Religion, Waterloo Lutheran Univ.; Shiraz, Iran, Asia Inst. of Pahlavi Univ., 1973. 207p. (Bibliographic studies in religion, 1; Asia Inst. of Pahlavi Univ. Monograph ser., 3) **BB609**

"Lists 1808 articles," chiefly in Western languages, "which have appeared in 421 Festschriften between 1875 and 1973."—*Introd.* Classified subject arrangement with author index and list of the *Festschriften* fully identified. Outline of subject headings defines topics and aids in reference use. Besides religion, includes history, archaeology, and language. Z7835.Z8O95

Zaehner, Robert Charles. The dawn and twilight of Zoroastrianism. London, Weidenfeld and Nicolson; N.Y., Putnam, [1961]. 371p. **BB610**

Scholarly in tone, but intended as a work for the nonspecialist reader on the history and essential features of Zoroastrianism. Bibliography; index. BL1571.Z3

B C

Linguistics and Philology

❖This section includes works dealing with the study of language: survey histories such as Mencken's *American language* (BC81), Brunot's *Histoire de la langue française* (BC122), and Cejador y Frauca's *Historia de la lengua y literatura castellana* (BC136); guides to groups of languages, e.g., De Bray's *Guide to the Slavonic languages* (BC162); bibliographies of language groups, e.g., Loewenthal's *Turkic languages and literatures of Central Asia* (BC171) and Hospers' *Basic bibliography for the study of Semitic languages* (BC174); and, of particular importance, the various annual bibliographies. Von Ostermann's *Manual of foreign languages* (BC56) is very useful to the worker who needs to know the alphabets, transliteration, and basic grammatical rules of many languages.

Many of the bibliographies of literature include works on language. For these consult Section BD, Literature. Dictionaries and bibliographies of dictionaries will be found in Section AD, Dictionaries.

INTERNATIONAL

Bibliography

Abrahamsen, Adele A. Child language; an interdisciplinary guide to theory and research. Baltimore, University Park Pr., [1977]. 381p. **BC1**

A topically arranged, annotated bibliography of about 1,500 items. Author and subject indexes. Z7004.C45A27

Akademiia Nauk SSSR. Fundamental'naia Biblioteka Obshchestvennykh Nauk. Obshchee iazykoznanie; bibliograficheskii ukazatel' literatury, izdannoi v SSSR s 1918 po 1962 g. Moskva, Nauka, 1965. 275p. **BC2**

A bibliography of Russian writings on general linguistics. Z7001.A35

—— Strukturnoe i prikladnoe iazykoznanie; bibliograficheskii ukazatel' literatury, izdannoi v SSSR s 1918 po 1962 g. Moskva, Nauka, 1965. 193p. **BC3**

A bibliography of structural and applied linguistics. Limited to materials published in the USSR, but including items in non-Slavic languages. Classed arrangement with name and title index. There is a separate list of books and articles published abroad which were the subject of Soviet reviews. Z7001.A36

Malinskaia, B. A. and **Shabat, M. TS.** Obshchee i prikladnoe iazykoznanie. Ukaz. literatury, izd. v SSSR s 1963 po 1967 g. Moskva, "Nauka," 1972. 295p. **BC4**

At head of title: Akademiia Nauk SSSR. Institut Nauchnoi Informatsii i Fundamental'naia Biblioteka po Obshchestvennym Naukam.

Serves as a supplement to both the *Obshchee iazykoznanie* (1965; BC2) and *Strukturnoe i prikladnoe iazykoznanie; bibliograficheskii ukazatel' literatury* (1965; BC3) Z7001.M33

Akademiia Nauk SSSR. Institut IAzykoznaniia. Bibliograficheskii ukazatel' literatury po iazykoznaniiu, izdannoi v SSSR s 1918 po 1957 god. Sost.: N.P. Debets i dr. Moskva, 1958. v.1. **BC5**

Ceased publication.

A bibliographic index, planned in 5v., of the literature in all branches of linguistics published in the USSR between 1918 and 1957. v.1 covers books, collections, and doctoral dissertations in Russian, to 1955. Z7001.A37

—— Bibliograficheskii ukazatel' literatury po russkomu iazykoznaniiu s 1825 po 1880 god. Glav. redaktor V. V. Vinogradov. Moskva, 1954–59. 8v. **BC6**

An annotated bibliographic index to the literature on linguistics published in Russia between 1825 and 1880. v.8 contains a general index. Z2505.A55

Allen, Harold Byron. Linguistics and English linguistics. 2d ed. Arlington Heights, Ill., AHM Pub. Corp., 1977. 184p. **BC7**

1st ed. 1966.

Intended as a guide "for graduate and advanced undergraduate students in linguistics, English, education, psychology, sociology, speech, and anthropology" (*Pref.*), listing materials through early 1975. Nearly 2,900 entries in classed arrangement with author index. Citations are to books and periodical articles in English. Z7001.A4

Blass, Birgit A., Johnson, Dora E. and **Gage, William W.** A provisional survey of materials for the study of neglected languages. Wash., Center for Applied Linguistics, [1969]. 414p.   **BC8**

An annotated list of more than 2,000 items representing 382 languages and dialects. Arrangement is by language or language group within large geographical areas. Includes teaching materials, readers, grammars, and dictionaries. Works listed are those intended primarily "for use by the beginning adult learner whose native language is English."—*Introd.*   Z7001.B59

Center for Applied Linguistics. Library. Dictionary catalog of the Library of the Center for Applied Linguistics, Washington, D.C. Boston, G. K. Hall, 1974. 4v.   **BC9**

Reproduces the catalog cards for the Center's collection. The library maintains "a predominantly contemporary acquisitions policy with only limited retrospective purchase and limited systematic book selection."—*Introd.*   Z7004.A6S46

Gazdar, Gerald, Klein, Ewan and **Pullum, Geoffrey K.** A bibliography of contemporary linguistic research. N.Y., Garland, 1978. 425p. (Garland reference library of the humanities, 119)   **BC10**

An author list of some 5,000 recent (i.e., 1970 and later) articles and short notes drawn from scholarly journals, conference proceedings, specialist anthologies and litho-printed books, chiefly on the central topics of linguistics: syntactic, semantic, philological and pragmatic theory. Language and subject indexes.   Z7001.G38

Gipper, Helmut and **Schwarz, Hans.** Bibliographisches Handbuch zur Sprachinhaltsforschung; Schrifttum zur Sprachinhaltsforschung in alphabetischer Folge nach Verfassern, mit Besprechungen und Inhaltshinweisen. Hrsg. [von] Leo Brandt. Köln, [1961?–84]. Lfg.1–29/30. (Wissenschaftliche Abhandlungen der Arbeitsgemeinschaft für Forschung des Landes Nordrhein-Westfalen, Bd.16a) (In progress)   **BC11**

"Die Arbeitsgemeinschaft für Forschung vorgelegt von Jost Trier und Leo Weisgerber."—*verso of title page.*
Contents: Lfg.1–29/30, A–Stutterheim.
An extensive annotated bibliography of works in various languages on semantics.

———— ———— Beiheft 1. [Opladen, 1974]

Contents: Proberegister (zu Teil I, Bd.1–2, A–K): Auswahl aus der Ordnung nach Sinnbezirken und dem Namenregister nebst Sprachenverzeichnis und Anhang. 81p.   Z7001.G56

Girke, Wolfgang, Jachnow, Helmut and **Schrenk, Josef.** Handbibliographie zur neueren Linguistik in Osteuropa. München, Wilhelm Fink Verlag, [1974]–80. Bd.1–2. (In progress)   **BC12**

Contents: Bd.1, 1963–65; Bd.2, 1966–71. (Bd.2 has title *Handbibliographie zur slavistischen und allgemeinen Linguistik in Osteuropa.*)
Table of contents and section headings in German, English, and Russian.
Nearly 6,000 items in Bd.1 and some 18,000 in Bd.2, mainly in the East European languages. Includes books and periodical articles. Classed arrangement with author index.   Z7001.G57

Gordon, W. Terrence. Semantics: a bibliography, 1965–1978. Metuchen, N.J., Scarecrow Pr., 1980. 307p.   **BC13**

A classed bibliography of more than 3,300 items. Includes materials from the fields of philosophy, linguistics, and psychology. "Lexical index" and author index.   Z7004.S4G67

Guiraud, Pierre. Bibliographie critique de la statistique linguistique. Revisée et complétée par Thomas D. Houchin, Jaan Puhvel et Calvert W. Watkins, sous la direction de Joshua Whatmough. Utrecht, Éd. Spectrum, 1954. 121p. (Comité International Permanent de Linguistes. Publications du Comité de la Statistique Linguistique. II)   **BC14**

A classified list of scholarly books and articles in many languages on a variety of statistical approaches to linguistic studies (e.g., word counts, rhyme frequencies, etc.).   P11.A1P45 no.2

Hammer, John H. and **Rice, Frank A.,** eds. A bibliography of contrastive linguistics. [Wash.], Center for Applied Linguistics, 1965. 41p.   **BC15**

A revised and expanded version of William W. Gage's *Contrastive studies in linguistics* (Wash., 1961). Lists studies which offer "a systematic comparison of selected linguistic features of two or more languages."—*Introd.* Arranged by languages (other than English), with an author index.   Z7004.G7H3

Hewes, Gordon Winant. Language origins: a bibliography. 2d rev. and enl. ed. The Hague, Mouton, 1975. 2v. (Approaches to semiotics, 44)   **BC16**

1st ed. 1971.
Aims "to cover all works on the origins of language, and related topics, to the middle of 1972."—*Foreword.* About 11,000 items, including works from the disciplines of psychology, anthropology, philosophy, speech pathology, animal communication behavior, anatomy of the larynx, and anatomy and neurophysiology of the brain, as well as linguistics. International in scope; entries are mainly for books and periodical articles, but a few manuscripts are included. Author listing with topical index; publication dates are included in the index citations to facilitate use.   Z7004.O75H46

Krenn, Herwig and **Müllner, Klaus.** Bibliographie zur Transformationsgrammatik. Heidelberg, Winter, 1968. 262p.   **BC17**

An author listing of books, periodical articles, research reports, dissertations, reviews. 2,459 entries.
A keyword index is provided by: Z7004.G7K72

Knoop, Ulrich, Kohrt, Manfred and **Küper, Christoph.** An index of Bibliographie zur Transformationsgrammatik by H. Krenn and K. Müllner. Heidelberg, C. Winter, 1971. 116p. (Bibliothek der allgemeinen Sprachwissenschaft, Reihe 2)   **BC18**

                                                     Z7004.G7K58

Kreuder, Hans-Dieter. Studienbibliographie Linguistik; mit einem Anhang zur Sprechwissenschaft von Lothar Berger. 2., völlig neubearb. Aufl. Wiesbaden, Steiner, 1982. 190p.   **BC19**

1st ed. 1974.
A bibliography for the study of linguistics, ranging from introductory texts to specialized sources; includes speech communication. Lists books and periodical articles in German or English. Classed arrangement with author index; brief annotations for monographs.   Z7001.K74

Mackey, William F., ed. Bibliographie internationale sur le bilinguisme. International bibliography on bilingualism. Québec, Presses de l'Université Laval, [1972]. 337p., 209p., 203p.   **BC20**

Prefatory matter in English and French.
Concerned with studies of "bilingualism as a phenomenon," and therefore omits "such things as bilingual dictionaries, materials for teaching foreign languages, and, as a rule, the professional literature of the language teacher, with the exception of studies on language learning and works on the education of bilingual children."—*Introd.* Includes some 11,000 entries in an alphabetical author listing, with separate subject indexes in English and in French.   7004.B5M3

Mayer, Stefan and **Weber, Michael.** Bibliographie zur linguistischen Gesprächsforschung. Hildesheim, Olms, 1983. 214p. (Germanistische Linguistik 1–2/81)   **BC21**

A "Sachlich-systematischer Teil" offering a classified approach to the bibliography precedes the alphabetical author listing of book and periodical citations. The author entries include reference to the appropriate subject classifications, thus providing "see also" references to related materials.

Moscow. Publichnaia Biblioteka. Otdel Spravochno-Bibliograficheskoi i Informatsionnoi Raboty. Bibliografiia bibliografii po iazykoznaniiu; annotirovannyi sistematicheskii ukazatel' otechestvennykh izdanii. [Sost.: E. I. Kukushkina i A. G. Stepanova] Moskva, 1963. 411p.   **BC22**

A bibliography of bibliographies published in Russia and the USSR in all fields of linguistic study. Z7001.M65

Pogarell, Reiner. Minority languages in Europe: a classified bibliography. Berlin [etc.], Mouton, [1983]. 208p. **BC23**

The subtitle not withstanding, this is a main-entry listing with indexes by (1) languages, regions, states, and (2) by keywords. About 2,400 entries in many languages for books, parts of books, and periodical articles. The compiler was particularly concerned to list important works from various periods in the hope "of making the fruits of past work accessible to the research of today."—*Introd.*
Z7004.L54P63

Pop, Sever. Bibliographie des questionnaires linguistiques. Louvain, Commission d'Enquête Linguistique, [1955]. 168p. (Comité International Permanent de Linguistes. Publications de la Commission d'Enquête Linguistique. VI) **BC24**

A chronological listing of questionnaires employed in linguistic field work, with annotations and sources of reference for each item. Indexes of names and subjects.

Schaller, Helmut Wilhelm. Bibliographie zur Balkanphilologie. Heidelberg, Winter, 1977. 109p. **BC25**

A topically arranged bibliography with author and subject indexes. In addition to general studies of the Balkans as a linguistic area, includes materials on Bulgarian, Macedonian, Serbo-Croatian, Albanian, Romanian, and Modern Greek. About 1,500 items.
Z2845.A2S32

Wares, Alan C. Bibliography of the Summer Institute of Linguistics. [Dallas], Summer Institute of Linguistics, 1979– . v.1– . (In progress) **BC26**

Contents: v.1, 1935–1975. 317p.
Based on earlier bibliographies of the Institute published 1947–76.
v.1 "is a compilation of works in linguistics, anthropology, and applied linguistics" (*Pref.*) comprising works published by members of the Institute and works published by the Institute. In two parts: (1) Technical articles (arranged by author) and (2) Vernacular works (arranged by country). Language, subject, and author indexes.
Z7001.W33

Wellisch, Hans (Hanan). Transcription and transliteration; an annotated bibliography on conversion of scripts. Silver Springs, Md., Inst. of Modern Languages, [1975]. 133p. **BC27**

Arrangement follows that of the *Bibliographie linguistique* (BC29); i.e., by language group, subdivided according to specific language. Author/title and subject indexes. Z7004.T73W44

Current

Analecta linguistica. v.1, no.1– . Amsterdam, J. Benjamins, 1971– . Semiannual. **BC28**

Publisher varies.
Title also in English (Informational bulletin of linguistics).
Issued by Magyar Tudományos Akadémia Nyelvtudományi Intezete.
A selected, international bibliography on linguistic subjects. Based on monographs and offprints received in Hungarian libraries or reported to the editorial office during the period preceding publication of the bibliography. Also reproduces tables of contents of current linguistic journals, and periodically publishes specialized bibliographies on linguistic subjects. Author index. Z7003.A5

Bibliographie linguistique des années 1939/1947– , publiée par le Comité International Permanent de Linguistes. Utrecht, Spectrum, 1949– . v.1– . Annual. **BC29**

Added title page in English: *Linguistic bibliography. . . .*
1939/47 in 2v.: v.1 lists books, reviews, and periodical articles on various branches of linguistics appearing in South Africa, Belgium (publications in Flemish), Czechoslovakia, Finland, France, Italy, the Netherlands, Norway, Poland, Spain, and Switzerland; v.2

includes contributions from Austria, Belgium (French), Denmark, England, Greece, India, Ireland, Portugal, Russia, Sweden, Turkey, and the U.S.A., etc., with an author index to both volumes.
Materials are grouped under large classes, with subdivisions, e.g., General linguistics: Indo-European, Asianic and Mediterranean, Finno-Ugrian, Basque, Hamito-Semitic, Negro-African, Caucasian, Turkish and Mongolian, Eastern Asia [and others]. Continued by annual volumes, with slightly enlarged coverage.
A bibliography of first importance, particularly valuable for the comprehensiveness of its listing of periodical articles. Lacks a subject index, but the detailed table of contents partially compensates as a subject approach. Z7001.P4

Bibliographie unselbständiger Literatur-Linguistik (BUL-L). Bd.1–3, 1971/75–77. Bearb. von Elke Suchan. Frankfurt am Main, V. Klostermann, [1976–78]. **BC30**

Published for the Sondersammelgebiet Linguistik of the Stadt- und Universitätsbibliothek, Frankfurt am Main.
A classed bibliography of periodical articles and essays in collective works, proceedings of congresses, etc. Arrangement is by language, with detailed subject breakdown within each language section. Author and subject indexes. Concerned with Western languages only.
The 1971/75 volume lists some 13,000 entries for items drawn from 123 frequently cited journals, plus references to collective works, congress proceedings, etc. Annual volumes cover 1976–77, with supplementary materials from earlier years.
Continued by:

Bibliographie linguistischer Literatur (BLL). Bd.4– , 1978– . Frankfurt am Main, V. Klostermann, 1979– . Annual. **BC31**

Subtitle: Bibliographie zur allgemeinen Linguistik und zur anglistischen, germanistischen und romanistischen Linguistik.
Issued by Sondersammelgebiet Linguistik der Stadt- und Universitätsbibliothek, Frankfurt am Main.
Introductory matter and section headings in English and German.
Continues *Bibliographie unselbständiger Literatur-Linguistik* (above) and assumes its numbering.
Now in four main sections: (1) General linguistics; (2) German linguistics; (3) English linguistics; and (4) Romance linguistics, with appropriate subdivisions for each. International in scope, with coverage of a long list of periodicals and analysis of numerous collective works.

Bulletin signalétique 524: Sciences du langage. Paris, Centre National de la Recherche Scientifique, 1947– . Quarterly. **BC32**

Title varies: 1947–60, *Bulletin signalétique: Philosophie, sciences humaines;* 1961–66, *Bulletin signalétique. Sec.21, Sociologie, sciences du langage;* 1967–68, *Bulletin signalétique 24, Sciences du langage.*
For fuller information on *Bulletin signalétique, see* AE277 and EA76.
Through 1968, an international abstract journal with very comprehensive coverage; beginning 1969, a bibliography only. Coverage of the language section has varied; it now includes the physiology, pathology, pychology and sociology of language, linguistic theory, historical linguistics and comparative grammar, philology, and stylistics in a classified arrangement with author and subject indexes. P2.B84●

LLBA; language and language behavior abstracts. v.1, no.1– , Jan. 1967– . N.Y., Appleton, 1967– . Quarterly. **BC33**

A sample issue, v.0, no.1, was published in advance of v.1, no.1.
Edited at the University of Michigan Center for Research on Language and Behavior in collaboration with the Bureau pour l'Enseignement de la Langue et de la Civilisation Françaises à l'Étranger. Publisher varies.
Designed to provide rapid access to scholarly articles relevant to language and language behavior, regardless of disciplinary focus. Abstracts are grouped under linguistics, psychology, communication sciences, and hearing, with appropriate subdivisions. Entries

are now drawn from more than 1,000 journals, reports, occasional papers, etc., in some 30 languages. Author index.   Z7001.L15●

Modern Language Association of America. MLA international bibliography, 1921– .   **BC34**

For full information *see* BD22.

Year's work in modern language studies, by a number of scholars. 1929/30– . London, Oxford Univ. Pr., 1931– . v.1– . Annual.   **BC35**

v.11 covers 1940–49 in one composite volume.

Coverage varies: usually includes material on language and literature in (1) Medieval Latin, (2) Romance languages, (3) Germanic languages, and (4) Slavonic languages. Concerned with developments from medieval times to the present day.

With v.35 (1974) a new section, "General linguistics," is introduced at the beginning of the volume.   PB1.Y45

Language-teaching

Centre for Information on Language Teaching and English-Teaching Information Centre of the British Council. A language-teaching bibliography. 2d ed. Cambridge, [Eng.], University Pr., 1972. 242p.   **BC36**

1st ed. 1968.

In eight main divisions: (1) Language; (2) Language teaching; (3–8) English for speakers of other languages, French, German, Italian, Russian, and Spanish.   Z5814.L26C45

Goldstein, Wallace L., comp. Teaching English as a second language: an annotated bibliography. N.Y., Garland, 1975. 218p.   **BC37**

A classed listing of 852 items, with descriptive annotations. Works are grouped under such headings as: Curriculum, Grammar, Reading, Spoken English, Teaching aids, Testing and evaluation, Texts, Writing. Key-word index and author index.   Z5818.E5G64

————— Teaching English as a second language 2; an annotated bibliography. N.Y., Garland, 1984. 323p. (Garland reference library of social science, v.181)   **BC38**

Serves as a supplement to the above, adding more than 900 items, primarily 1975–82 publications.   Z5818.E5G64

Language-teaching abstracts. v.1–7, 1968–74. London, Cambridge Univ. Pr., 1968–75. Quarterly.   **BC39**

Edited jointly by the English-Teaching Information Centre and the Centre for Information on Language Teaching.

International in coverage, but all abstracts appear in English. About 300 journals are regularly examined for materials pertinent to modern language teaching. Maintains the coverage of English as a second language previously appearing in *English-teaching abstracts* (1961–67). Classed arrangement, with author and subject indexes in the final number of the volume.

Superseded by: PB35.L32

Language teaching & linguistics: abstracts. v.8–14, 1975–81. London, Cambridge Univ. Pr., 1975–81. Quarterly.   **BC40**

Constitutes a change of title for *Language-teaching abstracts* (above) and assumes the volume numbering of that publication. "The inclusion of *Linguistics* in the new title indicates recognition of the importance of certain areas of this field to language teaching. The journal will continue to provide objective summaries in English of selected articles taken from nearly 400 journals."—*v.8, no.1.* Beginning with v.10 (1977) each issue includes a survey article on the state of scholarship in a particular area of the field of language teaching.

Continued by: PB35.L32

Language teaching. v.15, no.1– , Jan. 1982– . Cambridge, Cambridge Univ. Pr., 1982– . Quarterly.   **BC41**

Subtitle: The international abstracting journal for language teachers and applied linguists.

Supersedes *Language teaching & linguistics* and assumes its numbering.

Continues the plan and coverage of the earlier title, with increased emphasis on teaching methods and materials.   PB35.L32

Nostrand, Howard Lee, Foster, David William and **Christensen, Clay Benjamin.** Research on language teaching: an annotated international bibliography, 1945–1964. 2d ed. rev. Seattle, Univ. of Washington Pr., 1965. 373p.   **BC42**

1st ed. 1962.

An annotated, classified listing of books and periodical articles on methods, material, equipment, psychology of language learning, teaching at various levels, etc. Includes a list of bibliographies and one of periodicals and serials. In this edition a special effort was made to justify the "international" of the title by including more references to research outside the United States.   Z7001.N6

Petrov, Julia A. Foreign language, area, and other international studies: a bibliography of research and instructional materials completed under the National Defense Education Act of 1958, title VI, section 602: list no.9. Ed. by John Brosseau. [9th ed.] [Wash.], U.S. Dept. of Education, [1980]. 79p. (Publ. no. E-80-14017)   **BC43**

Citations are presented in two categories: (1) General reports (studies and surveys, conferences, linguistic studies, research in language-teaching methods) and (2) Specialized materials (commonly taught languages, uncommonly taught languages, foreign area studies). Indexed.   Z5818.L35P47

Robinson, Janet O. Annotated bibliography of modern language teaching: books and articles, 1946–1967. London, Oxford Univ. Pr., 1969. 231p. (Language and language learning, 23)   **BC44**

A guide for the teacher. Classed arrangement; author index. Includes selective lists of dictionaries, grammars, and studies of the individual languages, as well as works on teaching aids and methods, curriculum planning, etc.   Z5814.L26R63

Savard, Jean-Guy. Bibliographie analytique de tests de langues. Analytical bibliography of language tests. 2d ed., rev. & enl. Québec, Presses de l'Université Laval, 1977. 570p. (Pubns. of the Internat. Ctr. for Research on Bilingualism, F-1)   **BC45**

1st ed. 1969.

Prefatory matter in French and English.

Aims to "provide professors, students, researchers and all others in the field of testing and evaluation of language learning with an analytical book of tests" (*Introd.*) without critical evaluation thereof. Indexes of authors and titles. Some 275 tests were retained from the earlier edition, and about 220 new tests were added.

Z5818.L35S27

Periodicals

Maison des Sciences de l'Homme. Service d'Échange d'Informations Scientifiques. Liste mondiale des périodiques spécialisés: linguistique. World list of specialized periodicals: linguistics. Paris, Mouton, [1971]. 243p. (*Its* Publications, Série C, Catalogues et inventaires, 4)   **BC46**

Introductory matter, headings, and indexes in French and English.

Lists and describes 540 periodicals wholly or partly devoted to linguistics. Listing is by country of publication, with indexes by keyword, title, and sponsoring institution.   Z7003.M34

Ulving, Tor. Periodica philologica abbreviata; a list of initial abbreviations of periodicals in philology and related subjects. Stockholm, Almqvist & Wiksell, [1963]. 137p.   **BC47**

An international list of initial abbreviations for more than 3,000 periodicals, with full name of periodical and place of publication.   Z6945.A2U5513

Dissertations

Cooper, Stephen. Graduate theses and dissertations in English as a second language, 1975/76–1978/79. [Arlington, Va.], Center for Applied Linguistics, [1977–80]. 4v. Annual.
BC48

Vols. for 1976/77, 1978/79 publ. as *Language in education: theory and practice*, no. 3, 15.
Classed listing with author index. Brief abstract for many entries. Includes author's address current at time of compilation.
Continued by: Z5818.E5C66

—— ESL theses and dissertations, 1979/80– . Wash., Center for Applied Linguistics, 1981– . Annual. (Language in education, no.35, etc.) **BC49**

Rutherford, Phillip R. A bibliography of American doctoral dissertations in linguistics, 1900-1964. Wash., Center for Applied Linguistics, 1968. 139p. **BC50**

An author listing of more than 1,700 dissertations, with a subject index.
Supplemented in part by: Z7001.R8

Birdsong, David. American doctoral dissertations in foreign language education, 1965–1974: an annotated bibliography. Arlington, Va., ERIC Clearinghouse on Languages and Linguistics, Center for Applied Linguistics, 1976. 51p. (CAL-ERIC/CLL series on languages and linguistics, no.36)
BC51

Varnhagen, Hermann. Systematisches Verzeichnis der Programmabhandlungen, Dissertationen und Habilitationsschriften aus dem Gebiete der romanischen und englischen Philologie sowie der allgemeinen Sprach- und Litteraturwissenschaft und der Pädagogik und Methodik. 2. vollst. umgearb. Aufl. Besorgt von Johannes Martin. Leipzig, Koch, 1893. 296p. **BC52**

Lists German dissertations in literature and language.
Z7032.V32

Manuals

Allen, Charles Geoffry. A manual of European languages for librarians. [2d impression (with minor corrections)] London & N.Y., Bowker in assoc. with the London School of Economics, [1977]. 803p. **BC53**

1st impression 1975.
Intended as an aid to those librarians who, "even without the necessary expert knowledge . . . must accept and deal with books" (*Introd.*) in a variety of foreign languages. Includes sections for (1) Germanic languages, (2) Latin and the Romance languages, (3) Celtic, Greek and Albanian languages, (4) Slavonic languages, (5) Baltic languages, (6) Finno-Ugrian languages, and (7) Other languages. Includes transliteration of non-Roman alphabets.
P380.A4

Gleichen, *Lord* **Edward** and **Reynolds, John H.** Alphabets of foreign languages. 2d ed., 1933, repr. with incorporation of supplement of 1938 and certain revisions by Marcel Aurousseau. London, Permanent Committee on Geographical Names for British Official Use, 1956. 82p. **BC54**

1st ed. 1921.
Treats 78 languages in 11 groups. P213.G55

Voegelin, Charles Frederick and **Voegelin, Florence M.** Classification and index of the world's languages. N.Y., Elsevier, [1977]. 658p. **BC55**

"This volume is based in part upon our earlier survey of the literature, *Languages of the world*, published as twenty separate numbers of the journal *Anthropological Linguistics* (1964–66)."—*Acknowledgments.*
Arranged alphabetically by name of groups of related languages. Following a brief discussion of the language group there is a listing of generic units of the group. Bibliographic references are included in the discussions; list of references, p.359–83. Index of all names of groups, subgroups, languages, dialects, tribes and their alternate names which appear in the articles. P203.V6

Von Ostermann, Georg Frederick. Manual of foreign languages for the use of librarians, bibliographers, research workers, editors, translators, and printers. 4th ed. rev. and enl. N.Y., Central Book Co., 1952. 414p. **BC56**

A useful manual of concise information about some 130 languages and dialects, giving: the alphabet in the original letters or characters in varying forms, with transliteration into English and indication of pronunciation; brief rules for punctuation, capitalization, syllabication, transliteration, phonetics, and grammar; cardinal and ordinal numbers; years, seasons, months, days, etc.
3d ed. 1936, published by the U.S. Government Printing Office. "All portions of the third edition not requiring change have been reproduced in this new edition by the photographic process. Corrections and minor additions have been 'stripped' in, and all new material, set in type for the first time, is presented in a format approximating as closely as possible that used in the third and prior edition."—*Pref.* Some language sections have undergone extensive revisions, and Estonian has been added. Z253.V94

Wemyss, Stanley. The languages of the world, ancient and modern. Philadelphia, author, 1950. 237p. **BC57**

Subtitle: The alphabets, ideographs, and other written characters of the languages of the world, in sound and symbol. P213.W4

Surveys

Bodmer, Frederick. The loom of language. Lancelot Hogben, ed. N.Y., Norton, [1944]. 692p. il. **BC58**

A survey of the interrelationships of language in four main parts: (1) The natural history of language; (2) Our hybrid heritage; (3) The world language problem; (4) Language museum.
The last part includes word lists, giving basic vocabularies in Teutonic and Romance languages, and a list of Greek words with roots which survive in English and in international scientific terms.
P121.B6

Meillet, Antoine and **Cohen, Marcel.** Les langues du monde, par un groupe de linguistes. Nouv. éd. Paris, Centre National de la Recherche Scientifique, 1952. 1294p. maps (in pocket). **BC59**

1st ed. 1924.
At head of title: Société de Linguistique de Paris.
A basic work treating the languages and dialects of the world under language groupings. Under each section gives information on the locale, numbers of persons who speak the language, classification, characteristics, and, for each language, phonetics, morphology, vocabulary, etc. Extensive bibliographies with each group. *Index des langues,* p.1210–73.
Bibliography: (1) Classification des langues, p.xvii–xxxv; (2) Linguistique générale, p.xxxvi–xlii. (The bibliographies include titles in various languages from the 10th century to 1951.)
Atlas des langues du monde (folded maps in pocket) indicates the languages and language groupings of the various countries of the world. P201.M4

Pop, Sever. La dialectologie; aperçu historique et méthodes d'enquêtes linguistiques. Louvain, Bibliothèque de l'Université, Bureau du Recueil, 1950. 2v. (1334p.). maps. (Université de Louvain. Recueil de travaux d'histoire et de philologie, 3. sér., fasc. 38–39) **BC60**

Contents: 1.pt., Dialectologie romane: Le français, Le domaine franco-provençal, Le provençal, Le catalan, L'espagnol, Le portugais, L'italien, Le romanche, Le dalmate, Le roumain; 2.pt., Dialectologie non romane. Langues germaniques: Allemagne, Suisse, Grand-Duché de Luxembourg, Belgique et Pays-Bas. Les pays scandinaves, Grande-Bretagne, États-Unis et Canada. Langues celtiques, Langues slaves, Langues finno-ougriennes. Le grec modern.

L'albanais. Le domaine berbère. Le domaine bantou. Le domaine arabe. Le chinois. Les langues de l'Inde. Le coréen.

A comprehensive historical survey covering dialectal research and methods employed. Fully documented throughout text and in footnotes. Detailed indexes by year, place, persons, geographical names, and subjects. List of illustrations. Table of contents. Chronological list of linguistic atlases, 1880–1948, p.1194–97.   P375.P6

Dictionaries

Ambrose-Grillet, Jeanne. Glossary of transformational grammar. Rowley, Mass., Newbury House, [1978]. 166p.
BC61

". . . an attempt to provide students, teachers and other interested people with a tool which will help them proceed through the work of Noam Chomsky and other linguists who write in the field of transformational grammar."—*Introd.* An appendix explains basic transformations.   P158.A4

Crystal, David. A first dictionary of linguistics and phonetics. London, Deutsch; Boulder, Colo., Westview Pr., [1980]. 390p.   **BC62**

Intended for undergraduates and for those outside the field of linguistics who have an interest in or a need for information about the subject. Includes "only terms or senses which have arisen because of the influence of twentieth-century linguistics and phonetics" (*Pref.*) and does not attempt to cover the whole field or to include very common words which can be found in any good dictionary.   P29.C7

Dubois, Jean [and others]. Dictionnaire de linguistique. Paris, Larousse, [1973]. 516p.   **BC63**

Provides definitions (some in the form of articles of considerable length) of terms used in the science of linguistics.   P29.D5

Ducrot, Oswald and **Todorov, Tzvetan.** Encyclopedic dictionary of the sciences of language. Tr. by Catherine Porter. Baltimore, Johns Hopkins Univ. Pr., [1979]. 380p.   **BC64**

Translation based on the 2d ed. of *Dictionnaire encyclopédique des sciences du langage* (Paris, 1973).

An overview of the sciences of language "organized, not on the basis of a list of words, but according to a conceptual division of the domain under examination."—*Introd.* Thus, terms are defined and explained within topical essays on various aspects of language grouped in four main sections: (1) Schools; (2) Fields; (3) Methodological concepts; (4) Descriptive concepts. The French original has been revised as needed, bibliographical material updated, and English-language publications substituted for the French when practicable. Index of terms defined and index of authors cited in the text.
P29.D813

Greimas, Algirdas Julien and **Courtés, Joseph.** Semiotics and language; an analytical dictionary. Tr. by Larry Crist [and others]. Bloomington, Indiana Univ. Pr., [1982]. 409p.
BC65

Translation of *Sémiotique. Dictionnaire raisonné de la théorie du langage* (Paris, Hachette, 1979).

Aims "to review and evaluate the various theories of language, and simultaneously to present a synthesis—or at least a partial one—of the various attempts that have been made to establish this field of knowledge as a coherent theory."—*Pref.* Terms, with definitions and cross references, are presented in dictionary arrangement; the French term is given in parentheses following the English form. Bibliography, p.384–409.   P99.G6913

Hamp, Eric P. A glossary of American technical linguistic usage, 1925–1950. [3d ed.] Utrecht, Antwerp, Het Spectrum, 1966. 72p.   **BC66**

A publication of the Committee for Terminology, Permanent International Committee of Linguists.

The glossary is "designed to reflect terminology in use by linguists in America which may offer difficulty to linguistic workers in other countries. It includes technical terms which in form or in sense are peculiar to American usage."—*Introd.*   P29.H3

Handbuch der Linguistik; allgemeine und angewandte Sprachwissenschaft. [München], Nymphenburger Verlagshandlung, [1975]. 584p.   **BC67**

"Aus Beiträgen von Hans Arens [et al.] . . . unter Mitarbeit von Hildegard Janssen zusammengestellt von Harro Stammerjohann."
—*t.p.*

Employs a dictionary arrangement and provides definitions and discussion of linguistic terms, some of the entries running to several pages and including extensive bibliographies. There is an index of names of persons mentioned in the articles and those cited in the bibliographies.   P29.H33

Hartmann, R. R. K. and **Stork, F. C.** Dictionary of language and linguistics. N.Y., Wiley; London, Applied Science Pubs., [1972]. 302p.   **BC68**

Intended as an aid to language teachers and students of linguistics. Includes terminology from the various branches of linguistic scholarship, linguistic approaches and methods, etc., plus important terms from related and applied fields.   P29.H34

Nash, Rose. Multilingual lexicon of linguistics and philology: English, Russian, German, French. Coral Gables, Fla., Univ. of Miami Pr., [1968]. 390p. (Miami linguistics ser., no.3)   **BC69**

Arranged on an English base with indexes from the other languages.   P29.N34

Pei, Mario Andrew. Glossary of linguistic terminology. N.Y., Columbia Univ. Pr.; Garden City, N.Y., Anchor Books, 1966. 299p.   **BC70**

Although "originally aimed at the beginner in the field of linguistic studies," the glossary has been expanded "to include a fairly large number of more involved and technical terms and definitions, which will . . . make the work of value also to the more advanced student."—*Foreword.* Does not deal with purely grammatical and stylistic terms, or descriptions of languages, as did Pei and Gaynor's *Dictionary of linguistics* (N.Y., Philosophical Lib., 1954).
P29.P39

Welte, Werner. Moderne Linguistik: Terminologie/Bibliographie. Ein Handbuch und Nachschlagewerk auf der Basis der generativ-transformationellen Sprachtheorie. [München], Max Hueber Verlag, [1974]. 2v.   **BC71**

Terms are defined, with references to original and later usage. Bibliographical citations follow each entry. Arrangement is according to the German form of the term, with English and French equivalents given whenever there are corresponding terms in those languages.   P29.W38

Directories

Behrens, Sophia. Directory of foreign language service organizations, 2. Wash., Center for Applied Linguistics, [1981]. 58p. (Language in education, 33)   **BC72**

Prep. by ERIC Cleringhouse on Languages and Linguistics. 1st ed. 1978.

Aims "to provide foreign language educators with a convenient reference guide containing information on the availability of resources and services that can help them enrich classroom instruction."—*Introd.* Alphabetical listing of organizations (giving descriptions of programs and services) with language index.   P57.U7B4

Biography

Sebeok, Thomas Albert, ed. Portraits of linguists; a biographical source book for the history of western linguistics, 1746–1963. Bloomington, Indiana Univ. Pr., [1966]. 2v.
BC73

An anthology of 90 biographical studies of linguists born before 1900. Articles are reprinted from journals, yearbooks, etc.; some are in French or German. Index of names in v.2. **P83.S4**

Translation

Congrat-Butlar, Stefan. Translation & translators: an international directory and guide. N.Y., Bowker, 1979. 241p. **BC74**

Approximately half of the volume is a "Register of translators & interpreters" which lists: agencies; industrial, scientific and technical translators; humanistic/literary translators; conference translators; and conference interpreters. Individual translators are classified by language at the end of each category. Preliminary matter includes much information useful to translators and concerning translating as a profession. Annotated list of books and journals in the field, p.75–87. **P306.A2C6**

Delisle, Jean and **Albert, Lorraine.** Guide bibliographique du traducteur, rédacteur et terminologue. Bibliographic guide for translators, writers and terminologists. Ottawa, Éditions de l'Univ. d'Ottawa, 1979. 207p. (Cahiers de traductologie, no.1) **BC75**

Introductory matter in French and English.

An earlier version appeared in 1976 under title: *Répertoire bibliographique de la traduction.*

Intended for students of translation, professional translators, and those interested in the study of terminology and its methodology. Includes citations to general materials on translation and interpretation, theory and history of translation, automatic translation, French and English linguistics, etc. There is an extensive section (p.87–186) of specialized dictionaries (both mono- and multilingual) and thematic encyclopedias. Author index. **Z7004.T72D44**

Atlases

See also under individual languages.

Atlas linguarum Europae (ALE). Sous la rédaction de A. Weijnen [et al.]. Assen, Van Gorcum, 1975–79. [v.1–3] (In progress) **BC75a**

Contents: [v.1] Introduction (in French, English, Russian, German and Spanish); [v.2] Premier questionnaire; [v.3] Second questionnaire. Commentaires, v.1, fasc.1 by Mario Alinei [et al.], plus folded maps, was publ. 1983.

Working from the premise "that linguistic research must not be constrained by language boundaries . . . the *ALE* aims to reveal those aspects of language contact provided by the continent of Europe, and thus to enlarge the field of multilingual comparison.. . . The basic nature of the *ALE* will thus be that of presenting, side by side, comparable linguistic data taken from different languages, whether related or not."—*Introd., p.58.* **P380.A8**

ENGLISH

Bibliography and history

Alston, Robin Carfrae. A bibliography of the English language from the invention of printing to the year 1800. Leeds, Arnold, 1965–72. 10v. facsims. **BC76**

Contents: v.1, English grammars written in English and English grammars written in Latin by native speakers; v.2, Polyglot dictionaries and grammars; Treatises on English written for speakers of French, German, Dutch, Danish, Swedish, Portuguese, Spanish, Italian, Hungarian, Persian, Bengali, and Russian; v.3, pt.1, Old English, Middle English, early modern English miscellaneous works; Vocabulary; v.3, pt.2, Punctuation; Concordances; Works on language in general; Origin of language; Theory of grammar; v.4,

Spelling books; v.5, The English dictionary; v.6, Rhetoric, style, elocution, prosody, rhyme, pronunciation, spelling reform; v.7, Logic, philosophy, epistemology, universal language; v.8, Treatises on short-hand; v.9, English dialects; Scottish dialects; Cant and vulgar English; v.10, Education and language teaching.

Covers all aspects of the English language, including language-teaching. Lists and locates copies in libraries throughout the world, though chiefly in British and American collections.

A corrected reprint of v.1–10 "reproduced from the author's annotated copy with corrections to 1973" was published in 1974 in 1v. by Janus Pr., Ilkey, Eng. **Z2015.A1A4**

———— ———— Supplement. Additions and corrections, v.I–X; list of libraries; cumulative indexes. Leeds, Arnold, 1973. 117p.

Baugh, Albert Croll and **Cable, Thomas.** A history of the English language. 3d ed. Englewood Cliffs, N.J., Prentice-Hall, [1978]. 438p. il. **BC77**

1st ed. 1957 by A. C. Baugh.

Primarily a textbook for college students, which aims to present the historical development of the English language against a background of the political, social, and intellectual history of England from early times to the present. Includes English language in America. Along with minor additions and changes, this edition takes note of advances in scholarship and offers updated bibliographies.

Thomas Cable's *A companion to Baugh & Cable's History of the English language* (Englewood Cliffs, N.J., Prentice-Hall, 1983. 135p.) is a study aid with exercises. **PE1075.B3**

Kennedy, Arthur Garfield. A bibliography of writings on the English language from the beginning of printing to the end of 1922. Cambridge, Harvard Univ. Pr.; New Haven, Yale Univ. Pr., 1927. 517p. **BC78**

A very comprehensive list of 13,402 numbered items. Classified, with indexes to authors and reviewers and to subjects. A "Review with a list of additions and corrections" by Arvid Gabrielson was published in *Studia neophilologica* 2:117–68 (1929).
Z2015.A1K3

Leffall, Dolores C. and **Johnson, James P.** Black English; an annotated bibliography. Wash., Minority Research Center, [1973]. 75p. **BC79**

Includes books, parts of books, and periodical articles. Annotations for most of the book materials. **Z1234.D5L43**

McMillan, James B. Annotated bibliography of Southern American English. Coral Gables, Fla., Univ. of Miami Pr., [1971]. 173p. **BC80**

A classified listing of book materials, theses, and periodical articles. Author index. **Z1234.D5M32**

Mencken, Henry Louis. The American language; an inquiry into the development of English in the United States. 4th ed. corr., enl. and rewritten. N.Y., Knopf, 1936. 796p. **BC81**

———— ———— Supplements 1–2. N.Y., Knopf, 1945–48. 2v.

A historical treatment of the development of the English language in the United States covering such topics as: the two streams of English; the beginning and growth of the American language; pronunciation and spelling; the common speech; proper names in America; American slang, etc. Appendix: Non-English dialects in America. List of words and phrases. Index.

The supplements follow the same plan as the original work, the first containing supplemental material to chapters 1–6 and the second to chapters 7–11 and the appendix, with cross references to the main volume.

Each volume includes copious footnotes, references to sources, a list of words and phrases with reference to the text, and an index.
PE2808.M4

———— The American language; an inquiry into the development of English in the United States. The 4th ed. and the two supplements, abridged, with annotations and new material, by Raven I. McDavid, Jr. With the assistance of David W. Maurer. [1st abridged ed.] N.Y., Knopf, 1963. 777p., cxxiv p. **BC82**

Not a revision but a briefer form of the 3v. work with some modifications required by recent changes in the language "and in the civilization which the language reflects."—*Introd.* PE2808.M43

Scheurweghs, Gustave. Analytical bibliography of writings on modern English morphology and syntax, 1877–1960. Louvain, Belgium, Nauwelaerts, 1963–79. 5v. **BC83**

Publisher varies.

Contents: v.1, Periodical literature and miscellanies of the United States of America and western and northern Europe. With an appendix on Japanese publications by Hideo Yamaguchi (Fukui, Japan); v.2, Studies in book form, including dissertations and *Programmabhandlungen* published in the United States of America and western and northern Europe. With appendixes on Japanese publications by Hideo Yamaguchi, and on Czechoslovak publications by Ján Šimko (Bratislava); v.3, Soviet research on English morphology and syntax; English studies in Bulgaria, Poland, Rumania and Yugoslavia; v.4, Addenda and general indexes; v.5, Articles in periodicals, 1961–1970, comp. by E. Vorlat.

Annotated, classified bibliographies with author and subject indexes. v.5 is a listing by periodical (then chronologically by publication date of the articles) and includes abstracts. Z2015.A1S33

Wawrzyszko, Aleksandra K. Bibliography of general linguistics, English and American. [Hamden, Conn.], Archon Books, 1971. 120p. **BC84**

Over 300 annotated entries in classed arrangement. Includes a useful list of linguistic periodicals and series. Z7001.W35

Current bibliography

Abstracts of English studies: an official publication of the National Council of Teachers of English. Boulder, Colo., 1958– . v.1– . **BC85**

For full information *see* BD502.

Modern Humanities Research Association. Annual bibliography of English language and literature, 1920– . Cambridge, University Pr., 1921– . v.1– . **BC86**

For full information *see* BD503.

Handbooks

Hodges, John Cunyus and **Whitten, Mary E.** Harbrace college handbook. 1984 printing with the new MLA documentation style. 9th ed. San Diego, Harcourt Brace Jovanovich, [1984]. 586p. **BC87**

1st ed. 1941.

Intended both as a reference source for the individual writer and as a text book for class use. Offers sections on basic English grammar, punctuation, spelling and diction, sentence structure, planning and writing compositions (including library use and notetaking, footnotes, etc.). Frequently revised and updated. PE1112.H6

Maclin, Alice. Reference guide to English: a handbook of English as a second language. N.Y., Holt, Rinehart and Winston, [1981]. 405p. **BC88**

Intended either for classroom use or for independent study by non-native speakers and students of English. Employs a dictionary arrangement with the expectation that students can thus use it as a ready reference source to identify and correct their problems without consulting an instructor, but many of the headings (such as "determiners," "interrupters," "subordinating and reducing") seem

sufficiently unusual as to make reference to the index essential. Cross-references are also provided. PE1128.M3254

Atlases

Allen, Harold Byron. The linguistic atlas of the Upper Midwest. [Minneapolis], Univ. of Minnesota Pr., 1973–76. 3v. il. **BC89**

Includes Minnesota, Iowa, North Dakota, South Dakota, and Nebraska. PE2912.A4

Kurath, Hans. Linguistic atlas of New England . . . Hans Kurath, dir. and ed.; Miles L. Hanley, assoc. dir.; Bernard Bloch, asst. ed.; Guy S. Lowman, Jr., principal field investigator; Marcus L. Hansen, historian. Sponsored by the American Council of Learned Societies and assisted by universities and colleges in New England. Providence, R.I., Brown Univ., 1939–43. v.1–3 in 6v. 56cm. double maps. (Linguistic atlas of the U.S. and Canada) (Repr.: N.Y., AMS Pr., 1970) **BC90**

Each volume in two parts. Maps numbered consecutively, 1–734. PE2845.L5K8

——— ——— Handbook of the linguistic geography of New England. With the collaboration of Marcus L. Hansen, Bernard Bloch [and] Julia Bloch. 2d ed., with a new introd., word-index, and inventory of LANE maps and commentary by Audrey R. Duckert, and a reverse index of LANE maps to worksheets by Raven I. McDavid, Jr. N.Y., AMS Pr., [1973]. 527p. **BC91**

1st ed. 1939. 240p.
Bibliography of linguistic geography, p.54–61; Bibliography of New England history, p.105–21. PE2902.K78

The linguistic atlas of England. Ed. by Harold Orton, Stewart Sanderson and John Widdowson. London, Croom Helm, [1978]. approx. 450p., maps. **BC92**

First publ. 1977 by Humanities Pr., Atlantic Highlands, N.J.

Based on responses to "A questionnaire for a linguistic atlas of England" by Eugen Dieth and Harold Orton as published in Orton's "Introduction" to the *Survey of English dialects* (Leeds, 1962). That questionnaire "was designed with two interlinked purposes in mind. Firstly, it should elicit information about the current dialectal usages of the older members of the farming communities throughout rural England; and secondly, this information, when mapped, should illustrate the nature of the regional distributions of those features of their speech which had persisted from ancient times."— *Introd.* Includes phonological, lexical, morphological, and syntactical maps. PE1705.L56

Linguistic atlas of the Middle and South Atlantic states. Ed. in chief, Raven I. McDavid, Jr. Chicago, Univ. of Chicago Pr., [1980]– . Fasc.1–2. (In progress) **BC93**

At head of title: Linguistic atlas of the United States and Canada, Hans Kurath, Director.

"Sponsored by the American Council of Learned Societies."—*t.p.*

Based on field work performed in the 1930s and 1940s, and designed to provide examples of pronunciation and grammatical usage in specified communities. The first two fascicles give the results of the survey for the pronunciation of "New England," state names, "Philadelphia," "Baltimore," and "Washington," as well as the county name in which the informant resided. Transcriptions of pronunciations are given in a modified International Phonetic Alphabet. A handbook and an index to the completed work are promised.

Together with the *Linguistic atlas of New England* (BC90), the completed *LAMSAS* will offer "the full phonetic record of the primary dialect survey of the Atlantic States . . . where the chief varieties of our English developed during the colonial period, dialects that were carried westward in the nineteenth century."— *Pref.* PE2913.L55

OTHER GERMANIC LANGUAGES

General works

Althaus, Hans Peter, Henne, Helmut and **Wiegand, Herbert Ernst.** Lexikon der germanistischen Linguistik. 2. vollst. neu bearb. u. erw. Aufl. Tübingen, Niemeyer, [1980]. 870p. **BC94**

1st ed. 1973.
Articles by contributing scholars deal with the whole field of German linguistics and provide definitions of terms, historical background, discussions of problems, etc., together with bibliographical references. Includes social, ethnic, political, historical, and literary aspects of the language. Indexed. PF3071.A5

Hannich-Bode, Ingrid. Germanistik in Festschriften von den Anfängen (1877) bis 1973. Verzeichnis germanistischer Festschriften und Bibliographie der darin abgedruckten germanistischen Beiträge. Stuttgart, Metzler, [1976]. 441p. (Repertorien zur deutschen Literaturgeschichte, Bd.7; London. Univ. Inst. of Germanic Studies. Pubns., v.23) **BC95**

Lists and analyzes about 800 volumes of *Festschriften*. The analytical section is in nine main divisions, each with numerous subsections: (1) Allgemeines; (2) Allgemeine Sprachwissenschaft; (3) Germanische Sprachen; (4) Deutsche Sprache; (5) Allgemeine und deutsche Literaturwissenschaft; (6) Germanische Dichtung und Kultur; (7) Deutsche Literatur in einzelnen Zeitabschnitten; (8) Weltliteratur und vergleichende Literatur; (9) Nachbarwissenschaft. Indexes by author, title, broad subject, and personal names as subjects. Z7036.G47

Hansen, Erik and **Riemann, Nana.** Bibliografi over moderne dansk rigssprog, 1850–1978. [København], Gjellerup, [1979]. 94p. **BC96**

A classed bibliography of books, parts of books, and periodical articles. Detailed table of contents, but no index. Z2575.A2H36

Jahresbericht über die Erscheinungen auf dem Gebiete der germanischen Philologie hrsg. von der Gesellschaft für Deutsche Philologie in Berlin, 1879–1936/39. Berlin, W. de Gruyter, 1880–1954. 58v. **BC97**

Useful annual bibliography, listing the new book, pamphlet, and dissertation literature, and also indexing articles in a large number of important periodicals. The 1936/39 volume (publ. 1954) brings the record up to the beginning of World War II.
Superseded by *Jahresbericht für deutsche Sprache und Literatur* (BD834). Z7037.J25

Knobloch, Johann. Sprachwissenschaftliches Wörterbuch. Heidelberg, Winter, 1961–81. Lfg. 1–9. (Indogermanische Bibliothek. II. Reihe. Wörterbücher) (In progress) **BC98**

Contents: Lfg.1–9, a–Einheit.
A scholarly dictionary of general and comparative linguistics, with emphasis on German terms and scholarship.

Loewenthal, Fritz. Bibliographisches Handbuch zur deutschen Philologie. Halle, Niemeyer, 1932. 217p. **BC99**

A classified bibliography of more than 2,000 titles, some annotated. Name and subject index. Includes chapters on the Scandinavian languages. Z7036.L82

London. University. Institute of Germanic Studies. German language and literature; select bibliography of reference books. By L. M. Newman. 2d enl. ed. London, The Institute, 1979. 175p. (London. Univ. Inst. of Germanic Studies. Pubns., 9) **BC100**

1st ed. 1966.
A guide for the student and research worker, listing and annotating reference works for German language and literature and reflecting the trend toward German studies as a discipline. Sections for research method, German language and literature, German litera-

ture, German language and linguistics, Germanic subjects, general rapid reference books, and other subjects. In general the cut-off date is Dec. 1976. Indexed. Z2235.A2L6

Paul, Hermann. Grundriss der germanischen Philologie. 3. verb. und verm. Aufl. Strassburg, Trübner, 1911–16. 6v. **BC101**

1st ed. 1891–93; 2d ed. 1900–1909 in 3v.
For the advanced worker. Not alphabetically arranged, but in chapters with detailed alphabetical indexes, and many important bibliographical references. Covers the fields of language, literature, and allied subjects, e.g., myths, legends, manners and customs, etc.
A new edition is appearing as follows: PD71.P33

—— Grundriss der germanischen Philologie unter Mitwirkung zahlreicher Fachgelehrter, begründet von Hermann Paul. Berlin, W. de Gruyter, 1925–72. (v.1, 1926) **BC102**

Volumes published: v.1^1, 3–5$^{1-2}$, 7–8$^{1-5}$, 9–10$^{1-3}$, 11$^{1-3}$, 12$^{1-2}$, 13$^{1-5}$, 14–17$^{1-3}$, 18$^{1-3}$, 19–20. Some volumes have appeared in revised editions.
An extensive revision, now under the direction of Werner Betz. Each volume is edited by a specialist and covers a particular period or phase of Germanic philology.

Seymour, Richard K. A bibliography of word formations in the Germanic languages. Durham, Duke University Pr., 1968. 158p. **BC103**

An author listing of about 2,000 articles and monographs dealing with word formation in the Germanic languages (including English), through 1964. Omits studies on loan words, place-names, and personal names. Z7038.W6S4

Stroh, Fritz. Handbuch der germanischen Philologie. Berlin, W. de Gruyter, 1952. 820p. il. **BC104**

Includes a historical outline of Germanic philology in general, and studies of the philology of individual fields, such as law, religion, literature, art. A considerable amount of bibliographical material is included throughout, but there is no separate bibliography. Sources cited are included in the general index.

Atlases

Deutscher Sprachatlas; auf Grund des Sprachatlas des Deutschen Reichs von Georg Wenker begonnen von Ferdinand Wrede, fortgesetzt von Walther Mitzka und Bernhard Martin. Marburg (Lahn), N. G. Elwert, 1926–56. 335p. 25cm., and atlas of 128 maps, 63x68 cm. (in portfolio). **BC105**

Issued in parts.
Subtitle varies.
Mitzka has also prepared a *Handbuch zum deutschen Sprachatlas* (Marburg, Elwert, 1952. 180p.).

Eichhoff, Jürgen. Wortatlas der deutschen Umgangssprachen. Bern, München, Francke, [1977–78]. 2v. il., maps. 28cm. **BC106**

An atlas of German colloquial speech. 125 maps with explanatory text; word index in v.2. PF5005.E3

Dutch

Haeringen, Coenraad Bernardus van. Netherlandic language research; men and works in the study of Dutch. 2d ed. Leiden, Brill, 1960. 120p. **BC107**

1st ed. 1954.
A survey of 20th-century research on the history of the language of the Netherlands, with some critical evaluation of selected works in the field. Includes a chapter on reference works and periodicals.

Scandinavian

See also BD889.

Bibliography of Scandinavian philology. 1– , 1925/26– . (Appears annually in *Acta philologica scandinavica* or as supplements thereto)   **BC108**

Title varies; early issues called *Bibliographie der nordischen Philologie.*

A bibliography of Scandinavian philology and linguistics. Some issues cover more than one year. Lists books and periodical articles.

Haugen, Einar. A bibliography of Scandinavian languages and linguistics, 1900–1970. Oslo, Universitetsforlaget, [1974]. 527p.   **BC109**

Aims to present "a selection of articles, brochures, monographs, books, and series relating to the scientific and practical study of the Scandinavian languages" (*Pref.*), including "all the standard and non-standard forms of Danish, Faroese, Icelandic, Norwegian, and Swedish, as well as older attested and unattested forms of these." The body of the work is an alphabetical author listing. Each entry is followed by a set of "descriptors," i.e., letters and numerals used to indicate the language or languages dealt with and the type of subject matter (grammar, syntax, language teaching, etc.). The index follows the numerical/alphabetical sequence of the descriptors.   Z2555.H38

Jacobsen, Henrik Galberg. Dansk sprogrøgtslitteratur 1900–1955. København, [Gyldendal], 1974. 222p. (Dansk Sprognaevns skrifter, 7)   **BC110**

A bibliography of writings appearing in periodicals, collective volumes, and *Festschriften* on Danish language and linguistics. Chronological listing with author and subject indexes.   Z2575.A2J3

Yiddish

Weinreich, Uriel and **Weinreich, Beatrice.** Yiddish language and folklore; a selective bibliography for research. 'sGravenhage, Mouton, 1959. 66p. (Janua linguarum, no.10)   **BC111**

In two parts: pt.1, Yiddish language (253 items); pt.2, Yiddish folklore (items 254–481).   Z7070.W4

ROMANCE LANGUAGES

General works

Bach, Kathryn F. and **Price, Glanville.** Romance linguistics and the romance languages: a bibliography of bibliographies. [London], Grant & Cutler, 1977. 194p.   **BC112**

". . . lists, with brief critical or descriptive notes, some 650 bibliographical items relating to Romance linguistics in general or to one or more of the individual Romance languages or dialects."— *Pref.* Classed arrangement following the plan of the *Bibliographie linguistique* (BC29). Index of names.   Z7031.A1B33

Bal, Willy and **Germain, Jean.** Guide bibliographique de linguistique romane. Louvain, Éditions Peeters, 1978. 267p. (Louvain. Institut de Linguistique. Bibliothèque des cahiers, 12)   **BC113**

A selective bibliography and guide for the student of romance philology. Classed arrangement; author/title index.   Z7031.B34

Gröber, Gustav. Grundriss der romanischen Philologie. 1st– 2d ed. Strassburg, Trübner, 1897–1906. v.1–2 in 4.   **BC114**

v.1 is 2d ed., 1904–1906.

An important reference book on the history and development of

Romance philology and linguistics, for advanced workers. Not alphabetically arranged, but in chapters, with detailed indexes and many bibliographical references.   PC41.G7

—— —— Neue Folge. Abt. 1. Geschichte der französischen Literatur. Berlin, W. de Gruyter, 1933–38. v.3–5.   **BC115**

Contents: v.3–4, Geschichte der mittelfranzösischen Literatur: I, Vers- und Prosadichtung des 14. Jahrhundert, Drama des 14. und 15. Jahrhunderts. 2. Aufl. bearb. von Stefan Hofer; II, Vers- und Prosadichtung des 15. Jahrhundert. 2. Aufl. bearb. von Stefan Hofer; v.5, Frankreichs Literatur im 16. Jahrhundert, von Walter Mönch.

v.1–2 were to cover Altfranzösischen Dichtung; v.6– , 17. Jahrhundert– .   PC41.G7

Jahrbuch für romanische und englische Sprache und Literatur. Berlin, Brockhaus, 1859–76. 15v.   **BC116**

None published 1872–73. Publisher varies.

Contains a systematic bibliography of Romance languages and literatures.   PB3.J3

Kritischer Jahresbericht über die Fortschritte der romanischen Philologie, 1890–1912. Erlangen, Junge, 1892–1915. 13v.   **BC117**

An important bibliography of books and articles on Romance philology, i.e., language and literature. In chapters, not in list form, and so somewhat difficult to use for purposes of quick reference, but important for the large amount of material included and for the analysis of periodicals.   Z7032.K92

McKay, John C. A guide to romance reference grammars: the modern standard languages. Amsterdam, Benjamins, 1979. 126p. (Library and information sources in linguistics, v.6)   **BC118**

Describes and evaluates "the best reference grammars and comprehensive works on syntax of contemporary Catalan, French, Italian, Portuguese, Spanish, and Rumanian."—*Pref.* Indexed.   Z7031.M32

Mourin, Louis and **Pohl, Jacques.** Bibliographie de linguistique romane. 4ᵉ éd., remaniée et mise à jour. [Bruxelles, Presses Universitaires de Bruxelles], 1971. 178p.   **BC119**

A classified bibliography of works relating to the study of Romance languages. Based on bibliographic lists prepared for use in university courses.   Z7031.M68

Zeitschrift für romanische Philologie. Supplement: Romanische Bibliographie; Bibliographie romane; Romance bibliography. 1875– . Tübingen, Max Niemeyer, 1878– . Biennial.   **BC120**

Publisher varies. Title varies: to 1961/62 called *Supplementheft: Bibliographie.*

A significant current bibliography listing books and periodical articles on the language and literature of the various Romance languages.

v.39–43, 1914–23, never published. 1940–50 issued in 1v. (14 Lfg.), 1952–57; 1951–55 issued in 1v. (2 Lfg.), 1961; 1956–60 issued in 1v. (2 Lfg.), 1964. Beginning with the volume covering 1961–62 (publ. 1967) issued biennially in several volumes.   PC3.Z5

French

Bassan, Fernande, Breed, Paul F. and **Spinelli, Donald C.** An annotated bibliography of French language and literature. N.Y., Garland, 1976. 306p.   **BC121**

Intended as a guide for the student, the scholar, and the librarian, although emphasis is on general materials rather than scholarly studies. In three main sections: (1) General bibliographies and reference works; (2) General studies on the French language; and (3) Bibliographies and studies of literature. Items in the first section are annotated in some detail; most items in the other sections are not annotated. Nearly 1,600 entries; author/title index.

Z2175.A2B38

Brunot, Ferdinand. Histoire de la langue française des origines à nos jours. Préface de la nouvelle édition par Gerald Antoine. Paris, A. Colin, 1966–79. v.1–13. (In progress)
BC122

The 1905–53 edition has been reprinted, with the addition of a new preface and of complementary bibliographies for each literary period. v.11 and v.13 are published for the first time in this edition.
Contents: v.1, De l'époque latine à la Renaissance; v.2, Le seizième siècle; v.3, La formation de la langue classique (1600–1660); v.4, La langue classique (1660–1715). 2v.; v.5, Le français en France et hors de France au XVIIᵉ siècle; v.6, Le XVIIIᵉ siècle. 2pts. in 4v.; v.7, La propagation du français en France jusqu'à la fin de l'Ancien Régime; v.8, Le français hors de France au XVIIIᵉ siècle. 3 pts. in 2v.; v.9, La Révolution et l'Empire. 2v.; v.10, La langue classique dans la tourmente. 2v.; v.11, Le français au dehors sous la Révolution, le Consolat et l'Empire. 2v.; v.12, L'époque romantique (1815–1852), par Charles Bruneau; v.13, L'époque réaliste (1852–1886), par Charles Bruneau. 2v.; v.14, Le symbolisme (1886–1914), par Charles Bruneau (in prep.).
A monumental documented history of the French language.

PC2075.B7

Dulong, Gaston. Bibliographie linguistique du Canada français. Québec, Presses de l'Université Laval; Paris, Klincksieck, 1966. 166p. (Bibliothèque française et romane. Sér.E., Langue et littérature françaises au Canada, 1) **BC123**

A chronological listing of linguistic studies, glossaries, dictionaries, etc., relative to the French language in Canada. Author and subject indexes.

Z1365.D8

Griffin, Lloyd W., Clarke, Jack A. and **Kroff, Alexander Y.** Modern French literature and language; a bibliography of homage studies. [Madison], Univ. of Wisconsin Pr., [1976]. 175p.
BC124

For annotation *see* BD959.

Horluc, Pierre and **Marinet, Georges.** Bibliographie de la syntaxe du français (1840–1905). Lyon, A. Rey; Paris, A. Picard, 1908. 320p. (Annales de l'Université de Lyon. n.s. II. Droit, lettres, fasc.20) **BC125**

Lists materials published 1840–1905 on the history and treatment of French syntax from the Middle Ages through the 19th century.

Z2175.G7H8

Petit de Julleville, Louis. Histoire de la langue et de la littérature française des origines à 1900. Paris, Colin, 1896–99. 8v. il. **BC126**

For full information *see* BD1016.

Wagner, Robert-Léon. Introduction à la linguistique française. Genève, Droz; Lille, Giard, 1947. 142p. (Soc. de Publications Romanes et Françaises, v.27) **BC127**

Includes bibliographies, p.59–139.

—— —— Supplément bibliographique. 1955. 71p. (Soc. de Publications Romanes et Françaises, v.47)

PC2073.W3

Atlases

Atlas linguistiques de la France par régions. Paris, Éditions du Centre National de la Recherche Scientifique, 1961– . (In progress) **BC128**

A series of separately published works on specific regions of France. In general, the individual titles begin *Atlas linguistique et ethnographique. . .* , are edited by one or more scholars, and are unnumbered in the series; most run to two or more volumes. Areas covered to date include: Alsace (1969); Auvergne, Limousin (1975); Bourgogne (1975–80); Bretagne romane, Anjou, Maine (1975); Centre (1971–76); Champagne, Brie (1966–78); Franche-Comté

(1972–79); Gascogne (1965–73); Ile-de-France, Orléans (1973–79); Jura, Alpes du Nord (1971–82); Languedoc occidental (1978); Languedoc oriental (1982); Lorraine germanophone (1979); Lorraine romane (1980–82); Lyon (1967–76); Massif Central (1961–76); Normandie (1980); L'Ouest (Poitou, Aunis, Saintonge, Angoumois) (1971–74); Provence (1975–79).

Gilliéron, Jules and **Edmont, Edmond.** Atlas linguistique de la France . . . Paris, H. Champion, 1902–10. 1920 (i.e., 2048) maps in 17 portfolios. 55cm. **BC129**

Issued in 35 parts.

—— —— Notice servant à l'intelligence des cartes. Paris, H. Champion, 1902. 55p. 27cm.

—— —— Table. Paris, Champion, 1912. 519p.

—— —— Suppléments. Paris, Champion, 1920. 308p.

No more published.

G1841.E3G5

—— Atlas linguistique de la France . . . Corse. Paris, Champion, 1914–15. Pts.1–4. 800 maps. 56cm.

An appendix to the author's *Atlas linguistique de la France.*

G1841.E3G53

Italian

Golden, Herbert Hershel and **Simches, Seymour O.** Modern Italian language and literature; a bibliography of homage studies. Cambridge, Harvard Univ. Pr., 1959. 207p.
BC130

For full information *see* BD1058.

Hall, Robert Anderson. Bibliografia della linguistica italiana. 2. ed. riv. e aggiornata. Firenze, Sansoni, 1958. 3v. (Biblioteca bibliografica italica, 13–15) **BC131**

A major revision of the 1941 edition published as *Bibliography of Italian linguistics* (Baltimore, Linguistic Soc. of Amer.). This 2d ed. contains some 6,900 items, about twice the number in the first edition.
Includes material published since about 1860, arranged in four main sections: (1) History of the Italian language, (2) Description of the Italian language, (3) Italian dialectology, and (4) History of Italian linguistics. Five indexes: author and title; regions and dialects; words; etyma; and general subjects. Z2355.A2H315

—— —— Primo supplemento decennale (1956–1966). Firenze, Sansoni, 1969. 524p. (Biblioteca bibliografica italica, 35)

Supplements the 2d ed. of Hall's bibliography, listing about 2,500 items.

—— —— Secondo supplemento decennale (1966–1976). Pisa, Giardini, [1980]. 388p. (Orientamenti linguistici, 13)

About 3,500 entries numbered consecutively with the preceding supplement.

Atlases

Jaberg, Karl and **Jud, Jakob.** Sprach- und Sachatlas Italiens und der Südschweiz . . . ; die Mundartaufnahmen wurden durchgeführt von P. Scheuermeier, G. Rohlfs und M. L. Wagner . . . Zofingen (Schweiz.), Ringier, 1928–40. 8v. in 16. plates, fold.maps, tables. 46cm. **BC132**

PC1705.J3

Latin

Cousin, Jean. Bibliographie de la langue latine, 1880–1948. Paris, Soc. d'Édit. "Les Belles Lettres," 1951. 375p.

BC133

A classified bibliography, in many languages, of books and periodical articles on the Latin language. Z7026.C6

McGuire, Martin Rawson Patrick and **Dressler, Hermigild.** Introduction to medieval Latin studies: a syllabus and bibliographical guide. 2d ed. Wash., D.C., Catholic Univ. of Amer. Pr., 1977. 406p.

BC134

1st ed. 1964.

Aims "to give the beginning graduate student a comprehensive, solid, and up-to-date orientation" (*Pref.*) in the field. "The *Syllabus* and *Select Bibliography* are broader in scope than their titles might indicate, for they include references to, or even initial orientation in, a number of other disciplines—e.g., Classical, Patristic, Celtic, Germanic, Romance, Byzantine and Islamic Studies—insofar as these disciplines have connections with Medieval Latin Studies." Syllabus, with suggested readings, p.1–241; Select bibliographies, p.245–379. Indexed. PA2816.M24

Portuguese

Paiva Boléo, Manuel de. Introdução ao estudo da filologia portuguesa. Lisboa, Rev. de Portugal, 1946. 150p.

BC135

"Extr. dos nos. 34 a 43 da *Revista de Portugal.*"—*title page.*

Includes bibliographies on the various Romance languages, with emphasis on the Portuguese; covers phonetics, etymological dictionaries, historical grammars, etc.

Spanish

Cejador y Frauca, Julio. Historia de la lengua y literatura castellana. Madrid, 1915–22. 14v. il. **BC136**

For full information *see* BD1153. PC4027.C3

Enciclopedia lingüística hispánica, dirigida por M. Alvar [and others]. Madrid, Consejo Superior de Investigaciones Científicas, 1960–67. v.1–2 and suppl. to v.1. (In progress)

BC137

Contents: v.1, Antecedentes, onomástica; Suppl. to v.1, La fragmentación fonética peninsular; v.2, Elementos constitutivos, Fuentes.

To be in 6v.

A scholarly treatment of the Spanish language. Nonalphabetical; chapters by specialists with bibliographical footnotes. PC45.E5

Golden, Herbert Hershel and **Simches, Seymour O.** Modern Iberian language and literature: a bibliography of homage studies. Cambridge, Harvard Univ. Pr., 1958. 184p.

BC138

For full information *see* BD1136.

Hall, Pauline Cook. A bibliography of Spanish linguistics: articles in serial publications. Baltimore, Linguistic Soc. of Amer., [1957]. 162p. (Language dissertation, no.54. Suppl. to *Language*, v.32, no.4, pt.2, Oct.–Dec. 1956) **BC139**

Thesis, State University of Iowa.

"Articles on the Spanish language available to scholars in this country."—*Pref.* A classified list of 1,930 items, with indexes of authors, words, and subjects. Z2695.A1H17

Rohlfs, Gerhard. Manual de filología hispánica; guía bibliográfica, crítica y metódica. Traducción castellana del manuscrito alemán por Carlos Patiño Rosselli. Bogota, 1957. 377p. (Publicaciones del Instituto Caro y Cuervo, 12)

BC140

A survey of research materials for students of linguistics. Includes sections on South American Spanish and Portuguese.

Z2695.A1R6

Serís, Homero. Bibliografía de la lingüística española. Bogotá, 1964. 981p. (Publicaciones del Instituto Caro y Cuervo, XIX) **BC141**

Nearly 8,000 items (periodical and book materials) on all aspects of Spanish linguistics, including sections for individual dialects and for the various Spanish-American countries. Fully indexed. Item numbers continue in sequence from the author's *Manual de bibliografía de la literatura española* (BD1137) to emphasize the close relationship between language and literature and to facilitate cross references to the earlier work. Z2695.A1S4

Viñaza, Cipriano Muñoz y Manzano, *Conde* de la. Biblioteca histórica de la filología castellana. Madrid, Manuel Tello, 1893. 1112p. **BC142**

An extensive bibliography—covering the years 1492–1893—on Castilian philology. Classified arrangement, and then chronological. A valuable historical work. Z2695.A1V7

Woodbridge, Hensley Charles and **Olson, Paul Richard.** A tentative bibliography of Hispanic linguistics [based on the studies of Yakov Malkiel]. Urbana, Dept. of Spanish and Italian, Univ. of Illinois, 1952. 203p. **BC143**

Excludes Latin-American linguistics.

Lists 1,879 items covering Hispanic linguistics from the vulgar and medieval Latin period to the present day. Classified arrangement with author and word indexes. Includes both books and periodical articles. Z2695.A1W6

Atlases

Spain. Consejo Superior de Investigaciones Científicas. Atlas lingüístico de la Península Ibérica. Madrid, 1962– . v.1. (In progress) **BC144**

Contents: v.1, Fonética.

Only one volume published to date. Other recent linguistic mapping activity is represented by Manuel Alvar's *Atlas lingüístico y etnográfico de Andalucía* (Granada, Univ. de Granada y Consejo Superior de Investigaciones Científicas, 1961–73. 6v.) and his *Atlas lingüístico y etnográfico de Aragón, Navarra y Rioja* (Saragossa, Dept. de Geografía Lingüística, Inst. Fernando el Católico de la Excma, Diputación Provincial de Zaragoza, 1979– . v.1– ; in progress).

Spanish American

Marino Flores, Anselmo. Bibliografía lingüística de la República Mexicana. México, Inst. Indigenista Interamericano, 1957. 95p. **BC145**

Lists books and articles on the various languages and dialects of Mexico. Z7120.M3

Nichols, Madaline W. A bibliographical guide to materials on American Spanish. Cambridge, Harvard Univ. Pr., 1941. 114p. (Committee on Latin Amer. studies, Amer. Council of Learned Societies, Misc. pubn., no.2) **BC146**

1,201 annotated items—books and periodical articles—on the philology of American Spanish, including general material and material for each country. Records official philological academies and organizations and lists the learned journals. Z2695.D5N5

Solé, Carlos A. Bibliografía sobre el español en América 1920–1967. Wash., Georgetown Univ. Pr., [1970]. 175p.

BC147

Lists studies of Spanish linguistics and dialects in the Americas. General sections are followed by listings for individual countries. Author index; some descriptive notes. Z1609.L3S65

Tovar, Antonio. Catálogo de las lenguas de América del Sur; enumeración, con indicaciones tipológicas, bibliografía y mapas. Buenos Aires, Ed. Sudamericana, [1961]. 406p. il. **BC148**

A discussion of the languages and dialects of South America is followed by a bibliography, p.203–370. PM5008.T6

Atlases

Instituto Caro y Cuervo. Departamento de Dialectología. Atlas lingüístico-etnográfico de Colombia. [Director, Luis Flórez] Bogotá, Inst. Caro y Cuervo, 1981. 6v. **BC148a**

v.3 includes a supplement with two phonodiscs.
A less exhaustive work for Chile is Guillermo Araya's *Atlas lingüístico-etnográfico del sur de Chile* (Valdivia, Inst. de Filología de la Univ. Austral de Chile, 1973. 1v. in portfolio, chiefly maps). B1731.E3I5

CELTIC

Dublin. National Library of Ireland. Bibliography of Irish philology and of printed Irish literature. Dublin, Stat. Off., 1913. 307p. (Repr.: N.Y., Johnson, 1970) **BC149**

Compiled by R. I. Best and supplemented by: Z2037.D81

Best, Richard Irvine. Bibliography of Irish philology and manuscript literature; publications 1913–1941. Dublin, Dublin Inst. for Advanced Studies, 1942. 253p. **BC150**

Bibliographies of printed works relating to the Irish language and literature, comprising the works of native Irish writers down to the latter part of the 19th century.

Edwards, John. The Irish language: an annotated bibliography of sociolinguistic publications, 1772–1982. N.Y., Garland, 1983. 274p. (Garland reference library of the humanities, v.300) **BC151**

"Represented here are articles, chapters, books, and pamphlets bearing upon social, historical, psychological, and educational aspects of Irish—including the decline of the language, the restoration effort, the relationship of language to nationality and religion, and studies of important figures in the language movement."—*Introd.* Main entry listing, with subject, date, and journal indexes. Z7011.E38

Mather, J. Y. and **Speitel, H. H.** The linguistic atlas of Scotland: Scots section. Cartography by G. W. Leslie. Hamden, Conn., Archon Books, [1975–77]. 2v. maps. 28cm. **BC152**

Published in London by Croom Helm.
Based on the archives of the Scots section of the Linguistic Survey of Scotland in the Faculty of Arts at the University of Edinburgh. v.2 includes an index to the 2v. set. A Gaelic section is also planned. PE2102.M3

Woolley, John S. Bibliography for Scottish linguistic studies. Publ. for the University of Edinburgh, Linguistic Survey of Scotland. Edinburgh, James Thin, 1954. 37p. **BC153**

A list designed primarily "for those interested in the study of modern Scottish dialects."—*Pref.*

GREEK

Deltion vivliographias tēs Hellēnikēs glōssēs. Bibliographical bulletin of the Greek language. 1973– . Athens, 1974– . v.1– . Annual. **BC154**

At head of title: Spoudastērion Glōssologias tou Panepistēmiou Athēnōn.

George Babiniotis, ed. 1975/76 last publ.?
Introductory and explanatory matter in English and Greek.
Each issue is an international, classified listing (with author index) of the year's publications on "the entire Greek language (Ancient, Byzantine, Modern)."—*Pref.* Z7021.D44

Logos; monografías y síntesis bibliográfica de filología griega por Sebastian Cirac Estopañan. Barcelona, Univ. de Barcelona, 1960. v.1. (Facultad de Filosofía y Letras. Cátedra de Filología Griega. Sección de Filología Griega y Bizantinistica del C. S. de I. Científicas) **BC155**

No more published?
v.1 is an annotated listing of some 4,600 books and articles in various languages on Greek philology. Z7022.L6

Swanson, Donald Carl Eugene. Modern Greek studies in the West; a critical bibliography of studies on modern Greek linguistics, philology, and folklore, in languages other than Greek. N.Y., New York Pub. Lib., 1960. 93p. **BC156**

Includes books and periodical articles, with brief annotations and references to reviews. Indexes to authors, words discussed, Greek regions, etc. Z2291.S9

INDIC

Agesthialingom, S. and **Sakthivel, S.** A bibliography of Dravidian linguistics. Annamalainagar, Annamalai University, 1973. 362p. (Annamalai Univ. Dept. of Linguistics. Pubn., no.30) **BC157**

An author listing of about 3,700 articles and books is followed by sections citing dictionaries and book reviews. No index. Z7049.D7A35

Aggarwal, Narindar K. A bibliography of studies on Hindi language and linguistics. Gurgaon, Indian Documentation Service, [1978]. 184p. **BC158**

Aims to list "books, theses, dissertations, articles and published and unpublished papers written on Hindi language and linguistics" (*Introd.*); coverage begins with the early 1950s. More than 1,700 items in classed arrangement, with author index. Z7071.A34

Summer Institute of Linguistics (Nepal). A bibliographical index of the lesser known languages and dialects of India and Nepal. Richard D. Hugoniot, ed. Waxhaw, N.C., Wycliffe-Jaars Print Shop, 1970. 312p. **BC159**

A preliminary edition appeared under title: *The languages of India and Nepal.*
An alphabetical list of languages (with cross references from all variant names and spellings) indicates classification and location of the language and provides references to the extensive (more than 2,200 items) bibliography of linguistic and anthropological sources. Z7049.I3S9

SLAVIC

See also BC12.

Akademiia Nauk SSSR. Institut Russkogo IAzyka. Slavianskoe iazykoznanie; bibliograficheskii ukazatel' literatury, izdannoi v SSSR s 1918 po 1960 gg. Red. S. B. Bernshtein. Moskva, 1963. 2v. **BC160**

A bibliography of books, articles, surveys, and reviews published in the Soviet Union on the subject of Slavic linguistics. Z7041.A39

——— Slavianskoe iazykoznanie; bibliograficheskii ukazatel' literatury, izdannoi v SSSR s 1961 po 1965g. Moskva, Nauka, 1969. 465p. **BC161**

Continues the listings in the Academy's earlier publication (above) covering 1918–60. Z7041.A392

De Bray, R. G. A. Guide to the Slavonic languages. 3d ed., rev. and expanded. [Columbus, Ohio], Slavica Publishers, 1980. 3v.   **BC162**

Contents: pt.1, Guide to the south Slavonic languages; pt.2, Guide to the west Slavonic languages; pt.3, Guide to the east Slavonic languages. (Each volume may be purchased separately.)

1st ed. 1951.

An attempt to give an overall view of the Slavonic languages to those who are already familiar with one of the group. Each language is treated in a separate section, introduced by a brief history of the language and followed by a more-or-less detailed examination of the alphabet, pronunciation, morphology, word order, and features characteristic of the language, and brief passages from its literature. Each volume includes a selected bibliography listing grammars, dictionaries, and other aids to study for the languages under consideration in that particular volume. Detailed table of contents for each volume, but no indexes.   PG53.D4

Handke, Kwiryna and **Rzetelska-Feleszko, Ewa.** Przewodnik po językoznawstwie polskim. Wrocław, Zakl. Narodowy Imienia Ossolińskich Wydawnictwo, 1977. 474p.   **BC163**

Offers bibliographic essays on various aspects of Polish language and linguistics, with full citations to the works discussed. Indexed.   P81.P6H3

International Organization for Standardization. International system for the transliteration of Cyrillic characters. [Geneva], 1955. 7p. (ISO Recommendation, R9)   **BC164**

Presents a system resembling European practice, rather than the U.S. Library of Congress system, for transliteration into Latin characters from Russian, Bulgarian, Ukrainian, Belorussian, and Serbian. The recommendation was approved by 20 out of 34 member bodies of ISO as of 1953, and adopted by Unesco in 1956 for its bibliographical publications.

For discussion and tables of seven Anglo-American systems of transliteration from Russian, *see* R. Neiswender, *Guide to Russian reference and language aids,* p.63–66 (AA490).   AS4.I2 no.9

An introduction to Russian language and literature. Ed. by Robert Auty and Dimitri Obolensky. Cambridge, Cambridge Univ. Pr., [1977]. 300p. (Companion to Russian studies, 2)   **BC165**

Intended as a first guide for university students, but also meant to be useful to the general reader. Chapters on the Russian language and Russian writing and printing are followed by chapters on the main periods of Russian and Soviet literature, plus chapters on the theater. Each chapter was contributed by a specialist and ends with a select bibliography intended as a guide for further study (and listing both Russian and English sources). Indexed.   PG2051.I5

Sadnik, Linda and **Aitzemüller, Rudolf.** Vergleichendes Wörterbuch der slavischen Sprachen. Wiesbaden, Harrassowitz, 1963–75. v.1. (In progress?)   **BC166**

Contents: v.1, A–B (issued in 7 Lfg.).

A comparative dictionary for Slavic languages.   PG305.S2

Schaller, Helmut Wilhelm. Bibliographie zur russischen Sprache. Frankfurt a. M., Bern, etc., Lang, 1980. 204p. (Symbolae Slavicae, Bd.8)   **BC167**

A classed bibliography of more than 2,700 items with author and subject indexes. Includes books, periodical articles, and dissertations. Russian-language publications predominate, but other Western-language materials are well represented.   Z2505.A2S33

Stankiewicz, Edward and **Worth, Dean S.** A selected bibliography of Slavic linguistics. The Hague, Mouton, 1966–70. 2v. (Slavistic printings and reprintings, 49)   **BC168**

Intended as a bibliographical guide to all Slavic languages, but selective in that emphasis is on 20th-century linguistic research and on those studies "inspired by a structural approach."—*Introd.* v.1 deals with Slavic cultural pre-history, Balto-Slavic, Common Slavic, Comparative Slavic, Old Church Slavonic, and the South Slavic languages (Bulgarian, Macedonian, Serbo-Croatian, Slovenian); v.2 includes sections for general West Slavic linguistics, Polish, Pomeranian, Polabian, Lusatian, Czech, Slovak, general East Slavic linguis-

tics, Belorussian, Russian, Ukrainian, and a bibliography of bibliographies for the study of Slavic linguistics.   Z7041.S82

Unbegaun, Boris Ottokar. A bibliographical guide to the Russian language, with the collaboration of J. S. G. Simmons. Oxford, Clarendon Pr., 1953. 174p.   **BC169**

A practical guide to publications dealing with the Russian language and its history, listing 1,043 titles, many of them annotated, under three main divisions: (1) General (works of a general bibliographical nature); (2) Historical (works relating to the pre-history and history of the Russian language); and (3) Descriptive (grammar and vocabulary of modern literary Russian, and works on dialects, slang, jargon, etc.). Titles are given in full and in the original language. Index.   Z2505.U5

TURKIC

Allworth, Edward. Nationalities of the Soviet East: publications and writing systems. A bibliographical directory and transliteration tables for Iranian- and Turkic-language publications, 1818–1945, located in U. S. libraries. N.Y., Columbia Univ. Pr., 1971. 440p. (Modern Middle East ser., no.3)   **BC170**

A union list of Iranian and Turkic language publications (3,350 entries) in nine U.S. libraries. Arranged alphabetically by language, subdivided by subject field. An introductory essay surveys trends in American scholarship in this area, with a discussion of American library resources for such research.   Z3409.A43

Loewenthal, Rudolf. The Turkic languages and literatures of Central Asia; a bibliography. 'sGravenhage, Mouton, 1957. 212p. (Central Asiatic studies, I)   **BC171**

A classified list of 2,093 books and articles. Author index. Covers Old, Middle, and Modern Turkic languages.   Z7049.U5C4 no.1

Sovietico-Turcica: Beiträge zur Bibliographie der türkischen Sprachwissenschaft in rüssischer Sprache in der Sowjetunion, 1917–1957. Budapest, Akadémiai Kiadó, 1960. 319p. (Bibliotheca orientalis hungarica, IX)   **BC172**

"Mit Unterstützung der Ungarischen Akademie der Wissenschaften und unter Mitwirkung einer Arbeitsgemeinschaft des Turkologischen Instituts der Universität Budapest red. von Georg Hazai, übers. von A. T.-Varga . . ."—*verso of title page.*

More than 2,700 items, alphabetically listed by main entry in Russian, with German translation of title following each listing. Subject index in German.

SEMITIC

Bakalla, M. H. Arabic linguistics: an introduction and bibliography. [2d rev. ed.] [London], Mansell, [1983]. 741p.   **BC173**

1st ed. (1975) had title *Bibliography of Arabic linguistics.*

Lists about 5,500 items in some 20 languages, with separate sections for materials in Occidental and Oriental languages. Introductory essays on various aspects of Arabic linguistics precede the bibliography. Indexes of subjects and names.   Z7052.B35

A basic bibliography for the study of Semitic languages. J. H. Hospers, ed. Leiden, Brill, 1973–74. 2v.   **BC174**

Intends "to list as completely as possible and in the relevant contexts everything really needed by students in the Semitic languages, and other persons interested in these studies, in such a way that they can use the bibliographic information as an aid to discover for themselves more detailed material."—*Pref.*

In v.1 there are sections for each language or group of languages (e.g., Akkadian, Sumerian, Anatolian languages, Ancient Persian, Hebrew, Samaritan Hebrew, Syriac and Aramaic, etc.) compiled by specialists and each has subsections for philology, literature, cultural history, etc., as applicable. There is a final section on comparative Semitics.

v.2 brings together "the bibliographic material in the fields of the study of Pre-Classical, Classical and Modern Literary Arabic . . . and the Modern Arabic Dialects."—*Pref.* No indexes.

Z7049.S5B35

Leslau, Wolf. An annotated bibliography of the Semitic languages of Ethiopia. The Hague, Mouton, 1965. 336p. (Bibliographies on the Near East, 1)   **BC175**

A revised and expanded edition of the author's *Bibliography of the Semitic languages of Ethiopia* (1946).

In two main sections: North Ethiopic and South Ethiopic. Within these sections book and periodical references are grouped by language. Author and subject indexes. Includes useful notes on the individual languages at the beginning of the relevant subsections.

Z7049.S5L38

Sobelman, Harvey [and others]. Arabic dialect studies; a selected bibliography. Wash., Center for Applied Linguistics of the Modern Language Assoc. and the Middle East Inst., 1962. 100p.   **BC176**

Discussion and bibliography of studies on Syrian, Egyptian, Arabian Peninsula, Iraqi, North African, and Maltese Arabic.

Z7052.S6

AFRICAN LANGUAGES

Bibliographie analytique des langues parlées en Afrique subsaharienne: 1970–1980. Realisée par Jean-François Bourdin, Jean-Pierre Caprile, Michel Lafon. Paris, Assoc. d'Études Linguistiques Interculturelles Africaines, etc., [1983]. 555p.   **BC177**

At head of title: "Les langues parlées en Afrique: études, documents et bibliographies" et "Bulletin bibliographique du CIRELFA [Conseil International de Recherche et d'Étude en Linguistique Fondamentale et Appliquée]."

In three sections: (1) Sciences du language; (2) Ethnologie; (3) Sciences de l'éducation. Chronological arrangement within sections; indexes of authors, languages and ethnic groups, geographical names, and concepts. Entries include analytical notes; periodical citations predominate.   Z7106.B68

Meier, Wilma. Bibliography of African languages. Wiesbaden, Harrassowitz, 1984. 888p.   **BC178**

Title also in German, French, and Russian; introductory matter in English, German, French, and Russian.

An author listing (with titles in chronological order) is followed by two indexes, one being an alphabetical arrangement of languages with authors and abbreviated indication of their topics thereunder, the other an alphabetical arrangement of the languages with publication dates of the studies listed chronologically and indicating author's name and abbreviated topic.   Z7106.B53

Murphy, John D. and **Goff, Harry.** A bibliography of African languages and linguistics. Wash., Catholic Univ. of America Pr., 1969. 147p.   **BC179**

"Not only works relating to the so-called 'Negro African' languages are included, but also those dealing with the African varieties of Arabic, the Hamitic languages (Berber, etc.), Malagasy (an Indonesian language), Afrikaans (a development of Dutch), and the various Creoles. The greater part of the entries, however, relate to the indigenous languages of the African continent south of the Sahara."—*Introd.* Classed arrangement with index of languages and of authors. Very selective.   Z7106.M8

University of Rhodesia. Library. Catalogue of the C. M. Doke collection on African languages in the Library of the University of Rhodesia. Boston, G. K. Hall, 1972. 546p. (*Its* Bibliographical ser., no.2)   **BC180**

About 3,000 items. Separate author and subject sections.

Z7106.U54

Van Hoosen, Andrea M. African language materials available in the collection of Boston University's African Studies Library. Boston, Boston Univ., African Studies Ctr., 1979. 104p.   **BC181**

Arranged by individual language, plus a section for works dealing with entire families or groups of languages. 1,052 items.

Whiteley, Wilfred Howell and **Gutkind, A. E.** A linguistic bibliography of East Africa. Rev. ed. Kampala, East African Swahili Committee and East African Inst. of Social Research, 1958. lv. Looseleaf. (Suppl., 1960. 3p.)   **BC182**

The 1st ed. attempted to bring together "in one easily accessible publication a list of all that was known to have been written on the grammar and lexicon of the East African languages." This edition incorporates the listings from the 1954 volume and its supplements, with additional material: books, periodical articles, and manuscripts. Sections are devoted to the languages of Tanganyika, Kenya, and Uganda, with a special section for Swahili.   Z7106.W523

Atlases

Dalby, David. Language map of Africa and the adjacent islands. London, Internat. African Institute, 1977. 63p. plus 1 map in 4 sections (166x166cm.).   **BC183**

A provisional edition published in a limited number of copies; a revised edition is to have maps in color. The present map is drawn to a scale of 1:5,000,000 with insets of particularly complex areas greatly enlarged. Aims to show (1) "the approximate modern geographical distribution of home languages in Africa, based on majority first language usage in the home" and (2) "a revised classification of African languages, based on known levels of historical relationship."—*Introd.* A "Checklist of African languages" provides a classified index to the language and dialect names recorded on the map, and there is an alphabetical index to those names.

CHINESE

Kim, T. W. and **Wawrzyszko, A.** A bibliographical guide to the study of Chinese language and linguistics. Carbondale, Ill., Linguistic Research, Inc., 1980. 89p. (Current inquiry into language & linguistics, 39)   **BC184**

An annotated bibliography of textbooks, dictionaries, and works on linguistics, the Chinese writing system, and bibliographies of the subject. Author index.   Z3108.L5K55

Yang, Winston L. Y. and **Yang, Teresa S.** A bibliography of the Chinese language. N.Y., Amer. Assoc. of Teachers of Chinese Language and Culture, 1966. 171p.   **BC185**

A selective bibliography of "Western-language sources on the Chinese language, including materials on the various dialects and minority languages, but excluding works dealing with such essentially different languages as Tibetan and Mongolian."—*Pref.* More than 2,000 items in classed arrangement with author index. Another volume is planned for listing studies in Chinese and Japanese.

Z7059.Y3

JAPANESE

Yoshizaki, Yasuhiro. Studies in Japanese literature and language: a bibliography of English materials. Tokyo, Nichigai Associates (distr. by Kinokuniya Book Store), [1979]. 451p. (Nijisseiki bunken yōran taikei, 8)   **BC186**

For full information *see* BD1504.

OCEANIC

Hollyman, K. J. A checklist of Oceanic languages (Melanesia, Micronesia, New Guinea, Polynesia). Auckland, Linguistic Soc. of New Zealand, 1960. 32p. (Te reo monographs)　　　**BC187**

A list of more than 1,500 languages and dialects, with abbreviated references to the linguistic family from which derived, the areas in which spoken, and a bibliographic citation for further information.　　　PL5001.H6

Klieneberger, H. R. Bibliography of Oceanic linguistics. London, Oxford Univ. Pr., 1957. 143p. (London oriental bibliographies, v.1)　　　**BC188**

Includes "printed books, periodical articles, and reviews dealing with Oceanic (i.e., Polynesian, Micronesian, Melanesian, and Papuan) languages . . . [and] dictionaries, vocabularies, grammars, and other linguistic contributions but excludes writings in the individual languages themselves."—*Pref.* Arranged by region, subdivided by language.　　　Z7111.K5

Kunz, Egon F. An annotated bibliography of the languages of the Gilbert Islands, Ellice Islands and Nauru. Sydney, Trustees of the Pub. Lib. of New South Wales, 1959. 202p.　　　**BC189**

Locates copies, some in libraries outside Australia.　　　Z7111.K8

Teeuw, A. and **Emanuels, H. W.** A critical survey of studies on Malay and Bahasa Indonesia. 'sGravenhage, Nijhoff, 1961. 176p. (Koninklijk Instituut voor Taal-, Land- en Volkenkunde. Bibliographical ser., 5)　　　**BC190**

A survey with bibliography of linguistic materials, including a history of dictionaries, dialects, grammars, etc.

Atlases

Language atlas of the Pacific area. Gen. eds., S. A. Wurm and Shirô Hattori. Canberra, Australian Acad. of the Humanities in collaboration with the Japan Academy, 1981. 2 pts., looseleaf. maps. 41x57cm. (Pacific linguistics. Ser. C, no.66)　　　**BC191**

Contents: pt.1 (maps 1–24), New Guinea area, Oceania, Australia; pt.2 (maps 25–47), Japan area, Philippines and Formosa, Mainland and insular South-east Asia, additional maps.

Offers maps in color, showing distribution of languages, with explanatory notes and indexes.　　　G2861.E3L28

AMERINDIAN

Evans, G. Edward and **Clark, Jeffrey.** North American Indian language materials, 1890–1965: an annotated bibliography of monographic works. Los Angeles, Amer. Indian Studies Ctr., Univ. of Calif., [1980]. 154p. (American Indian bibliographic ser., 31)　　　**BC192**

Intended as an updating of Pilling's bibliographies (BC194) and as an aid in Native American education programs. Aims to list all "dictionaries, grammars, orthographies, primers, readers, and the like concerning those Native American languages whose main province lies north of the Mexican border."—*Introd.* Arranged by language, then by author; in addition to the annotation there is an indication of subject content (e.g., dictionary, grammar) and educational level. Indexed.

Marken, Jack W. The American Indian: language and literature. Arlington Heights, Ill., AHM Corp., [1978]. 204p.　　　**BC193**

A bibliography of the languages and literatures of the Indians of North America, excluding the Indians of Mexico and Central America, as well as the Eskimo. In the matter of literatures, focus is on the writings of Indians (although critical works discussing literary writings about Indians by non-Indian authors are included). General sections on bibliography, autobiography, general literature, and general language are followed by geographical sections with subdivisions for individual tribes. Indexed.　　　Z7118.M27

Pilling, James Constantine. Bibliographies of the languages of the North American Indians. N.Y., AMS Pr., [1973]. 3v.　　　**BC194**

Reprint of the 1887–94 editions of bibliographies which were separately published and issued as: Smithsonian Institution. Bureau of Ethnology. *Bulletin*, no.1, 5–6, 9, 13–16, 19.

Contents: v.1: pt.1, Eskimos, pt.2, Siouan, pt.3, Iroquoian, pt.4, Muskhogean; v.2: pt.5, Algonquian; v.3: pt.6, Athapascan, pt.7, Chinookan, pt.8, Salishan, pt.9, Wakashan.　　　Z7118.P6

B D

Literature

❖In the general library many of the questions asked at the reference desk pertain to some phase of literature, e.g., biographies of authors; reviews of books; quotations; identifications of partly remembered titles; characters; plots; location of poems, plays, short stories, essays; or the history and development of literature by form or by nationality. To answer these questions the general as well as the special reference works must be remembered. National bibliographies and biographical dictionaries, indexes to periodicals and book reviews, encyclopedias and dictionaries, are of basic importance. However, to supplement the general works, a large number of special aids are available, some international in scope and others devoted to the literature of a particular country.

The needs of libraries will vary, but basic equipment for an average American library would include: for **history and bibliography,** *New Cambridge bibliography of English literature* (BD497), *Cambridge history of English literature* (BD564), and *Literary history of the United States* (BD411); **dictionaries and handbooks,** *Columbia dictionary of modern European literature* (BD52), Kunitz and Haycraft's *Twentieth century authors* (BD107), *Oxford companion to American literature* (BD407), *Oxford companion to English literature* (BD556), *Princeton encyclopedia of poetry and poetics* (BD314); **plots,** *Thesaurus of book digests* (BD71), or Magill's *Masterpieces of world literature* (BD74); **quotations and proverbs,** Bartlett's *Familiar quotations* (BD120), *Oxford dictionary of quotations* (BD129), *Oxford dictionary of English proverbs* (BD183), Stevenson's *Home book of quotations* (BD132), and his *Home book of proverbs* (BD184); and the various **indexes** to poetry, plays, short stories, essays, etc.

Anthologies and collections of poetry, plays, short stories, and other forms of literature may be shelved in the reference room or may be made easily available elsewhere in the library. Materials in foreign literature should be acquired according to need. Libraries much used by students will need several of the annual bibliographical surveys, e.g., *MLA International bibliography* of the Modern Language

Association (BD22), *Annual bibliography* of the Modern Humanities Research Association (BD503), *Year's work in English studies* (BD504), and many of the more specialized works.

GENERAL WORKS

Bibliography of bibliography

Wortman, William A. A guide to serial bibliographies for modern literatures. N.Y., Modern Language Assoc. of Amer., 1982. 124p.   **BD1**

Lists and annotates about 950 "current serial bibliographies in modern literatures of use to students of literature."—*Pref.* Classed arrangement; author/title/subject index.   Z6519.W67

Bibliography

See also BD360.

Baldensperger, Fernand and **Friederich, Werner P.** Bibliography of comparative literature. Chapel Hill, Univ. of North Carolina Pr., 1950. 701p. (Univ. of North Carolina studies in comparative literature, no.1) (Repr.: N.Y., Russell & Russell, 1960)   **BD2**

An extensive compendium attempting to cover literary influences from early to modern times. Arranged in four books: the first and third dealing with generalities (including themes, motifs, genres, international literary relations, etc.); the second and fourth with specific literatures and their contributions, listed according to country or author exerting influence. Bibliographical citations are very brief. A detailed table of contents, but no index.

For continuation *see Yearbook of comparative and general literature* (BD28).   Z6514.C7B3

Betz, Louis Paul. La littérature comparée. Essai bibliographique. Introd. par Joseph Texte. 2. éd. augm., pub., avec un index méthodique, par Fernand Baldensperger. Strasbourg, Trübner, 1904. 386col., 389–410p. (Repr.: N.Y., Greenwood Pr., 1969)   **BD3**

A bibliography of books and periodical articles on comparative literature from the Middle Ages through the 19th century. Still useful for the large amount of 19th-century material not included in Baldensperger (BD2).   Z6514.C7B6

Bibliographie générale de littérature comparée, années 1949/1950–1957/1958. Paris, Boivin, 1951–59. Biennial.   **BD4**

Publiée avec le concours de l'UNESCO. Ceased publication.

Reprints of the quarterly bibliographies published in *Revue de littérature comparée,* issued in this form to supplement Baldensperger (BD2).   Z6514.C7B64

Doll, Howard D. Oral interpretation of literature: an annotated bibliography with multimedia listings. Metuchen, N.J., Scarecrow Pr., 1982. 489p.   **BD5**

About 4,200 entries. Chronological arrangement within separate sections for books, chapters in books, journal articles, specialized periodicals, theses and dissertations, filmstrips, and videotapes. Author and subject indexes. With the exception of theses and dissertations, entries are briefly annotated.   Z6514.S7D64

Dudley, Fred Adair. The relations of literature and science; a selected bibliography, 1930–1967. Ann Arbor, Mich., Univ. Microfilms, 1968. 137p.   **BD6**

"Combining annual bibliographies assembled by various hands for 'General Topic 7,' a discussion group of the Modern Language Association of America and published in *Symposium.*"—*title page.*

A compilation for the scholar interested in the literary impact of scientific thought. For a related annual *see* BD23.   Z6511.D8

Fisher, John Hurt, ed. The medieval literature of Western Europe; a review of research, mainly 1930–1960. [N.Y.], Publ. for the Modern Language Assoc. of America by New York Univ. Pr., 1966. 432p. (Modern Language Assoc. of America. Revolving fund ser., 22)   **BD7**

An MLA-sponsored survey of literary scholarship similar to those for later periods of English literature (BD538, BD626, BD648–BD650). Specialists have contributed chapters (with appropriate subdivisions which make for easy use) on Latin, Old English, Middle English, French, German, Old Norse, Italian, Spanish, Catalan, Portuguese, and Celtic medieval literatures. Chapters are "confined to the tools for research and the most important research produced between about 1930 and 1960" (*Foreword*), with evaluative comments. Indexed.   PN671.F5

Harvard University. Library. Literature: general and comparative; classification schedule, classified listing by call number, alphabetical listing by author or title, chronological listing. Cambridge, Harvard Univ. Lib., 1968. 189p. (Widener Library shelflist, 18)   **BD8**

For a note on the series *see* AA145.

Includes "general works on the art of literature, histories of comparative literature, and anthologies which contain a wide variety of literature."—*Pref.*

International Federation for Modern Languages and Literature. Répertoire chronologique des littératures modernes, publié par la Commission Internationale d'Histoire Littéraire Moderne. [Ed.], Paul Van Tieghem. Paris, Droz, 1935. 413p.   **BD9**

Issued in parts, 1935–37.

Arranged chronologically; under each year lists the principal writings and literary events by country. Covers 1455–1900. Index.   Z6519.I61

Jenkinson, Edward B. and **Daghlian, Philip B.** Books for teachers of English; an annotated bibliography. Bloomington, Indiana Univ. Pr., [1968]. 173p.   **BD10**

Survey chapters listing works useful to teachers of literary criticism, poetry, fiction, drama, rhetoric, etc., have been contributed by a number of scholars.   Z5814.E59J4

Kiell, Norman. Psychoanalysis, psychology, and literature; a bibliography. Metuchen, N.J., Scarecrow Pr., 1982. 2v. (1269p.)   **BD11**

1st ed. 1963.

Lists articles, monographs, and books which deal with literary writing from a psychological point of view. Classed arrangement with sections for various types of literary works (fiction, drama, autobiography, diaries, poetry, criticism, film, etc.). About 20,000 items in this edition, including many foreign-language entries. Author, title, and subject indexes in v.2.   Z6514.P78K53

Literature of the Renaissance. (*In* Studies in philology, v.14–66, 1917–69) Annual.   **BD12**

Title varies; some issues called *Recent literature of the Renaissance.*

Until 1938 covered works on the English Renaissance only. From 1939 covers English, French, Germanic, Italian, Neo-Latin, Spanish, and Portuguese (slight variations). Includes index of proper names.

Ceased publication 1969. "Because of the relatively heavy expense involved in publishing . . . and because other bibliographies now duplicate most of the information that has been given in 'Recent Literature of the Renaissance,' the present bibliography [i.e., that covering 1968 publications] will be the last."—*Studies in philology,* May 1969, prelim. note.

Magill, Frank Northen. Magill's bibliography of literary criticism; selected sources for the study of more than 2,500 outstanding works of Western literature. Englewood Cliffs, N.J., Salem Pr., [1979]. 4v.   **BD13**

A listing of studies—published as books, parts of books, and periodical articles—of works of fiction, drama, and poetry. Arrangement is by literary author, then by individual work, with studies listed alphabetically by author. "There are 613 authors represented, 2,546 literary works covered, and 36,137 individual citations listed. Major novels and plays usually have about twenty-five sources listed, while minor works average about a dozen."—*Pref.* Includes literary works of all periods, and foreign works available in English translation. Sources were selected with the undergraduate student and general reader in mind. Title index in v.4. Z6511.M25

McCormick, John O., ed. A syllabus of comparative literature. 2d ed. Comp. by the Faculty of Comparative Literature, Livingston College, Rutgers University. Metuchen, N.J., Scarecrow Pr., 1972. 220p. **BD14**

Previous ed. 1964.

A series of reading lists arranged by period for Western literature, plus brief sections for Indian, Chinese, and Japanese literatures. Z6511.L57

Natoli, Joseph P. and **Rusch, Frederick L.** Psychocriticism: an annotated bibliography. Westport, Conn., Greenwood Pr., [1984]. 267p. (Bibliographies and indexes in world literature, 1) **BD15**

"Unlike Kiell [BD11], we have restricted our coverage to articles and books in which a fairly recognizable school or method of psychology is applied to literature."—*Pref.* 1,435 citations published since 1969 are grouped by literary period from ancient and classical times to the twentieth century, with subdivisions for individual authors; an additional chapter lists general studies and essay collections. Subject and author indexes. Z6514.P78N38

Pownall, David E. Articles on twentieth century literature: an annotated bibliography, 1954 to 1970. N.Y., Kraus-Thomson, 1973–80. 7v. **BD16**

"An expanded cumulation of 'Current bibliography' in the journal Twentieth century literature. Volume one to volume sixteen, 1955 to 1970."—*title page.*

Arranged by name of literary author (the proposed section on general literary topics has not appeared); substantially expanded from the quarterly bibliographies on which it is based. "Current bibliography" continued to be a regular feature of *Twentieth century literature* through v.25, no.1 (Spr. 1979), then appeared sporadically through v.27, no.2 (Sum. 1981). Z6519.P66

The present state of scholarship in sixteenth-century literature. Ed. by William M. Jones. Columbia, Univ. of Missouri Pr., 1978. 257p. **BD17**

A series of essays, originally delivered as lectures in 1976–77, giving "a general overview of recent scholarship on the literature of Western Europe in the sixteenth century."—*Pref.* Each essay provides a select bibliography of recent publications, and each makes recommendations concerning areas for future study. No index. PN731.P7

Progress of medieval and Renaissance studies in the United States and Canada. Bull. no.1–25. Boulder, Colo., 1923–60. **BD18**

Title varies. Ceased publication.

Renaissance studies added with no.15. Each number contains lists of papers, publications, projects, doctoral dissertations, and a list of medieval and Renaissance scholars, with their publications. Z6203.P96

Reuss, Jeremias David. Repertorium commentationum a societatibus litterariis editarum. Secundum disciplinarum ordinem . . . T.8–9. Gottingae, Dieterich, 1810. (Repr.: N.Y., B. Franklin, 1961) **BD19**

Contents: T.8, Historia . . . Historia litteraria; T.9, Philologia, Linguae, Scriptores graeci, Scriptores latini, Litterae elegantiores, Poesis, Rhetorica, Ars antiqua, Pictura, Musica.

A valuable index to the publications of the learned societies of various countries up to 1800. Classed arrangement with author index.

For complete contents of v.8, *see* DA16; for description of complete set *see* EA22.

Thompson, George A. Key sources in comparative and world literature; an annotated guide to reference materials. N.Y., Ungar, [1982]. 383p. **BD20**

A bibliographic guide intended for the graduate student. Chapters for general and comparative literatures, classical, Romance, French, Italian, Hispanic, and German literatures, literature in English, other European literatures, Oriental literatures, and related fields. Lists many specialized bibliographies (e.g., of specific themes, genres, movements) and bibliographies and concordances for individual authors. Descriptive and evaluative annotations; citations to reviews. Classed arrangement within chapters (an outline preceding each chapter); index of editors, compilers, etc.; selective index of titles; subject index. Z6511.T47

Current

The eighteenth century; a current bibliography. n.s.1– , for 1975– . Philadelphia, Amer. Soc. for Eighteenth-Century Studies, 1978– . Annual. **BD21**

"A current bibliography incorporating English literature 1660–1800."—*verso of t.p.*

Represents a new series of the annual bibliography published in *Philological quarterly* 1971–75, covering scholarship of 1970–74; that series, in turn, superseded and incorporated the annual bibliography "English literature 1660–1800" (*see* BD526) which appeared in *PQ* 1926–70.

"The purpose of this bibliography is annually to record and evaluate the year's significant scholarship concerning the Enlightenment in Europe and the New World."—*Foreword.* Z5579.6.E36

Modern Language Association of America. MLA international bibliography of books and articles on the modern languages and literatures. 1921– . (Publ. as supplements to PMLA, v.37–) Annual. **BD22**

Title varies.

1921–1954/55 repr. as *MLA American bibliography;* 1956–68 repr. as *MLA International bibliography of books and articles on the modern languages and literatures* (N.Y., Kraus).

A very useful bibliography; from 1921 to 1955 entitled *American bibliography* and limited to writings by Americans on the literatures of various countries; coverage varied. 1956–62, title changed to *Annual bibliography* and coverage extended to include writers in other languages. 1963– , title changed to *MLA international bibliography* (this title used in reprint edition as noted above). Selections are made from various book sources and from a basic master list of many hundreds of periodicals in the field of modern languages and literatures. By 1963 the work listed books and articles in English, French, German, Spanish, Italian, Portuguese, Rumanian, Scandinavian, Netherlandic, Celtic, and a selection of East European languages. Beginning with the issue covering publications of 1969, the longer title as cited here has been used, and coverage further extended.

Within national literature sections there are subdivisions for literary periods, and names of authors treated appear in boldface type to facilitate searching. Author indexes have appeared in some volumes. No cumulations.

Beginning with the volumes covering 1981, published in 5v: I, British, American, Australian, English-Canadian, New Zealand, and English-Caribbean literatures; II, European, Asian, African, and South American literatures; III, Linguistics; IV, General literature and related topics; and V, Folklore. Subscriptions are available for individual volumes or any of the various "library editions": "Individual paperbound volumes include author and subject indexes. Library editions are available in four different combinations: all five volumes with [cumulated] author and subject indexes; Volumes I, II, and III with author and subject indexes; all five volumes with author index only; and Volumes I, II, and III with author index only."—*Guide for users 1981.* Although computer-produced, the subject indexes are not merely keyword-in-context, but "the indexers use terms that describe [an item's] content. These descriptors, based on the document author's own wording, are assigned to facets [of the structured index] pertinent to that item . . . ." Regarding scope, there are now no restrictions as to place of origin or publication or the original language of the works cited, nor is there a restriction on the physical type or medium of works. "Works limited to pedagogy, even as it relates to the teaching of language, literature, composition, and related subjects, are excluded . . . . There are no historical-period restrictions on language coverage; for literature, works exclusively on classical Greek and Latin literatures are excluded since those literatures are covered in *L'Année philologique*."

Availability of "library editions" as noted above has varied, but the one found in most research collections will be the first option bound in two physical volumes (i.e., the five numbered volumes bound together in 1v. with author index, and a separately bound volume containing the subject index to the five numbered volumes). Entries in the subject index give reference to volume and item numbers. Z7006.M64●

Relations of literature and science, 1979/80– . [Worcester, Mass.], Clark Univ. Pr., [1981]– . Annual. **BD23**

1979/80: ". . . ed. by Walter Schatzberg, chairman of the Bibliography Committee and published on behalf of the Division on Literature and Science of the Modern Language Association."

Lists books and periodical articles grouped by period.

Revue des revues, 1974– . (*In* Canadian review of comparative literature, v.1– , 1974–) Annual. **BD24**

An annotated bibliography of periodical articles on comparative literature; originally published as part of the Summer issue of the journal, it now constitutes a separate issue. In three sections: (1) Histoire et relations littéraires; (2) Théorie littéraire et méthodes d'études littéraires; (3) La littérature et les autres arts. International coverage; annotations appear in English or French; indexes of authors and subjects.

The Romantic movement: a selective and critical bibliography for 1936–78. (*In* ELH, a journal of English literary history, 1937–49; *in* Philological quarterly, 1950–64; *in* English language notes, 1965–79) Annual. **BD25**

Editors vary.

"Designed to cover a 'movement' " rather than a period. English section limited to 1800–37; other sections not so limited. Covers English, French, German, Spanish, and Portuguese.

For a reprint of the 1936–70 issues *see* BD27. Continued as numbered volumes within the "Garland reference library of the humanities" series:

The Romantic movement: a selective and critical bibliography for 1979– . N.Y., Garland, 1980– . Annual. (Garland reference library of the humanities, v.211 [etc.]) **BD26**

David V. Erdman, ed.

A continuation of the bibliography of the same title covering 1936–78 (above). Continues the plan and coverage of the earlier publications: i.e., "It is designed to cover a 'movement' rather than a period; though the English section, for example, is largely limited to the years 1789–1837, other sections extend over different spans of years."—[*p.v., 1979*] Sections for English, French, German, and Spanish, as well as a general section. No index. Z6514.R6R64

The Romantic movement bibliography, 1936–1970; a master cumulation from ELH, Philological quarterly and English language notes. Ed. by A. C. Elkins, Jr. and L. J. Forstner. [Ann Arbor, Mich.], Pierian Pr., [1973]. 7v. **BD27**

Not a true cumulation: the annual bibliographies have been reprinted in photo-offset with the addition of running heads to indicate year and original source of publication. In addition, the volumes have been paged continuously to facilitate indexing.

v.7 is devoted to a series of indexes: (1) Author/main entry/reviewer index; (2) Subject index: personal names; (3) Subject index: categories. A cumulated list of periodical title abbreviations is also included. Subject indexing is not sufficiently detailed to be wholly satisfactory.

David V. Erdman's Foreword to the set should be consulted for remarks on selectivity of the listings and shifts of emphasis over the years covered. Z6514.R6R65

Yearbook of comparative and general literature. Bloomington, Indiana Univ., 1952– . v.1– . Annual. **BD28**

Published in collaboration with the Comparative Literature Committee of the National Council of Teachers of English; the American Comparative Literature Association; and the Comparative Literature Section of the Modern Language Association.

Includes articles, news items, biographical sketches, and, in v.1–19, an *Annual bibliography* designed to serve as a supplement to Baldensperger, *Bibliography of comparative literature* (BD2). The bibliography was discontinued after v.19 (covering publications of 1969); thereafter, a list of English translations from other languages appeared annually through v.29 (1980) as the only regular bibliographic feature. PN851.Y4

Dissertations

Naaman, Antoine. Répertoire des thèses littéraires canadiennes de 1921 à 1976. Avec la collaboration de Léo A. Brodeur. Sherbrooke, Québec, Éditions Naaman, [1978]. 453p. **BD29**

Lists some 5,600 doctoral dissertations and master's theses on literature and language completed at Canadian universities 1921–76. Classed arrangement within seven broad categories (some of them further subdivided): (1) Civilisation, folklore et mouvement des idées; (2) Genres littéraires; (3) Histoire littéraire; (4) Écriture française dans le monde (hors de la France et du Québec); (5) Études comparées; (6) Traduction; (7) Sciences du langage. Indexes of authors, authors studied, and subjects. Includes theses in English as well as in French. Z6511.N26

Manuscripts

Henry E. Huntington Library and Art Gallery, San Marino, Calif. Guide to literary manuscripts in the Huntington Library. San Marino, Calif., Huntington Lib., 1979. 539p. **BD30**

Sue Hodson, comp.

"The two primary criteria for including an author in the guide are common identification as a literary figure and the appearance of his name in at least one standard biographical dictionary."—*Pref.* Reflects the library's strengths in British and American literature, but includes a few Canadian and European authors. (Manuscripts of authors who died before 1600 will be included in a separate volume devoted to medieval and renaissance manuscripts.) Arrangement is alphabetical by author, with type and extent of the manuscripts indicated; a few of the larger collections are described in some detail. Z6621.H527H46

Periodicals

See also BD79–BD83.

Modern Language Association of America. MLA directory of periodicals: a guide to journals and series in languages and literatures, 1978/79– . [N.Y.], Modern Language Assoc. of Amer., 1979– . Biennial. **BD31**

"A companion to the *MLA international bibliography*."—*t.p.*

Provides as full information as available on all journals and series included in the master list of the *MLA international bibliography* (BD22). Listing by title, with indexes of editorial personnel, languages, sponsoring organizations, and subjects. In addition to address, name of editor, first date of publication, ISSN and MLA acronym, information is given on subscriptions, editorial content, and submission requirements.

Also available in a paperbound edition which includes only those periodicals and series published in the United States and Canada. P1.A1M62a

Patterson, Margaret C. Author newsletters and journals: an international annotated bibliography of serial publications concerned with the life and works of individual authors. Detroit, Gale, [1979]. 497p. (American literature, English literature, and world literatures in English information guide ser., 19) **BD32**

Lists and annotates 1,129 titles of serial publications devoted to "collecting and distributing criticism, bibliographies, biographical information, textual studies, reviews, and related scholarship on the life and works of one author."—*Pref.* Includes both current and defunct publications. Arranged by author's name. Title index; numerous appendixes.　　　　Z6513.P37

Translations

Farrar, Clarissa Palmer and **Evans, Austin Patterson.** Bibliography of English translations from medieval sources. N.Y., Columbia Univ. Pr., 1946. 534p. (Records of civilization; sources and studies, no.39)　　　　**BD33**

"Aims to include English translations of important literary sources produced during the period from Constantine the Great to the year 1500 within an area roughly inclusive of Europe, northern Africa and western Asia."—*Pref.* Lists works published through 1942, with a few items published later which were inserted in proof.

An outstanding work including almost 4,000 entries arranged alphabetically by author, with many annotations describing content, translator's comment, editions or reprints of a given translation, adequacy of translation, etc. Extensive index to authors, translators, editors, titles, subjects, etc.　　　　Z6517.F3

Ferguson, Mary Anne Heyward. Bibliography of English translations from medieval sources, 1943-1967. N.Y., Columbia Univ. Pr., 1974. 274p. (Records of civilization; sources and studies, no.88)　　　　**BD34**

A supplement to Farrar and Evans's *Bibliography* (above), following the plan and principles of that work. 1,980 items. Annotations; index.　　　　Z6517.F47

Literatures of the world in English translation; a bibliography. N.Y., Ungar, [1967-70]. 3v. in 4.　　　　**BD35**

Contents: v.1, The Greek and Latin literatures, ed. by George B. Parks and Ruth Z. Temple; v.2, The Slavic literatures, comp. by Richard C. Lewanski; v.3, pt.1, Catalan, Italian, Portuguese and Brazilian, Provençal, Rumanian, Spanish and Spanish American literatures; pt.2, French literature (both parts ed. by George B. Parks and Ruth Z. Temple).

The series is an outgrowth of a project undertaken some 30 years ago by the National Council of Teachers of English in collaboration with the American Library Association. The aim is "to list for the first time the English translations of all works of foreign literatures." —*Pref., v.1.* Literature in the broad sense is encompassed, and the greater works of philosophy, history, science, and theology are included. All translations "of reasonable length" are listed except for a few frequently retranslated authors for whom only the more important and more recent translations are given. Each volume has an annotated bibliography of general literature (collective bibliographies of literature in translation, collective histories of literature, etc.), and individual sections of each volume are prefaced by lists of books on the general background, literary history, and literature of the country and period under consideration. The volumes can thus serve as guides to foreign literatures as well as bibliographies of translations into English. Further volumes were planned to deal with Celtic, Germanic, and other literatures of Europe; and with the literatures of Asia and Africa.

Indexes

Chicorel index series. N.Y., Chicorel Library Pub. Corp., [1970-78]. v.1-27.　　　　**BD36**

Contents: v.1-3, Chicorel theater index to plays in anthologies, periodicals, discs and tapes; v.3A, Chicorel bibliography to the performing arts; v.4, Chicorel index to poetry on discs, tapes, and cassettes; v.5A–C, Chicorel index to poetry in collections (Poetry-in-print); v.6A–C, Chicorel index to poetry; v.7-7A, Chicorel index to the spoken arts on discs, tapes, and cassettes; v.8, Chicorel theater index to plays in periodicals, discs, and tapes; v.9, Chicorel index to children's plays; v.10, Chicorel bibliography to books on music and musicians; v.11-11A, Chicorel index to abstracting and indexing

services: periodicals in humanities and the social sciences; v.12–12A, Chicorel index to short stories in anthologies and collections (with annual supplements beginning 1977); v.13-13C, Chicorel index to the crafts; v.14, Chicorel index to reading disabilities; v.14A, Chicorel index to reading and learning disabilities; v.15–15A, Chicorel index to biographies; v.16-16A, Chicorel index to environment and ecology; v.17-17A, Chicorel index to urban planning and environmental design; v.18-18A, Chicorel index to learning disorders: books; v.19, Chicorel abstracts to reading and learning disabilities (annual beginning 1976); v.20-20A, Chicorel index to poetry and poets; v.21, Chicorel theater index to drama literature; v.22-22A, Chicorel index to film literature; v.23-23B, Chicorel index to literary criticism; v.24, Chicorel index to parapsychology and occult books; v.25, Chicorel theater index to plays in anthologies and collections, 1970-76; v.26, Chicorel index to video tapes and cassettes; v.27, Chicorel index to mental health book reviews.

A series of computer-produced indexes to a wide range of materials published in anthologies, periodicals, etc.; focus was originally on literature and the performing arts.

Research methods

Thorpe, James. The use of manuscripts in literary research: problems of access and literary property rights. 2d ed. N.Y., Modern Language Assoc. of Amer., 1979. 40p.　　　　**BD37**

1st ed. 1974.

A guide written from the scholar's point of view. Includes information on locating manuscripts, obtaining access to collections, permissions to photocopy and publish, and literary property rights. This edition takes into account provisions of the 1976 United States copyright law.　　　　Z692.M28T47

Watson, George. The literary thesis; a guide to research. [London], Longmans, [1970]. 188p.　　　　**BD38**

A brief, readable guide to research problems and methods, ranging from selection of the thesis topic through publication of the finished work; includes some notes on bibliography, sources, and works of reference.　　　　LB2369.W33

General collections

Great books of the Western world and the great ideas. Ed. in chief, Robert Maynard Hutchins; assoc. ed., Mortimer J. Adler. Chicago, Encyclopaedia Britannica, [1952]. 54v. il.　　　　**BD39**

A collection of the great books from Homer to Freud, each given in English in its entirety (with three exceptions).

v.2-3, entitled *The great ideas: Syntopicon* (Mortimer J. Adler, ed. in chief), are an index and a guide to reading. The great ideas are arranged in 102 topical chapters, each with an introduction, an outline of topics, references, cross references, and additional readings. The citations under each topic are in chronological order, with references to specific parts of works dealing with the various phases of the topic.

v.3 closes with a bibliography of additional readings, a chapter on the principles and methods of syntopical construction, and an inventory of terms.

The Syntopicon may serve as an index to the set, a guide to writings on certain topics, or even as an index to quotations. However, its complex structure detracts from its use as a quick reference aid.　　　　AC1.G7

The Harvard classics, ed. by Charles W. Eliot. N.Y., Collier, 1909. 50 (i.e., 52)v. il.　　　　**BD40**

A collection of writings chosen as representations of the world's great literature in all fields. With a few exceptions, such as the Bible and Shakespeare, the works are complete, not selections. Chronologically the material covers from ancient to modern times: from the sacred books of the early religions, through the literature of Greece and Rome, the Middle Ages in the Orient and Europe, the Renaissance, and the 19th century in Europe and America.

v.50 contains an analytical author, subject, and title index to all of the material contained in the set, as well as an index to first lines of poems, songs and choruses, hymns, and psalms. There are two additional unnumbered volumes: (1) Reading guide and (2) Lectures on the Harvard Classics, edited by William Allan Nelson.

The set is useful in libraries particularly for its comprehensive index, and also because it may provide additional copies of standard works. A further index is provided by: AC1.A4

The idexicon, a guide to the great ideas of the Eastern and Western worlds. N.Y., Crowell-Collier, 1961. 470p. **BD41**

An index to the authors included and the ideas and subjects treated in the 50v. of the *Harvard classics.* Intended to aid in the tracing of the development of ideas and concepts by different writers through the centuries.

Warner library . . . Eds.: John W. Cunliffe, Ashley H. Thorndike. N.Y., Warner Lib. Co., 1917. 30v. il. **BD42**

Contents: v.1–26, World's best literature (sketches and selections); v.27, Book of songs and lyrics; v.28, Reader's dictionary of authors, ed. by H. M. Ayres; v.29, Reader's digest of books, ed. by H. R. Keller; v.30, Students' course in literature, by G. R. Lomer. General index: authors, titles, subjects, etc.

An old, but still useful, popular collection of representative selections from writers of all periods and countries, with considerable popular reference material in the way of critical notices, biographies, synopses of books, etc. Issued in three different editions. The 1st ed., ed. by Charles Dudley Warner (N.Y., Peale, 1896–97. 30v.), had title *Library of the world's best literature.* The 1917 edition is a reprint from plates of v.1–27 of the 1st ed., with changes and the addition of considerable new material on new pages inserted throughout in their proper places and fitted into the original paging by the use of subletters a,b,c, etc.; v.28–30 of this edition are entirely reset. A later, entirely rearranged edition, with the title *Columbia University course in literature, based on the World's best literature,* utilized considerable material from the 1917 edition; was arranged by countries and periods rather than by authors; and added selections and notices, but omitted the three special reference volumes of the 1917 edition.

The *Reader's digest* which forms v.29 of the 1917 edition is also published separately by Macmillan; for new, enlarged edition *see* BD73. The critical and biographical notices in v.1–26 of the 1917 edition and in the *Columbia University course in literature,* but not the selections, are indexed in the *Essay and general literature index.*
PN6013.W3

Criticism

Contemporary literary criticism; excerpts from criticism of the works of today's novelists, poets, playwrights, and other creative writers. Detroit, Gale, [1973–]. v.1– . (In progress) **BD43**

Subtitle varies; editors vary. Also called *CLC.*

An ongoing series of selected excerpts from critical writings on contemporary authors. Writers treated are "those who are either now living or who have died since January 1, 1960."—*Pref.* Critiques are drawn mainly from writings of the past 25 years. About 175 authors are treated in each volume (fewer in recent volumes), with an average of five excerpts (from books, reviews and periodical articles) about each. Full citations to source follow the excerpts. In addition to well-established authors, consideration is given to writers of current interest and authors of mystery and science fiction writings. 30v. were published through 1984; a "Cumulative index to critics" appears in each volume. PN771.C59

Literature criticism from 1400 to 1800. Dennis Poupard, ed. Detroit, Gale, [1984]– . v.1– . Irregular. il. **BD44**

Subtitle: Excerpts from criticism of the works of fifteenth, sixteenth, seventeenth, and eighteenth-century novelists, poets, playwrights, philosophers, and other creative writers, from the first published critical appraisals to current evaluations.

Similar to the publisher's other series of excerpts from literary

criticism (e.g., BD43). International coverage, with considerable emphasis on English authors; excludes Shakespeare. PN86.L53

Modern black writers. Comp. and ed. by Michael Popkin. N.Y., F. Ungar, [1978]. 519p. (A library of literary criticism) **BD45**

Like other volumes in the series (e.g., BD553), this is a compilation of excerpts from critical appraisals (originally published in books or periodicals) of the writers included. "The eighty writers discussed in this volume are all noted primarily for their work in either fiction, poetry, or drama."—*Introd.* Authors from some 23 countries (writing in English, French, and several African languages) are included. Index of critics, and a list of literary works mentioned.
PN841.M58

Nineteenth-century literature criticism. Detroit, Gale, [1981]– . v.1– . il. Irregular. **BD46**

Subtitle: Excerpts from criticism of the works of novelists, poets, playwrights, short story writers, and other creative writers who lived between 1800 and 1900, from the first published critical appraisals to current evaluations.

Laurie Lanzen Harris, ed.

A compilation of critical excerpts as indicated in the subtitle, following the plan of the publisher's *Contemporary literary criticism* (BD43) and *Twentieth-century literary criticism* (BD47). Each volume presents critical overviews of about 30 authors. PN761.N5

Twentieth-century literary criticism. Detroit, Gale, [1978]– . v.1– . Irregular. **BD47**

Subtitle (varies): Excerpts from criticism of the works of novelists, poets, playwrights, short story writers, and other creative writers who died between 1900 and 1960, from the first published critical appraisals to current evaluations.

Editors vary.

A companion to *Contemporary literary criticism,* but concerned only with deceased writers as indicated in the subtitle. For each author there is an identifying paragraph and a list of principal works followed by excerpts from criticism (with citations to sources). International coverage, with all critical excerpts in English. Originally included about 40 authors per volume; now limited to about 20. Cumulative indexes of authors, nationalities, and critics in each volume; the author index also includes references to authors treated in *Nineteenth-century literature criticism* (above) and *Contemporary literary criticism* (BD43), plus cross references to entries in other Gale series.

Dictionaries and encyclopedias

Barnet, Sylvan, Berman, Morton and **Burto, William.** A dictionary of literary, dramatic, and cinematic terms. 2d ed. Boston, Little, Brown, [1971]. 124p. **BD48**

1st ed., 1962, had title *A dictionary of literary terms.*

A brief handbook. Major literary forms and concepts are explained in some detail. Many cross references from specific terms to the longer articles. PN44.5.B3

Beckson, Karl and **Ganz, Arthur.** Literary terms; a dictionary. N.Y., Farrar, Straus and Giroux, [1975]. 280p. **BD49**

A revised and enlarged edition of the same authors' *Reader's guide to literary terms* (1960).

Gives definitions, cites examples, and frequently offers brief historical notes with bibliographic references. PN44.5.B334

Benét, William Rose. The reader's encyclopedia. 2d ed. N.Y., Crowell, [1965]. 1118p. il. **BD50**

1st ed. 1948.

A comprehensive work containing brief articles on writers, scientists, philosophers, etc., of all nations and all periods; allusions and literary expressions and terms; literary schools and movements; plots and characters; descriptions of musical compositions and works of art, etc.

The 2d ed. emphasizes world literature with special attention to areas of growing interest, e.g., the Orient, the Soviet Union, Latin America, and the Near East; and the literary developments since 1948 when the 1st ed. was published. PN41.B4

Cassell's Encyclopaedia of world literature. Rev. and enl. . . . Gen. ed.: J. Buchanan-Brown. London, Cassell, [1973]. 3v.
BD51

1st ed. 1953 in 2v., ed. by S. H. Steinberg, had title *Cassell's Encyclopaedia of literature.*
Contents: v.1, Histories and general articles; v.2–3, Biographies, A–Z.
The first volume includes entries for histories of national literatures, literary genres, literary movements, schools, and themes, and specific literary terms. v.2–3 contain brief biographical sketches of literary figures, plus the occasional entry for individual literary works. All biographical articles are signed with initials of the contributor, as are all but the briefest entries in v.1. There are selective bibliographies for a very high percentage of articles.
PN41.C3

Columbia dictionary of modern European literature. 2d ed., fully rev. & enl. Jean-Albert Bédé and William B. Edgerton, gen. eds. N.Y., Columbia Univ. Pr., 1980. 895p. **BD52**

The 1st ed. (1947) was a scholarly dictionary offering biographical sketches, with critical evaluations of modern European authors, together with articles on the many national literatures.
This is a thorough revision incorporating the contributions of some 500 scholars from the United States, Canada, and several European countries. Takes as its starting point "the period toward the end of the 19th century when Europe was swept by a wave of new literary movements" (*Pref.*), although writers were selected for inclusion "on the basis of their relevance to 20th-century literature." Survey articles on the various national literatures are again included along with articles on individual writers (which now total 1,853). Articles are signed with the initials of the contributors; many articles were newly prepared, and revisions by different hands of articles from the first edition are so indicated. Some entries from the earlier edition were dropped. The brief bibliographies appended to the articles were compiled "especially with a view to meeting the needs of readers who may not be specialists in the literature to which the writer belongs." PN771.C575

Cuddon, John A. A dictionary of literary terms. Garden City, N.Y., Doubleday, 1977. 745p. **BD53**

Aims "to provide a serviceable and fairly comprehensive dictionary of those literary terms which are in regular use in the world today; terms in which intelligent people may be expected to have some interest and about which they may wish to find out something more."—*Pref.* Numerous *see* and *see also* references. PN41.C83

Dictionnaire des oeuvres de tous les temps et de tous les pays: littérature, philosophie, musique, sciences par Laffont-Bompiani. [4. éd.] Paris, Soc. d'Édit. de Dictionnaires et Encyclopédies, [1962]. 4v. and index. il. **BD54**

1st ed. 1952–54.
An abridged French edition of Bompiani (BD57), omitting the section on literary movements and literary characters. Listing is by French form of the titles, with an author index volume.
AE25.D52

Dictionnaire des oeuvres contemporaines de tous les pays: littérature, philosophie, musique, sciences. Paris, Soc. d'Édit. de Dictionnaires et Encyclopédies, [1968]. 765p. il.
BD55

At head of title: Laffont-Bompiani.
Forms v.5 of the preceding work. Includes entries for works of authors who died after 1955 and of living writers born before 1910.
AG25.D522

Dictionnaire des personnages littéraires et dramatiques de tous les temps et de tous les pays: poésie, théâtre, roman, musique. Laffont-Bompiani. Paris, Soc. d'Édit. de Dictionnaires et Encyclopédies, [1960]. 668p. il. **BD56**

A companion volume to the *Dictionnaire des oeuvres de tous les temps et de tous les pays* (BD54). Identifies and describes characters

of fiction, poetry, music, and drama. Historical persons are included only if they have become literary characters. Cross references are made to works in the *Dictionnaire des oeuvres*. PN41.D485

Dizionario letterario Bompiani delle opere e dei personaggi di tutti i tempi e di tutte le letterature. Milan, Bompiani, 1947–50. 9v. il. **BD57**

Contents: v.1–7, A–Z; v.8, a dictionary of literary characters; v.9, indexes.
A dictionary, listing and describing the works of all times and all countries in literature, art, and music. Although the emphasis is on literature, musical works and many famous pictures are described. Lavishly illustrated with many colored plates and black-and-white illustrations. The first half of v.1 is devoted to 58 *movimenti spirituali,* arranged alphabetically, e.g., Dadaism, euphuism, mysticism. The main part of the work consists of signed articles, arranged alphabetically by the Italian form of the title of the work, followed by the original title in brackets. Brief biographical notes are usually included in the articles, but there are no author entries.
v.8 is a dictionary of literary characters alphabetized according to the Italian form of the name. The scope is broad, ranging from Adam to Superman. v.9 includes synoptic tables showing literary development in all parts of the world; a list of titles in the original languages with their Italian equivalents; an index of authors; and an index of illustrations by artist.

———— Appendice. Milan, Bompiani, 1964–79. 3v.

v.3 includes indexes to all three volumes of the appendix.
PN41.D5

Dizionario universale della letteratura contemporanea. [Direttore: Alberto Mondadori] Milano, Mondadori, 1959–63. 5v. il. **BD58**

An encyclopedia of world literature covering 1870–1960 and supplementing Bompiani. Arranged alphabetically, it includes authors ("non-literary" as well as men of letters), literary movements, periodicals, national literatures, etc. Bibliographies are generally substantial and include works by and about an author. Extensively illustrated in black-and-white and in color. v.5 includes chronological tables, 1870–1961, and various indexes: authors, titles both in Italian and in the original language; works not translated; illustrations, etc. PN41.D53

Elkhadem, Saad. The York dictionary of English-French-German-Spanish literary terms and their origin. Fredericton, N.B., Canada, York Pr., [1976]. 154p. **BD59**

The main section is an English-language dictionary of terms with equivalents in the other languages and a definition in English. Indexes from the other languages. PN41.E4

Encyclopedia of world literature in the 20th century. Rev. ed., Leonard S. Klein, gen. ed. Based on the 1st ed. by Wolfgang Bernard Fleischmann. N.Y., Ungar, [1981–84]. 4v. il.
BD60

The previous edition was published in 3v., 1967–71, with a supplement in 1975; Fleischman's edition, in turn, was based on the Herder *Lexikon der Weltliteratur im 20. Jahrhundert* (Freiburg, 1960–61. 2v.). This edition represents a thorough revision with a special effort to achieve uniformity and truly international coverage throughout the set. Articles are either revised and updated or completely new; none of those derived from the Herder work were retained; all articles are signed, and there is a list of contributors in each volume.
Biographical/critical articles predominate and include bibliographies of works by and about an author; there are topical articles on national literatures and literary movements; entries for literary genres have been excluded. No general index.
A favorable review of v.1 appears in *Booklist* 79:691–2 (Jan. 15, 1983). PN771.E5

Frenzel, Elisabeth. Motive der Weltliteratur: ein Lexikon dichtungsgeschichtlicher Längsschnitte. 2., verb. u. um ein Register erw. Aufl. Stuttgart, Kröner, [1980]. 867p.
BD61

1st ed. 1976.

Themes and motifs are treated at considerable length, with reference to occurrence in works throughout the range of world literature and brief bibliographies of relevant scholarly studies. Cross references; index.   PN43.F7

Holman, Clarence Hugh. A handbook to literature. Based on the original edition by William Flint Thrall and Addison Hibbard. 4th ed. Indianapolis, Bobbs-Merrill, [1980]. 537p.   **BD62**

One of the most useful works of this type offering explanations of terms, concepts, schools, and movements in literature. Alphabetically arranged, with many cross references. Appended are an "Outline of literary history, English and American" (p.471–526) and lists of Nobel Prizes for literature and Pulitzer Prizes for fiction, poetry and drama.

The original edition by Thrall and Hibbard appeared in 1936 and was revised and enlarged by Holman in 1960 and in 1972. This edition, again expanded, includes some 1,560 entries, none of which remains unchanged from the first edition.   PN41.H6

Kindlers Literatur Lexikon. Zürich, Kindler Verlag, [1965–74]. 7v. and Ergänzungsband. il.   **BD63**

Inspired by the *Dizionario letterario Bompiani* (BD57), but a completely new work. Entry is by title of the literary work (usually in the language of the original), and most articles include a brief history of the work, a précis of the plot, and a bibliography listing editions, critical works, adaptations, and translations as applicable. Includes Eastern as well as Western literature, with a certain emphasis on contemporary works. v.7 includes a series of essays on national literatures and literatures of specific historical periods; these were contributed by scholar specialists and include brief bibliographies. There are indexes of authors, of anonymous titles, and of titles in German translation, short titles, and variant titles; a separate index to the essays in v.7 is also included. A useful work, handsomely produced.   PN41.K53

Meyers Handbuch über die Literatur; ein Lexikon der Dichter und Schriftsteller aller Literaturen. Hrsg. von der Lexikonredaktion des Bibliographischen Instituts. Redaktionelle Leitung: Ingrid Adam und Gisela Preuss. 2., neu bearb. Aufl. Mannheim, Allgemeiner Verlag, [1970]. 987p. il.   **BD64**

1st ed. 1964.

Devoted to brief bio-bibliographical sketches of major (and some relatively minor) literary figures of all periods and from all countries. Includes entries for important anonymous works of literature; good coverage for contemporary writers. An appendix provides bibliographical references to histories of national literatures.   PN41.M45

The Penguin companion to world literature. N.Y., McGraw-Hill, [1969–71]. 4v.   **BD65**

British edition (Harmondsworth, Penguin, 1969–71) has title *Penguin companion to literature.*

Contents: [v.1] The Penguin companion to American literature, ed. by Malcolm Bradbury, Eric Mottram and Jean Franco; [v.2] The Penguin companion to classical, Oriental and African literature, ed. by D. M. Lang and D. R. Dudley (British rev. ed., 1971: Classical and Byzantine, ed. by D. R. Dudley; Oriental and African, ed. by D. M. Lang); [v.3] The Penguin companion to English literature, ed. by David Daiches (British ed. called Penguin companion to literature: Britain and the Commonwealth); [v.4] The Penguin companion to European literature, ed. by Anthony Thorlby (British rev. ed., 1971).

A useful series of handbooks consisting mainly of entries for individual authors. Articles are signed; some include select bibliographic references. The American literature volume has separate sections for the United States and for Latin America.

A review by Basil Cottle (*Review of English studies* 23:321–25, Aug. 1972) of the "Britain and the Commonwealth" handbook points out the strengths and weaknesses of that volume which may be considered fairly typical of the set.   PN41.P44

Ruttkowski, W. V. Nomenclator litterarius. Bern & München, Francke Verlag, [1980]. 548p.   **BD66**

Foreword in German, English, Dutch, French, Spanish, Italian, and Russian.

A multilingual dictionary of literary terms in seven languages. In the body of the work terms are usually entered under the German word, followed by equivalents in the other languages (although terms more or less universally used in the language of origin are entered under the well-known form), but there is an index in which terms in all languages are interfiled. About 2,600 entries. Bibliography of literary dictionaries arranged by language.

Sáinz de Robles, Federico Carlos. Ensayo de un diccionario de la literatura. [3. ed. corr. y aum.] Madrid, Aguilar, [1964–67]. 3v. (v.1, 1965)   **BD67**

1st ed. 1949–50.

Contents: v.1, Términos, conceptos, "ismos" literarios; v.2, Escritores españoles e hispanoamericanos; v.3, Autores extranjeros.

The entries in v.1 range from definitions of terms to extensive articles on literary concepts with bibliographies. The bio-bibliographical articles in v.2–3 include sketches of authors of all periods.   PN41.S2

Schneider, Georg. Die Schlüsselliteratur. Stuttgart, Hiersemann, 1951–53. 3v.   **BD68**

Contents: Bd.1, Das literarische Gesamtbild; Bd.2, Entschlüsselung deutscher Romane und Dramen; Bd.3, Entschlüsselung ausländischer Romane und Dramen.

A key to the identities of real characters and events appearing in literature under fictitious names. Not all-inclusive but treats the significant works of many literatures. v.1 gives general explanations and definitions, history, and discussion with indexes of authors and prototypes; v.2 is devoted to German fiction and drama; v.3, to non-German literature.   Z1026.S4

Shaw, Harry. Dictionary of literary terms. N.Y., McGraw-Hill, [1972]. 402p.   **BD69**

Defines and explains (often with illustrative examples) about 2,000 terms. Scope is fairly broad, embracing some terminology from magazines, newspapers, and other mass media. Includes numerous terms not found in Holman (BD62) but treatment of purely literary terms is generally briefer than in that work.   PN44.5.S46

Die Weltliteratur; biographisches, literarhistorisches und bibliographisches Lexikon in Übersichten und Stichwörten. Hrsg. von Erich Frauwallner, Hans Giebisch und E. Heinzel. Wien, Hollinek, [1951–54]. 3v.   **BD70**

A scholarly German encyclopedia of world literature from the earliest times to 1951, giving concise information about national literatures, literary forms, and outstanding authors, alphabetically arranged with many cross references. Articles include bibliographies; for personal names, these include both works by and about. v.3 includes an appendix and an index.   PN41.W4

———— Ergänzungsband. Wien, Hollinek, 1968–70. v.1–2.

Contents: v.1–2, A–O.

In addition to articles on authors not previously covered, additional information and new bibliographical citations are given for many writers previously treated. No more published.

Digests

❖Various handbooks and compilations which give plots of novels, and synopses and digests of well-known books, should be represented in the general reference collection, despite the fact that a student may often ask for an outline to save the trouble of reading assigned work. Synopses are found in many author dictionaries and handbooks: in such works as the *Oxford companions* (BD407, BD556) and in some encyclopedias such as Larousse, *Grand dictionnaire* (AC39). Critical reviews also often give outlines of the works reviewed. For other aids see the following:

Haydn, Hiram and **Fuller, Edmund.** Thesaurus of book digests: digests of the world's permanent writings from the ancient classics to current literature. N.Y., Crown, [1949]. 831p.   **BD71**

Very concise digests arranged by title, with an author index and an index to characters. In some cases, when authors are remembered for the body of their work rather than for a particular title, discussion is given under the author's name.

Supplemented by: PN44.H38

Weiss, Irving and **Weiss, Anne de la Vergne.** Thesaurus of book digests, 1950–1980. N.Y., Crown, [1981]. 531p.   **BD72**

Serves as a supplement to Haydn and Fuller's work (above), giving the plot, theme, or summary of the central thesis "of the most important books of all types and genres" *(Introd.)* from the 1950–80 period.   Z1035.A1W4

Keller, Helen Rex. Reader's digest of books. New and greatly enl. ed. N.Y., Macmillan, 1929. 1447p.   **BD73**

Frequently reprinted.

Earlier edition (1917. 941p.) was also issued as v.29 of the *Warner library* (BD42). Separately published in 1922.

Synopses of the outstanding works, fiction and nonfiction, of many countries and periods. In two alphabets; the supplementary alphabet, p.925–1423, contains the new material added in the 1929 edition, and is indexed in a separate index.   PN44.K4

Magill, Frank Northen. Masterpieces of world literature in digest form. N.Y., Harper, 1952–69. ser.1–4.   **BD74**

1st ser., 1952; 2d ser., 1956; 3d ser., 1960; 4th ser., 1969.

1st–4th ser. also published as *Masterplots . . . plots in story form from the world's fine literature* (N.Y., Salem Pr., 1954–68. 8v.)

Each volume arranged alphabetically by title of work. Indicates type of work, author, time, locale, date first published, principal characters, critique, the story.

Kept up-to-date by: PN44.M3

Masterplots annual volume, 1954–76. Ed. by Frank N. Magill. N.Y., Salem Pr., 1955–77. v.1–22.   **BD75**

Title varies: 1954, *Masterplots annual review.*

"Essay-reviews of 100 outstanding books published in the United States. . . ."—*title page.*

"Combined editions" were published from time to time, with a final cumulation as noted below.

Continued by: Z1219.M33

Magill's Literary annual. 1977– . Englewood Cliffs, N.J., Salem Pr., 1978– . Annual.   **BD76**

1977 ed. in 2v.

Frank N. Magill, ed.

"In a sense, the new series is a continuation of the MASTERPLOTS Annuals [above]—begun in 1954 and concluded with the 1976 volume, now all collected in SURVEY OF CONTEMPORARY LITERA-TURE (1977)."—*Pref. 1977.*   Z1219.M33

Magill, Frank Northen. Survey of contemporary literature. Rev. ed. Englewood Cliffs, N.J., Salem Pr., [1977]. 12v.   **BD77**

1st ed. 1972.

Subtitle: Updated reprints of 2,300 essay-reviews from Masterplots annuals, 1954–1976, and Survey of contemporary literature supplement; with 3,300 bibliographical reference sources.

Arranged by title of the work, with author index in v.12.   PN44.M34

Olbrich, Wilhelm. Der Romanführer. Stuttgart, Hiersemann, 1950–84. 17v.   **BD78**

A compilation of digests in German of novels and short stories from many countries. Index in v.15.   PN44.O5

Directories

Gerstenberger, Donna Lorine and **Hendrick, George.** Fourth directory of periodicals publishing articles on English and

American literature and language. Chicago, Swallow Pr., 1975. 234p.   **BD79**

1st ed. 1959.

A guide for scholars in placing manuscripts for publication. Indicates editorial policy of the journal, with notes on submitting manuscripts, etc.   Z2015.P4G4

Harmon, Gary L. and **Harmon, Susanna M.** Scholar's market: an international directory of periodicals publishing literary scholarship. Columbus, Publications Committee, Ohio State University Libraries, 1974. 703p.   **BD80**

A directory and guide for the literary scholar wishing to place a manuscript for publication in a periodical. Publications are grouped according to field of interest: e.g., periodicals devoted to a single author or group of writers, those concentrating on literature of a single country or period, those concerned with a specific literary genre, etc. Includes sections for American ethnic minorities, folklore, and film. Concerned only with periodicals which publish wholly or partly in English. Indexed. Now considerably in need of updating.   Z6513.H37

Literary market place, 1940– . The business directory of American book publishing. N.Y., Bowker, 1940– . Annual.   **BD81**

For full information *see* AA353.

Writers' and artists' year book. 1906– . A directory for writers, artists, playwrights, writers for film, radio and television, photographers and composers. London, Black; N.Y., Macmillan, 1906– . v.1– . Annual.   **BD82**

Subtitle varies slightly.

Contains lists of English, Commonwealth, and South African journals and magazines, with statement of kind of material accepted by each and rate of payment, lists of publishers, literary agents, markets for writers, plays, films, broadcasting artists, photographers, musicians, etc., and other kinds of directory material useful to writers desiring to place manuscripts.   PN12.W8

Writer's handbook. 1936– . Boston, Writer, 1936– . Annual.   **BD83**

Now in four parts, the first three made up of articles which appeared originally in *The writer,* on various phases of professional writing, including fiction, nonfiction, and specialties. Some articles are carried over from earlier editions, some are new, none are dated.

Pt.4 is a market guide, mainly to the periodical field, giving for each periodical: address, editor, and type of material accepted with indication of rate of payment. Also has section for radio and television, and for book publishers. Revised annually.   PN137.W73

Literary awards

Bufkin, E. C. Foreign literary prizes: Romance and Germanic languages. N.Y., Bowker, 1980. 300p.   **BD84**

A selected list of prizes with descriptive notes and full lists of recipients. Prizes included are meant to be "representative of the famous and the obscure, the old and the recent, the discontinued and the continuing."—*Pref.* Arranged by country; indexed.   PN171.P75B8

Literary and journalistic awards in Canada. Les prix de littérature et de journalisme au Canada. 1923–1973. Ottawa, Statistics Canada, Education, Science and Culture Div., Fine Arts and Media Section, 1976. 276p.   **BD85**

"Published by authority of the Minister of Industry, Trade and Commerce."—*t.p.*

Each award is described and a list of recipients is given in chronological order. Literary and journalistic awards are listed separately, each group arranged by type of award. Alphabetical lists of the awards and of names of recipients serve as indexes.   PR9184.8.C36

Literary and library prizes. 1935– . N.Y., Bowker, 1935– . Irregular. (10th ed. 1980)   **BD86**

Title varies. 1935 and 1939 editions were edited by Bessie Graham with title *Famous literary prizes and their winners*. [3d ed.], 1946, had title *Literary prizes and their winners*.

Lists literary and library awards, grants, etc., of the United States, Canada, and Great Britain, giving some explanation and background of the award and a record of the recipients for each since its establishment. (Library awards first appeared in the 4th ed., 1959.)
PN171.P75L5

World dictionary of awards and prizes. London, Europa, [1979]. 386p. **BD87**

For full information *see* CB314.

Handbooks

Ackermann, Alfred Seabold Eli. Popular fallacies; a book of common errors explained and corrected, with copious references to authorities. 4th ed. London, Old Westminster Pr., 1950. 843p. **BD88**

1st ed. 1907.
An informative and sometimes amusing potpourri of facts arranged under broad headings such as food, weather, literature, etc. Subject index. AZ999.A3

Brewer, Ebenezer Cobham. Brewer's [Dictionary of phrase and fable. Centenary ed., rev. by Ivor H. Evans. N.Y., Harper & Row, [1981]. 1213p. **BD89**

1st ed. 1870; "Centenary ed." 1970.
A useful and fascinating collection of brief entries for colloquial and proverbial phrases, biographical and mythological references, fictitious characters, titles, etc., giving origin, derivation or meaning, as appropriate. Much revised over the years, successive editors having "modified the text, deleted the obsolete or more trifling entries and added new material, especially contemporary phrases." —*Pref.* Older editions will prove occasionally useful since much material has been dropped in the course of numerous revisions.
PN43.B65

———— Reader's handbook of famous names in fiction, allusions, references, proverbs, plots, stories, and poems. New ed. rev. and greatly enl. London, Chatto; Philadelphia, Lippincott, 1899. 1243p. (Repr.: Detroit, Gale, 1966. 2v.) **BD90**

Still a useful handbook. An 1898 edition includes (p.1245–1501) two useful appendixes omitted from later issues: (1) List of English authors and their works, and (2) Title list of dramas and operas, giving authors and dates. PN43.B7

Freeman, William. Dictionary of fictional characters. Rev. by Fred Urquhart. With indexes of authors and titles by E. N. Pennell. London, Dent, 1973, Boston, The Writer, [1974]. 579p. **BD91**

1st ed. 1963; author and title indexes by J.M.F. Leaper separately issued 1965.
A listing of some 20,000 fictitious characters from approximately 2,000 books by some 500 British, Commonwealth, and American authors, written in the last 600 years. Covers novels, short stories, poems, and plays. This edition omits characters from numerous Victorian novels no longer read, and adds characters from various contemporary works and from older works previously ignored. The index enables one to find the names of principal characters when only the author or title of a work is known. PR19.F7

Magill, Frank N. Cyclopedia of literary characters. N.Y., Harper, [1963]. 1280p., xivp., 50p. **BD92**

"Also appears under title of *Masterplots cyclopedia of literary characters*."—*verso of title page*.
Arranged by title of work; gives the characters of each book with brief descriptions of each. Includes books of all periods from the ancient Greeks to the 20th century, with an author index and a character index. PN44.M3

Shankle, George Earlie. American nicknames, their origin and significance. 2d ed. N.Y., Wilson, 1955. 524p. **BD93**

1st ed. 1937.
Not limited to nicknames of persons, but includes also those applied to places, institutions, or objects, arranged by real names with cross references from nicknames. Information under the real names includes some explanation of the nicknames and their origin, and gives references to sources of information in footnotes.
E179.S545

❖The above are popular handbooks, useful mainly as first sources to check. Important information will also be found in periodicals of the "notes and queries" type. The following may be especially helpful:

American notes and queries. New Haven, Conn., 1962– . v.1– . Monthly (except July and Aug.). **BD94**

Lee Ash, ed.
A publication unrelated to the earlier *American notes and queries* ed. by Walter Pilkington and B. Asterlund (North Bennington, Vt., 1941–50. 8v.).
Includes questions and answers, mainly literary; book reviews; notes on foreign reference books; etc.
Subscription originally included an annual index, now no longer published. A cumulated author, title, and subject index for v.1–12 (1962–74) was published in eye-legible copy by General Microfilm Co., Cambridge, Mass., and a second decennial index for v.13–22 is promised; meanwhile, 2-year indexes may be purchased separately.

L'intermédiaire des chercheurs et curieux, correspondance littéraire, historique et artistique, questions et réponses, lettres et documents inédits . . . Paris, 1864–1940. v.1–103. il. Semimonthly; frequency varies. **BD95**

———— Table générale (t.1–34, 1864–96; t.35–82, 1897–1920; t.83–96, 1921–33). Paris, 1897, 1924, 1935. 3v.

Ceased publication. AG309.I6

L'intermédiaire des chercheurs et curieux; mensuel de questions et réponses historiques, littéraires, artistiques et sur toutes autres curiosités. Paris, Chercheurs et Curieux, 1951– . année 1– . Monthly. **BD96**

Title varies: 1951–55, *Chercheurs et curieux*.
A monthly, beginning with Apr. 1951, modeled on the preceding item. Designed to print answers to questions asked by readers. The Dec. issue includes an annual index by keywords. AG305.I64

———— Supplément 1960: Table décennale I (1951–1960), ed. by Joseph Valynseele. Paris, 1965. 316 col.

The first cumulative index for the new series.

Notes and queries, for readers and writers, collectors and librarians, 1849– . London, Oxford Univ. Pr., 1850– . v.1– . Monthly. **BD97**

Imprint and title vary; earlier subtitle: A medium of communication for literary men, artists, antiquarians and genealogists.
Weekly until June 1942; fortnightly July 1942–52. Formerly grouped in series of 12v. each, but since the beginning of the thirteenth series (1923) volumed continuously. An index to each volume, and a general index for each six years until 1935. The index for July 1935–Dec. 1947 was published in 1v. in 1955.
Contains a large amount of interesting and often very valuable information on out-of-the-way questions—usually small points in general and local history and literature, bibliography, manners, customs, folklore, local observances, quotations, proverbs, etc. Much of the information is in the form of signed answers to questions from readers, and sources of information are given. Indexes are well made and detailed, and should be used constantly as supplements to the handbooks of allusions, quotations, proverbs, etc. AG305.N7

❖Local periodicals of this type are also useful for small points in the literature, biography, history, etc., of their special localities. For titles of English county "notes and queries," *see Bibliography of British history: Tudor period*, ed. by Conyers Read, 2d ed. 1959, p.355–409 (DC267).

Biographies of authors

❖The main sources for biographical sketches of authors of any country are the encyclopedias and national biographical dictionaries of the country. For special dictionaries of authors of a particular country, *see* the name of that country in this section. *See also* Dictionaries and encyclopedias, p.411–13. Following is a brief list of author dictionaries which are international in scope:

The bibliophile dictionary; a biographical record of the great authors, with bibliographical notices of their principal works from the beginning of history. Detroit, Gale, 1966. 2v. in 1. unpaged.   **BD98**

Originally appeared as the final two volumes of the 30-volume *Bibliophile library of literature, art, and rare manuscripts* (N.Y., 1904).

The "bibliographical notices" offer critical or descriptive comments on the individual works of an author but no bibliographical details beyond date of publication.   PN41.B5

Contemporary authors; a bio-bibliographical guide to current authors and their works. Detroit, Gale, 1962– . v.1– .   **BD99**

For full information *see* AJ48.

Gives bio-bibliographical sketches of living authors who, for the most part, write in the English language. A few foreign writers are included.   Z1224.C6

Dizionario letterario Bompiani degli autori, di tutti i tempi e di tutti le letterature. Milano, Bompiani, 1956–57. 3v. il.   **BD100**

A companion set to the *Dizionario letterario Bompiani delle opere e dei personaggi* . . . (BD57). Contains biographical and critical sketches of some 6,000 authors, with listings of their important works but not works about them. Profusely illustrated.

An edition in French was published as: Z1010.D5

Dictionnaire biographique des auteurs de tous les temps et de tous les pays [par] Laffont-Bompiani. Paris, Soc. d'Édit. de Dictionnaires et Encyclopédies [1957–58]. 2v.   **BD101**

PN41.D48

European writers. William T. H. Jackson, ed., George Stade, ed. in chief. N.Y., Scribner, [1983–84]. v.1–4. (In progress)   **BD102**

Contents: v.1–2, The Middle Ages and the Renaissance (v.1, Prudentius to medieval drama; v.2, Petrarch to Renaissance short fiction); v.3–4, The age of reason and the enlightenment (v.3, René Descartes to Montesquieu; v.4, Voltaire to André Chénier).

These are the first volumes of what is to be an 11-volume set continuing the kind of coverage offered by *Ancient writers: Greece and Rome* (BD1391) and serving as a companion series to *American writers* (BD413) and *British writers* (BD573). Most of the signed essays which make up the volumes are concerned with individual authors but in v.1–2, for example, there are chapters such as "Arthurian legend," "Troubadours and trouvères," "Medieval satire," "Norse sagas," and "Renaissance short fiction." Articles of about 15,000 words were "written expressly for the general reader: that is, for high school, undergraduate, and graduate students, as well as for their teachers; for librarians and editors; for reviewers, scholars, and critics; for literary browsers; for people who want to repair either an erosion or a gap in their reservoir of knowledge." —*Pref.* Select bibliographies include editions, translations, background studies, and critical works.   PN501.E9

Great foreign language writers. Ed. by James Vinson and Daniel Kirkpatrick. N.Y., St. Martin's Pr., [1984]. 714p.   **BD103**

PN524.G74

Contemporary foreign language writers. Ed. by James Vinson and Daniel Kirkpatrick. N.Y., St. Martin's Pr., [1984]. 439p.   **BD103a**

The above are companion volumes in the publisher's "Great writers" series; both are highly selective as to authors included. For each writer there is a brief biographical note, a list of works by and about the writer, and a short critical essay signed by the contributor. Title index in each volume.   PN771.C585

Gubernatis, Angelo de. Dictionnaire international des écrivains du monde latin. Rome, Auteur, 1905. 1506p.   **BD104**

—— —— Supplément et index. Rome, Auteur, 1906. 254p.

Includes contemporary (at time of compilation) writers of Latin nationality—i.e., Belgian, French, Italian, Latin-American, Portuguese, Romanian, and Spanish, whatever the subject of their works —and non-Latin authors who have written on Latin subjects. Especially full for Italian names.

The supplement includes a subject index to both volumes.   Z1010.G93

Hargreaves-Mawdsley, William Norman. Everyman's dictionary of European writers. London, Dent; N.Y., Dutton, [1968]. 561p.   **BD105**

Offers brief biographical sketches of European writers of all periods (including some living authors). Influential writers on fields other than literature are also included.   PN451.H3

Kunitz, Stanley Jasspon and **Colby, Vineta.** European authors, 1000–1900; a biographical dictionary of European literature. N.Y., Wilson, 1967. 1016p. il.   **BD106**

967 biographies of European writers who were born after A.D. 1000 or died before 1925. Intended for the general reader. Brief bibliographies.   PN451.K8

Kunitz, Stanley Jasspon and **Haycraft, Howard.** Twentieth century authors, a biographical dictionary of modern literature; complete in one volume with 1850 biographies and 1700 portraits. N.Y., Wilson, 1942. 1577p. il.   **BD107**

Popularly written sketches, usually of some length, aiming to give information on "writers of this century of all nations, whose books are familiar to readers of English. No attempt has been made to include foreign authors on the basis of their reputation in their native lands or tongues; the criterion, in general, has been the degree of acceptance of their translated works in the United States and England."—*Pref.* Includes bibliographies by and about the author.   PN771.K86

—— and **Colby, Vineta.** Twentieth century authors . . . First supplement. N.Y., Wilson, 1955. 1123p.   **BD108**

700 new biographees have been added, and biographies and bibliographies in the basic volume have been brought up-to-date.

For companion volumes *see* BD111, BD113.

Magill, Frank N. Cyclopedia of world authors. [Rev. ed.] Englewood Cliffs, N.J., Salem Pr., 1974. 3v.   **BD109**

1st ed. 1958.

Treats the life and works of about 1,000 authors. Gives place and date of birth and death (when appropriate), list of works, a biographical sketch varying in length from 200 words to 1000, followed by a section of bibliographical references to biographical information.   PN41.M26

New Century cyclopedia of names, ed. by Clarence L. Barnhart with the assistance of William D. Halsey [and others]. N.Y., Appleton, 1954. 3v. (4342p.).   **BD110**

For full information *see* AJ37.

Wakeman, John, ed. World authors, 1950–1970; a companion to Twentieth century authors. N.Y., Wilson, 1975. 1594p. il.   **BD111**

A "companion" rather than a second "supplement" to *Twentieth century authors* (BD107) since it neither duplicates nor updates the biographical articles in that earlier work and its first supplement. Deals with 959 authors of literary importance or unusual popularity, "most of whom came to prominence between 1950 and 1970," but including "a number of writers whose reputations were made earlier, but who were absent from the previous volumes because of a lack of biographical information, or because their work was not then 'familiar to readers of English.' "—*Pref.*

As in the companion volumes, many of the authors provided autobiographical sketches; critical comment is generally fuller than in those earlier works. Bibliographies again list principal works and a selection of writings about each author. Articles are unsigned, but a list of contributors is supplied.

For a companion volume *see* BD113.　　　　　PN451.W3

Who was who among English and European authors. 1931–1949. Detroit, Gale, [1978]. 3v. (Gale composite biographical dictionary ser., 2)　　　　　**BD112**

"Based on entries which first appeared in 'The author's and writer's who's who & reference guide,' originally compiled by Edward Martell and E. G. Pine, and in 'Who's who among living authors of older nations,' originally compiled by Alberta Lawrence." —*t.p.*

The latest entry for each of the writers represented in the various volumes of *The author's & writer's who's who* have been reproduced, together with the entries from the 1931 Lawrence compilation. No attempt was made to establish death dates.　　　　PN451.W5

World authors, 1970–1975. Ed., John Wakeman. N.Y., Wilson, 1980. 894p. il.　　　　　**BD113**

"A volume in the Wilson authors series."—*t.p.*

A companion to *World authors 1950–1970* (BD111), not a supplement updating biographies found in that and earlier volumes of the series. "Most of the 348 authors included here are 'imaginative' writers—poets, novelists, dramatists—of literary importance and/or of exceptional popularity" (*Pref.*,) and most came to prominence in the 1970–75 period. Also included are "a number of philosophers, historians, biographers, critics, scientists, journalists, and others whose work seemed of sufficiently wide interest, influence, or literary merit." About a fifth of the authors have contributed autobiographical statements. Brief bibliographies.　　PN451.W67

The writers directory. [Ed.1]– , 1971/73– . London, St. James; N.Y., St. Martin's, [1970]– . Biennial (slightly irregular).　　　　　**BD114**

Gives "who's who" type information on "fiction and nonfiction writers, poets, dramatists, and others who have written and had published at least one full-length book in English."—*Pref., ed. 3.* A separate section lists the authors' names by "writing category." Includes many minor writers not found in other biographical sources.　　　　　PS1.W73

Indexes

Author biographies master index. 2d ed. Ed. by Barbara McNeil and Miranda C. Herbert. Detroit, Gale, [1984]. 2v.　　　　　**BD115**

Subtitle: A consolidated guide to biographical information concerning authors living and dead as it appears in a selection of the principal biographical dictionaries devoted to authors, poets, journalists, and other literary figures.

1st ed. 1978.

An index to some 650,000 entries in more than 225 biographical dictionaries and directories of writers. Much of the information in the *Children's authors and illustrators* volume of the same series is duplicated here.

The same publisher's *Twentieth-century author biographies master index,* ed. by Barbara McNeil (Detroit, Gale, 1984. 519p.) draws references from this work and adds new citations to later publications; it indexes some 170,000 biographical sketches.

Z5304.A8A88

Combs, Richard E. Authors: critical and biographical references; a guide to 4,700 critical and biographical passages in books. Metuchen, N.J., Scarecrow Pr., 1971. 221p.

BD116

Offers citations to critical and biographical passages in about 500

books and relating to more than 1,400 authors. Critical writings predominate.　　　　　PN524.C58

Havlice, Patricia Pate. Index to literary biography. Metuchen, N.J., Scarecrow Pr., 1975. 2v.　　　**BD117**

An index to biographical information on some 68,000 authors appearing in fifty volumes of collective biography and dictionaries of literature.　　　　　Z6511.H38

—— —— First supplement. Metuchen, N.J., Scarecrow Pr., 1983. 2v.

Provides references to about 53,000 authors in 57 volumes published 1969–81.

Literary criticism and authors' biographies; an annotated index. Comp. by Alison P. Seidel. Metuchen, N. J., Scarecrow Pr., 1978. 209p.　　　　　**BD118**

Provides references to biographical and critical materials appearing in collective works, volumes of literary history and criticism, etc. "Most entries refer to a chapter or discrete subchapter at least two pages long."—*Introd.* Aims not to duplicate indexing of volumes treated in Adelman and Dworkin (BD450), Bell and Baird (BD627), Combs (BD116), etc.　　　　　Z6511.L56

Weiner, Alan R. and **Means, Spencer.** Literary criticism index. Metuchen, N.J., Scarecrow Pr., 1984. 685p.

BD119

An index to bibliographies of literary criticism, giving references to the bibliographies and checklists, not direct citations to the critical studies (i.e., getting from this work to the actual criticism is a two-step process). Indexes 86 bibliographies and guides to criticism. Arranged by literary author with subdivisions for individual works.

Z6511.W44

Quotations

❖Books of quotations are important in any reference collection for: (1) identifying a given quotation and verifying the wording; (2) suggesting quotations about a particular subject or suitable for a special occasion; and (3) supplying quotable passages from the writings of given authors. The first is probably the most frequent need in libraries. As every book of quotations is necessarily selective, and as each includes something not given in others, the large library should keep the older works even when new and seemingly more comprehensive books are added to the reference collection. The small library, however, will find a much more limited supply quite adequate. If it has fairly recent editions of Bartlett's *Familiar quotations* (BD120) as the best chronological author list, and Stevenson's *Home book of quotations* (BD132) as a useful subject list, and one or two other volumes such as the *Oxford dictionary of quotations* (BD129), it is well equipped for ordinary reference work for English as well as for a general selection of foreign quotations.

The reference value of a book of quotations depends upon three things: (1) the comprehensiveness of the collection and the care and judgment with which the quotations have been chosen; (2) the exactness of reference with which the quotations are given, i.e., the reference should be not merely to the author, but to the special work and its chapter, section, stanza, etc.; and (3) the completeness of the index. Because the most frequent use of such books is for the purpose of locating a given quotation, the index should include every significant word in each quotation which a reader is at all likely to remember.

Additional sources for quotations which should not be overlooked are: (1) the unabridged dictionary which gives quotations to show the history and usage of words, e.g., the *Oxford English dictionary* (AD25), which is a prime source for quotations from medieval times to the 20th century; (2) question-and-answer periodicals, such as *Notes and queries* (BD97) and *L'intermédiaire des chercheurs* (BD96), through which many quotations are located; and (3) author concordances and dictionaries, helpful when the author is known or surmised.

Inasmuch as general collections of quotations so often include proverbs, maxims, aphorisms, etc., foreign-language collections of proverbs have been included in this section rather than in the "Proverbs" section which follows.

General collections

Bartlett, John. Familiar quotations: a collection of passages, phrases and proverbs traced to their sources in ancient and modern literature. 15th and 125th anniversary ed., rev. & enl. Ed. by Emily Morison Beck. Boston, Little, Brown, [1980]. 1540p.   **BD120**

1st ed. 1855; 11th ed., rev. by Christopher Morley and L. D. Everett, 1937; 12th ed., rev. and enl. by Morley and Everett, 1948; 13th and centennial ed., 1955.

A standard collection, comprehensive and well selected. Arranged by authors chronologically, with exact references. Includes many interesting footnotes, tracing history or usage of analogous thoughts, the circumstances under which a particular remark was made, etc. The index is especially fine, containing an average of four or five entries per quotation.

One of the best books of quotations with a long history. The 11th ed. almost doubled the size of the 10th ed.; the 12th ed. is the same as the 11th up to p.787, but after that it is re-edited to include new authors, particularly contemporary authors, additional quotations, etc. The miscellaneous section, Addenda, is also enlarged by the inclusion of both old and new quotations. The 13th, or Centennial, edition was thoroughly revised by the staff of the publishing firm. The chronological arrangement by author was maintained, and all quotations integrated into one listing except for quotations from anonymous works, the Bible, the Book of Common Prayer, and the Koran. The 14th ed. again showed extensive revision, adding quotations from both old and new sources and with additional subject indexing; it follows a single chronological sequence (the Book of Common Prayer being inserted after the Bible).

In recent editions many quotations previously included have been omitted, and many new ones added. Earlier editions should not be discarded, as they will include quotations not found in the latest edition.

The revised and updated 15th edition is presented in a larger format which accommodates more quotations per page, but it retains the arrangement of the previous edition. More than 400 new authors from periods throughout history have been added; both the "Anonymous" and Bible sections have been enlarged; and the number of quotations from the Koran and ancient Buddhist and Sanskrit writings have been increased; and some quotations are presented in new translations. Author and keyword indexes.
PN6801.B27

Benham, *Sir* **William Gurney.** Benham's Book of quotations, proverbs, and household words. New and rev. ed. with suppl. and full indexes. N.Y., Putnam, [1949]. 1384p.
BD121

1st ed. 1907; 2d rev. ed. 1936.

Contains: (1) Quotations, British and American, p.1–440; (2) Bible and Book of Common Prayer, p.441–65; (3) "Waifs and strays," e.g., political phrases, epitaphs, London street sayings, bell inscriptions, etc., p.466–512; (4) Foreign (Greek, Latin, German, Italian, Spanish, Dutch), p.513–764; (5) Proverbs, p.765–928; and (6) Index, p.929–1259.

Includes about 30,000 quotations. Frequently reprinted with little change. In the 1949 edition, the main part of the work is substantially the same as in the 1936 edition, with some errors corrected and dates of death added. A supplement with its own index has been added. While this supplement includes a few recent quotations of modern authors, it is largely devoted to additional quotations of authors included in the main work.   PN6080.B35

Brussell, Eugene E. Dictionary of quotable definitions. Englewood Cliffs, N.J., Prentice-Hall, [1970]. 627p.
BD122

A collection of definitions in which "aphorism and metaphor replace the straight dictionary meaning." Alphabetically arranged by subject categories. Author of the definition is indicated, but the specific source is not cited.   PN6081.B77

Evans, Bergen. Dictionary of quotations. N.Y., Delacorte, [1968]. 2029p.   **BD123**

Follows a topical arrangement similar to Stevenson's *Home book of quotations* (BD132). The "subject index" is basically a keyword index with the addition of references to names or terms which occur in the explanatory notes rather than in the actual quotations. An author index is also provided. A useful addition to the standard collections.   PN6081.E9

The dictionary of biographical quotation of British and American subjects. Ed. by Richard Kenin and Justin Wintle. N.Y., Knopf, 1978. 860p.   **BD124**

Intended "to give an impression of the rich diversity of the things people have written and said about one another."—*Introd.* Quotations have been drawn from a wide range of sources and are arranged under name of the person who is the subject of the quotation. Index of persons quoted.   CT773.D38

Great treasury of Western thought; a compendium of important statements on man and his institutions by the great thinkers in Western history. Ed. by Mortimer J. Adler and Charles Van Doren. N.Y., Bowker, 1977. 1771p.
BD125

A collection of quotations selected on the principle that each passage quoted should be "a seminal statement about one of the great ideas in the tradition of Western thought."—*Pref.* Quotations are often long ones, the average length being about 100 words. Functions as a companion to the *Syntopicon* volumes of the *Great books of the Western world* series (BD39). Arranged in twenty chapters (Man, Family, Love, Emotion, Mind, Knowledge, etc.) with introductory notes for each chapter and subsection. Overall subject and proper name index.   PN6331.G675

Hoyt, Jehiel Keeler. Hoyt's New cyclopedia of practical quotations drawn from the speech and literature of all nations, ancient and modern, classic and popular, in English and foreign text. With . . . copious indexes; compl. rev. and greatly enl. by Kate Louise Roberts. N.Y., London, Funk & Wagnalls, 1922. 1343p.   **BD126**

1st ed. 1882; 2d ed. enl. 1896. Reissued in 1940 with a few corrections and the addition of death dates for some authors in the author list. The "New 1947 Edition" published by Somerset Books, N.Y., is practically unchanged.

Contents: (1) Quotations, arranged alphabetically by general subjects; (2) Index of quoted authors, with brief biographical data; (3) Concordance of quotations.

A very comprehensive collection of some 21,000 quotations given with exact references. Omits quotations from the Bible. The indexes are excellent. Though now more than 50 years old, still useful except for contemporary writers.   PN6081.H7

Magill, Frank Northen, ed. Magill's Quotations in context. N.Y., Harper, 1966. 1230p., xxvip.   **BD127**

An attempt to go beyond mere identification of the source of a quotation and to elucidate the meaning by providing background remarks or summary of the original context. Some 2,000 quotations are included in alphabetical arrangement, with keyword and author indexes. Sources, author, date of first appearance, and type of work are indicated for each. Owing to the comparatively limited number of quotations dealt with, the work is chiefly useful as a supplement to the standard books of quotations.   PN6081.M29

——— ——— 2d ser. N.Y., Harper, [1969]. 1350p.

An extension rather than a revision of the earlier volume. Contains an additional 1,500 quotations. PN6081.M292

Mencken, Henry Louis. A new dictionary of quotations on historical principles from ancient and modern sources. N.Y., Knopf, 1942. 1347p. **BD128**

A comprehensive collection with emphasis on the lesser-known quotations. Includes many proverbs and some foreign quotations, mainly in English translation. Arranged by rubric with many cross references to allied headings. Quotations are dated whenever possible and arranged chronologically under rubric. An attempt has been made to trace each quotation to its earliest usage. No index. Gives name of author and title of work, but not exact reference. PN6081.M49

The Oxford dictionary of quotations. 3d ed. Oxford, Oxford Univ. Pr., 1979. 907p. **BD129**

1st ed. 1941.

A thorough revision with numerous deletions and many new authors represented; about 60 percent of the contents of the 2d ed. (1953) is retained. This is a comprehensive collection of quotations arranged in one alphabetical sequence of authors writing in English, foreign authors, the Bible, the Prayer Book, and anonymous works. "The claim that this is a dictionary of *familiar* quotations" (*Pref.*) is dropped with this edition. Proverbs and nursery rhymes are omitted, these being covered in the *Oxford dictionary of English proverbs* (BD183) and the *Oxford dictionary of nursery rhymes* (BD658). References to sources are sometimes more precise than in the previous edition. "In the interests of book-production economy the index is neither as intensive nor as extensive as in the second edition, but it still occupies over a third of the volume and contains nearly 70,000 entries." The index now includes an indication of the author's name as well as the page reference; there is again a separate Greek index.

An abridged version, *The concise Oxford dictionary of quotations* (2d ed., N.Y., Oxford Univ. Pr., 1982), offers about 5,800 quotations and is well suited to the home library and for student use. PN6081.O9

The quotable woman, 1800–1981. Comp. and ed. by Elaine Partnow. N.Y., Facts on File, [1982]. 602p. **BD130**

1st ed. (1977) had title: *The quotable woman, 1800–1975;* the new edition is basically a reprinting of that work with the addition of a supplement (pp.473–520) and indexes which incorporate references to the supplement.

A book of quotations by women. Contributors were chosen on the basis of "reputation, remarkability, quotability, and availability of their work" (*Pref.*), with an attempt to be as representative of as many professions and countries as possible; "usability" was one of the principal criteria for selecting the quotations. Arrangement is chronological by birth date of the women quoted, then alphabetically within each year. Rather than keyword indexing, a "subject index" is provided which attempts "to synthesize the meaning of each quotation into one or more classifications." Occupying only pages 563–602 of the volume, this index makes for a great deal of trial and error in locating a specific remembered (or half-remembered) quotation. PN6081.5.Q6

Quotations in black. Anita King, comp. and ed. Westport, Conn., Greenwood Pr., [1981]. 344p. **BD131**

Quotations by black persons are arranged by author in chronological sequence of date of birth, and there is a separate section of proverbs arranged by country. Author and subject/key word indexes. The Reference and Subscription Books Review Committee's review in *Booklist* 78:1189 (May 1, 1982) notes inconsistencies in the keyword indexing. PN6081.3.O67

Stevenson, Burton Egbert. The home book of quotations, classical and modern. 10th ed. rev. N.Y., Dodd, 1967. 2816p. **BD132**

1st ed. 1934.

A comprehensive and well-chosen collection of more than 50,000 quotations, arranged alphabetically by subject with subarrangement by smaller topics. Usually gives exact citation. Includes an index of authors—giving full name, identifying phrase, and dates of birth

and death, with references to all quotations cited—and a word index, which indexes the quotation by leading words, usually nouns, though in some cases verbs and adjectives are also used. Bold-face entries are given for some of the smaller subjects. The quotations under these are not indexed separately, and one must, therefore, turn to the subject and run through the entries. This practice must be remembered when using this index.

The 10th ed. includes two appendixes: I, p.2273–98j (for the most part, added in the 5th ed.); and II, p.2298k–z, p.2299a–z (added in later editions). The quotations on these pages are indexed in a separate section at the end of the main index, p.2811–16.

The 3d ed. (1937) was a thorough revision of the first two editions, with the addition of more than 1,000 quotations, revision of notes, etc., and a much enlarged index.

Of other editions, the 5th (1947) and the 9th include the most revision. The 9th adds over 500 new entries, with clarification of others. The changes are in the appendixes and the separate index. PN6081.S73

Tripp, Rhoda Thomas. The international thesaurus of quotations. N.Y., Crowell, [1970]. 1088p. **BD133**

An attempt to adapt the basic principles of Roget's *Thesaurus* to the classification of quotations. The volume "is primarily intended for those who want to use quotations, rather than simply to read them or recall them to mind."—*Pref.* Arrangement, however, is not greatly different from that found in Stevenson's *Home book of quotations* (above), since entries are grouped under "idea categories" arranged alphabetically—though Tripp includes various terms and concepts (some of them more precise), as well as numerous quotations, not found in Stevenson. Thorough cross-referencing. PN6081.T77

What they said. 1969– . [Beverly Hills, Calif.], Monitor Book Co., 1970– . Annual. **BD134**

Subtitle: The yearbook of spoken opinion.

1979–80 not yet publ.

Presents the statements, ideas, and opinions of persons prominent in the news during the year in question. Quotations are grouped in subject categories within three main sections: (1) National affairs; (2) International affairs; and (3) General. Indexes of speakers and of detailed subjects. For each quotation the speaker is briefly identified, the circumstances of the quotation are indicated, and (with a few exceptions) reference is given to published appearance of the statement in the newspaper or periodical press of the nation. D410.W46

❖It is often said that the reference collection cannot include too many quotation books. While this is not literally true, a wide selection of such works will certainly prove useful in the large and medium-sized libraries. In addition to the items noted above, the following are worth consideration: *FPA book of quotations: a new collection of famous sayings, reflecting the wisdom and the wit of times past and present . . .*, by Franklin Pierce Adams (N.Y., Funk & Wagnalls, 1952); *The home book of American quotations*, by Bruce Bohle (N.Y., Dodd, 1967); *The quotation dictionary*, by Robin Hyman (N.Y., Macmillan, 1965); *The Kenkyusha dictionary of English quotations*, by Sanki Ichikawa, Masami Nishikawa, and Mamoru Shimizu (Tokyo, Kenkyusha, 1952); *The great quotations*, by George Seldes (N.Y., Stuart, 1960); *Comtemporary quotations*, by James Beasley Simpson (N.Y., Crowell, 1964); *The world treasury of religious quotations; diverse beliefs, convictions, comments, dissents and opinions from ancient and modern sources*, by Ralph Louis Woods (N.Y., Hawthorn, 1966); and *Treasury of Jewish quotations*, by Leo C. Rosten (N.Y., McGraw-Hill, 1972).

Foreign and classical

❖For some questions concerned with foreign and classical quotations, the great dictionaries of the language, the special dialect or period dictionaries, and the dictionaries or concordances of individual authors are the most useful sources. For example, the *Thesaurus linguae latinae* (AD540) contains many more quotations than could be found in even a very comprehensive dictionary of Latin quotations. The books of foreign quotations listed below are the easy first aids; for material not found in them, dictionaries within the various fields should be consulted.

Arabic and Persian

Field, Claud. Dictionary of oriental quotations (Arabic and Persian). London, Sonnenschein; N.Y., Macmillan, 1911. 351p. (Repr.: Detroit, Gale, 1969) **BD135**

Gives quotations in transliteration, arranged alphabetically by first word, with translations. Index of authors and index of subjects and catchwords, the latter not very full. Includes 85 authors.

PN6095.O7F6

Canadian

The dictionary of Canadian quotations and phrases. Comp. by Robert M. Hamilton and Dorothy Shields. Rev. & enl. ed. Toronto, McClelland & Stewart, [1979]. 1063p. **BD136**

1952 ed. (repr. 1965) had title *Canadian quotations and phrases.* A topically arranged collection (with topics in alphabetical sequence) of "quotations and phrases selected from predominantly Canadian sources," but including "those which originated with outside observers of the Canadian scene—British, American, French—from the beginnings of our [i.e., Canadian] history up to the present."—*Pref.* Index of authors and anonymous titles, but no keyword indexing. PN6081.H24

Chinese

Ch'êng yü k'ao. A manual of Chinese quotations, being a translation of the Ch'êng yü k'ao. With the Chinese text, notes, explanations and English and Chinese indices for easy reference by J. H. Stewart Lockhart. [2d ed.] Hong Kong, Kelly and Walsh, 1903. 645p., cxviip. **BD137**
PN6095.C4C5

Scarborough, William. Collection of Chinese proverbs, rev. and enl. by the addition of some six hundred proverbs, by C. Wilfrid Allan. Shanghai, Presbyterian Mission Pr., 1926. 381p. **BD138**

Classified arrangement. Subject index. PN6519.C5S4

Dutch

Groot literair citatenboek van Nederlandse en Vlaamse auteurs uit de 19e en 20e eeuw. Samengesteld door Gerd de Ley. Amsterdam, Loeb, [1982?]. 205p. **BD139**

Arranged by author of the quotation, with only a very brief keyword index. Sources are given in a separate author listing at the back of the book rather than immediately following the quotation.
PN6095.D8G76

Laan, Kornelis ter. Nederlandse spreekwoorden, spreuken, en zegswijzen. 'sGravenhage, G. B. Van Goor Zonen's Uitgeversmaatsch, 1950. 332p. **BD140**

A collection of Dutch proverbs and sayings, including many translated from other languages. Arranged alphabetically by keyword. Reference is usually given to source.

Margadant, S. W. F. Twintigduizend citaten, aphorismen en spreekwoorden. [2. druk] 'sGravenhage, Leopolds Uitgeversmij, [1952]. 741p. **BD141**

1st ed. 1935.

Includes some 20,000 quotations in Dutch, many of them translations from other languages for which the original is usually given. Sources include ancient and modern literatures, proverbs, maxims, etc. Arranged by topic with some cross references. No word index.
PN6080.M3

French

Dictionnaire des citations françaises. [Sous la direction de Pierre Oster] Paris, Robert, [1979]. 1626p. il. **BD142**

Arrangement is by century (preceded by a section for the Middle Ages), then alphabetically by author. Source of the quotation is indicated, sometimes citing chapter, act/scene of a play, etc., but reference is often only to the title of the source work. 16,460 quotations. Subject index. PN6086.D455

Dournon, Jean-Yves. Le grand dictionnaire des citations françaises. Paris, Acropole, [1982]. 906p. **BD143**

Quotations are grouped by key word; reference is given to author and title of the quotation source. Index of authors cited.
PN6086.D68

Encyclopédie des citations, [par] Paul Dupré. Comité de Rédaction sous la présidence de Fernand Keller. Paris, Éd. de Trévise, [1959]. 701p. **BD144**

Includes quotations from many languages and periods, all translated into French. References are usually to exact sources. An index of personal names, one by keywords, and one by ideas.

Genest, Émile. Dictionnaire des citations; dictionnaire des phrases, vers et mots célèbres employés dans le langage courant, avec précision de l'origine. Paris, Nathan, [1954]. 423p. **BD145**

Arranged alphabetically by first word of quotation with indexes by author and by subject. Citation is usually to exact reference. Apparently a somewhat enlarged edition of the author's *Où est-ce donc?* (Paris, Nathan, 1925). Another of the author's earlier works is *Les belles citations de la littérature française* (Paris, Nathan, 1923–27. 2v.). PN6086.G43

Guerlac, Othon Goepp. Les citations françaises; recueil de passages célèbres, phrases familières, mots historiques. 2. éd. rev. et augm. Paris, Colin, 1933. 458p. **BD146**

Arranged in main by authors, chronologically, with two alphabetical indexes: (1) authors; (2) catchwords. Includes modern as well as older quotations, gives exact references, and has many footnotes giving additional facts, e.g., parallel passages in other writers, etc.
PN6086.G8

Guterman, Norbert. A book of French quotations with English translations. Garden City, N.Y., Doubleday, 1963. 442p. **BD147**

Arranged chronologically by author, French quotations and English translations on opposite pages. Brief descriptive notes in English are given for the authors. Indexes of authors, of first lines in French, and of first lines in English. PN6086.G85

Harbottle, Thomas Benfield and **Dalbiac, P. H.** Dictionary of quotations (French and Italian). London, Sonnenschein; N.Y., Macmillan, 1901. 565p. (Repr.: N.Y., Ungar, 1958) **BD148**

Under each language arranged alphabetically by first word of quotation. Gives exact references to sources. Index of authors and of subjects. PN6086.H3

German

Büchmann, Georg. Geflügelte Worte; der Zitatenschatz des deutschen Volkes. . . . Fortgesetzt von Walter Robert-tornow, [et al.]. 32. Aufl. vollständig neubearb. von Gunther Haupt und Winifred Hofmann. Berlin, Haude & Spener, [1972]. 1039p. **BD149**

1st ed. 1866.

Arranged by country of origin with a name index and word indexes. PN6090.B8

Dalbiac, Lilian. Dictionary of quotations (German) with author and subject indexes. London, Sonnenschein; N.Y., Macmillan, 1906. 485p. (Repr.: N.Y., Ungar, 1958)
BD150

German quotations arranged alphabetically, with English translations; indexes by subject in English and German, and by author. PN6090.D3

Geflügelte Worte: Zitate, Sentenzen und Begriffe in ihrem geschichtlichen Zusammenhang. Kurt Böttcher [et al.]. Leipzig, Bibliographisches Institut, [1981]. 778p. **BD151**

Arranged by historical period, then by country and author. Notes characterizing the author precede the quotation, and notes on context, meaning, etc., follow. Non-German quotations are given in the original language with German translation; sources are cited. Includes many coined and compound words, familiar phrases, book titles, etc. Index of personal names and a German keyword index. P305.G43

Peltzer, Karl. Das treffende Zitat: Gedankengut aus drei Jahrtausenden nach Stichwörten geordnet. Thun und München, Ott Verlag, [1957]. 740p. **BD152**

A general quotation book in German, arranged in one catchword alphabet. In most cases sources are indicated. Numerous reprintings. PN6092.P4

Puntsch, Eberhard. Zitatenhandbuch. 5., überarb. u. erw. Aufl. [München], Moderne Verlags-GmbH, [1971]. 1056p.
BD153

More than 10,500 maxims, proverbs, aphorisms, etc., in a subject arrangement. No keyword index, and citations are frequently to author only, not to a specific work. All quotations are given in German. PN6090.P8

Schiff, Michael. Das grosse Handbuch moderner Zitate des XX. Jahrhunderts. [München], Moderne Verlags-GmbH, [1968]. 1013p. **BD154**

Quotations are grouped in 19 chapters (e.g., Zeit; Der geistige Mensch; Soziale Umwelt; Literatur; Geld) with numerous subdivisions, plus a "Stichwortverzeichnis." Includes quotations from many non-German sources, but all quotations are given in German. Exact source of the quotation is not cited. PN6092.S4

Greek

See Latin and Greek.

Italian

See also BD148.

Finzi, Giuseppe. Dizionario di citazioni latine ed italiane. Milano, Sandron, [1902]. 967p. (Repr.: Sala Bolognese, Forni, 1979) **BD155**

Subtitle: Citazioni latine; Detti proverbiali; Frasi e versi curiosi; Versi leonini e salernitani; Detti e motti storici e allegorici; Massime di diritto romano; Citazioni italiane.
8,560 entries arranged by rubric. Keyword index. References are usually to exact sources. PN6080.F5

Fumagalli, Giuseppe. Chi l'ha detto? Tesoro di citazioni italiane e straniere, di origine letteraria e storica. Aggiunte le frasi storiche della guerra 1914–18. 9.ed. Milano, Hoepli, 1946. 841p. **BD156**

1st ed. 1894.
Covers quotations in different languages, arranged by subject, with references to exact sources and some explantory notes. Indexes: (1) authors; (2) quotations. PN6080.F8

Giusti, Giuseppe and **Capponi, Gino.** Dizionario dei proverbi italiani. Milano, Veronelli, [1956]. 483p. **BD157**

Earlier editions had title *Raccolta de' proverbi toscani.* 1st ed., 1852, frequently reprinted up to 1913. This reprinting, with different title, is without significant change; paging and indexing seem to check exactly with 1871 edition.

Palazzi, Fernando and **Spaventa Filippi, Silvio.** Il libro dei mille savi: massime, pensieri, aforismi, paradossi di tutti i tempi e di tutti i paesi, accompagnati dal testo originale e dalle citazione delle fonti. 4. ristampa della 2. ed. con l'aggiunta di circa altri mille aforismi. Milano, Hoepli, 1955. 1095p. **BD158**

All quotations given in Italian, with general source (not exact citation); quotations in original language given in footnotes. Index of authors but no word index. Arranged by subject.

Spagnol, Elena, comp. Dizionario di citazioni. Frasi famose, aforismi, sentenze, massime di autori italiani e stranieri, antichi e moderni. Milano, Feltrinelli, 1971. 975p.
BD159

Topical arrangement with author index. Reference is to author and title of a work, with chapter, scene, etc., only occasionally indicated. All quotations are given in Italian. PN6095.I7S6

Japanese

Buchanan, Daniel Crump, ed. and tr. Japanese proverbs and sayings. Norman, Univ. of Oklahoma Pr., [1965]. 280p.
BD160

Proverbs are grouped under what are termed "Japanese characteristics" ("Aesthetics" through "Women"), with a subject index. The quotation is given in romanized Japanese, followed by a translation and explanation of its meaning and usage. PN6519.J3B8

Latin and Greek

Cree, Anthony. Cree's Dictionary of Latin quotations. [Topsfield, Mass.], Newbury Books, [1978]. 226p. **BD161**

An earlier version appeared as *Cree's Shorter dictionary of useful and familiar Latin quotations* (Oxford, 1974); this work is greatly expanded. Quotations are mainly from classical sources (which are cited), but "a considerable number of modern, religious, medical and legal latin tags" (*Introd.*) are also included. Arranged alphabetically by first word of the Latin quotation, but unfortunately there are no subject or keyword indexes in either Latin or English. PN6080.C67

Guterman, Norbert, comp. A book of Latin quotations with English translations. Garden City, N.Y., Anchor Books, [1966]. 433p. **BD162**

Arranged by author with Latin and English on facing pages. English subject index and Latin keyword index. PN6080.G8

Harbottle, Thomas Benfield. Dictionary of quotations (classical). London, Sonnenschein, 1906. 678p. (Repr.: N.Y., Ungar, 1958) **BD163**

The best dictionary of Latin and Greek quotations. Gives each in the original, with exact reference to source, and an English translation with name of translator. Indexes: (1) authors; (2) subjects, Latin; (3) subjects, Greek; (4) subjects, English. This edition includes an appendix, p.649–78. PN6080.H2

Ramage, Craufurd Tait. Beautiful thoughts from Greek authors, with English translations. London, Routledge, 1895. 589p. **BD164**

Also published under title *Familiar quotations from Greek authors* (Repr.: Detroit, Gale, 1968).
Arranged alphabetically by author, with quotations in Greek and in English translation. Exact citations to sources. English index. PN6080.R33

——— Beautiful thoughts from Latin authors, with English translations. London, Routledge, 1895. 855p. **BD165**

Also published under title *Familiar quotations from Latin authors* (Repr.: Detroit, Gale, 1968?).

Arranged alphabetically by author, with quotations in Latin and in English translation. Exact citations to sources. Latin and English indexes.   PN6080.R35

Persian

See Arabic and Persian.

Scandinavian

Langlet, Valdemar. Bevingade ord och slagord; efter olika källor sammanställda och förklarade. Stockholm, Geber, 1925–28. 2v.   **BD166**

Contents: v.1, Citat från främmande sprak. 499p.; v.2, Svenska citat. 680p.

Norsk sitatleksikon. 6000 bevingede ord. 2. rev. utgave ved Fr. Voss. Stavanger, Stabenfeldt Forlag, [1955]. 680col.
BD167

A general quotation book including not only Norwegian quotations, but many from various languages translated into Norwegian, followed by the original. Alphabetical by catchword subject. First-line indexes in Norwegian and in each of the other languages. Author index.   PN6095.N6N67

Spanish

Borras y Bemejo, Tomás and **Sáinz de Robles, Federico Carlos.** Diccionario de sabiduría; frases y conceptos. [2. ed.] Madrid, Aguilar, 1956. 1369p.   **BD168**

1st ed. 1953.
Arranged by subject, giving only name of author and no further citation to source. Subject and author indexes.

Clarasó Daudí, Noel. Antología de textos, citas, frases, modismos, y decires. Barcelona, Acervo, [1970]. 1082p.
BD169

In three main sections: (1) "Antología de textos" (arranged by author, then topically within each author section); (2) "Antología de citas" (topically arranged, with indication of author, but not specific work); (3) "Antología de modismos, frases hechas y cedires." Except for a separate section of Latin phrases, all quotations are given in Spanish. Author index, but no overall subject index.
Luis Iscla Rovira's *Spanish proverbs: a survey of Spanish culture and civilization* (Lanham, Md., Univ. Pr. of America, 1984. 301p.) is designed as a work for students of Spanish language and culture; it groups proverbs according to unifying themes or ideas, giving the proverbs in Spanish with English translations in a separate section.   PN6095.S5C6

Harbottle, Thomas Benfield and **Hume, Martin.** Dictionary of quotations (Spanish) with subject and authors' index. London, Sonnenschein; N.Y., Macmillan, 1907. 462p. (Repr.: N.Y., Ungar, 1958)   **BD170**

PN6095.S5H3

Martínez Kleiser, Luis. Refranero general, ideológico español. Madrid, Real Academia Española, 1953. 783p.
BD171

More than 65,000 entries arranged under concepts; gathered from other collections of proverbs with references to the collections.
PN6491.M25

Mir y Noguera, Juan. Diccionario de frases de los autores clásicos españoles. 1. ed. argentina con más de 70,000 locuciones. Buenos Aires, Gil, 1942. 1328p.   **BD172**

This Argentinian edition of a work previously published in Madrid in 1899 was revised and an index of authors and works from

which the phrases were taken was added. Arranged by rubric. Gives exact references to sources.   PC4650.M5

Sbarbi y Osuna, José María. Gran diccionario de refranes de la lengua española; refranes, adagios, proverbios, modismos, locuciones y frases proverbiales . . . corr. y publ. bajo la dirección de Manuel J. García. Buenos Aires, Gil, [1943]. 1028p.   **BD173**

Published 1922 under title *Diccionario de refranes, adagios* [etc.]. Arranged by rubric. No indexes.   PC4689.S3

Vega, Vicente. Diccionario ilustrado de frases célebres y citas literarias. Barcelona, Gustavo Gili, 1952. 939p. il.
BD174

Quotations, in various languages, arranged alphabetically under subjects, with indexes by topic, first word of quotation, and author. When phrases are given in other languages, Spanish translations are included. In some cases quotations are translated into Spanish and are not given in the original. Citations to exact sources are given irregularly.   PN6095.S5V4

Proverbs

❖Many types of books of proverbs, like those of quotations, are available. A number of the older works may still prove useful for historical purposes, but the very comprehensive Stevenson, *Home book of proverbs, maxims and familiar phrases* (BD184), and the *Oxford dictionary of English proverbs* (BD183), will now answer most of the general questions in this field. For books of proverbs of particular countries, *see* books of quotations of the country.

Bibliography

Mieder, Wolfgang. International proverb scholarship: an annotated bibliography. N.Y., Garland, 1982. 613p. (Garland folklore bibliographies, 3)   **BD175**

An author listing of 2,142 book and periodical citations, with name, subject, and proverb indexes. Annotations are often evaluative as well as descriptive.   Z7191.M543

———— Proverbs in literature: an international bibliography. Berne, P. Land, [1978]. 150p. (European university papers. Ser.1, German language and literature, v.218)
BD176

1,166 entries (books, articles, and academic theses) in two main sections: (1) general studies of proverbs in literature (including relevant dictionaries of proverbs and works dealing with more than one author) and (2) studies of individual literary authors arranged alphabetically by name of the author under consideration. Index of scholars' names.   Z6514.P76M53

Moll, Otto E. Sprichwörterbibliographie. Frankfurt am Main, Klostermann, [1957–58]. 630p.   **BD177**

An extensive bibliography of more than 9,000 items, arranged first by language, then by period, locality, etc. Besides the languages of Europe and America, the work includes those of Asia, Africa, the Pacific islands, etc. Contains dialect dictionaries as well as collections of proverbs. Author index.

Stephens, Thomas Arthur. Proverb literature; a bibliography of works relating to proverbs, ed. by Wilfrid Bonser . . . comp. from materials left by the late T. A. Stephens. . . . London, W. Glaischer, 1930. 496p. (Folk-lore Society. Publ. 89) (Repr.: Norwood, Pa., Norwood Eds., 1976)   **BD178**

An annotated bibliography of more than 4,000 works on the proverbs of all nations, including collections of particular localities and special subjects.   Z7191.S83

Collections

Apperson, George Latimer. English proverbs and proverbial phrases; a historical dictionary. . . . London, Dent; N.Y., Dutton, [1929]. 721p. **BD179**

Traces the history of English proverbs and proverbial phrases, through references to the literature. In one alphabetical arrangement, but in a twofold manner: (1) all proverbs which classify naturally under such headings as months and seasons, animals, birds, God, the Devil, sun, moon, rain, time, war, etc., are listed under these headings; (2) all other proverbs are alphabetical under their first main word. PN6421.A7

Champion, Selwyn Gurney. Racial proverbs; a selection of the world's proverbs arranged linguistically . . . with authoritative introductions to the proverbs of 27 countries and races. London, Routledge; N.Y., Macmillan, 1938. cxxixp., 767p. **BD180**

"Embodies the first and second series of [his] 'Wayside sayings.' "
—*Introd.* Authorities consulted, p.cix–cxxix.

Arranged by country with the following four indexes: (1) Linguistic and geographical, (2) Subject-matter, (3) Race, and (4) Alternative chief-word. The introduction to the proverbs of each country or race is by a specialist. PN6405.C37

Davidoff, Henry. A world treasury of proverbs, from twenty-five languages. N.Y., Random, [1946]. 526p. **BD181**

More than 15,000 proverbs and sayings from 25 languages, arranged by rubric with subject and author indexes. PN6405.D3

Gluski, Jerzy, comp. Proverbs. Proverbes. Sprichwörter. Proverbi. Proverbios. Poslovits'i. A comparative book of English, French, German, Italian, Spanish and Russian proverbs with a Latin appendix. Amsterdam [etc.], Elsevier, 1971. 448p. **BD182**

About 1,100 proverbs are grouped in 48 topical sections. English is used as the base language, with equivalent forms of the proverbs given in the other languages, and a keyword index from each language is provided. PN6404.G6

Oxford dictionary of English proverbs. 3d ed.; rev. by F. P. Wilson. Oxford, Clarendon Pr., 1970. 930p. **BD183**

1st–2d eds. (1935–48) by W. G. Smith.

The 1st ed. (1935) contained about 10,000 proverbs, arranged alphabetically by first word, including "a," "an," "the." Successive editions have been somewhat enlarged and some earlier sources noted. Proverbs are now alphabetized under significant words (usually the first), with the preceding words, if any, transferred to the end or, occasionally, to an intermediate point. Liberal cross references are included from all other significant words, usually with enough of the phrase so that it is readily identifiable. Many proverbs and examples from Tilley's *Dictionary* (BD187) have been incorporated into the 3d ed.

Dated references are given for each proverb to the earliest uses and sources found, with variant usages at succeeding times, shown by examples from the literature in the manner of the *Oxford dictionary.*

An abridged version, ed. by J. A. Simpson, has appeared as *The concise Oxford dictionary of proverbs* (N.Y., Oxford Univ. Pr., 1983); it is limited to about a thousand entries. PN6421.O9

Stevenson, Burton. The home book of proverbs, maxims and familiar phrases. N.Y., Macmillan, 1948. 2957p. **BD184**

Reprinted 1965 with title *The Macmillan book of proverbs, maxims and famous phrases.*

Attempts to trace back to their sources, proverbs, maxims, and familiar phrases in ordinary English and American use and to show their development.

Follows the pattern of the author's *Home book of quotations* (BD132), with subject arrangement and detailed word index. Very comprehensive, including more than 73,000 expressions from many languages and periods; many of them might be considered quotations, as the interpretation of proverb and maxim is very broad. Dates for proverbs are noted, and those from foreign sources are given in English translation followed by the original language (except for the oriental). Indexes at least one and sometimes more keywords.

The relatively inexpensive *Penguin dictionary of proverbs* by Rosalind Fergusson (London, Allen Lane & Penguin Books, 1983. 331p.) includes some 6,000 proverbs grouped by category, with keyword index. PN6405.S8

Taylor, Archer. The proverb. Cambridge, Harvard Univ. Pr., 1931. 223p. **BD185**

—— —— Index. Helsinki, Suomalainen Tiedeakatemia, 1934. 105p. (FF [Folklore Fellows] communications, no.113) (Repr. in 1v.: Hatboro, Pa., Folklore Associates; Copenhagen, Rosenkilde & Bagger, 1962. 223p., 105p.)

The main volume discusses the origin, content, and style of proverbs. The index lists the proverbs mentioned with reference to page and also to the treatment in other collections of proverbs. PN6401.T3

—— and **Whiting, Bartlett Jere.** A dictionary of American proverbs and proverbial phrases, 1820–1880. Cambridge, Belknap Pr. of Harvard Univ. Pr., 1958. 418p. **BD186**

An alphabetically arranged dictionary, listing proverbs by what is considered the most important word, illustrated with many examples from American literature, 1820–80. PN6426.T28

Tilley, Morris Palmer. A dictionary of the proverbs in England in the 16th and 17th centuries; a collection of the proverbs found in English literature and the dictionaries of the period. Ann Arbor, Univ. of Michigan Pr., 1950. 854p. **BD187**

Contains some 11,780 proverbs arranged by catchword. Each proverb is followed by citations arranged chronologically. Contains a bibliography of the works cited, an index of Shakespearean quotations appearing in the text, and an index of significant words in the proverbs. PN6420.T5

Whiting, Bartlett Jere. Early American proverbs and proverbial phrases. Cambridge, Mass., Belknap Pr. of Harvard Univ. Pr., 1977. 555p. **BD188**

Serves as a chronological predecessor to Taylor and Whiting's *Dictionary of American proverbs and proverbial phrases* (BD186), covering the first decades of the 17th century to 1820. Although entries are derived from American sources, the compiler points out that prior to 1820, American proverbs were basically English and he states that "It is not to oversimplify to say that the contents of this book are English proverbs used by writers who happened to be in North America at the time."—*Introd.* Method of entry follows that of the Taylor/Whiting volume. Examples are drawn from the long list of works cited p.xxiii–lxiv. PN6426.W5

—— Proverbs, sentences, and proverbial phrases; from English writings mainly before 1500. Cambridge, Belknap Pr. of Harvard Univ. Pr., 1968. 733p. **BD189**

Drawn from published sources mainly written before 1500. A common form of the proverb or saying (entered alphabetically by keyword) is followed by variants, with reference to printed sources and date of usage. Index of important words. PN6083.W45

Children's literature

See also AA306–AA315, BD213, BD295–BD300, BD658.

Carpenter, Humphrey and **Prichard, Mari.** The Oxford companion to children's literature. Oxford & N.Y., Oxford Univ. Pr., 1984. 588p. il. **BD190**

Offers articles on authors and illustrators of children's books, genres of children's literature, characters, and individual titles, together with "very brief summaries of the state of children's literature in all languages, countries and continents" *(Pref.),* as well as accounts of early school books and entries for recurring subjects of children's reading matter. Emphasis is on English and American materials, with those of Asia and Africa least thoroughly covered. Occasional references to scholarly work in the field, but no bibliography as such. PN1008.5.C37

Children's literature review. [v.1]– . Detroit, Gale, 1976– . Irregular. **BD191**

"Excerpts from reviews, criticism, and commentary on books for children and young people."—*t.p.*

Editors vary.

Each volume offers excerpts from reviews and criticism (from both books and periodicals) of some 20 to 40 authors. International in scope. Cumulative indexes to authors and titles in successive volumes. PN1009.A1C5139

Doyle, Brian, comp. The who's who of children's literature. London, Evelyn; N.Y., Schocken, [1968]. 380p. il. **BD192**

300 biographical sketches of the most notable authors and illustrators of children's books, from the early 19th century to the present day, with a few earlier writers included. Authors and illustrators in separate sections. PN452.D6

Fisher, Margery Turner. Who's who in children's books: a treasury of familiar characters of childhood. N.Y., Holt, Rinehart and Winston, [1975]. 399p. il. **BD193**

An avowedly personal selection of memorable characters from children's literature, "not intended primarily as a reference book." —*Pref.* Includes "as many as possible of the characters who have now become household names, together with others less familiar" whom the compiler found particularly interesting. Entries usually run to half a column or more in length, placing the character in setting and circumstances of the story, with comment on the author's technique or approach to the character.

PN1009.A1F575

Kunitz, Stanley Jasspon and **Haycraft, Howard.** The junior book of authors. 2d ed. rev. N.Y., Wilson, 1951. 309p. il. **BD194**

The 1st ed., 1934, included biographical or autobiographical sketches of some 268 writers and illustrators (living and deceased) for younger readers. The 2d ed. contains 289 sketches, of which 160 are repeated with revisions; the remaining 129 are new names which came into prominence after 1934. The 108 names dropped are largely in the field of the classics, e.g., Louisa M. Alcott, and the borderline group of books between adult and juvenile. All of these names are to be found in other Wilson biographical dictionaries, but libraries may wish to keep both editions on their shelves.

PN1009.A1K8

Fuller, Muriel. More junior authors. N.Y., Wilson, 1963. 235p. portraits. **BD195**

A companion volume to the above.

Includes sketches, many of them autobiographical, of 268 authors and illustrators of books for children and young people.

PN1009.A1F8

De Montreville, Doris and **Hill, Donna.** Third book of junior authors. N.Y., Wilson, 1972. 320p. il. **BD196**

A companion to the two preceding items, offering biographical information on 255 authors and illustrators.

An ongoing series providing biographical information about authors and illustrators of books for young people is *Something about the author* (Detroit, Gale, 1971– . Irregular), 37 volumes of which have been published through 1984. The set is heavily illustrated and recent volumes include cumulative author and illustrator indexes.

PN1009.A1D45

LaBeau, Dennis. Children's authors and illustrators: an index to biographical dictionaries. Detroit, Gale, [1976]. 172p. **BD197**

Provides an index to biographical sketches contained in 26 collections; with the exception of *Contemporary authors,* all of the publications indexed are wholly concerned with children's authors and illustrators. Employs many of the same sources indexed in *Author biographies master index* (BD115). Z1037.A1C463

Lexikon der Kinder- und Jugendliteratur; Personen- , Länder- und Sachartikel zu Geschichte und Gegenwart der Kinder- und Jugendliteratur. Hrsg. von Klaus Doderer. Weinheim und Basel, Beltz Verlag, [1974–81]. 4v. il.

BD198

"Erarbeitet im Institut für Jugendbuchforschung der Johann Wolfgang Goethe-Universität in Frankfurt/Main. Bibliographische Angaben unter Mitwirkung der Internationalen Jugendbibliothek in München."—*t.p.*

Contents: v.1–3, A–Z; [v.4] Ergänzungs- und Registerband.

An international encyclopedia of the history of children's literature with articles on individual authors, types of children's literature (including comics), publishers, specific topics, and children's literature in countries throughout the world. Signed articles; bibliographies. PN1009.A1L49

Twentieth-century children's writers. D. L. Kirkpatrick, ed. 2d ed. N.Y., St. Martin's Pr., [1983]. 1024p. **BD199**

1st ed. 1978.

Provides brief biographical notes, bibliographies of published writings, references to critical studies (if any), locations of manuscript collections, and a signed critical evaluation for each of some 700 English-language authors of fiction, poetry and drama for children and young people. "The main part of the book covers writers most of whose work was published after 1900; the appendix [p.857–89] is of some important representative writers of the 19th century."—[*p.xvii.*] There is also a brief section (p.893–97) on foreign-language writers. Title index.

Drama

See also Theater and performing arts, p.574–98, and subhead "Drama" under the various national literatures.

Bibliography

Boyer, Robert D. Realism in European theatre and drama, 1870–1920; a bibliography. Westport, Conn., Greenwood Pr., [1979]. 236p. **BD200**

Includes 62 dramatists of Austria, Belgium and Holland, England, France, Germany, Ireland, Italy, Norway and Sweden, Russia, and Spain, with entries listing an author's plays, together with books, articles, and dissertations concerning those works. Index to authors cited. Z5784.R27B69

Drury, Francis Keese Wynkoop. Drury's Guide to best plays. 3d ed. by James M. Salem. Metuchen, N.J., Scarecrow Pr., 1978. 421p. **BD201**

1st ed. 1953.

Lists about 1,600 plays. Intended as a guide for those producing plays (e.g., amateur groups) as well as a selection guide for libraries. Gives dates of first production or printing, editions (including anthologies or collections), description, plot, number of characters, information on royalties, etc. Includes various indexes and special lists. Z5781.D8

Horn-Monval, Madeleine. Répertoire bibliographique des traductions et adaptations françaises du théâtre étranger du XVe siècle à nos jours. Paris, Centre National de la Recherche Scientifique, 1958–67. 8v. and index. **BD202**

Contents: v.1, Théâtre grec antique; v.2, Théâtre latin antique. Théâtre latin médiéval et moderne; v.3, Théâtre italien. Opéras italiens (livrets); v.4, Théâtre espagnol; Théâtre de l'Amérique latine; Théâtre portugais; v.5, Théâtre anglais; Théâtre américain; v.6, Théâtre allemand; Théâtre autrichien; Théâtre suisse; v.7, Théâtre scandinave (danois, norvégien, suédois). Théâtre flamand; Théâtre hollandais; Pays nordiques (Estonie, Finlande, Islande, Lettonie, Litaunie); v.8, Théâtres des pays slaves et autres pays européens. Théâtres des pays d'Asie et d'Afrique. Addenda au théâtre américain; [v.9], Index général des auteurs dramatiques étrangers traduits et cités dans les huit tomes du Répertoire.

The various sections have their own indexes in addition to the general index at the end of the set.   Z2174.D7H6

Schwanbeck, Gisela. Bibliographie der deutschsprachigen Hochschulschriften zur Theaterwissenschaft von 1885 bis 1952. Berlin, Selbstverlag der Gesellschaft für Theatergeschichte, 1956. 563p. (Gesellschaft für Theatergeschichte. Schriften. Bd.58)   **BD203**

A classified list of 3,309 German dissertations on the drama and theater from antiquity to the present. Author and catchword index.   Z5781.S4

Shipley, Joseph Twadell. The Crown guide to the world's great plays, from ancient Greece to modern times. Rev., updated ed. N.Y., Crown, [1984]. 866p.   **BD204**

1st ed. (1956) had title: *Guide to great plays.*

A listing, by author, of several hundred "great" plays of all periods. For each a plot synopsis is given, with additional information on the play's history and production, excerpts from reviews, notes on famous casts, etc. In this edition numerous older plays were dropped and newer ones added (along with a number of older plays previously omitted); new critical notes and information on recent revivals have been added to many of the earlier entries.   PN6112.5.S45

Stratman, Carl Joseph. Bibliography of medieval drama. 2d ed., rev. & enl. N.Y., Ungar, [1972]. 2v.   **BD205**

1st ed. 1954.

Covers early liturgical forms, mystery and miracle plays, moralities, interludes, etc. Lists manuscripts, published texts, and various editions of individual plays, with critical studies of them, including academic dissertations. Sections on general works and *Festschriften* are followed by chapters devoted to liturgical Latin drama, English, Byzantine, French, German, Italian, Low Countries, and Spanish drama. The sections on Continental medieval drama "have been included on a selective basis, as the material is intended primarily as an aid for students of the English drama."—*Pref.*

Library locations are given for manuscripts and for most of the book materials. More than 9,000 entries; indexed.   Z5782.A2S8

Indexes

Dramatic index for 1909–49, covering articles and illustrations concerning the stage and its players in the periodicals of America and England and including the dramatic books of the year. Boston, Faxon, 1910–52. 41v. Annual.   **BD206**

Ceased publication.

Issued separately, and also as pt.2 of the *Annual magazine subject index*, 1909–49 (AE243). Contains the cumulation of the *Dramatic index* published in the quarterly numbers of the *Bulletin of bibliography.* v.1–8, 11–41 have appendix *Dramatic books and plays (in English)* published 1912–16, 1919–49.

An annual subject index to articles about the drama, the theater, actors and actresses, playwrights, librettists, managers, etc.; to synopses of plays; to reviews; and to stage and dramatic portraits, scenes from plays, and other theatrical illustrations contained in English and American periodicals; and to texts of plays whether published in book or magazine form. Magazine articles are entered under subject only; texts of plays are under title, or under the form heading "Dramas" with cross reference from author; costume portraits are under both the actor and the character. While the index nominally begins with 1909, some retrospective indexing is included. From 1912, the dramatic books of the year are indexed both in the main index and in the appendix, *Dramatic books and plays,* which consists of (1) author list of books about the theater, (2) author list of play texts, and (3) title list of texts.

A cumulation has been published as: AI3.M26

Cumulated Dramatic index, 1909–1949. A cumulation of the F. W. Faxon Company's Dramatic index. Ed. by Frederick W. Faxon, Mary E. Bates and Anne C. Sutherland. Boston, G. K. Hall, 1965. 2v.   **BD207**

Cumulates the 41 volumes of the *Dramatic index* (above), including the three appendixes.   Z5781.C8

Firkins, Ina Ten Eyck. Index of plays, 1800–1926. N.Y., Wilson, 1927. 307p.   **BD208**

A comprehensive index of 7,872 plays by 2,203 authors, showing where the text of each can be found in collections or other publications. Indexes only plays in English but includes translations of foreign plays. In two parts: (1) author index, giving full bibliographical information about each play, and, in many cases, number of acts and brief characterizations, as comedy, tragedy, social, domestic, etc.; (2) title and subject index, referring to the author list.

————— ————— Supplement, [1927–34]. N.Y., Wilson, 1935. 140p.

Indexes 3,284 plays by 1,335 authors.   Z5781.A1F5

Index to the Best plays series, 1899–1950, 1949–1960. N.Y., Dodd, 1950–61. 147p., 46p.   **BD209**

For full information *see* BD432.

Ireland, Norma Olin. Index to full length plays, 1944 to 1964. Boston, Faxon, 1965. 296p. (Useful reference series, no.92)   **BD210**

A companion volume to Ruth Thomson's *Index to full length plays* (BD218). In this compilation, "952 books have been indexed including 154 collections and 798 individual plays."—*Foreword.* Instead of the separate author, subject, and title indexes in the Thomson work, all three types of entries are found in a single alphabet. Numerous new subject headings have been added. There is a "list of collections analyzed . . . and key to symbols used" and a bibliography of individual plays analyzed.   Z5781.T52

————— An index to skits and stunts. Boston, Faxon, 1958. 348p. (Useful reference ser., no.88)   **BD211**

An author, title, and subject index to 148 collections (books and pamphlets). Some 800 subject headings are used, and cross references are numerous.   Z5781.I7

Keller, Dean H. Index to plays in periodicals. Rev. & expanded ed. Metuchen, N.J., Scarecrow Pr., 1979. 824p.   **BD212**

1st ed. 1971.

A finding aid for plays published in periodicals. Indexes 267 periodicals, usually from the beginning through 1976. Author listing with title index.   Z5781.K43

Kreider, Barbara. Index to children's plays in collections. 2d ed. Metuchen, N.J., Scarecrow Pr., 1977. 227p.   **BD213**

1st ed. 1972.

Indexes 1,450 plays appearing in collections published 1965–74. Indexing is by author, title, and subject in a dictionary arrangement. Cast analysis tables, p.181–220.   PN167.K7

Logasa, Hannah and **Ver Nooy, Winifred.** An index to one-act plays. Boston, Faxon, 1924. 327p. (Useful reference ser., no.30)   **BD214**

————— ————— Supplement. [1st–5th] Boston, Faxon, 1933 –64. 5v. (Useful reference ser., no.46, 68, 78, 87, 94)

Basic volume: Plays written in English or translated into English, published since 1900; Suppl., 1924–31; 2d suppl., 1932–40; 3d suppl., 1941–48; 4th suppl., 1948–57; 5th suppl., 1956–64.

Title, author, and subject indexes to one-act plays in collections, and also to separately published pamphlets. The 3d supplement includes radio plays; the 4th and 5th, radio and television plays.   Z5781.L83

Ottemiller, John Henry. Ottemiller's Index to plays in collections: an author and title index to plays appearing in collections published between 1900 and early 1975. 6th ed., rev. and enl. by John M. Connor and Billie M. Connor. Metuchen, N.J., Scarecrow Pr., 1976. 523p.   **BD215**

1st ed. 1943.

Contents: (1) Author index, giving name and dates, title of play, date of first production (or of first publication if never performed), references from original titles and variant translated titles, references from joint authors and translators, etc.; (2) List of collections analyzed and key to symbols; and (3) Title index, referring from all forms of titles, translated titles, and subtitles.

Indexes 3,686 different plays by 1,937 authors in 1,237 collections published in England and the United States between 1900 and early 1975. Includes plays from ancient to modern times. All editions of the same collection have been included when the contents of successive editions vary. Does not include collections of children's plays, amateur plays, one-act plays, holiday and anniversary plays and pageants, and radio and television plays, but such plays are indexed if they appear in one of the collections that is included. Partial and selected texts are omitted. Chinese and Japanese plays in translation are included for the first time in this edition. Z5781.O8

Patterson, Charlotte A., comp. Plays in periodicals: an index to English language scripts in twentieth century journals. Boston, G. K. Hall, 1970. 240p. **BD216**

Indexes more than 4,000 plays appearing in 97 periodicals during the period 1900–68. Title listing with author index. Z5781.P3

Play index, 1949–1952, 1953–1960, 1961–1967, 1968–1972, 1973–1977, 1978–1982. N.Y., Wilson, 1953–83. 6v. **BD217**

1949–1952, an index to 2,616 plays in 1,138 volumes, ed. by Dorothy H. West and Dorothy M. Peake; 1953–1960, an index to 4,952 plays in 1,735 volumes, ed. by Estelle A. Fidell and Dorothy M. Peake; 1961–1967, an index to 4,793 plays, ed. by Estelle A. Fidell; 1968–1972, an index to 3,848 plays, ed. by Estelle A. Fidell; 1973–1977, an index to 3,878 plays, ed. by Estelle A. Fidell; 1978–1982, an index to 3,429 plays, ed. by Juliette Yaakov.

Each volume in four parts: (1) the main list, arranged by author, title, and subject; (2) a list of the collections indexed; (3) cast analysis, listing each play under type of cast (male, female, mixed, puppet) and further by number of characters; (4) directory of publishers. All types of plays are indexed, including translations into English. The dictionary catalog arrangement and the large amount of subject indexing are particularly helpful. Z5781.P53

Thomson, Ruth Gibbons. Index to full length plays, 1895 to 1925. Boston, Faxon, 1956. 172p. (Useful reference ser., no.85) **BD218**

————— ————— 1926–1944. Boston, Faxon, 1946. 305p. (Useful reference ser., no.71)

Each of these companion volumes includes a title index—giving author, translator, number of acts, number of characters, subject, and scene—followed by author and subject indexes referring to the title index and a bibliography giving publisher, date, etc.

For a continuation see Ireland's work of the same title (BD210). Z5781.T5

Criticism

Adelman, Irving and **Dworkin, Rita.** Modern drama; a checklist of critical literature on 20th century plays. Metuchen, N.J., Scarecrow Pr., 1967. 370p. **BD219**

Stresses critical articles rather than reviews of productions. Includes parts of books as well as periodical articles. Z5781.A35

Breed, Paul Francis and **Sniderman, Florence M.** Dramatic criticism index; a bibliography of commentaries on playwrights from Ibsen to the avant-garde. Detroit, Gale, [1972]. 1022p. **BD220**

Includes "nearly 12,000 entries in English on 300 or more American and foreign playwrights, the majority of them from the twentieth century" (Pref.) and drawn from more than 600 books and over 200 periodicals. Arrangement is alphabetical by name of the playwright; title and critic indexes. Z5781.B8

Coleman, Arthur and **Tyler, Gary R.** Drama criticism. Denver, Alan Swallow, [1966–71]. 2v. **BD221**

Contents: v.1, A checklist of interpretation since 1940 of English and American plays; v.2, A checklist of interpretation since 1940 of classical and continental plays.

Another in the publisher's series of bibliographies of criticism and interpretation. Lists book and periodical materials. v.1 covers publications of 1940–64; v.2, 1950 to about 1968. Z1231.D7C6

Contemporary dramatists. 3d ed. James Vinson, ed. [London], Macmillan; [N.Y.], St. Martin's Pr., [1982]. 1104p. **BD222**

1st ed. 1972.

Offers biographical and critical notes on more than 300 living playwrights (plus entries for dramatists who have died since the 1950s), together with lists of their plays and other publications, and references to critical studies. Separate sections (with briefer information; i.e., mainly lists of works) for screen writers, television writers, radio writers, and musical librettists. Title index. American and British dramatists predominate. PR737.C57

Major modern dramatists. Comp. and ed. by Rita Stein, Friedhelm Rickert. N.Y., Ungar, 1984– . v.1– . (In progress) **BD222a**

Contents: v.1, American, British, Irish, German, Austrian, and Swiss dramatists.

A collection of excerpts from critical writings similar to those found in other volumes of the "Library of literary criticism" series (e.g., BD553, BD1203), the difference here being that genre rather than nationality or language is the focal point. All excerpts are in English, some of them translated specifically for this compilation. A second volume is planned. PN1861.M27

Palmer, Helen H. European drama criticism, 1900–1975. 2d ed. Hamden, Conn., Shoe String Pr., 1977. 653p. **BD223**

1st ed. (1968) and its supplements 1–2 (1970–74) by H. H. Palmer and A. J. Dyson.

Cumulates the entries from the earlier edition and its supplements, and adds new material through 1975.

A companion to Eddleman's American drama criticism (BD430). Lists English and foreign-language criticisms (with heavy emphasis on English-language materials). Z5781.P2

Encyclopedias and handbooks

Crowell's Handbook of contemporary drama, by Michael Anderson [and others]. N.Y., Crowell, [1971]. 505p. **BD224**

Intended as a "guide to developments in the drama in Europe and the Americas since the Second World War."—Pref. Emphasis is on written drama rather than theater. Entries for playwrights, individual plays, national developments in specific countries, and some terms. The editors elected to present fairly lengthy discussions of a limited number of plays rather than brief descriptions of many. An international list of contributors is named, but articles are unsigned. Precise bibliographic information is disappointingly sparse. PN1861.C7

McGraw-Hill encyclopedia of world drama; an international reference work. [2d ed.] N.Y., McGraw-Hill, [1984]. 5v. il. **BD225**

For full information see BG62.

Matlaw, Myron. Modern world drama; an encyclopedia. N.Y., Dutton, 1972. 960p. il. **BD226**

Includes four types of articles in a single alphabetical sequence: (1) summary articles on the modern drama of individual countries; (2) biographical entries for playwrights who lived in the 20th century; (3) entries for specific dramatic works, including notes on publication, first production, and a synopsis; and (4) technical terms for recent or modern theater movements and developments. Character index and a general index.   PN1851.M36

Essays

Indexes

American Library Association. A.L.A. index . . . to general literature. 2d ed. enl. . . . Boston, Chicago, Amer. Lib. Assoc. Pub. Board, 1901–14. 679p. and suppl. 223p.
BD227

Basic volume, covering material to Jan. 1, 1900. 679p. (publ. 1901); Supplement, 1900–1910. 223p. (publ. 1914).

A subject index which attempts to do for books of essays and general literature what *Poole's Index* (AE227) does for periodicals. Indexes books belonging to the following classes: (1) Essays and similar collections of critical, biographical, and other monographs; (2) Books of travel and general history whose chapters or parts are worthy of separate reference; (3) Reports and publications of boards and associations dealing with sociological matters, and of historical and literary societies; and (4) Miscellaneous books and some public documents. Includes only books in English. Indexing is by catchword subject, not by modern catalog subject headings.

Continued by the *Essay index* (below), which indexes collections published since 1900. Some of the books indexed in the *Supplement*, 1900–1910, have been taken over by the *Essay index,* but others, particularly those on travel, have not been reindexed; therefore, the *Supplement* has not been entirely superseded. For a more detailed discussion of the relationship of the two indexes, *see* the preface to the *Essay index,* p.v–vi.   AI3.A32

Essay and general literature index, 1900–1933; an index to about 40,000 essays and articles in 2144 volumes of collections of essays and miscellaneous works, ed. by Minnie Earl Sears and Marian Shaw. N.Y., Wilson, 1934. 1952p.
BD228

Kept up-to-date by supplements: (1) 7-year cumulations, 1934–1940, 1941–1947, 1948–1954; (2) 5-year cumulations, 1955/1959– ; and (3) semiannual and annual cumulations.

Frequently cited as the *Essay index.*

The basic volume is a detailed index by authors, subjects, and some titles, to essays and articles published 1900–33 and also to earlier essays if included in collections published since 1900. Indexing is given with exact reference; in the case of many essays first printed in periodicals, the reference to the periodical is given also, and variant titles for the same essay are indicated.

A monumental work, useful in several departments of library service. In *cataloging,* it provides a usable substitute for a large amount of analysis, the cost of which would be prohibitive in the average card catalog. As a *reference* aid, it serves many purposes, showing, e.g., (1) list of essays by a given author, (2) authorship of an essay when only title is known, (3) analytical material on a given subject, particularly small, unusual, or intangible subjects not covered by whole books, (4) biographical and critical matter about persons, (5) criticisms of individual books, and (6) different places or collections in which an essay is printed (an important point in school or college libraries when it is necessary to supply many copies of some recommended reading). For purposes of *selection of books,* the list of books indexed serves as a good guide to the worthwhile essay and other composite-book material of the 20th century.

The permanently cumulated supplements, 1934–84, index more than 251,000 essays and articles in more than 14,200 collections.
AI3.E752

———— Works indexed 1900–1969. N.Y., Wilson, 1972. 437p.   **BD229**

A main entry and title listing of the 9,917 works which have been analyzed in the *Index* during the period indicated.

Fiction

Bibliography

Baker, Ernest Albert. Guide to historical fiction. London, Routledge; N.Y., Macmillan, 1914. 565p. (Repr.: N.Y., Argosy-Antiquarian, 1968)   **BD230**

Lists about 5,000 novels which in any way portray the life of the past, including medieval romances and novels of manners, as well as avowedly historical novels. Arrangement is first by country and then chronologically by the historical period; descriptive notes indicate briefly the plot and scene of each story, its historical characters, etc. Full index (148p.) of authors, titles, historical names, places, events, allusions, etc.   Z5917.H6B2

———— and **Packman, James.** Guide to the best fiction, English and American, including translations from foreign languages. New and enl. ed. London, Routledge; N.Y., Macmillan, 1932. 634p.   **BD231**

1st ed. 1903; 2d ed. 1913. The 3d ed. is much enlarged from the 2d by the addition of material from 1911 through 1930, and differs from the 2d ed. in arrangement, i.e., has one alphabetical list instead of national lists with chronological subdivisions.

An older but still useful work, with good annotations and a detailed general index of authors, titles, subjects, historical names, allusions, places, characters, etc.   Z5916.B18

Cumulated fiction index, 1945/60– . London, Assoc. of Assist. Librarians, [1960]– . Irregular.   **BD232**

Compilers: 1945/60, G. B. Cotton and A. Glencross; 1960/69, R. F. Smith; 1970/74, R. F. Smith and A. J. Gordon; 1975/79, M. E. Hicken.

The 1945/60 volume (also called "Fiction index three") superseded a 1953 volume entitled *Fiction index 1* (covering 1945/53) and its 1957 supplement. The subtitle to that volume reads: "A guide to more than 25,000 works of fiction, including short story collections, anthologies, omnibus volumes, extracts and condensed books, mainly available between January 1945 and February 1960, arranged under 3000 subject headings with numerous references, and intended for use in public and circulating libraries, schools and bookshops and by the general reader." Listings are limited to author and title, without publication information. Each of the three supplementary volumes (covering 1960/69, 1970/74 and 1975/79) adds some older titles not previously listed along with thousands of new titles from their respective periods.   Z5916.F52

Fiction, 1876–1983; a bibliography of United States editions. N.Y., Bowker, [1983]. 2v. (2328p.)   **BD233**

Contents: v.1, Classified author index; Main author index; v.2, Title index; Key to publishers and distributors abbreviations; Directory of publishers and distributors.

Derived from the Bowker databases for *Books in print* and *American book publishing record.* Lists about 170,000 titles of novels, novellas, short stories, and anthologies of fiction. The classified author index lists authors by country and period; full publication information appears in both the main author and title sections (though the amount of bibliographic detail varies considerably from entry to entry).   Z5916.F49

Fiction catalog. 10th ed., 1980. Ed. by Juliette Yaakov and Gary L. Bogart. N.Y., Wilson, 1981. 803p. (Standard catalog ser.)   **BD234**

Kept up-to-date by annual supplements; new editions are now issued quinquennially.

1st ed. 1908.

A standard work which lists and annotates a selection of the best fiction in English, along with a generous representation of foreign fiction that has been translated into English. The 5,056 titles in this edition were chosen with the assistance of consultant librarians, and include analytical entries for novelettes and composite works. Early editions were in dictionary form; now in two sections: (1) an author alphabet with full bibliographical information and annotations, and (2) a title and subject index. Annotations include notes on plot or content, along with excerpts from critical reviews. Availability of large-type editions is now noted; out-of-print titles are included; prices are given.

A companion to the *Public library catalog* (AA442; which includes works of fiction criticism), serving both as a book selection aid and a reference tool for identifying outstanding novels.   Z5916.F5

Hicken, Marilyn E. Sequels. [7th ed.] London, Assoc. of Assistant Librarians, 1982–84. 2v.   **BD235**

Contents: v.1, Adult books; v.2, Junior books, comp. by D. Fraser. 1st ed. 1922 by T. Aldred; 2d ed. 1928 by W. H. Parker; 3d–6th eds. 1947–74 by F. M. Gardner.

Includes (a) novels and stories in which the same character appears; (b) novels with a connected narrative or theme; (c) non-fiction, especially autobiography, where the connection between titles is not readily apparent; and (d) series of novels with a connection which is mainly historical or geographical. Listing is by author, with indication of series title or name of principal character, followed by individual titles; non-fiction is indicated. Paperbacks in series are included in this edition. Index of series titles and characters.   Z6514.S4H52

Husband, Janet. Sequels: an annotated guide to novels in series. Chicago, Amer. Lib. Assoc., 1982. 361p.   **BD236**

A bibliography of sequence novels, with brief commentary. Not limited to in-print materials, but probable availability in the medium-sized library was a criterion for selection. Arranged by author; title index.   Z5917.S44H87

Irwin, Leonard Bartram. A guide to historical fiction for the use of schools, libraries, and the general reader. 10th ed., new and rev. Brooklawn, N.J., McKinley, 1971. 255p.   **BD237**

1st–9th eds. (1930–68) by Hannah Logasa had title: *Historical fiction.*

In general, limited to books published since 1940, and to those which were favorably reviewed. Geographical/chronological arrangement; author and title indexes. Very brief annotations. 1st–6th eds. included some non-fiction titles; the latter are now listed in a separate publication, *A guide to historical reading: nonfiction for schools, libraries, and the general reader,* ed. by Fred R. Czarra (DA7).   Z5917.H6I7

Kerr, Elizabeth Margaret. Bibliography of the sequence novel. Minneapolis, Univ. of Minnesota Pr., [1950]. 126p.   **BD238**

Attempts to list all the novels in series in which the sequence of the volumes depends upon the development of characters and themes. Divides into the following language groups: British-American, Romance, Teutonic, and Slavic. The foreign sections of the bibliography are more selective than complete. For the 20th century, entries have been brought up to the end of 1948.   Z5917.S45K4

McGarry, Daniel D. and **White, Sarah Harriman.** World historical fiction guide: an annotated, chronological, geographical, and topical list of selected historical novels. 2d ed. Metuchen, N.J., Scarecrow Pr., 1973. 629p.   **BD239**

1st ed., 1963, had title *Historical fiction guide.*
Arranged by chronological period and then geographically; lists about 6,450 fictional works in English including translations into English. Covers from ancient times to 1900. Author and title but no subject index.   Z5917.H6M3

Negley, Glenn. Utopian literature; a bibliography, with a supplementary listing of works influential in Utopian thought. Lawrence, Regents Pr. of Kansas, [1977]. 228p.   **BD240**

An author listing of 1,232 items of Utopian literature, with indication of locations in eleven libraries in the United States, Great Britain and France (plus a few other locations for particularly rare items). The supplementary section of "influential works" lists and locates about 375 additional items. Short-title and chronological indexes.

Negley is also the compiler of *Utopia collection of the Duke University Library* (Durham, N.C., Friends of Duke Univ. Lib., 1965. 83p.).   Z7164.U8N43

Nield, Jonathan. Guide to the best historical novels and tales. [5th ed. rev., enl., rearranged, and mostly rewritten] London, Mathews; N.Y., Macmillan, [1929]. 424p. (Repr.: N.Y., B. Franklin, 1968)   **BD241**

1st ed. 1902.
An old but comprehensive list of 2,392 titles, mainly English but including some foreign material in English translation or in the original. Differs from the 1911 edition in the elimination of some 1,400 titles, and in the addition of 1,160 not previously included. Index of (1) authors, (2) titles, and (3) subjects.   Z5917.H6N6

Short story index: collections indexed 1900–1978. Ed. by Juliette Yaakov. N.Y., Wilson, 1979. 349p.   **BD242**

A listing of the 8,355 collections indexed in the seven cumulated volumes of the *Short story index,* 1900–78 (BD243). Main entry listing with *see* references from titles, joint authors, etc. Serves as a useful bibliography of short stories in English and English translation.   Z5917.S5S56

Indexes

Cook, Dorothy Elizabeth and **Monro, Isabel Stevenson.** Short story index; an index to 60,000 stories in 4320 collections. N.Y., Wilson, 1953. 1553p.   **BD243**

"Supersedes the *Index to short stories* compiled by Ina Ten Eyck Firkins (1923) and its Supplements (1929 and 1936)."—*Pref.*

Indexes—by author, title, and, in many cases, subject—some 60,000 stories published in 1949 or earlier. The list of collections indexed is given in pt.II, by author and title.

————— ————— Supplement, 1950–1954, 1955–1958, 1959–1963, 1964–1968, 1969–1973, 1974–1978, 1979–1983. N.Y., Wilson, 1956–84. 7v.

Contents: 1950–1954, comp. by D. E. Cook and Estelle A. Fidell (Indexes 9,575 stories in 549 collections); 1955–1958, comp. by Estelle A. Fidell and Esther V. Flory (Indexes 6,392 stories in 376 collections); 1959–1963, comp. by Estelle A. Fidell (Indexes 9,068 stories in 582 collections); 1964–1968, comp. by Estelle A. Fidell (Indexes 11,301 stories in 793 collections); 1969–1973, comp. by Estelle A. Fidell (Indexes 11,561 stories in 805 collections); 1974–1978, comp. by Gary L. Bogart (Indexes 16,519 stories in 930 collections and some 70 periodicals); 1979–1983, comp. by Juliette Yaakov (Indexes 16,633 stories in 904 collections and 67 periodicals).

Beginning with the 1959–63 supplement, authors' names are entered exactly as they appear for each story, "in accordance with newer cataloging practices which favor entry under names as given on the title-page."—*Pref., 1959–63.* With 1974, supplements have appeared annually (cumulating quinquennially) and coverage has been extended to include stories in selected periodicals.

For a bibliography of the collections indexed 1900–78 *see* BD242.   Z5917.S5C6

Eastman, Mary Huse. Index to fairy tales, myths and legends. 2d ed. rev. and enl. Boston, Faxon, 1926. 610p. (Useful reference ser., no.28)   **BD244**

————— ————— Supplement, 1937. 566p. (Useful reference ser., no.61)

————— ————— 2d Supplement, 1952. 370p. (Useful reference ser. no.82)

A title index—with entry under best-known title and cross references from variant titles—to the fairy tales and legends included in a large number of collections. Principally useful in public libraries and as a help to the children's librarian, but of some value also to the special student of folklore.   Z5983.F17E2

Hannigan, Francis J. Standard index of short stories, 1900–1914. Boston, Small, [1918]. 334p.   **BD245**

An author and title index to stories published in 24 American magazines, 1900–14. Contains some 35,000 entries for stories by about 3,000 authors. Although there is much duplication, it does include titles not found in the *Short story index* (BD243) or in the *Readers' guide* (AE231). Z5917.S5H2

Ireland, Norma Olin. Index to fairy tales, 1949–1972, including folklore, legends & myths, in collections. Westwood, Mass., Faxon, 1973. 741p. (Useful reference ser., 101) **BD246**

——— Index to fairy tales, 1973–1977, including folklore, legends and myths in collections, fourth supplement. Westwood, Mass., Faxon, [1979]. 259p. (Useful reference ser., 111) **BD247**

These two volumes constitute the third and fourth supplements to Eastman's index (BD244). They index 406 and 130 collections, respectively. Z5983.F17I732

Criticism

Contemporary novelists. 3d ed. James Vinson, ed. [Byfleet, Surrey, Macmillan, 1982] 750p. **BD248**

1st ed. 1972.
For each writer there is a brief biographical sketch, a bibliography of his published works, a comment by the writer if he chose to make one, and a critical essay by a contemporary scholar. References to other critical studies are limited to those suggested by the biographee. American and British writers predominate, but many Commonwealth novelists and Africans writing in English are included. Appendix of "nine novelists who have died since the 1950s but whose reputations are essentially contemporary."—*p.XV.*
PR737.V5

Critical survey of long fiction: English language series. Ed. by Frank N. Magill. Englewood Cliffs, N.J., Salem Pr., [1983]. 8v. (3352p.) **BD249**

Offers critical assessments of 272 authors noted primarily for their novels and novellas, plus 20 essays dealing with the history and development of the two forms. Alphabetical arrangement of authors in v.1–7; background essays and index in v.8. Signed articles.
A companion series is: PR821.C7

——— Foreign language series. Ed. by Frank N. Magill. Englewood Cliffs, N.J., Salem Pr., [1984]. 5v. (2396p.) **BD250**

A compilation of signed critical essays similar to the same publisher's set for English-language fiction writers. PN3451.C75

Critical survey of short fiction. Ed. by Frank N. Magill. Englewood Cliffs, N.J., Salem Pr., [1981]. 7v. **BD251**

Contents: v.1–2, Essays; v.3–6, Authors; v.7, Current writers, Index.
Aims to provide "an exhaustive examination of the history, characteristics, structure, and prime examples" (*p.v*) of short fiction from all periods. The signed essays consider many very specific aspects of short fiction and its literary devices; some include bibliographies. Author entries (also signed) follow a set form and consider the influence, story characteristics, and analysis of a writer's short fiction, and give brief biographical and bibliographical information. The "Current writers" section is often a statement by the writer concerning his own work. British and American authors predominate. PN3321.C7

Kearney, E. I. and **Fitzgerald, L. S.** The Continental novel; a checklist of criticism in English, 1900–1966. Metuchen, N.J., Scarecrow Pr., 1968. 460p. **BD252**

A bibliography of criticism published since 1900 in books and periodicals. Includes English-language criticism of the French, Spanish and Portuguese, Italian, German, Scandinavian, Russian and East European novel of all periods. Z5916.K4

Fitzgerald, L. S. and **Kearney, E. I.** The Continental novel: a checklist of criticism in English, 1967–1980. Metuchen, N.J., Scarecrow Pr., 1983. 496p. **BD253**

A continuation of the preceding item, extending coverage through

1980 and adding some pre-1967 publications. Arrangement is again by national/regional grouping, then by author and individual novel.
Z5916.F57

Walker, Warren S. Twentieth-century short story explication: interpretations 1900–1975, of short fiction since 1800. 3d ed. Hamden, Conn., Shoe String Pr., 1977. 880p. **BD254**

——— ——— Supplement I to 3d ed. [Hamden, Conn.], Shoe String Pr., 1980. 257p.

1st ed. 1961, with supplements 1963 and 1965.
A bibliography of interpretations which have appeared since 1900 in books, monographs and periodicals, of short stories published after 1800. Arranged by author, then by individual story. This edition, which supersedes the 2d ed. (1967) and its two supplements (1970–73), treats some 850 authors and covers through 1975; the supplement adds 186 authors and extends coverage mainly through 1978 (although the spine marking shows "1976–79").
Short fiction criticism: a checklist of interpretation since 1925 by Jarvis A. Thurston [and others] (Denver, Swallow, 1960) is now effectively superseded, although a supplement for American works was published 1982 (*see* BD453). Z5917.S5W33

Ward, William Smith. Literary reviews in British periodicals, 1789–1797; a bibliography, with a supplementary list of general (non-review) articles on literary subjects. N.Y., Garland, 1979. 342p. (Garland reference library of the humanities, v.172) **BD255**

A predecessor to the compiler's previously published volumes for the 1798–1820 and 1821–26 periods (below). Listing of reviews is by author of the work reviewed (with anonymous works entered by title under "Anonymous"). Z2013.W36

——— Literary reviews in British periodicals, 1798–1820; a bibliography, with a supplementary list of general (non-review) articles on literary subjects. N.Y., Garland, 1972. 2v. **BD256**

An index to reviews of literary works gleaned from a wide range of British periodicals and two newspapers (*The champion* and *The examiner*) for the period indicated. Arrangement is alphabetical by author, then chronological by publication date of the work under review. Appendixes of general (non-review) articles on authors and their works, general and genre criticism, and reviews of operas.
The two volumes are sometimes listed as supplementary to the same publisher's series, *The Romantics reviewed; contemporary reviews of British Romantic writers* (N.Y., 1972. 3v. in 9), compiled by Donald H. Reiman, which offers photographic reprints of reviews themselves. Z2013.W36

——— Literary reviews in British periodicals, 1821–1826: a bibliography with a supplementary list of general (non-review) articles on literary subjects. N.Y., Garland, 1977. 301p. (Garland reference library of the humanities, v.60) **BD257**

Continues the listing of reviews of literary works as indexed in the compiler's earlier volumes covering 1798–1820 (above).
Z2013.W36

Detective and mystery stories

Barzun, Jacques and **Taylor, Wendell Hertig.** A catalogue of crime. N.Y., Harper & Row, [1971]. 831p. **BD258**

A bibliography of nearly 3,500 works, with a brief critical commentary on each. Includes biographical notes on many authors. Indexed. Z5917.D5B37

Cook, Michael L. Mystery, detective, and espionage magazines. Westport, Conn., Greenwood Pr., [1983]. 795p. **BD259**

Intended as a tool for the serious study of popular culture. Magazines are presented alphabetically; for each there is a profile giving brief history, characteristics, and content, plus indication of indexing and locational sources, bibliographic references to additional information on publication history, and notes on editors, title changes, physical description, etc. Includes sections of notes on foreign magazines and on book clubs; numerous appendixes.

PN3448.D4C56

Hagen, Ordean A. Who done it? A guide to detective, mystery and suspense fiction. N.Y., Bowker, 1969. 834p.

BD260

An author listing of mystery fiction, 1841–1967, is followed by a subject guide, sections on mystery films and plays, and a selective listing of novels by locale, and a listing of characters in mystery fiction. Title index to the bibliography.   Z5913.D5H3

Hubin, Allen J. Crime fiction 1749–1980; a comprehensive bibliography. N.Y., Garland, 1984. 712p. (Garland reference library of the humanities, v.371)   **BD261**

Based on the compiler's *Bibliography of crime fiction, 1749–1975.* Includes mystery, detective, suspense, thriller, gothic, police, and spy fiction written for adults and "in which crime or the threat of crime is a major plot element."—*Introd.* Author listing, with title, series, and setting indexes. Lists about 60,000 titles.

Critical writings concerning the genre are listed in *Crime fiction criticism: an annotated bibliography,* edited by Timothy W. Johnson and Julia Johnson (N.Y., Garland, 1981. 423p.).

Spy fiction is dealt with more fully in Myron J. Smith's *Cloak and dagger fiction: an annotated guide to spy thrillers* (2d ed., Santa Barbara, Calif., ABC-Clio, 1982. 431p.).   Z2014.F4H82

Queen, Ellery, *pseud.* The detective short story: a bibliography. Boston, Little, 1942. 146p.   **BD262**

Lists, usually with brief annotations, short stories averaging 6,000–8,000 words in length, with some longer ones, dealing with crime and detection.   Z5917.D5Q4

Twentieth-century crime and mystery writers. Ed., John M. Reilly. London, Macmillan; N.Y., St. Martin's Pr., [1980]. 1568p.   **BD263**

Concerned primarily with "English-language writers of crime and mystery fiction whose work appeared during or since the time of Sir Arthur Conan Doyle."—*p. xxi.* There is a brief appendix of foreign-language writers well known to English readers. For each author is given a biographical note, a bibliography, and a signed critical essay.

PR888.D4T8

Science fiction, fantasy, and the Gothic

Bibliography

Anatomy of wonder: a critical guide to science fiction. 2d ed. Neil Barron, ed. N.Y., Bowker, 1981. 724p.   **BD264**

1st ed. 1976.
In two parts: (1) The literature; (2) Research aids. Chapters by various contributors provide a bibliographic essay and annotated bibliography on a specific period or special type of science fiction. Author and title indexes. Includes a section on foreign-language science fiction, p.379–506.   Z5917.S36A52

Bleiler, Everett Franklin. The checklist of science-fiction and supernatural fiction. Glen Rock, N.J., Firebell Books, [1978]. 266p.   **BD265**

Represents "an extensive revision and enlargement of a book first published in Chicago in 1948: *The Checklist of Fantastic Literature.*"—*Introd.* Aims to list first editions of adult English-language (including translations) fantastic fiction for the period 1800–1948. Author listing with a title section providing author's name. Abbreviations indicate subject content.   Z5917.F3B55

——— The guide to supernatural fiction. Kent, Ohio, Kent State Univ. Pr., [1983]. 723p.   **BD266**

"A full description of 1,775 books from 1750 to 1960, including ghost stories, weird fiction, stories of supernatural horror, fantasy,

Gothic novels, occult fiction, and similar literature. With author, title, and motif indexes."—*t.p.*

Gives notes on the authors and plot summaries as well as bibliographic information on the titles considered. The title index includes entries for individual stories in collections.

PN56.S8B57

Briney, Robert E. and **Wood, Edward.** SF bibliographies; an annotated bibliography of bibliographical works on science fiction and fantasy fiction. Chicago, Advent, 1972. 49p.

BD267

Includes bibliographies of individual science fiction writers as well as general bibliographies and indexes for the field.

Z5917.S36B75

Clareson, Thomas D. Science fiction criticism; an annotated checklist. [Kent, Ohio], Kent State Univ. Pr., [1972]. 225p.

BD268

Includes book materials and periodical articles.

Clareson is also the compiler of *Science fiction in America, 1870s–1930s; an annotated bibliography of primary sources* (Westport, Conn., Greenwood Pr., 1984. 305p.) which lists more than 800 items with extensive annotations.   Z5917.S36C55

Clarke, Ignatius Frederick. Tale of the future, from the beginning to the present day. 3d ed. London, Lib. Assoc., 1978. 357p.   **BD269**

1st ed. 1961.
"An annotated bibliography of those satires, ideal states, imaginary wars and invasions, coming catastrophes and end-of-the-world stories, political warnings and forecasts, inter-planetary voyages and scientific romances—all located in an imaginary future period—that have been published in the United Kingdom between 1644 and 1976."—*t.p.*

A chronological listing with brief annotations. Short-title and author indexes.   Z5917.S36C56

Currey, L. W. Science fiction and fantasy authors: a bibliography of first printings of their fiction and selected nonfiction. Boston, G. K. Hall, [1979]. 571p.   **BD270**

Designed "to meet the need for a one-volume bibliography which would provide up-to-date, comprehensive, and accurate checklists of book fiction by 215 authors identified with the science fiction and fantasy genres from the late nineteenth century to the present."—*Introd.* Each entry is meant to include "sufficient data to identify the first printing of the book, as well as subsequent printings and editions of interest to researchers and collectors."   Z1231.F5C87

Frank, Frederick S. Guide to the Gothic: an annotated bibliography of criticism. Metuchen, N.J., Scarecrow Pr., 1984. 421p.   **BD271**

Includes sections for English, Canadian, American, French, and German gothic literature, with subdivisions for individual writers. Also includes a section for "Special subject areas" (e.g., vampirism, werewolfism, etc.). Indexed.   Z5917.G66F7

McNutt, Dan J. The eighteenth-century Gothic novel: an annotated bibliography of criticism and selected texts. N.Y., Garland Pr., 1975. 330p.   **BD272**

Sections on the background, general history and specific aspects of the genre are followed by sections on the major practitioners: Horace Walpole, Clara Reeve, Charlotte Smith, Ann Radcliffe, Matthew Gregory Lewis, and William Beckford. In addition to annotations, excerpts from early reviews of individual novels are included.

The English gothic; a bibliographic guide to writers from Horace Walpole to Mary Shelley by Robert Donald Spector (Westport, Conn., Greenwood Pr., 1984. 269p.) provides bibliographic essays on the genre and the writers treated by McNutt, adding a section on Charles Robert Maturin and Mary Shelley.   Z2014.F5M3

Reginald, R. Science fiction and fantasy literature; a checklist, 1700–1974, with Contemporary science fiction authors II. Detroit, Gale, [1979]. 2v.   **BD273**

Contents: v.1, Author index, Title index, Series index, Awards index, Ace and Belmont doubles index; v.2, Contemporary science fiction authors II.

An earlier edition of v.2 was published 1974 under title: *Contemporary science fiction authors.*

The author section of v.1 "lists 15,884 English-language first editions of books and pamphlets published between 1700 and 1974 in the fields of science fiction, fantasy and weird supernatural fiction."—*Introd.* v.2 offers biographical sketches of 1,443 science fiction and fantasy authors of the 20th century.   Z5917.S36R42

Schlobin, Roger C. The literature of fantasy: a comprehensive, annotated bibliography of modern fantasy fiction. N.Y., Garland, 1979. 425p. (Garland reference library of the humanities, v.176)   **BD274**

"The titles selected are restricted to adult fantasy and juvenile fantasy with strong adult appeal" (*Pref.*) and except for those foreign-language authors and titles "that have conspicuously contributed to the Anglo-American literary tradition," only prose works published in English in book form are included.   Z2014.F4S33

Summers, Montague. A Gothic bibliography. London, Fortune Pr.; N.Y., Columbia Univ. Pr., 1941. 621p. il. (Repr.: N.Y., Russell & Russell, 1964)   **BD275**

Contents: Index of authors, p.1–219; Title index, p.220–568; Addenda, p.569–620.

A bibliography of the English Gothic novel from 1728 to 1916. Usually omits the well-known writers for whom there are already standard bibliographies. In addition to some peculiarities of arrangement, inclusion and exclusion, there are some questionable attributions of anonymous works, and the volume should be used with caution.   Z2014.F4S9

Tymn, Marshall B., Schlobin, Roger C. and **Currey, L. W.** A research guide to science fiction studies: an annotated checklist of primary and secondary sources for fantasy and science fiction. N.Y., Garland, 1977. 165p. (Garland reference library of the humanities, v.87)   **BD276**

Intends "to provide the reader—whether he be scholar, teacher, librarian, or fan—with a comprehensive listing of the important research tools that have been published in the United States and England through 1976."—*Pref.* About 400 annotated entries, plus a special listing of doctoral dissertations in the field. Arranged by type of material; author and title indexes.   Z5917.S36T93

The year's scholarship in science fiction and fantasy: 1972–1975. Marshall B. Tymn and Roger C. Schlobin [eds.]. [Kent, Ohio], Kent State Univ. Pr., [1979]. 222p. (Serif series, bibliographies and checklists, 36)   **BD277**

———— : 1976–1979. Marshall B. Tymn and Roger C. Schlobin [eds.]. [Kent, Ohio], Kent State Univ. Pr., [1982]. 251p. (Serif series, bibliographies and checklists, 41)

The two volumes above represent cumulations and revisions of the annual annotated bibliographies of secondary literature in the fields of science fiction and fantasy which appeared in issues of *Extrapolation.* Coverage is meant to be comprehensive for American scholarship, selective for British scholarship. Includes books, dissertations, articles, scholarly reprints and instructional audiovisual materials, but not book reviews. Indexed.

Continued by: Z5917.S36T95

The year's scholarship in science fiction, fantasy and horror literature, 1980– . Kent, Ohio, Kent State Univ. Pr., 1983– . Annual.   **BD278**

Z5917.S36Y4

Book reviews and criticism

Hall, Halbert W. Science fiction book review index, 1923–1973. Detroit, Gale, [1975]. 438p.   **BD279**

Indexes all books reviewed in selected science fiction magazines 1923–73, whether or not they are works of science fiction. For the period 1970–73, reviews of science fiction books appearing in a selection of non-science fiction magazines are also included. Full information appears in an author listing; title index. A "Directory of magazines indexed" gives complete bibliographic information on the science fiction magazines (including editors, changes of title, etc.) and tables of issue numbers and dates.

Continued by: Z5917.S36H35

———— Science fiction book review index, 1974–79. Detroit, Gale, [1981]. 391p.   **BD280**

Continues the policy of indexing all reviews appearing in the source magazines, and some reviews from magazines not regularly indexed are again included.   Z5917.S36H36

Science fiction writers; critical studies of the major authors from the early nineteenth century to the present day. E. F. Bleiler, ed. N.Y., Scribner's, [1982]. 623p.   **BD281**

Offers signed articles with selected bibliographies on about 75 writers grouped by period. Index of names and titles.

PS374.S35S36

Survey of modern fantasy literature. Ed. by Frank N. Magill. Englewood Cliffs, N.J., Salem Pr., [1983]. 4v.   **BD282**

Includes "high fantasy, low fantasy, horror, Gothic fantasy, science fantasy, psychological fantasy, avant-garde experiments, and various unclassified fantastic works."—*p.v.* Offers about 500 signed essay reviews (i.e., synopses plus background notes and critical commentary). Arranged by title of the work, with numerous entries on the short fiction of individual authors in v.4.

Diana Waggoner's *The hills of faraway; a guide to fantasy* (N.Y., Atheneum, 1978. 326p.) offers chapters on the theory of fantasy and trends in fantasy literature, followed by a bibliographic guide to the genre.   PN56.F34S97

Survey of science fiction literature. Ed. by Frank N. Magill. Englewood Cliffs, N.J., Salem Pr., [1979]. 5v.   **BD283**

Subtitle: Five hundred 2,000-word essay reviews of world-famous science fiction novels with 2,500 bibliographical references.

A compilation of signed review articles arranged by title with author index in v.5. A bibliographical supplement compiled by Marshall B. Tymn was published 1982 (183p.).   PN3448.S45S88

Twentieth-century science-fiction writers. Ed., Curtis C. Smith. N.Y., St. Martin's Pr., [1981]. 642p.   **BD284**

Offers brief biographical information, lists of publications, and signed commentary on English-language writers of science fiction.

PS374.S35T89

Indexes

Contento, William. Index to science fiction anthologies and collections. Boston, G. K. Hall, [1978]. 608p.   **BD285**

Attempting to include "all English language science fiction anthologies and collections published through June 1977," the index "covers over 2,000 book titles with full contents listings of over 1,900 books containing 12,000 different stories by 2,500 authors." —*Introd.* Concerned with science fiction stories which deal with "social and technical extrapolation and innovation while excluding stories that deal exclusively with horror, the weird, ghosts, mythology, sword and sorcery, the occult, and other fantasy."

Z1231.F4C65

———— Index to science fiction anthologies and collections, 1977–1983. Boston, G. K. Hall, [1984]. 503p.   **BD286**

Indexes about 1,000 additional collections.   Z1231.F4C65

Day, Donald Byrne. Index to the science fiction magazines, 1926–1950. Rev. ed. Boston, G. K. Hall, [1982]. 289p.   **BD287**

1st ed. 1952. The revision "incorporates several hundred corrections . . . collated from Day's own annotated copy of the original edition" (*Pref.*) and from other sources.

Indexes 55 American and three British periodicals from their first issue through 1950. Includes an index by authors, one by titles, and a checklist of the magazines indexed with a record of all issues.

Continued by: Z5917.S36D3

Strauss, Erwin S., comp. The MIT Science Fiction Society's Index to the S-F magazines, 1951–1965. [Cambridge, Mass.], 1966. 207p. **BD288**

Continues Day's index (above), and is continued by:

New England Science Fiction Association. Index to the science fiction magazines, 1966–1970. [West Hanover, Mass.], 1971. 82p. **BD289**

Continues the Strauss index (above). Z5917.S36N4

The NESFA index to the science fiction magazines and original anthologies. 1971/72– . Cambridge, Mass., New England Science Fiction Assoc., 1973– . Annual (some issues combined). **BD290**

A continuation of the above. The 1983 issue (publ. 1984) indexes ten magazines and 24 anthologies. Z5917.S36I55

Fletcher, Marilyn P. Science fiction story index, 1950–1979. 2d ed. Chicago, Amer. Lib. Assoc., 1981. 610p. **BD291**

Represents "an expanded and updated version of the *Science Fiction Story Index 1950–1968* [Chicago, 1971]."—*Pref.*

A computer-produced author and title index to anthologies published 1950 through 1979, both single- and multi-author collections. Each anthology is assigned a code number in the "List of anthologies indexed," and reference in the author and titles sections is to code number.

The Reference and Subscription Books Review Committee's review in *Booklist* 78:773 (Feb. 15, 1982) concludes that "Despite its flaws and omissions (not all volumes in numbered annuals were indexed), the second edition . . . will be valuable in public and academic libraries." Z5917.S36S5

Index to stories in thematic anthologies of science fiction. Ed. by Marshall B. Tymn [and others]. Boston, G. K. Hall, [1978]. 193p. **BD292**

Indexes 181 science fiction anthologies. Books are listed under subject headings such as: alien encounter, alternate worlds, business, corruption, drugs, freedom, history, mutation, religion, space travel, utopia, etc. Contents are listed for each anthology. Author and title indexes. Z5917.S36I53

Encyclopedias

The science fiction encyclopedia. Gen. ed., Peter Nicholls. Garden City, N.Y., Dolphin Books, Doubleday, 1979. 672p. il. **BD293**

An alphabetical arrangement of some 2,800 articles contributed by science fiction specialists. Includes entries for science fiction authors, themes, films, magazines, illustrators, editors, critics, filmmakers, publishers, pseudonyms, series, television programs, anthologies, comics, awards, terminology, etc. Numerous cross references. PN3348.S45S29

Versins, Pierre. Encyclopédie de l'utopie, des voyages extraordinaires, et de la science fiction. [Lausanne], L'Age d'Homme, [1972]. 999p. il. **BD294**

Dictionary arrangement. Entries for terms and names (real and fictional) in Utopian and science fiction literature; articles on writers in these genres concentrate on their contributions and influence in the field. Writers' works are cited with initial publication date, but there is no bibliography other than the table of sources of illustrations (p.987–95) which gives citations to several hundred publications. PN3448.S45V4

Poetry

Bibliography and indexes

American Library Association. Subject index to poetry for children and young people, comp. by Violet Sell [and

others]. Chicago, Assoc., 1957. 582p. (Repr.: Great Neck, N.Y., Core Collection Books, 1982) **BD295**

Intended for librarians and others for use with children and young people from kindergarten through high school; indexes poems in 157 collections on "specific topics, universal concepts, persons, places, and things, as well as . . . for special occasions or programs." —*Pref.* PN1023.A5

Smith, Dorothy B. Frizzell and **Andrews, Eva L.** Subject index to poetry for children and young people, 1957–1975. Chicago, Amer. Lib. Assoc., 1977. 1035p. **BD296**

A supplement to the 1957 edition (above). Indexes 263 new anthologies, and introduces numerous new subject headings. PN1023.S6

Brewton, John Edmund and **Brewton, Sara Westbrook.** Index to children's poetry; a title, subject, author, and first line index to poetry in collections for children and youth. N.Y., Wilson, 1942. 965p. **BD297**

"A dictionary index to 130 collections of poems for children and youth, with title, subject, author and first line entries. More than 15,000 poems by approximately 2500 different authors are classified under more than 1800 different subjects."—*Introd.* PN1023.B7

————— ————— First supplement. N.Y., Wilson, 1954. 405p.

Indexes 66 collections published between 1938 and 1951. "More than 7000 poems by approximately 1300 different authors are classified under more than 1250 different subjects."—*Introd.*

————— ————— Second supplement. N.Y., Wilson, 1965. 453p.

Indexes 85 collections published between 1949 and 1963, listing more than 8,000 poems by some 1,400 authors.

A smaller work, *Children's poetry index* by Maud R. Macpherson (Boston, Faxon, 1938. 453p.), indexes 50 collections, 18 of which are not included in Brewton, and therefore it may occasionally be useful.

————— and **Blackburn, G. Meredith.** Index to poetry for children and young people, 1964–1969. N.Y., Wilson, 1972. 575p. **BD298**

Subtitle: A title, subject, author, and first line index to poetry in collections for children and young people.

This is "in effect a supplement to *Index to Children's Poetry* [above] but because of the larger number of books at the 7–12 grade level, it seemed appropriate to give the present volume a new, more inclusive title."—*Introd.* Indexes more than 11,000 poems in 117 collections. PN1023.B72

Brewton, John Edmund, Blackburn, G. Meredith and **Blackburn, Lorraine A.** Index to poetry for children and young people, 1970–1975. N.Y., Wilson, 1978. 472p. **BD299**

Forms a supplement to the above, indexing "more than 10,000 poems by approximately 2,500 authors and translators" (*Introd.*) in 110 collections. PN1023.B722

————— Index to poetry for children and young people, 1976–1981. N.Y., Wilson, 1984. 320p. **BD300**

Indexes an additional 110 collections containing some 7,000 poems by about 2,000 authors. PN1023.B723

Bruncken, Herbert. Subject index to poetry; a guide for adult readers. Chicago, Amer. Lib. Assoc., 1940. 201p. **BD301**

Indexes 215 anthologies of prose and poetry under specific subjects. Attempts to supply material for "(1) the location of poetry on specific subjects, (2) the location of a poem, the topical matter or dominant idea of which is known, but not author, title or first line, (3) the location of a poem whose author, title or first line is not known, but a line or fragment of a line of which is known."—*Pref.* PN1021.B7

Granger, Edith. Granger's Index to poetry. 8th ed., completely rev. and enl., indexing anthologies published through June 30, 1985. Ed. by William F. Bernhardt. N.Y., Columbia Univ. Pr., 1986. 2014p.   **BD302**

1st ed. 1904; 2d ed. 1918; 3d ed. 1940; 4th ed. 1953; 5th ed. 1962; 6th ed. 1973; 7th ed. 1982, with intervening supplements.

A very useful index important in public, college, and school libraries as it indexes a large number of standard and popular collections of poetry (the 1st–3d eds. also indexed prose selections). In the 4th–8th eds. the title and first-line indexes are combined, followed by an author index and a subject index.

Each edition includes some anthologies previously indexed, drops some, and adds others. (The 7th ed. departed from the cumulative pattern of the 2d through 6th eds. and indexed only anthologies of the 1970–81 period.) The 8th ed. indexes a total of 405 volumes, 82 of which are new volumes or new editions of anthologies indexed here for the first time. Because of the number of titles indexed in earlier editions, but omitted in later ones, most libraries will find it advantageous to keep all.   PN1021.G7

Ireland, Norma Olin. An index to monologs and dialogs. Rev. and enl. ed. Boston, Faxon, 1949. 171p. (Useful reference ser., no. 77)   **BD304**

1st ed. 1939.

An author, subject, and title index to 140 collections—51 more than in the 1st ed.

——— ——— Supplement. Boston, Faxon, 1959. 133p. (Useful reference ser., no.89)

Indexes 127 additional collections.   PN4305.M6I64

Poetry index annual, 1982– ; a title, author, and subject index to poetry in anthologies. Great Neck, N.Y., Granger Book Co., [1982]– . Annual.   **BD305**

Each annual volume aims to index, by author, title, and subject, all anthologies of poetry published during the year preceding the date of issue (i.e., 1982 vol. indexes anthologies published 1981). Issues are not cumulative.   PN1022.P63

Sears, Minnie Earl. Song index. An index to more than 12,000 songs in 177 song collections. N.Y., Wilson, 1926–34. 2v.   **BD306**

For full information *see* BH272.

Includes poems which have been set to music. Indexes many titles not included in Granger (BD302), especially foreign poems in either original or translation.   ML128.S3S31

Spoken records

Hoffman, Herbert H. and **Hoffman, Rita Ludwig.** International index to recorded poetry. N.Y., Wilson, 1983. 529p.   **BD307**

The work "identifies and indexes—by author, title, first line, and reader—the contents of more than 1,700 recordings issued up through 1981 in the United States and abroad: some 15,000 poems by approximately 2,300 authors, read in upwards of twenty languages on phonodiscs, tapes, audio cassettes, film strips, and video cassettes."—*Pref.*   PN1022.H63

Roach, Helen Pauline. Spoken records. 3d ed. Metuchen, N.J., Scarecrow Pr., 1970. 288p.   **BD308**

1st ed. 1963.

A selected list with commentary rather than an attempt at a comprehensive bibliography. "Selections for inclusion have been made on the basis of excellence in execution, literary or historical merit, interest and entertainment value."—*Introd.* Indexed.   Z2011.R6

U.S. Library of Congress. Poetry Office. Literary recordings: a checklist of the Archive of Recorded Poetry and Literature in the Library of Congress. Rev., enl. ed. Wash., [Govt. Prt. Off., for sale by U.S. Supt. of Docs.], 1981. 299p.   **BD309**

Jennifer Whittington, comp.

Previous ed. 1966.

An inventory of the Archive's holdings through May 1975, listing recordings of nearly a thousand poets reading their own work. "It includes recordings of poetry readings and other literary events held in the Library's Coolidge Auditorium or the Whittall Pavilion, tapes of poets reading their poems in the Recording Laboratory or elsewhere for the archive, and recordings received through occasional gifts, exchanges, or purchases."—*Pref.*   PS306.5.Z9U53

Criticism

Critical survey of poetry: English language series. Ed. by Frank N. Magill. Englewood Cliffs, N.J., Salem Pr., [1982]. 8v.   **BD310**

v.1–7 (arranged by poet or anonymous title) offer critical essays about ten pages in length, with brief bibliographies, of poets and poetry in English from *Beowulf* to the present; v.8 presents longer essays on particular periods and various aspects of poetry criticism. All essays are signed; index in v.8.

A companion series is: PR502.C85

——— Foreign language series. Ed. by Frank N. Magill. Englewood Cliffs, N.J., Salem Pr., [1984]. 5v.   **BD311**

A compilation similar to the series for English-language poetry (above).   PN41.C7

Encyclopedias and handbooks

Deutsch, Babette. Poetry handbook; a dictionary of terms. 4th ed. N.Y., Funk & Wagnalls, [1974]. 203p.   **BD312**

A useful handbook for the student and practitioner. Employs a dictionary arrangement.   PN44.5.D4

Morier, Henri. Dictionnaire de poétique et de rhétorique. [3. éd. augm. et entièrement refondue] Paris, Presses Universitaires, [1981]. 1263p. il.   **BD313**

1st ed. 1961.

A dictionary of terms in modern poetry and rhetoric. Runs heavily to long, detailed articles, with numerous examples of use, and charts, diagrams, etc. to illustrate specific points. Particular attention is given to phonetics.   PN1021.M6

Princeton encyclopedia of poetry and poetics. Alex Preminger, ed. Enl. ed. Princeton, N.J., Princeton Univ. Pr., 1974. 992p.   **BD314**

Constitutes a reissue, with a supplement (p.909–92) bound in, of the *Encyclopedia of poetry and poetics* (Princeton, N.J., Princeton Univ. Pr., 1965. 906p.).

Includes "about 1,000 individual entries ranging from twenty to more than 20,000 words, dealing with the history, theory, technique, and criticism of poetry from earliest times to the present."—*Pref.* Most articles are signed with the initials of the contributor and carry bibliographical references. International in scope, with special articles on the poetry of various nationalities and ethnic groups. Authoritative and scholarly in tone, it is a valuable addition to the reference collection. The supplement adds entries for new developments and for topics previously omitted; it includes cross references to the main text.   PN1021.E5

Romances, epics, etc.

See also French—Bibliography—Medieval, p.487–88.

Ackerman, Robert William. An index of the Arthurian names in Middle English. Stanford, Calif., Stanford Univ. Pr., 1952. 250p. (Stanford Univ. publs. University ser. Language and literature, v.10)   **BD315**

Includes personal and place names. Names are briefly identified; variant spellings are noted; and citations are given to the works in which they appear.   PE1660.A23

British Museum. Dept. of Manuscripts. Catalogue of romances in the Dept. of Manuscripts in the British Museum. London, Trustees, 1883–1910. 3v. **BD316**

v.1–2, by H. L. D. Ward; v.3, by J. A. Herbert.

The most important reference book in English on the subject. For each romance it gives, in addition to the description of the manuscript in the British Museum, some account of the tale, its outlines, different versions, other manuscripts, authorship, history, etc., and important bibliographical references both to printed texts and to critical comment. Z6621.B87R7

Chapman, Coolidge Otis. An index of names in Pearl, Purity, Patience, and Gawain. Ithaca, N.Y., Cornell Univ. Pr., 1951. 66p. (Cornell studies in English, v.38) **BD317**

An index of proper names in four medieval poems, with line references and biographical and geographical information.

Barnet Kottler and Alan M. Markham have edited *A Concordance to five Middle English poems: Cleanness, St. Erkenwald, Sir Gawain and the Green Knight, Patience, Pearl* (Pittsburgh, Univ. of Pittsburgh Pr., 1966. 761p.). PR1203.C63

Coleman, Arthur. Epic and romance criticism. N.Y., Watermill, 1973–74. 2v. **BD318**

Contents: v.1, A checklist of interpretations, 1940–1972, of English and American epics and metrical romances; v.2, A checklist of interpretations, 1940–1973, of classical and continental epics and metrical romances.

Offers about 20,000 citations to criticisms in English appearing in periodicals, monographs, pamphlets, *Festschriften,* etc. ("Obvious" sources, i.e., those easily found through a library catalog, are not included in v.1.) Listing is by title of the epic or romance. No index of authors of the critical writings. Z7156.E6C64

Esdaile, Arundell. List of English tales and prose romances printed before 1740. London, pr. for the Bibliographical Society by Blades, East and Blades, 1912. 329p. (Repr.: Folcroft, Pa., Folcroft Pr., 1970) **BD319**

Pt.1, 1475–1642; pt.2, 1643–1739. Each part is arranged alphabetically by author and title, with plentiful cross references. Gives full title and imprint, list of editions, libraries in which the copies included were seen, and bibliographies in which the work is described. Scope of list includes both English tales and English translations of foreign works. Notes are bibliographical, not critical. Of value to the specialist, the bibliographer, and the cataloger. Z2014.F4E8

Guerber, Hélène Adeline. Book of the epic; the world's great epics told in story. London, Harrap, 1919. 631p. il. **BD320**

Gives synopses of the stories of the great Greek, Latin, French, Spanish, Portuguese, Italian, British, German, Dutch, Scandinavian, Russian and Finnish, Balkan, Hebrew and Early Christian, Arabian and Persian, Indian, Chinese and Japanese, and American epics. PN683.G8

International Arthurian Society. Bulletin bibliographique. Bibliographical bulletin. Paris, 1949– . no.1– . Annual. **BD321**

An international annual bibliography of Arthurian writings, including books, periodical articles, dissertations, works in progress, etc. References to reviews are frequently given. Listings are arranged by country of origin. For a cumulation *see* BD326.

Some numbers include special articles on Arthurian subjects and lists of members of the Society. Z8045.I5

Life, Page West. Sir Thomas Malory and the Morte Darthur: a survey of scholarship and annotated bibliography. Charlottesville, Publ. for the Bibliographical Soc. of the Univ. of Virginia by the Univ. Pr. of Virginia, [1980]. 297p. **BD322**

The bibliography, p.43–233, intends to be comprehensive through 1977, with a few later listings. 922 items. Indexes of names, titles, and subjects. Z8545.5.L53

Modern Language Association of America. A bibliography of critical Arthurian literature . . . 1922/29–1962. Ed. by John J. Parry . . . N.Y., 1931–63. **BD323**

v.1, 1922/29, ed. by John J. Parry; v.2, 1930/35, ed. by Parry and Margaret Schlauch. These two volumes were supplemented by lists appearing in the *Modern language quarterly,* the first covering 1936–39, annual thereafter and with editors varying. Ceased with volume covering 1962. For a cumulation *see* BD326.

A listing of books with references to reviews and periodical articles in various languages. Item numbers are consecutive from the beginning; in the 41 years, 1922–62, 5,328 items have been listed.

See also the *Critical bibliography of French literature,* v.1, The mediaeval period, chapters 6–11 (BD957). Z8045.M69

Newberry Library, Chicago. The Arthurian legend: a check list of books in the Newberry Library, comp. by Jane D. Harding. Chicago, Lib., 1933. 120p. **BD324**

Contents: Texts (classified by language) and critical works; Index to titles, editors, and translators of texts.

———— ———— Supplement. Chicago, 1938. 90p.

Z8045.N53

Northup, Clark Sutherland and **Parry, John J.** The Arthurian legends; modern retellings of the old stories, an annotated bibliography. (*In* Journal of English and Germanic philology 43:173–221, Apr. 1944) **BD325**

———— ———— Supplement, by Paul A. Brown. (*In* Journal of English and Germanic philology 49:208–16, Apr. 1950)

Lists bibliographies and discussions of modern versions; new versions of the Arthurian stories; doubtful items; and items rejected because the Arthurian connection is too slight or wholly lacking in spite of the titles.

Pickford, Cedric Edward and **Last, Rex.** The Arthurian bibliography. [Cambridge, Eng.], D. S. Brewer, [1981–83]. 2v. **BD326**

Contents: v.1, Author listing; v.2, Subject index.

A computer-produced work which merges the bibliographic entries from the annual Arthurian bibliographies in the *Modern language quarterly,* the *Bibliographical bulletin* of the International Arthurian Society, *Arthuriana,* the separate bibliographies by Parry and Schlauch, and the bibliographical material in J. D. Bruce's *Evolution of Arthurian romance.* v.1 lists the entries by author, with full citation and indication of the bibliography from which the citation was taken; references to reviews are included. v.2 includes a list of substantive corrections preceding the subject index. An updated edition is planned for publication in ten years' time, and various inconsistencies are to be reconciled therein. Z8045.P53

Reiss, Edmund, Reiss, Louise Horner and **Taylor, Beverly.** Arthurian legend and literature; an annotated bibliography. N.Y., Garland, 1984– . v.1– . (Garland reference library of the humanities, v. 415) (In progress) **BD327**

Contents: v.1, The Middle Ages.

v.1 covers "Arthurian works dating from the sixth through the fifteenth century, noting sixteenth century (and later) versions of earlier works when they are not significantly different from their medieval source."—*Pref.* Following sections for reference works, history and legend, and literary contexts, material is arranged by subject—mainly Arthurian figures; within subject divisions are listed editions, translations into English, and studies of the works (secondary works being selected to represent varying viewpoints, both old and new). For much-discussed writers and works the secondary listings concentrate on scholarship since the latest-published bibliography on the topic. Indexes of subjects and of scholars and critics. Z8045.R45

Spence, Lewis. Dictionary of medieval romance and romance writers. London, Routledge; N.Y., Dutton, 1913. 395p. (Repr.: N.Y., Humanities Pr., 1962) **BD328**

A list, in one alphabet, of the titles and characters of the principal British, Celtic, French, Italian, Scandinavian, Spanish, and Teutonic romances from the 11th to the 14th centuries. Gives: (1) under title, a fairly detailed synopsis of the story of the romance with some bibliographical references but no full list of editions, and (2) under character, a brief description of the character, and the title of the romance in which it appears.

An Arthurian dictionary by Charles and Ruth Moorman (Jackson, Univ. Pr. of Mississippi, 1978. 117p.) is a student's handbook to characters, places, and topics connected with the Arthur legend.

PN669.S6

Stylistics

Bailey, Richard W. and **Burton, Dolores M.** English stylistics; a bibliography. Cambridge, Mass., M.I.T. Pr., [1968]. 198p.   **BD329**

A classed bibliography of writings relating to the linguistic study of literary texts, chiefly English and American but including important stylistic studies of other literatures. Less selective than Milic's bibliography (below), although each contains citations not found in the other. Some annotations. Indexed.   Z2015.S7B2

Milic, Louis Tonko. Style and stylistics; an analytical bibliography. N.Y., Free Pr., [1967]. 199p.   **BD330**

A selective, classified bibliography of books and articles relating to the study of style in its various aspects. A series of "descriptors" is used rather than conventional annotations. Cross references; index.   Z6514.S8M49

Speech and rhetoric
Bibliography

See also BD515.

Cleary, James W. and **Haberman, Frederick W.** Rhetoric and public address: a bibliography, 1947–1961. Madison and Milwaukee, 1964. 487p.   **BD331**

Based on the annual bibliographies published in the *Quarterly journal of speech,* 1947–51, and in *Speech monographs,* 1952–61, but is not merely a cumulation of these. The entries were reviewed, some corrected, some dropped, and about 1,500 items added.

An alphabetically arranged list of 8,035 items with subject index. Also a list of practitioners and theorists, and an index of reviewers.

Continued by the *Bibliography of rhetoric and public address* appearing annually in *Speech monographs* through 1969 (covering 1968 publications).   Z6514.S7C5

Glenn, Robert W. Black rhetoric: a guide to Afro-American communication. Metuchen, N.J., Scarecrow Pr., 1976. 376p.   **BD332**

Intended as "a guide to available sources that would simplify the work of an instructor or a student interested in the content and communication of speeches and essays by Afro-Americans" (*Pref.*) from early to contemporary times. In four sections: (1) Bibliographies; (2) Anthologies; (3) History and criticism; (4) Speeches and essays.   Z1361.N39G55

Historical rhetoric: an annotated bibliography of selected sources in English. Ed. by Winifred Bryan Horner. Boston, G. K. Hall, [1980]. 294p.   **BD333**

" . . . an attempt to trace the tradition of rhetoric through its long history from ancient Greece to its evolution within the English-speaking world."—*Introd.* Five sections, each by a different scholar, and each having its own introduction followed by annotated lists of primary and secondary works, deal with the classical period, the Middle Ages, the Renaissance, the 18th century, and the 19th century. Indexed.

A complementary work, more limited in its period of coverage, is James J. Murphy's *Renaissance rhetoric; a short-title catalogue of works on rhetorical theory from the beginning of printing to A.D. 1700, with special attention to the holdings of the Bodleian Library, Oxford* (N.Y., Garland, 1981. 353p.). Murphy's *Medieval rhetoric; a*

select bibliography (Toronto, Univ. of Toronto Pr., 1971. 100p.) was published as no.[3] in the "Toronto medieval bibliographies" series.   Z7004.R5H57

The present state of scholarship in historical and contemporary rhetoric. Ed. by Winifred Bryan Horner. Columbia, Univ. of Missouri Pr., 1983. 230p.   **BD334**

Bibliographic essays by contributing scholars cover the classical period, the Middle Ages, the Renaissance, the 18th century, the 19th century, and contemporary rhetoric. Indexed.   PN183.P7

Dissertations

Abstracts of theses in the field of speech. (*In* Speech monographs, v.13–36, 1946–69) Annual.   **BD335**

An annual listing giving abstracts of doctoral dissertations and master's essays.

Doctoral dissertations in speech: work in progress, 1951–68. (*In* Speech monographs, v.18–35) Annual.   **BD336**

Lists dissertations in progress, arranged by subject.

Graduate theses; an index of graduate work in speech. (*In* Speech monographs, v.2–36, 1935–69) Annual.   **BD337**

The first installment covers 1902–34; annual thereafter. Includes both doctoral and master's theses completed.

Continued by *Bibliographic annual in speech communication,* 1970– .

Indexes

Manning, Beverley. Index to American women speakers, 1828–1978. Metuchen, N.J., Scarecrow Pr., 1980. 672p.   **BD338**

Indexes by author, subject, and title the speeches by women appearing in more than 200 publications (including collected works, proceedings of conferences and conventions, congressional committee hearings, etc.).   Z1231.O7M36

Sutton, Roberta Briggs. Speech index; an index to 259 collections of world famous orations and speeches for various occasions. 4th ed., rev. and enl. N.Y., Scarecrow Pr., 1966. 947p.   **BD339**

A dictionary catalog with entries for each oration under author, subject, and type of speech. The 4th ed. includes all the material from the three previous volumes (published 1935–62), and incorporates new materials and some older items previously overlooked. Covers through 1965.

Quinquennial supplements published 1972 and 1977 have been superseded by:

Mitchell, Charity. Speech index; an index to collections of world famous orations and speeches for various occasions. 4th ed., suppl., 1966–1980. Metuchen, N.J., Scarecrow Pr., 1982. 466p.   **BD340**

Cumulates the 1966/70 and 1971/75 supplements to the 4th ed. and adds indexing of speeches published in books during the 1975–80 period.   AI3.S85

Collections, handbooks, etc.

Ancient Greek and Roman rhetoricians; a biographical dictionary. Columbia, Mo., Artcraft Pr., 1968. 104p.   **BD341**

Comp. for the Speech Association of America by Robert W. Smith [and others]; ed. by Donald C. Bryant.

Includes biographies of figures who "contributed to the theory or pedagogy of public address or had taught rhetoric in the ancient Greek and Roman world."—*Pref.*   PA83.A5

Brewer, David Josiah [and others]. World's best orations; from the earliest period to the present time. St. Louis, Mo., Kaiser, [1901]. 10v. il.   **BD342**

Arranged alphabetically by author. Gives for each a brief biographical sketch and selected orations. Indexes: (1) orators; (2) subjects; (3) chronological index of orators; (4) chronological index of periods and events; (5) chronological indexes of law, government, and politics, of religion and philosophy, of literature; (6) general index of orators, subjects, events, etc.   PN6121.B85

Prochnow, Herbert Victor. 1400 ideas for speakers and toastmasters: how to speak with confidence. Natick, Mass., W. A. Wilde, 1964. 158p.   **BD343**

A collection of humorous stories, epigrams, unusual facts and illustrations, selections from speeches, quotations, and unusual comments, etc.

Prochnow has compiled a number of similar collections, including the *Speaker's handbook of epigrams and witticisms* (N.Y., Harper, 1955); *The successful toastmaster* (N.Y., Harper, 1966); and *The toastmaster's handbook* (N.Y., Prentice-Hall, 1949).
                                                       PN4193.I5P67

Representative American speeches. 1937/38– . N.Y., Wilson, 1938– . Annual.   **BD344**

Representative speeches of the year. Issued each year as a number of the *Reference shelf* (BD355).   PS668.B3

Speech Association of America. A history and criticism of American public address. 1st ed. N.Y., McGraw-Hill, 1943–55. 3v.   **BD345**

v.1–2, ed. by W. N. Brigance; v.3, ed. by M. K. Hochmuth and associates: W. N. Brigance and D. Bryant.

Chapters written by specialists treat the great speakers of America, from Jonathan Edwards to Franklin Delano Roosevelt, with extensive footnotes and bibliographies.   PS400.S66

Vital speeches of the day. v.1– , Oct. 8, 1934– . N.Y., City News Pub. Co., 1934– . Semi-monthly.   **BD346**

Prints in full the important addresses of contemporary leaders of public opinion in the fields of economics, politics, education, sociology, business, labor, etc.; heavy representation from government and big business.

—— 25 year index, Oct. 8, 1934–Oct. 1, 1959. Pelham, N.Y., City News Pub. Co., 1963. 137p.

                                                       PN6121.V52

Rhetorical terms

Lanham, Richard A. A handlist of rhetorical terms; a guide for students of English literature. Berkeley, Univ. of California Pr., 1968. 148p.   **BD347**

An alphabetical list of terms with definitions, followed by a number of classified lists of the terms.   PE1445.A2L3

Sonnino, Lee Ann. A handbook to sixteenth-century rhetoric. London, Routledge & Kegan Paul, [1968]. 278p.
                                                          BD348

Lists and defines (with examples) rhetorical terms of the period. A useful work for the student of Renaissance literature.   PN227.S6

Directories

Wasserman, Paul [and others]. Speakers and lecturers: how to find them. 2d ed. Detroit, Gale, [1981]. 2v.   **BD349**

Subtitle: A directory of booking agents, lecture bureaus, companies, professional and trade associations, universities, and other groups which organize and schedule lecture engagements for lecturers and public speakers on all subjects, with information on speakers, subjects, and arrangements, and biographical details on over 2,000 individuals.

Contents: v.1, Sources of speakers; v.2, Speaker biographies. 1st ed. 1979.   PN4007.W3

Debating

Bibliography

Kruger, Arthur N. Argumentation and debate: a classified bibliography. 2d ed. Metuchen, N.J., Scarecrow Pr., 1975. 520p.   **BD350**

1st ed. 1964.

A comprehensive, classified bibliography of books and articles in English, covering all aspects of debating and argument. About 6,000 entries in this edition, including doctoral dissertations and master's theses. Detailed subject index.

Rhetorik, Topik, Argumentation: Bibliographie zur Redelehre und Rhetorikforschung im deutschsprachigen Raum 1945–1979/80 by Robert Jamison and Joachim Dyck (Stuttgart-Bad Cannstatt, Frommann-Holzboog, 1983. 349p.) provides a listing of German publications.   Z7161.5.K75

Indexes

Debate index, comp. by Edith M. Phelps. New ed. rev. N.Y., Wilson, 1939. 130p. (Reference shelf, v.12, no.9)   **BD351**

—— Supplement, comp. by Julia E. Johnsen. N.Y., 1941. (Reference shelf, v.14, no.9)

—— 2d supplement, comp. by Joseph R. Dunlap and Martin A. Kuhn. N.Y., 1964. (Reference shelf, v.36, no.3)

A subject index of debates, briefs, bibliographies, and collections of articles on public questions.   Z7161.5.D28

Handbooks

❖Numerous manuals and texts on the conduct and technique of debates and discussions have been published. The following are representative examples; for others, *see* Kruger (BD350).

Eisenberg, Abné M. and **Ilardo, Joseph A.** Argument: a guide to formal and informal debate. 2d ed. Englewood Cliffs, N.J., Prentice-Hall, [1980]. 230p. il.   **BD352**

1st ed. 1972.

Intended to be useful "whenever and wherever advocates of change confront defenders of the status quo. It presents a plan for disciplined disagreement, rational rebuttal, and calm confrontation. In short, it is a manual for social transformation."—*Prologue.* In two main sections: (1) Rhetorical aspects of argument, and (2) Interpersonal aspects of argument. Bibliography; index.
                                                       PN4181.E49

Freeley, Austin J. Argumentation and debate: reasoned decision making. 5th ed. Belmont, Calif., Wadsworth, [1981]. 410p. il.   **BD353**

1st ed. 1961.

" . . . designed specifically for the undergraduate course in argumentation and debate, but . . . may be used in any broadly liberal course for students who seek self-realization and who desire to prepare themselves for effective participation in a democratic society."—*Pref.* Appendixes: The first Presidential debate; An intercollegiate debate; National intercollegiate debate propositions. Indexed.
                                                       PN4181.F68

Lyle, Guy Redvers and **Guinagh, Kevin.** I am happy to present; a book of introductions. 2d ed. N.Y., Wilson, 1968. 251p.   **BD354**

1st ed. 1953.

A brief essay on the art of introducing speakers precedes a selection of more than a hundred examples of introductory speeches made by well-known persons; introductions are grouped in broad professional categories.   PN4305.I7L9

Reference shelf. N.Y., Wilson, 1922– . v.1– .   **BD355**

Issued 6 numbers to a volume.

Each number is devoted to a timely controversial question, with reprints of selected articles from books and periodicals giving background information and pro and con arguments, followed by a comprehensive bibliography.

Summers, Harrison Boyd, Whan, Forest Livings and **Rousse, Thomas Andrew.** How to debate; a textbook for beginners. 3d ed. N.Y., Wilson, 1963. 355p.   **BD356**

1st ed. 1934.

A textbook for the beginning debater. Appendixes treat logical forms, preparing the debate brief, analysis of the proposition, speech development, and rules in debate. Indexed.   PN4181.S8

ENGLISH LANGUAGE

American

❖Although the distinction between "American" and "English" literatures effected in the following sections generally makes for easier use, it also offers a disadvantage in that a great many of the works cited deal with both American and English literature. Rather than duplicate a large number of entries throughout these sections, most works dealing with both fields have been placed in the "American" section without individual *see* references from the "English" section; exceptions have been made when the emphasis is predominantly English. Users of this *Guide* are urged to scan both sections for pertinent entries.

Guides

See also BD489–BD490.

Fenster, Valmai Kirkham. Guide to American literature. Littleton, Colo., Libraries Unlimited, 1983. 243p.
    BD357

Intended for students at both the graduate and undergraduate level. Pt. 1 is devoted to general guides and sources for the field, with brief annotations; pt.2 (p.67–226) offers bibliographic guides for the study of 100 individual authors. Author/title/subject index.
    Z1225.F46

Gohdes, Clarence Louis Frank and **Marovitz, Sanford E.** Bibliographical guide to the study of the literature of the U.S.A. 5th ed., completely rev. and enl. Durham, N.C., Duke Univ. Pr., 1984. 256p.   **BD358**

1st–4th eds. (1959–76) by C. L. F. Gohdes.

A standard guide for the student of American literature, with sections on such closely related topics as the book trade and publishing, the American language, literary relations with other countries, and literary aspects of women's studies and racial and minority studies. Classed arrangement; concise annotations; separate author and subject indexes.

Long a standard aid for students, the *Guide to American literature and its backgrounds since 1890* by Howard Mumford Jones and Richard M. Ludwig (4th ed., rev. and enl. Cambridge, Harvard Univ. Pr., 1972. 264p.) is now somewhat out of date.   Z1225.G6

Leary, Lewis. American literature; a study and research guide. With the collaboration of John Auchard. N.Y., St. Martin's Pr., [1976]. 185p.   **BD359**

"This guide attempts to chart a way through the maze of writings on American literature, most of which have appeared during the

past forty years, and to point toward those earlier writings that are still useful."—*Pref.* Essentially a series of bibliographic essays on various types of sources for research and study in the field of American literature. Chapter 10 is devoted to individual major authors. Includes a section on planning and writing a research paper.

A review by E. E. Chielens in *Criticism* (19:378, Fall 1977) points out various inaccuracies and suggests that Gohdes's *Bibliographical guide* (above) is a superior work.   Z1225.L47

Patterson, Margaret C. Literary research guide. 2d ed. N.Y., Modern Language Assoc. of Amer., 1983. 559p.   **BD360**

Subtitle: An evaluative, annotated bibliography of important reference books and periodicals on English, Irish, Scottish, Welsh, Commonwealth, American, Afro-American, American Indian, continental, classical, and world literatures, and sixty literature-related subject areas including bibliography, biography, book collecting, film, folklore, linguistics, little magazines, prosody, reviews, teaching resources, textual criticism, women's studies.

1st ed. 1976.

A guide for the student and independent research worker. Arranged by type of work (e.g., general guides to reference books, basic and ongoing bibliographies, bibliographies of bibliography, abstracting and indexing services) or field of literature as mentioned in the subtitle, most sections having a detailed subdivision. Includes notes on periodicals and suggestions for background reading on specific subject areas or literary forms. Annotations are evaluative and often make reference to related entries. Glossary of bibliographic terms; index.   Z6511.P37

Bibliography

❖In addition to the bibliographies listed below, those listed under United States, p.52, should be consulted. Besterman's *World bibliography of bibliographies* (AA16), and the *Bibliographic index* (AA17) refer to many individual bibliographies, either issued separately or included in periodicals or other composite works.

Nilon, Charles H. Bibliography of bibliographies in American literature. N.Y., Bowker, 1970. 483p.   **BD361**

Lists both separately published bibliographies and those appearing as periodical articles and parts of books. In four main sections: (1) Bibliography; (2) Authors; (3) Genre; (4) Ancillary. Index of names and titles.   Z1225.A1N5

American women writers: bibliographical essays. Ed. by Maurice Duke, Jackson R. Bryer and M. Thomas Inge. Westport, Conn., Greenwood Pr., [1983]. 434p.   **BD362**

Follows the pattern of *Eight American authors* (BD404), presenting bibliographical essays by contributing scholars on selected women writers or groups of writers from Colonial times to the present. In addition to providing a critical survey of scholarship through Fall, 1981, the essays frequently point out areas needing further investigation and research. Indexed.   Z1229.W8A44

A bibliographical guide to Midwestern literature. Gerald Nemanic, gen. ed. Iowa City, Univ. of Iowa Pr., [1981]. 380p.   **BD363**

Sections by contributing scholars deal with literature of the region as a whole, the individual states, history and society, folklore, architecture and graphics, blacks, Indians, literary periodicals, a special section on Chicago, and individual authors. No index.
    Z1251.W5B52

Blanck, Jacob Nathaniel. Bibliography of American literature, comp. . . . for the Bibliographical Society of America. New Haven, Yale Univ. Pr., 1955–83. v.1–7. (In progress)   **BD364**

Contents: v.1–7, Henry Adams–Frank Stockton.

A selective bibliography of American authors, which, when completed, will include the works published in book form of approximately 300 writers from the beginning of the Federal period up to and including persons who died before the end of 1930. Authors whose writings do not have literary interest or are not of the character of belles-lettres are excluded.

Material for each author is arranged chronologically and includes: (1) First editions of books and pamphlets, and any other book containing the first appearance of any work; (2) Reprints containing textual or other changes; and (3) A selected list of biographical, bibliographical, and critical works. Periodical and newspaper publications, later editions, translations, and volumes containing isolated correspondence are not included. Location is indicated for the copies examined. Z1225.B55

Etulain, Richard W. A bibliographical guide to the study of western American literature. Lincoln, Univ. of Nebraska Pr., [1982]. 317p. **BD365**

Sections for bibliographies, general works, and special topics are followed by lists of writings on individual authors. Index of authors of criticism.

The frontier experience: a reader's guide to the life and literature of the American West, ed. by Jon Tuska and Vicki Piekarski (DB131) devotes an extensive section to literature, while the same editors' *Encyclopedia of frontier and western fiction* is basically a biographical dictionary of authors of the genre with a few topical articles. Z1251.W5E8

First printings of American authors; contributions toward descriptive checklists. Matthew J. Bruccoli, series ed. Detroit, Gale, [1977–79]. 4v. **BD366**

" . . . planned as a field guide for scholars, dealers, librarians, researchers, students and collectors. The rationale for this work is to identify the first American printings and the first English printings of books by selected American authors."—*Introd.* About 500 authors are covered; selection is "admittedly impressionistic." Each list includes all separate publications wholly or substantially by the author; later printings are noted only when significant changes are incorporated. Some of the checklists are signed with initials of contributors, others were compiled by the editorial staff; some references to bibliographies and bibliocritical studies are noted; numerous illustrations. Each volume is an alphabetical sequence of checklists; v.4 includes an index of authors treated.
Z1231.F5F57

Gohdes, Clarence Louis Frank. Literature and theater of the states and regions of the U.S.A.; an historical bibliography. Durham, N.C., Duke Univ. Pr., 1967. 276p. **BD367**

Lists "monographs, anthologies, pamphlets, chapters of books, and periodical articles which will provide materials for the study of the local belles-lettres and theater of the United States, from earliest times to the present."—*Pref.* Arrangement is by state or region, with literature and theater treated in separate listings. Works on individual writers are generally excluded. Not indexed. Z1225.G63

Harvard University. Library. American literature. Cambridge, Harvard Univ. Lib., 1970. 2v. (Widener Library shelflist, v.26–27) **BD368**

For a note on the series *see* AA145.
Contents: v.1, Classification schedule, classified listing by call number, chronological listing; v.2, Author and title listing.
"The 50,000 books and periodicals in the AL, ALA, and ALB classes include literary histories, anthologies, and works by and about individual literary authors. To ensure full coverage of American authors, 8000 works of British and American fiction comprising the PZ and PZB classes have been added to the chronological and alphabetical lists. Since PZ and PZB represent strictly alphabetical arrangements, classified listings have not been included for them." —*Pref.* Z1225.H35

Hirschfelder, Arlene B., comp. American Indian and Eskimo authors; a comprehensive bibliography. N.Y., Assoc. on Amer. Indian Affairs, [1973]. 99p. **BD369**

An earlier bibliography by the same compiler was entitled *American Indian authors* (N.Y., 1970).

An author listing, plus a list of the authors by tribes. Brief annotations. Includes entries for some collective volumes.
Z1209.H55

Jacobson, Angeline. Contemporary native American literature; a selected & partially annotated bibliography. Metuchen, N.J., Scarecrow Pr., 1977. 262p. **BD370**

Aims to list "the literary works of Native American authors which have been written and published within the years from 1960 to mid-1976."—*Introd.* Arranged by literary genre, with index of authors and a title and first-line index of poems. Z1229.I52J32

Leary, Lewis Gaston. Articles on American literature, 1900–1950. Durham, N.C., Duke Univ. Pr., 1954. 437p.
BD371

A very useful bibliography—a revision and extension of the author's earlier work which covered 1920–45 (publ. 1947)—based on the bibliographies published quarterly in *American literature* since 1929, and annually in *PMLA* since 1922. The coverage has been broadened as well as extended backward to 1900 by the examination of periodicals and other bibliographies.
Continued by: Z1225.L49

—— —— 1950–1967. Comp. with the assistance of Carolyn Bartholet and Catharine Roth. Durham, N.C., Duke Univ. Pr., 1970. 751p. **BD372**

A continuation of Leary's bibliography for the 1900–50 period (above). Compiled on the same basic principles as the earlier volume and employing the same arrangement, this work is both "more inclusive (principally of articles appearing in foreign periodicals) and more selective (in assumptions by the compiler of the value or usefulness of some articles)."—*Introd.* Z1225.L492

Articles on American literature, 1968–1975. Comp. by Lewis Leary and John Auchard. Durham, N.C., Duke Univ. Pr., 1979. 745p. **BD373**

Forms a supplement to Leary's earlier volumes (above), and follows the plan of those compilations. Additions and corrections to the earlier volumes are included, and bibliographical essays are marked with an asterisk. Z1225.A77

Lepper, Gary M. A bibliographical introduction to seventy-five modern American authors. Berkeley, Serendipity Books, 1976. 428p. **BD374**

A series of checklists of "the writings of seventy-five American poets and novelists who have achieved literary prominence since 1945."—*Introd.* Does not include writings about the authors. The subscription books review in the *Booklist* 74:952 (Feb. 1, 1978) concludes that the volume "has only slight value for most libraries."
Z1227.L46

Libman, Valentina A. Russian studies of American literature; a bibliography. Tr. by Robert V. Allen. Ed. by Clarence Gohdes. Chapel Hill, Univ. of North Carolina Pr., 1969. 218p. (Univ. of North Carolina. Studies in comparative literature, no.46) **BD375**

The bibliography originally appeared in *Problemy istorii literatury SShA* (Moskva, Nauka, 1964; p.373–475) issued by the Institut Mirovoi Literatury of the Akademiia Nauk SSSR. Entries are here given in transliteration, with titles of books and periodical articles in both transliteration and English translation. A general section, chronologically arranged, is followed by sections for individual authors. Index of American authors, but none of critics. Makes a useful companion to the compiler's bibliography of Russian translations of American literary writings and studies (BD395).
Z1225.L5517

Literary history of the United States. 3d ed. rev. v.2, Bibliography. N.Y., Macmillan, 1963. 790p., 268p. **BD376**

For full information *see* BD411.

Literary writings in America: a bibliography. Millwood, N.Y., KTO Pr., 1977. 8v. **BD377**

Photoreproduction of a card file prepared at the University of

Pennsylvania under the auspices of the Works Progress Administration during 1938–42. "The primary purpose of the project was to establish bibliographical controls for materials hitherto inaccessible to researchers; specifically, to construct a complete listing of creative American literature written between 1850 and 1940."—*Pref.*

Arranged alphabetically by literary author, with sections for separate works, periodical publications, biography, and criticism as applicable. "The principal sources of material used in compiling *Literary Writings* are over 2,000 volumes of magazines, more than 500 volumes of literary history and criticism, and more than 100 bibliographies."—*Pref.* Signed book reviews are entered under the name of the reviewer as well as under the name of the author of the book reviewed.

A review by the Subscription Books Committee of A.L.A. in the *Booklist* 74:1571 (June 1, 1978) notes various inconsistencies, but recommends the set as a complement to *Poole's,* early volumes of the *Readers' guide,* etc.   Z1225.L58

Repertorio bibliografico della letteratura americana in Italia. A cura del Centro di Studi Americani. Roma, Edizioni di Storia e Letteratura, 1966. 2v. in 1. (Biblioteca di studi americani, 12/13)   **BD378**

Contents: v.1, 1945–1949. Coordinatore, Robert Perrault; v.2, 1950–1954. Coordinatore, Alessandra Pinto Surdi.

Lists Italian critical writings (books, parts of books, and periodical articles) on American literature and Italian translations of American literary works.   Z1225.R45

Rubin, Louis Decimus, ed. A bibliographical guide to the study of Southern literature. With an appendix containing sixty-eight additional writers of the colonial South by J. A. Leo Lemay. Baton Rouge, Louisiana State Univ. Pr., [1969]. 368p.   **BD379**

". . . an attempt to bring together, within the covers of a single book, a compilation of some of the most useful material available for the student who would begin work in the field of Southern literary study."—*Introd.* A section of more than 20 bibliographical surveys of general topics (literary periods, genres, etc.) is followed by checklists of biographical and critical writings on about 135 individual authors. About 100 scholars contributed to the volume.

Continued by: Z1225.R8

Society for the Study of Southern Literature. Committee on Bibliography. Southern literature, 1968–1975. Conflated, ed., and supplemented by Jerry T. Williams. Boston, G. K. Hall, [1978]. 271p.   **BD380**

"A continuation of A Bibliographical Guide to the Study of Southern Literature ed. [by] Louis D. Rubin, Jr. [above] conflated from the checklists published in the Spring issues of the Mississippi Quarterly."—*t.p.*

Cumulates the annotated entries from the *Mississippi quarterly* and adds new citations, cross references, and a name index.

Z1225.S63

Rusk, Ralph Leslie. The literature of the middle western frontier. N.Y., Columbia Univ. Pr., 1925. 2v. (Columbia Univ. studies in English and comparative literature, v.83) (Repr.: N.Y., Ungar, 1963)   **BD381**

v.1 is a history and survey to 1840; v.2 contains bibliographies classified according to the treatment in v.1, covering cultural beginnings, travel, newspapers and magazines, controversial writings, scholarly writings and school books, fiction, poetry and drama. Locates copies.   PS273.R8

Somer, John and **Cooper, Barbara Eck.** American & British literature, 1945–1975: an annotated bibliography of contemporary scholarship. Lawrence, Regents Pr. of Kansas, [1980]. 326p.   **BD382**

Intended primarily as an aid to the teacher and student. Deals with "books and monographs that study trends in American and British literature from 1945 to 1975."—*Introd.* The major portion of the book, "Studies of contemporary literature," is arranged in five categories (General studies; Drama; Fiction and prose; Poetry; Critical theory) plus a separate listing of studies published after

1975. A second section, "Study guides," lists bibliographies and indexes, directories, handbooks, etc.   Z1227.S65

Thompson, Ralph. American literary annuals and gift books, 1825–1865. N.Y., Wilson, 1936. 183p.   **BD383**

Contains a history and discussion of representative American annuals and gift books, and a catalog describing, with fuller data than that given in Faxon's *Literary annuals and gift-books* (Boston, Boston Book Co., 1912), some 230 titles with detailed information as to the different editions of each, location of copies, indication as to whether the annual is for juvenile or adult readers, and many notes as to reprints under changed titles. Index includes these variant titles. Largely supersedes the earlier list by Faxon.

AY10.T5

Current

American literary scholarship, 1963– . Durham, N.C., Duke Univ. Pr., 1965– . Annual.   **BD384**

On the plan of *The year's work in English studies* (BD504), this is a series of bibliographic essays by scholars providing an annual survey of published research in American literature. Chapters on individual authors or pairs of authors, American literature to 1800, fiction and poetry by period, the drama, folklore, etc., make up each volume. No index was published with the first volume, but the second includes separate indexes for 1963 and 1964; annual indexes thereafter.   PS3.A47

Dissertations

See also BD506.

Emerson, O. B. and **Michael, Marion C.** Southern literary culture; a bibliography of masters' and doctors' theses. Rev. & enl. ed. University, Univ. of Albama Pr., [1979]. 400p.

BD385

1st ed. (1955) by C. H. Cantrell and W. R. Patrick.

The earlier edition attempted to list all pertinent theses completed at United States institutions through the summer of 1948; this volume extends the period of coverage through 1969 (with some 1970 listings) and adds many Canadian and foreign theses. About 8,000 titles grouped in three main sections: (1) Individual writers; (2) Cultural, historical, and social backgrounds of Southern literature; (3) Literature. No index.   Z1251.S7C3

Gabel, Gernot U. and **Gabel, Gisela R.** Dissertations in English and American literature: theses accepted by Austrian, French, and Swiss universities, 1875–1970. Hamburg, Gabel, 1977. 198p.   **BD386**

2,169 entries. Arranged by period, general studies being followed by sections for individual literary authors; American literature is treated separately. Author and subject indexes.

———— ———— Suppl. 1971–1975 and additions. Köln, Edition Gemini, 1982. 56p.

Lists an additional 418 titles.   Z2011.G25

Howard, Patsy C., comp. Theses in American literature, 1896–1971. Ann Arbor, Mich., Pieran Pr., 1973. 307p.

BD387

Lists some 7,000 unpublished baccalaureate and master's theses from a wide range of American and foreign universities. Listing is by literary author treated, then alphabetically by author of the thesis. Index of authors of theses, and a brief subject index. Coverage is admittedly incomplete, but precise coverage for individual institutions is not indicated and appears to be spotty in various cases.

Z2011.H63

Woodress, James Leslie. Dissertations in American literature, 1891–1966. Newly rev. and enl. ed., with the assistance of Marian Koritz. Durham, N.C., Duke Univ. Pr., 1968. 185p.   **BD388**

1st ed. (1957) covered 1891–1955; it was reprinted 1962 with a supplement covering 1956–61. This is a complete resetting, incorporating into the main body of the work materials from the supplement to the 1962 ed. and new materials through 1966. About 4,600 entries, including many dissertations from foreign universities.
Z1225.W8

Manuscripts

Robbins, John Albert, ed. American literary manuscripts; a checklist of holdings in academic, historical, and public libraries, museums, and authors' homes in the United States. 2d ed. Athens, Univ. of Georgia Pr., [1977]. 387p.
BD389

1st ed., 1960, comp. by the Committee on Manuscript Holdings of the American Literature Group, Modern Language Association of America. This edition sponsored by the American Literature Section of the Modern Language Association.

Lists about 2,800 American writers indicating, by Library of Congress symbol for nearly 600 participating libraries, the holdings of manuscripts of creative works, journals or diaries, letters to and from the author, documents, memorabilia, etc. Type and extent of holdings are shown by "category-symbols," with, when possible, indications of the number of pieces. There is a separate list of "Authors for whom no holdings were reported."   Z6620.U5M6

Periodicals

Chielens, Edward E. The literary journal in America to 1900; a guide to information sources. Detroit, Gale, [1975]. 197p. (American literature, English literature, and world literatures in English, v.3)   **BD390**

An introductory essay is followed by a series of bibliographic listings (mainly annotated) of general studies, writings on literary periodicals of specific regions (including studies of individual magazines), bibliographies and checklists, and background studies. Indexed.   Z6951.C57

———— The literary journal in America, 1900–1950: a guide to information sources. Detroit, Gale, 1977. 186p.
BD391

Follows the guidelines of the author's guide for journals to 1900 (above). Includes chapters on general literary periodicals, little magazines, regional literary periodicals, politically radical literary periodicals, and academic quarterlies of scholarship and criticism. Indexed.   Z6951.C572

Kirkham, Edwin Bruce and **Fink, John W.** Indices to American literary annuals and gift books, 1825–1865. New Haven, Conn., Research Publs., Inc., 1975. 627p.   **BD392**

Serves as an index to the contents of the items listed in Ralph Thompson's *American literary annuals and gift books* (BD383) and to the microfilm edition of those books. Pt.1 lists each annual or gift book by title with a complete listing of the contents, giving editor's names, authors and titles of literary contributions, illustrations (with indication of painters and engravers), etc.; pt.2 indexes these lists by editor, publisher, city of publication, stereotypers, printers, titles of literary contributions, authors, engraving titles, painters, and engravers.   AY10.T52K57

Kribbs, Jayne K. An annotated bibliography of American literary periodicals, 1741–1850. Boston, G. K. Hall, [1977]. 285p.   **BD393**

An alphabetical listing of literary journals published during the period indicated. Gives full title (with indication of changes), place of publication, dates of first and last issue, editor, publisher, library locations, and notes on contents with names of contributors. Chro-

nological and geographical indexes as well as indexes of names, of editors and publishers, and of titles of tales, novels and dramas.
Z1219.K75

Translations

Brown, Glenora W. and **Brown, Deming B.** A guide to Soviet Russian translations of American literature. N.Y., King's Crown Pr., Columbia Univ., 1954. 243p.   **BD394**

Includes translations of American works—novels, short stories, poems, plays, biographies, memoirs, essays, movie scenarios, and certain journalistic and historical writings—published in book and periodical form in the USSR, 1917–47.

In two parts: (1) anthologies and (2) individual authors. Each entry includes Russian and American title, translator, publisher or periodical title, place and date of publication, pagination, number of copies published, and Russian source. Author and American title indexes.   Z1231.T7B7

Libman, Valentina Abramovna. Amerikanskaia literatura v russkikh perevodakh i kritike: bibliografiia 1776–1975. Moskva, "Nauka," 1977. 451p.   **BD395**

A bibliography of Russian translations of American literary writings, together with translations of critical studies and criticism originally published in Russian.   Z1231.T7L53

Moscow. Vsesoiuznaia Gosudarstvennaia Biblioteka Inostrannoi Literatury. Nauchno-bibliograficheskii otdel. Proizvedeniia amerikanskikh pisatelei v perevodakh na russkii iazyk (1918–1975); bibliograficheskii ukazatel'. Moskva, 1976. 370p.   **BD396**

A bibliography of Russian translations of American literary works. The main portion of the bibliography is arranged by individual author (filed according to the transliterated form of the name in the Cyrillic alphabet). Indexes of authors and of translators.
Z1231.T7M67

Mummendey, Richard. Die schöne Literatur der Vereinigten Staaten von Amerika in deutschen Übersetzungen; eine Bibliographie. Bonn, Bouvier; Charlottesville, Bibliographical Soc. of the Univ. of Virginia, 1961. 199p.   **BD397**

Title on spine: American belle-lettres in German translations; on added title page: Belle-lettres of the United States of America in German translations; a bibliography.

Prefatory matter in English and German.

"Lists the literary works of American authors published originally in the English language which have been translated into German and have appeared as separate volumes."—*Pref.* Covers from the early period through 1957 and lists as many translations as could be found.   Z1231.T7M8

Criticism

Borklund, Elmer. Contemporary literary critics. 2d ed. Detroit, Gale, 1982. 600p.   **BD398**

1st ed. 1977.

Intended as a guide to the work of about 125 modern British and American critics. For each, gives a brief biographical sketch, a bibliography of works by and about the critic, and a description of the writer's critical theories and position, together with representative quotations from his works.   PS78.B56

Curley, Dorothy Nyren, Kramer, Maurice and **Kramer, Elain Fialka.** Modern American literature. 4th enl. ed. N.Y., Ungar, [1969–76]. 4v. (A library of literary criticism)
BD399

1st ed. 1960.

An enlargement and updating of Dorothy Nyren's 1964 volume (3d ed.) of this title, which was designed as a successor, for American literature, to Moulton's *Library of literary criticism* (BD551). Gives excerpts from critical material found in popular and scholarly journals and in books, on American authors who wrote or became prominent after the turn of the century. Definite citation is given for each excerpt. "One hundred and fifteen authors have been added [in the 4th ed.] . . . , while more recent excerpts have also been added on two-thirds of the authors in the third edition; none of the excerpts previously included has been omitted."—*Foreword.* Additions include both older and newly established authors; this edition treats nearly 300 authors. v.3 includes an index of critics. v.4 is a supplement bringing up to date the criticism on about half the authors represented in v.1–3, and treating 49 additional writers.

PS221.C8

English and American studies in German; summaries of theses and monographs. 1968– . Tübingen, M. Niemeyer, 1969– . Annual. **BD400**

Issued as a supplement to *Anglia.*

Provides English-language abstracts of studies (doctoral dissertations, Habilitationsschriften, and independent monographs) completed in German-speaking countries. PE3.A6 Suppl.

Literary criticism register; a monthly listing of studies in English & American literature. v.1, no.1– , Feb. 1983– . [Deland, Fla., Lit. Crit. Reg.], 1983– . Monthly. **BD401**

Provides an up-to-date listing of new critical studies appearing in some 200 journals, plus references to *Dissertation abstracts international* and *American book publishing record.* Listing is by journal, with author and subject indexes (which cumulate semi-annually and annually).

Rees, Robert A. and **Harbert, Earl N.,** eds. Fifteen American authors before 1900; bibliographic essays on research and criticism. Madison, Univ. of Wisconsin Pr., [1971]. 442p. **BD402**

Similar in plan and purpose to *Eight American authors* (BD404) and *Sixteen modern American authors* (below). Scholars have contributed bibliographical essays on Henry Adams, William Cullen Bryant, James Fenimore Cooper, Stephen Crane, Emily Dickinson, Jonathan Edwards, Benjamin Franklin, Oliver Wendell Holmes, William Dean Howells, Washington Irving, Henry Wadsworth Longfellow, James Russell Lowell, Frank Norris, Edward Taylor, and John Greenleaf Whittier. In addition, there are survey chapters on the literature of the Old South and of the New South. Indexed.

PS201.R38

Sixteen modern American authors: a survey of research and criticism. Ed. by Jackson R. Bryer. Durham, N.C., Duke Univ. Pr., 1974. 673p. **BD403**

A rev. ed. of *Fifteen modern American authors* (1969).

Patterned after *Eight American authors* (below), this volume presents similar survey chapters by different scholars, each discussing bibliographies, editions, manuscripts and letters, biography, and critical studies of the individual author. Authors treated in the 1969 ed. were: Sherwood Anderson, Willa Cather, Hart Crane, Theodore Dreiser, T. S. Eliot, William Faulkner, F. Scott Fitzgerald, Robert Frost, Ernest Hemingway, Eugene O'Neill, Ezra Pound, Edwin Arlington Robinson, John Steinbeck, Wallace Stevens, and Thomas Wolfe. The new edition includes supplementary sections for each of the original 15 authors and adds a chapter on William Carlos Williams. Indexed. PS221.F45

Woodress, James, ed. Eight American authors; a review of research and criticism. Rev. ed. N.Y., Norton, [1971]. 392p. **BD404**

"Sponsored by the American Literature Section of the Modern Language Association."—*title page.*

The 1st ed. was edited by Floyd Stovall and appeared in 1956; a bibliographical supplement by J. Chesley Mathews was published 1963. As in the earlier edition, eight different scholars have contributed essays discussing the published bibliographies, editions, biographies, and critical studies of an individual author. Necessarily selective in regard to periodical articles. Bibliographical detail is minimal; cutoff date is generally 1969. Indexed.

Contents: Poe, by Jay B. Hubbell; Emerson, by Floyd Stovall; Hawthorne, by Walter Blair; Thoreau, by Lewis Leary; Melville, by Nathalia Wright; Whitman, by Roger Asselineau; Twain, by Harry Hayden Clark; Henry James, by Robert L. Gale. PS201.E4

Dictionaries and handbooks

Burke, William Jeremiah and **Howe, Will D.** American authors and books, 1640 to the present day. 3d rev. ed., rev. by Irving Weiss and Anne Weiss. N.Y., Crown, [1972]. 719p. **BD405**

1st ed. 1943.

"The purpose of this handbook is to present the most useful facts about the writing, illustrating, editing, publishing, reviewing, collecting, selling and preservation of American books from 1640 to 1940."—*Pref. to 1st ed.* The new edition brings the material up to 1970. It includes, in alphabetical order, concise articles—with cross references to related subjects—on authors, books, periodicals, newspapers, publishing firms, literary societies, regions and localities, etc. Limited to the continental United States. Biographical sketches, which include those of many minor writers, are brief, and usually give complete dates of birth and death, principal occupations, and titles of works. Lists many titles of novels, plays, short stories, poems, essays, orations, songs, hymns, etc., with author and publication date and sometimes brief synopses; and gives information on magazines, including "little magazines," and a selected list of newspapers. Coverage is wider than that in the *Oxford companion to American literature* (BD407), but the articles are much shorter.

Z1224.B87

Duyckinck, Evert Augustus and **Duyckinck, G. L.** Cyclopaedia of American literature. Ed. to date by M. L. Simons, Philadelphia, Baxter, 1875. 2v. il. **BD406**

1st ed. 1855. Various printings.

Subtitle: Embracing personal and critical notices of authors, and selections of their writings, from the earliest period to the present day, with portraits, autographs, and other illustrations.

Arranged chronologically, 1626–1875. Still useful for minor earlier writers. PS85.D7

Hart, James David. The Oxford companion to American literature. 5th ed. N.Y., Oxford Univ. Pr., 1983. 896p. **BD407**

1st ed. 1941.

A complete revision and resetting of this standard work. In dictionary arrangement, it includes short biographies of American authors, with lists of their major works and information regarding their style and subject matter; summaries and descriptions of the important American novels, stories, essays, poems and plays; definitions and historical outlines of literary societies, magazines, anthologies, co-operative publications, literary awards, book collectors, printers, etc. There are not so many entries as in Burke and Howe's *American authors and books* (BD405), but the articles are longer; likewise, the biographical sketches are longer and give more facts. But while Burke and Howe gives complete dates of birth and death (as does Herzberg, BD408), this gives years only; its synopses are also longer, and more space is given to the social and cultural background of American literature and to biographies and discussions of men and movements—social, economic, scientific, military, political, and religious—in their effects upon literature.

"The fifth edition contains full-scale entries on more than 240 authors not in the last edition. It also contains over 115 new entries devoted to detailed summaries of books that were either not in the fourth edition or but briefly noted in it. Of the authors and other subjects previously treated, in this edition over 590 have had extensive changes beyond mere updating made in the entries devoted to them."—*Pref.* Canadian writers previously treated have been deleted because Canadian literature now has its own "Oxford companion."

Chronological index gives, in parallel columns, the literary and social history of America from 1000 to 1982, p.861–96.

PS21.H3

The reader's encyclopedia of American literature, by Max J. Herzberg. N.Y., Crowell, [1962]. 1280p. il. **BD408**

A comprehensive dictionary of American authors, critics, literary movements, synopses of books, literary characters, periodicals, geographical features which have influenced literature, etc. Some of the longer articles (e.g., biographical sketches of major authors) are signed. References to full-length biographies and critical studies are sometimes given. Glossary of literary terms, p.1271–80. In general, articles are longer and more discursive than in the *Oxford companion* (BD407), but this work is also more inclusive though now somewhat out-of-date.   **PS21.R4**

Literary travel guides

Ehrlich, Eugene and **Carruth, Gorton.** The Oxford illustrated literary guide to the United States. N.Y., Oxford Univ. Pr., 1982. 464p. il.   **BD409**

Intended "to help travelers find places associated with the lives and works of writers."—*Pref.* Arranged by state within regional groupings, then by city or town. Includes brief comment on the site or the literary figure associated with it. Index of authors.

PS141.E74

History

Cambridge history of American literature, ed. by William Peterfield Trent, John Erskine, Stuart P. Sherman, Carl Van Doren. N.Y., Putnam, 1917–21. 4v. (Repr.: N.Y., Macmillan, 1972. 3v. in 1.)   **BD410**

Contents: v.1, Colonial and Revolutionary literature. Early national literature, pt.1; v.2, Early national literature, pt.2. Later national literature, pt.1; v.3–4, Later national literature, pts.2–3.

Still an important history of American literature. Covers the early period with unusual thoroughness; treats the ordinary literary forms and subjects, standard writers, etc., with great detail; and includes adequate treatment of many subjects not covered in the customary literary histories, e.g., accounts of the early travelers, explorers, and observers; colonial newspapers; literary annuals and gift books; later magazines and newspapers; children's literature; oral literature; the English language in America; non-English writings, i.e., German, French, Yiddish, aboriginal. Each chapter is by a specialist, and the bibliographies, arranged by chapters at the ends of v.1, 2, and 4, are very full, although not now up-to-date; in all, the bibliography covers more than 500 pages. Author, title, and subject index in v.1, 2, and 4 (the latter covers v.3–4).

A 1933 Macmillan reprint in 3v. and the 1972 reprint noted above omit the bibliographies.   **PS88.C3**

Literary history of the United States. Eds.: Robert E. Spiller [and others]. 4th ed. rev. N.Y., Macmillan, 1974. 2v.

BD411

1st ed. 1948 in 3v.; various reprintings; bibliography supplements issued 1959 and 1972.

Contents: v.1, History; v.2, Bibliography.

The first comprehensive history since the *Cambridge history of American literature* (above). v.1 (originally published in 2v.) presents a survey from colonial times to the present in a series of chapters written by authorities and integrated into a whole by a board of editors. The chapters are not signed, but a list of them with the author of each is given on p.1476–79. No footnotes. In the 4th ed., the main text remains the same except for minor corrections, but "new scholarship has made imperative . . . a wholly new chapter on Emily Dickinson. The chapter on the 'End of an Era,' dealing with the writers who survived World War II, has also been virtually rewritten as time has cleared perspective."—*Pref.* A final section entitled "Mid-Century and after" includes new subsections for poetry, drama, and fiction. The "Reader's bibliography" in v.1 (p.1480–1520) has been updated, and the history volume has its own index.

v.2, *Bibliography,* is a reprinting, with corrections, of the 1963 edition and the bibliography supplements of 1959 and 1972. Tables of contents of the three volumes have been combined, and a new consolidated index is supplied. The volume consists of bibliographical essays organized to develop the treatment of the text. Divided into four main sections: (1) Guide to resources; (2) Literature and culture; (3) Movements and influences; and (4) Individual authors. This fourth section furnishes information on about 240 authors, usually listing separate and collected works, edited texts and re-

prints, biography and criticism, primary sources (including location of manuscripts), and bibliographies. Gives valuable critical and evaluative comments on editions, biographies, etc. The index lists names of literary authors treated, titles of periodicals, and some subject and form headings, e.g., Anthologies, Negro writers and writing, Regionalism and local color, etc.; authors of periodical articles are specifically omitted.   **PS88.L522**

Biographies of authors

American women writers: a critical reference guide from colonial times to the present. Ed. by Lina Mainiero. N.Y., Ungar, [1979–82]. 4v.   **BD412**

Offers bio-bibliographical essays (with some critical comment) on a wide range of American women writers of all periods. Articles are signed by the contributors and carry lists of works by and about the authors treated. Aims to include all women writers of established literary reputation; a representative selection of popular writers, "nontraditional" writers (of diaries, letters, etc.), and children's writers; and a number of writers "best known for extraliterary achievements who have had wide general readership."—*Foreword.* Includes living authors.

An abridged edition was edited by Langdon Lynne Faust (N.Y., Ungar, 1983. 2v.).   **PS147.A4**

American writers: a collection of literary biographies. Leonard Unger, ed. in chief. N.Y., Scribner, [1974–81]. 4v. plus Suppl. 1–2 (in 4v.).   **BD413**

Contents: v.1, Henry Adams to T. S. Eliot; v.2, Ralph Waldo Emerson to Carson McCullers; v.3, Archibald MacLeish to George Santayana; v.4, Isaac Bashevis Singer to Richard Wright; Suppl. 1, pt.1, Jane Addams to Sidney Lanier; pt.2, Vachel Lindsay to Elinor Wylie; Suppl. 2, pt.1, W. H. Auden to O. Henry; pt.2, Robinson Jeffers to Yvor Winters.

The 4v. main set represents 97 of the pamphlets originally published in the "University of Minnesota pamphlets on American writers" series; some have been revised and updated. The supplements cover writers not included in the parent series. Thus, each author is treated in a separate signed essay designed to provide an introduction to the writer's life and work; essays "are aimed at people (general readers here and abroad, college students, etc.) who are interested in the writers concerned, but not familiar with their work."—*Introd.* Selected bibliographies of writings by and about the authors. Indexes in v.4 and in each of the supplements.

PS129.A55

American writers before 1800: a biographical and critical dictionary. Ed. by James A. Levernier and Douglas R. Wilmes. Westport, Conn., Greenwood Pr., [1983]. 3v. (1764p.)   **BD414**

Although the work has a literary bias, "American writers" has been broadly interpreted and figures from many fields of interest for American studies have been included (as have some non- Americans who have significantly influenced the development of American culture). Offers 786 biographical/critical sketches by some 250 scholars. Entries follow a standard pattern: (1) a list of the writer's major publications, with dates; (2) a biographical sketch; (3) a critical appraisal of the writer's work in its intellectual, social, religious, or political context; (4) a list of suggestions for further reading. Appendixes list writers by date of birth, place of birth, and place of principal residence. Chronology; index.   PS185.A4

American writers since 1900. Ed., James Vinson. Chicago, St. James Pr., [1983]. 668p.   **BD415**

For each writer there is a brief biographical sketch, a list of published books, a selected list of critical studies, and a signed critical essay. Includes some living authors.

Fred B. Millett's *Contemporary American authors; a critical survey and 219 bio-bibliographies* (N.Y., Harcourt, 1940. 716p.), though much out of date, is still occasionally useful.

Dictionary of literary biography. Detroit, Gale, 1978–84. v.1–33. il. (In progress)   **BD416**

Contents: v.1, The American renaissance in New England, ed. by

Joel Myerson; v.2, American novelists since World War II, ed. by Jeffrey Helterman and Richard Layman; v.3, Antebellum writers in New York and the South, ed. by Joel Myerson; v.4, American writers in Paris, 1920–1939, ed. by Karen Lane Rood; v.5, American poets since World War II, ed. by Donald J. Greiner (2v.); v.6, American novelists since World War II, 2d ser., ed. by James E. Kibler, Jr.; v.7, Twentieth-century American dramatists, ed. by John MacNicholas (2v.); v.8, Twentieth-century American science fiction writers, ed. by David Coward and Thomas Wymer (2v.); v.9, American novelists, 1910–1945, ed. by James J. Martine (3v.); v.10, Modern British dramatists, 1900–1945, ed. by Stanley Weintraub (2v.); v.11, American humorists, 1800–1950, ed. by Stanley Trachtenberg (2v.); v.12, American realists and naturalists, ed. by Earl Harbert and Donald Pizer; v.13, British dramatists since World War II, ed. by Stanley Weintraub (2v.); v.14, British novelists since 1960, ed. by Jay L. Halio (2v.); v.15, British novelists, 1930–1959, ed. by Bernard Oldsey (2v.);

v.16, The Beats: literary bohemians in postwar America, ed. by Ann Charters (2v.); v.17, Twentieth-century American historians, ed. by Clyde N. Wilson; v.18, Victorian novelists after 1885, ed. by Ira B. Nadel and William E. Fredeman; v.19, British poets, 1880–1914, ed. by Donald E. Stanford; v.20, British poets, 1914–1945, ed. by Donald E. Stanford; v.21, Victorian novelists before 1885, ed. by Ira B. Nadel and William E. Fredeman; v.22, American writers for children, 1900–1960, ed. by John Cech; v.23, American newspaper journalists, 1873–1900, ed. by Perry J. Ashley; v.24, American colonial writers, 1606–1734, ed. by Emory Elliott; v.25, American newspaper journalists, 1901–1925, ed. by Perry J. Ashley; v.26, American screenwriters, ed. by Robert E. Morsberger, Stephen O. Lesser and Randall Clark; v.27, Poets of Great Britain and Ireland, 1945–1960, ed. by Vincent B. Sherry, Jr.; v.28, Twentieth-century American Jewish fiction writers, ed. by Daniel Walden; v.29, American newspaper journalists, 1926–1950, ed. by Perry J. Ashley; v.30, American historians, 1607–1865, ed. by Clyde N. Wilson; v.31, American colonial writers, 1735–1781, ed. by Emory Elliott; v.32, Victorian poets before 1850, ed. by W. E. Fredeman and I. B. Nadel; v.33, Afro-American fiction writers after 1955, ed. by Trudier Harris and Thadious Davis.

"Entries range from brief notices of secondary figures (200 to 600 words) to comprehensive treatments (up to 15,000 words) of major figures. The major entries are written by authorities in their fields and are intended as permanent contributions to literary history. The purpose . . . is not only to provide reliable information in a clear format, but also to place literary figures in the larger perspective of North American literary history and to offer appraisals of their accomplishments by qualified scholars."—*Plan of the work.* Includes bibliographies of works by and about the authors.

A provisional judgment by the Reference and Subscription Books Review Committee is that, while the first three volumes (all published at the time the review was written) provide reliable information in a clear and attractive format, they are "not a necessary purchase for libraries owning *American Writers,* the *DAB,* or Robert E. Spiller's *Literary History of the United States. . . .* None of the three volumes . . . makes an important contribution to literary history."—*Booklist* 77:346–47.

Kept up to date and supplemented by the *Dictionary of literary biography yearbook,* 1980– (Detroit, Gale, 1981–).

The series is complemented by the same publisher's *Dictionary of literary biography: documentary series,* each volume of which deals with the major figures of a particular literary period, movement, or genre and offers a varied selection of documents, reproductions of manuscript pages, galley proofs, title pages, and photographs. Four volumes appeared 1982–84.

Kunitz, Stanley Jasspon and **Haycraft, Howard.** American authors, 1600–1900; a biographical dictionary of American literature, complete in one volume with 1300 biographies and 400 portraits. N.Y., Wilson, 1938. 846p. il. **BD417**

Popularly written biographies with brief bibliographies of works by and about the authors. PS21.K8

Southern writers: a biographical dictionary. Ed. by Robert Bain, Joseph M. Flora and Louis D. Rubin, Jr. Baton Rouge, Louisiana State Univ. Pr., [1979]. 515p. **BD418**

A project of the Society for the Study of Southern Literature.

Offers brief, signed "sketches of the lives of authors associated with the American South."—*Pref.* 379 authors are treated, a few being accorded sketches of about 1,000 words, a second group about 750 words, and the greatest number (including most of the contemporary figures) about 500 words. Bibliography of works by, but not about, each author. PS261.S59

Who was who among North American authors, 1921–1939. Detroit, Gale, [1976]. 2v. (1578p.) **BD419**

Represents a cumulation of the latest sketches of some 11,200 persons treated in the various volumes of *Who's who among North American authors* published 1921–39. Z1224.W6

General collections

Library of southern literature; comp. under the direct supervision of southern men of letters. E. A. Alderman, J. C. Harris, editors in chief. New Orleans, Martin and Hoyt, [c1908–23]. 17v. il. **BD420**

Contents: v.1–13, Biographical and critical sketches, and selected extracts arranged alphabetically by the authors discussed; v.14, Miscellanea: poems, anecdotes, letters, epitaphs and inscriptions, quotations, bibliography; v.15, Biographical dictionary, ed. by Lucian Lamar Knight, containing 3800 sketches; v.16, Historical side lights, 50 reading courses. Bibliography, references to bibliographies in v.1–13, and supplementary lists. Index of authors, titles, and subjects; v.17, Supplement.

A useful collection, but with various inaccuracies in the biographical sections. PS551.L5

Stedman, Edmund Clarence and **Hutchinson, Ellen Mackay.** Library of American literature from the earliest settlement to the present time. N.Y., Webster, 1891 [c1887–90]. 11v. il. **BD421**

Frequently reprinted.

Gives selections which are characteristic examples of the work of the principal American writers 1607–1889; a biographical dictionary of the writers included is given in v.11, and there is a general index of persons, subjects, and some titles, the latter grouped under form headings such as poetry, essays, etc.; quotations are brought out in the index under heading, "Noted sayings." PS504.S7

Drama

Bibliography

See also BD458.

Bergquist, G. William. Three centuries of English and American plays; a checklist. England, 1500–1800; United States, 1714–1830. N.Y., London, Hafner, 1963. 281p. **BD422**

For full information *see* BD579. Z2014.D7B45

Harris, Richard H. Modern drama in America and England, 1950–1970: a guide to information sources. Detroit, Gale, [1982]. 606p. (American literature, English literature, and world literatures in English, v.34) **BD423**

Lists of relevant bibliographies and selected critical writings are followed by lists of writings by and about 255 playwrights. Brief annotations; index. Z1231.D7H36

Hill, Frank Pierce. American plays printed 1714–1830; a bibliographical record. Stanford, Calif., Stanford Univ. Pr.; Oxford, Univ. Pr., 1934. 152p. (Repr.: N.Y., B. Blom, 1968) **BD424**

Based primarily upon the 2d ed. of Wegelin (BD429); and upon the typewritten catalog prepared by F. W. Atkinson, 1918, of published plays in his library. Arranged alphabetically by author and anonymous title, with title index and chronological list. Z1231.D7H6

Hixon, Donald L. and **Hennessee, Don A.** Nineteenth-century American drama: a finding guide. Metuchen, N.J., Scarecrow Pr., 1977. 579p.   **BD425**

Essentially a finding list to the "American plays, 1831–1900" portion of the Readex Corporation's microprint collection *English and American plays of the nineteenth century*. Lists about 4,500 plays, including plays of British and continental authors adapted or translated for the American stage. Author listing with three appendixes: (1) Series (which lists the contents of the many series analyzed in the main work); (2) Ethnic/racial (which lists those plays which include characters of a particular racial or ethnic origin); and (3) Subject/form (which "groups those plays dealing with particular broad subject areas, or representing specific literary and dramatic forms, into a variety of appropriate categories."—*Pref.*).

PS632.H57

Meserve, Walter J. American drama to 1900: a guide to information sources. Detroit, Gale, [1980]. 254p. (American literature, English literature, and world literatures in English, 28)   **BD426**

A bibliography of American drama, not American theater. Thus, "the entries deal with dramatists and their plays plus discussions of dramatic theory, dramatic criticism, and the critics themselves."—*Introd.* A section dealing with "Critical, historical, and reference resources" is followed by a section devoted to individual dramatists. Author, title, and subject indexes.   Z1231.D7M45

Roden, Robert F. Later American plays, 1831–1900; being a compilation of the titles of plays by American authors published and performed in America since 1831. N.Y., Dunlap Soc., 1900. 132p. (Publ. of the Dunlap Soc., n.s. 12) (Repr.: N.Y., B. Franklin, 1964)   **BD427**

Gives brief biographical notes, followed by a listing of published plays.   Z1231.D7W5

U.S. Copyright Office. Dramatic compositions copyrighted in the United States, 1870 to 1916. Wash., Govt. Prt. Off., 1918. 2v. (3547p.)   **BD428**

A list of about 60,000 plays registered for copyright July 21, 1870–Dec. 31, 1916. The main list is arranged alphabetically by title and gives, for each title, author's name, number of acts, number of pages, place published and date of a published play (or the word "typewritten" to indicate the typed manuscript of an unpublished play), date of copyright, holder of copyright, number of copies deposited, etc. Cross references from alternate, secondary, and translated titles are given in the main alphabet. Also includes a supplementary alphabet of recent titles (1915–16), and a detailed author index containing names of authors, joint authors, editors, translators, and copyright proprietors, pseudonyms, etc.

For titles of plays copyrighted later than 1916, the *Catalog of copyright entries* (AA596) should be consulted.   Z5781.U55

Wegelin, Oscar. Early American plays, 1714–1830; a compilation of titles of plays and dramatic poems written by authors born in or residing in North America previous to 1830. 2d ed. rev. N.Y., Literary Collector Pr., 1905. 94p.   **BD429**

The 1900 edition was reprinted by Haskell House, N.Y., 1968. Brief biographical sketches are followed by titles of plays.   Z1231.D7W41

Criticism

Eddleman, Floyd Eugene. American drama criticism: interpretations, 1890–1977. 2d ed. Hamden, Conn., Shoe String Pr., 1979. 488p.   **BD430**

1st ed. and supplements (1967–76) by Helen H. Palmer and Anne Jane Dyson.

A listing of "interpretations of American plays published primarily between 1890 and 1977 in books, periodicals, and monographs. . . . The dramatists are, or were, citizens of the United States, except for a few Canadian and Caribbean dramatists whose works have been or are being performed in this country."—*Pref.* Arranged by

dramatist, then by title of the play; date of first production is noted. Indexed.   Z1231.D7P3

—— —— Supplement I to the 2d ed. Hamden, Conn., Shoe String Pr., 1984. 255p.

Includes citations through 1982. For many playwrights a "general" section is now included preceding the entries for individual plays.

Marks, Patricia. American literary and drama reviews; an index to late nineteenth century periodicals. Boston, G. K. Hall, [1984]. 313p.   **BD431**

Cites reviews published in some thirteen periodicals during the period 1880–1900. Drama reviews and literary reviews are listed in separate sections, the first by title of the drama reviewed, the second by author of the book reviewed. Only "domestic presentations by American and foreign playwrights" (*Pref.*) are indexed in the drama section; United States publications predominate in the literary reviews section, but other works are not excluded. Indexed.

PN2256.M37

Annuals

Best plays of 1894/99– and year book of the drama in America. Boston, Small, 1920–25; N.Y., Dodd, 1926– . il. Annual.   **BD432**

Title varies: 1899/1909–1946/47, *Best plays . . .* ; 1947/48–1949/50, *Burns Mantle best plays.*

1894/99 (publ. 1955), 1899/1909 (publ. 1944), and 1909/19 (publ. 1933) are basic volumes edited by Burns Mantle and G. P. Sherwood, giving selected plays, and chronological lists of plays produced, with date, theater, and cast.

Contents of the annual volumes vary somewhat but include such sections as: (1) Digests with critical comment on selected plays of the year; (2) Title list of plays produced in New York during the year, giving for each: title, author, number of performances, theater, cast of characters, and brief outline of plot; (3) Plays produced outside of New York; (4) Shakespeare festivals; (5) Statistics of runs; (6) List of actors with place and date of birth of each; (7) Prizes and awards; and (8) Index of authors, Index of plays and casts, Index of producers, directors, designers.

—— Index, 1899–1950, 1949–60. N.Y., Dodd, 1950–61. 147p., 46p.

Include indexes, by title, to the plays appearing in the annual volumes, and indexes to authors, adapters, composers, and lyricists. Symbols indicate one of the "ten best," a Pulitzer-prize play, and a New York Drama Critics Circle award play.

A cumulative index has appeared as: PN6112.B45

Guernsey, Otis L. Directory of the American theater, 1894–1971; indexed to the complete series of *Best plays* theater yearbooks. N.Y., Dodd, Mead, [1971]. 343p.   **BD433**

Subtitle: Titles, authors, and composers of Broadway, off-Broadway, and off-off-Broadway shows and their sources.

An author, title, composer index to the Burns Mantle *Best plays* series (above) rather than a directory in its own right.

PN6112.B4524

History

Bogard, Travis, Moody, Richard and **Meserve, Walter J.** American drama. London, Methuen; N.Y., Barnes & Noble, [1977]. 324p. il. (The Revels history of drama in English, v.8)   **BD434**

For other volumes of the *Revels history* see BD615.

A chronological table of historical and theatrical events, 1492–1975, precedes the history proper; bibliographic essay, p.297–310. Indexed.   PR625.R44

Quinn, Arthur Hobson. History of the American drama, from the beginning to the Civil War. 2d ed. N.Y., Crofts, 1943. 530p.   **BD435**

1st ed. 1923.

Includes "A list of American plays," p.423–97; bibliography, p.393–421.   PS332.Q5

———— A history of the American drama from the Civil War to the present day. [Rev. ed.] N.Y., London, Crofts, 1937. 2v. in 1. (296p., 432p.) il.   **BD436**

Contains the text of the 2v. ed. of 1927 plus a chapter on the 1927–36 period. General bibliography and list of American plays, 1860–1936, p.305–402.   PS332.Q55

Fiction

Bibliography

Coan, Otis Welton and **Lillard, Richard Gordon.** America in fiction; an annotated list of novels that interpret aspects of life in the United States, Canada, and Mexico. 5th ed. Palo Alto, Calif., Pacific Books, 1967. 232p.   **BD437**

1st ed. 1941.

Lists novels and collections of short stories by phase or aspect of American life, with brief annotations indicating subject matter and treatment. Recommended titles are starred.   Z1361.C6C6

Dickinson, Arthur Taylor. Dickinson's American historical fiction. 4th ed. [by] Virginia Brokaw Gerhardstein. Metuchen, N.J., Scarecrow Pr., 1981. 312p.   **BD438**

1st ed. 1958.

This edition updated to include works published through 1977. "A total of 2755 novels casting light on some aspect of American history are classified into natural chronological periods from Colonial days to the 1970's. The brief annotations are designed to place the books in historical perspective rather than to make any critical judgment on the quality or the historical accuracy of the writing."— *Pref.*   Z1231.F4D47

Grimes, Janet and **Daims, Diva.** Novels in English by women, 1891–1920; a preliminary checklist. N.Y., Garland, 1981. 805p. (Garland reference library of the humanities, v.202)   **BD439**

Lists some 15,000 novels by more than 5,000 authors published in England and the United States. In three sections: (1) alphabetical listing of authors with their novels, verified; (2) anonymous and pseudonymous works, also verified; (3) citations to books not seen. Most entries are annotated. Title index.   Z2013.5.W6G75

Johannsen, Albert. The House of Beadle and Adams and its dime and nickel novels: the story of a vanished literature. Norman, Univ. of Oklahoma Pr., [1950–62]. 3v. il.

                                                        BD440

Contents: v.1, A history of the firm. Numerical lists of the various series of Beadle novels; v.2, The authors and their novels. Appendix. (Gives biographical sketches of the authors, and lists of their books; general alphabetical index of titles and subtitles; index of principal localities, characters, etc.); v.3, Supplement, Addenda, Corrigenda. (Includes an index of songs, giving the titles of the songs in the Beadle *Songsters*.)   Z1231.F4J68

Johnson, James Gibson. Southern fiction prior to 1860; an attempt at a first hand bibliography. Charlottesville, Va., Michie Co., 1909. 126p. (Repr.: N.Y., Johnson, 1967; N.Y., Phaeton, 1968)   **BD441**

Thesis (Ph.D.), Univ. of Virginia.

Arranged alphabetically, followed by a chronological list, 1765–1860.   Z1231.F4J7

Kirby, David K. American fiction to 1900; a guide to information sources. Detroit, Gale, [1975]. 296p. (American literature, English literature, and world literatures in English, v.4)   **BD442**

A brief section of general aids is followed by sections on individual authors of the period. For individual authors, lists principal works, bibliographies, biographies, and a selection of critical studies. Uneven in coverage.   Z1231.F4K57

New York. Public Library. Beadle collection of dime novels given to the . . . library by Dr. Frank P. O'Brien. N.Y., 1922. 99p. il.   **BD443**

A list of some 1,400 novels, arranged alphabetically by series, with indexes of: (1) authors, and (2) titles.   Z1231.F4N5

Rosa, Alfred F. and **Eschholz, Paul A.** Contemporary fiction in America and England, 1950–1970; a guide to information sources. Detroit, Gale, [1976]. 454p. (American literature, English literature, and world literatures in English, v.10)

                                                        BD444

A brief section of "Studies and reference works" is followed by a series of bibliographies of writings by and about some 136 contemporary authors.   Z1231.F4R57

Van Derhoof, Jack Warner. A bibliography of novels related to American frontier and colonial history. Troy, N.Y., Whitston, 1971. 501p.   **BD445**

An author listing without subject approach. Brief annotations are provided except where the title or subtitle obviates the need for such.   Z1231.F4V3

Woodress, James Leslie. American fiction, 1900–1950; a guide to information sources. Detroit, Gale, [1974]. 260p. (American literature, English literature, and world literatures in English, v.1)   **BD446**

Pt.1, General bibliography, contains four brief sections: one listing general background source material; the others, specialized source materials on the novel, the short story, and interviews with authors. Pt.2 comprises 44 individual bibliographical essays on those writers "who seem in 1973 to be the most significant producers of fiction during the first half of the twentieth century. They have been selected on the basis of the critical esteem accorded them during the 23 years that have passed since 1950."—*Introd.* The bibliographical essays include notes on bibliography and manuscripts, editions and reprints, biography, and criticism. Indexed.

                                                        Z1231.F4W64

Wright, Lyle Henry. American fiction, 1774–1850: a contribution toward a bibliography. 2d rev. ed. San Marino, Calif., Huntington Lib., 1969. 411p.   **BD447**

1st ed. 1939; rev. ed. 1948.

Lists novels, romances, short stories, fictitious biographies, travels, allegories, and tractlike tales, written by Americans. This edition includes about 3,500 items. Locates copies in 22 libraries.

                                                        Z1231.F4W9

———— American fiction, 1851–1875; a contribution toward a bibliography. Additions and corrections appended. San Marino, Calif., Huntington Lib., 1965. 438p.   **BD448**

First published 1957; this is a reprint with additions and corrections, p.417–38.

A companion volume to the above, listing more than 2,800 titles. Locates copies in 18 libraries and 1 private collection.

                                                        Z1231.F4W92

———— American fiction, 1876–1900; a contribution toward a bibliography. San Marino, Calif., Huntington Lib., 1966. 683p.   **BD449**

A companion to the two preceding items. Lists copies of the first or earliest located United States edition of works of fiction written for adults. 6,175 items, with locations (representing 15 libraries) given for most.   Z1231.F4W93

Criticism

Adelman, Irving and **Dworkin, Rita.** The contemporary novel; a checklist of critical literature on the British and American novel since 1945. Metuchen, N.J., Scarecrow Pr., 1972. 614p.   **BD450**

"Novelists are included if they wrote after 1945 . . . , if they wrote before 1945 but achieved their most significant recognition after 1945 . . . , or if they wrote before 1945 but continued with major publications after 1945."—*Pref.* Includes book materials and periodical articles; cutoff date is 1968 for periodicals and 1969 for books.   Z1231.F4A34

Eichelberger, Clayton L. A guide to critical reviews of United States fiction, 1870–1910. Metuchen, N.J., Scarecrow Pr., 1971–74. 2v.   **BD451**

v.1 provides references to reviews of works of both major and minor authors, drawn from about 30 periodicals of the period; v.2 covers another 10 periodicals.   Z1225.E35

Gerstenberger, Donna Lorine and **Hendrick, George.** The American novel; a checklist of twentieth-century criticism. Denver, Alan Swallow, [1961–70]. 2v.   **BD452**

Contents: [v.1] The American novel, 1789–1959; v.2, Criticism written 1960–1968.

Lists criticism on novels written since 1789. Arranged alphabetically by novelist, with listings of criticism arranged under individual novels, general studies, and bibliographies.   Z1231.F4G4

Weixlmann, Joseph. American short-fiction criticism and scholarship, 1959–1977: a checklist. Athens, Ohio, Swallow Pr./Ohio Univ. Pr., [1982]. 625p.   **BD453**

Serves as a supplement to Thurston's *Short fiction criticism* (BD254n) for American writings, but is less selective in the type of material included. Treats some 500 authors.   Z1231.F4W43

Annuals

Best American short stories of 1915– , and the Yearbook of the American short story. Boston, Houghton, 1915– . v.1– . Annual.   **BD454**

Title varies: 1915–41, *Best short stories.*

Each volume contains: (1) Text of selected short stories of the year, and (2) Yearbook. Contents of yearbooks vary; in recent years are much reduced in extent.   PZ1.B446235

History

Quinn, Arthur Hobson. American fiction; an historical and critical survey. N.Y., Appleton, [1936]. 805p.   **BD455**

A chronological treatment of the novel and short story from 1770 to 1935. Bibliography, p.726–72.   PS371.Q5

Poetry

Bibliography and indexes

See also BD647, BD653, BD662.

Alexander, Harriet Semmes. American and British poetry: a guide to the criticism, 1925–1978. Athens, Ohio, Swallow Pr., [1984]. 486p.   **BD456**

Similar in scope and purpose to *Poetry explication* (BD653), principal differences being that this includes criticism of poems of up to 1,000 lines in length whereas 500 lines is the upper limit for the other compilation, and periodical titles are not abbreviated herein. While there is considerable overlap between the two works, each contains citations not found in the other.   Z1231.P7A44

American poetry index. v.1– , 1981/82– . Great Neck, N.Y., Granger Book Co., [1983]– . Annual.   **BD457**

Subtitle: An author and title index to poetry by Americans in single-author collections.

Authors and titles appear in a single alphabetical sequence. 190 collections are indexed in v.1.

Brown University. Library. Dictionary catalog of the Harris collection of American poetry and plays. Boston, G. K. Hall, 1972. 13v.   **BD458**

Reproduction of the catalog cards for more than 150,000 printed books and pamphlets by American and Canadian authors. The library attempts to acquire every volume of American and Canadian

verse and every play of similar origin. (Latin American poetry and plays were collected up to the 1950s, but since that time only Mexican authors are collected.) The catalog does not include the extensive collections of broadsides, manuscripts, and sheet music in the library.

An earlier catalog of the collection was published by the Brown University Library as *The Anthony memorial; a catalogue of the Harris collection of American poetry with biographical and bibliographical notes by John C. Stockbridge* (Providence, R.I., 1886. 320p.).   Z1231.P7B72

Congdon, Kirby. Contemporary poets in American anthologies, 1960–1977. Metuchen, N.J., Scarecrow Pr., 1978. 228p.   **BD459**

Some 400 anthologies published during the 1960–77 period are cited and a list of contributors to each is given. A second section lists the poets alphabetically with reference to the anthologies in which their works appear. Individual titles of poems are not given. About 6,500 poets are represented.   Z1231.P7C65

Index of American periodical verse, 1971– . Metuchen, N.J., Scarecrow Pr., 1973– . Annual.   **BD460**

Editors vary.

An author listing giving full citation to each poem; title index. Computer-produced beginning with the volume covering 1982; now indexes poems in nearly 200 periodicals.

The *Anthology of magazine verse . . . and Yearbook of American poetry* (N.Y., Gomme, etc., 1913–29) included in the yearbook section of most volumes an author index to poems published in magazines, an author list of reviews and articles on poetry, an author list of new books of verse, and a selected list of books about poets and poetry.   Z1231.P7I47

Irish, Wynot R. The modern American muse; a complete bibliography of American verse, 1900–1925. Syracuse, N.Y., Syracuse Univ. Pr., [1950]. 259p.   **BD461**

Lists 6,906 separately published books of verse appearing in the first quarter of this century. Many of them are books of fugitive verse which were privately printed in small editions, and in many cases not listed in the usual publications of the book trade. Also included are the works of the better-known American poets published by the standard publishers.

Items are arranged chronologically by year of publication, and alphabetically by author under the year. Unfortunately there is no index, either by author or by title.   Z1231.P7I7

Lemay, Joseph A. Leo. A calendar of American poetry in the colonial newspapers and magazines and in the major English magazines through 1765. Worcester, Mass., American Antiquarian Soc., [c1970]. 353p.   **BD462**

Originally published in parts in the *Proceedings* of the American Antiquarian Society, Worcester, Mass.

For each poem is given: date and place of publication; first line; title; number of lines; author or pseudonym; and a note on the poem (including reprintings, accounts of the author, or other useful information). Indexes of first lines; names, pseudonyms, and titles; and subjects and genres.   Z1231.P7L44

Wegelin, Oscar. Early American poetry; a compilation of the titles of volumes of verse and broadsides by writers born or residing in North America, north of the Mexican border. 2d ed. rev. and enl. N.Y., Peter Smith, 1930. 2v. in 1. il.   **BD463**

Covers 1650–1820, listing 1,379 titles.
Supplemented by: Z1231.P7W4

Stoddard, Roger E., comp. A catalogue of books and pamphlets unrecorded in Oscar Wegelin's Early American poetry, 1650–1820. Providence, R.I., Friends of the Library of Brown Univ., 1969. 84p.   **BD464**

Reprinted from *Books at Brown*, v.23 (1969).

Describes and locates more than 250 books and pamphlets not recorded in Wegelin's bibliography (above) or not fully described therein.

Handbooks

Malkoff, Karl. Crowell's Handbook of contemporary American poetry. N.Y., T. Y. Crowell, [1973]. 338p. **BD465**

Includes biographical and bibliographical information, but intended mainly "as a guide to the actual process of reading contemporary American poetry."—*Pref.* Entries for individual poets, schools, and movements. PS3235.M3

Anthologies

The new Oxford book of American verse, chosen and ed. by Richard Ellmann. N.Y., Oxford Univ. Pr., 1976. 1076p. **BD466**

Earlier selections published 1927 and 1950, compiled by Bliss Carman and F. O. Matthiessen respectively, had title *Oxford book of American verse.* In this edition Ellmann has "attempted to select poems on the basis of intrinsic merit rather than the tendencies they represent."—*Introd.* Covers from Ann Bradstreet to Amiri Baraka (LeRoi Jones). PS584.N4

Stedman, Edmund Clarence. An American anthology, 1787–1900; selections illustrating the editor's critical review of American poetry in the nineteenth century. Cambridge, Mass., Houghton, 1900. 878p. **BD467**

Includes biographical notes, index of first lines, and index of titles. PS586.S7

Stevenson, Burton Egbert. The home book of verse, American and English; with an appendix containing a few well-known poems in other languages. 9th ed. N.Y., Holt, 1953. 2v. (lxxxiv p., 4013p.) **BD468**

PR1175.S76

———— Home book of modern verse. 2d ed. rev. N.Y., Holt, [1953]. 1124p. **BD469**

For full information on the above two items *see* BD659–BD660. PR1175.S762

Untermeyer, Louis. Modern American poetry, a critical anthology. New and enl. ed. [i.e., 8th]. N.Y., Harcourt, [1962]. 701p. **BD470**

1st ed. 1919.
A revised edition including biographical and critical paragraphs, with selections of poems from 76 poets from Walt Whitman to Anne Sexton, including 13 who appear for the first time in this edition.
Published also in a combined edition with the editor's *Modern British poetry* (N.Y., 1962). PS611.U6

Diaries, letters, and autobiography

First person female American: a selected and annotated bibliography of the autobiographies of American women living after 1950. Ed. by Carolyn H. Rhodes. Troy, N.Y., Whiston, 1980. 404p. (American notes & queries supplement, v.2) **BD471**

Lists 330 published autobiographies, journals, diaries, and collections of letters of 224 women living after 1950. Lengthy annotations. Z7963.A8F57

Matthews, William. American diaries, an annotated bibliography of American diaries written prior to the year 1861, . . . with the assistance of Roy Harvey Pearce. Berkeley, Los Angeles, Univ. of California Pr., 1945. 383p. (Univ. of California pubn. in English, v.16, 1945) (Repr.: Boston, J. S. Canner, 1959) **BD472**

A chronological list of diaries written prior to 1861 with annotations giving full name, occupation, dates, and home of author, and brief notes as to subject content of diary and record of printed source. Manuscript diaries are listed in a companion volume (BD474).
A new edition is in progress: Z1247.M3

Arksey, Laura, Pries, Nancy and **Reed, Marcia.** American diaries: an annotated bibliography of published American diaries and journals. Detroit, Gale, [1983]– . v.1– . (In progress) **BD473**

Contents: v.1, Diaries written from 1492 to 1844.
A revised and greatly expanded edition of Matthews' *American diaries* (above). Arrangement is by beginning date of the diary, then alphabetically by diarist; publication information is given in full, including references to extracts published in periodicals, etc. Annotations indicate period of coverage, content, special events described, or field of particular interest. Includes all diaries listed in Matthews "with the exception of a few Canadian diaries containing no evidence of any American content" (*Introd.*), a few foreign diaries for which no English translation could be found, and a few items cited in Harriette M. Forbes's *New England diaries, 1602–1800* (1923) of which no copy could be located. Detailed subject and geographic indexes.
Not only is the period of coverage extended beyond that treated by Matthews, but the definition of "American" now includes Alaskan, Hawaiian, and much Spanish-American material previously omitted. A second volume is to carry the record to 1980. Z5305.U5A74

Matthews, William. American diaries in manuscript, 1580–1954; a descriptive bibliography. Athens, Univ. of Georgia Pr., 1974. 176p. **BD474**

A chronological listing of more than 5,000 unpublished diaries (including those published only in part). Gives name, date of diary, brief statement of contents if known, and location. Author index. Z5305.U5M32

Weiss, Harry Bischoff. American letter-writers, 1698–1943. N.Y., New York Pub. Lib., 1945. 54p. **BD475**

"Reprinted from the *Bulletin* of the New York Public Library of Dec. 1944 and Jan. 1945."—*verso of title page.*
A bibliography of handbooks of model letter-writing for the "average" person. Locates copies. Z2014.L4W4

Afro-American literature

Bibliography

Black American writers: bibliographical essays. Ed. by M. Thomas Inge, Maurice Duke, Jackson R. Bryer. N.Y., St. Martin's Pr., [1978]. 2v. **BD476**

Contents: v.1, The beginnings through the Harlem renaissance and Langston Hughes; v.2, Richard Wright, Ralph Ellison, James Baldwin, and Amiri Baraka.
" . . . intended as an appraisal of the best biographical and critical writings about America's seminal black writers, as well as identification of manuscript and special resources for continued study."—*Pref.* Essays by contributing scholars deal with an individual writer, a group of writers, or a specific genre. Name index.

PS153.N5B55

Matthews, Geraldine O., comp. Black American writers, 1773–1949: a bibliography and union list. Boston, G. K. Hall, 1975. 221p. **BD477**

A classed bibliography listing monographic works by more than 1,600 authors. As far as possible, locates copies in 65 libraries in the South. Author index. Z1361.N39M35

Peavy, Charles D. Afro-American literature and culture since World War II: a guide to information sources. Detroit, Gale, [1979]. 302p. (American studies information guide ser., 6) **BD478**

In two parts: (1) Subjects (including general materials, literary genres, aspects of culture, sections for Black Muslims, Black Panthers, Civil Rights movement, etc.) and (2) Individual authors. Indexed. Z1229.N39P4

Rush, Theressa Gunnels, Myers, Carol Fairbanks and **Arata, Esther Spring.** Black American writers, past and present: a biographical and bibliographical dictionary. Metuchen, N.J., Scarecrow Pr., 1975. 2v. (865p.) il. **BD479**

Aims to present biographical, bibliographical and critical information on about 2,000 black writers. (In some instances only a record of publications is available.) In general, a biographical sketch is followed by a list of published books, representative references to contributions to periodicals and anthologies, and references to biographical and critical studies on the writer. Z1229.N39R87

Drama

Arata, Esther Spring and **Rotoli, Nicholas John.** Black American playwrights, 1800 to the present; a bibliography. Metuchen, N.J., Scarecrow Pr., 1976. 295p. **BD480**

Arranged alphabetically by name of playwright. Lists published and unpublished works (including filmscripts, musicals, theater criticism, etc.), together with references to reviews and criticism of the writers' works. Contributions to anthologies and periodicals are noted. Title index. Z1229.N39A7

—— More black American playwrights: a bibliography. Metuchen, N.J., Scarecrow Pr., 1978. 321p. **BD481**

"With the assistance of Marlene J. Erickson, Sandra Dewitz, Mary Linse Alexander."—*t.p.*

Forms a supplement to Arata and Rotoli's *Black American playwrights* (above). "Approximately 490 playwrights appear in this bibliography, of which 190 appeared in the 1976 edition."—*Pref.* Z1229.N39A73

Hatch, James V. and **Abdullah, Omanii.** Black playwrights, 1823–1977: an annotated bibliography of plays. N.Y., Bowker, 1977. 319p. **BD482**

An author listing of some 2,700 plays by approximately 900 black American playwrights. As far as possible, the following information is given for each title: date of composition or copyright, genre, brief description of theme or story line, cast (number, race, sex), length, date and place of production, publication information, library location or agent, and where to apply for permission to produce the play. Title index; various useful supplementary bibliographies and appendixes. Z1231.D7H37

Fiction

Fairbanks, Carol and **Engeldinger, Eugene A.** Black American fiction: a bibliography. Metuchen, N.J., Scarecrow Pr., 1978. 351p. **BD483**

Includes citations to short fiction appearing in periodicals and collections as well as separately published works; citations to reviews, biography, and criticism are also given. Does not include non-fiction or works for children and young people. General bibliography of the subject, p.327–51. Z1229.N39F34

Houston, Helen Ruth. The Afro-American novel, 1965–1975; a descriptive bibliography of primary and secondary material. Troy, N.Y., Whitston, 1977. 214p. **BD484**

Treats some 56 Afro-Americans who have published novels since 1964. A brief biographical note is followed by a listing of the writer's recent novels, a section of critical books by and about the author, and a listing of reviews of the post-1964 novels. Z1229.N39H68

Margolies, Edward and **Bakish, David.** Afro-American fiction, 1853–1976: a guide to information sources. Detroit, Gale, [1979]. 161p. (American literature, English literature, and world literatures in English, 25) **BD485**

In four sections: (1) Checklist of novels; (2) Short story collections; (3) Major authors—secondary sources; (4) Bibliographies and general studies. Author, title, and subject indexes. Z1229.N39M37

Poetry

Afro-American poetry and drama, 1760–1975: a guide to information sources. Detroit, Gale, [1979]. 493p. (American literature, English literature, and world literatures in English, 17) **BD486**

Contents: Afro-American poetry, 1760–1975, by W. P. French, M. J. Fabre, A. Singh; Afro-American drama, 1850–1975, by G. E. Fabre.

In each section a listing of general studies is followed by bibliographies of writings by and about individual authors. Z1229.N39A37

Chapman, Dorothy H. Index to black poetry. Boston, G. K. Hall, 1974. 541p. **BD487**

"Black poetry is here defined in the broadest manner . . . . References are included for the work not only of black poets but also of those poets who have in some way dealt with the black experience or written within the black tradition, regardless of their racial origins."—*Foreword.* Indexes about 125 collections. A title and first line index is followed by separate author and subject indexes. PS153.N5C45

Porter, Dorothy Burnett. North American Negro poets; a bibliographical checklist of their writings, 1760–1944. Hattiesburg, Miss., The Book Farm, 1945. 90p. (Heartman's Historical ser., no.70) **BD488**

An expansion of *A bibliographical checklist of American Negro poetry,* by Arthur A. Schomburg, 1916, listing writings of American Negro poets and indicating location of copies. Z1361.N39P6

English

Guides

Altick, Richard Daniel and **Wright, Andrew.** Selective bibliography for the study of English and American literature. 6th ed. N.Y., Macmillan; London, Collier Macmillan, [1979]. 180p. **BD489**

1st ed. 1960.

A highly respected and very useful compilation which aims "to provide students of English and American literature with a convenient and reasonably authoritative guide to research materials."—*Pref.* About 636 numbered items in this edition; some are briefly annotated. "A glossary of useful terms," p.147–61. Indexed. Z2011.A1A47

Bateson, Frederick Wilse and **Meserole, Harrison T.** A guide to English and American literature. 3d ed. London & N.Y., Longman, [1976]. 334p. **BD490**

Previous editions (1965–67) had title *A guide to English literature.*

"This modest handbook is intended for the reader of any age who is entering or re-entering, the serious study of English and American literature. Here are the principal editions and commentaries that such a reader may reasonably be expected to want to know about if he is to explore at all thoroughly any of the classics or the classical areas of our literature down to the present day."—*Pref.* A general section is followed by chapters for medieval, Renaissance, Augustan, Romantic, and modern English literature, with reading lists for each of the early periods. There is a separate chapter on American literature, and one on "Literary scholarship: an introduction to research in English literature." Indexed. Z2011.B32

Bond, Donald Frederic. A reference guide to English studies. 2d ed. Chicago, Univ. of Chicago Pr., [1971]. 198p. **BD491**

1st ed. 1962.

A manual designed for the graduate student. A successor to Tom Peete Cross's *Bibliographical guide to English studies* (10th ed. Univ. of Chicago Pr., 1951), following the same plan, with slight variations, but greatly increasing the number of entries. Z1002.B72

Kennedy, Arthur Garfield and **Sands, Donald B.** A concise bibliography for students of English. 5th ed. rev. by William E. Colburn. Stanford, Stanford Univ. Pr., 1972. 300p.
BD492

1st ed. 1940.

A classified bibliography without annotations; intended for advanced undergraduates and graduate students. This edition is more selective than the previous one (1960) and puts greater emphasis on recent publications. Author and subject indexes.   Z2011.K35

Sanders, Chauncey. An introduction to research in English literary history; with a chapter on research in folklore by Stith Thompson. N.Y., Macmillan, [1952]. 423p. il.
BD493

A manual and textbook for courses in bibliography and method, dealing with such subjects as the materials, the tools, and the methods of research; covers problems of editing, biography, authenticity and attribution, source study, chronology, success and influence, interpretation, technique, and the history of ideas and folklore, with a final chapter of suggestions on thesis writing.
PR56.S3

Bibliography

❖In addition to the guides and bibliographies listed here, those listed under Great Britain, p.74, should be consulted. The bibliographies in the *Dictionary of national biography* (AJ217) will also be helpful. Besterman's *World bibliography of bibliographies* (AA16), and the *Bibliographic index* (AA17) refer to many individual bibliographies, either issued separately or (except for Besterman) included in periodicals or other composite works.

Bibliography of bibliography

Howard-Hill, Trevor Howard. Index to British literary bibliography. Oxford, Clarendon Pr.; N.Y., Oxford Univ. Pr., 1969–80. v.1–2, 4–6. (In progress)   **BD494**

Contents: v.1, Bibliography of British literary bibliographies; v.2, Shakespearian bibliography and textual criticism; v.4–5, British bibliography and textual criticism; v.6, British literary bibliography and textual criticism, 1890–1969: an index.

"The *Bibliography of British Literary Bibliographies* forms the first volume of the *Index to British [Literary] Bibliography* which is intended to cover books, substantial parts of books, and periodical articles written in English and published in the English-speaking Commonwealth and the United States after 1890, on the bibliographical and textual examination of English manuscripts, books, printing and publishing, and any other books published in Great Britain or by British authors abroad, from the establishment of printing in England, except for material on modern (post-1890) printing and publishing not primarily of bibliographical or literary interest.

"The second volume will record the bibliographies of the work of Shakespeare (which have been excluded from the present volume [*see* BD703]) and bibliographical and textual discussions of them. The final volume, the *Bibliography of British Bibliography and Textual Criticism* [i.e., v.4–5], will list material not included in the prior volumes."—*Introd.*

The two-volume *British literary and textual criticism* (publ. 1979) constitutes v.4–5 of the series. It lists "writings in English published from 1890 [through 1969] which discuss bibliographical aspects of works printed or published in Britain from 1475 to the present day, and the circumstances of production and distribution of books in Britain during that period. From the literary viewpoint, the bibliography provides access to the literature of which a student or editor must take account when he attempts to determine the authority and correctness of a text which interests him."—*Introd.* v.4 has sections (with numerous subdivisions) for bibliography and textual criticism, general and period bibliography, regional bibliography, book production and distribution, and forms, genres, and subjects; v.5 is devoted to individual authors.

A combined index (designated as v.6 of the series) to v.1–2 and v.4–5 was published 1980 (409p.). v.3 of the series, *British bibliography to 1890,* is still in preparation, and a new index to the full set is promised when v.3 is finally published. Meanwhile, it is important to note that in the present v.6 (or interim index) indexing of v.1 refers to a revised and enlarged 2d ed. not yet published at the time the index appeared and not available for examination when this annotation was prepared. Moreover, Shakespeare entries in v.5, p.374–88, are supplementary to v.2 and are indexed as though they appear in that volume.   Z2011.A1H68

General

Allibone, Samuel Austin. Critical dictionary of English literature and British and American authors, living and deceased, from the earliest accounts to the latter half of the nineteenth century. Containing over 46,000 articles (authors), with forty indexes of subjects. Philadelphia, Lippincott, 1858. 3v. (3140p.) (Repr.: Detroit, Gale, 1965, with suppl.)   **BD495**

A standard, older work very useful in spite of the fact that it is not entirely accurate and so must often be checked for important points. Based in part upon Watt's *Bibliotheca Britannica* (AA793) and reflects Watt's inaccuracies. Arranged alphabetically by authors, giving for each: brief biographical sketch, list of works with dates, and references to critical comments or reviews.

———— ———— Supplement ... containing over 37,000 articles (authors), and enumerating over 93,000 titles by John Foster Kirk. Philadelphia, Lippincott, 1891. 2v. (1562p.)

Z1224.A43

Cambridge bibliography of English literature, ed. by F. W. Bateson.... Cambridge, Univ. Pr., 1940–57; N.Y., Macmillan, 1941–57. 5v.   **BD496**

Contents: v.1–3, 600–1900; v.4, Index; v.5, Supplement.

Covers with fullness and considerable detail, though avowedly not with actual completeness, the Old English, Middle English, modern English, and Latin literature of the British Isles, with comparatively brief treatment of the English literature of the Dominions and India; does not include American literature or the French literature of Canada, and gives only incidental inclusion of Welsh, Gaelic, or Celtic material.

Arranged chronologically, and under periods by literary forms, e.g., Poetry, Drama, Periodicals, etc., and large class groups, such as History, Philosophy, etc., with further subdivision under forms and groups by special topics and by the individual authors treated. References given under each author vary according to his importance or to the amount of material available, but generally include: bibliographies of that author, either separately published or included in some periodical or other work; collected editions of his works; separate works, with date of first edition and of subsequent editions within the next 50 years, with references to later editions having special features or editing; and a selection of biographical and critical works about the author.

Within the Drama sections, a useful reference feature is the analytical reference to texts of separate plays as printed in the standard collections of plays, such as Dodsley, Bell, French, Lacy, etc. The *Supplement* lists publications on the study of English language and literature, down to 1900, which appeared approximately from 1940 to 1955; it has no index, but sections are roughly keyed to comparable sections in v.1–3.

Now largely superseded by the revised edition (below), but some of the background chapters not carried forward to the new work will continue to be useful.   Z2011.B28

The new Cambridge bibliography of English literature. Cambridge, Univ. Pr., 1969–77. 5v.   **BD497**

Contents: v.1, 600–1600, ed. by George Watson; v.2, 1660–1800, ed. by George Watson; v.3, 1800–1900, ed. by George Watson; v.4, 1900–1950, ed. by I. R. Willison; v.5, Index, comp. by J. D. Pickles.

The volume for the 19th century (v.3) was given priority in this reworking of the *Cambridge bibliography of English literature* (above) mainly because the study of Victorian literature has advanced more rapidly and undergone greater changes than that of most other periods. Thus, v.3 appeared in 1969; v.2 and v.4 followed in 1971–72; and v.1 in 1974. Cutoff date for the inclusion of new publications varies from volume to volume: v.1 includes numerous 1970–71 items; 1969 is the terminal date for v.2 and v.4; v.3 includes some items as late as 1968. Basic design of the work remains the same, and the task of the contributors "has been to revise and integrate the existing lists of 1940 and 1957, to add materials of the past ten years, to correct and refine the bibliographical details already available, and to reshape the whole according to the new conventions which have been designed to give the Bibliography a clearer and more consistent air."—*Pref., v.3.* Various nonliterary sections (such as those for political and social backgrounds) have been omitted as impractical to update, but sections for travel, sport, education, and the press have been retained and revised. Sections on the literatures of certain Commonwealth nations (Anglo-Indian, Canadian, South African, Australian, and New Zealand) have been dropped; Celtic literature is excluded. Individual author listings are now confined to "literary authors native to or mainly resident in the British Isles"; the scope of the listings themselves is largely unchanged. Bibliographic citations again are very brief; analytics for separate plays in standard collections (as noted for *CBEL,* above) are given; a list of the principal abbreviations used is provided in each volume (with slight variations in the lists).

Period divisions remain the same, with a new, separate volume for the earlier 20th century (v.4). The final volume is "a general index to all four volumes, listing primary authors and major anonymous works, as well as certain headings from the Bibliography as a whole."—*Pref.* (Provisional indexes giving names of primary authors and selected subject categories appeared in each volume as published.) Because of changes and omissions in the new set, most libraries will want to retain the earlier edition in the reference collection.

Indispensable as a first reference bibliography in all college, university, and large public libraries, and also in medium-sized public libraries doing much work in English literature. For research work it will naturally need to be supplemented by various specialized works. Its value as a guide to the selection of books in the building of library collections is obvious.

For an early appraisal of v.3, *see TLS* Dec. 11, 1969, p.1432 (and letter from F. W. Bateson, *TLS* Dec. 18, 1969, p.1472). A review of v.2 in *Modern philology* 71:176–86 (Nov. 1973) draws attention to various inconsistencies, and peculiarities of arrangement, points out some errors, and offers a list of "omissions and false inclusions."

Z2011.N45

Church, Elihu Dwight. A catalogue of books, consisting of English literature and miscellanea, including many original editions of Shakespeare, forming a part of the library of E. D. Church, comp. and annotated by George Watson Cole. ... N.Y., Dodd, 1909. 2v. il. **BD498**

An admirably made catalog of rare books, especially important for its very fine bibliographical notes, and location of copies of the books described. Includes examples from the time of Caxton to the latter part of the 19th century. Z2011.C55

Folger Shakespeare Library, Wash., D.C. Catalog of printed books. Boston, G. K. Hall, 1970. 28v. **BD499**

In addition to its outstanding collection of materials for Shakespeare studies, the Library has "an exceptional collection of English printed books of the STC period, from 1475 to 1640. Additional holdings of rare books and manuscripts of the Continental Renaissance and the Wing period (1641–1700), make the Library a center not only of Shakespeare studies but also of every aspect of the English and Continental Renaissance."—*Foreword.* A dictionary catalog reproducing the catalog cards for the collection. v.28 includes two appendixes: (A) Periodical collection; (B) Chronological catalog of foreign language pamphlets.

The Library's manuscripts are listed in a separate catalog published by G. K. Hall, Boston, 1971 (3v.).

Harvard University. Library. English literature. Cambridge, Publ. by Harvard Univ. Lib., distr. by Harvard Univ. Pr., 1971. 4v. (Widener Library shelflist, 35–38) **BD500**

Contents: v.1, Classification schedule; Classified listing by call number; v.2, Chronological listing; v.3–4, Author and title listing.

"The 112,000 books, pamphlets, and periodicals in the *10441–23899* and *ELB* classes include literary histories, anthologies, and works by and about individual literary authors. To ensure more complete coverage of British authors, 8000 works of American and British fiction comprising the *PZ* and *PZB* classes have been added to the chronological and alphabetical lists."—*Pref.*

For a note on the series *see* AA145. Z2011.H36

The shorter new Cambridge bibliography of English literature. George Watson, ed. Cambridge, Cambridge Univ. Pr., [1981]. 1622 col. **BD501**

Essentially an abridgment of the *New CBEL,* but with some additions (mainly newly published items) and corrections. "All the major authors in *New CBEL,* and many minor ones, have been included . . . . In each case the primary section, or the canon of an author's works, has been wholly or largely kept; the secondary section, however, which consists of books and articles concerning that author, has usually been reduced substantially . . . ."—*Pref.*

Peter Davison's review in *The library* (ser.6, v.4, no.2, p.188–89, June 1982) terms this "an unimaginative scissors-and-paste job which shows little thought for the needs of the student and private person." Z2011.S5

Current

Abstracts of English studies: an official publication of the National Council of Teachers of English. Boulder, Colo., 1958– . v.1– . Quarterly (varies). **BD502**

Abstracts of articles in American and foreign periodicals on English, Commonwealth, and American literature and on English philology. Originally a monthly; from 1981 issued quarterly with annual cumulated subject and author indexes in the final issue of the year.

Modern Humanities Research Association. Annual bibliography of English language and literature. 1920– . Cambridge, Univ. Pr., 1921– . v.1– . Annual (some volumes cover 2–3 yrs.) **BD503**

An excellent annual bibliography of English and American literature, including books, pamphlets, and periodical articles, with references to reviews of books listed. The language section is arranged according to subject; the literature section is arranged chronologically. Indexes of authors and subjects treated, and of scholars.

Some reservations about the arrangement, indexing, and general editing of recent volumes are expressed in J. Gerritsen's review of the 1970 volume in *English studies* 55:152–54 (April 1974).

Z2011.M69

The year's work in English studies. 1919/20– . Publ. for the English Association. London, Murray, 1921– . v.1– . Annual. **BD504**

A selective, critical survey of studies of English literature appearing in books and articles published in Britain, Europe, and America, grouped by chronological periods. Also includes material on English language, and, since 1954, chapters on American literature. Indexes by author and subject. Covers much the same ground as the MHRA *Annual bibliography* (above), listing fewer titles, but giving running comment on their importance or character. Indexed. PE58.E6

Dissertations

Howard, Patsy C. Theses in English literature, 1894–1970. Ann Arbor, Mich., Pierian Pr., 1973. 387p. **BD505**

Lists some 9,000 unpublished baccalaureate and master's theses from a wide range of American and foreign universities. Listing is by literary author treated, then alphabetically by author of the thesis. Index of authors of theses, and a brief subject index. Coverage is

admittedly incomplete, but precise coverage for individual institutions is not indicated and appears to be spotty in various instances.
           Z2011.H63

McNamee, Lawrence F. Dissertations in English and American literature; theses accepted by American, British and German universities, 1865–1964. N.Y., Bowker, 1968. 1124p.   **BD506**

A computer-produced bibliography. Dissertations are listed in a subject arrangement which includes chapters on language and linguistics, teaching of English, and "creative" dissertations, as well as the expected sections for literary periods, genres, individual authors, etc. Index of authors of dissertations. A "Cross-index of Authors" compensates for the fact that studies dealing with two or more literary figures appear only once in the main listing. Does not wholly supersede the Altick and Matthews volume for Victorian literature (BD542) which includes Austrian, French, and Swiss dissertations.

—————— Supplement 1–2. N.Y., Bowker, 1969–74. 450p.; 690p.

Provides coverage of American, British, and German dissertations for the period 1964–73.   Z5053.M32

Mummendey, Richard. Language and literature of the Anglo-Saxon nations as presented in German doctoral dissertations, 1885–1950; a bibliography. Bonn, Bouvier; Charlottesville, Bibliographical Soc. of the Univ. of Virginia, 1954. 200p.   **BD507**

Added title page in German; prefatory matter and captions in English and German.

Lists 2,989 items arranged by subject field, with a name and subject index.   Z2011.M8

Periodicals

British literary magazines. Ed. by Alvin Sullivan. Westport, Conn., Greenwood Pr., [1983]– . [v.1]– . (In progress)
           BD508

Contents: [v.1] The Augustan age and the age of Johnson, 1698–1788; [v.2] The romantic age, 1789–1836.

To be in 4v., future volumes to cover the Victorian and Edwardian eras and the modern period.

Volumes 1 and 2 each contain 80 to 90 "profiles" of individual magazines; selection of titles is meant to reflect the range and variety of reviews, journals, essay periodicals and illustrated magazines published during the period. Signed essays offer information on the history, content, contributors, and significance of each title; bibliographic references to information sources, notes on indexes, reprints, library locations, and details of publishing history are given for each. Each volume ends with a chronology and other useful appendixes, and an index.   PN5124.L6B74

Stanton, Michael N. English literary journals, 1900–1950: a guide to information sources. Detroit, Gale, [1982]. 119p. (American literature, English literature, and world literatures in English, v.32)   **BD509**

About 135 literary journals of the period are listed with publication dates, frequency, and names of editors, plus an annotation characterizing the publication and listing notable contributors. A bibliography lists background readings, general works, and studies of individual journals. Indexed.   Z2005.S73

White, Robert B. The English literary journal to 1900; a guide to information sources. Detroit, Gale, [1977]. 311p. (American literature, English literature, and world literatures in English, v.8)   **BD510**

Aims to present "a bibliography of what has been written since about 1890 and what is now accessible to the general reader concerning pre-1900 British literary periodicals."—*Pref.* Sections for bibliographies and general studies are followed by sections for specific periodicals, persons, and places. Indexed.
         Z6956.G6W47

Old and Middle English

Beale, Walter H. Old and Middle English poetry to 1500; a guide to information sources. Detroit, Gale, [1976]. 454p. (American literature, English literature, and world literatures in English, v.7)   **BD511**

An annotated bibliography of texts, translations, and critical writings.   Z2014.P7B34

Greenfield, Stanley B. and **Robinson, Fred C.** A bibliography of publications on Old English literature to the end of 1972. Toronto, Univ. of Toronto Pr., [1980]. 437p. **BD512**

Intends to be an exhaustive listing of the published writings on Old English literature through 1972; "studies of Anglo-Saxon social, political, and economic history, art history, archaeology, and linguistic questions" are omitted "except where such studies deal specifically with a literary aspect of a literary work in Old English." —*Pref.* About 6,550 items in classed arrangement, with author/reviewer and subject indexes.   Z2012.G83

Middle English prose: a critical guide to major authors and genres. Ed. by A. S. G. Edwards. New Brunswick, N.J., Rutgers Univ. Pr., [1984]. 452p.   **BD513**

Similar to the M.L.A. reviews of research, this work aims "to provide an authoritative guide to a number of important authors and genres of Middle English prose."—*Pref.* Eighteen scholars have contributed chapters on individual writers and on groups or types of prose writings, each chapter offering "a survey of modern scholarship, a statement of desiderata and suggestions for possible avenues of future inquiry, and a bibliography of primary and secondary sources." Indexed.   PR255.M52

Robinson, Fred C. Old English literature; a select bibliography. [Toronto], Univ. of Toronto Pr., [1970]. 68p. (Toronto medieval bibliographies, 2)   **BD514**

Undertakes to list the most important and useful writings on each literary work of the period and on the literature in general. Brief descriptive notes or references to critical reviews follow most citations.

No.5 of the Toronto series is Rachel Bromwich's *Medieval Celtic literature* (Toronto, 1974. 109p.).   Z2012.R6

Simms, Norman Toby. Ritual and rhetoric: intellectual and ceremonial backgrounds to Middle English literature; a critical survey of relevant scholarship. [Norwood, Pa.], Norwood Editions, 1973. 358p.   **BD515**

Nearly 1,500 entries grouped under such headings as: The court, The church, Schools, The city, rhetorical parts, literary genres, etc. Some annotations; no index.   Z2012.S55

Wells, John Edwin. A manual of the writings in Middle English, 1050–1400, publ. under the auspices of the Connecticut Academy of Arts and Sciences. New Haven, Yale Univ. Pr., 1916–51. 941p. and suppl. 1–9. **BD516**

Main work, covering bibliography to Sept. 1915, 941p.; Suppl. 1–9, Additions and rectifications, Sept. 1915–Dec. 1945, paged continuously with main work, p.947–1938. Suppl. 8 includes an index to pieces first treated in Suppl. 1–8.

"This manual makes the first attempt to treat all the extant writings in print, from single lines to the most extensive pieces, composed in English between 1050 and 1400. At times, as with the Romances, the Legends, and the Drama, a desire for greater completeness has led to the inclusion of pieces later than 1400.

"The work is not a history, but a handbook. It seeks to record the generally accepted views of scholars on pertinent matters, and does not pretend to offer new theories or investigations."—*Pref.*

Gives for each piece listed: its probable date, MS or MSS, form and extent, dialect in which first composed, source or sources when known, bibliography, and—in case of the longer works—comment and abstract as well. An important handbook, indispensable in any library doing reference work in this field.

A new edition is in progress as: PR255.W4

A manual of the writings in Middle English, 1050–1500, by members of the Middle English Group of the Modern

Language Association of America. New Haven, Connecticut Academy of Arts and Sciences, 1967–80. v.1–6. (In progress)   **BD517**

General ed., v.1–2, J. B. Severs; v.3–6, A. E. Hartung.

"Based upon *A manual of the writings in Middle English 1050–1400* by John Edwin Wells, New Haven, 1916, and Supplements 1–9, 1919–1951."—*title page.*

[v.1] originally designated as "fasc.1."

Contents: [v.]1, Romances, by M. J. Donovan [et al.]; v.2, The Pearl poet, by M. P. Hamilton; Wyclyf and his followers, by E. W. Talbert and S. H. Thomson; Translations and paraphrases of the Bible, and commentaries, by L. Muir; Saints' legends, by C. D'Evelyn and F. A. Foster; Instructions for religious, by C. D'Evelyn; v.3, Dialogues, debates and catechisms, by F. L. Utley; Thomas Hoccleve, by W. Matthews; Malory and Caxton, by R. H. Wilson; v.4, Middle Scots writers, by F. H. Ridley; The Chaucerian apocrypha, by R. H. Robbins; v.5, Dramatic pieces (The miracle plays and mysteries, by A. J. Mill; The morality plays, by S. Lindenbaum; The folk drama, by F. L. Utley and B. Ward); Poems dealing with contemporary conditions, by R. H. Robbins; v.6, Carols, by R. L. Greene; Ballads, by D. C. Fowler; John Lydgate, by A. Renoir and C. D. Benson.

It is expected that the work will be complete in 10v. (including an index to the full set). Future volumes are to deal with: tales, chronicles; homilies; proverbs, precepts, and monitory pieces; Piers Plowman; works of religious information and instruction; science, information, and documents; geography and travel; letters; legal writings; Rolle and his followers; lyrics; Gower; undistributed prose (i.e., prose works suitable for inclusion but not assigned to the categories already treated).

Represents both a rewriting and an expansion of Wells's *Manual* (above). Bibliographies are updated; scope is broadened to include the 15th century; and the commentary is a fresh evaluation of the literature and of the scholarship of its critics. Follows the plan of the Wells work; each volume has its own index. Each section is by a specialist scholar, and a bibliography complements each survey. Cutoff date for the initial volumes is 1955, with some later listings of important studies down to press time; for the recent volumes coverage extends as late as 1978. In the tradition of its predecessor, this will be an indispensable work for the field.   PR255.M3

To 1700

Barker, Arthur E. The seventeenth century, Bacon through Marvell. Arlington Heights, Ill., AHM Publ. Corp., [1979]. 132p.   **BD518**

". . . intended for graduate and advanced undergraduate students in courses about the poetry and prose of the seventeenth century in England."—*Pref.* Drama is excluded, as are Shakespeare and Milton. Sections on general background and literary history of the period are followed by lists of editions, studies, etc., of individual authors. Indexed.   Z2012.B27

Harner, James L. English Renaissance prose fiction, 1500–1660; an annotated bibliography of criticism. Boston, G. K. Hall, [1978]. 556p.   **BD518a**

A bibliography of more than 3,200 items covering "editions and studies (published between 1800 and 1976) of prose fiction in English—both original works and translations—written or printed in England from 1500 to 1660. Works and translations included are limited to those which may be classified as novelle, romances, histories, anatomies, or jest books (or some combination of these)." —*Introd.* In four main sections: (1) Bibliographies; (2) Anthologies; (3) General studies; (4) Authors/translators/titles. When applicable, the latter section is subdivided for bibliographies, editions, and studies. Most entries are briefly annotated. Indexed.

Z2014.F4H37

Hazlitt, William Carew. Handbook to the popular, poetical, and dramatic literature of Great Britain, from the invention of printing to the Restoration. London, J. R. Smith, 1867. 701p. (Repr.: N.Y., B. Franklin, 1961)   **BD519**

Revised and supplemented by: Z2012.H3

—— Bibliographical collections and notes on early English literature, 1474–1700. London Quaritch, 1876–1903. 6v. (Repr.: N.Y., B. Franklin, 1961)   **BD520**

1st series has title, *Collections and notes.*

1st ser., 498p. (1876); 2d ser., 717p. (1882); 3d ser., 315p. (1887); suppl. to 3d ser., 181p. (1889); 2d suppl. to 3d ser., 106p. (1892); 4th ser., 446p. (1903).

Bibliography and notes on English literature comprising many thousands of titles.   Z2012.H31

—— General index to Hazlitt's Handbook and his Bibliographical collections (1867–1889), by G. J. Gray. London, Quaritch, 1893. 866p. (Repr.: N.Y., B. Franklin, 1961)   **BD521**

Indexes the *Handbook* (BD519) and all volumes of the *Bibliographical collections* (BD520), except the 4th series and the 2d supplement to the 3rd series.   Z2012.H3

Heninger, S. K. English prose, prose fiction, and criticism to 1660; a guide to information sources. Detroit, Gale, [1975]. 255p. (American literature, English literature, and world literatures in English, v.2)   **BD522**

Lists primary and secondary works by type (e.g., religious writings, travel literature, essays, narrative fiction, literary criticism, etc.). Nearly 800 items. Indexed.   Z2014.P795H45

Tannenbaum, Samuel A. and **Tannenbaum, Dorothy R.** Elizabethan bibliographies. [Concise bibliographies] N.Y., Author, 1937–50. no.1–41 and suppls. (Repr.: Port Washington, N.Y., Kennikat Pr., 1967. 10v.)   **BD523**

Contents: no.1, Christopher Marlowe (1937) and Suppl. 1–2 (1937–47); no.2, Ben Jonson (1938); no.3, Beaumont and Fletcher (1938) and Suppl. (1946); no.4, Philip Massinger (1938); no.5, George Chapman (1938) and Suppl. (1946); no. 6, Thomas Heywood (1939); no.7, Thomas Dekker (1939) and Suppl. (1945); no.8, Robert Greene (1939) and Suppl. (1945); no.9, Shakspere's Macbeth (1939); no.10, Shakspere's sonnets (1940); no.11, Thomas Lodge (1940); no.12, John Lyly (1940); no.13, Thomas Middleton (1940); no.14, John Marston (1940); no.15, George Peele (1940); no.16, Shakspere's King Lear (1940); no.17, Shakspere's The Merchant of Venice (1941); no.20, John Ford (1941); no.21, Thomas Nashe (1941); no.22, Michael Drayton (1941); no.23, Sir Philip Sidney (1941); no.24, Michel Eyquem de Montaigne (1942); no.25, Samuel Daniel (1942); no.26, George Gascoigne (1942); no.27, Anthony Mundy, including the play of "Sir Thomas Moore," (1942); no.28, Shakspere's Othello (1943); no.29, Shakspere's Troilus and Cressida (1943); no.30–32, Marie Stuart, Queen of Scots (1944–46. 3v.); no.33, Cyril Tourneur (1946); no.34, James Shirley (1946); no.35, George Herbert (1946); no.36, John Heywood (1946); no.37, Roger Ascham (1946); no.38, Thomas Randolph (1946); no.39, Nicholas Breton (1947); no.40, Robert Herrick (1949); no.41, Shakspere's Romeo and Juliet (1950). (Reprint numbering differs from original.)

A new series of supplements appeared as: Z2012.T3

Elizabethan bibliographies supplements. no.1–12, 15, 17–18. London, Nether Pr., 1967–71.   **BD524**

Contents: no.1, Thomas Middleton, John Webster, comp. by Dennis Donovan; no.2, Thomas Dekker, Thomas Heywood, Cyril Tourneur, comp. by Dennis Donovan; no.3, Robert Herrick, Ben Jonson, Thomas Randolph, comp. by George R. Guffey; no.4, George Chapman, John Marston, comp. by Charles A. Pennel and William P. Williams; no.5, Robert Greene, Thomas Lodge, John Lyly, Thomas Nashe, George Peele, comp. by Robert C. Johnson; no.6, Christopher Marlowe, comp. by Robert C. Johnson; no.7, Samuel Daniel, Michael Drayton, Sir Philip Sidney, comp. by George R. Guffey; no.8, Francis Beaumont, John Fletcher, Philip Massinger, John Ford, James Shirley, comp. by Charles A. Pennel and William P. Williams; no.9, Roger Ascham, George Gascoigne, John Heywood, Thomas Kyd, Anthony Munday, comp. by Robert C. Johnson; no.10, Sir Thomas Browne, Robert Burton, comp. by Dennis G. Donovan; no.11, Traherne and the seventeenth-century Platonists, comp. by George R. Guffey; no.12, Andrew Marvell, comp. by Dennis G. Donovan; no.15, Francis Bacon, comp. by J. K. Houck; no.17, Sir Walter Raleigh, comp. by Humphrey Tonkin; no.18, John Evelyn, Samuel Pepys, comp. by Dennis G. Donovan.

These issues supplement the Tannenbaum bibliographies (above), listing new editions and critical studies, and the series also includes certain Elizabethan authors not covered by Tannenbaum. Nos.13–14, 16 not published. Z2012.E38

18th century

Cordasco, Francesco. Eighteenth century bibliographies; handlists of critical studies relating to Smollett, Richardson, Sterne, Fielding, Dibdin, 18th century medicine, the 18th century novel, Godwin, Gibbon, Young, and Burke. To which is added John P. Anderson's bibliography of Smollett. Metuchen, N.J., Scarecrow Pr., 1970. 230p. **BD525**

Reprints, without updating, the bibliographies as they appeared in the series *18th century bibliographical pamphlets,* no.1–12 (Brooklyn, Long Island Univ. Pr., 1947–50), plus the Smollett bibliography which appeared in David Hannay's *Life of Tobias George Smollett* (London, Scott, 1887). Z2013.C67

English literature, 1660–1800; a bibliography of modern studies comp. for Philological quarterly, by Ronald S. Crane [and others]. Princeton, Princeton Univ. Pr., 1950–72. v.1–6. **BD526**

Contents: Studies published: v.1, 1925–1937; v.2, 1938–1949; v.3, 1950–1955; v.4, 1956–1959; v.5, 1960–1965; v.6, 1966–1969.

Reprints of the annual bibliographies published in *Philological quarterly,* 1926–70. Many entries include reviews or annotations. v.2 includes a name, subject, and topical index to v.1–2; vols. 4 and 6 include similar indexes to v.3–4 and v.5–6 respectively.

Ceased publication; incorporated into *The eighteenth century; a current bibliography,* 1970– (BD21). Z2011.E6

Glock, Waldo Sumner. Eighteenth-century English literary studies: a bibliography. Metuchen, N.J., Scarecrow Pr., 1984. 847p. **BD527**

Aims "to provide the undergraduate and graduate student and the scholar, . . . a comprehensive but not exhaustive survey of the critical literature on the most important writers of the eighteenth century."—*Pref.* Arranged by literary author, with subdivisions for individual works. Annotations; index of authors of the studies. Z2012.G56

Lund, Roger D. Restoration and early eighteenth-century English literature, 1660–1740; a selected bibliography of resource materials. N.Y., Modern Language Assoc. of America, 1980. 42p. (Selected bibliographies in language and literature, 1) **BD528**

A highly selective "guide to current periodicals, bibliographies, concordances, and other resource materials readily available" (*Pref.*) for the study of the literature of the period. Some brief annotations; index. Z2012.L88

Tobin, James Edward. Eighteenth century English literature and its cultural background; a bibliography. N.Y., Fordham Univ. Pr., 1939. 190p. **BD529**

Contents: pt.1, Cultural and critical background; pt.2, Bibliographies of individual authors.

The individual bibliographies list works by the author in very brief form, and books and articles about the author. No annotations. Z2013.T62

Translations

Rochedieu, Charles Alfred. Bibliography of French translations of English works, 1700–1800. Chicago, Univ. of Chicago Pr., [1948]. 387p. **BD530**

Lists the works of some 900 authors under the author's name and the English title, with cross reference from the French title. Z2014.T7R6

19th century

Annual bibliography of Victorian studies, 1976– . Edmonton, Alberta, LITIR Database, [1980]– . Annual. **BD531**

Brahma Chaudhuri, ed.

An annual bibliography of books, periodical articles, and reviews relating to the Victorian period ("from about 1830 to the beginning of the War of 1914"—*Pref.*), including writings on non-literary subjects. Books and articles are classified under seven broad categories (with appropriate subdivisions): general and reference works; fine arts; philosophy and religion; history; social sciences; science and technology; language and literature (with sections for individual authors); reviews are cited following the entry for the work reviewed. Detailed subject index; author, title, and reviewer indexes. Only English-language materials are included.

A cumulative volume has appeared as:

Cumulative bibliography of Victorian studies: 1976–1980. Edmonton, Alberta, LITIR Database, [1982]. 948p. **BD532**

Represents a cumulation of the main entries and the subject, author, and title indexes from the annual volumes (above); review citations and the reviewer index are not included. Although called "a single comprehensive index to all five volumes . . . from 1976 to 1980" (*Pref.*), the volume does not function effectively as such: i.e., the six-digit ID number (intended for online searching and updating) at the end of a citation provides an indication of the date of the annual, but it may be necessary to consult the index to the annual volume in order to locate the citation therein and, as already noted, review citations are not cumulated. Moreover, an errata slip points out a computer error which necessitates an adjustment of most of the item numbers in the cumulated index.

A new cumulation designated as *Comprehensive bibliography of Victorian studies, 1970–1984* was announced for 1985 publication in 3v.; it is to be hoped that the errors and shortcomings of the earlier cumulation will be overcome therein.

Bibliographies of studies in Victorian literature for the thirteen years 1932–1944, ed. by William Darby Templeman. Urbana, Univ. of Illinois Pr., 1945. 450p. **BD533**

A photoprint of bibliographies published originally in the May issues of *Modern philology,* 1933–45, and therefore arranged by year. Includes an index of Victorian authors mentioned in Sec.IV of each year and in the first three sections of the bibliography for 1932, which was differently arranged.

Continued by: Z2013.B59

————— for the ten years 1945–54, ed. by Austin Wright. Urbana, Univ. of Illinois Pr., 1956. 310p. **BD534**

Reprints of the annual *Victorian bibliographies,* 1945–54, published in *Modern philology.*

Continued by:

————— for the ten years 1955–1964, ed. by Robert C. Slack. Urbana, Univ. of Illinois Pr., 1967. 461p. **BD535**

Reprints the annual *Victorian bibliographies* for 1955–56 as published in *Modern philology* and 1957–64 as published in *Victorian studies.*

Continued by:

————— for the ten years 1965–1974, ed. by Ronald E. Freeman. N.Y., AMS Pr., [1981]. 876p. **BD536**

Reprints the annual *Victorian bibliographies* for 1965–74 published in *Victorian studies,* adding an errata list and a cumulated index.

Continued by: Z2013.B59

Victorian bibliography. Francis G. Townsend, ed. 1957– . (*In* Victorian studies, v.1– , June 1958–) **BD537**

Continues the list previously published in *Modern Philology.* Annual issues have been reprinted as noted above.

Lists books, usually with references to reviews, and periodical articles. Covers all aspects of the Victorian period, not literature alone.

De Laura, David J., ed. Victorian prose; a guide to research. N.Y., Modern Language Assoc. of America, 1973. 560p.
BD538

A survey of research designed as a companion to Stevenson's *Victorian fiction* (BD625) and Faverty's *Victorian poets* (BD648). Chapters cover: general materials, Macaulay, the Carlyles, Newman, Mill, Ruskin, Arnold, Pater, the Oxford Movement, Victorian churches, Critics, Unbelievers. PR785.D4

Fredeman, William Evan. Pre-Raphaelitism; a bibliocritical study. Cambridge, Harvard Univ. Pr., 1965. 327p.
BD539

A "critical reference guide" which provides "an annotated check list of both primary and secondary sources, covering all aspects of literary and visual Pre-Raphaelitism."—*Pref.* Includes descriptions of major collections, catalogs or exhibitions, bibliographies of individual figures, and a bibliography of the movement in general. Detailed index. Z5948.P9F7

The Romantic movement: a selective and critical bibliography. (*In* ELH, a journal of English literary history, 1937–49, etc.)
BD540

For full record *see* BD25.

Tobias, Richard C. Guide to the year's work in Victorian poetry and prose. [1967/72]. [Morgantown], West Virginia Univ., [1974]. 128p.
BD541

Intended as a supplement to Faverty's *The Victorian poets* (BD648) and DeLaura's *Victorian prose* (BD538); therefore, includes publications since the closing date of those volumes. Comprises bibliographic surveys by scholar specialists on individual writers or groups of writers. Not indexed.

Kept up to date by an annual article by Tobias in the periodical *Victorian poetry.*

Dissertations

Altick, Richard Daniel and **Matthews, William R.** Guide to doctoral dissertations in Victorian literature, 1886–1958. Urbana, Univ. of Illinois Pr., 1960. 119p.
BD542

2,105 dissertations from universities in the United States, United Kingdom, Germany, France, Austria, and Switzerland. Classifications include generalities, literary forms, literary criticism, and then individual authors. Author index. Z2013.A4

20th century

Mellown, Elgin W. A descriptive catalogue of the bibliographies of twentieth century British poets, novelists, and dramatists. 2d ed., rev. & enl. Troy, N.Y., Whitston, 1978. 414p.
BD543

1st ed. 1972.

A revision and expansion, extending coverage through 1977. Lists bibliographies of works by and about 20th-century British authors. Provides references to bibliographies appearing as parts of books, as periodical articles, and as separate publications, plus indication of bibliographic information appearing in biographical dictionaries and standard reference sources. Numerous annotations.
Z2011.A1M43

Temple, Ruth Zabriskie and **Tucker, Martin.** Twentieth century British literature; a reference guide and bibliography. N.Y., Ungar, [1968]. 261p.
BD544

Pt.1 lists (and frequently annotates) general literary histories, collections of critical essays, special studies on literary genres and theory, etc.; pt.2 consists of author bibliographies. The latter is primarily a reprint from the authors' *Modern British literature* (BD553) with some updating. Index of authors mentioned in pt.1.

Although there is a checklist of journals, citations are limited to book materials. Z2013.3.T4

Manuscript sources

Early English manuscripts in facsimile. Copenhagen, Rosenkilde & Bagger; Baltimore, Johns Hopkins Pr., [1951]–83. v.1–21. (In progress)
BD545

v.1, Beowulf (British Museum. MS. Cotton. Vitellius A.XV). The Thorkelin transcripts. Ed. by Kemp Malone. 1951.

v.2, Beda Venerabilis. Historia ecclesiastica gentis anglorum. (Leningrad. Public Library. MS. Q.V.I.18) The Leningrad Bede, an eighth century manuscript. Ed. by O. Arngart. 1952.

v.3, Orosius, Paulus. Historia adversum paganos. English. (British Museum. Add. MS. 47967) The Tollemache Orosius. Ed. by Alistair Campbell. 1953.

v.4, Anglo-Saxon Chronicle. (Oxford. Bodleian Library. MS. Laud misc. 636) The Peterborough chronicle. Ed. by Dorothy Whitelock. 1954.

v.5, Laece boc. (British Museum. Royal MS. 12D.XVII) Bald's Leechbook. Ed. by C. E. Wright with an appendix by Randolph Quirk. 1955.

v.6, Gregorius I, the Great, Saint, Pope. Regula pastoralis. English. (Oxford. Bodleian Library. MS. Hatton 20; British Museum. MS. Cotton. Tiberius. B.XI; Kassel. Landesbibliothek. MS. Anhang 19) The pastoral care; King Alfred's translation. Ed. by N. R. Ker. 1956.

v.7, Textus Roffensis. (Rochester Cathedral. Library. MS. A.3.5. pt.I) Textus Roffensis. Ed. by Peter Sawyer. 1957. For pt.II *see* no.11.

v.8, Catholic Church. Liturgy and ritual. Psalter. "Paris Psalter." (Paris. Bibliothèque Nationale. Fonds latin. MS. 8824) The Paris psalter. Pref. by various contributors. Collected by Bertram Colgrave. 1958.

v.9, Beda Venerabilis. Historia ecclesiastica gentis anglorum. (Cambridge. University Library. MS. Kk.5.16) The Moore Bede, an eighth century manuscript. Ed. by Peter Hunter Blair with contribution by Roger A. B. Mynors. 1959.

v.10, Blickling Homilies. (Princeton, N.J., Scheide Library. MS. 66) The Blickling homilies. Ed. by Rudolph Willard. 1960.

v.11, Textus Roffensis. (Rochester Cathedral. Library. MS. A.3.5. pt.II) Textus Roffensis. Ed. by Peter Sawyer. 1957. For pt.I *see* no.7.

v.12, Nowell Codex. (British Museum. MS. Cotton. Vitellius A.XV. 2d MS) The Nowell codex. Ed. by Kemp Malone. 1963.

v.13, Aelfric, Abbot of Eynsham. Homilies. (British Museum. Royal MS. 7C.XII) Aelfric's first series of Catholic homilies. Ed. by N. Eliason and P. Clemoes. 1966.

v.14, Catholic Church. Liturgy and ritual. Psalter. (British Museum. Cotton Vespasian MS. A.I) The Vespasian psalter. Ed. by D. H. Wright. 1967.

v.15, Benedict, Saint, Abbot of Monte Cassino. Regula. (Oxford. Bodleian Library. MS. Hatton 48). The rule of St. Benedict. Ed. by D. H. Farmer. 1968.

v.16, Catholic Church. Liturgy and ritual. Collectarium. (Durham. Cathedral Library. MS. A.IV.19) The Durham ritual. Ed. by T. J. Brown [et al.]. 1969.

v.17, Wulfstan II, Abp. of York. (British Museum. Cotton Nero MS. A.I) A Wulfstan manuscript containing institutes, laws and homilies. Ed. by H. R. Loyn. 1971.

v.18, Bible. O.T. Hexateuch. Anglo-Saxon. (British Museum. Cotton Claudius MS. B.IV) The Old English illustrated Hexateuch. Ed. by C. R. Dodwell and P. Clemoes. 1974.

v.19, Vercelli book. (Vercelli Biblioteca Capitolare MS. CXVII) The Vercelli book: a late tenth-century manuscript containing prose and verse. Ed. by C. Sisam. 1976.

v.20, Durham Gospels. (Durham. Cathedral Library. MS. A.II.17) The Durham Gospels; together with fragments of a gospel book in uncial. Ed. by C. D. Verey, T. J. Brown and E. Coatsworth. 1980.

v.21, An eleventh-century Anglo-Saxon illustrated miscellany. (British Museum. Cotton Tiberius MS. B.V pt.1) Ed. by P. McGurk. 1983.

Index of English literary manuscripts. Editorial board: P. J. Croft, Theodore Hofmann and John Horden. London, Mansell; N.Y., Bowker, 1980–82. v.1,4¹. (In progress)   **BD546**

Contents: v.1 (in 2 pts.), 1450–1625, comp. by Peter Beal; v.4, 1800–1900, pt.1, Arnold-Gissing, comp. by B. Rosenbaum and P. White.

Aims "to list and describe briefly the extant manuscripts of literary works by a select number of British and Irish authors who flourished between 1450 and 1900. The year 1450 was chosen as a starting point since it coincides approximately with the invention of printing and because the manuscripts of earlier date have already received close special attention."—*Gen. Introd.* Includes "authors' corrected proofsheets, diaries and notebooks, their marginal notes in printed books and, especially for the period to c.1700, scribal copies; in short, most materials which the textual scholar or editor may consider relevant to the text, as well as certain other manuscripts which may be rather of critical or biographical interest."

Selection of authors to be included was originally based on those chosen for the *Concise Cambridge bibliography of English literature,* but is not confined to that list and fairly radical departures will be noted in later volumes. Some 400 "British, North American, European, Russian, Australian, New Zealand, and South African repositories and private collectors were initially approached with written enquiries" regarding pertinent manuscripts. Volumes are arranged alphabetically by name of individual author; for each author there is an introduction indicating the extent and importance of existing manuscripts, followed by a descriptive listing of the individual manuscripts with their locations; letters are omitted as outside the scope of this index.

Further volumes are to include: v.2, 1625–1700; v.3, 1700–1800; v.4, pts.2–3, 1800–1900; v.5, Indexes of titles, first lines, names, repositories. The completed work promises to be of major importance to scholarship and fills a definite need.   Z6611.L7I15

Storey, Richard and **Madden, Lionel.** Primary sources for Victorian studies: a guide to the location and use of unpublished materials. [London], Phillimore, [1977]. 81p.
   BD547

". . . concentrates on collections within Britain, but a short section is included as an introduction to the problems of discovering collections of relevant materials outside Britain."—*Pref.* Bibliographic references; index.   Z2019.S86

Stratford, Jenny. The Arts Council collection of modern literary manuscripts, 1963–1972. [London], Turret Books, 1974. 168p.   **BD548**

With the 1967 exhibition catalog *Poetry in the making* (ed. by Jenny Lewis; London, Turret Books, 68p.), provides a record of some of the more impressive results of the Council's efforts to collect and preserve in British repositories the manuscripts of contemporary writers. Originally restricted to poetry, the collecting policy has been extended to include prose writers. In addition to items added to the British Museum collections, this volume includes some manuscripts purchased by other libraries with Council support. Gives a brief description of each manuscript (relating it to a published version when possible) and frequently indicates where related manuscripts are to be found. Indexed.   Z6611.L7S77

Criticism

The critical temper; a survey of modern criticism on English and American literature from the beginnings to the twentieth century. Martin Tucker, gen. ed. N.Y., Ungar, [1969–79]. 4v.   **BD549**

Contents: v.1, From Old English to Shakespeare; v.2, From Milton to romantic literature; v.3, Victorian literature and American literature; v.4, Supplement.

A further addition to the series entitled *A library of literary criticism* (BD399, BD843, BD1270, etc.). Serves also as a supplement to Moulton's *Library of literary criticism* (BD551). Like the other works in the series, it presents excerpts from critical studies appearing in books and periodicals. About 220 authors are considered. Index of critics in v.3. The supplement updates the earlier

volumes and adds sections for a few authors not previously accorded separate treatment.   PR83.C764

Juchhoff, Rudolf. Sammelkatalog der biographischen und literarkritischen Werke zu englischen Schriftstellern des 19. und 20. Jahrhunderts (1830–1958). Verzeichnis der Bestände in deutschen Bibliotheken. Unter Mitarbeit von Hildegard Föhl. Krefeld, Scherpe Verlag, [1959?]. 272p.
   BD550

A listing of several hundred English authors (1830–1958) with indication of biographical and critical material about them. Includes books, dissertations, essays, and chapters in books, but not periodical articles. Coverage is international for critical and biographical references, with a large number of German items.

Moulton, Charles Wells. Library of literary criticism of English and American authors. Buffalo, Moulton Pub. Co., 1901–05. 8v. il. (Repr.: Gloucester, Mass., Peter Smith, 1959)   **BD551**

A compilation of quoted material, not an encyclopedia of original articles. Covers the years 680–1904. For each author treated gives brief biographical data and then selected quotations from criticisms of his work, grouped as: (1) personal, (2) individual works, (3) general. Extracts are of some length and are given with exact references, so that the work serves both as an encyclopedia of critical comment and as an index of literary criticisms.

Dorothy N. Curley's *Modern American literature* (BD399) and Temple and Tucker's *Modern British literature* (BD553) serve as continuations. An abridged and updated version has appeared as: PR83.M73

———— Library of literary criticism of English and American authors through the beginning of the twentieth century. Abr., rev. and with additions by Martin Tucker. N.Y., Ungar, [1966]. 4v.   **BD552**

Contents: v.1, The beginnings to the seventeenth century; v.2, Neo-classicism to the romantic period; v.3, The romantic period to the Victorian age; v.4, The mid-nineteenth century to Edwardianism.

Both abridges and updates Moulton's earlier compilation (above), but the coverage differs—some authors not previously treated are added and some of only marginal literary interest have been dropped. Excerpts from critical appraisals are drawn from publications through 1964. Critic index in the final volume.   PR83.M73

Temple, Ruth Zabriskie and **Tucker, Martin.** Modern British literature. N.Y., Ungar, [1966–75]. 4v. (A library of literary criticism)   **BD553**

Like Dorothy Nyren Curley's volume for modern American literature (BD399), this work serves as a sequel to Moulton's *Library of literary criticism* (BD551). Excerpts from critical writings on each author are arranged in chronological order to reflect as far as possible the rise or decline of an author's fame, and "have been chosen to describe his qualities, define his status, indicate, if he is well known, something of his life and personality, and specify, if he is notable otherwise than as an author, his other pursuits."—*Introd.* At the end of each volume are bibliographies of the authors' separately published works, and in v.3 there is a cross reference index and an index of critics. v.4 is a supplement updating the criticism on about one-third of the authors previously treated and adding 49 "new" writers.   PR473.T4

Dictionaries and handbooks

The Cambridge guide to English literature. [By] Michael Stapleton. [Cambridge & N.Y.], Cambridge Univ. Pr., Newnes Books, [1983]. 992p. il.   **BD554**

A handbook or "companion" rather than a "guide" in the usual bibliographic sense. Includes entries for authors, titles, literary characters, literary terms and movements (although names and titles predominate). Covers English writing of the United States, Australia, Canada, New Zealand, Ireland, and South Africa as well as Great Britain. In addition to *see* and *see also* references, names and titles mentioned in the text are printed in boldface if accorded a separate entry. Articles often include editorial comment as well as factual information. Includes selected living authors. PR85.C28

A guide to twentieth century literature in English. Ed. by Harry Blamires. London & N.Y., Methuen, [1983]. 312p.
BD555

The editor and two other contributors provide some 500 articles on individual authors (writing in English) from the United Kingdom, Ireland, Australia, Canada, New Zealand, the Caribbean, the Gambia, Ghana, India, Kenya, Nigeria, Pakistan, Southern Africa, Sri Lanka, and Uganda. Articles offer brief biographical sketches, commentary on the writer's work as a whole, and frequently summaries of major works. PR471.G78

Harvey, Sir Paul. The Oxford companion to English literature. 4th ed. rev. by Dorothy Eagle. Oxford, Clarendon Pr., 1967. 961p.
BD556

1st ed. 1932.
A very useful dictionary of brief articles on authors, literary works, characters in fiction, drama, etc., and literary allusions commonly met with in English literature.
"The main work in preparing this new edition has been to bring the entries for the twentieth century up to date."—*Pref.* New entries were added for a number of 20th-century writers and works. Some entries (mainly common allusions) were dropped or shortened from the previous edition.
A 5th ed., ed. by Margaret Drabble, was published in 1985 (Oxford & N.Y., Oxford Univ. Pr. 1155p.); it is a thorough revision, but retains the principal characteristics of the original work.
PR19.H3

Concise Oxford dictionary of English literature. 2d ed. [rev. by Dorothy Eagle]. Oxford, Clarendon Pr., 1970. 628p.
BD557

An abridgment of the above. It retains the entries which deal with the main aspects of English literature, though often in shortened form. Articles have been added which summarize, concisely, periods of literary history and general literary subjects. The first edition, prepared by John Mulgan, appeared in 1939. The new volume is fully revised, with much new material added, particularly in regard to the literature of the 20th century. PR19.C65

Myers, Robin. A dictionary of literature in the English language, from Chaucer to 1940. Comp. for the National Book League. Oxford [etc.], Pergamon, [1970]. 2v. (1497p.)
BD558

Offers biographical and bibliographical information on about 3,500 authors writing in English. Biographical information is sketchy, and the bulk of v.1 is made up of lists of the individual writers' works, with publication dates. v.2 provides a title-author index—possibly the most useful aspect of the work. Z2010.M9

——— A dictionary of literature in the English language from 1940 to 1970, complete with alphabetical title-author index and a geographical-chronological index to authors. Oxford, etc., Pergamon, [1978]. 519p.
BD559

A continuation of the above. Z2010.M92

New Century handbook of English literature. Ed. by Clarence L. Barnhart, with the assistance of William D. Halsey. Rev. ed. N.Y., Appleton, [1967]. 1167p.
BD560

1st ed. 1956.
An encyclopedia in dictionary form comprising 14,000 entries for authors, titles, plots, characters, place-names, movements, literary terms, etc. Many of the articles are taken from the *New Century cyclopedia of names* (AJ37) and give detailed information; in others there seems little relevance to the subject and often a curious imbalance in relative length of articles.
While some new entries have been inserted in the new edition, and new information supplied in certain existing articles, the revision was done with a minimum of resetting and at the expense of deleting entries or portions of articles from the first edition.
PR19.N4

Outlines

Annals of English literature, 1475–1950; the principal publications of each year together with an alphabetical index of authors and their works. 2d ed. Oxford, Clarendon Pr., 1961. 380p.
BD561

1st ed. 1935, comp. by J. G. Ghosh and E. G. Withycombe; 2d ed. rev. and brought up to date by R. W. Chapman.
A chronological list giving, under each year, authors and brief titles of outstanding books published that year, and, in parallel columns, important literary or historical events of the same year. Detailed author index, p.268–340. Z2011.A5

Rogal, Samuel J. A chronological outline of British literature. Westport, Conn., Greenwood Pr., [1980]. 341p.
BD562

Lists significant births, deaths, events, and literary works as an aid "in determining the extent of literary activity and literary related events in England, Scotland, Ireland, and Wales during a specific year, decade, or century."—*Introd.* Indexed. PR87.R57

History

Baugh, Albert Croll. A literary history of England. 2d ed. London, Routledge & K. Paul; N.Y., Appleton-Century-Crofts, [1967]. [1796p.], 1xxxp.
BD563

Also issued in a 4v. ed.
1st ed. 1948.
Contents: I, The Middle Ages: the Old English period (to 1100) by K. Malone; The Middle English period (1100–1500) by A. C. Baugh; II, The Renaissance (1500–1660) by T. Brooke and M. A. Shaaber; III, The Restoration and eighteenth century (1660–1789) by G. Sherburne and D. F. Bond; IV, The nineteenth century and after (1789–1939) by S. C. Chew and R. D. Altick; Bibliographical supplement; Index.
A scholarly history, with bibliographical footnotes in the text. The "Bibliographical supplement" (unpaged) of the new edition provides extensive listings of books and periodical articles extending the scope of the footnote references and bringing the record up to date. PR83.B3

Cambridge history of English literature, ed. by A. W. Ward and A. R. Waller. Cambridge, Univ. Pr.; N.Y., Putnam, 1907–33. 15v.
BD564

An important general history of the literature, covering from the earliest times to the end of the 19th century; each chapter is by a specialist. Includes extended and very useful bibliographies.
Available in different editions which show some variations in text and content. The English edition has made corrections in text from time to time, and has issued errata sheets containing further corrections and also additions to the bibliographies; the American edition (originally Putnam, now Macmillan) differs in paging and lacks the corrections in text and the errata lists of the English edition, except that some of these errata, but not the additions to the bibliographies, have been listed in the index volume published in 1933. Inexpensive reprints of both the English and the American editions are reprints of the full text and index, but omit the bibliographies, thus losing much of their value for reference purposes. However, these reprints are useful in the small library unable to afford either of the complete editions, and in the large library as an extra set for circulation. PR83.C22

Garnett, Richard and **Gosse, Edmund.** English literature, an illustrated record. London, Heinemann; N.Y., Macmillan, 1903. 4v. il. (Repr.: 4v. in 2, 1935)
BD565

Gives literary history, biographical and critical sketches of authors, account and criticism of various works of literature, some illustrative extracts and quotations, and many illustrations—some in color, largely from contemporary prints—illuminations, portraits, etc. The special reference value of the work is in these illustrations.
A new edition, 1923, differs only in having a supplementary

chapter by John Erskine on the literature of 1902–22. This is the edition reprinted in 1935. **PR83.G3**

Oxford history of English literature, ed. by Frank Percy Wilson and Bonamy Dobrée. Oxford, Clarendon Pr., 1945–79. v.2¹⁻², 3–4¹, 5–10, 12. (In progress) **BD566**

A standard reference history. Each volume includes extensive bibliographies, but these are not indexed in each volume.

Contents: v.1, pt.1, Before the Norman Conquest (In prep.); v.1, pt.2, Middle English literature (In prep.); v.2, pt.1, Chaucer and the 15th century, by H. S. Bennett (1947; repr. with corrections, 1948, 1954); v.2, pt.2, The close of the Middle Ages, by E. K. Chambers (1945; 2d impr., with corrections, 1947); v.3, The 16th century, excluding drama, by C. S. Lewis (1954); v.4, pt.1, The English drama, 1485–1585, by F. P. Wilson (1969); v.5, The earlier 17th century, 1600–1660, by Douglas Bush (1945; 2d ed. rev., 1962); v.6, English literature of the late 17th century, by James Sutherland (1969); v.7, The early 18th century, 1700–1740, by Bonamy Dobrée (1959); v.8, The mid-18th century, by J. E. Butt and G. Carnall (1979); v.9, 1789–1815, by W. L. Renwick (1963); v.10, 1815–1832, by Ian Jack (1963); v.11, The mid-19th century (In prep.); v.12, Eight modern writers, by J. I. M. Stewart (1963).

Atlases, gazetteers, and guidebooks

Briscoe, John D'Auby, Sharp, Robert Lathrop and **Borish, Murray Eugene.** A mapbook of English literature. N.Y., Holt, [1936]. 47p. **BD567**

Maps of Great Britain and London by chronological period with biographical and literary notes. Special maps of the Lake country, Hardy's Wessex, Oxford, Cambridge, Ireland, and the travels of English writers on the continent of Europe. **PR109.B7**

Eagle, Dorothy and **Carnell, Hilary.** The Oxford illustrated literary guide to Great Britain and Ireland. 2d ed., rev. by Dorothy Eagle. Oxford & N.Y., Oxford Univ. Pr., 1981. 312p. plates, maps, il. **BD568**

1st ed. (1977) had title: *The Oxford literary guide to the British Isles.*

Most of the text is drawn directly from the earlier edition, with a few additional entries and expansion of some of the existing entries. In two sections: (1) List of place names (giving location of each place and its literary associations) and (2) Index of authors (which enables the user to follow a writer's career from place to place and to identify pertinent places in the previous section). Fictitious names of real places are entered as cross references. **PR109.E18**

Fisher, Lois H. A literary gazetteer of England. N.Y., McGraw-Hill, [1980]. 740p. il. **BD569**

Intends to provide "a comprehensive survey of the 'literary associations' of more than 500 English (and occasionally foreign) authors with more than 1,200 English localities."—*Pref.* Arranged alphabetically by place name, with entries for towns, villages, rivers, mountains, etc. Includes relevant information on the history, geography, and archaeology of the place; many quotations from literary works are included. The London entry, p.322–477, consists mainly of entries for individual writers (arranged by birth date) detailing their association with the city. Index of personal names and a few titles. **PR109.F5**

Goode, Clement Tyson and **Shannon, Edgar Finley.** An atlas of English literature. N.Y., Century, 1925. 136p., incl. maps. (Repr.: Norwood, Pa., Norwood Eds., 1976) **BD570**

Gives outline maps by periods, with tables of authors and place-names associated with them. **PR109.G6**

Hardwick, John Michael Drinkrow. A literary atlas & gazetteer of the British Isles. Cartography by Alan G. Hodgkiss. Newton Abbot, David & Charles; Detroit, Gale, [1973]. 216p. maps. **BD571**

Offers a series of county maps with sites and literary landmarks numbered thereon, each map preceded by a page or more of gazetteer entries keyed to the maps; there is a separate map for London. Alphabetical index of people and an index of people grouped by county.

Frank Morley's *Literary Britain: a reader's guide to its writers and landmarks* (N.Y., Harper & Row, 1980. 510p.) takes the form of a tour guide with background information and commentary on literary associations of various places. **PR109.H25**

Biographies of authors

❖In many cases the best biographical sketches of English authors will be found in the *Dictionary of national biography* (AJ217) and other works listed under Great Britain, p.298. In the absence of those works, or for names or information not included in them, the following smaller works may be useful:

Allibone, Samuel Austin. Critical dictionary of English literature and British and American authors. Philadelphia, Lippincott, 1858–91. 5v. **BD572**

For full information *see* BD495.

British writers. Ed. under the auspices of the British Council; Ian Scott-Kilvert, gen. ed. N.Y., Scribner, [1979–84]. 8v. **BD573**

Contents: v.1, William Langland to the English Bible; v.2, Thomas Middleton to George Farquhar; v.3, Daniel Defoe to the Gothic novel; v.4, William Wordsworth to Robert Browning; v.5, Elizabeth Gaskell to Francis Thompson; v.6, Thomas Hardy to Wilfred Owen; v.7, Sean O'Casey to poets of World War II; v.8, Index.

A companion set to the same publisher's *American writers* (BD413), "the British collection originates from a series of separate articles entitled *Writers and their work*" (*Introd.*) initiated by the British Council in 1950. Offers signed essays with bibliographies of works by and about the writers. "The articles are intended to appeal to a wide readership, including students in secondary and advanced education, teachers, librarians, scholars, editors, and critics, as well as the general public." **PR85.B688**

Browning, David Clayton. Everyman's dictionary of literary biography, English and American, comp. after John W. Cousin . . . [Rev. ed.] London, Dent; N.Y., Dutton, [1960]. 769p. (Everyman's reference library) **BD574**

1st ed. 1958.

Substantially a new work, although based on Cousin's *Short biographical dictionary of English literature* (1910). Brief biographical sketches of more than 2,000 authors, including contemporary figures. Principal works with dates are noted, but no critical references. **PR19.B7**

Great writers of the English language. Ed., James Vinson. London, Macmillan; N.Y., St. Martin's, [1979]. 3v. **BD575**

Contents: [v.1] Poets; [v.2] Novelists and prose writers; [v.3] Dramatists.

Represents a selection of writers from all periods. For each writer is given brief biographical notes, a list of published works, a select list of bibliographies and critical studies, and a signed critical essay on the works. **PR106.G69**

Kunitz, Stanley J. and **Haycraft, Howard.** British authors before 1800; a biographical dictionary. Complete in one volume with 650 biographies and 220 portraits. N.Y., Wilson, 1952. 584p. il. **BD576**

PR105.K9

———— British authors of the 19th century. Complete in one volume with 1000 biographies and 350 portraits. N.Y., Wilson, 1936. 677p. il. **BD577**

Both volumes contain sketches which are informal and popular in nature, the length of the articles ranging from 300 to 1,500 words, depending on the importance of the writer. Bibliographies of principal works are included with brief citations for works about the author. **PR451.K8**

Russell, Josiah Cox. Dictionary of writers of thirteenth century England. London, N.Y., Longmans, [1936]. 210p. (London. Univ. Inst. of Historical Research. Bull. Special suppl. 3) **BD578**

Offers fairly detailed sketches with many bibliographical references to sources.

Drama

Bibliography

Bergquist, G. William. Three centuries of English and American plays; a checklist. England, 1500–1800; United States, 1714–1830. N.Y., London, Hafner, 1963. 281p. **BD579**

". . . originally compiled to serve as an index to the contents of the microprint edition of the *Three centuries of English and American plays* . . ."—*Foreword.* This is a more complete listing of the dramatic literature of the period than can be found in other works. Arranged alphabetically by author and title; notes approximately 5,500 plays. Z2014.D7B45

British Museum. Dept. of Manuscripts. Catalogue of additions to the manuscripts: plays submitted to the Lord Chamberlain, 1824–1851. London, Museum, 1964. 359p. **BD580**

A continuation of the chronological listing of plays contained in the Larpent collection (BD591). The plays submitted 1824–1900 are in the British Museum, and this is the record of some 4,250 plays submitted to the Lord Chamberlain, 1824–1851. Arranged chronologically; author and title indexes.

Caldwell, Harry B. and **Middleton, David L.** English tragedy, 1370–1600: fifty years of criticism. San Antonio, Tex., Trinity Univ. Pr., [1971]. 89p. **BD581**

Critical studies are cited in two main sections: (1) Non-dramatic tragedy, and (2) Dramatic tragedy [exclusive of Marlowe and Shakespeare]. About 800 entries; indexed. Z2014.D7C3

Carpenter, Charles A. Modern British drama. Arlington Heights, Ill., AHM Publ. Corp., [1979]. 120p. **BD582**

A select bibliography for the graduate and undergraduate student. Sections of general works are followed by bibliographies of individual modern English and Irish dramatists. Author index.

The compiler's annual checklist "Modern drama studies" in the journal *Modern drama* serves to update the bibliography and extends coverage worldwide. Z2014.D7C35

Coleman, Edward Davidson. The Jew in English drama; an annotated bibliography. The Jew in Western drama; an essay and a check list (1968), by Edgar Rosenberg. N.Y., New York Pub. Lib., [1970]. 50p., 265p. **BD583**

A reprint of the 1943 edition of Coleman's bibliography, with the addition of Rosenberg's contribution from the Sept. 1968 *Bulletin* of the New York Public Library. Z5784.J6C6

Conolly, Leonard W. and **Wearing, J. P.** English drama and theatre, 1800–1900; a guide to information sources. Detroit, Gale, [1978]. 508p. (American literature, English literature, and world literatures in English, 12) **BD584**

Aims to cover "all important aspects of nineteenth-century English drama and theatre."—*Introd.* Includes sections for contemporary history and criticism; modern history and criticism; individual authors; bibliographies and reference works; anthologies of plays; the theaters; acting and management; stage design, scenic art, and costume; periodicals. Brief annotations; index. Z2014.D7C72

Fordyce, Rachel. Caroline drama: a bibliographic history of criticism. Boston, G. K. Hall, [1978]. 203p. **BD585**

Aims "to survey the major critical issues related to Caroline Drama as they have emerged over approximately the last 100 years, although there are necessary extensions into earlier criticism."—*Introd.* More than 800 items. Annotations; index. Z2014.D7F67

Greg, *Sir* **Walter Wilson.** A bibliography of the English printed drama to the Restoration. London, pr. for the Bibliographical Society at the Univ. Pr., Oxford, 1939–59. 4v. (1752p.). il. facsim. (Illustrated monographs, no.24) **BD586**

Contents: v.1, Stationers' records. Plays to 1616, no.1–349; v.2, Plays, 1617–1689, no.350–836. Latin plays. Lost plays; v.3, Collections, appendix, reference lists; v.4, Introduction, additions, corrections, index of titles.

Arranged according to the supposed date of the earliest surviving edition. Locates copies in British and American libraries. Z2014.D7G78

—— A list of English plays written before 1643 and printed before 1700. London, Bibliographical Soc., 1900. 158p. **BD587**

Arranged alphabetically by author with indexes by author and by title. Locates copies. Z2014.D7G8

—— List of masques, pageants, etc., supplementary to a List of English plays. London, Bibliographical Soc., 1902. 35p., cxxxip. (Repr.: N.Y., Haskell House, 1969) **BD588**

List of masques, pageants, etc.; Index of authors; Index of titles; Appendixes; Advertisement lists; The early play lists; A list of English plays (Addenda and corrigenda). Z2014.D7G81

Harbage, Alfred. Annals of English drama, 975–1700; an analytical record of all plays, extant or lost, chronologically arranged and indexed by authors, titles, dramatic companies, etc. Rev. by S. Schoenbaum. London, Methuen, [1964]. 321p. **BD589**

1st ed. 1940.

Chronologically arranged in tabular form, indicating author, title, date of first performance, type (i.e., masque, tragedy, tragi-comedy, etc.), auspices, first edition, and last edition. Indexes of playwrights, English plays, foreign plays translated or adapted, dramatic companies. List of theaters. Appendix: Extant play manuscripts, 975–1700, their location and catalog numbers. About 100 new entries were added in the revised edition, and the indexes made fuller and more detailed.

—— —— Supplement to the rev. ed. [by] S. Schoenbaum. Evanston, Ill., Dept. of English, Northwestern Univ., [1966]. 19p.

Lists additions and corrections. Z2014.D7H25

Hazlitt, William Carew. Manual for the collector and amateur of old English plays. Ed. from the material formed by Kirkman, Langbaine, Downes, Oldys, and Halliwell-Phillipps, with extensive additions and corrections. London, Pickering and Chatto, 1892. 284p. (Repr.: N.Y., Johnson, 1967) **BD590**

A listing of plays, alphabetically by title, and index of names, theaters, theatrical companies, city guilds, etc. Z2014.D7H4

Henry E. Huntington Library. Catalogue of the Larpent plays in the Huntington Library, comp. by Dougald MacMillan. San Marino, Calif., 1939. 422p. (Huntington Library lists, no.4) **BD591**

"The licensing act of 1737 required that copies of all plays and other entertainments designed to be performed on the stage in Great Britain be submitted . . . for license." John Larpent was appointed Examiner on Nov. 20, 1778, and "died in office on Jan. 18, 1824. The official copies of plays submitted to the Examiner between 1737 and Jan. 1824, in Larpent's possession at the time of his death were bought about 1832 by John Payne Collier and Thomas Amyot."—*Pref. note.* These copies are now in the Huntington Library.

The list is chronological with author and title indexes.

For continuation *see* BD580. Z2014.D7H525

King, Kimball. Twenty modern British playwrights: a bibliography, 1956 to 1976. N.Y., Garland, 1977. 289p. (Garland reference library of the humanities, v.96) **BD592**

Includes contemporary playwrights such as Alan Ayckbourn, Edward Bond, Simon Gray, Joe Orton, John Osborne, Harold

Pinter, together with a number of less well-known figures. Lists of the dramatists' own works (including plays staged but not published; work for television and films, etc.) are followed by annotated bibliographies of critical writings and lists of reviews. Indexed.

Z2014.D7K47

Link, Frederick M. English drama, 1660–1800; a guide to information sources. Detroit, Gale, [1976]. 374p. (American literature, English literature, and world literatures in English, v.9)   **BD593**

In two parts, the first listing reference materials, works on the stage, and theater biography, dramatic history, and general drama criticism of the period. The second part offers brief biographical sketches of individual dramatists, with references to biographical and critical studies and editions of the plays.   Z2014.D7L55

Logan, Terence P. and **Smith, Denzell S.,** eds. The predecessors of Shakespeare; a survey and bibliography of recent studies in English Renaissance drama. Lincoln, Univ. of Nebraska Pr., [1973]. 348p.   **BD594**

Bibliographic surveys, by scholar specialists, on individual major dramatists are followed by a section on anonymous plays, and one on other dramatists. Indexed.   Z2014.D7L83

———— The popular school; a survey and bibliography of recent studies in English Renaissance drama. Lincoln, Univ. of Nebraska Pr., [1975]. 299p.   **BD595**

"This volume is the second in Recent Studies in English Renaissance Drama, a series which in its entirety will provide a detailed account of both the historical development and current state of scholarship on playwrights and plays from 1580 to 1642, exclusive of Shakespeare."—*Pref.* (The preceding volume of the series is *The predecessors of Shakespeare.*)

Includes dramatists who wrote primarily for the open-air public theaters, and anonymous plays first performed in such theaters. Sections by contributing scholars on Thomas Dekker, Thomas Middle-ton, John Webster, Thomas Heywood, Anthony Munday, Michael Drayton, and the anonymous plays. Indexes of persons and of titles.   Z2014.D7L82

———— The new intellectuals: a survey and bibliography of recent studies in English Renaissance drama. Lincoln, Univ. of Nebraska Pr., [1977]. 370p.   **BD596**

Forms the third volume of the series designated by the subtitle. Together with [v.2] *The popular school,* covers drama of the 1593–1616 period. This volume "treats dramatists who either wrote principally for the private theaters or were significantly influenced by them, and the anonymous plays first performed in them."—*Pref.*   Z2014.D7L817

———— The later Jacobean and Caroline dramatists: a survey and bibliography of recent studies in English Renaissance drama. Lincoln, Univ. of Nebraska Pr., [1978]. 279p.   **BD597**

Fourth and last in the compilers' series, this volume includes material on plays and playwrights of both popular and private theaters from 1616 to 1642.   Z2014.D7L816

The London stage, 1660–1800; a calendar of plays, entertainments and afterpieces, together with casts, box-receipts and contemporary comment, comp. from the playbills, newspapers and theatrical diaries of the period. Carbondale, Ill., Southern Illinois Univ. Pr., 1960–68. 5v. in 11.   **BD598**

For full information *see* BG78.   PN2592.L6

Nicoll, Allardyce. A short-title alphabetical catalogue of plays produced or printed in England from 1660–1900. Cambridge, Univ. Pr., 1959. 564p. (v.6 of his History of English drama)   **BD599**

For full information *see* BD613.

Penninger, Frieda Elaine. English drama to 1660 (excluding Shakespeare); a guide to information sources. Detroit, Gale, [1976]. 370p. (American literature, English literature, and world literatures in English, v.5)   **BD600**

Intended primarily for "undergraduate and graduate students who seek direction towards editions and discussions which will enable them to initiate and pursue a study of a given area of the drama."—*Foreword.* A section of general works (bibliographies, collections and editions, general histories and studies, histories and studies of specific periods, theater and stagecraft, etc.) is followed by sections on individual dramatists. Index of authors, editors, compilers, and anonymous titles.   Z2014.D7P46

Sibley, Gertrude Marian. The lost plays and masques, 1500–1642. Ithaca, N.Y., Cornell Univ. Pr., 1933. 205p. (Cornell studies in English, v.19)   **BD601**

Contents: The lost plays and masques; Lost masques with known titles; English plays with known titles acted in Germany; Index of playwrights.   PR651.S6

Steele, Mary Susan. Plays and masques at court during the reigns of Elizabeth, James and Charles. New Haven, Yale Univ. Pr.; London, Milford, 1926. 300p. (Cornell studies in English, [10]) (Repr.: N.Y., Russell & Russell, 1968)   **BD602**

Lists court plays and masques for the years 1558–1642.

PR651.S73

Stratman, Carl Joseph, comp. Bibliography of English printed tragedy, 1565–1900. Carbondale, Southern Illinois Univ. Pr., [1966]. 843p.   **BD603**

"Restricted to English printed tragedies written in England, Scotland, or Ireland, from the beginnings of formal tragedy in England, to the end of the Nineteenth Century, together with the various adaptations of each work."—*Introd.* (Adaptations of Shakespeare's tragedies are included, but not editions of his works.) Lists 1,483 tragedies in 6,852 entries. Includes a section of anthologies; locates copies. References to standard bibliographies (*STC,* Greg, *CBEL,* etc.) are given, as are notes on production where relevant. There is a chronological table, a title index, and an appendix of manuscript locations.   Z2014.D7S83

Thompson, Lawrence S. Nineteenth and twentieth century drama: a selective bibliography of English language works. Numbers 1–3029. Boston, G. K. Hall, [1975]. 456p.

BD604

"The present catalog is the first part of what will ultimately be a bibliography of the dramatic literature of the English-speaking peoples of the nineteenth century, as comprehensive as possible, and of the twentieth century selectively. While each volume will be in a separate alphabet, the numbers of the items will be consecutive, and the indexes cumulative."—*Introd.*

Author listing with title index. All material listed is available in microform from General Microfilm Co., Watertown, Mass. (Microform publication is ongoing—about 375 fiches per year—but no further volumes of the bibliography have appeared.) Includes variant editions of some works, English translations of foreign-language plays, etc.   Z2014.D7T5

Woodward, Gertrude Loop and **McManaway, James Gilmer.** A check list of English plays, 1641–1700. Chicago, Newberry Lib., 1945. 155p.   **BD605**

"Its purpose is to record the plays and masques, with the variant editions and issues, printed in the English language in the British Isles or in other countries during the years 1641 to 1700, inclusive, and to give the location of copies in [15] American libraries."—*Pref.*

———— ———— Supplement, comp. by Fredson Bowers. Charlottesville, Univ. of Virginia, 1949. 22p.

Locates copies.   Z2014.D7W6

Handbooks

Berger, Thomas L. and **Bradford, William C.** An index of characters in English printed drama to the Restoration. [Englewood, Colo.], Microcard Editions Books, 1975. 222p.   **BD606**

An index to all the characters in the plays listed in Greg's

Bibliography of English printed drama to the Restoration (BD586). Indexing is by name, character types, nationalities, occupations, religious proclivities, psychological states. Reference is to Greg number only; a "Finding list" provides the title, author, dates, and *STC* reference.   PR1265.3.B4

History and biography

Baker, David Erskine. Biographia dramatica. . . . London, Longmans, 1812. 3v. in 4. (Repr.: N.Y., AMS Pr., 1966) **BD607**

Subtitle: A companion to the playhouse: containing historical and critical memoirs, and original anecdotes, of British and Irish dramatic writers, from the commencement of our theatrical exhibitions; among whom are some of the most celebrated actors. Originally comp. to the year 1764, by D. E. Baker. Continued to 1782, by Isaac Reed, and brought down to the end of November, 1811, with very considerable additions and improvements throughout, by Stephen Jones.

Contents: v.1, pts.1–2, Authors and actors, A–Z; v.2, Names of dramas, A–L; v.3, Names of dramas, M–Z. Latin plays by English authors. Oratorios.

An older work, but still important for its biographies of dramatists and long lists of their works.   Z2014.D7B2

Bentley, Gerald Eades. The Jacobean and Caroline stage. Oxford, Clarendon Pr., 1941–68. 7v.   **BD608**

Contents: v.1–2, Dramatic companies and players; v.3–5, Plays and playwrights; v.6, Theatres; v.7, Appendixes to v.6. General index.   PN2592.B4

Chambers, Edmund Kerchever. The mediaeval stage. Oxford, Clarendon Pr., 1903. 2v. (Reissued 1967)   **BD609**

Contents: v.1, Minstrelsy. Folk drama; v.2, Religious drama. The interlude. Appendices. Subject index.   PN2152.C4

—— The Elizabethan stage. Oxford, Clarendon Pr., 1923. 4v. il. (Repr. with corrections, 1951)   **BD610**

Partial contents: v.1, The court. The control of the stage; v.2, The companies. The play-houses; v.3, Plays and playwrights; v.4, Anonymous works. Appendices. Indexes (by plays, persons, places, subjects).   PN2589.C4

—— —— Index, comp. by Beatrice White, to "The Elizabethan stage" and "William Shakespeare: A study of facts and problems." Oxford, Clarendon Pr., 1934. 161p.

Published by arrangement with the Shakespeare Association for whose members the index was made.   PR2894.C442

Fleay, Frederick Gard. Biographical chronicle of the English drama, 1559–1642. London, Reeves, 1891. 2v. (Repr.: N.Y., B. Franklin, 1962)   **BD611**

A list of authors, arranged alphabetically, giving for each: (1) brief biographical data, and (2) a list of plays in the order of original production. Appendixes in v.2 cover: Plays by anonymous authors, Masques by anonymous authors, University plays in English, University plays in Latin, Translations.   PR651.F5

Genest, John. Some account of the English stage, from the Restoration in 1660 to 1830. Bath, pr. by H. E. Carrington, 1832. 10v. (Repr.: N.Y., B. Franklin, 1966)   **BD612**

A valuable early history of plays, players, and playwrights of the period covered.   PN2581.G4

Nicoll, Allardyce. A history of English drama, 1660–1900. Cambridge, Univ. Pr., 1952–59. 6v.   **BD613**

Contents: v.1, Restoration drama, 1660–1700. 4th ed.; v.2, Early 18th century drama [1700–1750]. 3d ed.; v.3, Late 18th century drama, 1750–1800. 2d ed.; v.4, Early 19th century drama, 1800–1850. [2d ed.]; v.5, Late 19th century drama, 1850–1900. [2d ed.]; v.6, A short-title alphabetical catalogue of plays produced or printed in England from 1660–1900.

Each historical volume is on the same general plan, giving: (1) history, and (2) appendixes, containing such useful reference materi-

al as lists of theaters and handlists of plays produced during the period covered.

v.6 not only serves as a title index to plays recorded in the earlier volumes, but provides additional information on some plays and lists others not previously mentioned; includes numerous cross references from alternate titles.

Continued chronologically by: PR625.N52

—— English drama, 1900–1930; the beginnings of the modern period. Cambridge, Univ. Pr., 1973. 1083p.   **BD614**

"The present book . . . both is and is not a continuation of the more extended 'history' concerned with the years 1660–1900 [above]. It is a separate volume: yet it could not have come into being if the theatrical activities of the preceding ages had not already been examined."—*Pref.* Includes a "Handlist of plays" for the period, p.452–1053. Indexed.   PR721.N45

The Revels history of drama in English. Gen. eds., Clifford Leech and T. W. Craik. London, Methuen; N.Y., Barnes and Noble, etc., 1975–1983. 8v. il.   **BD615**

Contents: v.1, Medieval drama, by A. C. Cawley [and others]; v.2, 1500–1576, by N. Sanders [and others]; v.3, 1576–1613, by J. L. Barroll [and others]; v.4, 1613–1660, by P. Edwards [and others]; v.5, 1660–1750, by J. Loftis [and others]; v.6, 1750–1880, by M. R. Booth [and others]; v.7, 1880 to the present day, by H. Hunt [and others]; v.8, American drama, by T. Bogard [and others].

A new work giving much attention to social background, the theaters, actors and repertory, etc., as well as to the dramatic literature. Each volume has its own bibliography and index.   PR625.R44

Fiction

Bibliography

Beasley, Jerry C. English fiction, 1660–1800; a guide to information sources. Detroit, Gale, [1978]. 313p. (American literature, English literature, and world literatures in English, 14)   **BD616**

A section on general bibliographic sources for the period is followed by sections on individual authors.   Z2014.F5B42

Block, Andrew. The English novel, 1740–1850; a catalogue including prose romances, short stories, and translations of foreign fiction. [New and rev. ed., i.e., 2d ed.] London, Dawsons of Pall Mall, 1961; N.Y., Oceana, 1962. 349p.   **BD617**

1st ed. 1939.

Arranged alphabetically by author or, if anonymous or pseudonymous, by title. Title index.   Z2014.F4B6

McBurney, William Harlin. A check list of English prose fiction, 1700–1739. Cambridge, Harvard Univ. Pr., 1960. 154p.   **BD618**

A listing of some 400 titles of works comprising the prose-fiction background from which the English novel grew. Arrangement is chronological by year, with, for each item, author, full title and imprint, price (where available), later editions to 1739, and at least one library location if possible, here or abroad.

Continued chronologically by: Z2014.F4M3

Beasley, Jerry C. A check list of prose fiction published in England, 1740–1749. Charlottesville, publ. for the Bibliographical Society of the Univ. of Virginia by the Univ. Pr. of Virginia, [1972]. 213p.   **BD619**

Serves as a continuation of W. H. McBurney's *Check list of English prose fiction, 1700–1739* (above). Chronological arrangement with name and title index. Locates copies.   Z2014.F4B37

Orr, Leonard. A catalogue checklist of English prose fiction, 1750–1800. Troy, N.Y., Whitston, 1979. 204p.   **BD620**

Attempts "to list chronologically most of the first editions of English prose fiction first published in London between 1750 and

1800."—*Pref.* Serves as a continuation of Beasley's checklist for 1740–49 (above). Nearly 1,200 items. Locates copies. Author and title indexes.   Z2014.F4O77

McBurney, William Harlin and **Taylor, Charlene M.** English prose fiction, 1700–1800, in the University of Illinois library. Urbana, Univ. of Illinois Pr., 1965. 162p.   **BD621**

An author listing of fiction items published 1700–1800. Limited to the holdings of a single library, and therefore not a successor to, or continuation of, the previous items.   Z2014.F4M33

O'Dell, Sterg. A chronological list of prose fiction in English printed in England and other countries, 1475–1640. Cambridge, Mass., Technology Pr. of M.I.T., 1954. 147p.
                                                                BD622

Author index. Locates copies and includes references to *STC* numbers.

Sargent, Lyman Tower. British and American utopian literature, 1516–1975; an annotated bibliography. Boston, G. K. Hall, [1979]. 324p.   **BD623**

A chronological listing of works of utopian literature is followed by a list of secondary works (books and articles in separate sections). Author and title indexes to the chronological list. Library locations; brief annotations.   Z2014.U8S27

Stanton, Robert J. A bibliography of modern British novelists. Troy, N.Y., Whitston, 1978. 2v. (1123p.)   **BD624**

Contents: v.1, Kingsley Amis, Elizabeth Bowen, Margaret Drabble, William Golding, L. P. Hartley, Richard Hughes, Rosamond Lehmann, Doris Lessing, Brian Moore; v.2, Iris Murdoch, V. S. Naipaul, Anthony Powell, Jean Rhys, Alan Sillitoe, C. P. Snow, Muriel Spark, Angus Wilson.

For each novelist there is a list of works subdivided by genre (novels, short stories, poems, plays, "other"); a section of general secondary studies, interviews, biographical sketches and other miscellaneous items; and a list of studies and reviews of individual works. A separate section lists works referring to two or more novelists and is subdivided as (1) books and dissertations, and (2) periodical articles; cross references to this section are provided in the individual author sections.

Stevenson, Lionel [and others]. Victorian fiction; a guide to research. Cambridge, Harvard Univ. Pr., 1964. 440p.
                                                                BD625

A companion to Faverty's *Victorian poets* (BD648) and De Laura's *Victorian prose* (BD538). Separate chapters on each of the principal novelists provide a survey of research and a critical evaluation of selected writings in the field.   PR873.S8

Ford, George H., ed. Victorian fiction; a second guide to research. N.Y., Modern Language Assoc. of America, 1978. 401p.   **BD626**

Intended as a companion to Lionel Stevenson's *Victorian fiction* (above) which covers publications through 1962. This volume aims "to supply complete coverage from 1963 through 1974" (*Pref.*) with occasional mention of works published 1975 or later, plus chapters on Robert Louis Stevenson and Samuel Butler reviewing the scholarly writing on those two figures from the beginning through 1974. Some pre-1962 items are also mentioned. Chapters are by scholar specialists, and there has been an effort "to provide some fresh emphasis" regarding "the availability of manuscripts and the record of film versions of Victorian novels."—*Pref.* Neglected areas of research are also noted. Fully indexed.   PR871.V5

Criticism

Bell, Inglis Freeman and **Baird, Donald.** The English novel, 1578–1956: a checklist of twentieth-century criticisms. Denver, Alan Swallow, [1959]. 169p.   **BD627**

A selective listing of 20th-century criticisms of English novels from Lyly to mid-20th century, including citations to books and periodicals. Arrangement is alphabetical by novelist's name, then by title of the novel.   Z2014.F4B4

Cassis, A. F. The twentieth-century English novel; an annotated bibliography of general criticism. N.Y., Garland Pr., 1977. 413p.   **BD628**

A bibliography of general criticism on the English novel. About 2,800 items in three main sections: (1) Bibliographies and checklists; (2) Criticism (books and articles in separate listings); (3) Dissertations and theses. Indexes of novelists and of selected topics and themes.   Z2014.F5C35

The English novel: twentieth century criticism. Chicago, Swallow Pr., [1976–82]. 2v.   **BD629**

Contents: v.1, Defoe through Hardy, ed. by Richard J. Dunn; v.2, Twentieth century novelists, ed. by Paul Schlueter and June Schlueter.

v.1 offers checklists of critical writings on the works of some 45 British novelists; v.2 treats an additional 80 novelists. For most authors there is a section of general studies plus lists of works relating to individual novels. There is also a general bibliography in each volume.   Z2014.F4E53

Palmer, Helen H. and **Dyson, Anne Jane.** English novel explication; criticisms to 1972. [Hamden, Conn.], Shoe String Pr., 1973. 329p.   **BD630**

Serves as a continuation of Bell and Baird's *The English novel* (BD627), listing criticisms from 1958 to 1972.   Z2014.F5P26

———— ———— Suppl. I, comp. by Peter L. Abernethy, Christian J. W. Kloesel and Jeffrey R. Smitten. [Hamden, Conn.], Shoe String Pr., 1976. 305p.

Emphasis is on material published 1972–74, with some earlier citations and a few 1975 publications.   Z2014.F5P26

History

Baker, Ernest Albert. The history of the English novel. London, Witherby, 1924–39. 10v. (Repr.: N.Y., Barnes & Noble, 1950)   **BD631**

Covers from the beginnings to the early 20th century. Brief bibliographies and an index in each volume.

An additional volume has been published as: PR821.B3

Stevenson, Lionel. The history of the English novel; volume XI: Yesterday and after. N.Y., Barnes & Noble, [1967]. 431p.   **BD632**

Bibliography, p.406–16.   PR881.S7

Poetry

Bibliography

Anderson, Emily Ann. English poetry, 1900–1950: a guide to information sources. Detroit, Gale, [1982]. 315p. (American literature, English literature, and world literatures in English, v.33)   **BD633**

Lists general bibliographic and research aids as well as works by and about modern British poets. Many annotations; indexed.
                                                         Z2014.P7A54

Boys, Richard Charles. A finding-list of English poetical miscellanies 1700–48 in selected American libraries. [Baltimore, 1940] (Repr. from ELH, a journal of English literary history 7:144–62, June 1940)   **BD634**

Based on Case's *Bibliography* (BD638); a chronological list showing location in 14 American libraries, with the addition of some other libraries not checked systematically.   Z2014.P7B7

Brogan, Terry V. F. English versification, 1570–1980: a reference guide with a global appendix. Baltimore, Johns Hopkins Univ. Pr., [1981]. 794p.   **BD635**

Intends "to collect, list, classify by subject, summarize, describe, generally evaluate, cross-reference, and index by poet and author all known printed studies of English versification from . . . 1570, up to

January 1980."—*Introd.* A classified bibliography, chiefly of English versification, but including appendixes of many other languages. Long annotations for most entries.

A list of addenda and corrigenda appears in *Modern philology* 81:50–52 (Aug. 1983).   Z2015.V37B76

Brown, Carleton Fairchild. Register of Middle English religious and didactic verse. Oxford, pr. for the Bibliographical Society at the Univ. Pr., 1916–20. 2v. [Bibliographical Soc., London Pubn.]   **BD636**

Contents: Pt.1, List of manuscripts; pt.2, Index of first lines and index of subjects and titles.

Manuscripts are listed according to the library in which they are found. Includes religious and didactic verse written between 1200 and 1500.   Z2012.B87

———— and **Robbins, Rossell Hope.** Index of Middle English verse. N.Y., pr. for the Index Society, by Columbia Univ. Pr., 1943. 785p.   **BD637**

A scholarly index to all poems published in England before 1500. Designed to complete the work by Carleton Brown, above. The 2,273 entries in the *Register* (for about 1,100 manuscripts) have been increased in this *Index* to 4,365 entries in more than 2,000 manuscripts. Includes a subject and title index and a list of locations of privately owned manuscripts.   Z2012.B86

———— ———— Supplement . . . [by] Rossell Hope Robbins [and] John L. Cutler. Lexington, Univ. of Kentucky Pr., 1965. 551p.

The supplement "expands some 2,300 of the 4,365 entries in the original *Index* and adds some 1,500 new entries."—*Introd.* Changes in ownership and location of manuscripts are recorded, and cataloging is completed for manuscripts not available for examination at the time the basic work was published. Editions of poems published since 1943 are also noted.

Case, Arthur Ellicott. Bibliography of English poetical miscellanies, 1521–1750. Oxford, pr. for the Bibliographical Society at the Univ. Pr., 1935 (for 1929). 386p.   **BD638**

Arranged chronologically by date of the earliest-known edition, with descriptions of subsequent editions to 1750. Indexes by title, by year, and by persons. Locates copies in British and American libraries.   Z2014.P7C3

Contemporary poets. 3d ed. James Vinson, ed. London, Macmillan; N.Y., St. Martin's Pr., [1980]. 1804p.   **BD639**

1st ed. (1970) had title: *Contemporary poets of the English language.*

Offers biobibliographical information on more than 1,100 poets writing in English; the selection of poets has varied from edition to edition, some being dropped and new names added. Includes an appendix of poets "who have died since 1950 but whose reputations are essentially contemporary."—*Editor's note.*   Z2014.P7C62

English poetry; select bibliographical guides. A. E. Dyson, ed. [London], Oxford Univ. Pr., 1971. 375p.   **BD640**

Scholar specialists have contributed bibliographic essays on 20 English poets from Chaucer to Eliot. Each includes a section on texts, critical studies and commentary, biographies and letters, bibliographies, and background reading. A section of "References" follows each chapter, providing full citations to the works mentioned in the earlier sections. A useful guide for the graduate student.   Z2014.P7E53

Foxon, David Fairweather. English verse 1701–1750; a catalogue of separately printed poems with notes on contemporary collected editions. [London & N.Y.], Cambridge Univ. Pr., [1975]. 2v.   **BD641**

Contents: v.1, Catalogue; v.2, Indexes.

"The catalogue attempts to list all separately published verse written in English, as well as works written in other languages and printed in the British Isles, but it omits all works printed in America. . . . "—*Introd.* A short-title catalog by author or first word of anonymous title; includes valuable descriptive notes; locates

copies. There are indexes of first lines, imprints, and subjects, plus a chronological index.   Z2014.P7F69

Marcan, Peter. Poetry themes; a bibliographical index to subject anthologies and related criticism in the English language, 1875–1975. London, Bingley; Hamden, Conn., Linnet Books, [1977]. 301p.   **BD642**

Intends to index "subject anthologies which bring together poetry on one subject or a group of related subjects."—*Introd.* Includes some anthologies of poetry and prose. Critical literature (books, periodical articles, academic theses) are also listed as being useful for their bibliographies and footnote references providing sources for thematic and comparative studies. Arranged according to a classification scheme outlined p.x–xvi, but there is no alphabetical subject index. Brief notes regarding coverage, period, emphasis, etc., frequently follow the bibliographic citations; studies and criticism are separately listed within each subject category. Index of authors and compilers. Anthologies indexed are mainly British imprints.   PN1022.M3

Mell, Donald C. English poetry, 1660–1800: a guide to information sources. Detroit, Gale, [1982]. 501p. (American literature, English literature, and world literatures in English, v.40)   **BD643**

A general section (including background resources, genre studies, etc.) is followed by sections on individual authors. Indexed.   Z2014.P7M44

Reilly, Catherine W. English poetry of the first World War. London, George Prior; N.Y., St. Martin's, 1978. 402p.   **BD644**

A listing of "poetry and verse on the theme of the First World War, written by English poets (i.e., poets of England, Ireland, Scotland and Wales), servicemen and civilians, who experienced the war. It is restricted to printed material in the form of book, pamphlet, card, or broadside."—*Abstract.* In two main sections: (1) Anthologies; (2) Individual authors. Title index. Supplementary list of names of war poets of other English-speaking nations.   Z2014.P7R44

Reiman, Donald H. English romantic poetry, 1800–1835: a guide to information sources. Detroit, Gale, [1979]. 294p. (American literature, English literature, and world literatures in English, 27)   **BD645**

Concentrates on "important modern studies of all kinds devoted primarily to or containing significant discussions of five major poets—Wordsworth, Coleridge, Byron, Shelley, and Keats—and twelve secondary poets."—*p.xv.* Also includes general works on Romanticism in England, the social and literary background, etc. Limited mainly to English-language materials. Indexed.   Z2014.P7R46

Indexes

See also BD637.

First-line index of English poetry, 1500–1800, in manuscripts of the Bodleian Library, Oxford; ed. by Margaret Crum. Oxford, Clarendon Pr., 1969. 2v. (1257p.)   **BD646**

Gives first line in modernized spelling, with indication of variants in wording; last line of the usual version of the poem; author's name, if known; title; and a list of Bodleian manuscripts in which the poem is found. Editorial notes provide references to printed versions of the poem. Index of authors.   Z2014.P7F5

Criticism

See also BD310.

Cline, Gloria Stark and **Baker, Jeffrey A.** An index to criticisms of British and American poetry. Metuchen, N.J., Scarecrow Pr., 1973. 307p.   **BD647**

Indexes critiques appearing in books and periodicals "selected primarily on the basis of their availability in college and university libraries."—*Pref.* Only collections of criticism are included among the books indexed. PR89.C5

Faverty, Frederic Everett. The Victorian poets; a guide to research. 2d ed. Cambridge, Harvard Univ. Pr., 1968. 433p. **BD648**

1st ed. 1956.

A handbook of bibliography, scholarship and criticism in the field; similar to Stevenson's *Victorian fiction* (BD625) and De Laura's *Victorian prose* (BD538). Chapters by specialists treat major poets separately, minor poets and movements collectively. In general, the closing date for publications considered is 1966.

PR593.F3

Houtchens, Carolyn Washburn and **Houtchens, Lawrence Huston,** eds. The English romantic poets and essayists; a review of research and criticism. Rev. ed. [N.Y.], publ. for the Modern Language Assoc. of America by New York Univ. Pr., 1966. 395p. **BD649**

1st ed. 1957.

A companion volume to Jordan's *The English romantic poets* (below). A critical evaluation of the material about 11 romantic poets and essayists, covering as pertinent, bibliographies, editions, biographies, and criticism. PR590.H6

Jordan, Frank. The English romantic poets; a review of research and criticism. 3d rev. ed. N.Y., Modern Language Assoc. of America, 1972. 468p. **BD650**

1st and 2d eds. (1950, 1956) ed. by Thomas M. Raysor.

A companion volume to Houtchens (above), with a general chapter on the romantic movement and special chapters on Wordsworth, Coleridge, Byron, Shelley, and Keats. This edition updated to include publications through 1970, with a few early 1971 items.

PR590.J6

Keats-Shelley journal. Keats, Shelley, Byron, Hunt, and their circles; a bibliography, July 1, 1950–June 30, 1962. Ed. by David Bonnell Green and Edwin Graves Wilson. Lincoln, Univ. of Nebraska Pr., [1964]. 323p. **BD651**

A collection of the first 12 annual bibliographies originally published in the *Keats-Shelley journal,* reprinted with a cumulated index. The intent has been to include all new editions, reprints, translations, etc., and all books and articles relating to any or all of these poets and of the contemporaries in their circles.

An annual bibliography (now compiled by Clement Dunbar) continues to be a feature of the *Keats-Shelley journal.*

Supplemented by: Z2013.K4

Keats, Shelley, Byron, Hunt, and their circles: a bibliography, July 1, 1962–December 31, 1974. Ed. by Robert A. Hartley; comp. by David Bonnell Green [and others]. Lincoln, Univ. of Nebraska Pr., [1978]. 487p. **BD652**

Cumulates the annual bibliographies which appeared in v.13–25 of the *Keats-Shelley journal.* Z2013.K42

Kuntz, Joseph Marshall and **Martinez, Nancy C.** Poetry explication: a checklist of interpretation since 1925 of British and American poems, past and present. [3d ed.] Boston, G. K. Hall, [1980]. 570p. **BD653**

1st ed. 1950 by J. M. Kuntz and G. Arms.

Now "presents a comprehensive index of poetry explications printed [in selected composite works and literary periodicals] during the period 1925–1977. It incorporates the checklists of 1950 and 1962 and, following the aim, scope, and limitations established for the first editions, lists explications printed through 1977, with an occasional excursion into 1978."—*Introd.* Z2014.P7K8

History

Courthope, William John. A history of English poetry. N.Y., London, Macmillan, 1895–1910. 6v. **BD654**

A standard work covering from the Middle Ages to the romantic movement. Each volume includes an analytical table of contents, and there is a cumulated index in v.6. PR502.C8

Perkins, David. A history of modern poetry: from the 1890's to the high modernist mode. Cambridge, Mass., Belknap Pr. of Harvard Univ. Pr., 1976. 623p. **BD655**

Treats British and American poetry. Indexed.

A projected second volume, to be entitled *From the 1920s to the present,* has not yet appeared. PR610.P4

Anthologies

Arber, Edward. British anthologies. London, Frowde, 1900–1901. 10v. **BD656**

Contents: v.1, Dunbar anthology, 1401–1508; v.2, Surrey and Wyatt anthology, 1509–47; v.3, Spenser anthology, 1548–91; v.4, Shakespeare anthology, 1592–1616; v.5, Jonson anthology, 1617–37; v.6, Milton anthology, 1638–74; v.7, Dryden anthology, 1675–1700; v.8, Pope anthology, 1701–44; v.9, Goldsmith anthology, 1745–74; v.10, Cowper anthology, 1775–1800.

Includes about 2,500 entire poems, by about 300 authors. Each volume has an author index, and an index of first lines, with notes and a glossary; v.10 has also a general index of first lines for the 10v.

Gardner, Helen Louise, ed. The new Oxford book of English verse, 1250–1950. N.Y., Oxford Univ. Pr., 1972. 974p. **BD657**

Earlier editions (1900; 1939) edited by Sir Arthur Quiller-Couch had title: *Oxford book of English verse.* The 1st ed. stopped with 1900; the second extended coverage to 1918 and included 966 poems as against 883 in the previous edition, with some changes in the selection from poets previously included as well as the addition of new names. Emphasis was on lyrical verse.

"The present edition is not a revision of Q's revision but a new anthology."—*Pref.* It is not confined to lyric verse, but "attempts to represent the range of English non-dramatic poetry from 1250 to 1950." There are 884 poems, including some excerpts from long poems; some brief notes and references are provided at the back of the book. With the exception of Pound and Eliot, American poets are excluded.

Complemented by a series of "Oxford books" each devoted to a particular period or century as follows: *Medieval English verse,* chosen by Celia and Kenneth Sisam, 1970. 617p.; *English mystical verse,* chosen by D. H. S. Nicholson and A. H. E. Lee, 1916. 644p; *Sixteenth century verse,* chosen by E. K. Chambers, 1932. 905p.; *Seventeenth century verse,* chosen by H. J. C. Grierson and G. Bullough, 1934. 974p.; *Eighteenth century verse,* chosen by David Nichol Smith, 1926. 727p.; *Regency verse, 1798–1837,* chosen by H. S. Milford, 1928. 888p.; *Nineteenth-century English verse,* chosen by John Hayward, 1964. 969p.; *Victorian verse,* chosen by Arthur Quiller-Couch, 1912. 1023p.; *Modern verse, 1892–1935,* chosen by W. B. Yeats, 1936. 454p.; *Twentieth-century English verse,* chosen by Philip Larkin, 1973. 641p.; *Contemporary verse, 1945–1980,* chosen by D. J. Enright, 1980. 299p.; *Light verse,* chosen by W. H. Auden, 1938, 533p.; and *Narrative verse,* chosen by Iona and Peter Opie, 1983. 407p. These are useful volumes which serve a number of purposes in the reference collection, even though they have little reference apparatus beyond indexes of authors and first lines, and inevitably reflect certain personal preferences of the compilers.

PR1174.G3

Opie, Iona and **Opie, Peter,** eds. Oxford dictionary of nursery rhymes. Oxford, Clarendon Pr., 1951. 467p. il. **BD658**

Said to be the most comprehensive and authoritative work ever published on English nursery rhymes; includes 550 rhymes (all current today or until recently), arranged alphabetically by the most prominent word or, in the case of nonsense jingles, by the opening phrase. The standard version of each nursery rhyme is given first, followed by the earliest recorded version (where available), and bibliographical references. Two indexes: (1) "notable figures associated with the invention, diffusion or illustration of nursery rhymes," and (2) first lines of both standard and other versions. Contains many prints of drawings and texts taken from famous old nursery-rhyme books, and a 45-page introduction.   PZ8.3.O6Ox

Stevenson, Burton Egbert. Home book of verse, American and English; with an appendix containing a few well-known poems in other languages. 9th ed. N.Y., Holt, [1953]. 2v. (lxxxiv p., 4012p.)   **BD659**

1st ed. 1912.

One of the most extensive collections, with coverage from the last part of the 16th century to the first part of the 20th century. Arranged by large subjects, with full indexes of authors, titles, and first lines.

Supplemented by: PR1175.S76

———— Home book of modern verse; an extension of The home book of verse, being a selection from American and English poetry of the 20th century. 2d ed., rev. N.Y., Holt, [1953]. 1124p.   **BD660**

1st ed. 1925. The 2d ed. is not noticeably changed except by the addition of "Corrigenda to Index of authors," p.1123–24.

A well-selected collection from early 20th-century poets. Arranged by large subjects with indexes by authors, first lines, and titles.   PR1175.S762

Untermeyer, Louis. A treasury of great poems, English and American, from the foundations of the English spirit to the outstanding poetry of our own time, with lives of the poets and historical settings selected and integrated. Rev. and enl. N.Y., Simon & Schuster, 1955. 1286p.   **BD661**

An anthology of almost 1,000 poems with interspersed comments on the poets, the origin and source of a poem, seeming obscurities, etc. Index of authors and titles. Index of first lines.   PR1175.U65

Ballads

Bibliography

Coffin, Tristram Potter. The British traditional ballad in North America. Rev. ed., with a supplement by Roger deV. Renwick. Austin, Univ. of Texas Pr., [1977]. 297p. (American Folklore Society. Bibliographical and special ser.)   **BD662**

1st ed. 1950.

The main portion of the work is "A bibliographical guide to story variation in the traditional ballad of America," presenting the published scholarship on the Child ballad in America, with citations to texts of the ballads. Index of standard titles of the ballads and songs.   ML3553.C6

Crawford, James Ludovic Lindsay, *26th Earl of.* Bibliotheca Lindesiana. Catalogue of a collection of English ballads of the XVIIth and XVIIIth centuries, printed for the most part in black letter. [Aberdeen], priv. pr. [Aberdeen Univ. Pr.], 1890. 686p.   **BD663**

Records more than 1,400 ballads by first line, with list of printers and index.   Z2014.B2L7

London. Stationers' Company. An analytical index to the ballad-entries (1557–1709) in the Registers of the Company of Stationers of London, comp. by Hyder E. Rollins. Chapel Hill, Univ. of North Carolina Pr., 1924. 324p.   **BD664**

Indexes ballads by title, by first line, and by names and subjects.   Z2014.B2L8

Anthologies

Child, Francis James. English and Scottish popular ballads. Boston, Houghton, 1883–98. 5v. (Repr. 1956. 5v. in 3)   **BD665**

The great collection of English ballads. Contains text of 305 distinct ballads, each given in all its extant versions. For each ballad includes a historical and bibliographical introduction, with full account of parallels in other languages, the diffusion of the story, etc. Appendix in v.5 contains: Glossary, Sources of the text, Index of published airs of English and Scottish ballads, Ballad airs [46] from manuscript, Index of ballad titles, Titles of collections of ballads briefly noted in this work, Index of matters, Bibliography. For the tunes of these ballads *see* BH292.

For the large reference or university library; for the smaller library the following abridgment is sufficient: PR1181.C5

———— English and Scottish popular ballads, ed. from the collection of Francis James Child by Helen Child Sargent and George Lyman Kittredge. Boston, Houghton, [1904]. 729p.   **BD666**

An abridgment of the above, sufficient for ordinary purposes. Gives each of the 305 ballads (except no.33, 279, 281, 290, and 299) in one or more versions, without the *apparatus criticus,* and with briefer notes. Contains a briefer glossary, full list of sources, and an index of titles.   PR1181.C5

Kinsley, James, comp. Oxford book of ballads, newly selected and edited. Oxford, Clarendon Pr., 1969. 711p.   **BD667**

Previous ed., 1910, ed. by Sir Arthur Quiller-Couch.

A collection of 150 ballads representing quite a different selection from that of the earlier edition. Tunes for about 80 of the ballads are given. Alphabetical index of titles, but no first-line index.   PR1181.K55

Parodies

Hamilton, Walter, comp. Parodies of the works of English and American authors, collected and annotated. London, Reeves, 1884–89. 6v. il.   **BD668**

A very comprehensive collection; many parodies are given in full, some only mentioned. Includes bibliographies. Index in each volume.   PN6110.P3H3

Lowrey, Burling. Twentieth century parody: American and British. N.Y., Harcourt, [1960]. 304p.   **BD669**

PN6231.P3L6

Macdonald, Dwight. Parodies: an anthology from Chaucer to Beerbohm—and after. N.Y., Random House, [1960]. 574p.   **BD670**

British and American parodists grouped in three periods, and a section of "Specialties."

A more recent collection is *The Faber book of parodies,* ed. by Simon Brett (London, Faber & Faber, 1984).   PN6231.P3M3

Diaries

Batts, John Stuart. British manuscript diaries of the nineteenth century: an annotated listing. Fontwell, Centaur Pr.; Totowa, N.J., Rowman and Littlefield, 1976. 345p.   **BD671**

Serves as a companion to Matthews' *British diaries* (below), listing unpublished diaries of the 19th century. Arranged by year, then alphabetically by diarist. Index of diarists and subject index.   Z6611.B6B38

Matthews, William. British diaries; an annotated bibliography of British diaries written between 1442 and 1942. Berkeley, Univ. of California Pr., 1950. 339p.   **BD672**

Diaries, both in published and manuscript form (and including those reproduced in periodicals) are listed chronologically by year of first entry. Brief annotations suggest the contents: religious, military, personal, social, etc. Author index. For unpublished items, owner or library location is given.   Z2014.D5M3

Individual authors

❖In this edition of the *Guide* the listings of bibliographies, dictionaries, concordances, and handbooks of individual authors have been limited to a few indisputably major figures. The types of works listed here for Chaucer, Milton, and Shakespeare may be regarded as typical of the kind of publications one might find for many lesser literary figures. A similar practice is followed for French, German and Italian literatures. In recent years the use of computers has resulted in publication of a remarkable number of concordances, and photo-offset printing from typescript has led to a similar increase in the number of author bibliographies now available. For additional titles consult the bibliographies listed under the subdivision "Bibliography" within the various national literature sections.

Chaucer

A Chaucer glossary. Comp. by Norman Davis [and others]. Oxford, Clarendon Pr.; N.Y., Oxford Univ. Pr., 1979. 185p. **BD673**

"The primary aim of this Glossary is to explain the meanings of words and phrases in Chaucer's works which are used in ways unfamiliar in modern English, and to refer them to a number (necessarily limited) of typical instances. It also illustrates Chaucer's use of many expressions not necessarily unfamiliar but characteristic of his language."—*Introd.* PR1941.C5

Dillon, Bert. A Chaucer dictionary: proper names and allusions, excluding place names. Boston, G. K. Hall, 1974. 266p. **BD674**

Names are explained, and citations to appearances in Chaucer's works are given. References to special studies relating to the names are frequently provided. Bibliography, p.246–66. PR1903.D5

French, Robert Dudley. A Chaucer handbook. 2d ed. N.Y., Crofts, 1947. 402p. **BD675**

1st ed. 1929. The revision is mainly in the bibliography and in the footnotes, with occasional changes in the text. The bibliography has been increased from about 12 to 29 pages. PR1905.F7

Hammond, Eleanor Prescott. Chaucer: a bibliographical manual. N.Y., Macmillan, 1908. 579p. **BD676**

Describes sources, manuscripts, editions, modernizations, translations, etc. Z8164.H29

Griffith, Dudley David. Bibliography of Chaucer, 1908–1953. Seattle, Univ. of Washington Pr., 1955. 398p. **BD677**

Planned as a supplement to Hammond (above). The section on "Influence and allusions" supplements C. F. E. Spurgeon's work (BD681).
Supersedes the author's earlier bibliography, which covered 1908–24.
Continued by: Z8164.G85

Crawford, William R. Bibliography of Chaucer, 1954–63. Seattle, Univ. of Washington Pr., [1967]. 144p. (Univ. of Washington pubn. in language and literature, v.17) **BD678**

Provides a supplement to D. D. Griffith's *Bibliography of Chaucer* (above). Z8164.C79

Baird, Lorrayne Y. A bibliography of Chaucer, 1964–1973. Boston, G. K. Hall, [1977]. 287p. **BD679**

Intended as a continuation of W. R. Crawford's Chaucer bibliography covering 1954–63 (above). Z8164.B27

Magoun, Francis Peabody. A Chaucer gazetteer. Chicago, Univ. of Chicago Pr., [1961]. 173p. **BD680**

"A listing and discussion of all geographical names and names

(uncapitalized) of geographical origin or with geographical connections . . . used by Chaucer."—*Pref.* PR1941.M3

Spurgeon, Caroline Frances Eleanor. Five hundred years of Chaucer criticism and allusion (1357–1900). London, pubn. for the Chaucer Society by K. Paul, 1914–[25]. 7v. (Chaucer Soc. [Pubn.], 2d ser., 48–50, 52–56) **BD681**

Issued also in 3v. by the Cambridge University Press, 1925. (Repr.: N.Y., Russell & Russell, 1960)
Contents: pt.1, Foreword to pt.1. Text of allusions (1357–1800); pt.2, Text of allusions (1801–1850); pt.3, Text of allusions (1851–1900); pt.4, Appendix A: Additional English and Latin references, with notes on the debt of some writers to Chaucer; pt.5, Appendixes B and C: French and German allusions; [pt.6], Introductions; [pt.7], Index.

——— ——— Supplement containing additional entries 1868–1900. London, priv. pr., 1920. 171p.

PR1924.A2

Tatlock, John Strong Perry and **Kennedy, Arthur G.** Concordance to the complete works of Geoffrey Chaucer and to the Romaunt of the Rose. Wash., Carnegie Inst., 1927. 1110p. (Carnegie Inst. pubn. 353) (Repr.: Gloucester, Mass., P. Smith, 1963) **BD682**

Complete, except in the case of about 150 very common words, for which only selected references are given. Based upon the text of the Globe edition. PR1941.T3

Milton

Bibliography

Hanford, James Holly and **McQueen, William A.** Milton. 2d ed. Arlington Heights, Ill., AHM Publ. Corp., [1979]. 111p. (Goldentree bibliographies) **BD683**

1st ed. 1966.
A selective bibliography and guide to Milton scholarship. Intended for the graduate student and advanced undergraduate.

Z8578.H35

Stevens, David Harrison. Reference guide to Milton; from 1800 to the present day. Chicago, Univ. of Chicago Pr., [1930]. 302p. **BD684**

Lists editions, translations, biography, criticism, etc., from 1800 to about 1928.
Supplemented by: Z8578.S84

Fletcher, Harris Francis. Contributions to a Milton bibliography, 1800–1930, being a list of addenda to Stevens' Reference guide to Milton. [Urbana], Univ. of Illinois Pr., 1931. 166p. (Univ. of Illinois studies in language and literature, v.16, no.1) **BD685**

Z8578.S84F

Huckabay, Calvin. John Milton: an annotated bibliography, 1929–1968. Rev. ed. Pittsburgh, Duquesne Univ. Pr., [1969]. 392p. (Duquesne studies. Philological ser., 1) **BD686**

An updating and revision of the author's earlier bibliography covering 1929–57 (publ. 1960).
Designed to supplement the bibliographies by David H. Stevens, *Reference guide to Milton* (BD684) and Harris F. Fletcher, *Contributions to a Milton bibliography* (BD685). Lists significant books and articles of the period covered, editions of Milton's works, and Milton studies. Includes doctoral dissertations, but omits many of the master's essays listed in the earlier edition. Z8578.H82

Shawcross, John T. Milton: a bibliography for the years 1624–1700. Binghamton, N.Y., Medieval & Renaissance Texts & Studies, 1984. 452p. (Medieval & Renaissance texts & studies, v.30) **BD687**

Attempts to list "all manuscripts and editions of the works and all studies and critical statements concerning Milton's life and works, all allusions and quotations, and all significant imitations during the years 1624–1700."—*Pref.* Indexed.   Z8578.S52

Variorum editions

A variorum commentary on the poems of John Milton. [Merritt Y. Hughes, gen. ed.] N.Y., Columbia Univ. Pr., 1970–75. v.1–2[1–3], 4. (In progress)   **BD688**

Contents: v.1, The Latin and Greek poems, by Douglas Bush; The Italian poems, by J. E. Shaw and A. Bartlett Giamatti; v.2[1–3], The minor English poems, by A. S. P. Woodhouse and Douglas Bush (3v.); v.4, Paradise regained, by W. MacKellar.

An attempt to provide a variorum edition of critical commentary on Milton's complete poems. The text used is that of the *Works of John Milton* in the Columbia edition and is not reprinted in the variorum volumes.   PR3593.V3

Concordances and indexes

Bradshaw, John. Concordance to the poetical works of John Milton. London, Sonnenschein, 1894. 412p. (Repr.: Hamden, Conn., Archon Books, 1965)   **BD689**

Based upon the Aldine edition (Bell, 1894); includes all the poems except the Psalms and the translations in the prose works; omits the commoner pronouns, conjunctions, adverbs, and prepositions.   PR3580.B8

Hudson, Gladys W., comp. Paradise lost; a concordance. Detroit, Gale, [1970]. 361p.   **BD690**

A computer-produced work. Employs the text of the second edition, 1674, as reproduced in v.3 of Milton's *Complete poetical works* (facsimile ed., Urbana, Univ. of Illinois Pr., 1948).   PR3562.H8

Ingram, William and **Swaim, Kathleen,** eds. A concordance to Milton's English poetry. Oxford, Clarendon Pr., 1972. 683p.   **BD691**

A computer-generated concordance "based on texts of Milton's poems that were published in his lifetime, on certain authoritative manuscripts of the same period, and in a few instances on later-seventeenth-century texts as well."—*Introd.*   PR3595.I55

Dictionaries and handbooks

Johnson, William C. Milton criticism: a subject index. [Folkestone, Kent, Eng.], Dawson, [1978]. 450p.   **BD692**

Not a bibliography as such, but rather "a detailed and relatively complete index to subjects referred to, or covered in, a carefully selected group of 150 books of criticism pertaining to the life and writings of John Milton."—*Introd.* A computer-produced compilation based on the indexes of the selected volumes, augmented by additional entries, it enables the user to determine whether a given topic is treated in any of the critical studies without consulting the volume itself.   PR3587.3.J6

Patterson, Frank Allen. An index to the Columbia edition of the Works of John Milton, by Frank Allen Patterson assisted by French Rowe Fogle. N.Y., Columbia Univ. Pr., 1940. 2v. (2141p.)   **BD693**

Uniform with the Columbia *Works of John Milton* but sold separately. A detailed, analytical index to the works of Milton, including references to names, ideas, and subjects. Serves also as a word index. May be used with other editions of Milton, although the page references are to the Columbia edition.   PR3550.F31

Gilbert, Allan H. Geographical dictionary of Milton. New Haven, Yale Univ. Pr., 1919. 322p. (Repr.: N.Y., Russell & Russell, 1968)   **BD694**

Gives all place-names mentioned in all of Milton's prose and poetry (except the addresses of the *Letters of state* and the biblical quotations in *De doctrina christiana*), with exact references to all passages where they occur and explanation of what they meant to

Milton. References are to the Oxford edition of the *Poems,* edited by Beeching, and to the edition of the *Prose works* published by Pickering, 1851.   PR3580.G5

Hanford, James Holly and **Taaffe, James G.** A Milton handbook. 5th ed. N.Y., Appleton, [1970]. 374p.   **BD695**

1st ed. 1926; 4th ed. 1946.

A survey companion to Milton studies for the advanced student. Discusses Milton's life and works with references to source materials. Bibliography, p.343–64.

"In the present edition . . . a necessary compromise has been made between the old and new in Milton scholarship. Many articles which elaborate or clarify accepted conclusions or which deal with minor points have been included without comment in the bibliography. Some material deserving of full discussion but not easily incorporated into the present format has been alluded to in the text and notes. Essential corrections have been made, however, and the present trends in research and interpretation have been in one way or another indicated."—*Pref.*   PR3588.H2

A Milton encyclopedia. William B. Hunter, Jr., gen. ed. Lewisburg, Pa., Bucknell Univ. Pr., [1978–83]. 9v.   **BD696**

Attempts "to bring together all of the important information and opinion concerning the life and works of John Milton."—*Pref.* Signed articles by specialists were written with the general reader in mind and represent the point of view of the contributor. There are occasional bibliographic references provided within the articles, but these are limited to book citations, and there are no bibliographies at the end of the articles. *See* references are provided from alternate forms of entry, and references to related terms are signaled by use of an asterisk in the text. v.9 is devoted mainly to bibliographies and indexes (of names, citations from the Bible, subjects), but includes some additional articles.   PR3580.M5

Shakespeare

See also BG76, BG83.

Bibliography

Bartlett, Henrietta C. Mr. William Shakespeare; original and early editions of his quartos and folios, his source books and those containing contemporary notices. New Haven, Yale Univ. Pr., 1922. 217p.   **BD697**

Z8811.B29

—— and **Pollard, Alfred W.** A census of Shakespeare's plays in quarto, 1594–1709, rev. and extended. New Haven, Yale Univ. Pr.; London, Milford, 1939. 165p.   **BD698**

Records and describes all separate editions and issues before 1709. Every known copy of each edition and issue is described, and its history from publication to Jan. 1939 given as fully as possible. The index includes all names of owners, booksellers, auctioneers, and binders found in the census.   Z8811.B28

Bevington, David. Shakespeare, Arlington Heights, Ill., AHM Publ. Corp., [1978]. 259p.   **BD699**

A selective bibliography which aims "to provide the names of various books and articles that cannot safely be ignored by anyone intending to survey the state of Shakespearean criticism and contribute something further to our understanding of Shakespeare."—*Pref.* Emphasis is on materials from 1930 through Feb. 1977. Items considered "most nearly indispensable" are marked with an asterisk. Topical arrangement, with sections on the individual plays. Indexed.   Z8811.B47

Birmingham [Eng.] Shakespeare Library. A Shakespeare bibliography; the catalogue of the Birmingham Shakespeare Library. [London], Mansell, 1971. 7v.   **BD700**

Contents: pt.1, Accessions pre-1932: v.1–2, English editions, English Shakespeariana; v.3, Foreign editions and Shakespeariana, Index of editors, translators, illustrators and series; pt.2, Accessions post 1931: v.4–6, English editions, English Shakespeariana; v.7,

Foreign editions and Shakespeariana, Index of editors, translators, illustrators and series.

Reproduces the catalogs of one of the world's major Shakespeare collections. The Shakespeariana sections include vast numbers of analytics for items in periodicals, collections of essays, anthologies, etc. Division of the bibliography into two parts, while unfortunate, results from the decision to avoid the massive expense and the long delay in publication foreseen if the two types of records—the original guard book catalog complete to 1932, and the card catalog which has served to record the Library's accessions since 1932—were to have been combined. Z8813.B5

Ebisch, Walther and **Schücking, Levin L.** Shakespeare bibliography. . . . Oxford, Clarendon Pr., 1931. 294p. [Sächsische Forschungsinstitut in Leipzig. Forschungsinstitut für Neuere Philologie. III. Anglistische Abt. Extra volume] **BD701**

A selective bibliography of material about Shakespeare, his times, life, personality, texts, sources, literary influences, language, art, production, influence, individual plays, etc.

———— ———— Supplement for the years 1930–35. Oxford, Clarendon Pr., 1937. 104p.

Z8811.E18

Folger Shakespeare Library, Wash., D.C. Catalog of the Shakespeare collection. Boston, G. K. Hall, 1972. 2v. **BD702**

Contents: v.1, Works; works in translation; selections; separate plays; v.2, Shakespeare as subject; titles.
For a note on the complete catalog of the library *see* BD499.

Z8811.F65

Howard-Hill, Trevor Howard. Shakespearian bibliography and textual criticism; a bibliography. Oxford, Clarendon Pr., 1971. 322p. (Index to British literary bibliography, v.2) **BD703**

Nearly 2,000 entries for bibliographies and checklists of Shakespeare's works, Shakespeare studies, and books and articles on bibliographical and textual investigation of Shakespeare's works. Regarding the latter, "only studies which relate to the physical features of the manuscript and printed sources of the text and its transmission from the author to the reader have been listed here."—*Introd.*
This volume also includes a supplement to v.1 of the series (BD494), bringing the record down to the end of 1969.

Z8811.H67

Jaggard, William. Shakespeare bibliography; a dictionary of every known issue of the writings of our national poet and of recorded opinion thereon in the English language, with historical introduction. Stratford-on-Avon, Shakespeare Pr., 1911. 729p. il. **BD704**

Z8811.J21

McManaway, James Gilmer and **Roberts, Jeanne Addison.** A selective bibliography of Shakespeare: editions, textual studies, commentary. Charlottesville, publ. for the Folger Shakespeare Lib. by Univ. Pr. of Virginia, [1975]. 309p.

BD705

A selective bibliography of about 4,500 items which "attempts to draw attention to the best and most important publications since 1930. A scattering of representative works of earlier date is given to serve as background."—*Pref.* Almost exclusively English-language materials; cutoff date is 1970, with a few important items of later date. Topical arrangement; sections on the individual plays usually include sub-sections for editions, textual commentary, and commentary on the plays. Author index. Particularly useful for work with undergraduates. Z8811.M23

A new variorum edition of Shakespeare. Supplementary bibliographies for Henry the Fourth, part one; Henry the Fourth, part two; The tragedy of Julius Caesar; The life and death of King Richard II. [N.Y., Modern Language Assoc. of America, 1977] 15p., 18p., 58p., 31p. **BD706**

For the *New variorum edition* see BD713.
Each bibliography is separately paged and has its own title page and index. (Each is also available in a separate, paperbound edition.) Compiled by divers hands. Period of coverage varies, the cutoff date being mainly 1972 or 1973.
A bibliographical supplement to "Twelfth night," comp. by W. C. McAvoy, was published 1984 (80p.).

Shattuck, Charles Harlen. The Shakespeare promptbooks; a descriptive catalogue. Urbana, Univ. of Illinois Pr., 1965. 553p. **BD707**

Intended "to promote new studies in the history of staged Shakespeare."—*Introd.* Lists, locates, and briefly describes promptbooks marked for stage use by actors, directors, etc. from Shakespearean times through 1961. Arrangement is by play, then chronological. Name index. A useful section explaining the symbols and abbreviations used in older promptbooks, and a register of libraries with promptbook holdings are included. PR3091.S4

Smith, Gordon Ross. A classified Shakespeare bibliography, 1936–1958. University Park, Pa., State Univ. Pr., 1963. 784p. **BD708**

In effect, a continuation of Ebisch and Schücking (BD701).

Z8811.S64

Velz, John W. Shakespeare and the classical tradition; a critical guide to commentary: 1660–1960. Minneapolis, Univ. of Minnesota Pr., [1968]. 459p. **BD709**

An annotated bibliography of writings on Shakespeare's classicism. Z8811.V4

Wells, Stanley, ed. Shakespeare; select bibliographical guides. [London], Oxford Univ. Pr., 1973. 300p. **BD710**

Intended as a "selective guide to the best in Shakespeare scholarship and criticism."—*Introd.* Bibliographic essays by various scholars on the background, problems, groups of plays, and some of the individual plays of Shakespeare. Z8811.W44

Shakespeare Association of America. [Annual bibliography of Shakespeariana] 1925– . **BD711**

Bibliographies for 1925–48 appeared under varying titles in the *Shakespeare Association bulletin,* v.1–24, 1926–49. Bibliographies for 1949– have title *Shakespeare: an annotated bibliography* (varies slightly), and are continued in the *Shakespeare quarterly,* v.1– , 1950– .
A bibliography of books, dissertations, pamphlets, and periodical material, including much analysis of periodicals. Before 1949, the bibliography was not annotated.

Shakespeare survey; an annual survey of Shakespearian study and production. v.1– , 1948– . Cambridge, Univ. Pr., 1948– . il. **BD712**

"Issued under the sponsorship of the University of Birmingham, the University of Manchester, the Royal Shakespeare Theatre, [and] the Shakespeare Birthplace Trust" (varies).
Each volume has a specific theme and includes articles related to some particular aspect of Shakespeare study. International in scope, with information on productions, etc., and an annual critical survey of "The year's contributions to Shakespearian study."
v.17, published in honor of the quartercentenary year, has special title *Shakespeare in his own age.* Intended to stand as an independent study of the Elizabethan period, it dispenses with such usual features as "International notes" and the reviews. PR2888.C3

Variorum editions

Shakespeare, William. A new variorum edition of Shakespeare, ed. by Horace Howard Furness . . . Philadelphia, Lippincott, 1871–1980. v.1–29. (In progress) il. **BD713**

Editors vary. Now publ. N.Y., Modern Language Assoc. of America.
Earlier variorum editions appeared in 1803, 1813, and 1821.

A monumental work of scholarship including, in addition to text with variant readings, much annotation and critical commentary.

PR2753.F5

Concordances

Bartlett, John. New and complete concordance or verbal index to words, phrases, and passages in the dramatic works of Shakespeare with a supplementary concordance to the poems. London, Macmillan, 1894. 1910p. (Repr.: N.Y., St. Martin's Pr., 1953, with title *A complete concordance . . .*)

BD714

Based upon the text of the Globe edition; gives full context for each word listed, with exact reference to act, scene, and line as numbered in the Globe edition, 1891. PR2892.B34

Oxford Shakespeare concordances; a concordance to the text . . . Oxford, Clarendon Pr., 1969–72. 37v. **BD715**

"In this series . . . a separate volume is devoted to each of the plays. The text for each concordance is the one chosen as copy-text by Dr. Alice Walker for the Oxford Old Spelling Shakespeare now in preparation."—*Gen. Introd.*

Some problems relating to the choice of text, together with brief comparison to the Spevack concordances (below), are noted in a review in *TLS* Aug. 14, 1969, p.903; a further review appears in *TLS* April 23, 1970, p.450.

Spevack, Marvin. A complete and systematic concordance to the works of Shakespeare. Hildesheim, Ger., G. Olms, 1968–80. 9v. **BD716**

Contents: v.1, Drama and character concordances to the folio comedies; v.2, Drama and character concordances to the folio histories; Concordances to the non-dramatic works; v.3, Drama and character concordances to the folio tragedies and Pericles, The two noble kinsmen, Sir Thomas More; v.4–6, "A"–Zwagger'd; Appendices; v.7, Concordances to stage directions and speech-prefixes; v.8, Concordances to the "bad" quartos and The taming of a shrew and The troublesome reign of King John; v.9, Substantive variants.

Aims to present "a complete and accurate computer-generated concordance to all of Shakespeare."—*Pref.* Text used is that of *The Riverside Shakespeare* (Boston, Houghton Mifflin, 1974), edited by G. Blakemore Evans. Appendixes include a word-frequency index, reverse-word index, hyphenated words, homographs, etc.

PR2892.S6

——— The Harvard concordance to Shakespeare. Cambridge, Belknap Pr., 1973. 1600p. **BD717**

A computer-generated concordance covering all the plays and poems. This is a slightly abbreviated version of v.4–6 of the compiler's *Complete and systematic concordance* (above). Uses the modern-spelling text of *The Riverside Shakespeare* (Boston, Houghton Mifflin, 1974) edited by G. Blakemore Evans. PR2892.S62

Stevenson, Burton Egbert. Home book of Shakespeare quotations, being also a concordance and a glossary of the unique words and phrases in the plays and poems. N.Y., London, Scribner, 1937. 2055p. **BD718**

PR2892.S63

Dictionaries and handbooks

Baker, Arthur Ernest. A Shakespeare commentary . . . v.1. Taunton, Eng., Author, 1938. 965p. tables. **BD719**

Subtitle: Dates of composition and first publication; sources of the plots and detailed outlines of the plays; together with the characters, place-names, classical, geographical, topographical and curious historical and folk allusions, with glosses; to which are added appendices, giving extracts from Holinshed, Plutarch, and the various romances, novels, poems and histories used by Shakespeare in the formation of the dramas.

Published in 15 pts., 1917–38. Pts. 1–13 had title *Shakespeare dictionary.*

A popular dictionary of characters, place-names, and allusions,

each part dealing with a different play and in a separate alphabet. Not completed. The plays dealt with are: Julius Caesar, As you like it, Macbeth, The tempest, Hamlet, King Lear, King John, Merchant of Venice, King Richard II, King Henry IV, King Henry V, King Henry VI, pts.1–3. PR2892.B2

Berman, Ronald. A reader's guide to Shakespeare's plays; a discursive bibliography. Chicago, Scott, Foresman, [1965]. 151p. **BD720**

Lists some 3,000 works about the plays, many with annotations or descriptive notes. There is a section for each play, with subsections for text, editions, sources, criticism, and staging. Z8811.B45

Campbell, Oscar James, ed. The reader's encyclopedia of Shakespeare. Assoc. ed., Edward G. Quinn. N.Y., Crowell, [1966]. 1014p. il. **BD721**

An impressive compilation of information on all aspects of Shakespeare's life and works. The articles, intended for the general reader as well as the specialist, are generally based on scholarly studies. Many of the longer articles are signed with the initials of contributing scholars; some include selected bibliographies. Entries for the individual plays include notes on the text, dating, and sources of the play; a plot summary; stage history; and excerpts from critical studies of the work. PR2892.C3

Halliday, Frank Ernest. A Shakespeare companion. 1564–1964. N.Y. Schocken, [1964]. 569p. il. **BD722**

1st ed. 1952.

A thoroughly revised edition of this detailed dictionary to the plots and characters of Shakespeare's plays; the productions; sources, spelling, and pronunciation of Elizabethan English; Shakespeare's life, etc. PR2892.H3

Muir, Kenneth and **Schoenbaum, Samuel,** eds. A new companion to Shakespeare studies. Cambridge, Univ. Pr., 1971. 297p. **BD723**

An earlier edition by Harley Granville-Barker and G. B. Harrison was entitled *A companion to Shakespeare studies* (Cambridge, 1934). Chapters on various aspects of Shakespeare's life and work, and surveys of Shakespeare criticism and scholarship have been contributed by British and American scholars. Chapters consider Shakespeare's life, reading, use of rhetoric and the English language; the social, historical, and philosophical background; playhouses, actors, and staging of Shakespeare's time; textual problems; and Shakespeare criticism through the ages. Reading lists, a chronological table, and an index complete the volume. PR2890.M8

Onions, Charles Talbut. Shakespeare glossary. 2d ed. rev. Oxford, Clarendon Pr., 1919. 259p. (Repr., with enl. addenda, 1963. 264p.) **BD724**

An excellent small dictionary, by a man who was for many years on the staff of the *New English dictionary.* The aim of the glossary is to supply: (1) definitions or illustrations of words or senses now obsolete or surviving only in archaic or provincial use; (2) explanations of other words involving allusions not generally familiar; and (3) explanations of proper names carrying with them some connotative significance, etc. Includes also obsolete and technical terms which occur only in the stage directions. PR2892.O6

Shakespearean criticism: excerpts from the criticism of William Shakespeare's plays and poetry, from the first published appraisals to current evaluations. Laurie Lanzen Harris, ed. Detroit, Gale, [1984]– . v.1– . (In progress) **BD725**

Similar to the publisher's collections of excerpts from criticism of 19th and 20th century literature (BD46, BD47). v.1 deals with "Hamlet," "Timon of Athens," "Twelfth Night," "The Comedy of Errors," and "Henry IV, Parts I and II"; four more volumes (each of which will, presumably, offer a similar mix of major and minor tragedies and comedies, and the histories) are to be devoted to the individual plays; further volumes are planned for performance criticism and other special topics. PR2965.S43

Stokes, Francis Griffin. Dictionary of the characters and proper names in the works of Shakespeare, with notes on the sources and dates of the plays and poems. London, Harrap;

Boston, Houghton, 1924. 359p. (Repr.: N.Y., Peter Smith, 1949) **BD726**

Includes, in one alphabet, titles of Shakespeare's works, with brief account of first editions, sources, etc.; names of all characters—historical, legendary, and fictitious—with brief analysis of the dramatic action of each; names used as allusions; place-names; and miscellaneous names, such as seasons, planets, etc. Gives exact reference to play, act, and line, and some bibliographical references to sources of further information. PR2892.S67

Sugden, Edward Holdsworth. Topographical dictionary to the works of Shakespeare and his fellow dramatists. Manchester, Univ. Pr.; London, N.Y., Longmans, 1925. 580p. il. maps. (Publ. of the University of Manchester, 168) **BD727**

Offers lists of place-names, i.e., countries, towns, rivers, and streets, with brief article about each and exact reference to the play in which it occurs, and references to sources of further information. Includes also the place-names of Milton and some references to Spenser. PR2892.S8

Irish

Anglo-Irish literature; a review of research. Ed. by Richard J. Finneran. N.Y., Modern Language Assoc. of America, 1976. 596p. **BD728**

A bibliographic survey similar to the MLA-sponsored publications by Faverty, Jordan, De Laura, etc. (BD648, BD650, BD538).

"The primary purpose of this volume is to provide essays on writers of Anglo-Irish background whose careers have been completed and who have been the subject of a substantial body of published research. A liberal definition of 'background' accounts for the inclusion of Wilde and Shaw, whose credentials are otherwise open to some debate. The other criteria explain the lack of any detailed discussion of writers such as Beckett, Clarke, Colum, O'Faolain, and many others."—*Pref.* Includes chapters (each by a specialist) on general works, 19th-century writers, Oscar Wilde, George Moore, Bernard Shaw, W. B. Yeats, J. M. Synge, James Joyce, "Four revival figures" (Lady Gregory, A.E., Gogarty, James Stephens), Sean O'Casey, and modern drama. Indexed. PR8712.A5

Recent research on Anglo-Irish writers. A supplement to Anglo-Irish literature: a review of research. Ed. by Richard J. Finneran. N.Y., Modern Language Assoc. of Amer., 1983. 361p. **BD729**

Updates the chapters of the 1976 publication through 1980 (with the exception of the George Moore section which ends with 1979) and adds new chapters on modern fiction and modern poetry. PR8712.R4

Brown, Stephen James. A guide to books on Ireland. Pt.1, Prose literature, poetry, music and plays. Dublin, Figgis; London, Longmans, 1912. 371p. (Repr.: N.Y., Lemma, 1970) **BD730**

No more published.
An annotated bibliography of Irish literature. Z2031.B86

———— Ireland in fiction; a guide to Irish novels, tales, romances, and folk-lore. New ed. ... Dublin, London, Maunsel, 1919. 362p. **BD731**

"Includes all works of fiction published in volume form, and dealing with Ireland or with the Irish abroad, and such works only."—*Pref.*
An author list of 1,713 novels in the English language, with descriptive annotations and brief biographical notes. Appendixes contain: some useful works of reference; publishers and series; classified lists of novels (e.g., historical fiction, legends, Catholic clerical life, etc.); Irish fiction in periodicals. Index of titles and subjects. Has more titles, and about 550 more notes, than the edition of 1916. Z2039.F4B8

Dictionary of Irish literature. Robert Hogan, ed. in chief. Westport, Conn., Greenwood Pr., [1979]. 815p. **BD732**

"The bulk of the dictionary is made up of biographical and critical essays on approximately five hundred Irish authors who wrote mainly in the English language."—*Pref.* A few foreign authors who "have made a rich and lasting contribution to Irish literature" are included; there are "a handful of general articles on topics such as folklore, which have been of major importance to literature"; and a number of entries for literary organizations or publications. Bibliographies of works by and about the authors are included; many of the articles are signed by contributors. A special section on "Gaelic literature" by Seamus O'Neill, and "A note on the history of Irish writing in English" precede the dictionary proper. There is a chronology, a general bibliography, and an index. PR8706.D5

Harmon, Maurice. Select bibliography for the study of Anglo-Irish literature and its backgrounds. An Irish studies handbook. [Portmarnock], Wolfhound Pr., [1977]. 187p. maps. **BD733**

In three main sections, each subdivided by form or genre: (1) Background: general reference; (2) Background: Ireland; (3) Anglo-Irish literature. Items are briefly annotated. Chronology, p.148–87. Table of contents, but no index. Z2037.H32

Hyde, Douglas. A literary history of Ireland from earliest times to the present day. New ed. with introd. by Brian Ó Cuív. London, Benn; N.Y., Barnes & Noble, [1967]. 654p. **BD734**

1st ed. 1899. This is not a new edition, but a reprinting with a new introduction.
A standard history. Bibliographical footnotes. PB1306.H8

Mikhail, E. H. An annotated bibliography of modern Anglo-Irish drama. Troy, N.Y., Whitston, 1981. 300p. **BD735**

A bibliography of general criticism on Anglo-Irish drama from 1899 through 1977, with a few items of later date. The 1,775 items are listed by type (bibliographies, reference works, books, periodical articles, dissertations, collections in libraries). Indexed. Z2039.D7M528

O'Donoghue, David James. The poets of Ireland; a biographical and bibliographical dictionary of Irish writers of English verse. Dublin, Figgis; London, Frowde, 1912. 504p. **BD736**

Biographical sketches with bibliographies. Restricted to Irish poets who wrote in the English language. Z2037.O26

Scottish

Aitken, William Russell. Scottish literature in English and Scots: a guide to information sources. Detroit, Gale, [1982]. 421p. (American literature, English literature, and world literatures in English, v.37) **BD737**

A bibliography supporting the study of an independent Scottish literary tradition. A section listing general works is followed by four chronological sections (medieval through 20th century, each subdivided for general works and individual authors), and a final section for popular and folk literature.

Beginning 1969, the *Annual bibliography of Scottish literature* issued as a supplement to the periodical *The bibliotheck* and *The year's work in Scottish literary and linguistic studies* published in *Scottish literary journal* (previously *Scottish literary news*) have provided ongoing bibliographic coverage of Scottish literature. Z2057.A35

Geddie, William. A bibliography of middle Scots poets; with an introduction on the history of their reputations. Edinburgh, pr. for the Scottish Text Society by Blackwood, 1912. 364p. (Scottish Text Soc. [Pubn. 61]) **BD738**

Lists editions, citations to biography and criticism, etc. PR8633.S4

Royle, Trevor. The Macmillan companion to Scottish literature. [London], Macmillan (distr. in U.S. by Gale, Detroit), [1983]. 322p. **BD739**

Aims "to provide an alphabetical list of references to Scotland's literature from earliest times to the present day. Its backbone is supplied by the biographical essays devoted to the principal poets, novelists, dramatists, critics and men of letters who have written in English, Scots or Gaelic and whose work constitutes the main corpus of Scottish literature."—*Introd.* Also includes entries for individual literary works, periodicals, terms, etc. Bibliographies of authors' works; some references to biographical and critical studies.

PR8511.R67

Welsh

Jones, Brynmor. A bibliography of Anglo-Welsh literature, 1900–1965. [Swansea], Wales and Monmouthshire Branch of the Lib. Assoc., 1970. 139p.   **BD740**

Includes "writers of Welsh birth or extraction who write imaginative literature in English, locating their narratives against a Welsh background and portraying Welsh characters and idiom" and works "set in a Welsh locale, though their authors are not necessarily of Welsh birth."—*Introd.* Separate sections for the literature and for bibliographical and critical materials.   Z2013.3.J64

Commonwealth

❖The term "Commonwealth" is here loosely applied: this section includes a few works concerning authors writing in English from areas outside what was, strictly speaking, the British Commonwealth.

General

Annual bibliography of Commonwealth literature. (*In* Journal of Commonwealth literature, 1965– ; Dec. issue) Annual.   **BD741**

Each issue usually includes sections for the Commonwealth in general, East and Central Africa, Western Africa, Australia, Canada, India, Malaysia and Singapore, New Zealand, Sri Lanka, the West Indies, Pakistan, and South Africa. A brief essay on significant publications and developments introduces each section.

Modern Commonwealth literature. Comp. and ed. by John H. Ferres and Martin Tucker. [N.Y., Ungar, 1977] 561p. (A library of literary criticism)   **BD742**

Offers excerpts from critical writings on authors from Commonwealth countries (including some former Commonwealth nations) throughout the world. Authors are grouped by region: Africa, Australia, Canada, the Caribbean, the Indian subcontinent, New Zealand. Selection was "based on four principal considerations: modernity (writers whose works and influence belong wholly or predominantly to the twentieth century), the author's general reputation at home as well as in Britain and the United States; the existence of worthwhile criticism, particularly in English; and availability of the author's work in the original or in English translation."—*Introd.* Similar to other volumes in the series (e.g., BD553). Index of critics.   PR9080.M6

New, William H., comp. Critical writings on Commonwealth literatures: a selective bibliography to 1970, with a list of theses and dissertations. University Park, Pennsylvania State Univ. Pr., [1975]. 333p.   **BD743**

A general section is followed by sections for Africa (East and West), Australia, Canada, New Zealand, South Africa and Rhodesia, South Asia, Southeast Asia, and West Indies. A separate "Theses and dissertations" section is also subdivided by geographic area. Includes research aids, general studies, and studies of individual major authors. United Kingdom is omitted. Index of critics, editors, translators.   Z2000.9.N48

African

Abrash, Barbara. Black African literature in English since 1952; works and criticism. N.Y., Johnson Reprint, 1967. 92p.   **BD744**

A bibliography of writings by and about black Africans writing in English.   Z3508.L5A25

Gorman, G. E. The South African novel in English since 1950; an information and resource guide. Boston, G. K. Hall, [1978]. 238p.   **BD745**

The work's approach is "functional" and aims "to assist in the development of that bibliographical expertise which will allow one to answer the basic 'who, what, where' questions arising in the study and provision of South African literary materials."—*Introd.* Pt.I covers "the literature itself and problems of definition, content and control; the second part, which arises out of this background discussion, presents a critical bibliographical survey of the various types of resource materials available to the investigator or collector of South African fiction."   PR9362.5.G6

Lindfors, Bernth. Black African literature in English: a guide to information sources. Detroit, Gale, [1979]. 482p. (American literature, English literature, and world literatures in English, 23)   **BD746**

". . . attempts to list all the important works produced on black African literature in English up to the end of 1976."—*Introd.* Pt.1, "Genre and topical studies and reference sources," is subdivided by genre and special topic (e.g., language and style, audience, publishing, censorship); pt.2 is concerned with individual authors. Brief annotations. Author, title, subject, and geographical indexes.   Z3508.L5L56

Saint-Andre-Utudjian, Eliane. A bibliography of West African life and literature. Waltham, Mass., African Studies Assoc., Brandeis Univ., [1977]. 146p.   **BD747**

Classed arrangement with author index. Concerned with the literary output of English-speaking West Africa, covering "background studies, bibliographies of creative works in English by West Africans, and a wide range of critical writing by either the African writers themselves or by African as well as non-African critics."—*Foreword.*

Australian

Andrews, Barry G. and **Wilde, William H.** Australian literature to 1900: a guide to information sources. Detroit, Gale, [1980]. 472p. (American literature, English literature, and world literatures in English, 22)   **BD748**

A general section for bibliographies, reference works, literary histories, periodicals, etc., is followed by sections on individual authors. Includes a section on non-fiction prose and a brief section on Australian English.   Z4021.A54

Annual bibliography of studies in Australian literature. (*In* Australian literary studies, 1964– .) Annual.   **BD749**

A general section is followed by a section on individual authors.

Blake, Leslie James. Australian writers. [Adelaide], Rigby, [1968]. 268p.   **BD750**

A survey of Australian writing from 1788 to 1966. Offers very limited bibliographical detail, but the many biographical and critical notes and the commentary on Australian literary journals make it a useful reference aid.   Z4021.B55

Cuthbert, Eleanora Isabel. Index of Australian and New Zealand poetry. N.Y., Scarecrow Pr., 1963. 453p.   **BD751**

In three parts: (1) authors, (2) titles, and (3) first lines. Indexes 22 collections.   Z4024.P7C8

Day, Arthur Grove. Modern Australian prose, 1901–1975: a guide to information sources. Detroit, Gale, [1980]. 462p.

(American literature, English literature, and world literatures in English, 29) **BD752**

Includes fiction, selected non-fiction, and drama. Classed arrangement with author, title, and subject indexes. 2,463 items, many of them annotated. Z4011.D38

Johnston, Grahame. Annals of Australian literature. Melbourne, etc., Oxford Univ. Pr., 1970. 147p. **BD753**

Modeled after the *Annals of English literature* (BD561). The main section of the work consists of yearly lists of noteworthy Australian books, with a parallel column noting births and deaths of authors, plus miscellaneous notes such as the founding of newspapers and periodicals. Index references are provided to both columns. Covers 1789–1968. Z4021.J6

Lock, Fred and **Lawson, Alan.** Australian literature—a reference guide. 2d ed. Melbourne, Oxford Univ. Pr., [1980]. 120p. **BD754**

1st ed. 1977.
A guide to sources of information for the study of Australian literature. More than 400 annotated entries in seven main sections: (1) Bibliographical aids; (2) Other reference sources (e.g., encyclopedias, dictionaries, biographical dictionaries); (3) Authors (i.e., a listing of bibliographies of individual authors); (4) Periodicals; (5) Library resources; (6) Literary studies; (7) Organizations. Index of authors, and one of titles and subjects. Z4011.L6

Miller, Edmund Morris. Australian literature; a bibliography to 1938. Extended to 1950, ed. with a historical outline and descriptive commentaries by Frederick T. Macartney. Sydney, Angus and Robertson, [1956]. 503p. **BD755**

An extensive revision of the author's *Australian literature . . .* (1940). Historical treatment of the writers and literature of Australia with extensive bibliographies. Arranged alphabetically by author. Contains considerable biographical material. Indexes that were useful because of the chronological arrangement have been omitted from this edition.
Although the rearrangement of contents makes this edition easier to use, the earlier edition remains a standard source and has been reissued in a "facsimile edition with addendum of corrections and additions" (Sydney, Sydney Univ. Pr., 1975. 2v.). Z4021.M5

The Oxford history of Australian literature. Ed. by Leonie Kramer. Melbourne & N.Y., Oxford Univ. Pr., [1981]. 509p. **BD756**

Following an introductory essay by the general editor, there are contributed chapters on "Fiction" by Adrian Mitchell, "Drama" by Terry Sturm, "Poetry" by Vivian Smith, and a general bibliography in essay form (p.429–90) by Joy Hooton. Index to the text, but not to the bibliography.
An *Oxford companion to Australian literature,* ed. by William H. Wilde and others, was scheduled for 1985 publication. PR9604.3.O9

Stuart, Lurline. Nineteenth century Australian periodicals: an annotated bibliography. Sydney, Hale & Iremonger, 1979. 200p. il. **BD757**

An alphabetical listing of those periodicals which "contain literary features in the form of essays, articles, fiction, poetry and minor literary items."—*Introd.* Locations are given for most titles, but some titles have been entered and described on the basis of information found in published sources. Indexed. Z6962.A8S78

Canadian

For Canadian authors writing in French *see* BD946–BD951.

The annotated bibliography of Canada's major authors. Ed. by Robert Lecker and Jack David. Downsview, Ont., ECW Pr. (distr. in U.S. by G. K. Hall), 1979–84. v.1–5. (In progress) **BD758**

To be in 10v., five to be devoted to prose writers, five to poets. Each volume is to be a collection of "comprehensive, annotated bibliographies of works by and on Canada's major French and English authors from the nineteenth and twentieth centuries" (*Introd.*), and each is to deal with five specific writers. Arrangement of authors is alphabetical within volumes, but not alphabetical throughout the series. There is an index to critics at the end of each individual bibliography, but no general index to each volume. Z1375.A56

The Brock bibliography of published Canadian plays in English, 1766–1978. Ed. by Anton Wagner. [Toronto], Playwrights Pr., [1980]. 375p. **BD759**

Lists both Canadian plays in English and French-Canadian plays translated into English. Plays are grouped by century, then listed alphabetically by author. Gives publication data for each play, number of scenes, cast requirements, and a statement of the theme of the play. Short-title index. Z1377.D7B75

Canada's playwrights: a biographical guide. Ed. by Don Rubin and Alison Cranmer-Byng. Toronto, Canadian Theatre Review Pubns., [1980]. 191p. il. **BD760**

Offers biographical sketches of contemporary playwrights, with lists of stage works (including publication and production data as applicable), other writings, and secondary sources as available. PR9191.5.C3

Canadian essay and literature index. 1973–75. Toronto, Univ. of Toronto Pr., [1975–77]. Annual. **BD761**

An author-title-subject index to essays, book reviews, poems, plays and short stories appearing in anthologies, collections, and magazines published in Canada during the year of coverage. Separate sections for each genre; full lists of books and periodicals indexed at the end of the volume. The initial volume covers 91 anthologies and collections and 38 magazines.
Ceased publication. AI3.C238

Canadian essays and collections index, 1971–1972. Ottawa, Canadian Lib. Assoc., [1976]. 219p. **BD762**

Editors: Joyce Sowby [and others].
Provides indexing of some 70 Canadian collective publications. Serves as a predecessor to *Canadian essay and literature index* (above). Z1365.C224

Fee, Margery and **Cawker, Ruth.** Canadian fiction: an annotated bibliography. [Toronto], Peter Martin Associates, [1976]. 170p. **BD763**

A bibliography of "Canadian literary prose" for the teacher, student, librarian and general reader. A section on secondary sources is followed by separate sections for "Novel annotations" and "Short story annotations." There is a title index and a "subject guide" to the novels, and separate author and title indexes for the short stories. Z1377.F4F4

Gnarowski, Michael. A concise bibliography of English-Canadian literature. Rev. ed. [Toronto], McClelland & Stewart, [1978]. 145p. **BD764**

1st ed. 1973.
Aims "to provide a concise and ready reference work for the student and interested reader."—*Pref.* Arrangement is alphabetical by author, with works listed chronologically within subdivisions for literary genres. References to reviews and critical studies are included. Z1375.G53

Harvard University. Library. Canadian history and literature . . . Cambridge, Harvard Univ. Lib., 1968. 411p. **BD765**

For full information *see* DB184.

Klinck, Carl Frederick. Literary history of Canada: Canadian literature in English. 2d ed. Toronto, Univ. of Toronto Pr., [1976]. 3v. **BD766**

The 1st ed. (1965) was a single-volume work providing the first comprehensive history of Canadian literature in English from earliest times to 1960. In the new edition that work has been revised and republished in 2v., the first covering mainly to 1920, the second to 1960; new chapters concerned with the years 1960–73 make up v.3. More than forty scholars have contributed the signed chapters;

notes on the contributors appear in v.2 and v.3. Index in each volume.

Admirable as the work is, the bibliographic apparatus is not wholly satisfactory from the reference librarian's point of view; that is, the bibliographical notes which are provided at the end of each volume "are brief and highly selective; they were appended only if the author of a chapter felt that they were essential. The entire omission of notes for certain other chapters means only that these contributors rely on the reader to seek out the numerous sources recorded in bibliographies of Canadian literature. . . . "—*Introd.* Watters' *Checklist of Canadian literature* (BD773) is recommended as virtually a companion volume, and *On Canadian literature* (BD774) is also mentioned as a useful and complementary volume.
PR9184.3.K5

—— and **Watters, Reginald E.** Canadian anthology. 3d ed., rev. and enl. Toronto, Gage Educational Pub., [1974]. 724p. il. **BD767**

1st ed. 1956.
Includes notes on the authors; bibliography, p.645–721.
PR9194.4.K5

Moyles, R. G. English-Canadian literature to 1900; a guide to information sources. Detroit, Gale, [1976]. 346p. (American literature, English literature, and world literatures in English, v.6) **BD768**

Attempts "to provide a list of all the important primary and secondary sources necessary for a thorough study of this literature." —*Introd.* Includes general reference aids, literary histories and criticism, anthologies, plus sections for individual authors and for the literature of exploration and travel. Z1375.M68

Naaman, Antoine Youssef. Guide bibliographique des thèses littéraires canadiennes de 1921 à 1969. Montréal, Éditions Cosmos, [1970]. 338p. **BD769**

A bibliography of doctoral dissertations and master's theses on literary subjects (and including folklore, language and linguistics) completed at Canadian universities. An introductory section, "Étude documentaire," offers an extensive bibliography on research methods and tools of research. Z6511.N25

The Oxford companion to Canadian literature. Gen. ed., William Toye. Toronto [etc.], Oxford Univ. Pr., 1983. 843p. **BD770**

Based on the literary component of the *Oxford companion to Canadian history and literature* (1967), but greatly expanded both as to range and depth of coverage. Entries for writers and genres predominate, the former including novelists, poets, dramatists, biographers, philosophers, and some authors of children's books; the latter extending to criticism, essays, translations, humor and satire, mystery and crime fiction, science fiction, and travel literature as well as the many expected categories (and including extensive surveys of novels in English, novels in French, and regional literature). French-Canadian literature and writers are treated at length; there is emphasis on modern writing, particularly that of the last forty years. Articles are signed; bibliographies are provided.
PS8015.O93

Sedgwick, Dorothy. A bibliography of English-language theatre and drama in Canada 1800–1914. Edmonton, Alberta, 1976. 48p. (Nineteenth century theatre research. Occasional pubns., 1) **BD771**

A bibliography of Canadian dramatic writings and works on the theater and dramatists of Canada. Items are grouped under the following headings: Canadian drama, Canadian dramatists, Canadian dramatic criticism, Canadian theatres, Canadian theatre history, Canadian stage-tours and visits, Reference and bibliography. Locates copies. Indexed. Z1377.D7S43

Sylvestre, Guy, Conron, Brandon and **Klink, Carl F.** Canadian writers; Écrivains canadiens. New ed., rev. and enl. Montreal, Éditions HMH, [1966]. 186p. **BD772**

A biographical dictionary containing information on about 350 Canadian authors. Articles appear in English or French according to the language of the biographee's writings. Includes a literary chronology, a brief general bibliography, and a useful index of titles of literary works mentioned in the biographies. PR9127.S9

Watters, Reginald Eyre. A checklist of Canadian literature and background materials, 1628–1960. 2d ed., rev. and enl. [Toronto], Univ. of Toronto Pr., [1972]. 1085p. **BD773**

1st ed., 1959, covered through 1950.
"In two parts: first, a comprehensive list of books which constitute Canadian literature written in English; and second, a selective list of other books by Canadian authors which reveal the backgrounds of that literature."—*title page.*
Pt.1 "attempts to record all known titles in the recognized forms of poetry, fiction, and drama that were produced by English-speaking Canadians"—*Pref.*; pt.2 is a selective listing of books by Canadians on biography, literary criticism, local history, religion, bibliography, etc., which might serve as background material.
Z1375.W3

—— and **Bell, Inglis Freeman.** On Canadian literature, 1806–1960; a check list of articles, books, and theses on English-Canadian literature, its authors, and language. Toronto, Univ. of Toronto Pr., [1966]. 165p. **BD774**

A Canadian equivalent (but adding book and thesis materials) of Lewis Leary's *Articles on American literature* (BD371), listing biographical, critical, and scholarly writings on English-Canadian belles-lettres and closely related categories. The first part groups works by literary form, history, background, etc.; the second lists works on individual authors in alphabetical sequence. Annual bibliographies in the spring issue of *Canadian literature* and the fall issue of *Canadian journal of linguistics* are suggested as means of keeping up-to-date on post-1960 publications. Z1375.W33

Indian

Central Institute of English and Foreign Languages, Hyderabad. A bibliography of Indian English. Hyderabad, 1972. 219p., 23p. **BD775**

Contents: pt.1, Indian English literature; pt.2, Indian English.
Lists publications from 1827 to date and includes literary works as well as critical writings and works on Indian English as a language. Z3208.L5C36

Singh, Amritjit, Verma, Rajiva and **Joshi, Irene M.** Indian literature in English, 1827–1979: a guide to information sources. Detroit, Gale, [1981]. 631p. (American literature, English literature, and world literatures in English information guide ser., v.36) **BD776**

A bibliography of creative writing in English by Indian authors, including works originally written in Indian languages and translated into English by their authors (i.e., "Indo-Anglian" or "Indo-English" literature as opposed to "Anglo-Indian literature"—works with an Indian setting written by Englishmen who lived in India). General sections are followed by sections for individual authors grouped by literary form. Indexed. Z3208.L5S56

Singh, Bhupal. Survey of Anglo-Indian fiction. Oxford, Univ. Pr., 1934. 344p. **BD777**

A survey and criticism of the Anglo-Indian novel is followed by a bibliography in three parts: (1) Anglo-Indian novels; (2) criticism and biography; and (3) articles and reviews. PR830.A5S5

Spencer, Dorothy Mary. Indian fiction in English: an annotated bibliography. Philadelphia, Univ. of Pennsylvania Pr., [1960]. 98p. **BD778**

Contents: Introductory essay on Indian society, culture and fiction; Annotated list of fiction and autobiography written by Indians in English or translated into English.
Lists some 200 works of fiction and about 45 autobiographies, about three quarters of which are written in English. Z3208.L5S6

New Zealand

Burns, James. New Zealand novels and novelists, 1861–1979; an annotated bibliography. [Auckland], Heinemann, [1981]. 71p. **BD779**

A chronological listing with author and title indexes. Annotations give a brief indication of contents, not critical evaluations.
Z4114.F4B83

McNaughton, Howard Douglas. New Zealand drama; a bibliographical guide. Interim ed. [Christchurch], Univ. of Canterbury Lib., 1974. 112p. (Reference and bibliographical ser., Univ. of Canterbury Lib., 5) **BD780**

Attempts to list every New Zealand play which has been published and/or produced, of which a copy can be traced. Includes radio and television as well as stage productions. Arranged by author, with title index. Z4114.D7M3

Thomson, John E. New Zealand literature to 1977: a guide to information sources. Detroit, Gale, [1980]. 272p. (American literature, English literature, and world literatures in English, 30) **BD781**

Chapters on bibliographies and reference works, literary history and criticism, and anthologies are followed by sections on individual authors. Indexed. Z4111.T45

West Indian

Allis, Jeannette B. West Indian literature: an index to criticism, 1930–1975. Boston, G. K. Hall, [1981]. 353p. **BD782**

Indexes relevant materials in selected American and British periodicals as well as in West Indian magazines and newspapers; five collections of literary essays are also indexed. In three sections: (1) Index of authors; (2) Index of general articles; (3) Index of critics and reviewers. Appendix of books on West Indian literature.
Z1502.B5A38

GERMANIC LANGUAGES

Dutch

Baur, Frank [and others]. Geschiedenis van de letterkunde der Nederlanden. 'sHertogenbosch, Teulings' Uitgevers-Maatschappij L. C. G. Malmberg, 1939–75. v.1–7, 9. il. (In progress) **BD783**

To be in 9v.
Each volume by a specialist. An illustrated history with bibliographies throughout. PT5060.B3

Brussels. Bibliothèque Royale de Belgique. De Nederlandsche letterkunde in België, 1830–1930. [Ronse], Leherte-Courtin, [1932]. 172p. il. **BD784**

Includes brief biographical sketches with bibliographies, and a list of 189 periodicals. Z2424.F5B9

Buisman, M. Populaire prozaschrijvers van 1600 tot 1815: romans, novellen, verhalen, levensbeschrijvingen, Arcadia's, sprookjes. Alphabetische naamlijst. Amsterdam, B. M. Israël, [1960]. 508p. **BD785**

A comprehensive bibliography of novels, short stories, biographies, Utopias, and fairy tales, published from 1600 to 1815, in Dutch as well as translations into Dutch. Z2444.F4B8

Frederiks, Johannes Godefridus and **Branden, F. J. van den.** Biographisch woordenboek der Noord- en Zuidnederlandsche letterkunde. 2. omgew. druk. Amsterdam, Veen, [1888–92]. 918p. **BD786**

A biographical dictionary useful especially for the 18th and 19th centuries and including writers from both Holland and Belgium.
Z2440.F85

Jong, Dirk de. Het vrije boek in onvrije tijd; bibliografie van illegale en clandestiene bellettrie. Leiden, Sijthoff, 1958. 341p. **BD787**

An author listing of more than 1,000 items of belles-lettres published clandestinely in the Netherlands during the German occupation in World War II. Z6514.U5J63

Knuvelder, Gerard Petrus Maria. Handboek tot de geschiedenis der Nederlandse letterkunde. 6. druk. Den Bosch, Malmberg, [1973–77]. 4v. (v.1 publ. 1976) **BD788**

1st ed. 1948–53.
Covers Dutch literary history and criticism from the Middle Ages through 1916. Bibliographical footnotes; each volume has its own index. PT5060.K62

Kritisch lexicon van de Nederlandstalige literatuur na 1945. Brussel, Samsom; Groningen, Wolters-Noordhoff, 1980– . 1v., looseleaf. (In progress) **BD789**

Offers biographical/critical accounts, with bibliographies, of contemporary Dutch authors.

Lectuur-Repertorium . . . 2. en definitieve uitgave. Uitgave van het Algemeen Secretariaat voor Katholieke Boekerijen. Antwerpen, Vlaamsche Boekcentrale, 1952–54. 3v. **BD790**

Subtitle: Auteurslijst bevattende 23,000 bio-bibliografische nota's en 3000 portretten van auteurs behorende tot de nederlandse en de algemene literatuur, met waarde- en vakaanduiding van 90,000 literaire en vulgariserende werken, samengesteld door het A.S.K.B. onder redactie van Joris Baers.
Supersedes the earlier edition (1932–36) and its supplements (1939–46). A detailed bio-bibliography of major authors writing in or translated into Dutch. Individual titles are keyed to a classification scheme to indicate moral values and literary type.
Z1010.L43

—— Supplement, 1952–1966. Antwerpen, 1968–70. 3v.

Lexicon van de moderne Nederlandse literatuur. Samengesteld door J. van Geelen [and others]. [2. herziene en uitgebreide druk.] Amsterdam, Meulenhoff, [1981]. 219p. il. **BD791**

1st printing 1978.
A biographical dictionary of contemporary writers. Includes a list of literary prizes and their recipients. PT5180.L4

Meijer, Reinder P. Literature of the low countries; a short history of Dutch literature in the Netherlands and Belgium. Assen, Van Gorcum, 1971. 384p. **BD792**

A brief history covering from the 12th and 13th centuries to the mid-20th century. Select bibliography. PT5061.M4

Petit, Louis David. Bibliographie der Middelnederlandsche taal- en letterkunde. Leiden, Brill, 1888–1910. 2v. **BD793**

Contents: v.1, Works appearing before 1888; v.2, Works appearing from 1888–1910.
A bibliography of Middle Dutch language and literature.
Z2411.P48

Winkel, Jan te. De ontwikkelingsgang der Nederlandsche letterkunde. 2. druk. Haarlem, Bohn, 1922–27. 7v. **BD794**

1st ed. 1908–21.
An important reference history. PT5060.W5

Afrikaans

Nienaber, Petrus Johannes. Bronnegids by die studie van die Afrikaanse taal en letterkunde. Johannesburg, Nienaber, 1947. 422p. **BD795**

—— —— Deel II–VIc, 1947/51–67. Johannesburg, 1952–68.

A bibliography of Afrikaans literature and language.

Z3601.N52

Flemish

Arents, Prosper. De Vlaamse schrijvers in het Engels vertaald, 1481–1949. Gent, Erasmus, [1950]. 466p. (Koninklijke Vlaamse Academie voor Taal- en Letterkunde) **BD796**

A bibliography of translations into English from the Flemish, with detailed bibliographical information and location of copies in American and European libraries.

—— Flemish writers translated (1830–1931); bibliographical essay. The Hague, Nijhoff, 1931. 191p. **BD797**

A listing of Flemish works translated into various languages; classified arrangement with indexes of authors, translators, illustrators, etc. Z2414.T7A6

Roemans, Robert. Bibliographie van de moderne Vlaamsche literatuur, 1893–1930. 1. deel. Kortrijk, 1930–34. Afl. 1–10. **BD798**

—— and **Assche, Hilda van.** Bibliografie van de Vlaamse tijdschriften. Reeks I: Vlaamse literaire tijdschriften van 1930 tot en met 1958. Hasselt, Heideland, 1960–71. Reeks I–III.

For full information *see* AE264–AE265. Z2424.F5R7

Friesian

Aarhus, Denmark. Statsbiblioteket. Friserne, Land og Folk Sprog og Litteratur. Aarhus, 1933–59. 2v. il. **BD799**

Contents: v.1, To 1933; v.2, 1934–59.
Lists works on the history, language, and literature of Friesland.

Friesland. Provinciale Bibliotheek. Catalogus der Friesche taal- en letterkunde en overige Friesche geschriften. Leeuwarden, Noordnederlandsche Boekhandel, 1941. 859p. **BD800**

A classified catalog with extensive indexes. Z2454.F8F7

Wumkes, G. A. Bodders yn de Fryske striid. Boalsert, Osinga, 1926. 751p. il. **BD801**

A collection of bio-bibliographical articles with extracts from writings.

—— Paden fen Fryslan; samle opstellen. Boalsert, Osinga, 1932–43. 4v. il. **BD802**

A history of Friesian literature, with bibliographical notes interspersed.

German
Guides

Faulhaber, Uwe K. and **Goff, Penrith B.** German literature: an annotated reference guide. N.Y., Garland, 1979. 398p. (Garland reference library of the humanities, v.108) **BD803**

An annotated bibliography of the major reference and research tools, works of literary criticism, and periodicals in the field of German literature. Includes a section on related fields, a checklist (without annotations) of information on German art, music, philosophy, history, geography, folklore, philology, and language teaching. Indexed. Z2231.F38

Hansel, Johannes. Bücherkunde für Germanisten. Studienausg. 8., neubearb. Aufl., bearb. von Lydia Tschakert. Berlin, Erich Schmidt Verlag, 1983. 209p. **BD804**

A guide to basic works for research in Germanic philology and literature, including guides, bibliographies, general histories, annual surveys, etc.; author/title and subject indexes. German-language works predominate, but a few titles in other languages are cited. The original edition (1959) included a section on manuscripts. Z2235.A2H3

Richardson, Larry L. Introduction to library research in German studies: language, literature, and civilization. Boulder, Colo., Westview Pr., [1984]. 227p. **BD805**

A guide for the English-speaking student with considerable emphasis on the use of libraries and bibliographic searching techniques and methods. About 250 reference sources are annotated at some length; many general sources are included, with indication of their relevance to research in German studies. Special section on computerized literature searches. Indexed. Z2235.A2R5

Bibliography

Albrecht, Günter and **Dahlke, Günther.** Internationale Bibliographie zur Geschichte der deutschen Literatur von den Anfängen bis zur Gegenwart, erarbeitet von deutschen, sowjetischen, bulgarischen, jugoslawischen, polnischen, rumänischen, tschechoslowakischen und ungarischen Wissenschaftlern. Berlin, Volk und Wissen, 1969–84. 4v. in 6. **BD806**

Preface in German and English.
Contents: v.1, Von den Anfängen bis 1789; v.2, Von 1789 bis zur Gegenwart. 2v.; v.3, Sachregister; Personen-Werk-Register; v.4, Zehnjahres-Ergängsungsband; Berichtzeitraum: 1965 bis 1974. 2v.

An international bibliography of the history of German literature, representing "the first effort to systematically bring together the results of Russian and Soviet research in German letters as well as those of the other socialist countries in the same field."—*Pref.* Although the work is necessarily selective, all aspects of literature are represented, and coverage is very broad; books, periodical articles, and dissertations are included. Cutoff date is 1964, with some important later items listed. v.2, pt.2 includes "Nachträge, Errata und Ergänzungen," p.857–1109. v.4 brings the record down through 1974; it has its own indexes. Z2231.A4

Arnold, Robert Franz. Allgemeine Bücherkunde zur neueren deutschen Literaturgeschichte. 4. Aufl. neubearb. von Herbert Jacob. Berlin, W. de Gruyter, 1966. 395p. **BD807**

1st ed. 1910.
A useful small bibliography, covering more than the field of German literature as it is ordinarily understood. In addition to editions, histories, criticisms, etc., it treats more general reference books—such as encyclopedias, biographical dictionaries, special encyclopedias—and attempts to indicate their special value to the student of German literature. Z2231.A87

Batts, Michael S. The bibliography of German literature: an historical and critical survey. Bern, P. Lang, [1978]. 239p. (Canadian studies in German language and literature, no.19) **BD808**

"The first purpose of the present study is . . . to provide a succinct historical survey of the bibliographical sources available to those who study the history of German literature in all its aspects."—*Introd.* Discusses bibliographic sources from the period before printing to the present, offering a critical examination of current bibliographic sources, and suggesting future developments. List of works cited and consulted, p.201–30. Indexed. Z2231.A1B37

Bode, Ingrid. Die Autobiographien zur deutschen Literatur, Kunst und Musik 1900–1965; Bibliographie und Nachweise der persönlichen Begegnungen und Charakteristiken. Stuttgart, Metzler, [1966]. 308p. **BD809**

More than 500 autobiographies and diaries are listed in the first section. A second section offers an index to the names of persons appearing in the autobiographies cited.

Dünnhaupt, Gerhard. Bibliographisches Handbuch der Barockliteratur. Hundert Personalbiographien deutscher Autoren des Siebzehnten Jahrhunderts. Stuttgart, Hiersemann, 1980–81. 3v. (Hiersemanns bibliographische Handbücher, Bd.2) **BD810**

A brief biographical sketch is followed by a list of 18th–20th century editions of the author's works and of monographic works about the author. Individual works are then listed chronologically, with full bibliographical information and references to other standard bibliographies and catalogs. Z2232.D85

Goedeke, Karl. Grundriss zur Geschichte der deutschen Dichtung aus den Quellen. 2. ganz neubearb. Aufl. Dresden, Ehlermann, 1884–1966. 15v. **BD811**

Contents: v.1, Das Mittelalter (1884); v.2, Reformationszeitalter (1886); v.3, Vom dreissigjährigen bis zum siebenjährigen Kriege (1887); v.4–5, Vom siebenjährigen bis zum Weltkriege (1891–93); v.6–7, Zeit des Weltkrieges (1898–1900); v.8–15, Vom Weltfrieden, 1815 bis zur französischen Revolution 1830 (1905–66).

The most complete bibliography of German literature, indispensable in the large reference library or for university work, but too exhaustive and special for the small library. Gives some biographical and critical comment on authors; critical and other notes on individual works, sources, etc.; and exhaustive bibliographies of editions, treatises, histories, biographical and critical articles, etc. No cumulated index but detailed index in each volume. PT85.G7

———— ———— Index bearb. von Hartmut Rambaldo. Nendeln, Liechtenstein, 1975. 393p.

An alphabetical index of the authors treated in Bd. 1–15, 1884–1966 (3. Aufl. of Bd. 4), of the 2d ed. of Goedeke (above). PT85.G72

———— ———— 3. neubearb. Aufl. nach dem Tode des Verfassers in Verbindung mit Fachgelehrten fortgeführt von Edmund Goetze. Dresden, Ehlermann, 1906–60. v.4, pts.1–5. **BD812**

This is the only volume published in a 3d ed.

Issued in parts; pts.1–4 (1906–13); pt.5 publ. Berlin, Akademie Verlag, 1957–60.

Contents: Bd.4, Abt.1, Vom siebenjährigen bis zum Weltkriege: Nationale Dichtung; Bd.4, Abt. 2–5, Goethe: Abt. 2, Goethe's Leben, Allgemeine Bibliographie; Abt. 3, Bibliographie der Werke Goethe; Abt.4, Nachträge, Berichtigungen und Register zu Abt.2–3; Abt.5, Goethe-Bibliographie, 1912–1950.

An extensive bibliography on Goethe's life and works. Abt.5 is *Goethe-Bibliographie, 1912–1950*, by Carl Diesch and Paul Schlager. For materials after 1950, *see* the Goethe-Gesellschaft's *Goethe* (BD878). PT85.G72

———— ———— Neue Folge. (Fortführung von 1830 bis 1880), hrsg. von der Deutschen Akademie der Wissenschaften zu Berlin unter Leitung von Leopold Magon . . . bearb. von Georg Minde-Pouet und Eva Rothe. Berlin, Akademie Verlag, 1955–62. Bd.1. **BD813**

Contents: Bd.1, Bibliographie der Literatur über die deutsche Dichtung im Zeitraum 1830 bis 1880; Die Schriftsteller in alphabetischer Folge, A–Ays. 733p.

Handbuch der deutschen Literaturgeschichte. 2. Abt.: Bibliographien. Hrsg. von Paul Stapf. Bern, Francke Verlag, [1969–74]. v.1–6, 8–12. (In progress) **BD814**

Contents: v.1, Frühes Mittelalter, von Henry Kratz; v.2, Hohes Mittelalter, von Michael Batts; v.3, Spätes Mittelalter, von G. F. Jones; v.4, Renaissance, Humanismus, Reformation, von James E. Engel; v.5, Barock, von Ingrid Merkel; v.6, Das Zeitalter der Aufklärung, von E. K. Grotegut und G. F. Leneaux; v.8, Romantik, von John Osborne; v.9, Neunzehntes Jahrhundert, 1830–1880, von Roy C. Cowen; v.10, Wilhelminisches Zeitalter, von Penrith Goff; v.11, Deutsches Schrifttum zwischen den Beiden Weltkriegen

(1918–1945), von Gertrud B. Pickar; v.12, Deutsches Schrifttum der Gegenwart (ab 1945), von Jerry Glenn.

Abt. 1 is "Darstellungen."

The completed series will offer select bibliographies for the individual periods, including bibliographies of individual authors. v.7 is to be "Goethezeit. Sturm und Drang," by Kathleen Harris.

Handbuch der Editionen: deutschsprachige Schriftsteller, Ausgang des 15. Jahrhunderts bis zur Gegenwart. Bearb. von Waltraud Hagen [et al.]. Berlin, Volk und Wissen, 1979. 607p. **BD815**

For some 240 writers (drawn from all periods), identifies and annotates the collected and selected editions of their works, collections of letters, etc., giving contents notes and indicating historical, textual, and comparative commentary, indexes, and other scholarly apparatus. Z2234.F55H36

Harvard University. Library. German literature. Cambridge, Mass., publ. by Harvard Univ. Lib., distr. by the Harvard Univ. Pr., 1974. 2v. (Widener library shelflist, 49–50) **BD816**

Contents: v.1, Classification schedule; Classified listing by call number; Chronological listing; v.2, Author and title listing.

Lists "more than 46,000 titles of works on the history of German language literature, literary anthologies, and works by and about individual European authors writing in German and its dialects."—*Pref.* Z2249.H37

Index Expressionismus; Bibliographie der Beiträge in den Zeitschriften und Jahrbüchern des literarischen Expressionismus, 1910–1925. Im Auftrage des Seminars für deutsche Philologie der Universität Göttingen und Zusammenarbeit mit dem Deutschen Rechenzentrum Darmstadt hrsg. von Paul Raabe. Nendeln, Liechtenstein, Kraus-Thomson, 1972. 18v. **BD817**

Contents: v.1–4, Ser.A, Alphabetischer Index; v.5–9, Ser.B, Systematischer Index; v.10–14, Ser.C, Index nach Zeitschriften; v.15–16, Ser.D, Titelregister; v.17–18, Ser.E, Gattungsregister.

A computer-produced index to 100 periodicals and 5 yearbooks associated with the German expressionist movement and reflecting its influence on the whole range of literature, the arts, and culture. A full citation to each article, poem, etc., is given in *Serie A,* the alphabetical author index, and in *Serie B* which offers a subject approach. The indexes by title (*Serie D*) and by genre (*Serie E*) give briefer information, and it is necessary to refer to the author index for the full citation. *Serie C* is arranged by title of the serial and offers a printout of the contents of the full run of each publication indexed, with contributions arranged alphabetically by author; the full citation is given in each entry. Z5936.E9R3

Körner, Josef. Bibliographisches Handbuch des deutschen Schrifttums. 3. völlig umgearb. und wesentlich verm. Aufl. Bern, Francke, 1949. 644p. (Reissued 1966) **BD818**

Previously published as an appendix to Wilhelm Scherer and Oskar Walzel's *Geschichte der deutschen Literatur* (4. Aufl. Berlin, Askanischer Verlag, 1928). Lists books and periodical articles dealing with German literature and authors from ancient times to World War II. Arrangement is chronological by periods, each subdivided by subject. Subject and name indexes, though the latter lists only the names treated, not the authors of critical and biographical studies.

In the research library this will not be a substitute for Goedeke (BD811), but will supplement it for more recent materials. Should be useful in the smaller library not needing the wealth of detail given in Goedeke. Z2231.K6

Köttelwesch, Clemens. Bibliographisches Handbuch der deutschen Literaturwissenschaft, 1945–1969. Frankfurt am Main, V. Klostermann, 1971–79. 3v. **BD819**

With v.2 dates of coverage appear as 1945–1972.

Designed as a select bibliography of works on German literature, including books, articles, contributions to collections, theses, and reprints of books originally published before 1945. In addition to German-language materials, French, English, Russian, Polish, Italian, and Dutch sources are represented. Classed arrangement; v.3 offers name and subject indexes. Z2231.K63

Melzwig, Brigitte. Deutsche sozialistische Literatur, 1918–1945: Bibliographie der Buchveröffentlichungen. Berlin, Aufbau-Verlag, [1975]. 616p. **BD820**

Lists writers' works published 1918–45, and reprints and translations through 1969. Chronological index, title index, and index of names. Z2233.3.M44

Olzien, Otto. Bibliographie zur deutschen Literaturgeschichte. Stuttgart, Metzler, 1953. 156p. (Annalen der deutschen Literatur. Ergänzungsheft 2) **BD821**

Includes some sources covered by more comprehensive bibliographies, but emphasis is here placed on work published since Körner's *Bibliographisches Handbuch des deutschen Schrifttums* (1949; BD818)—through the end of 1952. Includes bibliographies of individual authors arranged alphabetically.

—— —— Nachträge, 1953–1954, mit Ergänzungen und Berichtigungen. Stuttgart, Metzler, 1955. 24p.

Z2231.O4

Schmitt, Franz Anselm. Stoff- und Motivgeschichte der deutschen Literatur; eine Bibliographie. 3., völlig neu bearb. und erw. Aufl. Berlin, W. de Gruyter, 1976. 437p. **BD822**

1st ed. 1959.
A thorough revision and updating of this useful work, the 1st ed. of which was based on the *Bibliographie der Stoff- und Motivgeschichte der deutschen Literatur* by Kurt Bauerhorst (Berlin, 1932). Lists scholarly studies, mostly in German, on the use of themes and motifs in German literature. Arrangement is alphabetical by *Stoff* or *Motiv*. Includes books, periodical articles, dissertations, chapters in books, and *Festschriften*. Author index. Z2231.S35

Sternfeld, Wilhelm and **Tiedemann, Eva.** Deutsche Exil-Literatur, 1933–1945; eine Bio-bibliographie. 2. verb. u. stark erw. Aufl. Heidelberg, Lambert Schneider, 1970. 606p. (Deutsche Akademie für Sprache und Dichtung. Veröffentlichungen, 29a) **BD823**

1st ed. 1962.
Very brief biographical sketches of German exiles are followed by lists of books and periodical articles.
Another bibliography of German exile literature is: *Exil-Literatur 1933–1945; Eine Austellung aus Beständen der Deutschen Bibliothek, Frankfurt am Main,* comp. by Werner Berthold (3. erw. und verb. Aufl., Frankfurt a.M., 1967. 352p.). Z2233.S7

Stock, Karl Franz, Heilinger, Rudolf and **Stock, Marylène.** Personalbibliographien österreichischer Dichter und Schriftsteller; von den Anfängen bis zur Gegenwart. Pullach bei München, Verlag Dokumentation, 1972. 703p. **BD824**

"Mit Auswahl einschlägiger Bibliographien, Nachschlagewerke, Sammelbiographien, Literaturgeschichten und Anthologien."—*title page.* Z2111.A1S76

Wiesner, Herbert, Živsa, Irena and **Stoll, Christoph.** Bibliographie der Personalbibliographien zur deutschen Gegenwartsliteratur. München, Nymphenburger Verlagshandlung, 1970. 358p. **BD825**

Provides references to primary and secondary bibliographies of about 500 German-language writers of the 20th century. Z2221.A1W54

Wilpert, Gero von and **Gühring, Adolf.** Erstausgaben deutscher Dichtung; eine Bibliographie zur deutschen Literatur, 1600–1960. Stuttgart, Alfred Kröner, [1967]. 1468p. **BD826**

Lists some 47,000 first editions of about 1,360 German authors. Gives pagination, place, publisher, and date. Z2231.W74

Yale University. Library. Yale Collection of German Literature. German Baroque literature; a catalogue of the collection in the Yale University Library, by Curt von Faber du Faur. New Haven, Yale Univ. Pr., 1958–69. 2v. il. (Bibliographical ser. from the Yale University Library collections) **BD827**

". . . an attempt to present an outline of literary history based on a catalogue of a collection of books" for the period (*ca.* 1575–1740).—*Pref.* Classified arrangement with detailed bibliographic information. Indexes of authors, composers, and illustrators. v.2 represents additions to the collection since the publication of v.1.

Z2232.Y35

—— Bibliography-index to the microfilm edition of the Yale University Library Collection of German Baroque Literature. New Haven, Research Publs., 1971. 216p.

BD828

Research Publications Inc. has produced a microfilm series entitled "German baroque literature" which is based on the Yale Collection and reproduces 2,363 or the 3,087 titles in the Faber du Faur bibliography and its supplement (the remaining items not being filmed because of physical condition or incompleteness). This volume is primarily an index to the microfilm series (since it reproduces in author sequence the catalog cards provided by the microfilm publisher), but also serves as a cumulated author index to the Faber du Faur bibliographies. Z2232.Y353

Current

Bibliographie der deutschen Sprach- und Literaturwissenschaft. Bd.1– , 1945/53– . Frankfurt am Main, Klostermann, 1957– . Annual. **BD829**

Frequency varies. Editors vary: H. W. Eppelsheimer, C. Köttelwesch.
Title varies: Bd. 1–8, *Bibliographie der deutschen Literaturwissenschaft.*
A comprehensive bibliography of Western-language materials: books, pamphlets, articles, dissertations, reviews, etc. Basic arrangement is by literary period, with author and subject indexes.
Z2231.B5

Germanistik: internationales Referatenorgan mit bibliographischen Hinweisen. Jahrg.1– , Jan. 1960– . Tübingen, Niemeyer, 1960– . v.1– . Quarterly. **BD830**

An international bibliography of materials, from many countries, on German literature. Lists books, periodical articles, and parts of books. Arranged chronologically by period; some entries carry annotations. Annual author-subject index. Z2235.A2G4

Internationale germanistische Bibliographie, 1980– . München, K. G. Saur, 1981– . Annual. **BD831**

Hrsg. Hans-Albrecht Koch, Uta Koch.
A comprehensive bibliography for the whole range of German language, linguistics, and literature. Includes books, parts of books, periodical articles, and dissertations. Classed arrangement with detailed table of contents and a name index.

Jahresberichte für neuere deutsche Literaturgeschichte, 1890–1915. Berlin, Behr, 1892–1919. v.1–26, pt.1.

BD832

An important annual survey, including books, pamphlets, theses, and periodical articles. Continued by: Z2231.J25

Jahresbericht über die wissenschaftlichen Erscheinungen auf dem Gebiete der neueren deutschen Literatur, hrsg. von der Literaturarchivgesellschaft in Berlin, 1921–36/39. Berlin, W. de Gruyter, 1924–56. n.F., v.1–16/19. **BD833**

Continued by: Z2231.J26

Jahresbericht für deutsche Sprache und Literatur, bearb. unter Leitung von Gerhard Marx. Berlin, Akademie-Verlag, 1960–66. Bd.1–2. (Deutsche Akademie der Wissenschaften zu Berlin. Inst. für Deutsche Sprache und Literatur) **BD834**

Contents: Bd.1, 1940–45; Bd.2, 1946–50.
A continuation in combined form of two bibliographical series, the *Jahresbericht über die Erscheinungen auf dem Gebiete der germanischen Philologie* (BC97) and the *Jahresbericht über die wissenschaftlichen Erscheinungen auf dem Gebiete der neueren deutschen Literatur* (above).

A comprehensive bibliography of books and periodical articles on German language and literature of all periods. Includes works in European languages (except Slavic) from European and American periodicals. Classified arrangement with extensive indexes.

Z2235.A2J3

Dissertations

London. University. Institute of Germanic Studies. Theses in Germanic studies; a catalogue of theses and dissertations in the field of Germanic studies, excluding English, approved for higher degrees in the universities of Great Britain and Ireland between 1903 and 1961. Ed. by F. Norman, director. London, 1962. 46p. (*Its* Publications, 4) **BD835**

Z7036.L58

———— Theses in Germanic studies, 1962–67 . . . Ed. by S. S. Prawer and V. J. Riley. London, 1968. 18p. (*Its* Publications, 10)

Author listings, with subject indexes, of theses relating to Germanic literature and language. Z7036.L59

Manuscripts

Frels, Wilhelm. Deutsche Dichterhandschriften von 1400 bis 1900. Leipzig, Hiersemann, 1934. 382p. (Bibliographical pubn. Germanic section. Modern Language Assoc. of America. v.2) **BD836**

Subtitle: Gesamtkatalog der eigenhändigen Handschriften deutscher Dichter in den Bibliotheken und Archiven Deutschlands, Österreichs, der Schweiz und der ČSR. Z2231.F86

Translations into English

Goodnight, Scott Holland. German literature in American magazines prior to 1846. Madison, 1907. 264p. (Bull. of the Univ. of Wisconsin, no.188. Philology and literature ser., v.4, no.1) **BD837**

Includes a bibliography, arranged chronologically and by magazines, p.108–242; and index of (1) authors, and (2) magazines. PT123.U6G6

Haertel, Martin Henry. German literature in American magazines, 1846 to 1880. Madison, 1908. 188p. (Bull. of the Univ. of Wisconsin, no.263. Philology and literature ser., v.4, no.2) **BD838**

Includes a bibliography, p.95–178, and indexes of authors and of magazines. PT123.U6H3

Morgan, Bayard Quincy. A critical bibliography of German literature in English translation, 1481–1927. 2d ed., completely rev. and greatly augm. N.Y., Scarecrow Pr., 1965. 690p. **BD839**

———— ———— Supplement embracing the years 1928–1955. N.Y., Scarecrow Pr., 1965. 601p.

1st ed. 1922. A 2d ed. with supplement for 1928–35 was published 1938 (Stanford, Calif., Stanford Univ. Pr.; London, Milford. 773p.). The basic volume has been reprinted from the 1938 edition, omitting the supplement. The main list contains 10,797 numbered titles, and is followed by List A, Anonyms (587 titles); List B, Bibliographies (50 titles); List C, Collections (577 titles); and an index of translators. The new supplement incorporates the 1928–35 listings with new material for the longer period. In this supplement the list of translators has been dropped, as has the system of rating the quality of translations by diacritical marks. Further supplemented by BD842. Z2234.T7M8

———— and **Hohlfeld, A. R.** German literature in British magazines, 1750–1860. Madison, Univ. of Wisconsin Pr., 1949. 364p. **BD840**

1750–1810 by Walter Roloff; 1811–35 by Morton E. Mix; 1836–60 by Martha Nicolai.

A chronological list of magazine references with an alphabetical list of the German authors named. Preceded by a historical introduction giving a survey of magazine reflection of the British reception of German literature, 1750–1860. PT123.G7M6

O'Neill, Patrick. German literature in English translation: a select bibliography. Toronto, Univ. of Toronto Pr., [1981]. 242p. **BD841**

Intended "for the teaching scholar in the humanities, the student of comparative literature, and the educated general reader" (*Pref.*), the list reflects the compiler's "personal conception of what the canon of German literature (as available in translation) is at the beginning of the 1980s" and his "impression of what is best, most lasting, and most interesting to the English-speaking reader who has a taste for literature." Arranged by period, then alphabetically by author; introductory section of general collections. Indexes of authors and of translators. Z2234.T7O5

Smith, Murray F. A selected bibliography of German literature in English translation, 1956–1960. Metuchen, N.J., Scarecrow Pr., 1972. 398p. **BD842**

Subtitle: A second supplement to Bayard Quincy Morgan's *A critical bibliography of German literature in English translation* [BD839].

Scope has been broadened to include translations from the German in all fields, not merely belles-lettres. Z2234.T7S6

Criticism

Domandi, Agnes Körner, *comp.* Modern German literature. N.Y., Ungar, [1972]. 2v. (A library of literary criticism) **BD843**

For other volumes in the series *see* BD399, BD553, BD1270.

"For the purposes of these volumes 'modern German literature' includes works written since 1900 by authors from East and West Germany, Austria, and Switzerland."—*Introd.* Includes critical excerpts from literary magazines, newspaper book reviews, academic and scholarly periodicals, and scholarly books. Excerpts from German-language sources are presented in English translation. More than 200 authors are considered. Index of critics.

PT401.D6

Dictionaries of authors and literature

Brümmer, Franz. Lexikon der deutschen Dichter und Prosaisten vom Beginn des 19. Jahrhunderts bis zur Gegenwart. 6. völlig neubearb. Aufl. Leipzig, Reclam, [1913]. 8v. **BD844**

A useful handbook containing brief biographical sketches and lists of works of some 9,900 German, Austrian, and Swiss authors. Very strong in pseudonyms. Supplement in v.8 brings the work down to the end of 1912. Z2230.B894

Frenzel, Herbert Alfred and **Frenzel, E.** Daten deutscher Dichtung: chronologischer Abriss der deutschen Literaturgeschichte. [Neubearb. Ausg.] München, Deutscher Taschenbuch Verlag, 1980. 2v. **BD845**

1st ed. 1953; various printings. (1979 called "5. völlig neu bearb. Aufl.")

Arranged under broad period divisions, followed by an alphabetical list of authors of the period, and then a chronological list of outstanding works. Brief biographical notes are given for authors, with a résumé for each title. PT103.F72

Garland, Henry Burnand and **Garland, Mary.** The Oxford companion to German literature. Oxford, Clarendon Pr., 1976. 977p. **BD846**

Follows the familiar plan and arrangement of the various "Oxford companions" to literature, "although exigencies of space finally made it necessary to drop such entries as conspicuous characters in literary works."—*Pref.* Covers from about 800 to the early 1970's and attempts to provide "reasonably representative" coverage of each period of the literature of each German-speaking country.

A review by S. S. Prawer in *TLS,* May 21, 1976, p.607–8 discusses in some detail the various virtues and shortcomings of the work; similarly, the review by Roy Pascal in *Modern language review* 72:479–82 (Apr. 1977). The "collective verdict" of a group of specialists invited to review portions of the work for the *Journal of English and Germanic philology* (76:392–96, July 1977) is that the *Companion,* "while a most welcome tool, does not possess a sufficient degree of accuracy in detail and is often suspect in its emphases."   PT41.G3

Kosch, Wilhelm. Deutsches Literatur-Lexikon; biographisches und bibliographisches Handbuch. 2. vollständig neubearb. und stark erw. Aufl. Bern, Francke, 1947–58. 4v.
          BD847

1st ed. 1927–30.
Primarily a dictionary of German authors of all periods. Includes living persons. Extensive bibliographies cite both original and critical works. Includes entries on literary forms, titles, allusions, places, etc.
A new edition is in progress: Z2230.K862

────── ────── 3. völlig neubearb. Aufl. hrsg. von Bruno Berger und Heinz Rupp. Bern, Francke Verlag, 1966–84. Bd.1–9. (In progress)   **BD848**

Bd.1 published in parts.
Contents: Bd.1–9, A–Lucidarius.
This revision concentrates on entries for authors and anonymous titles, omitting such material from the previous edition as placenames, characters from classical literature, and terms and allusions easily found in other literary encyclopedias. Within the limits established for the new edition, it is very comprehensive as well as reasonably up-to-date (e.g., bibliographies include citations up to press time for successive volumes).   Z2231.K663

────── Deutsches Literatur-Lexikon. Ausgabe in einem Band. Bearb. von Bruno Berger. Bern, München, Francke Verlag, 1963, 511p.   **BD849**

Derived from the 2d ed. of the larger work. Consists almost entirely of biographical sketches of German writers, omitting most of the subject entries found in the 4-volume work. The biographical articles give brief biographical facts and often extensive bibliographies, both by and about the writers. Occasional inaccuracies in dates, etc.   Z2231.K66

Kritisches Lexikon zur deutschsprachigen Gegenwartsliteratur. Hrsg. von Heinz Ludwig Arnold. München, Edition Text + Kritik, 1978– . 4v. (looseleaf)   **BD850**

At head of title: KLG.
For each author treated there is a brief biographical sketch, followed by a signed critical essay on the writer and his work, plus a bibliography of writings by and about the author. Looseleaf format allows updating of individual entries at irregular intervals.

Kunisch, Hermann. Handbuch der deutschen Gegenwartsliteratur. 2., verb. und erw. Aufl. München, Nymphenburger Verlagshandlung, [1968–70]. 3v.   **BD851**

1st ed. 1965.
A revised and greatly expanded edition of this guide to contemporary German literature and literary criticism. v.1–2 comprise alphabetical author listings, followed by articles on literary movements and genres. v.3 is a "Bibliographie der Personalbibliographien" providing references to author bibliographies in other publications.
Partially superseded by: PT155.K82

Lexikon der deutschsprachigen Gegenwartsliteratur, begründet von Hermann Kunisch; neu bearb. und hrsg. von Herbert Wiesner. München, Nymphenburger, [1981]. 568p.
          BD852

Although based on Kunisch's *Handbuch* (above), this volume does not fully supersede that work: i.e., it does not include the articles on literary movements and genres, nor the "Bibliographie der Personalbibliographien" found therein. Biographical articles have been revised and expanded, and bibliographies updated; many

new writers are included, but some from the earlier edition were omitted.   PT155.L48

Kürschners deutscher Literatur-Kalender, hrsg. von Gerhard Lüdtke. Berlin, W. de Gruyter, 1879– . v.1– . Annual.
          BD853

Title and imprint vary.
Some years not issued. v.39, 1917; v.40, 1922; v.41, 1924. Beginning with v.42, 1925, the work is issued in two series, one continuing the *Literatur-Kalender,* the other becoming *Kürschners deutscher Gelehrten-Kalender* (AJ210).
A useful biographical record of German authors. Includes Austrian and Swiss authors writing in German.   Z2230.K92

Kürschner Nekrolog, 1901–1935, hrsg. von Gerhard Lüdtke. Berlin, W. de Gruyter, 1936. 976col.   **BD854**

Contents: Biographies reprinted from the *Literatur-Kalender* (above)—with date and place of death added—of some 3,700 authors who died 1901–35; two chronological lists, arranged by years of (1) births, and (2) deaths.

────── 1936–1970. Hrsg. von Werner Schuder. Berlin, W. de Gruyter, 1973. 871p.

          Z2230.K921

Kutzbach, Karl August. Autorenlexikon der Gegenwart. Bonn, Bouvier, 1950. v.1.   **BD855**

Contents: v.1, Schöne Literatur verfasst in deutscher Sprache mit einer Chronik seit 1945.
Bio-bibliographical sketches of about 1,000 contemporary writers of German-language belles-lettres, with indexes by form of writing, religious or philosophical outlook, etc. Annual records (1945–49) of obituaries, anniversaries, awards, and foundation or reinstatement of societies and publications. A second volume was planned for writers in other fields, but has not been published.   Z2230.K95

Lennartz, Franz. Deutsche Schriftsteller der Gegenwart: Einzeldarstellungen zur Schönen Literatur in deutscher Sprache. 11., erw. Aufl. Stuttgart, Kröner, [1978]. 825p. (Kröners Taschenausgabe Bd.151)   **BD856**

1st ed. 1938 (title varies).
Includes biographical and critical sketches, averaging two to three pages in length, with bibliographies.   PT155.L4

Lexikon deutschsprachiger Schriftsteller, von den Anfängen bis zur Gegenwart. [Hrsg. von] Günter Albrecht [et al.]. Kronberg Ts., Scriptor Verlag, 1974. 2v.   **BD857**

1st–4th eds., 1960–63, had title *Deutsches Schriftsteller Lexikon.* An earlier edition with the new title was published 1967–68.
Offers biographical sketches, with bibliographies, of about 1,500 German writers of all periods. Includes some living persons.
Austrian writers are dealt with in *Bio-bibliographisches Literaturlexikon Österreichs, von Anfängen bis zur Gegenwart* by Hans Giebisch and Gustav Gugitz (Wien, Hollinek, 1964. 516p.).
          PT41.A4

Lexikon sozialistischer deutscher Literatur, von den Anfängen bis 1945; monographisch-biographische Darstellungen. Halle, Verlag Sprache und Literatur, 1963. 592p.   **BD858**

An alphabetically arranged dictionary of articles on socialist writers, newspapers, collections, etc. Articles include bibliographies.
          Z2230.L46

Reallexikon der deutschen Literaturgeschichte, begründet von Paul Merker und Wolfgang Stammler. 2. Aufl. Berlin, W. de Gruyter, 1955–84. 4v.   **BD859**

1st ed. 1925–31 in 4v.
Issued in parts. Editors vary.
An alphabetically arranged dictionary with signed articles and extensive bibliographies on periods, types, schools, and kinds of German literature. No entries under personal names.   PT41.R4

Schmitt, Fritz. Deutsche Literaturgeschichte in Tabellen. Bonn, Athenäum-Verlag, 1949–52. 3v.   **BD860**

Contents: v.1, Die Literatur des Mittelalters, 750–1450; v.2,

Renaissance, Barock, Klassizismus, 1450–1770; v.3, 1770 bis zur Gegenwart.

A detailed outline of German literature, giving brief biographical and bibliographical facts, with references to manuscripts, source materials, and critical studies. Includes information on comparative literature and the influence of foreign literatures on the German.

PT103.S39

Schneider, Max. Deutsches Titelbuch. Ein Hilfsmittel zum Nachweis von Verfassern deutscher Literaturwerke. 2. verb. und wesentlich verm. Aufl. Berlin, Paschke, 1927. 798p.

BD861

1st ed. had title *Von wem ist das doch?* (1907–1909).

German titles and first lines of poems arranged alphabetically with attribution to author. Primarily of the 19th century with occasional 18th- and 20th-century titles. Index of subjects.

Continued by: Z2231.S37

Ahnert, Heinz Jörg. Deutsches Titelbuch 2; ein Hilfsmittel zum Nachweis von Verfassern deutscher Literaturwerke 1915–1965, mit Nachträgen und Berichtigungen zum Deutschen Titelbuch 1 für die Zeit von 1900 bis 1914. Berlin, Haude & Spener, [1966]. 636p. **BD862**

Z2231.A55

Schriftsteller der DDR. [Hrsg. Günter Albrecht u. a.] Leipzig, VEB Bibliographisches Institut, 1974. 656p. **BD863**

About 400 biographical sketches of DDR authors, mainly living persons but including some deceased persons who were still active in the last quarter century. Includes lists of publications.

PT3713.S3

Stammler, Wolfgang. Die deutsche Literatur des Mittelalters: Verfasserlexikon, unter Mitarbeit zahlreicher Fachgenossen. Berlin, de Gruyter, 1931–55. 5v. **BD864**

Issued in parts. v.3–5 edited by Karl Langosch.

Long, scholarly articles signed by specialists, with detailed bibliographies of works by and about German medieval authors and writings. Includes works in medieval Latin of significance in German literature, and also anonymous works.

A new edition is in progress. Z2230.S78

——— Die deutsche Literatur des Mittelalters: Verfasserlexikon. 2., völlig neu bearb. Aufl. Berlin, W. de Gruyter, [1977–84]. Bd.1–5$^{1-2}$. (In progress) **BD865**

On cover, Lfg.1: Begründet von Wolfgang Stammler, fortgeführt von Karl Langosch . . . hrsg. von Kurt Ruh . . . Redaktion, Kurt Illing, Christine Stöllinger.

Contents: Bd.1–5$^{1-2}$, A–Lebenter.

This edition revised and expanded in the light of recent scholarship. Signed articles with bibliographies. Writers of antiquity and medieval Latin writers continue to be treated if they have had an impact on German literature.

History

Boor, Helmut Anton Wilhelm de and **Newald, Richard,** eds. Geschichte der deutschen Literatur von den Anfängen bis zur Gegenwart. München, Beck, 1949–83. v.1–2, 3$^{1-2}$, 4$^{1-2}$, 5–6$^{1-2}$, 7^1. (In progress) **BD866**

Some volumes have appeared in revised editions.

Contents: v.1, Die deutsche Literatur von Karl dem Grossen bis zum Beginn der höfischen Dichtung, 770–1170, von H. de Boor; v.2, Die höfische Literatur, Vorbereitung, Blüte, Ausklang, 1170–1250, von U. Henning; v.3^1, Die deutsche Literatur im späten Mittelalter, 1250–1350, von H. de Boor; v.3^2, Zerfall und Neubeginn, 1350–1400, von H. de Boor; v.4^1, Das ausgehende Mittelalter, Humanismus und Renaissance, 1370–1520, von H. Rupprich; v.4^2, Das Zeitalter der Reformation, 1520–1570, von H. Rupprich; v.5, Die deutsche Literatur vom Späthumanismus zur Empfindsamkeit, 1570–1750, von R. Newald; v.6^1, Von Klopstock bis zu Goethes Tod, 1750–1832: Ende der Aufklärung und Vorbereitung der Klassik, von R. Newald; v.6^2, Klassik und Romantik, von H. E. Hass;

v.7^1, Die deutsche Literatur zwischen französischen Revolution und Restauration: Das Zeitalter der französischen Revolution, 1789–1806. PT85.B64

Könnecke, Gustav. Bilderatlas zur Geschichte der deutschen Nationallitteratur. Eine Ergänzung zu jeder deutschen Litteraturgeschichte. 2. verb. und verm. Aufl. Marburg, Elwert, [1895]. 423p. il. **BD867**

Various printings.

German literature from earliest times to the end of the 19th century, depicted in illustrations and facsimiles. Includes pictures of authors—many of them with autographs and samples of handwriting—biographical sketches, etc. PT43.K7

Drama

Allgayer, Wilhelm. Dramenlexikon: ein Wegweiser zu etwa 10,000 urheberrechtlich geschützten Bühnenwerken der Jahre 1945–1957; 1957–1960. Begründet von Friedrich Ernst Schulz. Köln, Berlin, Kiepenheuer und Witsch, [1958–62]. 2v. **BD868**

Original ed., 1942, ed. by F. E. Schulz.

A listing of German plays or plays translated into German. Alphabetical by title, with various data on production and publication. Author indexes. Z2234.D7S372

Binger, Norman. A bibliography of German plays on microcards. Hamden, Conn., Shoe String, 1970. 224p. **BD869**

An author listing of those plays which have been published (presumably through 1968) in Microcard editions by Falls City Microcards, Louisville, Ky. Title index. Z2234.D7B55

Gabel, Gernot U. Drama und Theater des deutschen Barock: eine Handbibliographie d. Sekundärliteratur. Hamburg, [Selbstverlag], 1974. 182p. **BD870**

A bibliography of works about the drama and theater of the German baroque era, 1580–1700. Classed arrangement with author index. Z2232.G3

Gregor, Joseph [and others]. Der Schauspielführer. Stuttgart, Hiersemann, 1953–82. 12v. **BD871**

Contents: Bd.1, Das deutsche Schauspiel vom Mittelalter bis zum Expressionismus; Bd.2, Das deutsche Schauspiel der Gegenwart; Das Schauspiel der romanischen Völker, T.1; Bd.3, Das Schauspiel der romanischen Völker, T.2; Das niederländische Schauspiel, Das englische Schauspiel, T.1–2; Bd.4, Das englische Schauspiel, T.3: Nordamerika; Das Schauspiel der nordischen Völker; Das Schauspiel der slavischen Völker: Russland, Ukraine; Bd.5, Das Schauspiel von slavischen Völker: Polen, Tschechoslowakei, Kroatien, Dalmatien, Slowenien, Serbien; Das Schauspiel Ungarns und Griechenlands, des Nahen und Fernen Ostens; Die antiken dramatischen Kulturen; Bd.6, Nachträge zu Bd.I–V; vergleichender Abriss der dramatischen Weltliteratur; Gesamtregister zu Bd.I–VI; Bd.7, Ergänzungen zu Band I–VI: Das Schauspiel bis 1956; Bd.8, Das Schauspiel der Gegenwart von 1956 bis 1965; Bd.9, Das Schauspiel der Gegenwart von 1966 bis 1970 der Inhalt der Wichtigsten Zeitgenössischen Theaterstücke aus aller Welt; Bd.10, Das Schauspiel der Gegenwart von 1971 bis 1973; v.11, Das Schauspiel von 1974–1976; v.12, Das Schauspiel von 1977–1979.

A guide to more than 1,000 years of German drama, and German translations of foreign drama, giving outlines of individual works with critical and historical notes. Arrangement is by period or school, with indexes by author, title, and date of first publication. PN6114.G7

Johns Hopkins University. Library. Fifty years of German drama; a bibliography of modern German drama, 1880–1930, based on the Loewenberg collection. Baltimore, Johns Hopkins Pr., 1941. 111p. **BD872**

A collection of some 3,000 volumes, nearly all first editions.

Z2234.D7J6

Fiction

Luther, Arthur and **Friesenhahn, Heinz.** Land und Leute in deutscher Erzählung. Ein bibliographisches Literaturlexikon neubearb. . . . 3. gänzlich veränd. und erg. Aufl. Stuttgart, Hiersemann, 1954. 555p.   **BD873**

A complete revision of Luther's *Deutsches Land in deutscher Erzählung* (2d ed. 1936) and his *Deutsche Geschichte in deutscher Erzählung* (2d ed. 1943).

In two parts: pt.1, approximately 8,000 novels are listed under 440 place-names; pt.2, some 2,200 novels are listed under the names of 680 historical personages. Indexes of places and of authors; chronological list of the historical characters.   Z5917.H6L97

Schmitt, Franz Anselm. Beruf und Arbeit in deutscher Erzählung; ein literarisches Lexikon. Stuttgart, Hiersemann, 1952. 668col.   **BD874**

German novels of the last two centuries arranged according to the protagonist's trade or profession, with alphabetical author index.   Z2234.F4S35

Poetry

Paulus, Rolf and **Steuler, Ursula.** Bibliographie zur deutschen Lyrik nach 1945. Frankfurt am Main, Athenaion, 1974. 157p.   **BD875**

A bibliography of modern German poetry with a classified section of general background and critical studies followed by sections for the principal practitioners. Index of names.   Z2234.P7P38

Individual authors

See note p.465.

Goethe

Bibliography

Bahr, Ehrhard and **Stewart, Walter K.** Internationales Verzeichnis der Goethe-Dissertationen, 1952–1976. [Ann Arbor, Mich.], Publ. for Amer. Soc. for Eighteenth-Century Studies by University Microfilms Internat., 1978. 85p.   **BD876**

A classed list (with author index) of European and American dissertations. "Besides the dissertations, simultaneously published books, masters theses, and *Habilitationsschriften* are taken into consideration."—*Pref.*   Z8350.B24

Goedeke, Karl. Grundriss zur Geschichte der deutschen Dichtung aus den Quellen. 3. neubearb. Aufl. Dresden, Ehlermann, 1906–60. v.4, pts.1–5.   **BD877**

An extensive bibliography on Goethe. For full information *see* BD812.

Goethe. Bd.1–33. Weimar, Böhlaus, 1936–71. 33v.   **BD878**

Frequency varies; subtitle varies. None published 1945–46.
"Neue Folge des Jahrbuchs der Goethe-Gesellschaft."
Supplements, with the title *Goethe-Bibliographie,* accompany each issue, 1952/53–1971.
Ceased publication with Bd.33, 1971; absorbed by *Goethe Jahrbuch* (v.89– , 1972–) which includes an annual bibliography.   PT2045.G63

Goethe-Bibliographie. 1970– . (*In* Goethe Jahrbuch, v.89– , 1972–) Annual.   **BD879**

Bearb. von Hans Henning.
Includes editions and studies in classed arrangement, with author index in each annual issue.   PT2045.G632

Kippenberg, Anton. Katalog der Sammlung Kippenberg. 2. Ausg. Leipzig, Insel-Verlag, 1928. 2v. and index. il.   **BD880**

Includes Goethe manuscripts, editions, translations, etc.   Z8350.K57

Pyritz, Hans Werner. Goethe-Bibliographie . . . unter redaktioneller Mitarbeit von Paul Raabe. Heidelberg, Carl Winter, 1955–68. 2v.   **BD881**

v.1 issued in parts, 1955–65.
Classified listing of scholarly materials useful for Goethe research, more selective than Goedeke (BD877). Includes books, parts of books, articles, theses, etc., with excellent bibliographic information and some brief annotations. v.2 adds new materials through 1964, using the classed arrangement of the earlier volume, and provides an author index to both parts.

Yale University. Library. William A. Speck Collection of Goetheana. Goethe's works with the exception of Faust; a catalogue comp. by members of the Yale University Library Staff, ed., arr., and supplied with literary notes and preceded by an introduction and a biographical sketch of William A. Speck by Carl Frederick Schreiber. . . . New Haven, Yale Univ. Pr., 1940. 239p. facsim.   **BD882**

The first volume of a comprehensive catalog of the William A. Speck collection of Goetheana. As planned, v.2 was to contain the record of the material on Faust; v.3, biographical material; and v.4, addenda and general index.   Z8350.Y18

Dictionaries and handbooks

Dobel, Richard. Lexikon der Goethe Zitate. [Zürich and Stuttgart], Artemis, [1968]. 1308col.   **BD883**

Quotations from Goethe's literary works and letters are arranged by keywords, with an index of other significant words, concepts, and names.   PT1892.A2D6

Fischer, Paul. Goethe-Wortschatz, ein sprachgeschichtliches Wörterbuch zu Goethes sämtlichen Werken. Leipzig, E. Rohmkopf, 1929. 905p.   **BD884**

PT2239.F5

Goethe-Handbuch: Goethe, seine Welt und Zeit in Werk und Wirkung. 2. vollkommen neugestaltete Aufl. unter Mitwirkung zahlreicher Fachgelehrter, hrsg. von Alfred Zastrau. Stuttgart, Metzler, 1955–61. v.1, v.4.   **BD885**

Contents: v.1, Aachen–Farbenlehre (issued in 14 Lfg.); v.4, Karten der Reisen Goethes (Index and maps in portfolio).
A new and considerably expanded reworking of the 1916–18 edition by Julius Zeitler. Signed articles with bibliographies.   PT2048.Z35

Goethe-Wörterbuch. Hrsg. von der Deutschen Akademie der Wissenschaften zu Berlin, der Akademie der Wissenschaften zu Göttingen, und der Heidelberger Akademie der Wissenschaften. Stuttgart, Kohlhammer, 1966–83. v.1–2⁶. (In progress)   **BD886**

Editors: Wolfgang Schadewaldt, Werner Simon, Wilhelm Wissmann.
Contents: v.1–2, A–Bleich.
This dictionary of Goethe's vocabulary, to be in 5v., shows grammatical and stylistic characteristics and gives references to usage in Goethe's works.   PT2239.G6

Scandinavian

See also under the individual languages: Danish, Icelandic, Norwegian, Swedish.

Bibliography

Arntz, Helmut. Bibliographie der Runenkunde: mit Unterstützung des Archäologischen Instituts des Deutschen Reiches. Leipzig, Harrassowitz, 1937. 293p. **BD887**

An extensive bibliography of materials in various languages on runic antiquities, inscriptions, etc., in Scandinavia, Iceland, England, and elsewhere. "Zeitschriften und (bio)- bibliographische Hilfsmittel," p.265–76. Z2556.A2A7

Bekker-Nielsen, Hans. Old Norse-Icelandic studies; a select bibliography. [Toronto], Univ. of Toronto Pr., [1967]. 94p. **BD888**

Intended as "an intelligent student's guide to Old Norse-Icelandic studies" and includes "a fairly wide range of different kinds of material relevant for the study of the language, literature, and other aspects of civilization in Norway and Iceland in the Middle Ages." —*Pref.* English- and German-language listings are included for the benefit of students with limited knowledge of modern Scandinavian languages. A useful complement to the annual *Bibliography of Old Norse-Icelandic studies* (below). Z2556.B4

Bibliography of Old Norse-Icelandic studies, 1963– . v.1– . Copenhagen, Munksgaard, 1964– . Annual. **BD889**

Selective bibliography catering to the interests of students "of Old Norse language and literature, medieval Norwegian and Icelandic history and related subjects."—*Pref.* Arrangement is alphabetical by author with a subject index. Preface and introductory essay in English. Z2556.B5

Budd, John. Eight Scandinavian novelists: criticism and reviews in English. Westport, Conn., Greenwood Pr., [1981]. 180p. **BD890**

Treats Jonas Lie, Arne Garborg, Selma Lagerlöf, Knut Hamsun, Sigrid Undset, Pär Lagerkvist, Vilhelm Moberg, Halldór Laxness. Indexed. Z2559.F52B82

Göttingen. Universität. Skandinavisches Seminar. Bibliographie der Runeninschriften nach Fundorten, hrsg. . . . im Auftrag von Wolfgang Krause. Göttingen, Vandenhoeck & Ruprecht, 1961–73. v.1–2. (Abhandlungen der Akademie der Wissenschaften in Göttingen. Phil.-Hist. Kl., 3. Folge, Nr. 48, 80) **BD891**

Contents: v.1, Die Runeninschriften der britischen Inseln, von Hertha Marquardt; v.2, Die Runeninschriften des europäischen Kontinents, von Uwe Schnall.

An extensive bibliography of books and articles on runic inscriptions and allied archaeological remains.

Hollander, Lee Milton. A bibliography of skaldic studies. Copenhagen, Munksgaard, [1958]. 117p. **BD892**

Lists editions and collections of skaldic verse, as well as books and articles about it. Index of authors, editors, and translators. Z2555.H6

Nordische Bibliographie, hrsg. von dem Nordischen Institut der Universität Greifswald. I. Reihe, Norwegen; II. Reihe, Schweden. Braunschweig, Westermann, 1928–31. v.1¹⁻³–2¹. **BD893**

Contents: I. Reihe, Norwegen: 1.Hft., Ibsen-Bibliographie, bearb. von Fritz Meyen (1928); 2.Hft., Norwegische Literatur (ausser Ibsen), bearb. von Fritz Meyen (1928); 3.Hft., Hamsun-Bibliographie, bearb. von Fritz Meyen (1931); II. Reihe, Schweden: 1.Hft., Lagerlöf-Bibliographie (1930).

No more published.

Dictionaries of authors

Ehrencron-Müller, Holger. Forfatterlexikon omfattende Danmark, Norge og Island indtil 1814. København, Aschehoug, 1924–39. v.1–12; Suppl.2. **BD894**

v.1–8, A–Weg; v.9, Wei–Ø. Supplement; v.10–12, Bibliografi over Holbergs Skrifter. Supplement 2. The latter includes corrections and additions to all volumes, including the Holberg bibliography.

An authoritative work, giving brief biographical data and full lists of writings for each author. Similar in plan to the dictionaries by Erslew (BD904) and Halvorsen (BD916), and linked to those two works by cross references in the case of many authors whose activity extended into the period after 1814. Z2570.E33

History

Blankner, Frederika. The history of the Scandinavian literatures . . . based in part on the work of Giovanni Bach with additional sections by Richard Beck, Adolph B. Benson, Axel Johan Uppvall and others. N.Y., Dial, 1938. 407p. (Repr.: Port Washington, N.Y., Kennikat, 1966) **BD895**

Subtitle: A survey of the literatures of Norway, Sweden, Denmark, Iceland and Finland, from their origins to the present day, including Scandinavian-American authors, and selected bibliographies.

The sections on Norwegian, Swedish, and Danish literature are based on the work of Giovanni Bach, translated and enlarged by Frederika Blankner. Other sections are by other specialists. Selected bibliographies of books and articles emphasize works in English. PT7063.B5

Rossel, Sven Hakon. A history of Scandinavian literature, 1870–1980. Tr. by Anne C. Ulmer in assoc. with the Univ. of Minnesota Pr. Minneapolis, The Press, [1982]. 492p. (Nordic ser., v.5) **BD896**

Translation and extension of Rossel's *Skandinavische Literatur, 1870–1970* (Stuttgart, W. Kohlhammer, 1973. 232p.). Brief bibliography; index of names. PT7065.R6

Danish

Bibliography

Bredsdorff, Elias. Danish literature in English translation; with a special Hans Christian Andersen supplement: a bibliography. Copenhagen, Munksgaard, 1950. 198p. **BD897**

Covers translations of Danish literature into English from 1533 to 1949 and also lists materials in English about Danish literature. The Supplement, p.119–98, is "A bibliography of Hans Christian Andersen's works in English translation, and of books and articles relating to H. C. Andersen."

Supplemented by: Z2574.T7B7

Schroeder, Carol L. A bibliography of Danish literature in English translation, 1950–1980, with a selection of books about Denmark. [Copenhagen], Det Danske Selskab, [1982]. 197p. **BD898**

Includes sections for individual authors, individual genres, and anthologies. The "Books about Denmark" section is a classed listing of relevant English-language materials in many fields intended for the general reader. Z2574.T7S37

Elkjaer, Kjeld [and others]. Skønlitteratur i danske Tidsskrifter, 1913–1942; en Bibliografi. København, Folkebibliotekernes Bibliografiske Kontor, 1946. 236p. **BD899**

Largely devoted to Danish literature, but also includes references to articles that have appeared in Danish periodicals on foreign literatures.

Lindtner, Niels Christian. Danske klassikere: en selektiv bibliografi. København, Danmarks Biblioteksskole, 1976. 200p. (Copenhagen. Danmarks Biblioteksskole. Skrifter, no. 11) **BD900**

A selective bibliography of the writings of Denmark's major authors. Z2571.L45

Mitchell, Philip Marshall. A bibliographical guide to Danish literature. Copenhagen, Munksgaard, 1951. 62p. **BD901**

A bibliography intended to indicate the most important works of Danish literature, literary history, and criticism, showing standard editions, translations, biographical and critical works, etc. The works considered most significant are starred.   Z2571.M5

Dictionaries of authors

Dansk skønlitteraert Forfatterleksikon, 1900–1950. Bibliografisk red., Svend Dahl; Medredaktører, Ludvig Bramsen og Mogens Haugsted; Biografisk red., Povl Engelstoft. København, Grønholt Pedersen, 1959–64. 3v.   **BD902**

A bio-bibliographical dictionary which treats some 3,500 20th-century Danish literary figures. The bibliographies, though presented in abbreviated form, appear to be very comprehensive. Data are meant to be complete through 1950, with some later listings.   Z2573.3.D3

Danske Digtere i det 20. Arhundrede. Ny forøget og revideret Udgave redigeret af Frederik Nielsen og Ole Restrup. København, Gads Forlag, 1965–66. 3v. il.   **BD903**

Previous ed., 1951, ed. by Ernst Frandsen.

Contents: Bd.1, Tiden fra Johannes V. Jensen til første Verdenskrig; Bd.2, Tiden fra Tom Kristensen til anden Verdenskrig; Bd.3, Tiden fra H. C. Branner til i Dag.

A biographical dictionary of modern Danish poets. Long, signed articles, but without bibliographies. General index in v.3.
PT7760.N53

Erslew, Thomas Hansen. Almindeligt Forfatter-Lexicon for Kongeriget Danmark med tilhørende Bilande, fra 1814 til 1840. Kjøbenhavn, Forlagsforeningens Forlag, 1843–53. 3v.   **BD904**

———— ———— Supplement . . . indtil Udgangen of Aaret 1853. Kjøbenhavn, 1858–68. 3v.

An older, but still standard, dictionary giving biographical sketches of Danish authors with bibliographies, for the period 1814–53.
Z2570.E73

Woel, Cai Mogens. Dansk Forfatterleksikon; 338 Biografier over nulevende danske Forfattere. [København], Nordiske Landes Bogforlag, 1945. 360p. il.   **BD905**

Biographical sketches with bibliographies of living authors.

History

Dansk litteraturhistorie. Copenhagen, Gyldendal, 1983–84. v.2–4, 7. (In progress)   **BD906**

Contents: v.2, Laerdom og magi 1480–1620; v.3, Staenderkultur og enevaelde 1620–1746; v.4, Patriotismens tid 1746–1807; v.7, Demokrati og kulturkamp 1901–45.

An extensive new history, each volume edited by a different scholar; to be complete in 9v. Includes bibliographical references and indexes.

Petersen, Carl Sophus and **Andersen, Vilhelm.** Illustreret dansk Litteraturhistorie. Kjøbenhavn, Gyldendal, 1924–34. 4v. il.   **BD907**

Issued in parts: v.1, 1929; v.2, 1934; v.3, 1924; v.4, 1925.

Planned as a third revised edition of Peter Hansen's *Illustreret dansk Litteraturhistorie,* the standard illustrated history of Danish literature, with extensive bibliographies at the end of each volume.
PT7660.P35

Finnish

Ahokas, Jaakko. A history of Finnish literature. [Bloomington], Publ. for the American-Scandinavian Foundation by Indiana Univ., Research Center for the Language Sciences, [1973]. 568p. ports.   **BD908**

Covers from the beginnings to the mid-20th century. Bibliographic notes; index of names and titles.   PH301.A35

Suomen kirjailijat 1945–1970: pienoiselämäkerrat: teosbibliografiat: tutkimusviitteet. Toim., Hannu Launonen [et al.]. [Helsinki], SKS, 1977. 438p. il. (Suomalaisen Kirjallisuuden Seura. Toimituksia, 332)   **BD909**

A dictionary arrangement of entries for 20th-century Finnish writers. Brief biographical data is followed by detailed lists of works by and about the authors. Title index.   Z2520.S945

Icelandic

See also AA872–AA874, BD887–BD896.

Hall, Gunnar. Bókaskrá Gunnars Hall. Catalogue of the library of Gunnar Hall. Akureyri, Prentad i Prentsmidju Björns Jónssonar, 1956. 520p.   **BD910**

A classified listing of an extensive collection of Icelandic and old Norse literature.

Leeds, Eng. University. Library. Icelandic Collection. A catalogue of the Icelandic collection. Leeds, The Library, 1978. 166p.   **BD911**

A main entry listing, with subject index, of a collection of more than 10,000 items.   Z2590.A3L43

Mitchell, Phillip Marshall and **Ober, Kenneth H.** Bibliography of modern Icelandic literature in translation, including works written by Icelanders in other languages. Ithaca, N.Y., Cornell Univ. Pr., 1975. 317p. (Islandica XL)   **BD912**

In two main sections: (1) Anthologies (grouped by language of translation), and (2) Works by individual authors (arranged alphabetically by author's name; translations of individual works are entered alphabetically by language of translation). Includes references to translations (including selections from longer works) appearing in periodicals, as parts of books, etc. Index of translators, editors and compilers.   Z2551.M57

Norwegian

Bibliography

See also AA990.

Næss, Harald S. Norwegian literary bibliography, 1956–1970. Red. Kaare Haukaas. Oslo, Universitetsforlaget, [1975]. 128p. (Norsk bibliografisk bibliotek, Bd. 50)   **BD913**

Added title page in Norwegian: *Norsk litteraturhistorisk bibliografi.*

Meant to be looked upon as a continuation of Øksnevad's *Norsk litteraturhistorisk bibliografi 1946–1955* (below).   Z2601.N33

Øksnevad, Reidar. Norsk litteraturhistorisk bibliografi, 1900–1945. Oslo, Gyldendal Norsk Forlag, 1951. 378p.   **BD914**

———— ———— 1946–1955. 1958. 139p.

A bibliography of books and periodical articles in various languages published in the 20th century on Norwegian literature and authors.   Z2601.O3

Dictionaries of authors

Bryan, George B. An Ibsen companion: a dictionary-guide to the life, works, and critical reception of Henrik Ibsen. Westport, Conn., Greenwood Pr., [1984]. 437p.   **BD915**

Offers entries for the individual plays (with stage histories, detailed synopses, bibliographic references) and characters, actors and actresses associated with various roles, translators, directors, etc. Chronology; select bibliography.   PT8887.B79

Halvorsen, Jens Braage. Norsk forfatter-lexikon, 1814–1880. Paa grundlag af J. E. Krafts og Chr. Langes "Norsk forfatterlexikon 1814–1856" samlet, redig. og udg. med understøttelse af statskassen. Kristiania, Norske Forlagsforening, 1885–1908. 6v. **BD916**

Biographical sketches with bibliographies of Norwegian authors. Preceded in time by Ehrencron-Müller (BD894). Z2600.H19

History

Beyer, Harald. A history of Norwegian literature. Tr. and ed. by Einar Haugen. [N.Y.], New York Univ. Pr. for the American-Scandinavian Foundation, [1957]. 370p. il. **BD917**

A translation of Beyer's *Norsk litteratur historie* (Oslo, Aschehoug, 1952). Bibliography, p.339–44. PT6360.B42

Elster, Kristian. Illustreret norsk litteratur historie. 2. utg. Oslo, Gyldendal, 1934–35. 6v. il. **BD918**

A standard illustrated history with bio-bibliographies. PT8360.E5

Swedish

Bibliography

Hagström, Tore, comp. Svensk litteraturhistorisk bibliografi intill ar 1900. Uppsala, Svenska Litteratursällskapet, 1964–82. (In progress) (Skrifter utgivna av Svenska litteratursällskapet, 34, H.1–6) **BD919**

A retrospective bibliography which will cover the period prior to the beginning of the *Svensk litteraturhistorisk bibliografi* 1900–35 (below). Z2621.H3

Svensk litteraturhistorisk bibliografi 1900–1935. Uppsala, Svenska Litteratursällskapet, 1939–50. 522p. (Skrifter utg. av Svenska Litteratursällskapet 29:1–6) **BD920**

Issued in 6 pts. Jonas Samzelius, ed.
A cumulation of the annual bibliographies appearing as a separately paged supplement of the Svenska Litteratursällskapet's journal *Samlaren,* below. Z2631.S8

Svensk litteraturhistorisk bibliografi. no.1– , 1880– . (Issued as a separately paged supplement to Samlaren: Tidskrift för svensk litteraturhistorisk forskning, 1880–) **BD921**

An annual classified bibliography; publication has been slightly irregular in recent years.

———— 1951–1960. Monografier. Lund, 1965. 243p.

Entries from the annual bibliographies have been clipped and rearranged alphabetically by name of the author treated. Z2631.S8

Dictionaries of authors

Åhlén, Bengt. Svenskt författarlexikon, 1900–1940: biobibliografisk handbok till Sveriges moderna litteratur. . . . Stockholm, Svenskt Författarlexikons Förlag, [1942.] 3v. **BD922**

v.1–2 are an alphabetical biographical dictionary with brief biographical sketches and lists of works by and about the authors. v.3 is a title index to works mentioned in the first 2v. Z2630.A15

———— ———— 1941–1950, 1951–1955, 1956–1960, 1961–1965, 1966–1970, 1971–1975. Stockholm, Rabén & Sjögren, [1953–81]. 6v. and Register 1941–1955.

Editors vary. Z2630.A152

Runnquist, Åke. Moderna svenska författare. En samblad översikt över svensk litteratur under fyra årtionden. 2. omarb., utökade uppl. Stockholm, Forum, 1967. 255p. il. **BD923**

An earlier edition (1959) grouped writers by period—the 'Thir-

ties, 'Forties, and 'Fifties. This is a dictionary arrangement of brief biographical sketches of modern Swedish writers, with an index of names and titles. PT9368.R8

Svenskt litteraturlexikon. 2. utvidgáde uppl. Lund, Gleerup, 1970. 643p. **BD924**

A handbook offering biographical sketches of Swedish authors together with definitions of literary terms. Some articles include bibliographical references. Contains an index of titles mentioned in the biographical sketches. PT9217.S9

History

Gustafson, Alrik. A history of Swedish literature. Minneapolis, Publ. for the American-Scandinavian Foundation by Univ. of Minnesota Pr., [1961]. 708p. il. **BD925**

Includes "A bibliographical guide for additional readings and studies," p.567–644, and "A list of translations into English, with some critical and explanatory notes," p.645–60. Indexed. PT9263.G8

Ny illustrerad svensk litteraturhistoria. Huvudredaktör E. N. Tigerstedt. [2. bearbetade uppl.] Stockholm, Natur och Kultur, [1967]. 4v. **BD926**

Contents: v.1, Forntiden. Medeltiden. Vasatiden; v.2, Karolinska tiden. Frihetstiden. Gustavianska tiden; v.3, Romantiken. Liberalismen; v.4, Attiotal. Nittiotal.
An illustrated history of Swedish literature, the first edition (1955–58 in 5v.) of which was designed to supersede the standard *Illustrerad svensk litteraturhistoria* by Henrik Schück and Karl Warburg (3. uppl. 1926–32. 7v.). Although not numbered in the series, Erik H. Linder's *Fem decennier av nittonhundratalet* (Stockholm, Natur och Kultur, 1965–66. 2v.) is a revision, updating, and expansion of the same author's *Fyra decennier av nittonhundratalet* (1958) which makes up v.5 of the 1955–58 edition of the history.
Each section is by a specialist, with substantial bibliographies at the end of each volume. PT9260.N9

Svenska litteraturens historia, av Fredrik Böök [et al.]. Ny omarb. uppl. Stockholm, Norstedt, 1929. 3v. il. **BD927**

A general history with bibliographies. PT9260.S7

Sveriges national-litteratur, 1500–1900, planlagdt af Oscar Levertin, utg. af Henrik Schück och Ruben G:son Berg. Stockholm, Bonnier, [1907–19]. v.1–25$^{1-2}$. il. **BD928**

An extensive collection of prose, poetical, and dramatic selections, with biographies of some of the authors represented. The arrangement is roughly chronological, some volumes being devoted to only one author, others including a number of authors. The lack of a general index makes the set difficult to use for quick reference.

ROMANCE LANGUAGES

General works

Guides

Palfrey, Thomas Rossman, Fucilla, Joseph Guerin and **Holbrook, William Collar.** A bibliographical guide to the Romance languages and literatures. 8th ed. Evanston, Ill., Chandler, 1971. 122p. **BD929**

1st ed. 1939.
Contents: (1) General Romance bibliography; (2) French language and literature (including Provençal, French-Swiss, Belgian); (3) Italian; (4) Portuguese and Brazilian; (5) Spanish, Catalan, Spanish-American; (6) Roumanian. Z7031.P15

Bibliography

Flasche, Hans. Die Sprachen und Literaturen der Romanen im Spiegel der deutschen Universitätsschriften, 1885–1950; eine Bibliographie. Bonn, Bouvier, 1958. 299p. (Bonner Beiträge zur Bibliotheks- und Bücherkunde, Bd.3)
BD930

In German, French, and English.

Published also by the Bibliographical Society of the University of Virginia under the title *Romance languages and literatures as presented in German doctoral dissertations, 1885–1950; a bibliography.*

A listing of more than 4,600 German dissertations from the 1885–1950 period; classified arrangement with author and subject indexes.

A companion volume to Mummendey's bibliography (BD507).
Z7031.F55

Hatzfeld, Helmut. Bibliografía crítica de la nueva estilística, aplicada a las literaturas románicas. Madrid, Ed. Gredos, 1955. 660p. (Biblioteca románica hispánica. I. Tratados y monografías. 6)
BD931

A survey bibliography of style investigation, treating general studies, stylistic comparison, the language of individual authors, history of style, theory of style, and many specialized aspects of stylistics. Two indexes: (1) style investigators; and (2) proper names, titles, problems, terms, etc.

The first edition in English was entitled *A critical bibliography of the new stylistics applied to the Romance literatures, 1900–1952* (Chapel Hill, N.C., 1953. 302p.; Repr.: N.Y., Johnson, 1970). This Spanish version is equivalent to a considerably expanded 2d ed.

—— A critical bibliography of the new stylistics applied to the Romance literatures, 1953–1965. Chapel Hill, [Univ. of North Carolina Pr.], 1966. 184p. (Univ. of North Carolina studies in comparative literature, 37) **BD932**

Intended as a supplement to the 1953 American edition of the same title. However, since this is a more selective work than the Spanish enlarged edition (above) and the 1955–60 supplementary volume (below), none of the earlier editions is fully superseded.
Z6514.S8H35

—— and **Le Hir, Yves.** Essai de bibliographie critique de stylistique française et romane (1955–1960). Paris, Presses Universitaires de France, 1961. 313p. (Université de Grenoble. Faculté des Lettres et Sciences Humaines. Pubn.26)
BD933

Serves as a supplement to the Spanish enlarged edition (BD931) of Hatzfeld's bibliography of stylistics, covering publications of the years 1955–60.
Z7031.H33

Translations

Parks, George B. and **Temple, Ruth Z.,** eds. The Romance literatures. N.Y., Ungar, [1970]. 1v. in 2. (Literatures of the world in English translation, v.3)
BD934

For a note on the series *see* BD35.

Contents: pt.1, Catalan, Italian, Portuguese and Brazilian, Provençal, Rumanian, Spanish and Spanish American literatures; pt.2, French literature.

Follows the plan of v.1 of the series (BD1389), with contributing scholars assuming responsibility for various sections. Includes entries through 1968.
Z7033.T7E56

Criticism

Curley, Dorothy Nyren and **Curley, Arthur,** comps. Modern Romance literatures. N.Y., Ungar, [1967]. 510p. (A library of literary criticism)
BD935

Like D. N. Curley's volume for modern American literature (BD399) and Temple and Tucker's work for modern British literature (BD553), this is a compilation of excerpts from critical writings

appearing in journals and books of both a scholarly and a popular nature. Authors were selected "both because of their intrinsic merit and because of the extent of American interest in them."— *Foreword.* Mainly writers of the 20th century are included. Index to critics.
PN813.C8

African writers (French)

Baratte-Eno Belinga, Thérèse, Chauveau-Rabut, Jacqueline and **Kadima-Nzuji, Mukala.** Bibliographie des auteurs africains de langue française. 4ᵉ éd. [Paris], Fernand Nathan, [1979]. 245p.
BD936

1st ed. 1965.

Lists French-language writings by African authors, including numerous publications outside the field of literature. Arranged by country, with subdivisions for bibliographies, anthologies, and individual authors. About 2,300 entries; index of authors.

Déjeux, Jean. Bibliographie de la littérature "algérienne" des Français. Paris, Éditions du Centre National de la Recherche Scientifique, 1978. 116p. (Centre de Recherches et d'Études sur les Sociétés Méditerranéennes. Cahiers, 7)
BD937

Subtitle: Bibliographie des romans, récits et recueils de nouvelles écrits par des Français inspirés par l'Algérie 1896–1975, précédée de la bibliographie des études sur la littérature "algérienne" des Français.

In two parts, as indicated in the subtitle, the first listing some 430 items; the second, 652 items. The two parts are separately indexed.
Z2174.P795D44

—— Bibliographie méthodique et critique de la littérature algérienne de langue française, 1945–1977. Alger, Société Nationale d'Édition et de Diffusion, [1979]. 307p.
BD938

Publications prior to Algerian independence (July 1, 1962) are listed in the first section, those following independence in the second; both have subsections for general studies and for studies of individual genres, with further subdivision as appropriate. Annotations; index.
Z3684.L5D44

—— Dictionnaire des auteurs maghrebins de langue française. Paris, Karthala, [1984]. 400p.
BD939

"Algérie: littérature de fiction et d'essais, histoire, sciences humaines, arts (1880–1982); Maroc: littérature de fiction et d'essais (1920–1982); Tunisie: littérature de fiction et d'essais (1900–1982)." —*t.p.*

Offers brief biographical notes with lists of works; separate section for each country. Appendixes; index.

Dugas, Guy. Bibliographie de la littérature "Tunisienne" des Français, 1881–1980. Paris, Éds. du Centre National de la Recherche Scientifique, 1981. 86p. (Cahiers du C.R.E.S.M., 13)
BD940

At head of title: Centre de Recherches et d'Études sur les Sociétés Méditerranéennes.

Includes a section of studies of the literature as well as editions of works of belles lettres and books of travel. Author index.
Z2174.P795D83

Belgian writers

Charlier, Gustave and **Hanse, Joseph.** Histoire illustrée des lettres françaises de Belgique. Bruxelles, Renaissance du Livre, [1958]. 656p. il.
BD941

A lavishly illustrated history of the literature of Belgium, in French, from the earliest times to the present day. Chapters are written by specialists and include bibliographies.
PQ3814.C5

Coppe, Paul and **Pirsoul, Léon.** Dictionnaire bio-bibliographique des littérateurs d'expression wallonne, 1622 à 1950. Gembloux, Duculot, [1951]. 415p. **BD942**

Includes 1,325 sketches and lists some 25,000 titles of works in the Walloon dialect. The sketch of each author indicates place and date of birth and death; pseudonym, if any; profession; and a concise critical note on the value of his contribution and the titles of his works. Bibliographical information is brief, usually consisting of title and date (in some cases dates are omitted). Z2424.W3C6

Culot, Jean-Marie. Bibliographie des écrivains français de Belgique, 1881–1950. Bruxelles, Palais des Académies, 1958–72. v.1–4. (In progress) **BD943**

Contents: v.1, Ouvrages d'histoire littéraire et de critique d'une portée générale ou relatifs à plusieurs écrivains, 1880–1950. Anthologies et ouvrages collectifs; Auteurs, A–Destrée; v.2–4, Det–N. (With v.2 the period of coverage was extended to 1960, and a section of general works for the period 1950–60 is included in that volume.)

Planned to continue the *Bibliographie nationale* (AA624) for writers in the field of literature. For each writer gives: dates, works by, and periodicals and collections to which he has contributed, with a list of works to consult. Z2413.C8

Hanlet, Camille. Les écrivains belges contemporains de langue française, 1800–1946. Liège, Dessain, 1946. 2v. (1302p.). il. **BD944**

An extensive survey of all Belgian authors writing in French from the 18th century to 1946. The length of the biography and critical annotation varies from a few lines to several pages. For many writers, bibliographies of works about the person are included. PQ3814.H3

Seyn, Eugène de. Dictionnaire des écrivains belges, bio-bibliographie. Bruges, Éd. "Excelsior," 1930–31. 2v. il. **BD945**

Includes bio-bibliographical sketches of writers considered to be Belgian, from early to modern times. Gives little or no bibliography about the writers. Z2410.S52

Canadian writers (French)

Barbeau, Victor and **Fortier, André.** Dictionnaire bibliographique du Canada français. Montréal, Académie Canadienne-française, [1974]. 246p. **BD946**

A bibliography of the writings of French Canadian authors, together with writings on Canada by French authors. Brief biographical notes are provided in most instances. Z1365.B3

British Columbia. University. Library. A checklist of printed materials relating to French-Canadian literature, 1763–1968. 2d ed. Vancouver, Univ. of British Columbia Pr., [1973]. 174p. **BD947**

Title also in French. Prefatory matter in English and French.
1st ed. 1958.
Gérard Tougas, comp.
Lists works by and about French-Canadian authors.
Z1377.F8B72

Drolet, Antonio. Bibliographie du roman canadien-français, 1900–1950. Québec, Presses Universitaires de Laval, 1955. 125p. **BD948**

An author listing of 886 titles of French-Canadian novels, preceded by a list of critical studies on the subject. Title index.
Z1377.F8D7

Grandpré, Pierre de. Histoire de la littérature française du Québec. Montréal, Librairie Beauchemin, 1967–69. 4v. il. **BD949**

A collaborative history consisting mainly of bio-bibliographies of

authors with selections from their works. Includes historians, journalists, and critics as well as literary figures. Profusely illustrated.
PQ3917.G7

Hayne, David M. and **Tirol, Marcel.** Bibliographie critique du roman canadien-français, 1837–1900. [Toronto], Univ. of Toronto Pr., [1968]. 144p. **BD950**

Concerned with the work of Canadian authors writing in French, this bibliography lists the editions (including serializations and published extracts), English translations, and significant studies of French-Canadian prose fiction. Many helpful notes and annotations. Indexed. Z1377.F8H3

Tougas, Gérard. Histoire de la littérature canadienne-française. 4. éd. Paris, Presses Universitaires de France, 1967. 312p. **BD951**

1st ed. 1960.
Also published in English: *History of French-Canadian literature,* tr. by Alta Lind Cook (2d ed. Toronto, Ryerson Pr., 1966).
A critical survey arranged by period and genre. Includes excerpts from major authors and analyses of their work. Bibliographical references in footnotes; author and title index. PQ3901.R6

French

Guides

Beugnot, Bernard and **Moureaux, J. M.** Manuel bibliographique des études littéraires; les bases de l'histoire littéraire, les voies nouvelles de l'analyse critique. [Paris], Nathan, [1982]. 478p. **BD952**

A bibliographic guide for the graduate student of French literature. Treats the basic tools of literary research, the principal areas of research (including the relationships of literature and the arts, psychoanalysis, sociology, etc.), and new trends in literary research (including French literature outside France). Z6511.B48

Kempton, Richard. French literature: an annotated guide to selected bibliographies. N.Y., Modern Language Assoc. of America, 1981. 42p. (Selected bibliographies in language and literature, 2) **BD953**

An annotated "selected listing of major bibliographies on French literature, most of which can be found in the libraries of institutions where graduate instruction in French is offered."—*Introd.* Indexed.
Z2171.A1C34

Osburn, Charles B. Research and reference guide to French studies. 2d ed. Metuchen, N.J., Scarecrow Pr., 1981. 532p. **BD954**

1st ed. 1968; suppl., 1972.
The earlier edition attempted to cover the whole range of French studies; this revision concentrates on French literature, with limited attention to peripheral fields. About 6,000 citations to "concordances, literary and language dictionaries, iconographies, filmographies, encyclopedias, surveys of scholarship, and especially, bibliographies" (*Introd.*) are grouped in five main sections: French literature (subdivided by period), French language, French language and literature outside France, Romance philology and Occitan studies, general background and related areas. Author and subject indexes.
Z2175.A2O8

Sources

Gallet-Guerne, Danielle. Les sources de l'histoire littéraire aux Archives Nationales. Paris, Impr. Nationale, 1961. 161p. **BD955**

At head of title: Ministère d'État Chargé des Affaires Culturelles. Direction des Archives de France. Archives Nationales.
A guide to the manuscript materials concerning French authors to be found in the various archives of France.

Bibliography

General

Arbour, Roméo. L'ère baroque en France; répertoire chronologique des éditions de textes littéraires. Première partie, 1585–1615. Genève, Droz, 1977. 2v. (Histoire des idées et critique littéraire, v.165) **BD956**

A year-by-year listing of literary texts published in France (whether in French or foreign languages, and including translations) and of French literary texts published abroad. Library locations (including many American locations and European libraries outside France) are given whenever possible, with source of the citation provided when there is no known location. More than 7,900 entries; indexes of names of persons, of editors, and of places of publication. The compiler presumably intends to extend the work through 1640.

Z2162.A72

A critical bibliography of French literature. Syracuse, N.Y., Syracuse Univ. Pr., 1947–85. v.1–4 and suppl., v.6, pts.1–3. (In progress) **BD957**

David Clark Cabeen was the original editor and the set is often referred to as "Cabeen"; Jules Brody became joint general editor with v.3; and with v.6 Richard A. Brooks became general editor.

Contents: v.1, The mediaeval period, ed. by Urban T. Holmes (1947; enl. ed. 1952); v.2, The sixteenth century, ed. by Alexander H. Schutz (1956); v.2, rev., The sixteenth century, ed. by Raymond C. La Charité (1985); v.3, The seventeenth century, ed. by Nathan Edelman (1961); v.3A, The seventeenth century; supplement, ed. by H. Gaston Hall (1983); v.4, The eighteenth century, ed. by George R. Havens and Donald F. Bond (1951); Supplement [to v.4], ed. by Richard A. Brooks (1968); v.6, The twentieth century, ed. by Douglas W. Alden and Richard A. Brooks (pt.1, General subjects and principally the novel before 1940; pt.2, Principally poetry, theater, and criticism before 1940, and essay; pt.3, All genres since 1940; index. 1980).

A work of first importance, this is a selective, evaluative, and annotated bibliography compiled by contributing specialists. Arranged by chronological periods; lists books, dissertations, and periodical articles, with references to reviews. Each volume has its own index.

In view of the greatly accelerated scholarly activity in the field of 16th-century French literature since publication of the original v.2, it was decided to make the new v.2 a thorough re-examination and re-evaluation. Although designated "revised" on the title page, the introduction to the 1985 volume states that "this volume is neither a revised edition of the 1956 publication nor a mere supplement to it. It is an entirely new and comprehensive work. The 1956 publication is not to be dismissed, however. Numerous entries in this volume refer specifically by number to assessments in the 1956 volume, and readers will no doubt profit from cross-references and comparisons that are both explicit and implicit." There has also been some reorganization of content in the new volume.

v.3A is a supplement to the 1961 volume for the 17th century, extending the listings of editions and critical works through 1979. However, owing to various delays and editorial decisions, "the user may be less assured that exclusions for 1977–78 are deliberate than for the earlier years, while partial coverage of 1979 is offered for future convenience and not for completeness."—*Introd.*

The volume covering the 19th century is still unpublished, and users of v.6 "should assume that any significant turn-of-the-century author who does not appear in this volume has been relegated to the nineteenth century."—*Introd.* Z2171.C74

Giraud, Jeanne. Manuel de bibliographie littéraire pour les XVIe, XVIIe et XVIIIe siècles français, 1921–1935. 2. éd., conforme à la première. Paris, Vrin, 1958. 304p. (Publications de la Faculté des Lettres de l'Université de Lille, II) **BD958**

Reprint of the work originally published 1939.

——— ——— 1936–1945. Paris, Nizet, 1956. 270p.

——— ——— 1946–1955. Paris, Nizet, 1970. 493p.

The basic volume and its supplements are designed to serve as continuations of the listings in Lanson (BD961) and Thième (BD987) for the 1931–55 period.

Griffin, Lloyd W., Clarke, Jack A. and Kroff, Alexander Y. Modern French literature and language; a bibliography of homage studies. [Madison], Univ. of Wisconsin Pr., [1976]. 175p. **BD959**

"Produced and distributed *on demand* by Xerox University Microfilms, Ann Arbor, Mich."—*verso of t.p.*

Both supersedes and extends the coverage of the 1953 bibliography of the same title by H. H. Golden and S. O. Simches. Includes references to articles pertinent to French language and literature appearing in some 588 homage volumes; a listing of the *Festschriften* is followed by a classified listing of the relevant contributions. Cutoff date is 1974 with some 1975 items included. Name index with reference both to authors of the articles analyzed and to literary authors as subjects (the latter designated by an asterisk).

Z2175.F45G74

Harvard University. Library. French literature. Cambridge, Mass., Harvard Univ. Lib., 1973. 2v. (Widener Library shelflist, 47–48) **BD960**

Contents: v.1, Classification schedule; classified listing by call number; chronological listing; v.2, Author and title listing.

These volumes "list nearly 52,000 titles representing historical and critical works on French literature, anthologies, and individual literary works written in French. Histories and anthologies of global scope appear, but the focus of this collection is on European literature in French."—*Pref.*

For a note on the series *see* AA145. Z2189.H3

Lanson, Gustave. Manuel bibliographique de la littérature française moderne, XVIe, XVIIe, XVIIIe, et XIXe siècles. Nouv. éd., rev. et augm. Paris, Hachette, 1921. 1820p. **BD961**

1st ed. in 5v., 1909–12; rev. ed. with suppl., 1v., 1914. The 1921 edition contains a brief section on the beginning of the 20th century and the "littérature de la guerre."

An important bibliography of French literature—selective, not complete—comprising more than 23,000 entries. Indexes a considerable amount of analytical material, including articles from more than 800 periodicals.

For continuation *see* BD958. Z2171.L22

Osburn, Charles B., ed. The present state of French studies: a collection of research reviews. Metuchen, N.J., Scarecrow Pr., 1971. 995p. **BD962**

Reprints from various sources bibliographic essays on some 40 topics in French literature from medieval through modern times. Since some of the essays originally appeared as early as the 1950s, the editor has provided an appendix of supplementary bibliographic essays to bring the coverage up through the late 1960s. Index of topics. PQ51.O8

Current

Bibliographie de la littérature française du Moyen Âge à nos jours. Année 1953–80. Paris, A. Colin, 1953–81. Annual. **BD963**

At head of title: René Rancoeur.

Title varies: 1953–61, *Bibliographie littéraire*; 1962–65, *Bibliographie de la littérature française moderne (XVIe–XXe siècles)*.

1953–61 published as reprints of bibliographies appearing in *Revue d'histoire littéraire de la France.* Indexes: 1953–55 in 1955; 1956–58 in 1958; 1959–61 in 1961. Ceased publication.

A general section is followed by period divisions arranged according to author treated. Indexes of author and of topical subjects.

Z2171.B54

Bibliographie der französischen Literaturwissenschaft, hrsg. von Otto Klapp. Bd.1– , 1956/58- . Frankfurt am Main, Klostermann, 1960– . v.1– . Annual. **BD964**

Frequency varies; v.1–6, biennial.

Added title page in French: Bibliographie d'histoire littéraire française. Introduction and headings in French.

Planned as a companion to H. W. Eppelsheimer, *Bibliographie der deutschen Literaturwissenschaft* (BD829*n*), this work interprets French literature in a broad sense. Lists books, articles, and theses published during the period covered, analyzing in each volume some 400 periodicals and more than 150 collections. Arrangement is chronological, from the Middle Ages to the 20th century, with indexes by name and by subject.　　Z2171.B56

—— Supplement zu den Bänden I–VI (1956–1968); Sachregister bearb. von Friedrich-Albert Klapp. Frankfurt am Main, Klostermann, 1970. 111p.

Current research in French studies at universities and polytechnics in the United Kingdom, 1970/71– . [London, Birkbeck College Library, 1971–] Annual.　　**BD965**

Title varies slightly.

Comp. for the Association of University Professors of French in association with the Modern Humanities Research Association by A. Carey Taylor.

A subject list in three sections: (1) Linguistic studies and stylistics; (2) Literary, historical and sociological studies not referring to a specific writer, historical figure, or anonymous work; (3) Alphabetical list of writers, historical figures, and anonymous works.

Dissertations

Gabel, Gernot U. Répertoire bibliographique des thèses françaises (1885–1975) concernant la littérature française des origines à nos jours. Köln, Gemini, 1984. (Bibliographien zur Romanistik, 3)　　**BD966**

4,100 entries grouped chronologically by century; within each period a general section is followed by an alphabetical arrangement of authors treated. Indexes of authors of the theses and of subjects.

Periodicals

Admussen, Richard L. Les petites revues littéraires, 1914–1939; répertoire descriptif. Paris, Nizet; St. Louis, Washington Univ. Pr., 1970. 158p.　　**BD967**

A title listing of literary "little magazines" appearing between the wars. Gives notes on dates of publication, contents, principal contributors, etc. Index of names cited.

Place, Jean Michel and **Vasseur, André** Bibliographie des revues et journaux littéraires des XIXᵉ et XXᵉ siècles. Paris, Éditions de la Chronique des Lettres Françaises, 1973–77. 3v.　　**BD968**

Gives for each title: history, complete publication information, list of important collaborators, excerpts, and table of contents of each number. Intends to be a complete listing of all literary journals published in France during the period covered.

v.1–2 are concerned with journals which began publication before 1900. v.3 treats a group of periodicals which began publication during the period 1915–30; it includes an index of names cited.　　PQ2.P5

Translations

See also BD934.

Bowe, Forrest. French literature in early American translation; a bibliographical survey of books and pamphlets printed in the United States from 1668 through 1820. Ed. by Mary Daniels. N.Y., Garland Pr., 1977. 528p.　　**BD969**

The bibliography is "limited to translations of works written in French which were published in the United States from the colonial period through the year 1820. It includes books and pamphlets, as well as some broadside material. . . . In general, unless a printed text in French which served as a basis for an English translation has been located, . . . problematical works have been omitted."—*p.xxiii.* Arranged in sections according to the general subject content of the

works translated (e.g., philosophy and religion, social sciences, history and biography, fiction and verse, drama, etc.); index of authors, translators and editors, and of French and English titles. Numerous descriptive and explanatory notes. Locates copies (many of the works being in the Bowe collection now at Cornell).　　Z1215.B66

Medieval

See also Provençal, p.497.

Bossuat, Robert. Manuel bibliographique de la littérature française du Moyen Âge. Melun, Librairie d'Argences, 1951. 638p. (Bibliothèque Elzévirienne. Nouv. sér. Études et documents)　　**BD970**

A bibliographical manual of the French literature of the Middle Ages, listing material in French and other western European languages. After an introduction giving general works, the book is divided into two sections: *L'ancien français* and *Le moyen français*. For each work, the principal editions are listed, followed by translations and adaptations, and critical works. The latter include both books and periodical articles.

—— —— Supplément, 1949–1953, avec le concours de Jacques Monfrin. 1955. 150p.

—— —— 2d supplément, 1954–1960. 1961. 132p.　　Z2172.B7

Duggan, Joseph J. A guide to studies on the *Chanson de Roland*. [London], Grant & Cutler, 1976. 133p.　　**BD971**

A bibliography for students and scholars, concentrating on publications of the period 1955–74. "For the period preceding 1955, items of overriding critical or historical significance have been included, as well as those which provide extensive bibliographies or outstanding surveys of the subjects to which they are devoted."—*Pref.* Includes editions of the text as well as critical studies. Classed arrangement with index of scholars and translators.　　Z6521.R7D83

Gautier, Léon. Bibliographie des chansons de geste. (Complément des Épopées françaises) Paris, Welter, 1897. 315p.　　**BD972**

Forms v.5 of the author's *Les épopées françaises* (BD1007).

A valuable comprehensive bibliography in two parts. The first part is a classed list of general works; the second is devoted to works about individual *chansons*.　　Z2172.G27

Linker, Robert White. A bibliography of old French lyrics. University, Miss., Romance Monographs, Inc., 1979. 401p. (Romance monographs, 31)　　**BD973**

Constitutes a reworking and updating of the material in Gaston Raynaud's *Bibliographie des chansonniers français* (Paris, 1884) and subsequent corrections and additions to that work.

In two main parts, the first listing bibliographies of manuscripts, descriptions of major manuscripts, a general bibliography of lyrics published in anthologies, periodicals, etc., and works on types of lyrics and on metrics and music of the poems; the second part is the bibliography of the lyrics themselves, arranged by name of the trouvère, then by initial word (anonymous poems are listed separately by first word). There is a cross-index of Raynaud and Linker entry numbers.　　Z2174.P7L55

Société Rencesvals. Bulletin bibliographique. Paris, 1958– . fasc.1– . Irregular.　　**BD974**

An annotated listing of books and articles on the *Chanson de Roland* and other medieval epics.　　PQ201.S66a

Woledge, Brian. Bibliographie des romans et nouvelles en prose française antérieurs à 1500. Genève, Droz, 1954. 180p. (Société de Publications romanes et françaises sous la direction de Mario Roques, 42)　　**BD975**

Lists 190 early French romances, with indication of manuscripts,

printings, sources, etc. Supplementary lists of manuscripts are arranged by city, printers, authors, titles, literary themes, etc.
Z2174.F4W64

—— —— Supplément, 1954–1973. Genève, Droz, 1975. 139p. (Publications romanes et françaises, 42)

—— Répertoire des plus anciens textes en prose française, depuis 842 jusqu'aux premières années du XIIIe siècle. Genève, Droz, 1964. 155p. (Publications romanes et françaises, 79)   **BD976**

A title listing of all recorded French prose texts to 1210, with date, place, manuscripts, incipit, published editions, and secondary sources. Indexes by manuscripts, place, dialect, and incipit.
PQ607.W6

16th–18th centuries

Cioranescu, Alexandre. Bibliographie de la littérature française du seizième siècle. Collaboration et préface de V.-L. Saulnier. Paris, Klincksieck, 1959. 745p.   **BD977**

In two parts: (1) *Généralités,* and (2) individual authors. Pt.2, the larger section, is arranged alphabetically by 16th-century author, listing works by him followed by a record of studies about him, including books and articles published through 1950. The explanation of the coverage of the index should be noted. In general, it includes the names of authors or persons *not* included in alphabetical order in the main work, names of places, anonymous works, literary themes, etc. It does not index the main entries for 16th-century works or the names of the modern authors of books and periodical articles.   Z2172.C5

—— Bibliographie de la littérature française du dix-septième siècle. Paris, Centre National de la Recherche Scientifique, 1965–66. 3v.   **BD978**

Similar in plan to the author's bibliography for 16th-century French literature (above), but confining itself more closely to literature alone. Again, a general section—with subdivisions for literary history, social and religious background, literary forms, etc.—is followed by the bibliographies of individual authors. Author and subject indexes. More comprehensive than the corresponding volume of Cabeen (BD957), but without the annotations as found in that work.   Z2172.C52

—— Bibliographie de la littérature française du dix-huitième siècle . . . Paris, Éditions du Centre National de la Recherches Scientifique, 1969. 3v.   **BD979**

Similar to the compiler's bibliographies for the 16th and 17th centuries (BD977, BD978), and following the plan of those works (i.e., a general section followed by bibliographies of 18th-century authors in alphabetical order, plus index). Closing date is 1960 for publications listed.   Z2172.C48

Modern Language Association of America. French III. Bibliography of French seventeenth century studies. no.1–25, 1952/53–77. Publ. for the French III Committee, Modern Language Assoc. of America, Bloomington, Ind., 1953–77. Annual.   **BD980**

Lists books and articles.
Continued by: Z2172.M6

French 17; an annual descriptive bibliography of French seventeenth century studies. no.26– , 1978– . Fort Collins, Colo., Publ. for Seventeenth Century French Div., Modern Language Assoc., by Colorado State Univ., 1978– . Annual.   **BD981**

Represents a change of title for the *Bibliography of French seventeenth century studies* (above) and continues its numbering.
Z2172.M6

Will, Samuel F. A bibliography of American studies on the French Renaissance (1500–1600). Urbana, Univ. of Illinois Pr., 1940. 151p. (Illinois studies in language and literature, v.26, no.2)   **BD982**

Includes books and periodical articles, published in America or by Americans from 1886 to 1937, on France in the 16th century. Lists 1,895 items.   Z2178.W55

19th–20th centuries

Escoffier, Maurice. Le mouvement romantique, 1788–1850: essai de bibliographie synchronique et méthodique. Paris, Maison du Bibliophile, 1934. 428p.   **BD983**

Arranged chronologically. Under each year works are listed by type: poetry, fiction, religion, philosophy, history, science, etc. Indexes of authors, anonymous works, collections and keepsakes, periodicals, and binders.   Z2174.R75E7

Lachèvre, Frédéric. Bibliographie sommaire des keepsakes et autres recueils collectifs de la période romantique, 1823–1848. Paris, Giraud-Badin, 1929. 2v. (Les bibliographies nouvelles. Collection du Bulletin du bibliophile)   **BD984**

A bibliography of French keepsakes or gift books, which include the early writings of many authors (often difficult to find elsewhere), with comprehensive indexes by title and by author.   Z6520.G4L2

Modern Language Association of America. French VI Bibliography Committee. French VI bibliography: critical and biographical references for the study of nineteenth-century French literature. 1954/55–1966/67. N.Y.?, 1956–68. no.1–7. Biennial.   **BD985**

Title varies. Frequency varies.

Ceased publication.

Patterned on the *French VII bibliography* (BD990). Lists books and periodical articles by general subjects and by author-subjects. v.1, no.4, covers 1958–61.

Talvart, Hector and **Place, Joseph.** Bibliographie des auteurs modernes de langue française (1801–1975). Paris, Éd. de la Chronique des Lettres Françaises, 1928–76. v.1–22. (In progress)   **BD986**

Contents: v.1–22, A–Morgan; Index des illustrateurs des ouvrages décrits, t.I–XXII.

An invaluable bibliography of French authors, planned on a large scale. Arranged alphabetically by author, giving generally for each: (1) a biographical sketch; (2) list of writings and editions; (3) minor literary works, i.e., addresses, prefaces, journals edited, etc.; and (4) lists of biographical and critical works and articles about the author, including a large amount of analytical material.

Each volume comprises material published up to the year of its publication and the dates on the title pages vary accordingly; i.e., v.1 covers 1801–1927; v.22, 1801–1975.

v.16–17 comprise a title index to works treated in v.1–15 (which covered through Mirbeau).   Z2171.T16

Thieme, Hugo Paul. Bibliographie de la littérature française de 1800 à 1930. . . . Paris, E. Droz, 1933. 3v. (Repr.: Geneva, Slatkine, 1971)   **BD987**

1st ed. 1907.

Contents: v.1–2, A–Z; v.3, Civilization.

An important reference bibliography, arranged alphabetically by author, listing both works by an author and extensive bibliographies of biographical and critical material about him. v.3 lists books and articles on the history of the language, literature, and culture of France.

See also Giraud (BD958).
Continued by: Z2171.T43

Dreher, Silpelitt and **Rolli, Madeline.** Bibliographie de la littérature française, 1930–1939. Complément à la Bibliographie de H. P. Thieme. Genève, Droz, 1948–49. 438p.   **BD988**

Includes material published 1930–39 on the authors treated by Thieme (above).
Continued by: Z2171.D7

Drevet, Marguerite L. Bibliographie de la littérature française, 1940–1949. Complément à la Bibliographie de H. P. Thieme. Genève, Droz, 1954–55. 644p. **BD989**

Z2171.D73

French VII bibliography; critical and biographical references for the study of contemporary French literature. v.[1]–4. N.Y., Stechert-Hafner, 1949–68. Annual. v.1–4 (whole no.1–20). **BD990**

v.1, numbered in retrospect, consists of five numbers, the last four of which are called "supplements" to the original number. v.1 covered "Books and articles published from 1940 to 1948;" subsequent issues are annual supplements.

Title varies: v.1, *Bibliography of critical and biographical references for the study of contemporary French literature,* by Douglas W. Alden and others.

Issued by the Bibliography Committee, French VII of the Modern Language Association (with the French Institute).

Indexes: v.1–2 (whole no.1–10); v.3–4 (whole no.11–20). Indexes are in two parts: (1) Index to author-subjects; (2) Index to authors of books and articles.

A very useful bibliography of material on 20th-century French literature. In two parts: pt.1, General subjects in a classified arrangement; pt.2, Author-subjects arranged alphabetically. Includes both books and periodical articles. Items are numbered consecutively throughout, and cross references by item number link materials under authors' names and those under subject fields.

Superseded by: Z2173.F7

French XX bibliography; critical and biographical references for French literature since 1885. v.5, no.1– (whole no.21–). N.Y., French Institute, 1969– . Annual. **BD991**

Continues the Modern Language Association's *French VII* bibliography and assumes its numbering. Scope and arrangement remain the same. Z2171.F7

Criticism

Modern French literature, comp. and ed. by Debra Popkin and Michael Popkin. N.Y., F. Ungar, [1977]. 2v. (A library of literary criticism) **BD992**

A collection of excerpts from critical writings on 168 modern French authors considered to be "the ones who are most read, taught, and written about today in France, the United States, and Britain."—*Introd.* Excerpts are given in English, many of them translated specifically for this publication. Index to critics in v.2. Similar to other volumes in the series, e.g., BD843. PQ306.M57

Dictionaries of authors and literature

Boisdeffre, Pierre de. Dictionnaire de littérature contemporaine [par] R. M. Albérès [pseud., et al.]. Nouv. éd. mise à jour. Paris. Éd. Universitaires, [1963]. 687p. **BD993**

1st ed. 1962.
Bio-bibliographies of 20th-century French writers, preceded by several introductory chapters on various literary forms and movements. PQ305.B54

Bonnefoy, Claude, Cartano, Tony and **Oster, Daniel.** Dictionnaire de littérature française contemporaine. Paris, Delarge, [1977]. 411p. il. **BD994**

A dictionary of selected writers of French literature who were alive as of Jan. 1, 1976, and those who, among older writers, had continued to publish new works in their late years. In most instances biographical information is very brief (sometimes minimal) and the bulk of the entry is devoted to commentary on the writer's works, themes, ideas, and place in the contemporary literary scene. A bibliography follows each entry, but this is usually limited to a list of the writer's own works. Appendixes deal with literary movements, regional literatures, and literary magazines. PQ305.B584

The concise Oxford dictionary of French literature. Ed. by Joyce M. H. Reid. Oxford, Clarendon Pr., 1976. 669p. **BD995**

An abridgement and revision of *The Oxford companion to French literature* (1959; BD999). "Abridgement has been effected by condensation and amalgamation rather than omission. . . . Many new articles have been added, and a great many existing articles revised or expanded, in an attempt to bring the whole work more nearly up to date . . . ; a few articles have also been added to fill gaps in the coverage of earlier periods."—*Pref.* PQ41.C6

Dictionnaire des lettres françaises, publié sous la direction du Cardinal Georges Grente. Paris, Arthème Fayard, 1951–72. 5v. in 7. **BD996**

Contents: Le Moyen Âge (1964); Le seizième siècle (1951); Le dix-septième siècle (1954); Le dix-huitième siècle (1960); Le dix-neuvième siècle (1972). (v.[4–5] in 2v. each)

Each period alphabetically arranged. This scholarly dictionary includes articles, varying from a few lines to several pages, on persons, academies, universities, and literary subjects. Articles are signed and contain extensive bibliographies of the works of the authors and of materials to consult concerning persons or subjects. PQ41.D53

Dictionnaire des littératures de langue française. [Éd. par] J. P. Beaumarchais, Daniel Couty, Alain Rey. [Paris], Bordas, [1984–85]. 3v. il. **BD997**

Covers French literature from medieval to contemporary times, with entries for authors, terms, titles of anonymous works and important literary reviews, for other national literatures as they influenced French literature, and for French literature written outside France (e.g., in Belgium, Quebec, etc.). Entries for major authors are very full, providing discussion of a writer's life and works (with chronological tables thereof), critiques and synopses of important individual writings. Articles are signed; most include bibliographies. Illustrations are grouped topically under headings which are generally not directly adjacent to other terms in the alphabetical sequence. "Index dex oeuvres" in v.3. PQ41.B4

Dizionario critico della letteratura francese diretto da Franco Simone. Torino, Unione Tipografico-Editrice Torinese, 1972. 2v. **BD998**

Articles on authors and selected topics by outstanding specialists, with extensive bibliographies.

Harvey, *Sir* **Paul** and **Heseltine, Janet E.** The Oxford companion to French literature. Oxford, Clarendon Pr., 1959. 771p. (Repr. with corrections, 1961) **BD999**

Covers French literature from medieval times to approximately 1939, in the manner of other Oxford "companions," including: (1) articles on authors, critics, historians, religious writers, savants, scientists, etc.; (2) articles on individual works, allusions, places, and institutions; and (3) general survey articles on phases or aspects of French literary life, movements, etc. PQ41.H3

Le Sage, Laurent and **Yon, André.** Dictionnaire des critiques littéraires; guide de la critique française du XXe siècle. University Park, Pennsylvania State Univ. Pr., [1969]. 218p. **BD1000**

Offers biographical sketches of French literary critics of this century, together with notes on the critical theories and concepts of each. Each sketch is followed by a bibliography of works by and about the critic. PQ67.A2L4

Niceron, Jean-Pierre. Mémoires pour servir à l'histoire des hommes illustres dans la république des lettres, avec un catalogue raisonné de leurs ouvrages. Paris, Briasson, 1727–45. 43v. **BD1001**

Beginning with v.31, each volume contains an index which includes articles in the preceding volumes. Z1010.N59

Pingaud, Bernard. Écrivains d'aujourd'hui, 1940–1960. Dictionnaire anthologique et critique. Paris, Grasset, 1960. 539p. il. **BD1002**

Gives brief biographical sketches, brief bibliographies of works by the authors, two or three pages of extracts of writings, and sometimes a few references to works about the writers.   PQ305.P5

Redfern, James. A glossary of French literary expression. N.Y., Harcourt, [1970]. 241p.   **BD1003**

"This book is intended for the student of French who is beginning to write compositions on literary selections he is reading. . . . Its purpose is to present the elements of a basic critical vocabulary in contexts which can serve as models of expression for the student's own ideas."—*Pref.* Entry is under the English form of the term, with the French equivalent defined in French or used in French context.
PC2680.R4

Indexes of names

Flutre, Fernand. Table des noms propres avec toutes leurs variantes figurant dans les romans du Moyen Âge écrits en français ou en provençal et actuellement publiés ou analysés. Poitiers, Centre d'Études Supérieures de Civilisation Médiévale, 1962. 324p. (Publications du C.E.S.C.M., II)
BD1004

A listing of proper names, in their variant forms, appearing in medieval romances written in French and Provençal, in two parts: (1) personal names, and (2) geographic, including ethnic, names. Gives citations to texts and a bibliography of the editions used.
PQ155.N2F55

Langlois, Ernest. Table des noms propres de toute nature compris dans les chansons de geste imprimées. Paris, Bouillon, 1904. 674p. (Repr.: N.Y., B. Franklin, 1971)
BD1005

A useful list of personal and geographical names arranged in one alphabet.   PQ155.N2L3

West, G. D. An index of proper names in French Arthurian verse romances, 1150–1300. [Toronto], Univ. of Toronto Pr., [1969]. 168p. (Univ. of Toronto romance ser., 15)
BD1006

Gives variants, exact citations to texts, and brief descriptions of the contexts in which the names occur.   PQ203.W4

History

Gautier, Léon. Les épopées françaises. Étude sur les origines et l'histoire de la littérature nationale. 2. éd., entièrement refondue. Paris, Palme, 1878–97. 5v. (Repr.: Osnabrück, Zeller, 1966)   **BD1007**

Contents: t.1–2, 1.pt., Origine et histoire; t.3–4, 2.pt., Légende et héros. Livre 1, Geste du roi. Livre 2, Geste de Guillaume; t.5, Bibliographie des chansons de geste.
A well-documented history.   PQ201.G3

Godefroy, Frédéric Eugène. Histoire de la littérature française depuis le 16ᵉ siècle jusqu'à nos jours. 2. éd. Paris, Gaume, 1878–1881. 10v.   **BD1008**

A standard 19th-century history.

Histoire de la littérature française, publiée sous la direction de J. Calvet. [Nouvelle éd.] Paris, de Gigord, 1955–64. 10v. il.   **BD1009**

Contents: v.1, Le Moyen Âge, par Robert Bossuat (1955); v.2, La Renaissance, par Raoul Morçay and Armand Müller (1960); v.3, Le préclassicisme, d'après Raoul Morçay, par Pierre Sage (1962); v.4, Les écrivains classiques, par H. Gaillard de Champris (1960); v.5, La littérature religieuse de François de Sales à Fénelon, par J. Calvet (1956); v.6, De Télémaque à Candide, par Albert Cherel (1958); v.7, De Candide à Atala, par Henri Berthaut (1958); v.8, Le romantisme, par Pierre Moreau (1957); v.9, Le réalisme et le naturalisme, par René Dumesnil (1955); v.10, Les lettres contemporains, par Louis Chaigne (1964).

Originally published 1931–38; all volumes have been revised, some completely rewritten. A valuable survey from the Catholic point of view, with much bibliography.

Histoire littéraire de la France; ouvrage commencé par des religieux bénédictins de la Congrégation de Saint Maur, et continué par des membres de l'Institut (Académie des Inscriptions et Belles-Lettres). Paris, Impr. Nationale, 1733–1981. v.1–41. (In progress)   **BD1010**

Title and imprint vary.

12v. of this work were published by the Maurists, 1733–63. v.11 and 12 were reprinted in 1841 and 1830.

Index to v.9–15 in v.15; to v.16–23 in v.23; to v.25–32 in v.32; to v.33–38 in v.38.

The most detailed history of French literature, beginning with the earliest period and so full that v.41 has advanced only through the 14th century. Comprises signed contributions by specialists, containing very detailed information and, especially in the later volumes, very full bibliographical references. Includes some articles on literary subjects, forms, movements, etc., but consists in the main of biographical and critical articles on individual authors, including many not treated in other histories.   PQ101.A2H6

Lanson, Gustave. Histoire de la littérature française. Remaniée et complétée pour la période 1850–1950 par Paul Tuffrau. Paris, Hachette, [1952]. 1441p.   **BD1011**

A standard work frequently reprinted.   PQ101.L3

——— Histoire illustrée de la littérature française; le Moyen Âge, du Moyen Âge à la Renaissance, le XVIᵉ siècle, le XVIIᵉ siècle, le XVIIIᵉ siècle, époque contemporaine. Paris, Hachette, [c1923]. 2v. il.   **BD1012**

This edition profusely illustrated. Also frequently reprinted, without the illustrations, in a 1v. edition. A standard work.
PQ101.L32

A literary history of France. Gen. ed., P. E. Charvet. London, Benn; N.Y., Barnes & Noble, 1967–74. 6v.   **BD1013**

Contents: [v.1] The Middle Ages, J. Fox; [v.2] Renaissance France, 1470–1589, I. D. McFarlane; v.2 [i.e., v.3], The seventeenth century, 1600–1715, P. J. Yarrow; [v.4] The eighteenth century, 1715–1789, R. Niklaus; v.4 [i.e., v.5], The nineteenth century, 1789–1870, P. E. Charvet; v.5 [i.e., v.6], The nineteenth and twentieth centuries, 1870–1940, P. E. Charvet.

A recent history in English. Footnotes; relatively brief bibliography in each volume; each volume has its own index.   PQ103.L5

Littérature française, par Joseph Bédier et Paul Hazard. Nouv. éd. ref. et augm. sous la direction de Pierre Martino. Paris, Larousse, 1948–49. 2v. il.   **BD1014**

1st ed., 1923, had title *Histoire de la littérature française illustrée.* This edition thoroughly revised and reset. Lavishly illustrated.
PQ101.H52

Littérature française; collection dirigée par Claude Pichois. [Paris], Arthaud, [1968–79]. 16v. il.   **BD1015**

Contents: v.1–2, Le Moyen Âge, by J. C. Payen and D. Poiron (1970–71); v.3–5, La Renaissance, by Y. Giraud [and others] (1972–74); v.6–8, L'Age classique, by A. Adam, P. Clarac and R. Pomeau (1968–71); v.9–11, Le XVIIIᵉ siècle, by Jean Erhard, R. Mauzi and B. Didier (1974–77); v.12–14, Le romantisme, by M. Milner, C. Pichois and R. Pouilliart (1968–79); v.15–16, Le XXᵉ siècle, by P. W. Walzer and G. Brée (1975–78).

Each volume includes a "Dictionnaire des auteurs," a bibliography (often very extensive), and a "Tableau synoptique" which lists literary, historical, and cultural events chronologically in parallel columns.   PQ101.P56

Petit de Julleville, Louis. Histoire de la langue et de la littérature française des origines à 1900. Paris, Colin, 1896–99. 8v. il.   **BD1016**

A history still useful for reference; chapters written by various authorities. Bibliographies; many good illustrations.   PQ101.P5

Drama

Brenner, Clarence Dietz. A bibliographical list of plays in the French language, 1700–1789. Berkeley, Calif., 1947. 229p. **BD1017**

Lists more than 11,000 dramatic compositions by author and title. Analyzes many collections. Z2174.D7B7

Champion, Edouard. La Comédie-Française, 1927–37. Nogent-le-Rotrou, Daupeley-Gouveneur, 1934–39. v.1–5. il. **BD1018**

The volumes cover 1927–32, 1933–34, 1935, 1936, 1937.
A continuation of Joannidès (below).

Joannidès, A. La Comédie-Française de 1680 à 1900. Dictionnaire général des pièces et des auteurs, avec une préface de Jules Claretie. Paris, Plon-Nourrit, 1901. 136p., 274p. facsims. **BD1019**

Contents: (1) Alphabetical title list of plays, giving title, author's name, date of first performance; (2) Alphabetical list of authors with short-title list of their works; (3) Chronological list, showing plays given each year and number of performances of each; and (4) Appendixes, giving plays of the Comédie Française presented at the Odéon, in the provinces, or in London; list of poems recited at the Comédie, etc. PN2636.P4C46

—— La Comédie-Française, 1680 à 1920. Tableau des représentations par auteurs et par pièces. Paris. Plon-Nourrit, 1921. 138p. **BD1020**

Contents: (1) Author list, giving short titles of plays, date of first performance, and total number of times each has been played down to 1920; (2) Title index. PN2636.P4C47

Lancaster, Henry Carrington. The Comédie Française, 1680–1701; plays, actors, spectators, finances. Baltimore, Johns Hopkins Pr.; London, Milford; Paris, Les Belles-Lettres, 1941. 210p. (Johns Hopkins studies in Romance literatures and languages. Extra v.17) **BD1021**

Arranged chronologically, giving in tabular form: name of play, number of spectators, receipts, etc.
Continued by: PN2636.P4C495

—— The Comédie Française, 1701–74; plays, actors, spectators, finances. (*In* American Philosophical Society. Transactions. n.s., v.41 [1951], p.593–849) **BD1022**

—— History of French dramatic literature in the 17th century. Baltimore, Johns Hopkins Pr.; Paris, Presses Universitaires, 1929–42. 5v. in 9. (Repr.: N.Y., Gordian Pr., 1966) **BD1023**

A detailed history with lists of plays, bibliographical footnotes, etc. v.5 includes a subject index, a finding list of plays, and a general index to all 5v. PQ526.L3

—— Sunset, a history of Parisian drama in the last years of Louis XIV, 1701–1715. Baltimore, Johns Hopkins Pr.; London, Milford; Paris, Les Belles-Lettres, 1945. 365p. **BD1024**

A sequel to the foregoing, compiled on the same plan, devoted primarily to plays acted or published in or near Paris. Includes additions and corrections to the *History . . . in the 17th century* (above), and a list of plays acted at the Comédie Française, 1701–Sept. 1715, supplementing the author's work on the Comédie Française (BD1021, BD1022).
Continued by: PQ536.L3

—— French tragedy in the time of Louis XV and Voltaire, 1715–1774. Baltimore, Johns Hopkins Pr.; London, Oxford Univ. Pr., 1950. 2v. **BD1025**
Continued by: PQ563.L3

—— French tragedy in the reign of Louis XVI and the early years of the French Revolution, 1774–1792. Baltimore, Johns Hopkins Pr., 1953. 181p. **BD1026**
PQ561.L28

Soleinne, Martineau de. Bibliothèque dramatique de Monsieur de Soleinne. Catalogue rédigé par P. L. Jacob, bibliophile. Paris, Alliance des Arts, 1843–45. 6v. (Repr.: N.Y., B. Franklin, 1965) **BD1027**

Contents: t.1, Théâtre oriental; grec et romain; latin moderne; ancien théâtre français; théâtre français moderne depuis Jodelle jusqu'à Racine. Supplément; t.2, Théâtre français depuis Racine jusqu'à Victor Hugo, théâtre des provinces, théâtre français à l'étranger; t.3, Suite du théâtre français; recueils manuscrits; recueils divers; théâtre de la cour; ballets; répertoires des théâtres de Paris; théâtre burlesque; théâtre de société; proverbes dramatiques; théâtre d'éducation; pièces satiriques; pièces en patois; dialogues. Appendice. Autographes; t.4, Théâtre italien; espagnol et portugais; allemand; anglais; suédois, flamand et hollandais, russe et polonais, turc, grec et valaque; t.5, 1.pt., Écrits relatifs au théâtre. 2.pt., Estampes et dessins. [3.pt.] Autographes. [4.pt.] Livres doubles et livres omis; [t.6] Table générale. (v.5, pts.1–2 and [3–4] publ. in 1v. in reprint edition; *Table* called "v.6" in reprint edition)

A useful catalog of an extensive collection covering the theater from ancient times through the first part of the 19th century. Particularly strong in all forms of the French theater, including drama, ballets, burlesque, etc. Also includes works of the theater in many other European countries. Z2174.D7S62

—— —— Table des pièces de théâtre décrites dans le catalogue de la bibliothèque de M. de Soleinne, par Charles Brunet. Pub. par Henri de Rothschild. Paris, D. Morgand, 1914. 491p. **BD1028**

Useful title index to more than 5,000 plays giving for each title brief information: whether prose or verse, kind of play (comedy, tragedy, etc.), number of acts, author's name, and reference to its number in the Soleinne catalog.

Two related bibliographies, old but still useful, are: *Essai d'une bibliographie générale du théâtre; ou, Catalogue raisonné de la bibliothèque d'un amateur, complétant le catalogue Soleinne*, by Joseph de Filippi (Paris, Tresse, 1861; repr.: N.Y., B. Franklin, 1967) and *Bibliothèque dramatique de Pont de Vesle. Forniée avec les débris des bibliothèques de Saint-Ange, de Crozat, de Mme. de Pompadour, etc., continuée par Mme. de Montesson, possédée depuis par M. de Soleinne*, by Paul Lacroix (Paris, Administration de l'Alliance des Arts, 1847; repr.: N.Y., B. Franklin, 1965).

Thompson, Lawrence Sidney. A bibliography of French plays on microcards. Hamden, Conn., Shoe String, 1967. 689p. **BD1029**

About 7,000 items arranged by author or anonymous title. Intended primarily as a guide to the microcard edition of the plays, but useful as a checklist of French plays published prior to about 1910. Z2174.D7T48

Wicks, Charles Beaumont. The Parisian stage: alphabetical indexes of plays and authors. University, Ala., Univ. of Alabama Pr., 1950–79. 5 pts. (Univ. of Alabama studies, no.6, 8, 14, 17) **BD1030**

Contents: pt.1, 1800–1815 (1950); pt.2, 1816–1830 (1953); pt.3, 1831–1850 (1961); pt.4, 1851–1875 (1967); pt.5, 1876–1900, with cumulative author index 1800–1900 (1979; not designated as part of the series).

Each part is in two sections: (1) an alphabetical list by title, and (2) an author index. Attempts to be a complete list of dramatic productions presented in Paris in the 19th century, giving where possible: title, subtitle, type of play, number of acts, whether in prose or verse, real names of authors, theater and date of first performance in Paris. PN2636.P3W5

Fiction

DeJongh, William Frederick Jekel. A bibliography of the novel and short story in French from the beginning of printing till 1600. Albuquerque, Univ. of New Mexico Pr., 1944. 79p. (Univ. of New Mexico. Bull. Bibliographical ser., v.1, no.1) **BD1031**

336 items arranged chronologically. Z2174.F4D4

Jones, Silas Paul. A list of French prose fiction from 1700 to 1750, with a brief introduction. N.Y., Wilson, 1939. 150p.
BD1032

Annotated, chronological list with detailed index to authors, titles, and pseudonyms. Locates copies.
See BD1034 for the 1751–1800 period. Z2174.F4J7

Lever, Maurice. La fiction narrative en prose au XVIIème siècle: répertoire bibliographique du genre romanesque en France (1600–1700). Paris, Éditions du Centre National de la Recherche Scientifique, 1976. 645p. **BD1033**

At head of title: Centre d'Étude de la Littérature française du XVIIème et du XVIIIème siècle (Paris-Sorbonne).
Interpreting "narrative fiction" as broadly as possible, the compiler aims to transcend the limitations of R. C. Williams' *Bibliography of the seventeenth-century novel in France* (N.Y., 1931) and to overcome the errors and deficiencies of R. W. Baldner's revision of that work (N.Y., 1967). The main listing is by title, and full bibliographic information, library locations, attribution of anonymous works, references to later editions, and the "incipit" of each work are given in that section. An author list (including pseudonyms) provides an author approach. Z5918.L47

Martin, Angus, Mylne, Vivienne G. and **Frautschi, Richard.** Bibliographie du genre romanesque français, 1751–1800. London, Mansell; Paris, France Expansion, 1977. 529p. il.
BD1034

"Genre romanesque" is here defined as including novels, short stories, and other prose writings (such as dialogues) that embody some element of narrative fiction. In general the plan and scope of the bibliography follow that of S. P. Jones's *A list of French prose fiction from 1700 to 1750* (BD1032), except that French translations of works originally published in other languages are included herein, as are new editions of older works. Arrangement is chronological, then alphabetical by author, with an index of authors and titles. In addition to information on variant editions, serialization in periodicals, and library locations, there are often useful notes on form and content. About 6,750 entries. Z2174.F5M37

Poetry

Lachèvre, Frédéric. Bibliographie des recueils collectifs de poésies du XVIᵉ siècle (du Jardin de plaisance, 1502, aux Recueils de Toussaint du Bray, 1609). . . . Paris, Champion, 1922. 613p. il. (Repr.: Geneva, Slatkine, 1967) **BD1035**

Subtitle: Donnant: (1) La description et le contenu des recueils; (2) Une table générale des pièces anonymes ou signées d'initiales de ces recueils (titre et premier vers), avec l'indication du nom des auteurs pour celles qui ont pu être attribuées.
A description of the contents of a large number of collections of poetry, with identification of many anonymous items.
Z2174.P7L15

—— Bibliographie des recueils collectifs de poésies publiés de 1597 à 1700. . . . Paris, Leclerc, 1901–05. 4v. (Repr.: Geneva, Slatkine, 1967) **BD1036**

Subtitle: Donnant: (1) La description et le contenu des recueils; (2) Les pièces de chaque auteur classées dans l'ordre alphabétique de premier vers, precedées d'une notice bio-bibliographique, etc.; (3) Une table générale des pièces anonymes ou signées d'initiales (titre et premier vers) avec l'indication des noms des auteurs pour celles qui ont pu leur être attribuées; (4) La reproduction des pièces qui n'ont pas été relevées par les derniers éditeurs des poètes figurant dans les recueils collectifs; (5) Une table des noms cités dans le texte et le premier vers des pièces des recueils collectifs. Etc., etc.
v.1–3 arranged chronologically, 1597–1700; v.4, Supplément, additions, corrections, tables générales.
A monumental work describing the collections, giving bio-bibliographical notices of the authors, with attributions for many anonymous poems, some of which have been disputed. Z2174.P7L2

—— Les recueils collectifs de poésies libres et satiriques publiés depuis 1600 jusqu'à la mort de Théophile (1626). Bibliographie de ces recueils et bio-bibliographie des auteurs qui y figurent. . . . Paris, Champion, 1914–22. 597p. and suppl., 95p. (The author's Le libertinage au XVIIᵉ siècle.—IV) **BD1037**

Supplements the preceding work. PQ1130.L5

—— Bibliographie sommaire de l'Almanach des muses (1765–1833). . . . Paris, Giraud-Badin, 1928. 206p. (Les bibliographies nouvelles. Collection du Bulletin du bibliophile. no.12) **BD1038**

Arranged chronologically; lists literary almanacs of this period, with detailed indexes. Z2174.P7L21

Mendès, Catulle. Le mouvement poétique français de 1867 à 1900. Rapport . . . suivi d'un Dictionnaire bibliographique et critique et d'une Nomenclature chronologique de la plupart des poètes français du XIXᵉ siècle. Paris, Impr. Nationale, E. Fasquelle, 1903. 218p., 340p. **BD1039**

The survey report is followed by the *Dictionnaire,* arranged alphabetically, and listing for each poet the titles of his works and extracts from critical opinions with references to sources.
Z2174.P7M5

Individual authors

See note p.465.

Corneille

Picot, Émile. Bibliographie cornélienne; ou, Description raisonnée de toutes les éditions des oeuvres de Pierre Corneille, des imitations ou traductions qui en ont été faites, et des ouvrages relatifs à Corneille et à ses écrits. Paris, Fontaine, 1876. 552p. (Repr.: Nendeln, Liechtenstein, Kraus, 1967) **BD1040**

Z8194.P6

Le Verdier, Pierre and **Pelay, E.** Additions à la Bibliographie cornélienne. Rouen, Lestringant, 1908. 251p. (Repr.: N.Y., B. Franklin, 1970) **BD1041**

Z8194.L65

Ritter, Ada. Bibliographie zu Pierre Corneille von 1958 bis 1983. Erfstadt, Lukassen, [1983]. 229p. **BD1042**

Arranged by year of publication, with author and subject indexes.
Z8194.R57

Marty-Laveaux, Charles Joseph. Lexique de la langue de Pierre Corneille. Paris, Hachette, 1868. 2v. **BD1043**

v.11–12 of the *Grands écrivains* edition of Corneille.
PQ1742.M3

Molière

Desfeuilles, Arthur. Notice bibliographique. Paris, Hachette, 1893. 326p. **BD1044**

v.11 of the *Grands écrivains* edition of Molière.

—— and **Desfeuilles, Paul.** Lexique de la langue de Molière, avec une introduction grammaticale. Paris, Hachette, 1900. 2v. **BD1045**

v.12–13 of the *Grands écrivains* edition of Molière.

Guibert, Albert-Jean. Bibliographie des oeuvres de Molière publiées au XVIIᵉ siècle. Paris, Éd. du Centre National de la Recherche Scientifique, 1961–73. 2v. and suppl. 1–2. il.
BD1046

A detailed and scholarly listing of separate plays, collected works, Dutch editions, ballets, poems, miscellaneous works, etc. Full bibliographic information and many explanatory notes. The supplement provides descriptions of several editions not described in the earlier volumes, and adds a section of references to library locations and bibliographic sources for previously described editions.

Z8586.G8

Saintonge, Paul Frédéric and Christ, Robert Wilson. Fifty years of Molière studies, a bibliography, 1892–1941. Baltimore, Johns Hopkins Pr.; London, Milford, 1942. 313p. (Johns Hopkins studies in Romance literatures and languages. Extra v.19) **BD1047**

3,316 numbered items. Z8586.S3

Racine

Guibert, Albert-Jean. Bibliographie des oeuvres de Jean Racine publiées au XVIIᵉ siècle et oeuvres posthumes. Paris, Éditions du Centre National de la Recherche Scientifique, 1968. 319p. il. **BD1048**

Lists both separately published and collected editions, with full bibliographical description. Z8730.2.G83

Williams, Edwin E. Racine depuis 1885; bibliographie raisonnée des livres—articles—comptes-rendus critiques relatifs à la vie et l'ouevre de Jean Racine, 1885–1939. Baltimore, Johns Hopkins Pr.; London, Milford, 1940. 279p. (Johns Hopkins studies in Romance literatures and languages. Extra v.16) **BD1049**

Z8730.2.W72

Freeman, Bryant C., ed. Concordance du théâtre et des poésies de Jean Racine. Alan Batson, programmeur. Ithaca, N.Y., Cornell Univ. Pr., [1968]. 2v. **BD1050**

In general, the text followed is that of the 1885 edition by Paul Mesnard. PQ1903.F7

Marty-Laveaux, Charles Joseph. Lexique de la langue de J. Racine, avec une introduction grammaticale, précédé d'une étude sur le style de Racine par P. Mesnard et suivi des tableaux des représentations de Corneille et de Racine par E. Despois. Paris, Hachette, 1873. cxlivp., 616p. **BD1051**

v.8 of the *Grands écrivains* edition of Racine.

Italian

Guides

Beccaro, Felice del. Guida allo studio della letteratura italiana. [Milano], Mursia, [1975]. 350p. **BD1052**

A general section is followed by chapters for the literature of each century, with sub-sections for major writers of each period. Editions and studies are treated in essay form; index of names.

Z2354.C8B4

Mazzoni, Guido. Avviamento allo studio critico delle lettere italiane. 4. ed. riv. e aggiorn. per cura di Carmine Jannaco, con prefazione di Francesco Maggini e appendici di Pio Rajna e Ernesto Giacomo Parodi. Firenze, Sansoni, [1951]. 238p. (Manuali di filologia e storia. ser. II, v.3) **BD1053**

1st ed. 1892.

A bibliographical handbook, still useful primarily for its comments on older materials. Z2351.M47

Puppo, Mario. Manuale critico-bibliografico per lo studio della letteratura italiana. 13. ed. riveduta e aggiornata. [Torino], Società Editrice Internazionale, [1980]. 432p. **BD1054**

A student's manual consisting of surveys of the scholarship on important authors and literary questions, followed by bibliographies of books and important articles. PQ4037.P8

Bibliography

Contributo a una bibliografia del futurismo letterario italiano, a cura di Anna Baldazzi [et al.]. [Roma, Cooperativa Scrittori, 1977] 629p. **BD1055**

A bibliography of writings on the futurist movement in Italian literature and of writings by authors of the movement. Includes a listing of the contents of the Italian futurist literary magazines. Lacks an index. Z2354.F87C65

Fucilla, Joseph Guerin. Universal author repertoire of Italian essay literature. N.Y., Vanni, [1941]. 534p. **BD1056**

An index to biographical and critical articles on authors, primarily Italian, but also including non-Italian writers of many countries, contained in 1,697 collections of Italian essays. Arranged alphabetically by subject.

Continued by: Z6511.F8

——— Saggistica letteraria italiana; bibliografia per soggetti: 1938–1952. Firenze, Sansoni, 1956. 281p. **BD1057**

A bibliography of studies on Italian and foreign authors and their works, contained in collections of miscellaneous essays printed in Italy 1938–52. Z2354.E7F8

Golden, Herbert Hershel and Simches, Seymour O. Modern Italian language and literature; a bibliography of homage studies. Cambridge, Harvard Univ. Pr., 1959. 207p. **BD1058**

Indexes 1,966 *Festschriften,* in 474 collections, on modern Italian language and literature from the Renaissance to 1957. Index of authors of the articles and of persons, works, and subjects treated.

Z2355.A2G6

Harvard University. Library. Italian history and literature: classification schedule, classified listing by call number, chronological listing, author and title listing. Cambridge, publ. by Harvard Univ. Lib., distr. by Harvard Univ. Pr., 1974. 2v. (Widener Library shelflist, 51–52). **BD1059**

For full information *see* DC394.

Prezzolini, Giuseppe. Repertorio bibliografico della storia e della critica della letteratura italiana dal 1902 al 1932, prep. nella Casa Italiana della Columbia University e con l'aiuto del Council on Research in the Humanities, New York, 1930–1936. Roma, Ed. Roma, [1937–39]. 2v. **BD1060**

Arranged alphabetically by names of authors written about or commented on, and by literary forms and subjects, with exact references to an enormous amount of critical and biographical material in books, periodicals, society publications, etc.

Z2351.P93

——— Repertorio bibliografico della storia e della critica della letteratura italiana dal 1933 al 1942. N.Y., Vanni, 1946–48. 2v. **BD1061**

This section follows the same general plan as the first 2v., giving references under authors, literary forms, etc. Many form headings have geographical subdivisions.

Repertorio bibliografico della letteratura italiana, 1943–1947. A cura della Facoltà di Magistero di Roma, sotto la direzione di Umberto Bosco. Firenze, Sansoni, [1969]. 138p. **BD1062**

Fills the gap between Prezzolini's bibliography (above) and the 1948–49 volume of the *Repertorio* as edited by Bosco (below).

Z2341.R4

Repertorio bibliografico della letteratura italiana, a cura della Facoltà di Magistero di Roma, sotto la direzione di Umberto Bosco. Firenze, Sansoni, 1953–60. 2v. **BD1063**

Contents: v.1, 1948–1949; v.2, 1950–1953.

With the 1943–47 *Repertorio* volume (above), provides a continuation of Prezzolini (BD1060). These volumes are arranged alphabetically by author, with subject indexes. Both books and periodical articles are listed. Z2341.B6

Translations

See also BD934, BD1085.

Shields, Nancy Catchings. Italian translations in America. N.Y., [1931]. 410p. (Inst. of French Studies. Comparative literature ser.)   **BD1064**

Translations of Italian works arranged chronologically by date of publication, covering the period 1751–1928. Each title is located in one library or, if not found, the original source of entry is indicated.   Z2354.T7S51

Dictionaries

Dictionary of Italian literature. Peter Bondanella and Julia Conway Bondanella, co-eds. Westport, Conn., Greenwood Pr., [1979]. 621p.   **BD1065**

An English-language guide to Italian literature which means to provide "an introduction to major and minor Italian writers from the twelfth century to the present, to Italian metrics and poetic forms or genres, and to literary or critical schools, periods, problems, and movements."—*Pref.* Entries for authors predominate; attention is given to relationships with other national literatures, cultures, and art forms. Many articles are signed; contributors' credentials are given, p.xv–xxi. Bibliographies include English translations of primary texts, as well as critical studies (books and articles) in various languages. Indexed.   PQ4006.D45

Dizionario critico della letteratura italiana. Diretto da Vittore Branca. Torino, Unione Tipografico Editrice Torinese, [1973]. 3v. plates.   **BD1066**

Offers signed articles, most of them several pages in length. A high percentage of articles is biocritical in nature, but there are entries for literary terms, movements, etc. Substantial bibliographies, those for individual authors including both works by and about the writer. Cross references; index of names in v.3.   PQ4057.D59

Dizionario enciclopedico della letteratura italiana. [Direttore: Giuseppe Petronio] Laterza, UNEDI, [1966–70]. 6v. il.   **BD1067**

Contents: v.1–5, A–Z; v.6, Appendice, Indici.

The main part of the dictionary is devoted to entries for: (1) major and minor Italian authors together with classical and foreign authors who have influenced Italian letters; (2) politicians, princes, and popes who have patronized the literature; (3) movements, cultural institutions, libraries, journals, and magazines; and (4) the language and terms of literary criticism. Bibliographies; general index.   PQ4006.D5

Dizionario generale degli autori italiani contemporanei. [Coordinamento Enzo Ronconi] [Firenze], Vallecchi, [1974]. 2v. (1551p.) il.   **BD1068**

Contents: v.1, Movimenti letterari, Abba-Luzzato Fegiz; v.2, Maccari-Zumbini, Influenze e corrispondenze.

Primarily a dictionary arrangement of biographical sketches of contemporary Italian authors (with bibliographies) and articles on literary journals; the alphabetical sequence is preceded by an essay on literary movements and followed by essays on relationships of Italian and foreign literatures, philosophy, art, and the cinema.   PQ4113.D58

Fusco, Enrico M. Scrittori e idee: dizionario critico della letteratura italiana. [Torino], Società Ed. Internazionale, [1956]. 626p.   **BD1069**

Includes biographical sketches, with bibliographies, of writers of all periods, and brief articles on movements, literary forms, etc.   PQ4006.F8

Renda, Umberto and **Operti, Piero.** Dizionario storico della letteratura italiana. Ed. riv. e aggiorn. sul testo originale di Vittorio Turri. [4 ed.] Torino, Paravia, [1959]. 1241p.   **BD1070**

1st ed. 1900; nuova ed., 1941, by Vittorio Turri and U. Renda.

A bio-bibliographical dictionary containing some 1,400 entries, many quite extensive, including living Italian writers, as well as articles on literary forms and movements, etc.

History

Cecchi, Emilio and **Sapegno, Natalino.** Storia della letteratura italiana. [Milano], Garzanti, [1965–69]. 9v. il.   **BD1071**

Contents: v.1, Le origini e il duecento; v.2, Il trecento; v.3, Il quattrocento e l'Ariosto; v.4, Il cinquecento; v.5, Il seicento; v.6, Il settecento; v.7, L'ottocento; v.8, Dall'ottocento al novecento; v.9, Il novecento.

Chapters are contributed by scholars specializing in various aspects of each period, with a bibliography at the end of each chapter.   PQ4037.C4

Flora, Francesco. Storia della letteratura italiana. [4 ed.] Verona, Mondadori, 1972. 5v.   **BD1072**

1st ed. 1940–46 in 3v.; various reprintings.

Contents: Dal Medio Evo alla fine del Trecento; v.2, Il Quattrocento e il primo Cinquecento; v.3, Il secondo Cinquecento e il Seicento; v.4, Il Settocento e il primo Ottocento; v.5, Il secondo Ottocento e il Novecento.

Each volume has a bibliography and its own index of names.   PQ4037.F63

Momigliano, Attilio, ed. Problemi ed orientamenti critici di lingua e di letteratura italiana. Milano, C. Marzorati, [1948–61] v.1–5 in 7.   **BD1073**

Some volumes have appeared in revised editions.

Contents: v.1¹⁻³, Notizie introduttive e sussidi bibliografici; v.2, Tecnica e teoria letteraria; v.3, Questioni e correnti di storia letteraria; v.4, Letterature comparate; v.5, Momenti e problemi di storia dell' estetica.

Articles by specialists, with extensive bibliographies. Generous sections on foreign literatures, literary movements, archives and libraries, as well as Italian literature proper.

Sanctis, Francesco de. Storia della letteratura italiana, a cura di Benedetto Croce. 6. ed. Bari, Laterza, 1958. 2v.   **BD1074**

A standard history published in many editions. English translation by Joan Redfern (N.Y., Basic Books, 1960; N.Y., Barnes & Noble, 1968).   PQ4037.S2

Wilkins, Ernest Hatch. A history of Italian literature. Rev. by Thomas G. Bergin. Cambridge, Harvard Univ. Pr., 1974. 570p.   **BD1075**

1st ed. 1954.

Illustrative passages and quotations from the literature are either given in English or accompanied by an English translation. "A list of English translations and books in English dealing with Italian literature," p.539–48; chronological chart; index.   PQ4038.W5

Biography

Chi scrive; repertorio bio-bibliografico e per specializzazioni degli scrittori italiani. [2. ed.] Milano, Igap Editrice, [1966]. 699p.   **BD1076**

1st ed. 1962.

In addition to the bio-bibliographies (of journalists, academic writers, translators, etc., as well as of writers of belles-lettres) there are lists of publishers, libraries, national and provincial newspapers, etc., plus a grouping of biographees by field of specialization and a list of pseudonyms.

Cosenza, Mario Emilio. Biographical and bibliographical dictionary of the Italian humanists and of the world of classical scholarship in Italy, 1300–1800. [2d ed., rev. and enl.] Boston, G. K. Hall, 1962–67. 6v.   **BD1077**

1st ed., 1954, appeared in microform.

Includes Italian scholars and those who studied in Italy, together with patrons and others concerned with the revival of classical studies. Gives for each humanist, where possible, brief biographical information, a list of variant names, teachers, pupils, works, and occasionally citations to secondary sources. Contains much information not easily available elsewhere, but is difficult to use because of its format—an unedited photoreproduction of Prof. Cosenza's handwritten cards. The fifth volume contains an edited synopsis of the first four and a very selective bibliography of secondary materials on humanism. v.6 is a supplement. Z7128.H9C6

Dizionario degli scrittori italiani d'oggi. Cosenza, Pellegrini, [1969]. 269p. il. **BD1078**

Brief biographies of contemporary Italian writers. Z2350.D58

Dizionario degli scrittori italiani d'oggi. 2. ed. Cosenza, Pellegrini, [1975]. 240p. il. **BD1079**

Preface signed: Peppino Rota.

A supplement to, rather than a new edition of, the 1969 work of the same title (above). Some of the sketches from the 1969 volume have been revised or updated, but most of the biographies are new. Z2350.D58

Ferrari, Luigi. Onomasticon; repertorio biobibliografico degli scrittori italiani dal 1501 al 1850. Milano, Hoepli, 1947. 708p. (Bibliotheca veneta, collana di opere erudite a cura della Scuola Storico-Filologica della Venezie . . . della R. Università di Padova. [v.1]) (Repr.: Nendeln, Liechtenstein, Kraus, 1973) **BD1080**

An index to almost 50,000 individual biographies of authors contained in some 375 collections, general and local. The list of these collections, p.xxi–xliv, forms a bibliography of collected works of Italian biography, with indication of location in Italian libraries. Z2350.F4

Gastaldi, Mario and **Scano, Carmen.** Dizionario delle scrittrici italiane contemporanee (arte, lettere, scienze). Milano, Gastaldi Editore, [1957]. 247p. il. **BD1081**

A dictionary of Italian women writers, usually giving place of birth, educational degrees, position or occupation, and bibliography of writings. CT3450.G3

Drama

Clubb, Louise George. Italian plays (1500–1700) in the Folger Library; a bibliography. Firenze, Olschki, 1968. 267p. (Biblioteca di bibliografia italiana, 52) **BD1082**

890 items. Full collation and numerous descriptive notes are given. Editions listed in M. T. Herrick's *Italian plays, 1500–1700* (below) and in Beatrice Corrigan's *Catalogue of Italian plays, 1500–1700* (BD1084) and its supplements are so indicated. Z2354.D7C55

Herrick, Marvin Theodore, comp. Italian plays, 1500–1700, in the University of Illinois Library. Urbana, Univ. of Illinois Pr., 1966. 92p. **BD1083**

Primarily concerned with plays by 16th-century authors. An author listing with title index. Z2354.D7H4

Toronto. University. Library. Catalogue of Italian plays, 1500–1700, in the Library of the University of Toronto, comp. by Beatrice Corrigan. [Toronto], Univ. of Toronto Pr., [1961]. 134p. **BD1084**

Arranged alphabetically by author, with title index. Gives bibliographical information, form, dedication, and (in many cases) brief annotations. Two supplements have appeared in *Renaissance news:* v.16 (1963), p.298–307; and v.19 (1966), p.219–28. Z2354.D7T6

Poetry

Molinaro, Julius A. American studies and translations of contemporary Italian poetry, 1945–1965: an historical survey and a bibliography. *In* New York Public Library bulletin, v.72, p.522–58 (Oct. 1968). **BD1085**

Bibliography of books, periodical articles, and poems in translation, p.529–58. Numerous annotations and notes on contents.

Supplemented by:

——— ——— 1965–1970; a supplementary survey and bibliography. *In* New York Public Library bulletin, v.78, p.351–72 (Spr. 1975).

Toronto. University. Library. A bibliography of sixteenth-century Italian verse collections in the University of Toronto Library. Comp. by Julius A. Molinaro. [Toronto], Univ. of Toronto Pr., [1969]. 124p. il. **BD1086**

Provides full title and imprint for each collection and the names of the poets represented in each volume. Indexes of authors and of first lines of anonymous poems. Z2354.P7T6

Individual authors

See note p.465.

Dante

Bibliography

Cornell University. Library. Catalogue of the Dante collection presented by Willard Fiske, comp. by Theodore Wesley Koch. Ithaca, N.Y., Lib., 1898–1921. 2v. and suppl. **BD1087**

Contents: v.1, Dante's works, Works on Dante (A–G); v.2, Works on Dante (H–Z), supplement, indexes, appendix; Supplement, additions 1898–1920.

Supplemented for some points by the following: Z8215.C81

Koch, Theodore Wesley. List of Danteiana in American libraries supplementing the catalogue of the Cornell collection. Boston, Ginn, 1901. 67p. **BD1088**

Repr. from the 18th *Annual report* of the Dante Society, Cambridge, Mass. Z8215.C811

——— Dante in America; a historical and bibliographical study. Boston, Ginn, 1896. 150p. **BD1089**

Repr. from the 15th *Annual report* of the Dante Society, Cambridge, Mass. Z8215.K76

——— ——— [Supplement] May 1896–May 1908. (*In* Dante Society, Cambridge, Mass. 28th Annual report, 1909. Boston, Ginn, 1910. p.11–35)

Evola, Niccolò Domenico. Bibliografia dantesca (1920–1930). Firenze, Olschki, 1932. 260p. (Giornale dantesco . . . v.33, n.s. 3. Annuario dantesco 1930. Supplemento) **BD1090**

Supplemented by *Bibliografia dantesca, 1931/37–1938/39,* published in *Il giornale dantesco,* v.39–41, and by:

Vallone, Aldo. Gli studi danteschi dal 1940 al 1949. Firenze, Olschki, 1950. 138p. (Biblioteca di bibliografia italiana. 19) **BD1091**

Supplemented by: Z8215.V3

Esposito, Enzo. Gli studi danteschi dal 1950 al 1964. Roma, Centro Editoriale Internazionale, 1965. 537p. **BD1092**

A bibliography of critical studies. Z8215.E85

Rome. Centro Nazionale per il Catalogo Unico delle Biblioteche Italiane e per le Informazioni Bibliografiche. Dante Alighieri, MCCLXV-MCMLXV. Roma, 1965. 191p. **BD1093**

A reprinting of the Dante section of v.3 of the Centro's *Primo catalogo collettivo . . .* (AA143), with an appendix (p.137–58) of additional items, plus numerous plates, and indexes of editors, illustrators, printers, and places of publication.   Z8215.R65

Concordances

Rand, Edward Kennard and **Wilkins, Ernest Hatch.** Dantis Alagherii opervm latinorvm concordantiae. Oxford, Clarendon Pr., 1912. 577p.   **BD1094**

Based on the text of the 3d Oxford edition, 1904.

PQ4311.A5R3

Sheldon, Edward Stevens and **White, A. C.** Concordanza delle opere italiane in prosa e del Canzoniere di Dante Alighieri pubblicata per la Società Dantesca di Cambridge, Mass. Oxford, Univ. Pr., 1905. 740p.   **BD1095**

PQ4308.Z5S5

Gordon, Lewis H. Supplementary concordance to the minor Italian works of Dante. Cambridge, publ. for the Dante Society, Harvard Univ. Pr., 1936. 38p.   **BD1096**

Supplementary to the preceding work.   PQ4464.G6

Wilkins, Ernest Hatch and **Bergin, Thomas Goddard.** A concordance to the Divine comedy of Dante Alighieri. Ed. for the Dante Society of America. Cambridge, Belknap Pr. of Harvard Univ. Pr., 1965. 636p.   **BD1097**

Based on the authoritative text prepared by Giuseppe Vandelli and issued by the Società Dantesca Italiana (rev. ed.; Florence, 1960). It therefore is to be preferred over the concordance edited by Edward Allen Fay (Cambridge, Mass., Dante Soc.; Oxford, Univ. Pr., 1888. 819p.), although the latter is also available in a 1966 reprint.   PQ4464.W5

Dictionaries and encyclopedias

Enciclopedia dantesca. Roma, Istituto della Enciclopedia Italiana, [1970–78]. 6v.   **BD1098**

Direttore: Umberto Bosco.

Includes in one alphabet a register of the vocabulary of Dante's vernacular works, citing instances in the texts and discussing forms, meanings, and the interpretations of previous commentators; foreign words in the vernacular texts; proper names in the Italian and Latin works; and Latin terms having cultural or doctrinal significance. v.6, "Appendice: biografia, lingua e stile, opere," offers articles on phonetics, grammar, morphology, and syntax, followed by a bibliography of Dante's works and of Dante studies, plus the text of the works. Articles are by specialists and many include references to secondary sources.

Effectively supersedes Giovanni A. Scartazzini's *Enciclopedia dantesca* (Milano, Hoepli, 1896–1905. 3v.).   PQ4333.E5

Grandgent, Charles Hall. Companion to the Divine comedy. Commentary by C. H. Grandgent as edited by Charles S. Singleton. Cambridge, Mass., Harvard Univ. Pr., 1975. 316p. il.   **BD1099**

Intended for those "who are obliged to read their Dante in English."—*Pref.* Offers generous extracts from "those parts of Grandgent's well-known edition of the poem [i.e., *La Divina Commedia*, ed. and annotated by C. H. Grandgent, rev. by C. S. Singleton; Harvard Univ. Pr., 1972] which can be understood by a reader who has little or no Italian (and quite possibly no Latin)."   PQ4464.G7

Siebzehner-Vivanti, Giorgio. Dizionario della Divina commedia, a cura di Michele Messina. Milano, Feltrinelli, [1965]. 721p.   **BD1100**

An earlier edition appeared in 1954 (Firenze, Olschki. 655p.). Primarily a dictionary of the vocabulary of the *Divine comedy*, with definitions and examples from the text.   PQ4464.S5

Toynbee, Paget. A dictionary of proper names and notable matters in the works of Dante. [New ed.] rev. by Charles S. Singleton. N.Y., Oxford Univ. Pr., 1968. 722p.   **BD1101**

A revision of Toynbee's 1898 *Dictionary* (of which a *Concise* edition appeared in 1914). References to Dante's works have been changed from the "Oxford Dante" edited by Toynbee to that sponsored by the Società Dantesca Italiana, which is now the standard edition. Additional entries have been supplied, mainly from Mario Casella's "Indici analitico" published with the 1921 edition of the *Opere di Dante* by the Società. Biographical and historical data have been revised or corrected as necessary in light of new research, and modern critical versions of other texts referred to have been substituted whenever pertinent.   PQ4333.T7

Portuguese
(including Brazilian)

See also BD1456.

Bibliography

Bibliografia de dramaturgia brasileira. São Paulo, Escola de Comunicações e Artes da USP, Associação Museu Lasar Segall, 1981–83. 2v.   **BD1102**

v.2 has title: Bibliografia da dramaturgia brasileira.

Contents: v.1, A–M; v.2, N–Z.

An author listing of dramatic works (more than 3,000 entries) giving publication information, together with indication of library locations and the number of acts and number of performers in each piece. The two volumes have separate title indexes.   Z1684.D7B5

Carpeaux, Otto Maria. Pequena bibliografia crítica da literatura brasileira. Nova edição [i.e., 4. ed.], com um apêndice de Assis Brasil, incluindo 47 novos escritores. [Rio de Janeiro], Edições de Ouro, [1980?]. 470p.   **BD1103**

1st ed. 1951.

Arranged chronologically by literary periods and movements, with bibliographical listings of works by and about individual authors. Covers from the colonial period to modern times. Apart from the appendix of new writers, the text of this edition is unchanged from the 3d ed. of 1964.   Z1681.C3

Gomes, Celuta Moreira. O conto brasileiro e sua crítica. Bibliografia (1841–1974). Rio de Janeiro, Biblioteca Nacional, 1977. 2v. (654p.)   **BD1104**

An earlier work by the same author, *Bibliografia do conto brasileiro* (publ. 1968–69 in 2v.) covered 1841–1967.

A bibliography of the Brazilian short story, together with critical studies of the writers and their works. Arranged by literary author, with listings of their own works followed by references to critical writings. Indexes of titles and of critics.   Z1684.S5G65

Moisés, Massaud [et al.]. Bibliografia da literatura portuguêsa. São Paulo, Ed. Saraiva, Ed. da Universidade, 1968. 383p.   **BD1105**

A bibliographic guide to Portuguese literature from earliest to modern times. Arranged by period, then by literary genre. The subsections on individual authors include both their own writings and critical works about the authors.

Moisés is also the compiler of *Literatura portuguesa moderna: guia biográfico, crítico e bibliográfico* (São Paulo, Editora Cultrix, 1973. 202p.) which presents biobibliographical sketches of contemporary writers.   Z2721.M63

Newberry Library, Chicago. A catalog of the William B. Greenlee collection of Portuguese history and literature and the Portuguese materials in the Newberry Library, comp. by Doris Varner Welsh. Chicago, Newberry Library, 1953. 342p.   **BD1106**

For full information *see* DC463.   Z2739.N48

Reis, Antônio Simões dos. Bibliografia da História da literatura brasileira de Sílvio Romero. Rio [de Janeiro], Zélio Valverde, 1944. 305p.   **BD1107**

No more published.

Bibliography to accompany Sylvio Romero's *História da literatura brasileira* (3. ed. Rio de Janeiro, Olympio, 1943. 5v.).

Contents: Fatores da literatura brasileira: v.1, Trabalhos estrangeiros e nacionais sobre a literatura brasileira.   Z1681.R4

Topete, José Manuel. A working bibliography of Brazilian literature. Gainesville, Univ. of Florida Pr., 1957. 114p.   **BD1108**

Aims "to present a complete picture of its major writers both bibliographically and critically, to bring together all known critical works on the subject, and to include as many of the contemporary writers as space and economy permit."—*Pref.*   Z1681.T6

Wogan, Daniel S. A literatura hispano-americana no Brasil: 1877–1944; bibliografia de crítica, história literária e traduçoes. Baton Rouge, Louisiana State Univ. Pr., [1948]. 98p.   **BD1109**

An annotated bibliography of 822 items, listing the contributions that Brazilians have made to the history and criticism of the literatures of Spanish America. Arranged by country; includes books and articles published from 1877 to 1945. Portuguese translations of Spanish-American novels, plays, short stories, and poems are included under each country division.   Z1609.L7W6

Dictionaries

Brasil, Assis. Dicionário prático de literatura brasileira. [Rio de Janeiro], Edições de Ouro, [1979]. 324p. il.   **BD1110**

A brief biographical sketch is followed by a list of each writer's work and a critical note. Entry is under the author's first name.   PQ9527.B7

Brinches, Victor Manuel Fernandes. Dicionário biobibliográfico luso-brasileiro. [Rio de Janeiro], Editora Fundo de Cultura, [1965]. 509p.   **BD1111**

In two main sections: (1) Autores portuguêses; (2) Autores brasileiros. Includes both living and deceased writers.   PQ9027.B7

Dicionário de literatura: literatura portuguesa, literatura brasileira, literatura galega, estilística literária. Direccão de Jacinto do Prado Coelho. 3. ed. Porto, Figueirinhas, 1978. 5v. (1526p.) il.   **BD1112**

1960 ed. had title: *Dicionário das literaturas portuguesa, galega e brasileira.*

Offers entries for authors, terms, movements, genres, etc. Signed articles; bibliographies. v.5 provides indexes of authors and titles.   PQ9006.C65

Foster, David William and **Reis, Roberto.** A dictionary of contemporary Brazilian authors. Tempe, Center for Latin American Studies, Arizona State Univ., 1981. 152p.   **BD1113**

Offers bio-critical sketches by some 34 contributors; those originally submitted in Portuguese have been translated into English. Entries "are more critical than biographic in nature" (*Introd.*) and emphasis is on younger writers. List of principal works at the end of each article.   PQ9506.F6

Gonçalves, Augusto de Freitas Lopes. Dicionário histórico e literário do teatro no Brasil. Rio de Janeiro, Livraria Editora Cátedra, 1975–82. v.1–4. (In progress)   **BD1114**

Contents: v.1–4, A–D.

A dictionary of dramatists, actors, actresses and others in various performing arts professions, together with entries for individual theater pieces (comedies, tragedies, operas, zarzuelas, etc.).   PN2471.G6

Luft, Celso Pedro. Dicionário de literatura portuguêsa e brasileira. Pôrto Alegre, Editôra Globo, [1967]. 316p.   **BD1115**

Intended for the student and teacher. Runs mainly to entries for individual authors, but includes entries for literary movements and genres. Bibliographies.   PQ9006.L8

Menezes, Raimundo de. Dicionário literário brasileiro. 2. ed., rev., aumentada e atualizada. Rio de Janeiro, Livros Técnicos e Científicos Editora, [1978]. 803p.   **BD1116**

A section of biographical sketches (with bibliographies of works by and about individual authors) is followed by an alphabetically arranged section of articles designated "Ismos literários, escolas e academias" (p.717–84); there is also a dictionary of pseudonyms and a select general bibliography.   PQ9527.M39

Pequeno dicionário de literatura brasileira. Organizado e dirigido por José Paulo Paes e Massaud Moisés. 2a. ed. rev. e ampl. São Paulo, Editora Cultrix, [1980]. 462p.   **BD1117**

1st ed. 1967.

Offers brief, signed articles contributed by some 30 scholars. Author entries predominate, but literary terms, movements, etc., are included. Bibliographies.   PQ9506.P4

History

Coutinho, Afrânio. A literatura no Brasil. 2. ed. atual. rev. Rio de Janeiro, Ed. Sul Americana, 1968–72. 6v.   **BD1118**

1st ed. 1955–59

A detailed history with extensive bibliographical footnotes.   PQ9511.C66

Forjaz de Sampaio, Albino. História da literatura portuguesa ilustrada, publicada . . . com a colaboração dos senhores Afonso Lopes Vieira, Agostinho de Campos, [e outros]. Paris, Aillaud, [1929–42]. 4v. il.   **BD1119**

A lavishly illustrated history, covering from medieval times to the 19th century with a brief chapter on the 20th century. Each chapter begins with an extensive bibliography. Illustrations include many facsimiles of title pages, manuscripts, etc.   PQ9011.F6

Saraiva, António José and **Lopes, Óscar.** História da literatura portuguêsa. 11. ed. corrigida e actualizada. Pôrto, Pôrto Editôra, 1979. 1218p.   **BD1120**

1st ed. 1955?

Includes bibliographies and index. A briefer work of the same title by Saraiva alone has also appeared in many editions.   PQ9012.S3

Provençal

See also BD1004–BD1005.

Brunel, Clovis. Bibliographie des manuscrits littéraires en ancien provençal. Paris, Droz, 1935. 146p. (Société de publications romanes et françaises. [Publications] XIII)   **BD1121**

Arranged geographically by depository. For each manuscript gives date, region, a brief description of contents, and editions. Indexes by depository, place of origin, title, and author. Includes a list of works classified by genre.   Z6605.P96B8

French XX bibliography. Provençal supplement. no.1. N.Y., French Institute–Alliance Française and the Camargo Foundation, 1976. 111p.   **BD1122**

Joseph D. Gauthier, comp.

Follows the style of the parent series (BD991), "but because of the founding of the Félibrige in 1854 and the importance of the second half of the 19th century in the history of Provençal literature" (*Editor's note*), the period of coverage goes back to 1850; as in the main series, publications from 1940 are listed.

A series of bibliographies bearing the title *Bibliographie occitane* compiled by Pierre Louis Berthaud and others (Paris, Les Belles Lettres; Montpellier, Centre d'Études Occitanes, Univ. Paul-Valery, etc., 1946–73) lists writings in or treating of the "langue d'Oc"; volumes published to date cover 1919/42, 1943/56, 1957/66 and 1967/71.

Jeanroy, Alfred. Bibliographie sommaire des chansonniers provençaux (manuscrits et éditions). . . . Paris, Champion, 1916. 86p. (Les classiques français du moyen âge. 2. série: Manuels [16])   **BD1123**

Lists manuscripts, giving date, provenance, contents, published editions, and citations to fuller descriptions.   Z7033.P8J4

—— La poésie lyrique des troubadours. Toulouse, Privat; Paris, Didier, 1934. 2v.   **BD1124**

Contents: v.1, Histoire externe. Diffusion à l'étranger. Liste de troubadours classés par régions. Notices bio-bibliographiques; v.2, Histoire interne. Les genres: leur évolution et leurs plus notables représentants.

A classic study. v.1 contains an alphabetical list of troubadours, giving biographical information, number of compositions, and bibliographical references. v.2 includes a chronology of the various genres. Bibliographies at the ends of chapters.   PC3315.J4

New York. Public Library. Provençal literature and language including the local history of southern France; a list of references in the New York Public Library, comp. by Daniel C. Haskell . . . N.Y., 1925. 885p.   **BD1125**

"Reprinted with additions October 1925 from the Bulletin of the New York Public Library of June to December 1921, January to April and June to December 1922."—*verso of title page.*

Classified catalog of a collection numbering about 25,000 items. Includes a section on modern Provençal.   Z7033.P8N5

Pillet, Alfred. Bibliographie der Troubadours . . . ergänzt, weitergeführt und hrsg. von dr. Henry Carstens . . . Haale (Saale), M. Niemeyer, 1933. 518p. (Schriften der Königsberger Gelehrten Gesellschaft. Sonderreihe, Bd.3)   **BD1126**

An author listing giving titles of poems, manuscripts, and editions, with citations to secondary sources. Includes a separate section on manuscripts, giving date, contents, and provenance; a list of anonymous compositions; and a rhyme index.

François Zufferey's *Bibliographie des poètes provençaux des XIVᵉ et XVᵉ siècles* (Genève, Droz, 1981. 91p.) lists manuscripts, editions, and studies of poets of the period following that dealt with by Pillet.   Z7033.P8P6

Taylor, Robert Allen. La littérature occitane du Moyen Age: bibliographie sélective et critique. Toronto, Univ. of Toronto Pr., [1977]. 166p. (Toronto medieval bibliographies, 7)   **BD1127**

A selected, annotated bibliography of the medieval literature of the "langue d'oc." In five main sections: (1) Instruments de travail; (2) Études de critique littéraire; (3) La poésie lyrique des troubadours (with subsections for individual authors); (4) La littérature non-lyrique; (5) Guide d'orientation aux matières contiguës. Indexed.   Z7033.P8T38

Spanish

Guides

Arnaud, Émile and **Tusón, Vicente.** Guide de bibliographie hispanique. [Toulouse], Privat-Didier, [1967]. 353p.   **BD1128**

A selective bibliographic guide for the beginner in Hispanic studies, with emphasis on language and literature. Some annotations.   Z2681.A75

Bleznick, Donald W. A sourcebook for Hispanic literature and language: a selected, annotated guide to Spanish, Spanish-American, and Chicano bibliography, literature, linguistics, journals, and other source materials. 2d ed. Metuchen, N.J., Scarecrow Pr., 1983. 304p.   **BD1129**

1st ed. 1974.

More than 1,400 entries in classed arrangement, with author and title indexes.   Z2695.A2B55

Foster, David William and **Foster, Virginia Ramos.** Manual of Hispanic bibliography. 2d ed., rev. and expanded. N.Y., Garland Pr., 1977. 329p.   **BD1130**

1st ed. 1970.

" . . . represents an attempt at providing Spanish and Spanish-American literary scholars with a comprehensive bibliographical guide to primary and important secondary sources of investigation."—*Introd.* Includes annotated listings of both literary and national bibliographies, plus works relating to library resources.   Z2691.A1F68

Bibliography

Bibliographie hispanique, 1905–17. N.Y., Hispanic Soc., [1909–19]. 13v. (Publications of the Hispanic Society of America) (Repr.: N.Y., Kraus, 1962)   **BD1131**

Annual bibliography including both books and periodical articles, and covering the languages, literature, and history of the Spanish- and Portuguese-speaking countries, both in Europe and elsewhere. No more published.   Z2685.B61

Bibliography of Old Spanish texts. Literary texts, ed. 2. Comp. by Anthony Cárdenas [and others]. [Madison, Wis., Hispanic Seminary of Medieval Studies], 1977. 128p.   **BD1132**

1st ed. 1975.

The bibliography "was originally conceived as a necessary first step in the change-over to computer-assisted techniques in the compilation of the Old Spanish dictionary, a project ongoing at the University of Wisconsin-Madison for nearly half a century."—*Introd.* Its aim is to create "an exhaustive descriptive inventory of the relevant pre-1501 Old Spanish texts" from which a selection can be made of the most lexically promising material to use in compiling the dictionary. This edition provides full citation (with indication of present location) of 1,869 items.   Z2682.B52

Cuadernos bibliográficos. v.1– . Madrid, C.S.I.C., 1961– . Irregular.   **BD1133**

Each issue is devoted to a special topic, e.g., no.1, Cervantes: bibliografía fundamental (1900–1959), by Alberto Sanchez; no.12, 14, 15, 19, 21, Impresos del siglo XVI, by José Simón Díaz; no.27, Romancero popular del siglo XVIII, by Francisco Aguilar Piñal; no.43, Indice de las poesías publicadas en los periódicos españoles del siglo XVIII, by Francisco Aguilar Piñal.

Fitzmaurice-Kelly, James. Spanish bibliography. [London], Oxford Univ. Pr., 1925. 389p. (Hispanic notes and monographs issued by the Hispanic Society of America. Bibliography ser. II)   **BD1134**

A much expanded English edition of the author's *Bibliographie de l'histoire de la littérature espagnole* (Paris, Colin, 1913. 78p.). Lists general works, collections, etc., then works by and critical studies about Spanish literary authors.   Z2691.F557

Foulché-Delbosc, Raymond and **Barrau-Dihigo, Louis.** Manuel de l'hispanisant. N.Y., Putnam, 1920; Hispanic Soc. of America, 1925. v.1–2.   **BD1135**

For full information *see* AA96.

Golden, Herbert Hershel and **Simches, Seymour O.** Modern Iberian language and literature: a bibliography of homage studies. Cambridge, Harvard Univ. Pr., 1958. 184p.   **BD1136**

Indexes articles in *Festschriften* and homage volumes; concerned primarily with Catalan, Portuguese, and Spanish languages and literatures, with some articles relating to Spanish America and Brazil. Covers studies from approximately 1500. 424 books in various languages, published through 1956, are indexed.   Z7031.G6

Serís, Homero. Manual de bibliografía de la literatura española. Syracuse, N.Y., Centro de Estudios Hispánicos, 1948–54. v.1 in 2v. (Publicaciones del Centro de Estudios Hispánicos, 2)   **BD1137**

Pt.1: fasc.1, Obras generales. 422p. (1948); fasc.2, p.423–1086 (1954). No more published.

The first volume of a very comprehensive bibliographical manual of Spanish literature. Includes 8,779 numbered items with a full alphabetical index and a general table of contents. Lists both books and periodical articles, some with annotations.

Later parts were announced to cover: (2) Lengua; (3) Edad media; (4) Siglos XVI y XVII; (5) Siglo XVIII; (6) Siglo XIX; and (7) Siglo XX, suplemento e índices.

The *Bibliografía de la lingüística española* by Serís (Bogotá, 1964; BC141) is not part of this series, but items therein have been numbered in sequence with the *Manual* to emphasize the close relationship between language and literature and to facilitate cross references from the *Bibliografía* to the *Manual*.   Z2691.S47

Simón Díaz, José. Bibliografía de la literatura hispánica. Madrid, Consejo Superior de Investigaciones Científicas, Inst. "Miguel de Cervantes" de Filología Hispánica, 1950–84. v.1–13. (In progress)   **BD1138**

Contents: v.1, Literatura castellana; Literatura catalana; Literatura gallega; Literatura vasca (1950); v.2, Bibliografías de bibliografías; Bio-bibliografías; Índices de publicaciones periódicas; Historia de la imprenta (1951); v.3, Literatura castellana: Edad media, Siglos XI–XV (1953); v.4, Siglos de oro: Fuentes generales: Autores, A–Agustin (1955); v.5–13, Autores, Alaba–Llusas (1958–84).

A comprehensive bibliography of all the Hispanic literatures. Books, periodical articles, and unpublished works such as theses and lectures are included; in some cases, references are given to reviews of books. Library locations, chiefly in Spanish libraries, are noted in many instances. v.2 contains 2,124 entries, mainly general bibliographies in the field of literature; bio-bibliographies; a list of periodical indexes, etc. The third and subsequent volumes are devoted to bibliographies of specific periods and individual authors. Comprehensive indexes in each volume.

An unnumbered volume termed "Tomos V y VI (apéndices)", published 1973, provides interim updating of the material in v.5–6 until such time as the 2d ed. of those volumes is published. It describes early editions of works which have come to light since publication of v.5–6, and indicates additional locations for rare books described in those volumes.

Several volumes of a new edition have appeared: Z2691.S5

———— ———— 2. ed., corr. y aum. Madrid, Consejo Superior de Investigaciones Científicas, Instituto "Miguel de Cervantes" de Filología Hispánica, 1960–72. v.1–4. (In progress)   **BD1139**

Contents: v.1, General: Literatura castellana; Literatura catalana; Literatura gallega; Literatura vasca (1960); v.2, [Bibliografías]; v.3¹⁻², Literatura castellana: Edad media, Siglos XI–XV (1963–65); v.4, Literatura castellana: Siglos de oro (1972).

In addition, v.1 of a "3. edición corregida y actualizada" was published 1983 (911p.).

———— Manual de bibliografía de la literatura española. 3a ed. refundida, corr. y aum. Madrid, Gredos, [1980]. 1156p. (Biblioteca románica hispánica. III. Manuales, 47)   **BD1140**

1st ed. 1963; *Adiciones 1962–64* (publ. 1966); *Adiciones 1965–70* (publ. 1972). The 1st ed. was reprinted 1966 and 1970 with the 1962–64 suppl. bound at back and designated as a 2d ed.

A bibliography of nearly 27,000 entries for books and periodical articles covering the whole range of Spanish literature. Not an abridgment of the author's larger work, but highly selective and more limited in scope.

A general section is followed by chronologically arranged sections covering one or more centuries. Within period divisions general works are followed by the names of individual authors, arranged alphabetically, with titles of their works and of biographical and critical works about them. Name and subject indexes.

Z2691.S54

Siracusa, Joseph. Relaciones literarias entre España e Italia; ensayo de una bibliografía de literatura comparada. Boston, G. K. Hall, 1972. 252p.   **BD1141**

An author listing of books, articles, and essays. Indexed by name, but not by topic.   Z2691.S57

Turkevich, Ludmilla Buketoff. Spanish literature in Russia and in the Soviet Union, 1735–1964. Metuchen, N.J., Scarecrow Pr., 1967. 273p.   **BD1142**

Includes listings of Russian translations of works by Spanish authors and of Russian writings about them.   Z2694.T7T8

Vera, Francisco. La cultura española medieval. Datos bio-bibliográficos para su historia. Madrid, Victoriano Suárez, 1933–34. 2v.   **BD1143**

A bio-bibliographical dictionary of the writers of medieval Spain.   DP99.V4

Dissertations

Chatham, James R. and **Ruiz-Fornells, Enrique.** Dissertations in Hispanic languages and literatures; an index of dissertations completed in the United States and Canada, 1876–1966. [Lexington], Univ. Pr. of Kentucky, [1970]. 120p.   **BD1144**

A classed list with author-subject index. Relevant dissertations completed in departments other than Hispanic languages and literatures are included.   Z2695.A2C46

Chatham, James R. and **McClendon, Carmen C.** Dissertations in Hispanic languages and literatures; an index of dissertations completed in the United States and Canada. Volume 2: 1967–1977. [Lexington], Univ. Pr. of Kentucky, [1981]. 162p.   **BD1145**

Lists an additional 3,527 dissertations. Alphabetical author listing with separate indexes for Catalan, Luso-Brazilian, and Spanish/Spanish American languages and literatures.   Z2695.A2C46

Translations into English

Pane, Remigio Ugo. English translations from the Spanish, 1484–1943, a bibliography. New Brunswick, N.J., Rutgers Univ. Pr., 1944. 218p. (Rutgers Univ. studies in Spanish, no.2)   **BD1146**

An unannotated, alphabetical list of 2,682 items of peninsular-Spanish literature and history. A review with corrections and additions by W. K. Jones was published in *Hispanic review* 13:174–77 (April 1945).   Z2694.T7P2

Rudder, Robert S. The literature of Spain in English translation; a bibliography. N.Y., F. Ungar, [1975]. 637p.   **BD1147**

Lists translations appearing in periodicals and in collections, as well as separately published works. Listing is by literary period (medieval, Renaissance, etc.), then by author; individual poems and stories are given separate entries. "Literature" is broadly interpreted to include historical writings, etc., of literary merit. "Spain" of the title refers to the country rather than the language, so that translations from Catalan, Basque, etc., are included, as are translations from the Latin of early Spanish writers. Indexes of authors and of anonymous works.   Z2694.T7R83

Dictionaries and encyclopedias

Diccionari de la literatura catalana, sota la direcció de Joaquim Molas i Josep Massot i Muntaner. Barcelona, Edicions 62, [1979]. 762p. (Cultura catalana contemporània, 9)   **BD1148**

Entries for Catalan authors predominate, but consideration is given to literary forms, terms, and genres, as well as some individual works and literary journals. Bibliographic notes at the end of many articles.   PC3901.D5

Diccionario de literatura española. Dirigido por Germán Bleiberg [y] Julián Marías. 4. ed., corr. y aum. Madrid, Ediciones de la Revista de Occidente, [1972]. 1197p., [70]p. **BD1149**

1st ed. 1949.
An extensive dictionary covering all periods of Spanish literature. Includes biographies (with bibliographies), articles on forms of literature, literary terms, etc. All articles are signed. An index of titles mentioned in the text and a chronological index. This edition revised, expanded and updated: some new articles have been added (e.g., "lingüística"), and there is a new appendix on palaeography.
PQ6006.D5

The Oxford companion to Spanish literature. Ed. by Philip Ward. Oxford, Clarendon Pr., 1978. 629p. **BD1150**

Follows the plan of the publisher's "companions" to other literatures, devoting most space to authors (not only creative writers, but also critics, historians, philosophers, etc.), but including some titles, terms, institutions, and literary movements. An important difference stems from the fact that "a great deal of literature in Spanish has been written beyond the geographical confines of Spain, and this necessitates the inclusion of entries on the more important authors and books, not only of Spain, but also of Argentina, Bolivia, Chile, Colombia, Costa Rica, Cuba, Dominican Republic, Ecuador, El Salvador, Guatemala, Honduras, Mexico, Nicaragua, Panama, Paraguay, Peru, Philippines, Puerto Rico, Uruguay, and Venezuela. The literatures of Portugal and Brazil are excluded, but languages of Spain other than Castilian are represented: Basque, Catalan, and Galician."—*Pref.* Frequently provides bibliographic citations to works offering fuller information. PQ6006.O95

Redfern, James. A glossary of Spanish literary composition. N.Y., Harcourt Brace Jovanovich, 1972. 224p. **BD1151**

Gives Spanish equivalents of English literary terms, with examples. PC4680.R4

History

Alborg, Juan Luis. Historia de la literatura española. Madrid, Editorial Gredos, [1966–80]. v.1–4. (In progress) **BD1152**

Contents: v.1, Edad Media y Renacimiento; v.2, Epoca barroca; v.3, Siglo XVIII; v.4, El romanticismo.
A detailed critical history with lengthy bibliographical footnotes and an author and title index in each volume.
The first 2v. have appeared in a "2.ed. ampliada" (1970–72).
PQ6032.A45

Cejador y Frauca, Julio. Historia de la lengua y literatura castellana. Madrid, "Revista de Archivos, Bibliotecas y Museos," 1915–22. 14v. il. **BD1153**

v.1–4 have appeared in a 2d ed., 1927–35, and v.1 in a 3d ed., 1932–33.
A standard history covering the time from Charles V to 1920. Includes bibliographies. PQ6032.C3

Díaz Plaja, Guillermo. Historia general de las literaturas hispánicas. Con una introducción de Ramón Menéndez Pidal. Barcelona, Ed. Barna, 1949–58. 5v. il. **BD1154**

Each section written by a specialist, with extensive bibliographies. Covers not only Spanish literature but others, such as Arab, Catalan, Hebrew, and Latin which have flourished in Spain, and the literatures of other Spanish-speaking countries in the Americas, Philippines, etc. PQ6032.D5

Valbuena Prat, Angel. Historia de la literatura española. 8. ed. corr. y ampliada. Barcelona, G. Gili, [1968]. 4v. **BD1155**

An important scholarly history. Bibliographical references in footnotes; author and title indexes in v.4.
Literatura hispanoamericana, by Angel Valbuena Briones (4. ed. ampliada. Barcelona, G. Gili, 1969. 624p), forms v.5 of this set.
PQ6032.V3

Biography

Instituto Nacional del Libro Español. Quién es quién en las letras españolas. 3. ed. [Madrid], Instituto Nacional del Libro Español, Ministerio de Cultura, [1979]. 495p. **BD1156**

1st ed. 1969.
Bio-bibliographical sketches of nearly 2,000 writers. Includes journalists, essayists, and critics, as well as poets, novelists, dramatists, etc. Z2690.I55

Drama

Ashcom, Benjamin Bowles. A descriptive catalogue of the Spanish comedias sueltas in the Wayne State University Library and the private library of Professor B. B. Ashcom. Detroit, Wayne State Univ. Libraries, 1965. 103p. **BD1157**

805 entries embracing 566 titles. Z2694.D7A8

Bergman, Hannah E. and **Szmuk, Szilvia E.** A catalogue of comedias sueltas in The New York Public Library. [London], Grant & Cutler, 1980–81. 2v. (309p.) **BD1158**

Provides full bibliographic descriptions of an extensive collection of *sueltas.* Alphabetical title listing. Z2694.D7B47

Boyer, Mildred Vinson. The Texas collection of *comedias sueltas*: a descriptive bibliography. Boston, G. K. Hall, [1978]. 620p. **BD1159**

"This volume has been designed to describe The University of Texas [at Austin] holdings in Spanish dramatic literature in suelta editions prior to 1834."—*Introd.* Arranged by author, with anonymous works listed first. 1,119 items representing some 750 different titles. Indexed. Z2694.D7B7

Cambridge. University. Library. *Comedias sueltas* in Cambridge University Library: a descriptive catalog, comp. by A. J. C. Bainton. Cambridge, The Library, 1977. 281p. (Cambridge Univ. Lib. Historical bibliography ser., 2) **BD1160**

Catalog of a collection of more than 900 separate editions of single plays, with full bibliographic description. Z2694.D7C35

Coe, Ada May. Catálogo bibliográfico y crítico de las comedias anunciadas en los periódicos de Madrid desde 1661 hasta 1819. Baltimore, Johns Hopkins Pr.; London, Milford, 1935. 270p. (Johns Hopkins studies in Romance literatures and languages, extra v.9) **BD1161**

A list of plays noted in the periodicals of Madrid from 1661 to 1819, arranged alphabetically by title, with author index.
Z2694.D7C6

Cotarelo y Mori, Emilio. Catálogo descriptivo de la gran colección de Comedias escogidas que consta de cuarenta y ocho volúmenes, impresos de 1652 a 1704. Madrid, Tipografía de Archivos, 1932. 266p. **BD1162**

Contains full descriptions of each volume of the *Comedias nuevas escogidas de los mejores ingenios de España,* with contents and author and title indexes. Z2694.D7C75

———— Teatro español; catálogo abreviado de una colección dramática española, hasta fines del siglo XIX y de obras relativas al teatro español. Madrid, V. e H. de J. Ratés, 1930. 164p. **BD1163**

A listing of more than 1,800 plays and works about the Spanish theater. Z2694.D7T2

McCready, Warren T. Bibliografía temática de estudios sobre el teatro español antiguo. [Toronto], Univ. of Toronto Pr., [1966]. 445p. **BD1164**

Lists books and periodical articles published 1850–1950 on the Spanish theater from the formative period through mid-18th century. Nearly 4,000 items; author index. Z2694.D7M15

Oberlin College. Library. Spanish drama collection in the Oberlin College Library; a descriptive catalogue. Paul P. Rogers, ed. Oberlin, Ohio, Oberlin College, 1940. 468p. **BD1165**

Covers the period from the last quarter of the 17th century to the year 1924. Includes 7,530 numbered items, arranged alphabetically by author.

—— —— Supplementary volume, containing reference lists. 1946. 157p.

Contents: no.7531–7644, Anonymous plays; Title list; Composers; Printers; List of theaters. Z2694.D7O2

O'Brien, Robert Alfred. Spanish plays in English translation; an annotated bibliography. N.Y., publ. for the American Educational Theatre Association by Las Américas Pub. Co., 1963. 70p. **BD1166**

Annotations on authors and plays. Includes information for producers on number of acts, number of men and women in cast, royalty requirements, etc. Z2694.D7O3

Regueiro, José M. Spanish drama of the golden age; a catalogue of the comedia collection in the University of Pennsylvania Libraries. [New Haven, Research Publications, 1971] 106p. **BD1167**

Guide to a collection of about 3,000 titles which have been issued on microfilm by Research Publications, New Haven, Conn. Z2694.D7R37

Thompson, Lawrence Sidney. A bibliography of Spanish plays on microcards. Hamden, Conn., Shoe String, 1968. 490p. **BD1168**

An author (or anonymous title) listing of some 6,000 "Spanish, Catalonian, and Spanish-American plays from the sixteenth century to the present, all published in Microcard editions by Falls City Microcards, Louisville, Kentucky, from 1957 through 1966."— *Introd.* Original texts are in the University of Kentucky Library. Spanish plays predominate. Z2694.D7T48

Toronto. University Library. A bibliography of *comedias sueltas* in the University of Toronto library, comp. by J. A. Molinaro, J. H. Parker and Evelyn Rugg. [Toronto], Univ. of Toronto Pr., 1959. 149p. **BD1169**

Lists the *sueltas* in a special collection presented to the university; includes principally 18th-century editions of more than 700 Spanish plays from 1703 to 1825. Arrangement is alphabetical by title, with indexes by author, and by publishers and booksellers. Z2694.D7T66

Fiction

Brown, Reginald F. La novela española, 1700–1850. Madrid, Dirección General de Archivos y Bibliotecas, Servicio de Publicaciones del Ministerio de Educación Nacional, 1953. 221p. (Bibliografías de archivos y bibliotecas) **BD1170**

Arranged chronologically with an author index.

Ferreras, Juan Ignacio. Catálogo de novelas y novelistas españoles del siglo XIX. Madrid, Ediciones Cátedra, [1979]. 454p. **BD1171**

Includes some 2,150 entries for authors and anonymous titles. Dates, a brief identifying statement, and notes on the major work or overall achievement are given for most authors, along with a list of novels. Z2694.F4F47

Laurenti, Joseph L. Bibliografía de la literatura picaresca: desde sus orígenes hasta el presente. Metuchen, N.J., Scarecrow Pr., 1973. 262p. **BD1172**

A chronological listing of picaresque novels, giving editions,

translations, and citations to secondary material. A preliminary section lists works on the picaresque genre in general. Z5917.P5L35

—— —— Suplemento. N.Y., AMS Pr., [1981]. 163p.

Title also in English: *A bibliography of picaresque literature. Supplement.*

Adds citations to publications of the 1973–early 1978 period, with some items omitted from the basic volume. Z5917.P5L35

Ricapito, J. V. Bibliografía razonada y anotada de las obras maestras de la picaresca española. [Madrid], Editorial Castalia, [1980]. 613p. **BD1173**

A general section of studies of the Spanish picaresque novel is followed by special sections on "La vida de Lazarillo de Tormes," "Guzmán de Alfarache," and "Vida del Buscón." Annotations are of some length. Cross references; index. Z2694.P5R53

Poetry

Cano, José Luis. Antología de la nueva poesía española. 2. ed., aumentada. [Madrid, Gredos, 1963] 438p. **BD1174**

1st ed. 1958.

An anthology of works of about 65 poets, with brief bio-bibliographical notes. PQ6187.C3

Rodriguez Moñino, Antonio R. and **Brey Mariño, Maria,** eds. Catálogo de los manuscritos poéticos castellanos existentes en la Biblioteca de The Hispanic Society of America (siglos XV, XVI y XVII). N.Y., Hispanic Society, 1965–66. 3v. il. **BD1175**

Descriptive notes and contents of the collections are given; v.3 contains detailed indexes. Z6621.N5257

Steunou, Jacqueline and **Knapp, Lothar.** Bibliografía de los cancioneros castellanos del siglo XV y repertorio de sus géneros poéticos. Paris, Centre National de la Recherche Scientifique, 1975–78. 2v. (France. Institut de Recherche et d'Histoire des Textes. Documents, études et répertoires, 22) **BD1176**

Introductory matter (including a bibliography of the manuscripts and early editions of the *Cancioneros*) is followed by five computer-generated sections: (A) Inventario de los manuscritos y antiguas ediciones; (B) Inventario por orden numerico de las poesías de cada manuscrito y edición; (C) Indice de los autores; (D) Clasificación de las poesías por orden alfabético [i.e., according to *incipit*]; (E) Clasificación de las poesías según los autores. Z2694.P7S74

Individual authors

See note p.465.

Cervantes

Drake, Dana B. Don Quijote (1894–1970): a selective annotated bibliography. Chapel Hill, U.N.C. Dept. of Romance Languages, 1974. 267p. (North Carolina studies in the romance languages and literatures, no.138) **BD1177**

Intended to continue the work of Leopoldo Rius y de Llosellas, *Bibliografia critica de las obras de Miguel de Cervantes Saavedra* (BD1181). A second volume was published as: Z8158.D69

—— —— Volume two, with an index to volumes one and two. Miami, Ediciones Universal, [1978]. 269p.

The following has been designated as v.3 of the set:

—— Don Quijote in world literature: a selective, annotated bibliography. N.Y., Garland, 1980. 272p. (Don Quijote, 1894–1970: a selective, annotated bibliography, v.3; Garland reference library of the humanities, v.187) **BD1178**

Taken together, the three volumes provide extensive annotations on the leading books and articles concerning *Don Quijote*. v.3

groups together references to works dealing with influences in a given country or region.   Z8158.D694

Grismer, Raymond Leonard. Cervantes: a bibliography. Books, essays, articles and other studies on the life of Cervantes, his works, and his imitators. N.Y., Wilson, 1946. 183p.   **BD1179**

Z8158.G7

Madrid. Biblioteca Nacional. Catálogo bibliográfico de la sección de Cervantes de la Biblioteca Nacional, por Gabriel-Martín del Río y Rico. . . . Madrid, "Revista de Archivos, Bibliotecas y Museos," 1930. 915p.   **BD1180**

Z8158.M24

Rius y de Llosellas, Leopoldo. Bibliografía crítica de las obras de Miguel de Cervantes Saavedra. Madrid, Murillo, 1895–1905. 3v. il.   **BD1181**

Z8158.R61

Sedó Peris-Mencheta, Juan. Catálogo de la colección cervantina Sedó (redactado por Luis María Plaza Escudero). Barcelona, José Porter, 1953–55. 3v.   **BD1182**

Contents: v.1, Ediciones del Quijote; v.2, Obras de Cervantes (excepto Don Quijote), Obras de Cervantes completas y selectas, Obras de inspiración cervantina, Novelística caballeresca y sentimental; v.3, Crítica cervantina, catálogos, conmemoraciones, varia. Índices.

A "Suplemento" (27p.), a "Guía del lector; Resumen estadístico de las ediciones del Quijote; Adiciones últimas" (8p.) and a "Fe de erratas" (6p.) have also been issued.   Z8158.S453

Suñé Benages, Juan and **Suñé Fonbuena, Juan.** Bibliografía crítica de ediciones del Quijote impresas desde 1605 hasta 1917 . . . Barcelona, Editorial Perelló, 1917. 485p. il.   **BD1183**

Z8158.S96

────── ────── Continuado hasta 1937 por el primero de los citados autores y ahora redactada por J. D. M. Ford y C. T. Keller. Cambridge, Harvard Univ. Pr., 1939. 73p.

Z8158.S96

Predmore, Richard L. An index to Don Quijote including proper names and notable matters. New Brunswick, N.J., Rutgers Univ. Pr., 1938. 102p. (Rutgers Univ. studies in Spanish, 1)   **BD1184**

More recent, but more limited in scope, is Eugene C. Torbert's *Cervantes' place-names: a lexicon* (Metuchen, N.J., Scarecrow Pr., 1978. 181p.).   PQ6361.Z9P7

Spanish American

Guides

Rela, Walter. Guía bibliográfica de la literatura hispanoamericana desde siglo XIX hasta 1970. Buenos Aires, Casa Pardo, 1971. 613p.   **BD1185**

A listing of more than 6,000 items without annotations. There are sections for general and national bibliography, literary history and criticism, anthologies, and biographical works. Within most sections there are subdivisions for the individual Latin American nations. Index of names.   Z1609.L7R44

────── Spanish American literature: a selected bibliography. Literatura hispanoamericana: bibliografía selecta, 1970–1980. [East Lansing], Michigan State Univ., Dept. of Romance and Classical Languages, [1982]. 231p.   **BD1186**

Similar in plan to the preceding item, bringing the listing up to date through 1980. Indexes of authors, critics, and translators.   Z1609.L7R45

Rodríguez, Mario and **Peloso, Vincent C.** A guide for the study of culture in Central America (humanities and social sciences). Wash., Pan American Union, 1968. 88p. (Pan American Union. Division of Philosophy and Letters. Basic bibliographies, 5)   **BD1187**

More than 900 items, about a quarter of them bibliographies and reference works.

Bibliography

Anderson, Robert Roland. Spanish American modernism; a selected bibliography. Tucson, Univ. of Arizona Pr., [1970]. 167p.   **BD1188**

A general section on Spanish American modernism is followed by select bibliographies on 18 representative authors. Includes books and articles. Index.   Z1609.L7A66

Bibliografía general de la literatura latinoamericana. Coordinador, Jorge Carrera Andrade; revisor, Héctor Luis Arena. Paris, Unesco, 1972. 187p.   **BD1189**

A bibliography of more than 3,100 items in three chronological sections: (1) Periodo colonial; (2) Siglo XIX; (3) Época contemporánea. Each section is subdivided for general works and individual countries.   Z1609.L7B5

Bryant, Shasta M., comp. A selective bibliography of bibliographies of Hispanic American literature. 2d ed., greatly expanded and rev. Austin, Inst. of Latin American Studies, Univ. of Texas at Austin, 1976. 100p. (Guides and bibliographies ser., 8)   **BD1190**

1st ed., 1966, published by Pan American Union as its "Basic bibliography," no.3.

A guide for the student. Arranged by author or other main entry. Index of names, plus topical subjects. 662 items.   Z1609.L7B77

Flores, Angel. Bibliografía de escritores hispanoamericanos, 1609–1974. A bibliography of Spanish-American writers. N.Y., Gordian Pr., 1975. 318p.   **BD1191**

In two sections, the first devoted to major writers of all periods, the second to other notable writers 1883–1974. Lists editions of each writer's works and critical/biographical references. Index of authors treated (about 190 in all).   Z1609.L7F55

Grismer, Raymond Leonard. A reference index to twelve thousand Spanish American authors; a guide to the literature of Spanish America. N.Y., Wilson, 1939. 150p. (Inter-American Bibliographical and Library Assoc. publ. ser.3, v.1)   **BD1192**

An index to more than 125 books of literary history, biography, bibliography, etc., containing material about Spanish-American authors. Arranged alphabetically by author.

Grismer's *New bibliography of the literatures of Spain and Spanish America* (Minneapolis, Perine, 1941–46. v.1–7) remains incomplete, covering only through "Cez".   Z1601.G86

Handbook of Latin American studies, 1935– . Gainesville, Univ. of Florida Pr., 1936– . v.1– . Annual.   **BD1193**

Each volume through 1963 includes a section on literature; beginning with v.26, literature appears in alternate years in the *Humanities* volume. For full information see DB241.

Z1605.H26

Harvard University. Library. Latin American literature: classification schedule, classified listing by call number; author and title listing; chronological listing. Cambridge, Harvard Univ. Lib., 1969. 498p. (Widener Library shelflist, 21)   **BD1194**

For a note on the series see AA145.

"Briefly, the *SAL* class provides for nearly all literary works—poetry, drama, fiction, essays, etc.—by Latin American authors and for writings about these authors and their work. Literary histories and anthologies are included. . . . Approximately 16,500 titles are listed."—*Pref.*   Z1609.L7H33

Leguizamón, Julio A. Bibliografía general de la literatura hispanoamericana. Buenos Aires, Ed. Reunidas, [1954]. 213p. **BD1195**

A much expanded revision of the bibliography which appeared originally in the author's *Historia de la literatura hispanoamericana* (Buenos Aires, Ed. Reunidas, 1945. 2v.). Classed arrangement with name index.

Simmons, Merle Edwin. A bibliography of the *romance* and related forms in Spanish America. Bloomington, Indiana Univ. Pr., 1963. 396p. (Indiana Univ. folklore ser., no.18) **BD1196**

A bibliography of books and articles on the romances, ballads, and folklore of South American countries. Lists more than 2,100 items. Z1609.P6S5

Yale University. Library. Spanish American literature in the Yale University Library; a bibliography [by] Frederick Bliss Luquiens. . . . New Haven, Yale Univ. Pr.; London, Milford, 1939. 335p. **BD1197**

Contains 5,668 numbered entries. "The word *literature* . . . is to be understood in the broad sense of 'good writing.' "—*Introd.* Arranged by the countries of Spanish America, with index to the whole. Z1601.Y16

Periodicals

Carter, Boyd George. Las revistas literarias de Hispanoamérica: breve historia y contenido. México, Ed. de Andrea, 1959. 282p. (Colección studium, 24) **BD1198**

Contents: pt.1, A brief history of literary periodicals of Spanish America; pt.2, Short studies of 50 literary periodicals; pt.3, A selected bibliography of articles from 125 literary periodicals; pt.4, General bibliography. Z6954.S8C3

Translations into English

Freudenthal, Juan R. and Freudenthal, Patricia M. Index to anthologies of Latin American literature in English translation. Boston, G. K. Hall, [1977]. 199p. **BD1199**

An index to writings in English translation of some 1,122 Spanish-American and Brazilian authors in 116 anthologies. Arranged by author, with translator and geographic indexes. Works are identified as poetry, fiction, drama, or "other." Z1609.T7F74

Jones, Willis Knapp. Latin American writers in English translation; a tentative bibliography. Wash., Pan Amer. Union, 1944. 141 (i.e., 142)p. ([Pan American Union. Columbus Memorial Library] Bibliographic ser., no.30) **BD1200**

"This bibliography is intended to list all Latin American writing from the time of Columbus and Cortes to the present, that has been translated into English."—*Introd.* Arranged by class with country subdivision. Includes history and travel, essays, poetry, drama, and fiction. Author index. Z1609.T7J6

Leavitt, Sturgis E. Hispano-American literature in the United States; a bibliography of translations and criticisms. Cambridge, Harvard Univ. Pr., 1932. 54p. (Harvard Council on Hispano-American Studies) **BD1201**

A chronological listing of books and periodical articles published in the United States on Hispano-American literature, as well as translations from the literature, 1827–1931. Author index. Z1601.L4

Shaw, Bradley A. Latin American literature in English translation; an annotated bibliography. N.Y., New York Univ. Pr., 1976. 144p. **BD1202**

"A Center for Inter-American Relations book."—*t.p.*
" . . . the scope of the bibliography is limited to published books which include fiction, poetry, drama or the literary essay in English translation. . . . Periodical literature and literary criticism are not included."—*Pref.* Sections for Spanish American literature, Brazil-

ian literature, and non-Hispanic literature of the Caribbean Islands and Guyanas, each sub-divided by genre. Indexes by author, English title, original title, and by country. Z1609.T7S47

Criticism

Foster, David William and Foster, Virginia Ramos. Modern Latin American literature. N.Y., Ungar, [1975]. 2v. (A library of literary criticism) **BD1203**

Like other volumes in the series (e.g., BD843), these volumes present critical commentary on 20th-century Latin American authors. Commentary is drawn from book and periodical materials; about half is translated from Spanish and Portuguese sources. 137 writers are treated. Index of critics in v.2. A subscription books review in the *Booklist* 73:275 notes the omission of a number of important authors. PQ7081.F63

Dictionaries of authors

See also BD1150.

Caribbean writers: a bio-bibliographical-critical encyclopedia. Ed., Donald E. Herdeck. Wash., Three Continents Pr., [1979]. 943p. il. **BD1204**

In four main sections: (1) Anglophone literature from the Caribbean; (2) Francophone literature from the Caribbean; (3) Literatures of the Netherlands Antilles and Surinam; (4) Spanish-language literature from the Caribbean. Each section includes one or more introductory essays, biographical/critical entries for individual authors, and supplementary lists of bibliographies, critical studies, selected journals, etc. No general index. PN849.C3C3

Foster, David William. A dictionary of contemporary Latin American authors. Tempe, Center for Latin American Studies, Arizona State Univ., 1975. 110p. **BD1205**

24 contributors have provided articles which are meant to offer "a characterization of the literary works of the authors, with as little reference to individual biography as possible."—*Pref.* Principal works of the author are listed at the end of each article. Brazilian writers are omitted here and treated in a separate volume (*see* BD1113). PQ7081.3.F6

Pan American Union. Division of Philosophy and Letters. Diccionario de la literatura latinoamericana. [Ed. provisional] Wash., Unión Panamericana, [1958–63]. [v.1–6] **BD1206**

Contents: v.1, Bolivia; v.2, Chile; v.3, Colombia; v.4, Argentina; v.5, Ecuador; v.6, America Central: pt.1, Costa Rica, El Salvador y Guatemala; pt.2, Honduras, Nicaragua y Panama. No more published.

Aims to present a comprehensive encyclopedia of Latin-American literature with emphasis on the critical evaluation of each writer. Each fascicle is a dictionary of authors, giving for each a biographical sketch, an evaluative critical summary, and a bibliography of works by and about. PQ7081.P27

Reichardt, Dieter. Lateinamerikanische Autoren; Literaturlexikon und Bibliographie der deutschen Übersetzungen. Tübingen, H. Erdmann, [1972]. 718p. **BD1207**

Brief bio-bibliographies of authors are arranged by country. Gives lists of published German translations. Z1607.R43

History

Hamilton, Carlos Depassier. Historia de la literatura hispanoamericana. 2. ed. corr y aumentada. Madrid, Ediciones y Publicaciones Españolas, 1966. 397p. **BD1208**

1st ed. 1960–61.

Covers from the colonial period to the 20th century.

PQ7081.H3

Sánchez, Luis Alberto. Nueva historia de la literatura americana. [6a ed.] Valparaíso, Ediciones Universitarias de Valparaíso, Univ. Católica de Valparaíso, [1982]. 615p.   **BD1209**

1st ed. 1944.
Bibliography p.499–568. Indexed.   PQ7081.S265

Drama

Hoffman, Herbert H. Latin American play index. Metuchen, N.J., Scarecrow Pr., 1983–84. 2v.   **BD1210**

Contents: v.1, 1920–1962; v.2, 1962–1980.
Includes references to separately published plays, plays in collections and anthologies, and plays published in periodicals. Arranged by author, with title index.   Z1609.D7H63

Lyday, Leon F. and **Woodyard, George W.** A bibliography of Latin American theater criticism, 1940–1974. Austin, Inst. of Latin American Studies, Univ. of Texas at Austin, 1976. 243p. (Texas. Univ. Inst. of Latin American Studies. Guides and bibliographies ser., 10)   **BD1211**

The period covered "corresponds to the establishment and development of a truly national theater movement in most areas of Latin America."—Introd. Author listing with subject index. 2,360 items.   Z1609.D7L9

Neglia, Erminio Giuseppe and **Ordaz, Luis.** Repertorio selecto del teatro hispanoamericano contemporaneo. 2. ed., rev. y ampl. Tempe, Ariz., Center for Latin American Studies, Arizona State Univ., 1980. 110p.   **BD1212**

1st ed. 1976.
Listing is by country, then by dramatist, giving titles of plays with dates of first performance, plus publication information for printed works. Author index.   Z1609.D7N43

Fiction

Coll, Edna. Indice informativo de la novela hispanoamericana. [Rio Piedras], Editorial Universitaria, Universidad de Puerto Rico, 1974–80. v.1–4. (In progress)   **BD1213**

Contents: v.1, Las Antillas; v.2, Centroamerica; v.3, Venezuela; v.4, Colombia.
The completed series should offer a comprehensive bibliography of the Spanish American novel. Within each country section the listing is alphabetical by novelist's name. Most entries include a biographical note on the author, together with a list of his novels (often including a note on the character of the work) and bibliographic references to biographical and critical works.   Z1609.F4C65

Foster, David William. The 20th century Spanish-American novel: a bibliographic guide. Metuchen, N.J., Scarecrow Pr., 1975. 227p.   **BD1214**

Arranged by names of the novelists; cites both periodical and book materials. Index of critics.   Z1609.F4F68

Individual countries

❖Only selected Spanish-American countries are listed here —those for which fairly recent bibliographies of literature have been found. For other material on these and on the other countries, consult the general bibliographies, BD1129–BD1145, BD1185 and the *Handbook of Latin American studies,* DB241.

Argentinian

Arrieta, Rafael Alberto. Historia de la literatura argentina. Buenos Aires, Ed. Peuser, 1958–60. 6v. il.   **BD1215**

Includes bibliography.   PQ7611.A7

Foster, David William. Argentine literature: a research guide. 2d ed., rev. and expanded. N.Y., Garland, 1982. 778p. (Garland reference library of the humanities, v.338)   **BD1216**

1st ed. 1970 by D. W. Foster and V. R. Foster had title: *Research guide to Argentine literature.*
A section of 30 general and special topics is followed by listings for 73 individual authors. "The general criterion has been to list those items considered useful to serious scholarly research and opinion—articles in all types of scholarly journals and the most important cultural ones, and all monographic studies—and those likely to be easily accessible in Latin America and the United States . . . ."—Introd. Also includes review articles and doctoral dissertations. Index of critics.   Z1621.F66

Orgambide, Pedro G. and **Yahni, Roberto.** Enciclopedia de la literatura argentina. Buenos Aires, Editorial Sudamericana, [1970]. 639p.   **BD1217**

Primarily a dictionary of authors, with some articles on general topics.   PQ7606.O7

Quienes son los escritores argentinos. Buenos Aires, Ediciones Crisol, 1980. 206p.   **BD1218**

Offers biographical sketches of contemporary Argentinian writers.   Z1620.Q53

Bolivian

Ortega, José and **Caceres Romero, Adolfo.** Diccionario de la literatura boliviana. La Paz, Editorial Los Amigos del Libro, 1977. 337p.   **BD1219**

A dictionary of Bolivian writers, giving brief biographical information, bibliographies of works by and about the authors, and often a brief critical note.   Z1650.O77

Chilean

California. University. Library. Contemporary Chilean literature in the University Library at Berkeley; a bibliography with introduction, biographical notes, and commentaries. Berkeley, Center for Latin American Studies, Univ. of California, 1975. 161p.   **BD1220**

Comp. by Gaston Somoshegyi-Szokol.
In three parts: (1) bibliography of selected 20th-century authors; (2) bibliographical guide to histories of Chilean literature; (3) biographical sketches of "selected contemporary Chilean writers whose works are considered to be the most significant in Chilean letters."—Introd. Index of authors.   Z1713.C25

Castillo, Homero and **Silva Castro, Raúl.** Historia bibliográfica de la novela chilena. México, Ed. de Andrea; Charlottesville, Bibliographical Soc. of the Univ. of Virginia, 1961. 214p.   **BD1221**

Added title page in English: Bibliography of the Chilean novel.
Arranged alphabetically by author; lists more than 4,000 titles, including short stories in collections.   Z1714.F4C33

Durán Cerda, Julio. Repertorio del teatro chileno; bibliografía, obras inéditas y estrenadas. Santiago de Chile, [Ed. Universitaria], 1962. 247p. (Universidad de Chile. Facultad de Filosofía y Educación. Publicaciones del Inst. de Literatura Chilena. ser.C, no.1)   **BD1222**

The "works" section lists 1,710 items alphabetically by author; a selective list of studies, and author and title indexes are appended.   Z1714.D7D8

Foster, David William. Chilean literature; a working bibliography of secondary sources. Boston, G. K. Hall, [1978]. 236p. **BD1223**

A section of general references on literary history, genres, etc., is followed by sections on individual Chilean authors. Z1711.F67

Szmulewicz, Efraín. Diccionario de la literatura chilena. Santiago de Chile, Selecciones Lautaro, 1977. 563p. **BD1224**

A biocritical note on the author is followed by a list of his works with dates of publication. Z1710.S95

Colombian

Ayala Poveda, Fernando. Manual de literatura colombiana. Bogotá, Educar Editores, [1984]. 405p. il. **BD1225**

Treats Colombian literature period-by-period, from earliest to modern times, with attention to individual authors and literary movements. Disappointingly little bibliography. PQ8161.A9

Englekirk, John Eugene and **Wade, Gerald E.** Bibliografía de la novela colombiana. México, Impr. Universitaria, 1950. 131p. **BD1226**

An annotated bibliography of the Colombian novel from about 1836. Z1744.F4E6

Orjuela, Héctor H. Bibliografía de la poesía colombiana. Bogotá, Instituto Caro y Cuervo, 1971. 486p. (Inst. Caro y Cuervo. Publ. Ser. bibliográfica, 9) **BD1227**

An author listing of the works of Colombian poets published as books, pamphlets or broadsides. Locates copies in numerous Colombian and foreign libraries. Z1744.P7

——— Bibliografía del teatro colombiano. Bogotá, [Instituto Caro y Cuervo], 1974. 312p. (Inst. Caro y Cuervo. Publ. Ser. bibliográfica, 10) **BD1228**

The main section is an author listing of Colombian dramatic literature. The "Secciones complementarias," p.209–76, offer lists of sources for the study of the Colombian theater, for the study of Latin American theater, and for the study of theater in general. Index of titles of the dramas. Many bibliographical and descriptive notes. Library locations are frequently given, including copies in selected United States libraries. Z1744.D7

——— Fuentes generales para el studio de la literatura colombiana; guía bibliográfica. Bogotá, 1968. 863p. (Inst. Caro y Cuervo. Publ. Ser. bibliográfica, 7) **BD1229**

A comprehensive bibliographical guide for the study of Colombian literature, with sections for bibliographies, dictionaries and guides, biographical works, anthologies and collections, history and criticism, literary movements and periods, literary genres, translations, etc. Library locations are given. Indexed. Z1008.C685

Ortega Torres, José Joaquin. Historia de la literatura colombiana, con prólogos de Antonio Gómez Restrepo y de Daniel Samper Ortega. 2. ed. aum. . . . Bogotá, Ed. Cromos, 1935. 1214p. il. **BD1230**

Contains some general literary history, but the greater part of the work consists of biographies and bibliographies, with extracts from the works of some 180 Colombian authors.

José Nuñez Segura's *Literatura colombiana: sinopsis y comentarios de autores representativos* (14a ed. Medellín, Editorial Bedout, 1976. 893p.) also offers biographical notes on authors, together with excerpts from their writings. PQ8161.O67

Porras Collantes, Ernesto. Bibliografía de la novela en Colombia, con notas de contenido y crítica de las obras y guías de comentarios sobre los autores. Bogotá, Inst. Caro y Cuervo, 1976. 888p. (Inst. Caro y Cuervo. Publ. Ser. bibliográfica, 11) **BD1231**

Based on the bibliography in A. Curcio Altamar's *Evolución de la novela en Colombia* (Bogotá, 1957). Forms a useful companion to H. H. Orjuela's bibliographies (in the same series) covering Colombian poetry and drama (*see* BD1227–BD1228).

More than 2,300 entries. Arranged alphabetically by author; title and chronological indexes. Bibliographical information is very full, including details of serialization where relevant; reprints and translations are included; library locations are given (including a number of libraries outside Colombia). Numerous notes on contents, and excerpts from critical evaluations; citations to critical studies are frequently given. Z1008.C685

Sanchez Lopez, Luis Maria. Diccionario de escritores colombianos. [Bogotà], Plaza & Janes, [1978]. 547p. il. **BD1232**

Offers brief biographical notes and commentary (often no more than an identifying phrase) on Colombian writers both living and deceased, together with lists of their works. Includes a list of pseudonyms with the author's real name given. Z1740.S26

Cuban

Arrom, José Juan. Historia de la literatura dramática cubana. New Haven, Yale Univ. Pr., 1944. 132p. il. (Yale Romanic studies, v.23) (Repr.: N.Y., AMS Pr., 1973) **BD1233**

Bibliografía general, p.93–94; Apéndice bibliográfico de obras dramáticas cubanas, p.95–127. This appendix is a useful bibliography of the Cuban theater. Locates copies in four libraries in the United States and five in Cuba. PQ7381.A7

Diccionario de la literatura cubana. Redactora: Marina García. Habana, Editorial Letras Cubanas, 1980– . v.1– . il. (In progress) **BD1234**

At head of title: Instituto de Literatura y Linguística de la Academia de Ciencias de Cuba.

Contents: v.1, A–L.

Biographical articles predominate, but there are entries for many literary journals, organizations, terms, etc. Bibliographies. PQ7371.D5

Foster, David William. Cuban literature: a research guide. N.Y., Garland, 1985. 522p. (Garland reference library of the humanities, v.511) **BD1235**

A bibliography of general works, works on special forms and topics, and writings on individual authors; in the latter case "the overriding principle has been to include those authors who have attracted a measurable degree of criticism of interest to research scholars in literature."—*Introd.* Lists books, periodical articles, and dissertations. Index of critics. Z1521.F694

Remos y Rubio, Juan Nepomuceno José. Historia de la literatura cubana. [Habana], Cardenas, 1945. 3v. **BD1236**

A comprehensive history of Cuban literature from its origin to recent times. Includes biographies and bibliographies.

PQ7371.R4

Ecuadorian

Barriga López, Franklin and **Barriga López, Leonardo.** Diccionario de la literatura ecuatoriana. 2a ed., corr. y aum. Quito, Editorial Casa de la Cultura Ecuatoriana, [1980]. 5v. **BD1237**

Primarily a biographical dictionary of Ecuadorian writers, with a few entries for literary societies and institutions. Very little bibliography. PQ8201.B35

Luzuriaga, Gerardo. Bibliografía del teatro ecuatoriano, 1900–1982. Quito, Casa de la Cultura Ecuatoriana, 1984. 131p. **BD1238**

The main portion of the work is an author listing of dramatic works; it is preceded by a list of reference sources and followed by a selection of citations to critical writings.

Rodríguez Castelo, Hernán. Literatura ecuatoriana, 1830–1980. [Otavala], Instituto Otavaleño de Antropologia, 1980. 171p. il. **BD1239**

A brief history of Ecuadorian literature for the period indicated, by one who has written extensively on various aspects of the literature.

Rolando, Carlos A. Las bellas letras en el Ecuador. Guayaquil, Impr. i Talleres Municipales, 1944. 157p.   **BD1240**

Running title: Bibliografía de autores nacionales-literatura.

A bibliography of literary works printed in Ecuador from colonial times to time of compilation. Arranged by class, including bibliography, library economy, periodicals, poetry, fiction, drama, essays, etc. Author index.   Z1771.R75

Mexican

Forster, Merlin H. An index to Mexican literary periodicals. N.Y., Scarecrow Pr., 1966. 276p.   **BD1241**

Indexes 16 Mexican literary periodicals which began and ceased publication during the general period 1920–60, most of them not indexed elsewhere. In two parts: (1) alphabetical author list; (2) index to that list offering a subject approach.   Z1421.F6

Foster, David William. Mexican literature: a bibliography of secondary sources. Metuchen, N.J., Scarecrow Pr., 1981. 386p.   **BD1242**

In two parts: (1) General references; (2) Authors. The first part is topically subdivided, with sections for literary genres and periods. Aims to list "those items considered useful to serious scholarly research and opinion—articles in all types of scholarly journals and the most important cultural ones, and all monographic studies— and those likely to be accessible in Latin America and the United States."—*Pref.* Mexican indigenous literature is excluded. Index of critics.   Z1421.F63

González Peña, Carlos. Historia de la literatura mexicana desde los orígenes hasta nuestros días. 12. ed. México, Ed. Porrúa, 1975. 362p.   **BD1243**

"Con un apendice elaborado por el Centro de Estudios Literarios de la Universidad Nacional Autonoma de México."—*t.p.*
1st ed. 1928.
An English translation has appeared as: *History of Mexican literature,* translated by Gusta Barfield Nance and Florence Johnson Dunstan (3d ed., rev. and enl. Dallas, Southern Methodist Univ. Pr., 1968. 540p.).   PQ7111.G6

Hoffman, Herbert H. Cuento mexicano index. Newport Beach, Calif., Headway Pubns., 1978. 599p.   **BD1244**

An index to Mexican short stories in some 674 collections (a few of them in English). An "Author & story" section gives reference to the numbered list of anthologies; a listing of titles refers to the "Author & story" section.   Z1424.S54H63

Iguiniz, Juan Bautista. Bibliografía de novelistas mexicanos. Ensayo biográfico, bibliográfico y crítico. Precedido de un estudio histórico de la novela mexicana por Francisco Monterde García Icazbalceta. México, Impr. de la Secretaría de Relaciones Exteriores, 1926. 432p. (Monografías bibliográficas mexicanas, núm.3)   **BD1245**

Bio-bibliographies of Mexican novelists, with a title index and a list of pseudonyms.   Z1424.F4I2

Lamb, Ruth S. Bibliografía del teatro mexicano del siglo XX. Claremont, Calif., Claremont Colleges; México, Ed. de Andrea, 1962. 143p. (Colección studium, 33)   **BD1246**

An alphabetical listing by author. No title index.

Leal, Luis. Bibliografía del cuento mexicano. Emory, Ga., Emory Univ.; México, Ed. de Andrea, 1958. 162p. (Colección studium, 21)   **BD1247**

A bibliography of the Mexican short story arranged alphabetically by author. Indexes various collections of stories and lists separately published stories and those published in periodicals.   Z1424.F4L4

Monterde García Icazbalceta, Francisco. Bibliografía del teatro en México. México, Impr. de la Secretaría de Rela-

ciones Exteriores, 1933 (i.e., 1934). 1xxxp., 649p. facsim. (Monografías mexicanas, 28)   **BD1248**

A bibliography of works by Mexican authors and by others who lived in Mexico, including original works, translations and adaptations, foreign works printed in Mexico or on Mexican subjects, and works containing studies on the Mexican theater.   Z1424.D7M7

Ocampo de Gómez, Aurora Maura and **Prado Velázquez, Ernesto.** Diccionario de escritores mexicanos. [México], Universidad Nacional Autonoma de México, Centro de Estudios Literarios, [1967]. 422p. il.   **BD1249**

Treats both living and deceased persons. In addition to writers of belles-lettres, prominent historians, biographers, philosophers, etc., are included, as are writers of other nationalities who have lived in Mexico and contributed significantly to Mexican letters. Biographical sketches are followed by bibliographies of works by and about the authors.   PQ7106.O24

Peruvian

Arriola Grande, F. Maurilio. Diccionario literario del Perú; nomenclatura por autores. [2a. ed.] Lima, Editorial Universo, [1983]. 2v. il.   **BD1250**

Biographical sketches of Peruvian authors and authors who have resided in Peru, most sketches including some critical commentary. Both deceased and living persons are considered.

Cabel, Jesús. Bibliografía de la poesía peruana, 65/79. [Lima], Amaru, [1980]. 142p.   **BD1251**

A listing of volumes of poetry published in Peru during the 1965–79 period. Separate sections for books by individual poets, anthologies, and *plaquetas;* index of names.   Z1864.P7C33

Foster, David William. Peruvian literature: a bibliography of secondary sources. Westport, Conn., Greenwood Pr., [1981]. 324p.   **BD1252**

A section of general references is followed by a section on individual authors, listing bibliographies, monographs and dissertations, and critical studies in books and periodicals. Index to authors of secondary sources.   Z1861.F67

Romero de Valle, Emilia. Diccionario manual de literatura peruana y materias afines. Lima, Univ. Nacional Mayor de San Marcos, [1966]. 356p.   **BD1253**

Limited for the most part to entries for individual authors but with some attention to literary genres, periodicals, etc.

PQ8306.R6

Puerto Rican

Foster, David William. Puerto Rican literature: a bibliography of secondary sources. Westport, Conn., Greenwood Pr., [1982]. 232p.   **BD1254**

A section of general references, subdivided topically, is followed by sections on individual authors. Index of authors of critical works.   Z1557.L56F67

Hill, Marnesba D. and **Schleifer, Harold B.** Puerto Rican authors: a biobibliographical handbook. Metuchen, N.J., Scarecrow Pr., 1974. 267p.   **BD1255**

Brief bio-bibliographies in English and Spanish on 251 Puerto Rican authors, from 1493 to the present. Includes living authors.   Z1556.H55

Rivera de Alvarez, Josefina. Diccionario de literatura puertorriqueña. 2. ed. rev. y aumentada y puesta al día hasta 1967. San Juan, P.R., Instituto de Cultura Puertorriqueña, 1970–74. 2v. in 3.   **BD1256**

1st ed. 1955.
The first volume (578p.), designated as "Introducción: Panorama histórico de la literatura puertorriqueña," is essentially a literary history of Puerto Rico with a brief general bibliography. v.2 (in 2v.) is an alphabetically arranged series of articles (with bibliographies)

on individual authors, literary terms, movements, etc. Entries for individual writers stress critical evaluation and literary status as much as biographical detail. PQ7421.R48

Uruguayan

Rela, Walter. Fuentes para el estudio de la literatura uruguaya, 1835–1968. [Montevideo], Ediciones de la Banda Oriental, [1969]. 134p. **BD1257**

More than 900 items in classed arrangement with name index. Largely supersedes the compiler's *Contribución a la bibliografía de la literatura uruguaya* (Montevideo, 1963). Z1891.R42

———— Repertorio bibliográfico del teatro uruguayo, 1816–1964. Montevideo, Editorial Síntesis, 1965. 35p. **BD1258**

A companion to the author's *Contribución a la bibliografía de la literatura uruguaya* (Montevideo, 1963), listing plays and works on the theater. Z1894.D7R4

Venezuelan

Becco, Horacio Jorge. Fuentes para el estudio de la literatura venezolana. Caracas, Ediciones Centauro, 1978. 2v. **BD1259**

A bibliography of published sources for the study of Venezuelan literature. Includes sections for bibliography, biography, literary history and criticism, theater, anthologies, etc. More than 1,800 items; indexed. Z1921.B4

Cardozo, Lubio. Bibliografía de bibliografías sobre la literatura venezolana en las bibliotecas de Madrid, Paris y Londres. Maracaibo, Centro de Estudios Literarios de la Univ. del Zulia [y] Centro de Investigaciones Literarias de la Univ. de Los Andes, [1975]. 67p. **BD1260**

An annotated bibliography of about 100 bibliographies. Z1911.A1C37

Diccionario general de la literatura venezolana (Autores). Mérida, Centro de Investigaciones Literarias, Univ. de Los Andes, Facultad de Humanidades y Educación, 1974. 829p. **BD1261**

Biographical sketches are followed by bibliographies—frequently extensive—which cite works by and about the authors. Foreign-born authors working in Venezuela or writing about Venezuela are included. A second volume of "Obras" was to deal with the most significant works in Venezuelan literature. PQ8531.D54

Hirshbein, Cesia Ziona. Hemerografía venezolana, 1890–1930. Caracas, Ediciones de la Facultad de Humanidades y Educación, Instituto de Estudios Hispanoamericanos, Univ. Central de Venezuela, 1978. 574p. **BD1262**

A bibliography of literary writings appearing in Venezuelan periodicals during the period indicated. Entries are grouped by genre, then entered alphabetically by author. Writings of foreign authors are listed in separate sections. Z1923.H57

Lovera De Sola, Roberto J. Bibliografía de la crítica literaria venezolana, 1847–1977. [Caracas], Instituto Autónomo Biblioteca Nacional y de Servicios de Bibliotecas, [1982]. 489p. **BD1263**

A bibliography of literary criticism published in Venezuela and therefore not limited to works on Venezuelan literature. Arranged by author, with indexes of authors, editors, etc., and of titles, but not of specific subjects. Brief annotations for most entries; special section on theater criticism. Z1921.L68

Rojas Uzcátegui, José de la Cruz and **Cardozo, Lubio.** Bibliografía del teatro venezolano. Mérida, Univ. de Los Andes, Facultad de Humanidades y Educación, Inst. de Investigaciones Literarias "Gonzalo Picón Febres," Consejo de Publicaciones, 1980. 199p. **BD1264**

An author listing (949 entries) of published dramas is followed by

appendixes listing unpublished plays (and those for which only incomplete information was available), of translations, and a chronology. Title index. Z1924.D7R64

Sambrano Urdaneta, Oscar. Contribución a una bibliografía general de la poesía venezolana en el siglo XX. Caracas, Ediciones de la Facultad de Humanidades y Educación, Escuela de Letras, Univ. Central de Venezuela, 1979. 367p. **BD1265**

A section for individual poets and their works is followed by a list of anthologies and a section on critical studies. Indexed. Z1923.S35

SLAVIC AND EAST EUROPEAN LANGUAGES

❖Only a few works in these literatures can be listed here. For more detailed bibliographies, *see* Horecky, *Basic Russian publications* (DC530) and *Russia and the Soviet Union* (DC531), as well as his *East Central Europe* (DC25) and *Southeastern Europe* (DC26); the *Columbia dictionary of modern European literature* (BD52), etc.

General works

Guides

Jena. Universität. Bibliothek. Slavica-Auswahl-Katalog der Universitätsbibliothek Jena; ein Hilfsbuch für Slawisten und Germanoslavica-Forscher. Weimar, H. Böhlaus Nachfolger, 1956–59. 2v. in 3. (Claves Jenenses 4–6) **BD1266**

Contents: v.1, Allgemeine Literatur, Tschechoslowakei und Polen; v.2, pt.1, Russland und Sowjetunion; pt.2, Jugoslawien und Bulgarien. Hochschul- Gymnasial- und Gelegenheitsschriften der UB Jena vom 16. bis 18. Jahrhundert, mit persönlichem oder sachlichem Bezug auf Südost- und Osteuropa. Nachträge.

A catalog of 7,400 of the Slavic and Germano-Slavic holdings of Jena University Library, particularly strong in 17th- and 18th-century literature. Arrangement is in the form of a bibliographic handbook for Slavic studies. Appendix and author index in v.3. Z929.J43

Bibliography

Wytrzens, Günther. Bibliographische Einführung in das Studium der slavischen Literaturen. Frankfurt a. M., Klostermann, 1972. 348p. (Zeitschrift für Bibliothekswesen und Bibliographie. Sonderheft 13) **BD1267**

A bibliography of more than 5,000 items for the study of the whole range of Slavic literatures. Classified arrangement with name index and detailed table of contents. Includes works in Western European languages as well as those in the Slavic languages.
Supplemented by: Z7041.W9

———— Bibliographie der literarwissenschaftlichen Slawistik, 1970–1980. Frankfurt am Main, Klostermann, [1982]. 348p. (Zeitschrift für Bibliothekswesen und Bibliographie. Sonderheft, 36) **BD1268**

Adds another 5,000 items in similar arrangement and again covering all the Slavic literatures on an international basis.
The same series includes Wytrzens' *Bibliographie der russischen Autoren und anonymen Werke* (no.19, 1975) and a supplement thereto for the 1975–80 period (no.37, 1982). Z7041.W89

Translations

Lewanski, Richard Casimir, comp. The Slavic literatures. N.Y., New York Pub. Lib. and Ungar, [1967]. 630p. (Literatures of the world in English translation; a bibliography. v.2) **BD1269**

For a note on the series *see* BD35.

This volume was in the final stages of publication under the New York Public Library imprint when it was decided to incorporate it into the series in preparation by Ungar. It therefore differs from the overall plan for other volumes of the series (e.g., scope is confined to belles-lettres; background materials and bibliographies are not listed, etc.). Arrangement is by language of the original work, then by author. References to translations appearing in periodicals are included. Closing date is 1960. Index of authors and translated titles. Z7041.L59

Criticism

Modern Slavic literatures. Comp. and ed. by Vasa D. Mihailovich [and others]. N.Y., Ungar, 1972–76. 2v. (A library of literary criticism) **BD1270**

Contents: v.1, Russian literature (424p.); v.2, Bulgarian, Czechoslovak, Polish, Ukrainian, and Yugoslav literatures (720p.).

v.1 presents excerpts from critical writings on 69 of "the most significant authors of the twentieth century" (*Introd.*) writing in Russian. In addition to English-language evaluations, excerpts from Russian critical writings are presented in translation. Similar treatment is accorded 196 writers in v.2, which is arranged alphabetically by literature, then by author. Index of critics in each volume. PG501.M518

Czech

Balášová, Olga [and others]. Bibliografie české literární vědy, 1945–1955. Práce o české literatuře. Praha, Státní Pedagogické Nakl., [1964]. 693p. **BD1271**

Lists 5,590 items on Czech literature of all periods published 1945–55. Z2138.L5B3

Čeští spisovatelé 19. a počátku 20. století; slovníková příručka. Napsal autorský kolektiv za redakse Květy Homolové, Mojmíra Otruby a Zdeňka Pešata. Vyd. 3. Praha, Československý Spisovatel, [1982]. 371p. **BD1272**

1st ed. 1972.

Offers biographical sketches and brief commentary on the publications of Czech writers of the 19th and first half of the 20th centuries. Index of names and titles cited in the text. PG5006.C44

Jelinek, Hanus. Histoire de la littérature tchèque. 4. éd. Paris, Éd. du Sagittaire, 1930–35. 3v. **BD1273**

v.1–3, Des origines à nos jours. PG5001.J4

Kunc, Jaroslav. Česká literární bibliografie, 1945–1966. Soupis článků, statí a kritik z knižních publikací a periodického tisku let 1945–1966 o dílech soudobých českých spisovatelů. Praha, Státní Knihovna ČSR Národní Knihovna, 1963–68. 4v. ports. **BD1274**

(Bibliografický katalog ČSSR, České knihy. Zvláštní sešit)

v.1–2 list works by and about Czech literary authors for the period 1945–63; v.3 continues the listings for 1945–66; v.4 is an index. Z2138.L5K8

—— Slovník soudobých českých spisovatelů; krásné písemnictví v letech 1918–45. Praha, Orbis, 1945–46. 2v. il. **BD1275**

A dictionary of Bohemian writers of the period 1918–45. Restricted to belles-lettres.
Continued by: Z2131.K8

—— Slovník českých spisovatelů beletristů, 1945–1956. Praha, Státní Pedagogické Nakl., 1957. 483p. (Ed. Národní Knihovny v Praze. Sv.6) **BD1276**

A biographical dictionary of 478 Czech literary figures. PG5004.K8

Slovník českých spisovatelů; pokus o rekonstrukci dějin české literatury 1948–1979. Uspořádali Jiří Brabec [et al.]. [Toronto, Sixty-Eight Publishers Corp., 1982] 537p. il. **BD1277**

Biographical sketches are followed by lists of writings by and about the authors. Z2138.L5S58

Estonian

Eesti kirjanduse biograafiline leksikon. Toimetanud E. Nirk ja E. Sõgel. Tallinn, Eesti Raamat, 1975. 462p. il. **BD1278**

At head of title: Eesti NSV Teaduste Akadeemia, Keele ja Kirjanduse Instituut.

Offers bio-bibliographical sketches of Estonian writers of all periods. PH633.E3

Mauer, Mare. Eesti kirjandus võõrkeeltes. Bibliograafianimestik. Tallinn, 1978. 244p. **BD1279**

At head of title: Eesti NSV Kultuuriministeerium. Fr. R. Kreutzwaldi nim. Eesti NSV Riiklik Raamatukogu.

Added title page in English (*Estonian literature in foreign languages: a bibliography*) and Russian.

A section of collections of folk tales and anthologies in translation is followed by listings of foreign-language translations of works by individual authors. Indexed.

Russian translations are listed in Osvald Kivi's three volumes covering 1940–55, 1956–65, and 1966–75, *Estonskaia khudozhestvennaia literatura, fol'klor i kritika na russkom i drugikh iazykakh narodov SSSR* (Tallinn, Eesti Raamat, 1956–78). Z2533.M28

—— Estonskaia literatura; rekomendatel'nyii ukazatel' literatury. Moskva, Kniga, 1975. 223p. il. **BD1280**

At head of title: Gosudarstvennaia Biblioteka SSSR imeni V. I. Lenina. Gosudarstvennaia Biblioteka Estonskoi SSR imeni Fr. R. Kreitsval'da.

Bio-bibliographies of Estonian authors. Z2533.M3

Nirk, Endel. Estonian literature; historical survey with bio-bibliographical appendix. [Translated from the Estonian by V. Hain, A. R. Hone and O. Mutt. Tallinn], Eesti Raamat, 1970. 414p. il. **BD1281**

A brief history for the person unfamiliar with the language, drawn mainly from *Eesti kirjanduse ajalugu*, ed. by Endel Sõgel (Tallinn, 1965–69. 3v.). A brief history in German is Henno Jänes's *Geschichte der estnischen Literatur* (Stockholm, Almqvist & Wiksell, 1965. 188p.).

Endel Mallene's *Estonian literature in the early 1970s: authors, books, and trends of development* (Tallinn, Eesti Raamat, 1978. 115p.) is primarily a series of biobibliographical sketches. PH631.N5

Hungarian

Bibliography

Budapest. Országos Széchényi Könyvtár. Irodalomtörténeti munkásság, 1939–44. Összeállitotta Kozocsa Sándor. Budapest, 1941–46. 6v. **BD1282**

Continued by:

A Magyar irodalom bibliográfiája, 1945/49–61/65. Összeállitotta Kozocsa Sándor. Budapest, 1950–78. Irregular. **BD1283**

Publisher varies. To have been continued on an annual basis following the 1945/49 issue, but volumes appear irregularly.

Includes literary criticism, linguistics, bibliographies, collections, works by and about Hungarian authors. Z2141.M22

Harvard University. Library. Hungarian history and literature: classification schedule, classified listing by call number, chronological listing, author and title listing. Cambridge, publ. by Harvard Univ. Lib., distr. by Harvard Univ. Pr., 1974. 186p. (Widener Library shelflist, 44) **BD1284**

For full information *see* DC357.

A Magyar irodalom és irodalomtudomány bibliográfiája. 1976– . Budapest, Országos Széchényi Könyvtár, 1979– . Annual. **BD1285**

"Készült a Könyvtár Olvasószolgálati és Tájékoztató Osztályán." —*verso of t.p.*

A bibliography of periodical articles relating to Hungarian literature. Classed arrangement with author index. Includes a section of writings on foreign literatures by Hungarian critics.

Magyarországi irodalom idegen nyelven: a hazai szépirodalom fordításainak bibliográfiája 1945–1968 közötti kiadások. Budapest, Országos Széchényi Könyvtár, 1975. 797p. **BD1286**

Title also in English *(Hungary's literature in translation: a bibliography of belles-lettres in foreign languages . . .)* and Russian; introductory matter in Hungarian, English and Russian.

Anthologies are grouped by genre (poetry, short stories, etc.), then by language of translation; all authors represented in a given work are listed with the title. A section for individual authors is arranged by literary category, then by author's name, followed by titles grouped by foreign languages. Name, language, and publisher indexes. Z2148.T7M34

Tezla, Albert. Hungarian authors; a bibliographical handbook. Cambridge, Belknap Pr. of Harvard Univ. Pr., 1970. 792p. **BD1287**

A companion to the author's *Introductory bibliography* . . . (below). Treats 162 "representative writers from the beginnings of Hungarian literature to the present."—*Pref.* Intends to give a complete record of first editions of each author's works, together with references to important biographical, bibliographical, and critical studies. Indexed. Z2148.L5T39

—— An introductory bibliography to the study of Hungarian literature. Cambridge, Harvard Univ. Pr., 1964. 290p. **BD1288**

1,295 numbered entries of secondary and primary sources published through 1960, designed primarily for students in the United States. Classified arrangement with name index. Titles are annotated, and there are numerous cross references. Locates copies in American and European libraries.

Tezla's *Hungarian authors* (above) is a companion work. Z2148.L5T4

Dictionaries

Benedek, Marcell, ed. Magyar irodalmi lexikon. Budapest, Akadémiai Kiadó, 1963–65. 3v. il. **BD1289**

Biographical sketches of Hungarian authors predominate, but there are entries for literary terms, journals, etc. Some of the longer articles are signed; bibliographic references. PH3007.B4

History

Czigány, Lóránt. The Oxford history of Hungarian literature from the earliest times to the present. Oxford, Clarendon Pr.; N.Y., Oxford Univ. Pr., [1984]. 582p. **BD1290**

An important new historical survey. Glossary; bibliography. Another recent one-volume history is Tibor Klaniczay's *A magyar*

irodalom története (Budapest, 1982) which has been translated into English as *A history of Hungarian literature* (Budapest, 1983). PH3012.C94

Pintér, Jenö. . . . Magyar irodalomtörténete. Tudományos rendszerezés . . . Budapest, [Magyar Irodalomtörténeti Társaság], 1930–41. 8v. in 13. **BD1291**

A standard history with extensive bibliography—both a general bibliography in v.1 and special bibliographies at the end of each chapter.

The Hungarian Academy's *A magyar irodalom története* under the general editorship of Istvan Sötér and others (Budapest, Akadémiai Kiadó, 1964–66. 6v.) is a relatively recent history from the Marxist point of view; it includes bibliographies. PH3012.P55

Latvian

Istoriia latyshskoi literatury. V 2-kh t. [Red. kollegiia . . . IA. Kalnyn (otv. red.) i dr.] Riga, "Zinatne," 1971. 2v. il. **BD1292**

On leaf preceding t.p.: Akademiia Nauk Latviiskoi SSR. Institut IAzyka i Literatury.

Contents: t.1, Do 1917 goda; t.2, S 1917 goda.

A history of Latvian literature presented mainly in terms of chapters by contributing scholars on individual writers. Bibliography at the end of v.2.

Latvian literature under the Soviets, 1940–1975 by Rolfs Ekmanis (Belmont, Mass., Nordland Pub. Co., 1978. 533p.) is a study of the effects of Soviet rule on Latvian literature; it includes an extensive classed bibliography, p.441–515. PG9005.I8

Latviešu pirmspadomju literatūra: biobibliogrāfisks rādītājs. Sastādītāji: Edgars Timbra [et al.]. Riga, 1980. 744p. **BD1293**

At head of title: Vila Lāča Latvijas PSR Valsts Bibliotēka. Zinātniski Metodiskā un Bibliogrāfiskā Darba Nodaļa.

Added title page in Russian.

A biobibliography of pre-Soviet literature.

Riga. Valsts Biblioteka. Bibliografijas un Metodiskā Darba Nodaļa. Latviešu rakstnieki; literaturs rādītājs. [Sastādītāji O. Pūce un J. Veinbergs] Rīgā, 1955. 247p. **BD1294**

Offers bio-bibliographies of about 80 Latvian authors from early 19th to mid-20th century. Z2535.R58

Lithuanian

Biržiška, Vaclovas. Lietuvių bibliografija, [1517–1904]. Kaunas, Švietmo Ministerijos Leidinys, 1924–29. 3v. **BD1295**

A bibliography of Lithuanian literature and related publications.

Lietuvos TSR Mokslų Akademija. Lietuvių Kalbos ir Literatūros Institutas. Tarybinė lietuvių literatūra ir kritika; bibliografiné rodyklé. 1945/1955– . Vilnius, 1957– . Irregular. **BD1296**

Subtitle varies slightly.

A bibliography of Soviet-Lithuanian literature and literary criticism, in Lithuanian and Russian. Z2537.L5

Lietuvių rašytojai; biobibliografinis žodynas. Vilnius, Vaga, 1979– . v.1– . (In progress) **BD1297**

Offers bio-bibliographies of Lithuanian writers (including living authors). Lists periodical contributions as well as separately published works, and includes writings about the authors. PG8709.L486

Stancikas, Eugenijus. Tarybinis lietuvių literatūros mokslas ir kritika apie literatūrini palikimą, 1959–1970: bibliografiné rodyklé. Vilnius, Vaga, 1975. 430p. **BD1298**

Continued by: Z2537.S75

—— Lietuvių literatūros mokslas ir kritika, 1971–1973. Bibliografine rodyklė. Vilnius, [Vaga], 1976. 428p.
BD1299

At head of title: Lietuvos TSR Mokslų Akademija. Lietuvių Kalbos ir literatūros Institutas.

A classed bibliography of critical writings on Lithuanian literature, together with Lithuanian writings on foreign literatures. Indexed.   Z2537.S74

Tarybu lietuvos rašytojai. Vilnius, [Vaga], 1977. 2v. il.
BD1300

Juozas Baltusis, ed.

A similar work with the same title appeared 1967. Offers autobiographical sketches of contemporary Lithuanian authors.
PG8701.T34

Polish

Bibliography

Bartelski, Lesław M. Polscy pisarze współcześni: informator 1944–1974. Wyd. 3, nowe. poszerzone. Warszawa, Wydawnictwa Artystyczne i Filmowe, 1977. 428p.   **BD1301**

1st ed. 1970.
Offers brief biographical sketches of contemporary Polish writers, with lists of published works.   Z2528.L5B37

Czachowski, Kasimierz. Obraz współczesnej literatury polskiej, 1884–[1934]. Lwów, Nakł. Państwowego Wydawnictwa Książek Szkolnych, 1934–36. 3v.   **BD1302**

Includes extensive bibliographies, chronology, and index.
PG7051.C9

—— Najnowsza twórczość literacka, 1935–37. Lwów, 1938. 273p. il.

Korbut, Gabrjel. Literatura polska od początków do wojny światowej; książka podręczna informacyjna dla stujujących naukowo dzieje rozwoju piśmiennictwa polskiego. . . . Wyd. 2., powiększone. Warszawa, Skład Główny w Kasie Im. Mianowskiego, 1929–31. 4v.   **BD1303**

1st ed. 1917–21 in 3v.
Contents: v.1, 10th–17th centuries; v.2, 18th century–1820; v.3, 1820–63; v.4, 1864–1914.
A continuation for the 20th century is provided by Korzeniewska (BD1305). A new and expanded edition of the original work is in progress as: Z2526.K84

Bibliografia literatury polskiej. Nowy Korbut. Redaktor naczelny Kazimierz Budzyk. Komitet redakcyjny Ewa Korzeniewska [et al.]. [Kraków, etc.], Wydawn. Literackie [etc., 1963–83]. v.1–9, 12–17. (In progress)   **BD1304**

Issued by Instytut Badan Literackich, Polska Akademia Nauk.
Includes general bibliography of Polish literature and bio-bibliographies of Polish writers. Represents the contributions of many scholars.   Z2521.B55

Korzeniewska, Ewa. Słownik współczesnych pisarzy polskich. Opracował zespół. Warszawa, Państwowe Wydawnictwo Naukowe, 1963–66. 4v. (Instytut Badań Literackich Polskiej Akademii Nauk. Bibliografia literatury polskiej "Nowy Korbut")   **BD1305**

A continuation of Korbut (BD1303).
A bio-bibliographical work of 20th-century Polish authors, giving brief biographical sketches followed by lists of works by and about the authors. v.4 is an index.   Z2528.L5K6

Lorentowicz, Jan. La Pologne en France; essai d'une bibliographie raisonnée . . . avec la collaboration de A. M. Chmurski. . . . Paris, Champion, 1935–41. 3v. (v.2, Institut d'Études Slaves de l'Université de Paris. Bibliothèque Polonaise. IV)   **BD1306**

Contents: v.1, Littérature, théâtre, beaux-arts; v.2, Encyclopédies,

langue, voyages, histoire; v.3, Géographie, sciences, droit; suppléments.
Lists French writings concerning Poland, including both book and periodical articles. Classified, with author and title indexes.
Z2526.L86

Polska Akademia Nauk. Instytut Badań Literackich. Bibliografia literatury polskiej okresu odrodzenia (materiały). Opracowali: Kazimierz Budzyk, Roman Pollak, Stanisław Stupkiewicz. [Warszawa], Państwowy Inst. Wydawniczy, 1954. 463p.   **BD1307**

A bibliography of Polish literature during the Renaissance and Reformation, and of later studies of the subject in all languages. Biographical articles on the major authors.

Słownik współczesnych pisarzy polskich: seria II. Opracował zespół pod red. Jadwigi Czachowskiej. Warszawa, Państwowe Wydawn. Naukowe, 1977–80. 3v. (Bibliografia literatury polskiej Nowy Korbut)   **BD1308**

Serves as a continuation of the work with the same title edited by Ewa Korzeniewska (BD1305). Offers bio-bibliographical information on contemporary writers not treated in the early set.
Z2528.L5S56

Starnawski, Jerzy. Warsztat bibliograficzny historyka literatury polskiej (na tle dyscyplin pokrewnych). [Wyd. 3] [Warszawa], Państwowe Wydawnictwo Naukowe, [1982]. 524p.
BD1309

A working bibliography of Polish literary history and related fields, including comparative literature.   Z2528.L5S68

Translations

Coleman, Marion Moore. Polish literature in English translation; a bibliography. Cheshire, Conn., Cherry Hill Books, 1963. 180p.   **BD1310**

Arranged by author; lists translations of novels, poems, short stories, dramas, etc., dating from the 16th century to 1960. Some references to reviews. Index of translators included.
Z2528.T7C6

Ryll, Ludomira and **Wilgat, Janina.** Polska literatura w przekładach; bibliografia 1945–1970. Warszawa, Agencja Autorska, 1972. 369p.   **BD1311**

Lists translations of Polish literary works into various languages. Includes a section of translations in anthologies. Indexes of authors, translators, editors, etc., and an index by country of publication.
Supersedes an earlier bibliography by J. Wilgat, *Literatura polska w świecie* (Warszawa, PEN Club, 1965) which covered translations 1945–61.   Z2528.T7R93

Taborski, Boleslaw. Polish plays in English translations; a bibliography. N.Y., Polish Inst. of Arts and Sciences in America, 1968. 79p.   **BD1312**

Lists translations in manuscript as well as printed translations. Includes a biographical note on the author and gives information on casts, sets, and a brief comment on each play.   Z2528.L5T3

Dictionaries

Słownik terminów literackich. Michał Głowiński [et al.]. Pod red. Janusza Sławińskiego. Wrocław, Zakład Narodowy Imienia Ossolińskich, 1976. 577p.   **BD1313**

A dictionary of literary terms, including terms from classical and foreign literatures.   PN41.S56

History

Kridl, Manfred. A survey of Polish literature and culture. Tr. from the Polish by Olga Scherer-Virski. N.Y., Columbia Univ. Pr., 1956. 525p. (Repr. 1967)   **BD1314**

A "thoroughly reworked and revised version" (*Pref.*) of the author's *Literatura polska na tle rozwoju kultury* (1945). Select bibliography; index.

Miłosz Czesław's *The history of Polish literature* (2d ed. Berkeley, Univ. of Calif. Pr., 1983. 583p.) emphasizes the 19th century and after.   PG7012.K713

Krzyżanowski, Julian. Historia literatury polskiej: alegoryzmpreromantyzm. Warszawa, Państw. Instytut Wydawn., 1974. 694p. il.   **BD1315**

1st ed. 1953; 1974 ed. called "Wyd. 4."
A standard university-level textbook. Bibliography, p.553–633.   PG7012.K78

Romanian

Academia Republicii Popular Romîne. Biblioteca. Bibliografia literaturii romîne, 1948–1960. Sub redacţis Acad. Tudor Vianu. Bucureşti, Editura Academiei Republicii Populare Romîne, 1965. 1123p.   **BD1316**

Provides bibliographies of individual authors, listing both separately published works and contributions to periodicals, as well as writings about the author. Includes a section on Romanian folklore. Index of names.   Z2921.A17

Adamescu, Gheorghe. Contribuţiune la bibliografia românească. Fasc.1–3. Bucureşti, Cartea Românească, 1921–28. 3 pts.   **BD1317**

Fasc.1–3, Istoria literaturii romăne. Texte şi autori, 1500–1921/25.
An important bibliography of Romanian literature, in chronological order by the birth dates of the writers.   Z2921.A19

Biblioteca Centrală Universitară Bucureşti. Literatura romănă: ghid bibliografic. Bucureşti, La Biblioteca, 1979– . v.1– . (In progress)   **BD1318**

Contents: v.1, Surse (714p.).
v.1 lists general reference works for literary research (encyclopedias, dictionaries, bibliographies, journals, etc.), with sections for aesthetics, literary theory, stylistics, literary history, literary movements, etc. Special sections for German literature and Hungarian literature in Romania. Includes a dictionary of terms in aesthetics, literary theory, and stylistics with references to an extensive bibliography on those topics (p.228–332). Fully indexed.

Călinescu, George. Istoria literaturii romăne dela origini până in prezent. Bucureşti, Fundaţia Regală Pentru Literatură şi Artă, 1941. 948p. il.   **BD1319**

A comprehensive survey of Romanian literature from the 16th to the early 20th centuries, arranged by periods. Treats many authors at length. Copiously illustrated. Extensive bibliography; alphabetical index of authors.

Dicţionarul literaturii romăne de la origini pînâ la 1900. Bucureşti, Editura Academici Republicii Socialiste Romănia, 1979. 976p. il.   **BD1320**

At head of title: Academia Republicii Socialiste Romănia. Institutul de Lingvistică, Istorie Literară şi Folclor al Universităţii "Al. I. Cuza" Iaşi.
Biographical entries predominate, but there is good coverage of individual literary periodicals, and literary societies, types of folklore, etc., are also treated. Extensive bibliographies.   PC801.D5

Istoria literaturii romăne. [Bucureşti], Editura Academiei Republicii Populare Romîne, [1964]–73. 3v. il.   **BD1321**

At head of title: v.1, Academia Republicii Populare Romîne; v.2–3, Academia Republicii Socialiste Romănia.
v.2–3 have title: Istoria literaturii romăne.
Contents: v.1, Folclorul. Literatura romînă în perioada feudală (1400–1780); v.2, De la şcoala ardeleană la junimea; v.3, Epica marilor clasici.
Bibliographies and indexes in each volume.   PC801.I8

Russian

Guides

Fomin, Aleksandr Grigor'evich. Putevoditel' po bibliografii, biobibliografii, istoriografii, khronologii i entsiklopedii literatury; sistematicheskii, annotirovannyi ukazatel' russkikh knig i zhurnal'nykh rabot, napechatannykh v 1736–1932 gg. Leningrad, Goslitizdat, 1934. 335p. (Repr.: N.Y., Johnson, 1966)   **BD1322**

An important guide to Russian bibliographies and reference works in the field of literature.   Z2501.F67

An introduction to Russian language and literature. Ed. by Robert Auty and Dimitri Obolensky. Cambridge, Cambridge Univ. Pr., [1977]. 300p. (Companion to Russian studies, 2)   **BD1323**

For full information *see* BC165.

Zenkovsky, Serge A. and **Armbruster, David L.** Guide to the bibliographies of Russian literature. Nashville, Tenn., Vanderbilt Univ. Pr., 1970. 62p.   **BD1324**

More than 300 items. A general section is followed by listings by period and by literary form. Author index.   Z2501.A1Z4

Bibliography

Akademiia Nauk SSSR. Biblioteka. Sovetskii roman, ego teoriia i istoriia; bibliograficheskii ukazatel', 1917–1964. Sost. N. A. Groznova. Leningrad, 1966. 256p.   **BD1325**

At head of title: Biblioteka Akademii Nauk SSSR. Institut Russkoi Literatury (Pushkinskii Dom) Akademii Nauk SSSR.
A briefly annotated bibliography on the history and theory of Soviet fiction, chronologically arranged.   Z2504.F5A52

Akademiia Nauk SSSR. Fundamental'naia Biblioteka Obshchestvennykh Nauk. Sovetskoe literaturovedenie i kritika: Russkaia sovetskaia literatura (obshchie raboty); knigi i stat'i 1917–1962 godov. Bibliograficheskii ukazatel'. Moskva, Nauka, 1966. 586p.   **BD1326**

An annotated bibliography of critical and historical materials on Soviet literature in general. A separate volume was planned for writings on individual authors.
Continued in three supplements ed. by A. S. Blazer and others, covering 1963–67 (publ. 1970. 180p.), 1968–70 (publ. 1975. 397p.), and 1971–73 (publ. 1979. 460p.).   Z2503.A45

Akademiia Nauk SSSR. Institut Russkoi Literatury. Bibliografiia drevnerusskoi povesti. Sost. A. A. Nazarevskii. Moskva, 1955. 191p.   **BD1327**

A bibliography of the early Russian folktale, listing manuscripts, published texts, and research.   Z2504.F5A53

Cross, Anthony Glenn and **Smith, Gerald Stanton.** Eighteenth century Russian literature, culture and thought: a bibliography of English-language scholarship and translations. Newtonville, Oriental Research Partners, 1984. 130p.   **BD1328**

"This book brings together and updates the bibliographies that the authors have been publishing together at intervals since 1976, and adds to them a bibliography of translations into English of eighteenth-century Russian literary works."—*Introd.* Classed arrangement with author and subject indexes, plus chronological lists of scholarly works and translations.

Droblenkova, Nadezhda Feotitovna. Bibliografiia sovetskikh russkikh rabot po literature XI–XVII vv. za 1917–1957 gg. Moskva, 1961. 434p.   **BD1329**

At head of title: Akademiia Nauk SSSR. Institut Russkoi Literatury.
Chronologically arranged by year of publication; lists Soviet research published in Russian on the history of Russian literature of

the 11th through the 17th centuries, and 18th-century manuscript material relevant to the earlier period. Name and subject indexes.
Continued for the 18th century by: Z2502.D7

Stepanov, V. P. and **Stennik, IU. V.** Istoriia russkoi literatury XVIII veka; bibliograficheskii ukazatel'. Leningrad, Nauka, 1968. 500p. **BD1330**

At head of title: Akademiia Nauk SSSR. Institut Russkoi Literatury.

Fills the gap between the Institute's previously published bibliographies for the 11th–17th centuries (above) and the 19th century (below). Z2502.S76

Akademiia Nauk SSSR. Institut Russkoi Literatury. Istoriia russkoi literatury XIX veka; bibliograficheskii ukazatel'. Pod red. K. D. Muratovoi. Leningrad, Izd-vo Akademii Nauk SSSR, 1962. 965p. **BD1331**

Z2503.A47

———— Istoriia russkoi literatury kontsa XIX nachala XX veka; bibliograficheskii ukazatel'. Pod red. K. D. Muratovoi. Leningrad, Izd-vo Akademii Nauk SSSR, 1963. 516p. **BD1332**

Two major bibliographies for Russian literature of the 19th and 20th centuries. Introductory sections deal with history of Russian literature and criticism, journalism, censorship, and related themes. Personal bibliographies for more than 450 authors are given, listing editions of complete works, and published letters, biographical materials, critical literature, and additional bibliographic and reference materials. Name and subject indexes. Z2503.A474

Foster, Ludmilla A., comp. Bibliography of Russian émigré literature, 1918–1968. Boston, G. K. Hall, 1970. 2v. **BD1333**

Added title page in Russian.
Lists "Russian literature written by Russian émigrés and published outside the Soviet Union."—*Pref.* Includes creative literature, memoirs, and literary criticism written in Russian or translated into Russian, whether appearing as separate publications or published in collections or journals. Main entry listing according to the Cyrillic alphabet; index. Library locations indicated. Z2513.F66

Harvard University. Library. The Kilgour collection of Russian literature, 1750–1920, with notes on early books and manuscripts of the 16th and 17th centuries. Cambridge, Harvard College Lib., 1959. 1v., unpaged. il. **BD1334**

A catalog of 1,348 first editions ". . . from Lomonosov to Blok . . . the holdings of Pushkin being particularly notable."—*Pref.* All title pages are reproduced in facsimile, with translations, collation, and notes to facilitate comparison and identification of editions by persons with limited knowledge of the language. Bookplates, labels, and stamps are also reproduced. Z2491.5.H3

———— Twentieth century Russian literature: classified listing by call number, alphabetical listing by author or title, chronological listing. Cambridge, Harvard Univ. Library, 1965. 142p., 139p., 140p. (Widener Library shelflist, no.3) **BD1335**

For a note on the series *see* AA145.
"This volume, unlike most others in the series, contains only a segment of a classification . . . , the portion of Twentieth Century Russian Literature that is devoted to individual authors."—*Pref.* Includes 9,430 titles of works by and about Russian literary authors whose main work was done after 1917. Z2503.3.H3

Kandel', Boris L'vovich, Fediushina, L. M. and **Benina, M. A.** Russkaia khudozhestvennaia literatura i literaturovedenie: ukazatel' spravochno-bibliograficheskikh posobii s kontsa XVIII veka po 1974 god. Moskva, Kniga, 1976. 492p. **BD1336**

At head of title: Gosudarstvennaia Publichnaia Biblioteka im. M. E. Saltykova-Shchedrina.
A classed bibliography of bibliographies of literature and literary criticism from the end of the 18th century to 1974. About 2,500 entries. Indexed. Z2501.A1K36

Leningrad. Publichnaia Biblioteka. Russkie sovetskie pisateli-prozaiki: bio-bibliograficheskii ukazatel'. [Sost.: V. M. Akimov i dr.] Leningrad, 1959–72. 7v. in 9. **BD1337**

Offers biography and extensive bibliography for a wide selection of Russian prose writers of the Soviet period. Z2503.L4

Matsuev, Nikolai Ivanovich. Khudozhestvennaia literatura, russkaia i perevodnaia; bibliografiia 1917/25–1938/53. Moskva, Gos. Izd-vo Khudozh. Lit-ry, 1926–59. 6v. **BD1338**

The four volumes for the years 1917–37 cover belles-lettres, criticism, and studies in literature written in Russian or translated into Russian from any other language. With the establishment of *Sovetskaia khudozhestvennaia literatura i kritika* (BD1349), the two volumes continuing the present title are limited to pre-Revolutionary Russian authors in current editions and literary studies, and translations into Russian from foreign literatures. Z2503.M26

Moscow. Publichnaia Biblioteka. Russkie pisateli vtoroi poloviny XIX nachala XX vv. (do 1917 g.); rekomendatel'nyi ukazatel' literatury. Moskva, 1958–63. 3v. **BD1339**

A selective, annotated bibliography of writings by and about Russian authors of the second half of the 19th century up to 1917, useful for listing of editions and Soviet criticism. Continues chronologically *Russkie pisateli XVIII veka* (1954) and *Russkie pisateli pervoi poloviny XIX veka* (1951). Z2503.M7

———— Velikaia Oktiabr'skaia sotsialisticheskaia revoliutsiia v proizvedeniiakh sovetskikh pisatelei; k istorii sovetskoi literatury. Bibliograficheskii ukazatel' dlia nauchnykh rabotnikov, 1917–1966. Moskva, Kniga, 1967. 407p. **BD1340**

A bibliography of belles-lettres by Soviet writers on the theme of the Russian Revolution. More than 3,600 items in chronological arrangement. Indexed. Z2503.M72

———— **Otdel Rukopisei.** Vospominaniia i dnevniki XVIII–XX vv.: ukazatel' rukopisei. Red. S. V. Zhitomirskaia. Moskva, "Kniga," 1976. 619p. **BD1341**

For full information *see* DC556.

Russkie pisateli. Biobibliograficheskii slovar'. Red. kollegiia: D. S. Likhachev [i dr.]. Moskva, Izd. "Prosveshchenie," 1971. 728p. il. **BD1342**

About 300 bio-bibliographies of Russian writers from the medieval period to the early 20th century. Z2500.R86

Russkie sovetskie pisateli. Poety. Biobibliograficheskii ukazatel'. Moskva, "Kniga," 1977–84. v.1–7. (In progress) **BD1343**

Contents: v.1–7, Avramenko-Evtushenko.
A biographical sketch of each writer is followed by a list of published works (including references for individual poems, etc.) and extensive listings of critical writings about the author.
Z2505.P7R87

Schanzer, George O. Russian literature in the Hispanic world: a bibliography. [Toronto], Univ. of Toronto Pr., [1972]. 312p. **BD1344**

Title also in Spanish.
A bibliography of publications documenting the spread and influence of Russian literature in Spain and Spanish America. The more than 3,700 items include "Spanish collections and anthologies of Russian literature, individual translations, criticisms both general and specific, and sections of semi-literary writings."—*p.xxxiii.* Listing is by author or other main entry, with numerous indexes.
Z2504.T7S3

Smirnov-Sokol'skii, Nikolai Pavlovich. Russkie literaturnye al'manakhi i sborniki XVIII–XIX vv.; [bibliografiia]. Moskva, Kniga, 1965. 590p. **BD1345**

A preliminary edition was published 1956.
Lists Russian literary almanacs of the 18th and 19th centuries, including humorous almanacs after 1867 and children's almanacs and collections. Includes 1,607 entries, chronologically arranged,

with author and title indexes. Detailed contents notes for many items.   Z2504.C6S52

Startsev, Ivan Ivanovich. Khudozhestvennaia literatura narodov SSSR v perevodakh na russkii iazyk; bibliografiia. Moskva, Gos. Izd-vo Khudozh Lit-ry, 1957–64. 2v.   **BD1346**

Contents: v.1, 1934–54; v.2, 1955–59.
A bibliography of the literature of language groups of the USSR as translated into Russian.   Z6514.T7S75

Vsesoiuznaia Knizhnaia Palata. Literaturno-khudozhestvennye al'manakhi i sborniki; bibliograficheskii ukazatel'. Moskva, 1957–60. v.1–4.   **BD1347**

Contents: v.1, 1900–11, comp. by O. D. Golubeva; v.2, 1912–17, and v.3, 1918–27, comp. by N. P. Rogozhin; v.4, 1928–37, comp. by O. D. Golubeva.
Analyzes the contents of Russian literary almanacs and related works; chronologically arranged, with various indexes.
                                                              Z2504.C6V7

Woll, Josephine. Soviet dissident literature: a critical guide. Boston, G. K. Hall, [1983]. 241p.   **BD1348**

An author listing of some 1,300 items with broad subject index. Includes "all belletristic samizdat that could be found in Western periodicals or books (poems, songs, stories, novels, novellas, dramas); all nonfiction books; articles and essays, as well as substantial pieces of documentation, which seem to the editor to contribute information, views, insights or analyses of some significance."— *Pref.* Some annotations.   Z2511.U5W64

Current

Sovetskaia khudozhestvennaia literatura i kritika, 1938/48; 1949/51– ; bibliografiia. Moskva, Sovetskii Pisatel', 1952– . Biennial after 1949/51.   **BD1349**

Current bibliography, with reviews, for contemporary Russian literature and criticism, and the literatures of other nationalities of the Soviet Union as translated into Russian.
Continues, in part, *Khudozhestvennaia literatura, russkaia i perevodnaia* (BD1338).   Z2503.S6

Dissertations

See also DC548.

Dossick, Jesse John. Doctoral research on Russia and the Soviet Union, 1960–1975; a classified list of 3,150 American, Canadian, and British dissertations with some critical and statistical analysis. N.Y., Garland, 1976. 345p. (Garland reference library of social science, 7)   **BD1350**

For full information *see* DC549.

Magner, Thomas F. Soviet dissertations for advanced degrees in Russian literature and Slavic linguistics, 1934–1962. University Park, Pa., Dept. of Slavic Languages, Pennsylvania State Univ., 1966. 100p.   **BD1351**

1,313 items in classed arrangement. Index of authors as subjects, but none of authors of the dissertations.   Z2505.A2M3

Translations

Bibliography of Russian literature in English translation to 1945. Bringing together: A bibliography of Russian literature in English translation to 1900, by Maurice B. Line and Russian literature, theatre, and art; a bibliography of works in English published between 1900–1945, by Amrei Ettlinger and Joan M. Gladstone. Totowa, N.J., Rowman and Littlefield, [1972]. 74p., 96p.   **BD1352**

The Line bibliography was first published in London in 1963; the Ettlinger and Gladstone compilation, also London, 1947. The latter was designed to supplement Philip Grierson's *Books on Soviet Russia, 1917–1942* (London, 1943).   Z2504.T8B53

Gibian, George. Soviet Russian literature in English: a checklist bibliography. Ithaca, N.Y., Center for International Studies, Cornell Univ., 1967. 118p.   **BD1353**

"A selective bibliography of Soviet Russian literary works in English and of articles and books in English about Soviet Russian literature."—*title page.*
Includes sections on 33 individual authors, plus sections on Soviet literature in general and on periodicals.   Z2504.T8G5

Proizvedeniia sovetskikh pisatelei v perevodakh na inostrannye iazyki; otdel'nye zarubezhnye izdaniia. Bibliograficheskii ukazatel'. 1945/53– . Moskva, 1959– .   **BD1354**

At head of title: Soiuz Pisatelei SSSR i Vsesoiuznaia Gosudarstvennaia Biblioteka Inostrannoi Literatury.
Contents: 1945/53, 1954/57, 1958/64, 1965/70, 1971/75.
Bibliography of translations of the works of Soviet Russian and other Soviet writers published abroad as separate books. Does not include translations in anthologies or collections or in periodical literature.   Z2504.T8P84

Dictionaries and encyclopedias

Handbook of Russian literature. Ed. by Victor Terras. New Haven, Yale Univ. Pr., [1985]. 558p.   **BD1355**

A useful handbook for the student of Russian literature, scholars in related areas, and the general reader. Each of 106 scholar-contributors was asked to write one or two major articles and a number of briefer ones from his general area of specialization. Articles on individual writers (including a few prominent living persons) predominate, but the nearly 1,000 entries encompass literary terms, genres, societies, periodicals, and important anonymous works, together with many useful topical articles. Since it is assumed that many users of the work do not read Russian, names are given in familiar spellings and titles of literary works are given in translation, usually followed by the transliterated Russian title; the bibliographies appended to most articles cite non-English secondary works only when they contain information not available in English. General classed bibliography (p.535–41); cross references; detailed index.   PG2940.H29

Kratkaia literaturnaia entsiklopediia. Glav. red. A. A. Surkov. Moskva, Sovetskaia Entsiklopediia, 1962–78. 9v. (Entsiklopedii, slovari, spravochniki)   **BD1356**

A general literary encyclopedia, particularly useful for the inclusion of writers of the Soviet period and those of the various national minority groups of the Soviet Union. v.9 contains supplementary articles in alphabetical sequence, plus a name/subject index to the full set.
An extensive review by John Glad appears in *Slavic and East European journal* 25,no.2:80–90 (Summer 1981).   PN41.K7

Literaturnaia entsiklopediia. Redaktsionnaia kollegiia: P. I. Lebedev-Polianskii, I. M. Nusinov. Moskva, "Khudozhestvennaia Literatura," 1929–39. v.1–9, 11. il. (Repr. 1948: American Council of Learned Societies reprints. Russian ser., no.20)   **BD1357**

An extensive treatment of world literature from a Marxist-Leninist standpoint, with special emphasis on the literatures of Russia and other portions of the USSR.   PN41.L46

The modern encyclopedia of Russian and Soviet literature. Ed. by Harry B. Weber. [Gulf Breeze, Fla.], Academic International Pr., 1977–84. v.1–7. (In progress)   **BD1358**

Contents: v.1–7, Abaginskii–Fonvizin.
"The coverage envisioned for this series goes beyond writers and their works to include those aspects of Russian and Soviet cultural life which impinge in one way or another on literature in a broad sense: literary criticism, the contributions of past literary scholars (no living scholar is represented), a number of selected linguistic problems, dramatic literature (but not the theater as such), literary genres, literary movements, literary journals, and folklore. . . . The encyclopedia strives, ultimately, to arrive at a cultural profile of Russia and the Soviet Union, as revealed in Russian literature, in the

many other national Soviet literatures, and in their literary traditions and literary history. This has entailed translating authoritative articles in older reference works, or combining information from many sources into a comprehensive article, or including entries by knowledgeable specialists."—*v.1,p.vi.* Longer articles are signed; most include bibliographies. Material translated from other sources seems not to be so identified. PG2940.M6

Timofeev, Leonid Ivanovich and **Turaev, S. V.** Slovar' literaturovedcheskikh terminov. Moskva, "Prosveshchenie," 1974. 509p. **BD1359**

A dictionary of general literary terms. Derivation is indicated for terms of Latin, Greek, or other Western-language origin. Entries are signed; many include bibliographies. PN44.5.T5

Vengerov, Semen Afanas'evich. Istochniki slovaria russkikh pisatelei. Sanktpeterburg, Tip. Imp. Akademiia Nauk, 1900–1917. v.1–4. **BD1360**

Contents: v.1–4, A–Nekrasov. No more published.
A dictionary of Russian writers, with references to sources.
Z2500.V95

History

Akademiia Nauk SSSR. Institut Russkoi Literatury. Istoriia russkoi literatury. Moskva, Izd-vo Akademii Nauk SSSR, 1941–56. 10v. in 13. il. **BD1361**

The work of many scholars, covering from the 11th century to 1917. Bibliographic footnotes, but no general bibliography or index.
PG2950.A47

Mirskii, Dmitrii Petrovich. A history of Russian literature from the earliest times to the death of Dostoevsky (1881). London, Routledge; N.Y., Knopf, 1927. 388p. **BD1362**
PG2951.M5

——— Contemporary Russian literature, 1881–1925. London, Routledge; N.Y., Knopf, 1926. 372p. **BD1363**

These two titles comprise a good concise history. A one-volume, abridged edition, edited by Francis J. Whitfield, was published 1949 (N.Y., Knopf. 518p.), but is considered inferior to the earlier versions. PG2951.M52

Struve, Gleb. Russian literature under Lenin and Stalin, 1917–1953. Norman, Univ. of Oklahoma Pr., [1971]. 454p. **BD1364**

A revision of the 1951 edition of the author's *Soviet Russian literature* which, in turn, was based on his 1935 work of that title. A reliable history, with extensive bibliography (p.396–432).
Deming Brown's *Soviet Russian literature since Stalin* (Cambridge, Cambridge Univ. Pr., 1978. 394p.) brings the record further up to date. PG3022.S82

Ukrainian

Hol'denberh, Lev Izrailevych. Ukrains'ka radians'ka literaturna bibliohrafiia. Ky'iv, Nauk. dumka, 1971. 177p. **BD1365**

A bibliographic essay is followed by a bibliography for the period 1918–69 (p.107–70). Indexed. Z2514.U5H62

Istoriia ukrains'koi literatury. Holova redkolegii IE. P. Kyryliuk. Ky'iv, "Naukova dumka," 1968–71. 8v. in 9. il. **BD1366**

On leaf preceding t.p.: Akademiia Nauk Ukrains'koi RSR. Instytut Literatury im. T. T. Shevchenka.
A work by many contributors, covering from earliest times to 1967. Bibliographical footnotes, but no general bibliography. Each volume has its own index.
A history of Ukrainian literature, from the 11th to the end of the 19th century (Littleton, Colo., Ukrainian Academic Pr., 1975. 681p.) is a translation of Dmytro Chyzhevskyi's *Istoriia ukrains'koi*

literatury vid pochatkiv do doby realizmu (1956); it includes a selected bibliography, p.619–40. PG3905.I8

Ukrains'ki pys'mennyky; bio-bibliohrafichnyi slovnyk. Red. O. I. Bilets'kyi. Ky'iv, Derzh. Vyd-vo Khudozh. Lit-ry, 1960–65. 5v. **BD1367**

Bio-bibliography, with a wide range of early texts, source materials, and criticism for Ukrainian and related literature of the 11th–18th centuries cited in the first volume. v.2–3 contain alphabetical lists of authors of the 19th and early 20th centuries. v.4–5 offer similar lists for 20th-century Ukrainian (Soviet) writers.
Z2514.U5U42

Yugoslav

See also Bibliografija rasprava (AE315).

Barac, Antun. Jugoslavenska književnost. 3. izd. Zagreb, Matica Hrvatska, 1963. 277p. **BD1368**

The 1st ed. (1954) was translated by Petar Mijušković and published as *A history of Yugoslav literature* (Beograd, 1955).
Includes Serbian, Croatian and Slovenian literature.
A German translation has appeared as *Geschichte der jugoslavischen Literaturen von den Anfängen bis zur Gegenwart,* translated and edited by Rolf-Dieter Kluge (Wiesbaden, Harrassowitz, 1977).
PG561.B3

Leksikon pisaca Jugoslavije. [Glavni urednik Zivojin Boškov. Novi sad], Matica Srpska, 1972–79. v.1–2. il. (In progress). **BD1369**

Contents: v.1–2, A–J.
Bio-bibliographies of Yugoslav writers, including living persons. Some very extensive lists of works by and about the authors.
PG564.L4

Mihailovich, Vasa D. and **Matejic, Mateja.** Yugoslav literature in English; a bibliography of translations and criticism (1821–1975). Cambridge, Mass., Slavica Publishers, [1976]. 328p. **BD1370**

Includes translations of anonymous folk literature as well as works of individual authors. The section of critical writings includes entries in reference works, books, articles, reviews, and dissertations. Indexed. Z2958.L5Y83

CLASSICAL LANGUAGES

General works

Bibliography

Engelmann, Wilhelm. Bibliotheca scriptorum classicorum; 8. Aufl. umfassend die Literatur von 1700 bis 1878, neubearb. von E. Preuss. Leipzig, Engelmann, 1880–82. 2v. (Repr.: Hildesheim, G. Olms, 1959). **BD1371**

Contents: v.1, Greek; v.2, Latin.
The standard bibliography, useful for information about editions of collected works and separate works, translations, and works about classical authors. Of first importance in the large reference or college library. Continued by: Z7016.E58

Klussmann, Rudolf. Bibliotheca scriptorum classicorum et graecorum et latinorum. Die Literatur von 1878 bis 1896 einschliesslich umfassend. Leipzig, Reisland, 1909–13. 2v. in 4. (Repr.: Hildesheim, Olms, 1961) **BD1372**

Contents: v.1, Greek; v.2, Latin.
Also published as v.146, 151, 156, and 165 of *Jahresbericht über die Fortschritte der klassischen Altertumswissenschaft* (Berlin, 1909, 1911–13). Z7016.E592

Fabricius, Johann Albert. Bibliotheca graeca . . . Ed. 4 variorum curis emendatior atque auctior. Hamburgi, Bohn, 1790–1809. 12v. **BD1373**

———— ———— Index. Lipsiae, Cnobloch, 1838. 94p.

Z7021.F12

———— Bibliotheca latina, mediae et infimae aetatis, cum supplemento Christiani Schoettgenii jam a p. Joanne Dominico Mansi. Florentiae, Baracchi, 1858–59. 6v. in 3. **BD1374**

Still useful bio-bibliographical dictionaries of Greek authors and Latin authors of the Middle Ages. Z7026.F13

Fifty years (and twelve) of classical scholarship; being Fifty years of classical scholarship, rev. with appendices. Oxford, Blackwell; N.Y., Barnes & Noble, 1968. 523p. il. **BD1375**

A revision and extension of *Fifty years of classical scholarship,* ed. by Maurice Platnauer (1954).
Chapters by contributing scholars survey the advances in various areas of classical scholarship since the founding of the Classical Association. An appendix to each chapter (usually by the original contributor) updates the original edition. Lacks an index.

PA3001.F5

Gwinup, Thomas and **Dickinson, Fidelia.** Greek and Roman authors: a checklist of criticism. 2d ed. Metuchen, N.J., Scarecrow Pr., 1982. 280p. **BD1376**

1st ed. 1973.
A bibliography of English-language studies intended mainly "for the use of students in the increasingly popular courses in comparative and world literature as well as other courses in the humanities." —*Introd.* A brief section of general works is followed by sections for individual authors. Z7016.G9

Harvard University. Library. Classical studies: classification schedules; classified listing by call number; chronological listing; author and title listing. Cambridge, Publ. by Harvard Univ. Lib.; distr. by Harvard Univ. Pr., 1979. 215p. (Widener Library shelflist, 57) **BD1377**

For a note on the series *see* AA145.
Includes about 6,700 shelflist entries for the Widener *Class* class which "provides for much of what is usually thought of as Classical Greek and Roman studies. The class includes works on the history and theory of classical scholarship, the history of classical literature (but not works about individual authors), classical arts and sciences, classical rhetoric, classical prosody, classical inscriptions, and classical mythology and religion."—*p.3.* Z6207.G7H37

Lambrino, Scarlat. Bibliographie de l'antiquité classique, 1896–1914. Paris, Soc. d'Édit. "Les Belles-Lettres," 1951. pt.1 (Collection de bibliographie classique) **BD1378**

Contents: 1.pt., Auteurs et textes.
A valuable work designed to fill the gap in the bibliographical record of classical studies between the works of Englemann (BD1371) and Klussman (BD1372), which together cover 1700–1896, and the *Dix années de bibliographie classique* of Marouzeau, 1914–24 (BD1379). Following the same plan as the latter, v.1, *Auteurs et textes,* 1896–1914, lists editions, translations, and works about classical writers in books and periodicals. The coverage is not limited to literature but includes all phases of Greco-Latin antiquity from prehistory to the Byzantine and Gallo-Roman periods. As in Marouzeau, the second volume was to be concerned with *Matières et disciplines.* Z7016.L2

Marouzeau, Jules. Dix années de bibliographie classique; bibliographie critique et analytique de l'antiquité gréco-latine pour la période 1914–1924. Paris, Soc. d'Édit. "Les Belles-Lettres," 1927–28. 2v. (Repr.: N.Y., B. Franklin, 1969) **BD1379**

Contents: v.1, Auteurs et textes; v.2, Matières et disciplines.
The subject volume covers the whole field of history and culture of the classical world.
Continued by *L'année philologique* (BD1382). Z7016.M35

Nairn, John Arbuthnot. Classical hand-list, ed. by B. H. Blackwell, Ltd. 3d ed. rev. and enl. Oxford, Blackwell, 1953. 164p. **BD1380**

1st ed., 1931, had title *A hand-list of books relating to the classics and classical antiquity.*
A convenient listing of texts and translations of Greek and Latin authors and books relating to classical antiquity. Z7016.N17

Ooteghem, Jules van. Bibliotheca graeca et latina à l'usage des professeurs des humanités gréco-latines. 2. éd. rev. et aug. Namur, Éd. de la Revue "Les études classiques," [1946]. 386p. **BD1381**

The 1st ed. appeared in *Les études classiques* in April and Oct. 1936. Compiled especially for teachers in the secondary schools and, therefore, treats mainly the authors taught in the schools, with other authors receiving less attention. Lists editions, translations, dictionaries, and critical studies under each author. Z7106.O5

Current bibliography and annual surveys

L'année philologique; bibliographie critique et analytique de l'antiquité gréco-latine, pub. sous la direction de J. Marouzeau [and others]. 1924/26– . Paris, Soc. d'Édit. "Les Belles-Lettres," 1928– . Annual. **BD1382**

A very useful bibliographic survey, in classified arrangement. Some volumes cover more than one year, and all include additional references to previous years. A continuation of Marouzeau (BD1379).
Beginning with v.36, United States, British, and Commonwealth publications (monographs, reviews, etc.) are reported by a newly established American branch of *L'année philologique* at Chapel Hill, North Carolina. Notes accompanying such entries appear in English. With v.42 (1971), a geographical index was added.

Z7016.M35A

Bibliotheca philologica classica, 1874–1938. Leipzig, Reisland, 1875–1941. 65v. Annual. (Beiblatt zum Jahresbericht über die Fortschritte der klassischen Altertumswissenschaft) **BD1383**

An annual survey, wider in scope than Engelmann (BD1371) and Klussmann (BD1372). No more published. PA3.J3

Klassieke bibliographie. 1.–22. jaarg., 1929–1950. Maandlijsten van tijdschriftartikelen met driemaandelijksche lijsten van nieuwe boekwerken in die Buma-Bibliotheek en in andere Nederlandsche bibliotheken. Utrecht, 1930–50. Annual. **BD1384**

Ceased publication.
Lists books and periodical articles, arranged by subject. The bibliography was also published on cards. Z7016.K64

Year's work in classical studies. v.1–34, 1906–1945/47. Ed. for the Classical Journals Board. London, Arrowsmith, 1907–50. Annual. **BD1385**

Ceased publication.
An annual survey in English, not so comprehensive as the *Bibliotheca philologica classica* (BD1383) or *L'année philologique* (BD1382). PA11.C7

Dissertations

Thompson, Lawrence Sidney. A bibliography of American doctoral dissertations in classical studies and related fields. [Hamden, Conn.], Shoe String Pr., 1968. 250p. **BD1386**

For full information *see* DA119; *see also* its complementary volume, DA120. Z7016.T48

Periodicals

Southan, Joyce E. A survey of classical periodicals; union catalogue of periodicals relevant to classical studies in certain British libraries. London, Univ. of London Inst. of

Classical Studies, 1962. 181p. (London University Inst. of Classical Studies. Bull. suppl. 13) **BD1387**

A union list of classical periodicals in some 50 British libraries, giving dates of publication, changes of title, etc. Z2260.S67

Translations into English

Foster, Finley Melville Kendall. English translations from the Greek, a bibliographical survey. N.Y., Columbia Univ. Pr., 1918. 146p. (Columbia Univ. studies in English and comparative literature [62]) **BD1388**

A list of translations from 1476 to 1917. Z7018.T7E71

Parks, George B. and **Temple, Ruth Z.**, eds. The Greek and Latin literatures. N.Y., Ungar, [1968]. 442p. (Literatures of the world in English translation, v.1) **BD1389**

For a note on the series see BD35.

Separate sections for Greek and for Latin literature, each arranged by chronological period. Within periods translations are listed by author, then by translated title. Scholars specializing in the various periods have assisted in compilation of the lists. Publications through 1965 are included. Index of authors and anonymous titles, but not of editors and translators. Z7018.T7E85

Smith, F. Seymour. The classics in translation; an annotated guide to the best translations of the Greek and Latin classics into English. London, N.Y., Scribner, 1930. 307p. **BD1390**

An annotated guide. Translations especially recommended are starred. Z7018.T7E87

Criticism

Ancient writers: Greece and Rome. T. James Luce, ed. in chief. N.Y., Scribner's, [1982]. 2v. (1148p.) **BD1391**

Contents: v.1, Homer to Caesar; v.2, Lucretius to Ammianus Marcellinus.

Offers 47 essays by contributing scholars mainly on individual authors or pairs of authors, chronologically arranged. Contributors were invited to write "personal, even idiosyncratic, essays in order to show what in their eyes constitute the significant achievements of the writers of the ancient world" (*Introd.*): biographical information and literary background are subordinate features of the essays. Intended for a wide range of readers, "from students in secondary school to advanced classical scholars." Bibliographies of texts and studies. Index in v.2. PA3002.A5

Handbooks

See also DA125.

Feder, Lillian. Crowell's Handbook of classical literature. N.Y., Crowell, [1964]. 448p. maps. **BD1392**

Subtitle on jacket: A modern guide to the drama, poetry, and prose of Greece and Rome, with biographies of their authors.

An alphabetical dictionary of names, titles, mythological characters, etc. Gives detailed summaries of individual works, occasional commentaries, etc. PA31.F4

Harsh, Philip Whaley. A handbook of classical drama. Stanford, Calif., Stanford Univ. Pr., 1944. 526p. (Repr. 1967) **BD1393**

Offers discussions of Greek and Roman dramatists and their plays, "designed to be a modern appreciation of the plays as literature and a convenient brief guide to further critical material." —*Pref.* Bibliography (p.497–511) lists texts in the original language and English translations with annotations. Recommended translations are starred. PA3024.H3

Harvey, Sir Paul. Oxford companion to classical literature. Oxford, Clarendon Pr., 1937. 468p. **BD1394**

Reprinted with corrections at frequent intervals.

A useful handbook of concise information on classical writers, literary forms and subjects, individual works, names and subjects in Greek and Roman history, institutions, religion, etc., about which the student or reader of classical literature may need information. DE5.H3

Hathorn, Richmond Yancey. Crowell's Handbook of classical drama. N.Y., Crowell, 1967. 350p. **BD1395**

A work in dictionary form, concentrating on Greek classical drama. Includes entries for dramatists, dramatic forms, terms in classical drama, individual plays (with brief background notes and summaries), and characters from extant dramas and from mythology. A more convenient ready-reference tool than the Harsh *Handbook* (BD1393), but without the bibliographic apparatus of that work. PA3024.H35

Thompson, Sir Edward Maunde. An introduction to Greek and Latin palaeography. Oxford, Clarendon Pr., 1912. 600p. il., facsims. **BD1396**

An enlarged edition of the author's *Handbook of Greek and Latin palaeography* (3d ed. 1906).

For full information see AA260. Z114.T472

Wellington, Jean Susorney. Dictionary of bibliographic abbreviations found in the scholarship of classical studies and related disciplines. Westport, Conn., Greenwood Pr., [1983]. 393p. **BD1397**

Aims to bring together the many abbreviations (and their variants) for journals, series, and standard works in the broad range of classical studies, plus some other abbreviations often encountered in scholarly publications in that field. Abbreviations are listed alphabetically (with separate sections for Greek and Cyrillic); for abbreviations of journals, serials, etc., reference is given to an item number in the section of "Bibliographic descriptions" where one must turn to find the full form. Includes some abbreviations not found in Leistner (AE14). PA99.W44

History

The Cambridge history of classical literature. Cambridge, Cambridge Univ. Pr., [1982]– . v.2– . plates. (In progress) **BD1398**

Contents: v.2, Latin literature, ed. by E. J. Kenney.

A critical history, with chapters by contributing scholars, intending "to make available to the widest possible public the results of recent and current scholarship in this field."—*Pref.* In v.2 (the first to be published), material relating to biography, chronology of a writer's works, and bibliography are confined mainly to the "Appendix of authors and works" at the end of the volume. Indexed.

Biography

Biographisches Jahrbuch für Altertumskunde, 1878–1943. Berlin, Calvary, 1879–98; Leipzig, Reisland, 1899–1944. v.1–63. **BD1399**

Annual, except that no volume was published for 1912. Issued as part of the *Jahresbericht über die Fortschritte der klassischen Altertumswissenschaft.* No biographical section since 1943.

Contains signed obituaries of classical philologists; articles are of some length, with bibliographies. PA3.J3

Grant, Michael. Greek and Latin authors, 800 B.C.–A.D. 1000; a biographical dictionary. N.Y., Wilson, 1980. 490p. il. **BD1400**

"A volume in the Wilson authors series."—*t.p.*

Includes sketches of some 370 writers. As far as possible, gives an account of the writer's life, a description and critical commentary on the works, and, where relevant, some discussion of the author's influence. Bibliography of useful editions of the works (including translations) and of selected critical studies. PA31.G7

Collections

Loeb classical library. founded by James Loeb. Cambridge, Harvard Univ. Pr., 1912– . v.1– . (In progress) **BD1401**

Publisher varies.

An extensive collection of several hundred volumes in two series: (1) Greek and (2) Latin. Each volume gives parallel texts of original and English translation, has a brief introduction, and a bibliography. No general index as yet, but indexes to individual authors, though varying in kind and value, are frequently useful for locating a subject or specific passage.

Greek

Bibliography

Harvard University. Library. Ancient Greek literature: classification schedules; classified listing by call number; chronological listing; author and title listing. Cambridge, Publ. by Harvard Univ. Lib., distr. by Harvard Univ. Pr., 1979. 638p. (Widener Library shelflist, 58) **BD1402**

For a note on the series *see* AA145.

Includes some 19,800 shelflist entries comprising the Widener *G* class. "It includes anthologies of literature and works by and about individual authors. Literary histories are in the *Class* class."—*p.3.*
Z7025.H37

Kessels, A. H. M. and **Verdenius, W. J.** A concise bibliography of Greek language and literature. Apeldoorn, Administratief Centrum, 1979. 287p. **BD1403**

A bibliography for students and teachers of the classics. Classed arrangement, with topical sections (e.g., dictionaries, grammar, epigraphy, tragedy) interspersed with sections on individual authors and schools. Lists editions of classical texts together with secondary studies. Brief index.

Riesenfeld, Harald and **Riesenfeld, Blenda.** Repertorium lexicographicum graecum: a catalogue of indexes and dictionaries to Greek authors. Stockholm, Almqvist and Wiksell, [1954]. 95p. **BD1404**

A companion volume to Paul Faider's *Répertoire des index et lexiques d'auteurs latins* (BD1421), listing indexes and dictionaries "bearing upon Greek literature from its beginning to the end of the Byzantine epoch," including the Greek Bible. Both separately published works and parts of volumes are listed. Preface and notes are in English. Z7021.R5

History

Croiset, Alfred and **Croiset, Maurice.** Histoire de la littérature grecque. 3.–4. éd. Paris, Boccard, 1914–47. 5v. **BD1405**

Edition note varies: v.1, 4th ed., 1928; v.2–3, 3d ed., 1914–29; v.4, 4th ed., 1947; v.5, 3d ed., 1928.

An important reference history; many bibliographies. PA3055.C8

Schmid, Wilhelm and **Stählin, Otto.** Geschichte der griechischen Literatur. München, Beck, 1929–48. v.1¹⁻⁵. (Handbuch der Altertumswissenschaft, begründet von Iwan von Müller . . . 7 Abt.) **BD1406**

A well-documented history, based on the standard German work, *Geschichte der griechischen Literatur,* by Wilhelm von Christ (6. Aufl. München, Beck, 1912–24. 2v. in 3). PA3057.S3

Individual authors

For other indexes and dictionaries *see* Riesenfeld, BD1404.

Aeschylus

Italie, Gabriel. Index Aeschyleus. Editio altera, correcta et aucta, curavit S. L. Radt. Leiden, Brill, 1964. 345p. **BD1407**

Wartelle, André. Bibliographie historique et critique d'Eschyle et de la tragédie grecque, 1518–1974. Paris, "Les Belles Lettres," 1978. 685p. **BD1408**

A bibliography of editions of the works of Aeschylus (including translations) and of critical studies on Aeschylus and Greek tragedy in general. Chronologically arranged by publication date, with indexes of editions, translations, authors, and principal subjects. Z8017.5.W37

Aristophanes

Dunbar, Henry. Complete concordance to the comedies and fragments of Aristophanes. Oxford, Clarendon Pr., 1883. 342p. (Repr.: Hildesheim, Olms, 1973) **BD1409**

Based upon the text of Dindorf's edition of Aristophanes (Oxford, 1835), and Meineke's edition of the *Fragments* (Berlin, 1840). PA3888.Z8D8

Todd, Otis Johnson. Index Aristophanevs. Cambridge, Harvard Univ. Pr.; Oxford, Univ. Pr., 1932. 275p. **BD1410**
PA3888.Z8T6

Euripides

Allen, James Turney and **Italie, Gabriel.** A concordance to Euripides. Berkeley, Los Angeles, Univ. of California Pr.; London, Cambridge Univ. Pr., 1954. 686p. (Repr.: Groningen, Bouma's Boekhuis, 1970) **BD1411**

Based on various texts; includes all occurrences of every word except for the very common prepositions, conjunctions, etc. PA3992.Z8

Homer

Cunliffe, Richard John. Lexicon of the Homeric dialect. London, Blackie, 1924. 445p. (Repr.: Norman, Univ. of Oklahoma Pr., 1963) **BD1412**

Supplemented by: PA4209.C8

—— Homeric proper and place names. London, Blackie, 1931. 42p. **BD1413**

Dunbar, Henry. A complete concordance to the Odyssey of Homer. New ed., compl. rev. and enl. by Benedetto Marzullo. Hildesheim, G. Olms, 1962. 398p. **BD1414**

1st ed. 1880.

A companion to Prendergast (BD1416), intended to form with that work a complete concordance to Homer. PA4209.D7

Packard, David W. and **Meyers, Tania.** A bibliography of Homeric scholarship. Prelim. ed. 1930–1970. Malibu, Calif., Undena Publn., 1974. 183p. **BD1415**

Cumulates into an author listing the Homer entries from *L'année philologique* of the period 1930–1970. Annotations are not included, but there is a subject index, with special sections for references to passages in the *Iliad* and the *Odyssey,* and for "Homeric words." Z8414.84.P32

Prendergast, Guy Lushington. Complete concordance to the Iliad of Homer. New ed., compl. rev. and enl. by Benedetto Marzullo. Hildesheim, G. Olms, 1962. 427p. **BD1416**

1st ed. 1875.
Compiled from Priestley's edition of Heyne's *Homer*, 1834.

Pindar

Gerber, Douglas E. A bibliography of Pindar, 1513–1966. [Cleveland, Ohio], publ. for the Amer. Philological Assoc. by the Press of Case Western Reserve Univ., 1969. 160p. (Philological monographs, no.28)   **BD1417**

Includes editions, translations, and commentaries, together with critical studies.   Z8692.3.G45

Rico, María. Ensayo de bibliografía pindárica. Madrid, Instituto Antonio de Nebrija, 1969. 354p. (Consejo Superior de Investigaciones Científicas. Manuales y anejos de "Emérita," 24)   **BD1418**

Includes editions, translations in various languages, and textual and critical studies.   Z8692.3.R5

Sophocles

Ellendt, Friedrich Theodor. Lexicon Sophocleum, adhibitis veterum interpretum explicationibus, grammaticorum notationibus, recentiorum doctorum commentariis. Ed. altera emendata. Curavit Hermannus Genthe. Berlin, Borntraeger, 1872. 812p. (Repr.: Hildesheim, Olms, 1958)   **BD1419**

PA4434.Z8

——— ——— Index commentationum Sophoclearum ab A. 1836 editarum triplex. Berlin, Borntraeger, 1874. 134p.

Latin

Bibliography

Caes, Lucien and **Henrion, R.** Collectio bibliographica operum ad ius romanum pertinentium. Bruxelles, Office Internat. de Librairie, 1949– . (In progress)   **BD1420**

For full information *see* CK13.

Faider, Paul. Répertoire des index et lexiques d'auteurs latins. Paris, Soc. d'Édit. "Les Belles-Lettres," 1926. 56p.   **BD1421**

Lists dictionaries and indexes of Latin authors.
For a similar list of Greek dictionaries *see* Riesenfeld, BD1404.
Z7028.D6F2

Harvard University. Library. Latin literature: classification schedules; classified listing by call number; chronological listing; author and title listing. Cambridge, Publ. by Harvard Univ. Lib., distr. by Harvard Univ. Pr., 1979. 610p. (Widener Library shelflist, 59)   **BD1422**

For a note on the series *see* AA145.
Includes some 18,600 shelflist entries comprising the Widener *L* and *ML* classes. The *L* class is for ancient Latin literature, including anthologies of literature and works by and about individual authors. (Literary histories are found in the *Class* class.) Inasmuch as literature is taken in its broadest sense, "writings of all Latin authors of the ancient period are included here regardless of subject. The only major exceptions are the few Latin authors whose works are entirely mathematical in content; they are in the *Math* class. Medieval and modern Latin belles lettres are in the *ML* class."—*p.3*.
Z7030.H37

Herescu, Niculae I. Bibliographie de la littérature latine. Paris, Soc. d'Édit. "Les Belles-Lettres," 1943. 426p. (Collection de bibliographie classique, pub. sous la direction de J. Marouzeau)   **BD1423**

An analytical, selective bibliography of materials on Latin subjects. Arranged by period with an alphabetical index to Latin authors. No index to secondary authors. Under each author, material is arranged under such subheadings as manuscripts, editions, extracts, translations, dictionaries and indexes, studies. In works of voluminous authors these may be further subdivided.
Useful because it brings together in a convenient form a large amount of material that is otherwise scattered. Covers to approximately 1940.

——— ——— Notes additionelles. Paris, Inst. Roumain d'Études Latines, 1951. 15p.

Z7026.H4

IJsewijn, Jozef. Companion to neo-Latin studies. Amsterdam, North-Holland, 1977. 370p.   **BD1424**

"Aims to pave the way to, and serve as a guide in, the immense field of Renaissance, Baroque and modern Latin" (*Pref.*) for beginners, and to provide "a compendium of basic factual and bibliographic information" for scholars in the field. "Neo-Latin" is defined as covering from about 1300 A.D. to the present. Chapters include: Classical, medieval and neo-Latin; Bibliographical aids; Historical survey of neo-Latin literature (with country subdivisions); Texts and editions; Language and style; Prosody and metrics; Literary forms and genres; Scholarly and scientific studies in neo-Latin; Historical survey of neo-Latin studies. Brief "Anthology of neo-Latin texts." Index of names.   PA8020.I37

Kristeller, Paul Oskar, ed. Catalogus translationum et commentariorum: medieval and Renaissance Latin translations and commentaries. Annotated lists and guides. Wash., Catholic Univ. of America Pr., 1960–80. v.1–4. (In progress)   **BD1425**

At head of title: Union Académique Internationale.
With v.3, F. Edward Cranz became editor in chief.
This series "will list and describe the Latin translations of ancient Greek authors and the Latin commentaries on ancient Latin (and Greek) authors up to the year 1600 . . ."—*Pref.*
The first issue includes extensive lists of the extant Greek and Latin authors (most of whom the series intends to treat), followed by a first group of bio-bibliographical sketches on specific classical writers. Chapters appear as they are completed, rather than in any alphabetical or chronological sequence, and "alphabetical indices of ancient authors will be added when necessary." v.4 includes an "Index of ancient authors treated in volumes I–IV."   Z701.K96

——— Latin manuscript books before 1600; a list of the printed catalogues and unpublished inventories of extant collections. 3d ed. N.Y., Fordham Univ. Pr., [1965]. 284p.   **BD1426**

For full information *see* AA241.   Z6601.A1K7

Menéndez y Pelayo, Marcelino. Bibliografía hispano-latina clásica, edición prep. por Enrique Sánchez Reyes. Santander, Aldus S. A. de Artes Gráficas, 1950–53. 10v. (Edición nacional de las obras completas de Menéndez Pelayo dir. por Angel González Palencia. t.44–53)   **BD1427**

A bibliography listing Spanish editions of Latin classics including: manuscripts, editions, commentaries, translations, critical works, imitations, and works showing the influence of Latin classics on Spanish literature. Comments, extracts, etc., are given throughout. Actual bibliographical information is not always complete. Indexes in last volume.

Munk Olsen, B. L'étude des auteurs classiques latins aux XIᵉ et XIIᵉ siècles. Paris, Éditions du Centre National de la Recherche Scientifique, 1982– . v.1– . (In progress)   **BD1428**

At head of title: Documents, études et répertoires publiés par l'Institut de Recherche et d'Histoire des Textes.
Contents: v.1, Catalogue des manuscrits classiques latins copiés du IXᵉ au XIIᵉ siècles: Apicius–Juvénal.
An aid for the study of the transmission of texts. Arranged by classical author, then by repository, with descriptions of the manuscripts and select bibliography. Includes information on some manuscripts of the 9th and 10th centuries.   PA2045.M86

Indexes

Swanson, Donald Carl Eugene. The names in Roman verse; a lexicon and reverse index of all proper names of history, mythology, and geography found in the classical Roman poets. Madison, Univ. of Wisconsin Pr., 1967. **BD1429**

A computer-produced index. PA2379.S9

History

See also BD1398.

Manitius, Maximilianus. Geschichte der lateinischen Literatur des Mittelalters. München, Beck, 1911–31. 3v. (Handbuch der Klassischen Altertumswissenschaft . . . hrsg. von I. von Müller. 9. Bd., 2. Abt., 1.–3. Teil) (Reissued 1964–65) **BD1430**

Contents: v.1, Von Justinian bis zur Mitte des 10. Jahrh.; v.2, Von der Mitte des 10. Jahrh. bis zum Ausbruch des Kampfes zwischen Kirche u. Staat; v.3, Vom Ausbruch des Kirchenstreites bis zum Ende des 12. Jahrh.
The standard history of medieval Latin literature, indispensable in the large reference library. PA8035.M3

Schanz, Martin. Geschichte der römischen Literatur bis zum Gesetzgebungswerk des Kaisers Justinian. Neubearb. Aufl. von Carl Hosius. München, Beck, 1935–66. 4v. in 5. (Handbuch der klassischen Altertumswissenschaft . . . hrsg. von I. von Müller. 8. Bd.) **BD1431**

Edition number varies: v.1, 1966: 4. Aufl. (Nachdruck); v.2, 1935: 4. Aufl.; v.3, 1959: 3.Aufl. (Nachdruck); v.4, 1959: 2.Aufl. (Nachdruck).
Contents: v.1, Die römische Literatur in der Zeit der Republik; v.2 Die römische Literatur in der Zeit der Monarchie bis auf Hadrian; v.3, Die Zeit von Hadrian 117 bis auf Constantin 324; v.4, Von Constantin bis zum Gesetzgebungswerk Justinians: 1. Hälfte, Die Literatur des vierten Jahrhunderts; 2. Hälfte, Die Literatur des fünften und sechsten Jahrhunderts.
An extensively documented history. Continued by Manitius (above). PA6007.S32

Teuffel, Wilhelm Sigismund. History of Roman literature, rev. and enl. by Ludwig Schwabe. Authorized tr. from the 5th German ed. by George C. W. Warr. London, Bell, 1891–92. 2v. **BD1432**

Contents: v.1, The Republican period; v.2, The Imperial period.
A bibliographical account of Roman history from earliest times to the 16th century A.D.
A 6th German edition, *Geschichte der römischen Literatur,* was published 1910–16 (Leipzig, Teubner. 3v.). PA6007.T55

Individual authors

See also the "Appendix of authors and works" in *The Cambridge history of classical literature,* v.2, p.799–935 (BD1398). For other dictionaries and indexes *see* Faider, BD1421.

Caesar

Merguet, Hugo. Lexikon zu den Schriften Cäsars und seiner Fortsetzer mit Angabe samtlicher Stellen. Jena, Fischer, 1886. 1142p. **BD1433**

Catullus

Harrauer, Hermann. A bibliography to Catullus. Hildesheim, Gerstenberg Verlag, 1979. 206p. (Bibliography to the Augustan poetry, 3) **BD1434**

A bibliography of editions, translations, commentaries, and studies. Nearly 3,000 items; indexed. Z8156.4.H37

Holoka, James P. Gaius Valerius Catullus; a systematic bibliography. N.Y., Garland, 1985. 324p. (Garland reference library of the humanities, v.513) **BD1435**

A classified bibliography of more than 3,000 entries, covering from 1878 through 1981 (with a few later listings). Author index. Z8156.4.H65

McCarren, V. P. A critical concordance to Catullus. Leiden, Brill, 1977. 210p. **BD1436**

A computer-produced concordance using the edition of R. A. B. Mynors (Oxford, 1958) as the basic text, but including variant readings. Effectively supersedes M. N. Wetmore's *Index verborum Catullianus* (New Haven, Yale Univ. Pr., 1912). PA6276.Z8

Cicero

Abbott, Kenneth Morgan, Oldfather, William Abbott and **Canter, Howard Vernon.** Index verborum in Ciceronis Rhetorica; necnon incerti auctoris libros Ad Herennium. Urbana, Univ. of Illinois Pr., 1964. 1160p. **BD1437**

"Based on the editions of Cicero's *Rhetorica* by A. S. Wilkins, *De inventione* by Eduard Stroebel, and the 2d ed. of *Ad Herennium* by Friedrich Marx."—*title page.*
Includes a bibliography of critical materials and an *"Additamentum ad Apparatum Criticum"* which attempts "to record the critical contributions or comments on the text which have been published since the appearance of the earliest of our basic texts in 1900." PA6366.A2

Oldfather, William Abbott, Canter, Howard Vernon and **Abbott, Kenneth Morgan.** Index verborum Ciceronis Epistularum. Urbana, Univ. of Illinois Pr., 1938. 583p. **BD1438**

Based on the edition by L. C. Purser in Oxford Classical Texts, 1901–1903. PA6366.O4

Spaeth, John William. Index verborum Ciceronis Poeticorum fragmentorum. Urbana, Univ. of Illinois Pr., 1955. 130p. **BD1439**

"Based on the text of Aemilius Baehrens."—*title page.* PA6305.P5S6

Horace

Bo, Domenico. Lexicon Horatianum. Hildesheim, G. Olms, 1965–66. 2v. (Alpha–Omega, 1:1–2) **BD1440**

Brings together the different uses of a word and offers brief explanations of doubtful readings. Based on the "Corpus scriptorum Latinorum Paravianum" edition (Torino, Paravia, 1958–60) of which Bo was an editor. PA6444.B6

Cooper, Lane. Concordance to the works of Horace. Wash., Carnegie Inst., 1916. 593p. (Repr.: N.Y., Barnes & Noble, 1961) **BD1441**

PA6444.C6

Livy

Packard, David W. A concordance to Livy. Cambridge, Harvard Univ. Pr., 1968. 4v. **BD1442**

A computer-produced concordance using "the texts available in 1967: the Oxford Classical Text through book 35, and the Teubner edition for the remainder."—*Introd.* PA6475.Z8

Ovid

Deferrari, Roy Joseph, Barry, *Sister* **M. Inviolata and Mc-Guire, Martin Rawson Patrick.** A concordance of Ovid. Wash., Catholic Univ. of America Pr., 1939. 2220p.   **BD1443**

"A combination of a concordance and an index verborum . . . based exclusively on the Teubner edition of Ovid."—*Pref.*   PA6553.D4

Paratore, Ettore, comp. Bibliografia Ovidiana. Sulmona, Comitato per le Celebrazioni del Bimillenario, [1958]. 169p.   **BD1444**

Lists incunabula, editions, translations, dissertations, critical works, articles, and dictionaries. Each section arranged chronologically. No index.   Z8649.P37

Petrarch

Cornell University. Libraries. Petrarch: catalogue of the Petrarch collection in Cornell University Library. Millwood, N.Y., Kraus-Thomson, 1974. 737p.   **BD1445**

A revised and expanded version of the 1916 *Catalogue of the Petrarch collection* edited by Mary Fowler. However, since many of the analytic notes from the earlier work have not been carried forward (and *see* references to that work are provided), libraries holding the earlier volume will want to retain it in the reference collection.   Z8676.C75

Vergil

The Classical world bibliography of Vergil, with a new introd. by Walter Donlan. N.Y., Garland, 1978. 176p. (Garland reference library of the humanities, v.96)   **BD1446**

Reprints three surveys of Vergilian scholarship which appeared in the *Classical world,* covering 1940–56, 1957–63 and 1964–73, plus J. E. Heffner's "Bibliographical handlist on Vergil's *Aeneid*" which also appeared in that journal.   Z8932.C58

Mambelli, Giuliano. Gli studi Virgiliani nel secolo XX. Contributo ad una bibliografia generale. Firenze, Sansoni, 1940. 2v. (Guide bibliografiche dell' Istit. Nazionale di Cultura Fascista. VII)   **BD1447**

An annotated bibliography of books and periodical articles in many languages.   Z8932.M18

Warwick, Henrietta Holm. A Vergil concordance. Minneapolis, Univ. of Minnesota Pr., [1975]. 962p.   **BD1448**

A keyword-in-context concordance based on the "Oxford classical texts" edition, *P. Vergili Maronis opera,* ed. by R. A. B. Mynors (Oxford, Clarendon Pr., 1969).   PA6952.W3

Wetmore, Monroe Nichols. Index verborum Vergilianus. [2d printing] New Haven, Yale Univ. Pr., 1930. 554p.   **BD1449**

Originally publ. 1911.

A word index to the *Eclogues,* the *Georgics,* the *Aeneid,* and the poems usually included in the *Appendix Vergiliana.*   PA6952.W4

AFRICAN LITERATURE

Bibliography

See also BD744–BD747 and BD936–BD940.

Baldwin, Claudia. Nigerian literature: a bibliography of criticism, 1952–1976. Boston, G. K. Hall, [1980]. 147p.   **BD1450**

About 1,500 entries; general criticism is followed by sections for individual authors. Indexes of critics and of titles.   PR9387.B34

East, N. B. African theatre: a checklist of critical materials. N.Y., Africana, [1970]. 47p.   **BD1451**

Lists books and periodical articles. Sections for bibliographies and general works are followed by regional listings. No index. "The bibliography originally appeared in the Spring, 1969, issue of *Afro-Asian Theatre Bulletin* but has been updated since its initial publication."—*Introd.*   Z3508.T4E3

Harvard University. Library. African history and literatures; classification schedule, classified listing by call number, chronological listing, author and title listing. Cambridge, distr. by Harvard Univ. Pr., 1971. (Widener Library shelf-list, 34)   **BD1452**

For full information *see* DD10.

Howard University, Washington, D.C. Library. Dictionary catalog of the Arthur B. Spingarn collection of Negro authors. Boston, G. K. Hall, 1970. 2v.   **BD1453**

Reproduction of the catalog cards for this collection of writings by Negroes. In addition to works by African-born and Afro-American authors, works by Caribbean, Afro-Cuban, and Afro-Brazilian authors are included.   Z1361.N39H78

Jahn, Janheinz. A bibliography of neo-African literature from Africa, America, and the Caribbean. N.Y., Praeger, [1965]. 359p.   **BD1454**

Also published as *Die neoafrikanische Literatur; Gesamtbibliographie von den Anfängen bis zur Gegenwart* (Düsseldorf, E. Diedrichs Verlag, 1965).

Introduction in German, English, and French.

"Neo-African literature can be defined as the new literature of African culture, and manifests the overlapping of two historically different literatures: (1) traditional Negro-African literature, and (2) Western literature."—*Introd.* Emphasis in the bibliography is on "creative" literature, but essays and autobiographical writings are frequently included. Works by Afro-Americans are also included as being necessary to the study of neo-African literature. Arrangement is by geographical area, then by author. Indexed.   Z3508.L5J3

—— and **Dressler, Claus Peter.** Bibliography of creative African writing. Nendeln, Liechtenstein, Kraus-Thomson, 1971. 446p.   **BD1455**

An expansion and updating of the African section of Jahn's *Bibliography of neo-African literature . . .* (above), with the addition of references to secondary sources.   Z3508.L5J28

Moser, Gerald M. A tentative Portuguese-African bibliography: Portuguese literature in Africa and African literature in the Portuguese language. University Park, Pennsylvania State Univ. Libraries, 1970. 148p. (Pennsylvania. State Univ. Libs. Bibliographical ser., 3)   **BD1456**

In three main sections: (1) oral folk literature; (2) written literature; and (3) literary history and criticism. Each section is subdivided by the major regions of Portuguese Africa. Includes books, pamphlets, contributions to periodicals, and some manuscripts.   Z3874.L5M6

Ramsaran, John A. New approaches to African literature; a guide to Negro-African writing and related studies. 2d ed. [Ibadan], Ibadan Univ. Pr., 1970. 168p.   **BD1457**

1st ed. 1965.

Primarily a select bibliography of African literary works, with some attention to critical works and background studies. Has sections for oral literature (vernacular and translated), modern African literature (including writings in English, French, and Portuguese), West Indian and French Caribbean literature, and the American Negro novel.   Z3508.L5R3

Zell, Hans M., Bundy, Carol and **Coulon, Virginia.** A new reader's guide to African literature. 2d completely rev. and expanded ed. London, Heinemann; N.Y., Africana Publ. Co., [1983]. 553p. il.   **BD1458**

1st ed. (1971) by Zell and Helene Silver had title *A reader's guide to African literature.*

" . . . lists 3091 works by black African authors south of the Sahara writing in English, French and Portuguese. Reference material, critical works and anthologies (many by non-African authors) are also included, as is a section on children's books by African authors."—*Introd.* There are separate sections for the literature of English-speaking Africa, Francophone Africa, and Lusophone Africa; those sections are further subdivided by region and country. Entries are annotated and sometimes include references from reviews. An annotated list of magazines and a section of biographical sketches of about 100 African writers follow the bibliographical sections; and there are directories of publishers and book dealers and of libraries with African literature collections. Indexed.

PN849.A35Z44

Biography

Herdeck, Donald E. African authors; a companion to black African writing. Wash., D.C., Black Orpheus Pr., 1973. v.1. il. **BD1459**

Contents: v.1, 1300–1973. 605p.

Biographical sketches on nearly 600 authors, mainly of sub-Saharan Africa, from all periods, but primarily 20th century. Lists of writings are included (with place and date of separately published works), and sources of biographical and critical information are sometimes given. Writings in 37 African vernacular languages are represented. Appendixes include a chronological list of authors; lists of authors by genre, by country of origin, by African and European languages employed; a list of major publishers of African literature; and bibliographies, p.591–601. PL8010.H38

Jahn, Janheinz, Schild, Ulla and **Nordmann, Almut.** Who's who in African literature: biographies, works, commentaries. Tübingen, Horst Erdmann Verlag, 1972. 406p. il. **BD1460**

Concerned with "sub-Saharan" or "Black African" writers (thus excluding North African and Ethiopian writers) writing in either European or African languages. Mainly contemporary figures, but includes some writers of earlier periods. In most instances full bibliographical details of an author's works and citations to critical studies are not given, but a cross reference to Jahn's *Bibliography of creative African writing* (BD1455) is provided instead.

PL8010.J33

ORIENTAL LANGUAGES
General works
Guides

Anderson, George Lincoln. Asian literature in English: a guide to information sources. Detroit, Gale, [1981]. 336p. (American literature, English literature, and world literatures in English, v.31) **BD1461**

Intended as "a guide to translations into English and to major scholarship and criticism in English of the literatures of East Asia."—*Introd.* Indian literature is omitted, having been treated in a separate volume of the series (BD776). Chapters are devoted to: Far East, China, Japan, Korea, Southeast Asia, Burma, Cambodia, Indonesia, Laos, Malaysia and Singapore, Thailand, Vietnam, Mongolia, Tibet, and Turkic and other literatures. For China and Japan the emphasis is on books; for other countries there is a heavy reliance on periodical materials. Indexed. Z3001.A655

Columbia University. Columbia College. A guide to Oriental classics. . . . , ed. by Wm. Theodore De Bary and Ainslie T. Embree. 2d ed. N.Y., Columbia Univ. Pr., 1975. 257p.
BD1462

1st ed. 1964.

" . . . compiled as an aid to students and teachers taking up for the first time the major works of Oriental literature and thought. It is designed especially for general education, which emphasizes a careful reading of single whole works and discussion of them in a group."—*Introd.* Sections for the Islamic, Indian, Chinese, and Japanese traditions. For each of the classics considered, provides lists of English translations, selected secondary readings in English, and a list of topics for discussion; brief evaluative notes accompany most citations. Z7046.C65

Bibliography

Jenner, Philip N. Southeast Asian literatures in translation; a preliminary bibliography. [Honolulu], Univ. Pr. of Hawaii, 1973. 198p. (Asian studies at Hawaii, no.9)
BD1463

Includes sections for Burma, Cambodia, Champa, Indonesia, Laos, Malaysia and Singapore, Philippines, Thailand, Vietnam, and a section of regional and general works. Includes folk literature, inscriptions, etc., as well as belles-lettres.

Lang, David Marshall, ed. A guide to Eastern literatures. London, Weidenfeld and Nicolson, [1971]. 501p.
BD1464

Specialists have contributed chapters on Arabic, Jewish, Persian, Turkish, Armenian and Georgian, Ethiopic, Indian and Pakistani, Sinhalese, Indonesian and Malaysian, Chinese, Tibetan, Mongolian, Korean, Burmese, and Japanese literatures. Most chapters include sections on the historical background, main trends in the literature, individual writers, and a bibliography. Indexed. PJ307.L3

Senny, Jacqueline. Contributions à l'appréciation des valeurs culturelles de l'Orient: traductions françaises de littératures orientales. Bruxelles, Commission Belge de Bibliographie, 1958. 299p. (Bibliographia belgica, 37) **BD1465**

Mémoire présenté à l'École Provinciale de Bibliothécaires du Brabant, session 1954.

A list of 2,466 Oriental works translated into French since the 17th century. Includes all of the Orient—the Near East as well as the Far East.

Arabic

Altoma, Salih J. Modern Arabic literature: a bibliography of articles, books, dissertations, and translations in English. Bloomington, Indiana Univ., 1975. 73p. (Indiana Univ., Asian Studies Research Inst. Occasional papers, no.3)
BD1466

A guide to materials in English. Classed listing with author index; dissertations appear in a separate listing without subject approach. About 850 items.

Brockelmann, Carl. Geschichte der arabischen Litteratur. 2. den Supplementbände angepasste Aufl. Leiden, Brill, 1943–49. 2v. **BD1467**

A new edition of this standard work "fitted to the *Supplementband*" (Leiden, Brill, 1937–42. 3v.). PJ7510.B7

The Cambridge history of Arabic literature. Cambridge & N.Y., Cambridge Univ. Pr., 1983– . [v.1]– . (In progress)
BD1468

Contents: [v.1] Arabic literature to the end of the Umayyad period, ed. by A. F. L. Beeston [et al.] (547p.).

The series is designed to replace Reynold A. Nicholson's *The literary history of the Arabs* (first publ. 1907), providing more extensive coverage than that long-standard work and offering an up-to-date survey of modern scholarship.

[v.1] presents chapters by an international roster of scholars; it includes a "Bibliography of translations of the Qur'ān into European languages," a glossary, a list of sources quoted, and an index.

Chauvin, Victor. Bibliographie des ouvrages arabes ou relatifs aux arabes publiés dans l'Europe chrétienne de 1810 à 1885. Liége, Vaillant-Carmanne, 1892–1922. 12 pts. **BD1469**

Contents: (1) Préface. Table de Schnurrer. Les proverbes; (2) Kalilah; (3) Louqmâne et les fabulistes. Barlaam. 'Antar et les romans de chevalerie; (4–7) Les mille et une nuits; (8) Syntipas; (9) Pierre Alphonse. Secundus. Recueils orientaux. Tables de Henning et de Mardrus. Contes occidentaux. Les maqâmes; (10) Le Coran et la tradition; (11) Mahomet; (12) Le Mahométisme.

No general index but some parts have alphabetical or subject indexes, some are arranged alphabetically. Z7052.C511

Chinese

Bailey, Roger B. Guide to Chinese poetry and drama. Boston, G. K. Hall, 1973. 100p. **BD1470**

A bibliographic guide to works in English translation. "The bibliography addresses itself to those who are approaching the study of Chinese poetry for the first time. Individually, the annotations describe and make judgments on specific works. Taken as a whole, however, the bibliography should enable the reader to acquire as good a fundamental knowledge of Chinese poetry as is available to the English-speaking reader."—*Introd.: Poetry.* There is a separate, briefer section on the drama. Z3108.L5B34

Davidson, Martha. A list of published translations from Chinese into English, French and German . . . (Tentative edition). Ann Arbor, Mich., J. W. Edwards for the Amer. Council of Learned Societies, [1952–57]. Pts.1–2. **BD1471**

Contents: pt.1, Literature, exclusive of poetry; pt.2, Poetry. No more published.

The series was planned to cover all fields in the humanities and the social sciences. Z7059.D38

Gibbs, Donald A. and **Li, Yun-chen.** A bibliography of studies and translations of modern Chinese literature, 1918–1942. Cambridge, Mass., East Asian Research Center, Harvard Univ.; distr. by Harvard Univ. Pr., 1975. 239p. (Harvard East Asian monographs, 61) **BD1472**

In three main sections: (1) Sources; (2) Studies of modern Chinese literature; (3) Studies and translations of individual authors. Concentrates on the period 1918–1942. Index of authors, translators, etc. Z3108.L5G52

Legge, James. Chinese classics; with a translation, critical and exegetical notes, prolegomena and copious indexes. 2d ed. rev. Oxford, Clarendon Pr., 1893–95. 5v. in 8. maps. (Repr.: Hong Kong, Hong Kong Univ. Pr., 1960. 5v.) **BD1473**

v.1–2, 2d ed., rev., 1893–95, printed at the Clarendon Press, Oxford; v.3–5—printed at the London Missionary Society's Printing Office, Hong Kong—are a reissue of the older edition with new title page and imprint: London, H. Frowde, [n.d.].

The volumes originally planned were "to embrace all the books in 'The thirteen king'," but v.6–7 were never published. English translations of the *Yih king* and the *Li ki* appeared, respectively, as v.16 and v.27–28 of the series *Sacred books of the East* (BB75). A translation of the *Hsiao king* appeared in v.3 of the same series.

Contents: v.1, Confucian analects, the Great learning, and the Doctrine of the mean; v.2, The works of Mencius; v.3, The Shoo-king, or the Book of historical documents: pt.1, The first parts of the Shoo-king, or the Books of T'ang, the Books of Yu, the Books of Hea, the Books of Shang, and the Prolegomena; pt.2, The fifth part of the Shoo-king, or the Books of Chow, and the indexes; v.4, The She-king, or the Book of poetry: pt.1, The first part of the She-king, or the Lessons from the states, and the Prolegomena; pt.2, The second, third, and fourth parts of the She-king, or the Minor odes of the kingdom, the Greater odes of the kingdom, the Sacrificial odes and praise-songs, and the indexes; v.5, The Ch'un ts'ew, with the Tso chuen: pt.1, Dukes Yin, Hwan, Chwang, Min, He, Wan, Seuen,

and Ch'ing, and the Prolegomena; pt.2, Dukes Seang, Ch'aou, Ting, and Gae, with Tso's appendix, and the indexes. PL2948.L5

Li, Tien-Yi. Chinese fiction; a bibliography of books and articles in Chinese and English. New Haven, Far Eastern Publ., Yale Univ., 1968. 356p. **BD1474**

A selective listing "of books and articles in Chinese and English that have been published in the field of Chinese fiction over the past few decades."—*Pref.* Chinese contributions predominate. There is a section for general studies and reference works, and important English translations of Chinese works of fiction are noted.
Z3108.L5L4

Lynn, Richard John. Chinese literature: a draft bibliography in Western European languages. Canberra, Faculty of Asian Studies in assoc. with Australian National Univ. Pr., 1979. 102p. (Oriental monograph ser., 24) **BD1475**

A classed bibliography of Western-language studies (monographs and dissertations) on various aspects of Chinese literature, including studies of individual literary figures. Indexed. Z3118.L5L96

Paper, Jordan D. Guide to Chinese prose. 2d ed. Boston, G. K. Hall, 1984. 149p. **BD1476**

1st ed. 1973.

Essentially an annotated listing of about 200 items (Chinese prose works available in English translation, together with some English-language studies) in classed arrangement. Suggestions for further reading; glossary; index. Z3108.L5P34

Schyns, Joseph. 1500 modern Chinese novels and plays. Peiping, Catholic Univ. Pr., 1948. 484p. **BD1477**

Subtitle: Present day fiction and drama in China by Su Hsueh-Lin; Short biographies of authors by Chao Yen-Sheng.

A study of contemporary Chinese literature; gives reviews in English of 1,500 novels and plays and about 200 biographies. Names and titles are given in romanized form and in Chinese characters.
PL2934.S4

Tsai, Meishi. Contemporary Chinese novels and short stories, 1949–1974: an annotated bibliography. Cambridge, Mass., Council on East Asian Studies, Harvard Univ.; distr. by Harvard Univ. Pr., 1979. 408p. (Harvard East Asia monographs, 78) **BD1478**

An author listing (arranged alphabetically according to the Wade-Giles romanization), with titles given in romanization and in Chinese characters, followed by an English translation of the title. Includes publications in book form and in periodicals; English translations of the works are noted. "The rationale for choosing which stories and novels to annotate . . . is one of informing the reader of the themes and sociopolitical realities reflected in the work."—*Pref.* Biographical notes on the authors are frequently given. Indexes of titles and of selected topics. Z3108.L5T78

Yang, Winston L. Y., Li, Peter and **Mao, Nathan K.** Classical Chinese fiction: a guide to its study and appreciation; essays and bibliographies. Boston, G. K. Hall, [1978]. 302p. **BD1479**

A guide for the student, teacher, scholar, or general reader. "The term 'classical Chinese fiction' is used to refer to traditional or pre-modern works ranging from the fictional writings of the Chou and the Han periods to novels of the late Ch'ing period. The emphasis, however, is on the major novels and short stories of the Ming and Ch'ing dynasties."—*Pref.* In two parts: (1) Essays (providing an introduction to the major classical Chinese novels and short stories) and (2) Bibliographies (which offer additional guidance through the annotated listings of bibliographies and critical studies). The bibliographies are limited to titles in English, French, and German. Glossary; index. Z3108.L5Y29

Coptic

The future of Coptic studies. Ed. by R. McL. Wilson. Leiden, Brill, 1978. 253p. (Coptic studies, v.1) **BD1480**

A selection of papers presented at the First International Congress of Coptology (Cairo, 1976), providing a survey of numerous aspects of Coptic studies. Bibliographical footnotes. PJ2015.F88

Kammerer, Winifred. A Coptic bibliography, comp. . . . with the collaboration of Elinor Mullet Husselman and Louise A. Shier. Ann Arbor, Univ. of Michigan Pr., 1950. 205p. (Univ. of Mich. General library publ., no.7) **BD1481**

Contains more than 3,000 references to Coptic texts and to books and periodicals on Coptic philology, literature, history, religion, and art published in all countries through 1948. Early works are included, although most items are from the late-19th and the 20th centuries. Many entries contain brief descriptive annotations, and some references to important reviews. Arrangement is classified, with an author index. Z7061.K3

Hebrew and Yiddish

Benjacob, Isaac. Ozar Ha-Sepharim (Bücherschatz). Bibliographie der gesammten hebraeischen Literatur mit Einschluss der Handschriften (bis 1863). Wilna, Benjacob, 1880. 678p. **BD1482**

For full information see BB529.

Brisman, Shimeon. A history and guide to Judaic bibliography. Cincinnati, Hebrew Union College Pr.; N.Y., Ktav Publ. House, 1977. 352p. **BD1483**

For full information see BB535.

Goell, Yohai. Bibliography of modern Hebrew literature in English translation. Jerusalem, Executive of the World Zionist Organization, Youth and Hechalutz Dept.; Jerusalem and N.Y., Israel Universities Pr., 1968. 110p. **BD1484**

"The present work lists translations of post-*Haskalah* literature only, a period in Hebrew letters dating roughly from the beginning of the penultimate decade of the nineteenth century."—*Introd.* About 7,500 items in classed arrangement with author and translator indexes, and a Hebrew title index of authors and titles. Z7070.G57

———— Bibliography of modern Hebrew literature in translation. Tel Aviv, Inst. for the Translation of Hebrew Literature, Ltd., 1975. 117p. **BD1485**

Mainly a listing of separately published translations, although a few translations appearing in periodicals or general anthologies have been included in cases where "special issues or sections have been devoted to modern Hebrew literature."—*Introd.* Translations are listed by language, subdivided by literary form. Appendix of monographs on modern Hebrew literature. Index of Hebrew authors, and one of translators, editors and authors of monographs. Z7070.G58

Bibliography of modern Hebrew literature in translation. no.1– , 1972/76– . Tel Aviv, Inst. for the Translation of Hebrew Literature, 1979– . Semiannual. **BD1486**

Isaac Goldberg, comp.

Provides an ongoing supplement to Goell's bibliography (above). The first issue of each year is devoted to translations into English, the second to translations into other languages. Includes translations appearing in periodicals and collections as well as separately published books.

Reisen, Zalman. Leksikon fun der yidisher literatur. . . . Wilno, Kleckin, 1927–29. 4v. il. **BD1487**

A dictionary in Yiddish.

Schwab, Moïse. Répertoire des articles relatifs à l'histoire et à la littérature juives, parus dans les périodiques, de 1665 à 1900. Paris, Geuthner, 1914–23. 539p. **BD1488**

For full information see BB564.

Shunami, Shlomo. Bibliography of Jewish bibliographies. 2d ed. enl. Jerusalem, Magnes Pr., 1965. 992p. **BD1489**

For full record see BB565.

Waxman, Meyer. A history of Jewish literature. N.Y., T. Yoseloff, [1960]. 5v. in 6. il. **BD1490**

First publ. 1930–41 in 4v. with title *A history of Jewish literature from the close of the Bible to our own days;* v.2 and v.4 appeared in enlarged and corrected eds. 1943–47.

A detailed history of Jewish literature in its various forms and in various countries from about 200 B.C. to 1960. Includes bibliography. PJ5008.W323

Indic

Emeneau, Murray Barnson. A union list of printed Indic texts and translations in American libraries. New Haven, Amer. Oriental Soc., 1935. 540p. (American Oriental ser., v.7) **BD1491**

"List includes all books in Sanskrit, Pali, Prakrit, and Apabhramśa, and most of the books in the older stages of the vernaculars . . . Translations of the texts are also included."—*Introd.* Does not include secondary works. Locates copies in 15 American libraries. Z7049.I3E5

Roadarmel, Gordon C. A bibliography of English source materials for the study of modern Hindi literature. Berkeley, Univ. of California, Center for South and Southeast Asia Studies, 1969. 96p. (Occasional paper, 4) **BD1492**

Lists English translations of Hindi poetry, fiction, dramas and essays, as well as English-language writings about modern Hindi literature. Z3208.L5R6

Who's who of Indian writers, 1983. Comp. and ed. by S. Balu Rao. New Delhi, Sahitya Akademi, 1983. 731p. **BD1493**

"Contains biographical and bibliographical information about nearly 6,000 living writers in 22 Indian languages including English."—*Half t.p. verso.*

An earlier edition was published 1961; this is essentially a new work, not a revision. Based mainly on information supplied by the biographees; limited to literary authors. PK2908.W49

Winternitz, Moriz. A history of Indian literature . . . Calcutta, Univ. of Calcutta, 1927–67. 3v. in 4. **BD1494**

Translated from the author's *Geschichte der indischen Litteratur* (Leipzig, Amelang, 1908–22). v.1–2 of the 1927–33 ed. have been reprinted: N.Y., Russell & Russell, 1971; New Delhi, Oriental Books, 1972 (called "2d ed.").

Contents: v.1, Introduction, Veda, National epics, Purānas, and Tantras (1927); v.2, Buddhist literature and Jaina literature (1933); v.3, pt.1, Classical Sanskrit literature (1963); v.3, pt.2, The scientific literature (1967).

A heavily documented history. PK2903.W62

Iranian

Afshar, Iraj. A bibliography of bibliographies on Iranian studies. [Tihrān, 1964?] 217p. **BD1495**

Main title page and text in Iranian, with some titles in Western languages, and indexes in both.

Browne, Edward Granville. A literary history of Persia. Cambridge, Univ. Pr., 1953–56. (v.1, 1956) 4v. il. **BD1496**

Contents: v.1, From the earliest times to Firdawsí; v.2, From Firdawsí to Sa'dí; v.3, The Tartar dominion (1265–1502); v.4, Modern times (1500–1924).

A reissue, not a new edition, of volumes originally published separately, some with slightly different title. PK6097.B7

Storey, Charles Ambrose. Persian literature; a bio-bibliographical survey. London, Luzac, 1927–71. v.1 in 2v.; v.2, pts.1–2.   **BD1497**

Contents: v.1, Qur'anic literature. History and biography: pt.1, General history, The prophets and early Islam. History of India (1927–39); pt.2, Biography. Additions and corrections. Indexes (1953); v.2, pt.1, Mathematics. Weights and measures. Astronomy and astrology. Geography (1958); v.2, pt.2, Medicine (1971).
Z7085.S88

Japanese

Bibliography

Bonneau, Georges. Bibliographie de la littérature japonaise contemporaine. Paris, Geuthner; Tôkyô, Mitsukoshi, [1938]. 280p. (Bull. de la Maison Franco-Japonaise, t.9, no.1–4, 1937)   **BD1498**

"5ème supplément à la *Bibliographie des principales publications editées dans l'Empire japonais.*"

A valuable bibliography. Pt.1, *Introduction*, gives important sources, Japanese and Western; list of translations from Western works into Japanese; and classification of authors as to type or school. Pt.2, *Bibliographie des oeuvres représentatives originales de la littérature japonaise contemporaine,* arranged alphabetically by author, gives transliteration; Japanese characters; date and place of birth and death; subject arrangement of works with title in transliteration, Japanese characters, and translation into French; place and date. Includes magazine articles. Pt.3, Index to names in the introduction and the bibliography.

The series *20-seiki bunken yōran taikei* (Tokyo, Nichigai Asoshietsu, 1976–) offers a variety of bibliographies and indexes on Japanese language, literature, and comparative literature (e.g., no.16, publ. 1984, *Hikaku bungaku kenkyū bunken yōran, 1945–1980,* is a bibliography of comparative literature in Japan).
Z7072.B72

Kokubungaku nenkan. Bibliography of research in Japanese literature. 1977– . [Tokyo, Kokubungaku Kenkyū Shiryōkan, 1978–] Annual.   **BD1499**

An annual bibliography and yearbook of Japanese literature. The bibliographic section is followed by lists of prizes and grants, and a necrology. Author index.

An older yearbook of literature and the arts is *Bungei nenkan/Bungei Nenkan Hensabu* (37th ed.: Tokyo, Shinchosa, 1984); it includes a who's who section, a chronology, etc., along with the annual bibliographical survey.

Kokusai Bunka Kaikan, Tokyo. Toshoshitsu. Modern Japanese literature in translation: a bibliography, comp. by the International House of Japan Library. Tokyo, Kodansha Internat. [distr. in U.S. by Harper & Row], [1979]. 311p.   **BD1500**

Arranged alphabetically by authors' names, then by title. Titles appear in Romaji, followed by the title in Japanese characters; translations are given in the language of translation, followed by the translator's name and bibliographic information. Includes references to works published in anthologies, collections, and periodicals. Indexes of titles and of translators.

Earlier, briefer bibliographies of translations are *Modern Japanese literature in Western translations* (Tokyo, International House of Japan Library, 1972. 190p.) and Hide Ikehara's *Bibliography of translations from the Japanese; from the 16th century to 1912* (Tokyo, Sophia Univ., 1971. 112p.).   Z3308.L5K66

Marks, Alfred H. and **Bort, Barry D.** Guide to Japanese prose. 2d ed. Boston, G. K. Hall, 1984. 186p.   **BD1501**

1st ed. 1975.

A guide to Japanese literary prose available in English translation. The annotated bibliography is in two sections: (1) Pre-Meiji literature (beginnings to 1867) and (2) Meiji literature and after (1868 to present). An introductory essay places the works in their historical and literary context. Author/title index.   Z3308.L5M37

Pronko, Leonard Cabell. Guide to Japanese drama. 2d ed. Boston, G. K. Hall, 1984. 149p.   **BD1502**

1st ed. 1975.

Offers an annotated bibliography of historical and critical works available in English on the Japanese theater, and of texts of the plays available in English translation. Introductory essay on the Japanese theater, its history and traditions, and a brief chronology. Author/title index.   Z3308.L5P76

Rimer, J. Thomas and **Morrell, Robert E.** Guide to Japanese poetry. 2d ed. Boston, G. K. Hall, 1984. 189p.   **BD1503**

1st ed. 1975.

A "Historical sketch and bibliographic outline" is followed by an annotated bibliography of historical and critical works and of Japanese texts available in English translation.   Z3308.L5R54

Yoshizaki, Yasuhiro. Studies in Japanese literature and language: a bibliography of English materials. Tokyo, Nichigai Associates (distr. by Kinokuniya Book Store), [1979]. 451p. (Nijisseiki bunken yōran taikei, 8)   **BD1504**

Added title page in Japanese.

In three parts: (1) Studies in Japanese literature; (2) Studies in Japanese language; and (3) Materials for further information. Follows a classed arrangement within each section. Aims to cover "most of the studies in Japanese literature and language that have ever been published in the English language."—*Foreword.* Includes books, periodical articles and dissertations. Index of names and titles.   Z7072.Y67

Dictionaries of authors and literature

Biographical dictionary of Japanese literature. [Ed. by] Sen'ichi Hisamatsu. Tokyo, Kodansha Internat. in collaboration with the Internat. Soc. for Educational Information [distr. by Harper & Row, N.Y.], 1976. 437p.   **BD1505**

Includes authors from all periods and genres. Glossary; bibliographies. Index by title, genre, organization, etc. Includes Japanese character version of proper names and titles.   PL723.B5

Gendai Nihon shippitsusha daijiten. Contemporary writers of Japan. [Ed. by] Jun'ichiro Kida [et al.]. Tokyo, Nichigai Asoshietsu, 1984. 5v.   **BD1506**

1st ed. 1978–79.

Provides biographical information about 13,000 contemporary writers in all fields, including the media, foreign writers active in Japan, and scientists who write for the general public. Gives citations to works by and about the authors.

Japan. Mombushō. Nihon Yunesuko Kokunai Iinkai. Who's who among Japanese writers. [Tokyo, Kasai Pub. and Prt. Co., 1957]. 140p.   **BD1507**

Issued by the National Commission for Unesco in cooperation with the Japan P.E.N. Centre.

Biographical sketches of contemporary Japanese writers.
PL723.J3

Nihon kindai bungaku meicho jiten. Nihon Kindai Bungakkan hen. Tokyo, Dō Bungakkan, 1982. 603p. il.   **BD1508**

A guide to outstanding works of modern Japanese literature presented in the form of essays by writers and critics. Includes biographical information on the authors, together with background information and critical comment on the works.   Z3308.L5N485

Nihon koten bungaku daijiten. [Kanshū Ichiko teiji, Noma Kōshin; henshūsha Nihon Koten Bungaku Daijiten Henshū Iinkai] Tokyo, Iwanami Shoten, 1983–85. 6v.   **BD1509**

An authoritative dictionary of Japanese literature covering up to the end of the Tokugawa regime. Some 13,000 items incorporate recent research on topics, people, and works in literature and allied fields such as religion, history and the arts. Signed articles with bibliographies. v.6 is a general index.

History

Keene, Donald. Dawn to the west: Japanese literature of the modern era. N.Y., Holt, Rinehart & Winston, [1984]. 2v.   **BD1510**

Contents: v.1, Fiction; v.2, Poetry, drama, criticism.

These first-published volumes of a projected 4-volume history of Japanese literature cover from the Meiji restoration (1868) to the present. Footnotes and bibliography at the end of each chapter; glossary, selected list of translations into English, and index in each volume.   PL726.55.K39

Philippine

Philippine literature in English. Esperanza V. Manuel, Resil B. Mojares, eds. Cebu City, E. Q. Cornejo, [1973]. 282p.   **BD1511**

Essentially an anthology of Philippine fiction, poetry, drama, and essays in English, but with useful introductory notes preceding the selections from each genre, biographical notes on the authors represented, and a brief bibliography.   PR9550.5.P5

Yabes, Leopoldo Y. Philippine literature in English: 1898–1957; a bibliographical survey. Quezon City, Univ. of the Philippines, 1958. p.343–434. (Repr. from Philippine social sciences and humanities review 22:343–434, Dec. 1957)   **BD1512**

Syriac

British Museum. Dept. of Oriental Printed Books and Manuscripts. Catalogue of Syriac printed books and related literature in the British Museum. Comp. by Cyril Moss. London, Museum, 1962. 1174col., 206col., 272col.   **BD1513**

Not merely a catalog but an extensive listing of Syriac texts and of books and periodical articles on Syriac studies. The first published record of Syriac materials in the British Museum.   Z7094.B74

Wright, William. A short history of Syriac literature. London, Black, 1894. 296p. (Repr.: Amsterdam, Philo Pr., 1966; Folcroft, Pa., Folcroft Lib. Eds., 1978)   **BD1514**

A brief history with bibliographic footnotes and index.   PJ5601.W7

B E

Fine Arts

❖The field of the Fine Arts is one in which the specialized library rather than the general library is often needed, because while the general library provides many reference books—bibliographies, dictionaries, indexes, etc., in painting, sculpture, and architecture—many times the large textbooks, histories, and collections of plates will be wanted. Because of their size and expense, these will usually be found only in the special library.

A general reference collection will need such works as: *Art index* (BE68); *Encyclopedia of world art* (BE96) or *McGraw-Hill dictionary of art* (BE101); *American art directory* (BE134); some histories of art, e.g., Gardner's *Art through the ages* (BE151), Janson's *History of art* (BE154), and Robb and Garrison's *Art in the Western world* (BE157); *Who's who in American art* (BE186); one or more of the works on symbolism in art (BE188–BE214); and perhaps one of the catalogs of art reproductions (BE220–BE224).

For additional titles and further information, the *Guide to the literature of art history* by Etta Arntzen and Robert Rainwater (BE1) should be consulted.

GENERAL WORKS

Guides

Arntzen, Etta Mae and **Rainwater, Robert.** Guide to the literature of art history. Chicago, Amer. Lib. Assoc.; London, Art Book Co., 1980. 616p.   **BE1**

A complete revision and updating of Mary Walls Chamberlin's *Guide to art reference books* (1959), this is an extremely useful guide to some 4,037 reference and research tools in the field of art. About 40 percent of the Chamberlin entries were retained, but annotations were rewritten or updated. Newer bibliographies, indexes, catalogs, and periodicals published through 1977 were added. Arrangement is in four main sections subdivided by subject or geographical area: (1) General reference sources; (2) General primary and secondary sources; (3) The particular arts (painting, sculpture, architecture, prints, drawings, photography, the decorative arts); (4) Serials. Archaeology is treated selectively, as are aesthetics, the philosophy of art, and art criticism. Monographs on individual artists are omitted, but major exhibition catalogs are included. Annotations are descriptive and often give the tables of contents. Indexes for author/title and for subject.   Z5931.A67

Ehresmann, Donald L. Fine arts: a bibliographic guide to basic reference works, histories, and handbooks. 2d ed. Littleton, Colo., Libraries Unlimited, 1979. 349p.   **BE2**

1st ed. 1975.

Aims to "cover the major books in the Western languages, published in the past hundred years, and available in major libraries of the United States."—*Pref.* In order to be included, a title must discuss two or more genres—architecture, sculpture, painting. 1,670 entries. In two sections: (1) Reference works (arranged by form—e.g., bibliographies, indexes, iconography—and covering books and periodical articles) and (2) Histories and handbooks (subdivided by periods and geographical areas, and citing only books). Dissertations, exhibition and museum catalogs are excluded. Good indexes of authors, editors, main entries, and detailed subjects.   Z5931.E47

Jones, Lois Swan. Art research methods and resources: a guide to finding art information. 2d ed., rev. and enl. Dubuque, Ia., Kendall/Hunt, [1984]. 332p.   **BE3**

1st ed. 1978.

Intended for everyone interested in art research, from student to specialist; thus materials included range from general reference works to specialized tools in foreign languages. This edition not only includes some new chapters, earlier sections were largely rewritten to reflect recent developments (e.g., online bibliographic searching) and new materials. In four parts: (1) "Before research begins" (intended for the beginner, and providing first steps such as use of the library); (2) "Art research methods" (step-by-step procedures for research projects and specialized problems); (3) "Art research resources" (an annotated list of some 1,500 tools, including microforms and online databases); (4) "Deciphering and obtaining the needed material" (the resources of the great research libraries and the possibility of interlibrary loan). Appendixes of art terms in several languages, and various useful lists. Indexed.   N85.J64

Kleinbauer, W. Eugene and **Slavens, Thomas P.** Research guide to the history of Western art. Chicago, Amer. Lib. Assoc., 1982. 229p. (Sources of information in the humanities, 2) **BE4**

In two main sections: (1) The field of art history; and (2) Reference works. The first and major portion of the book is a series of bibliographic essays on specific aspects of art history grouped under headings such as "Art history and its related disciplines," "Studying the art object," "Psychological approaches." The reference works section offers annotated listings of selected sources. Indexed. N380.K56

Muehsam, Gerd. Guide to basic information sources in the visual arts. Santa Barbara, Calif., ABC-Clio; Oxford, Eng., Jeffrey Norton Publ., 1978. 266p. **BE5**

A series of bibliographical essays followed by an alphabetical list of materials cited. Essays are intended for art and art history students, and discuss techniques of art research, important general art reference materials, primary sources, research materials for specific periods and forms in Western art; briefer essays are devoted to individual national schools of art (including oriental and primitive art). Name/title/subject index. N7425.M88

Bibliography

Allen, Jelisaveta S., ed. Literature on Byzantine art, 1892–1967. [London], Mansell for Dumbarton Oaks Center for Byzantine Studies, 1973–76. 2v. in 3. (Dumbarton Oaks bibliographies. Ser.I) **BE6**

Contents: v.1, By location: pt.1, Africa, Asia, Europe (A–Ireland); pt.2, Europe (Italy–Z), Indices; v.2, By categories.

v.1 is a topographically arranged cumulation of items pertinent to the history of art of specific places as drawn from the semiannual lists published 1892–1967 in III. Abteilung, "Bibliographische Notizien und Mitteilungen," of the *Byzantinische Zeitschrift* (DA175), primarily from the subdivision "Kunstgeschichte: Einzelne Orte." Entries appear as in the original *BZ* listing, with full bibliographic details, *BZ* citations and, usually, critical annotation. Author and place-name indexes.

In v.2 the cumulated entries are arranged topically within broad divisions on history of Byzantine art in general, and by art form (the "Iconography" section is by far the largest). For the most part, entries with a "purely regional or local orientation" have not been repeated in v.2, but this does not hold true of certain categories: the introduction spells out the policy and exceptions. Long critical annotations for entries in v.1 have not been repeated in v.2. Index of topics (including iconographic themes, museums and other owners of collections and manuscripts); index of modern authors.

Z5933.3.A45

Andreoli-deVillers, Jean-Pierre. Futurism and the arts: a bibliography, 1959–1973. Toronto, Univ. of Toronto Pr., [1975]. 189p. **BE7**

A year-by-year listing of "everything of importance on or about Futurism" (*Introd.*) and other avant-garde movements as they relate to Futurism. Name and topical subject index. For earlier works on the subject see the bibliographies by M. Drudi Gambillo in *Archivi del futurismo*, v.1–2 (Rome, 1958–62). Z5936.F85A62

Archives of American Art. Collection of exhibition catalogs. Boston, G. K. Hall, 1979. 851p. **BE8**

Photographic reproduction of catalog cards for some 15,000 exhibition catalogs located through a survey made in the mid-1960s. Represents the holdings of major public, museum, and historical society libraries in the United States, as well as the Archives' own collection. Catalogs are listed under name of gallery or museum and under artist. Covers 19th–20th centuries, but is apparently strongest for the 1900–45 period. Z5939.A73

Art books, 1876–1949; including an international index of current serial publications. N.Y., Bowker, [1981]. 780p. **BE9**

Derived from the database from which the *American book pub-*

lishing record cumulative, 1876–1949 (AA574) was produced, with the addition of serial records from the Bowker Serials Bibliography database from which *Ulrich's* (AE10) is generated.

Forms a chronological predecessor to the following:
Z695.1.A7A77

Bowker (R. R.) Company, New York. Art books, 1950–1979; including an international directory of museum permanent collection catalogs. N.Y., Bowker, [1979]. 1500p. **BE10**

Lists some 37,000 books drawn from the 1979/80 database developed for Bowker's *Books in print* and from questionnaires sent to 7,000 art museums throughout the world requesting lists of published catalogs. Arranged in four sections: (1) Subject index (providing the most complete entry); (2) Author index; (3) Title index; and (4) In print index (giving title and purchasing information in each entry). In addition, there is a "Geographic guide to museums" (arranged by country) and a "Permanent collection catalog index" (arranged alphabetically by name of museum).

A further record, *Art books 1980–1984* was published 1985 (N.Y., Bowker. 571p.). Z695.1.A7B68

Arts in America: a bibliography. Bernard Karpel, ed. Wash., Smithsonian Inst. Pr., [1979]. 4v. **BE11**

At head of title: Archives of American Art, Smithsonian Institution.

Contents: v.1, Sect. A–G: Art of the Native Americans; architecture; decorative arts; design; sculpture; art of the West; v.2, Sect. H–M: Painting; graphic arts; v.3, Sect. N–U: Photography; film; theater; dance; music; serials and periodicals; dissertations and theses; visual resources; v.4, Index.

About 25,000 entries for various aspects of the arts in America and their relationship to American life and culture. Each of the 21 sections is the work of an individual contributor or team of contributors; as such, they exhibit considerable variation in selectivity, length, and detail of the annotations. (A review by Janis Ekdahl in *ARLIS/NA newsletter*, 9:66–67, Feb. 1981, explains the particular focus of each section.) Most sections include entries for individual practitioners of the art in question (i.e., architects, painters, sculptors, photographers, dancers, actors, etc.); the section on periodicals in v.3 provides lengthy annotations on 253 individual serials in the visual arts. Bibliographic entries include books, parts of books, periodical articles, and academic theses (the list of dissertations and theses in v.3 is confined to the visual arts and is not annotated). Includes publications through 1975. "A survey of pictorial materials on Americana available for study and purchase in institutions in the United States" takes the form of a directory, with notes on special collections, holdings, etc.; it constitutes the "Visual resources" section in v.3. Index of authors and subjects. Z5961.U5A77

Bachmann, Donna G. and **Piland, Sherry.** Women artists: an historical, contemporary, and feminist bibliography. Metuchen, N. J., Scarecrow Pr., 1978. 323p. il. **BE12**

A partially annotated section of general books, periodical articles, and exhibition catalogs on women artists is followed by a lengthy section on individual artists grouped by century. For each artist is given a short biographical sketch, a note on collections containing her works, and a list of additional sources. Z7963.A75B32

Bell, Doris L. Contemporary art trends, 1960–1980: a guide to sources. Metuchen, N.J., Scarecrow Pr., 1981. 171p. **BE13**

Brief bibliographic essays on specific trends and trends in individual countries are followed by a bibliography of the works cited. Z5935.5.B44

Best, James J. American popular illustration; a reference guide. Westport, Conn., Greenwood Pr., [1984]. 171p. **BE14**

A guide to "sources that are reasonably accessible, dealing with American illustrators who have made a significant contribution to the body of American illustration."—*Pref.* Books and articles are cited in six major sections: historical overview; history and aesthetics; most noteworthy books on American illustrators; biographical materials on major illustrators; social and artistic context; book illustration techniques and sources of publication. Each section takes the form of a bibliographical essay, followed by a list of works cited. An appendix cites research collections. Indexed.

NC975.B45

Bibliografía del arte en España: articulos de revistas, por María Paz Aguilo [et al.]. Madrid, Consejo Superior de Investigaciones Científicas, Instituto Diego Velázquez, 1976–78. 2v. **BE15**

Contents: [v.1] Articulos de revistas clasificados por materias; [v.2] Articulos de revistas ordenados por autores.

An extensive bibliography of articles from 57 Spanish-language journals on the fine arts and applied arts of Spain. Topical arrangement (usually by form and period, with geographical subdivisions). Includes sections on archaeology, musical instruments, biography, conservation and restoration, ethnology and folklore, as well as the usual divisions of the fine and decorative arts. v.2 is an index by author's name giving reference to page number in v.1.

Z5944.S8B52

Bibliografia del libro d'arte italiano. Roma, Bestetti, [1952–64]. 2v. in 3. il. **BE16**

v.1 comp. by Erardo Aeschlimann; v.2, by C. E. Tanfani.
Contents: v.1, 1940–52; v.2, 1952–62. 2v.

Classified arrangement, with author and subject index in each volume. Includes exhibition catalogs, guide books, proceedings of congresses held in Italy, etc. Z5961.I8B5

Bibliographie zu Kunst und Kunstgeschichte; Veröffentlichungen im Gebiet der Deutschen Demokratischen Republik. Leipzig, Verlag für Buch- und Bibliothekswesen, [1956–61]. v.1–2. **BE17**

v.1, 1945/53; v.2, 1954/56. No more published?
Classified lists of books and periodical articles published in East Germany. Indexes in each volume for: periodicals, artists, place-names, catchwords, personal names, and authors. v.2 also contains a supplement of 1945–53 publications. Z5931.B5

Borroni, Fabia. "Il Cicognara"; bibliografia dell' archeologia classica e dell' arte italiana. Firenze, Sansoni, 1954–67. 2v. in 12. il. (Biblioteca bibliografica italica, 6–7, 10–11, 19, 23, 25, 27, 29, 31–32, 34) **BE18**

A comprehensive, annotated bibliography of classical archaeology and Italian art. Arranged under large form categories and then chronologically. v.1 includes: bibliography, catalogs of art libraries and of art books, encyclopedias and dictionaries, aesthetics, academic dissertations and conferences, didactic poems, technical aspects, and conservation and restoration, with an analytical index and an index to facsimiles. v.2 has title *Archeologia classica* and includes: treatises and descriptive literature, methods, manuals and general works, congresses and conferences, catalogs, museums, periodicals, travels, topography, numismatics, epigraphy, and costume. The final part of v.2 is an index. Z2357.B6

Buckley, Mary L. and **Baum, David W.** Color theory: a guide to information sources. Detroit, Gale, [1974]. 173p. (Art and architecture information guide ser., 2) **BE19**

An annotated basic bibliography of books on color studies "in science, in psychology (especially perception of color), in chemistry, in painting, and in the artists' writings and observations."—*Introd.* Emphasis is on books that "have influenced the concepts, theories, and particularly the painting of practicing artists." Indexed.

Z7144.C7B8

Coulson, Anthony J. A bibliography of design in Britain, 1851–1970. London, Design Council, [1979]. 290p. **BE20**

Intended as an introductory bibliography of relatively accessible works, but embracing "a very wide range of books and articles on many different subjects, including a lot that have scarcely been studied hitherto."—*Introd.* Topical arrangement within three main sections: (1) Fostering design; (2) Design and designers; (3) Areas of design activity. Includes a brief list of journals, and another of "Bibliographies, indexes, abstracts and catalogues." There is a

"Subject finder" which indexes the sections and major subjects of the bibliography, but no author/title or detailed subject index.

Z5956.D5C68

Creswell, Keppel Archibald Cameron. A bibliography of the architecture, arts, and crafts of Islam to 1st Jan. 1960. [Cairo], American Univ. at Cairo Pr., 1961. 1330p., xxv p. **BE21**

Contents: pt.1, Architecture (divided by country), p.1–478; pt.2, Arts and crafts (divided by craft or material, each subdivided by country), p.479–1330. Index of authors, p.i–xxv. Z5961.M6C7

————— ————— Supplement, Jan. 1960 to Jan. 1972. [Cairo], American Univ. in Cairo Pr., 1973. 366p.

Davis, Lenwood G. and **Sims, Janet.** Black artists in the United States: an annotated bibliography of books, articles, and dissertations on black artists, 1779–1979. Westport, Conn., Greenwood Pr., [1980]. 138p. **BE22**

Lists 476 books, catalogs, articles, reviews, and dissertations on black artists and their work in the United States. Annotated entries are grouped as major and general books, major and general articles, and dissertations. Includes a listing of "Black artworks in the National Archives." Indexed. Z5956.A47D38

Findlay, James A. Modern Latin American art; a bibliography. Westport, Conn., Greenwood Pr., [1983]. 301p. (Art reference collection, 3) **BE23**

Strongly reflective of the collection at the Museum of Modern Art Library in New York City. Covers monographs, exhibition catalogs, journal titles (but not articles) in a topical arrangement within geographical divisions. "Modern" includes the transitional period of the 19th century to the present. Includes Central America and the Caribbean; works on individual artists are omitted. Name index; numerous cross references. Z5961.L3F56

Freitag, Wolfgang M. Art books: a basic bibliography of monographs on artists. N.Y., Garland, 1985. 351p. (Garland reference library of the humanities, v.574) **BE24**

A listing by artist's name of more than 10,500 monographs on individual artists of all periods. Author index. Might be considered a new edition of Lucas's *Art books* (BE42) except that the whole emphasis here is on works on individual artists, with a very limited selection of general works. Z5938.F73

Georgi, Charlotte. The arts and the world of business. 2d ed. Metuchen, N.J., Scarecrow Pr., 1979. 175p. **BE25**

1st ed. 1973; suppl. 1–2, 1974–76.
An annotated bibliography of books, articles, government publications (state and federal), research papers (usually unpublished) dealing with arts management. Arranged by subject (e.g., Labor unions and the arts; Legal aspects of the arts) or by form (journals, newsletters, and newspapers). Includes an annotated directory of associations, councils, and other relevant organizations. Indexed by author. Z5956.A7G46

German expressionism in the fine arts: a bibliography by John M. Spalek, [et al.]. Los Angeles, Hennessey & Ingalls, 1977. 272p. (Art and architecture bibliographies, 3) **BE26**

A bibliography of more than 4,000 books, pamphlets, special journal issues, and exhibition catalogs covering the major art movements and artists in Germany, 1900–30. Includes materials in all Western languages, although most items are in German. Cutoff date is 1972. Author, gallery, and subject indexes.

Z5961.G4G47

Gettens, Rutherford John and **Usilton, Bertha M.** Abstracts of technical studies in art and archaeology, 1943–1952. Wash., 1955. 408p. (Freer Gallery of Art. Occasional papers, v.2, no.2) **BE27**

Preceded by *Technical studies in the field of the fine arts* (quarterly), published for the Fogg Art Museum, Harvard University, 1932–42. 10v.

Lists some 1,400 books and periodical articles in various languages dealing with the application of science and technology to the fields of art and archaeology. The abstracts are signed and are of varying length. Author and subject index.

Continued by BE53.   N7428.G44

Goldman, Bernard. Reading and writing in the arts. Rev. ed. Detroit, Wayne State Univ. Pr., 1978. 191p.   **BE28**

1st ed. 1972.

Intended as a bibliographic guide for the undergraduate, but useful for the non-specialist reading public. Aims to direct the user to an appropriate reference work or text likely to be found in a college or large public library. Materials chosen for inclusion are, therefore, usually in English, authoritative, not more than 75 years old, and emphasize those subjects popular with the undergraduate or the layman. Arranged by type of reference source (e.g., bibliographies, dictionaries) with a "Reference key by subject." Annotated. A periodicals section lists the "most responsible" journals and those that "report primarily on the current art scene."—*Introd.* Brief section on writing for art history journals. Index of authors and series.   Z5931.G6

Hammond, William Alexander. A bibliography of aesthetics and of the philosophy of the fine arts, 1900–1932. Rev. and enl. ed. N.Y., Longmans, 1934. 205p. (Repr.: N.Y., Russell & Russell, 1967)   **BE29**

1st ed. published as a supplement to the May 1933 issue of the *Philosophical review.*

Classified and annotated; author index.   Z5870.H22

Handbook of Latin American art. Manual de arte latino-americano. A bibliographic compilation. Joyce Waddell Bailey, gen. ed. Santa Barbara, Calif., ABC-Clio, [1984]. v.1, pts.1–2. (In progress)   **BE30**

Contents: v.1, General references and art of the nineteenth & twentieth centuries: pt.1, North America; pt.2, South America. (2v.)

Represents the cooperative efforts of an international group of scholars. Aims to identify "books, articles, anthologies, exhibition catalogs, and reports (both published and unpublished) written from the nineteenth century through July of 1983 on Latin American art and artists . . . in English, Spanish, Portuguese, French, German, Italian, Russian and other languages that cover ancient, colonial and contemporary art."—*Pref.* Format follows that of the *Handbook of Latin American studies* (DB241), and relevant citations from the first 44 volumes of that set are interfiled here. In v.1, the "General references" section is followed by a geographical arrangement subdivided topically; there are indexes of personal and corporate authors and of artists in each volume.

v.2 (announced for 1986 publication) will cover "Art of the colonial period"; v.3, "Art of ancient times." No plans are indicated for providing subject indexing of the individual volumes or for the set as a whole.   Z5961.L3H36

Hanks, Elizabeth Flinn. Bibliography of Australian art. Melbourne, Library Council of Victoria, 1976. 2v.   **BE31**

Contents: v.1, To 1900; v.2, 1901–1925.

"Based on the holdings of the State Library of Victoria, supplemented by the collections in the Mitchell Library, Sydney and the Art Gallery of New South Wales."—*Pref.*

A bibliography of books, periodical articles, exhibition catalogs, and book illustrations relating to Australian art. Each volume includes subject and artist entries, with artist entries arranged by form (e.g., books by; books illustrated by; books about).

Z5961.A85H35

Holmes, Oakley N. The complete annotated resource guide to black American art. Spring Valley, N.Y., Black Artists in America, [1978]. 275p.   **BE32**

A very personal compilation of materials on Afro-American art. In four sections: (1) an annotated bibliography by form (books and dissertations, exhibition catalogs, periodical articles); (2) a directory of companies which make available large prints, slides and filmstrips, motion pictures and videotapes, and audiotapes on Afro-American art; (3) a directory of Afro-American art organizations, museums and galleries, cultural and historical organizations and

museums, professional speakers and lecturers on the black experience in art; (4) a chronology of major events. No index.

Z5961.N4H64

Igoe, Lynn Moody. 250 years of Afro-American art: an annotated bibliography. N.Y., Bowker, 1981. 1266p.

BE33

A comprehensive bibliography of about 25,000 citations ranging from the popular to the scholarly, and including crafts as well as fine arts. In three main sections: (1) "Basic bibliography," arranged by author and including works relating to more than one artist; (2) "Subject bibliography," topically arranged; and (3) "Artist bibliography," arranged alphabetically by individual artist. Brief annotations.   Z5956.A47I38

International African Institute. A bibliography of African art. Comp. by L. J. P. Gaskin. London, The Institute, 1965. 120p. (Africa bibliography series B)   **BE34**

Nearly 5,000 entries in geographical arrangement, with subdivisions for the major genres. Includes an extensive listing of published catalogs and guides to museums, exhibitions, and collections, plus a section on bibliographies of Africana. Author and geographical-ethnic indexes.   Z5938.A3I5

Internationale Bibliographie der Kunstwissenschaft, 1902–17/18. Berlin, Behr, 1903–20. 15v. Annual.   **BE35**

Useful classified bibliography for the large or special library. Includes books and periodical articles in various languages. Author and subject indexes for each year.   Z5931.I61

Jagdish Chandra. Bibliography of Indian art, history & archaeology. Delhi, Delhi Printers Prakashan, 1978– . v.1– . (In progress?)   **BE36**

Contents: v.1, Indian art (316p.).

Intended to be in 3v. v.1 is a comprehensive bibliography of books, essays, exhibition catalogs, periodical articles, and annual reports on all aspects of Indian art and architecture (including handicrafts). There is a special section on the art of countries composing Greater India from Afghanistan to Borneo and Sarawak. Most publications cited are in Hindi or English. Lacks an index.

Z3206.J33

Kempton, Richard. Art nouveau: an annotated bibliography. Los Angeles, Hennessey & Ingalls, 1977– . v.1– . (Art & architecture bibliographies, 4–) (In progress?)   **BE37**

Contents: v.1, General, Austria, Belgium and France.

A bibliography of books, articles, exhibition catalogs, etc., published through 1971, concerning the movement in Europe and the United States. Each section (general and national) divided by form, then by individual artists or groups. Indexed. No more published?

Z5936.N6K45

Kendall, Aubyn. The art and archaeology of pre-Columbian Middle America: an annotated bibliography of works in English. Boston, G. K. Hall, 1977. 324p.   **BE38**

An expanded edition of the same author's *The art of pre-Columbian Mexico: an annotated bibliography . . .* (Austin, Tex., 1973).

Presents more than 2,000 annotated entries for books, exhibition catalogs, and periodical articles published through Dec. 1976. Alphabetical author listing within separate sections for books and periodicals. Appendix of selected dissertation titles. Subject index.

Z1208.M4K45

Kiell, Norman. Psychiatry and psychology in the visual arts and aesthetics; a bibliography. Madison, Univ. of Wisconsin Pr., 1965. 250p.   **BE39**

A companion to the author's *Psychoanalysis, psychology, and literature* (BD11), this volume being concerned with the writings of psychologists, psychoanalysts, philosophers, aestheticians, art critics, and educators on their findings and insights relative to the visual arts and aesthetics. Lists 7,208 books and periodical articles in subject categories such as aesthetics and art criticism, architecture, art therapy, color, graphic art, psychology and art, psychoses and art, etc. Author index.   Z5931.K5

Lietzmann, Hilda. Bibliographie zur Kunstgeschichte des 19. Jahrhunderts; Publikationen der Jahre 1940–1966. München, Prestel-Verlag, 1968. 234p. (Studien zur Kunst des neunzehnten Jahrhunderts, Bd.4) **BE40**

A classified bibliography of writings on 19th-century art, prefaced by three short essays. Z5935.L4

London. University. Courtauld Institute of Art. Bibliography of the history of British art. v.1–6, 1934–1946/48. Cambridge, Univ. Pr., 1936–56. 6v. **BE41**

Title varies: 1934–37, *Annual bibliography of the history of British art.*

Lists books and periodical articles in subject arrangement with an index in each volume. Includes Celtic and Viking art but not Roman. Covers architecture, painting, sculpture, the graphic arts, and applied arts. Writings on British museums and private collections are included, though the arts discussed may not be British; also includes writings on foreign artists working in Great Britain. After v.3, sections are omitted or curtailed when the subjects are covered by other bibliographical publications. Z5961.G7L8

Lucas, Edna Louise. Art books; a basic bibliography on the fine arts. Greenwich, Conn., New York Graphic Soc., [1968]. 245p. **BE42**

A classed list for the undergraduate art library. Though not so stated, this is generally considered to be a revision of the compiler's *Harvard list of books on art* (Cambridge, Harvard Univ. Pr., 1952), but as such it is somewhat disappointing because of various omissions. *The Harvard list,* in turn, was a revision of the compiler's *Books on art* (1936); although considerably out of date, these works may still be useful for references to some of the older titles and background materials. Z5931.L92

Mayer, Leo Ary. Bibliography of Jewish art. Ed. by Otto Kurz. Jerusalem, Magnes Pr.; London, Oxford Univ. Pr., 1967. 374p. **BE43**

An author listing of more than 3,000 items, with subject index. Includes publications to Spring 1965. Z5956.J4M3

Rath, Frederick L. and **O'Connell, Merrilyn Rogers.** A bibliography on historical organization practices. Nashville, Amer. Assoc. for State and Local History, [1975–84]. 6v. **BE44**

v.2–6 comp. by Rosemary S. Reese.

Contents: v.1, Historic preservation; v.2, Care and conservation of collections; v.3, Interpretation; v.4, Documentation of collections; v.5, Administration; v.6, Research.

Represents a new edition of the compilers' *Guide to historic preservation, historical agencies, and museum practices* (1970).

A selective bibliography of books, pamphlets, and periodical articles, most of them published since 1945. v.1 concentrates on five major areas: (1) Preservation law; (2) Urban development and redevelopment; (3) Preservation research and planning; (4) Preservation action; (5) Historical preservation in perspective. v.2 is arranged by type of conservation (e.g., conservation of works of art on paper), philosophy and principles, laboratories and instrumentation, training, environmental factors.

v.3 is "designed to help anyone involved in the myriad of educational activities conducted by historical organizations" (*Pref.*) by offering citations to important materials on visitor surveys, museum programs, museums and the schools, museum exhibits, museums in the media age, and the role of interpretation. v.4 aims to provide "a guide to the sources of information on artifacts, decorative arts, fine arts, and folk arts and crafts" for curators and directors who lack specialized knowledge and for dealers and private collectors. v.5 cites more than 2,400 sources of information on every aspect of the administration of institutions which "seek to preserve the cultural and historical heritage" (e.g., governing boards, ethics, personnel, fund-raising, insurance problems, public relations). v.6 offers classed bibliographies of historical organization practices in the areas of history, archaeology, architecture, and technology and crafts. Z1251.A2R35

Rave, Paul Ortwin. Kunstgeschichte in Festschriften; allgemeine Bibliographie kunstwissenschaftlicher Abhandlungen in den bis 1960 erschienenen Festschriften . . . unter Mitarbeit von Barbara Stein. Berlin, Mann, 1962. 314p. **BE45**

Contains (1) a list of the *Festschriften;* (2) a list, arranged by subject, of the 5,865 essays on art included in them; and (3) indexes of the titles of the *Festschriften,* of the authors of the art essays, of artists and others, and of places written about. Z5931.R35

Reisner, Robert George. Fakes and forgeries in the fine arts; a bibliography. N.Y., Special Libraries Assoc., 1950. 58p. **BE46**

Arranged mainly by field, i.e., painting, prints, sculptures, etc., with a general section on fakes and forgeries in more than one art form, and works on the moral, ethical, philosophical, and psychological aspects of forgery. Covers books and periodical articles published 1848–1948. Separate bibliography of articles from the *New York times,* 1897–1950 (p.37–54). Author index. Z5939.5.R4

Rowland, Benjamin. The Harvard outline and reading lists for Oriental art. 3d ed. Cambridge, Harvard Univ. Pr., 1967. 77p. **BE47**

First published in 1938 under title: *Outline and bibliographies of Oriental art.* Rev. ed. 1958.

Very brief chronological outlines by country are followed by the bibliographical lists. N7260.R6

Schlosser, Julius, *Ritter von.* La letteratura artistica, manuale delle fonti della storia dell' arte moderna. Trad. di Filippo Rossi. 3. ed. italiana aggiorn. da Otto Kurz. Firenze, Nuova Italia, [1964]. 792p. (Il pensiero storico, 12) **BE48**

Translation of *Die Kunstliteratur; ein Handbuch zur Quellenkunde der neueren Kunstgeschichte* (Wien, Schroll, 1924). Originally published under title *Materialen zur Quellenkunde der Kunstgeschichte* (Wien, 1914–20). An Italian translation with additions by the author was published in 1935, and an appendix by Otto Kurz in 1937; a 2d Italian edition appeared in 1956.

A valuable manual for the literature of art history up to the early-19th century. Kurz's additions of later material are enclosed in brackets. Indexes of artists and authors. N5300.S3316

South Kensington Museum, London. National Art Library. First proofs of the Universal catalogue of books on art. London, Chapman & Hall, 1870. 2v. (Repr.: N.Y., Burt Franklin, 1964. 2v. and suppl.) **BE49**

—— —— Supplement to the Universal catalogue of books on art. London, Eyre & Spottiswoode, 1877. 654p.

"Not only the books in the library, but all books printed and published at the date of the issue of the Catalogue, that could be required to make the library perfect."—*v.1, p.i.* Z5931.S72

Volz, John. Paint bibliography. Ottawa, Assoc. for Preservation Technology, 1975. 25*l.* (APT newsletter, v.4, no.1 suppl.) **BE50**

An author listing of about 450 books and periodical articles concerning "paint, its technology as well as tastes and philosophy with regard to the use of color."—*Foreword.* Based mainly on the collections at the New York Public Library and the Avery Library, Columbia University. No index.

Western, Dominique Coulet. A bibliography of the arts of Africa. Waltham, Mass., African Studies Assoc., [1975]. 123p. **BE51**

Lists books, articles, and exhibition catalogs "on art, architecture, oral literature, music and dance in Sub-Saharan Africa. Each of these major categories has been subdivided into both a general listing . . . as well as broad geographical areas . . . further into ethnic groups and some nations."—*Note.* Some annotations; author index. Z5961.S85W47

Yüan, Tung Li. The T. L. Yüan bibliography of Western writings on Chinese art and archaeology. Harrie A. Vanderstappen, ed. [London], Mansell, 1975. 606p. **BE52**

A subject listing, with detailed subdivisions; author index. The work was begun by T. L. Yüan and is intended as a companion volume to his *China in Western literature* (DE170); it "now contains over 15,000 items [including reviews] of a variety of materials on Chinese art and archaeology in English, German, Dutch, Scandinavian, Slavic, and French and other Romance languages published between 1920 and 1965."—*Foreword*. Books and articles are listed in separate sections; detailed outline of each section, but no alphabetical subject index. Z5961.C5Y9

Current

Art and archaeology technical abstracts. v.1– , 1955– . [New York], 1955– . Semiannual (irregular). **BE53**

Title varies: 1955–57, *Studies in conservation;* 1958–65, *I.I.C. abstracts.*

Publisher varies; now published by the Getty Trust in association with the International Institute for Conservation of Historic and Artistic Works, London.

A classed bibliography, with abstracts in English or language of the original. Author index in each issue; combined subject index in the second issue of the year. AM1.A7

Artbibliographies: current titles, v.1, no.1– , Sept. 1972– . Santa Barbara, Calif., ABC-Clio, 1972– . Bimonthly. **BE54**

Provides reproductions of the table of contents from about 60 journals, museum publications, annuals and irregular serials in each issue. The serials selected are those to be indexed in *Artbibliographies modern,* with this publication serving as a current-awareness tool. Z5937.A793

Artbibliographies modern, v.4, no.1– , Spr. 1973– . Oxford, European Bibliographic Center; Santa Barbara, Calif., Clio Pr., 1973– . Semiannual. **BE55**

Supersedes *LOMA: literature of modern art,* 1969–71 (BE56) and assumes its numbering.

Offers abstracts of books, exhibition catalogs, and periodical articles dealing with art and design throughout the world from about 1800 to the present. Coverage began with publications of 1972, and each issue includes any material currently published together with any important items omitted from earlier volumes. Alphabetical listing by topical subjects and artists' names in a single alphabet. English-language translations of foreign titles are given in parentheses following the original titles. Author index and museum/gallery index.

Three spinoffs from the database for this publication have been issued in the "Modern art bibliographical series": v.1, *Tribal and ethnic art* (1982. 99p.); v.2, *Photography* (1982. 284p.); v.3, *Design* (1984. 333p.). Z5935.L64●

LOMA: Literature on modern art; an annual bibliography. 1969–71. London, Lund Humphries, [1971–73]. Annual. **BE56**

Alexander Davis, ed.

Title and introductory matter also in French and German.

An international bibliography of books, periodical articles, exhibition catalogs, etc., on 20th-century art and artists. Includes painting, sculpture, drawing, prints, ceramics, textiles, graphic design. In two parts: (1) artists; (2) subjects. Also has an index. Includes about 5,000 entries per year.

Ceased publication with volume covering 1971. *Artbibliographies modern* (above) was announced as superseding this publication and the first issue was designated as v.4 in continuation of the *LOMA* series. However, *Art, design, photo* (1972–76/77) also laid claim to being the successor to *LOMA:* its editor was Alexander Davis, and coverage began with 1972, thus continuing *LOMA* coverage without a gap. Z5935.L64

Netherlands. Rijksbureau voor Kunsthistorische Documentatie. Bibliography of the Netherlands Institute for Art History. v.1, 1943/45– . Hague, 1943– . v.1– . **BE57**

Intended "as a supplement to the '*Mededeelingen*' of the Rijksbureau voor Kunsthistorische Documentatie. . . . A continuation . . . of the work done by van Hall."—*Note in v.1, no.1.* (H. van Hall's

Repertorium voor de geschiedenis der Nederlandsche schilder- en graveerkunst, sedert het begin der 12de eeuw. appeared 1936–49 in 2v.)

Each volume—in several parts, irregularly issued—has classed and annotated lists of books and periodical articles on Dutch and Flemish art of every period (not including architecture).

New York. Public Library. Art and Architecture Division. Bibliographic guide to art and architecture. 1975– . Boston, G. K. Hall, 1976– . Annual. **BE58**

Serves as a supplement to the Division's *Dictionary catalog* (BE64). In addition to the materials cataloged for the Art and Architecture Division, lists entries from Library of Congress MARC tapes. Z5939.N56a

Répertoire d'art et d'archéologie, dépouillement des périodiques et des catalogues de ventes, bibliographie des ouvrages d'art français et étrangers, t.1–67, 1910–63; nouv. sér., t.1– , 1965– . Paris, Morancé, 1910– . v.1– . **BE59**

Frequency varies: annual, 1910–72, except for 1914/19; quarterly (some issues combined) beginning 1973. Subtitle varies.

Indexes: for 1910–1914/19, 1925, and 1934–72, each volume has an index of authors, subjects, places; 1926–33 have author index only; for 1920–25, a combined index was published as fasc.29, 1927.

Published under the auspices of the Bibliothèque d'Art et d'Archéologie of the University of Paris and, later, of the Comité International d'Histoire de l'Art; most recently under the direction of the Comité Français d'Histoire de l'Art and Unesco.

A bibliography of periodical articles and, from 1920, books from various countries, classified by large subject (mainly period and country), with indexes of authors and of places. Format is greatly changed beginning with the issues for 1973. The work continues to be a classified index, but each issue includes an index of artists, an author index, and a detailed subject index (with code letters supplied to indicate country, as appropriate). Annual cumulated indexes beginning with n.s.v.10 (1974). Continues to omit Oriental and primitive art; these are covered in *Bulletin signalétique 526: art et archéologie; Proche Orient, Asie, Amérique* (v.24– , 1970– . Quarterly). Z5937.R4●

RILA, Répertoire international de la littérature de l'art. RILA, International repertory of the literature of art. [N.Y., College Art Assoc. of America], 1975– . v.1– . Semiannual. **BE60**

Publisher varies; now publ. by the Getty Trust; frequency varies (originally annual).

Volume for 1975 preceded by a number dated 1973 (called "Demonstration issue"). v.1 issued in two parts: Abstracts, and Index; v.2– , 1976– , published in two issues per year, with each issue containing abstracts and index; a cumulative index merging author and subject entries was published for v.1–5 (1975–79).

A major bibliography and abstract service covering books, dissertations, museum publications, exhibition catalogs, and articles in periodicals, *Festschriften* and conference proceedings concerned with post-classical European and post-Columbian American art. Abstracts are arranged topically under broad subject headings: Reference works, General works, Medieval art, Renaissance and baroque art, Modern art, Collections and exhibitions. (An "Exhibition list" within the latter section is a city-by-city listing of exhibits with reference to the item number in the relevant topical section where an abstract appears.) Detailed author and subject index. Z5937.R16●

Library catalogs

Freer Gallery of Art, Washington, D.C. Library. Dictionary catalog of the library. Boston, G. K. Hall, 1967. 6v. **BE61**

Contents: v.1–4, Western languages; v.5–6, Oriental languages.

Photoreproduction of the catalog cards for the collection of about 40,000 books, pamphlets, and periodicals. Includes analytics for periodical articles pertinent to the collection, which is almost exclusively Oriental, Near Eastern, and 19th-century American art.

New York. Metropolitan Museum of Art. Library. Library catalog of the Metropolitan Museum of Art. 2d ed., rev. & enl. Boston, G. K. Hall, 1980. 48v. **BE62**

1st ed. 1960, with 8 suppls., 1962–80.

This is a dictionary catalog with certain special filing rules: subject entries precede main or added entries, and chronological subdivisions precede other subdivisions. Sales catalogs are cited in v.46–48, cataloged by subject and by collector or auction house.

For this edition much of the collection was recataloged to make headings uniform and to update terminology and spelling; new headings have been added to reflect trends and new art movements; explanatory notes and cross references have been increased; items from the supplements have been incorporated; and new materials have been added. Z881.N6624

———— ———— First supplement. Boston, G. K. Hall, 1982. 840p.

Adds reproductions of some 17,844 cards representing cataloging through Sept. 1980.

The 8th supplement to the 1st ed. was published more or less simultaneously with the 2d ed. (i.e., 1980, in 3v.) and is available to libraries owning the earlier edition but not prepared to purchase the new one; cards represented in the 1980 supplement are included in the 2d ed. of the catalog.

New York. Museum of Modern Art. Library. Catalog of the Library. Boston, G. K. Hall, 1976. 14v. **BE63**

Photographic reproduction of the dictionary catalog of this library which is especially strong in the "visual arts from around 1850 to the present."—*Introd.* Includes citations to articles in periodicals not covered by the *Art index* and the *Répertoire d'art et d'archéologie;* exhibition catalogs are also represented. "Latin American ephemeral material (exhibition catalogs and artists' files)" are listed separately in v.7, as are periodical titles. Z5939.N557

New York. Public Library. Art and Architecture Division. Dictionary catalog. . . . Boston, G. K. Hall, 1975. 30v. **BE64**

Photographic reproduction of the card catalog; includes materials cataloged through Dec. 1971. Covers "painting, drawing, sculpture, and the history and design aspects of architecture and the applied arts."—*Introd.* Also lists relevant materials in the Cyrillic, Hebrew, and Oriental collections, the Local History and Rare Book divisions, and citations to periodical articles in journals in all parts of the library.

———— ———— Supplement 1974. Boston, G. K. Hall, 1976. 556p.

Covers material added Jan. 1972–Sept. 1974 to the Art and Architecture Division and the Prints Division. For current listings *see* BE58. Z5939.N56

Museum publications

The bibliography of museum and art gallery publications and audiovisual aids in Great Britain and Ireland, 1977– . Cambridge, Chadwyck-Healey; Teaneck, N.J., Somerset House, [1978]– . Irregular. **BE65**

Editor varies. 1979/80 latest published?

Information was derived from questionnaires completed by 811 museums and art galleries regarding material published and distributed (i.e., books, guides, catalogs, newsletters, slides, postcards, photographs, films, records and tapes, etc.). Institutions are listed alphabetically by name, with a list of publications, giving bibliographical information and price. Z2001.B54

Catalog of museum publications & media; a directory and index of publications and audiovisuals available from United States and Canadian institutions. 2d ed. Paul Wasserman, managing ed. Detroit, Gale, 1980. 1044p. **BE66**

1st ed. 1973 had title: *Museum media.*

Intends "to provide bibliographic control of books, booklets, periodicals, monographs, catalogs, pamphlets and leaflets, films and filmstrips, videotape programs, and other media which are prepared and distributed by museums, art galleries and related institutions in the United States and Canada."—*Pref.* Listing is by museum, with indexes by titles and keywords, periodical titles, subjects, and geographic locations. Z5052.M94

Periodicals

Lebel, Gustave. Bibliographie des revues et périodiques d'art parus en France de 1746 à 1914. Introd. par Georges Wildenstein. Paris & N.Y., 1951. 64p. il. (Gazette des beaux-arts, janv.–mars 1951. 6ᵉ pér., t.38) **BE67**

Arranged by title; includes date of first issue, frequency, editor, location (Bibliothèque Nationale or Bibliothèque d'Art et d'Archéologie de l'Université de Paris). Many entries have annotations. Chronological index.

Indexes

Art index, Jan. 1929– . N.Y., Wilson, 1930– . v.1– . Quarterly with annual cumulations. **BE68**

Subtitle (varies): A quarterly author & subject index to publications in the fields of archaeology, architecture, art history, city planning, crafts, graphic arts, industrial design, interior design, landscape architecture, museology, photography & films, and related subjects.

First permanent cumulation Jan. 1929–Sept. 1932; triennial cumulations, Oct. 1932–Oct. 1950; biennial cumulations Nov. 1950–Oct. 1967; annual cumulations Nov. 1967/Oct. 1968– .

Fields covered vary; now indexes about 190 American and foreign periodicals in the fields indicated in the subtitle. Method of indexing, which differs somewhat from that followed in the other special indexes issued by the same publisher, is as follows: (1) ordinary articles are indexed under author and subject or subjects; (2) book reviews are indexed under the author *reviewed* and under subject or subjects (Beginning with v.22, Nov. 1973–Oct. 1974, book reviews are listed in a separate section following the main body of the index.); (3) exhibitions are indexed under the artist or appropriate form heading; (4) illustrations accompanying an article are listed in the entry for that article but not indexed individually; illustrations without text are indexed under the artist's name. Z5937.A78●

Chicago. Art Institute. Ryerson Library. Index to art periodicals. Boston, G. K. Hall, 1962. 11v. **BE69**

Photographic reproduction of the library's card file. All entries are by subject, alphabeted within the subject by periodical. Material which appears in the *Art index* (BE68) is excluded. Z5937.C55

———— ———— First supplement. Boston, G. K. Hall, 1975. 573p.

Covers "indexing activity from 1961 to October, 1974."—*Pref.* Some retrospective indexing was also added.

Ellis, Jessie Croft. Index to illustrations. Boston, Faxon, 1966. 682p. **BE70**

"Includes references to picture material in all fields, exclusive of nature" (*Pref.*), drawn from a highly selective list of books and periodicals. NC996.E62

———— Nature and its applications; over 200,000 selected references to nature forms and illustrations of nature as used in every way. Boston, Faxon, 1949. 861p. (Useful reference series, no.74) **BE71**

A revised and very much enlarged edition of the author's *Nature index* (1930), broader in scope and in coverage. Indexes illustrations in about 130 books and periodicals, including some encyclopedias. Indexed works are mainly in English, but a few foreign works are included. Z5956.D3E53

———— Travel through pictures: references to pictures, in books and periodicals, of interesting sites all over the world. Boston, Faxon, 1935. 699p. (Useful reference series, no.53) **BE72**

Z6020.E47

Frick Art Reference Library. Original index to art periodicals. Boston, G. K. Hall, 1983. 12v. **BE73**

Reproduces the catalog cards of a file compiled in the Library between 1923 and 1969, indexing 27 French, English and (from 1928 on), Italian journals of the 19th and 20th centuries, some not analyzed elsewhere. Content reflects the Library's concentration at the time on "Western European and American painting, sculpture, and some decorative arts from the fourth century A.D. to 1860."— *Introd.* Imprint dates range from 1850 to 1960. The main strength of the index "is the extremely thorough coverage of individual artists cited in the articles indexed," extending "to individual works of art, . . . reproductions, exhibitions, provenance and location at the time of indexing." Entries for authors, artists, galleries, exhibitions, portraits, etc., with complete bibliographical details, in one alphabetical sequence. Should not be considered as offering comprehensive coverage of the Library's interests and holdings. Z5937.F74

Hewlett-Woodmere Public Library. Index to art reproductions in books. Comp. by the professional staff of the Hewlett-Woodmere Public Library [Hewlett, N.Y.] under the direction of Elizabeth W. Thomson. Metuchen, N.J., Scarecrow Pr., 1974. 372p. **BE74**

An index to reproductions in 65 art books published 1956–71. Approach is through the artist's name, with a title index; no subject approach. N7525.H48

Monro, Isabel Stevenson and **Monro, Kate M.** Index to reproductions of American paintings; a guide to pictures occurring in more than eight hundred books. N.Y., Wilson, 1948. 731p. **BE75**

———— ———— First supplement. 1964. 480p.

The main work "lists the work of artists of the United States occurring in 520 books and in more than 300 catalogues of annual exhibitions held by art museums. The paintings are entered (1) under name of the artist, followed by his dates when obtainable, by title of the picture, and by an abbreviated entry for the book in which the reproduction may be found; (2) under titles; and (3) in some cases under subjects. Locations of pictures in permanent collections have also been included whenever this information was available."—*Pref.*

The first supplement lists paintings in more than 400 books and catalogs, most of these published between 1948 and 1961.

A continuation is provided by BE78. ND205.M57

———— Index to reproductions of European paintings; a guide to pictures in more than three hundred books. N.Y., Wilson, 1956. 668p. **BE76**

"A guide to pictures by European artists that are reproduced in 328 books. The paintings are entered (1) under name of artist, followed by his dates when obtainable, by the title of the picture, and by an abbreviated entry of the book in which the reproduction may be found; (2) under titles; and (3) in some cases under subjects. Whenever permanent locations could be determined this information has been recorded by symbols."—*Pref.* ND45.M6

Parry, Pamela Jeffcott. Contemporary art and artists: an index to reproductions. Westport, Conn., Greenwood Pr., 1978. 327p. **BE77**

Some 60 major books and exhibition catalogs are indexed for "paintings, sculpture, drawings, prints, happenings, actions, environments, assemblages, conceptual pieces, earthworks, and video art" (*Pref.*) dating from about 1940 to the present. Complete information (i.e., title of work, date, media, location of work, publication in which reproduction appears) is given under artist's name; subject and title indexes. N6490.P3234

Smith, Lyn Wall and **Moure, Nancy Dustin Wall.** Index to reproductions of American paintings appearing in more than 400 books, mostly published since 1960. Metuchen, N.J., Scarecrow Pr., 1977. 931p. **BE78**

Intended as a continuation of Monro's *Index to reproductions of American paintings* (BE75), and similar in arrangement. "Under each artist's name, titles of his paintings are listed alphabetically and under those are placed the abbreviations for the books in which a reproduction occurs. Beside or just below the title is an abbreviation signifying the owner of a painting. Only permanent collections —no private owners are cited."—*Pref.* Index of titles arranged by general categories (e.g., allegories, animals, architectural subjects). ND205.S575

Vance, Lucile E. and **Tracey, Esther M.** Illustration index. 2d ed. N.Y., Scarecrow Pr., 1966. 527p. **BE79**

1st ed. 1957; suppl. 1961.

A subject index to illustrations in a number of popular periodicals and a few selected books. Incorporates the listings from the earlier edition and its supplement with new material, so that the period covered is 1950 through June 1963.

Continued by: N7525.V3

Greer, Roger C. Illustration index. 3d ed. Metuchen, N.J., Scarecrow Pr., 1973. 164p. **BE80**

N7525.G72

Appel, Marsha C. Illustration index. 4th ed. Metuchen, N.J., Scarecrow Pr., 1980. 458p. **BE81**

N7525.V3

———— Illustration index V, 1977–1981. Metuchen, N.J., Scarecrow Pr., 1984. 411p. **BE82**

Although termed "editions," the three items above are actually supplements to the Vance and Tracey volume. The "3d ed." covers July 1963–Dec. 1971; the "4th ed." 1972–76, with scope widened to include furniture, wildlife, art works and some personalities; and the final volume covers 1977–81. Indexing is of illustrations in eight to ten popular magazines. N7525.A66

Portraits

A.L.A. portrait index; index to portraits contained in printed books and periodicals; ed. by W. C. Lane and N. E. Browne. Wash., Lib. of Congress, 1906. 1601p. **BE83**

An index to portraits contained in 1,181 sets (6,216 volumes), including both books and periodicals through the year 1904. Indexes some 120,000 portraits of about 40,000 persons. Information given includes: (1) dates of birth and death, and brief characterization of the person, artist, engraver, etc., of the portrait; and (2) volume and page of the work where the portrait may be found. Does not index portraits in local histories, genealogical works, or collections of engravings as such, or portraits of writers included in sets of their collected works. N7620.A2

Cirker, Hayward and **Cirker, Blanche.** Dictionary of American portraits; 4045 pictures of important Americans from earliest times to the beginning of the twentieth century. N.Y., Dover, [1967]. 756p. il. **BE84**

Presents portraits of notable Americans with brief identifying captions. Painter, engraver, or source of portrait is often given. Index by profession or occupation. N7593.C53

Dictionary of British portraiture. Ed. by Richard Ormond and Malcolm Rogers. London, B. T. Batsford in assoc. with the National Portrait Gallery; N.Y., Oxford Univ. Pr., 1979–81. 4v. **BE85**

Contents: v.1, The Middle Ages to the early Georgians, by Adriana Davies; v.2, Later Georgians and early Victorians, by Elaine Kilmurray; v.3, The Victorians: historical figures born between 1800 and 1860, by Elaine Kilmurray; v.4, The twentieth century: historical figures born before 1900, by Adriana Davies.

Provides a listing of portraits of some 5,000 "famous figures in British history that are either in galleries and institutions or in collections accessible to the public."—*Introd.* Each volume covers a different historical period, and within volumes the arrangement is by name of sitter. Dates and identifying word or phrase are given for the sitter, and information on the portraits appears in abbreviated form. N7598.D5

Lee, Cuthbert. Portrait register. [Asheville, N.C.], Biltmore Pr., [1968]. v.1 (725p.) **BE86**

Lists some 8,000 portraits with indication of institutional or private ownership in the United States. Listings by subject and by painter. A further volume listing additions and corrections was planned, but has not been published. N7620.L4

Singer, Hans Wolfgang. Allgemeiner Bildniskatalog. Leipzig, Hiersemann, 1930–36. 14v. **BE87**

An index to engraved portraits from 17 German public collections. N7575.S55

——— Neuer Bildniskatalog. Leipzig, Hiersemann, 1937–38. 5v. **BE88**

A continuation of the above, including painted and sculpted portraits. N7575.S56

Archives

Archives of American Art. The card catalog of the manuscript collections of the Archives of American Art. Wilmington, Del., Scholarly Resources, [1981]. 10v. **BE89**

Reproduction of the catalog cards for this extensive collection of papers (18th century to the present) of artists, art critics and historians, collectors, galleries and museums, and art societies of the United States. Holdings of the Archives include about 5,000 collections, or about six million items, ranging from letters, journals and diaries, notebooks, scrapbooks and clippings, to business records, photographs, and oral histories. Indexing is primarily by personal name "since most . . . users conduct their research within the context of individuals."—*Introd.* Each entry includes a statement regarding content and indicates the named collection to which it belongs. Entries are keyed to microfilms of the Archives, sets of which are available at regional centers or through interlibrary loan. Microfilms of papers still in private hands or located at other institutions are available at the Archives of American Art in Washington (now part of the Smithsonian Institution). Z6611.A7A72

——— The card catalog of the oral history collections of the Archives of American Art. Wilmington, Del., Scholarly Resources, [1984]. 343p. **BE90**

Reproduces about 2,500 catalog cards for the Archives' collection of tape recordings (both transcribed and untranscribed, restricted and unrestricted materials) of interviews, lectures, panel discussions, symposia, etc., involving 20th-century American artists or presenting their reminiscences, views, etc. N6536.A73

McCoy, Garnett. Archives of American Art; a directory of resources. N.Y., Bowker, 1972. 163p. **BE91**

The Archives of American Art was founded in Detroit, Mich., in 1954, "to gather, preserve, and make available to scholars collections of personal papers, specifically the personal papers of painters and sculptors, of art dealers, critics, collectors, and curators."—*Pref.* The Archives became a bureau of the Smithsonian Institution in 1970.

This directory lists and briefly describes 555 groups of papers, all of which have been microfilmed and are thus available for on-site use at each of five regional centers (New York, Washington, Boston, Detroit, San Francisco) or through interlibrary loan. Arrangement is alphabetical by name of artist, organization, or institution, with an index which includes references to names mentioned in the descriptive notes. Z6611.A7M3

Dictionaries and encyclopedias

Baigell, Matthew. Dictionary of American art. N.Y., Harper & Row, [1979]; London, John Murray, 1980. 390p. (Repr. with corrections 1982) **BE92**

Treats almost 650 major American painters, sculptors, printmakers and photographers, together with movements and topics relating to art in the United States from the 16th century to the present. Each biographical entry is about a column in length, emphasizes artistic achievement and stylistic development, and usually ends with a reference to another printed source. Topical entries tend to be much longer, and again a single reference source is cited. N6505.B34

The Britannica encyclopedia of American art. Chicago, Encyclopaedia Britannica Educational Corp., [1973]. 669p. il. **BE93**

A heavily illustrated work dealing with American painting, sculpture, architecture, glass, silver, furniture, printmaking, folk art, photography, and handcrafts. Articles were contributed by 32 critics, historians, and curators of art, and are signed with initials; they are generally brief and well written, though fairly popular in tone. Bibliographies are not included with individual articles. There is a guide to entries by art genre; a guide to museums and public collections; a glossary of terms; and a bibliography (p.638–68). N6505.B73

Dizionario enciclopedico Bolaffi dei pittori e degli incisori italiani. Dall' XI al XX secolo . . . Torino, G. Bolaffi, [1972–76]. 11v. il. **BE94**

A generously illustrated biographical dictionary which includes entries for many minor Italian artists as well as the major figures. Many of the articles are signed. Bibliographies—some of considerable length—are included. N6922.D59

Enciclopedia dell' arte antica, classica e orientale. Roma, Istit. della Enciclopedia Italiana, 1958–73. 8v. il., maps. **BE95**

Ed. in chief, Ranuccio Bianchi Bandinelli.

A handsomely illustrated encyclopedia with signed articles and bibliographies, treating the art history and iconography of the countries of classical antiquity, i.e., Asia, Northern Africa, and Europe, from prehistory to about 500 A.D. [v.8] is entitled "Atlante dei complessi figurati e degli ordini architettonici." A 1970 supplement was published 1973. N31.E48

Encyclopedia of world art. N.Y., McGraw-Hill, 1959–83. 16v. il. **BE96**

Published simultaneously in Italian (*Enciclopedia universale dell' arte.* Firenze, Sansoni, 1958–67) and English; the original articles were written in various languages and translated into English.

The English-language edition corresponds to the Italian, with some minor changes and three major differences: (1) more cross references; (2) a more extensive article on the art of the Americas; (3) some 300 separate, short biographies added to give more ready access to information about persons treated in longer monographic articles.

Contributors are specialists from many parts of the world. Articles are signed and include extensive bibliographies. The subject matter covers "architecture, sculpture, and painting, and every other man-made object that, regardless of its purpose or technique, enters the field of esthetic judgment because of its form or decoration."—*Pref.* Includes all countries and all periods.

Approximately the last half of each volume consists of plates arranged to illustrate the articles in the first half. v.15 is an index; v.16 is a supplement, "World art in our time," ed. by Bernard S. Myers. N31.E4833

Harper's Encyclopedia of art; architecture, sculpture, painting, decorative arts, based on the work of Louis Hourticq . . . and tr. under the supervision of Tancred Borenius . . . fully rev. under the supervision of J. Leroy Davidson and Philippa Gerry, with the assistance of the staff of the Index of Twentieth-Century Artists, College Art Association, New York City. . . . N.Y., London, Harper, 1937. 2v. il. **BE97**

Reprinted as *New standard encyclopedia of art* (N.Y., Garden City Pub. Co., 1939. 2v. in 1).

Based on Louis Hourticq's *Bibliothèque omnium* (1925). Comprises short articles, brief bibliographies, and biographies (including living persons). N31.H3

The illustrated dictionary of art and artists. David Piper, ed. N.Y., Random House, [1984]. 448p. il. **BE98**

Primarily a biographical dictionary of painters, sculptors and graphic artists, but includes "entries on art movements, groups, techniques and critical terms, and on prominent patrons and writers on art."—*Pref.* Architecture and decorative arts are treated only in connection with painting and sculpture. Cross references; no bibliographies. Black-and-white portraits are scattered throughout the text; color illustrations are grouped by period. N5300.I45

Lexikon der Kunst. Architektur, bildende Kunst, angewandte Kunst, Industrieformgestaltung, Kunsttheorie. Hrsg. von Ludger Alscher [u.a.]. Leipzig, Seemann, 1968–78. 5v. il. **BE99**

Articles, some of substantial length, on a wide range of topics relating to art and architecture. Includes numerous biographical entries, some of contemporary figures. Bibliographic references at the end of many articles. N33.L45

McCulloch, Alan. Encyclopedia of Australian art. London, Hutchinson, 1968. 668p. il. **BE100**

Treats the visual arts in Australia from 1770 to the present. Dictionary arrangement of names of artists, galleries, prizes, societies, and exhibitions. Liberally illustrated. A new edition was published 1984 in 2v. N7400.M27

McGraw-Hill dictionary of art. Ed. by Bernard S. Myers. N.Y., McGraw-Hill, [1969]. 5v. il. **BE101**

Relatively long articles by more than 125 contributors deal with artists' lives and careers, artistic styles, periods, buildings, museums, and art terms. Bibliographies are included. Special attention is given to primitive art, to art of the Far East and Near East, and to descriptions of important monuments and museums in major cities of the world. Lack of an index is offset by numerous and useful cross references. A good alternative purchase for the smaller library unable to afford the same publisher's *Encyclopedia of world art* (BE96).

Entries on movements in modern art and on artists active since 1905 were drawn from this compilation to make up the *Dictionary of 20th century art,* edited by Bernard S. and Shirley D. Myers (N.Y., McGraw-Hill, 1974. 440p.); some entries were updated for the newer work. N33.M23

The Oxford companion to art. Harold Osborne, ed. Oxford, Clarendon Pr., 1970. 1277p. il. **BE102**

A typical addition to the "Oxford companion" series, this volume is "designed as a non-specialist introduction to the fine arts. In planning what to include . . . the word 'art' has been given the narrower meaning in which it denotes the visual arts generally but excludes the arts of theatre and cinema and the arts of movement such as dance."—*Pref.* Practical arts and handicrafts have also been largely excluded. Individual articles are meant to be merely introductory to the subject under consideration; although contributed by specialists, they are unsigned. Cross references are signaled by the use of small capitals within articles. Bibliographies are not provided at the end of articles; rather, a selective bibliography of more than 3,000 numbered items is appended, and references to the bibliography are indicated by numbers at the end of an article. N33.O9

The Oxford companion to twentieth-century art. Ed. by Harold Osborne. Oxford & N.Y., Oxford Univ. Pr., 1981. 656p. [128]p. of plates. il. **BE103**

Patterned after the *Oxford companion to art* (above), but planned and executed independently. Intended "as a handbook and a guide for students and others who wish to find their way intelligently through the exuberant jungle of contemporary art."—*Pref.* Forerun-

ners of modern art movements are generally excluded except as treated in articles concerning movements which they influenced significantly. "In the case of living artists articles purport to summarize their achievement and to indicate the nature of their performance up to the mid 1970s." Selective bibliography and list of illustrations at end of the volume; cross references. N6490.O94

Phaidon dictionary of twentieth-century art. London & N.Y., Phaidon, [1973]. 420p. il. **BE104**

"This dictionary covers fully all those artists whose major creative phases fall within this century, including those active at the present time."—*Foreword.* Includes terms in modern art as well as biographical sketches. Bibliographic citations appended to many articles. A useful ready-reference volume.

A "2d ed." 1977 is a reprinting in paperback without the plates. N6490.P46

Praeger encyclopedia of art. N.Y., Praeger, [1971]. 5v. (2139p.) il. **BE105**

Constitutes an English translation, revised and updated, with the addition of about 400 new articles, of the *Dictionnaire universel de l'art et des artistes* (Paris, Hazan, 1967).

Articles include biographies, periods, styles, schools, the art of individual nations and of various civilizations; additions for the English-language edition are chiefly in the areas of American, British, and German art. Articles are signed with initials of the contributor; illustrations are placed close to the relevant text. Bibliographies; cross references; index.

An abridged version, *Phaidon encyclopedia of art and artists* (Oxford, Phaidon; N.Y., Dutton. 704p.) was published 1978. N33.P68

Reallexikon zur byzantinischen Kunst. Hrsg. von Klaus Wessel, unter Mitwirkung von Marcell Restle. Stuttgart, A. Hiersemann, 1963–84. v.1–4² (Lfg.1–26). il. (In progress) **BE106**

Contents: v.1–4², Abendmahl–Kilikien.

A scholarly encyclopedia of Byzantine art, with long, signed articles. Bibliographies. N6250.W45

Reallexikon zur deutschen Kunstgeschichte. Stuttgart, Metzler, 1937–85. Bd.1–8⁸ (Lfg. 1–92). il. (In progress) **BE107**

Ed. by Otto Schmitt and others.

Imprint varies: Bd.2– , Stuttgart, Druckenmüller.

Contents: A–Figurine.

Long, signed articles, with bibliographies and many illustrations, on subjects in art history and on specific works of art. Biographies are excluded. Covers countries and regions with predominantly German culture from the early Middle Ages to the mid-19th century. v.3 contains an index of catchwords in German, French, English, and Italian covering the first 3v; beginning with v.4, each volume contains such an index covering the single volume. v.4 also contains a supplement (columns 1443–1544), as does v.6 (columns 1493–1512). N6861.R4

The Thames and Hudson dictionary of art and artists. Consulting ed., Herbert Read. Rev. ed. / Nikos Stangos. London, Thames and Hudson, [1985]. 352p. il. **BE108**

1st ed. 1966 ed. by Peter and Linda Murray, with title *A dictionary of art and artists.*

"The major part of the material in this dictionary was first published by Thames and Hudson Ltd in 1966 in the *Encyclopaedia of the arts. . . .* "—*verso of t.p.*

Aims to provide "comprehensive coverage of the fine arts, with entries on paintings, sculptures, drawings and prints, and the artists who have made them throughout the world."—*Foreword.* About 2,500 entries; 376 illustrations. N31.T47

Visual dictionary of art. Greenwich, Conn., New York Graphic Society, [1974]. 640p. il. **BE109**

Gen. ed., Ann Hill.

A dictionary of painting and sculpture featuring concise entries and with emphasis on artists. Includes brief survey articles on the art of various periods and countries. Heavily illustrated. Name index; brief bibliography. N33.V56

Terms

Adeline, Jules. The Adeline art dictionary, including terms in architecture, heraldry, and archaeology. Tr. from the French. With a supplement of new terms by Hugo G. Beigel. N.Y., Ungar, [1966]. 459p. **BE110**

Original French edition published 1884 under title *Lexique des termes d'art.*

A standard work which has appeared in many editions since its first appearance in English in 1891. "A large amount of information has been incorporated from F. W. Fairholt's *Dictionary of terms in art* [London, Virtue, 1854]."—*Introd.* This reprinting has a section of new terms appended, p.423–59. N33.A223

Hansford, Sidney Howard. A glossary of Chinese art and archaeology. [2d ed. rev.] London, China Soc., 1961. 104p. il. (China Soc. Sinological ser., no.4) **BE111**

1st ed. 1954.

A small dictionary of technical terms covering a wide variety of fields, including bronzes, gems and gem stones, sculpture in stone, painting, ceramics, lacquer, etc. Words are given in Chinese characters, Chinese transliteration, and English equivalent, with (in many cases) an explanation or definition. N7340.H3

Lucie-Smith, Edward. The Thames and Hudson dictionary of art terms. London & N.Y., Thames and Hudson, [1984]. 208p. il. **BE112**

"More than 2000 entries . . . define and explain terms from painting, sculpture, architecture, the decorative and applied arts, and the graphic arts, together with techniques of photography."— *Pref.* Brief definitions; 375 illustrations; cross references. N33.L75

Mayer, Ralph. A dictionary of art terms and techniques. N.Y., Crowell, [1969] 447p. il. (Repr.: N.Y., Barnes & Noble, 1981) **BE113**

Defines "terms encountered in the study and practice of the visual arts and in their literature" (*Pref.*) and includes descriptions of art periods, schools, and styles. Excluded are purely architectural terms, terms in Oriental art, and biographies. Whereas Quick's work (BE116) gives very technical discussions of processes and materials, Mayer merely defines and indicates the historical background. N33.M36

Mollett, John William. An illustrated dictionary of art and archaeology, including terms used in architecture, jewelry, heraldry, costume, music, ornament, weaving, furniture, pottery, ecclesiastical ritual. N.Y., American Archives of World Art, [1966]. 350p. il. **BE114**

A reprint of the work first published in 1883 under title *An illustrated dictionary of words used in art and archaeology,* which was "based on an amended edition of a dictionary by Ernest Bosc of Paris, but completely revised, [and] rewritten. . . . Contains 450 engravings from Bosc and 250 additional ones. A few Indian, Chinese, and Japanese terms in ordinary use in art are included" (Chamberlin's *Guide to art reference books,* p.34). N33.M6

Palmer, Frederick. Encyclopaedia of oil painting: materials and techniques. London, Batsford; Cincinnati, North Light, [1984]. 288p., [16]p. il. **BE115**

Explains "in simple terms the purposes of the equipment and materials along with some of the basic concepts of painting which are the concern of the intelligent amateur as well as the student and professional painter. . . . Discussion of technique is aimed at the amateur."—*Introd.* In two parts: (1) Equipment and materials (treating easels, palettes, brushes, canvas, solvents, pigments, color, etc.); (2) Techniques (dealing with glazes, encaustic, serigraphy, painting from photography, techniques of individual painters, etc.). Emphasis throughout is on practical advice to the beginning painter. Index of artists; general index. ND1500.P27

Quick, John. Artists' and illustrators' encyclopedia. 2d ed. N.Y., McGraw-Hill, [1977]. 327p. il. **BE116**

1st ed. 1969.

Aims to describe the wide range of methods and materials used in the arts and graphic arts. Alphabetical arrangement. Much technical information is presented in concise form. Numerous line drawings. N33.Q5

Réau, Louis. Dictionnaire polyglotte des termes d'art et d'archéologie. Paris, Presses Universitaires de France, 1953. 247p. (Repr.: Osnabrück, Zeller, 1977) **BE117**

At head of title: Comité International d'Histoire de l'Art. "Ouvrage publié avec le concours de l'UNESCO."

Unlike the 1928 edition (*Lexique polyglotte*), which was grouped by 12 languages with the equivalent French term for each entry, this edition has a single alphabet of common French terms (technical and iconographical) with the equivalent terms for each in Greek, Latin, Italian, Spanish, Portuguese, English, German, Dutch, Danish, Swedish, Czech, Polish, and Russian. No definitions are given. N33.R42

Reynolds, Kimberley and **Seddon, Richard.** Illustrated dictionary of art terms: a handbook for the artist and art lover. N.Y., Peter Bedrick Books, 1984. 190p. il. **BE118**

First published London, Ebury, 1981.

Aims "to provide a simple guide to terms frequently encountered in books, magazine articles, catalogues and even television programmes on making and looking at works of art."—*Pref.* Terms, selected chiefly from painting and sculpture, include styles, methods, materials, schools of art, abbreviations, etc. Appropriately placed illustrations illuminate the verbal explanations. Cross references; brief bibliography. N33.R49

Walker, John Albert. Glossary of art, architecture and design since 1945: terms and labels describing movements, styles, and groups, derived from the vocabulary of artists and critics. 2d rev. ed. London, Bingley; Hamden, Conn., Linnet Books, [1977]. 352p. **BE119**

1st ed. 1973.

Concerned mainly with Anglo-American terms derived from the published literature on art since 1945. Revision includes updating of articles and of the bibliographies, plus the addition of new entries for terms which gained currency since publication of the earlier edition. N34.W34

Directories

International

Abse, Joan. The art galleries of Britain and Ireland; a guide to their collections. London, Sidgwick & Jackson, 1975; Rutherford, N.J., Fairleigh Dickinson Pr., 1976. 248p. il. **BE120**

Offers descriptions of public museums and their major collections of paintings (with some attention to sculpture), together with address, telephone number, and hours of opening. Museums are listed alphabetically under name of city; index of artists and museum names. A few surprising omissions were noted (e.g., the Imperial War Museum).

A revised edition was published 1985 (London, Robson Books. 383p.). N1020.A27

Canada. Statistics Canada. Cultural Information Section. Directory of museums, art galleries and related institutions, 1972. Répertoire des musées, galeries d'art et des établissements connexes, 1972. Ottawa, Information Canada, 1973. 216p. **BE121**

A geographically arranged directory of museums, art galleries (noncommercial), archives, botanical gardens, zoos and aquariums, historic houses and sites, planetariums and observatories. Gives brief description, hours and dates of opening, price of admission, governing authority, but not address of institution. English and French in parallel columns. Institutional name index. AM21.A1D57

Fedden, Robin and **Joekes, Rosemary.** The National Trust guide to England, Wales, and Northern Ireland. 3d. ed. rev. & ed. by R. Joekes. London, Cape, [1984]. 691p. il., maps. **BE122**

1st ed. 1973.

Offers descriptions of properties owned by the National Trust, arranged alphabetically by type of property: houses; gardens and landscape parks; temples, follies, monuments, villages, dovecotes, churches, chapels, buildings of useful intent and public houses; medieval buildings; industrial monuments; archaeological sites; coast and country. Each section has an introductory essay; for each site are given: location, history, important features. Glossary; list of National Trust properties not described in the text (with location and brief notes); index.

A related volume is: DA660.F33

National Trust atlas. 2d ed. [London], National Trust/G. Philip, [1984]. 224p. il., maps. **BE123**

Sponsored by the National Trust for Places of Historic Interest or National Beauty and by the National Trust of Scotland.

1st ed. 1964.

Serves as a "guide to the properties of the Trusts throughout the United Kingdom, including Scotland and Northern Ireland as well as England and Wales."—*Introd.* Within each of ten regions information is presented in four sections: Coasts and countryside (for open spaces and wildlife refuges); Houses, gardens and parks; Castles, abbeys and other buildings; Archaeological and industrial sites. Gives a brief history of each place, with indication of significance and a map reference. Copiously illustrated. Glossary; list of architects and craftsmen with mention of sites associated with each; index to text; county index to properties; map index.

The Trusts issue annual booklets which give practical, but changing, information excluded from the *Atlas*: admission fees, hours of opening, and special facilities available at each property.

G1812.21.G5N3

Germaine, Max. Artists and galleries of Australia. [Rev. ed.] Brisbane, Boolarong Pubns., 1984. 595p. il. **BE124**

1st ed. (1979) had title: *Artists and galleries of Australia and New Zealand.*

A directory of Australian galleries and artists, with information to mid-1984. More than 3,000 artists in this edition, giving place and date of birth, genre or specialty, education, awards, exhibitions, and galleries where represented. N7404.G47

Guide to exhibited artists. Oxford, Eng. & Santa Barbara, Calif., Clio Pr., [1985]. 5v. **BE125**

Contents: [v.1] European painters; [v.2] North American painters; [v.3] Printmakers; [v.4] Sculptors; [v.5] Craftsmen.

Derived from computerized files based mainly on exhibition records. In each volume listing is by artist with the following information given, as available: date and place of birth, media, art education, mailing address, dates and places of exhibitions. An "Index" in each volume is an alphabetical listing of galleries with addresses.

Handbuch der Museen. Handbook of museums: Bundesrepublic Deutschland, Deutsche Demokratische Republik, Österreich, Schweiz, Liechtenstein. 2., neubearb. Aufl. München & N.Y., Saur, 1981. 779p. **BE126**

Ed. by Harald Gläser and others.

1st ed. 1971 ed. by Gudrun Birgit-Kloster.

Within country sections the listing is alphabetical by city. Includes art museums and galleries, natural science museums, technical museums, anthropological and archaeological museums, local history museums, and natural history museums. Indexes by place, by museum name, and by subject.

IFAR reports. v.6, no.1– , Jan./Feb. 1985– . N.Y., Internat. Foundation for Art Research, 1985– . 10 nos. per yr. **BE127**

Formed by the union of *Stolen art alert* (1980–84) and *Art research news* (1981–84); continues the numbering of the former, which was a reporting service for stolen art works. Reports on art thefts continue to be a feature of the new publication. N8554.I34

International directory of arts. Internationales Kunst-Adressbuch. . . . 1952/53– . Berlin, Deutsche Zentraldruckerei, [1952–]. v.1– . Annual. **BE128**

Absorbed *Deutsches Kunst-Adressbuch* which began publication in autumn of 1949.

Title also in French, Italian, and Spanish. Order and number of languages vary. Prefatory text and table of contents in German, English, French, and variously in Italian or Spanish.

Imprint varies; recent editions in 2v. Beginning with the 8th ed. (1965/66) the two volumes were sometimes published in alternate years.

Includes lists, with addresses, arranged by country, of: museums, art galleries, associations, universities, colleges and academies offering art courses, auctioneers, restorers, dealers, booksellers, numismatics, collectors, publishers, and periodicals. Content has varied over the years. The most useful of the international directories.

N50.I6

I musei italiani: informazioni, indirizzi, orari; testo italiano e inglese, a cura di Giorgio Riva. Milano, Bibliografica, [1977]. 253p. **BE129**

A brief, geographically arranged guide to Italian museums, giving for each: address, director, hours of opening (including summer and holiday schedules), and a short statement regarding any special collection strengths or notable holdings. Hours and descriptions are in English and Italian. "Index of localities by region."

AM54.A2M87

Museums in Africa; a directory. [Bonn, German Africa Society]; N.Y., Africana, [1970]. 594p. **BE130**

A first attempt at a comprehensive museum directory for this continent. AM80.A2M8

Museums of the world. 3d rev. ed. München & N.Y., Saur, 1981. 623p. (Handbook of international documentation and information, v.16) **BE131**

1st ed. 1973.

A listing by country and city of museums of all types in 163 countries. Gives address, year of founding, and indication of kinds of collections or strengths. Name and subject indexes. AM1.M76

Schweers, Hans F. Gemälde in deutschen Museen: Katalog der in der Bundesrepublik Deutschland ausgestellten Werke. Paintings in German museums: catalogue of works on exhibition in the Federal Republic of Germany. München & N.Y., Saur, 1981–82. 2v. il. **BE132**

Introductory matter in German and English.

" . . . provides the specialist with a general overview of approximately 60,000 paintings on exhibit in more than 350 museums" *(Foreword)*, and is thus useful to the curator planning an exhibition and to the museum visitor seeking works of a specific artist. In general, includes only items owned by a museum or on permanent or temporary loan. Entries are arranged by painter and give title, date of completion, type of material, size, and location. Supplement in v.2. N2210.S27

Year's art, 1880–1947, a concise epitome of all matters relating to the arts of painting, sculpture, engraving and architecture, and to schools of design, which have occurred during the year, together with information respecting the events of the year. London, Macmillan, 1880–1947. 64v. il. Annual. **BE133**

Publisher varies.

v.63 covers 1942–44; v.64, 1945–47.

Includes lists of museums, associations, and schools in Great Britain and the major ones in the Dominions and the United States; information on sales and exhibitions; a directory of artists and dealers; obituaries; and information on a variety of other pertinent subjects. N9.Y4

United States

American art directory. v.1– , 1898– . N.Y., Bowker, 1899– . il. Triennial, 1952– . **BE134**

Frequency varies.

Title varies: v.1–37, 1898–1945/48, *American art annual.* Volumes for 1913–73 published by or for the American Federation of Arts. *Who's who in American art,* v.1–4, 1936–47 (BE186), was issued as pt.2 of v.33–36 of the *American art annual* which, in v.1–32, 1898–1935, had included various biographical lists.

Now in three main sections: (1) Art organizations (national and regional associations, museums, and libraries of the United States and Canada); (2) Art schools (U.S. and Canada); (3) Art information (major museums and art schools abroad, state arts councils, art magazines, newspapers carrying art notes and their critics, scholarships and fellowships, etc.). Indexes of organizations, personnel, and subjects. N50.A54

Art in America. Annual guide to galleries, museums, artists. Comp. by the editors of Art in America. N.Y., Neal-Schuman, [1982]– . il. Annual. **BE135**

A reprinting, without advertisements, of the August issue of *Art in America.*

" . . . a comprehensive alphabetical listing, arranged by state and city, of U.S. museums, galleries and alternative spaces. Included are addresses, phone numbers, business hours, key staff members and a short description of the type of art shown."—*1984/85 ed.*

Faison, Samson Lane. The art museums of New England. Boston, D. R. Godine, 1982. 463p. il. **BE136**

A revised and expanded edition of Faison's *Guide to the art museums of New England* (1958).

Provides information concerning more than 100 art museums, historical societies and libraries open to the public in the six New England states, with critical and historical comment on about 550 works of art in their permanent collections. Arranged by state, south to north, then by city. Indexed.

The work is also available as three paperback volumes, each with its own index, covering (1) Connecticut and Rhode Island; (2) Massachusetts; (3) New Hampshire, Vermont, and Maine. N510.5.N4F2

Hobbie, Margaret. Museums, sites, and collections of Germanic culture in North America: an annotated directory of German immigrant culture in the United States and Canada. Westport, Conn., Greenwood Pr., [1980]. 155p. **BE137**

Attempts "to make material culture, and other nonbibliographic sources more readily available to students of German-American and German-Canadian history, through a descriptive listing of locations where such materials can be found."—*Pref.* In three sections: (1) Collections (describing German-American holdings of museums, historical societies, archives, and libraries); (2) National register sites (describing selected sites from the *National register of historic places*; BE228); and (3) Selected list of European sources (i.e., important foreign collections with useful material on European antecedents). Indexed. E184.G3H58

Hoffberg, Judith A. and **Hess, Stanley W.** Directory of art libraries and visual resource collections in North America. Comp. for the Art Libraries Soc. of North America (ARLIS/NA). [N.Y.], Neal-Schuman (distr. by ABC-Clio), [1978]. 298p. **BE138**

A directory of libraries, museums, galleries, art schools, colleges and universities in the United States and Canada; historical societies and film libraries are excluded. Information was derived from questionnaires. Pt.I is a directory of art libraries arranged by state or province, giving for each: address, hours, head, and brief statements concerning circulation, reference service, reprographic services, interlibrary loan, networks/consortia, special programs, holdings, and subject strengths. It is indexed according to more than 500 subject categories. Pt.II covers visual resource collections, similarly arranged and giving similar information on collections and services; it has three indexes: collection emphases, subscription series, special collections. Pt.III is an index to institutions.

——— ——— Addendum. N.Y., Neal-Schuman, [1979]. 36p.

This supplement was designed to correct the omission of a number of institutions from the art library section, although their questionnaires had been returned. It adds entries for every province in Canada and for 13 states of the United States. Z675.A85H63

McDarrah, Fred W. Museums in New York. 4th ed. N.Y., Simon & Schuster, 1983. 335p. il. **BE139**

1st ed. 1967.

A guide to the city's "museums, mansions, and mausoleums."—*Foreword.* Gives directory information (location, times of opening, facilities, etc.) plus brisk commentary on the collections, special features, etc. Geographical arrangement with alphabetical list of museums. AM13.N5M33

The official museum directory. 1971– . [N.Y., Amer. Assoc. of Museums and Crowell-Collier Educ. Corp., 1971]– . Annual. **BE140**

Frequency varies; annual since 1980.

Supersedes *Museums directory of the United States and Canada* (ed.1–2, 1961–65).

Provides information (address, principal staff, type of museum and scope of collection, notes on facilities, activities and publications, hours of opening) on over 6,000 museums of art, history, and science. In four main sections: (1) Institutions by state (alphabetically by city or town and then by institution); (2) Institutions by name alphabetically; (3) Institution directors and department heads by name alphabetically; (4) Institutions by category. Canada was included through 1983. AM10.A2O4

Robl, Ernest H. Picture sources 4. [4th ed.] N.Y., Special Libraries Assoc., 1983. 180p. il. **BE141**

Earlier eds. (entitled *Picture sources*) appeared 1959, 1964, 1975.

A directory intended for picture researchers, librarians, editors, artists, and all other professional users of pictures. This edition offers revised information, adds more than 200 collections (for a total of over 900), and is arranged in a single alphabetical listing of collections (rather than by broad subjects as in the previous editions). Entry gives name of collection, contact person, contents, subject and chronological coverage, and terms of access. Now produced by computer, so that more frequent updates are planned. Collections index; geographic index; subject index. N4000.N68

Sherman, Lila. Art museums of America: a guide to collections in the United States and Canada. N.Y., Morrow, 1980. 416p. il. **BE141a**

An alphabetical listing by state and city of fine arts museums and galleries giving a general description of collections and notes on admission (hours, fees, etc.); descriptions are usually one or two long paragraphs. An appendix lists museums according to subject strengths, with the large museums grouped under "general." Index of museum names. N510.S45

Sales

Art prices current . . . a record of sale prices at the principal London, Continental and American auction rooms. London, Art Trade Pr., 1908–73. v.1–9 (1907/08–1915/16); n.s. v.1–50 (1921/22–72/73). **BE142**

Subtitle varies. Publication suspended 1917–20.

Arranged by medium: pt.A, Paintings, drawings, and miniatures; pt.B, Engravings and prints. Each part is arranged chronologically by sales, with items within the part consecutively numbered and covering artist, title, size, purchaser, price, sometimes condition. Indexes of artists, engravers, and collectors.

Cote des tableux; ou, Annuaire des ventes de tableaux, dessins, aquarelles, pastels, gouaches, miniatures; guide du marchand, de l'amateur (Paris, L. Maurice, 1919–31. 11v.) provides a chronological record of sales for the period Oct. 1918–July 1929. Michèle Bérard's *Encyclopedia of modern art auction prices* (N.Y., Arco, 1971. 417p.) records the prices paid for modern paintings during the Sept. 1961–July 1969 period. N8670.A7

Lancour, Harold. American art auction catalogues, 1785–1942; a union list. N.Y., New York Pub. Lib., 1944. 377p. **BE143**

"Reprinted with revisions and additions from the *Bulletin* of the New York Public Library, Jan. 1943–Feb. 1944."—*verso of title page.*

A union checklist of more than 7,000 catalogs of auction sales of art objects including paintings, drawings, statuary, furniture, rugs, jewelry, textiles, musical instruments, curios, etc. Excludes books, maps, bookplates, stamps, and coins. Locates copies in 21 libraries. Includes a list of auction houses and an index of owners.

Z5939.A1L3

Lugt, Frits. Répertoire des catalogues de ventes publiques intéressant l'art ou la curiosité. ... La Haye, Nijhoff, 1938–53. v.1–3. (Publications du Rijksbureau voor Kunsthistorische en Ikonografische Documentatie)   **BE144**

A chronological list of more than 58,000 catalogs of art sales held throughout Europe: v.1 covers 1600–1825; v.2, 1826–60; v.3, 1861–1900. Information for each entry includes: date and place of sale, provenance, contents, number of items and pages, auctioneers, and location of copies in libraries. Index of names of collections sold. No more published?   N8650.L8

Print prices current; being a complete alphabetical record of all engravings, etchings and Baxter prints sold by auction in Great Britain and America, each item annotated with the date of sale, price realised and the quality and condition of the prints. v.1–21, Oct. 1918–Aug. 1939. London, F. L. Wilder, 1919–40. 21v. Annual.   **BE145**

Subtitle varies slightly.
American prices included for the first time in v.13, 1930/31. Arranged by engravers, with index by artists.   NE85.P7

World collectors annuary. v.1, 1946/49– . Delft, Brouwer [etc.], 1950– . il. Annual.   **BE146**

Lists alphabetically by artist the paintings, watercolors, and drawings sold at auction in Europe and the United States, giving description, provenance, place and date of sale, price paid, and bibliographic notes. Some volumes list prints; furniture, porcelain, etc., are listed only in v.5–10. Early volumes include a section of reproductions of selected works sold during the year.

A cumulative index to v.1–24, comp. by J.J.B. van Eijk van Voorthuijsen, was published as *World collectors index 1946–1972* (Voorburg, 1976. 256p.).   ND47.W6

Handbooks

Chamberlain, Betty. The artist's guide to the art market. 4th ed. N.Y., Watson-Guptil, [1983]. 252p.   **BE147**

1st ed. 1970.
A practical guide for the artist seeking a place to exhibit his works and channels for selling them. Includes sections on galleries and how they function, shopping for a gallery, showing work to dealers, business terms and agreements, pricing and selling, publicity, cooperatives, career opportunities, taxes and the self-employed artist, thefts. Indexed.   N8600.C48

Christie's Guide to collecting. Ed. by Robert Cumming. Oxford, Phaidon; Englewood Cliffs, N.J., Prentice-Hall, [1984]. 224p. il.   **BE148**

Aims "to encourage the spirit and traditions of private collecting and to offer down-to-earth advice on questions which are frequently asked."—*Foreword.* Brief chapters by specialist contributors on individual aspects of collecting are grouped in three sections: (1) Becoming a collector; (2) Looking after a collection; (3) Buying and selling. Appendixes include a select bibliography, a list of professional associations, directories of auction houses and dealers and of museums, galleries, etc. Indexed.   N5200.C48

Evans, Hilary. The art of picture research; a guide to current practice, procedure, techniques and resources. Newton Abbot, Devon, David & Charles, [1979]. 208p.   **BE149**

A clear and readable guide for the picture researcher, explaining the work of the researcher, what kinds of resources are available and how to use them, how to select an appropriate picture, and the technical aspects of an assignment (e.g., budgeting, copyright, insurance). Although the examples and illustrations are British, the discussion is applicable to picture research in any country.

Evans is also the author of *Picture librarianship* (N.Y., Saur; London, Bingley, 1980. 136p.).   Z692.P5E82

———— **Evans, Mary** and **Nelki, Andrea.** The picture researcher's handbook: an international guide to picture sources and how to use them. 2d ed. London, Saturday Ventures, 1979. 328p. il.   **BE149a**

1st ed. 1975.
A directory of libraries, museums, government agencies, commercial firms, and studios, providing brief descriptions of picture collections, scope, address, hours, availability, etc. Information is based on replies to questionnaires. Index of topics, names of collections, and of countries. A 3d ed. by Hilary and Mary Evans was announced for 1986 publication by Van Nostrand Reinhold (U.K.).   N4000.E8

Gealt, Adelheid M. Looking at art: a visitor's guide to museum collections. N.Y., Bowker, 1983. 609p. il.   **BE150**

Intends "to provide basic information that would aid museum-goers . . . in understanding what they see."—*Pref.* Not a guide to specific museums as such, but a survey of "the types of art produced by period, outlining the influences that are thought to have informed the artistic production of that age." Chapters on the history of collecting and growth of museums, how museums build collections, and the functions and organization of museums precede chronological chapters (with subdivisions for the art of individual countries) and chapters for Asian art, Pre-Columbian art, and tribal arts. Lists of artists (grouped by genre or medium) and of major representative collections conclude most chapters. Bibliography; index.

N5200.G4

History

❖Good histories of art range from introductory surveys such as the Gardner and Janson volumes noted below to the highly specialized and very scholarly multivolume series. In the special collection, the excellent *Pelican history of art* will be supplemented by various other series, essentially monographic in nature, both in English and foreign languages.

Gardner, Helen. Art through the ages. 7th ed. Rev. by Horst de la Croix and Richard G. Tansey. N.Y., Harcourt, [1980]. 2v. il.   **BE151**

1st ed. 1926.
A standard work, intended for students and the general reader; widely used as a basic textbook. Bibliography, p.897–903.

N5300.G25

Hauser, Arnold. The social history of art. [Tr. in collaboration with the author by Stanley Godman] N.Y., Knopf, 1951. 2v. (1022p.) il. (Repr.: N.Y., Vintage, 1958–60. 4v.)   **BE152**

Bibliography given in brief form as "Notes" to chapters at the end of each volume, with no systematic arrangement. Indexes of subjects and names at the end of v.2.   N72.H353

Honour, Hugh and **Fleming, John.** The visual arts: a history. Englewood Cliffs, N.J., Prentice-Hall, [1982]. 639p. il.   **BE153**

British ed. has title: *A world history of art* (London, Macmillan, 1982).

A good recent survey which aims to be "exploratory rather than critical"; i.e., the work "seeks to explore the different ways in which men and women have given visual expression to perennial human impulses and concerns. . . . "—*Introd.* Chronological treatment over a broad geographical range. Many illustrations; glossary; brief bibliography; index.   N5300.H68

Janson, Horst Woldemar and **Janson, Dora Jane.** History of art; a survey of the major visual arts from the dawn of history to the present day. 2d ed. Englewood Cliffs, N.J. Prentice-Hall; N.Y., Abrams [1977]. 767p. il. **BE154**

1st ed. 1962.

A handsomely illustrated summary of Western painting, sculpture, and architecture, up to the 19th century, with a brief postscript on Oriental and pre-Columbian art. Basically a textbook.

This is a revised and expanded edition with many new illustrations. The most extensive revision and enlargement is in the prehistoric section and in coverage of the modern period to the late 1960s. The bibliography has been expanded and updated.

A 3d ed. is scheduled for publication in 1986.   N5300.J3

——— Key monuments of the history of art: a visual survey. Englewood Cliffs, N.J., Prentice-Hall; N.Y., Abrams, [1959]. 1068p. il.   **BE155**

A selection of more than 1,200 reproductions of historically significant works covering architecture, sculpture, and painting throughout the world, from prehistoric to modern times.

N5301.J3

Pelican history of art, ed. by Nikolaus Pevsner. [Baltimore], Penguin, 1953–80. v.1–44. il. (In progress?)   **BE156**

A series expected to be in 50v., covering world art and architecture of all periods, each written by a specialist and containing substantial bibliographies and many plates. Volumes are not published in chronological or regional sequence of subject matter. Volumes published after v.31 do not carry a volume number. Many volumes have been issued in revised editions; the series is also published in paperback. The series numbering is in order of publication:

Contents: v.1, Painting in Britain, 1530 to 1790, by E. K. Waterhouse; v.2, The art and architecture of India: Buddhist, Hindu, Jain, by B. Rowland; v.3, Architecture in Britain, 1530 to 1830, by J. N. Summerson; v.4, Art and architecture in France, 1500–1700, by A. Blunt; v.5, Painting in Britain: the Middle Ages, by M. Rickert; v.6, The art and architecture of Russia, by G. H. Hamilton; v.7, The art and architecture of the ancient Orient, by H. Frankfort; v.8, The art and architecture of Japan, by R. T. Paine and A. Soper; v.9, Sculpture in Britain: the Middle Ages, by L. Stone; v.10, The art and architecture of China, by L. C. S. Sickman and A. Soper; v.11, Greek architecture, by A. W. Lawrence; v.12, Architecture in Britain: the Middle Ages, by G. F. Webb; v.13, Carolingian and Romanesque architecture, 800 to 1200, by K. J. Conant; v.14, The art and architecture of ancient Egypt, by W. S. Smith; v.15, Architecture: nineteenth and twentieth centuries, by H. R. Hitchcock; v.16, Art and architecture in Italy, 1600 to 1750, by R. Wittkower; v.17, Art and architecture in Spain and Portugal and their American dominions, 1500 to 1800, by G. Kubler and M. Soria; v.18, Art and architecture in Belgium, 1600 to 1800, by H. Gerson and E. H. ter Kuile; v.19, Gothic architecture, by P. Frankl; v.20, Painting and sculpture in Europe, 1780 to 1880, by F. Novotny; v.21, The art and architecture of ancient America: the Mexican, Maya and Andean peoples, by G. Kubler; v.22, Baroque art and architecture in Central Europe, by E. Hempel; v.23, Sculpture in Britain, 1530 to 1830, by M. Whinney; v.24, Early Christian and Byzantine architecture, by R. Krautheimer; v.25, Sculpture in the Netherlands, Germany, France, and Spain, 1400 to 1500, by T. Müller; v.26, Sculpture in Italy, 1400 to 1500, by C. Seymour; v.27, Dutch art and architecture, 1600 to 1800, by J. Rosenberg, S. Slive, E. H. ter Kuile; v.28, Art and architecture in Italy, 1250 to 1400, by J. White; v.29, Painting and sculpture in Europe, 1880 to 1940, by G. H. Hamilton; v.30, Prehistoric art in Europe, by N. K. Sandars; v.31, Painting and sculpture in Germany and the Netherlands, 1500 to 1600, by G. von der Osten and H. Vey; v.32, Etruscan and Roman architecture, by A. Boëthius and J. B. Ward-Perkins; v.33, Early Christian and Byzantine art, by J. Beckwith; v.34, Painting in Europe, 800 to 1200, by C. R. Dodwell; v.35, Painting in Italy, 1500 to 1600, by S. J. Freedberg; v.36, Ars sacra: 800–1200, by P. Lasko; v.37, Art and architecture of the eighteenth century in France, by W. G. Kalnein and M. Levey; v.38, Architecture in Italy, 1400–1600, by L. H. Heydenreich and W. Lotz; v.39, Roman art, by D. Strong; v.40, American art, by J. Wilmerding; v.41, The arts of prehistoric Greece, by S. Hood; v.42, Etruscan art, by O. Brendel; v.43,

Etruscan and early Roman architecture, by A. Boethius (a rev. ed. of v.32); v.44, Roman imperial architecture, by J. B. Ward-Perkins.

Robb, David Metheny and **Garrison, Jessie J.** Art in the Western world. 4th ed. N.Y., Harper, [1963]. 782p. il.   **BE157**

1st ed. 1935.

A standard introduction to the whole field of art. Separate sections on architecture, sculpture, painting, and the minor arts. Also contains: a chronological and topical concordance, glossary, bibliography, chronological table, index to the 652 illustrations, and a general index. Basically a textbook.   N5300.R56

Upjohn, Everard Miller, Wingert, Paul Stover and **Mahler, Jane Gaston.** History of world art. 2d ed. rev. and enl. N.Y., Oxford, 1958. 876p. 671 il., 17 pl.(col.)   **BE158**

1st ed. 1949.

A survey history of painting, sculpture, and architecture designed for introductory college courses. In this edition the chapters on the 20th century have been rewritten; chapters added on prehistoric, primitive, and pre-Columbian art; and reproductions put at the point of discussion of the works of art. Suggested readings, p.841–50; glossary, p.831–39; index. Primarily a textbook.   N5300.U6

Chronology

Clapp, Jane. Art censorship; a chronology of proscribed and prescribed art. Metuchen, N.J., Scarecrow Pr., 1972. 582p. il.   **BE159**

Incidents of art censorship ("artists or art works restricted for economic, social, political, moral or aesthetic reasons by state and church officials, and also by citizen or other groups, individuals, or society as a whole"—*Pref.*) are briefly reported in chronological sequence, with references to sources of information on the incident. Indexed.   N8740.C55

Biography

❖Here are listed some of the more important biographical dictionaries, mainly general in scope and international in coverage. Dictionaries devoted to a particular country, except for those of the United States, are largely omitted. For lists of these *see* Arntzen and Rainwater, *Guide to the literature of art history* (BE1), p.47–57.

Bénézit, Emmanuel. Dictionnaire critique et documentaire des sculpteurs, dessinateurs et graveurs de tous les temps. . . . Nouvelle éd. ent. refondue, revue et corrigée. Paris, Gründ, 1976. 10v. port.   **BE160**

1st ed. 1911–23. 3v.

A comprehensive work, covering artists from the 5th century B.C. to the mid-20th century A.D., including many minor names. Includes both Western and Eastern art. Entries, varying in length from a few lines to several columns, usually include a list of chief works, museums where displayed, and (in some instances) prices paid for works. Symbols and signatures are reproduced in facsimile, and at the end of each key letter of the alphabet a list of the signatures used by anonymous artists appears.

This is a complete updating and expansion of the previous edition (1948–55. 8v.), but using the same format and presenting the same type of information. Brief bibliography of sources at end of v.10. An unusual feature is the inclusion of tables of 20th-century rates of exchange for pounds, dollars and francs.   N40.B47

Berman, Esmé. Art & artists of South Africa: an illustrated biographical dictionary and historical survey of painters, sculptors & graphic artists since 1875. New updated & enl. ed. Cape Town, Balkema, 1983. 545p. il.   **BE161**

1st ed. 1970.

Runs heavily to biographical entries, but includes articles on genres and survey articles such as "Early painting activity in Kimberley." This edition retains all the earlier entries, adds many new ones, and expands "the number of sub-references and lists of names assembled under generic headings, such as *Graphic Artists, Landscape Artists, Water-colourists*, etc."—*Foreword*. References to sculpture and sculptors (not treated in the earlier edition) have also been added. Bibliography; index. **N7392.B47**

A biographical dictionary of artists. Sir Lawrence Gowing, gen. ed. London, Macmillan; Englewood Cliffs, N.J., Prentice-Hall, [1983]. 784p. il. (The encyclopedia of visual art, v.2) **BE162**

An alphabetical arrangement of biographical sketches from which "no major western artist is missing" (*Pref.*) and in which artists of other cultures are also represented. Selection runs heavily to painters, but other artists (and a few critics) are included. Accounts include dates, education, career, achievements, influence; many entries carry bibliographies. Less important names not dealt with in the body of the work appear in the index with a one-line identification. Chronology; illustrated glossary; index.

v.1 of *The encyclopedia of visual art* is entitled *History of art* and is a lavishly illustrated work of 54 brief chapters by specialists, covering from paleolithic times to the present. **N25.E53**

Biographical dictionary of Japanese art. Yutaka Tazawa, supervising ed. [Tokyo], Kodansha Internat., [1981]. 825p. il. **BE163**

Biographical sketches are grouped by categories (which include calligraphy, graphic design, tea ceremony, gardens, ceramics, swords, metalwork, textiles, and lacquer as well as the expected areas such as painting, prints, sculpture and architecture). Glossary; bibliography; index. **N7358.B55**

Contemporary artists. Muriel Emanuel [and others], eds. 2d ed. N.Y., St. Martin's Pr., [1983]. 1041p. il. **BE164**

1st ed. 1977 ed. by Colin Naylor.

While "no rigid criteria were imposed" on the advisory board responsible for the selection of artists treated, guidelines "proposed that all entrants should have worked as professional artists for at least five years, have exhibited their work in several individual important galleries, and have been included in large-scale museum survey shows—and be represented in the permanent collections of major museums throughout the world."—*Introd.* In general, excludes artists who died before World War II; includes artists from many countries. Entries comprise brief biography; individual exhibitions; selected group exhibitions; and collections in which the artist's work is included; bibliography by and about the person is followed by signed commentary. Information as late as 1982 is included. Although many specialties are represented, painting predominates. **N6490.C6567**

Contemporary British artists. Charlotte Parry-Crooke, ed. London, Bergstrom & Boyle Books; N.Y., St. Martin's Pr., [1979]. unpaged. il. **BE165**

For each artist gives a brief career chronology, a statement by the artist about his work, and one or two small black-and-white reproductions; address of dealer or other contact is also given. Includes a section of photographs of the artists, reproductions of signatures, and a directory of galleries in Great Britain, Ireland, the United States, Japan, and Western Europe. **N6768.C63**

Édouard-Joseph, René. Dictionnaire biographique des artistes contemporains, 1910–1930, avec nombreux portraits, signatures et reproductions. Paris, Art & Édition, 1930–34. 3v. il. **BE166**

Publisher varies.

Intended to include primarily artists living or exhibited in France from 1910 to 1930. Useful for minor figures not found elsewhere.

————— ————— Supplément. Paris, 1936. 162p. il.

N40.E4

Havlice, Patricia Pate. Index to artistic biography. Metuchen, N.J., Scarecrow Pr., 1973. 2v. **BE167**

An index to biographical material on artists appearing in 64 works (primarily dictionaries of artists and works of collective biography) in 10 languages. Entry gives artist's name, dates, nationality, media

employed, and code reference to work in which biographical information appears (references are to volume only, not to specific pages). **N40.H38**

————— ————— Supplement. Metuchen, N.J., Scarecrow Pr., 1981. 953p.

Indexes 70 additional titles.

Kaltenbach, Gustave Émile. Dictionary of pronunciation of artists' names, with their schools and dates, for American readers and students. [2d ed.] Chicago, Art Inst., [1938]. 74p. **BE168**

1st ed. 1934.

Includes more than 1,500 names. A very useful work. **N40.K3**

Khudozhniki narodov SSSR. Biobibliograficheskii slovar' v shesti tomakh. Red. Kollegiia: T. N. Gorina [i dr.]. Moskva, Izd. Iskusstvo, 1970–83. v.1–4¹. (In progress) **BE169**

Contents: v.1–4¹, Aavik–Kadyshev.

To be in 6v. Short bio-bibliographical entries for Russian artists, art critics, and art historians from earliest times to the present. Includes foreign artists who worked in Russia to the second half of the 19th century. The finished work will cover about 20,000 artists. **N6998.K47**

Kindlers Malerei Lexikon. Hrsg.: Germain Bazin [et al.]. Zürich, Kindler Verlag, [1964–71]. 6v. il. **BE170**

The first 5v. are devoted to biographies of individual artists, with lists of their works and selective bibliographies of works about them; v.6 includes essays on various periods and styles, etc., together with an index. Scope is international and covers all periods. Lavishly illustrated. Not on the same scholarly plane as Thieme-Becker (BE177), but the inclusion of contemporary figures and the relatively up-to-date bibliographies make it a useful complement thereto. **ND35.K5**

Mallett, Daniel Trowbridge. Index of artists; international—biographical; including painters, sculptors, illustrators, engravers and etchers of the past and the present. N.Y., Bowker, 1935. 493p. (Repr.: N.Y., Peter Smith, 1948, with suppl.) **BE171**

————— ————— Supplement. 1940. 319p.

"Covers all the artists whose works are exhibited in leading galleries or inquired about by modern students."—*Foreword*. Entries give basic biographical data. For further information, entries also include a key to one or more of the 22 general reference works and more than 1,000 specialized works listed as "Sources of biographical information." The Supplement includes entries for artists of all countries and periods not in the 1935 volume; a Necrology, 1935–40; and a list of early American silversmiths. The entries, in cases of artists not found in the listed sources, refer to the art gallery, museum, library, etc., from which data may be obtained.

Useful as a first source in biographical search, but should be used with some caution as it contains various inaccuracies. **N40.M3**

Marks, Claude. World artists, 1950–1980. N.Y., Wilson, 1984. 912p. ports. **BE172**

"An H. W. Wilson biographical dictionary."—*t.p.*

Offers biographies of 312 artists "who both worked and were influential" (*Pref.*) in the fields of painting, sculpture, and graphic arts; international coverage. Factual and critical essay on each artist, with lists of major exhibitions and collections, and a brief bibliography of books and articles about the artist. **N6489.M37**

Müller, Hermann Alexander and **Singer, Hans W.** Allgemeines Künstler-Lexicon. Leben und Werke der berühmtesten bildenden Künstler. 3. umgearb. u. bis auf die neueste Zeit ergänzte Aufl. Frankfurt a. M., Rütten & Loening, 1895–1901. 5v. **BE173**

————— ————— Nachträge und Berichtigungen. 1906. 295p.

Short biographical entries. A 5th ed. (not revised) was issued in 1921–22 in 6v., the final volume containing a second supplement with corrections. **N40.M94**

Osterwalder, Marcus. Dictionnaire des illustrateurs, 1800–1914 (illustrateurs, caricaturistes et affichistes). Paris, Hubschmid et Bouret, [1983]. 1221p. il. **BE174**

For each of 1,086 artists from throughout the world there is a biographical sketch and a representative illustration. Index of literary works cited, with names of illustrators. Two further volumes are planned to deal with illustrators of the 1500–1800 and 1914–1984 periods. NC961.6.O88

Petteys, Chris. Dictionary of women artists: an international dictionary of women artists born before 1900. Boston, G. K. Hall, [1985]. 851p. il. **BE175**

Includes biographical sketches of "more than 21,000 women painters, sculptors, printmakers, and illustrators born before 1900, regardless of the scarcity of information about them."—*Pref.* Gives references to sources of information at the end of each entry. Bibliography, p.781–851. N43.P47

Roberts, Laurance P. A dictionary of Japanese artists: painting, sculpture, ceramics, prints, lacquer. Foreword by John M. Rosenfield. Tokyo and N.Y., Weatherhill, [1976]. 299p. **BE176**

"This dictionary limits itself to artists who were born before 1900, or, if born later, who died before 1972."—*Pref.* Entry is by the most common form of the artist's name, with an index of alternate forms and one of Japanese characters. For each artist is given: all forms of name, dates, education, career, public collections in which represented, references to items in the bibliography (p.223–32) which provide fuller information. Brief glossary of terms. N7358.R6

Thieme, Ulrich and **Becker, Felix.** Allgemeines Lexikon der bildenden Künstler von der Antike bis zur Gegenwart, unter Mitwirkung von etwa 400 Fachgelehrten des In- und Auslandes. Leipzig, Seemann, 1907–50. 37v. **BE177**

Binder's title: Künstler Lexikon.
Imprint varies: v.1–4, Leipzig, Engelmann. Statement of contributors varies. v.16–37 ed. by Hans Vollmer.
Contents: v.1–36, A–Z; v.37, Meister mit Notnamen und Monogrammisten.
The most complete and authoritative dictionary of painters, sculptors, engravers, etchers, and architects. Locations of works of art are frequently given. Good bibliographies; the longer articles are signed. Some 400 contributing specialists.
Includes some figures who were living at time of compilation, but Vollmer (below) is the principal source for 20th-century artists. N40.T4

Vollmer, Hans. Allgemeines Lexikon der bildenden Künstler des XX. Jahrhunderts. Unter Mitwirkung von Fachgelehrten des In- und Auslandes. Leipzig, Seemann, 1953–62. 6v. **BE178**

Half-title: Künstlerlexikon des XX. Jahrhunderts.
Contents: Bd.1–5, A–Z. Nachträge, A–G; Bd.6, Nachträge, H–Z.
A continuation of Thieme, above. Includes some overlap from the 19th century. Gives brief biographical notes, lists of works, and bibliographical references. N40.V6

Who's who in art. Biographies of leading men and women in the world of art today. 1st ed.– . London, Art Trade Pr., 1927– . Biennial. **BE179**

Frequency of early editions varies: 1st–3d ed., 1927, 1929, 1934; 4th ed. 1948.
Includes artists, designers, craftsmen, critics, writers, teachers, collectors, and curators, with appendixes of monograms and signatures, and obituary. British names predominate. N40.W6

United States

Cederholm, Theresa Dickason, comp. Afro-American artists: a bio-bibliographical directory. [Boston], Boston Pub. Lib., 1973, 348p. **BE180**

Covers contemporary and earlier artists "from the slave craftsman of the 18th century to the present."—*Pref.* Gives biographical data, lists of works (with dates when known), exhibits, and sources of further information. Bibliography of sources, p.325–48.
N6538.N5C42

Cummings, Paul. A dictionary of contemporary American artists. 4th ed. N.Y., St. Martin's Pr., [1982]. 653p. **BE181**

1st ed. 1966.
Brief information on 923 artists, the majority of them still living. Indicates where and with whom the artist studied, awards, exhibitions and group shows, collections in which his works are found, and selected bibliographical references. Pronunciation of unusual names is given in the index of artists. Bibliography, p.611–53.
N6536.C8

Dawdy, Doris Ostrander. Artists of the American West: a biographical dictionary. Chicago, Sage Books, [1974–85]. 3v. **BE182**

Publisher varies; subtitle varies.
Identifies more than 4,000 artists, both American and foreign, all born before 1900, who worked in the West, are known to be painters, illustrators or printmakers, or who traveled in the West and made pictorial records of what they saw. Entries give date and place of birth and death (when known), standard art reference work which includes information on the individual, brief biography, and collection which includes the artist's work. Bibliography in each volume; index to the set in v.3. N6536.D38

Fielding, Mantle. Mantle Fielding's Dictionary of American painters, sculptors & engravers. New completely rev., enl. and updated ed. Ed. by Glenn B. Opitz. [Poughkeepsie, N.Y.], Apollo, [1983]. 1041p. **BE183**

1st ed. 1926; repr. with addenda, 1965.
A compendium of biographical sketches ranging from the very briefest information to fairly detailed lists of exhibitions and specific works in the collections of individual museums, etc. About 10,000 entries in this edition, covering major and minor American artists of the 18th–20th centuries. N6536.F5

Index of twentieth century artists. v.1–4, no.7, Oct. 1933–April 1937. N.Y., College Art Assoc., 1933–37. 4v. **BE184**

Each monthly number contains detailed information about one or more American artists, including for each artist: biographical data, awards and honors, membership in associations, museums containing his work, exhibitions in which he was represented, and bibliographical references—with reproductions of his work—in books and periodicals. The last number (Sept.) of each year is called a supplement, and consists of additions and revisions of material previously published. Cumulated index to v.1–3 in v.3. Total number of artists in the set, 120.
An "authorized reprint edition" (N.Y., Arno Pr., 1970) in 1v. includes a new cumulative index. N1.I5

New York Historical Society. Dictionary of artists in America, 1564–1860, by George C. Groce and David H. Wallace. New Haven, Yale Univ. Pr., 1957. 759p. **BE185**

"A documented biographical dictionary of painters, draftsmen, sculptors, engravers, lithographers, and allied artists, either amateur or professional, native or foreign-born, who worked within the present continental limits of the United States between the years 1564 and 1860 inclusive."—*Introd.* Includes almost 11,000 names. Bibliography, p.713–59. N6536.N4

Who's who in American art. v.1– , 1936/37– . N.Y., Bowker, 1935– . Biennial (irregular). **BE186**

Originally issued by the American Federation of Arts; from 1978, prep. by Jaques Cattell Press.
v.1–4, 1936/37–1940/47, published as pt.2 of the *American art annual* (v.33–36, 1936–1940/47; BE134*n*).
Early issues had subtitle (varies): A biographical directory of selected artists in the United States working in the media of painting, sculpture, graphic arts, illustration, design, and the handicrafts.
A biographical directory of painters, sculptors, graphic artists,

craftsmen, historians, critics, editors, museum personnel, educators, lecturers, etc. v.2 contains a Necrology, Oct. 1927–Oct. 1935, which continues the Necrology, 1897–1927, in v.25 of the *American art annual.* The Obituaries sections continue that record. v.4, p.611–53, contains a bibliography of American art by Elizabeth McCausland. Now includes art personalities of the United States, Canada, and Mexico. Arrangement has varied; from 1978 the biographies are in a single alphabet, with geographical and professional indexes, and a necrology. N6536.W5

Artists' signatures

Caplan, H. H. The classified directory of artists' signatures, symbols and monograms. [Enl. and rev. ed.] London, George Prior; Detroit, Gale, 1982. 873p. **BE187**

1st ed. 1976.

Introductory matter in English, French, German, Spanish, Italian.

Intended as a comprehensive dictionary offering (1) facsimiles of artists' signatures arranged alphabetically by name; (2) facsimiles of monograms arranged alphabetically under the first or uppermost letter of the monogram, plus an unclassified section of monograms; (3) reproductions of illegible or misleading signatures arranged under the first recognizable letter, again with an unclassified section; and (4) symbols arranged by general shape, with irregular ones entered at the end of the section.

The review in *Booklist* (80:411) concludes that "Libraries owning the first edition must decide whether or not their patrons are likely to need to consult a new edition of a work which has a heavy emphasis on lesser-known British artists and a very steep price." N45.C36

Symbolism in art

❖Works on symbolism in art are many and various, and a generous selection is given below. Libraries holding the older works by Anna Brownell Jameson, *The history of Our Lord as exemplified in works of art* (2d ed. London, Longmans, 1865. 2v.), *Legends of the Madonna* (Boston, Houghton, 1896. 372p.), *Legends of the monastic orders as represented in the fine arts* (2d ed. London, Longmans, 1900. 461p.), and *Sacred and legendary art* (Boston, Houghton, 1896. 2v.), will continue to find them useful for questions on Christian symbols, but will want to supplement them with one or more of the titles listed here. For related works *see also* Mythology, p.744; Classical Antiquities, p.983; Saints, p.364.

General

Bernen, Satia and **Bernen, Robert.** Myth & religion in European painting, 1270–1700. The stories as the artists knew them. N.Y., Braziller, [1973]. 280p. **BE188**

Treats, in dictionary arrangement, "stories of 850 common subjects of museum painting . . .: mythology, ancient history, Italian poetry, saints' lives, the Bible."—*Pref.* Stories are summarized briefly, with reference to biblical source or classical author usually indicated. ND1288.B47

Daniel, Howard. Encyclopedia of themes and subjects in painting; mythological, biblical, historical, literary, allegorical and topical. N.Y., Abrams, [1971]. 252p. il. **BE189**

"The largest part of this book comprises a dictionary of the most common recurring subjects to be found in European painting from the early Renaissance to the mid-19th century."—*Introd.* Most of the entries are illustrated by paintings reproduced in black-and-white. ND1288.D3

Droulers, Eug. [pseud. of Eugène de Seyn]. Dictionnaire des attributs, allégories, emblèmes et symboles. Turnhout, Brepols, [1948?]. 281p. il. **BE190**

Alphabetical arrangement, including names of people, attributes, allegorical figures, etc. Definitions vary in length from a few sentences to several paragraphs. The illustrations in the text and in a section at the end are indexed, and there is a bibliography of sources. AZ108.S7

Hall, James. Dictionary of subjects and symbols in art. Rev. ed. London, Murray; N.Y., Harper & Row, 1979. 349p. **BE191**

1st ed. 1974.

A basic dictionary offering entries for persons, picture titles, and objects and attributes in Christian and classical art. Clear definitions; liberal use of cross references. Except for some additions to the bibliography and a 4-page supplementary index, this edition differs little from the first. N7560.H34

Henkel, Arthur and **Schöne, Albrecht.** Emblemata; Handbuch zur Sinnbildkunst des XVI. und XVII. Jahrhunderts. Im Auftrage der Göttinger Akad. d. Wissenschaften. Stuttgart, J. B. Metzler, 1967. 2196col. il. **BE192**

———— ———— Supplement der Erstausgabe. Stuttgart, 1976. ccxvii p.

Reissued 1976 as "Erg. Neuausg." with supplement at front.

Reproduces emblems drawn from 45 collections published during the 16th and 17th centuries. Emblems are grouped by category (e.g., macrocosm, the four elements, plants, animals); reference is given to original source. Motto Register; Bild Register; Bedeutungs-Register. The supplement is a "Bibliographie zur Emblemforschung." N7740.H53

Lexicon iconographicum mythologiae classicae (LIMC). [Rédaction, Hans Christoph Ackermann, Jean-Robert Gisler] Zurich, Artemis, [1981–84]. v.1–2 (in 4v.) il. (In progress) **BE193**

To be in 7v. of two parts each (text and plates), plus a supplement.

To answer the need "for a collective work devoted to the iconography of classical mythology in the widest sense of the term," this exhaustive and splendidly produced dictionary "is designed to give an account of the present state of knowledge about the iconography of Greek, Etruscan, and Roman mythology" (*Introd.*) as well as that of neighboring cultures. Covers from the end of the Mycenean period to the beginning of the Christian era.

An alphabetical arrangement of signed articles in English, German, French or Italian. Entry comprises: introduction (myth and literary sources); bibliography; catalog (classification, description, date, museum references, etc.); iconographical commentary. Cross references. Excellent plates; line drawings. The final volume is to include an index. N7760.L49

Marle, Raimond van. Iconographie de l'art profane au Moyen-Âge et à la Renaissance, et la décoration des demeures. La Haye, Nijhoff, 1931–32. 2v. il. **BE194**

Contents: [v.1], La vie quotidienne; [v.2], Allégories et symboles. Includes bibliographies and many illustrations. N5970.M35

Pigler, Andor. Barockthemen: eine Auswahl von Verzeichnissen zur Ikonographie des 17. und 18. Jahrhunderts. 2., erw. Aufl. Budapest, Verlag der Ungarischen Akademie der Wissenschaften, 1974. 3v. il. **BE195**

1st ed. 1956.

A listing of themes represented in the baroque art of the 17th and 18th centuries, with references to the artists who have treated them (including artists of the 15th and 16th centuries); indication of where the work may be found; and notation where an illustration may be located in book or periodical. Usually includes the artists of Italy, France, Germany, and the Netherlands.

v.1 contains religious representations; v.2, secular representations in Greek and Roman history, legends, and folklore, and in general history, allegories, etc. Index to v.1–2 in v.2; v.3 is devoted to plates. N6410.P5

Sill, Gertrude Grace. A handbook of symbols in Christian art. N.Y., Macmillan, 1975. 241p. il. **BE196**

A dictionary of Christian symbols arranged under broad headings such as "Angels," "Vices and virtues," etc. Intended as a basic reference guide for museum visitors, tourists, and students, and for the home library. Indexed. N8010.S54

Vries, Ad de. Dictionary of symbols and imagery. 2d ed. Amsterdam, North-Holland Publ. Co., [1976]. 515p. **BE197**

1st ed. 1974. A 1981 issue (515p.) is termed "3d, rev. ed."

Intends to supply "associations which have been evoked by certain words, signs, etc. in Western civilization in the past, and which may float to the surface again tomorrow."—*Pref.* Includes allegories, metaphors, signs, images, etc. Emphasis is on literary, mythological, religious, and proverbial use rather than graphic representation. BL600.V74

Waters, Clara (Erskine) Clement. Handbook of legendary and mythological art. 23d ed. Boston, Houghton, 1892 [c1871–86]. 575p. il. (Repr.: Detroit, Gale, 1969) **BE198**

1st ed. 1871.

Contents: Symbolism in art; Legends and stories illustrated in art; Legends of place; Ancient myths illustrated in art. Catalogue of pictures.

The first two parts incorporate the text of the author's *Handbook of Christian symbols and stories of the saints as illustrated in art* (1886). N7760.W4

Whittlesey, Eunice S. Symbols and legends in Western art; a museum guide. N.Y., Scribner's, [1972]. 367p. il. **BE199**

A handbook "for the layman who wishes to have with him [on visits to art galleries and museums] a quick explanation, or refresher, of the subject matter that he is most likely to encounter" (*Introd.*)—Greek and Roman myths and legends, biblical and religious subjects, etc. Brief entries in dictionary arrangement. Cross references. M7740.W53

Christian

Bles, Arthur de. How to distinguish the saints in art by their costumes, symbols and attributes. N.Y., Art Culture Publ., 1925. 168p. il. **BE200**

Contents: (1) Chapters 1–12, symbolism in general and for different groups, e.g., Virgin Mary, Evangelists, monastic orders, etc., with illustrations and explanations of pictures showing symbols; (2) Appendixes: Alphabetical table of martyrdoms; Tables of saints classified by habitual costume; Saints classified by categories; Alphabetical table of symbols and attributes with names of those who bear them; Chronological tables of bishops and popes of Rome; List of illustrations; General index. N8080.B5

Child, Heather and **Colles, Dorothy.** Christian symbols, ancient & modern: a handbook for students. London, Bell; N.Y., Scribner, 1971. 270p. il. **BE201**

Concerned with "the use of visual Christian symbols in the service of the Church."—*Introd.* Uses background and descriptive text with line drawings and photographs. Includes chapters on: The Cross; The Trinity; Images of Christ; The Virgin Mary; The Nativity of Jesus Christ; The Holy Spirit; The Eucharist; Angels; Good and evil, etc. Indexed. BV150.C53

Drake, Maurice and **Drake, Wilfred.** Saints and their emblems. London, Laurie; Philadelphia, Lippincott, 1916. 235p. il. **BE202**

Includes: (1) Dictionary of saints; (2) Dictionary of emblems; (3) Appendixes: Patriarchs and prophets; Sibyls; Patron saints of arts, trades, and professions; Other patron saints. N8080.D7

Ferguson, George Wells. Signs & symbols in Christian art. With illustrations from paintings of the Renaissance. [2d ed.] London, Zwemmer, [1955]. 346p. il. **BE203**

First published N.Y., Oxford Univ. Pr., [1954] (346p.).

A basic work for the student or for quick reference. Uses simple, direct language, line drawings, and reproductions of works of art to explain the symbols and illustrate their use. Indexed. N7830.F37

Künstle, Karl. Ikonographie der christlichen Kunst. Freiburg im Breisgau, Herder, 1926–28. 2v. il. (v.1, 1928) **BE204**

v.1 discusses: (1) the history of symbolism in Christian art from the early church through the Middle Ages; (2) animal and other nature symbolism; (3) representations of subjects from the Old and New Testaments. v.2, which has a separate title page, *Ikonographie der Heiligen,* is a dictionary of saints, with brief biographical data; indication of saints' emblems; how and where depicted in mosaics, paintings, etc.; and bibliographical references to printed descriptions of these representations. N7830.K93

Lexikon der christlichen Ikonographie. Hrsg. von Engelbert Kirschbaum, in Zusammenarbeit mit Günter Bandmann [et al.]. Rom, Herder, 1968–76. 8v. il. **BE205**

Contents: v.1–4, Allgemeine Ikonographie, A–Z (Nachträge in v.4); v.5–8, Ikonographie der Heiligen: A–Z, Register.

v.5–8 ed. by Wolfgang Braunfels.

An impressive work with signed articles, bibliographies, and numerous illustrations.

Hans Aurenhammer's *Lexikon der christlichen Ikonographie,* which was being published in parts (Wien, Hollinek, 1959–67), was abandoned after Lfg.6, which covered through "Christus." BV150.L4

Réau, Louis. Iconographie de l'art chrétien. Paris, Presses Universitaires de France, 1955–59. 3v. in 6. il. **BE206**

Contents: v.1, Introduction générale; v.2, Iconographie de la Bible: pt.1, Ancien Testament. pt.2, Nouveau Testament; v.3, Iconographie des saints (in 3v.).

Classifies iconographic themes, indicates their variations and evolution, and lists principal works of art representing them. Covers medieval Western and Byzantine art. Includes bibliographies and many illustrations. N7830.R37

Schiller, Gertrud. Ikonographie der christlichen Kunst. [Gütersloh], Gütersloher Verlagshaus G. Mohn, [1966–80]. v.1–4$^{1-2}$. il. (In progress?) **BE207**

Contents: Bd.1, Inkarnation, Kindheit, Taufe, Versuchung, Verklärung, Wirken und Wunder Christi; Bd.2, Die Passion Jesu Christi; Bd.3, Die Auferstehung und Erhörung Christi; Bd.4^1, Die Kirche; Bd.4^2, Maria.

Text and illustrations (600 to 700 in each volume) in separate sections. The text of v.1–2 deals chronologically, and in some detail, with the background and events of the life of Christ, providing references to the biblical sources together with discussion of treatment of the various themes in art. Bibliographical footnotes provide references to specialized studies. The two parts of v.4 treat the Church and Mary. A "Registerbeiheft zu den Bänden 1 bis 4, 2" ed. by Rupert Schreiner, was published in 1980. v.1 is now available in a "3. durchges. Aufl." (1981); v.2 in a "2. Aufl." (1983).

An English translation of v.1–2 appeared as:

——— Iconography of Christian art. Tr. by Janet Seligman. Greenwich, Conn., N.Y. Graphic Soc., [1971–72]. 2v. il. **BE208**

Contents: v.1, Christ's incarnation, childhood, baptism, temptation, transfiguration, works, and miracles; v.2, The passion of Christ.

v.1 is a translation of the 2d ed. (1969) of *Ikonographie der christlichen Kunst* (above); v.2 is translated from the German edition of 1968. N7830.S35132

Webber, Frederick Roth. Church symbolism; an explanation of the more important symbols of the Old and New Testament, the primitive, the mediaeval and the modern church . . . introd. by Ralph Adams Cram. 2d ed. rev. Cleveland, J. H. Jansen, 1938. 413p. il. (Repr: Detroit, Gale, 1971) **BE209**

Glossary of the more important symbols, p.357–88; bibliography, p.389–94. BV150.W4

Buddhist

Akiyama, Aisaburo. Buddhist hand-symbol. Yokohama, Yoshikawa Book Store, 1939. 86p. il.   **BE210**

Text in English and Japanese. An illustration is given for each symbol.

Bhattacharyya, Benoytosh. The Indian Buddhist iconography, mainly based on the Sādhanamālā and cognate Tāntric texts of rituals. [2d ed rev. and enl.] Calcutta, Mukhopadhyay, 1958. 478p. il.   **BE211**

1st ed., Oxford Univ. Pr., 1924.
This comprehensive work is illustrated by more than 350 pictures and line drawings.

Chinese

Williams, Charles Alfred Speed. Encyclopedia of Chinese symbolism and art motives; an alphabetical compendium of legends and beliefs as reflected in the manners and customs of the Chinese throughout history. N.Y., Julian, 1960. 468p.   **BE212**

"A re-issue of the . . . work originally titled *Outlines of Chinese symbolism and art motives* published 1931, rev. 1932."
GR335.W53

Hindu

Banerjea, Jitendra Nath. The development of Hindu iconography. [2d ed. rev. and enl. Calcutta], Univ. of Calcutta, 1956. 653p. il.   **BE213**

1st ed. 1941.
A comprehensive history dealing with the development and manifestations of Hindu iconography from ancient times.

Gopinātha Rāu, T. A. Elements of Hindu iconography. Madras, Law Printing House, 1914–16. 2v. in 4. il.   **BE214**

In Sanskrit and English.   BL1201.G7

Other signs and symbols

Dictionnaire des symboles: mythes, rêves, coutumes, gestes, formes, figures, couleurs, nombres. Sous la direction de Jean Chevalier. [Paris], Robert Laffont, [1982]. 842p. il.   **BE215**

For full information *see* CF53.

Dreyfuss, Henry. Symbol sourcebook; an authoritative guide to international graphic symbols. N.Y., McGraw-Hill, [1972]. 292p.   **BE216**

Symbols are grouped according to subject areas with an index by objects and ideas represented.   AZ108.D74

Lehner, Ernst. Symbols, signs and signets. Cleveland, World, [1950]. 221p. il.   **BE217**

No attempt at completeness is claimed. Clear reproductions of signs and symbols are given under such headings as "Symbolic gods and deities," "Astronomy and astrology," "Heraldry," "Monsters," etc.; each section is preceded by a brief introduction. Some sections are indexed, but there is no general index. Bibliography, p.217–21.
AZ108.L4

Shepherd, Walter. Shepherd's Glossary of graphic signs and symbols. London, Dent, [1971]. 597p.   **BE218**

An attempt at formal classification of "the written marks by which mankind records ideas."—*Pref.* Emphasis is on signs used in technical literature, but attention is given to signs encountered in inscriptions, manuscripts, maps, charts, and various alphabets.
AZ108.S53

Whittick, Arnold. Symbols: signs and their meaning and uses in design. 2d ed. London, L. Hill, 1971. 383p. 78 pl. il.   **BE219**

1st ed. (1960) had title: *Symbols, signs and their meaning.*
Introductory discussion of the types and meaning of symbolism is followed by sections on "Symbolism in its precise and applied forms, and its practical uses," "Individual and collective expression—instinctive, creative and imaginative symbolism," and an "Encyclopaedic dictionary" of traditional and familiar symbols. Confined mainly to Western symbols and uses. This edition adds a chapter on postage stamps. Indexed.   AZ108.W45

Art reproductions

New York Graphic Society. Fine art reproductions of old & modern masters; a comprehensive illustrated catalog of art through the ages. Greenwich, Conn., New York Graphic Society, [1980]. 576p., 17p. il. (Repr. 1984)   **BE220**

1st ed. 1946.
A catalog of color prints published by this company. Arranged by broad group (i.e., Old masters, 20th-century painting, American painting, etc.), with index by artist and selected subject categories for anonymous works. Each entry includes: a small color reproduction, name and dates of the artist, his nationality if not indicated by group, title with date and location of the original painting, catalog number, size and price of the print. Indexes of classified subject matter and of artists.
The 1984 reprint includes a supplement of more than 70 new reproductions.   NE1860.N4A32

Pierson, William Harvey and **Davidson, Martha.** Arts of the United States: a pictorial survey. N.Y., McGraw-Hill, [1960]. 452p. il.   **BE221**

"Based on a collection of color slides assembled by the University of Georgia under a grant by Carnegie Corporation of New York."—*title page.*
The Carnegie project undertook: (1) to compile and document material representing the history of American art in most of its phases from the beginning to the present; (2) to select from this material some 4,000 works to be reproduced in high-quality color slides, intended for use in schools, museums, and libraries here and abroad. The catalog of these slides—arranged by subject and giving number, identifying information, and a small reproduction in black-and-white for each entry—is preceded by essays on each subject group written by the specialists who chose the material. An index of artists, titles, and subjects.   N6505.P55

United Nations Educational, Scientific and Cultural Organization. Catalogue de reproductions de peintures antérieures à 1860 et quinze plans d'expositions. Catalogue of reproductions of paintings prior to 1860 with fifteen projects for exhibitions. Catalogo de reproducciones de pinturas anteriores a 1860 y quinze proyectos de exposiciones. 10th ed. Paris, Unesco, [1979]. 346p.   **BE222**

1st ed. 1950. Revised irregularly.   ND49.C37

——— Catalogue de reproductions de peintures 1860 à 1979 et dix-sept plans d'expositions. Catalogue of reproductions of paintings 1860 to 1979 with seventeen projects of exhibitions. 11ᵉ éd. mise à jour. Paris, Presses de l'Unesco, 1981. 275p. il.   **BE223**

1st ed. 1949. Revised irregularly. Early editions had title *Catalogue de reproductions en couleurs de peintures.*
Title page and preface in French, English, and Spanish.
Choice of prints in the above catalogs is based on fidelity of color reproduction, significance of artist, and importance of the painting. The entries, arranged by artist, include a small reproduction in black-and-white; the name of the painter; dates and places of birth and death; the title of the original and its date, medium, size, and location. For the reproductions are given: the printing process, size, publisher, price and Unesco archives number. Index of painters and lists of publishers and printers.   ND47.U53

—— Répertoire international des archives photographiques d'oeuvres d'art. International directory of photographic archives of works of art. Paris, Dunod, 1950–54. 2v. **BE224**

v.1, 1950, gives information on 1,195 photographic collections from 87 countries with a supplement listing 19 additional collections. v.2 adds 100 collections in 24 countries not mentioned in v.1. Each volume is arranged by the French names of the countries, and includes indexes of subjects and of countries. N4000.U5

Restoration and conservation

See also BE44.

Bullock, Orin M. The restoration manual; an illustrated guide to the preservation and restoration of old buildings. Norwalk, Conn., Silvermine Publ., [1966]. 181p. il. **BE225**

"Written for the Committee on Historic Buildings of the American Institute of Architects."—*title page.*

Outlines procedures which "apply in general to the restoration of structures of any period, in any location, and of any magnitude."—*Introd.* An appendix reprints a series of papers on specific aspects of restoration. Also includes a glossary of selected terms, and a bibliography.

A 1983 reprint in paperback (N.Y., Van Nostrand Reinhold) adds a brief index, p.181–82. NA705.B77

The historic preservation yearbook. Ed.1– , 1984/85– . Bethesda, Md., Adler & Adler, [1984]– . Annual. **BE226**

Publ. in cooperation with National Trust for Historic Preservation.

Subtitle: A documentary record of significant policy developments and issues.

Documents are interspersed with surveys and summaries of developments on a wide range of preservation issues. Various contributors. Appendixes include a directory of degree programs in preservation. Indexed.

Markowitz, Arnold L. Historic preservation: a guide to information sources. Detroit, Gale, [1980]. 279p. (Art and architecture information guide ser., v.13) **BE227**

An annotated bibliography of books, pamphlets, dissertations, and whole issues of journals. Aims to cite, "fairly comprehensively, the classic works and the indispensable works, and, selectively, examples of the wide variety of publications related to the many aspects of the topic."—*Introd.* Primarily English-language publications of the 20th century (to 1978). Author, organization, title, and subject indexes. A favorable review appears in *Booklist* 77:991 (Mar. 1, 1981). Z1251.A2M37

National register of historic places, 1969– . Wash., National Park Service, [1969–]. Irregular. **BE228**

Prep. in the Office of Archeology and Historic Preservation.

Describes places designated as national historic landmarks or preserved by the National Park Service. Gives name, location, historical connection, etc. Geographical arrangement by state, then by county.

Detailed information and photographs from the files amassed for preparation of the register have been reproduced on microfiche by Chadwyck-Healey Inc., Alexandria, Va. Covering material through 1982, the set comprises about 3,200 fiches and carries the title *National register of historic places.* All types of properties of historical significance are included—archeological sites, neighborhoods, buildings, etc. E159.N34

New York University. Institute of Fine Arts. Conservation Center. Library catalog of the Conservation Center. . . . Boston, G. K. Hall, 1980. 934p. **BE229**

Reproduces the catalog cards for a major collection of resources on the restoration and conservation of works of art. Z5945.N49

Smith, John F. A critical bibliography of building conservation: historic towns, buildings, their furnishings and fittings. London, Mansell, 1978. **BE229a**

Comp. at the Institute of Advanced Architectural Studies, University of York, with a grant from the Radcliffe Trust.

A classed listing of books, journal articles, technical reports, and legislative documents dealing with the conservation of the "built environment" (*Foreword*), from towns to landscaping and gardens. Emphasis is on the situation in Great Britain; cutoff date is 1976. Annotations; place name index; author index.

Tubesing, Richard L. Architectural preservation in the United States, 1941–1975: a bibliography of federal, state, and local government publications. N.Y., Garland, 1978. 452p. **BE230**

"Developed from a publication of similar title but more limited scope published in 1975 by the Council of Planning Librarians as Exchange bibliography, 811–12."—*Pref.* The present bibliography deals with scholarly works, statistical reports, manuals and guides, tourist brochures published by federal, state, and local governments, Jan. 1, 1941–Dec. 31, 1975. (Congressional publications are excluded.) "Preservation" is here restricted to "those structures or their ruins which are still standing or which have been at least partially reconstructed." Topical arrangement (e.g., "Historic preservation plans, programs, policies and procedures," "Preservation technology bibliography, graphics, and audio-visual material," "Historic site brochures and maps"), usually subdivided geographically. An appendix gives names and addresses of federal and state agencies concerned with historic preservation. Indexed. Z5942.T82

ARCHITECTURE

Bibliography

American Association of Architectural Bibliographers. Papers. Charlottesville, Univ. Pr. of Virginia, 1965–79. v.1–13. Annual (irregular). **BE231**

Publisher varies.

A bibliographical series superseding the Association's *Publications* (no.1–27, 1954–64). Presents bibliographies of individual architects and of specific eras and aspects of architecture. Ceased publication. Z5941.A5

—— —— Index, v.1–10, 1965–1973. Charlottesville, Univ. Pr. of Virginia, 1975. 311p.

Issued as v.11 of the *Papers* series (above).

Mainly an index of authors and titles of works cited in the bibliographies.

Archer, John. The literature of British domestic architecture, 1715–1842. Cambridge, Mass., MIT Pr., [1985]. 1078p. il. **BE232**

" . . . approaches British domestic architecture in the eighteenth and early nineteenth centuries through the literary output of architects and others concerned with domestic design."—*Introd.* A lengthy introductory essay is followed by detailed bibliographic descriptions of the books, with commentary on the text and plates. Locates copies. Includes a short-title list of additional publications; list of printers, publishers, and booksellers. Indexed.

Z5944.G7A7

Bibliographie zur Architektur im 19 Jahrhundert; die Aufsätze in den deutschsprachigen Architektur-Zeitschriften 1789–1918. Ed., Stephen Waetzoldt; comp., Verena Haas. Nendeln, Liechtenstein, KTO Pr., 1977. 8v. **BE233**

"The bibliography lists all contributions on construction projects, reconstruction, renovation, design contests, architectural theory and criticism, as well as the technical aspects of building, which appeared in the 129 most important German-language journals on architecture and the construction industry published between 1789 and 1918 in the German and Austro-Hungarian empires and in

Switzerland."—*Pref.* Topically arranged by type of architecture. v.8 is an index by authors, by architects, and by places.

Columbia University. Libraries. Avery Architectural Library. Catalog. 2d ed., enl. [Adolf K. Placzek, Avery Librarian] Boston, G. K. Hall, 1968. 19v. **BE234**

———— ———— Supplement 1–3. Boston, G. K. Hall, 1972–77. 4v., 4v., 3v.

A printed catalog of the collection first appeared in 1895; an earlier photoreproduction of the catalog cards was published in 1958 in 6v.

The Avery Library is one of the outstanding architectural collections in the United States. This photographic reproduction of all cards in the Library's catalog includes not only the Avery collection but all architectural and art books on the Columbia University campus. With the three supplements, reflects books and periodicals cataloged through May 1977. Z5945.C652

Cuthbert, John A., Ward, Barry and **Keeler, Maggie.** Vernacular architecture in America: a selective bibliography. Boston, G. K. Hall, 1985. 145p. il. **BE235**

Focuses on "modern literature pertaining to architecture in the American folk tradition."—*Pref.* An alphabetical author listing of books and periodicals, with index of authors, abbreviated titles, and subjects. Z5944.U5C87

Ehresmann, Donald L. Architecture: a bibliographic guide to basic reference works, histories, and handbooks. Littleton, Colo., Libraries Unlimited, 1984. 338p. **BE236**

An annotated bibliography of "books written in English and Western European languages that were published between 1875 and 1980 and are accessible in libraries in the United States. . . . Books for the general reader and undergraduate are included together with exhaustive reference works and scholarly histories, handbooks, and special studies."—*Pref.* Sections for reference works and for general histories and handbooks are followed by chronological (primitive and prehistoric through modern) and geographical (European, Oriental, New World, Africa and Oceania) sections. Author/title and subject indexes. Forms a companion to the compiler's *Fine arts* (BE2) and *Applied and decorative arts* (BF3) bibliographies. Z5941.E38

Hall, Robert de Zouche. A bibliography on vernacular architecture. Newton Abbot, [Eng.], David & Charles, [1972]. 191p. **BE237**

An extensive classified bibliography on "the study of houses and other buildings, which, in their form and materials, represent the unselfconscious tradition of a region rather than ideas of architectural style."—*Introd.* Regional and local studies listed are confined to the British Isles. Author index. Z5944.G7H3

A current bibliography of vernacular architecture. v.1– , 1970/76– . [York, North Yorkshire], Vernacular Architecture Group, 1979– . Irregular. **BE238**

D. J. H. Michelmore, ed.
Planned as an occasional supplement to Hall's bibliography (above); follows the classified arrangement of that work.

Hitchcock, Henry Russell. American architectural books; a list of books, portfolios, and pamphlets on architecture and related subjects published in America before 1895. New expanded ed., with a new introduction by Adolf K. Placzek. N.Y., DaCapo Pr., 1976. 150p. **BE239**

1st ed. 1938–39. A 1962 ed. was a reprint of a 3d revised edition, 1946, which listed 1,461 items, distinguishing editions and locating copies in more than 130 public and private libraries. It included a new preface offering 30 emendations (8 being new titles or editions, the rest minor corrections of collations and imprints).

The 1976 ed. reprints the text of the 1962 ed. with a new introduction and "A listing of architectural periodicals before 1895" by Adolf K. Placzek, and an appendix, "Chronological short-title list of Henry Russell Hitchcock's 'American architectural books'" comp. under the direction of William H. Jordy (originally issued as *Publication* no.4 [Oct. 1955] of the American Association of Architectural Bibliographers). Z5941.H67

Information sources in architecture. Valerie J. Bradfield, ed. London, Butterworths, [1983]. 419p. il. **BE240**

Intended for the professional architect and researcher, the work "attempts to review the coverage of information over the whole of the construction processes, showing the appropriate sources of information and access to them."—*Pref.* Includes contributed chapters on libraries, information retrieval techniques, computerized information retrieval, trade literature, government publications, developing and executing a design, managing the design and the office, conservation, etc. Indexed. NA2540.I53

Kamen, Ruth H. British and Irish architectural history: a bibliography and guide to sources of information. London, Architectural Pr., [1981]. 249p. **BE241**

Offers "descriptions of books, periodicals and periodical articles, indexes and abstracts, collections, organisations and services . . . designed to assist students, scholars, researchers, teachers in schools and universities, librarians, local historians, picture researchers and the general public in identifying and using the sources available when seeking information about British and Irish architecture."—*p.1.* Topical arrangement with index of authors, organizations, subjects, and titles.

King, David James Cathcart. Castellarium Anglicanum: an index and bibliography of the castles in England, Wales, and the Islands. Millwood, N.Y., Kraus Internat. Pubns., 1983. 2v. (676p.) il. **BE242**

An inventory of all castles of England and Wales (including "possible" and vanished as well as extant ones), arranged by county. Each is described; reference to a contemporary source is given; and a bibliography of secondary sources to 1979 is provided. Name and place indexes; glossary. DA660.K54

Marshall, Howard Wight. American folk architecture; a selected bibliography. [Wash.], American Folklife Ctr., Library of Congress, 1981. 79p. (Pubns. of the American Folklife Ctr., 8) **BE243**

A bibliography of books and periodical articles in classed arrangement (including regional divisions). Fieldwork, museums and preservation are also considered, and there is a list of relevant periodicals. Not indexed. Z5944.U5M38

Phillips, Margaret. Guide to architectural information. Lansdale, Pa., Design Data Center, 1971. 89p. **BE244**

A guide to the most useful and essential reference materials in architecture much of it of interest to art historians and urban planners. Arranged by type of reference work: indexes, bibliographies, dictionaries, directories, handbooks, and some unconventional sources. Subject index. Z7914.B9P47

Roos, Frank John. Bibliography of early American architecture; writings on architecture constructed before 1860 in eastern and central United States. Urbana, Univ. of Illinois Pr., 1968. 389p. **BE245**

A revised and updated edition of the author's *Writings on early American architecture* (Columbus, Ohio, 1943). This edition includes 4,377 items. Z5944.U5R6

Royal Institute of British Architects, London. Library. Catalogue of the . . . library. London, 1937–38. 2v. **BE246**

Contents: v.1, Authors; v.2, Classified index and alphabetical subject index of books and manuscripts.

The catalog of an important library which had trebled in size since its preceding general catalog was published, 1889–99.
Z5945.R88

Senkevitch, Anatole. Soviet architecture, 1917–1962: a bibliographical guide to source material. Charlottesville, Univ. Pr. of Virginia, [1974]. 284p. **BE247**

A selective bibliography listing more than 1,000 titles of books and articles on the history and theory of Soviet architecture, especially in the R.S.F.S.R. Although Western-language materials are included, the emphasis is on Russian-language publications. Topical arrangement, with names and titles index. Annotated.

Especially useful is the introductory discussion of resources available in American libraries.   Z5944.R9S45

Sharp, Dennis. Sources of modern architecture: a critical bibliography. [2d ed., rev. and enl.] London, Granada, [1981]. 192p. il.   **BE248**

1st ed. 1967.

In three sections: (1) "Biographical bibliography," which provides biographical sketches of individual architects and references to writings about them; (2) "Subject bibliography," subdivided by period and concerned with general works on modern architecture and theory; and (3) "National bibliography," which lists books about national trends in modern architecture. Select list of architectural periodicals; index of architects and authors.   Z5941.5.S47

Sokol, David M. American architecture and art; a guide to information sources. Detroit, Gale, 1976. 341p. (American studies information guide ser., v.2)   **BE249**

For the general reader. An annotated listing of books, articles, serials, and exhibition catalogs; topically arranged, with author, title, and subject indexes. Includes the decorative arts, and sections on individual artists, as well as general materials on movements, period surveys, etc.   Z5961.U5S64

Wodehouse, Lawrence. American architects from the Civil War to the First World War: a guide to information sources. Detroit, Gale, [1976]. 343p. (Art and architecture information guide ser., v.3)   **BE250**

Intended as a continuation of Roos's *Bibliography of early American architecture* (BE245). A general section is followed by an annotated listing of books and articles concerning individual architects active within the period. Provides a brief biography (with reference to published writings and known repositories of his drawings) for each of the 175 architects. A third section is concerned with significant architects about whom little has been written. Detailed general index; building location index.   Z5944.U5W63

———— American architects from the first World War to the present; a guide to information sources. Detroit, Gale, [1977]. 305p. (Art and architecture information guide ser., v.4)   **BE251**

A companion to the same author's *American architects from the Civil War to the first World War* (above).

An annotated listing of "General reference works on American architects and their architecture" is followed by an annotated bibliography for 174 American architects active since the first World War. Subject and name index; building index.   Z5944.U5W635

———— Indigenous architecture worldwide: a guide to information sources. Detroit, Gale, [1980]. 392p. (Art and architecture information guide ser., v.12)   **BE252**

"Indigenous architecture is reliant upon local materials, microclimatic conditions, the economic basis of the society and on occasion one of a variety of other influences which could be religious, social, cultural, defensive, or symbolic."—*Introd.* This is a briefly annotated bibliography with entries arranged by continent, then by country. Separate section for "the vernacular as a nineteenth-century revival style and an influence in twentieth century architecture." Indexed.   Z5943.V47W62

Indexes

Columbia University. Libraries. Avery Architectural Library. Avery index to architectural periodicals. 2d ed. Boston, G. K. Hall, 1973. 15v.   **BE253**

1st ed. 1963 in 12v. plus 7 supplements, 1965–72.

Photographic reproduction of the Library's card file. Indexes articles on architecture in its widest sense, including archaeology, decorative arts, interior decoration, furniture, landscape architecture, city planning, and housing. Periodicals in non-Western alphabets are not included. In addition to integration of the entries from the supplements into the main listing in the new edition, corrections

and refinements have been made, plus back indexing of certain periodicals not previously included.   Z5945.C653●

———— ———— Suppl. 1–3. Boston, G. K. Hall, 1975–79. 3v.

Suppl. 1 covers the years 1973–74; Suppl. 2 covers 1975–76; Suppl. 3, 1977–78, with some back indexing of older periodicals. A fourth supplement was publ. 1986.

Royal Institute of British Architects, London. Comprehensive index to architectural periodicals, 1956–1970. [London, World Microfilms, 1973] 20 reels of microfilm (16mm.).   **BE255**

Photographic reproduction of a card file forming an international index to selected articles from some 200 architecture and planning journals of the 1956–70 period. Topical arrangement, with alpabetical listing by English-language title thereunder. The last reel contains the list of subject headings used. Much of the index was published in the quarterly issues of the *RIBA library bulletin*. For a detailed review *see* M. R. Whiteman's article in *Microform review* (3:48–50, Jan. 1974).

———— RIBA annual review, 1965/66–1971/July 1972. London, 1967–73. 7v.   **BE256**

The set offers annual cumulations of the bibliography appearing in each quarterly issue of the *RIBA library bulletin*. Subject arrangement with author index. Superseded by: Z5941.R68a

Architectural periodicals index, v.1– , Aug.1972/Dec. 1973– . London, 1974– . Quarterly, the 4th issue being the annual cumulation.   **BE257**

v.1 appeared quarterly with a fifth issue as the annual cumulation.

Represents the published version of the British Architectural Library's subject index to periodicals. Subject headings are derived from the controlled vocabulary found in *Architectural keywords* (London, RIBA Pubns., 1982). "Special fields indexed include architecture and allied arts, constructional techniques, design, environmental studies, planning."—*Pref.* Indexes some 450 journals. Classed arrangement with alphabetical listing by English-language title within subject categories; foreign-language articles carry a note as to language and presence of English summary. Name index; a topographical and building names index was added beginning with the annual cumulation of v.6.   Z5941.A69●

Dictionaries and encyclopedias

Architectural Publication Society. Dictionary of architecture. London, Richards, [1892]. 6v. il. (Repr.: N.Y., DaCapo, 1969)   **BE258**

Issued in 8v., 1852–92.

Still an important work, including terms; architectural forms and subjects; places, with some account of their architectural features; and biographies of architects. Bibliographical references.   NA31.A8

Briggs, Martin Shaw. Everyman's concise encyclopaedia of architecture. London, Dent; N.Y., Dutton, [1959]. 372p. il.   **BE259**

An alphabetically arranged dictionary of terms and biographies, with line drawings and a section of 32 plates.   NA31.B74

Brunskill, R. W. Illustrated handbook of vernacular architecture. [Rev. & expanded ed.] London, Faber & Faber, [1978]. 249p. il., maps.   **BE260**

1st ed. 1971.

Combines diagrams, photographs, and explanatory text to illustrate and describe various aspects of the subject. An introductory section is followed by sections on walling; roofing; plan and section; architectural details; farm buildings; urban vernacular and minor industrial buildings. Concerned mainly with vernacular architecture of the British Isles. Bibliography; index.

"Additions have been made to nearly all sections of the book but the sections on house plans, both rural and urban, have been very considerably extended. The American pages have been altered to bring them more closely to English precedent."—*Pref.*

NA7328.B83

Cowan, Henry J. Dictionary of architectural science. N.Y., Wiley, [1973]. 354p. il. **BE261**

"The dictionary aims to be comprehensive within the field of architectural science proper, i.e., structures, materials, acoustics, lighting, thermal environment and building services."—*Pref.* The terms were culled from the indexes of standard textbooks, with a few terms drawn from related fields. Brief definitions; illustrations are mainly for geometry and structural terms. Appendixes include a discussion of information processing, mathematical tables, directory of organizations, and "A survey of the literature of architectural science." NA31.C64

Curl, James Stevens. English architecture, an illustrated glossary; with a foreword by Lord Muirshiel and drawings by John J. Sambrook. Newton Abbot, Eng., North Pomfret, Vt., David & Charles, [1977]. 192p. il. **BE262**

A heavily illustrated dictionary of English (and some Scottish) terms in historical architecture. Succinct definitions; short bibliography. A related volume is Glen L. Pride's *Glossary of Scottish building* (Glasgow, Scottish Civic Trust, 1976). NA961.C87

Dictionnaire illustré multilingue de l'architecture du Proche Orient ancien. Ed., Olivier Aurenche. Lyon, Maison de l'Orient, 1977. 391p. il. **BE263**

The main portion of the work (p.11–185) is a dictionary in French giving definitions of, and usually some commentary on, terms used in describing the technology and archaeology of the Middle East from the Neolithic period to middle of the first millenium. The rest of the volume is devoted to glossaries giving French equivalents for the terms in German, English, Arabic, Greek, Italian, Persian, Russian, and Turkish. The dictionary section is heavily illustrated with drawings and photographs (a few in color). NA31.D524

Encyclopedia of architectural technology. Pedro Guedes, ed. in chief. N.Y., McGraw-Hill, [1979]. 313p. il. **BE264**

Publ. in Britain as *The Macmillan encyclopedia of architecture and technological change* (London, Macmillan, 1979).

Offers a series of essays arranged in five major sections: (1) Stylistic periods and geographical adaptations; (2) Built forms and building types; (3) Structures, services, mechanical and environmental systems; (4) Building materials; (5) Tools, techniques and fixings. Concentrates on technology and use of architecture; illustrations are well chosen. The index should be more detailed (e.g., the illustrations are not indexed). NA31.E58

Fleming, John, Honour, Hugh and **Pevsner, Nikolaus.** The Penguin dictionary of architecture. 3d ed. [Harmondsworth, Eng.; Baltimore], Penguin, [1980]. 356p. il. **BE265**

1st ed. 1966.

In addition to definitions of terms, includes biographical notes on leading architects. NA31.F55

Harris, Cyril M., ed. Dictionary of architecture and construction. N.Y., McGraw-Hill, 1975. 553p. il. **BE266**

Offers "definitions of terms which are encountered in the everyday practice of architecture and construction and in their associated fields, as, for example, terms found on drawings and in specifications."—*Pref.* Includes terms relating to products and materials, tools and equipment used in the building trades, "the control of the environment in buildings," history of architecture and restoration, urban planning and landscape architecture. Definitions are brief, but the work is profusely illustrated with very helpful line drawings. NA31.H32

Harris, John and **Lever, Jill.** Illustrated glossary of architecture, 850–1830. London, Faber, 1966; N.Y., Crown, 1967. 79p. 224pl. **BE267**

Defines and illustrates "the terms of architecture in general use for the study of British architecture until about 1830."—*Introd.* Definitions are brief; most of them are followed by reference to a photograph illustrating the term. NA31.H34

Hatje, Gerd. Encyclopaedia of modern architecture. London, Thames & Hudson, [1963]. 336p. il. **BE268**

Originally published as *Knaurs Lexikon der modernen Architektur* (München, Droemersche Verlagsanstalt. T. Knaur Nachf., 1963).

Articles, except very brief ones, are signed, and many include bibliographical references. They present those architects, schools, styles, associations, countries, construction terms, and materials which, since the mid-19th century, have contributed to the development of modern architecture. NA31.H37

Historic architecture sourcebook, ed. by Cyril M. Harris. N.Y., McGraw-Hill, [1977]. 581p. il. **BE269**

Offers brief definitions of some 5,000 architectural terms; features more than 2,000 illustrations—mainly line drawings.

An "unabridged and unaltered" reprint was issued in paperback with the title *Illustrated dictionary of historic architecture* (N.Y., Dover, 1983). NA31.H56

Hunt, William Dudley. Encyclopedia of American architecture. N.Y., McGraw-Hill, [1980]. 612p. il. **BE270**

Offers some 202 articles on major elements in American architecture from "Airport" to "Zoological garden" and including entries for fifty of the most important architects and architectural firms. Each term is discussed "in enough depth to explain the general facts and principles . . . but not to become so complete or technical that only experts would require or understand so much information."—*Pref.* Short bibliographies; index.

A review in *Library journal* (Nov. 1, 1980, p.2316) concludes that this volume is "most appropriate for the general reader," while the review in *ARLIS/NA newsletter* (Feb. 1981, p.63) states that the *Dictionary of architecture and construction* by C. Harris (BE266) provides better value for technical terms and that the architects included are easily found elsewhere. NA705.H86

Macmillan encyclopedia of architects. Adolf K. Placzek, ed. in chief. N.Y., Free Pr.; London, Collier Macmillan, [1982]. 4v. il. **BE271**

"Begun in 1979, the encyclopedia includes more than twenty-four hundred biographies of architects from ancient times to the present and from all geographical regions."—*Introd.* Includes only those architects born before the end of 1930 or who are deceased; engineers, bridge builders, landscape architects, town planners, "a few patrons, and a handful of writers, [are included] if their contributions were so influential as to have changed the face of the human environment." Signed articles range from 50 to 10,000 words; lists of works and bibliographies (some very extensive) conclude most entries. "Chronological table of contents"; glossary; index of names; and index of works in v.4. An important and impressive compilation. NA40.M25

Osborne, Arthur Leslie. A dictionary of English domestic architecture. London, Country Life, [1954]. 111p. il. **BE272**

Dictionary of terms. Articles range from brief definitions to encyclopedic length. Line drawings are clear and attractive.

NA31.O8

Planat, Paul Amédée. Encyclopédie de l'architecture et de la construction. Paris, Dujardin, [1888–92]. 6v. in 12. il. **BE273**

At head of title: Bibliothèque de la construction moderne, publiée sous la direction de M. P. Planat.

Intended as a summing up of the whole of architectural knowledge at the end of the 19th century, covering architectural history, principles, and legislation, and the technical phases of construction. Contributors were architectural scholars and practicing architects. Articles on broad subjects are long and signed. Brief biographies of great architects and builders are included. NA31.P6

Sturgis, Russell. Dictionary of architecture and building, biographical, historical, and descriptive. N.Y., Macmillan, 1901–02. 3v. il. (Repr.: Detroit, Gale, 1966) **BE274**

A standard dictionary in English, in spite of its age. Written in collaboration with many specialists, American and foreign. Longer articles and biographies are signed. Illustrations consist of line drawings, and plates which reproduce photographs. Bibliographies at the ends of many entries, and a bibliography of sources at end of v.3. NA31.S84

Viollet-Le-Duc, Eugène Emmanuel. Dictionnaire raisonné de l'architecture française du XIᵉ au XVIᵉ siècle. Paris, Bance, 1854–68. 10v. il. **BE275**

Imprint varies: v.7–10 publ. by A. Morel.

—— —— Table analytique et synthétique, avec table alphabétique des noms de lieux par départements, pour la France et par contrées, pour l'étranger, [par] Henri Sabine. Paris, Librairie des Imprimeries Réunies, 1889. 387p.

Long articles in dictionary arrangement, including some on sculpture. NA1041.V7

Ware, Dora and **Beatty, Betty.** A short dictionary of architecture, including some common building terms; with an introduction on the study of architecture by John Gloag. [3d ed. rev. and enl.] London, Allen & Unwin, [1953]. 136p. il. **BE276**

1st ed. 1944.
A useful small dictionary of terms commonly used in classical and modern architecture, well-illustrated with line drawings.
NA31.W27

Wasmuths Lexikon der Baukunst. Berlin, Wasmuth, [1929–37]. 5v. il. **BE277**

"Unter Mitwirkung zahlreicher Fachleute hrsg. von Günther Wasmuth . . ."—*title page.*
Covers both the practical and the art aspects of architecture, including terms, encyclopedic articles (often signed), many biographies, and excellent illustrations. No exhaustive bibliographies, but many short bibliographical references. NA31.W3

Directories

Pro file: 1978– . Philadelphia, Archimedia, 1978– . Irregular. **BE278**

Subtitle: The official directory of the American Institute of Architects (varies).
Henry W. Schirmer, ed.
A directory of members of the American Institute of Architects and their practices. Principal listing is by name of firm in a geographical arrangement. Gives addresses of all offices, type of firm, name of parent organization, personnel, work distribution by percentage of gross income (both current and projected), geographical distribution of work, awards. Indexes of firms and of principals, plus an alphabetical list of AIA members.

Handbooks

Architect's handbook of professional practice. Wash., Amer. Inst. of Architects, 1969– . 3v., looseleaf **BE279**

v.1 consists of chapters issued separately in pamphlet form and covering matters such as the construction industry, careers in architecture, selection of an architect, insurance and bonds of suretyship, the architect's office; v.2–3 are concerned with contracts and forms.

Harvey, John Hooper. Sources for the history of houses. [London], British Records Assoc., [1974]. 61p. (Archives and the user, no.3) **BE280**

An extremely helpful manual to guide those beginning a search into the history of English houses built before 1850; also potentially useful to researchers in more general areas of local history.
DA660.H34

McAlester, Virginia and **McAlester, Lee.** A field guide to American houses. N.Y., Knopf, 1984. 525p. il. **BE281**

"Each chapter treats one of the major architectural fashions, or *styles,* that have been popular over our country's past. The chapters are arranged chronologically, with the earliest styles first."—*p.ix.* Identifying features, the most common shapes (or principal subtypes) are illustrated with line drawings and photographs. Origin and history of each style is discussed, with indication of where examples are to be found. Bibliography; index. NA7205.M35

Reid, Richard. The book of buildings: a panorama of ancient, medieval, Renaissance, and modern structures. Chicago, Rand McNally, [1980]. 448p. il. **BE282**

Designed as "a topographical guide to building and architecture in Europe and North America."—*Introd.* Covers domestic and utilitarian structures as well as public buildings and monumental architecture. In four sections (Ancient classical world, Byzantine and medieval world, Modern classical world, and Modern world), with subsections for specific countries or regions. Architectural characteristics of various periods and regions are noted, as are features of specific buildings. A high percentage of buildings discussed is illustrated. Glossary; index of buildings. NA950.R44

Rifkind, Carole. A field guide to American architecture. N.Y., New American Library, 1980. 322p. il **BE283**

A chronological presentation of the development of architectural styles in the United States. In four sections: (1) residential; (2) ecclesiastical; (3) civic and commercial; (4) utilitarian. Terms are defined at first mention, and 450 line drawings and building plans illustrate the work. The brief index is not entirely satisfactory.
NA705.R53

Royal Institute of British Architects. RIBA handbook of architectural practice and management. 4th rev. ed. [London], RIBA Pubns., [1980]. 438p. **BE284**

1st ed. 1965.
In three main sections: (1) Principles and general information; (2) Office procedures; (3) Job procedures. Each section is subdivided for specific aspects of procedures and practices in the architectural profession. Indexed. NA1996.R65

Whiffen, Marcus. American architecture since 1780: a guide to the styles. Cambridge, Mass., M.I.T. Pr., [1969]. 313p. il. **BE285**

Chronological arrangement (i.e., groupings of "Styles that reached their zenith in 1780–1820"; "Styles that reached their zenith in 1820–1860"; etc.). For each style there is a note on its characteristics, a brief history, and a few illustrations. Indexed.
NA705.W47

History

Fletcher, *Sir* **Banister Flight.** A history of architecture. 18th ed. rev. by J. C. Palmes. London, Athlone; N.Y., Scribner, 1975. 1390p. il. **BE286**

A profusely illustrated reference history first published 1896. This edition continues the extensive revision and updating begun with the 17th ed. (1961) with an eye to offering "a much broader conspectus of the world's architecture" (*Pref.*) while retaining the single-volume format. By eliminating the "comparative analysis" sections which had long been a feature of the work it was possible to cover a good deal of new ground (e.g., additional chapters on non-Western architectures, and developments since World War I); also, the majority of existing chapters were "substantially recast, extended or rewritten." Includes bibliographies and index. NA200.F63

Gloag, John. Guide to Western architecture; with over 400 illustrations. 2d ed., rev. Feltham, Eng., Spring Books, 1969. 407p. il. **BE287**

1st ed. 1958.
A summary outline from the sixth century B.C. to the present. Includes bibliography. NA200.G6

Hamlin, Talbot Faulkner. The American spirit in architecture. New Haven, Yale Univ. Pr., 1926. 353p. il. (Pageant of America, v.13) **BE288**

Useful as a pictorial history. The first half of the book is in chronological arrangement. The second half concerns types of buildings. Each chapter has many architectural illustrations with explanatory captions, preceded by one to three pages of text summarizing social and architectural developments. NA705.H3

—— Architecture through the ages. [Rev. ed.] N.Y., Putnam, [1953]. 684p. il. **BE289**

1st ed. 1940.

An excellent survey history from the social point of view. The introduction, p.vii–viii, contains a selection of postwar publications describing recent discoveries and illuminating new evaluations and interpretations. NA200.H43

—— Forms and functions of twentieth-century architecture. N.Y., Columbia Univ. Pr., 1952. 4v. il. **BE290**

"Prepared under the auspices of the School of Architecture of Columbia University."—*verso of title page.*

Contents: v.1, The elements of building; v.2, The principles of composition; v.3–4, Building types.

An important work, which largely supersedes Julien Guadet's *Éléments et théorie de l'architecture* (3.éd. 1909). Many specialists collaborated, and each building type is dealt with by an outstanding architect. Each chapter has a list of suggested additional readings; v.4 includes a general index and also one of architectural works described or illustrated. More than 2,500 illustrations. NA680.H3

Histoire générale des églises de France, Belgique, Luxembourg, Suisse. Préface d'André Chastel. [Paris], R. Laffont, [1966–71]. 5v. il. **BE291**

v.2–5 have title: *Dictionnaire des églises de France, Belgique, Luxembourg, Suisse.*

Contents: v.1, Histoire génerale des églises; v.2, France: Centre et Sud-est; v.3, France: Sud-ouest; v.4, France: Ouest et Île-de-France; v.5, France: Nord, Est; Belgique, Luxembourg, Suisse.

The first volume presents a general history of the churches and church architecture of the area, with chapters contributed by a number of French scholars; a glossary of terms is included. Each successive volume offers signed articles, in dictionary arrangement according to commune, dealing with each of the churches in the area under consideration. Most articles include bibliographical references; numerous black-and-white and color illustrations are used throughout. NA4800.H55

Biography

American architects directory. Ed.1–3, 1956–70. N.Y., Bowker, 1955–70. **BE292**

"Published under the sponsorship of American Institute of Architects."—*title page.*

Alphabetical listing of names and addresses with brief biographical information when available. Members of the American Institute of Architects are included automatically; other architects of established reputation from whom biographical details have been obtained are also included. Contains a geographical index; lists of officers and regional directors of the Institute, its honorary members, fellows, and award winners. NA53.A37

Columbia University. Libraries. Avery Architectural Library. Avery obituary index of architects. 2d ed. Boston, G.K. Hall, 1980. 530p. **BE293**

Represents a new edition of the *Avery obituary index of architects and artists* (1963); obituaries of artists have not been indexed since 1960—hence the change of title. Begun in 1934, the index cites obituary notices appearing in the approximately 500 periodicals currently indexed in the *Avery index to architectural periodicals* (BE253) and in some newspapers (mainly the *New York times*). In addition, there is back-indexing of obituaries in four leading American architectural periodicals to the dates of their founding and some retrospective indexing of selected English, French, and German periodicals. About 17,000 references. Z5943.A69A93

Colvin, Howard Montagu. A biographical dictionary of British architects, 1600–1840. [London], Murray, 1978. 1080p. **BE294**

A completely revised edition of Colvin's 1954 dictionary which covered about 1,000 architects of the 1660–1840 period. Includes new sketches of 250 Scottish and Welsh architects as well as 400 additional biographies of English architects. Many sketches from the earlier edition have been expanded, but some have been dropped (*see* "Appendix B"). NA996.C6

Contemporary architects. Ed., Muriel Emanuel. London, Macmillan; N.Y., St. Martin's Pr., [1980]. 933p. il. **BE295**

Some 600 major architects and architectural firms are included. For each are given brief biographical details, chronological list of architectural works and publications, secondary works and bibliographies, a statement of purpose written by the architect, and a brief evaluation contributed by an expert. International in scope; most of the entries are for living architects or those recently deceased, with a few influential figures from the 1920–50 period selected for inclusion. NA680.C625

Harvey, John Hooper. English mediaeval architects, a biographical dictionary down to 1550. London, Batsford, [1954]. 411p. **BE296**

Subtitle: . . . including master masons, carpenters, carvers, building contractors and others responsible for design.

Painstaking details about some 1,300 persons, with references to sources. NA996.H3

Ware, Dora. A short dictionary of British architects. London, Allen & Unwin, [1967]. 312p. il. **BE297**

An index of places which exemplify the works of the biographees is a useful feature. NA996.W3

Who's who in architecture: from 1400 to the present day. Ed. by J. M. Richards. American consultant: Adolf K. Placzek. London, Weidenfeld and Nicolson; N.Y., Holt, Rinehart & Winston, [1977]. 368p. il. **BE298**

The word "architect" is here used "in the accepted modern sense of a professional man to whom the promoter of a building goes for the conception . . . and design and for overseeing the construction; and therefore the volume begins at the time when this notion of an architect first emerges—in the early days of the Italian Renaissance."—*Introd.* Geographical scope is "the Western world, plus those other parts of the world whose culture is derived from the West." About 50 major architects were accorded fairly long, signed articles and another 450 are given briefer treatment. Cross references are given from names of architects mentioned in passing but not treated in separate articles. NA40.W48

Withey, Henry F. and **Withey, Elsie Rathburn.** Biographical dictionary of American architects (deceased). Los Angeles, New Age Pub. Co., [1956]. 678p. **BE299**

Brief biographical sketches of nearly 2,000 men and women, working *ca.*1740–1952, now deceased. Usually indicates best-known works, and cites references at the end of the articles.

Wodehouse, Lawrence. British architects, 1840–1976; a guide to information sources. Detroit, Gale, [1978]. 353p. (Art and architecture information guide ser., v.8) **BE300**

A selective, annotated bibliography of the history of British architecture, with special chapters on Irish and Scottish architecture. The longest and most complete section is the "Selected annotated biographical bibliography of British architects, 1840–1976." Indexes of names, titles, subjects, and building locations. Z5944.G7W66

City planning

Alexander, Ernest R., Catanese, Anthony James and **Sawicki, David S.** Urban planning: a guide to information sources. Detroit, Gale, [1979]. 165p. (Urban studies information guide ser., v.2) **BE301**

Lists books and articles of "classical or of highest significance" (*Introd.*) in the area of comprehensive urban planning. Topically arranged within three large sections: (1) History and development; (2) Theory and context of planning; (3) Methods and techniques. Only English-language publications are included; all entries are briefly annotated. Author, title, and subject indexes. Z5942.A45

Bestor, George Clinton and **Jones, Holway R.** City planning bibliography; a basic bibliography of sources and trends. 3d ed. N.Y., Amer. Soc. of Civil Engineers, 1972. 518p. **BE302**

1st ed. 1962.
A classified bibliography of 1,837 books, pamphlets, reports, etc., about three-quarters of them annotated. Major sections include the nature and form of cities, history of cities and city planning, contemporary comprehensive planning, and education for planning, plus a list of general bibliographies and one of selected services and periodicals. A "b" following the item number indicates inclusion of a bibliography in that item. Indexed. Z5942.B42

Branch, Melville Campbell. Comprehensive urban planning; a selective annotated bibliography with related materials. Beverly Hills, Calif., Sage, [1970]. 477p. **BE303**

For full information *see* CC270. Z5942.B7

Council of Planning Librarians. Exchange bibliography. [Monticello, Ill., The Council], 1959–78. no.1–1564/65. **BE304**

For full information *see* CC274.

Ekistic index. no.1– , Jan. 1968– . Athens, Athens Technological Organization, Center of Ekistics, 1968– . Semiannual. **BE304a**

Frequency varies.
Articles are selected from journals from a wide range of countries, selection being based on the interest to planners, architects, social scientists, and others concerned with ekistics (i.e., with the science of city and area planning in relation to basic needs of the individual and the entire community). The index, computer-produced, lists articles by author, broad topic, and country or region to which the article refers. Z5942.E38

Golany, Gideon. New towns planning and development: a world-wide bibliography. Wash., Urban Land Inst., [1973]. 256p. (ULI research report 20) **BE305**

For full information *see* CC276.

Dictionaries and encyclopedias

Akademie für Raumforschung und Landesplanung. Handwörterbuch der Raumforschung und Raumordnung. 2. Aufl. Hannover, Jänecke, 1970. 3v. **BE306**

1st ed. 1966 in 1v.
An encyclopedia of regional and city planning in their broad aspects. Signed articles; bibliographies. *Sachregister* in v.3. HT391.A4

Encyclopedia of urban planning. Arnold Whittick, ed. N.Y., McGraw-Hill, 1974. 1218p. il. (Repr.: Huntington, N.Y., Krieger, 1980) **BE307**

For full information *see* CC298.

International Federation for Housing and Planning. International glossary of technical terms used in housing and town planning . . . 2d rev. and enl. ed. Ed., H. J. Spiwak. Amsterdam, [1951]. 144p. **BE308**

1st ed. 1934.
Title page and text in English, French, German, Italian, and Spanish. HD7287.I5

Vocabulaire international des termes d'urbanisme et d'architecture. . . . Présenté par Jean-Henri Calsat et Jean-Pierre Sydler. Paris, Société de Diffusion des Techniques du Bâtiment et des Travaux Publics, 1970. 350p. il. **BE309**

Title also in German and English (*International vocabulary of town planning and architecture*).
In French, German, and English. Words are given in a classed arrangement, with equivalent terms (and definitions) in parallel columns. Alphabetical index from each language. NA31.V6

PAINTING

Bibliography

Doumato, Lamia. American painting; a guide to information sources. Detroit, Gale, [1979]. 246p. (Art and architecture information guide ser., 11) **BE310**

An annotated bibliography of books, relevant sections of books, exhibition catalogs, and periodical articles on "American artists actively working either in the United States or abroad in the 1890s to the present, and [a few] prominent illustrators, whose role in the development of art in this country was a vital one."—*Introd.* (The illustrators include Sendak, Flagg, Kent, Rockwell, etc.) A general section is followed by sections on individual artists and illustrators, plus chapters on "Important library research collections" and "Museums with important collections for the study of American drawing." Z5956.D7D68

Keaveney, Sydney Starr. American painting; a guide to information sources. Detroit, Gale, [1974]. 260p. (Art and architecture information guide ser., v.1) **BE311**

A selective bibliography of recent (post-World War II through July 1973) books, exhibition catalogs, and journal articles. Topical arrangement; brief annotations. Includes a directory of periodical publications, publishers, research libraries, national art organizations, and museums of importance to the researcher in the field of American painting. Well indexed. Z5949.A45K4

Catalogs

Bernhard, Marianne. Verlorene Werke der Malerei in Deutschland in der Zeit von 1939 bis 1945 zerstörte und verschollene Gemälde aus Museen und Galerien. München, Friedrich Adolf Ackermann, [1965]. 231p. il. **BE312**

An illustrated catalog of paintings lost or destroyed during the war years. Listings by museum and by artist. ND1249.B4

Boston. Museum of Fine Arts. American paintings in the Museum of Fine Arts, Boston. Boston; distr. by New York Graphic Soc., Greenwich, Conn., [1969]. 2v. il. **BE313**

Contents: v.1, Text; v.2, Plates.
A scholarly catalog listing all American paintings (including those on loan) in the museum. The text is arranged alphabetically by artist; then the pictures are listed chronologically. Each painting is described, and bibliographical references are provided. Plates are arranged chronologically according to painters' dates, so that all of one individual's works are together. The text volume includes an index of titles and an index by collections. ND205.B58

Fredericksen, Burton B. and **Zeri, Federico.** Census of pre-nineteenth-century Italian paintings in North American public collections. Cambridge, Harvard Univ. Pr., 1972. 678p. **BE314**

A listing by artist gives title or subject of the painting and its location. This is followed by a classified "Index of subjects" in which the principal divisions are (1) religious subjects, (2) secular subjects, (3) portraits and donors, (4) unidentified subjects, and (5) fragments. ND611.F73

The Frick Collection, New York. The Frick collection; an illustrated catalogue. N.Y., distr. by Princeton Univ. Pr., 1968–77, v.1–4, 7–8. il. (In progress)   **BE315**

Contents: v.1, Paintings: American, British, Flemish and German; v.2, Paintings: French, Italian and Spanish; v.3, Sculpture: Italian; v.4, Sculpture: German, Netherlandish, French and British; v.7, Porcelains: Oriental and French; v.8, Limoges painted enamels, Oriental rugs and English silver.

A handsomely produced set which is to include all the works of art in this important collection. Based on the collection's folio catalog (1949–56) with the addition of new information. (v.5–6, 9 not yet published.)   N620.F6A6

Morse, John D. Old masters in America, a comprehensive guide; more than two-thousand paintings in United States and Canada by forty famous artists. Chicago, Rand McNally, [1955]. 192p. il.   **BE316**

"A complete listing of every picture now on display in America by forty of Europe's old masters."—*Foreword.* Arranged by artist. Under each a biographical sketch, brief comment on his work, and a list of his paintings in America, arranged by place and art gallery. A geographical index to the galleries is by state and city.
     ND1242.M6

New York. Metropolitan Museum of Art. American paintings; a catalogue of the collection of the Metropolitan Museum of Art. By Albert Ten Eyck Gardner and Stuart P. Feld. [N.Y.], Metropolitan Museum of Art; distr. by New York Graphic Soc., Greenwich, Conn., [1965]. v.1. il.
     BE317

Contents: v.1, Painters born by 1815 (292p.).

Planned as a 3-volume work, of which this is the only one published. For v.3 of a new catalog with a slightly different title *see* below. Arrangement is chronological by birth dates of the painters. Biographical notices of the painters are followed by descriptions of the paintings (which are illustrated in black-and-white), again in chronological sequence.

This is but one of the catalogs of important segments of the Museum's collections. Others include: *A catalogue of French paintings* . . . by Charles Sterling (Cambridge, Harvard Univ. Pr., 1955–67. 3v.); *Catalogue of Greek sculptures,* by Gisela M.A. Richter (Cambridge, Harvard Univ. Pr., 1954. 123p.); *Catalog of . . . paintings,* by Harry B. Wehle (v.1, Italian, Spanish and Byzantine; v.2, Early Flemish, Dutch and German. N.Y., Publishers Prt. Co., 1940–47); *Italian paintings . . . Florentine school,* by Federico Zeri (N.Y., N.Y. Graphic Soc., 1971. 234p.); *American sculpture . . .* by Albert Ten Eyck Gardner (Greenwich, Conn., N.Y. Graphic Soc., 1965. 192p.).   ND205.N364

—— American paintings in the Metropolitan Museum of Art. Ed. by Kathleen Luhrs. N.Y., The Museum, 1980. v.3. (In progress)   **BE318**

Contents: v.3, A catalogue of works by artists born between 1846 and 1864, by Doreen Bolger Burke.

The first published volume of what might be considered a new series of the catalog noted above. This volume covers painters most active during the last 30 years of the 19th century and includes paintings accessioned by the Museum before Jan. 1979. Sources are included for biographical facts and for quotations; a list of related works is given for each artist; and works mentioned but not illustrated are located in a museum or reference is given to a published reproduction. There is a master index of artists and titles and of former owners.   ND205.N373

Waterhouse, Ellis Kirkham. Roman baroque painting: a list of principal painters and their works in and around Rome, with an introductory essay. [Oxford], Phaidon Pr., [1976]. 163p. il.   **BE319**

Lists paintings of 79 artists "who executed commissions of some importance for the decoration of churches or palaces in Rome" (*Note*), but omitting easel pictures and painters "whose work was more domestic." Arranged alphabetically by painter's name; gives a brief note on each artist's career, a list (by location) of individual works with indication of subject and printed source of attribution,

and reference to those works in the bibliography which offer further information. Topographical index.   ND620.W37

Dictionaries and encyclopedias

Berckelaers, Ferdinand Louis. A dictionary of abstract painting, with a history of abstract painting [by] Michel Seuphor [pseud.]. N.Y., Tudor, 1957; London, Methuen, 1958. 305p. il.   **BE320**

Translated from the French *Dictionnaire de la peinture abstraite* (Paris, Hazan, 1957).

The history is followed by a "Chronological table of abstract art," p.[106–13], and the Dictionary, p.117–294, which gives brief biographical entries for some 500 artists. Many small, colored illustrations. Bibliography, p.297–[305].

Dictionary of modern painting. General eds.: Carlton Lake and Robert Maillard. [3d ed. rev. and enl.] N.Y., Tudor, [1964]. 416p. il.   **BE321**

1st American edition 1955.

Original French edition: *Dictionnaire de la peinture moderne* (Paris, Hazan, 1954), German translation: *Knaurs Lexikon moderner Kunst* (München, Knaur, 1955).

Includes, in alphabetical order, articles on persons, schools of painting, art movements, places, etc. The English version has some additional entries and illustrations. Covers the period from the Impressionists to approximately World War II, i.e., the only living painters to be included are those who had made their mark before the outbreak of the second World War.   ND30.D515

Encyclopedia of painting: painters and painting of the world from prehistoric times to the present day. Bernard S. Myers, ed. 4th rev. ed. N.Y., Crown, 1979. 511p. il.   **BE322**

Attempts in a "portable and not too costly volume . . . to give an over-all picture of the outstanding painters, movements, styles and techniques from the most ancient times to the present day."—*Pref.* Dictionary arrangement. Runs heavily to biographical entries. Includes almost 1,000 illustrations, many in color. No bibliography.   ND30.E5

Gaunt, William. Everyman's dictionary of pictorial art. London, Dent; N.Y., Dutton, [1962]. 2v. il.   **BE323**

"The aim is to provide in concise form and within the limits of 250,000 words and 1,000 illustrations a handy reference to painters and periods, forms and techniques of pictorial art in all parts of the world . . . from the earliest times to the present."—*Introd.* Includes biographical sketches of some 1,200 artists; descriptions of the main periods and schools of art; galleries; definitions of terms; descriptions of some famous paintings, etc. Supplementary lists of British and American artists are included in v.2.   N31.G3

Mayer, Ralph. The artist's handbook of materials and techniques. 1982 ed., rev. and updated. N.Y., Viking Pr., [1981]. 733p. il.   **BE324**

1st ed. 1940.

Aims to give the artist "a complete and up-to-date account of the materials and methods of his craft."—*Pref.* Chapters on pigments, oil painting, tempera painting, watercolor and gouache, pastel, mural painting, solvents and thinners, new materials, conservation of pictures, etc. Miscellaneous notes; bibliographies; appendix; index.   ND1500.M3

Taubes, Frederic. The painter's dictionary of materials and methods. N.Y., Watson-Guptill Publs., [1971]. 253p. il.   **BE325**

"The book is intended primarily for the painter, and the emphasis is, accordingly, on drawing and painting materials and techniques."—*Foreword.* Concerned with current practices, methods, and materials, with only occasional brief mention of obsolete terms and products no longer used. References to chemistry, formulas, etc., are also kept to a minimum. Many cross references.   ND1505.T38

History

Barker, Virgil. American painting, history and interpretation. N.Y., Macmillan, 1950. 717p. il. **BE326**

Covers the history to the end of the 19th century. Bibliographical references are given for each chapter at the end of the volume, and there is a brief list of general sources. The index includes a section on the owners of the paintings mentioned. ND205.B29

Haftmann, Werner. Painting in the twentieth century. [Trans. by Ralph Manheim. Newly designed and expanded ed.] N.Y., Praeger, [1965]. 2v. il. **BE327**

Translation of *Malerei im 20. Jahrhundert* (1954–55); 1st English ed. 1961.

Contents: v.1, An analysis of the artists and their work; v.2, [A pictorial survey with 1011 reproductions].

A good general survey. v.1 includes a section of biographies of the artists discussed. ND195.H323

Isham, Samuel. The history of American painting. New ed. with supplementary chapters by Royal Cortissoz. N.Y., Macmillan, 1927. 608p. il. (Reissue 1942) **BE328**

A standard work first published 1905, as v.3 of *The history of American art,* ed. by J. C. Van Dyke. Traces the development and the appreciation of painting in America to the latter part of the 19th century. The five chapters by Cortissoz continue the history for another quarter century. Bibliography compiled by Henry Meier, p.593–600. ND205.I7

Mather, Frank Jewett. Western European painting of the Renaissance. N.Y., Holt [1939]. 873p. il. (Repr.: N.Y., Tudor, 1948) **BE329**

A comprehensive survey. ND170.M3

Read, *Sir* **Herbert Edward.** A concise history of modern painting. Enl. and updated 3d ed. Additional material by Caroline Tisdall and William Feaver. N.Y., Praeger, [1975]. 392p. il. **BE330**

1st ed. 1959.

A brief survey covering painting from Cezanne to the mid-20th century. Because of its illustrations, documentation, and selected bibliography it should be useful for reference purposes. ND195.R4

Richardson, Edgar Preston. Painting in America, from 1502 to the present. N.Y., Crowell, [1965]. 456p. il. **BE331**

1956 ed. had subtitle "the story of 450 years."

A historical survey from the time of the artist-explorer to modern times, including a good deal of biographical information and critical comment. Select bibliography; index. ND205.R53

Biography

Aeschlimann, Erardo and **Ancona, Paola d'.** Dictionnaire des miniaturistes du Moyen Âge et de la Renaissance dans les différentes contrées de l'Europe. 2. éd. rev. et augm. Milan, Hoepli, 1949. 239 p. 155pl. (part col.) **BE332**

Brief biographical notes with bibliographical references. The 2d ed. has been revised, with some new names and additional references. 13 new plates have been added, but the plates in the 1st ed. seem superior to those in the 2d. An index, arranged by epochs subdivided by country, is new in the 2d ed. The 1st ed. was published in 1940 under the name of Aeschlimann; "Le nom de M. Paolo D'Ancona ne pouvait figurer en raison des lois raciales qui étaient en rigueur en Italie à cette époque."—*Pref., 2d ed.* N7616.A4

Bradley, John William. A dictionary of miniaturists, illuminators, calligraphers, and copyists, with references to their works, and notices of their patrons, from the establishment of Christianity to the eighteenth century. Comp. from various sources, many hitherto unedited. London, Quaritch, 1887–89. 3v. (Repr.: N.Y., B. Franklin, 1958) **BE333**

Entries include: name of artist, his century, his designation (whether miniaturist or other), and brief comment on his work, with sources. An appendix lists supplementary names. ND2890.B8

Bryan, Michael. Bryan's Dictionary of painters and engravers. [4th ed.] rev. and enl. under the supervision of G. C. Williamson. London, Bell; N.Y., Macmillan, 1903–05. 5v. il. (Repr: London, Bell, 1926–34 [v.1, 1930]; Port Washington, N.Y., Kennikat, 1964) **BE334**

1st ed. 1816. 2v.; 2d ed. rev. 1849. 1v.; Supplement 1876; new ed. rev. 1884–89. 2v.

A standard biographical dictionary which usually lists works and frequently indicates location. Monograms of painters and engravers, v.5, p.421–25. N40.B94

Cahill, James Francis. An index of early Chinese painters and paintings, . . . incorporating the work of Osvald Sirén and Ellen Johnston Laing. Berkeley, Univ. of California Pr., [1980]– . v.1– . (In progress) **BE335**

Contents: [v.1] T'ang, Sung and Yüan.

To be in 3v., the next two to cover Ming and Ch'ing periods.

Artists are grouped by dynasty; entries give brief biographical information (with references to published sources) and a listing of every known extant painting, together with indication of present location of the work and source of any reproductions. An asterisk indicates a painting of special importance, and a brief note tries to assess the genuineness of the painting. At the end of each dynasty section there is a list of anonymous paintings. General bibliography, p.379–91.

The "incorporated" works referred to in the title are Osvald Sirén's *Chinese painting* (N.Y. & London, 1956–58. 7v.) and Ellen Johnston Laing's *Chinese paintings in Chinese publications* (Ann Arbor, 1969). ND1043.3.C3

Canaday, John Edwin. The lives of the painters. N.Y., Norton, [1969]. 4v. il. **BE336**

Contents: v.1, Late Gothic to High Renaissance; v.2, Baroque; v.3, Neoclassic to Post-impressionist; v.4, Plates and index.

"The history of painting from the end of the Middle Ages to the eve of the twentieth century . . . is told in the form of several hundred biographies strung together on a historical cord."—*Pref.* Beginning with Cimabue, the author carries the history through painters born before 1840—thus ending with Cezanne and his contemporaries, but not including the neo-impressionists. Quality of the plates is disappointing. ND35.C35

Champlin, John Denison and **Perkins, Charles C.** Cyclopedia of painters and paintings. N.Y., Scribner, 1892 [c1885–87]. 4v. il. (Repr.: N.Y., Empire State Book Co., 1927) **BE337**

Gives, in one alphabet, biographical articles on painters and descriptive articles on famous paintings. The biographies give main facts of the artist's life; list of his paintings, with reference to the museums or collections where they are located; and some bibliography. Articles on paintings give brief description, some facts of history, museum, a statement of whether engraved and by whom, and some bibliographical references. Illustrated by outline drawings and plates. Includes numerous facsimiles of monograms and signatures. ND30.C4

Fisher, Stanley W. A dictionary of watercolour painters, 1750–1900. London, N.Y., Foulsham, 1972. 245p. il. **BE338**

Provides very brief biographical information on British painters who worked in watercolor, the majority of the entries being for artists of the period 1750–1900. Indicates dates of birth and death, birthplace (if known), career highlights, types of subjects usually painted, number of exhibited works, and names of galleries where typical examples may be found. ND1928.F54

Foskett, Daphne. A dictionary of British miniature painters. London, Faber & Faber; N.Y., Praeger, [1972]. 2v. il. **BE339**

Contents: v.1, Text; v.2, Illustrations.

"This Dictionary covers the years from c.1520–1910 and records the names or initials of all miniaturists who have come to my notice and who were born in, or worked in Great Britain and Ireland."— *Pref.* Builds on Basil Long's *British miniaturists* (London, 1929) which covered to 1860, and includes, along with other additional information and the extended period, matters recorded in Long's own annotated copy of his book.   N1337.G7F463

Harper, J. Russell. Early painters and engravers in Canada. [Toronto], Univ. of Toronto Pr., [1970]. 376p.   **BE340**

Offers such biographical data as are available for artists who worked in Canada, whose birth dates were before 1867. Includes artists who visited Canada and painted Canadian subject matter during the early period. For each artist gives date and place of birth and death, known details of the artist's life, list of public exhibitions where works have appeared, collections in which the artist is represented, and reference to biographical sources. Bibliography, p.343–76.   N6548.H37

Johnson, Jane and **Greutzner, A.** The dictionary of British artists, 1880–1940: an Antique Collectors' Club research project listing 41,000 artists. [Suffolk, Eng.], Antique Collectors' Club, [1976]. 567p.   **BE341**

An extension and updating of A. Graves's *Dictionary of British artists, 1760–1893* (London, 1901).

A listing of every artist (including architects and foreigners) who exhibited in any of 47 selected galleries (the selection intended to provide a representative view of art in London and across Great Britain) during 1880–1940. Gives for each: birth and/or death dates (if unknown, first and last exhibition years); towns of residence; memberships and honors; places exhibited and number of times; and, occasionally, art schools attended; an asterisk indicates that at least one picture by the artist brought more than £100 at auction during 1970–75.   N6767.J63

Norman, Geraldine. Nineteenth century painters and painting; a dictionary. Berkeley, Univ. of California Pr.; London, Thames & Hudson, [1977]. 240p. il.   **BE342**

A brief discussion of various art movements (with colored illustrations) is followed by an alphabetical arrangement of some 700 biographies. For each artist is given a note on historical context and type of work, information on influences, career, honors received, prominence during lifetime, and location of representative works in public museums. References to standard works on the artist are provided, and there are often black-and-white reproductions of a typical painting by the artist. Entries for prominent schools and art movements are also included in the dictionary.   ND190.N57

Waters, Grant M. Dictionary of British artists, working 1900–1950. Eastbourne, Eastbourne Fine Art, 1975. 368p.   **BE343**

Offers brief biographies of some 5,500 British, Irish, and foreign-born artists active in England during the period 1900–50. Most entries give artist's dates, memberships, education, and a sentence or two about his career.   N6768.W26

Witt Library. A checklist of painters, c.1200–1976, represented in the Witt Library, Courtauld Institute of Art, London. London, Mansell, 1978. 337p.   **BE344**

A listing of some 50,000 names of artists, European or European inspired, active from about 1200 to the present. Nationality and dates are given for each name. Although the library concentrates on painting and drawing, many decorative artists and engravers are included, as are a few sculptors and architects. Liberal use of cross references from variant forms of the names. Choice of nationality is somewhat arbitrary: care is taken to distinguish between Flemish and Dutch, but not between German and Austrian.   ND35.W5

Wood, Christopher. Dictionary of Victorian painters. Research by Christopher Newell. 2d ed., rev. and enl. Woodbridge, Eng., Antique Collectors' Club, [1978]. 764p. il.   **BE345**

1st ed. 1971.
Aims to list every British artist from the 1837–1901 period, with biographical information (although, in many instances, little more is

known than the date and place of a single exhibited painting). About 500 illustrations in a separate section of plates.

This is but one example of the many biographical dictionaries of British genre artists. Similar works include: *The dictionary of British book illustrators and caricaturists, 1800–1914,* by Simon Houfe (Rev. ed. Woodbridge, Eng., Antique Collectors' Club, 1981); *The dictionary of British 18th century painters in oils and crayons,* by Ellis K. Waterhouse (Woodbridge, Eng., Antique Collectors' Club, 1981); *A dictionary of British equestrian artists,* by Sally Mitchell (Woodbridge, Eng., Antique Collectors' Club, 1984); *A dictionary of British flower, fruit, and still life painters,* by Robert B. Burbidge (Leigh-on-Sea, F. Lewis, 1974); *Dictionary of British landscape painters,* by Maurice H. Grant (Leigh-on-Sea, F. Lewis, 1952); *A dictionary of British marine painters,* by Arnold Wilson (Leigh-on-Sea, F. Lewis, 1967); *A dictionary of British military painters,* by Arnold Wilson (Leigh-on-Sea, F. Lewis, 1972); *A dictionary of British sporting painters,* by Sidney H. Pavière (Leigh-on-Sea, F. Lewis, 1980); *Dictionary of Victorian engravers, print publishers and their works,* by Rodney K. Engen (Cambridge, Eng. & Teaneck, N.J., Chadwyck-Healey, 1979) and its companion volume by the same compiler, *Dictionary of Victorian wood engravers* (Cambridge, Eng. & Teaneck, N.J., Chadwyck-Healey, 1985).   ND467.W65

PRINTS AND ENGRAVINGS

Bibliography

Ludman, Joan and **Mason, Lauris.** Fine print references: a selected bibliography of print-related literature. Millwood, N.Y., Kraus Internat., [1982]. 227p.   **BE346**

A classed bibliography of "the published writings on prints from all historical periods and every part of the world. All possible references are cited on the history and technique of fine and historic prints. Entries on photographs, posters, bookplates, illustrations or ephemera are not included. . . . "—*p.xv.* 3,215 entries. Author and museum/gallery indexes. Detailed table of contents, but a good subject index would have been helpful.   Z5947.A3L82

Mason, Lauris and **Ludman, Joan.** Print reference sources: a selected bibliography, 18th–20th centuries. 2d ed., rev. & enl. Millwood, N.Y., KTO Pr., 1979. 363p.   **BE347**

1st ed. 1975.
Aims to provide "a selected bibliography of the literature on printmakers of the 18th through 20th centuries."—*Note.* Includes citations to "catalogues raisonnés, *oeuvre*-catalogues, museum and dealer publications, and checklists and essays from books and periodicals." About 5,000 citations to some 1,800 artists in this edition.   Z5947.A3M37

New York. Public Library. Prints Division. Dictionary catalog of the Prints Division. Boston, G. K. Hall, 1975. 5v.   **BE348**

Photographic reproduction of "entries for book and book-like materials, including pamphlets, clipping files, and other items of an ephemeral nature, that have been added to the collection through July 1975. Cataloging for individual prints does not appear."—*Foreword.* However, the catalog does analyze some collections of prints, scrapbooks of cartoonists, and periodicals (for biographical articles and reproductions).   Z5950.N562

Riggs, Timothy A. The Print Council index to oeuvre-catalogues of prints by European and American artists. Millwood, N.Y., Kraus Internat. Pubns., [1983]. 834p.   **BE349**

Comp. under the sponsorship of the Print Council of America.
An "oeuvre-catalogue" is here defined as "any listing of the artist's total output in prints or some clearly defined section of that output" (*Note to user*); bibliographies of books illustrated by a given artist are also included. Arranged by artist, with catalogs listed chronologically thereunder. Locates copies of hard-to-find items. Cut-off date is 1972.   Z5947.A3R53

Catalogs

U.S. Library of Congress. Prints and Photographs Division.
American prints in the Library of Congress; a catalog of the
collection. Comp. by Karen F. Beall . . . Baltimore, publ. for
the Lib. of Congress by Johns Hopkins Pr., [1970]. 568p. il.
BE350

"The book, with entries for about 1,250 artists, includes approximately 12,000 prints, arranged alphabetically by artist's name, and
if an artist is represented by more than one print, by title of the
print."—*Introd.* Brief facts on the artist's life are provided when
available. NE505.A47

U.S. Library of Congress. Reference Dept. Guide to the
special collections of prints and photographs in the Library
of Congress, comp. by Paul Vanderbilt. Wash., 1955. 200p.
BE351

Lists 802 collections arranged alphabetically by name of originator or subject designation, with sufficient annotation to make clear
each collection's origin, nature, and scope. Index of proper names
and broad subjects.
Lynda Corey Claasen has compiled a *Finders' guide to prints and
drawings in the Smithsonian Institution* (Wash., Smithsonian Inst.
Pr., 1981. 210p.). NE53.W3A52

Indexes

Parry, Pamela Jeffcott and **Chipman, Kathe.** Print index: a
guide to reproductions. Westport, Conn., Greenwood Pr.,
[1983]. 310p. (Art reference collection, 4) **BE352**

Intended as an aid for "locating illustrations of prints dating from
the early eighteenth century through the mid-1970s."—*Pref.* Lists
references to prints in 100 English-language monographs, exhibition
catalogs, and collection catalogs. Main listing is by artist, with
subject and title index. NE90.P17

Handbooks

Donson, Theodore B. Prints and the print market, a handbook for buyers, collectors, and connoisseurs. N.Y., Thomas
Y. Crowell, [1977]. 493p. **BE353**

Intended to "arm the novice with enough information and savvy
to venture courageously into the print market and provide the
professional with fresh insights and information."—*Foreword.*
Omits any consideration of Japanese woodblock prints and art
photographs. Appendix provides a directory of public print institutions, print clubs and societies, print publishers in the United States
and Great Britain, print conservators and restorers, print dealers
and galleries, bookstores. Lexicon of French-German-English terms.
NE62.D66

Printworld directory of prints and prices. Ed.1– , 1982– .
[Bala-Cynwyd, Pa.], Printworld, [1982]– . il. Irregular.
BE354

Concerned with "original, signed and numbered editions up to
and including editions of 500 with a current retail value of $100 or
more."—*1982 ed.* Arranged by artist, giving brief biographical data,
medium, galleries, and mailing address, along with a photograph of
one print and a list of current and sold out editions of the artist's
work, with prices.
A 3d ed., 1985/86 (publ. 1985) is distributed by Gale, Detroit.
NE491.P77

Shapiro, Cecile and **Mason, Lauris.** Fine prints: collecting,
buying, and selling; with glossaries of French and German
terms by Joan Ludman. N.Y., Harper & Row, 1976. 256p. il.
BE355

A good general handbook for the amateur or beginning collector

of prints. Covers all aspects of the subject from how to buy and sell,
to how to catalog a collection and building a reference library. The
glossaries define the French and German terms most often encountered in the field. Includes a directory of museums, clubs, and
dealers. NE885.S42

History

Castleman, Riva. Prints of the twentieth century: a history;
with illustrations from the collection of The Museum of
Modern Art. N.Y., The Museum, 1976. 216p. il. **BE356**

British ed. publ. without subtitle (London, Thames and Hudson,
1976).
A historical survey with many illustrations. Brief bibliography;
index. NE490.C39

Delteil, Löys. Manuel de l'amateur d'estampes au XVIIIe
siècle. Paris, Dorbon-Aîné, [1910]. 447p. 106pl. **BE357**

Manuel, p.1–364; Table alphabétique des ventes publiques, avec
noms des propriétaires, mentionnées au cours du Manuel, p.365–
68; Table des noms d'artistes et des estampes cités, p.369–442.
A detailed history of 18th-century engraving, chiefly in France but
including other European work. Prints cited in the text are noted at
the bottom of the page, often with information on sales and prices.
NE885.D4

——— Manuel de l'amateur d'estampes des XIXe et XXe
siècles (1801–1924). Paris, Dorbon-Aîné, [1925]. 2v. il.
BE358

A history of 19th- and 20th-century engraving. In organization
and format similar to the previous title. v.2 contains a bibliography,
p.[547]–56, and indexes of sales mentioned in the text, and of artists
and titles cited. NE885.D43

——— ——— 700 reproductions d'estampes des XIXe et
XXe siècles pour servir de complément au *Manuel* . . .
[Paris, 1925] 2v. il. **BE359**

Plates are chronologically arranged, each marked with name of
artist, title, and page reference to the *Manuel.* Index of artists and
titles.

Eichenberg, Fritz. The art of the print: art, masterpieces,
history, techniques. N.Y., Abrams, [1976]. 611p. il.
BE360

A history and survey with chapters by various contributors.
Numerous illustrations; glossary; select bibliography; index.
NE400.E32

Hind, Arthur Mayger. History of engraving and etching,
from the 15th century to the year 1914; being the 3d and
fully rev. ed. of "A short history of engraving and etching."
Boston, Houghton, [1923]. 487p. il. (Repr.: N.Y., Dover,
1963) **BE361**

Appendixes: (1) Classified list of engravers; (2) General bibliography; and (3) Index of engravers and individual bibliography.
A standard history of engraving. NE400.H66

——— An introduction to a history of woodcut, with a
detailed survey of work done in the fifteenth century . . .
with frontispiece and 483 illustrations in the text. London,
Constable; Boston, Houghton, 1935. 2v. il. (Repr.: N.Y.,
Dover, 1963) **BE362**

A standard work with clear and detailed treatment. Includes
chapters on technique, and historical surveys of the work in various
countries. Includes bibliography. NE1030.H55

❖Hind is also the author of other important works in this
field: *Early Italian engraving, a critical catalogue with complete reproduction of all the prints described* (London, Quaritch, 1938–48. 7v.); *Engraving in England in the sixteenth &*

seventeenth centuries; a descriptive catalogue with introductions (Cambridge, Univ. Pr., 1955–64. 3v.).

Biography

Bartsch, Adam von. Le peintre graveur. Nouv. éd. Leipzig, J. A. Barth, 1854–76. 21v. in 19. il.   **BE363**

Contents: v.1–5, [Dutch and Flemish engravers]; v.6–11, Les vieux maîtres allemands; v.12, Les clair-obscurs des maîtres italiens; v.13, Les vieux maîtres italiens; v.14, Oeuvres de Marc-Antoine et de ses deux principaux élèves Augustin de Venise et Marc de Ravenne; v.15, Les graveurs de l'école de Marc-Antoine Raimondi; v.16–18, Peintres ou dessinateurs italiens: Maîtres du seizième siècle; v.19–20, Peintres ou dessinateurs italiens: Maîtres du dix-septième siècle.

—— —— Suppléments . . . récueillis et publiés par Rudolph Weigel . . . t.1, Peintres et dessinateurs néerlandais. Leipzig, Weigel, 1843. 350p.

This important compilation is complemented and supplemented by the following works: *Der deutsche Peintre-graveur, oder Die deutschen Maler als Kupferstecher nach ihrem Leben und ihren Werken, von dem letzten Drittel des 16. Jahrhunderts bis zum Schluss des 18. Jahrhunderts . . .*, by Andreas Andresen (Leipzig, Weigel, 1872–78. 5v.); *Le peintre-graveur français, ou Catalogue raisonné des estampes gravées par les peintres et les dessinateurs de l'école française*, by A. P. F. Robert-Dumesnil (Paris, G. Warée, 1835–71. 11v.); *Le peintre-graveur français continué, ou Catalogue raisonné des estampes gravées par les peintres et les dessinateurs de l'école française nés dans le XVIIIᵉ siècle . . .*, by Prosper de Baudicour (Paris, Bouchard-Huzard, 1859–61. 2v.); and *Dutch and Flemish etchings, engravings and woodcuts, ca.1450–1700*, by F. W. H. Hollstein (Amsterdam, M. Hertzberger, 1949–84. 29v.).

NE90.B2

Beraldi, Henri. Les graveurs du XIXᵉ siècle; guide de l'amateur d'estampes modernes. Paris, Conquet, 1885–92. 12v. il.   **BE364**

Intended as an inventory of 19th-century prints. Some 2,000 artists are listed alphabetically with very brief biographical information, lists of their prints as complete as possible, and critical comment on the more important works.   NE149.B5

Fielding, Mantle. American engravers upon copper and steel; biographical sketches and check lists of engravings, a supplement to David McNeely Stauffer's American engravers. Philadelphia, priv. pr., 1917. 365p. il. (Repr.: N.Y., B. Franklin, 1964)   **BE365**

Checklists of 1,932 engravings with biographical information not found in Stauffer (BE367). Includes an index by subject of engraving.   NE505.F5

Monod, Lucien. Aide-mémoire de l'amateur et du professionnel. Le prix des estampes, anciennes et modernes, prix atteints dans les ventes, suites et états, biographies et bibliographies. Paris, Morancé, [1920–31]. 9v.   **BE366**

A dictionary of artists and their works with very brief biographical data, bibliography, and record of prices realized at various sales.

v.1–9, A–Z; v.9 also contains: Graveurs identifiés par leurs monogrammes ou par des désignations particulières (XVᵉ et XVIᵉ siècles), p.61–73; Bibliographie générale, p.77–109; Nomenclature des estampes par catégories et par sujets (indication des planches typiques, bibliographies, planches anonymes), p.113–281.   NE85.M6

Stauffer, David McNeely. American engravers upon copper and steel. N.Y., Grolier Club, 1907. 2v. il. (Repr.: N.Y., B. Franklin, 1964)   **BE367**

A pioneer work on engravers working in America before 1825. v.1 includes some 700 biographical sketches and an index of the engravings described, also a brief introduction on copperplate

engraving in the United States, and a short section of advertisements about prints found in early American newspapers. v.2 is a checklist of 3,438 works arranged by engraver.

—— —— An artist's index to Stauffer's "American engravers," by Thomas Hovey Gage. Worcester, Mass., Amer. Antiquarian Soc., 1921. 49p. (Repr. from *Proceedings of the American Antiquarian Soc.*, Oct. 1920)

See also Mantle Fielding, *American engravers upon copper and steel . . . a supplement to . . . Stauffer's American engravers* (BE365).   NE505.S8

SCULPTURE

Bibliography

Ekdahl, Janis. American sculpture: a guide to information sources. Detroit, Gale, 1977. 260p. (Art and architecture information guide ser., v.5)   **BE368**

A general section of research materials is followed by chronological sections and one for individual sculptors. Annotated. "American" is taken to mean artists "who have lived and worked in the United States for a significant portion of their careers and have contributed substantially to the art of America."—*Introd.* Appended is a directory of major sculpture collections in public institutions. Author, title, and subject indexes.   Z5954.U5E37

Indexes

Clapp, Jane. Sculpture index. Metuchen, N.J., Scarecrow Pr., [1970–71]. 2v. in 3.   **BE369**

Contents: v.1, Sculpture of Europe and the contemporary Middle East; v.2, Sculpture of the Americas, the Orient, Africa, the Pacific area, and the classical world. 2v.

Offers "a guide to pictures of sculptures in a selected number of around 950 publications that may be found in public, college, school and special libraries."—*Pref.* Works indexed are mainly in English. Indexing is by artist's name, by distinctive title, and by selected subjects.   NB36.C55

History

Bazin, Germain. The history of world sculpture. [Tr. from the French by Madeline Jay] Greenwich, Conn., New York Graphic Soc., [1968]. 459p. il.   **BE370**

The historical essay, p.7–87, is followed by a section of color illustrations, p.89–448, with descriptive notes for each of the more than 1,000 works illustrated.   NB60.B3813

A history of Western sculpture. Consultant ed., John Pope-Hennessy. Greenwich, Conn., New York Graphic Soc., [1967–69]. 4v. il.   **BE371**

Contents: [v.1] Classical sculpture, by George M. A. Hanfmann; [v.2] Medieval sculpture, by Roberta Salvini; [v.3] Sculpture: Renaissance to rococo, by Herbert Keutner; [v.4] Sculpture, 19th & 20th centuries, by Fred Licht.

These four volumes (separately cataloged in most libraries) of an unnumbered series constitute a good, brief survey of sculpture from classical times to the mid-twentieth century. Each offers a generous selection of illustrations (with notes thereon), a bibliography, and index.

Post, Chandler Rathfon. History of European and American sculpture from the early Christian period to the present day. Cambridge, Harvard Univ. Pr., 1921. 2v. il.   **BE372**

A standard work. Bibliography, v.2, p.271–89.   NB60.P6

Biography

Dictionary of modern sculpture. Gen. ed. Robert Maillard. N.Y., Tudor; London, Methuen, [1962, c1960]. 310p. il.   **BE373**

Translated from the French *Dictionnaire de la sculpture moderne* (Paris, Hazan, 1960).

Biographical and critical sketches of 412 sculptors representing the principal movements since Rodin. 453 works reproduced.   NB50.D53

Gunnis, Rupert. Dictionary of British sculptors, 1660–1851. New rev. ed. London, Abbey Lib., [1968]. 515p. il.   **BE374**

1st ed. 1953.

Gives the lives and known work of more than 1,700 sculptors; more attention given, when possible, to the lesser-known men than to those for whom biographies already exist. Includes indexes of places and names.   NB496.G85

Lami, Stanislas. Dictionnaire des sculpteurs de l'école française . . . Paris, Champion, 1898–1921. 8v.   **BE375**

Contents (not volumed as a set): Du moyen âge au règne de Louis XIV (1898. 581p.); Sous le règne de Louis XIV (1906. 504p.); Au 18ᵉ siècle (1910–11. 2v.); Au 19ᵉ siècle (1914–21. 4v.).

Each period arranged alphabetically by artist, giving biographical sketch, list of works, and bibliography. The volumes for the 19th century include only artists deceased before 1914.

Opitz, Glenn B. Dictionary of American sculptors: "18th century to the present." Poughkeepsie, N.Y., Apollo, 1984. 656p. il.   **BE376**

"Illustrated with over 200 photographs."—*t.p.*

Offers biographical sketches of more than 5,000 American sculptors, both living and deceased. "Selection criteria included the presence of the artist's work in exhibitions or collections in major cultural centers of the U.S. Artists of strictly local significance have generally been omitted."—*Pref.*   NB236.O64

B F

Applied Arts

❖Many of the subjects in this grouping of Applied Arts are highly specialized, and often the publications consist of illustrated texts rather than the more usual dictionary or handbook material. General libraries will want to acquire such works on a limited, selective basis, referring the more specialized questions to the special library. Only a small selection is listed here, including a few popular works for the hobbyist and amateur collector.

GENERAL WORKS

See also BF103.

American folk art: a guide to sources. Ed. by Simon J. Bronner. N.Y., Garland, 1984. 313p. il. (Garland reference library of the humanities, v.464)   **BF1**

Aims to guide the student and scholar through the field of folk art study "identifying the basic sources and the common topics" and "probing the relation of sources to topics of current concern, thus placing folk art study in the context of broader cultural studies."—*Introd.* Essays by specialists give an overview of the field and a sampling of its subfields. Annotated bibliographies for each chapter include books, articles, museum catalogs, dissertations, and films; the lists are introduced by commentary. Author and subject indexes.   Z5956.F6A53

Contemporary designers. Ann Lee Morgan, ed.; Colin Naylor, asst. ed. London, Macmillan; Detroit, Gale, [1984]. 658p. il.   **BF2**

"The international designers in this book come from virtually every area of the profession, including graphic, industrial/product, fashion, textile, and interior design as well as the design of sets and costumes for theatre and film."—*Introd.* 600 entries, about 80% of which are for living persons. Includes signed critical comment, and lists of exhibitions and publications along with the biographical information.   BF789.D4K8

Ehresmann, Donald L. Applied and decorative arts: a bibliographic guide to basic reference works, histories, and handbooks. Littleton, Colo., Libraries Unlimited, 1977. 232p.   **BF3**

A classified, annotated bibliography of books in Western European languages, primarily publications from the period 1875–1975. General sections on applied and decorative arts and on ornament are followed by sections for folk art, arms and armor, ceramics, clocks, watches and automata, costume, enamels, furniture, glass, ivory, jewelry, lacquer, leather and bookbinding, medals and seals, metalwork, musical instruments, textiles, toys and dolls. Author and subject indexes. 1,240 items.   Z5956.A68E47

Haslam, Malcolm. Marks and monograms of the modern movement, 1875–1930; a guide to the marks of artists, designers, retailers, and manufacturers from the period of the Aesthetic Movement to Art Deco and Style Moderne. Guildford, Eng., Lutterworth; N.Y., Scribner, 1977. 192p. il.   **BF4**

Marks are geographically arranged under five major headings: ceramics; glass; metalwork and jewelry; graphics; furniture and textiles. A brief paragraph adjacent to each mark identifies the artist or workshop. Name index.   N45.H37

Jervis, Simon. The Facts on File dictionary of design and designers. N.Y., Facts on File, [1984]. 533p.   **BF5**

Aims "to provide brief biographies of leading designers, mainly from about 1450 to the present day, and briefer accounts of some minor and a few insignificant figures."—*Pref.* Includes figures from the fields of ceramics, furniture, glass, interior decoration, ornament and textile, with little or no attention given to graphic design, heavy industrial design, theater and dress design. Concentrates on figures from Europe and North America. Includes definitions of terms and entries for styles and a few important periodicals and other publications in the field.   NK1165.J47

The Oxford companion to the decorative arts. Ed. by Harold Osborne. Oxford, Clarendon Pr., 1975. 865p. il.   **BF6**

Aims to provide an introduction "to those arts which are made to serve a practical purpose but are nevertheless prized for the quality of their workmanship and the beauty of their appearance. The Companion includes . . . leather-working, ceramics, textiles, costume, wood-working, metal-working, glass-making . . . , bell-founding, paper-making, clock-making, typography, landscape gardening, photography; . . . arms and armour, enamels, lacquer, jewellery, toys, lace-making and embroidery."—*Pref.* Unsigned articles, some of considerable length. Bibliography, p.851–65; references to the bibliography are indicated by numbers at the end of an article.

A review by Simon Jervis in *TLS,* Mar. 19, 1976, p.321, points out strengths and weaknesses of the work and laments the fact that it was not executed more specifically as a companion volume to the *Oxford companion to art* (BE102), with *see* references to that work.

NK30.O93

Stafford, Maureen and **Ware, Dora.** An illustrated dictionary of ornament. London, Allen & Unwin, 1974; N.Y., St. Martin's Pr., 1975. 246p. il.   **BF7**

A dictionary of terms used in architecture, the decorative arts, coins, games, heraldry, etc., for *ornament,* which is defined as "an accessory to, but not the substitute of the useful . . . ; a decoration or adornment."—*Introd.* Profusely illustrated with well-produced line drawings.   NK1165.S72

ANTIQUES

Benedictus, David. The antique collector's guide. 1st Amer. ed. N.Y., Atheneum, 1981. 264p. il.   **BF8**

First publ. London, Macmillan, 1980.
A dictionary of about 500 entries for popular antiques, styles, materials, designers, craftsmen, etc. Readable descriptions and identifications incorporating historical and anecdotal information, often with a book reference and indication of a museum collection where an example can be seen. British in origin and emphasis. Cross references; bibliography; glossary of names; index.   NK30.B37

Boger, Louise Ade and **Boger, H. Batterson.** The dictionary of antiques and the decorative arts. N.Y., Scribner, [1967]. 662p. il.   **BF9**

An earlier edition appeared in 1957 (566p.).
Subtitle: A book of reference for glass, furniture, ceramics, silver, periods, styles, technical terms, etc.   NK30.B57

Bridgeman, Harriet and **Drury, Elizabeth.** The encyclopedia of Victoriana. London, Hamlyn; N.Y., Macmillan, [1975]. 368p. il.   **BF10**

A topical presentation of "definitions and descriptions of Victorian artifacts and biographies of the principal designers and makers [thereof]."—*Editors' note.* For each type of material (furniture, photographs, glass, etc.) a survey of developments in Britain is followed by a survey for America, a glossary of terms, and a brief bibliography. Indexed. Illustrations are well chosen and attractively presented.   NK928.B66

The complete color encyclopedia of antiques, comp. by the Connoisseur; ed. by L. G. G. Ramsey. Rev. and expanded ed. N.Y., Hawthorn Books, [1975]. 704p. il.   **BF11**

Published in London as *The Connoisseur complete color encyclopedia of antiques.*
1st ed. 1962.
The 1st ed. (1962) was adapted from the Connoisseur's *Concise encyclopaedia of antiques* (5v. 1954–61) and *The concise encyclopaedia of American antiques,* by Helen Comstock (2v. 1958). The random grouping of chapters by some 100 contributors in those volumes was changed to bring like subject material together under 17 headings and that arrangement is followed in this edition. Many of the chapters contain glossaries. Includes a list of major museums in Great Britain, Europe, and the United States arranged under the 17 subjects represented. Incorporates articles on Art Nouveau and Art Deco, "the two collecting subjects which succeeded Victoriana as the avant-garde in collecting during the 1960s."—*Pref.* The bibliography (p.669–78) has also been updated.   NK1125.R343

Coysh, Arthur Wilfred. The antique buyer's dictionary of names. Newton Abbot, David & Charles; N.Y., Praeger, [1970]. 278p.   **BF12**

A biographical dictionary intended for quick reference over a wide range of fields. "It lists many craftsmen, decorators, and designers who worked in America, Britain, Europe and Japan, and

special care has been taken to include names that appear frequently in auction sale catalogues and dealers' advertisements."—*Pref.* Entries are grouped in sections such as "Art nouveau," "Bronzes," "Firearms," "Netsuke," etc. Indexed.   N40.C67

Durant, Mary B. The American Heritage guide to antiques. N.Y., American Heritage, [1970]. 1v., unpaged. il.   **BF13**

A brief section on "Colonial crafts" is followed by a glossary of about 800 terms with many illustrations. A section of "Style charts" illustrating furniture styles is also included.   NK30.D87

Franklin, Linda Campbell. Antiques and collectibles: a bibliography of works in English, 16th century to 1976. Metuchen, N.J., Scarecrow Pr., 1978. 1091p. il.   **BF14**

Aims "to provide the researcher, the serious collector and the librarian with a comprehensive listing of English language books and exhibition catalogues dealing with objects now considered 'antiques' or 'collectibles.'"—*Pref.* More than 10,000 items (books, pamphlets, dissertations, periodicals) in classified order. For books published before 1925, library locations are given.   Z5956.A68F7

Das grosse Fachwörterbuch für Kunst und Antiquitäten. Hrsg. von Christian Müller. München, Weltkunst Verlag, [1982]– . v.1– . (In progress)   **BF15**

Added title pages in English *(The art and antiques dictionary)* and in French.
A dictionary of technical terms "used in the art and antiques trade in English, French and German to meet the needs . . . of scientists, collectors . . . dealers . . . specialized experts and translators."—*Pref.* Terms are drawn from Eastern and Western art, architecture, textiles, book illustration, medals, heraldry, etc. Arranged on an English base with French and German equivalents, but without definitions.   N33.G76

Jackson, Albert and **Day, David.** The antiques care & repair handbook. N.Y., Knopf, 1984. 255p. il.   **BF16**

Describes and illustrates processes of repair and restoration for many categories of antiques. Addressed chiefly to beginners, with difficulty of procedure indicated. Classified arrangement. Index, glossary, and several useful appendixes.   NK1127.5.J32

Ketchum, William C. The catalog of world antiques: a fully illustrated collector's guide to styles and prices. [London], Windward; N.Y., Rutledge Pr., [1981]. 320p. il.   **BF17**

Aims "to provide . . . collectors with a general price and identification guide to the major areas of world antiques and collectibles." —*Introd.* Emphasis is on "those items that collectors can actually find" rather than on museum examples. Arranged in 14 chapters, each comprising a short introductory historical survey with a note on the current market, and a selection of good, detailed photographs with description and price range. Includes the major subjects of furniture, pottery, glass, textiles, etc., and the newer interests such as primitive and folk art, toys, woodenware. Glossary; bibliography; index.   NK1125.K47

——— The new and revised catalog of American antiques; photography by John Garetti. N.Y., Rutledge Books, [1980]. 384p. il.   **BF18**

1st ed. 1977.
A price guide for American antiques based on information from auctioneers, dealers, and knowledgeable collectors. The prices, updated from the 1st ed., "are presented not as a single figure but as a range" (*Introd.*) in view of the difficulty of pinpointing a single price for a given object. Photographs of representative items are grouped by type, briefly described, and the price range indicated. Brief bibliography (unchanged from the 1st ed.); index.
NK806.K4

Mackay, James Alexander. Turn-of-the-century antiques: an encyclopedia. N.Y., Dutton, 1974. 320p. il.   **BF19**

Published in London by Ward Lock as *Dictionary of turn of the century antiques.*
Concentrates on the period 1890–1910. Dictionary arrangement of articles on movements, events, styles, furnishings, art objects,

craftsmen, designers, etc., from many countries. Numerous illustrations. NK775.5.A7M32

Phillips, Phoebe. The collectors' encyclopedia of antiques. N.Y., Crown, [1973]. 703p. il. **BF20**

Entries are by large categories such as: arms and armor, bottles and boxes, carpets and rugs, ceramics, clocks, furniture, glass, metalwork, etc. Some bibliographic references. Brief index. NK28.P494

Phipps, Frances. The collector's complete dictionary of American antiques. Garden City, N.Y., Doubleday, 1974. 640p. il. **BF21**

Employs a dictionary arrangement within topical sections such as: historic periods and styles; rooms—their placement and use; crafts, trades, and useful professions; weights and measures; terms used by joiners and cabinetmakers; woods and their preferred uses; paints, dyes, finishes, varnishes, etc. A general index would have facilitated use. NK805.P52

The Random House collector's encyclopedia: Victoriana to Art Deco. N.Y., Random House, [1974]. 302p. il. **BF22**

Published in London by Collins, 1974, with title *The collector's encyclopedia.*
A companion to the *Encyclopedia of antiques* (below) which covers to 1875. This volume is concerned with the period 1851 to 1939, treating decorative arts of the time and "items which are collected in the same way as antiques."—*p.9.* Aims "to compress the maximum amount of information into the available space, employing a highly condensed style to avoid relying on abbreviations." Cross references are indicated by asterisks; numerous illustrations, many in color. Appendix of ceramic marks and silver date letters. Brief bibliography. NK775.R36

Random House encyclopedia of antiques. N.Y., Random House, [1973]. 400p. il. **BF23**

British edition entitled *Collins encyclopedia of antiques* (London, Collins, 1973).
Brief entries for a wide range of names and terms in the field of antiques. Many illustrations in black-and-white and in color. Cross references; brief bibliography. NK1125.R35

Savage, George. Dictionary of antiques. 2d ed. London, Barrie & Jenkins; N.Y., Mayflower, 1978. 534p. il. **BF24**

1st ed. 1970.
" . . . devised primarily to help both collectors and dealers in antiques of one kind or another to date and attribute those specimens which come their way. To this end considerable emphasis has been laid on styles or fashions in art at various periods because these are of great assistance in dating."—*Pref.* Covers from the Renaissance to the 20th century, but the user is referred to the author's *Dictionary of 19th century antiques* (1977) for fuller treatment of that period. NK30.S27

Wills, Geoffrey. A concise encyclopedia of antiques. N.Y., Van Nostrand, [1976]. 304p. il. **BF25**

"The subjects discussed and illustrated are furniture, pottery and porcelain, glass, silver, and pewter and other metals, made between 1500 and 1890."—*Foreword.* Deals almost exclusively with English antiques. NK928.W53

Directories

Kovel, Ralph M. and **Kovel, Terry.** The Kovels' Antiques & collectibles price list. Ed.15– , 1982/83– . N.Y., Crown, [1982]– . il. Annual. **BF26**

Continues the authors' *Kovels' Antiques price list, Kovels' Complete antiques price list,* etc.
Subtitle: A guide to the [year's] market for professionals, dealers, and collectors.
Lists alphabetically by category or object the antique or collectible, giving a one-line description and price asked by seller as reported from American sales and shows of the preceding 12-month

period. About 45,000 entries. Paragraph headings provide some background information. Paintings, books, stamps and coins are excluded. NK1125.A39

Miller, Judith and **Miller, Martin.** Miller's International antiques price guide. 1st Amer. ed. N.Y., Viking, [1985]. 735p. il. **BF27**

Eds.1–5 published in Britain 1979–84.
Offers the collector and professional "a guide to the market, not just a theoretical survey."—*Introd.* More than 10,000 objects are listed, each with photographic illustration, description, and price range based on previous year's sales. Arranged by category of antique (furniture, pottery, silver, toys, etc.). Directory of auctioneers; index. NK1133.M54

Warman's Americana & collectibles. Ed.1– . Elkins Park, Pa., Warman, [1984]– . il. Biennial. **BF28**

Subtitle: A price guide devoted to today's collectibles, with collecting hints, histories, references, clubs, museums.
Harry L. Rinker, ed.
Lists, describes, and prices "collectibles," which are defined as twentieth century, mass produced items made or heavily collected in America and selling for a few cents up to one hundred dollars. Arranged by categories (baseball cards, dolls, newspapers, watch fobs, etc.) with prices in the low to middle range. "Emphasis is on those items which are actively being sold in the marketplace."—*Introd.* AM303.9.W37

CERAMICS AND GLASS

Barber, Edwin Atlee. Ceramic collectors' glossary. N.Y., Walpole Soc., 1914. 119p. il. (Repr.: N.Y., DaCapo Pr., 1967) **BF29**

A dictionary of terms only, frequently with small line drawings. NK3370.B3

Boger, Louise Ade. The dictionary of world pottery and porcelain. N.Y., Scribner, [1971]. 533p. il. **BF30**

An A–Z arrangement giving "an account of the meaning and significance of the names and terms most frequently encountered in the study of pottery and porcelain over a span of almost 7000 years."—*Foreword.* Material on ceramics has been adapted from the author's *Dictionary of antiques and the decorative arts* (BF9). Numerous line drawings and renderings of specific pottery marks illustrate the text, and there is an extensive section of photographic plates. Numerous references to bibliographic sources, plus a selected bibliography. NK3770.B64

Campbell, James Edward. Pottery and ceramics; a guide to information sources. Detroit, Gale, [1978]. 241p. (Art and architecture information guide ser., v.7) **BF31**

An annotated bibliography of specialized works, mainly in English, dealing with ceramic techniques or historical periods. Includes lists of ceramic organizations and societies and museum collections. Intended for the artist, collector, or ceramic historian. Indexed. Z7179.C35

Chaffers, William. Marks & monograms on European and Oriental pottery and porcelain. The British section ed. by Geoffrey A. Godden. The European and Oriental sections ed. by Frederick Litchfield & R. L. Hobson. 15th rev. ed. London, Reeves, [1965]. 2v. il. **BF32**

1st ed. 1863?
The standard work in English, identifying more than 5,000 potter's marks. In this edition the British section has been completely revised; the others have been corrected, but are substantially unchanged. NK4215.C46

———— Collector's handbook of marks and monograms on pottery and porcelain. Rev. by Frederick Litchfield. 4th ed. London, Reeves, 1968. 367p. il. **BF33**

1st ed. 1874.
An abridgment of the above.   NK4215.C47

—— New keramic gallery, containing 700 illustrations of rare, curious and choice examples of pottery and porcelain from early times to the beginning of the twentieth century . . . 3d ed., enl. by over 100 additional illustrations, with descriptions . . . rev. and ed. by H. M. Cundall. London, Reeves, 1926. 2v. il.   **BF34**

1st ed. 1872, with title *The keramic gallery.*
A pictorial supplement to the 13th ed. of the author's *Marks and monograms on . . . pottery and porcelain.*   NK4225.C4

Corning Museum of Glass, Corning, N.Y. The history and art of glass: index of periodical articles, 1956–1979. Comp. by Louise K. Bush and Paul N. Perrot, ed. by Gail P. Bardhan. Boston, G. K. Hall, 1982. 876p.   **BF35**

—— The history and art of glass: index of periodical articles, 1980–1982. Comp. by Louise K. Bush, ed. by Gail P. Bardhan. Boston, G. K. Hall, 1984. 298p.

The basic volume lists more than 10,000 articles in many languages drawn from periodicals, conference proceedings, annuals and yearbooks. Arranged in three sections: (1) General publications; (2) Technological publications (including preservation); (3) Historical publications; each section is appropriately subdivided. Entries give full bibliographic data. The work is compiled from the annual checklists published in the Museum's *Journal of glass studies.* Author index.
The 1980–82 volume adds almost 4,000 articles in similar arrangement.   Z6046.C69

Cushion, John Patrick. Handbook of pottery and porcelain marks. 4th ed., rev. and exp. In collaboration with W. B. Honey. London, Faber, [1980]. 272p. il.   **BF36**

1st ed. 1956.
An aid to the identification of pottery and porcelain. "Marks recorded here are restricted to true factory marks and those others which . . . are of actual use in identifying the place of manufacture of a piece."—*Introd.* This edition expanded to include more than 3,850 marks. Especially strong in British marks, but includes marks of China and Japan; coverage of European countries is considerably enlarged over previous editions. Indexed.
The author's *Pocket book of British ceramic marks* (3d ed. London, Faber, 1976. 431p.) is a similar work limited to ceramic marks of Great Britain and Ireland.   NK4215.C80

The encyclopedia of glass. Ed. by Phoebe Phillips. N.Y., Crown, [1981]. 320p. il.   **BF37**

In two main sections: (1) History (offering historical overviews by country or region, plus sections on ancient glass and stained glass); (2) Techniques (with sections on glass melting, flat glass, paperweights, bottles, tableware, etc.). Glossary; bibliography; index. Heavily illustrated.   NK5104.E5

Fournier, Robert L. Illustrated dictionary of pottery form. N.Y., Van Nostrand Reinhold, [1981]. 256p. il.   **BF38**

"The prime objective . . . is to be a source of ideas, inspiration, and interest to the craftsman."—*Introd.* Employs a dictionary arrangement (name of the artifact, feature or shape of the vessel, etc.). Numerous photographs and line drawings. No bibliography.   TT919.5.F67

Garnier, Édouard. Dictionnaire de la céramique; faïences—grès—poteries . . . Aquarelles, marques et monogrammes d'après les dessins de l'auteur. Paris, Librairie de l'Art, [1893]. 258p. il. (Bibliothèque Internat. de l'Art. Guides du collectionneur)   **BF39**

Includes biography.   NK3770.G3

Godden, Geoffrey A. Encyclopaedia of British pottery and porcelain marks. London, Jenkins; N.Y., Crown, [1964]. 765p. il.   **BF40**

Includes, in alphabetical arrangement, more than 4,000 British china marks ranging in date from 1050 to the present.   NK4085.G63

Hamer, Frank. The potter's dictionary of materials and techniques. London, Pitman; N.Y., Watson-Guptill, [1975]. 349p. il.   **BF41**

A work for the potter, the teacher, and the student. Articles are in dictionary arrangement according to key words and phrases, with cross references to related terms. Generously illustrated with line drawings and photographs. Appendix of tables; brief bibliography.   TT919.5.H35

Hamilton, David. The Thames and Hudson manual of pottery and ceramics. N.Y., Thames and Hudson, 1982. 188p. il.   **BF42**

A reissue of the London, 1974, publication of that title which also appeared as *Van Nostrand Reinhold manual of pottery and ceramics* (N.Y., 1974).
A manual with many illustrations which aims to provide an introduction to the processes and techniques of ceramics. Glossary; index.   TT920.H33

Honey, William Bowyer. European ceramic art, from the end of the Middle Ages to about 1815. London, Faber & Faber, [1949–52]. 2v. il.   **BF43**

Contents: [v.1] Illustrated historical survey; [v.2] A dictionary of factories, artists, technical terms, etc.
A very useful work. Bibliography, [v.2].   NK4083.H62

Kämpfer, Fritz and **Beyer, Klaus G.** Glass: a world history; the story of 4000 years of fine glass-making. Tr. and rev. by Edmund Launert. London, Studio Vista, [1966]; Greenwich, Conn., New York Graphic Soc., [1967]. 314p. il.   **BF44**

A revised translation of *Viertausend Jahre Glas* (Dresden, 1966).
Chronological presentation of photographs (many in color) and text representing various periods and techniques in the history of glassmaking. A glossary (p.295–314) includes brief notes on outstanding glass artists, engravers, etc.   NK5106.K313

Nelson, Glenn C. Ceramics: a potter's handbook. 5th ed. N.Y., Holt, Rinehart, and Winston, [1984]. 350p. il.   **BF45**

1st ed. 1960.
Constitutes "a basic how-to manual for the beginning and intermediate potter as well as a reference source for the more sophisticated craftsperson."—*Pref.* Includes chapters on clays, ceramic history, techniques, decorating and glazing, kilns and firing. Reference tables; glossary; brief bibliography; index.   TP807.N363

Newman, Harold. An illustrated dictionary of glass. London, Thames & Hudson, [1977]. 315p. il.   **BF46**

Subtitle: 2,442 entries, including definitions of wares, materials, processes, forms, and decorative styles, and entries on principal glass-makers, decorators, and designers, from antiquity to the present, with an introductory survey on the history of glass-making by Robert J. Charleston.
The work is "intended primarily to define terms relating to glass and glassware, such as the constituent elements, the methods of production and decoration, and the styles in various regions and periods, and also to describe some pieces that bear recognized names."—*Pref.* Cross references; occasional bibliographic references.   TP788.N48

Savage, George and **Newman, Harold.** An illustrated dictionary of ceramics; defining 3,054 terms relating to wares, materials, processes, styles, patterns, and shapes from antiquity to the present day. London, Thames & Hudson; N.Y., Van Nostrand, [1974]. 319p. il.   **BF47**

A dictionary of terms, with many illustrations (some in color). Includes a list of "Principal European factories and their marks."   NK3770.S38

Solon, Louis Marc Emmanuel. Ceramic literature; an analytical index to the works published in all languages on the history and the technology of the ceramic art; also to the catalogues of public museums, private collections, and of auction sales . . . and to the most important price-lists of the ancient and modern manufactories. . . . London, Griffin, 1910. 660p. **BF48**

Pt.1, Author list, annotated; pt.2, Classified list. Z7179.S68

Strong, Susan R. History of American ceramics: an annotated bibliography. Metuchen, N.J., Scarecrow Pr., 1983. 184p. **BF49**

A classified, annotated bibliography of more than 600 items. A section for regional and local history lists accounts of potteries and related developments in specific states and regions; there are also sections for individual potteries and potters. Indexed.
Z7179.S85

CLOCKS AND WATCHES

Baillie, Granville Hugh. Clocks and watches; an historical bibliography. London, N.A.G. Pr., [1951]. 414p. il. (Repr.: London, Holland Pr., 1978) **BF50**

Comprehensive chronological list of books, pamphlets, manuscripts, and periodical articles—published up to 1800—on mechanical timepieces only. Introductory section gives a brief history of horology, with a list of earlier bibliographies on the subject and indications of London libraries rich in the field. Annotations are exceptionally full, with biographical notes on authors, locations of copies, outlines of contents, and quotations and illustrations from many items listed. Z7876.B33

———— Watchmakers and clockmakers of the world. [3d ed.] London, N.A.G. Pr., [1951]. 388p. maps. (Repr. 1966) **BF51**

1st ed. 1929.
An alphabetical directory giving name, place, dates, type of clock or watch, and sometimes other brief information. Lists makers to 1825 with a few outstanding later names. The 2d ed. included some 35,000 names—10,000 more than the 1st ed. The 3d ed. reproduces this text with an "Addenda" of some 600 new entries in a separate section. NK7486.B26

Britten, Frederick James. Britten's Old clocks and watches and their makers . . . 8th ed. by Cecil Clutton, and the late G. H. Baillie, and C. A. Ilbert. Rev. and enl. by Cecil Clutton. London, Methuen; N.Y., Dutton, 1973. 532p. il. **BF52**

Subtitle: A historical and descriptive account of the different styles of clocks and watches of the past in England and abroad, containing a list of nearly fourteen thousand makers.
1st ed. 1899; 7th ed. 1956.
The standard work in this field. A chronological history of the measurement of time to 1830, with a final, brief chapter (new to this edition) bringing the record forward to the present, and an extensive list of clock and watch makers (with dates and places of work). While there have been a few minor changes in the text, and the bibliography has been updated for this revision, the Subscription Books Committee review (*The booklist* 70:748, Mar. 15, 1974) concludes that "the library owning the seventh edition need not replace it with the eighth." TS542.B8

The Country life international dictionary of clocks. Consultant ed., Alan Smith. N.Y., Putnam, [1979]. 350p. il. **BF53**

Repr. with title *International dictionary of clocks* (N.Y., Exeter Books, 1984).
In five main sections: (1) The history and styles of clocks; (2) The mechanical parts of clocks; (3) Tools, materials, and workshop methods; (4) International clockmaking, with a selection of important makers (arranged by country); and (5) Sundials and astronomical instruments. Articles are signed with the initials of the contributor. Bibliography; index. TS540.7.C68

Distin, William H. and **Bishop, Robert.** The American clock; a comprehensive pictorial survey 1723–1900, with a listing of 6153 clockmakers. N.Y., E. P. Dutton, 1976. 359p. il. **BF54**

About 700 photographs of American clocks arranged chronologically within sections for types of clocks (e.g., tower clocks, tall case clocks, shelf clocks, novelty clocks), with indication of kind of movement, maker (if known), place and approximate date made. The "List of clockmakers" (p.283–347) gives location and working dates for each. Index to the illustrations. TS543.U6D57

Drepperd, Carl William. American clocks and clockmakers. Enl. [i.e., 2d] ed. Boston, Branford, 1958 [c1947]. 312p. 52p. il. **BF55**

Reproduces the 1st ed. of 1947 (which includes historical chapters; a list of American clockmakers, p.196–293; a list of terms with explanations, p.[295]–312; and a bibliography, p.312), and inserts at the end a 52p. supplement, "Additional names of clockmakers." NK7492.D7

London. Clockmakers' Company. The clockmakers' library: the catalogue of the books and manuscripts in the library of the Worshipful Company of Clockmakers, comp. by John Bromley. [London], Sotheby Parke Bernet Publs., [1977]. 136p. il. **BF56**

A revised version of the catalog of the Company's library produced by G. H. Baillie in 1951.
"Today the library comprises more than one thousand printed items, mainly in the field of historical horology; unique manuscript material, including the records of the Company from its incorporation in 1631; and a small collection of prints, portraits and photographs."—*Pref.* Separate sections for printed books, for manuscripts, for portraits, and for prints, drawings, etc. Includes accessions through Sept. 1975. Z7876.L85

COSTUME AND FASHION

See also BG113, BG119, BG121.

Bibliography

Colas, René. Bibliographie générale du costume et de la mode. Description des suites, recueils, séries, revues et livres français et étrangers relatifs au costume civil, militaire et religieux, aux modes, aux coiffures et aux divers accessoires de l'habillement. Avec une table méthodique et un index alphabétique. Paris, Colas, 1933. 2v. (Repr.: N.Y., Hacker Art Books, 1963) **BF57**

The 3,121 entries are listed by author. The bibliographical information for each item includes references to important bibliographies in which it appears. Z5691.C68

Hiler, Hilaire and **Hiler, Meyer.** Bibliography of costume; a dictionary catalog of about eight thousand books and pericdicals . . . ed. by Helen Grant Cushing, assisted by Adah V. Morris. N.Y., Wilson, 1939. 911p. (Repr.: N.Y., Blom, 1967) **BF58**

Lists "approximately eighty-four hundred works on costume and adornment, including books in all languages."—*Pref.*
More recent materials, 1957 to mid-1970s, are to be found in Kesler's *Theatrical costume* (BG119). Z5691.H64

Lipperheide, Franz Joseph, *Freiherr von.* Katalog der Freiherrlich von Lipperheide'schen Kostümbibliothek. Berlin, Lipperheide, 1896–1905. 2v. il. (Repr.: N.Y., Hacker Art Books, 1963) **BF59**

Classed catalog of an important collection which became the property of the Staatliche Kunstbibliothek, Berlin. Z5691.L76

Indexes

Monro, Isabel Stevenson and **Cook, Dorothy E.** Costume index; a subject index to plates and to illustrated texts. N.Y., Wilson, 1937. 338p.   **BF60**

———— ———— Supplement. Ed. by I. S. Monro and K. M. Monro. 1957. 210p.

An index to more than 600 works either wholly on costume or containing much material on the subject. Indexing is specific and detailed: under countries and localities, under classes of persons having special types of costume, and under details of costume—e.g., shoes, hats, etc.—with chronological subdivisions under important or large classes. The list of books indexed marks location of copies in some 33 libraries. The supplement indexes 347 books.

Z5691.M75

Dictionaries and encyclopedias

Calasibetta, Charlotte Mankey. Fairchild's Dictionary of fashion. N.Y., Fairchild, [1975]. 693p. il.   **BF61**

Aims to present "clothing terminology from both historical and contemporary viewpoints" (*Pref.*) and is meant to be used with *Fairchild's Dictionary of textiles* ed. by I. B. Wingate (N.Y., 1967), since "fabrics are included in this book but are not discussed in depth." Concise definitions; pronunciation is indicated when it differs "radically from a phonetic reading of the English word."— *p.xi.* Words or terms from the same basic category are grouped together and cross references made from the individual terms. Numerous line drawings and a few color plates. Following the main alphabetic arrangement there is a separate section on fashion designers grouped by country and giving brief biographical sketches; portraits and photographs of typical "designer styles" are also included.   TT503.C34

Cunnington, Cecil Willett, Cunnington, Phillis and **Beard, Charles.** A dictionary of English costume [900–1900]. London, A. & C. Black; Philadelphia, Dufour, [1960]. 281p. il. (Repr. 1976)   **BF62**

An alphabetically arranged dictionary of terms illustrated with numerous line drawings. Has a separate "glossary of materials," p.241–80, and one page of "obsolete colour names (prior to 1800)." The medieval items are chosen from material collected by Charles Beard. The 1976 reprint adds a "Glossary of laces" (p.281–83).

GT507.C8

Houck, Catherine. The fashion encyclopedia: an essential guide to everything you need to know about clothes. N.Y., St. Martin's, [1982]. 236p. il.   **BF63**

Defines and describes, in dictionary arrangement, many aspects of fashion: language, styles, fabrics, designers, manufacturers, processes, products, etc. Incorporates historical, technical and biographical information in entries varying from a line to several pages. Indexed.   TT503.H68

Ladbury, Ann. Dressmaking explained: A to Z of terms, processes, stitches. N.Y., Arco, [1985]. 358p. il.   **BF64**

Previously publ. (1982) under title: *The dressmaker's dictionary.*
Offers detailed explanations of terms, processes, and stitches, most with illustrations. Includes useful tables; dictionary arrangement.
Vogue sewing (N.Y., Harper & Row, 1982. 511p.) is a well-illustrated how-to book on the fundamentals of sewing, offering chapters on fashion, sewing techniques and technical needs, fabrics, tailoring, finishing, etc., and a glossary of fashion terminology.   TT503.L333

Picken, Mary (Brooks). The fashion dictionary: fabric, sewing, and apparel as expressed in the language of fashion. Rev. and enl. N.Y., Funk & Wagnalls, [1973]. 434p. il.   **BF65**

Based on the author's *Language of fashion* (1939). Includes more than 10,000 terms and names associated with wearing apparel, with many line drawings and photographic illustrations. Indicates pronunciation.   TT503.P5

Schoeffler, O. E. and **Gale, William.** Esquire's Encyclopedia of 20th century men's fashions. N.Y., McGraw-Hill, [1973]. 709p. il.   **BF66**

". . . a lavishly illustrated encyclopedia that, in seminarrative style, covers in detail every item of apparel worn by the American man of this century while exploring the society of which his clothes are a reflection."—*Introd.* Items of apparel are treated in categories (suits, topcoats and overcoats, formal day wear, dress shirts, neckwear, jewelry, socks, underwear, fishing clothes, toiletries, luggage, etc.), and chronologically within categories. Glossary; detailed index.   TT617.S36

Wilcox, Ruth Turner. The dictionary of costume. N.Y., Scribner, [1969]; London, Batsford, 1970. 406p. il.   **BF67**

Attempts to describe all facets of costume and fashion, from names of garments, fabrics, and designs, to fashion fads and personal names associated with specific articles of clothing or styles. Especially useful are the line drawings accompanying many of the definitions.   GT507.W5

Yarwood, Doreen. Encyclopaedia of world costume. London, Batsford; N.Y., Scribner, [1978]. 471p. il.   **BF68**

Articles are presented in a dictionary arrangement, with closely related topics considered together in a single, longer article. Discusses history and development of individual garments, fabrics, accessories, etc. Numerous black-and-white drawings in proximity to the text. The volume "is intended for use in the English-speaking world so is geared primarily to those needs, though the coverage of other regions is fairly wide."—*Pref.* Bibliography; index.   GT507.Y37

Directories

Huenefeld, Irene Pennington. International directory of historical clothing. Metuchen, N.J., Scarecrow Pr., 1967. 175p.   **BF69**

Lists historical-clothing collections and provides references thereto from individual types of garments and accessories.

NK4700.H8

History and illustration

Boucher, François Léon Louis. Histoire du costume en occident, de l'antiquité à nos jours. [Paris], Flammarion, [1965]. 447p. il.   **BF70**

English translation by John Ross published as *A history of costume in the West* (London, Thames & Hudson, 1967) and *20,000 years of fashion* (N.Y., Abrams, 1967).
Both men's and women's garments and accessories are illustrated and described, and the historical, political, and social background of each era is sketched. Some attention is given to children's clothing. Indexed.   GT510.B67

Brooke, Iris. Western European costume and its relation to the theatre. London, Harrap, [1939–40]. 2v., il., col.pl. (Repr.: N.Y., Theatre Arts Books, 1964–66)   **BF71**

Contents: v.1, 13th to 17th century; v.2, 17th to mid-19th century.
"The aim and scope of this book is to point out differences in costume, and the manner in which those costumes were worn at corresponding dates in the more important countries of Western Europe . . . also to give their connexions in relations to the theatre and dramatists contemporary with them."—*v.1, p.17.*

GT720.B73

Cunnington, Cecil Willett and **Cunnington, Phillis.** Handbook of English costume in the eighteenth century. Rev. ed. Boston, Plays; London, Faber, [1972]. 453p. il.   **BF72**

1st ed. 1957.

Drawings and descriptive text are used to describe men's, women's, and children's costume, period by period. Attention is given to head-gear and accessories. Quotations from writings contemporary to a given era attest to the currency, popularity, etc. of the various fashions.

Similar compilations by the same authors are: *Handbook of English mediaeval costume* (2d ed. London, Faber, 1969); *Handbook of English costume in the sixteenth century* (London, Faber, 1962); *Handbook of English costume in the seventeenth century* (2d ed. London, Faber, 1967); *Handbook of English costume in the nineteenth century* (2d ed. London, Faber, 1966). GT36.C8

Cunnington, Phillis Emily and **Buck, Anne.** Children's costume in England, from the fourteenth to the end of the nineteenth century. London, Black; N.Y., Barnes & Noble, [1965]. 236p. il. **BF73**

A century-by-century survey of English children's clothing based on references in writings and illustrations contemporary to the period. Individual items and details of apparel are described and usually illustrated. Indexed. GT1730.C8

Cunnington, Phillis Emily and **Lucas, Catherine.** Occupational costume in England, from the eleventh century to 1914, with chapters by Alan Mansfield. London, Black; N.Y., Barnes & Noble, [1967]. 427p. il. **BF74**

Descriptions of the clothing worn by people at work, with illustrations from contemporary sources. Indexed. GT730.C88

Davenport, Millia. The book of costume. N.Y., Crown, [1948]. 2v. (958p.) il. (Repr. 1979) **BF75**

A chronological survey from early times to the end of the American Civil War. The almost 3,000 illustrations (partly in color) are mainly from contemporary paintings, engravings, sculpture, etc. Location of the originals is usually given. GT513.D38

Glynn, Prudence. In fashion: dress in the twentieth century. Illus. by Madeleine Ginsburg. N.Y., Oxford Univ. Pr., 1978. 243p. il. **BF76**

A discussion of 20th-century fashion chronologically presented and treating the themes "Fashion as an art," "Special clothes," and "Fashion as a trade." Heavily illustrated with black-and-white photographs and drawings. TT504.G55

Harrold, Robert. Folk costumes of the world in colour. Poole [Eng.], Blandford Pr., [1978]. 255p. il. **BF77**

A country-by-country description of folk costumes, with regional subdivisions for many countries. Line drawings illustrate various accessories and details of costume; 80 color plates. Indexed. GT511.H38

Hill, Margot Hamilton and **Bucknell, Peter A.** The evolution of fashion; pattern and cut from 1066 to 1930. London, Batsford; N.Y., Reinhold, 1967. 225p. il. **BF78**

Presented in 56 chronological sections, each illustrating a man and woman in the typical attire of the upper middle class; following each illustration the patterns for the various garments and accessories are shown. GT510.H5

Laver, James. Costume and fashion: a concise history. Concluding chapter by Christina Probert. New ed. London, Thames and Hudson, [1982]; N.Y., Oxford Univ. Pr., 1983. 288p. il. **BF79**

1st ed. 1969 had title: *A concise history of costume.*

Offers a historical survey of fashion and social change from earliest times through the 1970s. Illustrations are placed close to pertinent text and their sources are identified. Select bibliography. GT511.L39

Lester, Katherine Morris and **Oerke, Bess Viola.** Illustrated history of those frills and furbelows of fashion which have come to be known as: accessories of dress. Peoria, Ill., Manual Arts, [1940]. 587p. il. **BF80**

Cover title: Accessories of dress.

Treats in groups the accessories worn or carried in connection with the costume: hats, veils, earrings, combs, fans, bracelets, walking sticks, muffs, buttons, buckles, etc. GT2050.L4

Levi Pisetzky, Rosita. Storia del costume in Italia. [Milano], Istituto Editoriale Italiano, [1964–69]. 5v. il. **BF81**

A detailed history with illustrations from works of art contemporary to the period treated. Covers through the 19th century. GT960.L4

Lister, Margot. Costume; an illustrated survey from ancient times to the twentieth century. London, Jenkins, 1967; Boston, Plays, [1968]. 346p. il. **BF82**

A chronological survey illustrated with many black-and-white drawings. GT513.L5

McClellan, Elisabeth. History of American costume, 1607–1870. N.Y., Tudor, 1937. 661p. il. (Repr. with a new introd.: N.Y., Tudor, 1969) **BF83**

First published as *Historic dress in America 1607–1800* (Philadelphia, Jacobs, [1904]) and *Historic dress in America 1800–1870* (Philadelphia, Jacobs, [1910]). GT607.M22

Payne, Blanche. History of costume, from the ancient Egyptians to the twentieth century. N.Y., Harper, [1965]. 607p. il. **BF84**

For each period there is brief consideration of the historical background, followed by descriptions—with many photographs and line drawings—of both men's and women's costumes. Some attention is given to footwear, hair styles, and accessories. Bibliography; index. GT510.P35

Planché, James Robinson. A cyclopaedia of costume; or, Dictionary of dress. London, Chatto and Windus, 1876–79. 2v. il. **BF85**

Subtitle: Including notices of contemporaneous fashions on the Continent; a general chronological history of the costumes of the principal countries of Europe, from the commencement of the Christian era to the accession of George the Third.

v.1, Dictionary of terms, garments, weapons, fabrics, etc.; v.2, History of costume in Europe to 1760. Many illustrations, some in color. GT510.P699

Racinet, Albert Charles Auguste. Le costume historique. Paris, Firmin-Didot, 1888. 6v. 500pl. (part col.) **BF86**

v.1 is mainly text: a general introduction; a summary of the four parts (L'antiquité classique, Le monde en dehors de l'Europe, Le monde européen à partir du moyen âge, L'Europe des temps modernes); an index of plates; a geographical and ethnographical index; a bibliography; etc. v.2–6 are plates with explanatory text covering clothing, furniture, arms, etc. GT513.R2

Rubens, Alfred. A history of Jewish costume. New and enl. ed. London, Weidenfeld and Nicolson; N.Y., Crown, [1973]. 221p. il. **BF87**

1st ed. 1967.

The traditional dress of Jewish peoples from biblical times is discussed and illustrated, with attention given to costumes of Jews in individual countries of the Western world. This edition in larger format, with additions and corrections and many color illustrations. GT540.R73

Sichel, Marion. Costume reference. Boston, Plays, Inc., 1977–79. 10v. il. **BF88**

Contents: v.1, Roman Britain and the Middle Ages; v.2, Tudors and Elizabethans; v.3, Jacobean, Stuart and Restoration; v.4, The eighteenth century; v.5, The Regency; v.6, The Victorians; v.7, The Edwardians; v.8, 1918–1939; v.9, 1939–1950; v.10, 1950 to present day.

A series of brief volumes each surveying English dress of a given period and indicating the principal trends of costume design. Includes both male and female attire, with attention to hairstyles and accessories. Illustrations in both black-and-white and in color. Indexed. The Subscription Books Committee review in the *Booklist* 74:1572 concludes that "Keeping in mind their limitations [e.g., brevity of the factual information and lack of specific detail], these volumes would be useful in a public library developing a collection on British costume. . . . " GT730.S48

Tilke, Max. National costumes from East Europe, Africa and Asia. N.Y., Hastings House, [1978]. 38p., 128p. il. **BF89**

British ed. (London, A. Zwemmer, 1978) has title *Folk costumes from East Europe, Africa, and Asia.*

Translation of *Trachten und Kostüme aus Europa, Afrika und Asien in Form, Schnitt und Farbe* (Tübingen, 1978) which, in turn, is based on Tilke's *Orientalische Kostüme* (1923) and *Osteuropäische Volkstrachten* (1925). Incorporates the plates from those volumes with some previously unpublished costume illustrations.

128 pages of colored plates are preceded by descriptive text concerning each of the costumes and individual garments illustrated. Lacks an index. GT1370.T5313

Truman, Nevil. Historic costuming. 2d ed. London, Pitman, 1966. 170p. il. **BF90**

1st ed. 1936.

Planned for the theatrical costumer but useful also for anyone interested in accurate details of historical costume, as it describes details of costumes of ancient Greece and Rome and of Britain from the 5th-century Saxons to 1910. Includes ecclesiastical costume, and armor. GT730.T7

Wilcox, Ruth Turner. Folk and festival costume of the world. N.Y., Scribner, [1965]. unpaged. il. **BF91**

Traditional costumes are described and illustrated on facing pages. GT510.W54

Yarwood, Doreen. Costume of the western world: pictorial guide and glossary. N.Y., St. Martin's Pr., [1980]. 192p. il. **BF92**

A brief history of the development of costume in Britain, western Europe and North America is followed by a glossary of terms, most of them illustrated by drawings.

Biography

Stegemeyer, Anne. Who's who in fashion. N.Y., Fairchild, [1980]. 179p. il. (Repr. 1984) **BF93**

"The emphasis here is on today's established designers, with a brief survey of influential figures in related fields and of the past."—*Pref.* In three sections: (1) Names to know; (2) Foreign designers; (3) American designers. Includes comments on the designer's works as well as biographical information; photographs and drawings are often included to depict a designer's work. Bibliography; index.

Who's who in fashion. Ed.1– . Zurich, Who's Who the Internat. Red Series Verlag, 1982– . il. Triennial? (1st ed., 3v. in 2) **BF94**

Subtitle: A biographical encyclopedia . . . containing some 6,000 biographies of living prominent personalities in the fields of fashion, beauty and jewellery.

Contains "who's who" type sketches comprising personal and professional information on Europeans in the fashion, cosmetics/perfume, and jewelry industries. Arranged alphabetically with an index of specialties. Directories of related institutions and organizations, and of wholesalers and retailers are appended.

FURNITURE AND INTERIOR DESIGN

Bibliography

Lackschewitz, Gertrud. Interior design and decoration; a bibliography, comp. for the American Institute of Decorators. N.Y., New York Pub. Lib., 1961. 86p. **BF95**

A selective list covering the history of architecture and the applied arts as well as 20th-century concepts of design. Arranged by subject with author index. Some entries have a brief descriptive comment. Z5956.D3L3

Paris. Bibliothèque Forney. Catalogue matières: arts-décoratifs, beaux-arts, métiers, techniques. Paris, Société des Amis de la Bibliothèque Forney, 1970–75. 4v. **BF96**

Reproduction of the subject catalog cards for the Library's collection of some 100,000 books and more than 1,300 periodical titles.

———— ———— Index alphabétique des auteurs. Paris, Société des Amis de la Bibliothèque Forney, 1974–75. 4 pts. in 1v. (367p.)

———— Supplément au Catalogue matières, arts-décoratifs, beaux-arts, métiers, techniques. Paris, Société des Amis de la Bibliothèque Forney, 1979–80. 2v.

Adds ten years of acquisitions—some 12,563 volumes. Dictionary arrangement. Z5939.P225

Viaux, Jacqueline. Bibliographie du meuble (mobilier civil français). Paris, Société des Amis de la Bibliothèque Forney, 1966. 589p. **BF97**

A classed bibliography, mainly periodical articles, on French furniture and furnishings. More than 5,000 items. Indexed. Z5995.3.F7V5

Dictionaries and encyclopedias

Aronson, Joseph. The encyclopedia of furniture. 3d ed., completely rev. N.Y., Crown, [1965]. 484p. il. **BF98**

1st ed. 1938. (Repr. 1967, with new title page, as *The new encyclpedia of furniture.*)

Alphabetical arrangement of short articles, illustrated with about 1,400 photographs and numerous line drawings. Increased coverage for the 19th century in this edition. NK2205.A7

Bajot, Édouard. Encyclopédie du meuble du XVᵉ siècle jusqu'à nos jours. Recueil de planches contenant des meubles de style de toutes les époques et de tous les pays, depuis le XVᵉ siècle . . . classées par ordre alphabétique . . . 2000 meubles de style reproduits à grande échelle. Paris, C. Schmid, [1901–09]. 20 pts. in 19v. 600pl. **BF99**

The many plates are arranged by type of furniture. Text is limited to very brief captions on the plates—identifying material, country, and period—and a "Table analytique des planches" and a "Notice" in v.1. Both list the 54 types of furniture alphabetically, the "Notice" giving a short historical paragraph for each type. NK2260.B3

Boger, Louise Ade. The complete guide to furniture styles. Enl. ed. N.Y., Scribner, [1969]. 500p. il. **BF100**

Previous edition 1959.

For the student and general reader. " . . . material was selected to provide the practical knowledge for following the development of the styles of furniture in Italy, France, The Netherlands, Spain, England and America. Chinese furniture of the Ming dynasty has also been included."—*Foreword.* Four new chapters on cabinetwork of the 19th and 20th centuries were added in the new edition. NK2270.B63

Connoisseur. The Connoisseur period guides to the houses, decoration, furnishing and chattels of the classic periods. Ed. by Ralph Edwards and L. G. G. Ramsey. [London, 1956–58] 6v. il. **BF101**

Also issued in a 1v. ed. (London, Connoisseur; N.Y., Bonanza, 1968. 1536p.)

Each volume has special title page: [v.1], The Tudor period, 1500–1603; [v.2], The Stuart period, 1603–1714; [v.3], The early Georgian period, 1714–1760; [v.4], The late Georgian period, 1760–1810; [v.5], The Regency period, 1810–1830; [v.6], The early Victorian period, 1830–1860. NK928.C6

Filbee, Marjorie. Dictionary of country furniture. N.Y., Hearst Books, [1977]. 200p. il. **BF102**

Concerned with furniture of smaller country homes, farmhouses and cottages of the 17th–19th centuries, with the aim of helping owners and prospective buyers "to identify various pieces and styles and to give some idea of their history."—*Introd.* Illustrated with photographs and line drawings. Brief bibliography; index.

NK2205.F54

Fleming, John and **Honour, Hugh.** Dictionary of the decorative arts. N.Y., Harper & Row, [1977]. 896p. il. **BF103**

British ed. (1977) has title: *The Penguin dictionary of decorative arts.*

Planned as a companion to the *Penguin dictionary of architecture* (BE265), the work is "concerned with furniture and furnishings— i.e., movable objects other than paintings and sculpture—in Europe from the Middle Ages onwards and in North America from the Colonial Period to the present day."—*Foreword.* Excludes articles of personal adornment, musical and scientific instruments, clocks (but not their cases), and printed books (although their bindings are considered). Cross references; bibliographic notes. NK30.F55

Gloag, John. A short dictionary of furniture, containing over 2,600 entries that include terms and names used in Britain and the United States of America. Rev. and enl. ed. London, Allen & Unwin, [1969]. 813p. il. **BF104**

Subtitle: With over 1,000 illustrations reproduced from contemporary sources or drawn by Ronald Escott, Marcelle Barton and Maureen Stafford.

1st ed. 1952.

Brief but clear definitions and descriptions, with many line drawings. Preliminary sections cover: (1) description and (2) design of furniture. The dictionary is followed by lists of British and American furniture makers and designers, and British clockmakers; bibliography; and tabulated lists of periods, types of furniture, materials, and craftsmen from 1100 to 1950. Emphasis is mainly British. Bibliography has been updated. NK2205.G55

Heal, *Sir* **Ambrose.** The London furniture makers from the Restoration to the Victorian era, 1660–1840 . . . London, Batsford, [1953]. 276p. il. **BF105**

Subtitle: A record of 2500 cabinet-makers, upholsterers, carvers and gilders with their addresses and working dates illustrated by 165 reproductions of makers' trade-cards, with a chapter by R. W. Symonds on the problem of identification of the furniture they produced illustrated by some hitherto unpublished examples of authenticated pieces. NK2529.H45

Henry Francis du Pont Winterthur Museum. American furniture, Queen Anne and Chippendale periods, in the Henry Francis du Pont Winterthur Museum, by Joseph Downs. N.Y., Viking, [1967, c1952] 1v., various pagings. il. **BF106**

First published N.Y., Macmillan, 1952. NK2406.H4

——— American furniture, the Federal period, in the Henry Francis du Pont Winterthur Museum, by Charles F. Montgomery. N.Y., Viking, [1966]. 497p. il. **BF107**

Although these companion volumes are basically catalogs of the impressive collection of American furniture at the Winterthur Museum, the fact that each piece is illustrated and described, plus the inclusion of background information and bibliography, makes them highly valuable for the study of these important periods in American furniture. NK2406.H4

Hoffman, Emmanuel. Fairchild's Dictionary of home furnishings: furniture and bedding, accessories, curtains and draperies, fabrics and fibers, floor coverings. N.Y., Fairchild Pubns., [1974]. 365p. il. **BF108**

Terms are grouped in sections corresponding to the categories mentioned in the subtitle, plus a "Retail appendix." Concise definitions; cross references are signaled by use of small capital letters within the text.

Hornung, Clarence Pearson. Treasury of American design; a pictorial survey of popular folk arts based upon watercolor renderings in the Index of American Design, at the National Gallery of Art. N.Y., Abrams, [1972]. 2v. il. **BF109**

"The collection in the Index of American Design contains over 17,000 renderings of American decorative arts ranging from before 1700 to about 1900. The selections in this book have been carefully made to show the most representative specimens of these works from various regions and cultures of our country. The watercolors here reproduced were rendered . . . by American artists in many states during the years 1935–41 under grants from the Federal and State governments."—*Foreword.*

Illustrations are grouped by type of object (furniture, glassware, ships' figureheads, toys, dolls, harness pieces, etc.). Index of artists and general index. NK805.H67

Kovel, Ralph M. and **Kovel, Terry H.** American country furniture, 1780–1875. N.Y., Crown, [1965]. 248p. il. **BF110**

About 700 items are illustrated and briefly described.

NK2406.K6

Macquoid, Percy and **Edwards, Ralph.** Dictionary of English furniture, from the Middle Ages to the late Georgian period. [2d ed.] rev. and enl. by Ralph Edwards. London, Country Life, [1954]. 3v. il. **BF111**

Of first importance. "A drastic revision of the former text, [1924–27. 3v.] with the addition of numerous sections and a very large *corpus* of illustrations."—*Foreword.*

An abridged edition "concerned only with domestic furniture" *(Foreword)* and omitting minor accessories was published as *The shorter dictionary of English furniture*, by Ralph Edwards (London, Country Life, 1964. 684p.; repr. 1972). NK2529.M32

Montgomery, Florence M. Textiles in America, 1650–1870. N.Y., Norton, [1984]. 412p., [32] leaves of plates. il. **BF112**

Subtitle: A dictionary based on original documents, prints and paintings, commercial records, American merchants' papers, shopkeepers' advertisements, and pattern books with original swatches of cloth.

In addition to the dictionary proper (p.141–377) there are explanatory sections on furnishing practices in England and America, bed hangings, window curtains, upholstery, and textiles for the period room in America. Numerous illustrations, many in color; bibliography, p.379–412. TS1767.M66

Nutting, Wallace. Furniture treasury (mostly of American origin). All periods of American furniture with some foreign examples in America, also American hardware and household utensils. Framingham, Mass., Old America Co., [1928–33]. 3v. il. **BF113**

v.1–2 reissued: N.Y., Macmillan, 1948. 2v.; also reissued as 2v. in 1: N.Y., Macmillan, 1954.

v.1–2 include 5,000 plates, arranged by type with descriptions and often dimensions and owners, covering styles to the end of the Empire period; index in v.2. v.3 has subtitle: Being a record of designers, details of designs and structure, with lists of clock makers in America, and a glossary of furniture terms, richly illustrated. It is intended to supplement the first two volumes by supplying fuller details. NK2406.N73

Pegler, Martin. The dictionary of interior design. N.Y., Crown, [1966]. 500p. il. **BF114**

Includes terms relating to furniture and period styles, architecture, woods, fabrics, ornament, etc., plus biographical notes on famous designers and architects. Illustrations are numerous, but very small.

Reprinted 1983 in a changed format and with a reduction in the number of illustrations (N.Y., Fairchild. 217p.). NK1165.P4

Penderel-Brodhurst, James George Joseph and **Layton, Edwin J.** Glossary of English furniture of the historic periods. London, Murray, [1925]. 196p. **BF115**

Defines terms and identifies prominent cabinetmakers and authors (French and English). Bibliographical sources are included in entries. NK2205.P4

Pictorial dictionary of British 19th century furniture design: an Antique Collectors' Club research project. Woodbridge, Eng., Antique Collectors' Club, [1977]. 583p. il. **BF116**

Aims "to show the complete range of Victorian furniture in illustrations drawn from contemporary sources."—*Introd.* Also includes antecedents of the Victorian era and examples of very early "modern" furniture, so that coverage ranges from 1800 to 1914. The bulk of the work is made up of small black-and-white illustrations of furniture arranged according to broad categories (bedroom furniture, cabinets, chairs, chests, couches, desks, hall stands, mantelpieces, mirrors, screens, shelves, sideboards, tables, and miscellaneous) appropriately subdivided. Illustrations are dated and name of designer or firm is indicated. A section on "The designers and design books" provides background notes on individual designers, firms, and styles. Chronology and list of contemporary sources quoted. NK2530.P5

Salaman, R. A. Dictionary of tools used in the woodworking and allied trades, *c.* 1700–1970. London, Allen & Unwin, [1975]; N.Y., Scribner, 1976. 545p. il. **BF117**

Tools and trades are entered alphabetically, with "families" of tools and tools of a particular trade grouped together; cross references are provided from the name of the specific tool when it is treated with tools of a trade. Many illustrations; bibliography. TT186.S24

Studio dictionary of design and decoration. Ed., Robert Harling. Rev. and enl. ed. N.Y., Viking Pr., [1973]. 538p. il. **BF118**

British ed. had title *House and Garden* dictionary . . . (London, Collins, 1973).

Based on a series by Robert Harling published in *House and garden* over a period of years.

A copiously illustrated work with entries for terms, styles, architects, and designers, etc. Articles are generally brief; no bibliography. NK1165.S78

Thornton, Peter. Authentic decor: the domestic interior, 1620–1920. [1st American ed.] N.Y., Viking, [1984]. 408p. il. **BF119**

Publ. in Great Britain by Weidenfeld & Nicolson.

Offers a survey, through illustrations and descriptive text, of how people arranged and decorated their rooms through the centuries. In general, the numerous illustrations (many in color, and including paintings, drawings, floor plans, details of decoration, etc.) were made when the decoration was new; restorations were avoided as misleading. Arranged in six 50-year periods with background notes to each. Illustrations are described in considerable detail, with attention given to materials and fabrics. International in scope; interiors range from the homes of aristocrats to those of the middle classes. Bibliographic notes; index. NK1860.T49

Viollet-Le-Duc, Eugène Emmanuel. Dictionnaire raisonné du mobilier français de l'époque carlovingienne à la Renaissance. Paris, Morel, 1858–75. 6v. il. **BF120**

Issued in parts. Imprint varies.

Contents: v.1: pt.1, Meubles; v.2: pt.2, Ustensiles; pt.3, Orfèvrerie; pt.4, Instruments de musique; pt.5, Jeux, passetemps; pt.6, Outils, outillages; v.3–4: pt.7, Vêtements, bijoux de corps, objets de toilette; v.5–6: pt.8, Armes de guerre offensives et défensives.

Index in each volume, with one for the whole work in v.6. NK30.V7

JEWELRY

Mason, Anita Frances. An illustrated dictionary of jewellery. N.Y., Harper & Row, [1974]. 389p. il. **BF121**

First published 1973 by Osprey Publishing, Reading, Eng.

Intended "both for those involved in the jewellery trade and for those with a less specialized interest in jewellery."—*Pref.* Attempts to cover the whole field concisely, dealing with "gemstones and their identification, with the techniques of jewellery-manufacture, with the history of jewellery, and with subjects of interest to the retail jeweller such as hallmarking." Cross references; brief bibliography. NK7304.M37

Newman, Harold. An illustrated dictionary of jewelry: 2,530 entries, including definitions of jewels, gemstones, materials, processes, and styles, and entries on principal designers and makers from antiquity to the present day. N.Y., Thames and Hudson, [1981]. 334p. il. **BF122**

Encompasses the types of entries indicated in the subtitle, with the basic definition of jewelry given as "any decorative article that is made of metal, gemstones and/or hard organic material of high quality, contrived with artistry or superior craftsmanship, and intended to be worn on a person (such as a necklace, bracelet, earrings or brooch), including such articles that are functional as well as decorative (e.g. cuff links, buckles, tie clips)."—*Pref.* Numerous illustrations; cross references. No bibliography.

NK7304.N43

LACE

Jackson, Emily. A history of hand-made lace. Dealing with the origin of lace, the growth of the great lace centres, the mode of manufacture, the methods of distinguishing and the care of various kinds of lace. With suppl. information by Ernesto Jesurum. London, Gill; N.Y., Scribner, 1900. 245p. il. (Repr.: Detroit, Tower Books, 1971) **BF123**

Bibliography, p.98–105; "Dictionary of lace," p.[107]–206; "Glossary relating to hand-made lace," p.[207]–19. NK9406.J3

Pfannschmidt, Ernst Erik. Twentieth-century lace. London, Mills and Boon; N.Y., Scribner, [1975]. 216p. il. **BF124**

Neither a handbook of techniques nor a full history of the subject, but, rather, a series of historical notes that "point the way to recent developments that have . . . not been systematically recorded hitherto." The bulk of the book (p.34–209) is devoted to illustrations. Indexed. NK9410.P42

Powys, Marian. Lace and lace-making. Boston, Branford, 1953. 219p. il. **BF125**

A practical handbook, giving descriptions of various types of lace with methods of identification; also directions for making, mending, and cleaning lace. NK9404.P75

Whiting, Gertrude, Lace guide for makers and collectors; with bibliography and five-language nomenclature, profusely illustrated with halftone plates and key designs. N.Y., Dutton, [1920]. 415p. il. **BF126**

Nomenclature in English, French, Italian, Spanish, and German. p.38–68. Bibliography, p.243–401. Illustrations and instructions for making various types of lace. TT800.W5

METAL ARTS
Gold and silver

Chaffers, William. Hall marks on gold and silver plate, illus. with revised tables of annual date letters employed in the assay offices of England, Scotland and Ireland. 10th ed. extended and enl. and with the addition of new date letters and marks, and a bibliography. Also incorporating makers' marks from the *"Gilda aurifabrorum."* Ed. by C. A. Markham. London, Reeves, 1922. 395p. il. **BF127**

1st ed. 1863.

Title varies slightly from edition to edition.

Includes also material on English gold- and silversmiths, tables of statutes and ordinances, chronological list of English plate, etc., bibliography, and a general index. NK7210.C45

Fales, Martha Gandy. Early American silver. Rev. and enl. ed. N.Y., Dutton, 1973. 336p. il. **BF128**

1st ed., 1970, had subtitle "for the cautious collector."
Historical survey of American silver from the 17th to the early 19th centuries. NK7112.F3

Jackson, *Sir* **Charles James.** English goldsmiths and their marks: a history of the goldsmiths and plate workers of England, Scotland, and Ireland; with over thirteen thousand marks, reproduced in facsimile from authentic examples of plate, and tables of date-letters and other hallmarks used in the assay offices of the United Kingdom. 2d ed. rev. and enl. London, Macmillan, 1921. 747p. il. (Repr.: N.Y., Dover, 1964) **BF129**

1st ed. 1905.
"The term 'Goldsmith' is used, as it formerly was, not only with reference to the worker in gold, but as comprising the Silversmith and the worker in both gold and silver."—*Introd.* NK7143.J15

Nocq, Henry. Le poinçon de Paris; répertoire des maîtres-orfèvres de la juridiction de Paris depuis le Moyen-Âge jusqu'à la fin du XVIIIᵉ siècle. Paris, H. Floury, 1926–31. 5v. il. **BF130**

Arranged alphabetically by name of the gold- or silversmith, giving brief information and mark. v.1–4, A–Z; v.4 includes a *"Résumé chronologique"* and other historical lists and notes; v.5 contains "Errata et addenda" and three indexes. NK7210.N6

Okie, Howard Pitcher. Old silver and old Sheffield plate. . . . Garden City, N.Y., Doubleday, 1928. 420p. il. **BF131**

Subtitle: A history of the silversmith's art in Great Britain and Ireland, with reproductions in facsimile of about thirteen thousand marks; tables of date letters and other marks; American silversmiths and their marks; Paris marks and Paris date letters with a description of the methods of marking employed by the Paris Guild of Silversmiths; hallmarks, and date letters when used, of nearly all the countries of continental Europe, reproduced in facsimile; a history of Old Sheffield plate and a description of the method of its production, with the names and marks in facsimile of every known maker. NK7143.O4

Rosenberg, Marc, Der goldschmiede Merkzeichen. 3. erweit. u. illus. Aufl. Frankfurt a. M., Frankfurter Verlags-Anstalt, 1922–28. 4v. il. (Repr. 1955) **BF132**

1st ed. 1890.
v.1–3, *Deutsches Reich,* are arranged by city with its goldsmiths chronologically listed. v.4, *Das europäische Ausland,* is arranged by country, then city. It includes Byzantine goldsmiths. Index of marks and names in each volume. NK7210.R6

Pewter

Cotterell, Howard Herschel. Old pewter; its makers and marks in England, Scotland and Ireland. An account of the old pewterer and his craft, illustrating all known marks and secondary marks of the old pewterers with a series of plates showing the chief types of their wares. London, Batsford; N.Y., Scribner, 1929. 432p. il. (Repr.: London, Batsford; Rutland, Vt., Tuttle, 1963) **BF133**

Alphabetical list of pewterers with illustrations of their marks where known, p.145–344; Initialled marks, alphabetical list, p.345–83; Illustrations of those marks which bear neither their owner's names nor initials, p.384–89; Index to the devices, p.390–415; Index to the "Hallmarks," p.416–21; General index, p.425–32. NK8415.G7C6

Ebert, Katherine. Collecting American pewter. N.Y., Scribner's, [1973]. 163p. il. **BF134**

Intended "to help the beginner and moderately advanced collector of American pewter."—*Introd.* Includes a section of "American

pewterers and their marks" and a list of "American makers of pewter or britannia without reported examples." Brief bibliography. NK8412.E23

Laughlin, Ledlie Irwin. Pewter in America, its makers and their marks. Barre, Mass., Barre Publ., 1969–71. 3v. il. 115pl. **BF135**

First publ. 1940 in 2v. In the 1969–71 ed. v.1–2 are reprinted unchanged; v.3 corrects and supplements those volumes, following the same format and chapter headings, adding "all pertinent available material" *(Pref., v.3)* which has accumulated in the thirty years following 1940. This ed. reprinted, 3v. in 1, by American Legacy Pr., N.Y., 1981 (687p.).
A standard work, giving history, problems for the collector, and biographical sketches of pewterers working in America prior to 1850, grouped geographically, then chronologically. Contains a "Check list of American makers of pewter, britannia or block tin . . . prior to 1850"; a list of "Dethroned pewterers" (names from previous lists omitted for cause). Index and bibliography in v.2 and v.3. NK8412.L3

RUGS

Arthur D. Jenkins Library. Rug and textile arts: a periodical index, 1890–1982. The Textile Museum, Arthur D. Jenkins Library. Boston, G. K. Hall, 1983. 472p. **BF136**

"Represents the selective indexing of textile and rug articles found in over 300 periodical titles owned by the Museum."—*Pref.* While the earliest dates from 1890, the majority of articles were published from 1920 to the early 1980s. Reproduces the catalog cards arranged in two sections: (1) author and (2) subject/title. Bibliographical information is complete for each entry; inclusion of tracings aids in use of the subject section. Z7914.T3A77

Eiland, Murray L. Oriental rugs: a new comprehensive guide. 3d ed. Boston, Little, Brown, [1981]. 294p. il. **BF137**

1st ed. 1973.
Concentrates "on presenting and evaluating the findings of recent scholarship and at the same time on providing a foundation for the beginner in rug studies."—*Pref.* Chapters deal with history and development of rugs and carpets, elements of design, dyes, construction, rugs of Persia, Turkish rugs, Turkoman rugs, and rugs of the Caucasus. Numerous illustrations (many in color); brief notes on sources; index. NK2808.E44

Erdmann, Kurt. Seven hundred years of oriental carpets; ed. by Hanna Erdmann & tr. from the German by May H. Beattie & Hildegard Herzog. London, Faber; Berkeley, Univ. of California Pr., 1970. 238p. il. **BF138**

Translation of *Siebenhundert Jahre Orientteppich* (Herford, Busse, 1966).
An illustrated historical survey treating the various types of oriental carpets by country and period. A brief account by the same author is: NK2808.E7513

——— Oriental carpets: an essay on their history. Tr. by Charles Grant Ellis. [2d ed. in English] London, Zwemmer; N.Y., Universe Books, [1962]. 80p. **BF139**

Translation of *Der orientalische Knüpfteppich* (2. Aufl., Tübingen, Wasmuth, 1960). NK2808.E743

Faraday, Cornelia Bateman. European and American carpets and rugs. . . . With more than 400 illustrations of antique and modern European and American carpets and rugs, with 32 plates in full color. Grand Rapids, Mich., Dean-Hicks Co., 1929. 382p. il. **BF140**

Subtitle: A history of the hand-woven decorative floor coverings of Spain, France, Great Britain, Scandinavia, Belgium, Holland, Italy, the Balkans, Germany, Austria, and early America; and of the machine-made carpets and rugs of modern Europe and of the United States.

A standard work on carpets other than the Oriental.

NK2795.F3

Herbert, Janice Summers. Oriental rugs: the illustrated guide. Rev. and expanded ed. N.Y., Macmillan; London, Collier Macmillan, [1982]. 175p. il.   **BF141**

1st ed. 1978.

A brief, somewhat superficial survey with illustrations in color. Includes a short section on buying and caring for oriental rugs. Useful at the beginning level. Glossary; index.   NK2808.H52

Lewis, George Griffin. The practical book of Oriental rugs. . . . [6th] rev. ed., with 32 color plates, 80 halftones and numerous line designs. Philadelphia, Lippincott, [1945]. 317p. il.   **BF142**

1st ed. 1911.

A useful handbook on the classification of Oriental rugs and their identification, materials, dyes, weaving, designs and their symbolism, etc.   NK2808.L65

Neff, Ivan C. and **Maggs, Carol V.** Dictionary of oriental rugs, with a monograph on identification by weave. N.Y., Van Nostrand Reinhold, [1979]. 238p. il.   **BF143**

First published London, Donker, 1977.

A dictionary of some 600 rug names with an explanation of the name and an attempt "to indicate in which way the rug is related to its name."—*p.16.* Bibliography; 84 color plates illustrating 42 rugs.   NK2808.N27

COINS, MEDALS, AND CURRENCY

See also BF180.

Guides

Coffin, Joseph. The complete book of coin collecting. 6th rev. ed. N.Y., Coward, McCann & Geohegan, [1979]. 251p. il.   **BF144**

1st ed. 1938.

Offers an introduction to coin collecting "to those who know little or nothing about it" *(Pref.),* but includes background material useful for the more advanced collector. Chapters cover beginning a collection, United States money, foreign and ancient coins, making a profit from coin collecting, and care and cleaning of coins. Emphasis is on American coins. Brief chapter bibliographies; no index. Includes a glossary and lists of dealers, clubs, and exhibitions.

An older, valuable guide, C. C. Chamberlain's *Teach yourself guide to numismatics* (London, English Universities Pr., 1960. 180p.) is a non-technical dictionary of readable, informative entries written "for the beginner . . . [and] small collector."—*Introd.* An American edition, with title *Coin dictionary and guide,* by Chamberlain and Fred Reinfeld (N.Y., Sterling, 1960. 251p.), expanded the British original to include terms peculiar to American coinage and coin collecting.   CJ81.C6

Bibliography

American Numismatic Society. Library. Dictionary catalogue. Boston, G. K. Hall, 1962. 7v. (5920p.)   **BF145**

[v.7], unnumbered, has title *Auction catalogue.*

———— ———— Suppl. 1–3. Boston, G. K. Hall, 1967–78. 4v.

Reproduces the catalog cards of "the most comprehensive numismatic library in America" *(Pref.),* encompassing every branch of the subject. Includes books, periodical articles, pamphlets, microforms and manuscripts in one alphabetic sequence. Supplements add the acquisitions of 1962 through 1977. More than 70,000 items in all.

Auction catalogs, both American and foreign, are listed in the last volume of the basic set, appearing under dealer and under owner; in the supplements they are in a separate section, listed by dealer.

Another large collection (20,000 items) is that of the American Numismatic Association, which published its *Library catalogue* (2d ed. Colorado Springs, The Association, 1977. 768p.) as a classified list of books, periodicals and auction catalogs, with an author index. Those materials circulate on a "borrow by mail" basis to Association members and member libraries.   Z6870.A52

Clain-Stefanelli, Elvira Eliza. Numismatic bibliography. München, Battenberg [distr. in U.S. by K. G. Saur, N.Y.], [1985]. 1848p. il.   **BF146**

1st ed., 1967, had title *Select numismatic bibliography.*

Preface in English, German, and French.

A classed, international bibliography of more than 18,300 entries covering books, periodical articles, conference proceedings, etc. Includes works on monetary theory and evolution of money, as well as coinages (by period and country/region), collections and collecting, tokens, medals, and many special topics. Indexed.

Z6866.C44

Coole, Arthur Braddan. A bibliography on Far Eastern numismatology and a coin index. [With the assistance of] Hitoshi Kozono [and] Howard F. Bowker. [Denver, 1967] 581p. il. (Encyclopedia of Chinese coins, v.1)   **BF147**

Presents an extensive bibliography in three sections: works in Chinese, in Japanese, and in Western languages; the first and second parts are alphabetical by romanized title; Western language materials are listed alphabetically by author (the latter part incorporating Bowker's *A numismatic bibliography of the Far East,* 1943).

Grierson, Philip. Bibliographie numismatique. 2e ed. rev. et aug. Bruxelles, 1979. 359p. (Cercle d'Études Numismatiques. Travaux, 9)   **BF148**

1st ed. 1954 had title *Coins and medals.*

Within period divisions the listings are by country and by peoples. Introductory notes for the various sections and subsections. Bibliographies include essential reference works and selected monographs and articles illustrating research trends. Indexed.

Lipsius, Johann Gottfried. A bibliography of numismatic books printed before 1800. With the supplement to 1866 by J[ohan Jakob] Leitzmann. Colchester, Essex, John Drury, 1977. 558p., 189p.   **BF149**

Reprints, unchanged, Lipsius' *Bibliotheca numaria* (1801), the standard pre-1800 numismatic bibliography (an author list with subject index) together with Leitzmann's *Schriften über Münzkunde* (1867), which added works of 1801 to 1866.

Mayer, Leo Ary. Bibliography of Moslem numismatics, India excepted. 2d considerably enl. ed. London, Royal Asiatic Soc., 1954. 283p. (Oriental Translation Fund. Pubn. New ser. v.35)   **BF150**

Lists more than 2,000 titles arranged alphabetically. The annotation after each title gives the names of the dynasties mentioned in the relevant book or article. In many cases references are given to reviews.

Mayer is also the author of *A bibliography of Jewish numismatics* (Jerusalem, Magnes Pr., Hebrew Univ., 1966. 78p.).

Numismatic literature. no.1– , Oct. 1947– . N.Y., American Numismatic Society, 1947– . Semiannual.   **BF151**

Frequency varies.

A classified listing of book and periodical publications with abstracts; separate sections of reviews and obituaries. Author and subject indexes.   Z6866.A53

Suetens, Ivo. Bibliographie numismatique. Supplément: ordres et decorations. Bruxelles, 1969–77. 2v. (Cercle d'Études Numismatiques. Travaux, 4, 8)   **BF152**

Intended as supplements to the 1954 ed. of Grierson's bibliography (BF148).

General bibliographic listings are followed by sections of specialized works on the orders of individual countries. Indexed.

Vermeule, Cornelius Clarkson. A bibliography of applied numismatics in the fields of Greek and Roman archaeology and the fine arts. London, Spink, 1956. 172p. **BF153**

1,309 numbered items, both books and periodical articles.
Z6869.G8V4

Catalogs, dictionaries, etc.

International

Coin world almanac. Ed.1– , 1976– . Sidney, Ohio, Amos Pr., 1976– . il. Irregular. **BF154**

Offers a "compact source of numismatic information" (*Foreword, 4th ed., 1984*), presenting general, historical and technical information arranged under such headings as: gold and silver, U.S. coins, paper money, rarities, coins as investments, organizations, etc. Bibliography; glossary; index. CJ1.C576

Coins: an illustrated survey, 650 BC to the present day. Martin J. Price, gen. ed. N.Y., Methuen, [1980]. 320p. il. **BF155**

Without pretending to be a complete history of coinage "this volume sets out to illustrate through more than 2000 photographs the main trends of coinage in its many different facets; and the accompanying essays [by various authors] show how the coins relate to their cultural and historical background."—*Foreword*. Short essays treat the nature of coinage, money before coinage, many periods of Western history, paper money, ancient Near East, Islam, India, and the Far East. Size of coin is indicated in the "List of illustrations." Brief bibliography and an index, chiefly of names and places. CJ59.C64

Craig, William D. Coins of the world, 1750–1850. 3d ed. Ed. by Holland Wallace. Racine, Wis., Western Pub. Co., Whitman Coin Supply Div., [1976]. 478p. il. **BF156**

1st ed. 1966.
"This catalog is designed to extend Richard S. Yeoman's *A Catalog of Modern World Coins* [BF172] backward another century."—*Introd.* Estimated values are given. CJ1751.C7

Doty, Richard G. The Macmillan encyclopedic dictionary of numismatics. N.Y., Macmillan; London, Collier Macmillan, [1982]. 355p. il. **BF157**

A "general dictionary of numismatic terms, ranging from the basic to the specialized" (*Introd.*) and intended for use by hobbyist and specialist alike. Each entry offers a brief definition of the term, followed by an account of its history, purpose, physical appearance, etc., as applicable. Cross references; bibliography, p.349–55.
CJ69.D67

Forrer, Leonard. Biographical dictionary of medallists: coin, gem, and seal-engravers, mint-masters, etc., ancient and modern, with references to their works B.C.500–A.D.1900. London, Spink, 1902–30. 8v. il. (Repr.: London, Baldwin, 1979–80) **BF158**

v.1–6, A–Z; v.7–8, Supplement A–Z. v.8 also contains a 2d supplement and an index of illustrations. CJ5535.F7

Frey, Albert Romer. Dictionary of numismatic names, with Glossary of numismatic terms in English, French, German, Italian, Swedish, by Mark M. Salton. [N.Y.], Barnes & Noble, [1947]. 311p., 94p. (Repr.: London, Spink, 1973) **BF159**

A reprint of a work originally published in 1917 as v.50 of the *American journal of numismatics;* gives information about terms used in numismatic works in English and foreign languages. Includes a list of principal authorities cited, p.[vii]–ix; a geographical index; and a paper money index. The Glossary lists numismatic terms alphabetically in each of the five languages, with equivalents in the other four, but without definitions. CJ67.F7

Friedberg, Robert. Gold coins of the world. 5th ed. Rev. & ed. by Arthur L. Friedberg and Ira S. Friedberg. N.Y., Coin and Currency Inst., [1980]. 484p. il. **BF160**

Subtitle: Complete from 600 A.D. to the present. An illustrated standard catalogue with valuations.
1st ed. 1958.
Preface in English, French, German, Italian, and Spanish.
"The aim has been to start the coin issues of each place with the first distinctive coins that positively identify the place as we know its name today."—*Pref.* In two parts, each alphabetical by country, then chronological by issue: pt.1, from earliest date to 1960; pt.2, recent issues beginning 1960. Geographical index. CJ1545.F74

Grierson, Philip. Byzantine coins. London, Methuen; Berkeley, Univ. of California Pr., [1982]. 411p. il. **BF161**

Aims to provide "a handbook giving in one volume a general history of Byzantine coinage and a descriptive guide to the coins which will serve the general reader and the historian . . . and the numismatist and collector."—*Pref.* Describes and illustrates most of the known types of Byzantine coins, 498 to 1453, without giving "details of dates, officinae and minor varieties provided by . . . catalogues of major collections." Notes and plates bound at back of volume. Indexed. CJ1229.G7

——— Numismatics. London & N.Y., Oxford Univ. Pr., 1975. 211p. **BF162**

A useful survey of the field of numismatics for the student and collector. Traces the history of coinage with attention to both Eastern and Western traditions from earliest times to the modern period. Includes a chapter on numismatic scholarship. Glossary; brief bibliography; index. CJ75.G74

Hobson, Burton and **Obojski, Robert.** Illustrated encyclopedia of world coins. Rev. and expanded ed. Garden City, N.Y., Doubleday, [1983]; London, Hale, [1984]. 528p. il. **BF163**

1st ed. 1970.
Articles appear in an alphabetical arrangement, with entries running heavily to names of countries or regions, but with entries such as "Biblical coins," "Byzantine coinage," "Cut money," "Free imperial cities," "Platinum coins," and "Rarities." There is a guide to inscriptions on coins, notes on collecting and investing in gold coins, a table of valuations, and an index. Many photographic illustrations. CJ67.H6

Holtz, Walter. Lexikon der Münzabkürzungen mit geschlichtlich–geographischen Erläuterungen. München, Klinkhardt & Biermann, [1981]. 606p. il. **BF164**

Provides the coin collector and historian with a key to decipher abbreviated Latin inscriptions of medieval and modern European coins. In three alphabetical lists: Neuzeit [since c1500]; Religiös-kirchliche Abkürzungen [medieval and modern]; Mittelalter [c800 to c1500]. A three-column page gives abbreviation, expanded Latin term, and German translation. Includes a section of background notes of historical and geographical information; list of Latin place names with modern German equivalents. Bibliography, p.605–06. CJ2455.H64

Junge, Ewald. World coin encyclopedia. London, Barrie & Jenkins; N.Y., Morrow, 1984. 297p. il. **BF165**

Entries for terms, denominations, coinmakers and medalists, mints, place names and their significance in numismatics, collectors and collections. Cross references; bibliography, p.283–97.
CJ67.J86

Krause, Chester L. and **Mishler, Clifford.** Standard catalog of world coins. Colin R. Bruce II, ed. 11th ed. [Iola, Wis., Krause Pubns., 1985] 2048p. il. **BF166**

1st ed. 1972.
A catalog of national coin issues. This edition includes "over 77,000 coin issues listed by date and mint, from more than 1300 coin-issuing countries, states, provinces, and cities" (*Introd.*), with some 42,000 coin photographs. Scope has been enlarged to extend from 1720 to the present. Glossary; index of coin denominations;

mint index; illustrated guide to Eastern mint names for Arabic, Persian and Turkish coinage.

Another Krause catalog, similar in format, is *Standard catalog of world gold coins* (1986 ed. Iola, Wis., Krause Pubns. [1985]. 640p.).
CJ1755.K72

Kroha, Tyll. Lexikon der Numismatik. [Gütersloh], Bertelsmann Lexikon-Verlag, [1977]. 512p. il. **BF167**

Entries for personal and place names, names of specific coins, and terms in numismatics. Bibliography, p.506–12. CJ69.K76

Reinfeld, Fred and **Hobson, Burton.** Catalogue of the world's most popular coins. 11th ed. Ed. by Robert Obojski. N.Y., Sterling, [1983]. 580p. il. **BF168**

1st ed. 1956.
Coins are listed by country or issuing region, with illustrations of both obverse and reverse sides. Prices are quoted for coins "in the condition in which the particular issue is usually encountered."— *p.10.* CJ63.R4

Schlickeysen, F. W. A. and **Pallmann, Reinhold.** Erklärung der Abkürzungen auf Münzen der neueren Zeit, des Mittelalters und des Altertums, sowie auf Denkmünzen und münzartigen Zeichen. 4. Aufl. Graz, Akademische Druck-u. Verlagsanstalt, 1961. 511p. **BF169**

Reprint of the "3. verb. und verm. Aufl. bearb. von Reinhold Pallmann" (Berlin, Spemann, 1896). 1st ed. 1855; 2d ed. 1882.
The section on medieval and modern coins includes information on marks on Russian coins. The section on antiquity concerns Greek and Roman coins. CJ71.S3

Schrötter, Friedrich, *Freiherr von.* Wörterbuch der Münzkunde, in Verbindung mit N. Bauer, K. Regling [u. A.]. Berlin, W. de Gruyter, 1930. 777p. il. (Repr. 1970) **BF170**

An encyclopedia of numismatics from ancient to modern times.
CJ67.S3

Seaby, Herbert Allen and **Rayner, P. Alan.** The English silver coinage from 1649. [4th rev. ed.] London, Seaby, [1974]. 240p. il. **BF171**

1st ed. 1949; 3d ed. 1968.
Aims "to provide collectors with a standard work of reference . . . , giving details of dates, varieties, comparative rarity, patterns and proofs, etc."—*Introd.*
Coins of England and the United Kingdom, 20th ed., ed. by P. Frank Purvey (London, Seaby, 1984. 320p.; *Standard catalogue of British coins,* v.1), is an illustrated catalog for both collectors and historians, covering coins from Celtic and Roman eras to the present. Values given represent the retail scale at Seaby's. Issued annually. CJ2485.S4

Yeoman, Richard S. A catalog of modern world coins 1850–1964. Rev. and ed. by Arthur L. Friedberg and Ira S. Friedberg. 13th ed. Fort Lee, N.J., Coin & Currency Inst., [1983]. 507p. **BF172**

1st ed. 1957.
Includes coins of all countries, in all metals, issued from 1850 to 1964. Gives estimated values in multiple conditions; Yeoman and Friedberg numbers.
A companion series, *Current coins of the world* (ed.1–7, 1966–76) served as a reference for coins currently in circulation (i.e., from about 1955). CJ1753.Y4

United States

Friedberg, Robert. Paper money of the United States; a complete illustrated guide with valuations. 10th ed., with additions and revisions by Ira S. and Arthur L. Friedberg. Fort Lee, N.J., Coin and Currency Institute, [1981]. 327p. il. **BF173**

"Large size notes, fractional currency, small size notes, encased postage stamps from the first year of paper money, 1861, to the present."—*t.p.*

1st ed. 1953; 9th ed. 1978.
Revisions include updated valuations. HG591.F7

A guide book of United States coins: fully illustrated catalog and valuation list, 1616 to date. Ed.1– , 1947– . Racine, Wis., Western Pub. Co., [1946?]– . il. Annual. (39th rev. ed. 1985) **BF174**

Subtitle varies slightly.
At head of title: The official red book of United States coins.
By Richard S. Yeoman; ed. by Kenneth Bressett.
An illustrated catalog and retail price list.
The same publisher issues the *Handbook of United States coins* by Richard Yeoman (43d ed., ed. by Kenneth Bressett. 1985. 191p.); it is known as the "Official blue book of United States coins" and contains dealer buying prices. CJ1826.G785

Hessler, Gene. The comprehensive catalog of U.S. paper money. 4th ed. Port Clinton, Ohio, [1983]. 502p. il. **BF175**

1st ed. 1974.
Includes both large- and small-sized notes, U.S. military payment certificates, and "all the notes circulated under U.S. authority in the districts, territories, and possessions outside the continental United States."—*Pref. 1st ed. (1974).* Some sections revised and expanded in this edition, and a list of national bank cities with the charter numbers of the banks has been added. A chapter on the history of paper money, and one on types of U.S. paper money precede the catalog proper. "The values listed throughout this catalog are suggested or average prices." HG591.H47

Krause, Chester L. and **Lemke, Robert F.** Standard catalog of U.S. paper money. 3d ed. [Iola, Wis., Krause Pubns., 1983] 212p. il. **BF176**

1st ed. 1981.
Intended as "a guide to those paper money issues since 1861 of the Government of the United States of America, along with several related currency issues which are traditionally collected by paper money hobbyists."—*Introd.* Gives brief background information on large size notes, national bank notes, small size notes, etc., selected illustrations, and lists of notes and their current values.
HG591.K7

Reed, Fred Morton. Cowles complete encyclopedia of U.S. coins. N.Y., Cowles, [1969]. 300p. il. **BF177**

In addition to descriptions and illustrations of United States seals and coinage, there is both historical and technical background information relating to the coins, and sections on counterfeit coins and on the condition and grading of coins. Indexed. CJ1830.R42

Swiatek, Anthony and **Breen, Walter.** The encyclopedia of United States silver & gold commemorative coins 1892–1954. N.Y., Arco Pub./F.C.I. Pr., [1981]. 362p. **BF178**

Intends to cover the field of commemorative coin collecting, "its origins, its history, its rules, objects and makers."—*Foreword.* For each coin gives historical background of event, person or place commemorated, circumstances of issue, designer, mintage and (often) place in today's coin world. Many good illustrations, those of coins greatly enlarged to show design detail. List of rare proof commemorative coinage and an "Investment section" with author's five- and ten-year price projections. Indexed.
A less elaborately produced, but equally informative catalog is Arlie R. Slabaugh's *United States commemorative coins* (2d ed. Racine, Wis., Western Pub. Co., 1975. 160p.). CJ1839.S9

POSTAGE STAMPS

Guides

Cabeen, Richard McP. Standard handbook of stamp collecting. New rev. ed. N.Y., Crowell, [1979]. 630p. il. **BF179**

Rev. by the Committee on Publications, Collectors Club of Chicago.

1st ed. 1957.

A thorough and wide-ranging guide in five main sections: (1) Introduction to stamp collecting; (2) Postal history and cover collecting; (3) Miscellaneous subjects; (4) Technical matters; (5) Classification and identification.

A review by the A.L.A. Reference and Subscription Books Review Committee judges this "as basic for libraries as either *Scott's* or *Minkus's* stamp catalogs. Public and school libraries will also need this very informative and useful philatelic enchiridion."—*Booklist* 76:1004.　　　　　　　　HE6215.C2

Rosichan, Richard H. Stamps and coins. Littleton, Colo., Libraries Unlimited, 1974. 404p. (Spare time guides, no.5) **BF180**

A bibliographic guide to works in the fields of numismatics and philately. Emphasis is on books, but includes information on periodicals, organizations, and libraries in the fields. Title, author, and subject indexes.　　　　　　Z7164.P85R56

Bibliography

Collectors Club, New York. Library. Philately: a catalog of the Collectors Club Library, New York City. Boston, G. K. Hall, 1974. 682p.　　　　　　**BF181**

Contents: Author catalog; Subject catalog; Title catalog; Periodicals catalog.

Reproduction of the catalog cards for one of the world's largest philatelic collections.　　　　Z7164.P85C64

Crawford, James Ludovic Lindsay, *26th Earl of.* Catalogue of the philatelic library of the Earl of Crawford, by E. D. Bacon. London, Philatelic Literature Soc., 1911. 924col. (Repr., with Suppl. and Addenda, N.Y., B. Franklin, 1969) **BF182**

———　——— Supplement. 1926. 136col.

———　——— Addenda to the Supplement. 1938. 8p.

The *Catalogue* was originally published for private distribution: J. L. L. Crawford. *Bibliotheca Lindesiana,* v.7: *A bibliography of the writings, general, special, and periodical, forming the literature of philately* (Aberdeen, Univ. Pr., 1911. 924col. [AA148]). The Supplement contains corrections and additions of separate works published to the end of 1908, and of periodicals and auction catalogs to the end of 1906, the same closing dates as those of the *Catalogue.* The Addenda was issued as a supplement to the March 1938 issue of the *London philatelist,* official journal of the Philatelic Literature Society.　　　　　　Z7164.P85L8

Smith, Chester M. American philatelic periodicals. State College, Pa., Amer. Philatelic Research Lib., 1978. 79p. **BF183**

A title listing of American philatelic journals, giving as far as possible: title (with cross references for changes, variants, etc.), publisher, dates, and number of volumes or issues published, Index of publishers, and a state-by-state geographic index. Does not locate files.　　　　　　Z7164.P85S63

Catalogs, dictionaries, etc.

Brookman, Lester G. The 19th century postage stamps of the United States. [1st ed.] N.Y., Lindquist, 1947. 2v. il. **BF184**

Historical and technical information with many illustrations of stamps.　　　　　　HE6185.U5B748

Konwiser, Harry Myron. American philatelic dictionary and Colonial and Revolutionary posts. N.Y., Minkus, 1947. 152p., 56p. il.　　　　　　**BF185**

Defines the "words and phrases that carry a definite meaning to the philatelist."—*Foreword.*

Colonial and Revolutionary posts, a history of the American postal

systems (56p., at end) is a partial reprint of a work with the same title published in 1931 (Richmond, Va., Dietz Publ. Co.).　　　　　　HE6196.K6

Lehnus, Donald J. Angels to zeppelins: a guide to the persons, objects, topics, and themes on United States postage stamps, 1847–1980. Westport, Conn., Greenwood Pr., 1982. 279p. il.　　　　　　**BF186**

Analyzes U.S. postage issues for the "persons, objects, topics, and themes" of the subtitle and presents the data derived in lists and tables, followed by chapters of text. Discusses such topics as nationality and birthplace, professions, persons honored while alive, etc., incorporating brief identification of person or theme, but information on categories and statistics predominates. Scott and Minkus numbers given in an appendix. Bibliography; index.　　　　　　HE6185.U5L34

Linn's World stamp almanac. Ed.1– , 1977– . Sidney, Ohio, Amos Pr., 1977– . il. Irregular.　　　**BF187**

Subtitle: A handbook for stamp collectors.

Comp. and ed. by the staff of Linn's Stamp news. 3d ed. 1980 (757p.).

Offered as a "compendium of the factual materials most essential for a full understanding and appreciation of stamp collecting."—*Foreword.* Contains a wide range of information arranged in 30 sections (history of philately, glossary of terms, directory information on museums and organizations, postal regulations, auctions, etc.). Bibliography; index.　　　　HE6194.L56

New American stamp catalog. Ed.1– , 1954– . N.Y., Minkus Pubns., 1953– . il. Annual.　　　**BF188**

Title varies; editor varies.

Covers all types of American stamps: regular postal issues, commemoratives, air mail, revenue stamps, Confederate States, etc., as well as stamps of United States possessions. Quotes Minkus' prices. The multivolume *Minkus new wide world stamp catalog* (1955– ; title varies) covers postage stamps of the rest of the world.　　　　　　HE6185.U5N4

Partington, Paul G. Who's who on the postage stamps of Eastern Europe. Metuchen, N.J., Scarecrow Pr., 1979. 498p. il.　　　　　　**BF189**

In two sections: (1) Native personalities and (2) Foreign personalities. Full biographical sketches are provided in the first category; dates and brief identification in the second. References to *Scott's Standard postage stamp catalogue* are given, as are sources of biographical information. Useful to the general reader as well as to the philatelist.　　　　　　CT759.P37

Scott Publications, Inc., N.Y. Standard postage stamp catalogue (The encyclopedia of philately). 16th ed.– . 1868– . N.Y., Scott Publ., 1867– . Annual. (140th ed. 1984) **BF190**

Title varies slightly. Publisher's name varies: Scott and Co.; Scott Stamp and Coin Co., Ltd.; etc.

Since 1974 each issue is in 4v. Contents for 1984: v.1, United States and affiliated territories, United Nations, British Commonwealth of Nations; v.2–4, European countries and colonies, independent nations of Africa, Asia, Latin America [arranged alphabetically, A–Z].

Gives illustrations, description, denominations, and value of the principal stamps, used and unused, of all countries. Supplementary material appears in *Scott's Monthly stamp journal.*　　HE6226.S48

Stanley Gibbons postage stamp catalogue. London, S. Gibbons, 1865– .　　　　　　**BF191**

Title varies: *Stanley Gibbons priced postage stamp catalogue,* etc.

Issued in a varying number of parts (at present, 22), each with edition numbering in its own sequence. Not all parts are issued annually. Supplementary information appears in *Stamp monthly* (formerly *Gibbons stamp monthly*).

The standard British catalog; quotes the estimated selling price at Stanley Gibbons Ltd. at time of publication.

The publisher also issues a "simplified catalogue," the *Stanley Gibbons stamps of the world,* "an illustrated and priced two-volume guide to the postage stamps of the world, excluding changes of paper, perforation, shade and watermark." HE6226.G5

United States Postal Service. Postage stamps of the United States. Wash., U.S. Govt. Prt. Off., 1970– . Looseleaf. il. (*Its Publication 9*) **BF192**

Cover title: United States postage stamps.

Subtitle: An illustrated description of all United States postage and special service stamps.

Supersedes the publication of the same title issued by the U.S. Post Office Dept., Division of Philately, 1927–68.

The original 1970 publication (241p., 39p.) covered from July 1, 1874 through June 30, 1970. New and revised pages are issued annually (slightly irregular) as "Transmittal letters" supplementary to the Service's *Publication 9.* HE6311.A312

PHOTOGRAPHY

See also Reprography, p.131.

Bibliography

Boni, Albert. Photographic literature; an international bibliographic guide to general and specialized literature on photographic processes; techniques; theory; chemistry; physics; apparatus; materials and applications; industry; history, biography; aesthetics. Associate eds., Hubbard Ballou [and others]. N.Y., Morgan and Morgan, [1962]. 335p. **BF193**

A listing under subject headings, with numerous cross references, of some 12,000 books, pamphlets, and periodical articles on the many technical aspects of photography noted in the title. Author index. Material is mainly in English, German, and French. Z7134.B6

———— ————, 1960–1970. N.Y., Morgan and Morgan, [1972]. 535p.

A supplementary volume following the earlier pattern and encompassing many new developments and additional subject headings.

Columbia University. Libraries. A catalogue of the Epstean collection on the history and science of photography and its applications especially to the graphic arts. N.Y., Columbia Univ. Pr., 1937. 109p. il. **BF194**

———— ———— Authors and short title index. Corrected, with additions, to May 1, 1938. 31p.

———— ———— Accessions, May 1938–Dec. 1941 with addenda 1942. N.Y., 1942. 29p.

The catalog of a comprehensive collection of scientific and applied photography. All three titles, together with a bibliography of Edward Epstean, by Beaumont Newhall, were reprinted in 1v. (Pawlet, Vt., Helios, 1972). Z7137.C72

International Museum of Photography at George Eastman House. Library. Library catalog. . . . Boston, G. K. Hall, 1982. 4v. **BF195**

Contents: v.1–2, Author/title; v.3–4, Subject.

Reproduces the catalog cards of the 30,000 volume reference library of the Museum. Rich in the "history, aesthetics, and technology of photography and cinematography from its earliest developments to the present day."—*Introd.* Lists books in two sequences: author/title, and subject. Includes many rarities; excludes manuscripts and periodicals. Z7134.I58

New York. Public Library. Research Libraries. Photographica: a subject catalog of books on photography. Boston, G. K. Hall, 1984. 380p. **BF196**

"Includes books, pamphlets, and selected periodical articles on

still photography and allied topics drawn from the holdings of the Research Libraries of the New York Public Libraries, Astor, Lenox, and Tilden Foundations."—*t.p.*

A subject catalog only, reproducing the catalog cards for the types of materials noted above. Nearly 8,000 entries under some 120 subject headings; drawn from collections throughout the Research Libraries of the New York Public Library. Does not list individual photographs or collections of individual photographers; cinematography and television are also excluded. Z7137.N48

Indexes and abstract journals

Abstracts of photographic science and engineering literature, publ. by the Society of Photographic Scientists and Engineers. N.Y., Engineering Index, 1962–72. v.1–11. Monthly. **BF197**

Supersedes *Ansco abstracts* and *Kodak monthly abstract bulletin.* Publisher varies. Ceased with v.11, no.12, Dec. 1972.

Aimed to present abstracts of "world literature dealing with the science, engineering and technology of photography, motion pictures, television, photogrammetry and related fields . . ."—*Introd.* TR1.A22

International photography index. 1979– . Boston, G. K. Hall, 1983– . Annual. **BF198**

Ed. by William S. Johnson.

Continues: *Index to articles on photography,* 1977–78 (2v.).

Offers in subject arrangement a listing of articles "that focus on photography as a medium of creative expression, or a vehicle for communication, or that deal with the history of photography and its practitioners."—*Pref. 1979.* How-to articles are excluded. The 1981 volume (publ. 1984) indexes about 100 periodicals, American and foreign, and contains 6,910 entries. About two thirds of them fall into the "By artist" section (i.e., are listed under name of the photographer). Indexes of authors of articles, authors of book reviews, and of institutions. Z134.I53

Moss, Martha. Photography books index: a subject guide to photo anthologies. Metuchen, N.J., Scarecrow Pr., 1980. 286p. **BF199**

Provides access by subject and photographer to the photographs reproduced in a selected list (22 titles) of photography books. Separate sections for photographers and subjects, with a third section for portraits of named individuals.

———— ———— II. Metuchen, N.J., Scarecrow Pr., 1985. 261p.

A supplement to the above, adding 28 more anthologies. TR199.M67

Parry, Pamela Jeffcott. Photography index: a guide to reproductions. Westport, Conn., Greenwood Pr., 1979. 372p. **BF200**

Indexes some 80 books and exhibition catalogs dealing with artistic, journalistic, and documentary photography. Major listing is by name of photographer or firm (or, if photographer is unknown, by title); subject and title indexes. TR199.P37

Photographic abstracts. London, Royal Photographic Society of Great Britain, 1921– . v.1– . Bimonthly. **BF201**

Frequency varies.

Indexes: v.1–10, 1921–30; v.11–20, 1931–40; v.21–30, 1941–50; v.31–40, 1951–60; and annual.

Abstracts in English on technical aspects of photography. Includes above 4,500 abstracts a year "from both technical journals and patent specifications."—*Aims and scope.*

Encyclopedias

Focal encyclopedia of photography. [Fully rev. ed.] London, N.Y., Focal Pr., [1965]. 2v. (1699p.) il. **BF202**

Also publ. in a 1v. ed.

1st ed. 1956.

A combination dictionary and encyclopedia bringing together definitions of terms and articles on the history, techniques, art, and application of photography. A panel of some 275 authors, representing many countries, contributed the longer, signed articles. Although the work is British in origin, attention is called to American variants in terms and practice. Illustrated with plates and line drawings.

The revised edition is almost one-third larger than the first edition. Most of the additional material is concerned with new techniques and terminology, but articles dealing with historical and statistical aspects of the subject have also been strengthened. TR9.F6

ICP encyclopedia of photography. N.Y., Crown, [1984]. 607p. il. (Pound Pr. book) **BF203**

At head of title: International Center of Photography.

A handsomely produced work which "is intended to give the general reader a comprehensive view of the medium in a single volume. The view provided by some 1,300 entries describes the current state of the aesthetic, communicative, scientific, technical, and commercial applications of photography; it describes how the medium developed; and it identifies the photographers, scientists, and inventors who have been and are responsible for this development."—*Pref.* Articles are unsigned, although there is a list of contributors (without credentials) and an international board of advisers for photographer inclusion. Photographs appear in close proximity to the pertinent articles and are carefully labeled; line drawings illustrate various processes and devices. A "Biographical supplement of photographers" briefly identifies some 2,000 photographers not accorded articles in the main text. Classified bibliography, p.600–07. TR9.I24

Dictionaries

Elsevier's Dictionary of photography in three languages: English, French, and German. Comp. and arr. by A. S. H. Craeybeckx. Amsterdam & N.Y., Elsevier, 1965. 660p. **BF204**

English base with German and French indexes. TR9.E46

Spencer, Douglas Arthur. The Focal dictionary of photographic technologies. London, Focal Pr.; Englewood Cliffs, N.J., Prentice-Hall, [1973]. 725p. il. **BF205**

Covers the whole range of photographic technologies. Intended "to assist young newcomers, to any branch of photographic science technology and their applications, to grasp the meaning of the frequently used but specialised terms in the particular field they are entering and whose significance writers in that field tend to take for granted."—*Introd.* Numerous diagrams and line drawings. Cross references; selected bibliography. TR9.S77

Stroebel, Leslie D. and **Todd, Hollis N.** Dictionary of contemporary photography. Dobbs Ferry, N.Y., Morgan & Morgan; London, Fountain Pr., [1974]. 217p. il. **BF206**

Intended as "a record of current usage in professional and illustrative photography, cinematography (including animation), and photographic engineering and science. In addition, terms have been included from disciplines that relate to photography, such as art, electronics, photomechanical reproduction, physics, psychology, television, and applied statistics."—*Pref.* Illustrated with line drawings and photographs. TR9.S88

Directories

Gadney, Alan. How to enter and win color photography contests. N.Y., Facts on File, [1982]. 204p. **BF207**

TR510.G25

——— How to enter and win black & white photography contests. N.Y., Facts on File, [1982]. 204p. **BF208**

These volumes are part of a series that expands and revises *Gadney's Guide to 1800 international festivals & grants . . .* (1980). They offer information on (1) award events and sales outlets, and (2) benefit programs to which individuals and organizations may apply for some type of aid or service. Entries include directory information on event or program, specifying as appropriate, award, entry rules, fee, description of entries permitted, contact person. Indexed. TR6.A1G3

McQuaid, James. An index to American photographic collections: comp. at the International Museum of Photography at George Eastman House. Boston, G. K. Hall, 1982. 407p. **BF209**

Intends to provide a "first broad and factual record of public collections of photography" *(Introd.)*, listing 458 sources throughout the country. Arranged by state, then city and institution. Some entries include a brief description of holdings; most name the photographers whose work they own. The "Photographer index" includes 19,000 names with references to the collections in which the photographer's work is represented. TR12.M4

National Photographic Record. Directory of British photographic collections. Comp. by John Wall. London, Heinemann, 1977. 266p. **BF210**

Some 1,600 photographic collections are described. Classified arrangement with indexes by subject, owners, photographers, and locations. TR12.N37

Photo-lab-index; the cumulative formulary of standard recommended photographic procedures. [Ed.1–] Dobbs Ferry, N.Y., Morgan and Morgan, 1939– . Looseleaf annual with quarterly supplements (irregular). (38th ed., 1981–) **BF211**

Publisher varies.

Each new edition consists of the previous edition amended by the intervening quarterly supplements.

A basic manual of "recommended photographic procedures in a standardized form," divided into 15 sections. Sec.1–8 treat photographic materials by their manufacturers; sec.9–15 contain general facts and data by subject area.

Stock photo and assignment source book: where to find photographs instantly. Fred W. McDarrah, ed. N.Y., Bowker, 1977. 481p. **BF212**

An extensive listing of American and European historical societies, libraries, freelance photographers, and government bodies which are sources for photographs. Arrangement is by type of organization, with each entry giving name, address, personnel, date the files begin, number of color and black-and-white photos (with broad subject designation), restrictions on use, and reference to any published catalogs, etc. A section entitled "Reference sources" gives name and address of researchers and consultants, photo publications, and photographers' associations. Name index. TR12.S86

World photography sources. David N. Bradshaw, ed. N.Y., Directories, [1982]. 1v., various pagings. **BF213**

Aims "to provide the picture searcher with sources for finding any kind of picture needed and to give him an overview of the subject in brief essays on the various elements met in this work."—*Introd.* Sources are grouped according to 12 specialties (Agriculture through Visual arts), plus a "general" category for non-specialist sources. Entries give name and address, indication of size and type of collection, subject specialties, procedure for ordering, and type of fees charged. Indexed.

Handbooks

Blaker, Alfred A. Handbook for scientific photography. San Francisco, W. H. Freeman, [1977]. 319p. il. **BF214**

A completely revised, expanded, and reorganized edition of *Photography for scientific publication* (1965).

Contents: A review of essentials; General techniques; Solutions to problems; Related techniques; Final preparation for publication and viewing.

"Throughout the book the approach is pragmatic, being in terms of what one *needs* to know to accomplish the stated ends, rather than in terms of theory or ideal circumstances. The coverage of basic photography is skeletal, on the assumption that most readers will have some general knowledge of the field."—*Pref.*   TR692.5.B55

Blodgett, Richard E. Photographs: a collector's guide. N.Y., Ballantine Books, [1979]. 248p. il.   **BF215**

A guide for those just becoming interested in collecting photographs; it thus features discussions on how to learn about the field, where to buy, what to buy, how much to pay. Chapters are also devoted to problems of authentication, rarity, physical care, and the kinds of photographs available. An appendix offers a glossary of terms, a dictionary of dealers, and a checklist of auction catalogs, dealers' catalogs, periodicals, organizations, and books to read.
TR6.5.B46

Hedgecoe, John. The photographer's handbook; a complete reference manual of techniques, procedures, equipment and style. 2d ed., fully rev. N.Y., Knopf, 1982. 352p. il.
BF216

1st ed. 1977.
About 600 topically arranged entries ranging from basic information about cameras and equipment to advanced techniques and special processes. Copiously illustrated with photographs and drawings. Updated to incorporate changes and developments in the tools of photography. Cross references; glossary; index.   TR150.H36

Holloway, Adrian. The handbook of photographic equipment. N.Y., Knopf, 1981. 216p. il.   **BF217**

Aims to provide "a clear, comprehensive guide to choosing and using the right tools" in photography, covering "the whole range of cameras, lenses and accessories, in all formats, lighting, studio, and darkroom equipment, and films and darkroom materials."—*Introd.*
TR197.H64

Photographer's market. 1978– . Cincinnati, [Writer's Digest Books], 1978– . il. Annual.   **BF218**

Subtitle: Where to sell your photographs.
Robert D. Lutz, ed.
Aims to be an "up-to-date source of information concerning the needs and policies of freelance photography buyers."—*Introd.* Includes directories of many types of business firms (e.g., advertising agencies, galleries, book and periodical publishers, record companies) with their photographic requirements and name of contact person. Data on contests, foundations and grants, workshops, plus feature articles on the profession and the business of freelancing. Bibliography; glossary; index.   TR12.P515

Thomas, Woodlief, ed. SPSE handbook of photographic science and engineering. N.Y., Wiley, [1973]. 1416p. il.
BF219

At head of title: Society of Photographic Scientists and Engineers.
A reference source for experienced photographic scientists and engineers. Chapters, by specialists, include bibliographic references. Sec.23 is a "Guide to photographic information," p.1329–91. Indexed.   TR150.T48

Witkin, Lee D. and **London, Barbara.** The photograph collector's guide. Boston, New York Graphic Soc., [1979]. 438p. il.   **BF220**

Aims to provide "concise biographies of the most important figures in photographic history, lucid discussions of the major questions about collecting, conservation, and value, and explanations of the many historical photographic processes."—*Foreword.* Major sections include: (1) The art of collecting; (2) A collector's chronology; (3) A collector's glossary; (4) The care and restoration of photographs; (5) Selected photographers; (6) Limited-edition portfolios; (7) Contemporary group exhibitions and catalogues. Appendix of "museums, galleries, auction houses, exhibition spaces." Bibliography; index.   TR6.5.W47

Biography

See also BF203.

Browne, Turner and **Partnow, Elaine.** Macmillan biographical encyclopedia of photographic artists & innovators. N.Y., Macmillan; London, Collier Macmillan, [1983]. 722p. [104]p. of plates.   **BF221**

Inasmuch as the work "strives to inform the reader about the world of photography as well as the photographers," it includes "persons, other than photographers, whose contributions to the field have proved vital to its growth and advancement."—*Pref.* Thus, there are entries for photographic curators, inventors, photography critics, etc., as well as for photographers living and deceased. The 144 plates appear in roughly chronological sequence on unnumbered pages at center of the volume, with *see* references from the names of the photographers. Lists of museums and photographic galleries appended.   TR139.B767

Contemporary photographers. Eds., George Walsh, Colin Naylor, Michael Held. N.Y., St. Martin's Pr., [1982]. 837p. il.   **BF222**

"The choice of 650 entrants is intended to reflect the best and most prominent of contemporary photographers (those who are living and those who have died in the recent past); photographers from earlier generations whose reputations are essentially contemporary; and photographers from the inter-war years and after who continue to be important influences."—*Introd.* Entries include a biographical sketch, list of exhibitions, listing of galleries and museums having the entrant's work in their collections, bibliography, and a signed critical essay. Representative photos were chosen by the entrants.   TR139.C66

B G

Theater and Performing Arts

❖Many libraries have had a long-standing interest in the theater, both professional and amateur, historical and current. Recent years have shown widespread interest in dance —particularly ballet—and fascination with motion pictures and television seems almost universal. In this section of the *Guide* are listed works dealing with the performing arts: (1) the theater itself—production, staging, management, players, etc.—as opposed to plays and history of the drama, which are treated in Section BD, Literature; (2) the dance; (3) motion pictures; and (4) the performance and entertainment aspects of radio and television. For works concerning opera and musical comedy, *see* Section BH, Music. Interest in cinema as an art form, coupled with easy access to films via television and videocassettes has led to a remarkable proliferation of reference works concerning that medium. Many of those works are of indifferent quality, but because the individual items so often include useful information not easily found elsewhere, the selection of works on motion pictures included here is somewhat more generous than for many topics covered in other sections of the *Guide*.

A basic collection might include the *Oxford companion to the theatre* (BG63); *Who's who in the theatre* (BG105);

Chujoy's *The dance encyclopedia* (BG144); Halliwell's *The filmgoer's companion* (BG243); and for those libraries which can afford them, the *Enciclopedia dello spettacolo* (BG11), and the New York times "directories" of the theater (BG46) and of the film (BG190).

GENERAL WORKS

Guides

Whalon, Marion K. Performing arts research; a guide to information sources. Detroit, Gale, [1976]. 280p. (Performing arts information guide ser., v.1) **BG1**

An annotated guide in six main sections: (1) Guides; (2) Dictionaries, encyclopedias, and handbooks; (3) Directories; (4) Play indexes and finding lists; (5) Sources for reviews of plays and motion pictures; (6) Bibliographies, indexes, and abstracts; (7) Illustrative and audiovisual sources. Author-title-subject index.   Z6935.W5

Wilmeth, Don B. American and English popular entertainment: a guide to information sources, Detroit, Gale, [1980]. 465p. (Performing arts information guide ser., v.7)   **BG2**

"In general, popular entertainment in the context of this guide refers to live amusements created by professional showmen for profit and aimed at broad, relatively unsophisticated audiences. A small section is devoted to precinematic optical entertainments. . . ."—*Pref.* Includes fairs, circuses, carnivals, minstrel shows, dime museums, burlesque, lyceum and chautauqua, stage magic, puppetry, popular theater, etc. Topical arrangement, with author, title, and subject indexes. Nearly 2,500 items (books, periodical articles, and dissertations) with brief annotations.

Wilmeth is also the compiler of *Variety entertainment and outdoor amusements: a reference guide* (Westport, Conn., Greenwood Pr., 1982. 242p.).   Z7511.W53

Bibliography

Becco, Horacio Jorge. Bibliografía general de las artes del espectáculo en América Latina. [Paris], Unesco, [1977]. 118p.   **BG3**

A bibliography of some 1,800 items on theater and performing arts of Latin America. Includes sections on regional theater of individual countries. Indexed.   Z1609.D7B42

Performing arts books, 1876–1981: including an international index of current serial publications. N.Y., Bowker, [1981]. 1656p.   **BG4**

The main section is derived from Bowker's American Book Publishing Record database; about 50,000 entries for books (with full bibliographic information) are classified according to Library of Congress subject headings; author and title indexes. The serials section is based on the Bowker Serials Bibliography database, with entries conforming to those found in *Ulrichs*.   Z6935.P43

Schoolcraft, Ralph Newman. Performing arts books in print: an annotated bibliography. N.Y., Drama Book Specialists, [1973]. 761p.   **BG5**

A successor to A.E. Santaniello's *Theatre books in print* (N.Y., 1963; 2d ed., N.Y., 1966), with expanded coverage for new categories and necessary general updating.

Covers theater and drama; technical arts of the theater, motion pictures, television, and radio; mass media and related popular arts. In general, plays and collections of plays are omitted. Classified listing with author and title indexes. Most works are in English. The

main listing covers in-print items published prior to the end of 1970; a supplement adds 1971 imprints plus some earlier items.

Kept up-to-date by: Z6935.S34

Annotated bibliography of new publications in the performing arts. no.1– , Jan./June 1970– . N.Y., Drama Book Shop, 1970– . Quarterly.   **BG6**

A classified listing with detailed table of contents, but no index. Suspended after no.42 (1985)?   Z6935.S34 suppl.

Stott, Raymond Toole. Circus and allied arts; a world bibliography, 1500–1957: based mainly on circus literature in the British Museum, the Library of Congress, the Bibliothèque Nationale and on his own collection. Derby, Eng., Harpur & Sons, [1958–71]. 4v. il.   **BG7**

Title page of v.4 gives the dates of coverage as "1500–1970" and includes the Universiteitsbibliotheek van Amsterdam among the basic collections.

Lists books and pamphlets in various languages dealing with circus history and biography; technical aspects of performances; and the circus in drama, literature, art, and fiction. v.3 has an index to v.1–3; v.4 has its own index.   Z7514.C6S7

Library resources

International Federation of Library Associations. Section for Theatrical Libraries and Museums. Performing arts libraries and museums of the world. Under the direction of André Veinstein. 2d ed. rev. and enl. by Cécile Giteau. Paris, Éditions du Centre National de la Recherche Scientifique, 1967. 801p.   **BG8**

Added title page in French: *Bibliothèques et musées des arts du spectacle dans le monde.* Text in English and French.

1st ed. 1960.

Gives detailed information about the performing arts collections in public and private libraries and museums in 37 countries. Indicates size and nature of holdings, regulations for use, hours, etc. Index of names of persons, places, and institutions.   Z675.T36I5

Performing arts resources. v.1– , 1974– . [N.Y.], Drama Book Specialists, [1975]– . Annual.   **BG9**

Ed. by Ted Perry.

A series sponsored by the Theatre Library Association. "Each annual volume . . . is envisioned as a collection of articles which will enable the performing arts student, scholar, and archivist to locate, identify, and classify information about theatre, film, broadcasting, and popular entertainments."—*Pref.*

v.1 includes "Performing arts research collections in New York City" by L. A. Rachow; "Film/broadcasting resources in the Los Angeles area" by A. G. Schlosser; "The Wisconsin Center for Theatre Research" by K. Johnson; "The Motion Picture Section of the Library of Congress" by J. B. Kuiper; "Vanderbilt Television News Archive" by J. B. Pilkington, etc.

Later volumes tend to be concerned with collections on very specific topics, occasional descriptions of foreign library resources, essays on aspects of performance, etc. Of considerable interest, however, is v.6 (1980) which is mainly devoted to "Federal Theatre Project records at George Mason University" by Laraine Correll and "Research materials of the Federal Theatre Project in the Theatre Collection of the New York Public Library" by Dorothy L. Swerdlove.   Z6935.P46

Young, William C. American theatrical arts: a guide to manuscripts in the United States and Canada. Chicago, Amer. Lib. Assoc., 1971. 166p.   **BG10**

Designed "to help scholars and students to locate manuscripts and other primary materials relating to the American and Canadian theatrical arts in the possession of institutions in the United States and Canada."—*Introd.* Manuscripts and special collections are briefly described under repository arranged according to National Union Catalog symbol. Index of persons and subjects.

Z6935.Y68

Encyclopedias and handbooks

Enciclopedia dello spettacolo. Roma, Casa Ed. le Maschere, [1954–62]. 9v. il.   **BG11**

Similar in format and in profusion of illustration to the *Enciclopedia italiana* (AC58), and designed to cover the "grand spectacle" from antiquity to the present. Includes the theater, opera, ballet, motion pictures, vaudeville, the circus, etc. Treats performers, authors, composers, directors, designers, etc.; types of entertainment; dramatic themes; historical and technical subjects; organizations and acting companies; and pertinent place-names. International roster of contributors; good bibliographies.   PN1625.E7

————— Appendice di aggiornamento. Cinema. [Venezia, Istit. per Collaborazione Culturale, 1963] 178col. il.

————— Aggiornamento 1955–1965. Roma, Unione Editoriale, [1966]. 1292col. il.

This supplement mainly devoted to biographical sketches of contemporary figures not found in the basic set. Although the text of the 1963 *Cinema* appendix is superseded by this volume, different illustrations have been used, and in the large cinema collection, at least, the 1963 work should be retained.

————— Indice repertorio. Roma, Unione Editoriale, [1968]. 1024p.

An index of titles of works mentioned in the main set and in the *Aggiornamento*, giving reference to the author, composer, etc., but not to volume or page.

Leonard, William Torbert. Theatre: stage to screen to television. Metuchen, N.J., Scarecrow Pr., 1981. 2v. (1804p.)   **BG12**

Documents productions of those works which have been presented in all three media. Entry is by title of the play; a synopsis is followed by a section giving comments on the original and subsequent productions and notes on critical reception. Stage, screen, and television credits are given for each, including revivals, re-makes under variant titles, etc. Limited to American and British stage productions; excludes Greek classics, Gilbert and Sullivan, and Shakespearean plays.   PN2189.L44

Sharp, Harold S. and **Sharp, Marjorie Z.,** comps. Index to characters in the performing arts. N.Y., Scarecrow Pr., 1966–73. 4v. in 6.   **BG13**

Contents: pt.1, Non-musical plays; an alphabetical listing of 30,000 characters. 2v.; pt.2, Operas and musical productions. 2v.; pt.3, Ballets; pt.4, Radio and television.

A dictionary of major and minor characters in stage works from earliest times to the present.   PN1579.S45

Variety international showbusiness reference. Mike Kaplan, ed. N.Y., Garland, 1981. 1135p. (Garland reference library of the humanities, v.292)   **BG14**

A compilation of information relating to the entertainment field derived from the files of *Variety* and "selected on the basis of possible reference need, judged by the queries which the publication receives daily for specific showbusiness information."—*Foreword.* Offers biographical notes (mainly film, stage, and TV credits) on some 6,000 figures in the entertainment world (including persons who died during 1980–81); full tabulations of winners and nominees of Oscar, Tony, Emmy, and Grammy awards; film, TV, Broadway and foreign play credits 1976–80 (listed by title and including the date when a review appeared in *Variety*); lists of festivals, long-running plays, platinum records, etc.; necrology 1976–80.   PN1579.V3

Variety major U.S. showbusiness awards. Mike Kaplan, ed. N.Y., Garland, 1982. 571p. (Garland reference library of the humanities, v.337)   **BG15**

Covers Oscars, Emmys, Tonys, Grammys, and Pulitzer Prize plays. Lists both nominees and award winners as applicable. Indexed.   PN2270.A93V37

Directories

Merin, Jennifer and **Burdick, Elizabeth B.** International directory of theatre, dance and folklore festivals. Westport, Conn., Greenwood Pr., [1979]. 480p.   **BG16**

"A project of the International Theatre Institute of the United States."—*t.p.*

Covers some 850 festivals in 56 countries. Listing is by country, then by name of the festival. Does not include United States festivals. Index of festival names; calendar of festivals by country.   PN1590.F47M47

Pride, Leo Bryan, ed. and comp. International theatre directory; a world directory of the theatre and performing arts. N.Y., Simon and Schuster, [1973]. 577p. il.   **BG17**

"The entries in this book consist chiefly of professional theatres, the great acting and opera companies, and the leading ballet and dance troupes of the world."—*Foreword.* Arrangement is geographical by country, then by city and name of theater or performance group. Some entries include historical or background notes, but these are very uneven and no pattern is evident for selection of those to be accorded this fuller treatment.   PN2052.P7

Simon's Directory of theatrical materials, services and information, comp. by Bernard Simon. 4th ed. N.Y., Package Publicity Service, [1970]. 320p.   **BG18**

1st ed. 1956.

A miscellany of information giving United States and Canadian sources of personnel and supplies used in stage productions and the management of theaters, e.g., actors' agents, ticket brokers, publishers, costumes, wigs, tents, etc.

Biography and history

Contemporary theatre, film, and television. v.1– . Detroit, Gale, [1984]– . v.1– . il. Irregular?   **BG19**

Subtitle: A biographical guide featuring performers, directors, writers, producers, designers, managers, choreographers, technicians, composers, executives, dancers, and critics in the United States and Great Britain.

Monica M. O'Donnell, ed.

With the abandonment of *Who's who in the theatre* (17th ed., 1981; BG105), this series is intended as an ongoing supplement to the final edition of that work, extending the scope to film and television, and adding new categories of persons included as indicated in the subtitle. Modelled on the same publisher's *Contemporary authors* (AJ48), each volume is to include new biographies of both new and established talents, and revised or updated sketches of persons included in the predecessor publication (including biographees who died since 1960). Information is derived mainly from questionnaires completed by biographees or their agents, with resulting unevenness and a notable absence of dates in some entries. Although meant to cover figures from the United States and Great Britain, v.1 seems almost wholly devoted to the former.   PN2285.C58

La Beau, Dennis. Theatre, film and television biographies master index. Detroit, Gale, [1979]. 477p. (Gale biographical index ser., no.5)   **BG20**

Subtitle: A consolidated guide to over 100,000 biographical sketches of persons living and dead, as they appear in over 40 of the principal biographical dictionaries devoted to the theatre, film and television.   PN1583.L3

Perry, Jeb H. Variety obits: an index to obituaries in Variety, 1905–1978. Metuchen, N.J., Scarecrow Pr., 1980. 311p.   **BG21**

Provides references to obituary notices published in *Variety* for "those people who worked in the production-related areas of motion pictures, television, radio, the legitimate stage, minstrelsy and vaudeville."—*Foreword.*   PN1583.P4

THEATER

Guides

Bailey, Claudia Jean. A guide to reference and bibliography for theatre research. 2d ed. rev. and exp. Columbus, Ohio State Univ. Libs., Pubns. Comm., 1983. 149p.   **BG22**

1st ed. 1971.

An annotated guide for the student and research worker. In two main sections: (1) General reference, and (2) Theatre and drama. The first part is very wide-ranging, covering national bibliography, library catalogs, general periodical and newspaper indexes, dissertation lists, etc.; the second deals with more specialized materials. Emphasis is on American and British theater. Author-title index.
Z5781.B15

Bibliography

Acuña, René. El teatro popular en Hispanoamérica: una bibliografía anotada. México, Univ. Nacional Autónoma de México, 1979. 114p.   **BG23**

380 items in classed arrangement within two main sections: (1) España; (2) Hispanoamérica. Concerned with works about the theater and the types of dramas performed rather than texts and studies of specific plays. Indexed.   Z2694.F6A25

Arnott, James Fullarton and **Robinson, John William.** English theatrical literature, 1559–1900; a bibliography, incorporating Robert W. Lowe's *A bibliographical account of English theatrical literature* published in 1888. London, Soc. for Theatre Research, 1970. 486p.   **BG24**

A revised and expanded edition of Lowe's work (London, 1888), which was an annotated listing of theatrical literature as distinguished from dramatic literature, thus omitting plays and critical accounts of them. The subject arrangement is much improved in the new edition, the period of coverage is extended, and American and other overseas editions are noted. All items from Lowe have been retained as, for the most part, have his notes. Indexes by author, title, and place of publication.   Z2014.D7A74

Asian theatre: a study guide and annotated bibliography. James R. Brandon, ed. Wash., D.C., University and College Theatre Assoc., 1979. 197p. (Theatre perspectives, no.1)
BG25

A briefly annotated bibliography for the English-language reader. Arranged by country, with subdivisions for (1) history, theory, practice; (2) plays; (3) audiovisual materials; (4) reference works. 1,348 items (books, periodical articles, and doctoral dissertations). No index.   Z3008.D7A84

Baker, Blanch M. Theatre and allied arts: a guide to books dealing with the history, criticism, and technic of the drama and theatre and related arts and crafts. N.Y., Wilson, 1952. 536p. (Reissued 1967)   **BG26**

Based on the author's *Dramatic bibliography* (N.Y., Wilson, 1933). An annotated listing of about 6,000 titles in three parts: (1) Drama, theatre and actors; (2) Stagecraft and allied arts of the theatre; (3) Miscellaneous reference material. Each part is subdivided by subject or geographical region. Items included were published between 1885 and 1948, with a few later titles, and almost all are available in English. Indexes by author and subject.   Z5781.B18

Ball, John Leslie and **Plant, Richard.** A bibliography of Canadian theatre history, 1583–1975. Toronto, Playwrights Co-op, 1976. 160p. il.   **BG27**

A classed bibliography of about 2,000 items, with author and subject index. Includes books, periodical articles, and unpublished theses. French-Canadian materials are included mainly as supplementary to the study of English-Canadian theater history.

———— ———— Supplement, 1975–1976. [Toronto], Playwrights Co-op, [1979]. 75p.

Lists new items from mid-1975 through 1976, plus additional works brought to the compilers' attention since publication of the original volume. A new listing of Canadian items concerning stagecraft has been added.   Z1377.D7B33

Boston. Public Library. Allen A. Brown Collection. Catalogue of the Allen A. Brown collection of books relating to the stage. Boston, 1919. 952p.   **BG28**

A dictionary catalog of a rich collection of works relating to the history of the stage, followed by an author list of works on the drama, and a brief supplementary list of titles added during the printing of the catalog.   Z5785.B72

British Drama League. Library. Player's library, the catalogue of the Library of the British Drama League, with an introd. by Frederick S. Boas. London, Faber & Faber, [1950]. 1115p.   **BG29**

Supersedes the Library's first catalog (1930) and its supplement (1934), and includes also the majority of books added to the Library through 1950. Arrangement of the catalog of plays is by author, with brief descriptive information. This is followed by a subject listing of books on the theater, a title index of plays, and an author index to the bibliography of the theater.

———— ———— 1st–3d supplements, 1951–56. 128p.; 256p.; 256p.

Z2014.D7B8

Dubois, William R., comp. English and American stage productions; an annotated checklist of prompt books 1800–1900. Boston, G. K. Hall, 1973. 524p.   **BG30**

Catalog of a collection of some 2,000 prompt books and prompters' editions of plays from the Nisbet-Snyder Drama Collection, Northern Illinois University Libraries.   Z5781.D85

Fordyce, Rachel. Children's theatre and creative dramatics: an annotated bibliography of critical works. Boston, G. K. Hall, 1975. 275p.   **BG31**

Lists some 2,269 items in a subject arrangement within three main sections: (1) Children's theatre and creative dramatics [i.e., materials covering both fields]; (2) Children's theatre; and (3) Creative dramatics. Does not include anthologies of children's plays "unless they are prefaced by or include some type of critical material."—*Pref.* Author index.   Z5784.C5F67

Hatch, James Vernon. Black image on the American stage; a bibliography of plays and musicals, 1770–1970. N.Y., DBS Publs., [1970]. 162p.   **BG32**

Lists full-length and one-act plays, musicals, revues, and operas written or produced in America between 1767 and 1970; each work must contain at least one black character or be written by a black playwright or on a black theme. Listing is by period, then alphabetically by author. Author index. Locates copies of many works, but there is no documentation for unlocated unpublished works.

Z5784.N4H35

Hebblethwaite, Frank P. A bibliographical guide to the Spanish American theater. Wash., Pan American Union, 1969. 84p. (Pan American Union. Div. of Philosophy and Letters. Dept. of Cultural Affairs. Basic bibliographies, 6)
BG33

An annotated list of books and articles arranged by country. Author index.   Z1609.D7H42

Larson, Carl F. W. American regional theatre history to 1900: a bibliography. Metuchen, N.J., Scarecrow Pr., 1979. 187p.   **BG34**

Concerned with regional theater exclusive of New York City. Arrangement is by state, then by city. Nearly 1,500 items. Lists books, parts of books, theses, periodical and newspaper articles, and some manuscript sources. Indexed.   Z5781.L34

NCTE Liaison Committee. Guide to play selection; a selective bibliography for production and study of modern plays. 3d ed. N.Y., Bowker, [1975]. 292p.   **BG35**

"Comp. by the NCTE Liaison Committee with the Speech Communication Association and the American Theatre Association, Joseph Mersand, Editorial Chairman. Distr. jointly by the National Council of Teachers of English, Urbana, Ill., and the R. R. Bowker Co., N.Y."—*t.p.*

1st ed. 1934.

About 850 plays are described in this edition, giving a brief summary and notes on staging needs, royalties, etc. A guide to play production precedes the sections listing short plays, full-length plays, plays by Afro-Americans, musical plays and television plays. Besides the author and title indexes there is a topical index plus a "player index" which lists the titles according to the number and sex of the players required. Z5781.N13

New York. Public Library. Research Libraries. Catalog of the theatre and drama collections. Boston, G. K. Hall, 1967–76. 51v. **BG36**

Contents: pt.1 [A], Drama collection: author listing. 6v.; [B] Drama collection: listing by cultural origin. 6v.; pt.2, Theatre collection: books on the theatre. 9v; pt.3, Theatre collection: non-book collection. 30v.

Pt.1 includes entries for editions of some 120,000 plays in Western languages (including translations), plus translations from Cyrillic, Hebrew, and Oriental languages. Plays in anthologies and periodicals are included along with separately published works. Pt.2 contains about 121,000 entries for more than 23,500 volumes of works relating to all aspects of the theater (stage history, biography, criticism, acting, stage management, etc.). Pt.3 reproduces about 744,000 cards for non-book materials such as programs, photographs of productions, portraits of theater personalities, reviews, press clippings, etc.

Separate supplements to pt.1 (Drama collection. 548p.) and pt.2 (Theatre collection. 2v.) were published in 1973. Pts.1 and 2 are supplemented by: Z5785.N56

———— Bibliographic guide to theatre arts. 1975– . Boston, G. K. Hall, 1976– . Annual. **BG37**

Serves as a supplement to the Library's *Catalog of the theatre and drama collections* (above), pts.1–2, listing materials newly cataloged by the New York Public Library, with additional entries from Library of Congress MARC tapes. Z6935.N46a

Samples, Gordon. The drama scholars' index to plays and filmscripts: a guide to plays and filmscripts in selected anthologies, series and periodicals. Metuchen, N.J., Scarecrow Pr., 1974–80. 2v. **BG38**

Attempts to present a "balanced selection" of plays of all periods (including texts in foreign languages); many of the anthologies, multivolume sets, and periodicals covered here are not indexed in the standard play indexes. Full information appears under the author's name, with cross reference from the title. "Indexing for the second volume goes back to the beginning of recorded literature and continues through 1977."—*Introd.* v.2 includes a title list of the anthologies indexed in both v.1 and 2. Z5781.S17

Stratman, Carl Joseph. Bibliography of the American theatre, excluding New York City. [Chicago], Loyola Univ. Pr., [1965]. 397p. **BG39**

Lists books, periodical articles, and theses and dissertations on all phases of the American theater (including ballet, opera, children's theater, secondary school theatrical work, scenery, lighting, etc.) outside New York City. Arranged by state, then by city, with author-subject index. At least one location is indicated for each book. Z1231.D7S8

———— **Spencer, David G.** and **Devine, Mary Elizabeth.** Restoration and eighteenth century theatre research: a bibliographical guide, 1900–1968. Carbondale, Ill., Southern Illinois Univ. Pr., [1971]. 811p. **BG40**

An alphabetical subject arrangement of more than 6,500 twentieth-century writings on Restoration and 18th-century theater research. Brief annotations for most entries. Indexed. Supersedes Stratman's *Restoration and 18th century theatre research bibliography, 1961–68* (Troy, N.Y., 1969). Z2014.D7S854

Wilmeth, Don B. The American stage to World War I; a guide to information sources. Detroit, Gale, [1978]. 269p. (Performing arts information guide ser., v.4) **BG41**

Concerned with aspects of the American theater "other than the literature of the stage. Thus, the major thrust of this collection of sources is the legitimate stage as a purveyor of entertainment, a business, and a producer of drama."—*Pref.* Includes sections for general reference sources, bibliographies, indexes, histories, individual theater personalities, stagecraft, theater collections, etc. Brief annotations; author, title, and subject indexes. Z1231.D7W55

Dissertations

Hoerstel, Karin and **Schlenker, Ingrid.** Verzeichnis der Hochschulschriften, Diplom- und Staatsexamensarbeiten der DDR zum Drama und Theater (1949–1970). [Berlin], Akademie der Künste der Deutschen Demokratischen Republik, 1973. 368p. **BG42**

Lists more than 2,000 research papers on various aspects of the theater and on dramatists of all countries and their works. Alphabetical author listing with subject index. Z5781.H64

Litto, Fredric M. American dissertations on the drama and the theatre; a bibliography. [Kent, Ohio], Kent State Univ. Pr., [1969]. 519p. **BG43**

Attempts to list "references to all doctoral dissertations on subjects related to theatre and drama completed in *all* academic departments of American (the United States and Canada) universities."—*Pref.* Computer-produced; the arrangement is by "reference code," with author, keyword-in-context, and subject indexes. Cutoff date is 1965. Z5781.L56

Periodicals

See also BG4.

Stratman, Carl Joseph. American theatrical periodicals, 1789–1967; a bibliographical guide. Durham, N.C., Duke Univ. Pr., 1970. 133p. **BG44**

Lists nearly 700 titles in chronological sequence. Indicates library locations whenever possible, with notes on missing issues. Index of titles, names of editors, etc.

Stratman is also the compiler of *A bibliography of British dramatic periodicals, 1720–1960* (N.Y., New York Pub. Lib., 1962. 58p.) which lists and locates files of 674 publications. Z6935.S75

Indexes

Guide to the performing arts, 1957–68. N.Y., Scarecrow Pr., 1960–72. Annual. **BG45**

1957–67 comp. by S. Yancey Belknap; 1968 by Louis Rachow and Katherine Hartley.

Indexes articles and illustrations in 30–45 periodicals, primarily United States and Canadian publications, although early volumes included a few titles in French, Italian, and Spanish. Began as a supplement to *Guide to the musical arts,* 1953–56 (BH101). Through 1963 included a separate section for television arts; this was later incorporated into the main listing. ML118.G8

The New York times directory of the theater. [N.Y.], Arno Pr., [1973]. 1009p. il. **BG46**

Not a directory in the usual sense, but rather an index to theater reviews published in the *New York times* during the period 1920–70; it is a by-product of the reprinting of those reviews (BG48), but is independently useful since reference is to date and page of the newspaper. There are separate indexes by title and by personal name. An unpaged section at front lists major theater awards and reprints the *New York times* articles announcing those awards. (The volume is really a separate issue of v.9–10 of the *New York times theater reviews* [BG48], with the addition of some material from v.1 of that set and a limited amount of new text.) Z6935.N48

Theatre magazine (indexes): A selective index to Theatre magazine, by Stan Cornyn. N.Y., Scarecrow Pr., 1964. 289p. **BG47**

Indexes *Theatre magazine* from 1900 to 1930. PN2000.T512

Reviews

The New York times theater reviews, 1870/1919– . N.Y., New York Times, 1971– . il. **BG48**

The 1870–1919 segment was issued 1976 in 5v. plus index. Volumes covering 1920–70 were the first segment published, appearing in 1971 in 10v. (including appendix and indexes). The series is continued on a biennial basis covering the years 1971/72– . (A set covering 1920–80 is currently listed as available in 13v. plus 2v. index.)

A reprinting in chronological sequence of reviews of theater productions as they appeared in the *New York times.* Appendixes of awards and prizes, and of productions and runs by season. Indexes of titles, production companies, and of personal names.

PN2266.N48

Salem, James M. A guide to critical reviews. 3d ed. Metuchen, N.J., Scarecrow Pr., 1984– . pt.1– . (In progress) **BG49**

Contents: pt.1, American drama, 1909–1982 (657p.).

Originally published in 4 pts., 1966–71. Pts.1–3 were issued in a second edition (1973–79) with the following contents: pt.1, American drama, 1909–1969; pt.2, The musical, 1909–1974; pt.3, Foreign drama, 1909–1977. No second edition of pt.4 ("The screenplay from The jazz singer to Dr. Strangelove") was published, but a supplementary volume designated as "The screenplay, supplement I, 1963–1980" was published 1982 (698p.).

Provides citations to reviews of staged productions, not to scholarly studies of the plays themselves. Reviews are drawn from popular and easily available American and Canadian periodicals and include those appearing in the *New York times* and the *New York theatre critics reviews.* Listing is by playwright; title index. Similar popular coverage is provided for the screenplays. Z5781.S16

Samples, Gordon. How to locate reviews of plays and films; a bibliography of criticism from the beginnings to the present. Metuchen, N.J., Scarecrow Pr., 1976. 114p. **BG50**

An annotated guide to indexes, checklists and bibliographies of reviews and critiques of plays and films. Separate sections for plays and films, subdivided by type of reference tool; within subsections the arrangement is mainly chronological by period covered. Author/title index. Unfortunately, numerous inaccuracies.

Z5781.S19

Stanley, William T. Broadway in the West End; an index of reviews of American theatre in London, 1950–1975. Westport, Conn., Greenwood Pr., [1978]. 206p. **BG51**

Aims to present "the essential facts of American theatrical works produced in London from 1950 through 1975" (*Pref.*), together with references to critical reviews appearing in some 17 review media. Entry is under author or adapter of the theater piece, and for each title is given the name of the theater, inclusive dates of the run, and number of performances, followed by citations to reviews. Title index; chronology; list of longest-running American productions in London during the period, etc. Z2014.D7S77

Annuals

See also BG262–BG263.

Annales du théâtre et de la musique. 1.–41. année, 1875–1916. Paris, Charpentier, 1876–1916. 41v. **BG52**

An annual survey of the plays, operas, and concerts of Paris, giving for each theater a record, with some comment, of the works produced there during the year and, in case of new works, cast of characters and synopsis of plot. PN2620.A6

Theatre world. 1944/45– . N.Y., Theatre World, 1945– . v.1– . il. Annual. **BG53**

Publisher varies. Title varies: 1950/51–1964/65 called *Daniel Blum's Theatre world.*

Annual survey of the American theater, with many illustrations. Emphasis is on Broadway productions, but attention is given to off-Broadway, regional theater, and touring companies. Lists casts, dates of opening and closing, etc., but gives no critical comment. Includes biographical sketches of outstanding players, producers, directors, designers, etc. Obituaries.

The *New York theatre annual* and its successor the *American theatre annual,* provided more ambitious coverage (e.g., including synopses of the plays and excerpts from reviews) for the 1976/77–1979/80 seasons only. PN2277.N5A17

Theatre world annual (London); a pictorial review of West End productions with a record of plays and players. no.1–16, 1949/50–1964/65. London, Rockliff; N.Y., Macmillan, 1950–65. il. Annual. **BG54**

Subtitle varies. PN2596.L6T542

World premières. v.1–15, Oct.1949–Nov./Dec. 1964. Paris, Internat. Theatre Inst., 1949–64. Monthly. **BG55**

Also called *ITI world premières.*

Subtitle: Monthly bulletin of the International Theatre Institute.

Contains brief accounts of new theatrical productions, including plays, operas, and ballets, as reported by the national centers of some 50 countries.

Dictionaries and encyclopedias

See also BH247–BH252.

Bordman, Gerald. The Oxford companion to American theatre. N.Y., Oxford Univ. Pr., 1984. 734p. **BG56**

Covers some of the same matter as the *Oxford companion to the theatre* (BG63), but often in a complementary way or using a somewhat different approach. An important difference is the inclusion here of entries for individual plays (selected chiefly on the basis of length of the New York run and varying according to the period); some foreign plays are included, as are a number of non-American figures who were prominent in the American theater. Emphasis is on Broadway and the New York stage. PN2220.B6

Bronner, Edwin. The encyclopedia of the American theatre, 1900–1975. San Diego & N.Y., A. S. Barnes; London, Tantivy Pr., [1980]. 659p. il. **BG57**

Not an encyclopedia in the usual sense, but rather a dictionary arrangement of entries for titles of individual plays "written (or adapted) by American or Anglo-American authors" (*Introd.*) and produced on Broadway or off-Broadway during the 1900–75 period. (The single exception is an omnibus entry for the Federal Theatre Project.) Entries include date of opening, theater, number of performances in the original run, a brief synopsis or statement of the play's theme (usually including references to the stars, critical judgment of the compiler, and often brief quotations from contemporary reviews), principal players, author, producer, director, and notes on revivals. Musicals are not included, although references to musical versions of the plays are included in the notes; screen versions are also noted, but no cross reference or index entry is provided when the title of the musical or screen version differs from the original.

Six appendixes help to justify the "encyclopedia" designation: (1) a calendar of notable premieres (including musicals and foreign plays); (2–3) Broadway debuts of actors and playwrights; (4) the 100 longest-running Broadway productions, 1900–75; (5) statistical record of Broadway productions by season; (6) awards. The index is of personal names only, but includes all names mentioned in the entries and in the appendixes. PN2266.B68

The concise Oxford companion to the theatre. Ed. by Phyllis Hartnoll. London, Oxford Univ. Pr., 1972. 640p. **BG58**

Although based on the *Oxford companion to the theatre* (1967 ed.), this is "something more than a cut and watered-down version of the original. Every article, however short, has been reconsidered, and in most cases recast and rewritten in minature in such a way as to retain the essential facts and still leave room, where necessary, for new material. The loss of the long articles on individual countries has been offset by the inclusion of more short articles on actors, dramatists, and directors who are important in the theatrical history of those countries."—*Pref.*   PN2035.C63

The encyclopedia of world theater, with 420 illustrations and an index of play titles. N.Y., Scribner, [1977]. 320p. il.   **BG59**

"Based on *Friedrichs Theaterlexikon* [Hanover, Friedrich, 1969] by Karl Gröning and Werner Kliess ... this English-language edition has been translated by Estella Schmid, and adapted and amplified under the general editorship of Martin Esslin."—*verso of t.p.*

Brief entries for actors and actresses, playwrights, directors, designers, types of drama, theatrical institutions, awards, etc.   PN2035.E52

Gassner, John and **Quinn, Edward.** The reader's encyclopedia of world drama. N.Y., Crowell, [1969]. 1030p. il.   **BG60**

In addition to entries for playwrights, selected titles, and types of drama, there are articles giving brief historical surveys of the development of the theater in individual countries. Articles are signed with the initials of the contributor, and there are some bibliographical references. Appendix of "Basic documents in dramatic theory."   PN1625.G3

Leiter, Samuel L. Kabuki encyclopedia: an English-language adaptation of *Kabuki jiten.* Westport, Conn., Greenwood Pr., [1979]. 572p. il.   **BG61**

A dictionary arrangement of entries for terms, names, titles, etc., related to Kabuki. Appendixes include "A brief chronology of Kabuki" and a list of major plays. Selected bibliography; subject guide to the principal entries; cross references; general index.   PN2924.5.K3L44

McGraw-Hill encyclopedia of world drama: an international reference work. Stanley Hochman, ed. in chief. [2d ed.] N.Y., McGraw-Hill, [1984]. 5v. il.   **BG62**

1st ed. 1972.

The 1st ed. was concerned almost exclusively with dramatists and the literature of the theater; aspects of production and stagecraft were virtually ignored. Whereas entries for playwrights continue to predominate, the 2d ed. offers extensive articles on national and ethnic theater traditions and on theater in individual countries or areas, with frequent emphasis on performance-related topics; moreover, title entries for anonymous plays, and articles on theater companies have been added. For each major dramatist there is a biographical sketch, a brief critique of his work, synopses of selected plays, and a bibliography of editions (including references to individual plays published in anthologies) and, usually, a list of critical and biographical works. For the lesser dramatist there is a brief account of his career, achievement, and dramatic output, and occasionally a synopsis of one or more plays. Nearly all articles are signed by contributing scholars; bibliographies are extensive and up-to-date. Glossary of terms (p.215–64), play title list (of all plays included in the lists of plays at the end of major articles), and a general index (including all play titles mentioned in the articles) in v.5. There are hundreds of good-quality illustrations, though players and dates are too often unidentified.   PN1625.M3

The Oxford companion to the theatre. Ed. by Phyllis Hartnoll. 4th ed. Oxford, Oxford Univ. Pr., 1983. 934p. il.   **BG63**

1st ed. 1951.

Offers definitions or explanations of theater terms, biographical sketches of theater personalities (including many living performers, playwrights, etc.), articles on specific theater companies and theater buildings, and historical sketches of theater in individual countries and cities. International in scope, with some emphasis on British

and American theater. This edition concentrates on "what is known as 'legitimate' theatre throughout its history" *(Pref.),* with little attention paid to popular genres such as music hall, and omitting ballet and opera. No attempt is made toward comprehensive coverage of recent technology as applied to theater buildings and staging. Contributors are listed, but articles are unsigned. Line drawings accompany a few articles, but the 96 plates are grouped in six chronological or topical sections.   PN2035.H3

Taylor, John Russell. The Penguin dictionary of the theatre. Rev. ed. Harmondsworth, Eng.; Baltimore, Penguin, 1974. 304p.   **BG64**

1st ed. 1966; various printings.

A handy little volume with a certain emphasis on contemporary plays and playwrights. Despite necessary selectivity, it should be useful in the small library and in the student's personal collection. Plays, players, playwrights, theater terms, etc., are all included.   PN2035.T3

Woll, Allen. Dictionary of the black theatre: Broadway, off-Broadway, and selected Harlem theatre. Westport, Conn., Greenwood Pr., [1983]. 359p.   **BG65**

In two main sections: (1) "The shows," a dictionary arrangement of the plays, revues, etc., "by, about, with, for and related to blacks" *(Pref.)* from 1898 to 1981, giving information on place and date of opening, number of performances, author, producer, director, cast, and notes on content and reception; (2) a section of biographical and historical notes on "Personalities and organizations." Chronology; discography; selected bibliography; index.   PN2270.A35W64

Terms

Bowman, Walter Parker and **Ball, Robert Hamilton.** Theatre language: a dictionary of terms in English of the drama and stage from medieval to modern times. N.Y., Theatre Arts, [1961]. 428p.   **BG66**

Contains more than 3,500 definitions of words and phrases. For the most part, excludes terms peculiar to grand opera and ballet.   PN2035.B6

Rae, Kenneth and **Southern, Richard.** An international vocabulary of technical theatre terms in eight languages (American, Dutch, English, French, German, Italian, Spanish, Swedish). Bruxelles, Elsevier; N.Y., Theatre Arts Books, [1959]. 139p.   **BG67**

Added title page in French: *Lexique international de termes techniques de théâtre en huit langues.*

In two parts: pt.1, numbered list of terms in English, alphabetically arranged, with equivalent terms in other languages; pt.2, indexes in the other seven languages.   PN2035.R3

Vaughn, Jack A. Drama A to Z; a handbook. N.Y., Ungar, [1978]. 239p.   **BG68**

Offers "an alphabetical listing of articles defining and discussing approximately 500 words and phrases commonly found in writings on the drama, from Aristotle to the present."—*Pref.* "A chronology of dramatic theory and criticism" (p.219–33) is an annotated list of major works in the field. "Suggestions for further reading," p.235–39.   PN1625.V3

Handbooks

American Theatre Planning Board. Theatre check list: a guide to the planning and construction of proscenium and open stage theatres. Middletown, Conn., Wesleyan Univ. Pr., [1983]. 123p. il.   **BG69**

1st ed. 1969.

Intends to "point out most of the possibilities and dangers inherent in each area of the structure to be built" *(Foreword),* giving "enough precise information to forestall the worst mistakes" without being so rigid as to restrict creative imagination. Indexed.   NA6830.A7

Herman, Lewis and **Herman, Marguerite Shalett.** Foreign dialects; a manual for actors, directors and writers. N.Y., Theatre Arts Books, [1959]. 415p. il. **BG70**

First published in 1943 as *Manual of foreign dialects for radio, stage and screen.* PN2071.F6H4

———— American dialects; a manual for actors, directors and writers. N.Y., Theatre Arts Books, [1959]. 328p. **BG71**

First published in 1947 as *Manual of American dialects for radio, stage, screen and television.* PE2841.H4

Kienzle, Siegfried. Modern world theater; a guide to productions in Europe and the United States since 1945. Tr. by Alexander and Elizabeth Henderson. N. Y., Ungar, [1970]. 509p. **BG72**

Tr. from the German *Modernes Welttheater* (1966).

"Of the 755 plays discussed in the original German work . . . this English version includes 563, and another 15 have been added by the author for this English edition."—*Translator's foreword.* Offers synopses, plus brief critical and interpretive comment. Dates of publication and production are indicated for each play. Arrangement is alphabetical by author. Index of play titles.

PN6112.5.K513

Langley, Stephen. Theatre managment in America: principle and practice; producing for the commercial, stock, resident, college, and community theatre. Rev. ed. N.Y., Drama Book Specialists, [1980]. 490p. **BG73**

1st ed. 1974.

". . . attempts to outline a comprehensive view of theatrical producing in America: its history, theory and practice. It deals exclusively with live theatre."—*Pref.* In four main parts: (1) Fundamentals of theatrical producing; (2) Methods of theatrical producing; (3) Business management in the theatre; (4) The theatre and its audience. Appendixes include sample forms and reports; bibliography, p.463–76. Indexed. PN2291.L3

Sobel, Bernard. The new theatre handbook and digest of plays. [8th ed. compl. rev.] N.Y., Crown, 1959. 749p. **BG74**

1st ed., 1940, had title: *The theatre handbook and digest of plays.*

Includes, in one alphabetical arrangement, theatrical terms, biographical notices, and digests of plays. Covers all periods and all countries.

In this edition many articles remain unchanged, a few have been updated, and a few new entries have been added, but comparatively few digests of plays of the 1950s have been included. The short essays signed by specialists, which appeared in earlier editions, have been omitted. Bibliography, comp. by George Freedley, p.727–49, largely unchanged; it includes only a scattering of works published later than 1950. PN1625.S6

History

Brockett, Oscar Gross. History of the theatre. 4th ed. Boston, Allyn and Bacon, 1982. 768p. il. **BG75**

1st ed. 1968.

A good general history tracing the development of the theater from primitive times to the present. Emphasizes European theater and American theater as an extension thereof; treats scenic and performance practices, stage architecture, theatrical conditions, etc. Select bibliography; index. PN2101.B68

Hogan, Charles Beecher. Shakespeare in the theatre, 1701–1800. Oxford, Univ. Pr., 1952–57. 2v. **BG76**

Contents: v.1, A record of performances in London, 1701–1750; v.2, A record of performances in London, 1751–1800.

Each volume is in two parts: pt.1, List of performances arranged chronologically; pt.2, An alphabetical list of the plays, giving insofar as possible the complete casts for every performance. Appendixes in each volume include, for the period covered: Shakespeare's popularity in the theatre; Order of popularity of Shakespeare's plays; and London theatres in use.

Indexes in each volume: (1) Actors (giving full name of each, dates when he was "flourishing" as a Shakespearean actor, or of birth and death, and parts he performed); (2) Characters, with names of all actors who played the parts. PR3097.H6

Howard, Diana. London theatres and music halls, 1850–1950. London, Lib. Assoc., 1970. 291p. il. **BG77**

Pt.1, "The directory of theatres, music halls, and pleasure gardens," attempts to list every commercial stage (more than 900 of them) in London during the period 1850–1950. Each entry includes the name, address, dates, building details, management, official records, contemporary accounts, historical accounts (i.e., accounts written at least 12 months after the event), and location of other pertinent materials. A second part offers a bibliography of bibliographies, a calendar of official records, a list of newspapers and periodicals, and a list of monographs on the history of the theater.

British music-hall, 1840–1923; a bibliography and guide to sources by Laurence Senelick, David F. Cheshire and Ulrich Schneider (Hamden, Conn., Archon Books, 1981. 361p.) lists works on all aspects of the music-hall (architecture, regulation, operation, performers, etc.) and includes a directory of pertinent collections.

PN2596.L6H595

The London stage, 1660–1800: a calendar of plays, entertainments and afterpieces, together with casts, box-receipts and contemporary comment, comp. from the playbills, newspapers and theatrical diaries of the period. Carbondale, Ill., Southern Illinois Univ. Pr., 1960–68. 5 pts. in 11v. il. **BG78**

Contents: pt.1, 1660–1700, ed. by William Van Lennep; pt.2, 1700–1729, ed. by E. L. Avery. 2v.; pt.3, 1729–1747, ed. by A. H. Scouten. 2v.; pt.4, 1747–1776, ed. by G. W. Stone. 3v.; pt.5, 1776–1800, ed. by C. B. Hogan. 3v.

An important, scholarly work providing a vast amount of information on the stage productions of the period. The theatrical seasons are arranged chronologically, listing plays, casts, etc., with an index in each volume.

An index to the full set is provided by: PN2592.L6

Schneider, Ben Ross. Index to The London stage, 1660–1800. Carbondale, Southern Illinois Univ. Pr., [1979]. 939p. **BG79**

A computer-produced index containing "all references to each name and title appearing in the calendar of *The London Stage, 1660–1800* [above], listed alphabetically in one merged index. References are to the date and theatre of the calendar entry containing the item, rather than to page, because it was felt that index entries would thus convey more information and that citations would be easier to locate in the volumes themselves, since they are arranged chronologically."—*Introd.* PN2592.L63S3

Loney, Glenn Meredith. 20th century theatre. N.Y., Facts on File, [1983]. 2v. il. **BG80**

Presented as a chronological record, the work intends "to offer an overview of theatre activity in North America and the British Isles since 1900, and to provide a 'date-finder' for those who want to obtain capsule information about a particular theatre event, production, personality, or playhouse."—*Pref.* Each year includes sections for: American premieres, British premieres, revivals/repertories, births/deaths/debuts, and theaters/productions. Index of names, titles, theaters. PN2189.L65

Mander, Raymond and **Mitchenson, Joe.** The theatres of London. London, Hart-Davis, 1961. 292p. il. **BG81**

Offers descriptions and histories of the theaters existing in London at time of compilation. PN2596.L6M35

Mantzius, Karl. A history of theatrical art in ancient and modern times, with an introd. by William Archer; authorized translation by Louise von Cossel. London, Duckworth; Philadelphia, Lippincott, 1903–21. 6v. il. (Repr.: N.Y., Peter Smith, 1937) **BG82**

Translation of *Skuespilkunstens historie* . . . (København, 1897–1916).

Contents: v.1, Earliest times; v.2, Middle Ages and Renaissance; v.3, Shakespearean period in England; v.4, Molière and his times; the theatre in France in the 17th century; v.5, The great actors of the 18th century; v.6, Classicism and romanticism (tr. by C. Archer).

PN2104.M3

Mullin, Michael and **Muriello, Karen Morris.** Theatre at Stratford-upon-Avon: a catalogue-index to productions of the Shakespeare Memorial/Royal Shakespeare Theatre, 1879–1978. Westport, Conn., Greenwood Pr., [1980]. 2v. (1038p.)   **BG83**

Contents: v.1, Catalogue of productions; v.2, Indexes and calendars.

A computer-generated catalog and index of virtually all Stratford productions (including non-Shakespearean plays) since 1879, prepared at the Univerity of Illinois from microfilm of the archives in the Shakespeare Centre Library, Stratford-upon-Avon. v.1 lists the plays by title, then chronologically by production, giving cast, director, designer, light designer, and theater at which performed; references to reviews are given when available, as are pertinent references to Shattuck's *The Shakespeare promptbooks* (BD707). v.2 provides indexes to (1) playwrights, (2) directors, designers, actors, and (3) reviewers. A year-by-year calendar of productions completes the work.   PN2596.S82S86

Nagler, Alois Maria. Sources of theatrical history. N.Y., Theatre Annual, [1952]. 611p. il. (Repr.: N.Y., Dover, 1959)

BG84

Lists primary sources, with long annotations, from the Greek classical theater to the end of the 19th century.   PN2101.N3

Nicoll, Allardyce. The development of the theatre: a study of theatrical art from the beginnings to the present day. 5th ed. rev. London, Harrap, 1966. 292p. il.   **BG85**

Concerned mainly with theatrical buildings, designs, arrangements, and equipment. Particular attention is given to the English stage. Good illustrations.   PN2101.N5

———— Masks, mimes and miracles: studies in the popular art. N.Y., Harcourt, 1931. 407p. il. (Repr.: N.Y., Cooper Square, 1963)   **BG86**

A historical survey from the earliest times through the 17th century, with special emphasis on the *commedia dell' arte.* Excellent illustrations. Appendix (p.351–90), devoted to the *commedia dell' arte,* includes lists of chief character parts and chief actors with bibliographical references, and alphabetical list of scenarii.

PN2071.G4N5

Odell, George Clinton Densmore. Annals of the New York stage. N.Y., Columbia Univ Pr., 1927–49. 15v. il.   **BG87**

A very full account of the history of the stage in New York City, covering actors, plays, theaters, etc., with the historical background of each period from about 1699–1894.

———— ———— Index to the portraits in Odell's Annals of the New York stage, transcribed from the file in the Theatre Collection at Princeton University. [N.Y.?], Amer. Soc. for Theatre Research, [1963]. 179p.

PN2277.N5O4

Stevens, David. English Renaissance theatre history: a reference guide. Boston, G. K. Hall, [1982]. 342p.   **BG88**

Offers "an annotated, chronological list of the scholarship from 1664 through 1979 on Elizabethan theatrical history."—*Pref.* Does not intend to include items which are purely literary. Index of authors and subjects.   Z2014.D7S78

Wearing, J. P. The London stage, 1890–1899: a calendar of plays and players. Metuchen, N.J., Scarecrow Pr., 1976. 2v. (1229p.)   **BG89**

Contents: v.1, 1890–1896; v.2, 1897–1899, Index.

Aims "to furnish a daily listing of the plays and players on the London stage from 1890–1899."—*Introd.* Information (in slightly

abbreviated form) was gleaned from a variety of sources and is presented in the form of a series of playbills. Arrangement is chronological by date of opening night performance (by theater when there was more than one opening production on the same day). Information includes: full title, author (including details of adaptation or translation as applicable), genre of play, theater at which performed, length of run and number of performances, cast (including changes), production staff, references to reviews of first performances. Index of titles, authors, performers, theaters, managers, etc. No doubt inspired by the series of the same title covering the 1660–1800 period (BG78).   PN2596.L6W37

———— The London stage, 1900–1909: a calendar of plays and players. Metuchen, N.J., Scarecrow Pr., 1981. 2v.

BG90

Contents: v.1, 1900–1907; v.2, 1908–1909, Index.

Continues the compiler's earlier listings of plays and players, thus providing a complete record from 1890 through 1909.

Continued by: PN2596.L6W38

———— The London stage, 1910–1919: a calendar of plays and players. Metuchen, N.J., Scarecrow Pr., 1982. 2v.

BG91

Provides details of some 3,278 productions at 39 theaters.

PN2596.L6W383

Young, William C. Famous American playhouses, 1716–1899. Chicago, Amer. Lib. Assoc., 1973. 327p. il. (Documents of American theater history, v.1)   **BG92**

NA6830.Y67

———— Famous American playhouses, 1900–1971. Chicago, Amer. Lib. Assoc., 1973. 297p. il. (Documents of American theater history, v.2)   **BG93**

The series was planned as "a multivolume anthology of primary and secondary source reading, . . . intended as a basic reference tool for librarians, scholars, students, and others interested in the American theater."—*Pref.* Types of documents include diaries, letters, journals, autobiographies, newspaper articles and reviews, magazine articles, playbills, publicity materials, and architectural descriptions. Most sources are contemporary with the event or matter under consideration, but more modern sources are sometimes quoted. Verbatim transcripts of the documents are given.

These volumes are concerned with the physical structure of 199 American playhouses, criteria for selection having been historical, architectural, and social and cultural importance. Within the overall chronological arrangement there are sections for New York theaters, regional theaters, etc., with chronological arrangement therein. Each volume has three indexes: alphabetical by name, geographical by location, and personal name and theatrical specialties.

For a companion volume *see* BG107.   NA6830.Y68

Biography

Archer, Stephen M. American actors and actresses: a guide to information sources. Detroit, Gale, [1983]. 710p. (Performing arts information guide ser., v.8)   **BG94**

Concerned with actors and actresses in the professional theater (i.e., the legitimate stage). Sections of reference works and general sources are followed by sections for individual performers. Entries are mainly for periodical articles; reviews of specific performances are not included. Author, title, and subject indexes.

Z5784.M9A7

Eisenberg, Ludwig Julius. Grosses biographisches Lexikon der deutschen Bühne im XIX Jahrhundert. Leipzig, List, 1903. 1180p.   **BG95**

Fairly long sketches, but no references to sources.   PN2657.E3

Highfill, Philip H., Burnim, Kalman A. and **Langhans, Edward A.** A biographical dictionary of actors, actresses, musicians, dancers, managers & other stage personnel in

London, 1660–1800. Carbondale, Southern Illinois Univ. Pr., [1973–84]. v.1–10. il. (In progress) **BG96**

Contents: v.1–10, Abaco–Nash.

"The purpose of these volumes is to provide brief biographical notices of all persons who were members of theatrical companies or occasional performers or were patentees or servants of the patent theatres, opera houses, amphitheatres, pleasure gardens, theatrical taverns, music rooms, fair booths, and other places of public entertainment in London and its immediate environs from the Restoration of Charles II in 1660 until the end of the season 1799–1800."—*Pref.*

An ambitious undertaking, the finished work promises to be a mine of information. Biographical data have been gleaned from a wide range of sources, but bibliographic references are confined to occasional mention within the text. Sketches vary in length from a few lines to several pages, and often include an impressive amount of detail. Cross references from variant forms of names.

PN2597.H5

Johnson, Claudia D. and **Johnson, Vernon E.** Nineteenth-century theatrical memoirs. Westport, Conn., Greenwood Pr., [1982]. 269p. **BG97**

Lists published memoirs of "those individuals of every nationality who performed in England and America for all or much of their careers."—*Introd.* (19th century in the title refers to the period of activity of the individuals, not to date of publication; the work thus supplements Arnott and Robinson's *English theatrical literature* [BG24] for many figures from the last half of the century.) Many annotations; author and subject index. Z6935.J63

Kaye, Phyllis Johnson. National playwrights directory. 2d ed. Waterford, Conn., O'Neill Theater Center, [1981]. 507p. il. **BG98**

1st ed. 1977.

Gives brief biographical information (obtained by questionnaire) on about 500 contemporary American playwrights, including address, and (usually) agent's name and address, titles of plays with indication of productions and availability of scripts; synopses of one or more plays of a given writer are often given. Index of play titles. PS129.K3

Kosch, Wilhelm. Deutsches Theater-Lexikon; biographisches und bibliographisches Handbuch. Klagenfurt, Kleinmayr, 1951–71. Lfg. 1–21. (In progress) **BG99**

Contents: Lfg.1–21, A–Schlettow. (v.1–2 complete in 18 Lfg.)

Bio-bibliographical information on persons connected with the theater, together with articles on dramatic theory, history, and themes. Bibliographical notes include material in newspapers and periodicals as well as books. PN2035.K6

Lyonnet, Henry. Dictionnaire des comédiens français (ceux d'hier): biographie, bibliographie, iconographie. Genève, Bibliothèque de la Revue Universelle Internationale Illustrée, [1911–12]. 2v. il. **BG100**

At head of title: Histoire du théâtre.
Issued in 80 pts., 1902–12.
Biographies are of some length, with many bibliographical references. Some portraits and facsimiles of autographs included. Persons living at time of compilation were omitted. PN2637.L8

Mongrédien, Georges. Dictionnaire biographique des comédiens français du XVIIe siècle; suivi d'un inventaire des troupes (1590–1710), d'après des documents inédits. Paris, Centre National de la Recherche Scientifique, 1961. 239p. **BG101**

Brief listings of actors, with numbered references to items in an extensive supplementary bibliography. Lists and gives information concerning acting companies sponsored by French royal houses, foreign royal houses, independent companies, and companies in various French cities. PN2637.M6

—— —— Supplément, par Georges Mongrédien et Jean Robert. Paris, CNRS, 1971. 62p.

Contains corrections and additions.

Notable names in the American theatre. [New and rev. ed.] Clifton, N.J., James T. White & Co., 1976. 1250p. **BG102**

Represents a second edition of Walter Rigdon's *Biographical encyclopaedia and who's who of the American theatre* (1966).

Contents: New York productions; Premieres in America; Premieres of American plays abroad; Theatre group biographies; Theatre building biographies; Awards; Biographical bibliography; Necrology; Notable names in the American theatre [i.e., the "who's who" section].

The "Notable names" section offers detailed biographical sketches of living persons (actors, directors, playwrights, designers, etc.) who have been active in the American theater, and also of Americans who have made their theater careers abroad and foreigners who have made a definite contribution to the American stage. The necrology section is also international in scope.

The section of "Theatre playbills," 1959–64, appearing in the earlier work is not carried forward to this edition. PN2285.N6

Nungezer, Edwin. Dictionary of actors and of other persons associated with the public representation of plays in England before 1642. New Haven, Conn., Yale Univ. Pr.; London, Milford, 1929. 438p. (Cornell studies in English, 13) **BG103**

Brings together information on early players, with references to sources. PN2597.N8

Rasi, Luigi. I comici italiani; biografia, bibliografia, iconografia. Firenze, Bocca, 1897–1905. 2v. il. **BG104**

A comprehensive work, covering the mid-16th through the 19th centuries, and containing many articles of considerable length. Copiously illustrated with portraits, stage designs, etc. PN2687.R3

Who's who in the theatre; a biographical record of the contemporary stage. Ed.1–17. London, Pitman, 1912–81. Irregular. **BG105**

Originally comp. by John Parker. Ed.17 publ. by Gale, Detroit.

Presents fairly detailed biographies of persons connected with the modern theater, including actors, actresses, dramatists, composers, critics, managers, scenic artists, historians, and biographers. Emphasis in early editions was on London stage personalities, but the most recent editions give good coverage for New York and include both London and New York playbills. Item BG19 is intended as a supplement. PN2012.W5

Who was who in the theatre, 1912–1976. Detroit, Gale, [1978]. 4v. (Gale composite biographical dictionary ser., no.3) **BG106**

Subtitle: A biographical dictionary of actors, actresses, directors, playwrights, and producers of the English-speaking theatre, comp. from *Who's who in the theatre,* volumes 1–15 (1912–72).

Reproduces the latest biographical sketch of any personality "dropped from *Who's Who in the Theatre* because of death or inactivity in the theatre."—*Foreword.* Death dates through 1976 have been added for individuals known to be deceased, although this aspect of the publication appears not to have been thoroughly researched. About 4,100 entries. PN2597.W52

Young, William C. Famous actors and actresses on the American stage. N.Y., Bowker, 1975. 2v. (1298p.) il. (Documents of American theater history) **BG107**

Intended as a companion to the same author's *Famous American playhouses* (BG92–BG93).

Aims "(1) to present contemporary evaluations of the abilities of a certain actor or actress; and (2) to relate a performer's philosophy of acting and approach to certain roles."—*Pref.* 225 actors and actresses (not necessarily Americans) are treated. For each performer there is a portrait, brief biographical data, and a number of extracts from contemporary criticism (reviews of plays, interviews, memoirs of fellow actors, etc.). Sources of the excerpts are given in full. Index of persons, plays, and characters mentioned in the extracts.

PN2285.Y6

Bibliography

Moyer, Ronald L. American actors, 1861–1910: an annotated bibliography of books published in the United States in English from 1861 through 1976. Troy, N.Y., Whitston, 1979. 268p. **BG108**

Aims to provide a complete record of those books "which contain substantial information" (*Pref.*) on American actors of the 1861–1910 period, and which were published in English in the United States. More than 350 entries. Indexed. Z5784.A27M65

Indexes

Wearing, J. P. American and British theatrical biography: a directory. Metuchen, N.J., Scarecrow Pr., 1979. 1007p. **BG109**

A guide to biographical information appearing in works of collective biography, theater yearbooks, encyclopedias of the theater, etc. For each person listed gives "name (with cross-references to stage names, pseudonyms, etc.), dates of birth and death, nationality, theatrical occupation(s), and a code to the source(s) containing fuller biographical information."—*Introd.* Focus is on American and British personalities, but others are included if "the sources surveyed make some mention of their contribution to the American or British theatre." PN2285.W42

Play production and dramatic technique

Allensworth, Carl, Allensworth, Dorothy and **Rawson, Clayton.** The complete play production handbook. Rev. ed. N.Y., Harper & Row, [1982]. 384p. il. **BG110**

1st ed. 1973.
Attempts "to present . . . all of the information a dedicated but inexperienced person or group will require to mount a creditable production of an average play on the average stage to be found in the average community center, high school, or college."—*Pref.* Includes a glossary of terms; a brief directory of sources of theatrical supplies and services; a bibliography; and an index. PN2053.A53

Baker, Hendrik. Stage management and theatrecraft: a stage manager's handbook. 3d ed. N.Y., Theatre Arts, 1981. 384p. il. **BG111**

1st ed. 1968.
A practical manual with definitions, explanations, and recommendations on various aspects of stage production. Includes chapters on rehearsals, scenery, properties, lighting, wardrobe, etc. PN2085.B3

Baygan, Lee. Makeup for theatre, film & television; a step by step photographic guide. N.Y., Drama Book Publishers, [1982]. 182p. il. **BG112**

Addressed to the performer. Each chapter deals with a certain type of makeup and each is meant to be complete in itself, repeating steps and procedures used in earlier chapters as necessary. Takes account of differences of skin colors of black and white actors. Glossary often gives reference to pertinent chapters, but there is no index. PN2068.B39

Burris-Meyer, Harold and **Cole, Edward C.** Scenery for the theatre; the organization, processes, materials, and techniques used to set the stage. Rev. ed. Boston, Little, Brown, [1972]. 518p. il. **BG112a**

1st ed. 1938.
Includes sections on planning, types of scenery, materials, tools and equipment for the scene shop, scene construction and painting, stage equipment, properties, assembling and running the show, processes and techniques. Lighting, acoustics, and costume are considered only as they impinge on or relate to scenery. Numerous illustrations, charts and graphs; definitions of terms; bibliography; index. Six contributing authors are named on the title page.

Willard F. Bellman's *Scene design, stage lighting, sound, costume & makeup: a scenographic approach* (N.Y., Harper & Row, 1983. 474p. il) aims to provide an integrated plan for the many physical aspects of a stage production. PN2091.S8B8

Cassin-Scott, Jack. Costumes and settings for staging historical plays. Boston, Plays Inc., [1979]. 4v. il. **BG113**

British ed. (London, Batsford, 1979) has title: *Costumes and settings for historical plays.*

Contents: v.1, The classical period; v.2, Medieval; v.3, The Elizabethan and Restoration periods; v.4, The Georgian period.

Each volume includes a general introduction to the period, followed by descriptions (with many sketches and pictorial aids) of subdivisions of the overall period, discussion and illustration of stage properties, and brief discussion of stage settings, stage lighting, and choosing a play. Each volume has its own index. PN2067.C33

Corson, Richard. Stage makeup. 6th ed. Englewood Cliffs, N.J., Prentice-Hall, [1981]. 420p. il. **BG114**

1st ed. 1942.
". . . intended to be used as a text and as a reference by actors and prospective actors who are or expect to be responsible for their own makeup—and also by those who might in some way be involved with the makeup, whether as designers, directors, makeup artists, or teachers."—*Pref.* In four main sections: (1) Basic principles; (2) Planning the makeup; (3) Applying the makeup; (4) Appendices. Chapters are subdivided to deal with very specific topics or problems; the many illustrations include numerous step-by-step procedures. Indexed. PN2068.C65

Farber, Donald C. Producing theatre: a comprehensive legal and business guide. N.Y., Drama Book Specialists, [1981]. 382p. **BG115**

An updating and extension of the author's *Producing on Broadway* (1969), now "intended as a text covering the business of producing theatre anywhere in the United States—that is, on Broadway, in resident theatres, stock, or other productions."—*Pref.* Chapters range from "Obtaining a property," "Movie deals," "The producing company," and "Raising money" through contracts with the theater and with the producers, and theater licenses. Appendixes (p.255–352) give sample agreements, contracts, etc. Indexed. KF4296.F37

Green, Joann. The small theatre handbook: a guide to management and production. [Harvard, Mass.], Harvard Common Pr., [1981]. 163p. il. **BG116**

Offers practical advice for managing a theater with a yearly budget of less than $100,000. Brief chapters deal with administration and budget, raising money, choosing the play, the director, the actor, rehearsals, publicity, etc. Appendix includes a select bibliography and a compilation of directory information. Indexed. PN2053.G688

Heffner, Hubert C. [and others]. Modern theatre practice. With an expansion of the scenery section by Tom Rezzuto and a chapter on sound by Kenneth K. Jones. 5th ed. N.Y., Appleton, [1973]. 660p. il. **BG117**

1st ed. 1935.
A standard, authoritative text treating play selection, production, direction, stage scenery, lighting, sound, costuming, etc. Contains glossaries, annotated bibliography, and index. PN3151.H4

Howard, John T. A bibliography of theatre technology: acoustics and sound, lighting, properties, and scenery. Westport, Conn., Greenwood Pr., [1982]. 345p. **BG118**

Lists some 5,700 items—books, periodical articles, theses—arranged by title within the categories noted in the subtitle (plus a brief section on research materials and collections). Subject and author indexes. Derived from an ongoing computer database at the University of Massachusetts Computing Center. Z5784.S8H68

Kesler, Jackson. Theatrical costume: a guide to information sources. Detroit, Gale, [1979]. 308p. (Performing arts information guide ser., v.6)   **BG119**

Aims "to provide for costume-designers, primarily, a practical, utilitarian listing, mostly of English-title books in the field" (*Pref.,*) mainly publications which have appeared since 1957. Classed arrangement with author, title, and subject indexes. About 1,700 items; annotations.   Z5691.K47

Lounsbury, Warren C. Theatre backstage from A to Z. Rev. ed. Seattle, Univ. of Washington Pr., [1972]. 191p. il.   **BG120**

First publ. 1967 as a revised and expanded version of the author's *Backstage from A to Z* (1959); this edition incorporates minor corrections and updatings, and adds a supplement of new material, p.168–85.
A manual in dictionary form of the technical aspects of theatrical production.   PN2035.L6

O'Donnol, Shirley Miles. American costume, 1915–1970: a source book for the stage costumer. Bloomington, Indiana Univ. Pr., [1982]. 270p. il.   **BG121**

A decade-by-decade presentation of written descriptions and illustrations (both photographs and line drawings) of American costumes as they occurred in everyday life. Includes suggestions for adaptation to stage use; hair styles and make-up are discussed. Select bibliography.   PN2067.O3

Reid, Francis. The stage lighting handbook. 2d ed. N.Y., Theatre Arts Books, 1982. 145p. il.   **BG122**

1st ed. 1976.
Discusses aims, equipment, rigging and wiring, basic steps in lighting design, differences to be considered in lighting plays and musicals, thrust and proscenium stages, etc. Glossary; index.   PN2091.E4R4

Stagecraft: the complete guide to theatrical practice. [Oxford], Phaidon, [1982]. 192p. il.   **BG123**

Trevor R. Griffiths, consultant ed.
A practical guide, with chapters on directing, stage management, acting, set design, lighting, costume design, etc. Aims to "show how to achieve the best possible production with the least number of pitfalls."—*Foreword.* Numerous illustrations. Indexed.   PN2053.S7

Stoddard, Richard. Stage scenery, machinery, and lighting: a guide to information sources. Detroit, Gale, [1977]. 274p. (Performing arts information guide ser., v.2)   **BG124**

Lists books, articles, pamphlets, selected exhibition catalogs, and unpublished doctoral dissertations on stage scenery and lighting throughout the world, whether for drama, opera or dance. Covers all historical periods; emphasis is on English-language materials. Classed arrangement with author and subject indexes. About 1,600 items; brief annotations.
Stoddard is also the compiler of *Theatre and cinema architecture: a guide to information sources* (Detroit, Gale, 1978. 368p.).   Z5784.S8S79

Warre, Michael. Designing and making stage scenery. London, Studio Vista; N.Y., Reinhold, [1966]. 104p. il.   **BG125**

A brief section on the historical background of scenic design is followed by chapters on the practical aspects of making stage sets.   PN2091.S8W34

THE DANCE

Bibliography

Beaumont, Cyril William. A bibliography of dancing. London, Dancing Times, 1929. (Repr.: N.Y., Blom, 1963)   **BG126**

An annotated list, arranged by author, selected from the holdings of the British Museum Library. Includes a detailed subject index.   Z7514.D2B3

Forrester, Felicitée Sheila. Ballet in England: a bibliography and survey, c.1700–June 1966. [London], Lib. Assoc., 1968. 224p. (Lib. Assoc. Bibliographies, no.9)   **BG127**

Classed bibliography with many annotations. Index.   Z7514.D2F6

Leslie, Serge and **Niles, Doris.** A bibliography of the dance collection of Doris Niles and Serge Leslie; annotated by Serge Leslie, ed. by Cyril Beaumont. London, C. W. Beaumont ["Dancing Times, Ltd."], 1966–68. 2v.   **BG128**

The collection runs to nearly 2,000 volumes. Main-entry listing; although the two volumes are continuously paged, each has its own index which groups the titles by fairly broad subject categories.   Z7514.D2L4

Magriel, Paul David. A bibliography of dancing; a list of books and articles on the dance and related subjects. N.Y., Wilson, 1936. 229p. il. (Repr.: N.Y., Blom, 1966)   **BG129**

———— ———— 4th cumulated supplement, 1936–40. 1941. 104p.

"A comprehensive list of references on the dance in all of its phases, and of the arts relating to it, as music, decor, costume, masques, mime and pantomime."—*Pref.* Locates copies.   Z7514.D2M2

New York. Public Library. Dance Collection. Dictionary catalog of the Dance Collection; a list of authors, titles, and subjects of multi-media materials in the Dance Collection of the Performing Arts Research Center of the New York Public Library. Boston, New York Pub. Lib. and G. K. Hall, 1974. 10v.   **BG130**

A book catalog produced by automated techniques listing materials cataloged for the collection prior to Oct. 1, 1973 (about 300,000 entries for some 96,000 items), and including entries for relevant materials in other divisions of the Research Libraries of the New York Public Library.
Supplemented by: Z7514.D2N462

———— Bibliographic guide to dance. 1st– , 1975– . Boston, G. K. Hall, 1976– . Annual.   **BG131**

Each annual issued in two or more volumes.
Represents an ongoing supplement to the *Dictionary catalog of the Dance Collection* (above), listing materials newly cataloged for the collection. A computer-produced catalog in dictionary form like the parent work.   Z7514.D2N462a

Petermann, Kurt. Tanzbibliographie; Verzeichnis der in deutscher Sprache veröffentlichten Schriften und Aufsätze zum Bühnen-, Gesellschafts-, Kinder-, Volks- und Turniertanz sowie zur Tanzwissenschaft, Tanzmusik und zum Jazz. Hrsg. vom Institut für Volkskunstforschung beim Zentralhaus für Kulturarbeit, Leipzig. Leipzig, VEB Bibliographisches Institut, 1966–79. Lfg.1–30. (In progress)   **BG132**

Lists book and periodical materials in German on all aspects of the dance—social, cultural, and artistic—and on all forms of dancing. In addition, there will be sections on music for the dance, on costumes, décor, etc., for dance productions, and on pantomime. A classed arrangement (outlined in Lfg.1) is employed, and there is to be an author and name index, and one of subjects. Most entries are briefly annotated, and a library location is given.
Lfg.30, the latest part received, carries the work through only 9 of the 17 subject categories outlined in the preface. Meanwhile, a "2. unveränderte Aufl." has been published in 3v. (München & N.Y., K.G. Saur, 1981–82), and an index volume is reported in preparation.   Z7314.D2P44

Ten years of films on ballet and classical dance, 1956–1965; catalogue. [Paris], UNESCO, [1968]. 105p.   **BG133**

Lists films on ballet, classical and modern dance in which the art of choreography is considered to be the main subject. For each title is indicated producing firm, choreographer, music, dancers, director, characteristics of the film, and distributor (with address). Indexes by country, by choreographer, and by composer.

GV1790.A1T4

Indexes

Guide to dance periodicals. v.1–10, 1931/35–1961/62. Gainesville, Univ. of Florida Pr., 1948–63. 10v. **BG134**

Frequency varies: quinquennial, 1931/35–1946/50; biennial, 1951/52–1961/62.

Comp. by S. Y. Belknap.

Publisher varies.

Indexes by author and subject some 18 periodicals devoted to the dance.

Z7514.D2G8

Minneapolis. Public Library. Music Dept. An index to folk dances and singing games. Chicago, Amer. Lib. Assoc., 1936. 202p. **BG135**

Includes folk dances, singing games, classic dances, tap and clog dances, and some earlier square- and contradances.

—— —— Supplement. 1949. 98p.

Indexes 60 collections published 1936–48.   ML128.D3M5

Annuals

Ballet annual; a record and year book of the ballet. 1st–18th, 1947–63. N.Y., Macmillan; London, A. & C. Black, 1947–63. 18v. il. Annual. **BG136**

Ceased publication.

Contains a list of "outstanding events of the year"; articles on various aspects of the ballet by well-known authorities and critics; and a checklist of ballet performances in European centers and America (chiefly New York).   GV1787.B25

Dance world. v.1–14. N.Y., Crown, 1966–79. il. Annual. **BG137**

John Willis, ed.

An annual similar to Blum's *Theatre world* (BG53), offering a pictorial survey of the New York dance season. Lists personnel of the various companies, repertories, opening and closing dates, etc. Includes a section on regional United States companies, and a biographical section. Indexed. Ceased publication.

GV1580.D335

Encylopedias and handbooks

Balanchine, George and **Mason, Francis.** Balanchine's Complete stories of the great ballets. Rev. and enl. ed. N.Y., Doubleday, [1977]. 838p. il. **BG138**

1954 ed. entitled *Complete stories of the great ballets;* 1968 ed. called *Balanchine's New complete stories of the great ballets.*

Deals with 404 ballets, both those deemed "of lasting importance in the history of the art" *(Pref.)* and significant works of the 25 years prior to compilation of the book; includes works in the contemporary repertory and those which made a deep impression at the time they were introduced. Gives notes on first productions and notable revivals as well as the stories, often with first-person commentary by Balanchine. Includes sections on "How to enjoy ballet," history and chronology, careers in ballet, and notes on dancers, dancing, and choreography. Glossary; index.   MT95.B3

Balet: entsiklopediia. Gl. red. IU. N. Grigorovich. Moskva, Sovetskaia Entsiklopediia, 1981. 623p. il. **BG139**

Offers articles (most of them signed) on dancers, choreographers, composers, designers, ballet terms, individual ballets, etc. Living persons are included. Brief bibliographies for a high percentage of articles. Numerous illustrations, some in color, represent stage views, dancers in specific roles, portraits, costume and set designs. International coverage, but recent Russian "defectors to the West" (e.g., Nureyev, Makarova) are not included.   GV1585.B27

Beaumont, Cyril William. Complete book of ballets; a guide to the principal ballets of the nineteenth and twentieth centuries. [Rev.] London, Putnam, [1951]. 1106p. il. **BG140**

1st ed. 1938.

Gives stories of ballets, including information concerning first productions and excerpts from reviews.

—— —— Supplement. 1945. [Repr. 1952] 212p. il.

Includes works not in the main volume.

—— Ballets of today . . . 2d supplement. London, Putnam, [1954]. 250p. il. **BG141**

—— Ballets past and present . . . 3d supplement. London, Putnam, [1955]. 259p. il. **BG142**

GV1787.B35

Bowers, Faubion. Theatre in the East; a survey of Asian dance and drama. N.Y., Nelson, [1956]. 374p. il. (Repr.: Salem, N.H., Ayer, 1980) **BG143**

Arranged in 14 chapters devoted to the countries of: India, Ceylon, Burma, Thailand, Cambodia, Laos, Malaya, Indonesia, Philippines, China, Vietnam, Hong Kong, Okinawa, and Japan. Gives history of the dance, and describes folk, traditional, and modern forms. Well illustrated.   GV1689.B6

Chujoy, Anatole and **Manchester, P. W.,** comps. The dance encyclopedia. Rev. and enl. ed. N.Y., Simon & Schuster, [1967]. 992p. il. **BG144**

1st ed. 1949.

Includes long, encyclopedic articles on various forms of the dance, written by specialists, in the same alphabet with briefer articles covering biography, special ballets, types of dances, terms used in dancing, ballet, etc. The bibliography of books on the dance and the discography included in the first edition have been omitted.

GV1585.C5

Cohen-Stratyner, Barbara Naomi. Biographical dictionary of dance. N.Y., Schirmer Books; London, Collier Macmillan, [1982]. 970p. **BG145**

Offers brief biographical sketches of some 2,900 figures from "the last four centuries of dance history in Europe and the Americas, embracing a wide range of theatrical genres, from the *opéra-ballet* to the Broadway musical, from the burlesque striptease to the television variety show."—*Pref.* Includes impressarios, composers, artists, etc., associated with dance, as well as performers and choreographers. Entries emphasize roles danced and works choreographed.

GV1785.A1C58

De Mille, Agnes. The book of the dance. N.Y., Golden Pr., [1963]. 252p. il. **BG146**

An encyclopedic work on the development of the dance, with examples from all periods and many countries. Gives definitions, types, and methods of choreography. Treats the classical ballet and modern dance in detail, including brief biographies of performers. Excellent photographs, many in color. Includes a list of principal ballets of leading choreographers and an index.   GV1601.D4

Dictionary of modern ballet. Gen. eds., Francis Gadan and Robert Maillard; American ed., Selma Jeanne Cohen. [Tr. from the French by John Montague and Peggie Cochrane] N.Y., Tudor, [1959]. 360p. il. **BG147**

Originally published as *Dictionnaire du ballet moderne* (Paris, 1957).

In one alphabet gives descriptions of ballets; famous ballet organizations and companies, etc.; and biographical sketches of dancers, composers, designers, choreographers, etc.   GV1787.D513

The encyclopedia of dance & ballet. Ed. by Mary Clarke & David Vaughan. London, Pitman; N.Y., Putnam's, [1977]. 376p. il. **BG148**

The title is meant "to indicate that the entries are not confined to classical ballet but record also activity in contemporary dance styles."—*Introd.* The work is, however, concerned "only with dance raised to a theatrical level as a performing art in any of the media of the twentieth century." Entries for dancers, companies, choreographers, individual ballets and types of dances. "Glossary of technical terms," p.368–72.   GV1585.E53

Koegler, Horst. The concise Oxford dictionary of ballet. 2d ed. London, Oxford Univ. Pr., 1982. 459p. il.   **BG149**

Original German edition (1972) had title *Friedrichs Ballettlexikon von A–Z;* first English edition 1977.

Although based on a German work, focus has been shifted to matters of Anglo-American interest, with much new material added. Attempts "to cover the whole ballet scene, past and present, its personalities, works, companies, places of performance, and technical terms, with some consideration of modern dance, ethnic dance, and ballroom dance."—*Foreword.*   GV1585.K6313

Lawrence, Robert. The Victor book of ballets and ballet music. N.Y., Simon & Schuster, 1950. 531p. il.   **BG150**

A brief, general outline of the history of ballet, followed by the stories of individual ballets, alphabetically arranged, and including musical themes. Indexes of choreographers and composers as well as a general index.   MT95.L48

McDonagh, Don The complete guide to modern dance. Garden City, N.Y., Doubleday, [1976]. 534p. il.   **BG151**

A survey of modern dance in terms of its leading choreographers—forerunners, founders and contemporary practitioners. For each choreographer there is a brief biographical sketch followed by a description of one or more selected, representative works and a "choreochronicle" which gives titles and dates of all known works of that individual. Bibliography; index.   GV1783.M26

Parker, David L. and **Siegel, Esther.** Guide to dance in film: a catalog of U.S. productions including dance sequences, with names of dancers, choreographers, directors, and other details. Detroit, Gale, [1978]. 220p. (Performing arts information guide ser., v.3)   **BG152**

A title listing of films, providing the kind of information noted in the subtitle. 1,750 items; name index.   GV1779.P37

Sachs, Curt. World history of the dance. Tr. by Bessie Schönberg. N.Y., Norton, [1937]. 469p. il.   **BG153**

Published in Germany under title: *Eine Weltgeschichte des Tanzes* (Berlin, 1933).   GV1601.S27

Shaw, Lloyd. Cowboy dances, a collection of western square dances; with a foreword by Sherwood Anderson. Caldwell, Idaho, Caxton, 1948. 411p. il.   **BG154**

Offers history and description of the dances, directions, and calls. Includes a glossary of terms. Appendix contains cowboy dance tunes.   GV1767.S5

Terry, Walter. Ballet guide: background, listings, credits, and descriptions of more than five hundred of the world's major ballets. N.Y., Dodd, Mead, [1976]. 388p. il.   **BG155**

Based in part on Terry's *Ballet, a new guide to the liveliest art* (N.Y., 1959).

Listing is alphabetical by title of the ballet. Gives choreographer, music, scenery and costume designers, company and date of first performance, principal dancers in first performance and important recreations of the roles, together with a description of the ballet. Index; glossary.   GV1790.A1T47

Wilson, George Buckley. A dictionary of ballet. 3d ed. London, Cassell, [1974]. 539p. il.   **BG156**

1st ed. 1957.

Gives definitions of terms; history; information on individual ballets; companies, and brief biographies of leading dancers, composers, and choreographers. Concerned chiefly with classical ballet but includes some information on modern, Spanish, and Indian dances.   GV1585.W5

Dictionaries of terms

Grant, Gail. Technical manual and dictionary of classical ballet. 3d rev. ed. N.Y., Dover, [1982]. 139p. il.   **BG157**

1st ed. 1950.

Gives brief definitions and pronunciation of dance terms, with small line drawings of main positions.   GV1787.G68

Kersley, Leo and **Sinclair, Janet.** A dictionary of ballet terms. [3d rev. ed.] London, Black, [1977]. 112p. il.   **BG158**

1st ed. 1952.

Originally intended mainly for the layman, but now including a number of more technical terms. Some definitions are of considerable length; closely related terms are often treated under a single heading. Numerous *see* and *see also* references; helpful line drawings. Pronunciation is not indicated.

A briefer work is Cyril Beaumont's *French-English dictionary of technical terms used in classical ballet* (Rev. ed. London, Beaumont, 1972. 43p.), a work for the student of dance.   GV1585.K45

Mara, Thalia. The language of ballet; an informal dictionary. Cleveland, World, [1966]. 120p. il.   **BG159**

A glossary of ballet terms with pronunciation indicated. Definitions are generally briefer than in the Kersley and Sinclair work (above), but it includes some entries not found there.   GV1585.M37

Raffé, Walter George. Dictionary of the dance. N.Y., Barnes; London, T. Yoseloff, [1964]. 583p. il.   **BG160**

Defines numerous terms relating to dances and dancing in all countries and periods. Describes in some detail specific dances and types of dances. No entries for individual dancers, choreographers, etc. A geographical index lists dances by country and culture of origin.   GV1585.R3

MOTION PICTURES

Guides

Armour, Robert A. Film: a reference guide. Westport, Conn., Greenwood Pr., [1980]. 251p.   **BG161**

Aims "to provide a reference guide to film for the person beginning the serious study of the medium or for the viewer wanting to pursue in depth what has been a casual interest."—*Pref.* Each chapter is a bibliographic essay on some aspect of film, e.g., history of film; film production; film criticism; film and society; major actors and directors; reference works and periodicals. Only books available in English are discussed. Indexed.   PN1993.45.A75

McClure, Arthur F. Research guide to film history. [Saratoga, Calif., R & E Publishers, 1983] 90p., [26]p.   **BG162**

Introductory essays on the historical and cultural significance of the American entertainment film and notes on historical analysis of a film are followed by a classed bibliography of works on various aspects of the film. No index.   PN1993.7.M33

Manchel, Frank. Film study; a resource guide. Rutherford, N.J., Fairleigh Dickinson Univ. Pr., [1973]. 422p.   **BG163**

Not a book on teaching methods, nor a comprehensive bibliography for study of the film, but "a survey designed to describe six popular approaches to the study of the cinema, along with a practical analysis of selected books, materials and information about motion picture rentals."—*Introd.* Includes many bibliographical footnotes. Indexed.   Z5784.M9M34

Sheahan, Eileen. Moving pictures; an annotated guide to selected film literature, with suggestions for the study of film. South Brunswick, N.J., A. S. Barnes, 1979. 146p.   **BG164**

A selective, carefully annotated guide to resources for film research. Emphasis is on English-language materials of a reference nature—encyclopedias, bibliographies, indexes, histories—but some major foreign-language works are included, as are some general reference works which offer film-related information. Works are grouped broadly by type, with subject and author/title indexes. Annotations are descriptive rather than evaluative. The guide is based on an earlier compilation prepared primarily for students at Yale University (1973).   Z5784.M9S5

Bibliography

Academy of Motion Picture Arts & Sciences and Writers Guild of America, West. Who wrote the movie and what else did he write? An index of screen writers and their film works, 1936–1969. Los Angeles, The Academy, 1970. 491p.   **BG165**

Leonard Spigelgass, ed.
In three sections: (1) a writer's index, which lists about 2,000 authors, their screen credits, and their other published works; (2) a film title index (about 13,000 listings), with indication of writing credits; and (3) an awards index, listing awards chronologically.   PN1998.A53

Austin, Bruce A. The film audience: an international bibliography of research, with annotations and an essay. Metuchen, N.J., Scarecrow Pr., 1983. 179p.   **BG166**

Lists non-book materials concerning the relationship of commercial cinema to its audience. Author listing with subject and title indexes.   Z5784.M9A87

Cohen, Louis Harris. The Soviet cinema, film and photography: a selected annotated bibliography. Rev. and expanded. Edwards Air Force Base, Calif., DOETC, Air Force Flight Test Center, 1976. 492p. il.   **BG167**

Preliminary ed. 1974. Based on the author's doctoral dissertation submitted at University of Southern California.
Topically arranged in chapters, with introductory notes for each chapter. Extensive annotations; numerous appendixes, including a "Dictionary of cinematography terms" which gives the Russian term in Cyrillic characters, in transliteration, and in English translation. Index of names and selected subjects.   Z5784.M9C64

Dyment, Alan R. The literature of the film; a bibliographical guide to the film as art and entertainment, 1936–1970. London & N.Y., White Lion, [1975]. 398p.   **BG168**

An annotated bibliography of English-language books on the film published since Jan. 1936 (the approximate closing date of the *Film index* [BG181]). Classed listing with index of names and titles. About 1,300 items.   Z5784.M9D9

Ellis, Jack C., Derry, Charles and **Kern, Sharon.** The film book bibliography, 1940–1975. Metuchen, N.J., Scarecrow Pr., 1979. 752p.   **BG169**

A classified listing of some 5,400 books "published in English between 1940 and 1975 which deal with various aspects of the motion picture."—*p.III.* Notes on contents are given for many items. Indexed.   Z5784.M9E44

Emmens, Carol A. Short stories on film. Littleton, Colo., Libraries Unlimited, 1978. 345p.   **BG170**

An aid for locating the short story which served as the basis for a movie. Identifies about 1,300 films from the 1920–76 period which were based on short stories. Arranged by author of the story; gives story and film titles, production information, director, cast, etc., as available. Indexes of story titles and of film titles.   Z5784.M9E46

Enser, A. G. S. Filmed books and plays: a list of books and plays from which films have been made, 1928–83. Aldershot, Hampshire & Brookfield, Vt., Gower, [1985]. 705p.   **BG171**

The compiler's original list (publ. 1951) covered 1928–49; there

have been a number of intervening supplements and cumulated editions, this representing the most recent cumulation.
Offers approaches from the film title, the original title when the film title differs from the published work, and from author's name. Date of film and film company or distributor are indicated; nearly all films listed are British or American.   Z5784.M9E55

Hoffer, Thomas W. Animation: a reference guide. Westport, Conn., Greenwood Pr., [1981]. 385p.   **BG172**

Offers essays, with bibliographies, on the history, development, and production of animated films. Includes a section on "Personalities in animation." Appendixes list major research centers, sources of films and videotapes about animation, relevant periodicals, etc. Indexed.   TR897.5.H63

Internationale Filmbibliographie, 1952–1962. Ed., H. P. Manz. Zürich, H. Rohr, 1963. 262p. (Schriftenreihe der Schweizerischen Gesellschaft für Filmwissenschaft und Filmrecht, Bd.1)   **BG173**

——— Nachtrag, 1–2. Zürich, H. Rohr, 1963–65. 2v.

A classified listing of books on all aspects of film and the film industry (including biographies of film personalities, etc.) published during the 1952–64 period. Author/subject index.   Z5784.M9I5

Internationale Filmbibliographie. Bibliographie internationale du cinéma. International motion-picture bibliography. [n.s.v.1]– , 1979/80– . München, Verlagsbuchhandlung für Filmliteratur, 1981– . Annual.   **BG174**

H. P. Manz, ed.
A successor to the 1952–64 series (above); uncumulated quarterly bulletins were issued by Manz through mid-1979. The first volume of this new series lists books published July 1979 through Dec. 1980. Follows the plan of the earlier series, but now focuses on the purely cinematic.

McCarty, Clifford. Published screenplays; a checklist. [Kent, Ohio], Kent State Univ. Pr., [1971]. 127p.   **BG175**

388 items. Alphabetical title listing, with index of names, sources, etc.   Z5784.M9M3

Mitry, Jean. Bibliographie internationale du cinéma et de la télévision. Paris, Institut des Hautes Études Cinématographiques, 1966–68. pt.1–3. (In progress?)   **BG175a**

Contents: pt.1, France et pays de langue française: t.1, Ouvrages de référence et histoire du cinéma; t.2, Histoire du cinéma (suite); t.3, Esthétique et technique; t.4, Administration, législation, exploitation, biographies, index des auteurs cités; pt.2, Italie: t.1, Bibliographie, histoire du cinéma, sociologie; t.2, Esthétique, technique, administration, manifestations, biographies; pt.3, Espagne-Portugal et pays de langue espagnole et portugaise.
Further volumes were to deal with the United States; England, Germany, Hungary, and German-language countries; Sweden, Denmark, and Scandinavian countries; USSR, Poland, Czechoslovakia, and Yugoslavia. Brief annotations are provided for many items.   Z5784.M9M55

Phillips, Leona Rasmussen. Silent cinema: annotated critical bibliography. N.Y., Gordon Pr., 1978. 149p.   **BG176**

Offers critical annotations for about 90 books on the silent film (including autobiographies and biographies of directors, actors and actresses, etc.). There is a selected list of additional titles and a few references to periodical articles.   Z5784.M9P5

Prichard, Susan Perez. Film costume; an annotated bibliography. Metuchen, N.J., Scarecrow Pr., 1981. 563p.   **BG177**

More than 3,600 entries for "literally any literature relevant to film costume . . . , even the most trivial."—*Introd.* Entry is by author or anonymous title, with a subject index. Includes references to biographical sketches of costume designers. Annotations not only indicate content but mention illustrations of costumes worn in specific films.   Z5691.P75

Rehrauer, George. The Macmillan film bibliography. N.Y., Macmillan, [1982]. 2v.   **BG178**

An earlier bibliography by Rehrauer had title *Cinema booklist* (Metuchen, N.J., Scarecrow Pr., 1972; supplements, 1974 and 1977).

An alphabetical title listing of books about film—critical works, biographies, published film scripts, histories, handbooks and directories, etc. Annotations (termed "Reviews") are often of considerable length and usually indicate the compiler's assessment of worth. About 6,700 entries. The separate index volume has subject, author, and script indexes.   Z5784.M9R423

Traub, Hans and **Lavies, Hanns Wilhelm.** Das deutsche Filmschrifttum: Bibliographie der Bücher und Zeitschriften über das Filmwesen 1896–1939. Nachdruck der Ausgabe von 1940 mit einem Nachtrag 1940–1960 von Herbert Birett. Stuttgart, Hiersemann, [1980]. 247p., 84p.   **BG179**

A reprinting of the 1940 publication and its 1962 supplement in their original form.

A classed bibliography of about 5,500 book and periodical references. Author and subject indexes to the basic work.
                                            Z5784.M9T7

Vincent, Carl, Redi, Riccardo and **Venturini, Franco.** Bibliografia generale del cinema. Bibliographie générale du cinéma. General bibliography of motion pictures. Roma, Ateneo, [1953]. 251p.   **BG180**

"Compiled by a group of members of the Cinematographic Centre of the University of Padua."—*p.5.*

Classified arrangement with name index. A general bibliography of works in various languages from the origin of motion pictures to approximately 1952.   Z5784.M9V5

Writers' Program, *New York.* The film index: a bibliography. v.1, The film as art, comp. by workers of the Writers' Program of the Work Projects Administration in the City of New York. N.Y., Museum of Modern Art Film Lib. and the Wilson Co., 1941. 723p.   **BG181**

An extensive, annotated, classified bibliography of books and articles on the history and technique, and the types of motion-picture films. Based on the collection in the Museum of Modern Art, the New York Public Library, and other libraries. Index of names and titles.

The *Index* was conceived as a three-volume work and while compilation of v.2–3 was carried out under WPA auspices, publication of the later volumes had to be abandoned when that agency went out of existence in 1942. However, working from the original index cards and in cooperation with the Museum of Modern Art, N.Y. (where the cards were deposited after the demise of the WPA), Kraus International Publications, Millwood, N.Y., has recently issued v.2, "The film as industry" (1985. 587p.). It lists periodical articles, books and pamphlets in classed arrangement with annotations for most entries. Kraus has announced v.3, "The film in society," for future publication; it is to include a name index. Cut-off date for publications included is 1935.   Z5784.M9W75

Dissertations

Fielding, Raymond. A bibliography of theses and dissertations on the subject of film: 1916–1979. Houston, Tex., Univ. Film Assoc., School of Communication, Univ. of Houston, [1979]. 72p. (Univ. Film Assoc. Monograph, 3)
                                            BG182

An author listing of some 1,420 master's theses and doctoral dissertations with broad subject index. (A subject category designated as "Critical and biographical studies of particular writers, directors, producers, and performers" provides references to individual names, but there are no index entries for specific film titles.)

Periodicals

Brady, Anna, Wall, Richard and **Weiner, Carolynn Newitt.** Union list of film periodicals: holdings of selected American collections. Westport, Conn., Greenwood Pr., [1984]. 316p.
                                            BG183

A union list for 35 libraries throughout the United States. Alphabetical title listing with index of title changes and geographical index. Holdings are indicated for most collections.
                                            Z5784.M9B76

Brussels. Cinémathèque de Belgique. Répertoire mondial des périodiques cinématographiques. World list of film periodicals and serials. 2. éd. [Bruxelles], 1960. 1v., unpaged.   **BG184**

1st ed. 1955; suppl. 1957.

Arranged by country, then by title; author and subject indexes. Indicates address, beginning date, frequency, etc. Brief descriptive notes in French and English. 769 titles.

Il cinema nelle riviste italiane by Davide Turconi and Camillo Bassotto (Venezia, Mostracinema, 1973. 321p.) lists about 600 Italian film periodicals with full publication information.
                                            Z5784.M9B8813

Indexes

Batty, Linda. Retrospective index to film periodicals, 1930–1971. N.Y., Bowker, 1975. 425p.   **BG185**

Indexes 14 film journals plus articles on the film appearing in the *Village voice.* Only two of the journals covered pre-date 1950. In three sections: film titles, subjects, book reviews.   Z5784.M9B39

Film literature index. v.1– , 1973– . Albany, N.Y., Filmdex, Inc., 1974– . Quarterly, with annual cumulation.   **BG186**

Subtitle (varies): A quarterly author-subject index to the international literature of film with expanded coverage of television periodical literature.

An index to periodical literature on the film. Some 300 periodicals are scanned for pertinent articles (many of the journals, of course, are indexed only selectively). Reviews of books on the film are listed under "Book reviews." There are entries for individual film titles, as well as for personal names and subjects.   Z5784.M9F45

Gerlach, John C. and **Gerlach, Lana.** The critical index; a bibliography of articles on film in English, 1946–1973, arranged by names and topics. N.Y., Teachers College Pr., [1974]. 726p.   **BG187**

Indexes articles from 22 American, British, and Canadian film periodicals on directors, producers, actors, critics, screenwriters, cinematographers, specific films, and on the history, aesthetics, influence, and economics of the film industry. Separate sections for names and topics; author index. About 5,000 items.
                                            Z5784.M9G47

International index to film periodicals, 1972– . N.Y., Bowker, [1973–]. Annual.   **BG188**

A project of the International Federation of Film Archives (FIAF), this is a cooperative effort of indexers in film archives throughout Europe and North America. The annual volumes represent a cumulation of entries originally reproduced on cards and distributed to subscribers to the card service at frequent intervals throughout the year. Indexes about 60 to 85 periodicals devoted exclusively to the film, and selected "as being representative of the countries where they are published, and as containing articles, reviews, etc., likely to be of lasting interest from an aesthetic or critical point of view."—*Pref., 1972.* Classed listing, with separate sections for reviews and studies of individual films and for biography. Index of subject headings used.   Z5784.M9I49

MacCann, Richard Dyer and **Perry, Edward S.** The new film index; a bibliography of magazine articles in English, 1930–1970. N.Y., Dutton, 1975. 522p.   **BG189**

Intended as a supplement to the *Film index* (BG181), although differing from that work in that only magazine articles are covered herein. Indexes some 12,000 articles arranged in 278 subject categories, with an author index. Brief annotations for most items. "Biography" section, p.241–326, is an index to biographical articles. Does not attempt to index film reviews and book reviews.
                                            Z5784.M9M29

The New York times directory of the film. N.Y., Arno Pr., 1971. 1243p. il.   **BG190**

Essentially a reprinting of the personal name and corporate index sections from the index volume of the *New York times film reviews* (BG198), but independently useful since reference is to the date and page of the newspaper. The list of awards and reviews of yearly "Ten best" films have been updated through 1970.   PN1995.N39

Reviews and criticism

See also BG50.

Alvarez, Max Joseph. Index to motion pictures reviewed by Variety, 1907–1980. Metuchen, N.J., Scarecrow Pr., 1982. 510p.   **BG191**

A title index to the thousands of reviews of films appearing in *Variety,* including reviews of "short subjects," re-releases, etc.   PN1995.A39

Bowles, Stephen E., comp. Index to critical film reviews in British and American film periodicals, together with: Index to critical reviews of books about film. N.Y., Burt Franklin, [1974–75]. 3v. in 2.   **BG192**

Contents: v.1–2, Critical film reviews, A–Z; v.3, Critical reviews of books about film, A–Z, and indexes.

Indexes "all articles designated as 'reviews,' and includes, as well, those articles which deal with the entirety of a film (rather than a restricted aspect)" (*Introd.*) appearing in some 31 British and American film journals. In general, a full run of the journal is indexed through 1971; 1939 is the earliest publication date. Entry is by title of the film, with indexes by directors and film reviewers. The separate section of "Critical reviews of books about film" is arranged by book title, with author, reviewer, and subject indexes.   Z5784.M9B64

Film review annual. 1981– . [Englewood, N.J.], J. S. Ozer, [1982]– . Annual.   **BG193**

Reprints complete reviews "of full-length films released in major markets in the United States during the course of the year."—*Pref.* Reviews are drawn from a wide range of newspapers and magazines —from dailies to quarterlies—and date and page of the original is given; citations are also given to reviews in publications (e.g., the *New York times, New Yorker*) from which reprint rights could not be obtained. Arranged by title of film; credits, playing time, etc., are given for each film; indexes of critics, casts, producers, directors, screenwriters, etc.   PN1995.F465

Hochman, Stanley, comp. and ed. American film directors. With filmographies and index of critics and films. N.Y., Ungar, [1974]. 590p.   **BG194**

At head of title: A library of film criticism.

Modeled on the volumes in the "Library of literary criticism" series (BD560, etc.). Offers excerpts from reviews and critical writings on the work of 65 American film directors. "Filmographies," p.531–63. Indexed.   PN1995.9.P7H57

Magill's Survey of cinema: silent films. Ed. by Frank N. Magill. Englewood Cliffs, N.J., Salem Pr., [1982]. 3v.   **BG194a**

Offers signed articles on individual silent films produced 1902–36; a group of essays on important people, developments and events influential in film history precedes the alphabetical title arrangement of articles. Includes numerous "lost" films with whatever information could be provided from available sources. Indexes of titles, directors, screenwriters, cinematographers, editors, and performers in v.3.   PN1995.75.M33

Magill's Survey of cinema: English language films, first series. Ed. by Frank N. Magill; assoc. eds., Patricia King Hanson, Stephen L. Hanson. Englewood Cliffs, N.J., Salem Pr., [1980]. 4v.   **BG195**

—— English language films, second series. Ed. by Frank N. Magill; assoc. eds., Stephen L. Hanson, Patricia King Hanson. Englewood Cliffs, N.J., Salem Pr., [1981]. 6v.   **BG196**

These are companion series to the compilation on silent films (above). "Together, the two series provide a broad overview of films in English—including works of American, British, Canadian, Australian, and Jamaican cinema—with extensive treatment given to major genres, directors, and performers."—*p.v,ser.2,v.1.* Entries for the individual films (arranged alphabetically by title) give release date, credits, and principal characters/cast, followed by a signed essay (1,000 to 2,500 words) which includes a plot summary and critical comment. Cumulative indexes (of titles, directors, screenwriters, cinematographers, editors, performers, and chronological list of titles) for both series in the final volume of the second series.   PN1993.45.M3

Magill's Cinema annual, 1982– . Englewood Cliffs, N.J., Salem Pr., [1982]– . Annual.   **BG197**

Ed. by Frank N. Magill.

Serves as an annual supplement to *Magill's Survey of cinema* (above), each volume dealing with films of the previous year (i.e., the 1982 volume surveys films of 1981). International coverage. For each film, gives credits and cast, a signed critique, and references to reviews. Indexes of directors, screenwriters, performers, and subjects.   PN1993.3.M34

New York times film reviews, 1913–1968. N.Y., New York Times and Arno Pr., 1970. 6v. (4961p.)   **BG198**

Contents: v.1–5, Reviews; v.6, Appendix and Index.

Offers photographic reprints of film reviews as they appeared in the *New York times* newspaper for the long period indicated. About 16,000 reviews. Indexes of titles, persons, and corporations. The appendix includes a section of reviews inadvertently omitted from earlier volumes, lists of film awards, and a selection of portraits.

Biennial supplements are being issued, with the 1969–70 volume published 1971 and that for 1981/82 in 1984.   PN1995.N4

Variety film reviews, 1907–1980. N.Y., Garland, 1983–85. 16v.   **BG199**

Contents: v.1, 1907–20; v.2, 1921–25; v.3, 1926–29; v.4, 1930–33; v.5, 1934–37; v.6, 1938–42; v.7, 1943–48; v.8, 1949–53; v.9, 1954–58; v.10, 1959–63; v.11, 1964–67; v.12, 1968–70; v.13, 1971–74; v.14, 1975–77; v.15, 1978–80; v.16, Index of titles.

Reproduces in chronological sequence the complete reviews as they appeared in *Variety.* Inasmuch as feature films were not distinguished from short subjects until July 1927, all film reviews are included up to that time; after that date only reviews of feature-length films are reproduced. It should be noted that *Variety* did not carry film reviews from March 1911 through December 1912. The title index includes cross references from English titles of foreign-language films.   PN1995.V34

Catalogs and filmography

American Film Institute. The American Film Institute catalog of motion pictures produced in the United States. N.Y., Bowker, 1971–76. (In progress)   **BG200**

Contents: v.F2, Feature films, 1921–1930. 2v.; v.F6, Feature films, 1961–70. 2v.

To be in 19v., covering feature films, short films, and newsreels from 1893 through 1970.

Feature films are listed alphabetically by title. For each film is given, as applicable: (1) identification and physical description; (2) production credits; (3) cast credits; (4) description of contents (i.e., genre, source, and summary of the film). Each segment has an index of credits, and an index by subject.   PN1998.A57

—— Catalog of holdings: The American Film Institute Collection and the United Artists Collection at the Library of Congress. Wash., The Institute, [1978]. 214p.   **BG201**

"Nitrate films of major American motion picture companies and supplementary collections—acquisitions of The American Film

Institute on behalf of the Library of Congress and the donation of United Artists Corporation."—*t.p.*

A title listing, indicating date, producer, director, principal actor (insofar as that information is available). PN1998.A575

Annual index to motion picture credits. 1978– . Westport, Conn., Greenwood Pr., 1979– . Annual. **BG202**

Comp. by the Academy of Motion Picture Arts and Sciences. Verna Ramsey, ed.

Continues *Screen achievement records bulletin* (1976–77) and the Academy's earlier publications of similar title. Two interim indexes covering films released in the Los Angeles area between Jan. 1 and Apr. 30, and those released between May 1 and Aug. 31 are also issued and are available to subscribers to the *Annual*. The *Annual* consists of credits from the two interim issues plus new credits from Sept. 1–Dec. 31.

In four sections: (1) Film titles (with full list of credits for each film); (2) Credits (grouped as actors, art direction, cinematographers, costume designers, directors, film editors, music, producers, sound, writers); (3) Releasing companies; (4) Alphabetical index of individual credits. Information is derived from the Academy's master list of films released in the Los Angeles area during the year of coverage (eligibility for an Academy award requiring "that a film must open in a commercial motion picture theatre in the Los Angeles area for a consecutive run of not less than a week"—*Introd.*). PN1993.A48a

British Film Institute, London. Library. Catalogue of the book library of the British Film Institute. Boston, G. K. Hall, 1975. 3v. **BG203**

Contents: v.1, Author catalogue; Title catalogue, A–F; v.2, Title catalogue, G–Z; Script catalogue; Subject catalogue: personality index; film index; v.3, Subject catalogue: alphabetical subject index.

Reproduction of the cards from the Library's catalog. About 20,000 titles, including some 4,000 film scripts. International in scope. Z5784.M9B85

—— —— First supplement. Boston, G. K. Hall, 1983. 2v.

Adds about 25,000 cards.

Buache, Freddy. Le cinéma italien, 1945–1979. [Lausanne], Éditions l'Age d'Homme, [1979]. 401p. il. **BG204**

Basic arrangement is by director or group of directors, with brief introductory remarks for each chapter followed by a list of individual films. For each film gives the date, French title if it differs from the original, brief credits, and a plot summary with background notes and critical comment on the film. Indexed. PN1997.8.B8

California. University. University at Los Angeles. Library. Motion pictures: a catalog of books, periodicals, screenplays, television scripts and production stills. [2d ed., rev. and expanded] Boston, G. K. Hall, 1976. 775p. **BG205**

1st ed. 1972.

Reproduction of the catalog cards for this special library which aims "to acquire books, periodicals, and journals covering the historical, critical, aesthetic, biographical and technical aspects, as well as the non-book and primary source material that will provide the information and knowledge sought by scholars and researchers [in the whole range of theater arts]."—*Pref.*

This edition includes accessions through Mar. 1976. Separate sections for: (1) Books and periodicals; (2) Published screenplays; (3) Unpublished screenplays; (4) Unpublished television scripts; (5) Production stills. Z5784.M9C3

Chirat, Raymond. Catalogue des films français de long métrage: films de fiction, 1919–1929. [Toulouse], Cinémathèque de Toulouse, [1984]. Unpaged. **BG206**

"Avec la collaboration de Roger Icart."—*t.p.*

A title listing of 1,055 films with credits, brief synopsis, etc. Chronological index and index of names. PN1998.C453

—— Catalogue des films français de long métrage: films sonores de fiction, 1929–1939. [2ᵉ éd.] Éd. complétée et illustrée. [Bruxelles, Cinémathèque Royale, 1981] [319p.] il. **BG207**

"Filmographie de base: Raymond Chirat. Rédaction, synopsis, illustration: Cinémathèque Royale."—*t.p.*

1st ed. 1975.

An alphabetical listing of sound films made between 1929 and 1939, with a running time in excess of 60 minutes; documentaries are not included. For each film gives date, technical credits, running time, cast, summary of the story, and additional notes; a still from the film is usually included. Chronological index of titles; index of secondary titles and series; index of names. PN1998.C453

—— Catalogue des films français de long métrage: films de fiction, 1940–1950. Luxembourg, Impr. Saint-Paul, S.A., [1981]. unpaged. il. **BG207a**

A title listing of more than 800 films, with a name index. Provides the same kind of information as do the volumes for the earlier periods. Forms an important record of French films from the years of World War II and the time of the German occupation. Gives references to published scripts.

Dimmitt, Richard Bertrand. An actor guide to the talkies. Metuchen, N.J., Scarecrow Pr., 1967–68. 2v. **BG208**

Subtitle: A comprehensive listing of 8,000 feature-length films from Jan. 1949 until Dec. 1964.

v.1 is a title listing of films giving cast and date; v.2 is an index by actors' names; indexing is to page number only. PN1998.D53

—— A title guide to the talkies, a comprehensive listing of 16,000 feature-length films from October, 1927 until December, 1963. N.Y., Scarecrow Pr., 1965. 2v. **BG209**

Purpose of the work is to indicate the title and author of the novel, play, short story, or original screen play used as the basis for the film. Since this information is not always included in the U.S. Copyright Office *Motion pictures* volumes (BG225), the work should prove useful in the large or specialized collection, even though the former publication is more comprehensive in coverage and is less expensive. PN1998.D55

Aros, Andrew A. A title guide to the talkies, 1964 through 1974. (As conceived by Richard B. Dimmitt.) Metuchen, N.J., Scarecrow Pr., 1977. 336p. **BG210**

A continuation of the Dimmitt compilation of the same title (above). The producer credit has been dropped in this listing and the director's name substituted. PN1998.A6695

Garbicz, Adam and **Klinowski, Jacek.** Cinema, the magic vehicle: a guide to its achievement. Metuchen, N.J., Scarecrow Pr., 1975–79. 2v. **BG211**

Contents: v.1, The cinema through 1949; v.2, The cinema in the fifties.

Attempts "to give a panoramic view of the achievement of the cinema through the 'film-by-film' approach" (*Pref.*) and "to include all films which anyone seriously interested in the cinema would consider worth seeing, wherever they come from." Chronological arrangement, with indexes of directors and of films. Screen credits and running time are given for each film, the plot is briefly outlined, and there is a critique of the film relating it to other examples of the director's work, its place in the development of a genre, etc. PN1995.8.G35

Garfield, Brian. Western films: a complete guide. N.Y., Rawson Assoc., [1982]. 386p. il. **BG212**

Chapters, mainly in essay form, deal with the genre, directors, writers, crews, actors, etc. The bulk of the work (p.99–358) is an alphabetical title list of films with information regarding date, credits, etc., and a one- or two-sentence synopsis followed by critical comment. Selective bibliography; no index. PN1995.9.W4G3

Gifford, Denis. The British film catalogue, 1895–1970; a reference guide. Newton Abbot, David and Charles; N.Y., etc., McGraw-Hill, [1973]. unpaged. **BG213**

Intended as a comprehensive record of the British "entertainment film" (i.e., newsreels, documentaries, etc., are excluded), but since British companies were not required to register productions prior to the Cinematograph Films Act of 1927, some few early films may have been missed.

Arrangement is by year, then by exhibition date within months. Title index. Information given includes length in footage or running time, whether silent or sound, color system employed, producer, director, distributor, story source, cast and characters, subject descriptor, brief plot summary, etc.   PN1993.5.G7G5

Klotman, Phyllis Rauch. Frame by frame: a black filmography. Bloomington, Indiana Univ. Pr., [1979]. 700p.   **BG214**

Provides information on more than 3,000 films "with black themes or subject matter . . . ; films that have substantial participation by Blacks as writers, actors, producers, directors, musicians, animators, or consultants; and films in which Blacks appeared in ancillary or walk-on roles."—*p.XIII.* As far as possible, each entry indicates: film title/series title; narrator/cast; writer; producer; director; studio/company; technical information; date/country of origin; type; distributor/archive; annotation. Annotations emphasize the participation or presence of blacks in the film. Arranged by film title; index of names of black actors, authors, directors, etc., but no subject index.   PN1995.9.N4K57

Lauritzen, Einar and **Lundquist, Gunnar.** American film-index, 1908–1915. Stockholm, Film-Index (distr. by Akademibokhandeln), [1976]. 704p. il.   **BG215**

"(Motion pictures: July 1908–December 1915)"—*t.p.*
A title listing of some 23,000 American films with indication of date, producer, director, author, cast, etc., as available.
     PN1998.L26

—— American film-index, 1916–1920: motion pictures, January 1916–December 1920. Stockholm, Film-Index, [1984]. 612p. il.   **BG216**

A title listing as in the preceding volume; credits are generally fuller in this volume. Includes "Additions and corrections to American Film-Index 1908–1915," p.550–612.   PN1998.L262

National Film Archive (Great Britain). National Film Archive catalogue. [London, British Film Institute, 1980–] v.1– . (In progress)   **BG217**

At head of title: The British Film Institute.
Contents: v.1, Non-fiction films.
Earlier catalogs of the archive appeared 1936–66.
Aims to include "some information about every film in the collection, whether fully examined or not."—*Introd.* Films are listed chronologically under country of origin, then by title; title and subject indexes. A synopsis or other notes accompany most entries; films for which viewing, descriptive cataloging and research have been completed are so marked.   PN1998.N4932

Niver, Kemp R. Motion pictures from the Library of Congress paper print collection, 1894–1912. Berkeley, Univ. of California Pr., 1967. 402p.   **BG218**

Offers "an index of films produced throughout the world between 1894 and 1912, paper-positive prints of which were deposited with the Library of Congress during those years for copyright purposes." —*Introd.* Lists some 3,000 films by title according to type. Cast is given where known, followed by producer, copyright date, footage, condition, and synopsis or significant technical information. Subject and title indexes. Prints of the restored films may be ordered from the Library of Congress.   Z5784.M9N58

Quinlan, David. British sound films: the studio years, 1928–1959. London, Batsford, 1984; Totowa, N.J., Barnes & Noble, 1985. 406p. il.   **BG219**

"This book is both an attempt to look at an era of filmmaking through its product, and a record of the product itself."—*Foreword.* Feature films are presented alphabetically, decade by decade, with introductory essays on the decade, the "star of the decade," and the "film of the decade." Credits are given as far as possible, and films are rated on a scale of 1 to 6 (poor to outstanding). Not indexed.
     PN1993.5.G7Q56

Stadt- und Universitätsbibliothek Frankfurt am Main. Fachkatalog Film. Bearb. von Norbert Ruecker und Thomas Siedhoff. München, K. G. Saur, 1982– . v.1– . (In progress)   **BG220**

Title also in English: *Subject catalog film.*
Contents: v.1, Literature on persons; holdings as of July 1981.
v.1 reproduces the catalog cards (greatly reduced in size) for the library's "monographic publications on the life and work of persons involved with film."—*Introd.* Arranged by personal name with a separate section for collective biography.   PN1998.A2S62

U.S. Library of Congress. Library of Congress catalog—Motion pictures and filmstrips, 1953–1957, 1958–1962, 1963–1967, 1968–1972. Ann Arbor, Mich., Edwards, 1958–73. Quinquennial.   **BG221**

Subtitle: A cumulative list of works represented by Library of Congress printed cards.
1953–57 published as v.28 of the *National union catalog* (AA126); 1958–62 as v.53–54 of the *Catalog;* 1963–67 and 1968–72 not numbered as part of the *Catalog* although included in the series.
Reprints cumulations of the title published quarterly, cumulating annually, and then cumulating quinquennially in the *National union catalog.* Preceded by v.24 (Films) of *Library of Congress author catalog,* 1948–52 (AA124).
"Includes entries for all motion pictures and filmstrips (but not for microfilms) currently cataloged or recataloged on L.C. printed cards. . . . Attempts to cover all educational motion pictures and filmstrips released in the United States and Canada . . ."—*Introd.* Other coverage varies.
Superseded by: Z881.U49A25

—— Films and other materials for projection. Oct. 1972/June 1973–78. Wash., 1974–79. 3 quarterly issues per yr., with annual and quinquennial cumulations.   **BG222**

Oct. 1972/June 1973 is a combined issue.
Supersedes the Library's *Motion pictures and filmstrips* (above).
The change of title is intended "to reflect the inclusion in 1973 of cataloging data for sets of slides and other transparencies."—*Foreword.*
Films are now listed in *NUC. Audiovisual materials* (AA539).
     Z881.U49A25

—— Motion Picture, Broadcasting, and Recorded Sound Division. The George Kleine collection of early motion pictures in the Library of Congress. Wash., The Library, 1980. 270p. il.   **BG223**

Prep. by Rita Horwitz and Harriet Harrison.
Acquired by the Library in 1947, the Kleine Collection "consisted of 456 titles, with approximately nine hundred reels of nitrate film on both negative and positive stock. Production dates of the films ranged from 1898 to 1926. The collection included many films produced by Thomas A. Edison, several imports from French companies, including Gaumont and Pathé, and from Italian companies, including Cines and Ambrosio, and some films produced by George Kleine himself. . . . "—*Introd.* The catalog provides detailed description of the individual films, with multiple access points through the indexes.   PN1998.A1U57

Walls, Howard Lamarr. Motion pictures 1894–1912 identified from the records of the United States Copyright Office. Wash., Copyright Off., Lib. of Congress, 1953. 92p.
     BG224

Lists 8,506 works, representing about 6,000 titles registered in the Copyright Office.
Continued by: PN1998.W25

U.S. Copyright Office. Motion pictures, 1912–1939 (publ. 1951); 1940–1949 (publ. 1953); 1950–1959 (publ. 1960); 1960–1969 (publ. 1971). (Catalog of copyright entries. Cumulative ser.)   **BG225**

Each catalog consists of three parts: (1) a title list of all motion pictures copyrighted, with full information on date of production, number of reels, source of story, credits, and name of company owning the copyright; (2) an index of names; and (3) a series list.
     PN1998.U615

Weaver, John T., comp. Forty years of screen credits, 1929–1969. Metuchen, N.J., Scarecrow Pr., 1970. 2v. (1458p.)
     BG226

Arrangement is by actor's name, with a listing of picture credits and dates. PN1998.A2W37

—— Twenty years of silents, 1908–1928. Metuchen, N.J., Scarecrow Pr., 1971. 514p. **BG227**

The volume is primarily devoted to an alphabetical list of motion picture players with titles of films in which they appeared, and a similar list of directors and producers with their credits.

PN1998.A2W38

Library resources

Allen, Nancy. Film study collections: a guide to their development and use. N.Y., Ungar, [1979]. 194p. **BG228**

Offers a brief guide to many aspects of film study collections: collection development, evaluation of materials, cataloging and classification, reference services, library instruction, and a survey of major archives and film study libraries. Focus is on English-language materials. Indexed. Z688.F54A44

Mehr, Linda Harris. Motion pictures, television and radio: a union catalogue of manuscript and special collections in the western United States. Boston, G. K. Hall, [1977]. 201p.
BG229

"Sponsored by The Film and Television Study Center, Inc."—*t.p.*
The work is "designed to locate, identify and describe research collections currently available for use in established institutions, libraries, museums, and historical societies in the eleven western United States: Arizona, California, Colorado, Idaho, Montana, Nevada, New Mexico, Oregon, Utah, Washington, and Wyoming."
—*Foreword.* Arranged alphabetically by name of institution, with a general index and an index by occupation. Collections include production and personal papers of directors, writers, producers, actors, etc.; screenplays and scripts; advertising material and posters; photographs and stills; clipping files; scrapbooks; props, costumes and equipment, etc. Primary focus is on paper materials; collections of films, television and radio tapes are included only when part of a general collection. PN1993.4.M37

Rose, Ernest D. World film and television study resources; a reference guide to major training centers and archives. Bonn-Bad Godesberg, Friedrich-Ebert-Stiftung, 1974. 421p.
BG230

A directory of film and television archives in 75 countries. There is usually a historical and descriptive note on film activity in each country, followed by a list of that nation's archives, institutes, etc., devoted to the film, with notes on the activities, collections, facilities, etc., of each. Arranged by continent, then by country.
PN1993.7.R6

Rowan, Bonnie G. Scholars' guide to Washington, D.C.: film and video collections. Wash., Smithsonian Inst. Pr., 1980. 282p. (Scholars' guide to Washington, D.C., no.6)
BG231

Published for the Woodrow Wilson International Center for Scholars.
The main section of the guide is a listing of "Collections, referral services, academic programs" arranged alphabetically by name of the repository, service organization, or institution, and giving notes on types and extent of services offered, descriptions of collections or programs, eligibility, etc. Numerous appendixes, including a "Bibliographic guide for film and video studies." Indexed.
PN1998.A1R68

Dictionaries, encyclopedias, and handbooks

The Aurum film encyclopedia. Ed. by Phil Hardy. [London], Aurum Pr., [1983–84]. v.1–2. il. (In progress) **BG232**

Contents: v.1, The Western; v.2, Science fiction.

Each volume is presented in a chronological arrangement, with films listed alphabetically by year and an introductory note for each decade. Gives production information, casts, etc., and a synopsis of each film. Each volume has its own index.

Bessy, Maurice and **Chardans, Jean-Louis.** Dictionnaire du cinéma et de la télévision. [Paris], Jean-Jacques Pauvert, [1965–71]. 4v. il. **BG233**

An important work for the study of the cinema, with particularly good coverage for the history and technology of motion-picture art. Coverage of television is less thorough and somewhat uneven. Includes many entries for film and television personalities, but these are confined largely to chronological listings of film work of the individuals, with some reference to television appearances.
PN1993.45.B4

Blackaby, Linda, Georgakas, Dan and **Margolis, Barbara.** In focus: a guide to using films. [N.Y.], New York Zoetrope, [1980]. 206p. il. **BG234**

"A project of Cine Information, Latin American Film Project and Neighborhood Film Project."—*t.p.*
A practical manual "designed to help groups use film resources more effectively, especially local sources of films and information, such as public libraries."—*Pref.* Chapters discuss program goals and objectives, program planning, publicizing the event, common problems and concerns in showing films, film and information sources, etc. TR890.B5

Boussinot, Roger. L'encyclopédie du cinéma. [2ᵉ éd.] [Paris], Bordas, [1980]. 2v. (1332p.; [192]p. of plates) il. **BG235**

1st ed. 1967–70.
International in scope, offering articles on film personalities, important individual films, terms, genres, film companies and organizations, and the history and current state of film in individual countries. Lists of principal films are given for major actors, actresses, directors, etc.; occasional bibliographic references. Photographs (many in color) are mainly grouped topically and placed without regard to alphabetical sequence of the text; unfortunately there is no index to the plates other than a brief "Table des horstexte" at the end of v.2. PN1993.45.B6

Cawkwell, Tim and **Smith, John Milton,** eds. The World encyclopedia of the film. N.Y., World; London, Studio Vista, [1972]. 444p. il. **BG236**

Offers short biographical sketches of directors, actors, writers, cameramen, set designers, etc. An index of titles of films gives references to sketches in which the film is mentioned; date of film is indicated in the index as is, in many cases, producing company and running time. PN1993.45.C3

Cinema, a critical dictionary: the major film-makers. Ed. by Richard Roud. N.Y., Viking Pr., [1980]. 2v. (1121p.) il.
BG237

A collection of signed articles by an international roster of film critics. Most of the articles are devoted to directors, but there are some entries for individual actors, and a few topical entries such as "American film noir" and "Polish cinema since the War." Although the articles are signed by the contributors, the editor has seen fit to append his own comments (sometimes in disagreement with the contributor) at the end of each article; suggestions for further reading are often included. Index of names, film titles, and illustrations. PN1993.45.C5

Dictionnaire du cinéma, sous la direction de Raymond Bellour et Jean-Jacques Brochier. Paris, Éditions Universitaires, [1966]. 763p. **BG238**

An international biographical dictionary of film directors, producers, and scriptwriters. Introductory essays on historical and cultural aspects of the cinema precede the dictionary proper. Index of principal names cited in the text. PN1998.A2D55

Filmlexicon degli autori e delle opere. Roma, Bianco e Nero, 1958–74. 9v. il. **BG239**

Introduction in Italian, French, English, German, and Spanish. Text in Italian.

Contents: v.1–7, Autori, A–Z; v.8–9, Aggiornamenti (1958–71).

International in scope. Planned to be in two sections: (1) authors, and (2) works; the latter section has not been published. The term "authors" includes "directors, story and scriptwriters, producers, actors, cameramen, composers, art directors and costume designers" of both silent and sound cinematography of the world. Entries contain biographical sketches, filmographies (which list film titles, principals, and dates), and, for the more important names, bibliographies.

Focal encyclopedia of film and television techniques. Raymond Spottiswoode, gen. ed. London, N.Y., Focal, 1969. 1100p. il.   **BG240**

Concentrates on the tools of film and television making. The longer articles are signed, and many include bibliographical references.   TR847.F62

Gregory, Mollie. Making films your business. N.Y., Schocken Books, [1979]. 256p.   **BG241**

A practical handbook on the business and economic aspects of film-making. Chapters deal with financing and budgeting, selling and distributing, legal aspects of film production, etc. Indexed.   PN1995.9.P75G7

Halliwell, Leslie. Halliwell's Film guide. 4th ed. N.Y., Scribner, [1983]. 936p. il.   **BG242**

1st ed. 1977.

May be considered a complementary volume to Halliwell's *Filmgoer's companion* (below) inasmuch as it both elaborates the information on the selection of films accorded entries there, and treats hundreds of other films omitted from that volume. About 10,000 films treated in this edition, including releases as late as 1982.

An alphabetical title listing of English-language and some foreign-language feature-length films, giving the compiler's rating for those of merit, country of origin, year of release, running time, credits, cast, a note on content or story line, assessment or indication of significance, and, for about a quarter of the items, brief comment from well-known critics. Includes many silent films as well as a number of films of marginal interest; television movies were included in the first edition only. The compiler's original aim was "to include every film which seemed likely or worthy of remembrance by the keen filmgoer or student, whether with affection for its own sake as good entertainment, for showcasing memorable work by a particular talent, for sheer curiosity value or for box office success." —*Introd.* Pressures to expand coverage in successive editions has led to greater compression of summaries and content notes. In the 4th edition the use of a 3-column page and smaller illustrations has allowed for more information in fewer pages.   PN1993.45.H27

———— Halliwell's Filmgoer's companion. 8th ed. N.Y., Scribner's, [1984]. 704p. il.   **BG243**

1st ed. 1965.

Intended for the general movie-goer rather than for the specialist or student of the cinema. Whereas the compiler's *Film guide* (above) concentrates on individual films, this work covers a broad range of topics relating to film: a high percentage of entries refers to actors and actresses; there are notes on directors, producers, photographers, etc.; some terms are defined; and outstanding films or those frequently remade are accorded individual entries—all in a single alphabetical sequence. This edition is revised through 1983, incorporates most of the information from Halliwell's *Filmgoer's book of quotes* (1973), and introduces a three column format which crowds more information into fewer pages.   PN1993.45.H3

International encyclopedia of film. Roger Manvell, gen. ed. N.Y., Crown, [1972]. 574p. il.   **BG244**

Emphasis is on biographies, but there are brief histories of film production in individual countries, definitions of technical terms, and articles of some length on general topics associated with the film industry. Bibliography, p.514–41. Index of film titles mentioned in the text.   PN1993.45.I5

Katz, Ephraim. The film encyclopedia. N.Y., Thomas Y. Crowell, [1979]. 1266p.   **BG245**

Aims to provide comprehensive coverage of world cinema, concentrating "on a broad range on entries about filmmakers and filmmaking with . . . a good balance of American, United Kingdom, and international subjects. Country by country, the history of major film industries is covered from its inception to the present day. Important film-related organizations and events are discussed; inventions, techniques, processes, equipment, and technical terms are explained. . . ."—*Pref.* Numerous biographies of directors, producers, screenwriters, cinematographers, art directors, composers, film editors, actors and actresses, with filmographies for directors and major stars. No entries for individual film titles.   PN1993.45.K34

Kinoslovar'. S. I. IUtkevich, glav. redaktor. Moskva, Sovetskaia Entsiklopediia, 1966–70. 2v. il.   **BG246**

Includes terms and technical aspects of cinematography as well as biographical articles on motion-picture players, directors, etc. International in coverage; many articles carry bibliographies.   PN1995.9.D5K5

The New York times encyclopedia of film, 1896–1979. Gene Brown, ed. [New York], Times Books, [1984]. 13v. il.   **BG247**

Reproduces in chronological sequence the complete text of articles from the *New York times* newspaper relating to all aspects of the film, film industry, personalities, etc. (except reviews, which are separately collected [*see* BG198]). v.13 provides an index of names, titles, and subjects, giving reference to date of the article. An invaluable source for the film historian.   PN1993.45.N4

The Oxford companion to film. Ed. by Liz-Anne Bawden. N.Y., Oxford Univ. Pr., 1976. 767p. il.   **BG248**

Aims "to answer any query which may occur to the amateur of film in the course of reading or film-going, and to lead him on to topics of related interest."—*Pref.* Entries for individual films, actors and actresses, directors and other motion picture personnel, film genres, and selected technical terms, etc., and brief surveys of the history of cinema art in individual countries.   PN1993.45.O9

Pickard, Roy. The award movies: a complete guide from A to Z. N.Y., Schocken Books, [1981]. 294p. il.   **BG249**

Aims to list "every 'best picture' named in the last fifty years by the top award organizations in America, Britain and Europe."—*Pref.* A title listing of the films (with credits, awards, and a brief synopsis of each) is followed by a section listing the awards by granting organization, festival, etc. Indexed.

Lists of awards (offering varying amounts of detail) are a feature of many of the handbooks listed in this section. A volume devoted exclusively to "the Oscars" is Richard Shale's *Academy awards* (2d ed. N.Y., Ungar, 1982. 691p. il.); it provides a historical note on the Academy and the awards along with the listing of winners by Academy Award categories from earliest year through 1977; a supplement lists winners through 1981.   PN1993.45.P47

Robertson, Patrick. Movie facts and feats: a Guinness record book. N.Y., Sterling, [1980]. 288p. il.   **BG250**

A collection of miscellaneous facts and figures, including "'firsts,' records [longest, shortest, oldest, youngest, etc.], oddities, remarkable achievements, historic landmarks and the wilder extravagances of the motion picture business."—*Pref.* Indexed.   PN1993.45.R58

Sadoul, Georges. Dictionary of films. Tr., ed., and updated by Peter Morris. Berkeley, Univ. of California. Pr., [1972]. 432p.   **BG251**

A translation, revision and expansion of *Dictionnaire des films* (Paris, 1965).

Lists films by title, indicating country of origin, date, principal credits, and cast, together with a brief statement regarding the plot and some critical comment. International in scope; covers the whole range of cinema history, though necessarily on a selective basis. Films are listed under the original-language title with cross references from all known release titles. Serves as a companion to Sadoul's *Dictionary of film makers* (BG283).   PN1993.45.S3213

—— Dictionnaire des films. [Nouv. éd.] remis à jour par Émile Breton en 1981. [Paris], Microcosme/Seuil, [1982]. 345p. il. **BG252**

1st ed. 1965; repr. with suppl. 1978.

A title listing, with date and brief credits for each film, followed by a note on the plot and critical comment. International coverage; most films are entered under the French title, with cross references from English, German, etc., titles. Index of directors.

PN1993.45.S32

Steinberg, Cobbett S. Film facts. N.Y., Facts on File, [1980]. 476p. **BG254**

Information (usually in lists or in tabular form) is presented in seven broad categories: (1) The marketplace; (2) The stars; (3) The studios; (4) The festivals; (5) The "ten best" lists; (6) The awards; (7) The codes and regulations. Indexed. PN1993.45.S75

Thiery, Herman. Dictionnaire filmographique de la littérature mondiale. Filmographic dictionary of world literature. Filmographisches Lexikon der Weltliteratur. Filmografisch lexicon der wereldliteratuur. [Par] Johan Daisne. Gand, E. Story-Scientia, 1971–77. 2v. and suppl. il. **BG255**

Introduction in French, English, German, and Flemish.

Contents: v.1, A–K; v.2, L–Z; [v.3] Suppl., A–Z.

The intention is "to illustrate how the whole of literature forms the basis of the seventh art" (*Introd.*) by identifying the works of world literature with the films derived from them. Each volume is in three parts: (1) a filmography arranged by author's name and giving film title, original book title if different from that of the film, country and year of production, re-makes (if any), directory, and principal cast members; (2) an extensive section of illustrations; and (3) an index of titles of both films and books. Truly international in coverage. PN1997.85.T5

Tulard, Jean. Dictionnaire du cinéma. Paris, Laffont, [1982–84]. 2v. **BG256**

Contents: [v.1] Les réalisateurs; [v.2] Acteurs-producteurs, scénaristes-techniciens.

v.1 offers filmographies and notes on the careers and works of directors and film-makers throughout the world; there are occasional bibliographic notes. v.2 has separate sections for scriptwriters, producers and film companies, actors, scenic designers, costumers, special effects creators, makeup artists, choreographers, etc., again listing films and providing brief comment on achievements and career of the individual. There is an index to both volumes in v.2, an asterisk signifying reference to the first volume. PN1998.A2T84

Terms

Beaver, Frank E. Dictionary of film terms. N.Y., McGraw-Hill, [1983]. 392p. il. **BG257**

Terms, with definitions, are presented in alphabetical arrangement; a topical index brings together terms relating to larger concepts. Chronological outline of film history; index of terms and film titles. Numerous illustrations. TR847.B43

Elsevier's Dictionary of cinema, sound and music, in six languages: English/American, French, Spanish, Italian, Dutch, and German. Comp. and arr. on an English alphabetical base by W. E. Clason. Amsterdam, N.Y., Elsevier, 1956. 948p. **BG258**

TR847.E4

Geduld, Harry M. and **Gottesman, Ronald.** An illustrated glossary of film terms. N.Y., Holt, Rinehart and Winston, [1973]. 179p. il. **BG259**

Intended for the layman and beginning student, definitions avoid technical jargon and use of highly technical terms. Both line drawings and photographs are used as illustrations.

PN1993.45.G38

Oakey, Virginia. Dictionary of film and television terms. N.Y., Barnes & Noble, [1983]. 206p. **BG260**

Offers brief definitions of technical and artistic terms, jargon and informal usages, and business terms of the industries.

PN1993.45.O34

Directories and annuals

The American Film Institute guide to college courses in film and television. 7th ed. Charles Granade, Jr., ed. Princeton, N.J., Peterson's Guides, [1980]. 334p. **BG261**

[Ed.1] 1969/70 called *Guide to college film courses*. Frequency varies; not all issues carry edition statement.

This edition "lists in alphabetical order by state all the institutions of higher education that responded to the American Film Institute survey by indicating that they offer opportunities for film or television study."—*Introd.* Includes 2-year institutions through graduate school. Also has lists of foreign film and television schools, grants and scholarships, festivals and awards, and relevant organizations. Index of graduate degrees and a general index.

PN1993.8.U5A453

Annuaire du spectacle: théâtre, cinéma, musique, radio, télévision. v.1–27, 1942/43–72/73. Paris, Raoult, 1943–73. il. Annual. **BG262**

Title varies: 1945–1955, *Annuaire du théâtre* . . .

A directory of theaters, producers, directors, actors, etc., in the categories of the subtitle, in France, Belgium, French-speaking Switzerland, etc.

Superseded by: PN2620.A67

AS. Annuaire du spectacle. 1974– . Paris, Éditions Raoult, [1974]– . Annual. **BG263**

A continuation of the above. Issues for 1974– published in three or more volumes, with contents covering the areas mentioned in the earlier subtitle and appearing in varying combinations (e.g., 1984 publ. in 3v.: [v.1] Comédiens & théatre; [v.2] Musique, variétés, radio; [v.3] Cinéma, T.V., video).

Each part offers directory information concerning official organizations and associations, publicity, distribution, suppliers, facilities, artists, etc. PN2620.A18

Gadney, Alan. How to enter & win film contests. N.Y., Facts on File, [1981]. 195p. **BG264**

One of a series of books by the same compiler covering film, video-audio-TV/radio broadcasting, fiction writing, nonfiction writing and journalism, photography, etc. Provides information for those wishing to enter their work in national and international contests, festivals, exhibitions, trade fairs, and the like, together with information on where and how to apply for grants, loans, scholarships, training programs, etc. PN1993.4.G32

International film guide, 1964– . London, Tantivy Pr.; N.Y., A. S. Barnes, 1963– . Annual. il. **BG265**

Peter Cowie, ed.

Offers an annual survey of film production in countries throughout the world (51 countries in the 1985 volume) and other features which vary: reviews of outstanding films, biographical sketches of prominent directors, directories of film festivals, archives, services, magazines, etc. Table of contents, but no general index.

PN1993.3.I544

International motion picture almanac, 1929– . N.Y., Quigley, 1929– . il. Annual. **BG266**

Title varies: 1929–1935/36, *The motion picture almanac;* 1952/53–55, *Motion picture and television almanac.*

The 1984 volume includes sections on: who's who in motion pictures; corporations; theater circuits; pictures; services; equipment and supplies; talent and literary agencies; organizations; advertising codes; statistics; world market; the press; non-theatrical motion pictures, etc. PN1993.3.I55

Kemps international film & television year book. Ed. 1– . London, Kemp's, 1956– . Annual. **BG267**

Title varies: *Kemp's Film & television directory; Kemp's International film & television directory.*

A directory of agencies, suppliers, and services for the film and television industries. In two sections: (1) Great Britain (employing a classified arrangement with a separate "Technicians section") and (2) International (arranged by country, then classified).

PN1998.A1K39

Screen world, 1949– . N.Y., Greenberg, 1950– . v.1– . il. Annual.   **BG268**

Publisher varies. Title varies: 1949–65, *Daniel Blum's Screen world.*

An annual survey of the pictures of the year, with many illustrations and listing of casts and credits. No critical commentary. Section of obituaries.   PN1993.3.D3

Spilsbury, Christina and **Boutchard, Deborah Davidson.** Film/video festivals and awards. 2d ed. Wash., Amer. Film Inst., 1981. 88p. (Factfile #3)   **BG268a**

1st ed. 1977.

A directory in four sections: (1) U.S. festivals and awards; (2) U.S. festivals and awards—films entered by invitation only; (3) Bibliography; (4) Periodicals with calendars of film/video events. An appendix lists selected foreign festivals. Indexed.

Biography

See also BG220.

Coursodon, Jean-Pierre and **Sauvage, Pierre.** American directors. N.Y., McGraw-Hill, [1983]. 2v.   **BG269**

Offers 118 critical essays (59 in each volume, in separate alphabets and with separate indexes for the two volumes) "on virtually every American film director of recognized (and, in quite a few instances, underrecognized) stature."—*Pref.* More than half of the essays are by Coursodon, but 21 other contributors are represented; each essay is preceded by a filmography. v.2 includes a general index.

PN1998.A2C657

Dizionario Bolaffi del cinema italiano, a cura di Gianni Rondolino. [Torino], Bolaffi, [1979]– . v.1– . il. (In progress)   **BG270**

Contents: v.1, Registi.

v.1 offers brief biographical sketches of Italian film personalities, listing titles and dates of their films from 1945 to 1979.

PN1993.5.I88D5

Dolmatovskaia, Galina Evgen'evna and **Shilova, Irina.** Who's who in the Soviet cinema. Moscow, Progress, 1979. 684p. il.   **BG271**

An English translation of *Kto est' kto v sovetskom kino.*

Offers biographical sketches of selected Soviet directors and actors, with representation from the individual Soviet Republics. Lists of film credits conclude the biographies.   PN1998.A2D613

Film directors: a complete guide. [Ed.1]– . [Beverly Hills, Calif.], Lone Eagle, [1983?]– . Annual.   **BG272**

1984 called "Second annual international edition."
Michael Singer, comp. and ed.

An alphabetical listing of directors with, when available, birth date, address, and a list of credits.   PN1998.A2D568

Gifford, Denis. The illustrated who's who in British films. London, Batsford, [1978]. 334p. il.   **BG273**

An earlier version was published 1968 as *British cinema.*

Basically a listing of about 1,000 British film personalities with choronological lists of their films. Other information is limited to little more than place and date of birth, death date for deceased persons, real name if different from career name, brief characterizing statement, and indication of Hollywood career if any.

PN1998.A2G485

The illustrated who's who of the cinema. Ed. by Ann Lloyd and Graham Fuller. London, Orbis; N.Y., Macmillan, [1983]. 480p. il.   **BG274**

A necessarily selective biographical dictionary of film personalities (actors, actresses, directors, screenwriters, etc.). Admittedly "an encyclopedia of mainstream cinema" *(Introd.)* with fullest coverage of figures from the '20s, '30s and '40s. Brief biographical sketches are followed by lists of films which aim to list the earliest and latest films together with a representative sampling of those between.

PN1998.A2I48

International directory of cinematographers, set- and costume designers in film. München, K. G. Saur, 1981–84. v.1–4. (In progress)   **BG275**

At head of title: International Federation of Film Archives (FIAF). Alfred Krautz, ed.

Contents: v.1, German Democratic Republic (1946–1978), Poland (from the beginnings to 1978); v.2, France (from the beginnings to 1980); v.3, Albania, Bulgaria, Greece, Rumania, Yugoslavia (from the beginnings to 1980); v.4, Germany (from the beginnings to 1945).

For each person there is an identifying word or phrase, brief biographical data as available, and a list of film credits. Indexes of names and film titles in each volume.   PN1998.A1I55

Langman, Larry. A guide to American film directors: the sound era, 1929–1979. Metuchen, N.J., Scarecrow Pr., 1981. 2v.   **BG276**

v.1 is a listing by director giving titles and dates of the films; v.2 is a title index.   PN1998.A2L34

———— A guide to American screenwriters: the sound era, 1929–1982. N.Y., Garland, 1984. 2v.   **BG277**

Contents: v.1, Screenwriters; v.2, Films.

v.1 is an alphabetical listing of about 5,000 screenwriters, with titles and dates of their films; co-directors are noted. v.2 is a title listing giving date of the film and name of director.   PN1998.L24

Michael, Paul. The American movies reference book: the sound era. Englewood Cliffs, N.J., Prentice-Hall, [1969]. 629p. il.   **BG278**

Includes separate, alphabetically arranged sections on players, films, directors, and producers. About 600 entries for actors and actresses (a brief biographical note followed by a list of feature films with dates), about 50 entries for directors, 50 for producers, and about 1,000 entries for films, giving casts and credits. Also a brief history of the American film, a chronological listing of awards, a selected bibliography, and an index of names.

PN1993.5.U6M53

Palmer, Scott. A who's who of British film actors. Metuchen, N.J., Scarecrow Pr., 1981. 561p.   **BG279**

About 1,400 entries for actors and actresses, giving birth (and death) dates, a brief identifying statement, and a chronological list of film appearances with dates. Mainly English personalities, but includes "Scottish, Irish, Welsh, Australian, Canadian, South African, and many other British Commonwealth personalities."—*p.v.*

PN1998.A2P365

Parish, James Robert. Film actors guide: Western Europe. Metuchen, N.J., Scarecrow Pr., 1977. 606p. il.   **BG280**

Covers motion-picture actors and actresses "based in Western Europe exclusive of Scandinavia" *(Pref.)* who played in feature-length films. Gives name, place and date of birth, and a list of films with dates.   PN1998.A2P389

Quinlan, David. The illustrated directory of film stars. London, Batsford; N.Y., Hippocrene Books, [1981]. 497p. il.   **BG281**

Aims to provide complete filmographies for some 1,600 film stars, mainly British and American, with emphasis on those who seemed "more interesting than most: because they made films over a long period, because they have been seriously neglected; because they have turned screen-writer or director, because they made films under a series of names, or had separate careers at different times in the cinema's history."—*Pref.* Biographical information is relatively brief.   PN1998.A2Q84

────── The illustrated guide to film directors. London, Batsford; Totowa, N.J., Barnes & Noble, [1983]. 335p. il.
BG282

Includes "as many British and American directors as possible, as well as some major directors from elsewhere in the world who have made a reputation for themselves outside their own countries."—*Introd.* Concentrates on "the journeyman working director of mainline feature films." Articles are concerned with directorial careers and achievements, with a minimum of personal biographical detail. Filmographies.   PN1998.A2Q85

Sadoul, Georges. Dictionary of film makers. Tr., ed., and updated by Peter Morris. Berkeley, Univ. of California Pr., [1972]. 288p.   **BG283**

A translation, revision, and expansion of *Dictionnaire des cinéastes* (Paris, 1965) and a companion to Sadoul's *Dictionary of films* (BG251).

A biographical dictionary, international in scope (though admittedly selective), of producers, directors, scenarists, photographers, designers, etc., but excluding actors and actresses.

A much updated edition of the original French publication has appeared as: PN1993.45.S313

────── Dictionnaire des cinéastes. [Nouv. éd.] remis à jour par Émile Breton et Michel Marie en 1981. [Paris], Microcosme/Seuil, [1982]. 302p. il.   **BG284**

1st ed. 1965; repr. 1977 with a suppl.

There is a 10-page bibliography (unpaged) at the end of the volume.   PN1998.A2S14

Schuster, Mel, comp. Motion picture directors: a bibliography of magazine and periodical articles, 1900–1972. Metuchen, N.J., Scarecrow Pr., 1973. 418p.   **BG285**

Lists English-language material of a "biographical or career-oriented" nature (i.e., reviews *per se* are not indexed) on directors, filmmakers and animators.   Z5784.M9S34

Shipman, David. The great movie stars. New rev. ed. [N.Y.], Hill and Wang, [1979–80]. 2v. il.   **BG286**

1st ed. 1970–72.

Contents: [v.1] The golden years; [v.2] The international years.

Presents biographical sketches, usually of some length, incorporating critical comment on the films, performances, etc. Choices for inclusion were "guided by the box-office figures, by popularity polls and by the reputation that remains."—*Introd. [v.1]* Brief bibliography and index to title changes in each volume.   PN1998.A2S54

Thomson, David. A biographical dictionary of film. 2d ed., rev. N.Y., Wm. Morrow, 1981. 682p.   **BG287**

First published with title: *A biographical dictionary of the cinema* (London, Secker & Warburg, 1975); American ed. with new title 1976.

Admittedly "a Personal, Opinionated and Obsessive" work which includes "the sharp expression of personal taste; jokes; digressions; insults and eulogies" (*Introd.*) along with expected factual information.   PN1998.A2T55

Truitt, Evelyn Mack. Who was who on screen. 3d ed. N.Y., Bowker, 1983. 788p.   **BG288**

1st ed. 1974.

About 13,000 entries for screen personalities (mainly American, British, French, and German) who died 1905–82. Entries are limited to birth and death dates (with places, when known), brief identifying information, and a list of films (with dates) in which the person appeared; cause or circumstances of death is sometimes indicated. Directors, writers, etc., are included only if they actually appeared in films.   PN1998.A2T73

Vizcaíno Casas, Fernando. Diccionario del cine español, 1896–1968. 3.ed. Madrid, Editora Nacional, 1970. 359p. il.
BG289

1st ed. 1966.

Offers brief biographical sketches of Spanish cinema personalities (actors, directors, etc.).   PN1993.45.V5

RADIO AND TELEVISION

See also BG229–BG230, BG233.

Guides

Schreibman, Fay C. Broadcast television: a research guide. Ed. by Peter J. Bukalski. Los Angeles, Calif., American Film Inst., Education Services, 1983. 62p. (Factfile, no.15)
BG290

A useful guide for an area not well covered bibliographically.

Bibliography

McCavitt, William E. Radio and television: a selected, annotated bibliography. Metuchen, N.J., Scarecrow Pr., 1978. 229p.; Suppl. one, 1977–81. Metuchen, N.J., 1982. 155p.   **BG291**

For full information *see* CH503.

NAB broadcasting bibliography: a guide to the literature of radio & television. Comp. by the staff of the NAB Library and Information Center, Public Affairs Dept. 2d ed. Wash., Nat. Assoc. of Broadcasters, [1984]. 66p.   **BG292**

1st ed. 1982.

Lists 360 books, most of them published since 1975, under seven categories (with numerous subdivisions): fundamentals of broadcasting, the business of broadcasting, broadcasting and the law, the technology and technique of broadcasting, broadcasting and society, comparative broadcasting, related technologies. Also includes a list of periodicals and a publishers directory. Author/title index.

Dissertations

Kittross, John M. A bibliography of theses & dissertations in broadcasting, 1920–1973. Wash., Broadcast Education Assoc., 1978. [238]p.   **BG293**

An author listing of some 4,300 dissertations and master's theses completed at American universities, with keyword-in-title index plus an index by year of completion and another by broad topics.

Sparks, Kenneth R. A bibliography of doctoral dissertations in television and radio. [3d ed.] Syracuse, N.Y., School of Journalism, Syracuse Univ., [1971]. 119p.   **BG294**

A classified listing of some 900 dissertations completed through June 1970. Author index.   Z7221.S65

Indexes

International index to television periodicals; an annotated guide. 1979/80– . London, Internat. Federation of Film Archives, [1983]– . Biennial.   **BG295**

Michael Moulds, ed.

Cumulates the entries from an index service in card form initiated in 1979. Selectively indexes nearly a hundred periodicals. "The periodicals covered have been selected from suggestions made by people working in the field. The items indexed are chosen as being of lasting interest from a social, economic, political, critical or aesthetic point of view. News and other items of ephemeral concern are generally not included."—*Pref.* In four sections: (1) General subjects; (2) Individual programmes and TV films; (3) Biography; (4) Author index. Brief annotations indicate scope or content of the article.

Encyclopedias and handbooks

See also BG240.

Brooks, Tim and **Marsh, Earle.** The complete directory to prime time network TV shows, 1946–present. 3d ed. N.Y., Ballantine Books, [1985]. 1123p. il.   **BG296**

1st ed. 1979.

Aims to provide information on "all network series that aired [on the four commercial networks] after 6 p.m., and also the top syndicated programs that ran predominantly in the evening or late night."—*Pref.* Entry is by title of series; gives inclusive dates of showing, broadcast history, cast (regulars, plus notable guests), notes on the story line, memorable episodes, etc. This edition updated through 1984. Numerous appendixes; index of names.

A similar work covering a somewhat broader range of programs, but offering less detail on individual series is Alex McNeil's *Total television: a comprehensive guide to programming from 1948 to the present* (2d ed. N.Y., Penguin, 1984. 1027p.). One more limited in scope is *Television comedy series: an episode guide to 153 sitcoms in syndication* by Joel Eisner and David Krinsky (Jefferson, N.C., McFarland, 1984. 866p.).   PN1992.18.B68

Brown, Les. Les Brown's Encyclopedia of television. N.Y., Zoetrope, 1982. 496p. il.   **BG297**

Constitutes an expanded edition of *The New York times encyclopedia of television* (1977).

Offers brief articles on various aspects of television: stars and programs, history, technology, special language, personnel, laws, networks, etc. Short bibliography.   PN1992.18.B7

Gianakos, Larry James. Television drama series programming: a comprehensive chronicle, 1947–1959. Metuchen, N.J., Scarecrow Pr., 1980. 565p.   **BG298**

PN1992.3.U5G48

———— Television drama series programming: a comprehensive chronicle, 1959–1975. Metuchen, N.J., Scarecrow Pr., 1978. 794p.   **BG299**

PN1992.3.U5G5

———— Television drama series programming: a comprehensive chronicle, 1975–1980. Metuchen, N.J., Scarecrow Pr., 1981. 457p.   **BG300**

PN1992.3.U5G49

———— Television drama series programming: a comprehensive chronicle, 1980–1982. Metuchen, N.J., Scarecrow Pr., 1983. 678p.   **BG301**

Although there are some variations in manner of presentation from volume to volume, the four items above follow the same general plan, offering a season-by-season listing of the individual television drama series and enumerating the episodes as an aid to "finding that particular drama which has somehow made a lasting impression upon the memory."—*Pref., 1959–75.* Most volumes include an overview of the season; each has its own index of series titles. The volume covering 1980–82 includes six "literary appendixes" giving retrospective listings of television adaptations, 1947–82, of various categories of literary works (e.g., classic Greek drama, Shakespearean plays, works of 19th century writers). That same

volume includes an extensive addenda section relating to all the earlier volumes.   PN1992.3.U5G53

Halliwell, Leslie and **Purser, Philip.** Halliwell's Television companion. 2d ed. London [etc.], Granada, [1982]. 713p. il.   **BG302**

1st ed. (1979) had title: *Halliwell's Teleguide.*

Combines characteristics of Halliwell's *Film guide* (BG242) and *Filmgoer's companion* (BG243), offering entries for television films, series, and personalities, and giving dates, credits, and critical comments.   PN1992.3.G7

Marill, Alvin H. Movies made for television: the telefeature and the mini-series, 1964–1984. N.Y., Zoetrope, 1984. 452p. il.   **BG303**

1st ed. 1980.

Films are listed chronologically, season by season, with full credits, a one- or two-sentence summary, and occasional notes on outstanding performances, awards, etc. Indexes of titles, casts, producers, and writers.   PN1992.8.F5M35

Terrace, Vincent. The complete encyclopedia of television programs, 1947–1979. 2d ed., rev. South Brunswick, N.J., A. S. Barnes, [1979]. 2v. (1211p.) il.   **BG304**

1st ed. 1976.

An alphabetical title listing of television serials and shows televised on a continuing basis. Gives a description of the show format or summary of the principal action of a series, performers (with indication of character played), playing time, inclusive dates when televised, music credits, etc. Aims to include information on "every known entertainment program, no matter how obscure, from 1947 to 1979."—*Pref.* About 3,500 network and syndicated programs are listed. Name index.   PN1992.U5T46

———— Radio's golden years: encyclopedia of radio programs, 1930–1960. San Diego, A. S. Barnes; London, Tantivy Pr., [1981]. 308p. il.   **BG305**

About 1,500 nationally broadcast network and syndicated entertainment programs are listed by title, with information on story line or program format, cast, announcer, sponsor, dates, etc. Index of names.   PN1991.3.U6T47

Directories

See also BG261–BG263, BG267.

International television almanac. [Ed.1]– , 1956– . N.Y., Quigley, 1956– . il. Annual.   **BG306**

A compendium containing information on television performers, producers, distributors, feature releases, directories of services, stations and agencies, television in Great Britain and Ireland, the world market, statistics, etc.   HE8698.I55

History and biography

Barnouw, Erik. A history of broadcasting in the United States. N.Y., Oxford Univ. Pr., 1966–70. 3v. il.   **BG307**

A carefully documented history. Bibliography, index.
HE8689.8.B36

Who's who in television and cable. Steven H. Scheuer, ed. N.Y., Facts on File, [1983]. 579p. il.   **BG308**

"A majority of the entries are devoted to the leading executives of the three commercial networks—ABC, CBS and NBC—public television and the major national cable services such as Home Box Office and the Cable News Network" *(Pref.)*, but numerous journalists, actors, actresses, and executives of important local TV stations are also included.   PN1992.4.A2W44

B H

Music

❖In this specialized field an excellent guide is available: *Music reference and research materials: an annotated bibliography,* by V. H. Duckles (BH2), which should be consulted for extensive and detailed information.

An attempt has been made to list here a substantial selection of works from which information may be sought in a general library. Bibliographical sources both for books about music and for music itself are abundant, as are various encyclopedias and biographical dictionaries, e.g., *The new Grove dictionary of music and musicians* (BH129), long the standard work in English; Baker's *Biographical dictionary of musicians* (BH187); and *The new Oxford companion to music* (BH130).

Most libraries will need at least one or two books on the opera and opera plots, e.g., Ewen's *Encyclopedia of the opera* (BH228); Rosenthal's *Concise Oxford dictionary of opera* (BH235); and *The new Kobbé's complete opera book* (BH243).

Sears's *Song index* (BH272) is essential; and some of the catalogs of recorded music, those of historical interest as well as those of current listings, will probably be needed. Public libraries in particular are likely to want a selection of reference works on popular music and guides to recordings.

GENERAL WORKS

Guides

Druesedow, John E. Library research guide to music: illustrated search strategy and sources. Ann Arbor, Mich., Pierian Pr., [1982]. 86p. il. (Library research guide ser., 6) **BH1**

A brief guide intended "primarily for the undergraduate music student who is preparing to write on the subject of music, perhaps for the first time."—*Pref.* ML111.D78

Duckles, Vincent Harris, comp. Music reference and research materials; an annotated bibliography. 3d ed. N.Y., Free Pr., [1974] 526p. **BH2**

1st ed. 1964.

An indispensable work for the teacher and student as well as for the librarian in this field. Lists (with annotations) more than 1,900 items in the following principal categories: Dictionaries and encyclopedias; Histories and chronologies; Guides to systematic and historical musicology; Bibliographies of music literature; Bibliographies of music; Catalogs of music libraries and collections; Catalogs of musical instrument collections; Histories and bibliographies of music printing and publishing; Discographies; Yearbooks and directories; Miscellaneous bibliographical tools. Appropriate subdivisions within most sections; useful headnotes to the sections. Indexes of authors, editors, and reviewers; of subjects; and of titles.
ML113.D83

Harris, Ernest E. Music education: a guide to information sources. Detroit, Gale, [1978]. 566p. (Education information guide ser., 1) **BH3**

Aims "to represent both works which reflect current thought and those older sources whose content remains pertinent and useful to today's practitioner."—*Introd.* Offers annotated listings in five main categories with numerous subdivisions: (1) General reference sources; (2) Music in education; (3) Subject matter areas; (4) Special uses of music; (5) Technology, multimedia resources, and equipment. Author, title, and subject indexes. ML19.H37

Haydon, Glen. Introduction to musicology; a survey of the fields, systematic and historical, of musical knowledge and research. N.Y., Prentice-Hall, 1941. 329p. (Repr.: Univ. of North Carolina Pr., 1959; Westport Conn., Greenwood Pr., 1978) **BH4**

Bibliographies at the end of each chapter and a general bibliography, p.301–13. ML3797.H29I6

Marco, Guy A. Information on music: a handbook of reference sources in European languages. Littleton, Colo., Libraries Unlimited, 1975–84. v.1–3. (In progress) **BH5**

Contents: v.1, Basic and universal sources; v.2, The Americas; v.3, Europe.

An annotated listing of books considered to be the most useful to students of music. Designed to supplement and extend Duckles (BH2) rather than supersede that work. In addition to the listing of sources relevant to the study of European music, v.3 offers an update to v.2, and there is an appendix of revisions to v.1–2. Each volume has its own index. ML113.M33

Phelps, Roger P. A guide to research in music education. 2d ed. Metuchen, N.J., Scarecrow Pr., 1980. 385p. il. **BH6**

1st ed. 1969.

A bibliographic and procedural guide prepared with needs of the graduate music student particularly in mind. A third edition is scheduled for publication in 1986. MT1.P5

Spiess, Lincoln Bunce. Historical musicology; a reference manual for research in music, with articles by Ernst C. Krohn [and others]. Brooklyn, Inst. of Mediaeval Music, [1963]. 294p. (Musicological studies, 4) (Repr.: Westport, Conn., Greenwood Pr., 1980) **BH7**

Intended as a guide for students of musicology. Includes 1,980 numbered items in its bibliography; not annotated. List of American and foreign music publishers. ML3797.S7

Watanabe, Ruth Taiko. Introduction to music research. Englewood Cliffs, N.J., Prentice-Hall, [1967]. 237p. **BH8**

A guide for the student. Includes information on use of the music library, general library card catalogs, selection and development of a research topic, and a brief survey of music bibliography and related research materials. ML3797.W37

Bibliography

Books

See also BH59.

Blum, Fred. Music monographs in series. N.Y., Scarecrow Pr., 1964. 197p. **BH9**

Subtitle: A bibliography of numbered monograph series in the field of music current since 1945.

Lists more than 250 series from some 30 countries, arranged alphabetically by title of series or issuing organization. Entries for each volume give author, title, and date. Includes list of publishers and their agents; alphabetical list of series and issuing organizations; index of names. ML113.B63

Boston. Public Library. Dictionary catalog of the music collection. Boston, G. K. Hall, 1972. 20v. **BH10**

Reproduction of the catalog cards (author, title, subject, and added entries) for the collection. Includes the Allen A. Brown collection, but not sheet music, recordings in the Sound Archives, or the Koussevitsky Archives.   ML136.B7B73

———— ———— 1st supplement. Boston, G. K. Hall, 1976. 4v.

This supplement lists the musical scores, books, pamphlets, and periodicals cataloged since Jan. 1972, together with corrections to the basic catalog.

———— **Allen A. Brown Collection of Music.** Catalogue . . . Boston, Lib., 1908–16. 4v.   **BH11**

Contents: v.1–3, A–Z; v.4, Suppl.
A dictionary catalog of an important collection especially strong in 19th-century music. Includes many analytics.   ML136.B7B7

British Museum. Dept. of Printed Books. Hirsch Library. Books in the Hirsch Library, with supplementary list of music. London, Trustees, 1959. 542p. (Catalogue of printed books in the British Museum. Accessions, 3d ser., pt.291B)   **BH12**

A catalog of more than 12,000 books, forming part of the Hirsch Library acquired in 1946. Entries are brief but generally adequate, with German titles most strongly represented. For the German catalog see BH21.
A catalog of the music in the collection was issued in 1951 (BH65). A supplement to that catalog is included as an appendix in the present volume.

Charles, Sydney Robinson. A handbook of music and music literature in sets and series. N.Y., Free Pr., [1972]. 497p.   **BH13**

Intended to complement rather than duplicate the works of Blum (BH9) and Heyer (BH74). In four sections: (1) sets and series containing music of several composers and sets and series containing both music and music literature; (2) sets and series devoted to one composer; (3) music literature monograph and facsimile series; (4) music periodicals and yearbooks. Indexed.   ML113.C45

Chase, Gilbert. A guide to the music of Latin America. 2d ed. rev. and enl. A joint publication of the Pan American Union and the Library of Congress. Wash., Pan Amer. Union, 1962. 411p. (Repr.: N.Y., AMS Pr., 1972)   **BH14**

1st ed. had title: *Guide to Latin American music* (1945).
An annotated bibliography with introductory comments for each country. Subheadings for each country vary somewhat but usually include: Introduction; General and miscellaneous; Biography and criticism; National anthem; Folk and primitive music.   ML120.S7C47

Coover, James B. Music lexicography; including a study of lacunae in music lexicography and a bibliography of music dictionaries. 3d ed., rev. and enl. Carlisle, Pa., Carlisle Books, [1971]. 175p.   **BH15**

1st ed., 1952, had title: *A bibliography of music dictionaries.*
Lists biographical as well as terminological works. Includes an essay on lacunae in music bibliography between 1500 and 1700, and has been enlarged to include about 1800 "lexicographic works," including autonomous works as well as portions and appendixes of larger works and some periodical articles. Indexes of personal names and of "topics and types of dictionaries."   ML128.D5C6

De Lerma, Dominique-René. Bibliography of black music. Westport, Conn., Greenwood Pr., 1981–84. 4v. (Greenwood encyclopedia of black music)   **BH16**

Contents: v.1, Reference materials; v.2, Afro-American idioms; v.3, Geographical studies; v.4, Theory, education, and related studies.
An extensive, international bibliography of many areas of black musical culture. "The arrangement . . . is patterned after that of *RILM* abstracts, with changes made to satisfy the specific needs of the subject and breaks in the numerical sequence to permit the inclusion of new subject areas at a later date."—*Introd.* Rather than using cross references, items are repeated in all relevant sections.

Includes "articles, graduate papers, journals, and monographs." Indexes in v.3 and 4 only.   ML128.B45D44

Eitner, Robert. Biographisch-bibliographisches Quellen-Lexikon der Musiker und Musikgelehrten der christlichen Zeitrechnung bis zur Mitte des neunzehnten Jahrhunderts. Leipzig, Breitkopf, 1900–04. 10v. (Repr.: N.Y., Musurgia, 1947. 10v.)   **BH17**

Gives brief biographies and full bibliographies; the most important work for bibliographies of manuscripts, early editions, etc., of authors and composers. In many cases indicates location of the items in European libraries. A criticism by Michel Brenet (Marie Bobillier) in *La revue musicale* (1905), p.480–89, contains various corrections. Corrections and additions are also included in the *Miscellanea musicae bio-bibliographica* . . . by Hermann Springer and others (published quarterly, 1912–16; repr.: N.Y., Musurgia, 1947. 435p.). The latter volume is also reprinted along with Giuseppe Radiciotti's "Aggiunte e correzioni ai Dizionari biografici dei musicisti" (first published in *Sammelbände der Internationalen Musikgesellschaft*, v.14–15) as the final volume of the 11v. reprint edition (termed "2. verb. Aufl.") published by Akademische Druck- und Verlagsanstalt, Graz, 1959.
Will be superseded by *Répertoire international des sources musicales* (BH34) when that work is completed.   Z6811.E363

Floyd, Samuel A. and **Reisser, Marsha J.** Black music in the United States: an annotated bibliography of selected reference and research materials. Millwood, N.Y., Kraus Internat. Pubns., 1983. 234p.   **BH18**

Offers a survey of all types of reference materials—bibliographies and indexes, catalogs, discographies, biographical dictionaries, and anthologies pertinent to the study of black music. Also includes a directory of relevant archives. Indexes of titles, names, and subjects.   ML128.B45F6

Ford, Wyn Kelson. Music in England before 1800: a select bibliography. London, Lib. Assoc., [1967]. 128p. (Lib. Assoc. bibliographies, no.7)   **BH19**

Lists works on "music and music-making in England by both native and foreign musicians, up to the year 1800."—*Introd.* In two main sections: (1) Music and its environment; and (2) Persons. Indexed.   ML120.E5F7

Gerboth, Walter. An index to musical *Festschriften* and similar publications. N.Y., Norton, [1969]. 188p.   **BH20**

Based on an earlier version appearing in a commemorative volume, *Aspects of medieval and renaissance music* (N.Y., Norton, 1966), the work has been expanded to include *Festschriften* published through 1967, earlier volumes previously overlooked, and works published in the Slavic languages. In three parts: (1) a list of the *Festschriften;* (2) a subject listing of the articles appearing in those volumes; and (3) an index by author and specific subject.   ML128.M8G4

Hirsch, Paul. Katalog der Musikbibliothek Paul Hirsch, Frankfurt am Main, hrsg. von Kathi Meyer und Paul Hirsch. Berlin, M. Breslauer, 1928–47. 4v.   **BH21**

v.4 has imprint: Cambridge Univ. Pr.
Contents: Bd.1, Theoretische Drucke bis 1800; Bd.2, Opern-Partituren; Bd.3, Instrumental- und Vokalmusik bis etwa 1830; Bd.4, Erstausgaben, Chorwerke in Partitur, Gesamtausgaben, Nachschlagewerke, etc. Ergänzungen zu Bd.1–3.
A catalog of one of the largest and finest libraries of music of Europe, acquired by the British Museum in 1946 (see BH12, BH65). For description see P. H. Muir, "The Hirsch catalogue," in *Music review* 9:102–107 (1948).   ML138.H64

Horn, David. The literature of American music in books and folk music collections; a fully annotated bibliography. Metuchen, N.J., Scarecrow Pr., 1977. 556p.   **BH22**

Nearly 1,500 books relating to any aspect of American musical life are cited and carefully annotated. Arrangement is chronological, then by type or form. Indexed. Based on *The literature of American music; a fully annotated catalogue of the books and song collections in Exeter University Library* (Exeter, 1972).   ML120.U5H7

Hughes, Andrew. Medieval music: the sixth liberal art. [Rev. ed.] Toronto, Univ. of Toronto Pr., [1980]. 360p. (Toronto medieval bibliographies, 4) **BH23**

1st ed. 1974; this is a corrected re-issue of the 1974 work with interpolation of new numbers referring to the "1980 supplement," p.270–94 in the 1980 ed.

A bibliography of secondary works published as books and periodical articles, in collections of essays, dictionaries, encyclopedias, catalogs, etc., on all aspects of medieval music. Intended for the beginning student, readers without formal training in the field, and for librarians developing a collection of these materials. Topical/geographical arrangement; brief annotations; separate subject indexes and indexes of authors and editors for the main work and for the supplement. ML114.H8

International African Institute. A select bibliography of music in Africa. Comp. by L. J. P. Gaskin. London, 1965. 83p. (Africa bibliography series, B) **BH24**

More than 3,000 items in regional groupings, with author index. ML120.A35I6

Jackson, Irene V. Afro-American religious music: a bibliography and catalogue of gospel music. Westport, Conn., Greenwood Pr., [1979]. 210p. **BH25**

In two parts, the first offering a bibliography of books, essays, magazine and newspaper articles, and dissertations on "the music of the established Black churches or denominations in the United States and the Caribbean as well as Afro-American cults in the Caribbean and South America" (*Pref.*) and also including entries on West African music, particularly in the area of religious ritual. The second part is a catalog, by composer, of the compositions of Afro-Americans (1938–65) based on the collection at the Library of Congress. Subject index to the bibliography; list of composers.

A review appears in *Journal of Negro history* 65:89–90 (Winter 1980). ML128.S4J3

Jackson, Richard. U.S. music; sources of bibliography and collective biography. Brooklyn, Inst. for Studies in Amer. Music, 1973. 80p. (ISAM monographs, no.1) **BH26**

An annotated listing of books which are "of practical aid to students engaged in American-music studies."—*Introd.* Arranged by broad topics (historical, regional) or by type (folk, 20th-century). Author/compiler index. ML120.U5J2

Kahl, Willi and **Luther, Wilhelm-Martin.** Repertorium der Musikwissenschaft, Musikschrifttum, Denkmäler und Gesamtausgaben in Auswahl (1800–1950). Mit Besitzvermerken deutscher Bibliotheken und Musikwissenschaftlicher Institute. Im Auftr. der Gesellschaft für Musikforschung bearb.... Kassel, Bärenreiter, 1953. 271p. **BH27**

A list of 2,795 items, in classified arrangement, representing holdings of German libraries. Includes name and subject indexes, and an index to national and folk music.

Kassel. Deutsches Musikgeschichtliches Archiv. Katalog der Filmsammlung. Nr.1–17. Kassel, Bärenreiter, 1955–81. Bd.1–3[1-5]. (In progress) **BH28**

Catalog of music and treatises on the history of German music for the period ca.1450–1700 now available on microfilm. For description of the *Archiv, see* Music Library Association, *Notes,* 2d ser., 16:38–39 (1958). ML120.G3K3

Kostka, Stefan M. A bibliography of computer applications in music. Hackensack, N.J., Joseph Boonin, 1974. 58p. (Music indexes and bibliographies, no.7) **BH29**

An author listing of 641 books, essays, periodical articles, dissertations, and mimeographed reports which discuss the application of computers to musical problems. Works cited are mainly in English, French, or German. No index. ML113.K685B5

Lieberman, Fredric. Chinese music; an annotated bibliography. 2d ed., rev. & enl. N.Y., Garland, 1979. 257p. (Garland reference library of the humanities, v.75) **BH30**

1st ed. 1970.

Provides exhaustive coverage of some 2,441 books and articles in Western-language publications containing critical commentary on Chinese music, dance, and drama. Arrangement is by author in a single alphabet. Index of serial titles; index of names. A topical outline of Chinese music serves as a kind of subject index since item numbers of relevant entries are given under each heading in the outline. ML120.C5L5

Mathiesen, Thomas J. Bibliography of sources for the study of ancient Greek music. Hackensack, N.J., Joseph Boonin, [1974]. 59p. (Music indexes and bibliographies, no.10) **BH31**

Lists some 949 books and articles dealing with the ancient Greek theory of music. Includes material on relationship between theories of metrics and music. Author listing; no index. ML114.M3

New York. Public Library. Research Libraries. Dictionary catalog of the Music Collection. 2d ed. Boston, G. K. Hall, 1982. 44v. **BH32**

1st ed. 1964, with supplements 1973 and 1976.

Photographic reproduction of the catalog cards for one of the great music collections, one particularly strong in folk song, 18th- and 19th-century librettos, full scores of operas, complete works, historical editions, Beethoven materials, Americana, music periodicals, vocal music, literature on the voice, programs, record catalogs, and manuscripts. Offers detailed cataloging for books, pamphlets, essays, periodical articles, microforms, scores and librettos; recordings are not included. More than 3,500,000 items are represented, including imprints through 1971.

Supplemented by BH47.

Pierpont Morgan Library, New York. The Mary Flagler Cary music collection; printed books and music, manuscripts, autograph letters, documents, portraits. N.Y., [1970]. 108p. il. **BH33**

A descriptive catalog of one of the important music collections in the United States. ML136.N52P5

Répertoire international des sources musicales. International inventory of musical sources. München, G. Henle, 1960–80. [2v. unnumbered, now called BI[1], BIII[1]] AI[1-[10]], BII, BIII[2], BIV[1-4], BV[1], BVI[1-2], BVII, BVIII[1-2], BIX[2], BX. (In progress) **BH34**

"Publié par la Société Internationale de Musicologie et l'Association Internationale des Bibliothèques Musicales."—*half title page.*

Title and introductory matter also in German and English.

Contents: *Série alphabetique,* AI[1-[10]], Einzeldrucke vor 1800. Redaktion Karlheinz Schlager (v.1–9, Aarts–Zwingmann; Anhang 1–2; [v.10] Text- und Musikincipit-Register zu den Anhängen 1 und 2 in RISM A/1 Band 9.); *Série systématique,* [BI[1]], Recueils imprimés, XVIe–XVIIe siècles; liste chronologique... sous la direction de François Lesure; BII, Recueils imprimés, XVIIIe siècle; ouvrage publié sous la direction de François Lesure; [BIII[1]], The theory of music from the Carolingian era up to 1400; a descriptive catalogue of manuscripts... ed. by Joseph Smits van Waesberghe [and others]; BIII[2], The theory of music from the Carolingian era up to 1400... Italy, ed. by Pieter Fischer; BIV[1], Manuscripts of polyphonic music, 11th–early 14th century, ed. by Gilbert Reaney; BIV[2], Manuscripts of polyphonic music, ca.1320–1400, by Gilbert Reaney; BIV[3-4], Handschriften mit Mehrstimmiger Musik des 14., 15. und 16. Jahrhunderts, hrsg. Max Lütolf. 2v.; BV[1], Tropen- und Sequenzenhandschriften, von Heinrich Husmann; BVI[1-2], Écrits imprimés concernant la musique; ouvrage publié sous la direction de François Lesure. 2v.; BVII, Handschriftlichen überlieferte Lauten- und Gitarrentabulauturen des 15. bis 18. Jahrhunderts, by Wolfgang Boetticher; BVIII[1-2], Das deutsche Kirchenlied, DKL: krit. Gesamtausg. d. Melodien, hrsg. Konrad Ameln, Marcus Jenny, Walther Lipphardt: pt.1: Verzeichnis der Drucke, pt.2, Register; BIX[2], Hebrew writings concerning music, its manuscripts and printed books from Geonic times up to 1800, by I. Adler; BX, The theory of music in Arabic writings (c.900–1900): descriptive catalogue of manuscripts in libraries of Europe and the U.S.A., by Amnon Shiloah.

Referred to as *RISM,* the work is "intended to provide a catalogue of all available bibliographical musical works, writings about music and textbooks on music from all countries of the world . . . from the earliest times to the year 1800."—*Foreword.*

The first 2v. to be published were unnumbered. It was announced in v.BII that the volumes of the general alphabetical series would be denoted by the symbol A, followed by the number of the volume in roman figures. The volumes of the classified series would bear the symbol B, followed by the number of the volume in roman figures.

Bibliographical descriptions are full; copies are located. Indexes are included with each volume or group of volumes.

Sendrey, Alfred. Bibliography of Jewish music. N.Y., Columbia Univ. Pr., 1951. 404p. (Repr.: N.Y., Kraus, 1969)   **BH35**

This comprehensive bibliography of almost 10,000 items is in two separate listings: (1) literature on the subject, and (2) the music itself, including recordings. Author indexes for both sections.
ML113.S5

Tyrrell, John and **Wise, Rosemary.** A guide to international music congress reports in musicology, 1900–1975. N.Y., Garland, 1979. 353p. (Garland reference library of the humanities, v.118)   **BH36**

A chronological listing of general congresses of music, anthropology, poetry, etc., but not specialized ones such as those concerned with music education, music therapy, dance, or music copyright. For each congress gives the name in the language of its publications, place, date, published proceedings, and a listing of the papers relating specifically to music. There are a number of useful indexes: places; titles, series, and sponsors; authors and editors; subjects.
ML128.M8T9

Warfield, Gerald. Writings on contemporary music notation: an annotated bibliography. [Ann Arbor], Music Lib. Assoc., 1976. 93p. (MLA index and bibliography ser., no.16)   **BH37**

Aims to be comprehensive in citing books and articles on new notation published 1950–75, but is selective in coverage of writings on music notation generally, new performance techniques, music copying, autographing and printing, ethnomusicology, and writings published 1900–50. Author arrangement, with subject index. Brief annotations.   ML128.N7W37

Weisser, Albert, comp. Bibliography of publications and other resources on Jewish music. N.Y., Nat. Jewish Music Council, Nat. Jewish Welfare Board, 1969. 117p.   **BH38**

"A revised and enlarged edition based in part upon 'The Bibliography of books and articles on Jewish music' prepared by Dr. Joseph Yasser and published in 1955."—*title page.* Adds new material through 1967.   ML128.J4W4

Wenk, Arthur B. Analyses of nineteenth-century music: 1940–1980. 2d ed. Boston, Music Library Assoc., [1984]. 83p. (MLA index and bibliography ser., no.15)   **BH39**

1st ed. 1975 with suppl. 1976.

"The present edition includes some ninety composers represented in sixty-six periodicals, and covers material appearing between 1940 and 1980."—*Pref.* Also lists analyses appearing in "biographies, book-length surveys, doctoral dissertations, and *Festschriften,*" though completeness is not claimed for those areas. Arranged by composer; author index.

A companion work is: ML118.W43

——— Analyses of twentieth-century music, 1940–1970. [Ann Arbor, Mich.], Music Library Assoc., 1975. 94p. (MLA index and bibliography ser., no.13)   **BH40**

Provides quick access to analytical articles on about 150 composers in 39 periodicals, plus coverage of biographies, book-length surveys, doctoral dissertations, and *Festschriften.*

——— ——— Supplement, 2d ed. Boston, Music Library Assoc., [1984]. 132p. (MLA index and bibliography ser., no.14)

"This supplement . . . includes all of the material published in the previous supplement [i.e., 1970–75 suppl. publ. 1975] as well as material of an analytical nature which has appeared since that

time."—*Pref.* Also indexes 41 periodicals and numerous *Festschriften* not previously included. Covers through 1980.   ML118.W462

Winick, Steven O. Rhythm; an annotated bibliography. Metuchen, N.J., Scarecrow Pr., 1974. 157p.   **BH41**

An annotated listing of almost 500 English-language books, theses, and periodical articles written during the 1900–72 period and considered useful to music educators. Topically arranged in three sections: (1) General background; (2) Psychology of rhythm; (3) Pedagogy of rhythm. Index of authors, editors and reviewers.
ML128.L3W53

Wood, David A. Music in Harvard libraries: a catalogue of early printed music and books on music in the Houghton Library and the Eda Kuhn Loeb Music Library. Cambridge, Mass., Houghton Lib. of the Harvard College Lib.; distr. by Harvard Univ. Pr., 1980. 306p.   **BH42**

A descriptive bibliography of the music and books on music printed before 1801 which had been cataloged for the Harvard libraries by Jan. 1967. Includes scores, sets of parts, part-books, songbooks with music, monographs, treatises and pamphlets on music, music periodicals, dance manuals with music. Listing is alphabetical by author or composer; name index.
ML136.C23H33

Current

Bibliographie des Musikschrifttums. 1936– . Frankfurt am Main, Hofmeister, 1936– . Annual.   **BH43**

Frequency varies; publication runs well behind date of coverage. Not published 1940–49. v.1936–39 called "1–4. Jahrg."

A classified bibliography of books and "serious" periodical articles. Author and subject indexes. Though emphasis is on German publications, coverage is international.   ML113.B54

British catalogue of music, Jan./March, 1957– . London, Council of the British National Bibliography, 1957– . 2 interim issues, with annual cumulation.   **BH44**

"A record of music and books about music recently published in Great Britain, based upon the material deposited at the Copyright Receipt Office of the British Museum."—*title page.* Classified arrangement, with index of composers and titles, and a subject index. Includes a list of music publishers. Excludes various types of modern popular music.   ML120.G7B7

Jahresverzeichnis der deutschen Musikalien und Musikschriften. Leipzig, Hofmeister, 1852–1968. v.1–117. Annual.   **BH45**

Title varies: 1852–53, *Kurzes Verzeichnis sämmtlicher in Deutschland und den angrenzenden Ländern gedruckter Musikalien . . . ;* 1854–1928, *Verzeichnis der im Jahre . . . erschienen Musikalien;* 1929–42, *Hofmeisters Jahresverzeichnis.*

In three sections: (1) Musikalien, Musikschriften, Zeitschriften und Jahrbücher in one alphabet; (2) Systematischer und Register-Teil; (3) Titel und Textregister.

Superseded by: ML113.H715

Jahresverzeichnis der Musikalien und Musikschriften. Jahrg.118– . Leipzig, VEF Friedrich Hofmeister Musikverlag, 1969– . v.118– . Annual.   **BH46**

"Veröffentlichungen der DDR, der BRD und Westberlins sowie der deutschsprachigen Werke anderer Länder."—*t.p.*

Continues the *Jahresverzeichnis der deutschen Musikalien und Musikschriften* (above). Issued in two parts: Alphabetischer Teil, and Systematischer und Register-Teil.

New York. Public Library. Research Libraries. Music Division. Bibliographic guide to music. 1975– . Boston, G. K. Hall, 1976– . Annual.   **BH47**

Serves as an ongoing supplement to the *Dictionary catalog of the Music Collection* (BH32) in that it includes all publications cataloged by the Research Libraries of the New York Public Library in the field of music, but also includes additional entries from Library of Congress MARC tapes in "such areas as literature of music (bibliography, history and criticism, philosophy of music), and music instruction and study (composition, orchestration, singing and voice culture)."—*Introd., 1975.* ML136.N5N5732

Dissertations

Adkins, Cecil and **Dickinson, Alis.** Doctoral dissertations in musicology. 7th North American ed., 2d Internat. ed. Philadelphia, Amer. Musicological Soc.; [Basel], Internat. Musicological Soc., 1984. 545p. **BH48**

"The second combined publication of the American-Canadian *Doctoral Dissertations in Musicology* (seventh cumulative edition) and the *International Doctoral Dissertations in Musicology* (second cumulative edition)."—*Pref.*

Doctoral dissertations in musicology was separately published in five editions 1952–71. The previous edition of this work was published 1977 as *International index of dissertations and musicological works in progress.*

About 6,500 titles in this edition, approximately 63% of which are American-Canadian works, the remainder being from universities in 30 other countries (non-American dissertations having been included only since 1972). Following a "General-Miscellaneous" section, dissertations are listed by period with topical subdivisions. References to abstracts in *Dissertation abstracts* (AH19) and in *RILM abstracts* (BH102) follow the bibliographic citations; an asterisk preceding the classification number indicates that the work is still in progress. Separate author and subject indexes. Non-student works are no longer listed, but are to appear from time to time in *Acta musicologica.*

An older list, more limited in scope, is W. S. Larson's *Bibliography of research studies in music education, 1932–1948* (Rev. ed. Chicago, Music Educators' Nat. Conference, 1949). It was continued on an irregular basis by lists of "Doctoral dissertations in music and music education," first compiled by Larson (later by Roderick D. Gordon) and appearing in the *Journal of research in music education:* 1949–56 (Fall 1957), 1957–63 (Spr. 1964), 1963–67 (Sum. 1968), 1968–71 (Spr. 1972), 1972 (Sum. 1974), 1972–77 (Fall 1978).

Records of research work for graduate degrees in music at British universities may be found in two lists compiled by Paul Doe, entitled "Register of theses on music" and appearing in *R.M.A.* [Royal Musical Association] *research chronicle,* no.3 (1963, with "Amendments and addenda" in no.4, 1964) and no.11 (1973); a third list by N. Sandon appears in no.15 (1979). ML128.M8A43

Gribenski, Jean. Thèses en doctorat en langue française relatives à la musique; French language dissertations in music. N.Y., Pendragon Pr., [1979]. 270p. **BH49**

Lists some 438 dissertations at the doctoral level written in French and accepted by universities in Belgium, Switzerland, Canada, and France during the 1883–1976 period. Brief annotations frequently point out chapters in which music is discussed. Classed arrangement based on the RILM scheme, with indexes by author, subject, date of degree, and university. ML128.L3G7

Heintze, James R. American music studies: a classified bibliography of master's theses. Detroit, Publ. for the College Music Society [by] Information Coordinators, 1984. 312p. il. (Bibliographies in American music, no.8) **BH50**

A topical listing of some 2,370 master's theses completed at colleges and universities throughout the United States, in whatever discipline so long as the topic relates to music. Entries are "based on both published and unpublished lists of master's theses, responses to requests for titles of theses sent to schools throughout the United States, and an examination of a number of college and university card catalogs."—*Introd.* Author, geographic, and subject indexes. ML128.M8H44

Mead, Rita H. Doctoral dissertations in American music: a classified bibliography. Brooklyn, Inst. for Studies in Amer. Music, 1974. 155p. (ISAM monographs, no.3) **BH51**

Topically arranged within six major sections: (1) Reference and research materials; (2) Historical studies; (3) Theory; (4) Ethnomusicology; (5) Organology; (6) Related fields. Lists dissertations accepted at United States universities on American music from 1890 through 1973 (i.e., includes dissertations listed in the Fall 1973 *Journal* of the American Musicological Society and the Dec. 1973 issue of *Dissertation abstracts international*). Author and subject indexes. ML128.M8M4

Schaal, Richard. Verzeichnis deutschsprachiger musikwissenschaftlicher Dissertationen 1861–1960. Kassel, Bärenreiter, 1963. 167p. (Musikwissenschaftliche Arbeiten, no.19) **BH52**

Cites 2,819 dissertations in German, listed alphabetically by author. Subject index. ML128.M8S3

❖Specialized dissertation lists include: *Ethnomusicology and folk music: an international bibliography of dissertations and theses* by Frank Gillis and Alan P. Merriam (Middletown, Conn., publ. for the Society for Ethnomusicology by the Wesleyan Univ. Pr., 1966. 148p.) and *Bibliography of theses and dissertations in sacred music* by Kenneth R. Hartley (Detroit, Information Coordinators, 1966. 127p.).

Periodicals

Fellinger, Imogen. Verzeichnis der Musikzeitschriften des 19. Jahrhunderts. Regensburg, Bosse, 1968. 557p. (Studien zur Musikgeschichte des 19. Jahrhunderts, 10) **BH53**

A chronological listing of 19th-century music periodicals, with indexes by title, editor, and subject. ML117.F44

Meggett, Joan M. Music periodical literature: an annotated bibliography of indexes and bibliographies. Metuchen, N.J., Scarecrow Pr., 1978. 116p. **BH54**

"Intended primarily for college and university music students as an aid to their research through music periodical literature . . . ."—*Pref.* An annotated listing of periodical indexes and bibliographies (the latter appearing in book form or as an essay or periodical article which includes references to periodical literature) on music and music-related topics. Indexes of authors/editors/compilers, subjects, and titles. ML128.P24M43

Thoumin, Jean-Adrien. Bibliographie rétrospective des périodiques français de littérature musicale, 1870–1954. Paris, Éd. Documentaires Industrielles et Techniques, 1957. 179p. **BH55**

On cover: Union Française des Organismes de Documentation.
A list of 600 titles with locations indicated. Indexes by date and by editors.

Manuscripts and printed music

See also BH33 and BH44.

Albrecht, Otto Edwin. A census of autograph music manuscripts of European composers in American libraries. Philadelphia, Univ. of Pennsylvania Pr., 1953. 331p. **BH56**

Lists 2,017 manuscripts by more than 500 European composers. Gives full bibliographical information. Includes list of owners. ML135.A2A4

American music before 1865 in print and on records: bibliodiscography; pref. by H. Wiley Hitchcock. Brooklyn, Inst. for Studies in Amer. Music, Brooklyn College, 1976. 113p. (ISAM monographs, no.6) **BH57**

This is both a "classified and annotated bibliography of pre-1865 American music . . . in print and available for purchase in 1976" and a "discography listing phonorecordings of pre-1865 American music that had been issued on 33⅓ r.p.m. discs up to 1976."—*Pref.* The bibliography is in three sections: (1) Music in performance editions; (2) Music in facsimile reprints; (3) Music in books. In all sections the arrangement is alphabetical by author or, if anonymous, by title. Index of composers, compilers, and titles for both the bibliography and the discography. ML120.U5A467

American Society of Composers, Authors and Publishers. ASCAP index of performed compositions. N.Y., ASCAP, 1978. 1423p. **BH58**

"The material in this volume is an unedited alphabetical listing of compositions in the ASCAP repertory which have appeared in the Society's survey of radio, television and wired music performances [through March 1977]."—*Pref.* Listing is by title, with name of performer and publisher.

A 99p. supplement was published 1981. ML120.U5A53

A basic music library: essential scores and books. Comp. by the Music Library Association Committee on Basic Music Collection under the direction of Pauline S. Bayne. Ed. by Robert Michael Fling. 2d ed. Chicago, Amer. Lib. Assoc., 1983. 357p. **BH59**

1st ed. 1978.

A thorough revision of a work "designed as a buying guide or selection tool for those who have responsibility for collecting music materials in small and medium-sized libraries, whether public or academic."—*Pref.* Principal sections: Score anthologies; Study scores; Performing editions; Vocal scores; Instrumental methods and studies; Music literature. Appendix of selected music dealers. Indexed. ML113.B3

The Boston composers project: a bibliography of contemporary music. Boston Area Music Libraries; Linda I. Solow, ed. Cambridge, MIT Pr., [1983]. 775p. **BH60**

Aims "to list every composition, published or unpublished, by every art music and jazz composer resident in the greater Boston area during the latter half of the 1970s" *(Pref.)*, thus serving as a prototype work to meet the needs of music researchers and cultural historians and to encourage similar work in other geographical areas. Listing is by composer, with index of names and titles.

ML125.B66B67

British Broadcasting Corporation. Central Music Library. [Catalogues] [London], British Broadcasting Corp., 1965–67. **BH61**

An unnumbered series of catalogs listing printed and manuscript materials in the BBC's vast collection. The published volumes include: *Chamber music catalogue* (1965. 1v.); *Choral and opera catalogue* (1967. 2v.); *Piano and organ catalogue* (1965. 2v.); *Song catalogue* (1966. 4v.).

British Museum. Dept. of Manuscripts. Catalogue of manuscript music in the British Museum, by Augustus Hughes-Hughes. London, Trustees, 1906–09. 3v. **BH62**

Contents: v.1, Sacred vocal music; v.2, Secular vocal music; v.3, Instrumental music, treatises, etc.

Classified list, with author, subject, and title indexes in each volume. ML136.L8B72

British Museum. Dept. of Printed Books. The catalogue of printed music in the British Library to 1980. [Laureen Baillie, ed.] London & N.Y., K. G. Saur, 1981–85. v.1–39. (In progress) **BH63**

Contents: v.1–39, A–Minay.

" . . . unites in a single sequence the various music catalogues maintained for the use of readers in the British Library Reading Rooms, and for the first time makes the full range of the collection accessible to an international public."—*Pref.* A main-entry listing with cross references from various alternative entry points.

ML136.L8B62

———— Catalogue of printed music published between 1487 and 1800 now in the British Museum, by W. Barclay Squire. London, Trustees, 1912. 2v. **BH64**

v.2 includes 1st supplement.

———— ———— 2d supplement, by William C. Smith. Cambridge, Univ. Pr., 1940. 85p.

ML136.L8B71

———— Hirsch Library. Music in the Hirsch Library. London, Trustees, 1951. 438p. (British Museum. Dept. of Print-

ed Books. Catalogue of printed music in the British Museum. Accessions. Pt.53) **BH65**

Lists vocal scores, operas, orchestral scores, chamber music, and collections of early editions, totaling nearly 9,000 entries, many of which are not included in the original 4v. catalog (BH21).

British union-catalogue of early music printed before the year 1801: a record of the holdings of over one hundred libraries throughout the British Isles; ed., Edith B. Schnapper. London, Butterworth, 1957. 2v. **BH66**

A scholarly bibliography which has drawn on the 1912 British Museum (Squire's) *Catalogue* . . . (BH64), but which is essentially an entirely new work. Listing is generally by composer or anonymous title; periodicals are grouped under "Periodical publications." Extensive index of song titles. ML116.B7

Brown, Howard Mayer. Instrumental music printed before 1600; a bibliography. Cambridge, Harvard Univ. Pr., 1965. 559p. **BH67**

A chronological, descriptive bibliography with contents notes. Locates copies. Lists works known to have existed but now lost, as well as extant volumes. Thorough indexing. ML128.I65B77

Composium directory of new music: annual index of contemporary compositions, 1970– . Los Angeles, Crystal Record Co., 1971– . Biennial. **BH68**

Frequency varies; title varies: *Directory of new music.*

Arranged by composer, giving a brief biographical sketch and a list of recent compositions (both published and unpublished); includes composer's address or name of publishing house from which copies of the works may be obtained. Ensemble and instrument listing.

Corbin, Solange, ed. Répertoire de manuscrits médiévaux contenant des notations musicales. Paris, Éditions du Centre National de la Recherche Scientifique, 1965–74. 3v. **BH69**

At head of title: École pratique des hautes-études, Sorbonne. 4. section: Sciences historiques et philologiques.

Madeleine Bernard, ed.

Contents: v.1, Bibliothèque Sainte-Geneviève, Paris; v.2, Bibliothèque Mazarine, Paris; v.3, Bibliothèques parisiennes: Arsenal, Nationale (Musique), Universitaire, École des Beaux Arts et fonds privés.

A listing and description of each medieval manuscript containing notation of a chant. Arrangement within volumes is by type of notation (e.g., neume, square note, etc.). Indexes by manuscript numbers, by original owner of manuscript, by form of manuscript (hymnal, the offices), by type of lines on the page, and by neume. v.1–2 include a listing of manuscripts with pictures of musical instruments, though only the folio number is listed, not the name of the instrument pictured. Indexes of repositories and of incipits in v.3. M135.A2C67

Davidsson, Åke. Bibliographie zur Geschichte des Musikdrucks. Uppsala, Swed., [Almquist & Wiksells], 1965. 86p. (Studia Musicologia Upsaliensia. Nova ser., 1) **BH70**

Nearly 600 items on the history of music printing and publishing. ML112.D16

Dichter, Harry and **Shapiro, Elliott.** Handbook of early American sheet music, 1768–1889. N.Y., Dover, 1977. 287p. il. **BH71**

A reprint, with corrections, of the 1941 edition published under title *Early American sheet music, its lure and its lore.*

Arranged by class in chronological periods. Each piece is described with bibliographical details, illustrations, etc. Includes "Famous American musical firsts," p.xxv–xxvii; and pt.3, "Lithographers and artists working on American sheet music before 1870," by Edith A. Wright and Josephine A. McDevitt, p.249–57.

A complementary work is Dichter's *Handbook of American sheet music; a catalog of sheet music for sale by the compiler* (Philadelphia, Dichter, 1947. 100p.), a catalog of about 2,000 items in classified arrangement without index; although designated as "First annual issue," nothing further was published. ML112.D53

Eagon, Angelo. Catalog of published concert music by American composers. 2d ed. Metuchen, N.J., Scarecrow Pr., 1969. 348p. **BH72**

1st ed. 1964 prep. by Music Branch, Information Center, U.S. Information Agency.

"Designed as a current reference for the extensive repertory of concert music by American composers, this catalog includes works in various categories which are generally available in some printed form for purchase."—*Foreword.* Entries are meant to be current as of June 1968. ML120.U5E23

————— ————— Supplement 1–2. Metuchen, N.J., Scarecrow Pr., 1971–74. 2v.

The supplements bring the coverage up to Nov. 1973.

Forsyth, Ella Marie. Building a chamber music collection; a descriptive guide to published scores. Metuchen, N.J., Scarecrow Pr., 1979. 191p. **BH73**

Some 300 published chamber music compositions are arranged by instrumentation, and within each section works are listed "by priority of selection, beginning with the most essential to a basic collection."—*Introd.* (Priority evaluations are the compiler's, who is a performer and teacher.) Citation for each work gives publication and performance information, level of difficulty, and sources for music analysis and commentary (i.e., those sources included in the annotated bibliography). Directory of publishers; popular title index; composer index. ML128.C4F7

Heyer, Anna Harriet. Historical sets, collected editions, and monuments of music: a guide to their contents. 3d ed. Chicago, Amer. Lib. Assoc., 1980. 2v. (1105p.) **BH74**

1st ed. 1957.
Contents: v.1, Text; v.2, Index.

v.1 lists, with contents and bibliographical information, "the complete editions of the music of individual composers and the major collections of music that have been published or are in the process of publication."—*Pref.* Encompasses "collections, anthologies, or monumental sets of music considered by the author to have historical value, musical worth, reliable editing, or significance to music research"; aims to be as complete as possible for the 19th and 20th centuries, with some emphasis on current publications (through June 1979). About 1,300 entries in this edition. Index lists entries by composers, compilers, editors, and by titles for title entries. ML113.H52

Hilton, Ruth B. An index to early music in selected anthologies. Clifton, N.J., European American Music Corp., [1978]. 127p. (Music indexes and bibliographies, no.13) **BH75**

The anthologies indexed were selected because they were available in most music libraries and are not devoted to a particular period, form, country, etc. "Early music" is defined as music "from antiquity to the end of the Baroque."—*Introd.* Main listing is under composer, anonymous title, or first line of an untitled text, and includes date and country of origin, type of work, performing medium, thematic-catalog number, and anthology citation; there are cross references from titles as added entries. Index by genre or medium. ML116.H54

Hixon, Donald L. Music in early America: a bibliography of music in Evans. Metuchen, N.J., Scarecrow Pr., 1970. 607p. **BH76**

Provides an index to "the music published in seventeenth and eighteenth century America as represented by Charles Evans' *American Bibliography* [AA557] and the Readex Corporation's microprint edition of *Early American Imprints, 1639–1800.*"—*Pref.* ML120.U5H6

Hofmeisters Handbuch der Musikliteratur; oder, Allgemeines systematisch-geordnetes Verzeichniss der in Deutschland und in den angrenzenden Ländern gedruckten Musikalien auch musikalischen Schriften und Abbildungen, mit Anzeige der Verleger und Preise. 3., bis zum Anfang des Jahres 1884 ergänzte Aufl., bearb, und hrsg. von Adolf Hofmeister. Leipzig, Hofmeister, [1844–45]. 3v. **BH77**

First published in Leipzig by Anton Meysel, 1817, covering music and music literature to 1815, with nine supplements to 1825. Karl Friedrich Whistling issued a revised 2d ed. in 1828 with three supplements: 1829, 1834, and 1839.

Adolf Hofmeister edited this 3d ed., called *C. F. Whistling's Handbuch* (varies), with supplementary volumes, as follows: *Handbuch der musikalischen Literatur; oder, Verzeichnis der im Deutschen Reiche, in den Ländern deutschen Sprachgebietes, sowie der für den Vertrieb im Deutschen Reiche wichtigen, im Auslande erschienenen Musikalien auch musikalischen Schriften, Abbildungen und plastichen Darstellungen, mit Anzeige der Verleger und Preise.* Bd.4–19 (incompl.), 1844–1940 (Leipzig, Hofmeister, 1852–1943). (Bd.19, Lfg.1–8 includes only A–L; no more published.) ML113.H71

Deutsche Musikbibliographie. Jahrg. 1– . Leipzig, Hofmeister, 1829– . Monthly. **BH78**

Supersedes *Handbuch der musikalischen Literatur,* 1817–29.
Title varies: 1829–1907, *Musikalisch-literarischer Monatsbericht;* 1908–42, *Hofmeisters Musikalisch-literarischer Monatsbericht.*

An alphabetical list, by composer or author, of music and musical writings published in German. Gives place of publication, publisher, and price. Indexed by subject and by publisher. Cumulated in Hofmeister's *Jahresverzeichnis der deutschen Musikalien und Musikschriften* (BH45). ML113.H72

Jarman, Lynn. Canadian music, a selected checklist, 1950–1973; a selective listing of Canadian music from *Fontes artis musicae,* 1954–73 based on the catalogued entries of *Canadiana* from 1950. Toronto, Univ. of Toronto Pr., 1976. 170p. **BH79**

A bibliographical project of the Canadian Association of Music Libraries.

A cumulation in classed arrangement of entries for Canadian music cited in *Fontes artis musicae.* (Items selected for inclusion in *Fontes* are those "of serious intent and of a certain length or substance."—*Pref.*) Index by composer/author, subarranged by title of works. ML120.C2J4

Lesure, François. Catalogue de la musique imprimée avant 1800 conservée dans les bibliothèques publiques de Paris. Paris, Bibliothèque Nationale, 1981. 708p. **BH80**

An author catalog (with a separate section for anonymous works, p.657–708) of early printed music in the Bibliothèque National and other public libraries of Paris. Gives full bibliographic information, library location, and shelfmark. ML125.P27L5

Newberry Library, Chicago. Bibliographical inventory of the early music in the Newberry Library, Chicago, Ill.; ed. by D. W. Krummel. Boston, G. K. Hall, 1977. 587p. **BH81**

Reproduction of the relevant catalog cards from this library which is particularly strong in medieval, Renaissance, and American music. Sections for manuscripts and for printed music and treatises are followed by eight geographical sections (with subdivisions, usually chronologically arranged). Index of composers, editors, and musical subjects; index of printers, engravers, artists, copyists, and publishers. ML136.C5N43

————— The Newberry Library catalog of early American printed sheet music. Comp. by Bernard E. Wilson. Boston, G. K. Hall, 1983. 3v. **BH82**

Contents: v.1, Main entries; Added entries, A–G; v.2, Added entries, H–Z; Chronology; v.3, Places; Title index.

Reproduces the catalog cards for the Library's Driscoll collection and other early American sheet music at Newberry—about 9,450 main entry cards and 11,550 added entries. The chronology runs to about 9,150 cards; the "Places" index to 9,500; and the title index to 4,800. ML136.C5N434

Olmsted, Elizabeth H. Music Library Association catalog of cards for printed music, 1953–1972; a supplement to the Library of Congress catalogs. Totowa, N.J., Rowman & Littlefield, 1974. 2v. **BH83**

Includes entries for printed music reported to the National Union Catalog for the period 1956–72, thus supplementing the *Library of Congress catalog—Music and phonorecords* (BH91). Much editing was done for this publication, but cards were not retyped and a considerable number of them are virtually unreadable. Name of the library supplying the card was not included, therefore the catalog cannot be used as a tool for locating copies. ML113.O42

Philadelphia. Free Library. The Edwin A. Fleischer Collection of Orchestral Music; a cumulative catalog, 1929–1977. Boston, G. K. Hall, [1979]. 956p. **BH84**

1st ed. 1933–45, suppl. 1966.

The collection has been completely recataloged since 1975 and new materials integrated to form this catalog of a major collection containing more than 13,000 scores (including about 2,500 scores for orchestra and solo instrument or voice). Arranged alphabetically by composer, each entry giving brief information about instrumentation, publisher, performing time, dates, pagination, incipit, and commentary. Three indexes: (1) ensembles other than standard orchestra (e.g., brass ensemble, string orchestra); (2) works requiring one or more solo or featured instrument; (3) works requiring voice. The scores in the public domain are available for loan to recognized organizations. ML136.P4F68

Saltonstall, Cecilia Drinker and **Saltonstall, Henry.** A new catalog of music for small orchestra. Clifton, N.J., European American Music Corp., [1978]. 323p. (Music indexes and bibliographies, no.14) **BH85**

1st ed. 1940.

"Compiled almost entirely from current retail catalogs sent to us by more than 200 publishers from 30 countries."—*Pref.* To be included, a work must have a minimum of ten parts, at least three string parts, and a wind section of two to twelve parts. Listing is by composer, giving title of work, publisher, instrumentation, duration. A directory of publishers is included. ML128.O5S33

Sonneck, Oscar George Theodore. Bibliography of early secular American music (18th century). Rev. and enl. by William Treat Upton. Wash., Lib. of Congress, Music Division, 1945. 616p. il. (Repr.: N.Y., Da Capo Pr., 1964) **BH86**

1st ed. 1905.

Revised edition adds much new material. Lists by title—with complete bibliographical information, including first lines—secular music issued by the American press prior to the 19th century. Also contains a list of articles and essays relating to music, and a list of composers, with their works. Locates copies. ML120.U5S6

U.S. Copyright Office. Catalog of copyright entries . . . pt.3: Musical compositions. Wash., Govt. Prt. Off., 1906–46. n.s. v.1–41. Monthly, 1906–45; annual, 1946. **BH87**

Through 1945, all musical compositions (published and unpublished) were entered by title in one alphabet in each monthly issue, followed by the list of renewals, with an annual index. In 1946 the *Catalog* was divided into four groups: (1) Unpublished music; (2) Published music; (3) Renewals; (4) Title index to groups 1 and 2.

Ceased publication; superseded by:

——— Catalog of copyright entries. 3d ser. Pt.5: Music. v.1–31, Jan./June 1947–July/Dec. 1977. Wash., Govt. Prt. Off., 1947–77. Semiannual. **BH88**

Issued in three parts, 1947–56: pt.5A, Published music; pt.5B, Unpublished music; pt.5C, Renewal registrations. (Pt.C issued as pt.14B, 1947–50.) Each part published in two numbers per year: (1) Jan./June, and (2) July/Dec.

Beginning with Jan./June 1957 (3d ser. v.11, pt.5, no.1), the three parts are combined and issued as pt.5, in three groupings: (1) current registrations, (2) renewal registrations, and (3) name index.

Lists all music published in the United States and foreign countries deposited for copyright registration during the period covered. Arrangement is by title. The index to names lists names of composers, authors of words, editors, compilers, arrangers, etc. as given in the main entry.

The most comprehensive bibliography of music available for the period of coverage.

For the 4th series (which includes pt.3, Performing Arts, and pt.7, Sound recordings) see AA596.

Wolfe, Richard J. Secular music in America, 1801–1825; a bibliography. N.Y., New York Pub. Lib., 1964. 3v. **BH89**

Lists approximately 10,000 titles and editions of secular music published in America, though not confined to American composers. Includes sacred music when printed in secular collections or in series, and religious pieces written by American composers and published in sheet-music form. Arranged alphabetically by composer or anonymous title with detailed bibliographical information. Gives short biographical sketches of lesser-known composers. Indexes of titles, first lines, publishers, etc., and a general index. Locates copies.

A scholarly work useful to research workers and students of American history, as well as to music scholars. ML120.U5W57

Current

Music-in-print series. Philadelphia, Musicdata, 1974– . v.1–6. (In progress) **BH90**

Contents: v.1, Sacred choral music in print, by Gary S. Eslinger (2d ed. 1985); v.2, Secular choral music in print, by Nancy K. Nardone (1982); v.3, Organ music in print, by Walter A. Frankel (2d ed., 1984); v.4, Classical vocal music in print, by Thomas R. Nardone (1976); v.5, Orchestral music in print, by Margaret K. Farish (1979); v.6, String music in print, by Margaret K. Farish (2d ed., 1980).

Compiled from publishers' catalogs with the aim of providing an ongoing record of music in print. Revised editions and interim supplements for individual volumes are published from time to time, and the full series is kept up-to-date on an annual basis by:

Music in print annual supplement. 1979– . Philadelphia, Musicdata, 1979– . Annual. **BH90a**

"Each year's Supplement contains a separate section updating each volume already published in the . . . series. The updates are cumulative, so that only the latest Supplement is needed, in addition to the base volumes of the series. . . . When special supplements or revised editions of the base volumes are published, the listings from the Annual Supplement are incorporated in them and dropped from the Supplement. . . . "—*Guide to use.* ML118.M83

U.S. Library of Congress. Library of Congress catalog—Music and phonorecords, 1953–72. Wash., 1953–72. Semiannual. **BH91**

Subtitle: A cumulative list of works represented by Library of Congress printed cards.

Issued semiannually with annual and quinquennial cumulations, the latter now forming part of the *National union catalog* cumulation, but independently numbered and available separately.

"*Music and Phonorecords* contains entries for music in the broadest sense. It includes music, phonorecords (i.e., sound recordings, musical and nonmusical), libretti, and books about music and musicians."—*Introd., 1963–67 cumulation.*

Superseded by: Z881.A1C328

National union catalog. Music, books on music, and sound recordings. Jan./ June 1973– . Wash., 1973– . Semiannual, the 2d issue of the yr. being the annual cumulation. **BH92**

At head of title: Library of Congress catalogs.

Supersedes the Library's *Music and phonorecords* (above).

"Music in the broadest sense, including music scores, sheet music, libretti, and books about music and musicians, is covered in this catalog. It also contains entries for sound recordings of all kinds, whether these are musical, educational, literary, or political."—*Foreword.* In addition to Library of Congress printed cards, cards supplied by seven cooperating libraries with extensive music collections are reproduced in the catalog.

Cumulations have been published for 1973–77 (8v.) and 1978–80 (7v.).

Keyboard instruments

Bedford, Frances and **Conant, Robert.** 20th century harpsichord music: a classified catalog. Hackensack, N.J., Joseph Boonin, [1974]. 95p. (Music indexes and bibliographies, no. 8) **BH93**

Works for solo harpsichord are listed by composer, followed by 33 sections for combinations of other instruments with harpsichord. Each entry gives composer, title, year composed, length of performance, and source for obtaining the music. Composer index; title index; list of composers' addresses. ML128.H35B4

Chang, Frederic Ming and **Faurot, Albert.** Team piano repertoire, a manual of music for multiple players at one or more pianos. Metuchen, N.J., Scarecrow Pr., 1976. 184p. **BH94**

An annotated listing of music available for two to four piano players, presented according to number of performers. Includes a list of recordings.

Cameron McGraw's *Piano duet repertoire* (Bloomington, Indiana Univ. Pr., 1981. 334p.) lists music originally written for one piano, four hands. ML128.P3C48

Hinson, Maurice. Guide to the pianist's repertoire. Ed. by Irwin Freundlich. Bloomington, Indiana Univ. Pr., [1973]. 831p. **BH95**

An alphabetical listing by composer, indicating available editions of the solo piano works. Anthologies and collections available are also listed by period and by country. Index of composers by nationality; lists of black composers and of women composers. Index of editors, arrangers, transcribers. ML128.P3H5

———— ———— Supplement. Bloomington, Indiana Univ. Pr., [1979]. 413p.

Lists new works, new editions of standard works, and earlier works inadvertently omitted from the 1973 volume. "Certain outstanding ragtime works are included as this type of music is a unique American contribution."—*Pref.* Besides the types of indexes provided in the earlier volume there is an index of compositions for piano and tape and one of compositions for prepared piano.

Hinson is also the compiler of *Music for more than one piano: an annotated guide* (Bloomington, Indiana Univ. Pr., 1983. 218p.). ML128.P3H5

———— The piano in chamber ensemble: an annotated guide. Bloomington, Indiana Univ. Pr., [1978]. 570p. **BH96**

A listing of compositions "requiring no more than 8 instruments" but involving "the piano on an equal basis."—*Pref.* Lists mainly works written after 1700 up to and including contemporary times. Arranged by number and combinations of instruments required, then by composer; publishers are indicated. Index of composers. ML128.C4H5

Kratzenstein, Marilou. Survey of organ literature and editions. Ames, Iowa State Univ. Pr., [1980]. 246p. **BH97**

"This book originally appeared as a series of articles in *The Diapason* (1971–1977) ... but with the list of editions [now] substantially augmented."—*Pref.* Offers a survey of the organ music of Western Europe and the United States, country by country, giving some history of the development of the music and the instrument, major composers for the organ, and schools. Each country essay concludes with a list of editions arranged by composer and collections arranged by title. Bibliography, p.216–30; name and subject indexes. ML600.K73

Vocal

Edwards, J. Michele. Literature for voices in combination with electronic and tape music, an annotated bibliography. Ann Arbor, Music Lib. Assoc., 1977. 194p. (MLA index and bibliography ser., no.17) **BH98**

A listing of 400 compositions for at least three live performers who sing or speak "in combination with electronic and tape music ... from the earliest known works through 1975 .... Second, the bibliography is a finding list of compositions currently available to performers."—*Pref.* Arranged by composer, with "Index by medium" (e.g., mixed choir, mixed choir and keyboard, etc.). Directory of addresses for publishers, non-score sources, foreign and hard-to-

find record labels, studios. Selected bibliography of sources, p.179–82. ML128.E4E37

Espina, Noni. Repertoire for the solo voice; a fully annotated guide to works for the solo voice published in modern editions and covering material from the 13th century to the present. Metuchen, N.J., Scarecrow Pr., 1977. 2v. (1290p.) **BH99**

The solos cited are mainly based on the voice-piano editions available through the fall of 1975. Arranged by nationality, then by special forms—opera, display songs, traditional songs and spirituals. Most sections are subdivided by type of voice. "Indices of the sources of the texts and the composers." ML128.S3E8

May, James D. Avant-garde choral music; an annotated selected bibliography. Metuchen, N.J., Scarecrow Pr., 1977. 258p. **BH100**

An "annotated bibliography of avant-garde choral compositions readily available from the music publishers of the United States" (*Pref.*) intended for use of high school, church, college and university choral directors. Gives full publishing information, voice requirements, accompaniment, supplementary requirements. Indexed. ML128.V7M43

Indexes and abstracts

Belknap, Sara Yancey. Guide to the musical arts; an analytical index of articles and illustrations, 1953–56. N.Y., Scarecrow Pr., 1957. 1v., unpaged. **BH101**

Lists some 15,000 articles and 6,000 illustrations, the former under both author and subject, in journals dealing with music, opera, the dance, and the theater. A considerable amount of the material, unfortunately, duplicates listings in the *Music index* (BH105).

For continuation, *see Guide to the performing arts* (BG45). ML113.B37

International Repertory of Music Literature. RILM abstracts of music literature. v.1– , Jan./Apr. 1967– . [Flushing, N.Y.], 1967– . Quarterly. **BH102**

"*RILM Abstracts* . . . publishes abstracts indexed by computer of all significant literature in music that has appeared since 1 January 1967."—*v.1, no.2.* Includes abstracts of books, articles (in periodicals or as parts of books), reviews, dissertations, iconographies, catalogs, etc. Classed arrangement with annual author-subject index. ML1.I83●

Krohn, Ernst Christopher. The history of music; an index to the literature available in a selected group of musicological publications. St. Louis, Mo., Washington Univ., 1952. 463p. (Washington Univ. Library studies, no.3) (Repr.: St. Louis, Baton Music Co., 1958) **BH103**

An index to material on the history of music appearing in some 40 periodicals, mainly German and English. Arrangement is by broad period divisions, further subdivided under such headings as "General studies," "Composers," and the various musical forms. Includes book reviews. Indexes by authors and composers. The material was collected in card-index form by the compiler over 25 years, but the periodicals covered are not confined to that period. ML113.K77

Music article guide. v.[1]– , Winter 1966– . Philadelphia, Information Services, Inc., 1966– . Quarterly. **BH104**

Subtitle varies; 1983: The nation's only annotated quarterly reference guide to selected, significant signed feature articles in American music periodicals geared exclusively to the special needs of school and college music educators.

Arrangement has varied; currently offers subject and author approaches, with full information appearing under the subject entry.

The short-lived *Popular music periodicals index* (Metuchen, N.J., Scarecrow Pr., 1973–76. 4v.) indexed relevant articles in 65 to 70 publications. ML1.M22795

Music index; the key to current music periodical literature. 1949– . Detroit, Information Service, 1950– . Monthly (cumulating annually).   **BH105**

Now indexes, by author and subject, about 350 periodicals, some of them selectively, representing various aspects of the music field, ranging from musicology to the retailing of music. Gives complete indexing for musical periodicals, and indexes articles pertinent to music in some more general publications. Includes obituaries, book reviews, and reviews of music performances and recordings.
ML118.M84

Zeitschriftendienst Musik; ZD Musik. Bd.1, no.1– , Jan. 1966– . Berlin, Deutscher Bücherverband, 1966– . Monthly, with cumulations.   **BH106**

A subject index to articles in about 60 music periodicals (mainly German publications, but some in other languages) with author index at back. Entries are cumulated from month to month; the final issue for the year includes all entries for that year, with cumulated author index and "Systematisches Register."   ML118.Z43

Encyclopedias and dictionaries

Algemene muziek encyclopedie. [Hoofredactie] J. Robijns en Miep Zijlstra. Haarlem, De Haan, [1979–84]. 10v. il.
BH107

1st ed. 1957–72 had title: *Algemene muziekencyclopedie.*
A dictionary of terms, musical forms, musicians, instruments, etc., covering all types of music from all periods and countries. Most of the entries are short and unsigned, an exception being coverage of the musical life of an individual country (e.g., 8½ columns are devoted to Belgium) and the history of a type of music (e.g., ballet music) or a musical style (e.g., baroque). These more extensive articles are signed and a brief bibliography is often appended. Handsomely and profusely illustrated. v.10 includes lists of musical terms and instruments with equivalents in several languages, and a section of corrections.   ML100.A4

Blom, Eric. Everyman's dictionary of music. 5th ed. Rev. by Sir Jack Westrup, with collaboration of [others]. London, Dent; N.Y., St. Martin's Pr., [1971]. 793p.   **BH108**

1st ed. 1946.
An excellent popular dictionary for quick reference, not for the specialist. Deals with Western music of the Christian era. Entries for terms, works, places, and biographical sketches (including living composers in this edition). Includes music examples.
ML100.B47

Britannica book of music. Benjamin Hadley, ed. N.Y., Doubleday/Britannica Books, [1980]. 881p. il.   **BH109**

From the wealth of material on music in various editions of the *Encyclopaedia Britannica* and from newly commissioned materials, the compilers have produced a dictionary of definitions; biographies of musicians, composers, critics; lengthy articles on musical forms or movements; descriptions of musical instruments, etc. Longer articles often include a brief bibliography or discography. Articles are unsigned; lacks an index.
The review in *Booklist* 77:1117 (Apr. 1, 1981) concludes that this item "is recommended as a quick-reference work for libraries serving the general reader" and that it serves as "a very good starting point" for serious investigation.   ML100.B848

Brockhaus-Riemann-Musiklexikon. Carl Dahlhaus und Hans Heinrich Eggebrecht, Hrsg. Wiesbaden, Brockhaus; Mainz, B. Schott's Söhne, 1978–79. 2v. il.   **BH110**

Offers short articles with brief bibliographies on people, terms, instruments, types of music (e.g., Arbeiterlied), etc. Especially useful for questions relating to German music.   ML100.B849

Dictionnaire de la musique; publié sous la direction de Marc Honegger. [Paris], Bordas, [1970–76]. 4v. il.   **BH111**

Contents: v.1–2, Les hommes et leurs oeuvres; v.3–4, Science de la musique: techniques, formes, instruments.
v.1–2 form an alphabetical biographical dictionary of composers

and others associated with music (e.g., music publishers, instrument makers, librettists, conductors, musicologists), both living and dead. Longer articles are signed; bibliographies are included.
v.3–4 comprise an alphabetical arrangement of survey articles on the music of individual countries, specific instruments and their development, forms of music, problems of acoustics, definitions of terms. Signed articles with bibliographies.   ML100.D65

Enciclopédia da música brasileira: erudita, folclórica, popular. São Paulo, Art Editora, 1977. 2v. (1190p.) and 2 records.   **BH112**

A dictionary devoted primarily to people involved with Brazilian music—popular, folkloric, or scholarly—but including entries for instruments, terms, etc. Most articles include a bibliography and/or a discography. Appendixes: discography of long-playing classical recordings by Brazilians; list of symphony orchestras in Brazil; music periodicals; list of Brazilian theaters (with a brief history). Title index; bibliography, p.1163–90.   ML106.B7E5

Enciclopedia della musica. Milano, Rizzoli, 1972–74. 6v. il.
BH113

At head of title: Rizzoli Ricordi.
A short-entry dictionary giving definitions, biographies, histories, etc., of music and musicians of all countries and periods, but strongest for European-based music. Each volume has an appendix giving for selected major composers a complete listing of all works (e.g., v.4 contains listings of the works of Liszt, Mozart, and Palestrina).
Another work of the same title under the editorial direction of Claudio Sertori was published by Ricordi, 1963–64 in 4v.

Encyclopedia of music in Canada. Ed. by Helmut Kallmann, Gilles Potvin, Kenneth Winters. Toronto, Univ. of Toronto Pr., [1981]. 1076p. il.   **BH114**

Concerned with "music in Canada and Canada's musical relations with the rest of the world" *(Introd.),* this compilation details "the activities and contributions of Canadian individuals and organizations in their great diversity" and discusses general topics in their Canadian aspects. Method of preparation and criteria for inclusion are carefully set forth in the introduction. Articles are signed with the initials of contributors (listed in the front matter). One or more bibliographic citations are included with many articles, and there are some discographies. General bibliography; list of abbreviations and acronyms used. Biographies include living persons. Index of "persons, organizations, companies, radio stations, churches, periodicals, schools, etc. that do *not* have their own entries."   ML106.C3E5

Encyclopedia of quotations about music. Comp. and ed. by Nat Shapiro. Garden City, N.Y., Doubleday, 1978. 418p.
BH115

A topical arrangement of more than 2,000 "wise, witty, and beautiful quotations about music."—*Introd.* Index of names and sources; index of keywords and phrases.   ML66.E6

Encyclopédie de la musique. [Publié sous la direction de François Michel en collaboration avec François Lesure et Vladimir Féderov et un comité de rédaction composé de Nadia Boulanger et al.] Paris, Fasquelle, 1958–61. 3v. il.
BH116

A general music encyclopedia particularly strong in biography, including contemporary Europeans. The biographical articles are not only more numerous but are usually longer than in Larousse (BH123). Illustrations in black-and-white and in color include facsimiles of music and manuscripts. Bibliographies are included with the articles; longer articles are signed. v.1 includes much "preliminary matter" (e.g., sections on the work of contemporary composers, discography, music libraries, institutions, organizations, chronologies, etc.).   ML100.E48

Encyclopédie des musiques sacrées, publiée sous la direction de Jacques Porte. Paris, Éditions Labergerie, [1968–70]. 4v. il.   **BH117**

Contents: v.1, L'expression du sacré en Orient, Afrique, Amérique du Sud; v.2–3, Traditions chrétiennes; v.4, Documents sonores [avec] commentaires.

Chapters on the sacred music of individual countries and various religious groups have been contributed by specialists; many include bibliographies or bibliographical footnotes. v.4 consists of eight recordings. ML102.E53

Entsiklopedicheskii muzykal'nyi slovar'. Avtor'i-sostaviteli B. S. Shteinpress i I. M. IAmpol'skii. Izd. 2-e., ispr. i dop. Moskva, Sovetskaiia Entsiklopediia, 1966. 631p. il. **BH118**

1st ed. 1959.
Brief articles on musical terms, forms, and instruments, and numerous biographical sketches. Many entries include bibliographies. ML100.E58

Grosse Lexikon der Musik in acht Bänden. Hrsg. von Marc Honegger und Günther Massenkeil. Freiburg i. Br., Basel, Herder, [1978–82]. 8v. **BH119**

This is a revised translation of *Dictionnaire de la musique* (BH111). Articles from the French edition have been translated, revised, and in some cases expanded (e.g., articles on harmony and music theory). Bibliographies at the end of articles have been revised and updated, with very current citations given.
A German translation of Gerald Abraham's *Concise Oxford history of music* has been published as v.9–10 of the set, with title *Geschichte der Musik.* ML105.D5515

The international cyclopedia of music and musicians. 11th ed. N.Y., Dodd, Mead, [1985]. 2609p. il. **BH120**

"Editor in chief, Oscar Thompson; editor, fifth–eighth editions, Nicolas Slonimsky; editor, ninth edition, Robert Sabin; editor, tenth and eleventh editions, Bruce Bohle."—*t.p.*
1st ed. 1939. Later editions show spotty revision, adding dates of death, making some corrections, and sometimes offering additional material in the appendixes. The 11th ed. represents a reprinting of the previous edition (2511p.), with the addition of an addenda section (p.2513–2609) consisting of about a thousand entries which revise and extend the articles in the earlier pages or add new entries for items not previously treated. ML100.I57

Jablonski, Edward. The encyclopedia of American music. Garden City, N.Y., Doubleday, 1981. 629p. **BH121**

Entries are arranged alphabetically within seven chronological sections, each with a brief historical introduction. Biographical sketches predominate, but there are entries for individual works, terms, etc. Brief appendix of "American music on records"; index. ML100.J28

Kennedy, Michael. The Oxford dictionary of music. Oxford & N.Y., Oxford Univ. Pr., 1985. 810p. **BH122**

This is a revised and enlarged edition of Kennedy's *Concise Oxford dictionary of music* (1980), which was in turn a third edition of Percy A. Scholes' first and second editions of that title (1952–64). It is the work of a single compiler, not a condensed version of the *New Oxford companion to music* (BH130). Includes entries for composers and musicians (including living persons), individual compositions, musical instruments, terms, firms and organizations, etc. Lists of compositions are given for composers. ML100.K35

Larousse de la musique. Publié sous la direction de Norbert Dufourcq avec la collaboration de Félix Raugel et Armand Machabey. Paris, Larousse, [1957]. 2v. il. **BH123**

An international encyclopedia with articles on musical terminology, subjects, places, performing groups (such as orchestras), etc. Primarily a dictionary of subjects rather than of persons, although there are many biographical sketches, usually brief. Little on contemporary musicians or artists; for these the *Encyclopédie de la musique* (BH116) is much fuller. Articles are well balanced in length, and some are signed. Illustrations in black-and-white and in color are numerous and well reproduced. Lists of works by a composer are given under his name; other bibliographic references are at the end of each volume. ML100.L28

Mayer-Serra, Otto. Música y músicos de Latinoamérica. México, Ed. Atlante, 1947. 2v. il. **BH124**

An alphabetical encyclopedia covering history, biography (including living persons), folklore, religious music, musical instruments, terminology, legislation, etc., of all the countries of Spanish America. In some cases full bibliographies are given for composers. Includes portraits; musical examples; words and music of the national hymns of the various countries, etc. ML199.M3

Michaelides, Solon. The music of ancient Greece; an encyclopedia. London, Faber & Faber, [1978]. 365p. il. **BH125**

A dictionary of musical terms, instruments, dances, composers, critics, theorists, and poets and philosophers of classical Greek music. Bibliographies for most articles give both classical Greek sources and modern studies. Alphabetical index of entries in Greek characters. ML167.M5

La musica. Sotto la direzione di Guido M. Gatti; a cura di Alberto Basso. [Torino], Unione Tipografico-Editrice Torinese, [1966–71]. 2v. in 6. **BH126**

Contents: [pt.1] Enciclopedia storica. 4v.; pt.2, Dizionario. 2v.
A handsomely produced set with long, signed articles—chiefly biographical entries in the historical section, but including articles on musical forms and instruments and survey articles on the history of music in individual countries. The "Dizionario" includes hundreds of briefer, unsigned entries for persons and terms not accorded the fuller treatment in pt.1; cross references are given to entries in the first part. Bibliographies are provided in both sections. ML100.M895

Die Musik in Geschichte und Gegenwart. Allgemeine Enzyklopädie der Musik. Unter Mitarbeit zahlreicher Musikforscher des In- und Auslandes. Kassel, Bärenreiter, 1949–79. 16v. il. **BH127**

Friedrich Blume, ed.
Contents: v.1–14, A–Z; v.15–16, Suppl., A–Z.
A scholarly, comprehensive work, international in scope, with long, signed articles by specialists. Includes extensive bibliographical notes. Profusely illustrated. An indispensable reference work for research in this field.
A general index was promised, but has not yet appeared. ML100.M92

Muzykal'naia entsiklopediia. Gl. red. Iurii Vsevolodovich Keldysh. Moskva, "Sov. Entsiklopediia–Sov. Kommozitor," 1973–82. 6v. il. **BH128**

Offers signed articles with bibliographies. Includes much biographical material. ML100.M97

The new Grove dictionary of music and musicians. Ed. by Stanley Sadie. [London, Macmillan, 1980] 20v. il. **BH129**

Based on *A dictionary of music and musicians* by Sir George Grove (1st ed. 1878; 5th ed. and suppls. 1954–75), but virtually a new work retaining only about 3 percent of the material from earlier editions. No longer emphasizing the 19th century, the *New Grove* "seeks to discuss everything that can be reckoned to bear on music in history and on present-day musical life."—*Pref.* More than half of the entries are for composers, but performers, scholars, theorists, patrons and publishers of music, and people in other arts whose work was important to music are included. Terminology, musical genres, and forms are fully treated; and there are entries for institutions, orchestras, and societies, as well as for cities and towns with significant musical traditions. "The biggest departure [from previous editions] . . . lies in the dictionary's treatment of non-Western and folk music, far more extensive and more methodical than anything of the kind attempted before."
Most articles are signed (the approximately 2,500 contributors are listed in v.20); longer articles generally follow a uniform structure; and bibliographies include both studies used as source materials and recommended readings. Both older and fairly recent publications are listed in the bibliographies. The "work lists" for individual composers "are designed not only to show a composer's output . . . , but also to serve as a starting-point for its study."—*Introd.* British terminological usage may present occasional difficulty for the American user. There is adequate cross-referencing for most entries, and

Appendix A (in v.20) provides an "Index of terms used in articles on Non-Western music, folk music and kindred topics."

A series of reviews of individual volumes of the *New Grove* appeared in *Musical times,* v.122 (Mar.–June 1981).

ML100.N48

The new Oxford companion to music. Gen. ed., Denis Arnold. Oxford, Oxford Univ. Pr., 1983. 2v. il.   **BH130**

Although based on *The Oxford companion to music* originally edited by Percy Scholes and published in ten editions 1938–70, this is essentially a new work. Both broader in scope and more comprehensive in coverage than its predecessor, it is truly international without pretending to offer exhaustive treatment of non-Western music. Intended for the general reader; frequent suggestions for further reading are given. Articles, often many pages in length, concern the people who make music (mainly composers, including living persons), their careers and achievements; the musical environment or history of music in individual countries or geographic areas; and the music itself—individual works, instruments, forms, scales and modal patterns, music theory, etc. Many articles are signed; numerous cross references; illustrations appear in proximity to relevant text.

A review by Christopher Wintle in *TLS* (12-30-83, p.1451) asserts that "although the balance of entries is not yet right, and the quality of the material is disconcertingly variable, the framework has nevertheless been established for a small, modern encyclopedia, suitable for all those who have an essentially academic interest in music, and whose resources do not stretch to *The New Grove*."

ML100.N5

Orovio, Helio. Diccionario de la música cubana: biográfico y técnico. Ciudad de la Habana, Editorial Letras Cubanas, 1981. 442p. il.   **BH131**

Biographical sketches predominate, but there are entries for music organizations, instruments, and terms in Cuban music.

ML106.C8O7

Randel, Don Michael. Harvard concise dictionary of music. Cambridge, Mass., Belknap Pr., 1978. 577p.   **BH132**

A dictionary for the amateur musician and the general public, providing short definitions of musical terms, instruments, and compositions, together with about 2,000 brief biographies of composers and performers. Most of the non-biographical information is taken from Apel's *Harvard dictionary of music,* 2d ed. (BH138). Coverage runs heavily to Western concert music, but there are entries for non-Western music and for Western music outside the "classical" tradition (e.g., blues). Current popular music is not covered. No bibliography.

ML100.R28

Riemann, Hugo. Riemann musik Lexikon. 12. völlig neubearb. Aufl., hrsg. von Wilibald Gurlitt. Mainz, B. Schott's Söhne; N.Y., Schott Music Corp., 1959–67. 3v.   **BH133**

1st ed. 1882.

Contents: v.1, Personenteil, A–K; v.2, Personenteil, L–Z; [v.3] Sachteil.

A considerably revised edition of a standard work, with text and bibliographies brought up-to-date. The first 2v. include articles on persons only; v.3 is devoted to musical subjects. Covers all periods and places with strong emphasis on German music. Includes lists of works throughout the text, and also bibliographies.   ML100.R52

———— ———— Erganzungsband: Personenteil. Hrsg. von Carl Dahlhaus. Mainz, Schott, 1972–75. 2v.

Includes new articles and additions and corrections to articles in the 12th edition.

Sohlmans Musiklexikon. 2 revid. och utv. uppl. [Huvudred. Hans Åastrand]. [Stockholm], Sohlmans Forläg, [1975–79]. 5v. il.   **BH134**

1st ed. 1948–52.

A revised edition of this major Scandinavian music encyclopedia, offering signed articles on composers, performers, institutions, works, and movements of Scandinavian music. Many bibliographies. v.5 includes a list, arranged by broad topics, of articles in the encyclopedia (e.g., Popmusik, Scenisk Musik).   ML100.S66

South African music encyclopedia. Gen. ed., Jacques P. Malan. Cape Town, Oxford Univ. Pr., 1979–[84]. v.1–3. maps. (In progress)   **BH135**

Contents: v.1–3, A–O.

An effort to provide a comprehensive, scholarly account of music in South Africa from 1652 to 1960, with some later information supplied. Offers signed articles on music, both European and native (although coverage of the latter is admittedly not as full as could be desired), musicians, "accounts of music in cities and towns, church music, theatres and concert halls, music education, musical instruments, Afrikaans folk music, visiting artists from overseas, the early years of the gramophone industry and musical societies. . . . "—*Introd.* Bibliographies; cross references.   ML106.S66S7

Vinton, John, ed. Dictionary of contemporary music. N.Y., Dutton, [1974]. 834p.   **BH136**

British ed. has title: *Dictionary of twentieth-century music* (London, Thames and Hudson, 1974).

The work is "confined to [contemporary] concert music in the Western tradition" (*Pref.*) with jazz and popular music confined to general articles under those entries, and Asian music and folk music also confined to general surveys. Biographical entries are limited to composers. Many of the articles are signed; many include bibliographic references.   ML100.V55

Dictionaries of terms

See also BH15.

Ammer, Christine. Harper's Dictionary of music. N.Y., Harper & Row, [1972]. 414p. il.   **BH137**

Entries for musical terms (often with some brief historical background provided) and for composers. The Subscription Books Committee review in *The booklist* (69:1) recommends the work as a "systematic presentation of musical facts at a fairly basic level."

ML100.A48

Apel, Willi. Harvard dictionary of music. 2d. ed., rev. and enl. Cambridge, Belknap Pr. of Harvard Univ. Pr., 1969. 935p. il.   **BH138**

1st ed. 1944.

Emphasis is on the historical point of view. Omits biographical articles because other dictionaries cover that field. Contains definitions of all kinds, including many used in musical performance, and articles on music history, aesthetics, theory, etc. The bibliographies list books, periodical articles, and references to examples of music.

ML100.A64

———— and **Daniel, Ralph T.** The Harvard brief dictionary of music. Cambridge, Harvard Univ. Pr., 1960. 341p. il.   **BH139**

Brief articles for the non-specialist who does not require the lengthier explanations of the *Harvard dictionary of music* (above). Includes opera plots, songs, and compositions, but no entries for composers.   ML100.A63

Baker, Theodore. A dictionary of musical terms . . . with a supplement containing an English-Italian vocabulary for composers. N.Y., Schirmer, 1923. 257p. (Repr.: N.Y., AMS Pr., 1970)   **BH140**

Subtitle: Containing upwards of 9,000 English, French, German, Italian, Latin and Greek words and phrases used in the art and science of music, carefully defined, and with the accent of the foreign words marked; preceded by rules for the pronunciation of Italian, German and French.

At head of title: 24th issue thoroughly revised, and augmented by an appendix of 700 additional words and phrases.   ML108.B165

Bobillier, Marie. Diccionario de la música, histórica y técnico. Traducción de la última edición francesa, rev. y notablemente ampliada con multitud de artículos nuevos . . . Terminología y folklore español y americano . . . Barcelona, Iberia, [1946]. 548p. il.   **BH141**

Translation of the author's *Dictionnaire pratique et historique de la musique* par Michel Brenet [pseud.] (Paris, Colin, 1926).

This profusely illustrated edition includes many terms not in the French edition.

Fink, Robert and **Ricci, Robert.** The language of twentieth century music: a dictionary of terms. N.Y., Schirmer Books, 1975. 125p. **BH142**

A dictionary offering brief definitions of "the basic terminologies of chance music, computer music, electronic music, film music, jazz, musique concrète, multimedia, rock, twelve-tone music and other more traditional styles of music composition . . . , as well as . . . a number of instruments and performance practices that have developed as composers have searched for new means of expression. Also, new tools for musical analysis have been included along with many of the important movements in contemporary plastic and graphic arts which employ techniques and aesthetic points of view similar to those found in twentieth century music."—*Pref.* Appendix: "A topical listing of terms included." Brief bibliography.

ML100.F55

Katayen, Lelia and **Telberg, Val.** Russian-English dictionary of musical terms. N.Y., Telberg Book Corp., [1965]. 125p. **BH143**

Russian-English only. ML108.K33

Levarie, Siegmund and **Levy, Ernst.** Musical morphology: a discourse and a dictionary. Kent, Ohio, Kent State Univ. Pr., [1983]. 344p. il. **BH144**

"An earlier edition of this work was published by the Institute of Mediaeval Music, Binningen, Switzerland, [1980] despite the objections of the authors, who took the position that it was unauthorized, incorrect, and not truly representative of their work. The present edition is fully authorized."—*verso of t.p.*

The dictionary portion consists of long, discursive entries and constitutes p. 49–305. Appendixes of illustrations and quotations. Bibliography; index of composers and compositions cited.

ML108.L48

Picerno, Vincent J. Dictionary of musical terms. Brooklyn, Haskell House, 1976. 453p. (Studies in music, no.42) **BH145**

Intended for the undergraduate or the interested amateur. Terms are drawn from all forms of music (jazz, electronic, classical, etc.). "A selected annotated bibliography" is appended to direct the user to further information. ML108.P57

Read, Gardner. Thesaurus of orchestral devices. N.Y., London, Pitman, [1953]. 631p. **BH146**

A lexicon of instrumentation, including index of nomenclature and terminology in English, Italian, French, and German; abbreviations; list of composers and works; and list of music publishers.

MT70.R37

Roche, Jerome and **Roche, Elizabeth.** A dictionary of early music: from the troubadours to Monteverdi. N.Y., Oxford Univ. Pr., 1981. 208p. il. **BH147**

Concerned with music of the Middle Ages, Renaissance and early Baroque period—areas which the compilers feel are generally slighted in works on early music (which tend to stress the Middle Baroque and later periods). "The aim . . . is to deal, as fully as possible within a compact format, with the instruments, musical forms, technical terms and composers" *(Introd.)* of the designated periods. Some brief bibliographical notes; cross references. ML100.R695

Terminorum musicae index septem lingus redactus. Budapest, Akadémiai Kiadó, 1978. 798p. **BH148**

Title also in English: *Polyglot dictionary of musical terms.*
Horst Leuchtmann, ed. in chief.
Terms in English, German, French, Italian, Spanish, Hungarian, and Russian are given in a single alphabetical sequence, with equivalents in each of the other languages. The base word is in the language from which the word originated or, if not in one of the seven languages of the dictionary, in German; cross references are given from terms in the other languages to the base word. Separate

Cyrillic alphabet section. An appendix gives equivalents in all seven languages and a large range of instruments through drawings and diagrams. ML108.T4

Vannes, René. Essai de terminologie musicale. Dictionnaire universel comprenant plus de 15,000 termes de musique en italien, espagnol, portugais, français, anglais, allemand, latin et grec, disposés en un alphabet unique. Thann, "Alsatia," 1925. 230p. **BH149**

Terms arranged in one alphabet by original language, with brief definitions and equivalents in the other languages. ML108.V18

Wörterbuch Musik/Dictionary of terms in music. Hrsg. von Horst Leuchtmann. 2. erw. Aufl. Munich, Verlag Dokumentation, 1977. 493p. **BH150**

"Englisch-Deutsch/Deutsch-Englisch; English-German/German-English."—*t.p.*
1st ed. 1964.
A dictionary of equivalent terms with separate sections for English-German and German-English. This edition expanded to include terms from music psychology and sociology, instrument-making, electronic music, acoustics, and dance as well as practical and theoretical music terms. ML108.W73

Directories

Benton, Rita. Directory of music research libraries, including contributors to the international inventory of musical sources (RISM). Prelim. ed. Iowa City, Univ. of Iowa, 1967–79. 4v. **BH151**

At head of title: International Association of Music Libraries. Commission of Research Libraries. v.4 publ. by Bärenreiter, Kassel.
Contents: pt.1, Canada and the United States; pt.2, Thirteen European countries; pt.3, Spain, France, Italy, Portugal; v.4, Australia, Israel, Japan, New Zealand.
The European nations covered in pt.2 are: Austria, Belgium, Denmark, Finland, Germany (East and West), Great Britain, Ireland, Luxembourg, Netherlands, Norway, Sweden, Switzerland.
v.1 appeared in a revised edition as: ML12.B45

Directory of music research libraries. Rita Benton, gen. ed. v.1, 2d rev. ed.: Canada: Marian Kahn and Helmut Kallmann; United States: Charles Lindahl. Kassel, Bärenreiter, 1983. 282p. (RISM. Ser.C) **BH152**

Bibliographies of relevant literature precede the directory sections. Combined index to the Canada and U.S. sections.

Brody, Elaine and **Brook, Claire.** The music guide to Austria and Germany. N.Y., Dodd, Mead & Co., 1975. 271p. **BH153**

ML21.B77

—— The music guide to Belgium, Luxembourg, Holland and Switzerland. N.Y., Dodd, Mead & Co., 1977. 156p. **BH154**

ML21.B773

—— The music guide to Great Britain: England, Scotland, Wales, Ireland. N.Y., Dodd, Mead & Co., [1975]. 240p. **BH155**

ML21.B78

—— The music guide to Italy. N.Y., Dodd, Mead, 1978. 233p. **BH156**

The above volumes are companion publications all following a similar plan. A summary discussion of music developments in each country is followed by notes for each major city, indicating guides and services available, opera houses and concert halls, libraries and museums, conservatories and schools, and musical organizations. Music festivals and competitions are also noted. Volumes are separately indexed. ML21.B783

Directory of music faculties in colleges and universities, U.S. and Canada, [Ed.4]– , 1972/74– . Comp. and ed. by Craig

R. Short. [Binghamton, N.Y.], College Music Soc., [1974]– . Irregular. (9th ed. 1982/84 publ. 1983)   **BH157**

Ed. 1–3 entitled *Directory of music faculties in American colleges and universities* (publ. 1967–70).

Lists music faculty members at institutions of higher learning. In four sections: (1) alphabetical listing by state of names and addresses of colleges and universities, with list of faculty members and area of teaching interest; (2) list of faculty members by area of interest; (3) alphabetical listing by name of faculty member; (4) listing of schools by type of degree offered (e.g., M.A. in ethnomusicology).   ML13.D57

Gusikoff, Lynne. Guide to musical America. N.Y., Facts on File, [1984]. 347p. il., maps.   **BH158**

Aims "to present historic highlights of different styles of music as they developed in particular regions of the United States at various times; and to specify certain geographic locations where one may hear different styles of music today."—*Introd.* Arranged by region, with brief introductory notes on types and development of music therein, and state/city directories of performing arts centers, festivals, etc. Indexed.   ML200.G95

International music guide, 1977– . London, Tantivy Pr.; Cranbury, N.J., A. S. Barnes, [1976–]. il. Annual.   **BH159**

Derek Elley, ed.

Similar to, and produced by, the same group as the *International film guide* (BG265), "surveying internationally all points of interest to the modern concertgoer and general music-lover."—*Introd.* Includes a survey of music of the year in various countries, a review of recordings, directories of festivals, music magazines, music shops, and music schools.

Music industry directory. Ed.7– , 1983– . Chicago, Marquis Professional Pubns., 1983– . Irregular.   **BH160**

Continues *The musician's guide,* 1st–6th eds., 1954–80.

Provides directory information on many aspects of the music profession and industry. 7th ed. in seven sections: (1) Organizations and councils; (2) Competitions, awards and grants; (3) Education; (4) Resources (including publications, reference works, etc.); (5) Performance (orchestras, opera companies, etc.); (6) Profession; (7) Trade and industry. Sections are separately indexed.

Pavlakis, Christopher. The American music handbook. N.Y., Free Pr., [1974]. 836p.   **BH161**

Intends "to bring together information on all areas of organized musical activity in the United States."—*Introd.* About 5,000 entries for service organizations and institutions, performing groups and ensembles, music societies, schools of music, music libraries and archives, individual composers, conductors, performers, etc. Arranged by broad groupings, with index of names, institutions, etc.   ML13.P39

Penney, Barbara. Music in British libraries: a directory of resources. 3d ed. London, Lib. Assoc., [1981]. 452p.   **BH162**

1st–2d eds. (1971–74) by Maureen W. Long.

A directory of music collections in British libraries. Information was derived from questionnaires and includes library address, chief personnel, hours of opening, restrictions on use (if any), type and size of collections, services offered, etc. Greater emphasis in this edition on special collections of books, printed music, manuscripts, and sound recordings. Index of place names and names of libraries; index of composers, types of music, and names of collections.   ML21.G7P4

Rabin, Carol Price. A guide to music festivals in America. Rev. and enl. Stockbridge, Mass., Berkshire Traveller, [1983]. 286p. il.   **BH163**

Describes 170 music festivals, classical and popular, held in 43 states, giving something of the history and flavor of each event, and name of director. Entries include information on where to write for tickets and for accommodations. Indexed by name of festival. Rock festivals have not been included.   ML35.R2

—— Music festivals in Europe and Britain. Stockbridge, Mass., Berkshire Traveller, [1984]. 191p. il.   **BH164**

A listing by country of the major European music festivals. Entries are similar to those for the compiler's book on music festivals in America.   ML35.R23

Resources of American music history: a directory of source materials from Colonial times to World War II. D. W. Krummel [and others, eds.]. Urbana, Univ. of Illinois Pr., [1981]. 463p.   **BH165**

Offers a survey of the evidence of American musical life and activity "as recorded in documents located in 3000 repositories in the United States and abroad."—*Introd.* In soliciting information from repositories, ten general types of documents were mentioned: sheet music; songbooks; other printed music (opera scores, band or orchestra music, etc.); manuscript music; programs for concerts, etc.; catalogs of music publishers and dealers; organizational papers and archives of music groups, clubs, orchestras, opera houses, commercial firms, etc.; personal papers; pictures; sound recordings (including oral history tapes). Entries give name and address of the repository, with notes on types of collections and extent of holdings; criteria for the descriptive notes are carefully set out, and names of respondents to the editorial inquiries are given. Geographical arrangement (i.e., by states of the United States, U.S. territories, Canada, other countries). Index of personal and institutional names and subjects.   ML120.U5R47

Handbooks

Berkowitz, Freda Pastor. Popular titles and subtitles of musical compositions. 2d ed. Metuchen, N.J., Scarecrow Pr., 1975. 209p.   **BH166**

A listing of titles associated with works of serious music from 1600 to the present, with notes as to origin of name. Arranged alphabetically in English except where the foreign-language title is well known. Includes bibliography and list of composers.   ML113.B39

Burbank, Richard. Twentieth century music. Introd. by Nicolas Slonimsky. N.Y., Facts on File, [1984]. 485p. il.   **BH167**

A chronology of musical events from Jan. 1900 through Dec. 1979, tracing "evolutionary changes that have taken place in twentieth century music."—*Author's pref.* Includes opera, dance, instrumental and vocal musical events; births, deaths, debuts, etc., of relevant figures; and selected statements and quotations about music. Indexed.   ML197.B85

Dearling, Robert and **Dearling, Celia.** Guinness book of music. Enfield, Middlesex, Guinness Superlatives, [1981]. 288p. il.   **BH168**

A revised, expanded, and updated edition of the compilers' *Guinness book of music facts and feats* (1976). Emphasis is somewhat more on factual information, both general and esoteric, than on "firsts" and various extremes as is often the focus of Guinness volumes (though there is a great deal of out-of-the-way information to intrigue the browser). Topically arranged, with indexes of names and of instruments.   ML160.D27

Hodgson, Julian. Music titles in translation: a checklist of musical compositions. London, Bingley; Hamden, Conn., Linnet Books, 1976. 370p.   **BH169**

"The list gives in one alphabetical sequence the original or English language translation followed by the translation or original as the case may be."—*Pref.* No index.   ML111.H7

Johnson, Harold Earle. First performances in America to 1900: works with orchestra. Detroit, Publ. for the College Music Soc. by Information Coordinators, 1979. 446p. (Bibliographies in American music, no.4)   **BH170**

Under name of composer works are listed by type (overture, incidental music, etc.), with place and date of first performance of each work anywhere in the United States; also given are performing organization and conductor or soloist, together with extracts from contemporary reviews. Form and media indexes. An appendix gives a list of leading music critics prior to 1900 with name of newspaper and dates of affiliation; there is also a list of major auditoriums, theaters, and concert halls arranged by city. ML120.U5J6

Krummel, Donald William. Guide for dating early published music; a manual of bibliographical practices. Hackensack, N.J., Joseph Boonin; Kassel, Bärenreiter Verlag, 1974. 267p. il., facsims. **BH171**

At head of title: International Association of Music Libraries. Commission for Bibliographical Research.

"A summary of the 'state of the art' of dating early music" (*p.15*) issued between 1700 and 1860. In two parts: (1) "Synopsis," a summary of the methodology of dating; and (2) "National reports," a country-by-country summary of music publishing therein. Index of music cited. A perceptive review by Peter Davison appears in *The library,* 5th ser., 32:75–78 (Mar. 1977). ML111.K78

Norris, Gerald. A musical gazetteer of Great Britain & Ireland. Newton Abbot, Eng. & North Pomfret, Vt., David & Charles, [1981]. 352p. il. **BH172**

Similar in concept to literary gazetteers, but concerned with the places where composers, conductors, singers, pianists, etc., lived, stayed, worked or performed. Arranged by region, then by county and place. Indexed. ML285.N67

Priest, Daniel B. American sheet music: a guide to collecting sheet music from 1775 to 1975, with prices. Des Moines, Wallace-Homestead, 1978. 82p. **BH173**

Considers the history, the form, the covers, etc., of popular sheet music in the United States from the middle of the 18th century to 1975. The price list, p.40–80, gives (by title only) the cost of obtaining a copy based on late 1976 prices. Brief bibliography. ML112.5.P74

Music business

See also BH160.

Baskerville, David. Music business handbook and career guide. 3d ed. Los Angeles, Sherwood Co., [1982]. 553p. **BH174**

1st ed. 1979.

Presents a discussion of music as a profession; in six sections: (1) an overview; (2) songwriting, publishing, copyright; (3) business affairs (including agents, licensing, concert promotion); (4) the record industry (contracts, distribution, etc.); (5) music in broadcasting and film (including music for advertising); (6) career planning and development. The appendix reprints forms used by the Copyright Office and ASCAP, and there is a brief directory of professional organizations and trade associations. Indexed. A 4th ed. was scheduled for publication in 1985. ML3795.B33

Rachlin, Harvey. The encyclopedia of the music business. N.Y., Harper & Row, [1981]. 524p. il. **BH175**

The music business is defined as "the business of selling music" (*Introd.*), and this alphabetical arrangement of more than 400 articles treats a wide range of topics relating thereto, including contracts, copyright, awards, types of music, organizations and associations, "the artist's image," and terms having special meaning in the field. Cross references; useful appendixes of award winners, etc.

More about this business of music, by Sidney Shemel and M. William Krasilovsky (rev. & enl. 3d ed. N.Y., Billboard Pubns., 1982. 214p.) is designed "to help participants in the music and recording industries comprehend the intricacies of the business and their rights and obligations."—*Pref.* ML102.M85R3

Weissman, Dick. The music business: career opportunities and self-defense. N.Y., Crown, [1979]. 246p. **BH176**

Presents a discussion of the music business with much practical advice for the person wanting a career in music. Together with sections on the various aspects of the music industry (e.g., record

companies), agents and unions, contracts and lawyers, it describes the numerous career opportunities such as music therapy work, arts management, studio work, etc. An appendix lists colleges offering various kinds of music programs, and a directory of music business organizations. Glossary; annotated bibliography (p.218–42); index. ML3790.W4

History

Abraham, Gerald Ernest Heal. The concise Oxford history of music. London & N.Y., Oxford Univ. Pr., 1979. 968p. il. **BH177**

Not a condensation of the *New Oxford history of music* (BH182), but an attempt to present in one volume a history of the "main stream of Western music" (*Pref.*) from the music of Mesopotamia to "cross-currents after 1945." Except for the 19th century, there is some emphasis on less familiar compositions. The "Suggestions for further reading" section is arranged according to the chapter divisions, and is the work of specialist scholars. ML160.A27

Collaer, Paul and **Linden, Albert vander.** Atlas historique de la musique. Paris, Elsevier, [1960]. 179p. il. maps. **BH178**

Maps and plates, with accompanying text, to illustrate the history of music from primitive times to the present. ML160.C68

Grout, Donald Jay. A history of Western music. 3d ed. N.Y., Norton, [1980]. 849p. il. **BH179**

1st ed. 1960.

A survey intended as a text for music students, or for the general reader. Contains glossary, bibliography (p.761–99), and music chronology. Numerous illustrations. Title, subject, and name index. ML160.G87

Kinsky, Georg, ed. A history of music in pictures, ed. . . . with the cooperation of Robert Haas, Hans Schnoor and other experts, with an introd. by Eric Blom. N.Y., Dover, [1951]. 363p. **BH180**

A collection of approximately 1,500 illustrations—portraits, instruments, facsimiles, etc.—forming a pictorial history of music from the earliest times to the present. The pictures constitute the main part of the work, the brief text consisting merely of: (1) explanatory notes on each plate of illustrations, (2) indexes and contents, and (3) introduction and foreword. Issued in three editions: (1) original German edition, with title *Geschichte der Musik in Bildern* (Leipzig, Breitkopf, 1930); (2) French edition, *Album musical* (Paris, Delagrave, 1930), printed from the same plates of pictures with notes, indexes, etc., translated into French and a new French introduction; and (3) the English edition originally published in London (Dent, 1930), also printed from the original German plates with translation of text. ML89.K62

Oxford history of music. 2d ed. Oxford, Univ. Pr., 1929–38. v.1–7 and introductory volume. il. **BH181**

Contents: Introductory volume, ed. by Percy C. Buck. Early history, Middle Ages, Folk song, etc. 1929; v.1–2, Polyphonic period, by H. E. Woolridge. 2d ed. rev. by Percy C. Buck. 1929–32; v.3, Music of the 17th century, by C. H. H. Parry. 2d ed. with revisions and introd. note by E. J. Dent. 1938; v.4, Age of Bach and Handel, by J. A. Fuller-Maitland. 2d ed. 1931.; v.5, Viennese period, by Sir W. H. Hadow. 2d ed. 1931; v.6, Romantic period, by E. Dannreuther. 2d ed. 1931; v.7, Symphony and drama, 1850–1900, by H. C. Colles. 1934.

Originally published 1901–1905, 6v.; v.1–3 revised and reissued, 2d ed., 1929–38; the new *Introductory volume* was issued with the 2d ed. to serve as an introduction to the study of the history of music; v.7 is new, but other volumes (i.e., v.4–6), though called 2d editions, are virtual reprints of original editions.

An important history, indispensable in any library doing much reference work in musical history. A new edition is nearing completion: ML160.O98

New Oxford history of music. London, Oxford Univ. Pr., 1954–82. (v.1, 1957) v.1–5, 7–8, 10. il., pl. (In progress)
BH182

Contents: v.1, Ancient and oriental music, ed. by Egon Wellesz (1957); v.2, Early medieval music up to 1300, ed. by Dom Anselm Hughes (1954); v.3, Ars nova and the Renaissance, 1300–1540, ed. by Dom Anselm Hughes and Gerald Abraham (1960); v.4, The age of humanism, 1540–1630, ed. by Gerald Abraham (1968); v.5, Opera and church music 1630–1750, ed. by Nigel Fortune and Anthony Lewis (1975); v.7, The age of enlightenment, 1745–1790, ed. by Egon Wellesz and Frederick Sternfeld (1973); v.8, The age of Beethoven, 1790–1830, ed. by Gerald Abraham (1982); v.10, The modern age, ed. by Martin Cooper (1974).

Planned to be in 10v., plus an index volume, as an entirely new survey of music from the earliest times to the present. Written by outstanding authorities in their fields.   ML160.N44

Slonimsky, Nicolas. Music since 1900. 4th ed. N.Y., Scribner's, [1971]. 1595p.   **BH183**

1st ed. 1938.
Partial contents: Descriptive chronology, 1900–1969; Letters and documents; Dictionary of terms.

A chronology of musical events (with commentary on the events listed) makes up the bulk of the volume. Fully indexed.
ML197.S634

Biography

See also BH240.

American Society of Composers, Authors and Publishers. ASCAP biographical dictionary. 4th ed. Comp. for the American Society of Composers, Authors and Publishers. N.Y., Jacques Cattell Pr./Bowker, 1980. 589p.   **BH184**

1st ed. 1948.
More than 8,000 biographical sketches of individual members (both living and deceased) of ASCAP in this edition. List of publisher members, p.563–89.   ML106.U3A5

Anderson, Ruth. Contemporary American composers: a biographical dictionary. 2d ed. Boston, G. K. Hall, 1982. 578p.   **BH185**

1st ed. 1976.
Offers biographical sketches with information derived from questionnaires. Criteria for inclusion were "Birth date no earlier than 1870 and American citizenship or extended residence in the United States."—*Pref.* Those who have written only one or two pieces or those who write only teaching pieces, jazz, popular, rock, or folk music are omitted.   ML390.A54

Australian composition in the twentieth century. Frank Callaway and David Tunley, eds. Melbourne, Oxford Univ. Pr., [1978]. 248p. il.   **BH186**

Each of 22 chapters is devoted to a prominent Australian composer of the 20th century, discussing the composer's contribution and ending with a list of works and a discography. A final chapter presents an overall view of Australian composition and considers teachers, composers recently arrived in Australia, and expatriates.
ML360.5.A9

Baker, Theodore. Baker's Biographical dictionary of musicians. 7th ed., rev. by Nicolas Slonimsky. N.Y., Schirmer Books; London, Collier Macmillan, [1984]. 2577p.
BH187

1st ed. 1900.
A useful and reliable dictionary, giving compact biographies—varying from a few lines to several pages—of musicians of all ages and nations, with bibliographies of the musician's own works and works about him. New editions have appeared at irregular intervals (with some interim supplements) through the work's long history,

and it has grown steadily in number of musicians treated. This is a revised, expanded, and updated edition; it now includes selected popular singers, rock and roll musicians, singers in movie musicals, etc.   ML105.B16

Butterworth, Neil. A dictionary of American composers. N.Y., Garland, 1984. 523p. (Garland reference library of the humanities, v.296)   **BH188**

Offers biographical sketches of American composers who "have their music performed widely beyond their own immediate circle." —*Introd.* Does not include composers of light music and jazz unless they have produced music in other media. Foreign-born composers who have become American citizens are included. Biographies of living composers were submitted to the biographees for correction whenever possible. Appendix lists teachers and their pupils.
ML106.U3B87

Canadian Broadcasting Corporation. Catalogue of Canadian composers. Ed. by Helmut Kallmann. Rev. and enl. ed. [Toronto], Corporation [1952]. 254p.   **BH189**

Previous ed. 1947.
Bio-bibliographical notes on 356 composers, many of whom were living at time of compilation. Contains a historical outline of music in Canada; bibliographies of musical biography and the folk song in Canada; and a directory of musical publications.   ML205.C3C3

Claghorn, Charles Eugene. Biographical dictionary of American music. West Nyack, N.Y., Parker, [1973]. 491p.
BH190

About 5,200 brief biographical notes on American composers, lyricists, musicians, singers and teachers. Includes both living and deceased persons.   ML106.U3C6

———— Women composers & hymnists: a concise biographical dictionary. Metuchen, N.J., Scarecrow Pr., 1984. 272p.
BH191

Aims to be a "comprehensive biographical dictionary of women hymnists and composers of church and sacred music covering all leading Protestant denominations, many Roman Catholics and a few Jewish hymnists."—*Introd.* About 755 entries.

Jane W. LePage's *Women composers, conductors, and musicians of the twentieth century; selected biographies* (Metuchen, N.J., Scarecrow Pr., 1980. 293p.) is limited to essays on 17 women musicians.   BV325.C58

Cohen, Aaron I. International encyclopedia of women composers. N.Y., Bowker, 1981. 597p. ports.   **BH192**

Offers information on "5,000 women composers from nearly 70 countries, with complete biographies of 3,700 composers."—*Pref.* Includes lists of compositions. An appendix lists composers by country and century.

Cohen is also the compiler of the *International discography of women composers* (Westport, Conn., Greenwood Pr., 1984. 254p.).
ML105.C7

Contemporary Canadian composers, ed. by Keith Macmillan and John Beckwith. N.Y., Oxford Univ. Pr., 1975. 248p. il.
BH193

Sponsored by the Canadian Music Centre.
144 Canadian composers who have produced most of their works since 1920 are listed alphabetically, with a survey of their output and a list of musical works and bibliography.   ML106.C3C66

Ewen, David. American composers: a biographical dictionary. N.Y., Putnam's, [1982]. 793p.   **BH194**

Treats 300 composers from Colonial times to the present. Aims to provide in-depth treatment (especially of living composers), with greater biographical detail than is usually found in other dictionaries and encyclopedias, plus "a succinct description of each composer's musical style" (*Foreword*) and notes on the development thereof. Often includes a statement of the composer's artistic creed. Lists of principal works and brief bibliography for each composer. Index of programmatic titles.   ML390.E815

———— Composers since 1900; a biographical and critical guide. N.Y., Wilson, 1969. 639p. il.   **BH195**

Designed to serve as a replacement for three of the compiler's earlier publications: *Composers of today, American composers today,* and *European composers today* (originally published 1934, 1949, and 1954, respectively). Covers 220 composers, living and deceased, who have been writing music since the beginning of this century.   ML390.E833

———— Great composers, 1300–1900; a biographical and critical guide. N.Y., Wilson, 1966. 429p. il.   **BH196**

Intended as a "replacement" for the author's *Composers of yesterday* (1937), not merely a revision of that work. Includes biographies of about 200 composers, a number of whom did not appear in the earlier work.   ML105.E944

———— Musicians since 1900: performers in concert and opera. N.Y., Wilson, 1978. 974p. ports.   **BH197**

Replaces *Living musicians* and its supplement (1940–57).

Gives "detailed biographical, critical and personal information about 432 of the most distinguished performing musicians in concert and opera since 1900."—*Introd.* Musicians born in the 19th century are included if their major careers were in the 20th century; both living and deceased musicians are included. A few bibliographical references are given at the end of each biography; a classified list of musicians concludes the volume.   ML105.E97

———— The world of twentieth-century music. Englewood Cliffs, N.J., Prentice-Hall, [1968]. 989p.   **BH198**

Designed to replace the author's *Complete book of 20th century music* (1952). Arranged by composer, with a brief analysis of his style, biographical information on the composer, and a chronological listing of his works with programmatic and analytical information on each. Indexed.   ML390.E87

Fétis, François Joseph. Biographie universelle des musiciens et bibliographie générale de la musique. 2. éd. entièrement refondue et augm. de plus de moitié. Paris, Didot, 1867–70. 8v.   **BH199**

———— ———— Supplément et complément publiés sous la direction de Arthur Pougin. Paris, Didot, 1878–80. 2v.

Repr. of the complete 10v. series: Bruxelles, Culture et Civilisation, 1964.   ML105.F42

Harris, Sheldon. Blues who's who; a biographical dictionary of blues singers. New Rochelle, N.Y., Arlington House, [1979]. 775p. ports. (Repr.: N.Y., DaCapo Pr., 1981.)   **BH200**

Offers some 571 biographies of blues singers active between 1900 and 1977. For each gives a chronology incorporating personal and career information, a listing of major songs and influences, and brief quotations from articles assessing the singer's style plus references to other biographical sources (usually a periodical article or record jacket). Selected bibliography; film index; radio index; television index; theater index; song index; names and places index.   ML102.B6H3

Historical Records Survey, District of Columbia. Bio-bibliographical index of musicians in the United States of America since colonial times. 2d ed. Wash., Music Section, Pan Amer. Union, 1956. 439p. (Repr.: N.Y., AMS Pr., 1972)   **BH201**

1st ed. 1941; 2d ed. shows little change.

Title, foreword, and introduction in English, Spanish, and Portuguese.

Indexes biographical material in about 65 books giving biographies of musicians in the United States. Names are given in as complete a form as possible, followed by dates of birth and death when ascertainable and references to works in which biographical material is to be found.

"A list of special studies, biographies and autobiographies pertaining to the persons whose names appear in the Index," p.421–39.   ML106.U3H6

Hughes, Charles William. American hymns old and new: notes on the hymns and biographies of the authors and composers. N.Y., Columbia Univ. Pr., 1980. 621p.   **BH202**

Forms a companion to the collection of representative hymns from the 17th to 20th centuries, *American hymns old and new,* edited by C. W. Hughes, Albert Christ-Janer, and Carleton Sprague Smith (N.Y., Columbia Univ. Pr., 1980). That volume has its own indexes of first lines/titles, authors and composers, tunes, meters, and Bible verses, whereas this offers information about the hymns and their originators. Notes on the hymns are presented alphabetically by first line, followed by a separate section of biographical sketches of the authors and composers.   ML3270.H8

Humphries, Charles and **Smith, William C.** Music publishing in the British Isles from the beginning until the middle of the nineteenth century. 2d ed., with suppl. Oxford, B. Blackwell, 1970. 392p.   **BH203**

Subtitle: A dictionary of engravers, printers, publishers and music sellers, with a historical introduction.

A reprinting of the 1st ed. (1954) with the addition of a supplement of addenda and errata, p.357–90.

There are similar compilations for Paris and Vienna: *A dictionary of Parisian music publishers, 1700–1950,* by Cecil Hopkinson (London, Author, 1954. 131p.); and *Der Wiener Musikaleinhandel von 1700 bis 1778,* by Hannelore Gericke (Graz, Böhlaus, 1960. 150p.).   ML112.H8

The illustrated encyclopedia of black music. Consultant, Mike Clifford; authors, Jon Futrell [and others]; ed., Ray Bonds. N.Y. Harmony Books, [1982]. 224p. il.   **BH204**

Concentrates mainly on performers, but includes song writers and producers who have made an important contribution to black music. Lists selected recordings.   ML105.I39

International who's who in music and musicians' directory. Ed. by Ernest Kay. 7th ed.– . Cambridge, Melrose Pr. (distr. in U.S. by Rowman & Littlefield), 1975– . Irregular.   **BH205**

Publisher varies.

Represents a change of title for *Who's who in music and musicians' international directory* (eds.1–6, 1935–72). The 10th ed. (1984) includes biographical sketches of about 8,000 musicians. Scope has been expanded to make the work truly international, but no selection criteria are indicated. Appendixes now list professional orchestras, organizations, major competitions and awards, music libraries, conservatories, etc.   ML106.G7W4

Kürschners deutscher Musiker-Kalender, 1954. 2. Ausg. des Deutschen Musiker-Lexikons. Hrsg.: Hedwig und E. H. Mueller von Asow. Berlin, de Gruyter, 1954. 1702col.   **BH206**

1st ed., *Deutsches Musiker-Lexikon,* by Erich Hermann Müller, was published in 1929.

Gives brief biographical data on approximately 4,500 musicians —primarily German, Swiss, and Austrian—whose birth dates range from 1854 to 1939. Performing artists and composers of international reputation are included. An appendix lists 1,500 musicians who had died since the 1st ed.   ML106.G3D4

Kutsch, K. J. and **Riemens, Leo.** A concise biographical dictionary of singers; from the beginning of recorded sound to the present. Tr. from the German; expanded and annotated by Harry Earl Jones. Philadelphia, Chilton, [1969]. 487p.   **BH207**

A translation of *Unvergängliche Stimmen* (2. Aufl. Bern, Francke, 1966), with additions and corrections. Offers brief biographies, plus notes on the singers' recordings.   ML400.K9813

Pena, Joaquín. Diccionario de la música Labor; iniciado por Joaquín Pena, continuado por Higinio Anglés, con la colaboración de Miguel Querol . . . Barcelona, Labor, 1954. 2v. il.   **BH208**

Bio-bibliographical dictionary, covering all periods, places and persons, but especially strong on Spanish and Latin-American musical life. Articles are fairly extensive, including lists of works and bibliographies. Contains numerous portraits.   ML105.P4

Southern, Eileen. Biographical dictionary of Afro-American and African musicians. Westport, Conn., Greenwood Pr., [1982]. 478p. (Greenwood encyclopedia of black music)   **BH209**

" . . . draws together widely dispersed and, in many instances, heretofore unpublished information on more than 1500 musicians of African descent, including living persons as well as figures of the past."—*Pref.* Bibliographical sources are cited at the end of each article; much information was derived from questionnaires. References to discographies appearing in works cited in the select bibliography (p.447–52) are also given.   ML105.S67

Who's who in American music: classical. Ed. by Jaques Cattell Pr. N.Y., Bowker, [1983]. 582p.   **BH210**

Offers "biographical data on 6,800 members of the music community who are currently active and influential contributors to the creation, preservation, performance, or promotion of serious music in America."—*Pref.* Thus, biographees include educators, librarians, writers, editors, organization administrators and executives, directors, patrons, etc., as well as composers and performers. Information was obtained mainly from questionnaires and concentrates on career and achievements, with current position and address. Geographic and professional classification indexes.

A 2d ed. with more than 9,000 biographical sketches was scheduled for publication at the end of 1985.

Bibliographies and indexes

Bull, Storm. Index to biographies of contemporary composers. Metuchen, N.J., Scarecrow Pr., 1964–74. 2v.   **BH211**

Concerned with composers who were "alive or born 1900, or later, or died in 1950 or later."—*v.1.* Information is given in columns: name, country with which the composer is identified, year of birth, country of birth (if different from the previous listing), date of death if known, indication (by abbreviation) of sources of further biographical information. About 4,000 composers listed in v.1; the second volume adds some 4,000 more names, plus further information on some of those included in v.1.   ML105.B9

Moldon, David. A bibliography of Russian composers. London, White Lion Publ., [1976]; Totowa, N.J., Rowman & Littlefield, 1977. 364p.   **BH212**

A bibliography of English-language books, essays, periodical articles, and some theses relating to Russian composers, i.e., "all composers born in countries comprising the present U.S.S.R."—*Pref.* Following a general section, arrangement is by name of composer, then chronologically by date of publication. Index of authors, editors and compilers, and a subject index.   ML120.R8M6

Skowronski, JoAnn. Women in American music, a bibliography. Metuchen, N.J., Scarecrow Pr., 1978. 183p.   **BH213**

Lists 1,305 books and periodical articles which treat any aspect of women as composers or musicians. Topical arrangement with name index. Most entries are briefly annotated.   ML128.W7S6

MUSICAL FORMS

American Society of Composers, Authors and Publishers. ASCAP symphonic catalog. 3d ed. N.Y., Bowker, [1977]. 511p.   **BH214**

1st ed. 1959.
A listing of "26,000 symphonic, chamber orchestra, chamber ensemble (10 instruments or more) and choral works" (*Pref.*) by ASCAP members and foreign composers whose United States performances are licensed through ASCAP. Listing is by name of composer or arranger, with each entry indicating title, date, publish-

er, instrumentation, name of librettist if given, performance time, source of sheet music or manuscript.   ML128.05.A55

Bryden, John Rennie and **Hughes, David G.** An index of Gregorian chant. Cambridge, Harvard Univ. Pr., 1969. 2v.   **BH215**

Contents: v.1, Alphabetical index; v.2, Thematic index.
"The *Index* attempts to cover that portion of the chant that was in general use for a considerable period of time" and "draws its material from the modern printed chant books, from five selected manuscripts, and from certain special studies dealing with specific categories of chant."—*Introd.*   ML102.C45B8

Cobbett, Walter Wilson. Cyclopedic survey of chamber music . . . with supplementary material ed. by Colin Mason. 2d ed. N.Y., Oxford, 1963. 3v.   **BH216**

1st ed. 1929–30. 2v.
v.1–2 of the 2d ed. are reissues of the 1929–30 edition except for a few amendments to the text, and the insertion of symbols in the margin to indicate a further reference in v.3.
The first two volumes contain signed articles (in alphabetical arrangement) on subjects concerned with chamber music: topics, persons, instruments, organizations, etc.; biographies, with lists of composers' works, are included. v.3 is a selective survey of chamber music since 1929, with a bibliography, additions and corrections to the original edition, and an index of composers.   ML1100.C7

Davidson, James Robert. A dictionary of Protestant church music. Metuchen, N.J., Scarecrow Pr., 1975. 349p.   **BH217**

Terms evaluated as relevant to Protestant church music are defined and treated from the historical point of view. Includes many short bibliographies; index of personal names and institutions mentioned in the text. No biographical entries. This is the first phase of a "Dictionary of church music" projected by the author.   ML102.C5D33

Drone, Jeanette Marie. Index to opera, operetta and musical comedy synopses in collections and periodicals. Metuchen, N.J., Scarecrow Pr., 1978. 171p.   **BH218**

Indexes plot synopses appearing in 74 collections and four periodical series. In four sections: (1) collections indexed; (2) title index, with indication of collection or periodical in which a synopsis may be found; (3) composer index, with reference to the title section; (4) bibliography of additional sources. Intended as an extension of Rieck's *Opera plots* (BH246).   ML128.O4D76

Edson, Jean Slater. Organ-preludes. Metuchen, N.J., Scarecrow Pr., 1970. 2v.   **BH219**

Subtitle: An index to compositions on hymn tunes, chorales, plainsong melodies, Gregorian tunes and carols.
Contents: v.1, Composer index; v.2, Tune-name index.
The "tune-name index" includes, in musical notation, the first few measures of the tune.

———— ———— Supplement. Metuchen, N.J., Scarecrow Pr., 1974. 315p.

    ML128.O6E4

Ewen, David. Encyclopedia of concert music. N.Y., Hill & Wang, 1959. 566p.   **BH220**

A companion volume to the author's *Encyclopedia of the opera* (BH228), addressed primarily to the amateur concert-goer and record collector. Includes, in a dictionary arrangement, some "1500 of the best known compositions in all branches of instrumental music, past and present" (*Pref.*); biographies of composers, conductors, and performers; information on famous orchestras, ensembles, festivals, etc.; musical terms, forms, styles, and literary sources.   ML100.E85

Frankenstein, Alfred Victory. A modern guide to symphonic music. N.Y., Meredith, [1966]. 667p. il.   **BH221**

Designed "as a general guide to the orchestral literature commonly performed in the United States today" (*Foreword*), the work is based on the author's program notes for the San Francisco Symphony Orchestra. MT125.F83M6

Yeats-Edwards, Paul. English church music: a bibliography. London, White Lion Publ., [1975]. 217p. **BH222**

A classed arrangement of books, pamphlets, tracts, and theses published in England, 1500–1973, and dealing with music used in the "choral worship of the church" (*Pref.*), but excluding the oratorio as dramatic music, or 'programme' music."

Represents a revision of a Library Association Fellowship thesis originally accepted 1970. ML128.C54Y4

❖There are a number of compilations listing compositions available for specific instruments or types of instruments, voices, etc. Examples of such publications are: *Klarinetten Bibliographie* by Eugen Brixel (Wilhelmshaven, Heinrichshofen, 1977. 493p.); *Singer's repertoire,* by Berton Coffin (2d ed. N.Y., Scarecrow Pr., 1960–62. 5v.); *Concert piano repertoire; a manual of solo literature for artists and performers,* by Albert Faurot (Metuchen, N.J., Scarecrow Pr., 1974. 338p.); *Music for the voice; a descriptive list of concert and teaching material,* by Sergius Kagen (Rev. ed. Bloomington, Indiana Univ. Pr., 1968. 780p.); and *Violin and keyboard: the duo repertoire,* by Abram Loft (N.Y., Grossman, 1973. 2v.).

Themes

Barlow, Harold and **Morgenstern, Sam.** A dictionary of musical themes. Rev. ed. N.Y., Crown, [1975]. 642p. **BH223**

1st ed. 1948.
The "Bartlett" for musical themes; contains some 10,000 themes of instrumental music arranged by composers, with a notation index arranged alphabetically by the first notes of the themes. Index of titles. ML128.I65B3

——— A dictionary of opera and song themes, including cantatas, oratorios, lieder, and art songs. N.Y., Crown, [1966]. 547p. **BH224**

A reprint of the work originally published under the title: *A dictionary of vocal themes* (1950). 1976 issue called "Rev. ed." (547p.).
Companion volume to the above. Contains themes from operas, oratorios, cantatas, art songs, and miscellaneous vocal works. Includes index to songs and first lines. ML128.V7B3

Brook, Barry S. Thematic catalogues in music. Hillsdale, N.Y., Pendragon Pr., [1972]. 347p. (RILM retrospectives, no.1) **BH225**

Subtitle: An annotated bibliography including printed, manuscript and in-preparation catalogues; related literature and reviews; an essay on the definitions, history, functions, historiography, and future of the thematic catalogue.
Supersedes the Music Library Association's *Checklist of thematic catalogues* (N.Y., 1954).
More than 1,400 items arranged by individual composer, compiler, publisher, or library collection. Index of names and subjects. ML113.B86

Opera

Eaton, Quaintance. Opera production, a handbook. Minneapolis, Univ. of Minnesota Pr., [1961–74]. 2v. **BH226**

v.1 gives information on the production of 259 contemporary and standard operas, with brief information on some 260 in the supplementary list. The second volume treats about 350 more operas. Each volume is divided as to "Long operas" and "Short operas" (90 minutes or less), and arrangement is alphabetical by title within each section. Includes synopsis, time, requirements of roles, chorus, orchestra, sources of scores, list of performing companies, etc. MT955.E25

The encyclopedia of opera. Ed. by Leslie Orrey. N.Y., Scribner, 1976. 376p. il. **BH227**

Offers short entries for operas and characters from opera as well as performers, composers, conductors, and designers selected for their "relevance to the contemporary scene . . . of music theater—opera, operetta, musical" (*Introd.*); emphasis, however, is on opera. Entries for music houses are found under name of the city in which located; there are also brief surveys of the history of opera in individual countries. Articles are signed with the initials of the contributor. ML102.O6E6

Ewen, David. Encyclopedia of the opera. New enl. ed. N.Y., Hill & Wang, [1963]. 594p. **BH228**

1st ed. 1955; this edition is identical to the earlier one except for a supplement of 19 pages preceding the text.
Aims to be a comprehensive source book about opera and opera performance. In one alphabet it covers: stories of the operas; characters; excerpts from operas; biographies (composers, librettists, singers, conductors, stage directors, impresarios, teachers, critics, musicologists, etc.); history of opera; opera houses and festivals; literary sources; special types of opera; technical terms. Pronunciation guide, p.557–94. ML102.O6E9

Grout, Donald Jay. A short history of opera. 2d ed. N.Y., Columbia Univ. Pr., 1965. 852p. il. **BH229**

1st ed. 1947. Also issued in 2v.
"The present edition aims to incorporate the results of recent research and to bring the history of opera forward to about 1960."—*Pref.* Bibliographies have been updated; new illustrations and musical examples are provided. ML1700.G83

Johnson, Harold Earle. Operas on American subjects. N.Y., Coleman-Ross, 1964. 125p. **BH230**

Covers operas on American subjects, written in America and abroad from 1658 to 1964. Arranged alphabetically by composer. Gives title, date, librettist, source, story, first performance with conductor, cast; cites reviews; includes publisher of vocal score. Subject index by topic and locale, and an index to titles. ML128.O4J6

Loewenberg, Alfred. Annals of opera, 1597–1940. 3d ed. rev. & corr. Totowa, N.J., Roman & Littlefield, 1978. 1756col. **BH231**

1st ed. 1943; 2d ed. 1955 (2v.) repr. 1970.
Lists nearly 4,000 operas, arranged chronologically according to dates of first performance, followed by the name of the composer and title of the opera (titles are given in the form in which they first appeared and in the original language; except for Italian, French, and German titles, a translation has been included), name of town where first performed, sometimes name of theater, and a history of performances. References to translations, revivals, etc.
Indexes: (1) Operas; (2) Composers, with dates of birth and death, giving the names of operas by each and dates; (3) Librettists; and (4) General index.
The review in *Booklist* 77:119–20 (Apr. 1, 1981) notes that this is "scarcely more than a reprint of the 1970 volume," and concludes that "those having the 1955 edition would do well to wait for the promised supplement, which will list premieres and revivals from 1940 to date. But libraries not having an earlier edition might wish to acquire this . . . and add the supplement when it appears." Unfortunately the supplement has yet to appear. ML102.O6L6

Martin, George Whitney. The opera companion to twentieth-century opera. N.Y., Dodd, Mead & Co., [1979]. 653p. **BH232**

In three parts: (1) Introductory essays; (2) Synopses; (3) Statistics. The essays discuss various aspects of 20th-century opera, with separate essays on Janáček, Puccini, Stravinsky, and Prokofiev. Synopses of 78 operas are given, selection having been based on "which twentieth-century operas are most performed, which have been recorded, and which seem to be gaining rather than losing popularity."—*Pref.* The statistics section presents a record of "what has been and is being performed in some of the world's opera houses." Indexed. MT95.M253

Mattfeld, Julius. A handbook of American operatic premières, 1731–1962. [Detroit, Mich., Information Service], 1963. 142p. (Detroit studies in music bibliography, no.5) **BH233**

Listing is alphabetical by title; gives dates of United States premières of nearly 2,000 operas. Index of composers. ML128.O4M3

Northouse, Cameron. Twentieth century opera in England and the United States. Boston, G. K. Hall, 1976. 400p. **BH234**

"Attempts to trace some of the basic details of the twentieth century opera subculture" (*Pref.*) by listing first performances of 1,612 20th-century English and American operas, an additional 941 operas for which complete performance information was not available, operas based on literary works, and published operas. Index of composers, librettists, opera titles, literary titles, and literary authors. ML128.O4N79

Rosenthal, Harold D. and **Warrack, John Hamilton**. The concise Oxford dictionary of opera. 2d ed. London, Oxford Univ. Pr., 1979. 561p. **BH235**

1st ed. 1964.

Includes entries for terms and characters in opera; brief synopses of operas; and biographical notes on composers, conductors, directors, producers, and singers.

Intended as a "concise but comprehensive work of reference— and perhaps also one of some entertainment."—*Foreword.* A thorough revision and updating, with facts rechecked and errors corrected. Coverage of operatic activities is extended to all countries; more biographies of singers and composers are included; and the number of literary references has been expanded. Articles often cite standard works on the subject. ML102.O6R67

Seltsam, William H. Metropolitan opera annals; a chronicle of artists and performances. N.Y., Wilson, 1947. 751p. il. **BH236**

A chronological record of the casts and of the operas performed from the first season of the Metropolitan in 1883/84 through 1946/47. Includes excerpts from press reviews for each season, especially those covering important debuts and first performances. Illustrated with photographs of the leading singers in typical roles. The index traces all references to artists, performances, reviews, and portraits. An 8p. "Index to composers" and list of errata was published in 1949.

———— ———— Supplement 1–3, 1947/57, 1957/66, 1966/76. N.Y., Wilson, 1957–78. 3v.

"Annals of the New York City Opera, 1944–1981," by George Louis Mayer and Martin L. Sokol, makes up a major portion of Sokol's *The New York City Opera: an American adventure* (N.Y., Macmillan, 1981. 562p.). It offers a season-by-season record similar to Seltsam's work for the Metropolitan Opera and has its own index. ML1711.8.N32M48

Simon and Schuster book of the opera: a complete reference guide. N.Y., Simon & Schuster, [1978]. 512p. il. **BH237**

A translation of *Opera: repertorio della lirico dal 1597,* ed. by R. Mezzanotte (Milan, 1977).

A guide to some 800 operas selected for their importance in the history of opera, their artistic quality, their popularity or acceptance by the public. Arranged chronologically by date of first presentation, beginning with "La Dafne" (1597) and ending with "Napoli Milionaria" (1977); amount of coverage increases for the more recent operas. Each entry includes synopsis, first performance information (including singers), short history and commentary, and, for later operas, critical reception. Indexes of titles, of composers and librettists, and of literary sources.

The review in *Booklist* 77:416 (Nov. 1, 1980) concludes that this "is an excellent supplement to, but not a replacement for, other reference books on the opera." ML102.O6O63

U.S. Library of Congress. Music Division. Catalogue of opera librettos printed before 1800, prep. by O. G. T. Sonneck. Wash., Govt. Prt. Off., 1914. 2v. (Repr.: N.Y., B. Franklin, 1967) **BH238**

Contents: v.1, Title catalogue; v.2, Author list, composer list, and aria index.

A detailed catalog giving for each libretto: full cataloging information, date and place of first performance, and valuable bibliographical and historical notes. Entry is first by original title, and then by replicas and translations, with reference from alternate, later, and translated titles. ML136.U55C45

———— Dramatic music . . . catalogue of full scores, comp. by O. G. T. Sonneck. Wash., Govt. Prt. Off., 1908. 170p. (Repr.: N.Y., DaCapo Pr., 1969) **BH239**

Arrangement is alphabetical by composer. ML136.U55D7

Who's who in opera: an international biographical directory of singers, conductors, directors, designers, and administrators. Also including profiles of 101 opera companies. Maria F. Rich, ed. N.Y., Arno Pr., 1976. 684p. **BH240**

A biographical directory of opera personnel active at the time of compilation. Inclusion was according to the following criteria: "Since the beginning of the 1971–72 season: singers must have sung at least five major roles with one or more of the designated companies [i.e., some 140 opera companies and festivals in 33 countries]; conductors must have conducted at least five operas with one or more of the designated companies; stage directors/producers must have staged at least two new opera productions with one or more of the designated companies; designers must have designed sets, costumes or lighting for at least two new opera productions with one or more of the designated companies. Administrators must have been in key administrative positions with any of the designated companies. . . . "—*Pref.* Includes 2,350 biographical sketches; information is meant to be current as of the 1974–75 season. ML102.O6W5

Discography

Celletti, Rodolfo, ed. Le grandi voci; dizionario critico-biografico dei cantanti con discografia operistica. [A cura del Centro-Studi Enciclopedia dello Spettacolo] Roma, Istituto per la Collaborazione Culturale, [1964]. 1044col. il. **BH241**

A dictionary of celebrated opera singers who have made phonograph recordings. Articles, most of which are signed, give biographical information with emphasis on roles sung, quality of the voice, etc. No bibliographies, but a discography of the singer's recordings of complete operas, individual arias, and selections from operas accompanies each article; these listings are generally very comprehensive. In addition, there is a list of complete opera recordings, and another of selections from opera. Despite the omission of certain notable singers, a useful volume, handsomely produced. ML400.C44

Harris, Kenn. Opera recordings; a critical guide. N.Y., Drake; Newton Abbot, David & Charles, [1973]. 328p. **BH242**

A guide for the collector. Operas are listed alphabetically by title, and a list of recordings available at press time is given for each (though not all those listed are evaluated in the text), followed by critical evaluation. Reference to older, out-of-print recordings is sometimes made. Evaluations admittedly reflect the compiler's personal taste. Index of artists, etc.

The Metropolitan Opera on record; a discography of the commercial recordings, comp. by Frederick P. Fellers (Westport, Conn., Greenwood Pr., 1984. 101p.), lists recordings from 1906 through 1972. ML156.4.O46H36

Plots

❖Many books, old and new, give plots or synopses of operas. They vary considerably as to the operas covered and in general treatment: some have short notes, some long ones; some discuss the music, some the performances, etc. Only a few of the most comprehensive and more recent are listed here. Various others, however, will be found in many libraries. *See also BH218.*

Kobbé, Gustav. The new Kobbé's complete opera book. Ed. and rev. by the Earl of Harewood. London & N.Y., Putnam, [1976]. 1694p. **BH243**

1st ed. 1919 entitled *The complete opera book;* rev. 1954, with later printings showing minor revisions. 1972 ed. entitled *Kobbé's Complete opera book.* This ed. (variously referred to as "4th rev. ed." and "9th ed.") reset and considerably expanded—new composers are represented, as are various operas not previously summarized.

The most complete general opera guide available. Discusses the development of opera, giving the stories of more than 300 operas, brief notes on the composers, illustrative musical phrases, dates of first performances, important revivals (with names of principal singers), etc. Includes older operas which are still being performed and modern works by contemporary composers. Indexed.
MT95.K52

Lubbock, Mark Hugh. The complete book of light opera. With an American section by David Ewen. London, Putnam, [1962]; N.Y., Appleton, [1963]. 953p. il. **BH244**

Intended to serve as a companion volume to Kobbé's *Complete opera book (see* above). Selection is limited to lightest genre of light opera, dating from mid-19th century to 1961. Contains some 300 "musicals" which "the visitor is likely to encounter" in Paris, Vienna, Berlin, London, and New York. Arranged by these places. Gives title, composer, story, source, and first-production information.
MT95.L85

Martens, Frederick Herman. A thousand and one nights of opera. N.Y., London, Appleton, 1926. 487p. (Repr.: N.Y., DaCapo Pr., 1978) **BH245**

A comprehensive book of opera synopses, including some 1,550 operas and ballets. Arranged chronologically by historical period of the subject. Synopses vary in length, some being very brief. Indexed by composer and title.
MT95.M23

Rieck, Waldemar. Opera plots. An index to the stories of operas, operettas, ballets, etc., from the 16th to the 20th century. N.Y., New York Pub. Lib., 1927. 102p. (Repr. from the New York Public Library. Bull., Jan.–April 1926)
BH246

An index by composers' names—with added detailed index of titles—to the outlines of plots contained in more than 200 books of synopses published in English, French, German, and Danish. The list of books indexed forms a useful bibliography of books of synopses.
ML128.L4R4

Musical theater

Bordman, Gerald Martin. The American musical theatre: a chronicle. N.Y., Oxford Univ. Pr., 1978. 749p. **BH247**

Describes in lively style almost every musical to appear on Broadway through the 1977/78 season; for the period before World War I, coverage includes the musical theater in Boston, Philadelphia, and Chicago. The pre-1866 period is merely summarized, but the arrangement thereafter is by theater season. Following an overview of the season pointing out developments, "hits," etc., musicals are listed by date of opening, with plot synopsis, performers' names, principal songs, and some estimate of the work's place in the history of the musical. Interspersed are brief biographical sketches of composers, playwrights, lyricists, actors, producers, and directors. An index of "shows and sources" lists the musicals with

the titles of works on which they are based and gives a separate list of sources and the musicals based on them. Index of songs; index of personal names. An exhaustive and enjoyable chronicle.
ML1711.B67

Ewen, David. Complete book of the American musical theater . . . N.Y., Holt, [1958]. 447p. il. **BH248**

Subtitle: A guide to more than 300 productions of the American musical theater from *The black crook* (1866) to the present, with plot, production history, stars, songs, composers, librettists and lyricists, illustrated with photographs.

Presented in textual form arranged alphabetically by composer. Lists of shows and songs; full index. ML1711.E9

Green, Stanley. Encyclopaedia of the musical theatre. N.Y., Dodd, Mead, [1976]. 488p. **BH249**

Offers "succinct information regarding the most prominent people, productions, and songs of the musical theatre, both in New York (incl. off-Bway) and London."—*Pref.* Includes a list of awards and prizes (with recipients), a table of "long runs," a brief bibliography, and a discography. ML102.M88G7

——— The world of musical comedy: the story of the American musical stage as told through the careers of its foremost composers and lyricists. 4th ed., rev. & enl. San Diego, A. S. Barnes, 1980. 480p. il. **BH250**

1st ed. 1960.

Each chapter is devoted to one or more composers and lyricists, with detailed record of productions of works. Appendixes include a list of shows with data on production, casts, and discography. Index of names and titles.

Principal changes in this edition involve chapters 22–31, and reflect the rise of composers and lyricists who have made significant contributions since the previous revision. The appendix has been extensively revised and updated to include new shows and important new recordings of scores.

Green is also the compiler of the *Rodgers and Hammerstein fact book* (N.Y., Lynn Farnal Group, 1980. 726p.). ML1711.G74

Lewine, Richard and **Simon, Alfred.** Songs of the theater. N.Y., H. W. Wilson, 1984. 897p. **BH251**

Effectively supersedes the compilers' *Encyclopedia of theater music* (1961) and *Songs of the American theater* (1973). Covers songs, both published and unpublished, from 1891 through 1983. "In the early period . . . lists all the important shows and scores of the era, the balance of our musical stage at the time still being devoted to vaudeville and imported operetta. Beginning with the mid-teens the book includes the songs from virtually every theater piece seen on Broadway" (*Pref.*), plus songs from Off-Broadway shows that ran 15 or more performances, or that were of unusual interest. Title listing with name of composer and lyricist, plus name and date of the show in which the song appeared. Index of composers, lyricists and authors; alphabetical list of shows, with dates and musical numbers; chronology of shows; index of films and television productions. ML128.S3L55

Lynch, Richard Chigley. Musicals! A directory of musical properties available for production. Chicago, Amer. Lib. Assoc., 1984. 197p. **BH252**

Intended as an aid to the amateur group wishing to choose a musical for stage presentation. Lists nearly 400 musical properties which were available at time of compilation, giving title, date of original production, playwright, composer, lyricist, plot summary, cast requirements, licensing agent, and available recordings. Indexed. ML19.L9

Discography

Hummel, David. The collector's guide to the American musical theatre. Metuchen, N.J., Scarecrow Pr., 1984. 2v.
BH253

An earlier version with the same title appeared 1978.

Contents: v.1, The shows; v.2, Index.

Aims to include "any musical presented on stage in the United

States."—*Introd.* Includes "musical comedy; musical drama; operettas; revues, including burlesque . . . ; one person shows; plays with songs; and a few plays with scores or musical background and no songs." Title listing of the shows, giving composer, lyricist, date and place of first performance, length of run, revivals, list of songs, notes on original cast, and a listing of all known recorded versions (including private tapes). Index of all personal names.

ML156.4.O46H85

Rust, Brian Arthur Lovell. London musical shows on record, 1897–1976. Harrow, Eng., General Gramophone Pubns. Ltd., 1977. 672p.   **BH254**

"An account of the recordings made between the beginning of disc-records in the 1890s and 1975 . . . of the work of artists appearing in musical productions on the London stage during those eight decades."—*Introd.* Pt.I is a chronological listing of all London musicals, including operettas and revues, regardless of whether any recordings were made; theater name and opening date are given for each. Pt.II is an alphabetical listing of shows from which recordings were made; for each show gives the name of the theater, opening night date, brief general description, list of principal cast members, and name of recording, its number and contents. Pt.III is a listing by performers of all recordings of each, whether or not from a musical show; an exception is made for performers from other musical forms (e.g., opera, radio) and only recordings of show music are listed for those individuals. Lacks an index.   ML156.4.O46R83

Gilbert and Sullivan

Dunn, George E. A Gilbert & Sullivan dictionary. N.Y., Oxford Univ. Pr., 1936. 175p. (Repr.: N.Y., Da Capo Pr., 1971)   **BH255**

Includes obscure words, phrases, allusions, foreign and colloquial words, names of persons, places and incidents, characters, original creators, successors, etc. Lists the operas with dates and theaters of first productions, etc.   ML410.S95D83

Hardwick, John Michael Drinkow. The Drake guide to Gilbert and Sullivan. N.Y., Drake, [1973]. 284p.   **BH256**

British ed., 1972, had title *The Osprey guide to Gilbert and Sullivan.*

Includes an index of characters, synopsis of each of the works (with quotations therefrom), index of first lines of songs, a glossary, and a discography.   MT100.S9747H3

Poladian, Sirvart. Sir Arthur Sullivan: an index to the texts of his vocal works. [Detroit, Information Service], 1961. 91p. (Detroit studies in music bibliography, no.2)

     BH257

In two parts: pt.1, index to operettas and other large vocal works by title, repeated catchy refrains, and important musical sections; pt.2, index to single songs, hymns, and miscellanea by title, first line, and tune name.   ML134.S97P6

Searle, Townley. Sir William Schwenck Gilbert; a topsy-turvy adventure. London, Alexander-Ousley, 1931. 105p.

     BH258

A bibliography of the works of Gilbert and of the Gilbert and Sullivan operas.   ML134.G4S3

Songs

Chipman, John H. Index to top-hit tunes, 1900–1950. Boston, B. Humphries, [1962]. 249p.   **BH259**

Contains 3,000 titles of American popular songs which have sold at least 100,000 copies of sheet music or 100,000 records. Listed by title alphabetically, and chronologically. Gives composer, publisher, and date; also indicates if featured in a film or musical.

ML128.V7C54

Day, Cyrus Lawrence and **Murrie, Eleanore Boswell.** English song-books, 1651–1702; a bibliography with a first-line

index of songs. London, pr. for the Bibliographical Society at the Univ. Pr., Oxford, 1940. 439p. il.   **BH260**

"The aim of this volume is to list, describe and index all the secular song-books published in England and Scotland between 1651 and 1702. The term secular song-book, as it is here somewhat arbitrarily used, means any publication containing the words and music of two or more secular songs."—*Introd.*

A detailed chronological bibliography of 252 numbered items, with indexes by first lines and by composers, authors, singers and actors, tunes and airs, sources, songbooks, printers, publishers, and booksellers.   ML120.G7D31

Ewen, David, ed. American popular songs from the Revolutionary War to the present. N.Y., Random House, [1966]. 507p.   **BH261**

A title listing of more than 3,600 popular songs, with indication of composer, lyricist, date, and films or musical productions in which the song may have been featured. A list of American performers and some of the songs associated with them is appended.

ML128.N3E9

Gooch, Bryan N. S. and **Thatcher, David S.** Musical settings of early and mid-Victorian literature: a catalogue. N.Y., Garland, 1979. 946p. (Garland reference library of the humanities, v.149)   **BH262**

A companion to the same compilers' *Musical settings of late Victorian and modern British literature* (below), but covering "published and unpublished settings of texts by prominent British authors who were, for the most part, born after 1800 and who lived to 1850 or later."—*Pref.* Follows the plan of the earlier volume; cut-off date for published settings is 1977. Index of composers and one of titles and first lines.   ML128.V7G58

——— ——— Musical settings of late Victorian and modern British literature: a catalogue. N.Y., Garland, 1976. 1112p. (Garland reference library of the humanities, v.31)

     BH263

A listing of texts set to music (both published and unpublished) up to July 1975. All authors included are British or "sufficiently identified with the English literary tradition" (*Pref.*), and all were "born after 1840 and lived to 1900 or later." Arranged by literary author, with each text identified by title, first line or literary form, and date of first publication; this is followed by the composer's name, the setting and publication information thereof, vocal specifications, and accompaniment. Indexes of authors and composers.

ML120.G7G66

Lax, Roger and **Smith, Frederick.** The great song thesaurus. N.Y., Oxford Univ. Pr., 1984. 665p.   **BH264**

A compendium of various lists (e.g., a chronology of "greatest" songs from the 16th century to the present; award winners; lyricists and composers with titles of their songs), the most extensive being of song titles (with a separate section for British titles). The "thesaurus" aspect of the work is provided by section IX, "Thesaurus of song titles by subject, key word, and category," which enables the user to find the full title, date and composer of a song of which only a portion of the title or the subject is known.   ML128.S3L4

Lowens, Irving. A bibliography of songsters printed in America before 1821. Worcester, Mass., Amer. Antiquarian Soc., 1976. 229p.   **BH265**

A songster is defined as "a collection of three or more secular poems intended to be sung."—*Introd.* These 650 collections are listed chronologically by title, alphabetically within each year. Geographical directory of printers, publishers, booksellers, engravers; index of compilers, authors, proprietors, and editors; title index. Locations are indicated for each collection.   ML128.S3L7

Rabson, Carolyn and **Keller, Kate Van Winkle.** National tune index microfiche: 18th-century secular music. N.Y., University Music Editions, 1980. 80 microfiche.   **BH266**

Includes a user's guide.

Almost 40,000 examples of British and American secular tunes gathered from 500 18th-century sources have been indexed by computer to "help identify the tunes and song texts, to suggest their relationship to one another, and to lead the researcher directly to the original sources."—*Pref.* The index has been issued on microfiche and is arranged as follows: (1) text index (title, first line, indicated tune name, burden index—usually the first line of the refrain or chorus); (2) music index (scale degrees, stressed notes, interval sequence); (3) source index (ballad operas, dance collections, instrumental collections, manuscripts, Playford's *Dancing master* 1651–1728, song collections, song sheets, theater works).

Further indexes are planned to cover sacred and folk tunes of the Americas. ML120.U5R12

Stecheson, Anthony and **Stecheson, Anne.** The Stecheson classified song directory. Hollywood, Calif., Music Industry Pr., [1961]. 503p. **BH267**

Arranged under some 400 catchwords and composers; gives titles, publishers, and sometimes dates, of about 100,000 popular songs. Includes list of publishers with addresses. Does not include a title index.

A supplement (69p.) was published in 1978. ML128.V7S83

Indexes

See also BB336–BB345, BH202.

Cushing, Helen Grant. Children's song index; an index to more than 22,000 songs in 189 collections comprising 222 volumes . . . N.Y., Wilson, 1936. xliip., 798p. **BH268**

In general, similar in plan to Sears's *Song index* (BH272), except that subject entries are added. Main entry, with full information, is under title, with cross references from alternate titles, different titles in different collections, translated titles, and original titles in certain languages (e.g., Russian), and from first lines and sometimes first line of chorus; and with added entries under composer of music, author of words, and subject. ML128.S3C9

DeCharms, Désirée and **Breed, Paul F.** Songs in collections: an index. [Detroit], Information Service, 1966. 588p. **BH269**

Indexes 9,493 songs in 411 collections, with separate sections for composed songs, anonymous and folk songs, carols, and sea chanteys. Index to all titles and first lines, and an author index. A useful complement to the Sears *Song index* (BH272). ML128.S3D37

Havlice, Patricia Pate. Popular song index. Metuchen, N.J., Scarecrow Pr., 1975. 933p. **BH270**

301 song books published between 1940 and 1972 have been indexed as an aid to finding both the words and music of folk songs, popular tunes, spirituals, hymns, children's songs, sea chanteys, and blues. Index by title, first line of song, and first line of chorus; index of composers and lyricists. ML128.S3H4

—— —— 1st–2d supplement. Metuchen, N.J., Scarecrow Pr., 1978–84. 2v. (368p., 530p.)

The supplements follow the plan of the basic volume, covering song books published to 1981 and picking up a few titles from the 1950s and 1960s.

Leigh, Robert. Index to song books. Stockton, Calif., Author, 1964. 237p. (Repr.: N.Y., DaCapo Pr., 1973) **BH271**

Subtitle: A title index to over 11,000 copies of almost 6,800 songs in 111 song books published [in the United States] between 1933 and 1962.

A title index to songs in books containing words and music. No entries for authors or composers. Serves as a partial continuation of Sears's *Song index* (below). ML128.S3L45

Sears, Minnie Earl. Song index. An index to more than 12,000 songs in 177 song collections comprising 262 volumes. Ed. by M. E. Sears, assisted by Phyllis Crawford. N.Y., Wilson, 1926. 650p. (Repr. with suppl.: Hamden, Conn., Shoe String Pr., 1966) **BH272**

—— —— Supplement; an index to more than 7,000 songs in 104 song collections comprising 124 volumes. N.Y., Wilson, 1934. 367p.

An important index, useful in the public, college, or school library, as well as in the music library. Contains titles, first lines, authors' names, and composers' names in one alphabet. Each song is indexed fully under its title, with added entry under composer and author, and cross references from first line and from variant or translated titles. Useful for finding: (1) words and music of a wanted song; (2) lists of songs by a given author or composer; (3) authorship of a poem when only its title or first line is known; and (4) whether or not a song has been translated, or is itself a translation, etc.

As many songs were originally poems which have been set to music, this index serves also as an index to poetry, especially for poems and translations not included in *Granger's Index to poetry* (BD302). ML128.S3S31

❖Various reference works listed elsewhere in this book, while not primarily concerned with songs, are frequently useful for supplementing the above indexes. *Notes and queries* (BD97) lists songs under the heading "Songs and ballads" in its indexes, and gives a considerable amount of information about these, sometimes with references to their location in collections not included in Sears's *Song index* (BH272). Larousse, *Grand dictionnaire universel* (AC39), has separate articles on about 600 songs entered under the French title, usually giving some information about the song and its author, the words in French, and the music (air only). The fine catalog of the Allen A. Brown collection of the Boston Public Library (BH11) analyzes many songs included in song collections. Two printed catalogs of the British Museum are very useful: its *Catalogue of printed music . . . 1487–1800* (BH64) analyzes many songs printed in periodicals, and its *Catalogue of manuscript music* (BH62) has two important indexes—one of sacred vocal music, and the other of secular vocal music—which give title and first-line indexing for many thousand songs. The Library of Congress *Catalogue of opera librettos* (BH238) has an aria index which serves as a key to songs included in operas.

Discography

Stahl, Dorothy. A selected discography of solo song: a cumulation through 1971. Detroit, Information Coordinators, 1972. 137p. (Detroit studies in music bibliography, 24) **BH273**

—— —— Supplement, 1971–1974. Detroit, 1976. 99p. (Detroit studies in music bibliography, 34)

1st ed. publ. 1968 as *Detroit studies in music bibliography,* 13.

Provides a listing by composer, title, and first line, of recordings featuring classical songs for the solo voice. ML156.4.V7S8

Jazz

Carl Gregor, *Duke of Mecklenburg.* International jazz bibliography; jazz books from 1919 to 1968. Strasbourg, P. H. Heitz, 1969. 198p. (Sammlung musikwissenschaftlicher Abhandlungen, Bd.49) **BH274**

Intended for "the serious friend of Jazz, the Jazz musician and the musicologist."—*Introd.* An author listing of more than 1,500 items, with indexes of names, countries, and subjects.

Supplements for 1970 and 1971–73 were published as Bd.3 and Bd.6, respectively, of *Beiträge zur Jazzforschung; studies in jazz research* (Graz, Universal Edition, 1971–75). ML128.J3C4

Case, Brian and **Britt, Stan.** The illustrated encyclopedia of jazz. London, Salamander Books; N.Y., Harmony House, 1978. 224p. il. **BH275**

Offers about 400 biographical sketches of jazz musicians from the last 50 years, giving brief biographical information, a discussion of the career, and a selected discography. Index of names mentioned within the articles. The review in *Booklist* 75:1390 (May 1, 1979) concludes that "Libraries owning Chilton's *Who's Who of Jazz* and Feather's and Gitler's encyclopedias of jazz for both the sixties and the seventies may not need *The Illustrated Encyclopedia of Jazz.* By itself, however, this is a good tool, especially for the small public library." ML102.J3C34

Feather, Leonard G. The encyclopedia of jazz. Rev. and enl. N.Y., Horizon Pr., [1960]. 527p. il. (Repr.: N.Y., DaCapo Pr., 1984) **BH276**

1st ed. 1955; supplementary yearbooks were issued 1956–58, with varying titles.

Contains biographical sketches of more than 2,000 jazzmen, with a guide to their recordings, history of jazz on records, recommended jazz records, bibliography, and discography. ML102.J3F4

——— The encyclopedia of jazz in the sixties. N.Y., Horizon Pr., [1966]. 1v., unpaged. **BH277**

Serves as a companion to the compiler's *Encyclopedia of jazz* (above), updating many biographies from that volume and adding new ones. ML105.F35

——— and **Gitler, Ira.** The encyclopedia of jazz in the seventies. N.Y., Horizon Pr., [1976]. 393p. il. **BH278**

Forms a companion volume to the two perceding items, extending the coverage through the 1966–75 period, adding some new names as well as updating biographical sketches in the earlier volumes. Adds results of polls published in *Down beat* and *Swing journal,* 1965–75; lists of jazz films and recommended recordings; and a brief bibliography. ML105.F36

Gold, Robert S. A jazz lexicon. N.Y., Knopf, 1964. 363p. **BH279**

Current and obsolete terms relating to jazz, with definitions according to historical usage. ML102.J3G6

Hefele, Bernhard. Jazz-bibliography . . . Jazz- Bibliographie. München & N.Y., Saur, 1981. 368p. **BH280**

Subtitle: International literature on jazz, blues, spirituals, gospel and ragtime music with a selected list of works on the social and cultural background from the beginning to the present.

Introductory matter in English and German; section headings in German.

A classed arrangement of about 6,600 items—books and periodical articles, predominantly English and German. Name index. ML128.J3H43

Jazz index: bibliography of jazz literature in periodicals and collections; Bibliographie unselbständiger Jazzliteratur. v.1, no.1– , Jan./Mar. 1977– . [Frankfurt/M., Norbert Ruecker], 1977– . Annual. **BH281**

Frequency varies.

Comp. by Norbert Ruecker and Christa Reggentin-Scheidt.

Introductory matter in English and German; subject headings in English only beginning with v.2.

Regularly indexes articles and reviews on jazz in more than fifty journals, with selective indexing of other journals which carry occasional articles on jazz. Beginning with v.2, record reviews were dropped, but book and concert reviews continue to be included. Articles on "blues" are listed in a separate section beginning with v.2.

Kennington, Donald and **Read, Danny L.** The literature of jazz: a critical guide. 2d ed., rev. Chicago, Amer. Lib. Assoc., 1980. 236p. **BH282**

1st ed. 1971.

Selective, but aims to list "all the significant material published in English up to the end of 1979."—*Introd.* Periodical articles are not included, but there is a list of jazz periodicals. Chapters are presented in the form of bibliographic essays on specific aspects of the literature, with a full bibliography at the end of each chapter. Name and title indexes. Chapters on blues and on jazz education are new to this edition. ML128.J3K45

Meeker, David. Jazz in the movies. [New enl. ed.] London, Talisman Books, [1981]; N.Y., DaCapo Pr., 1982. [336]p. il. **BH283**

1st ed. 1977.

Arranged by film title, with an index of jazz musicians. Notes on each film indicate jazz performers and numbers included. This edition incorporates information on films produced for television. ML128.M7M38

Merriam, Alan P. A bibliography of jazz . . . with the assistance of Robert J. Brenford. Philadelphia, Amer. Folklore Soc., 1954. 145p. (Pubn. of the American Folklore Soc. Bibliographical ser., v.4) (Repr.: N.Y., DaCapo Pr., 1970; N.Y., Kraus, 1970) **BH284**

Contains 3,324 items, arranged alphabetically by author, followed by a list of periodicals devoted to jazz, a subject index, and an index to periodical entries cited. ML128.J3M4

Discography

Tulane University. William Ransom Hogan Jazz Archive. Catalog of the William Ransom Hogan Jazz Archive: the collection of seventy-eight RPM phonograph recordings, Howard-Tilton Memorial Library, Tulane University. Boston, G. K. Hall, 1984. 2v. **BH285**

Reproduces the catalog cards (main and added entries) for the 78 RPM records in the Archive (which also has extensive holdings of relevant sheet music, oral history tapes, books, photographs, and manuscripts).

Charles Delaunay's *New hot discography: the standard directory of recorded jazz* (N.Y., Criterion, 1948. 608p.) is an older work which remains useful. ML156.2.T84

Electronic music

Cross, Lowell M., comp. A bibliography of electronic music. [Toronto], Univ. of Toronto Pr., [1967]. 126p. **BH286**

More than 1,500 entries; author listing with subject index. ML128.E4C76

Davies, Hugh. Répertoire international des musiques électroacoustiques. International electronic music catalog. Cambridge, Mass., distr. by M.I.T. Pr., [1968]. 330p. **BH287**

Intends as far as possible "to document all the electronic music ever composed in the almost twenty years since composers first began to work in this medium."—*Compiler's pref.* Listing is by country, then by city and studio. ML128.E4D39

Schwartz, Elliott Shelling. Electronic music: a listener's guide. Rev. ed. N.Y., Praeger, [1975]. 306p. il. **BH288**

1st ed. 1973.

Aims "to make the basic facts of electronic music as clear as possible for the typical 'listener'—the person who cares about music and its development but has little or no background in either the art of music or the science of electronics."—*Pref.* In addition to historical and introductory material includes a section of "Observations by composers," a section on tape composition at home, and a selected bibliography and discography. Indexed. ML1092.S37

Tjepkema, Sandra L. A bibliography of computer music: a reference for composers. Iowa City, Univ. of Iowa Pr., [1981]. 276p. **BH289**

Intended as "a comprehensive listing of books, articles, dissertations, and papers relating to the use of computers by composers of music."—*Pref.* Alphabetical author listing; index of subjects and of names other than those in the alphabetical sequence. Over 1,000 items. *See also* BH29. ML128.E4T55

Folk and popular music

Akademiia Nauk SSSR. Institut Mirovoi Literatury. Russkaia narodnaia pesnia; bibliograficheskii ukazatel' 1735–

1945 gg. Sost. V. M. Sidel'nikov. Moskva, Izd. Akademii Nauk SSSR, 1962. 169p. **BH290**

In two parts, chronologically arranged: pt.1, list of folk songs and poetry; pt.2, books and articles about Russian folk songs (in Russian). ML128.F75A4

Booth, Mark W. American popular music: a reference guide. Westport, Conn., Greenwood Pr., [1983]. 212p. **BH291**

An "inventory of resources for studying American popular music," offering "brief descriptions of books, periodicals, and special library collections" (*Pref.*) concerning various types of music (e.g., Tin Pan Alley, blues, ragtime, rock) from many periods. A historical sketch precedes sections on popular music in general and popular music before the twentieth century; subsequent chapters deal with specific types of music. Bibliography for each chapter; index.
ML102.P66B65

Bronson, Bertrand Harris. The traditional tunes of the Child ballads, with their texts according to the extant records of Great Britain and America. Princeton, N.J., Princeton Univ. Pr., 1959–72. 4v. **BH292**

An exhaustive, scholarly work including all known variants of the texts. Each ballad preceded by historical notes. v.4 includes a section of addenda to v.1–4 (p.437–513); a list of printed works and manuscripts referred to in the compilation; and indexes of sources, of tunes and ballads quoted, of singers, of authors and titles cited, and of persons referred to in various other capacities.
For Child's *English and Scottish popular ballads, see* BD665.
ML3650.B82

Brunnings, Florence E. Folk song index: a comprehensive guide to the Florence E. Brunnings collection. N.Y., Garland, 1981. 357p. (Garland reference library of the humanities, v.252) **BH293**

A title index of some 49,399 songs in the compiler's personal collection of 1,115 books and journals and 695 records. Includes references from variant titles. ML128.F75B83

Dean-Smith, Margaret. A guide to English folk song collections, 1822–1952, with an index to their contents, historical annotations, and an introduction. Liverpool, Univ. Pr. of Liverpool, in assoc. with the English Folk Dance and Song Soc., 1954. 120p. **BH294**

Indexes some 60 collections. ML128.F75D4

Fuld, James J. The book of world-famous music; classical, popular and folk. Rev. and enl. ed. N.Y., Crown, [1971]. 688p. il. **BH295**

1st ed. 1966.
Attempts to "trace each of the well-known melodies back to its original printed source."—*Introd.* With each entry a good deal of historical information is briefly presented, including biographical notes on composers and lyricists, many of whom are little known. Arrangement is by title, with the opening bars of the music given. Indexed. ML113.F8

Hoffmann, Frank W. The literature of rock, 1954–1978. Metuchen, N.J., Scarecrow Pr., 1981. 337p. il. **BH296**

A selective, annotated bibliography of books and periodical articles concerned with rock music arranged in chronological sections to reflect the historical development of the genre. Select discography. Indexed. ML128.R6H6

Kinkle, Roger D. The complete encyclopedia of popular music and jazz, 1900–1950. New Rochelle, N.Y., Arlington House, [1974]. 4v. (2644p.) il. **BH297**

Contents: v.1, Music year by year, 1900–1950; v.2–3, Biographies; v.4, Indexes and appendices.
v.1 offers year-by-year listings of Broadway musicals, movie musicals, and representative popular music (the last by year of greatest popularity, not by year of copyright). v.2–3 give brief career sketches (with discographies) of noted performers, lyricists and composers, bandleaders and sidemen, etc., in the field of popular music and jazz, with lesser coverage of light opera, blues, and country and western personalities. v.4 includes indexes of personal names, Broadway musicals, movie musicals, popular songs; appendixes offer lists of important recordings, *Down beat* poll winners, and Academy Award winners and nominees for music, 1934–72.
ML102.P66K55

Kunst, Jaap. Ethnomusicology, a study of its nature, its problems, methods and representative personalities. 3d enl. ed. The Hague, Nijhoff, 1959. 303p. il. (Repr. with suppl. 1974) **BH298**

1st ed., 1950, publ. under title *Musicologica.*
Contains bibliography (p.79–215) consisting of books and articles published before Sept. 1958 on music and musical instruments of non-Western people, on ancient and early European music and music instruments, and on Western folk music. Includes some 5,000 entries. Locates copies. Has indexes of subjects; peoples and regions studied; authors; collectors; musicians; and periodicals.

———— ———— Supplement. The Hague, Nijhoff, 1960. 45p.

Adds additional titles to the bibliography, all issued before Sept. 1958. ML3797.K8

Laforte, Conrad. Le catalogue de la chanson folklorique française. Nouv. éd. augm. et entièrement refondue. Québec, Presses de l'Université Laval, 1977–83. v.1–4, 6. (Les archives de folklore, 18–21, 23) (In progress) **BH298a**

Contents: v.1, Chansons en laisse; v.2, Chansons strophiques; v.3, Chansons en forme de dialogue; v.4, Chansons énumératives; v.6, Chansons sur des timbres.

To be in six parts, covering folk songs of the French-speaking people of Canada, the United States, and Europe. v.1 indexes the "chansons en laisse" by theme within 17 groups, referring to the list of sources (p.xxi–cxi) in manuscript, published form, and recordings. Indexes by title and subject. ML120.F7

Lawless, Ray McKinley. Folksingers and folksongs in America; a handbook of biography, bibliography, and discography. New rev. ed. with special suppl. N.Y., Duell, [1965]. 750p. (Repr.: Westport, Conn., Greenwood Pr., 1981) **BH299**

Previous ed. 1960.
The original volume is here reprinted, with a supplement which updates the earlier material and is separately indexed.
Offers a variety of useful material on the subject, including biographical sketches of singers; an annotated bibliography of collections of folk songs; checklists of titles and discography; and chapters on instruments, societies, and festivals. Indexes of names, titles, and subjects. ML3550.L4

Lomax, Alan and **Cowell, Sidney Robertson.** American folk song and folk lore, a regional bibliography . . . [N.Y., Progressive Educ. Assoc., 1942] 59p. (P.E.A. Service Center pamphlet, no.8) **BH300**

An annotated list of books and articles, arranged by regions and by work, dance, and worship songs. Included is a list of periodicals and of bibliographies. ML120.U5L7

McLean, Mervyn. An annotated bibliography of Oceanic music and dance. Wellington, Polynesian Soc., 1977. 252p. (Polynesian Society. Memoir, 41) **BH301**

Lists nearly 2,200 books, journals, articles, reviews, record notes, theses, and manuscripts relating to music, musical instruments, song texts, and dance in Oceania (i.e., "all islands of the Pacific, together with New Guinea and nearby islands including Torres Strait"—*Introd.*). Excludes Australia, Malaysia, the Philippines, and Indonesia. Materials are in English, French, German, Italian, and Spanish. Arranged alphabetically by author; the annotation includes a geographic or cultural area code based on Murdock's *Outline of world cultures* (1963). Area index.

———— Supplement: an annotated bibliography of Oceanic music and dance. Auckland, Polynesian Soc., 1981. 74p. (Polynesian Soc., Wellington. Memoirs, no.41, suppl.)

Adds more than 500 citations.

Mattfeld, Julius. Variety music cavalcade, 1620–1961; a chronology of vocal and instrumental music popular in the United States. Rev. ed. Englewood Cliffs, N.J., Prentice-Hall, [1962]. 713p.   **BH302**

Originally published (in a different form) first in the *Variety radio directory*, 1938–39, then in weekly issues of *Variety*. Lists popular music chronologically, with a brief account of various events occurring each year. Also includes hymns; secular and sacred songs; choral compositions; and instrumental and orchestral works. Only the musical items are indexed.   ML128.V7M4

Nettl, Bruno. Reference materials in ethnomusicology; a bibliographic essay. 2d ed., rev. Detroit, Information Coordinators, 1967. 54p. (Detroit studies in music bibliography, no.1)   **BH303**

1st ed. 1961.

" . . . not a survey of research studies but rather a summary of surveys and compendia, and an attempt to provide substitutes where surveys do not exist."—*Pref.* Full citations to the publications mentioned in the essay are listed at the end of the work.
ML128.E8N5

Nite, Norm N. Rock on: the illustrated encyclopedia of rock n' roll. N.Y., Harper & Row, [1978–85]. 3v. il.   **BH304**

Contents: v.1, The solid gold years (1st ed. 1974; updated ed. 1982); v.2, The modern years, 1964–present (1978); v.3, The video revolution, 1979–1984 (1985).

Each volume comprises biographical sketches (with discographies) of individuals and performing groups. Index of song titles.
ML105.N49

The Rolling Stone encyclopedia of rock & roll. Ed. by Jon Pareles; Consulting ed., Patty Romanowski. N.Y., Rolling Stone Pr./Summit Books, [1983]. 615p. il.   **BH305**

Intended as "a guide to the people who have made rock & roll. Each of the alphabetically arranged entries provides basic biographical information and, where appropriate, a selective discography or a discography plus group personnel chronology, followed by an essay that sums up the subject's life and career in music."—*Introd.*
ML102.R6R64

Roxon, Lillian. Lillian Roxon's Rock encyclopedia. Comp. by Ed Naha. Rev. ed. N.Y., Grosset & Dunlap, [1978]. 565p. il.   **BH306**

1st ed. 1969 entitled *Rock encyclopedia*.

An updated edition which tries "to reflect rock and roll as it is today, spotlighting the contemporary artists as well as the prototypical ravers."—*Introd.* Entries are mainly concerned with individuals and performing groups (with lists of recordings), but there are some definitions of terms in rock parlance.

The international encyclopedia of hard rock & heavy metal, by Tony Jasper and others (London, Sidgwick & Jackson, 1983. 400p.), is an alphabetical arrangement of entries for performing groups and individuals.   ML102.P66R7

Sandburg, Larry and **Weissman, Dick.** The folk music sourcebook. N.Y., Knopf, 1976. 260p. il.   **BH307**

Sponsored by the Denver Folklore Center.

Aims to "provide the reader with information about all aspects of North American folk and folk-based music."—*Pref.* Includes an annotated listing of records, books, and other instructional materials currently in print; information on buying and caring for folk instruments; lists of important folk festivals, archives, periodicals, films, folklore centers; and a glossary. Index of names, with a few topical entries.   ML19.S26

Shapiro, Nat. Popular music; an annotated index of American popular songs. N.Y., Adrian Pr., [1964–73]. v.1–6. (In progress?)   **BH308**

Contents: v.1, 1950–59; v.2, 1940–49; v.3, 1960–64; v.4, 1930–39; v.5, 1920–29; v.6, 1965–69.

Each volume presents a selective list of popular songs published during the period covered. Arranged by year, then alphabetically by title; gives author, composer, publisher, and first or best-selling record, with indication of performer and recording company.

Popular music, 1920–1979; a revised cumulation, by Shapiro and Bruce Pollock, was published 1985 (Detroit, Gale) in 3v.
ML120.U5S5

Simpson, Claude Mitchell. The British broadside ballad and its music. New Brunswick, N.J., Rutgers Univ. Pr., [1966]. 922p.   **BH309**

"The purpose of this book is to relate broadside ballads to the tunes for which they were designed."—*Introd.* Title entries (with music) for more than 400 tunes, followed by information on the origin of the musical setting and the uses to which it has been put. Index of titles, first lines, tune names, and refrains of ballads.
ML2831.S39

Stambler, Irwin and **Landon, Grelun.** The encyclopedia of folk, country, & western music. 2d ed. N.Y., St. Martin's Pr., [1983]. 902p. il.   **BH310**

1st ed. 1969.

An alphabetical arrangement of articles on individual performers and performing groups is followed by a section listing awards and a selected bibliography.   ML102.F66S7

Taylor, Paul. Popular music since 1955; a critical guide to the literature. London & N.Y., Mansell, [1985]. 533p.
BH311

Aims "to provide a critical, bibliographical guide to the literature of contemporary popular music published in English since 1955."—*Pref.* In eight main sections with numerous subdivisions: (1) General works; (2) Social aspects of popular music; (3) Artistic aspects of popular music; (4) The popular-music business; (5) Forms of popular music; (6) Lives and works; (7) Fiction; (8) Periodicals. Annotations; glossary; indexes.   ML128.P63T39

Vaughan Williams Memorial Library, London. The Vaughan Williams Memorial Library catalogue of the English Folk Dance and Song Society. [London], Mansell, 1973. 769p.
BH312

For full information *see* CF97.

Discography

Indiana. University. Archives of Traditional Music. A catalog of phonorecordings of music and oral data held by the Archives of Traditional Music. Boston, G. K. Hall, [1975]. 541p.   **BH313**

Photoreproduction of the classified catalog for a collection of materials "transmitted in the main by performance or word of mouth," which in music features "folk music, music of non-literate societies, non-European classical or art music, and popular music. Among the verbal forms . . . are folktales, jokes, proverbs, interviews. . . . "—*Pref.* Listing is by code (i.e., classification) number, with a note for each entry indicating geographic area or culture group, name of collector and date, and HRAF number based on Murdock's *Outline of world cultures* (1969). Indexes of geographic or cultural areas, subjects, collectors, performers, informants, and recording companies.   ML156.2.I53

International Folk Music Council. International catalogue of recorded folk music; ed. by Norman Fraser. London, publ. for UNESCO by Oxford Univ. Pr., 1954. 201p. (Archives of recorded music, ser. C: Ethnographical and folk music, v.4)
BH314

Text in English and French.

In two parts: pt.1, Commercial records, i.e., records that may be purchased; pt.2, Recordings held by institutions. Locates collections of authentic folk music in various countries.   ML156.4.F5I55

Lee, Dorothy Sara. Native North American music and oral data: a catalogue of sound recordings, 1893–1976. Bloomington, Indiana Univ. Pr., 1979. 463p.   **BH315**

Offers descriptions of 500 field, broadcast, and commercial recordings which feature the music of North American Indians (including Indians of Central America) and are available at the Indiana University Archives of Traditional Music. That collection includes transcripts from recordings collected at other museums and libraries such as the American Museum of Natural History. Each entry gives name of collector, culture group and area, year recorded, medium of recording, record company, number of hours, quality, documentation available, and subject descriptors. Index to subjects and to culture groups. The catalog is produced from computer printout and is sometimes difficult to read; indexing is not always precise and is not well explained. ML156.2.I55

Morthland, John. The best of country music. N.Y., Doubleday, 1984. 436p. **BH316**

Offers extended discussions of what the compiler considers to be the 100 most significant albums, plus briefer mention of about 650 others deemed of particular interest. Entries are grouped in sections such as "Early string bands and balladeers," "The depression years," "Singing cowboys," "Bluegrass," "The Nashville sound." Indexed. ML156.4.C7M67

Stone, Ruth M. and **Gillis, Frank J.** African music and oral data, a catalog of field recordings, 1902–1975. Bloomington, Indiana Univ. Pr., 1976. 412p. **BH317**

"The present catalog, based on the African Field Recordings Survey, provides concise summaries of collections of phonorecordings of music and oral data held by individuals and institutions throughout the world."—*Pref.* Information was derived from questionnaires, and the results are categorized by collector or repository, by country, and by culture group. Cross references; subject index. ML156.4.P7S8

Tudor, Dean. Popular music; an annotated guide to recordings. Littleton, Colo., Libraries Unlimited, 1983. 647p. **BH318**

" . . . represents a thorough updating and revision of the four separate volumes published by Libraries Unlimited in 1979 as *Jazz, Black Music, Grass Roots Music,* and *Contemporary Popular Music.*" —*Pref.*
Intended as a survey and buying guide for American popular music available on long-playing records. Arranged by categories, with numerous subdivisions: Black music; Folk music; Jazz music; Mainstream music; Popular religious music; Rock music. Annotations; performing artists index. ML156.4.P6T85

U.S. Library of Congress. Music Division. Folk music; catalog of folk songs, ballads, dances, instrumental pieces, and folk tales of United States and Latin America on phonograph records. Wash., [1964]. 110p. **BH319**

Similar catalogs were issued at irregular intervals beginning 1943. Lists 166 discs containing 1,240 titles, representative of the best of more than 16,000 records in the collection of the Archive of American Folk Song. These records are sold only by the Library of Congress. ML156.4.F5U5

————— Archive of American Folk Song. Check-list of recorded songs in the English language in the Archive of American Folk Song to July, 1940. Alphabetical list with geographical index. Wash., Lib., 1942. 3v. **BH320**

The alphabetical list, comprising v.1–2, gives title, name of singer, collector, and place and date of recording. v.3 is a geographical index of titles, arranged by state and county. ML156.U5A72

Music in motion pictures

International Music Centre, Vienna (IMZ). Music in film and television, an international selective catalogue, 1964–1974: opera, concert, documentation. Paris, UNESCO Pr., [1975]. 197p. **BH321**

Film and video-tape productions "shown between 1964–1974 at international IMZ events were taken as the basic stock . . . supplemented with representative international productions from the same period which the authors considered important."—*Pref.* In four sections: (1) music theater and opera productions; (2) concert music productions; (3) educational programs; (4) experimental programs. Indexes of titles, composers, producers, directors, performing artists, orchestra or performing groups, conductors, organi-

zations and companies (by country), title, production company (with addresses). ML128.M7I63

Limbacher, James L. Film music: from violins to video. Metuchen, N.J., Scarecrow Pr., 1974. 835p. **BH322**

A section of notes and comment on film music by various composers and writers is followed by an alphabetical list of film titles and dates, a chronological list of films and their composers, an alphabetical list of composers and their films (with dates), and a list of recorded musical scores arranged by film title. Covers through 1972. ML2075.L54

————— Keeping score: film music 1972–1979. Metuchen, N.J., Scarecrow Pr., 1981. 510p. **BH323**

Continues the listings in the preceding compilation. In three main sections: (1) Films and their composers/adaptors; (2) Composers and their films; (3) Recorded musical scores (a discography). ML128.M7L5

Pitts, Michael R. and **Harrison, Louis H.** Hollywood on record: the film stars' discography. Metuchen, N.J., Scarecrow Pr., 1978. 410p. il. **BH324**

Aims to "list recorded work of motion picture performers since the introduction of the modern long-playing record in 1948."—*Introd.* Listing is by performer; no index. Limited to musical performances. ML156.4.M6P58

Woll, Allen L. Songs from Hollywood musical comedies, 1927 to the present; a dictionary. N.Y., Garland, 1976. 251p. (Garland reference library in the humanities, v.44) **BH325**

" . . . provides a guide for . . . nostalgia buffs, allowing them to identify their favorite movie musical show tunes, and, if possible, find soundtrack recordings of them."—*How to use this book.* In four alphabetically arranged sections: (1) title listing of songs (with name of film); (2) title listing of musicals (with date of release, name of principal players, director, song writers, and, when available, recorded songs with name of record company and number; (3) chronological listing of musicals; (4) composers and lyricists. Name index. ML102.P66W64

INSTRUMENTS

Boston. Museum of Fine Arts. Leslie Lindsey Mason Collection. Ancient European musical instruments . . . by Nicholas Bessaraboff. [Cambridge], publ. for the Museum of Fine Arts by Harvard Univ. Pr., 1941. 503p. il. **BH326**

An authoritative historical study with excellent illustrations. Includes a useful bibliography of books about musical instruments and catalogs of collections. ML462.B6M22

Bowers, Q. David. Encyclopedia of automatic musical instruments. Vestal, N.Y., Vestal Pr., [1972]. 1008p. il. **BH327**

Subtitle: Cylinder music boxes, disc music boxes, piano players and player pianos, coin-operated pianos, orchestrions, photoplayers, organettes, fairground organs, calliopes, and other self-playing instruments mainly of the 1750–1940 era; including a dictionary of automatic musical instrument terms.
Arranged by types as mentioned in the subtitle; indexed. The dictionary of terms is on p.947–81. ML1050.B6

Coover, James. Musical instrument collections: catalogs and cognate literature. Detroit, Information Coordinators, 1981. 464p. (Detroit studies in music bibliography, 47) **BH328**

In two main sections: (1) Institutions and expositions (arranged by place); and (2) Private collections (arranged by owner). Appendixes provide a chronological listing of early inventories to 1825, and one of expositions and exhibitions, 1818–1978. The index includes names of auctioneers, antiquarians, and firms. ML155.C63

Farrell, Susan Caust. Directory of contemporary American musical instrument makers. Columbia, Univ. of Missouri Pr., 1981. 216p. il.   **BH329**

Aims to include "all contemporary American makers of musical instruments, regardless of the number of instruments they produce, the size of their shop, or whether they work full-time or part-time."—*Introd.* Does not include Canadians or Americans working abroad. Information (obtained mainly by questionnaires) includes address, beginning date of instrument-making, instruments available (or made to order), specific types of instruments made and number produced, etc. The main alphabetical listing is followed by lists by type of instrument and by state.   ML17.F37

Marcuse, Sibyl. Musical instruments, a comprehensive dictionary. Garden City, N.Y., Doubleday, 1964. 608p. il.   **BH330**

Describes musical instruments used throughout the world from earliest times to the present. Gives names in English with foreign equivalents. Includes numbered list of sources referred to throughout the text. Excellent illustrations, though limited to 24 plates.   ML102.I5M37

——— A survey of musical instruments. N.Y., Harper & Row; Newton Abbot, [Eng.], David & Charles, [1975]. 863p. il.   **BH331**

Known musical instruments of all periods are discussed within appropriate "family" sections—idiophone, membranophone, chordophone, aerophone. Glossary; brief bibliography; name and topic indexes.   ML460.M365S94

Music Library Association. A survey of musical instrument collections in the United States and Canada, conducted by a Committee of the Music Library Association: William Lichtenwanger, chairman and compiler. [Ann Arbor], Music Lib. Assoc., 1974. 137p.   **BH332**

Through questionnaires and personal visits, 572 collections (each having at least 15 items) were identified. That number includes 334 institutions, "mostly museums and historical societies, in which musical instruments are not segregated into identifiable collections but are rather scattered amongst many other artifacts on a geographic or other non-musical basis; . . . 41 other institutions that have either a single and separate musical instrument collection . . . or a multiplicity of more-or-less separate collections; and 197 private collections."—*Pref.* Not included are collections of replicas or of phonographs.

Arranged geographically, giving for each collection: name, address, curator, hours, brief description, any finding aids or brief descriptions. Index of collectors or institutions; index of instruments and classes of instruments; index of cultural, geographical, and historical origins.   ML19.M87

The New Grove dictionary of musical instruments. Ed. by Stanley Sadie. N.Y., Grove's Dictionaries of Music, 1984. 3v. il.   **BH333**

Although this work "takes its title, its method and approach, and some of its material" (*Pref.*) from the *New Grove* (BH129), much new material appears here, and there has been substantial revision of many articles derived from the larger work. Five broad categories of articles are included: (1) instruments of classical Western music; (2) makers of those instruments; (3) modern Western instruments (including electronic ones) and their makers; (4) performing practice; and (5) non-Western and folk or traditional instruments—the latter category being particularly well represented. Signed articles, with bibliographies; cross references; numerous illustrations, diagrams, and examples of music. List of contributors in v.3.   ML102.I5N48

Sachs, Curt. The history of musical instruments. N.Y., Norton, [1940]. 505p. il.   **BH334**

Bibliography, p.469–87.   ML460.S2H5

——— Real-Lexikon der Musikinstrumente, zugleich ein Polyglossar für das gesamte Instrumentengebiet; mit 200 Abbildungen. Berlin, Bard, 1913. 442p. il. (Repr.: Hildesheim, G. Olms, 1962; N.Y., Dover, 1964)   **BH335**

A comprehensive historical dictionary of instruments of all countries.   ML102.I5S2

Victoria and Albert Museum, South Kensington. Catalogue of musical instruments, by Raymond Russell and Anthony Baines. London, H.M.S.O., 1968. 2v. il.   **BH336**

Contents: v.1, Keyboard instruments, by R. Russell; v.2, Non-keyboard instruments, by A. Baines.

Catalog of an important collection of musical instruments dating from about 1530 to 1880.   ML462.L6S77

RECORDED MUSIC

Catalogs and discography

❖In addition to the items for which full information is given below, numerous older discographies and guides for the record collector are occasionally useful. These include: *Guide to long-playing records* (N.Y., Knopf, 1955. 3v.); *The record book; international edition. A guide to the world of the phonograph,* by David Hall (N.Y., Durrell, 1948. 1394p.); *Collectors' guide to American recordings, 1895–1925,* by Julian M. Moses (N.Y., Amer. Record Collectors Exchange, 1949. 199p.); *The complete entertainment discography from the mid-1890s to 1942,* by Brian Rust (New Rochelle, N.Y., Arlington House, 1973. 677p.).

Discographies of the musical theater, songs, jazz, folk and popular music are entered under those genres in the sections preceding this list. Other specialized discographies include: *Discopaedia of the violin, 1889–1971,* by James L. Creighton (Toronto, Univ. of Toronto Pr., 1974. 987p.); *Conductors on record,* by John L. Holmes (Westport, Conn., Greenwood Pr., 1982. 734p.); *Four centuries of organ music: from the Robertsbridge Codex through the Baroque era: an annotated discography,* by Marilou Kratzenstein and Jerald Hamilton (Detroit, Information Coordinators, 1984. 300p.; Detroit studies in music bibliography, 5); *American organ music on records,* by Lois Rowell (Braintree, Mass., Organ Literature Foundation, 1976. 105p.); *The American dance band discography, 1917–1942,* by Brian Rust (New Rochelle, N.Y., Arlington House, 1975. 2v.); *V-discs: a history and discography,* by Richard S. Sears (Westport, Conn., Greenwood Pr., 1980. 1166p.).

Bauer, Robert. The new catalogue of historical records, 1898–1908/09. [2d ed.] London, Sidgwick and Jackson, [1947]. 494p.   **BH337**

1st ed. 1937 had title: *Historical records.*

A listing of recordings of internationally famous opera and concert singers, arranged by name of performer. Includes brief listings of: the Cappella Sistina, talking records, instrumentalists, and complete operas.   ML156.B33

Clough, Francis F. and **Cuming, G. J.** The world's encyclopaedia of recorded music. London, Sidgwick and Jackson; N.Y., London Gramophone Corp., [1952]. 890p.   **BH338**

Based on Darrell's *Gramophone Shop encyclopedia of recorded music* (1936). A comprehensive listing of all electrically recorded music of interest to June 1951, and of pre-electrical recordings of unique value. Information is detailed, and the arrangement convenient. A useful historical record.

——— ——— 1st supplement (April 1950–May/June 1951). p.725–80. (Bound with main volume.)

——— ——— 2d supplement (1951–1952). 1953. 262p.

——— ——— 3d supplement (1953–1955). [1957]. 564p.   ML156.2.C6

Cohn, Arthur. Recorded classical music: a critical guide to compositions and performances. N.Y., Schirmer; London, Collier Macmillan, [1981]. 2164p.   **BH339**

Concerned with evaluating classical records, not cassettes and tapes. Presents the compiler's choice of the single best performance of each work (about 12,000 compositions by some 1,600 composers) with critical comment; each piece is judged individually, not the overall quality of a collection in the case of several short pieces included on a single disc. Covers all periods and performing media. Arranged by composer; no index of performing artists.

                ML156.9.C63

Felton, Gary S. The record collector's international directory. N.Y., Crown, [1980]. 365p.   **BH340**

A directory of record dealers, giving name, address, services, specialties, mail order arrangements, etc. Concentrates on the English-speaking world, with the largest number of entries from the United States. Includes a list of magazines, newsletters, etc., and a brief bibliography of directories and guides. Index of dealers by record category.   ML12.F44

Greenfield, Edward, Layton, Robert and **March, Ivan.** The complete Penguin stereo record and cassette guide. Harmondsworth, Eng.; N.Y., Penguin Books, 1984. 1386p.   **BH341**

1st ed. 1952 had title: *The new Penguin stereo record and cassette guide.*

Aims "to provide the serious collector with a comprehensive guide to the finest stereo records, cassettes and compact discs of permanent music available in the United Kingdom."—*Introd.* In four main sections: (1) Composer index; (2) Concerts of orchestral and concertante music; (3) Instrumental recitals; (4) Vocal recitals and choir collections. Includes full information on the recording and critical comment on both performance and quality of the recording.

Haggin, Bernard H. The new listener's companion and record guide. 5th ed. N.Y., Horizon Pr., 1978. 456p.   **BH342**

1st ed. 1956.

Introductory chapters on musical procedures and forms are followed by a critical survey of the literature of music, designed to help the reader in listening to music and evaluating it. The second part of the work is a guide to recorded performances of past and present.

This is a reprinting of the 1971 edition with the addition of two sections: (1) Additional recorded performances issued through 1973 (p.365–97) and (2) Additional recorded performances 1974 to Apr. 1978 (p.398–456).   MT6.H142

Halsey, Richard Sweeney. Classical music recordings: for home and library. Chicago, Amer. Lib. Assoc., 1970. 340p.   **BH343**

Intended as a "guide for organizations and individuals concerned with collecting and organizing, playing and caring for sound recordings."—*Pref.* The main section provides a comprehensive listing of recordings by composer and title, indicating record number, an "aesthetic significance" rating, a minimum age level, and designation of those recordings with a high percentage of favorable reviews. A second section lists works by recording company and record number, with name of performers given. Glossary of audio terms; title index to composer list; subject, proper name and composer index.   ML111.5.H34

New York Library Association. Children's and Young Adult Services Section. Recordings for children: a selected list of records and cassettes. 4th ed. N.Y., The Assoc., 1980. 25p.   **BH344**

1st ed. 1961.

Selection was made on the basis of "effectiveness, aesthetics and broad appeal, as well as being executed with integrity and respect for children" (*Introd.*), and the list aims to accommodate a broad range of informational and recreational requirements. Listing is by type of recording—children's songs and folk music, folk and fairy tales, orchestral music, popular music, holidays, etc.   ML156.4.C5N5

Bibliography

Bibliography of discographies. N.Y., Bowker, 1977–[83]. v.1–3. (In progress)   **BH345**

Contents: v.1, Classical music, 1925–1975, by Michael H. Gray and Gerald D. Gibson; v.2, Jazz, by Daniel Allen; v.3, Popular music, by Michael H. Gray.

To be in 5v. (v.4 is to cover ethnic and folk music; v.5, general discographies of music, plus label lists and speech recordings and animal sounds). Includes references to discographies appearing in periodicals and as monographs. Each volume has its own index.

            ML156.2.B49

Cooper, David Edwin. International bibliography of discographies: classical music and jazz and blues, 1962–1972; a reference book for record collectors, dealers, and libraries. Littleton, Colo., Libraries Unlimited, 1972. 272p. (Keys to music bibliography, no.2)   **BH346**

Restricted to Western classical music, jazz and blues. Lists discographies appearing in books and periodical articles published 1962–72. Arranged by period, subject or genre, composer and performer. Includes a "Summary of national discographies, catalogs and major review sources." Index of authors, titles, series, subjects.

            ML113.C655I6

Rust, Brian. Brian Rust's Guide to discography. Westport, Conn., Greenwood Pr., [1980]. 133p. (Discographies, no.4)   **BH347**

An introduction to the task of compiling a discography. Includes a brief history of major record labels, a bibliography of "booklength" discographies, and a directory of organizations and magazines.

            ML111.5.R87

Current

The new Schwann. [v.35, no.12]– , Dec. 1983– . Boston, ABC Schwann Pubns., 1983– . Monthly.   **BH348**

Supersedes *Schwann-1, records and tapes* (1972–Nov. 1983) and its semiannual supplement (called *Schwann-2*), which in turn superseded the *Schwann record and tape guide* (1949–71; title has varied; volume numbering was continuous throughout).

A useful guide to currently available records and tapes.

Reviews

Index to record and tape reviews. 1975– . San Anselmo, Calif., Chulainn Pr., [1976]– . Annual.   **BH349**

Continues *Record and tape reviews index* (1972–74).

Now indexes reviews appearing in about forty of the principal reviewing periodicals of the United States, England, and Canada. In three sections: (1) Composers; (2) Music in collections; (3) Anonymous works. Each citation gives as full information as is available concerning performers, disc and label number, variant labels, cassette or tape numbers, etc., as well as name of reviewer and location of the review.   ML156.9.R32

Index to record reviews, comp. by Kurtz Myers [and others]. March 1948– . (In *Notes*, 2d ser., v.5, no.2–) Quarterly.   **BH350**

Title varies: *Index of record reviews.*

Indexes reviews of recordings in some 15–30 American and English periodicals, with indication of the reviewer's opinion of the quality of the performance: excellent, adequate, or inadequate.

Cumulated as:

Myers, Kurtz. Index to record reviews. Boston, G. K. Hall, 1978. 5v.   **BH351**

A cumulation of the "Index to record reviews" which appeared in the periodical *Notes* (above) from 1948 through early 1977.

———— Index to record reviews 1978–1983. Boston, G. K. Hall, 1985. 873p.   **BH352**

Forms a first supplement to the above. "Based on material originally published in *Notes* . . . between 1978 and 1983."—*t.p.*
ML156.9.M89

Records in review. v.1–25, 1955–81. Great Barrington, Mass., Wyeth, [1955]–81. Annual.   **BH353**

Title and publisher vary: *High fidelity record annual* (Philadelphia, Lippincott), 1955–56. Ceased publication.

Long, critical, signed reviews of serious musical recordings, compiled from *High fidelity* magazine. Arranged by composer; includes section of "Recitals and miscellany." Index of performers.

B J

Sports, Recreation, and Travel

Reference works relating to sports, recreation and hobbies are wide-ranging both as to subject matter and quality of content: there are encyclopedias and handbooks for almost every individual sport, for countless crafts (pursued as pastime or for profit), and for various other forms of recreation. The following selection of titles for specific sports is limited mainly to the major, currently popular pursuits; books listed here emphasize the history, terminology, and playing records of the sports, not techniques for improving one's game.

Public libraries of all sizes, and most academic libraries, will need at least a few basic sports reference sources such as Menke's *Encyclopedia of sports* (BJ24) or *The Oxford companion to world sports and games* (BJ26), backed up by works such as *The way to play* (BJ28) and *The complete Hoyle* (BJ29). Libraries with a clientele showing particular interest in crafts will find *The encyclopedia of crafts* (BJ98) a useful acquisition. The importance of travel guides in the library collection is discussed under the subhead "Guidebooks" below.

SPORTS AND GAMES

Bibliography

Davis, Lenwood G. and **Daniels, Belinda S.** Black athletes in the United States: a bibliography of books, articles, autobiographies, and biographies on black professional athletes in the United States, 1800–1981. Westport, Conn., Greenwood Pr., [1981]. 265p.   **BJ1**

Focuses on the first, or the major and best-known professional black athletes in baseball, basketball, boxing, football, golf, and tennis. Lists reference books, monographs, and articles by form, subdivided by type of sport and by personality. More than 3,800 entries. Indexed.   Z7515.U5D38

Gratch, Bonnie, Chan, Betty and **Lingenfelter, Judith.** Sports and physical education; a guide to the reference resources. Westport, Conn., Greenwood Pr., [1983]. 198p.   **BJ2**

Lists English-language monographs published since 1970 and ongoing, regularly published reference serials. Classified arrangement in three parts: (1) individual sports; (2) sports and physical education: general and topical; (3) indexes, data bases, and information centers. Personal and corporate author, title, and subject indexes.   Z7511.G7

Henderson, Robert William. Early American sport; a checklist of books by American and foreign authors published in America prior to 1860, including sporting songs. 3d ed. rev. and enl. Rutherford, N.J., Fairleigh Dickinson Univ. Pr., [1977]. 309p. il.   **BJ3**

1st ed., 1937.

Arranged alphabetically by author (or title, if anonymous) with a subject index. Based on the collection in the Racquet and Tennis Club of New York City. Locates copies.   Z7511.H49

Henry E. Huntington Library and Art Gallery, San Marino, Calif. Sporting books in the Huntington Library, comp. by Lyle H. Wright. San Marino, Calif., 1937. 132p. (Huntington Library lists, no.2)   **BJ4**

A classed list, with author and title index.   Z7516.H52

Higginson, Alexander Henry. British and American sporting authors, their writings and biographies . . . with a bibliography by Sydney R. Smith. . . . Berryville, Va., Blue Ridge Pr., 1949. 443p. il.   **BJ5**

Biographical sketches, in chronological order, are followed by an alphabetical bibliography (p.399–437), which includes author and title entries. Alphabetical index of authors.   Z7511.H55

Mallon, Bill. The Olympics: a bibliography. N.Y., Garland, 1984. 258p. (Garland reference library of social science, v.246)   **BJ6**

Listings of official reports and publications of the various Olympic committees are followed by writings about the Olympics (arranged by country of publication, then by date). Not indexed.
Z7514.O5M35

Nunn, Marshall E. Sports. Littleton, Colo., Libraries Unlimited, 1976. 217p. (Spare time guides, no.10)   **BJ7**

A classed, annotated bibliography of 649 books on American sports, such as baseball, football, hockey, golf, self-defense, motorcycling, tennis, equestrian sports, the Olympics, etc.; within each subject chapter there are reference and non-reference sections. Also gives an annotated listing of 93 sports periodicals arranged by subject, and lists of associations and publishers. The "Spare time guide" series is designed "to provide sufficient information to enable librarians and hobbyists to distinguish between books of varying quality."—*Pref.* A review in the *Booklist* (73:1596, June 15, 1977) treats this volume and no.9 in the series, R. G. Schipf's *Outdoor recreation* (1976; 278p.), which performs a similar bibliographic service for non-competitive sports.   Z7511.N86

Turner, Pearl. Index to outdoor sports, games, and activities. Westwood, Mass., Faxon, [1978]. 409p. (Useful reference ser., 105)   **BJ8**

A subject index to the contents of 497 books and seven periodicals relating to "92 outdoor pursuits, including both competitive and noncompetitive individual and team sports."—*Pref.* Publications indexed are from the 1970–75 period.   GV191.6.T87

Current

Physical education index. v.1– . Cape Girardeau, Mo., [Ben Oak Publ. Co.], 1978– . Quarterly, the 4th issue being an annual cumulation.   **BJ9**

Indexes by subject domestic and foreign periodicals published in English or that contain English summaries. Covers dance, health, physical education, physical therapy, recreation, sports and sports medicine, plus articles that discuss pertinent legislation, relevant reports of national and international associations and conventions, and biographies, reports and obituaries of outstanding individuals.
GV201.P534

Dictionaries and encyclopedias

Avis, Frederick Compton. The sportsman's glossary. London, Souvenir Pr.; Toronto, Ryerson Pr., [1961]. 301p. **BJ10**

Brief definitions listed under 15 different sports; almost exclusively British usage. No index. GV567.A8

Clark, Patrick. Sports firsts. N.Y., Facts on File, [1981]. 262p. il. **BJ11**

"Firsts" are grouped by sport or sports category (baseball, football, basketball, hockey, racing, golf, racquet sports, water sports, winter sports, track and field, target sports, combat sports, soccer, flying, indoor sports, Olympics, and "other sports") with information provided on the origin of the various sports, teams, competitions, awards and trophies. Bibliography; index. GV571.C56

Considine, Tim. The language of sport. N.Y., Facts on File/World Almanac Pubns., [1982]. 355p. **BJ12**

Terms and phrases are grouped by sport (baseball, basketball, bowling, boxing, football, golf, ice hockey, soccer, and tennis) with a historical sketch of the sport at the beginning of each section. Includes entries for associations, tournaments, etc. Indexed. GV567.C59

Cuddon, John A. The international dictionary of sports and games. N.Y., Schocken Books, [1980]. 870p. il. **BJ13**

Covers the major sports and games, and some of the minor ones, giving a historical summary, synopsis of the rules, etc. Also includes "a selection of technical, semi-technical, jargon, colloquial and slang terms."—*Pref.* Does not include biographies or bibliographies. Has a certain British emphasis. GV567.C8

Cummings, Parke. The dictionary of sports. N.Y., Barnes, [1949]. 572p. il. **BJ14**

A dictionary of terms used in sports. GV567.C85

Dictionnaire des jeux, publié sous la direction de René Alleau, avec la collaboration de Renaud Matignon. [Paris], Tchou, [1964]. 544p. il. **BJ15**

A comprehensive work describing in detail ancient and modern games and amusements of all countries. Gives history of each game and rules of play. Contains excellent illustrations, some in color. GV1200.D5

Encyclopedia of physical education, fitness, and sports. Thomas K. Cureton, Jr., series ed.; sponsored by the Amer. Alliance for Health, Physical Education, and Recreation. Salt Lake City, Utah, Brighton Pub. Co., [1977–81]. 3v. il. **BJ16**

v.3 publ. by Addison-Wesley, Reading, Mass.
Contents: [v.1] Philosophy, programs, and history; [v.2] Training, environment, nutrition, and fitness; [v.3] Sports, dance, and related activities.
Each volume consists of chapters by contributing editors on various aspects of physical education, physical fitness, and sports (including information on the origin and early development of individual sports, etc.). Each volume has its own index. GV567.E49

Friedman, Arthur. The world of sports statistics. N.Y., Atheneum, 1978. 302p. **BJ17**

Subtitle: How the fans and professionals record, compile and use information.
Offers sections on baseball, hockey, football, basketball, "Betting and stats," and "Numbers for fun and profit." Includes samples of professional statistical reports and scoresheets, with information on how to compile and read them. GV741.F73

Frommer, Harvey. Sports lingo: a dictionary of the language of sports. N.Y., Atheneum, 1979. 302p. **BJ18**

Terms are grouped by individual sport ("Archery" through "Wrestling") and a general index is provided. GV567.F76

——— Sports roots: how nicknames, namesakes, trophies, competitions, and expressions in the world of sports came to be. N.Y., Atheneum, 1979. 191p. il. **BJ19**

A dictionary arrangement of names, terms, and expressions, with an explanation of the origin of each. GV706.8.F76

Gomme, Alice Bertha. Traditional games of England, Scotland, and Ireland; with tunes, singing-rhymes and methods of playing according to the variants extant and recorded in different parts of the Kingdom. London, Nutt, 1894–98. 2v. (Dictionary of British folk-lore, ed. by G. Laurence Gomme, pt.1) (Repr.: London, Thames & Hudson, 1984) **BJ20**

"The games included in this collection bear the important qualification of being nearly all Children's Games: that is to say, they were either originally children's games since developed into games for adults, or they were the more serious avocations of adults, which have since become children's games only."—*Pref.* Dictionary arrangement. Sources are cited for many of the descriptions.
GR141.G5

Hickok, Ralph. New encyclopedia of sports. N.Y., McGraw-Hill, [1977]. 543p. il. **BJ21**

Intends to provide information "about all North American competitive sports."—*Pref.* Entries are mainly for specific sports, but some terms applicable to or encompassing a number of sports (e.g., handicap, Olympic Games) are also used as entries. Articles for individual sports usually include notes on the history of the sport, a summary of its rules, and a list of results and records; some include biographical sections for outstanding athletes, and glossaries.
A Reference and Subscription Books Committee review in the *Booklist* (74:1699, July 1, 1978) concludes: "Libraries that have acquired Frank Menke's *The Encyclopedia of Sports,* 5th ed., 1975, and John Arlott's *Oxford Companion to World Sports and Games,* 1975, may have sufficient coverage to serve their clientele."
GV567.H52

Kamper, Erich. Encyclopedia of the Olympic games. N.Y., McGraw-Hill, [1972]. 360p. **BJ22**

In English, French, and German.
As far as possible, gives the names of the top six competitors in all Olympic events from 1896 through 1972. GV721.5.K34

McWhirter, Norris. Guinness book of sports records, winners & champions. Peter Matthews, ed. N.Y., Sterling Pub. Co., [1982]. 352p. il. **BJ23**

Organized by specific sport, with a note on origins of the sport preceding the entries for "first," "most," "longest," "shortest," etc. Includes many lists of champions and holders of world records. Index is by sport with indication of type of record; does not include names. GV741.M28

Menke, Frank Grant. The encyclopedia of sports. 6th rev. ed. Revisions by Pete Palmer. South Brunswick, N.J., A. S. Barnes, [1978]. 1132p. **BJ24**

1st ed. 1939. Title varies slightly.
Covers a wide variety of sports, giving: history, description, basic rules, names and records of champions, and financial statistics, with special attention to the United States. In general, information has been updated through 1976. GV567.M46

Norback, Craig T. and **Norback, Peter G.** The New American guide to athletics, sports, & recreation. [N.Y.], New American Library, [1979]. 659p. **BJ25**

An alphabetical arrangement of entries for some 60 of today's most popular sports, both professional and amateur sports and "recreational sports" such as hiking. Gives general information on the sport itself; background and history; professional and amateur organizations; leagues, clubs, and playing facilities; recent rule changes; etc. GV583.N63

The Oxford companion to world sports and games. Ed. by John Arlott. London & N.Y., Oxford Univ. Pr., 1975. 1143p. il. **BJ26**

Aims to provide an introduction to sports and games "which are the subject of national or international competition" (*Pref.*), but omits blood sports and board and table games. Intends "to help the reader to understand a sport when he watches it for the first time. The descriptive section explains how it is played—as distinct from how to play it." Does not print the rules of each game, but provides a digest thereof, together with a diagram of the playing field, etc., as applicable. Entries for individual sports figures and champions, and for specific sporting events and competitions. Articles are unsigned, but a list of contributors is provided. Cross references; occasional bibliographic citations. GV207.O93

Wallechinsky, David. The complete book of the Olympics. N.Y., Viking, [1984]. 628p. il. **BJ27**

Summer games and winter games are treated in separate sections. Within those sections sports are considered individually, with information on each event, lists of winners (with times, scores, etc.) by year, often with commentary on specific contests and notes on the contestants. Includes discontinued events. Covers through 1980. Detailed table of contents, but no index. GV721.5.W25

Rules

Diagram Group. The way to play; the illustrated encyclopedia of the games of the world. N.Y., Paddington Pr., [1975]. 320p. il. **BJ28**

Covers "family games and social games, games played for fun, and games played for profit" (*Foreword*), including games from foreign countries and from ancient times. Gives a note on the history or origin of each game, concise rules, players and equipment needed. Games are grouped by type, such as race board games, general card games, target games, dice games, word and picture games, children's party games, etc. Indexed. GV1201.D48

Foster, Robert Frederick. Complete Hoyle. Rev. and enl. Philadelphia, Lippincott, [1963]. 697p. il. **BJ29**

Subtitle: an encyclopedia of games, including all indoor games played to-day, with suggestions for good play, illustrative hands and all official laws to date . . . with the complete laws of contract bridge and canasta. GV1243.F77

The rule book: the authoritative, up-to-date, illustrated guide to the regulations, history, and object of all major sports. The Diagram Group. N.Y., St. Martin's Pr., [1983]. 430p. il. **BJ30**

This is a new edition of *The rules of the game* (N.Y. & London, Paddington Pr., 1974) which the Diagram Group also edited, and which attempted to explain through diagrams and drawings the features of each game and its international rules. A *Library journal* review (Apr. 1, 1983, p.731) concludes that the revision "suffers greatly from a reduction in both content and format." GV731.R75

Directories

The big book of halls of fame in the United States and Canada: sports. Comp. and ed. by Paul Soderberg and Helen Washington. N.Y., Bowker, 1977. 1042p. **BJ31**

Arranged alphabetically by particular fields of sport ("Angling" through "Wrestling," plus a separate section for "Special fields"). Entries include directory and general information about each hall of fame, followed by a list of members with a biographical sketch of each intended to give enough information to indicate why the biographee was worthy of inclusion in the hall of fame. Indexed. CT215.B53

Individual sports

Baseball

The baseball encyclopedia: the complete and official record of major league baseball. Ed. by Joseph L. Reichler. 6th ed.

rev. updated, and expanded. N.Y., Macmillan; London, Collier Macmillan, [1985]. 2733p. **BJ32**

1st ed. 1969.

An exhaustive record of individual player, team, and league statistics, lists, rosters, etc., derived from a computerized databank. Updated through the 1984 World Series. Not indexed. GV877.B27

Grobani, Anton. Guide to baseball literature. Detroit, Gale, [1975]. 363p. il. **BJ33**

A classed bibliography of works on various aspects of the game—histories, instructional manuals, rule books, record books, team histories, biographies of individual players, etc.—including lists of periodicals, anthologies of writings on the sport, fiction and other literary treatments. Z7514.B3G76

Reichler, Joseph L. The great all-time baseball record book. N.Y., Macmillan; London, Collier Macmillan, 1981. 544p. il. **BJ34**

A well-organized compendium of baseball statistics from earliest period through 1980. Major sections for individual batting, pitching, and fielding records, rookie records, and team records. Player index. GV877.R39

Thompson, Sherley Clark. All-time rosters of major league baseball clubs. Rev. ed. South Brunswick, N.J., Barnes, [1973]. 723p. **BJ35**

Revisions by Pete Palmer.

1st ed. 1967.

Gives club records and yearly rosters, 1882–1972, with batting averages, etc., for individual players. GV862.T47

Turkin, Hy and **Thompson, S. C.** The official encyclopedia of baseball. 10th rev. ed. Garden City, N.Y., Dolphin/Doubleday, [1979]. 633p. il. **BJ36**

Revisions by Pete Palmer.

1st ed. 1951.

Chapters on the history of the game and its major leagues are followed by chapters on: register of all players and their records since 1871, World Series records, special records, honored players, umpires, administration, miscellany, and stadium diagrams. Updated through 1978. GV867.T8

Basketball

The NBA's Official encyclopedia of pro basketball. Ed. by Zander Hollander. N.Y., New American Library, [1981]. 532p. il. **BJ37**

A revised and updated edition of *The pro basketball encyclopedia* (1977), the main difference between the two volumes being the addition of statistics for the 1978–81 period. In five main sections: (1) The early game (i.e., history of the sport, early teams and leagues); (2) The major leagues; (3) All part of the game (i.e., sections on the Globetrotters, officials, Hall of fame); (4) Official NBA rules; (5) All-time player directory. Indexed. GV885.7.N37

Boxing

The ring record book and boxing encyclopedia, 1983. Bert Randolph Sugar, ed. in chief. Ring Publishing Corp., 1983. 1125p. il. **BJ38**

1st ed. 1941; usually updated annually, occasionally biennially.

Lists title bouts of the previous year on a month-by-month basis; provides updated records of active fighters in the Americas and elsewhere; and various other records, lists, and statistics. Indexed.

Football

Grobani, Anton. Guide to football literature. Detroit, Gale, [1975]. 319p. il. **BJ39**

A bibliography of works on all aspects of the sport, arranged by categories such as: general works, early British works, record books, general histories, team histories, biographies, anthologies, periodicals, yearbooks, rule books, dictionaries and spectators' guides, etc. Indexed. Z7514.F7G76

NFL's Official encyclopedic history of professional football. [2d ed.] N.Y., Macmillan, 1977. 512p. il. **BJ40**

1st ed. 1973.

Based on official records of the National Football League. Includes individual team histories and rosters, team standings and records, records of championship and bowl games, etc.

GV954.N37

Treat, Roger L. The encyclopedia of football. 16th rev. ed. Revisions ed. by Pete Palmer. South Brunswick, N.J., A. S. Barnes, 1979. 738p. il. **BJ41**

1st ed. 1952.

In five main sections: (1) The story of the game; (2) Year-by-year history from 1919 to the present; (3) The players (with lists of individual and championship game records); (4) The coaches; (5) The teams (with lists of records, etc.). No index.

Updated to include information through 1978. GV954.T7

Golf

Davies, Peter. Davies' Dictionary of golfing terms. N.Y., Simon and Schuster, [1980]. 188p. il. **BJ42**

"In this dictionary, historical development and continuity are shown by the copious use of dated citations. Etymologies, where appropriate, are given in brackets before the definitions."—*Foreword.* GV965.D37

The encyclopedia of golf, ed. by Donald Steel and Peter Ryde. N.Y., Viking, [1975]. 480p. il. **BJ43**

The main portion of the work is an alphabetical arrangement of entries for players, terms, courses, clubs and associations, tournaments and championships, etc. Tables of results of championships and cup matches, p.427–73. GV965.E5

Evans, Webster. Encyclopaedia of golf. [3d ed.] London, Hale, [1980]. 320p. il. **BJ44**

1st ed. 1971.

An alphabetical arrangement of entries covering all aspects of golf: "its history, leading personalities, origin and meaning of terms used, evolution of clubs and balls, records, championships and championship courses, details of all countries where golf is played, rules and definitions, other golf-like and kindred games."—*Introd.* About 1,500 entries; cross references. Although the book is of British origin, particular attention is given to the sport in the United States. GV965.E84

Golf magazine's Encyclopedia of golf. Ed. by John M. Ross and the eds. of Golf magazine. Updated and rev. ed. N.Y., Harper & Row, [1979]. 437p. il. **BJ45**

1st ed. 1970.

Covers the history of the game, tournament and championship records, equipment, rules, and terms; includes a biographical section. Indexed. GV965.G5455

Kennington, Donald. The sourcebook of golf. With an appendix on collecting golfiana by Sarah Baddiel. [London], Lib. Assoc., 1981. 255p. il. **BJ46**

Brief bibliographic essays on the history of golf; golfers; how to play; essays, fiction and humor; the golf business; reference sources and periodicals; golfing organizations, each followed by pertinent bibliography. Title index; name and subject index. GV965.K43

Murdoch, Joseph S. F. The library of golf, 1743–1966; a bibliography of golf books, indexed alphabetically, chronologically, and by subject matter. Detroit, Gale, 1968. 314p. il. **BJ47**

Many entries are annotated. Z7514.G6M8

——— and **Seagle, Janet.** Golf: a guide to information sources. Detroit, Gale, [1979]. 232p. (Sports, games, and pastimes information guide ser., v.7) **BJ48**

In two parts, the first being a selected, annotated list of books on various aspects of golf (most of them published after 1965), and the second a guide to other sources of information such as golf periodicals, organizations, libraries, equipment dealers, instructional programs, etc. Indexed. Z7514.G6M79

Hockey

Fischler, Stan and **Fischler, Shirley Walton.** The hockey encyclopedia: the complete record of professional ice hockey. N.Y., Macmillan, [1983]. 720p. **BJ49**

A compendium of registers of players and teams, giving year-by-year statistics from 1917/18 through the 1982/83 season.

A 1975 publication entitled *Fischler's Hockey encyclopedia* (N.Y., Crowell. 628p.) runs heavily to entries for individual players, but includes terms, teams, equipment, etc. GV847.5.F57

Ronberg, Gary. The illustrated hockey encyclopedia. N.Y., Balsam Pr./Rutledge Book, [1984]. 399p. il. **BJ50**

Non-alphabetical arrangement. Emphasis is on teams and players. Numerous statistical tables. No index. GV848.4.N7R66

Martial arts

Martial arts encyclopedia. Ed. by Larry Winderbaum. Wash., Inscape (distr. by Gale), [1977]. 215p. il. **BJ51**

"This . . . is neither a how-to book nor a detailed history. It attempts to present both the rich cultural heritage of the arts and to survey their contemporary impact . . . , but nowhere in the book is there a guide to practicing any single art presented."—*Introd.* Includes general information "on all of the martial arts, including aikido, iaido, judo, jujutsu, karate, kendo, kung fu, kyudo, sumo, tae kwon do, t'ai chi ch'uan, bando, jodo, and pentjak-silat." Dictionary arrangement of terms, names, places, etc. Lists of relevant books and magazines. GV1112.M34

Skiing

Ski magazine's Encyclopedia of skiing. Rev. and updated. Ed. by Richard Needham. N.Y., Harper & Row, [1979]. 452p. il. **BJ52**

1st ed. 1970 by R. Scharff.

In six sections: (1) The history of skiing; (2) Ski equipment; (3) Principles of skiing; (4) Ski competition; (5) Where to ski; (6) Glossary, lexicon, and ski associations. Indexed. GV854.E53

Soccer

Henshaw, Richard. The encyclopedia of world soccer. Wash., New Republic Books, [1979]. 828p. il. **BJ53**

A comprehensive treatment of the game, including entries (in dictionary arrangement) for terms and equipment; history; individual players and clubs; tournaments and championships (with statistics); and status of the game in countries throughout the world.

GV943.H367

Hollander, Zander. The American encyclopedia of soccer. N.Y., Everest House, [1980]. 544p. il. **BJ54**

Concerned with both American college and professional soccer, giving attention to the history and development of the game, statistics of team standings, individual players' records, etc. Indexed. GV944.U5A42

Rosenthal, Gary. Everybody's soccer book. N.Y., Scribner's, [1981]. 354p. il. **BJ55**

Although much of the book is concerned with individual skills,

tactics and systems of play, there are good sections on history of the sport, United States and Canadian soccer, and World Cup soccer. Also includes the 1980 NCAA soccer rules, a glossary, and an index.
GV943.R66

Swimming

Besford, Pat. Encyclopedia of swimming. 2d ed. London, Robert Hale; N.Y., St. Martin's Pr., [1976]. 302p. il. **BJ56**

1st ed. 1971.

An alphabetical arrangement of entries for persons and topics associated with the sport. Includes numerous lists of champions, trophy winners, world records, etc.

Council for National Cooperation in Aquatics. Swimming and diving; a bibliography. N.Y., Association Pr., [1968]. 264p. **BJ57**

Classed bibliography with author index. Includes published and unpublished materials through 1966. Z7631.C6

Greenwood, Frances Anderson. Bibliography of swimming. N.Y., Wilson, 1940. 308p. **BJ58**

A dictionary catalog of books and periodical articles on swimming and allied subjects, containing approximately 10,000 titles listed by author and classified under 608 subjects. Includes material in various languages published up to June 1938. Z7631.G79

Tennis

Collins, Bud and **Hollander, Zander.** Bud Collins' Modern encyclopedia of tennis. Garden City, N.Y., Doubleday, 1980. 389p. il. **BJ59**

Chapters by Collins and other contributors cover the history of tennis, the 1919–45 era and the 25 greatest players of those years, the 1946–67 and 1968–79 periods and their greatest players, the officials, equipment, International Tennis Hall of Fame, and "tennis lingo." Appendixes of rules and records. Indexed. GV993.C6

Robertson, Maxwell. The encyclopedia of tennis. N.Y., Viking, [1974]. 392p. il. **BJ60**

In three main sections: (1) background information on the history and development of the game, rules and their interpretation, courts and equipment, playing the game; (2) an alphabetical arrangement of entries for individual players, developments in specific countries, terms, championships, etc.; (3) tables of records of championships and cup matches. GV990.R62

United States Tennis Association official encyclopedia of tennis. Centennial ed., rev. and updated. Ed. by Bill Shannon, with the staff of the USTA. N.Y., Harper & Row, [1981]. 558p. il. **BJ61**

"Revision of: Official encyclopedia of tennis. Rev. and updated 1st ed., c1979."—*verso of t.p.*

In seven sections: History of tennis; Tennis equipment; Principles of tennis; Rules and etiquette of lawn tennis; Results of major tournaments and championships; Tennis greats; Glossary of tennis terms. Indexed. GV995.U54

Wrestling

Clayton, Thompson. A handbook of wrestling terms and holds. Comp. . . . with the help of Doug Parker [and others]. New and rev. ed. South Brunswick, N.J., A. S. Barnes, [1974]. 192p. il. **BJ62**

1st ed. 1968.

Aims to provide a common language for wrestling coaches. Lists and illustrates 445 maneuvers, with alternate terms given for each; illustrations are captioned with the most popular name of the maneuver. Indexed. GV1195.C55

Other outdoor sports and recreation

General works

Pinkerton, James R. and **Pinkerton, Marjorie J.** Outdoor recreation and leisure; a reference guide and selected bibliography. Columbia, Univ. of Missouri, Research Center, School of Business and Public Administration, 1969. 332p. **BJ63**

Classed arrangement with author and title indexes. Z7511.P52

Recreation and outdoor life directory: a guide to national and international organizations. Steven R. Wasserman, ed. 2d ed. Detroit, Gale, [1983]. 1020p. **BJ64**

1st ed. 1979.

In two main parts, the first covering general sources such as organizations, state and federal agencies, consultants, special libraries and information centers. The second part provides information concerning parks, scenic trails, shorelines, fish and game reserves, and similar outdoor recreational facilities under federal and state auspices. Indexed. GV191.35.R4

U.S. Children's Bureau. Handbook for recreation. [Rev. ed. Wash.], U.S. Dept. of Health, Education, and Welfare. Social Security Admin., Children's Bureau, 1960. 148p. il. (*Its* Pubn. no.231) (Repr.: Detroit, Gale, 1976) **BJ65**

Contains information on games, dances, music, storytelling, etc. Especially useful for nonprofessional recreational leaders in charge of group activities. Includes a title index and a classified game and activity index; also, a list of references with brief annotations. GV1201.U5

Van der Smissen, Betty and **Joyce, Donald V.** Bibliography of theses and dissertations in recreation, parks, camping and outdoor education, 1970. [Wash.], Nat. Recreation and Park Assoc., [1970]. 555p. **BJ66**

" . . . updates, as well as integrates, the 1962 *Bibliography Related to Recreation Research* . . . and its supplement, 1965 *Research in Recreation. Part I* compiled . . . by the National Recreation Association; and the theses and dissertations section of the 1962 *Bibliography Related to Camping and Outdoor Education* and its 1965 supplement, both compiled . . . by the American Camping Association."—*Foreword.*

An author listing of more than 3,800 theses and dissertations, many with annotations. Institutional and subject indexes.

Continued by:

Van der Smissen, Betty. Bibliography of theses and dissertations in recreation and parks, 1979. [Wash.], Nat. Recreation and Park Assoc., 1979. [162]p. **BJ67**

Lists nearly 2,800 additional items.

Camping

Campground & trailer park directory. United States, Canada, Mexico. [Skokie, Ill.], Rand McNally, [1984]– . il., maps. Annual. **BJ68**

Continues *Rand McNally campground & trailer park guide* (1971–83), which was formed by the union of Rand McNally's *Guidebook to campgrounds* and *Travel trailer guide.*

Gives information on size, elevation, facilities, activities available, etc.

Landi, Val. The Bantam great outdoors guide to the United States and Canada: the complete travel encyclopedia and wilderness guide. N.Y., Bantam, [1978]. 854p. il., maps. **BJ69**

Arranged by region, then by state or province. A map and an introduction for each region are followed by an "encyclopedia" section (giving information on accommodations for tourists, fishing and hunting, camping, canoeing, highways, etc.) and a "travel and recreation guide" for each state and province. Indexed.

GV191.4.L36

Parents' guide to accredited camps, 1982– . [Martinsville, Ind., Amer. Camping Assoc.], 1982– . Annual. **BJ70**

Supersedes directories for 1977–81 issued in four regional editions. Those editions, in turn, superseded the Association's *National directory of accredited camps for boys and girls* (1971–76), which superseded the *Directory of accredited camps . . .* (1961–70), etc.

Lists and provides information on camps accredited by the American Camping Association (camps being visited every three years to assure that ACA standards are maintained). State-by-state listing. Tabular guide to activities; a "special clientele" section lists camps serving specific groups (asthmatics, blind, deaf, etc.).

Woodall's Campground directory. North American ed. Ed.11– , 1977– . Highland Park, Ill., Woodall, 1977– . il., maps. Annual. **BJ71**

Continues *Woodall's Trailering parks and campgrounds* (varies; 1967–76); also issued in regional editions.

Includes facilities in the United States and Canada.

GV198.56.W66

Hunting and fishing

Acerrano, Anthony J. The practical hunter's handbook. N.Y., Winchester Pr., [1978]. 246p. il. **BJ72**

Intended for "the outdoorsman who manages to slip away to the woods or fields whenever a spare-time opportunity arises."—*Introd.* A chapter on places to hunt is followed by chapters on specific types of game (e.g., rabbits, squirrels, pheasants, ducks, regional birds, regional big game). Includes chapters on care of the kill and game cookery. Indexed. SK33.A23

Clotfelter, Cecil F. Hunting and fishing. Littleton, Colo., Libraries Unlimited, 1974. 118p. (Spare time guides: information sources for hobbies and recreation, 2) **BJ73**

Includes sections for hunting, fishing, firearms, and archery, as well as more general sections for encyclopedias and dictionaries, periodicals, and national organizations relating to the fields mentioned. Indexed. Z7514.H9C6

Elman, Robert. The hunter's field guide to the game birds and animals of North America. Rev. ed. N.Y., Knopf, 1982. 655p. il. **BJ74**

1st ed. 1974.

Aims to give information about the life, habitat, and behavior of all North American game species. Sections for upland birds, ducks, geese, swans, shore and marsh birds, small game, deer, medium game, and big game. Many illustrations. Indexed. SK40.E45

New hunter's encyclopedia. Compl. rev. 3d ed. Harrisburg, Pa., Stackpole, [1966]. 1131p. il. (Updated new printing: N.Y., Gallahad Books, 1974?) **BJ75**

A revision and updating of the *Hunter's encyclopedia* (1948) edited by R. R. Camp.

Contents: Big game; Small game; Animal predators; Winged predators; Small mammals; Upland game birds; Shorebirds; Waterfowl; Color section (colored plates of upland game birds and waterfowl); Firearms; Ammunition; Dogs; The complete hunter (including sections on camping, clothing, various methods of hunting, regulations and laws, etc.).

A comprehensive work dealing with the game animals and birds of this continent, describing their appearance, characteristics, history, range, etc., with methods of hunting, firearms, game laws, etc. Arranged by groups indicated above, with detailed index.

SK33.H945

Phillips, John Charles. American game mammals and birds; a catalogue of books, 1582–1925, sport, natural history and conservation. Boston, Houghton, 1930. 638p. **BJ76**

Also published under title: *A bibliography of American sporting books* (Boston, Morrill, 1930).

Most of the titles are from the Charles Sheldon Library which now belongs to Yale University. Gives complete bibliographical information and frequently a brief descriptive note. Z7408.N6P5

Mountaineering

Noyce, Wilfrid and **McMorrin, Ian.** World atlas of mountaineering. London, Nelson, 1969; [N.Y.], Macmillan, [1970]. 224p. il. **BJ77**

Intended as a concise summary of mountaineering activity, the work is meant to be read through as well as to serve as a reference book. "The main concern throughout has been with general tendencies, with the result that some peaks and some personalities are not mentioned."—*Pref.* Signed contributions offer descriptive, factual accounts of specific peaks, ranges, and geographical regions, followed by highlights of mountaineering activity in the area. Indexed.

GB511.N67

Unsworth, Walter. Encyclopaedia of mountaineering. London, Robert Hale; N.Y., St. Martin's Pr., [1975]. 272p. il. **BJ78**

An alphabetical arrangement of entries for places (i.e., "all the important mountain areas of the world and most of the lesser ones"—*Pref.*), people (about 400 climbers from various countries and periods), techniques and equipment, terms, and topics from other fields which have some bearing on mountain climbing. Indexed. GV199.85.U57

Sailing and water sports

See also Swimming.

Encyclopedia of sailing. Rev. and updated by the eds. of Yacht racing/cruising, with Robert Scharff and Richard Henderson. N.Y., Harper & Row, [1978]. 468p. il. **BJ79**

1st ed. 1971.

Information is presented within eight topical sections: (1) The history of sailing; (2) Sailboats and sailing gear; (3) Catalog of one-design and offshore sailboats; (4) The art of sailing; (5) Sailing is fun [concerned with cruising]; (6) The lure of racing; (7) Sailing competition; (8) Glossary of sailing terms. Detailed table of contents, but no index. GV811.E52

Noel, John V. The boating dictionary, sail and power. N.Y., Van Nostrand Reinhold, [1981]. 295p. **BJ80**

Offers very brief definitions of about 3,000 terms related to powerboats, sailboats, the ocean environment, boat construction, and electronic navigational aids. GV775.N58

Richey, Michael W., ed. The sailing encyclopedia. N.Y., Lippincott & Crowell, 1980. 288p. il. **BJ81**

Aims to treat "every subject likely to interest those concerned with sail" (*Pref.*) and is meant for the general reader rather than the specialist. Dictionary arrangement; cross references; useful line drawings and diagrams as well as photographs. GV811.S255

Tate, William Henry. A mariner's guide to the rules of the road. 2d ed. Annapolis, Md., Naval Inst. Pr., [1982]. 159p. il. **BJ82**

1st ed. 1974.

A guide for the professional mariner and the serious marine hobbyist.

A similar work is William P. Crawford's *Mariner's rules of the road* (N.Y., Norton, 1983. 336p. il.). VK371.T37

Ziegler, Ronald M. Wilderness waterways: a guide to information sources. Detroit, Gale, [1979]. 317p. (Sports, games, and pastimes information guide ser., v.1) **BJ83**

In four parts: (1) Books (an annotated listing of books on canoeing, kayaking and rafting, waterways environment and guides to the waterways, camping skills, etc.); (2) Other media (films, periodicals, pamphlets); (3) Organizations and government agencies which can provide information on wilderness waterways; and (4) Publishers, book dealers, libraries, and other sources of information. Indexed.   Z7514.C3Z53

Parks and protected areas

Index, National Park System and related areas . . . [Wash., Nat. Park Service, U.S. Dept. of the Interior, 1979–] Irregular. (1982 latest publ.)   **BJ84**

Continues *Index of the national park system and affiliated areas* (1975), which in turn superseded *National parks and landmarks* (title varies; 1946–74).

Each edition supersedes the previous one. National parks, monuments, memorials, rivers, lake- and seashores, etc., are listed and briefly described on a state-by-state basis. A "related areas" section lists and describes areas not part of the National Park System: "Affiliated areas" which include various properties that preserve significant resources; the "Wild and scenic rivers system;" and the "National trail system." Alphabetical index.   E160.N25

International Union for Conservation of Nature and Natural Resources. Commission on National Parks and Protected Areas. United Nations list of national parks and equivalent reserves. 1980 ed. [Gland, Switz.], The Union, [1980]. 121p. il., maps.   **BJ85**

In English and French.
1st ed. 1961–62.
Describes 1,204 national parks; country arrangement. Gives information on number of areas, background of legal basis, administration, land tenure, tourism, research conducted, area, staff, budget, date established, tourist facilities, etc. Country maps show park locations.

Riley, Laura and **Riley, William.** Guide to the national wildlife refuges. Garden City, N.Y., Anchor Pr./Doubleday, 1979. 653p.   **BJ86**

A guide to the approximately 380 wildlife refuges throughout the United States, telling "how to get there, what there is to see and do, where a visitor can stay or camp nearby, best times to visit, any special equipment needed, and how to get more information."—*p.1.* Arranged by region, then by name of the refuge. Indexed.
                                                              QH76.R54

World directory of national parks and other protected areas. Morges, Switz., International Union for Conservation of Nature and Natural Resources, 1977– . 2v. (looseleaf) maps.   **BJ87**

Publ. with the financial assistance of the World Wildlife Fund and the United Nations Educational, Scientific and Cultural Organization.

Describes national and provincial parks, nature reserves, multiple-use reserves, marine reserves, and certain anthropological, archaeological, and historical reserves. Country arrangement. Entries include bibliographic references, mention of noteworthy fauna and vegetation, problems, scientific research being conducted, etc.

Board and card games

Bibliographies of works on playing cards and gaming. Montclair, N.J., Patterson Smith, 1972. 311, 79p. (Patterson Smith reprint series in criminology, law enforcement, and social problems. Pubn. no.132)   **BJ88**

Subtitle: A reprint of A bibliography of works in English on playing cards and gaming, by Frederick Jessel [1905] and A bibliography of card-games and of the history of playing-cards, by Norton T. Horr [1892].

Both reprinted works are main-entry listings; the Horr bibliography lacks a subject index.   Z5481.B5

Hargrave, Catherine Perry. A history of playing cards and a bibliography of cards and gaming. Comp. and il. from the old cards and books in the collection of the United States Playing Card Company in Cincinnati. Boston, Houghton; London, Allen and Unwin, 1930. 468p. il. (Repr.: N.Y., Dover, 1966)   **BJ89**

Bibliography, p.369–449.   GV1233.H3

Bridge

The official encyclopedia of bridge. Newly rev. 4th ed. Henry G. Francis, ed. in chief. N.Y., Crown, [1984]. 922p. il.
                                                              BJ90

"Authorized by the American Contract Bridge League and prepared by its staff."—*t.p.*
1st ed. 1964.
A general information section offers an alphabetical arrangement of entries for technical, historical, procedural, and terminological information. There are separate sections for biographies, tournament results, and bibliography.   GV1282.22.O35

Chess

Betts, Douglas A. Chess; an annotated bibliography of works published in the English language, 1850–1968. Boston, G. K. Hall, 1974. 659p.   **BJ91**

Lists and annotates English-language works on the game of chess published 1850–1968. Classed arrangement with index of authors, titles, and subjects.   Z5541.B47

Graham, John. The literature of chess. Jefferson, N.C., McFarland, [1984]. 250p. il.   **BJ92**

"This book surveys the literature in a number of areas, reviews recommended books and provides a basis for choice" *(Pref.)* among the hundreds of titles available. Chapters deal with introductory works, works on openings, middle game, endings, chess lore, etc., each chapter preceded by a list of titles (136 in all, with bibliographic information) to be discussed. Indexed.   GV1445.G74

The Hague. Koninklijke Bibliotheek. Bibliotheca Van der Linde-Niemeijeriana; a catalogue of the chess collection in the Royal Library, The Hague. The Hague, 1955. 342p.
                                                              BJ93

A catalog of several rich collections on chess in the Royal Library, particularly those originally owned by Antonius Van der Linde and M. Niemeijer. Classed, with author index.   Z936.H139

Hooper, David and **Whyld, Kenneth.** The Oxford companion to chess. N.Y., Oxford Univ. Pr., [1984]. 407p. il.   **BJ94**

" . . . embraces all branches of chess including its history and gives recommended books for further reading. All terms commonly used by players are explained, about 570 biographies are given, and there are entries for about 650 names representing some 700 openings or variations."—*Pref.* Includes more than 220 games and more than 190 compositions. Index of named openings; multilingual glossary of chess terminology.   GV1445.H616

Sunnucks, Anne. The encyclopaedia of chess. 2d ed. London, Hale; N.Y., St. Martin's Pr., 1976. 619p. il.   **BJ95**

1st ed. 1970.
Provides information on chess as played throughout the world, lists of national champions, results of major international tournaments, biographies of leading players, etc. A Subscription Books Committee review in the *Booklist* (74:1573, June 1, 1978) terms the work "an excellent informational source . . . appropriate for all types of libraries." Some information in the 1st ed. was not carried over into the new work.   GV1314.5.S93

CRAFTS

Bibliography

Lovell, Eleanor Cook and **Hall, Ruth Mason.** Index to handicrafts, model-making, and workshop projects. Boston, Faxon, 1936. 476p. (Useful reference ser., no.57)   **BJ96**

———— ———— Supplement, 1–5. . . . Boston, Faxon, 1943–75. 527p., 593p., 914p., 468p., 629p.

Compilers vary.

An index to books and periodical articles for use in school and home craftwork.   Z7911.L89

Shields, Joyce F. Make it: an index to projects and materials. Metuchen, N.J., Scarecrow Pr., 1975. 477p.   **BJ97**

". . . an index to hand-crafted projects described in 475 English language volumes published between January 1, 1968 and January 1, 1974."—*p.v.* The first part of the work is an alphabetical index by specific type of project or craft; the second section provides an index by materials from which the projects are crafted.   Z7911.S54

Encyclopedias

The encyclopedia of crafts. Laura Torbet, ed. N.Y., Scribner, 1980. 3v. il.   **BJ98**

A dictionary arrangement of entries for individual crafts and the terms, materials, tools, etc., relevant to those crafts. About 50 crafts are accorded lengthy articles and there are about 12,000 entries for specific terms identified with those crafts. Definitions and explanations are clear and concise, and the numerous diagrams and line drawings are effectively used. There are many *see* and *see also* references, and use of boldface type for terms within an article indicates that the word or phrase in boldface has its own individual entry.   TT9.S37

Directories

Glassman, Judith. National guide to craft supplies. N.Y., Van Nostrand Reinhold, [1975]. 224p.   **BJ99**

Identifies about 600 sources of supply by craft area, e.g., basket and seat weaving, ceramics, dolls, yarn, etc. Under each craft area suppliers are listed by state. Each entry includes address, description and cost of catalogs, purchase requirements, shipping information, etc. Also has sections on bookstores, societies, galleries and museums, instruction, fairs, periodicals. Subject bibliography of about 800 titles. Indexed.   TT153.7.G48

"How-to" books

Katz, William A. and **Katz, Linda Sternberg.** How-to: 1400 best books on doing almost everything. N.Y., Bowker, 1985. 377p.   **BJ100**

A classified, annotated listing "of the best how-to-do-it books, including some government publications, published primarily between 1980 and 1984."—*Pref.* Gives full publication information and price. Author, title, and subject indexes. Intended as a companion to the compilers' *Self-help: 1400 best books on personal growth* (N.Y., Bowker, 1985. 379p.).

Older lists include *How-to-do-it books; a selected guide* (3d ed. rev. N.Y., Bowker, 1963. 265p.) and *Know-how books; an annotated bibliography of do it yourself books for the handyman and of introductions to science, art, history and literature for the beginner and home student,* by Frank Seymour Smith (London, Thames & Hudson, 1956; N.Y., Bowker, 1957. 306p.).   Z6151.K38

Nueckel, Susan, ed. Selected guide to make-it, fix-it, do-it-yourself books. N.Y., Fleet Pr., [1973]. 213p.   **BJ101**

2,178 items listed alphabetically by subject category. Brief descriptive annotations. Directory of publishers; topical index.

TRAVEL AND TOURISM

Bibliography

Corley, Nora Teresa. Travel in Canada: a guide to information sources. Detroit, Gale, [1983]. 294p. (Geography and travel information guide ser., v.4)   **BJ102**

About 800 entries, most of them annotated, for books, periodicals, series, and agencies which are sources of information about travel in Canada. In three main sections (1) Canada; (2) Canada by region; (3) Canada by province and territory. Each section is appropriately subdivided by focus of publication (e.g., guidebooks, periodicals, atlases and maps, transportation, accommodations, cities, recreation). Fully indexed.   Z1382.C67

Edgar, Neal L. and **Ma, Wendy Yu.** Travel in Asia; a guide to information sources. Detroit, Gale, [1983]. 413p. (Geography and travel information guide ser., v.6)   **BJ103**

An annotated listing of materials in English, with emphasis on publications since 1969. Arranged by country, with author, title, and subject indexes. Nearly 1,200 entries.   Z3001.E22

Goeldner, Charles R. and **Dicke, Karen.** Bibliography of tourism and travel research studies, reports, and articles. Boulder, Colo., Business Research Div., Graduate School of Business Admin., Univ. of Colo. [Salt Lake City, Utah], Travel Research Assoc., [1980]. 9v. (762*l.*)   **BJ104**

Contents: v.1, Information sources; v.2, Economics; v.3, International tourism; v.4, Lodging; v.5, Recreation; v.6, Transportation; v.7, Advertising-Planning; v.8, Statistics-Visitors; v.9, Index.

Aims "to provide a ready source of research references on travel, recreation, and tourism for use in business, government, and academic fields."—*Pref.* Entries are mainly for post-1970 publications.   Z6004.T6G63

Kaul, H. K. Travels in South Asia: a selected and annotated bibliography of guide-books and travel-books on South Asia. Delhi, Arnold-Heinemann; [Atlantic Highlands, N.J.], Humanities Pr., [1979]. 215p.   **BJ105**

In two parts: (1) Guide-books; (2) Travel-books (i.e., accounts written by travelers). Author, title, and geographical indexes. Extensive annotations.   Z3185.K38

Post, Joyce A. and **Post, Jeremiah B.** Travel in the United States: a guide to information sources. Detroit, Gale, [1981]. 578p. (Geography and travel information guide ser., 3)   **BJ106**

Provides references to printed sources (books, atlases, magazines, maps) and to organizations, information centers, which offer information on various aspects of travel in the United States. General and regional sections are followed by sections for the individual states. Annotations; indexes.   Z1245.P67

Dictionaries and encyclopedias

Encyclopedia of world travel. Ed. by Nelson Doubleday and C. Earl Cooley. Rev. by John J. Corris and Seth Goldstein. 3d rev. ed. Garden City, N.Y., Doubleday, [1979]. 2v. (1292p.) il.   **BJ107**

1st ed. 1961.

Contents: v.1, United States, Canada, Mexico, Central America, Bermuda, the Bahamas, the Caribbean, South America; v.2, Europe, Africa, the Middle East, Asia, the Pacific.

Each article sketches the geography, climate, history, agriculture, industry, cities, special events, sports and recreation facilities, and dining and shopping opportunities. Most articles are country guides; the United States and Canada are covered on the state and provincial level. Indexed. G153.4.E52

Metelka, Charles J. The dictionary of tourism. Wheaton, Ill., Merton House, 1981. 87p. **BJ108**

"Entries were selected from among words and terms that 1. are in contemporary use by more than one part of the tourism industry; 2. are frequently used and considered important by at least one part of the tourism industry; 3. are specific to tourism; 4. are used in the academic study of tourism."—*Introd.* G155.A1M443

Guidebooks

❖Guidebooks prepared for the use of travelers are very useful in a reference department for historical and geographical information. For certain kinds of local information they are fuller than either the general or the special gazetteers, giving more local maps, plans of cities, etc. They are especially helpful for information about the art museums, collections, etc., of any given place, its architectural and historical monuments, scenic features, railroads, highways and other communications, hotels, literary and historical associations, etc.

Old guidebooks have a definite reference function and should not be discarded when a later work or edition is acquired. For geographical and travel questions, the most recent work must be used, but the older books will often have historical information not given in the later ones: they will show the location of an old street no longer in existence; describe a building no longer standing; or furnish general descriptive information for an earlier period. For such questions the older guidebook is a most convenient source.

With the increase in travel and tourism, literally thousands of current guidebooks are now available. It will be possible to list here only some of the important standard series, e.g., (1) **Baedeker** series, published in English, French, and German editions, and originating in Germany, has long been regarded as the most authentic and complete guide for the serious traveler, although many volumes are now out-of-date. The handbooks, written in a concise, informative style, cover mainly countries, regions, and cities of Europe, and parts of North and South America, the Near East, and Egypt. Since 1958, a new series of touring guides ("Autoguides") has been issued covering most of the same areas. The Baedekers are especially useful for their maps, city plans, and diagrams; (2) **Muirhead's Blue guides** (London, Benn) are mainly guides to European countries, cities, and environs. Similar to *Baedeker* in style and coverage, they include excellent maps and plans; (3) **Nagel's Travel guide** series (also called *Nagel's Encyclopedia-guides*), formerly part of the Muirhead series *Guides bleues* (Paris, Hachette), and now published in Geneva by Nagel, have recent editions for most of the countries of Europe, some of the cities of Europe, and parts of Africa, Asia, and North America. They are published in various languages, including English, German, Spanish, Italian, French, Swedish, and Danish; (4) **Fodor's Travel guides,** edited by Eugene Fodor (N.Y., Mc-Kay, 1936– ; series title and publisher have varied), illustrated and revised annually, are modern in format and style, and include volumes for various areas of the U.S.; for numerous countries of Europe, Asia, South America, and the Caribbean; and guides to individual cities.

Other popular series, most volumes of which are issued in paperback and are relatively inexpensive, include **Frommer's** guides, the **Mobil** guides, and the **Shell** guides. The Mobil series is concerned primarily with travel in the United States, while the Shell guides emphasize the British Isles (with many volumes for individual counties of England), but

each includes volumes devoted to other countries. The Frommer series is wide-ranging in coverage, many of the titles being designated as "$-a-day guides"; an interesting inclusion is *Frommer's A guide for the disabled traveler: the United States, Canada & Europe* by Frances Barish (N.Y., Frommer/Pasmantier, 1984. 362p.).

General

Cure, Karen. The travel catalogue. N.Y., Holt, Rinehart & Winston, [1978]. 191p. il. **BJ109**

A guide to recreation and travel in the United States, Canada, and the Caribbean, arranged in four main divisions: (1) resorts, inns, and lodgings; (2) historic sites and attractions; (3) crafts, music, dance activities; (4) miscellaneous vacation ideas and activities. A preliminary chapter deals with the mechanics of travel; a directory of travel bureaus, tourist boards, etc., is appended. Guidebook references are noted throughout the text. Indexed. G151.C67

Fielding's Europe. Ed.32– , 1979– . N.Y., Fielding Pubns., 1979– . il. Annual. **BJ110**

1st–31st eds. (1948–78) had title *Fielding's Travel guide to Europe* (varies slightly).

A popular, practical guide addressed particularly to the American tourist. Information on hotels, restaurants, night life, shopping, etc., is generally fuller than that for museums and similar places of interest to the traveler. D909.F45

Bibliography

Hachette, *firm, publishers, Paris.* Avec les "Guides bleues" à travers la France et le monde. (Bibliothèque des voyages) Paris, Hachette, 1959. 304p. il. **BJ111**

A listing of some 4,000 titles (published in French, and in print at the time of compilation of the list) of guidebooks and volumes of geographical and artistic description of interest to tourists.

———— Supplément, 1960–62. Paris, Hachette, 1962. 116p.

Z6019.H3

Hinrichsen, Alex. Baedeker's Reisehandbücher, 1832–1944: Bibliographie der deutschen, französischen und englischen Ausgabe. Holzminden, Hinrichsen, 1981. 72p. il. **BJ112**

A 1979 ed. (67p.) had title: *Baedeker's Reisehandbücher: 1828–1945.*

A bibliography of the German, English, and French editions of the Baedeker travel guides.

Baedeker's Handbook(s) for travellers; a bibliography of English editions published prior to World War II (Westport, Conn., Greenwood Pr., 1975. 38p.) serves as the basis for the microfiche edition of *Baedeker's Handbooks* issued by Greenwood Press.

Z6011.H48

Neal, Jack A., comp. Reference guide for travellers. N.Y., Bowker, 1969. 674p. **BJ113**

An annotated list of English-language guidebooks and background readings for the traveler, most items drawn from in-print lists of 1968. Geographical arrangement, with author/title and place-name indexes. Z6011.N4

Nueckel, Susan. Selected guide to travel books. N.Y., Fleet Pr. Corp., [1974]. 117p. **BJ114**

Works are grouped under such headings as: Backpacking and hiking, Bicycling, Camping, Countries, Currency conversion, Foreign language aids, Mountaineering, etc. About 700 items; brief annotations; subject index. Z6011.N83

Travel guidebooks in review. Ed. by Jon O. Heise. 3d ed., rev. Syracuse, N.Y., Gaylord Professional Pubns. 1978. 187p. **BJ115**

Eds.1–2 (1974–75), publ. by the International Center of the University of Michigan, had title: *Suit your spirit.*

78 travel guides and series of guidebooks are grouped by continent, then by type: the European section includes annually revised guides; specialty guides; series guides about specific countries, cities or regions; accommodation and restaurant guides; train guides; motoring and camping guides; and bicycling and walking guides. Individual guides to countries or cities, and North American guides are excluded. Each entry indicates the purpose, audience, what information is included, and gives an evaluation. Various appendixes serve as indexes to the books, publishers' directories, guidebooks published in series, etc. Z6016.T7S9

United States Travel Data Center. Travel data locator index: a reference guide to current data on travel and recreation. 2d ed. Wash., The Center, 1978. 223p. **BJ116**

Prep. by Joan Betto.
1st ed. 1973.
A subject index to about 100 statistical series covering travel and recreation, produced by the federal government, trade associations, and consulting firms. Z6004.T6U54

United States

American guide series, comp. by the Federal Writers' Project (later called Writers' Program). [Publ. variously by different publishers], 1937–49. il. **BJ117**

Includes guides to each state, many cities and regions, and some special subjects. The state guidebooks are particularly useful, giving accurate information about points of interest with some historical and background material and sidelights on the unusual.

Many of these guides are out-of-print. Some have been reprinted, and a number have been revised and published in new editions by various publishers, notably Hastings House, N.Y.

Yearbooks

Travel market yearbook, 1965– . N.Y., Travel and Tourism Consultant Internat. [etc.], 1965– . Annual. **BJ118**

Subtitle: The yearbook of travel facts, figures and trends.
Title varies: *Travel marketing,* 1978.
Presents statistics of particular interest to the travel industry and its marketing executives in the United States on the tourism market, transportation, accommodations, destinations, travel services, traveler characteristics, advertising, and demographics.
G155.A1T66

Hotels

Financial Times Ltd. Financial Times world hotel directory. 1975/76– . [London, Financial Times, 1975]– . il., maps. Annual. **BJ119**

Publisher varies.
Arranged by country, then by city. Geographical index; numerous city maps. TX907.F47a

Hotel and motel red book, 1886– . N.Y., Amer. Hotel Assoc. Directory Corp., 1886– . il., maps. Annual. **BJ120**

At head of title: Official directory of American hotel and motel association members including hotels, motels, resorts in the United States and other countries (varies).

Title varies: 1886–1902, *United States official hotel directory;* 1903–1953/54, *The official hotel red book and directory;* 1954/55–1962/63, *Hotel red book.*

Arranged by state and city; separate sections for Canada, Caribbean, etc., and a brief international section. Gives credit card information, indicates facilities available (e.g., swimming pool); rates are not always given. TX907.O45

Timetables

Official airline guide. 1943– . Chicago, [Amer. Aviation Publs.], 1943– . il., maps. Monthly. **BJ121**

Publisher varies.
Combines *American aviation air traffic guide* and *Official aviation guide of the airways.*
Published in various editions: (1) North American edition, for United States and possessions (with supplement for ground transportation services); (2) World-wide edition, for United States, possessions, Canada, and all other countries. TL720.8.O38

The official guide of the railways and steam navigation lines of the United States, Canada, and Mexico. N.Y., National Railway Pubn. Co., 1868– . maps. Bimonthly. **BJ122**

Title varies: *The official railway guide, North American travel edition,* etc. Publisher varies. Frequency varies.
Gives current passenger timetables, including principal connecting rail, bus and water service. HE2727.O3

Official steamship guide; international. v.1– . N.Y., Transportation Guides, 1932– . il., maps. Monthly. **BJ123**

Title varies: *Official steamship and airways guide,* v.1–64 (1932–Aug.1963).
Steamship schedules and fares; entry requirements for international travel; passport and visa summary.

Russell's Official national motor coach guide. Cedar Rapids, Iowa, Russell's Guides, 1927– . maps. Monthly. **BJ124**

Now offers timetables "of the majority of intercity motor bus operators in the United States, Canada, Mexico, and Central America."—*Dec.1985 issue.* HE5623.A1R8

C

Social and Behavioral Sciences

❖The term "social sciences" embraces a large number of subjects which deal with the relationship of man to society. In this *Guide* the term is used to cover the works concerned with education; sociology, including social welfare and social conditions; anthropology; psychology; mythology; folklore and popular customs; statistics; economics and business; political science and government; law; and geography.

Only a few reference works deal with the social sciences as a whole, but Carl M. White's *Sources of information in the social sciences* (CA9) is a guide to the literature in most of the above fields. This (or, preferably, its 1986 successor) should be consulted for many sources not listed here. Both the *London bibliography of the social sciences* (CA34), the most extensive bibliography in English in this area, and its French counterpart by Grandin (CA17) will be needed in the large library. The *Encyclopaedia of the social sciences* (CA46), long an authoritative work, is still useful for many purposes and is complemented by the *International encyclopedia of the social sciences* (CA51); both are invaluable in academic and research libraries.

Although not yet as widely applied as in the fields of pure science and technology, computer techniques are becoming an important aspect of information retrieval in various areas of the social sciences. Foremost among the rapidly increasing number of bibliographic data files available for machine searching are the *Social sciences citation index* (CA36), the ERIC databases (*see* the introductory note to the Education section, p.653), *Public Affairs Information Service bulletin* (CA35), *Sociological abstracts* (CC16), and *Psychological abstracts* (CD69). Libraries offering access to these and similar databases will have specially trained information librarians knowledgeable about the strengths and weaknesses of a given data file to assist the research worker and to direct the computer search.

C A

General Works

GUIDES

Freides, Thelma. Literature and bibliography of the social sciences. Los Angeles, Melville, [1973]. 284p.　　**CA1**

A collection of essays stressing the parallel communication systems of scholarly literature and bibliography in the social sciences. Bibliographic review essays discuss types of literature (research reports, handbooks, histories, encyclopedias, dictionaries), and bibliographies for their retrieval. Encompasses anthropology, economics, geography, history, political science, psychology, sociology, and education.　　Z7161.F73

Hoselitz, Berthold Frank. A reader's guide to the social sciences. [Rev. ed.] N.Y., Free Pr., [1970]. 425p.　　**CA2**

1st ed. 1959.

Designed to present a general introduction to the literature of the social sciences, and deals with "the differences in the literary output in major disciplines and the nature of available tools, in the form of books, journals, pamphlets, and reference works, that are consulted and used by social scientists in their research and teaching."—*Pref., 1st ed.* Scholar specialists have contributed chapters on sociology, anthropology, psychology, political science, economics, and geography. A general bibliography lists most of the titles mentioned in the essays and serves in lieu of an index since it includes page references to the text. H61.H69

Lewis, Peter R. The literature of the social sciences; an introductory survey and guide. London, Lib. Assoc., 1960. 222p. **CA3**

A student's guide to the literature of the field (history as such excluded), listing important texts as well as bibliographic and reference tools, with emphasis on British materials. Governmental and international documents are well represented. Annotations are generally brief. Z7161.L45

Li, Tze-chung. Social science reference sources: a practical guide. Westport, Conn., Greenwood Pr., [1980]. 315p. (Contributions in librarianship and information science, no. 30) **CA4**

An outgrowth of the syllabus for a course on information sources in the social sciences, this work is in three parts: (1) the nature of the social sciences, their research methodology and basic reference sources; (2) chapters on the reference and periodical literature pertaining to cultural anthropology, economics and business, education, history, law, political science, psychology and sociology; (3) summary. Provides detailed, critical and comparative descriptions of major reference sources. Covers unpublished materials and data archives, and database bibliographic services as well as printed materials. Name and title indexes. Z7161.A1L5

Mason, John Brown. Research resources: annotated guide to the social sciences. Santa Barbara, Calif., ABC-Clio, 1968–71. 2v. **CA5**

Contents: v.1, International relations and recent history: indexes, abstracts and periodicals; v.2, Official publications: U.S. government, United Nations, international organizations, and statistical sources.

Intended mainly for the student. The first volume lists and provides annotations on a wide range of indexing and abstracting services, reference guides, bibliographies, directories, periodicals, and newspapers useful for social science research. The second volume is a guide to official publications and statistical sources. Z7161.M36

Maunier, René. Manuel bibliographique des sciences sociales et économiques. Paris, Sirey, 1920. 228p. (Repr.: N.Y., Burt Franklin, 1968) **CA6**

An older guide to bibliographies and reference books of the social sciences and economics, particularly useful for historical purposes as it includes many 18th- and 19th-century publications. Includes works in French, English, German, and Italian.

Use of social sciences literature. N. Roberts, ed. London, Butterworth, [1977]. 326p. **CA7**

A series of bibliographic essays by a group of British librarians and academics. Includes chapters on the literature, sources, and needs in the fields of economics, sociology, politics, social anthropology, management research, education, environmental planning, public administration, and criminology. Special chapters on use of the official publications of the United Kingdom, foreign countries, and international organizations. Index of "subjects, institutions and *types* of literature" but none of individual authors and titles. H62.U63

Walford's Guide to reference material. 4th ed., ed. by A. J. Walford. [London], Lib. Assoc., [1982]. v.2. **CA8**

For full information *see* AA507.

v.2, comp. with the assistance of Joan M. Harvey and L. J. Taylor (812p.), covers the social and historical sciences, philosophy and religion.

White, Carl M. and associates. Sources of information in the social sciences; a guide to the literature. 2d ed. Chicago, Amer. Lib. Assoc., 1973. 702p. **CA9**

1st ed. 1964.

A new and greatly enlarged edition of this now standard guide to the literature of the social sciences. Although originally designed primarily for graduate library school students, the work is widely useful to research workers as well. Nine principal chapters treat, respectively: social science in general; history; geography; economics and business administration; sociology; anthropology; psychology; education; and political science. Each consists of two main sections: (1) a bibliographic essay written by a specialist to explain the history and methodology of the discipline, and to cite, as applicable, a substantial number of pertinent, significant monographs; (2) annotated lists of reference sources, grouped by form, type, or specialized aspect, e.g., guides to the literature, abstracts, bibliographies, encyclopedias, handbooks, etc. Periodicals are listed in each category. Detailed table of contents and index of authors, titles and subjects.

Although it is now considerably out of date, *Sources of information in the social sciences* should be consulted for many specialized sources not included in this *Guide*. A 3d ed., ed. by William H. Webb, was published 1986. Z7161.W49

BIBLIOGRAPHY

American Behavioral Scientist. The ABS guide to recent publications in the social and behavioral sciences. N.Y., 1965. 781p. **CA10**

Cumulates the monthly bibliography section, "New studies," as it appeared in the *American behavioral scientist* from 1957 to late 1964. This is, therefore, a selective bibliography of books and periodical articles in the whole range of the social and behavioral sciences. Most entries are annotated. Arranged by author or other main entry, with indexes by title, by proper name, and by "subject." The latter is termed a "topical and methodological index" and is a broad topical classification according to the system devised by Alfred de Grazia for the social and behavioral sciences. Owing to the lack of a conventional subject approach, and because of the relative selectivity, the bibliography's usefulness as a reference work is somewhat limited.

Supplemented by: Z7161.A4

Recent publications in the social and behavioral sciences. 1966–75. N.Y., American Behavioral Scientist, 1966–75. Annual. **CA11**

A series supplementing the *ABS guide* (above). Continues the listings from "New studies" as in the parent work. All entries are annotated; title and subject indexes. Z7161.A42

Belson, William A. and **Thompson, Beryl-Anne.** Bibliography on methods of social and business research. London, Crosby Lockwood [for] London School of Economics and Political Science, [1973]. 300p. **CA12**

"The papers dealt with . . . are principally those journal articles, published research reports and conference papers that deal with the techniques of gathering information from population samples in the context of social and business research."—*Introd.* Alphabetical author listing with detailed subject index. About 2,100 items. Z7161.B44

Berkowitz, Morris I. and **Johnson, J. Edmund.** Social scientific studies of religion: a bibliography. [Pittsburgh], Univ. of Pittsburgh Pr., [1967]. 258p. **CA13**

For full information *see* BB6. Z7751.B47

Bower, Robert T. and **DeGasparis, Priscilla.** Ethics in social research; protecting the interests of human subjects. N.Y., Praeger, [1978]. 207p. **CA14**

The text of this work (p.1–80) discusses risks to the subject of social research, the principle of informed consent, risks and benefits, and regulation. The bibliography (p.85–220) is an annotated main-entry list of relevant books, periodical articles, reports and papers published between 1965 and 1976. Author and subject indexes. H62.B625

Comfort, A. F. and **Loveless, Christina.** Guide to government data: a survey of unpublished social science material in libraries of government departments in London. London, Macmillan, 1974. 404p. **CA15**

Publ. for the British Library of Political and Economic Science.
For each department, provides a brief selection of published materials (especially those about departmental functions, organization, and research), followed by brief descriptions of unpublished materials produced from 1940 onwards; the latter material was originally compiled for internal use, or was prepared as ephemeral material for public distribution.   Z7165.G8C72

Goehlert, Robert U. and **Martin, Fenton S.** Policy analysis and management, a bibliography. Santa Barbara, Calif., ABC-Clio, [1985]. 398p.   **CA16**

A detailed classed bibliography of almost 10,000 English-language journal articles, books, research reports, and selected essays; author and subject indexes. Complemented by John S. Robey's *Analysis of public policy: a bibliography of dissertations, 1977–1982* (Westport, Conn., Greenwood Pr., 1984).   Z7161.G587

Grandin, A. Bibliographie générale des sciences juridiques, politiques, économiques et sociales de 1800 à 1925/26. Paris, Recueil Sirey, 1926. 3v.   **CA17**

v.1–2, classified bibliography; v.3, indexes of authors, titles, and subjects.

———— ———— 1.–19. Suppléments, 1926–50. Paris, Recueil Sirey, 1928–51. v.1–19.

No more published?
A very comprehensive bibliography of French monographic works in the fields of law, and of the political, economic, and social sciences. International in scope, with special emphasis on French-speaking countries.
Continued for economic materials by Mossé, *Bibliographie d'économie politique* (CH18).   Z6458.F8G7

International Committee for Social Sciences Documentation. Retrospective bibliography of social science works published in the Middle East: U.A.R., Iraq, Jordan, Lebanon, 1945–1955. Cairo, UNESCO Middle East Science Cooperation Off., 1959. 299p.   **CA18**

Title and headings in English and French.
Prep. with the cooperation of the United Arab Republic National Commission for Unesco.
Classified arrangement under each country. Covers sociology, sociocultural anthropology, social psychology, political science, and economics. Author index.
Continued by:

United Nations Educational, Scientific and Cultural Organization. Middle East Science Cooperation Office. Middle East social science bibliography; books and articles on the social sciences publ. in Arab countries of the Middle East in 1955–1960. Cairo, 1961. 152p.   **CA19**

Cover title: Social science bibliography: Arab countries of the Middle East.
A classified listing of some 1,200 items, in Western languages and in Arabic (transliterated). Author index.   Z7165.N35U5

Heiliger, William S. Bibliography of the Soviet social sciences 1965–1975. Troy, N.Y., Whitston, 1978. 2v.   **CA20**

Lists over 9,300 books, periodical articles, conference proceedings, theses and dissertations by issuing institute or journal; journal articles are further subdivided by broad topic. All titles are translated into English. Institutional publications, conference papers, theses and dissertations are cross-referenced to their listing in the *Bibliografiia izdanii* of the Akademiia Nauk SSSR (CA165) for ordering information and availability. Author index; inadequate subject index.   Z7165.R9H45

Lu, Joseph K. U.S. government publications relating to the social sciences: a selected annotated guide. Beverly Hills, Calif., Sage, [1975]. 260p.   **CA21**

A detailed table of contents serves as the subject index to some 750 entries, arranged in chapters, e.g., bibliographic sources, American history, business and economics, Communism. Each entry includes the Superintendent of Documents classification number; cutoff date for entries is mid-1973. Appendixes provide brief lists of

background reading and guides, order information, and a list of depository libraries. Personal name and title indexes.
                   Z1223.Z7L8

McInnis, Raymond G. and **Scott, James William.** Social science research handbook. N.Y., Barnes and Noble, [1975]. 395p. (Repr.: N.Y., Garland, 1985)   **CA22**

A bibliography of about 1,500 reference works. In two sections: pt.A defines the disciplines in the social sciences—anthropology, demography, economics, geography, history, political science, and sociology—and discusses reference sources arranged by type, and reference works on specialized subfields; pt.B follows a similar arrangement for areas of the world. A bibliography section gives full information for all titles cited in pts.A and B.   Z7161.A1M3

Ouvrages cyrilliques concernant les sciences sociales; liste des reproductions disponibles. Cyrillic publications concerning the social sciences; current list of reproductions. Paris, Mouton, 1964–65. 2v. (Cahiers du monde russe et soviétique. Suppl.1–2)   **CA23**

Compiled from publishers' catalogs to provide comparative information on hard-copy reprint and microform reproductions of books and periodicals, primarily in Russian. In addition to social sciences, includes literature, linguistics, early texts, and criticism. Classified arrangement in v.1; v.2 provides both a supplement and an index to the two volumes. The supplement includes Cyrillic works in Bulgarian, Belorussian, Serbian, and Ukrainian as well as Russian. It was announced that "a complete card file of available cyrillic reproductions will be maintained and kept up to date at the Centre de Documentation sur l'URSS et les Pays Slaves."—*Introd., v.2.*
                   Z2519.O85

Social science abstracts; a comprehensive abstracting and indexing journal of the world's periodical literature in the social sciences. N.Y., Social Science Abstracts, Columbia Univ., 1929–33. 5v.   **CA24**

Ceased publication.
Contents: v.1–4, Abstracts, 1929–32; v.5, Indexes: Subject, p.1–548; Authors, p.551–677; List of periodicals and serials in the social sciences, p.681–725.
An extensive bibliography with abstracts written by specialists. Covers practically the same fields as the *Encyclopaedia of the social sciences* (CA46).   H1.S6

Southern Asia social science bibliography (with annotations and abstracts). no.8–14, 1959–65. Calcutta, Research Centre on the Social Implications of Industrialization in Southern Asia, 1960–65. Annual.   **CA25**

Formed by the merger, and continuing the numbering of: *Social science bibliography: India* (1952–58) and *South Asia social science abstracts* (1954–58), both formerly published by Unesco, Field Service Cooperation Office for South Asia. Ceased publication.
A combination bibliography and abstract journal listing books, pamphlets, and periodical articles published in English in South Asia, and, in the case of Vietnam, those published in French. Countries covered: India, Pakistan, Ceylon, Burma, Indonesia, Malaya and Singapore, the Philippines, Thailand, and Vietnam. Classed arrangement with author and subject indexes.
Continued by *Asian social science bibliography.*   Z7165.I6U5

Woronitzin, Sergej. Bibliographie der Sozialforschung in der Sowjetunion (1960–1970). Bibliography of social research in the Soviet Union (1960–1970). Pullach bei München, Verlag Dokumentation, 1973. 215p.   **CA26**

Includes approximately 700 books and periodical articles published in Russian or Ukrainian, with titles also translated into German and English. Lists collected and periodically issued compilations, works on theory and methodology, and empirical research by subject area. Author index.

Current

APAIS, Australian public affairs information service; a subject index to current literature. no.1– , July 1945– . Canberra, National Lib. of Australia, 1945– . Monthly except Dec.; 1955– , cumulated annually.　　　**CA27**

A subject index of selected articles on Australian political, economic, social, and cultural affairs. "It indexes relevant articles in a wide range of periodicals published both in Australia and overseas . . . [and] all articles, whatever their subject, in a selected list of Australian periodicals which have been chosen for indexing because of their importance in the social sciences and humanities. Sections on Australian subjects from books published outside Australia which do not qualify for *Australian national bibliography* [AA618] are included in APAIS. Some annual reports of government agencies and other important organizations are also indexed."—*Introd., 1970 cum.* Conference proceedings and selected newspaper articles have also been indexed in recent years.　　　Z7165.A8A8

Bibliographie der Sozialwissenschaften; internationale Dokumentation der Buch- und Zeitschriftenliteratur des Gesamtgebiets der Sozialwissenschaften, 1905–67. Göttingen, Vandenhoeck & Ruprecht, 1906–68. Annual (previously monthly).　　　**CA28**

Frequency varies. Publisher varies.

Title varies: usually *Bibliographie der Sozialwissenschaften,* with variant subtitles, through 1936; *Bibliographie der Staats- und Wirtschaftswissenschaften,* 1937–43; suspended, 1944–49; *Bibliographie der Sozialwissenschaften,* 1950–67.

Jahrg. 42–59 also called N.F., Jahrg. 1–18; Jahrg. 42 covers 1948/49.

1950–63 published in parts bound with the *Jahrbuch für Sozialwissenschaft;* later years issued separately in conjunction with the *Jahrbuch.*

A classified list with author and subject indexes, listing both books and periodicals in a large range of the political and social sciences in various languages. A comprehensive and very valuable bibliography in these fields.

Continued as:　　　Z7163.K852

Bibliographie der Wirtschaftswissenschaften (vormals Bibliographie der Sozialwissenschaften), 1968– . Göttingen, Vandenhoeck & Ruprecht, [1971–]. Jahrg. 60– (N.F., Jahrg. 19–). Annual.　　　**CA29**

Supersedes the *Bibliographie der Sozialwissenschaften* and continues its numbering.

Continues to be a classified listing of books, parts of books, and periodical articles in many languages. Separate indexes of subjects and of names and titles. Several hundred periodicals and series are regularly gleaned for relevant articles. Each annual volume is published in two parts, with individual subject and name indexes.
　　　Z7164.E2B5187

Bulletin signalétique 521: Sociologie-ethnologie. v.24– , 1970– . Paris, Centre du Documentation Sciences Humaines, 1970– . Quarterly.　　　**CA30**

A comprehensive, international abstract journal. For complete information on the *Bulletin* series *see* EA76.

Current contents: social & behavioral sciences. v.6, no.2– , Jan. 2, 1974– . Philadelphia, Inst. for Scientific Information, 1974– . Weekly.　　　**CA31**

Continues *Current contents. Behavioral, social & educational sciences* and assumes its numbering.

Reproduces contents tables of about 1,300 international journals as well as articles from multi-authored books; each issue is indexed by title keyword and author (with current address). A cumulative journal index locating the contents table of each journal appears on a triannual basis. Tables of contents are grouped within 13 broad subject categories. The publisher provides similar *Current contents* volumes for the physical, chemical and earth sciences; agriculture, biology and environmental sciences; clinical practice; engineering, technology and applied sciences; arts and humanities.
　　　Z1219.C98

Fondation Nationale des Sciences Politiques. Bulletin analytique de documentation politique, économique et social contemporaine. 1. année– . Paris, Presses Universitaires de France, 1946– . Monthly.　　　**CA32**

Frequency varies.

Selective indexing from about 2,200 French and foreign periodicals on political, economic, and social questions, frequently with a brief descriptive note. Gives exact citations with inclusive paging. Arranged by class with annual subject index; no author index.
　　　Z7163.F7

Foreign language index. v.1– , 1968/71– . N.Y., Public Affairs Information Service 1972– . Quarterly with annual cumulations.　　　**CA33**

v.1, covering 1968/71, was issued in a single cumulated volume; the first quarterly issue, v.2, no.1, was published in Spring 1973 and covers late 1971–early 1972 materials. Publication continues on a quarterly basis thereafter, the fourth issue of the year being an annual cumulation.

A companion to the *PAIS bulletin* (CA35), this "is an indexing service for selected library materials in the fields of economic and public affairs published in languages other than English."—*Pref.* Covers materials in French, German, Italian, Portuguese, and Spanish, with expanded coverage for other languages anticipated. Like *PAIS bulletin,* it is a subject listing, but within subject categories the listing is by author rather than title, and there is an author index which repeats the bibliographic citation. v.1 is limited to periodicals, but with v.2 selected books, pamphlets, and government publications are included.　　　Z7164.E2P8●

London bibliography of the social sciences . . . comp. under the direction of B. M. Headicar and C. Fuller, with an introd. by Sidney Webb (Lord Passfield). London, London School of Economics, 1931–32. 4v., and suppl. (v.5–41), 1934–84. (London School of Economics. Studies in economics and political science: Bibliographies, no.8)　　　**CA34**

At head of title, v.15–41: British Library of Political and Economic Science.

Publisher varies.

The most extensive subject bibliography in its field; important to all large libraries and research workers. International in scope, recording books, pamphlets, and documents in many languages. Arranged alphabetically by subject, with brief but adequate information: author, title (often abbreviated), paging, date, location, and information as to whether the work contains a bibliography; has many cross references.

Author indexes are included in v.4 (to v.1–3) and in v.5 and v.6 but not in later volumes. A list of periodicals appeared in v.4, with supplementary lists (up to 1936) in v.5 and v.6.

Coverage varies. v.1–5 include holdings of nine London libraries and special collections; the supplements, 1931–36, 1936–50, 1950–55, list additions—other than works in the Russian language—to the British Library of Political and Economic Science, and the Edward Fry Library of International Law (some variation). v.10–11, 1950–55, include additions in Russian, 1936–50, to the two libraries noted. v.12–14 list all additions for 1956–62 to the two libraries; and v.15–21 list similar additions for 1962–68; v.22–31 cover 1969–73. Each subsequent volume includes annual additions.

The 6th to 8th supplements (v.15–21, 22–28, 29–31 of the series) are produced photographically from cards (and published by Mansell), providing more bibliographical information than formerly appeared. "Indexes" in v.21, 28, and 31 are lists of subject headings, alphabetically and in classified order.　　　Z7161.L84

Public Affairs Information Service. Public Affairs Information Service bulletin. 1st– , annual cumulations. N.Y., Service, 1915– . v.1– .　　　**CA35**

Usually cited as *PAIS.* Now issued in three forms: (1) semimonthly bulletins; (2) cumulations published three times a year; (3) the permanent annual volume, with author index.

A subject index to the current literature relating to economic and social conditions: books, documents, pamphlets, reports of public and private agencies, articles in periodicals, multigraphed material, etc. Includes selective indexing to more than 1,000 periodicals published in English throughout the world.

A very useful index for political science, government, legislation, economics, sociology, etc. Indispensable in the large library.
　　　Z7163.P9●

—— —— Cumulative author index 1965–1969. Comp. and ed. by C. Edward Wall. Ann Arbor, Mich., Pierian Pr., 1973. 490p.

Offers an author approach to *PAIS* for the period indicated. Similar indexes are planned for earlier periods.

—— —— Cumulative subject index to the P.A.I.S. annual bulletin, 1915–1974. Arlington, Va., Carrollton Pr., [1977–78]. 15v.

References listed under subject headings give reference to the years, pages, and columns of the *Bulletin* where the complete entries can be found. General, subject, and geographical sub-headings have been combined in one alphabet under the major heading, rather than listed separately as in the annual volumes. Geographical entries appear under each of the various names by which the area has been known during the sixty-year period covered.

Social sciences citation index, 1972– . Philadelphia, Institute for Scientific Information, 1973– .   **CA36**

"An international interdisciplinary index to the literature of the social sciences."—*title page.*

Issued three times a year, the third issue being the annual bound cumulation. Began publication with the issue covering [Jan.–April] 1973; a cumulated issue giving retrospective coverage for 1972 was published 1974. Five-year cumulations have been published for 1966–70, 1971–75, and 1976–80; they offer expanded journal coverage beyond the annual volumes.

Patterned after the same publisher's *Science citation index* (EA72), this service enables the user to identify related writings (periodical articles, reviews, etc.) by indicating sources in which a known work by a given author has been cited. A subject search may also be made through use of the "Permuterm subject index." Covers about 2,000 journals, many of them selectively (i.e., relevant articles from journals in the physical, chemical and life sciences are included since the index draws on material in the total Institute for Scientific Information database).

Each issue is in three main parts: (1) Citation index (arranged alphabetically by cited author, with references to articles in which a work is cited; there are separate sections for corporate authors and anonymous publications); (2) Source index (arranged alphabetically by author and giving full bibliographic citations plus the author's address if available); and (3) Permuterm subject index (offering a subject approach through a system of indexing which "involves the permutation of all significant words within each sentence of the title and subtitle of an article to form all possible pairs of terms"; reference here is to names appearing in the "Source index"). There is also a "Corporate address index."   Z7161.S65●

Social sciences in socialist countries. v.1 (1978/79)– . Moscow, Ed. by INION of the Academy of Sciences of the USSR under the direction of Dr. R. Mdivani on behalf of the ECSSID Programme (European Cooperation in Social Science Information and Documentation), 1981– . Annual?   **CA37**

Sponsored by the European Coordination Centre for Research and Documentation in Social Sciences (Vienna Centre).

Provides English-language title translations and abstracts for books published in East European countries and the Soviet Union. "Social sciences" has been interpreted to include relevant aspects of philosophy, history, literary theory, science and technology. Broad subject arrangement; indexed by names, geographic area, and subject.

Social sciences in the USSR, annotated bibliography for 1979– . Academy of Sciences of the USSR, Institute of Scientific Information on Social Sciences. Moscow, The Institute, 1982– . Annual.   **CA38**

Title also in Russian: Sovetskoe obshchestvovedenie, Ukazatel' literatury.

A selective bibliography of monographs written by Soviet scholars in the main fields of social science research. Bibliographic descriptions in the vernacular, with English-language titles and abstracts. Topical arrangement; no author index.   Z7165.R9S6

Social sciences index. v.1, no.1– , June 1974– . N.Y., Wilson, 1974– . Quarterly with annual cumulations.   **CA39**

For full information *see* AE236.

Dissertations

See also AH11.

United Nations Educational, Scientific and Cultural Organization. Thèses de sciences sociales; catalogue analytique international de thèses inédites de doctorat, 1940–1950. Theses in the social sciences; an international analytical catalogue of unpublished doctorate theses, 1940–1950. [Paris, 1952] 236p.   **CA40**

Contains listings from 30 member states and from Germany (which was not a member at the time of the survey). Titles have been translated, when necessary, into French or English. Listings are under broad subject, and then alphabetical by the French version of a country's name. An index to authors and an index to the broad subjects used.   Z7161.U4

Periodicals

Unesco Social Science Documentation Centre. World list of social science periodicals. Prep. with the co-operation of the International Committee for Social Science Information and Documentation. 5th ed., rev. [Paris], Unesco, [1980]. 447p. (World social science information services, 1)   **CA41**

1st ed. 1953.
Also publ. in French and Spanish.

3,191 social sciences periodicals, serial bibliographies, and abstracting services are arranged by country of publication, with title and subject indexes; publications of international organizations are listed separately. Updated semiannually in the *International social science journal.*   Z7163.U52

U.S. Bureau of the Census. Bibliography of social science periodicals and monograph series, . . . under grant from Office of Science Information Service, National Science Foundation. Wash., 1961–65. no. 1–22. (*Its* Foreign social science bibliographies, ser. P–92, no.1–22)   **CA42**

Contents: no.1, Rumania, 1947–1960. 1961. 27p.; no.2, Bulgaria, 1944–1960. 1961. 36p.; no.3, Mainland China, 1949–1960. 1961. 32p.; no.4, Republic of China, 1949–1961. 1962. 24p.; no.5, Greece, 1950–1961. 1962. 19p.; no.6, Albania, 1944–1961. 1962. 12p.; no.7, Hong Kong, 1950–1961. 1962. 13p.; no.8, North Korea, 1945–1961. 1962. 12p.; no.9, Republic of Korea, 1945–1961. 1962. 48p.; no.10, Iceland, 1950–1962. 1962. 10p.; no.11, Denmark, 1945–1961. 1963. 111p.; no.12, Finland, 1950–1962. 1963. 85p.; no.13, Hungary, 1947–1962. 1964. 137p.; no.14, Turkey, 1950–1962. 1964. 88p.; no.15, Norway, 1945–1962. 1964. 59p.; no.16, Poland, 1945–1962. 1964. 312p.; no.17, U.S.S.R., 1950–1963. 1965. 443p.; no.18, Yugoslavia, 1945–1963. 1963. 152p.; no.19, Czechoslovakia, 1948–1963. 1964. 129p.; no.20, Japan, 1950–1963. 1965. 346p.; no.21, Soviet Zone of Germany, 1948–1963. 1965. 190p.; no.22, Sweden, 1950–1963. 1964. 83p.

Covers countries in the Communist bloc or other areas using "difficult languages." Each number is a classified listing of titles available in the Library of Congress. Annotations (or tables of contents), and indexes by subject, title, and issuing agency, are supplied.   Z7161.U43

Book reviews

Book review index to social science periodicals. [Ann Arbor, Mich.], Pierian Pr., 1978–81. 4v.   **CA43**

Arnold M. Rzepecki, ed.

Contents: v.1, 1964–1970; v.2, 1971; v.3, 1972; v.4, 1973–Mar. 1974.

The set fulfills "a commitment made in 1970 to provide book review coverage of social science journals to complement the *Index to Book Reviews in the Humanities*" (*Introd.*), thus filling "the lacuna of social science periodicals book reviews until the appearance of *Social Sciences Index* in April 1974." The term "social science" is broadly interpreted "to include not only history titles, but also archaeology and journals dealing with the sociological aspects of religion," and therefore indexes reviews in the history journals dropped from *Index to book reviews in the humanities* (*see* AA520, note). It should be kept in mind that *all* reviews in a given periodical are indexed, not only those on social science topics.

Z7161.A15B65

DICTIONARIES AND ENCYCLOPEDIAS

Branciard, Michel. Dictionnaire économique et social: dictionnaire Thomas Suavet. 11. éd., entièrement rev. et corr. Paris, Économie et Humanisme, [1978]. 582, 17p. il. **CA44**

For full information *see* CH45.

Dictionnaire de sociologie, familiale, politique, économique, spirituelle, générale, publié sous la direction de G. Jacquemet avec le concours de nombreux collaborateurs. Paris, Letouzey, 1931–39. v.1–4 (incompl.). **CA45**

No more published.

Contents: v.1–3, A–Bouclier; v.4 (fasc.19–22), Boud–Cercles.

A scholarly encyclopedia with long, signed articles, often with bibliographies. Contains biographies, and many short articles on tribes, clans, etc. Written from the Catholic point of view.

HM17.D5

Encyclopaedia of the social sciences; ed. in chief, E. R. A. Seligman; assoc. ed., Alvin Johnson. N.Y., Macmillan, 1930–35. 15v. **CA46**

v.1 includes Introductions: I, Development of social thought and institutions (12 articles), p.3–228; II, The social sciences as disciplines by country (11 articles), p.231–49. Index in v.15.

The first comprehensive encyclopedia of the whole field of the social sciences, projected and prepared under the auspices of ten learned societies. Aims to cover all important topics in the fields of political science, economics, law, anthropology, sociology, penology, and social work, and the social aspects of ethics, education, philosophy, psychology, biology, geography, medicine, art, etc. International in scope and treatment, but fuller for the English-speaking world and western Europe than for other regions or interests. Articles are by specialists and signed; bibliographies in the main are adequate and in unusually good form. About 50 percent of the articles are biographical; includes many biographies of deceased persons.

The *International encyclopedia of the social sciences* (CA51) complements, but does not supersede this work. H41.E6

Encyclopedia of policy studies. Ed. by Stuart S. Nagel. N.Y., Dekker, [1983]. 914p. **CA47**

Defines policy studies as "the study of the nature, causes, and effects of alternative public policies for dealing with specific social problems."—*p.xv.* Consists of chapters providing surveys and bibliographic references on nine general approaches and 23 specific policy problems. Indexed. H97.E6

Foulquié, Paul. Vocabulaire des sciences sociales. Paris, Presses Universitaires de France, [1978]. 378p. **CA48**

Entry for each term includes: brief etymology; definition according to various social science fields; usage examples quoted from a variety of sources. Source bibiliography. H43.F68

Gould, Julius and **Kolb, William L.,** eds. A dictionary of the social sciences. N.Y., Free Pr., [1964]. 761p. **CA49**

Comp. under the auspices of Unesco.

Includes terms from "the fields of political science, social anthropology, economics, social psychology, and sociology—the aim being to select terms that were general and/or in some way basic to the disciplines concerned."—*Introd.* (Terms about whose meaning there is little dispute and which are adequately defined in standard dictionaries were generally omitted.) Fairly full and comprehensive treatment is given for a term, with a concise definition or definitions followed by historical background, discussion of controversies or divergences of meanings, special significance which the term may have in the social sciences, etc. Articles are signed and were contributed by scholars from the British Commonwealth and the United States. Bibliographical references are included in many articles. H41.G6

Handwörterbuch der Sozialwissenschaften. Hrsg. von E. von Beckerath [et al.]. Stuttgart, Fischer, [1952–68]. 12v. and Registerband. **CA50**

Published in parts.

Represents a revised and expanded edition of the *Handwörterbuch der Staatswissenschaften* which appeared in four editions: 1st ed. 1890–94. 6v.; 2d ed. 1898–1901. 7v.; 3d ed. 1909–11. 8v.; 4th ed. 1923–29. 8v. and suppl. The 1st–3d ed., edited by J. Conrad, L. Elster [and others], often cited as *Conrad's Handwörterbuch;* 4th ed. edited by L. Elster, A. Weber, F. Wieser.

A standard, comprehensive work. Long, signed articles by specialists on places, persons, and subjects, with extensive bibliographies.

H45.H18

International encyclopedia of the social sciences. David L. Sills, ed. [N.Y.], Macmillan and the Free Pr., [1968–80]. 18v. **CA51**

Not a mere revision of the *Encyclopaedia of the social sciences* (CA46), but a completely new work "designed to complement, not to supplant, its predecessor."—*Introd.* Planned to represent the social sciences in the 1960s, it reflects the development and recent rapid expansion in this area. Topical articles are devoted to concepts, principles, theories, and methods in the disciplines of anthropology, economics, geography, history, law, political science, psychiatry, psychology, sociology, and statistics. Contributors were asked to emphasize the analytical and comparative aspects of a topic rather than the historical and descriptive material. Biographical sketches in v.1–16 have been limited to about 600 (in contrast to the 4,000 in the earlier set), and only living persons born before 1890 were eligible for inclusion; for full information on v.18, "Biographical supplement," *see* CA77. Scholars from more than 30 countries contributed the signed articles; bibliographies are provided. The dictionary arrangement is strengthened by *see* and *see also* references as well as by a complete index. H40.A2I5

Karrenberg, Friedrich. Evangelisches Soziallexikon. Hrsg. von Theodor Schober, Martin Honecker, Horst Dahlhaus. [7-vollständig neu bearb. u. erw. Aufl.] Stuttgart, Kreuz-Verlag, 1980. 1560col. **CA52**

1st ed. 1954.

Prepared by 160 German-Protestant social scientists who attempt to trace historical developments, presenting Catholic and secular viewpoints as well as Protestant. Covers such topics as sociology and social work, and the social aspects of biology, economics, law, medicine, etc. Includes bibliographies. H45.K3

Miller, P. McC. and **Wilson, M. J.** A dictionary of social science methods. Chichester, [Eng., etc.], Wiley, [1983]. 124p. il. **CA53**

Defines terms used in research in the empirical social sciences; many statistical models and terms are included. H41.M54

Reading, Hugo F. A dictionary of the social sciences. [London, Sociologia Publs., 1976] 231p. **CA54**

Also published by Routledge & Kegan Paul, 1977.

Offers very brief definitions of more than 7,500 terms covering "all the social sciences with the exception of economics and linguistics."—*Pref.* Cross references are indicated by use of italics.

H41.R42

Smith, Robert E. F. A Russian-English dictionary of social science terms. London, Butterworth, 1962. 495p. **CA55**

Aims to provide an aid to the translation of Russian social science texts in the fields of sociology, politics, economics, accounting, public administration, welfare, and education.　　　H49.S55

Thinès, Georges and **Lempereur, Agnès.** Dictionnaire général des sciences humaines. Paris, Éditions Universitaires, [1975]. 1033p.　　　**CA56**

"Sciences humaines" is broadly interpreted so that there are terms from anthropology, biology, criminology, demography, esthetics, linguistics, literature, mathematics, pedagogy, physiology, political science, psychiatry, psychology, sociology, statistics, etc. Field of usage is indicated for each term defined, with two or more definitions given for terms having specialized meanings in different fields. *See* and *see also* references; occasional bibliographic citations; charts and diagrams. Includes some name entries, mainly for psychologists and sociologists.　　　BF31.T47

United Nations Educational, Scientific and Cultural Organization. Glossary of conference terms: English, French, Arabic. 2d rev. ed. [Paris], Unesco, [1978]. 90p.　　　**CA57**

1st ed. 1974.
This edition incorporates "a number of minor amendments and a few additions."—*Pref.* A 1–volume edition of the three glossaries (based on English, French, or Arabic), with organizational charts of the United Nations, the Food and Agriculture Organization, the International Labour Organisation, and Unesco is also available.　　　AS6.U57

Zadrozny, John Thomas. Dictionary of social science. Wash., Public Affairs Pr., [1959]. 367p.　　　**CA58**

Brief definitions of several thousand terms, primarily in sociology, political science, and economics, with lesser listings in related fields.　　　H41.Z3

DIRECTORIES AND HANDBOOKS

Canadian social science data catalog. 2d ed. Downsview, Ont., York Univ., Inst. for Behavioural Research, Data Bank/Information Systems, Nov. 1976. 341p. Looseleaf.　　　**CA59**

1st ed. 1974.
A catalog of the numeric data sets at the Data Bank of the Institute for Behavioural Research which may be distributed to users outside the University; the first edition included all sets available at the Data Bank. Data set descriptions contain full summaries of the individual data sets, and are chronologically arranged; there are KWIC, principal investigator, title of study, and geographic indexes.　　　Z7166.C35

Conference of Social Science Councils and Analogous Bodies. International directory of social science research councils and analogous bodies, CNSSC. 1978/79. N.Y. [etc.], K. G. Saur, [1978]. 159p.　　　**CA60**

Contains entries from 28 national and five regional organizations, with quite detailed information on history, structure, revenue and expenditures, grants, international cooperative programs, and publications.
Continued by:　　　H62.A1C58a

International directory of social science organizations. Comp. and ed. by International Federation of Social Science Organizations. 1981/82– . Stockholm, Almqvist & Wiksell, [1981]– . Irregular.　　　**CA61**

The 1981/82 ed. expands coverage to 40 national and ten regional and international organizations.　　　H62.A1C58a

Gabrovska, Svobodozarya, Biskup, Manfred and **Bossilkova, Anna.** European guide to social science information and documentation services. Comp. for the European Cooperation in Social Science Information and Documentation. N.Y., Pergamon, [1982]. 234p.　　　**CA62**

A directory of 215 institutions and libraries providing social

science information services (data or bibliographic) in 22 countries, including the Soviet Union and Eastern Europe. Services are grouped by country, then alphabetically under the English name. Subject index.　　　H61.9.G3

Information services on research in progress: a worldwide inventory. Ed. by the Smithsonian Science Information Exchange, Inc. and comp. with the support of Unesco within its General Information Programme and UNISIST. 2d ed. [Paris], Unesco, [1982]. 320p. il.　　　**CA63**

1st ed. 1978.
Presents profiles of 230 information systems, international, regional, and national. Indexed by subject, country, organization, system and individual names.　　　Q179.96.I55

Levine, Herbert M. and **Owen, Dolores B.** An American guide to British social science resources. Metuchen, N.J., Scarecrow Pr., 1976. 281p.　　　**CA64**

Organized into three chapters: (1) basic information on British information sources in the United States and the realities of British life for the American academic; (2) a description of the major British library and record office resources for the social scientist, detailing subject coverage, access, publications, and services; and (3) descriptions of relevant professional associations and political parties. Index by subject, type of material, and institution.　　　H62.L443

Miller, Delbert Charles. Handbook of research design and social measurement. 4th ed. N.Y., Longman, [1983]. 678p.　　　**CA65**

1st ed. 1964.
In five main parts: (1) guide to research design, including the research grant proposal; (2) collection of data in library, field, and laboratory, with a directory of social science data libraries and international social science research centers; (3) guides to statistical analysis; (4) selected sociometric scales and indexes, grouped by subject; (5) material on research budgeting, funding, and reporting in scholarly meetings and journals. Personal name index.　　　H62.M44

Mullins, Carolyn J. A guide to writing and publishing in the social and behavioral sciences. N.Y., John Wiley, [1977]. 431p.　　　**CA66**

Intended "primarily for students and professionals in the social and behavioral sciences, but also for their typists, editors, and publishers."—*Pref.* Includes sections on writing outlines, first drafts, revisions; information on preparing and placing scholarly articles for journal publication; instructions for preparing a book manuscript; and information on "publishers, prospectuses, and contracts." Bibliography; illustrative examples; index.　　　H91.M8

Neave, Henry R. Statistics tables for mathematicians, engineers, economists and the behavioural and management sciences. London, Allen & Unwin, [1978]. 87p.　　　**CA67**

Presents a collection of tables relating to standard statistical techniques considered in an introductory course in statistical methods; includes tables relevant to probability, distributions, estimation, hypothesis-testing, regression, correlation and analysis of variance, non-parametric methods, quality control, and basic operations research.　　　QA276.25N43

SSRC Survey Archive data catalogue: guide to the Survey Archive's social science data holdings and allied services. Colchester, Eng., Social Science Research Council Survey Archive, Univ. of Essex, [1979?]. lxxi, 268p.　　　**CA68**

Describes the more than 1,300 data sets held by the SSRC Survey Archive, the largest national repository of machine-readable social science data in Great Britain. Data sets are grouped by subject, with a preliminary chapter listing large-scale continuous and longitudinal surveys, such as the 1971 United Kingdom census, the Gallup political polls, etc. Information for each data set entry includes: purpose, list of variables, publications, sponsor, depositor, principal investigator, sample details, and date. Indexed by depositor, survey title, geographical area, and population sampled. New data set acquisitions are noted in the tri-annual Survey Archive *Bulletin*.

Sessions, Vivian S., ed. Directory of data bases in the social and behavioral sciences. [N.Y.], Science Associates/Internat., [1974]. 300p. **CA69**

Arranged alphabetically by name of sponsoring institution, with indexes by major categories and keywords, by distinctive names and acronyms, plus personnel and geographic indexes. Lists 685 databases, with information (derived from questionnaires) on address, staff, subject field, scope and sources of data, storage media, hardware, software, output media, etc. Includes some foreign as well as United States institutions. Z699.5.S65S47

United Nations Educational, Scientific and Cultural Organization. Social Science Clearing House. International organizations in the social sciences: a summary description of the structure and activities of nongovernmental organizations specialized in the social sciences and in consultative relationship with Unesco (categories A and B). 3d rev. ed. [Paris], UNESCO, [1964]. 147p. (*Its* Reports and papers in the social sciences, no.21) **CA70**

1st ed. 1956; 2d ed. 1961

Since this edition is strictly limited to those organizations having consultative relationships with Unesco in the categories A ("consultative and associate") and B ("information and consultative"), the total number of bodies treated is confined to 14. Organizations of category C ("mutual information"), some of which appeared in the previous edition, are omitted. H62.U475

—— Research councils in the social sciences. [Paris, UNESCO, 1955] 54p. (*Its* Reports and papers in the social sciences, no.3) **CA71**

Gives information about the social science research councils, arranged by country. H62.U475

U.S. Library of Congress. National Referral Center. A directory of information resources in the United States: social sciences. Rev. ed. Wash., Lib. of Congress, 1973. 700p. **CA72**

1st ed. 1965.

Briefly describes the collections, services, facilities, accessibility, etc., of various libraries, government agencies, and societies in the whole range of social sciences. Alphabetical listing, with subject index. AS25.A46

University of Bath. Inventory of information resources in the social sciences. [Farnborough, Hants], Saxon House; Lexington, Mass., Lexington Books, [1975]. 239p. **CA73**

Prep. by the University of Bath for the Organisation for Economic Co-operation and Development.

J. M. Brittain and S. A. Roberts, eds.

Added title page in French; introductory matter in English and French.

In two main sections: (1) Information services and (2) Information sources. "The information services recorded are those organisations or activities, existing independently or within some other organisation, whose integral function and distinguishing feature is the management of information on given topics and the supply of that information to those who need or request it. . . . The information sources are reference or bibliographical publications providing details of the types of information potentially available to social science information users."—*Introd.* A third section, information research, contains details of research projects dealing with information activities in the social sciences. Entries are arranged by subject, and within each subject by country. General, subject, and country indexes. H61.U575

World directory of social science institutions. Research, advanced training, documentation, professional bodies. 3d ed., rev. [Paris], Unesco, [1982]. 535p. (World social sciences information services, 2) **CA74**

1st ed. 1977. A 1970 ed. had title: *World index of social science institutions.*

In English, French, and Spanish.

Provides descriptions for more than 2,300 international and national organizations. Arranged by country; indexed by name and subject. H62.W673

BIOGRAPHY

American men and women of science: Social and behavioral sciences. 13th ed. N.Y., Jaques Cattell Pr./Bowker, 1978. 1545p. **CA75**

Represents a change of title for *American men of science,* 1st–11th eds., 1906–68. "The social and behavioral sciences" formed a numbered volume of the series in eds. 9–10; in both the 11th and 12th eds. "The social and behavioral sciences" section has been in 2v. without whole numbering within the set.

The 13th ed. contains biographical sketches of some 24,000 figures prominent in the fields of economics, sociology, political science, statistics, psychology, geography, and anthropology.

For a note on the physical and biological sciences section *see* EA221. H50.A47

Current bibliographic directory of the arts & sciences, 1978– . Philadelphia, Inst. for Scientific Information, 1979– . Annual. **CA76**

Subtitle: An international directory of scientists and scholars.

Earlier directories had titles: *International directory of research & development scientists* (1967–69); *ISI's Who is publishing in science* (1971–78).

In three main sections: (1) Author (giving full address and abbreviated citations to book and journal publications in that year; book and journal lists indicate which ISI service covers the publication so the complete citation can be found); (2) Organization (providing city and state or city and country address); (3) Geographic (listing all organizations within an area and all publishing authors within the organizations, by state or country, then city).

Q145.I56

International encyclopedia of the social sciences. v.18, Biographical supplement. N.Y., Free Pr.; London, Macmillan, [1980]. 820p. **CA77**

For the basic set *see* CA51.

Offers signed biographical sketches, with bibliographies, of 215 social scientists who either had died since preparation of the earlier volumes of the set or were born no later than Dec. 31, 1908 (i.e., were past age 70 at the time work began on this supplement). H40.A2I5

Internationales Soziologenlexikon. Hrsg. von Wilhelm Bernsdorf and Horst Knospe. 2., neubearb. Aufl. Stuttgart, Enke, 1980– . Bd.1– . (In progress) **CA78**

Contents: Bd.1, Beiträge über bis Ende 1969 verstorbene Soziologen.

1st ed. 1959.

To be in 2v. Maintains the broad interpretation of *Soziologen* offered in the 1st ed. Biographies are signed and include bibliographies of primary and secondary materials. HM19.I6

National register of social scientists in India. [Comp. by] Indian Council of Social Science Research. Ed. by N. K. Nijhawan. New Delhi, Concept Pub. Co., [1983]. 976p. **CA79**

A register of 7,527 teaching faculty and researchers listed according to 17 subdisciplines, anthropology through social work and communications. Entries provide birthdate, educational background, publications, and position as of 1980. Detailed specialization index, but no comprehensive name index. H57.N37

Rentz, Sophie Bassili. A directory of social scientists in the Middle East. [Cairo, Organization for the Promotion of Social Sciences in the Middle East, 1977?] 249p. **CA80**

For more than 200 social scientists, provides information on educational background, fields of interest, current research, dissertations, and publications. Emphasizes behavioral sciences such as sociology, anthropology, psychology. Country listings, indexed by field of subject specialization. H57.R4

United Nations Educational, Scientific and Cultural Organization. Secretariat. Social scientists specializing in African studies; directory. Africanistes spécialistes de sciences sociales; répertoire. Paris, La Haye, Mouton, 1963. 375p. (École Pratique des Hautes Études, 6. sec., Sciences économiques et sociales: 4. sér. v.5. Bibliographies et instruments de travail. Monde d'outre-mer passé et présent)   **CA81**

A biographical dictionary of 2,072 social scientists from the whole African continent, and from countries all over the world, who specialize in African studies. The term "social science" is interpreted in its broadest aspects. A geographical index and one by subject speciality.   DT19.5.U5

Who's who in Soviet social sciences, humanities, art and government, comp. by Ina Telberg. [N.Y., Telberg Book Co., 1961] 147p.   **CA82**

"Based on the information in the 3d ed. of 'Malaia sovetskaia entsiklopediia,' Moscow, 1958–61."—*Pref.* Provides brief biographical sketches in English of some 700 living persons. Alphabetical by transliterated form of the name, with a Russian index and an index by professions.   DK275.A1W5

FOUNDATIONS AND PHILANTHROPIC ORGANIZATIONS

Bibliography

Bibliography of fund raising and philanthropy. Exec. ed., George T. Holloway; ed., Rosy B. Gonzales. 2d ed. Rockville Centre, N.Y., National Catholic Development Conference, [1982]. 76p.   **CA83**

1st ed. 1975.
Lists books in print and out of print (or available through special libraries), periodical titles, and selected titles grouped by seven subject areas. Gives prices; publishers directory.   Z7164.C4B54

Georgi, Charlotte and **Fate, Terry.** Fund-raising, grants, and foundations: a comprehensive bibliography. Littleton, Colo., Libraries Unlimited, 1985. 194p.   **CA84**

1976 ed. had title: *Foundations, grants & fund-raising.*
In three sections: reference titles subdivided by form; subject sources on accounting, computers, foundations, fund-raising, grantsmanship, etc.; a basic "library" of the best titles arranged by publisher. About 1,500 titles, including periodicals and online databases. Indexed.   Z7164.F5G46

Handbooks

Coleman, William E. Grants in the humanities: a scholar's guide to funding sources. 2d ed. [N.Y., Neal-Schuman, 1984] 175p.   **CA85**

Concerned mainly with grants for individuals undertaking postdoctoral research. Information on "the art of grantsmanship," writing the proposal, sample proposals and budgets, and the grant recipient's income tax is followed by descriptive listings of granting agencies, directories of federal information centers and state humanities centers, and information on the Foundation Center. Indexed.   AZ507.C58

Des Marais, Philip H. How to get government grants. [N.Y.], Public Service Materials Center, [1975]. 160p.   **CA86**

Describes (1) how an eligible institution organizes to qualify for government funding; (2) how the institution identifies the programs and sources of government funds for which it can apply; (3) how proposals and applications for grants and contracts are developed; (4) how grants received should be managed.   HJ275.D48

Hillman, Howard and **Abarbanel, Karin.** The art of winning foundation grants. N.Y., Vanguard, [1975]. 188p.   **CA87**

A step-by-step guide for grant applicants. Includes a sample proposal.   HV41.H55

Hillman, Howard and **Natale, Kathryn.** The art of winning government grants. N.Y., Vanguard Pr., [1977]. 246p.   **CA88**

In three parts: (1) The six grant-seeking phases; (2) Where the money is (a discussion of federal, state, and local governmental and quasi-governmental agencies and their programs); (3) Information sources (both printed and institutional). Appendixes; bibliography; index.   HJ275.H49

—— and **Chamberlain, Marjorie.** The art of winning corporate grants. N.Y., Vanguard, [1980]. 180p.   **CA89**

The third and final volume in the authors' "Art of winning grants" series. This is a guide to researching the grant patterns of corporations, writing grant proposals, presenting them, and following through on the corporate response. Outlines questions asked by evaluators and presents a sample proposal. Annotated list of further information on sources is provided, as well as a bibliography.   HG177.H47

Human Resources Network. User's guide to funding resources. Radnor, Pa., Chilton, [1975]. 860p. in various pagings.   **CA90**

Subtitle: How to get money for: education, fellowships, scholarships, youth, the elderly, the handicapped, women, civil liberties, conservation, community development, arts and humanities, drug and alcohol abuse, health.
"Our intention has been to provide funding information for all fund seekers, from the largest hospital to the smallest radical-change organization. Our prejudices, however, have led us to place emphasis on the needs of individuals and grassroots community organizations."—*Introd.* General information on funding and fund-raising is followed by sections for each of the categories mentioned in the subtitle. Within each category a listing of national grant-giving foundations, organizations, institutions, etc., is followed by state listings grouped by region. Separate index for each group of related categories.   HG174.H85

Kurzig, Carol M. Foundation fundamentals: a guide for grantseekers. [N.Y.], Foundation Center, [1980]. 148p. il.   **CA91**

A concise guide to the mechanics of grantsmanship. Illustrated by examples taken from, but not limited to, titles published by this principal publisher and information resource on foundations. Features a valuable bibliography of area foundation directories, as well as sources for further reading.   HV41.K87

Lefferts, Robert. Getting a grant in the 1980s: how to write successful grant proposals. 2d ed. Englewood Cliffs, N.J., Prentice-Hall, [1982]. 168p.   **CA92**

A rev. ed. of the author's *Getting a grant* (1978).
"The intention of this book is to help demystify proposal writing and grant seeking by providing a set of principles, methods, and guidelines that are accessible to anyone who has basic writing skills and an understanding of the human service field."—*Pref.* Includes a section on "Resources for locating funding sources and presenting proposals," a sample program proposal and critique, a glossary, and an index.   HV41.L413

Smith, Craig W. and **Skjei, Eric W.** Getting grants. N.Y., Harper & Row, [1980]. 286p.   **CA93**

Offers an overview of the world of grants and grant-making as well as information on procedures and techniques for obtaining grants. ". . . rather than focus immediately on where to go and what to do, we precede that practical advice with a description of the principles and processes of the unique world of grants."—*Introd.*   HJ275.S55

White, Virginia P. Grants: How to find out about them and what to do next. N.Y., Plenum, [1975]. 354p.   **CA94**

In two main sections: (1) How to find out about grants and who gives them (basic sources of information; government grants; foundation grants; business and industry grants) and (2) The application (what to do before you apply; writing the proposal; how grants are awarded). Numerous appendixes; index.   Q180.U5W47

White, Virginia P. Grants for the arts. N.Y., Plenum, [1980]. 360p.   **CA95**

Provides a good deal of background information as well as information on government, corporate, and foundation funding. Includes instructions regarding applications, proposals, etc. Indexed.   NX398.W46

Directories

International

Directory of grant-making trusts. London, Nat. Council of Social Service, 1968– . (8th comp. 1983)   **CA96**

Publisher varies.
At head of title: Charities Aid Foundation.
A directory of registered charities and foundations of Britain compiled from official records of the Charity Commissioners and the Department of Education and Science.   AS911.A2D5

Guide to European foundations, 1973– . Milano, Franco Agnelli, 1973– .   **CA98**

Supersedes the *Directory of European foundations* (Milano, 1969).
The 1973 volume provides information on 296 foundations from 16 European countries. Emphasis is on "foundations that undertake or support activities in the sciences, arts or education, thereby leaving aside the vast majority of foundations that support strictly religious or charitable causes."—*Introd.* Information was derived from questionnaires completed by the foundations. Arrangement is by country, with indexes of persons, of foundation names, and by broad field of activity.   AS911.A2D532

Hart, Eric Keith, comp. Directory of philanthropic trusts in Australia. [Hawthorn, Victoria], Australian Council for Educational Research, [1968]. 274p.   **CA99**

A directory of philanthropic foundations for Australia. Trusts disbursing less than $1,000 (Austral.) per year are excluded.   HV473.A2H3

The international foundation directory. Consultant ed., H. V. Hodson. 3d ed. Detroit, Gale; [London, London Publs., 1983]. 401p.   **CA100**

1st ed. 1974.
Intends "to present a picture of foundations as an international phenomenon and force" (*Introd.*) and, in order to be included, a foundation must operate internationally in some way. (Exceptions to the latter restriction are those institutions "of such wealth that although they may be restricted to regional or national boundaries their activities are on so great a scale as to have an international impact," and "national and international organizations serving the common purposes of institutions which themselves may figure in the list.") Arrangement is by country. Indexes by name of foundation and by activity.   HV7.I57

Neuhoff, Klaus and **Vinken, Horst.** Deutsche Stiftungen für Wissenschaft, Bildung und Kultur. Baden-Baden, Nomos, [1969]. 428p. (Schriftenreihe zum Stiftungswesen, 1)   **CA101**

A directory of German foundations and charitable endowments in the areas of science, education, and culture. Geographical arrangement, with indexes by foundation name and by subject.   AS178.N43

Stromberg, Ann. Philanthropic foundations in Latin America. N.Y., Russell Sage Foundation, 1968. 215p.   **CA102**

Provides a directory of existing Latin-American foundations (with information similar to that given in the *Foundation directory,* CA110), together with summaries of relevant legislation and information on administration and organization of foundations in the individual Latin-American nations.   HV110.5.S87

United States

Annual register of grant support, 1969– . Los Angeles, Academic Media, 1969– . Annual.   **CA103**

Subtitle: A guide to grant support programs of government agencies, foundations, and business and professional organizations.
Supersedes *Grant data quarterly* (v.1–2, 1967–68).
Support programs are listed in four main categories (general, humanities, social sciences, sciences), with subsections for each of the latter three. Subject, organizational, and geographic indexes.   AS911.A2A67

Corporate 500: the directory of corporate philanthropy [1980]– . [San Francisco], Public Management Institute (distr. by Gale), [1980]– . Irregular.   **CA104**

3d ed. 1984.
For the top 500 corporations in the United States, a 1- to 2-page entry provides: address, telephone number, and name of any associated foundation; areas of interest; eligibility requirements; policy statement; financial profile, including data on high and low grant, average range, and number; application process; list of recent sample grants. Indexed by areas of interest, eligible activities, geographic location, and names of corporate personnel and grant recipients.   HV97.A3C63

Directory of research grants, 1975– . [Phoenix], Oryx Pr., [1975]– . Annual.   **CA105**

Place of publication varies.
Aims to offer "up-to-date information about grant, contract and fellowship support programs available for Federal and State governments, private foundations, associations, and corporations for research, training and innovative efforts."—*Pref.* A few programs sponsored by countries other than the United States are also included. Arrangement is alphabetical by subject field, "Accident prevention" through "Water resources and pollution." Indexes of grant names and of sponsoring bodies.   LB2338.D57●

Federal Council on the Arts and the Humanities. Cultural directory II: federal funds and services for the arts and humanities. [Wash.], Smithsonian Inst. Pr., 1980. unpaged.   **CA106**

". . . an updated edition of the original guide published in 1975."—[*p.5*]. Now includes descriptions of federal government support programs and activities for the humanities as well as the arts. About 300 programs are described. Listing is by federal agency. Appendixes list regional offices of the agencies. Indexed.   NX735.F42

Foundation Center. The Foundation Center source book. 1975/76– . N.Y., Foundation Center, 1975– .   **CA107**

"Documentation on large grant-making foundations: entity descriptions; policies, programs, application procedures; grants."—*t.p.*
". . . seeks to relate the needs of fund seekers to the activities of foundations and to assist foundations in making their programs known to a wider public . . . [and brings together] detailed and up-to-date information on the larger grant-making foundations in the United States operating on a regional or national basis. Fund seekers will find the essential data needed to determine if particular proposals fall within the scope of the foundation programs described."—*Introd.*
Foundations are listed alphabetically, with the following information presented for each: (1) descriptive and fiscal data (based on the entry in the *Foundation directory,* revised and updated as necessary); (2) statement of policy, programs, application procedures, etc.; (3) a listing of recent grants illustrating the current program.   HV97.F65F67a

——— The Foundation Center source book profiles, 1977/78– . N.Y., Foundation Center, 1977– . Looseleaf. Quarterly.   **CA108**

Frequency varies.

Each foundation profile includes: address, telephone number, and executive staff; background data and purpose; grant analysis by subject area, recipient, geographic distribution; a list of recent grants arranged by subject; policies, guidelines, and application procedures. About 125 profiles are included in each installment; since individual profiles are revised biennially, each volume, or series, supersedes the previous one. Focuses on foundations with national and regional grant patterns in excess of $200,000 annually. Indexes —by subject, types of support, geographic area, and foundation name—cumulate with each issue or installment.

———— National data book. Ed.1– , 1975– . N.Y., The Center, 1975– . Annual.   **CA109**

Title varies: 1st–4th eds. called *The Foundation Center national data book.*

For more than 22,000 smaller non-profit organizations in the United States, identifies name, location, principal officer, grants paid for the year, assets and gifts received, and whether it is a community foundation or publishes an annual report. The "Data book" (v.1) is arranged by state, and within each state, in descending order of annual grant amounts. The "Index" (v.2) provides alphabetical access by foundation name.   AS911.A2F64●

Foundation directory. 10th ed. Comp. by the Foundation Center. N.Y., Foundation Ctr., 1985. 885p.   **CA110**

1st ed. 1960. Frequency varies; ed.5– , biennial with annual supplements.

Replaces *American foundations and their fields* (eds.1–7, 1930–55, published by the Twentieth Century Fund and Raymond Rich Associates).

The series offers an invaluable compilation of detailed information on foundations. Geographical arrangement, with indexes by field of interest, personal names, and corporate titles. Prefatory material in the various editions offers useful statistics and information on foundation organization and operation.

Inasmuch as the assets criterion has been raised over the years ($1 million or more, or grants of $100,000 or more during the last year of record for the 10 ed.), early editions included listings for many smaller foundations not found in the latest edition and those volumes continue to be useful for identification, locations, and matters of historical interest.   AS911.A2F65●

Foundation grants index, 1970/71– ; a cumulative listing of foundation grants. Comp. by the Foundation Center. N.Y., 1972– . Annual.   **CA111**

Produced from a computerized data bank maintained by the Foundation Center. Provides a cumulated record of grants as reported in issues of *Foundation grants index bimonthly* (formerly listed in the bimonthly "Grants index" section of *Foundation news*). Includes grants of $5,000 or more, usually as reported by the donating foundation.

Beginning with the 1972 volume, in four sections: (1) Grants, listed by state, then alphabetically by donating foundation and recipient, with amount and description of the grant; (2) Donating foundations; (3) Index of recipients; (4) Subject categories.   AS911.A2F66●

Foundation grants to individuals. Ed. by Claude Barilleaux and Alexis Teitz Gersumky. [3d ed.] N.Y., Foundation Center, 1982. 203p.   **CA112**

1st ed. 1977.

Provides data on scholarships and loans, fellowships, internships, awards, etc., from foundations or companies which accept applications directly from individuals. Useful bibliographic essay on sources of information on grants to individuals. Indexed.

LB2336.F598

Foundations. Editors in chief, Harold M. Keele and Joseph C. Kiger. Westport, Conn., Greenwood Pr., [1984]. 516p. (Greenwood encyclopedia of American institutions, 8)   **CA113**

Offers brief histories of about 230 American foundations which each have assets in excess of $30 million; many histories have been written by the foundations' personnel, and provide bibliographic

references. Those foundations which do not make grants to other organizations and individuals, but use their own staff to complete projects, may be found in *Research institutions and learned societies* (CA129).   HV88.F68

Guide to corporate giving 3. Ed. by Robert A. Porter. N.Y., American Council for the Arts, 1983. 567p.   **CA114**

1st ed. (1978) publ. as *A guide to corporate giving in the arts* by Susan Wagner.

Describes the contributions programs and application procedures of more than 700 American corporations. Arranged alphabetically by corporation; indexed by geographic location, subject interest, and type of support given.   NX711.U5G8

Millsaps, Daniel. National directory of arts and education support by business corporations, 2. 2d ed. [Wash., Washington International Arts Letter, 1982] 234p. (Arts patronage ser., 10)   **CA115**

1980 ed. had title: *National directory of arts support by business corporations, 1.*

Data is presented alphabetically by name of corporation, with geographic and subject indexes.

Other titles in the series include *National directory of grants and aid to individuals in the arts, international* (4th ed., 1980) and *National directory of arts support by private foundations, 5* (1983). Additional information appears in the monthly publication *Washington international arts letter.*

ASSOCIATIONS, SOCIETIES, AND ACADEMIES

See also EA179–EA183.

❖Information is frequently requested in libraries on the organization, officers, publications, addresses, and history of various associations and societies, and for such purposes the directories listed in this section may be useful. The *Encyclopedia of associations* (CA125) is the most comprehensive list for the United States, giving details about associations in many fields. Lists of international associations are also much in demand, and the larger library will need directories for countries other than the United States.

For society directories in particular fields, *see* subhead "Directories" under the subject, e.g., Social sciences—Directories.

Bibliography

Associations' publications in print. [Ed.1]– , 1981– . N.Y., Bowker, [1981]– . Annual.   **CA116**

1st ed. in 2v. (2497p.).

Lists newsletters, journals, bulletins, books, pamphlets, and ephemeral material produced by associations in the United States and Canada. v.1 is a subject index; v.2 contains title and publisher/title indexes, an associations directory, and acronym and abbreviation indexes; full bibliographic data are provided in both the subject and title indexes.   Z1215.A75

British Museum. Dept. of Printed Books. Catalogue of printed books: Academies. London, Clowes, 1885. 1018col., 100col.   **CA117**

Published as part of the Museum's *Catalogue of printed books;* included in alphabetical sequence under "Academies" in v.1 of the Edwards reprint of the *Catalogue* (see AA132n).

A useful historical record. In two parts: (1) Catalogue of the publications of societies, arranged alphabetically by place with subarrangement by name of society; (2) Alphabetical index of names of societies.

The listings for academies in the new British Museum *Catalogue* (AA132) are scattered throughout rather than being collected in a single volume.

Directory of published proceedings. Series SSH: Social sciences/Humanities. v.1, no.1– , Jan. 1968– . White Plains, N.Y., InterDok Corp., 1968– . Quarterly.   **CA118**

At head of title: InterDok.

A companion to the series for science and technology (EA192), this one covering proceedings of congresses, conferences, symposia, etc., in all areas of the social sciences and humanities. Within each issue the arrangement is chronological by date of the conference, with editor, location, and subject/sponsor indexes which cumulate annually. Four-year cumulations are available for 1968/71, 1972/75, and 1976/79.   Z7161.D56

Index to social sciences and humanities proceedings. no.1– , Jan./Mar. 1979– . Philadelphia, Institute for Scientific Information, 1979– . Quarterly, with annual cumulation.   **CA119**

An index to published proceedings which appear as books, reports, preprint sets, or journal literature. In seven sections: (1) contents of proceedings, which provides full bibliographic information; (2) category index (a broad subject index); (3) keyword index to the titles of papers, conferences, and books; (4) sponsor index; (5) author/editor index; (6) meeting location index; (7) corporate index, listed by geographic location and by organization.

International

See also CA125, CB205, CK431.

Directory of European associations. Répertoire des associations européennes. Handbuch der europäischen Verbände. 1971– . Beckenham, Eng., CBD Research; Detroit, Gale, 1971– .   **CA120**

Contents: Pt. 1 National industrial, trade and professional associations; Pt. 2, National learned, scientific and technical societies.

Pt. 2 is a classed directory of voluntary associations in the natural sciences, technology, engineering and architecture, economics, finance, management, medicine, social sciences, law, history, archaeology, literature and the arts. Indexed by subject, abbreviation, and name of organization.   AS98.D55

International research centers directory. Ed.1, no.1– , Jan. 1982– . Detroit, Gale, 1982– . Irregular.   **CA121**

Subtitle: A world guide to government, university, independent nonprofit, and commercial research and development centers, institutes, laboratories, bureaus, test facilities, experiment stations, and data collection and analysis centers, as well as foundations, councils, and other organizations which support research.

Country arrangement, with alphabetical index by organization name and subject keyword. Ed.1 is published in three parts at 4 to 6 month intervals, each issue listing about 500 research centers; the index is cumulated in successive issues.   AS25.I8

World guide to scientific associations and learned societies. Internationales Verzeichnis wissenschaftlicher Verbände und Gesellschaften. 4th ed. [Barbara Verrel, managing ed.] N.Y., Saur, 1984. 947p. (Handbook of international documentation and information, v.13)   **CA122**

Title, prefatory matter, and headings in English and German.

Title varies; 1st ed., 1974, had title: *World guide to scientific organizations.*

A directory of more than 22,000 national and international associations and societies in various fields of science, technology, the humanities, and the social sciences. Information on each association includes founding date, address, name of executive head and secretary, and number of members. Arranged by country; indexed by subject, name, and abbreviation.

Meetings

See also CA118–CA119.

World meetings: social & behavioral sciences, education, & management; a two year registry of future meetings. v.1, no.1– , Jan. 1971– . Chestnut Hill, Mass., World Meetings Information Center, 1971– . Quarterly.   **CA123**

In each issue the complete data on meetings is presented in eight sections, one for each quarter of the 2-year period. Each new issue drops the first quarter of the preceding issue and adds a new quarter; changes and new listings are added in all other sections as necessary. There are indexes by date of meeting, by keyword, by location, by deadline for papers or abstracts, and by sponsor.   AS471.W65

United States

Bowker, Richard Rogers. Publications of societies; a provisional list of the publications of American scientific, literary, and other societies from their organization. N.Y., Publishers' Weekly, 1899. 181p.   **CA124**

Gives name of society, institution, or college, with date of founding, address, and lists of publications. Still occasionally useful for historical information about 19th-century organizations.   Z5065.U39B7

Encyclopedia of associations. Ed.1– . Detroit, Gale, 1956– . Annual.   **CA125**

Contents: v.1, National organizations of the United States; v.2, Geographic and executive index; v.3, New associations and projects (quarterly); v.4, International organizations; v.5, Research activities and funding programs.

Subtitle, v.1 (varies): A guide to national and international organizations including: trade, business and commercial; agricultural and commodity; governmental, public administration, legal and military; scientific, engineering and technical; educational; cultural; social welfare; health and medical; public affairs; fraternal, foreign interest, nationality and ethnic; religious; veteran, hereditary and patriotic; hobby and avocational; athletic and sports; labor unions, associations, and federations; chambers of commerce; and Greek letter related organizations.

Associations are grouped according to the categories mentioned in the subtitle, with an alphabetical and keyword index. About 18,000 associations in the 19th ed. (1985). Now volumes are in preparation for regional, state and local organizations, and association periodicals.   HS17.G334●

Government research centers directory. Ed.1–2, 1980–82. Detroit, Gale, 1980–82. Biennial.   **CA126**

Subtitle: A guide to U.S. government research and development centers, institutes, laboratories, bureaus, test facilities, experiment stations, data collection and analysis centers, and grants management and research coordinating offices in agriculture, art, business, education, energy, engineering, environment, medicine, military science, and basic and applied sciences.

Indexed by name, keyword, acronym, and classified arrangement of government agencies following the sequence used in the *United States government manual* (CJ112). Updated between editions by *Government research centers directory supplement.* Continued by *Government research directory,* which assumed its edition numbering (3d– , 1985–).   Q179.98.G68

Research centers directory. Ed.1– , 1960– . Detroit, Gale, 1960– . Biennial.   **CA127**

Title varies: 1st ed. called *Directory of university research bureaus and institutes.*

"A guide to university-related and other nonprofit research organizations established on a permanent basis and carrying on continuing research programs in agriculture, business, conservation, education, engineering and technology, government, law, life sciences, mathematics, area studies, physical and earth sciences, social sciences, and humanities."—*title page, 4th ed.*

Classified arrangement, with alphabetical index and index of sponsoring institutions. *New research centers* (below) serves as a periodic supplement between editions.   AS25.D5

New research centers. Supplement, no.1– , May 1965– . Detroit, Gale, 1965– .   **CA128**

Offers a periodic supplement and updating between editions of *Research centers directory* (above). Entries follow the pattern of those in the *Directory*, providing information on new centers or those which for some reason may have been omitted from the previous edition. In addition, significant changes in status, new or expanded information, etc., on previously listed centers are given. Cumulative alphabetical name index and institutional index in each issue.   AS25.D5

Research institutions and learned societies. Joseph C. Kiger, ed. Westport, Conn., Greenwood Pr., [1982]. 551p. (Greenwood encyclopedia of American institutions, 5)   **CA129**

Presents historical sketches of 164 American non-governmental, non-profit organizations, excluding business, university, and professional organizations; future volumes in the series will cover foundations and professional organizations. Entries range in length from two to four pages, with suggestions for further reading; many are signed by one of the 68 contributors. Appendixes provide subject classification, chronology, institutional affiliation. Indexed.   AS25.R47

Research services directory. no.1– , Sept. 1981– . Detroit, Gale, 1981– .   **CA130**

Subtitle: A guide to laboratories, consultants, firms, data collection and analysis centers, individuals, and other facilities in the private sector which conduct research in such fields as business, education, energy and the environment, agriculture, government, public affairs, social sciences, art and the humanities, physical and earth sciences, life sciences, and energy and technology.

Covers United States for-profit organizations providing research services on a contract or fee basis. Alphabetical listing, with geographical and subject indexes.   Q180.U5R397

Schmidt, Alvin J. Fraternal organizations. Westport, Conn., Greenwood Pr., [1980]. 410p. (Greenwood encyclopedia of American institutions, v.3)   **CA131**

Provides information on more than 450 fraternal organizations, both active and defunct, of the United States and Canada. Much of the information was supplied by the organizations themselves; notes on the extinct societies rely to a large degree on the *Cyclopedia of fraternities* by A. C. Stevens (1907) and the *Dictionary of secret and other societies* by A. Preuss (1924; CA167), with credit given to those sources. Citations to additional sources of information are included in many entries.   HS17.S3

Washington information directory. 1975/76– . [Wash.], Congressional Quarterly Inc., 1975– . Annual.   **CA132**

Subject chapters (e.g., Congress and politics; employment and business; energy) list executive agencies, congressional committees and subcommittees, and private organizations as information sources. Each entry gives address, telephone number, director, and brief description of the agency. Appendixes give directory information for Congress, executive agencies, foreign embassies, national labor unions, religious organizations, state and local officials, and regional federal information sources. Subject and agency indexes. A very useful handbook.   F192.3.W33

Africa

Abréviations en Afrique. Abkürzungen. Abbreviations in Africa. München, [Deutsche Afrika-Gesellschaft], 1969. 260p.   **CA133**

Introductory matter in German, English, and French.

About 4,000 abbreviations used for organizations, societies, institutions, agencies, etc., in Africa. In addition to the full meaning, country of origin is often indicated.   AS600.A7A2

Austria

Handbuch der österreichischen Wissenschaft, 1947/48– . Wien, Österreichischer Bundesverlag für Unterricht, Wissenschaft und Kunst, 1948– . Biennial (irregular).   **CA134**

At head of title: Österreichische Akademie der Wissenschaft.

Title varies: some issues called *Jahrbuch der österreichischen Wissenschaft.*

Lists academies, universities, libraries, museums, societies, etc., with their officers, address, history, and general information; there is also a classed listing of learned journals giving addresses, but no bibliographical data.

Belgium

Belgium. Service des Échanges Internationaux. Liste des sociétés savantes et littéraires de Belgique. Bruxelles, 1960. 141p. (*Its* Publication, 9)   **CA135**

Gives information on officers, membership, publications, purposes, etc.   AS238.A5

Brazil

Brazil. Secretaria Especial do Meio Ambiente. Catálogo nacional das instituições que atuam na área do meio ambiente 1981/82. 2a ed. Brasília, Ministério do Interior, Secretaria Especial do Meio Ambiente, Secretaria Adjunta de Planejamento, 1982. 473p.   **CA136**

1st ed. 1980 had title: *Cadastro nacional das instituições que atuam na área do meio ambiente.*

A directory of associations and scientific institutions, arranged by region of the country; indexed by institution, subject, and abbreviation.

França, Marilena de Castro and **Almeida, Walkiria de.** Siglas brasileiras; dicionário de entidades e publicações. Rio de Janeiro, 1970. 517p. (Instituto Brasileiro de Bibliografia e Documentação. Fontes de informação, 3)   **CA137**

A listing of abbreviations and acronyms for Brazilian organizations, commissions, agencies, associations, etc., with addresses; index by full name of the organization.   AS80.A6F7

Bulgaria

Bulgarska Akademiia na Naukite, Sofia. Biblioteka. Opis na izdaniiata na Bulgarskata Akademiia na Naukite, 1869–1953. Sofiia, 1956. 535p.   **CA138**

Added title page in French: Bibliographie des publications de l'Académie des Sciences de Bulgarie, 1869–1953. An updated 3v. ed. was published 1984.   Z5055.B9B8

Canada

Directory of associations in Canada. Répertoire des associations du Canada. [Ed.1–], 1973– . [Toronto], Univ. of Toronto Pr., 1973– . Biennial.   **CA139**

Introductory and explanatory matter in English and French.

1st ed. 1974; 5th ed. 1984.

Gives brief directory information on non-governmental, non-profit organizations. Detailed subject index to specialized interests of the associations. Lists about 11,000 associations.   AS40.D49

Czechoslovakia

Kulturní adresáiř CSR. [Praha, Ústav pro Výskum Kultury, 1973] 501p. **CA140**

Milan Hromádka, ed.

Title and table of contents also in Russian, German, French, and English (*Cultural directory of the Czech Socialistic Republic*).

Gives directory information on a wide range of agencies, organizations, and institutions relating to cultural life and activities: government organizations and committees, libraries, museums, educational institutions, press, publishing, music and theater arts, mass communication, national parks, etc. DB194.H76

France

Caron, Pierre and **Jaryc, Marc.** Répertoire des sociétés françaises de sciences philosophiques, historiques, philologiques et juridiques. Publié par la Fédération des Sociétés Françaises de Sciences Philosophiques, Historiques, Philologiques et Juridiques. Paris, Maison du Livre Français, 1938. 280p. **CA141**

Gives name, date of founding, address, officers, number of members, publications, etc. Arranged geographically with indexes of persons, places, etc. AS155.C3

France. Comité des Travaux Historiques et Scientifiques. Liste des sociétés savantes et littéraires. Paris, 1975. 114p. **CA142**

Revision and updating of an edition which appeared in 1958.
Geographical listing of French societies with indexes by title of publication, name of society, broad subject, and area (for local history societies). AS158.F72

Manfrass, Klaus. Politik und politische Wissenschaft in Frankreich: politische Organisationen, Publikationen, Presseorgane, Dokumentationsstätten, Forschungseinrichtungen. München, K. G. Saur, 1979. 234p. (Dokumentation Westeuropa, Bd.3) **CA143**

A directory of associations, administrative agencies, learned institutions, and publishing enterprises which have impact on the political situation in France. Arranged by type of activity; indexed by personal name and publication title. JN2728.M27

Soulis, Jean-Jacques. Les fondations reconnues d'utilité publique en France. [Paris], Vieux Logis, [1970]. 653p. **CA144**

A selective, classed directory of endowed French associations and learned societies. Indexed by foundation, subject, and personal name. HV265.S66

Germany

Domay, Friedrich. Handbuch der deutschen Wissenschaftlichen Akademien und Gesellschaften, einschliesslich zahlreicher Vereine, Forschungsinstitute und Arbeitsgemeinschaften in der Bundesrepublik Deutschland. Mit einer Bibliographie deutscher Akademie- und Gesellschafts-publikationen. 2., völlig neu bearb. u. erw. Aufl. Wiesbaden, F. Steiner Verlag, 1977. 1209p. **CA145**

Represents a new and greatly expanded edition of Domay's *Handbuch der deutschen wissenschaftlichen Gesellschaften* (1964). In addition to added information for scientific academies as noted in the title, there are new sections for information science and documentation and for the arts. Indexed. AS175.D59

Müller, Johannes. Die wissenschaftlichen Vereine und Gesellschaften Deutschlands im neunzehnten Jahrhundert; Bibliographie ihrer Veröffentlichungen seit ihrer Begründung bis auf die Gegenwart. Berlin, Asher, 1883–87; Behrend, 1917. v.1–2. **CA146**

A useful record of 19th-century societies and their publications. Contents: v.1, to about 1882; v.2, 1882–1914.

Each volume contains: (1) a short classified list of societies; (2) a main list arranged alphabetically by place and under place by society, giving for each society a list of its publications (with record of what constitutes a complete set for the period covered, note of indexes, names of editors, etc., and, for monographic sets, contents by author and title); (3) an alphabetical index of titles of periodicals, names of societies, editors, and authors. Z5055.G29M9

Stifterverband für die Deutsche Wissenschaft. Vademecum deutscher Lehr- und Forschungsstätten. Überarbeitete Ausg. Essen, 1964. 432p. **CA147**

1st and 2nd eds. had title: *Vademecum deutscher Forschungsstätten;* 3d ed.: *Taschenbuch für das Wissenschaftliche Leben.*

Lists German research institutes and learned societies in various fields, arranged by class, giving name, address, chief officer, subject area, etc. Indexes by names, places, and subjects. AS178.S7

Vezényi, Pál. Bibliographia academica Germaniae. Abhandlungen und Sitzungsberichte; Reports and proceedings. München-Pullach, Verlag Dokumentation, [1971–]. Bd.1– . **CA148**

Contents: Bd.1, Königliche Gesellschaft der Wissenschaften (Akademie der Wissenschaften) Göttingen; Bayerische Akademie der Wissenschaften München (Abhandlungen, Sitzungsberichte, Forschungen zur Deutschen Geschichte).

Preface and text headings in both German and English.

The series intends to index "all the independent articles and reports of all academies in Germany (Federal Republic and German Democratic Republic), in Switzerland and in Austria; a special supplement will include German-language publications of foreign academies in neighboring countries (Denmark, Finland, Russia, Hungary, etc.)."—*Pref.* Omits book reviews and business reports of individual classes and commissions. Classed arrangement with author index. Z5055.G29V46

Wirtschafts- , Rechts- und Sozialwissenschaften: Fakultäten, Institutionen, Personen. [München], Consultverlag, [1970]. 345p. **CA149**

At head of title: Dokumentation der Wissenschaft, Bd.2.

A directory of East and West German universities and faculty members, as well as research institutes with administrative personnel. Indexed by personal name and subject specialty.

Great Britain

Anderson, Ian Gibson. Councils, committees, and boards: a handbook of advisory, consultative, executive & similar bodies in British public life. 3d ed. Beckenham, Kent, Eng., CBD Research (distr. in U.S.A. by Gale), [1977]. 402p. **CA150**

1st ed. 1970.

A directory of national or regional bodies in the United Kingdom which exist as government advisory committees, departmental committees of inquiry, public boards and authorities, royal and other forms of commissions, and other groups of experts brought together in a similar advisory capacity. Provides name, address, description, activities, and publications. Alphabetically arranged; indexed by abbreviations, executive personnel, and subject. Conceived as a companion volume to the *Directory of British associations* (below). AS118.A5

Directory of British associations. Ed.1– . [Beckenham, Eng., etc.], C.B.D. Research, 1965–] **CA151**

Frequently revised; ed.7, 1982.

Provides brief information on national organizations, associations, societies, institutes, etc., in the United Kingdom and the Republic of Ireland. Alphabetical by name of the association, with indexes of abbreviations, publications, and subjects. AS118.D56

Wilkes, Ian H. British initials and abbreviations. 3d ed. London, Leonard Hill, 1971. 346p. **CA152**

1st ed. 1963.

". . . lists all organizations in Great Britain and Ireland known by their initials, and also all international organisations to which Britain belongs on a governmental, institutional, or individual level."—*Pref.*   AS118.W5

Italy

Doc Italia. Ed. 2– , 1978– . [Rome], Editoriale Italiana, [1979]– . Irregular (ed. 3, 1982 publ. 1983).   **CA153**

Subtitle: Anuario degli enti di studio, ricerca cultura e informazione.
At head of title: Istituto Nazionale dell'Informazione.
Continues *Doc; documentazione.*
A directory of learned societies, institutions, and associations in Italy; includes founding date, description of activities, officers, periodical publications, etc. Subject index.   AS218.D6

Maylender, Michele. Storia delle accademie d'Italia. Bologna, Cappelli, [1926–30]. 5v.   **CA154**

A dictionary of Italian academies of all periods and kinds, arranged alphabetically by the significant word in the academy's name. Fuller for historical than for bibliographical information; useful particularly for material about old or obscure organizations.
                                                                        AS215.M3

———— ———— "Repertorio alfabetico e bibliografico" by Giuseppe Gabrieli. (*In* Accademie e biblioteche d'Italia 10:71–99, marzo–aprile 1936)

Latin America

See also names of individual countries.

Latinamerican guide CBA. CBA guía Latinoamericana, 1973/74– . Montevideo, CBA, 1974– . No more publ.?
                                                                        CA155

For Spanish-speaking Caribbean and Latin American countries, provides directory data on academies, archives, associations, libraries, publishers, museums, and other cultural institutions. Country arrangement, subdivided by types of institution. No index.

Sable, Martin Howard. Master directory for Latin America. Los Angeles, Latin American Center, Univ. of California, 1965. 438p. (Calif. Univ., Los Angeles. Latin American Center. Reference ser., no.2)   **CA156**

Subtitle: Containing ten directories covering organizations, associations, and institutions in the fields of agriculture, business-industry-finance, communications, education-research, government, international cooperation, labor-cooperatives, publishing and religion, and professional, social and social service organizations and associations.   F1406.5.S3

United Nations. Economic Commission for Latin America. Library. Lista de siglas latinoamericanas; Latin American initialisms and acronyms with English translations. Santiago de Chile, 1970. Detroit, repr. by Blaine Ethridge, 1974. 157p. (United Nations Document E/CN.12/Lib.3)
                                                                        CA157

Provides initials for national and regional (but not international) organizations; only official English translations are given.
                                                                        AS60.A7U54

Mexico

Salas Ortega, Guadalupe, ed. Directorio de asociaciones e institutos científicos y culturales de la República Mexicana. México, Dirección General de Publicaciones, 1959. 242p.
                                                                        CA158

At head of title: Universidad Nacional Autónoma de México. Departamento de Psicopedagogía.
A directory of cultural and scientific associations, universities, institutions, etc., in alphabetical arrangement, with a geographical index and supplementary lists of libraries and museums.
                                                                        AS63.A7S3

Velásquez Gallardo, Pablo and **Zamora, Pedro.** Guía de asociaciones de la República Mexicana. México, Universidad Nacional Autónoma de México, 1970. 419p.   **CA159**

At head of title: Instituto de Investigaciones Sociales.
The main listing is by field of interest or specialization. Alphabetical and geographical indexes.   AS63.V4

Poland

Informator nauki polskiej, 1958– . Warszawa, Państwowe Wydawnictwo Naukowe, 1958– . Annual.   **CA160**

A directory of Poland's learned societies, universities, scientific institutes, museums, and archives, giving addresses, names of directors and other personnel, and title and periodicity of serial publications. The name index, with addresses, is a substantial directory of Polish scientists. Recent volumes also include an index to names of institutions.
An English-language edition is entitled *Polish research guide.*
                                                                        AS256.P7I5

Polska Akademia Nauk. Directory, 1957– . [Wrocław], Ossolineum, [1957–]. Irregular.   **CA161**

A directory in English of the Polish Academy of Sciences and its subdivisions and allied societies as established in 1952, with a list of serial and periodical publications and name index.
                                                                        AS262.P6224

Research guide to Polish social sciences and humanities. Warsaw, National Center for Scientific, Technical, and Economic Information, 1979. 799p.   **CA162**

A directory of teaching and research centers, providing listings of personnel and major recent publications. Indexed by abbreviations, personal and corporate names.   H62.5.P6R47

Słownik polskich towarzystw naukowych. Wrocław, Zakład Narodowy imienia Ossolińskich, 1978– . v.1– . (In progress)
                                                                        CA163

At head of title: Polska Akademia Nauk. Biblioteka PAN w Warszawie.
Redaktor naukowy, Leon Łoś.
Contents: v.1, Towarzystwa naukowe działające obecnie w Polsce.
A directory of learned societies and institutions in Poland. Arranged by broad subject fields, with lengthy, signed entries for the 172 institutions, providing: basic data on history, location, areas of subject specialization; library and archives, and staff officers; a comprehensive history; list of publications; statutes, bibliographies, and catalogs; and secondary literature on the institution. Indexed by institution and personnel.   AS248.A7S58

Portugal

Centro de Documentaçao Cientifica, Lisbon. Instituições cientificas, literárias e artísticas portuguesas. 4. ed. Lisboa, Inst. de Alte Cultura, 1958. 237p. (*Its* Publ. no. 55)
                                                                        CA164

An alphabetical listing followed by a classified arrangement by Universal Decimal Classification.   Z6660.C38 no.55

Union of Soviet Socialist Republics

Akademiia Nauk SSSR. Bibliografiia izdanii, v.1– , 1956– . Moskva, 1957– . Annual.   **CA165**

Added title page in English: *Bibliography of publications of the Academy of Sciences of the USSR: a yearbook.*

All publications of the USSR Academy of Sciences for a given year are recorded under departments and institutes of the Union Academy and its affiliates. Publications of republic academies are not included. Articles in symposia and irregular serials (transactions, learned papers, etc.) are analyzed by author and title. The name index includes authors of articles in regularly appearing journals, with abbreviation of periodical title and number.

Z5055.R8A3726

Secret societies

Whalen, William Joseph. Handbook of secret organizations. Milwaukee, Bruce, [1966]. 169p.   **CA166**

For purposes of this work the "definition of secret organization includes the criterion of a secret ritual and initiation ceremony."—*Pref.* Largely concerned with 45 major organizations (plus entries for "Fraternities, College" and "Negro lodges") but providing incidental references to various other groups. An older, but still useful work is: HS204.W45

Preuss, Arthur, comp. A dictionary of secret and other societies. St. Louis, Herder, 1924. 543p. (Repr.: Detroit, Gale, 1966)   **CA167**

Subtitle: Comprising Masonic rites, lodges, and clubs; concordant, clandestine, and spurious Masonic bodies; non-Masonic organizations to which only Freemasons are admitted; mystical and occult societies; fraternal, benevolent and beneficiary societies; political, patriotic, and civic brotherhoods; Greek letter fraternities and sororities; military and ancestral orders; revolutionary brotherhoods, and many other organizations.

Includes some bibliographical references.   HS122.P7

C B

Education

❖A useful guide in the field of education is Woodbury's *Guide to sources of educational information* (CB5). The general library, even a small library, will need one or more of the many educational directories, e.g., the four publications which now make up the *Education directory* (CB206, CB207, CB228, CB190) provide a broad range of coverage at nominal cost. Other very useful directories include *American universities and colleges* (CB214), its companion publication, *American community, technical, and junior colleges* (CB213), and *Patterson's American education* (CB210). In the larger library the *World of learning* (CB205), which gives information about educational institutions and societies in all countries, will be needed.

Bibliographies, indexes—particularly the *Education index* (CB131)—and dictionaries and encyclopedias should be added as required. Among the latter types, Good's *Dictionary of education* (CB148), although somewhat out of date in certain areas, remains a reputable and useful work; larger libraries will want to include the *Encyclopedia of education* (CB143) and the *Encyclopedia of educational*

research (CB145). The *Digest of educational statistics* (CB258) and *The condition of education* (CB257) are useful statistical sources.

For materials in the audio-visual field *see* items AA528–AA541. Children's literature sources are dealt with in section BD, items BD190–BD199.

Computer-assisted bibliographic searching and information retrieval have become an integral part of educational research. The U.S. Educational Research Information Center (ERIC) data files are among the most extensive databases adapted to machine searching, offering access to the materials listed in the *Current index to journals in education* (CB130) and *Resources in education* (formerly *Research in education,* CB132–CB133), and carefully developed search strategies yield highly satisfactory results.

In the section which follows there is considerable emphasis on recent publications, but a number of older works have been retained because they seem an important part of the historical record or because they cover areas not adequately dealt with elsewhere. Balancing historical interest with current needs has made for some difficult choices, and no doubt some users of this *Guide* will question the omission of certain older works which are still occasionally useful: e.g., *Documentation in education* by Arvid and Mary Burke (N.Y., 1967); *Sources in educational research* by Theodore Manheim and others (Detroit, 1969); *The New York University list of books in education* by Barbara S. Marks (N.Y., 1968); and *Bibliographies and summaries in education to July 1935* by Walter S. Monroe and Louis Shores (N.Y., 1936).

GENERAL WORKS

Guides

Berry, Dorothea M. A bibliographic guide to educational research. 2d ed. Metuchen, N.J., Scarecrow Pr., 1980. 215p.   **CB1**

1st ed. 1975.

Intended "as a concise guide to assist the student in education courses to make effective use of the resources of the library of his college or university."—*Pref.* An annotated listing of over 700 items arranged by type (periodicals, research studies, government publications, reference materials, etc.), with author, title, and subject indexes.   Z5811.B39

Current bibliographical sources in education. Sources d'information bibliographiques courantes sur l'education. Fuentes bibliográficas actuales en materia de educación. Prep. by International Bureau of Education. 2d ed. [Paris], Unesco, [1984]. 53p.   **CB2**

Originally issued as *Educational documentation and information* no.203 (1977).

In English, French, and Spanish.

Based mainly on the reference collection at the IBE Documentation Centre, it includes current bibliographies, indexes of periodicals, and registers of research. Arrangement is alphabetical by country, with separate listings for the publications of international and regional organizations.   Z5811.C78

Humby, Michael. A guide to the literature of education. 3d ed. London, Univ. of London, Inst. of Education Lib., 1975. 142p. (Education libraries bulletin. Suppl. 1)   **CB3**

Based on *A guide to the literature of education* by S. K. Kimmance (2d ed. 1961).

Aims "to give selected examples of the various types of printed material to be found in an education library."—*Introd.* 572 annotated entries arranged by type: guides to the literature of education, bibliographies, encyclopedias, dictionaries, directories and yearbooks, periodicals, biographies, statistics, etc. Indexed.

Z5811.H85

Kennedy, James R. Library research guide to education: illustrated search strategy and sources. Ann Arbor, Mich., Pierian Pr., [1979]. 80p. (Library research guides ser., no.3) **CB4**

A guide to locating and using appropriate materials for writing term papers in the field of education. Assumes a knowledge of basic library tools and mechanics of preparing term papers, and concentrates on the information gathering process and evaluating the information.   LB1028.K38

Woodbury, Marda. A guide to sources of educational information. 2d ed., completely rev. Arlington, Va., Information Resources Pr., 1982. 430p.   **CB5**

1st ed. 1976.

Selects, describes, and often evaluates the major print and nonprint and organizational sources for educational research. Emphasis is on current and widely useful tools. Arrangement is basically by form (dictionaries, directories, bibliography, nonprint, etc.) with four subject chapters: finance and government; special education; instructional materials; tests and assessment instruments. An explanation of the steps in effective research and a guide for writers are also included. Subject index.   Z5811.W65

Bibliography

General

Altbach, Philip G., Kelly, Gail P. and **Kelly, David H.** International bibliography of comparative education. [N.Y.], Praeger, [1981]. 300p.   **CB6**

More than 3,000 citations to Western-language books and articles in three sections: (1) bibliographic essay; (2) comprehensive bibliography on comparative education as a field of study; (3) selective national bibliographies on education. Subject index.

Z5814.C76A46

Baatz, Charles Albert. The philosophy of education: a guide to information sources. Detroit, Gale, [1980]. 344p. (Education information guide ser., v.6)   **CB7**

A classed bibliography intended for both the beginner and the specialist. Includes both books and periodical articles; most entries are annotated. Author, title, and subject indexes.   LB885.B22A36

Baatz, Olga K. and **Baatz, Charles Albert.** The psychological foundations of education. Detroit, Gale, [1981]. 441p. (Education information guide ser., v.10)   **CB8**

Considered by the author to be a natural outcome of *The philosophy of education* (above). Introductory chapters explain the structure and scope of the work. The bibliography is arranged in six broad categories: education and psychology; intellectual education; moral education; affective education; poietic education; and the acting person. Some annotations; author, title, and subject indexes.

Z5811.B2

Columbia University. Teachers College. Library. Dictionary catalog of the Teachers College Library. Boston, G. K. Hall, 1970. 36v.   **CB9**

Offers a photoreproduction of the catalog cards for this collection of more than 400,000 items.   Z5819.C73

—— —— 1st–3d supplements. Boston, G. K. Hall, 1971–77. 17v.

1st suppl. (1971), 5v.; 2d suppl. (1973), 2v.; 3d suppl. (1977), 10v. Cover materials added to the Library for the period 1970–76. Supplemented by *Bibliographic guide to education* (CB21).

Drazen, Joseph Gerald. An annotated bibliography of ERIC bibliographies, 1966–1980. Westport, Conn., Greenwood Pr., [1982]. 520p.   **CB10**

Provides citations to more than 3,200 individual bibliographies listed in *Resources in education* (CB133) under the headings "bibliographies," "annotated bibliographies," "reference materials" plus some from the "information resources" category. Arranged in about 600 subject categories; some cross references. Full bibliographic information with brief evaluative annotations; author and subject indexes.   Z5811.D73

Durnin, Richard G. American education; a guide to information sources. Detroit, Gale, [1982]. 247p. (American studies information guide ser., v.14)   **CB11**

"This bibliography encompasses the general and specific books relating to the backgrounds (historical, biographical, philosophical, political, and sociological) of the theory, practice, and organization of the American school ... elementary, secondary, and higher education."—*Pref.* Broad subject arrangement; name index.

Z5815.U5D87

Education literature 1907–1932. N.Y., Garland, 1979. 25v. in 12.   **CB12**

A reproduction of the 117 published indexes to periodical articles, books, conference proceedings, government publications, pamphlets, and other material received by the U.S. Office of Education (Bureau of Education to 1929) Library from 1907 to 1932. v.12 is a cumulative index expanded by entries for the previously unindexed v.15–16 and edited to eliminate inconsistencies.   Z5811.E415

France. Ministère de l'Éducation Nationale. Répertoire des ouvrages pédagogiques du XVIᵉ siècle. (Bibliothèques de Paris et des départements) Nieuwkoop, B. de Graaf, 1962. 733p.   **CB13**

"Unchanged photomechanical reprint of the edition Paris, 1886." —*verso of title page.*

Arranged by author with broad subject index. Brief note of author's life and work often included with an entry.   Z5811.F8

Harvard University. Library. Education and education periodicals. Cambridge, Harvard Univ. Lib.; distr. by Harvard Univ. Pr., 1968. 2v. (Widener Library shelflist, 16–17) **CB14**

Contents: v.1, Classification schedule; classified listing by call number; v.2, Alphabetical listing by author or title; chronological listing.

For a note on the series see AA145.

Lists more than 30,000 works housed in the Widener Library; it does not include holdings of the Harvard Graduate School of Education Library.   Z5817.H33

Higson, Constance Winifred Jane. Sources for the history of education. . . . London, Lib. Assoc., 1967. 196p.   **CB14a**

Subtitle: A list of material (including school books) contained in the libraries of the institutes and schools of education, together with works from the libraries of the Universities of Nottingham and Reading.

Listing is alphabetical within chronological sections, 15th century to 1870, with special sections for children's books published 1801–70 and for government publications through 1918. Subject index.

Z5811.H5

—— Supplement to Sources for the history of education. [London], Library Assoc., 1976. 221p.

Subtitle: A list of materials added to the libraries of the institutes and schools of education, 1965–1974, together with works from certain university libraries.

The history of American education; a guide to information sources. Francesco Cordasco with David N. Alloway and Marjorie Scilken Friedman. Detroit, Gale, [1979]. 313p. (Education information guide series, v.7)   **CB14b**

Lists nearly 2,500 entries for books, periodical articles, and source collections. Arranged by broad subject category and time period; author, title, and subject indexes.   LA212.H57

Paulston, Rolland G. Non-formal education; an annotated international bibliography. N.Y., Praeger, [1972]. 332p.

CB15

A classed bibliography with author and area indexes. Includes pertinent materials on both underdeveloped and developed areas. Z5811.P27

Pedagogicheskaia bibliografiia. Sost. V. A. Il'ina [et al.]. Moskva, Izdatel'stvo "Proveshchenie," 1967–73. v.1–3. **CB16**

Contents: v.1, 1924–1930; v.2, 1931–1935; v.3, 1936–1940.

At head of title: Akademiia Pedagogicheskikh Nauk SSSR. Gosudarstvennaia Nauchnaia Biblioteka.

A comprehensive, classed bibliography with indexes of authors, editors, etc., in each volume. Includes publications on all aspects of education. The series was to cover through 1950; no more published. Z5811.P38

Quay, Richard H. Index to anthologies on postsecondary education, 1960–1978. Westport, Conn., Greenwood Pr., [1980]. 342p. **CB17**

A subject and author index to some 3,600 essays appearing in 218 anthologies of the 1960–78 period. Essays are grouped in 31 topical sections, with indication of whether the work originally appeared in the anthology or, if previously published in a periodical, reference to the earlier source. Some annotations; author index. LB2305.Q39

Richmond, William Kenneth. The literature of education; a critical bibliography, 1945–1970. London, Methuen, [1972]. 206p. **CB18**

A selective, classed bibliography. Z5811.R53

United Nations Educational, Scientific and Cultural Organization. International guide to educational documentation, 1955–1960. Paris, 1963. 700p. **CB19**

Covers books, pamphlets, periodicals, occasional papers, film and sound recordings, etc., published from 1955 to 1960. Pt.1 is a list of international sources and international organizations issuing educational material. Pt.2 (the main section) is an alphabetical arrangement under the 95 countries and territories included. Gives complete bibliographical information with annotations of varying length. Most countries which publish a considerable volume of documentation are included, notable exceptions being Canada, China, Indonesia, and Italy. Author, title, and name index. Z5811.U32

—— —— 1960–65. Paris, 1971. 575p.

Continues the bibliographic record as in the earlier volume. Canada, China, and Italy are now included. Lacks the indexes mentioned above.

U.S. Dept. of Health, Education, and Welfare. Library. Author/title catalog of the Department Library. Boston, G. K. Hall, 1965–67. 29v.; Suppl. 1, 1973. 7v. **CB20**

—— Subject catalog of the Department Library. Boston, G. K. Hall, 1965. 20v.; Suppl. 1, 1973. 7v.

Both of the above sets offer photoreproduction of the cards from the Library's catalogs. The collection of more than 500,000 volumes is strong in the fields of education and the social sciences, and is particularly notable as having "the most complete set of the Departmental and operating agencies' publications."—*Foreword.* The subject catalog reproduces about 350,000 cards with another 109,000 in the supplements; the author/title catalog about 540,000 entries with 61,700 added in the supplement.

Current

Bibliographic guide to education. 1978– . Boston, G. K. Hall, 1979– . Annual. **CB21**

Serves as a supplement to the *Dictionary catalog* of the Teachers College Library, Columbia University (CB9).

Lists, in dictionary arrangement, materials cataloged by the Teachers College Library during the year of coverage, together with selected publications in the field of education cataloged by the Research Libraries of the New York Public Library. Z5813.B4

International bulletin of bibliography on education. Boletin internacional de bibliografia sobre educacion. no.0; v.1– , 1971/80– . Madrid, Bibliografías Internationales Badesco, 1981– . Quarterly with annual summary. **CB21a**

At head of title: B.I.B.E. Project.

Title also in French, German, Italian and Portuguese.

In English, French, German, Italian, Portuguese and Spanish.

An international listing of books arranged according to the Universal Decimal Classification. No.0, covering 1971–80, provides bibliographic data only; subsequent issues include tables of contents or summaries. Annual summary number indicates the quarterly issue in which an item appears and includes the full citation; the latter feature makes the summary number independently useful and it may be subscribed to separately. Includes alphabetical author list and an alphabetical list of the most important descriptors used, with UDC number.

The *Bibliographie pädagogik; educational bibliography* (München & N.Y., K. G. Saur, 1966– . Annual) is another international bibliography, but there is heavy emphasis on German-language materials. Beginning 1982, it is published in three series: A, periodicals; B, books; C, educational research.

Higher education

Altbach, Philip G. Comparative higher education: research trends and bibliography. London, Mansell, 1979. 206p. **CB22**

A survey/essay (p.1–113) precedes the bibliography (more than 1,100 items) which aims "to present some of the best literature currently available on higher education in a comparative perspective and to provide some key references on higher education in many individual nations."—*p.117.* Indexed. LB2324.A43

—— Comparative higher education abroad: bibliography and analysis. N.Y., Praeger, [1976]. 274p. **CB23**

"Publ. in cooperation with the International Council for Educational Development."—*t.p.*

A bibliography of more than 1,700 items (books, articles, and dissertations, mainly from 1974) is followed by a section of "Book notes" on significant books of 1974, and two bibliographic essays on aspects of higher education. The bibliography is arranged by continent, then by country. A "cross reference index" offers a broad subject approach. Z5814.U7A39

—— Higher education in developing countries: a select bibliography. [Cambridge], Harvard Univ., Center for International Affairs, 1970. 118p. (Occasional papers in international affairs, no.24) **CB24**

Lists books and periodical articles organized by country or geographical areas. Items considered of particular importance are marked with an asterisk. No index. Z5814.U7A4

—— and **Kelly, David H.** American students: a selected bibliography on student activism and related topics. Lexington, Mass., Lexington Books, [1973]. 537p. **CB25**

A revised and greatly expanded version of Altbach's *Student politics and higher education in the United States* (1968). Lists books, periodical articles, and doctoral dissertations in classed arrangement. Detailed table of contents, but no index. Items of special importance are starred. Z5814.S86A55

—— Higher education in developing nations: a selected bibliography, 1969–1974. N.Y., Praeger, [1975]. 229p. **CB26**

"Publ. in cooperation with the International Council for Educational Development."—*t.p.*

2,400 items supplementing Altbach's 1970 work of similar title (CB24). Arranged by country; "cross reference index." Z5814.U7A42

Beach, Mark. A bibliographic guide to American colleges and universities, from colonial times to the present. Westport, Conn., Greenwood Pr., 1975. 314p. **CB27**

". . . an effort to bring together in one source citations to major books, articles and dissertations relating to the history of specific institutions of higher learning."—*Introd.* Listing is by state, with general works followed by histories of specific institutions. Subject index. 2,806 entries.   Z5815.U5B4

Bengelsdorf, Winnie. Ethnic studies in higher education; state of the art and bibliography. Wash., Amer. Assoc. of State Colleges and Universities, 1972. 260p. (Repr.: N.Y., Arno Pr., 1978)   **CB28**

A bibliographic report with summaries of recent materials. Includes sections for Asian-American studies, Black studies, Chicano studies, Indian studies, Puerto-Rican and other Spanish-speaking American studies, White ethnic studies, Multi-ethnic studies, and Teacher training.   Z1361.E4B45

Bibliographie internationale de l'histoire des universités. Genève, Droz, 1973–74. v.1–2. (Études et documents publiés par la Section d'histoire de la Faculté des lettres de l'Université de Genève, 9, 10; Commission internationale pour l'histoire des universités. Études et travaux, 2, 5)   **CB29**

Contents: v.1, Espagne, Louvain, Copenhague, Prague; v.2, Portugal, Leiden, Pécs, Franeker, Basel. No more published.

A project of the Commission Internationale pour l'Histoire des Universités. "The original purpose of the project was, first, to complete and bring up to date the bibliographical references given in the new edition of H. Rashdall *The Universities of Europe in the Middle Ages* by F. M. Powicke and A. B. Emden (Oxford: Oxford University Press, 3 volumes [1936]); second to list publications related to the history of universities during the 16th, 17th and 18th centuries."—*Pref., v.2.*

Represents contributions of various scholars toward a comprehensive international bibliography of the history of universities. The general plan proposed for each national section groups the citations as: (1) sources (archives, etc.); (2) general histories; (3) administrative history; (4) social history; (5) intellectual history; (6) iconography and topography of the universities. Individual contributions exhibit certain variations from this scheme.

Related publications sponsored by the Commission (e.g., the Gabriel and Hassinger bibliographies listed below, CB34, CB37) are cited in the prefaces to v.1 and 2.   Z5814.U7B483

Blaug, Mark. Economics of education: a selected annotated bibliography. 3d ed. Oxford & N.Y., Pergamon Pr., 1978. 421p.   **CB30**

1st ed. 1964.

A classed bibliography of about 1,940 items, chronological within sections. International coverage, although the majority of items is in English. Includes works published to Sept. 1975. Author index.   Z5814.F5B55

Blessing, James Hartman. Graduate education; an annotated bibliography. [Wash.], U.S. Dept. of Health, Education, and Welfare, Office of Education, [1961]. 151p. (*Its* Bull. 1961, no.26)   **CB31**

Lists almost 900 books, pamphlets, and periodical articles in classified arrangement, with index of names, institutions, and principal topics.   Z5814.U7B53

Eells, Walter Crosby. College teachers and college teaching; an annotated bibliography on college and university faculty members and instructional methods. Atlanta, Ga., Southern Regional Educ. Board, 1957. 282p.   **CB32**

Contains nearly 2,700 entries for books, monographs, and periodical articles, published 1945 and later, with a few exceptions. Arranged by subject with author index.

——— ——— Supplement 1–3. 1959–67. 134p., 192p.; 124p.

     Z5814.U7E3

——— and **Hollis, Ernest V.** The college presidency, 1900–1960; an annotated bibliography. [Wash.], Dept. of Health,

Education, and Welfare, Office of Education, [1961]. 143p. (*Its* Bull. 1961, no.9)   **CB33**

Contains 700 numbered references to books, periodicals, theses, reports, etc., with annotations. Arranged in six broad topics. Includes index of names and subjects.   Z5814.U7E297

Gabriel, Astrik. Summary bibliography of the history of the universities of Great Britain and Ireland up to 1800, covering publications between 1900 and 1968. Notre Dame, Ind., Mediaeval Inst., Univ. of Notre Dame, 1974. 154p. (Texts and studies in the history of mediaeval education, 14)   **CB34**

About 1,500 items. Sections on the history of education in Europe and in England to 1800 are followed by sections on the history of universities in England, Scotland, Wales and Ireland. Author and subject indexes.   Z5815.G5G3

Harris, Robin S. and **Tremblay, Arthur.** A bibliography of higher education in Canada. [Toronto], Univ. of Toronto Pr., [1960]. 158p. (Studies in higher education in Canada, no.1)   **CB35**

Title page, introduction, and captions in English and French.

Pt.1 provides references on the Canadian cultural and educational background; pt.2 has sections on history and organization of the institutions; curriculum and teaching (with subdivisions for specific fields of study); the professor; and the student.   Z5815.C3H3

——— ——— Supplement [1–3]. [Toronto], Univ. of Toronto Pr., [1965–81]. 3v. (Studies in higher education in Canada, no.3, 5; Studies in the history of higher education in Canada, no.8)   **CB36**

Title pages, introductions, and captions in English and French.

The first supplement (1965. 170p.) includes publications from the 1959–63 period; the second (1971. 311p.) from 1964–69; and the third (1981. 193p.) from 1970–74.

Hassinger, Erich, ed. Bibliographie zur Universitätsgeschichte; Verzeichnis der im Gebiet der Bundesrepublik Deutschland 1945–1971 veröffentlichen Literatur. Bearb. von Edwin Stark. Freiburg, Verlag Karl Alber, [1974]. 316p.   **CB37**

More than 3,200 items. A general classified section is followed by studies on individual universities arranged alphabetically by city. Author and subject indexes.   Z5814.U7H35

Higher education; a bibliographic handbook. Ed. by D. Kent Halstead. Wash., U.S. Dept. of Education, Office of Educational Research and Improvement, Nat. Inst. of Education, 1981–84. 2v.   **CB38**

v.2 publ. 1981. A prototype of v.1 was publ. 1979 with the title *Higher education planning: a bibliographic handbook.*

"The purpose of this bibliography and future editions is to identify and publicize on a continuing basis high-quality references in higher education."—*Introd.*

v.1 approaches subjects from an aggregate state or national perspective; v.2 deals with topics usually approached at the individual institutional level. Covers mainly the period 1968–81. Arranged by 38 topical categories with lengthy annotations (some evaluative); author and title indexes.   Z5814.U7H63

Moscow. Universitet. Biblioteka. Universitetskoe obrazovanie v SSSR i za rubezhom. [Moskva], Izdat. Moskovskogo Universiteta, 1966–81. vyp.1–3.   **CB39**

Added title page in English: University studies in the USSR and abroad.

Contents: vyp.1, Bibliograficheskii ukazatel' russkoi i inostrannoi literatura za 1950–1960, G. G. Krichevski and E. A. Nersesova, eds.; vyp. 2, Ukazatel' russkoi i inostrannoi literatury za 1961–1967, V. L. Birzovitch and E. A. Nersesova, eds.; vyp.3, Ukazatel' russkoi i inostrannoi literatury za 1973–1977, V. L. Birzovitch and K. S. Kuibysheva, eds.

Lists books and periodical materials relating to history, administration, aims, policies, etc., of universities throughout the world.

Classed arrangement within geographical divisions. Index of authors and detailed table of contents in each volume.

Z5814.U7M6

Nitsch, Wolfgang and **Weller, Walter.** Social science research on higher education and universities. Pt.II: Annotated bibliography. The Hague, Mouton, 1970. 802p. (Confluence 10) **CB40**

Pt.I (1973) is a "Trend report." The annotated bibliography is a classed listing of nearly 8,300 items. Lacks an index.

Z5814.U7N58

Parker, Franklin and **Parker, Betty June.** U.S. higher education; a guide to information sources. Detroit, Gale, [1980]. 675p. (Education information guide ser., v.9) **CB41**

An annotated bibliography of books and reports on U.S. higher education. Attempts comprehensive coverage for the twentieth century and includes major works from the nineteenth. Arranged by author, with author, title, and subject indexes. LA227.3.P35

Quay, Richard H. and **Olevnik, Peter P.** The financing of American higher education: a bibliographic handbook. [Phoenix, Ariz.], Oryx Pr., 1984. 142p. **CB42**

Offers annotated entries for works on principal issues and trends in financing higher education for the period 1960–81. Emphasis is on the last decade. Broad subject classification with author and subject indexes. Appendixes include related bibliographic sources and financial data sources for higher education. Z5814.U7Q382

Sovetskie i zarubezhnye universitety: annotirovanni ukazatel' literatury, 1968–1972. Moskva, Izd-va Moskovskogo Universiteta, 1975. 298p. **CB43**

Eds., E. A. Nersesova and G. G. Tolstikova.

At head of title: Moskovskii gosudarstvennyi universitet imeni M. V. Lomonosova. Kafedra nauchnoi informatsii.

Added title page in English: Soviet and foreign universities: annotated bibliography.

Prefatory matter, section headings, etc., in Russian and English.

Lists books and articles on various aspects of Soviet and foreign universities. Separate sections for the USSR and for foreign universities, with author/editor indexes for each. Z5814.U7S68

A subject bibliography of the history of American higher education. Comp. by Mark Beach. Westport, Conn., Greenwood Pr., [1984]. 165p. **CB44**

Designed as a companion to Beach's *Bibliographic guide to American colleges and universities* (CB27), this bibliography lists major books, articles, and dissertations concerned with the history of higher education. Classed arrangement with author and subject indexes. Z5814.U7S89

Swanson, Kathryn. Affirmative action and preferential admissions in higher education: an annotated bibliography. Metuchen, N.J., Scarecrow Pr., 1981. 336p. **CB45**

In three parts: (1) The law and the courts (containing government and legal sources); (2) The academic community response; (3) The philosophical debate. Pts. 2 and 3 are arranged by author, with no detailed subject access. Name and title indexes. Z5814.U7S93

White, Jane N. and **Burnett, Collins W.** Higher education literature: an annotated bibliography. [Phoenix], Oryx Pr., 1981. 177p. **CB46**

A classified bibliography of more than 1,600 citations to monograph and report literature on 2– and 4–year accredited colleges and universities in the United States. Appendixes list reference sources, professional journals, important legislation, etc. Author and subject indexes. Z5814.U7W53

Willingham, Warren W. [and others]. The source book for higher education; a critical guide to literature and information on access to higher education. N.Y., College Entrance Examination Board, 1973. 481p. **CB47**

An extensive annotated bibliography, together with short bibliographical essays on all phases of higher education in the United States. Z5814.U7W55

Minorities and disadvantaged

Benítez, Mario A. and **Villarreal, Lupita G.** The education of the Mexican American: a selected bibliography. Rosslyn, Va., Nat. Clearinghouse for Bilingual Education; Austin, Tex., Dissemination and Assessment Ctr. for Bilingual Education, [1979]. 270p. **CB48**

Provides comprehensive coverage of the significant research works directly related to the education of the Mexican American. Includes books, monographs, journals, theses, dissertations, ERIC documents, federal laws, court decisions, and other government documents from 1896–1976. Arranged chronologically within the following broad topics: bibliographies; general; Mexican American students; schools; curriculum; migrant education; bilingual education; higher education; adult education; and community. Author and chronological indexes. Z5815.U5B45

Brooks, Ian R. and **Marshall, A. M.** Native education in Canada and the United States: a bibliography. [Alberta], Office of Educational Development, Indian Students University Program Services, Univ. of Calgary, [1976]. 298p. **CB49**

A classed, annotated bibliography of about 3,000 references on the pedagogy, psychology, sociology, and politics of Native education, written during the period 1900–75. Author index.

Z1209.2.N67B76

Chambers, Fredrick. Black higher education in the United States: a selected bibliography on Negro higher education and historically black colleges and universities. Westport, Conn., Greenwood Pr., [1978]. 268p. **CB50**

Materials are grouped according to type: (1) Doctoral dissertations, 1918–1976; (2) Institutional histories, 1867–1976; (3) Periodical literature, 1857–1976; (4) Masters' theses, 1922–1974; (5) Selected books and general references; (6) Miscellaneous. Subject index. Z5814.B44C45

Cordasco, Francesco and **Bernstein, George.** Bilingual education in American schools: a guide to information sources. Detroit, Gale, [1979]. 307p. (Education information guide ser., v.3) **CB51**

" . . . intended as a selective guide to the vast extant resources of bilingual education in the United States, its history, programs, curricula, administration, staff and teacher training, and the federal and state legislation which have governed its evolution as well as the indices of tests, evaluation and measurement which have been employed."—*Introd.* "Bilingual education has been defined as introduction in two languages: the child's native language and English." Includes a section on "English as a second language" although that is not technically bilingual education. Annotated; indexed.

LC3731.C667

Jones, Leon. From Brown to Boston: desegregation in education, 1954–1974. Metuchen, N.J., Scarecrow Pr., [1979]. 2v. (2175p.) **CB52**

A bibliography of desegregation in education from the period of the 1954 case of *Brown v. Board of Education of Topeka* to the 1974 *Miliken v. Bradley* case and the Boston school crisis which followed. Books, articles, and legal cases are treated in separate sections; items are grouped by year within sections, then listed alphabetically by author or other main entry. Lengthy annotations. Indexes of authors/titles, cases/legal issues, and subjects. Closer subject indexing would have added to the utility of the work. Z5814.D5J65

Mallea, John R. and **Shea, Edward C.** Multiculturalism and education: a select bibliography. [Toronto], Ontario Inst. for Studies in Education and Ontario Ministry of Culture and Recreation, [1979]. 292p. (Informal ser., 9) **CB53**

A classed bibliography with sections (appropriately subdivided) for: plural societies, culture and education, language and education, minorities and education, race and education, ethnicity and education, immigration and education, multicultural education, audiovisual materials. Author index. Z5814.E2M34

Quay, Richard H. In pursuit of equality of educational opportunity: a selective bibliography and guide to the research literature. N.Y., Garland, 1977. 173p. (Garland reference library of social science, v.41)　　**CB54**

In four sections: (1) the bibliography, an author listing of 1,435 entries serving as "a representative cross section of the literature [since the early 1960s] within reasonable quantitative limits."— *p.xix*; (2) a bibliography of bibliographies (about 250 titles) for those wishing more comprehensive coverage; (3) bibliography of sources consulted; and (4) topical index.　　Z5814.E68Q38

Weinberg, Meyer. The education of poor and minority children: a working bibliography. Westport, Conn., Greenwood Pr., 1981. 2v. (1563p.)　　**CB55**

An unannotated bibliography of about 40,000 entries, three-quarters of which deal with the United States. v.1 deals mainly with American ethnic groups (e.g., Spanish-speaking peoples, American Indians, Asian Americans, Afro-Americans, etc.). Subjects considered in other sections include school policies, legislation and public finance, community studies, higher education, and world education studies by country and area. Author index.

Occupational education

Hall, Jack and **Lessard, Victoria C.** The vocational-technical core collection. [N.Y.], Neal-Schuman, [1981–84]. 2v.　　**CB56**

Contents: [v.1] Books; [v.2] Films and video.

The first volume is a broadly classed subject bibliography and selection guide offering bibliographic data and brief descriptive annotations for 2,451 books; broad vocational fields are subdivided for more specific topics. The second volume is an annotated bibliography of films and videotapes for vocational-technical institutions; annotations are meant to help the non-specialist select materials in technical subject areas. Each volume has its own indexes.　　Z1039.C65H34

Mapp, Edward. Books for occupational education programs; a list for community colleges, technical institutes and vocational schools. N. Y., Bowker, 1971. 308p.　　**CB57**

Books are grouped by occupation within four main sections: Commercial programs; Community service programs; Engineering programs; Health service programs. Lists English-language materials with imprint date of 1960 or later. Index of authors and other main entries.　　Z5814.T4M34

Resources in vocational education. 1977–82/83. Columbus, Ohio State Univ., Center for Vocational Education, 1977–83. Bimonthly.　　**CB58**

A continuation of *AIM/ARM abstracts of instructional and research materials in vocational and technical education* (1974–76) which was formed by the merger of *Abstracts of instructional materials in vocational and technical education* and *Abstracts of research and related materials in vocational and technical education,* continuing the numbering of the latter. Ceased with v.15, no.1. Topical arrangement, with author and subject indexes.

Schuman, Patricia Glass, Rodriguez, Sue A. and **Jacobs, Denise M.** Materials for occupational education; an annotated source guide. 2d ed. N.Y., Neal-Schuman, [1983]. 384p.　　**CB59**

1st ed. 1971.

Aims to facilitate the location of learning materials for community and junior college programs. Lists 800 organizations, associations, agencies, and companies that provide sources for occupational training.　　HF5381.S423

Special education

Anthony, John B. and **Anthony, Margaret M.** The gifted and talented: a bibliography and resource guide. [Pittsfield, Mass., Berkshire Community Pr., 1981] 200p.　　**CB60**

A bibliography and resource directory for the field of education of the gifted and talented. The approximately 3,200 items (books, articles, dissertations, etc.) in the bibliography are arranged in six broad categories (e.g., identification, characteristics, special issues). The resources section lists diagnostic instruments, media aids, relevant organizations, etc. No index.

Baskin, Barbara Holland and **Harris, Karen H.** Books for the gifted child. N.Y., Bowker, 1980. 263p.　　**CB61**

Scope is limited to "juvenile literature, a category that includes toddlers at the lower end and youngsters of about twelve or those below the teenage years at the upper."—*Pref.* Chapters on "The gifted in society," "Identification of gifted children and academic responses," and "Intellectual aspects of the reading experience" are followed by "A selected guide to intellectually demanding books," an extensively annotated list of books deemed to have special utility and value for gifted youngsters. Indexed.　　Z1039.G55B37

Evans, Martha M. Dyslexia; an annotated bibliography. Westport, Conn., Greenwood Pr., [1982]. 644p. (Contemporary problems of childhood, no.5)　　**CB62**

Citations to more than 2,400 English-language publications are organized by a detailed subject classification, with descriptive abstracts and indexed by author and selective key-word subjects. Includes bibliographies, directories, dictionaries, glossaries, and serial publications devoted entirely to dyslexia. Glossary of terms.　　Z6671.52.D97E9

Exceptional child education abstracts. v.1, no.1– , Apr. 1969– . Arlington, Va., Council for Exceptional Children, 1969– . Quarterly.　　**CB63**

Contains abstracts stored in the computer file of the Council for Exceptional Children Information Center as part of the ERIC program. Abstracts relate to education of the handicapped and gifted children and youth. Arrangement is by numerical sequence of the abstracts, with author and subject indexes. Indexes were cumulative within each volume through 1975; beginning 1976 there are author, title, subject indexes which cumulate in the final issue of the year. Includes abstracts of books, periodical articles, government documents, etc.　　Z5814.C52E9●

Lake, Sara. Gifted education; a special interest resource guide in education. [Phoenix, Ariz.], Oryx Pr., 1981. 110p.　　**CB64**

Addressed mainly to educators, this bibliography covers gifted education from preschool through grade 12. Annotated entries cover the period 1976–Fall 1980 and are arranged in the following categories: characteristics of the gifted; gifted education; current issues and efforts; program planning and administration; curriculum and instruction; counseling and guidance; parents. Indexed.　　LC3993.9.L34

Laubenfels, Jean. The gifted student: an annotated bibliography. Westport, Conn., Greenwood Pr., 1977. 220p. (Contemporary problems of childhood, no.1)　　**CB65**

A classified, annotated bibliography of about 1,300 items (including books, periodical articles, government publications, and dissertations). Emphasis is on publications "of the past fifteen years since the 1961 publication of John Gowan's *Annotated Bibliography on the Academically Talented Student.*"—*Pref.* Appendixes: (A) Some individuals and organizations concerned with the gifted; (B) List of instruments useful in identifying the gifted; (C) Audio-visual materials for professional use. Indexed.　　LC3993.L35

Teachers and teaching

Fraser, Barry J. Annotated bibliography of curriculum evaluation literature. [Jerusalem], Israel Curriculum Center, Ministry of Education and Culture, [1982]. 210p.　　**CB66**

Provides abstracts for North American and European items from the period 1963–81. Arrangement is alphabetical; author and topical indexes.　　Z5814.C9F73

Hill, Phyliss M., ed. The teachers' library. Wash., Nat. Education Assoc., [1977]. 151p. **CB67**

1st ed. 1966. Previous eds. comp. by AASL-TEPS Coordinating Committee for the Teachers' Library Project.

Much of the volume is devoted to annotated lists of books and pamphlets, films, filmstrips, and journals recommended for inclusion in a professional library intended to give teachers ready access to recent and helpful ideas in their specific fields. Z5811.A25

Powell, Marjorie and **Beard, Joseph W.** Teacher effectiveness; an annotated bibliography and guide to research. N.Y., Garland, 1984. 730p. (Garland reference library of social science, v.116) **CB68**

Provides brief annotations for books, journal articles, research reports, conference papers, and dissertations concerning teacher characteristics, expectations, perceptions, and behavior; the influence of teacher behavior; teacher-student relations; student perceptions and behavior; and methodology. Covers preschool through secondary schools for the period 1965–80. Indexed.

Z5814.T3P68

Tyler, Louise L. A selected guide to curriculum literature; an annotated bibliography. [Wash.], Nat. Education Assoc., Center for the Study of Instruction, [1970]. 135p. **CB69**

Limited to about 70 items with extensive annotations.

Z5814.C9T9

Wayne State University, Detroit. Archives of Labor and Urban Affairs. An American Federation of Teachers bibliography. Detroit, Wayne State Univ. Pr., 1980. 222p. **CB70**

An annotated bibliography of 1,475 titles in five sections: (1) books; (2) articles, arranged by decade; (3) dissertations and theses; (4) selected documents and pamphlets from the union; (5) archival materials located throughout the United States. Selective subject index. Z5815.U5W38

Teaching aids

See also Audiovisual materials, p.49.

The guide to simulations/games for education and training. Robert E. Horn and Anne Cleaves, eds. 4th ed. Beverly Hills, Calif., Sage, [1980]. 692p. **CB71**

Previous ed. 1974.

Describes about 1,400 games and simulations used for educational purposes, suitable for teenagers and adults. Academic games are grouped under 25 broad subject categories; business listings are grouped under six categories. Each entry provides name, originator, copyright date, age level, number of players, playing time, producer, and description. Indexed by author, game, and producer. A collection of 24 essays evaluating games in the various subject areas is new to this edition. LB1029.G3H67

T.E.S.S.; the educational software selector, 1984– . [By] EPIE Institute. N.Y., Teachers College Pr., 1984– . CB72

The first edition contains more than 5,000 descriptions of educational software being marketed to schools and colleges for use on microcomputers. Broad subject arrangement covering all educational levels from nursery school through graduate school, plus management aids for teachers and administrators. Entries include type of program, scope, grade level, intended group or individual usage, description, configuration, price, components, availability, plus citations to reviews and ratings. Indexed. LB1028.5.T47

Truett, Carol and **Gillespie, Lori.** Choosing educational software: a buyer's guide. Littleton, Colo., Libraries Unlimited, 1984. 202p. **CB73**

Designed to assist the non-programming educator in selecting and evaluating microcomputer software. Summarizes use of microcomputers in education, provides information on evaluation and evaluation forms, and lists sources for obtaining software and aids for selection. Includes an annotated bibliography. Indexed.

LB1028.5.T69

Other special topics

Apanasewicz, Nellie Mary. Education in the U.S.S.R.; an annotated bibliography of English-language materials, 1965–1973. [Wash.], U.S. Dept. of Health, Education, and Welfare, [1974]. 92p. **CB74**

An earlier bibliography by Apanasewicz and S. M. Rosen, *Soviet education: a bibliography of English-language materials,* was published 1964. The present work serves as a supplement to that volume and "lists 347 titles indexed in 224 subject categories."—*Foreword.*

Z5815.R9A76

Auster, Ethel. Reference sources on Canadian education; an annotated bibliography. [Toronto], Ontario Institute for Studies in Education, [1978]. 114p. (OISE bibliography ser., no.3) **CB75**

Serves as a guide to the study of education in Canada. Chapters are arranged by type of publication, with an introductory explanation. Indexed. Z5815.C3A9

Baron, George. A bibliographical guide to the English educational system. 3d ed. [London], Univ. of London, Athlone Pr., 1965. 124p. **CB76**

1st ed. 1951.

A selective bibliography presented in essay form under type of school, and covering the whole range of English education. This edition adds new material through Sept. 1964. Index of authors, but none of subjects. Z5815.G5B37

A bibliography of American educational history: an annotated and classified guide. Ed. by Francesco Cordasco and William W. Brickman. N.Y., AMS Pr., [1975]. 394p.

CB77

Listings of general bibliographies, encyclopedic works, collections of source materials, and comprehensive histories are followed by sections on elementary, secondary, and vocational education; education in the individual states; higher education; school books and instructional materials; the teaching profession; church, state and education; the federal government and education; education of women; biographies of American educators; foreign influences; contemporary issues; and separate sections for specific periods in American education. Sections have been contributed by various scholars. Author index. Z5815.U5B5

Blyth, Dale A. and **Karnes, Elizabeth Leuder,** comps. Philosophy, policies and programs for early adolescent education; an annotated bibliography. Westport, Conn., Greenwood Pr., [1981]. 689p. **CB78**

Provides detailed annotations for over 1,600 items arranged under twelve basic themes: philosophy and theory of schools for early adolescents; prescriptions for and descriptions of middle schools; prescriptions for and descriptions of junior high schools; guidance programs; design and renovation of schools; internal organization of schools; curriculum; cocurricular and extracurricular activities; policy analyses; research; teacher preparation and in-service training; and discipline and problem behavior. Author and subject indexes. LB1623.B49

Bunch, Clarence. Art education: a guide to information sources. Detroit, Gale, [1978]. 331p. (Art and architecture information guide ser., v.6) **CB79**

A bibliography of books and pamphlets about art or art methods which are concerned with "using the book's content with children and/or adults."—*Pref.* Introductory chapters on general reference sources, periodicals and serials, and organizations and publishers precede the basic topical arrangement; entries are alphabetical by author within the latter broad categories. Author, title, and subject indexes. Z5818.A8B85

Cantwell, Zita M. and **Doyle, Hortense A.** Instructional technology: an annotated bibliography. Metuchen, N.J., Scarecrow Pr., 1974. 387p. **CB80**

An annotated bibliography of English-language materials (mainly publications of the 1960–73 period), arranged by author, with a subject index. "Emphasis in the selection has been given to studies of the actual use of an aspect of Instructional Technology in a learning situation."—*Introd.* 958 items.　　　　　Z5814.A85C35

Cordasco, Francesco and **Alloway, David Nelson.** Sociology of education: a guide to information sources. Detroit, Gale, [1979]. 266p. (Education information guide ser., v.2)
CB81

An annotated bibliography of more than 1,500 references drawn from studies of the 1960s and 1970s on American education. In four chapters which are further subdivided by topic: (1) reference works, bibliography, and basic texts; (2) teaching, teaching personnel, and administration of the schools; (3) levels of education, from pre-school through the university; (4) special education of adults, the disadvantaged, exceptional children, minorities, etc. Author, title, and subject indexes.　　　　　LC191.C583

Craigie, James. Bibliography of Scottish education, 1872–1972. [London], Univ. of London Pr., 1974. 279p. (Publications of the Scottish Council for Research in Education, 65)
CB82

Supplements the Council's *A bibliography of Scottish education before 1872* (1970). A classed listing in four parts: (1) general reference works, histories, and periodicals on the topic; (2) Parliamentary materials; (3) materials on more detailed aspects of education; (4) Scottish universities. Indexes of authors, subjects, and places.　　　　　Z5815.S3C72

Fraser, Stewart E. and **Hsu, Kuang-liang.** Chinese education and society, a bibliographic guide; the cultural revolution and its aftermath. White Plains, N.Y., International Arts & Sciences, 1972. 204p.　　　　　**CB83**

A classed bibliography on Chinese education and closely related topics since 1966. English-language materials predominate, although some writings in Chinese and certain other languages are included. Lacks an index.　　　　　Z5815.C54F7

Graff, Harvey J. Literacy in history; an interdisciplinary research bibliography. N.Y., Garland, 1981. 422p. (Garland reference library of the humanities, v.254)　　　　　**CB84**

An introductory section on primary sources for the historical study of literacy (censuses, wills, deeds, criminal records, military records, etc.) is followed by a classed bibliography of secondary sources (books and periodical articles). Author index.

Z5814.I3G73

Greaves, Monica Alice. Education in British India, 1698–1947; a bibliography and guide to the sources of information in London. [London, Univ. of London, Inst. of Education], 1967. 182p. (Education libraries bull., Suppl. 13)　　**CB85**

1,379 items. Main-entry listing with subject index. Includes a brief section on manuscripts and records.　　　　　Z5815.I4G7

Hanson, John Wagner and **Gibson, Geoffrey W.** African education and development since 1960; a select and annotated bibliography. East Lansing, Inst. for International Studies in Education and African Studies Center, Michigan State Univ., 1966. 327p. (Education in Africa ser., 2)
CB86

Nearly 1,600 items in classed arrangement; author index.

Z5815.A3H3

Karnes, Elizabeth Lueder, Block, Donald D. and **Downs, John.** Discipline in our schools; an annotated bibliography. Westport, Conn., Greenwood Pr., [1983]. 700p.　　**CB87**

Lists about 400 items by form: books, dissertations and papers, journal articles, and school district publications and nonprint materials. Complete bibliographic citations with annotations. Indexed.

Z5814.D49K37

Lauerhass, Ludwig and **Oliveira de Araujo Haugse, Vera Lucia.** Education in Latin America; a bibliography. [Los Angeles], UCLA Latin American Center Pubns., Univ. of Calif., Los Angeles; Boston, G. K. Hall, [1980]. 431p. (UCLA Latin American Ctr. Pubns. reference ser., v.9)
CB88

"Designed as an introductory reference volume for research on education in Latin America in all its formal and nonformal aspects from its beginning in pre-Columbian times to the mid-1970s in all areas of Latin America and the Caribbean."—*Introd.* Emphasis is on formal, in-school aspects of education from the period 1945–75. A companion volume for nonformal education is Susan L. Poston's *Nonformal education in Latin America,* published by the Center in 1976.　　　　　Z5815.L3L46

Leming, James S. Contemporary approaches to moral education: an annotated bibliography and guide to research. N.Y., Garland, 1983. 451p. (Garland bibliographies in contemporary education, v.2; Garland reference library of social science, v.117)　　　　　**CB89**

Presents citations to material on "the important thinking and research surrounding the practical side of the moral education movement of the 60's and 70's."—*Introd.* Classed arrangement with author and subject indexes. Covers publications of the mid-1960s to 1981.　　　　　Z5814.M7L45

——— Foundations of moral education: an annotated bibliography. Westport, Conn., Greenwood Pr., [1983]. 325p.
CB90

Nearly 1,500 entries in classed arrangement within two main sections: (1) "Reflections on the domain of moral education" and (2) "Moralization: the learning of morality." Author and subject indexes.　　　　　Z5873.L45

Little, Lawrence Calvin, comp. Religion and public education: a bibliography. 3d ed., rev. and enl. Pittsburgh, Univ. of Pittsburgh Book Center, 1968. 214p.　　**CB91**

1st ed. 1966.
More than 3,200 items grouped as books and pamphlets, publications of religious bodies and public school systems, doctoral dissertations, master's theses, and periodical articles. No detailed subject approach.　　　　　Z5814.C57L5

Londoño Benveniste, Felipe and **Ochoa Núñez, Hernando.** Bibliografía de la educación en Colombia. Bogotá, Instituto Caro y Cuervo, 1976. 678p. (Publicaciones del Instituto Caro y Cuervo: Serie bibliográfica, 12)　　　**CB92**

A detailed subject classification of more than 4,600 citations. Name index.

Pantelidis, Veronica S. Arab education, 1956–1978: a bibliography. [London], Mansell, [1982]. 552p.　　　**CB93**

A classed, partially annotated listing of more than 5,600 journal articles, dissertations, reports, conference papers, etc., written in English or for which an English-language summary is available. Geographical arrangement, subdivided by subject. Indexed.

Z5815.A68P3

Passin, Herbert. Japanese education: a bibliography of materials in the English language. N.Y., Teachers College Pr., [1970]. 135p.　　　　　**CB94**

Topical arrangement with author index.　　　　　Z5815.J3P37

Rosenstiel, Annette. Education and anthropology; an annotated bibliography. N.Y., Garland, 1977. 646p. (Garland reference library of social science, v.20)　　　　　**CB95**

Designed to reflect historical influences, current trends, theoretical concerns, and practical methodology. Over 3,400 entries for books, articles, conference papers, and dissertations in English, French, Spanish, German, Italian, and Portuguese, covering the period 1689–1976. Annotations in English. Arranged by author, with topical and regional indexes.　　　　　Z5814.E2R67

Russ-Eft, Darlene F., Rubin, David P. and **Holmen, Rachel E.** Issues in adult basic education and other adult education; an annotated bibliography and guide to research. N.Y., Garland, 1981. 180p. (Garland bibliographies in contemporary education, v.1; Garland reference library of social science, v.67)　　　　　**CB96**

Focuses on major issues during the five years prior to compilation.

In two parts: a discussion of major issues, and an annotated bibliography of the literature in adult basic education and related topics. Indexed. Z5814.A24R87

Schantz, Maria E. and **Brunner, Joseph F.** Reading in American schools: a guide to information sources. Detroit, Gale, [1980]. 266p. (Education information guide ser., v.5) **CB97**

In five main parts: (1) Theory, practice, and programs; (2) Literature; (3) Diagnosis and remediation; (4) Bilingualism; (5) Law, leisure, literacy. Appendix of relevant journals. Lists about 1,050 items, mainly books, but some periodicals articles. Annotations; author, title, and subject indexes. Z5818.L3S29

Sedlak, Michael W. and **Walch, Timothy.** American educational history: a guide to information sources. Detroit, Gale, [1981]. 265p. (American government and history information guide ser., v.10) **CB98**

An annotated, selective bibliography of books and periodical titles, with preference given "to those items which . . . have enduring value; to items which have not appeared previously in other bibliographies, to periodical literature which has not appeared in other bibliographies; and to periodical literature which is not ordinarily found in library card catalogs. We have also emphasized materials published since 1965."—*Pref.* "Guides to further research" (p.227–39) lists general histories of American education, historiographical studies, and reference bibliographies and guides. Broad subject arrangement; author and subject indexes. LA205.S42

Seruya, Flora C., Losher, Susan and **Ellis, Albert.** Sex and sex education: a bibliography. N.Y., Bowker, 1972. 336p. **CB99**

A classed bibliography with author, title, and subject indexes; some annotations. Includes sections on sex attitudes, customs and behavior, sex diseases and disorders, social-sexual problems, sex in literature, etc. Z7164.S42S38

Songe, Alice H. Private school education in the U.S.; an annotated bibliography, 1950–1980. Jefferson, N.C., Mc-Farland, 1982. 89p. **CB100**

"Covers all aspects of the independent and church-related school . . . [and seeks] to present recent and contemporary views on the controversies that seem to remain centered on nonpublic education."—*Introd.* Arranged by type of publication; indexed. Z5814.P65S58

Spear, George E. and **Mocker, Donald W.** Urban education: a guide to information sources. Detroit, Gale, [1978]. 203p. (Urban studies information guide ser., v.3) **CB101**

An annotated bibliography in three main sections: (1) Preschool, elementary, and secondary schools; (2) Urban higher education; (3) Adult education. Includes references on changing population patterns, improvement of instruction, training and recruitment of teachers, community control, etc., as they relate to urban schools. Publications are mainly from the period after 1965. Author, title, and subject indexes. Z5814.U8S64

Spencer, Richard Edward and **Awe, Ruth.** International educational exchange; a bibliography. [N.Y., Inst. of International Education, 1970] 156p. **CB102**

Includes entries for books and articles on all aspects of the international exchange of students, teachers, and specialists: selection, scholarships, attitudes, academic achievement, follow-up studies, curriculum, etc. Topical arrangement; no index. Z5814.E23S5

Taggart, Dorothy T. A guide to sources in educational media and technology. Metuchen, N.J., Scarecrow Pr., 1975. 156p. **CB103**

An annotated bibliography for teachers and students, particularly concerned with providing the basis for a "well-balanced and up-to-date collection for the university library in the field of educational media and technology."—*Pref.* Topically arranged, with author and title indexes. Z5814.V8T33

Teichler, Ulrich and **Voss, Friedrich.** Bibliography on Japanese education: postwar publications in Western languages. Pullach, Verlag Dokumentation, 1974. 294p. **CB104**

Title also in German; preface and section headings in English and German.

A bibliographic record of the literature for non-Japanese-speaking persons; publications listed are mainly in English, with some in German and a few in other Western languages. Classed arrangement, with index of authors and institutions; detailed table of contents, but no subject index. Includes books, periodical articles, and doctoral dissertations. Z5815.J3T44

Tysse, Agnes N. International education: the American experience; a bibliography. Metuchen, N.J., Scarecrow Pr., 1974–77. 2v. in 3. **CB105**

Contents: v.1, Dissertations and theses (169p.); v.2, Periodical articles: pt.1, General; pt.2, Area studies and indexes. (1094p.)

A bibliography covering all aspects of foreign student study in the United States. v.1 lists 553 doctoral dissertations, most with annotations, and 139 masters' theses. Z5814.E23T93

Umbima, W. E. Research in education on East Africa (Kenya, Tanzania, Uganda)—periodical articles, theses, and research papers, 1900–1976. Nairobi, Univ. of Nairobi Lib., [1977]. 198p. **CB106**

Within six sections—East Africa, Kenya, Tanzania, Uganda, Supplement, Research in progress—materials are classed by form; periodical articles section also includes essays within books, and theses and research papers sections include government publications and conference papers. Some emphasis on Kenya. Subject index. Z5815.K4U47

Von Klemperer, Lily. International education: a directory of resource materials on comparative education and study in another country. [Garrett Park, Md., Garrett Park Pr., 1973] 202p. **CB107**

A bibliography in two main sections: (1) Description and comparison of education systems of the world, and (2) International exchange of persons. Author index; annotations. Z5814.C76V66

Yoo, Yushin. Soviet education: an annotated bibliography and readers' guide to works in English, 1893–1978. Westport, Conn., Greenwood Pr., [1980]. 408p. **CB108**

A classed bibliography of 1,587 items, both books and periodical articles. A high percentage of entries is drawn from the periodical *Soviet education.* Author and title indexes. Z5815.R9Y66

Dissertations

See also CB105, CB275.

Beauchamp, Edward R. Dissertations in the history of education, 1970–1980. Metuchen, N.J., Scarecrow Pr., 1985. 259p. **CB109**

Lists 2,443 dissertations which "treat education in an historical dimension."—*Introd.* Selection was made on the basis of a thorough manual search of *Dissertation abstracts international* and the abstracts included therein. Sections on history of education in America, Canada, Europe, etc., are topically subdivided. Subject index. Z5811.B382

Blackwell, Annie Margaret. A list of researches in education and educational psychology, presented for higher degrees in the universities of the United Kingdom, Northern Ireland, and the Irish Republic . . . classified according to a modification of the Dewey Decimal System. . . . London, publ. for the Foundation by Newnes Educ. Pub. Co., [1950–52]. 2v. (National Foundation for Educational Research in England and Wales. Pubn. no.1, 5) **CB110**

v.1, 1918–48; v.2, 1949–51.

————— ————— Supplement, no.1–3. London, [1954–58]. (Pubn. no.7, 9, 11)

Z5811.B62

Cordasco, Francesco and **Covello, Leonard,** comps. Educational sociology: a subject index of doctoral dissertations completed at American universities, 1941–1963. N.Y., Scarecrow Pr., 1965. 226p. **CB111**

2,146 entries in classed arrangement. Author index, but no detailed subject approach. Z5055.U49C6

Gilbert, Victor F. and **Holmes, Colin.** Theses and dissertations on the history of education, presented at British and Irish universities between 1900 and 1976. [Lancaster, Eng.], History of Education Society, 1979. 376p. (Guides to sources in the history of education, no.6) **CB112**

Nearly 2,400 academic theses in classed arrangement; indexes of persons, places, subjects, and authors. Z5811.G48

Gray, Ruth A. Doctors' theses in education; a list of 797 theses deposited with the Office of Education and available for loan. Wash., Govt. Prt. Off., 1935. 69p. (U.S. Office of Education. Pamphlet no.60) **CB113**

"Includes all doctors' theses in Education deposited in the Office of Education prior to September 15, 1934. Arranged alphabetically by author, subject and institution."—*Foreword.* Z5055.U5A63

Iowa. University of Northern Iowa, Cedar Falls. Bureau of Research and Examination Services. Master's theses in education, 1951/52– . Cedar Falls, Research Pubns., 1953– . Annual. **CB114**

Editor varies.
A general list of master's essays in education from many institutions. Z5816.I6M3

Kirschner, Charlene D., Mapes, Joseph L. and **Anderton, Ray L.** Doctoral research in educational media, 1969–1972. [2d ed.] Stanford, Calif., ERIC Clearinghouse on Information Resources, Stanford Center for Research and Development in Teaching, School of Education, Stanford Univ., 1975. 96p. **CB115**

1970 ed. had title: *Doctoral research in library media.*
An annotated listing of dissertations from the 1969–72 period, topically arranged within categories such as "Audio," "Audiovisual," "Computers in instruction," "Library," etc. No index. LB1028.5.K535

Little, Lawrence C. A bibliography of doctoral dissertations on adults and adult education. Rev. ed. Pittsburgh, Univ. of Pittsburgh Pr., 1963. 163p. **CB116**

A list of some 2,500 doctoral dissertations, arranged alphabetically by author. No subject approach. Z5814.A24L5

Parker, Franklin. American dissertations on foreign education; a bibliography with abstracts. Troy, N.Y., Whitston, 1971–77. v.1–15. (In progress) **CB117**

v.5– ed. with Betty June Parker.
Contents: v.1, Canada; v.2, India; v.3, Japan; v.4, Africa; v.5, Scandinavia; v.6, China (in 2v.); v.7, Korea; v.8, Mexico; v.9, South America; v.10, Central America; v.11, Pakistan and Bangladesh; v.12, Iran and Iraq; v.13, Israel; v.14, Middle East; v.15, Thailand.
Each volume is an author listing, with subject index. Abstracts are quoted from *Dissertation abstracts* (AH19) or from an abstract published by the degree-granting institution. Not all entries include an abstract. Further volumes are planned for works on education in Japan, Latin America, USSR, Africa, and Israel.
The Parkers are also compilers of *Education in Puerto Rico and of Puerto Ricans in the U.S.A.; abstracts of American doctoral dissertations* (San Juan, Inter American Univ. Pr., 1978. 601p.). Z5815.C3P28

Research studies in education; a subject and author index of doctoral dissertations, reports and field studies; and a research methods bibliography, 1941/51–70. Bloomington, Ind., Phi Delta Kappa, 1953–72. Annual 1952–70. **CB118**

Subtitle varies.
1953/63 cumulation publ. 1965.

Includes doctoral dissertations completed and under way. Z5811.R4

Periodicals

See also CB14.

Arnold, Darlene Baden and **Doyle, Kenneth O.** Education/psychology journals: a scholar's guide. Metuchen, N.J., Scarecrow Pr., 1975. 143p. **CB119**

A listing of 122 journals "of professional interest to many psychologists, educationists, educational psychologists, and educators."—*Introd.* Intended "to help these people decide which journals to read and subscribe to and to which to submit their professional manuscripts." In addition to directory information, gives a description of content, indication of typical disciplines served, intended audience, criteria for accepting articles, style requirements for manuscripts, etc. LB1051.A732

Camp, William L. and **Schwark, Bryan L.** Guide to periodicals in education and its academic disciplines. 2d ed. Metuchen, N.J., Scarecrow Pr., 1975. 552p. **CB120**

1968 ed. had title: *Guide to periodicals in education.*
Provides subscription data, address, editorial policy, and notes on manuscript preparation and disposition for 602 nationally distributed United States education and education-related periodicals. Based on information obtained from the editors. Z5813.C28

Dyer, Thomas and **Davis, Margaret.** Higher education periodicals: a directory. [Athens, Ga.], Inst. of Higher Education, Univ. of Georgia, [1981]. 148p. **CB121**

Successor to a 1969 publication entitled *An annotated guide to periodical literature: higher education.*
"An annotated directory to 269 periodicals which regularly publish articles and other items of interest to higher education professionals, students, and professors."—*Pref.* Arranged alphabetically by name of publication. Brief descriptions include title and any former titles; publisher, editor, address; distinguishing characteristics; subscription information; circulation; and publication policies. Title index. L900.D93

Educational Press Association of America. America's education press: a classified list of educational publications issued in the United States and Canada. 1925–76. Wash., 1926–76. 33v. **CB122**

Frequency varies: annual, 1925–48; biennial, 1950–76.
Title varies; subtitle varies.
Coverage varies; 1963 is the 2d ed. of *An international list of educational periodicals* and the 28th *Yearbook* of the Educational Press Association. Ceased with 33d ed., 1976; a successor publication, *Edpress directory* (title varies) is a membership list only. Z5813.E24

Krepel, Wayne J. and **DuVall, Charles R.** Education and education-related serials: a directory. Littleton, Colo., Libraries Unlimited, 1977. 255p. **CB123**

Offers directory information and descriptions of "501 journals and newsletters, all related in some way to the field of education" (*Introd.*), and whose contents deal with teaching and learning. Entries include information about submitting articles for publication, style requirements for manuscripts, etc. Appendix lists indexing and abstracting services in the field. Z5813.K74

Levin, Joel. Getting published: the educators' resource book. N.Y., Arco, [1983]. 281p. **CB124**

Intended for those who want "to sell educational material or contribute articles to educational journals."—*Pref.* Pt.I provides introductory information and advice on publishing; pt.II is an alphabetical list of publishers; pt.III lists 274 educational periodicals by category. Indexed. Z286.E3L48

Manera, Elizabeth S. and **Wright, Robert E.** Annotated writer's guide to professional educational journals. Scottsdale, Ariz., Bobets Publ. Co., [1982]. 188p. il. **CB125**

Surveys 162 education and psychology journals, providing address of editor and publisher, copyright holder, publishing data, and guidelines for authors who want to submit articles for publication.

Z286.P4M36

La presse d'éducation et d'enseignement, XVIIIᵉ siècle—1940. Répertoire analytique établi sous la direction de Pierre Caspard. [Paris], Institut National de Recherche Pédagogique, Éditions du CNRS, 1981–84. v.1–2. (In progress) **CB126**

Contents: v.1–2, A–J.

Promises to provide an exhaustive bibliography of French periodicals relating to education and teaching. Journals are entered by title, with notes on dates of beginning and cessation, frequency, place of publication, size, approximate number of pages per issue, statement of policies and purpose, typical content, Bibliothèque Nationale class mark or other Parisian library location. LA692.P7

Indexes and abstracts

British education index. v.1– , 1954/58– . London, Lib. Assoc., 1961– . Quarterly with annual cumulation. **CB127**

Imprint varies; v.7– issued by British Library Bibliographic Services Div.

Frequency of cumulation varies: v.1, Aug. 1954–Nov. 1958; v.2, Dec. 1958–Dec. 1961; v.3–7, 1962/63–1970/71, biennial; v.8, 1972– , annual.

Selectively indexes some 312 British periodicals by subject. Includes an author index which repeats the full citation. Z5813.B7

Canadian education index. Répertoire canadien sur l'éducation. v.[1]– , Jan./Mar. 1965– . Toronto, Canadian Education Assoc., 1965– . 3 issues per yr.; annual cumulation. **CB128**

Frequency varies; period of cumulation varies; publisher varies (1965–72 issued by Canadian Council for Research in Education).

Provides an author and subject index to selected periodicals, books, pamphlets, and reports concerning Canadian education.

Z5813.C3

Complete guide and index to ERIC reports: thru December 1969. Englewood Cliffs, N.J., Prentice-Hall, 1970. 1338p. **CB129**

"This volume will serve primarily as a *cumulative index* to the vast body of literature on change in curricula, in educational media, and in teaching methods collected and disseminated by the Educational Resources Information Center—ERIC."—*Pref.* Provides a subject index, author index, clearinghouse index, and a numerical title list. Z5814.R4C6

Current index to journals in education. v.1, no.1/2– , Jan./Feb. 1969– . Phoenix, Ariz., Oryx Pr., 1969– . Monthly, with semiannual cumulations. **CB130**

Publisher varies.

Annual cumulations v.1–6, 1969–74; semiannual v.7– , 1975– .

Published in cooperation with the U.S. Office of Education's Educational Resources Information Center (ERIC) program, this service now provides detailed indexing for articles in more than 700 education and education-related journals. Currency of coverage is an important feature, though there are inevitable delays of many months in the case of some journals. Classed arrangement, with subject and author indexes which cumulate semiannually and annually. Serves as a companion to ERIC's monthly *Resources in education* (CB133).

A cumulated *CIJE author/title index, 1969–1984* has been announced for publication (Phoenix, Oryx Pr., 1985., 2v.).

Education index, Jan. 1929– ; a cumulative author subject index to a selected list of educational periodicals and yearbooks. N.Y., Wilson, 1932– . Monthly (except July and Aug.), cumulating throughout the year, with annual bound cumulation. **CB131**

v.1–8, 1929–May 1953, issued with triennial cumulations; v.9–13, June 1953–June 1963, biennial cumulations.

Subtitle varies.

Now indexes by author and subject about 325 periodicals, proceedings, yearbooks, etc., covering all phases of education, varying somewhat from volume to volume and, until June 1961, including many references to books, pamphlets, and analytics in books and society transactions; non-periodical material is not included after June 1961. During the period July 1961–June 1969 (v.13–19) indexing was by subject only. Z5813.E23●

Research in education. v.1–9, Nov. 1966–Dec. 1974. [Wash., U.S. Dept. of Health, Education, and Welfare], 1966–74. Monthly. **CB132**

At head of title: Educational Research Information Center—ERIC.

Lists and provides résumés of educational research reports of interest to the educational community. Beginning 1968, semiannual and annual cumulated indexes (subject, author, and institution indexes) are available.

Title changed to *Resources in education* beginning with v.10 (1975).

Resources in education. v.10, no.1– , Jan. 1975– . [Wash., U.S. Dept. of Health, Education, and Welfare, Nat. Inst. of Education], 1975– . Monthly. **CB133**

Supersedes *Research in education* (above) and continues its numbering. Follows the plan of the earlier title (i.e., documents are listed in numerical order by ED number, with subject, author, and institution indexes in each issue); indexes cumulate semiannually.

Beginning 1979, an annual cumulation has been published by Oryx Pr., Phoenix, Ariz., in 2v. (v.1, Abstracts; v.2, Index).

Z5813.R4●

State education journal index. v.1, no.1– , Sept./Dec., 1963– . Westminster, Colo., 1964– . Semiannual. **CB134**

Subtitle (varies): An annotated index of state education journals.

Indexes about 45 to 50 state and association publications, most of which are not indexed in the *Education index*. Subject arrangement. Z5811.S845

Dictionaries and encyclopedias

Anderson, Scarvia B., Ball, Samuel and **Murphy, Richard T.** Encyclopedia of educational evaluation. San Francisco, Jossey-Bass, 1975. 515p. il. **CB135**

Attempts to present the major concepts and techniques for evaluating education and training programs in a single alphabetical arrangement of articles "and in terms that are generally comprehensible to program administrators, funding agents, and students coming new to the field, as well as to the social scientists and measurement specialists who have tended to dominate it."—*Pref.* Bibliographic references; charts and diagrams; index.

LB2823.A65

Bush, Clifford L. and **Andrews, Robert C.** Dictionary of reading and learning disability. Los Angeles, Western Psychological Services, [1978]. 179p. **CB136**

Designed as a handy reference guide, this dictionary gives brief definitions of terms in the fields of reading and learning disabilities. Appendixes include a list of evaluation instruments arranged by category. LC4019.B87

Davis, William E. Educator's resource guide to special education: terms—laws—tests—organizations. Boston, Allyn and Bacon, [1980]. 259p. **CB137**

A practical, basic guide arranged in five sections, the first and most extensive of which provides definitions of terms in special education. Other sections include: acronyms; tests, surveys, and inventories; federal legislation and litigation; and organizations concerned with exceptional persons. LB15.D33

Dejnozka, Edward L. Educational administration glossary. Westport, Conn., Greenwood Pr., [1983]. 247p. **CB138**

Offers short definitions of about 1,400 terms that are used in administration of elementary and secondary schools. Contains a bibliography and several appendixes, including names and addresses of organizations and associations, pertinent periodicals, and accredited education programs. LB15.D373

—— and **Kapel, David E.** American educators' encyclopedia. Westport, Conn., Greenwood Pr., [1982]. 634p.

CB139

Comprises nearly 2,000 short entries for names and terms frequently found in the literature of professional education. Bibliographic references are provided for most entries. Useful appendixes; detailed index. LB15.D37

Demnard, Dimitri and **Fourment, Dominique.** Dictionnaire d'histoire de l'enseignement. [Paris], J.-P. Delarge, [1981]. 896p. **CB140**

A dictionary of terms, concepts, persons, etc., important to the history of education. Concerned primarily with developments in France, but includes entries for many international figures and related movements. LB15.D38

A dictionary of education. Ed. by P. J. Hills. London & Boston, Routledge & Kegan Paul, [1982]. 284p. **CB141**

Brief essays on fifteen areas of education are followed by an alphabetical listing of terms. Substantial definitions, with cross references and citations to further reading. Emphasis on British terms. LB15.D48

Educational Resources Information Center. Thesaurus of ERIC descriptors. 10th ed. Phoenix, Ariz., Oryx Pr., [1984]. 614p. **CB142**

Consists of three main sections: "Alphabetical descriptor display," an alphabetical list of all terms existing in the *Thesaurus* file, including the number of postings in *Current index to journals in education* (CB130) and *Resources in education* (CB133); "Rotated descriptor display," an alphabetical index to all significant words that form descriptors; and the "Two-way hierarchical term display," showing the broader-narrower relationships of all main terms.
Z695.1.E3E34

Encyclopedia of education. Lee C. Deighton, ed. in chief. [N.Y.,] Macmillan, [1971]. 10v. **CB143**

A work offering "a view of the institutions and people, of the processes and products, found in educational practice. The articles deal with history, theory, research, and philosophy, as well as with the structure and fabric of education."—*Pref.* Emphasis is on American education, but attention is given to comparative education, exchange programs, and the educational systems of more than 100 countries. Biographies have been kept to a bare minimum, but individual contributions to educational thought and practice are dealt with.

Limited to slightly more than 1,000 articles, most of which are several pages in length; closely related articles by different contributors are often grouped under a broad heading for convenience of use. Articles are signed, and include bibliographies. Intended for all adults engaged in some way in educational practice or decision-making, and, except where the subject matter dictates otherwise, articles are written in non-technical language. The separate index volume offers a "Directory of contributors" and, in addition to the detailed subject index, includes a "Guide to Articles" which lists each article in alphabetical sequence, followed by a list of *see* and *see also* references to related entries. LB15.E47

The encyclopaedia of educational media communications and technology. Ed. by Derek Unwin and Ray McAleese. London, Macmillan; Westport, Conn., Greenwood Pr., [1978]. 800p. il. **CB144**

Represents the work of an international roster of scholars. Alphabetically arranged entries vary in length from a single-line definition to signed articles of many pages with extensive bibliographies. Covers terms, concepts, techniques, technical equipment, etc.
LB1042.5.E52

Encyclopedia of educational research. 5th ed. Harold E. Mitzel, ed. in chief. N.Y., Free Pr., [1982]. 4v. il. **CB145**

1st ed. 1941.
"Sponsored by the American Educational Research Association." —*t.p.*

Designed to present "a critical synthesis and interpretation of reported educational research" and intended "for the use of students, scholars, critics, and advocates for education."—*Pref.* Signed articles with bibliographies offer well-documented discussions of recent trends and developments as well as traditional topics. Language is that of the non-specialist. Charts and tables; *see* and *see also* references; index. L901.E57

Entsiklopedyah hinukhit. Educational encyclopedia; thesaurus of Jewish and general education. Martin M. Buber, ed. in chief. [Jerusalem, Ministry of Education and Culture and the Bialik Inst., 1959–69] 5v. il. **CB146**

Added title page in English; text in Hebrew.
Contents: v.1, Principles of education; v.2, Ways of education; v.3, Organization of education; v.4, History of education; v.5, Auxiliary sciences of education.
Each volume arranged in alphabetical order, and with a different editor or team of editors. Bibliographies refer to works in various languages. LB15.E55

Gatti, Richard D. and **Gatti, Daniel J.** New encyclopedic dictionary of school law. West Nyack, N.Y., Parker Pub. Co., [1983]. 400p. **CB147**

A comprehensive encyclopedia intended for administrators, teachers, school trustees, board members and educators dealing with legal issues. Dictionary arrangement with table of cases, categorical index, and subject index. KF4117.G32

Good, Carter V., ed. Dictionary of education. 3d ed. N.Y., McGraw-Hill, [1973]. 681p. **CB148**

Prep. under the auspices of Phi Delta Kappa.
1st ed. 1945.
A scholarly dictionary of terms and words that have special meaning in the educational field. For the 1st ed. more than 100 specialists and some 100 reviewing committees selected, wrote, and evaluated the definitions. Nearly 200 coordinators, associates, and reviewers are listed in this latest edition, and the number of entries (terms and cross references) has been increased to 33,000. Educational terms used in Canada and in England and Wales are defined in separate sections at the end of the book. Similar sections for France, Germany, and Italy which were previously included have been dropped from this edition. LB15.G6

Grandpré, Marcel de. Termes d'usage courant en matière de certificats d'études secondaires et de diplômes et grades de l'enseignement supérieur dans quarante-cinq pays. [Paris], UNESCO, [1969]. 207p. (Études sur les équivalances internationales de diplômes) **CB149**

At head of title: Glossaire international.
Provides a basis for determining equivalency of academic degrees and diplomas among various countries. In two parts: "Nomenclature générale," which is a single alphabetical listing of the terms with indication of the country or countries in which each term is officially accepted; and "Glossaire par pays," which lists and defines the terms in use on a country-by-country basis. LB2381.G7

Hawes, Gene R. and **Hawes, Lynne S.** The concise dictionary of education. N.Y., Van Nostrand, [1982]. 249p.

CB150

Offers brief definitions of education terms of interest to a wide audience. Includes recent terms not found in Good's *Dictionary of education* (CB148). LB15.H38

The international encyclopedia of education: research and studies. Oxford & N.Y., Pergamon Pr., [1985]. 10v. il.

CB151

Torsten Husen and T. Neville Postlethwaite, editors in chief.
An impressive new work which represents "the first major attempt to present an up-to-date overview of scholarship brought to bear on educational problems, practices, and institutions all over the world."—*Pref.* Covers scholarly and professional work in education in the broad sense, surveying the state of the art in the various

branches of education, the availability of scientifically sound and valid information relating thereto, and the types of further research needed. Articles are signed and include bibliographies; most entries are several pages in length. Country articles review the system of education in individual nations throughout the world. Alphabetical arrangement of articles; cross references; numerous charts and tables.

v.10 offers a classified list of entries, grouping the article titles according to broad subject fields; that list is complementary to the detailed subject index in the same volume. In addition, there is an author index for works cited in the text and the bibliographies, and a list of contributors with indication of academic affiliation and titles of articles contributed to the encyclopedia. LB15.I569

The international encyclopedia of higher education. Asa S. Knowles, ed. in chief. San Francisco, Jossey-Bass, 1977. 10v. **CB152**

Contents: v.1, Contents, contributors, acronyms, glossary; v.2–9, [Entries] A–Z; v.10, Indexes.

Represents the contributions of an international roster of scholars (listed with their current positions in v.1, p.119a–79a). Entries are presented in an alphabetical arrangement, but with some grouping of materials in order to "reduce duplication of data and give readers easier access to related subjects."—*Pref.* Types of entries may be broadly categorized as: (1) national systems of higher education; (2) topical essays; (3) fields of study; (4) educational associations; (5) research centers and institutes; (6) reports on higher education; (7) documentation centers; plus the sections for acronyms and glossary of terms in v.1. No biographical entries are included. Articles are signed and bibliographies are appended. Intended for the layman as well as the specialist, with basic information in each article meant to be understandable to the non-specialist. *See* and *see also* references in addition to the name and subject indexes in v.10. LB15.I57

Lexikon der Pädagogik. Bern, A. Francke, [1950–52]. 3v. il. **CB153**

Contents: v.1–2, Systematischer Teil, A–Z; v.3, Überblick über die Geschichte der Pädagogik. Biographien in alphabetischer Reihenfolge. Erziehungswesen einzelner Staaten. Nach Autoren geordnetes Artikel-Register.

An extensive encyclopedia with signed articles and bibliographies. v.3 includes a biographical section, p.19–496, giving sketches of 1,277 personalities of all periods and countries. LB17.L4

Lexikon der Pädagogik. Neue Ausgabe. [Hrsg. vom Willmann-Institut München, Wien. Leitung der Herausgabe: Heinrich Rombach] Freiburg, Herder, [1970–71]. 4v. **CB154**

An earlier edition appeared in 5v., 1913–17; this is a complete reworking, not restricted by the contents of the earlier publication. Includes biographical sketches as well as entries for terms, etc., in education and closely related fields. Signed articles with bibliographies. Index in v.4. (Not a revision of the Swiss work of the same title [above].) LB15.L495

Monroe, Paul. A cyclopedia of education, ed. . . . with the assistance of departmental editors and more than 1000 individual contributors. N.Y., Macmillan, 1911–13. 5v. il. **CB155**

A 1968 reprint (Detroit, Gale) includes "a new introductory essay by William W. Brickman, Francesco Cordasco, [and] Thomas H. Richardson."

Excellent when issued; now out-of-date, but still useful, particularly for historical and biographical articles. Has signed articles by specialists, good bibliographies, and excellent illustrations, some in color. The scope of the work is general, including education in all countries and all periods, but American subjects receive somewhat fuller treatment than foreign topics. Analytical index in v.5 groups articles by larger subjects than those used in the main alphabet. LB15.M6

Moore, Byron C., Abraham, Willard and **Laing, Clarence R.** A dictionary of special education terms. Springfield, Ill., Thomas, [1980]. 117p. **CB156**

"The major areas with which this dictionary is concerned include

mental retardation, emotional handicaps, hearing, vision and learning disability, speech, physical handicaps and giftedness."—*Introd.* Brief, clear definitions; pronunciation is indicated. LB15.M63

Page, G. Terry, Thomas, John Bernard and **Marshall, Alan R.** International dictionary of education. London, Kogan Page; N.Y., Nichols, [1977]. 381p. il. **CB157**

More than 10,000 entries covering expressions and terms, international organizations, major national institutions and associations, educators, etc. Appendixes list abbreviations for associations and organizations, as well as United States honor societies, fraternities and sororities. LB15.P34

Palmer, James C. and **Colby, Anita Y.** Dictionary of educational acronyms, abbreviations, and initialisms. [Phoenix, Ariz.], Oryx Pr., 1982. 88p. **CB158**

About 3,600 acronyms, abbreviations, and initialisms were submitted by personnel from the ERIC Clearinghouses or gleaned from a review of educational journals. Pt.I lists them alphabetically; pt.II is a "reverse list," with entries arranged by their unabbreviated forms. LB15.P35

Rowntree, Derek. A dictionary of education. Totowa, N.J., Barnes & Noble, [1982]. 354p. **CB159**

Presents short definitions of English-language terms in alphabetical order. Includes some names of prominent educators and educational theorists. LB15.R64

Songe, Alice H. American universities and colleges: a dictionary of name changes. Metuchen, N.J., Scarecrow Pr., 1978. 264p. **CB160**

Records information on name changes undergone by 1,120 of the existing 1,618 4-year colleges and universities identified in the *Education directory: colleges and universities,* 1976–77 (CB228); also includes institutions that have closed since the 1964/65 school year. L901.S57

Teacher's encyclopedia. Prep. by thirty-six contributors; ed. by the Prentice-Hall editorial staff. Englewood Cliffs, N.J., [1966]. 1116p. il. **CB161**

Intends to present information on practical learning situations and teaching experiences. Chapters by specialists are grouped in seven main sections, e.g., "How to appraise—and improve—your classroom technique"; "Sources and resources for a total learning environment"; "Meeting the needs of exceptional children." Chapter outlines, boldface subheadings within chapters, and a detailed subject index make for efficient use. Bibliographies are included. LB1025.T3

Handbooks

Bilingual special education resource guide. Ed. by Carol H. Thomas and James L. Thomas. [Phoenix, Ariz.], Oryx Pr., 1982. 189p. **CB162**

" . . . intended as a resource guide for individuals involved with educational programming for the bilingual special child."—*Pref.* Consists of two parts: (1) a series of essays that discuss assessment, curriculum and methodology, social and emotional needs, parent involvement, career education, and teacher education; (2) lists of information sources such as agencies and centers involved with special education, teacher training programs, indexes, databases and journals, plus a directory of experts. Bibliography; index. LC3719.B54

Borich, Gary D. and **Madden, Susan K.** Evaluating classroom instruction; a sourcebook of instruments. Reading, Mass., Addison-Wesley, [1977]. 496p. **CB163**

Reviews currently available evaluation instruments. Arranged according to type of evaluation: of teachers, pupils, and the classroom by teachers, pupils, and observers. Entries include type of measure, availability, description, sample items, reliability, validity, norms, administration and scoring, comments, and references. Indexed.   LB2823.B67

Council of Chief State School Officers. Education in the states. Ed. by Jim B. Pearson and Edgar Fuller. Wash., Nat. Education Assoc., [1969]. 2v. il.   **CB164**

Contents: v.1, Historical development and outlook; v.2, Nationwide development since 1900.

The first volume traces the historical development since 1900 of each of the 50 state departments of education and the central school agencies of Puerto Rico, American Samoa, Guam, the Panama Canal Zone, and the Virgin Islands. v.2 presents chapters by specialists on 16 areas of concern to all state departments of education (e.g., state financing of elementary education, school curriculum, teacher education, school food services, etc.). Includes bibliographies.   LA205.C58

Goodman, Steven E., ed. Handbook on contemporary education. Comp. and ed. in association with Reference Development Corp. N.Y., Bowker, 1976. 622p.   **CB165**

A collection of papers by specialists on contemporary topics in education, each paper "designed to provide the user with needed 'state-of-the-art' information as well as further sources of information."—*Pref.* In eight sections: (1) Educational change and planning; (2) Administration and management of education; (3) Teacher/faculty issues; (4) Education and training of teachers and administrators; (5) Students and parents; (6) Special interest groups; (7) Teaching and learning strategies; (8) Some alternatives and options in education. Indexed.   LB17.H27

Handbook of adult education. Ed. by Robert M. Smith, George F. Aker, J. R. Kidd. [5th ed. N.Y.], Macmillan, [1970]. 594p.   **CB166**

Earlier editions (1934–60) had title *Handbook of adult education in the United States.*

Editors and sponsor vary.

Includes survey articles by specialists on various aspects and areas of adult education, directory information of adult education agencies, a list of general information sources on adult education, and a list of the contents of past handbooks. Each article has a list of suggested readings. Indexed.   LC5251.H28

The handbook of school psychology. Ed. by Cecil R. Reynolds and Terry B. Gutkin. N.Y., Wiley, [1982]. 1284p., 30p. il.   **CB167**

Intended for practicing school psychologists. Provides both current scientific knowledge and practical suggestions. Covers current perspectives, psychological and educational assessment, intervention, evaluation and training, medical problems, legal issues, and international approaches. Includes a 111-page list of references to items cited in the body of the work.   LB1051.H2356

Handbook of special education. Ed. by James M. Kauffman and Daniel P. Hallahan. Englewood Cliffs, N.J., Prentice-Hall, [1981]. 807p. il.   **CB168**

Attempts to bring together in one source the most basic information in the field of special education. 34 chapters by 49 contributors are arranged in five major sections: (1) Introduction; (2) Conceptual foundations; (3) Service delivery systems; (4) Curriculum and methods; (5) Child and environmental management. Chapters include comprehensive bibliographies. Indexed.   LC3965.H26

Hoover, Kenneth H. The professional teacher's handbook; a guide for improving instruction in today's middle and secondary schools. 3d ed. Boston, Allyn and Bacon, [1982]. 672p.   **CB169**

1st ed. 1973.

"Provides a basic conceptual framework for using instructional methodologies. . . . "—*Pref.* Surveys preinstructional and instruction-related activities; discusses methods and techniques for the individual and small groups, for large groups, and for affective learning; describes assessment techniques; and provides information on working with special individuals and groups. Appendixes include sample evaluation forms for student teachers, examples of a

teaching unit and a learning activity package, and a list of selected films, filmstrips, etc. Indexed.   LB1607.H665

International guide to qualifications in education. N.Y. & London, Mansell, [1984]. 675p.   **CB170**

At head of title: The British Council. National Equivalence Information Centre.

Surveys the educational systems of 141 countries. Chapters are arranged by country and include the general aspects of the educational system, the type of recognition usually accorded in the United Kingdom to particular qualifications, an explanation of each country's marking system, and a discussion of the types of education in each country: teacher education, further education, higher education, technical and vocational education.   LB2350.I55

International handbook of education systems. Ed. by J. Cameron [and others]. Chichester, [Eng.] & N.Y., Wiley [1983–84]. 3v. il.   **CB171**

Contents: v.1, Europe and Canada, ed. by Brian Holmes; v.2, Sub-Saharan Africa, ed. by John Cameron; North Africa and the Middle East, ed. by Paul Hurst; v.3, Asia, Australasia and Latin America, ed. by Robert Cowen and Martin McLean.

Offers profiles of educational systems worldwide, except the United States, U.S.S.R., and the United Kingdom. Entries include information on geography, population, society and culture, history and politics, the economy, the education system, educational administration, educational finance, and development and planning of the education system. References and suggestions for further reading are included in volumes 1 and 2.   LB15.I58

Knowles, Asa Smallidge, ed. Handbook of college and university administration. N.Y., McGraw-Hill, [1970]. 2v.   **CB172**

Contents: v.1, General; v.2, Academic administration.

The first volume is meant for administrators and business managers handling the non-academic activities of colleges and universities; it includes sections on legal aspects, planning and space requirements, public relations, business and financial administration, etc. v.2 is for those who administer the academic functions of the university, with sections on admissions, library and instructional resources, athletics and health programs, etc. Each volume has its own detailed index.   LB2341.K63

Mamchak, P. Susan and **Mamchak, Steven R.** Complete school communications manual with sample letters, forms, bulletins, policies, and memos. Englewood Cliffs, N.J., Prentice-Hall, [1984]. 486p.   **CB173**

Provides sample letters, memos, bulletins, and forms for handling a variety of administrative concerns. Topics include absenteeism, academic freedom, budgets, child abuse, dismissal, due process, medical forms, zones and zoning.   LB2801.A2M34

Sasnett, Martena and **Sepmeyer, Inez.** Educational systems of Africa; interpretations for use in the evaluation of academic credentials. Berkeley, Univ. of California Pr., [1967]. 1550p.   **CB174**

"Constitutes the first step in a 6-part revision and expansion of *Educational Systems of the World* [1952]."—*Pref.*

Summarizes the educational patterns of 44 African nations and offers recommendations on granting of credit for African credentials and proposals for academic placement of African students in United States institutions. Bibliography, p.1509–50.   L971.A2S3

Second handbook of research on teaching; a project of the American Educational Research Association. Ed. by Robert M. W. Travers. Chicago, Rand McNally, [1973]. 1400p.   **CB175**

1st ed. 1963 ed. by N. L. Gage with title: *Handbook of research on teaching.*

A scholarly work designed especially for the advanced student preparing to do research on teaching. Summarizes and critically analyzes research in the field. Lengthy articles, written by specialists, are grouped in four main parts: an introduction to the history and theory of research on teaching; methods and techniques of research and development; research on special problems of teaching; research on the training in school subjects. Extensive bibliographies; name and subject index. LB1028.S39

U.S. Office of Education. Accreditation in higher education, organized and ed. by Lloyd E. Blauch. [Wash., Govt. Prt. Off., 1959] 247p. **CB176**

A discussion of the nature and standards of accreditation, and of state and regional agencies of accreditation, with chapters on accreditation of education for the professions. Includes bibliographies. LB2355.U5

World guide to higher education; a comparative survey of systems, degrees, and qualifications/Unesco. 2d ed. [Epping, Eng.], Bowker; [N.Y.], Unipub, Unesco Pr., [1982]. 369p. **CB177**

1st English ed. 1976. Also available in French and Spanish eds. Prep. by the International Association of Universities.

Presents a summary of the university systems and their governance, access to higher education and its stages, a table of duration of studies, and a glossary of titles, degrees, certificates, etc., for 142 countries. Alphabetical arrangement.

World survey of education. v.1–5. Paris, UNESCO, 1955–71. **CB178**

Supersedes *World handbook of educational organization and statistics* (1951).

Contents: v.1, Handbook of educational organization and statistics. 1955. 943p.; v.2, Primary education. 1958. 1387p.; v.3, Secondary education. 1961. 1482p; v.4, Higher education. 1966. 1433p.; v.5, Educational policy, legislation and administration. 1971. 1418p.

Covers some 200 countries, including states not members of Unesco. Each volume arranged by country. Includes surveys, statistics, bibliographies, etc. v.1 has a glossary of terms in various languages. L900.W56

Yearbooks

Educational media yearbook. 1973– . Littleton, Colo., Libraries Unlimited, [1973]– . Annual. **CB179**

Publisher varies: 1973–78 publ. N.Y., Bowker; 1979 not publ. James W. Brown, ed.

Cosponsored by Association for Educational Communications and Technology, 1981– ; cosponsored by American Society for Training and Development, 1983– .

Summarizes important developments and indicates current sources of information in the fields of instructional technology and educational media. 10th ed. (1984) in six main sections: (1) Trends in instructional technology; (2) Status reports; (3) Guide to organizations and associations; (4) Doctoral and master's programs; (5) Directory of funding sources; (6) Mediagraphy. LB1028.3.E37

International yearbook of education. 10th– , 1948– . [Paris], UNESCO, 1948–69, 1980– . Annual. **CB180**

Assumed the volume numbering of the *Annuaire international de l'éducation et de l'enseignement,* 1933–47 (suspended publication, 1940–45). Issued jointly by Unesco and the International Bureau of Education 1948–69; "Suspended for a decade after the IBE became an integral part of Unesco in 1969" *(Pref., 1980);* an experimental volume was published 1979 with the title *International guide to education systems,* ed. by Brian Holmes.

Surveys current educational conditions in United Nations member states and summarizes recent developments. Statistical tables are included. Beginning 1980, content of the yearbook originates in the sessions of the International Conference on Education. L101.A2A63

The NASDTEC manual; manual on certification and preparation of educational personnel in the United States. Ed. by Robert A. Roth and Richard Mastain. [Sacramento, Calif.], Nat. Assoc. of State Directors of Teacher Education and Certification, 1984. 1v., looseleaf. **CB181**

A comprehensive compilation of data on teacher preparation and certification. Presented mainly as a variety of tables that offer information on state certification requirements; assignment or misassignment of personnel; credential holders and applicants; substandard, limited, or emergency credentials; use of examinations; noneducational and special requirements; minimum requirements for elementary and secondary accreditation; out-of-state institutions offering coursework; reciprocity and acceptance of out-of-state certification and credits; institutions and approved programs; state standards for initial, second stage certification; state standards for continuing education; support systems for beginning teachers. Periodic updates are planned.

Requirements for certification of teachers, counselors, librarians, and administrators for elementary schools, secondary schools, junior colleges. v.1– , 1935– . Chicago, Univ. of Chicago Pr., 1935– . Annual. (49th ed. 1984–85) **CB182**

Title varies.

Covers initial certification requirements for the several states and recommendations of regional and national accrediting associations. Includes requirements for junior colleges, administrators, counselors and librarians, as well as those for elementary and secondary school teachers. LB1771.W6

Standard education almanac. 1968– . Chicago, Professional Pubns., Marquis Who's Who, 1968– . Biennial. (17th ed., 1984/85) **CB183**

Subtitle: A comprehensive, up-to-date guide to educational facts and statistics.

Publisher varies.

A reference source which brings together discussions of current issues, statistics, specially selected articles and reports, and lists of resources relating to all levels and aspects of education in the United States and Canada.

The World year book of education. 1931–74. N.Y., Harcourt, 1931–74. Annual. **CB184**

Issued under the auspices of the University of London, Institute of Education, and Teachers College, Columbia University, 1953–74. Publisher varies.

Title varies: 1931–64, *The year book of education.* Publication suspended 1941–47.

Long articles dealing with selected problems of higher education throughout the world, written by authorities from various countries. Volumes from 1953– have distinctive titles: e.g., Status and position of teachers; Education and technological development; Guidance and counseling; Higher education in a changing world.

Continued by: L101.G8Y4

World yearbook of education, 1979– . London, Kogan Page; N.Y., Nichols, [1979]– . Annual. **CB185**

Editors vary.

Resumed publication on an annual basis. Each annual volume is again devoted to an overview of issues and developments, and trend reports on a given topic (e.g., 1979 is "Recurrent education and lifelong learning"; 1980 is "Professional development of teachers"; 1981 is "Education of minorities"; 1982/83 is "Computers and education"; 1984 is "Women and education"). L101.G8Y4

Yearbook of adult and continuing education. Ed.1– , 1975/76– . Chicago, Marquis, [1975]– . **CB186**

Each edition offers "government and private agency statistics and general information on a variety of problems related to adult basic, adult continuing and career-related adult education."–*Introd., 2d ed.* Subject and geographical indexes.

Yearbook of higher education; a directory of colleges and universities. 1969– . Chicago, Marquis Professional Pubns., [1969]– . Annual. **CB187**

Publisher varies.

1984/85 ed. (publ. 1984) in three main sections: (1) Directory of institutions of higher education; (2) Resources; (3) Statistics. The directory includes names of major administrative officials and departmental chairmen. Institutional and subject indexes to the last two sections. LB2300.Y4

Yearbook of special education. 1975/76–81/82. Chicago, Marquis, 1975–81. Annual.   **CB188**

The 1st ed. "presented government and private agency statistics on a variety of educational problems within the field of special education. The second edition was intended to complement the first by offering evaluative studies related to the various handicaps, current status reports of federal and state legislation, and listings of on-going research. Included are programs and associations of interest to professionals and families of people requiring special educational assistance and data on career education."—*Introd.,2d ed.* Includes sections for the mentally retarded, speech and hearing handicapped, physically handicapped, blind and visually impaired, gifted and talented. Indexed.   LC4001.Y4

Associations

American Council on Education. Overseas Liaison Committee. International directory for educational liaison. Wash., The Committee, [1973]. 474p.   **CB189**

In four sections: (1) International, giving addresses and descriptions of organizations, donor agencies, foundations, and other nonprofit organizations; and (2–4) geographical sections on Africa, Asia, and Latin America/Caribbean, with information on national and regional organizations, research institutes, and universities.

L900.A47

Directory of education associations, 1977– . [Wash.], U.S. Dept. of Education, for sale by Supt. of Docs., U.S. Govt. Prt. Off., 1977– . Annual.   **CB190**

Continues: U.S. Office of Education. *Education directory: education associations,* 1969/70–76. Previously published as pt.4 of the Office's *Education directory.* Volumes for 1977–78/79 issued by U.S. Dept. of Health, Education and Welfare, Office of Education.

Contents of 1980/81 ed.: (1) National and regional education associations; (2) National honor and professional associations; (3) State education associations; (4) Foundations; (5) Religious education associations; (6) International education associations. Indexed.

L901.D598

Private organizations and associations: information resources for education. Arlington, Va., Consortium of Associations for Educational Dissemination, 1978. 186p.   **CB191**

Describes some of the private-sector resources in "educational dissemination." Arranged according to seven general categories: education associations; professional membership organizations; educational laboratories and centers; advocacy groups; education-related organizations; multimedia organizations; foundations. Indexed.

World Confederation of Organizations of the Teaching Profession. Directory of member organizations. Morges, Switz., The Confederation, 1976. 225p.   **CB192**

In English, French, German, Portuguese, or Spanish.

A list, by country, of the associations and institutions that are members of the Confederation. Entries include address, history, membership, purposes, governing body, international relations, meetings, officers, major current activities, central trade union (if applicable), decision-making bodies, and publications of the organizations.   L10.W5

Directories

Bibliography

Guide to American educational directories. Ed.1– . N.Y., B. Klein, 1963– . (5th ed. 1980)   **CB193**

B. Klein, ed.
Publisher varies.
Directories are listed under subject, then alphabetically by title, with annotations. "Directory" is broadly interpreted, so that the

work includes a wide range of yearbooks, biographical dictionaries and registers, bibliographies, fact books, etc., as well as standard general and special directories, membership lists, etc.   Z5813.G8

International

Garraty, John A., Von Klemperer, Lily and Taylor, Cyril J. H. The new guide to study abroad: summer and full year programs for high-school students, college and university students, and teachers. 1981–82 ed. N.Y., Harper & Row, [1981]. 464p. il.   **CB194**

1st ed. (1962) had title *A guide to study abroad.*

A useful source of information in five major sections: (1) Planning for study abroad; (2) The college and graduate student abroad; (3) The post-secondary and secondary school student abroad; (4) The teacher abroad; (5) Foreign experience outside the classroom. Indexed.   LB2376.G33

Handbook on international study. 1955–65. N.Y., Inst. of Internat. Education, 1955–65. Irregular.   **CB195**

A directory of study, training, and exchange opportunities which has had an erratic publishing history, some editions appearing in separate volumes providing information for (1) U.S. nationals, and (2) foreign nationals. Superseded by two separate publications, *Handbook on U.S. study for foreign nationals* (1973), and *Handbook on international study for U.S. nationals* (1970–77). The so-called 6th ed. of the latter was to have been in five volumes covering different areas of the world, but only the volumes entitled *Study in Europe* (1976), *Study in the American republics area* (1976), and *Study in Asia, Africa, and Oceania* (1977) were ever published. The Institute's *Learning traveler* series (CB199–CB201) offers some of the same types of information for U.S. nationals, but does not truly supersede the *Handbook.*   LB2376.H3

Hoopes, David S. and **Hoopes, Kathleen R.** Global guide to international education. N.Y., Facts on File, [1984]. 704p.   **CB196**

Provides information on organizations, academic programs, and available resources in the field of international education. Names, addresses and phone numbers of most programs, organizations and institutions are included. Indexed by organization, publication, and topic.   L900.H66

Index generalis, 1st–21st year, 1919–1939; 1952/53–1954/55; general yearbook of universities and of higher educational institutions, academies, archives, libraries, scientific institutes, botanical and zoological gardens, museums, observatories, learned societies . . . Paris, Dunod, 1919–39; 1953–55. Annual.   **CB197**

Title varies; 1919–39 in French. Publisher varies. Publication suspended after 1939; resumed 1953; ceased 1955. (A special "extrait" called "France 1958" was published 1959.)

In six main parts: (1) Universities and schools of science and technology grouped by countries; (2) Observatories; (3) Libraries and archives; (4) Scientific institutes arranged by place; (5) Learned societies and academies arranged by subject; (6) Indexes (geographical and personal).

Gives for each institution: name and address; brief general and statistical information; list of principal professors, directors, etc. Indispensable for the period between the World Wars; especially useful for its name indexes.   L101.A2I52

International handbook of universities and other institutions of higher education. [Ed.1–] Paris, International Assoc. of Universities, 1959– . Triennial. (9th ed. 1983)   **CB198**

Imprint varies.
In effect, this series supersedes M. M. Chambers's *Universities of the world outside U.S.A.* (Wash., 1950). Although the three are separate and independent publications, this handbook serves as a companion to the *Commonwealth universities yearbook* (CB253) and *American universities and colleges* (CB214) and therefore excludes Commonwealth and United States institutions.

The descriptions of the individual institutions generally include: name, location, history, administration, academic year, fees, academic staff, enrollment, degrees and diplomas, library, publications, chief administrative officers. Index of institutions, but no personal or subject indexes. L900.I58

The learning traveler: v.1, U.S. college-sponsored programs abroad; academic year. N.Y., Inst. of Internat. Education, 1980– . Annual. **CB199**

Gail A. Cohen, ed.

Continues *Undergraduate study abroad,* last publ. 1966.

Lists programs sponsored by recognized U.S. colleges and universities that offer regular U.S. academic credit. Most courses are for undergraduates. Programs are listed alphabetically by region, country, and city. Entries include name and address of the sponsoring school and brief information about the program.

———— v.2, Vacation study abroad. N.Y., Inst. of Internat. Education, 1980– . Annual. **CB200**

Gail A. Cohen, ed.

Continues *Summer study abroad.*

Lists courses for students of college age and above who wish to study abroad during late spring, summer, and early fall. About half of the programs are sponsored by U.S. colleges and universities. Arranged by region, country, and city with indexes by sponsoring institutions and by fields of study.

———— v.3, Teaching abroad. N.Y., Inst. of Internat. Education, 1984– . Annual? **CB201**

Barbara Cahn Connotillo, ed.

Describes faculty needs and opportunities for U.S. teachers at institutions abroad. Provides information on the individual school, teacher requirements thereat, duration of appointments, benefits, and person to contact regarding applications. Listing of embassies; bibliography.

Minerva. Jahrbuch der gelehrten Welt. Jahrg. 1–35, 1891/–92–1913/14, 1920–38, 1952–70. Strassburg, Trubner, 1891–1914; Berlin, W. de Gruyter, 1920–38; 1952–70. **CB202**

Frequency varies. Suspended 1915–19, 1939–51. (35. Jahrg., Bd.1–2, publ. 1966–70)

Before World War II this work was a convenient and reliable international directory, arranged by names of towns, giving under each town the names of universities, colleges, technical schools, libraries, museums, archives, and learned societies with information as to their income, size, name of principal officials, publications, etc. Index of personal names. Contents vary, but the wealth of detail given in the prewar volumes is still useful for historical purposes.

Beginning with v.31, issued in two parts: (1) Universitäten und Fachhochschulen; (2) Forschungsinstitute, Observatorien, Bibliotheken. Only the first of those parts was resumed during the postwar period. A new series entitled *Minerva. Internationales Verzeichnis wissenschaftlicher Institutionen* appeared in 1972, continuing the numbering of pt.2 (i.e., called "Ausg. 33") and consisting of two volumes: [v.1] Forschungsinstitute; and [v.2] Wissenschaftliche Gesellschaften. Each volume has its own index. AS2.M6

Schools abroad of interest to Americans. 5th ed. Boston, Porter Sargent, [1982]. 513p. **CB203**

Aims "to objectively describe some 950 elementary and secondary schools in 126 countries of interest to young Americans and others seeking pre-college programs of study abroad."—*Pref.* Schools are grouped by continent or other geographical area. Includes a section for post-secondary and specialized opportunities. Index of names of schools. L900.S3

World guide to universities. Internationales Universitäts-Handbuch. 2d ed. N.Y., Bowker; München, Verlag Dokumentation, 1976. 2pts. in 4v. **CB204**

Contents: pt.1, v.1–2, Europe; index; pt.2, v.1, America; pt.2, v.2, Africa, Asia, Oceania; index.

Ed. by Michael Zils.

1st ed. 1971–72.

Prefatory matter and textual headings in German and English.

Within continental sections, presents information country-by-country, then by university, on universities and other institutions of

higher education. For each institution gives: address, telephone, founding date, enrollment, principal administrative officers, address of library and name of director, faculties or departments (with affiliated schools and institutes), names of academic staff members (with indication of subject field). Subject and personal name indexes for each part.

A new edition of pt.2, v.1, was published as *Directory of North and South American Universities* (N.Y., K.G. Saur, 1978. 1084p.).

World of learning, 1947– . London, Europa Pubns., 1947– . Annual. **CB205**

Continues the section on institutions of learning formerly published in *Europa year book* (CJ205). Arranged alphabetically by country. Lists learned societies and research institutions, libraries, museums, universities, and other institutions of higher education. For most institutions gives date of founding, administrative officers, faculties, etc. Fullness of information varies. An international section contains information on Unesco and international councils and organizations. AS2.W6

United States

General

Education directory: public school systems, 1969/70– . [Wash.], Nat. Center for Education Statistics, 1970– . Irregular. **CB206**

Cover title, 1969/70– : *Elementary and secondary education.*

Continues in part the *Education directory* issued by the U.S. Office of Education.

Provides a list of local public school systems arranged by state. Includes location of superintendent, name of county, grade span, number of pupils, and number of schools. L901.E35

Education directory: state education agency officials, 1976/77– . Wash., U.S. Govt. Prt. Off. for Nat. Center for Educational Statistics, 1977– . **CB207**

Issue for 1969/70 had title *Education directory: state governments,* which continued in part the *Education directory* issued by the U.S. Office of Education.

Lists principal officials responsible for state-level administration of elementary, secondary and vocational-technical education.

Eisenberg, Gerson G. Learning vacations, 1980–81. 3d ed. Baltimore, Eisenberg Educational Enterprises, [1980]. 337p. **CB208**

1st ed. 1977.

A directory of learning opportunities, arranged by sections on: (1) campus programs; (2) travel programs; (3) wilderness programs; (4) arts and crafts programs; (5) museums and historical societies programs; (6) music, dance, and folk festivals and schools; (7) food and wine courses; (8) writers conferences; (9) campus programs for those over 60 years old. Provides program title, dates, description, accommodations, cost, and information contact. Indexed by institution, location, subject. L901.E48

Learning independently: a directory of self-instruction resources, including correspondence courses, programmed learning products, audio and videocassettes, multi-media kits, and conventional learning materials such as books intended for non-formal education. 2d ed. Paul Wasserman, managing ed. Detroit, Gale, 1982. 452p. **CB209**

1st ed. 1979.

Nearly 3,500 entries for the types of materials and programs mentioned in the subtitle are arranged by specific subject categories, with indexes of titles/keywords, authors, and producers/distributors. Addresses and prices are included in the listings. LC32.L42

Patterson's American education. v.[1]– , 1904– . Mount Prospect, Ill., Educ. Directories, 1904– . Annual. (v.80, 1984) **CB210**

Coverage and arrangement vary. Title varies.

A comprehensive list of public and private schools, colleges, universities, and other special schools in two main parts: (1) school systems, arranged first by states, then by towns; (2) directory of schools, colleges, and universities classified by specialty.

Includes officers of state, county, and city educational systems, etc., and a list of educational associations. An alphabetical index to private schools, colleges, and universities classified by specialty refers to the geographical section. L901.P3

School universe data book. Library edition. 1976/77– . [Denver], Curriculum Information Center, 1977– . Annual. **CB211**

1976/77 ed. in 5v. (Also available in a "Marketing edition" of 51v. for the individual states.)

Offers "a complete reference file, in printed form, of all the information about schools stored in the computer bank created and maintained by the Curriculum Information Center . . . [providing] comprehensive, verified data about public schools, Catholic schools, and other independent schools in all 50 states and the District of Columbia."—*Introd.* A state-by-state compilation, giving names of state and district-level administrators, street addresses and phone numbers of school districts, data on enrollment, statistical summaries by county and district, etc. L901.S473

Higher education

❖Directories designed to assist prospective students and their parents in choosing a college are many and varied, offering a wide range of selection criteria beyond the mere choice of curricula. Only a limited number of such directories could be included in this section. "College directories: a 1985 overview" in the "Reference books bulletin" section of *Booklist,* Sept. 15, 1985 (p.116–20) surveys 18 representative titles recommended for a basic collection.

A work which college students often consult is the *Gourman report,* a publication which ranks programs of study at American colleges and universities. Compiled by Jack Gourman, it first appeared in 1967 (Los Angeles, National Education Standards) and is now published in separate editions for undergraduate and graduate programs. The compiler's failure to provide information about methodology for establishing the rankings leaves the authority of the work open to serious questioning. Concern about that matter is voiced in Beverly T. Watkins' article in *The chronicle of higher education* (Feb. 15, 1984, p.12–13) and again in David Webster's article, "Who is Jack Gourman and why is he saying all those things about my college?" in *Change* (Nov./Dec. 1984, p.14–19).

Accredited institutions of postsecondary education; programs, candidates, 1976/77– . Wash., American Council on Education, 1976– . Annual. **CB212**

"A directory of accredited institutions, professionally accredited programs, and candidates for accreditation."—*t.p.*

A state-by-state listing of institutions and programs whose names were supplied by national and regional accrediting groups that have been accepted by the Council on Postsecondary Accreditation (COPA). Entries include dates of first accreditation or of admission to candidacy category, and of latest renewal, with name of accrediting body; specialized accreditation by any of 53 professional agencies in 102 fields is also indicated. Candidates for accreditation are listed in a separate section. L901.A48

American community, technical, and junior colleges. Ed. 9– . N.Y., American Council on Education/Macmillan; London, Collier Macmillan, 1984– . Irregular. **CB213**

Continues *American junior colleges* (ed.1–8, 1940–71) and assumes its numbering.

9th ed., ed. by Dale Parnell and Jack W. Peltason as a joint effort of the American Council on Education and the American Association of Community and Junior Colleges.

A companion to the Council's *American universities and colleges* (below). The 9th ed. provides information on more than 1,500 institutions that offer associate degrees and are accredited by a

recognized accrediting agency. Covers location, general description of purpose and offerings, detailed information on government, history, physical plant, administration, academic calendar, admission requirements, curricula, faculty, degree requirements, special training facilities, enrollment, student activities, fees, student aid, and institutional finance. Indexed. L901.A53

American universities and colleges. 12th ed. N.Y., W. deGruyter, 1983. 2156p. **CB214**

Publ. quadrennially since 1928 (except 1944). Publisher varies. Sponsored by the American Council on Education.

The most generally useful educational directory for higher education, presenting a summary of the present resources of American colleges and universities in three main sections: (1) Survey articles on higher education in the United States, including chapters on undergraduate, graduate, and professional education; the federal government and higher education; the foreign student, etc.; (2) Professional education; (3) Descriptions of more than 1,400 institutions arranged alphabetically by state, giving for each: definite information about each institution's history, organization, calendar, admission and degree requirements, fees, graduate work, departments and teaching staff, distinctive educational programs and activities, degrees conferred, enrollment, foreign students, library resources, publications, student financial aid, finances, buildings and grounds, administrative officers, etc. Institutional index.

Appendixes include: accreditation in higher education; academic costume code; degree abbreviations; tables of earned doctorates conferred, 1861–1980, etc. LA226.A65

Barron's Profiles of American colleges. Comp. and ed. by the College Division of Barron's Educational Series. [13th ed.] Woodbury, N.Y., Barron's Educational Series, [1982]. 2v. **CB215**

Contents: v.1, Description of colleges; v.2, Index of college majors.

1st ed. 1964, frequently reprinted with revisions.

A comprehensive guide to about 1,350 American colleges and universities. In addition to giving information as to location, faculty, enrollment, courses offered, financial aid, etc., this directory includes a statement of the college's aims, living arrangements, regulations regarding student life, religious affiliation, and special programs. Especially useful to guidance officers. Arranged alphabetically by state with index of colleges. L901.P72

Bayerl, Elizabeth. Interdisciplinary studies in the humanities: a directory. Metuchen, N.J., Scarecrow Pr., 1977. 1091p. **CB216**

"The programs in the directory are intended to be inclusive of the main kinds of formal academic programs in colleges and universities in the United States fitting within the context of interdisciplinary studies in the humanities. . . ."—*Foreword.* Program descriptions are drawn mainly from college catalogs. In two main sections: (1) Senior institutions; (2) Two-year colleges. Listing in each section is by state, then by name of institution. Index by names of formal curricular offerings. AZ183.U5B29

Bear, John Bjorn. The alternative guide to college degrees & non-traditional higher education. N.Y., Stonesong Pr., [1980]. 192p. **CB217**

Discusses important issues in alternative education such as evaluating a school, accreditation, equivalency exams, correspondence courses, and credit for life experience. Offers a list of regular degree-granting alternative schools plus specialized lists for medical schools, law schools, and Bible schools. Includes information on honorary degrees and diploma mills. Indexed. LB2360.B4

Blaze, Wayne and **Nero, John.** College degrees for adults: a comprehensive guide to over 120 programs featuring options for self-directed learning, credit for learning through life experience, and off-campus learning. Boston, Beacon Pr., [1979]. 140p. **CB218**

"Focusing on the more nontraditional new degree programs, those which allow maximum opportunity for self-directed learning," the work describes "the variety of programs that exist and provide[s] suggestions for planning a program of study within them."—*Introd.*

Pt.1 outlines the various options and programs, with suggestions for pursuing them; pt.2 offers descriptions, in a state-by-state arrangement, of more than 100 adult-oriented degree programs. Glossary; index.   LC5251.B57

Cass, James and **Birnbaum, Max.** Comparative guide to two-year colleges and career programs. N.Y., Harper & Row, [1976]. 549p.   **CB219**

Describes, state-by-state, about 1,740 institutions in terms of admission requirements, programs and degrees offered, and costs. Indexed by field of study and religious affiliation of church-related institutions. Makes a special attempt to identify programs related to those occupations which promise to offer above-average job opportunities in the foreseeable future.

College blue book. Ed.1– . Yonkers, N.Y., C. E. Burckel, 1923– . Irregular. (19th ed. 1983)   **CB220**

Publisher and editors vary.

A comprehensive fact book, giving directory and statistical information, much of it in tabular form.

19th ed. in 3v.: [v.1] Narrative descriptions; [v.2] Tabular data; [v.3] Degrees offered by colleges and subjects. In addition, two supplementary volumes are issued: *Occupational education* (CB282) and *Scholarships, fellowships, grants, and loans* (CB288).

                                                                              LA226.C685

College Entrance Examination Board. The college handbook. 1941– . N.Y., Board, 1941– . Biennial. (22d ed., 1984/85)   **CB221**

Title varies. Frequency varies.

Detailed descriptions of more than 3,000 institutions, giving information about location, size, programs of study, terms of admission, costs, financial assistance, and where to write for further information.   LB2351.A1C6

Comparative guide to American colleges, for students, parents, and counselors. Ed.1– . N.Y., Harper, 1964– . (11th ed. 1983)   **CB222**

Frequently revised.

Compilers: James Cass and Max Birnbaum.

A useful directory offering much analytical and comparative data intended to serve as a basis for college selection. Includes information on admissions, academic environment, faculty, student body, campus life, religious affiliation, costs, etc. Arrangement is alphabetical by name of institution, with geographical, selectivity, and religious indexes. Comparative list of majors included.

                                                                                 L901.C33

Continuing education: a guide to career development programs. 2d ed. [Syracuse, N.Y.], Gaylord in assoc. with Neal-Schuman Publ., [1981]. 680p.   **CB223**

A directory of institutions and organizations offering programs in continuing education. Information is based on "questionnaires, catalogs, brochures, and announcements submitted by the nearly 2500 institutions and organizations that are included."—*Pref.* Institutions are grouped by state; organizations are listed alphabetically by name in a separate section. A "Guide to career areas" provides a subject approach to the programs; index of institutions and organizations.   L901.C835

Crocker, John R. The student guide to Catholic colleges & universities. San Francisco, Harper & Row, [1982]. 468p. il.
                                                                                  CB224

Lists 225 colleges or universities that were founded historically by a Catholic religious order or congregation, etc., describe themselves as "Catholic" or "rooted in the Catholic tradition," or are members of the Association of Catholic Colleges and Universities. Descriptions are based on questionnaires completed by the school and include information on student enrollment, degrees conferred, curricular requirements, campus services, campus activities, admissions requirements, financial aid, tuition and fees. Indexed.

                                                                                   L901.C9

Directory of graduate programs, 1984/85– . Princeton, N.J., Educational Testing Service, 1985– . Biennial.   **CB225**

At head of title: The official GRE/CGS directory of graduate programs.

Supersedes *The graduate programs and admissions manual,* 1972/73–81/83.

Contents: pt.A, Agriculture, biological sciences, psychology, health sciences, home economics; pt.B, Arts, humanities; pt.C, Physical sciences, mathematics, engineering; pt.D, Social sciences, education.

Provides statistical data from responding institutions concerning approximate number of graduate degrees awarded, approximate number of faculty, approximate number of students, departmental prerequisites, financial aid. Lists highest degree awarded and applicable foreign language requirement.   L901.G72

Directory of United States traditional and alternative colleges and universities, 1984/86– . Wash., NASACU-DATA and Information Center, ACUPAE Nat. Directory Committee, [1984]– . Irregular?   **CB226**

At head of title: The National Association of State Approved Colleges and Universities (NASACU) and the American Council for University Planning and Academic Excellence (ACUPAE).

Lists institutions "which are legally licensed, approved, registered and authorized by any form of the law or under any provisions to grant academic degrees whether they are accredited or not."—*Introd.* Includes traditional degree programs and nontraditional programs such as nonresidential degree programs, independent study, external degree programs, programs requiring short campus attendance or optional class attendance, correspondence schools, evening courses, etc. Indexed.   L901.D514

Doughty, Harold R. and **Livesey, Herbert B.** Guide to American graduate schools. 4th ed., completely rev. [N.Y.], Penguin Books, [1982]. 559p.   **CB227**

1st ed. 1967. Compilers have varied.

" . . . describes more than six hundred institutions throughout the United States providing graduate and professional study. All have been surveyed once again for this fourth edition."—*Pref.* Covers all areas of the liberal arts and sciences, education, medicine, dentistry, veterinary medicine, pharmacy, nursing, law, social work, agriculture, theology, the applied arts, engineering, and business.

                                                                                 L901.D65

Education directory: colleges and universities, 1975/76– . Wash., Nat. Center for Educational Statistics, 1976– . Annual.   **CB228**

Continues *Education directory: higher education* (1969/70–74/75).

A listing of changes with title *Supplement to the Education directory, colleges and universities, 1982–83* was issued in lieu of a complete directory for 1982/83.

" . . . lists those institutions in the United States and its outlying areas that are legally authorized to offer and are offering at least a 1-year program of college-level studies leading toward a degree."—*Foreword, 1983/84 ed.*   L901.E34

Graduate and professional school opportunities for minority students. Ed. 1– . [1969]– . Princeton, N.J., Educational Testing Serv., 1969– . (6th ed., 1975/77)   **CB229**

1st–2d eds. publ. by Harvard-Yale-Columbia Intensive Summer Studies Program, with title: *Graduate study opportunities for minority group students.*

Sections on professional schools (business, law, medical, etc.) are followed by a listing of graduate programs by subject area, ranging from agriculture to zoology.

Grupenhoff, John T. National education directory, 1982. Rockville, Md., [Aspen Systems Corp., 1982]. 483p. il., maps.   **CB230**

A directory of Congressional committees, federal agencies, state officials and associations, national and regional associations, and honor and professional associations relevant to education. Name indexes.   L901.G78

Guide to external degree programs in the United States. Ed. by Eugene Sullivan. 2d ed. N.Y., American Council on Education and Macmillan, [1983]. 124p.   **CB231**

Designed to meet the needs of working persons and other part-time students who are unable to complete an undergraduate or graduate degree program in the traditional way. Educational methods range from independent study projects and correspondence courses to computer-assisted learning and telecommunications technology. Information is provided for each school concerning accreditation, acceptance of out-of-state students and tuition differential, minimum campus time, instructional methods provided for off-campus learning, and student support services.   LB2381.G84

HEP higher education directory, 1983– . Wash., Higher Education Publishers, 1983– . Annual.   **CB232**

Lists "accredited institutions of postsecondary education which meet the U.S. Department of Education eligibility requirements."—*Foreword.* Entries are arranged alphabetically by state and include address, phone number, date established, affiliation, highest degree offered, program, accreditation, and administrative officers. Provides lists of agencies, associations and consortia of higher education and indexes to key administrators and to institutions according to accrediting body.   L901.E34

Independent study catalog: NUCEA's guide to independent study through correspondence instruction, 1983/1985– . Princeton, N.J., publ. for the Nat. Univ. Continuing Education Assoc. by Peterson Guides, 1983– . Biennial.   **CB233**

Lists 12,000 correspondence courses in 1,000 subject areas at 72 colleges and universities in the United States and Canada. Includes courses for high school, college, and graduate credit, as well as noncredit courses. Arranged by institution. Entries include course title, department offering the course, course number, number of credits, and level. Indexed.   LC5951.N34a

Lovejoy's College guide, comp. by Clarence Earle Lovejoy. 1940– . N.Y., Simon & Schuster, 1940– . Biennial (irregular). (16th ed. 1983)   **CB234**

Title varies: 1940–41, *So you're going to college*; 1948–50/51, *Complete guide to American colleges and universities.*

Publisher varies; editor varies.

Subtitle (varies): A complete reference book to ... American colleges and universities for use by students, parents, teachers.

Gives concise information on accreditation, type, enrollment, equipment, expenses, scholarships, degrees, etc. Advice on how to choose a college, and how to get scholarships, loans, etc., is included.   LA226.L6

Macmillan guide to correspondence study. Comp. and ed. by Modoc Press, Inc. N.Y., Macmillan; London, Collier Macmillan, [1983]. 497p.   **CB235**

Describes courses offered by accredited schools, giving only details of admission requirements and procedures, tuition and fees. In three main sections: pt.1 lists college and university courses that can be transferred to a formal degree program, plus "professional" noncredit courses and courses developed for career enrichment; pt.2 lists proprietary home study schools, primarily vocational; pt.3 is a comprehensive general index.   L901.M26

National Academy of Sciences. An assessment of research doctorate programs in the United States. Wash., Nat. Acad. of Sci. Pr., 1982. 5v.   **CB236**

Contents: [v.1] Humanities; [v.2] Social & behavioral sciences; [v.3] Biological sciences; [v.4] Engineering; [v.5] Mathematical & physical sciences.

"The present assessment, sponsored by the Conference Board of Associated Research Councils . . . , continues a tradition pioneered by the American Council on Education, which in 1966 published *An Assessment of Quality in Graduate Education,* the report of a study conducted by Allan M. Cartter, and in 1970 published *A Rating of Graduate Programs,* by Kenneth D. Roose and Charles J. Andersen [CB240]."—*Pref.*

The 5v. offer a comparative study of the quality of programs in 32 disciplines at some 228 doctorate-granting universities. Gives information on program size at each university, characteristics of graduates, reputational survey results, and university library size. The reputational surveys were conducted among faculty members in the various disciplines.   H62.A1A8

Ohles, John F. and **Ohles, Shirley M.** Private colleges and universities. Westport, Conn., Greenwood Pr., [1982]. 2v. (Greenwood encyclopedia of American institutions, 6)   **CB237**

Offers "institutional sketches of 1,291 American private colleges and universities listed in 1977–78 directories published through the U.S. Department of Education and Marquis Educational Media."—*Introd.* Gives historical information and institutional profile. Bibliographical references at the end of many articles; indexed.   L901.O33

Peterson's Annual guides to graduate study. 1976– . Princeton, N.J., Peterson's Guides, 1976– . Annual.   **CB238**

Continues *The annual guides to graduate study,* 1971–75.

Issued in five books (titles vary slightly): bk.1, Graduate and professional programs: an overview; bk.2, Graduate programs in the humanities and social sciences; bk.3, Graduate programs in the biological, agricultural, and health sciences; bk.4, Graduate programs in the physical sciences and mathematics; bk.5, Graduate programs in engineering and applied sciences.

The institutional profiles appearing in the first volume provide basic information about colleges and universities in the United States, Canada, and American territories offering graduate work; that volume serves both as a basic reference source and as foundation for the other volumes in the series. It also provides a list of graduate and professional programs by field; institutions and their offerings; and combined degree programs. "In Books 2 through 5, directories for each academic area give the names and addresses of all institutions offering degrees in the field, plus, in most cases, a capsule summary of the program's faculty, size, student body, tuition, specific degrees offered, tests required, and professional accreditation. The information comes directly from each institution. . . ."—*How to Use.* . . . In addition, 2-page descriptions contributed by the schools give fuller information about programs offered in various individual academic areas.   L901.P46

Peterson's Annual guides to undergraduate study: guide to four-year colleges. 1976– . Princeton, N.J., Peterson's Guides, [1976–]. Annual.   **CB239**

Continues the same publisher's *Annual guide to undergraduate study,* 1971–75.

College profiles include general information, undergraduate profiles, freshmen data, enrollment patterns, and information on admissions, graduation requirements, expenses, financial aid, special programs, career services, housing, athletics, and majors. Indexed.   L901.A55●

Roose, Kenneth D. and **Andersen, Charles J.** A rating of graduate programs. [Wash.], American Council on Education, [1970]. 115p.   **CB240**

A follow-up study to A. M. Cartter's *Assessment of quality in graduate education* (Wash., 1966). Although not specifically intended as a reference tool (there is no index), the various tables showing ranking of graduate departments, etc., have considerable reference value. Questionnaires on which the tables are based were circulated in the spring of 1969. Continued by CB236.   LA227.3.R65

U.S. Office of Education. Accredited postsecondary institutions and programs including institutions holding preaccredited status . . . 1970– . [Wash., U.S. Govt. Prt. Off., 1971–] Annual.   **CB241**

Supersedes the same agency's *Accredited higher institutions,* 1917–64.

Publication suspended 1973–78. v. for 1972/79 issued by U.S. Office of Education; 1980– , by U.S. Dept. of Education.

Lists institutions by state, with indication of initial date of accreditation and date of latest renewal or reaffirmation. Includes post-secondary and vocational institutions as well as institutions of higher education accredited or preaccredited by regional or specialized agencies recognized by the U.S. Commissioner of Education.   LA226.A263

Elementary and secondary education

Handbook of private schools. Ed.1– . Boston, Sargent, 1915– . il. Annual. (65th ed. 1984) **CB242**

Title varies. Popularly known as "Porter Sargent."
Subtitle: An annual descriptive survey of independent education.
Lists and describes nearly 2,000 private elementary and secondary schools in the United States. Gives information on type, tuition, staff, enrollment, facilities, etc. Contains a directory of summer academic programs and camps; classified directories of firms and agencies; and an alphabetical index of schools. L901.H3

Lovejoy, Clarence Earle. Lovejoy's Prep and private school guide: independent private nonpublic institutions, boarding and day. 5th ed. N.Y., Simon & Schuster, [1980]. 218p. **CB243**

Editions of 1958–74 published under title: *Lovejoy's Prep school guide.*
Subtitle: A complete reference book that gives facts about private elementary and secondary schools and is designed for students, parents, teachers, guidance counselors, libraries, churches, parish houses, youth agencies, industrial corporations, foundations, and U.S. and foreign government bureaus and departments, including embassies.
Offers brief information on more than 2,300 college preparatory schools—independent, private, non-public institutions, boarding and day schools. The main listing is by state and there is a listing of schools by special programs or curricula. Indexed. L901.L65

Peterson's Annual guide to independent secondary schools, 1980– . Princeton, N.J., Peterson's Guides, 1980– . Annual. **CB244**

Provides information on independent American and Canadian secondary schools and similar foreign schools that use English in the classroom. Aims to include schools (1) whose standards have been recognized by a legitimate outside group; (2) whose curricula are probably free of undue religious or political influence; and (3) that principally offer curricula tailored for college bound students. Indexed. L900.P48

Private independent schools; the American private schools for boys and girls . . . Ed.1– . Wallingford, Conn., Bunting, 1943– . il. Annual since 1951. **CB245**

Title varies: 1943, *Independent schools, a directory.*
Subtitle varies.
Gives fairly lengthy descriptions of more than 1,000 private schools and brief listings of others. Includes a list of educational associations.

Specialized education

Axford, Lavonne B. A directory of educational programs for the gifted. Metuchen, N.J., Scarecrow Pr., 1971. 282p. **CB246**

Listing is by state. Includes both public and private institutions, and summer programs. L901.A95

Directory for exceptional children, a listing of educational and training facilities . . . Ed.1– . Boston, Sargent, 1954– . Biennial (irregular). (10th ed. 1984–85) **CB247**

Subtitle varies.
Gives information on academic programs for the learning disabled, facilities for the emotionally disturbed and socially maladjusted; programs for the autistic; psychiatric guidance clinics; facilities for orthopedic and neurological handicaps; facilities for the mentally retarded; schools for the blind, the partially sighted, the deaf and hard of hearing; speech and hearing clinics, etc. Separate list of Canadian facilities. Includes list of associations, societies, and foundations. LC4007.D5

Directory of college facilities and services for the handicapped. Ed. by Charles S. McGeough, Barbara Jungjohan and James L. Thomas. Phoenix, Ariz., Oryx Pr., 1983. 373p. **CB248**

Compiled "to serve as a basic guide for disabled individuals and for high school and college counselors who seek to assist the population in locating postsecondary educational opportunities."— *Introd.* Provides an overview of more than 2,000 programs and services in the United States and Canada. Includes information on special services, auxiliary aids, and access, plus demographic data on the institutions, degree or certificate granted, information on the physical terrain and the name of a resource person. Indexed.
L901.D474

Directory of facilities and services for learning disabled. Ed.9– , 1981/82– . Novato, Calif., Academic Therapy Pubns., [1981]– . Annual. **CB249**

Continues *Directory of educational facilities for the learning disabled* (1967/68–79/80).
Listing is by state; information is derived from questionnaires completed by the agencies represented. Inclusion does not constitute an endorsement. L901.D5115

Directory of learning resources for the gifted and talented. 1981/82– . [Waterford, Conn., Bureau of Business Practice, 1981–] Biennial? **CB250**

" . . . designed to help you find expert help and advice, identify the latest thinking and research in the field, and locate the resources you need for program development, program funding, and staff training."—*p.2.* Offers the same type of information as is found in the *Directory of learning resources for the handicapped* (below).

Directory of learning resources for the handicapped. 1979/80– . [Waterford, Conn., Bureau of Business Practice, 1979–] Biennial? **CB251**

Intended as an information resource for those working with the handicapped. Includes sections on periodicals; information centers; professional training centers; federal programs, agencies and officials; state agencies and officials; national and state organizations and associations; publishers and sources of special materials.
LC4001.D57

Gollay, Elinor and **Bennett, Alwina.** The college guide for students with disabilities. Cambridge, Mass., Abt Publs.; Boulder, Colo., Westview Pr., [1976]. 545p. **CB251a**

Subtitle: A detailed directory of higher education services, programs, and facilities accessible to handicapped students in the United States.
Provides information on college-based, state, and national resources. Brief chapters cover legal rights, handbooks and directories, financial aid, and private, federal, and state agencies relevant to the disabled. College summary tables and individual college descriptions are followed by accessibility tables on over 7,000 buildings surveyed. Index of colleges. L901.G68

Canada

Directory of Canadian universities. Répertoire des universités canadiennes. 1977– . Ottawa, Statistics Canada, 1978– . Annual. **CB252**

Represents a change of title from *Universities and colleges of Canada* (1948–77). Published jointly by the Association of Universities and Colleges of Canada and Statistics Canada.
Provides information on history and governance, programs and degrees, admission requirements, costs, academic year, grading system, buildings and grounds, libraries, student aid, student life and services, etc. Includes a list of diploma, degree and certificate programs which indicates the institutions and levels at which the programs are offered. L905.D5

Great Britain

Commonwealth universities yearbook; a directory to the universities of the British Commonwealth and the handbook of their Association, 1914– . London, Assoc. of Commonwealth Universities, 1914– . v.1– . Annual. **CB253**

Publication suspended 1941–46.

Title varies: 1914–47, *Yearbook of the universities of the Empire;* 1948–57, *Yearbook of the universities of the Commonwealth.*

Gives fairly detailed information about the universities of the British Commonwealth, including names of administrative officers and faculties; general information as to history, library, and museums; requirements for admission and degrees; scholarships, etc. Index of names. LB2310.Y5

The education authorities directory and annual. 1903– . London, School Govt. Pub. Co., 1903– . Annual. **CB254**

Title varies slightly.

Published as *School government handbook,* no.4, 1903–1929/30. With the issue of 1930/31, the Directory ceased to form part of the series.

Includes a large amount of official, institutional, and local directory material. L915.E3

Girls' school year book (public schools). The official book of reference of the Association of Head Mistresses. London, Black, 1906– . v.1– . Annual. **CB255**

Title varies slightly.

Counterpart to the *Public and preparatory schools year book* (below).

Public and preparatory schools year book. The official book of reference of the Headmasters' Conference and of the Incorporated Association of Preparatory Schools. London, Black, 1889– . v.1– . Annual. **CB256**

Title varies; subtitle varies.

Gives descriptive information, teaching staffs, etc., of public and preparatory schools for boys in Great Britain. Briefer information is included on universities and colleges and non-university educational institutions. Beginning with v.92 (1982), includes most of the major preparatory schools for girls. Contains a section on careers: Navy, Army, Air Force, Civil Service, Church, Teaching, Law, and other professions.

Statistics

The condition of education, 1975– . Wash., U.S. Dept. of Education, Office of Educational Research and Improvement, Nat. Center for Educational Statistics, 1975– . Annual. **CB257**

1975–79 issued by Dept. of Health, Education and Welfare, Education Division, Nat. Center for Educational Statistics; 1977–[82] issued in parts. ERIC version for 1981–82 distributed to depository libraries on microfiche.

A statistical survey and overview of trends in elementary, secondary, and higher education. Chapters are devoted to specific topics of concern and include text, tables, and charts. A cumulative four-year statistical summary concludes each volume. L112.N377a

Digest of educational statistics. 1962– . Wash., Govt. Prt. Off., 1962– . Annual. **CB258**

1962–65 issued as U.S. Office of Education *Bulletin;* 1966– published by U.S. Office of Education, National Center for Educational Statistics.

A very useful compilation, giving current statistical information on schools, enrollments, teachers, graduates, educational attainment, finances, federal programs in the field of education, libraries, international education, and research and development.

Replaces the "Statistical summary of education," formerly chapter 1 in the *Biennial survey* (CB265). L111.A6

Hamilton, Malcolm C. Directory of educational statistics: a guide to sources. Ann Arbor, Mich., Pierian Pr., 1974. 71p. il. **CB259**

99 bibliographic sources are grouped by subject—general, public elementary and secondary schools, public school expenditures and revenues, salaries, nonpublic schools, higher education, degrees and enrollment, international education, education in Great Britain,

miscellaneous. The entry for each source gives a brief description and publication history. Title and subject indexes. L901.H28

Harris, Seymour Edwin. A statistical portrait of higher education. A report for the Carnegie Commission on Higher Education. N.Y., McGraw-Hill, [1972]. 978p. **CB260**

About 700 tables with explanatory text representing all aspects of higher education. Detailed table of contents, but no index. LA227.3.H25

McCoy, Marilyn and **Halstead, D. Kent.** Higher education financing in the fifty states: interstate comparisons fiscal year 1981. 3d ed. Boulder, Colo., Nat. Center for Higher Education Management Systems for Nat. Inst of Education, [1984]. 546p. il. **CB261**

1st ed. 1979.

Combines the broad view of financing at the state budget level with detailed information on institutional revenues and expenditures. State profiles include data on population and enrollment, tax structure, the amount allocated to higher education and the distribution of state and local appropriations followed by detailed statistics concerning state and local government support of higher education, tax capacity, institutional revenues and expenditures, and trends. Appendixes. LB2342.M18

National Research Council. Board on Human-Resource Data and Analysis. A century of doctorates; data analyses of growth and change. Wash., Nat. Academy of Sciences, 1978. 173p. il. **CB262**

Added subtitle: U.S. PhD's—their numbers, origins, characteristics, and the institutions from which they come.

Lindsay R. Harmon, project director.

Offers statistical data showing production of "third-level research degrees such as PhD, ScD, EngD, and EdD; professional degrees such as MD, DDS and DVM are not included."—*Pref.*

Tabular arrangement by field, institution, etc. This volume is the sixth in a series, and cumulates data from the five earlier volumes. LB2386.N32

United Nations Educational, Scientific and Cultural Organization. Manual of educational statistics. [Paris], UNESCO, [1961]. 241p. **CB263**

Definitions, classifications, and tabulations of educational statistics, as described by the Committee on the International Standardization of Educational Statistics. LB2846.M37

—— Statistical yearbook. Annuaire statistique. Ed.1– , 1963– . [Paris], 1964– . Annual. **CB264**

Title page and text in English and French.

Supersedes United Nations Educational, Scientific and Cultural Organization's *Basic facts and figures.*

Contains international statistical tables on education, educational expenditures, science and technology, libraries, book production, newspapers and periodicals, film and cinema, and radio and television broadcasting.

U.S. Office of Education. Biennial survey of education, 1916/18–1956/58. Wash., Govt. Prt. Off., 1921–63. **CB265**

Chapter 3 of 1956/58 issue not published.

Ceased publication; superseded by a variety of statistical publications covering special subject fields.

Contains basic data and statistics on education in the United States from kindergarten through graduate school. L111.A6

School law

Gee, E. Gordon and **Sperry, David J.** Education law and the public schools: a compendium. Boston, Allyn and Bacon, [1978]. 1v., looseleaf. **CB266**

A comprehensive list of educational terms having potential legal application. Attempts "(1) to define the term or to describe the nature of the problem . . . (2) to describe, explore, and summarize the current legal status of the subject in question; and (3) to provide specific guidelines, suggestions or help."—*How to use the compendium.* Includes a glossary of legal terms used and a table of cases.

KF4119.G43

Hollander, Patricia A. Legal handbook for educators. Boulder, Colo., Westview Pr., [1978]. 287p. **CB267**

A practical overview of the legal issues faced by today's educators. Provides information on prevailing judicial decisions, statutes, and regulations. Topics include due process and personal liability; recruitment, admission, and financial obligations of students; treatment of students; faculty and administrative recruitment, hiring, and collective bargaining; treatment of faculty; and funding and facilities. Index of cases. KF4119.H64

Rezny, Arthur Adolph. A schoolman in the law library. Danville, Ill., Interstate Printers and Pub., [1968]. 68p.

CB268

Subtitle: Problems, bibliography, research tools, analysis of a case, glossary of legal terms.

A brief guide to the use of legal research materials, especially useful to school administrators and advanced students of education.

Yearbook of school law. 1950– . Danville, Ill., Interstate Printers and Pub., 1950– . Annual. **CB269**

Publisher varies; editor varies.

Supersedes the *Yearbook of school law,* ed.1–10, 1932–42.

Contains digests and analyses of court decisions affecting schools. Has an index and a table of cases; also indexed in the *Education index* (CB131).

Biography

Biographical dictionary of American educators. Ed. by John F. Ohles. Westport, Conn., Greenwood Pr., [1978]. 3v. (1666p.) **CB270**

Aims "to provide a ready source of biographical information about those people who have shaped American education from colonial times to the American bicentennial of 1976. Because education in the United States developed on the state level, leaders in education in the states have been included, as well as national figures and those who have been leaders in subject matter fields. Basic criteria for selection were persons who had been engaged in education, were eminent, and had reached the age of sixty, had retired, or had died by January 1, 1975."—*Pref.* Signed articles, averaging about a page in length, are mainly by educators and concentrate on the biographee's education, employment, contributions to the field of education, and participation in professional associations and activities. Bibliographic sources are cited. General index in v.3. Appendixes include lists of biographees by place of birth, by state of major service, by field of work, and by year of birth.

LA2311.B54

Directory of American scholars; a biographical directory. 8th ed. N.Y., Jaques Cattell Pr./Bowker, 1982. 4v. CB271

For full information *see* AJ90.

Leaders in education. 5th ed. Ed. by Jaques Cattell Pr. N.Y., Bowker, 1974. 1309p. **CB272**

1st ed. 1932.

About 17,000 biographical sketches. ". . . includes officers and deans of accredited institutions of higher learning, professors of education, directors and staff of educational research institutes, state and provincial commissioners of education and certain members of their staffs, leading figures in the public and private school fields, officers of foundations concerned with education, officials of the Office of Education and major educational associations, and authors of important pedagogical books."—*Pref.* This edition includes a new "specialty" index to biographees, as well as a geographic index. LA2311.L4

National faculty directory, 1970– . Detroit, Gale, [1970–]. Annual (slightly irregular). **CB273**

Subtitle (varies): An alphabetical list, with addresses, of . . . members of teaching faculty at junior colleges, colleges, and universities in the United States and at selected Canadian institutions.

Gives department and institutional affiliation only, not faculty rank or other biographical information. L901.N34

Who's who in American education; an illustrated biographical dictionary of eminent living educators of the United States and Canada. Nashville, Tenn., Who's Who in Amer. Education, 1928–68. Ed.1–23. il. Biennial. **CB274**

Ceased publication.

Contains sketches of persons active in higher education, and primary and secondary school administrative officers, as well as some persons not directly connected with education, e.g., public relations executives, librarians of public libraries, etc.

LA2311.W45

GUIDANCE

Bibliography

Career education: a dissertation index. Ann Arbor, Mich., University Microfilms International, 1976. 333p. **CB275**

The main portion of the work is a keyword index to "career education titles accepted by North American universities between 1972 and 1975."—*Introd.* About 2,700 titles; all are abstracted in *Dissertation abstracts international* (and citations to that publication are included along with information for ordering copies from University Microfilms). The author index repeats the full citation. Expands and updates Edwin G. York's *1900 doctoral dissertations on career education* (1975).

Egelston, Roberta R. Career planning materials: a guide to sources and their use. Chicago, Amer. Lib. Assoc., 1981. 177p. il. **CB276**

The first four chapters provide an annotated bibliography of titles which identify and describe occupations and forecast employment, describe education and training, provide directory data on where jobs are available, and discuss job search skills; titles of special interest to women, minorities, and the handicapped are highlighted by graphic symbols. The final chapter describes the organization of a library collection of career planning materials. Appendixes feature directories of relevant organizations, publishers, and state employment security agencies. Indexed. Z7164.V6E46

Goodman, Leonard H. Current career and occupational literature, 1973/77– . N.Y., Wilson, 1978– . Biennial.

CB277

The first issue covers 1973–77; subsequent volumes cover two years and are published at two-year intervals. Designed to replace Gertrude Forrester's *Occupational literature; an annotated bibliography* (N.Y., Wilson, 1971).

1984 ed. in two main sections: pt.1, Annotated bibliography of books and pamphlets arranged by career; pt.2, Career planning and education books and other materials that describe more than one occupation. Indexed. Z7164.V6G65

Lovejoy's Career & vocational school guide. [Ed.1–] N.Y., Simon and Schuster, 1955– . (6th ed. 1982) **CB278**

1st–2d ed. had title: *Vocational school guide.*

Subtitle, ed.4– : A source book, clue book and directory of institutions training for job opportunities.

Provides introductory information on careers and jobs; a list of associations by trade or profession that provide career information; a list of schools offering a particular career program; and capsule descriptions of the schools. L901.L6

Rockcastle, Madeline T. "Where to start"; an annotated career planning bibliography, 1983–1985. 4th ed. Ithaca, Cornell Univ. Career Center, [1983]. 206p. **CB279**

1st ed. 1979.

About 1,500 books and pamphlets are arranged by type of career or subject interest. Includes chapters on financial aids. overseas travel and employment, study and work options, study abroad, summer and short-term employment, and women. Appendixes provide lists of periodicals which feature job listings, and series of career information titles.   Z7164.V6R63

Directories and handbooks

Career guidance; a handbook of methods, by Robert E. Campbell [and others]. Columbus, Ohio, Merrill, [1973]. 421p.   **CB280**

Includes sections on (1) Educational level considerations relating to career guidance; (2) Population subgroups for whom special guidance procedures are desirable; (3) Types of career guidance methods; (4) Designing career guidance approaches; (5) Guidelines for career guidance program development; and (6) Compendium of career guidance methods. The latter is a collection of 643 abstracts of publications on guidance methods. Indexed.   HF5831.C2657

Careers encyclopedia. Ed. by Craig Norback. Homewood, Ill., Dow Jones-Irwin, [1980]. 456p.   **CB281**

An alphabetical arrangement of entries for 187 careers, giving for each a job description plus information on place of employment, working conditions, qualifications necessary, opportunities for advancement, and salary range. One or more sources of information (with addresses) also included. Indexed.   HF5382.5.U5C337

College blue book: occupational education, 1972– . N.Y., Macmillan, 1972– . Irregular.   **CB282**

v. for 1972– issued as a supplement to the *College blue book* (CB220).
A state-by-state listing of occupational schools is followed by a subject listing of curricula and programs of instruction.   L901.O3

Directory of counseling services. 1973– . [Wash.], Internat. Assoc. of Counseling Services, [1973]– . Irregular.   **CB283**

Continues *Directory of approved counseling agencies* (1950–69/70).
A tool for counselors making referrals and for individuals seeking competent counseling. Lists accredited member agencies on a state-by-state basis.   HF5381.A1N4273

The encyclopedia of careers and vocational guidance. William E. Hopke, ed. in chief. 6th ed. Chicago, J. G. Ferguson, 1984. 3v.   **CB284**

1st ed. 1967.
Contents: v.1, Reviewing career fields; v.2, Selecting a career; v.3, Selecting a technician's career.
Intended for junior and senior high school students, their parents, teachers and counselors. v.1 presents guidelines for planning, test results, the future, finding a job, and career fields; v.2 and 3 contain articles on specific occupations, following the classification system of the *Dictionary of occupational titles* (CH775).   HF5381.E52

Gale, Barry and **Gale, Linda.** The national career directory: an occupational information handbook. N.Y., Arco, [1979]. 240p.   **CB285**

On cover: Over 2000 references to free or inexpensive printed materials and information available on hundreds of careers for today and tomorrow—includes names, addresses, and career relationships.
Arranged alphabetically by name of occupation, with an index and lists of "career clusters" to further aid the user.   HF5382.5.U5G3

Technician education yearbook. Ed.1– , 1963/64– . Ann Arbor, Mich., Prakken Pub., [1963]– . il. Annual.   **CB286**

Now contains a directory of more than 2,000 United States institutions offering technician training. Also includes sections for new issues, problems, and proposals in technical training; case studies of outstanding programs; occupational information, etc.   T73.T4

FELLOWSHIPS AND SCHOLARSHIPS

Coleman, William E. Grants in the humanities; a scholar's guide to funding sources. 2d ed. [N.Y., Neal-Schuman, 1984] 175p.   **CB287**

1st ed. 1980.
Lists 197 programs, including "facilities" appointments that do not include financial assistance. Provides useful information on obtaining grants and writing the proposal. Includes a sample proposal, a sample budget, and a list of granting agencies. Indexed.   AZ507.C58

The college blue book: scholarships, fellowships, grants, and loans. M. Lorraine Mathies, ed. N.Y., Macmillan Information, [1975–]. Irregular.   **CB288**

Awards are grouped as (1) General, (2) Area studies; (3) Environmental studies; (4) Humanities; (5) Life sciences; (6) Medical sciences; (7) Minorities; (8) Physical sciences; (9) Social sciences; (10) Technology, with numerous subdivisions in categories 2–10. Within categories, listing is by name of agency giving the award; information is quite full. Indexed.   LB2338.S36

Davis, Jerry S. and **Van Dusen, William D.** Guide to the literature of student financial aid. N.Y., College Entrance Examination Board, 1978. 166p.   **CB289**

A classed bibliography with annotations. Lacks an index.   LB2337.4.D38

Directory of financial aids for minorities. 1984/85– . Santa Barbara, Calif., ABC-Clio, [1984]– . Irregular?   **CB290**

Gail A. Schlachter, ed.
The 1984/85 volume lists about 900 financial aid programs (scholarships, fellowships, loans, grants, awards and internships) available to Asians, blacks, Hispanics and Native Americans. Includes bibliography and indexes.   LB2338.D56

Directory of financial aids for women. Ed.1– . Santa Barbara, Calif., ABC-Clio, 1978– . Irregular.   **CB291**

Gail A. Schlachter, ed.
Publisher varies.
Lists scholarships, fellowships, loans, grants, awards, and internships designed primarily or exclusively for women, state sources of educational benefits for women, etc. Programs which have broadened their scope to include men have been dropped from the third edition (publ. 1985). Indexed.

Feingold, S. Norman and **Feingold, Marie.** Scholarships, fellowships, and loans. Arlington, Mass., Bellman Publ. Co., [1949–82]. 7v.   **CB292**

v.1–4 of this title (publ. 1949–62) constituted a first edition of the series, with v.5 (publ. 1972) serving as a kind of transition volume; the two latest volumes are those which are currently useful. Like v.6 (publ. 1977), v.7 "concentrates on those financial aids which are awarded by the donor or a designated administering agency other than the training/educational institutions to be attended. Volumes VI and VII should be used together. The information contained in Volume VII does not duplicate the data contained in Volume VI."—*Introd.* In both volumes the fund descriptions are listed alphabetically by funding agency, and in each there is a "Vocational goals index" and an alphabetical index which provides references from names of all administering agencies, donors, and awards.   LB2338.S46

A foreign student's selected guide to financial assistance for study and research in the United States. Ed. by Joseph Lurie with Jonathon Miller. Garden City, N.Y., Adelphi Univ. Pr., [1983]. 327p.   **CB293**

Describes financial award programs from 232 undergraduate and 173 graduate schools in the United States. Includes awards reserved for foreign nationals and those available to both U.S. citizens and foreign nationals. Indexed by institution, nationality, and region of the world.   LB2338.F674

Foundation directory, comp. by the Foundation Library Center. Ed.1– . N.Y., Foundation Center, 1960– . **CB294**

Publisher varies.

An extensive listing of foundations, many of which award grants or fellowships.

For complete entry *see* CA110.

Grants register, 1969/70– . N.Y., St. James Pr., [1969–]. Biennial. **CB295**

An international directory of scholarships, fellowships, grants, and similar financial aids available to graduate students and advanced scholars throughout the English-speaking world. Grant-giving foundations, institutions, etc., are listed alphabetically with brief information on type of assistance offered. There is a subject index subdivided by country, and an index of awarding bodies.

LB2338.G7

Keesler, Oreon. Financial aids for higher education; a catalog for undergraduates. [Ed.6]– , 1974/75– . Dubuque, Ia., William C. Brown, 1975– . Annual? **CB296**

Continues *A national catalog of financial aids for students entering college.*

Intended for high school seniors and undergraduates, the 1984 edition lists more than 3,200 programs for financial assistance. A special feature, "The program finder," lists special aid programs for specific groups of individuals. LB2338.K39

Public Management Institute. The complete grants sourcebook for higher education. [Wash.], American Council on Education, [1980]. 605p. **CB297**

Pt.1 provides information on successful grantsmanship; pt.2 is a directory of more than 500 federal, foundation, and corporate sources of support. Entries include the funding source's area of interest, financial data, eligibility requirements, application information, policy, and sample grants. LB2336.P8

Study abroad; études à l'étranger; estudios en la extranjero. v.1– , 1948– . Paris, UNESCO, 1948– . **CB298**

Subtitle varies. Title and introductory matter also in French and Spanish; text in English, French, or Spanish.

Frequency varies: originally annual; from v.15, mainly biennial.

Beginning with issue for 1968/70, continues *Vacations abroad* which was issued as a separate publication 1948–66.

Gives details of available fellowships and scholarships for international study, including: name, field of study, value, duration, number available, where to send application, and date limit. Arranged according to donors of awards, by administering agency or by country in which donor is located. Includes a list of organizations, arranged alphabetically. LB2338.S86

Von Hahman, Gail. Directory of financial aid in higher education: for Africans and for Americans studying about Africa. 2d ed. Waltham, Mass., African Studies Assoc., Brandeis Univ., [1975]. 155p. **CB299**

1973 ed. comp. by S. Shapiro.

An alphabetically arranged directory of more than 230 programs and grants sponsored by U.S. governmental or private agencies, foreign countries, and international organizations, providing description of grants, eligibility requirements, and financial data. No index. LB2338.S46

ACADEMIC CUSTOMS

Costume and protocol

Gunn, Mary Kemper. A guide to academic protocol. N.Y., Columbia Univ. Pr., 1969. 112p. **CB300**

Concerned with entertainment and social occasions on campus as well as with academic ceremonies. LB2379.G8

Hargreaves-Mawdsley, W. N. A history of academical dress in Europe until the end of the eighteenth century. Oxford, Clarendon Pr., 1963. 235p. il. **CB301**

Gives detailed, historical descriptions of academic costumes in European universities, arranged chronologically by country. Emphasis is on Great Britain but most other countries, except the empires of Russia and Turkey, are included. Contains copious notes, many illustrations, glossary of terms, and bibliography. Index to subjects and names. LB2389.H26

Haycraft, Frank W. The degrees and hoods of the world's universities and colleges. [4th ed.] compl. rev. and enl. by E. W. Scobie Stringer. Cheshunt, Herts., Eng., Cheshunt Pr., 1948. 159p. il. **CB302**

1st ed. 1923.

A useful guide to academic costume with strong British emphasis. For each institution gives date of founding; list of degrees offered; and descriptions of gowns, cowls, and hoods, with illustrations, some in color. Includes a history of academic dress, and a list of abbreviations of degrees. LB2389.H3

Shaw, George Wenham. Academical dress of British universities. Cambridge, Heffer, [1966]. 120p. il. **CB303**

Describes the gowns, hoods, robes, and caps worn by graduates and undergraduates of British universities. Includes a good section of illustrations of the various types of gowns and hoods.

LB2389.S47

Sheard, Kevin. Academic heraldry in America. Marquette, Mich., Northern Michigan College Pr., [1962]. 78p. il. **CB304**

Gives descriptions of hoods worn at colleges and universities in the United States. Arranged first by institution, then by color. Includes brief information on academic ceremonies, seals, and flags. Not a complete listing and not always accurate but useful, as it brings together information in convenient form for ready reference. LB2389.S5

Smith, Hugh. Academic dress and insignia of the world: gowns, hats, chains of office, hoods, rings, medals and other degree insignia of universities and other institutions of learning. Cape Town, A. A. Balkema, 1970. 3v. il. **CB305**

Contents: v.1, British Commonwealth, Irish Republic, and Republic of South Africa; v.2, Europe, Africa, Asia, United States of America, Central and South America; v.3, Glossary and definitions; Hood identification tables; U.S.A. Inter Collegiate code; Abbreviations; Index.

Detailed descriptions and illustrations of academic costume of individual institutions throughout the world. LB2389.S6

Academic degrees

Eells, Walter Crosby and **Haswell, Harold A.** Academic degrees: earned and honorary degrees conferred by institutions of higher education in the United States. [Wash., Govt. Prt. Off., 1960] 324p. il. (U.S. Office of Education. Bull. 1960, no.28) (Repr.: Detroit, Gale, 1970) **CB306**

Provides information on some 2,400 degrees (1,600 currently in use) conferred by American universities and colleges. Arranged in three principal lists: (1) classified by field, (2) alphabetical by name of degree, and (3) alphabetical by abbreviation. LB2381.E4

College colors

Snyder, Henry L. Our college colors. [Kutztown, Pa., Kutztown Pub. Co., 1949] 260p. **CB307**

Gives the colors for each American college and university with date of adoption and brief history, where ascertainable, of the reason for the choice. LB3630.S6

Fraternities

Baird's Manual of American college fraternities. Ed.1– .
Menasha, Wis., George Banta, 1879– .   **CB308**

Title varies.

19th ed., 1977, ed. by John Robson. Founded and originally
edited by William R. Baird.

The standard manual of American college fraternities. Gives a
descriptive analysis, with a detailed account of each fraternity.
Includes men's and women's social and professional fraternities,
honor societies, and recognition societies.   LJ31.B2

Prizes and awards

Brook, Herbert. The blue book of awards; a compilation of
major prizes, medals, honors and distinctions, including
significant graduate scholarships and fellowships, open to
citizens of the United States and Canada, indexed by donors
and classified by fields. Chicago, Marquis-Who's Who,
[1956]. 186p.   **CB309**

Lists many types of awards, prizes, medals, competitive scholarships, etc. The main section is arranged alphabetically, giving, where
pertinent: date of establishment, purpose, eligibility, what the award
consists of, when given, address from whom information may be
obtained. Index by donor and a classified index by field.   AS8.B7

Hohenberg, John. The Pulitzer Prizes; a history of the
awards in books, drama, music, and journalism, based on
the private files over six decades. N.Y., Columbia Univ. Pr.,
1974. 434p.   **CB310**

A history of the prizes, with appendixes listing members of the
advisory board and terms of service, and recipients of the awards in
chronological order. Indexed.   AS911.P8H83

Stuart, Sandra Lee. Who won what when: the record book of
winners. 1980 ed. Secaucus, N.J., Lyle Stuart, [1980]. 513p.
          CB311

1st ed. 1977.

Limited to winners of American or major foreign prizes awarded
since 1900. Listed by broad subject area, then by name of award.
Indexed.   AS8.S83

Walter, Claire. Winners: the blue ribbon encyclopedia of
awards. Rev. ed. N.Y., Facts on File, 1982. 916p.   **CB312**

1st ed. 1978.

Covers a wide selection of "major American honors in various
fields of endeavor . . . [and] important awards given abroad, particularly those of international scope."—*Pref.* Entries, in classified
arrangement, give title of the award, issuing body with address and
telephone number, statement explaining basis of award, chronological list of winners from earliest year to 1977. Indexed, but spot
checking shows many inconsistencies in indexing. To be updated
every three years.   AS8.W34

Wasserman, Paul and **McLean, Janice.** Awards, honors, &
prizes. 5th ed. Detroit, Gale, [1982]. 2v.   **CB313**

Subtitle: An international directory of awards and their donors,
recognizing achievement in advertising and public relations, art,
business, government, finance, science, education, engineering, literature, technology, sports, religion, public affairs, radio and television, politics, librarianship, fashion, medicine, law, publishing,
international affairs, transportation, architecture, journalism, motion pictures, music, photography, theatre and performing arts.

1st ed. 1969.

Contents: v.1, United States and Canada; v.2, International and
foreign.

Coverage has been expanded with each successive edition, with a
separate volume for international awards and national awards given

in foreign countries having been added for the 3d ed. (1975).
Includes information on some important awards which are no
longer made.

v.1 (U.S. and Canada) of a 6th ed. appeared in 1985.   AS8.W38

World dictionary of awards and prizes. London, Europa,
[1979]. 386p.   **CB314**

An alphabetical arrangement of entries for some "2,000 international and national awards from 62 countries," with emphasis in
selection "on achievement of an intellectual nature and of truly
national and international standing."—*Foreword.* Includes "prestigious lectureships" but not prizes for heroism, voluntary service, or
sport. Gives descriptive information, awarding body, and selected
list of recipients. Indexed. Numerous omissions noted.

          AS911.A2W58

C C

Sociology

❖This section deals mainly with reference materials pertinent to the disciplines of sociology and social work (including social conditions and problems), and to the study of
individual social, racial, and ethnic groups. Selected reference sources are cited for topics such as alcoholism, drug
abuse, death and dying, marriage and the family, poverty,
sexual behavior, and urbanization. Social groups such as the
aging, children and youth, and the disabled are also included. Sections on race relations and minorities, as well as
women, reflect the publishing explosion in these fields since
the appearance of the previous edition of this *Guide.*

Reference materials concerned with criminology are listed in section CK (Law), and titles concerned with native
populations outside North America will be found in section
CE (Anthropology and Ethnology). The CA section (General
works in the Social Sciences) lists major titles such as the
London bibliography of the social sciences (CA34) and the
International encyclopedia of the social sciences (CA51).
Titles listed in the "Guides" subdivision of section CA, as
well as Bart's *Student sociologist's handbook* (CC1), should
be used for direction toward more specialized sources.

GENERAL WORKS

Guides

Bart, Pauline and **Frankel, Linda.** The student sociologist's
handbook. 3d ed. Glenview, Ill., Scott, Foresman, [1981].
249p.   **CC1**

1st ed. 1971.

A guide to: the field of sociology; the methodology of writing
papers; periodical titles grouped by subject; research and resource
materials; governmental and nongovernmental data sources. Contains a new chapter on alternative careers. Indexed.   HM68.B37

Bibliography

Abramson, Harold J. and **Sofios, Nicholas.** Index to sociology readers, 1960–1965. Metuchen, N.J., Scarecrow Pr., 1973. 2v. (1125p.) **CC2**

Provides an index by author and subject to 227 readers (a "reader" is defined as "an edited collection of different authors' works") published in English during 1960–65. Reprintings of periodical articles are so indicated, with reference to the original source given. Z7164.S68A22

Barbano, Filippo and **Viterbi, Mario.** Bibliografia della sociologia italiana (1948–1958). Torino, Ramella, 1959. 168p. (Torino. Università. Istituto di Scienze Politiche. Pubblicazioni. VI) **CC3**

At head of title: Centro Nazionale di Prevenzione e Difesa Sociale [e] Associazione Italiana di Scienze Sociali.

A classified bibliography of more than 1,600 books and periodical articles on general sociology and the sociology of law, religion, education, industry, human relations, public relations, and rural and urban sociology. Author index.

Bibliographie zur deutschen Soziologie, 1945–1977. Bibliography of German sociology, 1945–1977. Göttingen, Schwartz, [1980]. 800p. **CC4**

"Center for International Comparative Studies (CICS), University of Illinois, Urbana, und Informationszentrum Sozialwissenschaften, Bonn. Hrsg. u. eingel. von Karl-Heinrich Bette, Matthias Herfurth, Günther Lüschen, unter Mitarbeit von Gerhard Schönfeld [et al.]."—*t.p.*

In German and English.

A topically arranged bibliography of 9,922 citations to German-language literature and foreign-language contributions of German-speaking authors (excluding GDR publications in sociology, and unpublished theses). Author and subject indexes. Z7164.S68B53

C.R.I.S.: Combined retrospective index set to journals in sociology, 1895–1974. With an introd. and user's guide by Evan I. Farber. Annadel N. Wile, exec. ed. Wash., Carrollton Pr., 1978. 6v. **CC5**

Contents: v.1, Anthropology, applied sociology, culture, death and death rates, differentiation and stratification, group interactions; v.2–3, Institutions: in general; bureaucratic structures; family; formal voluntary organizations; health; medical systems and structures; industrial systems and structures; law and legal systems; military (personnel) systems and structures; political institutions; religion; v.4, Knowledge, research in sociology, rural systems and structures, sex roles, social change and economic development; v.5, Social disorganization, social ecology, sociology as a profession, theorists, theory of sociology, urban systems and structures; v.6, Authors.

About 85,000 articles from 118 English-language sociology journals are arranged in 137 subject categories, each with date and keyword indexes. Each entry provides keyword, brief title, author's name, year, volume and code number for journal title, and beginning page number.

Harvard University. Library. Sociology. Cambridge, Mass., Harvard Univ. Lib., distr. by Harvard Univ. Pr., 1973. 2v. (Widener Library shelflist, no.45–46) **CC6**

For a note on the series *see* AA145.

Contents: v.1, Classification schedule; Classified listing by call number; Chronological listing; v.2, Author and title listing.

"The 49,000 titles included in the *Soc* classification cover sociological history and theory, social groups and institutions, social problems and reform, and social psychology."—*Pref.*

Z7164.S68H36

Holland, Janet and **Steuer, Max D.** Mathematical sociology; a selective annotated bibliography. N.Y., Schocken, [1970]. 109p. **CC7**

An annotated bibliography of English-language articles and books (mainly published since 1950) concerned with the use of mathematical techniques in sociology. Z7164.S68H6

Instituto Fe y Secularidad. Sociología de la religión y teología; estudio bibliográfico. Sociology of religion and theology: a bibliography. Madrid, Editorial Cuadernos para el Diálogo, 1975–78. v.1–[2]. (In progress?) **CC8**

Prefatory matter and headings in Spanish and English.

v.1 (474p.) is in two main sections: (1) a topically arranged bibliography with lengthy abstracts or reviews of about 100 seminal works in this field; (2) a detailed, systematically classed, international bibliography of more than 16,200 works; translations and book reviews are noted. Author index.

v.[2] (designated on the title page as "v.B"; 215p.) omits the preliminary section of book annotations and reviews, and adds about 8,000 entries for items published between 1974 and 1976, employing the classified subject arrangement and adding a subject index. Z7164.S685.I58

Kurtz, Lester R. Evaluating Chicago sociology: a guide to the literature, with an annotated bibliography. Chicago, Univ. of Chicago Pr., [1984]. 303p. **CC9**

A critical analysis and bibliography of the "Chicago school" of sociology, including such figures as W. I. Thomas, Robert Park, Ernest W. Burgess, John Dewey, George Herbert Mead, and Thorstein Veblen. A review appeared in *Contemporary sociology* 14:369–70 (May 1985). Z7165.U6C474

Mark, Charles. Sociology of America: a guide to information sources. Detroit, Gale, 1976. 454p. (American studies information guide series, v.1) **CC10**

A classed listing of almost 1,900 English-language books on the sociological study of American life. Most titles were published since 1960, and most are annotated. Chapters 1–3 deal with bibliographic resources, general reference works, and journal titles; remaining chapters list empirical studies on various subjects. Author, title, subject, and periodical title indexes. Z7164.S66M37

Matthews, Mervyn and **Jones, Thomas A.** Soviet sociology, 1964–75: a bibliography. N.Y., Praeger, [1978]. 269p. **CC11**

A classed bibliography of about 2,500 books and articles emphasizing empirical works on Soviet society; excludes Marxist-Leninist theory, critiques of "bourgeois" sociology, Soviet social psychology, and short periodical articles. The introduction provides an excellent historical survey of the discipline and suggests current awareness sources for the post-1975 period. No index. Z7164.S68M28

Nandan, Yash. Durkheimian school: a systematic and comprehensive bibliography. Westport, Conn., Greenwood Pr., [1977]. 457p. **CC12**

A classified list of over 7,000 entries divided into three parts: (1) bibliographies of the periodicals produced by the Durkheimian school; (2) bibliography of members' works published outside of the *Année sociologique;* and (3) bibliography of works on the Durkheimian school. Within most of these divisions the arrangement is chronological. Includes all available English translations. Appendixes. Author index to pt.I. Z7164.S68N36

Thomas, Lucienne E. and **Cep, Primerose.** Sociologie et psychologie sociale en France (1945–1965); bibliographie. . . . [Paris, Association pour la Diffusion de la Pensée Française, 1966] 252p. **CC13**

"Bibliographie établie et annotée par la Bibliothèque du Centre d'Études Sociologiques."—*title page.*

1,195 items in classed arrangement with author index. Many annotations. Z7164.S68T45

Current

Current sociology. La sociologie contemporaine. v.1– , 1952– . [Paris], UNESCO, 1952– . Quarterly (varies). **CC14**

Each issue is a monograph (usually designated as "A trend report and bibliography") offering a survey and bibliography of recent research and publications in some specific area of sociology.

Z7161.C8

International bibliography of sociology. Bibliographie internationale de sociologie. [1951]– . London, Tavistock; Chicago, Aldine, 1952– . [v.1]– . Annual.   **CC15**

Publisher varies: [v.1–4] published as issues of *Current sociology* (CC14); v.5–9 Paris, UNESCO; v.10, 1960– , issued as *Publications* of the international Committee for Social Sciences Documentation, as one of the series of the "International bibliography of the social sciences" (series title varies slightly).

Introductory matter, headings, etc., in English and French.

An extensive classified listing of books, pamphlets, periodical articles, and official government publications in many languages, including Slavic and Asian languages. Indexes by author and subject (in English and French).

For other bibliographies in the series *see* CH36 (Economics); CJ39 (Political science); CE29 (Social and cultural anthropology).

Z7161.I594

Sociological abstracts. v.1, no.1– , Nov. 1952– . N.Y., Sociological Abstracts, 1952– . v.1– .   **CC16**

Frequency varies. Now published six times a year, the last issue being the cumulative index issue for the year. Most volumes include supplements which publish abstracts of papers presented at meetings of sociological societies. Book reviews and abstracts appear since 1980 in a separate section, "International review of publications in sociology," which is also available as a separate publication.

Co-sponsored by the American Sociological Association, Eastern Sociological Society, International Sociological Association, and Midwest Sociological Society.

A classified abstract journal, covering a broad range of sociological articles in periodicals in various languages.   HM1.S67●

Dissertations

Lunday, G. Albert. Sociology dissertations in American universities, 1893–1966. Commerce, East Texas State Univ., 1969. 277p.   **CC17**

Arranged under 26 topical headings; author index. The university at which the dissertation was done is indicated by code number.

Z7164.S68L9

Sociology theses register. Ed.1– . [London?], Social Science Research Council [and] British Sociological Assoc., [1976–]. Annual.   **CC18**

Frances Wakeford, ed.

A pilot issue, *Register of post-graduate theses,* was published 1974.

Lists research "using a sociological perspective" in progress for higher degrees at United Kingdom institutions, mainly in departments of sociology, education, social administration and management studies. Classified listing with subject index.

Periodicals

Sussman, Marvin B. Author's guide to journals in sociology & related fields. N.Y., Haworth Pr., [1978]. 214p.   **CC19**

For more than 350 journals listed in *Sociological abstracts* and the "Sociology" section of *Ulrich's International periodicals directory,* provides a profile which includes: manuscript and subscription addresses; price, frequency, indexing/abstracting sources; general interest areas, and appropriate and inappropriate topics; style sheet, review period, publication lag, acceptance rates, reprint policy, etc. Subject, title, and keyword index.   Z7163.S87

Wepsiec, Jan. Sociology: an international bibliography of serial publications, 1880–1980. [London], Mansell, [1983]. 183p.   **CC20**

An alphabetical listing of 2,311 journals, monograph series, transactions and numbered reports from institutions, and directories; full bibliographic reference includes abstracting or indexing

source. Indexed by subject and form (e.g., abstracts, bibliographies, indexes).   Z7164.S68W46

Dictionaries and encyclopedias

Bernsdorf, Wilhelm. Wörterbuch der Soziologie. 2. neubearb. u. erw. Ausg. Stuttgart, F. Enke Verlag, 1969. 1317p.   **CC21**

1st ed. 1955.

An encyclopedic dictionary of sociological terms with fairly long, signed contributions by 165 scholars from about 20 countries. Most articles include brief bibliographies.   HM17.B44

Encyclopedia of sociology. New and updated. [Guilford, Conn., DPG Reference Pub., 1981] 317p. il.   **CC22**

1st ed. 1974.

Brief definitions or descriptions (some signed) of "the language of sociology, the full range of its theories, the institutions of society, and the leading figures in both historical and contemporary sociology."—*Pref.* More than 1,300 articles, ranging in length from 25 to 2,500 words. Classified bibliography of approximately 700 recent publications for "nonprofessionals in the field."   HM17.E5

Gallino, Luciano. Dizionario di sociologia. Torino, UTET, [1978]. 820p.   **CC23**

Lengthy articles, usually presented in five sections: (1) general definition; (2) historical evolution; (3) subfields and variations; (4) factors affecting development; (5) present situation. Bibliography, including journal titles. Index.   HM17.G34

Hoult, Thomas Ford. Dictionary of modern sociology. Totowa, N.J., Littlefield, Adams, 1969. 408p.   **CC24**

Intended to reflect "current concept usage" as found in sociological and related literature. Many definitions are followed by examples of usage. Extensive bibliography of works and authors cited.

HM17.H63

International encyclopedia of sociology. Ed. by Michael Mann. N.Y., Continuum, [1984]. 434p.   **CC25**

Also publ. under title *The Macmillan student encyclopedia of sociology.*

About 750 short, signed entries for terms, phrases, persons, and schools of thought; some bibliographic references. Editors and contributors are affiliated with the London School of Economics, resulting in some British emphasis.   HM17.I53

Lexikon zur Soziologie. Hrsg. von Werner Fuchs [et al.]. 2., verb. u. erw. Aufl. Opladen, Westdeutscher Verlag, 1978. 890p.   **CC26**

Brief definitions of sociological terms; most entries are signed with the initials of the contributors. Equivalent English terms are given in many instances.   HM17.L483

Mitchell, Geoffrey Duncan. A new dictionary of the social sciences. Hawthorne, N.Y., Aldine, [1979]. 244p.   **CC27**

1968 ed. had title: *A dictionary of sociology.*

An introductory dictionary for the student of sociology. Articles have been increased in number from approximately 300 to 350; about half the additions are biographical sketches. Some 20 definitions were revised or expanded. Signed articles include bibliographical references. A review appears in *Contemporary sociology* 10:603 (July 1981).   HM17.M56

Theodorson, George A. and **Theodorson, Achilles G.** A modern dictionary of sociology. N.Y., Crowell, [1969]. 469p.   **CC28**

Brief definitions intended for the student, the general reader, and professional workers in related fields.   HM17.T5

Willems, Emilio. Dictionnaire de sociologie; adaptation française par Armand Cuvillier. 2. éd., aug. Paris, Marcel Rivière, 1970. 315p.   **CC29**

Originally published in 1950 in Portuguese as *Dicionário de sociologia.* The French translation has been revised and brought up-to-date. A combination, in one alphabet, of definitions of sociological terms and concepts with biographical sketches of world social scientists. About half of the entries are biographical.

Wörterbuch der marxistisch-leninistischen Soziologie. 2., überarbeitete und erweiterte Aufl. [Opladen], Westdeutschen Verlag, [1978]. 758p. **CC30**

1st ed. 1969.
Offers fairly lengthy definitions of sociopolitical terms as interpreted within a Marxist context. HM17.W63

Handbooks

Handbook of contemporary developments in world sociology. Ed. by Raj P. Mohan and Don Martindale. Westport, Conn., Greenwood Pr., 1975. 493p. (Contributions in sociology, 17) **CC31**

Analyzes, on a regional and an individual country basis, the status of post-World War II sociology. Each article, written by a scholar in the field, discusses historical and intellectual background of the discipline, teaching and research, methodology, and fields of specialization; some articles also treat organizations, research centers, and periodicals in the field. Bibliographical notes. HM19.H23

Directories

Guide to graduate departments of sociology, 1965– . Wash., Amer. Sociological Assoc., [1965–]. Annual. **CC32**

Lists graduate sociology departments by university, with teaching staffs. Includes tables of course offerings and of financial information.

SOCIAL CONDITIONS AND SOCIAL WELFARE

Bibliography

Aldcroft, Derek H. and **Rodger, Richard.** Bibliography of European economic and social history. Manchester, Eng., Manchester Univ. Pr., [1984]. 243p. **CC33**

A companion to Chaloner and Richardson's *Bibliography of British economic and social history* (CC37). Covers all of continental Europe for the period 1700–1939 and "includes most of the literature published during the twentieth century and a small selection of the important, and still relevant, writings which appeared in the nineteenth century."—*Pref.* Geographical/topical arrangement with author index. Detailed table of contents, but no alphabetical subject index. Z7165.E8A4

Bahr, Howard M. Disaffiliated man; essays and bibliography on skid row, vagrancy, and outsiders. [Toronto], Univ. of Toronto Pr., [1970]. 428p. **CC34**

The bulk of the volume (p.94–394) is an annotated bibliography topically arranged. Author and subject indexes. Z7164.S66B35

Blackstone, Tessa. Social policy and administration in Britain: a bibliography. London, F. Pinter, 1975. 130p. **CC35**

Designed for undergraduate students of social policy, as a work complementary to *Modern British society* by John Westergaard and others (CC61). Emphasizes British books on the current status of

social services. Subject classification with detailed table of contents; no index. Z7165.G8B56

Brode, John. The process of modernization; an annotated bibliography on the sociocultural aspects of development. Cambridge, Harvard Univ. Pr., 1969. 378p. **CC36**

A classified bibliography with author and area indexes.
Z7164.U5B7

Chaloner, William Henry and **Richardson, R. C.** Bibliography of British economic and social history. [Rev. ed.] Manchester, Eng., Manchester Univ. Pr., [1984]. 208p. **CC37**

1st ed. 1976 had title: *British economic and social history.*
A select bibliographic guide to books and periodical articles in English. A brief general section is followed by four main chronological sections (1066–1300; 1300–1500; 1500–1700; 1700–1970), plus separate sections for Wales, Scotland, and Ireland, each with appropriate subdivisions. Detailed table of contents, but no alphabetical subject index. About 5,800 items; some brief annotations.
Z7165.G8C46

Cutcliffe, Stephen H., Mistichelli, Judith A. and **Roysdon, Christine M.** Technology and values in American civilization: a guide to information sources. Detroit, Gale, [1980]. 704p. (American studies information guide ser., v.9) **CC38**

An annotated selection of more than 2,400 books, articles, bibliographies, symposia proceedings, government publications, and journals which discuss man's confrontation with the tangible aspects of civilian technology, from the mid-19th century through late 1978. 22 broad subject chapters are subdivided by more specific topical areas. Treats historical, economic, social, and cultural aspects of technology. Author, title, and subject indexes. Z5579.C87

Emezi, Herbert O. Nigerian population and urbanization, 1911–1974; a bibliography. Los Angeles, African Studies Center, Univ. of California, 1975. 145p. (Calif. Univ. at Los Angeles. African Studies Center. Occasional paper, 10) **CC39**

More than 1,600 items arranged under headings such as urbanization, settlement, migration, population, family planning, etc. Author index. DT1.C12 no.10

Flaherty, David H., Hanis, Edward H. and **Mitchell, S. Paula.** Privacy and access to government data for research: an international bibliography. London, Mansell, 1979. 197p. **CC40**

In six main sections: (1) Privacy, computers, and data banks: general issues and public concern; (2) Government statistical data banks; (3) Uses of government microdata for research and statistical purposes; (4) Legal aspects of privacy and data protection; (5) Data security measures in computer systems; (6) Selected bibliographic materials. In all but the last two categories, citations are grouped by the five countries studied: Canada, Federal Republic of Germany, Great Britain, Sweden, and the United States. Author and title indexes.

The bibliography is a by-product of the research project sponsored by the Ford Foundation and entitled "Information Privacy and Access to Government Microdata Files for Social Science Research." A companion publication resulting from the project is *Privacy and government data banks: an international perspective,* ed. by D. H. Flaherty (London, Mansell, 1979). Z7164.L6F56

Flaherty, David H. Privacy and data protection: an international bibliography. White Plains, N.Y., Knowledge Industry, [1984]. 276p. **CC41**

A selective, annotated bibliography of 1,862 citations to books, periodical articles, and government reports. France is a new addition to geographical coverage; format remains the same as the earlier volume; author indexing only. Z7164.L6F57

Frey, Frederick W. Survey research on comparative social change; a bibliography. Cambridge, Mass., M.I.T. Pr., [1969]. unpaged. **CC42**

About 1,600 items on survey research in developing nations, drawn from about 260 journals. Classed arrangement within geographical sections; author-subject index. Annotations emphasize the survey methods and methodological information to be found in the articles. Z7164.U5F73

Glenn, Norval D., Alston, Jon P. and **Weiner, David.** Social stratification; a research bibliography. Berkeley, Calif., Glendessary, [1970]. 466p. **CC43**

Lists book and journal publications in classed arrangement with author index. Confined to writings in English, chiefly from the period 1940 to early 1968, and drawn from the field of sociology and many related areas. Z7164.S64G55

Hoerder, Dirk. Protest, direct action, repression: dissent in American society from colonial times to the present; a bibliography. München, Verlag Dokumentation, 1977. 434p. **CC44**

A classed bibliography of English-language books, periodical articles, and doctoral dissertations. In three parts, with appropriate topical and chronological subdivisions: (1) General literature on direct action and social change; (2) Social protest and repression in mainstream American history; (3) Minorities in the United States, rebellion against discrimination and oppression. Chronological register of events cited (with references to bibliographic citations); author index. An earlier bibliography by Hoerder is *Violence in the United States, riots, strikes, protest and suppression* (Berlin, 1973).
Z7165.U5H63

Institute of Development Studies. Village Studies Programme. Village studies data analysis and bibliography. [Epping, Essex, Eng.], Publ. for the Inst. of Development Studies at the Univ. of Sussex by Bowker, 1976–78. 2v. **CC45**

Contents: v.1, India, 1950–1975 (329p.); v.2, Africa, Middle East and North Africa, Asia (excluding India), Pacific Islands, Latin America, West Indies and the Caribbean, 1950–1975 (319p.).

A bibliography of all single village studies undertaken between 1950 and 1975; "the focus has been on the range of information contained in the primary studies . . . not on the theoretical value or technical analysis of these data by the original author."—*p.xi.* Each entry is annotated briefly and coded according to which of about 60 possible data elements are available in the study. Geographical arrangement, with author, institution, and topic indexes. Some works produced before 1950 are listed in appendixes.
Z7165.I6I54

Kotz, Arnold and **Lear, Julia Graham.** The policy analysis source book for social programs. [Wash.], National Planning Assoc. (for sale by Govt Prt. Off.), 1975. 2v. **CC46**

An annotated bibliography consisting of about 3,750 abstracts of books, articles, and reports, with a list of an additional 775 titles organized topically in 16 major categories and about 130 subsections. Selected documents emphasize human resources programs such as income maintenance, manpower training, housing, health, etc.; abstracts include qualitative and quantitative results and methodologies used. Author and subject indexes. HN56.K68

Lange, Peter. Studies on Italy, 1943–1975. [Turin], Fondazione Giovanni Agnelli, [1977]. 183p. **CC47**

Subtitle: Select bibliography of American and British materials in political science, economics, sociology and anthropology.

A classed bibliography of books, chapters in books, periodical articles, government documents, doctoral dissertations, and research in progress. Future volumes are planned to include materials in Italian, French, German, and East European languages. Author "index" repeats the citations. Z7165.I8L35

Latin, Howard A. Privacy: a selected bibliography and topical index of social science materials. South Hackensack, N.J., F. B. Rothman, 1976. 93p. **CC48**

Sponsored by the Earl Warren Legal Institute, University of California.

An author listing of books, essays, symposia proceedings, and scholarly journal articles from social science disciplines relevant to the study of privacy. Topical subject index, without cross references.
Z7161.L38

Marien, Michael. Societal directions and alternatives: a critical guide to the literature. LaFayette, N.Y., Information for Policy Design, [1976]. 400p. **CC49**

A classed bibliography of more than 1,000 English-language books and articles intended "to identify, categorize, and comment upon much of the contemporary literature addressing four central . . . questions: Where are we? Where are we headed? What kind of society could we have? What are the possible strategies for achieving the desirable society?"—*Introd.* Annotations are lengthy, critical, and indicate audience level. Nine indexes: author, organization, chronological book title, titles for our present society, evolutionary stage theories, alternative societies, selected proposals, selected criticism, selected subjects and ideas. Z5579.M36

Miller, Albert Jay. Confrontation, conflict, and dissent: a bibliography of a decade of controversy, 1960–1970. Metuchen, N.J., Scarecrow Pr., 1972. 567p. **CC50**

About 5,400 entries grouped under such headings as "Firearms, control and regulation," "The gap in generations and the drug dilemma," "Police-community relations," "Student dissent." Author and subject indexes. Includes references from many "underground" or "alternative" publications. Z7165.U5M53

Monie, Joanna and **Wise, Adrienne.** Social policy and its administration: a survey of the Australian literature, 1950–1975. [Rushcutters Bay, N.S.W., etc.], Pergamon, [1977]. 594p. **CC51**

A topically arranged, annotated bibliography of about 4,000 references to monographic, report, series, and serial titles; journal articles are excluded. Each of ten major sections provides brief introduction to the literature and a "table of contents"; sections include social welfare economics, family and social services, education, public health, social justice, recreation, labor, urban and rural communities, demography and social statistics, and minorities and pressure groups. Author and subject index. Z7165.A8M65

Morrison, Denton E. and **Hornback, Kenneth E.** Collective behavior: a bibliography. N.Y., Garland, 1976. 534p. (Reference library of social science, v.15) **CC52**

"'Collective behavior' is the . . . term sociologists use to cover a range of . . . 'noninstitutionalized' phenomena including revolutions, social movement, protests, riots, panics, mobs, crowds, fads, crazes, rumor—and more."—*Introd.* More than 5,000 entries are listed by author, with classed subject/title index and proper names index. Emphasis is on material published within the last 20 years, focusing on the movements and protests of the 1960s as seen from a theoretical, methodological, or empirical viewpoint.
Z7204.S67M67

Oberg, Larry R. Human services in postrevolutionary Cuba: an annotated international bibliography. Westport, Conn., Greenwood Pr., [1984]. 433p. **CC53**

Cites 2,027 titles published 1959–82 on education, housing and services to the elderly, ethnic minorities, public health and medicine, and women and the family; introductory materials include general works, histories, and bibliographies. Strong emphasis on education and youth. Author, title, and subject indexes.
Z7165.C85O23

Parish, David W. Changes in American society, 1960–1978: an annotated bibliography of official government publications. Metuchen, N.J., Scarecrow Pr., 1980. 438p. **CC54**

Presents a broad subject arrangement (71 categories) of 1,335 annotated titles. Within each category, federal publications are listed first, according to Superintendent of Documents classification; state documents follow, arranged by state and by agency. Descriptive annotations include price and Library of Congress call number when available. Federal and state serials are arranged by topic in an appendix; other appendixes list agency addresses, federal depositories, documents sales centers and dealers. Author, title, and subject indexes. Z7165.U5P37

Project Share. The Project Share Collection, 1976–1979. Rockville, Md., Dept. of Health, Education, and Welfare, Office of the Assistant Secretary for Planning and Evaluation, Project Share, 1979. 891p.   **CC55**

A cumulative volume of abstracts published by Project Share, a clearinghouse for improving the management of human services. About 1,800 abstracts are arranged within 14 broad subject categories, such as administration, evaluation, relations with governments, legislation/regulation and federally funded programs, management technology, forecasting and needs assessment, etc. Information on availability of the abstracted item is provided; many of the reports are available from NTIS. Indexed by Project Share or NTIS order number and title, and by detailed subject.   HV91.P763

Social indicators: an annotated bibliography of current literature. Kevin J. Gilmartin [and others, eds.]; American Institutes for Research. N.Y., Garland, 1979. 123p. (Garland reference library of social science, v.62)   **CC56**

Supplements *Social indicators and societal monitoring* by L. D. Wilcox and others (1972), focusing on literature published during 1972–78. About 600 items are grouped as key historical works, state-of-the-art, theory, methodology, analysis and reporting, examples, and bibliographies. Author and subject indexes.

Z7164.S66S52

Social reform and reaction in America: an annotated bibliography. Santa Barbara, Calif., ABC-Clio, [1984]. 375p. (Clio bibliography ser., 13)   **CC57**

A classed bibliography of 2,993 articles, with abstracts, published during the 1973–82 period and drawn from the history database of the ABC-Clio Information Services. Includes materials on the United States and Canada. Author and subject indexes.

Z7164.S66A543

Spitz, Allan A. Developmental change; an annotated bibliography. Lexington, Univ. of Kentucky Pr., [1969]. 316p.   **CC58**

An annotated, classified bibliography of nearly 2,500 articles appearing in scholarly journals, symposia, and conference reports since 1960. Deals mainly with "political, social and economic factors of modernization and development."—*Pref.* Relevant books are listed in an appendix, but without annotation.

Z7164.E15S615

Stogdill, Ralph Melvin. Stogdill's Handbook of leadership; a survey of theory and research. Rev. and exp. ed. by Bernard M. Bass. N.Y., Free Pr.; London, Collier Macmillan, [1981]. 856p.   **CC59**

1974 ed. publ. as *Handbook of leadership.*
The original 3,000 references in the 1974 *Handbook* have been expanded to about 5,000; 525 titles were published between 1974 and 1978, and the remainder were derived from a search of the literature of the 1960–79 period. Author arrangement. Subject approach is only through the research and review essays which constitute the main body of the work (p.5–617).   HM141.S83

Wehler, Hans-Ulrich. Bibliographie zur modernen deutschen Sozialgeschichte (18.–20. Jahrhundert). Göttingen, Vandenhoeck & Ruprecht, [1976]. 269p. (Arbeitsbücher zur modernen Geschichte, Bd.1)   **CC60**

A classed bibliography in 50 subject sections. Includes reference works and secondary sources on the theory of social history, its subject themes, and its application to specific historical periods and events. Covers books, chapters in collective works, and periodical articles; international in scope. No index.   Z7165.G3W44

Westergaard, John H., Weyman, Anne and **Wiles, Paul.** Modern British society; a bibliography. N.Y., St. Martin's Pr., [1977]. 199p.   **CC61**

A revised and updated edition of a work by the same authors and with the same title published in London, 1974. Classed arrangement with author index. Detailed table of contents, but no subject index. Mainly books, with relatively few periodical articles listed.

Z7165.G8W48

Handbooks and directories

The futures directory. Comp. by John McHale and Magda Cordell McHale with Guy Streatfield and Laurence Tobias. [Guildford, Surrey, Eng.], IPC Science and Technology Pr.; [Boulder, Colo.], Westview Pr., [1977]. 396p.   **CC62**

Subtitle: An international listing and description of organizations and individuals active in future studies and long-range planning.
Presents results of survey studies carried out at the Center for Integrative Studies, State University of New York at Binghamton, in cosponsorship with the United Nations Institute for Training and Research. Provides information on orientation of work, methods used, time range of work, funding sources, for whom work is done, etc. Separately indexed for organizations and individuals by geographic location, method, and subject.   CB158.F871

Handbook of futures research. Ed. by Jib Fowles. Westport, Conn., Greenwood Pr., [1978]. 822p. il.   **CC63**

Consists of 41 articles by futurists on issues relating to the development of futures research, its procedures, problems, and areas of application; each chapter has a substantial bibliography. Appendix lists relevant journals, graduate programs, and organizations. Indexed.   CB158.H35

World Future Society. The future: a guide to information sources. 2d ed. Wash., World Future Society, [1979]. 722p.   **CC64**

1st ed. 1977.
About 200 new sources have been added to this directory of organizations, individuals, research projects, books and reports, periodicals, audiovisual materials, and educational courses and programs.   CB158.W67

Social work

Bibliography

Columbia University. Whitney M. Young, Jr. Memorial Library of Social Work. Dictionary catalog of the Whitney M. Young, Jr. Memorial Library of Social Work. Boston, G. K. Hall, 1980. 10v.   **CC65**

Contents: v.1–8, Dictionary catalog; v.9, Agency catalog; v.10, Projects catalog.
A photographic reproduction of the catalog cards of the largest single library in the United States supporting professional social work education. The collection focuses on English-language materials published since 1795, and comprises over 60,000 volumes, including about 700 current periodicals, as well as government documents, dissertations and master's essays, and the publications of voluntary agencies; the latter materials are accessible through the "Agency catalog." The "Projects catalog" covers more than 5,000 master's essays and reports from the Columbia University School of Social Work and the New York School of Social Work.

Z7164.C4C5

Conrad, James H. Reference sources in social work: an annotated bibliography. Metuchen, N.J., Scarecrow Pr., 1982. 201p.   **CC66**

More than 600 citations are classed by subject and subdivisions corresponding to those used in *Social work research and abstracts* (CC73), e.g., "Fields of Service—Adoption, Aging, Alcoholism," etc. Within subdivisions, reference works are grouped according to type. Focuses on works published between 1970 and 1981. Appendixes list relevant journals, organizations, and libraries. Indexed.

HV40.C66

Li, Hong-Chan. Social work education: a bibliography. Metuchen, N.J., Scarecrow Pr., 1978. 341p.   **CC67**

A classed bibliography, listing more than 3,000 books, periodicals, proceedings, reports, government documents, ERIC materials, and doctoral dissertations. International in scope, but limited to

English-language materials, principally from 1960 to the present. Author index.   Z7164.C4L49

Loavenbruck, Grant and **Crecca, Carol.** Continuing social work education: an annotated bibliography. N.Y., Council on Social Work Education, [1980]. 113p.   **CC68**

144 citations to books, articles, papers, documents, and dissertations written since 1970 are grouped in four parts: (1) overviews; (2) theory; (3) methodology; (4) policies and regulations; each part is further subdivided into 18 subject sections. Substantive annotations. Author index.   Z7164.C4L62

Minnesota. University. Social Welfare History Archives Center. Descriptive inventories of collections in the Social Welfare History Archives Center. Westport, Conn., Greenwood Pr., [1970]. 846p.   **CC69**

The Social Welfare History Archives Center "concentrates particularly on collecting and preserving the records of national voluntary associations in the social service fields and the personal papers of their leaders."—*Introd.* This volume reproduces inventories of 24 collections (about a quarter of the Center's holdings as of 1969).   Z7164.C4M55

Moscovitch, Allan. The welfare state in Canada: a selected bibliography, 1840 to 1978. [Waterloo, Ont.], Wilfrid Laurier Univ. Pr., [1983]. 246p.   **CC70**

A detailed classed bibliography. Appendixes describe primary materials in the Public Archives of Canada, list periodicals and bibliographies, and provide a chronology of significant welfare legislation. Subject and author indexes.   Z7164.C4M6

Social planning, policy & development abstracts. v.1, no.1– , June, 1979– . San Diego, Sociological Abstracts, 1979– . Semiannual.   **CC71**

Subtitle: An international data base.

Formerly titled: Social welfare, social planning/policy & social development.

Selects and abstracts items from some 1,300 serials and national and international conference proceedings. Also lists book reviews appearing in the serials. Publisher notes "less than 2% selection overlap with *Sociological abstracts* [CC16]." Author, subject, and source (periodical) indexes.

Social welfare in America: an annotated bibliography. Ed. by Walter I. Trattner and W. Andrew Achenbaum. Westport, Conn., Greenwood, [1983]. 324p.   **CC72**

Provides 1,410 citations to "general surveys, major monographs, scholarly articles, and dissertations written since 1945, as well as some documentaries and a number of older works . . . concerning social welfare . . . from the early 1600s to the early 1980s."—*Introd.* Topical arrangement by age group, further subdivided chronologically and topically. Author and subject indexes.   Z7164.C4S6

Social work research & abstracts. v.13, no.2– , Summer 1977– . N.Y., Nat. Assoc. of Social Workers, 1977– . Quarterly.   **CC73**

Supersedes *Abstracts for social workers* which ceased with v.13, no.1 (Spr. 1977), and continues its numbering.

Each issue presents five or six research papers, followed by abstracts of articles grouped within six main sections: (1) fields of service; (2) social policy and action; (3) service methods; (4) the profession; (5) history; (6) related fields of knowledge. Quarterly author and subject indexes cumulate annually.

Tighe, Leo W. A classified bibliography for the field of social work. Santa Clara, Calif., Premier Publ., 1959. 235p.   **CC74**

Treats counseling, guidance, and social work. Lists some 5,500 books, articles, government documents, dissertations, and audiovisual aids.   Z7164.C4T5

Dissertations

Doctoral dissertations in social work. (*In* Social service review, Sept. 1954–74) Annual.   **CC75**

Gives abstracts of completed dissertations and lists of those in preparation. Includes only dissertations submitted at graduate schools of social work. Inasmuch as doctoral dissertations were included in *Abstracts for social workers* beginning 1975 and are continued in *Social work research & abstracts,* the annual listing of dissertations in *Social service review* was discontinued after the Dec. 1974 issue (v.48, no.4).

Dictionaries and encyclopedias

Encyclopedia of social work: successor to the Social work year book. N.Y., Nat. Assoc. of Social Workers, 1965– . v.15– . (Irregular; v.17 publ. 1977 in 2v.)   **CC76**

The *Social work year book* was issued, 1929–49, by the Russell Sage Foundation; 1951–54, by the American Association of Social Workers; 1957–60, by the National Association of Social Workers. The new title indicates a broadening of the scope and an increase in the number of articles, including biographies of outstanding social workers.

The articles and biographies are signed and of some length, with bibliographies. Closely related articles are grouped together to emphasize interrelationships. A detailed index complements the alphabetical arrangement of the articles.   HV35.S6

1983–84 supplement to the Encyclopedia of social work, 17th ed. Encyclopedia Supplement Sub-Committee, Scott Briar [and others]. Silver Springs, Md., Nat. Assoc. of Social Workers, [1983]. 274p.

The first in a series of interim supplements before an 18th ed. is to be published in 1987. Articles are either updated from the 1977 ed. or completely new. Statistical and demographic tables have been almost doubled in number.   HV91.A18

Social service organizations. Ed. in chief, Peter Romanofsky. Westport, Conn., Greenwood Pr., [1978]. 2v. (843p.)   **CC77**

A dictionary arrangement of historical sketches of nearly 200 national and local voluntary social service agencies, particularly those that have been listed in the *Encyclopedia of social work* (CC76) and the *Social work year book.* Sketches run three to five pages in length, and mention archives, publications, and scholarly secondary sources. Appendixes provide: (1) list of religiously affiliated social service organizations; (2) chronology of founding dates; (3) subject index of agency functions; (4) "genealogy" of name changes, mergers, dissolutions, etc. Indexed.   HV88.S59

Timms, Noel and **Timms, Rita.** Dictionary of social welfare. London, Routledge & Kegan Paul, [1982]. 217p.   **CC78**

A student's dictionary of terms, phrases, and some organizations, outlining the applications in welfare legislation, policy, and use by welfare practitioners. Most entries provide bibliographical references. British orientation.   HV12.T54

Directories

Barkas, J. L. The help book. N.Y., Scribner's, [1979]. 667p. il.   **CC79**

A layman's guide to organizations offering information or direct assistance within the broad areas of health, the family, counseling, education, women's issues, crime, citizen action, emergencies, and employment. Arranged by 52 subject areas. Free or inexpensive literature is noted, with brief annotations.   HV41.B268

Community resources directory: a guide to U.S. volunteer organizations and other resource groups, services, training events and courses, and local program models. 2d ed. Ed. by Harriet Clyde Kipps. Detroit, Gale, 1984. 943p.   **CC80**

Forms a 2d ed. of *411: community resource tie line* and *Community green sheets* (1980).

"Covers such management areas as funding, public relations, information and referral, business and industry involvement, leadership development, special volunteer groups, and central recruitment operations. Describes programs in the arts; business assistance; civic affairs; consumer services; day care; drug abuse and alcoholism; education; employment; family, youth, and children; the handicapped; health; housing; law enforcement and crime prevention; mental health; nutrition; the older person; physical environment, recreation; and transportation."—*t.p.*

In three parts: (1) resource groups and publications listed by "management areas" and programs described on the title page; (2) training programs listed by state and city; (3) profiles of specific programs. Indexed by organization name and broad subjects.

HN90.V64C65

Estes, Richard J. Directory of social welfare research capabilities: a working guide to organizations engaged in social work and social welfare research. Ardmore, Pa., Dorrance & Co., [1981]. 129p. **CC81**

A state-by-state arrangement of 75 social welfare related research units in the United States and Puerto Rico, with details on administrative relationship to universities, agencies, or professional associations, budget, staffing, research purposes and activities, publications, and areas of interest. Indexed by name, affiliation, administrative officer, and areas of interest. HN29.E87

Greenstone, James L. and **Leviton, Sharon.** Hotline: crisis intervention directory. N.Y., Facts on File, [1981]. 310p. **CC82**

A classified directory of more than 700 crisis intervention agencies throughout the United States, giving for each: sponsor, purpose, services, hours, staffing, fees, eligibility requirements, available transportation, and referral and follow-up services; those offering telephone hotline services are highlighted. Bibliography. Indexed by geographic location and agency name. RC480.6.G72

Kruzas, Anthony T. Social service organizations and agencies directory. Detroit, Gale, [1982]. 525p. **CC83**

Subtitle: A reference guide to national and regional social service organizations, including advocacy groups, voluntary associations, professional societies, federal and state agencies, clearinghouses and information centers.

More than 6,700 directory entries are classified into 47 subject chapters, from adoption to youth; these chapters are subdivided according to type of organization (national, state, government, clearinghouse). State government agency entries are neither annotated nor indexed. Name and keyword indexes. HV89.K78

National Association of Social Workers. Directory of agencies: U.S. voluntary, international voluntary, intergovernmental. Wash., The Association, [1978]. 96p. **CC84**

Provides information on the membership, purpose and activities, and publications of more than 300 national voluntary agencies, international voluntary agencies, and intergovernmental agencies whose programs are related to the social work field. Excludes national governmental agencies and foundations lacking a service program. Alphabetical list; no subject access. HV89.N223

—— NASW professional social workers' directory, 1978– . Wash., The Association, [1978]– . Irregular. **CC85**

Continues the *NASW directory of professional social workers* (eds.1–3, 1960–72).

A membership directory providing information on education, position, professional licenses, etc. HV89.N2

—— NASW register of clinical social workers. Ed.1– . Wash., The Association, 1976– . Irregular. (3d ed., 1982) **CC86**

In two sections: (1) list of clinical social workers arranged alphabetically, with name, address, qualifying state license, employer, educational background, and specialization; (2) geographic index by state and city, with an alphabetical listing of names. HV89.N223a

National directory of private social agencies. Flushing, N.Y., Social Service Publications, [1964–]. **CC87**

Subtitle: A loose-leaf directory of private social agencies in the

United States, classified by services offered and listed by states and cities.

Helga A. Croner, ed.

Now lists about 15,000 agencies, homes, and organizations which "give direct help to individual applicants, or refer them to the proper address."—*Introd.* Monthly "amendments" keep the directory up-to-date. HV89.N27

Pinson, William M. Resource guide to current social issues. Waco, Tex., Word Books, [1968]. 272p. **CC88**

Includes sections on some 40 topics of wide concern. Lists agencies and organizations as well as printed sources of information. Z7164.S66P47

Public welfare directory, 1940– . Chicago, Amer. Public Welfare Assoc., 1940– . il. Annual. **CC89**

Lists federal, state, and local public assistance and welfare agencies, with directors. For each state includes an introductory statement on its administration of public welfare and on "Where to write" for information on assistance, birth and death records, marriage and divorce records, mental health, correctional institutions, etc. Includes Canadian federal, provincial, and territorial human service programs. HV89.A55

Stickney, Patricia J. and **Resnick, Rosa Perla.** World guide to social work education. N.Y., Internatl. Assoc. of Schools of Social Work, [1974]. 297p. **CC90**

This volume "describes the major features of 79 schools of social work, illustrates programs of social work education in 65 countries, and provides general information on 19 national associations of schools of social work, three regional associations, and the International Association of Schools of Social Work."—*Pref.* HV11.S83

Aging

Guides

Place, Linna F., Parker, Linda and **Berghorn, Forrest J.** Aging and the aged: an annotated bibliography and library research guide. Boulder, Colo., Westview Pr., [1980]. 128p. **CC91**

A selective, "teaching" bibliography, intended for the student desiring an introduction to the field. The first chapter outlines use of the library, relevant reference sources, journals, associations, and federal agencies and programs. The remaining four chapters are compilations of book and journal literature citations related to general perspectives on aging, physiological, psychological, and social aspects of aging, and the environment and the elderly. Brief annotations for many titles; author and title indexes. Z7164.O4P52

Bibliography

See also CC135, CC211, CC266.

Abuse of the elderly: a guide to resources and services. [Ed. by] Joseph J. Costa. Lexington, Mass., Lexington Books, [1984]. 289p. **CC92**

Pt.1 (p.3–95) consists of essays on physical abuse and crimes against the aged in the United States; pt.2 (p.99–289) provides directory information and a partially annotated bibliography (arranged alphabetically by main entry, with no subject access). HV1461.A28

Aging; a guide to resources. Ed. by John B. Balkema. [N.Y.], Gaylord Professional Pubns. in assoc. with Neal-Schuman, [1983]. 232p. **CC93**

An annotated bibliography of reference sources and "working tools" for professionals in social gerontology. Emphasizes bibliographies, directories, statistics, periodicals, guides, handbooks and manuals; English-language books, pamphlets, periodicals. Broad subject arrangement; each chapter is further subdivided by topics and formats. Name and subject indexes.   Z7164.O4A33

Allyn, Mildred V. About aging: a catalog of films, with a special section on videocassettes, 1979. 4th ed. Los Angeles, Ethel Percy Andrus Gerontology Center, Univ. of Southern Calif., 1979. 249p.   **CC94**

An annotated catalog of more than 450 16mm. and feature films, with subject index and distributors' directory.

HQ1064.U5A64

———— ———— 1981 supplement. Los Angeles, [1981]. 100p.

HQ1064.U5A644

Alternatives to institutionalization: an annotated research bibliography on housing and services for the aged. By Wendy Garen [and others]. [Urbana], Housing Research and Development, Univ. of Illinois at Urbana-Champaign, 1976. 137p.   **CC95**

Presents citations to a wide variety of materials grouped under seven categories: households; housing; support services; health services; environment; methodology; and functional ability. No author or detailed subject approach.

Borenstein, Audrey. Older women in 20th-century America; a selected annotated bibliography. N.Y., Garland, 1982. 351p. (Women's studies facts and issues, 3; Garland reference library of social science, 122)   **CC96**

Provides lengthy annotations for more than 800 books, essays, journal articles and dissertations concerned with the woman over 40. Includes literary works, oral histories, and published personal documents as well as social science materials and bibliographies. Subject arrangement; name index.

The mature woman in America: a selected annotated bibliography, 1979–1982, by Eleanor F. Dolan and Dorothy M. Gropp (Wash., Nat. Council on the Aging, 1984. 122p.) is intended to include non-literary works not listed in the Borenstein bibliography for the 1979–82 period; 423 citations are entered under author, with subject index.   Z7164.O4B67

Davis, Lenwood G. The black aged in the United States: an annotated bibliography. Westport, Conn., Greenwood Pr., [1980]. 200p.   **CC97**

The first chapter covers the black aged and slavery, and is subdivided by form and more specific subjects. The remaining five chapters of bibliographic citations are grouped by form (books, dissertations and theses, government publications, and articles), and subdivided by subject. There is also a directory of homes for the black aged, 1860–1980, and a list of relevant journal titles. Indexed.

Z7164.O4D38

DeLuca, Lucy, McIlvaine, B. and **Mundkur, Mohini.** Aging: an annotated guide to government publications. Storrs, Conn., Univ. of Connecticut Library, 1975. 68p. (*Its* Bibliography ser., 3)   **CC98**

Selective coverage of federal, state, foreign and international documents for the period 1960–74. Classed by broad subject, with title and series indexes. SuDocs classification numbers are provided.

Z7164.O4D44

Edwards, Willie M. and **Flynn, Frances.** Gerontology: a core list of significant works. [Ann Arbor, Mich.], Inst. of Gerontology, [1978]. 160p.   **CC99**

Comp. with a national panel of consultants.

A subject classed bibliography of articles and books. "Emphasis is on the areas broadly termed 'social' gerontology."—*Pref.* Author and title indexes.   Z7164.O4E38

Ethel Percy Andrus Gerontology Center. Library. Catalogs of the Ethel Percy Andrus Gerontology Center, University of Southern California, Los Angeles. Boston, G. K. Hall, 1976. 2v. (1193p.)   **CC100**

Contents: v.1, Author-title catalog; v.2, Subject catalog.

A photographic reproduction of the card catalog of the Library,

which consists of about 5,500 monographs, as well as documents, agency publications, conference proceedings, microfilm doctoral dissertations, reprints, and 97 serial subscriptions.

The Ethel Percy Andrus Gerontology Center compiles its *Technical bibliographies on aging* series from commercially available databases and published announcement series for books, government documents, dissertations, etc. Titles range from 30 to 60 pages and include such topics as: black and Mexican American aging; sexuality; the older worker; depression; nutrition; environmental planning; intergenerational relations; middle age, etc.

Z7164.O4E84

Ethnicity and aging: a bibliography. Comp. by Edward Murguia [and others]. San Antonio, Tex., Trinity Univ. Pr., [1984]. 132p. (Checklists in the humanities and education, 8)   **CC101**

A selective listing of 1,432 citations on the minority elderly in the United States, divided by ethnic and racial categories and, within these, into topical areas. Author index.   Z7164.O4E85

Fecher, Vincent John. Religion & aging: an annotated bibliography. San Antonio, Tex., Trinity Univ. Pr., [1982]. 119p.   **CC102**

Citations to more than 500 items are grouped by broad topics; indexed by subject and author.   Z7761.F42

Harris, Diana K. The sociology of aging: an annotated bibliography and sourcebook. N.Y., Garland, 1985. 283p. (Garland bibliographies in sociology, v.5; Garland reference library of social science, v.206)   **CC103**

A topically arranged bibliography of English-language titles on American elderly, published 1960–80; includes reference works and a directory of associations. Author index.   Z7164.O4H374

Krout, John H. The rural elderly: an annotated bibliography of social science research. Westport, Conn., Greenwood Pr., [1983]. 123p.   **CC104**

Classed arrangement of 590 individual citations published mainly 1970–82, including dissertations, theses, conference papers, and unpublished manuscripts. Author and geographic area indexes (limited to the United States).   Z7164.O4K76

Lyndon B. Johnson School of Public Affairs. Alternate care for the elderly: an annotated bibliography. [Austin, The School], 1977. 79p. (Policy research project report, no.22)   **CC105**

Prep. under faculty advisers Lodis Rhodes and John P. Hamilton.

A selective review of the literature on needs of the elderly, adult day care services, homemaker services, institutional care, alternative housing, information and referral services, meals programs, protective services, transportation and the elderly. No index.

Z7165.U5L86

McIlvaine, B. and **Mundkur, Mohini.** Aging: a guide to reference sources, journals and government publications. Storrs, Univ. of Connecticut Lib., [1978]. 162p. (*Its* Bibliography ser., no.11)   **CC106**

"Sponsored by the Program and Center for Gerontology."—*t.p.*

In three main sections: (1) annotated reference sources — library catalogs, handbooks, statistical sources, laws, indexes, abstracts, and bibliographies published in the United States since 1970; (2) U.S., state, foreign and international government documents published from 1975 to 1977 (an earlier bibliography covered government publications from 1960 to 1975; *see* CC98); (3) important journals in the field. Indexed.   Z7164.O4M33

Monroe, Margaret Ellen and **Rubin, Rhea Joyce.** Challenge of aging: a bibliography. Littleton, Colo., Libraries Unlimited, 1983. 209p.   **CC107**

An annotated, topically arranged guide to non-technical books, including literary works, for the layperson concerned with the adjustment to, and lifetasks of, aging. Nonprint materials available from the National Library Service for the Blind and Physically Handicapped are indicated. Author/title and subject indexes.

Z7164.O4M66

Mubarak, Jill, Sapienza, Diane and **Shimane, Robert.** Gerontology and the law: a selected bibliography. Los Angeles, Univ. of Southern California Law Center, 1979. 102p. (Asa V. Call Law Library bibliography ser., no.85) **CC108**

Subject arrangement, subdivided according to form of publication. Covers crime and criminal victimization of the aged; employment, age discrimination, and mandatory retirement; health, health care, and Medicare; housing; income maintenance; legal services; political activity; special social services. Similar topics are treated in the section on foreign and comparative works. Includes books, articles, documents, and conference proceedings. KF390.A4M8

Rooke, M. Leigh and **Wingrove, C. Ray.** Gerontology: an annotated bibliography. Wash., University Pr. of America, [1978]. 262p. **CC109**

"Only books, monographs and substantial papers are referenced in this bibliography, with the exception of some government publications. . . . The references included have been published between 1966 and early 1977, with exceptions made in some instances because of the continuing relevance of the publication or the paucity of materials on the topic."—*Pref.* A section of general references is followed by a topical section arranged alphabetically by topic; within each category government publications are listed separately (and are not annotated, the titles being descriptive of the content). Z7164.O4R56

Shock, Nathan W. A classified bibliography of gerontology and geriatrics. Stanford, Calif., Stanford Univ. Pr., [1951]. 599p. **CC110**

———— ———— Supplement I, 1949–1955. 1957. 525p.

———— ———— Supplement II, 1956–1961. 1963. 624p.

Includes monographs and periodical articles—more than 51,000 items—in all languages. Attempts to cover the whole field, from biochemistry to social science and social work as they concern the aged.

Supplements appeared in the *Journal of gerontology* through 1980. Z7164.O4S5

U.S. Dept. of Health, Education, and Welfare. Library. Selected references on aging: an annotated bibliography. Comp. for the Special Staff on Aging. Wash., Govt. Prt. Off., 1959. 110p. **CC111**

On cover: 1961 White House Conference edition.
Earlier editions were issued by the Federal Security Agency Library.
A classified listing with brief annotations. Z7164.O4U48

———— Words on aging; a bibliography of selected annotated references, comp. for the Administration on Aging. Wash., U.S. Admin. on Aging, [1970]. 190p. **CC112**

The seventh in a series of similar listings published since 1950 (the previous edition, 1963, was entitled *Aging in the modern world*). Offers a selective, classified list of periodical articles published 1963–67 and books from 1900 through 1967. Author index.

———— More words on aging. Supplement. Wash., U.S. Admin. on Aging, 1971. 107p. **CC113**

Z7164.O4U5

Current

Current literature on aging. v.1, no.1– . [Wash.], Nat. Council on the Aging, 1957– . Quarterly. **CC114**

An annotated subject bibliography of books, periodical articles, government documents, conference proceedings, etc. Annual author and subject indexes. Z7164.O4N37a

Gerontological abstracts. v.1, no.1– , Nov. 1976– . [Ann Arbor, Mich., University Information Services], 1976– . 6 nos. per yr. **CC115**

Each issue is classed broadly into biological, clinical, and social aspects of aging, then further subdivided by topic. No cumulative indexing. Z7164.O4G38

Index to periodical literature on aging. v.1, no.1– . Detroit, Lorraine Pubns., 1982– . Quarterly. **CC116**

Title varies: v.1 (1982–83), *Areco's quarterly index to periodical literature on aging.*
Bibliographic citations to English-language articles are repeated in three indexes: subject, author, and book review. Z7164.O4I4

Periodicals

Gibson, Mary Jo, Heath, Angela and **Nusberg, Charlotte.** International survey of periodicals in gerontology. 2d ed. Wash., Internat. Federation on Ageing, 1982. 92p. **CC117**

1st ed. 1978.
A directory, alphabetically arranged by country of publication; entries are coded by intended audience, but not priced. Title index. HQ1060.I58

Handbooks

Dickinson, Peter A. Sunbelt retirement: the complete state-by-state guide to retiring in the South and West of the United States. N.Y., Dutton, [1980]. 338p. il., maps. **CC118**

Surveys climate and environment, medical facilities, housing availability and costs, cost of living, recreation and culture, and special senior services for regions and communities. Dickinson is also the author of *Retirement Edens outside the Sunbelt* (N.Y., Dutton, 1981. 302p.), *Travel and retirement Edens abroad* (N.Y., Dutton, 1983. 365p.) and *The complete retirement planning book* (Rev. 2d ed., N.Y., Dutton, 1984. 258p.). HQ1063.D5

Handbook of aging and the social sciences. 2d ed. Editors, Robert H. Binstock [and] Ethel Shanas. N.Y., Van Nostrand Reinhold, [1985]. 809p. il. **CC119**

A review of research, organized in broad sections. Chapters by specialists cover the social aspects of aging; aging and social structure (including the status of the aged in various societies); aging and social systems; the study of aging; aging and social intervention. Extensive bibliographies for each chapter, with author index and subject indexes.
Other titles in the publisher's "Handbooks of aging" series are *Handbook of the biology of aging* by Caleb L. Finch and Leonard Hayflick (1977) and *Handbook of the psychology of aging* by James E. Birren and K. Warner Schaie (1977). HQ1061.H336

Handbook on the aged in the United States. Ed. by Erdman B. Palmore. Westport, Conn., Greenwood Pr., [1984]. 458p. il. **CC120**

Presents 26 chapters written by specialists and grouped in four main parts: demographic, religious, ethnic, and "special concerns" groups (addicts, criminals, the disabled, homosexuals, etc.); extensive bibliographic references. Directory of research centers; statistical tables; author and subject indexes. HQ1064.U5H23

International handbook on aging: contemporary developments and research. Ed. by Erdman Palmore. Westport, Conn., Greenwood Pr., [1980]. 529p. **CC121**

Chapters by specialists provide information on the state of gerontology in 28 countries throughout the world, giving a brief survey of the history of gerontology in each case, notes on the aged population, legislation, research and study, programs for the aged, etc. Bibliographies, tables, index. HQ1061.I535

National Council on the Aging. Research and Evaluation Dept. Fact book on aging: a profile of America's older population. Wash., The Council, 1978. 263p. il. **CC122**

Charles S. Harris, Research Coordinator.
Designed as a reference source for the practitioner in order to consolidate basic information about the elderly from federal government publications, books and articles, and national surveys and studies. Eight chapters treat demography, income, employment,

health (physical and mental), housing, transportation, and criminal victimizations; each chapter begins with highlights and charts, and is heavily statistical. Sources are identified; bibliographical notes.

HQ1064.U5N254

Norback, Craig T. and **Norback, Peter G.** The older American's handbook. N.Y., Van Nostrand Reinhold, [1977]. 311p.   **CC123**

Subtitle: Practical information and help on ... medical and nursing care, housing, recreation, legal services, employment, in-home services, food associations and organizations, transportation, mental health and counseling ... for older and retired Americans.

Bernard E. Nash, consulting ed.

A subject listing of agencies, programs, and publications serving the areas mentioned in the subtitle. Stresses the "do-it-yourself" approach for older Americans who wish to take care of themselves. No index.   HQ1064.U5N58

Sourcebook on aging. 2d ed. Chicago, Marquis Academic Media, [1979]. 539p.   **CC124**

1st ed. 1977.

Material for this edition has been organized into four parts — selected readings, legislation, statistics, and resources — with subject, organization, and geographic indexes. Statistics is the longest section, with two articles focusing on the black aged. Includes an extensive bibliography on middle-aged and aging families.

HQ1064.U5S63

Directories

American Association of Homes for the Aging. Membership directory, 1981– . Wash., The Association, 1980– . Irregular.   **CC125**

Lists homes for the aging, skilled nursing facilities, intermediate care facilities, housing programs, and at-home services offered by non-profit organizations. In four sections: state directories of member homes and facilities; associate members; state associations; sponsors of more than one facility. Personal name index.

HV1461.A562a

Cohen, Lilly, Oppedisano-Reich, Marie and **Gerardi, Kathleen Hamilton.** Funding in aging: public, private and voluntary. 2d ed., rev. & enl. Garden City, N.Y., Adelphi Univ. Pr., [1979]. 308p.   **CC126**

1st ed., 1977, had title: *A national guide to government and foundation funding sources in the field of aging.*

Updates information provided in the 1977 edition and adds a section on voluntary assistance which provides directory information for major national gerontological associations, denominational organizations, and professional, service, and fraternal organizations.   HV1465.C57

Directory of nursing homes: a state-by-state listing of facilities and services. Ed. by Sam Mongeau. 2d ed. [Phoenix], Oryx Pr., 1984. 1301p.   **CC127**

A listing of 16,139 state-licensed long-term facilities in the United States and its possessions, arranged by state and then by city. Entries include level of care provided, number of beds, and Medicaid/Medicare certification; many entries provide data on personnel, ownership, special activities, and languages spoken. Indexed by institutional name.   RA997.A2D49

Directory of senior centers and clubs. Wash., Nat. Council on the Aging, 1966– . Irregular.   **CC128**

Title varies: 1966, *National directory of senior centers;* 1970, *Senior centers in the United States.*

A state-by-state listing of about 5,000 programs offering regularly scheduled educational, recreational, or social activities directed to older adults.   HQ1060.D56

Gerontological Society. International directory of gerontology. Bethesda, Md., U.S. Dept. of Health, Education and Welfare, Nat. Inst. of Child Health and Human Development, [1969]. 330p.   **CC129**

Provides biographical sketches, descriptions of institutions, and special research sources by country, with a listing of persons by discipline within country.   HV1450.G46

Huff, Robert L. National directory of retirement facilities. Wash., Housing, Program Dept., Nat. Retired Teachers Assoc.-Amer. Assoc. of Retired Persons, 1979. 3v. (208p.)   **CC130**

A directory of government-funded housing projects, and private non-profit agencies providing housing for the elderly. Arranged by state, then by city within the above categories; very brief descriptions of facilities.   HQ1063.H83

National continuing care directory: comprehensive information on retirement facilities and communities offering pre-paid contracts for long-term care (also called life care). Ed. by Ann Trueblood Raper for the Amer. Assoc. of Homes for the Aging. Wash., Amer. Assoc. of Retired Persons; Glenview, Ill., Scott, Foresman, [1984]. 618p. maps.   **CC131**

Describes 277 retirement communities and facilities which offer continuing care, i.e., contracted, guaranteed housing and services such as meals, transportation, and health care. Listed by state; indexed by metropolitan area and special features.

HV1465.N273

United Nations. Dept. of Economic and Social Affairs. International directory of organizations concerned with the aging. N.Y., United Nations, 1977. 54p.   **CC132**

Contains information on 117 international, regional, and national institutions. Gives name, address, executive officer, brief description of the organization, its structure, personnel, and programs. Includes a list of periodicals.   HV1451.U55

United Nations. Dept. of International Economic and Social Affairs. International directory of organizations concerned with the aging. 1978 supplement. N.Y., United Nations, 1978. 45, 3p.   **CC132a**

Contains information on 70 international, regional, and national institutions, covering organizations not included in the original directory as well as those which appeared in the original without detailed information.

Alcoholism

Bibliography

See also CC451.

Abel, Ernest L. Alcohol and reproduction: a bibliography. Westport, Conn., Greenwood Pr., [1982]. 219p.   **CC133**

An author arrangement of 2,120 citations; international coverage of materials in various formats on topics such as sexual effects of alcohol, fetal alcohol syndrome, etc. Subject index.

Z6671.2.F46A26

Barnes, Grace M. Alcoholism and youth: a comprehensive bibliography. Westport, Conn., Greenwood Pr., [1982]. 452p.   **CC134**

An international bibliography of books, articles, theses, reports, and government documents; English translations have been provided for foreign titles. Author arrangement of 4,666 entries. Subject index.   Z7721.B37

—— **Abel, Ernest L.** and **Ernst, Charles A. S.** Alcohol and the elderly: a comprehensive bibliography. Westport, Conn., Greenwood Pr., [1980]. 138p.   **CC135**

An international selection of more than 1,200 citations to articles, books, reports, and monographs, the majority of which were written since 1970. Subject index.   Z7721.B36

Chalfant, H. Paul and **Roper, Brent S.** Social and behavioral aspects of female alcoholism: an annotated bibliography. Westport, Conn., Greenwood Pr., [1980]. 145p.   **CC136**

A total of 488 periodical articles written during the 1970s are arranged by broad topics, such as rates, psychological aspects, social and cultural aspects, death, deviant behavior, the family, and treatment. Author index.   HV5824.W6C46

Dorn, Nicholas and **South, Nigel.** Message in a bottle: theoretical overview and annotated bibliography on the mass media and alcohol. [Aldershot, Hants., England], Gower, [1983]. 178p.   **CC137**

About 400 articles, reports, books, etc., are listed and annotated. International in scope.   Z7721.D67

Gold, Robert S., Zimmerli, William H. and **Austin, Winnifred K.** Comprehensive bibliography of existing literature on alcohol, 1969 to 1974. Dubuque, Ia., Kendall/Hunt, [1975]. 470p.   **CC138**

Intends to list materials both of research and general periodical nature. Separate sections for periodical articles, books, pamphlets, and dissertations. Classed arrangement within each section. Author index and a "subject index" which offers a list of titles to be found under each topical category.   Z7721.G64

Heath, Dwight B. and **Cooper, A. M.** Alcohol use and world cultures. Toronto, Addiction Research Foundation, [1981]. 248p. (Addiction Research Foundation bibliography ser., 15)   **CC139**

Subtitle: A comprehensive bibliography of anthropological sources.

Aims to provide "easier and more comprehensive access to the large, diverse and widely scattered literature that deals with alcoholic beverages in relation to human behavior among various populations throughout the world."—*Introd.* Covers prehistoric times to mid-1978. Appendix of research in progress. Indexed by author and subject, including concept, theory, nation, and tribe or other special population.   Z7721.H4

International bibliography of studies on alcohol. New Brunswick, N.J., Rutgers Center of Alcohol Studies, [1966–80]. v.1–3.   **CC140**

Mark Keller, ed.

Contents: v.1, References, 1901–1950, prep. by Sarah Spock Jordy; v.2, Indexes to v.1, 1901–1950 (pt.1, Subjects, prep. by Vera Efron; pt.2, Authors, prep. by Sarah Spock Jordy); v.3, References and indexes, 1951–1960.

Designed as "a broad multidisciplinary and interprofessional bibliography" (*Introd.*) for the study of phenomena related to the uses of alcohol, whether medical, social, psychological, legal, or economic. References are given to abstracts in the *Journal of studies on alcohol* and the *Classified Abstract Archive of the Alcohol Literature,* located at the Rutgers Center of Alcohol Studies.   Z7721.I5

Kurtz, Norman R., Googins, Bradley and **Howard, William.** Occupational alcoholism: an annotated bibliography. Toronto, Addiction Research Fndn., [1984]. 218p. (*Its* Bibliographic ser., no. 17)   **CC141**

481 citations to a wide variety of formats are grouped within 20 subject categories, focusing on the North American experience; author and category indexes.   Z7164.C81K88

Milgram, Gail Gleason. Alcohol education materials: an annotated bibliography. New Brunswick, N.J., Pubns. Div., Rutgers Ctr. of Alcohol Studies, [1975]. 304p.   **CC142**

A summary and evaluation of 873 titles published in North America between 1950 and early 1973. An additional 686 citations are given in: Z7721.M54

———— Alcohol education materials, 1973–1978: an annotated bibliography. New Brunswick, N.J., Pubns. Div., Rutgers Ctr. of Alcohol Studies, [1980]. 257p.

Continued for 1978–79 by a listing in the Summer 1979 issue of the *Journal of alcohol and drug education.*   Z7721.M543

Dictionaries and encyclopedias

Keller, Mark, McCormick, Mairi and **Efron, Vera.** A dictionary of words about alcohol. 2d ed. New Brunswick, N.J., Pubns. Div., Rutgers Ctr. of Alcohol Studies, [1982]. 291p.   **CC143**

1st ed. 1968.

An international dictionary with some etymologies; bibliographic references.   HV5017.K42

Lender, Mark Edward. Dictionary of American temperance biography; from temperance reform to alcohol research, the 1600s to the 1980s. Westport, Conn., Greenwood Pr., [1984]. 572p.   **CC144**

Provides brief narrative biographies of about 2,000 figures; bibliographic references include primary and secondary sources, and citations to standard biographical reference works. Indexed.   HV5239.A2L46

O'Brien, Robert and **Chafetz, Morris.** The encyclopedia of alcoholism. N.Y., Facts on File, [1982]. 378p.   **CC145**

A concise reference work in dictionary form; about 500 entries, many including bibliographic references. Appendixes provide United States statistical data and international directory information. Bibliography; index.   HV5017.E5

Directories

The alcohol and drug abuse yearbook/directory, 1979/80. N.Y., Van Nostrand Reinhold, [1979].   **CC146**

Only 1v. publ.?

Provides directory information for alcoholism associations, occupational programs, state alcoholism authorities and treatment centers, state drug abuse authorities and treatment programs. Under each state, organizations are listed alphabetically. No index.

Children and youth
Bibliography

See also CC134, CC383, CC404.

Adolescent mental health abstracts. v.1, no.1– , [Summer 1983]– . St. Louis, Mo., Center for Adolescent Mental Health, Washington Univ., 1983– . Quarterly.   **CC147**

Abstracts English-language periodical articles pertaining to research, policy, theory, and service delivery regarding mental health in the 12–18 year-old group; education and juvenile delinquency items are selectively abstracted. Selected books are treated separately. Author and subject indexes.

Child abuse and neglect research: projects and publications. Feb. 1976– . Wash., U.S. Dept. of Health, Education, and Welfare, Office of Human Development, Office of Child Development, Children's Bureau, Nat. Center on Child Abuse and Neglect, 1976– . Irregular.   **CC148**

Frequency varies.

Identifies and describes current research projects and publications, dated 1965 and later, selected from journals, books, and other "readily accessible" sources. Projects and publications are listed in separate sections, alphabetically by investigator and author; projects are indexed by investigator, organization, financial sponsor, and subject; publications are indexed by author and subject. A companion publication, *Child abuse and neglect programs* (1976) identifies about 2,000 private and public agencies with programs in the field; it is arranged geographically, with program director, organization, and subject index. Both are produced from the National Center on Child Abuse and Neglect's data base, *Child abuse and neglect,* which covers 1965 to date and is available for online searching.   HV741.C456●

Child development abstracts and bibliography. v.1– , June/
Dec. 1927– . Lafayette, Ind., Purdue Univ., Soc. for Re-
search in Child Development, 1927– . 3 times a year.
CC149

Title varies slightly. Frequency varies. Publisher varies.
Contains abstracts of articles from American and foreign periodicals; abstracts are usually signed. Also includes a section of book
notices. Arrangement is by subject. Author and subject index
cumulates annually.   HQ750.A1C47

Derrick, Deborah. Selected and annotated bibliography of
youth, youth work, and provision for youth. Leicester,
National Youth Bureau, 1976. 411p.   **CC150**

A bibliography of books, reports, documents, and pamphlets on
youth, from infancy through adolescence. Classified into 19 chapters, with appropriate subdivisions, dealing with social studies,
psychology, social services, community development, education,
work and leisure, delinquency and social problems, youth services,
counseling, etc. Author and subject indexes.   Z7164.Y8D35

ERIC Clearinghouse on Early Childhood Education. Research relating to children. Bulletin [1]–42, Dec. 1948/June
1949–Feb. 1979. [Wash., Govt. Prt. Off.], 1950–79. Irregular.   **CC151**

Bulletins 1–27 issued by the U.S. Children's Bureau. Clearinghouse for Research in Child Life.
Each issue reports research in progress or very recently completed. Does not repeat studies included in earlier issues. Contains
abstracts of studies arranged by broad subjects, and indexes of
organizations, investigators, and subjects.   HQ768.8.U5

Garoogian, Andrew and **Garoogian, Rhoda.** Child care issues
for parents and society: a guide to information sources.
Detroit, Gale, [1977]. 367p. (Social issues and social problems information guide ser., 2)   **CC152**

An annotated guide to "books and periodicals of a nontechnical
nature, . . . audiovisual aids, sources of free and inexpensive materials, and organizations . . . that have emerged in the field of child care
during the past five years [1970–75]."—*Introd.* Organized by subject, with books, pamphlets, audiovisual materials, etc., listed by
form under each subject. Author, title, organization, and subject
indexes.   Z7164.C5G37

Gottlieb, David, Reeves, Jon and **TenHouten, Warren D.** The
emergence of youth societies; a cross-cultural approach.
N.Y., Free Pr., [1966]. 416p.   **CC153**

The bulk of the volume is devoted to a bibliography of materials
relating to adolescent behavior and training throughout the world.
Arranged by country; many items are annotated.   Z7164.Y8G62

Hirsch, Elisabeth S. Problems of early childhood: an annotated bibliography and guide. N.Y., Garland, 1983. 253p.
CC154

A series of topical bibliographic essays are followed by briefly
annotated entries subdivided by form and audience level: books and
pamphlets for adults, studies and articles (including essays and
ERIC reports), and books for children. Topics include: separation,
illness, death, divorce, single-parent families, working mothers,
siblings, discipline, social relations, etc.; handicapping problems are
excluded. Author and subject indexes.   Z5814.C5H57

Kalisch, Beatrice J. Child abuse and neglect: an annotated
bibliography. Westport, Conn., Greenwood Pr., [1978].
535p. (Contemporary problems of childhood, 2)   **CC155**

Includes more than 2,000 English-language sources (most of them
from the 1960–77 period) in classed arrangement. Introductory
section is followed by broad subject sections, subdivided as necessary, on: prediction, detection, and prevention; causative factors;
manifestations; treatment; sexual abuse; legal issues. Appendixes
note bibliographic tools, selected organizations, and text of the
Child Abuse Prevention and Treatment Act. Author and keyword
subject indexes.   Z7164.C5K34

Menefee, Louise Arnold and **Chambers, Merritt Madison.**
American youth, an annotated bibliography, prep. for the

American Youth Commission. Wash., Amer. Council on
Education, 1938. 492p.   **CC156**

Annotated and classified, with alphabetical index.
Supplemented by: Z7164.Y8M5

Chambers, Merritt Madison and **Exton, Elaine.** Youth—key
to America's future; an annotated bibliography. Wash.,
Amer. Council on Education, [1949]. 117p.   **CC157**

          Z7164.Y8C5

Scheffler, Hannah Nuba. Resources for early childhood: an
annotated bibliography and guide for educators, librarians,
health care professionals, and parents. N.Y., Garland, 1983.
584p. (Garland reference library of social science, v.118)
CC158

Topically organized into 16 chapters, each preceded by an essay
and concluded with an evaluative bibliography, based on the collection at the New York Public Library Early Childhood Resource and
Information Center. Author and title indexes.   HQ767.9.S3

van Why, Elizabeth Wharton. Adoption bibliography and
multi-ethnic sourcebook. Hartford, Conn., Open Door Soc.
of Connecticut, [1977]. 320p.   **CC159**

Consists of (1) a bibliography including articles, books, audiovisual materials, periodicals, and bibliographies; (2) a "multi-ethnic"
source-book describing organizations and their available materials;
and (3) appendixes. The bibliography is indexed by geographic
locations, peoples, and languages.   Z7164.A23V35

Wells, Dorothy P. Child abuse: an annotated bibliography.
Metuchen, N.J., Scarecrow Pr., 1980. 450p.   **CC160**

A review in *Wilson library bulletin* (Sept. 1980, p.66) notes the
similarities between this work and B. J. Kalisch's *Child abuse and
neglect* (CC155). Although concluding that the Kalisch work is
superior overall, the reviewer indicates that Wells's coverage of
foreign-language material is stronger.   Z7164.C5W37

Winchell, Carol Ann. The hyperkinetic child: a bibliography
of medical, educational, and behavioral studies. Westport,
Conn., Greenwood Pr., [1975]. 182p.   **CC161**

A comprehensive bibliography of almost 1,900 citations from a
wide variety of materials, arranged by subject: etiology, diagnosis,
clinical, educational, and parental management, and related psychological and sociological studies. Author and selective keyword subject indexes.   Z5814.C52W53

————— The hyperkinetic child; an annotated bibliography,
1974–1979. Westport, Conn., Greenwood Pr., [1981]. 451p.
(Contemporary problems of childhood, no.4)   **CC161a**

Updates the author's earlier volume by the addition of more than
2,000 English-language materials arranged in a detailed subject
classification. Appendixes feature drug tables, glossary, list of audiovisual materials, and directory of service organizations. Author and
key-word indexes.   Z5814.C52W53

Woodbury, Marda. Childhood information resources. Arlington, Va., Information Resources, 1985. 593p.   **CC162**

An international, annotated bibliography focusing on American
children through age 12. Thirteen chapters are arranged by type or
form of information resource—printed, audiovisual, computerized,
etc.; four chapters deal with subjects such as tests, statistics, and
parent education. Indexed.   Z5814.C5W6

Directories

National directory of children & youth services, 1979– .
Wash., CPR Directory Services Co., 1979– . Annual.
CC163

Comp. by the editors of *Child protection report.*
Pt. I, "Guide to state, county and major city agencies and
services," summarizes state and county administration of social
services and provides names, addresses, and telephone numbers for
program administrators for over 3,100 counties and major cities;

information on private agencies is also provided for about 200 large population centers. Pt. II, "Quick reference guides," provides directory information for federal programs, runaway youth centers, information clearinghouses and resource centers, and private and professional organizations.

Urban Information Interpreters. The national children's directory: an organizational directory and reference guide for changing conditions for children and youth. Ed. by Mary Lee Bundy and Rebecca Glenn Whaley. College Park, Md., Urban Information Interpreters, [1977]. 303p. **CC164**

Identifies about 700 national and local groups concerned with improving conditions for children and youth in the United States. Each entry describes objectives, activities, publications, background and membership. National groups are listed alphabetically; local groups by state. Title and classified subject indexes. Includes sections on "alternative" children and youth programs, and federal government activities in this area. Classed, annotated bibliography of about 300 items. HV741.U7

Youth-serving organizations directory. Detroit, Gale, [1978]. 476p. **CC165**

Annie M. Brewer, comp.

Based on entries appearing in the 12th ed. of the *Encyclopedia of associations* (CA125). "Youth" generally refers to persons between 12 and 20 years of age. Includes organizations to which the young belong, those with adult members who teach, heal, or administer to the young, those whose membership is indirectly involved with programs related to the young, and those whose scope is so large that youth services are included. Indexed by name and keyword. A 2d ed., expanded to 1179p., was published in 1980. HS17.Y68

Death and dying

Bibliography

Comprehensive bibliography of the thanatology literature. Ed. by Martin L. Kutscher [and others]. N.Y., MSS Information Corp., [1975]. 285p. **CC166**

An author listing of 4,844 books, periodical articles, essays, reports, government documents, and unpublished materials. The broad subject terms used in the index (e.g., death, hospitals, children) impair the usefulness of the work. Z5725.C65

Death education: an annotated resource guide. Wash., Hemisphere Publ. Corp., [1980]. 303p. **CC167**

Hannelore Wass, Charles A. Corr, Richard A. Pacholski, Catherine M. Sanders, comps.

A series of annotated lists with introductory comments and narrative passages, covering: books and journal articles, textbooks and reference works, with more detailed descriptions and evaluations; bibliographies; journals; research methods; audiovisual resources; organizations. Indexed. HQ1073.D42

Miller, Albert Jay and **Acri, Michael James.** Death: a bibliographical guide. Metuchen, N.J., Scarecrow Pr., 1977. 420p. **CC168**

Nearly 3,850 items in classed arrangement, with author and subject indexes. Sections for general works, education, humanities, medical profession and nursing experiences, religion and theology, science, social sciences, and audiovisual media. Brief annotations. Includes suicide. Z5725.M54

Poteet, G. Howard. Death and dying; a bibliography (1950–1974). Troy, N.Y., Whitston, 1976. 192p. **CC169**

Concentrates "almost exclusively on the psychology of death" *(Pref.)*, omitting materials on suicide, legal interpretations of death, and most materials on euthanasia. Books are separately listed in an author arrangement; periodical articles appear in an alphabetical subject listing. Author index. Z7204.D4P68

Sell, Irene L. Dying and death: an annotated bibliography. N.Y., Tiresias Pr., [1977]. 144p. **CC170**

506 annotated items are grouped in three sections: (1) 328 articles in journals or collected papers; (2) 71 books; (3) 53 audiovisual aids. Within each section items are arranged by author. Author and title indexes. The bibliography "was prepared primarily for nursing practitioners, educators, and students involved with providing care for dying patients."—*Pref.* Z6675.T4S44

Simpson, Michael A. Dying, death, and grief: a critically annotated bibliography and source book of thanatology and terminal care. [4th ed.] N.Y., Plenum Pr., [1979]. 288p. **CC171**

Lists "over 750 [in-print] books—as well as over 200 films, audio- and video-tapes and cassettes, teaching materials, journals and other relevant publications and resources" *(Introd.)* relating to dying, death, grief, etc. Annotations; author and subject indexes to the book lists. Z5725.S55

Strugnell, Cécile. Adjustment to widowhood and some related problems; a selective & annotated bibliography. N.Y., Health Sciences Publ. Corp., 1974. 201p. **CC172**

English-language materials (books, parts of books, periodical articles) on bereavement, widowhood (general and cross-cultural), the elderly widowed, children's bereavement, loneliness, etc., are listed and annotated. Lacks an index. Z7961.S78

Triche, Charles W. and **Triche, Diane Samson.** The euthanasia controversy, 1812–1974; a bibliography with select annotations. Troy, N.Y., Whitston, 1975. 242p. **CC173**

About 1,350 items; includes book materials, periodical articles, and newspaper accounts. Subject arrangement of the periodical literature; author index. Z6675.E95T74

Handbooks

Bleckman, Isaac A. Death and dying A to Z; a loose-leaf encyclopedic handbook on death and dying and related subjects. Queens Village, N.Y., Croner Pubns., [1980]– . Looseleaf. **CC174**

Kurt J. Guggenheim, project director and ed. in chief.

"This handbook is designed to serve as a comprehensive guide . . . , providing concise explanations of current ideas and trends as well as historical background. It contains a dictionary of special terms, lists and tables of facts and figures, directories of organizations and services, and bibliographies of publications and audiovisual materials."—*Introd.* Kept up-to-date by a quarterly "Amendment service" beginning Jan. 1981. GT3150.B58

Sourcebook on death and dying. James A. Fruehling, consulting ed. Chicago, Marquis Professional Pubns., [1982]. 788p. il. **CC175**

In five parts: pt.I, "Current issues," reprints articles on euthanasia, living wills, definitions of death, etc.; pt.II, "Facts and figures," provides mortality statistics, data on the funeral industry, information on organ donations, survivors' benefits, etc.; pt.III gives directory information on associations, memorial societies, self-help groups, hospices, and publications; the final two sections are a glossary and an index. HQ1073.5.U6S68

Disabled

Bibliography

Bauman, Mary Kinsey. Blindness, visual impairment, deaf-blindness: annotated listing of the literature, 1953–75. Philadelphia, Temple Univ. Pr., [1976]. 537p. **CC176**

Serves as a supplement to Helga Lende's *Books about the blind* (CC183). About 3,750 items in classed arrangement, with author and analytical subject indexes. Includes a directory of associations and agencies.

Kept up to date by a semiannual bibliography of the same title: Z5346.B38

Blindness, visual impairment, deaf-blindness: semiannual listing of current literature. v.1, no.1– , Summer 1976– . Philadelphia, Nevil Interagency Referral Service, 1976–'. Semiannual.   **CC177**

An author listing of English-language material of "professional relevance," excluding medical literature. Annotations. Analytical subject index, cumulative within each year.   Z5346.A2B54

DSH abstracts. v.1– , Oct. 1960– . [Wash.,] Deafness, Speech and Hearing Pub., 1960– . v.1– . Quarterly.
                                                        CC178

Sponsored by the American Speech and Hearing Association and Gallaudet College.
Offers abstracts of articles in the major languages on deafness, speech, and hearing. Titles are given in the original language (except Russian and Oriental languages), with English translation. Classified arrangement with author index. Annual author and subject indexes.
                                                          RF1.D45

Fellendorf, George W. Bibliography on deafness: *The Volta review,* 1899–1976, *American annals of the deaf,* 1847– 1976. [Rev. ed.] [Wash., Alexander Graham Bell Assoc. for the Deaf, 1977] 272p.   **CC179**

1st ed. 1966; supplement 1973.
A subject listing of articles and research reports printed in these journals during the periods indicated. Under each topic articles from the journals are listed separately, in chronological order. Author index.   Z5721.F4

Flint, Richard W., Higgins, Francis C. and **Padden, Donald A.** Doctors' dissertations and masters' theses on the education of the deaf, 1897–1955. Wash., 1955. p.343–417. (*In* Amer. annals of the deaf, v.100, no.4, Sept. 1955)
                                                        CC180

Lists more than 1,000 theses by author, with indexes by subject and by college.

Graham, Milton D. Social research on blindness: present status and future potentials. N.Y., Amer. Foundation for the Blind, 1960. 177p.   **CC181**

Arranged by sections concerning types of activity with the blind. In each, major research projects are outlined in some detail, followed by extensive lists of relevant publications.   HV1598.G7

Harvard University. Psycho-Acoustic Laboratory. Bibliography on hearing . . . S. S. Stevens, dir.; J. G. C. Loring, comp.; Dorothy Cohen, tech. ed. Cambridge, Mass., Harvard Univ. Pr., 1955. 599p.   **CC182**

An enlargement of *A bibliography in audition,* comp. by George A. Miller [and others], 1950.
This edition contains more than 10,000 titles with emphasis on the period 1938–52, with important materials before 1938. All titles listed in the 1st ed. are repeated here, and the coverage has been expanded, particularly in the fields of psychology and the acoustics of music, deafness and the deafened, ultrasonics, and the effects of drugs on human and animal hearing. Arranged alphabetically by author with subject index. Titles are given in the original language with English translation of foreign titles in brackets.
                                                        Z6663.H4H3

Lende, Helga. Books about the blind; a bibliographical guide to literature relating to the blind. New rev. ed. N.Y., Amer. Foundation for the Blind, 1953. 357p.   **CC183**

1st ed. 1940.
An annotated bibliography of about 4,200 references, more than half of which were not listed in the first edition. The main classes cover: work with the blind; education; psychology; vocations and economic adjustment; social adjustment; literature and reading; special groups; biographies and autobiographies; author index.
                                                          Z5346.L4

Microfilming Corporation of America. Rehabilitation & handicapped literature, 1950–1978: a bibliographic guide to the microfiche collection. Ed. by Allene Goforth [and others]. Sanford, N.C., The Corporation, [1981]. 438p.   **CC184**

A guide to the collection of reports and studies funded by federal grants and located at the National Rehabilitation Information Center, Catholic University of America. Author, title, and subject indexes.
Supplemented by: Z6122.M52

Rehabilitation & handicapped literature, 1979– update. Sanford, N.C., Microfilming Corp. of America, [1981]– . Annual.

Pearman, William A. and **Starr, Philip.** The physically handicapped; an annotated bibliography of empirical research studies, 1970–1979. N.Y., Garland, 1981. 132p. (Garland reference library of social science, v.76)   **CC185**

An author arrangement of 330 citations to periodical articles. There is an introductory literature review on measurement and methodological problems in physical disability research. Indexed by subject and additional authors.   Z6675.R4P4

Physical disability, an annotated literature guide. Ed. by Phyllis C. Self. N.Y., Dekker, [1984]. 474p.   **CC186**

Twelve chapters on varying aspects of disability and rehabilitation (blindness, deafness, communication, legal rights, etc.) begin with bibliographic review essays and conclude with annotated monograph entries; three chapters deal with federal government publications, journals, and audiovisual reference services. Author and title indexes.   RD797.P483

Recording for the Blind, Inc. Catalog of tape recorded books, 1971. [N.Y., 1971?] 592p.   **CC187**

On cover: 1971–72.
Lists more than 14,000 titles, including books in 14 foreign languages available on tape as of April 30, 1971. 350 to 400 new titles are recorded each month.
"Recording for the Blind, Inc. is a national, non-profit voluntary organization, supported by public contributions, which provides recorded educational books free-on-loan to visual and physically handicapped elementary, high school, college and graduate students as well as adults who require reading material in the pursuit of their professions or vocations."—[*Introd. note*]

Talking books: Adult. N.Y., publ. for the Library of Congress by the American Foundation for the Blind, 1956– . Biennial?   **CC188**

"A catalog of talking book records for adults provided by the Library of Congress and announced in *Talking book topics* . . . as available from the cooperating regional libraries."—*title page.* Supersedes the Library's *Talking books for the blind.*
Comp. by the Division for the Blind and Physically Handicapped of the Library of Congress.
Listing is by broad Dewey classes, with an author-title-subject index. Descriptive annotation for each entry. Recordings are available on free loan to eligible handicapped persons.
The Foundation, in cooperation with the Library of Congress, also issues periodic catalogs of *Press braille adult* books, and of braille and talking books *For younger readers.*   Z5347.T3

Dictionaries and encyclopedias

Butterworth, Rod R. The Perigee visual dictionary of signing; an A to Z guide to over 1,200 signs of American sign language. [N.Y.], Putnam, [1983]. 450p. il.   **CC189**

"The purpose of this work is to provide a basic and adequate vocabulary in American Sign Language which the student can use to learn to communicate with the deaf." Each sign is both illustrated and verbally explained.   HV2475.B87

World Federation of the Deaf. Unification of Sign Commission. Gestuno: international sign language of the deaf. Carlisle, Eng., British Deaf Assn., 1975. unpaged. il.
                                                        CC191

In English and French.
Illustrates about 1,500 sign-language gestures for words, numbers,

and letters, grouped by categories such as people and relationships, environment, weather, etc. English and French word indexes.

HV2474.W67

Directories

Directory of agencies serving the visually handicapped in the United States. Ed.17– , 1971– . N.Y., Amer. Foundation for the Blind, 1971– . (Ed. 22, 1984) **CC192**

Supersedes *Directory of agencies serving blind persons in the United States* (1st ed. 1926) and continues its numbering.

A state-by-state listing of statewide and local services, followed by supplementary lists of specialized agencies and organizations. Gives address, executive officer, etc., plus a statement regarding types of service or assistance offered. HV1790.A4

Directory of library resources for the blind and physically handicapped. 1970– . Wash., Lib. of Congress, Div. for the Blind and Physically Handicapped, 1970– . **CC193**

Lists the regional libraries which distribute through the mail the books and magazines in braille and on records provided by the Library of Congress, Division for the Blind and Physically Handicapped. Also lists the machine lending agencies for each area.

The Division publishes *Braille book review,* "a magazine of news about braille materials and related matter" (1932–) which is distributed free of charge to blind and physically handicapped persons who borrow books from libraries and other agencies cooperating in the Library of Congress program. Z675.B6D5

Directory of national information sources on handicapping conditions and related services. [3d ed.] Wash., U.S. Dept. of Education, Office of Special Education and Rehabilitative Services, Clearinghouse on the Handicapped, 1982. 263p. (Publ. no. E–82–22007) **CC194**

1st ed. 1976.

Identifies and describes federal and private organizations providing information or direct service relevant to handicapped individuals (mental health, alcoholism and drug abuse are not fully represented). Each entry describes the organization's activities, clientele, and services in terms of user eligibility, fees, etc. In two sections: national organizations; federal information sources. Indexed by disorder, special "target" populations, and subject areas in which organizations have information relative to handicaps.

HV1553.D544

Eckstein, Burton J. Handicapped funding directory: a guide to sources of funding in the United States for handicapped programs and services. 1980/81 ed. Oceanside, N.Y., Research Grant Guides, 1980. 173p. **CC195**

Lists about 400 foundations, associations, federal and state agencies which grant funds to institutions and agencies for handicapped programs and services. Entries provide only brief notes as to areas of interest, with the exception of those for federal agencies, which are taken from the *Catalog of federal domestic assistance* (CH119). Indexed by name and state, but no subject access.

HV3006.A4E27

Ready Reference Press. Directory of information resources for the handicapped: a guide to information resources and services for the handicapped. Santa Barbara, Calif., Ready Reference Pr., [1980]. 236p. **CC196**

In six parts: (1) advocacy, consumer, voluntary health organizations; (2) information/data banks; (3) federal government agencies other than information units; (4) professional and trade organizations; (5) facilities, schools, clinics; (6) service organizations. Each entry provides a description of the agency's activities and information services, including publications. Appendixes list relevant religious and sports organizations, and provide an annotated list of directories. Indexed by subject and by specific disorder.

HV1553.R4

U.S. Office for Handicapped Individuals. Federal assistance for programs serving the handicapped. Wash., U.S. Dept. of Health, Education, and Welfare, Office of the Asst. Secretary for Human Development, Office for Handicapped Individuals, 1977. 333p. (DHEW publ.; no.(OHD) 77–22001) **CC197**

First issued 1976.

Describes about 200 programs and activities for people with disabilities, including programs to alleviate the problems of alcoholism and drug abuse; information on the majority of programs was derived from the *Catalog of federal domestic assistance* (CH119), augmented by surveys conducted by the Office for Handicapped Individuals. Does not include general programs for the financially disadvantaged or aged persons. Program descriptions include restrictions, eligibility requirements, application procedure, contacts, enabling legislation, appropriations. Indexed by agency, subject, and applicant eligibility. Appendixes include related programs, resource centers and bibliography, and state agencies serving the handicapped. HV3001.A1O36

Handbooks

Cruzic, Kathleen. Disabled? yes. Defeated? no: resources for the disabled and their families, friends, and therapists. Englewood Cliffs, N.J., Prentice-Hall, 1982. 212p. il. **CC198**

A self-help book with suggestions, lists of sources for products, clothing, and equipment, bibliographies of printed and audiovisual materials, directories of organizations, etc. Indexed.

HV1568.C77

Hale, Glorya. The source book for the disabled: an illustrated guide to easier and more independent living for physically disabled people, their families and friends. N.Y. & London, Paddington Pr. (distr. by Grosset & Dunlap), [1979]. 288p. il. **CC199**

Focuses on attitudes toward situations, available options, and describes and illustrates aids for use in the home, for leisure activities, and for personal needs. Chapters on communication, relations with the "outside world," the home, personal needs, sexuality, the disabled parent and the disabled child, and leisure and recreation. Resources section suggests organizations, printed sources, and companies supplying various aids. HV3011.H26

Katz, Alfred Hyman and **Martin, Knute.** A handbook of services for the handicapped. Westport, Conn., Greenwood Pr., [1982]. 291p. **CC200**

Designed "to provide a general overview of common problems and needs of the handicapped, and of the resources [i.e., remedial programs] available . . . ."—*Introd.* Seven chapters, with factual, directory, and bibliographic data, on: physical care services, housing, financial aids, employment and vocational rehabilitation, counseling, children's services, recreation and social activities.

HV1553.K37

Kreisler, Nancy and **Kreisler, Jack.** Catalog of aids for the disabled. N.Y., McGraw-Hill, [1982]. 246p. il. **CC201**

More than 700 types of equipment and aids are grouped in 13 main categories according to purpose, e.g., transportation, household activities, communication, recreation, travel; descriptions of each aid include a photograph (when necessary), price category, and supplier. Directory of agencies and organizations, suppliers, and periodicals. Indexed. RD755.K73

Sourcebook of aid for the mentally and physically handicapped. Judith Norback, ed. N.Y., Van Nostrand Reinhold, [1983]. 506p. **CC202**

A directory of federal, state, and private agencies and associations; printed and database information sources; comparative data on state laws and college services; and text information. Indexed.

HV1553.S66

Velleman, Ruth A. Serving physically disabled people: an information handbook for all libraries. N.Y., Bowker, 1979. 392p. il. **CC203**

Intended as an aid to librarians, educators, and students in library service, education, and rehabilitation counseling, to enable them "to explore the informational needs of physically disabled people, to determine the role of the librarian in meeting these needs, and to offer pertinent sources of information."—*Introd.* Offers valuable information on equipment, printed sources, organizations, and core library collections. Indexed. Z711.92.P5V44

Drug abuse

Bibliography

Andrews, Theodora. A bibliography of drug abuse, including alcohol and tobacco. Littleton, Colo., Libraries Unlimited, 1977. 306p. **CC204**

An annotated listing of 725 works, mostly English-language books published since about 1960. Pt.I lists general reference sources, including periodical titles. Pt.II is a classed list of source material by subject area, e.g., psychology, education, the law, medical aspects, religion, hallucinogens, marijuana, stimulants. The sections on alcohol and tobacco cover thirty pages. Author/title and subject indexes. Z7164.N17A52

——— A bibliography of drug abuse. Supplement, 1977–1980. Littleton, Colo., Libraries Unlimited, 1981. 312p. **CC205**

Includes annotations for an additional 741 works, mostly English-language monographs, with some emphasis on alcohol and tobacco, self-help materials, and the problems of special groups such as the elderly, women, physicians, minorities, etc. Author/title index. Z7164.N17A52

Austin, Gregory A. and **Prendergast, Michael L.** Drug use and abuse: a guide to research findings. Santa Barbara, Calif., ABC-Clio, [1984]. 2v. (955p.) **CC206**

Contents: v.1, Adults; v.2, Adolescents.
Presents detailed abstracts of 238 federally funded research studies carried out between 1970 and 1980 on the psychosocial aspects of drug use and abuse. Within each volume, abstracts are grouped by broad topics, e.g., treatment, crime, drug use among women or ethnic minority youth. Includes published and unpublished research reports. Indexes in v.2 cover both volumes: author, topic, drug, sample type, sex, age, ethnicity, location, methodology, and instrument. RC564.A95

Charles, Sharon Ashenbrenner and **Feldman, Sari.** Drugs: a multimedia sourcebook for children and young adults. N.Y., Neal Schuman; Santa Barbara, ABC-Clio, [1980]. 200p. (Selection guide ser., 4) **CC207**

Evaluates books and audiovisual materials which can be used with or by young adults (grades 6–12) in drug education programs. Z7164.N17C47

Gold, Robert S., Zimmerli, William H. and **Austin, Winnifred K.** Comprehensive bibliography of existing literature on drugs, 1969 to 1974. Dubuque, Ia., Kendall Hunt, [1975]. 808p. **CC208**

Citations grouped by form—articles, books, pamphlets, dissertations—are further subdivided by topic; government documents are also included. Indexed by author and form, subdivided by topic. Z6675.P5G64

Iiyama, Patti, Nishi, Setsuko Matsunaga and **Johnson, Bruce D.** Drug use and abuse among U.S. minorities; an annotated bibliography. N.Y., Praeger, [1976]. 247p. **CC209**

Outgrowth of "a document originally prepared by Patti Iiyama of the Metropolitan Applied Research Center (MARC), as source material for the National Conference on Drug Abuse (Washington, December 1972), which focused on narcotics addiction among minorities" *(Pref.)* — i.e., blacks, Asian Americans, Mexican Americans, Puerto Ricans, and Native Americans. As used here, "drug abuse" refers "primarily to opiate, in the main heroin, addiction." Entries are grouped by minority. Lengthy annotations. Name and subject indexes. Z7164.N17I37

Menditto, Joseph. Drugs of addiction and non-addiction, their use and abuse; a comprehensive bibliography, 1960–1969. Troy, N.Y., Whitston, 1970. 315p. **CC209a**

A classified listing (using headings such as Amphetamines and stimulants, Marijuana, Narcotic rehabilitation, Narcotics and crime), with separate listings in each section for books, periodical articles, and dissertations. Author index.
Supplemented by: Z7164.N17M45

Drug abuse bibliography. 1970– . Troy, N.Y., Whitston, 1971– . Annual. **CC209b**

J. C. Advena, comp. Z7164.N17D75

National Institute on Drug Abuse. Findings of drug abuse research. Rockville, Md., The Institute, 1975. 2v. (762p.) (*Its* Research monograph ser., 1) **CC210**

"An annotated bibliography of NIMH and NIDA-supported extramural grant research 1967–74. . . ."—*t.p.*
v.1 "offers three sections of entries pertaining to the methodology of drug abuse research and findings of basic research into the chemical and metabolic characteristics of drugs and their mechanisms of action."—*Introd.* v.2 "includes entries on the behavioral and clinical aspects of drug abuse research including results of studies of adverse effects, prevention and treatment systems and the literature on human and psychosocial factors of drug abuse research." Author/editor and subject/drug indexes for each volume. Heavy biomedical emphasis. Z7164.N17N38

Ruben, Douglas H. Drug abuse and the elderly: an annotated bibliography. Metuchen, N.J., Scarecrow Pr., 1984. 247p. **CC211**

An international, topically arranged bibliography of 787 annotated citations to books, articles, and government documents; indexed by journal, author, and subject. Z7164.N17R82

Dictionaries and encyclopedias

Abel, Ernest L. A dictionary of drug abuse terms and terminology. Westport, Conn., Greenwood Pr., [1984]. 187p. **CC212**

Emphasizes slang words and expressions; a glossary offers a thesaurus approach. Omits alcohol- and tobacco-related terms. Bibliography. HV5804.A23

——— A marijuana dictionary: words, terms, events, and persons relating to cannabis. Westport, Conn., Greenwood Pr., 1982. 136p. **CC213**

Definitions of slang terms are accompanied by illustrative quotations, chronologically arranged. Also includes terms referring to the use of the plant as a source of the fiber, hemp. Appendix lists foreign words and expressions about marijuana. Bibliography of about 150 titles. Cross references; index. HV5822.M3A2

O'Brien, Robert and **Cohen, Sidney.** The encyclopedia of drug abuse. N.Y., Facts on File, [1984]. 454p. **CC214**

Provides international coverage of the medical, physical, psychological, political, and legal aspects of drug abuse, with extensive tabular appendixes, glossary, directory, and bibliography. Designed as a companion to O'Brien and Chafetz's *Encyclopedia of alcoholism* (CC145). HV5804.O24

Handbooks

Guggenheimer, Kurt J. Narcotics and drug abuse, A to Z. Queens Village, N.Y., Social Service Pubns., [1971]– . 3v., looseleaf. **CC215**

In several sections: dictionary; profiles of narcotics and abused drugs; directory of pharmaceutical companies and their drug products; main-entry bibliography; history, directory of organizations, survey of the foreign drug scene; state-by-state directory of facilities and organizations providing services related to drug abuse. HV5804.G8

Marriage and the family

Bibliography

See also CC364, CC371.

Aldous, Joan and **Hill, Reuben.** International bibliography of research in marriage and the family, 1900–1964. [Minneapolis], Minnesota Family Study Center and the Inst. of Life Insurance, [1967]. 508p. **CC216**

A computer-produced bibliography of books and articles. 12,850 references.

A second volume covering 1965–72 (1530p.) was published 1974; the first volume of a new supplementary series, *Inventory of marriage and family literature,* covering 1973/74 (publ. 1975) has been designated as v.3, and continues on an annual basis.
Z7164.M2A48

American family history: a historical bibliography. Santa Barbara, Calif., ABC-Clio, [1984]. 282p. (ABC Clio research guide, 12) **CC217**

More than 1,100 citations, with abstracts, drawn from the history database of the ABC-Clio Information Services. In four sections: (1) The family in historical perspective; (2) The family and other social institutions; (3) Familial roles and relationships; and (4) Individual family histories. Author and subject indexes. HQ535.A587

August, Eugene R. Men's studies: a selected and annotated interdisciplinary bibliography. Littleton, Colo., Libraries Unlimited, 1985. 215p. **CC218**

Cites 591 English-language books "about males as males" (*Introd.*), exploring topics such as men's rights, divorce and custody, masculine gender role, men in families, literary works, autobiographies and biographies, etc. Subject arrangement; author and title indexes. Z7164.M49A84

History of the family and kinship: a select international bibliography. Ed. by Gerald L. Soliday [and others]. Millwood, N.Y., Kraus Internat. Pubns., [1980]. 410p. **CC219**

"A project of the *Journal of Family History* [and] the National Council on Family Relations."—*t.p.*

About 6,200 entries, representing Western-language sources published through 1976. Arrangement is by region; further subdivisions are usually based on form of material (general surveys and bibliographies), individual country, or historic period. Chapters on classical antiquity and the Middle East and North Africa offer broad subject approach. Index of names. Z7164.M2H57

Israel, Stan. A bibliography on divorce. N.Y., Bloch, [1974]. 300p. **CC220**

An international bibliography classed by broad topics—legal, religious, and sociological aspects of divorce. About 160 citations, including tables of contents and annotations. Additional titles are noted without annotation. Z7164.M2I76

McKenney, Mary. Divorce: a selected annotated bibliography. Metuchen, N.J., Scarecrow Pr., 1975. 157p. **CC221**

About 600 items in classed arrangement; subject and author indexes. Most entries are briefly annotated. 1972 cutoff date, with a few later publications noted. Appendixes for relevant organizations and state divorce laws. Z7164.M2M34

Milden, James Wallace. The family in past time; a guide to the literature. N.Y., Garland, 1977. 200p. **CC222**

An annotated bibliography of English-language materials published prior to Dec. 31, 1975, including books, articles, unpublished papers and theses. Classified arrangement with author index. Sections for methodology and theory; family in European history, in American history, and in non-Western history; and family history projects. Z5118.F2M54

Peck, Theodore P. The troubled family: sources of information. Jefferson, N.C., McFarland, 1982. 258p. **CC223**

Pts.1–3 are directories of organizations concerned with families; pt.4 is a bibliography of publications issued 1973–81, topically arranged; pt.5 lists more general information sources. Focus is on the United States. Indexed. HV699.P35

Sage family studies abstracts. v.1, no.1– , Feb. 1979– . Beverly Hills, Sage Pubns., 1979– . Quarterly. **CC224**

Each issue abstracts about 250 books, articles, pamphlets, government publications, etc. Abstracts are grouped by broad topic; author and subject index in each issue. An additional 40 to 60 "related citations" are listed by author in each issue, without abstracts.
HQ536.S23

Schlesinger, Benjamin. The Jewish family; a survey and annotated bibliography. [Toronto], Univ. of Toronto Pr., [1971]. 175p. **CC225**

The classified, annotated bibliography occupies p.73–146. Intermarriage and life in the kibbutz are among the aspects considered. Not indexed. HQ525.J4S4

—— The multi-problem family; a review and annotated bibliography. 3d ed. [Toronto], Univ. of Toronto Pr., [1970]. 191p. **CC226**

1st ed. 1963.
The annotated bibliography is arranged by country with author index. An appendix listing works published Dec. 1962–April 1965 appeared in the 2d ed. (1965) and has not been further updated for this edition; an essay on "The multi-problem family in Canada" is the principal addition. Z5118.F2S3

—— The one-parent family: perspectives and annotated bibliography. 4th ed. Toronto, Univ. of Toronto Pr., [1978]. 224p. **CC227**

1st ed. 1969.
A survey of various aspects of the problem is followed by an annotated bibliography (p.77–193) in three chronological sections: 1930–69, 1970–74, 1975–78. Within sections, references are grouped under such headings as: Divorced, Widowed, Unmarried, Remarriage, etc. Author index. A 5th ed. was published 1985.
HQ535.S27

Sell, Kenneth D. and **Sell, Betty H.** Divorce in the United States, Canada, and Great Britain: a guide to information sources. Detroit, Gale, [1978]. 298p. (Social issues and social problems information guide ser., 1) **CC228**

Not a list of selected publications on the subject of divorce, but an annotated guide to basic general reference sources, showing how each may be used to identify materials on divorce. Special features include: a checklist of doctoral dissertations on divorce, 1891–Apr. 1978; detailed analyses of American, British, and Canadian statistical reports; and a list of published newspaper indexes. Name, title, and subject indexes. Z7164.M2S4

—— Divorce in the 70s: a subject bibliography. [Phoenix], Oryx Pr., 1981. 191p. **CC229**

Lists more than 4,700 books, articles, government documents, dissertations and theses, and audiovisual titles produced in the United States between 1970 and 1979. Broad topical arrangement, e.g., legal literature, subdivided by chapters on alimony, annulment, etc. Indexed by author, subject, and geographic area.
Z7164.M2S396

Straus, Murray A. and **Brown, Bruce W.** Family measurement techniques: abstracts of published instruments, 1935–1974. Rev. ed. Minneapolis, Univ. of Minnesota Pr., [1978]. 668p. **CC230**

1st ed. 1969.
A classed arrangement of abstracts for 813 test measures for husband-wife, parent-child, and sibling-to-sibling relationships. Each abstract provides variables measured, test description, availability, and bibliographic references to the test. References section cites other sources for sociological and psychological measures. Author, test title, and subject indexes. HQ728.S86

Handbooks

Family factbook. Consulting ed., Helena Znaniecki Lopata. Chicago, Marquis Academic Media, [1978]. 676p. il.
CC231

In six sections, combining articles and statistics: (1) the family in general; (2) adults and marriage; (3) children; (4) health; (5) work and income; (6) housing. Most of the material has been reprinted, with original source indicated. Subject index.   HQ536.F366

Population planning

Bilsborrow, Richard E. Population in development planning: background and bibliography. Chapel Hill, N.C., Laboratories for Population Statistics-Technical Information Service, Univ. of North Carolina, 1976. 216p. (TIS bibliography ser., 11)
CC232

A classed bibliography of the published literature dealing with "relationships between population factors and social and economic factors, particularly in developing countries."—*Pref.* Chapters cover macroeconomic models and capital formation and the main themes in planning: regional, labor, agricultural, educational, health, and housing. Author index.   Z7164.D3B54

Freedman, Ronald. The sociology of human fertility; an annotated bibliography. N.Y., Irvington Publishers, [1975]. 283p.
CC233

An earlier compilation by the same author appeared as "The sociology of human fertility: a trend report and annotated bibliography" in *Current sociology,* v.10/11, no.2, 1961–62. "The present work consists mainly of an annotated and classified bibliography of the literature on fertility published since 1961. It also includes a reworking of that portion of the original essay which dealt with the basis for the recent interest in the sociology of human fertility and a descriptive model of the classes of variables that affect fertility."—*Pref.* More than 1,650 English-language items, plus an appendix of some 430 additional recent publications listed alphabetically by author and without annotation. Geographical index only.
Z7164.D3F7

International family-planning programs, 1966–1975: a bibliography. Ed. by Katherine Ch'iu Lyle, Sheldon J. Segal. University, Ala., Univ. of Alabama Pr., [1977]. 207p.
CC234

". . . covers sociological, medical and behavioral literature, including books, chapters of books, conference papers, and journal articles."—*p.ix.* Arrangement is by country, with an introductory section on general aspects; within each country section entries are listed alphabetically by author. Subject and author indexes.
Z7164.B5I57

Konoshima, Sumiye, Radel, David and **Buck, Elizabeth Bentzel.** Sources of information on population/family planning: a handbook for Asia. Honolulu, East-West Communication Institute, 1975. 263p.
CC235

"This Handbook contains profiles of sixty-four national, regional, and international information sources. . . . The profile . . . describes its general activities, its information and materials services, its resource base, and the subject and geographical coverage."—*Abstract.* Six indexes: classed subject, keyword subject, institutional name, geographical location, geographic area as subject, audiovisual services.   HQ766.K66

Lucas, Caroline and **Osburn, Margaret.** Population/family planning thesaurus: an alphabetical and hierarchical display of terms drawn from population-related literature in the social sciences. Rev. by Karen Long and Carann Turner. 2d ed. Chapel Hill, Lib., Carolina Population Center, Univ. of North Carolina, 1978. 286p.
CC236

1st ed. 1975.
Lists and indicates relationships among 3,900 terms in population

literature, including equivalent terms in the National Library of Medicine's *Medical subject headings* (MeSH) and the International Institute for the Study of Human Reproduction's *Fertility modification thesaurus.* Intended to be used for information retrieval with the Library's database, which is available to the public through a commercial vendor as *Population bibliography.*   Z695.1.B55L83●

Stettner, Allison G. and **Cowan, Anita P.** Health aspects of family planning: a guide to resources in the United States. N.Y., Human Sciences Pr., [1982]. 247p.   **CC237**

In two sections: pt.1 is an annotated bibliography arranged by subject (e.g., contraceptive methods, adolescents, the handicapped); pt.2 lists reference works by type, together with private and government agencies in the field. Indexed.   Z7164.B5S75

Trzyna, Thaddeus C. Population: an international directory of organizations and information resources. Claremont, Calif., Public Affairs Clearinghouse, 1976. 132p. (Who's doing what ser., 3)
CC238

Aims to provide "in convenient reference form a central source of information about organizations concerned with population and family planning, their programs and activities, key personnel, publications, and other information resources."—*Introd.*   HB850.T79

Union list of population/family planning periodicals: a serial holdings list of 36 North American APLIC member libraries and information centers. Susan Kingsley Pasquariella, ed. and comp. Clarion, Pa., Assoc. for Population/Family Planning Libraries and Information Centers, Internat. (APLIC), 1978. 135p.
CC239

An alphabetical list of approximately 2,500 serial titles held by member libraries; includes all serial titles reported, not only those relevant to population and family planning.   Z6945.U4414

Poverty

Cameron, Colin. Attitudes of the poor and attitudes toward the poor: an annotated bibliography. [Madison], Inst. for Research on Poverty, Univ. of Wisconsin–Madison, [1975]. 182p.
CC240

Emphasis is on publications of the 1965–73 period. Classed arrangement. Author and subject indexes.   Z7164.U5C34

————— ————— Supplement I. [Madison], Inst. for Research on Poverty, Univ. of Wisconsin-Madison, 1977. 157p.

Updates the basic volume through mid-1976. The author's bibliography, *Food stamps,* was issued by the Institute in 1977 (51p.), as was his *Statistics of poverty: a bibliography* (170p.).

Oster, Sharon M., Lake, Elizabeth E. and **Oksman, Conchita Gene.** The definition and measurement of poverty. Boulder, Colo., Westview Pr., [1978]. 2v.   **CC242**

Contents: v.1, A review; v.2, Annotated bibliography.
v.1 serves as a review of the American literature produced since 1950 on factors involved in the definition and measurement of poverty, such as historical definitions, index numbers, family size and composition, regional cost-of-living differences, etc. v.2 presents abstracts of about 1,000 books, articles, government documents, and dissertations, arranged by author and keyed according to the corresponding chapters of v.1; its index lists the literature in the bibliography according to those chapters.   HC110.P5O88

Partington, Martin, Hull, John and **Knight, Susan.** Welfare rights: a bibliography on law and the poor, 1970–1975. London, [Pinter], 1976. 167p.   **CC243**

Within two main divisions—British legal periodical literature, and books—titles are listed according to subject, e.g., legal services, social security law, family law, housing, consumer law, ombudsmen, etc. Civil liberties and labor law are not discussed.
KD3310.A1P37

Poverty and health in the United States; a bibliography with abstracts. N.Y., Medical and Health Research Assoc. of New York City, 1967. 292p. **CC244**

A selective list of studies "which appraise the health status of the poor, analyze the availability and quality of health services, investigate possible causes and effects of medical deprivation and proposals and programs for improving the health care of the disadvantaged."—*Pref.* Author and subject indexes. Semiannual supplements were issued in 1968. RA418.P6

Poverty and human resources abstracts. v.1, no.1–9, no.4, Jan./ Feb. 1966–Dec. 1974. [Ann Arbor, Mich.], 1966–74. Quarterly. **CC245**

Publisher varies. Frequency varies; originally bimonthly.

Published with the cooperation of the Institute of Labor and Industrial Relations, an institute jointly supported by the University of Michigan and Wayne State University.

At head of title: *PHRA.*

Format and content have varied considerably. Latterly an abstracting service covering book and periodical materials relating to "human, social, and manpower problems and solutions ranging from slum rehabilitation and job development training to compensatory education, minority group problems, and rural poverty."— *v.6, no.1–2.* Abstracts are grouped topically, and in later volumes there are author and detailed subject indexes in each issue, with annual cumulated index.

Title changed to: Z7165.U5P2

Human resources abstracts. v.10, no.1– , Mar. 1975– . Beverly Hills, Calif., Sage Publs., 1975– . Quarterly. **CC246**

HD4802.H85

Schlesinger, Benjamin. Poverty in Canada and the United States; overview and annotated bibliography. [Toronto], Univ. of Toronto Pr., [1966]. 211p. **CC247**

The bibliography employs a subject arrangement; author index. Z7164.C4S37

Tompkins, Dorothy Campbell. Poverty in the United States during the sixties: a bibliography. Berkeley, Inst. of Governmental Studies, Univ. of California, 1970. 542p. **CC248**

A topically arranged bibliography of 8,338 citations to a wide variety of materials. Indexed. Z7165.U5T62

Sex and sexual behavior

An annotated bibliography of homosexuality. Vern L. Bullough [and others]. N.Y., Garland, 1976. 2v. **CC249**

Sponsored by the Institute for the Study of Human Resources, Los Angeles.

"The . . . aim has been to bring together representative entries from a multidisciplinary point of view."—*p.xv.* More than 12,700 citations are classed under broad subject headings, e.g., behavioral sciences, education and children, law and its enforcement, novels, the homophile movement, transvestism and transsexualism. Author index and index of pseudonyms for each volume, but no detailed subject approach. Despite the title, annotations are few and exceedingly brief. Z7164.S42A66

Astin, Helen S., Parelman, Allison and **Fisher, Anne.** Sex roles: a research bibliography. Rockville, Md., Nat. Inst. of Mental Health, [1975]. 362p. **CC250**

About 450 entries in classed arrangement, with author and subject indexes. Covers publications of 1960–72. Abstracts are provided. Emphasis is on psychological and sociological attitudes of contemporary "developed" nations. BF692.A87

Barnes, Dorothy L. Rape: a bibliography, 1965–1975. Troy, N.Y., Whitston, 1977. 154p. **CC251**

In three main sections: (1) books, arranged by author; (2) periodical articles, arranged by title; and (3) periodical articles, arranged by subject and repeating the complete entries from the previous section. English-language material only. Author index. Z5703.4.R35B37

A bibliography of prostitution. N.Y., Garland, 1977. 419p. **CC252**

Ed. by Vern Bullough, Barrett Elcano, Margaret Deacon, Bonnie Bullough.

Includes more than 6,400 books and periodical articles arranged by broad topics such as anthropology, area studies (subdivided by country or region), biography, fiction, law, males, war, etc. No detailed subject approach. Author index. Z7164.P95B52

Byerly, Greg and **Rubin, Rick.** Pornography, the conflict over sexually explicit materials in the United States; an annotated bibliography. N.Y., Garland, 1980. 188p. (Garland reference library of social science, v.64) **CC253**

A selective bibliography of 444 citations to English-language monographs, dissertations, government documents, and journal articles, most of them produced in the 1970s. Arrangement is by form and broad subject, with author and subject indexes. Excludes works on art censorship, general censorship, or literary criticism of pornographic works. Z7164.P84B93

Friedman, Leslie. Sex role stereotyping in the mass media: an annotated bibliography. N.Y., Garland, 1977. 324p. **CC254**

Concerns sex role stereotyping in the American mass media. Arranged by broad topic, with more detailed subdivisions. Covers the mass media in general, advertising, broadcast media, film, print media, popular culture (music, humor, comic strips and books, science fiction, pornography), media image of minority group women, media image of men, children's media, impact of media stereotypes on occupational choices. Author and subject indexes. Z7164.S42F74

Grady, Kathleen E., Brannon, Robert W. and **Pleck, Joseph H.** The male sex role: a selected and annotated bibliography. Rockville, Md., Dept. of Health, Education and Welfare, Public Health Service, National Institutes of Health, National Institute of Mental Health. Wash., [for sale by Govt. Prt. Off., 1979]. 196p. (DHEW Pubn. no. (ADM)79–790) **CC254a**

Presents citations to some 250 books and articles organized within 14 topical categories; annotations indicate the population under study, methodology, results, and comments. Author index. Z7164.S42G7

Herzer, Manfred. Bibliographie zur Homosexualität. Verzeichnis des deutschsprachigen nichtbelletristischen Schrifttums zur weiblichen und männlichen Homosexualität aus den Jahren 1466 bis 1975 in chronologischer Reihenfolge zusammengestellt. Berlin, Verlag Rosa Winkel, 1982. 255p. **CC255**

A chronological listing of book and periodical citations, with author and subject indexes. Includes references to reviews of the books cited. Z7164.S42H47

Indiana. University. Institute for Sex Research. Library. Catalog of the social and behavioral sciences monograph section of the Library of the Institute for Sex Research, Indiana University, Bloomington, Indiana. Boston, G. K. Hall, 1975. 4v. **CC256**

Reproduces about 36,500 cards representing some 30,000 books cataloged through Sept. 1973. The Institute was founded in 1947 by Alfred C. Kinsey, and the library contains principally Western-language works from the 19th and 20th centuries in such areas as marriage, women's rights, sex education, sex ethics and religion, abortion, contraception, venereal disease, etc.

Continued and complemented by:

—— Catalog of periodical literature in the social and behavioral sciences section, . . . including supplement to monographs, 1973–1975. Boston, G. K. Hall, 1976. 4v. **CC257**

Reproduces about 68,800 cards in dictionary arrangement, giving citations to some 14,000 journal and reprint articles, 200 doctoral dissertations, and 1,000 monographs (these last added to the collection 1973–75). Subject headings are taken from the Institute's *Sexual nomenclature: a thesaurus,* comp. by JoAnn Brooks and Helen C. Hofer (Boston, G. K. Hall, 1976. 403p.).

Institute for Sex Research. Sex research: bibliographies from the Institute for Sex Research. Comp. by Joan Scherer Brewer and Rod W. Wright. [Phoenix], Oryx Pr. in assoc. with Neal-Schuman Publishers, [1979]. 212p.   **CC258**

"These are not comprehensive bibliographies, but represent basic works, other bibliographies, and literature reviews" (*Introd.*), as well as conference papers, dissertations, and other sources published mainly through 1977. Broad subject arrangement, with author and subject indexes.   Z7164.S42I57

Kemmer, Elizabeth Jane. Rape and rape-related issues: an annotated bibliography. N.Y., Garland, 1977. 174p.   **CC259**

Includes literature on rape published in English for the period 1965–76. Author arrangement; subject index.   Z7164.S44K45

Lesbian studies: present and future. [Ed. by] Margaret Cruikshank. Old Westbury, N.Y., Feminist Pr., [1982]. 286p.   **CC260**

Essays on lesbian studies in the curriculum; numerous bibliographic references. Also provides resource directory, sample syllabi, and annotated bibliography (p.199–273).   HQ75.3.L48

Parker, William. Homosexuality; a selective bibliography of over 3,000 items. Metuchen, N. J., Scarecrow Pr., 1971. 323p.   **CC261**

Intends to include all significant writings on the subject in English (or translated into English) published through 1969. Arranged by type of publication (e.g., books, articles in popular magazines, articles in legal journals, articles in medical and scientific journals, etc.) with author and subject indexes. Meant for the layman as well as for the researcher and professional.   Z7164.S42P35

——— Homosexuality bibliography: supplement, 1970–1975. Metuchen, N.J., Scarecrow Pr., 1977. 337p.   **CC262**

Lists more than 3,100 entries by type—books (non-fiction), pamphlets and documents, theses and dissertations, etc.—with subject and author indexes. Appendixes list: movies; television programs; audiovisual aids; American laws applicable to consensual adult homosexuals. A second supplement covering publications of 1976–82 appeared in 1985 (395p.).   Z7164.S42P35 suppl.

Rubin, Rick and **Byerly, Greg.** Incest, the last taboo: an annotated bibliography. N.Y., Garland, 1983. 169p. (Garland reference library of social science, v.143)   **CC263**

419 citations are grouped by form, including books, dissertations, articles, and audiovisual materials. Emphasis is on English-language titles published since 1970. Indexed by periodical title, author, and subject.   HQ72.U53R8

Schlesinger, Benjamin. Sexual abuse of children; a resource guide and annotated bibliography. Toronto, Univ. of Toronto Pr., [1982]. 200p.   **CC264**

The resource guide provides several chapters on the current knowledge about incest and other forms of sexual abuse of children; the selected annotated bibliography consists of about 180 items arranged by topic; audiovisual resources are listed separately, as are relevant associations. Author index.   HQ72.C3S35

Sex studies index, 1980– . Boston, G. K. Hall, 1982– . Annual.   **CC265**

Comp. at Indiana University, Alfred C. Kinsey Institute for Sex Research.

Indexes articles in periodicals and collective works by author and by subject headings derived from the Institute's *Sexual nomenclature* (CC257n).   Z7164.S42S39

Wharton, George F. Sexuality and aging: an annotated bibliography. Metuchen, N.J., Scarecrow Pr., 1981. 251p.   **CC266**

A 1978 ed. without annotations had title: *A bibliography of sexuality and aging.*

1,106 citations to a wide variety of literature are grouped in broad subject classifications, with author and title indexes. Some foreign language titles are included.   Z7164.S42W48

Urbanization

Bibliography

See also City planning, BE301–BE309.

Alexander, Ernest R., Catanese, Anthony James and **Sawicki, David S.** Urban planning: a guide to information sources. Detroit, Gale, [1979]. 165p. (Urban studies information guide ser., v.2)   **CC267**

For full information *see* BE301.

Bell, Gwen, Randall, Edwina and **Roeder, Judith E. R.** Urban environments and human behavior: an annotated bibliography. Stroudsburg, Pa., Dowden, Hutchinson & Ross, [1973]. 271p. (Community development ser., 2)   **CC268**

Lists a selection of books, essays, and periodical articles which discuss behavior and urban forms in terms of: (1) the design viewpoint; (2) the social science viewpoint; and (3) parts of the urban environment, from a room to a new town. International in scope; English-language materials only. Author and subject indexes.   Z5942.B35

Bestor, George Clinton and **Jones, Holway R.** City planning bibliography; a basic bibliography of sources and trends. 3d ed. N.Y., American Society of Civil Engineers in cooperation with the California Council of Civil Engineers and Land Surveyors, 1972. 518p.   **CC269**

For full information *see* BE302.

Branch, Melville Campbell. Comprehensive urban planning; a selective annotated bibliography with related materials. Beverly Hills, Calif., Sage, [1970]. 477p.   **CC270**

Focus is almost entirely on U.S. planning experience, problems and future cities. References relate to comprehensive urban planning and thus include land use, economic geography, public administration, environment, and technological trends. Includes periodical articles, conference papers, books, reports, pamphlets, and bibliographies. Subject, author, and title indexes.   Z5942.B7

Breese, Gerald William. Urban Southeast Asia: a selected bibliography of accessible research, reports, and related materials on urbanism and urbanization in Hong Kong, Indonesia, Malaysia, the Philippines, Singapore, Thailand, Vietnam. [N.Y., Southeast Asia Development Advisory Group, 1973] 165p.   **CC271**

An international bibliography, excluding census publications, newspapers, and maps; is not concerned with the areas of history, political science, public administration, and geography. Author index.   Z7164.U7B68

Brunn, Stanley D. Urbanization in developing countries: an international bibliography. East Lansing, Latin American Studies Center and the Center for Urban Affairs, Michigan State Univ., 1971. 693p. (Latin American Studies Center. Research report, 8)   **CC272**

More than 7,000 items arranged by country. Index by broad subject field only.   Z7164.U7B7

Buenker, John D., Greenfield, Gerald Michael and **Murin, William J.** Urban history: a guide to information sources. Detroit, Gale, [1981]. 448p. (American government and history information guide ser., v.9)   **CC273**

An annotated, topically arranged bibliography of published sources and dissertations on United States urban history prior to the 1960s. Author, title, and subject indexes. Z5942.B88

Council of Planning Librarians. Exchange bibliography. no.1–1564/65. [Monticello, Ill., The Council], 1959–78. **CC274**

Place of publication varies.

Each bibliography is on a specific topic touching on some aspect of city planning, urbanization, and related problems. Range of topics is very wide, international in scope, and some deal with historical or background information on urban affairs.

Continued by the Council's *CPL bibliography* (1978–), the first three numbers of which index the entire set of *Exchange bibliographies*.

Filipovitch, Anthony J. and **Reeves, Earl J.** Urban community: a guide to information sources. Detroit, Gale, [1978]. 286p. (Urban studies information guide ser., v.4) **CC275**

A selection of the research done between 1970 and mid-1976 on urban sociology, primarily dealing with American and British experiences. Annotated entries are grouped by subject, e.g., theories of community, physical aspects, social groups and classes, size and density, safety, quality of life, etc. Lists of cited journals, bibliographies, abstracts and indexes. Author, title, and subject indexes.
Z7164.S68F54

Golany, Gideon. New towns planning and development: a world-wide bibliography. Wash., Urban Land Inst., [1973]. 256p. (ULI research report 20) **CC276**

A classified listing of more than 4,500 items on the development of towns from early times to the present, written in the 20th century. Emphasis is on developments in the United States and England, but there is coverage for some other countries as well. Detailed table of contents, but no index. Z5942.G64

Hardoy, Jorge Enrique. Urbanización en América Latina: una bibliografía sobre su historia. [Buenos Aires, Centro de Estudios Urbanos y Regionales, Inst. Torcuato di Tella, 1975–77] 3v. **CC277**

Covers the pre-Columbian period through the 1920s. Partially annotated. Arranged by chronological era, then by topic or geographic area. No index. Z7165.L3H26

Hoover, Dwight W. Cities. N.Y., Bowker, 1976. 231p. **CC278**

More than 1,000 items in classed arrangement, with author and title indexes. "The basic criteria for inclusion . . . were contemporaneity and availability of materials."—*Pref.* Includes books, films, filmstrips, and other media. Annotated. Z7164.U7H66

Kline, Paula. Urban needs: a bibliography and directory for community resource centers. Metuchen, N.J., Scarecrow Pr., 1978. 257p. **CC279**

A bibliography of directories, manuals, guides, and handbooks providing information on programs and agencies in the areas of education, employment, housing, community development, consumer protection, legal services, health care, recreation, and social services. Focuses on material published between 1969 and 1977, on the national level. Classed subject arrangement, with author, title, and subject indexes. Z7165.U5K57

Meyer, Jon K. Bibliography on the urban crisis: the behavioral, psychological, and sociological aspects of the urban crisis. Chevy Chase, Md., Nat. Inst. of Mental Health, 1969. 452p. (Public Health Service publ. no.1948) **CC280**

Attempts to provide "a comprehensive listing of the literature, both academic and popular, on the causes, effects, and responses to urban disorders."—*Pref.* Within broad subject categories, items are listed in reverse chronological order; author and keyword-in-title indexes. Emphasis is on publications of 1954–68.
Z7165.U5M43

Murphy, Thomas P. Urban indicators: a guide to information sources. Detroit, Gale, [1980]. 234p. (Urban studies information guide ser., v.10) **CC281**

A selective, annotated bibliography of research literature on social indicators applied to urban situations. In six chapters, dealing with: development of urban indicators; types (policy oriented, descriptive, analytic); methodology; applications; program evaluation; future directions. Lists of relevant journals, abstracts and indexes, and associations. Author, title, and subject indexes. HT167.M87

O'Connor, Anthony M. Urbanization in tropical Africa; an annotated bibliography. Boston, G. K. Hall, [1981]. 381p. **CC282**

Focuses on English- or French-language publications and doctoral dissertations produced since 1960 on the urbanization process, excluding public administration and labor relations. Geographical arrangement; only the general African items are subdivided by topic. Indexed by place names and authors. Z7165.A47O26

Palumbo, Dennis James and **Taylor, George Albert.** Urban policy: a guide to information sources. Detroit, Gale, [1978]. 198p. (Urban studies information guide ser., v.6) **CC283**

Annotations focus on books, chapters in books, and scholarly articles published within the last 20 years. In five chapters, with appropriate topical subdivisions: (1) models and analytical theories; (2) community characteristics which determine policy; (3) policy goals; (4) policy formulation and implementation; (5) policy evaluation methods. Author, title, and subject indexes. Z7164.S68P34

Quarterly digest of urban and regional research. v.15– , Fall 1968– . Urbana, Univ. of Illinois, Bureau of Planning, [1968–]. **CC284**

Supersedes the Bureau's *Research digest* (v.1–14, 1954–67) and continues its numbering. Research projects, both completed and in progress, in the United States and Canada are listed under six broad headings—Physical environment; Demography and human behavior; Urban and regional economy; Social services; Land use and transportation; and Government—with appropriate subdivisions. Each issue is indexed by subject, agency, place, and name.

Ross, Bernard H. and **Fritschler, A. Lee.** Urban affairs bibliography; an annotated guide to the literature in the field. 3d ed. Wash., School of Govt. and Pub. Admin., College of Pub. Affairs, American Univ., 1974. 85p. **CC285**

1st ed. 1969.
Limited to books. Classed arrangement; no index.

Z7165.U5F74

Sable, Martin Howard. Latin American urbanization: a guide to the literature, organizations, and personnel. Metuchen, N.J., Scarecrow Pr., 1971. 1077p. **CC286**

Intended as a partial supplement to Sable's *Guide to Latin American studies* (DB225n). A classed bibliography on the problems of urbanization and allied fields is followed by a directory of research institutes and organizations. Indexed. Z7165.L3S28

Shumsky, Neil L. and **Crimmins, Timothy.** Urban America: a historical bibliography. Santa Barbara, ABC-Clio, [1983]. 422p. **CC287**

A classed bibliography of 4,068 items; subject and author indexes.
HT123.U725

Sutcliffe, Anthony. The history of urban and regional planning: an annotated bibliography. London, Mansell, [1981]. 284p. **CC288**

About 1,400 citations to secondary materials are grouped into eight major subject chapters, subdivided by detailed topics. General sections on planning and pertinent reference titles are followed by chapters on planning in individual countries and in towns and cities, individual planners, 19th-century antecedents, and various aspects, such as new towns. Indexed by names and authors. Z5942.S931

Town Planning Institute, London. Planning research; a register of research of interest to those concerned with town and country planning. 1st–3d ed. London, 1961–68. 3v. **CC289**

Ed.1 records work commenced or completed 1948–58; ed.2, 1948–63; ed.3, 1964–67.

Lists research work, completed or in progress, "carried out in the United Kingdom in town and country planning, landscape architecture, surveying and related fields."—*Pref., 2d ed.* Descriptive notes on the projects are given, and details of publications are provided as applicable. Classed arrangement with indexes.   Z5942.T6

Van Willigen, John. The Indian city: a bibliographic guide to the literature on urban India. New Haven, Human Relations Area Files, 1979. 2v.   **CC290**

A list of over 3,800 books, essays, periodical articles, conference papers, theses and dissertations published between the mid-19th century and 1973. Arranged by name of geographic entity (city, state, region), then by broad subject area. No author index. For a more topical, though chronologically more limited approach, the user is referred to Ashish Bose's *Bibliography on urbanization in India, 1947–1976* (New Delhi, Tata McGraw-Hill, 1976).   Z5942.V36

White, Paul M. Soviet urban and regional planning: a bibliography with abstracts. N.Y., St. Martin's, [1980]. 276p.   **CC291**

A topically arranged bibliography of 370 citations, fully annotated, to English-, French- and German-language sources and translations of Soviet works. Author and subject indexes.   Z5942.W48

Zikmund, Joseph and **Dennis, Deborah Ellis.** Suburbia: a guide to information sources. Detroit, Gale, [1979]. 142p. (Urban studies information guide ser., v.9)   **CC292**

An annotated, topically arranged bibliography of 392 references published since 1965; popular periodical articles, doctoral dissertations, and government documents have been excluded. Chapters on demography, education, politics, economics, sociology, and minorities. Author, title, and subject indexes.   Z7164.U7Z54

Current

Sage urban studies abstracts. v.1, no.1– , Feb. 1973– . Beverly Hills, Calif., Sage Publs., 1973– . Quarterly.   **CC293**

Each issue offers some 250 abstracts of English-language books, periodical articles, reports, and documents. A section for "related citations" includes similar materials (some in foreign languages) without annotations. Author and subject indexes.   HT51.S24

Urban affairs abstracts. Aug. 1971– . Wash., National League of Cities, 1971– . Weekly with semiannual and annual cumulations.   **CC294**

A selective abstracting service based on about 350 titles received in the National League of Cities Library. Abstracts are grouped according to about fifty broad subjects. Semiannual and annual cumulations are indexed by author, geographic area (states, cities, counties, foreign countries), and subject descriptors. Emphasis is on the United States, Canada, and Great Britain.   HT123.U7

Dictionaries and encyclopedias

Abrams, Charles. The language of cities; a glossary of terms. N.Y., Viking, [1971]. 365p.   **CC295**

An attempt to identify and define terms used in the various disciplines concerned with urban affairs. Includes terms from the fields of housing, city planning, land economics, real estate, public administration, architecture, social welfare, transportation, public law, government, and race relations.   HT108.5.A24

Akademie für Raumforschung und Landesplanung. Handwörterbuch der Raumforschung und Raumordnung. 2. Aufl. Hannover, Jänecke, 1970. 3v.   **CC296**

For full information *see* BE306.

Clapp, James A. The city; a dictionary of quotable thought on cities and urban life. [New Brunswick, N.J., Rutgers Univ.], Center for Urban Policy Research, [1984]. 288p. il.   **CC297**

Author arrangement; indexed by city and subject.

HT111.C576

Encyclopedia of urban planning. Arnold Whittick, ed. N.Y., McGraw-Hill, 1974. 1218p. il. (Repr.: Huntington, N.Y., R. E. Krieger, 1980)   **CC298**

An international encyclopedia on the various aspects of urban planning and closely related subjects (e.g., transportation, sociology, economics and aesthetics), with articles contributed by specialists. Covers "48 of the principal countries of the world where systems of planning legislation and administration are maintained" (*Pref.*), with indication of professional practice, education and training, institutions, geographical and climatic conditions, traditions in planning, etc. Includes short articles on well-known planners, architects, sociologists, etc., who have made distinctive contributions in this field. Some brief bibliographies. Index of topics and of personal and geographical names.   HT166.E5

Schultz, Marilyn Spigel and **Kassen, Vivian Loeb.** Encyclopedia of community planning and environmental management. N.Y., Facts on File, [1984]. 475p. il., maps.   **CC299**

About 2,000 articles, including biographies, entries for legislation, governmental and private agencies, etc., concerned with planning and the environment in the United States, Canada, and Western Europe. Thematic index.   HD108.6.S38

Vocabulaire international des termes d'urbanisme et d'architecture . . . . Présenté par Jean-Henri Calsat et Jean-Pierre Sydler. Paris, Société de Diffusion des Techniques du Bâtiment et des Travaux Publics, 1970. 350p. il.   **CC300**

For full information *see* BE309.

Directories

University urban research centers. [Ed.1]–2. Wash., Urban Institute, [1969–72].   **CC301**

Title varies: 1st ed. called *A directory of university urban research centers.*

In addition to address and name of the director for each center, there is a statement of purpose, indication of past and current projects, staff size, publications, etc.

Winston, Eric V. A. Directory of urban affairs information and research centers. Metuchen, N.J., Scarecrow Pr., 1970. 175p.   **CC302**

Provides information on more than 250 organizations, agencies, and institutions "actively involved in the eradication of our urban ills."—*Introd.* Alphabetical listing with geographical and subject indexes.   HT110.W5

RACE RELATIONS AND MINORITIES

Bibliography

See also CC101.

Allworth, Edward. Soviet Asia, bibliographies: a compilation of social science and humanities sources on the Iranian, Mongolian, and Turkic nationalities, with an essay on the Soviet-Asian controversy. N.Y., Praeger, [1975]. 686p.   **CC303**

Lists about 5,200 bibliographies, in book and periodical format, published in Czarist Russia and the Soviet Union between 1850 and 1970. Classified by five geographical divisions, and further subdivided into national groups, entries are listed under broad subject categories. Annotations indicate: language of the book, main languages of the entries and number of entries, period covered and dates within which the entries were published, and pagination.

Z3414.M54A44

Ascolani, Augusto and **Birindelli, Anna Maria.** Introduzione bibliografica ai problemi delle migrazioni . . . con appendici: Sugli aspetti della criminalità fra i lavoratori migranti a cura di Giorgio Marbach. Roma, 1971. 457p.   **CC304**

At head of title: Comitato Italiano per lo Studio dei Problemi della Popolazione.

An international bibliography in classed arrangement. Most entries are annotated. Geographical index, but none of authors.

Z7164.I3A78

Bailey, J. P. and **Headlam, Freya.** Intercontinental migration to Latin America: a select bibliography. London, Inst. of Latin American Studies, 1980. 62p.   **CC305**

Covers the 1830–1950 migration of about 50 to 70 million Europeans and Asians to Latin America. Section A, "Latin America in general," and Section B, "Individual countries of settlement," are further subdivided for general migration, and migration from specific regions and ethnic groups. 570 citations; author index.

Z7164.I3B433

Bentley, G. Carter. Ethnicity and nationality: a bibliographic guide. Seattle, Univ. of Washington Pr., [1981]. 381, [53]p. (Pubns. on ethnicity and nationality of the School of Internat. Studies, Univ. of Wash., v.3)   **CC306**

A selective, partially annotated bibliography of more than 2,300 English-language items published through 1979; excludes "ethnic studies" literature (e.g., biographies, literature, folklore, music, dance and drama, newspapers and periodicals, and histories), as well as ethnographies of individual groups. The first 308 entries are annotated; all entries are coded as to content, geographical area covered, and group under study. Alphabetical author arrangement; indexed by geographical area and content.   Z5118.E84B46

Brana-Shute, Rosemary. A bibliography of Caribbean migration and Caribbean immigrant communities. Gainesville, Fla., Reference and Bibliographic Dept., Univ. of Florida Libs. in coop. with the Center for Latin American Studies, Univ. of Florida, 1983. 339p. (Univ. of Florida. Libs. Reference and Bibliographic Dept. Bibliographic ser., no.9)   **CC307**

Almost 2,600 citations on emigration and immigration to the Caribbean islands, Belize, Guyana, Suriname, and French Guiana. International in scope; includes published materials, theses and government reports. Author listing; indexed by location, topic, and names.   Z7164.I3B7

Briani, Vittorio. Italian immigrants abroad: a bibliography on the Italian experience outside Italy in Europe, the Americas, Australia, and Africa. Ed., with a new introd. and supplemental bibliography by Francesco Cordasco. Detroit, Blaine Ethridge, [1979]. xlix, 229p.   **CC308**

1967 ed. publ. as: *Emigrazione a lavoro italiano all' estero* (Rome, Ministero degli Affari Esteri).

The original work consists of more than 2,000 entries arranged in chronological sequence within the following subject categories: (1) general emigration history; (2) Argentina; (3) Brazil; (4) United States; (5) other American countries; (6) Belgium; (7) France; (8) Switzerland; (9) other European countries; (10) the European Community and international organizations; (11) Australia; (12) Africa; and (13) internal migrations. Indexed by author, regions of Italy, countries, and subjects. Cordasco's supplement is a partially annotated bibliography of about 350 titles dealing with the Italian experience in the United States.   Z7165.I8B73

Buenker, John D. and **Burckel, Nicholas C.** Immigration and ethnicity: a guide to information sources. Detroit, Gale, [1977]. 305p. (American government and history information guide ser., 1)   **CC309**

A selected, annotated bibliography of more than 1,400 English-language books, periodical articles, and doctoral dissertations, em-phasizing post-1945 imprints. Excludes Afro-Americans and Native Americans, fiction, autobiographical and audiovisual material. Topical arrangement includes general accounts, "old" and "new" immigration, Orientals, "recent" ethnics after the 1920s, acculturation and restriction, private centers and federal government information sources. Author and subject indexes.   Z7165.U5B83

Centro Paraguayo de Documentación Social. Las migraciones en America Latina: bibliografía. Centro Paraguayo de Estudios Sociológicos, Centro Paraguayo de Documentación Social, Grupo de Trabajo de Migraciones Internas, Comisión de Población y Desarrollo, Consejo Latinoamericano de Ciencias Sociales. Buenos Aires, El Consejo, 1976. 76p.   **CC310**

1,556 entries are arranged by author or main entry; indexed by topical subject, country, and chronological period. Lists other relevant bibliographies.   Z7165.L3C44

Cordasco, Francesco. Italian Americans: a guide to information sources. Detroit, Gale, [1978]. 222p. (Ethnic studies information guide ser., 2)   **CC311**

Some 2,000 English- and Italian-language sources are grouped under five main headings: (1) General reference works; (2) Social sciences; (3) History and regional studies; (4) Applied sciences; (5) Humanities. Two separate chapters deal with newspapers and periodicals, and fraternal, professional, and religious organizations. A very brief appendix treats audiovisual materials. Locations are indicated for rare items.

Cordasco is the author of two earlier, related publications: *Italians in the United States: a bibliography* (N.Y., Oriole, 1972) and *The Italian American experience: an annotated and classified bibliographical guide* (N.Y., B. Franklin, 1974).   Z1361.I8C659

Doezema, Linda Pegman. Dutch Americans: a guide to information sources. Detroit, Gale, 1979. 314p. (Ethnic studies information guide ser., v.3)   **CC312**

An annotated bibliography of about 800 English- and Dutch-language sources in four main sections: (1) reference works; (2) general works on the Dutch in America; (3) the Colonial period; (4) the new immigration, from 1846 to the present. Appendixes list archives and libraries, newspapers and periodicals, and audiovisual materials and curriculum aids. Author, title, and subject indexes.

Z1361.D8D64

European immigration and ethnicity in the United States and Canada: a historical bibliography. David L. Brye, ed. [Santa Barbara, Calif., ABC-Clio, 1983] 458p. (Clio bibliography ser., 7)   **CC313**

4,066 abstracts of periodical articles derived from the database of *America: history and life,* v.11–17 (1973–79). Excludes English settlement before 1783 and early Spanish immigration (which is to be covered in a future volume). Under separate sections for United States and Canada, entries are grouped by national group or subject area. Subject and author indexes.   Z1361.E4E9

Gakovich, Robert P. and **Radovich, Milan M.** Serbs in the United States and Canada: a comprehensive bibliography. [Minneapolis], Immigration History Research Center, Univ. of Minnesota, 1976. 129p. il. (IHRC ethnic bibliography, no.1)   **CC314**

A bibliography and partial union catalog for nearly 800 archival collections, books, pamphlets, and articles; also lists current and historical newspapers and periodicals. Author index.

Other titles in the series include: no.2, *Hungarians in the United States and Canada,* comp. and ed. by Joseph Szeplaki (1977. 113p.); and no.3, *Slovenes in the United States and Canada,* by Joseph D. Dwyer (1981. 196p.).   Z1361.S4G34

Guide to Swedish-American archival and manuscript sources in the United States. Chicago, Swedish-American Historical Society, [1983]. 600p.   **CC315**

A survey of 3,090 collections of personal and private papers, records of businesses, churches, and fraternal organizations relating to Swedish immigration to, as well as life in, the United States.

Arranged by state and city; collections are briefly described. Indexed.   Z1361.S9G8

Haines, David W. Refugee resettlement in the United States: an annotated bibliography on the adjustment of Cuban, Soviet and Southeast Asian refugees. Wash., Office of Refugee Resettlement, Dept. of Health and Human Services, 1981. 104p.   **CC316**

Cites 304 titles relevant to refugee resettlement within the past 20 years; includes printed materials, and unpublished papers and reports. Author listing; subject index.   HV640.4.U54H15

Horak, Stephan M. Eastern European national minorities, 1919–1980: a handbook. Littleton, Colo., Libraries Unlimited, 1985. 353p.   **CC317**

A selective, annotated international bibliography of 982 items. Each country chapter includes a historical summary followed by bibliographic citations on minority groups. Includes Slovene and Croat minorities in Italy and Austria, 1945–1980. Statistical data are tabulated, and research centers in Eastern European countries are described. Author/title index.   Z2483.H53

International Development Research Centre. Migration Task Force. Social change and internal migration; a review of research findings from Africa, Asia, and Latin America. [Ottawa, IDRC, 1977] 128p.   **CC317a**

Alan Simmons, Sergio Diaz-Briquets, Aprodício A. Laquian, comps.

Literature reviews for the three areas mentioned in the title cover determinants of migration, migrant characteristics, consequences of migration, and policy implications. Text citations refer to a bibliography (p.113–28) for complete information.   HB2121.I57

Jerabek, Esther. Czechs and Slovaks in North America: a bibliography. N.Y., Czechoslovak Soc. of Arts & Sciences in America; Chicago, Czechoslovak Nat. Council of America, 1976. 448p.   **CC318**

A classed bibliography of more than 7,600 items relating to Czechs and Slovaks in North America. Useful list of periodicals and newspapers, p.314–64. Fully indexed.

Johnson, Harry Alleyn. Ethnic American minorities: a guide to media and materials. N.Y., Bowker, 1976. 304p.   **CC319**

"The primary purpose of this book . . . is . . . to present a highly documented, annotated source of instructional materials and media on four major minorities—Afro-Americans, Asian Americans, Native Indian Americans, and Spanish-speaking Americans."—*Pref.* Chapters by a specialist on each minority conclude with annotated entries for multimedia resources, classed by type. A fifth chapter treats other ethnic minorities. Directory of producers and distributors. Title index for media, as well as a general index.   E184.A1J58

Keresztesi, Michael and **Cocozzoli, Gary.** German-American history and life; a guide to information sources. Detroit, Gale, [1980]. 372p. (Ethnic studies information guide ser., v.4)   **CC320**

About 1,000 English-language monographs are grouped by broad subjects. Biographies, scholarly series titles, and journals are noted. There is a directory of archival and literary resources. Author, title, and subject indexes.   Z1361.G37K47

Kinloch, Graham Charles. Race and ethnic relations: an annotated bibliography. N.Y., Garland, 1984. 250p. (Garland bibliographies in sociology, v.3; Garland reference library of social science, v.226)   **CC321**

A classed bibliography of English-language books and articles published 1960–80 on intergroup relations, primarily in the United States but with some attention to other societies. Emphasis on social science literature; 1,068 items. Author and subject indexes.   Z1361.E4K54

Kinton, Jack F. American ethnic groups and the revival of cultural pluralism: evaluative sourcebook for the 1970's. 4th

ed. [Aurora, Ill., Social Science & Sociological Resources], 1974. 206p.   **CC322**

Lists books and articles in a classed arrangement. No index.   Z1361.E4K55

Madan, Raj. Colored minorities in Great Britain; a comprehensive bibliography, 1970–1977. Westport, Conn., Greenwood Pr., [1979]. 199p.   **CC323**

A subject arrangement of more than 1,800 English-language titles on the "non-white" peoples of Asia, Africa, and the West Indies, both immigrants and citizens, living in Great Britain. Includes books, government publications, theses and dissertations, pamphlets, and periodical articles. Author, title, and subject indexes. For retrospective coverage, the user is referred to Ambalavaner Sivanandan's *Coloured minorities in Britain* (3d ed., London, Institute of Race Relations, 1969).   Z2027.N4M3

Mangalam, J. J. Human migration; a guide to migration literature in English, 1955–1962. Lexington, Univ. of Kentucky Pr., 1968. 194p.   **CC324**

In three sections: (1) an annotated bibliography of articles, chapters of books, and dissertations; (2) an unannotated listing of books and reports; and (3) an unannotated listing of migration entries from *Industry and labour, International labour review,* and *Population index* for the period indicated. Subject index.   Z7164.D3M36

Metress, Seamus P. The Irish-American experience: a guide to the literature. [Wash.], University Pr. of America, [1981]. 220p.   **CC325**

A topically arranged bibliography of social science literature on the Irish in the United States and Canada.   Z1361.I7M47

Miller, Wayne Charles [and others]. Comprehensive bibliography for the study of American minorities. N.Y., New York Univ. Pr., 1976. 2v. (1380p.)   **CC326**

A classified, briefly annotated bibliography of approximately 29,300 entries; mainly monographs are cited, with articles and pamphlets included for those ethnic groups with less coverage (exceptions being made for American Indian artists and the black American civil rights movement). Good coverage of many ethnic groups not represented elsewhere. Includes other bibliographies, periodicals and indexes, as well as works in social sciences and humanities. Historical-bibliographical essays preceding each group have been reprinted in Miller's *Handbook of American minorities* (1976). Author and title indexes.   Z1361.E4M529

Myroniuk, Halyna and **Worobec, Christine.** Ukrainians in North America: a select bibliography. St. Paul, Minn., Immigration History Research Center, Univ. of Minn.; Toronto, Multicultural History Society of Ontario, [1981]. 236p.   **CC327**

A classed bibliography of about 2,000 titles. Name index.   Z1395.U47M9

North, Jeannette H. and **Grodsky, Susan J.** Immigration literature: abstracts of demographic, economic, and policy studies. [Wash., U.S. Dept of Justice, Immigration and Naturalization Service, Office of Planning, Evaluation, and Budgeting; for sale by Supt. of Docs.;], 1979. 89p.   **CC328**

English-language sources, published since the 1960s, are grouped by broad subject area, then by type of publication. The subject focus is on immigration to the United States from 1965 to the present, with special attention to "brain drain" studies, political refugees, undocumented aliens, and the enforcement and administration of the 1965 Immigration and Nationality Act. A large number of the articles were retrieved from a search of 16 databases of the Lockheed DIALOG system.   JV6455.N67

Oaks, Priscilla. Minority studies: a selective annotated bibliography. Boston, G. K. Hall, [1975]. 303p.   **CC329**

A section of general studies is followed by sections (with appropriate subdivisions by type of material and subject) on Native Americans, Spanish Americans, Afro-Americans, and Asian Americans. Author/title index. Includes popular as well as scholarly materials. 1,800 items.   Z1361.E4O24

Pap, Leo. The Portuguese in the United States: a bibliography. [N.Y.], Center for Migration Studies, 1976. 80p.   **CC330**

A classed bibliography of books, periodical articles, master's theses, doctoral dissertations, and federal government publications. 800 items; no index.   Z1361.P65P36

Pochmann, Henry August. Bibliography of German culture in America to 1940. Rev. and corrected by Arthur R. Schultz with addenda, errata, and expanded index. Millwood, N.Y., Kraus Internat. Pubns., 1982. 489p.   **CC331**

1st ed. 1953.

The approximately 13,400 entries of the first edition are reprinted and an additional 4,900 entries are collected in the addenda section of this edition; corrections and changes to the old material are presented in the errata section. New materials are strongest in the fields of Pennsylvania German culture, emigration, World War I, and genealogies. Author arrangement; the index includes entries in both the bibliography and addenda.   Z1361.G37P6

Schultz, Arthur R. German-American relations and German culture in America: a subject bibliography, 1941–1980. Millwood, N.Y., Kraus Internat. Pubns., [1984]. 2v.   **CC331a**

Forms a supplement to Pochmann's *German culture in America* (above), listing "works on German ethnic culture and history in America, as well as sources dealing with German-American literary, philosophical, and cultural relations. Included here are books, monographs, articles, and dissertations from the past forty years, and the reviews thereof."—*Pref.* Some annotations; index. Appendix of academic programs, festivals, historic sites, museums, etc.

Emil Meynen's *Bibliographie des Deutschtums der kolonialzeitlichen Einwanderung in Nordamerika . . . 1683–1933* (Leipzig, Harrassowitz, 1937) has been reprinted under an English title, *Bibliography on the colonial Germans of North America, especially the Pennsylvania Germans and their descendants* (Baltimore, Genealogical Pub. Co., 1982. 636p.).   Z1361.G37S38

Potgieter, Pieter Jacobus Johannes Stephanus. Index to literature on race relations in South Africa, 1910–1975. Boston, G. K. Hall, [1979]. 555p.   **CC332**

Comp. for the Potchefstroom University for Christian Higher Education.

A list of books, periodical articles, and some South African official publications (usually non-parliamentary). In two parts: (1) subject index, with brief author-title information, and (2) author index, with full bibliographic information. Subject index lacks consistency in use of headings. A review pointing out other shortcomings of this work appears in *Africana journal,* v.11, no.4 (1980), p.368–69.   Z3608.R3P67

Race relations abstracts. v.1–2, no.2. London, Inst. of Race Relations, 1968–70.   **CC333**

Ceased publication.

Abstracts of periodical articles in subject arrangement; author index in each issue. Emphasis on the British situation, but includes some material from Europe, the United States, Australia, and New Zealand.

Continued by:

Sage race relations abstracts. v.1, no.1– , Nov. 1975– . London & Beverly Hills, Calif., Sage, 1976– . Quarterly.   **CC334**

Published on behalf of the Institute of Race Relations, London.

Abstracts European and American periodical literature on immigration and race relations, with some books, essays, and "grass-roots and other fugitive literature" included. Some British emphasis. Each issue contains a bibliographical essay, e.g., "The Netherlands as a multi-racial society." Author and subject, but no geographical, indexes.   HT1521.S15

Recent immigration to the United States: the literature of the social sciences. Wash., Smithsonian Institution Pr., 1976. 112p. RIIES bibliographic studies, 1)   **CC335**

Prep. for the Research Institute on Immigration and Ethnic Studies, Smithsonian Institution, by Paul Meadows, Mark LaGory, Linda Leue and Peter Meadows.

A bibliography on post-World War II immigration to the United States, emphasizing the themes of general migration theory, world immigration trends, the impact of immigration on the home country and on the United States, immigration policy in countries of origin and settlement, the settlement process, and comparison of the "old" and "new" immigrants. No index. An extract from this work was published as a special essay in *Sage race relations abstracts,* v.2, no.3 (June 1977), p.1–30.   Z7164.I3R38

Schlachter, Gail A. and **Belli, Donna.** Minorities and women: a guide to reference literature in the social sciences. Los Angeles, Reference Services Pr., 1977. 349p.   **CC336**

Descriptive annotations for over 800 English-language reference materials on minorities and women in America. Divided into information sources (fact-books, biographies, documentary sources, directories, and statistical materials) and citation sources (bibliographies, indexes, abstracts, etc.). Further subdivided by group: minorities, American Indians, Asian Americans, black Americans, Spanish Americans, and women. Author, title, and subject indexes.   Z7964.U49S34

Spalek, John M. Guide to the archival materials of the German-speaking emigration to the United States after 1933. Charlottesville, Publ. for the Bibliographical Soc. of the Univ. of Virginia by the Univ. Pr. of Virginia, [1978]. 1133p.   **CC337**

For full information *see* DB66.

Tolzmann, Don Heinrich. German-Americana: a bibliography. Metuchen, N.J., Scarecrow Pr., 1975. 384p.   **CC338**

A classed bibliography of more than 5,300 entries on German-American history, language and literature, press and book trade, religious and cultural life, business and industry, radicalism, biography, and genealogy. Includes books, newspaper and periodical articles, pamphlets, dissertations, government documents, and audiovisual materials, most of them produced since 1941. Also includes many directory entries. Indexed.   Z1361.G37T64

U.S. Library of Congress. Congressional Research Service. Illegal aliens and alien labor: a bibliography and compilation of background materials (1970–June 1977). Wash., Govt. Prt. Off., 1977. 58p.   **CC339**

Prep. at the request of the Committee on the Judiciary, U.S. House of Representatives. 95th Congress, 1st Session, Committee print no.9.

A list of congressional and other government documents (federal, state and local), monographs, periodical and newspaper articles and editorials, arranged by form. Also includes state laws relating to the employment of illegal aliens and brief summaries of relevant U.S. Supreme Court cases.   Z7165.U5U65

U.S. National Institute of Mental Health. Center for Minority Group Mental Health Programs. Bibliography on racism. Rockville, Md., The Center [for sale by Govt. Prt. Off.], 1972–78. 2v.   **CC340**

Contents: v.1, Bibliography on racism; v.2, Bibliography on racism, 1972–75.

Each volume contains a listing of all abstracts available at time of publication from the database of the National Clearinghouse for Mental Health Information. The second volume is organized by ethnic group, then by broad subject, and includes books, periodical articles, reports, and doctoral dissertations. Author and keyword subject indexes.   Z7164.R12U52

Zurawski, Joseph W. Polish American history and culture: a classified bibliography. Chicago, Polish Museum of America, 1975. 218p.   **CC341**

About 1,700 English-language sources are organized within a

detailed subject classification. Includes citations on American-Polish foreign relations. Indexed by organization and personal name.
Z1361.P6Z87

Periodicals

Ethnic serials at selected University of California libraries: a union list. Ed. by Barbara Kuhn al-Bayati [and others]. Los Angeles, Univ. of California, [1977]. 368p. il.　　**CC342**

Provides locations and holdings for 1,817 current and retrospective newspapers and periodicals at all of the University of California campuses except Berkeley. In five sections: (1) multi-ethnic studies; (2) Chicano studies; (3) Asian American studies; (4) Afro-American studies; (5) American Indian studies. Each of the last four sections has its own index.　　Z1361.E4E83

The Oxbridge directory of ethnic periodicals. N.Y., Oxbridge Communications, [1979]. 247p.　　**CC343**

A directory of some 3,500 ethnic periodicals, newspapers, newsletters, directories, etc. Arranged according to about 70 ethnic groups; title index. Information was derived from the Standard Periodical Data Base augmented by data from questionnaires.
Z6953.5.A1O9

Dissertations

Cordasco, Francesco and **Alloway, David N.** American ethnic groups, the European heritage; a bibliography of doctoral dissertations completed at American universities. Metuchen, N.J., Scarecrow Pr., 1981. 365p.　　**CC344**

More than 1,400 doctoral dissertations are arranged in two major geographical areas of ethnic origin (western and northern Europe; central, southern and eastern Europe), then by nation or region. Other sections deal with multigroup studies, emigration/immigration, history, politics, economics, policy; th¯re is a checklist of selected bibliographies. Descriptive annotations; author and subject indexes.　　Z1361.E97C67

Gilbert, Victor Francis and **Tatla, Darshan Singh.** Immigrants, minorities and race relations: a bibliography of theses and dissertations presented at British and Irish universities, 1900–1981. London, Mansell, [1984]. 153p.　　**CC345**

In two main sections: general studies, subdivided by topic; national and regional studies, subdivided by country and subject as appropriate. Subject and author indexes.　　Z7164.I3G5

Dictionaries and encyclopedias

Cashmore, Ernest Ellis. Dictionary of race and ethnic relations. London, Routledge & Kegan Paul, [1984]. 294p.
CC346

Offers essay-length articles on schools of thought, major persons, theories, concepts, and empirical studies, with emphasis on the United Kingdom and the United States. Bibliographical references; index.　　DA125.A1C35

Harvard encyclopedia of American ethnic groups. Stephan Thernstrom, ed. Cambridge, Mass., Belknap Pr. of Harvard Univ. Pr., 1980. 1076p. maps.　　**CC347**

The core of this encyclopedia consists of 106 signed essays on ethnic groups, ranging in length from 3,000 to 40,000 words, "based on the estimated size of the group, the length and complexity of its history in the United States, and the availability and nature of source material."—*Introd.* "Ethnic" should not be interpreted as "foreign," since there are essays on Mormons, Appalachians, Amish, Hutterites, Southerners, and Yankees. Each essay touches on origins, migration, arrival, settlement, economic and social life, religion, culture, education, politics, maintenance of ethnicity; bibliographies are brief and stress readily available works. In addition to

the group essays, there are 29 thematic essays on such topics as federal policy toward American Indians, concepts of ethnicity, folklore, health beliefs and practices, politics, prejudice, etc. A series of 87 maps and numerous statistical tables complete the work.
E184.A1H35

Levine, Robert M. Race and ethnic relations in Latin America and the Caribbean: an historical dictionary and bibliography. Metuchen, N.J., Scarecrow Pr., 1980. 252p.　　**CC348**

A dictionary of terms, names, and events, which emphasizes relations among ethnic groups and races more than terms relating to individual groups. Some entries are keyed to the bibliography for further information; selected bibliography of 1,342 books and articles arranged by region and country. Indexed.　　F1419.A1L48

Directories and handbooks

Akiner, Shirin. Islamic peoples of the Soviet Union (with an appendix on the non-Muslim Turkic peoples of the Soviet Union). London, Kegan Paul, [1983]. 462p. maps.
CC349

For each ethnic group, provides historical background, population data, and information on educational levels, language, religion, and distribution outside the Soviet Union. Chronology; bibliography; index.　　DK34.M8A35

Bernardo, Stephanie. The ethnic almanac. Garden City, N.Y., Doubleday, 1981. 560p. il.　　**CC350**

A fact book about American ethnic groups—historical background, contributions in various subject areas, biographical sketches, statistics, organizations. Indexed.　　E184.A1B426

Directory of special programs for minority group members: career information services, employment skills banks, financial aid. 1974– . [Garrett Park, Md., Garrett Park Pr.], 1974– . Annual.　　**CC351**

Includes information on general employment and educational assistance programs, federal aid programs, women's programs, college and university awards.　　HD5724.D56

Handbook of major Soviet nationalities. Zev Katz, ed. N.Y., Free Pr., [1975]. 481p.　　**CC352**

Groups 17 Soviet nationalities by geographical and/or cultural area: the Slavs, the Baltics, the Transcaucasus, Central Asia, and other nationalities (Jews, Tatars, and Moldavians). The chapter on each nationality includes general information (territory, economy, history, demography, culture, external relations), media (language, media, and educational institutions), and national attitudes. Each chapter is written by a specialist and includes bibliography. Appendix of comparative tables for the nationalities. Subject index.
DK33.H35

Hobbie, Margaret. Museums, sites, and collections of Germanic culture in North America: an annotated directory of German immigrant culture in the United States and Canada. Westport, Conn., Greenwood Pr., [1980]. 155p.
CC353

Focuses on the material culture and non-bibliographic resources for German-American and German-Canadian history through descriptive listings of repositories where such material can be found: museums, historical societies, libraries and archives; historic houses and sites; European collections. Bibliography; name and general indexes.　　E184.G3H58

Joramo, Marjorie K. Directory of ethnic publishers and resource organizations. 2d ed. Chicago, Office for Library Service to the Disadvantaged, Amer. Lib. Assoc., 1979. 102p.　　**CC354**

1st ed., 1976, ed. by Beth J. Shapiro.

Emphasizes material available on Afro-Americans, Asian Americans, Hispanic Americans, and Native Americans from non-traditional publishers and organizations. A total of 279 entries, arranged

alphabetically, provide notes on the purpose of the organizations and price lists of publications. Indexed by subject and ethnic group.
E184.A1S57

Minority organizations: a national directory. Ed.1– , 1978– . Garrett Park, Md., Garrett Park Pr., 1978– . Irregular. (Ed. 2, 1982) **CC355**

Katherine W. Cole, ed.

The 2d ed. provides name, address, telephone number, brief description, and list of publications for 7,186 organizations established by or for Native Americans and black, Hispanic, and Asian Americans; also lists 1,358 organizations for which no current information was available. Indexed by name, geographical location, and function.

Wasserman, Paul and **Morgan, Jean.** Ethnic information sources of the United States. 2d ed. Detroit, Gale, [1983]. 2v. **CC356**

Subtitle: A guide to organizations, agencies, foundations, institutions, media, commercial and trade bodies, government programs, research institutes, libraries and museums, religious organizations, banking firms, festivals and fairs, travel and tourist offices, airlines and ship lines, bookdealers and publishers' representatives, and books, pamphlets and audiovisuals on specific ethnic groups.

1st ed. 1976.

Sections on more than 100 ethnic peoples are arranged alphabetically by group name, with information sources indicated in the subtitle grouped under 26 major headings within each group. Blacks, American Indians, and Eskimos are not included. Organization index. E184.A1W27

Wixman, Ronald. The peoples of the USSR: an ethnographic handbook. Armonk, N.Y., M. E. Sharpe, [1984]. 246p. maps. **CC357**

Designed as a quick reference guide. Entry for each group of people provides name variants, ethnic background, language, population (1926–79), religious affiliation, and location (keyed to 15 maps). No detailed historical, cultural, literary, or political information. DK33.W59

Wynar, Lubomyr R. Encyclopedic directory of ethnic organizations in the United States. Littleton, Colo., Libraries Unlimited, 1975. 414p. **CC358**

Aims "to identify major ethnic organizations in terms of their objectives, publications, and activities."—*Pref.* Lists 1,475 organizations arranged under 73 categories representing separate ethnic groups. Indexed. E184.A1W94

Afro-Americans
Bibliography

See also CC97.

Abajian, James. Blacks and their contributions to the American West; a bibliography and union list of library holdings through 1970. Boston, G. K. Hall, 1974. 487p. **CC359**

"Compiled by James de T. Abajian for the Friends of the San Francisco Public Library in cooperation with the American Library Association."

A classed list of some 4,300 items with detailed author/subject index. Z1361.N39A27

Alves, Henrique L. Bibliografia afro-brasileira: estudos sobre o negro. 2. ed., rev. e ampliada. Rio de Janeiro, Livraria Editora Cátedra, 1979. 181p. **CC360**

"Em convênio com o Instituto Nacional do Libro."—*t.p.*

1st ed. 1976.

Lists 2,283 works (books, periodical and newspaper articles, essays, reports, government documents) by author; no subject approach. Z1697.N4A56

Amistad Research Center. Author and added entry catalog of the American Missionary Association Archives, with references to schools and mission stations. Westport, Conn., Greenwood, [1970]. 3v. **CC361**

For full information *see* BB315.

Blacks in America; bibliographical essays, by James M. McPherson [and others]. Garden City, N.Y., Doubleday, 1971. 430p. **CC362**

". . . an attempt to combine narrative, interpretation, and bibliography in a chronological and topical framework that will provide teachers, students, and interested readers with an up-to-date guide to Afro-American history and culture."—*Pref.* Material is arranged under 100 topical headings, with name and subject index.
Z1361.N39B56

Brignano, Russell Carl. Black Americans in autobiography; an annotated bibliography of autobiographies and autobiographical books written since the Civil War. Rev. and expanded ed. Durham, N.C., Duke Univ. Pr., 1984. 193p.
CC363

In two main sections: (1) Autobiographies ("volumes describing appreciable spans of the authors' lives") and (2) Autobiographical books (diaries, journals, collections of essays, eyewitness accounts of important events, etc.). Locates copies. Occupational, institutional, organizational, geographical, chronological and title indexes.
Z1361.N39B67

Davis, Lenwood G. The black family in the United States: a selected bibliography of annotated books, articles, and dissertations on black families in America. Westport, Conn., Greenwood Pr., [1978]. 132p. **CC364**

More than 380 annotated entries are grouped by type (books, articles, dissertations), and subdivided by subject (slavery, poverty, economic status, religion, education, health, sex, etc.). There are author and "selective" keyword subject indexes.
Z1361.N39D355

—— Black-Jewish relations in the United States, 1752–1984: a selected bibliography. Westport, Conn., Greenwood Pr., [1984]. 130p. (Bibliographies and indexes in Afro-American and African studies, no.1) **CC365**

1,241 citations are grouped first by form (major books and pamphlets, general works, dissertations and theses, newspaper and periodical articles), then by subject. Indexed. Z1361.N39D357

—— The black woman in American society; a selected annotated bibliography. Boston, G. K. Hall, [1975]. 159p.
CC366

Entries are grouped according to type: books, articles, general reference works, etc. Author and subject index. Includes a directory of selected black periodicals, lists of pertinent national organizations, elected officials, etc., and some brief tables of statistics on black women. Z1361.N39D36

—— Malcolm X: a selected bibliography. Comp. with the assistance of Marsha L. Moore. Westport, Conn., Greenwood Pr., [1984]. 146p. **CC367**

Includes primary and secondary materials classed by type, with contents notes. Index. Z8989.7.D38

—— and **Sims-Wood, Janet L.** The Ku Klux Klan: a bibliography. Westport, Conn., Greenwood Pr., 1984. 643p.
CC368

Expands the coverage of W. H. Fisher's *Invisible empire* (CC373) to include newspaper articles and materials on Klan activities in foreign countries; some classification by state within form subdivisions. Appendixes; author index. Z1249.K8D38

—— Marcus Garvey: an annotated bibliography. Westport, Conn., Greenwood Pr., [1980]. 192p. **CC369**

Offers 562 references in eight parts: (1–2) books and selected articles by Garvey; (3–7) books, periodical and newspaper articles, theses and dissertations about Garvey; (8) documents. Unpublished material is not included. Indexed. Z8324.49.D38

Dumond, Dwight Lowell. A bibliography of antislavery in America. Ann Arbor, Univ. of Michigan Pr., [1961]. 119p.
CC370

Prepared to accompany the author's *Antislavery; the crusade for freedom in America* (1961), "this is the literature written and circulated by those active in the antislavery movement and used by the author."—*Note.* Includes works published up to the time of the Civil War.　　　　　　　　　　　　　　　Z1249.S6D8

Dunmore, Charlotte. Black children and their families: a bibliography. San Francisco, R & E Research Associates, 1976. 103p.　　　　　　　　　　　　　　**CC371**

Lists published materials on the black American child in sections on adoption, education, health, family life, ghetto life, mental health, sex and family planning. Separate sections include bibliographies and reference works, a periodicals directory, source directory for films and filmstrips, and a list of selected library collections. No index.　　　　　　　　　　　　　　Z1361.N39D898

Fisher, William Harvey. Free at last; a bibliography of Martin Luther King, Jr. Metuchen, N.J., Scarecrow Pr., 1977. 169p.　　　　　　　　　　　　　　**CC372**

A bibliography of primary and secondary sources, arranged in four sections: (1) works written by King, including manuscript collections; (2) books, articles, dissertations, documents and manuscript collections primarily about King; (3) similar materials about his family, associates, and death; (4) reviews of books by King. Some entries are briefly annotated. Author index.　　　Z8464.44.F57

———— The invisible empire: a bibliography of the Ku Klux Klan. Metuchen, N.J., Scarecrow Pr., 1980. 202p.
CC373

English-language materials are grouped chronologically (the Klan in the 19th and 20th centuries), then by form (dissertations, manuscripts/archives, government documents, books, and articles). Annotated. Author and subject indexes.　　　Z1249.K8F54

Hampton Institute, Hampton, Va. Collis P. Huntington Library. A classified catalogue of the Negro collection, comp. by the Writers' Program of the Work Projects Administration in the state of Virginia. Sponsored by Hampton Institute. [n.p.], 1940. 255p., [35]p.　　　　**CC374**

More than 5,000 titles on the Negro in Africa and in America. Particularly strong in material on slavery and reconstruction. Classified, with author and title index.　　　　　Z1361.N39H3

Helmreich, William B. Afro-Americans and Africa: black nationalism at the crossroads. Westport, Conn., Greenwood Pr., 1977. 74p. (African Bibliographic Center. Special bibliographic ser., n.s., no.2)　　　　　　　**CC375**

An annotated list of about 400 books and articles (including some newspaper pieces) from the period 1960–73. Also provides a general bibliography of works on Afro-Americans and Africans in which further titles are grouped by subject. Introductory essays review the literature of African and black nationalism both historically and in a social science context. Subject index.　　　Z3501.Af852 no.2

Howard University. Library. Moorland Foundation. Dictionary catalog of the Jesse E. Moorland Collection of Negro life and history. Boston, G. K. Hall, 1970. 9v.　　**CC376**

An earlier, classified catalog ed. by Dorothy B. Porter was published 1958.

Reproduction of the catalog cards for a collection of more than 100,000 books, pamphlets, periodical titles, master's theses, manuscripts, music, newspaper clippings and pictures. Particularly strong in publications relating to American Colonization Society, African slave trade and its suppression, and abolition of slavery.

———————— 1st supplement. Boston, G. K. Hall, 1976. 3v.

Lists additions to the book collection since 1970, but excludes manuscript, photographic, music, and oral history resources since the Library's Manuscript Division plans to issue a separate catalog of those additions.　　　　　　　　　Z1361.N39H82

Indiana. University. Libraries. The black family and the black woman: a bibliography. N.Y., Arno, 1978. 231p.
CC378

Comp. by Phyllis Rauch Klobnan and Wilmer H. Baatz.

"A bibliography of the holdings in the Indiana University Library."—*verso of t.p.*

An earlier version appeared in 1972 as a resource guide for students and faculty at Indiana University. This edition has added 600 new entries, a separate category on psychology/sociology of the black woman, a new section on ERIC materials, a separate category on films, and an enlarged children's literature section. Subject arrangement. No index.　　　　　　　Z1361.N39I45

Jenkins, Betty Lanier and **Phillis, Susan.** Black separatism: a bibliography. Westport, Conn., Greenwood Pr., [1976]. 163p.　　　　　　　　　　　　　　**CC379**

A classified, annotated list of books and articles arranged in two parts: (1) The separatism vs. integration controversy; (2) Institutional and psychological dimensions. Pt.I is organized historically; pt.II by subject (identity, education, politics, economics, and religion). Name and title indexes.　　　　　　　Z1361.N39J45

Miller, Elizabeth W. The Negro in America: a bibliography. 2d ed., rev. and enl., comp. by Mary L. Fisher. Cambridge, Harvard Univ. Pr., 1970. 351p.　　　　　　**CC380**

1st ed. 1966.

A listing of books and periodical articles grouped under such headings as "History," "Intergroup relations," "Urban problems," "Employment," "Education," "Political rights and suffrage," with new sections added in the revised edition to cover music, literature and the arts. Emphasis is on materials published since 1954. Author index. A useful and thorough compilation, and a needed complement to Work's bibliography (CC403).　　　　Z1361.N39M5

Miller, Joseph C. Slavery: a comparative teaching bibliography. [Waltham, Mass.], Crossroads Pr., [1977]. 122p.
CC381

Designed as an introductory bibliography for students, listing secondary literature relating to slavery. More than 1,600 entries are grouped by broad geographic or subject area (French North America, the Muslim world, the slave trade, etc.), with author and geographical keyword indexes.　　　　　Z7164.S6M5

Momeni, Jamshid A. Demography of the black population in the United States: an annotated bibliography with a review essay. Westport, Conn., Greenwood Pr., [1983]. 354p.　　　　　　　　　　　　　　**CC382**

A classed bibliography of more than 650 titles on aspects of fertility, marriage, birth control, health, migration, population growth, etc. Primarily relates to twentieth-century situations. Author index.　　　　　　　　　　　Z1361.N39M6

Myers, Hector F., Rana, Phyllis G. and **Harris, Marcia.** Black child development in America, 1927–1977: an annotated bibliography. Westport, Conn., Greenwood Pr., [1979]. 470p.　　　　　　　　　　　　**CC383**

More than 1,200 citations from social sciences monographic and professional journal literature are grouped in five areas: language development, physical development, cognitive development, personality development, and social development. Most abstracts are quoted directly from the eight original abstract sources surveyed for this bibliography. Author and subject indexes.　　Z1361.N39M94

Negro in print. v.1–7, no.2, May 1965–Sept. 1971. Wash., Negro Bibliographic and Research Center, 1965–71. Bimonthly.　　　　　　　　　　　　　**CC384**

At head of title: Bibliographic survey.

Listings, with annotations, of publications on the Negro and, to a lesser extent, other minority groups. Most issues have sections for nonfiction, fiction, paperbacks, books for young readers, and periodical articles. Emphasis was on current material, but earlier publications were included from time to time. Some issues are devoted to a specific topic (e.g., Jan. 1966 is a "Negro history issue") or stress a particular feature. Individual issues not indexed; a 5-year subject index, 1965–70, was published 1971.

Ceased publication.   Z1361.N39N39

New York. Public Library. Schomburg Collection of Negro Literature and History. Dictionary catalog. Boston, G. K. Hall, 1962. 9v.   **CC385**

A photographic reproduction of the cards of a dictionary catalog of "a library and archive of materials devoted to Negro life and history . . . international in scope . . . includes books by authors of African descent, regardless of subject matter or language . . . and all significant materials about peoples of African descent."—*Pref.* Includes more than 36,000 bound volumes.   Z881.N592S35

———— ———— Supplement. 1st–3d. Boston, 1967–76. 2v.; 4v.; 5v.

The quinquennial supplements include all acquisitions, old and new, for which cards were printed after publication of the basic set. Many major microform holdings are not yet represented. Materials processed after 1974 appear in:

Schomburg Center for Research and Black Culture. Bibliographic guide to black studies, 1975– . Boston, G. K. Hall, 1976– . Annual.   **CC386**

The 1975 volume covers materials acquired by the New York Public Library's Schomburg Collection between Sept. 1974 and Sept. 1975. Later volumes include some additional entries from Library of Congress MARC tapes. Dictionary catalog arrangement; employs some subject headings developed especially for the Schomburg Collection.   Z1361.N39S373a

Newman, Richard. Black access; a bibliography of Afro-American bibliographies. Westport, Conn., Greenwood Pr., [1984]. 249p.   **CC387**

Lists bibliographies which have "an independent existence as a book, pamphlet, article, or chapter in a book."—*Pref.* Covers a broad range of topics relating to Afro-Americans; includes Canadian material. Main-entry listing with subject and chronological indexes.

                                      Z1361.N39N578

———— Black index: Afro-Americana in selected periodicals, 1907–1949. N.Y., Garland, 1981. 266p. (Garland reference library of social science, v.65; Critical studies on black life and culture, v.4)   **CC388**

An author and subject guide in dictionary arrangement to more than 1,000 articles from some 350 periodicals published in the United States, Canada, and Great Britain. Articles are drawn from the *Annual magazine subject index* (AE243), and new indexing is provided by author and book reviewer, plus expanded subject access. Does not include citations from the *Journal of negro history,* for which a separate index is available.   Z1361.N39N58

Obudho, Constance E. Black-white racial attitudes: an annotated bibliography. Westport, Conn., Greenwood Pr., 1976. 180p.   **CC389**

An annotated, classified bibliography of books and periodical articles published between 1950 and 1974 on attitude formation and change and associated factors in the United States. Articles include doctoral dissertation abstracts in *Dissertation abstracts international.* Author and subject indexes.   Z1361.N39O28

Partington, Paul G. W. E. B. Du Bois: a bibliography of his published writings. [Rev. ed.] Whittier, Calif., Partington, [1979]. 202p.   **CC390**

1st ed. 1977.

About ten pages of corrections and new entries have been added for this edition, bringing the total number of entries from 2,365 to 2,591.   Z8244.9.P37

Porter, Dorothy Burnett. Afro-Braziliana; a working bibliography. Boston, G. K. Hall, [1978]. 294p.   **CC391**

A selective bibliography which intends "to make known a selection of published works written by Afro-Brazilians and their contribution to the life and history of Brazil . . . . Works listed are those to be found in American repositories . . . ."—*Pref.* In two parts: (1) a

classified section; (2) writings of selected authors, with critical and biographical references. More than 5,200 items; some annotations. Indexed.   Z1697.N4P67

———— The Negro in the United States; a selected bibliography. Wash., Lib. of Congress, 1970. 313p.   **CC392**

A selective bibliography (1,781 entries) "designed to meet the current needs of students, teachers, librarians, researchers, and the general public for introductory guidance to the study of the Negro in the United States."—*Pref.* Although slightly more selective than the same author's *Working bibliography on the Negro* (below), it includes numerous items not found in that work; it also has the advantage of a more detailed subject approach through the author-subject index. Some brief descriptive notes.   Z1361.N39P59

———— A working bibliography on the Negro in the United States. [Ann Arbor, Mich.], Xerox Univ. Microfilms, 1969. 202p.   **CC393**

A classed list of nearly 2,000 items (mainly books, with a few periodical citations) intended to facilitate book selection "for public, private and university collections of Afro-Americana."—*Introd.* Some brief annotations. Author index.   Z1361.N39P62

Ramos Guédez, José Marcial. Bibliografía Afrovenezolana. Caracas, Instituto Autónomo Biblioteca Nacional y de Servicios de Bibliotecas, 1980. 125p. (Colección bibliográfica y documental venezolana, 1; Serie bibliográfica, Instituto Autónomo Biblioteca Nacional y de Servicios de Bibliotecas, 2)   **CC394**

A classed bibliography of nearly 1,000 titles, with some contents notes. Name index.   Z1937.N4R35

Salk, Erwin A. A layman's guide to Negro history. New enl. ed. N.Y., McGraw-Hill, [1967]. 196p.   **CC395**

1st ed. 1966.

"A fact book on the history of the Negro people in the United States" (p.1–79) is followed by a series of chronological and topical bibliographies. A brief descriptive note follows many of the citations. Not indexed.   Z1361.N39S23

Sims, Janet L. The progress of Afro-American women: a selected bibliography and resource guide. Westport, Conn., Greenwood Pr., [1980]. 378p.   **CC396**

A classed bibliography of 19th and 20th century materials on all aspects of the life of the Afro-American woman, from slavery to participation in the women's rights movement. Author index. About 4,000 items.   Z1361.N39S52

Smith, Dwight La Vern. Afro-American history: a bibliography. Santa Barbara, Calif., ABC-Clio, [1974–81]. 2v. (Clio bibliography ser., 2, 8)   **CC397**

Offers 6,387 abstracts drawn from the database of *America: history and life* (DB47) from 1953–78. Classed arrangement, with author/subject indexes.   Z1361.N39S53

Smith, John David. Black slavery in the Americas: an interdisciplinary bibliography, 1865–1980. Westport, Conn., Greenwood Pr., [1982]. 2v. (1847p.)   **CC398**

A classed bibliography with author and subject indexes; 15,667 citations in 25 chapters (both topical and geographical) with many subdivisions. Limited to English-language materials: books, articles, theses and dissertations, review articles. Covers all aspects of slavery, except that political aspects (including antislavery and abolition movements) are largely omitted. Citations are reproduced from computer printout.   Z7164.S6S63

Thompson, Edgar Tristram and **Thompson, Alma Macy.** Race and region; a descriptive bibliography. Chapel Hill, Univ. of North Carolina Pr., 1949. 194p.   **CC399**

A comprehensive, annotated, classified bibliography on race relations compiled with special reference to the relations between whites and Negroes in the United States. Based on collections in Duke University, the University of North Carolina, and North Carolina College in Durham, with indication of location of copies in these libraries.   Z1361.N39T5

Walton, Hanes. The study and analysis of black politics; a bibliography. Metuchen, N.J., Scarecrow Pr., 1973. 110p.   **CC400**

A classed listing of more than 1,000 books and articles on the American black political experience. Each of 13 subject chapters begins with a brief introduction, then lists materials by type. Treats political parties and candidates, voting patterns, international politics, urban politics, the Supreme Court, etc. Author index.

Z1361.N39W29

Westmoreland, Guy T. An annotated guide to basic reference books on the black American experience. Wilmington, Del., Scholarly Resources Inc., [1974]. 98p.   **CC401**

A classified, annotated guide to reference works "which deal primarily or completely" with the black American experience. Author, title, and subject indexes.   Z1361.N39W528

Williams, Ora. American black women in the arts and social sciences: a bibliographic survey. Rev. and expanded ed. Metuchen, N.J., Scarecrow Pr., 1978. 197p. il.   **CC402**

1st ed. 1973.

Pt.1, "Comprehensive listing," includes reference works, autobiographies and biographies, anthologies, literature, feminist issues, miscellaneous subjects, art (including art and musical works), and audiovisual material. Pt.2, "Selected individual bibliographies," includes portraits, and primary and secondary works. Pt.3, "Ideas and achievements of some American black women," is followed by a list of black periodicals and publishing houses. Indexed.

Z1361.N39W56

Work, Monroe Nathan. Bibliography of the Negro in Africa and America. N.Y., Wilson, 1928. 698p. (Repr.: N.Y., Octagon, 1965)   **CC403**

A comprehensive bibliography of more than 17,000 selected titles of books, pamphlets, and periodical articles. Classified, with author index.   Z1361.N39W8

Dissertations

Research in black child development: doctoral dissertation abstracts, 1927–1979. Comp. by Hector F. Myers [and others]. Westport, Conn., Greenwood Pr., [1982]. 737p.   **CC404**

Groups 627 abstracts drawn directly from *Dissertation abstracts international* in five areas of development: language, physical, cognitive, social, and personality. Author and subject indexes.

E185.86.R44

West, Earle H. A bibliography of doctoral research on the Negro, 1933–1966. [Ann Arbor, Mich.], Xerox Univ. Microfilms, 1969. 134p.   **CC405**

Lists 1,452 dissertations in classified arrangement. The author index provides references to *Dissertation abstracts* (AH19), together with University Microfilms order numbers and prices.

Continued by: Z1361.N39W44

Peebles, Joan B. A bibliography of doctoral research on the Negro, 1967–1977. Ann Arbor, Mich., University Microfilms Internatl., [1978?]. 65p.   **CC406**

Cover title: *Black studies: a dissertation bibliography.*

Supplements E. H. West's *Bibliography of doctoral research* (above) and supersedes an earlier supplement covering 1967–69. Retains the classified arrangement and provides similar information as in the West volume.   E29.N393

—— Black studies II: a dissertation bibliography. Ann Arbor, Mich., University Microfilms Internat., [1981?] 59p.   **CC407**

A supplement to the author's *Bibliography of doctoral research on the Negro, 1967-1977* (above). Lists new dissertations from 1976 to 1980, additional dissertations from 1940 to 1976, and master's theses from 1948 to 1979. Classed arrangement; author index. Citations to *Dissertation abstracts international* and *Masters abstracts* are given.

Periodicals

Daniel, Walter C. Black journals of the United States. Westport, Conn., Greenwood Pr., [1982]. 432p.   **CC408**

Provides historical/descriptive sketches of more than 100 black journals (excluding newspapers) selected "on the basis of available periodicals and a mix of those that seem to reflect the broad scope of the black American experience from 1827 to the 1980s."—*Introd.* Each sketch concludes with a bibliography of sources for further information and details of publication history in uniform format. Index includes names of contributors mentioned in the sketches.

PN4882.5.D36

Wisconsin. University-Madison. Library. Black periodicals and newspapers: a union list of holdings in libraries of the University of Wisconsin and the Library of the State Historical Society of Wisconsin. 2d ed., rev. Madison, State Historical Soc. of Wisconsin, 1979. 83p.   **CC409**

Comp. by Neil E. Strache and others.

1st ed. 1975.

An alphabetical title listing with geographic and subject indexes. Limited to the holdings of the libraries mentioned in the subtitle, but serves as a guide to what is believed to be "one of the strongest collections in this field."—*Introd.* Gives holdings and locations for more than 600 periodicals and newspapers, both current and defunct, and representing "all phases of black thought and action."

Z1361.N39W59

Dictionaries and encyclopedias

See also DB114.

Burke, Joan Martin. Civil rights; a current guide to the people, organizations, and events. 2d ed. N.Y., Bowker, 1974. 266p.   **CC410**

At head of title: A CBS news reference book.

1st ed., 1970, by A. John Adams and J. M. Burke.

An alphabetical section giving information on individuals and organizations is followed by a number of appendixes: lists of Congressional voting records on civil rights acts; a list of federal and state agencies with civil rights responsibilities; a civil rights chronology; a list of leading black elected officials; a directory of civil rights resources; a selected bibliography; and an index. Originally prepared as a quick reference source for correspondents and editors of CBS News, the guide has as its criterion "information that the well-informed newsman or citizen needs to know—not the specialist."—*Foreword.*   JC599.U5B85

Encyclopedia of black America. W. Augustus Low, ed., Virgil A. Clift, assoc. ed. N.Y., McGraw-Hill, [1981]. 921p. il., maps.   **CC411**

A dictionary arrangement of about 325 articles and 1,400 biographies written by approximately 100 scholars and authorities; articles are unsigned, but are listed under the author's name in the list of contributors. Most articles range up to a page in length, although 11 "clusters" contain 61 major, related articles; most major articles list bibliographic references. Data extend to the 1976–77 period. Numerous cross references; index.   E185.E55

Nunez, Benjamin. Dictionary of Afro-Latin American civilization. Westport, Conn., Greenwood Pr., [1980]. xxxv, 525p. il., maps.   **CC412**

Comp. with the assistance of the African Bibliographic Center.

Offers more than 4,500 multilingual entries for words and phrases, biographies, and historical events; sources are given for some entries. Focus is on the Caribbean, with lesser attention to Latin America. Selected bibliography; subject index and name index organized by country or region.   F1408.3.N86

U.S. Bureau of the Census. The social and economic status of the black population in the United States: an historical view, 1790–1978. [Wash., for sale by Supt. of Docs.], 1979. 271p. il. (Current population reports: Special studies: Ser. P-23, no.80)   **CC413**

A statistical presentation of changes in population distribution, income levels, labor force, employment, education, family composition, mortality, fertility, housing, voting, public office holding, armed forces personnel, etc. In two parts: (1) historical trends, 1790 to 1975; (2) recent trends, 1975-78. "The historical profile is the distinguishing feature of this report, which is the ninth in the series on Black Americans."—*Introd.*   HA203.A218 no.80

Directories

Black list. [2d ed.] N.Y., Black List, [1975]. 2v.   **CC414**

Subtitle: The concise and comprehensive reference guide to black journalism, radio and television, educational and cultural organizations in the USA, Africa and the Caribbean.

Contents: v.1, Afroamerica (USA); v.2, Africa, the Caribbean, Latin America.

1st ed. 1970.

Lists television and radio networks, cable television networks, newspapers, magazines, and educational and cultural institutions, with address and person in charge.   P88.B6

The black resource guide. 1983 national ed. [Wash., Ben Johnson], 1983. 119p. il.   **CC415**

1st ed. 1981.

A national directory of organizations important to Afro-Americans. Also lists Afro-American federal, state, and local political figures, celebrities, news columnists, etc. Some statistical data is included. Plans call for annual publication.   E185.5.B568

Directory of African and Afro-American studies in the U.S. 1976–79. Waltham, Mass., African Studies Assoc., 1976–79.   **CC416**

Continued the *Directory of African studies in the U.S., 1971–1974/75.* Ceased publication.

Offers brief descriptions and lists of courses for 623 colleges and universities offering at least one course in relevant areas. Lists an additional 295 institutions known to offer pertinent courses, but which failed to answer the questionnaire. Indexes by institution, discipline, language, and faculty.   DT19.9.U5D561

Race Relations Information Center, Nashville. Directory of Afro-American resources. Ed. by Walter Schatz. N.Y., Bowker, [1970]. 485p.   **CC417**

Lists and briefly describes 5,365 collections of resource materials at 2,108 institutions: "college, university, public, governmental and business libraries; federal, state, local and private agencies; and organizations with civil rights programs and responsibilities, or with substantive interests in black America."—*Pref.* Collections are mainly of primary source materials and supporting documents. Geographical arrangement, with an index of subjects, persons, places, and institutions mentioned, and a separate personnel index. Bibliography of secondary sources, p.347–56.

Black studies; select catalog of National Archives and Records Service microfilm publications (Wash., 1973. 71p.) lists and briefly describes material in the National Archives which is important for the study of black history and which is available on microfilm.   Z1361.N39R3

Handbooks

Bergman, Peter M. The chronological history of the Negro in America. N.Y., Harper, [1969]. 698p.   **CC418**

A year-by-year presentation of facts and miscellaneous information relating to the Negro in America (mainly United States, but including occasional references to other parts of the Americas). Offers an impressive gathering of information, but dates, etc., are often too inexact or statements too sketchy to be truly satisfactory; some inaccuracies have been noted. Detailed index, but no subheads nor strict pattern of arrangement within yearly listings to make for easy scanning.   E185.B46

The black American reference book. Ed. by Mabel M. Smythe. Englewood Cliffs, N.J., Prentice-Hall, 1976. 1026p.   **CC419**

Sponsored by the Phelps-Stokes Fund.

A revised and updated edition of *The American Negro reference book* edited by J. P. Davis (1966).

Scholars and specialists have contributed 30 chapters intended to provide "a reliable summary of current information on the main aspects of Negro life in America, and to present this information in sufficient historical depth to provide the reader with a true perspective."—*Pref.* Some chapters carry bibliographies; others employ bibliographic footnotes; several include useful tables. Reference value and depth of coverage of the individual chapters vary considerably. Detailed index.   E185.D25

Diggs, Ellen Irene. Black chronology from 4000 B.C. to the abolition of the slave trade. Boston, G. K. Hall, [1983]. 312p.   **CC420**

Rev. ed. of *Chronology of notable events and dates in the history of the African . . .* (1970).

A chronology from the beginning of the first Egyptian empire to the emancipation of Brazilian slaves in 1888. Bibliographic references; index.   DT17.D5

The Ebony handbook, by the Editors of Ebony. [Editor: Doris E. Saunders] Chicago, Johnson, 1974. 553p.   **CC421**

1966 ed. had title: *The Negro handbook.*

While this work covers much of the same ground as the *Black American reference book* (above), the general presentation, together with a good deal of directory-type information and the inclusion of considerably more statistical tables, makes this handbook more useful as a ready reference tool. In addition to general updating in the new edition, there has been extensive rearrangement and much of the text is new or considerably revised.   E185.E22

Garrett, Romeo B. Famous first facts about Negroes. N.Y., Arno Pr., 1972. 212p.   **CC422**

A topical listing of American Negro "firsts." Index of names and subjects.   E185.G22

The Negro almanac; a reference work on the Afro-American. Comp. and ed. by Harry A. Ploski and James Williams. 4th ed. N.Y., Wiley, [1983]. 1550p. il.   **CC423**

1st ed. 1967.

Covers a wide range of topics in the social sciences, with numerous statistical tables and charts illustrating various aspects of Negro life, history, and culture. Selected bibliography; index.

E185.N385

Annuals

National Urban League. The state of black America, 1976– . [N.Y.], The League, 1976– . Annual. il.   **CC424**

Offers essays, statistics, chronology, etc.   E185.5.N317

Negro year book, 1912–52. Tuskegee Inst., Ala., Dept. of Records and Research, 1912–52. 11v.   **CC425**

Publ. 1912, 1913, 1914/15, 1916/17, 1918/19, 1921/22, 1925/26, 1931/32, 1937/38, 1941/46, 1952. Ceased publication.

1st–9th ed. edited by Monroe N. Work; 10th–11th ed. edited by Jessie P. Guzman.

Contains statistics and survey articles on the Negro in the United States—his conditions and achievements.   E185.5.N41

Biography

D'Emilio, John. The civil rights struggle: leaders in profile. N.Y., Facts on File, [1979]. 191p.   **CC426**

Presents biographies of 83 men and women whose careers have

been focused on the Afro-American civil rights struggle since 1945, either as leaders of the movement or of the opposition. Chronology covers 1941–77; bibliography is organized by broad subject divisions. Indexed. Biographies are derived from the same publisher's *Political profiles* series (CJ180).   E185.96.D38

Logan, Rayford Whittingham. Dictionary of American Negro biography. N.Y., Norton, [1982]. 680p.   **CC427**

For full information *see* AJ67.

Who's who in colored America; a biographical dictionary of notable living persons of Negro descent in America. Brooklyn, N.Y., Who's Who in Colored America, 1927–50.
    CC428

For full record *see* AJ93.

Asian-Americans

Doi, Mary L., Lin, Chien and **Vohra-Sahu, Indu.** Pacific/Asian American research: an annotated bibliography. Chicago, Pacific/Asian American Mental Health Research Ctr., [1981]. 267p. (*Its* Bibliography ser., no.1)   **CC429**

Cites 556 journal articles, essays, etc., mostly published since 1969; dissertations are excluded. Alphabetical main-entry arrangement; indexed by 19 ethnic groups, geographic regions, and subjects.
    No.3 in the Center's *Bibliography series* is: Z1361.O7D64

Yu, Elena S. H., Murata, Alice K. and **Lin, Chien.** Bibliography of Pacific/Asian American materials in the Library of Congress. Chicago, [1982]. 254p.   **CC430**

In two parts, Roman and non-Roman alphabet materials; each part is subdivided by ethnic groups, but lacks a detailed subject index.   Z1361.O7Y8

Hansen, Gladys C. The Chinese in California; a brief bibliographic history. Annotated by William F. Heintz. [Portland, Ore.], Abel, 1970. 140p.   **CC431**

Based on material in the Californiana Collection, Dept. of Rare Books and Special Collections, San Francisco Public Library.
    Represents a sampling of books from the period 1850–1968, largely historical in content. Author listing with subject index.
    Z1261.H25

Matsuda, Mitsugu. The Japanese in Hawaii; an annotated bibliography of Japanese Americans. Rev. by Dennis M. Ogawa with Jerry Y. Fujioka. Honolulu, Social Sciences and Linguistics Inst., Univ. of Hawaii, [1975]. 304p. (Hawaii ser., no. 5)   **CC432**

Publication supported by the Japanese American Research Center (JARC).
    Matsuda's original bibliography covering 1868–1967 was published 1968.
    An author listing of more than 750 published English-language items, plus a list of newspapers and periodicals and a separate section of Japanese materials. Subject index to the English-language materials. Intended for undergraduate student use.   Z4708.J3M3

Norell, Irene P. Literature of the Filipino-American in the United States: a selective and annotated bibliography. San Francisco, [R and E Research Associates], 1976. 84p.
    CC433

Classed arrangement; no index. Includes books, periodical articles, and academic theses.   E184.F4N67

Ong, Paul M. and **Lum, William Wong.** Theses and dissertations on Asians in the United States, with selected references to other overseas Asians. Davis, Calif., Asian American Studies, Dept. of Applied Behavioral Sciences, Univ. of California, 1974. 113p.   **CC434**

A major revision and expansion of Lum's *Asians in America*

(1970). Lists 1,372 items in topical arrangement, with keyword and author indexes.   Z1361.O7L84

Rj Associates. Asian American reference data directory. [Wash.], U.S. Dept. of Health, Education, and Welfare, Office of Special Concerns, Office for Asian American Affairs, 1976. 482, [93]p.   **CC434a**

Canta Pian, project director.
    Focuses on data developed by federal and state agencies, universities and individuals on topics "relevant to the Department" (*Introd.*), such as the current health, education, and social welfare of the Asian American population. Most of the 480 abstracts cover material produced within the five years preceding compilation. Indexed by subject area, ethnic group, and author.   Z1361.O7R57

Saito, Shiro. Filipinos overseas: a bibliography. N.Y., Center for Migration Studies, 1977. 156p.   **CC435**

An updating and expansion of the author's "Bibliographic considerations and research status of the overseas Filipinos," a working paper submitted at the first Conference on International Migration from the Philippines, June 10–14, 1974. Entries are arranged according to the conference agenda: Demographic overview of migration; U.S. immigration policy; Views from the barrios; The brain drain; and Destinations of migration, with a section on each area. Includes published and unpublished English-language materials. Appendixes list papers presented at the first and second Conferences on International Migration from the Philippines, relevant dissertations and theses done at the University of Hawaii, and a list of Filipino newspapers and periodicals published in Hawaii and located in the University of Hawaii Library. Author index.
    Z3298.I3S24

Gypsies

Leeds. University. Library. Brotherton Library. Catalogue of the Romany collection formed by D. U. McGrigor Phillips and presented to the University of Leeds. Edinburgh, publ. for the Brotherton collection by Nelson, 1962. 227p.
    CC436

A classified bibliography of more than 1,200 items, including books and pamphlets, manuscripts, music, letters, playbills, pictures, engravings, etc., relating to Gypsies in many countries. Author and title index.

Native Americans

Guides

Haas, Marilyn L. Indians of North America; methods and sources for library research. [Hamden, Conn.], Library Professional Pubns., 1983. 163p. il.   **CC437**

In three parts: (1) a guide to library methodology and relevant reference works; (2) an annotated, topical bibliography of standard monographs, subject bibliographies, and journal titles; (3) an unannotated list of books on individual tribes. Most titles have been published in English since 1960. For the beginning researcher.
    Z1209.H22

Hirschfelder, Arlene B., Byler, Mary Gloyne and **Dorris, Michael A.** Guide to research on North American Indians. Chicago, Amer. Lib. Assoc., 1983. 330p. map.   **CC438**

A selective, classed bibliography of about 1,100 published English-language works, with lengthy annotations. 27 subject chapters provide: introductory essay followed by citations to general works, titles on geographic areas, and bibliographies. Ethnographies of particular groups and dissertations have been excluded (users being referred to Murdock [CC453] and Dockstader [CC461] for those materials). Author-title and subject indexes.   Z1209.2.N67H57

Bibliography

See also CD30.

Abler, Thomas S. and **Weaver, Sally M.** A Canadian Indian bibliography 1960–1970. [Toronto], Univ. of Toronto Pr., [1974]. 732p. **CC439**

An annotated listing of material "of scholarly interest published between 1960 and 1970 on the Canadian Indian and Metis."—*Introd.* More than 3,000 entries (for books, periodical articles, reports, theses) in classed arrangement. A "case law digest" section (p.306–62) attempts "to bring together all case law relating to Indian legal questions decided since 1 July 1867." Z1209.2.C2A24

American Indian index. Chicago, J. A. Huebner, 1953–68. no.1–147. **CC440**

Contents: no.1–103, A–Z; no.104–147, sec.2, A–Ger.
Ceased publication.
A subject index to books, periodicals, and documents.

California State University, Northridge. Libraries. Native Americans of North America: a bibliography based on collections in the Libraries of California State University, Northridge. Comp. by David Perkins and Norman Tanis. Metuchen, N.J., Scarecrow Pr., 1975. 558p. il. **CC441**

"This book was first published by California State University, Northridge."—*verso of t.p.*
A classed bibliography of books, with author/title and series indexes. About 3,400 items. Z1209.2.N67C34

Hippler, Arthur E. and **Wood, John Richard.** The Alaska Eskimos: a selected, annotated bibliography. [Fairbanks], Inst. of Social and Economic Research, Univ. of Alaska, [1977]. 334p. in various pagings. (ISER report ser., no.45) **CC442**

Pt.1 lists materials by author; full bibliographic information, including annotation, is provided in pt.2. Entries are arranged by linguistic groups in pt.3, and by time of observation in pt.4.
The Institute has also issued bibliographies on Eskimo acculturation (1970), the Subarctic Athabascans (1974), and the Aleut (CC449). Z1210.E8H49

Hirschfelder, Arlene B. Annotated bibliography of the literature on American Indians; published in state historical society publications: New England and Middle Atlantic states. Millwood, N.Y., Kraus Internat. Pubns., [1982]. 356p. **CC443**

Cites and annotates "those materials by and about American Indians that have appeared in publications of thirteen state-level historical societies in eleven New England and Middle Atlantic states" (*Introd.*) from first volume of each series through 1979. Listing is by author (or other main entry) with indexes of subjects, of persons, places and titles, and of Indian nations. Z1209.2.U5H57

Hodge, William H. A bibliography of contemporary North American Indians. Selected and partially annotated with study guide. N.Y., Interland Publ., 1976. 310p. **CC444**

Materials included must meet one or more of the following criteria: "(1) They have not been published, e.g., state and federal reports such as committee hearings, position papers, procedural guides, tribal government documents, etc.; (2) For one or a combination of reasons, they have not been widely circulated; (3) They contain significant amounts of ethnographic data which also have immediate implications for important theoretical questions now current within the society sciences; (4) Their chief focus is upon current Indian activity."—*Introd.* Intended to complement rather than supplant existing guides and bibliographies of the subject. Separate study guides for "Indian life prior to 1875" and "Contemporary American Indians" are followed by topical sections such as "History—overview," "Social organization," "Migration patterns," "City living," "Anthropology of development," "Religion," "Health-disease-poverty." Author index; subject index is limited to entries for geographic areas and names of tribes. Z1209.2.N67H6

Huntington Free Library and Reading Room, New York. Dictionary catalog of the American Indian collection. Boston, G. K. Hall, 1977. 4v. **CC445**

Photoreproduction of the catalog cards for the collection which serves as the library for the Museum of the American Indian, Heye Foundation, New York City. Represents more than "35,000 volumes relating to the anthropology, art, history and current affairs of all the Native Peoples of the Western Hemisphere."—*Introd.* Z1209.H85

Index to literature on the American Indian, 1970– . San Francisco, Indian Historian Pr., 1972– . Annual (1973 last publ.?). **CC446**

Sponsored by the American Indian Historical Society.
An alphabetical author and subject index of book and periodical materials, both popular and scholarly. About 300 periodicals (mainly from the U.S. and Canada) were searched for the 1971 volume.

Indians of the United States and Canada; a bibliography. Dwight L. Smith, ed. Santa Barbara, ABC-Clio, [1974–83]. v.1–2. (Clio bibliography ser., 3, 9) (In progress?) **CC447**

These two volumes have drawn together more than 4,900 annotated entries from the periodical literature abstracted in *America: history and life* (DB47) from 1954 through 1978. In each volume, regional and tribal sections are grouped within four main sections: (1) Pre-Columbian Indian history; (2) Tribal history, 1492–1900; (3) General Indian history, 1492–1900; (4) The Indian in the twentieth century. Indexed by subject and author; list of periodicals abstracted. Z1209.2.N67I52

Johnson, Steven L. Guide to American Indian documents in the Congressional serial set: 1817–1899. N.Y., Clearwater Publ. Co., [1977]. 503p. **CC448**

"A project of the Institute for the Development of Indian Law."—*t.p.*
Lists some 10,649 documents relating to Indian affairs "which were located in the Serial Set volumes from 1817 through 1899."—*p.xv.* A chronological section lists the documents sequentially, giving title and date, citation to the Serial Set, and a brief description of the contents of the document. A subject index, organized mainly by tribal headings, is intended as "an index to the listings and not to the contents of the documents." KF8201.A1J63

Jones, Dorothy Miriam and **Wood, John R.** An Aleut bibliography. [Fairbanks], Inst. of Social, Economic and Govt. Research, Univ. of Alaska, [1975]. 195p. in various pagings. maps. (ISEGR report ser., 44) **CC449**

A selective, annotated survey of English-language materials on Aleut cultural and social life. In four sections: (1) alphabetical list of Aleut literature by author; (2) complete bibliographic information, including annotation; (3) list of literature arranged by time of observation (precontact and aboriginal period, Russian administration to 1867, American administration, 1867 to 1940, contemporary); (4) list organized by broad subject and type of publication. Z1210.A4J6

Laird, W. David. Hopi bibliography, comprehensive and annotated. Tucson, Univ. of Arizona Pr., [1977]. 735p. **CC450**

An alphabetical listing of over 2,900 published books, articles, and government and church reports on all aspects of Hopi life; excludes book reviews, newspaper articles, audiovisual materials, and most foreign-language publications. Title index and subject index; the latter refers to entries which include in their title the subject named, not necessarily to content of the items listed. Z1210.H6L33

Mail, Patricia D. and **McDonald, David R.** Tulapai to Tokay: a bibliography of alcohol use and abuse among native Americans of North America. New Haven, Conn., HRAF Pr., 1980. 356p. **CC451**

An annotated bibliography of 369 titles, including unpublished materials, from 1900 to 1976. Author listing; subject index; introductory literature review. Z1209.2.N67M34

Marken, Jack Walter and **Hoover, Herbert T.** Bibliography of the Sioux. Metuchen, N.J., Scarecrow Pr., 1980. 370p. (Native American bibliography ser., no.1) **CC452**

Lists 3,367 books, journal articles, published and unpublished dissertations and theses which have appeared since the publication of Dockstader's *The American Indian in graduate studies* (CC461). Alphabetical subject arrangement, with name and subject indexes. Z1210.D3M37

Murdock, George Peter and **O'Leary, Timothy J.** Ethnographic bibliography of North America. 4th ed. New Haven, Human Relations Area Files Pr., 1975. 5v. **CC453**

Contents: v.1, General North America; v.2, Arctic and subarctic; v.3, Far West and Pacific coast; v.4, Eastern United States; v.5, Plains and Southwest.

1st ed. 1941.

Computer produced; contains about 40,000 entries for books and articles on the native ethnic groups of North America. This edition shows an expanded number of ethnic group bibliographies (especially for the North Mexican area) which have been added to correspond to the *Handbook of North American Indians* (CC470). New bibliographies on Pan-Indianism, urban Indians, Canadian Indians, and United States and Canadian government relations with the native peoples. The "General introduction" supplies excellent discussion of sources of materials not included: government publications, ERIC documents, theses and dissertations, manuscripts and archives, nonprint materials and maps, and general bibliographic sources. Z1209.2.N67M87

Newberry Library, Chicago. Center for the History of the American Indian. The Newberry Library Center for the History of the American Indian bibliographical series. [Chicago,1976–83] [v.1–] (In progress) **CC454**

Contents: Native American historical demography, by Henry F. Dobyns (95p.); The Indians of California, by Robert F. Heizer (68p.); The Indians of the Subarctic, by June Helm (91p.); The Plains Indians, by E. Adamson Hoebel (75p.); The Navajos, by Peter Iverson (64p.); The Ojibwas, by Helen Hornbeck Tanner (78p.); The Apaches, by Michael E. Melody (86p.); United States Indian policy, by Francis Paul Prucha (54p.); The Cherokees, by R. D. Fogelson (98p.); Indian missions, by J. P. Ronda and J. L. Axtell (85p.); The Indians of the Northeast, by E. Tooker (77p.); The Delawares, by C. A. Weslager (84p.); The Creeks, by M. D. Green (114p.); Native Americans of the Northwest coast, by R. S. Grumet (108p.); The Sioux, by H. T. Hoover (78p.); Indians in Maryland and Delaware, by F. W. Porter III (107p.); Native American prehistory, by D. R. Snow (75p.); The emigrant Indians of Kansas, by W. E. Unrau (78p.); The Pawnees, by M. R. Blaine (96p.); The Indians of the Southwest, by H. B. Dobyns and R. C. Euler (192p.); The Choctaws, by C. S. Kidwell and C. Roberts (96p.); The Cheyennes, Maheoo's people, by P. J. Powell (128p.); Sociology of American Indians, by R. Thornton and M. K. Grasmick (96p.); Southeastern frontiers: Europeans, Africans, and American Indians, 1513–1840, by J. H. O'Donnell (118p.); The Indians of New England, by N. Salisbury (109p.); The Yakimas, by H. H. Schuster (158p.); Indians of the Great Basin, by O. C. Stewart (138p.); Canadian Indian policy, by R. J. Surtees (107p.); The urbanization of American Indians, by R. Thornton, G. D. Sandefur and H. G. Grasmick (87p.); Native American women: a contextual bibliography, by R. Green (120p.).

Subtitle: A critical bibliography.

Each volume has two main parts: a bibliographical essay and an alphabetical list of all works cited. There are also two sets of recommended titles: (1) books for beginners; (2) books for a basic library collection. The alphabetical list of all works cited is keyed as to level of suitability, and includes books and periodical articles.

Prucha, Francis Paul. A bibliographical guide to the history of Indian-white relations in the United States. Chicago, Univ. of Chicago Pr., [1977]. 454p. **CC455**

"A publication of the Center for the History of the American Indian of the Newberry Library."—*t.p.*

A classed bibliography of about 9,700 items; author/subject index. "Emphasis is on United States history, but British colonial Indian affairs have been included."—*Pref.* In two parts: (1) Guides to sources (i.e., reference works on archives, government documents,

manuscripts, and similar materials); (2) Classified bibliography of published works through 1974.

Continued by: Z1209.2.U5P67

—— Indian-white relations in the United States: a bibliography of works published 1975–1980. Lincoln, Univ. of Nebraska Pr., [1982]. 179p. **CC456**

Follows the plan of the earlier volume. While British colonial Indian affairs have been included, Canadian items have been excluded, and no attempt has been made to provide materials on Spanish-Indian relations. Author/subject index. Z1209.2.U5P67

Sutton, Imre. Indian land tenure: bibliographical essays and a guide to the literature. N.Y., Clearwater, [1975]. 290p. il. **CC457**

Presents a series of bibliographical essays in seven areas: (1) Aboriginal occupancy and territoriality; (2) Land cessions and the establishment of reservations; (3) Land administration and land utilization; (4) Aboriginal title and land claims; (5) Title clarification and change; (6) Tenure and jurisdiction; (7) Land tenure and culture change. A final essay compares the Native American experience with that of other post-colonial indigenous groups. Chapter bibliographies refer to the main bibliography, p.221–76; this is indexed by tribal and geographical indexes. Subject index to the essays. Z1209.2.U5S95

U.S. Dept. of the Interior. Library. Biographical and historical index of American Indians and persons involved in Indian affairs. Boston, G. K. Hall, 1966. 8v. **CC458**

A reproduction of the card file developed in the Bureau of Indian Affairs and now incorporated into the library of the Dept. of the Interior. It is a subject catalog only and, having been reproduced without editing, exhibits numerous irregularities in filing, forms of names, subject headings, etc. Includes references to some materials not in the Departmental collections. Z1209.U494

Whiteside, Don. Aboriginal people: a selected bibliography concerning Canada's first people. Ottawa, Nat. Indian Brotherhood, [1973]. 345p. **CC459**

Emphasizes unpublished speeches, reports, conference proceedings, newspaper articles, works by aboriginal people (indicated by an asterisk in the author index), and includes a section on the philosophy of aboriginal resistance. A classed list, with author and subject indexes. Z1209.2.C2W46

Wolf, Carolyn E. and **Folk, Karen R.** Indians of North and South America: a bibliography based on the collection at the Willard E. Yager Library-Museum, Hartwick College, Oneonta, N.Y. Metuchen, N.J., Scarecrow Pr., 1977. 576p. **CC460**

A main-entry list of over 4,000 books, periodical articles or issues, essays, and analyzed series published before late spring 1976, together with a description of the Yager collection of newspaper clippings. Title, series, and subject indexes. Z1209.W82

Dissertations

Dockstader, Frederick J. and **Dockstader, Alice W.** The American Indian in graduate studies; a bibliography of theses and dissertations. N.Y., Museum of the American Indian, Heye Foundation, 1973–74. 2v. (Museum of the American Indian, Heye Foundation. Contributions, v.25, pts.1–2) **CC461**

Pt.1 of the bibliography, covering theses of 1890–1955, was originally published 1957. It was reprinted 1973 in a 2d ed. omitting the "Addenda," p.362–64 and the index. Pt.2 covers the period 1955–70; it continues the item numbering from the main section of pt.1 (i.e., beginning with item 3660) and incorporates the addenda from the original volume into the alphabetical author sequence of pt.2. A new index to both volumes is provided. The total number of entries is now 7,446. Dissertations known to be available from University Microfilms are marked with an *M* following the citation. Z1209.D62

North American Indians: a dissertation index. Ann Arbor, Mich., University Microfilms Internat., 1977. 169p.
                                                            CC462

A keyword index listing over 1,700 doctoral dissertations written between 1904 and 1976, with an author index; both parts supply full bibliographic information. References to abstracts in *Dissertation abstracts international* and order information for dissertations available from University Microfilms are provided.   Z1209.N67N67

——— Supplement I. Ann Arbor, University Microfilms Internat., 1979. 56p.

Provides keyword title and author indexes to an additional 455 dissertations written 1977–78, and 102 masters theses published by University Microfilms 1962–78.   Z1209.2.N67U54

Periodicals

Native American periodicals and newspapers, 1828–1982; bibliography, publishing record, and holdings. Ed. by James P. Danky; comp. by Maureen E. Hady. Westport, Conn., Greenwood Pr., [1984]. 532p. il.   **CC464**

"In association with the State Historical Society of Wisconsin."—*t.p.*

A guide to the holdings and locations of 1,164 periodical and newspaper titles by and about Native Americans in the United States and Canada; 71% of the titles are held by the State Historical Society. Detailed bibliographic descriptions include information on indexes, editors, microform availability, library locations, and detailed holdings. Indexed by subject, editor, geographical area, and chronological period.

A complementary work is: Z1209.2.U5N37

Littlefield, Daniel F. and **Parins, James W.** American Indian and Alaskan native newspapers and periodicals. Westport, Conn., Greenwood Pr., [1984]– . v.1– . (In progress)
                                                            CC465

Contents: v.1, 1826–1924.

v.1 is a bibliography of about 200 titles "published by American Indians or Alaska Natives and those whose primary purpose was to publish information about *contemporary* Indians or Alaska Natives."—*p.vii.* Excludes Canadian and Mexican titles, as well as those focusing on archaeological, ethnological, and historical topics. Alphabetically arranged entries provide description, publication history, bibliographic information, bibliography, and selected locations. Appendixes list titles chronologically, by location, and by tribal interest or affiliation. Subject index.

Future volumes are to cover an additional 1,300 titles.
                                                            PN4883.L57

Archives

Chepesiuk, Ronald and **Shankman, Arnold M.** American Indian archival material; a guide to holdings in the Southeast. Westport, Conn., Greenwood Pr., [1982]. 325p.
                                                            CC466

A guide to materials held by 174 repositories in Alabama, Florida, Georgia, Kentucky, Louisiana, Mississippi, the Carolinas, Tennessee, Virginia, and West Virginia, principally on the Creek, Seminole, Cherokee, Chickasaw, Choctaw, and Lumbee tribes. List of repositories reporting no holdings or not responding, p.171–265. Indexed.
                                                            Z1209.2.U52S663

Hill, Edward E. Guide to records in the National Archives of the United States relating to American Indians. Wash., General Services Admin., Nat. Archives and Records Serv., 1981. 467p. il.   **CC467**

A "specialized supplement" to the *Guide to the National Archives . . .* (DB70), this volume is also arranged by record groups issued by particular agencies. Includes pre-federal, federal, and non-federal records such as those of the Confederacy, Russian agencies, personal papers, etc. Indexed.

The American Indian (Wash., 1972. 50p.) in the National Archives' "Select catalog of National Archives microfilm publications" series lists relevant records available on microfilm.
                                                            Z1209.2.U5H54

Dictionaries and encyclopedias

Klein, Barry. Reference encyclopedia of the American Indian. 3d ed. Rye, N.Y., Todd Publs., [1978]. 2v.   **CC468**

1st ed. 1967.

v.1 is a classified directory listing relevant government agencies and associations, museums, and cultural institutions, reservations and tribal councils, educational courses and materials, and an extensive bibliography (arranged by author and subject). v.2 offers biographical sketches of individuals named in the first volume— American Indians prominent in Indian affairs, business, the arts and professions, and non-Indians active in fields related to the study of American Indians.   E76.2.R8

Leitch, Barbara A. A concise dictionary of Indian tribes of North America. [Algonac, Mich.], Reference Pubns., [1979]. 646p. il.   **CC469**

Offers articles on individual tribes, giving geographic base, meaning of the tribal name and its variants, language, related groups, brief historical notes, information on tribal organization, religion, customs, crafts, etc. Brief bibliographies accompany most articles. Entries for languages consist only of *see* references to tribes of that language family, but serve to link the tribes. Indexed.   E76.2.L44

Handbooks and directories

Handbook of North American Indians. Wash., Smithsonian Inst., 1978–84. v.5, 6, 8–10, 15. il., maps. (In progress)
                                                            CC470

William C. Sturtevant, gen. ed.

Contents: v.5, Arctic, ed. by D. Damas; v.6, Subarctic, ed. by J. Helm; v.8, California, ed. by R. F. Heizer; v.9–10, Southwest, ed. by A. Ortiz; v.15, Northeast, ed. by B. G. Trigger.

These are the first published parts of a 20v. set planned to give "an encyclopedic summary of what is known about the prehistory, history, and cultures of the aboriginal peoples of North America who lived to the north of the urban civilizations of central Mexico." —*Pref.* Each volume comprises essays by specialists on specific aspects of Indian life, with extensive bibliography and detailed index.

Other volumes are to cover: [1] Introduction, methodology, sources, and continental summaries; [2] Indian and Eskimo communities in the twentieth century; [3] Environmental and biological backgrounds, physical anthropology, and earliest prehistoric cultures; [4] History of Indian-white relations; [5–7] and [9–15] will deal with major culture areas other than California; [16] Technology and the visual arts; [17] Native languages; [18–19] Biographical dictionary; [20] Cumulated index.   E77.H25

Hodge, Frederick Webb. Handbook of American Indians north of Mexico. Wash., Govt. Prt. Off., 1907–10. [Reissued 1912] 2v. il. (U.S. Bureau of American Ethnology. Bull. 30) (Repr.: N.Y., Pageant Books, 1959)   **CC471**

"Contains a descriptive list of the stocks, confederacies, tribes, tribal divisions and settlements north of Mexico, accompanied with the various names by which these have been known, together with biographies of Indians of note, sketches of their history, archeology, manners, arts, customs and institutions, and the aboriginal words incorporated in the English language . . . . Accompanying each synonym (the earliest known date always being given) a reference to the authority is noted, and these references form practically a bibliography of the tribe for those who wish to pursue the subject further."—*Pref.*   E77.H69

——— Handbook of Indians of Canada. Publ. as an appendix to the Tenth report of the Geographic Board of Canada. Ottawa, Parmelee, 1913. 632p. maps. **CC471a**

A reprint, with some additional material, of the articles in the author's *Handbook of American Indians north of Mexico* (above) which relate to Canada. E78.C2H6

Marquis, Arnold. A guide to America's Indians; ceremonials, reservations, and museums. Norman, Univ. of Oklahoma Pr., [1974]. 267p. il. **CC472**

A brief reference guide to many aspects of American Indian life. Useful maps, tables of tribes and reservations, etc. Bibliography; index. E76.2.M37

Swanton, John Reed. The Indian tribes of North America. Wash., Govt. Prt. Off., 1952. 726p. maps. (Smithsonian Inst. Bureau of American Ethnology. Bull. 145) (Repr. 1958) **CC474**

Arranged by state and then by other countries of North America. Gives extensive information on Indian tribes: their location, history, population, connection in which they have become noted, villages, meanings of names, etc. Detailed index. Bibliography, p.643–82. E77.S94

Terrell, John Upton. American Indian almanac. N.Y., World, [1971]. 494p. maps. **CC475**

An attempt to present to the general reader facts about prehistoric American Indians. Individual tribes, etc., are treated under ten geographical divisions of the United States. Employs an essay style, but an index, a glossary of terms, a select bibliography, and bibliographical notes make the work useful as a reference source. E77.T34

U.S. Dept. of Commerce. Federal and state Indian reservations and Indian trust areas. [Rev. ed.] [Wash., Govt. Prt. Off., 1974] 604p. **CC476**

1st ed., 1971, prep. by U.S. Economic Development Administration.

Gives basic information about Indian tribes and Alaskan natives. Arrangement is by state, then by native village or reservation. For each reservation usually gives: population, land status, culture, climate, government, community facilities, vital statistics. E93.U6553

Spanish-speaking Americans

Bibliography

Bravo, Enrique R., comp. Bibliografía puertorriqueña selecta y anotada. An annotated, selected Puerto Rican bibliography. N.Y., Urban Center of Columbia University, [1972]. 115p., 114p. **CC477**

A classed bibliography of more than 300 items on the anthropological, social, cultural, economic, and political history of Puerto Ricans. The works are first cited with annotations in Spanish and an index, then repeated in a separate section with English annotations and index. Z1551.B7

Cordasco, Francesco, Bucchioni, Eugene and **Castellanos, Diego.** Puerto Ricans on the United States mainland; a bibliography of reports, texts, critical studies and related materials. Totowa, N.J., Rowman & Littlefield, [1972]. 146p. **CC478**

A selective bibliography with some annotations. About 750 entries in broad subject categories with author index. Z1361.P8C67

Herrera, Diane. Puerto Ricans and other minority groups in the continental United States: an annotated bibliography, with a new foreword and supplemental bibliography by Francesco Cordasco. Detroit, Blaine Ethridge Books, [1979]. xxxi, 397p. **CC479**

Originally publ. as *Puerto Ricans in the United States* (1973).

Focuses on bilingual and bicultural education of Puerto Rican and other non-English-speaking students; also includes sociological, psychological, and literary studies of the Puerto Rican experience. More than 2,500 citations arranged by subject; author index. Z1361.E4H42

MacCorkle, Lyn. Cubans in the United States: a bibliography for research in the social and behavioral sciences, 1960–1983. Westport, Conn., Greenwood Pr., [1984]. 227p. (Bibliographies and indexes in sociology, no.1) **CC480**

Cites English-language literature within seven broad subject areas; arranged chronologically within subject sections. Author index. Z1361.C65M32

Meier, Matt S. Bibliography of Mexican American history. Westport, Conn., Greenwood Pr., [1984]. 500p. **CC481**

4,372 citations are organized within two broad categories: six chapters follow chronological periods from colonial times to the present; three chapters treat topics of labor, politics, and culture; and the concluding three chapters list reference works, libraries and archives, and journals. Within the chronological/topical chapters works are grouped by form—books, dissertations, articles—with many contents notes. Author and subject indexes. Z1361.M4M414

Pino, Frank. Mexican Americans; a research bibliography. [East Lansing], Latin American Studies Center, Michigan State Univ., 1974. 2v. **CC482**

The work "is intended as an interdisciplinary guide to the study of the Mexican American" and "includes materials ranging from the early Spanish settlements to the present day activities of the Hispano, Mexican-American and Chicano."—*p.ix*. Lists books, monographs, master's theses, doctoral dissertations, articles in journals, and government publications. Arranged in 35 subject categories, with extensive cross-referencing. Author index, but no detailed subject index. Z1361.M4P55

Puerto Rican Research and Resources Center. The Puerto Ricans: an annotated bibliography. Paquita Vivó, ed. N.Y., Bowker, 1973. 299p. **CC483**

A selective bibliography on all aspects of Puerto Rican history, life, and culture. In four main sections: (1) Books, pamphlets, and dissertations; (2) Government documents; (3) Periodical literature (i.e., a list of periodicals, plus a selection of periodical articles); (4) Audiovisual materials. The first three sections are subdivided by subject field; there are author, subject, and title indexes. Emphasis is on recent materials, and English-language publication is given preference where both English and Spanish versions exist. Z1551.P84

Robinson, Barbara J. and **Robinson, Joy C.** The Mexican American: a critical guide to research aids. Greenwich, Conn., JAI Pr., [1980]. 287p. (Foundations in library and information science, v.1) **CC484**

An annotated bibliography of more than 660 bibliographies and other reference sources, grouped in two parts: general works, and subject bibliographies. Selections include books, book chapters, government publications, periodical articles, pamphlets, theses and dissertations, and mimeographed materials. Author, title, and subject indexes. Z1361.M4R63

Sourcebook of Hispanic culture in the United States. Ed. by David William Foster. Chicago, Amer. Lib. Assoc., 1982. 352p. **CC485**

In four main parts: (1) Mexican Americans; (2) Continental Puerto Ricans; (3) Cuban Americans; (4) General. Subsections by contributing scholars offer introductory essays and annotated bibliographies on the history, anthropology, sociology, literature, etc., of the group concerned. Bibliographies are meant to include "the most important monographs, essays, journals, and reports on the topic" (*Introd.*) and "the bibliographies should be able to serve as guides for collection development in large public, research [and] university libraries." Author-title index. Z1361.S7S64

Talbot, Jane Mitchell and **Cruz, Gilbert R.** A comprehensive Chicano bibliography, 1960–1972. Austin, Tex., Jenkins Publ. Co., 1973. 375p. **CC486**

A classed bibliography (books, articles, theses and dissertations, government documents, reports) with author index and a "cross index" indicating materials which relate to other topics in addition to the category in which the citation is placed. Includes audiovisual materials and children's literature. Z1361.M4T34

Tatum, Charles M. A selected and annotated bibliography of Chicano studies. 2d ed. [Lincoln, Nebr.], Soc. of Spanish and Spanish-American Studies, [1979]. 121p. (SSSAS bibliographies, 101) **CC487**

1st ed. 1976.

Intended for the secondary school or college teacher. Emphasizes material produced by Chicanos. Sections on art, folklore, audiovisual materials, journals and newspapers, music, language instruction, and a series of chapters on forms of literature and literary criticism. Name index. Z1361.M4T36

Trejo, Arnulfo D. Bibliografía chicana; a guide to information sources. Detroit, Gale, [1975]. 193p. (Ethnic studies information guide ser., 1) **CC488**

An annotated guide to more than 300 publications concerning Chicano life and experience. Subject arrangement with author and title indexes. Includes directories of relevant newspapers, periodicals, and publishers. Z1361.M4T73

Woods, Richard D. Reference materials on Mexican Americans: an annotated bibliography. Metuchen, N.J., Scarecrow Pr., 1976. 190p. **CC489**

Lists separately published bibliographies and reference-type works (dictionaries, collective biographies, etc.) on Mexican Americans in the United States. 387 entries in classed arrangement, with author, subject, and title indexes. E184.M5W66

Indexes

Chicano periodical index; a cumulative index to selected Chicano periodicals published between 1967 and 1978. Boston, G. K. Hall, 1981. 972p. **CC490**

"Produced by the Committee for the Development of Subject Access to Chicano Literatures. Director, Richard Chabrán . . . . Coordinating Center, Chicano Studies Library, Univ. of California, Berkeley; Operational Center, Chicano Studies Research Library, Univ. of California, Los Angeles."—*t.p.*

A subject index to more than 4,900 articles appearing in some 18 Chicano academic journals, literary publications, popular magazines, and special interest periodicals. Author/title index. Z1361.M4C47

————; a cumulative index to selected periodicals, 1979–81 (with selected serials indexed retrospectively). Ed. by Francisco García-Ayvens, Richard Chabrán; comp. by the Chicano Periodical Indexing Project. Boston, G. K. Hall, 1983. 648p. **CC491**

Adds about 4,500 citations to articles from 23 periodicals. Z1361.M4C474

Dictionaries

Meier, Matt S. and **Rivera, Feliciano.** Dictionary of Mexican American history. Westport, Conn., Greenwood Pr., [1981]. 498p. il., maps. **CC492**

An alphabetically arranged dictionary of Chicano culture, covering the period 1519 to 1980. Brief entries sometimes include suggestions for further reading. Appendixes offer general bibliography, chronology, glossary of Chicano terms, list of Mexican American journals, statistical tables, and maps. Indexed. E184.M5M453

Directories

U.S. Cabinet Committee on Opportunity for the Spanish Speaking. Directory of Spanish speaking organizations in the United States. Wash., 1970. 224p. **CC493**

Provides information on slightly more than 200 organizations. E184.S75A44

Biography

Martínez, Julio A. Chicano scholars and writers: a bio-bibliographical directory. Metuchen, N.J., Scarecrow Pr., 1979. 579p. **CC494**

Provides biographical information and lists of publications for more than 500 scholars and writers in the humanities, social sciences, and education. Critical works on the biographies are also noted. Subject index by field of interest. E184.M5M385

WOMEN

Guides

Lynn, Naomi B., Matasar, Ann B. and **Rosenberg, Marie Barovic.** Research guide in women's studies. Morristown, N.J., General Learning Pr., [1974]. 194p. **CC495**

A basic guide, mainly at the undergraduate level. Only four chapters deal specifically with women's studies and courses; the remaining six deal with general reference works and subjects such as how to research and write a paper, how to use statistics, etc. Subject index. HQ1206.L96

McKee, Kathleen Burke. Women's studies; a guide to reference sources. Storrs, Conn., Univ. of Connecticut Lib., [1977]. 112p. (Bibliography ser., no.6) **CC496**

"With a supplement on feminist serials in the University of Connecticut Library's Alternative Press Collection, by Joanne V. Akeroyd."—*t.p.*

Arranged by type of publication (guides; library catalogs; handbooks; directories; statistics; indexes, abstracts and bibliographies) with topical subdivisions as appropriate. Author, title, and subject indexes. Based on the collection at the University of Connecticut Library, Storrs. 364 items with annotations. Z7965.M33

Warren, Mary Anne. The nature of woman: an encyclopedia & guide to the literature. Inverness, Calif., Edgepress, [1979]. 708p. **CC497**

Offers a series of author and topical entries concerned with the following issues: "(1) moral, psychological, theological and other 'intrinsic' differences between women and men (apart from the obvious biological ones); (2) causal explanations of sex dominance, where it occurs; (3) the moral implications of sex roles, and the moral aspects of other issues of special relevance to women, e.g. abortion; and (4) possible means of engineering social change with respect to sex roles."—*p.i.* Cross references are provided from the topical articles to the author entries. Bibliography; glossary; index. HQ1115.W37

Bibliography

Bibliography of bibliography

Ballou, Patricia K. Women: a bibliography of bibliographies. Boston, G. K. Hall, [1980]. 155p. **CC498**

An annotated bibliography of 557 English-language books, pamphlets, essays, journal articles, and dissertations of a bibliographic nature produced since 1970. Classed arrangement: publications of

one type of format; geographical subjects; topical subjects. Cross references and personal names index. A 2d ed. is in preparation.
Z7961.A1B34

Ritchie, Maureen. Women's studies: a checklist of bibliographies. London, Mansell, 1980. 107p.   **CC499**

A bibliography of 489 English-language bibliographies published as books, articles, or pamphlets. 19 broad subject groups are usually further subdivided. Price and ordering information are given. Author and keyword indexes.   Z7961.A1R58

Williamson, Jane, ed. New feminist scholarship: a guide to bibliographies. Old Westbury, N.Y., Feminist Pr., [1979]. 139p.   **CC500**

A bibliography of 391 English-language bibliographies, resource lists, and literature reviews in monograph or article form, arranged in 30 subject sections. Literary bibliographies of individual women writers are excluded, as are lists of non-sexist books for children and young adults. About half of the entries are annotated. Author and title indexes.   Z7161.A1W54

Current

Studies on women abstracts. v.1, no.1– . [Abingdon, Oxfordshire], Carfax, [1983]– . Quarterly.   **CC501**

An international abstracting source, with some British emphasis. Separate journal article and book sections are arranged by periodical title and author, respectively. Author and subject indexing appears only in the final quarterly issue and covers the full year.

Women studies abstracts. v.1, no.1– , Winter 1972– . Rush, N.Y., 1972– . Quarterly, with annual index.   **CC502**

Abstracts are grouped under headings such as: Education, Sex characteristics and differences, Employment, etc. Articles from a wide range of periodicals (including some foreign-language journals) are abstracted, along with some books and pamphlets. There is an additional listing of articles not abstracted, and a listing of book reviews. Subject index.   Z7962.W65

General

See also CC136, CC172, CC260.

Astin, Helen S., Suniewick, Nancy and **Dweck, Susan.** Women; a bibliography on their education and careers. Wash., Human Service Pr., [1971]. 243p.   **CC503**

"Sponsored by University Research Corp. and the Institute of Life Insurance."—*title page.*
A classed bibliography with abstracts. 352 items: books, pamphlets, theses, and periodical articles. Author and subject indexes.
Z7963.E7A86

Bibliographic guide to studies on the status of women, development and population trends. [Paris, etc.], Bowker, UNIPUB, Unesco, [1983]. 284p.   **CC504**

A general introduction dealing with women's work and labor force participation, family and household, education, and demographic forces in Africa, the Arab states, Asia, Eastern Europe, Latin America, North America and western Europe is followed by annotated bibliographies on each region; these are subdivided by topic and include special journal issues and research institutes. Indexed by country, subject, and author.   Z7963.E7B5

Bickner, Mei Liang. Women at work; an annotated bibliography. Los Angeles, Manpower Research Center, Inst. of Industrial Relations, Univ. of California, [1974–77]. 2v.   **CC505**

A selective bibliography intended "primarily for persons who teach, conduct research, or are serious students in the general area of working women."—*Introd.* Classed arrangement of books, journal articles, government documents, reports, and court decisions; author, title, classed category, and subject indexes. Special attention is paid to minority women, women employed outside the professions,

and relevant legal developments. v.1 includes material published 1959–73; v.2 covers the literature from 1973 to 1975.
Z7963.E7B52

Cantor, Aviva. A bibliography on the Jewish woman: a comprehensive and annotated listing of works published, 1900–1978. Fresh Meadows, N.Y., Biblio Pr., [1979]. 53p.   **CC506**

1st version publ. 1972; this is the 6th version.
A broadly classed subject bibliography of in-print English-language books, pamphlets, serial titles, and articles. Includes reference sources, anthologies, poetry, children's books; materials relate to the Jewish woman historically, in the Holocaust, in resistance movements, and in various countries. No index.   Z7964.J4C36

Diner, Hasia R. Women and urban society: a guide to information sources. Detroit, Gale, [1979]. 138p. (Urban studies information guide ser., v.7)   **CC507**

Most of the literature listed here dates from the 1940s to the late 1970s and concerns women in Africa, Asia, and Latin America. Issues include urban family structure, fertility, women's employment, social interaction among urban women, etc. Appendixes present a core collection, list of abstracts and indexes, and periodical titles. Author, title, and subject indexes.   Z7961.D55

Faunce, Patricia S. Women and ambition: a bibliography. Metuchen, N.J., Scarecrow Pr., 1980. 695p.   **CC508**

A classed list of a wide variety of materials published from 1960 to 1976 on the social, psychological, educational, and occupational forces shaping women's achievement and ambition. Social/psychological forces include fear of success and failure; occupational forces are subdivided by subject area. A separate section treats black, Latin, and Native American women. Author index.   Z7961.F38

Goodwater, Leanna. Women in antiquity: an annotated bibliography. Metuchen, N.J., Scarecrow Pr., 1975. 171p.   **CC509**

"Intended as a guide to the political, social, legal, and literary achievements and treatment of women in antiquity . . . specifically ancient Greece and Rome, . . . the Minoans, Etruscans, the Hellenistic kingdoms, and some provinces of the Roman Empire" (*Pref.*), this work omits material on women in Africa or the Near East, as well as Cleopatra, Christian saints, and literary material on Sappho. Its two main sections cover (1) ancient sources by and about women and women authors and (2) modern works. Indexes by personal names of classical women, and by authors, editors, and translators.
Z7961.G66

Hughes, Marija Matich. The sexual barrier: legal, medical, economic and social aspects of sex discrimination. Wash., Hughes Pr., [1977]. 843p.   **CC510**

A revised and enlarged ed. of the author's earlier volumes of similar title (San Francisco, 1970; Suppl. 1–2, 1971–72). It groups more than 8,000 English-language books, articles, pamphlets and documents of the 1960–75 period into 17 subject chapters which are further subdivided by specific topic and/or geographic region. Many brief annotations. Principal strength is the comprehensive treatment of legal issues affecting women; the detailed listing of materials on women in specific occupations is another distinctive and useful feature.   KF4758.A1H83

Internationaal Archief voor de Vrouwenbeweging. Library. Catalogue of the library of the International Archives for the Women's Movement. Boston, G. K. Hall, 1980. 4v.   **CC511**

Contents: v.1–2, Author catalogue; v.3–4, Systematic catalogue.
Reproduces the catalog cards for a collection of some 15,000 books and pamphlets and about 280 feminist and women's magazines. "Part of the collection consists of archives (i.e., that of the National Exhibition of Women at Work of 1898), posters, badges, photos, and other visual material."—*Pref.*   Z7965.I7

Jacobs, Sue-Ellen. Women in perspective; a guide for cross-cultural studies. Urbana, Univ. of Illinois Pr., [1974]. 299p.   **CC512**

An extensive and important bibliography of book and periodical materials, dissertations, etc. In two main sections: (1) Geographical topics and (2) Subject topics, the first section subdivided by country or region, the second by specific subject. Author index and detailed table of contents, but no subject index. Z7961.J33

Jarrard, Mary E. W. and **Randall, Phyllis R.** Women speaking; an annotated bibliography of verbal and nonverbal communication, 1970–1980. N.Y., Garland, 1982. 478p. (Garland reference library of social science, v.108) **CC513**

1,327 entries for English-language publications (excluding theses and dissertations) are classed according to subject in three broad areas—settings, characteristics, and means (verbal, nonverbal) of communication, then further subdivided by topic. Subject index. HQ1426.J37

Krichmar, Albert. The women's movement in the seventies; an international English-language bibliography. [With the assistance of] Virginia Carlson Smith and Ann E. Wiederrecht. Metuchen, N.J., Scarecrow Pr., 1977. 875p. **CC514**

Lists some 8,600 "English-language publications concerning the status of women in nearly 100 countries. . . . The emphasis is on change, attempted change, and continuing problems confronting women in the countries in which they live."—*Introd.* Includes doctoral dissertations, books, pamphlets, research reports, periodical articles, and government documents published or reprinted 1970–75," plus some 1976 publications. Geographical arrangement, with topical subdivisions under those countries or areas about which there is a considerable quantity of literature. Author and subject indexes; numerous annotations. Z7961.K57

McFeely, Mary Drake. Women's work in Britain and America from the nineties to World War I; an annotated bibliography. Boston, G. K. Hall, [1982]. 140p. **CC515**

In two sections, "Women's work in Great Britain" and "Women's work in America," with more than 500 entries for books (including fiction), pamphlets, and articles written between 1890 and 1914, plus later material dealing with that period. Includes both paid employment and voluntary work in social welfare, etc. For material on American women and trade unions, the user is referred to *American women and the labor movement* by M. J. Soltow and M. K. Wery (CC548). Author, title, and subject indexes. Z7963.E7M43

Moore, Kathryn M. and **Wollitzer, Peter A.** Women in higher education: a contemporary bibliography. Wash., Nat. Assoc. of Women Deans, Administrators and Counselors, [1979]. 114p. **CC516**

Prep. by Pennsylvania State University.

An annotated subject bibliography of about 400 entries published during the 1970s on women as students, faculty, and administrators. Author index. Z5815.U5M66

Oakes, Elizabeth H. and **Sheldon, Kathleen E.** Guide to social science resources in women's studies. Santa Barbara, Calif., ABC-Clio, [1978]. 162p. **CC517**

An annotated bibliography of books and special collections of articles in journals and books which are current, readily available, interdisciplinary and international in scope. Materials have been included which would be useful as readings for undergraduate women's studies courses. Organized by academic discipline—anthropology, economics, history, psychology, sociology, feminist thought—with appropriate subdivisions. Lists of bibliographies, journals, and other resources. Author and subject indexes. Z7961.O23

Parker, Franklin and **Parker, Betty June.** Women's education—a world view: annotated bibliography of doctoral dissertations. Westport, Conn., Greenwood Pr., [1979]. 470p. **CC518**

An attempt to list and annotate "all locatable U.S. and Canadian doctoral dissertations in English that concern the education of girls and women at all ages and school levels in public and private

institutions worldwide."—*Pref.* Alphabetical author listing with subject index. Z7963.E2W65

Rosenberg, Marie Barovic and **Bergstrom, Len V.** Women and society: a critical review of the literature with a selected annotated bibliography. Beverly Hills, Sage Publs., [1975]. 345p. **CC519**

The "Introduction: a selective review of the literature" is a 20-page survey of classic books on women in history, women at work, and women in politics; the remainder of the volume cites 3,600 books, articles, documents, periodicals and newspapers, and women's collections and libraries grouped into large subject areas; most chapters have more detailed subject breakdowns. Brief annotations. Indexed by authors, journal issues devoted to women, persons, places, subjects.
Continued by: Z7961.R67

Een, JoAnn Delores and **Rosenberg-Dishman, Marie B.** Women and society, citations 3601 to 6000: an annotated bibliography. Beverly Hills, Sage Publs., [1978]. 275p. **CC520**

Retains the basic organization of the preceding work while adding sections on the political status of women and women's handbooks and almanacs, and omitting sections on women's collections and libraries and women's periodicals and newspapers. Indexed by authors, places and topics, with a special index of journal issues or sections devoted to women. Z7961.E4

Sophia Smith Collection. Catalogs of the Sophia Smith Collection women's history archive, Smith College, Northampton, Massachusetts. Boston, G. K. Hall, 1975. 7v. **CC521**

Contents: v.1–2, Author catalog; v.3–5, Subject catalog; v.6–7, Manuscript catalog; Photographs.

Photoreproduction of the catalog cards for a collection emphasizing the history of women in the United States, but with international materials as well. Numerous analytics for essays and periodical articles. Z7965.S65

Stineman, Esther. Women's studies: a recommended core bibliography. Littleton, Colo., Libraries Unlimited, 1979. 670p. **CC522**

"Underlying this bibliography is the intent to provide an annotated and indexed collection, organized around traditional disciplines, of English-language, mainly in-print publications that support research on women."—*Introd.* 1,763 items. Z7961.S75

Sullivan, Kaye. Films for, by, and about women. Metuchen, N.J., Scarecrow Pr., 1980. 552p. **CC523**

An international, annotated title listing of about 4,000 films—feature, documentary, educational, etc. Directory of film sources. Indexed by women filmmakers and subject. PN1995.9.W6S95

Wheeler, Helen Rippier. Womanhood media: current resources about women. Metuchen, N.J., Scarecrow Pr., 1972. 335p. **CC524**

Includes sections on reference works, a basic book collection (with annotations), women's movement periodicals, audiovisual materials, and a directory of sources. Z7961.W48

——— Womanhood media supplement: additional current resources about women. Metuchen, N.J., Scarecrow Pr., 1975. 482p. **CC525**

". . . continues the media and other resource parts of the 1972 volume, i.e., its Part III, 'A Basic Book Collection,' IV, 'Non-Book Resources,' and V, 'Directory of Sources.' "—*Introd.*
Z7961.W48

Women in medicine; a bibliography of the literature on women physicians. Comp. and ed. by Sandra L. Chaff [and others]. Metuchen, N.J., Scarecrow Pr., 1977. 1124p. **CC526**

"This work provides citations to literature which documents [the] increasing involvement of women in medicine, and examines the causes and future course of this trend. It includes, also, material about the lives of specific women physicians and helps provide insight into how the careers of most women physicians have differed from those of their male colleagues."—*Introd.* About 4,000 entries in classed arrangement, representing literature from the 18th century through 1975. International in scope. Author, subject, and personal name indexes.   Z7963.M43W65

Women, 1965–1975. Cynthia Crippen, ed. [Glen Rock, N.J., Microfilming Corp. of America, 1978] 1150p. il. (The New York times cumulative subject & personal name index)
CC527

A topically arranged cumulation of selected material from the *New York times index* from 1965 to 1975. Detailed subject classification; under each heading abstracts are arranged chronologically, with complete citations to the *New York times* articles. Geographic, subject, organization, and personal names indexes. Chronology and bibliography.   Z7961.W62

Women's work and women's studies, 1971–73/74. N.Y., Women's Center, Barnard College, 1972–75. Annual.
CC528

An interdisciplinary bibliography of published research, dissertations, pamphlets, and research in progress; omits articles appearing in popular magazines. Classed arrangement with author index; some brief annotations.   Z7961.W64

United States

See also CC96, CC366, CC396, CC402, CC515.

Addis, Patricia K. Through a woman's I: an annotated bibliography of American women's autobiographical writings, 1946–1976. Metuchen, N.J., Scarecrow Pr., 1983. 607p.   **CC529**

Supplements Kaplan's *Bibliography of American autobiographies* (AJ96). An author listing of more than 2,200 autobiographies, diaries, published collections of letters, travel narratives, etc. Indexed by profession, subject or narrative type, and title.
Z7963.B6A32

Arthur and Elizabeth Schlesinger Library on the History of Women in America. The manuscript inventories and the catalogs of manuscripts, books and pictures. 2d rev. and enl. ed. Boston, G. K. Hall, 1984. 10v.   **CC530**

Contents: v.1–8, Book catalog; v.9–10, Manuscript inventories. 1st ed. 1973.
Reproduces the subject, title, and author cards for some 18,000 volumes, over 200 collections of personal papers, and 31 archives of women's organizations located at Radcliffe College; books from the Widener Library at Harvard are also listed.   Z7965.A78

Buhle, Mari Jo. Women and the American Left: a guide to sources. Boston, G. K. Hall, [1983]. 281p.   **CC531**

An annotated bibliography of 595 items arranged by historical periods from 1871 to 1981, subdivided by form (histories, biographies, books and pamphlets on "the woman question," periodicals, fiction and poetry). Indexed.   Z7964.U49B84

Conway, Jill K., Kealey, Linda and **Schulte, Janet E.** The female experience in eighteenth- and nineteenth-century America: a guide to the history of American women. N.Y., Garland, 1982. 290p. (Garland reference library of social science, v.35)   **CC532**

Bibliographical citations to primary and secondary works are preceded by introductory review essays in more than 40 subject chapters. Arranged in six principal sections: culture and society, work, education, religion, politics, health. Author index. A future volume is to cover the twentieth century.   Z7961.C64

Davis, Nanette J. and **Keith, Jone M.** Women and deviance: issues in social conflict and change: an annotated bibliography. N.Y., Garland, [1984]. 236p. (Applied social science

bibliographies, v.1; Garland reference library of social science, v.157)   **CC533**

A selection of 516 titles on crimes by and crimes against women in the United States, as well as such "social control" topics as abortion, substance abuse, lesbianism, poverty, suicide, teenage pregnancy, etc. Subject and name indexes.   Z7964.U49D38

Equal Rights Amendment Project. The equal rights amendment: a bibliographic study. Westport, Conn., Greenwood Pr., [1976]. 367p.   **CC534**

About 5,800 items arranged by type of media, with author and organization indexes. Provides references to pertinent materials in the microfilm series *Herstory* and *Women and the law* (reel 1).
KF4758.A1E6

Feinberg, Renee. Women, education, and employment; a bibliography of periodical citations, pamphlets, newspapers and government documents, 1970–1980. [Hamden, Conn.], Library Professional Pubns., 1982. 274p.   **CC535**

A detailed subject classification of more than 2,500 entries for English-language items pertaining to the United States; includes ERIC documents. Author and subject indexes.   Z5815.U5F44

Fishburn, Katherine. Women in popular culture: a reference guide. Westport, Conn., Greenwood Pr., [1982]. 267p.
CC536

Presents seven bibliographical review essays on the histories and theories of women in American popular culture, and women in popular literature, magazines, film, television, advertising, fashion, sports, and comics; each essay concludes with a list of titles cited. Also lists selected periodical titles and special issues, reference works, chronology of principal dates, and major research centers.
HQ1426.F685

Franzosa, Susan Douglas and **Mazza, Karen A.** Integrating women's studies into the curriculum: an annotated bibliography. Westport, Conn., Greenwood Pr., [1984]. 100p. (Bibliographies and indexes in education, no.1}   **CC537**

Nine subject chapters corresponding to academic disciplines (literature, science, fine arts, etc.) are subdivided for sections on women in the field, reconceptualizing the discipline, thematic guides, and curriculum strategies. Author index.   Z7964.U49F73

Haber, Barbara. Women in America: a guide to books, 1963–1975; with an appendix on books published 1976–1979. Urbana, Ill., Univ. of Illinois Pr., [1981]. 262p.
CC538

An updated ed. of the author's 1978 work publ. by G. K. Hall.
The basic text features full annotations of nonfiction works grouped by broad subject; the appendix entries (p.191–246) are arranged by subject, but are listed as references cited in bibliographic essays. Indexed.   Z7964.U49H3

Harrison, Cynthia E. Women in American history: a bibliography. Santa Barbara, Calif., [ABC-Clio, 1979]. 374p. (Clio bibliography ser., 5)   **CC539**

Offers 3,395 abstracts of articles from about 550 periodicals and five collected works published between 1963 and 1976; about 3,000 of the abstracts were drawn from *America: history and life* (DB47), but the others are new to this work. Broad subject organization, with detailed subject and author indexes. Also includes material on Canadian women.   Z7962.H37

———— Women's movement media: a source guide. N.Y., Bowker, 1975. 269p.   **CC540**

". . . includes approximately 550 descriptions of organizations, arranged by function, type or main interest of the group, which supply books, periodicals, films, tapes, records, services, and information on and for women."—*Pref.* Sections for: (1) Publishers, distributors, news services, and products; (2) Women's research centers and library research collections; (3) Women's organizations and centers; (4) Governmental and quasi-governmental organizations and agencies; (5) Special interests. Geographic index; media title index; name index of groups; subject index of groups.
Z7964.U49H37

Kennedy, Susan E. America's white working-class women; a historical bibliography. N.Y., Garland, 1981. 253p. (Women's studies: facts and issues, v.2; Garland reference library of the humanities, v.260) **CC541**

An annotated bibliography of more than 1,000 citations to English-language materials, including dissertations and government documents. General works are followed by sections organized by historical period, subdivided by topic. Author and subject indexes.

Z7903.E7K45

Krichmar, Albert. The women's rights movement in the United States, 1848–1970; a bibliography and sourcebook. Metuchen, N.J., Scarecrow Pr., 1972. 436p. **CC542**

A topically arranged bibliography on "the legal, political, economic, religious, educational, and professional status of women since 1848."—*Introd.* In addition to the more than 5,100 references to book, periodical, and pamphlet materials, there are sections on manuscript sources and women's liberation serial publications. Some annotations; indexed. Z7964.U49K75

Leonard, Eugenie Andruss, Drinker, Sophie Hutchinson and **Holden, Miriam Young.** The American woman in colonial and revolutionary times, 1565–1800; a syllabus with bibliography. Philadelphia, Univ. of Pennsylvania Pr., 1962. 169p. **CC543**

A syllabus, with references grouped under headings and subheadings, organized to show all aspects of the life and work of the colonial woman, followed by a bibliography of 1,082 items (books and articles). Z7964.U49L4

McCaghy, M. Dawn. Sexual harassment: a guide to resources. Boston, G. K. Hall, [1985]. 181p. **CC544**

299 citations to a wide variety of materials published since the mid-1970s, primarily concerning the situation in the United States. Arranged in topical chapters preceded by short review essays; full annotations. Author/title and subject indexes. Z7963.E7M427

Nelson, Barbara J. American women and politics: a selected bibliography and resource guide. N.Y., Garland, 1984. 255p. (Garland reference library of social science, v.174) **CC545**

A topically arranged list of about 1,600 citations, emphasizing work published 1970–82. "Politics" has been broadly interpreted to include social movements, political socialization, women's role in the welfare state, and feminist/political theory. Author and subject indexes. Z7964.U49N38

Phelps, Ann T., Farmer, Helen S. and **Backer, Thomas E.** New career options for women: a selected annotated bibliography. N.Y., Human Sciences Pr., [1977]. 144p. **CC546**

A classed bibliography of 240 English-language books, journal articles and government reports published since 1970, designed to complement *New career options for women; a counselor's sourcebook* (N.Y., Human Sciences Pr., 1977). Stresses information useful to career counselors for women, covering topics such as types of work (professional, part-time, crafts, management), education and apprenticeship programs, effects on children of a working mother, other social, biological and psychological factors, and legal issues. Author and title indexes. Z7164.V6P48

Sahli, Nancy Ann. Women and sexuality in America: a bibliography. Boston, G. K. Hall, [1984]. 404p. **CC547**

An annotated bibliography of 1,684 citations. Broad topical arrangement; author/title and subject indexes. Z7964.U49S26

Soltow, Martha Jane and **Wery, Mary K.** American women and the labor movement, 1825–1974: an annotated bibliography. Metuchen, N.J., Scarecrow Pr., 1976. 247p. **CC548**

A revised edition of *Women in American labor history* (East Lansing, Mich., 1972).

Classed arrangement under the following main headings: (1) Employment; (2) Trade unions; (3) Working conditions; (4) Strikes; (5) Legislation; (6) Worker education; (7) Labor leaders; (8) Supportive efforts. Author and subject indexes. Z7963.E7S635

Stanwick, Kathy and **Li, Christine.** The political participation of women in the United States: a selected bibliography, 1950–1976. Metuchen, N.J., Scarecrow Pr., 1977. 160p. **CC549**

Comp. by Center for the American Woman and Politics, Eagleton Institute of Politics, Rutgers–The State University of New Jersey.

Expansion and updating of the Center's *Women and American politics; a selected bibliography, 1965–1974* (New Brunswick, N.J., 1974). More than 1,500 entries grouped by type, with biographical and author indexes, but no topical subject approach. Includes substantial amounts of unpublished material and research in progress at the time of publication. Z7961.S74

Terris, Virginia R. Woman in America: a guide to information sources. Detroit, Gale, [1980]. 520p. (American studies information guide ser., v.7) **CC550**

A classified, annotated bibliography of more than 2,400 entries. Particularly strong section on women in the arts (p.281–342); notes source collections, microform and audiovisual materials, and oral history resources. Appendixes list centers and collections, film and audiovisual sources, government agencies, news services, organizations, periodicals, and presses. Author, title, and subject indexes. Z7964.U49T45

Tingley, Elizabeth and **Tingley, Donald F.** Women and feminism in American history; a guide to information sources. Detroit, Gale, [1981]. 289p. (American government and history information guide ser., v.12) **CC551**

An annotated bibliography of English-language works on suffragism, equal rights, and "any activity or analysis which concerns itself with women and the action necessary for women to obtain their rightful status as full human beings, including . . . the creation of a women's culture . . . ."—*Pref.* Eleven chapters provide reference sources and a historical approach; the remaining 22 chapters deal with topics such as antifeminist writing since 1940. Author, title, and subject indexes. Z7964.U49T52

Wilkins, Kay S. Women's education in the United States: a guide to information sources. Detroit, Gale, [1979]. 217p. (Education information guide ser., v.4) **CC552**

A classified, annotated bibliography of more than 1,100 items, with author, title, and subject indexes. Z7963.E2W53

Wilson, Carolyn F. Violence against women: an annotated bibliography. Boston, G. K. Hall, [1981]. 111p. **CC553**

A selection of 213 books and articles, most written since 1975, on battered women, rape, sexual abuse of children, and pornography. Topical arrangement; author/title and subject indexes.

HV6250.4.W65W54

Women's history sources: a guide to archives and manuscript collections in the United States. Ed. by Andrea Hinding. N.Y., Bowker, 1979. 2v. **CC554**

"In association with the University of Minnesota."—*t.p.*

Contents: v.1, Collections; v.2, Index.

Records the results of the "Women's History Sources Survey" conducted under auspices of the Social Welfare History Archives at the University of Minnesota with additional funding from the National Endowment for the Humanities. Entries describe "18,026 collections in 1,586 repositories, arranged geographically by state and city."—*Pref.* The bulk of the information was obtained by questionnaire, but field workers conducted on-site surveys at various institutions which were unable to report their own holdings. Included are collections devoted to: (1) Papers of a woman; (2) Records of a women's organization; (3) Records of an organization, institution, or movement in which women played a significant but not exclusive part; (4) Records of an organization, institution, or movement that significantly affected women; (5) Groups of materials assembled around a theme or type of record that relates to women; (6) Papers of a family (in which there are papers of female members); (7) Collections with "hidden" women. Descriptions are good; indexing is detailed; but unfortunately there are some surprising omissions. Z7964.U49W64

Women in specific countries, regions, or ethnic groups

❖The African Training and Research Centre for Women of the United Nations Economic Commission for Africa has published several useful titles in its annotated *Bibliography series,* including *Women and development in Africa* by Nancy J. Hafkin (1977. 177p. no.1); *Women and development in Tanzania* by Ophelia Mascarenhas (1980. 135p. no.2; later included in *Women in Tanzania* by Mascarenhas and Marjorie Mbilinyi [N.Y., Africana, 1983. 256p.]); *Women and development in Mali* by Susan Caughman (1982. 34p. no.6); and *Women and development in Zimbabwe* (1984. 50p. no.9). The Centre has also issued *Women and development in Ethiopia* by Alasebu Gebre Selassie (1981. 58p.).

Aren, Munise. Türk toplumunda kadin: bibliyografya: 16–19 Mayis 1978 İstanbul semineri için Sosyal Bilimler Derneği adina derlenmiştir. Women in Turkish society: prep. under the auspices of the Turkish Social Science Assoc. for the Istanbul seminar, May 16–19, 1978. Ankara, [Dernek], 1978. 123p. **CC556**

In Turkish.
A broadly classed subject listing of 1,049 titles, with author and title indexes. Predominantly Turkish-language studies. Elizabeth E. Lytle's *Women in Turkey* (Monticello, Ill., Vance Bibliographies, 1979. 14p. Public admin. ser., Bibliography P-172) lists more Western-language sources. Z7964.T8A73

Bailey, Susan F. Women and the British empire: an annotated guide to sources. N.Y., Garland, 1983. 185p. (Themes in European expansion, v.3; Garland reference library of social science, v.159) **CC557**

In four main sections: wives of administrators; settlers; missionaries; native women. Each section begins with a lengthy bibliographic essay, concludes with critically annotated citations to primary and secondary sources (including unpublished materials). Indexed. Z7964.G7B34

Barrow, Margaret. Women, 1870–1928: a select guide to printed and archival sources in the United Kingdom. London, Mansell; N.Y., Garland, [1981]. 249p. **CC558**

In four parts: (1) archives, arranged by subject and then by holding institution; (2) printed works, divided by type of publication and then by subject; (3) non-book materials, such as films, photographs, newspaper clippings, and oral history; (4) directory of libraries and record offices. Indexed. Z7964.G7B37

Cohen Stuart, Bertie A. Women in the Caribbean: a bibliography. [The Hague], Smits; Leiden, Dept. of Caribbean Studies, Royal Inst. of Linguistics and Anthropology, 1979. 167p. **CC559**

An annotated, classified bibliography of over 650 items dealing with Suriname, French Guiana and Guyana, the Bahamas and Bermuda, and the islands of the Antillean archipelago. Entries are coded according to the geographical codes used in Comitas' *Complete Carribbeana* (DB408). Author index. Z7964.C38C64

Fan, Kok-sim. Women in southeast Asia: a bibliography. Boston, G. K. Hall, [1982]. 415p. **CC560**

3,865 entries are grouped by broad subject and subdivided by country—Brunei, Burma, Indochina, Indonesia, Malaysia, Philippines, Singapore, and Thailand. Includes published and unpublished materials in English, Malay, Indonesian, Dutch, and French. Author index. Z7961.F35

Frey, Linda, Frey, Marsha and **Schneider, Joanne.** Women in Western European history; a select chronological, geographical, and topical bibliography. Westport, Conn., Greenwood Pr., [1982–84]. 2v. **CC561**

Contents: [v.1] From antiquity to the French Revolution; [v.2] The nineteenth and twentieth centuries.
A selective bibliography of 17,381 references to Western language books and periodical articles; primary and literary sources have been excluded. As the subtitle suggests, arrangement is by period, further subdivided by country, then by subject. Detailed tables of contents with subject, name, and author indexes. Z7961.F74

Knaster, Meri. Women in Spanish America: an annotated bibliography from pre-conquest to contemporary times. Boston, G. K. Hall, [1977]. 696p. **CC562**

More than 2,500 items in classed arrangement, with author and subject indexes. Unpublished doctoral dissertations and master's theses are separately listed without annotations. A geographic index would have been helpful. Z7964.L3K525

Koh, Hesung Chun. Korean and Japanese women: an analytic bibliographical guide. Westport, Conn., Greenwood Pr., [1982]. 903p. maps. **CC563**

"Publ. under the auspices of the Human Relations Area Files."—*t.p.*
About 600 items in a wide variety of formats, issued between 1789 and 1979 in the Korean, Japanese, and English languages, are listed first by historical period and then by subject. Annotated entries. Coverage for Japan is selective. Indexed. Z7964.K6K63

Kratochvil, Laura and **Shaw, Shauna.** African women: a select bibliography. Cambridge, Eng., African Studies Centre, [1974]. [74p.] **CC564**

A classed list of more than 1,200 items. International in scope. Items are keyed as to regions covered. Regional and author indexes. Z7964.A3K7

Meghdessian, Samira Rafidi. The status of the Arab woman: a select bibliography. Westport, Conn., Greenwood Pr., [1980]. 176p. **CC565**

"Compiled . . . under the auspices of the Institute for Women's Studies in the Arab World, Beirut University College, Lebanon."—*t.p.*
A bibliography of over 1,600 entries, primarily English- and French-language books, articles, conference proceedings, master's theses, doctoral dissertations, and bibliographies, most of them published since 1950. Arrangement is by general subjects and individual countries, with no subject subdivision under country. Author and broad subject index. Z7964.A7M43

Otto, Ingeborg and **Schmidt-Dumont, Marianne.** Frauenfragen im Modernen Orient: eine Auswahlbibliographie. Women in the Middle East and North Africa: a selected bibliography. Hamburg, Deutsches Orient-Institut, Dokumentations Leitstelle Moderner Orient, 1982. 247p. (Dokumentationsdienst Moderner Orient. Reihe A; Middle East documentation service. Ser. A, 12) **CC566**

In addition to Arab countries, includes Israel, Turkey, Iran, Afghanistan, and Pakistan. International scope, wide variety of formats, some German-language contents notes. Country arrangement with subject, personal and corporate author indexes. Z7964.N42O88

al-Qazzaz, Ayad. Women in the Middle East and North Africa: an annotated bibliography. Austin, Center for Middle Eastern Studies, [1977]. 178p. (Middle East monographs, no.2) **CC567**

Includes English-language books, essays in books, periodical articles, conference reports, pamphlets, and unpublished papers. Author listing with country and subject indexes. Z7964.N42Q38

Raccagni, Michelle. The modern Arab woman; a bibliography. Metuchen, N.J., Scarecrow Pr., 1978. 262p. **CC568**

Nearly 3,000 books, articles, reports, and dissertations in Western languages and Arabic are grouped in general or country sections, then subdivided by more detailed subject areas. Some titles are briefly annotated. Author and broad subject index. Z7964.A7R32

Rihani, May and **Joy, Jody.** Development as if women mattered: an annotated bibliography with a Third World focus. [Wash.], New TransCentury Foundation, [1978]. 137p. (Overseas Development Council. Occasional paper, no.10)   **CC569**

"Prep. under the auspices of the Secretariat for Women in Development of the New TransCentury Foundation."

Descriptions of 287 works are arranged topically, then by geographic area; topics include socioeconomic participation, migration, education, rural development, health, communications, etc. Author index. Most titles were produced 1976–77; the volume thus complements another work published by the Overseas Development Council, Mayra Buvinic's *Women and world development* (1976. 162p.), which consists of annotations for about 400 studies arranged according to subject categories and geographic focus. A good deal of unpublished material is included in both works.

Sakala, Carol. Women of South Asia: a guide to resources. Millwood, N.Y., Kraus Internat. Pubns., [1980]. 517p.   **CC570**

In two parts: Pt.I, "Published resources," is a classified, annotated bibliography of about 4,600 Western-language books, essays, articles, serials, dissertations, and audiovisual materials for the areas of India, Pakistan, Bangladesh, Sri Lanka, and Nepal; Pt.II, "Libraries, archives, and other local resources," is a series of reports by individual scholars on libraries, government archives, and records of women's organizations in India, Pakistan, Bangladesh, and Sri Lanka. Author and subject indexes.   Z7964.S65S23

Wei, Karen T. Women in China: a selected and annotated bibliography. Westport, Conn., Greenwood, [1984]. 250p. (Bibliographies and indexes in women's studies, no.1)   **CC571**

More than 1,100 citations to Western-language sources are presented in topical arrangement. Focuses on China and Taiwan from the mid-nineteenth century to the present. Separate chapters on bibliographies and special journal issues. Author and title indexes.   Z7964.C5W44

Weitz, Margaret Collins. Femmes: recent writings on French women. Boston, G. K. Hall, [1985]. 245p.   **CC572**

Annotated entries focus on French monographs of 1970–79 and are arranged by subject; earlier works (1830–1969) are listed by author without annotations. Lengthy chapter introductions and annotations; subject, author, and title indexes.   Z7964.F8W44

The women of England from Anglo-Saxon times to the present; interpretive bibliographical essays. Ed. with an introd. by Barbara Kanner. Hamden, Conn., Archon Books, 1979. 429p.   **CC573**

Bibliographic essays by contributing scholars on women in specific periods of English history (e.g., Anglo-Saxon, Norman, and Plantagenet, 18th century) or specific aspects of English women's studies (e.g., "Women under the law in medieval England," "Demographic contributions to the history of Victorian women," "Using novels to study Victorian women"). Includes references to both primary and secondary sources. Subject index; bibliographies at the end of each chapter are arranged alphabetically.

HQ1599.E5W65

Handbooks

Beere, Carole A. Women and women's issues: a handbook of measurements and tests. San Francisco [etc.], Jossey-Bass, 1979. 550p.   **CC574**

Identifies 235 oral or written instruments that measure variables pertinent to women's issues. Topically organized into 11 chapters, with instrument descriptions providing: title and author, year it first appeared in the literature, audience, summary, information about administration, scoring, reliability and validity, source, and a bibli-

ography of research studies in which the instrument was used. Indexed by instrument title, names, and variables measured.

HQ1180.B43

EveryWoman's legal guide: protecting your rights at home, in the workplace, and in the market place. Barbara A. Burnett, consulting ed. Garden City, Doubleday, 1983. 576p.   **CC575**

A guide to legal problems women may face as consumers, homemakers, family members, workers, and participants in the criminal legal system. Appendix of hot lines and organizations; suggested further reading; index.   KF390.W6E83

Handbook of international data on women. [By] Elise Boulding [and others]. [Los Angeles], Sage Publs.; N.Y., Halsted Pr., [1976]. 468p.   **CC576**

Presents data derived from the United Nations and the Institute of Behavioral Science, University of Colorado, on: general economic activity; economic activity by status; economic activity by industry; economic activity by occupation; literacy and education; migration; marital status; life, death, and reproduction; political and civic participation; and a world overview of national statistics. For much of the data 1968 is the mean year.   HQ1115.H36

Ross, Susan Deller and **Barcher, Ann.** The rights of women: the basic ACLU guide to a woman's rights. Rev. ed. Toronto & N.Y., Bantam, [1983]. 406p. charts.   **CC577**

1st ed. 1973.

One of a series of American Civil Liberties Union guides intended for the laypersons affected. Within subject areas (e.g., name changes), follows a question-and-answer format to raise major issues and inform the nonspecialist of the basic law on the subject. Appendixes provide comparative charts on state laws, as well as directories of women's organizations.

Similar ACLU guides are available for gay people, prisoners, the critically ill, etc.   KF478.Z9R67

U.S. Bureau of the Census. A statistical portrait of women in the U.S., 1978. Wash., 1980. 169p. (Current population reports: special studies: ser. P-23, no.100)   **CC578**

First publ. 1976.

The earlier report contained some historical data relating to women, beginning in 1900 when available. The statistics in this report update the earlier one for the 1970s, with an additional chapter on American Indian and Asian-American women.

HA203.A218 no.100

U.S. Women's Bureau. Handbook of facts on women workers. [Wash.], 1948– . (*Its* Bulletin 225–)   **CC579**

Title varies: 1983 ed. had title: *Time of change.*

The 1983 ed. (*Bulletin* 298; 192p.) is in two parts: (1) women in the labor force, their occupations, income, and training; (2) laws governing women's employment and status.   HD6093.A35

Weiser, Marjorie P. K. and **Arbeiter, Jean S.** Womanlist. N.Y., Atheneum, 1981. 500p.   **CC580**

A book of lists, miscellany, records, and statistics relevant to women. Brief bibliography; index.   HG1115.W43

Women's Action Alliance. Women's action almanac: a complete resource guide. N.Y., William Morrow, 1979. 432p. il.   **CC581**

Ed. by Jane Williamson, Diana Winston, and Wanda Wooten.

Entries on 84 issues of concern to women summarize the feminist perspective, with background information, historical context, and current status. Lists of pertinent women's organizations and selected, annotated print resources conclude each entry. A directory of national women's organizations is appended.   HQ1115.W64

The women's annual; the year in review, 1980– . Boston, G. K. Hall, [1981]– . Annual.   **CC582**

A sourcebook reviewing current topics of interest to women—domestic life, education, health, politics and law, popular culture, psychology, religion, violence against women, and work. Each essay provides an extensive bibliography, sometimes including a resource directory. HQ1402.W65

The women's book of world records and achievements. Garden City, N.Y., Anchor Pr./Doubleday, 1979. 798p. il. **CC583**

Lois Decker O'Neill, ed.

17 topically organized chapters describe "women with provable records . . . including 'firsts,' and . . . others generally acknowledged as leaders within particular fields of endeavor to produce a book celebrating women's world records and achievements in the late 19th and the 20th centuries."—*Introd.* Indexed. CT3234.W65

Directories

Directory of Indian women today. Chief ed., Ajeet Cour; ed., Arpana Cour. [New Delhi], India Internat. Publs., [1976]. various paging. il. **CC584**

Brief biographies and photographs of more than 6,000 living Indian women, arranged by professions, with a name index. A "Facts and views" section includes essays on Indian women in various professions; "Social welfare organisations" is a directory arranged by state. HQ1742.A3D55

National Council of Women of the United States. International directory of women's organizations. [N.Y., Research and Action Associates, 1963.] various pagings. il. **CC585**

Gives information on international and American women's organizations, including name, purpose, date of founding, officers, address, membership, affiliations, etc. No index. HQ1883.N3

Rutgers University, New Brunswick, N.J. Center for the American Woman and Politics. Women in public office: a biographical directory and statistical analysis. 2d ed. Metuchen, N.J., Scarecrow Pr., 1978. 510p. **CC586**

Kathy Stanwick, project director.

Comp. by Center for the American Woman and Politics, Eagleton Institute of Politics, Rutgers—The State University of New Jersey.

1st ed. 1976.

Identifies 17,000 women serving as public officials in local, state, and federal government during 1976–77. Federal executive appointments and members of the federal judiciary at the district and court levels are new to this edition, as is a statistical analysis comparing female and male officeholders. Arranged by federal, then by state offices, with name index. HQ1391.U5R88

Schlachter, Gail Ann. Directory of financial aids for women. 2d ed. Santa Barbara, ABC–Clio, 1982. 344p. **CC587**

Subtitle: A listing of: scholarships, fellowships, loans, grants, awards, and internships, designed primarily or exclusively for women; women's financial institutions, state sources of educational benefits; and reference sources on financial aids.

1st ed. 1978.

Aids are listed according to the categories mentioned in the subtitle; the "reference sources" section is an "Annotated bibliography of general financial aids directories." Subject, program, sponsor, and location indexes. A 1985/86 ed. was published 1985. HQ1381.S36

Who's who and where in women's studies. Ed. by Tamar Berkowitz, Jean Mangi and Jane Williamson. [Old Westbury, N.Y.], Feminist Pr., 1974. 308p. **CC588**

A directory of American colleges and universities with information on their course offerings in women's studies is followed by a faculty list with address and titles of courses taught. There is also a list of courses by academic department. Information is updated periodically in *Women's studies newsletter.* HQ1181.U5W48

Women's Action Alliance. Women helping women: a state-by-state directory of services. N.Y., [The Alliance], 1981. 179p. **CC589**

For each state and the District of Columbia, entries are grouped by service category: battered women and rape victim services, career counseling services, displaced homemaker programs, planned parenthood clinics, skilled trades training centers, women's centers, women's commissions, women's health centers. Within each category, services are listed alphabetically by city. More than 2,100 organizations are included. HV1445.W65

Women's organizations & leaders—1973 directory. Ed. by Myra E. Barrer. Wash., Today, [1973]. 1v., various pagings. **CC590**

". . . a current and comprehensive directory and guide to more than 8000 women's organizations and their leaders. Individual women, active in the women's movement, through their actions or writings are also listed."—*Abstract.*

C D

Psychology and Psychiatry

❖Psychology and psychiatry are very specialized fields, requiring for the research worker highly specialized and technical texts. Most of these would be found only in the special library. Here are listed some of the more general bibliographies and indexes which may be useful in a general library. Needed, also, would probably be one or two dictionaries of psychological terms and directories of psychologists. Bibliographies of tests and measurements are frequently consulted in both academic and public libraries. McInnis' *Research guide for psychology* (CD6) is an excellent, comprehensive guide to the literature.

GENERAL WORKS

Guides

Bell, James Edward. A guide to library research in psychology. Dubuque, Ia., W. C. Brown, [1971]. 211p. **CD1**

For the undergraduate student. Brief chapters on use of the library, library sources, and writing the research paper are followed by lists of psychology sources by type (dictionaries, encyclopedias, handbooks, etc.) and selected reading lists for various aspects of psychology. BF76.8.B43

Borchardt, D. H. and **Francis, R. D.** How to find out in psychology: a guide to the literature and methods of research. Oxford, Pergamon, [1984]. 189p. il. **CD2**

A selective annotated guide for the student, emphasizing basic international titles and English-language works published since the early 1970s. Chapters I–II deal with the field of psychology and its major theories; chapters III–VI discuss reference sources; chapters VII–IX treat the process of research and the presentation of results; the final chapter includes information on the profession. The bibliography, p.175–86, is a list of monographs and serial titles cited in the text. Subject index. BF76.8.B67

Daniel, Robert Strongman and **Louttit, Chauncey McKinley.** Professional problems in psychology. N.Y., Prentice-Hall, 1953. 416p. **CD3**

In part a revision and expansion of C. M. Louttit's *Handbook of psychological literature* (Bloomington, Ind., Principia Pr., 1932).

A manual intended primarily for the graduate student in psychology, the practicing psychologist, and the librarian, covering especially the literature search, the scientific report, and problems of the professional psychologist. Includes an annotated bibliography of reference books in psychology; a list of psychological journals; sources for books, tests, apparatus, etc.; a glossary of abbreviations; and name and subject indexes.   BF76.D35

Elliott, Charles Kenneth. A guide to the documentation of psychology. London, Bingley; [Hamden, Conn.], Linnet Books, [1971]. 134p.   **CD4**

Intended for the advanced undergraduate and the graduate student. Discusses library use, documentary aids, searching procedures, etc. Appendixes list reference sources of various kinds.
                     BF76.8.E4

Greenberg, Bette. How to find out in psychiatry. N.Y., Pergamon, [1978]. 113p.   **CD5**

Subtitle: A guide to sources of mental health information.

A bibliography arranged under broad headings, e.g., guides to libraries and the literature, primary sources, secondary sources, drug therapy, mental health statistics, etc. There is an appendix of classics in psychiatric literature. Indexed.   Z6664.N5G69

McInnis, Raymond G. Research guide for psychology. Westport, Conn., Greenwood Pr., [1982]. 604p. il. (Reference sources for the social sciences and humanities, no.1)
                     CD6

A critical guide to about 1,200 information sources. An introductory section on general works (arranged by type) is followed by 16 topically arranged subdivisions, each discussing research guides, "substantive information sources" (handbooks, encyclopedias, annuals, etc.), literature reviews, and bibliographic sources. Titles are listed with complete data in a concluding section. Indexed.
                     Z7201.M35

Reed, Jeffrey G. and **Baxter, Pam M.** Library use: a handbook for psychology. Wash., Amer. Psychological Assn., [1983]. 137p. il.   **CD7**

An introduction to undergraduate library resources. Includes subject, citation, and computer bibliographic searches, tests and measures, current awareness and specialized sources. Indexed.
                     BF76.8.R43

Bibliography

Andor, L. Eve. Psychological and sociological studies of the black people of Africa, south of the Sahara, 1960–1975; an annotated select bibliography. [Bramfontein, So.Afr., Nat. Inst. for Personnel Research, Council for Scientific and Industrial Research, 1983] 397p.   **CD8**

Intended as a continuation of the author's *Aptitudes and abilities of the black man in sub-Saharan Africa, 1784–1963* (Johannesburg, 1966). A detailed, classed bibliography of 3,122 entries on intellectual and personality attributes, attitudes toward, and behavior in, environmental change. Author, geographic area, comparative studies, and subject indexes.   Z3508.P8A66

Berlin, Irving Norman. Bibliography of child psychiatry and child mental health, with a selected list of films. [2d ed.] N.Y., Human Sciences, [1976]. 508p.   **CD9**

"An official publication of the Academy of Child Psychiatry."— *t.p.*

1st ed. 1963 had title: *Bibliography of child psychiatry.*

A topically arranged list of 4,257 citations, with asterisks marking the most important. Includes infant, child, and adolescent studies. Film titles also arranged by subject, with contents notes. Author and subject indexes.   Z6671.5.B4

Bibliography of world literature on mental retardation, January 1940–March 1963. [By] Rick Heber [research director of] the President's Panel on Mental Retardation [and oth-

ers]. [Wash., publ. for the Panel by the U.S. Dept. of Health, Education, and Welfare, Public Health Service, 1963] 564p. (Public Health Service pubn., 1316)   **CD10**

An author listing of 16,096 citations, with author/subject index. An additional 2,372 citations are found in: Z6677.B5

Supplement to Bibliography of world literature on mental retardation . . . . Rick F. Heber, Patrick J. Flanigan. Bethesda, Md., U.S. Dept. of Health, Education, and Welfare, Public Health Service, Nat. Institutes of Health, Nat. Inst. of Child Health and Human Development, [1965]. 99p.

Chandler, Albert Richard and **Barnhart, Edward N.** A bibliography of psychological and experimental aesthetics, 1864–1937. Berkeley, Univ. of California Pr., 1938. 190p.
                     CD11

An enlarged and rearranged edition of Chandler's *Bibliography of experimental aesthetics* (1933) and its supplements.

"This bibliography attempts to list all the books and articles dealing with the theoretical and experimental work of psychologists in the field of aesthetics appearing in English and the principal European languages."—*Pref.* 1,739 numbered references are arranged by topic. Author index.   Z5870.C45

Chicago. Institute for Psychoanalysis. Chicago psychoanalytic literature index, 1920–1970. Chicago, CPL Pub., [1971]. 3v.   **CD12**

Contents: v.1, Author and title; v.2–3, Subject.

The index (some 100,000 cards) has been maintained at the Chicago Institute for Psychoanalysis and is devoted to writings (mainly in English) on psychoanalysis, psychosomatic medicine, and related areas. Includes books, annual reviews, symposium proceedings, articles in professional journals.   Z6664.N5C485

———— ———— Supplement. Chicago, CPL Publ., 1975– . Quarterly, the 4th issue being an annual cumulation.

The supplements are produced by computer in subject arrangement; author references appear in the annual volume.
                     Z6664.N5C485

Core readings in psychiatry: an annotated guide to the literature. Ed. by Michael H. Sacks, William H. Sledge and Phyllis Rubinton. [N.Y., Praeger, 1984] 539p.   **CD13**

Presents 62 topical chapters by psychiatric specialists. "Core" is defined either as "classic in introducing a new concept, finding or methodology . . . or as highly relevant to a current understanding of the topic area."—*Introd.* Critical annotations; essential works are starred. Author and subject indexes.   RC454.C655

Davis, Martha. Understanding body movement, an annotated bibliography. N.Y., Arno, 1972. 190p.   **CD14**

Provides 931 abstracts of "published and unpublished literature on body movement style, facial expression, gaze behavior, symbolic actions, gestures, postures, movement interaction, and psychological aspects of coordination, motor development, and abnormal movement."—*Introd.* Concentrates on 20th century English-language titles; dissertations are included. Main-entry arrangement; subject index.   Z7201.D3

———— and **Skupien, Janet.** Body movement and nonverbal communication; an annotated bibliography, 1971–1981. Bloomington, Indiana Univ. Pr., [1982]. 294p. il.   **CD15**

A sequel to Davis' *Understanding body movement* (above). An international bibliography of more than 1,411 published works (including dissertations) on psychological and anthropological aspects of body movement. Subject and author indexes.
                     Z7204.M66D38

Driver, Edwin D. The sociology and anthropology of mental illness; a reference guide. Rev. & enl. ed. [Amherst], Univ. of Massachusetts Pr., 1972. 487p.   **CD16**

1st ed. 1965.

Intended for social scientists and the health professions; the work "attempts to systematically cover the literature on social and cultural aspects of mental illness and its treatment in Europe,

Africa, Asia and Latin America as well as in the United States."—*Pref.* Covers literature published 1956–68: more than 5,900 items in classed arrangement, with author-subject index. Z6664.N5D7

Family therapy and research: an annotated bibliography of articles, books, videotapes, and films published 1950–1979. 2d ed. Ira D. Glick [et al.]. N.Y., Grune & Stratton, 1982. 308p. **CD17**

1st ed. 1971; a 1965 ed. had title *Psychiatry and the family*.

A classed arrangement of titles relevant to psychiatry, psychology, and social work, excluding sociology and anthropology. Features a section on literature surveys. Author index. Z6664.N5F34

Farberow, Norman L. Bibliography on suicide and suicide prevention, 1897–1957, 1958–1970. Rockville, Md., Nat. Inst. of Mental Health, [1972]. 126p., 143p. (DHEW publ. no. [HSM] 72-9080) **CD18**

Revision and extension of Farberow's 1969 publication which covered through 1967 and was issued as Public Health Service publication no. 1970.

Entries are grouped in two periods: the 1897–1957 section (2,202 entries) incorporates and expands the bibliography published in Farberow and Shneidman's *The cry for help* (N.Y., McGraw-Hill, 1961); the 1958–70 section lists 2,542 additional items. Foreign-language titles are given in English translation and sometimes also in the original language. Author listing, with separate subject index for each section. Z7615.F38

Favazza, Armando R. and **Oman, Mary.** Anthropological and cross-cultural themes in mental health; an annotated bibliography, 1925–1974. Columbia, Univ. of Missouri Pr., 1977. 386p. (Univ. of Missouri studies, v.65) **CD19**

Includes over 3,600 English-language periodical articles. Chronological arrangement, with author and subject indexes. The introduction provides a most interesting review of the cultural areas and specific themes included.

Continued by: RC455.4.E8F38

Favazza, Armando R. and **Faheem, Ahmed D.** Themes in cultural psychiatry; an annotated bibliography, 1975–1980. Columbia, Univ. of Missouri Pr., 1982. 194p. **CD20**

Cites 1,643 periodical articles and books. Coverage of non-English language journals, anthropological journals, and books have been added to this volume. Author listing; subject index. Z6664.N5F37

Frye, Jerry K. FIND: Frye's Index to nonverbal data. Duluth, Univ. of Minnesota Computer Center, Univ. of Minnesota, [1980]. 344p. **CD21**

An author listing of 4,072 English-language titles from a wide variety of sources on human non-verbal communication. Seriously flawed by inadequate subject indexing, the headings used in the topical index being too broad or imprecise (e.g., the user is likely to be discouraged by finding nearly a page of item numbers following terms such as "Facial" or "Physical behavior/body language"). Z7204.C59F79

Golann, Stuart E. Coordinate index reference guide to community mental health. N.Y., Behavioral Publs., [1969]. 237p. **CD22**

". . . provides a bibliography of 1,510 references, most of which were published between 1960 and 1967. Each reference is coded as to content. In addition to the glossary used to code each document, a multiple access, coordinate type of index is provided to facilitate flexible and specific in-depth access to the community mental health literature."—*Pref.* Also includes a section on other sources of information. Z6664.N5G58

Gottsegen, Gloria Behar. Group behavior: a guide to information sources. Detroit, Gale, [1979]. 219p. (Psychology information guide ser., v.2) **CD23**

An annotated bibliography of English-language books and journal titles on small group dynamics, especially in clinical-therapeutic or industrial-organizational settings. Author, title, and subject indexes. Other titles in the series include: v.1, *History of psychology* by

Wayne Viney, Michael Wertheimer and Marilyn Lou Wertheimer (1979. 502p.); v.3, *Communication* by A. George Gitter and Robert Grunin (1980. 157p.); v.4, *Human motivation* by Charles N. Cofer (1980. 176p.); v.5, *Abnormal behavior* by Henry Leland and Marilyn W. Deutsch (1980. 261p.); v.6, *Humanistic psychology* by Gloria Gottsegen and Abby J. Gottsegen (1980. 185p.). Z7164.07.G67

Grinstein, Alexander. The index of psychoanalytic writings. N.Y., Internat. Universities Pr., [1956–75]. 14v. **CD24**

A revision and updating of John Rickman's *Index psychoanalyticus, 1893-1926* (London, Woolf, 1928).

Lists books, periodical articles, reviews, and abstracts, published in any language, 1900–69. Titles are given in the original language, frequently followed by an English translation. Arranged alphabetically by author; detailed subject index. Z7204.P8G7

Grobman, Jerald. Group psychotherapy for students and teachers: a selected bibliography, 1946–1979. N.Y., Garland, 1981. 113p. (Garland reference library of social science, v.102) **CD25**

A topical bibliography on group psychotherapy, for use by students and teachers. Comprises 758 references to journal articles and book chapters stressing the treatment of patients rather than theoretical material. Author and subject indexes. Z6664.N5G74

Hart, Henry Harper. Conceptual index to psychoanalytic technique and training. [Croton-on-Hudson, N.Y.], North River Pr., 1972. 5v. (1584p.) **CD26**

Contents: v.1, Code; v.2–5, A–W.

A subject index to some 330 psychoanalytic concepts, techniques and training methods as used in psychoanalytic therapeutic practice, as opposed to theory. Indexes about 300 books and 3,000 articles published 1896–1960. Includes ideas from Freud, Jung, Stekel, Adler, etc. A *Library journal* (98:524, Feb. 15, 1973) recommended purchase as a "valuable complementary set" to the "more inclusive" Grinstein work (above).

Harvard University. The Harvard list of books in psychology, comp. and annotated by the psychologists in Harvard University. 4th ed. Cambridge, Harvard Univ. Pr., [1971]. 108p. **CD27**

1st ed. 1949; 3d ed. 1964. The 1st ed. superseded *Books in psychology* (1938) and its supplement (1944).

744 titles selected for their importance and value in psychology at the present time; annotated and arranged by topic. In this edition new entries account for almost half the list. Includes publications as recent as 1970. Author index. Z7201.H28

—— **Library.** Philosophy and psychology. Cambridge, Mass., Harvard Univ. Lib., distr. by Harvard Univ. Pr., 1973. 2v. (Widener Library shelflist, 42–43) **CD28**

For full information *see* BA17.

Holmes, Thomas H. and **David, Ella M.** Life change events research, 1966–1978; an annotated bibliography of the periodical literature. N.Y., Praeger, [1984]. 331p. **CD29**

"Life change events research is the branch of stress research that attempts to identify, measure, and study the consequences of discrete life experiences."—*Pref.* Focuses on time prior to MEDLARS use of "life change events" as a subject heading. Includes a wide variety of English-language materials beyond periodical articles. Author and subject indexes. Z6665.5.H64

Kelso, Dianne R. and **Attneave, Carolyn L.** Bibliography of North American Indian mental health. Westport, Conn., Greenwood Pr., [1981]. 411p. map. **CD30**

"Prep. under the auspices of the White Cloud Center."—*t.p.*

Lists 1,363 English-language periodical articles, research reports, government documents, doctoral dissertations, conference papers, and book chapters; complete books are excluded. Author and descriptor indexes. Based on a computerized database at White Cloud Center, Portland, Ore. RC451.5.I5K44

Key, Mary Ritchie. Nonverbal communication: a research guide & bibliography. Metuchen, N.J., Scarecrow Pr., 1977. 439p. **CD31**

A companion volume (providing the complete bibliography) to the same author's *Paralanguage and kinesics (nonverbal communication): with a bibliography* (1975). Aims to be "fairly complete . . . on the communicative aspects of paralanguage and kinesics, together with contributing features in proxemics, tactile behavior, silence. . . . It is not complete in areas which are disciplines in themselves" (*p.140*), such as dance, psychology, and education. Text of 140 pages, although more thorough treatment of ideas is in the earlier work. Bibliography includes books, articles, some unpublished papers. Author listing with subject index.   P99.5.K4

Kiell, Norman. Psychiatry and psychology in the visual arts and aesthetics; a bibliography. Madison, Univ. of Wisconsin Pr., 1965. 250p.   **CD32**

For annotation *see* BE39.

—— Psychoanalysis, psychology, and literature; a bibliography. 2d ed. Metuchen, N.J., Scarecrow Pr., 1982. 2v. (1269p.)   **CD33**

For annotation *see* BD11.

Lester, David, Sell, Betty H. and **Sell, Kenneth D.** Suicide: a guide to information sources. Detroit, Gale, [1980]. 294p. (Social issues and social problems information guide ser., 3)   **CD34**

An annotated bibliography of specialized sources and a guide to the use of general reference sources for the study of suicide. Special features include a checklist of doctoral dissertations and a checklist of suicides in literature. Indexed.   RC569.L47

Menninger, Karl. A guide to psychiatric books in English. 3d ed. N.Y., Grune & Stratton, [1972]. 238p. (Menninger Clinic monograph ser., no.7)   **CD35**

1st ed. 1950 and 2d ed. 1956 had title *A guide to psychiatric books.*
A checklist of English-language books on psychiatry and related fields arranged by topic; this edition does not include the series of reading lists for specific groups. Name index.   Z6664.N5M48

Menninger Clinic, Topeka, Kansas. Library. Catalog of the Menninger Clinic Library, the Menninger Foundation . . . . Boston, G. K. Hall, 1971. 4v.   **CD36**

Contents: v.1–3, Author-title catalog; v.4, Subject catalog.
Photoreproduction of the catalog cards of a collection of about 30,000 volumes and 400 serials, with particular strength in psychiatry and clinical psychology, adjunctive therapy, psychiatric nursing, social work counseling, psychophysiology, and psychopharmacology. Updated by:

—— —— Supplement. Boston, G. K. Hall, 1978. 2v.

Mental Health Materials Center, Inc., New York. The selective guide to audiovisuals for mental health and family education. Ed. by Jack Neher. 4th ed. Chicago, Marquis Academic Media, [1979]. 511p.   **CD37**

1st ed. 1967. Title has varied; 1979 ed. had title *Current audiovisuals for mental health education.*
An annotated subject guide to about 400 films, videotapes, filmstrips, etc. Provides summary, evaluation, audience level, and ordering information. Title and detailed subject indexes. A companion volume to: RA790.85.Z9M45

—— The selective guide to publications for mental health and family life education. Ed. by Hal Rifken. 4th ed. Chicago, Marquis Academic Media, [1979]. 912p.   **CD38**

1st ed. 1968. 1973 and 1976 eds. had title *A selective guide to materials for mental health and family life education.*
A subject-classed bibliography of about 500 books, pamphlets and print resources; each entry provides summary, evaluation, ordering information, excerpt, and audience level. Title and detailed subject indexes.   Z6664.N5M497

Morrow, William R. Behavior therapy bibliography, 1950–1969; annotated and indexed. Columbia, Univ. of Missouri Pr., [1971]. 165p. (Univ. of Missouri studies, v.54)   **CD39**

An author listing of some 900 references; annotations are presented as a series of abbreviations or code symbols indicating experimental design, setting, subject, behavior, and modification procedures. Reference tables provide a classified index to each of the coded categories.   Z6664.N5M67

Mosak, Harold H. and **Mosak, Birdie.** A bibliography for Adlerian psychology. Wash., Hemisphere Pub. Co.; N.Y., Wiley, [1975]. 320p.   **CD40**

Approximately 10,000 citations, including: Adlerian references by Adlerian writers; references to topics of Adlerian interest written by non-Adlerians; writings by Adlerians on non-Adlerian topics. Author listing; indexed by subject and personal name. Includes review citations.   Z7204.P8M67

National Research Council. Research Information Service. Bibliography of bibliographies on psychology, 1900–1927. Comp. by C. M. Louttit. Wash., Nat. Research Council, 1928. 108p. (National Research Council. Bull., no.65)   **CD41**

Lists 2,134 bibliographies in books and journals, arranged by authors. Number of references is indicated for each entry. Subject index.

Natoli, Joseph P. and **Rusch, Frederik L.** Psychocriticism: an annotated bibliography. Westport, Conn., Greenwood Pr., [1984]. 267p. (Bibliographies and indexes in world literature, 1)   **CD42**

For full information *see* BD15.

Obudho, Constance E. Human nonverbal behavior: an annotated bibliography. Westport, Conn., Greenwood Pr., [1979]. 196p.   **CD43**

A compilation of 536 English-language books, articles, and dissertations written since 1940 on kinesics, personal space, facial expression, the relationship between body type and personality, and body postures and gestures. In two parts—studies with normal individuals, and studies with psychiatric subjects—with subject and author indexes.   Z7204.C59O25

Prentice, Ann E. Suicide: a selective bibliography of over 2,200 items. Metuchen, N.J., Scarecrow Pr., 1974. 227p.   **CD44**

Separate sections for books, theses and dissertations, articles in books, articles in religious journals, articles in medical and scientific journals, etc. Separate author and subject indexes.   Z7615.P73

Reden, C. W. van, Grondel, A. G. and **Geyer, R. F.** Bibliography, alienation. 3d enl. ed. Amsterdam, Stichting Interuniversitair Instituut voor Sociaal-Wetenschappelijk Onderzoek, 1980. 455p. (SISWO-publication, 208)   **CD45**

1st ed. 1972.
Provides citations to 4,723 articles, 1,010 books and chapters from books, 762 dissertations, 473 research reports, 409 congress papers, 17 bibliographies, and 9 audiovisual titles on alienation, anomie, and social isolation. In three main parts: literature published before 1978; literature published 1978–79 (both sections arranged by form); indexes (co-author, book reviews, book chapters, keyword).

Riggar, T. F. Stress burnout: an annotated bibliography. Carbondale and Edwardsville, Ill., Southern Illinois Univ. Pr., [1985]. 299p.   **CD46**

An alphabetical listing of more than 1,000 citations to books and articles, with lengthy annotations. Classed subject index.

BF481.R53

Rothenberg, Albert and **Greenberg, Bette.** The index of scientific writings on creativity: general, 1566–1974. [Hamden, Conn.], Archon, [1976]. 274p.   **CD47**

A companion volume to the authors' *Index of scientific writings on creativity: creative men and women* (Hamden, Archon, 1974), which is limited to works on specific persons in the arts. An international, topically arranged bibliography of 6,823 citations to scholarly works on: general creativity; creativity and psychopathology; developmental studies; creativity in the fine arts; scientific creativity; creativity in industry, engineering and business; creativity of women; facilitating creativity. Addendum-update. Author and subject indexes.

Z7204.C8R65

Schweizerische Philosophische Gesellschaft. Bibliographie der philosophischen, psychologischen und pädagogischen Literatur . . . 1900–1940.   **CD48**

For full record *see* BA62.

Stein, Morris Isaac and **Heinze, Shirley J.** Creativity and the individual: summaries of selected literature in psychology and psychiatry. Glencoe, Ill., Free Pr., [1960]. 428p. (McKinsey Foundation annotated bibliography, 3)   **CD49**

"A publication of the Graduate School of Business, University of Chicago. Third series."—*verso of title page.*

Summaries of selected 20th-century writings of psychologists and psychiatrists on the creativity of the individual.   Z7204.C8S72

Sternlicht, Manny and **Windholz, George.** Social behavior of the mentally retarded; an annotated bibliography. N.Y., Garland, 1984. 226p. (Developmental disabilities, v.1; Garland reference library of social science, v.175)   **CD50**

Presents 619 abstracts grouped by topics such as family and peer interactions, classroom adjustment, emotional disturbances, criminal behavior, adjustment in institutional, community and independent living settings. Author index.   Z6677.S74

Strupp, Hans H. and **Bergin, Allen E.** Research in individual psychotherapy; a bibliography. Chevy Chase, Md., U.S. Nat. Inst. of Mental Health, [1969]. 167p. (Public Health Service publ. no. 1944)   **CD51**

Lists "research reports pertaining to individual psychotherapy with adult patients as well as general references relevant to research in psychotherapy."—*Pref.* Includes 2,741 numbered entries arranged alphabetically by author. Each entry is letter coded to one or more "content categories" which indicate the major emphases of the research reports. Studies involving a research design and reporting quantitative results are emphasized.   Z6664.N5S8

Tavistock Joint Library. Catalogue of the Tavistock Joint Library, London, England. Boston, G. K. Hall, 1975. 2v.   **CD52**

Photoreproduction of the catalog cards from the combined Tavistock Clinic Library of pre-First World War psychiatric materials and the Tavistock Institute of Human Relations. "The main disciplines covered are psychology, psychiatry, psychoanalysis, sociology and the study of organsations. Areas in which the Library is particularly strong are group psychotherapy and experimental and sociological work on the family and other small groups."—*Pref.* About 10,000 books and 5,500 pamphlets in author arrangement; individual entries are given for chapters in multi-author works.

Tilton, James R., DeMyer, Marian K. and **Loew, Lois Hendrickson.** Annotated bibliography on childhood schizophrenia, 1955–1964. N.Y., Grune & Stratton, [1966]. 136p.   **CD53**

Brings up-to-date W. Goldfarb and M. M. Dorsen's *Annotated bibliography of childhood schizophrenia* (N.Y., 1956) which covered through 1954. Lists 346 English-language works classified by major themes: historical and general review articles; description and diagnosis; etiology; biochemical, neurological, and physiological studies; family characteristics; treatment and care; and follow-up studies. Nearly all items are annotated. Author index.

Z6664.N5T5

Vincie, Joseph F. and **Rathbauer-Vincie, Margreta.** C. G. Jung and analytical psychology: a comprehensive bibliography. N.Y., Garland, 1977. 297p. (Garland reference library of social science, v.38)   **CD54**

An international bibliography of works about C.G. Jung and the Jungian school of thought, arranged chronologically, from 1910 through 1976. Book reviews of Jung's works are listed separately. Subject and name indexes.   Z8458.75.V55

Voutsinas, Dimitri. Documentation sur la psychologie française. Paris, Group d'Études de Psychologie de l'Université de Paris, [1957–61]. fasc.1–5.   **CD55**

Fasc.1–4 are retrospective listings; fasc.5 covers the year 1960.

The first issue is entitled *Dix années de psychologie française (1947–1956)* and is a bibliography of articles appearing in some 120 French periodicals. Fasc.2 (1958) is in three parts: (1) Articles in French journals for 1957; (2) Monographs published since 1947; (3) An alphabetical index of authors mentioned in fasc.1. Fasc.3 includes a retrospective list of periodical articles 1843–1946, and lists books and articles of 1958. Fasc.4 continues and completes the retrospective listing and lists books and articles of 1959.

No more published.

Watson, Robert Irving. The history of psychology and the behavioral sciences: a bibliographic guide. N.Y., Springer, [1978]. 241p.   **CD56**

An annotated bibliography of about 800 citations on the interconnections between philosophy, medicine, literature, and the social sciences, and the development of psychology. Covers general resources, historical accounts, methods of historical research, historiographic fields and theories.   Z7201.W373

——— Eminent contributors to psychology. N.Y., Springer, 1974–76. 2v.   **CD57**

Contents: v.1, A bibliography of primary references; v.2, A bibliography of secondary references.

v.1 deals with references to the works of deceased eminent contributors to psychology. v.2 is a collection of references to sources in which the contributors and their contributions are discussed by others. Coverage is from the Renaissance to the present day. The major contributors to the study of mind and behavior are drawn from philosophy, biology, anthropology, medicine, psychology, etc.   Z7201.W37

Wohlwill, Joachim F. and **Weisman, Gerald D.** The physical environment and behavior: an annotated bibliography and guide to the literature. N.Y., Plenum, [1981]. 474p.   **CD58**

More than 1,400 citations to monographs, journal articles, conference proceedings, and doctoral dissertations in the field of environmental psychology are grouped by subject (e.g., noise, crowding, privacy, personal space). Also includes applied areas such as transportation, housing, institutional settings. Author index.

A complementary bibliography is: Z7204.E55W63

Kruse, Lenelis and **Arlt, Reiner.** Environment and behavior: an international and multidisciplinary bibliography, 1970–1981. Paris & N.Y., K. G. Saur, 1984. 2v. (1424p.)   **CD59**

Contents: v.1, Alphabetical listing by author, key word index; v.2, Abstracts.   Z7204.E55K77

Young, Morris N. Bibliography of memory. Philadelphia, N.Y., Chilton, [1961]. 436p.   **CD60**

A comprehensive bibliography of books, pamphlets, articles in periodicals, manuscripts, prints, circulars, games, and advertising devices. Arranged alphabetically by author, with a separate section of anonymous works. Lists works in many languages and of all periods. No index.   Z7204.M4Y6

Periodicals

Psychologie. Liste mondiale des périodiques spécialisés. Psychology. World list of specialized periodicals. La Haye, Mouton, 1967. 168p. (Maison des Sciences de l'Homme. Service d'Échange d'Informations Scientifiques. Publications. Sér C: Catalogues et inventaires, 2)   **CD61**

A select list similar to Unesco's *World list of social science periodicals* (CA41). For a companion list of philosophy periodicals, *see* BA41.

Covers more than 350 periodicals in psychology which were available in 1965. Periodicals are arranged by country, then alphabetically by title; a special section includes periodicals published by international organizations. A short analysis of each periodical provides editorial information, and a concise description of one issue notes average number and length of articles, number and average length of research notes, regular features, etc. Indexes by title, by institution, and by subject. Z7203.P974

Markle, Allen and **Rinn, Roger C.**, eds. Author's guide to journals in psychology, psychiatry and social work. N.Y., Haworth Pr., [1977]. 256p. **CD62**

A guide to help authors locate the professional journals in which acceptance of their articles is most probable. *Psychological abstracts* and the 1976 edition of *Ulrich's International guide to periodicals* were used as the guides for choosing the English-language journals for inclusion. The types of information given for the journals include: address, major content areas, type of articles usually accepted and inappropriate manuscripts, topics preferred, publication lag time, acceptance rate, style requirement, location of indexing and abstracting, and circulation. BF76.8.M37

Osier, Donald V. and **Wozniak, Robert H.** A century of serial publications in psychology, 1850-1950: an international bibliography. Millwood, N.Y., Kraus Internat. Pubns., [1984]. 805p. (Bibliographies in the history of psychology and psychiatry [2]) **CD63**

Some 1,107 serials are fully described in a chronological main-entry listing, with an appendix of 739 serials "not primarily psychological but which contain material relevant to psychology or written by psychologists" (*p.641*) grouped in 11 subject categories. Focus is historical and there is no data past 1950 on continuing publications; however, a number of pre-1850 publications have been included. Title and name indexes. Z7203.O8

Tompkins, Margaret and **Shirley, Norma.** Serials in psychology and allied fields. 2d ed. Troy, N.Y., Whitston, 1976. 472p. **CD64**

1st ed. (1969) had title: *A checklist of serials in psychology and allied fields.*

More than 800 current serials listed, with annotations. A title and subject index and a listing of serials by subject are added to this edition. Z7203.T65

Manuscripts

Sokal, Michael M. and **Rafail, Patrice A.** A guide to manuscript collections in the history of psychology and related areas. Millwood, N.Y., Kraus Internat., [1982]. 212p. **CD65**

In two main sections: the first describes more than 500 individual manuscript collections in the United States relating to psychology, psychiatry, psychoanalysis, child development, parapsychology, phrenology, neurology, and mental health; the second describes the most important archival repositories in the United States, Canada, and Western Europe. Indexed. BF81.S58

Abstract journals and indexes

L'année psychologique. v.1, 1894- . Paris, Presses Universitaires de France, 1895- . **CD66**

Includes signed abstracts of periodical articles and critical book reviews, with exact references to sources. International coverage. Periodical article abstracts were discontinued after v.65 (1965).

Author and subject indexes to v.1-25 are contained in v.26. BF2.A6

Bibliographic guide to psychology. 1975- . Boston, G. K. Hall, [1976]. Annual. **CD67**

Continues the same publisher's *Psychology book guide* (1974) which covered Library of Congress materials only.

A comprehensive annual subject bibliography which brings together "publications cataloged by The Research Libraries of the New York Public Library and the Library of Congress."—*Pref.* Arranged alphabetically by main entry and subject. Z7203.N47a

Developmental disabilities abstracts. v.12-13, Jan. 1977-Oct. 1978. [Wash], Developmental Disabilities Office, [1977-78]. Quarterly. **CD68**

Represents a continuation of two earlier publications, whose numbering it assumes: *Mental retardation abstracts*, v.1-10, 1964-73, and *Mental retardation & developmental disabilities abstracts*, v.11, 1974-76.

Prep. under a grant to the American Assoc. on Mental Deficiency, with support services provided by Herner and Co., Wash., D.C.

In 1978, abstracted about 3,600 scientific and professional articles dealing with the medical, developmental, training, programmatic, family, and personnel aspects of developmental disabilities. Author and subject indexes. RC570.M4

Psychological abstracts, 1927- . Lancaster, Pa., Amer. Psychological Assoc., 1927- . v.1- . Monthly. **CD69**

An important bibliography listing new books, journal articles, technical reports, and other scientific documents, with a signed abstract of each item. Abstracts are now arranged in 16 major classification categories, some with subsections. Author index, and, beginning with 1963, brief subject index to each number; cumulated author and subject indexes issued quarterly and annually.

BF1.P65●

——— Cumulative subject index to Psychological abstracts, 1927/60- . Boston, G. K. Hall, 1966- .

Title, publisher and frequency vary: 1927/60 (publ. in 2v.), Suppl.1 (1961/65) and Suppl.2 (1966/68 in 2v.) publ. by G. K. Hall, 1966-71; Suppls. for 1969/71- publ. triennially by American Psychological Assoc.

A cumulation of the subject indexes for the period indicated, with some revision and consolidation of headings. References are to year and abstract number only. BF1.P652

Columbia University. Libraries. Psychology Library. Author index to Psychological index, 1894 to 1935, and Psychological abstracts, 1927 to 1958. Boston, G. K. Hall, 1960. 5v. **CD70**

Reproduced photographically directly from the cards without further editing; consists of a cumulation of the author entries appearing in these two sets, combined with an earlier card file which preceded the *Psychological index.* These volumes, reproducing card files made by cutting out the actual entries, pasting them on cards, and filing them alphabetically, provide an author index to psychological books and articles in many languages from 1890 to 1958. Z7203.P975

——— Cumulative author index to Psychological abstracts. Supplement. 1st- . Boston, G. K. Hall, 1965- .

Publisher and frequency vary: Suppls. 1-2 (1959/63, 1964/68) publ. by G. K. Hall, 1965-69; Suppls. for 1969/71- publ. triennially by American Psychological Assoc. The 1981/83 cumulative author and subject indexes are to be the final volumes of the series.

Psychological index, 1894-1935, an annual bibliography of the literature of psychology and cognate subjects. Princeton, N.J., Psychological Review Co., 1895-1936. 42v. **CD71**

Lists original publications in all languages, both books and periodical articles, together with translations and new editions in English, French, German, and Italian. A classified subject list, with an alphabetical author index but no subject index. Lists about 5,000 titles each year, and indexes about 350 periodicals. The list of the principal periodicals indexed, with abbreviations used, is given in v.30. Very useful for advanced work.

Continued by *Psychological abstracts* (CD69). Z7203.P97

——— Abstract references. . . . Columbus, Ohio, Amer. Psychological Assoc., 1940-41. 2v. (v.1, 1941) **CD71a**

Contents: v.1, v.1-25, 1894-1918; v.2, v.26-35, 1919-28.

Editor, H. L. Ansbacher. Prepared by the American Psychological Association in cooperation with the Work Projects Administration of the City of New York.

These abstract references have been compiled to serve as a backward extension of *Psychological abstracts* (CD69), which was founded in 1927. The set provides a list of the numbers of those titles from the *Psychological index* (CD71) for which one or more abstracts were located in the periodicals examined, with reference to volume and page of the abstract. As numbers only are given, it must be used in conjunction with the *Psychological index*. References to abstracts have been supplied for 43 percent of the titles in the *Psychological index* (45,000 of the 107,000 titles from 1894 to 1928). Since more than one abstract was found for some titles, references are given to more than 75,000 abstracts.   Z7203.P972

Psychopharmacology abstracts. v.1–19, Jan. 1961–Apr. 1982. Chevy Chase, Md., U.S. Dept. of Health, Education and Welfare, Nat. Inst. of Mental Health, 1961–83. Quarterly, with annual cumulated index.   **CD72**

Prep. for the Psychopharmacology Service Center, National Institute of Mental Health.

Frequency varies.

"Designed to assist the Institute in meeting its obligation to foster and support laboratory and clinical research into the nature and causes of mental disorders and methods of treatment and prevention."—*Note.*

Abstracts are arranged in subject categories. Indexed by author and by subject.   RC475.P66

Book reviews

Contemporary psychology: a journal of reviews. v.1– , Jan. 1956– . Wash., Amer. Psychological Assoc., 1956– . Monthly.   **CD73**

Each issue provides critical reviews of about 70 books, films, tapes, and other media relevant to psychology. Annual author/reviewer index.   BF1.C53

Mental health book review index. N.Y., 1956–72. [v.1]–17.   **CD74**

Frequency varies; 1956–60, semiannual; 1961–72, annual.

No.1–6 were issued as supplements to *Psychological newsletter*, v.7, no.3–v.9, no.6, and have no volume numbering, but constitute v.1–3. Ceased publication.

Lists references to signed book reviews appearing in three or more of some 200 journals. Number of journals covered varies. "Since Issue No. 1 of the INDEX, 5,400 books have been listed, with a total of more than 34,000 references to reviews."—*Pref., 1972.*

"The fields represented include parts of the biomedical and social sciences and the humanities, with a concentration in the psychological sciences. The individual books range in scope from the study of an entire discipline to that of a particular problem; in presentation, from technical to general treatments; in size, from multi-volume works to pamphlets. Their one common characteristic is that they have been reviewed in journals in the English language which related to the behavioral sciences."—*Introd. to the Cumulative author-title index.*

—— Cumulative author-title index, v.1–12, 1956–1967. N.Y., Council on Research in Bibliography, 1969. 178p.

Continued by: Z6664.N5M49

Chicorel index to mental health book reviews, 1974– . N.Y., Chicorel Lib. Pub. Corp., 1977– . Annual. (Chicorel index ser., v.26)   **CD75**

Publication runs late (e.g., 1979 vol. covering reviews of 1978 was publ. 1981).

Subtitle: An annotated guide to books and book reviews in the behavioral sciences.

For each title provides brief description followed by citations to reviews appearing in some 200 English-language periodicals; reviewers' names are given. Author arrangement; indexed by author/editor and about 70 subject areas.   Z6664.N5C487

Dictionaries and encyclopedias

American Psychiatric Association. Joint Commission on Public Affairs. A psychiatric glossary. 5th ed. Boston, Little, Brown, [1980]. 142p.   **CD76**

1st ed. 1957.

This edition "incorporates the revised nomenclature of the American Psychiatric Association's new *Diagnostic and Statistical Manual (DSMIII).*"—*Introd.* An identical "trade edition" appeared as *The American Psychiatric Association's Psychiatric glossary* (Wash., Amer. Psychiatric Pr., 1984).   RC437.A5

Baüml, Betty J. and **Baüml, Franz H.** A dictionary of gestures. Metuchen, N.J., Scarecrow Pr., 1975. 249p. il.   **CD77**

Describes "culturally transmitted (semiotic) gestures" *(Introd.)* which are depicted in verifiable printed or artistic sources. Entries are by parts of the body, under which are given the significance of the gesture, its geographical identification, and its source of verification. Source list (bibliography) and list of art works cited. More illustrations would have been helpful.   BF591.B3

Campbell, Robert Jean. Psychiatric dictionary. 5th ed., N.Y., Oxford Univ. Pr., 1981. 704p.   **CD78**

4th ed. 1970 by L. E. Hinsie and R. J. Campbell.

". . . a continuing version of the Dictionary by Leland E. Hinsie and Jacob Shatzky, first published in 1940."—*t.p.*

About 600 entries "that seemed duplicative or of minimal usefulness to workers in the field" *(Pref.)* have been deleted. "Many of the older definitions were shortened, often by converting lengthy quotations into a summary sentence or two. As a result, it was possible to add over 800 entries without increasing the size of the volume itself."   RC437.H5

Chaplin, James Patrick. Dictionary of psychology. New rev. ed. [N.Y., Dell, 1975] 576p. il.   **CD79**

1st ed. 1968.

Aims to provide accurate, concise meanings of technical terms in the field of psychology. "Terms from the related disciplines of psychoanalysis, psychiatry, and biology have been freely included where these have found wide usage in the literature of psychology." —*Introd.*   BF31.C45

Dorsch, Friedrich [et al.]. Psychologisches Wörterbuch: Anhang, Tests und Testautoren, Bibliographie. 10., neubearb. Aufl. Bern, H. Huber, [1982]. 882p. il.   **CD80**

1st ed. 1921.

A standard German dictionary produced in cooperation with more than eighty contributors. Signed articles include etymologies and bibliographic references. Tests are arranged by author (p.769–813). Bibliography, p.814–82.   BF31.D6

Drever, James. A dictionary of psychology, rev. by Harvey Wallerstein. Baltimore, Penguin, [1964]. 320p.   **CD81**

1st ed. 1952.

An excellent, inexpensive dictionary, giving concise definitions of about 4,000 terms used in psychology.   BF31.D7

Eidelberg, Ludwig, ed. Encyclopedia of psychoanalysis. N.Y., Free Pr.; London, Collier-Macmillan, [1968]. 571p.   **CD82**

Presents definitions and interpretations of 642 terms and personalities in psychoanalysis. Most articles include bibliographies, references to related concepts, and suggestions for additional reading. Indexed.   BF173.E5

Encyclopedia of psychology. Raymond J. Corsini, ed.; Bonnie D. Ozaki, asst. ed. N.Y., Wiley, [1984]. 4v. il.   **CD83**

Contents: v.1–3, A–Z; v.4, Bibliography; name index; subject index.

Comprises about 2,100 signed articles, ranging in length from less than 200 to 9,000 words, on subjects and persons (living and deceased). Complete citations for bibliographic references are provided in the 280-page bibliography in v.4.   BF31.E52

Encyclopedia of psychology. Editors: H. J. Eysenck, W. Arnold and R. Meili. London, Search Pr.; [N.Y.], Herder and Herder, [1972]. 3v.   **CD84**

The work of an international roster of contributors. Includes concise definitions and 282 articles ranging in length up to 4,000 words covering important terms and concepts in psychology. Nearly all articles are signed; each major article and many of the shorter ones carry bibliographies. For the English-language edition (the work is also published in a number of foreign-language editions), the majority of bibliographic citations are in English. Includes a limited number of biographies. Cross references. Also issued in a 1v. (1187p.) ed. by Continuum (N.Y., 1979).   BF31.E52

The encyclopedia of psychology. New and updated. [Guilford, Conn., DPG Reference Pub., 1981] 320p. il.   **CD85**

1973 ed. had title: *Psychology encyclopedia.*
About 1,000 short articles for the nonspecialist are arranged alphabetically, with cross-references and *see* references. Includes biographies. Bibliography, p.302–20.   BF31.E52

The encyclopedic dictionary of psychology. Ed. by Rom Harré and Roger Lamb. [Oxford], Blackwell Reference, [1983]. 718p. il.   **CD86**

Offers definitions of terms, explanations of theories, processes, etc., in the areas of cognitive psychology, psycholinguistics, and neuropsychology, including entries for key personalities in the field. Signed articles; bibliographies; cross references; index.   BF31.E555

English, Horace Bidwell and **English, Ava C.** A comprehensive dictionary of psychological and psychoanalytical terms; a guide to usage. [N.Y.], Longmans, [1958]. 594p.   **CD87**

An excellent dictionary, containing some 12,000 terms "frequently used in a special or technical sense by psychologists."—*Pref.* Includes 287 longer articles which define and compare a group of related terms or comment on terminological problems. Gives pronunciation.   BF31.E58

Goldenson, Robert M. The encyclopedia of human behavior; psychology, psychiatry, and mental health. Garden City, N.Y., Doubleday, 1970. 2v. (1472p.) il.   **CD88**

Terms, theories, treatment techniques, and biographies of important figures in the fields of psychology, psychiatry, and mental health are dealt with in about 1,000 entries in dictionary arrangement. Bibliographies do not accompany individual articles, but references are frequently made to publications cited in full in the "References" section, p.1384–1432. Illustrative cases have been included in 165 articles on psychiatric disorders. Numerous cross references; index. A "Category index" lists articles grouped by related subject matter.   BF31.G6

Grzimek's Encyclopedia of ethology. Ed. in chief, Bernhard Grzimek. N.Y., Van Nostrand Reinhold, [1977]. 705p. il.   **CD89**

Comprises 43 topical chapters by an international group of specialists on animal habits and behavior and their relationships with ecology and comparative psychology. Supplementary readings; glossary; index.   QL751.G8945

Guttman, Samuel A., Jones, Randall L. and **Parrish, Stephen M.**, eds. The concordance to the Standard edition of the complete psychological works of Sigmund Freud. Boston, G. K. Hall, [1980]. 6v.   **CD90**

A KWIC (keyword in context) index based on the *Standard edition.* Also provides access to the quoted line in the *Gesammelte Werke.* About 100 frequently used words are omitted.   BF173.F85G87

Handbuch der Psychologie in 12 Bänden; hrsg. von Philipp Lersch [et al.]. Göttingen, Verlag für Psychologie, C. J. Hogrefe, [1959–78]. v.1–11. il. (In progress)   **CD91**

Each volume consists of long articles treating a different aspect of psychology: general psychology, perception and learning, developmental psychology, study and theories of personality, psychological

diagnosis, methods, educational psychology, industrial psychology. Articles, written by authorities, are signed and include lengthy bibliographies. Each volume has author and subject indexes.

Hehlmann, Wilhelm. Wörterbuch der Psychologie. 11. erg. Aufl. Stuttgart, A. Kröner, [1974]. 650p. il.   **CD92**

1st ed. 1959.
A dictionary of some 3,500 terms giving fairly long definitions. Contains brief biographical information on internationally known psychologists with partial list of their works and of works about them. Includes chronology of psychology from ancient times to 1945 and a bibliography of standard works in psychology.   BF31.H4

Heymer, Armin. Ethological dictionary: German, English, French. N.Y., Garland; Berlin, Verlag Paul Parey, [1977]. 237p.   **CD93**

Defines about 1,000 terms relevant to the biological study of behavior both in animals and humans. Definitions are given alphabetically by German term, with English and French definitions following; indexed in English and German. Bibliographical references.   QL750.3.H49

Howells, John G. and **Osborn, M. Livia.** A reference companion to the history of abnormal psychology. Westport, Conn., Greenwood Pr., [1984]. 2v. (1141p.) il.   **CD94**

About 4,200 entries on material of historical interest; "abnormal" is interpreted as unusual, as well as pathological. Includes biographies of deceased persons, and bibliographic references. List of entries by categories; index. A qualified review appeared in *Library journal,* 12-15-83, p.2324.   RC454.4.H68

International encyclopedia of psychiatry, psychology, psychoanalysis, and neurology. N.Y., Van Nostrand Reinhold (publ. for Aesculapius Pubs.), [1977]. 12v. il.   **CD95**

Ed. by Benjamin B. Wolman.
Authoritative survey articles include brief bibliographies. Cross references; index.   RC334.I57

———— Progress volume 1– . Benjamin B. Wolman, ed. [N.Y.], Aesculapius Pubs., [1983]– .   **CD95a**

More than 130 signed scholarly articles describe the most significant developments in the descriptive sciences and therapeutic techniques since the publication of the basic set; numerous cross references to articles in the parent work. Includes biographies. Name and subject indexes.   RC334.I573

Kaplan, Harold I., Freedman, Alfred M. and **Sadock, Benjamin J.** Comprehensive textbook of psychiatry, III. 3d ed. Baltimore, etc., Williams & Wilkins, [1980]. 3v. il.   **CD96**

1st ed. 1967.
An encyclopedic work by more than 230 contributors. "In addition to clinical material . . . this book includes germane biological, psychological, and sociological information; presentations of current concepts and theoretical models; and discussions of various aspects of community psychiatry and of the delivery of mental health services."—*Pref.* Bibliographic references; glossary, p.3306–65; index to all volumes.   RC454.F74

Longman dictionary of psychology and psychiatry. Robert M. Goldenson, ed. in chief. N.Y., Longman, [1984]. 815p. il.   **CD97**

Presents almost 16,000 entries for terms, phrases, drugs, and persons from the psychosciences; chemical formulae are indicated, and pronunciation of foreign terms and proper names is usually given. Appendixes outline the DSM-III classification and its entries in the dictionary, and list entries for psychological tests and therapies.   BF31.L66

Pieron, Henri. Vocabulaire de la psychologie. 6. éd., remaniée et augmentée. Paris, Presses Universitaires de France, 1979. 587p.   **CD98**

1st ed. 1951.

Comprises over 5,000 terms used in psychology with signed definitions. English and German terms are given when there is no satisfactory French equivalent. References are given to authors and dates of first use. Numerous appendixes provide lists of abbreviations, symbols, etc. Includes an index of names cited in the definitions.   BF31.P5

Die Psychologie des 20. Jahrhunderts. Zürich, Kindler, 1976–[81]. 15v. il.   **CD99**

Contents: Bd.1, Die Europäische Tradition, hrsg. Heinrich Balmer; Bd.2–3, Freund und die Folgen, hrsg. Dieter Eicke; Bd.4, Pawlaw und die Folgen, hrsg. Hans Zeier; Bd.5, Binet und die Folgen, hrsg. Gerhard Strube; Bd.6, Lorenz und die Folgen, hrsg. Roger A. Stamm; Bd.7, Piaget und die Folgen, hrsg. Gerhard Steiner; Bd.8, Lewin und die Folgen, hrsg. Annelise Heigl-Evers; Bd.9, Ergebnisse für die Medizin: Psychosomatik, hrsg. Peter Hahn; Bd.10, Ergebnisse für die Medizin: Psychiatrie, hrsg. Uwe H. Peters; Bd.11–12, Konsequenzen für die Pädagogik, hrsg. Walter Spiel; Bd.13, Anwendungen im Berufsleben, Arbeits-, Wirtschafts- und Verkehrpsychologie, hrsg. François Stoll; Bd.14, Auswirkungen auf die Kriminologie, hrsg. Ulrich Ehebald; Bd.15, Imagination, Kreativität und Transzendenz . . . , hrsg. Gion Condrau.

A massive and important encyclopedia of approximately 1200 pages per volume. Represents the work of more than 600 contributors, predominantly from Western Europe. Each volume deals with a specific dimension, subdiscipline, or allied field. Each volume has a separate subject and author index and a glossary.   BF105.P78

Rycroft, Charles. A critical dictionary of psychoanalysis. N.Y., Basic Books; London, Nelson, [1968]. 189p.   **CD100**

". . . entries consist not merely of formal dictionary definitions of technical terms used in the analytical literature, but also give some account of their origin, of their connexion with other terms and concepts used in analytical theory, and of the controversies relating to them that exist among analysts themselves."—*Introd.* Cross references help to establish relationships.   RC437.R9

Warren, Howard Crosby. Dictionary of psychology. Boston, Houghton, [1934]. 372p. il.   **CD101**

Consists of definitions of English terms and of foreign terms used in English literature. Includes 18 tables covering complexes, logical fallacies, phobias, statistical formulas, etc.; bibliography of technical dictionaries and vocabularies in philosophy, psychology, and cognate subjects; and glossaries of French and German terms with references to their English equivalents. An older work, but authoritative and generally reliable.   BF31.W3

Wolman, Benjamin B., comp. and ed. Dictionary of behavioral science. N.Y., Van Nostrand Reinhold, [1973]. 478p.   **CD102**

Covers all areas of psychology and closely related fields: experimental and developmental psychology, personality, learning, perception, motivation, intelligence, aspects of applied psychology (e.g., diagnosis and treatment of mental disorders; social, industrial, and educational psychology), psychiatry, psychoanalysis, biochemistry, psychopharmacology, clinical practice, neurology, neurosurgery, genetics, etc. Definitions are meant to be as simple and concise as possible. Cross references have been used very sparingly. Entries are unsigned, but are the work of many contributors. Appendixes: (A) Classification of mental disorders, by American Psychiatric Association; (B) Ethical standards of psychologists, by American Psychological Association.   BF31.W64

Handbooks

American handbook of psychiatry. Silvano Arieti, ed. in chief. 2d ed. N.Y., Basic Books, 1974–81. 7v.   **CD103**

Previous ed. 1959–60 in 3v.

Contents: v.1, The foundation of psychiatry; v.2, Child and adolescent psychiatry, sociocultural and community psychiatry; v.3,

Adult clinical psychiatry; v.4, Organic disorders and psychosomatic medicine; v.5, Treatment; v.6, New psychiatric frontiers; v.7, Advances and new directions.

The *Handbook* has been completely revised, updated, and expanded.   RC435.A562

Borgatta, Edgar F. and **Lambert, William W.** Handbook of personality theory and research. Chicago, Rand McNally, [1968]. 1232p.   **CD104**

Includes 24 chapters written by specialists. In five parts: (1) general bases of personality studies; (2) personality development; (3) adult behavior and personality; (4) special emphases; and (5) personality variables and polar types: the current status of some major variables of personality. Most chapters include extensive references. Author and subject indexes.   BF698.B623

Cattell, Raymond B., ed. Handbook of multivariate experimental psychology. Chicago, Rand McNally, [1966]. 959p.   **CD105**

Intended for "a new species of psychologist—the mathematician experimenter."—*Pref.* Pt.I deals with abstract method; pt.II with substantive psychological concepts and laws from the application of such methods. Includes a 1,601-item bibliography. Author and subject indexes.   BF181.C3

Comprehensive handbook of psychopathology. Ed. by Henry E. Adams and Patricia B. Sutker. N.Y., Plenum, [1984]. 1091p. il.   **CD106**

In six main parts: theoretical and methodological issues; major and minor variations in behavior; addictions and other disorders of biological functioning; psychological factors associated with medical and dental disorders; psychological factors in childhood disorders. Chapters by specialists focus on overviews of clinical description, research, and theories, with extensive references. Indexed.   RC454.C636

Eysenck, Hans Jürgen, ed. Handbook of abnormal psychology. [2d ed.] San Diego, Calif., R. R. Knapp; [London], Pitman, [1973]. 906p. il.   **CD107**

1st ed. 1960.

In four main parts: (1) description and measurement of abnormal behavior; (2) experimental study of abnormal behavior; (3) causes and determinants of abnormal behavior; and (4) modification of abnormal behavior. Chapters by specialists (mainly British) include extensive references. Indexes of authors and subjects.   RC454.4.E95

Gordon, Jesse E., ed. Handbook of clinical and experimental hypnosis. N.Y., Macmillan; London, Collier-Macmillan, [1967]. 653p.   **CD108**

Presents information on the background, research and clinical applications, theories, and new developments in hypnosis.   RC495.G6

Handbook of child psychology. Paul H. Mussen, ed. 4th ed. N.Y., Wiley, [1983]. 4v. il.   **CD109**

1st publ. as *Manual of psychology,* ed. by Leonard Carmichael (1946); 3d ed. publ. as *Carmichael's Manual of child psychology,* ed. by P. H. Mussen (1970).

Contents: v.1, History, theory, and methods, ed. by William Kessen (590p.); v.2, Infancy and developmental psychobiology, ed. by Marshall M. Haith and Joseph J. Campos (1244p.); v.3, Cognitive development, ed. by John H. Flavell and Ellen M. Markman (942p.); v.4, Socialization, personality, and social development, ed. by E. Mavis Hetherington (1043p.).

A sourcebook surveying the contemporary status of child psychology. Each volume consists of chapters by specialists, with bibliographic references and index.   BF721.H242

The handbook of clinical psychology: theory, research, and practice. Ed. by C. Eugene Walker. Homewood, Ill., Dow Jones-Irwin, [1983]. 2v. (1439p.) il.   **CD110**

A multi-authored volume which provides a scholarly review of current research literature and clinical practice. In six major sections: theoretical and experimental foundations; psychotherapy research; diagnosis and assessment; treatment methods; psychological profession; forensic psychology. Indexed. RC467.H27

Handbook of industrial and organizational psychology. Marvin D. Dunnette, ed. Chicago, Rand McNally, [1976]. 1740p. (Repr.: N.Y., Wiley, 1983) **CD111**

Contents: pt.1, Theoretical and methodological foundation of industrial and organizational psychology; pt.2, Individual and job measurement and the management of individual behavior in organizations; pt.3, Description and measurement of organizations and of behavioral processes in organizations.

". . . the plan is to produce a *Handbook* that is broad in scope, giving strong emphases to both conceptual and methodological issues relevant to the study of industrial and organizational behavior."—*Pref.* Contains 37 signed chapters; most include references. Subject index. HF5548.8.H265

The Harvard guide to modern psychiatry. Ed. by Armand M. Nicholi, Jr. Cambridge, Mass., Belknap Pr. of Harvard Univ. Pr., 1978. 691p. il. **CD112**

About 30 professors and subject specialists, most affiliated with Harvard University, have contributed to this guide which offers 31 signed chapters with bibliographic references. In six main sections: examination and evaluation; brain and behavior; psychopathology; treatment and management; special populations; psychiatry and society. Indexed. RC454.H36

The mental health almanac. Robert D. Allen, ed. N.Y., Garland STPM Pr., [1978]. 403p. **CD113**

A resource list and guide for professionals in the field. A brief overview of a topic (e.g., rape) is followed by a selective annotated list of books, articles, audio tapes and films, and a directory of relevant associations. Pt.III, "The profession," offers similar treatment of graduate programs, licensing, employment, funding, professional associations, and service organizations. No index. RA790.6.M39

The psychotherapy handbook. Ed. by Richie Herink. N.Y., New American Library, [1980]. 724p. **CD114**

Offers short signed descriptions of more than 250 varieties of psychotherapy; each description includes history, technique, applications, and bibliography. RC480.P826

Wolman, Benjamin B. Handbook of clinical psychology. N.Y., McGraw-Hill, [1965]. 1596p. **CD115**

Intended "to acquaint clinical psychologists and other professionals with the tremendous scope of research, experience, theory, and practice in this rapidly growing field."—*Pref.* Includes sections on research methods, theoretical foundations, diagnostic methods, clinical patterns, methods of treatment, and clinical psychology as a profession. Within each section chapters have been contributed by specialists, and extensive bibliographies are provided. Name and subject indexes. RC467.W6

—— Handbook of general psychology. Englewood Cliffs, N.J., Prentice-Hall, [1973]. 1006p. il. **CD116**

A review of psychology which "stresses the elements common to the highly diversified special areas . . . without pretending to cover all the common elements nor to be encyclopedic."—*Pref.* 45 chapters by specialists deal with the broad areas of history, theory, and methodology; the human organism; perception; learning; language, thought, and intelligence; motivation and emotion; personality; specialized areas. Bibliographic references; index. BF121.W63

Directories

Directory of mental health libraries and information centers. Barbara E. Epstein, ed. Wash., Amer. Psychiatric Pr., [1984]. 297p. **CD117**

Comp. under the auspices of the Assoc. of Mental Health Librarians.

Provides data on some 275 mental health library collections in the United States and Canada. Includes collection characteristics, services, publications, and access information. Arranged by state, then by city. Indexed by personnel, institution, and subject.

Z675.M43D57

Directory of outpatient psychiatric clinics . . . and other mental health resources in the United States and Territories. 1925– . Bethesda, Md., U.S. Dept. of Health, Education, and Welfare, 1925– . Irregular. **CD117a**

Issuing body varies; imprint varies. Continues the *Directory of psychiatric clinics,* published by the National Association for Mental Health in cooperation with the National Institute of Mental Health.

Includes psychiatric day-night services; state hospitals for mental disease; public institutions for mentally retarded; veterans administration hospitals; mental health associations; state departments dealing with mental health and mental retardation; regional offices, U.S. Dept. of Health, Education, and Welfare. Arranged alphabetically by state. Information for each establishment includes brief description, address, designation of service area, description of service limitations, days open, and number of attending staff.

RC443.D5

Graduate study in psychology and associated fields. 1968/69– . Amer. Psychological Assoc., [1967]– . Annual. **CD118**

Title varies.

Includes graduate programs in the United States and Canada. The list of programs is by degree offered. Indexed. BF77.G73

Gunn, John Charles. A directory of world psychiatry. [London], World Psychiatric Assoc., [1971]. 350p. maps. **CD119**

An international directory of hospitals and institutions dealing with the mentally ill. Within each entry for 89 countries provides: brief description of the country's psychiatric services; list of the main public psychiatric hospitals; list of university departments which teach psychiatry; list of psychiatric journals published there; data on the national psychiatric associations. RC335.G85

The mental health yearbook/directory. 1979/80– . N.Y., Van Nostrand Reinhold, [1979]– . Irregular? **CD120**

Judith Norback, ed.

A combined directory and sourcebook of explanations of various programs, agencies, facilities, information services, and publications. RA790.6.M465

Sourcebook of aid for the mentally and physically handicapped. Judith Norback, ed. N.Y., Van Nostrand Reinhold, [1983]. 506p. **CD121**

For full information *see* CC202.

U.S. National Institute of Mental Health. Mental health directory. Wash., Govt. Prt. Off., 1964–77. Annual. **CD122**

"NIMH has provided listings of treatment resources in every State and Territory . . . gathered from the Division's 1976 inventory of mental health facilities. . . . The Institute's National Clearinghouse for Mental Health Information has supplemented this material with information about Regional, State, and voluntary mental health agencies and in professional and private organizations."— *Pref., 1977.* Entries are arranged by state, then city, town, or county. Data include name, address, phone number, and services provided.

Wolman, Benjamin B. International directory of psychology. N.Y. & London, Plenum, [1979]. 279p. **CD123**

Subtitle: A guide to people, places, and policies.

"A compendium summarizing the highlights of psychology— country by country."—*Foreword.* Entries are arranged alphabetically by country, emphasizing national psychological organization, education and training, legal status, research, and opportunities for foreign psychologists. Not indexed. BF30.W64

Biography

American Psychological Association. Biographical directory. 1970– . Wash., 1970– . Triennial.   **CD124**

Supersedes the Association's *Directory* (1948–68), which in turn superseded its *Yearbook* (1916–47).

The 1981 edition lists some 54,000 names of Association members, giving brief biographical data. Contains a geographical index and a divisional membership roster. Introductory material includes background information and bylaws of the Association and "Ethical standards of psychologists."   BF11.A67

American Psychiatric Association. Biographical directory of fellows and members. [Ed.1]– , 1941– . N.Y., Bowker, 1941– . (7th ed. 1977)   **CD125**

Publisher varies; title varies.

The 7th ed. lists some 24,000 American psychiatrists, and a few from foreign countries. Gives information as to training, experience, specialty, publications, etc. Contains a geographical index. Introductory material includes information on the development of the Association.   RC326.A56

International Union of Psychological Science. International directory of psychologists: exclusive of the U.S.A. 3d. ed. Amsterdam & N.Y., North-Holland, 1980. 589p.   **CD126**

"Planned by the Committee on Publication and Communication of the International Union of Psychological Science and prepared by the Zentralstelle fuer Psychologische Information und Dokumentation at the University of Trier, West Germany."—*t.p.*

Eds., Eugene H. Jacobson and Guenther Reinert with assistance of Detlef Herrig.

1st ed. 1958.

A directory of psychologists arranged by country. Omits the United States. Entries provide brief biographical data, address, and field of interest. Index of associations.   BF30.I54

Nordby, Vernon and **Hall, Calvin S.** A guide to psychologists and their concepts. San Francisco, Freeman, 1974. 187p. ports.   **CD127**

"The aims of this book are twofold: first, to present brief biographies of [42] persons whose thinking has been influenced and sometimes decisive in establishing the conceptual horizons of contemporary psychology; second, to set forth as clearly and as succinctly as we can their principal concepts. This guide is written for the general reader. . . . "—*Introd.*   BF109.A1N67

Psychological register, ed. by Carl Murchison. Worcester, Mass., Clark Univ. Pr., 1929–32. v.2–3.   **CD128**

Includes brief biographies of psychologists throughout the world, with extensive bibliographies of their works. Arranged by country; v.2 (1929) includes 1,250 psychologists from 29 countries; v.3 (1932)—a revision and expansion of the 1929 volume—includes 2,400 psychologists from 40 countries. v.1 was announced to include persons deceased before the initiation of the series and to extend back to the time of the early Greek psychologists, but was not published.   BF109.P7

Watson, Robert Irving. The great psychologists, from Aristotle to Freud. 2d ed. Philadelphia, Lippincott, [1968]. 613p.   **CD129**

1st ed. 1963.

A useful, well-written summary, tracing the development of psychology through the lives and works of more than 50 great psychologists and some 100 of their famous associates. For the 2d ed., some chapters and portions of others were completely rewritten, and a chapter entitled "Psychology until 1945" was added. Includes bibliographies, with a high percentage of citations to primary sources. Indexes of names and subjects.   BF81.W35

Zusne, Leonard. Biographical dictionary of psychology. Westport, Conn., Greenwood Pr., [1984]. 563p.   **CD130**

A rev. ed. of the author's *Names in the history of psychology* (1975).

Presents biographical sketches for about 640 deceased psychologists and individuals who have made significant contributions to the development of psychology from antiquity to the present. Bibliographical references are included. Appendixes list biographees by birth date and institutional affiliation. Indexed.   BF109.A1Z85

Style manuals

Publication manual of the American Psychological Association. 3d ed. [Wash., Amer. Psychological Assoc., 1983] 208p.   **CD131**

1st ed. publ. as v.49, no.4, pt.2 (July 1952) of *Psychological bulletin.*

"This *Publication Manual* draws its rules from a large body of psychological literature, from editors and authors experienced in psychological practices. Writers who employ this Manual conscientiously will express their ideas in a form and style both accepted by and familiar to a broad readership in psychology."—*Introd.*   BF76.7.P83

Tests and measurements

Buros, Oscar Krisen, ed. Mental measurements yearbook. [1st]– . Highland Park, N.J., Gryphon, 1938– . (8th, 1978, in 2v.)   **CD132**

Title and publisher vary.

Supersedes *Educational, psychological, and personality tests,* 1933/34–1936, by Oscar K. Buros.

The yearbooks are "designed to assist users in education, psychology, and industry to make more intelligent use of standardized tests of every description."—*Introd.* Each yearbook follows much the same pattern and is meant to supplement rather than supersede the earlier volumes. References are numbered consecutively through each of the volumes and each has cross references to reviews, excerpts, and bibliographic references in earlier volumes.

The 8th yearbook, covering mainly the period 1971–77, is in three parts: (1) Tests and reviews, arranged in 15 major classifications, listing 1,184 educational, psychological, and vocational tests with 898 original reviews as well as excerpts from 140 test reviews from 29 journals, and 17,481 references on the construction, use, and validity of specific tests; (2) Books and reviews, listing 576 books on testing and assessment techniques and 381 book reviews (with excerpts) from 46 journals; and (3) Indexes by periodical, publisher, book title, test title, name, and test classification.

Information for each test entry includes title; description of groups for which the examination is intended; date of copyright or publication; acronym; part scores; availability of forms, parts, or levels; number of pages; factual statements concerning lack of data or norms; availability of machine-scorable answer sheets; cost, scoring, and reporting services; time necessary to administer; author and publisher. Test bibliographies cover English-language materials. The majority of tests covered in the yearbooks are or have been sold commercially in the United States.

An index to tests treated in the first six yearbooks is provided in Buros's *Personality tests and reviews* (below).

——— Personality tests and reviews; including an index to the Mental measurements yearbooks. Highland Park, N.J., Gryphon, [1970]. 1659p.   **CD133**

"The major purpose . . . is to make readily available to users of personality tests the wealth of information—original test reviews, excerpted test reviews, and references on the construction, use, and validity of specific tests—to be found in the first six *Mental Measurements Yearbooks.* The volume also includes a great deal of new material on personality testing: a comprehensive bibliography of 513 personality tests; 7,116 new references dealing with the construction, use, and validity of specific tests; separate author indexes for all tests having 25 or more references; and a scanning index to all personality tests in this volume."—*Pref.*

Also includes: the "Mental Measurements Yearbook test index"; a master index to the nonpersonality tests, reviews, and references in the first six yearbooks; an index to all reviews of measurement books excerpted in the yearbooks and in *Educational, psychological and personality tests* of 1936; "Standards for educational and psychological tests and manuals"; a title index to all tests listed in the yearbooks, in *Tests in print,* or in *Reading tests and reviews;* and an analytical name index. BF698.5.B87

—— Tests in print; a comprehensive bibliography of tests for use in education, psychology, and industry. Highland Park, N.J., Gryphon, [1961]. 479p. **CD134**

A comprehensive bibliography of standard tests, listing both tests in print and out of print as of 1961. Also serves as an index and supplement to the first five *Mental measurements yearbooks.* 487 of the 2,126 entries represent new tests not listed in any of the yearbooks. Entries for in-print tests include bibliographic and descriptive information (examinees and level, number of scores, etc.) and include, where appropriate, the most recent listing of a test in the yearbook series with information on its in-print status; the number of reviews it has received; the names of reviewers; the number of references on its construction, use, and validity; the number of references reprinted from reviews in journals; and cross references to the yearbooks. Entries for out-of-print titles include only the title with cross references to additional information and reviews in the yearbooks. Includes a publisher's directory and index, a distributor's directory and index, and name and title indexes. Z5814.E9B8

—— Tests in print II; an index to tests, test reviews, and the literature on specific tests. Highland Park, N.J., Gryphon, 1974. 1107p. **CD135**

A bibliography of 2,467 separately published tests for use with English-speaking subjects, accompanied by 16,574 English-language bibliographic references on the construction, use, and validity of these tests; also indexes the test section of all previously published *Mental measurements yearbooks* for an additional 39,371 references on these same tests. Broad classed arrangement; test title and name indexes are cumulative for all previously published volumes of the yearbooks, *Tests in print I, Personality tests and reviews,* and *Reading tests and reviews.* Publishers directory and index; the "scanning" index is an expanded table of contents, with intended populations listed for each test. Z5814.E9B82

Tests in print III: an index to tests, test reviews, and the literature on specific tests. Ed. by James V. Mitchell, Jr. Lincoln, Neb., Buros Inst. of Mental Measurements, Univ. of Nebraska-Lincoln, 1983. 714p. **CD136**

A bibliography of 2,672 test entries, with 12,170 references to reviews or articles related to the construction, validity, or use of the tests in specific settings (including references to previous editions of *Tests in print,* the *Mental measurements yearbooks,* or other separate monographs on types of tests which the Institute has published). Alphabetical arrangement; cumulative indexes by title, classified subject, publisher, and personal name. Z5814.E9T47

Goldman, Bert A. and **Saunders, John L.** Directory of unpublished experimental mental measures, 1974– . N.Y., Behavioral Publ., 1974– . Irregular. (v.1, 1974; v.2, 1978; v.3, 1982) **CD137**

"The *Directory of Unpublished Experimental Mental Measures* proposes to supplement the *Mental Measurements Yearbooks* by publishing periodic surveys of tests not available commercially, using as sources those journals that carry studies and reports employing experimental instruments. Its orientation is predominantly educational, but it includes material related to psychology, sociology, and personnel work as well."—*Foreword v.1.* v.3 is based on all tests in the 1973 issues of 46 journals. Broad subject arrangement. Each entry gives test name, purpose, author, article, and journal. Author and subject indexes. BF431.G625

Hildreth, Gertrude Howell. Bibliography of mental tests and rating scales. 2d ed. N.Y., Psychological Corp., 1939. 295p. **CD138**

1st ed. 1933.

A comprehensive list of more than 4,000 tests, classified by subject. Contains subject and author indexes.

—— —— 1945 supplement. N.Y., Psychological Corp., 1946. 86p.

Includes some 1,000 tests published 1940–Oct. 1945, and some earlier tests omitted from the basic list. Z5814.P8H6

Taulbee, Earl S., Wright, H. Wilkes and **Stenmark, David E.** The Minnesota multiphasic personality inventory (MMPI): a comprehensive annotated bibliography (1940–1965). Troy, N.Y., Whitston, 1977. 603p. **CD139**

A comprehensive, annotated bibliography of 2,144 references on the MMPI from 1940 to 1965. The overall coverage includes: abstracts of MMPI articles; non-abstracted MMPI articles; manifest anxiety references; foreign references; doctoral dissertations; master's theses, books, manuals, and test reviews. Author and subject indexes.

Tests: a comprehensive reference for assessments in psychology, education, and business. Richard C. Sweetland and Daniel J. Keyser, eds. Kansas City, Mo., Test Corp. of Amer., [1983]. lxxii, 890p. **CD140**

A "quick reference guide" to 3,000 available English-language tests; entry for each provides title, author, purpose, description, time and age limit, scoring, cost and publisher. Classed arrangement; indexed by title and author. BF176.T43

—— Supplement. Kansas City, Mo., Test Corp. of Amer., [1984]. 426p.

Adds more than 500 new and previously published tests; indexes cover both the supplement and the basic volume.

PARAPSYCHOLOGY AND OCCULTISM

Caillet, Albert Louis. Manuel bibliographique des sciences psychiques ou occultes. Paris, Dorbon, 1912. 3v. **CD141**

Subtitle: Sciences des mages. Hermétique. Astrologie. Kabbale. Franc-Maçonnerie. Médecine ancienne. Mesmérisme. Sorcellerie. Singularités. Aberrations de tout ordre. Curiosités. Sources bibliographiques et documentaires sur ces sujets.

Lists 11,648 items, with full title, imprint, and collation of each, and, in many cases, notes about the books and brief biographical data about the authors. Z6876.C25

Claire, Thomas C. Occult bibliography: an annotated list of books published in English, 1971 through 1975. Metuchen, N.J., Scarecrow Pr., 1978. 454p. **CD142**

1,850 books, arranged by author, published or reprinted during the period covered. Author/title/subject index.
Continued by: Z6876.C56

—— Occult/paranormal bibliography: an annotated list of books published in English, 1976 through 1981. Metuchen, N.J., Scarecrow Pr., 1984. 561p. **CD142a**

Contributes an additional 1,813 citations for books and periodical articles, either newly published or reissued. Attempts to list all American and British works, with some coverage of other English-language titles. Asterisks denote major works. Indexed by personal name, title, and subject. Z6876.C57

Cornell University. Libraries. Catalogue of the Witchcraft Collection in the Cornell University Library. Millwood, N.Y., KTO Pr., 1977. 644p. **CD143**

Introduction by Rossell Hope Robbins; ed. by Martha J. Crowe; index by Jane Marsh Dieckmann.

Reproduces approximately 12,000 catalog cards for the 2,900 printed works and manuscripts in the collection. "The main topics included are demonic possession, theological and legal disputation, witchcraft trials, and torture. Not included in the collection are materials dealing largely or solely with alchemy, astrology, cabala, magic, the occult, prophecies, and superstition."—*Pref.* Author/title list, with separate subject index.   Z6878.W8C67

Eberhardt, George M. A geo-bibliography of anomalies: primary access to observations of UFOs, ghosts, and other mysterious phenomena. Westport, Conn. & London, Greenwood Pr., [1980]. 1114p.   **CD144**

"The *Geo-Bibliography of Anomalies* is a comprehensive list of mysterious events, discoveries, people, and places in North America. Over 22,100 separate events are grouped under 10,500 geographic place-names. The types of events listed include: phenomena accepted by 20th-century science but which are incompletely understood (ball lightning, for example); phenomena not accepted by science but still relatively understandable given reality as we know it (lake monsters); phenomena not accepted by science which indicate that the world as we know it occasionally interacts with realities quite alien to it (close encounters with UFOs); and historical and archeological mysteries (European visits to North America in ancient times)."—*Introd.*

Covers only North America north of Mexico. Entries are arranged by geographic region and by state or province within regions. Subject, observer, ship, and ethnic group indexes.   Z5705.E23

Encyclopedia of occultism and parapsychology. Ed. by Leslie Shepard. 2d ed. Detroit, Gale, [1984]. 3v.   **CD145**

Subtitle: A compendium of information on the occult sciences, magic, demonology, superstitions, spiritism, mysticism, metaphysics, psychical science, and parapsychology, with biographical and bibliographical notes and comprehensive indexes.

1st ed. 1978.

"Based on *Encyclopedia of occultism* by Lewis Spence, London, 1920, and *Encyclopaedia of psychic science* by Nandor Fodor, London, 1934, substantially revised by Leslie Shepard and supplemented by new material written by him."—*verso of t.p.*

All articles from the first edition and the two inter-edition supplements, *Occultism update* (1980–81), have been integrated into one alphabetical sequence. Entries cover phenomena, individuals, terms, organizations, and publications, and range in length from a paragraph to two pages; most have bibliographic references. Indexed.   BF1407.E52

Handbook of parapsychology. Ed. by Benjamin B. Wolman. N.Y., Van Nostrand Reinhold, [1977]. 967p.   **CD146**

Contains 34 signed chapters on various aspects of parapsychology, all with extensive lists of references, followed by a list of suggested readings and a glossary. The chapters range from balanced treatments of research methods to some highly credulous chapters on alleged phenomena. Useful for references to the enormous recent literature. Indexed.   BF1031.H254

Melton, J. Gordon. Magic, witchcraft, and paganism in America; a bibliography. N.Y., Garland, 1982. 231p. (Garland bibliography on sects and cults, 1; Garland reference library of social science, 105)   **CD147**

Comp. from the files of the Institute for the Study of American Religion.

A subject listing of about 1,500 items by or about the "magical community" in America from colonial times to the present; includes folk magic religions such as voodoo, santería, hoodoo, hauna, and bruja. Indexed by author and periodical type. Material is available at the Institute for the Study of American Religion.   Z6878.M3M44

Parapsychology abstracts international. v.1, no.1– , Aug. 1983– . [Dix Hills, N.Y.], Parapsychology Sources of Information Ctr., 1983– . Semiannual.   **CD148**

Subtitle: Summaries of the literature of parapsychology from earliest times to date.

Rhea A. White, ed.

Each issue is comprised of about 250 abstracts organized by form: parapsychology journal articles, English; parapsychology journal articles, non-English; articles in nonparapsychological journals; articles in general interest magazines; conference proceedings; chapters in books; dissertations and theses; monographs; books. Author and subject indexes for each issue; a cumulative index is to be published every two years.   BF1001.P275

Research Publications, Inc. Witchcraft in Europe and America: guide to the microfilm collection. Ed. by Diane M. Del Cervo. Woodbridge, Conn., Research Pubns., 1983. 111p.   **CD149**

The collection comprises 1,045 titles drawn from the Witchcraft Collection at Cornell University, the Harry Price Library of Magical Literature at the University of London, Essex Institute at Salem, Mass., Lea Library at the University of Pennsylvania, Harvard and Yale University libraries. The guide is arranged both by author and title.   Z6878.W8R47

Robbins, Rossell Hope. The encyclopedia of witchcraft and demonology. N.Y., Crown, [1959]. 571p. il.   **CD150**

Concerned primarily with the witchcraft of 1450–1750 in various countries. Articles are generally brief, but some run to several pages. Although bibliographies are not appended to individual articles, there is a select bibliography of 1,140 items with its own subject index.   BF1503.R6

Spence, Lewis. Encyclopaedia of occultism, a compendium of information on the occult sciences, occult personalities, psychic science, magic, demonology, spiritism and mysticism. London, Routledge, 1920. 451p. il.   **CD151**

The 1960 reprint (New Hyde Park, N.Y., University Books) is "Verbatim except for an occasional correction of a misprint."—*Publisher's pref.*

Intended to provide the general reader with a conspectus of occult sciences as a whole. Contains some 2,500 entries, many of which are several pages in length.   BF1025.S7

Thorndike, Lynn. History of magic and experimental science. N.Y., Macmillan, 1923; Columbia Univ. Pr., 1934–58. 8v. (v.3–6, History of Science Soc. Publ., n.s.4)   **CD152**

Contents: v.1–2, First 13 centuries; v.3–4, 14th–15th centuries; v.5–6, 16th century; v.7–8, 17th century.

A well-documented history with chapters devoted to historical periods, personalities, the development of disciplines, and various practices. Separate indexes in v.1–4; a combined index to v.5–6 in v.6, and to v.7–8 in v.8.   Q125.T52

White, Rhea A. and **Dale, Laura A.** Parapsychology: sources of information. Metuchen, N.J., Scarecrow Pr., 1973. 302p.   **CD153**

Comp. under the auspices of the American Society for Psychical Research.

An annotated list of both recent and out-of-print books in English on parapsychology and related areas of study; about 300 items. In addition to the bibliography, there are sections for (1) parapsychology in encyclopedias; (2) parapsychological organizations; (3) periodicals; (4) a chronology; and (5) glossary of terms.   Z6878.P8W47

C E

Anthropology and Ethnology

❖Few general reference books in anthropology are available, as most works in this field treat specific countries or areas. The *International bibliography of social and cultural anthropology* (CE29) is a comprehensive annual bibliography; the library catalogs of Harvard's Peabody Museum of Archaeology and Ethnology (CE12) constitute an important retrospective bibliography; the *Atlas for anthropology* (CE53) is useful for its ethnic maps. In addition, research workers and students in this field will want to become familiar with the Human Relations Area Files, collections which are available in hard copy or in microform at numerous libraries throughout the country.

The Human Relations Area Files constitute a collection of data on approximately 325 primitive, historical, and contemporary cultures. Each culture is assigned a "Cultural file," within which source materials (books, articles, manuscripts, plus translations done especially for the Files) were developed for the study of specific cultures or areas, and also for the study of particular topics cross-culturally. The key to the cultural groups is George P. Murdock's *Outline of world cultures* (6th rev. ed. New Haven, Human Relations Area Files, 1983. 259p.). A companion volume, the Human Relations Area Files' *Outline of cultural materials* (5th rev. ed. New Haven, 1982. 247p.), groups the subject categories into 79 major and 637 minor subject divisions. While the introduction to the Files in the *Outline of cultural materials* is good, another and more comprehensive description is available in Robert O. Lagacé's *Nature and use of the HRAF files; a research and teaching guide* (New Haven, Human Relations Area Files, 1974. 49p.). This booklet also discusses related File programs such as the HRAF-Microfiles and the HRAF Collection, and other aspects of the HRAF system.

GUIDES

Frantz, Charles. The student anthropologist's handbook; a guide to research, training, and career. Cambridge, Mass., Schenkman, [1972]. 228p. **CE1**

Introductory chapters on the nature of anthropology and the field as a profession are followed by sections on field and laboratory research, use of libraries and museums, reference works and aids to library research, and a consideration of cultural areas and regional studies. Lacks an index and is disappointing as a bibliographic guide. GN42.F7

BIBLIOGRAPHY

Bibliography of bibliography

Anthropological bibliographies: a selected guide. Comp. by Library-Anthropology Resource Group, Margo L. Smith and Yvonne M. Damien, eds. South Salem, N.Y., Redgrave Pub. Co., [1981]. 307p. **CE2**

More than 3,200 bibliographic monographs, periodical articles, essays, filmographies, and discographies are organized geographically, with a separate section for topical bibliographies lacking geographical emphasis. Emphasizes recent publications and updates earlier guides to anthropological bibliographies for Africa, Asia, the Americas, and the Soviet Union. Some brief annotations. Indexed by personal name, geographic area, ethnic group, language, and subject areas.

General

Biennial review of anthropology, 1959–71. Ed. by Bernard J. Siegel. Stanford, Calif., Stanford Univ. Pr., 1959–71. **CE3**

Describes and evaluates noteworthy papers and monographs in anthropology. International in coverage. Arranged in chapters representing fields of interest; each chapter is written by a specialist and includes a bibliography. Contains a subject index.

Ceased with vol. for 1971; continued by the *Annual review of anthropology* (CE27). Z5112.B56

Comas, Juan. Historia y bibliografía de los congresos internacionales de ciencias antropológicas: 1865–1954. México, Dirección General de Publicaciones, 1956. 490p. il. (Univ. Nacional Autónoma de México. Inst. de Historia. Publ., 1.ser., núm.37) **CE4**

Covers the activities and publications of four major international organizations in anthropology, plus those of several smaller bodies. Includes a classified subject bibliography of some 3,000 papers which have been published in the reports of the more important congresses. GN17.C6

Conklin, Harold C. Folk classification: a topically arranged bibliography of contemporary and background references through 1971. Rev. reprinting with author index. New Haven, Conn., Dept. of Anthropology, Yale Univ., 1980. 521p. **CE5**

1st ed. 1972.

"This 1980 edition differs from the 1972 publication in two respects: a number of corrections have been made and a single Index to all authors, listed together with the Sections in which their works are cited, has been added at the end."—[*p.18*] A classed listing of about 5,000 entries. Includes "references to (1) analyses of specific systems of folk classification, (2) discussions and comparisons of such analyses, and (3) theoretical and practical background literature on classification in general and in various subject fields."—*Introd.* Includes publications only to 1972, as in the earlier edition. Z5118.P5C65

Divale, William Tulio. Warfare in primitive societies: a bibliography. [Rev. ed.] Santa Barbara, Calif., ABC-Clio, [1973]. 123p. (War/peace bibliography ser., 2) **CE6**

1st ed. 1971.

Pt.I is divided into sixteen theoretical or topical sections (biological factors, demographic factors, scalping, war ceremonies, etc.); pt.II comprises sections on seven major geographical regions (four of which are further subdivided by area), and lists sources on the warfare of the various peoples of these regions. Author and tribal name indexes. Z5118.W3D57

Driver, Edwin D. The sociology and anthropology of mental illness; a reference guide. Rev. & enl. ed. [Amherst], Univ. of Massachusetts Pr., 1972. 487p. **CE7**

For full information *see* CD16.

Favazza, Armando R. and **Oman, Mary.** Anthropological and cross-cultural themes in mental health; an annotated bibliography, 1925–1974. Columbia, Univ. of Missouri Pr., 1977. 386p. (Univ. of Missouri studies, v.65) **CE8**

For full information *see* CD19.

Favazza, Armando R. and **Faheem, Ahmed D.** Themes in cultural psychiatry; an annotated bibliography, 1975–1980. Columbia, Univ. of Missouri Pr., 1982. 194p. **CE9**

For full information *see* CD20.

Harrison, Ira E. and **Cosminsky, Sheila.** Traditional medicine: implications for ethnomedicine, ethnopharmacology, maternal and child health, mental health, and public health —an annotated bibliography of Africa, Latin America, and the Caribbean. N.Y., Garland, 1976. 229p. (Garland reference library of social science, v.19) **CE10**

1,135 citations are grouped by region—Africa, Latin America and the Caribbean—then by subjects noted in the subtitle, including health care delivery systems; there is also a general nonregional section subdivided by topic. Focuses on the 1940–75 period. Indexed by author and country.

Continued by: Z5118.M4H3

Cosminsky, Sheila and **Harrison, Ira E.** Traditional medicine, vol. II, 1976–1981: current research . . .: an annotated bibliography . . .. N.Y., Garland, 1984. 327p. (Garland reference library of social science, v.147) **CE11**

Adds 1,391 citations, with an appendix of dissertations and theses. Z5118.M4C67

Harvard University. Peabody Museum of Archaeology and Ethnology. Library. Catalogue: authors. Boston, G. K. Hall, 1963. 26v. **CE12**

———— ———— Supplement 1–4. Boston, 1970–79. 6v., 2v., 3v., 3v.

Z5119.H35

———— Catalogue: subjects. Boston, G. K. Hall, 1963. 27v.

———— ———— Supplement 1–4. Boston, 1970–79. 6v., 2v., 4v., 4v.

Photoreproduction of the catalog cards from this outstanding collection. "The 82,000 volumes and pamphlets . . . provide countless references to Europe, Africa, Asia and Oceania. The field of anthropology is here taken to include prehistoric archaeology, ethnology and physical anthropology."—*Pref.* An important feature is the inclusion of entries for journal articles, contributions to *Festschriften,* and proceedings of congresses.

The supplements of each part cover items added to the collection 1963–77. *Anthopological literature* (CE28) serves as a continuation. Z5119.H36

Tozzer Library. Tozzer Library index to anthropological subject headings. Boston, G. K. Hall, 1981. 177p. **CE12a**

1971 ed. publ. as *Index to subject headings,* under the Library's earlier name as entered above.

In the earlier ed. geographic and linguistic headings were given primacy; here emphasis is on ethnic groups, languages, and major archaeological sites. Nine new subfields of anthropology have been added as subject headings, and a list of "floating subheadings" has been provided. These subject headings will be used in the 5th suppl. to the catalog of the Library. Z695.1.A63T69

Heider, Karl G. Films for anthropological teaching. 7th ed. [Wash., American Anthropological Assoc., 1983] 312p. (*Its* Special publ., no.16) **CE13**

An annotated guide to 1,575 films, including price and distributor. Arranged by film title; indexed by geographical area, subject, distributor, and persons involved. GN42.3.Z9H44

International catalogue of scientific literature: P, Anthropology. 1st–14th annual issues, 1903–19. London, 1903–20. 14v. **CE14**

For full description *see* EA17.

Keesing, Felix Maxwell. Culture change; an analysis and bibliography of anthropological sources to 1952 . . . Stanford, Calif., Stanford Univ. Pr.; London, Oxford Univ. Pr., [1953]. 242p. (Stanford anthropological ser., no.1) **CE15**

The analytical survey (p.1–94) is divided by broad periods, and discusses the trends in research and outstanding publications in each period. The bibliography (p.104–242) is chronological from 1820, with items listed alphabetically for each year. Information given is very brief. Periodical articles are included. No index. Z5111.K4

Kemper, Robert V. and **Phinney, John F. S.** The history of anthropology: a research bibliography. N.Y., Garland, 1977. 212p. **CE16**

A classed bibliography of more than 2,400 entries arranged in five major sections: (1) general sources; (2) background (largely pre-1900); (3) modern anthropology; (4) related social sciences; (5) bibliographical sources. Each major section is further subdivided by subject, geographic area, and personality. Author index. Z5111.K44

Krogman, Wilton Marion. A bibliography of human morphology, 1914–1939. Chicago, Univ. of Chicago Pr., [1941]. 385p. **CE17**

Classed index to materials in more than 900 periodicals under such headings as: osteology, races of man, prehistory of man, craniology, human heredity, nervous system, etc. Author index. Z7994.M8K7

Lapointe, François H. and **Lapointe, Claire C.** Claude Lévi-Strauss and his critics: an international bibliography of criticism (1950–1976) followed by a bibliography of the writings of Claude Lévi-Strauss. N.Y., Garland, 1977. 219p. **CE18**

Pt.I lists books, reviews and unpublished theses and dissertations on Lévi-Strauss, works giving a "general presentation," titles devoted to a single work of Lévi-Strauss, materials comparing him with other figures, and works arranged by subject. Pt.II is a chronological bibliography of his writings, including translations. Covers through June 1975. Author and name index. Z8504.35.L36

Mead, Margaret. Margaret Mead: the complete bibliography, 1925–1975. Ed. by Joan Gordan. The Hague, Mouton, 1976. 202p. **CE19**

1,397 citations to printed sources are chronologically listed, with notes on variant language editions and reprints; separate notations for records, tapes and cassettes, films, and videotapes. Name and subject indexes. Z8561.3.M42

Miller, Mamie Ruth Tanquist. . . . An author, title, and subject check list of Smithsonian Institution publications relating to anthropology. Publ. in cooperation with the School of American Research. . . . Albuquerque, Univ. of New Mexico Pr., 1946. 218p. (Univ. of New Mexico. Bull. Bibliographical ser., v.1, no.2; whole no.405) **CE20**

For full list of publications of the Bureau of American Ethnology, *see* CE24. Z5111.M5

Rosenstiel, Annette. Education and anthropology: an annotated bibliography. N.Y., Garland, 1977. 646p. **CE21**

An international bibliography of 3,435 books, periodical articles, dissertations, papers, reprints, etc., "reflecting (1) historical influences, (2) current trends, (3) theoretical concerns, and (4) practical methodology at the interfaces of these two disciplines."—*Introd.* Author arrangement, with English translations provided for foreign-language titles. Covers the literature from 1689 to 1976. Topical subject and name indexes. Z5814.E2R67

Tippett, Alan Richard, comp. Bibliography for cross-cultural workers. South Pasadena, Calif., William Carey Library, [1971]. 252p. **CE22**

A classed bibliography of about 3,000 items (books and periodical articles) published to mid-1971. No index. Intended primarily for the use of graduate students in missionary studies but useful to cross-cultural workers and students of anthropology in general. Z5111.T54

U.S. Bureau of American Ethnology. Bulletin. Index to Bulletins 1–100, with index to Contributions to North American ethnology, Introductions, and Miscellaneous publications, by Biren Bonnerjea. Wash., Govt. Prt. Off., 1963. 726p. (U.S. Bureau of Amer. Ethnology. Bull. 178) **CE23**

Includes subject, author and title indexes and index to illustrations. Z1209.U49

———— List of publications of the Bureau of American Ethnology, with index to authors and titles. Wash., Smithsonian Inst. Pr., 1971. 134p. **CE24**

Provides a listing to all the various series published by the Bureau, with indication of "in print" status, and an author-title index.

———— General index: Annual reports of the Bureau, v.1–48 (1879–1931) . . . comp. by Biren Bonnerjea. Wash., Govt. Prt. Off., 1933. p.25–1220. (In *its* 48th Annual report, 1930/31) **CE25**

Pt.1, Subject index; pt.2, List of annual reports . . . with an index to authors and titles.

Current

Abstracts in anthropology. v.1– , Feb. 1970– . Westport, Conn., Greenwood Periodicals, 1970– . Quarterly. **CE26**

Abstracts are grouped in four sections—Archaeology, Cultural anthropology, Linguistics, and Physical anthropology—and include books, articles, and conference papers. Abstracts have been contributed by authors, by journals publishing the original articles, or by the editors. Beginning with v.1, no.4, both author and subject indexes are included in each issue. Annual cumulated author and subject indexes. GN1.A15

Annual review of anthropology. v.1– , 1972– . Palo Alto, Calif., Annual Reviews Inc., 1972– . Annual. **CE27**

Like its predecessor, the *Biennial review of anthropology* (CE3), this series describes and evaluates recent publications in the field. Chapters by specialists on topics of current interest and varying scope in physical, social, and cultural anthropology are followed by bibliographies giving full citations to the writings discussed. International in coverage, but with a high percentage of references in English. Author and subject indexes. Z5112.A5

Anthropological literature: an index to periodical articles and essays. v.1, no.1– , Winter 1979– . Pleasantville, N.Y., Redgrave Publ. Co., 1979– . Quarterly. **CE28**

"Comp. by Tozzer Library, Peabody Museum of Archaeology and Ethnology, Harvard University."—*t.p.*

A broad subject index to articles in about 1,000 serials, as well as colloquia and symposia publications, *Festschriften,* and collections of readings received by the Tozzer Library. Citations are grouped by author within five sections: cultural/social; archaeology; biological/ physical; linguistics; general/method/theory. Indexes by joint author, archaeological site and culture, ethnic and linguistic group, and geographic area appear in each issue, as well as on an annual and a proposed quinquennial basis. International in scope, with primary emphasis on materials published in English, French, German, Spanish, and the Slavic languages. v.6 (1984) is to be published in microfiche by the Tozzer Library. Z5112.A57

International bibliography of social and cultural anthropology. Bibliographie internationale d'anthropologie sociale et culturelle. v.1– , 1955– . Prep. by the International Committee for Social Sciences Documentation in cooperation with the International Congress of Anthropological and Ethnological Sciences. London, Tavistock; Chicago, Aldine, 1958– . v.1– . Annual. (International bibliography of the social sciences) **CE29**

Publisher varies. v.1–5 publ. as part of *Documentation in the social sciences* (Paris, UNESCO); v.6– , as a *Publication* of the International Committee for Social Sciences Documentation.

A companion to the other Unesco annual bibliographies in the social sciences: sociology (CC15), economics (CH36), and political science (CJ39). Attempts to list scientific works in many languages from many countries. Includes books, periodical articles, and duplicated materials but not unpublished typewritten theses, etc. Arranged by a special classification scheme, with an author index and subject indexes in both English and French. Z7161.I593

Museum of Mankind. Library. Anthropological index to current periodicals in the Museum of Mankind Library (incorporating the former Royal Anthropological Institute Library). v.15– , Jan./Mar. 1977– . London, Royal Anthropological Inst., 1977– . Quarterly. **CE30**

Continues the *Index to current periodicals received in the Library of the Royal Anthropological Institute* (1963–76) and assumes its numbering. Title varies.

Maintains the regional, classified approach of the previous title. A revised list of about 650 current periodicals held by the Library was

published in 1978, with additions listed in Pt.I of each index volume. A cumulative annual author index has been published since 1972. A cumulative author index to v.1–9 (1963–71) and a subject index to v.1–5 (1963–67) are available on cards at the Museum of Mankind Library.

Reviews in anthropology. v.1, no.1– , Feb. 1974– . Westport, Conn., Redgrave Information Resources Group, 1974– . Quarterly. **CE31**

Publishes long, detailed reviews of new books in the field. Z5111.R47

Dissertations

See also CE46.

Anthropology: a dissertation bibliography. [Ann Arbor, Mich.], University Microfilms Internat., [1978]. 65p. **CE32**

Lists about 3,400 American doctoral dissertations written between 1911–77 which are available from University Microfilms International; reference is made to abstracts appearing in *Dissertation abstracts international* through Sept. 1977. Broad subject classification subdivided by topical and regional subfields. Language and linguistics coverage is only partial. Name index.

———— Supplement [1]– . [Ann Arbor, Mich.], University Microfilms Internat., [1980]– . Irregular. **CE33**

Suppl. [1] lists 1,131 doctoral dissertations for which abstracts have appeared in *DAI* from Oct. 1977 through Jan. 1980. Follows the plan of the earlier compilation, with more coverage of linguistics than previously.

McDonald, David R. Masters' theses in anthropology: a bibliography of theses from United States colleges and universities. New Haven, HRAF Pr., 1977. 453p. **CE34**

A list of more than 3,700 titles, arranged by broad subjects—social/cultural anthropology, archaeology, physical anthropology, linguistics. Indexed by subject, ethnic group, geographical area, cross-cultural studies, author, and educational institution. Z5111.M26

Periodicals

Serial publications in anthropology. Comp. by Library-Anthropology Resource Group. F. X. Grollig and Sol Tax, eds. South Salem, N.Y., Redgrave, [1982]. 177p. **CE35**

1st ed. 1973.

An alphabetical main entry listing of current serial anthropological titles, including publisher's address and frequency. Indexed by topical and geographic subjects, and by corporate author.

Z5112.S47

Manuscripts and archives

National Anthropological Archives. Catalog to manuscripts at the National Anthropological Archives . . . , Smithsonian Institution, Wash., D.C. Boston, G. K. Hall, 1975. 4v. **CE36**

A photographic reproduction of catalog cards representing documents collected by the Bureau of American Ethnology between 1879 and 1965. In three divisions: (1) an alphabetical file on the Indians of North America north of Mexico; (2) a smaller geographical file on peoples of Mexico, Central America, and non-North American areas; (3) a numerical file indicating the subject under which cards have been filed in the other two divisions. Subject approach is by tribe, linguistic group, or name of individual. Z1209.2.N67N37

DICTIONARIES AND ENCYCLOPEDIAS

L'Anthropologie. [Réalisé sous la direction d'André Akoun. Verviers, Marabout, 1974.] 690p. il., maps.   **CE37**

A dictionary comprising about 400 brief articles and thirteen major summary articles. Some bibliographic notes.   GN11.A8

Encyclopedia of anthropology. Ed. by David E. Hunter and Phillip Whitten. N.Y., Harper & Row, [1976].   411p. il.   **CE38**

Intended for the student and instructor in anthropology. About 1,400 entries "ranging in length from 25 to 3,000 words."—*Pref.* Many articles are signed by the contributors; some have brief bibliographies appended. Includes biographies, but no ethnographic articles on cultural groups.   GN11.E52

International dictionary of regional European ethnology and folklore. Copenhagen, Rosenkilde & Bagger, 1960–65. 2v.   **CE39**

"Under the auspices of the International Council for Philosophy and Humanistic Studies and with the support of UNESCO published by CIAP (International Commission of Folk Arts and Folklore)."—*title page.*

Contents: v.1, General ethnological concepts, by Åke Hultkrantz; v.2, Folk literature (Germanic), by Laurits Bødker.

v.1 is an alphabetically arranged dictionary designed "to give definitions of ethnological and folkloristic technical terms and concepts."—*Introd.* Arranged by English term with synonyms in French, Spanish, German, and Swedish, and descriptive definitions and references to the literature of the subject. Bibliography, p.251–52.

v.2 differs in plan, the terms here being entered under the various national denominations rather than grouped under the English equivalent of the term. Entries include bibliographic references.   GN307.I5

Winick, Charles. Dictionary of anthropology. N.Y., Philosophical Lib., 1956. 579p. (Repr.: Paterson, N.J., Littlefield, Adams, 1964)   **CE40**

A dictionary of anthropological terms, uneven in coverage but useful for the definitions of unusual terms not usually found in general dictionaries.   GN11.W5

HANDBOOKS

Honigmann, John J. Handbook of social and cultural anthropology. Chicago, Rand McNally, [1973]. 1295p.   **CE41**

A survey and discussion of the state of knowledge and a review of research in the various branches of anthropology. Each chapter is by a specialist; extensive bibliographies; subject index.   GN315.H642

Muslim peoples; a world ethnographic survey. 2d ed., rev. and exp. Richard V. Weekes, ed. in chief. Westport, Conn., Greenwood Pr., [1984]. 2v. (953p.) maps.   **CE42**

An alphabetical arrangement of brief survey articles on some 190 ethnic groups throughout the world which have been identified as wholly or partly Muslim. Articles are signed, and each carries a bibliography of English-language materials. The work is "designed primarily for the English-speaking nonspecialist, whether academician or layman."—*Introd.* Bibliographic entries are " 'recent,' that is, since 1945," and the bibliographies "concentrate on works related to current patterns of living—the theme of this survey."   DS35.625.A1M87

Naroll, Raoul and **Cohen, Ronald,** eds. A handbook of method in cultural anthropology. Garden City, N.Y., publ.

for the Museum of Natural History [by] the Natural History Pr., 1970. 1017p.   **CE43**

Chapters by specialists on various aspects of methodology. Principal sections include: General problems; The field work process; Models of ethnographic analysis; Comparative approaches; and Problems of categorization. Bibliographies are included.   GN345.N37

Sixty cultures: a guide to the HRAF probability sample files. Robert O. Lagacé, ed. Appendix by David Levinson. New Haven, Human Relations Area Files, 1977– . Pt.A– . (In progress)   **CE44**

Pt.A consists of profiles of each of the sixty cultural groups which constitute the HRAF Probability Sample Files. Each profile includes a summary of information on the culture, a general review of the sources processed for that file (usually with evaluative comments), a bibliographic list of sources processed, and a list of other sources cited which have not been processed for the file. Pt.B will include an additional sixty cultures. Subject index.   GN307.S59

Textor, Robert B., comp. A cross-cultural summary. New Haven, Conn., HRAF Pr., [1967]. 208p. plus appendixes.   **CE45**

A 400-culture sample derived from G. P. Murdock's *Ethnographic atlas* (CE52n) has been analyzed according to 526 characteristics. Computer-produced, the analysis is set forth in the form of lengthy tables designed to show that for a given cultural characteristic, a series of other characteristics may be expected to occur with a specified degree of probability.   GN307.T4

DIRECTORIES

Guide to departments of anthropology. 1969/70– . [Wash.], Amer. Anthropological Assoc., [1969]– . Annual.   **CE46**

Continues *Guide to graduate departments of anthropology,* 1962/63–1968/69.

Covers academic, museum, and research departments in the United States, Canada, and selected foreign countries. Includes a list of completed doctoral dissertations. Name index.   GN43.A2G84

Hunter, John E. Inventory of ethnological collections in museums of the United States and Canada. 2d ed. (rev. and enl.). [Wash.], Committee on Anthropological Research in Museums of the American Anthropological Assoc.; [N.Y.], Wenner-Gren Foundation for Anthropological Research, 1967. 92l.   **CE47**

1st ed. 1967.

Describes collections and research facilities of 48 museums in the United States and 4 in Canada. Alphabetical arrangement by museum; indexed by culture area.   GN36.U6H8

International directory of anthropological institutions, ed. by William L. Thomas, Jr. and Anna M. Pikelis . . . N.Y., Wenner-Gren Foundation for Anthropological Research, 1953. 468p.   **CE48**

Arrangement is under geographical division, either individual countries or closely related groups of countries. For each of these sections a general outline of the history and scope of anthropological research is given, followed by detailed information on individual institutions. Alphabetical indexes of institutions and of cities and towns.   GN2.T45

International directory of anthropologists. Ed.5. Chicago, Univ. of Chicago Pr., 1975. 496p.   **CE49**

Ed.1–4 published 1938–67 with varying issuing bodies: 1938–40 issued by the National Research Council; 1950 by the Committee on International Relations in Anthropology of the Division of Anthropology and Psychology, National Research Council and the American Anthropological Association; 1967 by associates in *Current anthropology.* A "1970 revision" appeared in the periodical *Current anthropology,* v.11, p.249–400 (June 1970). Place of publication has varied.

Offers biographical data on more than 4,300 scholars in the field. "Other associates of *Current anthropology*" (i.e., those who did not respond to the questionnaire) are listed with name and address only in a separate section. Geographical index; Chronological index; Subject/methodological index.   GN20.I5

ATLASES

Atlas of man. N.Y., St. Martin's Pr., [1978]. 272p. il., maps.   **CE50**

John Gaisford, ed.

"The main body of the Atlas is divided into nine sections, corresponding to geographical divisions. . . . Each section begins with an introduction to the historical, geographic and cultural characteristics of the region, illustrated with appropriate maps. Then individual entries describe the countries and main groups of people living within the region, and on each double page there is a map showing their location."—*p.33*. Provides population estimates. Sketches of groups average 100 to 500 words. An introductory work for the non-specialist, heavily illustrated with colored maps and photographs. Indexed.   GN378.A84

Atlas of mankind. Chicago, Rand McNally, [1982]. 191, [15]p. il., maps.   **CE51**

"A global perspective" (p.10–55) provides a general, thematic background through world maps, diagrams and photographs on topics such as languages, food production, kinship, and taboo. Each topic is cross-referenced to ethnographic groups described in "Peoples of the world" (p.56–191). The latter section divides the world into 11 regions; for each region there are maps of language distribution and land use, diagrams of state populations and religious practices, and a history time bar providing key dates. Some ethnographic groups are described in essays of approximately 500 words. Glossary; index.   GN316.A85

Murdock, George Peter. Atlas of world cultures. [Pittsburgh], Univ. of Pittsburgh Pr., [1981]. 151p.   **CE52**

First publ. as *Ethnographic atlas* (1967).

Identifies 563 societies whose cultures are most fully described in the ethnographic literature, and lists up to two ethnographic sources as a guide to that literature. Presents in coded form data on 76 items of ethnographic information for each society, with a worldwide summary and conclusion. The sample is a significant reduction from the 1,264 cultures coded for the *Ethnographic atlas* and installments appearing in the journal *Ethnology* until 1971.   GN345.3.M86

Spencer, Robert F. and **Johnson, Elden.** Atlas for anthropology. 2d ed. Dubuque, Iowa, W. C. Brown, [1968]. 61*l*. fold. maps.   **CE53**

This series of maps, intended as a manual for beginning students, covers tribes and ethnic groups, language areas, Old World prehistory, and New World prehistory.   G1046.E1S7

THE AMERICAS

Bibliography

See also CC437–CC467, DB234.

Baldus, Herbert. Bibliografia crítica da etnologia brasileira. São Paulo, [Ed. São Nicolau Indústria Grafica], 1954–68. 2v.   **CE54**

v.2 has imprint: Hannover, Kommissionsverlag Münstermann-Druck, 1968.

An annotated bibliography of about 2,800 items in various languages.

Berg, Hans van den. Material bibliográfico para el estudio de las Aymaras, Callawayas, Chipayas, Urus. Cochabamba,

Facultad de Filosofía y Ciencias Religiosas, Universidad Católica Boliviana, 1980. 3v.   **CE55**

An annotated bibliography of more than 5,800 entries on the Bolivian and Peruvian ethnic groups named in the title. Author listing; the final volume is an index by ethnic group, subject, and author.   Z1209.2.B5B47

Bernal, Ignacio. Bibliografía de arqueología y etnografía; Mesoamérica y Norte de México, 1514–1960. México, Inst. Nacional de Antropología e Historia, 1962. 634p. maps. (Inst. Nacional de Antropología e Historia. Memorias, 7)   **CE56**

More than 13,000 numbered entries, including books, periodical articles, reports, etc., classified by region and then by subject. Author index.   Z1209.B45

Bernal Villa, Segunda. Guía bibliográfica de Colombia de interés para el antropólogo. Bogotá, Ediciones Universidad de los Andes, 1969. 782p. maps.   **CE57**

An extensive bibliography with emphasis on cultural anthropology but with some attention to archaeology, geography, history, and linguistics. A general section is followed by regional sections. Author index.   Z1731.B44

Boletín bibliográfico de antropología americana. México, D.F., Comité de Antropología del Instituto Panamericano de Geografía e Historia, 1937–80. v.1–40.   **CE58**

During its years of publication the *BBAA* not only carried critical reviews of current publications and reports on research activity, but included many bibliographies of specific topics.

Comas, Juan. Bibliografía selectiva de las culturas indígenas de América. México, 1953. 292p. maps. (Inst. Pan-Americano de Geografía e Historia. Comisión de Historia. Publ. núm. 166. Bibliografías, 1)   **CE59**

2,014 entries. Classed arrangement, with indexes to indigenous groups and to authors. Lists works in various languages, with a preponderance of English titles.   F1401.P153 no.166

González Martínez, José Luis and **Ronzelen, Teresa María van.** Religiosidad popular en el Perú; bibliografía antropología, historia, sociología y pastoral. Lima, Centro de Estudios y Publicaciones (CEP), [1983]. 375p. il.   **CE60**

A classed, annotated bibliography of 694 titles on Christian and folk beliefs and customs, indexed by geographic area and author.   Z7834.P4G66

Gregorovich, Andrew. Canadian ethnic groups bibliography; a selected bibliography of ethno-cultural groups in Canada and the province of Ontario. Toronto, Dept. of the Provincial Secretary and Citizenship of Ontario, 1972. 208p.   **CE61**

More than 2,100 items arranged by ethnic group treated. Some annotations.   Z1395.E4G74

Larrea, Carlos Manuel. Bibliografía científica del Ecuador: antropología, etnografía, arqueología, prehistoria, lingüística. 3.ed. Quito, Corporación de Estudios y Publicaciones, 1968. 289p.   **CE62**

1st ed. appeared as v.3 of the compiler's *Bibliografía científica del Ecuador* (Quito, 1948–53).

An author listing of book and periodical materials; subject index.   Z7407.S6L33

McGlynn, Eileen A. Middle American anthropology: directory, bibliography, and guide to the UCLA Library collections. Los Angeles, Latin American Center and University Library, Univ. of Calif., 1975. 131p. il. (Latin American collections in the UCLA Lib.: Guides, ser. B, no.1)   **CE63**

In two main sections: (1) international directories of individuals and institutions; (2) bibliography of reference works, serial titles, selected monographs, and rare and non-book materials. Based on, but not limited to, the UCLA library collections. Indexed.   Z1209.2.C45M32

Mareski, Sofía and **Ferraro, Oscar Humberto.** Bibliografía sobre datos y estudios etnográficos y antropológicos del Paraguay. Asunción, [Centro Paraguayo de Documentación Social], 1972. 143p. (Centro Paraguayo de Documentación Social. Documentos y estudios bibliográficos, 2)   **CE64**

An author listing of 975 items, with subject index.

Z1209.2.P3M37

Martínez, Héctor, Cameo C., Miguel and **Ramírez S., Jesús.** Bibliografía indígena andina peruana (1900–1968). [Lima, Centro de Estudios de Población y Desarrollo, 1969] 157p.   **CE65**

A multigraphed edition in 2v. was published 1968.

A classed bibliography of 1,700 items. A general section is followed by sections for northern, central, and southern areas of Peru, each with geographical and topical subdivisions. Indexes of authors, subjects, and places.   Z1209.M3

Méndez-Domínguez, Alfredo. Mesoamerica: directorio y bibliografía, 1950–1980. Guatemala, Universidad del Valle de Guatemala, [1982]. 313p.   **CE66**

An international bibliography of about 5,000 entries produced by some 700 scholars. Includes the fields of archaeology, cultural and social anthropology, folklore, linguistics, physical anthropology and demography. Author listing; no subject approach.

Z1209.2.C45M47

Myers, Robert A. Amerindians of the Lesser Antilles: a bibliography. New Haven, Conn., Human Relations Area Files, 1981. 158*l*. map.   **CE67**

A classed bibliography of about 1,300 references to archaeological, historical, and linguistic research on the Ciboney, Arawak, and Carib peoples of the eastern Caribbean. Geographical and author indexes.   Z1209.2.L47M93

O'Leary, Timothy J. Ethnographic bibliography of South America. New Haven, Conn., Human Relations Area Files, 1963. 387p. maps.   **CE68**

A listing of books, periodical articles, reports, etc., intended to cover ethnographic literature on continental South America through 1961. No coverage of Panama and the Caribbean Islands except where the latter belong to Colombia or Venezuela. The main part is arranged by areas, and within each area by tribal groups. Includes list of works on general South America and a list of bibliographic aids.   Z5114.O4

Parra, Manuel Germán and **Jiménez Moreno, Wigberto.** Bibliografía indigenista de México y Centroamerica (1850–1950). México, Inst. Nacional Indigenista, 1954. 342p. (Memorias del Inst. Nacional Indigenista, v.4)   **CE69**

A comprehensive bibliography of books and articles, in various languages, covering all aspects of the life of Indians of Mexico and Central America.   Z1029.P3

Pollak-Eltz, Angelina. Bibliografía antropológica venezolana, 1983. Caracas, Instituto de Lenguas Indígenas y Centro de Estudios Comparados de Religión, Universidad Católica Andrés Bello, [1983?]. 66p.   **CE70**

A main-entry list of 595 books, with contents notes and subject index.   Z1209.2.V4P64

Storck, Peter L. A preliminary bibliography of early man in eastern North America, 1839–1973. [Toronto], Royal Ontario Museum, [1975]. 110p. (Archaeology monograph, 4)   **CE71**

"This bibliography contains 1242 . . . journal articles, reviews, monographs, and books dealing in whole or in part with the subject of Early Man in eastern North America" (*Introd.*), i.e., early and late Palaeo-Indian and possible antecedent cultures in Canadian provinces east of Manitoba and the United States east of the Mississippi River. Author listing, with geographic, subject, and site-locality indexes.   Z1208.N6S77

Sued Badillo, Jalil. Bibliografía antropológica para el estudio de los pueblos indígenas en el Caribe. Santo Domingo, Fundación García-Arévalo, 1977. 579p. (Serie investigaciones, no.8)   **CE72**

An international bibliography in two main sections: (1) broad subject arrangement; (2) geographic arrangement. Covers the Caribbean islands and the surrounding countries of Central and South America. No index.   Z1209.2.C27S9

Valle, Rafael Heliodoro. Bibliografía maya . . . . México, [1937–41]. 404p. (Repr.: N.Y., B. Franklin, 1971)   **CE73**

At head of title: Instituto Panamericano de Geografía e Historia. Issued in parts as appendix to *Boletín bibliográfico de antropología americana*, v.1–5, 1937–41.

A comprehensive bibliography of materials about Mayan culture in various languages and of all periods.   Z1210.M4V3

Handbooks

Handbook of Middle American Indians. Robert Wauchope, gen. ed. Austin, Univ. of Texas Pr., [1964–76]. 16v. il. maps.   **CE74**

Contents: v.1, Natural environment and early cultures, ed. by R. C. West; v.2–3, Archaeology of Southern Mesoamerica, ed. by G. R. Willey; v.4, Archaeological frontiers and external connections, ed. by G. R. Willey and G. F. Ekholm; v.5, Linguistics, ed. by N. A. McQuown; v.6, Social anthropology, ed. by M. Nash; v.7–8, Ethnology, ed. by E. Z. Vogt; v.9, Physical anthropology, ed. by T. D. Stewart; v.10–11, Archaeology of Northern Mesoamerica, ed. by G. F. Ekholm and I. Bernal; v.12–15, Guide to ethno-historical sources, ed. by H. F. Cline [and others]; v.16, Sources cited and artifacts illustrated. ed. by M. A. Harrison.

Each volume or pair of volumes is made up of a series of essays by specialists on specific aspects of the life, customs, arts and culture, environmental influences, etc., of the various groups of Middle American Indians. Each has its own extensive bibliography and detailed index.

Supplemented by: F1434.H3

Archaeology. Ed. by Jeremy A. Sabloff. Series ed., Victoria Reifler Bricker. Austin, Univ. of Texas Pr., [1981]. 463p. il. (Supplement to the Handbook of Middle American Indians, v.1)   **CE75**

Future supplements are to cover language and literature, social organizations and cultural institutions, and physical anthropology.   F1219.A76

Steward, Julian Haynes. Handbook of South American Indians. . . . Prep. in cooperation with the United States Department of State as a project of the Interdepartmental Committee on Cultural and Scientific Cooperation. Wash., Govt. Prt. Off., 1946–59. 7v. il. (U.S. Bureau of American Ethnology. Bull. 143) (Repr.: N.Y., Cooper Square, 1963)   **CE76**

At head of title: Smithsonian Institution. Bureau of American Ethnology.

Contents: v.1, The marginal tribes; v.2, The Andean civilizations; v.3, The tropical forest tribes; v.4, The circum-Caribbean tribes; v.5, The comparative ethnology of South American Indians; v.6, Physical anthropology, linguistics, and cultural geography of South American Indians; v.7, Index.

Anthropological descriptions by American specialists of all phases of the life of the tribes considered, with especial attention to the time of a tribe's first contact with Europeans. Well illustrated; good ethnographical maps. Extensive bibliographies.   F2229.S75

❖For the *Handbook of North American Indians see* CC470.

Directories

Friedemann, Nina S. de and **Arocha, Jaime.** Bibliografía anotada y directorio de antropólogos colombianos. [Bogotá], Sociedad Anthropológica de Colombia, [1979]. 441p. il.   **CE77**

The directory section identifies educational background, affiliation, and address for 277 Colombian anthropologists, and codifies each of their works listed in the bibliography by subdiscipline, subject, indigenous group, chronological period, and geographic area. The annotated bibliographical entries are arranged by author and indexed by the codified categories noted. GN25.X1F75

AFRICA

Bibliography

See also DD91.

Amedekey, E. Y. The culture of Ghana; a bibliography. Accra, publ. for the Univ. of Ghana by Ghana Universities Pr., 1970. 215p. **CE78**

An annotated, classified bibliography of more than 1,600 items. Z3785.A7

Anafalu, Joseph C. The Ibo-speaking peoples of southern Nigeria: a selected annotated list of writings, 1627–1970. Munich, Kraus Internat. Pubns., [1981]. 321p. map. **CE79**

A subject arrangement of more than 3,000 entries for books, pamphlets, periodical articles, conference papers, dissertations, and Nigerian government reports. Some brief descriptive notes. Indexed. Z3597.A73

Anthropology of southern Africa in periodicals to 1950: an analysis and index. Comp. under direction of N. J. van Warmelo. Johannesburg, Witwatersrand Univ. Pr., 1977. 1484p. map. **CE80**

A chronological list of periodical articles, from 1795 to 1950; each entry gives bibliographic citation and list of subjects, tribes and ethnic groups, place-names, and persons covered, with coded notation as to fullness of information. Indexed by linguistic group, place-name, and author; the linguistic group index is further subdivided by subject, tribe and group, and person. "The field covered by indices is the history, anthropology, and linguistics of the Bantu ethnic groups of Southern Africa (South Africa, Botswana, Lesotho, and Swaziland), whilst only bibliographies [Pt.4 of the book] cover the adjacent areas."—*Introd.* Z5113.A56

Armer, Michael. African social psychology: a review and annotated bibliography. N.Y., Africana Publishing Co., [1975]. 321p. (African bibliography ser., 2) **CE81**

863 abstracts are grouped in five broad subject divisions: (1) Attitudes, values, and aspirations [covering such areas as occupation, education, politics, health, the family, religion]; (2) Personality types, traits, and abnormalities; (3) Personality development, change, and adjustment [acculturation, modernization, etc.]; (4) Psychological structures and processes; (5) Methods, techniques, and bibliographies. Author, country, and cross-classification (i.e., cross reference) indexes. Z7165.A4A75

Baldwin, David E. and **Baldwin, Charlene M.** The Yoruba of Southwestern Nigeria: an indexed bibliography. Boston, G. K. Hall, [1976]. 269p. **CE82**

Lists, alphabetically by author, articles, books, and other publications on Southwestern Nigeria of "geographical, geological, agricultural, zoological, biological, sociological, and anthropological" interest. Literary works by Yoruba authors are also included. Subject index. Z3597.B34

Hambly, Wilfrid Dyson. Source book for African anthropology. Chicago, 1937. 2v. (953p.) il. (Anthropological ser., Field Museum of Natural History, v.26. Publ.394, 396) (Repr.: N.Y., Kraus, 1968) **CE83**

Bibliographies, p.728–866.

—————— —————— Supplement. Bibliography of African anthropology, 1937–1949. Chicago, Natural History Museum, 1952. p.161–292. (*In* Fieldiana: Anthropology, v.37, no.2)

Selective but extensive bibliographies listing both books and periodical articles. DT15.H27

Hertefelt, Marcel d'. African governmental systems in static and changing conditions; a bibliographic contribution to political anthropology. Tervuren, Belg., Musée Royale de l'Afrique Centrale, 1968. 178p. **CE84**

At head of title: Koninklijk Museum voor Midden-Afrika, Tervuren, Belgie.

More than 1,200 items, mainly from the period 1940–66. Arrangement is alphabetical by author, with indexes of peoples and of subjects. Intended for anthropology teachers and students interested in the governmental processes of African peoples. Z5113.H47

Ita, Nduntuei O. Bibliography of Nigeria: a survey of anthropological and linguistic writings from the earliest times to 1966. London, Cass, [1971]. 273p. **CE85**

Lists "publications in archaeology, all branches of anthropology, linguistics and relevant historical and sociological studies and covers the period from the earliest times to 1966. Materials listed include books, pamphlets, government publications and articles in periodicals."—*Pref.* In two parts, the first listing in classed arrangement those works dealing with Nigeria in general; the second is arranged by individual ethnic groups. Author and ethnic indexes. Z3597.I8

Liniger-Goumaz, Max. Pygmées et autres races de petite taille (Boschimans—Hottentots—Negritos, etc.): bibliographie générale. Genève, Les Éditions du Temps, 1968. 335p. **CE86**

Title also in English: Pygmies and other short-sized races (Bushmen—Hottentots—Negritos, etc.).

Nearly 3,300 items. Author listing with subject/geographical index. Z5118.P9L5

Mylius, Norbert. Afrika Bibliographie, 1943–1951. Wien, Verein Freunde der Volkerkunde, 1952. 237p. (Repr.: N.Y., Kraus, 1969) **CE87**

Serves as a supplement to Wieschhoff (CE94). After general sections which list bibliographies and periodicals, the material is arranged by geographical region and subdivided by subject. Periodical articles are not included.

Neser, L. Zulu ethnography: a classified bibliography. [KwaDlangezwa], publ. for the KwaZula Documentation Centre by the Univ. of Zululand, 1976. 92l. (Publications, Univ. of Zululand: Ser.3, Specialized publications, 18) **CE88**

Includes books, articles, chapters in books, theses, dissertations and manuscripts. Author index. Z3608.E85N47

—————— Zulu ethnography: a supplementary bibliography. Kwa-Dlangezwa, Univ. of Zululand, 1980. 71p. (Univ. of Zululand. Pubns.: Ser. B, Research projects, no.6) **CE89**

Cites published and unpublished materials completed or in progress as of the middle of 1980, with additional articles not included in the 1976 volume. Z3608.E85N47

Rita-Ferreira, Antonio. Bibliografia etnológica de Moçambique (das origens a 1954). Lisboa, Junta de Investigações do Ultramar, 1961. 254p. **CE90**

Contains approximately 1,000 entries, mostly in English, with annotations in Portuguese. Includes books and periodical articles, arranged first by region and then by ethnic group. Z3884.E7R5

Salamone, Frank A. and **McCain, James A.** The Hausa people, a bibliography. New Haven, Human Relations Area Files, 1983. 2v. (295l.) (HRAFlex books, MS12-001. Bibliography ser.) **CE91**

A bibliographical essay (p.1–47) points out the major works by subject, followed by a main-entry listing of 1,271 titles. Focus is on English-language works on the Hausa in Nigeria. Z3597.S24

Schapera, Isaac. Select bibliography of South African native life and problems. Comp. for the Inter-University Committee for African Studies. London, Oxford Univ. Pr., 1941. 249p. (Repr.: N.Y., Kraus, 1969) **CE92**

Lists and briefly annotates the more important books, periodical articles and reports published prior to 1939. Arranged in sections: physical anthropology, archaeology, ethnology, modern status and conditions, and linguistics. Author index included.   Z3518.S3

—— —— Supplement. Modern status and conditions. Bibliography, 1939–49, by A. Holden and A. Jacoby. Cape Town, [Univ., School of Librarianship], 1950. 2 pts. in 1v.

—— —— 2d supplement. Modern status and conditions, 1950–58. A select bibliography, by R. Giffen and J. Back. Cape Town, Univ., School of Librarianship, 1958. 2 pts. in 1v.

—— —— [3d supplement] Modern status and conditions, 1958–63. A supplement . . . comp. by Cynthia Solomon. [Cape Town], Univ. of Cape Town, School of Librarianship, 1964. 51p.

—— —— [4th supplement] Modern status and conditions, 1964–80. A supplement . . . comp. by Stephanie Bernice Alman. [Cape Town], Univ. of Cape Town Libraries, 1974. 39p.

Strohmeyer, Eckhard and **Moritz, Walter.** Umfassende Bibliographie der Völker namibiens (Südwestafrikas) und Südwestangolas. Comprehensive bibliography of the peoples of Namibia (South West Africa) and Southwestern Angola. [Starnberg, Max-Planck–Institut zur Erforschung der Lebensbedingungen der Wissenschaftlichtechnischen Welt, 1975]–1982. 2v.   **CE93**

Title and subject headings in German and English.

An international bibliography of about 5,000 citations, arranged by ethnic group, subdivided by topic. Some brief contents notes are included. Author-title index.

Wieschhoff, Heinrich Albert. Anthropological bibliography of Negro Africa. New Haven, Conn., Amer. Oriental Soc., 1948. 461p. (American Oriental ser., v.23)   **CE94**

Arranged by name of tribe and geographical area, in alphabetical order.   Z5113.W5

Zaretsky, Irving I. and **Shambaugh, Cynthia.** Spirit possession and spirit mediumship in Africa and Afro-America: an annotated bibliography. N.Y., Garland 1978. (Garland reference library of social science, v.56)   **CE95**

An earlier edition appeared 1966 as *Bibliography on spirit possession and spirit mediumship.*

An international bibliography of 2,054 titles written between the mid-19th century and 1977. Author arrangement; indexed by 18 separate indexes. Portuguese citations from Brazil are listed separately, as are relevant serial titles.   Z6878.S8Z36

Films

Premier catalogue sélectif international de films ethnographiques sur l'Afrique noire. [Paris], UNESCO, [1967]. 408p.   **CE96**

Lists 467 films, many with detailed descriptive notes and critical appraisals.   GN342.P7

Dictionaries and encyclopedias

Balandier, Georges and **Maquet, Jacques.** Dictionnaire des civilisations africaines. Paris, Hazan, [1968]. 448p. il.   **CE97**

Deals with various aspects of black African culture and civilization. Articles are signed with the initials of contributing scholars but lack bibliographies. An English translation appeared as *Dictionary of black African civilization* (N.Y., L. Amiel, 1974).   DT352.4.B3

ASIA

Bibliography

Bibliography of anthropology of India (including index to current literature). Ed. by N. C. Choudhury; comp. by Shyamal Kumar Ray. Calcutta, Anthropological Survey of India, [1976]– . v.1– . (In progress)   **CE98**

Contents: v.1, 1960–1964.

An international classed bibliography of books and articles, largely in the English language, published during the period indicated. Broad subject arrangement, with items listed alphabetically by author within classes. Four indexes: author, ethnic or population group, geographical or Indian state, and regional (pertaining to more than one state). Further volumes are planned.   Z5119.R39

Calcutta. National Library. Indian anthropology, comp. by J. M. Kanitkar. Ed., rev. and enl. by D. L. Banerjee and A. K. Ohdedar. Calcutta, 1960. 290p. (A bibliography of Indology, v.1)   **CE99**

More than 2,000 books and articles on Indian anthropology and related subjects: sociology, history, geography, etc. Many annotations, some extensive. Arrangement is by geographical region, with a final section on India as a whole. Author and subject indexes.   Z3201.C3

Dessaint, Alain Y. Minorities of Southwest China: an introduction to the Yi (Lolo) and related peoples and an annotated bibliography. New Haven, HRAF Pr., 1980. 373p.   **CE100**

Offers a brief survey (p.1–34) of the linguistics, history, and ethnography of the Yi (Lolo) people, the fourth largest minority in China, and related tribes of Yunnan, Szechwan, Kweichow, and neighboring North Vietnam, Laos, Thailand, Burma, and India. Author listing of more than 1,000 titles in English, French, German, Russian, Spanish, Portuguese, Chinese, Japanese, and Thai. Annotations. Indexed by ethnic group, periodical title, and classed subject categories derived from G. P. Murdock's *Outline of cultural materials* (4th ed. New Haven, 1971).   DS730.D45

Fürer-Haimendorf, Elizabeth von. An anthropological bibliography of South Asia, together with a directory of recent anthropological field work. Paris, Mouton, 1958–70. v.1–3. (École Pratique des Hautes Études. 6e sec. Le monde d'outre-mer passé et présent. 4. sér.: Bibliographies III, IV, VIII)   **CE101**

Includes books, periodical articles, and unpublished dissertations in Western languages, dealing mainly with the cultural and social aspects of anthropology. Other fields are covered less completely. The geographic area comprises India, Pakistan, Nepal, Sikkim, Bhutan, and Ceylon. Arranged by regional sections with subject subdivisions, each including a directory of field research and an author index.

v.1 includes a select list of works published prior to 1940 and works issued 1940–54; v.2 covers 1955–59; v.3, 1960–64.

Continued by: Z5115.F83

Kanitkar, Helen A. An anthropological bibliography of South Asia . . . together with a directory of anthropological field research comp. by Elizabeth von Fürer-Haimendorf. The Hague, Mouton, [1976–]. New ser., v.1– . (In progress?)   **CE102**

Contents: v.1, 1965–1969.

Compiled and edited in the School of Oriental and African Studies, University of London. Arrangement remains the same, but physical anthropology and prehistoric archaeology have been dropped; tribal welfare and problems, urbanization and industrialization, values and attitudes, political sociology and sociolinguistics have been added. Appendixes on social and cultural anthropology of South Asians overseas, and ethnology of India as depicted in literature to 1750 A.D. Author and field research indexes.   Z5115.K35

Kennedy, Raymond. Bibliography of Indonesian peoples and cultures. 2d rev. ed. Rev. and ed. by Thomas W. Maretzki and H. Th. Fischer. New Haven, Conn., Human Relations Area Files, 1962. 207p. maps. **CE103**

For full information see DE219.

Koh, Hesung Chun. Korean family and kinship studies guide (with a section on women). New Haven, Conn., Human Relations Area Files, 1980. 548*l*. **CE104**

Some 840 citations are analyzed and/or indexed according to: historical time period; subject, time, and location; methodology; author and title. Includes a wide variety of materials, primarily written in Korean, Japanese, and English, between 1789 and 1978; annotated. Z7165.K6K63

Sharma, Rajendra Narayan and **Bakshi, Santosh.** Tribes and tribal development: a select bibliography. New Delhi, Uppal, [1984]. 489p. **CE105**

A topically arranged list of 4,431 citations to books and articles. Further subdivided by geographic regions of India, but with no approach by specific tribal group. Author index. Z7165.I6S523

Troisi, J. The Santals: a classified and annotated bibliography. [New Delhi], Manohar, 1976. 234p. **CE106**

Presents annotations for more than 500 books, monographs, articles, and government reports in English, Santali, or Italian on the Santals (the largest homogenous tribe in India, located mainly in Bihar and Bengal). Broad subject arrangement, with author and subject indexes. Z3208.E85T76

AUSTRALIA, NEW ZEALAND, AND OCEANIA

Bibliography

Australian National University, Canberra. Dept. of Anthropology and Sociology. An ethnographic bibliography of New Guinea. Canberra, Australian Nat. Univ. Pr., 1968. 3v. **CE107**

Contents: v.1, Author index; v.2, District index; v.3, Proper names index.

Lists references to books and periodical articles published through 1964. Z5116.A84

Bernice P. Bishop Museum. Library. Dictionary catalog of the library, Bernice P. Bishop Museum, Honolulu, Hawaii. Boston, G. K. Hall, 1964. 9v. **CE108**

Photoreproduction of the author, subject, and title cards from the Library's catalog. The Museum "confines its efforts entirely to study of the peoples and natural areas of the Pacific," and concentration of interest is "in cultural anthropology, archaeology, marine zoology, malacology, entomology, music, further recording of linguistic material, astronomy, bibliography."—Pref. Z881.H785

———— ———— Supplement 1–2. Boston, G. K. Hall, 1967–69. 2v.

Suppl.1 represents holdings added through Aug. 1967. Suppl.2 provides access to the "Fuller Library," a collection of about 2,500 volumes on Pacific history and exploration.

Coppell, William George. World catalogue of theses and dissertations about the Australian Aborigines and Torres Strait Islanders. Sydney, Sydney Univ. Pr., [1977]. 113p. **CE109**

A provisional edition appeared in the Australian Institute of Aboriginal Studies Newsletter, n.s., no.2:32–52 (1974).

"The catalogue is very largely confined to works presented at universities, except that several diploma theses presented at other tertiary education institutions have been included, where they are of particular interest in the field of Aboriginal studies."—Introd. Author listing with subject index; cutoff date is June 1976. Z5116.C66

Greenway, John. Bibliography of the Australian aborigines and the native peoples of Torres Strait to 1959. [Sydney], Angus & Robertson, [1963]. 420p. **CE110**

An alphabetical listing of 10,283 books and periodical articles, primarily in English but with some titles in other European languages. Indexes by subject and by aboriginal tribe. Z5116.G7

Hays, Terence A. Anthropology in the New Guinea highlands: an annotated bibliography. N.Y., Garland, 1976. 238p. **CE111**

Entries are grouped into broad subject chapters: (1) general, including reference works, surveys, and material by non-anthropologists; (2) social and cultural anthropology; (3) linguistics; (4) prehistory; (5) physical anthropology; (6) physical environment. Includes books, scholarly articles, master's theses, and doctoral dissertations completed through 1974. Author and ethnolinguistic group indexes. Z5116.H38

Marshall, Mac and **Nason, James D.** Micronesia 1944–1974; a bibliography of anthropological and related source materials. New Haven, HRAF Pr., 1975. 337p. **CE112**

An author listing of book and periodical materials, with a "Guide to topics and areas" serving as a topical index. The Gilbert Islands (because British-controlled rather than part of the Trust Territory administered by the United States) are omitted from the compilers' definition of Micronesia. Includes some unpublished papers and doctoral dissertations, but no government documents. Z5116.M37

Potter, Michelle. Traditional law in Papua New Guinea: an annotated and selected bibliography. Canberra, Australian Nat. Univ., Dept. of Law, Research School of Social Sciences, 1973. 132p. maps. **CE113**

An author arrangement of 283 periodical articles. Each entry contains a brief summary and shows which groups and subjects are discussed. Indexed by group, alphabetic subject, and systematic subject. All indexes are divided into "Index A," dealing with traditional law in general, and "Index B," dealing with changes in the traditional law as a result of outside influences. Cutoff date is 1970. KTA.P687

Saito, Shiro. Philippine ethnography; a critically annotated and selected bibliography. Honolulu, Univ. Pr. of Hawaii, [1972]. 512p. (East-West bibliographic series, 2) **CE114**

A classed bibliography of about 4,300 items. Concerned with cultural anthropology as distinct from physical anthropology, but includes items which deal with a specific cultural language group. Indexed. Z3296.S23

Taylor, Clyde Romer Hughes. A bibliography of publications on the New Zealand Maori and the Moriori of the Chatham Islands. Oxford, Clarendon Pr., 1972. 161p. **CE115**

A revision and updating of the New Zealand and Maori section of the compiler's Pacific bibliography (2d ed. 1965; DG9). Z4127.E85T38

Films

International Committee on Ethnographical and Sociological Films. Premier catalogue sélectif international de films ethnographiques sur la région du Pacifique. Paris, Unesco, 1970. 342p. **CE116**

Lists 341 films, arranged by country or area; approximately one-half receive detailed critical analysis. Indexed by film title, subject, personal and corporate names. GN342.I5

Handbooks

Tindale, Norman Barnett. Aboriginal tribes of Australia: their terrain, environmental controls, distribution, limits, and proper names. Berkeley, Univ. of California Pr., 1974. 404p. il., maps. **CE117**

"The principal theme of this book . . ., after first giving an outline picture of these people and their ways of life, is focused on telling as much as has been learned of the distribution, size, composition, and dynamics of the Australian tribes and the history of the aborigines. . . ."—*Introd.* Includes a lengthy bibliography. Appendix on Tasmanian tribes by Rhys Jones.   GN665.T56

EUROPE

Bibliography

Bunakova, O. V. and **Kamenetskaia, R. V.** Bibliografiia trudov Instituta etnografii im. N. N. Miklukho-Maklaia, 1900–1962. Leningrad, Nauka, 1967. 281p. **CE118**

Added t.p.: *Bibliographie des travaux de l'Institut d'ethnographie Mikloukho-Maclay.*
Table of contents in Russian and French.
A classed bibliography of 5,195 items; reviews are noted. Author and subject indexes.   Z511.B8

Niewiadomska, Maria. Bibliografia etnografii polskiej za lata 1961–1969. Wrocław, Zakł. Narodowy imienia Ossolińskich Wydawnictwo Polskiej Akademii Nauk, 1982–83. 2v. (Prace Komitetu Nauk Etnologicznych PAN, 3–4) **CE119**

Introduction in Polish and English.
Earlier periods were covered by Halina Bittner-Szewczykowa's "Materialy do bibliografii etnografii polskiej za lata 1945–54" which appeared as a supplement to *Lud,* v.43 (1958), and by Bolesław Gawin's "Bibliografia etnografii polskiej 1955–60" in *Lud,* v.44 (1960), v.46 (1962) and v.51 (1967).
Covers general works (bibliographies, reference works, periodicals, etc.), works on methodology and the theory of culture, the history and organization of ethnography, museum management and exhibitions relating to ethnography, works on the ethnography of Poland, and works on ethnography in other countries. Indexed.
Continued chronologically by: Z2528.E85N53

Karpińska, Grażyna Ewa. Bibliografia etnografii polskiej za lata 1970–1975. Wrocław, Zakł. Narodowy im. Ossolińskich, 1980. 430p. (Prace Komitetu Nauk Etnologicznych PAN, 2) **CE120**

Introduction in Polish and English.
Organized in the same manner as the preceding item. Author and geographical indexes.   Z5111.K36

O'Leary, Timothy J. and **Steffens, Joan.** Lapps ethnographic bibliography. New Haven, Human Relations Area Files, 1975. 2v. **CE121**

A computer-produced list of more than 1,421 books, periodical articles, and chapters from collected works. Each entry is composed of three parts: (1) the standard bibliographic citation; (2) coded descriptive notes on bibliography, cataloging source, format, language; (3) content analysis relative to dates covered, Lapps regional and cultural types discussed, geographic area and site, date of fieldwork, social unit involved, primary or secondary nature of data, author's background, and language used. Indexed by *Outline of cultural materials* (OCM); by author, sub-group, geographic location; by field date and bibliography date.   Z2617.E85O43

Pereira, Benjamim Enes. Bibliografia analítica de etnografia portuguesa. Lisboa, 1965. 670p. **CE122**

At head of title: Instituto de Alta Cultura. Centro de Estudos de Etnologia Peninsular.

An annotated bibliography of book and periodical materials. 3,834 items in subject arrangement with author index.   Z2737.E7P46

Ripley, William Zebina. Selected bibliography of the anthropology and ethnology of Europe. Boston, Pub. Lib., 1899. 160p. **CE123**

Also published as a supplement to the author's *Races of Europe* (N.Y., Appleton, 1899).
Contains nearly 2,000 entries, arranged by author, including books and serial publications. Subject index with references to main entries.   Z5117.R59

Sanders, Irwin Taylor, Whitaker, Roger and **Bisselle, Walter C.** East European peasantries: social relations; an annotated bibliography of periodical articles. Boston, G. K. Hall, [1976–81]. [v.1]–2. (In progress) **CE124**

Each volume represents citations to more than 800 periodical articles added to the Collection on East European Peasantries in the Mugar Memorial Library, Boston University, since 1972. Country arrangement (Albania is not included); no index.   Z7165.E82S26

Sweet, Louise Elizabeth and **O'Leary, Timothy J.** Circum-Mediterranean peasantry; introductory bibliographies. New Haven, Human Relations Area Files, 1969. 106p. **CE125**

Originally published in five issues of *Behavior science notes,* 1967–68.
Arrangement is by country, and includes North African and Middle Eastern countries as well as European areas. Lacks an index.   Z7165.M38S8

Theodoratus, Robert J. Europe: a selected ethnographic bibliography. New Haven, Conn., Human Relations Area Files, 1969. 544p. **CE126**

Listing is by ethnic groups. Includes all of Europe except "the Caucasus Mountain region and the Finno-Ugric and Turkish peoples of the eastern and northeastern regions of the European part of the Soviet Union."—*Pref.* Lacks an index.   Z5117.T5

Titova, Zoia Dmitrievna. Etnografiia; bibliografiia russkikh bibliografii po etnografii narodov SSSR (1851–1969). Moskva, "Kniga," 1970. 142p. **CE127**

An annotated listing of 734 items arranged by geographical area. Author and subject indexes.   Z5117.T53

C F

Mythology, Folklore, and Popular Culture

MYTHOLOGY

❖Such standard works as Gayley's *Classic myths* (CF25) and the *Mythology of all races* (CF14) have been joined more recently by the *New Larousse encyclopedia of mythology* (CF15) and *Crowell's Handbook of classical mythology* (CF35). More extensive listings than are provided here may be found in Diehl's *Religions, mythologies, folklores* (CF1) and Smith's *Mythologies of the world* (CF2).

International

Bibliography

See also BD244, BD246.

Diehl, Katharine Smith. Religions, mythologies, folklores: an annotated bibliography. 2d ed. N.Y., Scarecrow Pr., 1962. 573p. **CF1**

An extensive bibliography of materials on mythology and folklore is a feature of the work; for full information *see* BB10.

Z7751.D54

Smith, Ron. Mythologies of the world: a guide to sources. Urbana, Ill., Nat. Council of Teachers of English, [1981]. 346p. **CF2**

Comprises about 30 bibliographical essays on the mythologies of specific geographical areas, e.g., Mesopotamian, Biblical, Islamic, Celtic, Arthurian, Oceanic; comments on works such as collections of myths, analyses, works on religion, cultural history, relevant archaeology, art and architecture, language and its translation. No index. Z7836.S63

Dictionaries and encyclopedias

Campbell, Joseph. Historical atlas of world mythology. San Francisco, Harper & Row, [1983]– . v.1– . il., maps. (In progress) **CF3**

Contents: v.1, The way of the animal powers (301p.).
"The folkways and mythologies to be explored in the first two volumes of the present work are of two orders: (1) of hunting and gathering tribes, and (2) of the earliest planting cultures."—*p.49. The way of the animal powers* discusses the folklife and mythologies of the plains areas of Europe and Africa, the equatorial forest, and the hunting cultures of Asia, Australia, and North America; it is indexed by subject, place, and myth motif.

v.3, *The way of the celestial lights,* will trace the sky mythologies of the great ancient cities, and v.4, *The way of man,* will follow the transformation of mythological structures in the post-Renaissance world.

A lengthy review of v.1 (and interview with the author) in the *New York times* (Dec. 18, 1983, sect.VII, p.3), while pointing out that the work is neither an atlas nor an easily accessible reference source, describes it as "the most sumptuous and ambitious of all dictionaries and encyclopedias of mythology." BL311.C16

Carlyon, Richard. A guide to the gods. N.Y., Morrow, 1982. 401p. **CF4**

Provides brief descriptions of about 1,000 gods, goddesses, and divine figures. Geographical arrangement by continent, then by region or group; within each section, deities are described alphabetically. Includes some lesser-known pantheons (e.g., Slavonic, Haitian, Gnostic). Indexed. BL473.C37

Cotterell, Arthur. A dictionary of world mythology. N.Y., Putnam's [1980]. 256p. il. **CF5**

Arrangement is according to "the seven great traditions of world mythology: namely, West Asia, South and Central Asia, East Asia, Europe, America, Africa, and Oceania."—*Introd.* For each geographic area there is a brief introductory essay giving background information; this is followed by a dictionary arrangement of entries for the principal deities and mythological figures of the area. Select bibliography; index. BL303.C66

Dictionnaire des mythologies et des religions des sociétés traditionnelles et du monde antique. Sous la direction de Yves Bonnefoy. [Paris], Flammarion, [1981]. 2v. il. **CF6**

Offers signed articles on mythologies and religions of primitive peoples, terms, symbols, rituals, concepts, etc. Index of subjects, names of deities, etc. BL311.D5

Gottschalk, Herbert. Lexikon der Mythologie der europäischen Völker: Götter, Mysterien, Kulte und Symbole, Heroen und Sagengestalten der Mythen; 368 vritgenössische Bilder aus Mythen und Sagen. Berlin, Safari-Verlag, [1973]. 488p. il. (*His* Bebildertes Lexikon der Mythologie [Bd.1]) **CF7**

Essays on the mythologies are followed by dictionary entries for mythologies of the Greeks, Romans, Celts, Germans, Balts, Slavs, Hungarians, Finns, and Siberian peoples. Indexed. BL303.G65

Hamilton, Edith. Mythology. Boston, Little, 1942. 497p. il. **CF8**

Includes both classic and Norse myths with comparisons of the original and the later versions. Family charts, p.457–73.

BL310.H3

Haussig, Hans Wilhelm. Wörterbuch der Mythologie. Stuttgart, Ernst Klett, [1961–82]. Lfg.1–8. il. (In progress) **CF9**

Contents: Abt. 1, Die alten Kulturvölker: Teil 1, Götter und Mythen im Vorderen Orient (comprises Lfg.1–4); Teil 2, Das Alte Europa (Lfg.5–10); Teil 3, Die Iranischen Völker (Lfg. 11–12, 17); Teil 5, Götter und Mythen des indischen Subkontinents (Lfg. 8, 13–16, 18).

A work treating the mythologies of the world. Arranged by geographical area; each section is written by a specialist and includes a dictionary of names, terms, etc., pertinent to the mythology of the region. Further volumes are announced to cover East Asia and early America. BL383.W63

Hendricks, Rhoda A. Mythologies of the world: a concise encyclopedia. Max S. Shapiro, exec. ed. Garden City, N.Y., Doubleday, 1979. 216p. il. **CF10**

A dictionary arrangement of brief entries for deities, place names, terms, texts, etc., from mythologies throughout the world. Pronunciation is indicated. BL303.H45

Jobes, Gertrude and **Jobes, James.** Outer space: myths, name meanings, calendars from the emergence of history to the present day. N.Y., Scarecrow Pr., 1964. 479p. **CF11**

Discusses origins of astrological and astronomical myths and facts. Chapters on the moon, sun, zodiac, numerical symbolism, celestial phenomena, constellations, stars, and Chinese celestial beliefs. Bibliography; index. BL438.J6

Monaghan, Patricia. The book of goddesses and heroines. N.Y., Dutton, 1981. 318p. **CF12**

A glossary of approximately 1,000 goddesses and heroines, with brief factual descriptions and some legends included. A listing of the figures by geographic location precedes the text; bibliography.

BL473.5.M66

Mythology: an illustrated encyclopedia. Ed. by Richard Cavendish. N.Y., Rizzoli, [1980]. 303p. il. **CF13**

Essentially a series of essays by contributing scholars on the mythology of an individual country, area, or religious or ethnic group. Essays are grouped geographically within sections for Asia, the Middle East, the West, Africa, the Americas, the Pacific. Brief glossary; select bibliography; index. BL311.M95

Mythology of all races. Louis Herbert Gray, ed., v.1, 3, 6, 9–12; John Arnott Macculloch and G. F. Moore, eds., v.2, 4–5, 7–8, 13. Boston, Archaeological Inst. of America, Marshall Jones Co., 1916–32. 13v. il. **CF14**

Contents: v.1, Greek and Roman, by W. S. Fox; v.2, Eddic, by J. A. Macculloch; v.3, Celtic, by J. A. Macculloch; Slavic, by Jan Máchal; v.4, Finno-Ugric, Siberian, by Uno Holmberg; v.5, Semitic, by S. H. Langdon; v.6, Indian, by A. B. Keith; Iranian, by A. J. Carnoy; v.7, Armenian, by M. H. Ananikian; African, by Alice Werner; v.8, Chinese, by J. C. Ferguson; Japanese, by Masaharu Anesaki; v.9, Oceanic, by R. B. Dixon; v.10, North American, by H. B. Alexander; v.11, Latin-American, by H. B. Alexander; v.12, Egyptian, by W. Max Müller; Indo-Chinese, by J. G. Scott; v.13, Index.

An important set which contains valuable reference material in

both text and illustrations. The general index makes it the most useful single reference work in the field available in English.
BL25.M8

Myths. [By] Alexander Eliot, with contributions by Mircea Eliade [and] Joseph Campbell. N.Y., McGraw-Hill, [1976]. 320p. il., maps. **CF14a**

Brief accounts of myths are organized by theme (e.g., creation, cosmogeny, heroes, animals, quests, love, death). Heavily illustrated. Maps showing cultural areas and peoples are keyed to illustrations and myths appearing in the text. Bibliography; index.
BL315.M95

New Larousse encyclopedia of mythology. With an introd. by Robert Graves. [Tr. by Richard Aldington and Delano Ames, and rev. by a panel of editorial advisers from the Larousse mythologie générale, ed. by Felix Guirand. New ed. N.Y.], Putnam, [1969]. 500p. il. **CF15**

First published in France in 1935; first English edition, 1959. Presents articles on the mythologies of various countries and civilizations from prehistory to present times. Not an encyclopedia in the usual sense of the term, as the material is presented in essay form with no easy approach to specific points. Includes various aspects of folklore, legend, and religious customs.
BL311.N43

Sykes, Egerton. Everyman's dictionary of nonclassical mythology. [4th ed., rev.] London, Dent; N.Y., Dutton, [1968]. 282p. **CF16**

1st ed. 1952.
Several thousand personal and place-names, epithets, concepts, etc., are treated briefly but pointedly. Cross references are indicated, and there is a selective bibliography, arranged by geographical area.
BL303.S9

Walker, Barbara G. The woman's encyclopedia of myths and secrets. San Francisco, Harper & Row, [1983]. 1124p. il. **CF17**

A dictionary arrangement of 1,350 entries, ranging in length from 25 words to several pages. Bibliographic notes for each entry refer to citations in the bibliography, p.1105–18. Textual cross references and marginalia notes, but no index.
BL458.W34

Chinese

Werner, Edward Theodore Chalmers. Dictionary of Chinese mythology. Shanghai, Kelly, 1932. 627p. (Repr.: Dover, N.H., Longwood, 1976) **CF18**

"This dictionary has been written with the object of furnishing, in a compact form, information concerning the entities, animate and inanimate, constituting the Chinese supernal and infernal hierarchies."—*Pref.*
BL1801.W35

Egyptian

Bonnet, Hans. Reallexikon der ägyptischen Religionsgeschichte. 2., unveränderte Aufl. Berlin, W. de Gruyter, 1971. 883p. il. **CF19**

1st ed. 1952.
An encyclopedic dictionary, giving definitions and descriptions of persons, cults, concepts, etc., in Egyptian religious history and mythology. Bibliographical references are to available rather than to original sources.

Lurker, Manfred. The gods and symbols of ancient Egypt; an illustrated dictionary with 114 illustrations. [London], Thames & Hudson (distr. by Norton), [1980]. 142p. il., map. **CF20**

Translation of *Götter und Symbole der Alten Ägypter* (Bern, Scherz, 1974); English-language ed. rev. and enl. by Peter A. Clayton.

About 300 entries, with photographs and line drawings. Chronological table; select bibliography; index to illustrations.
BL2428.L8713

Mercatante, Anthony S. Who's who in Egyptian mythology. N.Y., C. N. Potter; distr. by Crown, [1978]. 231p. il. **CF21**

Primarily a dictionary of ancient Egyptian deities, but including entries for related signs, symbols, terms, etc. Annotated bibliography, p.219–31.
BL2428.M47

Greek and Roman

Bibliography

Peradotto, John Joseph. Classical mythology; an annotated bibliographical survey. Urbana, Ill., Amer. Philological Assoc., 1973. 76p. **CF22**

A "bibliographical survey, which is offered as a set of possible tools—for whatever kind of mythology course (even at the graduate level)."—*Introd.* Presented as a series of brief, evaluative essays on selected works covering various aspects of the study of mythology. Works are rated according to a code indicating suitability for college-level courses.

Dictionaries and encyclopedias

Bell, Robert E. Dictionary of classical mythology: symbols, attributes & associations. Santa Barbara, ABC-Clio, [1982]. 390p. il. **CF23**

Offers a topical approach to classical mythology: i.e., arrangement is according to about a thousand topical subjects under which are listed the mythological characters associated with each term, and for each of which is given a brief summary of the myth or reason why the particular attribute or symbol is associated therewith. Citations to sources in the *Loeb classical library* are often given. A "Guide to persona" enables the user to locate all topical entries associated with a given character.
BL715.B44

Boswell, Fred and **Boswell, Jeanetta.** What men or gods are these? A genealogical approach to classical mythology. Metuchen, N.J., Scarecrow Pr., 1980. 315p. **CF24**

Presents genealogical charts showing the family relationships of the gods and goddesses of classical mythology, with notes to the charts summarizing the stories and information about each character. "In addition to the family charts, there are four major lists of heroes who participated in (1) the voyage of the *Argo,* (2) the Calydonian Boar Hunt, (3) the Wars against Thebes, and (4) the Trojan War."—*Pref.* Index of names appearing on the genealogical charts, and a "subject index" which lists the gods according to their function or topical association; the latter index includes both Greek and Roman names, but no cross references are provided in the index to the charts. A brief bibliography provides "ample bibliographical material to engage the undergraduate student for some time."
BL782.B6

Gayley, Charles Mills. Classic myths in English literature and in art, based originally on Bulfinch's Age of fable (1855), accompanied by an interpretative and illustrative commentary. ... New ed. rev. and enl. Boston, Ginn, [1939]. 597p. il. **CF25**

A standard text frequently reprinted, treating the classical myths particularly in their relationship to English poetry and to art, with brief chapters on Norse and German mythology. Includes an extensive commentary and detailed indexes.
BL721.G3

Grant, Michael and **Hazel, John.** Gods and mortals in classical mythology. Springfield, Mass., G. & C. Merriam, [1973]. 447p. il. **CF26**

A dictionary of names in classical mythology. Attempts "to identify and describe the principal and best known and most influential incidents built into each mythological narrative over the ancient centuries" (*Introd.*), noting alternate and contradictory forms in many instances. BL715.G67

Grimal, Pierre. Dictionnaire de la mythologie grecque et romaine. 4ᵉ éd. rev. Paris, Presses Universitaires de France, 1969. 578p. il. **CF27**

1st ed. 1951.

A dictionary of the most generally known myths and legends, with bibliographical references and genealogical tables. An index of mythological, historical, and geographical proper names and another of legendary themes. An English translation is to be published 1985. BL715.G7

Harnsberger, Caroline Thomas. Gods and heroes: a quick guide to the occupations, associations and experiences of the Greek and Roman gods and heroes. Troy, N.Y., Whitston, 1977. 396p. **CF28**

The main body of the work is arranged alphabetically by terms denoting occupations, characteristics, attributes, etc., with the names of gods and goddesses associated with the term listed thereunder, together with a brief explanation of the association. An index of the names of the deities and heroes refers to the term associated with each. BL715.H29

Hunger, Herbert. Lexikon der griechischen und römischen Mythologie, mit Hinweisen auf das Fortwirken antiker Stoffe und Motive in der bildenden Kunst, Literatur und Musik des Abendlandes bis zur Gegenwart. 7., unveränderte. Aufl. Wien, Hollinek, [1975]. 464p. il. **CF29**

1st ed. 1953.

A concise dictionary of Greek and Roman mythology arranged alphabetically, with bibliographical references to the themes in art, literature, and music. BL303.H8

Kravitz, David. Who's who in Greek and Roman mythology. N.Y., C. N. Potter; distr. by Crown, [1976]. 246p. il. **CF30**

Published 1975 by New English Library, London, under title: *The dictionary of Greek & Roman mythology.*

A dictionary of very brief definitions of characters, places, themes, etc., associated with Greek and Roman mythology. Emphasizes the family relationships of its subjects, sometimes providing tables of "lovers" and "children of the union." For major deities, includes epithets, iconography, associations, festivals, and places of worship. BL715.K7

Lexicon iconographicum mythologiae classicae (LIMC). [Redaction, Hans Christoph Ackermann, Jean-Robert Gisler] Zurich, Artemis, [1981–84]. v.1–2. il. (In progress) **CF31**

Contents: v.1–2, A–Athena.

A scholarly encyclopedia on the iconography of Greek, Etruscan, and Roman mythology from the post-Mycenaean period to the beginning of the early Christian era; includes divinities and heroes of neighboring cultures. Each volume consists of two parts: texts and corresponding plates. Articles are in German, English, French, or Italian, and include introduction, bibliography, catalog of iconographical types and appearances, and iconographical commentary. To be in 7v. N7760.L49

Mayerson, Philip. Classical mythology in literature, art, and music. Waltham, Mass., Xerox College Pub., [1971]. 509p. il. **CF32**

Myths and legends are briefly recounted and explained, with references made to important variations in the stories as drawn from major classical sources. The summaries are followed by illustrations from the later literature (mainly English) and the arts. As aids to pronunciation, accents and long vowels are marked in the index. NX650.M9M38

Room, Adrian. Room's Classical dictionary: the origins of the names of characters in classical mythology. London, Routledge & Kegan Paul, [1983]. 343p. il. **CF33**

Emphasis is on the meaning of the names, but the story or identity

of each mythological figure is briefly told. Numerous appendixes; brief bibliography. BL727.R58

Roscher, Wilhelm Heinrich. Ausführliches Lexikon der griechischen und römischen Mythologie. Leipzig, Teubner, 1884–1937. 6v. and 4 suppl. il. (Repr.: Hildesheim, Olms, 1965. 7v. in 10) **CF34**

Contents: v.1–6, A–Z und Nachträge; Supplements: [1] Bruchmann, K. F. H. Epitheta deorum quae apud poetas graecos leguntur. 1893; [2] Carter, I. B. Epitheta deorum quae apud poetas latinos leguntur. 1902; [3] Berger, H. Mythische Kosmographie der Griechen. 1904. 2v.; [4] Gruppe, O. Geschichte der klassischen Mythologie und Religionsgeschichte. 1921.

Scholarly, signed articles with bibliographies and good illustrations. The most complete work of its kind; valuable for large reference or university libraries. BL715.R79

Tripp, Edward. Crowell's Handbook of classical mythology. [N.Y.], Crowell, [1970]. 631p. **CF35**

Primarily a retelling of the classical myths with their variant forms. The alphabetical arrangement (with entries for mythological characters, place names, and some related terms) makes for more convenient reference use than does Gayley's *Classic myths* (CF25). Each story is generally told in full only once, under the name of one of its principal characters; sources are indicated. Treats both Greek and Roman mythology, the former predominating. Numerous cross references; guide to pronunciation. BL303.T75

Oceanic

Poignant, Rosyln. Oceanic mythology; the myths of Polynesia, Micronesia, Melanesia, Australia. London, Hamlyn, [1967]. 141p. il. **CF36**

Notes on the background and development of the mythology of each area are followed by a brief recounting of various myths of the region. Indexed; many good illustrations. BL2600.P6

Teutonic

Guerber, Hélène Adeline. Myths of northern lands, narrated with special reference to literature and art. N.Y., Amer. Book Co., 1895. 319p. il. (Repr.: Detroit, Singing Tree Pr., 1970) **CF37**

A useful collection of the Norse myths written in a popular style. Includes numerous poetical quotations with index to same, in addition to glossary and index to names, places, keywords, etc.
BL860.G8

FOLKLORE AND POPULAR CULTURE

❖Libraries of all sizes will need some works on folklore. *Funk and Wagnalls standard dictionary of folklore, mythology and legend* (CF55) is a good, comprehensive encyclopedia for quick reference. Frazer's *Golden bough* (CF62), a great mine of information, is also available in a one-volume abridgment, *The new Golden bough* (CF64).

The *Internationale volkskundliche Bibliographie* (*International folklore bibliography;* CF49) presents a current record of folklore studies of many countries and of all periods, while Inge's *Handbook of American popular culture* (CF90) offers a wealth of background and bibliographical information on many aspects of what has come to be known as "popular culture."

General Works

Guides

Brunvand, Jan Harold. Folklore; a study and research guide. N.Y., St. Martin's Pr., [1976]. 144p.   **CF38**

Intended as a guide "for the beginner, chiefly the college undergraduate."—*Introd.* In three main sections: (1) The subject in context; (2) Reference guide; (3) The research paper. The "Reference guide" is a bibliographic essay on the tools for folklore research. Glossary; index.   Z5981.B78

Thompson, Stith. The folktale. N.Y., Dryden Pr., 1946. 510p.   **CF39**

Designed as a guide to the kinds of folktales and to methods of studying them. Extensive bibliographies and many bibliographical notes.   GR74.T47

Thematic indexes

Aarne, Antti Amatus. The types of the folktale; a classification and bibliography . . . tr. and enl. by Stith Thompson. 2d rev. ed. Helsinki, Suomalainen Tiedeakatemia, 1961. 588p. (FF communications, no.184)   **CF40**

Original title: *Verzeichnis der Märchentypen* (Helsinki, 1910; FF communications, no.3).   Z5983.F17A27

Baughman, Ernest Warren. Type and motif-index of the folktales of England and North America. The Hague, Mouton, 1966. 607p. (Indiana Univ. Folklore ser., 20)   **CF41**

Revision and expansion of a 1953 doctoral dissertation. Employs the motif number system used in the Stith Thompson *Motif-index* (CF42), and the alphabetical index for that work also serves for locating motif numbers in the present listing.   GR67.B3

Thompson, Stith. Motif-index of folk-literature; a classification of narrative elements in folktales, ballads, myths, fables, mediaeval romances, exempla, fabliaux, jest-books and local legends. Rev. and enl. ed. Bloomington, Indiana Univ. Pr., 1955–58. 6v.   **CF42**

1st ed. 1932–36.

A decimal classification scheme devised to index the motifs found in traditional narrative literature: the folktale, myth, ballad, fable, medieval romance, etc. References are usually furnished to one or more works where material about a motif may be found, but the work is planned primarily as an index and is only incidentally a bibliography. v.6 is a detailed alphabetical index of motifs.   GR67.T52

Bibliography

Abstracts of folklore studies. v.1–13, Jan. 1963–Wint. 1975. Austin, Tex., Amer. Folklore Soc., 1963–75. 13v.   **CF43**

Place of publication varies.

Listing is by periodical in which the article abstracted appears. Annual subject index. A supplement to v.6 (Winter 1968) is devoted to "Data on journals abstracted" and gives subscription information on some 150 journals devoted to folklore or which carry occasional articles on the subject.   GR1.A52

Cleveland. Public Library. John G. White Dept. Catalog of folklore, folklife, and folk songs. 2d ed. Boston, G. K. Hall, 1978. 3v.   **CF44**

1st ed. 1964 had title: *Catalog of folklore and folk songs.*

This edition revised, enlarged, and updated to include all materials added since 1965. Some 36,000 volumes are now covered; many new subject headings have been added.   Z5985.C5

De Caro, F. A. Women and folklore: a bibliographic survey. Westport, Conn., Greenwood Pr., [1983]. 170p.   **CF45**

In two parts: (1) "Essay guide," which discusses works listed in the

bibliography, divided by types of materials and topical areas; (2) bibliography of 1,664 citations to English-language publications. Subject index.   Z5983.W65D4

Hague. Koninklijke Bibliotheek. Catalogus van folklore in de Koninklijke Bibliotheek. Den Haag, Drukkerij "Humanitas," 1919–22. 3v. in 2.   **CF46**

Contents: 1. deel, Europa; 2. deel, Buiten Europa. Supplement. Registers.

A very rich collection for all countries.   Z5985.H27

Taylor, Archer. A bibliography of riddles. Helsinki, Suomalainen Tiedeakatemia, 1939. 173p. (FF communications, no.126)   **CF47**

A guide to the literature of the European traditional riddle. Topical arrangement, with author index.

Current

Folklore Fellows. FF communications. no.1– . Helsinki, Suomalaisen Tiedeakatemian Kustantama, 1911– . no.1– .   **CF48**

An important series of monographs for the whole field of folklore. Includes studies on classification of folktales and bibliographies of specific folk literatures.   GR1.F55

Internationale volkskundliche Bibliographie. International folklore bibliography. Bibliographie internationale des arts et traditions populaires. Ouvrage publié par la Commission Internationale des Arts et Traditions Populaires sous les auspices du Conseil International de la Philosophie et des Sciences Humaines et avec le concours de l'UNESCO. 1939/1941– . Bâle, Impr. G. Krebs; Bonn, Rudolf Habelt, 1949– . Biennial (1979/80 publ. 1985).   **CF49**

Frequency varies.

Title in German, English, and French; order on title page varies. Language of subtitle varies. Publisher varies.

Supersedes *Volkskundliche Bibliographie* (1917–37/38, publ. 1919–57 in 14v.).

Contents: 1939–1941 (publ. 1949); 1942–1947 (publ. 1950); 1948–1949 (publ. 1954); 1950–1951 (publ. 1955); 1952–1954 (publ. 1959); biennial thereafter.

An extensive bibliography covering folklore of all countries and of all periods. Classed arrangement with author index.   Z5982.I523

Simmons, Merle Edwin. Folklore bibliography. 1973– . Philadelphia, Inst. for the Study of Human Issues, 1975– . Annual.   **CF50**

Published for the Folklore Institute at Indiana University.

Continues the bibliographies covering 1937–72 published annually in the *Southern folklore quarterly.*

A bibliography of books and articles on folklore published in or relating to the folklore of the United States, Canada, Latin America, Spain, Portugal, and other Spanish or Portuguese-speaking regions of the world.   Z5981.S532

❖Other current bibliographies which include listings of folklore studies are: *Handbook of Latin American studies* (DB241); *MLA international bibliography* (BD22); and "Articles on American literature appearing in current periodicals" in quarterly issues of *American literature.*

Dissertations

Dundes, Alan. Folklore theses and dissertations in the United States. Austin, Tex., publ. for the Amer. Folklore Soc. by the Univ. of Texas Pr., [1976]. 610p. (Pubn. of the Amer. Folklore Soc., bibliographical and special ser., 27)   **CF51**

A chronological listing of doctoral dissertations and master's theses from 1860 through 1968. Indexed by author, subject, and institution. Z5981.D85

Dictionaries and encyclopedias

Briggs, Katharine Mary. Encyclopedia of fairies, hobgoblins, brownies, bogies, and other supernatural creatures. N.Y., Pantheon Books, [1976]. 481p. il. **CF52**

First published under title: *A dictionary of fairies.*

For the most part, treats fairies of the British Isles, with mention of foreign fairies "for comparison or elucidation."—*Pref.* Numerous cross references. Bibliography; index of types and motifs to the folktales recounted in the text. GR549.B74

Dictionnaire des symboles: mythes, rêves, coutumes, gestes, formes, figures, couleurs, nombres. Sous la direction de Jean Chevalier. Éd. rev. et augm. [Paris], Robert Laffont, [1982]. 842p. il. **CF53**

About 1,200 entries (most of them signed with the initials of the contributor) with explanation of the symbolism of the term, its mythological, legendary, or religious background, etc. Bibliographies are not included in the articles, but abbreviated references are made to the general bibliography at the end of the volume. GR931.D52

Enzyklopädie des Märchens: Handwörterbuch zur historischen und vergleichenden Erzählforschung. Berlin, W. de Gruyter, 1975–84. Bd.1–4. (In progress) **CF54**

Kurt Ranke, ed.

Contents: Bd.1–4, Aarne—Förster.

To be in 12v., each volume consisting of five *Lieferungen.* Includes material on methodology, types and motifs, figures, regional studies, biographies, seminal works, etc. Lengthy, signed articles with extensive bibliographies. GR72.E58

Funk and Wagnalls standard dictionary of folklore, mythology and legend. Maria Leach, ed. Jerome Fried, assoc. ed. N.Y., Funk & Wagnalls, [1973]. 1236p. **CF55**

This is a reissue in 1v., with minor corrections, of the 2v. edition published 1949–50. A "Key to countries, regions, cultures, culture areas, peoples, tribes, and ethnic groups" (p.1197–1236) has been added.

A comprehensive encyclopedia and dictionary dealing with the gods, heroes, tales, motifs, customs, beliefs, songs, dances, games, proverbs, etc., of the cultures of the world, including "survey articles" with bibliographies on regions and on special subjects (ballad, dance, fairy tale, national mythologies, etc.), written and signed by specialists.

The ALA Subscription Books Committee's review of the 1v. edition concludes that the work "remains a standard reference tool for all kinds of libraries. However, since the text of the 1972 edition is basically unchanged and the newly added key is not really an adequate index, this edition is desirable only if the original edition needs replacement or one simply prefers a single-volume edition."
—*The booklist* 70:253, Nov.1, 1973. GR35.F82

Jobes, Gertrude. Dictionary of mythology, folklore and symbols. N.Y., Scarecrow Pr., 1962. 3v. **CF56**

Lacks the lengthy survey articles in *Funk and Wagnall's Standard dictionary of folklore . . .* (above), but contains a greater number of brief entries, particularly names. v.3 is a subject index, tabulating the names and attributes of gods, mythological characters, animals, places, etc. N7640.J57

Legends of the world. Ed. by Richard Cavendish. N.Y., Schocken Books, [1982]. 432p. il. **CF57**

An encyclopedic sourcebook of the traditional narrative stories or epics focusing mainly on human characters. Divided into five sections—Far East, Middle East, West, Africa and the Americas, Pacific—which are subdivided by about 40 cultures. A comparative survey (p.393–409) serves as a motif-index to the legends. Bibliography; index. GR79.L43

Manguel, Alberto and **Guadalupi, Gianni.** The dictionary of imaginary places. N.Y., Macmillan, [1980]. 438p. il., maps. **CF58**

A "gazetteer" to more than 1,000 imaginary places of literature, restricted to places on earth which can be "visited" (i.e., no heavens, hells, places of the future, other planets, real places disguised in literature, etc.). Literary works include mythology, fables, epics, chronicles, classical histories and geographies, travellers' accounts, etc. Bibliography. GR650.M36

Radford, Edwin and **Radford, M. A.** Encyclopaedia of superstitions, ed. and rev. by Christina Hole. [Rev. and enl. ed.] London, Hutchinson, 1961. 384p. **CF59**

1st ed. 1948.

An alphabetically arranged work describing English superstitions. BF1775.R3

Rinzler, Carol Ann. The dictionary of medical folklore. N.Y., Crowell, [1979]. 243p. **CF60**

Attempts to discount or affirm various bits of folk advice, popular beliefs, and "old wives' tales" relating to health, medical problems, nutrition, etc. Entry is under key term, with various beliefs and propositions discussed thereunder. Scientific studies and reports are occasionally referred to within an entry, but bibliographical references or other documentation are not generally given. Indexed. RC81.A2R56

Walsh, William Shepard. Curiosities of popular customs and of rites, ceremonies, observances, and miscellaneous antiquities. Philadelphia, Lippincott, 1898. 1018p. il. (Repr.: Detroit, Gale, 1966) **CF61**

Descriptions of popular customs in various countries of the world. GT31.W2

Handbooks

Frazer, *Sir* **James George.** The golden bough; a study in magic and religion. 3d ed. London, Macmillan, 1907–15. 12v. (Repr.: London, Macmillan; N.Y., St. Martin's, 1955. 13v., including *Aftermath* [CF63]) **CF62**

Various printings and reprintings.

Contents: v.1–2, The magic art and the evolution of kings; v.3, Taboo and the perils of the soul; v.4, The dying god; v.5–6, Adonis, Attis, Osiris—studies in the history of oriental religion; v.7–8, Spirits of the corn and of the wild; v.9, The scapegoat; v.10–11, Balder the Beautiful—the fire festivals of Europe and the doctrine of the external soul; v.12, Bibliography and general index.

Not a reference book in the ordinary sense of the word, but a great storehouse of information about primitive religion. The very detailed general index makes it possible to use the set for ready reference, and the bibliography is extensive. BL310.F7

———— Aftermath; a supplement to the Golden bough. London, Macmillan, 1936. 494p. **CF63**

This supplementary volume contains new matter gathered from works published since 1915, and from some earlier sources not utilized in the basic work. BL310.F715

———— The new Golden bough; a new abridgment of the classic work. Ed., with notes and foreword, by Theodor H. Gaster. N.Y., Criterion, [1959]. 738p. **CF64**

An abridgment of Frazer's work, bringing it to date in the light of recent discoveries. Includes many of Frazer's original notes, keyed to additional notes by the new editor. Comprehensive index. BL310.F72

Gordon, Lesley. Green magic: flowers, plants & herbs in lore & legend. N.Y., Viking Pr., [1977]. 200p. il. **CF65**

Narrative chapters on such topics as: Christian flower legends; herbals and herbalists; plants of love, hate and blood; a few flowers from Shakespeare; political and historical flowers. Provides a cross-register for plants and the sentiments they express. Bibliography; index. GR780.G67

The Americas

Bibliography

American popular culture: a historical bibliography. Arthur Frank Wertheim, ed. Santa Barbara, Calif., ABC-Clio, [1984]. 246p. (Clio bibliography ser., no.14)   **CF66**

A classed bibliography (with abstracts) of more than 2,700 periodical citations drawn from the ABC-Clio database (from which *America: history and life,* etc. are derived). Author and subject indexes.   Z5961.U5A53

Bibliografía del folklore de Guatemala, 1892–1980. Guatemala, Dirección General de Antropología e Historia, 1980. 174p.   **CF67**

A classed bibliography of about 700 items on material, social, and intellectual folklore, with many descriptive notes. Author and title indexes.   Z5984.G9B52

Bibliografía folclórica. v.1– . 1977– . [Rio de Janeiro, Ministerio da Educacão e Cultura, Departamento de Assuntos Culturais, Fundacão Nacional de Arte, Campanha de Defesa do Folclore Brasileiro, 1977]– . Annual.   **CF68**

A classed list of materials on Brazilian folklore, with brief descriptive notes.   Z5984.B7B5

Boggs, Ralph Steele. Bibliography of Latin American folklore. N.Y., Wilson, 1940. 109p. (Inter-American bibliographical and Library Assoc. Publications. Ser. I, v.5)   **CF69**

A partially annotated bibliography of 643 titles, classed by subject and further, by country. Includes Central and South America, and the Caribbean islands. Mexican folklore receives a more detailed treatment in the compiler's *Bibliografía del folklore mexicano* (1939).   Z5984.L4B7

Center for Southern Folklore. American folklore films and videotapes: an index. Comp. by Carolyn Lipson. Memphis, Center for Southern Folklore, [1976]. 338p. il.   **CF70**

Since 1974 the Center for Southern Folklore has collected information on films and videotapes relating to folklore of the United States. This index provides data on some 1,800 titles, with indication of distributor, content, running time, etc. In five sections: (1) Subject index; (2) Film annotations; (3) Videotape annotations; (4) Special collections (listing materials not available for national distribution); and (5) Appendix (giving title listings by distributor and distributors' addresses).

A second volume was published as: Z5984.U6C45

American folklore films and videotapes: a catalog. Center for Southern Folklore. 2d ed. N.Y., Bowker, 1982. 355p. il.   **CF71**

Lists titles released between 1976 and Apr. 1982, together with works released earlier but omitted from the first volume. About 2,000 titles, with subject index and directory of distributors.   Z5984.U6A44

Clements, William M. and **Malpezzi, Frances M.** Native American folklore, 1879–1979; an annotated bibliography. Athens, Ohio, Swallow Pr., [1984]. 247p.   **CF72**

Folklore is here viewed as verbal art and its performance, so that the bibliography "includes books and articles which treat oral narratives, songs, chants, prayers, formulas, orations, proverbs, riddles, word play, music, dances, games, and ceremonials."—*Introd.* Entries are arranged by tribal groups within sections for cultural areas. Indexes of subjects and authors/editors/translators. 5,450 entries.   Z1209.C57

Colonelli, Cristina Argenton. Bibliografia do folclore brasileiro. São Paulo, Conselho Estadual de Artes e Ciências Humanas, 1979. 294p. (Coleção folclore, 20)   **CF73**

An author listing of books and periodical articles, with subject index. 4,919 entries.   Z5984.B7C6

Flanagan, Cathleen C. and **Flanagan, John T.** American folklore: a bibliography, 1950–1974. Metuchen, N.J., Scarecrow Pr., 1977. 406p.   **CF74**

Concerned "only with verbal folklore: more specifically ballads, folk songs, myths, legends, tales, superstitions, beliefs, cures, proverbs, riddles, and the like."—*Pref.* Sections for "Festschriften, symposia, collections," "Bibliography, dictionaries, archives," "Folklore: study and teaching," and "General folklore" are followed by sections arranged by type of material treated. Author index, but none of detailed subjects. About 3,600 items. Supplements Haywood's *Bibliography of North American folklore and folksong* (CF77).   Z5984.U6F55

Fowke, Edith F. and **Carpenter, Carole Henderson.** A bibliography of Canadian folklore in English. Toronto, Univ. of Toronto Pr., [1981]. 272p.   **CF75**

Preliminary ed. 1976.

Basic arrangement is by genre (e.g., folktales, folk music and dance, folk speech and naming, superstitions and popular beliefs, folklife and customs) with subdivisions for major ethnic groups. Separate sections for recordings, films, theses and dissertations. Author index.   Z5984.C33F68

Georges, Robert A. and **Stern, Stephen.** American and Canadian immigrant and ethnic folklore: an annotated bibliography. N.Y., Garland, 1982. 484p. (Garland folklore bibliographies, v.2)   **CF76**

A selective bibliography of 1,900 English-language books, essays, and articles published between 1888–1980 on the folklore of European and Asian immigrants and their North American descendants. Arrangement is by 56 ethnic groups and a general section; indexed by folklore form and topic, general subject, geographical occurrence, and author.   GR105.G43

Haywood, Charles. A bibliography of North American folklore and folksong. 2d rev. ed. N.Y., Dover, [1961]. 2v. (1301p.) maps.   **CF77**

1st ed. 1951.

Contents: v.1, The American people north of Mexico, including Canada; v.2, The American Indians north of Mexico, including the Eskimos.

This is a corrected republication of the 1951 edition, with the addition of a new "Index supplement: composers, arrangers, performers."

A comprehensive, classified bibliography. Covers material on folklore, folksong, legends, dance, etc., as well as music in printed form and on records. Includes some descriptive and evaluative annotations; detailed tables of contents; an author and subject index with title entries for individual songs; and a new index of composers, arrangers, and performers.   Z5984.U5H32

Heisley, Michael. An annotated bibliography of Chicano folklore from the Southwestern United States. Los Angeles, produced for and distr. by the Center for the Study of Comparative Folklore and Mythology, Univ. of California, [1977]. 188p.   **CF78**

A classed bibliography with author, geographical, and subject indexes. Each subject section is subdivided as (1) published works and (2) theses and dissertations. Slightly more than 1,000 items.   Z5984.U6H45

Jones, Steven Swann. Folklore and literature in the United States; an annotated bibliography of studies of folklore in American literature. N.Y., Garland, 1984. 262p. (Garland folklore bibliographies, 5)   **CF79**

Aims to review "scholarship directly and primarily concerned with examining folklore in American literature," specifically those studies published through 1980 "that in an explicit and central way examine the influence of folklore upon American literature."—*Introd.* A main-entry listing with an index subdivided for literary authors, folklore genres, general theory, regional and ethnic studies, humor, and general studies. Includes doctoral dissertations and master's theses. Z1225.J66

Landrum, Larry. American popular culture: a guide to information sources. Detroit, Gale, [1982]. 435p. (American studies information guide ser., v.12) **CF80**

A thematic, annotated bibliography of 2,173 titles focusing on lifestyles, ideology, material culture, leisure, games, sports, popular music, dance, public art, theater, literature, and media. Name and subject indexes. Z1361.C6L28

Leib, Amos Patten and **Day, A. Grove.** Hawaiian legends in English: an annotated bibliography. 2d ed. Honolulu, Univ. Pr. of Hawaii, [1979]. 162p. **CF81**

1st ed. 1949.
An introductory section (p.5–35) provides information on the early translators and "re-tellers" of Hawaiian legends. The bibliography is arranged alphabetically by author, and includes translations appearing in periodicals and brief extracts appearing in longer works as well as separately published translations. Z5984.H38L4

Nascimento, Braulio do. Bibliografia do folclore brasileiro. Rio de Janeiro, Biblioteca Nacional, Divisão de Publicações e Divulgação, 1971. 353p. **CF82**

An alphabetical author listing of more than 2,400 items, with index by broad subjects. Z5982.B7N38

Niles, Susan A. South American Indian narrative, theoretical and analytical approaches; an annotated bibliography. N.Y., Garland, 1981. 183p. (Garland folklore bibliographies, v.1; Garland reference library of the humanities, v.276) **CF83**

Includes references to about 600 works which analyze South American Indian narrative folklore or present summaries or collections of tales; excludes "folklorizations" and popular treatments of native beliefs, as well as material from the Afro-American and Ibero-American traditions. Author arrangement; indexed by tribal group and subject. Z1209.2.S77N54

Pan American Institute of Geography and History. Commission on History. Comité Interamericano de Folklore. Bibliografía del folklore peruano. México, Lima, 1960. 186p. (*Its* Pubn., 2) **CF84**

An annotated bibliography of 1,809 entries in broad subject arrangement, with author and detailed subject indexes. (Also issued as Pubn. 92 of Pan American Inst. of Geography and History, Commission on History, and as Pubn. 230 of Pan American Inst. of Geography and History.) F1401.P153 no.230

Pereira Salas, Eugenio. Guía bibliográfica para el estudio del folklore chileno. [Santiago], Inst. de Investigaciones Musicales, Univ. de Chile, [1952]. 112p. **CF85**

"Tirada aparte de los *Archivos del folklore chileno,* Fasc.4, 1952." —*t.p.*
A classed bibliography of 1,289 titles. Continued by:
Z5984.C45P4

Dannemann Rothstein, Manuel. Bibliografía del folklore chileno, 1952–1965. Austin, Center for Intercultural Studies in Folklore and Oral History, Univ. of Texas, 1970. 60p. (Latin American folklore ser., 2) **CF86**

425 items in subject arrangement. Most entries are briefly annotated. Author index. Z5984.C45D35

Szwed, John F. and **Abrahams, Roger D.** Afro-American folk culture: an annotated bibliography of materials from North, Central and South America and the West Indies. Philadelphia, Inst. for the Study of Human Issues, [1978]. 2v. (Pubns. of the American Folklore Soc., Bibliographical and special ser., v.31–32) **CF87**

Contents: pt.1, North America; pt.2, The West Indies, Central and South America.
Geographical arrangement; indexed by subject and specific locale.
Z5984.A44S95

Handbooks

Fowke, Edith. Folklore of Canada. [Toronto], McClelland and Stewart, [1976]. 349p. **CF88**

An anthology of fairy-tales, legends, jokes, myths, tall tales, riddles, and songs, grouped by ethnic source: native peoples, Canadians, Anglo-Canadians, and other groups. Sources are noted. Extensive bibliography. Indexed by tale types; motifs; contributors and informants; general index. GR113.F67

Handbook of American folklore. Ed. by Richard M. Dorson. Bloomington, Indiana Univ. Pr., [1983]. 584p. il. **CF89**

Provides "an introduction to American folklore as it has been studied in America" and "is intended to show established scholars, students, and the general public what the discipline of folkloristics is all about."—*Introd.* In four main sections: (1) Topics of research; (2) Interpretation of research; (3) Methods of research; (4) Presentation of research. Each section is made up of brief essays by contributing scholars on specific aspects of American folklore research—its content, history, methodology and current state. Bibliographic notes follow each essay and there is a classed bibliography, p.541–63. Detailed index. GR105.H36

Handbook of American popular culture. Ed. by M. Thomas Inge. Westport, Conn., Greenwood Pr., 1978–81. 3v. **CF90**

Offers an impressive body of articles on various aspects of American popular culture, past and present, including various genres of popular literature and arts, film and other mass media, advertising, the circus, games and toys, the occult, pop religion, and self-help theories. Each chapter was "prepared by an authority on the subject, provides a brief chronological survey of the development of the medium; a critical guide in essay form to the standard or most useful bibliographies, reference works, histories, critical studies, and journals; a description of the existing research centers and collections of primary and secondary materials; and a checklist of works cited in the text."—*Pref.* Each volume has its own index. E169.1.H2643

Europe

Bibliography

Bibliografia generală a etnografiei si folclorului românesc. Redactor: Adrian Fochi. [Bucharest], Editura Pentrŭ Literatură, 1968. v.1. **CF91**

Contents: v.1, 1800–1891. No more publ.?
Classed bibliography with author, subject, and geographical indexes. Z5984.R6B5

Danaher, Kevin D. A bibliography of Irish ethnology and folk tradition. Comp. by Caoimhin O'Danachair. Dublin, Mercier Pr., [1978]. 95p. **CF92**

In two sections, the first a listing according to the categories of O'Súilleabháin's *Handbook of Irish folklore;* the second, a listing by author. Full bibliographical information in both lists. Z5117.D35

Lönnqvist, Bo. Folklivsforskning: en bibliografi över Svenskfinland. [Borgå, Tryckeri- & Tidnings Ab, 1976] 180p. il. (Meddelanden från Folkkultursarkivet, 5; Skrifter uitgivna av Svenska Litteratursällskapet i Finland, no.473) **CF93**

A classed subject bibliography of Finnish folklore and Swedish folklore in Finland. Indexed by author and geographical area. Z5984.F5L63

Nederlandse volkskundige bibliografie; systematische registers op tijdschriften, reekswerken en gelegenheidsuitgaven. Antwerpen, Centrum voor Studie en Documentatie, 1964–82. Deel 1–33. (In progress) **CF94**

When complete this will be a very comprehensive record of Dutch periodical literature in the field. Each volume covers one or more periodicals, offering a classed listing of contents with author and subject indexes.   Z5984.N4N43

Russkii fol'klor; bibliograficheskii ukazatel', 1901/1916–1966/1975. Sost. M. IA. Mel'ts. Leningrad, 1961–84. (In progress)   **CF95**

At head of title: Akademiia Nauk SSSR. Institut Russkoi Literatura (Pushkinskii Dom). Ordena Trudovogo Krasnogo Znameni. Biblioteka Akademii Nauk.

Classed bibliography of folklore and writings on folklore in Russian, published in the Soviet Union, with author index. More than 22,000 items in the series.   Z5984.R9R8

Swanson, Donald Carl Eugene. Modern Greek studies in the West; a critical bibliography of studies on modern Greek linguistics, philology and folklore, in languages other than Greek. N.Y., New York Pub. Lib., 1960. 93p.   **CF96**

For full information *see* BC156.

Includes a list of books and monographs on folk literature and folklore, p.44–48; periodical articles, p.68–74.

Vaughan Williams Memorial Library, London. The Vaughan Williams Memorial Library catalogue of the English Folk Dance and Song Society. [London], Mansell, 1973. 769p.   **CF97**

Subtitle: Acquisitions to the library of books, pamphlets, periodicals, sheet music and manuscripts, from its inception to 1971.

"The Library contains 7,000 books, pamphlets and periodicals; 4,000 tape recordings and records; an extensive photograph collection; and a number of archival films dealing with the folk customs and dances of England."—*Introd.* Separate author and subject sections, with a table of subject classes, and an alphabetical index to the subject headings.   ML136.L8V4

Dictionaries and encyclopedias

Bächtold-Stäubli, Hanns. Handwörterbuch des deutschen Aberglaubens, hrsg. unter besonderer Mitwirkung von E. Hoffmann-Krayer . . . Berlin, W. de Gruyter, 1927–41. 9v. and Nachträge in v.9. (Handwörterbücher zur deutschen Volkskunde, hrsg. vom Verband Deutscher Vereine für Volkskunde. Abt.I)   **CF98**

A scholarly encyclopedia with long, signed articles by specialists, and extensive bibliographies. Treats German superstitions and popular beliefs, covering religious, sociological, and historical aspects.   GR166.H3 Abt.1

Bødker, Laurits. Folk literature (Germanic). Copenhagen, Rosenkilde & Bagger, 1965. 365p. (International dictionary of European ethnology and folklore, 2)   **CF99**

For full information on the *Dictionary, see* CE39.

Includes folk literature of the German-speaking parts of Europe, including Scandinavia and Holland. Entries include bibliographies; full bibliography, p.335–65.

Brand, John. Popular antiquities of Great Britain. Faiths and folklore . . . [ed.] by W. Carew Hazlitt. London, Reeves, 1905. 2v. il.   **CF100**

Subtitle: A dictionary of national beliefs, superstitions and popular customs, past and current, with their classical and foreign analogues, described and illustrated. Forming a new edition of "The Popular Antiquities of Great Britain" by Brand and Ellis, largely extended, corrected and brought down to the present time, and now first alphabetically arranged.

Reprinted as: DA110.B832

Hazlitt, William Carew. Faiths and folklore of the British Isles; a descriptive and historical dictionary . . . [N.Y.], B. Blom, [1965]. 2v.   **CF101**

Reprint of the 1905 edition of Brand's *Popular antiquities* (above) with a new introduction by Decherd Turner.   DA110.H38

Briggs, Katharine Mary. A dictionary of British folktales in the English language, incorporating the F. J. Norton collec-

tion. London, Routledge; Bloomington, Indiana Univ. Pr., [1970–71]. 2v. in 4.   **CF102**

Contents: pt.A, Folk narratives: v.1, Fables and exempla; Fairy tales; v.2, Jocular tales; Novelle; Nursery tales; pt.B, v.1–2, Folk legends.

"The main distinction between Folk Narratives and Folk Legends is clear enough: Folk Narrative is Folk Fiction, told for edification, delight or amusement, Folk Legend was once believed to be true."—*Introd., pt.A, v.1.*

Offers a transcription or a summary of each tale or legend. Within each subsection tales are arranged alphabetically by title, admittedly making for some difficulty since many of the tales have no real titles, the titles of others may vary in different collections, and different tales sometimes have the same title. To overcome these difficulties the editor has provided an "Index of tale-types and migratory legends" according to numbers of the Aarne-Thompson tale type index (CF40), with some suggested numbers and types interpolated. An alphabetical index of story titles appears in the first volume of each part; there is an impressive list of books quoted, cited, and consulted.

The F. J. Norton collection is a compilation in manuscript form of tales transcribed from printed sources; it is to be housed in the Library of the Folklore Society at the University College Library, London.   GR141.B69

Hole, Christina. British folk customs. London, Hutchinson, [1976]. 232p. il., map.   **CF103**

An alphabetical arrangement of brief articles on customs chosen on the basis of intrinsic interest, importance, length of their history, etc. Some articles have bibliographical references, and there is also a select bibliography. A calendar groups events by dates, and a map shows locations mentioned in the text, whether historic or contemporary. Index.   GT4843.H64

Mackensen, Lutz. Handwörterbuch des deutschen Märchens, hrsg. unter besonderer Mitwirkung von Johannes Bolte . . . Berlin, W. de Gruyter, 1930–40. v.1–2. (Handwörterbücher zur deutschen Volkskunde. . . . Abt.II, Märchen)   **CF104**

Contents: v.1–2, A–Gyges. No more published.

Long, signed articles by specialists—with extensive bibliographies —on the types and motifs of German fairy tales.   GR166.M3

Słownik folkloru polskiego. Pod. red. Juliana Krzyżanowski. [Warszawa], Wiedza Powszechna, 1965. 487p. il.   **CF105**

A dictionary of Polish folklore. Includes biographical sketches of scholars and specialists in this field. Bibliographies accompany most articles.   GR35.S45

Africa

Coughlan, Margaret N. Folklore from Africa to the United States: an annotated bibliography. Wash., Lib. of Congress, 1976. 161p. il.   **CF106**

A selective listing of folklore collections, linguistic, ethnological, and anthropological studies, travel accounts and government reports containing tales. The arrangement is geographical, from general sub-Saharan Africa through regions of Africa to the West Indies and the United States; within each region, the material is grouped as studies and collections for adults, and collections for children. Lengthy annotations. Author-title index.

Z5984.A35C68

Görög, Veronika. Littérature orale d'Afrique noire: bibliographie analytique. Paris, Maisonneuve et Larose, 1981. 394p.   **CF107**

"Ouvrage publié avec le concours de Centre National de la Recherche Scientifique, Centre d'Études Africaines, École des Hautes Études en Sciences Sociales, Ministère de la Coopération." —*t.p.*

A listing by author or editor of studies, collections, bibliographies, etc., of African oral literature. More than 2,800 items—periodical articles, monographs, anthologies, dissertations. Brief annotations; ethno-linguistic index and index of genres. Z5984.A35G67

Scheub, Harold. African oral narratives, proverbs, riddles, poetry, and song. Boston, G. K. Hall, [1977]. 393p. **CF108**

An earlier version was published as *Bibliography of African oral narratives* (Madison, Wis., 1971).

An international bibliography of more than 5,800 collections appearing either as separate publications or as contributions to periodicals. Listing is by author or other main entry; indexes provide approach by genre, culture, etc. Annotations frequently include quotations from the compiler of the collection.

Z5984.A35S3

Asia

Algarin, Joanne P. Japanese folk literature; a core collection and reference guide. N.Y., Bowker, 1982. 226p. **CF109**

In three main parts: (1) an annotated bibliography of works on Japanese folklore and folktales, arranged by author; (2) an annotated list of Japanese folktale anthologies, with brief descriptions of the stories included; (3) a section of brief synopses of 26 classic Japanese folktales. 138 citations, with detailed annotations. Appendixes list Japanese-language sources and provide a glossary. Indexed.

Z3308.L5A44

Bernardo, Gabriel Adriano. A critical and annotated bibliography of Philippine, Indonesian and other Malayan folklore. Ed. by Francisco Demetrio y Radaza, S.J. Cagayan de Oro City [Philippines], Xavier Univ., 1972. 150p. il. **CF110**

A posthumously published work based on a master's thesis presented in 1923, with some revision and updating. In two parts: (1) Philippine folklore; (2) Indonesian and other Malayan folklore. Each part is subdivided for (1) general and other expository works; (2) myths, legends, fairy tales and other folk stories; and (3) miscellaneous texts. Author and title index. Z5984.P45B47

Danandjaja, James. An annotated bibliography of Javanese folklore. Berkeley, Center for South and Southeast Asia Studies, Univ. of California, 1972. (*Its* Occasional paper, no.9) 162p. maps. **CF111**

Lists nearly 900 monographs and periodical articles arranged by topic, with author index. Descriptive annotations.

DS503.C35 no.9

Handoo, Jawaharlal. A bibliography of Indian folk literature. Mysore, Central Institute of Indian Languages, 1977. 421p. (CIIL folklore ser., 2). **CF112**

An author listing of texts and studies of Indian folk literature, i.e., items "such as myths, tales, legends, fables, . . . songs, ballads (or any form of verse), proverbs, riddles, etc."—*Introd.* About 4,250 entries. Lack of a subject index seriously limits the usefulness of the work. Z5984.I5H36

Kirkland, Edwin Capers. A bibliography of South Asian folklore. The Hague, publ. for Indiana Univ. Research Center in Anthropology, Folklore, and Linguistics by Mouton, [1966]. 291p. (Indiana Univ. folklore ser., 21; Asian folklore studies monographs, 4) **CF113**

Concerned with "all types of folklore, not just folk literature."—*Introd.* Citations to texts of songs, tales, legends, etc., are included, as well as writings about the folk literature, customs, dances, festivals, and the like. 6,852 items in an alphabetical author listing with subject index. A high percentage of entries is in English.

Z5984.S6K5

Sen Gupta, Sankar and **Parmar, Shyam.** A bibliography of Indian folklore and related subjects. Calcutta, Indian Publs., 1967. 196p. (Indian folklore series, no.11) **CF114**

A classed bibliography of English-language materials of the last 100 years. Many annotations; author index. Z3201.S42

Oceania

Kirtley, Bacil F. A motif-index of traditional Polynesian narratives. Honolulu, Univ. of Hawaii Pr., 1971. 486p. **CF115**

Follows the plan and classification system used in Stith Thompson's *Motif-index of folk-literature* (CF42), citing bibliographical sources of narratives containing specific story elements.

GR380.K5

HOLIDAYS

Banks, Mary Macleod. British calendar customs: Orkney and Shetland. London, Folk-Lore Soc., W. Glaisher, 1946. 110p. il. (Publ. of the Folk-Lore Soc., 112) **CF116**

GR145.O7B3

———— British calendar customs: Scotland. . . . London, Folk-Lore Soc., W. Glaisher, 1937–41. 3v. il. (Publ. of the Folk-Lore Soc., 100, 104, 108) **CF117**

Contents: v.1, Movable festivals, Harvest, March riding and Wapynshaws, Wells, Fairs; v.2, The Seasons, the Quarters, Hogmanay, Jan. to May; v.3, June to Dec., Christmas, the Yules.

Both of the above titles treat customs and observances of their respective regions, with descriptions and anecdotes.

For *British calendar customs: England, see* CF131.

GT4845.A2B3

Chambers, Robert. Book of days; a miscellany of popular antiquities in connection with the calendar, including anecdote, biography, and history, curiosities of literature, and oddities of human life and character. Philadelphia, Lippincott, 1899. 2v. **CF118**

1st ed. 1862—64. Later editions show little change.

Arranged by day, giving anecdotes and descriptions of popular customs and observances. A standard work. DA110.C52

Festivals sourcebook. 2d ed. Paul Wasserman, managing ed. Detroit, Gale, [1984]. 721p. **CF119**

Subtitle: A reference guide to fairs, festivals and celebrations in agriculture, antiques, the arts, theater and drama, arts and crafts, community, dance, ethnic events, film, folk, food and drink, history, Indians, marine, music, seasons, and wildlife.

1st ed. 1977.

Covers events in the United States and Canada. Arranged according to the categories mentioned in the subtitle, then by state and province. Includes a chronological listing of events, an event name index, geographic index, and subject index. GT4802.F47

Frewin, Anthony. The book of days. London, Collins, 1979; N.Y., Morrow, 1981. 414p. il. **CF120**

A separate page for each day is divided into three main sections: celebratory, historical, biographical; events are listed chronologically. Some British emphasis. Bibliography; no index. D11.5.F73

Gaster, Theodor Herzl. Festivals of the Jewish year; a modern interpretation and guide. N.Y., Sloane, [1953]. 308p. **CF121**

Gives historical outlines of the great Jewish festivals, with descriptions of their observation, comparing them with the customs and ceremonies of other peoples. A bibliography of further readings, but no index. BM690.G33

Gregory, Ruth W. Anniversaries and holidays. 4th ed. Chicago, Amer. Lib. Assoc., 1983. 262p. **CF122**

1st ed. (1928) by Mary E. Hazeltine.

In three main parts: (1) Calendar of fixed days (arranged by month and day); (2) Calendars of movable days (with sections for the Christian church calendar, the Islamic calendar, the Jewish calendar, and other "feasts, festivals, and special events days"); (3) Books related to anniversaries and holidays (in classed arrangement). The book citations are annotated. Indexed. A very useful guide.

GT3930.G74

Harper, Howard V. Days and customs of all faiths. N.Y., Fleet, [1957]. 399p.　　　**CF123**

Arranged by month and day, giving brief descriptions of the saints or the religious significance of the day. Includes Protestant, Catholic, and Jewish practices and beliefs.　　　GR930.H3

Hatch, Jane M. The American book of days. 3d ed. N.Y., Wilson, 1978. 1214p.　　　**CF124**

Based on George W. Douglas' work of the same title (1st ed. 1937).

"Like its predecessors, this new edition profiles the lives of many of the United States' distinguished citizens, explores the richness of its religious traditions, describes the variety of its holidays, customs and festivities, samples its folklore, and reports its ways . . . of marking anniversaries and commemorating achievements."—*Pref.* Aims "to tell what happens or did happen on every day of the year and how, where, and by whom these events are (and have been) observed in this country." Indexed.　　　GT4803.D6

Myers, Robert J. Celebrations; the complete book of American holidays. Garden City, N.Y., Doubleday, 1972. 386p. il.
CF125

Presents information on the origin and history of holidays currently observed in America and on the methods of past and present observance.　　　GT4803.A2M84

Samuelson, Sue. Christmas: an annotated bibliography. N.Y., Garland, 1982. 96p. (Garland folklore bibliographies, v.4; Garland reference library of the humanities, v.343)
CF126

A main entry listing of books, articles, dissertations, and theses on the historical, psychological, sociological, and folklore approaches to the study of Christmas; collections or "mere" descriptions of Christmas customs are generally not included. International scope; subject index.　　　Z5711.C5S25

Shemanski, Frances. A guide to fairs and festivals in the United States. Westport, Conn., Greenwood Pr., [1984]. 339p.　　　**CF127**

A selective guide to fairs and festivals in the fifty states and territories—American Samoa, Puerto Rico and the U.S. Virgin Islands. Narrative descriptions include history, special features, achievements, awards, financing, and date. Arranged by state and city; the calendar of fairs lists them chronologically within state, and an appendix lists fairs by broad type. Indexed. A companion guide to world festivals is in preparation.　　　GT3930.S4

Spicer, Dorothy Gladys. Festivals of western Europe. N.Y., Wilson, 1958. 275p.　　　**CF128**

Concerned with religious feasts and folk festivals having their basis in church holidays; national and political holidays are excluded. Arrangement is by country, then chronological. Includes notes on origins of many festivals, local customs of celebration, etc.

GT4842.S6

——— Yearbook of English festivals. N.Y., Wilson, 1954. 298p.　　　**CF129**

A calendar guide to the folk festivals of Great Britain, with a special section on the Easter cycle. Indexed by customs, counties, and regions. Includes a glossary of festival terms.　　　GT4843.S6

Weiser, Francis Xavier. Handbook of Christian feasts and customs; the year of the Lord in liturgy and folklore. N.Y., Harcourt, [1958]. 366p.　　　**CF130**

Attempts to explain the origin, history, development, and observances of Christian feasts with liturgical aspects and the celebration in folklore, including symbols, customs, and traditions. Includes many references to the literature of the field.　　　BV30.W4

Wright, Arthur Robinson. British calendar customs: England . . . ed. by T. E. Lones. London, Folk-Lore Soc., W. Glaish-

er, 1936–40. 3v. il. (Pubn. of the Folk-Lore Soc., 97, 102, 106)　　　**CF131**

Contents: v.1, Movable festivals; v.2–3, Fixed festivals, January–December.

Lists customs and observances, with descriptions and anecdotes. For other volumes of *British calendar customs see* CF116–CF117.

GT4843.W7

ETIQUETTE

Bibliography

Bobbitt, Mary Reed. A bibliography of etiquette books published in America before 1900. N.Y., New York Pub. Lib., 1947. 35p. (Repr. from the New York Public Library *Bull.,* Dec. 1947)　　　**CF132**

Arrangement is by author, or title when author is unknown. Includes title index. Locates copies.　　　Z5877.B6

Newberry Library, Chicago. A check list of courtesy books in the Newberry Library, comp. by Virgil B. Heltzel. Chicago, 1942. 161p.　　　**CF133**

Contains 1,539 entries, for various editions of works on "courtesy literature" written before 1775.　　　Z5873.N5

Handbooks

Debrett's Etiquette and modern manners. Elsie Burch Donald, ed. London, Debrett's Peerage; N.Y., Viking Pr., [1981]. 400p. il.　　　**CF134**

British orientation. Aims to give "detailed information about ceremonies and events which are part of the British tradition," to eliminate obsolete conventions, and to establish "as 'correct form' useful new practices that have emerged to suit new circumstances." —*Introd.* Indexed.　　　BJ1873.D34

Ford, Charlotte. Charlotte Ford's Book of modern manners. N.Y., Simon & Schuster, [1980]. 509p. il.　　　**CF135**

Emphasizes a flexible set of suggestions for "situations for which there are no longer exact standards of proper behavior."—*Introd.* Chapters on weddings and marriages are followed by "living together," divorce, and the single mother. Also discusses community relations, sports and games, pets, etc. Indexed. For a review, see "Mode code," *Time* 115:60 (Mar. 10, 1980).　　　BJ1853.F59

Latner, Helen. The book of modern Jewish etiquette: a guide for all occasions. N.Y., Schocken Books, [1981]. 373p. il.
CF136

Concerned with proper conduct in regard to the "details of daily living" as well as formal occasions, Jewish holidays, rites and procedures. Considers relations with the community and with non-Jewish friends and associates. Indexed.　　　BJ2019.5.J4L37

McCaffree, Mary Jane and **Innis, Pauline B.** Protocol: the complete handbook of diplomatic, official, and social usage. Englewood Cliffs, N.J., Prentice-Hall, [1977]. 414p. il.
CF137

"The purpose of this book is to help the newcomer to official life . . . to learn and understand the rules of protocol and to serve as a reference for the person whose life is governed . . . by the practices and policies of protocol."—*Pref.* Stresses everyday usage of protocol in the United States, covering order of precedence, titles and forms of address, calling and calling cards, invitations and replies, official entertaining and private parties, places to entertain, table seating arrangements, White House entertaining, the diplomatic corps, ceremonies, flag etiquette, and women in public and official life. Bibliography. Subject index.   BJ1853.M23

Martin, Judith. Miss Manners' Guide to excruciatingly correct behavior. N.Y., Atheneum, 1982. 745p. il.   **CF138**

A humorously presented, but determinedly correct, guide to modern social behavior. Incorporates questions and answers from the United Feature Syndicate column by "Miss Manners." Indexed.
BJ1853.M294

Post, Emily. Emily Post's Etiquette. 14th ed. rev. by Elizabeth L. Post. N.Y., Harper & Row, [1984]. 1018p. il.
CF139

First published in 1922 under title *Etiquette in society, in business, in politics, and at home.*
Long a standard work. Particularly useful for formal occasions.
BJ1853.P6

Swartz, Oretha D. Service etiquette. 3d ed. Annapolis, Naval Inst. Pr., [1977]. 582p. il.   **CF140**

1st ed. 1959.
A guide to service etiquette, or "aspects of everyday good manners combined with the traditions and customs of the various branches of the armed forces."—*Introd.* Includes male and female uniform charts, forms of military and civilian address, business and social correspondence, entertaining, traditional military ceremonies, flag etiquette, etc. Indexed.   U766.M2

Vanderbilt, Amy. The Amy Vanderbilt complete book of etiquette: a guide to contemporary living. Rev. and expanded by Letitia Baldrige. Garden City, N.Y., Doubleday, 1978. 879p. il.   **CF141**

1st ed., 1952, had title *Amy Vanderbilt's Etiquette*; 1972 ed. called *New complete book of etiquette.*
This latest revision emphasizes "good manners" in contemporary American society, offering options in many social situations rather than merely hard and fast rules (although attention is still given to formal etiquette). Includes a section "manners in business." Indexed.   BJ1853.V27

Forms of address

See also CJ569–CJ570, CJ572–CJ573a.

Montague-Smith, Patrick W. Debrett's Correct form; an inclusive guide to everything from drafting wedding invitations to addressing an archbishop. [Rev. ed.] [Kingston upon Thames], Debrett's Peerage Ltd., [1976]. 423p.
CF142

1st ed. 1970.
Besides revision of existing text, new sections have been added for "American usage" and "Usage in other foreign countries."
CR3891.M65

Titles and forms of address: a guide to their correct use. 17th ed. London, Black, [1980]. 190p.   **CF143**

First published 1918 as *Titles, being a guide to the right use of British titles and honours.*
A useful handbook to correct English usage for the titled classes and for the church, the armed services, the law, the universities, the government services, etc. Also includes lists of abbreviations and of the pronunciation of names.   CR3891.T58

❖Lists somewhat similar to the above are included in certain more comprehensive reference works, e.g.: modes of addressing persons of title are included regularly in the introductory parts of the peerages; sections on forms of address are included in various books on etiquette.

A useful list for American forms is found in L. Doris and B. M. Miller's *Complete secretary's handbook* (CH346); another is in *Webster's Third new international dictionary,* 1961, p.51a–54a (AD11), under "Forms of address."

C G

Statistics and Demography

❖Reference questions calling for statistics are frequent in any library, and books which furnish reliable and up-to-date statistics are of great importance in any reference collection, especially in libraries where original research in social, political, economic, or industrial questions is done.

Statistical reference works fall into six main classes: (1) general dictionaries or compends, (2) almanacs or annuals of miscellaneous statistics and general information, (3) census reports and bulletins, (4) national yearbooks and statistical annuals limited to the figures of one particular country, (5) periodicals, official and non-official, (6) statistics of a particular subject, e.g., agriculture, foreign commerce, etc.

Of these six classes, the first and second are of the easiest and most frequent use for popular questions and are useful within their limitations, although they are usually neither detailed nor authoritative enough for important questions. For reliable and authoritative statistics, works falling in the other classes must be used.

The third class is always official (i.e., prepared by a government), and no attempt has been made to list these here, except for guides to the U.S. census. For information about census reports in various other countries, consult the two bibliographies published by the Census Library Project of the Library of Congress (CG205 and CG84), and the bibliographies prepared by the Population Research Center at the University of Texas (CG16).

For statistical annuals and national yearbooks, *see* p.759. The *Population index* (CG27) and the *Public Affairs Information Service bulletin* (CA35) are both useful indexes to the statistical material to be found in periodicals.

For statistics on special subjects *see* names of individual subjects. Frequently recourse must also be had to government publications of varying kinds. Statistics for regions, states, and smaller subdivisions may be found in census publications, regional surveys, state and municipal handbooks, etc. For additional works on statistical method and mathematical statistics, *see* Mathematics, p.1216.

GENERAL WORKS

Guides

Burrington, Gillian A. How to find out about statistics. Oxford & N.Y., Pergamon, [1972]. 153p. il.   **CG1**

An introductory guide for the student. The first five chapters discuss education, training, and careers for statisticians, the use of libraries, statistical associations, and textbooks. Chapters 6–11 treat periodicals, bibliographies, general statistical serials and compendia, social and economic statistics, and national statistics of various countries. Emphasis is on the major international, British, and American sources. Indexed.   Z7551.B86

Bibliography

Ball, Joyce, ed. Foreign statistical documents; a bibliography of general, international trade, and agricultural statistics, including holdings of the Stanford University libraries. Comp. by Roberta Gardella. Stanford, Calif., Hoover Inst. on War, Revolution, and Peace, 1967. 173p. (Hoover Inst. bibliographical ser., 28)   **CG2**

A country-by-country listing concentrating "mainly on publications using a Western European language either as the first or second language."—*Introd.* Can be used effectively with Wasserman's *Statistics sources* (CG72). Lists both current and defunct series.
Z7551.B3

Buros, Oscar Krisen, ed. Statistical methodology reviews. 1933/38–1941/50. N.Y., Wiley, 1938–51. 3v   **CG3**

Title varies: [v.1] *Research and statistical methodology; books and reviews;* [v.2] *Yearbook of research and statistical methodology.* Imprint varies.
v.1–2 include books on research methods, scientific methods, social relations of science, collective biographies of scientists, general histories of science, and statistical methodology. v.3 lists only books on statistical methods, probability, and mathematics of statistics. Arrangement is alphabetical by author of the book reviewed. Includes indexes of: (1) publishers, (2) names of authors and reviewers, (3) titles, and (4) broad subjects.   Z7405.R4B9

Clausen, Gisela, Gärtner, Karla and **Otto, Johannes.** Bibliographie deutschsprachiger bevölkerungswissenschaftlicher Literatur, 1976–1982. Wiesbaden, Bundesinstitut für Bevölkerungsforschung, 1983. 611p. (Materialien zur Bevölkerungswissenschaft, Hft.31)   **CG4**

A classed bibliography with lengthy annotations; author index. Similar compilations covering 1945–65, 1966–75, and 1976–80 were published as *Hefte* 10, 23, and 26 of the series.

Cormier, Reine. Les sources des statistiques actuelles; guide de documentation. Paris, Gauthier-Villars, 1969. 287p.   **CG5**

An annotated guide to statistical sources: general, demographic and health, economic, cultural. Attention is given to Europe and to the world at large, but emphasis is on French sources. Subject index.
Z7551.C65

Driver, Edwin D. World population policy; an annotated bibliography. Lexington, Mass., Lexington Books, [1971]. 1280p.   **CG6**

More than 3,500 items, most of them annotated at some length. Restricted to works on general population policy and measures affecting fertility and family size; coverage is for the period 1940–69. Primarily English-language materials.   Z7164.D3D75

Duchesne, Jean-Louis and **Tobón, María-Victoria.** Bibliography of IUSSP conference proceedings from 1947 to 1973. [Liège, IUSSP, 1974] 362p. (IUSSP papers, no.3)   **CG7**

A chronological listing of more than 2,000 papers from the published conference proceedings of the International Union for the Scientific Study of Population. Author, subject, and geographical indexes.   Z7164.D3D35

Eldridge, Hope T. The materials of demography: a selected and annotated bibliography. N.Y., 1959. 222p. (Repr.: Westport, Conn., Greenwood Pr., 1975)   **CG8**

Published by the International Union for the Scientific Study of Population and the Population Association of America (Brown University, Providence, R.I.).
A classified listing of books, articles, and, especially, reports of conferences, special research committees, etc., in English. Many full annotations, and usually listings of individual papers contained in polygraphic works. Author index.   Z7164.D3E4

Golini, Antonio. Bibliografia delle opere demografiche in lingua italiana (1930–1965). Roma, Università di Roma, Istituto di Demografia, 1966. 172p.   **CG9**

A detailed, classed, annotated bibliography of books and periodical articles, with official sources listed separately. Excludes health statistics and studies of socioeconomic problems of population (e.g., labor, housing, and education). No cross references; works are cited under each appropriate subject category with annotations only under the principal category. No index.
Supplemented by: Z7164.D3G63

——— and **Caselli, Graziella.** Bibliografia delle opere demografiche italiane (1966–1972). Roma, Facoltà di Scienze Statistiche, Demografiche ed Attuariali, Università di Roma, 1973. 308p.   **CG9a**

Adds material by Italians published in a foreign language, works on the economically active population, labor force, employment, and health statistics in general. Author index.

Hatten tojō koku no tōkei shiryō mokuroku, 1968– . Tokyo, Ajia Keizai Kenkyūjo, [Ajia Keizai Shuppankai Hatsubai, 1968]– . Annual.   **CG10**

English title: Catalogue of statistical materials of developing countries.
In Japanese with some English, French, or Spanish.
Continues *Kaihatsu tojō koku no tōkei shiryō mokuroku.*
Lists statistical materials collected by the Statistics Dept. of the Institute of Economics. Arranged by region, country, and subject; appendix lists titles from intergovernmental agencies. Titles are translated into English. 1980 volume lists some 5,590 titles from 121 countries.   Z7164.U5H33

Institut International de Statistique. Revue. 1.–39. année. La Haye, 1933–71. Quarterly (slightly irregular).   **CG11**

Supersedes: Institut International de Statistique. Office Permanent. *Bulletin mensuel.*
Frequency varies. Ceased publication with v.39 (1971).
Title page also in English: *Revue of the International Statistical Institute.* Text in English, French, German, Italian, or Spanish, with summaries in English or French (occasionally in both).
Through v.34 (1966), each number included a section, "Bibliographie statistique internationale," an important bibliography, international in scope.
Superseded by the *International statistical review* (which continues the numbering of the *Revue*), v.40– , 1972– . The international bibliography is not a feature of each issue, but bibliographies on specific aspects of statistics frequently appear in the journal.
HA11.I505

International Statistical Institute. Bibliography of basic texts and monographs on statistical methods, 1945–1960. [2d ed. by William R. Buckland and Ronald A. Fox] Edinburgh, Oliver & Boyd; N.Y., Hafner, [1963]. 297p.   **CG12**

1st ed. 1951.
Lists nearly 200 books, written in English, with full bibliographical information, including chapter headings. Gives excerpts of reviews from statistical journals for each entry. Arranged by broad subject; author index.   Z7553.M48I55

Kendall, Maurice George and **Doig, Alison G.** Bibliography of statistical literature. Edinburgh, Oliver & Boyd; N.Y., Hafner, 1962–68. 3v. (v.1 repr.: N.Y., Arno, 1981)   **CG13**

Contents: v.[1] 1950–58; v.2, 1940–49; v.[3] Pre-1940, with supplements to the volumes for 1940–49 and 1950–58.
An author list of papers, mostly in Western languages, on statistical method, statistical theory, and probability from the 16th century up to the end of 1958. No books are included.   Z7551.K42

Koren, John. History of statistics, their development and progress in many countries; in memoirs to commemorate the seventy-fifth anniversary of the American Statistical Association. N.Y., Macmillan, 1918. 773p. (Repr.: N.Y., B. Franklin, 1970)   **CG14**

Especially useful for information about the history of official statistical publications.   HA19.K7

Podzimek, Jaroslav. Bibliografie československé statistiky a demografie, 1945–1968. Praha, Výzkum. Ústav Stat. a Účetnictví, [1969]. 2v.   **CG15**

A classed, annotated bibliography of books, articles, research reports and papers. v.1 lists statistical, theoretical, and methodological works, v.2, demographic studies. Introduction and tables of contents also in English. Indexed by personal name.

Z7551.A2P6

Texas. University. Population Research Center. International population census bibliography. Austin, Univ. of Texas, Bureau of Business Research, 1965–68. no.1–7.   **CG16**

Contents: no.1, Latin America and the Caribbean; no.2, Africa; no.3, Oceania; no.4, North America; no.5, Asia; no.6, Europe; no.7, Supplement [to v.1–6].

The series was issued in conjunction with the Center's census acquisition program and aims to provide a universal bibliography of census reports. Each number consists mainly of listings of separately published population census reports, though other types of series (e.g., housing and agriculture) are sometimes listed if population data are included therein. The entries, arranged alphabetically by area, then chronologically, indicate the contents of multivolume reports. Note is also taken of years in which censuses were known to have been conducted, but for which no published reports were found.

Continued by: Z7164.D3T45

Goyer, Doreen S. International population census bibliography, revision and update, 1945–1977. N.Y., Academic Pr., 1980. 576p. (Texas bibliography II)   **CG17**

1965–68 ed. by the Population Research Center, University of Texas (above).

Extends the coverage of the original work to national and territorial population censuses held through 1977, but excludes those taken before 1945. Arrangement is now alphabetical by individual country, rather than by region. Information given includes name of statistical agency and publications distributor, document entries with original and English-language title, and at least one library location. Notes censuses for which no publications are available, administrative changes, and sometimes date of next census.

Z7164.D3G69

——— National population censuses, 1945–1976: some holding libraries. Clarion, Pa., Assoc. for Population/Family Planning Libraries and Information Centers, Internat. (APLIC), 1979. 44p. (APLIC Special pubn., no.1)   **CG18**

Locates population census reports in 53 U.S. and Canadian libraries. Brief entries give only country, date of census, and library symbols (not those employed in the National Union Catalog).

Z7553.C3G69

International population census publications, series II, pre-1945: guide to the microfilm edition. Ed. by Diane M. Del Cervo. Woodbridge, Conn., Research Pubns., 1984. 454p.   **CG19**

Based on the *International population census bibliography* (CG16). Provides bibliographic citation and access to the microfilm reels in the publisher's collection of the same title. Arrangement is by country, then date of census. Excludes United States censuses, since these have been covered in the publisher's *United States decennial census publications* (CG107).   Z7164.D3I59

United Nations. Dept. of Economic and Social Affairs. Analytical bibliography of international migration statistics, selected countries, 1925–1950. N.Y., 1955. 195p. (Population studies, no.24)   **CG20**

An analytical bibliography for 24 selected countries, presenting a list of primary sources and other publications containing statistical data, and "within each major category of departures and arrivals the sources and years for which detailed classification and cross-classifications are available."—*Introd.*   Z7164.I3U55

United Nations. Statistical Office. Statistical papers: Series M. N.Y., 1949– . no.1– . Irregular.   **CG21**

This series contains papers on international statistics, e.g.: no.1, Nomenclature of geographic areas for statistical purposes (1949); no.4, International standard industrial classification of all economic activities (rev. 1958); no.8, International standard definitions for

transport statistics (1950); no.18, Bibliography of recent official demographic statistics (1954); no.21, World weights and measures: handbook for statisticians (1955); no.22, Directory of international standards for statistics, including a bibliography on methods (rev. 1960); no.36, Bibliography of industrial and distributive-trade statistics (rev. 1963); no.38, Commodity indexes for the Standard international trade classification (1963); no.39, 46, 55, Input-output bibliography, 1960–70 (1964–72).

U.S. Bureau of the Census. Library. Catalogs of the Bureau of the Census Library, Washington, D.C. Boston, G. K. Hall, 1976. 20v.   **CG22**

A dictionary catalog of a collection strong in the statistics of agriculture, business, construction, economics, foreign trade, governments, housing, industries, population, transportation, as well as in statistical methodology and data processing. Special collections include: an archival collection of U.S. census publications from 1790 to the present; the state and local government documents collection, principally serials on financial and governmental activities (cataloged in v.20); the electronic data processing–micrographics collection (cataloged in v.19); and the foreign and international statistical collection.

——— ——— First supplement. Boston, G. K. Hall, 1979. 5v.

Includes material cataloged or recataloged after Mar. 1976. Material in the state and local government documents and in the EDP–micrographics collections are now interfiled in the main sequence.   Z7555.U54

Zelinsky, Wilbur. A bibliographic guide to population geography. Chicago, 1962. 257p. (Chicago Univ. Dept. of Geography. Research paper no. 80)   **CG23**

A listing of 2,588 items on all phases of population geography, published in various parts of the world from the mid-19th century to mid-1961. Regional arrangement with author index.

H31.C514 no.80

Bibliography of bibliography

Lancaster, Henry Oliver. Bibliography of statistical bibliographies. Edinburgh and London, publ. for the International Statistical Institute by Oliver & Boyd, [1968]. 103p.   **CG24**

Has a section for bibliographies of statisticians and mathematicians and a section for subject bibliographies. Includes both book and periodical materials. Indexed.

Supplementary lists have appeared in the *Revue* of the Institut International de Statistique, 37:57–67 (1969); 38:258–67 (1970); 39:64–73 (1971) and in the *International statistical review* 40:73–81 (1972).   Z7551.L3

Indexes and current bibliography

DataMap, 1983– ; index of published tables of statistical data. N.Y., Longman, [1983]– . Annual.   **CG25**

The initial volume indexes the tables of 28 statistical sources that "would together provide the most parsimonious coverage of the widest possible variety of social, political, economic, technical, and other data."—*[p.xi]* Most are United States government or United Nations publications, as well as the major almanacs.   Z7552.D37

Goode, Stephen H. Population and the population explosion; a bibliography for 1970–76. Troy, N.Y., Whitston, 1973–81. Annual.   **CG26**

A listing of books, periodical articles, and pamphlets appearing during the year. Citations are drawn from a selection of standard bibliographic sources. Books and pamphlets appear in a separate author arrangement; periodical articles are listed in both a title and a subject listing, with full citation given in each section.

Z7164.D3G65

Population index. v.1– , 1935– . Princeton, N.J., Office of Population Research, Princeton Univ., and the Population Assoc. of America, 1935– . v.1– . Quarterly.   **CG27**

Title varies: Jan. 1935–Oct. 1936, *Population literature.* v.1, no.1 (rev. May 1, 1935) "replaces 'Review of current research, 1,' including all titles from that publication as well as additional foreign and American citations for 1933. (No 1934 or 1935 titles were added.) The period covered by this number begins Jan. 1, 1933, which terminates the period covered by *Social science abstracts* (1929–1932) [CA36]."—*Note, v.1, p.1.*

v.1–2 were published by the Population Association of America, Wash., D.C.

An annotated bibliography of books and periodical literature on all phases of population problems. Arranged by class, with annual cumulated indexes by author and country. Includes special articles and current items.

Bibliographic entries from issues of the period 1935–38 have been cumulated as: Z7164.D3P83

Princeton University. Office of Population Research. Population index bibliography. Cumulated 1935–1968, by authors and geographical areas. Boston, G. K. Hall, 1971. 9v.   **CG28**

Contents: Author index, 4v.; Geographical index, 5v. (v.1–3, 1935–1954; v.4–5, 1954–1968).

Cumulates the bibliographic entries from *Population index* (above), providing both an author and a geographical approach. Libraries will, of course, need to retain the issues of *Population index* for the survey articles, statistical tables, etc., appearing in the individual issues (and indexed in this cumulation of the bibliographic listings).

In the author part items are cited only once, with no added entries for joint authors or for individuals responsible for publications entered under corporate headings. In the geographical part entries are arranged by continent, then by country or region, with further subdivision by topics if there are more than 100 entries. There are no running heads nor any detailed table of contents to guide the user.

Continued by: Z7164.D3P852

Population index bibliography: cumulated 1969–1981 by authors and geographical areas. Office of Population Research, Princeton Univ. Boston, G. K. Hall, 1984. 4v.   **CG29**

Contents: v.1, 1969–1974, Author index; v.2, 1975–1977, Author, subject and geographical indexes; v.3, 1978–1981, Author index; v.4, 1978–1981, Subject and geographical indexes.

Indexes all citations in the quarterly bibliography of *Population index* for 1969 through 1981. v.1 is a photographic reproduction of catalog cards; v.2–4 are the true index, providing only basic bibliographic data and referring the user to the abstract in the appropriate volume of *Population index.*

Schweizerische Bibliographie für Statistik und Volkswirtschaft. Bibliographie suisse de statistique et d'économie politique, bearb. vom Eidgenössischen Statistischen Amt, Bern. 1. Jahrg.– , 1937– . Bern, Schweizerische Gesellschaft für Statistik und Volkswirtschaft, 1938– . Annual (slightly irregular)   **CG30**

Classified; beginning with v.7, has an author index. Includes books, reports, and articles on statistics, primarily by Swiss authors, plus a selection of works by foreign authors.   Z7552.S42

Dictionaries

Freund, John E. and **Williams, Frank J.** Dictionary/outline of basic statistics. N.Y., McGraw-Hill, [1966]. 195p.   **CG31**

Comprises a dictionary of statistical terms and an outline of statistical formulas.   HA17.F7

Hungary. Központi Statisztikai Hivatal. Statisztikai szótár; 1700 statisztikai kifejezés hét nyelven. Statistical dictiona-

ry; 1700 statistical terms in seven languages. [4. kiad.] Budapest, [Statisztikai Kiadó Vállalat], 1964. 171p.   **CG32**

1st published 1960.

Title and introductory material in seven languages: Russian, Hungarian, Bulgarian, Czech, Polish, German, and English. Main listing is in Russian with equivalents in other languages, followed by word indexes of the six non-Russian languages.   HA17.H8

Inter-American Statistical Institute. Statistical vocabulary. 2d ed. Wash., Pan Amer. Union, 1960. 83p. (Repr. 1967)   **CG33**

1st ed. 1950.

Title page and text in English, Spanish, Portuguese, and French.

Consists of (1) a "main list" of more than 1,300 English terms with equivalents in Spanish, Portuguese, and French, and (2) separate Spanish, Portuguese, and French alphabetical indexes, each keyed to the English equivalents.   HA17.I6

Kendall, Maurice George and **Buckland, William R.** A dictionary of statistical terms; prep. for the International Statistical Institute. 4th ed., rev. and enl. London & N.Y., Longman, 1982. 213p.   **CG34**

1st ed. 1957.

A dictionary of terms in current use, taking into account usage as found in book and journal literature.

Glossaries of equivalent terms in French, German, Italian, and Spanish were a feature of the earlier editions, but are omitted herein. A *Russian-English/English-Russian glossary of statistical terms* by Samuel Kotz (Edinburgh, Oliver & Boyd, 1971. 87p.) was issued as a companion volume to the 3d ed. (1971).   QA276.14.K46

Kurtz, Albert K. and **Edgerton, Harold A.** Statistical dictionary of terms and symbols. N.Y., Wiley; London, Chapman and Hall, 1939. 191p. (Repr. 1967)   **CG35**

A very good dictionary, giving clear and sometimes detailed definitions. Explanations of many symbols are included.   HA17.K83

Logie, Gordon. Glossary of population and housing: English-French-Italian-Dutch-German-Swedish. Amsterdam, Elsevier Scientific Publ. Co., 1978. 265p. (International planning glossaries, 1)   **CG36**

Terms in the major areas of population, demography, migration, households, housing policy, density, and living climate are given in tabular form with English as the base language and equivalents in each of the other five. Usage of the terms in each section is also given in a paragraph or two in English. Indexes in each of the other languages refer to page numbers in the glossary, making the work somewhat awkward to use.   HD7287.5.L63

Multilingual demographic dictionary. English section. 2d ed. Adapted by Etienne van de Walle from the French section by Louis Henry. Liège, Ordina, [1982]. 161p.   **CG37**

1st ed. 1958.

Issued also in Czech, Finnish, French, German, Italian, Spanish, and Swedish. Explanations of concepts and technical terms (numbered) used in demography. Alphabetical index is included, referring to the numbers for explanations.   HB849.2.M84

Paenson, Isaac. English-French-Spanish-Russian systematic glossary of the terminology of statistical methods. Spanish translation prep. by J. M. Doblado. Oxford, Pergamon, [1970]. 517p. il.   **CG38**

Added title page and introductory matter in each of the other languages.

Terms and definitions are grouped in chapters with the aim of placing the various terms in their logical context; full treatment of each term is given in all four languages. Alphabetical index in each language.   HA17.P34

Pressat, Roland. The dictionary of demography. Ed. by Christopher Wilson. [Oxford & N.Y.], Blackwell Reference, [1985]. 243p. il.   **CG39**

First published in French as *Dictionnaire de démographie* (Paris, P.U.F., 1979).

The English-language edition has utilized a broader encyclopedic approach than the French, but stresses technical concepts and measures. Signed definitions, many with bibliographic references.

HB849.2.P7413

Encyclopedias

International encyclopedia of population. N.Y., Free Pr., [1982]. 2v. il. **CG40**

John A. Ross, ed. in chief.

Sponsored by the Center for Population and Family Health of the International Institute for the Study of Human Reproduction, Columbia University.

Consists of 129 medium-length, signed articles on the current state of demography and population topics, and serves as a companion to the same publisher's *International encyclopedia of statistics* (below) and the *International encyclopedia of the social sciences* (CA51). Alphabetical arrangement by topic and country or geographic area. Limited treatment of historical aspects and specific organizations, with no biographies included. Bibliographies for individual articles are supplemented by articles on directories and publications. Alphabetical and topical lists of contents; indexed.

HB849.2.I55

International encyclopedia of statistics. Ed. by William H. Kruskal and Judith M. Tanur. N.Y., Free Pr., [1978]. 2v. (1350p.) **CG41**

This compilation "draws together, expands, and brings up to date the statistics articles of the *International Encyclopedia of the Social Sciences* [CA51]."—*Introd.* In addition to the approximately 70 articles "on statistics proper, numerous articles on social science topics with strong statistical flavor, and about 45 biographies of statisticians and others important in the development of statistics" from the parent work, five new articles and 12 new biographies have been introduced. Nearly all of the articles were revised, amended, or have postscripts added. Bibliographies were updated. The detailed index includes references from names of contributors.

HA17.I63

Directories

American Statistical Association. Directory of statisticians and others in allied professions, 1961– . Wash., Amer. Statistical Assoc., [1962–]. Irregular. **CG42**

A combined membership directory of the American Statistical Association, the Biometric Society (Eastern and Western North American regions), and the Institute of Mathematical Statistics. Arranged alphabetically; gives dates, address, position, and education. Includes a geographical listing. HA1.D52

Fogle, Catherine, Gleiter, Karin and **McIntyre, Marilyn.** International directory of population information and library resources. Chapel Hill, N.C., Carolina Population Center, 1972–75. 2v. **CG43**

A directory of agencies and institutes concerned with all aspects of population (e.g., population planning, family research, demography). HB850.F6

Statistical services directory. 1st ed., issue no. 1– , June 1982– . Detroit, Gale, [1982]– . 3 nos. per yr. with annual cumulation. **CG44**

Subtitle: A guide to the organizations, corporations, professional and trade associations, research centers, universities, publishers, foundations, and government agencies that provide statistical services.

Organization description is followed by information on statistical publications: format, period covered, release date, frequency, and cost. The first three issues profiled 1,129 services; subject index in each issue is cumulative. HA37.U137

Surveys, polls, censuses, and forecasts directory. [no.] 1– , Oct. 1983– . Detroit, Gale, 1983– . 3 nos. per yr. **CG45**

Subtitle: A guide to sources of statistical studies in the areas of business, social science, education, science, and technology.

Alphabetically arranged entries for polls or surveys provide sponsoring agency, description, frequency, time and geographic coverage, availability. Indexed by subject and sponsor. Heavy business orientation, with no individual poll data for organizations such as Gallup, Harris, etc. Z7554.U5S95

Handbooks

Goyer, Doreen S. and **Domschke, Eliane.** The handbook of national population censuses: Latin America and the Caribbean, North America, and Oceania. Westport, Conn., Greenwood Pr., 1983. 711p. il., maps. **CG46**

Describes each national census in terms of its definitions and concepts, special features, quality, and publication plan; also lists other national statistical publications. Provides population figures for total country, capital, large city, and metropolitan areas from 1945 to 1980. Subsequent volumes will cover Asia, Africa, and Europe. HA36.G67

Atlases

McEvedy, Colin and **Jones, Richard.** Atlas of world population history. [Harmondsworth], Penguin, [1978]. 368p. il., maps. **CG47**

Presents population figures in graph form for most countries of the world from prehistoric times to estimates for the year 2000. Short narrative summaries comment on the historical population changes and include bibliographic guides to primary sources and the most important secondary sources. Geographical arrangement by continent, subdivided by country. General bibliography; index.

HB851.M32

COMPENDIUMS

International

Alderson, Michael Rowland. International mortality statistics. N.Y., Facts on File, [1981]. 524p. **CG48**

Provides mortality statistics by sex, calendar period, cause of death, and country for the 1901–75 period for 22 European countries, Canada, Chile, the United States, Japan, Turkey, Australia and New Zealand; the Soviet Union is not included. Data are tabulated for 178 causes of death, including war deaths and immigration statistics; the collection, publication, validity, and uses of these statistics are discussed. Indexed by cause of death. HB1321.A43

Annuaire de statistique internationale des grandes villes. International statistical yearbook of large towns. v.1–6, 1961–72. La Haye, 1961–72. Biennial. **CG49**

Issued by the Permanent Office of the International Statistical Institute and the International Union of Local Authorities.

Brings up-to-date the various types of information appearing in separate volumes of the *Statistique internationale des grandes villes* (below). HA42.A55

Statistique internationale des grandes villes. 1927–34. La Haye, Van Stockum, 1927–40. v.1–3. **CG50**

Title varies.

——— Sér. A–E. The Hague, [International Statistical Institute, Committee on Statistics of Large Towns], 1954–65.

Title also in English: *International statistics of large towns.*

A series of volumes as follows: A1, Statistiques démographiques des grandes villes, 1946/51. 1954; A2, Statistiques démographiques des grandes villes, 1946/53. 1957; A3, Statistiques démographiques des grandes villes, 1952/57. 1963; A4, Comments. Including a social economic classification, 1960. 1965; B1, Statistique du logement et de la construction, 1946/53. 1956; B2, Statistique du logement; analyse et tableaux supplémentaires. 1960; C1, Données économiques des grandes villes, 1950/54. 1958; D1, Services publics et transports dans les grandes villes, 1950 et 1955. 1959; E1, Statistique culturelle et des sports, 1951/57. 1961.

Annuaire international de statistique. La Haye, Institut International de Statistique, Office Permanent, 1916–21. 8v. maps.   **CG51**

Contents: (1) État de la population (Europe), 1916; (2) Mouvement de la population (Europe), 1917; (3) État de la population (Amérique), 1919; (4) Mouvement de la population (Amérique), 1920; (5) État de la population (Afrique, Asie, Océanie), 1921; (6) Salaires et durée du travail, conventions, collectives, chômage, placement, syndicats ouvriers et patronaux, grèves et lock-outs; (7) Enseignement primaire, agriculture, postes, télégraphie et téléphonie, sociétés anonymes, coopératives, habitations, indices des prix de gros; (8) Finances d'états, production, cours des changes. No more published. v.1–5 continued by: HA42.A6

Institut International de Statistique. Office Permanent. Aperçu de la démographie des divers pays du monde, 1922–36. La Haye, Van Stockum, 1923–39. v.1–[6].   **CG51a**

v.6, publ. 1939, covers 1929–36.
Contents: (1) État de la population; (2) Mouvement de la population.

Demographic yearbook; Annuaire démographique, 1948– . N.Y., 1949– . Annual.   **CG52**

Prep. by the Statistical Office of the United Nations in collaboration with the Dept. of Economic and Social Affairs.
A compendium of international demographic data including official statistics from almost 250 geographic areas of the world. Covers population (distribution, characteristics, etc.), natality, mortality, marriage and divorce. Cumulative subject index.
The 1978 *Yearbook* is presented in two volumes: the basic yearbook presents the general annual tables on basic demographic statistics, size distribution, natality, mortality, nuptuality and divorce; the second volume or special issue is a historical supplement presenting time series from 1948 to 1978 on population size, age, sex and urban/rural residence, natality, mortality, and nuptuality. (Similar information from 1936 to 1947 was presented in the 1948 yearbook.)   HA17.D45

Handbook of economic statistics, 1975– . Wash., Nat. Foreign Assessment Ctr., 1975– . Annual. (*Its* Research aid)   **CG53**

Provides statistics for selected non-communist countries and all the communist countries on national accounts, foreign trade, foreign aid, energy, minerals and metals, agriculture, transportation, manufacturing, construction, communication, etc. Tables arranged by topic, with subject index.   HA155.U54a

Keyfitz, Nathan and **Flieger, Wilhelm.** World population: an analysis of vital data. Chicago, Univ. of Chicago Pr., [1968]. 672p.   **CG54**

Basic population data and vital statistics have been analyzed by computer techniques to produce a series of tables (some of them highly technical) useful for comparative demographic research. The basic data were derived from official national publications or from the United Nations *Demographic yearbook.* Tabular summary of contents, but no index.   HB881.K48

Kurian, George Thomas. The new book of world rankings. Rev. ed. N.Y., Facts on File, [1984]. 490p.   **CG55**

1st ed. (1979) had title: *The book of world rankings.*
"Designed as an international scorecard that compares and ranks over 190 nations of the world according to their performance in [343] areas."—*Pref.* 32 rankings have been weeded from the first ed.

and 49 added here. Also provides brief country profiles. Sources are indicated for most tables. Indexed.   HA155.K87

Mueller, Bernard. A statistical handbook of the North Atlantic area. Aperçu statistique de la région Atlantique-Nord. N.Y., Twentieth Century Fund, 1965. 239p.   **CG56**

Introductory matter in English and French.
Provides statistical tables and explanatory notes on population, labor force, agriculture, foreign trade, etc., of the North Atlantic nations. The base year is 1962. No index.   HA1107.M8

Mulhall, Michael George. Dictionary of statistics. 4th ed. rev. London, Routledge, 1899. 853p. (Repr.: Detroit, Gale, 1969)   **CG57**

Pt.1, Statistics from the time of Emperor Diocletian to 1890, arranged alphabetically. Pt.2, 1890–98; List of books of reference; Index to pts.1–2. Does not give authorities for statistics included.
Supplemented by: HA17.M8

Webb, Augustus Duncan. New dictionary of statistics. London, Routledge; N.Y., Dutton, 1911. 682p. (Repr.: Detroit, Gale, 1974)   **CG58**

A supplement, for 1899–1909, to Mulhall's *Dictionary of statistics* (above). Arranged on the same general plan as Mulhall, but superior to that work in that authorities for all statistics are given.   HA17.W38

Preston, Samuel H., Keyfitz, Nathan and **Schoen, Robert.** Causes of death: life tables for national populations. N.Y., London, Seminar Pr., 1972. 787p. tables.   **CG59**

Offers "data on mortality from recorded causes of death in 180 populations, with detail provided on age and sex."—*Pref.*   HB1321.P7

Showers, Victor. World facts and figures. N.Y., Wiley, [1979]. 757p. il., tables.   **CG60**

Subtitle: A unique, authoritative collection of comparative information about cities, countries, and geographic features of the world.
A revised and enlarged edition of the author's *The world in figures,* published 1973.
Comparative tables are presented in six main sections: (1) The physical base (largest seas and islands, longest rivers, highest mountains, etc.); (2) Country comparisons; (3) City comparisons; (4) Outstanding works of man (highest buildings, longest bridges, etc.); (5) Country gazetteer, by continent; (6) City gazetteer, by continent and country. Selected bibliography, p.679–88. Indexed.   G109.S52

Sovet ekonomicheskoi vzaimopomoshchi. Sekretariat. Statistical yearbook of member states of the Council for Mutual Economic Assistance, 1976–80. London, IPC Industrial Pr., [1977–81]. Annual.   **CG61**

A translation of the Council's *Statisticheskii ezhegodnik stranchlenov.*
Covers Bulgaria, Cuba, Czechoslovakia, the German Democratic Republic, Hungary, Mongolia, Poland, Romania, and the Soviet Union. Includes figures for 1960, 1965, 1970–75, etc. on area and population, cultural activities, public health and social security, and aspects of the national economy.   HA1107.S65a

Statesman's year-book; statistical and historical annual of the states of the world, 1864– . London, N.Y., Macmillan, 1864– . v.1– . Annual.   **CG62**

Not an almanac of miscellaneous statistics, but a concise and reliable manual of descriptive and statistical information about the governments of the world. Contents vary somewhat but usually cover: (1) British Commonwealth; (2) United States; (3) Other countries, arranged alphabetically. Recent issues have included a section on international organizations. For each country gives: information about its ruler, constitution and government, area, population, religion, social welfare, instruction, justice and crime, state finance, defense, production and industry, agriculture, commerce, navigation, communications, banking and credit, money, weights and measures, diplomatic representatives, etc. A valuable feature is the selected bibliography of statistical and other books of reference given for each country.

The most useful of all the general yearbooks; indispensable in any type of library. JA51.S7

Statistical Office of the European Communities. ACP: statistical yearbook. ACP: annuaire statistique, 1970/76– . Luxembourg-Kirchberg, 1977 [i.e., 1978]– . **CG63**

On cover: Eurostat.

In English and French.

Presents a selection of the main demographic, economic, and social indicators relating to those 52 countries which are signatories to the Lomé Convention (called the ACP countries); a smaller section provides data on similar topics for all developing countries (ACP and others). HA1955.A13

Statistical year-book of the League of Nations, 1926–1942/44. Geneva, 1927–45. Annual. (Publications of the League of Nations. II, Economic and financial) **CG64**

For continuation see the *Statistical yearbook* of the United Nations (below).

Title varies. 1935–1942/44 in French and English.

Annual survey of commerce, finance, and industry in the various countries of the world. Particularly useful for comparative purposes.

United Nations. Statistical Office. Statistical yearbook; Annuaire statistique, 1948– . N.Y., 1949– . v.1– . Annual. **CG65**

A summary of international statistics to continue the *Statistical year-book of the League of Nations* (above). Covers population, agriculture, mining, manufacturing, finance, trade, social statistics, education, etc., of the various countries of the world, the tables usually covering a number of years. References are given to sources.

A "World summary" was introduced beginning with v.15 (1963), summarizing tables appearing in various chapters.

Supplemented by: HA12.5.U63

———— Supplement to the Statistical yearbook and the Monthly bulletin of statistics; methodology and definitions. Issue 2, 1972. N.Y., United Nations, 1974. 424p. **CG65a**

"1st issue" 1967.

"The descriptive notes given in the *Supplement* relate to the tables published in the 1972 edition of the *Statistical Yearbook* and the March-June 1973 issues of the *Monthly Bulletin of Statistics*. New series and major revisions introduced in the *Bulletin* after June, 1973, are described in annex IV of each issue of the *Bulletin*."—*Introd.* HA36.U415

———— Statistical pocketbook. Ed. 1– . N.Y., United Nations, 1976– . Annual. (*Its* Statistical papers, ser. V, no.1–) **CG66**

Pt.1 provides basic statistical information (area, population density and growth rate, national accounts, education, etc.) for each member country of the United Nations. Pt.2 presents demographic, economic, and social statistics by subject, for the world as a whole, selected regions, and major countries.

The world in figures. [Comp. by] The Economist. [4th ed. London, The Economist, 1981] 294p. maps. **CG67**

Earlier editions appeared in 1976, 1978, and 1981.

In two parts: (1) general world section which ranks countries according to various subject headings and indicators; (2) a section on regions and countries which provides national data on geography, population, resources, production, finance, and trade. HA155.W66

World tables, 3d. ed. Baltimore, Publ. for the World Bank [by] Johns Hopkins Univ. Pr., [1984]. 2v. **CG68**

1st ed. publ. under title: *World tables 1976.*

Presents historical time series for individual countries in absolute numbers for the basic economic variables—population, national accounts, prices, balance of payments, external public debt, foreign trade indexes, and central government finance—as well as economic and social indicators in a form suitable for cross-country analysis

and comparison. Time series period has been extended from 1950 through 1981. HC59.W669

Guides and bibliographies

Harvey, Joan M. Sources of statistics. 2d ed., rev. and enl. [London], Linnet Books & Clive Bingley, [1971]. 126p. **CG69**

1st ed. 1969.

Attempts "to name and describe the main statistical publications of the United Kingdom, . . . some of the more important United States publications and those of the various international organisations."—*Introd.* Each chapter is essentially a bibliographic essay on statistical publications relating to population, social problems, education, labor, etc. Indexed. Z7554.G7H3

Legeard, Claude. Guide de recherches documentaires en démographie. Paris, Gauthier-Villars, 1966. 321p. **CG70**

Includes considerable historical and methodological information as well as a bibliographical survey of source materials. Emphasis is on France. Indexed. Z7164.D3L4

Population index. v.1– , 1935– . Princeton, N.J., Office of Population Research, Princeton Univ., and the Population Assoc. of America, 1935– . v.1– . Quarterly. **CG71**

For full information see CG27.

A special bibliography, "Governmental and intergovernmental serial publications containing vital or migration statistics," appeared in the Winter 1980 issue (v.46, no.4), p.617–783, a revised and expanded version of the original bibliographies which appeared in the issues of Oct. 1977 (v.43, no.4) and Jan. 1979 (v.45, no.1).

Statistics sources. Ed. by Paul Wasserman and Jacqueline O'Brien. 9th ed. Detroit, Gale, [1984]. 2v. **CG72**

Subtitle: A subject guide to data on industrial, business, social, educational, financial, and other topics for the United States and internationally.

1st ed. 1962.

Attempts to bring together "under specific subject headings information to guide its user to sources of numeric data about the United States and foreign countries."—*Pref.* The alphabetical subject approach places citations to sources for United States statistics directly under the topical heading, whereas sources for other countries are generally entered under the name of the country, with a topical subdivision. Z7551.S84

U.S. Library of Congress. Census Library Project. Statistical bulletins; an annotated bibliography of the general statistical bulletins of major political subdivisions of the world, prep. by Phyllis G. Carter. Wash., 1954. 93p. (Repr.: Westport, Conn., Greenwood Pr., 1978) **CG73**

At head of title: U.S. Library of Congress. Reference Dept.; U.S. Dept. of Commerce. Bureau of the Census.

Lists "periodicals issued by an official agency more frequently than annually," covering statistics in several subject fields. Arranged by continent and then by country. Indicates beginning date, frequency, categories of statistical data, holdings in Washington libraries, etc. Z7552.U64

———— Statistical yearbooks; an annotated bibliography of the general statistical yearbooks of major political subdivisions of the world. Prep. by Phyllis G. Carter . . . Wash., 1953. 123p. (Repr.: Westport, Conn., Greenwood Pr., 1978) **CG74**

At head of title: U.S. Library of Congress. Reference Dept.; U.S. Dept. of Commerce. Bureau of the Census.

Arranged by continents and then alphabetically by country. Gives full bibliographical data, including dates of first and most recent issues, types of statistics covered, frequency, etc. Z7552.U65

United Nations. Statistical Office. Directory of international statistics, [1973–]. N.Y., United Nations, 1975– . (*Its* Statistical papers, ser. M, no.56, etc.) **CG75**

Supersedes the Office's *A list of statistical series collected by international organizations* (1951, rev. 1955) and its *Directory of international standards for statistics* (1945, rev. 1960).

In two parts: pt.1 outlines the organization, statistical responsibilities, and statistical publications of the United Nations, its specialized agencies, and selected organizations outside the U.N. system, and provides a classed list of the statistical series published by the U.N. system, detailing issuing agency, source, frequency, and whether the series is in machine readable form; pt.2 is an inventory of databases and their organization in the system. A revision was published 1982.

Indexes

Index to international statistics; a guide to the statistical publications of international intergovernmental organizations. v.1, no.1– , Jan. 1983– . Wash., Congressional Information Service, 1983– . Monthly, with quarterly and annual cumulations.   **CG76**

"IIS is intended to be a master guide and index to current English language statistical publications of the world's major [intergovernmental organizations]. These 80–90 organizations include the United Nations system, the Organization for Economic Cooperation and Development, the European Community, the Organization of American States. . . . "—*User guide.* Similar in format to the publisher's *American statistics index* (CG108) and *Statistical reference index* (CG110), with abstracts arranged by issuing body and indexed by subject, name, geographic area, category (age, commodity, country, company, industry, sex), issuing source, title, and publication number. Both abstracts and indexes are cumulated on a quarterly and annual basis.

The "IIS Microfiche Library" includes about 90% of the titles noted in the *Index;* materials are shipped to subscribers on a monthly basis.   Z7552.I53

Pieper, Frank C. SISCIS: subject index to sources of comparative international statistics. Beckenham, Kent, Eng., CBD Research (distr. by Gale), [1978]. 745p.   **CG77**

A valuable index totalling over 53,000 entries extracted from 358 current sources, giving international coverage of comparative data. Under each subject, detailed descriptions of data available and territories for which the information is given is keyed to a title code; title codes are interpreted in a list at the end of the book; there is also an alphabetical list of titles indexed. Numerous cross references. Appendixes provide similar information for: (1) exports by product and destination; (2) imports by product and source; (3) index numbers; (4) global statistics.   Z7551.P54

The Americas

América en cifras. 1960–77. Wash., Pan Amer. Union, 1961–78. Irregular.   **CG78**

Early editions had introduction, explanatory notes, and preface in English and Spanish; 6th ed. (1970) and 7th ed. (1972) in Spanish only.

Provides basic statistical information on the American nations; early editions in 8 to 10 parts, with supplement; recent editions in 4 to 5 parts. Supplies statistics in the areas of demography, housing, agriculture, forestry, fishing, industrial production, transport, tourism, trade, finance, prices, wages, consumption, labor, politics, public administration, social and cultural affairs. Supplements contain: (1) tables of contents of all parts; (2) subject index; and (3) a general bibliography.

Mitchell, Brian R. International historical statistics, the Americas and Australasia. Detroit, Gale, [1983]. 949p.   **CG79**

A companion to the author's *European historical statistics* (CG201) and *International historical statistics, Africa and Asia* (CG118). Presents comparative statistics for 26 North, Central, and South American countries, as well as for Australia and New Zea-

land, mostly from the mid-nineteenth century to the early 1970s. Tables are grouped in 11 broad subject areas; sources are noted.   HA175.M55

Organization of American States. General Secretariat. Statistical bulletin of the OAS. v.1, no.1– , Jan. 1979– . Wash., The Organization, 1979– . Monthly.   **CG80**

In three parts: (1) analytical article: (2) regional statistical tables; (3) country tables of selected economic indicators.

South American handbook, 1924– ; a yearbook and guide to the countries and resources of South and Central America, Mexico and West Indies. London, Trade and Travel Publs., 1924– . maps. Annual.   **CG81**

Continues the *Anglo-South American handbook,* 1921–22. Title and publisher vary. Now issued without subtitle.

A very useful handbook giving travel and gazetteer information about each country; also offers information on natural resources, government, communications, and transportation, etc.
      F1401.S71

Bibliography

Harvey, Joan M. Statistics America: sources for social, economic and market research (North, Central & South America). Ed.2, rev. and enl. Beckenham, Kent, Eng., CBD Research, [1980]. 385p.   **CG82**

For each country, gives description of central statistical office, other major organizations publishing statistics, principal libraries of statistical material, libraries and information services abroad, bibliographies of statistics, and descriptions of major statistical publications arranged in the following groups: general, production, external trade, internal distribution, population, and standard of living. Title, organization, and subject indexes.   Z7554.A5H37

Inter American Statistical Institute. Bibliography of selected statistical sources of the American nations. Bibliografía de fuentes estadísticas escogidas de las naciones americanas. Wash., 1947. 689p. (Repr.: Detroit, Blaine-Ethridge Books, 1974)   **CG83**

Subtitle: A guide to the principal statistical materials of the 22 American nations, including data, analyses, methodology, and laws and organization of statistical agencies.

In English and Spanish.

A comprehensive, classified bibliography with annotations. Detailed alphabetical index and a classified index. Gives full information about the statistical publications of each country, including censuses, yearbooks, current serials, and works in special subjects, e.g., economics, labor, etc. Also includes a section on general statistical works.

Supplemented by quarterly bibliography in *Estadística; journal of the Inter American Statistical Institute,* v.6– , 1948– .
      Z7554.S75I4

U.S. Library of Congress. Census Library Project. General censuses and vital statistics in the Americas; prep. under the supervision of Irene B. Taeuber. Wash., Govt. Prt. Off., 1943. 151p. (Repr.: Detroit, Blaine-Ethridge Books, 1974)   **CG84**

Subtitle: An annotated bibliography of the historical censuses and current vital statistics of the 21 American republics, the American sections of the British Commonwealth of Nations, the American colonies of Denmark, France, and the Netherlands, and the American territories and possessions of the United States.
      Z7553.C3U5

United States

American year book; a record of events and progress, 1910–19, 1925–50. N.Y., Nelson, 1911–50. v.1–36.   **CG85**

Publisher varies. Ceased publication.

Long, signed articles, by specialists, give good narrative accounts

—including bibliographies and statistics—of the events of the year, covering national and international politics, American government, economics and business, social conditions, science, humanities, etc., with a chronology and a necrology.   E171.A585

Andriot, John L. Population abstract of the United States. [Enl. and rev. ed.] McLean, Va., Andriot Associates, [1983]. 2v. maps.   **CG86**

Produced as a companion volume to the *Township atlas of the United States* (CL341) to provide all available population totals for states, counties, and cities which had a 1980 population of 10,000 or more. "Each state section contains a brief history of the formation of the state; a map and index showing names and locations of counties as of 1980; historical population totals [including urban-rural distribution] for the state, counties, and cities; and the 1980 population for minor civil divisions."—*Foreword.* Indexes and maps to counties and smaller areas are in the *Township atlas.*

Bogue, Donald J. The population of the United States . . . with a special chapter on fertility by Wilson H. Grabill. Glencoe, Ill., Free Pr., [1959]. 873p. (Studies in population distribution, no.14)   **CG87**

Extensive tables, diagrams, and text on United States population: growth, distribution, age, sex, mortality, fertility, economics, etc. Includes estimates for 1960 and later.   HB3505.B62

———— The population of the United States: historical trends and future projections. N.Y., Free Pr., [1985]. 728p. il.   **CG88**

" . . . this volume is completely new and not a revision [of the 1959 volume]. The earlier volume will still be useful to anyone who needs more detailed data for the years preceding and immediately following World War II. The present book places greatest analytical effort on the years since 1960, and hence can be regarded as a sequel to the first."—*Pref.* Includes census data available as of July 1, 1984. Provides some comparative international statistics, as well as future estimates. Bibliographies.   HB3505.B63

Marlin, John Tepper and **Avery, James S.** The book of American city rankings. N.Y., Facts on File, [1983]. 369p.   **CG89**

Contains 267 thematic tables with information on the 100 largest cities in the United States; sources are indicated. The second part of the book summarizes selected rankings for each city. Indexed.   HT123.M2984

The new book of American rankings. FYI Information Services. N.Y., Facts on File, 1984. 312p.   **CG90**

Rev. ed. of *The book of American rankings* (1979) by C. S. Judge. Similar in form and intent to G. T. Kurian's *New book of world rankings* (CG55), this volume is designed as "a compendium, or scorecard, comparing the 50 states and major cities in over 300 key areas."—*Introd.* Each table includes: brief introduction; description of table, with date, source, and median and average data for the nation. The second section of the book presents state profiles, describing how each state stands in important rankings and listing its position in 20 of the most significant ones. Bibliography; index.   HA214.N49

Social indicators 1- , 1976- ; selected data on social conditions and trends in the United States. [Wash.], U.S. Dept. of Commerce, Office of Federal Statistical Policy and Standards, and Bureau of the Census, 1977- . Triennial.   **CG91**

An earlier ed. appeared in 1973.
Presents maps, charts, and tables illustrating statistical measures of well-being and public perception in eleven major social areas, such as population, the family, social security and welfare, health and nutrition, public safety, etc. Each chapter on these major areas contains: (1) introductory text and charts; (2) statistical tables, with source references; and (3) technical notes and definitions, with a brief bibliography. International comparisons are presented for each social area. "For lengthier and more authoritative interpretations, the reader is advised to consult the following publication: The American Academy of Political and Social Sciences, "America in the Seventies: some social indicators," *The Annals,* volume 435 (January 1978). The entire issue is devoted to a number of articles based on the chapters of *Social Indicators, 1976.*"—*Introd.*   HN52.S6

State and metropolitan area databook, 1979- . Wash., Govt. Prt. Off., 1980- . v.1- . maps, charts.   **CG92**

A *Statistical abstract* supplement (*see* CG94).
In three main parts: (1) statistical data for each state, arranged by census geographic division and region, and for the United States as a whole (2,008 statistical items are presented for each state, including data on population and vital statistics, health, education, employment, income, government, social welfare, crime, construction, housing, banking, elections, energy, transportation, natural resources, trade and services); (2) similar data for metropolitan areas arranged alphabetically; (3) data for metropolitan areas ranked by population-size categories. Five appendixes provide information on standard metropolitan statistical areas ranked by population size, effects of population change, estimates of states and congressional districts population and voting age population, etc. Subject index.   HA202.S84

U/S: a statistical portrait of the American people. Ed. by Andrew Hacker. N.Y., Viking, 1983. 500p.   **CG93**

Offers statistical tables with a short textual introduction for each. Based on "official figures, compiled by various government agencies" *(Pref.),* but exact sources of the tables are not noted.   HA214.U15

U.S. Bureau of the Census. Statistical abstract of the United States, 1878- . Wash., Govt. Prt. Off., 1879- . v.1- . Annual.   **CG94**

v.1–25, 1878–1902, prep. by the Bureau of Statistics (Treasury Dept.); v.26–34, 1903–11, by the Bureau of Statistics (Dept. of Commerce and Labor); 1912–37, by the Bureau of Foreign and Domestic Commerce.
A single-volume work presenting quantitative summary statistics on the political, social, and economic organization of the United States. Indispensable in any library; it serves not only as a first source for statistics of national importance but also as a guide to further information, as references are given to the sources of all tables.
Statistics given in the tables cover a period of several years, usually about 15 or 20; some tables run back to 1789 or 1800.   HA202

———— County and city data book, 1949- . Wash., Govt. Prt. Off., 1952- . (Irregular)   **CG95**

A *Statistical abstract supplement* which combines its *Cities supplement,* 1940, and its *County data book,* 1947.
Issued for 1949, 1952, 1956, 1962, 1967, 1972, 1977, 1983.
Presents the latest available census figures for each county, and for the larger cities in the United States. Also has summary figures for states, geographical regions, urbanized areas, standard metropolitan areas, and unincorporated places.   HA202.A36

———— City government finances, 1909- . Wash., Govt. Prt. Off., 1913- . Annual.   **CG96**

Title varies: 1909–41, *Financial statistics of cities*; 1942–64, *City finances.*
Includes summary of city government finances, and compendium of city government finances, with figures for the largest cities in some detail.   HJ9011.A4b

———— State government finances, 1915- . Wash., Govt. Prt. Off., 1916- . Annual.   **CG97**

Title varies: 1915–41, *Financial statistics of states*; 1942–65, *State finances.*
Issues usually include: individual state reports; topical reports (e.g., budgets, expenditures, debt, tax collections, etc.).   HJ275.S7

———— Historical statistics of the United States, colonial times to 1970. Bicentennial ed. Wash., U.S. Dept of Commerce, for sale by Supt. of Docs., 1975. 2v. (House document, 93d Congress, 1st session, no.93–78)   **CG98**

Represents a complete revision of the Bureau's *Historical statistics . . . colonial times to 1957* and its *Continuation to 1962*. Maintains the broad subject arrangement of the previous edition and includes almost all of its time series index which first appeared in *Historical statistics of the United States, 1789 to 1945*; the index indicates which statistics for particular subjects begin in the specified 10- or 20-year time segment.   HA202.B87

Vital statistics of the United States, 1937– . Wash., U.S. Bureau of the Census, 1939– . Annual.   **CG99**

Contains basic data on natality, marriage, divorce, and mortality. Issued in two volumes: v.1, Natality characteristics for each state, metropolitan area and other geographic areas of the United States, Puerto Rico and the Virgin Islands; v.2, in 2 pts., Mortality data for the United States, Puerto Rico and Virgin Islands.

Supersedes *Birth, stillbirth and infant mortality statistics* and *Mortality statistics* of the U.S. Bureau of the Census.

Complemented by: HA203.A22

U.S. National Vital Statistics Division. Special reports. Wash., 1936–65. v.1–54 (some nos. issued in rev. eds.)

Individual volumes include selected studies, state or national summaries, life tables, etc.

Guides and bibliography

Guide to U.S. government statistics, by John L. Andriot. 4th ed. McLean, Va., Documents Index, [1973]. 431p.   **CG100**

1st ed. 1956.

Title varies: 1956–57, *U.S. government statistics*.

Arranged by departments and agencies, listing the various publications containing statistical data according to Superintendent of Documents classification number. Information is given on frequency, availability, price, and ordering procedure. Annotations are pertinent and concise. Title and subject indexes.

The booklet *Statistical services of the United States government* issued by the U.S. Bureau of the Budget in 1968 is reprinted as p.1–44 of the 4th ed. of the *Guide*.   Z7554.U5G8

U.S. Bureau of the Census. Bureau of the Census catalog. Wash., Govt. Prt. Off., 1947– . Frequency varies; annual beginning 1980.   **CG101**

Title varies: *Census publications; catalog and subject guide,* 1946–51; *Catalog of United States census publications,* 1952–62; *Bureau of the Census catalog of publications,* 1963.

Provides abstracts and ordering information for Bureau publications, data files, and microfiche. New products are listed in the *Monthly product announcement*; the *Directory of data files* describes the Bureau summary statistics, microdata, geographic reference data, and software, and is updated periodically.

The *Census catalog and guide, 1985* continues the *Bureau of the Census catalog,* cumulates the 1980–84 volumes, and covers all reports and maps "in print," microfiche titles, and available data files.

A cumulative publication, *Bureau of the Census catalog of publications: 1790–1972* (Wash., 1974. 320p., 591p.) is based primarily on the annual issues for the period 1946–72 together with a reprint of the 1790–1945 catalog prepared by Henry J. Dubester (CG103); each of the two sections in that volume has its own index.   Z7554.U5U32

——— Guide to recurrent and special governmental statistics. Wash., Govt. Prt. Off., 1976. 205p. (State and local government special studies, no.78)   **CG102**

First published 1972.

The *Guide* "summarizes the tabular presentations produced as part of the Census Bureau's program of State and local government statistics. It is divided into two sections, one for recurrent reports and the other for special studies. Within these sections are chapters referring to the most recent issue of the various reports published in this statistical series. Each chapter is essentially a synthesis of the original report, and contains the title, table of contents, and a sample of every table published in the original report."—*Pref.*   JK2403.A35 no.78

U.S. Library of Congress. Census Library Project. Catalog of United States census publications, 1790–1945, prep. by Henry J. Dubester. Wash., Govt. Prt. Off., 1950. 320p.   **CG103**

Designed both to serve as a "guide to census statistics and to record the historical development of publication patterns."—*Pref.* Annotated. In two sections: pt.1, decennial census publications; pt.2, other publications, arranged by subject, e.g., agriculture, business, industry, religious bodies, etc. The index is to the subjects contained in titles and annotations. Reprinted in the 1790–1972 compilation noted above (CG101*n*).

For brief information largely supersedes earlier bibliographical surveys and indexes, but the following are sometimes useful for more detailed information: U.S. Bureau of Labor Statistics. *The history and growth of the United States census* (Wash., Govt. Prt. Off., 1900. 967p.); U.S. Office of the Census. *A century of population growth from the first census . . . to the twelfth, 1790–1900* (Wash., Govt. Prt. Off., 1909. 303p.); its *Circular of information concerning census publications, 1790–1916* (Jan. 1, 1917. 124p.); its *Topical index of population census reports, 1900–1930* (1934. 76p.); its *Periodic and special reports on population, 1930–1939* (1939. 12p.).

Supplemented by: Z7554.U5U62

——— State censuses; an annotated bibliography of censuses of population taken after the year 1790 by states and territories of the United States; prep. by Henry J. Dubester. Wash., Govt. Prt. Off., 1948. 73p.   **CG104**

Items from this list were reproduced in the *State censuses microfiche collection* (Millwood, N.Y., KTO Microform, 1976).   Z7554.U5U63

U.S. National Archives and Records Service. Federal population censuses, 1790–1890; a catalog of microfilm copies of the schedules. Wash., 1971. 90p. (National Archives pubn. no.71–3)   **CG105**

Previous editions issued by U.S. National Archives.

Positive microfilm copies of the original population schedules may be purchased from the National Archives and Records Service; this is a chronological list, with prices.

The following items are useful complements: HA37.U548

Brewer, Mary Marie. Index to census schedules in printed form; those available and where to obtain them. Huntsville, Ark., Century Enterprises, Genealogical Services, 1969. 63p.   **CG106**

A listing by state and county of early published censuses, with indication of availability and price.   Z7553.C3B7

Research Publications, Inc. Bibliography and reel index: a guide to the microfilm edition of United States decennial census publications, 1790–1970. Woodbridge, Conn., Research Pubns., 1975. 276p.   **CG107**

Serves both as a bibliography of U.S. decennial census publications and a reel index to the microfilm edition thereof. Final reports are taken from the *Catalog of United States census publications, 1790–1945* (CG103) and the *Bureau of the Census catalog of publications, 1946–1972* (CG101) and arranged according to the numbering system used in the *International population census bibliography* (CG16).   Z7554.U5R47

Indexes

American statistics index . . . A comprehensive guide and index to the statistical publications of the U.S. government, 1973– . Wash., Congressional Information Service, 1973– . Annual, with monthly supplements.   **CG108**

Contents: pt.1, Index; pt.2, Abstracts.

The 1974 "Annual and retrospective edition" covered federal government statistical publications in print, as well as significant publications issued since the early 1960s; in the case of serial publications, only the format and contents of the most recent edition were described, with notes characterizing any major changes throughout the years. The 1974 "Annual" supersedes the initial 1973 edition, which was limited to social statistics. Supplementary "Annual" editions cumulate coverage of publications originally provided by the monthly supplements from 1974 to date.

Attempts to list (with full bibliographical description and price) and index all federal government publications "which contain statistical data of probable research significance, whether published periodically, irregularly, or as monographs." Intends to list all relevant publications currently in print, and most publications issued during the ten years prior to 1974.

Indexed by: subjects and names; categories (geographic, economic, demographic, and standard classification systems); titles; agency report numbers. Monthly supplements, also issued in two parts, report changes on publications included in the preceding annual as well as new publications.

The "ASI Microfiche Library" includes almost all publications abstracted and indexed in *American statistics index;* it is available in a variety of purchase possibilities. Z7554.U5A46●

Schulze, Suzanne. Population information in nineteenth century census volumes. [Phoenix, Ariz.], Oryx Pr., 1983. 446p. **CG109**

On a census-by-census basis, provides an index to a wide range of population-related information in the publications resulting from each decennial census, 1790–1890. Includes numerous social and economic categories as well as the expected demographic and vital statistics aspects. Indicates microform availability of the census publications. A tabular subject guide appears on the end papers; a more detailed index would have been useful. Z7164.D3S44

Statistical reference index; a selective guide to American statistical publications from sources other than the U.S. government. v.1, no.1– , Jan. 1980– . Wash., Congressional Information Service, 1980– . Monthly with quarterly cumulative index, and annual cumulation. **CG110**

Frequency varies: bimonthly, 1984– .

Patterned on the publisher's *American statistics index*, this service presents abstracting and indexing of national and state data on business, industry, finance, economic and social conditions, government and politics, the environment, and population, derived from publications other than those of the U.S. federal government. Abstracts are grouped by source of information, e.g., associations, business organizations, commercial publishers, independent research organizations, state governments, and universities. Indexed by subject and name; geographic, economic, and demographic categories; issuing source; and title.

The "SRI Microfiche library" includes almost all publications abstracted and indexed in the *Statistical reference index* and is available from the same publisher on a monthly or annual subscription basis in a variety of purchase possibilities.

Directories

Directory of federal statistical data files, March 1981– . Prep. through the coordination of U.S. Dept. of Commerce, Nat. Technical Information Serv. and the U.S. Dept. of Commerce, Off. of Federal Statistical Policy and Standards. [Wash.], The Dept., [1981]– . Annual. **CG111**

Describes publicly accessible data files. Each abstract provides general description, geographical and chronological coverage, accompanying reference materials, related data files, etc. Organized by agency; indexed by title, subject, and agency/subject.

HA37.U113

Stemmons, John D. The United States census compendium: a directory of census records, tax lists, poll lists, petitions, directories, etc. which can be used as a census. Logan, Utah, Everton Publ., [1973]. 144p. **CG112**

Listing is by state, then by county, with indication of date of census or other type of record and a coded reference to source. Both printed and manuscript sources are considered. While the references to materials appearing in periodicals and special materials will be useful, there is a preponderance of references to National Archives and Records Service sources. The introduction fails to explain fully the source references. Z1250.S83

U.S. Bureau of the Census. Directory of federal statistics for local areas: a guide to sources, 1966–76. [Wash., Govt. Prt. Off.], 1966–78. 2v. **CG113**

An earlier version entitled, *Directory of federal statistics for metropolitan areas* was published 1962 by the Advisory Commission on Intergovernmental Relations. "Provides table-by-table descriptions of statistical reports on areas smaller than States . . . ; to be included, a table must provide statistics on a type of local area for the entire United States."—*p.[v]*. Arranged alphabetically by broad topic (agriculture, banking and finance, commerce and trade, etc.). Within each topic, information is presented in a five-column tabular format covering: subject; data items included; areas to which data apply; frequency; bibliographic source. Appendixes describe sources of unpublished data, give population and rank of SMSAs and of cities of 100,000 or more by rank (1970 and 1975), and list data sources for federal and municipal statistics. Bibliography; subject index.

Supplemented by: HB2175.U54

——— ——— Urban update, 1977–1978. [Wash., Govt. Prt. Off.], Dec. 1979. p.361–490.

Continues the pagination and retains the format of the 1976 volume (above), but focuses on cities, urbanized and metropolitan areas, and some towns and counties. Cumulative index and bibliography include references to the 1976 volume. HA37.U114

——— Directory of federal statistics for states; a guide to sources, 1967. Wash., Govt. Prt. Off., 1967. 372p. **CG114**

A companion to the Bureau's *Directory of federal statistics for local areas* (above). Intended as "a comprehensive finding guide to available [i.e., in-print] published sources of Federal statistics on social, political, and economic subjects."—*Introd.* HA37.U52

——— Directory of non-federal statistics for states and local areas; a guide to sources, 1969. [Wash., Govt. Prt. Off., 1970] 678p. **CG115**

A companion to the *Directory of federal statistics for local areas* and the *Directory of federal statistics for states* (above). "It is intended to direct the user to published sources of non-Federal statistics on social, political, and economic subjects."—*Introd.* HA37.U52

Handbooks

U.S. Office of Management and Budget. Statistical Policy Div. Statistical services of the United States government. Rev. ed. Wash., 1975. 234p. **CG116**

1st ed. 1959.

Describes the statistical system of the federal government, and the methods of collection, tabulation, and presentation of the data. Deals with economic and social statistics, with emphasis on that information which is made available to the public.

Atlases

U.S. Bureau of the Census. Urban atlas; tract data for standard metropolitan statistical areas. [Wash., Govt. Prt. Off., 1974–75] maps. (GE80–no.240 [etc.]) **CG117**

Prep. in cooperation with the Labor Department, Manpower Administration.

Contents: no.240, Allentown, Bethlehem, Easton; no.520, Atlanta; no.720, Baltimore; no.1000, Birmingham; no.1120, Boston; no.1280, Buffalo; no.1600, Chicago; no.1640, Cincinnati; no.1680, Cleveland; no.1920, Dallas; no.2000, Dayton; no.2080, Denver; no.2160, Detroit; no.3120, Greensboro, Winston-Salem, High Point; no. 3360, Houston; no. 3760, Kansas City; no.4480, Los Angeles, Long Beach; no.4920, Memphis; no.5120, Minneapolis, St.

Paul; no.5600, New York; no.5640, Newark; no.5720, Norfolk, Portsmouth; no.5880, Oklahoma City; no.5920, Omaha; no.6160, Philadelphia; no.6280, Pittsburgh; no.6760, Richmond; no. 6840, Rochester; no.7040, St. Louis; no.7280, San Bernardino, Riverside, Ontario; no.7320, San Diego; no.7360, San Francisco, Oakland; no.7400, San Jose; no.8160, Syracuse; no.8280, Tampa, St. Petersburg; no.8400, Toledo.

Provides a graphic presentation of selected census tract statistics for the largest SMSAs existing at the time of the 1970 census of population and housing. Each atlas contains twelve maps illustrating, by census tract, percentages, ratios, or medians for: population density; population under 18 years of age; population over 65 years of age; black population; high school graduates; median family income; interrelationship of family income and educational attainment; blue-collar labor force; median housing value; median contract rent; housing units which are owner occupied; occupied units built during 1960–70.

Africa

Mitchell, Brian R. International historical statistics: Africa and Asia. N.Y., New York Univ. Pr., 1982. 761p.   **CG118**

"Companion vol. to: European historical statistics, 1750–1975 [by] B. R. Mitchell. 2nd rev. ed. 1980 [CG201]."—*verso of t.p.*

Presents comparative statistics for 80 African and Asian countries (including Cyprus and the Near East), derived from official governmental and intergovernmental publications, and supplemented by unofficial sources. Dates of coverage vary, but the majority of tables begin during the first half of the nineteenth century. Topics include climate, population, labor force, agriculture, industry, external trade, transport and communications, finance, prices, education, and national accounts.   HA4675.M55

West Africa annual. 1962– . London, J. Clarke, 1962– . il. Annual.   **CG119**

Imprint varies.

Under each country gives information on the land and the people, history, population, government, constitution, finance, economic programs, education, etc.   DT471.W394

Bibliography

Boston University. African Studies Library. Censuses, development plans, and statistical abstracts: a working list of holdings in the Boston University documents collection. Comp. by Victoria K. Evalds. Boston, African Studies Ctr., Boston Univ., 1982. 49*l*. (Working papers, Boston Univ., African Studies Ctr., no.63)   **CG120**

Arranged in three sections, according to document type as indicated in the title, then by country and date. Lists materials on the national level only.   Z7554.A34B67

France. Institut National de la Statistique et des Études Économiques. Service de Cooperation. Bibliographie démographique 1945–1970. Travaux publiés par l'I.N.S.E.E. (Service de la Coopération), les services de statistique des états africains d'expression française ou de Madagascar, et le Secrétariat d'État aux Affaires Étrangères. Paris, 1972. 83p.   **CG121**

1st edition covering through 1962 published 1963.

Lists demographic works on the following French-African countries: Cameroun, Centrafique, Congo, Côte-d'Ivoire, Dahomey, Gabon, Guinée, Haute-Volta, Madagascar, Mali, Mauritanie, Niger, Sénégal, Tchad, Togo, Algérie, Maroc, Tunisie, Burundi, Zaïre, Rwanda.   Z7165.F8A48

Gregory, Joel W., Cordell, Dennis D. and **Gervais, Raymond.** African historical demography: a multidisciplinary bibliography. [Los Angeles], Crossroads Pr., [1984]. 248p.   **CG122**

Cites 2,550 works on pre-1960 African population—age and sex structure, fertility, marriage, divorce, mortality, morbidity, migra-

tion, and urbanization; excludes official statistical sources. Arranged by geographical region, then broad topic; indexed by personal and geographical names, and detailed subjects.   Z7164.D3G73

Harvey, Joan M. Statistics Africa: sources for social, economic, and market research. 2d ed., rev. and enl. Beckenham, Kent, Eng., CBD Research; [Detroit, Gale, 1978]. 374p.   **CG123**

1st ed. 1970.

A section on Africa as a whole precedes sections on individual countries. Each section contains: (1) information on the central statistical office and other organizations collecting or publishing statistical material; (2) principal libraries inside the country with statistical collections open to the public; (3) libraries and information services in other countries (particularly English-speaking countries) where the country's statistical publications are available; (4) statistical bibliographies; (5) the major statistical publications (grouped as general, production, external trade, internal distribution and service trades, population, social, finance, transport and communications). Indexed by organization, title, and subject.

Z7554.A34H37

Pinfold, John R. African population census reports; a bibliography and checklist. München, K. G. Saur, 1985. 100p.   **CG124**

A listing by country of the major national census publications, mid-nineteenth century to the present, of continental and island African countries; locations are indicated for major British, Belgian, French, German, Swedish, and Dutch libraries.   HA4672.P5

United Nations. Economic Commission for Africa. Library. Annuals received in the UNECA library. Addis Ababa, 1962. 194p. (United Nations [document] E/CN.14/LIB/ser.A/2)   **CG125**

A selected list of serials arranged in three parts: (1) non-governmental annuals; (2) governmental annuals; (3) United Nations and specialized agencies annuals. Includes main entry, subject, and title indexes. The statistical annuals listed are mainly from the African nations. Does not include dates.   JX1977.A2

U.S. Library of Congress. Census Library Project. Population censuses and other official demographic statistics of Africa (not including British Africa); an annotated bibliography, prep. by Henry J. Dubester. Wash., Govt. Prt. Off., 1950. 53p.   **CG126**

Z7554.A34U5

—— Population censuses and other official demographic statistics of British Africa; an annotated bibliography, prep. by Henry J. Dubester. Wash., Govt. Prt. Off., 1950. 78p.   **CG127**

Z7554.A35U5

Albania

Albania. Drejtoria e Statistikës. Anuari statistikor, 1958– . Tiranë, [1958]– . Annual? (1962 last publ.?)   **CG128**

Presents chapters of statistics on climate, geography, population, industry and investment, transportation and communications, education, etc. The same agency also publishes: HA1659.A4A3

Vjetari statistikor i R.P.Sh., 1958– . [Tiranë, Drejtoria e Statistikës, 1958]– . Irregular. il.   **CG129**

In addition to current data, also provides time series from 1938.

Algeria

Annuaire statistique de l'Algérie, 1926– . Alger, République Algerienne Démocratique et Populaire, Ministère de la Planification et de l'Amènagement du Territoire, Direction

des Statistiques et de la Comptabilité Nationale, 1928– .
Annual.   **CG130**

Issuing body varies.
Offers a comprehensive range of statistics, with detailed subject
index.   HA2071.A32

Arab States

See also CJ399.

al-Kitāb al-iḥṣa'ī al-sanawī lil-bilād al- 'Arabīyah, 1976– .
al-'Qāhirah, Majlis al-Waḥdah al-Iqtisadiyah al-'Arabīyah,
al-Amānah al-'Ammah, al-Maktab al-Markazī al-'Ārabī lil-
Iḥṣa', [1976]– . Annual.   **CG131**

Added title page: *Statistical yearbook for Arab countries.*
Comp. by the General Secretariat, Council of Arab Economic
Unity and Arab Central Statistical Bureau.
Provides data on geography, population, agriculture, industry,
economic aggregates, services (health, education, tourism), and the
Palestinians, usually with 5- or 10-year time series.
                                                              HA1950.5.K56

McCarthy, Justin. The Arab world, Turkey, and the Balkans
(1878–1914): a handbook of historical statistics. Boston, G.
K. Hall, [1982]. 309p. maps.   **CG132**

"The statistics in this book are Ottoman, published by the
Ottoman government or drawn from the Ottoman Archives. They
are intended to give a picture of the Ottoman state and people
during the last century of the empire."—*Pref.* Includes tables
relating to climate, population, education, justice, manufacturing,
transportation, etc. Indexed.   HA4556.M35

Statistical yearbook (Arab member States), 1982– . Paris,
Unesco, 1983– . il. Annual.   **CG133**

Title also in French; text in Arabic, English, and French.
Based on data in the *Unesco statistical yearbook* (CB264) for the
Arab member states of the organization. Preliminary tables of
statistics on population, literacy, and educational attainment are
followed by statistics on education, educational expenditure, science and technology, and culture and communication. Main section
arranged by subject, then country; tables of relevant statistics
arranged by country conclude the work.   DS36.88.S82

Bibliography

Cairo. Ma'had al-Takhṭīṭ al-Qawmī. Dalīl al-maṣādir al-
iḥṣā' īyah fī al-bilād al-'Arabīyah. Cairo, al-Ma'had, 1975.
416p.   **CG134**

A country-by-country listing of statistical sources of Arab countries, with subject subdivisions. Western-language sources are included. Indexed.   Z7554.A6A2

**Sirs el Laiyana, Egypt. Arab States Fundamental Education
Centre. Social Science Division.** Statistical sources of the
Arab states; a comprehensive list. Sirs-el-Layyan, Arab
States Training Centre for Education for Community Devel-
opment, 1961. 29p.   **CG135**

"A bibliography of official statistics issued regularly or occasionally by the governments of ten Arab states."—*Pref.*

Argentina

**Argentine Republic. Dirección Nacional de Estadística y
Censos.** Anuario. 1892–1914. Buenos Aires, Compania Sud-
americana de Billetes de Banco, 1892–1914?   **CG136**

—— Anuario estadístico. 1944– . Buenos Aires, 1947– .
Irregular.   **CG136a**

Publication suspended 1958–72; 1973– issued by Instituto Nacional de Estadística y Censos.   HA954.A57

Vázquez-Presedo, Vicente. Estadística históricas argentinas
(comparadas). Buenos Aires, Ediciones Macchi, 1971–76.
2v.   **CG137**

Contents: pt.1, 1875–1914; pt.2, 1914–39.
Offers statistical tables for population, immigration and emigration, production, foreign trade, finance, public services, etc. Detailed table of contents in each volume, but no indexes; bibliography
in pt.1.   HA957.V39

Asia

See also CG118.

Asia yearbook, 1963– . Hong Kong, Far Eastern Economic
Review, Ltd., 1963– . il. Annual.   **CG138**

Title varies: 1960–62, *Yearbook;* 1963–72, *Far Eastern Economic
Review yearbook.*
Introductory topical essays with statistics deal with the region as a
whole; economic aspects (population, fishing, development banks,
energy, investment, etc.) are emphasized. The country profiles
which follow deal with political/social affairs, foreign relations, the
economy and the infrastructure. There is a summary of the year's
events for each country.   HC411.F19

Statistical yearbook for Asia and the Pacific, 1968– . [Bang-
kok], Economic and Social Commission for Asia and the
Pacific, United Nations, 1969– . Annual.   **CG139**

Title varies: 1968–72, *Statistical yearbook for Asia and the Far
East.*
In English and French.
Detailed country tables include Afghanistan and Iran, and there
are comparative statistical indicator tables for the region and the
world. An appendix lists the principal source publications and
issuing agencies for each country. Updated by *Quarterly bulletin for
Asia and the Pacific.*   JX1977.A2

Bibliography

Harvey, Joan M. Statistics Asia & Australasia: sources for
social, economic and market research. 2d ed. Beckenham,
Kent, Eng., CBD Research, [1983]. 440p.   **CG140**

Describes the main statistical information sources for each country, including: directory information on the central statistical office
and other statistics-gathering organizations; principal libraries with
statistical sources open to the public; libraries and information
services in other countries (usually English-speaking) where such
materials are available; current statistical bibliographies; and major
statistical publications. Indexes of titles, organizations and subjects.
                                                               HA37.A775H37

Australia

See also CG140.

Year book, Australia, 1908– . Canberra, Australian Bureau
of Statistics, 1908– . v.1– . maps. Annual since v.41, 1955.
                                                                CG141

Title varies.
The 1908 volume includes statistics for the 1901–1907 period,
together with some figures for the period 1781–1900.
Includes chapters on physical geography and climate, general
government, defense, population, vital statistics, labor, overseas
transactions, transport and communication, public health, public
finance, education, industry, etc.
Kept to date by the Bureau's *Digest of current economic statistics*
(monthly), *Monthly review of business statistics,* and *Quarterly
summary of Australian statistics.* In addition, the individual Australian states publish statistical annuals.   HA3001.B5

Bibliography

Checklist of nineteenth century Australian colonial statistical sources: censuses, blue books, and statistical registers. Ed. by Ann E. Miller. [Kensington, N.S.W.], History Project, Inc., [1982]. 69p. (Historical bibliography monograph, no.7)   **CG142**

A list of individual parts of the colonial censuses, as well as musters, and statistical registers included in the British Parliamentary papers. Arranged by colony or state, then by format.

Z7554.A77C48

Finlayson, Jennifer Ann S. Historical statistics of Australia; a select list of official sources. Canberra, Dept. of Economic History, Research School of Social Sciences, Australian National Univ., 1970. 55p.   **CG143**

A listing of official serial publications which publish statistical data.   Z7554.A8F54

Hagger, A. J. A guide to Australian economic and social statistics. Sydney [etc.], Pergamon, [1983]. 116p. (Guides to Australian information sources)   **CG144**

A guide and bibliography to current statistical publications of the Australian Bureau of Statistics; should be used with that agency's *Catalogue of publications* for complete bibliographic information. The series is designed to extend Borchardt's *Australian bibliography* (AA39).

Austria

Austria. Statistisches Zentralamt. Statistisches Handbuch für die Republik Österreich. Wien, 1950– . 1. Jahrg., n.F., 1950– . Annual.   **CG145**

Continues *Statistisches Jahrbuch für Österreich* (Jahrg. 1–18, 1920–38), v.1–17 of which were published as *Statistisches Handbuch* by the Bundesamt für Österreich, and v.18 (1938) as *Statistisches Jahrbuch für Österreich* by the Statistisches Landesamt after the annexation of Austria by Germany.

Particularly strong in economic, commercial, and industrial statistics. Includes an international section.   HA1171.C3

Österreichisches Jahrbuch, 1919– , hrsg. vom Bundespressedienst. Wien, Staatsdruckerei, 1920– . v.1– . Annual.   **CG146**

Suspended 1937–44. Publisher varies.

A comprehensive summary of the political, economic, social, and cultural life, including statistical data.   HC261.O8

Bibliographie zur Bevölkerungsforschung in Österreich, 1945–1978. Von Karl Husa [et al.]. Mit einem Beitrag zur Entwicklung der Bevölkerungsforschung in Österreich nach dem Zweiten Weltkrieg von Karl Husa und Christian Vielhaber. Wien, A. Schendl, 1980. 167p. il., maps. (Abhandlungen zur Humangeographie, Bd.3)   **CG147**

A classed bibliography of 1,178 items; international in scope, although the great majority are in German. Papers and dissertations are included. Arranged by province, then by subject (e.g., minorities, refugees, guest workers, etc.). Author and subject indexes.

Bahamas

Bahamas. Dept. of Statistics. Statistical abstract, 1969– . Nassau, [1969?]– . il. Annual.   **CG148**

Offers very detailed statistics on a wide range of socioeconomic topics, usually with a ten-year time series.   HA861.A3

Bangladesh

Statistical yearbook of Bangladesh, 1963– . Dacca, Bangladesh Bureau of Statistics, Statistics Div., Ministry of Planning, Govt. of the People's Republic of Bangladesh, [1963]– . Annual.   **CG149**

Title and issuing body vary.

A detailed presentation of statistics in terms of land and geography, social and economic conditions. A more abbreviated presentation is available in the *Statistical pocket book of Bangladesh,* published by the same agency since 1977.   HA4590.6.A26

Belgium

Annuaire statistique de la Belgique, 1870– . Bruxelles, Institut National de Statistique, 1870– . v.1– . maps. Annual.   **CG150**

Issuing body and title vary slightly: v.42–80, 1912–59, called *Annuaire statistique de la Belgique et du Congo belge.*

Detailed statistics on a wide range of topics, most tables offering comparative figures for a number of years. Fully indexed.

HA1393.A34

Benin

Annuaire statistique (Institut National de la Statistique et de l'Analyse Économique), 1975– . Cotonou, Institut National de la Statistique et de l'Analyse Économique, 1974– . Annual.   **CG151**

Title varies: 1975–79, *Annuaire statistique de la République populaire du Bénin.* Preceded by *Annuaire statistique du Dahomey,* 1965–74.

Offers detailed statistics on various geographical, demographic, economic, medical, and cultural aspects of the country.

HA2111.D34A54

Bolivia

Bolivia en cifras, 1972– . [La Paz], Instituto Nacional de Estadística, [1973–]. il., maps. Annual.   **CG152**

A statistical compendium of general data and the principal statistical series on demography, economics, and social conditions. No index or detailed list of tables; no bibliographical sources cited.   HA965.B65

Resumen estadístico (Instituto Nacional de Estadística, Bolivia). La Paz, Instituto, [1980]– . il. Annual.   **CG153**

The Instituto is an agency of Bolivia's Ministerio de Planeamiento y Coordinación which is the source for most of the tables.

Offers figures on population, education, housing, health, employment, prices, trade, national accounts, etc.   HA961.R47

Botswana

Statistical abstract (Botswana. Central Statistics Office), 1966– . Gaberones, 1966– . Annual.   **CG154**

Prep. by Central Statistics Office, Ministry of Development Planning.

In addition to the usual range of statistical tables, a list of available statistical publications is included in an appendix.

A useful complementary handbook, with text and tables on geography, government, defense, the economy, health, education, transportation, housing, and employment, is: HA1977.B6A3

Botswana (Botswana. Dept. of Information and Broadcasting. Publications Section), 1982– . [Gaberones, 1982?]– . Annual? **CG155**

Subtitle: An official handbook.

Brazil

Anuário estatístico do Brasil. v.32– , 1971– . Rio de Janeiro, Instituto Brasileiro de Estatística, 1971– . Annual. **CG156**

Continues the publication of the same title issued by the Instituto Brasileiro de Geografia e Estatística, 1908/12–70, and assumes its numbering.

Offers statistical tables (usually with comparative figures for recent years) on physical characteristics, geography, economics, social and cultural conditions, and political and administrative affairs. HA971.A32

Brazil. Ministério das Relaçoes Exteriores. Brasil. Ed.1– , 1932– . Brasilia, 1932– . il., maps. Irregular. **CG157**

In Portuguese; some numbers also in English or Spanish.

Offers general information and statistics on area, demography, administration, and the economic, social, and cultural affairs of Brazil. Subject index. HC186.A332

Brazil. Conselho Nacional de Estatística. Bibliografia geográfico-estatística brasileira. Rio de Janeiro, 1956. v.1. **CG158**

Contents: v.1, 1936/1950. No more published?

A listing of the publications of the Brazilian Institute of Geography and Statistics from 1936 through 1950, arranged by subject. Devoted mainly to economic and geographical aspects of Latin America, but the area covered includes various countries of the world. Z1686.A5

Bulgaria

Statisticheski godishnik na Narodna Republika Bulgariia. 1947/48– . Sofia, 1948?– . Annual since 1960. **CG159**

Issued by Tsentralno Statistichesko Upravlenie, Bulgaria, 1960–68; by Durzhavno Upravlenie za Informatsiia, 1969– .

Supersedes *Statisticheski godishnik na Tsarstvo Bulgariia; Annuaire statistique de Royaume de Bulgarie,* v.1–34, 1909–42 (Sofia, 1910–42).

Russian and English translations of the text to be used with the tables were issued 1962 and 1964; an abridged translation including selected tables appeared in 1968 with title *Statisticheskii ezhegodnik; Statistical yearbook.*

Offers detailed statistical tables on population, labor, industry, scientific and technological developments, agriculture, finance, etc. HA1621.A45

Burundi

Annuaire statistiques, 1962/65– . République du Burundi, Ministère du Plan, Service National des Études et Statistiques, [1966?]– . Annual. **CG160**

Title varies slightly: 1977, *Annuaire statistique.* Issuing body varies.

A source for statistics on population, education, public health, economic conditions, etc. HA2124.B86A25a

Cameroon

Cameroon. Dept. of Statistics and National Accounts. Note annuelle de statistique—Direction de la Statistique et de la Comptabilité Nationale, 1973/74– . [Yaoundé], Direction de la Statistique et de la Comptabilité Nationale, Ministère du Plan et de l'Aménagement du Territoire, [1974?]– . Annual. **CG161**

In five main sections: production (agricultural, agro-industrial, manufacturing); prices; foreign trade; transport; finances, money and credit. HA2141.D46a

Canada

Canada handbook, 1930– . Ottawa, Statistics Canada, 1930– . il. Annual. **CG162**

Subtitle: The annual handbook of present conditions and recent progress. (varies).

Volumes for 1930–71 issued by the agency under its earlier name, Canada. Bureau of Statistics. Early volumes entitled *Canada* (English ed.)

Intended to provide a factual survey of recent economic, social and cultural developments, presented against a statistical background. HC115.A425

Canada year book, 1905– . Ottawa, Statistics Canada, 1906– . v.1– . il., maps. Annual. **CG163**

Subtitle (varies): Statistical annual of the resources, demography, institutions and social and economic conditions of Canada.

Some volumes cover two years.

Volumes for 1905–71 issued by the agency under its earlier name, Canada. Bureau of Statistics.

Presents official data on the physiography, history, constitution and government, institutions, population, production, industry, trade, transportation, finance, labor, administration, and general social and economic conditions. Includes a useful chapter, "Official sources of information and miscellaneous data," containing a "Directory of sources" and a bibliography of special materials published in earlier editions of the yearbook. HA744.S81

Canadian almanac and directory for 1847– . Toronto, Copp Clark Co., 1847– . Annual. **CG164**

Title varies. Publisher varies.

Contains reliable legal, commercial, governmental, statistical, astronomical, departmental, ecclesiastical, financial, educational, and general information. AY414.C2

Canadian annual review of politics and public affairs, 1960– . Ed. by John T. Saywell. Toronto, Univ. of Toronto Pr., 1961– . v.1– . Annual. **CG165**

Title varies.

A survey annual covering such fields as: parliament and politics, external affairs and defense, the national economy, life and leisure, obituaries. Some chapters are in French. F1001.C215

Historical statistics of Canada. 2d ed. F. H. Leacy, ed. [Ottawa], Statistics Canada, [1983]. ca.900p. **CG166**

1st ed. 1965 ed. by M. C. Urquhart and K. A. H. Buckley.

Sponsored by the Social Science Research Council of Canada.

Patterned on *Historical statistics of the United States* (CG98), with some variation in the arrangement of the sections. Most data are for national aggregates, though some are for region or province; the period of coverage is generally 1867 to the mid-1970s. Sources of statistics are indicated, and there are helpful explanatory notes and background information. Detailed index. HA745.H57

Perspective Canada. English ed. [1]– . [Ottawa], Office of the Senior Advisor on Integration, Statistics of Canada, 1974– . il., maps. Irregular. **CG167**

Title varies slightly: 1980, *Perspectives Canada III.*

Each volume consists of a set of descriptive essays on socioeconomic conditions. Statistical tables, maps, and charts.

HN104.P47

Bibliography

Canada. Statistics Canada. Catalogue—Statistics Canada, 1972– . Ottawa, Statistics Canada, [1972?]– . Annual.
        CG168

A sales catalog of publications released by the department; in the most recent volumes, out-of-print material, discontinued titles, and items older than ten years have been removed. Classed arrangement; indexed by title, subject, commodity, and census. Supersedes the *Catalogue of publications* issued by Canada's Bureau of Statistics.
        HA37.C24b

Chad

Annuaire statistique du Tchad, 1966– . [Fort Lamy], République du Tchad, Ministère d'État Chargé de l'Economie Moderne, du Plan, du Commerce et de la Coopération Internationale, Direction du Plan et du Développement, Sous-direction de la Statistique [etc., 1967]– . il. Annual.
        CG169

Issuing body varies.
Contains data on administration, geography, health, education, and various aspects of the economy.   HA4718.A74

Chile

Chile. Servicio Nacional de Estadística y Censos. Anuario estadístico de Chile. 1848/58–1951, 1976– . Santiago, 1860–1951, 1976– .   **CG170**

The general statistics of Chile first appeared in 1860, the initial volumes covering 1848/58, and ran until 1888/90 (27v). Next published were volumes for 1909 (3v.) and 1910 (3v.). From 1911–51, the statistics have appeared in several subseries, e.g., Demografía, Agricultura, Política y administración, etc., some of them issued without series title. The various subseries are continued after 1951 as independent publications (e.g., Chile. Dirección de Estadística y Censos. *Demografía,* 1952–).
Title varies; some volumes called *Estadística anual.* Publication suspended 1952–75; issued by Instituto Nacional de Estadísticas, 1976– .   HA991.B2

Chile. Instituto Nacional de Estadísticas. Compendio estadístico, 1971– . [Santiago, República de Chile, Ministerio de Economía, Fomento y Reconstrucción, Instituto Nacional de Estadísticas, 1971]– . Annual.   **CG171**

Title varies: 1976, *Anuario estadístico.*
Presents a wide variety of socioeconomic statistics. In 1980 the Instituto published *Chile: series estadísticas, 1981,* a synthesis drawn from its other annual statistical publications. Many time series were retrospective to 1950; sources, when noted, were usually the agency responsible, rather than a printed work.   HA991.I58a

Mamalakis, Markos. Historical statistics of Chile. Westport, Conn., Greenwood Pr., [1978–83]. 4v.   **CG172**

Contents: v.[1], National accounts; v.2, Demography and labor force; v.3, Forestry and related activities; v.4, Money, prices, and credit services.
Each volume consists of a lengthy introduction and bibliography, followed by statistical tables. The volume on national accounts covers the 1940–74 period; that on population varies according to the individual topic, but basic population figures are included from mid-19th-century to 1975.

China

Chen, Nai-ruenn. Chinese economic statistics; a handbook for mainland China. Chicago, Aldine, [1967]. 539p.
        CG173

". . . official statistics, both national and provincial, relating to the economy of mainland China since 1949 have been compiled from Communist Chinese sources; and whenever possible, statistics for missing years are computed on the basis of the Communist Chinese definitions."—*Pref.* The concept, coverage, and classification of Communist Chinese statistical data are also explained. Indexed.
        HA1706.C48

China (People's Republic of China, 1949–). Kuo Chia T'ung Chi Chü. Ten great years; statistics of the economic and cultural achievements of the People's Republic of China. [Tr. from the Chinese] Peking, Foreign Languages Pr., 1960. 223p. il.   **CG174**

Also published in Chinese.
"The aim of this book is to describe, through extensive statistical data presented systematically, the great economic and cultural achievements of the People's Republic of China during the past decade."—*Foreword.*   DS777.55.A53

China facts & figures annual, v.1– , 1978– . [Gulf Breeze, Fla.], Academic Internat. Pr., [1978]– . il. Annual.
        CG175

Presents statistical and factual data on the People's Republic of China, with sections on: government, foreign affairs, the Chinese Communist Party, armed forces, demography, economy, energy, industries, agriculture, foreign trade and aid, transportation, science, culture and communications, health, education and welfare. Printed sources are indicated for most information, generally official Chinese, Japanese, or American titles. Also offers a chronology of the year, and bibliography of the year's books, articles, government documents, and reports. No index.   DS779.15.C48

China official yearbook, 1983/84– . [Hong Kong, Dragon Pearl Pubns., 1983]– . il. Annual?   **CG176**

An almanac of factual data reflecting events of the previous year. Includes: chronology; introduction; political documents texts; texts of selected laws, regulations, and diplomatic documents; statistics; narrative review of the year by topical area; supplements pertaining to recent events and materials; gazetteer information in the appendix. Indexed.

China year book, 1912–1939. London, Routledge; N.Y., Dutton, 1912–19; Tientsin, Tientsin Pr., 1921–29; Shanghai, North China Daily News, 1931–39. Irregular.
        CG177

Ed. by H. G. W. Woodhead and H. T. Montague Bell.
Unofficial but of first importance, while published, for reliable, detailed information about the people, government, economic conditions, religion, education, products, etc., of China. Includes a "Who's who in China." Index to previous issues appears in the 20th issue (1939).   JQ1501.A16

Chinese year book . . . Issue 1–7, 1935/36–1944/45. Prep. from official and other public sources by the Council of International Affairs, Chungking. Bombay, London, Thacker, 1935–46.   **CG178**

Publisher varies.
Contains a large amount of historical, descriptive, industrial, ecomomic, and directory information, as well as statistical material. Differs from the *China year book* (above) primarily in being compiled by Chinese authorities; it also contains fuller discussions of some subjects. Does not have a biographical section.
Ceased publication with 1944/45 issue.   DS701.C73

Clarke, Christopher M. China's provinces: an organizational and statistical guide. Wash., Nat. Council for US-China Trade, 1982. 462p. il., maps.   **CG179**

Provides directory and statistical data for the 29 provinces, centrally administered municipalities (Beijing, Shanghai, Tianjin), and autonomous regions of the People's Republic of China.
        HC427.92.C59

Republic of China, May 1983– . Taipei, Taiwan, Union Pacific Internat.; N.Y., Collings, 1983– . il. Irregular?
        CG180

Sponsored by Government Information Office, Republic of China.

Supersedes *China handbook* (1937/43–1956/57; publication suspended 1947–49) and *China yearbook* (1958–80).

Attempts to cover the political, economic, social, and cultural activities of the Republic of China. Contains a who's who section.

DS777.53.C459

Statistical yearbook of China. Comp. by the State Statistical Bureau, PRC. English ed. 1981– . Hong Kong, Economic Information & Agency, 1982– . Annual. **CG181**

Contains statistical data from 1950 to date, with an appendix for the statistics for Taiwan. HA4631.S78

Statistical yearbook of the Republic of China, 1975– . [Taipei], Directorate-General of Budget, Accounting & Statistics, Executive Yuan, Republic of China, [1975–]. Annual. **CG182**

Pt.I consists of statistical tables which are, in numbering and format, identical to those used in the United Nations *Statistical yearbook* (CG65); comparative figures for the period from 1946 are given as appropriate. Pt.II contains definitions of terms, sources of data, statistical procedures used in censuses and surveys, etc.

HA1710.5.A183a

Taiwan statistical data book. [1962?]– . [Taipei], Council for International Economic Cooperation and Development, Executive Yuan, Republic of China, [1962?]– . Annual. **CG183**

Issuing body varies.

" 'Taiwan' includes both the municipality of Taipei and the province of Taiwan unless otherwise specified."—*Pref.*

HA1710.5.T35

Bibliography

U.S. Bureau of the Census. The population and manpower of China: an annotated bibliography, by Foreign Manpower Research Office, Bureau of the Census. [Wash., Govt. Prt. Off., 1958] 132p. (*Its* International population statistics reports, ser.P–90, no.8) **CG184**

Contains materials on Taiwan as well as on mainland China, and also on Chinese in other sections of southeast Asia.

Z7164.D3U52

Colombia

Colombia. Departamento Administrativo Nacional de Estadística. Anuario general de estadística, 1905–66/67. Bogotá, Impr. Nacional, 1905–68. Annual. **CG185**

Issuing body varies. Title varies.

Supersedes *Anuario estadístico,* 1875/76–1884, issued by Oficina de Estadística Nacional. Publication suspended 1906–14. 1966/67 last published. Continued in part by *Anuario demográfico; Anuario de precio y costos;* and *Anuario de transportes y comunicaciones.*

HA1011.A16

Urrutia Montoya, Miguel and **Arrubla, Mario.** Compendio de estadísticas históricas de Colombia. Bogotá, [Dirección de Divulgación Cultural, Universidad National de Colombia], 1970. 312p. **CG186**

Chapters by specialists present and discuss statistics on topics such as wages in Bogotá, censuses, trade, elections, etc.

The government of Colombia has also issued tables of historical statistics (mainly 19th century, and on broader areas such as education, health, etc.) in its *Estadísticas históricas* ([Bogotá], Departamento Administrativo Nacional de Estadística, [1975]. 200p.).

HA1016.U76

Costa Rica

Costa Rica. Dirección General de Estadística y Censos. Anuario estadístico, 1883– . San José, Impr. Nacional, 1884– . **CG187**

Title varies slightly.

Suspended 1894–1906, 1946–47. Discontinued volume numbering after v.49, 1945.

Offers detailed statistical tables on population, vital statistics, health, social security, child welfare, commerce, industry, transport, tourism, etc. HA802.A2

Cuba

See also CG286.

Anuario estadístico de Cuba, 1952– . [La Habana], Comité Estatal de Estadísticas, 1952– . Annual. **CG188**

Issuing body varies.

Presents an extensive range of national statistics, with some comparative international statistics. Indexed. HA871.A65

Rowe, Patricia M. and **O'Connor, Susan J.** Detailed statistics on the urban and rural population of Cuba: 1950 to 2010. Wash., Center for Internat. Research, U.S. Bureau of the Census, 1984. 297p. **CG189**

Presents statistics on population, fertility, mortality and migration, with summary data on marital status, foreign birth, health measures, education, literacy, labor force and households. Bibliographic sources cited.

Schroeder, Susan. Cuba: a handbook of historical statistics. Boston, G. K. Hall, [1982]. 589p. il., maps. **CG190**

Contains 22 chapters providing figures from the 15th century to the present on climate, demography, education, labor, production, foreign trade, finance, politics, government and the military; introductory texts are followed by statistical tables. Indexed.

F1778.S37

Cyprus

Cyprus. Financial Secretary's Office. Statistics Section. Statistical abstract. no.1– , 1955– . Nicosia, Govt. Prt. Off., [1955]– . Annual. **CG191**

Issuing agency varies.

Offers comprehensive data on geography and climate, population, migration and tourism, education, justice, social welfare, and a variety of economic areas, with comparative international statistics.

HA1950.C9A3

Czechoslovakia

Statistická ročenka Československé Socialistické Republiky. 1934– . Praha, Statní Nakl. Technické Literatury, 1934– . **CG192**

Title varies. Publication suspended 1939–56.

Continuation of *Statistická prírucka* issued by Státní Urad Statistický, which in turn superseded *Manuel statistique de la République Tchécoslovaque* (Statistisches Handbuch der Cechoslovakischen Republik), v.1–4, 1920–32, and *Annuaire statistique de la République Tchécoslovaque,* 1934–38.

Some issues also published in English as *Czechoslovak statistical abstract.* The 1958 volume was published in English by U.S. Joint Publication Research Service as *Translation and glossary of Czechoslovak statistical yearbook* (Wash., 1959). HA1191.A416

Denmark

Denmark. Danmarks Statistik. Statistisk aarbog. Statistical yearbook. 1892– . København, 1896– . v.1– . Annual.
CG193

Text in Danish and English, beginning with v.57, 1952; previously published with text in Danish and French.

Includes sections of statistics for Denmark proper, the Faroe Islands, Greenland, and an international section.   HA1477

Dominican Republic

Dominican Republic. Dirección General de Estadística y Censos. Anuario estadístico, 1936–54. Trujillo, 1937–57. Annual.   **CG194**

Ceased publication with issue for 1954.   HA886.A35

—— República Dominicana en cifras, v.[1]– , 1964– . Santo Domingo, Oficina Nacional de Estadística [1964?]– . il. Irregular.   **CG195**

Issuing body varies.

Provides statistics on geography, climate, natural resources, population, agriculture, industry, mining, manufacturing, etc. No sources indicated.   HA887.A5

Ecuador

Ecuador. Dirección General de Estadística y Censos. Síntesis estadística del Ecuador, 1955–62. [Quito, 1963]. 55p.
CG196

A similar volume covering 1955–60 appeared in 1962.
HA1022.A55

Instituto Nacional de Estadística (Ecuador). Anuario de estadística, 1963/68. Quito, [1968?]. il.   **CG197**

Includes data on population, vital statistics, industry, foreign trade, social statistics, etc.

Continued by: HA1025.I55

—— Serie estadística, 1967/72– . Quito, [1974?]– . Annual.   **CG198**

Annual issues cover overlapping 5-year periods.

Issuing body later called Instituto Nacional de Estadística y Censos.

Ethiopia

Ethiopia. Central Statistical Office. Statistical abstract, 1963– . Addis Ababa, [1963?]– . Irregular.   **CG199**

The first volume offers retrospective information to 1952. Includes an explanation of sources, methodology, limitations of data. Statistical data without methodological explanation is provided in the *Statistical pocket book of Ethiopia* published annually by the Central Statistical Office since 1968, with the initial volume offering retrospective data since 1961.   HA1961.A3

Europe, Western

Befolkningsstatistik. Bevölkerungsstatistik. Demographic statistics, 1960/76– . [Luxembourg-Kirchberg, De Europaeiske Faellesskabers Statistiske Kontor, 1978]– . Annual.
CG200

In Danish, German, English, French, Italian, and Dutch.

Presents statistics for the nine (later ten) countries of the European Communities. Separate country tables provide population by sex and age; number and rate of births, deaths, marriages, and divorces; population change and migration; reproduction and fertility rates; life expectancy; and population projections. Comparative tables for all countries are also provided.   HA1107.5.B43

Mitchell, Brian R. European historical statistics, 1750– 1975. 2d ed. N.Y., Facts on File, 1980. 868p.   **CG201**

1st ed. 1975 covered 1750–1970.

Official and unofficial statistical sources were used to provide comparative data for the 26 European countries treated. The 75 tables are arranged in 11 sections: Climate; Population and vital statistics; Labour force; Agriculture; Industry; External trade; Transport and communications; Finance; Prices; Education; National accounts. Understandably, coverage is uneven, but the editors have tried to complete the information provided by a given country's statistical office.

In addition to updating statistics to 1975, errors have been corrected, various tables (especially for Section K, National accounts) have been revised with the advice of authorities in foreign countries, and a table of "Mean temperature in January and July" has been added.   HA1107.M5

Statistical Office of the European Communities. Social indicators for the European Community, 1960–1978. Luxembourg, Office des Publications Officielles des Communautés Européennes, [1980]. 234p. il.   **CG202**

Title also in French; prefatory matter and headings in English and French.

"Contains a broadly comparable collection of data for the nine countries of the European Community on the following eight areas . . . : population, employment, working life, living standards, social security, health, education and housing."—*p.[235]*. Some comparisons are made with selected Third World countries. Some time series extend back to 1950 and 1960. Numerous graphs, charts, tables, etc.

Bibliography

Blake, Judith and **Donovan, Jerry J.** Western European censuses, 1960; an English language guide. Berkeley, Inst. of International Studies, Univ. of California, [1971]. 421p. (Population monograph ser., 8) (Repr.: Westport, Conn., Greenwood Pr., 1976)   **CG203**

Furnishes "the titles and page numbers of all statistical tables in every volume of every census . . .; a detailed glossary of technical terms that appear in more than one volume of that census . . .; [and] a bibliographically correct entry for every volume" (*Introd.*) of the 1960 census publications issued by the governments of western Europe (including Greece, but not the rest of the Balkans).
HA37.E93B5

Harvey, Joan M. Statistics Europe; sources for social, economic and market research. 4th ed., rev. and enl. Beckenham, Kent, Eng., CBD Research; [Detroit, Gale, 1981]. 508p.   **CG204**

1st ed. 1968.

Information presented for each country includes: directory information on the central statistical office and other major organizations publishing statistical information; principal libraries inside and outside the country where its statistical materials are available; current bibliographies and sales lists of statistics; list of the major statistical publications, arranged as general, production, external trade, internal distribution and service trades, population, social, finance, transport and communications (with appropriate subdivisions for most groups). Organization, title, and subject indexes.
Z7554.E8H35

U.S. Library of Congress. Census Library Project. National censuses and vital statistics in Europe, 1918–1939; an annotated bibliography. Wash., Govt. Prt. Off., 1948. 215p. (Repr. with suppl.: Detroit, Gale, 1967)   **CG205**

A very useful guide to the national censuses and official statistical publications of the various countries of Europe, for the period between the two World Wars.

───── ───── 1940–1948 Supplement. 1948. 48p.

Z7553.C3U46

Europe, Eastern

Länder der Erde; politisch-ökonomisches Handbuch. 7. völlig neubearb. und erw. Aufl. [Gesamtredaktion: Horst Seydewitz und Frank Zeller] Berlin, Verlag Die Wirtschaft, 1980. 720p. il. **CG206**

1st ed. 1959, translated from the Russian *Zarubezhnye strany.*
Economic and political statistical information on the countries of the world; especially useful for East European countries.

D40.Z3715

Finland

Suomen tilastollinen vuosikirja, uusi sarja. Statistisk arsbok för Finland, ny ser. Statistical yearbook of Finland, n.s., 1902– . Helsinki, 1903– . Ed.1– . Annual. **CG207**

Continues a publication of the same title, 1879–1902.
Title and text also in Swedish and French, 1934–52; in Swedish and English, 1953– . Some early issues in Russian and French.
Offers a wide range of detailed statistical tables with indication of sources; includes some comparative statistics for countries other than Finland. Each issue has a retrospective bibliography of Finnish statistical publications. HA1448.F537c

France

See also CG5, CG70.

Annuaire statistique de la ville de Paris et des communs suburbaines de la Seine. 1.– année, 1880– . Paris, 1881– . Annual. **CG208**

Title varies slightly. Some years in combined issues. Ceased publication with issue for 1967?
Published by Préfecture de la Seine. Direction du Cabinet du Préfet.
Statistical tables grouped under broad subjects as: démographie, climatologie, territoire, construction et logement, hygiène publique et hygiène sociale, travail, enseignement et beaux-arts, police et justice, finances et mouvement économique, elections. Most tables give figures for Paris and the communes. HA1229.P22

France. Institut National de la Statistique et des Études Économiques. Annuaire statistique de la France, 1878– . Paris, Impr. Nationale, 1878– . v.1– . Annual. **CG209**

Title varies slightly. v.56 covers 1940/45.
v.1–56 (1878–1940/45) issued by Statistique Générale de la France.
At head of title, v.78 (1973): Republique Française. Ministère de l'Économie et des Finances.
Offers a wide range of statistics for the individual départements as well as for France as a whole. Includes an international section.

HA1213.A4

France. Ministère de la France d'Outre-mer. Service de Statistique. Annuaire statistique de l'Union française outre-mer. 1939/46–1947/58. Paris, Impr. Nationale, [1951–59]. 3v. **CG210**

1958 volume published 1959 with title *Outre-mer.*
An "Édition provisoire" entitled *Annuaire statistique des possessions françaises: années antérieures à la guerre* was published 1944.
Continued by: HA1228.A23

France. Institut National de la Statistique et des Études Économiques. Annuaire statistique des territoires d'outre-mer. 1959– . **CG210a**

Paroisses et communes de France. Dictionnaire d'histoire administrative et démographique. Paris, Éditions du Centre National de la Recherche Scientifique, 1974–84. [v.1–75] il. (In progress) **CG211**

Ed. by Jacques Dupâquier and others.
Contents: [v.1] Région parisienne; [v.1a] Ain; [v.7] Ardèche; [v.10] Aube; [v.11] Aude; [v.26] Drôme; [v.38] Isère; [v.45] Loiret; [v.48] Lozère; [v.49] Maine-et-Loire; [v.51] Marne; [v.58] Nievre; [v.60] Oise; [v.62] Pas-de-Calais (in 2v.); [v.67] Bas-Rhin; [v.69] Rhône; [v.72] Sarthe; [v.73] Savoie; [v.74] Haute-Savoie; [v.75] Règion Parisienne; [v.87] Haute-Vienne.
An attempt to provide parish-by-parish demographic statistics from the 17th century to 1968. Includes bibliographic references.

JS5112.P37

Germany

Basisdaten: Zahlen zur sozio-ökonomischen Entwicklung der Bundesrepublik Deutschland. Bearb. von Roland Ermrich. Bonn-Bad Godesberg, Verl. Neue Gesellschaft, [1974]. 648p. il. **CG212**

A handbook of social indicators relating to population, employment, economy, raw materials, education, health, housing, working conditions, income and expenditure, leisure, mass media, political participation, etc. Most time series cover 1950–70. Sources indicated for all tables. Bibliography; list of tables; subject index.

HC286.6.B27

Germany (Federal Republic, 1949–). Statistisches Bundesamt, Wiesbaden. Statistisches Jahrbuch für die Bundesrepublik Deutschland, 1952– . Stuttgart-Mainz, Kohlhammer, 1952– . Annual. **CG213**

Continues the *Statistisches Jahrbuch für das Deutsche Reich,* 1880–1938 (57v.) for the territory under the Federal Republic of Germany. Has an added section for international statistics.

HA1232.A45

───── Handbook of statistics for the Federal Republic of Germany. Stuttgart, Kohlhammer, 1961– . il. Triennial. **CG214**

Supersedes in part the office's *Statistisches Taschenbuch; Pocketbook of statistics; Annuaire statistique de poche,* issued in 1958.
An English-language version of the agency's *Statistisches Taschenbuch für die Bundesrepublik Deutschland* (Stuttgart, 1958–). Also published in French and (beginning with the 1970 ed.) Spanish.
Offers a compact compendium of statistics on economic, social, and cultural matters drawn from the *Statistisches Jahrbuch* (above).

HA1232.A463

Germany (Territory under Allied Occupation, 1945–1955, U.S. Zone). Länderrat. Statistisches Handbuch von Deutschland, 1928–44. München, F. Ehrenwirth, 1949. 640p., 17p. **CG215**

Designed to provide some statistical information for the period following the 1938 issue of the *Statistisches Jahrbuch für das Deutsche Reich* (1880–1938. 57v.). 1928 was chosen as a "normal" year to compare with later available statistics. HA1241.A52

Statistisches Jahrbuch deutscher Gemeinden. 1.Jahrg.– , 1890– . Braunschweig, Waisenhaus-Buchdr., 1890– . Annual. **CG216**

Imprint varies.
Title varies: 1890–1933 called *Statistisches Jahrbuch deutscher Städte.* None issued 1917–26, 1939–48.
Detailed statistical tables for a wide range of economic, social, and cultural conditions and activities. HA1330.A1S8

Germany (Democratic Republic, 1949–). Staatliche Zentralverwaltung für Statistik. Statistisches Jahrbuch der Deutschen Demokratischen Republik. 1.– Jahrg., 1955– . Berlin, Deutscher Zentralverlag, 1956– . Annual. **CG217**

Publisher varies.

Offers a wide range of statistical tables, many with comparative figures for 15 to 20 years. Includes an international section.
HA1248.A2A33

Soziologischer Almanach: Handbuch gesellschaftspolitischer Daten und Indikatoren für die Bundesrepublik Deutschland. Eike Ballerstedt, Wolfgang Glatzer. 3.Aufl., völlig neu bearb. von Helga Cremer-Schäfer und Erich Wiegand. Frankfurt and N.Y., Campus Verlag, [1979]. 615p. (SPES-Projekt, Bd.5) **CG218**

A compendium of socioeconomic statistics for West Germany, in the areas of population, production, institutions, family, leisure, specific social groups, inequality, labor, crime, political participation, mass communications, taxation and public expenditure. Tables show historical data for the last 100 years, and comparative figures for other countries. HN445.S6

Statistical pocket book of the German Democratic Republic. v.1– , 1959– . Berlin, Staatsverlag, 1959– . Annual. **CG219**

Also published in German, French, and Russian.
A brief statistical summary in tabular form. HA1248.A2A335

Bibliography

Deutsche Statistische Gesellschaft. Bibliographie der amtlichen westdeutschen Statistik, 1945–1951. München, 1952. 91p. (Einzelschriften der Deutschen Statistischen Gesellschaft. Hft.Nr.3) **CG220**

Germany (West). Statistisches Bundesamt. Veröffentlichungsverzeichnis, 1951– . [Mainz, Kohlhammer, 1951?]– . Annual. **CG221**

Title varies: 1951–82, *Verzeichnis der Veröffentlichungen des Statistischen Bundesamtes.*
Lists all sales publications available at the beginning of the calendar year and describes various services of the Federal Statistical Office. New publications are announced weekly in the office's *Bundesanzeiger* and *Statistischer Wochendienst,* and in the monthly *Wirtschaft und Statistik.* Indexed.
Also available in English, French, and Spanish versions.
Z7554.G3A25

Ghana

Ghana. Central Bureau of Statistics. Statistical yearbook. 1st– ed., 1961– . Accra, 1962– . **CG222**
7th issue, 1969/70, published 1973. HA1977.G6A264

—— Statistical hand book of the Republic of Ghana. Ed.1– , 1967– . Accra, 1967– . Irregular. **CG223**

Statistical tables relative to the social structure and economic trends of the nation. HA1977.G5A23

Great Britain

Feinstein, C. H. Statistical tables of national income, expenditure, and output of the U.K., 1855–1965. Cambridge, Eng., Cambridge Univ. Pr., [1976]. 141p. **CG224**

First published as part of *National income, expenditure and output of the United Kingdom, 1855–1965* (1972); issued separately, with a new introduction, 1976.
Presents 65 tables of "estimates of national income, expenditure and output at current and constant prices . . . [and] series for the capital stock, population, employment and unemployment, prices and wages."—*Introd.* Original explanatory text from the 1972 edition has not been included. HC260.I5F42

Gt. Brit. Central Statistical Office. Annual abstract of statistics. v.1– , 1840/53– . London, Stat. Off., 1854– . v.1– . Annual. **CG225**

v.1–83 issued by the Board of Trade as *Statistical abstract for the United Kingdom.* Each of these volumes contained statistics for the preceding 15 years. Coverage varies slightly.
v.83, covering 1924 to 1938, was published in 1940. No volumes were published during World War II, but v.84, with a new title and under a new issuing body, appeared in 1948 and covers 1935–46; v.85, published 1949, covers 1938–48; v.87– , 1951– , published annually, cover the last ten years. HA1122.A33

Hey, John Denis. Britain in context. N.Y., St. Martin's Pr., [1979]. 189p. il. **CG226**

A statistical presentation of the United Kingdom for "the interested and intelligent layman"—*p.2.* 87 topics are organized into three main sections: (1) Britain as part of the world, offering economic comparisons with other countries; (2) Britain as an economic aggregate, focusing on key national economic issues; (3) Britain as a society of individuals, presenting vital, social, and economic statistics. Each topic is presented on two facing pages, one devoted to a verbal account and the other to graphic illustration. Sources are identified. Bibliography; index. HC256.6.H43 1979b

Mitchell, Brian R. Abstract of British historical statistics. With the collaboration of Phyllis Deane. Cambridge, Univ. Pr., 1962. 513p. **CG227**

Presents tables of economic statistics of the United Kingdom, with information on sources and coverage and with introduction and bibliographies for each section. In some cases figures go back to the 17th century and earlier, but most series begin with the 18th and 19th centuries and are taken only to 1938. HA1135.M5

—— and **Jones, H. G.** Second abstract of British historical statistics. Cambridge, Univ. Pr., 1971. 227p. **CG228**

Primarily a continuation of the earlier abstract, providing tables for 1938 onwards for most series, but adding some series not included in the earlier volume (with pre-1938 figures for these). Cutoff date is usually 1965 or 1966. HA1135.M52

Social trends. no.1– . London, H.M.S.O., 1970– . Annual. **CG229**

At head of title: Central Statistical Office.
"A publication of the Government Statistical Service."—*title page.*
"The purpose . . . is to bring together some of the more significant statistical series relating to social policies and conditions. The emphasis is on trends, though there are also tables showing distributions at particular times."—*no.4 (1973), p.5.* About half the tables are carried forward from issue to issue with only minor changes and updating, the others vary from issue to issue, being of less central or of passing interest. HA1134.S6

Bibliography

Edwards, Bernard. Sources of social statistics. London, Heinemann, [1974]. 276p. il. **CG230**

Serves as a companion volume to the author's *Sources of economic and business statistics* (CH265), and surveys statistical materials available from official British sources in the areas of population, vital statistics, health, welfare, social security, housing, education, crime and justice. Indexed. HA37.G7E43

Gt. Brit. Central Statistical Office. Guide to official statistics, no.1– . London, H.M.S.O., 1976– . Biennial. **CG231**

Each issue of the guide "tries . . . to give a good indication to the user of the likelihood of a particular subject's being included in a given source."—*No.3, 1980 [p.iv].* Covers official and significant non-official sources of statistics for the United Kingdon published within the last ten years. Classed subject arrangement, with keyword index. Brief introductory remarks for most sections; all sources are abstracted. HA37.G5816

Gt. Brit. Interdepartmental Committee on Social and Economic Research. Guides to official sources. London, Stat. Off., 1953–61. no.1–6.   **CG232**

Contents: no.1, Labour statistics (rev. May 1958). 1958; no.2, Census reports of Great Britain, 1801–1931. 1951; no.3, Local government statistics. 1953; no.4, Agricultural and food statistics. 1958; no.5, Social security statistics. 1961; no.6, Census of production reports. 1961.   Z7165.G8G7

Gt. Brit. Office of Population Censuses and Surveys. Guide to census reports: Great Britain 1801–1966. London, H.M.S.O., [1977]. 279p.   **CG233**

"The aim of this volume is to use, as a base, the *Guides to Official Sources No.2 Census Reports of Great Britain 1801–1931* which was published under the auspices of the Interdepartmental Committee on Social and Economic Research [*see* CG232], and develop it to include the censuses of 1951, 1961 and 1966."—*Foreword.* Provides information on the background, scope and organization of the census, the questions and schedules, special subjects of inquiry, use of the reports, etc. "List of census reports for Great Britain, 1801–1966," giving date of publication and reference to Parliamentary papers, p.1–10.

A useful complement is Catherine Hakim's *Census data and analysis* (London, Off. of Population Censuses and Surveys, 1978. *Its* Occasional paper, no.6).   HA37.G6

Gt. Brit. Permanent Consultative Committee on Official Statistics. Guide to current official statistics, . . . 1922–38. London, Stat. Off., 1923–39. v.1–17. Annual.   **CG234**

Subtitle: Being a systematic survey of the statistics appearing in all official publications.

No more published.   Z7554.G7G7

Maunder, W. F., ed. Reviews of United Kingdom statistical sources. London, Heinemann, [1974–81]. v.1–15. (In progress).   **CG235**

Publ. for the Royal Statistical Society and the Social Science Research Council.

Contents: v.1, [pt.1] Personal social services, by B. P. Davies; [pt.2] Voluntary organisations in the personal social service field, by G. J. Murray; v.2, [pt.3] Central government routine health statistics, by M. Alderson; [pt.4] Social security statistics, by F. Whitehead; v.3, [pt.5] Housing in Great Britain, by S. Farthing; [pt.6] Housing in Northern Ireland, by M. Fleming; v.4, [pt.7] Leisure, by F. M. M. Lewis and S. R. Parker; [pt.8] Tourism, by L. J. Lickorish; v.5, [pt.9] General sources of statistics, by G. F. Lock; v.6, Wealth and personal incomes, by A. B. Atkinson, A. J. Harrison and T. Stark; v.7, Road passenger transport and road goods transport, by D. L. Munby and A. H. Watson; v.8, Land use and town and country planning, by J. T. Coppock and L. F. Gebbett; v.9, Health surveys and related studies, by M. Alderson and R. Dowie; v.10, Ports and inland waterways and civil aviation, by R. E. Baxter and C. M. Phillips; v.11, Coal, gas, electricity, by D. J. Harris, H. Nabb and D. Nuttall; v.12, Construction and the related professions, by M. C. Fleming; v.13, Wages and earnings, by A. Dean; v.14, Railroad and sea transport, by D. H. Aldcroft and D. Mort; v.15, Crime, by M. A. Walker.

Constitutes a revised and expanded edition of *The sources and nature of the statistics of the United Kingdom,* ed. by Maurice Kendall (2v., 1952–57).

Each volume offers detailed reviews of official and non-official statistical sources on a national level. Factual and bibliographic data for statistical series are given in the "Quick reference list"; there is also a general bibliography. Illustrations of forms used in data collection are provided.   HA37.G7M38

Greece

Statistikē epetēris tēs Hellados. Statistical yearbook of Greece. 1930– . Athēnai, Ethnikon Typographeion, 1931– . Irregular.   **CG236**

Title varies.

Vols. for 1930–39 called v.1–10. Publication suspended 1940–53. Vols. for 1930–39 in Greek and French; 1954– in Greek and English.

Vols. for 1930–39 issued by Greece. Genikē Statistikē Hypēresia; 1954– by Greece. Ethnikē Statistikē Hypēresia.   HA1351.S75

Chouliarakēs, Michaël G. Statistikē vivliographia peri Hellados, 1821–1971. Athēnai, [Ethnikon Kentron Koinōnikōn Spoudōn], 1971. 78,[108]–118p.   **CG237**

Includes a supplement: *Statistikē dēmosieumata kai vivliographia statistikēs en Helladi, 1833–1932* (p.[108]–118) reprinted from S. Kladas' *Hē statistikē en Helladi* (Athēnai, 1932).

A classed bibliography of 688 numbered citations, principally in Greek, but with English, French, and Italian-language materials represented.   Z7165.G84C46

Guatemala

Guatemala. Dirección General de Estadística. Anuario estadístico, 1970– . [Guatemala, 1970]– . il. Annual.   **CG238**

Continues *Guatemala en cifras* (1955–69).

Provides data on geography, demography, social and economic conditions, usually with a 10-year time series. Agencies are listed as sources.   HA811.A37

Arias de Blois, Jorge. Demografía guatemalteca, 1960–1976; una bibliografía anotada. Guatemala, Univ. del Valle de Guatemala, 1978. 163p.   **CG239**

Cites 192 books, dissertations, and articles published after 1960. Annotations are often quite long; some include tables. Not indexed.   Z7164.D3A69

————— ————— Primer suplemento: 1977–79. [Guatemala City], Univ. del Valle de Guatemala, [1983]. 99p.

An author listing with comprehensive abstracts and subject index.

Honduras

Honduras. Dirección General de Estadística y Censos. Anuario estadístico, 1952– . Tegucigalpa, 1953– . il. Annual.   **CG240**

Issuing body varies.

Offers statistics on climate, population, social security, public health, education, and various aspects of the economy.   HA821.A43

Hungary

Hungary. Központi Statisztikai Hivatal. Statisztikai évkönyv. 1949/55– . Budapest, 1957– . Annual.   **CG241**

Also published in English and Russian as *Statistical yearbook; Statisticheskii ezhegodnik.*

Supersedes the Office's *Magyar statisztikai évkönyv . . . Statistisches Jahrbuch,* 1871–90; *Magyar statisztikai évkönyv. Új folyam,* 1893–1900; and *Annuaire statistique hongrois. Nouv. cours,* 1901–41.   HA1201.A52

Hungary. Könyvtár és Dokumentációs Szolgálat. Bibliográfiai Osztály. Statisztikai adatforrások 1945–1974: bibliográfia. Budapest, [Statisztikai Kiadó Vállalat], 1975. 209p.   **CG242**

Elemérné Hajdú, ed.

A classed bibliography of monographs, monographic series, periodical titles, and conference proceedings.   Z7554.H8H86

India

India (Republic). Central Statistical Organisation. Statistical abstract, India. n.s. no.1– , 1949– . Delhi, 1950– . Annual. **CG243**

Issuing body varies: n.s. no.1 issued by the Office of Economic Advisers.

Supersedes *Statistical abstract for British India,* 1911/12–1939/40, issued by the Dept. of Commercial Intelligence and Statistics, and the *Statistical abstract* for 1946/47 issued by the Office of the Economic Adviser.   HA1713.A732

India, a reference annual, 1953– . New Delhi, Pubns. Div., Ministry of Information and Broadcasting, [1954]– . il. Annual. **CG244**

Comp. by the Research and Reference Div., Ministry of Information and Broadcasting.

A fact book on Indian life, administration, and economy, compiled with the cooperation of national ministries and state administrations. Extensive, topically arranged bibliography. Indexed.   DS405.I64

India; a statistical outline. [Ed.1–] Bombay, Indian Oxygen Ltd., 1965– . Irregular. (7th ed. 1984)   **CG245**

Imprint varies.

Includes sections on national income and wealth; demography; agriculture; irrigation and power; food and consumption; industry; transport; labor; foreign trade; public finance; education; health and family planning, etc.   HA1724.I49

Times of India directory and year book including who's who, 1914– . Bombay and London, Bennett, Coleman, 1914– . Annual. **CG246**

Title varies: *Indian year book,* 1914–47; *The Indian and Pakistan year book and who's who,* 1949–1952/53.

Unofficial but very useful. Contains a large amount of descriptive and statistical information and, 1918– , a "Who's who in India."   DS405.I7

Bibliography

Guide to official statistics. [New Delhi], Central Statistical Organisation, Dept. of Statistics, Ministry of Planning, Govt. of India, 1979. 138p.   **CG247**

A guide to the major recurrent statistical publications of India. Topical arrangement; title index.   HA37.I4G78

India. Office of the Economic Adviser. Guide to current official statistics. . . . Prep. under instructions from the Economic Adviser by S. Subramanian, statistician. Delhi, Manager of Pubns., 1943–49. v.1–3.   **CG248**

Contents: v.1, Production and prices (2d ed.); v.2, Trade, transport and communications, and finance (excluding public finance); v.3, Public finance, education, public health, census, labour, consumption of commodities, and miscellaneous.   HA37.I382

India (Republic). Office of the Registrar General. Bibliography of census publications in India. C. G. Jadhav, comp. Ed. by B. R. Roy Burman. [Delhi, Manager of Publications, 1972] 520p. (Census centenary pubn., no.5)   **CG249**

A chronological listing for India in general is followed by similar lists of publications for the individual states, the union territories, and countries formerly covered by Indian censuses.   Z3205.I85

Indonesia

Dutch East Indies. Centraal Kantoor voor de Statistiek. Statistisch jaaroverzicht van Nederlandsch-Indie. Statistical abstract for the Netherlands East Indies; new ser. of the Statistical annual of the Netherlands (Colonies), 1922/23–39. Batavia, 1924–40. [17v.?]   **CG250**

Title page and text in Dutch and English.

1930–39 issues are pt.2 of *Indisch verlag,* 1931–40.   HA1811.A3

Indonesia. Biro Pusat Statistik. Statistical abstracts [1950–1955]. Djakarta, Central Bureau of Statistics, 1956. 138p.   **CG251**

—— Statistical pocket book of Indonesia. 1957– . Djakarta, 1957– . Irregular.   **CG252**

An earlier publication with the same title was issued by Dutch East Indies. Centraal Kantoor voor de Statistiek.

A volume for 1956 was issued in Indonesian only, with title *Statistik.* 1957–63 issued annually with text in English; 1964–67 not published. Beginning with volume for 1968/69, published biennially with text in Indonesian and English.

Offers basic statistical information on the economic and social conditions of the country.   HA1811.A34

Indonesia, an official handbook, 1970– . [Jarkarta], Dept. of Information, Republic of Indonesia, [1970?]– . il. Annual.   **CG253**

Comp. and produced by Dept. of Information, Directorate of Foreign Information Service.

Title varies: 1970–77, *Indonesia handbook.*

A handbook combining narrative and statistics in chapters on geography, demography, government, economics, social and cultural development, religion, defense, and the mass media.   DS611.A337

Statistik Indonesia. Statistical yearbook of Indonesia, 1975– . Jakarta, Biro Pusat Statistik, [1976?]– . Annual.   **CG254**

In Indonesian and English.

Presents data on geography, climate, population and manpower, education and culture, and a wide variety of economic topics, with some comparative international statistics.   HA1811.B57c

Iran

Iran almanac and book of facts. Ed.1– , 1961– . Tehran, Echo of Iran, 1961– . Annual.   **CG255**

Though not an official publication, this comprehensive book of general information on Iranian life and culture includes many tables of statistics. 15th ed. (1976) last published?   AY1185.I7

Statistical yearbook of Iran, 1966– . [Tehran], Plan and Budget Organization, Statistical Centre of Iran, [1967]– . il. Annual?   **CG256**

In English and Farsi.

The first volume included statistical data up to 1966; later volumes contain data for the current year. Covers geography, demography and social conditions, economic resources, economic organization, commerce, and political affairs.   HA1861.S73

Iraq

Iraq. Jihāz al-Markazī lil-Iḥsā'. Annual abstract of statistics. 1927/28–1937/38– . Baghdad, 1939– . Annual (slightly irregular).   **CG257**

At head of title: Ministry of Economics. Title varies. Issuing body varies.

Title and text in English and Arabic.   HA1950.I75A34

Ireland

Ireland (Eire). Central Statistics Office. Statistical abstract of Ireland. 1931– . Dublin, Stat. Off., 1931– . v.1– . Annual. **CG258**

1931–1947/48 issued by Dept. of Industry and Commerce.
"The area referred to as Ireland in this Volume is to be interpreted as meaning Ireland exclusive of the Six Counties [of Northern Ireland]."—*Pref.* Most tables include comparative figures for recent years. HA1141.A35

Irish historical statistics: population, 1821–1971. Ed. by William Edward Vaughan and André Jude Fitzpatrick. Dublin, Royal Irish Academy, 1978. 372p. (New history of Ireland: Ancillary pubns., 2) **CG259**

Covers statistics on population, age groups, religious denominations, ages and conjugal status, and births, marriages, and deaths for Northern Ireland and the Republic of Ireland, from 1672 to 1971. Sources for all tables are noted. Extensive bibliography. Future volumes are planned to cover statistics on agricultural production and prices, occupations and industry, communications, commerce, and finance. HA1146.I74

Kirwan, Frank and **McGilvray, J. W.** Irish economic statistics. [2d ed.] Dublin, Institute of Public Administration, 1983. 225p. il. **CG260**

1st ed. 1968.
A guide to the sources of Irish economic statistics and their methods of presentation and analysis. Ten chapters discuss population and vital statistics, manpower, agriculture, industry, foreign trade, national income and expenditure, prices and wages, taxation, transport and communication, and regional statistics. Bibliography; index. HC260.5.K57

Ireland, Northern

Northern Ireland. Ministry of Finance. Registrar-General's Division. Ulster year book, 1926– . Belfast, 1926– . Irregular. **CG261**

None published 1939–46.
The official handbook for Northern Ireland. Presents statistical and other information on social and economic conditions, health, education, etc. HC257.I6A5

Israel

Israel. ha-Lishkah ha-Merkazit li-Statistiskah. Statistical abstract of Israel. no.1– , 1949/50– . Jerusalem, Govt. Printer, 1951– . Annual. **CG262**

Title and text in Hebrew and English.
Offers statistics on population, social and economic aspects of the country. HA1931.A35

—— Society in Israel: selected statistics. 2d ed., ed. by U. O. Schmelz. Jerusalem, 1976. liv, 172, 42p. **CG263**

In English and Hebrew.
A compendium of statistics for the period from 1950 to the present, in the areas of population and vital statistics, immigration, households, employment, income and expenditure, social security, housing, health, education, leisure, and public order. Statistical data are preceded by explanatory chapters which include lists of published sources. Subject index. HA1932.L57

Israel yearbook, 1950/51– . [Tel Aviv], Israel Yearbook Pubns., 1951– . Annual. **CG264**

Publisher varies.
Succeeds the *Anglo-Palestine yearbook* (1946, 1947–48) and the *Palestine yearbook and Israeli annual.*
Offers a review of social and economic conditions, industrial and scientific developments, and cultural activities. DS101.I68

Italy

Associazione per lo Sviluppo dell' Industria nel Mezzogiorno. Statistiche sul Mezzogiorno d'Italia, 1861–1953. Roma, SVIMEZ, 1954. 1096p. **CG265**

Focuses on regionalism; gives economic, political, and social statistics for the south of Italy, which is less highly developed industrially than the north and center. Not all tables cover the whole period 1861–1953, but especially full treatment is given to population, transportation, emigration, internal migration, education, etc.

Italy. Istituto Centrale di Statistica. Annuario statistico italiano, 1878– . Roma, Istit. Poligrafico dello Stato, 1878– . Annual (irregular). **CG266**

1878–1955 called ser.1–5. Ser.1–2 issued by the Direzione Generale della Statistica.
Includes statistical tables for population, health and social welfare, education, cultural affairs, agriculture, commerce and industry, finance, economics, etc. HA1367.A3

—— Compendio statistico italiano, 1927– . Roma, Istit. Poligrafico dello Stato, 1927– . Annual. **CG267**

Publication suspended 1943–45.
1946 issue, called ser.2, v.1, serves as an abridged edition of the *Annuario* (above). HA1362.A32

—— Sommario statistico delle regioni d'Italia. Roma, 1947. 248p. maps, tables. **CG268**

Some tables give figures beginning with 1871. HA1365.A5

Bibliography

See also CG9.

Bonasera, Francesco. Le "fonti" nello studio della geografia economica. Padova, CEDAM, 1970. 134p. il., maps. **CG269**

At head of title: Università degli Studi di Palermo. Istituto di Geografia Economica.
An annotated bibliography of statistical sources, topically arranged. Appendix provides a chronological list of statistical publications from the 19th century to 1961. HF1025.B634

Istituto Central di Statistica (Italy). Catalogo delle pubblicazioni, [1953?]– . Roma, Istituto, [1953?]– . Annual. **CG270**

A classed catalog of official statistical publications arranged by type (current statistics, censuses, special studies), subdivided by specific topics. Subject index. Z7554.I8I85

Ivory Coast

La Côte d'Ivoire en chiffres; annuaire statistique de la Côte d'Ivoire, 1975– . [Dakar, Société Africaine d'Édition, 1975?]– . il. Annual. **CG271**

In four main parts, subdivided by topical chapters: general; agriculture; industry; infrastructure. HC547.I8C63

Jamaica

Handbook of Jamaica, 1881– . London, Crown Agents; Jamaica, Govt. Prt. Off., 1881– . v.1– . maps. Irregular. **CG272**

Subtitle: Comprising historical, statistical and general information . . . obtained from official and other reliable records and comp. by the Jamaica Information Service.
1967 last published? F1861.H23

Jamaica. Dept. of Statistics. Statistical abstract, 1947– . Kingston, Govt. Printer, [1948]– . Annual.　　**CG273**

Title varies: 1947–57, *Digest of statistics;* 1958–71, *Abstract of statistics.*

Offers detailed statistics for the latest year and one or two earlier years.　　HA891.A27

Statistical yearbook of Jamaica, 1973– . [Kingston, 1974]– . il. Annual.　　**CG274**

Prep. by the Information Section of the Central Planning and Development Div. of the Dept. of Statistics.

A factbook combining statistical tables and textual matter.
　　HA891.C45a

Japan

Japan. Okurasho. Financial and economic annual of Japan. Tokyo, Govt. Prt. Off., 1901–40. v.1–40. maps. Annual.
　　CG275

Includes information on area, population, agriculture, industry, and commerce for the Japanese Empire. Early volumes give figures from 1867/68.

No more published.　　HC461.A3

Japan. Sōrifu. Tōkeikyoku. Résumé statistique de l'Empire du Japon, 1884–1940. Tokyo, 1887–1940. v.1–54.
　　CG276

In Japanese and French.

A résumé of the Japanese statistical annual published in Japanese.　　HA1832.A28

Japan statistical yearbook, 1949– . [Tokyo], Statistics Bureau, Prime Minister's Office, 1949– . Annual.　　**CG277**

Volumes for 1949 and 1950 published by the Nihon Statistical Association.

In Japanese and English. To replace the *Statistical yearbook of the Empire of Japan,* which ceased with v.59, 1941. The 1949 issue attempts to fill the 8-year gap in statistics; from 1950 on, the issues concentrate on annual figures.　　HA1832.J36

Japan year book, 1933–1949/52. [Tokyo], Foreign Affairs Assoc. of Japan, [1933–52]. Annual (irregular).　　**CG278**

"This year book has no connection with that published by the late Prof. Takenobu under the same title, which is now defunct" (*Pref., 1933*), but which was published 1906–31 by the Japan Year Book Office.

A detailed review of the economic, social, political, and cultural life of Japan. Of special value for coverage during the war years, including much documentary material, e.g., the Constitution, Supreme Commander for the Allied Powers letters and memoranda, laws and ordinances, and text of the Japanese peace treaty signed Sept. 8, 1951.

Ceased publication.　　DS803.J52

The Oriental economist's Japan economic yearbook. [Tokyo], Oriental Economist, 1954– . Annual.　　**CG279**

On cover: Japan economic yearbook.

General economic information with statistical tables. Ceased publication.　　HC461.O65

Statistical handbook of Japan. [Tokyo], Bureau of Statistics, Office of the Prime Minister, 1964– . Annual.　　**CG280**

A brief description, with statistical charts and tables, of modern Japanese economic, social, and cultural activities.　　HA1832.S75

Taeuber, Irene B. The population of Japan. Princeton, N.J., Princeton Univ. Pr., 1958. 461p. il.　　**CG281**

A comprehensive work containing statistics from the 12th century to 1950, with projections to 1980. Annotated bibliography, p.395–461, includes references to statistics for Taiwan, Korea, and Manchoukuo.

See also Yoshiharu S. Matsumoto's *Demographic research in*

Japan, 1955–70 (Honolulu, East-West Ctr., 1974. 78p. Papers of the East-West Population Inst., no.30).　　HB3651.T3

Jordan

Jordan. Dā'irat al-Iḥṣa'at al-'Ammah. Statistical yearbook. no.1– . Amman, 1950?– . Annual.　　**CG282**

At head of title: The Hashemite Kingdom of Jordan.

Text in English and Arabic. Includes demographic, agricultural, and economic statistics.　　HA1950.J6A22a

Kenya

Kenya. Central Bureau of Statistics. Statistical abstract, 1955– . [Nairobi], 1955– . Annual.　　**CG283**

Issuing body varies.

Offers current statistics on a wide range of geographical, social, and economic topics, with the agency usually noted as the source. Updated by the quarterly *Kenya statistical digest.*
　　HA1977.K4A22

Obudho, Robert A. Demography, urbanization, and spatial planning in Kenya: a bibliographical survey. Westport, Conn., Greenwood Pr., [1985]. 285p. (African special bibliographic ser., no.7)　　**CG283a**

3,231 citations are grouped according to form in six sections: bibliography of bibliographies, books, articles, public documents, doctoral dissertations, and unpublished manuscripts. Arrangement within each section is alphabetical by author. Author index, but no subject approach.　　Z7164.D3O27

Korea, Republic of

Han'guk Ūnhaeng. Chosabu. Economic statistics yearbook. Ed.1– . Seoul, 1960– . Annual.　　**CG284**

Added title page in Korean. Text in Korean and English.

Besides economic data, gives statistical information on area, population, agriculture, minerals, education, communications, etc.

Korea statistical yearbook. [Ed.1]– , 1953– . [Seoul?], Economic Planning Board, Republic of Korea, [1953]– . Annual.　　**CG284a**

Title varies: *Statistical yearbook of the Republic of Korea.*

In English and Korean.

Includes basic statistical data on Korea—land, climate, population, economy, society, education, public health, etc.
　　HA4630.5.A34

Latin America

See also CG78–CG84, and names of individual countries.

Anuario estadístico de América Latina. Statistical yearbook for Latin America, 1973– . Santiago, Chile, United Nations Economic Commission for Latin America, 1974– .
　　CG285

Supersedes the Commission's *Boletín estadístico de América Latina; Statistical bulletin for Latin America* (1964–72).

In English and Spanish.

Each issue consists of a number of parts: (1) statistical series for region and regional associations (e.g., Latin American Free Trade Association, Andean Group, Central American Common Market, and Caribbean Free Trade Association); (2–4) statistical series for Latin American and Caribbean countries arranged alphabetically by country. Includes population, national accounts, agriculture, industry, transport, trade, prices, balance of payments, and social statistics.　　JX1977.A2

Statistical abstract of Latin America. [Ed.1–] 1955– . [Los Angeles, Univ. of California at Los Angeles, Center of Latin American Studies], 1956– . Annual (irregular). (Ed.23, 1984)   **CG286**

With ed. 17 (1976) of the main work several changes in content and format were made: (1) "Non-Latin American countries" (Barbados, Jamaica, Guyana, Trinidad and Tobago) were excluded; (2) a time-series dimension was added, rather than simply presenting material for the most current year; (3) the twenty Latin American countries are presented in alphabetical order in each table; (4) a cartogram series has been added to show the spatial extent of political units in terms of population size; (5) series which have not changed significantly since the previous edition, or which are scheduled for updating in the next edition, are not published.

HA935.S8

—— Supplement [1]– . Los Angeles, 1970– .

Contents: [no.1] Cuba 1968 (publ. 1970); [no.2] Latin American political statistics (publ. 1972); [no.3] Statistics and national policy (publ. 1974); [no.4] Urbanization in 19th century Latin America: statistics and sources (publ. 1973); [no.5] Measuring land reform (publ. 1974); [no.6] Quantitative Latin America studies: methods and findings (publ. 1977); [no.7] Money and politics in Latin America (publ. 1977); [no.8] Latin American population and urbanization analysis: maps and statistics, 1950–1982 (publ. 1984); [no.9] Statistical abstract of the United States–Mexico borderlands (publ. 1984).

Bibliography

Edmondston, Barry. Population research in Latin America and the Caribbean; a reference bibliography. [Ann Arbor, Mich.], Publ. for the Internat. Studies Program and the Latin American Studies Program, Cornell Univ., by University Microfilms Internat., 1979. 161p.   **CG287**

Cites monographs and articles readily available in large academic libraries. Topical arrangement subdivided by country. No index.

Z7164.D3E37

Resúmenes sobre población en América Latina. Latin American population abstracts. v.1, no.1– , June 1977– . Santiago, Chile, Centro Latinoamericano de Demografía, 1977– . 2 nos. per yr.   **CG288**

Other title: *DOCPAL Resúmenes de población en América Latina.* Vol. for June 1977 also called "Número experimental."

Each issue supplies about 700 Spanish-language abstracts of a wide variety of materials relating to Central and South America and the Caribbean. Detailed subject classification, with subject, geographic, and author indexes. Lists books, conferences, institutional publications, and journals indexed in each issue. The Latin American Population Documentation System maintains a computerized database on all Latin American and Caribbean population documents written since 1970; in 1979 the database included 10,000 entries, with 250 added each month. *Resúmenes* includes only the most important titles added since 1975. The entire database is available for searching and document delivery service through the Latin American Population Documentation System.

HB3350.5.R48●

Lebanon

Lebanon. Mudīrīyat al-Iḥṣā' al-Markazī. al-Majmū'ah al-iḥṣa'īyah al-Lubnānīyah; recueil de statistiques libanaises. v.1– , 1963– . Beyrouth, Direction Centrale de la Statistique, [1964?]– . Annual.   **CG289**

In Arabic and French.

Offers data on climate, population, housing, agriculture, industry, health, education, and various sectors of the economy, with long time series.   HA1950.L4A35

Libya

Libya. Maṣlaḥat al-Iḥṣa' wa-al-Ta'dād. Majmu'ah al-iḥṣā'i-yah, 1958/62– . Tripoli, Census and Statistics Dept., 1963– . Annual.   **CG290**

Title varies: *Statistical abstract of Libya.*
In Arabic and English.
Strongest in economic statistics, but also includes data on meteorology, demography, health statistics, and education.

HA2167.L5A34

Luxembourg

Luxemburg. Service Central de la Statistique et des Études Économiques. Annuaire statistique. 1955– . Luxembourg, 1956. v.1– . Annual.   **CG291**

Before 1940 the annual statistics were published as supplements to the *Annuaire officiel* of the Office de la Statistique Générale, 1925–30, under the title "Note statistique"; 1931–40 as "Aperçu statistique." Publication suspended 1941–45.

The present series gives comparative figures from 1938 and selected dates thereafter. Plans call for a large retrospective compilation to be issued as the 1973 annual.

Malawi

Malaŵi statistical yearbook, 1965– . Zomba, Nat. Statistical Office, [1966]– . Annual.   **CG292**

Title varies: 1965–70, *Compendium of statistics for Malawi.*
Presents statistics provided by government departments, statutory bodies, private firms, and the National Statistical Office. Some printed sources are given, but generally only the agency is listed.

HA1977.M3M33

Malaysia

Malaya (Federation). Official year book. v.1– , 1961– . Kuala Lumpur, Govt. Pr., 1961– . Annual.   **CG293**

At head of title: Ministry of the Interior.   DS591.A27

Malaysia official yearbook, v.1– , 1961– . Kuala Lumpur, Federal Dept. of Information, Ministry of Information, [1961?]– . il. Annual.   **CG294**

Cover title: *Buku rasmi tahunan. Official yearbook.*
A handbook with narrative and statistical data on all aspects of Malaysian society, politics, and economic conditions. Chronology; bibliography.

Another edition, *Malaysia, buku rasmi tahunan* began publication 1976.   DS591.A27

Mali

Annuaire statistique de la République du Mali, 1966– . [Bamako], Service de la Statistique Générale, de la Comptabilité Économique Nationale et de la Mécanographie, [1966?]– . il. Annual.   **CG295**

Introductory general statistics are followed by data on climate, population, economic resources, transportation and communications, prices, and finances.   HA2096.A15

Imperato, Pascal J. and **Imperato, Eleanor M.** Mali, a handbook of historical statistics. [Boston], G. K. Hall, [1982]. 339p. maps.   **CG296**

Presents a classed arrangement of statistics, mostly from the

period 1930–1973, with introductory essays and bibliographic references. Health statistics are especially comprehensive. Indexed.
HA4727.I56

Malta

Malta. Office of Statistics. Annual abstract of statistics. no.1– , 1946– . Valetta, 1947– . Annual.   **CG297**

Title varies; early volumes called *Statistical abstract of the Maltese islands.*
Statistical tables on demographic, economic, and cultural aspects of the area.   HA1117.M3A3

Malta year book for the year 1953–78. . . St. Julian's, St. Michael's College Publ., [1953–78]. il. Annual.   **CG298**

General information, with some summary statistics and articles on various aspects of Maltese history, culture, etc. Superseded by *The year book* (Sliema, De La Salle, 1979–).   DG987.M33

Mauritania

Mauritania. Direction de la Statistique et des Études Économiques. Annuaire statistique, 1968– . [Noakchott, 1969]– . Annual.   **CG299**

Issuing agency varies.
Early volumes provided brief chronology as well as statistics on socioeconomic aspects of the country. Emphasizes the current two years, with some ten-year time series.   HA2096.5.A2a

Mexico

México. Dirección General de Estadística. Anuario estadístico, 1893– . México, 1894– . Annual (irregular).   **CG300**

Title varies slightly.
None published 1908–29, 1931–37.
Covers population, education, labor, agriculture, industry, communication, commerce, finance, etc.   HA762.A3

Rowe, Patricia M. Detailed statistics on the urban and rural population of Mexico: 1950 to 2010. Wash., Internat. Demographic Data Center, U.S. Bureau of the Census, 1982. 242p. map.   **CG301**

Presents statistics on population, fertility, mortality, and migration, and summary data on family planning, marital status, health, religion, education, literacy, labor force, households, and gross national product. Glossary; bibliographic sources.   HA765.R68

Bibliography

México. Dirección de Estadística. Bibliografía mexicana de estadística. México, Talleres Gráficos de la Nación, [1942]. 2v.   **CG302**

Contents: t.1, Generalidades, teoría y aplicaciones metodológicas, demografía, estadística social, económica, administrativa geografía; t.2, Historia, lingüística, publicaciones periódicas, cartografía, titulos complementarios. Índice general geográfico. Índice onomástico de autores.   Z7554.M6M6

—— Catálogo general de las estadísticas nacionales. México, 1960. 127p.   **CG303**

1st ed., 1937, had title *Catálogo de estadística.*

A listing of Mexican statistical publications, arranged by subject, with general index. Dates are not indicated.   HA37.M7

—— —— Índice. México, 1960. 44p.

Morocco

Morocco. al-Maslahah al-Markazīyah lil-Ihṣa'iyat. Annuaire statistique du Maroc. [v.1]– , 1925– . Rabat, 1926– . Annual (irregular).   **CG304**

Volumes for 1925–54 in French; 1955/56– in French and Arabic. Some volumes cover 2-year periods; v.14 covers 1939–44. Title varies slightly. Issuing body varies.   HA2181.A3

Nepal

Nepal. Central Bureau of Statistics. Statistical pocket book, Nepal, 1974– . Kathmandu, [1974?]– . Irregular.   **CG305**

Includes the latest available data on area and population, agriculture, mineral production, education, health, etc., with some international comparative statistics.   HA1950.N5A14a

Netherlands

Netherlands. Centraal Bureau voor de Statistiek. Jaarcijfers voor Nederlanden. Statistical year book of the Netherlands. 1881–1967/68. 'sGravenhage, Bureau, [1882]–1970.
     CG306

Title varies.
Text in Dutch and French, 1884–1939; in Dutch and German, 1940–1941/42; in Dutch and English, 1943/46–1967/68.
From 1887 to 1921, each volume consisted of two parts: (1) "Rijk in Europa," and (2) "Kolonien"; from 1922 to 1939, the "Kolonien" section was continued as a separate publication by Netherlands East Indies (*see* CG250).
Most tables give comparative figures for a 5-year period or longer. Superseded by:

Statistical yearbook of the Netherlands, 1969/70– . The Hague, Staatsuitgeverij, 1971– . Annual.   **CG307**

At head of title: Netherlands Central Bureau of Statistics.
Supersedes *Jaarcijfers voor Nederlanden* (above).
Inasmuch as it was felt that the yearbook was most widely used in foreign countries, the decision was made to publish in English. Includes a bibliography of sources of statistics.   HA1381.S75

New Zealand

Bloomfield, Gerald T. New Zealand, a handbook of historical statistics. Boston, G. K. Hall, [1984]. 429p. maps.
     CG308

Based on published New Zealand official statistics from 1840 to 1975. Indexed.   HA3184.B55

New Zealand. Dept. of Statistics. Catalogue of New Zealand statistics. [4th ed.] [Wellington, 1977–79] 1v.   **CG309**

1st ed. 1962.
A guide to locating official statistics in government publications and to statistical data published elsewhere, not a compendium of statistical data.   Z7554.N5A47

—— New Zealand official year-book, 1892– . Wellington, 1892– . v.1– . Annual.   **CG310**

Covers a wide range of descriptive as well as statistical information. Recent volumes include a list of special articles appearing in previous issues, and a select bibliography of New Zealand publications.   DU400.A3

Nicaragua

Nicaragua. Dirección General de Estadística. Anuario estadístico, 1938– . Managua, Talleres Nacionales, 1939– . Annual. **CG311**

Title varies; issuing body varies. Publication suspended 1948–68.

———— Resumen estadístico, 1950–1960. Managua, 1960. 115p. il. **CG312**

Charts and tables relating to meteorology, demography, education, industry, transportation, commerce, banking and finance, etc.

Niger

Niger. Ministère du Développement et de la Coopération. Direction de la Statistique. Annuaire statistique, 1962– . [Niamey, 1963?]– . Annual. **CG313**

Presents data on geography, population, economic activities, finances, relations with foreign countries, planning and national accounts; most statistics have a 10-year time series. HA2097.A27

Nigeria

Nigeria. Federal Office of Statistics. Annual abstract of statistics. v.1– , 1960– . Lagos, Federal Govt. Printer, 1960– . Annual. **CG314**

Statistical tables on area and climate, population, manpower, agriculture, industry, trade, finance, education, etc. HA1977.N5A22

Norway

Norway. Statistisk Sentralbyrå. Statistisk årbok for Norge; Statistical yearbook of Norway, 1880– . Oslo, 1881– . v.1– . Annual. **CG315**

Title varies.
1886–1951 in Norwegian and French; 1952– in Norwegian and English. v.62–64, covering 1943–45, publ. in 1v. 1946.
Includes demographic, economic, social, and cultural data. Many tables include comparative figures from earlier years. Includes an international section. HA1502.A32

Pakistan

Pakistan statistical yearbook. Ed. 1– , 1952– . Karachi, Manager of Pubns., 1954– . Irregular. **CG316**

Issued by the Central Statistical Office of Pakistan.
Continues the *Statistical digest of Pakistan,* issued by the Dept. of Commercial Intelligence and Statistics, 1950.
1972 ed. includes comparative statistics for 1947–72; 1982 ed. for 1972–82. HA1730.5.P33

Statistical pocket-book of Pakistan. Ed.1– , 1962– . Karachi, Manager of Pubns., 1962– . Annual. **CG317**

Issued by the Central Statistical Office of Pakistan.
Offers a variety of statistics in concise form. HA1730.5.S7

Panama

Panama. Departamento de Estadística. Anuario de estadística, 1908–1934. Panama, 1909–36. Irregular. **CG318**

Name of issuing agency varies.

Title varies; 1908–10 called *Estadística anual.* Some years issued in the Department's *Boletin de estadística;* many years not published? HA851.A2

Panama. Dirección de Estadística y Censos. Panama en cifras. [Ed.1–] Panama, 1953– . Irregular. **CG319**

Title varies: *Nuestro progreso en cifras* (Ed.1–2, 1953–58). Most volumes cover a 5-year period. HA852.A57

Paraguay

Paraguay. Dirección General de Estadística y Censos. Anuario estadístico, 1886– . Asunción, Impr. Nacional, 1888– . Irregular. **CG320**

Name of issuing agency varies.
Statistical tables relating to climate, demography, education, health and social welfare, finance, agriculture, industry, commerce, etc. HA1041.A2

Peru

Perú. Dirección Nacional de Estadística y Censos. Anuario estadístico del Perú, 1918– . Lima, 1919– . Irregular. **CG321**

Name of issuing agency varies. Title varies: 1918–43, *Extracto estadístico del Peru.*
v.27 (n.s.v.11), covering 1958–66 (publ. 1969) last published?
Detailed tables for a wide range of demographic, economic, and social aspects of the country. HA1052.A452

Philippines

Philippine statistical yearbook. [Ed.1– , 1940– . Manila, Nat. Economic and Development Authority, 1941– . Irregular. **CG322**

Title and issuing body vary.
Not published 1941–45, 1947–56.

Poland

Poland. Glowny Urzad Statystyczny. Rocznik statystyczny, rok 1– , 1920/21– . Warsaw, 1922– . Annual (irregular). **CG323**

Title varies: 1920/21–38, in Polish and French, *Rocznik statystyki . . . Annuaire statistique de la République Polonaise.*
Now issued also in English (*Statistical yearbook of Poland*), French and German.
Offers a wide range of statistical tables, many with comparative figures for recent years. Includes an international section. HA1451.A46

———— Concise statistical yearbook of Poland. v.1– , 1930– . Warsaw, 1930– . Annual (irregular). **CG324**

At head of title: Central Statistical Office of the Polish People's Republic.
Title varies. Publication suspended 1940–46.
Some issues published in English, French, and Russian editions; recent years in English, German, and Russian. HA1451.A47

———— Bibliografia wydawnictw Głownego Urzędu Statystycznego, 1918–1968. Warszawa, 1968. 466p. **CG325**

A classified listing, chronological within sections, of Polish statistical publications. Z7554.P6A5

Portugal

Portugal. Instituto Nacional de Estatística. Anuário estatístico. Annuaire statistique. 1962– . Lisboa, [1963?]– . Annual.   **CG326**

Continues the Instituto's *Anuário estatístico* (1875–1960) and its *Anuário estatístico do ultramar* (1943–61), formerly issued separately.

In Portuguese and French.

1962–73 issued in two parts: (1) Continente e ilhas adjacentes; (2) Províncias ultramarinas. From 1974 covers only Portugal, the Azores, and Madeira, as indicated in the current subtitle: *Continente, Açores e Madeira*.   HA1575.A58

Romania

Anuarul statistic al Republicii Socialiste Romania. 1902– . Bucureşti, Direcţia Centrală de Statistică, 1902– . Annual.   **CG327**

Title varies.

The agency also publishes a concise version in English, German, French, and Spanish; the English edition is called *Statistical pocket book of the Socialist Republic of Romania* (1960–).   HA1641.A2

Rwanda

Rwanda. Direction de la Statistique et de la Documentation. Bulletin de statistique . . . Supplément annuel, no.1– , 1974– . Kigali, [1974]– . il. Annual.   **CG328**

Contains statistical data for the current year and some two years previous; a variety of social and agricultural statistics are unique to the annual supplement whereas the *Bulletin de statistique* presents primarily economic data.   HA2124.R8A15a

El Salvador

El Salvador. Dirección General de Estadística y Censos. Anuario estadístico, 1911–23, 1927– . San Salvador, Impr. Nacional, 1912– . Annual.   **CG329**

Most years issued in two parts; recent years in five volumes: (1) Comercio exterior (Importación; Exportación); (2) Demografía, Salud; (3) Industria, Comercio, Servicios; (4) Meteorología, Agricultura y ganadería, Costo de vida y comercio interior, Transporte y comunicaciones, Construcciones, Fisco, Banca; (5) Educación, Cultura, Justicia.   HA841.A2

Saudi Arabia

Saudi Arabia. Maṣlaḥat al-Iḥṣā'at al- 'Āmmah. al-Kitāb al-iḥṣā'ī al-sanawī, 1– , 1965– . [al-Riyāḍ], Wizārat al-Mālīyah wa-al- Iqtiṣād al-Watanī, Maṣlaḥat al-Iḥṣā'at al-'Āmmah, [1965]– . il. Annual.   **CG330**

Added title page: *Statistical yearbook—Central Department of Statistics.*

In Arabic and English.

Provides data for the most recent two years, with occasional 5- and 10-year time series. While most topical areas are covered, demographic statistics are notably absent.   HA1681.M37a

Senegal

Senegal. Direction de la Statistique. Situation économique du Sénégal, 1967– . [Dakar], République du Sénégal, Ministère des Finances et Affaires Économiques, Direction de la Statistique, [1968?]– . il. Annual.   **CG331**

Offers statistics on demography, education, health, and a variety of economic topics. Supplemented by a series which began publication in 1976 by the Société Africaine d'Édition, *Le Sénégal en chiffre; annuaire statistique du Sénégal.*   HA2099.A262

Sierra Leone

Sierra Leone. Central Statistics Office. Annual statistical digest, 1968– . [Freetown, 1969?]– . Annual.   **CG332**

Presents geographical data, social and demographic statistics, and economic/price statistics, all subdivided for detailed topics. Sources indicated are usually an agency or ministry, but some printed sources are cited.

Singapore

Yearbook of statistics: Singapore, 1967– . Singapore, Dept. of Statistics, [1967?]– . il. Annual.   **CG333**

Presents data on climate and land utilization, demography, labor, agriculture, industry, power, etc., usually with a ten-year time series.   HA1797.S5A35

Somalia

Statistical abstract (Somalia. Waaxda Dhexe ee Istaatistikada), no.1– , 1964– . Prep. and printed by the Government of the Democratic Republic of Somalia, Central Statistical Dept., Ministry of Planning and Co-ordination. Mogadishu, The Dept., 1964– . Annual.   **CG334**

In English and Italian (later in Somali).

Title varies.

Offers statistics in meteorology, population, education, foreign trade, agriculture, health, development program, banking, industry, etc.   HA2167.A2

South Africa

Johnson, Peter D. and **Campbell, Paul R.** Detailed statistics on the population of South Africa, by race and urban/rural residence: 1950 to 2010. Wash., Internat. Demographic Data Center, U.S. Bureau of the Census, 1982. 455p.   **CG335**

Presents statistics on population, fertility, mortality, and migration, with summary data on family planning, marital status, health, religion, education, literacy, labor force, households, and gross national product. Glossary; bibliographic sources.   HA4701.J64

South Africa. Dept. of Statistics. Suid-Afrikaanse statistieke. South African statistics. 1968– . Pretoria, 1968– . Biennial.   **CG336**

Continues the Bureau of Statistics' *Statistical yearbook* (1964–66).

In English and Afrikaans.

Includes tables (usually with comparative statistics for recent years) for population, health, education, labor, prices, agriculture, industry, trade, finance, etc.   HA1991.A232

South Africa. Office of Census and Statistics. Official year book of the Union and of Basutoland, Bechuanaland Protectorate and Swaziland, 1917–60. Pretoria, Govt. Printer, 1918–61. v.1–30. maps. Biennial.   **CG337**

An important yearbook, giving detailed statistical, descriptive,

and historical information, with bibliographies and lists of government publications. no.1–2, 1917–18, do not include Basutoland.
Ceased publication. DT752.A3

———— Uniestatistieke oor vyftig jaar; jubileumuitgawe, 1910–1960 . . . Union statistics for fifty years; jubilee issue. [Pretoria, 1960] lv., various pagings. **CG338**

Bilingual throughout. Tables for vital statistics, education, labor, agriculture, industry, etc. Table of contents and notes for each section, but no general index. HA1992.A5

State of South Africa; pictorial, social, economic, financial and statistical year-book for the Republic of South Africa. v.1– , 1957– . Johannesburg, Da Gama, [1957?]– . il. Annual. **CG339**

Title and publisher vary.
A comprehensive yearbook on conditions in the Union of South Africa. HC517.S7S82

Year book and guide to Southern Africa: Republic of South Africa, Federation of Rhodesia and Nyasaland, South West Africa, etc., ed. annually for the Union-Castle Mail Steamship Co., 1901–71. London, R. Hale, 1901–71. il., maps. Annual. **CG340**

Title varies. Not published 1941–46.
A useful yearbook containing a large amount of descriptive, statistical, and gazetteer information.
Covered South and East Africa 1913–49. In 1950, the former *South and East African year book and guide* was divided into two separate publications, of which this is one; the other, *Year book and guide to East Africa,* ceased publication in 1965.

Spain

Spain. Dirección General de Estadística (1938–). Zona de Protectorado y de los Territorios de Soberanía de España en el Norte de Africa. Anuario estadístico, 1941–55. Madrid, 1942–57. 13v. il. Annual. **CG341**

Detailed statistical tables for Spanish territories and protectorates.
Ceased publication. HA2231.A3

Spain. Instituto Nacional de Estadística. Anuario estadístico de España, 1858– . Madrid, 1859– . Annual (slightly irregular). **CG342**

Issuing agency varies.
Suspended publication 1868–1911, 1935–42. 1912 also called año 1.
In two parts: (1) Totales nacionales; (2) Detalle provincial. HA1543.A52

———— ———— Edición manual, 1941– . Irregular. **CG342a**

A concise version of the *Anuario.* Some issues cover two years.

Inventario de estadísticas de España, 1960–81. Barcelona, CIDC, Departamento de Documentación, [1981?]. 641p. **CG343**

Produced by the Consorcio d'Información y Documentación de Cataluña.
Earlier eds. publ. 1975, 1978.
A list of official statistical publications arranged by agency, indicating years or editions published; indexed by agency, title, and subject. A *Suplemento 1, 1982–83* adds an additional 95 publications. Z7165.S7I58

Sri Lanka

Śrī Lankā saṅkhyāta nibardhaya. Ilaṅkaip puḷḷiviparat tokuppu. Statistical abstract of Ceylon, 1949– . Colombo, Dept. of Census and Statistics, 1949– . Annual. **CG344**

Title varies; issuing agency varies.
In English, Sinhalese, and Tamil.
The 1949 volume covers 1937–48.
Contains, with additions, the types of information formerly appearing in the discontinued *Ceylon blue book* (Colombo, 1892–1938): statistics of population, commerce, industry, education, etc. HA1728.C43

Peebles, Patrick. Sri Lanka: a handbook of historical statistics. Boston, G. K. Hall, [1982]. 357p. **CG345**

19th and 20th-century statistics derived from colonial, commercial, and national government sources are grouped in subject chapters with prefatory essays. Subject index. HA4750.8.P43

Sweden

Sweden. Statistika Centralbyrån. Statistisk årsbok för Sverige. Statistical yearbook of Sweden. Stockholm, 1914– . Annual. **CG346**

Title and text in Swedish and English, 1952– ; previously in Swedish and French.
Continues *Sveriges officiella statistik i sammandrag,* 1870–1913.
Includes a section of comparative international statistics. HA1523.A46

Switzerland

See also CG30.

Switzerland. Statistisches Bureau. Statistisches Jahrbuch der Schweiz. Annuaire statistique de la Suisse, 1891– . Bern, 1891– . v.1– . Annual. **CG347**

In place of the yearbook for 1897, the *Graphischstatistischer Atlas der Schweiz, 1897,* was issued.
Some tables give figures for 30 years. HA1593.A4

Syria

Syria. al-Maktab al-Markazī lil-Iḥsā'. al-Majmū'a al-iḥsā'īya. Statistical abstract of Syria. Ed.1– , 1948– . Damascus, Govt. Printer, [1948?]– . Annual. **CG348**

Issuing agency varies.
In Arabic and English; 1st and 2d eds. in Arabic only. HA1941.A32

Tanzania

Handbook of Tanganyika. 2d ed. Ed. by J. P. Moffett, Commissioner for Social Development. [Dar-es-Salaam, Govt. Printer, 1958] 703p. il., maps. **CG349**

1st ed. 1930, issued by the Chief Secretary's Office, ed. by Gerald F. Sayers.
An historical and descriptive account of the territory, with statistics throughout the text. Although compiled in part from official sources, is not an official publication. Bibliography, p.567–677. DT438.H3

Tanzania. Bureau of Statistics. Statistical abstract. 1964– . [Dar es Salaam, 1965–] **CG350**

Supersedes: Tanganyika. Central Statistical Bureau. *Statistical abstract* (1961–63).
Includes tables for land and climate, population, trade, transport, agriculture, commerce and industry, finance, employment, public health, education, etc. HA2131.B87b

Thailand

Thailand. Samnakngān Sathiti hoeng-Chāt. Statistical bibliography. [Ed.1–] Bangkok, [1961]– . (1976/83 ed. publ. 1984) **CG351**

Early issues had subtitle: An annotated bibliography of Thai government statistical publications.   Z7554.T5S8

—— Statistical year book, Thailand. no.1– . [Bangkok], 1916– . Irregular. **CG352**

Publisher varies.
In Thai and English. Volumes cover two to ten years.
Presents statistical tables in the fields of economics, public administration, and social matters.   HA1781.A3

Wilson, Constance M. Thailand: a handbook of historical statistics. Boston, G. K. Hall, [1983]. 366p. **CG353**

Tables are topically arranged and are based mainly on published Thai government statistics. Sources are indicated; some figures are from the 1800s, but most tables include only 20th-century statistics. Indexed.   HA4600.55.W54

Togo

Annuaire statistique (Togo. Ministère des Finances, de l'Économie et du plan. Direction de la Statistique), 1966/69– . Lomé, La Direction, [1971]– . Annual. **CG354**

Continues in part the *Inventaire économique du Togo* issued by the Service de la Statistique et de la Comptabilité Nationale, 1956–[67].   HA4723.A22

Trinidad and Tobago

Trinidad and Tobago. Central Statistical Office. Annual statistical digest. no.1– , 1935/51– . [Port of Spain], 1951– . Annual. **CG355**

1951–68 issued by Trinidad Central Statistical Office. No.1 includes data for 1935–51. Sources of statistics indicated.   HA867.A35

Trinidad and Tobago year book, 1865– , containing information obtained from official records and reliable sources. Port of Spain, 1865– . Annual. **CG356**

   F2121.T833

Tunisia

Tunisia. Service des Statistiques. Annuaire statistique de la Tunisie, 1913– . Tunis, 1914– . Annual. **CG357**

Title and issuing body vary.
Early volumes focus on population, public works, agriculture, and mining; later volumes add a wider range of socioeconomic statistics, usually with a ten-year time series.   HA2071.T52

Turkey

See also CG132.

Spitler, James F. and **Roof, Michael K.** Detailed statistics on the urban and rural population of Turkey: 1950 to 2000. Wash., Internat. Demographic Data Center, U.S. Bureau of the Census, 1982. 496p. map. **CG358**

Presents statistics on size of population, and estimates of fertility, mortality, and migration for total, urban, and rural areas, as well as summary information on family planning, marital status, health, religion, education, literacy, labor force, household size, and gross national product. Glossary; bibliographic sources.

   HA4556.5.S64

Turkey. Devlet Istatistik Enstitüsü. Türkiye istatistik yilligi. Statistical yearbook of Turkey, 1928– . [Ankara], 1928– . v.1– . Annual. **CG359**

Title varies; issuing body varies.
Not published 1954–58; resumed 1959.
Volume for 1928 in French only; to 1968 in Turkish and French; 1968– have title also in English: *Statistical yearbook of Turkey,* with text in Turkish and English.
Provides a statistical summary of various geographical, social, and economic aspects of the country.   HA1911.A3

Uganda

Uganda. Office of the President. Statistics Division. Statistical abstract, 1957– . Entebbe, Govt. Printer, [1958?]– . Annual. **CG360**

Issuing agency varies.
Offers current figures on population, trade, transport and communications, agriculture, public health, education, justice, and sectors of the economy.   HA1977.U35A328

Union of Soviet Socialist Republics

Lewytzkyj, Borys. The Soviet Union: figures—facts—data. Die Sowjetunion: Zahlen—Fakten—Daten. München, K. G. Saur, 1979. 614p. **CG361**

Mainly lists and tables providing information "about size of territories, population, structure of administration, party and state apparat, national economy, science and education" (*Pref.*) and similar matters. "Systematic index" (i.e., detailed table of contents), but no alphabetical index.   DK17.L46

Mickiewicz, Ellen Propper, ed. Handbook of Soviet social science data. N.Y., Free Pr., [1973]. 225p. **CG362**

"This handbook is mainly oriented toward modern, post-Stalin data which . . . are both more abundant and more reliable than earlier data. The data here focus on the more recent problems of development, social, political, and economic; therefore, the bulk of the information relates to the decades beginning with the 1950's."— *Introd.*

Specialists have contributed sections (with introductory notes, tables, and bibliographic references) on demography, agriculture, production, health, housing, education, elite recruitment and mobilization, communications, and international interactions.

   HN523.5.M5

Narodnoe khoziaistvo SSSR; statisticheskii ezhegodnik, [1955]– . Moskva, Gos. Statisticheskoe Izd-vo, 1956– . Annual. **CG363**

Issued by Tsentral'noe Statisticheskoe Upravlenie SSSR.
The official statistical annual, giving data on area, population, economics, industry, agriculture, health, education, and cultural and social affairs. Most important data include comparative figures for the years 1913, 1928, and 1940, pre-Revolutionary and prewar years.
[1971] is a special issue: *K 50-letiiu obrazovaniia SSSR. Narodnoe Khoziaistvo SSSR 1922–1972* (publ. 1972).
For further information concerning USSR statistical materials, *see* Paul L. Horecky, *Basic Russian publications* (DC530).

   HA1432.N3

Shoup, Paul S. The East European and Soviet data handbook: political, social, and developmental indicators, 1945– 1975. N.Y., Columbia Univ. Pr., 1981. 482p. **CG364**

Stresses statistical data for historical and cross-national comparisons on subjects not covered in other sources, such as party membership, social classes, occupations, and levels of education;

also provides sections on population, national and religious affiliation, background of party leaders, developmental indicators and standard of living. Most economic statistics (which are readily available elsewhere) are not included here. Lengthy introduction analyzes problems in use and interpretation of statistics from this region. Appendixes; bibliography; summary of sources; sources for individual tables.   HA1446.S53

USSR: facts and figures annual. v.1– , 1977– . Gulf Breeze, Fla., Academic International Pr., 1977– . il. Annual.   **CG365**

Presents statistical and factual data on various areas of Soviet life: government, Communist Party, republics, demography, armed forces, economy, agriculture, foreign trade and aid, health, education and welfare, communications, transportation, institutions, labor, and special topics. Data are derived from Soviet, American, and international sources; bibliographic references are noted for all data. "Future annual editions are planned as revised continuation volumes to UFFA/1977 rather than another year of the same information."—*Introd.,v.1.* A very useful compendium.

Bibliography

Bibliografiia po problemam narodonaseleniia: sovetskaia i perevodnaia literatura, 1960–1971 gg. Pod red. D. I. Valenteia i E. IU. Burnasheva. Moskva, Statistika, 1974. 342p.   **CG366**

A classed bibliography of 3,299 citations, dealing principally with the demography of the Soviet Union. Supersedes an earlier volume with the same title and by the same editors covering the period 1965–68 (publ. 1971). The same publisher issued *Bibliografiia po problemam narodonaseleniia, 1972–1975 gg.,* by the same editors, in 1977.

Continued by: Z7164.D3B52

Davydova, A. G. Literatura o naselenii: bibliograficheskii ukazatel, 1975–1978 gg. [ukazatel lit-ry sost. A. G. Davydovoi]; pod red. D. I. Valenteia, E. IU. Burnasheva. Moskva, Statistika, 1981. 255p.   **CG367**

Z7164.D3D3

Izdatel'stvo "Statistika." Knigi izdatel'stva "Statistika": 1971–1975 gg: bibliograficheskii ukazatel. [Sost. N. I. Shatunova] Moskva, Statistika, 1976. 79p.   **CG368**

A classed bibliography of 798 citations to material on statistics and on electronic data processing. Indexed.   Z5640.I92

———— Statistika i uchet. Annotirovannyi katalog knig izd-va "Statistika." 1966–1970 gg. Moskva, Statistika, 1971. 423p.   **CG369**

At head of title: Komitet po Pechati pri Sovete Ministrov SSSR.
A classed bibliography of official statistical publications, materials on mathematical statistics, demography, and other areas of statistics. No index.   Z7551.I96

Mashikhin, Evgenii Aleksandrovich and **Simchera, V. M.** Statisticheskie publikatsii v SSSR: bibliogr. ukaz.: [1918–1972]. Moskva, Statistika, 1975. 279p.   **CG370**

Pt.I gives a historical survey of statistics in the Soviet Union during the period indicated, the organizations and agencies concerned with their collection, etc. Pt.II is a bibliography of monographic and serial statistical sources (with titles of special issues) on the national, republic, autonomous region, oblast, and city level. Pt.III lists serial statistical publications by geographic area, on national and republic bases. A final section lists Soviet conferences and symposia proceedings on the subject.   Z7554.R9M3

United Arab Republic

Egypt. Government Press. Almanac, 1902–39. Cairo, Govt. Pr., 1902–39. Annual.   **CG371**

Issuing office varies. 1913–26 had title: *Egyptian government almanac.*
General information, with some statistical tables.   DT43.A3

Egypt. Maṣlaḥat al-Iḥṣā' wa-al-Taʿdād. Annuaire statistique. Année [1]– , 1909– . Cairo, 1909– . Annual (irregular).   **CG372**

Title varies slightly. In Arabic and French.
1909–1955/56 issued by: Egypt. Ministry of Finance. Statistical Department. 1959 last published?
A wide range of statistical tables, many with comparative figures for five to ten years.   HA2042.A5

United Arab Republic. Maṣlaḥat al-Iḥṣā' wa-al-Taʿdād. Ten years of revolution; statistical atlas. Dix ans de révolution; atlas statistique. Cairo, United Arab Republic, Dept. of Statistics and Census, 1962. 1v., unpaged. il.   **CG373**

In English and French.
Statistics on population, national economy, agriculture, industry, transport and communications, trade, education, and health. Most tables include figures from 1951 through 1961, with some projected figures for 1962/63.   HC535.A5685

Uruguay

Rial Roade, Juan. Estadísticas históricas de Uruguay, 1850–1930: población, producción agropecuaria, comercio, industria, urbanización, comunicaciones, calidad de vida. Montevideo, Centro de Informaciones y Estudios del Uruguay, 1980. 168p. (Cuaderno [Centro de Informaciones y Estudios del Uruguay], no.40)   **CG374**

Offers statistical tables, graphs, maps, charts describing Uruguay, ranging from population (e.g., age, sex, region) to health and economics (exports, land use, occupations). List of sources at end of volume.   HA1084.R52

Uruguay. Dirección General de Estadística y Censos. Anuario estadístico, 1884– . Montevideo, Impr. Nacional, 1885– . Quadrennial (irregular).   **CG375**

Name of issuing body varies.
Published in parts.   HA1071

———— Síntesis estadística, 1918– . Annual (slightly irregular).   **CG376**

Ceased with 1941/42?

Venezuela

Venezuela. Dirección General de Estadística y Censos Nacionales. Anuario estadístico de Venezuela, 1877– . Caracas, Ed. Grafolit, 1878– . Irregular; annual since 1964.   **CG377**

Name of issuing agency varies.
Not published 1913–37.
Offers a wide range of detailed statistics. Source of many tables is indicated.   HA1091.A4

West Indies

Caribbean year book. [Ed.1]–50, 1926/27–79/80. London, Skinner, 1927–80. il. Annual.   **CG378**

Title varies: 1927–76, *West Indies and Caribbean year book.*
Covered: Bermuda, Bahamas, Barbados, Guyana, British Honduras, Jamaica, Cayman, Turks and Caicos Islands, Trinidad and Tobago, Leeward Islands, Windward Islands, Canal Zone (Panama), Colombia, Costa Rica, Cuba, Dominican Republic, El Salvador, French Guiana, French West Indies, Guatemala, Haiti, Honduras, Netherlands Antilles, Nicaragua, Panama, Puerto Rico, Surinam, Venezuela, Virgin Islands.

Includes general information, statistics, and trade directories.
F2131.W47

Yugoslavia

Statisticki godisnjak Jugoslavije. 1954– . Beograd, Savezni Zavod za Statistiku, 1954– . Annual. **CG379**

Title varies.

Name of issuing agency varies.

Detailed statistics on a wide range of topics, with comparative figures for recent years.

The Federal Statistical Office of Yugoslavia also issues a *Statistical yearbook of the Socialist Federal Republic of Yugoslavia . . .* English text (Beograd, 1955–). This is a translation key to be used with original tables in *Statisticki godisnjak;* no figures from the tables are reproduced therein. HA1631.A34

Yugoslavia. Direktsīja Drzhavne Statīstīke. Statisticki godisnjak. Annuaire statistique. Knjiga 1–9, 1929–38/39. Beograd, 1932–39. **CG380**

In Serbian and French. HA1631.A3

Statistical pocket-book of Yugoslavia. 1955– . Beograd, 1955– . Annual. **CG381**

At head of title: Federal Institute for Statistics.

Also published in Serbo-Croatian, Russian, German, and French.

Aims to present in concise form "the essential and general statistical information on Yugoslavia, socialist republics and socialist autonomous provinces."—[*p.3*]. HA1631.S8

Zambia

Zambia. Central Statistical Office. Statistical year-book, 1967– . Lusaka, [1968?]– . Annual. **CG382**

Includes tables on population and housing, health, education, labor, agriculture, transport, commerce and industry, trade, finance, etc. HA1977.R48A33

C H

Economics

❖This area is a large one under which many related subjects are grouped: business and business management, commerce, finance and banking, insurance, labor and industrial relations, and various others. Many large libraries, both public and academic, will have special departments devoted to one or several of these subject fields, and in most large cities there will be pertinent special libraries, usually connected with large business or banking concerns. These libraries will have many more specialized sources than can be listed here.

In this section are included some of the bibliographies, indexes, dictionaries, and handbooks from which, or about which, information may be sought in a large general library.

Documents issued by the federal government are particularly useful in the field of economics. Only a few of the many valuable publications of the various departments and bureaus can be listed here. The U.S. Bureau of Labor Statistics, the Bureau of the Census, the Department of Commerce and its various bureaus, including the now defunct Bureau of Foreign and Domestic Commerce, and many others are prolific publishers. For further information consult the *Monthly catalog of United States government publications* (AG51).

GENERAL WORKS

Guides

Information sources in economics. Ed., John Fletcher. 2d ed. London, Butterworths, [1984]. 339p. **CH1**

1st ed. (1971) had title: *The use of economics literature.*

An attempt by British librarians and economists "jointly to view the literature of economics and provide a guide to it."—*Introd.* Introductory chapters on libraries and literature searches are followed by chapters on types of resources—bibliographies, periodicals, documents of national governments and international organizations, statistics, bibliographic and numeric databases. Thirteen chapters on various subject areas of economics were written by economists to suggest the most useful sources. Strong British emphasis. HB71.I53

Maltby, Arthur. Economics and commerce: the sources of information and their organisation. London, Bingley; [Hamden, Conn.], Archon Books, 1968. 239p. **CH2**

A bibliographical survey intended primarily as a text for the British Library Association examination. Z7164.E2M38

Bibliography

Amstutz, Mark R. Economics and foreign policy: a guide to information sources. Detroit, Gale, [1977]. 179p. (International relations information guide ser., v.7) **CH3**

An annotated bibliography of over 750 English-language books and articles on the political economy of international relations, grouped into chapters on international political economy and economic relations, politics and trade, regional integration, politics and the international monetary system, politics and foreign aid, foreign private investment, imperialism, and the economics of war and defense. Final chapter covers bibliographies and journals. Author, title, and subject indexes. Z7164.E17A48

Batson, Harold Edward. A select bibliography of modern economic theory, 1870–1929. London, Routledge, 1930. 224p. (Repr.: N.Y., Kelley, 1968) **CH4**

An annotated bibliography of books and periodical articles; listing is by subject and by author. Z7164.E2B3

Black, Robert Dionysius Collison. A catalogue of pamphlets on economic subjects published between 1750 and 1900 and now housed in Irish libraries. N.Y., Kelley, 1969. 632p. **CH5**

Comprises a union catalog of "pamphlets of economic interest published anywhere between the 1st January, 1750 and the 31st December, 1900" (*Introd.*) and now housed in one or more of the 17 cooperating libraries. Chronological arrangement with author and title indexes. Z7164.E2B6

Braeuer, Walter. Handbuch zur Geschichte der Volkswirtschaftslehre; ein bibliographisches Nachschlagewerk. Frankfurt am Main, Klostermann, [1952]. 224p. **CH6**

An international bio-bibliography of the history of political economy from ancient and medieval times to the modern day, with biographical sketches of important economists. Includes books, dissertations, and periodical articles.

Frank, Geneviève. Women at work and in society; a selected bibliography, 1970–1978. Geneva, International Institute for Labour Studies, [1980]. 99p. (Internat. Inst. for Labour Studies. Bibliography ser., no.2) **CH7**

Title and prefatory material also in French.

Over 500 English- and French-language books, periodical articles, symposia proceedings, and documents grouped by topic: labor force participation, work and family, sexual division of work, education and training, women's role in the economy, etc. Author index.

Z7963.E7F72

Fundaburk, Emma Lila. Development of economic thought and analysis. Metuchen, N.J., Scarecrow Pr., 1973. 875p. (The history of economic thought & analysis: a selective international bibliography, v.1) **CH8**

In three main sections: general works; specific works on particular economists, countries and areas, method and scope, and supply, demand, value, price; works on historical periods and schools. Author/subject and short-title indexes. Z7164.E2F82

Goldsmiths'-Kress library of economic literature: a consolidated guide to Segment I–[II] of the microfilm collection. Woodbridge, Conn., Research Pubns., 1976–[83]. v.1–5. (In progress.) **CH9**

Contents: v.1, Through 1720; v.2, 1721–1776; v.3, 1777–1800; v.4, 1801–1820; v.5, 1920–1831.

Primarily an access tool to the microfilm collection published by Research Publications of the holdings of the Goldsmiths' Library of Economic Literature at the University of London and the Kress Library of Business and Economics at the Harvard Graduate School of Business.

Arranged chronologically, with topical headings within years.

Z7164.E2G64

London. University. Goldsmiths' Company's Library of Economic Literature. Catalogue of the Goldsmiths' Library.... Comp. by Margaret Canney and David Knott. Cambridge, University Pr., 1970–83. 4v. **CH10**

Contents: v.1, Printed books to 1800; v.2, Printed books 1801–1850; v.3, Additions to the printed books to 1850. Periodicals. Manuscripts; v.4, Index.

The completed set records about 40,000 books printed before 1851, periodicals which began publication before 1851, manuscripts and autograph letters. The collection is one of the world's finest for early works on economics. Z7164.E2L65

Harvard University. Graduate School of Business Administration. Baker Library. The Kress Library of Business and Economics. Catalogue, covering material published through 1776, with data upon cognate items in other Harvard libraries. Boston, Baker Lib., Harvard Graduate School of Business Admin., [1940]. 414p. (Repr.: N.Y., Kelley, 1964) **CH11**

Arranged chronologically, with alphabetical index of authors and anonymous titles. Z7166.H332

——— Catalogue, 1777–1817, giving data also upon cognate items in other Harvard libraries. Boston, 1957. 397p.

——— Catalogue, 1818–1848, giving data also upon cognate items in other Harvard libraries. Boston, 1964. 397p.

——— Catalogue supplement, 1473–1848, giving data also upon cognate items in other Harvard libraries. Boston, 1967. 453p.

Replaces the original (1956) supplement, incorporating the 2,569 entries from that volume into the present listing of 6,902 items.

Harvard University. Library. Economics and economics periodicals. Cambridge, distr. by Harvard Univ. Pr., 1970. 2v. (Widener Library shelflist, 23–24) **CH12**

For a note on the series *see* AA145.

Contents: v.1, Classification schedule, classified listing by call number, chronological listing; v.2, Author and title listing.

Lists "over 65,000 books and periodicals including works on economic theory, economic history and conditions, transportation and communications, commerce, and finance as well as on more specialized aspects of economics such as demography, corporations, money, taxation, insurance, etc."—*Pref.* Z7164.E2H37

Hollander, Jacob Harry. The economic library of Jacob H. Hollander, comp. by Elsie A. G. Marsh. Baltimore, 1937. 324p. **CH13**

3,860 titles, chronologically arranged, 1574–1936. Particularly rich in 18th-century English tracts. Z997.H73

Hutchinson, William Kenneth. History of economic analysis: a guide to information sources. Detroit, Gale, [1976]. 243p. (Economics information guide ser., 3) **CH14**

A "sourcebook for the neophyte" (*Introd.*), dealing with the period 1600–1940. Each chapter is devoted to a particular school of thought—the forerunners of classical economics, classical economics, inductivists, marginalists, American economists, and 20th-century British economic thought—and consists of introduction, major contributions, commentaries on the major contributions, and contributions of lesser importance; the last are not annotated. List of relevant journals and organizations. Author, title, and subject index. Z7164.E2H87

Krannert Library. A catalogue of rare books, pamphlets, and journals on business and economics in the Krannert Library special collection, 1500–1870. [West Lafayette, Ind.], Purdue Univ., 1979. 357p. **CH15**

Comp. by John M. Houkes and Ljudmila T. Mursec.
Preliminary eds. publ. 1970 and 1974.

A chronologically arranged bibliography of about 5,000 books, pamphlets, and serial titles from the Krannert collection and other Purdue University libraries; government documents have been excluded. Name and title index. Z7164.C81K75

McCulloch, John Ramsay. The literature of political economy; a classified catalogue of select publications in the different departments of that science, with historical, critical, and biographical notices. London, Longmans, 1845. 407p. (Repr.: London School of Economics and Political Science. Ser. of reprints of scarce works on political economy, no.5, 1938) **CH16**

Z7164.E2M2

Melnyk, Peter. Economics; bibliographic guide to reference books and information sources. Littleton, Colo., Libraries Unlimited, 1971. 263p. **CH17**

Includes sections on economic theory, economic conditions in various countries, private and public finance, commerce and marketing, international economics, economic geography, industry and transportation, labor economics, population and statistics, and a selected list of periodicals. Many annotations. Index.

Z7164.E2M45

Mossé, Robert. Bibliographie d'économie politique, 1945–1960; histoire des doctrines, statistique et économétrie, géographie économique, économie rurale, économie financière, travail, sociologie, démographie. Paris, Sirey, [1963]. 124p. **CH18**

A classed bibliography on political economy interpreted broadly. Continues for this area the work of Grandin (CA17).

——— ——— [Supplément 1–5] 1960/62–1972/74. Paris, Sirey, 1966–76. 5v.

Z7164.E2M69

Schleiffer, Hedwig and **Crandall, Ruth.** Index to economic history essays in Festschriften, 1900–1950. Cambridge, Mass., publ. by Arthur H. Cole and distr. by Harvard Univ. Pr., 1953. 68p. **CH19**

Arranged by broad subjects (period and geographical division, followed by history of economic thought and business economics, and economic historiography), with indexes of authors and of proper names. Z7164.E2S36

Shackelford, Jean A. Urban and regional economics: a guide to information sources. Detroit, Gale, [1980]. 192p. (Economics information guide ser., v.14)   **CH20**

An annotated bibliography of about 600 English-language books dealing with aspects of growth and development, planning and policy, location theory, spatial analysis, regional models and techniques, etc. Indexed.   Z7164.R33S48

Sivolgin, Vladimir Epifanovich. Ekonomika SSSR: annotirovannyi ukazatel' otechestvennykh bibliograficheskikh posobii za 1817–1977 gg. 2e izd., perer. i dop. Moskva, GBL, 1979. 194p.   **CH21**

At head of title: Gosudarstvennaia Biblioteka SSSR imeni V. I. Lenina. Informatsionno-bibliograficheskii Otdel.

1st ed. 1965.

An annotated bibliography of bibliographies. 733 entries. Indexed by personal and geographical names and by titles.

Z7164.E2S623

United Nations Library (Geneva, Switz.). League of Nations & United Nations monthly list of selected articles; cumulative, 1920–1970: economic questions. Ed. by Norman S. Field. Dobbs Ferry, N.Y., Oceana, 1973–75. 6v.   **CH22**

Contents: v.1, Economic conditions, 1920–1955; v.2, Economic conditions, 1956–1970, Economic conditions—Food and agriculture, 1920–1955; v.3, Economic conditions—Food and agriculture, 1956–1970, Economic conditions—Textiles, mining, coal, metals, 1920–1970; v.4, Economic conditions—Petroleum, 1920–1970, Economic conditions—Miscellaneous industries, 1920–1970; v.5, Commercial policy, 1920–1970; v.6, Economic policy, 1920–1970.

Arranged by subject and country in chronological order; compiled from the card file used to issue the Library's *Liste mensuelle d'articles sélectionnés.*   Z7164.E2U445

University of Kansas. Library. Descriptive catalog of the history of economics collection (1850–1930). Boston, G. K. Hall, 1984. 2v.   **CH23**

A dictionary catalog of the collection of some 10,000 titles, described by a former curator of Harvard University's Kress Library of Business and Economics as "unmatched elsewhere" (*Introd.*) for its post-1800 resources. Strong in international materials; about 65% in non-English languages.   HB85.Z99U54x

Washington, D.C. Joint Library of the International Monetary Fund and the International Bank for Reconstruction and Development. Economics and finance; index to periodical articles, 1947–1971, comp. by the staff of the Joint Bank-Fund Library for the International Monetary Fund and the World Bank Group. Boston, G. K. Hall, 1972. 4v.   **CH24**

Reproduction of entries from a card file maintained at the Joint Bank-Fund Library. Covers "both descriptive economics and theory, and includes such subjects as money and banking, fiscal policy, taxation, international finance, international commerce, commodities, and the economic aspects of, for example, agriculture, education, and transportation."—*Pref.*   Z7164.E2W34

——— ——— 1st–2d supplement, 1972/74–75/77. Boston, G. K. Hall, 1976–79. 2v.

Zaremba, Joseph. Mathematical economics and operations research: a guide to information sources. Detroit, Gale, [1978]. 606p. (Economics information guide ser., 10)   **CH25**

An annotated bibliography of more than 1,600 English-language books published before 1975 which have substantial portions of their analysis in terms of a well-defined branch of mathematics (differential calculus, matrix algebra, set theory, etc.) or which undertake analysis in terms of established analytical techniques (linear programming, dynamic programming, etc.). In three main sections, subdivided by topic—mathematics, economics, operations research—with appendixes on methodology and miscellaneous topics. Annotations are quite full; they include predicted audience, mathematical prerequisites for comprehension, presence of exercises, problems, references, and summaries. Author, title, and subject indexes.   Z7164.E2Z37

——— Statistics and econometrics: a guide to information sources. Detroit, Gale, [1980]. 701p. (Economics information guide ser., v.15)   **CH26**

An annotated bibliography of more than 1,700 English-language books, arranged topically in 17 chapters; emphasizes works published since 1960. Documents of international organizations are excluded. Annotations provide information on type of book, audience, summary of contents, mathematical and statistical prerequisites required for understanding, and availability of exercises, problems, etc. Complements the author's *Mathematical economics and operations research* (above). Author, title, and subject indexes.

Z7551.Z37

Current

Bibliographic guide to business and economics, 1975– . Boston, G. K. Hall, 1975– . Annual.   **CH27**

A dictionary catalog of all materials cataloged during the year by the Research Libraries of the New York Public Library, with additional entries from the Library of Congress MARC tapes. Full bibliographic information is given in the main entry, with abbreviated or condensed citations for added entries, titles, series, and subject headings. Includes print and non-book materials in the following major subject areas: economic theory, population, demography, economic history, land and agriculture, industry and labor, transportation and communication, commerce, business administration, finance, foreign exchange, insurance, revenue and taxation, and public finance.   Z7164.C81N353a

Ecodoc: revue bibliographique trimestrielle publiée par le Reseau d'Information en Économie Générale. no.1– , Mai/Juin 1981– . Paris, Centre de Documentation Sciences Humaines, 1981– . Quarterly.   **CH28**

Issued under the auspices of the Centre National de la Recherche Scientifique.

Continues *Documentation économique*, 1934–Mars/Avril 1981.

An international bibliography classed according to the system of the *Journal of economic literature* and corresponding to the ECODOC database (part of the French FRANCIS system). Offers about 350 French-language abstracts and descriptors per issue, with indexes by document type, personal and corporate authors, descriptors, and geographic names. No cumulative features. Excludes socioeconomic and health data, employment, energy, agriculture, and transportation (which are covered by other sections of FRANCIS).

Z7163.E27●

Economic books; current selections. v.1– , Mar. 1974– . Clifton, N.J., Kelley, 1974– . Quarterly.   **CH29**

A publication of the Dept. of Economics and the University Libraries of the University of Pittsburgh.

Annotates English-language books, and indicates suitability for libraries of various sizes. Classed subject arrangement; author index.

A companion publication is: Z7164.E2E2

Economics and business: an international annotated bibliography. v.21– , Jan. 1976– . N.Y., Gordon and Breach, 1976– . Quarterly.   **CH30**

Continues in part the University of Pittsburgh publication (below), and assumes its numbering.   Z7164.E2E252

Pittsburgh. University. Dept. of Economics. Economics selections. 1964–84. Pittsburgh, 1964–84. Quarterly.   **CH31**

Title varies.

Supersedes *Economics library selections*, Ser. I, New books in economics, issued by Johns Hopkins Univ., Dept. of Political Economy, 1954–62.

An annotated list of books published in English (German, French, and Spanish books were formerly included), arranged by subdivisions of economics.

A "Cumulative bibliography" containing the citations (without annotation) of the Johns Hopkins series, 1954–62, was published N.Y., Gordon & Breach, 1965.

———— Cumulative bibliography, series I and II, 1963–1970. N.Y., Gordon and Breach, [1974]. 393p.

———— Cumulative bibliography, volume III, 1971–1977. N.Y., Gordon & Breach, [1979]. 316p.

Economic titles/abstracts. v.1– , Jan. 1974– . The Hague, Nijhoff, 1974– . Semimonthly. **CH32**

Comp. by the Library and Documentation Center of the Economic Information Service (Ministry of Economic Affairs), The Netherlands.

Contains information taken from approximately 2,000 journals, as well as books and reports. Each issue consists of about 600 entries arranged by the Universal Decimal Classification. Entries consist of bibliographic data, English keywords, and brief abstract in the original language of the publication. Annual subject index.

A closely corresponding file is available for online searching. A more selective bibliography drawn from this database is:

Key to economic science and managerial sciences. v.21, no.1– , June 1953– . The Hague, Nijhoff, 1953– . Semimonthly. **CH33**

Title varies: 1953–75, *Economic abstracts;* 1976–77, *Key to economic science.*

Comp. by the Library and Documentation Center of the Economic Information Service (Ministry of Economic Affairs), The Netherlands.

Offers a selection from the abstracts of books, reports, and scholarly journal articles which were originally published in *Economic titles/abstracts* (above). Classed arrangement with annual author and subject indexes. HB1.A1E2

Economics working papers: a bibliography. Dobbs Ferry, N.Y., TRANS-Media Publ. Co., 1973– . Semiannual. **CH34**

Publ. in assoc. with the University of Warwick Library and the Center for International Studies, University of Pittsburgh.

From 1976 to 1980 all social science working papers received at the University of Warwick Library were included; since 1980, coverage has been restricted to economics, excluding management. International in scope; author and subject listings, with series index.

The papers listed have been reproduced in the publisher's microfilm series, to which this bibliography serves as a guide.

Index of economic articles in journals and collective volumes. v.1– , 1886/1924– . Homewood, Ill., R. D. Irwin, 1961– . Annual. **CH35**

Title varies: v.1–7 called *Index of economic journals.*
Frequency varies. v.20 covering 1978 publ. 1983.
Contents: v.1, 1886–1924; v.2, 1925–1939; v.3, 1940–1949; v.4, 1950–1954; v.5, 1954–1959; v.6, 1960–1963; v.6A, 1960–1963, Collective volumes; v.7, 1964–1965; v.7A, 1964–1965, Collective volumes; v.8– , 1966– , annual.

Now lists articles in English from the principal economics journals of various countries (about 200 titles in v.20). Arranged by a detailed classification scheme, with author index in each volume. Citations are full and precise.

Beginning with v.6A (covering 1960–63), indexes collective volumes such as *Festschriften,* conference reports and papers, collected essays, Congressional Committee hearings and special committee reports for United States and Canada, collections of English-language translations of foreign articles and essays.

Updated by "New books" and "Subject index of articles in current periodicals" sections of the *Journal of economic literature* (CH37*n*). Articles cited in the "Index" and the *Journal* are also searchable in the *Economic literature index* database.
Z7164.E2I4812●

International bibliography of economics. Bibliographie internationale de science économique, 1952– . London, Tavistock; Chicago, Aldine, 1955– . v.1– . Annual. **CH36**

Publisher varies. v.1–8, Paris, UNESCO; v.9, 1960– , issued as *Publications* of the International Committee for Social Sciences

Documentation, as one of the series of the *International bibliography of the social sciences* (series title varies slightly).
In English and French.
An extensive, classified list of books, pamphlets, periodical articles, and official government publications, in various languages, including Slavic and Asian. Indexes by author and subject (separate subject indexes in French and English). Z7164.E2I58

Journal of economic abstracts. v.1–6, 1963–68. Cambridge, Harvard Univ., 1963–68. Quarterly. **CH37**

"An international journal published cooperatively by the contributing journals under the auspices of the American Economic Association."—*title page.*

Offers rather lengthy abstracts selected from some 35 contributing journals. Arranged by journal, with subject index in each issue and author index appearing annually.

Title changed with v.7, 1969, to *Journal of economic literature,* which continues to carry selected abstracts, reviews of recent literature, book reviews, etc., but is no longer strictly an abstract journal. HB1.J6●

Dissertations

Wood, W. Donald, Kelly, L. A. and **Kumar, P.** Canadian graduate theses, 1919–1967; an annotated bibliography (covering economics, business and industrial relations). Kingston, Ont., Queen's Univ., Industrial Relations Centre, 1970. 483p. (*Its* Bibliography ser., no.4) **CH38**

A classed listing of both doctoral and master's theses, including theses written by Canadians at non-Canadian universities. Nearly 2,500 items. Author index.
Continued in part by: Z5055.C2W6

Perry, Elizabeth. Bibliography of masters and doctoral theses on Canadian industrial relations 1967 to 1978. Toronto, Ctr. for Industrial Relations, Univ. of Toronto, 1981. 93p. **CH39**

Lists Canadian theses and United States theses on Canadian topics. Separate lists for dissertations and for master's theses; subject index. Z7164.L1P395

Manuscripts and archives

Harvard University. Graduate School of Business Administration. Baker Library. Manuscripts in Baker Library: a guide to sources for business, economic and social history. Comp. by Robert W. Lovett and Eleanor C. Bishop. 4th ed. Boston, Baker Lib., 1978. 382p. **CH40**

1st ed. publ. 1932 as *List of business manuscripts in Baker Library.*

A description of more than 1,500 manuscript collections, arranged by subject area or, in the case of foreign manuscripts, by country. General index; donor index; chronological index.
Z7164.C81H276

Jones, Charles A. Britain and the dominions: a guide to business and related records in the United Kingdom concerning Australia, Canada, New Zealand, and South Africa. Boston, G. K. Hall, [1978]. 253p. **CH41**

Identifies archival records held by public repositories and about 500 private companies. Arranged by geographical location of the archive; indexed by title of material, geographic region, subject, etc. Bibliography. HF3504.J66●

Book reviews

Wall Street review of books. v.1– , Mar. 1973– . Pleasantville, N.Y., Redgrave Publ. Co., 1973– . Quarterly. **CH42**

Each issue contains from 15 to 20 signed reviews of current books in all fields relevant to business and economics. HG1.W28

Dictionaries and encyclopedias

See also CK125.

The American dictionary of economics. [Ed. by] Douglas A. L. Auld [and others]. N.Y., Facts on File, [1983]. 342p. il. **CH43**

A rev. ed. of *The Penguin dictionary of economics* by G. Bannock, R. E. Baxter and R. Rees (2d ed., 1978).

Much material from the earlier work has been rewritten to cover American institutions, statistical and illustrative matter. Emphasis on terms, phrases, personalities and organizations important to economic theory and history, econometrics, statistics, and business finance. Public finance, international trade and payments are more selectively covered.   HB61.A49

Ammer, Christine and **Ammer, D. S.** Dictionary of business and economics. Rev. and expanded ed. N.Y., Free Pr.; London, Collier Macmillan, [1984]. 507p. il.   **CH44**

1st ed. 1977.

Offers fairly lengthy entries for terms, associations, abbreviations, and economists, ranging "from economic theory of the past and present to its numerous applications in the world of business firms and consumers, from price and income theory to real estate, insurance, business law and accounting, from public finance and labor economics to the world of the small investor."—*Pref.* Bibliography.   HB61.A53

Branciard, Michel. Dictionnaire économique et social: dictionnaire Thomas Suavet. 11. éd., entièrement rev. et corr. Paris, Économie et Humanisme, [1978]. 582, 17p. il.   **CH45**

1st ed. 1962.

A revision of Suavet's dictionary of economic and sociological terms. Articles group related terms together, giving definitions, bibliographic references, statistical tables, and necessary mathematical formulae; different meanings are numbered separately, and there is an index of about 1,600 words (including personal name references) citing the subject article in which they appear. Chronology; abbreviations.   HB61.B73

A dictionary of economic quotations. Comp. by Simon James. 2d ed. London, C. Helm; Totowa, N.J., Barnes & Noble, [1984]. 240p.   **CH46**

1st ed. 1981.

Quotations are arranged according to more than 130 topics, with indexing by key word and source.   HB34.D53

The dictionary of modern economics. Rev. ed. Gen. ed., David W. Pearce. Cambridge, Mass., MIT Pr., [1983]. 481p. il.   **CH47**

1st ed. 1981.

More than 2,500 entries for terms, organizations, and economists have been prepared by Scottish professors. Some British emphasis.   HB61.D52

Dictionnaire des sciences économiques, publié sous la direction de Jean Romeuf, avec la collaboration de Gilles Pasqualaggi. Paris, Presses Universitaires de France, 1956–58. 2v.   **CH48**

A dictionary of terms used in the study of economics; international in scope. Includes biographical sketches of significant figures, excluding living persons. Many articles are signed; some have bibliographies.   HB61.D5

Elster, Ludwig, ed. Wörterbuch der Volkswirtschaft. 4. völlig umgearb. Aufl. Jena, Fischer, 1931–33. 3v. il.   **CH49**

1st ed. 1898 in 2v.

A standard German encyclopedia of economics, supplementary to the *Handwörterbuch der Staatswissenschaften* (CA50n) which covered political science. Signed articles, bibliographies, and biographies of deceased persons.   HB61.E5

Encyclopedia of American economic history: studies of the principal movements and ideas. N.Y., Scribner, [1980]. 3v. (1286p.) il.   **CH50**

Glenn Porter, ed.

72 signed articles by prominent scholars are grouped in five sections extending over the three volumes: historiography; chronology; economic growth; the institutional framework; the social framework. Most articles have extensive annotated bibliographies. List of contributors and general index in the final volume. Similar to the publisher's *Encyclopedia of American foreign policy* (DB149).   HC103.E52

Encyclopedia of economics. Douglas Greenwald, ed. in chief. N.Y., McGraw-Hill, [1982]. 1070p. il.   **CH51**

More than 170 prominent economists have contributed about 300 signed articles on topics from the fields of economics, econometrics, and statistics. Articles treat concepts (e.g., supply-side economics), institutions (e.g., International Monetary Fund), and historical periods (e.g., the Great Depression); biographical articles are not included. Bibliographies; cross references. A chronology of economic events, technological and financial developments, and economic thought is appended. Indexed. A useful, comprehensive work.   HB61.E55

The encyclopedia of economics. New and updated ed. [Guilford, Conn., DPG Reference Publishing, 1981] 304p. il.   **CH52**

1st ed. 1973.

More than 1,000 short articles, alphabetically arranged, with cross references and lists of related articles. Includes biographies. Classified bibliography of recent publications. Intended for the "nonprofessional" reader.   HB61.E552

Gilpin, Alan. Dictionary of economic terms. 4th ed. London, Butterworths, [1977]. 249p. il.   **CH53**

1st ed. 1966.

About 300 new entries have been added, bringing the total to more than 2,800 terms. Entries relating to the European Economic Community, North America, and Australasia have been increased, but the work retains its United Kingdom focus.   HB61.G47

Hanson, John Lloyd. A dictionary of economics and commerce. 5th ed. [Plymouth, Eng.], Macdonald & Evans, [1977]. 472p. il.   **CH54**

1st ed. 1965.

Provides explanations of terms from pure and applied economics and economic history; brief definitions of some of the more important commercial terms are also included. About 5,000 entries; some British emphasis.   HB61.H35

McGraw-Hill dictionary of modern economics; a handbook of terms and organizations. Douglas Greenwald, ed. 3d ed. N.Y., McGraw-Hill, [1983]. 632p.   **CH55**

1st ed. 1965.

Pt.1 lists and defines approximately 1,425 modern economic and related terms. Definitions were written for the non-specialist and are sometimes supplemented by charts, tables, or diagrams. Pt.2 alphabetically lists and describes about 235 private and public organizations concerned with economics and marketing.

A somewhat abridged paperback version was published as: HB61.M3

The concise McGraw-Hill dictionary of modern economics: a handbook of terms and organizations. [Ed. by] Douglas Greenwald [and others]. N.Y., McGraw-Hill, [1984]. 395p. il.   **CH56**

This version omits about 250 accounting and insurance terms which appear in the parent volume, as well as most public and private economics and research organizations.   HB61.M32

The Macmillan book of business and economic quotations. Ed. by Michael Jackman. N.Y., Macmillan, [1984]. 302p.   **CH57**

Quotations are grouped within about 60 broad subject categories, then arranged chronologically; indexed by person and key word.

PN6084.B87M33

Moffat, Donald W. Economics dictionary. 2d ed. N.Y., Elsevier, [1983]. 331p. il. **CH58**

Brief definitions, with extensive cross references and some repetition of the shorter definitions. Criteria for length of entry are: "for expressions found in the popular and trade press, but not in textbooks, give a full explanation; for expressions involved in controversy, give a summary of what both sides are saying; ordinary economics expressions found in textbooks should be included, but with only a brief explanation."—*Pref.* HB61.M54

Palgrave, Sir **Robert Harry Inglis.** Palgrave's Dictionary of political economy, ed. by Henry Higgs. London, N.Y., Macmillan, 1923–26. 3v. (Repr.: N.Y., Augustus M. Kelley, 1963) **CH59**

1st ed. 1894–96; reprinted 1910 without change in the text, but with a supplement of new articles in v.3, p.693–803; a reprint of the 1910 edition, issued 1915–18, contains the same supplement but with cross references to the supplement incorporated in the main alphabet. The 1923–26 edition is printed from the stereotyped plates of the 1st ed., with some changes in the plates, and with a supplement which uses some of the material from the earlier supplement and adds some new articles.

A standard English work, including some general and foreign aspects of the subject, but largely limited to developments of economic study in the English-speaking world. Signed articles by specialists, and bibliographies. Useful and authoritative, but unfortunately not up-to-date. HB61.P17

Foreign terms

Eichborn, Reinhart von. Cambridge-Eichborn German dictionary: economics, law, administration, business, general. Cambridge, Cambridge Univ. Pr., [1983]. 2v. **CH60**

Originally publ. as *Der grosse Eichborn* (Burscheid, Siebenpunkt Verlag, 1981–82).

Contents: v.1, English-German; v.2, German-English.

Based on the author's *Spezialwörterbuch für Handel und Wirtschaft* (Stuttgart, 1947–48) and its American edition, *Business dictionary* (Englewood Cliffs, N.J., Prentice-Hall, 1961–62). About 250,000 entries. H45.E36

Jong, Frits J. de. Quadrilingual economics dictionary: English/American, French, German, Dutch. The Hague, Nijhoff; Deventer, Kluwer Technical Books, 1980. 685p. **CH61**

Composed of four separate dictionary sections, with English/American, French, German and Dutch alternately serving as the base language, with equivalent terms given in the other three languages. HB61.J64

Paenson, Isaac. Systematic glossary English/French/Spanish/Russian of selected economic and social terms. English-French-Russian text comp. by Isaac Paenson; Spanish translation prep. by Luis de la Plaza. N.Y., Oxford, Pergamon Pr., 1963– . Looseleaf. **CH62**

Added title page in French, Spanish, and Russian; preface and introduction in all four languages.

Definitions of economic terms arranged according to the system of ideas they convey, proceeding from the general to the particular. Intended primarily for economists, social scientists, translators, government officials, international civil servants, etc. HB61.P14

Vaughan, Floyd Lamar and **Vaughan, M. Clifford.** Glossary of economics, including Soviet terminology, in English/American, French, German, Russian. Amsterdam, Elsevier, 1966. 201p. **CH63**

The main section gives the English term with French and German

equivalents; French, German, and Russian lists are keyed to this section. An appendix of "Soviet economic terminology" presents the Russian term with English, French, and German equivalents in parallel columns. HB61.V3

Directories

Guide to graduate study in economics, agricultural economics, and doctoral degrees in business and administration in the United States of America and Canada. 7th ed. Ed. by Wyn F. Owen and Larry R. Cross. Boulder, Colo., Economics Inst., [1984]. 518p. maps. **CH64**

"Prep. under the auspices of the American Economic Assoc. and the American Agricultural Economics Assoc."—*verso of t.p.*

Title has varied; first publ. as *Graduate study in economics* (1965).

A directory describing regular departmental and special academic programs. Also provides many qualitative rankings of graduate programs and statistical data. HB74.8.G84

World index of economic forecasts, industrial tendency surveys and development plans. 2d ed. Ed. by George Cyriax. N.Y., Facts on File, [1981]. 378p. **CH65**

Comp. by Cambridge Information and Research Services, Ltd. 1st ed. 1978.

Presents profiles of 370 organizations which provide forecasts, plans, and surveys for more than 100 countries; each profile includes a list of publications and descriptions of the coverage of the forecasts, their methodology, techniques, etc. Separate sections treat macroeconomic forecasters, specialist forecasters (commodity, exchange rate, energy, shipping, population, labor force), surveys, and the most recent national development plans. Indexed by organization, geographic focus, and subject. HB3730.W66

Biography

American Economic Association. Survey of members, including classification listings, 1978– . Nashville, Amer. Economic Assoc., 1978– . Irregular. **CH66**

Vols. for 1978– issued as a special number of the *American economic review* (usually in December). Dec. 1985 latest published.

Continues the Association's *Directory* (1974) and the biographical information included in its *Handbook* (publ. irregularly since 1890).

Biographical data gathered by questionnaires distributed to members, plus classification of members by fields of specialization, academic affiliation, etc.

Blaug, Mark and **Sturges, Paul.** Who's who in economics: a biographical dictionary of major economists, 1700–1981. [Brighton, Eng.], Wheatsheaf Books; Cambridge, Mass., MIT Pr., [1983]. 435p. **CH67**

Offers data on 397 deceased and 674 living economists (the latter selected on the basis of regular publication in the journal literature). Entries are comprised of name, year and place of birth, career history, degrees, professional affiliations and awards, major field of interest, brief statement of principal contributions to economics, and selected publications; those for living economists are based on information supplied by the biographees. Indexed by place of birth, place of residence, and major fields of interest. HB76.W46

Mai, Ludwig H. Men and ideas in economics: a dictionary of world economists past and present. Totowa, N.J., Littlefield, Adams, 1975. 270p. **CH68**

Offers brief profiles of the significant ideas and publications of more than 700 economists, philosophers, statesmen, and academicians. Appendixes list present-day economists and their publications (organized by country), and outline historical periods and schools of economic thought. HB76.M3

Atlases

ᴧrge. Economic atlas of the Soviet Union. 2d ed., ᴧn Arbor, Univ. of Michigan Pr., [1971]. 90p. maps. ᴧl. **CH69**

1st ed. 1960.

Arranged by region with agricultural, mineralogical, industrial, and transportation maps for each. Other maps treat economic aspects of the entire country. Brief text, bibliography, and index. Typography and layout good. G2111.G1K5

Oxford University Press. Oxford economic atlas of the world. Prep. by the Cartographic Dept. of the Clarendon Pr. 4th ed. [London], Oxford Univ. Pr., 1972. 239p. col. maps. 38cm. **CH70**

1st ed. 1954. Earlier editions prep. by the Economist Intelligence Unit and the Cartographic Dept. of the Clarendon Press.

In two main parts: (1) a section of world maps grouped by 13 subjects (e.g., environment, crops, livestock, energy, manufacturing industries, demography, society and politics), and (2) a statistical supplement arranged alphabetically by country. A list of sources of information is given, and a gazetteer section provides an index to the maps. Most maps are based on the 1963–65 period; comparative figures for 1953–55 are given in the statistical tables. A review of this edition appears in *The booklist* 69:653.

"The atlas is in series with the Oxford Regional Economic Atlases, which deal separately and in much greater detail with *Western Europe, North America, Africa,* the *U.S.S.R. and Eastern Europe,* and the *Middle East and North Africa.*"—Introd. G1046.G1O92

ECONOMIC CONDITIONS

International

United Nations. Dept. of International Economic and Social Affairs. World economic survey. no.1– , 1945/47– . N.Y., 1948– . il. **CH71**

Title varies: no.1, 1945/57, *Economic report*; no.2–7, 1948–1953/54, *World economic report*. Many issues in 2 pts.

A comprehensive review of world economic conditions and trends. Some issues have supplements. HC59.A169

Africa

Blauvelt, Euan and **Durlacher, Jennifer.** Sources of African and Middle-Eastern economic information. Westport, Conn., Greenwood Pr.; [Farnborough, Eng., Gower Pr., 1982]. 2v. **CH72**

"The objectives of these volumes are the same as those of the companion volumes, *Sources of European Economic Information* [CH96] ... and *Sources of Asian/Pacific Economic Information* [CH84]; to signal the availability of statistical and economic data and to furnish the reader with the necessary direction to obtain the material. [The work] provides not the information itself, but a synopsis and details of the issuing body."—*Introd.* The first volume treats Middle-Eastern countries; the second, continental Africa. In each volume, pt.I (the directory of source publications) gives bibliographic data and brief annotations for books, periodicals, government and international documents, reports, etc., from a wide variety of organizations and publishers; pt.II serves as a directory of issuing organizations. Both parts are arranged by country, and each volume is indexed by publication titles and by subjects, with country subdivision. Z7165.A4B55

Killick, Tony. The economies of East Africa. Boston, G. K. Hall, [1976]. 150p. **CH73**

An annotated bibliography of English-language materials published since 1963 on the economics of Kenya, Tanzania, and Uganda. Material is classed by topic (e.g., international trade, agriculture, industrial and service sectors, population, manpower, technologies). Indexed by subject, place, and author.

Continued by: Z7165.A42K54

—— **Rupley, Lawrence** and **Finucane, Brendan.** The economies of East Africa, a bibliography: 1974–1980. Boston, G. K. Hall, [1984]. 294p. **CH74**

Adds about 2,000 titles, including more unpublished works such as doctoral dissertations written since 1970. Z7165.A42K543

Scientific Council for Africa. Inventory of economic studies concerning Africa south of the Sahara; an annotated reading list of books, articles and official publications. [Ed., Peter Ady] London, Commission for Technical Cooperation in Africa South of the Sahara, 1960. 301p. (*Its* Pubn. no.30) **CH75**

Title also in French.

Includes books, articles, and documents published since 1945. Arranged first by geographical region, then by subject subdivision. Many items are annotated, in English or French, or both. A list of titles, by number, translated into Portuguese, is appended. Author index. AZ800.S35 no.30

Arab countries

American University of Beirut. Economic Research Institute. A selected and annotated bibliography of economic literature on the Arabic speaking countries of the Middle East, 1938/52–53/65. Beirut, 1954–67. **CH76**

Title varies slightly.

A basic volume covering 1938/52 was published 1954 (199p.), with annual supplements beginning 1953; a second cumulation covering 1953/65 appeared in 1967 (458p.). A cumulation for the period 1938/60 was published by G. K. Hall, Boston, 1967 (358p.); in addition to cumulating the entries from the basic work and the annual supplements, some 800 new entries were added in that volume.

Classified arrangement with author index. Includes works in Arabic, English, and French. Z7164.E15A6

Khan, Muhammad Akram. Islamic economics: annotated sources in English and Urdu. Leicester, [Eng.], Islamic Foundation, [1983]. 221p. (Islamic economics ser., 7) **CH77**

A classed bibliography of about 650 entries, with supplement; author and subject indexes.

A complementary work is Muhammad Nejatullah Siddiqi's *Muslim economic thinking: a survey of contemporary literature* (Leicester, Islamic Foundation, 1981. 130p. Islamic economic ser., 1). Z7935.M6K48

Kubursi, A. A. The economies of the Arabian Gulf: a statistical sourcebook. London & Dover, N.H., Croom Helm, [1984]. 206p. **CH78**

Provides statistics on national accounts, oil and gas, trade, population and employment, public finance, agriculture, industry, money and credit, and education, mainly for the 1970–81 period. Printed sources are given for most tables. Countries included are Saudi Arabia, Kuwait, Bahrain, Qatar, Oman, and the United Arab Emirates. Detailed table of contents, but no index. HC415.3.K8

Nicholas, David. The Middle East, its oil, economics and investment policies; a guide to sources of financial information. Westport, Conn., Greenwood Pr., 1981. 199p. **CH79**

Annotates English-language sources published since 1970 in the following areas: (1) economics and finance (general); (2) petroleum and energy (general); (3) Middle East oil and economics: historical, geographical, and political background; (4) Middle East economies and the petroleum industry; (5) economies of individual Middle Eastern countries; (6) economic relationships between the Middle East and other countries. Within each subject area sources are arranged by form: guides; directories, annuals, reference works; periodicals; books, reports, and pamphlets. Brief discussion of computer data bases and services. Indexed.   HD9576.N36N52

Sa'igh, Yūsuf 'Abd Allāh. The economies of the Arab world: development since 1945. N.Y., St. Martin's Pr., [1978]. 726p.   **CH80**

A detailed analytical and statistical study of economic development in Iraq, Kuwait, Saudi Arabia, Jordan, Syria, Lebanon, Egypt, Sudan, Libya, Tunisia, Algeria, and Morocco. Each chapter covers one national economy and explores the history of development, socio-political factors, finance, performance of specific sectors of the economy, and national planning; a concluding chapter deals with the region as a whole, the impact of petroleum on the Arab economies, and Arab economic cooperation. Sources for all statistical tables are identified; numerous footnotes to each chapter. Indexed.   HC498.S29

Asia

Almanac of China's economy, 1981– . Comp. by the Economic Research Centre, the State Council of the People's Republic of China, and the State Statistical Bureau. N.Y., Eurasia Pr., [1982]– . Annual.   **CH81**

A comprehensive survey of the economy of the People's Republic of China, with a basic introduction to the period since 1949. Provides translations of documents, lengthy surveys of sectors of the economy, economic statistics, and a chronology of major economic events. Appendixes provide directories of companies, associations, universities, periodicals, etc. Indexed.   HC427.92.A1A45

Annotated bibliography on the economic history of India (1500 A.D. to 1947 A.D.). Pune, Gokhale Inst. of Politics and Economics; New Delhi, Indian Council of Social Science Research, 1977–80. 5v.   **CH82**

Half-title: Economic history of India: a bibliography.

Contents: v.1, Selections from records; Survey and settlement reports; Gazetteers; Acts and regulations; v.2, British Parliamentary papers; Reports of committees and commissions; v.3, Census reports; serials; v.4A, Books; v.4B, Articles; theses; addenda.

A classified arrangement of English-language printed sources; each part has an introduction, as well as subject, region, and author indexes. Particular attention has been given to statistical material on economic history. A major bibliography.   Z7165.I6A8

Arief, Sritua and **Arief, Melanie Sritua.** The Indonesian economy, 1967–1977: a bibliography. [Hull, Eng.], Sritua Arief Associates, [1978]. 220p.   **CH83**

Lists 853 books, articles, reports, dissertations, and papers. International in scope. Author arrangement, with subject index.

Z7165.I65A74

Blauvelt, Euan and **Durlacher, Jennifer.** Sources of Asian/Pacific economic information. Westport, Conn., Greenwood Pr., [1981]. 2v.   **CH84**

An annotated bibliography of more than 5,000 entries, providing bibliographic details, language, date or frequency of publication, and summary of contents. Country arrangement; indexed by title, subject, and issuing organization.   Z7165.P26B53

Chen, Virginia. The economic conditions of East and Southeast Asia; a bibliography of English-language materials, 1965–1977. Westport, Conn., Greenwood Pr., [1978]. 788p.   **CH85**

Lists English-language books, periodical articles, theses and dissertations on the economies of Burma, Hong Kong, Indonesia, Japan, Malaysia, the Philippines, Singapore, South Korea, Taiwan, and Thailand; entries on Japan constitute almost half of the total. "At the beginning of each chapter is a brief introduction to the economy of each country and the recently published works on this

subject. The bibliographic citations are arranged alphabetically by Library of Congress subject headings; reference works and periodicals precede the main section of subject breakdown."—*Introd.* No index.   Z7165.A743C47

Hicks, George L. and **McNicoll, Geoffrey.** The Indonesian economy, 1950–1965; a bibliography. [New Haven], Southeast Asia Studies, Yale Univ., [1967]. 248p. (Yale Univ. Southeast Asia Studies. Bibliography ser., 9)   **CH86**

A classed bibliography of more than 1,200 English and Indonesian titles. Author and subject indexes.   Z7165.I65H5

———— The Indonesian economy, 1950–1967; bibliographic supplement. [New Haven, 1967] 211p. (Bibliography ser., 10)

Lee, Molly Kyung Sook Chang. East Asian economies: a guide to information sources. Detroit, Gale, 1979. 326p. (Economics information guide ser., v.1)   **CH87**

Emphasizes English-language monographs and doctoral dissertations written since 1945, with separate chapters on journals and bibliographies. Chapters are devoted to Asia in general, China, Japan, Korea, and Taiwan, with subject subdivisions. Author, title, and subject indexes.   Z7165.A743L43

Canada

The Browning directory of Canadian business information, 1984– . Toronto, Browning Associates, [1984]– . Looseleaf. Annual.   **CH88**

A bibliography of business directories, buyers guides, statistical sources, market surveys, and special issues of periodicals, arranged by broad subject/industry categories. Title and subject indexes.

Canadian business & economics: a guide to sources of information. Economique et commerce au Canada: sources d'informations. Barbara E. Brown, ed. Ottawa, Canadian Lib. Assoc., [1984]. 469p.   **CH89**

In English and French.

1st ed. 1976.

A comprehensive work, with many annotations, arranged by type (bibliography, directory, etc.) and subject. Omits trade journals, most annual reports of government agencies, and most publications listed in the Statistics Canada catalogs. English and French indexes by author, title, corporate author, and, occasionally, series.

Z7165.C2C225

Dick, Trevor J. O. Economic history of Canada: a guide to information sources. Detroit, Gale, [1978]. 174p. (Economics information guide ser., 9)   **CH90**

A classed bibliography of materials grouped in five chapters, with appropriate topical, geographical, and chronological subdivisions: (1) Interpretive and bibliographic sources; (2) From colonial times to the present; (3) The colonial period to 1867; (4) Confederation (1867) to 1920; (5) From 1920 to the present. Brief evaluative comments on the sources precede each subdivision. Author, title, and subject indexes.   Z7165.C2D5

Europe, Eastern

Birkos, Alexander S. and **Tambs, Lewis A.** East European and Soviet economic affairs; a bibliography (1965–1973). Littleton, Colo., Libraries Unlimited, 1975. 170p.   **CH91**

A selective bibliography of English-language books and articles from the period 1965–73. Classed arrangement within country divisions. About 1,200 items. Author, title, and periodical/publisher indexes.   Z7165.E8B55

COMECON data, 1979– . Ed. by the Vienna Institute for Comparative Economic Studies (Wiener Institut für International Wirtschaftsvergleiche); sponsored by the First Austrian Bank (Die Erste österreichische Spar-Casse). N.Y., Holmes & Meier, 1980– . Biennial.   **CH92**

1978 ed. had title *RGW in Zahlen/CMEA data.*

Presents statistical data on economic conditions in the CMEA (Council for Mutual Economic Assistance) as a whole, and for Bulgaria, Cuba, Czechoslovakia, German Democratic Republic, Hungary, Poland, Romania, and the USSR. Material is taken from the national statistical yearbooks, periodicals and newspapers, as well as from publications of international organizations and Western sources.

COMECON foreign trade data (CH402) is published in alternate years.   HC244.C186

Handbook of the economy of the German Democratic Republic. Prep. by Doris Cornelson [and others], a research team of the German Institute for Economic Research, West Berlin; ed. by Reinhard Pohl; trans. from the German by Lux Furtmüller. [Farnborough, Eng.], Saxon House, [1979]. 366p. il.   **CH93**

Translation of *Handbuch DDR–Wirtschaft* (1977).

A survey covering the period from 1945 through 1975. Chapters (with numerous subsections) cover seven broad areas: (1) basic factors of production and economic development; (2) economic policy; (3) national accounts; (4) production in individual economic sectors; (5) use and distribution of products and incomes; (6) foreign economic relations; (7) the GDR in the Council for Mutual Economic Assistance. Numerous figures, charts, and tables, with bibliographic sources. Indexed.   HC290.78.H2913

Horchler, Gabriel Francis. Hungarian economic reforms: a selective, partially annotated bibliography. [New Brunswick, N.J., Hungarian Research Center, American Hungarian Foundation, 1977] 182p.   **CH94**

A topical arrangement of 1,620 books, articles, and serial titles. "Economic reforms" refers to the limitation of central planning and encouragement of market forces, managerial initiative, increased foreign trade, agriculture, and consumerism. Author index.   Z7164.E2H67

O'Relley, Z. Edward. Soviet-type economic systems: a guide to information sources. Detroit, Gale, [1978]. 228p. (Economics information guide ser., 12)   **CH95**

A selective bibliography of English-language sources (including translations) on theories, models, and processes of the economies of Bulgaria, Czechoslovakia, East Germany, Hungary, Poland, Romania, and the Soviet Union. Material is arranged by category (e.g., planning theory, efficiency and productivity, sectoral problems and accomplishments), with very brief annotations. Author, title, and subject indexes.   Z7164.E2O66

Europe, Western

Blauvelt, Euan and **Durlacher, Jennifer.** Sources of European economic information. 4th ed. Cambridge, Mass., Ballinger, [1983]. 642p.   **CH96**

1st ed. 1974.

A bibliography of about 6,000 sources of economic and statistical information for Western and Eastern Europe. Pt.1, the directory of publications, is arranged by country; brief annotations are given. Pt.2 serves as a directory of issuing organizations or publishers. Indexed by publication title and by subject, subdivided by country.   Z7165.E8B59

European markets: a guide to company and industry information sources. By Washington Researchers. [Wash., Washington Researchers, 1983] 509p.   **CH97**

In three parts: (1) directory of relevant federal, state, international, and private sector organizations; (2) brief bibliography of publications and databases; (3) sources of information listed by individual country, including organizations and published sources. Coverage limited to Western Europe. Indexed.   HF3493.E825

Hall, Hubert. Select bibliography for the study, sources, and literature of English mediaeval economic history. London, King, 1914. 350p. (Studies in economics and political science . . . London School of Economics) (Repr.: N.Y., B. Franklin, 1960)   **CH98**

About 3,200 items. Topical arrangement with introductory notes and full index.   Z2018.H23

Hamilton, F. E. Ian. Regional economic analysis in Britain and the Commonwealth; a bibliographic guide. N.Y., Schocken, [1970]. 410p.   **CH99**

In seven main geographical sections with appropriate topical subdivisions: (1) The British Isles; (2) The British Commonwealth in general; (3) Africa; (4) Australia and New Zealand; (5) Canada; (6) South and South-east Asia; (7) The small territories.

Z7165.O7H25

Hanson, Laurence William. Contemporary printed sources for British and Irish economic history, 1701–1750. Cambridge, Univ. Pr., 1963. 978p.   **CH100**

Includes books, pamphlets, broadsides, etc., totaling more than 6,500 items, published 1701–50 inclusive. Represents the holdings of the principal libraries of Great Britain and eight important libraries of the United States. Locates copies.   Z7165.G8H35

An introduction to the sources of European economic history, 1500–1800. Ithaca, Cornell Univ. Pr., [1977]. 256p. il.   **CH101**

Ed. by Charles Henry Wilson and Geoffrey Parker.

A team of international economic historians have compiled the chapters herein, covering: Italy, Spain, Portugal, the Low Countries, the British Isles, France and Germany. The content of each chapter follows the same format: the country's population, agriculture, industry, trade and transport, currency and finance, prices and wages, and wealth and social structure. Numerous charts, graphs, and tables. Bibliographic notes and references; indexed.

HC240.I68

Kingston, Irene and **Benjamin, William A.** Directory of European business information. Wash., Center for Business Information, [1979]. 590p.   **CH102**

In four parts: (1) general sources, including monographs, research services and data bases, and statistical data; (2) eleven subject chapters subdivided by form; (3) national information sources, statistics, company information, professional and commercial organizations, with cross references to sources mentioned in pts.1 and 2; (4) subject/title index.

Overton, David. Common Market digest: an information guide to the European communities. N.Y., Facts on File, [1984]. xlvii, 387p.   **CH103**

Intended "to provide each enquirer on a Community topic with a starting point. It attempts to give a modicum of information [and also provides] references to both primary and secondary source material." Chapters are organized by broad subject (e.g., economic and agricultural development, external affairs), with detailed index. Also includes biographical sketches of outstanding figures.

HC241.2.O93

Palmer, Stanley H. Economic arithmetic: a guide to the statistical sources of English commerce, industry, and finance, 1700–1850. N.Y., Garland, 1977. 207p. (Garland reference library of social science, v.26)   **CH104**

A series of essays on the statistics of commerce, prices, the textile industries, mining industries, iron industry, banking and finance offer a guide to the statistical sources of the period prior to the appearance of official statistical bureaus and their publications; both primary sources (government documents, books, and pamphlets) and secondary materials are noted. Bibliography; index.

Z7554.G7P34

Latin America

See also DB345.

Business information sources of Latin America and the Caribbean. Wash., Organization of American States, General Secretariat, Columbus Memorial Lib., 1982. 60p. (Documentation and information ser., 5) **CH105**

Ellen G. Shaffer, comp.

Updates the Organization's 1977 *Guide to Latin American business information sources,* most citations being new to this edition. A bibliography of current, readily available titles, with brief descriptive notes and ordering information. Country arrangement with title index and directory of country embassies. HF3230.5.B87

Felipe Herrera Library. Index of periodical articles on the economics of Latin America. Inter-American Development Bank, Felipe Herrera Library. Boston, G. K. Hall, 1983. 4v. **CH106**

Contents: v.1, Author index; v.2, Title index; v.3–4, Subject index; Geographical index.

The Library receives over 1,200 current periodicals and 70 newspapers and has extensive holdings of official serial publications of international and regional organizations. The index covers articles published 1950–77. Spanish-language subject and geographical headings are used. Z7165.L3F44

Harvard University. Bureau for Economic Research in Latin America. Economic literature of Latin America, a tentative bibliography. Cambridge, Harvard Univ. Pr., 1935–36. 2v. **CH107**

An extensive bibliography of books, pamphlets, and periodical articles listing a total of 12,520 numbered items. Arranged geographically by country or region, with a subject arrangement under each and a general index of authors for each volume. Special features are the introductory notes at the head of important sections; the appendixes on the statistical sources of South America, Mexico, and the Caribbean; and notes on collections of Latin-American economic literature in leading libraries. Z7164.E2H36

Jones, Tom Bard, Warburton, Elizabeth Anne and **Kingsley, Anne.** A bibliography on South American economic affairs; articles in nineteenth-century periodicals. Minneapolis, Univ. of Minnesota Pr., [1955]. 146p. **CH108**

For each country, lists material under agriculture, commerce, communications, finance, immigration, industry, labor, mining, and transportation. Z7165.S75J6

Latin America; a guide to economic history, 1830–1930. Roberto Cortés Conde and Stanley J. Stein, eds. Berkeley, Univ. of California Pr., 1977. 685p. **CH109**

"Sponsored by the Joint Committee on Latin American Studies of the American Council of Learned Societies and the Social Science Research Council and by the Consejo Latinoamericano de Ciencias Sociales."—*t.p.*

A cooperative effort of an international group of scholars. A section for general bibliography is followed by separate sections for Argentina, Brazil, Chile, Colombia, Mexico, and Peru. Each country section begins with an interpretive essay, and the ensuing bibliography for each is topically subdivided under ten major headings: (1) General and reference works; (2) Demography, manpower, and living conditions; (3) Structures and institutions; (4) Macroeconomic growth and fluctuation; (5) Foreign trade and investment; (6) Regional economy; (7) Agriculture, ranching, forestry; (8) Industry: factory and artisan; (9) Extractive industry; (10) Transport, public utilities and services. Introductory essays and annotations are in the language of the contributor. Indexes of authors and of periodicals. Z7165.L3L32

Sable, Martin Howard. Periodicals for Latin American economic development, trade and finance; an annotated bibliography. Los Angeles, Latin American Center, Univ. of California, [1965]. 72p. (Calif. Univ., Los Angeles. Latin American Center. Reference Ser., no.3) **CH110**

A selected list of periodicals, chiefly from the United States and Latin America. Arranged by country, with subject index. Includes government publications. Z7165.L3S3

Seminar on the Acquisition of Latin American Library Materials (26th, 1981, Tulane University). Latin American economic issues: information needs and sources: papers of the twenty-sixth annual meeting . . . April 1–4, 1981. [Madison, Wis.], SALALM Secretariat, Univ. of Wisconsin, Madison, etc., [1984]. 354p. **CH111**

Presents 27 papers discussing printed and computerized information sources on Latin American economic conditions, including organizations and libraries with relevant special collections. Also includes the annual SALALM bibliographies, *Bibliography of bibliographies: 1981 supplement* and *Bibliography of microform projects, 1981.* Z688.L4S46

Wish, John R. Economic development in Latin America; an annotated bibliography. N.Y., Praeger, [1965]. 144p. **CH112**

Largely limited to items published since 1955. Arranged under such headings as "Economic development," "Marketing," "Agriculture," with appropriate subdivisions. Author index.

Z7165.L3W5

Union of Soviet Socialist Republics

Clarke, Roger A. and **Matko, Dubravko J. I.** Soviet economic facts, 1917–81. N.Y., St. Martin's Pr., [1983]. 228p. **CH113**

1st ed. (1972) had title *Soviet economic facts, 1917–1970.*

"The object of this volume . . . is to present . . . complete annual series for the main aggregate economic magnitudes, a list of industrial and agricultural products which is determined basically by availability, and . . . other more general data related to economic performance."—*Pref.* Compiled from official Soviet sources and Western estimates; sources noted. HC335.C519

Kazmer, Daniel R. and **Kazmer, Vera.** Russian economic history; a guide to information sources. Detroit, Gale, [1977]. 520p. **CH114**

A classified, annotated listing of books, pamphlets, and periodicals in English, with many references to Russian-language source material. Subject classification approximates arrangement used in *Index of economic articles* (CH35); chapters are subdivided into general materials or works dealing with the periods up to 1860; from 1860 to 1917; and post-1917. Author and title indexes.

See also CH91, CH95, CH96. Z7165.R9K34

United States

Gagala, Kenneth L. The economics of minorities: a guide to information sources. Detroit, Gale, [1976]. 212p. (Economics information guide ser., 2) **CH115**

An annotated bibliography of English-language sources, most of them published from 1965 to 1974, on the economic conditions of nonwhite peoples in the United States. Chapters deal with topics related to the black American: education, urbanization, housing, consumption, labor, economic development and inequality, governmental law and policy. Two chapters are devoted to American Indians and Spanish-Americans. Author, title, and subject indexes. Z1361.N39G26

Hasse, Adelaide Rosalie. Index of economic material in documents of the states of the United States. Prep. for the Dept. of Economics and Sociology of the Carnegie Institution of Washington. Wash., Carnegie Inst., 1907–22. 13v. in 16. **CH116**

Volumes issued are: California, 1849–1904 (1908); Delaware, 1789–1904 (1910); Illinois, 1809–1904 (1909); Kentucky, 1792–1904 (1910); Maine, 1820–1904 (1907); Massachusetts, 1789–1904 (1908); New Hampshire, 1789–1904 (1907); New Jersey, 1789–1904 (1914); New York, 1789–1904 (1907); Ohio, 1787–1904 (1912); Pennsylvania, 1790–1904 (1919–22); Rhode Island, 1789–1904 (1908); Vermont, 1789–1904 (1907). No more published.

Includes a comprehensive listing of all economic material (with definite reference to volume and page) to be found in the printed reports of administrative officers, legislative committees, and special commissions of the states, and in the governors' messages, for the period covered. The word "economic" has been interpreted very liberally to include almost any aspect of American history. Indexing is by general heading and broad subject.

Omits reports of bureaus of labor before 1902, as these are covered in the *Index to all reports issued by bureaus of labor statistics . . . to March 1902*, issued by the U.S. Bureau of Labor.

Hutchinson, William Kenneth. American economic history: a guide to information sources. Detroit, Gale, [1980]. 296p. (Economics information guide ser., v.16)　　**CH117**

An introductory bibliography for the student of the "new economic history [which] emphasizes the use of statistics, data processing . . . and the application of rigorous economic models to the available [historical] data."—*Introd.* Topical arrangement of more than 1,500 books and periodical articles covering the period from the colonial era to 1960; most entries are annotated. Brief appendixes list relevant organizations and journals. Author, title, and subject indexes.　　Z7165.U5H89

Orsagh, Thomas, ed. The economic history of the United States prior to 1860; an annotated bibliography. Santa Barbara, [Amer. Bibliog. Ctr.–Clio Pr., 1975]. 100p.　　**CH118**

About 800 entries. Brief annotations for most items. Classed arrangement; author and subject indexes.　　Z7165.U5O77

U.S. Office of Management and Budget. Catalog of federal domestic assistance. 1965– . Wash., Govt. Prt. Off., 1965– . Annual.　　**CH119**

Update publ. 6 mos. after the *Catalog.*

1965–70 issued by U.S. Office of Economic Opportunity.

Title varies: 1965, *Catalog of federal programs for individual and community improvement*; 1967, *Catalog of federal assistance programs.*

". . . a government-wide compendium of Federal programs, projects and activities which provide assistance or benefits to the American public. It contains 1,013 programs administered by 52 different Federal agencies."—*Introd., 1985.*　　HC110.P63U53a

ECONOMIC DEVELOPMENT

Bibliography

Frank, Geneviève and **Gaudier, Maryse.** Les implications sociales d'un nouvel ordre économique international bibliographie sélective. [Geneva, Internat. Inst. for Labour Studies, 1976] 101p.　　**CH120**

Title (*The social implications of a new international economic order: selective bibliography*) and supporting materials also in English.

Prep. for the World Symposium on the Social Implications of a New International Economic Order, Algiers, Jan. 19–23, 1976.

About 1,000 books, articles, and documents in English and French classed by subject: establishment of a new international economic order, development strategies, employment, science and technology, social policy, international organizations and international action. Author index.　　Z7164.E15F7

Geiger, H. Kent. National development, 1776–1966; a selective and annotated guide to the most important articles in English. Metuchen, N.J., Scarecrow Pr., 1969. 247p.　　**CH121**

A chronological, annotated listing of 350 books and articles on the cultural, economic, political, and social aspects of development. Author-title-subject index.　　Z7164.U5G43

Hazlewood, Arthur. The economics of "under-developed" areas; an annotated reading list of books, articles and official publications. 2d enl. ed. London, publ. for the Inst. of Commonwealth Studies by Oxford Univ. Pr., 1959. 156p.　　**CH122**

1st ed. 1954.

A classified list of 1,027 numbered items, mostly published between 1930 and 1958, with indexes by author and place.　　Z7161.H3

——— The economics of development; an annotated list of books and articles published 1958–1962. London, publ. for the Inst. of Commonwealth Studies by Oxford Univ. Pr., 1964. 104p.　　**CH123**

A sequel to the above, listing 732 entries in English in classified arrangement. Index by author and place.　　Z7164.U5H37

International development abstracts. 1982/1– . [Norwich, Eng., Geo Abstracts, 1982]– . Bimonthly.　　**CH124**

Intended to cover the world literature on developing countries in a format similar to *Geo abstracts* (CL57). Classed according to about 20 subject areas. *International development index* will serve as an annual author, keyword, regional, and journal index to all abstracts in *International development abstracts,* as well as to items from other Geo Abstracts titles that are relevant to development studies.　　HC59.69.I57

Katz, Saul M. and **McGowan, Frank.** A selected list of U.S. readings on development, prep. for the United Nations Conference on the Application of Science and Technology for the Benefit of the Less Developed Areas. Wash., Agency for Internat. Development, [1963]. 363p.　　**CH125**

Lists 1,195 numbered items including books, documents, and periodical articles, mostly published since 1950. Arranged by broad subject with author index.　　Z7164.U5K3

Nawaz, Tawfique. The new international economic order, a bibliography. Westport, Conn., Greenwood Pr., [1980]. 163p.　　**CH126**

Lists a wide spectrum of international research—books, articles, reports, documents, etc.—on commodities, trade, money and finance, transnational corporations, technology transfer, law and policy aspects, economic cooperation among developing countries, international organizations, and socialist countries in the world economy. Broad subject classification, with no detailed subject or author approach.　　Z7164.E17N48

Powelson, John P. A select bibliography on economic development: with annotations. Boulder, Colo., Westview Pr., [1979]. 450p.　　**CH127**

A selection of about 2,000 books and journal articles from the 1970s, classified by 48 subject categories and by individual country. Most entries are annotated. Also lists serials and reports dealing with global development, Africa, Asia, and Latin America. Cross references, but no index.　　Z7164.E15P68

ReQua, Eloise G. and **Statham, Jane.** The developing nations; a guide to information sources concerning their economic, political, technical, and social problems. Detroit, Gale, [1965]. 339p.　　**CH128**

Based on the holdings of the Library of International Relations in Chicago, this is chiefly an annotated bibliography of English-language books, periodical articles, government documents, etc., arranged under such headings as "Economic development," "Technical assistance," and "Social development," with appropriate subsections. Also includes a directory of agencies and institutions administering development, a select list of periodicals, and a directory of publishers. Z7164.U5R4

Verbic, Nada. Bibliography on economic cooperation among developing countries, 1981–1982: with annotations. Boulder, Colo., Westview Pr., [1984]. 299p. **CH129**

"Publ. in assoc. with the Research Centre for Cooperation with Developing Countries (RCCDC), Ljubljana, Yugoslavia."—*t.p.*

An international bibliography of more than 2,000 citations to a wide variety of sources. Topical and geographical arrangement, with author index, but no detailed subject approach. Some material dates from the 1978–80 period; two earlier publications covered the 1970–78 and 1979–80 periods. Z7164.U5V47

Directories

Directory of non-governmental organisations in OECD member countries active in development co-operation. [Paris], Development Centre of the Organisation for Economic Cooperation and Development, [1981]. 2v. **CH130**

Contents: v.1, Profiles; v.2, Index.

Title, introductory matter, indexes, and some entries also in French.

Presents data on more than 1,700 national and international non-profit organizations involved in development aid or education. Country arrangement; indexed by subject, recipient country and subject, and organization name. HC60.D524

Overseas Development Institute, London. Development guide: a directory of non-commercial organisations in Britain actively concerned in overseas development and training. 3d ed. [London], The Institute, 1978. 216p. **CH131**

1st ed. 1962

Describes 198 British organizations involved in development in less developed countries; excludes educational establishments, commercial organizations, foundations, and social or cultural organizations. Gives information on research, activities, education, scholarships, training and consultancy programs, and library of the organizations. HC60.O85

Technical Assistance Information Clearing House. U.S. non-profit organizations in development assistance abroad: TAICH directory 1983. Wynta Boynes, ed. 8th ed. N.Y., Technical Assistance Information Clearing House of the American Council of Voluntary Agencies for Foreign Service, [1983]. 584p. **CH132**

"This directory is an updated edition of part I (organization profile information) of the 1971 TAICH directory—U.S. non-profit organizations in development assistance abroad. Part II of the 1971 directory has been expanded and updated through a series of periodically revised country reports."—*Introd.* Describes organizations in terms of history and structure, objectives, programs and countries of assistance, organizational, financial and personnel resources, publications, and audiovisual materials. Indexed by subject field and country of assistance, and name of organization. "Directory changes" sheets are issued periodically. HC60.T4432

Handbooks

Handbook of national development plans. Metra Consulting. London, Graham & Trotman, 1983– . 1v., looseleaf. **CH133**

The basic volume provides digests of about 50 national development plans; an additional 20 plans are projected for the semiannual supplement service, with annual consolidated editions. Standard format includes comments on previous plans, summary, allocation of funds by sector, expected effect of plan on GDP, and recent performance of plan; a summary ranges from 5 to 10 pages. Title of each plan is given in English. HC59.7.H297

Source books

Group of 77. The Third World without superpowers: the collected documents of the Group of 77. Karl P. Sauvant, ed. N.Y., Oceana, [1981]. 6v. **CH134**

Presents texts of all formal materials issued by the group 1963–80 on the international economic program of the Third World at meetings of UNCTAD, UNIDO, IMF, World Bank, and United Nations conferences.

For a similar set of legal and political documents *see* CK356.

HF1413.G714

Annuals

World development report, 1978– . [N.Y.], Oxford Univ. Pr., [1978]– . Annual. **CH135**

Publ. for the World Bank.

Each volume is in two parts: (1) survey of a financial topic relevant to economic development (e.g., international flow of capital); (2) statistics on world development derived from World Bank information, generally over a 20-year time series. HC59.7.W659

ACCOUNTING

Bibliography

Bentley, Harry Clark and **Leonard, Ruth S.** Bibliography of works on accounting by American authors, 1796–1934. Boston, Author, 1934–35. 2v. **CH136**

Contents: v.1, Books published 1796–1900; v.2, 1901–1934.

Z7164.C81B5

Demarest, Rosemary R. Accounting: information sources. Detroit, Gale, [1970]. 420p. **CH137**

"An annotated guide to the literature, associations and federal agencies concerned with accounting."—*title page.*

The bibliography employs a classed arrangement; author and title indexes. Z7164.C81D28

Institute of Chartered Accountants in England and Wales, London. Library. Current accounting literature 1971; a catalogue of books, pamphlets, and periodicals of current interest in the members' library of the Institute of Chartered Accountants in England and Wales at 31 August 1971. Ed. by M. G. J. Harvey. London, Mansell, [1971]. 586p.

CH138

Mainly "confined to material of current interest, most of which has been published since 1960."—*p.xi.* Full information appears in an author section, with brief citations given in a classified subject section. Separate list of periodicals. Z7164.C81I42

—— Historical accounting literature. [London], Mansell, 1975. 360p. **CH139**

Subtitle: A catalogue of the collection of early works on bookkeeping and accounting in the Library of the Institute of Chartered Accountants in England and Wales, together with a bibliography of literature on the subject published before 1750 and not in the Institute Library. Z7164.C81I43

Current

Accountants' index; a bibliography of accounting literature. N.Y., Amer. Inst. of Certified Public Accountants, 1921– . Quarterly supplements with annual cumulation. **CH140**

Basic volume, 1912–20; Supplements, 1– , 1921/23– . Frequency varies.

A detailed author and subject bibliography of the English-language book, pamphlet, and periodical literature of the subject. Includes a large amount of indexing of periodicals, government documents, and references to parts of books dealing with specific subjects.   Z7164.C81A5●

Commerce Clearing House. Accounting articles, 1963– ; describing and indexing accounting articles published in accounting and business periodicals, books, and pamphlets. Chicago, 1963– . Monthly.   **CH141**

Entries, with brief abstracts are grouped by accounting area (e.g., auditing, budgeting, cost accounting). Indexes by topic and by author. Cumulative volumes have been issued for the years 1971–74 and 1975–79.   Z7164.C81C78

Dictionaries

Estes, Ralph W. Dictionary of accounting. 2d ed. Cambridge, Mass., MIT Pr., [1985]. 162p. il.   **CH142**

1st ed. 1981.
Offers brief, nontechnical definitions of acronyms, words, and phrases, with bibliographical references for the more technical terms.   HF5621.E77

Kohler, Eric Louis. Kohler's Dictionary for accountants. 6th ed. Ed. by W. W. Cooper, Yuji Ijiri. Englewood Cliffs, N.J., Prentice-Hall, [1983]. 574p.   **CH143**

1st ed., 1952, was an unofficial revision and expansion of the 1936 *Accounting terminology* of the American Institute of Accountants' Committee on Terminology, of which the author was chairman. Contains definitions and explanations of about 2,600 terms. The standard dictionary of the subject.   HF5621.K6

Directories

The national directory of certified public accountants. Diane Krauth, dir. of publishing. Princeton, N.J., Peter Norback, [1981]. 1002p.   **CH144**

In two main sections: (1) Biographical, with educational and occupational data on some 20,000 certified public accountants; (2) CPA firms, a listing by state and city. Also lists firms with more than one office, professional accounting associations, and higher education programs in accounting.

Who audits America. Ed.1– , 1976– . Menlo Park, Calif., Data Financial Pr., 1976– . Annual.   **CH145**

A directory of accounting firms which audit publicly-held corporations. Listings are by corporation, major and minor accounting firms, and state. Also lists mergers, acquisitions, name changes, and companies which have changed accounting firms.
                                                     HF5616.U5W5

Handbooks

Accountants' handbook. 6th ed., ed. by Lee J. Seidler and Douglas R. Carmichael. N.Y., Wiley, [1981]. 2v., various pagings (approx. 1700p.). il.   **CH146**

1st ed. 1923 ed. by William A. Paton.
The 28 chapters of the previous edition have been expanded to 45, written by financial executives and analysts and partners in accounting firms. Bibliographic references have been added for each chapter. Indexed. For many years the authoritative handbook in the field.
                                                     HF5621.A22

Ameiss, Albert P. and **Kargas, Nicholas A.** Accountant's desk handbook. 2d ed. Englewood Cliffs, N.J., Prentice-Hall, [1981]. 438p. il.   **CH147**

A sourcebook in four main parts: (1) financial accounting; (2) managerial accounting, financial and tax planning, and information control systems; (3) auditing standards and procedures; (4) regulato-

ry, contractual, fiduciary, and social responsibility topics. Many illustrative examples and forms. Bibliographic references.
                                                     HF5635.A474

Casey, William J. Accounting desk book: the accountant's everyday instant answer book. 7th ed., rev. by Douglas L. Blensly, Tom M. Plank. Englewood Cliffs, N.J., Inst. for Business Planning, [1983]. 472p. il.   **CH148**

1st ed. 1964.
A handbook in which 42 subject chapters are organized within three main sections: accounting, taxes, and management. References are made throughout to the American Institute of Accountants' looseleaf service, *Professional standards*. Useful appendixes; index. An 8th ed. under Blensley's editorship was announced for 1985 publication.   HF5635.C33

Encyclopedia of accounting systems. Rev. and enl. ed. Gen. ed., Jerome K. Pescow. Englewood Cliffs, N.J., Prentice-Hall, [1976]. 3v. (1859p.) il.   **CH149**

1st ed. 1958.
Each chapter, written by a specialist, covers the accounting system for a particular industry and discusses the following topics: the industry in brief, the accounting system, account classifications and books of account, data processing procedures, cost system, time and payroll system, plant and equipment records and depreciation, the reporting system, data processing applications, and time-saving techniques.   HF5635.E54

Handbook for auditors. James A. Cashin, ed. in chief. N.Y., McGraw-Hill, [1971]. 1v., various pagings.   **CH150**

Intends to cover all branches of auditing. Chapters by specialists are grouped in six sections: (1) Principles, standards, and responsibilities; (2) Evaluation and programming; (3) Objectives and audit procedures; (4) Reviews and reports; (5) Education and professional requirements; (6) Horizons for auditing. Bibliographies; index. New edition announced for 1986.   HF5667.H26

Handbook of accounting and auditing. Boston & N.Y., Warren, Gorham & Lamont, [1981]. 1v., various pagings.
                                                     CH151

Ed. by John C. Burton, Russell E. Palmer, and Robert S. Kay.
49 signed chapters by academics, government personnel, and professional practitioners (including many partners and management group personnel of Touche Ross & Co.) are organized in seven subject divisions: (1) general financial accounting; (2) general auditing; (3) specific areas of financial accounting, reporting, and auditing; (4) accounting for specialized industries; (5) major accounting institutions; (6) the legal environment; (7) recent research. Bibliography; index. A 1983/84 update was issued 1983.   HF5635.H22

Handbook of modern accounting. Sidney Davidson, ed.; Roman L. Weil, assoc. ed. 3d ed. N.Y., McGraw-Hill, [1983]. 1v., various pagings. il.   **CH152**

1st ed. 1970.
Offers 47 chapters by specialists on various accounting topics. New material includes use of the computer in accounting. Chapters have brief bibliographies. Appendix provides compound interest, annuity, and bond tables. Indexed.   HF5635.H23

The managerial and cost accountant's handbook. Homewood, Ill., Dow Jones-Irwin, [1979]. 1297p. il.   **CH153**

Ed. by Homer A. Black and James Don Edwards.
42 narrative chapters by accounting executives and educators are arranged in eight sections covering: historical background and basic concepts; accounting aspects of organizations; accounting aspects of manufacturing; cost accounting for other business enterprises, government, and non-profit organizations; recent developments and trends. Indexed.   HF5686.C8M263

The modern accountant's handbook. Homewood, Ill., Dow Jones–Irwin, [1976]. 1203p. il.   **CH154**

Ed. by James Don Edwards and Homer A. Black.
A compendium of current knowledge on practical accounting policies. Chapters written by authorities are organized into eight parts: (1) objectives of corporate financial accounting; (2) realization

and measurement of earnings; (3) special problems in accounting measurement; (4) special problems in administering corporate resources; (5) publication of financial information; (6) accounting policy and corporate liability; (7) accounting standards for special enterprises; (8) planning and control.   HF5635.M757

Muksian, Robert. Financial mathematics handbook. Englewood Cliffs, N.J., Prentice-Hall, [1984]. 486p.   **CH155**

Demonstrates formulas and tables for the calculation of interest, annuity values, bonds, loan payments, depreciation of assets, etc.; provides general tables of algorithms, exponentials, and compound interest at varying rates.   HF5691.M84

Prentice-Hall, Inc. Accountant's encyclopedia, revised. Jerome K. Pescow, gen. ed. Englewood Cliffs, N.J., Prentice-Hall, 1981. 2v.   **CH156**

A handbook with chapters contributed by more than 40 individuals, most of them CPA's. Includes business mathematics refresher course; index; guide to records retention.
1982 ed. called simply *Accountant's encyclopedia.*   HF5635.P93

————— Encyclopedia of auditing techniques. Jennie M. Palen, ed. Englewood Cliffs, N.J., [1967]. 2v. (1566p.)   **CH157**

Two introductory chapters (on typical auditing procedures and the particular problems of auditing electronically produced records) are followed by 38 chapters each dealing with a specific type of industry or business activity. Although the latter are in alphabetical sequence, an index and cross-reference system would have been helpful.   HF5667.P72

ADVERTISING AND PUBLIC RELATIONS

Guides

Richard, John M. A guide to advertising information sources. Scottsdale, Ariz., MacDougal, 1969. 59p.   **CH158**

An annotated list of 277 sources—yearbooks, directories, bibliographies, etc.

Bibliography

Cutlip, Scott M. A public relations bibliography. 2d ed. Madison, Univ. of Wisconsin Pr., 1965. 305p.   **CH159**

1st ed. 1957.
A classed bibliography with author-subject index. The new edition is a complete revision, updating the original work through 1963, with a few 1964 entries. Many entries from the earlier edition were dropped, but more than 2,000 new ones were added.   Z7164.P957C8

Lipstein, Benjamin and **McGuire, William J.** Evaluating advertising: a bibliography of the communications process. N.Y., Advertising Research Foundation, 1978. 362p.   **CH160**

A classified bibliography of more than 7,000 books and periodical articles published since 1960 on "the creation and evolution of persuasive communications" (*p.xxvii*), in terms of source, audience, policy, theory, media employed, etc. Arranged alphabetically by author; indexed by "access words" keyed to the relevant class number in the "Topic index" which lists item numbers of relevant entries.   Z7164.C81L734

Norton, Alice. Public relations: information sources. Detroit, Gale, [1970]. 153p. (Management information guide, 22)   **CH161**

An annotated bibliography of general sources, works on public

relations in special fields, public relations tools and methods, careers, and international studies. Directory of associations. Lists English-language books, pamphlets, and articles. Indexed.   Z7164.P957N63

Pollay, Richard W. Information sources in advertising history. Westport, Conn., Greenwood Pr., [1979]. 330p.   **CH162**

Three bibliographic essays treating economic data on advertising, commercial and professional sources of data, and the trade press of advertising are followed by a classified, annotated bibliography. Also provides directories of archives, manuscripts and special collections, and professional associations. Indexed.   Z7164.C81P66

Dictionaries and encyclopedias

Ayer glossary of advertising and related terms. 2d ed. Comp. and publ. by the Ayer Pr. Julie Moss, ed. Philadelphia, [1977]. 219p.   **CH163**

Terms are listed alphabetically and briefly defined in a general section; this is followed by classified sections (for TV and radio; Printing, photography, and graphic arts: Research terms; Association, union, government bureau terms) in which the terms relating to specific areas of communications are again listed and their definitions repeated.   HF5803.A84

Graham, Irvin. Encyclopedia of advertising. 2d ed. N.Y., Fairchild, [1969]. 494p. il.   **CH164**

Subtitle: An encyclopedia containing more than 1100 entries relating to advertising, marketing, publishing, law, research, public relations, publicity, and the graphic arts, combined with valuable reference material in one conveniently alphabetized working manual for everyday use by advertisers, agencies, advertising practitioners, businessmen and students.
1st ed. 1952.
Has an index to terms grouped according to general subject matter, and a directory of associations with brief descriptions of their make-up and work.   HF5803.G68

Paetzel, Hans W. Complete multilingual dictionary of advertising, marketing and communications: English, French, German. Lincolnwood, Ill., Passport Books, [1984]. 606p.   **CH165**

In three sections—German, English, French—which provide the equivalent word or phrase from each of the other two languages. About 8,000 terms.

Sharp, Harold S. Advertising slogans of America. Metuchen, N.J., Scarecrow Pr., 1984. 543p.   **CH166**

A dictionary of about 15,000 slogans used by some 6,000 businesses and organizations. Slogans, organizations, and products appear in one alphabetical listing; no keyword or thematic approach.   HF6135.S53

Tatham-Laird & Kudner. Dictionary of advertising terms. Ed. by Laurence Urdang. [Chicago], Tatham-Laird & Kudner, [1977]. 209p. il.   **CH167**

Over 4,000 very brief explanations of specialized terms, special meanings of ordinary words, names of devices, services and organizations, with cross references for abbreviations, acronyms, and synonyms.   HF5803.T37

Directories

O'Dwyer (J.R.) Company. O'Dwyer's Directory of public relations firms, 1970– . N.Y., O'Dwyer, 1970– . Annual.   **CH168**

For United States public relations firms and the public relations departments of advertising agencies, provides names of principal officers, number of employees, fee income, specialty, and account names. Indexed by specialty, account names, and geographical location. Some rankings tables.

The same publisher issues the annual *O'Dwyer's Directory of public relations executives.* HM263.O37

Standard directory of advertisers. 1964– . N.Y., National Register Pub. Co., 1964– . **CH169**

Frequency varies. In two annual editions: "Classified" (by product) and "Geographical" (by state and city), with annual geographical indexes, biweekly bulletin, and five cumulative supplements.

Supersedes in part the *Standard advertising register* (1915–63), and incorporates *McKittrick directory of advertisers* (1899–1960).

Now includes information on some 17,000 companies. The *Standard directory of international advertisers and advertising agencies* is a worldwide listing. HF5805.S7

Standard directory of advertising agencies. N.Y., National Register Pub. Co., 1964– . 3 times a yr. (Feb., June, Oct.) **CH170**

Supersedes the "Agency list" of the *Standard advertising register.* Now lists some 4,000 U.S. agencies and 400 foreign. A geographical index precedes the alphabetical listing of agencies. Supplemented in interim months by *Agency news.* HF5805.S72

Standard rate and data service. Skokie, Ill., Standard Rate and Data Service, 1919–50. v.1–32. **CH171**

Title varies; frequency varies.

Excellent source of information on rates and advertising media. Published in various sections with varying titles. Includes newspapers, magazines, radio and television, films, transportation. Gives Canadian and Mexican rates as well as those for United States.

Superseded by a series of separate publications of Standard Rate and Data Service, Inc., most of them beginning 1951 and assuming the volume numbering of the *Standard rate and data service;* most are monthly, some quarterly, some semiannual. Titles have varied; sections current in 1985 include: *Business publication rates and data,* 1951– ; *Canadian advertising rates and data,* 1953– ; *Community publication rates and data,* 1978– ; *Consumer magazine and farm publication rates and data,* 1951– ; *Co-op service directory,* 1981– ; *Direct mail list rates and data,* 1967– ; *Network rates and data,* 1951– ; *Newspaper rates and data,* 1951– ; *Print media production data,* 1968– ; *SRDS newspaper circulation analysis,* 1958– ; *Spot radio rates and data,* 1951– ; *Spot radio small markets edition of Spot television rates and data,* 1951– ; *Transit advertising rates and data,* 1951– . Several international editions are also available (e.g., England, France, Italy, Mexico, West Germany).

Weiner, Richard. Professional's guide to public relations services. 5th ed. [N.Y., R. Weiner, Inc., 1985] 532p. il. **CH172**

1st ed. 1968.

New chapters have been added on communications and image consultants, computerized news, printing, and telephone services; there also are more British and Canadian listings. Companies and services are grouped under functional categories; name, address, personnel names, branch offices, services, and fees are given for each. Indexed. HD59.W38

Handbooks

Barton, Roger, ed. Handbook of advertising management. N.Y., McGraw-Hill, 1970. 1v., various pagings. **CH173**

For the corporate advertising manager. Specialists have contributed chapters on aspects of the organization of the advertising department, planning, research, copy, legal matters, etc. Includes a glossary of advertising terms. Indexed. HF5823.B314

Concise guide to international markets, 1966– . London, Internat. Advertising Assoc., United Kingdom Chapter, 1966– . il., maps. Irregular. (4th ed. 1980/83) **CH174**

Leslie Stinton, ed. in chief.

Provides marketing information for 110 countries, grouped by continent or region. Profile of each country includes statistical information on income, expenditure, retail and wholesale outlets, advertising agencies and expenditure, regulations, available media, market research and public relations facilities, and advertising reference books. HF5801.C63

Darrow, Richard W. and **Forrestal, Dan J.** The Dartnell public relations handbook. [2d ed.] Chicago, Dartnell, [1979]. 1115p. il. **CH175**

1st ed. 1967.

Consists of 50 chapters authored by specialists and grouped in four main sections: (1) public relations field today; (2) external public relations; (3) internal communications; (4) public relations in the health sciences field. Numerous case studies. Indexed.

HD59.D28

European Data Index Ltd. European advertising & marketing handbook: a Eurodatex special report. [Ed.1–] [London, European Data Index Ltd., 1973–] maps. **CH176**

2d (1975/76) ed. publ. 1975.

Profiles of thirteen Western European nations (excluding Eire, Greece and Portugal) offer statistical data on age and structure of the population, size of households and their income, education, ownership of consumer durables, consumer spending, and employment. Detailed information on advertising conditions in each country is also supplied. HF5813.E79E84

European marketing data and statistics. Ed. 1– , 1962– . London, Euromonitor Pubns.; distr. in North America by Gale, [1963]– . Annual. **CH177**

Comprises statistical tables offering comparisons between 26 countries in Western and Eastern Europe in such areas as: population, employment, production, trade, the economy, standard of living, consumer expenditure, consumption, market size in particular industries, retailing, etc.

International marketing data and statistics. Ed.1– , 1975/76– . London, Euromonitor Pubns.; distr. by Gale, 1975– . Annual. **CH177a**

A companion volume to *European marketing data and statistics* (above), providing similar comparative statistical tables for 100 countries of the Americas, Asia, Africa, and Australasia on the subjects of: population, employment, production, trade, the economy, standard of living, consumption, housing, health, education, and communications. Indexed. HA42.I56

Public relations handbook. Lesly's Public relations handbook. 3d ed. Englewood Cliffs, N.J., Prentice-Hall, [1983]. 718p. il. **CH178**

Philip Lesly, ed.

1950–67 eds. had title: *Public relations handbook.*

Chapters by specialists are grouped in 7 sections: (1) What public relations is and does; (2) What public relations includes; (3) How an organization utilizes public relations; (4) Analysis and preparation; (5) The techniques of communication; (6) The practice of public relations; (7) Emerging principles and trends. Appendix includes bibliography, glossary, codes of ethics, and list of associations. Indexed. HM263.P7656

Stansfield, Richard H. The Dartnell advertising manager's handbook. 3d ed. Chicago, Dartnell, [1982]. 1088p. il. **CH179**

Includes sections on advertising-campaign planning, agency selection, copy writing, illustration, layout, media, corporate advertising, etc. Detailed index. HF5823.S78

Biography

Who's who in advertising. Ed.1– . N.Y., D. V. Morgan, 1963– . Irregular. **CH180**

A biographical dictionary of key executives of advertising agencies, corporations, and the media; cross-referenced by company name. A 2d ed. (1972) provided data on about 4,000 American and

Canadian executives; the 3d ed. (1980) expanded coverage to about 10,000 names.   HF5810.A2W46

BUSINESS

Guides

See also AB177.

The basic business library: core resources. Ed. by Bernard S. Schlessinger. [Phoenix], Oryx Pr., 1983. 232p.   **CH181**

In three parts: (1) core list of printed business reference sources for small and medium-size libraries (alphabetically arranged entries, critical annotations, subject and author indexes); (2) a bibliography of business reference and business libraries literature, 1976–81, with subject and source indexes; (3) state-of-the-art essays on business reference sources and services.   Z675.B8B37

Brownstone, David M. and **Carruth, Gorton.** Where to find business information: a worldwide guide for everyone who needs the answers to business questions. 2d ed. N.Y., Wiley, [1982]. 632p.   **CH182**

1st ed. 1979.
In three main sections: (1) a topical and geographical subject index to the current sources of business information in pt.3; (2) publishers index listing these sources by publisher; and (3) sources of business information, an annotated title list of about 5,000 English-language publications, emphasizing current sources—loose-leaf services, newsletters, trade periodicals, general business periodicals, computerized data bases, yearbooks, directories, and government publications.   HD30.35.B76

Daniells, Lorna M. Business information sources. [2d ed.] rev. Berkeley, Univ. of California Pr., [1985]. 673p.   **CH183**

1st ed. 1976.
The classic guide to business information, intended for the business person as well as the business student and librarian. Emphasizes resources published since the 1st ed.: current books, periodicals, newspapers, databases and services, as well as the traditional reference sources. Because of the many references to older titles treated in the earlier edition, that volume should be retained for reference purposes. Chapters 1–9 discuss basic reference sources; chapters 10–21, more specific areas such as management, accounting, computers and management information systems. The final chapter provides a "basic bookshelf" for the small office library. English-language sources only. Indexed.   Z7164.C81D16

Encyclopedia of business information sources. Paul Wasserman, managing ed. 5th ed. Detroit, Gale, 1983. 728p.   **CH184**

Subtitle: A detailed listing of primary subjects of interest to managerial personnel, with a record of sourcebooks, periodicals, organizations, directories, handbooks, bibliographies, on-line data-bases, and other sources of information on each topic.
An earlier version (1965) appeared under the title *Executive's guide to information sources.*
Lists primary and secondary sources of factual information of interest to business executives, researchers, scholars, and students of business. An alphabetical subject arrangement.   HF5035.E53

How to find information about companies; the corporate intelligence source book. By Washington Researchers. 4th ed. [Wash., The Researchers, 1985] 353p. (Washington Researchers business research ser., 3)   **CH185**

Lorna M. Daniells, Elizabeth M. Williams, Beth Gibber, contributing eds.
A "do-it-yourself guide to business research" (*Introd.*), suggesting information available from local, state, and federal government

agencies, the courts, trade associations and labor unions, credit reporting and bond rating services, databases, and libraries.   HD2785.H68

Bibliography

Bowman, James S., Elliston, Frederick A. and **Lockhart, Paula.** Professional dissent: an annotated bibliography and resource guide. N.Y., Garland, 1984. 322p. (Public affairs and administration ser., v.2; Garland reference library of social science, v.128)   **CH186**

A topical bibliography of 1,393 citations on "whistle-blowing" in government, business, and the professions; includes government documents, reference works, audiovisual resources, and directory data. Author index.   Z7164.C81B763

Business and economics books, 1876–1983. N.Y., Bowker, [1983]. 4v.   **CH187**

Contents: v.1–3, Subject index; v.4, Author index, Title index.
More than 143,000 titles published and distributed in the United States are organized by Library of Congress subject headings. Complete bibliographic information appears under subject; author and title indexes provide page references to the main entries in the subject section.   Z7164.C81B927

Business firms master index. Jennifer Mossman and Donna Wood, eds. Detroit, Gale, [1985]. 1124p.   **CH188**

Subtitle: A guide to sources of information on approximately 110,000 companies in the United States and including Canadian and other selected foreign firms.
The first edition is limited to firms in the communications field—publishers, advertising agencies, public relations firms, newspapers, computer companies, television and cable networks and services, online services and databases, etc. For each company reference is made to about 50 directory-type sources for further information. Arrangement is by company name. Future editions are to expand into other subject areas.   Z7164.T87B87

Fildes, Robert, Dews, David and **Howell, Syd.** A bibliography of business and economic forecasting. [Westmead, Farnborough, Eng.], Gower Pr., [1981]. 424p.   **CH189**

An author listing of more than 3,700 periodical articles and 300 books written between 1965 and 1978, with subject index.
A bibliography of business and economic forecasting: part 2, 1979–1981 by Fildes and Dews was published by the Manchester Business School in 1984 as its *Working paper,* no.87.

Frank, Nathalie D. and **Ganly, John V.** Data sources for business and market analysis. 3d ed. Metuchen, N.J., Scarecrow Pr., 1983. 470p.   **CH190**

1st ed. (1964) had title: *Market analysis: a handbook of current data sources.*
Lists and describes federal, regional, and local sources; university programs; advertising media; periodicals; abstracts and indexes; directories, etc. Emphasis is on "original sources of quantitative data and on continuing keys to business facts."—*Introd.*   HF5415.124F7

Harvard University. Graduate School of Business Administration. Baker Library. Core collection: an author and subject guide, 1970/71– . [Boston], 1971– . Revised annually.   **CH191**

Baker Library's Core Collection is intended for the student wishing to browse in a small, open-shelf collection of recent books in business and related fields. Based on reading and reserve lists from the School; regularly weeded and updated. Kept up to date by the monthly *Recent additions to Baker Library.*   Z7164.C81H32

Henderson, G. P., ed. European companies: a guide to sources of information. 3d ed. Beckenham, [Eng.], C. B. D. Research, 1972. 224p.   **CH192**

1st ed. 1962.
Lists and describes sources of information on companies and

business enterprises in countries of western Europe. For each country usually lists: official registers, forms of business organization, number of business enterprises, stock exchanges, credit reporting and information services, rates of exchange, and published sources of information about companies.   HC240.H458

Hill, George H. Black business and economics: a selected bibliography. N.Y., Garland, 1985. 351p. (Garland reference library of social science, v.267)   **CH193**

Gives citations to 100 books, 180 theses and dissertations, and articles from popular periodicals written since 1885. Book citations, arranged by author, are annotated. Government documents are listed by author, title, or department, and are followed by topically arranged listings of dissertations, theses, journal and newspaper articles. About 2,268 citations in all.   Z7164.C81H47

Humpert, Magdalene. Bibliographie der Kameralwissenschaften. Köln, Schroeder, 1937. 1184p. (Kölner bibliographischen Arbeiten, 1)   **CH194**

Published in parts, 1935–37.
Originally planned to include works published 1727–1835, but starting on p.105, the 16th and 17th centuries are also included, so that the greater part of the work covers 1520–1850.   Z7161.H92

Jones, Donald G. Business ethics bibliography, 1971–1975. Charlottesville, Va., Univ. Pr. of Virginia, [1977]. 207p.   **CH195**

Sponsored by the Center for the Study of Applied Ethics, Colgate Darden Graduate School of Business Administration, University of Virginia.
Continues in part D. L. Gothie's *Selected bibliography of applied ethics in the professions* (BA16), but selects only those books, essays, and articles dealing with management of particular services, issues relevant to the social responsibilities of business, theory, and religion and business ethics. Annotated. Updated by Jones's *Bibliography of business ethics, 1976–1980* (Charlottesville, Univ. Pr. of Virginia, 1982. 220p.)   Z7164.C81J59

McDermott, Beatrice S. and **Coleman, Freada A.** Government regulation of business, including antitrust: information sources. Detroit, Gale, [1967]. 229p.   **CH196**

"A comprehensive annotated bibliography of works pertaining to the Antitrust Division, Department of Justice, and to the major regulatory agencies of the federal government."—*title page*.   KF5406.A1M3

Marke, Julius J. and **Bander, Edward J.** Commercial law: information sources. Detroit, Gale, [1970]. 220p.   **CH197**

A classed bibliography with some annotations; intends to embrace the whole field of commercial law.   KF871.M3

Small business sourcebook. John Ganly, Diane Sciattara [and] Andrea Pedolsky, eds. Detroit, Gale, [1983]. 796p.   **CH198**

Subtitle: A guide to the information services and sources provided to 100 small businesses by associations, consultants, educational programs, franchisers, government agencies (federal, state, and local), reference works, statisticians, suppliers, trade shows, and venture capital firms.
Pt.1, arranged by store type, lists associations, reference works, sources of supply, statistical sources, trade periodicals, trade shows and conventions, franchises, consultants, etc. Pt.2 provides directory data and an annotated list of published information sources. Indexed. A supplement was published 1985.   HD2346.U5S65

U.S. Dept. of Commerce. Library. United States Dept. of Commerce publications. Wash., Govt. Prt. Off., 1952. 795p.   **CH199**

A selected list of publications dating from 1790 to 1950. Press releases and materials of similar nature are not usually included.

——— ——— Supplement. 1951/52– . Annual.

          Z1223.C75

Commerce publications update is a biweekly list of the Department's publication.

Woy, James B. Business trends and forecasting: information sources. Detroit, Gale, [1966]. 152p.   **CH200**

Subtitle: An annotated guide to theoretical and technical publications, and to sources data.
A selective bibliography on general economic forecasting. Emphasis is on recent material.   Z7164.C81W83

Current

See also AF82.

Business, economics books and serials in print. 1973– . N.Y., Bowker, 1973– . Annual.   **CH201**

Title varies: 1973–76, *Business books in print;* 1977–80, *Business books and serials in print.*
Author, title, and subject lists of U.S. books in economics, industry, finance, business, management, industrial psychology, and vocational guidance make up the bulk of the volume. A separate section includes information on serials and is reprinted from the various Bowker sources (i.e., *Ulrich's; Irregular serials and annuals; Ulrich's quarterly*). An annual midyear supplement (the first issue covering 1977/78) is a complementary volume, similar in format, which lists new titles and updates information from the basic volume when necessary. Publishers' addresses are provided.
          Z7164.C81B962

Business index [microform]. Jan. 1979– . Menlo Park, Calif., Information Access Corp., 1980– . Monthly; each issue is cumulative.   **CH202**

A complete COM (computer output microfilm) index to the contents of about 500 English-language business and financial periodicals, the *Wall Street journal, Barron's,* and the business section of the *New York times.* Selectively indexes another 1,100 general and legal periodicals, U.S. government reports, and books. Indexing is by subject, name, and title of reviewed material; reviews are critically graded.

Business periodicals index. N.Y., Wilson, 1958– . v.1– . Monthly (except Aug.), with annual cumulation.   **CH203**

One of the two indexes stemming from the *Industrial arts index* (EA66n). Now indexes, by subject, about 275 English-language periodicals.   Z7164.C81B983●

Business publications index and abstracts. v.1, no.1– , Jan. 1983– . Prep. by Management Contents. Detroit, Gale, 1983– . Monthly with annual cumulation.   **CH204**

Issued monthly in two parts (Abstracts, and Subject/author citations); both parts cumulate in annual volumes, and the subject/author citations also cumulate quarterly. Supersedes *Management contents* (1975–82).
This is the printed version of the *Management contents* database. The 1983 annual indexes about 650 English-language periodicals, as well as monographs, conference proceedings, and business course materials. Abstracts ranging from 50 to 300 words are provided for some 40,000 articles. Retrospective indexing to 1980 is planned.
          Z7164.C81B9853

Canadian business index. v.6, no.1– , Aug. 1980– . Toronto, Micromedia, 1980– . Monthly with annual cumulation.   **CH205**

Supersedes *Canadian business periodicals index* (1975–80) and continues its numbering.
Currently indexes about 170 Canadian periodicals, reports, and some newspapers (*Financial post, Financial times, Globe and mail*) in business, industry, and economics. In three sections: subject, corporate name, and personal name.   Z7164.C81C24●

Predicasts F&S index, 1968– . Cleveland, Predicasts, 1968– . Monthly, with quarterly and annual cumulation.   **CH206**

Predicasts currently indexes about 750 financial publications, business newspapers, trade magazines, and special reports for information on corporate acquisitions and mergers, new products, technological developments, and socio-political factors affecting business. Titles of the indexes have varied; indexes covering more than one country are arranged in three sections: industries and products; countries; and companies. Current titles are: *Predicasts F&S index: Europe*; *Predicasts F&S index: international*; *Predicasts F&S index: United States*; and *Predicasts F&S index of corporate change*. The United States index is in two sections: industries and products, general economic data; and companies. The *Index of corporate change* is in three sections: alphabetical by company; SIC-coded company guide; special tabulations (bankruptcies, foreign operations, etc.). There is a one-line summary of content for each citation; major articles are indicated typographically.   ●

Predicasts forecasts. no.1– , Oct. 1960– . Cleveland, Predicasts, Inc., 1960– . Quarterly, the 4th issue being an annual cumulation.   **CH207**

Title varies.
Volumes for 1960–66 published by Economic Index & Survey, Inc.
Gives short- and long-term statistical projections for United States basic economic indicators and products (by SIC number). For each statistic, gives bibliographic reference to the source, periodical article, government document, or private study.   HC101.P7●

Worldcasts. Product, Dec. 15, 1964?– . Cleveland, Predicasts, 1964?– . Quarterly.   **CH208**

Issued in four looseleaf binders called: P-1, General economics, utilities & services; P-2, Agriculture, mining, forestry, food, textiles, wood & paper; P-3, Chemicals, polymers, drugs, oil, rubber, stone, clay & glass; P-4, Primary metals, machinery, electronics, transportation equipment. Titles vary.   HC1040.P74●

Worldcasts. Regional, Dec. 15, 1964?– . Cleveland, Predicasts, 1964?– . Quarterly.   **CH209**

Issued in four looseleaf binders called: R-1, West Europe; R-2, East Europe, Africa, Middle East; R-3, North America, Canada, Central America, South America; R-4, Asia & Oceania. Titles vary.
The two titles above are supplementary to *Predicasts forecasts* The latter provides short- and long-term projections for basic economic and industrial statistics for countries other than the United States. Indicates citation to periodical article, government document, or other source from which the statistics are derived.   HF1040.P75●

Periodicals

See also AE21.

Cabell, David W. E. Cabell's Directory of publishing opportunities in business, administration, and economics. 2d ed. Beaumont, Tex., Cabell Pub. Co., [1981]. 557p.   **CH210**

An author's guide to more than 250 English-language periodical publications. For each publication, describes type of manuscript sought, editorial policy, review process, acceptance rate, review time, reviewer's comments, style guide, etc. If the publication has a set of published guidelines, it is included *in toto*. Alphabetical title listing; subject index. A 3d ed. was published 1985.   H91.C23

Harvard University. Graduate School of Business Administration. Baker Library. Current periodical publications in Baker Library. 1971/72– . [Boston], 1971– . Annual.   **CH211**

Supersedes its *Current journals in Baker Library* which, in turn, superseded its *Printed catalog of current journals*.
In three sections: (1) titles; (2) subjects; (3) geographic regions. Includes all currently received serial publications regardless of frequency.   Z7164.C81H266

Sicignano, Robert and **Prichard, Doris.** Special issues index; specialized contents of business, industrial, and consumer journals. Westport, Conn., Greenwood Pr., [1982]. 309p.   **CH212**

A title listing of 1,283 North American English-language journals. For each title, its special issues (such as buyer's guides, directories, statistical summaries, convention reports, and reviews/previews)

are listed chronologically as they appear during a year. Also provides a classified list of periodicals, and a subject/organization index.   Z7164.C81S624

Databases

The executive's sourcebook to marketing, company and demographic data. Chevy Chase, Md., Information USA, [1985]. 403p.   **CH213**

Subtitle: A directory to on-line, off-line, data tapes and diskettes from commercial vendors, state government offices, federal agencies, and non-profit organizations.
Describes about 2,500 data sources, with information on fee structures and off-hours discounts. Indexed by subject, vendor, and format.

Howitt, Doran and **Weinberger, Marvin I.** *Inc.* magazine's Databasics: your guide to online business information. N.Y., Garland, [1984]. 614p. il.   **CH214**

In five parts: background information on databases and searching, and electronic mail; a guide to selected business databases arranged by broad subject (e.g., news, demographics, companies); detailed profiles of vendors; discussions of hardware and software; the future of databases. Numerous appendixes of printed sources, information brokers, hardware and software. A detailed guide for the end-user, but useful for the librarian as well.   HF5548.2.H67

Mayros, Van and **Werner, D. Michael.** Business information: applications and sources. Radnor, Pa., Chilton, [1983]. 490p.   **CH215**

In two main sections: (1) "Applications," consisting of ten chapters dealing with areas of business (e.g., banking and finance) subdivided by six to twenty specific topics (e.g., interest rates), with information sources listed by category under each topic; (2) "Sources," providing complete bibliographic data for all information sources listed in the first section, grouped by type. There is also a subject index and directory of database vendors. Most useful for information on information services and databases.   HD30.35.M39

Business services

❖Business is a field which changes so rapidly that reference works pertaining to it soon become out-of-date, and many types of questions can be answered only by the use of current material. Fundamental for this purpose are the different business and financial "services," most of which are now issued in looseleaf form. In general, each service is devoted to one specialized subject, and consists of basic material kept up-to-date by revisions—supplied periodically—covering new laws, regulations, rulings, decisions, etc. Some services are completely factual; others include editorial explanations.

Since these services are quite expensive, they will be out of reach of the smaller library, but any large library which does much work in business will have to have at least some of them. Information about price, form, and frequency may be secured by writing directly to the company concerned.

Directory of business and financial services. 8th ed. Ed. by Mary McNierney Grant, Riva Berleant-Schiller. N.Y., Special Libraries Assoc., [1984]. 189p.   **CH216**

Earlier eds., 1924, 1931, 1939, 1944, 1956, 1963, 1976.
Title varies: 1924, *Handbook of commercial information services*.
Lists about 1,200 business and financial services (both printed and online), arranged by title. Describes each service giving type, scope, frequency of publication, format, and price. Includes an index of publishers, place of publication, and subject.
A 1985 supplement is planned.   HG151.7.D57

Dictionaries and encyclopedias

Brownstone, David M., Franck, Irene M. and **Carruth, Gorton.** The VNR dictionary of business and finance. N.Y., Van Nostrand Reinhold, [1980]. 288p.   **CH217**

Offers brief definitions of basic business and financial terms. In the case of variant meanings, the definitions are numbered in their general order of importance, with the most general meaning given first.   HF1001.B7

Giordano, Albert G. Concise dictionary of business terminology. Englewood Cliffs, N.J., Prentice-Hall, [1981]. 225p.   **CH218**

Offers very brief definitions for more than 8,000 terms and phrases (including slang); acronyms and abbreviations are listed in a separate section.   HF1001.G56

Greener, Michael. The Penguin dictionary of commerce. 2d ed. [Harmondsworth, Eng.], Penguin, [1980]. 329p.   **CH219**

1st ed. 1970.
A work of British origin which aims "to concentrate on terms which concern the man in the street in his dealings with the business world" (*Pref.*) rather than on the more highly specialized terminology of the business professions.   HF1002.G73

Handwörterbuch der Betriebswirtschaft. 4. völlig neugestaltete. Aufl. Hrsg. von Erwin Grochla und Waldemar Wittmann. Stuttgart, Poeschel, [1974–76]. 3v. il. (Enzyklopädie der Betriebswirtschaftslehre, Bd.1)   **CH220**

1st ed. 1926–28.
Signed articles, with bibliographies of some length. Not limited to material on German policies and practices.   HF1001.H33

Janis, J. Harold. Modern business language and usage in dictionary form. Garden City, N.Y., Doubleday, 1984. 506p. il.   **CH221**

In one alphabetical sequence, about 3,000 words and phrases are defined and topics such as usage, style, grammar, form and composition, and punctuation are discussed. Classified guide to topics; bibliography.   PE1115.J34

Oran, Daniel and **Shafritz, Jay M.** The MBA's dictionary. Reston, Va., Reston Pub. Co., [1983]. 431p. il.   **CH222**

A dictionary for undergraduate and graduate students of business management. Entries for abbreviations, terms, persons, organizations, laws, court cases, etc.; pronunciation indicated for foreign terms.   HD70.U5O68

Rice, Michael Downey. Prentice-Hall dictionary of business, finance and law. Englewood Cliffs, N.J., Prentice-Hall, [1983]. 362p.   **CH223**

Defines about 3,600 words, phrases, and abbreviations, with references to statutory materials and sources of terms, leading cases, and articles in legal and business literature.   KF887.R53

Rosenberg, Jerry Martin. Dictionary of business and management. 2d ed. N.Y., Wiley, [1983]. 631p.   **CH224**

1st ed. 1978.
Offers very brief definitions for more than 10,000 terms, phrases, symbols, acronyms, and abbreviations. Appendixes provide tables for various forms of measurement and interest, a list of graduate programs in business and management, quotations, and a chronology of major business and economic events in the United States.   HF1001.R79

Foreign terms

French

Anderla, Georges and **Schmidt-Anderla, Georgette.** Dictionnaire des affaires anglais-français, français-anglais; Delmas business dictionary English-French, French-English. [Paris], J. Delmas, [1972]. 587p.   **CH225**

Cover title: Delmas dictionnaire des affaires; Harrap business dictionary.
Consists of about 70,000 English or French phrases and their equivalents in the other language, with a separate section for abbreviations. Includes an appendix of basic weights, measures, and conversion coefficients.

Redfern, James. Basic terms of business and finance: French-English, English-French. Lanham, Md., University Pr. of America, [1984]. 575p.   **CH226**

Offers the briefest equivalent terms and abbreviations in both languages.   HF1002.R38

Japanese

Kenkyusha's English-Japanese dictionary of trade and industry. Enl. and rev. ed. Tokyo, Kenkyusha, [1957]. 1068p.   **CH227**

Title also in Japanese.
1st ed. 1955.
By Nintarō Fujita (who also edited earlier English-Japanese dictionaries of commercial and technical terms, published Tokyo, Kenkyusha, 1941 and 1948).

Polyglot

Appleby, Barry Léon. Elsevier's Dictionary of commercial terms and phrases: in five languages: English, German, Spanish, French, and Swedish. Amsterdam & N.Y., Elsevier, 1984. 1083p.   **CH228**

Base language is English, with equivalents given in the four other languages. Indexed in all five languages.   HF1002.A66

Herbst, Robert. Dictionary of commercial, financial and legal terms. 3d ed. Zug, Switz., Translegal, [1982–83]. 3v.   **CH229**

Contents: v.1, English-German-French; v.2, German-English-French; v.3, French-English-German.
Added title pages in German and French.
Subtitle: Comprising trade and industry, exporting and importing, manufacturing, distributing, and marketing terms, as well as those used in banking, stock exchange dealings, credit, foreign exchange, taxation and customs, traffic including land, sea, and air transport, insurance and mail services, economics, social science, and politics, and covering, in particular, the special terminology as used in all fields of private and public law including the legislative, executive, and judicial branches of government.
1st ed. 1955–66.   HB61.H46

Isaacs, Alan. The multilingual commercial dictionary. N.Y., Facts on File, [1980]. 486p.   **CH230**

First published in the United Kingdom by Pan Books, 1978.
Provides a selection of the most commonly used terms in international business in English, German, French, Spanish, Italian, and Portuguese. All terms from all languages are arranged alphabetically in the same list, with their equivalent terms in the other languages.   HF1002.I884

Portuguese

Gomes, Luiz Sousa. Dicionário econômico-comercial e financeiro. (Terminologia de econômia, finanças, comércio e contabilidade) 8. ed., rev., ampliada e atualizada. Rio de Janeiro, Ed. Civilização Brasileira, [1966]. 271p.   **CH231**

Subtitle: Com um apêndice bio-bibliográfico sôbre os principais economistas brasileiros e estrangeiros e um dicionário de moedas.   HB61.G6

Spanish

Robb, Louis Adams. Dictionary of modern business: Spanish-English and English-Spanish. Wash., Anderson Kramer Assoc., 1960. 610p. **CH232**

Added title page in Spanish.

A glossary of specialized words and phrases used in business, finance, accounting, manufacturing, etc., not generally found in English-Spanish dictionaries. Based on Spanish language as used in Latin America. HF1002.R62

Directories

Business organizations and agencies directory. Ed.1– . Detroit, Gale, [1980]– . Irregular. **CH233**

Anthony T. Kruzas and Robert C. Thomas, eds.

Subtitle: A guide to trade, business, and commercial organizations, government agencies, stock exchanges, labor unions, chambers of commerce, diplomatic representation, trade and convention centers, trade fairs, publishers, data banks and computerized services, educational institutions, business libraries and information centers, and research centers.

Organized in 26 broad categories, as suggested by the subtitle. Entries provide name, address, telephone number, and contact personnel; a brief description of organizations, grants, databases, libraries and franchise operations is usually given. Limited to the United States. A supplement was published 1985. HF3010.B87

Clapp, Jane. Professional ethics and insignia. Metuchen, N.J., Scarecrow Pr., 1974. 851p. il. **CH234**

205 United States professional organizations, in categories from accountants to zoologists, are listed with address, corresponding officer, and one or more of the following items: code of ethics, conduct, standards, or rules; emblem; accreditation program. Includes a few international organizations. HD6504.A194

Directory of corporate affiliations. Skokie, Ill., National Register Publ. Co., 1968– . Annual. **CH235**

"Who owns whom."—*t.p.*

Title varies slightly.

In two sections: (1) an alphabetical list of parent companies, giving address, telephone number, ticker symbol, stock exchange(s), legal firm, approximate sales, number of employees, type of business and officers; it also lists subsidiaries and affiliates, with similar information; (2) a cross-index of the subsidiaries, giving name of parent company. A separate geographical index listing the companies by state and city is also available. The *Corporate action bulletin* appears bimonthly as an updating service, reporting personnel changes, acquisitions, address changes, and proposed actions. A companion volume is the annual *International directory of corporate affiliations.* HG4057.A217

Dun's Business rankings, 1982– . Parsippany, N.J., Dun's Marketing Services, 1982– . Annual. **CH236**

Identifies leading U.S. public and private business and ranks them by annual sales volume and number of employees, in five separate sections: alphabetically by company name; by state; by industry category (SIC code); public businesses; private businesses. Concluding sections cross-index division names with headquarter companies, and list chief executives and other officers by function. HG4057.A237

Dun's Latin America's top 25,000. 1984– . Parsippany, N.J., Dun's Marketing Services, 1984– . Annual. **CH237**

In three sections: businesses listed geographically, with SIC code, sales, number of employees, and executives' names; by SIC code numbers; alphabetically by name of company. HG4091.5.A2

Europe's 15,000 largest companies, 1975– . Oslo, etc., A. S. Økonomisk Literatur, Bowker, 1975– . Annual. **CH238**

Title also in German and French. Text in English, German, and French. Title varies.

Publisher varies: 1977, A. S. Økonomisk Literatur, Dun & Bradstreet International.

For Western Europe, ranks companies within these categories: (1) all industrials; (2) the 500 largest industrials by profit; (3) the 250 most profitable industrials; (4) the money losers; (5) the largest industrials by activity group; (6) the largest industrials by country. Trading companies, banks, insurance companies, transport companies, advertising agencies, hotels and restaurants are also ranked. Appropriate statistics are provided for each company. Indexed. HD2356.E9E93

Franchise opportunities handbook. [Ed.14]– . Wash., Govt. Prt. Off., 1980– . Annual. **CH239**

Title and issuing body have varied. Eds.1–6 (1965–70) called *Franchise company data* . . . .

Identifies about 1,000 franchise operations and provides for each description of operation, number of franchises, founding date, capital needed, financial and managerial assistance available, and training programs. Arranged by type of business, with alphabetical corporate name index. Provides directory of government and private assistance programs, checklist for evaluating a franchise, and bibliography. Date when information was submitted is given in all cases.

Peter G. Norback and Craig T. Norback's *The Dow Jones-Irwin guide to franchises* (Rev. ed., Homewood, Ill., Dow Jones-Irwin, 1982. 308p.) offers an almost identical subject arrangement and descriptions for about 500 franchises; statistical data appears to date from 1981. This guide does provide telephone numbers, which the handbook does not, and its bibliography, while duplicating many titles from the handbook, appears to have been revised more recently. HF5429.3.F694

Jane's Major companies of Europe. 1970–79/80. London, Sampson, Low, Marston; N.Y., McGraw-Hill, 1970–79. Annual. **CH240**

Superseded *Beerman's Financial year book of Europe* (ed. 1–4, 1965–68).

Basic information on European companies is now presented in a classified listing of companies (Finance; Services; Light industry and industrial chemicals; Engineering; Building; Metals and minerals) with an alphabetical index by company name, and an index by country. Ceased publication. HG5421.J35

Lambert's World of trade, finance, & economic development: an international directory of government contacts. Wash., Lambert Pubns., 1984– . Semiannual. **CH241**

Contents: v.1, Africa/The Americas; v.2, Asia/Europe including Australasia & Oceania.

Provides names, titles, addresses, telephone and telex numbers for key personnel involved with national or international economic activities in more than 170 countries and international organizations.

Million dollar directory, 1979– . Parsippany, N.J., Dun's Marketing Services, 1979– . Annual. **CH242**

Formed by the union of *Dun & Bradstreet million dollar directory* and *Dun & Bradstreet middle market directory* (1959–78).

Lists all American businesses and domestic subsidiaries of foreign companies with a net worth of $500,000 or more, giving annual sales, number of employees, division names and functions, etc. Businesses are also listed geographically and by SIC code.

National trade and professional associations of the United States, and labor unions. Ed.1– , 1966– . Wash., Columbia Books, 1966– . Annual. **CH243**

Publisher varies.

Title varies: v.1–6, 1966–71, called *Directory of national trade and professional associations of the United States.*

Serves as a successor to C. Jay Judkins's *National associations of the United States* (Wash., U.S. Dept. of Commerce, 1949. 634p.) and its supplementary publications, *Directory of national trade associations* (Wash., U.S. Dept. of Commerce, Office of Technical Services, 1956) and the *Directory of national associations of businessmen* (Ed.1–2, 1960–61).

Now offers information on some 4,600 national trade associations, and professional and learned societies.   HD2425.D622

The official guide to MBA programs, admissions, & careers, 1971/72– . [Princeton, N.J.], Graduate Management Admission Council, [1971]– . Irregular.   **CH244**

Title varies. 1984 latest publ.

An international directory describing graduate management programs, admissions requirements, expenses, financial assistance, placement activities. Arranged alphabetically by university, with summary tables by country and state.   HF1131.O36

Principal international businesses, 1974– . N.Y., Dun & Bradstreet, 1974– . Annual.   **CH245**

Subtitle: A world marketing directory.

Introductory matter in English, French, German and Spanish.

Section I lists companies by country, providing for each: sales volume, indication of whether it exports or imports, number of employees, SIC and DUNS numbers, description of field of activity, and name and title of senior operating officer. Section II lists businesses by SIC number, and Section III lists them by name.   HF54.U5P74●

Professional organizations in the Commonwealth. Ed. by Norman Tett and John Chadwick. 2d rev. ed. London, publ. for the Commonwealth Foundation by Hutchinson, [1976]. 584p.   **CH246**

1st ed. 1970.

Lists and describes professional associations throughout the Commonwealth. Organizations are grouped by profession; index entries are also grouped by profession, then subdivided by country.   HD2421.P73

Standard & Poor's Register of corporations, directors and executives. N.Y., Standard & Poor's Corp., 1928– . Annual.   **CH247**

In three volumes: v.1, Corporation directory (an alphabetical list of about 45,000 corporations, giving names of executive personnel, number of employees, main products, etc.); v.2, Directors and executives (brief biographical data on corporate officers); v.3, Indexes (by SIC number, geographic location, corporate family, etc.).   HG4057.A4

Trade associations and professional bodies of the United Kingdom; a directory and classified index. Ed.1– , 1962– . Comp. by Patricia Millard. London, C.B.D. Research, 1962– .   **CH248**

Publisher varies. Revised every two or three years.

Now an alphabetical listing with subject and geographical indexes.   HD2429.G7M5

Ward's directory of 51,000 largest U.S. corporations. [No.1]– . By the editors of News Front Business Trends. [Petaluma, Calif., B. H. Ward Pubns., 1980]– . Annual.   **CH248a**

Title varies.

Analyzes public and private companies and ranks them by sales volume, with ranked lists arranged by SIC industries; also ranks them by geographical area. Preliminary sections list the most profitable large, medium, and small corporations. Companies are also listed alphabetically, with name, address, telephone number, sales volume, number of employees and plants, names of executive personnel, etc. 1984 ed. also designated as "v.1," two companion works being *Ward's Directory of 49,000 private U.S. companies* (v.2) and *Ward's Business directory of major international corporations* (v.3).

Who owns whom: United Kingdom and Republic of Ireland: a directory of parent, associate and subsidiary companies. Ed.1– . London, Roskill, 1958– . Annual.   **CH249**

Title varies.

In two main sections: (1) United Kingdom parent and associate companies showing subsidiary and associate companies; (2) United Kingdom subsidiary and associate companies showing parent and associate companies. A "Continental Europe" edition has been

published since 1961. A companion series for foreign subsidiaries of United States companies appeared in four editions, 1969–72, as *Who owns whom: international subsidiaries of U.S. companies*; it has been superseded by: HG4135.Z5W5

Who owns whom (North American edition). 1973– . London, Roskill, 1973– . Annual.   **CH249a**

World guide to trade associations. Internationales Verzeichnis der Wirtschaftsverbände. Ed.1– . Munich, K. G. Saur, 1973– . Irregular. (Ed.3 publ. 1985)   **CH250**

Issued as "Handbook of international documentation and information" ser., v.12.

A directory of more than 46,000 trade associations, arranged by trade category, then by country.   HD2421.W67

Bibliography

International

Anderson, Ian Gibson. Current African directories, incorporating "African companies—a guide to sources of information." Beckenham, Eng., C.B.D. Research Ltd., 1972. 187p.   **CH251**

Subtitle: A guide to directories published in or relating to Africa, and to sources of information on business enterprises in Africa.

In two parts: (1) African directories, listed alphabetically by title, with descriptive information; and (2) sources of information on African companies, on a country-by-country basis. The latter section was originally planned as a separate publication, but was not previously published in another form.   Z5771.4.A4A7

Henderson, George P. Current European directories. Ed.2. Beckenham, Eng., C.B.D. Research Ltd., [1981]. 413p.   **CH252**

1st ed. 1969.

Subtitle: A guide to international, national, city and specialised directories and similar reference works for all countries of Europe, excluding Great Britain and Ireland.   Z5771.H39

International bibliography of special directories. Ed.7– . München & N.Y., Saur, 1983– . Irregular. (Handbook of international documentation and information, v.5)   **CH253**

Continues *International bibliography of directories,* 1st–6th eds., 1962–78.

Title and prefatory matter also in German.

The 7th ed. lists more than 5,600 address books and membership lists published regularly or irregularly in about fifty countries. Detailed subject arrangement; under each subject, international directories are followed by national directories.   Z5771.I58

Trade directories of the world, comp. and ed. by Ulrich H. E. Croner. Queen's Village, N.Y., Croner Pub., 1952?– . 1v., looseleaf.   **CH254**

Title varies: *Croner's World register of trade directories.*

Lists general, trade, business, and professional directories of the United States and of more than 60 foreign countries. Most entries are annotated. Kept up-to-date by an amendment service.   Z5771.C7

United States

Davis, Marjorie Veith. American business directories. 2d ed. April 1947. Wash., Govt. Prt. Off., 1947. 198p. (U.S. Bureau of Foreign and Domestic Commerce. Industrial ser., no.67)   **CH255**

1st ed. 1942.

In two sections: (1) Classed list arranged alphabetically; (2) Names of "general" directories arranged geographically.

Substantially the same material in slightly different arrangement is given in the author's *Guide to American business directories* (Wash., Public Affairs Pr., 1948. 242p.).

Still useful for historical purposes; includes many titles not listed in *Guide to American directories* (CH257). Z5771.D33

The directory of directories: an annotated guide to business and industrial directories, professional and scientific rosters, and other lists and guides of all kinds. Detroit, Information Enterprises, [1980]– . Ed.1– . Biennial. **CH256**

James M. Ethridge, ed.

An outgrowth of the periodically published *Directory information service* (1977–78). Includes entries for directories arranged according to broad subject field. Indicates coverage of each directory, type of information included, arrangement, size, frequency, price, and ordering information. Title and subject indexes. Additional listings between editions are published in the *Directory information service* (3 issues per yr.). Z5771.D55

Guide to American directories. [1954]– . N.Y., McGraw-Hill, 1954– . Irregular. (11th ed., 1982) **CH257**

Publisher varies. Bernard Klein, ed.

Title varies: 1954–58, *Guide to American directories for compiling mailing lists.* Subtitle varies.

A very extensive listing under several hundred categories, with descriptive information and publication data for each title. Covers industrial, professional, and mercantile guides and directories. Z5771.G8

Spear, Dorothea N. Bibliography of American directories through 1860. Worcester, Mass., Amer. Antiquarian Soc., 1961. 389p. (Repr.: Westport, Conn., Greenwood Pr., 1978) **CH258**

A geographical listing, with locations of 1,647 business directories, city and county directories, etc. Many annotations. Works listed are available in the microfilm collection, *City directories of the United States* from Research Publications. Z5771.2S68

❖Many individual states or regions have industrial directories, e.g., *MacRae's state industrial directory, New York State*; *Directory of New England manufacturers.* These should be consulted for local information. The *Colt microfiche library of state directories* reproduces about 30 state industrial directories.

Great Britain

Current British directories. Ed.1– . Beckenham, Eng., C.B.D. Research Ltd., 1953– . (10th ed., 1985) **CH259**

Publisher varies.

Subtitle (varies): A guide to the directories published in Great Britain, Ireland, the British Commonwealth and South Africa.

In three main sections: (1) Local directories; (2) Specialized directories; (3) Directories of the British Commonwealth and South Africa. Z5771.C8

Goss, Charles William Frederick. The London directories, 1677–1855; a bibliography with notes on their origin and development. London, Archer, 1932. 146p. **CH260**

Z5771.G67

Norton, Jane Elizabeth. Guide to the national and provincial directories of England and Wales, excluding London, published before 1856. Repr. with corrections. London, Royal Historical Soc., 1984. 241p. (Royal Historical Soc. Guides and handbooks, 5) **CH261**

First published 1950.

Complements C. W. F. Goss, *The London directories, 1677–1855* (above). Includes national, local, and Welsh directories.

Z2034.N67

Statistics

Almanac of business and industrial financial ratios. By Leo Troy. Englewood Cliffs, N.J., Prentice-Hall, 1971– . Annual beginning 1974. **CH262**

For the industry as a whole and for corporations of similar size as measured by assets, gives comparative figures, percentages, and ratios for factors such as net sales, total receipts, cost of operations, compensation of officers, taxes, interest, depreciation, amortization, pensions and benefit plans, etc. 1978 edition is the first to show separate tables for each total industry and for those operating at a profit. Indexed by field of activity. HF5681.R25A45

Balachandran, M. A guide to trade and securities statistics. Ann Arbor, Pierian Pr., 1977. 185p. **CH263**

An alphabetically arranged subject guide to data found in about 30 heavily used serials in the field of trade and security statistics, such as *Best's Insurance reports, Commodity year book, Moody's Bond record, Standard and Poor's Industry surveys,* etc.

Z7165.U5B338

Economic almanac for 1940–67/68; a handbook of useful facts about business, labor and government in the United States and other areas. N.Y., Nat. Industrial Conference Board, [1940–68]. Biennial. **CH264**

Annual, 1940–50. Ceased with 18th ed., 1967/68.

A statistical compendium covering such subjects as: prices, banking, finance, national income, resources, manufacturing, communication and transportation, industries, agriculture, labor, foreign trade, international economic statistics, etc. Includes a glossary of terms used in business and economics. A general index is followed by a separate index for Canada. HC101.E38

Edwards, Bernard. Sources of economic and business statistics. London, Heinemann, [1972]. 272p. **CH265**

Introductory chapters on statistical collection and classification and the development of British government statistical services are followed by chapters discussing the origin, uses, and publication of several types of statistics: manpower and wages, production and industry, distribution, transport, GNP, overseas trade and balance of payment, family expenditure. Also discusses various indexes. Only British sources are considered. Indexed. HA37.G7E4

The handbook of economic and financial measures. Ed. by Frank J. Fabozzi and Harry I. Greenfield. Homewood, Ill., Dow Jones-Irwin, [1984]. 517p. il. **CH266**

21 chapters by subject specialists treat the most commonly used measures of economic activity, explaining their background, construction, uses, and limitations. In six sections: aggregate economic activity; government deficit and trade balance; money supply and capital market conditions; inflation; firms and consumers; forecasting. Bibliographic references; index. HC106.8.H36

Hoel, Arline Alchian, Clarkson, Kenneth W. and **Miller, Roger LeRoy.** Economics sourcebook of government statistics. Lexington, Mass., Lexington Books, [1983]. 271p. **CH267**

Describes more than fifty main statistical series published by the federal government in terms of how they are compiled, strengths and weaknesses, when they become available, primary and secondary sources of current and historical publications, references on the series, and agency to be contacted. In six chapters covering inflation, general business conditions, interest rates, employment and earnings, international finance and trade, the budget. Appendixes; glossary; index. HC106.8.H63

O'Hara, Frederick M. and **Sicignano, Robert.** Handbook of United States economic and financial indicators. Westport, Conn., Greenwood Pr., [1985]. 224p. **CH268**

Explains about 200 economic measures compiled and appearing in some 55 sources. Entry provides brief definition, source, where announced, frequency, historical cumulations. Includes bibliographic references. Alphabetical arrangement with subject index.

HC106.8.O47

Survey of current business. v.1– , Aug. 1921– . Wash., Govt. Prt. Off., 1921– . Monthly, with weekly supplements. **CH269**

A publication of the U.S. Office of Business Economics.
Descriptive and statistical material on basic income and trade developments in the United States. Covers prices, foreign trade, commodities, industries, etc. *Annual review* number issued in Feb., 1939–62; *National income and product accounts* number in July since 1948. HC101.A13

———— Business statistics. Wash., Govt. Prt. Off., 1932– . Biennial. **CH270**

Title varies: 1932–42 called *Supplement.* Publication suspended 1934, 1942–47.
Tables give monthly and quarterly data for 2,600 statistical series reported in the *Survey of current business.* HC101.A1322

U.S. Bureau of Economic Analysis. Long term economic growth, 1860–1965– ; a statistical compendium. [Wash., Govt. Prt. Off., 1966]– . Irregular. **CH271**

Issuing agency varies.
Charts, graphs, and statistical tables offer a comprehensive view of the growth of the American economy. HA203.A241

U.S. Council of Economic Advisers. Economic indicators. May, 1948– . Wash., Govt. Prt. Off., 1948– . Monthly. **CH272**

Prepared for the Joint Economic Committee by the Council of Economic Advisers.
Presents basic statistical series on total output, income, and spending; employment, unemployment, and wages; production and business activity; prices, currency, credit, and security markets; and federal finance.
Supplements, published in 1953 and revised 1955, 1957, 1960, 1962, 1964, and 1967, describe each series and give annual data. HC101.A186

U.S. President. The economic report of the President transmitted to Congress. Jan. 1947– . Wash., Govt. Prt. Off., 1947– . Annual. **CH273**

Title varies slightly.
Annual, accompanied by a supplementary report, dated July, with the title *The mid-year economic report,* 1947–52.
Reports for Jan. 1949– include *The annual economic report,* by the Council of Economic Advisers.
Offers a review of the nation's economic condition, documented by statistics. HC106.5.A272

History

Corporate America: a historical bibliography. Santa Barbara, Calif., ABC-Clio, [1984]. 341p. (ABC-Clio research guides, 5) **CH274**

Presents 1,368 abstracts of articles on American business history, published 1973–82 and drawn from the database of *America: history and life.* Broad subject arrangement; keyword subject and author indexing. Z7164.T87C66

Dallas. Public Library. Business and Technology Division. Business history collection: a checklist. Dallas, Tex., 1974. 236p. **CH275**

A listing of histories of particular firms, American and foreign, arranged by the name of the firm. No index. Z7165.U5D34

Hamburg. Welt-Wirtschafts-Archiv. Verzeichnis der Fest- und Denkschriften von Unternehmungen und Organisationen der Wirtschaft. [Hamburg], 1961. 566p. (*Its* Veröffentlichung) **CH276**

A listing of more than 4,000 *Festschriften* and histories of firms and companies. International in scope, but mainly German. Lists works published in this century that are found in the *Archiv.* In classified arrangement with indexes by: (1) author and personal name; (2) firm; and (3) geographical location.

Particularly strong in the histories of individual companies, many of which are not listed in general and national bibliographies. Z7165.G3H3

Harvard University. Graduate School of Business Administration. Baker Library. Studies in enterprise; a selected bibliography of American and Canadian company histories and biographies of businessmen. Lorna M. Daniells, comp. Boston, 1957. 169p. (*Its* Reference list, no.4) **CH277**

An expanded edition of the Library's *Business biographies and company histories* (1948).
Lists 2,080 items in a classified arrangement, with subject and author indexes. Z7164.C81H26

Larson, Henrietta Melia. Guide to business history; materials for the study of American business history and suggestions for their use. Cambridge, Harvard Univ. Pr., 1948. 1181p. (Harvard studies in business history, v.12) **CH278**

Contents: (1) Introduction; (2) Historical background and setting of American business; (3) Business administrators: Biographical and autobiographical books, pamphlets and articles; (4) The history of individual business units; (5) History of industries; (6) General topics in business history; (7) Research and reference materials. Index.
4,904 annotated entries. Dated, but still a useful guide to historical study. HC103.L3

Lovett, Robert Woodberry. American economic business history information sources. Detroit, Gale, [1971]. 323p. **CH279**

Subtitle: An annotated bibliography of recent works pertaining to economic, business, agricultural, and labor history and the history of science and technology for the United States and Canada.
Intended in part as a supplement to H. M. Larson's *Guide to business history* (above). Z7165.U5L66

Biography

See also CH247.

Dictionary of business biography: a biographical dictionary of business leaders active in Britain in the period 1860– 1980. Ed. by David J. Jeremy. London, Butterworths, 1984– 85. v.1–4. il. (In progress; to be in 5v.) **CH280**

Contents: v.1–4, A–R.
A project of the Business History Unit, London School of Economics and Imperial College. The completed work will present about 1,000 biographies of British entrepreneurs, excluding academics, civil servants, trade unionists and agriculturalists whose business involvement was not central to their careers. Bibliographies include works by and about the biographee, including unpublished sources.

Ingham, John N. Biographical dictionary of American business leaders. Westport, Conn., Greenwood Pr., [1983]. 4v. (2026p.) **CH281**

Presents 835 biographical entries, with information on 1,159 "most significant" business leaders of the United States from colonial times to the present; entries range in length from 750 to more than 3,000 words and conclude with bibliographic references. Appendixes arrange leaders by industry, company, birthplace and date, ethnic background and religion, place of business activity, and sex. Indexed. HC102.5.A2I53

International businessmen's who's who. Ed.1– . London, Burke's Peerage, 1967– . Irregular. **CH282**

2d ed. 1970; a 3d ed. is scheduled for 1986.
Intended as an aid to businessmen engaged in international trade, the work includes biographical sketches of prominent figures engaged in export, import, and related fields "from some sixty of the world's largest countries."—*Foreword, Ed.1.* HF5500.I614

Reference book of corporate managements. Ed.1– . N.Y., Dun & Bradstreet, 1967– . Annual.   **CH283**

Title varies: Ed.1–13, *Dun & Bradstreet reference book of corporate managements.*

Lists and provides brief biographical information on officers and directors of about 2,400 companies of great investor interest. Companies are listed in alphabetical sequence; index of principal officers.   HD2745.D85

Who's who in finance and industry. Ed.1– . Chicago, Marquis, 1936– . Biennial.   **CH284**

Title varies: 1936–59, *Who's who in commerce and industry;* 1961–68/69, *World who's who in commerce and industry;* 1970/71, *World who's who in finance and industry.*

Gives international coverage of businessmen. Includes index of firms with references to personnel for whom sketches are included.   HF3023.A2W5

Annuals

The Business week almanac, [1982]– . Ed. by J. Robert Connor and the staff of Business week. N.Y., McGraw-Hill, 1982– . il. Annual.   **CH285**

A ready-reference handbook on the American business scene. The 1982 volume is organized in 61 subject chapters, from advertising to women in business. Survey chapters present figures from 1980, although the "Economic diary" is a daily chronicle for 1981. Provides brief biographical sketches of business leaders, chronology of business in America, a survey of executive salaries, book reviews, glossary, investment outlook, personal business guide, etc. A useful and interesting compilation. Indexed.   HF3031.B83

Dow Jones–Irwin. Dow Jones–Irwin business and investment almanac. Ed. by Sumner N. Levine. Homewood, Ill., Dow Jones–Irwin, 1977– . il. Annual.   **CH286**

Title varies: 1977–81, *Dow Jones-Irwin business almanac.*

A quick-access source to a variety of current information in business, investment, finance, and economics. Emphasis on American domestic and international business. Index.   HF5003.D68a

BUSINESS MANAGEMENT

Guides

Information sources in management and business. Ed., K. D. C. Vernon. 2d ed. London, Butterworths, [1984]. 346p. il.   **CH287**

A rev. ed. of *The use of management and business literature* (1975).

In three parts: literature content, libraries and bibliographic tools; types of business information (companies, statistics, online services, market research, research in progress and unpublished materials); bibliographic review essays of the literature of six subject areas. Chapters by specialists; some British emphasis. Indexed.   Z7164.O7I413

Bibliography

Alred, Gerald J., Reep, Diana C. and **Limaye, Mohan R.** Business and technical writing: an annotated bibliography of books, 1880–1980. Metuchen, N.J., Scarecrow Pr., 1981. 240p.   **CH287a**

In three main sections: (1) previous bibliographies; (2) the main bibliography, arranged by author, followed by citations to related works (e.g., style guides, works on graphics, oral communication, and publishing); (3) addendum of additional titles. Author, title, and subject indexes.   Z7164.C81A413

American Management Association. Ten-year index of AMA publications, Jan. 1923/Jan. 1932–57/66. N.Y., Assoc., 1932–67.   **CH288**

Issued as follows: 1923/32, 1932/45, 1954/63, 1957/66. Title varies.

A detailed catalog of AMA publications, arranged by subject with author index.

Continued by:

——— Index to AMA resources of the seventies, 1970– 1976. N.Y., AMACOM, [1977]. 162p.   **CH289**

Elizabeth A. Keegan, comp.

A subject arrangement of all books, periodical articles, reports, studies and services published by the AMA during this period. Title-series and author indexes.

Continued by *Index to AMA resources, 1977–81* (N.Y., Amer. Mgmt. Assoc., 1982. 184p.).   Z7164.O7A49

Bakewell, K. G. B. Management principles and practices: a guide to information sources. Detroit, Gale, [1977]. 519p. (Management information guide ser., 32)   **CH290**

A selective, briefly annotated bibliography of books, periodical titles and articles, and audiovisual materials on management in general and its various functional areas. Appendixes provide directories of organizations, periodicals, and publishers/distributors. Proper name, title, and subject index.   Z7164.O7B25

Cannon, Joan Bartczak and **Smith, Ed.** Resources for affirmative action: an annotated directory of books, periodicals, films, training aids, and consultants on equal opportunity. [Garrett Park, Md., Garrett Park Pr., 1982]. 190p. il.   **CH291**

1,400 items indexed by personal name, title, and publisher/distributor. Appendixes.   Z7164.C81C243

Catalyst, Inc. Two-career families: an annotated bibliography of relevant readings. Comp. and updated through February 1, 1981. N.Y., Catalyst, 1981. 126p., 150p.   **CH292**

More than 900 citations to books, periodical articles, essays, conference papers, government documents, etc. Main entry arrangement with author and subject indexes. In two sections: (1) bibliographic list compiled through Mar. 1980; (2) Addendum compiled through Feb. 1, 1981. Later citations on the topic have been added to a commercially available bibliographic database.   Z7963.E7C37●

Cornell University. Graduate School of Business and Public Administration. Management; a subject listing of recommended books, pamphlets and journals, [by] Betsy Ann Olive. Ithaca, N.Y., 1965. 222p.   **CH293**

More than 4,200 numbered items. Author index.

    Z7164.A2C65

Dunphy, Dexter Colby and **Stening, Bruce W.** Japanese organization behaviour and management: an annotated bibliography. [Hong Kong], Asian Research Serv., [1984]. 214p.   **CH294**

Includes more than 500 citations to English-language material published 1970–83, emphasizing scholarly articles and first-hand case studies of Japanese operations at home and abroad. Author arrangement, with name, topical, and keyword subject indexing. Excludes employment systems.   Z7165.J3D86

Ford, Bill, Easther, Millicent and **Brewer, Ann.** Japanese employment and employee relations: an annotated bibliography. Canberra, Australian Govt. Publ. Serv., 1984. 180p.   **CH295**

At head of title: Dept. of Employment and Industrial Relations, Working Environment Branch, Program in Organizational Behaviour, Univ. of New South Wales.

Cites 536 English-language books, chapters, periodical articles, conference papers, etc., published 1970–83 in topical arrangement with author and subject indexes.

Franklin, Jerome L. Human resource development in the organization: a guide to information sources. Detroit, Gale, [1978]. 175p. (Management information guide, 35)   **CH296**

An annotated bibliography of books, parts of books, reports, and articles published since 1960. In three major divisions, with appropriate subdivisions: (1) background and overview of organizational development; (2) personnel development strategies and techniques; (3) case studies. Annotations often include lists of book contents. Author, title, and subject indexes.   Z7164.O7F72

Hanson, Agnes O. Executive and management development for business and government: a guide to information sources. Detroit, Gale, [1976]. 357p. (Management information guide ser., 31)   **CH297**

An annotated bibliography, principally of English-language books; selected sources emphasize "development of conceptual approaches and skills, imagination, and judgment, factors that contribute to flexibility and adaptability, rather than techniques, methods, and procedures."—*Pref.* The final three chapters list relevant reference sources, periodical titles, and organizations. Author, title, subject, and proper name indexes.   Z7164.O7H275

Hollander, Stanley C. Management consultants and clients. East Lansing, Div. of Research, Grad. School of Business Admin., Michigan State Univ., 1972. 541p.   **CH298**

1st ed. (1963) had title: *Business consultants and clients.*
An annotated bibliography of over 1,200 entries on the client-consultant relationship in the United States and abroad. Classed arrangement with author index.   Z7164.C81H6

Leavitt, Judith A. Women in management; an annotated bibliography and sourcelist. [Phoenix], Oryx Pr., 1982. 197p.   **CH299**

Includes more than 700 citations to books, papers, newspaper and journal articles, and dissertations written between 1970 and 1981, arranged in 20 subject chapters; appendixes list films, pamphlets, periodicals, professional organizations, networking directories, and other bibliographies. Author index.   Z7963.E7L43

Stogdill, Ralph Melvin. Leadership abstracts and bibliography, 1904 to 1974. Columbus, College of Administrative Science, Ohio State Univ., 1977. 829p. (College of Administrative Science monograph, no.AA10)   **CH300**

When the author's *Handbook of leadership* (N.Y., Free Pr., 1974) was published, *The booklist* review (71:1093) suggested that the most useful section for reference purposes was the bibliography. The abstracts of more than 3,000 books and journal articles from that bibliography are provided here; arrangement is alphabetical by author, with author and subject indexes.   Z7164.S68S86

Stout, Russell. Organizations, management, and control: an annotated bibliography. Bloomington, Indiana Univ. Pr., 1980. 189p.   **CH301**

Surveys the monographic and periodical literature produced from 1969 to 1979, grouping it within 11 main subject sections with appropriate subdivisions: accounting and budgeting; analytical methods and quantitative techniques; computers and information; control; decision; developing countries; evaluation; management; organization; planning and policy; and the contributions of R. E. D. Woolsey. Evaluative annotations, with recommended works noted. Author and subject indexes.   Z7164.C81S779

Thompson, Marilyn Taylor. Management information, where to find it. Metuchen, N.J., Scarecrow Pr., 1981. 272p.   **CH302**

Twenty topical chapters list resources on management in general, specific aspects of management (e.g., personnel management), and management in various fields (e.g., public administration, education, health care, social services, library administration). Within chapters, sources are grouped by format; associations and computerized information services are included. Limited to materials published in English in the 1970s. Very brief annotations; author/title index.   Z7164.C81T53

U.S. Office of Personnel Management. Library. Personnel bibliography series. no.1–129. Wash., 1960–81.   **CH303**

Issuing agency varies.
Each number is on a specific aspect of personnel work and each has a distinctive title.

Walsh, Ruth M. and **Birkin, Stanley J.** Business communications: an annotated bibliography. Westport, Conn., Greenwood Pr., [1980]. 686p.   **CH304**

More than 1,600 English-language books, periodical articles, and doctoral dissertations written within the past 20 years are cited in three sections: (1) author/title index; (2) keyword in context index; (3) abstracts and annotations.   Z7164.C81W24

Current

Personnel literature. Off. of Personnel Management, Lib. v.38, no.1– , Jan. 1979– . Wash., The Library [for sale by Govt. Prt. Off.], 1979– . Monthly.   **CH305**

Continues: U.S. Civil Service Commission. Library. *Personnel literature* (1941–78), and assumes its numbering.
A detailed subject index of books, reports, periodical articles, government documents, etc., received by the Library. About 250 titles are listed each month. Annual names/subject index.
    Z7164.C81U45683

Personnel management abstracts. v.1– , Jan./Feb. 1955– . Chelsea, Mich., Personnel Management Abstracts, 1955– . Quarterly.   **CH306**

Publisher varies.
An international bibliography of English-language literature. Currently abstracts articles from more than 80 periodicals, and includes reviews of current books. Broad subject arrangement with author index; no detailed subject approach nor cumulative indexing features.   HF5549.P452

Periodicals

Tega, Vasile. Management and economics journals: a guide to information sources. Detroit, Gale, [1977]. 370p. (Management information guide, 33)   **CH307**

A selection of over 160 journals, "academic and business oriented, [which] are internationally prestigious and generally regarded as 'core' journals."—*Introd.* Entries follow an alphabetical title arrangement, and provide publication information, a description of scope, purpose, and content, editorial policy on manuscript submission, notes on registers of doctoral dissertations and current research, and details of special issues published since 1960. An appendix lists by subject journals which include lists of doctoral dissertations and research in progress. Periodicals subject index; special issues subject index; and index of journals which deal with single attributes of top companies (e.g., *Business week's* "Highest paid executives" annual issue).   Z7164.O7T23

Dictionaries and encyclopedias

Banki, Ivan S. Dictionary of administration and management. [Los Angeles], Systems Research [Inst., 1981]. 752p.   **CH308**

In three sections: (1) acronyms and abbreviations; (2) brief definitions and discussions of terms, concepts, testing and evaluation tools, and national and international management associations, organizations and institutions; (3) bibliographic sources.
    HD30.15.B36

The encyclopedia of management. Ed. by Carl Heyel. 3d ed. N.Y., Van Nostrand Reinhold, [1982]. 1371p. il.   **CH309**

1st ed. 1963.
More than 300 signed articles by 203 contributors are alphabetically arranged and range in length from half a page to about 30

pages. 41 articles are new to this edition; they treat such topics as employee privacy, the quality of working life, robots in industry, women in management, and zero-base budgeting. Biographical sketches are included. Bibliographies; cross references. Appendixes list universities and colleges offering programs in business administration, and provide directory-type information for organizations and periodicals mentioned in the text. Indexed.   HD30.15.E49

French, Derek and **Saward, Heather.** Dictionary of management. 2d ed. Aldershot, Gower, 1983. 470p.   **CH310**

1st ed. 1975.

Brief explanations of about 4,000 terms, including abbreviations, associations, and foreign expressions. Variations between American and British usage are noted.   HD19.F73

Handbook for professional managers. N.Y., McGraw-Hill, [1985]. 1000p. il.   **CH311**

Lester R. Bittel and Jackson E. Ramsey, eds.

1978 ed. had title: *Encyclopedia of professional management.*

"In this work there are over 239 comprehensive entries, which contain nearly 17,500 specific definitions. In general, each entry provides: (1) a definition of the underlying principle or concept; (2) application opportunities, techniques, procedures, and examples; (3) an evaluation of the usefulness of the concept or technique; (4) a list of other sources of information. . . ."—*Pref.* Signed articles by 229 contributors. No biographical entries. Synoptic and general indexes.   HD31.H31245

Horton, Forest W. Reference guide to advanced management methods. [N.Y.], Amer. Management Assoc., [1972]. 333p. il.   **CH312**

Intends to provide an overview of modern management technology. Sections devoted to various concepts, methods, techniques, etc., are set forth in alphabetical sequence, with bibliographic references provided at the end of each section. Treats such topics as: Automation; Brainstorming; Budgeting systems; Conference methods; Decision making; Group dynamics; Linear programming; Manpower planning; Models; Personnel selection; Profit planning; Statistical methods, etc. Glossary; index.   HD31.H653

An international dictionary of personnel terms. [2d ed.] [London], European Assoc. of Personnel Management, [1980]. 157p.   **CH313**

Provides basic terms and phrases in French, with equivalents in Norwegian, English, Spanish, Finnish, German, Portuguese, Dutch, Swedish, and Danish. The Italian section appears separately. Classed arrangement; indexes in all languages.   HF5549.A23I57

Johannsen, Hano and **Page, G. Terry.** International dictionary of business. Englewood Cliffs, N.J., Prentice-Hall, [1981]. 376p.   **CH314**

Previous ed. (1975) had title: *International dictionary of management.*

A dictionary of about 5,800 terms, phrases, and names relevant to business management. United States coverage has been expanded in this edition and some appendix data omitted. A 3d ed. is to be published 1986.   HD30.I5J64

Shafritz, Jay M. Dictionary of personnel management and labor relations. Oak Park, Ill., Moore Publ. Co., [1980]. 429p. il.   **CH315**

Defines words, terms, phrases, processes, personal names, laws, organizations, and court cases. Offers separate lists of organizations in labor relations, business schools, personnel journals and textbooks, tests and test publishers.

A revised and expanded edition was scheduled for 1985 publication as the *Facts on File dictionary of personnel management and labor relations.*   HF5549.A23S52

Sommer, Werner and **Schönfeld, Hanns-Martin.** Management dictionary, German-English. 4th rev. & enl. ed. Berlin & N.Y., W. de Gruyter, 1978. 542p.   **CH316**

Prefatory material in German and English.

Offers American English equivalents for German terms. Intended as a comprehensive dictionary in the many related fields of business management for businessmen, accountants, and students.

A companion volume is: HF1002.S622

————Management dictionary, English-German. [5th rev. & enl. ed.] Berlin & N.Y., W. de Gruyter, 1979. 621p.

Prefatory material in English and German.   HF1002.S622

Wortman, Leon A. A deskbook of business management terms. [N.Y.], AMACOM, [1979]. 615p.   **CH317**

A dictionary which provides very brief definitions of acronyms, initialisms, personal and corporate names, legal instruments, and terms drawn from the fields of finance, economics, marketing, insurance, law, industrial relations, human behavior, industrial psychology, real estate, transportation and distribution, data processing, statistics, and management.   HD30.15.W67

Directories

Consultants and consulting organizations directory: a reference guide to concerns and individuals engaged in consultation for business and industry. Ed.1– . Detroit, Gale, [1966]– . Irregular (6th ed. 1984)   **CH318**

Title varies.

Janice McLean, ed.

Arranged by broad subject area; indexed by subject, industry, firm name and personal name. (For biographical data *see Who's who in consulting,* CH331.)

Kept up to date between editions by: HB69.C6C647

New consultants. Issue no.1– , June 1973– . Detroit, Gale, 1973– . Semiannual.   **CH318a**

Continuing education for business people; a guide to 30,000 courses, conferences, seminars, workshops, and independent study opportunities. Ed. by Andrea Pedolsky. Detroit, Neal-Schuman in assoc. with Gale, [1981]. 406p.   **CH319**

In four sections: (1) academic programs, in geographical arrangement; (2) programs offered by associations and organizations, with geographic index; (3) independent study programs, with geographic index; (4) a directory of publishers and distributors of continuing education learning materials. Indexed by subject and name.

HF1131.C7

Directory of career training and development programs: a guide to career training and development opportunities available through business and industry, government agencies, and professional organizations. Alvin Renetzky, ed. in chief. Santa Monica, Calif., Ready Reference Pr., [1979]. 286p.   **CH320**

Focuses on in-house training and development programs rather than those offered by outside organizations on a fee basis, which are included in *Training and development organizations directory* (CH330). Describes the type of training and benefits. Subject and geographic indexes.   HF5549.5.T7D53

———— Suppl.1. Santa Monica, Calif., Ready Reference Pr., [1981]. 351p.

Directory of internships, work experience programs, and on-the-job training opportunities. Ed.1. Thousand Oaks, Calif., Ready Reference Pr., [1976]. 371p.   **CH321**

Subtitle: A guide to internship, work experience, and on-the-job training opportunities sponsored by governmental agencies, business and industry, professional associations, foundations, and various social and community organizations.

Listing is alphabetical by sponsoring body, with program title, geographic, and subject indexes.

1st supplement to Directory of internships, work experience programs, and on-the-job training opportunities. Thousand Oaks, Calif., Ready Reference Pr., [1977]. 354p.

HD5715.2.D57

Directory of management consultants, 1986. 4th ed. Fitzwilliam, N.H., Consultants News, [1985]. 456p.   **CH322**

1st ed. 1977.

For each individual and corporate management consultant, provides address, telephone number, brief description of service, contact personnel, geographic areas served, founding date, staff, revenues, areas of interest, industries served. Alphabetically arranged, with subject, industrial, and geographical indexes.   HD69.C6D5

Directory of management education programs. [2d rev. ed. N.Y.], AMACOM, 1978. 2v.   **CH323**

Comp. by Management Development Resource Service of the American Management Association.

1st ed. 1977.

Contents: v.1, Academic sources; v.2, General sources.

Provides descriptions of about 3,200 non-credit programs offering management education. Each entry consists of a detailed program description, data on curriculum and teaching methods, financial information, staff and clientele profiles, and contact personnel. Programs have been classified into 16 major areas and 140 subdivisions, and indexed by sponsoring organization and program title.

HD30.42.U5D58

Dun's Consultants directory. 1986– . Parsippany, N.J., Dun's Marketing Services, 1985– . Annual.   **CH324**

A directory of the 25,000 largest United States consulting firms, in four sections: alphabetical (providing full directory information on specialty area, founding date, sales, number of employees); geographical (by state and city); specialty; and branch offices (by state and metropolitan area).

Gevers international consultants, world-wide professional directory 1981– . [Lausanne, Seminar Services, 1981–] Annual.   **CH325**

[3d ed.] 1983 publ. in 3v.

Country arrangement. Within country sections full details about consulting firm and members are supplied in the main listings which are organized by six types of firms. Indexes of personal and corporate names, plus a classified subject or professional index. More than 100 countries are included. Kept up-to-date by mid-year supplements.   HD69.C6G442

In-house training and development programs; a guide to schools and colleges offering training programs for businesses; seminar packages; consultants; and audiovisual producers and distributors. Andrea Pedolsky, ed. Detroit, Neal-Schuman in assoc. with Gale, [1981]. 328p.   **CH326**

Provides directory information on programs, individuals, and organizations. Listings within each section are indexed by subject and/or geographic area. Also lists additional sources of information, printed and organizational. Name index.   HF5549.5.T7I38

International business travel and relocation directory. Detroit, Gale, [1985]. 896p. maps.   **CH327**

Subtitle: The who, what, and where handbook for international business travel and operations, covering country characteristics, travel documents, currency, customs, pets, airports, hotels, tipping, holidays, health, housing, and further sources of information.

Title varies: 1st ed. 1980: *Directory of international business travel and relocation.*

"Taken from Overseas assignment directory service, prepared by the editors of Knowledge Industry Publications, Inc."—*verso of t.p.*

In two parts, the first giving general background information for personnel officers and employees going abroad. Pt.II presents chapters on individual countries, covering: country characteristics; predeparture regulations, documents, and procedures; airports, transportation, hotels; money and banks; communications; business hours and holidays; health; information for a long-term stay; background reading.   HF5549.5.E45I57

Management media directory; an annotated guide of commercially available audiovisual programs for business & management schools, in-house training & development programs, management consultants, and human resource managers. Jill Provan [and] Maryruth Phelps Glogowski, eds. Detroit, Neal-Schuman in assoc. with Gale, [1982]. 506p.   **CH328**

Describes 3,624 programs available for purchase from American distributors in 93 subject areas. The main section is arranged alphabetically by title of the program and provides for each title the year issued, format, color or black-and-white, distributor, and contents. Indexed by subject and series title. Directory of distributors. Purchase or rental costs are not indicated.   HD30.412.M36

The student guide to fellowships and internships. Written by the students of Amherst College. N.Y., Dutton, [1980]. 402p.   **CH329**

Internship programs are listed in chapters according to field, with a short introduction to each chapter. Program descriptions give basic information, general description, and candid comments by program administrators and students who have participated. National fellowship programs are described p.357–97. Select, annotated bibliography.   LB2338.S843

Training and development organizations directory; a reference work describing firms, institutes, and other agencies offering training, professional, and personal development programs for business, industry, and government. 3d ed. Paul Wasserman, managing ed. Detroit, Gale, [1983]. 1198p.   **CH330**

1st ed. 1978.

Pt.I is a geographically arranged directory of American organizations which present seminars, workshops, institutes, etc. Pts.II and III provide subject indexes, also arranged by state and city. The concluding sections are alphabetical indexes of individuals and organizations.

Kept up to date by: HD30.42.U5T72

New training organizations. no.1– , Mar. 1981– . Detroit, Gale, 1981. Semiannual.   **CH330a**

HD30.42.U5N48

Who's who in consulting; a reference guide to professional personnel engaged in consultation for business, industry, and government. 2d ed. Detroit, Gale, [1973]. 1011p.   **CH331**

Paul Wasserman, managing ed.

1st ed. 1968.

Supplements and serves as a companion to *Consultants and consulting organizations directory* (CH318) by offering biographical and career information on more than 7,500 individuals. Section I is the main body of the text, providing the biographical listings; Section II is a subject index of consultants arranged within field of activity by state, city, and consultant. Three supplements published Sept. 1982–Nov. 1983 included 2,934 new or updated entries.

HD69.C6W5

Handbooks

AMA management handbook. William K. Fallon, ed. 2d ed. [N.Y.], American Management Assoc., [1983]. 1v., various pagings. il.   **CH332**

1st ed. 1970.

Fourteen sections, with chapters contributed by about 200 specialists, analyze the subdisciplines of management, from finance through public relations. No bibliographic references. Indexed.

HD31.A418

The chief executive's handbook. Ed. by John Desmond Glover and Gerald A. Simon. Homewood, Ill., Dow Jones–Irwin, 1976. 1106p. il.   **CH333**

An attempt to provide a practical handbook for corporate chief executive officers, with chapters by specialists on organization, motivation, strategy, research and development, production, marketing, finance, international business, public relations, etc. Bibliographical footnotes.   HD31.C47

Craig, Robert L. Training and development handbook: a guide to human resource development. 2d ed. N.Y., McGraw-Hill, [1976]. 859p. in various pagings. il. **CH334**

Sponsored by the American Society for Training and Development.

A series of chapters by specialists on continuing education and training for work. New material includes: behavioral sciences applications to management practices and development training; the use of systematic and quantitative methods; instructional methods and media; training of specific employee groups (minority, international, secretarial and clerical); new concepts such as organization development. Most chapters include references and bibliography.

HF5549.5.T7C7

The Dartnell office administration handbook. Ed. by Robert S. Minor and Clark W. Fetridge. 6th ed., rev. and enl. Chicago, Dartnell, [1984]. 974p. il. **CH335**

Earlier editions had title *The Dartnell office manager's handbook* (1st ed. 1958).

A comprehensive treatment of the managerial, psychological, and physical aspects of office administration, with expanded coverage of personnel administration and computer/electronic technology. Appendix includes a glossary. HF5547.D251

The Dartnell personnel administration handbook. By Wilbert E. Scheer. 2d ed. [Chicago, Dartnell, 1979] 1088p. il. **CH336**

1st ed. 1969 had title: *Dartnell personnel director's handbook*.

Consists of 13 chapters, with contributions by specialists, on recruitment, employment, training and development, health and safety, employee services, wage and salary administration, benefits, labor relations, records and reports, and policies. Indexed.

HF5549.D3392

Famularo, Joseph J., ed. Handbook of modern personnel administration. N.Y., McGraw-Hill, [1972]. 1v., various pagings. il. **CH337**

Aims "to provide comprehensive, authoritative, and understandable information on all aspects of modern personnel administration."—*Pref.*

Chapters by specialists on training and development, wage and salary administration, employee benefits, government controls, labor relations, records and reports, etc. Fully indexed.

A 1986 edition is to be entitled *Handbook of human resources administration*. HF5549.F29

The foreman supervisor's handbook. 5th ed. N.Y., Van Nostrand Reinhold, [1984]. 625p. il. **CH338**

Carl Heyel, H. W. Nance, eds.

1st–4th eds. (1943–67) had title *The foreman's handbook*.

Practical handbook, with chapters written by authorities in management, personnel relations, and production. Indexed.

HF5549.F59195

Gumpert, David E. and **Timmons, Jeffry A.** The insider's guide to small business resources. Garden City, N.Y., Doubleday, 1982. 407p. il. **CH339**

A guide to programs, organizations, printed materials, and sources of assistance in education, management, financing, franchising, exporting, and lobbying; separate chapters on assistance for women and minority businesses. Glossary; index. Reprinted in 1984 under title *The encyclopedia of small business resources* (N.Y., Harper & Row). HD2346.U5G85

Handbook of work and organizational psychology. Ed. by P. J. D. Drenth [and others]. N.Y., Wiley, [1984]. 2v. **CH340**

Focuses on European developments; most contributors are from the Netherlands. Chapters discuss definitions, historical background, interactions between persons and work, persons and groups, etc. Bibliographic references. For a similar handbook from the American viewpoint *see* CD111. HF5548.8.H2655

Heyel, Carl. The encyclopedia of management. 3d ed. N.Y., Van Nostrand Reinhold, [1982]. 1371p. il. **CH341**

1st ed. 1963.

Arranged in dictionary form, this comprehensive work attempts to cover all aspects of management. Articles are written by specialists and are signed. Includes lengthy lists of references and suggested sources for further information. HD19.15.E49

Human resources management and development handbook. Ed. by William E. Tracey. [N.Y.], AMACOM, Amer. Management Assoc., [1985]. 1550p. il. **CH342**

Offers 108 chapters by specialists in personnel management and development arranged in 18 sections. Bibliographic references; index. HF5549.5.M3H85

Management handbook: operating guidelines, techniques and practices. Paul Mali, ed. in chief. N.Y., Wiley, [1981]. 1522p. il. **CH343**

An impressive collection of 67 chapters written by academic and corporate specialists, grouped in seven clusters: (1) management theory and practices; (2) organization management; (3) managing functions; (4) managing daily work; (5) employees; (6) resources; (7) personal self-development. Bibliographic footnotes and bibliographies. Indexed. HD31.M2924

Maynard, Harold Bright, ed. Handbook of business administration. N.Y., McGraw-Hill, [1967]. 1v., various pagings. il. **CH344**

Chapters have been contributed by specialists on all aspects of management, both general and special. Includes bibliographies. Indexed. HD31.M375

Vancil, Richard F., ed. Financial executive's handbook. Homewood, Ill., Dow Jones-Irwin, 1970. 1314p. **CH345**

Chapters by specialists on the whole range of responsibilities, duties, etc., of the financial executive are grouped under ten major headings, such as "Financial and economic analysis," "Planning and budgeting," "Asset management and control." Indexed.

HD31.V34

Secretary's handbooks

Doris, Lillian and **Miller, Besse May.** Complete secretary's handbook. 5th ed. Rev. by Mary A. De Vries. Englewood Cliffs, N.J., Prentice-Hall, [1983]. 596p. il. **CH346**

1st ed. 1951.

A standard handbook providing a range of practical techniques for general secretarial duties, guides to grammar and letter writing, techniques and forms for records and correspondence, and a collection of quick reference sources and facts. Takes into account modern office equipment and computer technology. Indexed.

HF5547.5.D6

Office automation: a glossary and guide. Ed. by Nancy MacLellan Edwards. [White Plains, N.Y.], Knowledge Industry Pubns., [1982]. 275p. **CH347**

A dictionary of terms relevant to data processing, micrographics and other record management systems, reprographics, telecommunications, and word processing. HF5548.2.O36

The professional secretary's handbook. Boston, Houghton Mifflin, [1984]. 583p. il. **CH348**

A guide to procedures in the conventional and the "electronic" office, with about one-third devoted to office automation. Features a chapter on the preparation of scientific and technical material.

HF5547.5.P7

Webster's New world secretarial handbook. New rev. ed. N.Y., Simon and Schuster, [1981]. 530p. il. **CH349**

1st ed. 1968; 1974 ed. had title: *New world secretarial handbook*.

Offers factual information on aspects of the secretary's functions, including word-processing, bookkeeping, business law. Appendix provides data on abbreviations, business terms, forms of address, travel, weights and measures, spelling and syllabication, index. HF5547.5.W39

COMMERCE

Commodities

See also CH411, CH571.

CRB commodity year book. v.1, 1939– . N.Y., Commodity Research Bureau, 1939– . v.1– . il. Annual.　　**CH350**

Title varies: 1939–84, *Commodity year book.* Publication suspended 1943–47.

Offers economic information with emphasis on statistical data for basic raw commodities and semifinished products.　　HC14.C6

────── Statistical abstract service. v.1, no.1– , Jan. 1964– .

Issued three times a year, each issue bringing most series up-to-date.

Commodity futures trading; bibliography, 1967/73– . [Chicago], Chicago Board of Trade, 1974– . Annual, with irregular cumulations.　　**CH351**

1967/76 cumulation publ. 1978.

In three sections: (1) books, monographs, and material provided by commodity exchanges; (2) resource material, i.e., scholarly journal articles and government documents; (3) trade, or popular press articles. Each section is subdivided by specific topics or commodity. No index.

A "Futures bibliography" appears in each quarterly issue of the *Journal of futures markets,* 1982– .　　Z7164.C83C64

Commodity review and outlook, 1982/83– . Rome, Food and Agriculture Organization of the United Nations, 1983– . il. Annual.　　**CH352**

Continues *FAO commodity review and outlook,* 1961–82.

Offers narrative and statistical overview of the agricultural commodity market situation and international action, plus overviews of specific commodities (including fisheries and forestry).　　HD1401.F63a

Guide to world commodity markets. 4th ed. Gerald Roberts, consultant ed. London, Kogan Page; N.Y., Nichols, [1985]. 409p. il., map.　　**CH353**

1st ed. 1977.

In three parts: (1) introductory essays on commodity markets; (2) data on price, production, and consumption of the principal commodities traded on the exchanges; (3) descriptions of individual commodity exchanges, regarding history, organization, contract particulars, volume of trading, etc. Appendixes list current membership of the larger exchanges and provide a glossary, time-zone map, and measurement-conversion tables. Indexed.　　HG6046.G84

Handbook of futures markets: commodity, financial, stock index, and options. Ed. by Perry J. Kaufman. N.Y., Wiley, [1984]. 1v., various pagings. il.　　**CH354**

In six parts: markets and operations; market influences; use of markets; forecasting methods and tools; risk and money management; commodities (chapters 25–49 treat specific commodities). Most chapters have bibliographies, and there is a major concluding bibliography of books, articles, and periodical titles. Glossary.　　HG6046.H36

Manthy, Robert S. Natural resource commodities — a century of statistics: prices, output, consumption, foreign trade, and employment in the United States, 1870–1973. [Ed. by Joan R. Tron]. Baltimore, Publ. for Resources for the Future by the Johns Hopkins Univ. Pr., 1978. 240p. graphs.　　**CH355**

An update of Resources for the Future's *Trends in natural resource commodities* by Neal Potter and Francis Christy, Jr. (1962).

In five sections: (1) methodology; (2) highlights; (3) detailed agricultural, mineral, and forest commodity summaries, emphasizing the post-1950 period; (4) individual data series for 200 natural resources commodities, from 1870 to 1973; (5) documented sources and explanatory notes for the data tables.　　HF1052.M35

Nicholas, David. Commodities futures trading: a guide to information sources and computerized services. London, Mansell, [1985]. 144p.　　**CH356**

In six sections: market trading and price distribution online systems; computerized news retrieval services from newspapers and newsletters; journals, magazines, and abstracting/indexing services; yearbooks, directories, and reference works; books. Directory of vendors; index.　　HG6046.N53

Schmitz, C. J. World non-ferrous metal production and prices, 1700–1976. [London], Cass; [Totowa, N.J., Biblio Distribution Centre, 1979]. 432p.　　**CH357**

Presents statistical information on mine and smelter production and average annual prices in major markets for the following metals: aluminum, antimony, chromium, copper, gold, lead, magnesium, manganese, mercury, molybdenum, nickel, silver, tin, tungsten, and zinc. Includes sources, notes to tables, and select bibliography. Country index.　　HD9539.A2S42

Wasserman, Paul and **Kemmerling, Diane.** Commodity prices: a source book and index. Detroit, Gale, [1974]. 200p.　　**CH358**

Subtitle: A source book and index providing references to wholesale and retail quotations for more than 5,000 agricultural, commercial, industrial, and consumer products.

An updated and revised ed. of Wasserman's *Sources of commodity prices* (1959).　　Z7164.P94W33

Woy, James B. Commodity futures trading: a bibliographic guide. N.Y., Bowker, 1976. 206p.　　**CH359**

The main text defines various commodity trading methods and related topics, and annotates information available on each subject in collected works, monographs, and periodical articles; the full bibliographic citation is included in the "Bibliography" section. Lists relevant federal government reports and periodicals. Author and subject indexes.　　Z7164.C83W69

Yearbook of international commodity statistics, 1984– . United Nations Conference on Trade and Development. N.Y., United Nations, 1984– . Annual.　　**CH360**

The work is "intended to provide statistical series at the regional and country levels for trade in selected agricultural primary commodities and minerals, ores and metals. In the case of the latter group of commodities, production and consumption series have also been included since comprehensive, disaggregated information is not available elsewhere."—*Foreword.* The 1984 volume provides many series retrospective to 1966.

Consumerism

Bibliography

See also CH370.

America buys. v.1, 1980– . Menlo Park, Calif., Information Access Corp., 1981– . Annual.　　**CH361**

Subtitle: The index to product evaluations.

Indexes product comparisons, descriptions and evaluations appearing in 375 magazines covered by the *Magazine index* (AE225), in the *Christian science monitor,* the *New York times,* and the *Wall Street journal,* and from books processed by the Library of Congress. Indexed by brand name and product type.

Updated by:

America buys updating service. Menlo Park, Calif., Information Access Corp., 1981– . Quarterly.

TX335.A49

Consumers index to product evaluations and information sources. v.1, no.1– , Winter 1974– . Ann Arbor, Mich., Pierian Pr., 1973– . Quarterly, with annual cumulation.　　**CH362**

A broad subject index to the contents of about 100 periodicals, intended for the consumer, library, business office, and educational instructor. Each item is briefly annotated; if specific products are included, the entry is coded to indicate description, evaluation, or test. A similarly classed section treats books, pamphlets, and consumer aids. TX335.C676

U.S. Office of Consumer Affairs. Consumer education bibliography. Prep. by the Office of Consumer Affairs and the New York Public Library. [Wash., distr. by U.S. Supt. of Docs.], 1971. 192p. **CH363**

An earlier version (1969) was prepared by the Yonkers Public Library. This edition lists more than 4,000 "books, pamphlets, periodical articles, audiovisual aids, and teachers' materials relating to consumer interests and consumer education."—*Introd.* Brief annotations. Classed arrangement, with detailed subject index.
Z5776.C65U5

Directories and handbooks

Consumer protection directory. 2d ed. Chicago, Marquis Academic Media, 1975. 466p. **CH364**

Subtitle: A comprehensive guide to consumer protection organizations in the United States and Canada.
Eds., Sally R. Osberg and Thaddeus C. Trzyna.
1st ed. published 1973 as part of the *Directory of consumer protection and environmental agencies.*
Gives addresses of organizations, names of chief administrative officers and, frequently, a statement of purpose or function. A "User's guide" is provided "to help readers identify organizations concerned with a specific area of interest, such as insurance or food and nutrition."—*Introd.* Subject index, organization index, personnel index, publication index. HC110.C63C635

David, Nina. Reference guide for consumers. N.Y., Bowker, 1975. 327p. **CH365**

In three parts: (1) "Multimedia materials," providing fairly lengthy annotations for more than 500 books, pamphlets, periodical titles and films published between 1960 and 1974; (2) "Organizations," giving directory information for United States federal, state, county and city agencies, private organizations, and Canadian national and provincial agencies; (3) "Newspapers," listing American and Canadian newspapers with consumer features, and syndicated columnists. Author, title, and subject indexes.
Z5776.C65D4

Dorfman, John. A consumer's arsenal. N.Y., Praeger, [1976]. 270p. **CH366**

In three main parts: (1) a "tactics manual," describing ten basic steps that should be taken in a complaint procedure; (2) a state-by-state evaluation of consumer agencies and laws, suggesting how good the consumer's chances of redress are; (3) a dictionary arrangement of common consumer complaints, with advice on their solutions.
HF5415.5.D66

Eiler, Andrew. Consumer protection manual. N.Y., Facts on File, [1984]. 658p. il. **CH367**

Describes consumer rights under federal and uniform state laws relating to purchasing goods, warranties, methods of payment, consumer credit collection, and small claims court. Appendixes; index. HC110.C63E38

Help, 1976/77– . Wash., Consumer News [distr. by Acropolis Books], [1976]– . Irregular. **CH368**

Subtitle varies; 1981, *The indispensable almanac of consumer information.*
A useful, up-to-date handbook for consumer education and protection. TX335.H445

Reader's Digest. Reader's Digest consumer adviser: an action guide to your rights. Pleasantville, N.Y., Reader's Digest Assn., [1984]. 416p. **CH369**

Designed to enable the user "to be a careful, informed, questioning buyer who accepts little or nothing on faith . . . [and] to be a determined activist who uses fully the economic and legal muscle

[he] now has to fight back when rights are violated."—*p.5.* Fifteen chapters deal with topics such as shopping, housing, medical care, etc. Directories of legal agencies, courts, consumer groups, etc. Indexed. TX355.R38

Wasserman, Paul and **Siegman, Gita.** Consumer sourcebook. 4th ed. Detroit, Gale, [1983]. 2v. (1427p.) **CH370**

Subtitle: A directory and guide to government organizations; information centers, clearinghouses, and toll-free numbers; associations, centers and institutes; media services; publications relating to consumer topics; sources of recourse and advisory information; and company and trade name information.
1st ed. 1974.
Offers directory and descriptive information arranged according to the categories indicated in the subtitle. HC110.C63W37

❖Guides to the purchasing of all types of products from the consumer point of view are given in various publications; they report the results of tests of the items, with indication of recommended and non-recommended brands. Two of the most used of these periodicals are:

Consumers' research magazine. Sept. 1931– . Washington, N.J., Consumers' Research, 1931– . il. Monthly. **CH371**

Title varies.
Each monthly issue includes an abridged cumulative index to the preceding issues of the current year. TX335.A1C68

Consumer reports. May 1936– . Mt. Vernon, N.Y., Consumer's Union of United States, 1936– . il. Monthly. **CH372**

Title varies.
The Dec. issue is the annual buying guide. TX335.A1C6

Foreign trade

Bibliography

See also CH748.

Brooke, Michael Z., Black, Mary and **Neville, Paul.** International business bibliography. N.Y., Garland, 1977. 480p. **CH373**

First published by Macmillan Pr., London, 1977.
Produced by the International Business Unit of the University of Manchester Institute of Science and Technology.
An author listing of books published in the last twenty years and articles and papers published in the last five years; brief summaries of many entries. Indexed by geographic area and broad subject; more specific subject indexing should have been provided and will be a necessary improvement in the proposed continuation. Directory of journals, book publishers, and institutions. Z7164.C81B86

Browndorf, Eric and **Riemer, Scott.** Bibliography of multinational corporations and foreign direct investment to March 1978. Dobbs Ferry, N.Y., Oceana Pubns., 1978. Looseleaf. **CH374**

The basic volume consists of citations to approximately 9,500 English-language publications written since 1970 and grouped in four major sections: (1) books, manuscripts, and government publications on the activities of the multinational corporation in general on a world scale; (2) periodical articles relating to the same topic; (3) case studies of foreign direct investment in specific countries; (4) studies of about 700 specific American multinational corporations operating abroad. A looseleaf service has provided two releases updating the material to Dec. 1979. Z7164.T87B76

European Centre for Study and Information on Multinational Corporations. Multinational corporations; the E.C.S.I.M. guide to information sources. Comp. and ed. by Joseph O. Mekeirle. Brussels, ECSIM, 1977. 454p. **CH375**

Title and prefatory material also in French and German.
In three main parts: (1) Primary information sources (i.e., com-

mercial book publishers, research sources and organizations, periodicals and special periodical issues); (2) Secondary information sources (i.e., bibliography of bibliographies, company information sources, current bibliographies, databases); (3) Indexes (author, title, periodical title, organizational, subject). Many annotations.

Z7164.T87E95

Hernes, Helga. The multinational corporation: a guide to information sources. Detroit, Gale, [1977]. 197p. (International relations information guide ser., 4)   **CH376**

An annotated bibliography of English-language books and periodical articles emphasizing the social aspects of multinational corporations, grouped into three parts: (1) the multinational corporation as a large organization; (2) the multinational corporation and the nation; (3) the role of the multinational corporation in the international system. Introductory bibliographic essays. Cutoff date is apparently 1974. Author, title, and subject indexes.

HD2755.5.H47

Hilbert, Roger and **Oehlmann, Christiane.** Foreign direct investments and multinational corporations in sub-Saharan Africa: a bibliography. Frankfurt & N.Y., Campus Verlag, [1980]. 699p.   **CH377**

Title and prefatory matter also in German.

In three main parts: general data and information sources pertaining to multinational corporations and to related non-African subjects; (reference and primary sources); selected secondary literature on multinational corporations and on related non-African subjects; primary and secondary literature on multinational corporations in Black Africa, arranged by region and country. International in scope. Detailed classified arrangement with author index.

Z7164.T87H54

Hoopes, David S. Global guide to international business. N.Y., Facts on File, [1983]. 847p.   **CH378**

An annotated sourcebook of organizations and publications (including databases) which is intended as a "first stop reference point" for questions about the practical aspects of international business operations. In four sections, subdivided by functional topic, area or country: (1) general information; (2) personnel information; (3) areas of the world; (4) individual countries. Indexed.

HF54.5.H66

International Trade Centre. A guide to the world's foreign trade statistics. Geneva, International Trade Centre, 1977. 155p.   **CH379**

Subtitle: A directory of the foreign trade statistical serials published by international organizations, governmental bodies, and selected semi-official agencies, with detailed bibliographical notes and practical advice to aid researchers and documentalists.

Lists international and national serials, with periodicity, classifications, brief notes on contents and time lag. Geographical arrangement; agency and title index.   Z7164.C8I64

Lall, Sanjaya. Foreign private manufacturing investment and multinational corporations: an annotated bibliography. N.Y., Praeger, [1975]. 196p.   **CH380**

Includes English-language publications on the manufacturing sector, written mostly between 1965 and 1973, and arranged in chapters by topic. One chapter deals specifically with Marxist and "dependence" school analysis of foreign investment, another with area studies. Cross references, but no subject index.

Z7164.F5L34

Lifschitz, Edgardo. Bibliografía analítica sobre empresas transnacionales. Analytical bibliography on transnational corporations. [México, D.F.], Instituto Latinoamericano de Estudios Transnacionales, [1980]. 607p.   **CH381**

Cites 3,815 books, articles, essays, documents and papers written before 1978. Arranged by main entry; indexed by subject, geographical area, and company name.   Z7164.C8L47

Mekeirle, Joseph O. The Arab world: a guide to business, economic and industrial information sources. [Dallas], Inter-Crescent Publ. Co., [1980]. 492p.   **CH382**

In four parts: (1) the Arab world as a whole; (2) individual Arab countries; (3) author, organization, and subject indexes; (4) source directory for publishers. Pts. 1 and 2 have sections listing: bibliographies; introductory books; books on the economic, business, and industrial aspects of the Arab world; directories, guides, and yearbooks; company information sources; periodicals; and periodical articles classified by topic.   Z7164.C8M44

Sagafi-nejad, Tagi and **Belfield, Robert.** Transnational corporations, technology transfer and development: a bibliographic sourcebook. N.Y., Pergamon, [1980]. 145p.

    CH383

Updates a 1976 version, but omits about 500 earlier references. Citations are arranged by author in eight chapters: (1) science and technology in development; (2) international technology gap and the NIEO; (3) transnational corporations and technology; (4) methods of corporate technology transfer; (5) technology transfer and host countries; (6) case studies of technology transfer; (7) technology transfer and the home country; (8) regulation of technology transfer. Author index.   T174.3.S23

Wheeler, Lora Jeanne. International business and foreign trade; information sources. Detroit, Gale, [1968]. 221p.

    CH384

Mainly a classed bibliography of books, pamphlets, and government publications serving as sources of information on the conduct of international business. Categories include theory of international trade, investment, financing, exporting and importing, legal aspects, taxation; there are sections for reference books, sources of statistics, periodicals, and directories. Also a list of schools and one of organizations assisting in international commerce.   Z7164.C8W5

Dictionaries

Eksportno-importnyi slovar'. Glavnyi red. B. T. Kolpakov. Moskva, Vneshtorgizdat, 1952–54. 3v. il.   **CH385**

An alphabetically arranged encyclopedia with articles ranging from a few lines to several pages. Gives translations of terms into a number of languages, as well as definitions in Russian. Many tables and figures are included in the text, and there are some colored plates. All kinds of commodities are listed.   HF1001.E4

Kohls, Siegfried. Dictionary of international economics: German, Russian, English, French, Spanish. Leiden, Sijthoff; Berlin, Verlag Die Wirtschaft, 1976. 619p.   **CH386**

Prefatory material in the five languages covered.

Originally published as *Ökonomisches Wörterbuch Aussenwirtschaft*.

The alphabetically arranged main section gives about 6,500 German terms and phrases with their equivalents in the other four languages; indexes from each of the other languages. Emphasizes terms of commerce, commercial law, payments system, carrying trade, and customs administration; largely exclusive of monetary systems, industrial and trade terminology.   HF1002.K6613

Motta, Giuseppe. Dizionario commerciale: inglese-italiano, italiano-inglese. Economia, legge, finanza (amministrazione, banca, borsa, assicurazione, scambi, commercio estero e marittimo, trasporti, dogane, ecc.). Milano, C. Signorelli, [1966]. 1050p.   **CH387**

HF1002.M6

Netto, Modestino Martins. Vocabulário de intercâmbio comercial: português-inglês; inglês-português. Com um apêndice contendo abreviaturas comerciais, pêsos e medidas, sistema monetário, modelo de cartas comerciais, etc. Rio de Janeiro, Ed. Civilização Brasileira, [1961]. 251p.   **CH388**

A practical glossary of commercial terms.   HF1002.N45

Servotte, Jozef V. Dictionnaire commercial et financier: français, néerlandais, anglais, allemand. 2. éd., rev. et augm. Bruxelles, Éd. Brepols, [1962]. 955p.   **CH389**

1st ed. 1956.

Added title page: Woordenboek voor handel en financien.

HF1002.S42

Directories

American export register. 1945/46– . N.Y., Thomas Internat. Pub. Co., 1946– . Annual. **CH390**

Title varies: 1945/46–78. *American register of exporters and importers.*

Lists some 25,000 active American export and import concerns and allied services. Product indexes in English, Spanish, French, German, Portuguese, Arabic, Chinese, and Japanese.

HF3010.A6

Angel, Juvenal Londoño. Directory of foreign firms operating in the United States. 4th ed. N.Y., World Trade Academy Pr., [1978]. 768p. **CH391**

1st ed. 1969.

In three parts: (1) Foreign firms in the United States (arranged by country and providing name and address of American subsidiary and foreign parent company); (2) Alphabetical listing of foreign parent companies and corresponding American subsidiaries; (3) Alphabetical listing of American subsidiaries, branches, or affiliates of foreign firms. A 5th ed. appeared 1986. HG4057.A155

Arpan, Jeffrey S. and **Ricks, David A.** Directory of foreign manufacturers in the United States. 3d ed. Atlanta, Georgia State Univ., College of Business Administration, Publishing Services Division, 1985. 384p. **CH392**

Lists about 4,300 foreign-owned United States companies, with address, SIC product classification numbers, major products, and parent company name and address. Arranged alphabetically by American subsidiary, and indexed by parent company, home country of parent company, state of location, and SIC product classification number. HD9723.A76

Custom house guide. N.Y., Import Publs., 1862– . Annual (with monthly supplements). **CH393**

United States tariff schedules, duty rates, ports, internal revenue code, customs, shipping and commerce regulations, and reciprocal trade agreements.

Monthly supplements called *American import/export management.* HE953.N5C8

Directory of American firms operating in foreign countries. Ed.1– . N.Y., Uniworld Business Pubns., [1955]– . Irregular. (10th ed., 1984) **CH394**

Eds.1–9 comp. by J. L. Angel.

Issued in 3v. v.1 lists, in alphabetical order, more than 3,200 U.S. firms operating overseas, with the U.S. address, names of executive staff, principal products or services, and the foreign countries of operation. v.2–3 list American firms by the country in which the firm has subsidiaries or branches, together with its home office address, the names and addresses of subsidiaries or branches, and their products and services. HG4538.A1D5

Directory of United States importers. 1967– . N.Y., Journal of Commerce, 1967– . Biennial. **CH395**

Continues *Directory of United States import concerns* (1948–66).

A geographical listing of importers is followed by a commodity index. HF3012.D53

Exporters' encyclopaedia. Ed.1– , 1904– . Containing full and authentic information relative to shipments for every country in the world. N.Y., T. Ashwell, 1904– . Annual, including supplementary bulletins which keep the Encyclopaedia up to date throughout the subscription year. **CH396**

Publisher varies. Title varies: *Dun & Bradstreet exporters' encyclopaedia.* Imprint varies.

Includes market information; import and exchange regulations; shipping services, communication data, etc., arranged alphabetically by country; general export information on law, insurance, export terms and practices, shipping and packing; communications data

(radio, cable, mail), time charts, weights and measures; information sources (government agencies, international organizations, etc.). The *Export documentation handbook* (annual, with quarterly updates) summarizes documentation required by each country, with examples. HF3011.E9

Kelly's Directory of merchants, manufacturers and shippers of the world. A guide to the export and import, shipping and manufacturing industries . . . London, Kelly's Directory, 1880– . Annual. **CH397**

Title varies: *Kelly's manufacturers and merchants directory,* etc.

Alphabetical and classified lists of British manufacturers, merchants, wholesalers and firms, with a section on brand and trade names. HF54.G7K4

Major companies of the Arab world, 1975– . London, Graham & Trotman (distr. in U.S.A. by Franklin Watts), 1976– . Irregular. **CH398**

Title varies: 1975 ed. had title *Major companies of the Arab world and Iran.*

Ed. by Giselle C. Bricault.

A directory of the major commercial and industrial companies (including non-Arab firms), foreign bank branches, shipping agents, etc., providing address, names of principal officers, description of activities, and data concerning agencies, subsidiaries, bankers, ownership, number of employees, and financial information. All information has been derived from questionnaires submitted to the companies. Indexed by company and business activity.

The publisher also issues *Major companies of Argentina, Brazil, Mexico and Venezuela, Major companies of Europe, Major companies of Nigeria,* and *Major companies of the Far East.*

HF3866.M332

Owen's Worldtrade. 1953/54– . London, Pan-African Commercial Directory, 1954– . il., maps. Annual. **CH399**

Title varies: 1953/54, *Pan-African commercial directory;* 1955, *Owen's Pan-African & Middle East directory;* 1960–67, *Owen's African and Middle East commerce & travel and international register;* 1968–72, *Owen's Commerce and travel and international register, Africa, Middle and Far East.*

32d ed. 1984/85 publ. in two sections: "Africa & Asia business directory" and "Middle East & Mediterranean business directory." An international register of manufacturers, merchants, and traders, with descriptive notes on population, finance, resources, commerce, etc., of each country.

Stopford, John M., Dunning, John H. and **Haberich, Klaus O.** World directory of multinational enterprises. [2d, updated and expanded ed.] Detroit, Gale, [1982–83]. 3v. **CH400**

1st ed. 1980.

For the 500 largest multinationals in the world, provides: a 5-year table of financial and operating statistics; background history; current situation; major shareholders; principal subsidiaries. Appendixes of statistical tables on overseas activity, diversification, etc.

HD2755.5.S844

Talib's OPEC trade directory. Ed. by Shamas Esamil. 2d ed. London, Macmillan, 1979. 679p. il. **CH401**

1st ed. 1976.

Provides a background summary (derived from the U.S. Dept. of State *Background notes*) and an SIC-based directory of companies for each of the OPEC countries: Saudi Arabia, Kuwait, Iran, Iraq, United Arab Emirates, Libya, Nigeria, Indonesia, Venezuela, Algeria, Qatar, Ecuador, and Gabon. HF54.U5T34

Handbooks and yearbooks

COMECON foreign trade data, 1980– . Westport, Conn., Greenwood Pr., 1981– . Annual? **CH402**

Ed. by the Vienna Institute for Comparative Economic Studies and sponsored by the First Austrian Bank.

A statistical handbook on the foreign economic relations of Bulgaria, Czechoslovakia, the German Democratic Republic, Hungary, Poland, Romania, the Soviet Union, and Yugoslavia, derived from their national statistics, OECD or other Western countries' national statistics, and from United Nations and unofficial Western sources.   HF3491.5.C65

East-West trade: a sourcebook on the international economic relations of socialist countries and their legal aspects. Comp. and ed. by Dietrich André Loeber. Dobbs Ferry, N.Y., Oceana, 1976. 4v.   **CH403**

Contents: v.1, Background material. Organization of international economic relations. Equality and discrimination in international economic relations; v.2, Foreign trade system. Foreign trade contracts; v.3, Industrial cooperation. Intellectual property; v.4, Financial relations. Transport. Dispute settlement.

Assembles international agreements, national statutes, administrative regulations, and documents of regional and international organizations dealing with the international economic relations of the Soviet Union, socialist East European countries, China, Mongolia, North Korea, North Vietnam, and Cuba. Bibliography of secondary literature and indexes of persons, subjects, and countries in the final volume.   HF1411.E14

Food and Agriculture Organization of the United Nations. FAO trade yearbook. v.12– , 1958– . Rome, [1959]– .
                                                      CH404

Formerly issued as pt.2 of *Yearbook of food and agricultural statistics,* and continues the yearbook's numbering.
Title varies: 1958–75, *Trade yearbook.* Title and text also in French and Spanish.
Offers a wide range of tables on external trade in food and agricultural commodities.   HD9000.4.F58

Foreign commerce handbook, 1922/23– . Wash., Foreign Commerce Dept., Chamber of Commerce of the U.S., 1922– . Irregular. (17th ed. 1981)   **CH405**

A guide to the sources of export and import services and information.   HF3011.F6

Foreign commerce yearbook, 1948–51. Wash., Govt. Prt. Off., 1950–53.   **CH406**

Issued by U.S. Dept. of Commerce, Office of International Trade. Ceased publication.
Preceded by: U.S. Bureau of Foreign and Domestic Commerce, *Commerce yearbook,* 1922–1932, which included pt.1, United States, and pt.2, Foreign countries. Pt.1 was discontinued in 1932. Pt.2 was continued by the Office's *Foreign commerce yearbook,* 1933–39; publication suspended 1934, 1940–47.
Gives detailed information on business conditions in the United States and foreign countries, summarizing statistical information originally collected by government bureaus, trade associations, and trade journals, with references to sources of information.
                                                      HF53.U72

Foreign trade marketplace. George J. Schultz, ed. Detroit, Gale, 1977. 662p.   **CH407**

Introductory chapters cover the operations aspects of international trade from the standpoint of American companies. The main text consists of 35 chapters providing directory information on exporting and importing, United States and foreign government agencies and organizations, marketing, advertising, transportation, communication, and regulations. Indexed by subject and by geographic area.   HF1010.F67

Handbook of international business. Ed. by Ingo Walter. N.Y., Wiley, [1982]. 1v., various pagings. il.   **CH408**

Presents survey articles by specialists on aspects of the environment of international business, finance, trade, marketing, management of international operations, and legal matters; bibliographic references and bibliographies conclude most of the 42 chapters. Appendixes provide subject classed bibliography and directory of international services in law, accounting, insurance, banking, advertising, etc. Indexes.   HD62.4.H36

International marketing handbook. 2d ed. Detroit, Gale, [1985]. 3v. (3637p.) maps.   **CH409**

Frank E. Bair, ed.
1st ed. 1981.
Contents: v.1, Afghanistan-India; v.2, Indonesia-Trinidad and Tobago; v.3, Tunisia-Zimbabwe and area guides and statistics.
Subtitle: Detailed marketing profiles for 138 nations, special information on doing business with Eastern Bloc countries and in the Near East and North Africa, and fundamental data for developing an export marketing effort.
Reprints the most recent *Overseas business reports* and other documents issued by the International Marketing Association of the U.S. Dept. of Commerce. Updated between editions by a supplement.
A review of the 1st ed. in *Wilson library bulletin* (Nov. 1981, p.222) points out similarities to the *Exporter's encyclopedia* (CH396), which it judged "superior" although more expensive.
                                                      HF1009.5.I538

International trade, 1952– . Geneva, Contracting Parties to the General Agreement on Tariffs and Trade, [1952]– . Annual.   **CH410**

In five main sections: summary of main trends and issues; trade in individual commodities; trade of industrial countries, by major areas and countries; trade of non-industrial areas, by major areas and countries; trade of the Eastern (i.e., Soviet Union and Eastern Europe) trading area. Provides analytical and statistical treatment.
                                                      HF499.C65

International trade statistics yearbook, 1950– . N.Y., 1951– . Annual.   **CH411**

Continues *International trade statistics,* issued by the League of Nations, 1933–39.
Title varies: 1950–82, *Yearbook of international trade statistics.*
In 2v.: v.1, Trade by country, contains detailed data by countries, with summary tables on trade relations of each with its region and the world; v.2, Trade by commodity [and] commodity matrix tables, shows the total economic world trade of certain commodities analysed by region and country.
Current quarterly statistics are published irregularly in *Commodity trade statistics* (United Nations. *Statistical papers,* ser. D).
                                                      HF91.U473

Middle East review, 1974– . Saffron Walden, Essex, Eng., Middle East Review Co., Ltd., 1974– . il., maps. Annual.
                                                      CH412

Title varies: 1974–80, *Middle East annual review.*
Also issued in an Arabic ed.
Distributed in the United States by Rand McNally.
In two main sections: (1) a series of introductory chapters by British and American journalists and researchers on various topics in areas of trade, industry, civil engineering and construction, services, finances, etc.; (2) a country-by-country survey contributed by individual authors; these surveys include politics, foreign relations, social conditions, development plans, budget, foreign investment, balance of payments, etc., and provide factual and analytical information. "Middle East" is defined to include North Africa, Somalia, and the Sudan. Similar volumes cover other geographic regions: *Africa review, Latin America and Caribbean review, Asia & Pacific review.*   HC410.7.A1M517

Newman, Dorothy M. and **Newman, Walter C.** Canadian business handbook. [3d ed.] Toronto, McGraw-Hill Ryerson, [1979]. 673p. il.   **CH413**

A compendium on practices and information arranged in 18 subject chapters, including: taxes, insurance, trade, communications, federal and provincial government aids to business, business information, etc. Indexed.   HF3227.N4

United Nations Conference on Trade and Development. Handbook of international trade and development statistics. N.Y., United Nations, 1969– . Irregular. (6th ed. 1983)
                                                      CH414

In English and French.
Offers a basic collection of statistical data on world trade and development. Sources of statistical tables are indicated. Kept up to date between editions by annual supplements.   HF1016.U54a

U.S. Bureau of the Census. Foreign commerce and navigation of the United States, 1821– . Wash., Govt. Prt. Off., [1820/21]– . Annual (irregular). **CH415**

Not published 1947–62; volume for 1946/63 (publ. 1965) contains summarized data for this period. Resumed with volume covering 1964 (publ. 1968). The 1965 issue (publ. 1970) is in 3v.: v.1, Standard international trade classification (SITC) commodity by country; v.2, Area and country by standard international trade classification; v.3, Schedule A and Schedule B commodity by country.

Gives official statistical data on foreign trade and navigation of the United States.

Publishing body varies; before 1865, published by the Register of Treasury. HF102.A2

—— Monthly summary of foreign commerce and navigation. 1866–April 1951. (Cumulated quarterly)

Both annual and monthly publications were temporarily replaced by:

—— Quarterly summary of foreign commerce. Jan. 1951–June 1961. Wash., Govt. Prt. Off., 1951–63. (Cumulated annually)

Ceased publication.

Contains information and statistical tables on imports and exports by commodities, countries, customs districts, economic classes, etc.

World trade annual. 1963– . N.Y., Walker, 1964– . Annual. **CH416**

Prep. by the Statistical Office of the United Nations.

1963–68 in 4v. per year; 1969– in 5v. per year.

Based on data provided by the 22 principal trading countries of the world, the series is designed to provide both summarized and detailed statistics of trade by commodity by country. Currently arranged by region and country, then by exports and imports according to Standard International Trade Classification number; values shown in U.S. dollars. HF53.W6

Money, weights, and measures

American International Investment Corporation, San Francisco. World currency charts. [Ed.1]– . San Francisco, Amer. Internat. Investment Corp., 1963– . Irregular (8th ed., 1977 last publ.?). **CH417**

Offers charts and statistics giving exchange rates based on the United States dollar for currencies from 147 countries, from 1929 to the most recent year available before publication of the chartbook. Sometimes par value is also included. HG3863.A65

Chisholm, L. J. Units of weight and measure; international (metric) and United States customary. Definitions and tables of equivalents. . . . Wash., U.S. Dept. of Commerce. Nat. Bur. of Standards. 1967. 251p. (Nat. Bur. of Standards misc. pubn., 286) **CH418**

Title of earlier eds. varies: 1903, *Table of equivalents of the customary and metric weights and measures*; 1906–13, *Tables of equivalents of the United States customary and metric weights and measures*. QC100.U57 no.286

Doursther, Horace. Dictionnaire universel des poids et mesures, anciens et modernes, contenant des tables des monnaies de tous les pays. Bruxelles, Hayez, 1840. 604p. (Repr.: Amsterdam, Meridian Pub. Co., 1965) **CH419**

Out-of-date, but useful for questions involving historical information, since it includes many old and unusual terms. QC82.D6

Elsevier's Lexicon of international and national units; English/American, German, Spanish, French, Italian, Japanese, Dutch, Portuguese, Polish, Swedish, Russian. Comp. and arr. by W. E. Clason. Amsterdam, Elsevier, 1964. 76p. **CH420**

A guide to the meaning and value of internationally and nationally used units. Includes: International units, arranged alphabetically by unit; Units used in different countries, arranged by country; Words and indexes; Bibliography. QC82.E37

McCusker, John J. Money and exchange in Europe and America, 1600–1775; a handbook. Chapel Hill, Univ. of North Carolina Pr. for Inst. of Early Amer. History and Culture, Williamsburg, Va., [1978]. 367p. il. **CH421**

"Aims to provide sufficient information of a technical and statistical nature to allow the reader to convert a sum stated in one money into its equivalent in another."—*p.[3].* HG219.M33

Naft, Stephen. International conversion tables: weights, measures, gauges, currencies, conversion equivalents and factors, technical units, alphabets, other useful information. Expanded and rev. by Ralph de Sola. N.Y., Duell, [1961]. 372p. **CH422**

1st ed. had title: *Conversion equivalents in international trade.* HF5714.N3

Pick, Franz and **Sédillot, René.** All the monies of the world; a chronicle of currency values. N.Y., Pick, [1971]. 613p. **CH423**

A translation, enlarged and updated, of Sédillot's *Toutes les monnaies du monde* (Paris, 1954).

Entries for monetary units and for countries issuing currencies appear in a dictionary arrangement. Entries for the monies include origin of the name, worth, and historical notes; entries for countries provide brief chronologies of events related to monetary systems and changes therein. HG216.P614

Tate, William. Tate's Modern cambist. Centenary ed. 28th ed. by W. F. Spalding. London, Wilson; N.Y., Bankers Publ. Co., 1929. 734p. **CH424**

Subtitle: A manual of the world's monetary systems, the foreign exchanges, the stamp duties on bills of exchange in foreign countries, the principal rules governing bills of exchange and promissory notes, foreign weights and measures, bullion and exchange operations. HG3863.T2

—— Tate's Money manual, being the 1st–2d annual editions of additions, alterations and amendments to the centenary edition of Tate's Modern cambist, by W. F. Spalding. London, Wilson; N.Y., Bankers Publ. Co., [1931–33]. v.1–2. **CH425**

World currency yearbook, 1984– . Brooklyn, Internat. Currency Analysis, [1985]– . Annual. **CH426**

Continues *Pick's Currency yearbook,* (ed.1–22, 1955–77/79) and assumes its numbering.

Descriptions of world currencies and monetary conditions yearbook. Includes official exchange rates. HG219.P5

The world measurement guide. [4th ed., rev. London, Economist Newspaper; Detroit, Gale, 1980] 240p. il. **CH427**

1st ed. (1954) had title *The Economist guide to weights and measures*; 3d ed. (1975) called *The Economist measurement guide and reckoner.*

Provides tables and data on: measurement systems for most countries; conversion tables; measurements in space and time, agriculture, fishing, forestry, and industry; definitions and formulae for accountancy, economics, finance, and mathematics; interest rate tables, etc. Indexed. HF5712.W67

Zupko, Ronald Edward. A dictionary of English weights and measures from Anglo-Saxon times to the nineteenth century. Madison, Univ. of Wisconsin Pr., 1968. 224p. **CH428**

Gives etymology of the term, explanation of the unit and its variants, and citations from medieval and modern sources illustrating use. QC82.Z8

—— French weights and measures before the Revolution: a dictionary of provincial and local units. Bloomington, Indiana Univ. Pr., [1978]. 208p. **CH429**

A dictionary of premetric terms giving definitions, periods and places of use, etymologies, equivalencies, and references (with dates) to manuscript and printed sources. Bibliography of sources cited, p. 189–208.   QC89.F8Z86

Tariff

Bibliography

Contracting Parties to the General Agreement on Tariffs and Trade. GATT bibliography, 1947–1953. Geneva, GATT Secretariat, 1954. 40p.   **CH430**

Contents: pt.1, Bibliography of texts of the GATT and governmental publications; pt.2, Selected GATT publications; pt.3, Chronological list of references to GATT, arranged alphabetically within each period.

Includes books, pamphlets, articles, periodicals, newspaper reports and editorials, and miscellaneous material.

————— ————— Supplement 1–16. Geneva, GATT Secretariat, 1955–70.

Z7164.T2C612

U.S. Tariff Commission. Publications of the U.S. Tariff Commission. 1920– . Wash., Govt. Prt. Off., 1920– . Irregular.   **CH431**

Title varies: *Subject index to tariff information surveys and reports, 1920; List of principal subjects investigated and reported by the United States Tariff Commission, 1921–27; List of publications of the United States Tariff Commission, 1929–34; Publications of the Tariff Commission, 1939–53.*   Z1223.T22

————— The tariff; a bibliography. A select list of references. Wash., Govt. Prt. Off., 1934. 980p. (Miscellaneous ser.) (Repr.: Westport, Conn., Greenwood Pr., 1976)   **CH432**

Classified and annotated list of almost 6,500 items, with (1) author index, and (2) subject and title index. Emphasis is on the tariff situation in the United States, but material listed furnishes information on the more important countries of the world.

Z7164.T2U63

Dictionaries and encyclopedias

U.S. Tariff Commission. Dictionary of tariff information. Wash., Govt. Prt. Off., 1924. 1036p.   **CH433**

Includes articles on tariff systems, methods, practices, history, biographical articles on men connected with American tariff history, and descriptive and statistical articles on all commodities mentioned in the tariff act of 1922. Contains some bibliography.

HF1705.U5

Transportation

Bibliography

Davis, Bob J. Information sources in transportation, material management, and physical distribution: an annotated bibliography and guide. Westport, Conn., Greenwood Pr., [1976]. 715p.   **CH434**

Materials are organized under 67 subjects, and within each subject, by type: book and pamphlet (including government publications); periodical titles (including directories, guides, and services); organizations; education (awards, libraries, programs, courses, scholarships, certification); and miscellaneous (analyses and statistics, atlases and maps). Indexed. An impressive compilation based in part on *An annotated bibliography of books, periodicals, films, and organizations of the oil pipeline industry* (1972) and *An annotated bibliography of the motor carrier industry* (1976).   Z7164.T8D25

Flood, Kenneth U. Research in transportation: legal/legislative and economic sources and procedure. Detroit, Gale, [1970]. 126p. (Management information guide, 20)
CH435

Describes and evaluates transportation information sources.
Z7164.T8F55

Metcalf, Kenneth Nolan. Transportation: information sources. Detroit, Gale, [1966]. 307p. (Management information guide, 8)   **CH436**

Subtitle: An annotated guide to publications, agencies, and other data sources concerning air, rail, water, road, and pipeline transportation.   Z7164.T8M4

Northwestern University. Transportation Center. Library. Catalog of the Transportation Center Library, Northwestern University. . . . Boston, G. K. Hall, 1972. 12v.   **CH437**

Contents: v.1–3, Author-title catalog; v.4–12, Subject catalog.

A photoreproduction of the catalog cards for this library of 80,000 books and reports and 52,000 journal articles on: transportation socioeconomics; highway traffic analysis; and highway police administration. Represents all materials processed since 1960 to time of publication. Author-title section includes books and reports; citations to periodical articles, conference papers, and pamphlets appear in the subject section.

Updated by: Z7164.T8N75

Current literature in traffic and transportation. v.1, no.1– , Jan./Feb. 1960– . Evanston, Ill., Library, Transportation Center at Northwestern Univ., 1960– . Monthly.   **CH438**

Supersedes *Current literature in transportation.*

A detailed subject-classed list of journal articles, books, conference proceedings, reports, government documents, etc. No index.
Z7164.T8C8

Rakowski, James P. Transportation economics: a guide to information sources. Detroit, Gale, [1976]. 215p. (Economics information guide ser., 5)   **CH439**

An annotated bibliography of the most widely available book and article literature produced between 1960 and 1974 on transportation economics and business logistics. Sources are arranged by the industry discussed—railroads, highways, air, water, and urban transportation. Books and articles are listed separately for each industry; book titles are annotated; articles are subdivided by topic and listed without annotation. Final chapter covers reference sources, periodical titles, private and government sources of information. Author, title, and subject indexes.   Z7164.T8R34

Reebie Associates. Transguide: a guide to sources of freight transportation information. Greenwich, Conn., Reebie Associates, 1980. 381p.   **CH440**

". . . the purpose of TRANSGUIDE is to emphasize the sources of freight transportation facts and statistics."—*Pref.* Eight subject sections — air transportation, commodity classifications, general transportation, highways and trucks, pipelines, railroads and rail, freight traffic flows, and waterways and marine transport — provide annotated entries for publications lists, bibliographies, guides and directories, maps, statistical presentations, and studies/services. Source availability and price are indicated, and the "Sponsors and vendors" section (p. 255–340) gives detailed ordering instructions for each supplier. Subject and title indexes.   Z7164.T8R44

U.S. Dept. of Transportation. Library Services Division. Bibliographic list, no.1–11. Wash., 1969–81.   **CH441**

Supersedes U.S. Federal Aviation Administration. Library Services Division. *Selected references; bibliographic list.*

Contents: no.1, Transportation and the handicapped (1969); no.2, Aircraft noise and sonic boom (1969); no.3, Department of Transportation; selected readings (1970); no.4, Airport problems (1971); no.5, Hijacking (1971); no.6, Urban mass transportation (1971); no.7, Aircraft and air pollution (1971).

U.S. Library of Congress. Reference Dept. Soviet transportation and communications; a bibliography comp. by Renee S. Janse. Wash., 1952. 330p.   **CH442**

Classified listing, with an author index and Library of Congress classification number if in that library. Holdings also indicated for 46 other libraries. Emphasis is on post-1930 publications, but entries are not limited as to date. Z7164.T8U55

Dissertations

Doctoral dissertations on transportation, 1961/67– . Evanston, Ill., Northwestern Univ. Transportation Ctr. Lib., [1968]– . Annual. **CH443**

A classed list of United States dissertations drawn from *Dissertation abstracts international, American economic review, Journal of business,* and *Transportation research.* Indexed by place, subject and author. Z7164.T7D6

Dictionaries and encyclopedias

Logie, Gordon. Glossary of transport: English, French, Italian, Dutch, German, Swedish. Amsterdam & N.Y., Elsevier, [1980]. 296p. (Internat. planning glossaries, 2) **CH444**

A polyglot dictionary giving equivalent terms in the broad subject areas of transport and transportation studies, roads and road traffic, parking and road vehicles, railways, water-borne transport, and aviation. Indexes in all six languages. HE141.L63

Rand McNally and Company. The Rand McNally encyclopedia of transportation. Chicago, Rand McNally, [1976]. 256p. il. **CH445**

Geoffrey Crow, ed.
Offers brief definitions and discussions of modes of travel, mechanics of engines, personalities, specific ships and planes, and other topics involved in or associated with transportation. Dictionary arrangement, with numerous cross references and illustrations. TA1009.R36

Transportation-logistics dictionary. Joseph L. Cavinato, ed. [2d ed.] Wash., Traffic Service Corp., [1982]. 323p. **CH446**

1st ed. 1977.
Provides succinct definitions for abbreviations, terms, and phrases used in the transportation industry, including materials management and distribution management. HE141.T69

Tuma, Jiri. The pictorial encyclopedia of transport. London & N.Y., Hamlyn, [1979]. 494p. il., maps. **CH447**

Translated from the Czech by Alena Einhornová.
In eight sections: (1) transport's role in the development of civilization; (2) the history of transport; (3) railways; (4) road transport; (5) water transport; (6) air transport; (7) public urban transport; (8) transportation of the future. Indexed. TA1145.T8513

Aviation

See also EJ83.

The complete illustrated encyclopedia of the world's aircraft. N.Y., A & W Publishers, [1978]. 320p. il. **CH448**

David Mondey, ed.
"This book was designed and produced by Quarto Publishing Limited . . . London, 1978."—*verso of t.p.*
Intended as a single-volume encyclopedia of aviation for the general reader. A brief history of aviation history is followed by an alphabetical listing of manufacturers of heavier-than-air, powered, production aircraft. Listings provide brief sketches of important technological contributions and aircraft models produced by the firms. Brief glossary; indexed by aircraft model. Heavily illustrated with color and black-and-white photographs.

Encyclopedia of aircraft. Ed. by Michael J. H. Taylor and John W. R. Taylor. N.Y., Putnam, [1978]. 256p. il. **CH449**

Descriptions of 244 aircraft are arranged alphabetically, with tables of technical data presented at the end of the book. Includes early aircraft and military aircraft of the World Wars as well as contemporary models. Many illustrations, some in color; brief glossary; index. TL670.3.E52

International encyclopedia of aviation. N.Y., Crown, [1977]. 480p. il. **CH450**

David Mondey, gen. ed.
A heavily illustrated encyclopedia on the history of aviation, rocketry, and space flight. Chapters by individual specialists are grouped in seven sections: origins and development; military aviation; civil and maritime aviation; lighter-than-air; specialized aircraft; rocketry and space exploration; facts, feats and records (including flying feats, air crimes, air disasters, aviation law, biographical sketches, chronology, and international directory of air museums). Indexed. TL509.I63

Taylor, John William Ransom, Taylor, Michael John Haddrick and **Mondey, David.** Air facts & feats. Rev. ed. [3d ed.] N.Y., Sterling, [1978]. 240p. il. **CH451**

2d ed. 1973 publ. as *The Guinness book of air facts and feats.*
A chronological survey of flight, from ancient times to the present day. Emphasizes pioneering flight efforts, the role of aircraft in the World Wars, and the current situation of civil and military aviation and research. Appendixes detail speed records and air disasters. Bibliography; index. TL515.M274

World encyclopedia of civil aircraft: from Leonardo da Vinci to the present. [Ed. by] Enzo Angelucci; English-language ed. supervised by John Stroud. N.Y., Crown, [1982]. 414p. il., maps. **CH452**

Italian ed. had title: *Atlante enciclopedico degli aerei civili del mondo da Leonardo a oggi* (Milano, Mondadori, 1981).
Provides technical data, color plates, scale views, photographs, and historical background for more than 400 civil (and some military) aircraft; numerous comparative tables. Chronological arrangement; chapters have introductory essays, plates, notes to plates, and photographs. Bibliography; country and general indexes. TL515.A8413

Wragg, David W. A dictionary of aviation. [Reading, Berkshire, Eng.], Osprey, [1973]; N.Y., F. Fell, 1974. 286p. **CH453**

Intended for the layperson. Provides brief definitions of terms and concepts, events and personalities, major airlines, guided weapons, aircraft, and aircraft manufacturers. "Aviation" is broadly defined to include lighter-than-air flight and space flight, to a lesser degree. Individual air forces and air arms are not treated in any detail. TL509.W67

Railroads

See also CL284.

Bureau of Railway Economics, Wash., D.C. Railway economics, a collective catalogue of books in fourteen American libraries. Chicago, Univ. of Chicago Pr., [1912]. 446p. **CH454**

A classified catalog, with index of names. Z7231.B87

Hollingsworth, John Brian. Atlas of the world's railways. N.Y., Everest, [1980]. 350p. il., maps. **CH455**

A country-by-country survey of the world's railways; each account begins with a short history, then provides narrative descriptions of major railways—their background, development, and statistics. Not a true atlas, since color maps produced by George Philip and Sons are from general atlases and do not emphasize railway lines. TF145.H75

Hubbard, Freeman H. Encyclopedia of North American railroading; 150 years of railroading in the United States and Canada. N.Y., McGraw-Hill, [1981]. 377p. il. **CH456**

A concise encyclopedia of articles on personalities, equipment, historical developments, and railroad lines and companies operating in the United States and Canada since the 1830s. Many articles have bibliographical references. Abundant illustrations. Dictionary arrangement, with cross-references and index. HE2751.H8

Jane's Urban transport systems. Ed.1– , 1982– . London, Jane's Pub. Co., 1982– . il., maps. Annual. **CH457**

For full information *see* EJ195.

Jane's World railways. Ed. 9– , 1965/66– . N.Y., Franklin Watts, 1965– . il., maps. Annual. **CH458**

Cover title: *Jane's World railways and rapid transit systems.*
Title varies: 1st–8th eds., 1950/51–65/66 called *World railways.* Frequency varies: biennial, 1965/66–74/75.
Contents: alphabetical directories of manufacturers, associations, consultant services; country summaries of railway systems; city reports on rapid transit; tabulated data arranged by country and company. TF1.J3

Morris, James Oliver. Bibliography of industrial relations in the railroad industry. Ithaca, New York State School of Industrial and Labor Relations, Cornell Univ., [1975]. 153p. (Cornell industrial and labor relations bibliography ser., 12) **CH459**

Attempts to identify published source material on the work environment, its influences, and its consequences within the intercity and interstate rail transportation system. Materials are categorized into sections by type, including: bibliographies; manuscripts, books and theses; periodical literature; government serial publications. Books, periodical literature, and government documents are further organized by topic and chronological period. No index. Z7164.T7M67

Ottley, George. A bibliography of British railway history. 2d ed. London, H.M.S.O., 1983. 683p. **CH460**

1st ed. 1965.
A classified bibliography, including books, parts of books, pamphlets, etc., on the history and description of rail transportation in Britain from earliest times through early 1964. Based largely on British Museum holdings, but with additional listings for types of materials not regularly deposited there (e.g., unpublished theses). 7,950 items; locates copies. Detailed index. Z7235.G7O8

Railway directory & year book. Ed. 73– , 1968– . London, Transport & Technical Pubns., 1967– . il., maps. Annual. **CH461**

"Comp. from official sources under the direction of the editor of *The railway gazette.*"
Continues the *Directory of railway officials & yearbook* (1895–1966) and assumes its numbering.
Provides international directory and statistical data for railways and rapid transit, associations, trade unions, government departments, etc. Also offers a trade directory for various manufactures and services. Indexed. HE1009.U6

Thomson, Thomas Richard. Check list of publications on American railroads before 1841; a union list of printed books and pamphlets, including state and federal documents, dealing with charters, by-laws, legislative acts, speeches, debates, land grants, officers' and engineers' reports, travel guides, maps, etc. N.Y., New York Pub. Lib., 1942. 250p. **CH462**

"Reprinted with additions from the *Bulletin* of the New York Public Library of January–July–October 1941."—*verso of title page.*
Includes 2,671 numbered entries, arranged chronologically, of works which are predominantly related to railroads, or which have the words "railroad" or "railway" on the title page. Includes books, pamphlets, broadsides (except stock or contract certificates or bonds), and maps. Locates copies in 36 libraries that cooperated in checking the list. Z7235.U5T5

Who's who in railroading and rail transit. Ed.17– . N.Y., Simmons-Boardman, 1971– . Irregular. **CH463**

Continues *Who's who in railroading in North America* (1885–1968) and assumes its numbering. Title varies. Prior to 1930, known as the *Biographical directory of railway officials of America.* HE2723.W5

Ships

Albion, Robert Greenhalgh. Five centuries of famous ships, from the Santa Maria to the Glomar Explorer. N.Y., McGraw-Hill, [1978]. 435p. il. **CH464**

Presents historical sketches of about 160 vessels, arranged chronologically from 1492 to 1660 through the 18th century, the transitional period between sail and steam, the age of steam, and the 20th century. Each entry, ranging from two to eight pages, is accompanied by an illustration and a suggested reading list. Index of ships. VM15.A5

The encyclopedia of ships and seafaring. Peter Kemp, ed. N.Y., Crown, [1980]. 256p. il. **CH465**

Nine narrative chapters present the history of ships, sea warfare, navigation, and man's use of the sea as a resource. These are followed by three alphabetically arranged sections featuring information on famous ships, a guide to ship and boat types, and biographies. Copiously illustrated; indexed. VK15.E53

Hocking, Charles. Dictionary of disasters at sea during the age of steam, including sailing ships and ships of war lost in action, 1824–1962. [London, Lloyd's Register of Shipping, 1969] 2v. **CH466**

Includes all shipping casualties occurring on the high seas and in territorial and inland waters during the period indicated. Listing is by name of ship. Particulars (tonnage, etc.) of the ship are given, as well as a brief account of the disaster. VK1250.H6

Howe, Octavius Thorndike and **Matthews, F. C.** American clipper ships, 1833–1858. Salem, Mass., Marine Research Soc., 1926–27. 2v. il. (Marine Research Soc., Salem, Mass. Pubn. 13) **CH467**

Arranged alphabetically by name of ship, giving description and history of each and often a picture. Index includes names of captains, owners, etc., and of ships not described separately. VM23.H6

Matthews, Frederick C. American merchant ships, 1850–1900. Salem, Mass., Marine Research Soc., 1930. 399p. il. (Marine Research Soc., Salem, Mass. Pubn. 21) **CH468**

A companion work to Howe (above), on the same general plan. VM23.M3

Lytle, William M. and **Holdcamper, Forrest R.** Merchant steam vessels of the United States, 1790–1868. "The Lytle-Holdcamper list," comp. from official merchant marine documents of the United States and other sources. Rev. and ed. by C. Bradford Mitchell. Staten Island, N.Y., Steamship Historical Soc. of America, 1975. 322p. **CH469**

A revision and enlargement of *Steam vessels built in the United States, 1807–1856,* comp. under the author's supervision and issued by the U.S. Bureau of Navigation in 1931. Precedes in date *Merchant vessels of the United States, 1866/67– ,* published by the U.S. Bureau of Customs (CH482).
Gives information on name, tonnage, year and place built, first home port, and disposition. A separate list of ships lost. HE745.L97

Noel, John V. The VNR dictionary of ships and the seas. N.Y., Van Nostrand Reinhold, [1981]. 393p. **CH470**

Offers very brief definitions, without pronunciation guide or illustration, of terms selected from the following areas: oceanography, ocean engineering, familiar sea mammals, fish, and plants, weather, ships and shipping, seamanship, cargo handling, commercial maritime terms, marine insurance, ocean fishing, yachting, and surfing. Includes acronyms and some British words. Intended for the layman and generalist. V23.N63

The Oxford companion to ships & the sea. London, Oxford Univ. Pr., 1976. 971p. il., maps. **CH471**

Peter Kemp, ed.

"The field to be covered is immense, ranging from the ships and the men who first opened up the world with their voyages into the unknown, through the struggles of nations as they developed and recognized that power and prosperity depended on the exercise of sea power, to those who wrote about, and painted, the sea scene."— *Pref.* Brief entries for personal, place, and ship names, nautical terms (including seamen's slang). Good illustrations. Cross references V23.O96

Smith, Eugene Waldo. Trans-Atlantic passenger ships, past and present. Boston, Dean, [1947]. 350p. il. **CH472**

Deals with the principal passenger ships operating in the North Atlantic 1840–1940. Lists alphabetically some 1,000 ships, giving: date of construction, name of builder and owner, tonnage, dimensions, activities, changes of name, and final disposition.

HE565.A3S5

────── Trans-Pacific passenger ships and Appendix to Trans-Atlantic passenger ships, past and present. Boston, Dean, [1953]. 266p. il. **CH473**

Attempts "to include all known trans-Pacific passenger ships built from 1860 up to the present time. Includes liners sailing from English ports to New Zealand . . . via the Panama Canal."—*Introd.*

Appendix brings the author's companion volume, *Trans-Atlantic passenger ships, past and present,* further up-to-date.

HE565.A3S52

Woollam, W. G. Shipping terms and abbreviations: maritime, insurance, international trade. Cambridge, Md., Cornell Maritime, 1963. 144p. **CH474**

Contains more than 2,000 abbreviations. The list of abbreviations, arranged alphabetically, is followed by an alphabetical index of terms. HE567.W6

Annuals

American Bureau of Shipping. Record of the American Bureau of Shipping, "American Lloyds," established 1867 to provide a standard American classification of vessels. N.Y., 1869– . Annual. **CH475**

────── Supplement, no.1– , 1949– . Semimonthly.

Title varies: 1869–1932, *Record of American and foreign shipping.*

HE565.U5A55

International shipping and shipbuilding directory. London, Benn; N.Y., Nichols, 1883–1981. **CH476**

Title varies: 1883–1950/51, *Shipping world year book*; 1952–64, *Shipping world year book and who's who.*

Provides directory information for the United Kingdom and other countries on: shipowners, managers, agents, and shipping lines; shipbuilders and repairers; towage and salvage; seaborne containers; maritime organizations; and products and services. Most sections follow a country arrangement; indexed by name of ship and firm.

Continued in part by:

Lloyd's Maritime directory, 1982– . Colchester, Essex, Lloyd's of London, [1982]– . il. Annual. **CH477**

An international directory of shipowners, shipbuilders, marine services, marine engine builders, maritime and related organizations. In most sections companies are listed alphabetically, with indexes to country, personnel, subsidiary companies, and vessels.

HE951.L56

Lloyd's Nautical year book, 1979– . London, Lloyd's, 1979– . il. Annual. **CH478**

Continues *Lloyd's Calendar* 1908–78.

A useful yearbook containing much miscellaneous commercial

shipping and navigation information: laws affecting commerce and navigation, lists of British chambers of commerce, weights and measures of various nations, legal holidays of the world, etc.

VK8.L6

Lloyd's Ports of the world. London, Shipping World, 1946– . v.1– . il. Annual. **CH479**

Arranged by continent, with a separate section for the United Kingdom. Ports are listed alphabetically by country. Usually includes: location, population, accommodations, charges, pilotage, imports, and exports.

Until 1946 issued as a section of the *Shipping world year book* (later *International shipping and shipbuilding directory,* CH476). 1946–81 entitled *Ports of the world.* HE552.P62

Lloyd's Register of shipping. Founded 1760, reconstituted 1834, united with the Underwriters' Registry for iron vessels in 1885. London, Lloyd's, 1834– . Annual. **CH480**

Recent issues in four or more volumes, with some variation in contents. The "Register of ships" gives the names, classes, and general information concerning the ships classed by *Lloyd's Register,* together with particulars of all known ocean-going merchant ships in the world of 100 tons gross and upwards. It also lists lighters carried on board ship, floating docks, liquefied gas carriers, ships carrying refrigerated cargo, refrigerated cargo containers, refrigerated stores and container terminals, and off-shore drilling rigs. The "Register" is kept up-to-date by means of cumulative monthly supplements containing the latest survey records for all classed ships, and changes of name, ownership, flag, tonnage, etc., for all ships, whether classed or not.

The "Shipowners" section gives a list of owners and managers of the ships recorded in the "Register" with their fleets, as well as lists of former and compound names of ships. An "Appendix" contains a list of shipbuilders with existing ships they have built; marine enginebuilders and boilermakers; dry and wet docks; telegraphic addresses and codes used by shipping firms; marine insurance companies and marine associations. HE565.A3L7

Merchant ships. Ed. by Eric Talbot-Booth. . . . London, S. Low & Marston; N.Y., Macmillan, 1936–59. il. Annual. **CH481**

Ceased publication.

Pictures and line drawings of the merchant ships of the various countries of the world, with pertinent information on tonnage, distinguishing features, history, etc. A continuation and extension of *British merchant ships,* ed. by E. C. Talbot-Booth (London, Rich and Cowan, 1934. 220p.). HE565.A3M4

U.S. Bureau of Customs. Merchant vessels of the United States (including yachts and government vessels). 1866/67– . Wash., Govt. Prt. Off., 1869– . v.1– . il. Annual. **CH482**

Title varies; issuing office varies.

Includes an alphabetical list of vessels, giving: name, tonnage, where built, name of owner, home port, etc.; former names of merchant vessels; owners of vessels, etc. HE565.U5A2

U.S. Naval Oceanographic Office. World port index; locations and general descriptions of maritime ports and shipping places, with reference to appropriate sailing directions and charts. Ed.1– . Wash., Govt. Prt. Off., 1953– . il. Biennial. **CH483**

Frequency varies; issuing agency varies.

" . . . shows locations, characteristics, facilities, and available services of maritime ports and shipping places in all parts of the world, and lists the applicable charts and Sailing Directions for each port."—*Pref.* HE552.W67

Atlases

Lloyd's Maritime atlas, including a comprehensive list of ports and shipping places of the world, comp. and ed. by . . .

Lloyd's Shipping Pubns. Ed.1– . London, Lloyd's, 1951– . Irregular. (14th ed. 1983) **CH484**

1st ed. 1951. G1060.L6

Tables of distances

Distances between ports. 5th ed. Wash., Govt. Prt. Off., 1985. 187p. **CH485**

Prep. by Defense Mapping Agency, Hydrographic Center.
Supersedes the U.S. Hydrographic Office, *Table of distances between ports,* first published in 1916. VK799.D57

National Ocean Survey. Distances between United States ports. 6th (1978) ed. Wash., U.S. Dept. of Commerce, National Oceanic and Atmospheric Admin., National Ocean Survey, 1978. 66p. in various pagings. maps. **CH486**

1st–4th eds., 1929–67, issued by U.S. Coast and Geodetic Survey.
Nautical mileage charts show distances for Atlantic and Pacific coasts, the Panama Canal, the Great Lakes and New York state waterways; a table for estimating transit time is given. Indexed. VK799.N35

Reed's Tables of distances between ports and places in all parts of the world, comprising over 31,000 distances with a table of contents and complete alphabetical index, comp. by A. B. Purbrick and W. R. Nedham. 12th ed. Sunderland, Eng., Reed, 1953. 176p. **CH487**

1st ed. 1931. G109.R4

Communications
Postal guides

United States Postal Service. Postal service manual. [Wash., Govt. Prt. Off.], 1970–79. Looseleaf. **CH488**

Supersedes the *Postal manual* of the U.S. Post Office Dept., 1954–69.
Contents: (1) Domestic mail (including Instructions for mailers); (2) Organization and administration; (3) Postal procedures; (4) Personnel; (5) Transportation; (6) Facilities.
Since 1979, superseded by five looseleaf volumes: *Postal operations manual, Domestic mail manual, Administrative support manual, Financial management manual,* and *Employer and labor relations manual.*

———— National five digit ZIP code and post office directory. Wash., Govt. Prt. Off., 1982– . Annual. **CH489**

Unites the *National zip code directory* (1965–78) and the *Directory of post offices with ZIP codes* (1955–78). HE6361.N37

———— International mail manual. Wash., [1955–]. 1v., looseleaf. **CH490**

Title varies.
Kept up-to-date by looseleaf sheets. Reconstitutes *United States official postal guide,* 1937–54, pt.2, *International postal service.*
"Contains rates and other conditions governing mail to individual foreign countries, arranged alphabetically by countries."—*Pref.*

Canada. Post Office Dept. Canada postal guide. Hull [i.e., Ottawa, R. Duhamel], Queen's printer, [1966]– . Looseleaf. Biennial. **CH491**

Supersedes the biennial publication with title: *Canada official postal guide* (1875–1965).
In 2v.: pt.1, Postal laws and regulations; pt.2, International mails, rates and conditions. HE6653.A3

———— List of post offices in Canada. Ottawa, Queen's Printer, 1955– . Looseleaf. **CH492**

HE6653.A562

Gt. Brit. Post Office. Post office guide. London, Stat. Off., 1856– . **CH493**

From 1856 to 1879, called *British postal guide;* published quarterly. Frequency thereafter varies, usually annually with supplements and, since 1937, associated volumes: *Post offices in the United Kingdom* (published irregularly), and *London post offices and streets* (published irregularly); *Postal addresses and index to postcode directories* (published irregularly). HE6933.A2

Nomenclature internationale des bureaux de poste: liste complète des bureaux de poste des pays et territoires compris dans le ressort de l'Union Postale Universelle. Éd. 1977. Berne, L'Union, 1977. liv, 1148p. **CH494**

1st ed. 1968. Previously published as *Dictionnaire des bureaux de poste* of the Union's Bureau International.
An alphabetical listing of post office names, including postal code, name of country, and territorial subdivision (county, state or province). Names of countries in French and in the official language are given at the beginning of the volume. HE6031.N65

Mass media
Bibliography

See also AA338, BG292–BG293.

Blum, Eleanor. Basic books in the mass media. 2d ed. Urbana, Univ. of Illinois Pr., [1980]. 426p. **CH495**

1962 edition had title: *Reference books in the mass media.*
Subtitle: An annotated, selected booklist covering general communications, book publishing, broadcasting, editorial journalism, film, magazines, and advertising.
Arranged according to the categories mentioned in the subtitle. Fully indexed. Z5630.B55

Chin, Felix. Cable television: a comprehensive bibliography. N.Y., IFI/Plenum, [1978]. 285p. **CH496**

A section for "general reference materials" (i.e., a listing of relevant periodicals, indexes, and legal digests) is followed by a classified, annotated bibliography of 650 items—mainly citations to periodical articles. Numerous useful appendixes (including a glossary of CATV terms); author and subject indexes. Z7711.C47

Communication abstracts. v.1, no.1– , Mar. 1978– . Beverly Hills, Calif., Sage, 1978– . Quarterly. **CH497**

Publ. with the cooperation of the School of Communications and Theater, Temple University.
Each issue offers about 250 abstracts of articles from about 100 journals and 50 recent books. Topically arranged, using headings such as: general communication, advertising, communication theory, mass communication, public communication, journalism, etc. Author and subject indexes in each issue cumulate annually. P87.C59733

Danielson, Wayne A. and **Wilhoit, G. C.** A computerized bibliography of mass communication research, 1944–1964. [N.Y., Magazine Publishers Assoc.], 1967. 399p. **CH498**

Offers a KWIC index approach to articles on mass communication appearing in 48 social science journals during the period indicated. Citations are arranged alphabetically by author in the bibliography section.

Gordon, Thomas F. and **Verna, Mary Ellen.** Mass communication effects and processes: a comprehensive bibliography, 1950–1975. Beverly Hills, Calif., Sage Pubns., [1978]. 229p. **CH499**

An author listing of about 2,700 titles emphasizing social-psychological aspects of the media; excludes the areas of law and regulation, historical development, economics and business, technical operations, management and training. Treats media influence and effects, content presentation, use by and effects on adolescents, children, blacks, the aged, the poor, and women. Subject index. Z5630.G67

Hachten, William A. Mass communication in Africa: an annotated bibliography. Madison, Center for International Communication Studies, Univ. of Wisconsin, 1971. 121p.   **CH500**

A classed bibliography of more than 500 items (books, periodical articles, academic theses). Author and country indexes.   Z5630.H28

Hansen, Donald A. and **Parsons, J. Herschel.** Mass communication: a research bibliography. [Santa Barbara, Calif., Glendessary Pr., 1968] 144p.   **CH501**

A selective, classified bibliography of writings published since 1945. Author index.   Z5630.H3

Hill, George H. Black media in America: a resource guide. Boston, G. K. Hall, [1984]. 333p.   **CH502**

An annotated bibliography of 4,069 citations to items relating to blacks as producers and consumers of mass media, excluding motion pictures. Arranged by form (books, dissertations, theses, journal articles, newspaper and magazine articles), subdivided by topic. Indexed.   Z5633.A37H55

McCavitt, William E. Radio and television: a selected, annotated bibliography. Metuchen, N.J., Scarecrow Pr., 1978. 229p.   **CH503**

An annotated listing of some 1,100 "selected books on broadcasting."—*Introd.* A topical listing (under such headings as: surveys, history, regulation, programming, production, criticism, audience, cable television, broadcasting careers) with author index.   Z7221.M23

———— ———— Supplement one, 1977–1981. Metuchen, N.J., Scarecrow Pr., 1982. 155p.

Mass communication in India; an annotated bibliography. Comp. at Indian Institute of Mass Communication. Singapore, Asian Mass Communication Research and Information Centre, [1976]. 216p. (Asian mass communications bibliography ser., 2)   **CH504**

A subject-classed, annotated list of over 800 English-language materials. Includes published materials (books, collections, conference reports, and government publications) from 1945 to 1973, and unpublished sources (M.A. and Ph.D. theses, seminar papers) from 1960 to 1973. Lists periodical titles but not articles. Author/title index.
See also Kalpana Dasgupta and Bhagwan K. Prasad's *Mass communication in India . . . 1974–77* (New Delhi, Indian Inst. of Mass Communication, 1982. 163p.).   Z5630.M36

Meyer, Manfred and **Nissen, Ursula.** Effects and functions of television: children and adolescents; a bibliography of selected research literature, 1970–1978. München [etc.], K. G. Saur, 1979. 172p. (Communication research and broadcasting, no.2)   **CH505**

Translation of *Wirkungen und Funktionen des Fernsehens.*
A classed bibliography of more than 900 titles based on empirical research findings; most are books and articles, though some ERIC documents are included. Citations on particular programs or series are provided. Author and subject indexes.   Z5814.T45M4913

Murray, John P. Television & youth; 25 years of research and controversy. Boys Town, Neb., Boys Town Center for the Study of Youth Development, [1980]. 278p.   **CH506**

In four parts: (1) a bibliographic review of the literature; (2) the "master" bibliography, chronologically arranged and coded by subject area; (3) thirteen specialized subject bibliographies; (4) bibliographies on policy guidelines, and other bibliographies.   Z7164.C5M87

Richstad, Jim and **McMillan, Michael.** Mass communication and journalism in the Pacific islands: a bibliography. Honolulu, Univ. Pr. of Hawaii, [1978]. 299p.   **CH507**

"An East-West Center book from the East-West Communication Institute."—*t.p.*
For each nation or territory, lists materials in the following areas:

reference works; newspapers; periodicals; biographies; government and international agency reports; divisions of the media (cinema, the press, radio, television); and related topics (news agencies, legal issues, printing, labor relations, etc.). Most entries are briefly annotated; indexed. Includes Hawaii.   P92.I78R5

Shearer, Benjamin F. and **Huxford, Marilyn.** Communications and society: a bibliography on communications technologies and their social impact. Westport, Conn., Greenwood Pr., [1983]. 242p.   **CH508**

A selective, classed bibliography of 2,732 citations to books, essays, periodical articles, and dissertations; international scope, but predominantly English-language materials. Author and subject indexes.   Z5630.S43

Smith, Myron J. U.S. television network news: a guide to sources in English. Jefferson, N.C., McFarland, 1984. 233p.   **CH509**

A classed bibliography of 3,215 citations to books, articles, government documents, and theses written since the late 1940s. Brief annotations for books; author and subject indexes. Includes material on specific networks and news programs; extensive coverage of relationships to politics, foreign affairs, and defense.   Z6951.S57

Sparks, Kenneth R. A bibliography of doctoral dissertations in television and radio. [3d ed.] Syracuse, N.Y., School of Journalism, Syracuse Univ., [1971]. 119p.   **CH510**

A classified listing of some 900 dissertations completed through June 1970. Author index.   Z7221.S65

Spiess, Volker. Bibliographie zu Rundfunk und Fernsehen. Hamburg, Hans-Bredow-Institut, [1966]. 206p. (Studien zur Massenkommunikation, 1)   **CH511**

A classed bibliography of 1,859 items.   Z5630.S68

Dictionaries and encyclopedias

Les Brown's Encyclopedia of television. N.Y., New York Zoetrope, [1982]. 496p. il.   **CH512**

For full information *see* BG297.

Diamant, Lincoln. The broadcast communications dictionary. Rev. and expanded ed. N.Y., Hastings House, [1978]. 201p.   **CH513**

1st ed. 1974.
Provides very brief definitions of some 2,000 technical, common, and slang terms; cross references are italicized. Not intended as a technical dictionary.   N1990.4.D5

Ellmore, R. Terry. Illustrated dictionary of broadcast—CATV—telecommunications. Blue Ridge Summit, Pa., Tab Books, [1977]. 396p. il.   **CH514**

A dictionary of words, phrases, acronyms and initials directly related to radio, television, and cable television. Brief definitions, with extensive use of cross references. "Advertising, production, and regulation . . . are covered extensively. The coverage of film, lighting and news is centered around the terms' relationship to radio, television and cable television."—*Introd.* Engineering terms are defined for the non-engineer. About 8,000 definitions.   TK6634.E37

Longman dictionary of mass media & communication. [Ed. by] Tracy Daniel Connors. N.Y., Longman, [1982]. 255p.   **CH515**

"Intended to . . . [bring] together the terms most often used between communications specialities and [to define] them indicating the specific area of communication in which a meaning is used."—*Pref.* Provides brief definitions with variant meanings in all fields included (e.g., advertising, film, graphic arts, computers, data processing, printing, photography, public relations, theater). A *Li-*

brary journal review (107:1451) questions the "imperative" need for such a dictionary, but recommends it for public libraries.

P87.5.L66

Handbooks and directories

See also AE38, BG308.

Broadcasting cablecasting yearbook, 1982– . [Wash.], Broadcasting Pubns., [1982]– . il. Annual.   **CH516**

Continues *Broadcasting cable yearbook* (1980–81), which was formed by the merger of *Broadcasting yearbook* (1968–79) and *Broadcasting, cable sourcebook* (1973–79).

An international directory in nine main sections: an overview of the fifth estate—broadcasting media, technology, regulations, and station ownership; radio; television; cable systems; satellites; programming; advertising and marketing; technology manufacturers; professional services, associations, and broadcasting educational programs. Some statistical rankings. Short annotated bibliography of recent books.   HE8689.B77

McCavitt, William E. Broadcasting around the world. Blue Ridge Summit, Pa., Tab Books, [1981]. 336p. il.   **CH517**

Chapters by country specialists or official sources survey radio and television broadcasting in the Republic of South Africa, Poland, USSR, Japan, South Korea, Israel, Canada, the United States, Brazil, Guyana, India, West Germany, Britain, Ireland, Italy, the Netherlands, Sweden and Australia. Select bibliography.

HE8689.4.M32

Media personnel directory: an alphabetical guide to names, addresses, and telephone numbers of key editorial and business personnel at over 700 United States and international periodicals. Detroit, Gale, [1979]. 262p.   **CH518**

Alan E. Abrams, ed.

Entries provide job title, last-reported place of service, and address and telephone number of the magazine; includes editors, publishers, columnists, art directors, book reviewers, sales and production managers, and foreign and domestic correspondents. Only magazine affiliations are given.   PN4820.M4

Norback, Craig T. and **Norback, Peter G.** TV Guide almanac. N.Y., Ballantine Books, [1980]. 680p.   **CH519**

Provides information on such television-related topics as: advertising, audience research, college and university programs in broadcasting, awards, history, broadcast libraries, politics and television, ratings, cable and public television, etc. Some articles have been written by the organizations concerned (e.g., A. C. Nielsen Company, National Association of Broadcasters). Indexed.

PN1992.3.U5N6

Steinberg, Cobbett S. TV facts. N.Y., Facts on File, [1980]. 541p.   **CH520**

In six chapters: (1) the programs; (2) the viewers; (3) the ratings; (4) the advertisers; (5) the awards, polls, and surveys; (6) the networks and stations. Much of the information presented here on advertising, the business aspects of the industry, and certain awards, is not conveniently available elsewhere; however, the "Prime time schedules" (p.3–129) have been reprinted from Brooks and Marsh's *Complete directory to prime time network TV shows* (BG296). Indexed.   PN1992.18.S75

Sterling, Christopher H. and **Haight, Timothy R.** The mass media: Aspen Institute guide to communication industry trends. [N.Y., Praeger, 1978] 457p.   **CH521**

A statistical compendium of more than 300 data tables describing communication trends in the United States since 1900. Organized by broad subject area—growth, ownership, economics, employment, content trends, audiences, and U.S. media abroad—and within these, by media categories. Sources of all tables are identified. Extensive, partially annotated bibliography. Subject index.

P92.U5S68

Telecommunications systems and services directory. no.1– , July 1983– . Detroit, Gale, [1983]– .   **CH522**

Subtitle: An international descriptive guide to new and established telecommunications organizations, systems, and services, covering voice and data communications, teleconferencing, electronic mail, local area networks, satellite services, videotex and teletext, interactive cable television, transactional services, telegram, telex, facsimile, and others, including related consultants, associations, research institutes, publishers and information services, and regulatory bodies, with a detailed glossary of terms, acronyms, standards, and issues in the field.

John Schmittroth, Jr. and Martin Connors, eds.

An international directory, alphabetically arranged, with indexes by name, function, geographic area, and personal name. The first edition is to be in three parts appearing at six-month intervals.

TK5102.5T3965

TV. The television annual. 1978/79– . N.Y., Macmillan, [1979]– . il. Annual.   **CH523**

"A complete record of American television from June 1, 1978 through May 31, 1979."—*t.p., 1978/79.*

Ed. by Steven H. Scheuer.

Includes sections for an overview of the season, prime-time viewing, daytime programs, broadcast news, sports programs, children's programs, television technology, the networks, television and the public interest. Indexed.   PN1992.3.U5T23

Television & cable factbook, 1946– . Wash., Television Digest, Inc., [1946–]. no.1– . Annual.   **CH524**

Subtitle: The authoritative reference for the advertising, television and electronics industries.

Frequency varies. Title varies (1946–50 called *TV directory;* 1951–81, *Television factbook*).

Now published in two volumes per year: the "Cable and services" volume covers all data other than stations; the "Stations" volume includes United States, Canadian, and international stations.

TK6540.T453

Toll-free digest, 1976– . [Claverack, N.Y., Toll-Free Digest Co., 1975–] Annual.   **CH525**

Lists toll-free telephone numbers according to category, with company name index; hotels, motels, etc., are listed in a separate section.   HE8811.T64

United Nations Educational, Scientific and Cultural Organization. Division of Free Flow of Information. Professional association in the mass media; handbook of press, film, radio, television organizations. [Paris], UNESCO, [1959]. 206p.   **CH526**

A directory giving detailed information on 1,049 national organizations in 93 states and territories, and 64 international associations. Includes history, purpose, membership, publications, etc.

P88.8.U5

U.S. Foreign Broadcast Information Service. Broadcasting stations of the world . . . 25th ed. [Wash., 1972]. 4 pts.   **CH527**

1st ed. 1946.

Contents: pt.1, Amplitude modulation broadcasting stations according to country and city; pt.2, Amplitude broadcasting stations, according to frequency; pt.3, Frequency modulation broadcasting stations; pt.4, Television stations.

The Service also publishes *Short wave broadcasting stations of the world according to frequency.*   TK6555.U615

World communications; a 200-country survey of press, radio, television and film. [5th ed. Epping, Eng., and N.Y.], Gower Pr., Unipub, [1975]. 533p.   **CH528**

1st ed. 1950.

"The purpose of this, as of previous editions, is to describe the situation of the four principal media (press, radio, television, film) in the various countries and territories of the world, indicating, with statistical support, the general structure, facilities, output, distribution and coverage of each. . . ."—*Pref.* New categories on space communications and professional training and association. Index of news agencies and a brief bibliography.   P90.W64

FINANCE AND BANKING

Bibliography

Aggarwal, Raj. The literature of international business finance: a bibliography of selected business and academic sources. N.Y., Praeger, [1984]. 297p.   **CH529**

Lists more than 3,600 English-language items relevant to financial management in the multinational company, within seven broad subject chapters, e.g., accounting, taxation, foreign investment decision. No detailed subject or author index.   Z7164.F5A38

Brealey, Richard A. and **Pyle, Connie.** A bibliography of finance and investment. Cambridge, Mass., MIT Pr., [1973]. 361p.   **CH530**

A classed bibliography of more than 3,600 books, periodical articles, dissertations, and unpublished papers, most appearing after 1962. Within each subject area materials are chronologically arranged. The author "index" repeats the full citation.   Z7164.F5B77

Heggestad, Arnold A. Public regulation of financial services: costs and benefits to consumers; a bibliography. Boulder, Colo., Westview Pr., [1977]. 246p.   **CH531**

A bibliography of books, periodical articles, government documents, and doctoral dissertations produced since 1960. Subjects include domestic monetary and financial theory and policy, commercial banking, thrift institutions, credit unions, and personal credit. Subject arrangement; no index.   Z7164.F5H43

International Association for Research in Income and Wealth. Bibliography on income and wealth, v.1–8, 1937/47–57/60. Cambridge, Bowes & Bowes, 1952–64. v.1–8.   **CH532**

v.1 ed. by Daniel Creamer; v.2–8, ed. by Phyllis Deane.

Ceased publication.

A cooperative work by contributors from many countries. Contains listings for books, pamphlets, and periodical articles, but only when they provide critical or descriptive analysis of the measures used. The arrangement is topical, with geographical subdivision when pertinent; otherwise, under each topic the arrangement is alphabetical by author. Author, geographical, and subject indexes.   Z7164.W4I57

Ladley, Barbara and **Wilford, Jane M.** Money and finance; sources of print and nonprint materials. [N.Y.], Neal-Schuman, [1980]. 208p. (Neal-Schuman sourcebook ser., 2)   **CH533**

A directory for the lay person describing more than 500 American organizations providing publications and information on aspects of personal finance. Arranged alphabetically within 17 subject categories ranging from general consumer information to transportation and travel. Indexed by organization, title, and subject.   HG151.7.L33

Lister, Roger and **Lister, Eva.** Annotated bibliography of corporate finance. Toronto, Macmillan Co. of Canada, [1979]. 240p.   **CH534**

A classified bibliography of 1,270 English-language monographs and periodical articles. Author and subject indexes.   Z7164.F5L57

Masui, Mitsuzo. A bibliography of finance. Kobe, International Finance Seminar in the Kobe Univ. of Commerce, 1935. 1614p., 116p. (Repr.: N.Y., B. Franklin, 1969)   **CH535**

Contents: British books and articles; Ouvrages françaises; Deutsche Literatur; American books and articles; Author index.

Includes works dating from the 15th century to 1933.   Z7164.F5M27

Published official sources of financial statistics. Sources officielles publiées des statistiques financières. Paris, Organisation for Economic Co-operation and Development, [1980]. 132p.   **CH536**

In English and French.

For each country the catalog provides two lists: (1) official institutions which publish financial statistics, with address, telephone and telex numbers, and a list of their publications; (2) financial subjects, keyed to the official publication which provides the data, and indicating frequency, chronological basis of the data, and brief description. Includes similar data for some international organizations: Bank for International Settlements, International Monetary Fund, European Communities and Organization for Economic Cooperation and Development.   Z7164.F5P824

Rees, Alan M. and **Janes, Jodith.** Money management information source book. N.Y., Bowker, 1983. 299p.   **CH537**

An annotated bibliography of the literature of financial planning and personal investment for the lay person. Evaluates more than 600 books (most of them published since 1978), as well as periodicals, investment newsletters, pamphlet literature, and technical sources. Glossary; subject, author, and title indexes.   Z7164.T4R43

Rock, James M. Money, banking, and macroeconomics; a guide to information sources. Detroit, Gale, 1977. 281p. (Economics information guide ser., 11)   **CH538**

An introductory, annotated survey of the literature on macro-monetary economics and its main fields; financial intermediation and commercial banking; macro-monetary theory; central banking; and stabilization policy. Concentrates on recent, widely available, English-language books and periodical articles. Author, title, and subject indexes.   Z7164.F5R63

Sources of world financial and banking information. G. R. Dicks, ed. Westport, Conn., Greenwood Pr., [1981]. 720p.   **CH539**

In three parts: (1) about 5,000 sources listed alphabetically by relevant country, with an international section for sources covering a number of countries; each entry has a brief summary of contents; (2) publishers' directory for these sources; (3) a series of seven topical indexes, subdivided by country, referring to sources listed in the first part.   Z7164.F5S713

Weiner, Richard and **Holt, Rena.** Investment newsletters. [N.Y.], Public Relations Publ. Co., [1982]. 186p.   **CH540**

A directory of more than 800 newsletters available on a subscription basis, with subscription information and brief descriptive notes. Title arrangement; indexed by editor, publisher and title, but not by subject.   Z7164.F5W47

Woy, James B. Investment information; a detailed guide to selected sources. Detroit, Gale, [1970]. 231p.   **CH541**

Intended as an index to regularly recurring financial statistics (i.e., those appearing in daily, weekly, or monthly publications). Arrangement is alphabetical by type of information sought.   Z7164.F5W93

—— Investment methods; a bibliographic guide. N.Y., Bowker, 1973. 220p.   **CH542**

The main part of the volume is an alphabetical listing of investment methods with a concise definition for each and one or more annotated bibliographic references to books which will provide further information on the method. There is also a selected bibliography, topically arranged, of periodical articles; a directory of periodicals; and an author index.   Z7164.F5W94

Zerden, Sheldon. Best books on the stock market: an analytical bibliography. N.Y., Bowker, 1972. 168p.   **CH543**

A listing of 150 books in seven main categories (methods of investing; history; biography; books for the beginner; how to beat the market; general works; textbooks and reference works), plus a supplementary list of recommended titles. Items in the main list are annotated in considerable detail. Indexed.   Z7164.F5Z46

Dictionaries and encyclopedias

Brownstone, David M. and **Franck, Irene M.** The VNR investor's dictionary. N.Y., Van Nostrand Reinhold, [1981]. 326p.   **CH544**

Defines words and phrases derived from the areas of securities, finance, banking, business, accounting, law, real estate, statistics, and government, as they relate to investment and finance. When meanings vary, the most general one is listed first.   HG4513.B76

Davids, Lewis E. Dictionary of banking and finance. Totowa, N.J., Littlefield, Adams, 1978. 229p.   **CH545**

Offers brief definitions of terms, phrases, and abbreviations from the fields of banking and finance, as well as selected vocabulary related to accounting, trust administration, taxation and government.   HG151.D365

Dorfman, John. The stock market directory. N.Y., Doubleday, 1982. 560p.   **CH546**

Provides basic data on about 1,500 stocks listed on the New York Stock Exchange, with more detailed "profiles" or analyses of about 500 stocks from large companies, very profitable companies, or companies with high investor interest. Indicates ten-year profits and losses.   HG4057.A233

Downes, John and **Goodman, Jordan Elliot.** Dictionary of finance and investment terms. Woodbury, N.Y., Barron's Educational Series, [1985]. 495p. il.   **CH547**

On cover: Over 2500 terms clearly defined and explained. Covers stocks and bonds, banking, corporate finance, and more.
An excellent dictionary of current terminology.   HG151.D69

Encyclopedia of investments. Ed. in chief, Marshall E. Blume. Boston, Warren, Gorham & Lamont, [1982]. 1041, 1–52p. il.   **CH548**

Presents some 60 articles about types of investment vehicles, written by specialists; most include glossary, directories of dealers or brokers, and bibliography. Indexed.   HG4527.E5

Enzyklopädisches Lexikon für das Geld-, Bank- und Börsenwesen. Zugleich 2. Aufl. vom Handwörterbuch des Bankwesens von M. Palyi und P. Quittner. In Gemeinschaft mit 150 Fachleuten aus dem In- und Ausland bearb. von Erich Achterbert [et al.]. Frankfurt am Main, F. Knapp, [1957]. 2v. (1732p.)   **CH549**

1st ed. 1933.
Includes bibliographies.

International Committee for the Study of the History of Banking and Credit. History of the principal public banks, accompanied by extensive bibliographies of the history of banking and credit in eleven European countries, collected by J. G. van Dillen. . . . The Hague, Nijhoff, 1934. 480p. (Repr.: London, Cass, 1964)   **CH550**

Covers banking history from the end of the 15th century to 1815 in Spain, Italy, Holland, Germany, Sweden, England, France, Poland, Russia, Belgium, and Denmark; chapters—written variously in French, German, English, or Italian—are by different authors. Extensive bibliographies.   HG1551.I5

Moffat, Donald W. A concise desk book of business finance. 2d ed. Englewood Cliffs, N.J., Prentice-Hall, [1984]. 381p. il.   **CH551**

1st ed. 1975.
A dictionary of financial terminology.   HG151.M7

The money encyclopedia. Ed. by Harvey Rachlin. N.Y., Harper & Row, [1984]. 669p. il.   **CH552**

An encyclopedia "to help [the general reader] in approaching the financial world—as both a consumer and investor—with greater awareness, understanding, and perspicacity."—*Pref.* Dictionary arrangement of signed articles, often several pages in length, by about 140 contributors.   HG181.M574

Munn, Glenn Gaywaine. Encyclopedia of banking and finance. 8th ed. rev. and expanded by F. L. Garcia. Boston, Bankers Pub. Co., [1983]. 1024p.   **CH553**

1st ed. 1924.
Definitions of terms and encyclopedic articles, with bibliographies, on: money; credit; banking practice, history, law, accounting, and organization; trusts and finance; foreign exchange; investments; securities; speculation; business organization; insurance; commodities; markets; brokerage.   HG151.M8

Pessin, Allan H. and **Ross, Joseph A.** Words of Wall Street; 2,000 investment terms defined. Homewood, Ill., Dow Jones-Irwin, [1983]. 297p.   **CH554**

A dictionary of securities industry terms, expressions, and delivery systems. A new edition, *More words of Wall Street,* is announced for 1986.   HG4513.P47

Prentice-Hall, Inc. Corporate treasurer's and controller's encyclopedia, revised. Englewood Cliffs, N.J., Prentice-Hall, [1975]. 2v. (1050p.) il.   **CH555**

Rev. by Sam R. Goodman.
Previous editions ed. by Lillian Doris.
A practical manual, with many illustrations of forms and procedures. No bibliography.   HG4061.P74

Rosenberg, Jerry M. Dictionary of banking and finance. N.Y., Wiley, [1982]. 690p.   **CH556**

Provides brief definitions for about 10,000 terms, phrases, symbols, acronyms, abbreviations, and commonly used foreign words and phrases. In cases of multiple definitions, general usage is given first, with other definitions listed by area of specialty (banking, law, finance, computers, etc.). Numerous statistical and factual appendixes. A new edition was announced for 1985 publication as *Dictionary of banking and financial services.*   HG151.R67

Standard and Poor's Corporation. Standard & Poor's Stock market encyclopedia. N.Y., [1961?]– . Ed.1– . Semiannual.   **CH557**

Stocks are listed alphabetically, with two pages of information on each, including pertinent income account and balance sheet statistics, recent developments, prospects, etc.   HG4921.S68

Thomson, William. Thomson's Dictionary of banking. 12th ed. [London], Pitman, [1974]. 669p. il.   **CH558**

F. R. Ryder, legal ed.; D. B. Jenkins, gen. ed.
1st ed. 1912.
More a one-volume encyclopedia than a dictionary. Deals with the business of banking as practiced in England; appendixes treat Scottish banking and Northern Ireland land laws relating to banking. Articles include sections from relevant laws, results of law cases, and law reports, if appropriate; historical development is usually traced. List of abbreviations; numerous tables and cross references.   HG151.T38

Thorndike, David. The Thorndike encyclopedia of banking and financial tables. Rev. ed. Boston & N.Y., Warren, Gorham & Lamont, [1980]. unpaged (approx. 1700p.).   **CH559**

Subtitle: Containing tables for real estate mortgage loans and depreciation, compound interest and annuity, interest and savings, installment loans, leasing and rebates, discount, mortgage and bond values.
1st ed. 1973.
A compilation of tables for use with various fixed income transactions where an interest rate is an integral part of the transaction, to determine amount, rate, term, and/or payment.   HG1626.T49

—— —— Yearbook, 1975– . Boston, Warren, Gorham & Lamont, 1975– . Annual.   **CH559a**

Prep. in conjunction with editorial staffs of the *Bankers magazine* and the *Banking law journal.*
Designed to supplement the main volume through the addition of tables and other materials reflecting changing economic conditions. Pt.I is made up of tables; pt.II is a narrative and tabular discussion

of new developments in finance, investment, laws and regulations, etc. Indexed.

Valentine, Stuart P. International dictionary of the securities industries. N.Y., Nichols, [1985]. 217p. **CH560**

Focuses on investment terminology used in the overseas markets of the United States, United Kingdom, Germany, Italy, France, the Netherlands, and Japan. About 2,500 words and phrases, with some bibliographic references. HG4513.V35

Walmsley, Julian. A dictionary of international finance. Westport, Conn., Greenwood Pr., [1979]. 270p. **CH561**

Offers definitions (with some British emphasis) of terms related to banking, capital markets, international trade and economics, commodity markets, and some aspects of insurance; tax and accountancy terminology is omitted, as are most foreign-language terms. Bibliographic references to monographs and articles are provided for most definitions. A new edition was announced for 1985.
HG151.W34

Wyckoff, Peter. The language of Wall Street. N.Y., Hopkinson & Blake, [1973]. 247p. il. **CH562**

The same author's *Dictionary of stock market terms* was published 1964 (Englewood Cliffs, N.J., Prentice-Hall. 301p.).
A dictionary of terms intended for the layman as well as the businessman involved with the stock market. HG4513.W92

Foreign terms

Elsevier's Banking dictionary in six languages: English/American, French, Italian, Spanish, Dutch, and German. Comp. and arr. by Julio Ricci. 2d, completely rev. ed. Amsterdam & N.Y., Elsevier, 1980. 286p. **CH563**

1st ed. 1966.
A polyglot dictionary arranged on an English base with equivalent terms in the other languages. More than 2,400 terms; indexed by terms in the other languages. HG151.E45

Elsevier's Dictionary of financial terms in English, German, Spanish, French, Italian, and Dutch. By Francis J. Thomson. Amsterdam [etc.], Elsevier Scientific Publ. Co., 1979. 496p. **CH564**

Originally intended as a revision of S. F. Horn's *Glossary of financial terms* (1965), with the inclusion of two additional languages, Italian and Dutch. For about 2,400 English terms, offers equivalents in the other languages and indexes from those languages.
HG151.E47

Elsevier's Lexicon of stock-market terms: English/American, French, German, Dutch. Comp. and arr. by B. L. L. M. Thole. N. Y., American Elsevier, 1965. 131p. **CH565**

Basic table in English, with indexes from the other languages.
HG4513.E4

Gunston, Charles Arthur and **Corner, Charles Morris.** Gunston & Corner's German-English glossary of financial and economic terms. 6th ed., greatly compressed, but in content much amplified. Frankfurt/Main, Knapp, [1972]. 1032p. **CH566**

1st ed. 1953.
London edition (1953) had title: *Glossary of German financial and economic terms.* HG151.G85

Handbooks

Bankers desk reference, [1978]– . Boston & N.Y., Warren, Gorham & Lamont, [1978]– . Annual since 1983. il. **CH567**

A handbook, with subject articles organized into chapters on: deposits, payments and collections; consumer credit; commercial lending; funds management; bank supervision and regulation; bank holding companies; international banking. Also includes mathemat-

ical tables and a glossary. Indexed. When the publication became an annual in 1983 it absorbed the *Bankers desk reference yearbook* which was first published 1980. HG1611.B19

Baughn, William Hubert and **Walker, Charles E.** The bankers' handbook. Rev. ed. Homewood, Ill., Dow Jones–Irwin, [1978]. 1205p. il. **CH568**

1st ed. 1966.
Presents a series of 87 essays by experts in the field, grouped into broad sections, e.g., organization, personnel, information and data systems, planning, investments and securities markets, credit, international banking. Indexed. HG2491.B3

Financial handbook. Ed. by Edward I. Altman. 5th ed. N.Y., Wiley, 1981. 1v., various pagings. **CH569**

1st ed. 1925.
A valuable handbook for detailed information on the financial management of a business. HG173.F49

Handbook of business finance and capital sources. 1979– . Minneapolis, Minn., Inter-Finance Corp., 1979– . Triennial? **CH570**

Ed. by Dileep Rao.
In four parts: (1) descriptive information on financial institutions and instruments, and the fundamentals of business finance; (2) names, addresses, contact officers, and investment criteria of private financial institutions, arranged by type of institution, then geographically; (3 and 4) similar information on state and federal programs. Pt.I is indexed.

Handbook of financial markets—securities, options, futures. Frank J. Fabozzi and Frank G. Zarb, eds. Homewood, Ill., Dow Jones-Irwin, [1981]. 794p. il. **CH571**

43 chapters by subject specialists are organized in three "books": the securities markets—environment, structure, instruments, and private financial intermediaries; the options market; the futures markets—commodity and financial. Bibliographic references; index. HG4527.H25

Herrick, Tracy G. Bank analyst's handbook. N.Y., Wiley, [1978]. 380p. il. **CH572**

A guide for those persons making business and investment decisions, including valuations, concerning banks. Examines sources of information, banking policies (liquidity, credit risk, interest rate, profitability, and capital), the impact of the environment (domestic and international banks, loan and securities markets, regulatory pressures), management, and types of valuation. Indexed.
HG1576.H47

The international banking handbook. Ed. by William H. Baughn and Donald R. Mandich. Homewood, Ill., Dow Jones-Irwin, [1983]. 853p. **CH573**

Fifty chapters on the major issues and functions of international banking contributed by individual specialists; some bibliographical references. Indexed. HG3881.I574

The international finance handbook. Ed. by Abraham M. George, Ian H. Giddy. N.Y., Wiley, [1983]. 2v. il.
CH574

Presents 54 chapters by specialists, grouped into eight main sections: introduction; foreign exchange markets; Eurocurrency markets; national banking, money, and bond markets; international bond market; international equity markets; special financing techniques and sources; management of international finance. Appendixes on mathematical formulae and current periodical sources of information. Glossary; index; bibliographic references.
A somewhat less technical book, "written by practicing professionals for practitioners" (*Pref.*) and stressing actual skills, concepts, and techniques, is the *Handbook of international financial management,* ed. by Allen Sweeny and Robert Rachlin (N.Y., McGraw-Hill, 1984). HG3881.I57633

The investment manager's handbook. Sumner N. Levine, ed. Homewood, Ill., Dow Jones-Irwin, [1980]. 1037p. il.
CH575

39 chapters by practitioners and academics cover subjects in seven principal areas of investment management: (1) administrative and theoretical fundamentals; (2) management strategies; (3) measuring and monitoring performance; (4) legal and regulatory aspects; (5) management by type of portfolio; (6) money market portfolio management; (7) computer services. Each chapter provides bibliographical references. Security analysis is covered in the *Financial analyst's handbook, 1: portfolio management* (Homewood, Ill., 1975). Indexed.   HG4527.I58

Kent, C. H. European stock exchange handbook. Park Ridge, N.J., Noyes Data Corp., 1973. 567p.   **CH576**

Provides relatively full information about the stock exchanges of 18 European countries. Arranged alphabetically by country.   HG4551.K45

Levine, Sumner N. Financial analyst's handbook. Homewood, Ill., Dow Jones–Irwin, 1975. 2v. il.   **CH577**

Contents: v.1, Methods, theory, and portfolio management; v.2, Analysis by industry.

A series of chapters written by specialists as "a comprehensive guide to the principles and procedures necessary for successful investment management."—*Pref.* v.1 provides a discipline oriented coverage of investments, treating investment vehicles, special investment vehicles, the analysis of financial reports, economic analysis and timing, mathematical aids, and portfolio management and theories. v.2 provides analyses of specific industries, and includes a section on information sources, with an essay by Sylvia Mechanic on "Key reference sources" (p.859–82) and a subject guide to industry publications (p.833–926). Overall index in both volumes.   HG4521.L625

Paine Webber Inc. The Paine Webber handbook of stock and bond analysis. Kiril Sokoloff, ed. in chief. N.Y., McGraw-Hill, [1979]. 1v., various pagings (approx. 600p.). graphs.   **CH578**

A handbook for investors indicating key questions to ask about a potential investment. In two parts: (1) equity analysis, with chapters on specific industries; (2) fixed-income analysis, with chapters on different types of fixed-income and tax-exempt securities. Each chapter is written by a Paine Webber analyst. Indexed.   HG4921.P3

Pratt's Guide to venture capital sources. 8th ed. [Wellesley Hills, Mass., Venture Economics, 1984] 531p.   **CH579**

Stanley E. Pratt, ed.

1st ed. 1970.

A number of essays by professionals are grouped in five areas: (1) Background; (2) Sources of business development financing; (3) How to raise venture capital; (4) When and how to go public; (5) Perspectives. Also provides directories of United States and Canadian venture capital companies and U.S. underwriters specializing in small companies. Company and name indexes for U.S. venture capital companies.   HG65.P73

Standard and Poor's Corporation. Standard & Poor's Ratings guide: corporate bonds, commercial paper, municipal bonds, international securities. N.Y., McGraw-Hill, [1979]. 417p. il.   **CH580**

An attempt to explain "what ratings are and what they are and are not intended to do, illustrate the key general areas of analysis that are intrinsic to most ratings, highlight certain new areas, and provide copies (in the exhibits) of some of the internal tools we employ."—*Pref.* Appendixes provide definitions and samples of reports, worksheets, analyses, etc.   HG4651.S7

The stock market handbook: reference manual for the securities industry. Ed. by Frank G. Zarb and Gabriel T. Kerekes. Homewood, Ill., Dow Jones-Irwin, 1970. 1073p.   **CH581**

In five main sections: (1) The scope of the securities industry; (2) Securities; (3) The integrated securities firm; (4) The specialty securities house; and (5) Elements of investment decision making. Within sections, chapters have been contributed by specialists on all aspects of the securities industry. Includes a select glossary of stock market terms. Index.   HG4921.S794

Treasurer's handbook. Ed. by J. Fred Weston and Maurice B. Goudzwaard. Homewood, Ill., Dow Jones–Irwin, [1976]. 1181p. il.   **CH582**

More than fifty contributing authors have supplied chapters on current theory and practices written for the practicing treasurer. Most chapters include selected reading lists. Appendix of compound interest tables.   HG4026.T73

Statistics

The Dow Jones averages, 1885–1980. Ed. by Phyllis S. Pierce. Homewood, Ill., Dow Jones-Irwin, [1982]. unpaged (ca.380p.). il.   **CH583**

Presents a chronological list of tables for the Dow Jones industrial and transportation averages as they have appeared on a daily basis in the *Wall Street journal* since 1896 (publication before that date was irregular).   HG4915.D64

Fisher, Lawrence and **Lorie, James Hirsch.** A half-century of returns on stocks and bonds; rates of return on investments in common stocks and on U.S. Treasury securities, 1926–1976. Chicago, Univ. of Chicago Grad. School of Business, 1977. 174p.   **CH584**

Presents 51 tables showing annual estimates of rates of return on investments in portfolios of common stocks listed on the New York Stock Exchange, and on investments in U.S. Treasury securities. Rates are presented in current dollars and adjusted for changes in the Consumer Price Index. Based on a machine-readable data file at the Center for Research in Security Prices.   HG4915.F47

U.S. Board of Governors of the Federal Reserve System. Banking and monetary statistics, 1914–1941. Pt. I. Wash., [1976]. 682p.   **CH585**

—— Banking and monetary statistics, 1941–1970. Wash., [1976]. 1168p.   **CH586**

     HG2493.U54

—— All-bank statistics, United States, 1896–1955. [Wash., 1959] 1229p.   **CH587**

A comprehensive revision, based on *Banking and monetary statistics* (1943), giving statistics for all banks by class of bank and by state, with explanatory text.   HG2493.A517

—— Annual statistical digest, 1971/75– . Wash., [1976–]. Annual.   **CH588**

The 1914–41 volume is a reprint of pt.1 of the original 1943 edition and includes "data on the condition and operation of all banks . . ., statistics of bank debits, bank earnings, bank suspensions, branch, group, and chain banking, currency, money rates, security markets, Treasury finance, production and movement of gold, and international financial developments."—*Pref.* Some statistical series predate 1914. (Pt.II, detailing member bank statistics for each Federal Reserve district, was not reprinted.) This basic volume is amended and updated by the 1941–70 volume and by the *Annual statistical digest.* The latter also contains data previously published in the *Federal Reserve bulletin,* and which will no longer appear in that publication.   HG181.A1U55a

—— Federal Reserve bulletin. v.1– , 1915– . Wash., 1915– . Monthly.   **CH589**

The most complete current information, including statistics, on financial conditions in the United States. Also reports on financial developments in foreign countries.   HG2401.A5

U.S. Internal Revenue Service. Statistics of income. 1916– . Wash., Govt. Prt. Off., 1918– . Annual.   **CH590**

Issued by the Service under earlier names: 1916–26, Office of Commissioner of Internal Revenue; 1927–47, Bureau of Internal Revenue.

Beginning 1953, issued in varying number of parts, e.g., (1) Individual income tax returns; (2) Corporation income tax returns; (3) Sole proprietorship and partnership returns; and (4) Fiduciary income returns. Many years include supplements. A special supplement, *International income and taxes; corporation income tax returns,* has been published irregularly beginning 1961. Updated by *Statistics of income. SOI bulletin* (1981– ; quarterly).

HJ4652.A24

Annuals and directories

Bankers' almanac and year book . . . full particulars of the principal banks of the world. The standard international banking work of reference. London, Skinner, 1844– . Annual. **CH591**

Subtitle varies.
Directory of banks by country, with emphasis on British banks.

HG2984.B3

The Dow Jones investor's handbook. Princeton, N.J., Dow Jones Books, [1966]– . Annual. **CH592**

The 1966 volume offers a brief explanation of the Dow Jones averages and provides figures for the long period they have covered. Also includes a variety of other information on security-market indicators. Later volumes provide updated tables and a review of stock market activity of the previous year. HG4921.F3

International stock & commodity exchange directory, 1974/75 ed. Canaan, N.H., Phoenix Publishing, [1974]. 340p. **CH593**

Peter Wyckoff, comp.
A listing by country and city of the major stock and commodity exchanges. Information provided for each includes officers, hours, regulatory laws, issues traded and volume, unit of trading, memberships, commissions, and historical background. Section on related information has time zone designations, glossary; indexes by person, commodity, and name of exchange.

——— 1976 supplement. Canaan, N.H., [1976]. 53p.

Notes changes since the 1974/75 edition. HG4512.I57

Polk's World bank directory. 1895– . Nashville, Tenn., R. L. Polk & Co., 1895– . **CH594**

Title varies: v.1–59, 1895–1924, *The bankers encyclopedia;* v.60–114, 1924–51, *Polk's Bankers encyclopedia.*
Beginning 1971, issued in two parts: (1) International section (annual); and (2) North American section (semiannual). Kept up-to-date by cumulative supplements which are superseded by each new edition.
Covers United States and foreign banks with branches, giving: name, address, officers, directors, financial statement, and other banking data.

Rand McNally international bankers directory; the bankers blue book, 1872– . Chicago, Rand McNally, 1872– . v.1– . Semiannual. **CH595**

Information on United States and foreign banks, giving: name, address, official personnel, financial statement, governmental banking agencies, and their officials. HG2441.R3

Standard & Poor's Security dealers of North America. 1922– . N.Y., Standard and Poor's Corp., 1922– . Semiannual. **CH596**

Title varies.
Aims to provide an up-to-date listing of all stock and bond dealers in the United States and Canada. HG4907.S4

Stock exchange official year-book. London, Skinner, 1934– . Annual. **CH597**

Publisher varies. Supersedes the *Stock exchange year-book* and the *Stock exchange official intelligence.*
Some editions issued in 2v. Contains details of securities quoted on the London and other Federated Stock Exchanges, a classified list of quoted securities, particulars relating to stamp duties, scales of minimum stock exchange commissions, charges for stock exchange

quotation, trustee investments, and various statistics. Some recent issues include a list of parent companies and their subsidiaries.

HG5431.S82

Who is where in world banking, 1975/76– . London, Banker Research Unit, [1975–]. Irregular. **CH598**

Subtitle: A guide to the overseas representation of the world's major banks classified by financial centre.
Eds., Philip Thorn and Jean Lack.
A list by country and then by city of the overseas offices of the world's leading banks, providing name, status, and address.
A companion volume is: HG1536.W48

Who owns what in world banking, 1975/76– . London, Banker Research Unit, [1975–]. Annual. **CH599**

Subtitle: A guide to the subsidiary and affiliated interests of the world's major banks.
Eds., Philip Thorn and Jean Lack.
An alphabetical list of major individual and consortia banks. For each bank, domestic and international subsidiaries and affiliates are given, with percentage figures for the parent bank holdings. Index for all banks.

Biography

American Banker. Directory of U.S. banking executives. N.Y., Amer. Banker, 1980. 824p. **CH600**

In two sections: (1) brief biographies elicited from the biographee and edited to conform to format; (2) a bank affiliation index arranged by state and name of bank. HG2441.A57

Silver, A. David. Who's who in venture capital. N.Y., Wiley, [1984]. 378p. **CH601**

A directory of individuals and firms providing venture capital funds, with chapters giving advice on the means of raising venture capital. A new edition is announced for 1986. HG4963.S56

Who's who in banking; the directory of the banking profession. 1966–72. N.Y., Business Pr., [1966–72]. 3v. **CH602**

Biographical sketches of financial executives—mainly from commercial banks—of the United States, Puerto Rico, and the Virgin Islands. HG2463.A1W55

Who's who in world banking, 1975/76– . London, Financial Times, 1975– . Annual. **CH603**

J. B. Bonham, ed.
A biographical dictionary of more than 2,500 executive officers. Arrangement is by name, with an index arranged by country and by banks in each country.

Public finance

Bibliography

Bird, Richard Miller and **Terán C., Juan M.,** comps. Bibliography on taxation in developing countries. Cambridge, Law School of Harvard Univ., 1968. 184p. **CH604**

The main part of the volume is arranged by country, with subject divisions thereunder.

Knox, Vera H. Public finance: information sources. Detroit, Gale, [1964]. 142p. **CH605**

Arranged in chapters covering various aspects of public finance: revenues, expenditures, taxation, fiscal administration, and international public finance. Lists books, periodical articles, and documents, mostly published since 1960, with short annotations when needed. Includes lists of periodicals, services, and indexes. Author and subject indexes.   Z7164.F5K65

Owens, Elisabeth A., comp. Bibliography on taxation of foreign operations and foreigners. Cambridge, Law School of Harvard Univ., 1968. 92p.   **CH606**

A classified bibliography on international taxation, listing articles and books on "U.S. tax policies and rules governing foreign income, foreign transactions, foreigners, relief of double taxation, tax treaties, and the prevention of international tax evasion and avoidance."—*Pref.*
Updated by: KF6419.A1O9

———— and **Hovemeyer, Gretchen A.** Bibliography on taxation of foreign operations and foreigners, 1968–1975. Cambridge, Mass., Law School of Harvard Univ., 1976. 107p.   **CH606a**

———— ———— 1976–1982. Cambridge, Mass., Internat. Tax Program, Law School of Harvard Univ., 1983. 190p.   **CH606b**

The supplements omit general references to English-language materials on foreign tax laws.

Statistics

Government finance statistics yearbook. 1977– . Wash., Internat. Monetary Fund, [1977]– . Annual.   **CH607**

Offers detailed tables for each country on central government revenue, expenditure, lending, financing, and debt, plus similar but less detailed data for state and local government. Comparative statistics are presented in the form of world tables arranged by topic. *See also* CH609.   HJ101.G68

International Monetary Fund. Balance of payments statistics. Yearbook. 1st– , 1946/47– . Wash., 1949– . Annual.   **CH608**

Continues the annual *Balance of payments* issued 1926–45 by the Secretariat of the League of Nations. Sections issued monthly are superseded by a bound volume.
In two parts: country figures, and world totals for balance of payments components and aggregates.   HF1014.I5●

———— International financial statistics. v.1– , 1948– . Wash., Internat. Monetary Fund, 1948– . Monthly (with yearbook vol.).   **CH609**

Contains summary tables by subject—e.g., exchange rates, gold production, world trade, etc.— followed by very detailed tables for each country, describing its financial and monetary condition.   HG3881.I626●

National accounts statistics, 1982– . N.Y., United Nations, 1985– . Annual.   **CH610**

Continues *Yearbook of national accounts statistics* (1957–81) which superseded *Statistics of national income and expenditure* (1952–57).
1982 issued in 3v.: Main aggregates and detailed tables; Analysis of main aggregates; and Government accounts and tables.
Provides analysis of national accounts (gross domestic product, expenditures, income and outlay, etc.) by individual country, an international summary, and by government sector. Kept up-to-date by the United Nations *Monthly bulletin of statistics.*

Tax Foundation, Inc., New York. Facts and figures on government finance, 1941– . Englewood Cliffs, N.J., Prentice-Hall, 1941– . Biennial.   **CH611**

Title varies. Publisher varies.
Information about taxes, expenditures, and debt at federal, state, and local levels. Statistics also cover selected national economic series, social insurance programs, and government enterprise operations.   HJ257.T25

INSURANCE

Bibliography

Annotated readings in social security. Wash., U.S. Dept. of Health and Human Services, Social Security Admin., Off. of Policy, Off. of Research and Statistics, 1982. 600p. (SSA pubn. 13–11754)   **CH612**

1936–70 eds. entitled *Basic readings in social security.*
Includes books, articles, and government publications in classed arrangement. Brief annotations; author index.   Z7164.L1A63

Ferguson, Elizabeth, ed. Sources of insurance statistics. N.Y., Special Libraries Assoc., 1965. 191p.   **CH613**

A project of the Insurance Division, Special Libraries Association.
Provides references to published sources which appear on a regular, continuing basis. Detailed subject approach within sections for major types of insurance.
A revised edition was announced for 1985.   HG8045.F45

Four decades of international social security research: a bibliography of studies by the Social Security Administration, 1937–80. Wash., U.S. Dept. of Health and Human Services, Social Security Administration, Office of Policy, Office of Research and Statistics, 1981. 68p.   **CH614**

A bibliography of articles, research reports, essays and books published by the Social Security Administration. Arranged by country and subject.   Z7164.L1F68

Insurance Society of New York. Library. Life insurance catalog of the Library of the Insurance Society of New York. Boston, G. K. Hall, 1960. 352p.   **CH615**

Subject catalog of a library established in 1901, which in 1960 contained about 80,000 books, pamphlets, and periodicals.   Z7164.I7I82

International Social Security Administration. Documentation Service. Recueil documentaire. Documentation series. Genève, 1963–71. 4v.   **CH616**

Title and prefatory matter in French, English, Spanish, and German.
Contents: no.1, Liste universelle des périodiques de sécurité sociale (1963); no.2, Bibliographie universelle de sécurité sociale, 1960–1963 (1964); no.3, Liste universelle des périodiques de sécurité sociale [2d ed.] (1966); no.4, Aspects économiques de la sécurité sociale, recherche en matière de sécurité sociale, bibliographie (1971).

Nelli, Humbert O. and **Ewedemi, Soga.** A bibliography of insurance history. 2d ed. Atlanta, Publishing Services Division, School of Business Administration, Georgia State Univ., 1976. 115p. (Research monograph, School of Business Admin., Georgia State Univ., no.70)   **CH617**

Comp. from the Insurance History Collection at the Center for Insurance Research, Georgia State University.
1st ed. 1971.
A wide variety of types of material—company histories, periodicals, clippings, photographs, policies, etc.—is arranged by broad topic: fire insurance, life insurance, marine insurance, general insurance, friendly societies, guilds, notarial activities. International in scope; no index.   Z7164.I7N37

Soltow, Martha Jane and **Gravelle, Susan.** Worker benefits, industrial welfare in America, 1900–1935; an annotated bibliography. Metuchen, N.J., Scarecrow Pr., 1983. 230p.   **CH618**

A selective bibliography of 712 citations to secondary materials in topical arrangement, with indexing by company, personal, and corporate names.   Z7164.F8S66

Thomas, Roy Edwin. Insurance information sources. Detroit, Gale, [1971]. 332p.   **CH619**

A combination of bibliographic and directory information on

various aspects and types of insurance. Directory listings include schools, libraries, professional and trade organizations, publishers. There is a listing of insurance reference books, a list of insurance periodicals, and selected bibliographies (of books and some academic dissertations) on specific types of insurance (health insurance, group insurance, government and social insurance, life insurance, etc.). Author and subject index. Poorly organized and needs to be supplemented by other sources for periodical and current materials.

Z7164.I7T48

Current

Bibliographie universelle de sécurité sociale. World bibliography of social security. v.1– , 1963– . Genève, 1963– . Quarterly.   **CH620**

Title also in Spanish and German.

Prep. by the Documentation Service of the International Social Security Association.

Supersedes the "World bibliography of social security" issued as a special section of the Association's *Bulletin.*

In three parts: (1) comprehensive bibliography of non-periodical literature on social security; (2) selected listing of important articles and studies from social security periodicals; and (3) notes on social security legislation. Each section is arranged by country with a subject index in each issue.   Z7164.L1B52

Insurance and employee benefits literature, no.374– . N.Y., July/Aug. 1981– . Bimonthly.   **CH621**

Issued by Insurance and Employees Division, Special Libraries Association. Imprint varies.

Continues *Insurance literature* (Nov. 1961–May/June 1981), which superseded *Insurance book reviews,* April 1933–Oct. 1961.

Includes books, pamphlets, reprints, statistical annuals, and association proceedings in all branches of insurance, including economics of aging and social insurance. Author and title index.

Insurance periodicals index. 1963– . Boston, Special Libraries Assoc., Insurance Div., 1964– . Annual.   **CH622**

A cumulation of the index published monthly in the periodical *Insurance* through 1968, and thereafter in *Best's review.* Offers a subject index to articles in some 40 insurance periodicals. Author and geographical indexes.   HG8011.I545

A list of worthwhile life and health insurance books, 1968– . Wash., Amer. Council of Life Insurance [etc.], 1968– . Annual.   **CH623**

A selected, annotated list of books, currently in print, of interest to the general public, librarians, students of insurance, and those within the insurance business.   Z7164.I7L58

Social security abstracts. v.1– , 1965– . Geneva, International Social Security Association, 1965– . Semiannual.   **CH624**

Provides abstracts of selected, important listings from the Association's *Bibliographie universelle de sécurité sociale* (CH620). Abstracts are grouped according to the main branches of social security. About 150 abstracts are published per year; annual country, subject, and author indexes.

University Microfilms International. UMI life insurance index. v.1– , Mar. 1979– . Ann Arbor, Mich., Univ. Microfilms Internat., 1979– . Quarterly with annual cumulation.   **CH625**

Prep. in cooperation with the Million Dollar Round Table Information Retrieval Committee.

Provides abstracts for articles drawn from about 75 American periodicals, Internal Revenue Service documents, and news service updates. Author index provides full bibliographic data; abstracts appear in a subject index. The same publisher produces *Property & liability insurance index* (1980– ; quarterly with annual cumulation).   HG8771.U54a●

Dictionaries and encyclopedias

Davids, Lewis E. Dictionary of insurance. 6th ed. [Totowa, N.J.], Rowman & Allanheld, 1983. 338p.   **CH626**

1st ed. 1959.

Definitions of terms and phrases selected for the layman, the insurance company employee, and the student of insurance. Includes abbreviations and addresses of state insurance commissioners and insurance-related organizations.   HG8025.D3

Green, Thomas E., Osler, Robert W. and **Bickley, John S.** Glossary of insurance terms. [Santa Monica, Calif.], Merritt, [1980]. 234p.   **CH627**

Offers brief definitions, indicating usage according to the type of insurance involved—automobile, aviation, crime, general, health, inland and ocean marine, legal, liability, life, property, reinsurance, surety, and workers' compensation.   HG8025.G73

Levy, Michael H. A handbook of personal insurance terminology. Lynbrook, N.Y., Farnsworth, 1968. 595p.   **CH628**

A dictionary of "the language used in, by, and about the life and health insurance industry."—*p.v.*   HG8759.L4

Manes, Alfred. Versicherungslexikon, ein Nachschlagewerk für alle Wissensgebiete der gesamten Individual- und Sozial-Versicherung. 3. wesentlich erw. u. umgearb. Aufl. Berlin, Mittler, 1930. 1934 col.   **CH629**

1st ed., Tübingen, Mohr, 1909; Ergänzungsband, 1913; 2d ed., Berlin, Mittler, 1924.

An outstanding encyclopedia of the whole subject of insurance, with signed articles by specialists and bibliographies. Includes biographies of deceased persons. Now out-of-date, but no other work fully supersedes it.   HG8025.M2

Sachs, Wolfgang and **Drude, Günther.** Lebensversicherungstechnisches Wörterbuch: Deutsch, Englisch, Französisch, Italienisch, Spanisch. 2. Aufl. Karlsruhe, Verlag Versicherungswirtschaft, 1964. 308p.   **CH630**

Added title page in each language; English title: *Dictionary of actuarial and life insurance terms.*

1st ed., Würzburg, 1954.

Handbooks

Gregg, Davis Weinert and **Lucas, Vane B.** Life and health insurance handbook. 3d ed. Homewood, Ill., Richard D. Irwin, 1973. 1336p. il.   **CH631**

1st ed. 1959.

A series of chapters by specialists on all major phases of life and health insurance, including pensions, profit sharing, and estate planning. Most chapters have selected bibliographic references.   HG8769.G7

Social security handbook. [Ed.1]– . [Wash.], U.S. Dept. of Health, Education, and Welfare, Social Security Admin., 1960– . il. Irregular. (8th ed. 1984)   **CH632**

Subtitle: Retirement insurance, survivors insurance, disability insurance, health insurance, Supplemental Security Income, black lung benefits, public assistance.

Reflects current provisions of the Social Security Act, its regulations and case decisions in summary form; explains how programs operate, who is entitled to benefits, and how the benefits may be obtained.

Social security programs throughout the world, 1958– . Wash., U.S. Dept. of Health, Education and Welfare, Social Security Admin., Div. of Program Research, [1958]– . Irregular. (U.S. Social Security Admin. Div. of Research and Statistics. Research report; 1983 is report no.59)   **CH633**

Summarizes the social security programs for each country in tabular form.   HD7091.U62

Webster, Bryce and **Perry, Robert L.** The complete social security handbook. N.Y., Dodd, Mead, [1983]. 346p. il.
CH634

A guide to the United States benefit programs of Social Security, Medicare, Supplemental Security Income, and Medicaid, as well as private income sources for retirement. Illustrative forms and directory information on Medicare carriers, organizations for the elderly and disabled, Social Security regional offices. Glossary; bibliography; index.   HD7125.W43

Annuals

Insurance almanac; who, what, when and where in insurance, an annual of insurance facts. Ed.1– , 1913– . N.Y., Underwriter Pr. and Pub. Co., 1912– . Annual.   **CH635**

Title varies.
Includes directory information on insurance agents, brokers, organizations, state officials, insurance groups, etc. Formerly included a section of "Who's who in insurance," which has been issued as a separate volume since 1948 (CH637).   HG8019.I5

Spectator insurance year book. 1874–1962. Philadelphia, Spectator Co., 1874–1962. Annual.   **CH636**

Title varies; formerly *Insurance year book.*
Coverage varies; sections on fire, marine, casualty, and surety ceased with 1953/54.
Contains much directory and statistical information, together with some historical data.
Ceased with issue for 1962.

Who's who in insurance; a section of the Insurance almanac. N.Y., Underwriter Pr. and Pub. Co., 1948– . v.1– . Annual.   **CH637**

A continuation of the biographical section formerly appearing in the *Insurance almanac* (CH635).   HG8523.W5

Statistics

Best's Insurance reports. Life-health edition. 1906– . Morristown, N.J., A. M. Best Co., 1906– . Annual.   **CH638**

Title varies.
Presents "comprehensive statistical reports upon the financial position, history, and operating results of legal reserve life insurance companies, fraternal benefit societies, and assessment associations operating in the United States and Canada."—*Pref., 1973 ed.*
Companies are listed alphabetically in the main section; there is a listing by states, and a separate section for mutual funds.
A similar annual is published for property-casualty insurance: HG8943.B3082

Best's Insurance reports. Property-casualty edition. 1899/1900– . Morristown, N.J., A. M. Best, 1900– . Annual.   **CH639**

Title varies.   HG9655.B5

Insurance directory and year book (Post magazine almanack) containing statistics and facts of ordinary life, industrial life, fire, accident and marine insurance. 1931– . London, Buckley Pr., 1931– . Annual.   **CH640**

Title varies. *Post magazine almanack* established 1840.
Statistical and directory information for the United Kingdom.   HG8596.I53

Life insurance fact book. 1946– . N.Y., Institute of Life Insurance, 1946– . Annual.   **CH641**

Publisher varies.
Offers statistical tables, charts, and interpretive text on the life insurance business in the United States. Includes some brief historical information and a glossary/index.
A similar publication for Canada is published by the Canadian

Life Insurance Association in English and in French (*Canadian life insurance facts* and *Faits sur l'assurance-vie au Canada*).
Insurance facts, published annually by the Insurance Information Institute, New York City, presents similar data of general interest relating to property and liability insurance.   HG8943.L5

Metropolitan Life Insurance Company. Statistical bulletin. Jan. 1920– . N.Y., 1920– . v.1– . Quarterly.   **CH642**

Frequency varies.
Each issue includes three or more statistical reports on selected aspects of morbidity and mortality, disability, birth rates, leading causes of death, etc. Some reports and projections are based on Metropolitan policyholder figures, others are from government or other standard sources. Annual index.   HG8963.M5A3

Social security bulletin. v.1– , Mar. 1938– . Wash., Social Security Administration, 1938– . Monthly.   **CH643**

Statistical data for each year, 1939–48, were published in the Administration's *Social security yearbooks,* 1940–49. Supplements, with data for each year, 1949–54, were included in the Sept. *Bulletin,* 1950–55; beginning with 1955 data, the *Supplement* is a separate publication: HD7123.S56

—— Annual statistical supplement. 1955– . Annual.

LABOR AND INDUSTRIAL RELATIONS

Guides

Soltow, Martha Jane and **Sokkar, Jo Ann Stehberger.** Industrial relations and personnel management: selected information sources. Metuchen, N.J., Scarecrow Pr., 1979. 286p.   **CH644**

An annotated bibliography of almost 800 reference sources. A section on general sources of information is followed by 16 topical subdivisions. Emphasizes U.S. publications. Personal name, title, and subject indexes.   Z7164.L1S684

Bibliography

Allen, Victor Leonard. International bibliography of trade unionism. [London], Merlin, [1968]. 180p.   **CH645**

More than 1,600 items in classed arrangement with author index. Includes only material published since 1940.   Z7164.T7A38

Azevedo, Ross E. Labor economics: a guide to information sources. Detroit, Gale, 1978. 261p. (Economics information guide ser., 8)   **CH646**

Focuses on labor economics in the United States. In three major parts: (1) textbooks and anthologies; (2) journals; (3) subject sections listing first books, then journal articles, in chronological order. Most publications date from 1950 to 1974. Indexed.   Z7164.L1A87

Bain, George Sayers and **Woolven, G. B.** Bibliography of British industrial relations. Cambridge & N.Y., Cambridge Univ. Pr., [1979]. 665p.   **CH647**

An impressive attempt to compile "all the secondary source material . . . published in English between 1880 and 1970 on British industrial relations. It includes books, pamphlets, articles . . . , theses, and government reports. The subject is broadly defined to cover . . . the traditional topics of trade unionism and labour-management relations . . . and relevant material from such disciplines as industrial psychology, industrial sociology, labour economics, labour history, labour law, personnel management, and social administration."—*Pref.* Includes material on England, Scotland, Wales, Northern Ireland, and the Republic of Ireland. Detailed subject classification; indexed by name and title. About 15,000 references. A supplement covering 1971–79 was published 1985.   Z7164.L1B26

Burnett, John, Vincent, David and **Mayall, David.** The autobiography of the working class: an annotated, critical bibliography. N.Y., New York Univ. Pr., 1984– . v.1– . (In progress) **CH648**

Contents: v.1, 1790–1900.

v.1 offers abstracts of 804 memoirs from England, Scotland and Wales; other types of life histories which are not strictly autobiographical are classed by occupation in an appendix. Author arrangement; indexed by place, occupation, education, and dates. A second volume is to cover 1900–45. Z7164.L1B95

Cayer, N. Joseph and **Dickerson, Sherry S.** Labor management relations in the public sector: an annotated bibliography. N.Y., Garland, 1984. 395p. (Public affairs and administration, v.7; Garland reference library of social science, v.168) **CH649**

A topical bibliography of 1,599 entries, classed first by form (articles, books and monographs), then by content. Focuses on scholarly literature published since 1962. Indexed by author and subject. Z7164.I7C39

Chamberlin, Waldo. Industrial relations in Germany, 1914–1939; annotated bibliography of materials in the Hoover Library on War, Revolution, and Peace and the Stanford University Library. Stanford, Calif., Stanford Univ. Pr., [1942]. 403p. (Repr.: N.Y., AMS Pr., 1974) **CH650**

Lists 1,720 items with full bibliographic information and detailed annotations. Includes sections for documents, society publications, newspaper and periodical publications, monographs, studies, articles. Indexed. Z7164.L1C5

Chan, Ming K. Historiography of the Chinese labor movement, 1895–1949: a critical survey and bibliography of selected Chinese source materials at the Hoover Institution. Stanford, Calif., Hoover Institution Pr., [1981]. 232p. (Hoover Pr. bibliographical ser., 60) **CH651**

Pts. I and II are bibliographical essays on the general labor situation and the history of the Chinese labor movement. Pt. III, "Selected bibliography," lists alphabetically the 728 titles covered in the survey; no periodical articles are cited. Author and subject indexes. Z3108.L3C4

Cornell University. New York State School of Industrial and Labor Relations. Library. Library catalog. Boston, G. K. Hall, 1967. 12v. **CH652**

The library's collection included some 78,000 volumes and bound periodicals and 80,000 pamphlets at the time of publication of the catalog. All of the books, a selected number of the more important pamphlets, and author and subject entries for selected articles from 150 periodicals since 1952 are represented in this photographic reproduction of the catalog cards. Periodical titles and holdings are not included.

All additions for the Aug. 1966–Sept. 1974 period are represented in *Cumulation of the library catalog supplements of the New York State School of Industrial and Labor Relations, Martin P. Catherwood Library, Cornell University* (Boston, G. K. Hall, 1976. 9v.). Annual supplements were published 1977–82. Z7164.L1C84

Dale, Leon Andrew. A bibliography of French labor, with a selection of documents on the French labor movement. N.Y., A. M. Kelley, 1969. 317p. **CH653**

Coverage is less comprehensive than would be expected. Includes some listings through 1967. Books and articles are listed by author in separate sections; subject index. Z7164.T7D3

Dowe, Dieter. Bibliographie zur Geschichte der deutschen Arbeiterbewegung, sozialistischen und kommunistischen Bewegung von den Anfängen bis 1863. Unter Berücksichtigung der politischen wirtschaftlichen und sozialen Rahmenbedingungen; mit einer Einleitung Berichtszeitraum 1945–1975. 3., wesentl. erw. u. verb. Aufl. bearb. von Volker Mettig. Bonn-Bad Godesberg, Verlag Neue Gesellschaft, [1981]. 358p. (Archiv für Sozialgeschichte, Beiheft 5) **CH654**

1st ed. 1976.

An international bibliography of 3,286 citations in classed arrangement with author and main-entry title indexes.

Continued by: Z7164.L1D68

Bibliographie zur Geschichte der deutschen Arbeiterschaft und Arbeiterbewegung 1863 bis 1914: Berichtszeitraum 1945 bis 1975; mit einer forschungsgeschichtlichen Einleitung. Hrsg. Klaus Tenfelde, Gerhard A. Ritter. Bonn, Verlag Neue Gesellschaft, [1981]. 687p. (Archiv für Sozialgeschichte, Beiheft 8) **CH655**

Offers 7,100 citations to articles, dissertations, monographs and essays in classed arrangement; indexed by place name and author.

Continued by: Z7164.L1B54

Klotzbach, Kurt. Bibliographie zur Geschichte der deutschen Arbeiterbewegung, 1914–1945: Sozialdemokratie, christlich-soziale Bewegungen, kommunistische Bewegung und linke Splittergruppen: mit einer forschungsgeschichtlichen Einleitung. 3. wesent. erw. und verb. Aufl., bearb. von Volker Mettig. Bonn, Verlag Neue Gesellschaft, 1981. 394p. (Archiv für Sozialgeschichte, Beiheft 2) **CH656**

1st ed. 1974.

An international bibliography of 3,945 citations arranged by chronological period, then topically; author index.

HD8450.Z99K58x

Dwyer, Richard E. Labor education in the U.S.: an annotated bibliography. Metuchen, N.J., Scarecrow Pr., 1977. 274p. **CH657**

A listing, with very brief annotations, of periodical articles, parts of conference proceedings and ERIC materials produced from 1914 to 1976 on the three stages of labor education: (1) worker's education (1900–1940s); (2) labor education (post-World War II to the late 1960s); (3) labor studies (late 1960s to the present). Also lists archival and oral history collections. Author and subject indexes. Z5184.A24D95

Ente per la Storia del Socialismo e del Movimento Operaio Italiano. Bibliografia del socialismo e del movimento operaio italiano. Roma, Torino, Ed. E.S.M.O.I., 1956–68. il. 2v. in 6. **CH658**

Contents: v.1, pts.1–2, Periodici; v.2, pts.1–4, Libri, opuscoli, articoli, almanacchi, numeri unici (pts.1–3, A–Z; pt.4, Appendix and indexes of names cited and of subjects).

v.1 is a comprehensive listing of the serial publications of Italian socialism, labor parties, workers' movements, unions, etc., issued from 1848 to 1950. Based entirely upon the holdings of the Biblioteca Nazionale Centrale di Firenze; includes 3,866 items with full bibliographical description. Arranged alphabetically with indexes by political parties, trades, date of founding, place of publication, personal names, etc. v.2 is an alphabetical list—by author or title—of books, pamphlets, articles, and unique items published from 1815 to 1952. Locates copies in 90 Italian libraries.

A projected third volume listing government documents has not been published. Z7164.S67E5

——— ——— Roma, Edizioni E.S.S.M.O.I., 1975–76. v.2 suppl. in 2v.

Contents: v.2, Libri, opuscoli, articoli, almanacchi, numeri unici (Supplemento 1953–67). In two parts: I, A–L; II, M–Z.

Continues the alphabetical arrangement—by author or title—of items published 1953–67; gives locations in Italian libraries.

Fink, Gary M. State labor proceedings: a bibliography of the AFL, CIO, and AFL-CIO proceedings, 1885–1974, held in the AFL-CIO Library. Westport, Conn., Greenwood Pr., [1975]. 291p. **CH659**

Mary Mills, comp.

A guide to the publisher's microfiche collection of the proceedings (which will be updated and made available on a continuing basis). Pt.1 of the guide provides brief chronological surveys of each state labor movement, with annotations of the types of issues discussed in convention proceedings. Pt.2 is the bibliography of convention proceedings, yearbooks, minutes of executive board meetings, etc., listed alphabetically by state.   HD8055.A6F55

Geneva. International Institute for Labour Studies. Bibliography on major aspects of the humanisation of work and the quality of working life. 2d ed. Geneva, International Labour Office, 1978. 300p.   **CH660**

1st ed. 1977.

Major bibliographic work undertaken by Rose Marie Greve.

Presents a subject arrangement of about 2,000 titles in the areas of job satisfaction, new forms of work organization (such as participation in management and flexible working hours), social indicators of the quality of working life, etc. Author index.   Z7164.L1G38

Gulick, Charles Adams, Ockert, Roy A. and **Wallace, Raymond J.** History and theories of working-class movements; a select bibliography. Berkeley, Calif., Bureau of Business and Economic Research and Inst. of Industrial Relations, Univ. of California, [1955]. 364p.   **CH661**

Lists articles, notes, and occasional documents in periodicals culled from the files of the University of California Library, covering the years 1800–1953. Area coverage is worldwide, but only articles in English are included.

Arrangement is by region and country (with approximately one third of the total devoted to Great Britain), subdivided by subject. No annotations and no indexes.   Z7164.L1G8

Hepple, B. A., Neeson, J. M. and **O'Higgins, Paul.** A bibliography of the literature on British and Irish labour law. [London], Mansell, 1975. 331p.   **CH662**

Attempts to cover "all the relevant literature concerned with the legal relationships of people at work" (*Introd.*) in England, Wales, Scotland, Northern Ireland and the Republic of Ireland. Includes "the individual relationship between worker and employer . . ., the payment of wages, hours, holidays and other conditions of employment . . .; protective legislation . . .; compensation for accidents and diseases . . .; training and vocational education . . .; unemployment . . .; collective bargaining . . .; industrial conflict . . .; organisation of employers and workers . . .; and certain international aspects of direct relevance to Great Britain and Ireland."—*Introd.* Classed arrangement with author and subject indexes. Mainly English-language materials (books and periodical articles) from the 18th century through the end of 1972. More than 4,500 items; library locations are given for books and pamphlets.

A supplement was published as *Labour law in Great Britain and Ireland to 1978*, by B. A. Hepple and others (London, Sweet and Maxwell, 1981. 131p.).   KD3001.H46

International Labour Office. Library. Bibliographic contributions, no.1– . Geneva, Internat. Labour Off., 1949– . Irregular.   **CH663**

Among the useful titles in this series are: *Catalogue of publications in English of the International Labour Office, 1919–1950* (no.5; 1955); *Subject guide to publications of the International Labour Office, 1919–1964* (no.25; 1967); *Bibliography on labour law* (no.13; 1958); *Bibliography on the International Labour Organisation* (no.19; 1959); *Bibliography on research sources on labour questions* (no.24; 1965); and *Bibliography of women workers* (no.26; 1970).

McBrearty, James C. American labor history and comparative labor movements; a selected bibliography. Tucson, Univ. of Arizona Pr., [1973]. 262p.   **CH664**

Pt.I, "Books," subdivides American labor history by chronological period and by topic, and comparative labor movements by country; pt.II, "Articles," follows the same format. There is a separate section for novels. Limited to English-language materials. Author index.   Z7164.L1M15

Martens, George R. African trade unionism: a bibliography with a guide to trade union organizations and publications. Boston, G. K. Hall, [1977]. 119p.   **CH665**

About 1,000 titles published from the mid-1940s through early 1977 are arranged by country studied, with some annotations. Also provides directory information for 82 national and pan-African

trade unions, and a survey of 57 labor newspapers and periodicals published by these organizations. Name index.   Z7164.T7M37

Morris, James Oliver and **Córdova, Efrén.** Bibliography of industrial relations in Latin America. Ithaca, New York State School of Industrial and Labor Relations, Cornell Univ., [1967]. 290p. (Cornell industrial and labor relations bibliography ser., 8)   **CH666**

In addition to industrial relations, the bibliography covers labor law and economics, manpower problems, aspects of union history, and social security. A general section is followed by a section for individual countries, each with topical subdivisions. Lacks an index.   Z7164.L1M69

Mouvements ouvriers et socialistes: chronologie et bibliographie. Collection dirigée par É. Dolléans et M. Crozier. Paris, Les Éditions Ouvrières, [1950–59]. 5v. in 6.   **CH667**

Contents: [v.1], Angleterre, France, Allemagne, États-Unis, 1750–1918, [par] Édouard Dolléans et Michel Crozier (1950); [v.2], L'Italie, des origines à 1922, [par] Alfonso Leonetti (1952); [v.3], L'Espagne, 1750–1936, [par] Renée Lamberet (1953); [v.4], La Russie, [par] Eugène Zaleski: t.1, 1725–1907; t.2, 1908–1917 (1956); [v.5], L'Amérique latine, 1492–1936, [par] Carlos M. Rama (1959).

Each volume is arranged chronologically by period. Under each period there is a chronology of events important to the labor movement, followed by a bibliography listing documents, newspapers, books, and pamphlets, including official publications. v.1 and v.4 have indexes of names cited; the other volumes have no indexes.   Z7161.M64

Naas, Bernard G. American labor unions' constitutions and proceedings: a guide to the microform edition, 1836–1978. Glen Rock, N.J., Microfilming Corp. of America, 1980. 128p.   **CH668**

Independently useful as a bibliography of constitutions and proceedings of American labor unions as well as serving as a key to the microform collection. Arranged by broad subject groups (e.g., clothing, transportation, communications, etc.), with keyword index. Kept up to date by annual supplements.   Z7164.L1M62

Neufeld, Maurice F., Leab, Daniel J. and **Swanson, Dorothy.** American working class history: a representative bibliography. N.Y., Bowker, 1983. 356p.   **CH669**

Rev. ed. of Neufeld's *A representative bibliography of American labor history* (1964).

An international bibliography of 7,261 entries on United States labor history. Chapters offer historical, regional, and topical approaches, including sections on 37 major specific occupations, trades, and industries. Sources cited include theses, films, and literary works, as well as books, articles, government reports, union documents. Name index.

Supplemented by an annual bibliography of articles and dissertations in the Fall issue of *Labor history.*   Z7164.L1N54

Peck, Theodore P. Employee counseling in industry and government: a guide to information sources. Detroit, Gale, [1979]. 121p. (Management information guide, 37)   **CH670**

In three main parts: (1) a directory of private organizations and government agencies concerned with management and personnel administration; (2) a bibliography of literature on personnel counseling, including the special areas of alcoholism, drug abuse, executive stress, retirement, career development, and women; (3) lists of related journals, abstracting and indexing services, directories, and databases. Subject index.   HF5549.5.C8P4

Pettman, B. O. Industrial democracy: a selected bibliography. Bradford, West Yorks., Eng., MCB Pubns., [1978]. 95p. (Institute of Scientific Business. Bibliography, no.11)   **CH671**

About 3,000 international references are grouped under 73 countries and further classified by form—books, articles, theses, or government documents. Author index.   Z7164.L1P438

Preisberg, Rolf-Dieter. Bevölkerung und Beschäftigung im Vorderen Orient: eine bibliographische Einführung. Population and labour in the Middle East: a bibliographic introduction. Hamburg, Deutsches Orient-Institut im Verbund der Stiftung Deutsches Übersee-Institut, Dokumentations-Leitstelle Moderner Orient, 1978. 160p. (Dokumentationsdienst moderner Orient; Reihe A, 9) **CH672**

An annotated bibliography of a wide variety of international literature produced during the last 20 years. Geographical arrangement includes countries of North Africa, the Middle East, Turkey, Iran, Afghanistan, and Pakistan. Subject and author indexes.
Z7164.D3P84

Raffa, Frederick A., Haulman, Clyde A. and **Hosni, Djehane A.** United States employment and training programs: a selected annotated bibliography. Westport, Conn., Greenwood Pr., [1983]. 154p. **CH673**

Major focus is on the Comprehensive Employment and Training Act (CETA), with some attention to pre-CETA programs and other programs from the mid-1960s to the present. 248 citations to books, journal articles, reports, and U.S. government documents (with SuDocs or NTIS number, as appropriate); main entry listing with author and subject indexes. Z7164.L1R33

Reynolds, Lloyd George and **Killingsworth, Charles C.** Trade union publications: the official journals, convention proceedings, and constitutions of international unions and federations, 1850–1941. Baltimore, Johns Hopkins Pr., 1944–45. 3v. **CH674**

Contents: v.1, Description and bibliography; v.2–3, Subject index, A–Z.
Based on the collections in the U.S. Dept. of Labor Library, the John Crerar Library, and the Johns Hopkins University Library.
Z7164.T7R4

Smith, Harold. The British labour movement to 1970; a bibliography. [London], Mansell, [1981]. 250p. **CH675**

A subject listing of books, pamphlets, and periodical articles published between 1945 and 1970 on British labor history, excluding works on industrial relations (for which *see* Bain and Woolven's *Bibliography of British industrial relations,* CH647). Chapters on general works, history and theory of socialism, early radicalism (Luddism, Peterloo, Chartism), the Labour Party and Labour governments, related organizations such as the Fabian Society, trade unionism, cooperative societies. More than 3,800 citations; name index. Z7164.L1S47

Tamiment Library. Catalog of the Tamiment Institute Library of New York University. Boston, G. K. Hall, 1980. 4v. **CH676**

Reproduction of the catalog cards for a rich collection of materials relating to American labor history, workers' education movements, socialism, communism, anarchism, and American radicalism. Lists books, pamphlets, and periodicals—mainly 19th and 20th century publications acquired by the Rand School during its period of existence, 1906–56. Books are entered by author and in a classified shelflist arrangement; pamphlets are listed in an author/title arrangement and in a separate subject arrangement. There are separate alphabetical listings of periodicals and of manuscript collections, as well as author and subject indexes to the *International socialist review* and *Mother earth.* A *Guide to the manuscript collection of the Tamiment Library* was published 1977 (N.Y., Garland; 82p.).

Tremblay, Louis-Marie. Bibliographie des relations du travail au Canada (1940–1967). Montréal, Presses de l'Université de Montréal, 1969. 242p. **CH677**

An annotated bibliography of 1,269 items. Classed arrangement; author and subject indexes. Z7165.C2T72

U.S. Bureau of Labor. Index of all reports issued by bureaus of labor statistics in the United States prior to March 1902, prep. by Carroll D. Wright. Wash., Govt. Prt. Off., 1902. 287p. (Repr.: N.Y., Johnson, 1970) **CH678**

Indexes the reports of the federal and various state bureaus, whatever their designation, which published labor statistics.
Z7164.L1U6

U.S. Bureau of Labor Statistics. BLS publications, 1886–1971. [By Rosalie K. Epstein] Wash., U.S. Dept. of Labor, Bureau of Labor Statistics, 1972. 184p. (*Its* Bulletin, no.1749) **CH679**

Contains a numerical listing of all bulletins since 1886 and all reports since 1953, a list of current periodicals, and a subject index of bulletins and reports.
Continued by: Z7164.L1U6672

———— ———— 1972–1977. [By Rosalie K. Epstein] Wash., U.S. Dept. of Labor, Bureau of Labor Statistics, 1978. 42p. (*Its* Bulletin, no. 1990)

U.S. Dept. of Labor. Library. United States Department of Labor library catalog. Boston, G. K. Hall, 1975. 38v.
CH680

A dictionary catalog representing more than 535,000 volumes, including books, periodicals, government reports, labor union publications, microforms, and cassettes. The collection deals with "the history of the labor movement; labor economics and industrial relations; arbitration, conciliation and mediation; labor laws; employment and unemployment; labor force and labor market; unemployment insurance; workmen's compensation; apprenticeship and training; wages and hours; working conditions; women's employment; industrial hygiene and safety; wholesale and retail prices; cost of living, productivity and other related subjects."—*Pref.* Extensive use of analytics. Z7164.L1U686

Walsh, Ruth M. and **Birkin, Stanley J.** Job satisfaction and motivation: an annotated bibliography. Westport, Conn., Greenwood Pr., 1979. 643p. **CH681**

Cites about 950 English-language books, periodical articles, dissertations, and research reports. In three parts: (1) author index; (2) keyword-in-context subject index; (3) abstracts. Most of the material was published in the late 1960s and 1970s. Z7164.C81W25

Wisconsin. State Historical Society. Library. Subject catalog; including the Pamphlet subject catalog beginning in volume 22. Westport, Conn., Greenwood Pr., [1971]. 23v.
CH682

"Pamphlets acquired through 1967 are listed in the Subject catalog; those acquired since 1967 are in the Pamphlet subject catalog."
Reproduces the subject catalog cards for works in the general collection, selected federal and state government publications, Wisconsin obituaries since 1846, biographical sketches in Wisconsin county histories published before 1955, and selected analytics for articles published in Wisconsin periodicals and learned journals; broadsides, street maps, paper manuscripts and photographs were excluded. The *Author-title catalog* (including City directory catalog, the Atlas catalogs—publishers and geographic, the Newspaper catalog and the Newspaper catalog (Labor) was produced by the same publisher on microfiche (1974; 600 sheets). Z1236.W57

Woodbridge, Mark E. American Federation of Labor and Congress of Industrial Organizations pamphlets, 1889–1955: a bibliography and subject index to the pamphlets held in the AFL-CIO Library. Westport, Conn., Greenwood Pr., [1977]. 73p. **CH683**

For each of the two unions, pamphlets are listed chronologically and alphabetically by title within the year; subject index covers both collections. Includes more than 1,300 pamphlets. Z7164.L1W66

Current

See also CC246.

Bibliographie zur Geschichte der deutschen Arbeiterbewegung. Jahrg. 1– , 1976– . Bonn-Bad Godesberg, Verlag Neue Gesellschaft GmbH., 1976– . Quarterly. **CH684**

Hrsg.: Bibliothek des Archivs der Sozialen Demokratie (Friedrich-Ebert-Stiftung).

A current international bibliography of writings (both book and periodical materials) on the German workers' movement. Classed arrangement with author and subject indexes. Citations are printed on perforated pages so that they can be re-arranged as a 3×5 card file or kept in bound-volume form.   Z7164.L1B53

Employment relations abstracts. 1958–72. Detroit, Information Service, 1958–72. Monthly. Looseleaf.   **CH685**

Frequency varies.

Continues *Labor-personnel index* (1950–58). Offers brief abstracts of current books and selected articles from approximately 250 journals in the field of labor relations. Arranged under 20 broad categories with separate, detailed subject guide.

Continued by: Z7164.C81L135

Work related abstracts, 1973– . Detroit, Information Coordinators, 1973– . Looseleaf. Monthly.   **CH686**

Provides abstracts for periodical articles only. The subject index cumulates quarterly and annually.   Z7164.L1W68

Periodicals

Harrison, Royden John, Woolven, Gillian B. and **Duncan, Robert.** The Warwick guide to British labour periodicals 1790–1970; a check list. [Hassocks, Eng.], Harvester Pr.; [Atlantic Highlands, N.J.], Humanities Pr., [1977]. 685p.
                                        CH687

"By a *Labour periodical* we understand one which falls into one or other of the following three categories: First, one which was produced by an organised body consisting wholly or mainly of wage-earners or collectively dependent employees. . . . Second, . . . all periodicals which were produced in the avowed interest of the working class. . . . Third, . . . those which were produced for wage-earners by members of other social classes who sought to improve them, instruct them, or entertain them."—*Introd.*

An alphabetical listing of some 4,125 titles, giving (as far as the information was available) dates of publication, volumes or issues published, sponsoring body, library locations, a code letter indicating character of the journal, and often, a descriptive or explanatory note. Subject index (which includes names of sponsoring agency or organization) and index of dates.   Z7164.L1H37

Milan. Istituto Giangiacomo Feltrinelli. Bibliografia della stampa periodica operaia e socialista italiana (1860–1926). Milano, Feltrinelli, 1956–61. 3v.   **CH688**

Contents: I periodici di Milano: bibliografia e storia, 1860–1904, 1905–1926 (publ. 1956–61 in 2v.; called v.3, pt.1–2); I periodici di Messina: bibliografia e storia, a cura di Gino Cerrito (publ. 1961).

Arranged chronologically, with full bibliographical detail and historical description of each periodical. Indexed by title, personal name, and place of publication.

Naas, Bernard G. and **Sakr, Carmelita S.** American labor union periodicals: a guide to their location. Ithaca, N.Y., Cornell Univ., 1956. 175p.   **CH689**

"Published by the New York State School of Industrial and Labor Relations . . . for the Committee of University Industrial Relations Librarians."—*verso of title page.*

A union list of more than 1,700 labor union periodicals to be found in about 20 cooperating libraries.   Z7164.L1N14

Wisconsin. State Historical Society. Labor papers on microfilm; a combined list. Madison, 1965. 66p.   **CH690**

First issued 1951 as a list of labor papers microfilmed by and available from the State Historical Society of Wisconsin; later editions enlarged to include films prepared by other libraries.

Locates master negatives from which positive copies may be ordered; does not include listings for positive copies. Generally limited to titles published in the United States. Includes official serial publications and journals of various labor unions, as well as a broad selection of local labor papers.   Z7164.L1W57

Dissertations

See also CH39.

Fox, Milden J. and **Howard, Patsy Cliffene.** Labor relations and collective bargaining; a bibliographic guide to doctoral research. Metuchen, N.J., Scarecrow Pr., 1983. 281p.
                                        CH691

An author list of 2,700 doctoral dissertations drawn from *Dissertation abstracts international* and the *Comprehensive dissertation index* with bibliographic references to citations in those volumes. Keyword and phrase index.   Z7164.L1F69

Gilbert, Victor F. Labour and social history theses: American, British and Irish university theses and dissertations in the field of British and Irish labour history, presented between 1900 and 1978. [London], Mansell, [1982]. 194p.
                                        CH692

A classed bibliography of North American doctoral dissertations and British and Irish doctoral theses, master's essays, and special studies; indexed by persons, places, subjects, and authors. Updated annually in the Autumn issue of the *Bulletin* of the Society for the Study of Labour History.   Z7164.L1G5

Indexes and abstract journals

Index to labor articles, v.1–27. N.Y., Rand School of Social Science, 1926–53. Monthly; bimonthly.   **CH693**

Ceased publication with Sept./Oct. 1953.

Classified arrangement with no cumulations and no author index. Indexes labor articles in general periodicals and in some labor papers not indexed elsewhere. From the labor point of view.
                                        Z7164.L1I38

The University of Michigan index to labor union periodicals: a cumulative subject index to materials from a selected list of newspapers and journals published by major labor unions. Jan. 1960–Feb. 1969. Ann Arbor, Univ. of Michigan, Bureau of Industrial Relations, 1960–69. Monthly, with annual cumulation.   **CH694**

An annotated subject index to 50 labor union periodicals. Ceased publication.   Z7164.T7U6

Encyclopedias and handbooks

American Federation of Labor. American Federation of Labor; history, encyclopedia, reference book . . . publ. by authority of the 1916 and 1917 conventions. Wash., 1919–60. 3v. in 4. il. (Repr.: Westport, Conn., Greenwood Pr., 1977)   **CH695**

Covers subjects considered at conventions of the AFL, with abstract of the actions taken or opinion expressed, and references to sources. v.1 includes 1881–1918; v.2, 1919–23; v.3, 1924–55, when the AFL merged with the CIO to form a new union. General index.
                                        HD8055.A5A42

First facts of American labor: a comprehensive collection of labor firsts in the United States. Arr. by subject, fully indexed, [and comp. by] Philip S. Foner. N.Y., Holmes & Meier, [1984]. 237p.   **CH696**

A dictionary of labor "firsts"; no cited sources or bibliographic references.   HD8066.F55

International handbook of industrial relations: contemporary developments and research. Westport, Conn., Greenwood Pr., [1981]. 698p.   **CH697**

Albert A. Blum, ed.

Presents 28 essays by scholars and specialists on worker-management relations in individual countries (one essay treats Scandinavia as a unit). Most chapters discuss historical background, labor law, conflicts and strikes, government's role, trade unions, employers' organizations, etc. Brief bibliographies; indexed.   HD6971.I62

International labor profiles. Detroit, Grand River Books, [1981]. 297p. il.   **CH698**

Subtitle: Comprehensive reports on the labor forces of 40 key nations, including data on wage and hour standards, labor organizations, social benefit programs, governmental regulations, and other labor-related topics.

Reprints reports from the *Country labor profiles* published periodically by the Bureau of International Labor Affairs, U.S. Dept. of Labor. A second volume or an expanded and updated second edition will be published when material is ready on the remaining countries. Sketches include data on government, population, education and training, public health, employment, industrial relations (labor and employer organizations, collective bargaining) labor standards, wages, hours and level of living, social security. Brief bibliographies.   HD4901.I56

Labor unions. Ed. in chief, Gary M. Fink. Westport, Conn., Greenwood Pr., [1977]. 520p. (Greenwood encyclopedia of American institutions, 1)   **CH699**

Offers "historical sketches of more than two hundred national unions and labor federations that have been part of the American labor movement."—*Pref.* Selection criteria included "longevity, historical significance, size and economic power, and the influence a particular union had in the development of organized labor in America. An effort was also made to include unions representative of most minority groups, trades and industries, chronological time periods, and ideological movements."—*Pref.* Includes bibliographic references.   HD6508.L234

Lees-Smith, Hastings Bertrand, ed. The encyclopaedia of the labour movement. London, Caxton, [1928]. 3v. il. (Repr.: Detroit, Gale, 1971)   **CH700**

Now out-of-date, but useful historically.   HD4839.L4

Marsh, Arthur Ivor. Concise encyclopedia of industrial relations: with bibliography. [Farnborough, Eng.], Gower Pr., [1979]. 423p.   **CH701**

First publ. 1973 as *Dictionary of industrial relations.*

A dictionary relating to industrial relations in the United Kingdom. Each entry usually includes a bibliographic reference; the references (about 1,200) are listed in the bibliography (p.355–423), grouped by form.   HD4839.M34

Marsh, Arthur I. and **Ryan, Victoria.** Historical directory of trade unions. [Westmead, Hants., Eng.], Gower, [1980]–84. v.1–2. (In progress)   **CH702**

Contents: v.1, Non-manual unions; v.2, Including unions in engineering, shipbuilding, and minor metal trades, coal mining, and iron and steel, agriculture, fishing, and chemicals.

As far as possible, the entry for each union intends to include: (1) Name; (2) Foundation date (together with name changes, amalgamations, cessation, etc.); (3) Characteristics (i.e., membership, leadership, policy, outstanding events, etc.); (4) Sources of information (books, articles, minutes, location of documentation).

Further volumes are to cover: v.3, Trade unions in transport and construction; v.4, Trade unions in textiles, printing, retail distribution, and miscellaneous industries.   HD6664.M26

Paradis, Adrian A. and **Paradis, Grace D.** The labor almanac. Littleton, Colo., Libraries Unlimited, 1983. 205p.   **CH703**

A compendium on the United States labor movement, including: historical chronology since 1636; directory of national unions and organizations; register of leaders; federal labor laws; federal government agencies; state agencies; bibliographic and statistical sources. Indexed.   HD8072.5.P37

Rifkin, Bernard and **Rifkin, Susan** American labor sourcebook. [N.Y.], McGraw-Hill, [1979]. 896p. il.   **CH704**

An effort to provide a 1-volume compendium on the subject matter of American labor. Offers directory information on labor organizations and government agencies concerned with labor; a chronology of labor developments in 1977 and 1978; significant legislative texts and summaries of legislation and court decisions; a brief history; information on labor in the public sector and in other countries; statistics. Much of the material is reprinted from Department of Labor and Bureau of Labor Statistics publications. Indexed.   HD8072.R53

Vetter, Betty M. and **Babco, Eleanor L.** Professional women and minorities: a manpower data resource service. 5th ed. Wash., Scientific Manpower Commission, 1984. 280p.   **CH705**

1st ed. 1975 in looseleaf format.

Detailed statistical information on the education, participation and availability of women and minorities. General information on enrollment, degrees, professions, workforce, and academic workforce is followed by information on specific subject fields. Recruitment resources lists registers of women and minority members in each subject field. Bibliography and index. Kept up-to-date by semiannual supplements.   HD6278.U5V47

World labour report. Geneva, Internat. Labour Office, [1984–85]. v.1–2. il. (In progress)   **CH706**

Contents: [v.1] Employment, incomes, social protection, new information technology; [v.2] Labour relations, international labour standards, training, conditions of work, women at work.

The work "is concerned mainly with facts, and aims at giving an overall picture of recent developments concerning major labor problems in the contemporary world."—*Pref.,[v.1].* Bibliographical references and selected bibliography of International Labour Office publications; statistical annex and tables. To be in 4v., the third of which will deal with pay.   HD5706.W68

Dictionaries

Jones, Jack and **Morris, Max.** A–Z of trade unionism and industrial relations. London, Heinemann, [1982]. 343p.   **CH707**

A dictionary of British trade unionism, intended for the general public; appendixes list unions and their membership, and provide a directory of relevant institutions.   HD8391.J66

Logie, Gordon. Glossary of employment and industry, English-French-Italian-Dutch-German-Swedish. Amsterdam [etc.], Elsevier Scientific Pub. Co., 1982. 290p. (International planning glossaries, 3)   **CH708**

A glossary of terms relating to employment, minerals, metals, extractive industries, energy resources, marketing, and water supply. Arranged by subject, with brief introductory remarks. Basic table is in English, with equivalents from the other languages. Indexes in all languages.   HD2324.L63

Roberts, Harold Selig. Roberts' Dictionary of industrial relations. Rev. ed. Wash., Bureau of National Affairs, [1971]. 599p.   **CH709**

First published in a preliminary edition (1957–63) under the title: *Dictionary of labor-management relations.* Another edition with that title appeared in 1966.

Aims "to provide a simple yet reasonably accurate explanation of terms and phrases currently used in the field of labor-management relations, brief summaries of important cases, short notes on international unions, and other items which might be of interest and help to a person seeking concise information."—*Introd.* Many entries include bibliographical "Source references." A new edition is scheduled for 1986.   HD4839.R612

Seide, Katharine, comp. A dictionary of arbitration and its terms; labor, commercial, international: a concise encyclopedia of peaceful dispute settlement. Dobbs Ferry, N.Y., publ. for the Eastman Library of the Amer. Arbitration Assoc. by Oceana Pubns., 1970. 334p.   **CH710**

Includes not only the vocabulary of arbitration, "but also a liberal sprinkling of legal terms, statutes, cases and concepts with which an arbitrator or student may be concerned."—*Introd.*

KF9085.A68S4

Directories

Coldrick, A. Percy and **Jones, Philip.** The international directory of the trade union movement. [N.Y., Facts on File, 1979] 1365p.   **CH711**

In two main parts: (1) international trade unions which are global in scope; (2) trade union organizations of each region of the world, and the trade unions of every country within each region. Each entry in pt.1 describes background, purposes, membership, finance, structure, activities, policies, publications, and gives a table with detailed directory information. National entries summarize the country's political situation and work force, history of the trade unions, labor legislation, and management relations; a listing follows for trade unions, giving date of establishment, international affiliation, membership, and officers. No index.   HD6475.2.C65

Directory of U.S. labor organizations. 1982/83– . Wash., Bureau of National Affairs, [1982]– . il. Biennial.

CH712

Continues a publication of the U.S. Bureau of Labor Statistics variously titled: *Directory of national unions and employee associations* (1971–80), *Directory of national and international labor unions in the United States* (1943–69), and *Directory of A.F.L. unions* and *Directory of C.I.O. unions* (1939–42).

Preliminary material on the structure of the A.F.L.-C.I.O. is followed by directory information on individual unions—officers, membership totals, convention dates. International unions are listed. Indexed by name of organization and officers.   HD6504.D64

Geneva. International Institute for Labour Studies. Directory of institutes for labour studies. Répertoire des instituts d'études sociales. Guía de institutos de estudios laborales. [Geneva], International Inst. for Labour Studies, [1978]. Looseleaf (approx. 760p.)   **CH713**

In English, French, or Spanish.

A revised version of the International Labour Office's *Directory of labour relations institutes* (1973).

Provides information on 264 institutes arranged under 74 countries. Each institute entry consists of information on the history, administration, staffing, purpose, educational and training activities, research, facilities, and publications. About one-third of the entries are to be updated each year, and new entries are to be added through the updating service issued annually in Oct.

HD4824.G44

Marsh, Arthur I. Trade union handbook: a guide and directory to the structure, membership, policy and personnel of the British trade unions. 3d ed. [Farnborough, Eng.], Gower, [1984]. 415p. il.   **CH714**

1st ed. 1979.

In addition to an introductory historical overview of the British trade union movement, provides data on addresses and officers, membership, district organization, historical background and current policies for British trade unions and other related organizations. Includes a bibliography of official trade union histories.

HD6663.M37

U.S. Bureau of International Labor Affairs. Directory of labor organizations. Wash., 1958– . Looseleaf.   **CH715**

Contents: Africa. [3d ed.?] 1966. 2v.; Asia and Australasia. Rev. ed., 1963. 2v.; Europe. [3d ed.] 1965. 2v.; Western hemisphere. Rev. ed., 1964. 2v.

Each volume contains "the best available data and information on the structure, composition, membership, and international affiliations of labor organizations" (*Foreword*) in the area covered.

Statistics

See also CG76, CG108.

Gt.Brit. Dept. of Employment and Productivity. British labour statistics: historical abstract 1886–1968. London, H.M.S.O., 1971. 436p.   **CH716**

Provides more than 200 tables drawn from original sources, e.g., *Abstract of labour statistics of the United Kingdom,* census reports, etc. Sources are indicated for all tables. Glossary; index.

HD8388.A5

International Labour Office. Labour force estimates and projections, 1950–2000. 2d ed. Geneva, The Office, 1977. 6v.   **CH717**

1st ed. 1971 had title *Labour force projections, 1965–1985.*

Contents: v.1, Asia; v.2, Africa; v.3, Latin America; v.4, Northern America, Europe, Oceania and the USSR; v.5, World summary; v.6, Methodological supplement. (Pts.1–5 in English, French and Spanish; pt.6 available separately in each language.)

Presents data on population, labor force and labor force activity by sex and age group for 1950–2000, plus data on the total labor force in agriculture, industry and services by sex and age group for 1950–1970.   HD5712.I58

Labor force statistics derived from the Current population survey: a databook. Wash., U.S. Dept. of Labor, Bureau of Labor Statistics, 1982. 2v. (U.S. Bureau of Labor Statistics. Bulletin, 2096)   **CH718**

A comprehensive collection of historical monthly, quarterly, and annual data, in many cases retrospective to 1948. Includes data on employment and unemployment classed by occupation, industry, age, sex, race, education, etc. Supplemented on a current basis by tables in the *Monthly labor review* (below) and *Employment and earnings* (CH720n).   HD5724.L19

U.S. Bureau of Labor Statistics. MLR, monthly labor review. v.1– , July 1915– . Wash., Bureau of Labor Statistics, 1915– . Monthly.   **CH719**

Title varies.

Contains special articles and summaries of special reports in the field of labor. Statistics cover employment, labor turnover, earnings, hours, work stoppages, prices and cost of living, etc. Each issue also contains a bibliography of recent labor literature. An annual statistical supplement was issued 1959–65.   HD8051.A78●

———— ———— Subject index. Wash., Govt. Prt. Off., 1941. 2v. (*Its* Bulletin no.695–96)

Covers v.1–11, July 1915–Dec. 1920; v.12–51, Jan. 1921–Dec. 1940. Continued by decennial indexes, 1941–50 (Bull. no.1080); 1951–60, (Bull. no.1335).

———— Employment and earnings, United States, 1909/60– . Wash., 1961– . Annual. (*Its* Bulletin no.1312 etc.)

CH720

Offers statistical tables "providing basic information on the nation's non-farm work force."—*Pref.*

Arranged by industry and by Standard Industrial Classification code number, then by year and by month, as statistics are available. Each new volume includes statistics from 1909 (e.g., 1909/84 published 1985; Bull. no.1312–12). Updated by the monthly *Employment and earnings.*   HD8051.A62●

———— Employment, hours and earnings, states and areas . . . 1939/82– . Wash., 1983– . Annual. (*Its* Bulletin no.1370)

CH721

Continues *Employment and earnings, states and areas,* 1939/62–1939/81.

"Employment data relate to the nonfarm sector of the economy, and exclude proprietors, the self-employed, domestic workers in private homes, and unpaid family workers."—*Introd.*

Groups together detailed industry data for states or area (usually Standard Metropolitan Statistical areas). Tables are by state or area, then by Standard Industrial Classification. Each successive issue includes figures from 1939 to date; supplementary reports are issued. HD8051.A62●

—— Handbook of labor statistics, 1924/26– . Wash., Govt. Prt. Off., 1927– . (*Its* Bulletin no.439, etc.) **CH722**

Supplement for 1950 published 1951; nothing further published until volume for 1967. Frequency varies; biennial 1982– . (1985 volume is Bull. no.2217)

Summarizes information and statistics from the various publications of the Bureau, and from some other government publications, on related subjects. Includes selected foreign labor statistics. HD8051.A62●

—— History of wages in the United States from colonial times to 1928. Revision of Bull. no.499 with suppl., 1929–1933. Wash., Govt. Prt. Off., 1934. 574p. tables. (*Its* Bulletin no.604) (Repr.: Detroit, Gale, 1966) **CH723**

HD8051.A62 no.604

Yearbook of labour statistics. 1935/36– . Geneva, Internat. Labour Off., 1936– . Annual. **CH724**

Frequency varies: 1936–42, annual; 1943/44–1951/52, biennial; 1952/53– , annual.

Preceded by: v.1, *Annual review*, 1930; v.2–5, *I.L.O. yearbook*, 1931–1934/35.

Text in French, Spanish, and English.

Now summarizes labor statistics for 180 countries or territories. As far as possible, data cover the last ten years. HD4826.I63

—— Bulletin of labour statistics. 1st– , March 1965– . Geneva, 1965– . Quarterly. **CH725**

Supplements the annual data presented in the Office's *Yearbook.* Supersedes the statistical supplement included with each monthly issue of the *International labour review* until Dec. 1964.

Annuals

Labor relations yearbook, 1965– . Wash., Bureau of National Affairs, [1966]– . Annual. **CH726**

Subtitle: Chronology of events, collective bargaining, labor relations conferences, labor organizations, role of federal government, selected analyses, economic data.

In addition to materials mentioned in the subtitle, provides coverage of the role of state government, and bibliographic citations and summaries of important literature. "Analyses" of selected cases are reprinted from the publisher's *Labor relations reporter.*

The Bureau also publishes a *Daily labor report, Labor relations reference manuals, Wage and hour cases, Labor arbitration reports,* and *Fair employment practice cases,* all searchable online. HD8059.L33●

Labor Research Association. Labor fact book. N.Y., Internat. Pub., 1931–65. il. Biennial (irregular). **CH727**

Information on political, economic, and social conditions that have affected the labor movement in America, supported by data largely drawn from standard government, business, and labor publications. Some volumes include a chapter on labor abroad. Name and subject index. Ceased publication with no.17, 1965.

HD8072.I253

History

Commons, John Rogers. History of labour in the United States. N.Y., Macmillan, 1935–36. 4v. (Repr.: N.Y., Kelley, 1966) **CH728**

First published 1918–35 in 4v.

A comprehensive survey of the development of labor organization and legislation in the United States, with introductions by John R. Commons; each part by a specialist. Based on the work following. Includes extensive bibliographies. HD8066.C7

A documentary history of American industrial society, ed. by John R. Commons [and others]. N.Y., A. H. Clark, 1910–11. 10v. in 11. (Repr. with new preface to v.1–2, by Louis Filler: N.Y., Russell & Russell, 1958) **CH729**

Prepared under the auspices of the American Bureau of Industrial Research with the cooperation of the Carnegie Institution of Washington.

Contents: v.1–2, Plantation and frontier; v.3–4, Labor conspiracy cases; Supplement to v.4 published separately 1910 (included in v.4 in the 1958 reprint); v.5–10, Labor movement and index.

A collection of source materials covering from the colonial period to 1880. Includes extensive bibliographies. HC103.D63

Biography

See also AJ270.

Biographical dictionary of American labor. Ed. in chief, Gary M. Fink. [2d ed., rev. and expanded] Westport, Conn., Greenwood Pr., [1984]. 767p. **CH730**

A revision of Fink's *Biographical dictionary of American labor leaders* (1974).

About 734 biographies. "It was determined that each individual included . . . should have had a substantial impact on the American labor movement in one way or another. . . . It was also considered important to include a broad sampling of leaders from different eras, from as many different industries, crafts and trades as possible, and from among those women, Afro-Americans, and Chicanos whose contributions to the labor movement were largely ignored until recently. Although the emphasis [in the 1st ed.] was on leaders of the trade-union movement, an effort was made to include a representative group of labor-oriented radicals, politicians, editors, staff members, lawyers, reformers, and intellectuals."—*Pref.* Bibliographical sources, including personal papers, are cited; many of the sketches are signed. Appendixes include lists by union affiliation, religious preference, place of birth, and major public offices, plus tables indicating formal education and political preference. Indexed. HD8073.A1B56

Who's who in labor; the authorized biographies of the men and women who lead labor in the United States and Canada and of those who deal with labor [ed. by Marion Dickerman and Ruth Taylor] . . . authorized ed. N.Y., Dryden, 1946. 480p. **CH731**

Contents: Men and women who lead labor, p.1–390; Men and women who deal with labor, p.391–443; List of international labor unions, p.445–51; Directory of the labor press, p.453–56; List of educational and research directors, p.457–65; Chronology of labor legislation, p.465–66; Glossary of labor terminology, ed. by J. R. Steelman, p.467–72; The constitution of the American Federation of Labor, p.473–78; The constitution of the Congress of Industrial Organizations, p.479–80. HD8073.A45

Who's who in labor. Ed.1– . N.Y., Arno Pr., 1976– . **CH732**

An earlier work with the same title, ed. by Marian Dickerman and Ruth Taylor, was published 1946 (above).

Ed.1 (807p.) presents biographical sketches of leaders "currently active in the labor movement" (*Pref.*), including persons involved in industrial relations as neutrals or government officials. In addition to the biographies, there are sections offering information on: (1) AFL-CIO and other federations; (2) National unions and employee associations; (3) Government offices serving labor; (4) Labor studies centers. There are also a glossary of labor terms, a bibliography of labor periodicals, and an index by organization. About 3,800 biographies.   HD8073.A1W5

MANUFACTURING INDUSTRIES

Bibliography

Directory of industry data sources. [Ed.1]– . [Cambridge, Mass.], Harfax, Ballinger, [1981]– . Annual.   **CH733**

William A. Benjamin, ed.

Contents: v.1–3, United States of America and Canada; v.4–5, Western Europe.

An annotated bibliography (more than 22,000 entries in Ed.2) of sources of marketing, or financial information sources. Each volume in five parts: (1) general secondary reference sources covering more than one industry; (2) data sources for each of 65 industries, arranged by type (e.g., marketing reports, statistical surveys, forecasts, directories, special journal issues, dissertations, numerical and bibliographic databases); (3) publishers, listed alphabetically and by document type; (4) subject indexes, by SIC Code and alphabetical; (5) title index. Corresponds to the commercially available bibliographic database "Industry data sources."

Z7165.U5D59●

Fundaburk, Emma Lila. Reference materials and periodicals in economics; an international list. Metuchen, N.J., Scarecrow Pr., 1971–72. v.1, 4.   **CH734**

Contents: v.1, Agriculture; v.4, Major manufacturing industries: automotive, chemical, iron and steel, petroleum and gas. No more published.

Within each volume works are grouped by type of publication, then alphabetically by author. Indexed.   Z7164.E2F83

Romaine, Lawrence B. A guide to American trade catalogs, 1744–1900. N.Y., Bowker, 1960. 422p. (Repr.: N.Y., Arno, 1976)   **CH735**

An extensive listing of trade catalogs in classified arrangement, indicating location of copies.   Z7164.C8R6

Dictionaries and encyclopedias

Room, Adrian. Dictionary of trade name origins. London, Routledge & Kegan Paul, [1982]. 217p. il.   **CH736**

Identifies more than 1,000 trade or brand names and gives brief etymologies; many illustrative logos. Appendix on significance of particular letters and suffixes. International, but British emphasis.   T324.R66

Top symbols and trademarks of the world. Ed. by Franco Maria Ricci and Corinna Ferrari. [Milan], Deco Pr., [1973]. 7v. il.   **CH737**

Contents: v.1, United States, pt.1; v.2, United States, pt.2, Canada; v.3, Japan, Spain, Latin America; v.4, Great Britain, Ireland, Benelux; v.5, France, Italy; v.6, Switzerland, West Germany, Austria; v.7, Scandinavia, Socialist countries.

A pictorial dictionary illustrating about 5,500 symbols and trademarks used since 1945 in more than 30 countries. Arranged alphabetically according to firm or organization within country or geographical region. Each entry lists artist, design company, and date of trademark. Volume indexes by designer and studio.

Continued by:

Top trademarks annual, 1977– . [Milan], Deco Pr., [1977]– . il. Annual.   **CH738**

Ed. by Franco Maria Ricci and Corinna Ferrari.

Recently established trademarks are listed by company within appropriate country section. Entry gives name of firm, address, type of firm, designer, year trademark was designed, and illustration. Indexed by designer and type of firm.

Trade names dictionary. Ed.1– . Detroit, Gale, [1976]– . Irregular. (4th ed. 1984 in 2v.)   **CH739**

Subtitle: A guide to trade names, brand names, product names, coined names, model names, and design names, with addresses of their manufacturers, importers, marketers, or distributors.

Prelim. ed. 1974.

An alphabetical listing of more than 194,000 entries for products, manufacturers, and distributors. Product entries provide the trade name, a brief description, name of the company which owns, markets, or distributes the item, and a code indicating the source of the information.

Supplemented by: T223.V4A22

———— Company index. Detroit, Gale, 1979– .

Each company appearing in the *Dictionary* is listed alphabetically, with a list of its products, each followed by a brief product description and the code for the source in which the trade name was noted; a special section provides company addresses.

The set is kept up-to-date by:

———— New trade names. 1976– . Detroit, Gale, 1977– . Annual.   **CH739a**

Each issue is cumulative in this inter-edition service.

Directories

Thomas' Register of American manufacturers and Thomas' Register catalog file. N.Y., Thomas Pub. Co., [190?]– . Annual.   **CH740**

Title varies.

1985 in 19v.: v.1–11, Products and services listed alphabetically; v.12–13, Company names, addresses with zip codes and telephone numbers, listed alphabetically with branch offices, capital ratings, company officials, trademark index, and index to products and services; v.14–19, Catalogs of companies appearing alphabetically and cross indexed in the first 13 volumes.   T12.T6

Trade shows and professional exhibits directory. Robert J. Elster, ed. Detroit, Gale, [1985]. 549p.   **CH741**

Subtitle: An international guide to scheduled events providing commercial display facilities, including conferences, conventions, meetings, congresses and councils, fairs and festivals, trade and industrial shows, merchandise marts, and expositions.

Provides trade show and exhibition dates and locations for the next four years. Broad industry arrangement; indexed by exhibition name, keyword in name, location, date, sponsoring and exhibition management organizations, and detailed subject.   T394.T717

❖Inasmuch as more than 450 specific types of manufacturing industries exist, coverage of their literature is beyond the scope of this *Guide*. Daniells (CH183) has a good chapter on "Industry statistics" (p.91–123); the most complete bibliography of specific industries is the *Directory of industry data sources* (CH733). The *United States census of manufactures,* first taken 1800 and issued somewhat irregularly by the U.S. Bureau of the Census, offers a wealth of statistics for industries and products.

Handbooks

Brady, George Stuart and **Clauser, Henry R.** Materials handbook; an encyclopedia for managers, technical professionals, purchasing and production managers, technicians, supervisors, and foremen. 11th ed. N.Y., McGraw-Hill, [1977]. 1011p. il. **CH742**

1st ed. 1929.

Gives chief characteristics, sources, substitutes, and uses of several thousands of materials. "General information, with the most commonly accepted comparative figures, is given on materials in their group classifications in order to give a general picture; selected processed materials and patented and trade-named materials are then described to give a more specific understanding of commercial applications."—*Foreword*. Groups of materials are entered alphabetically; detailed index. TA403.B75

Production handbook. Gordon B. Carson, Harold A. Bolz and Hewitt H. Young, editorial consultants. 3d ed. N.Y., Ronald Pr., [1972]. 1v., various pagings. il. **CH743**

1st ed. 1944.

Offers detailed information on the planning, organization, and operation of a manufacturing industry. TS155.P747

Purchasing handbook. Aljian's Purchasing handbook. 4th ed. N.Y., McGraw-Hill, [1982]. 1v., various pagings. **CH744**

1st ed. 1958.

Sponsored by the Nat. Assoc. of Purchasing Management. Paul V. Farrell, coordinating ed.

Each section contributed by specialists in the field.

HF5437.P795

U.S. Office of Management and Budget. Standard industrial classification manual. Wash., Govt. Prt. Off., [1939]– . Irregular. **CH745**

The 1972 ed. and its 1977 suppl. replace all previous eds. and suppls.

"The Standard Industrial Classification was developed for use in classification of establishments by type of activity in which engaged; for purposes of facilitating the collection, tabulation, presentation and analysis of data relating to establishments; and for promoting uniformity and comparability in the presentation of statistical data collected by various agencies of the United States Government, State agencies, trade associations, and private research organizations."—*Introd*. Titles and descriptions of industries are presented in 12 main divisions, with numerous subsections for each and alphabetical indexes of non-manufacturing and of manufacturing industries. HF1041.U613

Statistics

United Nations. Statistical Office. The growth of world industry, 1938–1961; national tables. La croissance de l'industrie mondiale, 1938–1961; tableaux par pays. N.Y., United Nations, 1963. 849p. **CH746**

Detailed statistical tables on various kinds of industrial production for about 100 countries and territories. Represents "A more current and expanded version of Pt.2 of [its] *Patterns of industrial growth, 1938-1959.*"—*Introd*. JX1977.A2

———— The growth of world industry, 1938–1961; international analysis and tables. N.Y., 1965. 345p.

Title also in French.

Both of the above were continued by annual volumes for 1967–73 (publ. 1969–75), which in turn were continued by:

Yearbook of industrial statistics, 1974– . N.Y., United Nations, 1976– . Annual. **CH747**

Continues *The growth of world industry* (1969–73) issued by the United Nations Statistical Office.

Issued in 2v. per year: v.1, General industrial statistics; v.2, Commodity production data.

Presents (1) national surveys for about 200 countries or areas on various indicators of industrial activity, classified by ISIC code, with a selection of indicators to measure global and regional trends in

industrial productivity and employment, and (2) production statistics on more than 527 industrial commodities. HA40.I6Y4

MARKETING

Bibliography

See also Advertising and public relations, p.799–800.

American Marketing Association. Bibliography series, no.1– . Chicago, The Association, 1954– . Irregular. **CH748**

Title varies: *Bibliography series* (1954–77); *AMA bibliography series* (1978–80). Issues unnumbered since no.38, 1980.

A useful series which has included such titles as *A basic bibliography on marketing research,* comp. by Robert Ferber and others (no.2; 3d ed. 1974); *Selling and sales management,* by L. B. Chonko and B. M. Enis (no.36; 1980); and *International marketing,* by S. T. Cavusgil and J. R. Nevin (1983).

Daniells, Lorna M. Note on sources of external marketing data. Boston, Harvard Business School (distr. by the Intercollegiate Case Clearing House), 1980. 64p. **CH749**

An annotated bibliography of sources for government and nongovernmental statistics, industry statistics, foreign statistics, market guides and services, advertising statistics, forecasting, together with reference sources such as bibliographies, periodical indexes, databases, directories, and marketing magazines.

The marketing information guide, 1954–82. [Wash., Trade Marketing Information Guide, 1954–82] 29v. **CH750**

Title varies: *Distribution data guide* (1954–60).

Publisher varies; frequency varies (originally monthly, then bimonthly).

Subtitle: The annotated bibliography.

Presented about 80 abstracts per issue of books, articles, market surveys, federal and state government documents, and reports. Broad subject arrangement; semiannual indexes.

Z7165.U5A362

Revzan, David Allen. A comprehensive classified marketing bibliography. Berkeley, Univ. of California Pr., 1951. v.1–2. (Univ. of Calif. Bureau of Business and Economics Research pubn.) **CH751**

Contents: Pt.1, Books published through 1949; pt.2, Government publications, university research monographs, and articles in professional journals, published through 1949. A third part, planned to cover material in technical and trade journals, has not been published.

Attempts to be comprehensive, but is not complete. Each volume has an author index. Z7164.M18R4

———— A geography of marketing; resource bibliography. [Berkeley], Inst. of Business and Economic Research, [Univ. of California, 1968]. 259p. **CH752**

A classified bibliography of more than 3,600 items with author index. Includes all aspects of marketing and related topics.

Z7164.M18R42

Thompson, Ralph B. and **Faricy, John H.** A selected and annotated bibliography of marketing theory. 2d rev. ed. Austin, Bureau of Business Research, Univ. of Texas at Austin, [1976]. 86p. (Bibliography ser., 18) **CH753**

1st rev. ed. 1970.

A classified list stressing material relevant for theorists or students of marketing, with emphasis on behavioral sciences concepts. Each section is on a particular theory (e.g., consumer behavior) and is subdivided by format (i.e., books and articles). No index.

Z7164.C81T4 no.18

Current

Journal of marketing. v.1– , July 1936– . N.Y., American Marketing Assoc., 1936– . Quarterly.   **CH754**

From 1937 through 1984 each issue offered a "Marketing abstracts" section with lengthy abstracts of current periodical articles. In 1985 this became a "Marketing literature review" section offering about 400 citations with brief descriptors for articles drawn from about 125 English-language journals; full abstracts are available from the ABI/INFORM database. Subject arrangement.

HF5415.A2J6●

Marketing information: a professional reference guide. [Ed.1]– . Atlanta, Business Publ. Div., College of Bus. Admin., Georgia State Univ., [1982]– . Biennial.   **CH755**

Jac L. Goldstucker, ed.

In two parts: (1) a guide to marketing associations, research organizations, advertising agencies, special libraries, continuing education programs, and U.S. government agencies, each section providing an alphabetical listing and, in most cases, detailed subject and geographic indexes; (2) an annotated guide to books, periodicals, audiovisual materials, and databases, arranged by 21 topical interest areas of marketing, giving prices, and indexed by title.

Dissertations

Clarke, George Timothy. Bibliography of advertising and marketing theses for the doctorate in United States colleges and universities, 1944 to 1959. N.Y., Advertising Educ. Foundation, [1961]. 28p.   **CH756**

A list of 393 doctoral theses from 38 educational institutions, arranged under 46 subjects. Entry is by title, followed by author, institution granting the degree, and date. No annotations; no author index.   Z7164.C81C53

Marketing doctoral dissertation abstracts, 1974/75– . Chicago, Amer. Marketing Assoc., [1977]– . Annual. (Bibliography ser. Amer. Marketing Assoc., no.24, etc.)   **CH757**

Presents abstracts of dissertations from about 80 United States and one Canadian university programs. Author listing with subject index.   HF5415.M29758

Dictionaries

MacMillan dictionary of marketing & advertising. Ed. by Michael J. Baker. N.Y., Nichols, [1984]. 217p. il.   **CH758**

Offers short, signed entries by 15 contributors, principally from the Department of Marketing, Strathclyde University. British emphasis.   HF5415.B273

Shapiro, Irving J. Dictionary of marketing terms. 4th ed. [Totowa, N.J.], Littlefield, Adams, [1981]. 276p.   **CH759**

3d ed. 1973 had title: *Marketing terms.*

A student's dictionary of approximately 5,000 entries, with special emphasis given to concepts from the behavioral sciences, marketing research, and managerial decision-making techniques.

HF5412.S52

Directories

Bradford's Directory of marketing research agencies and management consultants in the United States and the world. N.Y., C. E. Burckel, 1944– . Biennial.   **CH760**

Frequency varies.

Title varies: 1944, *Survey and directory, marketing research agencies in New York City;* 1945, *Survey and directory, marketing research agencies in the United States;* 1947–1954/55, *Bradford's*

Survey and directory of marketing research agencies in the United States and the world (varies).

Lists agencies and individuals engaged in marketing and economic research, etc.   HF5415.A2B7

Direct marketing market place, 1980– ; the directory of the direct marketing industry. Hewlett Harbor, N.Y., Hilary House (distr. by Bowker), [1979]– . Annual.   **CH761**

"Including a directory of names, addresses and phone numbers." —*t.p.*

A source similar in purpose and format to the *Literary market place* (AA353) for the direct marketing field. Classified section lists direct marketers of products and services (principally through mail order catalogs), service firms and suppliers, creative and consulting services, courses, associations, awards, etc. Primarily U.S. listings, with a chapter on Canadian and foreign firms. Names, addresses, and telephone numbers are given for companies and individuals.

HF5415.1.D57

Directory of U.S. and Canadian marketing surveys and services, 1976– . Fairfield, N.J., Charles H. Kline & Co., [1976]– . Annual.   **CH762**

An alphabetical list of marketing reports and syndicated continuing services available from American, Canadian, and European consulting firms. Each entry lists the firm's name, its syndicated services, individual surveys under $1,000, and individual surveys over $1,000. Subject index.   HF5415.3.D56

Editor and Publisher. Market guide. v.1– , 1924– . N.Y., 1924– . maps. Annual.   **CH763**

Each recent issue offers individual market surveys of some 1,500 United States and Canadian cities where a daily newspaper is published. Arranged by state and city; gives for each city such information as: population, location, trade area, banks, principal industries, colleges and universities, largest department stores, chain stores, retail outlets and sales, newspapers, etc.

HF5905.E38

FINDex: the directory of market research reports, studies and surveys. Ed.1– . N.Y., FIND/SVP, 1979– . Annual with semiannual suppl. Looseleaf.   **CH764**

The 1979 volume lists about 2,000 reports and studies currently available from domestic and international sources. Entries are arranged by industries and provide date, brief description, source, and price; market research reports on individual companies are also included. Publishers' directory and list of report titles by each publisher conclude the volume. The 1980 ed. expands coverage to some 4,000 reports, studies and surveys.

Handbooks

Dartnell Corporation. The Dartnell sales promotion handbook. 7th ed. Ovid Riso, ed. Chicago, Dartnell, [1979]. 1206p. il.   **CH765**

1st ed. 1950; earlier editions called *The sales promotion handbook.*

A desk-reference book detailing techniques and tools of sales promotion, distribution channels, evaluation of effectiveness, equipment, mail order selling, the role of computers, etc.

The Dartnell marketing manager's handbook. 2d ed. Ed. by Stuart Henderson Britt and Norman F. Guess. Chicago, Dartnell, [1983]. 1293p. il.   **CH766**

Chapters written by professors and marketing executives treat marketing management, organization and staffing, research, planning, consumer products and services, industrial products, promotion, international marketing, and program evaluation. Brief bibliographies.

The Dartnell sales manager's handbook, ed. by Ovid Riso. 13th ed. Chicago, Dartnell Corp., 1980. 1106p. il.

CH767

1st ed., 1934; early editions had title *The sales manager's handbook.*

A useful compilation emphasizing sales organizations, training, methods of selling, and marketing research. "Ready-reference sections" provide bibliography, glossary, legal data, postal rates, etc.

Ferber, Robert. Handbook of marketing research. N.Y., McGraw-Hill, [1974]. 1v., various pagings. il.　　**CH768**

Consists of chapters by specialists arranged in four sections: (1) Introduction, focusing on the history, function, and operations of marketing research; (2) Techniques, covering quantitative methods such as surveys, sampling, model building, and computer techniques; (3) Behavioral science techniques; (4) Major areas of application, subdivided by major types of marketing—new products, sales, advertising, industrial, international. Indexed.

HF5415.2.F419

Handbook of modern marketing. 2d ed. Ed. by Victor P. Buell. N.Y., McGraw-Hill, [1986]. 1v., various pagings. il.　　**CH769**

1st ed. 1970.

Chapters by specialists cover such topics as distribution, pricing, organization and staffing, marketing management, selling and sales management, customer services, packaging, ethical and legal aspects of marketing, etc. Detailed index.　　HF5415.H1867

Nelson, Theodore A. Measuring markets: a guide to the use of federal and state statistical data. [Updated version] [Wash.], Dept. of Commerce, Industry and Trade Admin., 1979. 101p.　　**CH770**

Updates a 1974 ed. of the same title.

Pt.I describes types of markets, sales goals, market potential, sales territories, and market research data. Pt.II, the major section, discusses population, income, employment, sales, and tax data, with tabular listing of data sources, giving geographic coverage, publication frequency, issuing agency, and SIC industry coverage. Bibliography of government and private publications.　　HF5415.3.N44

Statistics

Consumer Europe. [Ed.1]– . [London], Euromonitor Pubns., [1976]– . Irregular.　　**CH771**

5th ed. 1985.

Consists of statistical tables which tabulate for five-year periods the production, sales, distribution, and consumption of over 250 markets in 13 Western European countries: Austria, Belgium, Denmark, Finland, France, Germany, Great Britain, Italy, Netherlands, Norway, Spain, Sweden, and Switzerland.　　HD7022.C68

OCCUPATIONS

See also Guidance, p.675.

Angel, Juvenal Londoño. Looking for employment in foreign countries; reference handbook. 6th ed. rev. and enl. N.Y., World Trade Academy Pr., [1972]. 727p.　　**CH772**

Offers information on employment conditions in individual countries abroad, together with lists of "agencies offering possibilities of information about employment" in the various countries. A much abbreviated 7th ed. (139p.) was edited by June L. Aulick (1985).

HF5381.A7847

Bostwick, Burdette E. Résumé writing: a comprehensive how-to-do-it guide. 3d ed. N.Y., Wiley, [1985]. 323p.　　**CH773**

1st ed. 1976.

This edition includes new résumés from a wide variety of occupations and expanded treatment of letters, proposals, and other job search related writings. Includes sample résumés of many types.　　HF5383.B57

Dickhut, Harold W. Professional resume and job search guide. 5th ed. Englewood Cliffs, N.J., Prentice-Hall [1981]. 218p. il.　　**CH774**

1st–4th eds. had title *Professional resume/job search guide* (1972–78).

A guide to preparing the resumé; numerous sample resumés and cover letters. Index.　　HF5383.D47

Dictionary of occupational titles. U.S. Dept. of Labor, Employment and Training Admin., U.S. Employment Service. 4th ed. [Wash.], The Administration, 1977. 1371p.　　**CH775**

1st ed. 1939–44.

Offers standardized descriptions of job duties for about 20,000 occupations. Detailed classed arrangement indexed alphabetically by occupation and industry group. Occupations emerging since 1977 were included in a *Supplement* (1982. 36p.). More detailed descriptions of the physical demands, environmental conditions, and training time required for selected jobs are given in *Selected characteristics of occupations defined in the Dictionary of occupational titles* (1981. 479p.).　　HB2595.U543

Directory of career resources for women: a guide to career resources and opportunities for women. Alvin Renetzky, ed. in chief. Santa Monica, Calif., Ready Reference Pr., [1979]. 287p.　　**CH776**

Identifies private organizations, social service agencies, college and university centers, YWCAs, consulting services, and employment agencies which offer career information, resources, and training for women. Each entry provides background information, resources offered, special features, hours, and contact personnel. Alphabetical arrangement by organization, with subject and geographical indexes.　　HD6095.D57

Doss, Martha Merrill. The directory of special opportunities for women; a national guide of educational opportunities, career information, networks, and peer counseling assistance for entry or reentry into the work force. [Garrett Park, Md., Garrett Park Pr., 1981] 293p. il.　　**CH777**

In four sections: (1) an alphabetically arranged directory of national organizations, associations, government agencies and programs; (2) a directory of local organizations, arranged by state and then by zip code; (3) a list of women's colleges and universities; (4) resources, including books, pamphlets, newsletters and magazines, newspapers, and foundations. Indexed.　　HD6058.D8

Harrop, David. America's paychecks; who makes what. N.Y., Facts on File, [1980]. 254p.　　**CH778**

A narrative comparison of American occupations designed as entertainment rather than economic analysis, but which manages to provide useful information on the history and scale, employment levels, economic output, and wages of different occupations. Organized by occupation; inherited, entrepreneurial, and criminal wealth is discussed. Indexed. A revised ed., *America's paychecks II,* was published 1982.　　HD4975.H33

——— World paychecks; who makes what, where, and why. N.Y., Facts on File, [1982]. 176p.　　**CH779**

Compares salary ranges, perquisites, and standards of living for a variety of occupations, including international organizations, national governments, multinational organizations, criminals, etc. Organized by type of work; indexed.　　HD4906.H28

Hawes, Gene R. The encyclopedia of second careers. N.Y., Facts on File, [1984]. 444p. il.　　**CH780**

A vocational guide not limited in usefulness to those seeking second careers. The main part describes more than 200 occupations, including entry possibilities, income level, advancement, future growth, and sources of information. Also has sections on: career

selection; small businesses; growth regions; job searches and resumés; schools and colleges; career services offered by institutions.
HF5384.H382

Kocher, Eric. International jobs: where they are, how to get them. A handbook for over 500 career opportunities around the world. Rev. ed. Reading, Mass., Addison-Wesley, [1984]. 337p. il.   **CH781**

In two parts: (1) chapters on career planning, curriculum development, work permits and documentation, and job letters, résumés and interviews; (2) a directory of international career opportunities offered by the federal government, United Nations, non-profit organizations, businesses and banks, the communications field, teaching, and law. Bibliography; index.   HF5381.K596

The national job bank: a comprehensive guide to major employers in the nation's key job markets. Senior ed., Robert Lang Adams. Brighton, Mass., B. Adams, [1983]. 1432p.   **CH782**

A directory of most major businesses and some large non-profit organizations in the nation's ten "key" job markets—Atlanta, Boston, Chicago, New York, Northern California, Pennsylvania, Southern California, the Southwest, Texas, and Washington, D.C. Describes the nature of the business, prospective employment, types of available positions, personnel contact. Indexed by industry, subdivided by geographical location. Compiled from separately published "regional" job bank volumes.   HF5382.5.U5N34

Occupational index. v.1–33, Jan. 1936–1968. Jaffrey, N.H., Personnel Services, [1936]–68. v.1–33. Quarterly.
CH783

Publisher varies. Ceased publication.

Bibliography with abstracts of current publications on occupational information. Each volume has cumulated author, title, and subject indexes to the abstracts listed during the year.
Z7164.C81O2

U.S. Bureau of Labor Statistics. Occupational outlook handbook; employment information on major occupations for use in guidance. 1st ed.– . Wash., 1949– . Biennial. (*Its* Bull. no.940, etc.)   **CH784**

17th ed., 1984/85, is *Bulletin* no.2205.

Gives information on employment trends and outlook in more than 800 occupations. Indicates nature of work, qualifications, earnings and working conditions, how to enter, where to go for more information, etc. Updated by *Occupational outlook quarterly.*
HF5381.U62

U.S. Bureau of the Census. 1980 census of population. Alphabetical index of industries and occupations. Wash., Govt. Prt. Off., 1982. 473p.   **CH785**

Prepared for each decennial census, with occasional editions in between.   HC106.7.U542

——— 1980 census of population. Classified index of industries and occupations. Wash., Govt. Prt. Off., 1982. 293p.   **CH786**

HC106.7.U542

West, Jonathan P. Career planning, development, and management: an annotated bibliography. N.Y., Garland, 1983. 306p. (Public affairs and administration ser., 1; Garland reference library of social science, v.145)   **CH787**

973 citations to English-language books and articles are arranged in 27 topical chapters; 17 concentrate on the individual's role in career planning and development, 10 on the organization's efforts to manage careers. Focuses on 1960–82 publications. Author and title indexes.   Z7164.V6W45

Wright, John W. The American almanac of jobs and salaries. Completely rev. and updated. [N.Y.], Avon, [1984]. 824p.   **CH788**

1st ed. 1982.

A survey of occupations and their salaries. Sources are indicated for most tables, and some historical data is provided.
HD8038.U5W74

REAL ESTATE

Bibliography

Babb, Janice B. and **Dordick, Beverly F.** Real estate information sources. Detroit, Gale, [1963]. 317p.   **CH789**

An annotated list of books, periodicals, reports, and organization publications, mostly in English, arranged by subject. Includes author and subject index.   Z7164.L3B2

Haikalis, Peter D. and **Freeman, Jean K.** Real estate; a bibliography of the monographic literature. Westport, Conn., Greenwood Pr., [1983]. 317p.   **CH790**

"Prep. under the auspices of the California State University Real Estate Education Endowment, Office of the Chancellor, California State University, Long Beach, California."—*t.p.*

Based on the holdings of 19 California State University libraries, this is a list of more than 2,600 book and document titles arranged in a detailed classification covering land use, real estate business, housing, finance and insurance, taxation, and law. Author and title indexes.   Z7164.L3H18

MacBride, Dexter D. The bibliography of appraisal literature. Wash., American Soc. of Appraisers, 1974. 769p.
CH791

English-language sources (principally books and periodical articles) selected by specialists and arranged in fifteen subject chapters, each with sub-categories. Includes real property, personal property, intangibles, utilities, machinery and equipment, technical evaluation, appraisal administration. Author index.
Z7164.V3M3

Messner, Stephen D., ed. Minority groups and housing; a selected bibliography, 1950–67. Storrs, Center for Real Estate and Urban Economic Studies, Univ. of Connecticut, [1968]. 60p. (Univ. of Conn. Center for Real Estate and Urban Economic Studies. General ser., no.1)   **CH792**

A selected, classified listing of book, periodical, and some unpublished materials.

Continued by:

Boyce, Byrl N. and **Turoff, Sidney.** Minority groups and housing; a bibliography, 1950–1970. [Morristown, N.J.], General Learning Pr., [1972]. 202p.   **CH793**

Continues the Messner listing (above).

A topical listing with author and detailed subject indexes.
Z7164.H8B73

Paulus, Virginia. Housing: a bibliography, 1960–1972. N.Y., AMS Pr., [1974]. 339p.   **CH794**

A classed list of 3,625 entries on housing concerns in the United States, excluding architecture, vacation homes, and new towns. A wide variety of materials is grouped into six major categories or "frameworks": economic; legal; social/political; demographic; informational (i.e., reference works); and general works and anthologies. Detailed table of contents. Author index and "subject finding guide."   Z7164.H8P38

Real estate appraisal bibliography, 1973–1980. Chicago, American Institute of Real Estate Appraisers, [1981]. 146p.
CH795

A detailed classed bibliography emphasizing periodical literature from about ten major real estate appraisal journals, proceedings, and annual publications. Supplements the Institute's *Real estate appraisal bibliography* (Chicago, 1973), which covered works published 1945–72.   Z7164.L3R38

Rouse, John E. Urban housing: public and private; a guide to information sources. Detroit, Gale, [1978]. 319p. (Urban studies information guide ser., v.5)   **CH796**

Lists books, articles, essays, federal government publications, published mainly 1972–76, on urban housing issues in the United States. Topical arrangement under such headings as "Housing finance," "Housing subsidies," "Open housing," "Housing for the elderly." Author, title, and subject indexes. Annotations, some rather lengthy. An appendix lists housing periodicals (including those issued by the federal government), aids to understanding HUD, housing bibliographies, and housing associations and lobbies.   Z7164.H8R68

❖The Swedish Council for Building Research has issued three titles in its *Document* series: *Bibliography on human settlements in developing countries: references with relevance to eastern Africa,* by Mirina Curutchet (1982. 224p.; no.12); *Bibliography on human settlements with emphasis on households and residential environment—Kenya,* by Carin Boalt, Suzanne Grant Lewis and Dorothy Myers (1982. 101p.; no.13); and *Bibliography on human settlements with emphasis on households and residential environment—Zambia,* by Ann Schlyter and Jairus Chanda (1982. 137p.; no.14).

Current

Homes and homebuilding, 1967– . Produced by the Nat. Housing Ctr. Library. Wash., Nat. Assoc. of Home Builders, 1967– . Annual.   **CH798**

A subject index to the English-language periodicals received at the National Housing Center Library. About 4,500 articles from some 250 journals in 1985. Subject arrangement only.   Z5943.D7H65

Housing and planning references. no.1–127, 1948–May/June 1965; n.s., no.1– , July/Aug. 1965– . Wash., Dept. of Housing and Urban Development, 1948– . Bimonthly.   **CH799**

Lists a selection of books, government documents, private reports, and periodical articles received by the Library of the Dept. of Housing and Urban Development. International in scope. Topical arrangement, with geographic and author indexes.   Z7165.U5A3

Dictionaries and encyclopedias

Boyce, Byrl N. Real estate appraisal terminology. Rev. ed. Cambridge, Mass., Ballinger Pub. Co., [1981]. 367p.   **CH800**

Sponsored jointly by the American Institute of Real Estate Appraisers and the Society of Real Estate Appraisers.

Based on the Institute's *Appraisal terminology and handbook* (CH807) and the Society's *Real estate appraisal principles and terminology* (2d ed. Chicago, 1971), with new and expanded terminology in the areas of investment analysis, statistics, mathematics, and computers.   HD1387.B69

Brownstone, David M. and **Franck, Irene M.** The VNR real estate dictionary. N.Y., Van Nostrand Reinhold, [1981]. 335p.   **CH801**

Briefly defines terms and phrases drawn from real estate transactions, financing, law, accounting, construction, architecture, management, government regulation, personal financial planning, taxation, and investment.   HD1365.B76

Dumouchel, J. Robert. Dictionary of development terminology. N.Y., McGraw-Hill, [1976]. 278p.   **CH802**

Subtitle: The technical language of builders, lenders, architects and planners, investors, real estate brokers and attorneys, appraisers, land taxing and zoning authorities, government officials, community organizers, housing managers, urban renewal specialists.

Very brief definitions of terms used in urban renewal and the

housing industry, e.g., "Fannie Mae," Capehart-Wherry housing, New Community Development Program. List of abbreviations and acronyms precedes the definitions.   HT108.5.D84

Friedman, Jack P., Harris, Jack C. and **Lindeman, J. Bruce.** Dictionary of real estate terms. Woodbury, N.Y., Barron's Educational Ser., [1984]. 317p. il.   **CH803**

Provides one- or two-sentence definitions, with examples, of about 1,200 words, phrases, and organizations; numerous illustrative sketches. Appendixes: illustration of house sections, tables of measurement, mortgage costs, mathematical formulas, etc. The same text was issued with expanded tables for mortgage costs as *Barron's Real estate handbook* (1984. 569p.).   HD1365.F75

Gross, Jerome S. Illustrated encyclopedic dictionary of real estate. 2d ed. Englewood Cliffs, N.J., Prentice-Hall, [1978]. 418p. il.   **CH804**

1st ed., 1969, had title: *Illustrated encyclopedic dictionary of real estate terms.*

Provides very brief definitions of terms used in the field; this edition has expanded coverage of finance, construction, legal phraseology and jargon; 80 sample real estate and office forms have been shifted to a separate section. Appendixes provide organizations list, loan amortization schedule, illustration of architectural features of a house, etc.   HD1365.G76

Hemphill, Thomas and **Hemphill, Charles F.** The essential dictionary of real estate terminology. Englewood Cliffs, N.J., Prentice-Hall, [1982]. 193p.   **CH805**

Terms, phrases, abbreviations, and organizations drawn from the fields of accounting, appraisal, architecture, economics, law, marketing, money and banking, property management, sales management, surveying, taxation, and urban planning.   HD1365.H45

Reilly, John W. The language of real estate. Chicago, Real Estate Education Co., [1977]. 585p. il.   **CH806**

Defines about 1,700 real estate and building terms. Appendixes provide examples of documents used in real estate transactions, the realtors code of ethics, and a sample closing problem.   KF568.5.R44

Handbooks and statistical sources

American Institute of Real Estate Appraisers. Appraisal terminology and handbook. 5th ed. Chicago, [1967]. 268p.   **CH807**

First published 1948 under title: *Handbook for appraisers.*
A dictionary of terms, plus a section of tables, rules, etc.   HD1387.A58

Arnold, Alvin L. and **Kusnet, Jack.** The Arnold encyclopedia of real estate. Boston, Warren, Gorham & Lamont, [1978]. 901p., [154]p.   **CH808**

Provides basic definitions or explanations of terms used in the real estate industry, as well as related legal, tax, and banking terms. Appendix provides charts or statistical materials on construction, housing inventory, sales, interest rates and mortgage loans, nonresidential real estate, depreciation schedules, etc. "Topical entry finder" lists individual entries grouped under 12 broadly related subject categories.   HD1365.A76

———— ———— Yearbook, 1980– . Boston, Warren, Gorham & Lamont, 1980– . Annual.

Updates definitions and statistical materials presented in the main volume. Some new terms are supplied.

The McGraw-Hill construction business handbook: a practical guide to accounting, credit, finance, insurance, and law for the construction industry. Ed. by Robert F. Cushman and John P. Bigda. 2d ed. N.Y., McGraw-Hill, [1985]. 1079p.   **CH809**

Presents 59 chapters by individual specialists in areas such as: organization, accounting, taxes, and record-keeping; financing, insurance, and bonding; contract analysis and procurement; government regulations; contract performance and rights; collection procedures. Bibliographic footnotes; indexed.   HD9715.A2M27

The McGraw-Hill real estate handbook. Robert Irwin, ed. N.Y., McGraw-Hill, [1984]. 1v., various pagings. il.   **CH810**

Presents 36 chapters written by specialists in seven main areas—financing, investing, taxation, law, real estate exchanges, appraisal, and marketing. No bibliographic references. Indexed.
    HD1375.M17

Real estate almanac. N.Y., Wiley, [1980]. unpaged (approx. 460p.). il.   **CH811**

Ed. by Robert D. Allen and Thomas E. Wolfe.
Provides directory information for professional organizations and government agencies in the United States and foreign countries. Also offers sections on education and careers in real estate, license laws, home warranty and government financial programs. Lengthy section of sample forms for real estate transactions. No index.
    HD255.R34

Real estate handbook. Ed. by Maury Seldin. Homewood, Ill., Dow Jones-Irwin, [1980]. 1186p. il.   **CH812**

67 narrative chapters written by academics and professionals are grouped in five sections: (1) business and legal consequences of transactions; (2) variety of analyses—appraisal, feasibility, etc.; (3) marketing and regulation; (4) financing sources; (5) types of real estate investment. Appendix serves as a directory of organizations with licensing or membership requirements.   HD255.R38

United Nations. Statistical Office. Compendium of housing statistics, 1975–1977. Recueil des statistiques de l'habitation, 1975–1977. Dept. of International and Social Affairs, Statistical Office. 3d issue. N.Y., United Nations, 1980. 354p. ([Document] United Nations; ST/ESA/STAT/SER.N/3)   **CH813**

In English and French.
1st ed. 1974.
Presents official housing census data for 187 countries or areas, such as housing supply and size, density of occupation and tenure, facilities, rate of construction, costs, estimates of need, characteristics of population and households in urban and rural areas. Also presents data on land utilization and environmental pollution.
Continued by:

Compendium of human settlements statistics. Dept. of International Economic and Social Affairs, Statistical Office. Issue 4– , 1983– . N.Y., United Nations, 1985– . Quinquennial.   **CH814**

In English and French.

U.S. Bureau of the Census. Housing construction statistics, 1889 to 1964. [Wash., Govt. Prt. Off., 1966] 805p.   **CH815**

Presents historical statistics consisting mainly of "published data available in some 200 separate reports prepared by the Bureau of the Census, the Bureau of Labor Statistics, the National Bureau of Economic Research, Incorporated, and the Twentieth Century Fund."—*Introd.* Source notes are given for each table.
The Bureau's *1970 census of housing* (1972–73; 7v.) taken in conjunction with the 19th decennial census offers a wide range of statistical information.

Yearbook of construction statistics, 1963/72–74/81. N.Y., United Nations, 1974–83. Annual. (Series: United Nations. Document ST/ESA/STAT/Ser.U/)   **CH816**

At head of title, 1964/73– : Department of International Economic and Social Affairs, Statistical Office.
Presents country statistical data on employment, wages, value, stages of construction, types of building activity, etc. Also provides comparative international figures on dwelling construction and index numbers of construction activity.
Continued by: HD9715.A1Y4

Construction statistics yearbook, 1982– . Dept. of International Economic and Social Affairs, Statistical Office. N.Y., United Nations, 1984– . Annual.   **CH817**

    HD9715.A1Y4

C J

Political Science

❖Political science may be defined as the science dealing with the principles and conduct of government, and of politics. Holler's *Information sources of political science* (CJ3) is an excellent guide for the student, and there is a good chapter on political science in Carl White's *Sources of information in the social sciences* (CA9). Various interdisciplinary works of interest to the political scientist will be found in other Social Sciences sections of this *Guide* and in the History and Area Studies sections. This section also deals with the related topics of public opinion, the armed forces, and arms control and peace research.

GENERAL WORKS

Guides

Brock, Clifton. The literature of political science; a guide for students, librarians, and teachers. N.Y., Bowker, 1969. 232p.   **CJ1**

"This guide is intended primarily for the undergraduate major and beginning graduate student as an introduction to library materials and research methods in political science."—*Pref.* In two parts: (A) Information sources and how to use them, and (B) Bibliographies and other reference sources. Within sections, chapters are devoted to methods of research and special aspects of research in political science, with annotated bibliographies of reference sources. Indexed.   Z7161.B83

Harmon, Robert Bartlett. Political science; a bibliographical guide to the literature. N.Y., Scarecrow Pr., 1965. 388p.   **CJ2**

Includes sections on general research materials, political science and the study of politics, comparative government, state and local government, political theory, international relations, etc. In addition to general and specialized works, the various subsections include listings for reference materials, with annotations for many of the reference works. Author and subject indexes. A very uneven work.   Z7161.H27

——— ——— Supplement 1–3. Metuchen, N.J., Scarecrow Pr., 1968–74. 3v.

Holler, Frederick L. Information sources of political science. 3d ed. Santa Barbara, ABC-Clio, [1980]. 278p.   **CJ3**

1st ed. 1971.
A guide to more than 1,750 printed or computerized reference works in political science, including public administration. Offers lengthy, critical annotations and tables illustrating interrelation-

ships of titles. Subject, author, and title indexes. Considerable revision has made this edition better organized and more convenient to use than earlier editions. A new edition is to be published 1985. Z7161.H64

Information sources in politics and political science: a survey worldwide. Eds., Dermot Englefield and Gavin Drewry. London, Butterworths, [1984]. 509p. **CJ4**

British academicians, librarians, and specialists present bibliographic review essays on the topical and area studies aspects of politics; p.135–241 are devoted to the United Kingdom. Includes monographs and periodical titles as well as reference sources. Indexed. Z7161.I544

International relations theory: a bibliography. Ed. by A. J. R. Groom and Christopher Mitchell. London, Frances Pinter; N.Y., Nichols, [1978]. 222p. **CJ5**

". . . the aim has been to reflect and comment upon the present state of the literature in International Relations in . . . its theoretical and conceptual aspects and to point to both likely and desirable future directions."—*Introd.* Chapters by individual scholars compare English-language sources in areas such as methodology, research methods, strategy, foreign policy analysis, etc.; each essay concludes with a list of titles mentioned. Z6461.I49

Pfaltzgraff, Robert L. The study of international relations: a guide to information sources. Detroit, Gale, [1977]. 155p. (International relations information guide ser., v.5) **CJ6**

An annotated bibliography of English-language books (most published since 1945) on the theory and methodology of international relations. General introductory chapters on the nature of the discipline and approaches to it are followed by chapters listing works on the international system, diplomacy, power and theories of conflict, military strategy and theories of deterrence, and integration and alliance theories. Annotated list of important journals, and list of recommended books for the small library. Author, title, and subject indexes. Z6461.P53

Wynar, Lubomyr Roman. Guide to reference materials in political science; a selective bibliography. Denver, Colorado Bibliographic Institute, 1966–68. 2v. **CJ7**

v.1 covers: (1) Social science general reference sources; (2) Political science general reference sources; (3) Political theory; and (4) Ideology. v.2 deals with: (1) International relations; (2) Public administration; (3) Political behavior, public opinion, political parties and electoral processes; (4) Comparative political systems; (5) Government documents; and (6) Reference sources in law. Most entries are annotated. Z7161.W9

Bibliography

Ashford, Douglas Elliott, Katzenstein, Peter J. and **Pempel, T. J.** Comparative public policy, a cross-national bibliography. Beverly Hills, Sage Pubns., [1978]. 272p. **CJ8**

Organized by broad subject area, then by geographical region. Subjects include administrative reform, economic management, local and regional reorganization, labor relations, race and migration, social security, higher education, science and technology; countries include the United States, Great Britain, France, West Germany, and Japan. Emphasizes English-language material written in the last 20 years. No detailed subject or author index. Z7161.A84

Beaufays, Jean. Le fédéralisme, le régionalisme: bibliographie. Liège, Département de Science Politique, Université de Liège et Centre Universitaire de Droit Publique, 1976. 280*l*. (Études et recherches—Université de Liège, Département de science politique, no.10) **CJ9**

An author listing of more than 2,300 books and periodical articles, indexed by geographic area and subject. Z7164.F4B4

Beck, Carl and **McKechnie, J. Thomas.** Political elites: a select computerized bibliography. Cambridge, Mass., M.I.T. Pr., [1968]. 661p. **CJ10**

Attempts to include "a fair representation of the various conceptual and theoretical areas touched by the study of political elites."—*Introd.* In three sections: (1) a KWOC (keyword out of context) index; (2) a full citation listing; and (3) an author list. Z7164.E4B4

Bibliographie zur Politik in Theorie und Praxis. Bearb. von Albrecht Tyrell. Hrsg., Karl Dietrich Bracher, Hans-Adolf Jacobsen, Albrecht Tyrell. Vollständige Neubearbeitung. [Königstein], Athenäum; [Düsseldorf], Droste, 1982. 252p. (Bonner Schriften zur Politik und Zeitgeschichte, 20) **CJ11**

1st ed. 1970; suppl. 1973.
An international, classed bibliography of 4,724 citations. Z7161.A2B52

Bibliographies françaises de sciences sociales. Paris, Fondation Nationale des Sciences Politiques, 1960–67. v.1–4. (No more published?) **CJ12**

Contents: v.1, Jean Meyriat. La science politique en France, 1945–1958: bibliographie commentée (1960); v.2, Bernard Gournay. L'administration française: pt.1, Administrations centrales, bibliographie commentée (1961); v.3, France. Centre National de la Recherche Scientifique. Centre d'Études Sociologiques. Groupe de Sociologie Rurale. Les sociétés rurales françaises (1962); v.4, Bernard Gournay. L'administration française: pt.2, Administrations locales (1967).

From 1968 this series was to have been designated as "Bibliographies spéciales," complemented by two new supplementary series:

——— Guides de recherches. Paris, Colin, 1970–75. v.1–6. (In progress?)

Contents: v.1, J. L. Bodiguel. L'administration française (1970); v.2, Lilly Marcou. L'Union soviétique (1971); v.3, Aline Coutrot. Jeunesse et politique (1971); v.4, Henri Ménudier. L'Allemagne après 1945 (1972); v.5, Denis Martin. L'Afrique noire (1973); v.6, Guy Feuer. Le Moyen-Orient contemporain (1975).

——— Répertoire documentaires. Paris, Fondation, 1968–71. v.1–4. (In progress?)

Contents: v.1, Guide sommaire des ouvrages de référence en sciences sociales (1968); v.2, Catalogue général des périodiques reçus par la Fondation Nationale des Sciences Politiques (1968); v.3, Jean Charlot. Répertoire des publications des partis politiques français, 1944–1967 (1970); v.4, Supplément au Catalogue général des périodiques reçus par La Fondation Nationale des Sciences Politiques (1971).

Blackey, Robert. Revolutions and revolutionists; a comprehensive guide to the literature. Santa Barbara, Calif., ABC-Clio, [1982]. 488p. (War/peace bibliography ser., no.17) **CJ13**

1976 ed. had title: *Modern revolutions and revolutionists.*
A bibliographic guide to more than 6,200 printed sources in Western languages, on concepts and aspects of revolutions from ancient times through 1979. Also provides a brief chronology and selections of quotations on revolution. Chronological and geographical arrangement; indexed by author and subject. Z7164.R54B5

Blackstock, Paul W. and **Schaf, Frank L.** Intelligence, espionage, counterespionage, and covert operations: a guide to information sources. Detroit, Gale, [1978]. 255p. (International relations information guide ser., 2) **CJ14**

A highly selective, annotated bibliography, limited mainly to books and articles in the English language. Concentrates on the post-1945 period, with some attention to historical treatments. Author and title indexes. Z6724.I7B55

The combined retrospective index set to journals in political science, 1886–1974. Wash., Carrollton Pr., 1977. 8v. **CJ15**

At head of title: C.R.I.S.
Annadel N. Wile, exec. ed.
Contents: v.1, International law, international organizations, international relations, international trade and economics; v.2, Meth-

odology and theoretical approaches, political behavior and process, political ideologies, political systems, political thought; v.3, Administration in general, economics in general, financial administration, management in general, organization, departments and functions; v.4–5, Organization, departments and functions (cont'd.); v.6, Organization, departments and functions, personnel, population. v.7–8, Author indexes.

More than 115,000 articles from 179 English-language political science journals have been assigned to one or more of 95 subject categories, then computer-sorted by keyword and chronological coverage under each subject category. Each entry provides keyword, brief title, author's name, year, volume and code number for journal title, and beginning page.   Z7163.C65

Deutsch, Karl Wolfgang and **Merritt, Richard L.** Nationalism and national development; an interdisciplinary bibliography. Cambridge, Mass., M.I.T. Pr., [1970]. 519p.   **CJ16**

An earlier bibliography by Deutsch, *An interdisciplinary bibliography on nationalism* (Cambridge, 1956), covered the period 1935–53; this volume covers 1935–66. A classed bibliography of about 5,000 items, with author and keyword-in-context indexes. Includes books, pamphlets, and journal articles in the major Western languages, but with English-language materials predominating.

Supplements Pinson (CJ27).   Z7164.N2D43

Fondation Nationale des Sciences Politiques. Bibliographie courante d'articles de périodiques postérieurs à 1944 sur les problèmes politiques, économiques, et sociaux. Boston, G. K. Hall, 1968. 17v.   **CJ17**

Added title page in English: *Index to post-1944 periodical articles on political, economic, and social problems.*

Reproduces the catalog cards from a file maintained at the Foundation's Centre de Documentation Contemporaine, covering through 1967. Includes about 300,000 entries selected from more than 1,700 periodicals received at the Centre. Classed arrangement; classification schedule and list of periodical abbreviations (with indication of dates of coverage) in v.1.

————— ————— Supplement 1–11. Boston, 1969–78. 22v.

      AI7.F6

France. Institut National d'Études Démographiques. Economie et population; les doctrines françaises avant 1800. [v.2], Bibliographie générale commentée. Paris, Presses Universitaires de France, 1956. 688p. (*Its* Travaux et documents. Cahier no.28)   **CJ18**

An annotated bibliography of books published in France before 1800 on subjects relative to population, such as: economics, agriculture, commerce and industry, colonies, finance, labor, social questions, marriage, children, religion, health, law, etc. Most of the works were published in the 18th century, with fewer from the 17th and 16th centuries. (v.1, text by Joseph J. Spengler, was published as Cahier no.21 in 1954.)

Harvard University. Library. Government: classification schedule, classified listing by call number, author and title listing, chronological listing. Cambridge, Harvard Univ. Lib.; distr. by Harvard Univ. Pr., 1969. 263p. (Widener shelflist, 22)   **CJ19**

For a note on the series *see* AA145.

Includes historical and theoretical works on political science and the theory of the state; general and comparative works on constitutional law and on the government and administration of countries, local political divisions, and colonies; and general works on civil law.   Z7161.H284

Hawley, Willis D. and **Svara, James H.** The study of community power: a bibliographic review. Santa Barbara, Calif., ABC-Clio, [1972]. 123p.   **CJ20**

Emphasizes English-language materials published since 1920 on "the structure or pattern of community-wide decision making that is intended to authoritatively allocate significant privilege or resources among various institutions, groups and/or individuals" (*Pref.*), thus excluding studies of specific interests or subcommunities. Chapters on history of the field, field studies in communities,

methodology, and secondary analysis. Annotations; reviews are noted. Author index.   Z7164.C842H38

LaBarr, Dorothy F. and **Singer, Joel David.** The study of international politics: a guide to the sources for the student, teacher and researcher. Santa Barbara, Calif., Clio Books, [1976]. 211p.   **CJ21**

A bibliography of English-language materials grouped into eight main sections: (1) Approaches to the study and teaching; (2) Texts and general treatises; (3) American and comparative foreign policy; (4) Journals and annuals; (5) Special series; (6) Abstracts and book reviews; (7) Data sources and handbooks; (8) Bibliographies. The sections are subdivided by type, e.g., authored volumes, articles, edited volumes; contents of edited volumes are listed. Excludes material on international law and international organizations. Author index includes individual authors within the edited volumes.

      Z6461.L3

Leif, Irving P. Community power and decision-making: an international handbook. Metuchen, N.J., Scarecrow Pr., 1974. 170p.   **CJ22**

A classed bibliography of books, articles, dissertations, theses, and conference papers; chapters on theory, methodology, community power as a discipline, American community power studies (subdivided by topical issues such as education, labor, urban planning), and international community power studies. Author index. A selection from this bibliography, with annotations, was published as part of "Community power and decision-making; a trend report and bibliography" by Leif and T. N. Clark in *Current sociology* 20, no. 2 (1972).   Z7164.C842L43

Literatur-Verzeichnis der politischen Wissenschaften, 1952–70. Hrsg. von der Hochschule für Politische Wissenschaften, München, 1952–70. Annual.   **CJ23**

A comprehensive, annual bibliography of German writings on political science. Annotated and classified.   Z7163.L53

Menendez, Albert J. Church-state relations: an annotated bibliography. N.Y., Garland, 1976. 126p.   **CJ24**

A topically arranged listing of English-language books; brief annotations; author index. Emphasis is on developments in the United States and Great Britain.   Z7776.72.M45

Miewald, Robert D. The bureaucratic state: an annotated bibliography. N.Y., Garland, 1984. 601p. (Public affairs and administration ser., 6; Garland reference library of social science, 166)   **CJ25**

More than 2,700 English-language items written since the mid-19th century are grouped in subject chapters; includes historical, theoretical, national, and contemporary case studies. Author index.   Z7164.A2M53

Mishra, Sudhakanta. Economics of foreign aid: bibliography on foreign aid with special reference to India. Allahabad, Kitab Mahal, 1978– . v. 1– . (In progress)   **CJ26**

Contents: v.1, 1947–66.

v.1 is topically arranged, listing 1,150 English-language references under broad categories such as: assistance from individual countries (subdivided by country), assistance from international institutions, technical assistance, agriculture, industry, and foreign investment. There is a significant amount of material on countries other than India. No indexes.   Z7165.I6M57

Pinson, Koppel S. A bibliographical introduction to nationalism. N.Y., Columbia Univ. Pr., 1935. 70p.   **CJ27**

An annotated bibliography of works in English, French, and German dealing specifically with the problems of nationalism in various parts of the world.

Supplemented by Deutsch and Merritt (CJ16).   Z7164.N2P6

Scholar's guide to intelligence literature: bibliography of the Russell J. Bowen Collection in the Joseph Mark Lauinger Memorial Library, Georgetown University. Ed. by Marjorie W. Cline, Carla E. Christiansen and Judith M. Fontaine. Frederick, Md., University Pubns. of America, [1983]. 236p.

     CJ28

Publ. for the National Intelligence Study Center.

A classed international bibliography of about 6,000 books, documents, and articles on espionage, counterintelligence, covert action, subversion, etc., including histories of wars and warfare from the American Revolution to the Vietnamese conflict. Author and title indexes.

Tandon, J. C., Batra, Sunita and **Moley, Regina.** Nonalignment: a bibliography. [New Delhi], Lancers, [1983]. 116p. **CJ29**

"Publ. under the auspices of School of International Studies, Jawaharlal Nehru University, New Delhi."—t.p.

A classed bibliography of English-language documents, books, periodical and newspaper articles. Author index.

Z6464.N62T36

U.S. Library of Congress. General Reference and Bibliography Division. A guide to bibliographic tools for research in foreign affairs. 2d ed. with supplement, comp. by Helen F. Conover. Wash., 1958. 145p., 15p. (Repr.: Westport, Conn., Greenwood Pr., 1970) **CJ30**

1st ed. 1956.

The 2d ed. adds a 15p. supplement. 351 items are listed—with long annotations—in two sections, including bibliographies, manuals, indexes, etc. Z6461.U49

Universal Reference System. Political science, government and public policy series. Princeton, N.J., Princeton Research, [1965–69]. 10v. **CJ31**

Subtitle: An annotated and intensively indexed compilation of significant books, pamphlets, and articles, selected and processed by the Universal Reference System—a computerized information retrieval service in the social and behavioral sciences.

Contents: v.1, International affairs (2d ed., 1969); v.2, Legislative process, representation, and decision-making; v.3, Bibliography of bibliographies in political science, government, and public policy; v.4, Administrative management; v.5, Current events and problems of modern society; v.6, Public opinion, mass behavior, and political psychology; v.7, Law, jurisprudence, and judicial process; v.8, Economic regulation: business and government; v.9, Public policy and the management of science; v.10, Comparative government and cultures.

The series is a computer-produced bibliography with elaborate indexing for maximum retrievability. Represents a selection of classics and 20th-century writings, with heavy concentration on materials of recent years. Items are arranged in an arbitrary numerical sequence, with access through the index section of each volume. Updated by annual supplements.

Winkler, Heinrich August and **Schnabel, Thomas.** Bibliographie zum Nationalismus. Göttingen, Vandenhoeck & Ruprecht, [1979]. 155p. (Arbeitsbücher zur modernen Geschichte, Bd.7) **CJ32**

A classed bibliography of books, periodical articles, and dissertations. Sections for general, theoretical, and specialized studies are followed by a geographical arrangement for works relating to a specific country or region. No index. Z7164.N2W54

Wright, Moorhead, Davis, Jane and **Clarke, Michael.** Essay collections in international relations; a classified bibliography. N.Y. & London, Garland, 1977. 172p. **CJ33**

"This bibliography details original material on international relations since 1870 written in English and appearing in nonrecurrent multi-author works published between 1945 and 1975."—Introd. Selective inclusion of materials in "peripheral" areas of international economics, international law, and diplomatic history, and concentration on theoretical, analytical, and historical work rather than current events reporting. Main text is a classified bibliography of individual essays, referring to the list of essay collections for full bibliographic information. Author and subject indexes. Z6461.W7

Zawodny, Janusz Kazimierz. Guide to the study of international relations. San Francisco, Chandler, [1966]. 151p. **CJ34**

A selected bibliography of "sources which are useful for locating (and, in some instances, understanding) materials in the fields of International Relations."—Pref. About 500 entries, most of them annotated. Index. Serves to update, in many respects, Helen Conover's Guide to bibliographic tools for research in foreign affairs (CJ30). Z6461.Z3

Bibliography of bibliography

Harmon, Robert Bartlett. Political science bibliographies. Metuchen, N.J., Scarecrow Pr., 1973. v.1. **CJ35**

A classed list of nearly 800 separately published bibliographies makes up v.1. Author and title indexes. No more published.

Z7161.A1H35

Current

See also CJ31.

ABC pol sci; advance bibliography of contents: political science and government. v.1– , March 1969– . [Santa Barbara, Calif., ABC-Clio, 1969–] 6 nos. per yr. **CJ36**

A "current awareness" service listing the contents of the latest issues of journals in the fields of political science, government, international law, international relations, public policy, etc. Now has author and subject indexes in each issue, cumulating in the 6th issue of the year. Z7161.A214

Canadian review of studies in nationalism. Revue canadienne des études sur le nationalisme. Annual bibliography of works on nationalism: a regional selection. v.1– , 1974– . (Suppl. to the semiannual periodical Canadian review of studies in nationalism) **CJ37**

A selective guide to the contemporary (1970 to the present) literature on nationalism. Each section by an individual scholar includes a brief "state of the scholarship" survey on particular regions or cultures; entries for books and periodical articles are annotated. Z7164.N2C3

Fondation Nationale des Sciences Politiques. Bulletin analytique de documentation politique, économique et social contemporaine. Paris, 1946– , v.1– . **CJ38**

For full record see CA32.

International bibliography of political science. Bibliographie internationale des sciences sociales, 1953– . London, Tavistock; Chicago, Aldine, 1953– . v.1– . Annual. (International bibliography of the social sciences) **CJ39**

Publisher varies. v.1–8, Paris, UNESCO; v.9, 1960– , issued as Publications of the International Committee for Social Sciences Documentation, as one of the series of the International bibliography of the social sciences (series title varies slightly).

In English and French.

An extensive, classified listing of books, pamphlets, periodical articles, and official government publications in various languages, including Slavic and Asian languages. Indexes by author and subject (in English and French). Z7163.I64

International political science abstracts. Documentation politique internationale. v.1– , 1951– . Oxford, Blackwell, 1951– . Quarterly. **CJ40**

Publisher varies.

Prepared by the International Political Science Association in cooperation with the International Committee for Social Sciences Documentation and with the support of Unesco.

Abstracts are in English or French and are selected from a large number of periodicals published in various countries. Arrangement varies. Recent issues are classified by large groupings, with cumulated annual author and subject indexes. JA36.I5

Politische Dokumentation. Jahrg. 1– , Juni 1965– . München, Verlag Dokumentation, 1965– . 3 nos. per yr. **CJ41**

At head of title, Jahrg. 2– : *Pol-dok.*
Frequency varies.
Vols. for [1966–71] issued by Leitstelle Politische Dokumentation in association with Otto-Suhr-Institut of the Freie Universität, Berlin; [1978]– by Leitstelle Politische Dokumentation.
Abstracts articles from about 200 German-language periodicals. Author, geographical area, and subject indexes in each issue, cumulating annually.   JA14.P62

Recent publications on governmental problems. Chicago, Merriam Center Library, 1932– . Semimonthly, with annual cumulation.   **CJ42**

Sponsored by the American Planning Assoc., American Public Works Assoc., Council of Planning Librarians, Internat. Assoc. of Assessing Officers, Public Administration Service, Univ. of Chicago Computation Center.
English-language books, periodicals, reports, and documents are listed in about ten topical sections, subdivided by detailed subjects; some brief annotations. Annual cumulation indexed by personal and corporate author, subject, and title.   Z7164.A2R4

United States political science documents. v.1– , 1975– . Pittsburgh, Univ. of Pittsburgh, Univ. Center for International Studies, 1976– . Annual.   **CJ43**

Contents: pt.1, Indexes; pt.2, Document descriptions.
"Published by University Center for International Studies, University of Pittsburgh, in conjunction with the American Political Science Association."—*t.p.*
An abstracting service for more than 120 American journals in the political, social, and policy sciences. Pt.1 includes five indexes: Author/Contributor, Subject, Geographic area, Proper name, and Journal; all give complete bibliographic citations and reference to the abstract printed in pt.2. (The parts are available separately.) Abstracts in pt.2 are 100–200 words in length. Subject and geographic area indexes are based on descriptors from the *Political science thesaurus* by Carl Beck and others. The database established for *USPSD* has also been used for a number of "derivative publications": *Comparative studies documents, Ethnic studies bibliography, Intercultural studies reference guide, International studies documents, Public policy studies documents, Strategic studies documents, Russian and East European studies bibliography,* and *Asian studies bibliography.*   Z7163.U58●

Periodicals

Political and social science journals: a handbook for writers and reviewers. Santa Barbara, Calif., ABC-Clio, [1983]. 236p.   **CJ44**

A guide to 440 English-language journals' editorial policies and procedures for manuscripts and book reviews. Alphabetical title arrangement; subject index.   JA74.P62

Dictionaries and encyclopedias

Académie Diplomatique Internationale. Dictionnaire diplomatique . . . t.6–7. Pub. sous la direction de A.–F. Frangulis. Genève, Paris, N.Y., [etc.], Académie, 1957–68. 2v.   **CJ45**

v.6 is an alphabetical dictionary treating questions relating to diplomacy, with bibliographies. Includes articles on general subjects —e.g., atomic energy, colonialism, communism, prisoners of war, etc.—interfiled with articles on the countries of the world. The latter include descriptive notes; political and diplomatic history with documentation and bibliography; and, in *annexes,* the texts of the principal multilateral treaties concluded by them. v.7 supplements rather than supersedes the earlier dictionary, adding new entries and updating many of the earlier ones.
For v.5, a biographical volume, *see* CJ74.   JX1226.A3

Beck, Reinhart. Sachwörterbuch der Politik. Stuttgart, Kröner, [1977]. 1003p.   **CJ46**

A dictionary of about 1,500 terms broadly related to political science. Many definitions have brief bibliographical references.   JA63.B43

Becker, Carol A. International relations dictionary. 2d ed., rev. Wash., Govt. Prt. Off., 1980. 80p. (Dept. of State pub. 9172; Dept. and foreign service ser. 221)   **CJ46a**

1st ed. 1978.
An extremely useful dictionary of terms, phrases, acronyms, catch words and abbreviations which the Library Division has not located in other reference books. The "Notes" section for each entry lists bibliographic documentation; numerous cross references.   JX1226.B42

Buranelli, Vincent and **Buranelli, Nan.** Spy/counterspy: an encyclopedia of espionage. N.Y., McGraw-Hill, [1982]. 361p.   **CJ47**

Comprises about 400 articles on individual spies, organizations, incidents, and techniques from the 17th century until the present. International scope. Bibliographical references; index.   UB250.B87

Chandler, Ralph C. and **Plano, Jack C.** The public administration dictionary. N.Y., Wiley, 1982. 406p.   **CJ47a**

Key concepts are grouped within seven subject chapters; entries include definition, historical and contemporary comment on significance, and relevant cross references. Bibliography; index.   JA61.C47

Cutchin, D. A. Guide to public administration. Itasca, Ill., F. E. Peacock, [1981]. 159p. il.   **CJ48**

Principally a dictionary of terms, phrases, specific laws, and important personalities; also provides brief annotated bibliography of reference and periodical titles. Indexed.   JA61.C87

Diplomaticheskii slovar'. V trek tomakh. Glavnaia redaktsiia A. A. Gromyko i dr. 4-e perer. i dop. izd. Moskva, Nauka, 1984– . v.1– . (In progress)   **CJ49**

1st ed.: Moskva, Gospolitizdat, 1948–50. 2v.
A dictionary of modern diplomacy and international affairs. International in scope with emphasis on Russia. Includes definitions of diplomatic terms and a considerable amount of biography. Many articles on international conferences, treaties, diplomatic proceedings, and the foreign policies of countries. Some articles have bibliographies.   D205.D5212

Dizionario di politica. Diretto da Norberto Bobbio [et al.] 2a ed. [Turin], UTET, [1983]. 1268p.   **CJ50**

Lengthy, signed articles by an international group of scholars stress the variant definitions of political concepts and their historical development. Most articles have brief bibliographies.   JA64.I8D59

Dobson, Christopher and **Payne, Ronald.** The dictionary of espionage. London, Harrap, [1984]. 234p.   **CJ50a**

Provides biographical sketches of spies and spymasters since the Second World War; also outlines intelligence organizations and activities of 17 countries. Glossary; selected bibliography.   UB270.P38

Elliott, Florence. A dictionary of politics. [7th ed.] Harmondsworth, Penguin, [1973]. 522p.   **CJ51**

A compact dictionary of terms, places, and living persons important in current international affairs.   D419.E4

Geschichtliche Grundbegriffe; historisches Lexikon zur politischsozialen Sprache in Deutschland. Hrsg. von Otto Brunner, Werner Conze, Reinhart Koselleck. Stuttgart, Ernst Klett Verlag, [1972–84]. v.1–5. (In progress)   **CJ52**

Contents: v.1–5, Adel–Soziologie.
The completed work will comprise about 130 long, monographic articles on socio-political terms and concepts. Articles are signed and include many bibliographic references.   D9.G43

Görlitz, Axel. Handlexikon zur Politikwissenschaft. [München], Ehrenwirth, [1970]. 481p.   **CJ53**

Terms in the field of political science are treated in signed articles of some length, with bibliographies appended.   JA63.G63

Haensch, Günther. Wörterbuch der internationalen Beziehungen und der Politik, systematisch und alphabetisch; Deutsch, Englisch, Französisch, Spanisch. 2., völlig neubearb. u. erw. Aufl. [München], Max Hueber Verlag, [1975]. 781p.   **CJ54**

1st ed. 1965.

Title also in English (*Dictionary of international relations and politics*), French, and Spanish.

Grouped by subject, the words, phrases, and geographical names can be approached collectively through the detailed table of contents, or individually through the alphabetical index, both being quatrolingual. The section of "Names of states, territories, etc." has been omitted from this edition.   JX1226.H283

Kleines politisches Wörterbuch. 3., überarb. Aufl. Berlin, Dietz, 1978. 1075p.   **CJ55**

A political science dictionary with lengthy entries focusing on terms, events, and abbreviations relevant to East Germany and other Communist countries.   JA63.K54

Laqueur, Walter Ze'ev, ed. A dictionary of politics. Rev. ed. N.Y., Free Pr., 1974. 565p.   **CJ56**

1st ed. 1971.

Concentrating on developments since 1933, the work is designed "to present concise, up-to-date information about the facts, the changes in terminology and the historical background of contemporary politics for the student and general reader."—*Pref.* Includes entries for political figures as well as for terms.   D419.L36

Plano, Jack C., Riggs, Robert E. and **Robin, Helenan S.** The dictionary of political analysis. 2d ed. Santa Barbara, Calif., ABC-Clio, [1982]. 197p. (Clio dictionaries in political science, 3)   **CJ57**

1st ed. 1973.

Focuses on terms used in statistical and behavioral analyses of political data. Alphabetical arrangement of about 200 entries. Bibliography; index.   JA61.P57

Plano, Jack C. and **Olton, Roy.** The international relations dictionary. 3d ed. Santa Barbara, Calif., ABC- Clio, [1982]. 488p.   **CJ58**

1st ed. 1969.

Offers definitions of terms relating to international relations and foreign policy, together with comments on the significance of each term. Entries are grouped within topical sections rather than being in a single alphabetical sequence. Index of terms.   JX1226.P55

Scruton, Roger. A dictionary of political thought. N.Y., Harper & Row, [1982]. 499p.   **CJ59**

"The emphasis . . . is conceptual rather than factual, exploring the formulation of doctrines rather than their specific application. Political events are mentioned only when they cast light on intellectual conceptions . . . [and] the few proper names . . . are those of thinkers rather than those of political figures.—*Pref.* Numerous cross references.   JA61.S37

Staatslexikon; Recht, Wirtschaft, Gesellschaft, hrsg. von der Görres-Gesellschaft. 6. völlig neubearb. und erw. Aufl. Freiburg, Herder, 1957–63. 8v.   **CJ60**

1st ed. 1889–97; 5th ed. 1926–32.

A standard German work written from the Catholic viewpoint. This edition is enlarged and thoroughly revised, articles have been rewritten, and new ones added. Articles are signed and have good bibliographies listing works in various languages.   JA63.S82

Directories

Bundy, Mary L. and **Gilchrist, Irvin.** The national civil rights directory: an organizations directory. College Park, Md., Urban Information Interpreters, [1979]. 183p.   **CJ61**

In two main parts: national organizations, and local organizations listed by state. Includes religious, academic, legal, media, political, labor, and ethnic associations. Indexes by name of organization and subject focus; list of periodical publications; selected bibliography.   JC599.U5B84

Directory of organizations and individuals professionally engaged in governmental research and related activities. 1935– . Austin, Tex., Governmental Research Assoc., 1935– .   **CJ62**

Title varies slightly.

Arranged geographically, with alphabetical indexes by organization and individual. Includes local, state, and national agencies, as well as individual members of the Governmental Research Association.   JK3.G627

Duffy, David and **Jacobs, Barbara.** Directory of Third World studies in the United States. [Waltham, Mass.], Crossroads Pr., [1981]. 463p.   **CJ63**

In two parts: (1) formal Third World studies programs; (2) colleges and universities offering "at least a few courses on the Third World."—*Introd.* Institutional entries provide information on: faculty and courses, degrees, languages, affiliations with foreign institutions, library collections, number of students, special features, and publications. Updates African programs information presented in the *Directory of African and Afro-American studies in the United States* (CC416). No subject approach.   HC59.7.D78

European Consortium for Political Research. Directory of European political scientists. 3d fully rev. ed. N.Y., Holmes & Meier, [1979]. 461p.   **CJ64**

1st ed. 1972.

Provides the following information for some 2,100 academic political scientists working in Europe: date of birth and nationality; address; degrees awarded; title of doctoral dissertation; career appointments; selected publications; subject specialization. Indexed by subject field and area focus. A 4th ed. is to be published 1985.   JA84.E9E89

Murphy, Dennis D. Directory of conservative and libertarian serials, publishers, and freelance markets. 2d ed. [Tucson, Author], 1979. 64p.   **CJ65**

For full information *see* AE36.

Policy Studies Organization. [Directories. Urbana, Ill., The Organization, 1973–]   **CJ66**

This organization, publisher of *Policy studies journal,* now publishes six directories in this field. Each directory is available in paperback and is to be published on a serial basis. Titles include: *Policy studies directory* (1973– ; academic programs); *Policy research centers directory* (1978–); *Political science utilization directory* (1975– ; political science activities in government agencies); *Policy grants directory* (1977–); *Policy studies personnel directory* (1979–); and *Policy publishers and associations directory* (1980–).

Handbooks

Banks, Arthur S. and **Textor, Robert B.** A cross-polity survey. Cambridge, Mass., Massachusetts Inst. of Technology Pr., 1963. 118p., [1405p.]   **CJ67**

Consists of a computer printout designed to aid in cross-national research for demographic, economic, political, and social relationships, plus introductory and explanatory matter.

For a review *see American sociological review* 29:635–36, Aug. 1964.   JA73.B35

Brownlie, Ian, ed. Basic documents on human rights. 2d ed. Oxford, Clarendon Pr., 1981. 505p.   **CJ68**

1st ed. 1971.

A collection of representative documents, with introductory notes and bibliographical references.   K3238.A1B76

Greenstein, Fred I. and **Polsby, Nelson W.** Handbook of political science. Reading, Mass., Addison-Wesley, [1975]. 9v.   **CJ69**

Contents: v.1, Political science: scope and theory; v.2, Micropolitical theory; v.3, Macropolitical theory; v.4, Non-governmental politics; v.5, Governmental institutions and processes; v.6, Policies and policy-making; v.7, Strategies of inquiry; v.8, International politics; v.9, Cumulative index.

A collection of review articles by scholars representing the major areas of political science, similar in concept to the Gardner Lindzey and Elliot Aronson *Handbook of social psychology* (2d ed., 1968–69. 5v.). Each essay concludes with extensive references. Author and subject index. Extensive reviews of each volume appears in *American political science review* 71:1621–36 (Dec. 1977).   JA71.G752

International handbook of political science. Ed. by William G. Andrews. Westport, Conn., Greenwood Pr., 1982. 464p.   **CJ70**

An international survey of the discipline of political science. 26 chapters by political scientists discuss the evolution of the field in particular countries since 1945—intellectual structure, teaching, research, associations, relationship with politics—with footnotes and bibliographies. Appendixes and bibliography of works on political science in countries not included in this volume. Indexed.   JA71.I57

International handbook of the ombudsman. Ed. by Gerald E. Caiden. Westport, Conn., Greenwood Pr., [1983]. 2v.   **CJ71**

Contents: [v.1] Evolution and present function; [v.2] Country surveys.

Approximately 75 contributors have prepared essays with notes and bibliographies on the development of the ombudsman's role, its function in different organizations, and its history in about ninety countries and cities of the world. Indexed.   JF1525.O45I55

Research support for political scientists: a guide to sources of funds for research fellowships, grants and contracts. Comp. by Stephen F. Szabo. 2d ed. Wash., Departmental Services Program, Amer. Political Science Assoc., [1981]. 154p.   **CJ72**

1st ed. 1977.
In four main sections: (1) research fellowships; (2) doctoral dissertation research grants; (3) private foundations; (4) government grants. Coverage of research fellowships is the most comprehensive, and that of private foundations awards the least; state and local government grants are excluded. Each entry includes funding, description of award, application instructions, and contact personnel. Bibliography; no index.   JA88.U6S9

Taylor, Charles Lewis and **Jodice, David A.** World handbook of political and social indicators. 3d ed. New Haven, Yale Univ. Pr., [1983]. 2v.   **CJ73**

1st ed. 1964 by Bruce M. Russett and others.
Contents: v.1, Cross-national attributes and rates of change; v.2, Political protest and government change.

Assembles political, economic, social, and cultural series of quantitative data with which to rank nations. Limited to mid-twentieth century to the present. Information is presented mainly in tabular form with introductory and explanatory text.   HN25.T39

Biography

See also CJ71.

Académie Diplomatique Internationale. [t.5], Dictionnaire diplomatique, comprenant les biographies des diplomates, du Moyen Âge à nos jours, constituant un traité d'histoire diplomatique sur six siècles, publié sous la direction de A.-F. Frangulis. Genève, Paris, N.Y., [etc.], Académie, [1954?]. 1261p.   **CJ74**

A biographical dictionary of diplomats from the Middle Ages to mid-twentieth century, international in scope. Some articles signed; some bibliographies. Uneven in treatment.

For t.6–7, *Dictionnaire diplomatique, see* CJ45.   JX1226.A3

American Political Science Association. Biographical directory. Ed.1– . Wash., Assoc., 1945– . (6th ed., 1973)   **CJ75**

Title varies.
Serves as a who's who in political science, giving biographical information on members of the Association. Supplemented by the annual *American Political Science Association membership directory* which provides only names and addresses.   JA28.A56

Kuehl, Warren F. Biographical dictionary of internationalists. Westport, Conn., Greenwood Pr., [1983]. 934p.   **CJ76**

Offers signed biographical sketches of persons from many countries who "held important or leadership positions in national or international nongovernmental societies or associations to promote the concept of world organization or cooperation"; who "held important posts in functional international bodies"; who "gained public recognition as originators or exponents" of relevant ideas, plans, schemes, etc.; or who "sought actively to promote transnationalism in nonpolitical areas."—*Pref.* Includes only deceased persons who were still alive after 1800. Bibliographies; chronology; index. A companion volume is to be entitled *Biographical dictionary of modern peace leaders.*   JC361.K79

Atlases

Wheatcroft, Andrew. The world atlas of revolutions. N.Y., Simon and Schuster, [1983]. 208p. il., maps.   **CJ77**

A graphic presentation of modern revolutions from 1765 to the present; each situation is described in 3 or 4 pages of text, illustrations, and maps. Select bibliography; index.   G1035.W5

NATIONAL POLITICS AND GOVERNMENT

United States

Guides

Guide to American foreign relations since 1700. Ed. by Richard Dean Burns. Santa Barbara, Calif., ABC-Clio, [1983]. 1311p. maps.   **CJ78**

For full information *see* DB27.

Simpson, Antony E. Guide to library research in public administration. N.Y., John Jay College of Criminal Justice, Center for Productive Public Management, [1976]. 210p. il.   **CJ79**

Chapters on the field of public administration, and the definition of the research problem and search strategy, are followed by chapters on types of reference works, computer searches, archival resources, and suggestions on writing the research paper. Indexed.   Z7164.A2S5

Vose, Clement E. A guide to library sources in political science: American government. Wash., Amer. Pol. Sci. Assoc., [1975]. 135p. il. (Instructional resource monograph, no.1)   **CJ80**

A guide for students in three main sections: (1) American national government, discussing government publications, indexes, and reference sources for research relating to various branches of the government and their activities; (2) General reference books of interest to the research worker in political science; (3) The political scientist in the library, discussing basic library techniques, plus information on the use of manuscripts and archives. No index.   Z7165.U5V67

Bibliography

Brooks, Alexander D. Civil rights and liberties in the United States; an annotated bibliography . . . with a selected list of fiction and audio-visual materials collected by Albert A. Alexander and Virginia H. Ellison. N.Y., Civil Liberties Educ. Foundation, Inc., 1962. 151p. **CJ81**

An annotated bibliography of books on civil and political rights, most of them published since 1945. Prepared specifically for use with high school students; should be useful to the general reader as well. Classified, with no index. Z7164.L6B7

Iowa. University. Libraries. The right wing collection of the University of Iowa Libraries, 1918–1977: a guide to the microfilm collection. Glen Rock, N.J., Microfilming Corp. of America, 1978. 175p. **CJ82**

Designed to accompany the 177-reel microfilm collection published under the same title. Provides access by title or corporate author to the serials and ephemera collections at the University of Iowa Libraries, the B'nai B'rith Collection at Harvard University's Widener Library, and collections at California State University at Fullerton Library, Northern Arizona University Library, Tulane University Library, and the Kenneth Spencer Research Library of the University of Kansas. Each entry provides description of holdings, type of serial, and general information. Indexed by subject, place of publication, and year of publication. Z7163.I7

Kaid, Lynda Lee, Sanders, Keith R., and **Hirsch, Robert O.** Political campaign communication: a bibliography and guide to the literature. Metuchen, N.J., Scarecrow Pr., 1974. 206p. **CJ83**

A listing of over 1,500 books, articles, pamphlets, federal documents, and unpublished materials on political campaign communication in the United States between 1950 and 1972. Also includes a French- and German-language supplement, an annotated list of fifty "seminal" books on the topic, and a guide to the literature to keep the user abreast of research. Subject index. Z7165.U5K34

Manheim, Jarol B. and **Wallace, Melanie.** Political violence in the United States, 1875–1974: a bibliography. N.Y. & London, Garland, 1975. 116p. **CJ84**

A classed list of over 1,500 entries: books, articles, doctoral dissertations, and government documents covering strikes, race riots, gun control, assassinations, anarchism and terrorism, vigilantism, police violence, etc. Author index but no detailed subject approach. Z7165.U5M27

Maurer, David J. U.S. politics and elections: a guide to information sources. Detroit, Gale, [1978]. 213p. (American government and history information guide ser., v.2) **CJ85**

An introductory, annotated bibliography of monographic literature, arranged by historical period from colonial times to 1976; each section lists biographies separately. Author, title, and subject indexes. Z1236.M39

Miles, William. The image makers; a bibliography of American presidential campaign biographies. Metuchen, N.J., Scarecrow Pr., 1979. 254p. **CJ86**

Bibliographic descriptions of 1,283 "books, pamphlets, magazines, almanacs, speeches, [and] political compendia . . . which are or in which appear . . . campaign biographies, both favorable and unfavorable, dating from 1796 to 1976."—*Introd.* Arranged chronologically by campaign, then by candidates and those who unsuccessfully sought nomination. Indexed by author, title, and candidate. Z7164.R4M63

Plischke, Elmer. U.S. foreign relations: a guide to information sources. Detroit, Gale, [1980]. 715p. (American government and history information guide ser., v.6) **CJ87**

This compilation of "analytical, descriptive, and documentary sources . . . bibliographical guides, monographs, textbooks, essays [including periodical articles], and documentary materials . . . is concerned with the foreign affairs process, not with diplomatic history, current events, world politics, or substantive foreign policy development and analysis."—*Pref.* In four main segments: (1) diplomacy in general; (2) conduct of U.S. foreign relations (p.77–502), reference works and unofficial studies of governmental agencies and activities, and specialized aspects such as decision making, crisis diplomacy, policy formulation, etc.; (3) official sources and unofficial document collections (p.503–610); and (4) memoirs and biographical literature. Chapter introductions provide evaluative reviews of the literature; some brief, critical annotations. Detailed table of contents; author index. A valuable guide. Z6465.U5P52

Rouse, John Edward. Public administration in American society: a guide to information sources. Detroit, Gale, [1980]. 553p. (American government and history information guide ser., v.11) **CJ88**

An annotated bibliography of about 1,700 books and periodical articles covering the past 50 years, but focusing on the growing impact of the public bureaucracy in the 1970s. Chapters on federalism, governmental divisions and the administrative process, evaluation, policy making, accountability, human organization, personnel administration, productivity, budgeting, etc. Addendum of about 200 titles from 1979–80. Appendixes provide directory information on the American Society for Public Administration and the National Association of Schools of Public Affairs and Administration. Author, title, and subject indexes. JK421.R63

Smith, Myron J. Watergate: an annotated bibliography of sources in English, 1972–1982. Metuchen, N.J., Scarecrow Pr., 1983. 329p. **CJ89**

More than 2,500 items listed by main entry, with brief contents notes; reference works are listed separately. Includes a chronology, biographies, a list of audiovisual materials, and an index.

Kenyon C. Rosenberg and Judith K. Rosenberg's *Watergate: an annotated bibliography* (Littleton, Colo., Libraries Unlimited, 1975) provides a chronological approach to the literature (including news magazines and newspaper editorials) from 1972 through Aug. 1974. Z1245.S64

Unity in diversity: an index to the publications of conservative and libertarian institutions. The New American Foundation. Carol L. Birch, ed. Metuchen, N.J., Scarecrow Pr., 1983. 263p. **CJ90**

A subject index to about 3,000 monographic and article titles published between 1970 and 1981 by such organizations as the American Enterprise Institute for Public Policy Research, CATO Institute, Foreign Policy Research Institute, Hudson Institute, Heritage Foundation, Hoover Institution, etc. Author index. Z7161.U63

Wilson, David E. National planning in the United States: an annotated bibliography. Boulder, Colo., Westview Pr., [1979]. 279p. **CJ91**

A classed listing of about 2,000 citations relevant to the concept of national planning, or societal guidance, in the areas of public administration, political science, economics, and sociology. The period 1900–72 is treated in chronological segments; planning trends in the 1970s and the future are arranged by broad topics. No author or detailed subject approach. Z7165.U5W48

Dictionaries and encyclopedias

Cyclopedia of American government, ed. by Andrew C. McLaughlin and Albert Bushnell Hart. N.Y., Appleton, 1914. 3v. il. (Repr.: N.Y., Peter Smith, 1949) **CJ92**

A useful work although now much out-of-date. Covers topics in theory or philosophy of political society; forms of political organization and government; international and constitutional law; history of political parties; and other American political topics. Many biographies. Arranged alphabetically by small subjects, with an analytical index. Signed articles by specialists with bibliographies. For the earlier political history of the United States, J. J. Lalor's *Cyclopaedia of political science* (N.Y., Merrill, 1888–90. 3v.) is still occasionally useful. JK9.C9

Elliot, Jeffrey M. and **Ali, Sheikh Rustum.** The presidential-congressional political dictionary. Santa Barbara, Calif., ABC-Clio, [1984]. 365p. il. (Clio dictionaries in political science, 9)   **CJ93**

Entries are organized by subject-matter chapters, except for chapter 3, "The Presidency," where presidents are entered in chronological order. Appendix; bibliographic notes; index.

JK9.E4

Encyclopedia of American political history: studies of the principal movements and ideas. Jack P. Greene, ed. N.Y., Scribner, [1984]. 3v. (1420p.)   **CJ94**

For full information *see* DB151.

Encyclopedia of U.S. government benefits. New & rev. ed. N.Y., Everest House, [1981]. 1010p. il.   **CJ95**

Subtitle: A complete, practical, and convenient guide to United States government benefits available to the people of America, written by a group of government experts.

Ed. by Roy A. Grisham, Jr. and Paul D. McConaughy.

1st ed. 1965.

Presents a catalog of federal government services and programs arranged alphabetically by subject and by agency. Indexed. A new ed. is to be published 1985.   JK424.E55

Findling, John E. Dictionary of American diplomatic history. Westport, Conn., Greenwood Pr., [1980]. 622p.   **CJ96**

Offers biographical sketches of "more than five hundred persons associated with U.S. foreign policy from the Revolution through 1978 as well as descriptions or definitions of more than five hundred non-biographical items connected with American diplomacy, ranging from crises to catchwords."—*Pref.* Biographees were selected mainly from the roster of U.S. chiefs of mission, though other, non-diplomatic persons are also included. Brief bibliographical references. Various useful appendixes; index.   E183.7.F5

Government agencies. Donald R. Whitnah, ed. in chief. Westport, Conn., Greenwood Pr., [1983]. 683p. (Greenwood encyclopedia of American institutions, 7)   **CJ97**

A dictionary arrangement of signed articles on individual federal agencies, giving information on their history, functions, achievements, failures, etc., and placing them in their social and political contexts. Bibliographies; chronology; genealogy (i.e., detailing name changes); index.   JK421.G65

Plano, Jack C. and **Greenberg, Milton.** The American political dictionary. 7th ed. N.Y., Holt, Rinehart and Winston, [1985]. 606p.   **CJ98**

1st ed. 1962.

Terms are grouped under 14 topics, e.g., U.S. constitution, civil liberties, the legislative process, finance and taxation, foreign policy and international affairs. Each section includes definitions and explanations (as appropriate) of terms and important agencies, cases, and statutes. The index allows the work to be used as a dictionary. Cross references within articles.   JK9.P55

Safire, William L. Safire's Political dictionary. N.Y., Random House, [1978]. 845p.   **CJ99**

"An enlarged, up-to-date edition of *The new language of politics* [1968; 2d ed. 1972]."—*t.p.*

Despite the change of title, this is presented as the "third edition" of the 1968 work, considerably enlarged and updated. "As defined here, the language of politics does not include much of the language of government. If a word has a good definition available in most dictionaries, this is not the place to look for it. . . . In the same way, this dictionary concerns itself not with the historical event, but with the language that comes out of it. . . ."—*p.x.* Cross references; brief bibliography; index of names. Citations to sources of quotations are usually too imprecise to be genuinely useful.   JK9.S2

Smith, Edward Conrad and **Zurcher, Arnold John.** Dictionary of American politics. 2d ed. N.Y., Barnes & Noble, [1968]. 434p.   **CJ100**

1st ed., 1888, by Everit Brown and Albert Strauss; 2d ed., 1924, was almost completely rewritten by Edward C. Smith; 3d ed., 1944,

was revised by the present editors. 1949 edition had title: *New dictionary of American politics.* 1955 edition reverted to the earlier title and was published without edition number.

Represents a complete revision. Gives brief, concise definitions; includes slogans, political slang, nicknames, etc.   JK9.S5

Sperber, Hans and **Trittschuh, Travis.** American political terms; an historical dictionary. Detroit, Mich., Wayne State Univ. Pr., 1962. 516p.   **CJ101**

An alphabetical dictionary of political terms giving origins and various meanings, with references to sources, showing earliest and developing usage. Includes a bibliography of the literature searched.

JK9.S65

Whisker, James B. A dictionary of concepts on American politics. N.Y., Wiley, [1980]. 285p.   **CJ102**

Aims "to provide the student with a readable and useful source book that, in as little space as possible, tells what an idea, concept, event, or institution is and why it is important."—*Pref.* Terms are grouped thematically under headings such as "Political ideas," "Politics and political parties," "The presidency," "Congress," "The court system," "Civil liberties and civil rights." Indexed.

JK9.W47

Directories

Directory of registered federal and state lobbyists. Ed.1. Orange, N.J., Academic Media, [1973]. 865p.   **CJ103**

Aims "to provide a comprehensive survey of lobbyists (legislative advocates) who are working to influence officials and legislation."—*Introd.* Compiled from official state and federal sources. Listing is by state, with indexes by names of lobbyists and by organizations represented by the lobbyists. Includes full address and telephone numbers of lobbyists and names of the organizations they represent. An appendix gives the texts of the laws and rules governing registration of lobbyists in the various states.   JK1118.D56

Directory of registered lobbyists and lobbyist legislation. Ed. 2– . Chicago, Marquis Academic Media, 1975– .   **CJ104**

Continues the *Directory of registered federal and state lobbyists* (above).   JK1118.D561

Encyclopedia of governmental advisory organizations. Ed. 1– . Detroit, Gale, 1973– . Irregular.   **CJ105**

Subtitle: A reference guide to presidential advisory committees, public advisory committees, interagency committees and other government-related boards, panels, task forces, commissions, conferences, and other similar bodies serving in a consultative, coordinating, advisory, research, or investigative capacity.

Ed. by Linda E. Sullivan.

Describes over 3,400 committees of current and historic interest, including data on history and authority, program, membership, subsidiary units, staff, meetings, and publications. Material is grouped into ten broad subject areas, with alphabetical and keyword index. The index refers the user to the *U.S. government manual* (CJ112) or the *Congressional directory* (CJ141) for administrative agencies and congressional committees.

Between editions the *Encyclopedia* is updated by:

JK468.C7E52

New governmental advisory organizations. Detroit, Gale, 1976– . Irregular. Looseleaf.   **CJ106**

JK468.C7E521

Federal regulatory directory, 1979/80– . Wash., Congressional Quarterly, 1979– . ports. Annual.   **CJ107**

For 15 major regulatory agencies, provides material on agency's background, power and authority, biographies of important officers, detailed organizational description, information sources issued by the agency, details on public participation, a list of regional offices, and additional references. More abbreviated information is provided for an additional 63 regulatory agencies. Appendix gives data on the *Federal register, Code of federal regulations,* and relevant legislation. Indexed.   KF5406.A15F4

Researcher's guide to Washington experts. By Washington Researchers. Ed. 5– . Wash., The Researchers, [1981]– . Annual.   **CJ108**

Continues: *Researcher's guide to Washington,* 1977–80.

About one-half of the volume is devoted to a detailed telephone directory of federal offices and personnel, indexed by keyword and subject; names of personnel are supplied. "Federal document rooms" describes collections of unpublished materials, and includes information on access and copying facilities. Provides practical information on use of the Freedom of Information Act and the Privacy Act. The 1978 edition includes papers presented at a 1977 conference on Washington information sponsored by the publishers.

U.S. Civil Service Commission. Official register of the United States, 1933–59; persons occupying administrative and supervisory positions in the legislative, executive and judicial branches of the federal government, and in District of Columbia government. Wash., Govt. Prt. Off., 1933–59.   **CJ109**

Before 1861, published by the Dept. of State; 1861–1905, by the Dept. of the Interior; 1907–32, by the Bureau of the Census; 1933–59, by the Civil Service Commission. Biennial until 1921; not issued 1922–24; annual, 1925–59. Ceased publication.

The *Official register,* formerly known as the *Blue book,* was the official list of government employees. In two main parts: (1) a classified list, arranged by departments, agencies, offices, etc., in Washington, and in the territorial possessions, giving names of the principal officials and assistants, showing, for each, official title, salary, legal residence, and place of employment; (2) alphabetical index of names included in the classified list.

Until 1911 the *Official register* included the names of all government employees, including the postal service; from 1913 to 1921 it was complete except for the postal service. The issues from 1925 to 1959 were much reduced in size and included only principal officials.   JK5

U.S. Dept. of State. The biographic register, 1870– . Wash., Govt. Prt. Off., 1870– . Annual (some years not publ.; after 1974, classified ed. issued with limited distribution).   **CJ110**

Title varies: 1869–1942, *Register of the Department of State;* 1944–50, some years called *Biographic register;* 1951– , *Biographic register.*

Contents vary. The early *Register* usually contained sections on departmental organization; information about the foreign service of the United States; historical lists; lists of the clerical, administrative, and fiscal service; and a biographical section for administrative and professional employees. The *Biographic register,* published since 1944, includes only the biographical section, and in recent years has provided information on personnel of the State Department and other federal government agencies in the field of foreign affairs. It thus includes biographies of ambassadors, ministers, chiefs of missions, foreign service officers, foreign service information officers, foreign service staff officers (classes 1–4) and Civil Service employees of grade GS-12 and above. Also includes personnel of U.S. Mission to the U.N., Agency for International Development, Action (the Peace Corps), the U.S. Information Agency, the U.S. Arms Control and Disarmament Agency, and the Foreign Agricultural Service.   JK851.A3

U.S. Dept. of State. Historical Office. United States chiefs of mission, 1778–1982. 2d ed. [Wash., Govt. Prt. Off.], 1982. 394p. (Dept. of State pubn. 8738; Department and Foreign Service ser., 147)   **CJ111**

A register of the principal U.S. diplomatic personnel, arranged by country and date of service. Appendixes list chiefs of mission to international organizations and ambassadors at large.
                                                              JX1706.A59U54

United States government manual. ... 1935– . Wash., 1935– . Annual (earlier volumes irregular).   **CJ112**

Title varies: 1949–72, *United States government organization manual.* Publisher varies. Looseleaf, 1935–37.

The official organization handbook of the federal government, giving information on the organization, activities, and current officials of the various departments, bureaus, offices, commissions, etc., with descriptions of quasi-official agencies and selected international organizations; charts of the more complex agencies; and appendixes relating to abolished or transferred agencies, to government publications, etc.   JK421.Un34

Washington representatives. v.3– , 1979– . Wash., Columbia Books, 1979– . Annual.   **CJ113**

Continues *Directory of Washington representatives of American associations and industry* (1977–78) and assumes its numbering.

Subtitle: Who does what for whom in the nation's capital. A compilation of Washington representatives of the major national associations, labor unions and U.S. companies, registered foreign agents, lobbyists, lawyers, law firms and special interest groups, together with their clients and areas of legislative and regulatory concern.

The current volume provides name, address and telephone numbers for about 5,000 individuals, 500 law and public relations firms, and 4,000 companies with representation in Washington. Indexed by subject and foreign interests.   JK1118.D58

Weinberger, Marvin I. and **Greevy, David U.** The PAC directory: a complete guide to political action committees. Cambridge, Mass., Ballinger, [1982]. 1552p. in various pagings.   **CJ114**

Provides directory, financial, and statistical data on PACs from 1977 through 1980, including presidential and congressional candidate support; also lists ratings of congressional incumbents for the period by 26 groups and organizations. A 2v. ed. by Weinberger, Greevy and Chadwick R. Gore was published 1984.
                                                              JK1991.W44

❖Earlier, unofficial publications which are occasionally useful are: Charles Lanman, *Biographical annals of the civil government of the United States* (2d ed., 1887); R. B. Mosher, *Executive register of the United States, 1789–1902* (1903); and B. P. Poore, *Political register* (1878).

Bibliography

Wynkoop, Sally and **Parish, David W.** Directories of government agencies. Rochester, N.Y., Libraries Unlimited, 1969. 242p.   **CJ115**

An annotated listing of more than 400 directories "prepared by federal departments and their various offices and agencies [and] published by the United States Government or made possible through federal support."—*Introd.* Arranged by Superintendent of Documents classification number, with index of subjects and compilers (most titles appear under subject categories rather than in alphabetical sequence).   Z7165.U5W9

Handbooks

America's governments: a factbook of census data on the organization, finances, and employment of federal, state, and local governments. Comp. by Richard P. Nathan and Mary M. Nathan. N.Y., Wiley, [1979]. 332p.   **CJ116**

"Based on 1977 Census of Governments data and annual census data on finances and employment for the same year."—*t.p.*

A summary volume on the data produced by the U.S. Bureau of the Census for the *Census of governments,* 1977, and other reports. In four main sections: (1) governmental organization; (2) finances; (3) employment; (4) historical statistics. Covers federal, state, county, municipal, and township levels. Sources of reprinted text and tables are not identified. Appendix serves as a bibliography of relevant U.S. government documents.   JK464 1979.A46

Executive branch

Guides and bibliographies

The American presidency: a historical bibliography. Santa Barbara, Calif., ABC-Clio, [1984]. 376p. (Clio bibliography ser., no.15)   **CJ117**

Derived from the *America: history and life* database. Offers citations and abstracts to some 3,489 items from the journal literature of the 1973–82 period. Arranged by chronological period, plus a general section. Author and subject indexes.

           Z1249.P7A47

Davison, Kenneth E. The American presidency: a guide to information sources. Detroit, Gale, [1983]. 467p. (American studies information guide ser., v.11)   **CJ118**

Sections on the office, functions and powers, documents, problems, elections, etc., are followed by chapters on the individual presidents. Some annotations; author and title indexes.

           Z1249.P7D38

Goehlert, Robert U. and **Martin, Fenton S.** The presidency: a research guide. Santa Barbara, Calif., ABC-Clio, [1985]. 341p.   **CJ119**

In four main sections: the presidency as an institution, emphasizing official documents and secondary sources; individual presidents, their publications, presidential libraries, and secondary sources; campaigns and elections, with both primary and secondary titles; design and development of a research project and strategy on the presidency. Appendixes (p.219–98) present research information in tabular format. Author and title indexes.   Z1249.P7G63

Greenstein, Fred I., Berman, Larry and **Felzenberg, Alvin S.** Evolution of the modern presidency; a bibliographical survey. Wash., Amer. Enterprise Inst. for Public Policy Research, [1977]. unpaged. (AEI studies, 153; Studies in political and social processes)   **CJ120**

A classed listing of about 2,500 items; author index. Brief annotations for most entries. Emphasis on developments during the administrations of Franklin D. Roosevelt through Gerald Ford.

           Z7165.U5G74

Studying the presidency. Ed. by George C. Edwards III and Stephen J. Wayne. Knoxville, Univ. of Tennessee Pr., [1983]. 312p.   **CJ121**

Presents a series of essays (with bibliographic notes) by specialists on the methodology and various other aspects of the study of the United States presidency. In two sections: (1) "Approaches and analyses" and (2) "Data sources and techniques." The latter includes chapters on information sources (including online databases), use of legal sources, presidential libraries, and interviewing presidential aides. Indexed.   JK518.S78

Directories and biographical dictionaries

Biographical directory of the United States executive branch, 1774–1977. Robert Sobel, ed. Westport, Conn., Greenwood Pr., [1977]. 503p.   **CJ122**

A 1971 ed. covered 1774–1971.

Includes brief sketches of the careers of all cabinet heads, as well as of presidents, vice presidents, and presidents of the Continental Congress. An index section provides chronological lists, lists by cabinet post or other political office, etc.   E176.B576

DeGregorio, William A. The complete book of U.S. presidents. N.Y., Dembner Books, [1984]. 691p. il.   **CJ123**

Biographies take a more narrative form than those in Kane's compilation (CJ126); each is divided into about 40 headings, such as physical description, romantic affairs, praise, criticism, quotes, books by and about, etc. Also offers biographical sketches of cabinet members. Bibliographical notes. Coverage is through mid-1983. Indexed.   E176.1.D43

Federal staff directory, 1982– . Mt. Vernon, Va., Congressional Staff Directory, 1982– . Annual.   **CJ124**

Subtitle: Containing in convenient order useful information concerning the Executive Branch and its 27,000 key executives with their staff assistants. Carefully indexed by key word and individual with 1,400 staff biographies.

Charles B. Brownson, ed.

A useful companion to the publisher's *Congressional staff directory* (CJ137), providing staff names, addresses, and telephone numbers; also gives brief biographies for key officials. Indexed.

           JK723.E9F44

Federal yellow book. Wash., Washington Monitor, 1976– . Bimonthly.   **CJ125**

Subtitle: A loose-leaf directory of the federal departments and agencies.

A directory of executive departments, administrative agencies, and regional offices. Indexed by organization, but without personal name approach.   JK6.F45

Kane, Joseph Nathan. Facts about the presidents: a compilation of biographical and historical information. 4th ed. N.Y., H. W. Wilson, 1981. 456p.   **CJ126**

1st ed. 1959.

In two parts: pt.1 devotes a chapter to each president in chronological order, with data on family background, political career, and administration; pt.2 presents material in comparative form, with collective data and statistics. Indexed. A supplement covering the Reagan presidency is to be published 1985.   E176.1.K3

The presidents: a reference history. Henry F. Graff, ed. N.Y., Scribner, 1984. 700p.   **CJ126a**

Offers a chronological history of the presidency presented in the form of interpretive essays on the individual men who held the office, the events and developments of each adminstration, and the impact of the man and his policies on the course of American history. The essays (by 35 professional historians and political scientists) follow no rigid pattern, but typically provide an account of the president's early life and pre-presidency years before concentrating on his time in office. Select bibliography for each essay, often with evaluative comment, references to manuscript sources, and citations to editions of the writings of the president. Indexed.

           E176.1.P918

Southwick, Leslie H. Presidential also-rans and running mates, 1788–1980. Jefferson, N.C., McFarland, [1984]. 722p.   **CJ127**

Offers biographical sketches of those "nominated for president or vice president but who failed to achieve that goal."—*Introd.* Chronologically arranged by election year, with notes on the election preceding the biographies of the unsuccessful candidates. Indexed.

           E176.1.S695

Taylor, Tim. The book of presidents. N.Y., Arno Pr., 1972. 703p.   **CJ128**

A chronology of each presidential administration, together with a wide range of information about each president's background and early years, elections, party conventions, etc. Statistical summary and index of names.   E176.1.T226

Vexler, Robert I. The vice-presidents and cabinet members: biographies arranged chronologically by administration. Dobbs Ferry, N.Y., Oceana, 1975. 2v.   **CJ129**

Biographical sketches are followed by bibliographic citations to sources of further information. Name index in v.2.   E176.V48

Periodicals

National journal. v.1, no.1– , Aug. 18, 1969– . Wash., Center for Political Research, 1969– . Weekly.   **CJ130**

Each weekly issue offers a brief review of the previous week's actions and events throughout the federal government, reporting on the White House, federal departments and agencies, Congress (including tabulations of House and Senate votes on key issues), and the courts. Other features touch on parties and elections, national issues, in-depth reports on federal policy, and a report on the political situation in an individual state. Each weekly issue is indexed by personal and geographical names and by private organization; indexes cumulate monthly and semiannually, with subject and government-organization indexes added in the cumulations.

JK1.N28

Congress

Guides

Congressional Quarterly's Guide to Congress. 3d ed. [Wash., 1982] 1185p. il. **CJ131**

1st ed. 1971.

In seven sections: (1) Origins and development of Congress; (2) Powers of Congress; (3) Congressional procedures; (4) Housing and support of Congress; (5) Congress and the electorate; (6) Pressures on Congress; (7) Qualifications and conduct of members. Includes footnotes and selected bibliographies. Useful appendixes of biographical, statistical, and documentary materials. Indexed.

JK1021.C559

Goehlert, Robert. Congress and law-making: researching the legislative process. Santa Barbara, Calif., [ABC-Clio Pr., 1979]. 168p. il. **CJ132**

A guide designed to help users trace congressional legislation and to familiarize them with the basic reference sources for tracing legislation and for research work on Congress and legislators. Lengthy annotations; illustrations of the sources. Appendixes show how to cite government publications, and list federal depository libraries. Indexed. KF240.G63

Bibliography

Baker, Richard A. The United States Senate: a historical bibliography. [Wash., Govt. Prt. Off.], 1977. 78p. il. **CJ133**

A classed bibliography of approximately 1,000 books, articles, and dissertations on the Senate, its practices, customs, and former members. Includes a reference section for primary materials, directories, indexes, etc. State index of senators for the biographical section; index of authors and editors. Z7165.U5B335

Goehlert, Robert U. and **Sayre, John R.** The United States Congress: a bibliography. N.Y., Free Pr.; London, Collier Macmillan, [1982]. 376p. **CJ134**

A classed bibliography of more than 5,600 books, essays, articles, government documents, theses and dissertations organized in 14 topical chapters. Focuses on scholarly sources concerning the history, development, and legislative process of Congress published since 1782; a companion volume is to include biographical references to members of Congress. Subject and author indexes.

Z7165.U5G575

Guide to research collections of former United States senators, 1789–1982. Prep. under the direction of William F. Hildenbrand. Kathryn Allamong Jacob, ed. in chief. Wash., Historical Office, United States Senate, 1983. 362p. (U.S. Senate bicentennial pubn., 1; Senate Doc. 97–41, 97th Cong., 2d Sess.) **CJ135**

A catalog indicating location and scope of papers and oral history materials, arranged by member. Appendixes list collections by repository, and senators alphabetically by state. CD3043.G85

Directories

The almanac of American politics. Wash., Barone, 1972– . Biennial. **CJ136**

Subtitle: The Senators, the Representatives—their records, states and districts.

A political overview for each individual state is followed by a district-by-district summary of political background and information on the legislators. A very useful compilation. JK1012.A44

Congressional staff directory, 1959– . Indianapolis, New Bobbs-Merrill, 1959– . Annual. **CJ137**

Publisher varies.

A useful supplement to the *Official congressional directory* (CJ141) and the *United States government manual* (CJ112), for listing of congressional staffs, subcommittees, committee staffs, etc. Includes a list of major cities with population over 1,500, with the names of their representatives; biographical sketches of key staff personnel; and personal name index.

A "pre-publication supplement" called *Advance locator for Capitol Hill* has been published annually beginning 1965. A biennial companion volume, *Election index,* was published 1966–82.

JK1012.C65

Congressional yellow book. Wash., Washington Monitor, 1976– . Quarterly. **CJ138**

Subtitle: A loose-leaf directory of members of Congress, their committees and key aids.

Completely revised every three months. Provides names of state delegations, senators and representatives and their staffs, committee memberships, and data on leadership and membership organizations. No index.

Politics in America; members of Congress in Washington and at home, 1982– . Wash., Congressional Quarterly Pr., [1981]– . Biennial. **CJ139**

Profile articles summarize members' performances, issues in which they are interested, legislative influence, political alliances, elections, and voting records; statistical data on elections, campaign finances, voting records, interest group ratings, and committee memberships are appended. The politics of states and individual congressional districts are briefly sketched. Geographical arrangement, followed by directories of committee membership and members' offices; name index. JK1010.P64

U.S. Congress. Biographical directory of the American Congress, 1774–1971. [Wash.], Govt. Prt. Off., 1971. 1972p. (92d Cong., 1st sess. Senate doc. 92–8. Ser. set no.12938) **CJ140**

1st ed. 1928.

Contents: (1) Lists: Executive officers, 1789–1971; The Continental Congress; Representatives under each apportionment; Members of each Congress, 1st through 91st, arranged by Congress and then by state; (2) Biographies, arranged alphabetically.

Indispensable in any large library. JK1010.A5

————— Official congressional directory for the use of the U.S. Congress. 1809– . Wash., Govt. Prt. Off., 1809– . il. Irregular. **CJ141**

From 1865, printed at the Government Printing Office; before that by private firms.

Contents, approximately the same in recent volumes though sometimes varying the order: (1) Biographical sketches of members of Congress, arranged by states; (2) State delegations; (3) Alphabetical list of names; (4) Terms of service; (5) Committees, membership and days of meetings; (6) Congressional commissions, joint committees and boards; (7) Committee assignments; (8) Administrative assistants and secretaries; (9) Statistical information including sessions of Congress; votes cast for senators and representatives; number of states and territories, present list; Presidents and vice-presidents, 1789– ; (10) The Capitol: officers of the Senate, officers of the House, members' rooms, etc.; Miscellaneous officers; (11) Executive departments; (12) Independent agencies; (13) Judiciary: biographies of members of Supreme Court, lists of the courts; (14) District of Columbia government; (15) International organizations; (16) Foreign diplomatic representatives and foreign consular officers in the United States; (17) U.S. diplomatic and consular offices; (18) Press galleries: representatives of newspapers and periodicals, pho-

tographers, radio and television correspondents, members, rules, etc.; (19) Maps of congressional districts; (20) Individual index.
JK1011

—— The United States congressional directories, 1789–1840. Ed. by Perry M. Goldman and James S. Young. N.Y., Columbia Univ. Pr., 1973. 417p.   **CJ142**

Collates information provided in the early congressional directories, including names and addresses of state delegations, members of standing and select committees, and the boardinghouse groups (or fraternities) of congressional members. The cutoff date of 1840 was chosen because "most . . . libraries possess a complete series of the *Congressional Directories* from 1840 on, and . . . the earlier directories are rare items." No personal names index or biographical material; the user is referred to the *Biographical directory of the American Congress* (CJ140) for material on the state delegations.
JK1011.U53

Handbooks

Congressional sourcebook series, 1976– . Wash., Program Analysis Div., General Accounting Office, 1976– .
CJ143

1977 issue called 2d ed.
The series consists of three volumes per issue, each being "an indexed directory and guide, addressing the following areas: (1) *Requirements for Recurring Reports to the Congress*—describes the various requirements for recurring reports to the Congress from the executive, legislative, and judicial branches of the Federal Government. (2) *Federal Information Sources and Systems*—describes approximately 1,400 Federal sources and systems maintained by 91 executive agencies, which contain fiscal, budgeting, and program-related information. (3) *Federal Program Evaluation*—contains an inventory of program evaluation reports produced by and for most of the departments, agencies, and various commissions of the Federal Government."—*Foreword.* Titles and frequency of the individual parts vary; many libraries catalog each part separately.

Deschler, Lewis. Deschler's Precedents of the United States House of Representatives: including references to provisions of the Constitution and laws, and to decisions of the courts. Wash., Govt. Prt. Off., [1977–84]. v.1–7. (House document, 94th Cong., 2d sess.; no.94–661) (In progress)
CJ144

"It is the function of these volumes to review the precedents from 1936 through the first session of the 93d Congress. . . . Subsequent precedents will be found in supplements to this edition to be prepared for each Congress."—*Pref.* Precedents are defined as (1) rulings or decisions of the Speaker or Chairman on a point of order or parliamentary inquiry; (2) express or implied conclusions or decisions of the House itself; (3) practices or procedures of the House which are never specifically ruled on. Table of contents for each volume; each chapter begins with an index to precedents.
A condensed, up-to-date version is to be published for each Congress beginning with the 93d. This has begun to appear as :
KF4992.D486

—— Deschler's Procedure: a summary of the modern precedents and practices of the U.S. House of Representatives, 86th Congress– . Wash., Govt. Prt. Off., 1975– . Biennial.   **CJ145**

KF4992.D49

U.S. Congress. House. Constitution, Jefferson's Manual and Rules of the House of Representatives. . . . Wash., Govt. Prt. Off., 1824– .   **CJ146**

The House manual. Title varies. Issued for each session of Congress.   KF4992.U54

U.S. Congress. Senate. Senate manual, containing the standing rules, orders, laws, and resolutions affecting the business of the United States Senate; Jefferson's Manual; Declaration

of Independence; Articles of Confederation; Constitution of the United States, etc. Wash., Govt. Prt. Off., 1820– .
CJ147

Title varies. Issued for each session of Congress.
In addition to the items listed in the title, the *Senate manual* includes various tables, e.g., List of the presidents pro tempore of the Senate from the first Congress; Lists of senators from the first Congress; Electoral votes for president and vice-president from 1789; Justices of the Supreme Court, 1789– ; Cabinet officers, 1789– , etc.   JK1151

—— Senate procedure: precedents and practices, by Charles L. Watkins and Floyd M. Riddick. Wash., Govt. Prt. Off., 1964. 761p. (88th Cong., 1st sess. Senate doc. 44)
CJ148

". . . a compilation of the rules of the Senate, portions of laws affecting Senate procedure, rulings by the Presiding Officer, and established practices of the Senate."—*Pref.*
Divided into chapters and arranged alphabetically with a detailed index. Contains much, but not all, of the information included in the *Senate manual* and is arranged differently.   JK1266 1964a.A5

Vital statistics on Congress. Norman J. Ornstein [et al., comps.]. 1984–85 ed. Wash., Amer. Enterprise Inst. for Public Policy Research, [1984]. 261p. il. (AEI studies, 410)
CJ149

Constitutes a 2d updated ed. of the 1980 ed.
Presents statistics on congressional elections, campaign finance, party membership characteristics, committees, staff, costs, level of activity, and voting; statistical sources are identified. Time period varies, but most data series extend back to the 1940s and some are earlier. Brief introduction to each chapter of statistics.
JK1041.V57

Periodicals

See also CJ130.

Congressional Quarterly weekly report. v.1, no.1– , Sept. 9, 1946– . Wash., Congressional Quarterly, 1946– . Weekly.
CJ150

Title varies. Quarterly indexes cumulate annually.
Supplements accompany some numbers.
A reliable and extremely useful news service offering a weekly summary of congressional action and developments. Most issues include the following sections (with special features or supplements added as appropriate): National report; Political report; Executive branch; Lobby report; In committee; On the floor; Vote charts.
JK1.C15

Congressional Quarterly almanac. v.1– , Jan./Mar. 1945– . Wash., Congressional Quarterly, 1945– . Annual.   **CJ151**

Title varies. Frequency varies: 1945–47, quarterly.
Each volume now offers a survey of legislation for one session of Congress (e.g., v.40, 1984, covers the 98th Congress, 2d session). Major congressional action is summarized in sections dealing with categories of legislation (e.g., agriculture and labor, appropriations, consumer legislation, crime and justice, etc.) subdivided according to specific topics. Includes voting information on individual measures. Several useful appendixes. Fully indexed.   JK1.C66

Congressional Quarterly Service, Wash., D.C. Congress and the nation, 1945/1964– ; a review of government and politics in the postwar years. Wash., 1965– . v.1– . Quadrennial.   **CJ152**

Contents: v.1, 1945–1964; v.2, 1965–1968; v.3, 1969–1972.
Offers a survey of United States politics and government based on material from the *CQ almanac* (above), with the addition of information from other sources. Beginning with v.2, each volume covers one presidential term.
The same agency's publication, *Politics in America, 1945–1964* (Wash., 1965), is drawn principally from v.1 of this work.
KF49.C65

Congressional districts

Congressional districts in the 1980s. Wash., Congressional Quarterly, [1983]. 632p. maps. **CJ153**

Presents descriptive and statistical profiles of the 435 congressional districts based on the 1980 census and subsequent reapportionment and redistricting. Offers data on election returns, demographics, media, military installations, and industries. JK1341.C63

Martis, Kenneth C. The historical atlas of United States congressional districts, 1789–1983. N.Y., Free Pr.; London, Collier Macmillan, [1982]. 302p. maps. 34cm. **CJ154**

Based on *The atlas of congressional roll calls* prep. by the Historical Records Survey in New York City, 1938–39, and New Jersey, 1940–42.

In three parts: (1) Introduction; (2) 97 congressional district maps, one for each Congress, with alphabetical lists of all individuals elected to the Congress and indication of the member's state and district; and (3) descriptions of each congressional district's geographic composition, according to law. Bibliographical references; indexes.

This is the first volume in the "United States Congress Bicentennial Atlas Project" series. "Volume II, *The Historical Atlas of Political Party Representation in the United States Congress: 1789–1987,* will identify the political party membership/affiliation of every individual elected to Congress and will map the geographical patterns of political parties for each Congress. Volume III, *The Atlas of Critical Votes in the United States Congress,* will identify and map the most important roll-call votes taken in the first two hundred years of the United States Congress."—*Pref.* G1201.F9M3

Parsons, Stanley B., Beach, William W. and Hermann, Dan. United States congressional districts, 1788–1841. Westport, Conn., Greenwood Pr., [1978]. 416p. maps. **CJ154a**

Sets forth "the county compositions, boundaries, and selected statistical information relating to all of the congressional districts in the United States during the early national period."—*Introd.* Further volumes are planned for the 1842–1942 period. G1201.F7P3

U.S. Bureau of the Census. Congressional district data book. (Districts of the 87th– Congress) [1961/62–] Wash., Govt. Prt. Off., 1961– . maps. (A *Statistical abstract* suppl.) **CJ155**

An earlier report for congressional districts appeared as Appendix G of the 1956 *County and city data book* (CG95). [2d ed.] 1963, with supplements, *Redistricted states,* no.1–32, 1965–67.

Arranged by state; gives statistics on congressional districts covering such items as: population and housing; vote cast for president and representatives; vital statistics; race and nativity; education; income; employment status; industry; occupation. Appendixes include historical tables of apportionment. Contains maps of congressional districts. HA205.A5

—— Congressional district atlas. 86th– Congress, April 1, 1960– . Wash., Govt. Prt. Off., 1960– . maps. Biennial since 1964. **CJ156**

Maps showing the boundaries of the congressional districts for each Congress are arranged by state, and include maps of selected regions, counties, and cities. Revised maps are issued as changes are made. G1201.F7U5

Elections

America votes; a handbook of contemporary American election statistics. v.1– , [1954/55]– . N.Y., Macmillan, 1956– . Biennial. **CJ157**

Publisher varies. Ed., v.1– , Richard M. Scammon. Issued by Governmental Affairs Institute.

Arranged alphabetically by state. Statistics, by state, of vote since 1945 for president, governor, senator, congressman; statistics, by county and ward, of vote in most recent election for president, governor, senator; with maps of each state and of large cities and

congressional districts, and brief statements of basic political information and special situations in each state. JK1967.A8

The American electorate: a historical bibliography. Santa Barbara, Calif., ABC-Clio, [1984]. 388p. (ABC-Clio research guides, 8) **CJ158**

Sections on voters and voting behavior and the electoral process precede sections on the elections of 1619–1860, 1861–1919, 1920–1959, and 1960–1983. More than 1,400 citations (with abstracts) to periodical articles; author and subject indexes. Derived from the ABC-Clio database (which generates *America: history and life*). Z7164.R4A46

Burnham, Walter Dean. Presidential ballots, 1836–1892. Baltimore, Johns Hopkins Pr., [1955]. 956p. **CJ159**

A historical introduction is followed by tables showing distribution of votes by county, section, state, etc. A very useful compilation, followed in time by: JK524.B8

Robinson, Edgar Eugene. The presidential vote, 1896–1932. Stanford, Calif., Stanford Univ. Pr., [1934]. 403p. **CJ160**
JK524.R6

—— They voted for Roosevelt; the presidential vote, 1932–1944. Stanford, Calif., Stanford Univ. Pr., [1947]. 207p. (Repr.: N.Y., Octagon Books, 1970) **CJ161**
JK1967.R6

Congressional Quarterly. Congressional Quarterly's Guide to U.S. elections. Wash., Congressional Quarterly, 1975. 1103p. maps, il. **CJ162**

A narrative section on the history of the party system and nominating conventions is followed by four main sections listing popular vote returns: since 1824 for presidential, gubernatorial and House elections, since 1913 for Senate elections, and since 1919 for southern primaries. Also supplies biographical material for presidential and vice-presidential candidates, and lists of governors and senators since 1789. General index and special candidate indexes. An impressive compilation. A 2d ed. is to be published 1985. JK1967.C66

—— Congressional Quarterly's Guide to 1976 elections: a supplement to CQ's Guide to U.S. elections. Wash., Congressional Quarterly, 1977. 66p.

Follows the format of the parent work (above), presenting material on the 1976 elections. Narrative section on political party conventions is followed by sections giving voting statistics for presidential, gubernatorial and senatorial, and House elections. Lists corrections to the *Guide.* Bibliography; candidates index. JK1968 1976.C65

Congressional Quarterly, Inc. Presidential elections since 1789. 3d ed. [Wash.], Congressional Quarterly, [1983]. 211p. maps. **CJ163**

1st ed. 1975.
Presents statistics on electoral and popular votes for president, lists of political party nominees, 1831–1976, presidential primary returns, and a biographical directory of presidential and vice-presidential candidates. Chapters and bibliographies in essay form. JK524.C65

Cox, Edward Franklin. State and national voting in federal elections, 1910–1970. [Hamden, Conn.], Archon Books, 1972. 280p. **CJ164**

Aims to provide voting statistics on a state-by-state basis in all three types of federal elections (presidential, senatorial, representative). In each category figures are given for the Democratic, Republican, and "other" party votes, together with percentages. JK1965.C59

Elections Research Center. Governmental Affairs Institute. America at the polls; a handbook of American presidential election statistics 1920–1964. Comp. and ed. by Richard M. Scammon. Pittsburgh, Univ. of Pittsburgh Pr., 1965. 521p. **CJ165**

Follows the format of the Institute's *America votes* (CJ157), giving a state-by-state, county-by-county breakdown of election statistics.
                                                                    JK524.G6

Petersen, Svend. A statistical history of the American presidential elections; with supplementary tables covering 1968–1980. Westport, Conn., Greenwood Pr., 1981. 250, [25]p.
                                                                    CJ166

The main section of the work was first published 1963; reissued 1968; 1968 suppl. publ. 1971.

"Containing 133 statistical compilations, including a table of votes and percentages for each presidential election [1789–1960], by states and candidates; a table of votes and percentages for each state, by elections and candidates; a table of votes and percentages, by states and elections, for each historical party (Democratic, Republican, Whig, Prohibition, Socialist Labor, Socialist Workers, Populist, Greenback, Farmer Labor, Communist, and Socialist); and 28 other tables covering interesting sidelights."—*Note.*   JK1967.P4

Runyon, John H., Verdini, Jennefer and **Runyon, Sally S.** Source book of American presidential campaign and election statistics, 1948–1968. N.Y., Ungar, [1971]. 380p.
                                                                    CJ167

In addition to tables of election results, there are statistics relating to presidential primaries, national party conventions, opinion polls, and various aspects of the campaigns such as itineraries, costs, media exposure, etc.   JK524.R83

U.S. Congress. House. Statistics of the presidential and Congressional election of Nov. 2, 1920– . Wash., Govt. Prt. Off., 1921– . Biennial.   **CJ168**

Subtitle (varies slightly): Showing the highest vote for presidential electors, and the vote cast for each nominee for United States senator, representative, delegate, and resident commissioner to the 67th– Congress, together with a recapitulation thereof, including the electoral vote.   JK1967.A3

U.S. Congress. Senate. Library. Electoral and popular votes for president and congressional election statistics. Wash., Govt. Prt. Off., 1948. 24p.   **CJ169**

Subtitle: Record of popular and electoral vote for president and vice-president by principal political parties and states, 1900 to 1944, and votes for senators and representatives by parties and states in elections of November 1942, 1944 and 1946, together with excerpts from the Constitution and statutes relating to elections.

❖Electoral votes for the president and vice-president, from 1789– , are included in the *Senate manual* (CJ147). A bibliography on the Electoral College is:

Szekely, Kalman S., comp. Electoral college; a selective annotated bibliography. Littleton, Colo., Libraries Unlimited, 1970. 125p.   **CJ170**

Nearly 800 items relating to the history of the Electoral College, its organization, attempts at and proposals for reform, etc. Indexed.
                                                                    Z7165.U5S95

Political parties

❖The standard histories of political parties, and the campaign textbooks issued by the principal parties, are the main sources of information in this field. Contents of the campaign textbooks vary, but usually contain party platforms, statements of the party's stand on principal issues, acceptance speeches of candidates, committee members, etc. Political and election statistics, accounts of national conventions, and texts of party platforms were given in the *Tribune almanac and political register* (N.Y., 1938–1914). Statistics and chief points of party platforms are given in the *World almanac* (AC87). Summary election statistics on federal offices are given in *Historical statistics of the United States* (CG98) and in the *Statistical abstract* (CG94). State manu-

als and legislative handbooks often give statistics of state and local elections.

Bain, Richard C. and **Parris, Judith H.** Convention decisions and voting records. 2d ed. Wash., Brookings Institution, [1973]. 350p., plus tables.   **CJ171**

1st ed. 1960, by Richard C. Bain.

A handbook of presidential conventions, 1832–1972, with a section on each consisting of the political background, organization of the conventions, platforms adopted, nominations, balloting, etc. Appended are lists of nominees, convention officers, and voting records by state.   JK2255.B3

The Democratic and Republican parties in America: a historical bibliography. Santa Barbara, Calif., ABC-Clio, [1984]. 290p. (ABC-Clio research guides, 7)   **CJ172**

About 1,000 citations (with abstracts), mainly to periodical literature. Topical arrangement with author and subject indexes. Derived from the ABC-Clio database (which generates *America: history and life*).   Z7164.P8D45

Johnson, Donald Bruce and **Porter, Kirk H.** National party platforms. Rev. ed. Urbana, Univ. of Illinois Pr., [1978]. 2v. (1035p.)   **CJ173**

1st ed. 1936. An earlier work by Porter, with the same title, was published 1924.

Contents: v.1, 1840–1956; v.2, 1960–1976.

For each campaign, gives a brief history, lists of party candidates, voting totals, and the texts of platforms for all major and principal minor parties. Name and subject indexes in each volume.
                                                                    JK2255.J64

―――― National party platforms of 1980; supplement. . . . Urbana, Univ. of Illinois Pr., [1982]. 233p.

                                                                    JK2255.J643

McKee, Thomas Hudson. National conventions and platforms of all political parties, 1789–1905; convention, popular and electoral vote. Also the political complexion of both houses of Congress at each biennial period. 6th ed. rev. and enl. Baltimore, Friedenwald, 1906. 418p. 33p.   **CJ173a**
                                                                    JK2255.M2

National party conventions, 1831–1980. [3d ed.] Wash., Congressional Quarterly, [1983]. 245p. il.   **CJ174**

1976 ed. had title: *National party conventions, 1831–1972.*

Provides a brief summary of each party convention, the results of convention ballots, historical profiles of American political parties, lists of nominees, and a biographical directory of candidates. Most sections have bibliographies. Indexed.   JK2255.N37

Rockwood, D. Stephen [and others]. American third parties since the Civil War: an annotated bibliography. N.Y., Garland, 1985. 177p. (Garland reference library of social science, v.227)   **CJ175**

An introductory bibliography intended to supplement other bibliographic titles on progressivism, socialism, etc. Monographic coverage is stressed, with most periodical titles included in a section on third party movements of the last two decades. In six chapters: general theory and practice; the Populist (People's) Party; parties of the Left; Dixiecrats and American Independents; the Progressive Party; minor third parties. Author and title indexes.
                                                                    Z7164.P8R63

Schapsmeier, Edward L. and **Schapsmeier, Frederick H.** Political parties and civic action groups. Westport, Conn., Greenwood Pr., [1981]. 554p.   **CJ176**

Presents profiles of almost 300 national political organizations, about one-third of which are political parties; entries range in length from a brief paragraph to more than 20 pages, with bibliographical references. Alphabetical arrangement; keyword index. Appendixes list organizations by broad functional areas and founding dates. Tables of presidential candidates and votes for major political parties; glossary; index.   JK2260.S36

Wynar, Lubomyr Roman. American political parties; a selective guide to parties and movements of the 20th century. Littleton, Colo., Libraries Unlimited, 1969. 427p. **CJ177**

Lists books, monographs, and unpublished dissertations on American political parties and movements of the 20th century. Includes references to published platforms, proceedings of national conventions, etc., as well as secondary writings about the parties.
Z7165.U5W88

Biography

McMullin, Thomas A. and **Walker, David.** Biographical directory of American territorial governors. Westport, Conn., Meckler, [1984]. 353p. **CJ178**

Presents biographies of the governors of American incorporated territories (excluding Puerto Rico, Guam, the Philippines, and Samoa). Articles range from one to two pages in length, and include bibliographies. Arranged by state, with name index and chronology of office.
E176.M17

Morris, Dan and **Morris, Inez.** Who was who in American politics. N.Y., Hawthorn Books, [1974]. 637p. **CJ179**

Subtitle: A biographical dictionary of over 4,000 men and women who contributed to the United States political scene from colonial days up to and including the immediate past.

Includes some living persons no longer active in politics.
E176.M873

Political profiles. Ed., Nelson Lichtenstein; assoc. ed., Eleanora W. Schoenebaum. N.Y., Facts on File, [1976–79]. v.1–5. (In progress) **CJ180**

Contents: [v.1], The Truman years; [v.2], The Eisenhower years; v.3, The Kennedy years; v.4, The Johnson years; [v.5], The Nixon-Ford years.

The set will be complete in 6v., the final volume to cover *The Carter years.*

Each volume contains about 500 signed biographies, ranging from 400 to 2,000 words, of the most politically influential persons in each presidential administration. Includes officeholders, journalists, intellectuals, economic leaders, civil rights activists, etc. Figures with long political careers may be found in several volumes, with the text focusing on the person's activity during the period covered. Short bibliographies for some entries. Each volume has a chronology, appendixes of officeholders, general bibliography, and index.
E840.6.P64

Stineman, Esther. American political women: contemporary and historical profiles. Littleton, Colo., Libraries Unlimited, 1980. 228p. **CJ181**

Presents 60 biographies of congresswomen, ambassadors, special presidential assistants, governors and lieutenant governors, and mayors, emphasizing contemporary women serving in major positions since the late 1970s. Biographies are usually two or three pages in length, with references to selected speeches and writings, and bibliographies. General bibliography on women and politics, p. 161–89.
HQ1236.S74

Who's who in American politics; a biographical directory of United States political leaders. Ed.1– , 1967/68– . N.Y., Bowker, 1967– . Biennial. **CJ182**

Biographical sketches of political figures ranging from the president and nationally prominent personalities to local figures.
E176.W6424

Who's who in government. Ed.1–3, 1972/73–77. Chicago, Marquis, [1972–77]. 3v. **CJ183**

Offers biographical data on key men and women in all branches of the United States federal government, together with selected officials in local, state, and international government. Includes many names not found in *Who's who in America.* Index by field or subject specialty and by government department.

A publication with the same title was issued by the Biographical Research Bureau, 1930–32.
E747.W512

State and local government

Bibliography

See also AG79.

Bollens, John Constantinus, Bayes, John R. and **Utter, Kathryn L.** American county government; with an annotated bibliography. Beverly Hills, Calif., Sage, [1969]. 433p.
CJ184

A review of the literature, suggested approaches to new research, and bibliographical commentary on books, monographs, articles, and documents relating to American county government in general and to individual states.
JS411.B64

Council of State Governments. State blue books and reference publications (a selected bibliography). Rev. and annotated ed., March 1974. Lexington, Ky., The Council, [1974]. 86p.
CJ185

1st ed. 1972.

Lists state blue books (or nearest equivalent), legislative manuals and rules, digests of legislative action, etc., on a state-by-state basis. Only the blue books are annotated (by descriptive coding), but the list is useful as a directory (with addresses and price information) of a wide variety of other state publications.
Z7165.U5C68

Government Affairs Foundation. Metropolitan communities: a bibliography, with special emphasis upon government and politics. Chicago, Public Admin. Service, [1957]. 392p.
CJ186

5,120 numbered, annotated items. Pt.1, "Government and politics in metropolitan areas," deals with: (1) functions and problems; (2) governmental organization; and (3) politics in metropolitan communities. Pt.2, "Socioeconomic background," treats: (1) social structure and process; (2) population; and (3) the metropolitan economy. Author and subject index.

———— ———— Supplement, 1955/57, 1958/64, 1965/67, 1968/70. Chicago, 1960–72.

Z7164.L8G66

Hutcheson, John D. and **Shevin, Jann.** Citizen groups in local politics: a bibliographic review. Santa Barbara, Calif., Clio, 1976. 275p. **CJ187**

"Focuses on the organization, activities, strategies, and impacts of citizen groups attempting to influence local governmental decision-making processes in the United States."—*Introd.* Chapters present reviews of the literature of topics such as "Citizen groups in planning and community development," citing books, articles, reports, and doctoral dissertations written in English between 1950 and 1975; some book reviews are indicated. Author index.
Z7165.U5H87

International Union of Local Authorities. Metropolis; a select bibliography of administrative and other problems in metropolitan areas throughout the world. [2d ed.] Comp. and ed. by D. Halász. The Hague, Nijhoff, 1967. 265p.
CJ188

1st ed. 1961.

Arranged by country. Materials on the United States and Canada are omitted.
Z7164.L8I53

Murphy, Thomas P. Urban politics: a guide to information sources. Detroit, Gale, [1978]. 248p. (Urban information guide ser., 1) **CJ189**

A selective, annotated bibliography of English-language books and periodicals (most of them published since 1970), on American urban governmental structure, political parties and leaders, community participation, socio-ethnic politics, public policy issues, the reorganization of metropolitan governments and adjacent areas, and federal urban relations. Appendixes list bibliographies, abstracts and indexes, other reference books, textbooks, periodical titles, and associations. Author, title, and subject indexes.

Z7165.U5M85

Ross, Bernard H. Urban management: a guide to information sources. Detroit, Gale, [1979]. 288p. (Urban studies information guide ser., v.8)   **CJ190**

A systematic, annotated guide to English-language materials published between 1965 and 1976, with emphasis on scholarly journal articles and readily available monographs. Includes chapters on administrative leadership, management operations, personnel management, urban decentralization, bureaucracy, the budget, etc. Appendixes list relevant organizations, periodical titles, and bibliographies. Author, title, and subject indexes.   Z7164.L8R67

Selected bibliography on state government, 1959–1972. Comp. by Regis Koslofsky [and others]. Lexington, Ky., Council of State Governments, [1972]. 237p. (Council of State Govts. RM publ. 492)   **CJ191**

A selection of more than 1,000 items on state government. Entries with full bibliographical information appear in a numerical sequence without regard to chronology or alphabetization; access is through a keyword-in-context index and an author index.

Z7165.U5

MacManus, Susan A. Selected bibliography on state government, 1973–1978. Lexington, Ky., Council of State Governments, [1979]. 148p.   **CJ192**

Updates the Council's *Selected bibliography ... 1959–1972* (above). Books and periodical articles are arranged in 19 broad subject chapters, which are further subdivided. Author index. 1978 materials are listed and indexed in a separate appendix.

Z7165.U5M32

Tompkins, Dorothy Campbell. State government and administration; a bibliography. [Berkeley], Bureau of Public Admin., Univ. of California, [1954]. 269p.   **CJ193**

An annotated list of books and periodical articles issued, for the most part, since 1930, arranged by large subject field with author and title index. Covers such areas as state constitutions, laws and codes, documents, legislative organization, judicial administration, etc. Includes a list of state manuals, p.138–42, and other state publications.   Z7165.U5T63

White, Anthony G. Reforming metropolitan governments: a bibliography. N.Y., Garland, 1975. 116p.   **CJ194**

Treats reform in its literal sense, as the changing of form to deal with jurisdictional problems, mostly in relation to consolidated city-counties. The first section of the book includes survey and census data on this type of metropolitan area. The second section is an annotated bibliography of more than 580 sources, grouped by type: (1) books, documents, pamphlets; (2) periodicals, major news articles; (3) legal documents, decisions. Subject and author indexes.

Z7164.L8W47

Handbooks and yearbooks

Book of the states. v.1– , 1935– . Chicago, Council of State Governments, 1935– . il. Biennial.   **CJ195**

A comprehensive manual on state activities. Order of presentation varies. Contents 1984/85: (1) Intergovernmental affairs; (2) The governors and the executive branch; (3) The legislatures; (4) The judiciary; (5) Legislation, elections and constitutions; (6) Administration; (7) Finances; (8) Major state services; (9) The state pages (giving officers, statistics, and general information). Index.

Frequency varies. Now issued biennially in the spring of even-numbered years, with emphasis given to the developments of the two preceding years. Three supplements are usually issued in the odd-numbered years: state elective officials and legislators; administrative officials classified by functions; and state legislative leadership, committees, and staff.   JK2403.B62

The county year book. v.1– . Wash., Nat. Assoc. of Counties [and] Internat. City Management Assoc., [1975–]. Annual.   **CJ196**

Subtitle: The authoritative source book on county governments.

Similar in format and purpose to the *Municipal year book* (CJ198), this work presents survey chapters analyzing general and comparative data on administrative and legislative trends, management structure, administrative functions and services. A directory section provides information on associations, agencies and officials, and sources of information (a selected bibliography for major areas of county administration).   JS301.C67

Directory of recognized local governments. Wash., Internat. City Management Assoc., [1977]. 90p.   **CJ197**

Identifies cities, counties and councils of government in the United States and Canada which are recognized by the I.C.M.A. "as having established an appointed position of overall professional management."—*p.5.* Statistical tables on council-manager and general management counties and municipalities. Directory section arranged by state and then by municipality, with population, legal basis, form and year of recognition, executive, year of appointment. Directories of related agencies include state municipal leagues, provincial associations and unions, and state and provincial agencies for local affairs. Continued by the Association's *Who's who in local government management* (1985–).   JS323.D57

Municipal year book, 1934– ; the authoritative résumé of activities and statistical data of American cities. Chicago, Internat. City Managers' Assoc., 1934– . v.1– . Annual.   **CJ198**

Subtitle varies: currently reads "The authoritative source book of urban data and developments."

Contents vary. Beginning 1973 includes data and articles on Canadian municipalities.   JS344.C5A24

The national directory of state agencies, 1974/75– . Wash., Information Resources Pr., 1974– . Biennial.   **CJ199**

Comp. by Matthew J. Vellucci, Nancy D. Wright and Gene P. Allen.

In two main parts, the first listing the states and the District of Columbia, and for each identifying all agencies concerned with a particular function (administration, aging, etc.), giving title of administrator, name of agency and name of overall department, address and telephone number. The second section organizes the information by function, and under that provides identical information listed by state. Appendix lists associations of state officials by function.   JK2443.N37

State information book. 1975– . Wash., Potomac Books, [1975]– . Biennial.   **CJ200**

1973 volume had title: *State information and federal region book.*

For each state, provides names of state executive and legislative officers, justices, and Washington representatives, together with addresses of major state departments and federal agencies located in the state. Gives similar information for the District of Columbia, Puerto Rico, the Virgin Islands, American Samoa, Guam, the Trust Territory of the Pacific Islands, and the Northern Mariana Islands. Also gives addresses for the Federal Regional Councils.

Worldmark encyclopedia of the states. [N.Y.], Worldmark Pr.; Harper & Row, [1981]. 690p. il., maps.   **CJ201**

Patterned after the *Worldmark encyclopedia of the nations* (CJ218), this volume offers a wide range of political, social, and economic information on the states of the United States of America. "Each state ... is treated in an individual chapter, within a framework of 50 standard subject headings; generally, the more populous the state, the longer the article. The District of Columbia and the Commonwealth of Puerto Rico each has its own chapter, and two additional articles describe in summary form the other Caribbean and Pacific dependencies. The concluding chapter is a 50-page overview of the nation as a whole."—*Pref.* A headnote for each state gives information on the state name, date of entry into union, state flower, legal holidays, etc.; seals and flags are illustrated and described; a selected bibliography concludes each chapter. List of contributors. Not indexed, but uniform presentation of information in each chapter and use of boldface subheadings make for easy use.   E156.W67

Biography and elections

See also AJ62.

Bartley, Numan V. and **Graham, Hugh Davis.** Southern elections: county and precinct data, 1950–1972. Baton Rouge, Louisiana State Univ. Pr., [1978]. 407p. maps.
CJ202

Focuses on major primary elections (gubernatorial and senatorial) and pertinent referenda votes for Alabama, Arkansas, Florida, Georgia, Louisiana, Mississippi, North and South Carolina, Tennessee, Texas, and Virginia; also includes basic demographic and geographic analysis of the votes. Conceived as a continuation of A. Heard and D. S. Strong's *Southern primaries and elections, 1920–1949* (University, Ala., 1950).   JK1967.B37

Biographical dictionary of American mayors, 1820–1980: big city mayors, Baltimore, Boston, Buffalo, Chicago, Cincinnati, Cleveland, Detroit, Los Angeles, Milwaukee, New Orleans, New York, Philadelphia, Pittsburgh, San Francisco, St. Louis. Ed. by Melvin G. Holli and Peter d'A. Jones. Westport, Conn., Greenwood Pr., [1981]. 451p.   **CJ203**

Offers signed biographies with bibliographical sources for 679 mayors. Useful appendixes list mayors by city, party affiliation, ethnic background, religious affiliation, and birthplace, and give population data for the cities. Indexed.   E176.B5725

Glashan, Roy R. American governors and gubernatorial elections, 1775–1978. Westport, Conn., Meckler Books, [1979]. 370p.   **CJ204**

A listing by state of: (1) governors, providing date and place of birth, party, major occupations, residence, death date, and date at which he or she became governor; (2) gubernatorial elections, giving all significant voting totals by party and candidate. Bibliography of general and state sources; no index.   JK2447.G53

Kallenbach, Joseph E. and **Kallenbach, Jessamine S.** American state governors, 1776–1976. Dobbs Ferry, N.Y., Oceana, 1977–82. 3v.   **CJ205**

Contents: v.1, Electoral and personal data; v.2–3, Biographical data.

v.1 offers a state-by-state listing of governors and summaries of election results.   JK2447.K35

Raimo, John W. Biographical directory of American colonial and revolutionary governors, 1607–1789. Westport, Conn., Meckler Books, [1980]. 521p.   **CJ206**

"In this volume the word governor has been interpreted, broadly speaking, to include anyone who held effective executive power in those British colonies which in 1776 became the first thirteen states" (*Introd.*), though occasional exceptions are noted in the introduction. Arranged by colony, with biographical sketches entered chronologically by date of governorship. Chronology and select bibliography for each colony; bibliographies for individual articles; index of names.   E187.5.R34

General works
Bibliography

Korman, Roger I. Checklist of government directories, lists, and rosters. Westport, Conn., Meckler Publishing; Cambridge, Eng., Chadwyck-Healey, [1982]. 51p.   **CJ207**

About 300 titles owned by the Library of Congress are arranged by country and briefly annotated. Includes only directories published on the national level; 78 countries are represented.
Z7164.A2K67

Palic, Vladimir M. Government organization manuals: a bibliography. Wash., Lib. of Congress, 1975 [i.e., 1976]. 105p.   **CJ208**

"This bibliography is essentially a list of manuals and other publications that outline, in more or less detail, the organization of national governments."—*Pref.* Owing to the rarity of detailed and current manuals, there are also included "works of a more general scope that describe the history and often the legislative background of government agencies and bibliographies which may lead the researcher to other sources of information on governmental organization." General, regional, and individual country listings. Index.
Z7164.A2P33

Encyclopedias and handbooks

Day, Alan J. and **Degenhardt, Henry W.** Political parties of the world. Detroit, Gale, [1980]. 432p.   **CJ209**

For about 1,000 active political parties, provides brief history, orientation, structure, leadership, membership, publications, and international affiliations. Appendixes group parties by type or affiliation. Country arrangement; indexed by personal name and publication title.   JF2011.D39

Degenhardt, Henry W. Political dissent: an international guide to dissident, extra-parliamentary, guerrilla and illegal political movements. Gen. ed., Alan J. Day. [Burnt Mill, Harlow, Essex, Eng.], Longman, [1983]. 592p.   **CJ210**

Arranged by countries grouped under broad regional areas. Introductory survey of the political situation and relevant internal security developments in a country is followed by entries for dissident movements, describing history, purpose, specific activities, leadership, leading individual dissenters. Information is based on the resources of *Keesing's Contemporary archives.* Name indexes.

Peter Janke's *Guerrilla and terrorist organisations: a world directory and bibliography* (Brighton, Eng., Harvester Pr., 1983. 534p.) offers less detail on current dissident group activities, but more extensive, critical bibliographies.   JC328.3.D43

Hamburg. Welt-Wirtschafts-Archiv. Länderlexikon. Hamburg, Verlag Weltarchiv GmbH, 1953–60. 3v. il.   **CJ210a**

Published in parts. Lothar Berghändler, ed.
Contents: v.1, Western, Central, and Southern Europe; v.2, Northern and Eastern Europe, Africa, the Near East; v.3 [2.Aufl.], the Near East *(cont.),* Asia, Oceania, North America, Central America and the West Indies, South America, Antarctica.

Treats the social and economic structure of the countries of the world. Arrangement is by country with articles of substantial length, e.g., 150 pages for Great Britain. Emphasis is on the present. Topics include governmental structure, politics, social organization, geography, economics, finance, agriculture, trade, industry, and education. Includes tables, statistics, and extensive bibliographies.
JA63.H2

Herman, Valentine. Parliaments of the world; a reference compendium. Prep. . . . with the collaboration of Françoise Mendel. Berlin & N.Y., W. de Gruyter, [1976]. 985p.
CJ211

At head of title: Inter-Parliamentary Union.
Data on 56 parliaments as they existed Sept. 1, 1974, are presented in a series of 70 comparative tables. "Each table should not only enable the reader to ascertain the essential similarities and differences between various parliamentary systems in respect of a given question, but also to find detailed information concerning one or more individual Parliaments."—*Introd.* Tables are preceded by textual surveys of the matter in question. Indexed. A new edition is to be published 1986.   JF501.H45

Kurian, George Thomas. Encyclopedia of the Third World. Rev. ed. N.Y., Facts on File, [1982]. 3v. (2125p.) maps, il.
CJ212

1st ed. 1978.
A compendium which seeks "to identify all major components and sections of national life [for 122 countries] and present them within a clearly defined hierarchical structure and in a consistent sequence."—*Pref.* An extremely useful source for comparative study of countries. More than 30 categories are presented for each country, including: map and basic fact sheet; location and area; weather; population and ethnic composition; languages and reli-

gions; constitution and government; civil service; local government; foreign policy; parliament and political parties; economy, budget, and finance; agriculture; industry; energy; defense; education; health; food; media; social welfare; human rights; socioeconomic annual growth rates. Each country section also provides a chronology and selected bibliography. Indexed. A new edition is to be published 1986.   HC59.7.K87

———— Atlas of the Third World. N.Y., Facts on File, [1983]. 381p. il., maps.   **CJ213**

A companion to the above, using about 1,000 two-color maps, charts, and graphs to illustrate social, economic, and political indicators for the Third World as a whole and for individual countries. No sources indicated; indexed.   G1046.G1K8

Mackie, Thomas T. and **Rose, Richard.** The international almanac of electoral history. 2d ed. [London], Macmillan, [1982]. 422p.   **CJ214**

1st ed. 1974.
"The purpose of this book is to provide a complete and accurate compilation of election results in Western nations since the beginning of competitive national elections."—*Introd.* An introductory note precedes the statistical tables for each country. "The starting point chosen for each country is the first election in which the great majority of seats for the national parliament were contested, and most candidates fought under common cross-local labels." Covers through 1981.   JF1001.M17

Marxist governments: a world survey. Ed. by Bogdan Szajkowski. N.Y., St. Martin's Pr., 1981. 3v. maps.   **CJ215**

Twenty-five scholars have contributed profiles of 24 countries ruled by Marxist-Leninist parties. Arranged alphabetically by country, each profile consists of the party's history, structure, constitution, electoral system, mass organizations and membership, and data on the country's economy, domestic policies, and foreign relations; footnotes and bibliographies are included. Afghanistan, Madagascar, and San Marino are excluded. Subsequent editions are planned to include material on significant Communist local governments and parties in non-Marxist states. Cumulated index.
                                                          JC474.M3512

World encyclopedia of political systems & parties. Ed. by George E. Delury. N.Y., Facts on File, [1983]. 2v. (1296p.)
                                                          CJ216

Contents: v.1, A–M; v.2, N–Z, Smaller countries & microstates; index.
Country articles describe executive, legislative and judicial functions, regional and local structures, electoral systems; history, organization, policy, membership, financing, and leadership of individual parties; other political forces, national prospects. Bibliographies of suggested reading.   JF2011.W67

The world factbook/National Foreign Assessment Center. Apr. 1981– . [Wash.], Central Intelligence Agency, 1981– . maps. Semiannual.   **CJ217**

Continues the Central Intelligence Agency's *National basic intelligence factbook.*
For each country of the world the work provides brief data on geography, population, government, economy, communications, and defense forces. Small maps of each country; regional maps in color.   G122.U56a

Worldmark encyclopedia of the nations. [6th ed.] N.Y., Worldmark Pr., [1984]. 5v. il., maps.   **CJ218**

Contents: v.1, United Nations; v.2, Africa; v.3, Americas; v.4, Asia & Oceania; v.5, Europe.
The 1st ed., 1960, was in 1v., with all countries in one alphabet; later editions are divided by continents, with countries listed alphabetically in each volume.
Condensed factual information is given for each country, each new edition showing revision and updating throughout. Bibliographies are appended for each country. The volume on the United Nations treats its organization and operation and its various subsidiaries.   G63.W67

Yearbooks

Countries of the world and their leaders. [Ed.1–] Detroit, Gale, 1974– . Irregular. maps.   **CJ219**

Ed. 1 called *Countries of the world.*
Subtitle: The U.S. Department of State's report on Status of the world's nations, combined with its series of Background notes. . . . Includes Central Intelligence Agency's List of chiefs of state and cabinet ministers of foreign governments.
Gathers together and reprints the current *Background notes, Status of the world's nations, Chiefs of state and cabinet ministers of foreign governments,* and the *International organizations* series on CENTO, OAU, NATO, OECD, and the European Communities. Alphabetical and chronological lists of newly independent nations.
                                                          G122.C67

Europa year book. 1959– . Ed.1– . London, Europa Pubns., 1959– . Annual.   **CJ220**

History: (1) *Europa year book,* 1926–29; *Europa, the encyclopedia of Europe,* 1930–58. These were loose-leaf publications covering: international organizations, including the United Nations and its specialized agencies; world politics, giving the texts of international documents, etc.; and information on each European country. (2) *Orbis, encyclopaedia of extra-European countries,* 1938–59. Also looseleaf; gave the same type of information for the countries of Africa, the Americas, Asia, and Australasia, i.e., surveys and directories of political, industrial, financial, cultural, educational, and scientific organizations.
The new, bound volumes, starting in 1959, supersede the loose-leaf series; 1959 issue, in 1v., superseded *Europa.* Beginning with 1960, issued in 2v.: v.1, covering international organizations and Europe; v.2, covering Africa, the Americas, Asia, and Australasia. Beginning with 1963, information on educational and learned societies and institutions is omitted and carried only in *World of learning* (CB205).
Information on the United Nations, its agencies, and other international organizations is followed by detailed information about each country, arranged alphabetically in each volume, giving an introductory survey, a statistical survey, the government, political parties, the constitution, religion, press, publishers, radio and television, finance, trade and industry, transport and tourism, atomic energy, and brief list of universities.   JN1.E85

International yearbook and statesmen's who's who, 1953– . London, Burke's Peerage, 1953– . Annual.   **CJ221**

Coverage varies. Usually includes: (1) information on international organizations, and (2) political, statistical, and directory information about each country of the world. A biographical section gives sketches of world leaders in government, church, commerce, industry, and education.   JA51.I57

Political handbook of the world. 1975– . N.Y., McGraw-Hill, 1975– . Biennial.   **CJ222**

Arthur S. Banks, ed.
Publ. for the Center for Social Analysis of the State University of New York at Binghamton and for the Council on Foreign Relations.
Frequency varies; publisher varies.
Subtitle [varies]: Governments and intergovernmental organizations . . . .
Supersedes the *Political handbook and atlas of the world* (1927–74).
Treats the independent governments of the world; usually gives: chief government officials, party programs and leaders, political events, and the press (names of newspapers with political affiliation, proprietor or editor, and in some cases the circulation).
The atlas section found in the earlier title has been dropped, the information on intergovernmental organizations expanded, and a new section added for regional issues.   JF3.P6

Yearbook on human rights for 1946– . Lake Success, N.Y., United Nations, 1947– . v.1– . Annual (irregular). **CJ223**

Contents vary, but provide surveys of the constitutional and legal provisions of the various countries of the world in regard to the rights of the citizen, his status before the law, right of petition, property rights, rights of the press, assembly, education, religion, culture, status of women, etc. JC571.U4

Registers

Almanach de Gotha, annuaire généalogique, diplomatique et statistique, 1763–1959/60. Gotha, Perthes, 1763–1960. Annual. (Not published 1945–58) **CJ224**

A standard handbook in which coverage varies, with extensions and additions. For many years, until 1940, included two main sections: (1) Annuaire généalogique, which gave genealogies of the royal and princely houses of Europe, and (2) Annuaire diplomatique et statistique, which gave statistical and descriptive information about the various countries of the world, with lists of the principal executive, legislative, and diplomatic officials of each.

Publication began in 1763 as the French edition of the *Gothaischer Hof-Kalender zum Nutzen und Vergnügen eingericht.* Publisher varies: 1823–1944 by Justus Perthes.

Title varies: 1942–44, *Gothaisches Jahrbuch für Diplomatie, Verwaltung und Wirtschaft.*

Année 182, 1959/60, also called *Nouvel almanach du corps diplomatique,* issued in separately paged parts, each covering an individual country. Parts issued: Afghanistan (1960); Albanie (1960); Amérique, États-Unis (1959); Belgique (1959). These parts include general information about governmental organization, diplomatic and consular representatives, statistics, genealogies of the royal or governing houses, and biographical notices of government officials; also bibliographies. CS27.A2

Chiefs of state and cabinet members of foreign governments. [Wash.], Central Intelligence Agency, 1966?– . Monthly. **CJ225**

A country-by-country listing without biographical or other information. Each monthly issue supersedes the previous one. Includes "as many governments of the world as is considered practicable, some of them not yet fully independent and others not officially recognized by the United States."—*Pref.* JF37.U5

Henige, David P. Colonial governors from the fifteenth century to the present; a comprehensive list. Madison, Univ. of Wisconsin Pr., 1970. 461p. **CJ226**

Presents lists of the governors or other colonial administrators "of the European colonies [including American and Australian] from 1415, when the Portuguese occupied Ceuta, to the present time."—*Pref.* Arrangement is by name of the ruling country or "imperial system," with colonies listed alphabetically thereunder. For each colony there is a historical note followed by the chronological list of governors. Both a general index and an index of governors' names. JV431.H45

International guide to electoral statistics; guide international des statistiques électorales. Ed. by Stein Rokkan and Jean Meyriat. The Hague, Mouton, [1969–]. v.1– . (Maison des Sciences de l'Homme. Service d'Échange d'Informations Scientifiques. Publications. Sér. B: Guides et répertoires, 2–). (In progress?) **CJ227**

Contents: v.1, National elections in Western Europe. 351p.

Chapters (mainly in English, but some in French) by specialists provide notes on the background and development of electoral systems of 15 countries of Western Europe, with citations to published sources of electoral statistics and electoral studies. Some statistical tables are included for each country. JF1001.I55

Jameson, John Franklin. A provisional list of printed lists of ambassadors and other diplomatic representatives. . . . Paris, Presses Universitaires de France, [1928]. 16p. **CJ228**

Extract from the *Bulletin* of the International Committee of Historical Sciences (no.4, March 1928).

A convenient record of printed lists of diplomats, arranged by country. In some cases the record goes back to the Middle Ages. Z6464.R4J3

Repertorium der diplomatischen Vertreter aller Länder seit dem Westfälischen Frieden (1648). Repertory of the diplomatic representatives of all countries since the Peace of Westphalia (1648). Zürich, Fretz & Wasmuth, 1936–65. 3v. **CJ229**

Imprint varies. Title in German, English, French, Italian, and Spanish.

v.1, 1648–1715, by Ludwig Bittner and Lothar Gross (Berlin, G. Stalling, 1936.); v.2, 1716–1763, by Friedrich Hausmann (1950.); v.3, 1764–1815, by O. F. Winter (1965).

Arranged by country to which the envoys were sent; each volume has personal-name and country indexes. v.2 also has "Nachträge und Berichtigungen zum I Band," p.429–504.

Ross, Martha. Rulers and governments of the world. London & N.Y., Bowker, 1977–78. 3v. **CJ230**

Contents: v.1, Earliest times to 1491; v.2, 1492 to 1929; v.3, 1930 to 1975.

Volumes 2 and 3 corresponded to v.3–4 of Bertold Spuler's *Regenten und Regierungen der Welt* (Würzburg, 1962–64). v.1 is an entirely new compilation and lists important rulers of territories, ecclesiastical sees, dynasties, peoples, and hordes. All precolonial African regimes are included in this volume rather than in v.2–3, and several Islamic and other dynasties are continued in this volume beyond 1491. Index of territories, dynasties, sees, and hordes; table of forms of names in various languages. Name index; bibliography. D11.5.R67

Truhart, Peter. Regents of nations: a systematic chronology of states and their political representatives in past and present: a biographical reference book. München [etc.], Saur, 1984– . pt.1– . (In progress) **CJ231**

Title and prefatory matter also in German.

Contents: pt.1, Africa/America (980p.).

A register of heads of states, governors of dependent territories, foreign and colonial ministers, and some "counter-governments" and pretenders. Arranged by continent, region, and country. Pts. 2 and 3 will cover Asia, Australia and Oceania, and Europe; pt.3 will include an index to the whole work. JF37.T78

Africa

See also DD8.

Alderfer, Harold Freed. A bibliography of African government, 1950–1966. [2d ed.] Lincoln University, Pa., Lincoln Univ. Pr., [1967]. 163p. **CJ232**

An earlier edition in mimeographed form appeared in 1964.

Lists both books and articles. Arranged by country; author index. Z3501.A6

Annuaire de l'Afrique du Nord. v.1– , 1962– . Paris, Centre National de la Recherche Scientifique, 1964– . il., maps. Annual. **CJ233**

Covers Algeria, Libya, Morocco, Tunisia. Includes reports on various phases of constitutional and economic development; chronologies of diplomatic, political, and economic life; documents; bibliography. DT181.A74

—— Tables décennales, 1962–1971. Paris, Éditions du Centre National de la Recherche Scientifique, 1978. 135p. maps.

Contents: Table des auteurs; table des comptes rendus; table des sigles; table des documents [listed by country and then by topic]; table analytique [by subject, subdivided by country].

Asiedu, Edward Seth. Public administration in English-speaking West Africa: an annotated bibliography. Boston, G. K. Hall, [1977]. 365p. **CJ234**

Includes books, pamphlets, surveys, reports, theses, and periodical articles published between 1945 and 1969 on Gambia, Ghana, Liberia, Nigeria, and Sierra Leone; an addenda section covers materials published 1970–75. The bibliography "includes anything on the subject of the institutions of government at all levels, i.e., Federal, Regional, and local, and also anything on the process of administering public policy."—*Pref.* Indexed.   Z7165.A48A83

A bibliography for the study of African politics. [s.l.], Crossroads Pr., 1977–83. v.1–3. (In progress)   **CJ235**

v.1 was previously issued in 1973 as a monograph by R. B. Shaw and R. L. Sklar under the same title used for the series (*see* below). v.2, by Alan C. Solomon, is designed as a supplement and covers the 1971–75 period. Its more than 3,900 entries (mostly English-language materials) are grouped as: (1) general works, subdivided by form and subject; and (2) works on specific regions and states. Indexed.

The 1976–80 period is covered in v.3 (1983), by Eric R. Siegel, with 5,720 entries; Egypt has been omitted, and the language scope broadened to include more Western languages.   Z3508.P6B52

Shaw, Robert B. and **Sklar, Richard L.** A bibliography for the study of African politics. Los Angeles, African Studies Center, Univ. of California, 1973. 206p. (African Studies Center. Occasional paper, no.9)   **CJ236**

About 3,900 entries for works published through 1970. A section of general works is followed by sections for individual regions and states. Author index.   DT1.C34 no.9

Bidwell, Robin. Guide to African ministers. London, Collings, 1978. 79p.   **CJ237**

Gives in tabular form the names and dates of heads of state (including colonial governors), prime ministers, and ministers of foreign affairs, defense, interior or local government, and finance serving in African countries from 1950 through 1976. Each of the sections is subdivided into eight parts representing countries grouped together for geographical or historical reasons. Notes; no name index. Similar works by Bidwell include the following three volumes in his "Guide to government ministers" series: v.1, *The major powers and Western Europe, 1900–1971* (London, Cass, 1973); v.2, *The Arab world, 1900–1972* (London, Cass, 1973); and v.3, *The British Empire and successor states, 1900–1972* (London, Cass, 1974).   JQ1874.B53

Cook, Chris and **Killingray, David.** African political facts since 1945. N.Y., Facts on File, 1983. 263p.   **CJ238**

Covers the political history of the continent from 1945 to 1980. In addition to chronology, biographies, and political data, provides information on conflicts and coups, population, economy, and trade unions.   DT30.C594

Drabek, Anne Gordon and **Knapp, Wilfrid.** The politics of African and Middle Eastern states: an annotated bibliography. Oxford & N.Y., Pergamon, [1976]. 192p.   **CJ239**

A geographical listing of principally English-language books on post-independence political development and international politics; within each region, titles are further classed as dealing with: (A) Political history; (B) Political systems, government; (C) Political parties, interest groups and ideologies; (D) Biographies, memoirs, speeches, writings by political leaders; (E) External relations. No index.   Z3508.P6D7

Duic, Walter Zwonimir. Africa administration; directory of public life, administration and justice for the African states. N.Y. & Paris, K. G. Saur; München, Verlag Dokumentation Saur, 1978. 1285p. il., maps.   **CJ240**

Contents: v.1, Zaïre, Ivory Coast, Benin, Gabon, Guinea-Bissau, Ghana, Upper Volta, Liberia, Guinea, Senegal, Cameroon, Togo, Gambia, Sierra Leone, Nigeria, Zambia.

In English, German, French, Spanish, Italian, and Serbo-Croatian.

A systematically arranged directory providing data on state and regional government, public life, commerce, the judicial system, social affairs, education, and religion; gives addresses, telephone and telex numbers, and names of executive officers. Numerous country and city maps locate about 20,000 cities and towns. Similar in concept and format to Duic's *Europa-Administration* (CJ284). No more published.   DT2.D84

Kirk-Greene, A. H. M. A biographical dictionary of the British colonial governor. [Brighton, Eng.], Harvester Pr., [1980]– . v.1– . (In progress)   **CJ241**

Contents: v.1, Africa.

The first volume provides brief data (family background, birth and death dates, marriage and children, education, career, governorships, honors, publications, source material) for about 200 governors in Africa between 1875 and 1968. Appendix provides chronological list of governors by country. Reviewed in *African affairs* 81:587–8 (no.325, Oct. 1982).   JV1009.A2K57

Phillips, Claude S. The African political dictionary. Santa Barbara, Calif., ABC-Clio, [1984]. 245p. maps. (Clio dictionaries in political science, 6)   **CJ242**

Items are arranged alphabetically in ten topical chapters, with maps, tables, bibliography, and index.   DT30.5.P47

Segal, Ronald. Political Africa; a who's who of personalities and parties. London, Stevens & Sons; N.Y., Praeger, 1961. 475p.   **CJ243**

In two sections: (1) "Personalities," p.1–288, which gives biographical sketches of leaders in all parts of Africa, and (2) "Parties," p.291–475, which describes the political parties of the various countries, arranged alphabetically by country. At the head of each country division, information is given on area and population, with reference to the names of persons from that country who are listed in the first section.   DT18.S4

Vineberg, Robert A. Africa and the Middle East: a bibliography. [Jerusalem], Hebrew Univ. of Jerusalem, 1977. 125p. (Occasional papers, no.13)   **CJ244**

At head of title: The Harry S. Truman Research Institute. Library and Documentation Unit, Africa Research Unit.

A wide variety of sources have been arranged in three main sections: (1) Africa and the Middle East; (2) Israel and Africa (including material on developing countries on other continents); (3) Arab states and Africa. Sections are usually further subdivided by country. Hebrew and Arabic titles have been translated into English. No index.   Z3508.R4V56

Albania

U.S. Central Intelligence Agency. Directory of officials of the People's Socialist Republic of Albania. [Wash.], Central Intelligence Agency, 1970– . (*Its* Reference aid CR70-11 [etc.])   **CJ245**

Revised periodically (e.g., Reference aid CR77-10848, Mar. 1977).

Supersedes the *Directory of Albanian officials* issued by the U.S. Dept. of State, Bureau of Intelligence and Research (1966).

Identifies by office the officials of the national and district government, the Communist party, and other prominent public organizations. Name index.   JN9684.U54

Americas

See also names of individual countries.

Political parties of the Americas: Canada, Latin America, and the West Indies. Westport, Conn., Greenwood Pr., [1982]. 2v. (864p.)   **CJ246**

Robert J. Alexander, ed.

Contents: [v.1] Anguilla–Grenada; [v.2] Guadeloupe–Virgin Islands of the United States.

Each chapter by a specialist briefly describes the political history of a country, each political party which has existed there (with foundation date, orientation, leadership, electoral history), and concludes with a bibliography. United States parties are excluded since they are covered by Schapsmeier's *Political parties ...* (CJ176).   JL195.P64

Asia

See also names of individual countries.

The Far East and Australasia. Ed.1– , 1969– . London, Europa, [1969]– . Annual. **CJ247**

Subtitle: A survey and directory of Asia and the Pacific.

States and territories are discussed in four major units: (1) South Asia, (2) South East Asia, (3) East Asia, and (4) Australasia and the Pacific Islands. A general introduction to the regions, development problems, aid and investment, and major commodities is followed by chapters on regional cooperative organizations. A useful reference section at the end of the volume includes a "Who's Who in the Far East and Australasia." DS1.F3

Ferguson, Anthony. Far Eastern politics: China, Japan, Korea, 1950–1975. Paris, International Political Science Abstracts, 1978. 250p. **CJ248**

This is a special index to *International political science abstracts* (CJ40), v.1–25. Each entry provides full bibliographic information and the original abstract number for access to the *IPSA* volumes. Titles of articles in languages other than English have been translated. Arrangement is by country, subdivided by topic; author and detailed subject indexes. JA36.I5 Suppl.

Nationalism in East Asia: an annotated bibliography of selected works, ed. by F. Gilbert Chan. N.Y., Garland, 1981. 170p. (Canadian review of studies in nationalism, v.1; Garland reference library of social science, v.70) **CJ249**

The first three chapters ("Chinese nationalism: a bibliographical survey," "Communist nationalism in China," "Nationalism in China: Chinese and Japanese sources") were compiled by Chan; two chapters on Japan and one on Korea were contributed by other scholars. Z3001.N34

Southeast Asian politics, 1967–1979: a bibliography; Indonesia, Malaysia, the Philippines, Singapore, Thailand. Kuala Lumpur, Meta, [1980]. 468p. **CJ250**

Comp. by Research Staff of Sritua Arief Associates.

Almost 2,000 citations to books, articles, reports, theses and dissertations, etc., are arranged geographically by country and region. Author and subject indexes. Z3221.S675

Australia

Commonwealth government directory. 1977– . Canberra, Australian Government Publ. Service, 1977– . Annual. **CJ251**

Supersedes *Australian government directory* (1973–75) and *Commonwealth of Australia directory* (1961–72).

1976 ed. publ. under title: *A guide to Commonwealth government departments and authorities.*

For executive, parliamentary, judicial, and ministerial agencies, provides name, address, brief notes on creation, role, and function, and names of personnel. Indexed by organization and subject, and by personal names. JQ4021.C25

International Public Relations Party. The governments of Australia: a political and department guide. [4th ed.] Braddon, The Party, [1983]. 230p. (looseleaf) il., maps. **CJ252**

1st ed. 1972.

A register, with brief biographies and photographs of federal and state government officials, and of members of the "shadow ministries" of the opposition party. Directory data on legislatures and executive parties; electoral maps. JQ4021.I58

——— The Australian political handbook. Canberra City, Internat. Public Relations Pty., 1974. 210p. maps. **CJ253**

Subtitle: A handbook listing the executive structures of Australia's major political parties, trade union organisations and other politically important groups, with complete lists of federal and state parliamentarians, and federal and state electoral maps.

Identifies, with brief biographical information for major figures, the organization and executives of political parties and trade unions, both federal and state. Also lists federal and state cabinets and members of Parliament. JQ4021.I58

Mayer, Henry, Bettison, Margaret and **Keene, Judy.** A research guide to Australian politics and cognate subjects (ARGAP). [Melbourne], Cheshire, [1976]. 329p. **CJ254**

An annotated bibliography of bibliographies, with notes on standard works and yearbooks, together with mention of journal articles, mimeographed material, etc. Classed by type of publication and by subject; "cognate subjects" include the economy, domestic affairs, society, biography, and research. Both the main text and "Supplement 1" (p. 269–310) have author and title indexes. Checklist of relevant Australian periodicals, with index or abstracting source, and list of Australian newspaper indexes, 1800–1973. Z7165.A8M35

Parliamentary handbook of the Commonwealth of Australia. Ed.1– , 1901/15– . Canberra, Govt. Printer, 1915– . Irregular. **CJ255**

Title varies: v.1–7, *Biographical handbook and record of elections;* v.8–11, *Parliamentary handbook and record of elections;* Ed.18–19, Suppl.1, *Australian parliamentary handbook.*

Biographical sketches and lists of members of parliament, records of parliaments and ministries, records of elections, etc.

Rydon, Joan. A biographical register of the Commonwealth Parliament, 1901–1972. Canberra, Australian Nat. Univ. Pr., 1975. 229p. (Australian parliaments: Biographical notes, 5) **CJ256**

An alphabetical arrangement of entries which include personal biography, career outside Parliament, political career, and sources of further information. Details of ministries and dates of parliaments have been excluded, as they are available in the *Parliamentary handbook* (above). JQ4054.R93

Austria

Österreichischer Amtskalender. Jahrg.1– , 1922– . Wien, Staatsdruckerei, 1922– . Annual. **CJ257**

Combines the *Niederösterreichische Amtskalender* and the *Hof- und Staatshandbuch.* Title pages of each issue carry the volume numbering of each of the earlier series as well as the new series number.

Suspended publication 1938–48; resumed with v.17, 1949.

A detailed directory of the departments and personnel of the national and local governments of Austria. JN1604.A32

Belgium

Almanach royal officiel, publié depuis 1840. v.1–98. Bruxelles, Guyot, 1840–1939. Annual (not publ. 1915–19). **CJ258**

Ceased publication.

Detailed directory information of the government of Belgium.

Brazil

See also CJ461, DB313.

Javari, Jorge João Dodsworth. Organizações e programas ministeriais regime parlamentar no Império. 2. ed. Rio de Janeiro, Dept. de Impr. Nacional, 1962. 469p. **CJ259**

A historical register listing cabinet members, deputies to the national assembly, senators, etc., from 1822 to 1889, first issued in

1889 under title *Organizações e programas ministeriais desde 1822 a 1889.* This is a corrected edition.   JL2411.J33

Bulgaria

Directory of officials of the Bulgarian People's Republic. [Wash., Central Intelligence Agency], 1975– . charts. (*Its* Reference aid A(CR)75–38 [etc.])   **CJ260**

Revised periodically.

Supersedes the *Directory of Bulgarian officials* (1972), issued by the U.S. Dept. of State, Bureau of Intelligence and Research.

Lists officeholders of the central and regional governments, political parties, diplomatic posts, major public organizations, and mass media. Name index.   JN9604.U54

Canada

Campbell, Colin. Canadian political facts 1945–1976. Toronto, [etc.], Methuen, [1977]. 151p.   **CJ261**

A miscellaneous collection of statistical tables, lists of office holders, etc., grouped under such headings as: The executive, Parliament, Elections, Political parties and pressure groups, The Canadian economy, Population and language. Lacks an index.   JL65 1977.C35

Canadian parliamentary guide. (Ed. with the patronage of the Parliament of Canada and of the legislatures of the various provinces) by G. Pierre Normandin. Ottawa, Syndicat des Oeuvres Sociales Limité, 1912– .   **CJ262**

Imprint varies. Succeeds *Parliamentary companion, 1862–1911.*

Lists, with biographical sketches, the administrative officials, privy council, the senate, and the house of the government of Canada and of the provinces. Includes election statistics, etc., and lists of diplomatic representatives to and from Canada.   JL5.A4

Carrigan, D. Owen, comp. Canadian party platforms, 1867–1968. [Toronto], Copp Clark; Urbana, Univ. of Illinois Pr., [1968]. 363p.   **CJ263**

In addition to the party platforms, there are historical notes and a table of election results for each campaign.   JL195.C3

Clement, Wallace and **Drache, Daniel.** A practical guide to Canadian political economy. Toronto, Lorimer, 1978. 183p.   **CJ264**

A selective, annotated, topically arranged bibliography of about 1,500 titles emphasizing "radical scholarship with its roots in a broadly defined Marxist tradition."—*Pref.* Covers subjects such as dependency factors, uneven regional development, class formations, culture and nationalism, women, and Quebec. Author index.   Z7165.C2C58

Heggie, Grace F. Canadian political parties, 1867–1968; a historical bibliography. [Toronto], Macmillan, [1977]. 603p.   **CJ265**

An annotated bibliography on federal Canadian politics, with approximately 8,850 entries, including books, essays, historical societies' publications, theses, and journal articles. Pt.I, "The federal political parties of Canada," is arranged by chronological period and individual party; pt.II, "Government and political institutions," lists works on Dominion-Provincial relations, the constitution, government organization and administration, the executive, Parliament, and the judiciary. Appendixes list reference sources and periodicals. Author and subject indexes.   Z7165.C2H43

Lambert, Ronald D. The sociology of contemporary Quebec nationalism: an annotated bibliography and review. N.Y., Garland, 1981. 148p. (Canadian review of studies in nationalism, v.2; Garland reference library of social science, v.78)   **CJ266**

586 citations to books and periodical articles from the post-1945

period (most published since the 1960s) are annotated and preceded by a lengthy review of the literature.   Z1392.Q3L34

Organization of the government of Canada. June 1958– . Ottawa, Queen's Printer, 1958– . (13th ed., 1980)   **CJ267**

Published by authority of the Secretary of State.

Arranged by department, agency, etc. For each there is textual explanation, a list of principal officeholders, and usually an organizational chart.   JL5.O7

Chile

Urzua Valenzuela, Germán. Diccionario político institucional de Chile. Santiago, Editorial Ariete, 1979. 242p. (Colección ensayos, no.1)   **CJ268**

Offers brief definitions and histories of political parties, movements, institutions, etc., from the 19th century to the present. Electoral figures are presented for many parties and for the Chamber of Deputies.   JL2605.U79

China

China directory in Pinyin and Chinese, 1984– . [Tokyo], Radiopress, [1984]– . Annual.   **CJ269**

Title varies: *China directory, 1971–79; China directory in Pinyin, Wade-Giles, 1980; China directory in Pinyin and Wade-Giles, 1981–83.*

In English, Japanese and Chinese.

A comprehensive register of central, provincial, and local officials of agencies and organizations, with chronologies of party congresses and conferences. Name index.   JQ1507.C5291

Directory of Chinese officials: national level organizations. July 1980– . [Wash.], Nat. Foreign Assessment Ctr., 1980– . Irregular.   **CJ270**

Continues *Directory of officials of the People's Republic of China* (1972–80) and *Directory of Chinese Communist officials* (1953–69).

Identifies individuals who hold leading positions in the Communist party, government, legislature, economic and military organizations, judicial system, and selected mass organizations. Name index.   JQ1507.D55

Klein, Donald W. and **Clark, Anne B.** Biographic dictionary of Chinese communism, 1921–1965. Cambridge, Mass., Harvard Univ. Pr., 1971. 2v.   **CJ271**

Offers "433 biographies of men and women who contributed to the Chinese Communist movement from the establishment of the Chinese Communist Party in 1921 to 1965."—*Introd.* Bibliographic footnotes and a selected bibliography. Many useful appendixes.   DS778.A1K55

Lamb, Malcolm. Directory of officials and organizations in China, 1968–1983. [3d ed.] Armonk, N.Y., M. E. Sharpe, 1984. 717p. (Contemporary China papers/Contemporary China Centre, Research School of Pacific Studies, Australian National Univ., Canberra)   **CJ272**

1st ed. 1976.

A register of central organizations and officials, with data on key municipal and provincial positions. Personal name index.   JQ1507.L36

Perleberg, Max. Who's who in modern China . . . Hong Kong, Ye Olde Printerie, 1954. 428p. il.   **CJ273**

For full entry and annotation *see* AJ121.

Contains information on government organization and personnel for both Nationalist and Communist China.   DS734.P4

U.S. Central Intelligence Agency. National Foreign Assessment Center. Directory of Chinese scientific and educational officials. [Wash.], The Center, [available from National

Technical Information Service], 1979. 559p. (*Its* Reference aid CR 79–11870)   **CJ274**

Identifies members of ministries of the state council and its special agencies, selected national level offices and committees, international representation, selected mass organizations, provincial and administrative organizations, various academies, publishing houses, colleges and universities, hospitals, and industrial organizations. Name index.   Q149.C5U54

Cuba

U.S. Central Intelligence Agency. National Foreign Assessment Center. Directory of officials of the Republic of Cuba. [Wash.], The Center, 1979. 298p.   **CJ275**

Supersedes its *Directory of Cuban officials* formerly issued by the Central Intelligence Agency as *Directory of personalities of the Cuban government* . . . (1973–78).

A register of the Cuban government and the official and mass organizations, with names of key personalities. Name index. Revised periodically.   JL1007.U53

Czechoslovakia

U.S. Central Intelligence Agency. National Foreign Assessment Center. Directory of officials of the Czechoslovak Socialist Republic. [Wash.], The Center, 1980. 175p.   **CJ276**

Supersedes the *Directory of Czechoslovak officials* (1963–79) issued by the U.S. Central Intelligence Agency. Lists officials of government and political parties, diplomats, and officers of major public organizations; information is that received as of Apr. 30, 1980. Name index.   JN2217.U55

Denmark

Denmark. Kongelig dansk Hof- og Statskalender; Statshåndbog for kongeriget Danmark for Aaret 1734– . . . . København, Schultz, 1734– . Annual.   **CJ277**

Title varies: *Königlich dänischer hof- und staats-calender.*
A detailed directory of the departments and personnel of the Danish government. Indexes of personal names and of offices, agencies, etc.   JN7104.K554

Denmark, 1924– , publ. by the Royal Danish Ministry of Foreign Affairs. Copenhagen, 1924– . il. Irregular.   **CJ278**

Some years published in French, German, Spanish, and English.
Provides concise information on geography, history, occupations, science, art, and general culture. Profusely illustrated.

Europe

See also names of individual countries; for materials on the European Communities and European Parliament *see* CK441–CK458; *see also* CJ220.

Annuaire européen, European yearbook. Publié sous les auspices du Conseil de l'Europe. The Hague, Nijhoff, 1955– . v.1– . Annual.   **CJ279**

"Aim is to promote the scientific study of European organizations and their work" (*Note*), including their constitutions and functions. Includes the Council of Europe, European Coal and Steel Community, and other international communities and cooperative organizations.

Documents appear in French and English; articles in French with English summaries, or in English with French summaries. Bibliographies include a section of books, pamphlets, and periodical material of the year on European integration.   JN3.A5

Babuscio, Jack and **Dunn, Richard Minta.** European political facts, 1648–1789. N.Y., Facts on File, [1984]. 387p.   **CJ280**

Designed as a companion to the *European political facts* volumes by Cook and Paxton (below). In eight main sections: heads of state and key ministers; political chronology; the Enlightenment; defense and warfare; treaties and diplomacy; the Church; population; colonies and dependencies. Indexed.   JN9.B3

Cook, Chris and **Paxton, John.** European political facts, 1789–1848. N.Y., Facts on File, [1981]. 195p.   **CJ281**

Designed as a companion to the authors' volumes covering 1848–1918 and 1918–73. Provides chronologies, registers of heads of state and key ministers, descriptions of parliaments and systems of government, glossaries of people and terms, statistics, etc. Sources are not identified. Indexed.   JN10.C65

—— European political facts, 1848–1918. N.Y., Facts on File, [1978]. 342p.   **CJ282**

A companion to the same authors' volumes for 1918–73 (below) and 1789–1848 (above). Aims to bring together comparable information for all the countries of Europe: chronological tables; notes on parliaments; lists of heads of state, ministers, etc.; elections; political parties; statistics of population and urbanization, etc. Indexed.   JN10.C66

—— European political facts, 1918–73. [London, Macmillan]; N.Y., St. Martin's, [1975]. 363p.   **CJ283**

A volume covering 1918–84 is to be published 1985.   JN12.C64

Duic, Walter Zwonimir. Europa-Administration: Handbuch der Verwaltung und Justiz für die Europäischen Gemeinschaften. München, Verlag Dokumentation, 1976. 1161p. maps.   **CJ284**

In German, French, Dutch, English, Italian, and Serbo-Croatian.
Entries for all member states of the European Communities (Germany, France, Italy, the Netherlands, Belgium, the United Kingdom, Denmark, Republic of Ireland, Grand Duchy of Luxembourg, and the European Communities as such) have been standardized by identifying all comparable institutions concerned with the same subject area with the same code number; each entry provides name, address, telephone number, and name of executive officer. Includes more than 16,000 entries from national to county level. Covers state, regional, and local administrative institutions, police, judiciary, labor authority, social affairs, finance administration, transport, building construction and public works, commerce, tourism, education, and defense.   JN94.A12D84

Lexikon zur Geschichte der Parteien in Europa. Unter Mitarbeit zahlreicher Fachgelehrter hrsg. von Frank Wende. Stuttgart, A. Kröner, [1981]. 890p.   **CJ285**

Arranged alphabetically by country, each country section by a contributing scholar or team of scholars. A brief historical overview of the country's political parties is followed by an alphabetical listing of entries for individual parties. Bibliographic references; personal name index.   JN94.A979L49

McCrea, Barbara P., Plano, Jack C. and **Klein, George.** The Soviet and East European political dictionary. Santa Barbara, Calif., ABC-Clio, [1984]. 367p. (Clio dictionaries in political science, 4)   **CJ286**

Entries are grouped into chapters according to subject matter, with definitions, paragraphs on historical and contemporary significance, and cross references. Comprehensive index and country index.   DJK6.M33

Nationalism in the Balkans: an annotated bibliography. [Ed. by] Gale Stokes. N.Y., Garland, 1984. 243p. (Canadian review of studies in nationalism, v.3; Garland reference library of social science, v.160)   **CJ287**

" . . . authors were requested to write representative, not exhaustive, bibliographies of post-World-War II literature relating to nationalism and their country or national group."—*Introd.* 578 citations grouped by country or national group, excluding Albania. Author index.   Z2846.N37

Political parties in the European Community. Ed. by Stanley Henig. [London], Allen & Unwin, Policy Studies Inst., [1979]. 314p.   **CJ288**

At head of title: European Centre for Political Studies, European Cultural Foundation.

"Our purpose has been to recount the party political history of the last decade and to update material on party membership, finance, electoral support and internal power structure."—*Introd.* Chapters on Belgium, Denmark, France, the Federal Republic of Germany, Ireland, Italy, Luxembourg, the Netherlands, and the United Kingdom. Supplements an earlier study by Stanley Henig and John Pinder, *European political parties* (London, Allen & Unwin, 1969), which contains more historical data.   JN94.A979E85

Political parties of Europe. Ed. by Vincent E. McHale. Westport, Conn., Greenwood Pr., [1983]. 2v. (1295p.)   **CJ289**

Contents: [v.1] Albania–Norway; [v.2] Poland–Yugoslavia, European Parliament.

Country chapters offer introduction, bibliography, and historical data for parties represented in the national parliaments through 1982. Includes Eastern Europe, the Soviet Union, and formerly independent Estonia, Latvia, and Lithuania. Tabular data on electoral history, appendixes of party genealogies, and country chronologies. Indexed.   JF2011.P595

Rees, Philip. Fascism and pre-fascism in Europe, 1890–1945: a bibliography of the extreme right. [Brighton, Eng.], Sussex, Harvester; [Totowa], N.J., Barnes & Noble, [1984]. 330p.   **CJ290**

A selective bibliography of the "most cited and the most significant writings on the ideology and practice of the extreme right" *(Pref.)*, primarily books, dissertations, and articles of post-1945. Country arrangement includes Eastern Europe and the Soviet Union, but excludes Britain (which was covered in Rees's *Fascism in Britain,* CJ323). Also excludes foreign policies of fascist states, antifascist resistance movements, the Holocaust and concentration camps. Personal name index.   Z2000.7.R44

Sallnow, John and **John, Anna.** An electoral atlas of Europe, 1968–1981; a political geographic compendium including 76 maps. London, Butterworth Scientific, [1982]. 149p. maps.   **CJ291**

Offers maps and statistical tables to illustrate analytical text on European electoral systems and election results; bibliographic references are appended to each chapter on a particular country. Only national election results are indicated. Personal name and political party indexes.   JN94.A956S24

Who's who in European institutions and organizations. Ed.1– . Zurich, Who's Who, 1982– . Irregular.   **CJ292**

Subtitle: A biographical encyclopedia of the international red series containing some 4000 biographies of the top administrators, chairmen, politicians and other leading personalities working with European institutions and organizations and international institutions in Europe.

Finland

Suomen valtiokalenteri, 1869– . Helsinki, Weilin & Göös, 1869– . Annual.   **CJ293**

Publisher varies.

A Swedish edition is published as *Finlands statskalender,* 1811– . Directory information of the government of Finland.   JN6707

France

See also CA143, CJ12.

Annuaire diplomatique et consulaire de la République Française. Paris, Impr. Nationale, 1858–1954. Annual.   **CJ294**

Title varies. Ceased publication.

Includes a historical list of the ministers of foreign affairs since 1589, and directory information on the diplomatic and consular service of France, with biographical sketches.   JX1793.A2

Bottin administratif et documentaire. 1942– . Paris, Société Didot, Bottin, 1942– . Annual.   **CJ295**

Title varies. Originally published as part of *Bottin,* and continues its numbering. The "Étranger" section of *Bottin* was continued as *Bottin mondial* (later *Bottin international*).

Principal contents: Présidence de la République; Organisation et composition du gouvernement; Corps diplomatique; Assemblées; Grands corps de l'état; Premier ministre; Ministères et secrétariats d'état; Administrations centrales et régionales; Administration départementale; Table alphabétique des noms.   JN2303.B6

Coston, Henry. Dictionnaire de la politique française. Paris, Librairie Française, [1967]. 1088p.   **CJ296**

Includes entries for political terms, parties, institutions, journals, and political figures.   DC55.C72

Dictionnaire des parlementaires français: notices biographiques sur les ministres, sénateurs et députés français de 1889 à 1940. Publié sous la direction de Jean Jolly. . . . Paris, Presses Universitaires de France, 1960–77. 8v.   **CJ297**

Subtitle varies slightly.

Contents: t.1, Chronological and alphabetical lists of ministers from 1871; Alphabetical lists of senators, deputies, etc., 1871–1876; Biographical sketches, A–Azéman; t.2–8, Biographical sketches, B–Z.

Continues Robert (CJ298) and supersedes Samuel (CJ299). The biographical sketches vary in length, but generally are fairly full.   JN2785.D5

Robert, Adolphe, Bourloton, Edgar and **Cougny, Gaston.** Dictionnaire des parlementaires français, comprenant tous les membres des assemblées françaises et tous les ministres français depuis le 1er mai 1789 jusqu'au 1er mai 1889, avec leurs noms, état civil, états de services, actes politiques, votes parlementaires, etc. Paris, Bourloton, 1891. 5v. il.   **CJ298**

Fairly long biographical sketches of members of parliament and ministers, 1789–1889.

Samuel, René Claude Louis and **Bonét-Maury, Géo.** Les parlementaires français, II. 1900–1914.Dictionnaire biographique et bibliographique des sénateurs, députés, ministres ayant siège dans les assemblées législatives. Paris, Roustan, 1914. 479p.   **CJ299**

Begun as a continuation of the preceding work by Robert, but the volume covering 1889–1900 was never published. This volume called v.2. Now superseded by CJ297.   JN2771.S3

Dioudonnat, Pierre-Marie and **Bragadir, Sabine.** Dictionnaire des 10,000 dirigeants politiques français. Paris, SEDOPOLS, [1977]. 755p.   **CJ300**

Subtitle: Décrivant la carrière politique de toutes les personnes qui ont joué un rôle depuis 1967 (les candidats à l'Assemblée nationale, au Sénat et à la présidence de la République, les dirigeants des partis politiques, les membres des gouvernements et des cabinets ministériels et précédé d'un dictionnaire des organisations politiques, groupes parlementaires et étiquettes électorales.

Information in the biographical sketches is limited to the subject's political career. Entries for political and parliamentary groups provide history, dates of conferences, statistics on electoral results, membership, and lists of periodical publications. Useful appendixes on such topics as current political documents, composition of the government, the Senate, the Assemblée Nationale, and other subjects. **DC418.D56**

France. Almanach national; annuaire officiel de la République Française, 1872–1919. Paris, Berger-Levrault, 1872–1919. v.173– 217/221. **CJ301**

Published since 1693. Earlier volumes had title *Almanach royal, Almanach impérial,* etc. Imprint varies.

No more published.

Of first importance for information about the organization and personnel of the government of France to the end of World War I. Gives many official lists, e.g., cabinet, senate, and chamber; principal officers of the various government offices and bureaus; and outlines of the duties and functions of these bureaus. Includes also lists of the Legion of Honor, other orders, courts, departmental prefectures, universities, academies, societies, museums, chambers of commerce, etc. **JN2304**

Germany

Germany. Reichsministerium des Innern. Handbuch für das Deutsche Reich, 1874–1936. Berlin, Heymann, 1874–1936. 46v. Annual (irregular). **CJ302**

Contents vary but usually give a directory of governmental organizations with personnel. Useful for historical purposes.

Superseded by *Handbuch für die Bundesrepublik Deutschland,* 1953–54, issued by the Bundesministerium des Innern, which in turn was superseded by *Die Bundesrepublik* (CJ310). **JN3204**

Kosch, Wilhelm. Biographisches Staatshandbuch: Lexikon der Politik, Presse und Publizistik. Bern, Francke Verlag, [1963]. 2v. (1208p.) **CJ303**

Issued in parts, 1959–63.

An extensive biographical dictionary of past and present Germans, Austrians, and Swiss prominent in politics and journalism. Articles are brief and unsigned but include bibliographies. In addition to biographies, contains entries for newspaper and journal titles relating to political affairs. **DD85.K6**

Schwarz, Max. MdR; biographisches Handbuch der Reichstage. [Hannover], Verlag für Literatur und Zeitgeschehen GmbH, [1965]. 832p. **CJ304**

Lists members of the cabinets and of the parliaments of the First (1848–49), Second (1867–1918), and Third (1919–33) Reich, and gives brief biographical information for each. Includes a short parliamentary history of each period. The appendix offers useful statistics on the political parties. **JN3669 1965.S3**

Wahlstatistik in Deutschland: Bibliographie der deutschen Wahlstatistik, 1848–1975. Bearb. von Nils Diederich, Niedhard Fuchs, Irene Kullack und Horst W. Schmollinger. München, Verlag Dokumentation, 1976. 206p. (Berichte und Materialen des Zentralinstituts für sozialwissenschaftliche Forschung (ZI6) der Freien Universität Berlin, Bd.4) **CJ305**

Sources are arranged geographically by state (plus the city of West Berlin), then by type of election—Bundestag, Landtag, municipal, town, etc., for the period since 1945. A second section treats historical elections for the German Empire, Prussia, Bavaria, Hamburg, and other states. **Z7164.R4W33**

Germany, East

See also CJ55.

DDR Handbuch. Hrsg. vom Bundesministerium für innerdeutsche Beziehungen; wissenschaftliche Leitung, 2. völlig überarb. u. erw. Aufl. Peter Christian Ludz, unter Mitwirkung von Johannes Kuppe. Köln, Verlag Wissenschaft und Politik, [1979]. 1280p. il. **CJ306**

A dictionary arrangement of fairly lengthy articles on all major aspects of East German society, politics, economy, foreign policy, and legal system. Classified bibliography. **DD261.D17**

Germany (Dem. Repub. 1949–). Volkskammer. Die Volkskammer der Deutschen Demokratischen Republik. Wahlperiode 1– . 1957– . Berlin, Kongress-Verlag, [etc.], 1957– . Irregular. **CJ307**

Title varies: 1957–59, Handbuch der *Volkskammer der Deutschen Demokratischen Republik.*

A handbook giving the constitution and other documents of the German Democratic Republic, as well as biographical sketches and pictures of members of the chamber.

U.S. Central Intelligence Agency. Directory of officials of the German Democratic Republic. [Wash.], 1975– . (*Its* Reference aid A(CR)75–44 [etc.]) **CJ308**

Supersedes the *Directory of East German officials* (1960–74).

Germany, West

Bermbach, Udo. Hamburger Bibliographie zum parlamentarischen System der Bundesrepublik Deutschland 1945–1970. Opladen, Westdeutscher Verlag, 1973. 629p. **CJ309**

A comprehensive bibliography in topical arrangement. Index of authors and personal names, and of subject categories.

——— ——— Ergänzungslieferung 1–3. Opladen, 1974–77.

Contents: no.1, 1971–1972. 154p.; no.2, 1973–1974. 256p.; no.3, 1975–1976. 170p.

Die Bundesrepublik, Jahrg.65– , 1956/57– , vereinigt mit Handbuch für die Bundesrepublik Deutschland. Berlin, Carl Heymann, 1956– . Biennial (irregular). **CJ310**

Formed by the merger of the *Handbuch für die Bundesrepublik Deutschland,* 1953–54, and the *Taschenbuch für Verwaltungsbeamte,* and assumes the numbering of the latter.

Jahrg. 67– , issued in Hefte: one for the *Bund,* followed by others for the individual provinces.

A directory of West Germany and of its individual component provinces, listing not only government bodies, but also educational and cultural institutions, banks, etc. **JN4423**

Germany (Federal Republic, 1949–). Presse- und Informationsamt. Deutschland heute. 7. neu bearb. Aufl. Wiesbaden, Franz Steiner, 1965. 986p. **CJ311**

1st ed. 1953.

Also published in English and French.

A survey of current affairs in the German Federal Republic with chapters on political, economic, social, religious, and cultural affairs. Not a yearbook as such; each edition is complete in itself. The 7th ed. covers events through 1963. **DD259.A518**

Günther, Klaus and **Schmitz, Kurt Thomas.** SPD, KPD/DKP, DGB in den Westzonen und in der Bundesrepublik Deutschland, 1945–1975: eine Bibliographie. 2., wesentlich erw. u. verb. Aufl. Bonn-Bad Godesberg, Neue Gesellschaft GmbH, 1980. 222p. (Archiv für Sozialgeschichte, Beiheft 6) **CJ312**

1st ed. 1976.

A topically arranged list of scholarly books, periodical articles, and dissertations. Includes English-, French-, and German-language materials on the Social Democratic party, the German Communist party, and the German Trade Union Federation. Author index. **Z7164.P8G84**

Kürschners Volkshandbuch Deutscher Bundestag. 1. Wahlperiode, 1953/57– . Darmstadt, Neue Darmstädter Verlagsanstalt, 1954– . Irregular. **CJ313**

Supersedes *Kürschners Deutscher Reichstag,* 1890–1933. Published after each election; gives information on the Bundestag, with biographical sketches and pictures of the members.

JN3971.A78K8

Röhring, Hans-Helmut and **Sontheimer, Kurt.** Handbuch des deutschen Parlamentarismus; das Regierungssystem der Bundesrepublik in 270 Stichworten. München, R. Piper, [1970]. 598p.   **CJ314**

Signed articles, most of them with bibliography, on various aspects of the German governmental system and closely related matters.   JN3971.A7R6

Saur, Karl Otto, ed. Who's who in German politics; a biographical guide to 4,500 politicians in the Federal Republic of Germany. N.Y., Bowker, 1971. 342p.   **CJ315**

Also published with German title page: *Who's who in der Politik* (München, Verlag Dokumentation, 1971).
Introductory matter in English and German.
Information is very brief and is based on responses to questionnaires sent to all ministers and state secretaries of the federal and state governments, members of the Bundestag, the Landtage, and to various local and municipal representatives.   DD259.63.S277

Schramm, Friedrich Karl. Der Staatsbürger fragt; Lexikon für den Staatsbürger. 5. Aufl. Wiesbaden, Verlag Chmielorz GmbH, 1961. 372p. il.   **CJ316**

A dictionary of terms, agencies, institutions, organizations, etc., relating to the government of the West German republic.

Ghana

Ghana year book: a Daily Graphic publication. [Accra, Ghana Graphic Co.], 1958– . Annual.   **CJ317**

Continues the *Gold Coast year book,* 1953–56.
Includes general directory information of the government and organizations of Ghana, with a brief biographical section.

DT511.A17

Great Britain

Bibliography

Britain and Europe since 1945. A bibliographical guide. Comp. by James Hennessy. [Brighton, Eng.], Harvester Pr., 1973. 98p.   **CJ318**

Subtitle: An author, title and chronological index to British primary source material on European integration issued since 1945.
A guide to the publisher's microfiche collection of the same title, which reproduces 26,000 pages of literature produced by British pressure groups and other organizations on the topic of British integration into Europe. Participating organizations are briefly described. Includes material produced through 1972. The collection is updated annually and issued with: HC241.25.G7B675

Britain and Europe during 1973– ; a bibliographical guide. [Hassocks, Eng.], Harvester Pr., 1974– . Annual.   **CJ319**

Subtitle: An author, title and chronological index to British primary source material on European integration issued during 1973– .
1975 volume is entitled *Britain and Europe during 1975—year of the Referendum.*

Bryan, Gordon. Scottish nationalism and cultural identity in the twentieth century; an annotated bibliography of secondary sources. Westport, Conn., Greenwood Pr., [1984]. 180p. (Bibliographies and indexes in law and political science, 1)   **CJ320**

A classed bibliography of 894 citations on the political, literary, and linguistic aspects of Scottish nationalism; also lists relevant periodicals, and cultural and political organizations. Chronology; index.   Z2067.N35B79

Pidduck, William. The radical right and patriotic movements in Britain: a bibliographical guide: an author, title and chronological index to primary source material on the radical right and patriotic movements in Britain. [Hassocks, Eng.], Harvester Pr., 1978. 99p.   **CJ321**

A guide to the publisher's microfiche collection of the same title. This first volume indexes the publications of the Bow Group, the Monday Club, Pressure for Economic and Social Toryism, and Aims of Industry, as well as the journal *Solon.* Material published through 1974 is included. Supplementary annual indexes to new materials and materials from other groups have been published for 1976–78.

Z7165.G8P5

Pollock, Laurence and **McAllister, Ian.** A bibliography of United Kingdom politics: Scotland, Wales and Northern Ireland. Glasgow, Centre for the Study of Public Policy, Univ. of Strathclyde, 1980. 126p. (Studies in public policy, v.3)   **CJ322**

Focuses on the politics of the non-English parts of the United Kingdom since 1945; excludes journalistic articles, government documents, material published by political parties. In general, arranged by geographic area—Ireland, Isle of Man, Northern Ireland, Wales, etc.—then by main entry; no detailed subject approach or index.   Z7165.G8P64

Rees, Philip. Fascism in Britain. Sussex, [Eng.], Harvester Pr.; [Atlantic Highlands], N.J., Humanities Pr., [1979]. 243p.   **CJ323**

An annotated bibliography on fascist, pro-Nazi, anti-war, radical right, and anti-Semitic movements in Britain from 1923 to mid-1977. Arranged by historical period, with subject subdivisions; separate sections list writings by and about Sir Oswald Mosley. Indexed.   22021.F2R43

Registers

The civil service year book, 1974– . London, H.M.S.O., 1974– . Annual.   **CJ324**

Supersedes the *British imperial calendar and civil service list* (1809–1973).
In five chapters: (1) The royal households and offices; (2) Parliamentary offices; (3) Ministers and departments: England; (4) Libraries, museums and galleries, research councils and other organisations: England; (5) Departments and other organisations [separately listed for Northern Ireland, Scotland, and Wales]. Includes salary tables and indexes to officers and to departments and organizations. Kept up to date in part by the quarterly *Her Majesty's ministers and senior staff in public departments.*   JN106.B8

The diplomatic service list. 1966– . London, H.M.S.O., 1966– . Annual.   **CJ325**

Issued by the Diplomatic Service Administration Office.
Continues in part the *Foreign Office list and diplomatic and consular year book* (1806–1965).
In four parts: (1) Home departments (the Foreign and Commonwealth Office); (2) British missions overseas; (3) Chronological lists from 1957 of Secretaries of State, Ministers of State, Permanent Under-Secretaries, Ambassadors, and High Commissioners; (4) Biographical notes and lists of staff.   JX1783.A22

Office-holders in modern Britain. London, Institute of Historical Research, Univ. of London, 1972–84. v.1–9. (In progress)   **CJ326**

Contents: v.1, Treasury officials, 1660–1870, comp. by J. C. Sainty; v.2, Officials of the Secretaries of State, 1660–1782, comp. by J. C. Sainty; v.3, Officials of the Board of Trade, 1660–1870, comp. by J. C. Sainty; v.4, Admiralty officials, 1660–1870, comp. by J. C. Sainty; v.5, Home Office officials, 1782–1870, comp. by J. C. Sainty; v.6, Colonial Office officials, 1794–1870, comp. by J. C. Sainty; v.7, Navy Board officials, 1660–1832, comp. by J. M. Collinge; v.8, Foreign Office officials, 1782–1870, comp. by J. M. Collinge; v.9, Officials of royal commissions of inquiry, 1815–1870, comp. by J. M. Collinge.

"The immediate purpose of the series . . . is to provide lists of the officials who served in the departments of the central government between the Restoration and 1870."—*Pref.* The chronological lists of appointments by office are followed by an alphabetical list of officials.

Pickrill, D. A. Ministers of the Crown. London, Routledge & Kegan Paul, [1981]. 135p.   **CJ327**

Lists holders of ministerial posts in the central government from earliest times (or, in the case of Ireland, from 1801); includes both senior and junior ministers, as well as the Speaker of the House of Commons. A name index to the lists of office-holders would have made the volume more useful.   JN401.P5

Directories

Directory of pressure groups and representative associations. 2d ed. [by] Peter Shipley. [N.Y.], Bowker, [1979]. 123p.   **CJ328**

Represents a second edition of the *Guardian directory of pressure groups . . .* (1977). Information was gathered by questionnaire. The classified arrangement has been refined; more than 600 British organizations are included.   JN329.P7B39

Dod's Parliamentary companion, 1832– . London, Business Dictionaries, 1832– . Annual.   **CJ329**

Publisher varies.
Includes: biographies of the Royal family and the members of the House of Lords and the House of Commons; procedure; ministries and government departments, etc.   JN500.D7

Handbooks

Britain, 1948/49– , an official handbook, prep. by the Central Office of Information. London, Stat. Off., 1948– . Annual.   **CJ330**

Publisher varies.
Descriptive articles and figures from various official sources on the administration and the national economy of the United Kingdom. Covers government, social welfare, industry, labor, press and broadcasting, etc. Includes bibliography.   DA630.A17

Butler, David and **Sloman, Anne.** British political facts, 1900–1979. 5th ed. [London, etc., Macmillan, 1980] 492p.   **CJ331**

1st ed. 1963.
Provides lists of political personnel and tables of political statistics and assembles statistical data on many social, economic, and cultural factors. A review in *The economist* (Mar. 29, 1980, p.134) notes: "And it is scrupulous in its references—making it as valuable a political bibliography as it is an encyclopaedia in its own right." New ed. publ. 1985.   JN231.B8

Flackes, William D. Northern Ireland: a political directory, 1968–83. [London], British Broadcasting Corp., [1983]. 323p. map.   **CJ332**

A "concise guide to the political, pseudo-political, paramilitary and quasi-religious bodies active in the Ulster scene and the personalities associated with them" (*Introd.*); also includes relevant groups and personalities from the United Kingdom and the Irish Republic. Brief descriptions without bibliographic references. Chronology; summary of election results; section on the security system.   DA990.U46F49

Rose, Richard and **McAllister, Ian.** United Kingdom facts. [London, Macmillan, 1982] 168p.   **CJ333**

Presents "basic facts about public life in Scotland, Wales and Northern Ireland. English data and data for the United Kingdom as a whole are included when comparison is helpful."—*Introd.* Focuses on politics, media public opinion polls, and selected socio-economic trends from 1945 to 1979. Brief bibliographies and source notes.   JN231.R67

The Scottish government yearbook, 1978– . Edinburgh, P. Harris Publ.; Totowa, N.J., Rowman & Littlefield, [1978]– . il. Annual.   **CJ334**

In two sections: (1) scholarly essays on local, national, and international policy and politics of Scotland; (2) reference section providing directory and statistical data, and a bibliography of recent publications on Scottish government and politics. Indexed.   JN1187.S38

Staveley, Ronald and **Piggott, Mary.** Government information and the research worker. 2d rev. ed. London, Lib. Assoc., 1965. 267p.   **CJ335**

Previous ed. 1952.
Offers summaries of resources, facilities, and services available to researchers in British government agencies and ministries, each chapter presented by a librarian or an agency official. The sections on the Ministry of Education and the Central Statistical Office are omitted from this edition, but there are new chapters on the Board of Trade, the Foreign Office, the Naval Historical Branch of the Ministry of Defence, the Royal Commission on Historical Monuments (England), and the United Kingdom Atomic Energy Authority.   Z2009.S7

Parliament

Bibliography

Goehlert, Robert U. and **Martin, Fenton S.** The Parliament of Great Britain: a bibliography. Lexington, Mass., Lexington Books, [1983]. 209p.   **CJ336**

A bibliography of English-language reference works and secondary literature produced since the late 19th century on the history, development, and legislative process of Parliament, excluding national politics and government policy in general. Subject arrangement; indexed.   Z7164.R4G57

Dictionaries and encyclopedias

Abraham, Louis Arnold and **Hawtrey, Stephen Charles.** Abraham and Hawtrey's Parliamentary dictionary. 3d ed. London, Butterworth, 1970. 248p.   **CJ337**

1st ed. 1956.
A brief encyclopedia of British parliamentary terms and concepts, giving definitions and, in some cases, longer articles, with many cross references and a serviceable index.   JN594.A7

Wilding, Norman W. and **Laundy, Philip.** An encyclopaedia of Parliament. 4th ed., completely rev. N.Y., St. Martin's Pr., [1971]. 931p.   **CJ338**

1st ed. 1958.
A very useful, alphabetically arranged encyclopedia of parliamentary history and procedures. Many brief articles, some long ones. Covers all Commonwealth parliaments, but emphasis is on the Parliament at Westminster. 34 appendixes provide chronological lists of parliaments, ministers, secretaries, etc.; tables of salaries; and a bibliography (p.892–931).   JN555.W5

Handbooks

Craig, Fred W. S., comp. Boundaries of parliamentary constituencies, 1885–1972. Chichester, Eng., Political Reference Publs., 1972. 212p. maps.   **CJ339**

Serves as a companion to Craig's *British parliamentary election results* (CJ347–CJ350).   JN561.C7

——— British general election manifestos, 1900–1974. Rev. and enl. ed. London, Macmillan, 1975. 484p.   **CJ340**

1st ed. 1970.
A collection of the texts of the election manifestos of the three principal parties in Britain.   JN1121.C73

Crewe, Ivor and **Fox, Anthony.** British parliamentary constituencies: a statistical compendium. London, Faber and Faber, 1984. 397p. maps. **CJ341**

Consists of uniform entries for 650 British election districts, providing electoral, social, and demographic statistics with explanatory text. Appendixes list districts in rank order according to various electoral or socio-demographic characteristics. Data is from 1979 and 1983. JN561.C74

Dissension in the House of Commons: intra-party dissent in the House of Commons' division lobbies, 1945–1974. Comp. and ed. by Philip Norton. [London, Macmillan, 1975] 643p. **CJ342**

Attempts to record "all cross-votes and other occasions of intra-party dissent which have taken place in the House of Commons' division lobbies from 1945 to 1974. Each occasion in which Members of either the Conservative or Labour parties in Parliament entered a lobby against their party Whip, or, in exceptional cases, against the clearly expressed wishes of their Front Benches, is recorded. In each case, the names of those Members who voted against the Whip are listed, preceded by a short *précis* of the debate upon which the vote occurred, with particular emphasis upon the views (if any) by those who subsequently cast the dissenting votes." —*Introd.* JN675 1975.D57

Norton, Philip. Dissension in the House of Commons, 1974–1979. Oxford, Clarendon Pr., 1980. 524p. **CJ343**

Serves as a continuation of Norton's compilation covering 1945–74 (above). Follows the scheme of that earlier volume with only minor changes. The compiler's analysis of dissenting actions of the period is presented in a final chapter. Select bibliography; subject and name indexes. JN675 1980.N67

Kinnear, Michael. The British voter; an atlas and survey since 1885. N.Y., St. Martin's Pr., [1981]. 173p. il. **CJ344**

Illustrates social, economic, and organizational factors in British politics and elections from 1885 to 1979, through text, tables, and maps. Bibliography; index. G1811.F9K5

Waller, Robert. The almanac of British politics. London, Croom Helm; N.Y., St. Martin's Pr., [1983]. 608p. maps. **CJ345**

Offers socioeconomic profiles of individual parliamentary constituencies in a manner similar to the *Almanac of American politics* (CJ136), but without biographical data on the constituencies' parliamentary representatives. Statistics are provided from the most recent census and general election. JN561.W28

Election statistics

Craig, Fred W. S. British parliamentary election results, 1832–1885. [London, Macmillan, 1977] 692p. **CJ346**

JN1037.C67

——— British parliamentary election results, 1885–1918. [London, Macmillan, 1974] 698p. **CJ347**

——— British parliamentary election results, 1918–1949. 3d ed. Chichester, Parliamentary Research Serv., 1983. 785p. **CJ348**

1st ed. 1969.

——— British parliamentary election results, 1950–1973. 2d ed. Chichester, [Eng.], Parliamentary Research Serv., 1983. 780p. **CJ349**

An earler edition covered 1950–70.
Companion volumes for British election statistics. Arranged by constituency, then by date of the election. Index of candidates and of constituencies. JN1037.C7142

——— British parliamentary election results 1974–1983. [Chichester, Eng.], Parliamentary Research Services, [1984]. 382p. **CJ350**

Intended to be used in conjunction with the author's *British electoral facts, 1885–1975* (3d ed. London, Macmillan, 1976. 182p.). Constituencies are grouped under Greater London, England, Wales, Scotland, and Northern Ireland, with columns for each constituency providing: date of election; number of electors on the Register; number of electors voting; candidate's name, party, number of votes polled, and number of votes as a percentage of total votes cast. Indexed by candidates.

A volume entitled *Britain votes 3,* covering the 1983 election, was published 1984. JN1037.C7144

——— Minor parties at British parliamentary elections, 1885–1974. [London, Macmillan, 1975] 147p. **CJ351**

Serves as a companion to the compiler's several volumes of *British parliamentary election results* (above). Entries are arranged by name of party, outlining history, policy, sources of information, and electoral activity. Statistical summary. Party and personal name indexes. JN1037.C725

Registers and biographical dictionaries

See also CJ329.

Foster, Joseph. Members of Parliament, Scotland, including the minor barons, the commissioners for the shires, and the commissioners for the burghs, 1357–1882. On the basis of the parliamentary return 1880, with genealogical and biographical notices. 2d ed. rev. and corr. London, priv. pr. by Hazell, Watson and Viney, 1882. 360p. **CJ352**

JN1263.F7

Gt. Brit. Parliament. House of Commons. Members of Parliament . . . [Return of the name of every member of the Lower House of Parliament of England, Scotland and Ireland, with name of constituency represented and date of return, from 1213 to 1874]. London, Stat. Off., 1878–91. 2pts. in 4v. (House of Commons. Reports and papers, 1878. no.69, 69I, 69II; 1892. no.169, also numbered 69III) (Repr.: Index to pt.II, Hamden, Conn., Shoe String, 1961. 300p.) **JC353**

Contents: Pt.1, Parliaments of England, 1213–1702, arranged chronologically. Index to pt.1, with appendix and corrigenda; pt.2, Parliaments of Great Britain, 1705–96, Parliaments of the United Kingdom, 1801–74, Parliaments and Conventions of the Estates of Scotland, 1357–1707, Parliaments of Ireland, 1559–1800. Index to pt.2, with appendix, i.e., names and members 1880–1885, and corrigenda; Parliaments of Great Britain, 1705–1800; Parliaments of the United Kindgom, 1801–85.

A very important record. JN672.A55

Namier, *Sir* **Lewis Bernstein** and **Brooke, John.** The House of Commons, 1754–1790. N.Y., publ. for the History of Parliament Trust by Oxford Univ. Pr., 1964. 3v. **CJ354**

At head of title: The history of Parliament.
Contents: v.1, Introductory survey, constituencies, appendixes; v.2–3, Members, A–Y. The latter give brief biographical sketches, with histories of individual parliamentary careers. Includes references to sources. JN672.N2

Sedgwick, Romney. The House of Commons, 1715–1754. N.Y., publ. for the History of Parliament Trust by Oxford Univ. Pr., 1970. 2v. **CJ355**

At head of title: The history of Parliament.
Contents: v.1, Introductory survey, appendices, constituencies, members, A–D; v.2, Members, E–Y.

Although published later, this is the chronological predecessor of the Namier and Brooke volumes (above) and follows the general plan of that work. JN675 1715.S4

The Times, London. House of Commons . . . London, The Times, 1945– . [v.1]– . **CJ356**

Editions have been issued at intervals following general elections.
Subtitle: With full results of the polling, biographies of members and unsuccessful candidates, photographs of all members and a

complete analysis, statistical tables, and a map of the general election (varies slightly). JN672.T6

Wedgwood, Josiah Clement. History of Parliament, 1439–1509. London, Stat. Off., 1936–38. v.1–2. col. coats of arms, facsim. **CJ357**

Contents: v.1, Biographies of the members of the Commons House; v.2, Register of the ministers and of the members of both houses, 1439–1509.

The first two of a proposed set of 3v. dealing with the history of Parliament from 1439–1509. For a note on v.1 *see* AJ232.

v.2, *Register,* contains introductory chapters on treatment, sources, and analyses; time analysis and lists of parliaments, arranged chronologically; notes on each constituency with alphabetical lists of members; tables and appendixes. JN505.W4

Who's who of British Members of Parliament. [Ed. by] Michael Stenton. [Hassocks, Sussex, Eng.], Harvester Pr.; [Atlantic Highlands, N.J.], Humanities Pr., [1976]–81. 4v. **CJ358**

Contents: v.1, 1832–1885; v.2, 1886–1918; v.3, 1919–1945; v.4, 1945–1979.

"A biographical dictionary of the House of Commons based on annual volumes of 'Dod's Parliamentary companion' and other sources."—*t.p.*

The editor has selected "the fullest and most useful entries that Dod [CJ329] provides on each MP's parliamentary career" (*Pref.*) and rounded them out with additional information such as the reason for leaving Parliament, highlights of subsequent career, death date.

A review of v.1 in *TLS* Feb. 18, 1977, p.185, notes various shortcomings of the work. JN672.W47

Local government

Golding, Louis. Dictionary of local government in England and Wales. London, English Universities Pr., [1962]. 446p. **CJ359**

Alphabetically arranged, with brief explanations of a large number of terms, regulations, agencies, etc., pertinent to local government.

Martin, Geoffrey Haward and **McIntyre, Sylvia.** A bibliography of British and Irish municipal history. [Leicester], Leicester Univ. Pr., 1972– . v.1– . (In progress) **CJ360**

For full record *see* DC325.

Municipal year book and public services directory. London, Municipal Journal, 1897– . v.1– . **CJ361**

Title varies; subtitle varies.

Includes: (1) articles on all phases of English local government: finance, power, roads, education, parks, public health, town planning, water supply, etc.; (2) list of associations and societies concerned with local government; and (3) information about municipal corporations with lists of offices; county and district councils, with officers, etc. JS3003.M8

British Commonwealth

See also CJ241.

British Council. Public administration; a select list of books and periodicals. London, Longmans, 1964. 120p. **CJ362**

A classified list of 1,548 titles of books and documents on public administration in the British Commonwealth, primarily by British authors. Name index, including titles of periodicals and yearbooks. No annotations.

Carnell, Francis. The politics of the new states; a select annotated bibliography with special reference to the Commonwealth. London, publ. for the Institute of Commonwealth Studies by Oxford Univ. Pr., 1961. 171p. **CJ363**

Books, articles, and documents, principally on political affairs of new states and territories in Asia and Africa. Classed arrangement, with indexes by author and place. Some brief annotations. Z7164.C7C3

Cook, Chris and **Paxton, John.** Commonwealth political facts. N.Y., Facts on File, [1979]. 293p. **CJ364**

Follows the format and philosophy of the various editions of David Butler's *British political facts* (5th ed. CJ331), with chapters on: evolution of the Commonwealth; heads of state, governors general, governors and high commissioners; constitutional history and parliamentary organization; ministers; elections; political parties; justice; defense and treaties; population; trade unions. Indexed. JN248.C63

Gt.Brit. Overseas Development Administration. Technical co-operation: a monthly bibliography. v.1, no.1– , Jan. 1964– . London, 1964– . Monthly. **CJ365**

Name of issuing body varies.

Concerned with technical cooperation and public administration overseas. "Largely devoted to the official publications of the Commonwealth, but reports and bulletins from foreign institutes and organizations will also be listed when received."—*Introd. note.*

——— Supplement. no.1– , 1964– . (Irregular; usually 2 to 4 per yr.)

Lists bills and subsidary legislation of Commonwealth countries.

Bloomfield, Valerie. Commonwealth elections, 1945–1970: a bibliography. Westport, Conn., Greenwood Pr., [1976]. 306p. **CJ366**

"This bibliography developed out of the library and research activities of the Institute of Commonwealth Studies, University of London."—*Introd.* References to some 760 elections have been provided in some 5,600 citations. "Originally it was intended to restrict the survey to elections and referenda at the national level, but in response to suggestions from political scientists coverage has been extended to state and provincial elections as well." Includes unpublished sources, official reports, electoral studies, and political party documents. Academic theses are excluded. Author and name index. Z7164.R4B55

A year book of the Commonwealth. 1967– . London, H.M.S.O., 1967– . Annual. **CJ367**

Supersedes the *Colonial Office list* (1862–1966) and the *Commonwealth Relations Office year book* (1951–66).

Includes notes on the history and constitutional development of each of the Commonwealth member countries, as well as lists of government officials, diplomatic representatives, etc. British representatives in Commonwealth countries are also listed. JN248.C5912

Hungary

U.S. Central Intelligence Agency. National Foreign Assessment Center. Directory of officials of the Hungarian People's Republic. [Wash., Central Intelligence Agency], 1971– . charts. (*Its* Reference aid A71–18 [etc.]) **CJ368**

Revised periodically (e.g., Reference aid A(CR)75–1, 1975).

Supersedes the *Directory of Hungarian officials* issued by the U.S. Dept. of State, Bureau of Intelligence and Research (1964–70).

Lists officials of national and regional governments, Communist party, and major public organizations. Name index. JN2052.1979.U54

India

Attar Chand. Bibliography of Indo-Soviet relations, 1947–77: a book of readings with selected abstracts. New Delhi, Sterling, [1978]. 152p. **CJ369**

1,166 references to books, essays, newspaper and journal articles are classed by subject and indexed by personal name. Emphasizes Indian, Russian, and Communist sources.   Z3208.R4A77

India; a reference annual. 1953– . Delhi, Ministry of Information and Broadcasting, 1953– . Annual (irregular).   **CJ370**

A general governmental yearbook, comprising considerable directory-type, statistical, and textual information on the major services of the national government, and the activities of the country as a whole.   DS405.I64

Kohli, A. B. Councils of ministers in India, 1947–1982. New Delhi, Gitanjali, [1983]. 188p.   **CJ371**

In three parts: chronological register; list of "important" ministries and major personnel; biographical sketches of prime ministers. Name index.   JQ242.K63

Rana, Mahendra Singh. Indian government and politics: a bibliographical study, 1885–1980. New Delhi, Wiley Eastern, [1981]– . v.1– . (In progress)   **CJ372**

A subject-classed bibliography of English-language books, articles, proceedings, and doctoral theses. v.1 includes historical studies of political thought and institutions, biographies, and ideologies and movements. Includes a separately classified list of doctoral dissertations. To be complete in 2v., the second to treat the areas of state politics, public administration, political parties, general elections, and foreign affairs. There will be about 21,000 references in all.   Z3208.A4R36

Singh, V. B. and **Bose, Shankar.** Elections in India: data handbook on Lok Sabha elections, 1952–80. New Delhi [etc.], Sage Pubns., [1984]. 642p.   **CJ373**

Statistical data on elections to the lower house of the Union Parliament, and to the lower houses of the state legislatures, the Vidhan Sabhas, are presented at three levels: all-India, state, and constituency.   JQ294.S565

Indonesia

Arief, Sritua and **Arief, Melanie Sritua.** Indonesian politics, 1967–1977: a bibliography. [Jakarta], Sritua Arief Associates, [1978]. 125p.   **CJ374**

An author listing of 565 English- and Indonesian-language monographs, articles, papers, and dissertations. Author and subject indexes.   Z3278.A5A74

Iran

Directory of Iranian officials. [Wash.], Directorate of Intelligence, U.S. Central Intelligence Agency, 1985– . Irregular? (*Its* Reference aid CR85-10921, etc.)   **CJ375**

A register of officials of the government, political parties, dissident movements, religious groups, economic and commercial organizations, and information agencies; indexed by agency and personal name.

Ireland

Ford, Percy and **Ford, Grace.** A select list of reports of inquiries of the Irish Dáil and Senate, 1922–72. [Dublin], Irish Univ. Pr., [1974] 64p. (Southampton, Eng., Univ. Studies in parliamentary papers)   **CJ376**

Aims "to help students to follow the development of thought on Eire's main lines of domestic policy since the foundation of the State."—*Scope.* Lists reports and papers on policy in constitutional, economic, social and legal matters. Classed arrangement; index based on keywords in title, with addition of names of personal authors and chairmen.   Z7165.I68F67

Ireland: a directory and yearbook, 1976– . Dublin, Inst. of Public Administration, [1976–]. Annual.   **CJ377**

A specially prepared reference edition of the *Administration yearbook and diary* published by the Institute of Public Administration. Basic information on Irish government, associations, finance, communications, higher education, religion, and Northern Ireland's governmental structure. Yearbook section provides statistics on population, commerce, labor, trade, banking, agriculture, social services, etc. Also includes general information on maps, taxes, etc. Index.   JN400.I68

A source book of Irish government. Ed. by Basil Chubb, assisted by Geraldine O'Dea. Rev. ed. Dublin, Inst. of Public Administration, 1983. 255p. il., map.   **CJ378**

1st ed. 1964.
Describes the functions of the national and local governments, the courts, participation in the European Communities, etc., with excerpts from relevant documents. Bibliography; index.   JN1428.S68

Walker, Brian Mercer. Parliamentary election results in Ireland, 1801–1922. Dublin, Royal Irish Academy, 1978. 438p. maps. (New history of Ireland: Ancillary pubns., 4)   **CJ379**

Gives results of general and by-elections.   JN1541.W34

Italy

Bartolotta, Francesco. Governi d'Italia, 1848–1961. [Roma, 1962?] 330p.   **CJ380**

A chronological listing of the ministries and ministers of state of Italy, 1848–1961. No biographies.

I deputati e senatori del . . . Parlamento republicano. Roma, La Navicella, 1949– . v.1– .   **CJ381**

Biographical sketches of the members of each Italian Parliament.   JN5531.D4

Italia; annuario dell' economia, della politica, della cultura. Milano, Etas/Kompass, 1963–69. Annual.   **CJ382**

Title varies: 1963–65, *Annuario politico italiano.* Publisher varies.
A handbook of political and economic information. Includes directory material, documents, statistical tables, and biographical sketches of cabinet officers, deputies, and senators.   JN5203.A53

Italy. Parlamento. Annuario parlamentare, 1948/49– . Roma, Tipografia della Camera dei Deputati, 1948– . Annual.   **CJ383**

The official register of the Italian government with lists of officials, agencies, commissions, and local administrations, and information on other countries of the world, the United Nations and other international organizations.   JN5445.A33

Pallotta, Gino. Dizionario politico e parlamentare italiano. [Rome], Newton Compton, [1976]. 302p. (Paperbacks società d'oggi, 6)   **CJ384**

Offers brief definitions of political terms, abbreviations, organizations, movements, with longer articles on political parties and changes in the government. Includes tables of election statistics and lists of the Councils of Ministers.   JA64.I8P34

Ivory Coast

See also CJ237.

Les élites ivoiriennes: who's who in Ivory Coast; qui est qui en Côte d'Ivoire. [Ed.1–]. Paris, Ediafric, 1976– .   **CJ385**

Cover title: Numéro special du Bulletin de l'Afrique noire.
A register and biographical directory of the principal political figures of the Ivory Coast.   DT545.82.A2E43

Japan

U.S. Embassy. Japan. The government organization of Japan (with names of bureau, division and section chiefs) as of Nov. 20, 1962. Tokyo, Translation Services Branch, Political Section, Amer. Embassy, 1962. 232p.   **CJ386**

Previous edition 1959.   JQ1621.U5

Publications of political science in Japan. Nihon seijigaku bunken mokuroku. Prep. by Nihon Seiji Gakkai [Japanese Political Science Assoc.]. Tokyo, Daigaku Shuppankai, 1967–75. Annual.   **CJ387**

In Japanese and English.
Publication suspended.
Lists books and selected periodical articles on political science published in Japan during the year preceding publication of the annual volume.   Z7161.P94

Ward, Robert Edward and **Watanabe, Hajime.** Japanese political science; a guide to Japanese reference and research materials. Rev. ed. Ann Arbor, Univ. of Michigan Pr., 1961. 210p. (Univ. of Michigan. Center for Japanese Studies. Bibliographical ser., no.1, rev. ed.) (Repr.: Westport, Conn., Greenwood Pr., 1978)   **CJ388**

1st ed. 1950.
An annotated, classified list of 1,759 numbered items, "confined largely, although not exclusively to works written in Japanese" (*Introd.*), which deal with political science subjects in Japan since the Meiji Restoration (1868).   Z7165.J3W3

Korea, North

An, Tai Sung. North Korea: a political handbook. Wilmington, Del., Scholarly Resources, [1983]. 294p. map.   **CJ389**

Provides general, statistical, and directory-type information, with biographies of political leaders and texts of constitution and party rules. Extensive multilingual bibliography.   DS932.A76

Directory of officials of the Democratic People's Republic of Korea. [Wash., Nat. Foreign Assessment Center], 1978– . (*Its* Reference aid CR78–11396 [etc.]) Irregular.   **CJ390**

Supersedes the Central Intelligence Agency's *Directory of North Korean officials* (1972).
Identifies persons holding "key positions in the Korean Workers Party; national, provincial, and municipal governments; legislative bodies; military organizations; the diplomatic service; and selected mass, cultural and scientific organizations."—*Pref.* Name index.   JQ1729.5.A4D56

Suh, Dae-Sook. Korean Communism, 1945–1980: a reference guide to the political system. Honolulu, Univ. Pr. of Hawaii, [1981]. 592p.   **CJ391**

Provides an annotated bibliography of the writings of Kim Il Sung (with subject and chronological indexes), historical agendas and personnel registers for the Korean Communist party and legislative assemblies, cabinets, and court; also provides translations of constitutions and by-laws, and romanized glossary. Name and subject indexes.   JQ1729.5.A3 1981.S83

Latin America

See also names of individual countries; *see also* CJ246.

Kantor, Harry. Latin American political parties: a bibliography. [Gainesville], Reference and Bibliography Dept., Univ. of Florida Libraries, in cooperation with the Center for Latin American Studies, 1968. 113p. (Florida, Univ. Libraries. Bibliographic ser., 6)   **CJ392**

Listing is by country, with subdivisions for individuals or types of parties.   Z7165.L3K3

Latin American politics: a historical bibliography. Santa Barbara, Calif., ABC-Clio, [1984]. 290p. (Clio bibliography ser., no.16)   **CJ393**

Collects from the *America: history and life* database 3,006 abstracts of items published 1973–82 dealing with Latin American and Caribbean politics since 1914. A section on general and multicountry studies is followed by seven sections on regions and countries (some subdivided by topic). Subject and author indexes.   Z1609.P64L39

Rossi, Ernest E. and **Plano, Jack C.** The Latin American political dictionary. Santa Barbara, Calif., ABC-Clio, [1980]. 261p.   **CJ394**

A topically arranged work similar to Plano and Greenberg's *American political dictionary* (CJ98) or Plano and Olton's *International relations dictionary* (CJ58); some definitions from those works have been expanded in this volume, but most entries are new. Entries include basic definition, historical background and current relevance. Indexed.   F1406.R67

Who is who in government and politics in Latin America. Ed.1– . N.Y., Decade Media Books, 1984– . Biennial?   **CJ395**

A bilingual edition. Presents biographical sketches of prominent individuals from Latin American and Caribbean countries; country arrangement; name index.

Mexico

Alisky, Marvin. Who's who in Mexican government. Tempe, Arizona State Univ., Center for Latin American Studies, 1969. 64p.   **CJ396**

Although the information is generally very brief, the work helps to fill a gap in biographical coverage for this area.   F1235.5.A2A4

Camp, Roderic Ai. Mexican political biographies, 1935–1981. 2d ed., rev. and exp. Tucson, Univ. of Arizona Pr., [1982]. 447p.   **CJ397**

1st ed. 1976.
"Contains the biographies of public men, living or deceased, who have been prominent in Mexican political life from 1935 to mid 1980."—*p.ix*. The appendixes supply lists of Supreme Court justices, federal senators, directors of federal departments, governors, party executives, union executives, etc. List of sources consulted and selective bibliographical essay.   F1235.5.A2C35

González-Polo, Ignacio F. Bibliografía general de las agrupaciones y partidos políticos mexicanos, 1910–1970. México, Reforma Política, 1978. 317p. (Reforma política: serie bibliografías, 4)   **CJ398**

"Primera édicion en el *Boletín del Instituto de Investigaciones Bibliográficas*, núm. 8, julio-diciembre de 1972."—*p. [4]*.
An annotated bibliography in two parts: (1) 356 studies on Mexican political parties and groups; (2) 1,506 primary documents from these sources. Indexed.   Z7165.M45G66

Near East

See also CJ239, CJ244.

Middle East and North Africa. 1948– . London, Europa Pubns., 1948– . il. Annual (irregular).   **CJ399**

Coverage varies. Changed title with 11th ed., 1964/65; previously covered only the Middle East.
Similar in presentation to *Europa* (CJ220); i.e., a general survey of the area and a section on regional organizations is followed by surveys of individual countries.   DS49.M5

Schulz, Ann. International and regional politics in the Middle East and North Africa: a guide to information sources. Detroit, Gale, [1977]. 244p.   **CJ400**

Chapters begin with an essay on the literature, then list English-language books, with annotations. Concentrates on post-1945 situation, with chapters on regional issues, foreign policies of individual states, external powers, Arab-Israeli conflict, petroleum. Reference materials are listed in a separate chapter. Author, title, and subject indexes.   Z6465.N35S38

Ziring, Lawrence. The Middle East political dictionary. Santa Barbara, Calif., ABC-Clio, [1984]. 452p. maps. (Clio dictionaries in political science, 5)   **CJ401**

Terms are arranged alphabetically within subject chapters and indexed in a general index; also indexed by country. Appendixes include maps and statistical tables; selected bibliography.

D561.Z58

Netherlands

Parlement en kiezer, jaarboekje, 1911/12– . 'sGravenhage, Nijhoff, 1911– . Annual.   **CJ402**

A handbook and register of the government of the Netherlands. Includes brief biographies of members of Parliament.

Staatsalmanak voor het Koninkrijk der Nederlanden. 1808– . 'sGravenhage, Nijhoff, 1808– . Annual.   **CJ403**

Not published 1809–14.
Published by the Departement van Binnenlandsche Zaken. Serves as the official register of the Netherlands.   JN5704

New Zealand

New Zealand. Dept. of Statistics. Report on the local authority statistics of New Zealand, 1926– . Ed.1– . Wellington, 1926– . v.1– . Annual.   **CJ404**

Takes the place of the *Annual statistical report on local government* (issued annually from 1875; biennially, 1903–24) and the *Municipal handbook.*
Title varies: 1926–1959/60, *The local authorities handbook of New Zealand,* issued by the Dept. under its earlier name (to 1954/55), Census and Statistics Dept.
Offers detailed statistics of local governments in New Zealand.

JS10.N8

Norway

Norway. Norges statskalender for året 1815– . Oslo. Aschehoug, 1815– . Annual (irregular).   **CJ405**

A comprehensive, detailed register of the government and governmental departments of Norway.   JN7405

Pakistan

Jones, Garth N. and **Ali, Shaukat.** A comprehensive bibliography: Pakistan government and administration. [Lahore, All Pakistan Public Admin. Research Centre], 1970–83. v.1–4. (In progress)   **CJ406**

v.4 has title *Bibliography: Pakistan government and administration, 1970–1981,* and is ed. by Mohamed Jameelur Rehman Khan (Islamabad, Public Admin. Res. Ctr.).
Topical arrangement subdivided by form (books, articles, reports

and others). Principally English-language materials. Includes Pakistani newspaper articles, theses and dissertations. Author index.

Z7165.P3J65

Papua New Guinea

Faircloth, Susan, Holzknecht, Hartmut and **May, R. J.** Politics and government in Papua New Guinea. Boroko, Papua New Guinea, Inst. of Applied Social and Economic Research, 1978. 253p. (IASER bibliography 4)   **CJ407**

An introductory section on traditional politics attempts to extract, "from the vast anthropological literature of Papua New Guinea, those references which have a substantial concern with 'political' topics—social organization and control, dispute settlement, ceremonial exchange, warfare, and so on."—*p.5.* A second section on modern politics and government employs a classed arrangement. Intends to include "all books, accessible theses, official publications and substantial articles or papers which have been widely circulated or are held by the libraries of IASER or the University of Papua New Guinea."—*p.41.* Author index.

Z7165.P33F34

Papua New Guinea handbook and travel guide. [Ed.9]– . Sydney, Pacific Publications, [1978]– . Irregular.   **CJ408**

1st ed. 1954; earlier eds. called *Papua and New Guinea handbook.*
A handbook of current information, including a business directory, a directory of public officials, and a gazetteer.   DU740.T8

Persian Gulf countries

The Gulf handbook; a guide for businessmen and visitors. Ed.1– . Bath, Eng., Trade and Travel Pubns. (distr. in U.S.A. by Garrett Park Pr.), 1976– . il., maps. Annual.   **CJ409**

An introductory section on the region details travel information and social customs. Chapters on each of the Gulf countries (Bahrain, Iran, Iraq, Kuwait, Oman, Qatar, Saudi Arabia, and the United Arab Emirates) outline geography and climate, plants and wildlife, communications and social background, constitution and history, and the economy; there follows a survey of major towns (with some street maps), with descriptions of services and points of interest. Place index.   DS326.G83

Philippines

Philippines (Republic). Office of Public Information. Official directory of the Republic of the Philippines. Manila, Bureau of Printing, 1946?– . Irregular.   **CJ410**

1965 last published?
Lists the departments and agencies of the government, with names of personnel.   JQ1407.A3

Poland

Directory of officials of the Polish People's Republic. [Wash., Central Intelligence Agency], 1977– . (*Its* Reference aid CR 77–13209 [etc.]) Irregular.   **CJ411**

Supersedes the *Directory of Polish officials* (1960–76).
Lists prominent personalities in the national, provincial and municipal governments; political parties; mass, cultural, and economic organizations; diplomatic service; mass media. Name index.

JN6757.D55

Rhodesia

See Zimbabwe.

Romania

Directory of officials of the Socialist Republic of Romania. [Wash.], Nat. Foreign Assessment Center, 1976– . (*Its* Reference aid CR 76–12905 [etc.]) **CJ412**

Revised periodically (e.g., CR 77–15215, Nov. 1977). Ed. for 1976 published by the Central Intelligence Agency.

Supersedes the *Directory of Romanian officials* (1966–75).

Lists by office or organization the major officials of the national and local governments, the Romanian Communist party and its organizations, and other major public associations. Name index.
JN9627.D54

Sierra Leone

Sierra Leone year book. 1961– . Freetown, Freetown Daily Mail, 1961– . Irregular. **CJ413**

Miscellaneous governmental information. Includes a classified trade directory, and a brief who's who section. DT516.A2S5

South Africa

See also DD161.

Bibliographies on South African political history. Boston, G. K. Hall, [1979–82]. 3v. **CJ414**

Comp. for the Institute for Contemporary History, University of the Orange Free State.

Contents: v.1, Register of private document collections on the political history of South Africa since 1902, ed. by O. Geyser, P. W. Coetzer, J. H. Le Roux; v.2, General sources on South African political history since 1902, comp. by P. W. Coetzer, J. H. Le Roux; v.3, Index to periodical articles on South African political and social history since 1902.

Not a bibliography of bibliographies as the title suggests, but a register of collections of primary sources and a classed bibliography of secondary materials. v.1, the register, lists and describes the larger and more important collections (although some important collections not fully inventoried and arranged are excluded), and lists smaller collections in the "annexure." v.2 is a bibliography of monographic secondary sources classed in 20 subject areas; political history is broadly interpreted to include social welfare, justice, culture, and sport. v.3 follows the classification scheme of the previous volume. Z3608.A5B5

Davies, Robert, O'Meara, Dan and **Dlamini, Sipho.** The struggle for South Africa: a reference guide to movements, organizations and institutions. London, Zed Books, [1984]. 2v. map. **CJ415**

"Centre of African Studies, Eduardo Mondlane University."—*t.p.*

Consists of essays and directory entries for pressure groups in South Africa in the 1980s. The ten chapters begin with introductory essays, continue with individual entries, and conclude with bibliographies. Indexed. JQ1931.D38

Official South African municipal year book, 1909– . Cape Town, Juta; London, E. G. Allen, 1910– . v.1– . il.
CJ416

General information and statistics of South African municipalities. JS7531.A5

Wynne, Susan G. South African political materials: a catalogue of the Carter-Karis collection. Bloomington, Southern African Research Archives Project, 1977. 811p. **CJ417**

A classified catalog of mainly primary material collected in Southern Africa and used in preparing *From protest to challenge: a documentary history of African politics in South Africa, 1882–1964* (Stanford, Hoover Inst. Pr., 1977. 4v.). Also serves as a reel guide to the microfilm copy of the collection available through the Cooperative Africana Microfilm Project. Name index.

Spain

Guía de la administración del estado. Presidencia del Gobierno. 1960– . Madrid, Centro de Información Admin., 1960– . Irregular. **CJ418**

A guide to the organization of the government and its ministries. Does not include names of officials. Has a section giving addresses and telephone numbers of government agencies and of diplomatic representatives in Madrid. JN8104.A32

Sudan

Sudan almanac; an official handbook. Khartoum, Govt. Prt. Pr., 1948– . Biennial. **CJ419**

Publisher varies.

Gives information on the diplomatic missions to and from the Sudan, history, religion, geography and climate, government, finance, trade, industry, education, transport, press, etc.

Sweden

Sweden. Sveriges statskalender. 1877– . Utg. efter Kungl. Maj:ts nådigste förordnande av dess Vetenskapsakademi. Uppsala och Stockholm, Almquist, 1877– . Annual.
CJ420

Continues *Sveriges och norges statskalender,* 1764–1876.

A comprehensive register of the governmental departments and organizations of Sweden, including academies, learned societies, and universities. JN7724

Switzerland

Gruner, Erich. Die schweizerische Bundesversammlung, 1848–1920. Bern, Francke Verlag, [1966]. 2v. and portfolio of tables. (Helvetia politica, ser. A, v.1–2) **CJ421**

Added title page in French: L'Assemblée Fédérale Suisse. Introductory matter in German and French; text in German.

The first volume presents biographical information on the 1,467 deputies of the Swiss Federal Assembly from 1848 to 1920, grouped by canton. The second volume is a sociological and statistical study of the professional, educational, etc., backgrounds of the deputies, with illustrative graphs and tables. The portfolio of tables provides a chronological picture of membership by canton.

——— Die schweizerische Bundesversammlung, 1920–1968. Bern, Francke Verlag, [1970]. 287p. and portfolio of tables.

Extends the coverage of v.2 of the earlier set, but does not provide biographical sketches. JN8850.G7

Switzerland. Staatskalender der Schweizerischen Eidgenossenschaft. Annuaire de la Confédération Suisse. Annuario della Confederazione Svizzera. Hrsg. von der Bundeskanzlei. Bern, 1849– . Annual. **CJ422**

The official register of the departments and officials of Switzerland. JN8704

Thailand

Siam directory. Bangkok, Thai Co., 1947– . Annual.
　　　　　　　　　　　　　　　　　　　　CJ423

Title varies: *Thai directory.* 1963/64 last published?
A general directory covering government and diplomatic officials, trade and industry, education, religion, societies, etc.
　　　　　　　　　　　　　　　　　　　DS563.S53

Thailand official yearbook. 1964– . Bangkok, Govt. House Prt. Off., 1964– . Irregular.　　　　　　　**CJ424**

Offers general information on the government of Thailand, foreign affairs, national defense, social welfare and health services, judicial and legal system, national economy, education, etc. Includes some statistical tables.　　　　　　　DS586.T5

Thailand year book, 1964/65–69/70. Bangkok, Temple Publicity Services, 1964–69.　　　　　　　　　　**CJ425**

Presents an impressive amount of general and directory-type information on a wide range of Thai agencies, organizations, and activities, both governmental and non-governmental.
　　　　　　　　　　　　　　　　　　　DS561.T57

Turkey

Bodurgil, Abraham. Turkey—politics and government; a bibliography, 1938–1975. Wash., Lib. of Congress, 1978. 156p.　　　　　　　　　　　　　　　**CJ426**

For full information and annotation *see* DC507.　　Z2850.B64

Sturm, Albert Lee and **Mihçioglu, Cemal.** Bibliography on public administration in Turkey, 1928–1957, selective and annotated. Ankara, 1959. 224p.　　　　　**CJ427**

Joint publication of the Faculty of Political Sciences and the Institute of Administrative Sciences of the University of Ankara and the Graduate School of Public Administration and Social Service of New York University.
A classified list of 1,100 books and articles, in Western languages and Turkish. Brief annotations; author and subject indexes.
　　　　　　　　　　　　　　　　　　　Z7165.T9S7

Union of Soviet Socialist Republics

See also CJ286, CJ468.

Hodnett, Grey and **Ogareff, Val.** Leaders of the Soviet Republics, 1955–1972; a guide to posts and occupants. Canberra, Dept. of Pol. Sci., Research School of Social Sciences, Australian Nat. Univ., 1973. 454p.　　**CJ428**

A listing by republic and office of officials in republic-level party positions, positions in the republic Council of Ministers, and other high-ranking republic-level positions. Within each position category, the arrangement is chronological, indicating service dates of each official. Name index.
Continued by:　　　　　　　　　　　JN6521.H62

Ogareff, Val. Leaders of the Soviet republics, 1971–1980; a guide to posts and occupants. Canberra, Dept. of Political Science, Research School of Social Sciences, Australian Nat. Univ., 1980. 452p.　　　　　　　　　**CJ429**

Adds new material on RFSFR regional leaders of cities, oblasts, autonomous republics, etc. Name index.　　JN6521.O38

Institut zur Erforschung der UdSSR. Party and government officials of the Soviet Union, 1917–1967. Metuchen, N.J., Scarecrow Pr., [1969]. 214p.　　　　　　**CJ430**

Edward L. Crowley, Andrew I. Lebed and Heinrich E. Schulz, eds.
A revised and expanded edition of the Institute's earlier, mimeographed publication, *Key officials of the government of the USSR.* The first section, "Key officials of the Communist Party of the Soviet Union," lists party officials (congress by congress) for the 1st through the 23d congresses, 1898–1967. The second section lists government officials, 1917–67, arranged by groups of departments and offices. General index and index of names.　　JN6598.K7I54

Kraus, Herwig. The composition of leading organs of the CPSU (1952–1982): CPSU CC Politburo and Secretariat members, CPSU CC full and candidate members, CPSU Central Auditing Commission members (as of May 30, 1982). [s.1., s.n., 1982?]　　　　　　　**CJ431**

1st ed. 1976.
For each official, provides full name, birth date, present or latest-known position, and major status changes between Party congresses, such as appointments, expulsions, deaths, etc. Some sources noted. Lacks a name index.　　　　　　　　JN6598.K7K6625

Liber, George and **Mostovych, Anna.** Nonconformity and dissent in the Ukrainian SSR, 1955–1975: an annotated bibliography. Cambridge, Mass., Harvard Ukrainian Research Inst., [1978]. 245p.　　　　　　　　**CJ432**

Contains 1,242 entries pertaining to the Ukrainian national movement, as well as Jewish migration to Israel, religious developments among Catholics, Orthodox, and Protestants, and the Russian civil rights movement in the Ukraine. Includes primary sources published in the Ukraine, as well as *samydav* and secondary source materials.　　　　　　　　　　　　Z2514.U5L48

Moskva; kratkaia adresno-spravochnaia kniga. Moskva, 193–?– . Irregular.　　　　　　　　　　**CJ433**

Title varies.
Issued by Moskovskaia gorodskaia spravochno-informatsionnaia kontora "Mosgorspravka," Moscow.
Volume for 1938 called 2d ed. Annual, 1953–56.
A city directory for Moscow, listing addresses and telephone numbers of government offices, scientific and educational institutions, and other organizations in such fields as banking, trade, health and social service, transportation, and communication.
　　　　　　　　　　　　　　　　　　　DK595.M6

SSSR; administrativno-territorial'noe delenie soiuznykh respublik. 1924– . Moskva, 1924– . Irregular.　　**CJ434**

At head of title: Otdel po Voprosam Raboty Sovetov Presidiuma Verkhovnogo Soveta SSSR.
Official directory of the administrative divisions of the USSR from Union Republic to town, with some statistical information, including population and distances between points. Alphabetical index of place-names.
1971 edition covers changes from July 1, 1967 to July 1, 1971.
　　　　　　　　　　　　　　　　　　　JS6052.A13

U.S. Central Intelligence Agency. Directory of Soviet officials. Wash., 1973– . (*Its* Reference aid) Irregular.　**CJ435**

Supersedes the publication of the same title issued by the U.S. Dept. of State's Division of Biographic Information (1961–63) and its Bureau of Intelligence and Research (1966). An earlier directory, *Soviet political leaders,* appeared without imprint in 1957.
Beginning 1973, issued in 4v.: v.1, National organizations; v.2, R.S.F.S.R.; v.3, Union republics; v.4, science and education.

Who's who in the Soviet Union: a biographical encyclopedia of 5,000 leading personalities in the Soviet Union. Ed. by Borys Lewytzkyj. München, Saur, 1984. 428p.　　**CJ436**

For full information see AJ387.

Vietnam

Phan Thien Chau. Vietnamese communism; a research bibliography. Westport, Conn., Greenwood Pr., [1975]. 359p.　　　　　　　　　　　　　　　**CJ437**

"An attempt to present a systematic assessment of research materials available in North America as of June 1974 on Vietnamese nationalism, communism and revolution."—*Introd.* A classed, computer-produced list of books and articles in Vietnamese,

English, and French. The "Introductory bibliographic guide" (p.3–19) critically annotates major primary and secondary sources. Author and title indexes. Z7165.V5P48

U.S. Central Intelligence Agency. Council of ministers of the Socialist Republic of Vietnam. [Wash.], 1977. 103p. il. (*Its* Reference aid CR 77–10004) **CJ438**

Offers biographical material on the 38 members of the council. Each biography provides a photograph, current positions and previous posts, and miscellaneous information on party membership, family, education, etc.

U.S. Central Intelligence Agency. National Foreign Assessment Center. Directory of officials of the Socialist Republic of Vietnam. [Wash.], 1980– . (*Its* Reference aid CR80–15659 [etc.]) Irregular. **CJ439**

A register of officeholders in the Vietnamese Communist party, national, provincial and municipal governments, legislative bodies, military organizations, the diplomatic service, and selected mass, cultural and scientific organizations. Name index.

Yugoslavia

U.S. Central Intelligence Agency. Directory of officials of the Socialist Federal Republic of Yugoslavia. [Wash., Central Intelligence Agency], 1976– . charts. (*Its* Reference aid CR76–10408 [etc.]) **CJ440**

Revised periodically.
Supersedes the Agency's *Directory of Yugoslav officials* (1972).
Lists by office and organization the major personalities of federal and local governments; political parties; mass organizations; international relations, commercial, academic, and religious organizations; and the mass media. Name index.

Zimbabwe

Cary, Robert and **Mitchell, Diana.** African nationalist leaders in Rhodesia: who's who. Bulawayo, Books of Rhodesia, 1977. 310p. **CJ441**

In two main sections: (1) biographies of the principal nationalists (arranged chronologically according to when each individual made his appearance on the political scene) and (2) biographies of military leaders and other prominent persons connected with the guerrilla war. DT962.76.A2C37

PARLIAMENTARY PROCEDURE

Davidson, Henry Alexander. Handbook of parliamentary procedure. N.Y., Ronald, [1955]. 292p. **CJ442**

Rules and practices for small organizations. JF515.D32

Deschler, Lewis. Deschler's Rules of order. Englewood Cliffs, N.J., Prentice-Hall, [1976]. 221p. **CJ443**

A system of parliamentary procedure based on the author's experience as parliamentarian of the U.S. House of Representatives. "In preparing this book, I have taken the approach that the House parliamentary system is readily adaptable to any membership organization that needs some form of parliamentary procedure. I have simplified and generalized that system in such a way that it will be applicable to any membership organization, large or small, legislative or nonlegislative."—*Pref.* JF515.D45

Keesey, Ray E. Modern parliamentary procedure. Boston, Houghton Mifflin, [1974]. 176p. **CJ444**

"This is a textbook and manual of simplified parliamentary procedure, entirely compatible with accepted parliamentary principles but free of the traditional mysterious jargon of the professional parliamentarian."—*Pref.* Intends to simplify the conduct of meetings and to make for easier participation by members of a group. Includes a critically annotated bibliography of parliamentary procedure manuals. JF515.K395

Robert, Henry Martyn. The Scott, Foresman Robert's rules of order newly revised. A new & enl. ed. by Sarah Corbin Robert. [Glenview, Ill. Scott, Foresman and Co., 1981] x1ii, 594p. **CJ445**

First published in 1876 with the title *Pocket manual of rules of order for deliberative assemblies.* Frequently revised and reprinted. 1970 ed. publ. under title: *Robert's Rules of order newly revised.*

Represents the 8th ed. of this standard guide to parliamentary rules, with charts, tables, and lists. Indexed. JF515.R692

Sturgis, Alice Fleenor. Sturgis standard code of parliamentary procedure. 2d ed. N.Y., McGraw-Hill, [1966]. 283p. **CJ446**

1st ed. 1950.
Compiled with the advice of legal authorities, and with regard to court decisions and the common law. The new edition represents a thorough reworking, with additions and considerable rearrangement of materials. The appendix adds sections on governmental bodies and labor organizations, suggested by-law provisions for a local organization, and model minutes, as well as retaining the lists of references and of definitions found in the earlier edition. JF515.S88

PUBLIC OPINION

Smith, Bruce Lannes, Lasswell, Harold D. and **Casey, Ralph D.** Propaganda, communication, and public opinion; a comprehensive reference guide. Princeton, N. J., Princeton Univ. Pr., 1946. 435p. **CJ447**

An expansion of *Propaganda and promotional activities; an annotated bibliography,* published 1935.
This edition includes four essays on "The science of mass communication," followed by an annotated, selective bibliography of some 2,500 titles arranged by class. Includes books, periodicals, and articles which appeared between the middle of 1934 and early 1943, with a few titles of earlier dates. 150 titles have been starred as "outstanding" and given somewhat fuller annotations than most of the others.
Continued by: Z7204.S67S6

Bureau of Social Science Research, Washington, D. C. International communication and political opinion; a guide to the literature [by] Bruce Lannes Smith and Chitra M. Smith. Prep. for the Rand Corp. Princeton, N. J., Princeton Univ. Pr., [1956]. 325p. **CJ448**

A classified, annotated bibliography of 2,563 numbered items, in English, French, and German, covering publications from mid-1943 to mid-1955, with some materials up to mid-1956. Author and subject index. The work "concentrates on materials dealing with *international* propaganda, communication, and opinion, and cites works on *internal* matters only when they are of more than general relevance to international politics. It deals primarily with *political* propaganda and promotional activities."—*Introd.*

Z7204.S67B87

Index to international public opinion, 1978/79– . Westport, Conn., Greenwood Pr., [1980]– . Annual. **CJ449**

Elizabeth Hann Hastings and Philip K. Hastings, eds.
Prep. by Survey Consultants International, Inc.
In three main sections: (1) single nation surveys; (2) single nation surveys conducted by Gallup International Research Institutes; (3) multinational surveys. Within these sections, surveys are arranged by topic and then by country. Each survey entry lists date and organization responsible for conducting the survey, sample size, question, and response in percentages. List of sources. Indexed by

subject, country where survey was conducted, and country as subject of survey.   HM261.I552

The international Gallup polls: public opinion 1978–79. Wilmington, Del., Scholarly Resources, [1980–81]. 2v.
     CJ450

Reports the findings of recent public opinion and social research surveys conducted by member companies of Gallup International. Most are national surveys conducted in about 70 countries, although two multinational surveys, "European Economic Community polls" and "Youth of the world survey" are included. Indexed by subject and country. Lacks the sample size and bibliographical source information presented by the *Index to international public opinion.* Ceased publication.   HM261.G276

Gallup, George Horace. The Gallup poll: public opinion, 1935–1971. N.Y., Random House, [1972]. 3v. (2388p.)
     CJ451

Presents all the statistical data from more than 7,000 polls of American political and social opinion. Reports are listed chronologically by date when the information was released to newspapers; interviewing dates are also indicated. Subject index.
     HN90.P8G3

——— The Gallup poll: public opinion 1972–1977. Wilmington, Del., Scholarly Resources, 1978. 2v. (1334p.)
     CJ452

Contents: v.1, 1972–75; v.2, 1976–77.
A continuation of the volumes covering 1935–71 (above). Presents, in chronological order, the results of all the public opinion polls conducted by the American Institute of Public Opinion. Each volume begins with a chronology of the years covered. Indexed.
     HN90.P8G32

The Gallup poll: public opinion, 1978– . Wilmington, Del., Scholarly Resources, [1979]– . Annual.   **CJ453**

George H. Gallup, ed.
An annual compilation of public opinion polls conducted by the Gallup organization, providing date, question, and results; most results are analyzed by age, sex, race, income level, geographic region, political affiliation, etc. Summary notes are provided. Chronological arrangement; subject index.
Current polls are reported in the *Gallop report* (formerly *Gallup opinion index*) and *Gallup international reports.*   HN90.P8G35

The Gallup international public opinion polls, France, 1939, 1944–1975. George H. Gallup, gen. ed. N.Y., Random House, [1976]. 2v. (1257p.)   **CJ454**

Contents: v.1, 1939, 1944–1967; v.2, 1968–1975.
A compilation of the tabular data resulting from the French Gallup reports, chronologically arranged. Subject index.
     HN440.P8G35

The Gallup international public opinion polls, Great Britain, 1937–1975. George H. Gallup, gen. ed. N.Y., Random House, [1976]. 2v. (1578p.)   **CJ455**

Contents: v.1, 1937–1964; v.2, 1965–1975.
Statistical data from all British Gallup Poll reports; editorial and interpretive material has been omitted. Subject index.
     HN400.P8G34

Noelle, Elisabeth and **Neumann, Erich Peter.** The Germans: public opinion polls 1947–1966. Allensbach, Bonn, Verlag für Demoskopie, 1967. 630p. il.   **CJ456**

Presents the results of about 1,900 polls.
Continued by: DD259.2.N62

The Germans—public opinion polls, 1967–1980. Ed. by Elisabeth Noelle-Neumann, Institut für Demoskopie, Allensbach. Westport, Conn., Greenwood Pr., [1981]. 516p. il.
     CJ457

Offers the results of surveys conducted in the Federal Republic of Germany and West Berlin. Some results are presented by sex, age group, occupation, educational level, regional distribution, etc. Indexed.   HN460.P8G47

COMMUNISM AND SOCIALISM

Bibliography

Andréas, Bert. Le manifeste communiste de Marx et Engels; histoire et bibliographie, 1848–1918. Milano, Feltrinelli, [1963]. 429p., 23p. facsim. (Bibliographies par l'Institut Giangiacomo Feltrinelli, 6)   **CJ458**

Facsimile reproduction of the 1st ed. of the *Communist manifesto* (23p.) at end.
A bibliography of 544 items in various languages dealing with the *Communist manifesto.* Detailed notes on special editions.

Attar Chand. Lenin and India: a bibliography with selected abstracts, 1917–1980. New Delhi, Sterling, [1980]. 179p.
     CJ459

More than 600 titles on the influence of Lenin and the Soviet Revolution on India and its communist and socialist party movements. Classed subject arrangement, with personal name index. Emphasizes Indian, Russian, and communist sources.

Bravo, Gian Maria. Marx e Engels in lingua italiana, 1848–1960. Milano, Ed. Avanti, 1962. 176p. (Saggi e documentazioni, 10)   **CJ460**

A bibliography of almost 800 books and articles, in Italian, on Marx and Engels.   Z8551.67.B7

Chilcote, Ronald H. Brazil and its radical left; an annotated bibliography on the communist movement and the rise of Marxism, 1922–1972. Millwood, N.Y., Kraus Internat. Pubns., [1980]. 455p.   **CJ461**

In three sections: the first two are author listings of more than 3,000 books and pamphlets and periodical articles on the communist, socialist, anarchist, and leftist-oriented labor movements in Brazil since the founding of the Brazilian communist party in 1922; the third is a list of periodicals, with library locations. Index to periodicals cited and a general index.   Z7164.S67C54

Collotti, Enzo. Die Kommunistische Partei Deutschlands, 1918–1933; ein bibliographischer Beitrag. Milano, Feltrinelli, [1961]. 217p. (Milan. Ist. Giangiacomo Feltrinelli. Bibliografie, 4)   **CJ462**

Arranged by chronological periods. Introduction to each period is followed by bibliographic listings.   Z1009.M58 no.4

Delaney, Robert Finley. The literature of communism in America; a selected reference guide. Wash., Catholic Univ. of Amer. Pr., 1962. 433p.   **CJ463**

A classified, annotated bibliography. The annotations reflect the personal opinions of the writer.   Z7164.S67D4

Egan, David R. and **Egan, Melinda A.** V. I. Lenin, an annotated bibliography of English-language sources to 1980. Metuchen, N.J., Scarecrow Pr., 1982. 482p.   **CJ464**

An international bibliography of 2,926 citations to books, essays, chapters, periodical articles, and doctoral dissertations, including Soviet English-language periodicals and translations from Russian-language sources. Topical arrangement; author and subject indexes.
     Z8500.8.E36

Egbert, Donald Drew and **Persons, Stow.** Socialism and American life. Princeton, N.J., Princeton Univ. Pr., 1952. 2v. il. (Princeton studies in American civilization, no.4)
     CJ465

Contents: v.1, Essays by various authors; v.2, Bibliography, descriptive and critical; bibliographer, T. D. Seymour Bassett.
The bibliography, in essay form, gives references to materials on socialism in its various manifestations as developed in this country, from the early religious communism to the mid-20th century. Detailed table of contents and index to authors and subjects.
     HX83.E45

Eubanks, Cecil L. Karl Marx and Friedrich Engels: an analytical bibliography. 2d ed. N.Y., Garland, 1984. 299p. (Garland reference library of social science, v.100) **CJ466**

1st ed. 1977.

Intended to be "a comprehensive bibliography of those writings by and about Marx and Engels either written or translated into English, including books . . . , articles, chapters from books and doctoral dissertations . . . . Marx and Engels, not Lenin, not Mao and not the history of various communist revolutions were the primary focus of attention."—*Introd.* Introductory bibliographic essay, p.ix–l. Primary materials include individual and collected works of Marx, Engels, and Marx and Engels. Secondary literature is arranged by type—books, articles, and doctoral dissertations. Indexed. Z8551.67.E94

Goehlert, Robert and **Herczeg, Claire.** Anarchism: a bibliography. [Monticello, Ill.], Vance Bibliographies, [1982]. 122p. (Public administration ser.: bibliography P-902) **CJ467**

An international bibliography with 1,678 citations arranged by topic, geographic area and personal name, with author index. A complementary title, listing manuscripts, pamphlets, special collections, and periodicals, is *L'Anarchisme: catalogue de livres et brochures des XIXᵉ et XXᵉ siècles,* prep. under the direction of Denise Fauvel-Rouif (Paris, Saur, 1982. 170p.). Z7164.A52G63

Hammond, Thomas Taylor. Soviet foreign relations and world communism; a selected, annotated bibliography of 7,000 books in 30 languages. Princeton, N.J., Princeton Univ. Pr., 1965. 1240p. **CJ468**

Includes references to books, parts of books, periodical articles, and graduate theses on Soviet diplomatic and economic relations and on communist movements and tactics throughout the world since 1917. In three main parts: (1) "Soviet relations by chronological periods," listing works treating of Soviet dealings with more than one country; (2) "Soviet foreign relations and communism by regions and countries"; and (3) "Special topics." Most items are annotated. Index of authors, editors, compilers, and anonymous titles. Z2517.R4H3

Kehde, Ned. The American left, 1955–1970: a national union catalog of pamphlets published in the United States and Canada. Westport, Conn., Greenwood Pr., [1976]. 515p. **CJ469**

A main-entry listing of some 4,000 pamphlets, with index of subjects, joint authors, and publishers. Includes pamphlets in the Labadie Collection of the University of Michigan, the Bancroft Library of the University of California, the Kansas Collection of the University of Kansas, the Tamiment Library of New York University, and the Division of Archives and Manuscripts of the State Historical Society of Wisconsin, as well as pamphlet entries from the *National union catalog* and the New York Public Library card catalogs. Selection criteria extend to "any pamphlet written by an individual or a political or social organization advocating a liberal to radical position."—*Introd.* Z7165.U5K43

Kyriak, Theodore E. International communist developments, 1957–1961; an index and guide to a collection of U.S. JPRS translations emanating from Africa, Asia, Latin America and western Europe. Annapolis, Md., Research Microfilms, [1962]. 54p. **CJ470**

"The United States Joint Publications Research Service (JPRS) was established in early 1957 to service the various units of the federal government with translations of unclassified foreign documents, scholarly works, research reports, and other selected source material not available in English."—*Introd.*

This work lists the contents of such translations dealing with international communist developments, 1957–61.

Z7164.S67K9

Lachs, John. Marxist philosophy; a bibliographical guide. Chapel Hill, Univ. of North Carolina Pr., [1967]. 166p. **CJ471**

A bibliographical guide to the philosophy of Marxism, "the group of theories that is usually thought to constitute the world view of dialectical and historical materialism."—*Introd.* Includes both critical and expository works. Author index. Z7128.D5L3

Lauerhass, Ludwig. Communism in Latin America: a bibliography. The post-war years (1945–1960). Los Angeles, Calif., Center of Latin American Studies, 1962. 78p. **CJ472**

A listing of books, government publications, and articles, arranged under country. Includes works in English, Spanish, Portuguese, French, German, and Russian.

Supplemented by: Z7164.S67L28

Sable, Martin Howard and **Dennis, M. Wayne.** Communism in Latin America; an international bibliography, 1900–1945, 1960–1967. Los Angeles, Latin American Center, Univ. of California, 1968. 220p. **CJ473**

Extends the coverage of the work by L. Lauerhass (above) backward to 1900 and forward to 1967. Arrangement is again by country. Author index. Z7164.S67S2

Répertoire international des sources pour l'étude des mouvements sociaux aux XIXᵉ et XXᵉ siècles. Paris, Librairie Armand Colin, 1958–63. v.1–3. **CJ474**

At head of title: Comité International des Sciences Historiques. Commission Internationale d'Histoire des Mouvements Sociaux et des Structures Sociales.

"Publié avec le concours de l'Unesco et sous les auspices du Conseil International de la Philosophie et des Sciences Humaines."

v.1, *La première Internationale. Périodiques, 1864–77,* lists periodicals in various languages with full bibliographical detail, brief description, and location of copies in European and a few American libraries.

v.2, *La première Internationale. Imprimés, 1864–1876: Actes officiels du Conseil Général et des Congrès et Conférences de l'Association Internationale des Travailleurs,* is arranged by congress, with descriptive notes of contents of the publications and index of personal names. (A preliminary edition of this section, somewhat different in arrangement, appeared in 1959.)

v.3, *La première Internationale. Imprimés, 1864–1876: Actes officiels des fédérations et sections nationales de l'Association Internationale des Travailleurs,* is arranged by country; it includes descriptive notes, an index of names, and locates copies.

No more published. Z7164.S67I52

Rubel, Maximilien. Bibliographie des oeuvres de Karl Marx, avec en appendice un répertoire des oeuvres de Friedrich Engels. Paris, Marcel Rivière, 1956. 272p. **CJ475**

A comprehensive bibliography listing works by Marx including published works, correspondence, unpublished manuscripts, and *dubiosa,* followed by a bibliography of Engels's works.

———— ———— Supplément. Paris, Marcel Rivière, 1960. 74p.

Seidman, Joel Isaac. Communism in the United States; a bibliography. Ithaca, N.Y., Cornell Univ. Pr., [1969]. 526p. **CJ476**

A "substantial revision, along with an expansion and updating" (*Pref.*) of the Fund for the Republic's *Bibliography on the communist problem in the United States* (N.Y., 1955). Many annotations were revised or expanded; some items from the earlier work were omitted; and a special effort was made to fill gaps in the literature critical of the communist position—those gaps being a matter for which the earlier volume was criticized. Z7164.S67S38

Sharma, Jagdish Saran. Indian socialism; a descriptive bibliography. Delhi, Vikas, [1975]. 349p. **CJ477**

A classed list with author index. Intends to document the growth and development of Indian socialism, the role of national leaders and statesmen, etc. Books, periodical and newspaper articles, pamphlets, government documents, etc., are included. Some entries are briefly annotated. Z7164.S67S44

Spiers, John, Sexsmith, Ann and **Everitt, Alastair.** The left in Britain: a checklist and guide. [Hassocks, Sussex, Eng.], Harvester Pr., [1976]. 168p. **CJ478**

Subtitle: With historical notes to 37 left-wing political movements and groupings active in Britain between 1904–1972 whose publications comprise the Harvester/Primary Sources Microfilm Collection.

A checklist of the publications of about forty groups, which also serves as a guide to the 71,000 pages reproduced by the publishers in microform. Although the collection goes back to 1904 (largely based on materials from the Socialist Party of Great Britain), most of the material is from the 1950s and later. The background of each group is briefly sketched before the main text of the checklist, which is divided into four parts; each part has, when appropriate, an author, title, and chronological index, and consolidated author and title indexes are also provided. While a number of Marxist, Leninist, Trotskyist and Maoist groups are represented, the Communist Party of Great Britain is not included.

Updated by: Z7165.G8S65

Pidduck, William. The left in Britain during 1973 and 1974, parts one and two; a bibliographical guide. Hassocks, Harvester Pr., 1978. 61p. **CJ479**

Z7164.S67P48

Stammhammer, Josef. Bibliographie des Socialismus und Communismus. Jena, Fischer, 1893–1909. 3v. **CJ480**

A standard bibliography of materials in various languages on socialism and communism up to 1908. Z7164.S67S7

Sworakowski, Witold S. The Communist International and its front organizations; a research guide and checklist of holdings in American and European libraries. Stanford, Calif., Hoover Inst. on War, Revolution, and Peace, 1965. 493p. (Hoover Inst. bibliographical ser., 21) **CJ481**

A checklist of "holdings of 44 American and four European libraries of books and pamphlets published by and on . . . the principal organizations which, during the time of the operation of the Communist International, from March 1919 to June 1943, promoted, sustained, and directed the communist movement in all corners of the world."—*Pref.* More than 2,200 entries. Classed arrangement, with index. Z7164.S67S86

Trotsky bibliography: list of separately published titles, periodical articles and titles in collections treating L. D. Trotsky and Trotskyism. Ed. by Wolfgang Lubitz. Munich, K. G. Saur, 1982. 458p. **CJ482**

Title also in German; prefatory matter in English and German.

Lists 3,227 titles in European languages written between 1917 and 1982, including dissertations, book reviews, and belles-lettres. Main-entry arrangement, with subject, source, chronological, and dissertation indexes. Z8886.5.L8

Uyehara, Cecil H. Leftwing social movements in Japan, an annotated bibliography. Publ. for the Fletcher School of Law and Diplomacy, Tufts University. Tokyo, Rutland, Vt., Tuttle, [1959]. 444p. **CJ483**

An extensive listing of books, periodicals, and documents in Japanese. Arrangement is classified, within chapters, each with a textual introduction. Entries are transliterated, followed by Japanese characters. Locations indicated for 12 United States libraries and several in Japan. Author-title index. Z7164.S67U9

Vigor, Peter Hast. Books on communism and the communist countries; a selected bibliography. [3d ed.] London, Ampersand, [1971]. 444p. **CJ484**

1st ed. by R. N. Carew Hunt, 1959; 2d ed. by Walter Kolarz, 1964.

A selected, annotated bibliography of some 2,600 items in classed arrangement within three main sections: (1) Studies of communism in general and in the USSR; (2) Communism in other countries; and (3) Official documents and publications. Revision for this edition resulted in about 350 titles being dropped as against 500 added. Although "in print" status was a consideration in the selection,

many older, out-of-print works (including important books from the 20s and 30s) are included. Coverage extends into 1970.

Z7164.S67V5

Weinrich, Peter. Social protest from the left in Canada, 1870–1970. Toronto, Univ. of Toronto Pr., 1982. 627p. **CJ485**

A chronological listing, mostly of primary documents, from political parties, trade unions, cooperatives, leftist movements, and groups involved in riots, rebellions, and strikes. Excludes material relating to Quebec, and selectively includes secondary works and government documents. Canadian library locations are indicated. Separate lists of annual reports and serials. Indexed by author, organization, and title. Z7165.C2W44

Whetten, Lawrence L. Current research in comparative communism; an analysis and bibliographic guide to the Soviet system. N.Y., Praeger, [1976]. 159p. **CJ486**

Pt.I is a discussion of research design, methodology, evolution of themes in communism, and problem areas involving domestic change and reform. Pt.II is a selected bibliography on change in domestic policy in the USSR and East European states (excluding Albania). The bibliography is a classed list of English-language books and periodical articles published 1965–75 on topics such as economic development, social change, communist elites and interest groups, ideology, censorship, law, and agriculture. Entries are keyed to audience and nature of item (general, statistical, technical, conceptual). No index. Z7164.S67W47

Current

The left index. no.1– , Spr. 1982– . Santa Cruz, Calif., Left Index, [1982]– . Quarterly. **CJ487**

"Journals selected for inclusion . . . have a Marxist, radical or left perspective. . . . Newsletters and newspapers are not included."— *Pref.* Includes humanities, social sciences, and sciences topics. Author listing with book review index and subject index cumulating annually. Z7164.S67L34

Periodicals

Shaffer, Harry G. Periodicals on the socialist countries and on Marxism: a new annotated index of English-language publications. N.Y., Praeger, [1977]. 133p. **CJ488**

A 1971 edition had title: *English language periodic publications on communism.*

The "annotated index" of the subtitle might better read "annotated bibliography"; the volume offers a list of English-language periodicals which "concentrate on subject matter of concern to students of communism whose interest lies in the social sciences, in the humanities, or in related fields" *(Pref.)*, together with descriptions of their contents and publishing information. Arrangement is alphabetical by title, with a "geographic reference index."

Z7164.S67S435

Dictionaries, encyclopedias, and handbooks

See also CJ215.

Dekoster, Lester. The vocabulary of communism. Grand Rapids, Mich., Eerdmans, [1964]. 224p. **CJ489**

Subtitle: Definitions of key terms, summaries of central ideas, short biographies of leading figures, descriptions of significant things and events. Includes "The classics of Marxism," p.183–99, and "Anti-Marxist classics," p.203–23. HX17.D4

A dictionary of Marxist thought. Ed. by Tom Bottomore. Cambridge, Mass., Harvard Univ. Pr., 1983. 587p. **CJ490**

A dictionary of terms, topics, and biographies. Signed articles by about 75 contributors; most conclude with bibliographic references. Bibliography of works cited, p.533–66. Indexed. HX17.D5

Draper, Hal. The Marx-Engels cyclopedia. With the assistance of the Center for Socialist History. N.Y., Schocken, [1985]– . [v.1]– . (In progress) **CJ491**

Contents: [v.1] The Marx-Engels chronicle: a day-by-day chronology of Marx and Engels' life and activity.

v.1 covers the period from Marx's birth (1818) to Engels' death (1895), without an index. v.2, *The Marx-Engels register,* is to be a bibliography of their writings; v.3, *The Marx-Engels glossary,* will be a dictionary of all proper names mentioned in the first two volumes. HX39.5.D69

Fogarty, Robert S. Dictionary of American communal and utopian history. Westport, Conn., Greenwood Pr., [1980]. 271p. **CJ492**

Presents biographical sketches of more than 140 prominent leaders and descriptions of 59 of the most important or interesting colonies. An additional 270 settlements are briefly noted in an annotated chronology of communal and utopian societies established between 1787 and 1919. Each biographical and communal entry has a list of sources noted. An appendix provides a review of the literature. Selected bibliography; index. HX653.F65

Marxism, communism and Western society; a comparative encyclopedia. [N.Y.], Herder and Herder, [1972–73]. 8v. il. **CJ493**

C. D. Kernig, ed.

Long, signed articles by an international team of scholars attempt to survey "all the areas in which there is disagreement between East and West."—*Pref.* Emphasis is on "the differences as mirrored in the thought and language of the corresponding disciplines." Opposing views are presented and a comparison or a critical appraisal offered. Extensive bibliographies. AE5.M27

Russell, James. Marx-Engels dictionary. Westport, Conn., Greenwood Pr., [1980]. 140p. **CJ494**

Provides brief definitions of only those terms appearing in the writings of Marx and Engels which may present difficulty to the general reader because they are no longer commonly used, have a particular Marxian meaning, or are technical historical, economic, and philosophical terms. Where available, definitions given by Marx or Engels are provided. HX17.R87

Sworakowski, Witold S. World communism; a handbook, 1918–1965. Stanford, Calif., Hoover Inst. Pr., 1973. 576p. (Hoover Inst. pubn. 108) **CJ495**

Intended as a kind of companion to the *Yearbook on international communist affairs* (CJ500), providing historical background to the more detailed information found therein. Articles on "each of the 106 countries in which a communist party was or is active" (*Pref.*), plus survey articles on developments in Latin America and sub-Saharan Africa, were contributed by 53 scholars. Arrangement is alphabetical by country. An appendix lists "Communist parties by country with name changes, 1918–1965." Indexes of names and of subjects. HX40.S89

Trevisani, Giulio. Piccola enciclopedia del socialismo e del comunismo. 4. ed. Milano, Soc. Ed. de 'Il calendario del popolo,' [1958]. 735p. il. **CJ496**

1st ed. 1945.

Alphabetically arranged, with articles on people, places, movements, institutions, and book and journal titles. Articles are unsigned and vary in length, many with brief bibliographies appended. Emphasis on Italian subjects. Numerous cross references. HX17.T7

Wilczynski, Jozef. An encyclopedic dictionary of Marxism, socialism and communism: economic, philosophical, political and sociological theories, concepts, institutions and practices—classical and modern, East-West relations included. Berlin & N.Y., W. de Gruyter, [1981]. 660p. **CJ497**

More than 2,300 entries cover theories, writings, terms and doctrines, parties, organizations, and major personalities. HX17.W54

Biography

Lazic, Branko M. and **Drachkovitch, Milorad M.** Biographical dictionary of the Comintern. Stanford, Calif., Hoover Inst. Pr., 1973. 458p. **CJ498**

More than 700 biographies. In addition to biographical sketches of "those approximately three hundred individuals who comprised the Comintern's overall directorate" (*Introd.*), entries are included for (1) "Individuals who spoke at the Comintern congresses from 1919 to 1935" so long as they also played important roles in the communist movement in their own countries; (2) secret emissaries of the Comintern sent abroad; (3) leaders of international organizations such as the Red Trade Union International; and (4) graduates of the four principal Comintern schools. HX11.I5L3378

Osterroth, Franz. Biographisches Lexikon des Sozialismus. Hannover, Dietz, 1960. Bd.1. **CJ499**

Contents: Bd.1, Verstorbene Persönlichkeiten.

Brief biographical sketches of persons of German-area nationality concerned with any of various socialist movements. HX273.O74

Yearbooks

Yearbook on international communist affairs, 1966– . Stanford, Calif., Hoover Inst. on War, Revolution, and Peace, Stanford Univ., 1967– . Annual. **CJ500**

Intends to assemble in several sections "data concerning the individual communist parties and their activities, together with material pertaining to the international communist movement and its problems."—*Pref., 1966.* In addition to country-by country profiles of national communist parties, volumes usually include a section on international communist conferences, a section on international communist organizations, a bibliography, and an index. Some volumes include a section of documents; some have a biographical section. HX1.Y4

ARMED FORCES

❖For wars, battles, and specific aspects of military history *see* the History and Area Studies section.

Guides

Arkin, William M. Research guide to current military and strategic affairs. [Wash., Institute for Policy Studies, 1981] 232p. **CJ501**

An excellent guide, in five sections: (1) introduction; (2) general information sources; (3) U.S. government documents; (4) U.S. military; (5) worldwide military and strategic affairs. Within each section are listed bibliographies, recurrent statistical data sources, periodicals, other reference sources, and important monographs. Emphasizes current resources and periodicals; an appendix lists some 600 periodicals and serials. No index. UA10.5.A7

A short research guide on arms and armed forces. N.Y., Facts on File, [1980]. 112p. **CJ502**

Comp. by Ulrich Albrecht and others.

An evaluation of literature sources such as directories and reference works, documents, periodicals, monograph series, newsletters, books, research guides and bibliographies. Concentrates on Europe and the Third World. Also provides detailed analyses of the *Military balance, Jane's Fighting ships,* and the *SIPRI yearbook of world armaments and disarmament.*   Z6721.S53

Bibliography

Anderson, Martin and **Bloom, Valerie.** Conscription: a select and annotated bibliography. Stanford, Hoover Inst. Pr., 1976. 453p. (Hoover bibliographical ser., 57)   **CJ503**

Over 1,385 entries organized into 17 chapters representing major subjects; within most chapters writings are classified as books, unpublished manuscripts, articles, pamphlets, reprints, speeches, and government documents. Emphasis is on U.S. experience, "particularly from the viewpoint of public policy recommendations" *(Introd.),* but material relevant to England and other foreign countries is included. Separate chapter on bibliographies. Author and title indexes.   Z6724.C63A53

Copenhagen. Marinens Bibliothek. Katalog . . . udarb. . . . af H. A. Ø. Bistrup. København, Levin, 1933–36. 2v.   **CJ504**

Contents: v.1, Catalog of literature concerning the discoveries and the explorations of the polar environs and the oceans; whale and seal fisheries; biography; periodicals, annuals, and other periodical papers; v.2, Naval, nautical, and technical literature.

Catalog of an extensive collection of books and periodicals in many languages.   Z941.C73

———— ———— Tillaeg (Supplement). 1933– . København, 1934– .

1948/52– are 5-year cumulations of the Library's monthly and annual *Erhvervelser.*

Gordon, Colin. The Atlantic Alliance: a bibliography. London, Frances Pinter; N.Y., Nichols [1978]. 216p.   **CJ505**

A bibliography of about 3,000 English-language books, reports, pamphlets, papers, and articles on the Atlantic Alliance and its successor, the North Atlantic Treaty Organization. Divided into four main chronological periods, and within each by five subject subdivisions: legal, economic, national and regional, politico-military, and military-strategic. No index.   Z6464.N65G67

Lang, Kurt. Military institutions and the sociology of war; a review of the literature with annotated bibliography. Beverly Hills, Calif., Sage Pubns., [1972]. 337p.   **CJ506**

A long bibliographic essay (p.29–156) is followed by a classed bibliography of 1,325 items. (Although termed an "annotated bibliography," such notes as appear are very brief; entries are linked to the preceding discussion, however, through use of item number references in the text.) Separate author, title, and subject indexes.   U21.5.L35

NATO, a bibliography and resource guide. [Ed. by] Augustus Richard Norton [and others]. N.Y., Garland, 1985 [i.e., 1984]. 252p. (Garland reference library of social science, v.92)   **CJ507**

A topically arranged listing of about 4,000 English-language entries, with sections on chronological periods, member states, issues, strategies, alliance politics, and the Warsaw Pact. Author index.   UA646.3.N224

Pohler, Johann. Bibliotheca historico-militaris. Systematische Uebersicht der Erscheinungen aller Sprachen auf dem Gebiete der Geschichte der Kriege und Kriegswissenschaft seit Erfindung der Buchdruckerkunst bis zum Schluss des Jahres 1880. Leipzig, Lang, [1887]–99. 4v. (Repr.: N.Y., B. Franklin, 1961. 4v.)   **CJ508**

An extensive military bibliography of some 50,000 titles, including materials in many languages and covering 26 countries and all periods from ancient times to mid-19th century. Broad in scope; includes military history and science, tactics, weapons, etc., economics, politics, biography.   Z6721.P74

Smith, Myron J. The secret wars; a guide to sources in English. Santa Barbara, Calif., ABC-Clio, [1980]. 3v. (War/Peace bibliography ser., no. 12–14).   **CJ509**

Contents: v.1, Intelligence, propaganda, and psychological warfare, resistance movements, and secret operations, 1939–1945; v.2, Intelligence, propaganda and psychological warfare, covert operations 1945–1980; v.3, International terrorism, 1968–1980.

An impressive compilation of more than 9,000 books, papers, periodical articles, government documents, doctoral dissertations and master's theses. Detailed table of contents and chronologies. Author and subject indexes in v.1 and 2; author index only in v.3.   Z6724.I7S63

U.S. Dept. of the Army. National security, military power & the role of force in international relations; a bibliographic survey of literature. [Wash., Govt. Prt. Off.], 1976. 177p.   **CJ510**

Abstracts for some 850 books, periodical articles, reports, papers, and documents are grouped in broad subject divisions, with topical and geographical subdivisions. Concerned with the post-World War II period. No index.   Z6721.U542

U.S. Military Academy, West Point, N.Y. Library. Subject catalog of the military art and science collection . . . with selected author and added entries, including a preliminary guide to the manuscript collection. Westport, Conn., Greenwood Pr., [1969]. 4v.   **CJ511**

Photoreproduction of library catalog cards representing selections relative to military art from the library's general dictionary catalog. About 66,000 cards.

Current

Air University Library index to military periodicals. v.1– , Oct./Dec. 1949– . Maxwell Air Force Base, Ala., Air Univ. Lib., 1949– . v.1– . Quarterly, with annual cumulative issues.   **CJ512**

Title varies: 1949–62, *Air University periodical index.*

Triennial cumulations issued 1952–67.

Provides "a subject index to significant articles, news items, and editorials appearing in . . . English language military and aeronautical periodicals not indexed in readily available commercial indexing services."—*Pref.* Now indexes about 65 periodicals. Subject coverage is broad, including the technical aspects of military art and science, supplies, equipment, military history, military-civil relations, arms control, etc.

Current military literature: comment and abstracts & citations of important articles from international military and defence periodicals. v.1, no.1– , 1983– . Oxford, Military Pr., [1983]– . Bimonthly.   **CJ513**

Abstracts from about 200 journals are arranged in subject-classed order with author, geographic area, and source journal indexes.

Quarterly strategic bibliography. v.1, no.1– , Jan./Mar. 1977– . [Boston, Va.], Center for International Security Studies of the American Security Council Foundation, 1977– . Quarterly.   **CJ514**

Continues: *Current bibliographic survey of national defense.*

Arranged by form—periodicals (including newspapers), congressional documents, books, and other documents. Each issue is indexed by author and subject; no cumulation.   Z1361.D4.Q37

Dissertations

Millett, Allan R. and **Cooling, B. Franklin,** comps. Doctoral dissertations in military affairs; a bibliography. Manhattan, Kans., Kansas State Univ. Lib., 1972. 153p. (Kansas State Univ. Lib. Bibliography ser., no.10)   **CJ515**

In three main sections with appropriate subdivisions: (1) Studies of world military affairs; (2) Military affairs of the United States; and (3) Studies of war and the military. Kept up-to-date by annual lists appearing in the journal *Military affairs* (Manhattan, Kans.) beginning Feb. 1973. Z6721.M46

Periodicals

U.S. Air University. Libraries. Union list of foreign military periodicals. Preliminary ed. Ed. by Paul H. Spence and Helen J. Hopewell. Maxwell Air Force Base, Ala., Air Univ. Lib., 1957. 72p. **CJ516**

A union list of 356 titles in some 30 libraries in the United States and Canada, followed by a geographical index listing titles under country of origin. Z6723.U3

Dictionaries and encyclopedias

Air forces of the world; an illustrated directory of all the world's military air power. [By] Mark Hewish [and others]. N.Y., Simon and Schuster, [1979]. 264p. il., maps. **CJ517**

The organization, structure, inventory, combat experiences of national air forces (including those operated by army, navy, etc.) are described, followed by tables showing technical details of aircraft, number, basing, etc. Ten pages of maps locate major bases throughout the world. Indexed. UG630.A382

Air power: the world's air forces. Ed. by Anthony Robinson. London, Orbis (distr. in U.S.A. by McGraw-Hill), [1980]. 304p. il. **CJ518**

A heavily illustrated volume describing the history, organization, training, equipment, and aircraft of more than 60 nations. Three chapters are devoted to the United States forces, two to NATO, and one to the Warsaw Pact; other chapters concentrate on individual countries, often grouped by region. Indexed. UG630.A388

Atlante enciclopedico degli aerei militari del mondo dal 1914 a oggi. The Rand McNally encyclopedia of military aircraft, 1914–1980. Enzo Angelucci, ed. Chicago, Rand McNally, 1981. 546p. il. **CJ519**

Italian ed. publ. by Mondadori, 1980.

Provides color illustrations, photographs, silhouettes, and specifications for about 800 models, arranged by historical period (i.e., World Wars I and II, 1919–39, and the post-1945 period). Numerous charts and graphs complement the text. Bibliography; index. Designed as a companion to the editor's *World encyclopedia of civil aircraft* (CH452). A *Library journal* review (Mar. 1, 1982, p.553) called this "the most useful one-volume reference on military aircraft available." UG1240.A8413

The complete encyclopedia of arms & weapons. Ed. by Leonid Tarassuk and Claude Blair. N.Y., Simon and Schuster, [1982]. 544p. il. **CJ520**

Subtitle: The most comprehensive reference work ever published on arms and armor from prehistoric times to the present—with over 1,250 illustrations.

Tr. of *Enciclopedia ragionata delle armi* (Milano, Mondadori, 1979).

A dictionary arrangement of articles on individual weapons and types of armor, with emphasis on their component parts, and tracing developments through history. Sections of color plates group illustrations of arms and armor by periods; numerous black-and-white illustrations appear in proximity to the descriptive articles. Select bibliography, p.534–44. U815.E5313

Department of Defense dictionary of military and associated terms: incorporating the NATO and IADB dictionaries. Wash., Joint Chiefs of Staff [distr. U.S. Govt. Prt. Off.], 1984. 403p. (JCS pub. 1) **CJ521**

1st ed. 1972.

A glossary of standardized military and associated terms, including important modern weapons; each definition indicates whether it has been standardized and approved for use by the Department of

Defense, NATO, or IADB (member countries of the Inter-American System). U24.D46

Diagram Group. Weapons: an international encyclopedia from 5000 BC to 2000 AD. N.Y., St. Martin's Pr., [1980]. 320p. il. **CJ522**

Weapons are grouped by function, progressing from the simple (hand-held weapons) to the complex (biological weapons), with explanations of function and many illustrative examples. Chronological tables for major topics. "Visual indexes" arrange Western weapons by historical periods, and others by region. Bibliography; index. U800.D55

Gunston, Bill. The illustrated encyclopedia of rockets and missiles; a comprehensive technical directory and history of the military guided missile systems of the 20th century. N.Y., Crescent Books, [1979]. 264p. il. **CJ523**

Divided into 11 sections, according to the missile's function and deployment; e.g., surface-to-surface land tactical, air-to-surface strategic, anti-submarine, etc. Descriptions of the missiles are arranged chronologically by nation within each section and include historical development, use, specifications, and illustration. Indexed by name, code-name, missile type, country of origin, designer, and manufacturer. Brief glossary. UG1310.G86

Hanrieder, Wolfram F. and **Buel, Larry V.** Words and arms: a dictionary of security and defense terms, with supplementary data. Boulder, Colo., Westview Pr., [1979]. 265p. il. **CJ524**

Provides brief definitions for terms common to the field of U.S. strategic defense, with particular emphasis on strategic nuclear weapons systems. The "supplementary data" refers to reprinted texts on policy and comparative statistical information on strategic forces, military expenditures, and status of arms control agreements. U24.H33

Luttwak, Edward. A dictionary of modern war. N.Y., Harper & Row, [1971]. 224p. il. **CJ525**

Concerned with "the more important weapons currently in service as well as the terms, ideas and organizations of the military dimension of modern life."—*Foreword.* U24.L93

Parkinson, Roger. The encyclopedia of modern war. N.Y., Stein and Day, [1977]. 226p. maps. **CJ526**

An attempt to cover "battles . . . weapons [and] personalities, plus . . . conceptual topics such as strategy, tactics and various theories and principles."—*Pref.* Dictionary arrangement of brief entries covering the period 1793 to the present. Numerous cross references; index. U24.P37

Pretz, Bernhard. Dictionary of military and technological abbreviations and acronyms. London, Routledge & Kegan Paul, [1983]. 496p. **CJ527**

An international dictionary, including equipment model numbers. U26.P73

Quick, John. Dictionary of weapons and military terms. N.Y., McGraw-Hill, [1973]. 515p. il. **CJ528**

Intended as "a comprehensive record of the significant weapons and weapon systems developed over the centuries."—*Foreword.* Many illustrations. U24.Q5

Sovetskaia voennaia entsiklopediia: [V 8-mi t./In-t voen. istorii]; Gl. red. komis., Marshal Sov. Soiuza A. A. Grechko (pred.) . . . [i dr.]. Moskva, Voenizdat, 1976–80. 8v. il., maps. **CJ529**

On leaf preceding t.p.: Ministerstvo oborony SSSR.

Emphasizes post-revolutionary military history, biography, theory, and technology. Many articles are signed; brief bibliographies.

A useful single volume work is *Voennyi entsiklopedicheskii slovar',* ed. by V. V. Ogarkov (Moskva, Voenizdat, 1983. 863p.). U24.S72

Warry, John. Warfare in the classical world; an illustrated encyclopedia of weapons, warriors and warfare in the ancient civilisations of Greece and Rome. N.Y., St. Martin's, [1981]. 224p. il., maps.   **CJ530**

A handsomely illustrated, chronologically arranged survey of warfare as practiced by the Greeks, Romans, and those who came into conflict with them from Homeric times until the 5th century A.D. Illustrations include color photographs, original art work (especially of soldiers and their equipment), battle diagrams, etc. Glossary; index.   U33.W37

Bibliography

Craig, Hardin, Jr. A bibliography of encyclopedias and dictionaries dealing with military, naval and maritime affairs, 1577–1971. 4th ed. rev. & corr. Houston, Tex., Dept. of History, Rice Univ., 1971. 134p.   **CJ531**

1st ed. 1960.

A chronological listing of encyclopedias, dictionaries, and wordbooks, plus a few miscellaneous items of interest to the user. International in scope; numerous brief annotations. Author index.   Z6724.D5C7

Handbooks

Dupuy, Trevor Nevitt, Hayes, Grace P. and **Andrews, John A. C.** The almanac of world military power. 4th ed. San Rafael, Calif., Presidio Pr., [1980]. 418p. maps.   **CJ532**

Gay Hammerman, coordinating ed.

1st ed. 1970.

The first section provides regional surveys, including analyses of military geography, strategic significance, regional alliances, and recent conflicts. The main body of the work is given over to national studies consisting of: (1) power potential statistics; (2) summaries of the nation's defense structure, politico-military policies, and strategic problems; and (3) inventories of armed forces strength, organization, and equipment. Glossary of equipment.   UA15.D9

Jane's Fighting Ships. 1898– . London, S. Low, 1898– . v.1– . Annual.   **CJ532a**

Title varies: 1898–1904, *All the world's fighting ships;* 1905–15, *Fighting ships.*

Arranged by country with subdivisions according to type of ship. Gives numbers and names of ships within each class; builders; dates of laying down, launching, and completion; and a photograph of a ship within the class. Specifications for each class are also given. Summary information on statistics, names of naval personnel, and strength of fleet accompany entries for each country. Other features are identification silhouettes, a section on naval aircraft and missiles, a table of naval strengths, and indexes of named ships and classes.   VA40.F5

Knötel, Richard, Knötel, Herbert and **Sieg, Herbert.** Uniforms of the world: a compendium of army, navy, and air force uniforms, 1700–1937. Rev., brought up to date, and enl. by Herbert Knötel, Jr. and Herbert Sieg. N.Y., Scribner, [1980]. 483p. il.   **CJ533**

Translation of R. Knötel's *Handbuch der Uniformkunde;* based on a 1956 translation by R. G. Ball.

Organized by armed forces division—army, navy, air force—then by country. Narrative descriptions with line drawings; colors are carefully noted in the text.   UC480.K513

The military balance, 1959/60– . London, International Inst. for Strategic Studies, 1959– . Annual.   **CJ534**

Title varies: 1959/60–62/63, *The communist bloc and the western alliances; the military balance.* 1959/60–70/71 issued by the Institute under its earlier name: Institute for Strategic Studies.

A standard statistical assessment of military forces and defense expenditures, presented in tabular form for countries and regional organizations such as NATO and the Warsaw Pact.

Pemsel, Helmut. A history of war at sea: an atlas and chronology of conflict at sea from earliest times to the present. Tr. by G. D. G. Smith. [Annapolis, Md.], Naval Inst. Pr., [1978]. 176p. il., maps.   **CJ535**

Tr. from the 1975 German ed., *Von Salamis bis Okinawa.* 1st English-language ed., fully rev., publ. 1977.

A chronicle of armed conflicts at sea from the Persian Wars to the Yom Kippur War of 1973, stressing fleet engagements rather than single ship encounters. Many battle maps and line drawings of ships. Appendixes; index.   D27.P2713

Reference handbook of the armed forces of the world. 4th ed. Ed. by Robert C. Sellers. N.Y. & London, Praeger, 1977. 278p.   **CJ536**

1st ed. 1966.

A country-by-country listing giving figures on defense budget, manpower in armed forces, branches of military service, equipment, etc. New material in this edition includes data on national flag, official language, and combat effectiveness evaluation for each country, and appendixes on U.S.–Third World security assistance funding, Middle East procurements since 1971, and U.S.–U.S.S.R. military posture.   UA15.R43

Small, Melvin and **Singer, Joel David.** Resort to arms; international and civil wars, 1816–1980. Beverly Hills, Calif., Sage, [1982]. 373p.   **CJ537**

A rev. ed. of the authors' *The wages of War, 1816–1965* (N.Y., Wiley, 1972).

A statistical analysis of 224 international and civil wars; also includes chronological list of excluded wars, and bibliographical references.   U21.2.S6

Strategic survey, 1966– . London, Internat. Inst. for Strategic Studies, 1967– . Annual.   **CJ538**

1966–71 issued by the Institute under its earlier name: Institute for Strategic Studies.

Supplements *The military balance* (CJ534), giving narrative summaries of the strategic situation in countries and regions of the world; includes chronology.   U162.S77

World armies. [Ed. by] John Keegan. 2d ed. Detroit, Gale, [1983]. 688p. il., maps.   **CJ539**

Intends "to provide a portrait of each army in its domestic context, historical, social and political as well as military."—*Pref.* Editorial emphasis is on the domestic status of each army. Arranged by country. Main entry for each includes: history; strength and budget; command and constitutional status; role, commitment, deployment and recent operations; organization; recruitment, training, and reserves; equipment and arms industry; rank, dress and distinctions and current developments.   UA15.W68

World armaments and disarmament: SIPRI yearbook, 1968/69– . Stockholm, Almqvist & Wiksell; N.Y., Humanities Pr., [1970–]. Annual.   **CJ540**

Title varies: 1968/69–71, *SIPRI yearbook of world armaments and disarmament.*

Attempts to provide a factual and balanced survey of developments in the arms race and efforts to curb it. Comprises an extensive account of world military expenditures, disarmament measures, etc., of the period covered by each volume, and a reference section providing tables, charts, and background information on the world arms and disarmament questions. The subtitle derives from the Institute's former name: Stockholm International Peace Research Institute.   UA10.S69

World armaments and disarmament: SIPRI yearbooks 1968–1979: cumulative index. London, Taylor & Francis (distr. in U.S.A. by Crane, Russak & Co.), 1980. 90p.   **CJ541**

Zivkovic, Georg. Heer- und Flottenführer der Welt. Die Inhaber der höchsten militärischen Würden, Ämter, Kommandos, und Anzeichnungen. 2., neubearb. u. erw. Aufl. Wien, Author, 1980. 971p.   **CJ542**

Title and introductory matter also in English and French.

Provides country-by-country lists of the leaders, with dates of terms of service. UB200.Z58

Biography

World military leaders. Paul Martell and Grace P. Hayes, eds. N.Y., Bowker; Dunn Loring, Va., T. N. Dupuy Associates, [1974]. 268p. **CJ543**

Trevor N. Dupuy, exec. ed.

Intends to provide biographical sketches "of military and civilian personnel in senior positions in military establishments in all nations of the world."—*Pref.* Includes a list of "Military leaders by nation." U51.W69

Atlases

Kidron, Michael and **Smith, Dan.** The war atlas: armed conflict—armed peace. N.Y., Simon & Schuster, [1983]. [128]p. il., maps. **CJ544**

Graphic representation on forty two-page colored maps of the wars and military situation since 1945. Source notes and comments on sources; bibliography. G1046.R1K5

United States

Guides

A guide to the sources of United States military history. Ed., Robin Higham. Hamden, Conn., Archon Books, 1975. 559p. **CJ545**

For full information *see* DB28.

A guide to the study and use of military history. [By] John E. Jessup, Jr. and Robert W. Coakley. [Wash.], Center of Military History, U.S. Army, [1979]. 507p. **CJ546**

For full information *see* DB29.

Bibliography

Allard, Dean C., Crawley, Martha L. and **Edmison, Mary W.** U.S. naval history sources in the United States. Wash., Naval History Div., Dept. of the Navy, 1979. 235p. il. **CJ547**

Updates and expands the coverage of the Naval History Division's 1970 publication *U.S. naval history sources in the Washington area.* Aims "to aid students of naval history by identifying manuscript, archival, and other special collections deposited in more than 250 American archives and libraries. Most of these materials are the private papers of officers, men, and civilian officials of the U.S. Navy."—*Introd.* Arranged by state, then by repository. Index of names of persons, institutions, ships, etc. Z1249.N3A48

Dornbusch, Charles Emil. Histories, personal narratives: United States Army; a checklist. Cornwallville, N.Y., Hope Farm Pr., 1967. 399p. **CJ548**

1st ed., 1956, had title: *Histories of American army units, World Wars I and II and Korean conflict, with some earlier histories.* It was a listing of all types of unit histories of the Army, not including the Air Force or the Navy.

The new edition adds more than a thousand titles; items are numbered consecutively; library location is given for a high percentage of the works. Z1249.M5D6

———— Unit histories of the United States Air Forces, including privately printed personal narratives. Hampton Bays, N.Y., Hampton Books, 1958. 56p. il. **CJ549**

Covers World War I and World War II. Z6724.A3D66

Mahon, John K. and **Danysh, Romana.** Infantry. [2d ed.] Part I: Regular army. Wash., Office of the Chief of Military History, U.S. Army, 1972. 938p. il. **CJ550**

At head of title: Army lineage series.

An earlier volume on the infantry appeared in 1953. Pt.II is to cover Army National Guard and Army Reserve. Other volumes will be devoted to armor-cavalry, artillery, divisions and separate brigades.

v.1 provides lineage and heraldic data for each individual infantry unit. UA28.M352

Moran, John B. Creating a legend; the complete record of writing about the United States Marine Corps. Chicago, Moran Andrews, [1973]. 681p. **CJ551**

Z6725.U5M67

Paszek, Lawrence J. United States Air Force history: a guide to documentary sources. Wash., Off. of Air Force History, 1973. 245p. il. **CJ552**

Locates and describes more than 700 collections of primary and secondary documents on the Air Force. In five sections: (1) official Air Force depositories; (2) National Archives, Federal Records Centers, and presidential libraries; (3) university collections; (4) Library of Congress, federal and local government depositories and historical societies; (5) other sources on astronautics and aviation in general. Index to depositories and general index. CD3034.5.P37

Smith, Myron J. Navies in the American Revolution: a bibliography. Metuchen, N.J., Scarecrow Pr., 1973. 219p. (American naval bibliography, 1) **CJ553**

An author listing of approximately 1,600 items, including monographs, articles, papers, master's theses and doctoral dissertations. Subject index. This is the only volume of the series which includes foreign-language material. Z1238.S54

———— The American Navy, 1789–1860; a bibliography. Metuchen, N. J., Scarecrow Pr., 1974. 489p. (American naval bibliography, 2) **CJ554**

About 4,000 entries. A section of general works is followed by separate sections for (1) 1789–1815; (2) 1815–1860; and (3) government documents. Subject index. Z6835.U5S6

———— American Civil War navies: a bibliography. Metuchen, N. J., Scarecrow Pr., 1972. 347p. (American naval bibliography, 3) **CJ555**

Lists over 2,800 English-language items alphabetically by author, with a subject index. Z1242.S63

———— The American Navy, 1865–1918: a bibliography. Metuchen, N.J., Scarecrow Pr., 1974. 372p. (American naval bibliography, 4) **CJ556**

Roughly 3,500 entries alphabetically arranged in six sections: (1) General works; (2) 1865–1898: From the old Navy to the new; (3) 1898: The war with Spain; (4) 1898–1917: The "bully" years; (5) 1917–1918: The First World War; (6) Government documents. Subject index. Z6835.U5S62

———— The American Navy, 1918–1941: a bibliography. Metuchen, N. J., Scarecrow Pr., 1974. 429p. (American naval bibliography, 5) **CJ557**

More than 4,700 entries in an alphabetical arrangement; government documents have been included on a selective basis and are listed chronologically in a separate section. Subject index. Z6835.U5S63

———— The United States Navy and Coast Guard, 1946–1983: a bibliography of English-language works and 16mm films. Jefferson, N.C., McFarland, 1984. 539p. **CJ558**

10,057 citations, topically arranged. Includes books, periodical articles, reports, government documents, theses, dissertations, and research projects. Author and subject indexes.   Z1249.N3S63

U.S. Dept. of the Army. The role of the Reserve in the total Army: a bibliographic survey of the United States Army Reserve. Wash., [Headquarters, Dept. of the Army; for sale by Supt. of Docs.], 1977. 107p. il., maps.   **CJ559**

An annotated, subject-classed bibliography of books, articles, pamphlets, government documents, and other sources on the historical, organizational, operational, and legislative aspects of the Army Reserve. 29 appendixes feature maps, charts, and statistical tables.   Z6725.U5U4226

U.S. Dept. of the Army. Office of Military History. Unit histories of World War II. United States Army, Air Force, Marines, Navy. Reproduced in collaboration with the New York Public Library. [Wash.], Office of the Chief of Military History, [1950]. 141p.   **CJ560**

Lists 1,223 unit histories.

——— ——— Supplement, 1951. Reproduced in collaboration with the New York Public Library and Office of the Chief of Military History, Dept. of the Army, Wash., Library Section, Special Services Division, Dept. of the Army, Sept. 1951. 50p.

Lists items 1,230–1,673. Includes some official as well as nonofficial histories.   Z6207.W8U52

——— Check list of new unit histories, comp. by C. E. Dornbusch. Wash., 1952–56. 3v. in 1.   **CJ561**

U.S. Military Academy, West Point. The centennial of the U.S. Military Academy at West Point, N.Y., 1802–1902. v.2, Statistics and bibliographies. Wash., Govt. Prt. Off., 1904. 433p.   **CJ562**

Includes: Bibliographies of West Point, 1694–1902; Bibliography of the U.S. Military Academy, 1776–1902; Bibliography of the writings of graduates, 1802–1902; List of graduates (1802–1902).   U410.L1A2

U.S. Naval Academy, Annapolis. Library. Bibliography of naval literature in the United States Naval Academy Library, comp. by L. H. Bolander. [Annapolis, 1929] 3v. in 1.   **CJ563**

Contents: Pt.1, American naval biography; pt.2, Foreign naval biography; pt.3, Naval history.

"Works dealing with naval strategy, tactics, ordnance, and gunnery, seamanship, and navigation have not been included."—*title page.*   Z6834.B6U5

Dictionaries

Air University. Aerospace Studies Institute. The United States Air Force dictionary. Ed. by Woodford Agee Heflin. Princeton, N.J., Van Nostrand, 1956. 578p.   **CJ564**

Defines more than 16,500 words and abbreviations as used in the Air Force, including terms in the fields of aeronautics, aerodynamics, meteorology, electronics, atomic energy, supersonics, etc.   UG630.U637

Elting, John Robert, Cragg, Dan and **Deal, Ernest L.** A dictionary of soldier talk. N.Y., Scribner's, [1984]. 383p.   **CJ565**

Offers brief definitions of U.S. Army language, with appendix of naval and marine terms. Indicates historical usage. Bibliography.   U24.E38

Noel, John V. and **Beach, Edward L.** Naval terms dictionary. 4th ed. Annapolis, Naval Institute Pr., [1978]. 354p.   **CJ566**

1st ed. 1952.

Provides brief definitions for terms, phrases, and abbreviations in current usage. Appendixes explain the designation system for ships and service craft, aircraft, missiles, and electronic equipment, as well as the ranking structure for enlisted personnel.   V23.N6

Ruffner, Frederick G. and **Thomas, Robert C.** Code names dictionary. Detroit, Gale, [1963]. 555p.   **CJ567**

Subtitle: A guide to code names, slang, nicknames, journalese and similar terms: aviation, rockets and missiles, military, aerospace, meteorology, atomic energy, communications and others.   PE1693.R9

Wedertz, Bill. Dictionary of naval abbreviations. 3d ed. Annapolis, Md., Naval Institute Pr., [1984]. 330p.   **CJ568**

1st ed. 1970.

About 45,000 abbreviations "commonly used by the naval establishment and . . . unavailable in standard dictionaries . . . . All medical, chemical, educational, and religious abbreviations have been deleted, as have abbreviations dealing with computers and computer languages, foreign organizations, state and city designations, and the aerospace industry."—*Pref.*   V23.W43

Handbooks

See also CF140.

Ageton, Arthur Ainsley and **Mack, William P.** The naval officer's guide. [Ed.1]– . Annapolis, Md., U.S. Naval Inst., 1943– . (9th ed. 1983)   **CJ569**

Publisher varies.

A wide range of useful information for the new officer, with material on sea duty as well as on service at naval establishments on shore.   V133.A6

The air force officer's guide. By A. J. Kinney and John N. Napier. Ed. 23– . Harrisburg, Pa., Stackpole Books, [1979]– . il. Annual (irregular).   **CJ570**

Continues *Air officer's guide* (1923–78).   UG633.A1A49

Heinl, Robert Debs. The Marine officer's guide. 4th ed. Annapolis, Naval Institute Pr., 1977. 713p. il.   **CJ571**

1st ed. 1956.

Earlier editions by G. C. Thomas.

Describes the position and function of the Marine Corps within the national defense network; the history, traditions, social customs and usages of the Corps; career and professional matters for the new officer. Glossary; index. A 5th ed. is to be published 1985.   VE153.T5

Lovette, Leland Pearson. Naval ceremonies, customs, and traditions. Rev. by Royal W. Connell, William P. Mack. 5th ed. Annapolis, Md., Naval Inst. Pr., [1980]. 386p. il.   **CJ572**

1st ed. 1934; previous eds. had title: *Naval customs, traditions & usage.*

Traces the historical development and describes the modern status of various traditions, ceremonies, customs, and usages for the United States Navy and Marine Corps. A chapter is devoted to the derivation of nautical words and naval expressions. Useful appendixes offer biographical sketches and further rules of etiquette. Bibliography; index.   V310.L6

Officer's guide. [Ed.1–] Harrisburg, Pa., Stackpole, Military Service Div., [1930]– . Annual (irregular).   **CJ573**

Subtitle: A ready reference on customs and correct procedures which pertain to officers of the United States Army.   U133.O48

United States Naval Institute. Almanac of naval facts. Annapolis, [The Institute], 1964. 305p.   **CJ574**

Designed as a ready reference source on the United States Navy.

Offers a calendar of important dates and data on naval explorations and ship losses (all in chronological arrangement). Sections on "naval firsts" and "naval terms and phrases" are alphabetically arranged. Lacks an index. E182.U587

Decorations and insignia

Kerrigan, Evans E. American badges and insignia. N.Y., Viking, [1967]. 286p. il. **CJ575**

Descriptions and illustrations of military insignia of the United States. UC533.K45

——— American war medals and decorations. Newly rev. and expanded. N.Y., Viking, [1971]. 173p. il. **CJ576**

Descriptions and illustrations, some in color, of decorations, service medals, and awards to civilians. CJ5805.K4

National Geographic Society. Insignia and decorations of the United States armed forces, by Gilbert Grosvenor [and others] . . . Rev. ed., Dec. 1, 1944. Wash., Nat. Geographic Soc., 1945. 208p. il. **CJ577**

Descriptions and illustrations, many in color, of decorations, medals, service ribbons, badges, and other insignia of the United States armed forces. UC533.N3

Robles, Philip K. United States military medals and ribbons. Rutland, Vt., Tuttle, [1971]. 187p. il. **CJ578**

Provides answers (through descriptive and historical text and colored illustrations) to "most of the questions concerning eligibility for award and wear of the medals of the United States Armed Forces."—*Pref.* Merchant Marine awards are also included. UC533.R62

U.S. Adjutant General's Office. American decorations. A list of awards of the Congressional Medal of Honor, the Distinguished-Service Cross, and the Distinguished-Service Medal, awarded under authority of the Congress of the United States, 1862–1926. Wash., Govt. Prt. Off., 1927. 845p. **CJ579**

——— ——— Supplement 1–5, Jan. 1, 1927–June 30, 1941. Wash., 1937–41.

No more published. UB433.A5

Ships

U.S. Naval History Division. Dictionary of American naval fighting ships. Wash., 1959–81. 8v. il. **CJ580**

"An alphabetical arrangement of the ships of the Continental and United States navies, with a historical sketch of each one."—*Pref.* Appendixes appear in v.1–7: in v.1, chronological listings of battleships, cruisers, submarines, torpedo boats and destroyers, escort vessels; in v.2, aircraft carriers; Confederate forces afloat (historical sketches); in v.3, historic ship exhibits; monitors; Civil War naval ordnance; in v.4, amphibious warfare ships; aviation auxiliaries; destroyer tenders; ships of the line; classification of naval ships and service craft; in v.5, stone fleet; minecraft; new ships; aircraft; in v.6, submarine chasers; eagle-class patrol craft; in v.7, tank landing ships. VA61.A53

Biography

Callahan, Edward William. List of officers of the Navy of the United States and of the Marine Corps, from 1775 to 1900; comp. from the official records. N.Y., Hamersly, 1901. 749p. (Repr.: N.Y., Haskell House, 1969) **CJ581**

Subtitle: Comprising a complete register of all present and former commissioned, warranted, and appointed officers of the United States Navy, and of the Marine Corps, regular and volunteer. V11.U7C2

Cullum, George Washington. Biographical register of the officers and graduates of the U.S. Military Academy at West Point, N.Y., since its establishment in 1802 . . . 3d ed., rev. and extended. Boston, etc., 1891–[1950]. 9v. **CJ582**

Place and publisher vary.
Contents: v.1–3, 1802–90; v.4, 1890–1900, ed. by E. S. Holden; v.5, 1900–10, ed. by Lieut. Charles Braden; v.6, A and B, 1910–20, ed. by Col. Wirt Robinson; v.7, 1920–30, ed. by Capt. W. H. Donaldson; v.8, 1930–40, ed. by Lt.Col. E. E. Farman; v.9, 1940–50, ed. by Col. Charles N. Branham.
v.4–9 called supplements. U410.H52

Dictionary of American military biography. Roger J. Spiller, ed. Westport, Conn., Greenwood Pr., [1984]. 3v. (1368p.) **CJ583**

Presents biographical essays (about 1,500 words each) on some 400 living and deceased persons. Bibliographical references; numerous appendixes; index. U52.D53

DuPre, Flint O. U.S. Air Force biographical dictionary. N.Y., Watts, [1965]. 273p. **CJ584**

Includes sketches for outstanding living and deceased members of the Air Force. No bibliographical references or list of sources, but, like Karl Schuon's *U.S. Marine Corps biographical dictionary* (N.Y., Watts, 1963) and *U.S. Navy biographical dictionary* (N.Y., Watts, 1964), it is useful as a quick-reference source for information on Medal of Honor winners and other military figures not always found in standard biographical dictionaries. UG633.D8

Heitman, Francis Bernard. Historical register of officers of the Continental Army during the war of the Revolution, April 1775 to Dec. 1783. New, rev., and enl. ed. Wash., Rare Book Shop Pub. Co., 1914. 685p. (Repr.: Baltimore, Genealogical Pub. Co., 1973) **CJ585**

An alphabetical register of officers, with service records and various supplementary lists. E255.H48

——— Historical register and dictionary of the United States Army from its organization, Sept. 29, 1789, to March 2, 1903. Publ. under act of Congress approved March 2, 1903. Wash., Govt. Prt. Off., 1903. 2v. (57th Cong., 2d sess. House doc. 446) (Repr.: Urbana, Univ. of Illinois Pr., 1965) **CJ586**

v.1 is primarily an alphabetical dictionary of officers of the U.S. Army, giving their service records with some preliminary lists; v.2 includes an alphabetical list of officers of the regular army who were killed, wounded in action, or taken prisoner; strength of the army and losses in the several wars; dates of certain wars, campaigns; alphabetical list of battles, actions, etc., 1775–1902; chronological list of battles, actions; list of forts, batteries, camps . . . general hospitals, national cemeteries, etc.; and various statistical tables. U11.U5H6

Powell, William Henry. List of officers of the army of the United States from 1779–1900 embracing a register of all appointments . . . in the volunteer service during the Civil War and of volunteer officers in the service of the United States June 1, 1900, comp. from the official records. N.Y., Hamersly, 1900. 863p. **CJ587**

A list of officers, 1779–1815, is arranged by years, followed by the army list, 1815 to 1900, which is arranged alphabetically by name with brief biographical information; a list of officers of volunteers; general officers of the Revolution; etc. Index of names. Known also as the *United States army list.* U11.U5P7

——— Officers of the army and navy (volunteer) who served in the Civil War. Philadelphia, Hamersly, 1893. 419p. il. **CJ588**

E467.P88

———— and **Shippen, Edward.** Officers of the army and navy (regular) who served in the Civil War. Philadelphia, Hamersly, 1892. 487p. il.   **CJ589**

E467.P87

Webster's American military biographies. Springfield, Mass., G. & C. Merriam, 1978. 548p.   **CJ590**

Presents more than 1,000 biographies of persons important to the military history of the nation, including "not only the battlefield heroes and great commanders, but also the frontier scouts, nurses, Indian leaders, historians, explorers, shipbuilders, and inventors. . . ."—*Introd.* Biographies average 450 words and cover the entire career. Bibliographies are not provided. Addenda section offers lists of chief service officers, and chronological lists of wars, battles, expeditions, etc., for the Army, Navy, and Marine Corps.

U52.W4

Africa

Martin, Michel L. L'armée et la société en Afrique: essai de synthèse et d'investigation bibliographique. [Bordeaux, France], Centre d'Études d'Afrique Noire, 1975. 241*l*.

CJ591

A selection of more than 1,700 items on the history and structure of African military institutions, civil-military relations, the role of the army in the development process, etc.; includes material on these subjects pertaining to other Third World countries.

Z6725.A4M37

Asia

Guide to Far Eastern navies. Ed. by Barry M. Blechman and Robert P. Berman. Annapolis, Naval Institute Pr., [1978]. 586p. il.   **CJ592**

In two parts: (1) essays by naval officers and scholars describing the naval balance in the Western Pacific and the navies of the People's Republic of China, Japan, the Republic of China, the Republic of Korea, the Democratic People's Republic of Korea, and the Philippines; (2) detailed specifications for the individual ships and aircraft of those navies. Indexed.   VA620.G84

Canada

Cooke, O. A. The Canadian military experience, 1867–1983: a bibliography. Bibliographie de la vie militaire au Canada, 1867–1983. 2d ed. Ottawa, Directorate of History, Dept. of Nat. Defense, 1984. 329p. (Canada. Dept. Nat. Defense. Directorate of History. Monograph ser., 2)

CJ593

Prefatory matter in English and French.

Brief sections for bibliography and for "Defense policy and general works" are followed by major sections for naval forces, land forces, and air forces, each subdivided by period. Lists books, pamphlets, government publications, and journals, but not individual periodical articles. No index.   Z1387.M54C66

France

Taillemite, Etienne. Dictionnaire des marins français. [Paris], Editions Maritimes & d'Outre-Mer, [1982]. 357p. il.

CJ594

A biographical dictionary of 850 French maritime figures from the 17th century to the present day, with some earlier persons included. Chronological index.   DC49.5.T34

Germany

Witthöff, Hans Jürgen. Lexikon zur deutschen Marinegeschichte. Herford, Koehlers Verlagsgesellschaft, 1977–78. 2v. il., maps.   **CJ595**

An encyclopedia of naval strategy, battles, terminology, personnel, and craft. Many entries have bibliographies appended.

V23.W57

Great Britain

Carman, W. Y. A dictionary of military uniform. N.Y., Scribner's, [1977]. 140p. il.   **CJ596**

Brief entries for items of military dress, badges, etc. Many illustrations. "Unless otherwise stated the description refers to the British Army although possibly it could apply to other nations."—*Note.*   UC480.C27

Uden, Grant and **Cooper, Richard.** A dictionary of British ships and seamen. N.Y., St. Martin's, [1980]. 591p. il., maps.   **CJ597**

A heavily illustrated historical dictionary of the British naval heritage from early times to the present. Brief articles, including biographies. Alphabetical arrangement, with cross references.

VK57.U33

Latin America

English, Adrian J. Armed forces of Latin America: their histories, development, present strength and military potential. [London & N.Y.], Jane's Publishing, [1984]. 490p. il., maps.   **CJ598**

For each country, provides: vital statistics; geostrategic description; historical background; politico-strategic position; general structure of the armed forces (army, navy, air force, paramilitary); sources of defense supplies and current requirements; defense production; foreign influences; summary and prospects. Statistical appendixes; selected bibliography; index.   UA602.3.E54

La Mura, Enzo. Militär und Politik in Lateinamerika: Auswahlbibliographie. Fuerzas armadas y política: bibliografía selecta. Hamburg, Institut für Iberoamerika-kunde, Dokumentations-Leitstelle Lateinamerika, 1976. 80p. (Dokumentationsdienst Lateinamerika, Reihe A, Heft 2)

CJ599

Prefatory matter and headings in German and Spanish.

An international bibliography of materials available in West German libraries. Includes sections on bibliographical and statistical sources, the role of the military in foreign relations such as arms sales, and the political role of the military in specific Latin American countries, with special emphasis on Brazil, Chile, and Peru. Author index.   Z1609.P64L38

Union of Soviet Socialist Republics

Bibliography

Smith, Myron J. The Soviet navy, 1941–1978: a guide to sources in English. Santa Barbara, Calif., ABC-Clio, [1980]. 211p. (War/peace bibliography ser., no.9)   **CJ600**

A classed subject arrangement of 1,741 monographs, periodical articles, papers, government documents, doctoral dissertations, and master's theses. Each of the 11 main sections has a brief introduction and a concluding note on related sources in other sections of the bibliography; citations are to publications of the 1941–78 period. Includes reference works and audiovisual sources. Appendixes list late entries (to June 1979), journals consulted, and select Soviet naval biographies. Author index.   Z6835.R9S64

———— The Soviet air and strategic rocket forces, 1939–1980: a guide to sources in English. Santa Barbara, ABC-Clio, [1981]. 321p. il. (War/peace bibliography ser., no.10)   **CJ601**

A classified subject bibliography to English-language books, articles, government documents, dissertations, theses, and reports written between 1939 and 1980. Each of the seven main sections is preceded by an introduction and subdivided according to type of publication. Reference sources are noted. Author index.
    Z6724.A38S63

———— The Soviet army, 1939–1980; a guide to sources in English. Santa Barbara, Calif., ABC-Clio, [1982]. 551p. (War/peace bibliography ser., 11)   **CJ602**

A classed bibliography with more than 5,700 citations to English-language books, reports, periodical articles, government documents, dissertations and theses, and research projects. Provides very brief biographies for 120 Soviet military figures. Author index.
    Z6725.S68S54

Dictionaries and encyclopedias

Menaul, Stewart. The illustrated encyclopedia of the strategy, tactics and weapons of Russian military power. N.Y., St. Martin's Pr., [1980]. 249p. il., maps.   **CJ603**

Primarily useful for its organizational charts, color photographs, color illustrations and line drawings, and model specifications of Soviet military aircraft, ships, armored vehicles, missiles, and other weapons. There is a distinct textual and pictorial similarity between this work and *The Soviet war machine; an encyclopedia of Russian military equipment and strategy* (N.Y., Chartwell Books, 1976); the two works share many of the same contributors and were originally published by Salamander Books, London.   UA770.M46

The military-naval encyclopedia of Russia and the Soviet Union. Ed. by David R. Jones. [Gulf Breeze, Fla.], Academic Internat. Pr., 1978–84. v.1–4. il. (In progress)   **CJ604**

Contents: v.1–4, "A" (gliders)–Adzhariia.

Intended as a comprehensive encyclopedia of military leaders, ships, regiments, formations, weapons systems, battles, campaigns and wars, military institutions, armed forces, treaties, etc. Lengthy articles are signed; almost all have bibliographies. To be in about 50v., with indexes and supplements.   UA770.M56

Complemented by:

Soviet armed forces review annual. v.1– , 1977– . [Gulf Breeze, Fla.], Academic Internat. Pr., [1977]– . Annual. il.   **CJ605**

David R. Jones, ed.

Designed to assemble and organize in a standard format the available public information on Soviet military affairs, with analytical topical discussion, documentation, and bibliography. Consists of surveys of the current military situation, signed reviews by specialists, documents, and bibliography. No index.   UA770.S657

Polmar, Norman. Guide to the Soviet navy. 3d ed. Annapolis, Naval Inst. Pr., [1983]. 465p. il.   **CJ606**

1st ed. (1970) was an updated and expanded translation of *Die Seerüstung der Sowjetunion* (1964).

Each chapter covers a separate aspect of the Soviet navy: organization, personnel, weapons and equipment, warships and their construction, naval air force, infantry, coastal defense, bases and ports, shipbuilding industry. All ships, aircraft, and weapons are presented and illustrated chronologically. Bibliography; index.
    VA573.P598

ARMS CONTROL AND PEACE RESEARCH

Bibliography

Arms control and disarmament; a quarterly bibliography with abstracts and annotations. v.1–9[2]. Wash., Govt. Prt. Off., 1964–73. Quarterly.   **CJ607**

Comp. by the Arms Control and Disarmament Bibliography Section of the Library of Congress.

Originally included abstracts or brief annotations of books, periodical articles, government documents, and publications of international organizations "selected from a survey of the literature received by the Library of Congress that is likely to be available in the larger research and public libraries in the United States."—*Pref.* Beginning with v.2, no.1, Winter 1965/66, coverage was extended to include abstracts and annotations of current literature in French, German, and Russian, as well as of materials in English.

Classed arrangement within issues; cumulated subject and author indexes for each volume.

Ceased publication with issue for Spring 1973.   JX1974.A1A7

Boulding, Elise, Passmore, J. Robert and **Gassler, Robert Scott.** Bibliography on world conflict and peace. 2d ed. Boulder, Colo., Westview Pr., 1979. 168p.   **CJ608**

Publ. in cooperation with the Consortium on Peace Research and the Section on the Sociology of World Conflicts of the American Sociological Association.

In four main sections: author listing of about 1,000 English-language books, essays and articles, accompanied by subject key; collections, annuals, and series; periodical titles; and bibliographies. Focuses on works published between 1945 and 1978. No direct subject access.   Z6464.Z9B68

Burns, Grant. The atomic papers: a citizen's guide to selected books and articles on the bomb, the arms race, nuclear power, the peace movement, and related issues. Metuchen, N.J., Scarecrow Pr., 1984. 309p.   **CJ609**

A topically arranged, annotated bibliography of English-language books (published 1945–79) and periodical articles (published since 1980); includes a section on literature with nuclear themes. Subject and author index.   Z6464.D6B85

Burns, Richard Dean. Arms control and disarmament: a bibliography. Santa Barbara, Calif., ABC-Clio, [1977]. 430p. (War/peace bibliography ser., no.6)   **CJ610**

The series was developed in cooperation with the Center for the Study of Armament and Disarmament, California State University, Los Angeles.

Over 8,000 primary and secondary English-language sources on the theory and practice of arms control and disarmament, both historical and contemporary. Cutoff date appears to be 1976. Subject and author indexes.   Z6464.D6B87

Legault, Albert. Peace-keeping operations; bibliography. Paris, International Information Center of Peace-keeping Operations, [1967]. 203p.   **CJ611**

A bibliography of book and periodical materials with extensive annotations.   JX1981.P7L43

Lloyd, Lorna and **Sims, Nicholas A.** British writing on disarmament from 1914–1978: a bibliography. [London, F. Pinter; N.Y., Nichols, 1979] 117p.   **CJ612**

Complements R. D. Burns's *Arms control and disarmament* (above) by stressing titles written in Great Britain during this period. In two sections: pre-1914 to 1941, and 1941 to the present; subject subdivisions within sections. Author index.

    Z6465.G7L56

Reference Research Associates. Bibliography, nuclear proliferation. Wash., Govt. Prt. Off., 1978. 159p.   **CJ613**

Prep. for the Subcommittee on Energy, Nuclear Proliferation, and Federal Services of the Committee on Governmental Affairs, U.S.

Senate, and the Committee on International Relations, and Committee on Science and Technology, U.S. House of Representatives, by the Environment and Natural Resources Policy Div., Congressional Research Service, Library of Congress.

At head of title: 95th Congress, 2d session. Joint committee print. Comp. by Thomas W. Graham and Ridgely C. Evers.

A selective, annotated bibliography in two sections: (1) the annotations, arranged by form—books, articles, periodicals consulted, government documents, papers and other sources; (2) a classed subject index.   Z6464.D6R43

Repertory of disarmament research. United Nations Institute for Disarmament Research. Geneva, UNIDIR, 1982. 449p.   **CJ614**

In three main parts: (1) bibliography of reference works; (2) bibliography of documents and studies published between 1970 and 1980, classed by topic and publication date; (3) directory of research institutes and centers. International in scope; author index.
                         Z6464.D6R46

Review of research trends and an annotated bibliography: social and economic consequences of the arms race and of disarmament. [Paris], Unesco, [1978]. 44p. (Reports and papers in the social sciences, no.39)   **CJ615**

Presents a review of research trends in the field and an annotated subject bibliography of 174 titles.   H62.U475 no.39

United Nations. Dag Hammarskjöld Library. Disarmament: a select bibliography, 1973–1977. N.Y., United Nations, 1978. 139p. (Dag Hammarskjöld Library. Bibliographical ser., no.26)   **CJ616**

Previous volumes covered the literature of 1962–64 (1965. 95p.), 1964–67 (1968. 38p.), and 1967–72 (1973. 63p.).

An international subject-classed bibliography in two sections: (1) books and articles; (2) selected United Nations documents.
                         JX1977.A2

Bibliography of bibliography

Carroll, Berenice A., Fink, Clinton F. and **Mohraz, Jane E.** Peace and war; a guide to bibliographies. Santa Barbara, Calif., ABC-Clio, [1983]. 580p. (War/peace bibliography ser., 16)   **CJ617**

An annotated bibliography of 1,398 bibliographies published in a variety of formats, 1785 through 1980. International in scope; focuses on works of general application rather than particular conflicts (except for the two World Wars). Subject arrangement; author and subject indexes.   Z6464.Z9C55

Dictionaries

Disarmament terminology. Comp. by the Language Services Division of the Foreign Office of the Federal Republic of Germany. Berlin & N.Y., W. de Gruyter, 1982. 645p. (Terminological ser., v.1)   **CJ618**

Title also in German, French, Spanish, and Russian.

A polyglot dictionary of terms, phrases, organizations, conferences, and agreements. Base language is English, with indexes in all five languages.   JX1974.D548

Directories

Peace research: trend report and world directory. [Paris], Unesco, [1978]. 250p. (Reports and papers in the social sciences, no.43)   **CJ619**

1st ed. (1967) publ. as *International repertory of institutions specializing in research on peace and disarmament;* 2d ed. (1973) as *International repertory of institutions for peace and conflict research.*

Describes 310 institutions, organized by country, with an initial

international category. Indexed by name and director of organization.   H62.U475 no.43

Yearbooks

See also CJ540.

Unesco yearbook on peace and conflict studies, 1980– . Westport, Conn., Greenwood Pr.; Paris, Unesco, [1981]– . Annual.   **CJ620**

" . . . contents of this Yearbook are more general and international in scope than those of . . . periodicals and more methodological and documentary than . . . scientific journals."—*Pref.* The first volume contains surveys of peace research information systems, a literature review and bibliography on war, a bibliographical guide to disarmament, and an international review of peace research activities. Indexed.   JX1904.5.U52

United Nations disarmament yearbook. v.1– , 1976– . N.Y., United Nations, 1977– . Annual.   **CJ621**

Prep. by the United Nations Centre for Disarmament.

"The approach adopted is . . . to cover each question in the field of disarmament and arms control which was dealt with by the General Assembly during . . . 1976."—*Introd.* Later volumes include reports on the status of existing disarmament agreements, chronologies of events, and factual information on military expenditures, arms trade, armed forces, etc. Appendixes include documents, lists of resolutions, activities of U.N.-related organizations. Detailed table of contents, but no index.   JX1974.U546

C K

Law

❖Because law is such a highly specialized subject, most legal research is done in special law libraries. These may be independent or they may be connected with some institution, such as state, legislative research, or university libraries. Few general libraries can buy many law books, both because they are expensive and because they are so technical that they can be used satisfactorily only by those trained in the law. Although recent years have seen publication of a number of reference works on law intended for the lay person (e.g., *The guide to American law,* CK145), the smaller general library should buy only those books which are needed for supplying the less technical legal information and should refer complicated legal questions to a nearby law library.

The larger general library, however, will need at least a small collection to answer questions in the fields of history, economics, and political and social science, as well as the more general law questions. The minimum equipment should include: (1) a law dictionary; (2) a set of the *Revised statutes of the United States* (CK205), and either the *United States code* (CK207) or the *United States code annotated* (CK208); (3) the latest revision or compilation of the laws of the home state, with subsequent session laws; (4) the charter and ordinances of the home city; (5) the latest compilation of the United States *Treaties in force* (CK367) and the *Digest of international law* (CK318–CK321). To this minimum the library would add, as public demand or library funds justified, one of the large law encyclopedias and, if the library contained many legal periodicals, the indexes of legal periodicals. Commercial looseleaf services and reporters appropriate to law libraries are identified in the guides by Cohen (CK2–CK3), Jacobstein (CK5), and Price (CK7).

GENERAL WORKS

Guides

See also AB178.

Bander, Edward J. and **Bander, David F.** Legal research and education abridgment; a manual for law students, paralegals and researchers. Cambridge, Mass., Ballinger, [1978]. 214p. **CK1**

In two main parts: (1) legal research techniques, which briefly outlines the major titles and types of reference sources; (2) subject and topic research, which lists leading texts, journals, treatises, and bibliographies for various fields of law. Sources for New York state legal texts are appended to many subject sections. Indexed.
KF240.B26

Cohen, Morris L. Legal research in a nutshell. 4th ed. St. Paul, Minn., West Pub. Co., 1985. 452p. il. **CK2**

1st ed. 1965.
A manual for the student, intended as a brief introduction to the main areas of legal literature. For more detailed references *see* his *How to find the law* (below) or its abridgment, *Finding the law* (1984). Useful appendixes list state research guides, looseleaf services, official state reporters, and titles in the national reporter system.
KF240.C54

—— and **Berring, Robert C.** How to find the law. 8th ed. St. Paul, Minn., West, 1983. 790p. il. **CK3**

1st ed. 1931.
A classic, practical guide to legal bibliography, each chapter of which is written by a different law librarian or law professor. Intended as a teaching aid rather than as a reference work.
KF240.C538

Dane, Jean and **Thomas, Philip A.** How to use a law library. London, Sweet & Maxwell, 1979. 182p. il. **CK4**

A student's guide to locating the law relating to England and Wales, with chapters on sources of European Community law and public international law. Chapters on law reports, legislation, periodicals, government publications, and tracing cases on particular topics.
KD392.D36

Jacobstein, J. Myron and **Mersky, Roy M.** Fundamentals of legal research. 3d ed. Mineola, N.Y., Foundation Pr., 1985. 717p. il. **CK5**

1st ed. 1977.
Serves as a successor to E. H. Pollack's *Fundamentals of legal research* (4th ed., 1973).
Intended as an aid to students learning to do legal research, but summary and citation sections of each chapter are useful for reference purposes. Most useful for Anglo-American law. New material includes chapter on computers and microforms in legal research. Available in an abridged version as *Legal research illustrated* (2d ed. Mineola, N.Y., Foundation Pr., 1981. 386p.).
KF240.J3

Kling, Samuel G. The complete guide to everyday law. 3d ed. Chicago, Follett, [1973]. 709p. **CK6**

1st ed. 1966.
Intended for home and office use, "to provide the reader with a knowledge of the basic legal principles by which he lives and by

which society operates."—*Pref.* Arranged by question-and-answer method within topical sections; indexed. Includes a section of sample legal forms and a glossary of legal terms. A useful guide for the layman, though oversimplified in certain areas.

Price, Miles Oscar, Bitner, Harry and **Bysiewicz, Shirley R.** Effective legal research. 4th ed. Boston, Little, Brown, [1979]. 643p. **CK7**

1st ed. 1953.
A manual on legal research and bibliography which discusses procedures and literature. Of particular value to librarians will be chapters on special types of reference works, e.g., indexes, digests, encyclopedias, dictionaries, looseleaf services, etc.
Presents five new chapters on Australian materials, New Zealand materials, South African materials, international law, and automated legal research. The former chapter on English and Canadian materials has been divided into two separate chapters. The appendix listing abbreviations has been expanded.
KF240.P7

Bibliography

Association of American Law Schools. Law books recommended for libraries. South Hackensack, N.J., Rothman, 1967. 6v., looseleaf. **CK8**

Consists of 46 subject lists available as separate pamphlets or as a set. Intended as book selection aids for law libraries, the lists are useful as guides to the best in legal literature. Most of them were compiled by Miles O. Price, then checked and revised by law faculties and librarians throughout the country; those on certain specialized topics were prepared by experts in the subjects. In general, the lists include encyclopedias, dictionaries, periodicals, law reports, and selected treatises. Pt.47 is a general index.
Through 1976, kept up-to-date by looseleaf supplements. Updated by:
K38.A75

Recommended publications for legal research, 1979. Comp. by Oscar J. Miller and Mortimer D. Schwartz. Littleton, Colo., Rothman, 1985. 147p. **CK9**

A list of English-language books announced for 1979, keyed as to suitability for basic, intermediate, or research library collections. Subject arrangement, with author/title index. Further volumes are to appear on an annual basis.
KF1.R43

Akademie für Staats- und Rechtswissenschaft der DDR. Informationszentrum Staat und Recht. Katalog iuridicheskikh dokumentatsionnykh istochnikov sotsialisticheskikh stran. Register of legal documentation of socialist states. Potsdam-Babelsberg, [Informationszentrum Staat und Recht], 1976– . v.1– . (Spezialbibliographien zu Frage des Staates und des Rechts, Heft 16) (In progress) **CK10**

Contents: v.1, Union of Soviet Socialist Republics, German Democratic Republic; v.2, Hungary, Poland; v.3, Yugoslavia, Romania; v.4, People's Republic of Bulgaria, Czechoslovak Socialist Republic; v.5, Union of Soviet Socialist Republics, German Democratic Republic, Hungarian People's Republic, Socialist Republic [of] Romania, People's Republic of Poland.
Prefatory material in Russian, German, English and French.
For each country lists: (1) published texts of the constitution, codes and laws in force, collections of laws in various subjects, and collections of court decisions; (2) legal journals, bibliographies, and dictionaries; (3) directory information on juridical research and teaching institutions. v.5 records additions and changes in the legal documentation system for countries covered in the first three volumes of the set.

Bibliography of translations of codes and other laws of private law. [2d ed.] Strasbourg, Council of Europe, 1975. 314p. **CK11**

In French, English, and German.
1st ed. 1967.
Chapters for each of 27 countries are subdivided into sections listing sources of translations (French, English, and German) relating to civil law, commercial law, civil procedure, and special

legislative texts. Limited to European countries, with the following exceptions: Brazil, the United States, Israel, Japan, Egypt, and Turkey.

Bibliography on foreign and comparative law; books and articles in English. N.Y., Parker School of Foreign and Comparative Law, Columbia Univ., 1955. 526p.   **CK12**

Charles Szladits, comp.

Lists some 14,000 books and periodical articles in English in the broad fields of foreign and comparative law. Does not include the Anglo-American legal systems. Classified, with indexes by authors and by geographic areas.

——— 1953–1959. Dobbs Ferry, N.Y., Oceana, 1962. 559p.

——— 1960–1965. Dobbs Ferry, N.Y., Oceana, 1968. 855p.

——— 1966–1971. Dobbs Ferry, N.Y., Oceana, 1975. 2v.

——— 1972–1977. Dobbs Ferry, N.Y., Oceana, 1981. 3v.

Annual supplements continue to be published.

Caes, Lucien and **Henrion, R.** Collectio bibliographica operum ad ius romanum pertinentium. Bruxelles, Office Internat. de Librairie, 1949–78. Ser.I, v.1–25; ser.II, v.1–2. (In progress)   **CK13**

Contents: Ser.I, Opera edita in periodicis miscellaneis encyclopaediisque, v.1–25 (1949–78); Index notarum cumulativus, v.1–20 (called Suppl.I); Index rerum cumulativus, v.11–20 (called Suppl.II); Ser.II, Theses: v.1, Theses Galliae (1800–1848) (publ. 1950); v.2, Theses Germaniae (1885–1958) (publ. 1960).

An extensive listing of scholarly articles in periodicals, collections, miscellanies, *Festschriften,* theses, etc., dating approximately from the mid-19th century. "Law" is broadly interpreted so that a substantial body of classical Latin literature is included. Arrangement of each volume is alphabetical by author, with a subject index.

Columbia University. Libraries. Law Library. Dictionary catalog. Boston, G. K. Hall, 1969. 28v.   **CK14**

Reproduction of the catalog cards for this collection of about 470,000 volumes.

——— ——— Supplement 1. Boston, 1973. 7v.

Includes additions to the collection for the period 1967–Fall 1972 (about 30,000 titles).

——— ——— Supplement 2. Boston, G. K. Hall, 1977. 4v.

Represents titles cataloged (and recataloged) from the middle of 1972 through 1975—more than 50,000 cards. This is to be the final supplement.

Dau, Helmut. Bibliographie juristischer Festschriften und Festschriftenbeiträge 1864–1944: Deutschland, Schweiz, Österreich. Berlin, Berlin Verlag, 1984. 567p.   **CK15**

——— Bibliographie juristischer Festschriften und Festschriftenbeiträge 1945–1961. . . . Karlsruhe, Müller, 1962. 166p.

——— Bibliographie juristischer Festschriften und Festschriftenbeiträge 1962–1966. . . . Bielefeld, K. Runge, 1967. 195p.

——— Bibliographie juristischer Festschriften und Festschriftenbeiträge 1967–1974. . . . Bielefeld, K. Runge, 1977. 546p.

——— Bibliographie juristischer Festschriften und Festschriftenbeiträge 1975–1979. . . . Berlin, Berlin-Verlag, [1981]. 638p.

These volumes provide subject and author approaches to the contents of commemorative volumes for the period 1864–1979. The 1864/1944 volume includes an index to all five volumes.

Dias, Reginald Walter Michael. Bibliography of jurisprudence. 3d ed. London, Butterworths, 1979. 453p.   **CK16**

1st ed. 1957.

An annotated bibliography of English-language sources, arranged by 22 subject chapters corresponding to the author's textbook *Jurisprudence.* Includes books, essays, and periodical articles. Author, case, and general subject index.   K201.D5

Elliston, Frederick and **Schaick, Jane van.** Legal ethics: an annotated bibliography and resource guide. Littleton, Colo., Rothman, 1984. 199p.   **CK17**

A topically arranged bibliography of English-language books and periodicals on lawyers' professional responsibility, roles, the legal business, the courts, and related materials on ethics, professional ethics, and the philosophy of law. Author index.   KF305.A1E43

Hamburg. Max-Planck-Institut für Ausländisches u. Internationales Privatrecht. Aufsatzdokumentation zur Privatrechtsvergleichung, Privatrechtsvereinheitlichung sowie zum internationalen Privatrecht und ausländischen Privatrecht. Eine Bibliographie der Jahre 1968–1972. Tübingen, Mohr (Siebeck), 1975. 1133p.   **CK18**

Hrsg. vom Max-Planck-Institut für ausländisches und internationales Privatrecht.

Added title page in English: *Bibliography of articles on comparative private law, unification of private law, and on private international law and foreign private law. A bibliography of the years 1968–1972.*

In German and English.

Lists about 9,600 articles from periodicals, *Festschriften* and other collected works in a detailed classification scheme within each of the four legal areas noted in the title. Indexed by author, geographic area, and subject. For a detailed review, *see International journal of law libraries,* 4:257–60 (Nov. 1976).

Harvard University. Law School. Library. Annual legal bibliography. 1960/61–81. Cambridge, Mass., 1962–81. Annual.   **CK19**

Includes a listing of monographs and articles received in the Harvard Law School Library, cumulating the items which appeared in the *Current legal bibliography* (below) with some additional material.

——— Current legal bibliography. v.1– , Oct. 1960– . Cambridge, Mass., 1960– . 9 times a yr.   **CK20**

Subtitle: A selected accessions list of books and articles received.

International Association of Legal Science. Catalogue des sources de documentation juridique dans le monde. A register of legal documentation in the world. 2d ed. rev. and enl. Prep. by the International Association of Legal Science and the International Committee for Social Sciences Documentation. [Paris], UNESCO, [1957]. 423p. (Documentation in the social sciences)   **CK21**

1st ed. 1953.

Under country lists codes, collections, constitutions, legal periodicals, centers of documentation, legal bibliographies, etc. Extent of information varies from country to country.

London. University. Institute of Advanced Legal Studies. Library. Catalogue of the Library of the Institute of Advanced Legal Studies. Boston, G. K. Hall, 1978. 6v.   **CK22**

Contents: v.1–3, Author catalogue; v.4–6, Subject catalogue.

A photographic reproduction of catalog cards representing the holdings—about 130,000 volumes, with the main emphasis on serial publications. The Library issues the *Index to foreign legal periodicals* (CK167), and receives about 2,200 serial titles on a current basis.   K40.L66

United Nations Library (Geneva, Switzerland). League of Nations & United Nations monthly list of selected articles; cumulative, 1920–1970: legal questions. Ed. by Norman S. Field. Dobbs Ferry, N.Y., Oceana, 1972. 2v.   **CK23**

Contents: v.1, Public international law, private international law; v.2, National law—countries.

A compilation arranged by subject and country in chronological order. Based on the card file used to compile the Library's *Liste mensuelle d'articles sélectionnés*.

Bibliography of bibliography

Howell, Margaret A. A bibliography of bibliographies of legal material. Woodbridge, printed by the New Jersey Appellate Print. Co., [1969]. 2v. (851p.) **CK24**

———— ———— Supplement 1969–1971. Woodbridge, [1972]. 444p.

Based on the collection at Rutgers—The State University Law Library in Newark. Employs an alphabetical subject arrangement, listing both separately published bibliographies and books, and periodicals containing bibliographies.

Lansky, Ralph. Handbuch der Bibliographien zum Recht der Entwicklungsländer. Handbook of bibliographies on law in the developing countries. Frankfurt am Main, Klostermann, [1981]. 621p. map. **CK25**

Prelim. ed. 1977.

In German, English, French and Spanish.

An annotated bibliography of about 1,450 bibliographies and other legal reference sources supplying bibliographic information on the law of developing countries. Classed first by region and country, then by date of publication. Works of special importance are marked with an asterisk. Indexed. K37.L36

U.S. Library of Congress. Law Library. Anglo-American legal bibliographies; an annotated guide by William L. Friend. Wash., Govt. Prt. Off., 1944. 166p. **CK26**

A historical survey of Anglo-American legal bibliography is followed by an alphabetical list of all types of legal bibliographical publications except "works devoted exclusively to American statutory materials, and library and publishers' catalogues."—*Pref.* Z881.U5

Current

See also CK20.

Bibliographic guide to law, 1975– . Boston, G. K. Hall, 1975– . Annual. **CK27**

Serves as a successor to the *Law book guide* (1969–74).

Includes all material cataloged by the Library of Congress within each year specified, in the subject areas of U.S. law, international law, international arbitration, treaties, and foreign law; all unclassified works assigned to the Law Library of the Library of Congress are also identified. Dictionary arrangement; accessible through main and added entries, title, series, and subjects. Includes full cataloging information. KF38.B52

Law books, 1876–1981: books and serials on law and its related subjects. N.Y., Bowker, [1981]. 4v. **CK28**

Contents: v.1–3, Books—Subject index; v.4, Books—Author and title indexes, Serials—Subject and title indexes, Publishers, Online database producers and vendors.

Citations to about 130,000 books and 4,000 serials titles drawn from the *American book publishing record* database, *National union catalog,* and MARC tapes. Excludes looseleafs, pamphlets, juvenile literature, and materials published by the U.S. Government Printing Office and the United Nations.

Updated by: KF1.L36

Bowker's Law books and serials in print, 1984/85– . N.Y., Bowker, [1984]– . Annual. **CK29**

Contents: v.1, Books—Subject index; v.2, Books—Author index; v.3, Books—Title index; Subject index to cataloged titles; Serials—Subject index, Title index; Publishers and distributors abbreviations.

Continues *Law information* (1982–83) and *Law information update* (1983–84).

Lists English-language legal materials drawn from the Bowker databases, MARC tapes, and the Government Printing Office Publications Reference File; includes some materials from foreign publishers.

Kept up to date by:

Bowker's Law books and serials in print update: materials on law and related topics recently published and to be published. v.2, no.2– , Feb. 1984– . N.Y., Bowker, [1984]– . 10 nos. per yr., with annual cumulation. **CK30**

Continues *Law information update* (Jan. 1983–Jan. 1984) and assumes its numbering. KF1.L392

Buckwalter, Robert L. ed. Law books in print: books in English published throughout the world and in print through 1981. 4th ed. Dobbs Ferry, N.Y., Glanville, [1982–83]. 6v. **CK31**

1st–3d eds. (1957/61–76) ed. by J. M. Jacobstein and M. G. Pimsleur.

Contents: v.1–2, Authors/titles; v.3–4, Subjects; v.5, Publishers' series; v.6, Publishers' price list.

With the 3d ed. new features include listings of new periodical titles which began publication in 1973 or later, and of reprints, microfilms, and cassettes. LC card numbers are indicated when available. Updated by: KF1.B82

Law books published. v.1– . Dobbs Ferry, N.Y., Glanville, 1969– . Quarterly. **CK32**

A quarterly record of books published in English during the year. The fourth quarterly issue is an annual cumulation. KF1.L38

National legal bibliography. Recent acquisitions of major legal libraries. v.1, no.1– , Jan. 1984– . Buffalo, N.Y., W. S. Hein, 1984– . Monthly. **CK33**

v.1, no.1–[6?] are reprints of *National legal bibliography* publ. in Arlington, Mass., by P. D. Ward.

Includes books, serials, government and other documents, theses and dissertations cataloged by about 15 university and public libraries. Broad topical arrangement (U.S. and general; international; foreign jurisdiction by country). K38.N36

Periodicals

Hein, William S., Marmion, Kevin M. and **Hein, Ilene N.** Hein's Legal periodical check list. Buffalo, N.Y., W. S. Hein, 1977– . 2v. Looseleaf. **CK34**

For each Anglo-American title listed in the June 1976 (v.69, no.9) issue of the *Index to legal periodicals,* the work correlates volume and issue number with appropriate date, and notes any misprints, title changes, issue variations, cumulative indexes available, current publishing address, etc. Alphabetical index notes all title changes. K36.H43

Legal newsletters in print, 1985– . N.Y., Infosources Pub., [1985]– . Annual. **CK35**

A directory of newsletters published in the United States, complementing Stern's *Legal looseleafs in print* (CK38). Title listing, with publisher and subject indexes. KF1.L45

Mersky, Roy M., Berring, Robert and **McCue, James K.** Author's guide to journals in law, criminal justice, & criminology. N.Y., Haworth Pr., [1979]. 243p. **CK36**

Arranged in four sections: (1) general law school law reviews; (2) specialized law school law reviews; (3) association publications; (4) commercial publications. Provides publication information on review period, publication lag time, acceptance rate, style requirements, reprint policy, copyright holder, author remuneration, etc. Indexed by subject, title, and keyword. K36.M47

Oxbridge Communications, Inc. Legal & law enforcement periodicals: a directory. N.Y., Facts on File, [1981]. 238p. **CK37**

3,800 periodicals published in the United States and Canada are listed in 50 subject categories. Some entries include brief descriptive note, indexing, advertising rates. Title index. Information is drawn from the database of the *Standard periodical directory* (AE37).

Stern, Arlene L. Legal looseleafs in print 1981– . N.Y., Infosources Publ., [1981]– . Annual.   **CK38**

A title listing of legal looseleafs published in the United States which are currently in print. Each entry provides title, publisher, year of original publication, number of volumes, price, frequency and annual cost of supplements. Detailed subject index.

KF1.S73

Wypyski, Eugene M. Legal periodicals in English. Dobbs Ferry, N.Y., Glanville, 1976–83. 5v. Looseleaf.   **CK39**

Includes all periodical titles currently or formerly indexed in the *Index to legal periodicals* and the *Index to legal periodical literature* (CK170, CK169), with cumulative title, subject, and geographical indexes.

For each title, reproduces Library of Congress printed card or "original" catalog card, with information on title, publishing address, frequency, variations in title, subjects treated, indexing source, reprint editions, where cited in "Shepard's Citations." Attempts to "expand and restructure" (*Pref.*) L. W. Morse's *Checklist of Anglo-American periodicals* (Dobbs Ferry, N.Y., Glanville, 1962).   K36.W96

United States

Dahl, Richard C. and **Bolden, C. E.** The American judge; a bibliography. Vienna, Va., Coiner, [1968]. 330p.   **CK40**

A classed bibliography (with an extensive section for biographical references) of more than 9,100 items in English, a limited number of them from foreign sources.   KF8775.A1D3

Gasaway, Laura N., Hoover, James L. and **Warden, Dorothy M.** American Indian legal materials: a union list. Stanfordville, N.Y., E. M. Coleman, 1980. 152p.   **CK41**

A main-entry listing of about 3,500 monographic, government document, and serial titles held by the libraries of 28 U.S. law schools, government agencies, and law firms. Indexed by subject, geographic area, and tribe.   KF8201.A1G37

Hood, Howard A. and **Padgett, Kathi L.** Affirmative action: an annotated bibliography of recent periodical literature. Nashville, Vanderbilt Law Lib., 1978. 71p.   **CK42**

A subject arrangement, with chapters on general considerations, higher education, employment, labor unions and seniority rights, housing, and women; two chapters deal with the special cases of *Bakke v. Regents of the University of California* and *Defunis v. Odegaard.*   KF4755.5.A1H66

Jacobstein, J. Myron and **Mersky, Roy M.** Water law bibliography, 1847–1965. Source book on U.S. water and irrigation studies: legal, economic and political. Silver Spring, Md., Jefferson Law Book Co., 1966. 249p.   **CK43**

Limited to material dealing specifically with the law (items on water pollution, for example, are not included). Lists both book and periodical materials. Indexed. Supplements covering 1966–77 were published 1969–78.   KF5551.J6

Klein, Fannie J. The administration of justice in the courts; a selected annotated bibliography. Dobbs Ferry, N.Y., Oceana, 1976. 2v. (1152p.)   **CK44**

Publ. for the Institute of Judicial Administration and National Center for State Courts.

Updates and expands the author's *Judicial administration and the legal profession* (1963).

Contents: v.1, The courts; v.2, The administration of criminal justice in the courts.

A classed bibliography of more than 5,000 items, dealing with court systems, the judge, the administration and operation of courts, the trial process, the appellate process, the criminal justice system, the criminal trial, sentencing procedures, etc. "Selected

bibliographies, guidebooks, and handbooks," p.939–79. Table of cases. Personal name and subject indexes.   KF8700.A1K39

The law in the United States of America; a selective bibliographical guide. By Joseph L. Andrews [and others]. N.Y., New York Univ. Pr., 1965. 100p.   **CK45**

At head of title: International Association of Law Libraries.

Intended for law librarians in countries other than the United States; lists important treatises, textbooks, and monographs, with very brief annotations. Omits periodicals. Gives full bibliographical information in a subject arrangement. No index.   KF1.A5

National Indian Law Library. Catalogue; an index to Indian legal materials and resources. v.1– , 1973/74– . [Boulder, Colo.], 1974– . Looseleaf.   **CK46**

Cumulative eds. issued at irregular intervals. Each cumulative ed. has four cumulative supplements.

Publ. with the Native American Rights Fund.

The 1982 cumulative ed. includes about 3,400 items relating to "tribal existence, protection of tribal resources, promotion of human rights, advancement of tribal self-determination; and to the accountability of the dominant society."—*Introd.* A subject section, plaintiff/defendant, defendant/plaintiff table, and author/title table refer user to the numerical listing where complete bibliographic and file contents information are given.   KF8201.A1N38

Pimsleur, Meira G. Checklists of basic American legal publications. Publ. for American Association of Law Libraries. South Hackensack, N.J., Rothman, 1962– . 3v. Looseleaf. (AALL pubn. no.4)   **CK47**

Sec.1 covers *State statutes, revisions, compilations,* and is "a revision and updating of Grace E. Macdonald's *Checklist of statutes of states of the United States of America* (1937)." Sec.2 covers the *Session laws of the various states of the United States,* and is a revision of Grace E. Macdonald's *Checklist of session laws* (1936). Sec.3 is a *Checklist of reports and opinions of the attorneys-general,* and is based on Lewis W. Morse's "Historical outline and bibliography of Attorneys General reports and opinions" in *Law library journal* 30, no.2:39–248 (1937). Sec. 4 (1974–) lists reports of state judicial councils and conferences. Sec. 5 (1976–) lists American Law Institute restatements of the law and codifications. Meira G. Pimsleur was editor 1962–78; the 1983 supplements were edited by Marcia J. Zubrow.

Ritz, Wilfred J. American judicial proceedings first printed before 1801: an analytical bibliography. Westport, Conn., Greenwood Pr., [1984]. xlviii, 364p.   **CK48**

Attempts to list "every law report, trial, or separate event of judicial significance occurring in or relating to what was the United States in 1801, and for which there was something *printed* prior to that date (other than a newspaper account)."—*p.xvii.* Arranged by geographical area and subject. Citations include library locations and references in early American imprints bibliographies and microform projects.   KF3.R57

Schwartz, Mortimer D. Environmental law: a guide to information sources. Detroit, Gale, 1977. 191p. (Man and the environment information guide ser., 6)   **CK49**

Includes English-language monographs, U.S. Congressional materials, proceedings, and periodical titles dealing with environmental law "as a field intended to protect, preserve, or rehabilitate the physical environment."—*Pref.* Three main sections cover: (1) The legal process; (2) Pollution control; and (3) Conservation of resources. Existing bibliographies are noted for each topic discussed. Annotations are brief. Author, title, and subject indexes.

KF3775.A1S35

Stephenson, D. Grier. The Supreme Court and the American Republic: an annotated bibliography. N.Y., Garland, 1981. 281p. (Garland reference library of social science, v.85)   **CK50**

A selective bibliography of books, periodical articles, court cases, and reference materials. Sections on research aids, origins and development, and constitutional development; also offers many references to general and individual biographical and autobiographical materials. Author and court case indexes.   KF8741.A1S75

Tompkins, Dorothy Campbell. Court organization and administration; a bibliography. Berkeley, Inst. of Governmental Studies, Univ. of California, 1973. 200p.   **CK51**

Lists monographs and articles on the organization and reorganization of United States courts and on various aspects of the administration of those courts, published since 1956. Does not include materials on the U.S. Supreme Court, juvenile, or traffic courts.   KF8700.A1T64

——— The Supreme Court of the United States; a bibliography. Berkeley, Bureau of Public Admin., Univ. of California, 1959. 217p.   **CK52**

Includes a wide selection of monographs, articles, speeches, reports, etc., most of which have appeared since 1930. Items are grouped under such headings as: Organization, Work of the Court, Justices. Some are annotated. Author index.

Women's annotated legal bibliography. [v.1]– . Benjamin N. Cardozo School of Law, Yeshiva Univ. N.Y., Clark Boardman, [1984]– . Irregular?   **CK53**

v.1 provides synopses of law journal articles and student works published during 1978–83 from over 150 journals. Includes references to cases and statutes. Topical arrangement.
    KF477.A1W635

Ziegenfuss, James T. Law, medicine & health care: a bibliography. N.Y., Facts on File, [1984]. 265p.   **CK54**

Focuses on English-language literature produced since 1974. Broad subject arrangement, without detailed subject or author access. Includes directories of relevant journals and law firms practicing in these fields.   KF3821.A1Z53

Individual states

❖There are available a number of useful bibliographic guides to research in the law of individual states of the United States, as well as state law reporters and looseleaf services noted in Cohen's *Legal research in a nutshell* (CK2).

Foster, Lynn and **Boast, Carol.** Subject compilations of state laws; research guide and annotated bibliography. Westport, Conn., Greenwood Pr., [1981]. 473p.   **CK55**

Pt.I is a brief research guide on how to compile or locate a subject compilation of state laws. Pt.II is an annotated bibliography of more than 1,200 treatises, reference books, journal articles, state and federal documents, looseleaf services, and cases published between 1960 and 1979 that contain compilations of state laws. Subject arrangement, with cross references. Author and publisher indexes.
    Continued by: KF1.F67

Nyberg, Cheryl and **Boast, Carol.** Subject compilations of state laws, 1979–1983: research guide and annotated bibliography. Westport, Conn., Greenwood Pr., [1984]. 556p.   **CK56**

In two parts: an update to the state statutory research guide offered in the Foster/Boast volume (above), and a research guide to state administrative regulations; a subject-arranged, annotated bibliography of 1,466 compilations of state statutes published 1979–83. Author index.   KF1.N93

Guide to state legislative materials. Ed. by Mary L. Fisher. Rev. ed. Littleton, Colo., Publ. for the American Assoc. of Law Libraries by F. B. Rothman, 1983. 1v. (looseleaf) (AALL pubn. ser., no.15)   **CK57**

1st ed. 1979.
For each state, American Samoa, Guam, Puerto Rico, the U.S. Virgin Islands, and the District of Columbia, provides data in standardized format on bills, hearings, legislative digests, committee reports, debates, journals, legislative manuals and directories, slip laws, session laws, codes, attorney general opinions, executive or-

ders, administrative regulations, state law guide, etc. Includes notes on availability, source, indexing.   KF1.G8

Africa

Vanderlinden, Jacques. African law bibliography. Bibliographie de droit africain. 1947–1966. Bruxelles, Presses Universitaires, [1972]. 471p.   **CK58**

Introductory matter in English and French.
Includes books, periodicals, and government and official reports. Classed arrangement, with country subdivisions within each topical subject section. Author index and index of subject headings. Kept up to date by supplements.
A similar bibliography for 1967–68 appeared in the *Annual survey of African law* (v.2, London, Cass, 1971).

——— ——— First supplement, 1977–1980. [1981]. 340p.

Canada

Boult, Reynald. A bibliography of Canadian law. Bibliographie du droit canadien. New ed. Ottawa, Canadian Law Information Council, 1977. 661p.   **CK59**

Prefatory matter in English and French.
1st ed. 1966.
More than 11,000 items (book and periodical materials) in classed arrangement with author index.

——— ——— 1st supplement. Ottawa, Canadian Law Information Council, 1982. 271p.

The Canadian abridgment, second edition. Index to Canadian legal literature. Gen. eds., Gary P. Rodrigues [and] Laurie Grant. Toronto, Carswell, 1981– . v.1–2. (In progress)   **CK60**

Contents: v.1, Administrative law—immigration; v.2, Income tax—workmen's compensation; v.3, Subject key, author index (not yet publ.).
A classified bibliography of books and articles on legal matters published in Canada since 1956. To be updated by releases containing material originally published in *Canadian current law*.
    KE1.C36

China

Cho, Sung Yoon. Japanese writings on Communist Chinese law, 1946–1974: a selected annotated bibliography. Wash., Lib. of Congress, 1977. 223p.   **CK61**

"Law" has been interpreted to include politics, economics, land reform, communes, and international relations. A subject-arranged bibliography of almost 1,100 monographs, articles, and translations; title is given in romanized Japanese with English translation. Brief, descriptive annotations. Author index.

Hsia, Tao-tai. Guide to selected legal sources of Mainland China; a listing of laws and regulations and periodical literature, with a brief survey of the administration of justice. Wash., Library of Congress, Far Eastern Law Div., 1967. 357p.   **CK62**

"This *Guide,* which has been compiled to meet the research needs of the Government and the academic community, consists mainly of two lists: laws and regulations, 1949–63, and articles related to legal matters selected from Communist Chinese periodicals."— *Pref.* Indexed.   Z663.5.G8C53

Lin, Fu-shun. Chinese law, past and present; a bibliography of enactments and commentaries in English text. N.Y., East Asian Institute, Columbia Univ., [1966]. 419p.   **CK63**

Covers only materials in English, whether originally written in English or translated from other languages, and includes studies, statutes, official documents, court decisions, etc. Title of the original and the source are provided for each translation. Special emphasis on the law and legal system of Communist China. Classed arrangement with author index.

Pinard, Jeanette L. The People's Republic of China: a bibliography of selected English-language legal materials. 1985 ed. Wash., Law Library, Library of Congress, [1985]. 108p.   **CK64**

1st ed. 1983.

Lists secondary materials and translations of Chinese laws within 26 subject categories, then by book or article form. Most items were published since 1972.

Denmark

Søndergaard, Jens Korslund. Dansk juridisk bibliografi, 1950–1971. København, Juristforbundet, 1973. 760p.   **CK65**

Contents and preface also in English.

Supplements Torben Lund's *Juridiske literaturhenvisninger* (1950). Arranged by form, then alphabetically, with subject and author indexes. Includes references to Søndergaard's periodical articles on Danish and Scandinavian legal literature in English.

Continued by:

—— Dansk juridisk bibliografi, 1972–1980. København, Juristforbundet, 1983. 420p.

Title, contents and preface also in English.

Europe, Eastern

Leideritz, Paula M. Key to the study of East European law. Deventer, Kluwer, 1978. 168p.   **CK66**

"Under the auspices of the Law Institute of the University of Amsterdam."

In two sections: (1) bibliography of bibliographies, which lists for each country of Eastern Europe and the Soviet Union the general, legal, and specialized legal bibliographies (both retrospective and current), official law gazettes, collections of laws and court decisions, journals of translations, and law dictionaries; (2) location guide for Dutch libraries holding Western and East European periodicals, and monographic series specializing in East European law.

Mid-European Law Project. Legal sources and bibliography [of various Middle European countries]. N.Y., publ. for Free Europe Committee by F. A. Praeger, 1956–64.   **CK67**

A series of publications sponsored by the Mid-European Law Project, under the general editorship of Vladimir Gsovski, on the legal sources and bibliography of the Middle European nations.

Contents: *Legal sources and bibliography of Bulgaria*, by Ivan Sipkov (1956); *Legal sources and bibliography of Czechoslovakia*, by Alois Bohmer [and others] (1959); *Legal sources and bibliography of Hungary*, by Alexander K. Bedo and George Torzsay-Biber (1956); *Legal sources and bibliography of Poland*, by Peter Siekanowicz (1964); *Legal sources and bibliography of Romania*, by Virgiliu Stoicoiu (1964); *Legal sources and bibliography of the Baltic states (Estonia, Latvia, Lithuania)*, by Johannes Klesment [and others] (1963); *Legal sources and bibliography of Yugoslavia*, by Fran Gjupanovich and Alexander Adamovitch (1964).

Europe, Western

See also names of individual countries.

Guide to foreign legal materials: Belgium, Luxembourg, Netherlands, by Paul Graulich [and others]. Dobbs Ferry, N.Y., Oceana, 1968. 258p. (Parker School studies in foreign and comparative law. Parker School guides to foreign law, v.3)   **CK68**

Similar to the guides for French, German, and Swiss law (below) and for Italian law (CK84). Cutoff date is 1965, with a few later imprints listed.

Szladits, Charles. Guide to foreign legal materials; French, German, Swiss. [N.Y.], Oceana, 1959. 599p.   **CK69**

At head of title: Parker School studies in foreign and comparative law.

Lists laws, reports, and books, arranged in three parts: (1) French law, (2) German law, and (3) Swiss law. Includes all branches of the law. A list of legal abbreviations is given at the end of each part.

France

Grandin, A. Bibliographie générale des sciences juridiques, politiques, économiques et sociales de 1800 à 1925/26. Paris, Recueil Sirey, 1926. 3v.   **CK70**

v.1–2, classified bibliography; v.3, indexes of authors, titles, and subjects.

—— —— 1.–19. supplément, 1926–50. Paris, Recueil Sirey, 1928–51. 19v.

For full description *see* CA17.   Z6458.F8G7

Germany

See also CK69.

Akademie für Staats- und Rechtswissenschaft der DDR. Bibliothek. Bibliographie rechtswissenschaftlicher Literatur der DDR, 1949–1973. Potsdam-Babelsberg, Informationszentrum Staat und Recht, 1975. 176p.   **CK71**

"Vorbereitet auf Anforderung der UNESCO unter der Schirmherrschaft der Internationalen Vereinigung für Rechtswissenschaft." —*t.p.*

A classed bibliography of German-language materials.

Updated by:

—— —— 1974–1976. Potsdam-Babelsberg, Die Akademie, 1979. 2v.

—— —— 1977–1979. Potsdam-Babelsberg, Informationszentrum Staat und Recht, 1981. 2v. in 1 (376p.).

An international bibliography, adding articles and dissertations to the earlier coverage of books.

Deutsche Rechtsbibliographie, 1982– . Hrsg. [von] Gesellschaft für Rechtsvergleichung. Baden-Baden, Nomos Verlagsgesellschaft, [1984]– . Annual.   **CK72**

An annual bibliography of all legal titles published in the Federal Republic of Germany, including dissertations. Topical arrangement; author, title, and subject indexes.

Gesellschaft für Rechtsvergleichung. Bibliographie des deutschen Rechts in englischer und deutscher Sprache; eine Auswahl. Mit einer Einführung in das deutsche Recht von Fritz Baur; übers. von Courtland H. Peterson. Karlsruhe, Müller, 1964. 584p.   **CK73**

Added title page in English: German Association of Comparative Law. Bibliography of German law in English and German.

A representative cross section of German legal literature. With a few exceptions, the bibliography is limited to books and periodicals published in Germany since 1918. Selected works published in, and important statutes enacted by, the German Democratic Republic are included. Introduction, notes, and explanatory matter in German and English. Author index and bilingual subject index.

Updated by supplements:

—— —— Ergänzungsband 1964–1968. Karlsruhe, Müller, 1969. 221p.

—— —— Ergänzungsband 1969–1973. Karlsruhe, Müller, 1975. 282p.

Lansky, Ralph. Grundliteratur Recht: Bundesrepublik Deutschland: eine Auswahl-Bibliographie. Basic literature on law: Federal Republic of Germany: selective bibliography. 3. Aufl. München, J. Schweitzer, 1984. 172p.   **CK74**

1st ed. 1974 publ. as *Arbeitshefte der Arbeitsgemeinschaft für juristisches Bibliotheks- und Dokumentationswesen*, no.1.

Cites 876 books on the law of West Germany and West Berlin, and books published there on general and international law.

Great Britain

Beale, Joseph Henry. Bibliography of early English law books. Cambridge, Harvard Univ. Pr., 1926. 304p. **CK75**

—— —— Supplement, comp. for the Ames Foundation, by R. B. Anderson. Cambridge, Harvard Univ. Pr., 1943. 50p.

Arranged under statutes, decisions, treaties, printers and their law books. Material is listed in chronological order dating from the late 15th to the end of the 16th century. An appendix locates copies in 25 libraries. The supplement includes revisions and corrections of the original volume and adds new material.   Z6458.G7B365

A legal bibliography of the British Commonwealth of Nations. 2d ed. London, Sweet & Maxwell, 1955–64. 7v.
     CK76

1st ed. (1925–49 in 7v.) had title *Sweet & Maxwell's Complete law book catalogue*.

Contents: v.1, English law to 1800, including Wales, the Channel Islands and the Isle of Man (1955); v.2, English law from 1801 to 1954, including Wales, the Channel Islands and the Isle of Man (1957); v.3, Canadian and British-American colonial law from earliest times to Dec. 1956 (1957); v.4, Irish law to 1956 (1957); v.5, Scottish law to 1956, together with a list of Roman law books in the English language (1957); v.6, Australia, New Zealand and their dependencies, from earliest times to June 1958, with lists of reports of cases, digests, and collections of statutes and rules (1958); v.7, The British Commonwealth, excluding the United Kingdom, Australia, New Zealand, Canada, India and Pakistan (1964).

v.1 lists books printed from 1480 to 1954, and contains indexes by subject, places, authors and titles. v.2–7 are arranged alphabetically by author or anonymous title, with subject index.

Raistrick, Donald. Lawyers' law books; a practical index to legal literature. 2d ed. [Abingdon, Oxon, Eng.], Professional Books, 1985. 604p.   **CK77**

1st ed. 1977.

A bibliography of United Kingdom legal literature. Under detailed subject headings, lists encyclopedic statutory references, specialized reports and journals, and books. Bibliographic information is as minimal as possible for correct identification. Author and short title index.   KD51.R33

United Kingdom National Committee of Comparative Law. A bibliographical guide to the law of the United Kingdom, the Channel Islands and the Isle of Man. 2d ed. Editor: A. G. Chloros. London, Univ. of London, Inst. of Advanced Legal Studies, 1973. 301p.   **CK78**

1st ed. 1956.

A selective bibliography designed to introduce English law to foreign lawyers. Arranged by subject, with short introductions, drawing attention to unique features of the English legal system.
     KD51.U5

Hungary

Nagy, Lajos. Bibliography of Hungarian legal literature, 1945–1965. Budapest, Akadémiai Kiadó, 1966. 315p.
     CK79

Prefatory articles and notes translated by I. Gombocz, K. Veredy, and M. Zehery.

Published by the Institute for Legal and Administrative Sciences of the Hungarian Academy of Sciences, under the auspices of the International Association of Legal Science and the International Committee for Social Science Documentation.

A selective, classified bibliography with author and subject indexes.

India

Jain, Hem Chandra. Indian legal materials: a bibliographical guide. Bombay, N. M. Tripathi Ltd.; Dobbs Ferry, N.Y., Oceana, 1970. 123p.   **CK80**

Intended to aid law librarians in other countries "in selecting the Indian legal materials necessary for a basic workable collection of law reports, texts, and treatises on Indian law."—*Pref.* Includes both current and older materials; recommendations for a minimum collection are starred. Subject index.

Supplemented by C. C. Shah's *Indian law 1974–75: a comprehensive catalogue . . .* (Bombay, Tripathi, 1974. 96p.).

Ireland

O'Higgins, Paul. A bibliography of periodical literature relating to Irish law. Belfast, Northern Ireland Legal Quarterly, 1966. 401p.   **CK81**

Nearly 5,000 articles from more than 130 periodicals. Subject arrangement with author and detailed subject indexes.

—— —— First supplement. [Belfast, No. Ireland Legal Quarterly], 1973. 149p.

Israel

Livneh, Ernst. Israel legal bibliography in European languages, with 1965 supplement. Jerusalem, Academon, 1965. 118p. (Jerusalem. Hebrew Univ. Faculty of Law. Inst. for Legislative Research and Comparative Law. Pubn. 7a)
     CK82

A classified bibliography with index.

Wegner, Judith Romney. A bibliography of Israel law, in English and other European languages. Jerusalem, Inst. for Legislative Research and Comparative Law, 1972. 124p. (Jerusalem. Hebrew Univ. Inst. for Legislative Research and Comparative Law. Pubn. 24)   **CK83**

A classed bibliography with author and subject indexes.

Italy

Grisoli, Angelo. Guide to foreign legal materials: Italian. Dobbs Ferry, N.Y., publ. for the Parker School of Foreign and Comparative Law, Columbia Univ., by Oceana, 1965. 272p. (Parker School studies in foreign and comparative law. Parker School guides to foreign law, v.2)   **CK84**

A bibliographical survey of Italian legal materials with a descriptive introduction and a list of the most frequently used legal abbreviations. The cutoff date for materials included is 1962. Indexed.

Japan

Coleman, Rex and **Haley, John.** An index to Japanese law: a bibliography of Western language materials, 1867–1973. [Tokyo, Univ. of Tokyo Pr.], 1975. 167p.   **CK85**

On cover: *Law in Japan; an annual*, special issue, 1975.

A classed bibliography of Western-language translations of Japanese legal materials, as well as secondary literature in book, pamphlet, and article form. No index. Updates Coleman's *Index to Japanese law 1867-1961* (Cambridge, Mass., 1961).

Latin America

See also AG158 and names of individual countries.

American Association of Law Libraries. Committee on Foreign and International Law. Basic Latin American legal materials, 1970–1975. Eds., Juan F. Aguilar [and] Armando E. Gonzalez. South Hackensack, N.J., Rothman, 1977. 106p. (AALL pubn. ser., 13)   **CK86**

Updates K. Wallach's *Union list of basic Latin American legal materials* (1971; below). Lists, by country: constitutions, major codes, laws in specific subject areas, and secondary monographs published 1971–75.

———— Union list of basic Latin American legal materials. Kate Wallach, ed. South Hackensack, N.J., Rothman, 1971. 64p. (AALL pubn. ser., 10)   **CK87**

Concerned with the "latest editions of the constitutions, codes, statutes on civil, commercial, criminal, labor, mining and petroleum laws, procedure, taxation and official gazettes."—*Introd.* Represents holdings of 64 libraries.

Bayitch, Stojan A. Latin America; a bibliographical guide to economy, history, law, politics, and society. Coral Gables, Fla., Univ. of Miami Pr., 1961. 335p. (Interamerican legal studies, no.6)   **CK88**

A list of books and articles drawn from approximately 400 periodicals. Contains only works in English with emphasis given to law and related topics, excluding international law and foreign relations. Includes a guide by subjects, a guide by countries, and an alphabetical subject index.

An expanded and updated edition with less emphasis on law was published 1967 (*see* DB225n).   Z1601.B34

Medina, Rubens and **Medina-Quiroga, Cecilia.** Nomenclature and hierarchy—basic Latin American legal sources. Wash., Lib. of Congress, 1979. 123p.   **CK89**

Identifies and explains the differences between similarly titled legal instruments from different countries. For each of 20 Central and South American and Caribbean countries (including Haiti), describes the various legal instruments and ranks them hierarchically. Bibliographic references.

Schuster, Edward. Guide to law and legal literature of Central American republics. N.Y., 1937. 153p. (American Foreign Law Assoc., Bibliographies of foreign law ser., no.11)   **CK90**

A bibliographic survey of the general, comparative and national legal literature of Costa Rica, Guatemala, Honduras, Nicaragua, Panama, and El Salvador. Indexed.   Z6458.A1A5 no.11

U.S. Library of Congress. Law Library. Guide[s] to the law and legal literature of [Latin American countries]. Wash., Lib. of Congress, 1943–48.   **CK91**

Published as numbers of its Latin American series as follows: no.3, Cuba, the Dominican Republic, and Haiti (1944); no.4, Colombia (1943); no.6, Mexico (1945; *see also* CK94); no.12, Bolivia (1947); no.13, Mexican states (1947); no.14, Paraguay (1947); no.16, Venezuela (1947); no.18, Ecuador (1947); no.20, Peru (1947; *see also* CK97); no.26, Uruguay (1947); no.28, Chile, 1917–46 (1947); no.32, Argentina, 1917–46 (1948).

———— Legal codes of the Latin American republics. Wash., Lib. of Congress, 1942. 95p. (Latin Amer. ser., no.1)   **CK92**

Includes Spanish and Portuguese translations of the English texts.

Villalón Galdames, Alberto. Bibliografía jurídica de América Latina, 1810–1965. [Santiago de Chile], Editorial Jurídica de Chile, 1969–84. v.1–2. (In progress; to be in 5v.)   **CK93**

"Precedida de una introducción al estudio: la bibliografía; las bibliografías universales y nacionales; las bibliografías por temas y, en especial, las bibliografías jurídicas; los índices periódicos de artículos; las bibliografías de bibliografías; los métodos de investi-

gación; la técnica bibliográfica; la mecanización; la cooperación internacional, y la situación actual de la bibliografía en América Latina."—*title page.*

Contents: v.1, Introducción; Argentina; Bolivia; v.2, Brazil, Colombia, Costa Rica, Cuba.

In v.1 the extensive introduction (p.1–216) is followed by the bibliographies for Argentina and Bolivia, each being a main-entry listing. A separate volume (320p.) of "Indices provisorios del tomo I" provides subject approaches, etc. Successive volumes will provide bibliographies of the other Latin American countries in alphabetical order. The final volume will be a general index for the set.   KG1.V54

Mexico

Clagett, Helen Lord and **Valderama, David M.** A revised guide to the law and legal literature of Mexico. Wash., Lib. of Congress, 1973. 463p. (Latin American ser., no. 38)   **CK94**

1945 ed. by John T. Vance and Helen L. Clagett had title *A guide to the law and legal literature of Mexico* (CK91).

Includes chapters on constitutional, civil, commercial, criminal, and administrative law, civil procedure, criminal procedure, the judicial system, land laws, aliens, public finance and taxation, social legislation, etc., with additional sections for general works, indexes to legislation, court reports and digests, legal periodicals, legal dictionaries and encyclopedias. Bibliographic footnotes throughout; index.

New Zealand

Northey, John Frederick. Index to New Zealand legal writing. 2d ed. Auckland, Legal Research Foundation, 1982. 260p.   **CK95**

1st ed. 1977.

A classed bibliography of New Zealand legal literature published between 1954 and 1981. In two parts: books, articles, theses and dissertations; case notes.

Nigeria

Jegede, Oluremi. Nigerian legal bibliography: a classified list of legal materials related to Nigeria. 2d ed. Dobbs Ferry, N.Y., Publ. for the Nigerian Institute of Advanced Legal Studies, Lagos, by Oceana, [1983]. 332p.   **CK96**

1st ed. 1975.

About 2,000 citations. Broad subject arrangement subdivided by form: law texts, official reports, books, articles, and dissertations. Personal name index.

Peru

Valderrama, David M. Law & legal literature of Peru: a revised guide. Wash., Library of Congress, 1976. 296p.   **CK97**

Original ed. by H. L. Clagett publ. as *A guide to the law and legal literature of Peru* (CK91).

A major revision, representing a reorganization of the contents, updating of previous entries, and addition of new topics such as Indians, agrarian reform, territorial waters, etc. Covers legislative history from 1821 to 1972.

Sweden

Regner, Nils Ivan. Svensk juridisk litteratur. Stockholm, Norstedt, [1957–84]. v.1–4. (Institutet for Rattsvetenskaplig Forskning. [Skrifter] 16, 61, 100, 120, etc.)   **CK98**

A topically arranged bibliography, presently covering the 1865–

1982 period. International in scope, with emphasis on Scandinavian writings. Name index.

Switzerland

See also CK69.

Müller, Alfred. Bibliographie des schweizerischen Rechts. Bibliographie juridique suisse, 1970– . Basel, Helbing & Lichtenhahn, 1970– . Annual. **CK99**

A classed bibliography with author index. Originally issued as unnumbered supplements to *Zeitschrift für schweizerisches Recht.*

Turkey

Oehring, Otmar. Bibliographie zum türkischen Recht und den internationalen Beziehungen der Türkischen Republik. Titel in Fremdsprachen. Berlin, K. Schwarz, 1982. 233p. (Islamkundliche Materialien, Bd. 8) **CK100**

2,727 citations in classed arrangement; name index.

Union of Soviet Socialist Republics

See also AG188.

Butler, William Elliott. Russian and Soviet law: an annotated catalogue of reference works, legislation, court reports, serials, and monographs on Russian and Soviet law (including international law). Zug, Switz., InterDocumentation, [1976]. 122p. (Bibliotheca slavica, 8) **CK101**

Serves as the catalog of the publisher's microfiche collection of more than 1,100 titles. Within sections on Russian, Soviet, foreign, and international law, entries are arranged by form (reference works, legislation, periodicals, official gazettes, etc.), and then by subject if appropriate. "The collection does not aspire to 'completeness' nor to the inclusion of 'basic' materials; its object is to supply at modest cost whatever legal materials in this field scholars or libraries deem desirable or advisable to have available."—*Introd.*

———— Writings on Soviet law and Soviet international law; a bibliography of books and articles published since 1917 in languages other than East European. Cambridge, Mass., 1966. 165p. **CK102**

At head of title: Harvard Law School Library.

Books, pamphlets, dissertations, and periodical articles are arranged by subject under four main headings: (1) reference works; (2) Soviet legal system; (3) private international law; and (4) public international law. Author and subject indexes. (Excludes German-language literature on Soviet law published in the German Democratic Republic.)

Harvard University. Law School. Library. Soviet legal bibliography. Vaclav Mostecky and William E. Butler, eds. Cambridge, Mass., 1965. 288p. **CK103**

Subtitle: A classified and annotated listing of books and serials published in the Soviet Union since 1917 as represented in the collection of the Harvard Law School Library as of Jan. 1, 1965.

The classification closely follows the scheme of the *Annual legal bibliography* (CK19); there are author and analytical subject indexes. Soviet works on individual countries other than those of the USSR are not included. Entries are given in transliteration, and an English translation of the title is also provided. Annotations are meant to indicate the precise subject matter of the book; critical assessments are avoided.

Hazard, John Newbold and **Stern, William B.** Bibliography of the principal materials on Soviet law. N.Y., Foreign and Internat. Book Co., 1945. 46p. (American Foreign Law Assoc. Bibliographies of foreign law ser., no.12) **CK104**

Bibliography of the principal materials on Soviet law published in

the English, French, German, and Russian languages to Dec. 31, 1943.

Hazard, John Newbold, Butler, William E. and **Maggs, Peter B.** The Soviet legal system; fundamental principles and historical commentary. 3d ed. Dobbs Ferry, N.Y., Oceana, 1977. 621p. (Parker School studies in foreign and comparative law) **CK105**

1st ed. 1962.

In three main parts: (1) The Soviet state and its citizens; (2) Administering Soviet socialism; and (3) Private legal rights and obligations of Soviet citizens. In addition to the commentary and documentation, there is a bibliography of "Selected readings," p.561–74.

A companion volume, *The Soviet legal system; selected contemporary legislation and documents* (Dobbs Ferry, N.Y., Oceana, 1978. 733p.) contains the texts of most of the documents referred to, or excerpted, in the Hazard work.

Dictionaries

Ballentine, James Arthur. Ballentine's Law dictionary with pronunciations. 3d ed., ed. by William S. Anderson. Rochester, N.Y., Lawyers Co-operative Pub. Co., 1969. 1429p. **CK106**

1930 and 1948 editions had title *Law dictionary with pronunciations.*
About 30,000 terms. KF156.B3

Black, Henry Campbell. Black's Law dictionary; definitions of the terms and phrases of American and English jurisprudence, ancient and modern, with guide to pronunciation. 5th ed., by the publisher's editorial staff. St. Paul, Minn., West Pub. Co., 1979. 1511p. **CK107**

1st ed., 1891, had title *A dictionary of law.*
This comprehensive work is the standard law dictionary for ready reference. An abridged edition was published 1983. KF156.B53

Bouvier, John. Bouvier's Law dictionary and concise encyclopedia. 3d revision (being the 8th ed.) by Francis Rawle. Kansas City, Mo., Vernon; St. Paul, Minn., West Pub. Co., 1914. 3v. **CK108**

First published in 1839 and long regarded as the authoritative American legal dictionary; has gone through many printings. Now out-of-date but useful for obsolete terms.

Various revised and condensed editions have been issued for student use.

Burton, William C. Legal thesaurus. N.Y., Macmillan; London, Collier Macmillan, [1980]. 1058p. **CK109**

Alphabetically arranged entries provide very brief definitions (in the case of multiple meanings), parts of speech, synonyms, associated legal concepts in their full format, and foreign phrases and translations. Indexed. KF156.B856

A concise dictionary of law. [Oxford & N.Y.], Oxford Univ. Pr., 1983. 394p. **CK110**

A dictionary of English law; about 1,500 entries. Compiled by lawyers for use by laypersons. KD313.C66

Curzon, Leslie B. A dictionary of law. 2d ed. [Estover, Eng.], Macdonald and Evan, [1983]. 405p. **CK111**

Offers very brief definitions of English legal terms, with references to legal literature, statutes, and cases. KD313.C87

Egbert, Lawrence Deems and **Morales-Macedo, Fernando.** Multilingual law dictionary: English-Français-Español-Deutsch. Alphen aan den Rijn, Sijthoff; Dobbs Ferry, N.Y., Oceana; Baden-Baden, Nomos, 1978. 551p. **CK112**

For English legal terms and phrases, provides equivalents in French, German and Spanish, with indexes from each of those languages. Appendixes: (1) list of brief definitions of English legal terms and phrases; (2) bibliography of law dictionaries; (3) selective guide to legal literature; (4) list of member countries of the United Nations, and a list of U.N. organs and related agencies.   K54.E3

The encyclopedia of words and phrases, legal maxims: Canada 1825 to 1978. 3d ed. Gen. ed., Gerald D. Sanagan. Toronto, R. De Boo, [1979]. 4v.   **CK113**

1st ed. 1940.

A dictionary which attempts "to extract from Canadian judicial decisions . . . all material shedding light on the meaning of words and phrases, both legal and otherwise."—*Introd.* References to cases and decisions are provided, with notation indicating national or provincial courts.   KE180.E5

Gifis, Steven H. Law dictionary. 2d ed. Woodbury, N.Y., Barron's Educational Ser., [1984]. 618p. il., map.   **CK114**

1st ed. 1975.

Intended as a ready reference source in paperback for the student. More than 3,000 terms are defined, many with relevant legal citations. Pronunciation indicated for Latin and French terms. Appendixes provide American Bar Association Code (1969) and Rules (1983).   KF156.G53

Jowitt, William Allen Jowitt, *1st Earl.* The dictionary of English law. 2d ed. by John Burke. London, Sweet & Maxwell, 1977. 2v. (1935p.)   **CK115**

1st ed. 1959.

Changes in this edition reflect the exclusion of Scottish legal terms, reorganization of the court system, remodelling of local and central government, etc. A first supplement was published 1981.
KD313.J6

Le Docte, Edgard. Dictionnaire des termes juridiques en quatre langues. Viertalig juridisch woordenboek. Legal dictionary in four languages. 3e (bewerkte en vermeerderde) druk. London, Sweet & Maxwell, [1982]. 758p. diagrs.
CK116

For about 12,000 French legal terms the Dutch, English, and German equivalents are given, with indexes from those languages.
K54.L4

Legal secretary's encyclopedic dictionary. 3d ed. Rev. by Mary A. DeVries. Englewood Cliffs, N.J., Prentice-Hall, [1982]. 445p. il.   **CK117**

"By the Prentice-Hall Editorial Staff."—*t.p.*
1st ed. 1962.

An alphabetical dictionary of terms, situations, procedures, and sample forms with which the legal secretary will need to be familiar.
KF319.L36

Oran, Daniel. Oran's Dictionary of the law. St. Paul, West Pub. Co., [1983]. 500p. il., maps.   **CK118**

A basic dictionary, with standard pronunciation indicated for foreign terms. Appendix provides a brief guide to legal research.
KF156.O69

Redden, Kenneth R. and **Veron, Enid L.** Modern legal glossary. Charlottesville, Va., Michie Co., [1980]. 576p.
CK119

A dictionary "devoted exclusively to a definition of legal terms and related concepts, both old and new" (*Pref.*), as well as professional associations, government agencies, international organizations, foreign expressions, popular names of cases and statutes, trials, ancient codes, and biographies.   KF156.R43

Stroud, Frederick. Stroud's Judicial dictionary of words and phrases. 4th ed., by John S. James. London, Sweet & Maxwell, 1971–74. 5v.   **CK120**

1st ed. 1890.

Not a law lexicon but a "dictionary of the English language . . . so far as that language has received interpretation by the Judges."—*Pref.*   KD313.S77

Foreign terms

See also CK116.

Belgian

Wilkin, Robert. Dictionnaire du droit public. Bruxelles, E. Bruylant, 1963. 419p.   **CK121**

Gives long explanations of terms according to Belgian legal usage.

Chinese

Bilancia, Philip R. Dictionary of Chinese law and government: Chinese-English. Stanford, Stanford Univ. Pr., 1981. 822p.   **CK122**

About 25,000 legal and governmental terms used in the People's Republic of China and in the Chinese Soviet areas are entered under their Wade-Giles romanized equivalents. Each main entry consists of the romanized term, the simplified or traditional Chinese characters, pronunciation guide, definitions, cross references, and examples of usage. Transliteration conversion tables for Pinyin, Wade-Giles and other systems are provided, as well as a radical index.
KQK.B59

French

Dictionnaire juridique; nouveau Dictionnaire Th. A. Quemner: français-anglais: administration, assurances, bourse, commerce, douanes, droit, économie, exportation, finances et fiscalité. Jean Baleyte [et al.]. Paris, Ed. de Navarre, [1977]. 311p., 415p.   **CK123**

In two parts: v.1, Français-anglais; v.2, Anglais-français. First published 1953–55 in 2v.

Sprudzs, Adolf, comp. Foreign law abbreviations: French. Dobbs Ferry, N.Y., Oceana, 1967. 103p.   **CK124**

A dictionary of abbreviations and symbols used in contemporary French legal writing.

German

Dietl, Clara-Erika, Moss, Anneliese A. and **Lorenz, Egon.** Wörterbuch für Recht, Wirtschaft und Politik: mit erläuternden und rechtsvergleichenden Kommentaren. 3., völlig neubearb. und erw. Aufl. des von Gerhard Erdsiek und Clara-Erika Dietl begründeten "Erdsiek-Dietl." München, Beck; N.Y., Bender, 1985– . v.1– . (In progress)   **CK125**

Added title page: Dictionary of legal, commercial and political terms.
Contents: T.1, Englisch-Deutsch.
1st ed. 1964.
A major German dictionary, particularly important for terms, phrases, agreements and organizations in international law.
K52.G4D54

Jacobs, Barbara. Law dictionary; technical dictionary of the Anglo-American legal terminology. German-English. 3., completely new and rev. ed. Berlin and N.Y., W. de Gruyter, 1971. 385p.   **CK126**

At head of title: v. Beseler-Jacobs.
Added title page in German.
Previous ed. (1947) by Dora H. von Beseler had title: *An English-German and German-English pocket dictionary of law and business terminology.*

Kirchner, Hildebert and **Kastner, Fritz.** Abkürzungsverzeichnis der Rechtssprache. 3., erneuerte u. erw. Aufl. Berlin, W. de Gruyter, 1983. 412p.   **CK127**

1st ed. 1957.

Schlegelberger, Franz. Rechtsvergleichendes Handwörterbuch für das Zivil- und Handelsrecht des In- und Auslandes. Berlin, Vahlen, 1927–40. v.1–7, pts.1–3. **CK128**

Contents: v.1, Länderberichte; v.2–7³, A–Vermächtnis.

Encyclopedic dictionary of civil and commercial legal terms in various countries of the world with long, signed articles including bibliographies. v.1 treats the legal system of each country; v.2–7 give definitions of terms in alphabetic arrangement.

Italian

Fusi, Maurizio. Dizionario legale ad uso delli aziende, dei dirigenti e dei professionisti, con tavole sinottiche delle disposizioni fiscali. Milano, F. Angeli, [1960]. 593p. (Manuali Franco Angeli, editore, 3) **CK129**

Sprudzs, Adolf. Italian abbreviations and symbols: law and related subjects. Dobbs Ferry, N.Y., Oceana, 1969. 124p. **CK130**

About 2,600 abbreviations and symbols with expansion.

Japanese

Ito, Jujiro. A Japanese-English dictionary of legal terms with supplement. Tokyo, Daigaku Shobo, [1952]. 896p., 346p. **CK131**

Gives equivalents of the various meanings which may be attached to legal words and phrases, with many examples from actual laws, citing sources.

Latin

Berger, Adolf. Encyclopedic dictionary of Roman law. Philadelphia, Amer. Philosophical Soc., 1953. 303–809p. (Transactions of the American Philosophical Society, n.s. 43, pt.2, 1953) **CK132**

Purpose is "to explain technical Roman legal terms, to translate and elucidate those Latin words which have a specific connotation when used in a juristic context or in connection with a legal institution or question, and to provide a brief picture of Roman legal institutions and sources. . . ."—*Introd.*

Includes references to sources and to bibliographies. The main alphabet is followed by an English-Latin glossary, and a general bibliography, p.786–808.

Latin for lawyers. 3d ed. London, Sweet & Maxwell, 1960. 287p. **CK133**

1st ed. 1915.

Contains: (1) A course in Latin, with legal maxims and phrases as a basis of instruction; (2) A collection of over 1,000 Latin maxims, with English translations, explanatory notes, and cross references; (3) Vocabulary of Latin words.

Russian

Prischepenko, Nicholas P. Russian-English law dictionary. Completed and ed. by the New York University School of Law. N.Y., Praeger, [1969]. 146p. **CK134**

About 9,700 Russian terms with English equivalents.

Telberg, Ina. Soviet-English dictionary of legal terms and concepts. N.Y., Telberg, [1961]. 111p. **CK135**

Contains approximately 590 Russian terms with definitions in English. Terms are from constitutional and administrative, civil and procedural, housing, land, family, labor, criminal, and finance law.

Spanish

Fernández de León, Gonzalo. Diccionario jurídico. Buenos Aires, V. P. de Zavalía, 1955. 343p. **CK136**

Latin-American usage. Gives long definitions, usually followed by citations.

Robb, Louis Adams. Dictionary of legal terms, Spanish-English and English-Spanish. N.Y., Wiley, [1955]. 228p. **CK137**

Added title page and preface in Spanish.

A dictionary of equivalents: "definitions are given only when there is no equivalent or occasionally for a term that is somewhat unfamiliar."—*Pref.*

Tejada y Sainz, Juan de Dios. Spanish and English legal and commercial dictionary. A revision and enlargement of the Law translator's reference glossary. Santa María del Rosario, Cuba, Ed. Var-I-Tek, 1945. 158p. **CK138**

Subtitle: Contains over 10,000 terms . . . pertinent to: canon, civil, commercial, international, municipal and penal law; transportation, accounting, banking and finance; insurance, metrology; and numerous abbreviations.

Contents: pt.1, English-Spanish; pt.2, Spanish-English.

Encyclopedias

American jurisprudence; a modern comprehensive text statement of American law, state and federal. 2d ed. Compl. rev. and rewritten . . . by the editorial staff of the publishers. Rochester, N.Y., Lawyers Co-operative; San Francisco, Bancroft-Whitney, 1962–76. 82v. **CK139**

1st ed. 1936–62.
Kept up-to-date by supplements.
Each volume has subject index.

——— General index. Rochester, N.Y., 1977–78. 8v.

——— Desk book: historical and legal documents, facts, tables, charts, and statistics of special interest to attorneys. By the editorial staff of the publishers. Rochester, N.Y., Lawyers Co-operative; San Francisco, Bancroft-Whitney, 1979. 848p.

Pocket supplements issued from time to time.
A useful handbook for ready reference.

——— New topic service. Rochester, N.Y., Lawyers Co-operative; San Francisco, Bancroft-Whitney, 1973– .

Introduces material on rapidly changing or new topics; issued in pamphlet form or bound volumes, which are further supplemented by annual cumulative pamphlets (e.g., *New topic service: Federal rules of evidence.* 1975. 585p.; kept up-to-date by supplements).

——— Table of statutes and rules cited. N.Y., Lawyers Cooperative; San Francisco, Bancroft-Whitney, 1977. 384p.

KF154.A42

Australian and New Zealand commentary on Halsbury's Laws of England. 4th ed. Sydney, Butterworths, 1974– . Looseleaf. (In progress; to be in 18v.) **CK140**

Sir Garfield Barwick, ed. in chief.

Intended to "provide a concise and comprehensive statement of Australian and New Zealand Law on all those topics dealt with in Halsbury which have relevance to Australia or New Zealand" (*Pref.*) as a foundation for an encyclopedic text and counterpart to *Halsbury's Laws* for those countries. Published in chapters (pts. A–I issued to date) corresponding to the Titles in Halsbury, with paragraphs keyed to equivalent paragraphs. Each chapter is written by a specialist, with numerous citations to statute and case law.

Congressional Quarterly, Inc. Congressional Quarterly's Guide to the U.S. Supreme Court. [Wash., Congressional Quarterly, 1979] 1022p. **CK141**

The first five sections survey the origins and development of the court, its relationships with the federal system, the individual, and various "pressure groups." Pt.6 contains a survey of its membership, with brief biographies, and pt.7 consists of capsule summaries of major decisions. Appendix of relevant documents. Subject and case indexes.　　　　JK1571.C65

Corpus juris secundum; a complete restatement of the entire American law as developed by all reported cases, by William Mack and Donald J. Kiser, assisted by the combined editorial staffs of the American Law Book Co. and West Publishing Co. Brooklyn, N.Y., Amer. Law Book Co., 1936–83. 101v. in 146.　　　　**CK142**

Cited as *CJS.*

A new edition, superseding *Corpus juris (CJ)*, 1914–37, 72v. However, case citations refer to decisions handed down since the publication of *CJ*. For earlier authorities a specific reference to *CJ* cites all cases back to 1658. This makes the original work still valuable.

Kept up-to-date by cumulative annual parts and recompiled volumes.　　　　KF154.C56

———— General index. [1981] 5v.

Encyclopedia of Soviet law. Ed. by F. J. Feldbrugge, G. P. van den Berg and William B. Simons. 2d rev. ed. Dordrecht & Boston, Nijhoff, 1985. 964p. (Law in Eastern Europe, 28)　　　　**CK143**

1st ed. 1973.

Articles in A–Z arrangement with topical headings based on those used in the *Index to foreign legal periodicals* and corresponding Russian lists. Articles are signed; some of them include brief bibliographical notes.

Encyclopédie juridique de l'Afrique. [Abidjan], Nouvelles Éditions Africaines, [1982]. 10v. il., map.　　　　**CK144**

A legal encyclopedia for the countries of Francophone sub-Saharan Africa: Benin, Burundi, Cameroon, Central African Republic, Congo, Ivory Coast, Gabon, Guinea, Upper Volta, Mali, Mauritania, Niger, Rwanda, Senegal, Chad, Togo, and Zaire. Lengthy topical articles with bibliographical references.

The guide to American law: everyone's legal encyclopedia. St. Paul, Minn., West Pub. Co., [1983–84]. v.1–8. il. (In progress)　　　　**CK145**

Contents: v.1–8, Abortion–Remedy.

When complete in 12v., this set will offer a non-technical legal encyclopedia consisting of more than 4,600 entries and 420 major signed articles. Entries deal with legal principles and concepts, trial accounts, landmark documents, historical events, major deceased figures, legal organizations, federal departments and regulatory agencies, legal quotations, etc. Case and statutory citations are both to official reporters and those published by West. Volume appendixes provide tables of cited cases and popular name acts; the appendix for v.11 will give texts of important legal documents as well as sample legal forms. Each volume has topical lists of articles on American and British legal history, international law, jurisprudence, legal education, and legal organization. Separate indexes for quotations (speaker and topic), illustrations, names, and subjects in each volume.　　　　KF156.G77

Halsbury's Laws of England. 4th ed. London, Butterworth, 1973–84. v.1–50. (In progress)　　　　**CK146**

1st ed. (1901–17) had title *The laws of England.*

An encyclopedia of English law. Cumulative interim indexes are issued after every tenth volume; the master index will be the final two volumes of the set. Kept up-to-date by a monthly service and an annual cumulative supplement. An added feature is the *Monthly review,* which offers digests of reports and statutes, notices of white papers and similar documents, and references to articles published on legal topics; these are consolidated each year in the *Annual abridgment,* thus providing an annual record of the development of English law.　　　　KD310.H34

———— Index to volumes 1–42. London, Butterworth, 1984. 2v.

International encyclopaedia for labour law and industrial relations. Ed. in chief, R. Blanpain. Deventer, Neth., Klu-

wer, 1977–[81]. v.1–8. Looseleaf. ports. (In progress; to be in 10v.)　　　　**CK147**

Intended to provide surveys of the laws and systems governing individual workers and collective organizations for each country of the world, as well as for regional organizations such as the European Communities. Includes bibliographies and indexes. About six countries have been covered each year since 1977.　　　　K1705.I5

International encyclopedia of comparative law. Tübingen, Mohr (Siebeck); The Hague, Mouton, 1971– . v.1– . (In progress)　　　　**CK148**

Prep. under the auspices of the International Assoc. of Legal Science.

Contents: v.1, National reports, V. Knapp, ed.; v.2, The Legal systems of the world, D. René, ed.; v.3, Private international law, K. Lipstein, ed.; v.4, Persons and family, M. Rheinstein, ed.; v.5, Succession, K. H. Neumayer, ed.; v.6, Property and trust, F. H. Lawson, ed.; v.7, Contracts in general, A. T. von Mehren, ed.; v.8, Specific contracts, K. Zweigert, ed.; v.9, Letters of credit, B. Kozolchyk, ed.; v.10, Quasi-contracts, E. von Caemmerer, ed.; v.11, Torts, A. Tunc, ed.; v.12, Law of transport, R. Rodière, ed.; v.13, Business and private organizations, A. Conard, ed.; v.14, Copyright and industrial property, E. Ulmer, ed.; v.15, Labour law, O. Kahn-Freund, ed.; v.16, Civil procedure, M. Cappelletti, ed.; v.17, State and economy, B. T. Blagojevic, ed.

A major enterprise, intended to be complete in about 17,000 pages. Chapters in each volume are being issued in fascicles; v.1 will incorporate a detailed description of the legal system of about 140 nations; the remaining 16v. will offer comparative analyses of the main issues in civil and commercial law throughout the world. Each section is by an individual scholar, and is provided with extensive footnotes and bibliography.　　　　K530.I57

Modern legal systems cyclopedia. Gen. ed., Kenneth Robert Redden. Buffalo, N.Y., W.S. Hein, 1984–85. v.1–5. Looseleaf. (In progress)　　　　**CK149**

Contents: v.1, North America; v.2, Pacific basin; v.3, Western Europe (A): E.E.C. countries; v.4, Western Europe (B): Non-E.E.C. countries; v.5, Middle East. (To be in 10v.)

Intended to cover each of the legal systems of the world, including legal education, governmental systems, substantive and procedural law. Each volume is in two parts: country and general studies; annotated bibliographies for each chapter are to be updated by annual supplements.　　　　K530.M62

Reader's Digest family legal guide: a complete encyclopedia of law for the layman. Pleasantville, N.Y., Reader's Digest Assoc., [1981]. 1x, 1268p.　　　　**CK150**

Presents 2,600 articles of varying length, with illustrative brief case histories and highlight summaries for the longer articles. 34 charts and tables outline comparative laws of all states and the District of Columbia. 17 special articles on practical aspects of common legal situations. Numerous cross references; index.　　　　KF387.R4

Handbooks

See also EK207–EK208, EK210.

Alexander, Shana. Shana Alexander's State-by-state guide to women's legal rights. Barbara Brudno, legal consultant. Los Angeles, Wollstonecraft, distr. by Price/Stern/Sloan Publishers, [1975]. 224p.　　　　**CK151**

Marriage, children, adoption, abortion, divorce, rape, widowhood, work, crime, and legal age are covered in chapters with introductory essays and state-by-state summaries of the legal situation. Glossary.　　　　KF478.Z95A4

Environment regulation handbook. N.Y., Environment Information Center, 1973– . 3v. Looseleaf. il., maps.　　　　**CK152**

Arranged by subject—air pollution, land use, mobile sources, National Environmental Policy Act, etc. Each section has an introductory summary of relevant laws, regulations, and court decisions; this is followed by the texts of important laws, federal regulations, notices, policy guides, etc. Subject index. Although most sources are federal in origin, some chapters have summaries of state laws, and these laws pertaining to specific or local jurisdictions can be ordered from the publisher.

Kept up to date by monthly supplements. KF3775.A6E47

Environmental legislation: a sourcebook. Ed. by Mary Robinson Sive. N.Y., Praeger, 1976. 561p. **CK153**

Provides "a sampling of environmental laws at the federal and state levels, plus some state constitutional provisions, presidential executive orders, and administrative regulations."—*Introd.* Legislative excerpts are grouped in subject chapters, with brief introductions; criteria for inclusion are: (1) in force as of 1975; (2) historically significant; (3) have stringent requirements and sanctions; (4) regulate rather than simply promote study. Appendixes include: directory of organizations, government agencies, and public interest law firms; brief discussion on finding the law; index to legal excerpts by title and detailed subject; bibliography. KF3775.E54

Klein, Fannie J. Federal and state court systems—a guide. Cambridge, Mass., Ballinger, [1977]. 303p. **CK154**

Publ. for the Institute of Judicial Administration.

Presents chapters on the structure, personnel, internal operation, and administration of state and federal courts, including grand and petit jury and a detailed discussion of the court system in nine states. An appendix by Edward Bander gives a brief review of basic legal research sources. Glossary; index. KF8700.K6

Lawyer's desk book. 8th ed. Englewood Cliffs, N.J., Institute for Business Planning, 1985. 660p. **CK155**

1st ed. 1967.

A quick reference handbook and practical overview of those areas with which a lawyer most frequently deals. Comprehensive tables, charts, and directory information are provided in the appendix. Indexed. KF386.L39

Robinson, Joan. An American legal almanac. Law in all states: summary and update. Dobbs Ferry, N.Y., Oceana, 1978. 439p. charts. **CK157**

A popular statement of contemporary law in the areas of: family relationships, including marriage, divorce, inheritance, and estate planning; commercial law and laws governing workers and labor relations; laws for special groups—home owners and tenants, consumers, juvenile law, environmental law, women and the law; civil rights and duties, and criminal law. Numerous charts comparing state laws relevant to these topics. Also serves as an update to seventy numbers of the publisher's "Legal almanacs" series.

KF387.R55

Ross, Martin J. New encyclopedic dictionary of business law—with forms. 2d ed. Englewood Cliffs, N.J., Prentice-Hall [1981]. 349p. il. **CK158**

1st ed. 1975.

Offers definitions of commonly used legal terms, with examples of their uses in different contexts. Illustrations are given of typical situations, and more than forty specimen legal forms are reproduced. KF887.R67

Shepard's Acts and cases by popular names: federal and state . . . to January, 1968. Colorado Springs, Colo., Shepard's Citations, 1968– . **CK159**

Subtitle: A compilation of popular names by which federal and state acts and cases have been referred to or cited, together with an identification of each act in terms of its constitutional or statutory references and each case in terms of the volume and page reference where the text of the decision may be found.

Combines the listings previously appearing in the same publisher's separate volumes for federal acts (1957) and for federal and state cases (1964) with new material. Kept up-to-date by cumulative supplements. KF80.S5

Walker, David M. The Oxford companion to law. Oxford, Clarendon Pr.; [N.Y., Oxford Univ. Pr.], 1980. 1366p. **CK160**

Offers concise information and definitions for legal institutions, courts, judges and jurists, systems and branches of law, legal ideas and concepts, doctrines and principles. Emphasizes British law, but includes broad coverage of all Western legal systems. Excludes authority references for many statements. Appendixes provide lists of legal officeholders and selected bibliography. K48.W34

Webster's Legal secretaries handbook. Coleen K. Withgott, gen. ed. Springfield, Mass., G. & C. Merriam, [1981]. 660p. il. **CK161**

A practical handbook outlining law office administration, use of modern office technology, the preparation of legal documents, styles of written communication, and use of a law library. Extensive bibliography. KF319.W42

World Peace Through Law Center. Law and judicial systems of nations. 3d rev. ed. Ed. by Charles S. Rhyne. Wash., World Peace Through Law Center, 1978. 919p. **CK162**

1st ed. 1968.

Various legal scholars and practitioners have provided narrative sketches of the legal systems of 144 countries, covering the legal profession and organization of the bar, legal education, courts of justice, and the legal system. Tables of statutes index the sources mentioned in the text and footnotes; there is a bibliography.

K583.W64

Indexes

Blandford, Linda A. and **Evans, Patricia Russell.** Supreme Court of the United States, 1789–1980: an index to opinions arranged by Justice. Millwood, N.Y., Kraus Internat. Pubns., 1983. 2v. (1133p.) **CK163**

Sponsored by the Supreme Court Historical Society.

For each Justice (listed chronologically), opinions are organized by category, indicating majority, plurality, concurring, separate, or dissenting opinions, statements, or opinions as circuit judges; each listing provides name of case and citation to its appearance in the *United States reports.* Appendixes provide some biographical data and a chronology of succession of Justices from 1789 to 1980.

KF101.6.B57

Current law index. v.1, no.1– , Jan. 1980– . Menlo Park, Calif., Information Access Corp., 1980– . 8 nos. per yr. with quarterly and annual cumulations. **CK164**

Sponsored by the American Association of Law Libraries.

Indexes about 700 law periodicals by subject, author, title of book being reviewed, case, and statute. Corresponds to the database *Legal resource index.* K33.C87 ●

Guenther, Nancy Anderman. United States Supreme Court decisions: an index to excerpts, reprints, and discussions. 2d ed. Metuchen, N.J., Scarecrow Pr., 1983. 856p. **CK165**

1st ed. 1976.

"The objective . . . is to provide students a means of locating reprints, excerpts, and discussions of Supreme Court decisions available in publications printed from 1960 to 1980 that are generally accessible to undergraduate students."—*Pref.* Excludes newspapers and materials noted in the *Index to legal periodicals* (CK170). Arranged chronologically; indexed by case name and subject. KF101.6.G83

Index to Canadian legal periodical literature. 1963/65– . Montreal, [1966]– . Quarterly, with annual cumulation.

CK166

Originally bimonthly; in 1977 frequency of the *Index* changed to quarterly, with each issue cumulating all previous material for that year through the usual annual cumulation. Now indexes articles, case comments, and book reviews from about sixty Canadian periodicals; also includes relevant cassettes and essays published in book form. Two longer cumulations have been published: 1961–70 (1972) and 1971–75 (1977).

Index to foreign legal periodicals. v.1– , 1960– . London, publ. by the Inst. of Advanced Legal Studies, Univ. of

London, in cooperation with the American Assoc. of Law Libraries, 1960– . v.1– . Quarterly, cumulating annually and triennially. **CK167**

Indexes "the main legal periodicals dealing with international law (public and private), comparative law and the municipal law of all countries of the world other than the United States, the British Isles and the countries of the British Commonwealth. . . ."—*Pref.* Beginning with v.4 (1963) collections of legal essays such as *Festschriften* are also indexed.

Index to legal essays: English language legal essays in Festschriften, memorial volumes, conference papers and other collections, 1975–1979. Comp. for the British and Irish Association of Law Librarians under the editorship of Barbara Tearle. [London], Mansell, [1983]. 430p. **CK168**

Lists about 340 collections, with subject, geographical, and author indexing for about 6,000 essays. Other volumes are planned to cover 1945–74.   K38.I52

Index to legal periodical literature. Boston, Boston Book Co., 1888–1919; Chipman, 1924; Indianapolis, Bobbs-Merrill, 1933; Los Angeles, Parker and Baird, 1939. v.1–6.
CK169

v.1–2, ed. by Leonard A. Jones; v.3–6, by Frank E. Chipman.
Contents: v.1, To 1886; v.2, 1887–98; v.3, 1898–1908; v.4, 1908–22; v.5, 1923–32; v.6, 1932–37.
Each volume consists of a main subject index, with brief author index to the subject part. Indexes periodical literature in the English language on technical and historical law subjects; legal biography; and a considerable number of articles on political, economic, and sociological subjects. v.1 indexes practically all articles in 158 legal periodicals (1373v.); all articles on law subjects in 113 general periodicals (including a few sets published in the 18th century); and the proceedings of various bar associations. v.4 indexes 91 periodicals and is practically a consolidation of v.1–14 of the annual *Index to legal periodicals* (below). Useful in the general library as well as in the law library.   Z6453.I38

Index to legal periodicals, 1908– . Publ. for the American Association of Law Libraries. N.Y., Wilson, 1909– .
CK170

Monthly indexes (frequency varies), with annual cumulations and, from 1926, 3-year cumulations which supersede the annuals. The cumulated volumes consist of a subject and author index; a table of cases; and, since 1940, a book review index. Indexes periodicals published in the U.S., Canada, Great Britain, Ireland, Australia and New Zealand. Earlier volumes indexed bar association and judicial council reports.   K9.N32●

Index to periodical articles related to law. v.1– , Oct. 1, 1958– . Dobbs Ferry, N.Y., Glanville, 1958– . Quarterly with annual cumulation. **CK171**

Publisher varies. Frequency varies.
A selective index which covers important articles in journals not included in the *Index to legal periodicals* or the *Index to foreign legal periodicals.*

———— Ten-year index. Dobbs Ferry, N.Y., Oceana, 1970. 411p.

Cumulates the entries from v.1–10 (1958–68). 5-year cumulations of v.11–15 (1969–73) and v.16–20 (1974–78) are available.

Legal information management index. v.1, no.1– , Jan./Feb. 1984– . [Newton Highlands, Mass., Fox Information Consultants, 1984–] Bimonthly, with annual cumulation.
CK172

Indexes about 125 English-language periodicals for material relating to legal information management and law librarianship. Keyword subject, author, and review indexes.   Z675.L2L46

Legal periodical digest, 1928–1963/64. N.Y., Commerce Clearing House, 1964. v.1–29. **CK173**

Title varies.
A looseleaf abstracting service covering leading articles in United States, Canadian, Philippine, and Puerto Rican legal periodicals.

Digests are on sheets inserted in a binder according to subject. Annual cumulative subject and author indexes. Continued in part by *Business law articles* (Chicago, Commerce Clearing House, 1965–70. Looseleaf).

Directories

American Bar Association. Directory. [1937/38?]– . Chicago, Assoc., 1938– . Irregular. **CK174**

Lists officers, committees, etc.

Directory of corporate counsel, 1980/81– . N.Y., Law & Business, Inc., [1980–]. Annual. **CK175**

Kenneth B. Miller, managing ed.
For some 4,000 companies, subsidiaries, and divisions, provides details on: law department's address, telephone number, and staffing; area of legal specialization; biographical data on individuals listed. Companies include publicly held corporations, privately owned businesses, utilities, insurance companies, and financial institutions. Arranged by company name; indexed by subsidiary organizations and names of personnel.   KF195.C6D57

Directory of law libraries. 1940– . [N.Y.], publ. for the Amer. Assoc. of Law Libraries . . . by the Commerce Clearing House, 1940– . Biennial. **CK176**

Title varies: *Law libraries in the United States and Canada,* 1940–62/63.
Geographical listing of law libraries in the United States, Canada, and other foreign countries that are members of the Association. Gives name, librarian, and number of volumes. Personnel index.
     Z675.L2L384

Directory of legal aid and defender offices in the United States, 1933– . Wash., Legal Aid & Defender Assoc., 1933– . Annual. **CK177**

Name of issuing body varies. Title varies slightly.
Gives the names and addresses of all such known organizations in the United States, Canada, the Philippine Islands, and Puerto Rico, with a brief description of the types and limitations of the services provided by each.   KF336.A332

Epstein, Elliott M., Shostak, Jerome and **Troy, Lawrence.** Barron's Guide to law schools. 6th ed. Woodbury, N.Y., Barron's, [1984]. 461p. **CK178**

1st ed. 1967.
Provides information on all American Bar Association-approved law schools.   KF266.E6

International Association of Law Libraries. Directory, [1977]– . [Marburg, Ger.], Internat. Assoc. of Law Libraries, [1980]– . Irregular. **CK179**

A list, arranged by country, of personal and institutional members. Indexed.   Z675.L2I56b

International Association of Law Libraries. European law libraries guide. Guide européen des bibliothèques de droit. Prep. . . . under the auspices of the Council of Europe. [n.p., 1971] 678p. **CK180**

Introductory matter in English and French. Text in English (with section on France in English and French).
Information on size, subject interests, access and facilities, etc., of 522 European law libraries. Arranged by country, then by city.

International Legal Aid Association. Directory of legal aid and advice facilities available throughout the world. London, N.Y., The Association, 1966– . 3v., looseleaf.
CK181

Arranged by country.

Law and legal information directory. 3d ed. Paul Wasserman, managing ed. Detroit, Gale, [1984]. 902p. **CK182**

Subtitle: A guide to national and international organizations, bar associations, federal court system, federal regulatory agencies, law schools, continuing legal education, paralegal education, scholarships and grants, awards and prizes, special libraries, information systems and services, research centers, legal periodical publications, and book and media publishers.

1st ed. 1980.

Provides details on more than 7,700 sources of information. In 17 broad sections, 11 of which have individual indexes. Introduction suggests other reference sources for each section. Emphasis is on the United States and Canada, with select international sources given for organizations, scholarships and grants, awards and prizes, and information systems and services. KF190.L35

The lawyer's almanac, 1981/82– . N.Y., Law & Business, Inc.; Harcourt Brace Jovanovich, [1981]– . Annual. **CK183**

Subtitle: A cornucopia of information about law, lawyers, and the profession.

A handbook providing directory and factual data on American law. In six main sections: the legal profession; the judiciary; government departments and agencies; statutory summaries and checklists; texts of selected statutes and codes; commonly used abbreviations. Compiled from many other printed sources, without independent verification. Indexed. KF190.L3625

Lawyers directory. Charlottesville, Va., Lawyers Directory, 1883– . Annual. **CK184**

Semiannual, 1888–1925; annual, 1926– .

Title varies: until 1925, called *Sharp & Alleman Co.'s Lawyers and bankers directory.*

Contains digests of laws and a selection of leading lawyers with biographical data. Includes the United States, Canada, and principal foreign countries. Has a list of foreign embassies and legations.

Lawyer's register by specialties and fields of law including a list of corporate counsel. Cleveland, Lawyer to Lawyer Consultation Panel, 1978– . Annual. **CK185**

Under each of 158 fields of law, lists (by state and city) the lawyers specializing in that field, with name of affiliated firm and biographical information; there is a listee index by state and personal name. The corporate counsel section lists the corporate counsel for 1,020 counties, with a personal name index.

The legal connection: corporations and law firms. Ed.1– . Menlo Park, Calif., [S. P. Harris, 1979–]. Annual. **CK186**

Ed. by Spencer Phelps Harris.

Subtitle: A directory of 8,000 publicly held companies and the 4,000 law firms who are linked to them.

Provides abbreviated directory information in two main sections: (1) company list; (2) law firm list. There is also a list of law firms by city. Specifies type of relationship with the law firm.

KF195.C6L43

Martindale-Hubbell law directory (annual) . . . 1931– . [63d–] N.Y., Martindale-Hubbell, [c1931–]. **CK187**

Consolidation of *Martindale's American law directory,* 1868–1930 (continues its volume numbering) and *Hubbell's Legal directory,* 1870–1930. Now published annually in 7v.

v.1–6 are arranged geographically by state, then by city, and include: list of firms and lawyers of the United States and Canada; selected list of foreign lawyers, arranged by country; roster of registered patent attorneys; and a biographical section. v.7 includes digests of the laws of the states, territories and possessions of the United States, Canada and its provinces, and foreign countries; United States copyright, patent, and trademark laws; and court calendars and uniform acts. Contains no single alphabetical list of lawyers.

Tseng, Henry P. The law schools of the world. Buffalo, N.Y., W. S. Hein, 1977. 419p. **CK188**

Pt.I is a country-by-country survey of legal education systems; pt.II is a similarly arranged directory of law schools, providing name of school, address, telephone, degree offered, whether foreign students are admitted, language of instruction, names of admissions officer, dean, and law librarian. K100.A4T76

World legal directory. 2d ed. Wash., World Peace Through Law Center, 1974. 431p. **CK189**

Subtitle: A comprehensive computerized directory of judges, lawyers, teachers of law, courts, law schools, law libraries, and bar associations in 145 countries.

1st ed. 1969 publ. as *World law directory.*

This edition includes the first selective listing of members of law firms in the United States and Canada; this feature is to be expanded in future editions.

The first edition of the Center's *Law and judicial systems of nations* (Wash., 1965) included similar information.

Biography

Almanac of the federal judiciary: profiles of all active United States District Court judges. Susan Alexander, ed. Chicago, LawLetters, [1984]– . 1v., looseleaf. **CK190**

Judges are listed by the districts in which they sit. Biographical information includes noteworthy rulings, media comment, lawyers' evaluations, annual statistical workload, etc. Name index.

KF8700.A1A45●

The American bench: judges of the nation. Ed.1– , 1977– . Minneapolis, R. B. Forster & Associates, 1977– . Annual. **CK191**

Mary Reincke, exec. ed.

Offers biographical information on "judges from all levels of federal and state courts with jurisdictional and geographical information on the courts they serve."—*Foreword, 1977.* Arranged in fifty-two sections, one for the United States courts, and one for each of the fifty states and the District of Columbia. Each section includes descriptive information on each court in the state, followed by maps of the judicial divisions and subdivisions, then an alphabetically arranged series of biographies of the judges. An alphabetical name index at front indicates title, court and state of each judge.

KF8700.A19A47

Barnes, Catherine A. Men of the Supreme Court: profiles of the justices. N.Y., Facts on File, [1978]. 221p. il. **CK192**

Offers five- to ten-page biographies, with portraits and bibliographical references, of the 26 men who served as justices of the Supreme Court between 1945 and 1976. Most biographies have been revised since their initial appearance in the publisher's *Political profiles* series (CJ180). Concludes with a chronology of service, list of significant decisions, and bibliography (p.187–204). Indexed.

KF8744.B34

Biographical dictionary of the federal judiciary. Comp. by Harold Chase [and others]. Detroit, Gale, [1976]. 381p. **CK193**

Offers biographical sketches of United States federal judges, 1789–1974. Includes judges of the Supreme Court, U.S. Circuit Court, U.S. District Courts, U.S. Court of Claims, etc.; only judges with lifetime tenure were selected for inclusion. Biographies appearing in *Who's who in America* and *Who was who in America* are reproduced here; when no sketch was available in those works, one was compiled from other sources. KF353.B5

Directory of law teachers, 1922– . St. Paul, Minn., West Pub. Co., 1923– . Annual. **CK194**

Suspended 1943–45; resumed with issue for 1946/47.

Title varies: *Directory of teachers in member schools,* 1922–56; *Directory of law teachers in American Bar Association approved law schools,* 1957–69. Volumes for 1922–56 issued by the Association of American Law Schools.

Alphabetical list of U.S. and Canadian teachers with biographies.

KF266.D552

Friedman, Leon and **Israel, Fred L.,** eds. The justices of the United States Supreme Court, 1789–1969; their lives and major opinions. N.Y., Chelsea House in assoc. with Bowker, 1978. 5v. **CK195**

Scholars have contributed biographical essays on each of the justices; these are followed by a select bibliography for each, and the text of several of his representative opinions. v.4 includes some useful charts and tables, and a general index to the set. v.5 covers the Burger Court, 1969–78.   KF8744.F75

Judicial Conference of the United States. Bicentennial Committee. Judges of the United States. 2d ed. Wash., The Committee (for sale by Supt. of Docs.), 1983. 681p.   **CK196**

1st ed. 1978.

Provides biographical directory data for each person who sat as a judge of the United States from the 18th century to the present. Indexed by appointing president, year of appointment.
KF353.J83

Who's who in American law. Ed.1– . Chicago, Marquis, 1978– . Irregular.   **CK197**

The 1st ed. provides "biographical information on approximately 18,000 lawyers, judges, and educators. Included are attorneys for federal and state agencies; United States attorneys; presidents and key committee heads of federal, state and local bar associations; general counsel to America's largest corporations; and partners and members of major law firms. Among the judicial population are federal and supreme court justices; chief judges of each federal court; Judge Advocate Generals from each branch of the armed services; and hundreds of judges from state and local courts throughout the United States. Listed also are educators—deans and professors from America's foremost law schools."—*Pref.*
KF372.W48

STATUTES

United States

Indexes

Commerce Clearing House. Congressional index. 75th Congress, 1937/38– . Chicago, Commerce Clearing House, 1937– . Weekly throughout session. Looseleaf.   **CK198**

"Indexes all congressional bills and resolutions of general interest and lists their current status. It is designed to lay open to the user a complete record of federal legislation and its progress from initial introduction to final disposition."—*no.1.*

Contains section on voting records in which all roll-call votes on the progress of legislation are reported weekly.   J69.C6

Monthly digest of current legislation. v.1–9, May 3, 1963– Mar. 1972. Pittsburgh, Aspen Systems Corp., 1963–72. v.1–9.   **CK199**

Ceased publication.

Title varies: v.1–2, *Current state legislation index*; v.3–7, *Automated statutory reporter*; v.8, *Computerized law index.*

Originally concerned with state legislation; beginning 1965, included federal legislation.

Nabors, Eugene. Legislative reference checklist: the key to legislative histories from 1789–1903. Littleton, Colo., Rothman, 1982. 440p.   **CK200**

For all public laws passed during this period, provides references to bill and joint resolution numbers, public law numbers, appearance in printed congressional debates, and listing in *Statutes at large.*   KF49.L43

Schultz, Jon S. Comparative statutory sources. 2d ed. [Buffalo, N.Y., W. S. Hein, 1978] 68p.   **CK201**

1st ed. 1973.

A subject index to publications containing comparative statutory studies which are revised or supplemented annually or more frequently and those which are published in looseleaf services. Sources

indexed include various CCH and BNA reporters, *Constitutions of the United States, Book of the states,* various almanacs, etc.
KF1.S35

State law index; an index to the legislation of the states of the United States enacted . . . 1925/26–1947/48. Wash., Govt. Prt. Off., 1929–49. v.1–12. Biennial.   **CK202**

Ceased publication.
Title varies.
1925/26–1933/34, comp. by the Legislative Reference Service of the Library of Congress; 1935/36–1947/48, by the State Law Index, Library of Congress.   Z6457.A1S8

U.S. Laws, Statutes, etc. (Indexes). Index to the federal statutes [1789–1873, 1874–1931] general and permanent law. . . . Wash., Govt. Prt. Off., 1911–33. 2v.   **CK203**

The volume for 1789–1873 indexes v.1–17 of the *Statutes at large* (CK206); the volume for 1874–1931 indexes the *Revised statutes of 1874* (CK205) and the *Statutes at large,* v.18–46; this latter volume is a revision by W. H. McClenon and W. C. Gilbert of the Scott and Beaman *Index analysis of the federal statutes 1874–1907.*

These two volumes index all federal legislation of a public, general, and permanent nature through 1931.

U.S. Library of Congress. Legislative Reference Service. Digest of public general bills and selected resolutions with index. 74th Cong., 2d sess.– . Wash., Govt. Prt. Off., 1936– .   **CK204**

Normally published each session in two cumulative issues with occasional supplements and a final edition.

Provides "a brief synopsis, the essential features of public bills and resolutions and changes made therein during the legislative process."—*Foreword.*

A complementary title is *Major legislation of the Congress* (Wash., Lib. of Congress, Congressional Research Service, 1981– . Irregular, each issue cumulative within each Congress).   J52.A3

Texts

U.S. Laws, Statutes, etc. Revised statutes of the United States, passed at the first session of the Forty-third Congress, 1873–74; embracing the statutes of the United States, general and permanent in their nature, in force Dec. 1, 1873. 2d ed. Wash., Govt. Prt. Off., 1878. 1394p.   **CK205**

In 1867 a commission was appointed to compile all the general and permanent laws by subject. The first revision, accepted and published as the *Revised statutes of 1873,* contained in the texts certain liberties taken by the revisers. The *Revised statutes,* 2d ed. 1878, restored the original text, and is the edition usually cited. Supplements were made and published in 1891 and 1901, but these are now largely superseded by the *Code* (CK207).

———— The statutes at large of the United States of America . . . containing the laws and concurrent resolutions enacted . . . and reorganization plans and proclamations, 1789– 1873; 1873– . Boston, Little, 1845–73; Wash., Govt. Prt. Off., 1875– . v.1– .   **CK206**

Title varies slightly.

The present series of *Statutes at large* starts with v.18 (1873–75). It was preceded by the *Laws of the United States:* Folwell edition, for the first 13 Congresses, 1789–1813; Bioren and Duane edition, for the first 28 Congresses, 1789–1845; Little, Brown edition, called *Statutes at large,* covering the first 42 Congresses, 1789–1873, and ending with v.17. This series was taken over by the federal government, v.18– .

Contents vary, but beginning with v.65, 1951, each volume contains public laws, reorganization plans, private laws, and concurrent resolutions and proclamations. Arrangement is chronological by date of passage of the act under the divisions: Public laws, Private laws, etc. A subject index and a personal-name index in each volume.

Slip laws are published separately, as soon as enacted, in two series: (1) Public Acts (cited as Public Law), and (2) Private Acts (cited as Private Law), and are superseded upon publication of the

Statutes at large. Slip laws and resolutions are listed in the *Monthly catalog* (AG51) under "Congress" and then by number.

Treaties to which the United States was a party (1776–1949) were published in the *Statutes at large,* 1848–1949. Since Jan. 1, 1950, they have been contained in *United States treaties and other international agreements* (CK370).

————United States code. 1982 ed. Wash., Govt. Prt. Off., 1983. 17v. **CK207**

Supersedes previous editions published 1926, 1934, 1940, 1946, 1952, 1959, 1970, and 1976.

Cited as *USC.*

This code contains all general and permanent laws of the United States in force on Jan. 14, 1983, arranged under 50 titles, i.e., subjects, with many subdivisions called chapters.

Cumulative supplements issued annually.

———— ———— General index, [1983]. 5v.

———— ———— Tables, [1983]. 720p.

———— United States code annotated. St. Paul, Minn., West Pub. Co., 1927– . v.1– . **CK207a**

Cited as *USCA.*

Comprises all laws of a general and permanent nature under the same arrangement as that of the *Code* (above). Annotations are from federal and state court reports and opinions of the United States Attorney-General.

Kept up-to-date by cumulative, annual, pocket parts containing amendments and additions. Later replacement volumes are issued from time to time.

———— ———— 1985 general index. St. Paul, Minn., West Pub. Co., 1985. 8v.

———— Constitution of the United States annotated; annotated from federal and state courts [1949–1983]. 8v. **CK208**

———— United States code service. Lawyers edition. Rochester, N.Y., Lawyers Co-operative Pub. Co.; San Francisco, Bancroft-Whitney, 1972–85. **CK209**

Subtitle: All federal laws of a general and permanent nature arranged in accordance with the section numbering of the United States Code and the supplements thereto.

Supersedes the *Federal code annotated* (1937–70).

All laws of a permanent and general nature are grouped under the same fifty titles as in the *United States code,* with annotations as to the decisions of federal and state courts, executive orders, proclamations, Attorney General's opinions, and other titles by the publisher.

Code of federal regulations. 1949 ed., containing a codification of documents of general applicability and future effect as of Dec. 31, 1948, with ancillaries and index. Publ. by the Division of the Federal Register, National Archives. Wash., Govt. Prt. Off., 1949–72. 76v. **CK210**

Cited as *CFR.*

This is the second edition of the *Code* (1st ed. 1938), and contains a "codification of the Federal Administrative rules and regulations, general and permanent . . . duly promulgated on or before Dec. 31, 1948, and effective as to facts arising on and after Jan. 1, 1949."

The set forms basic volumes for the type of material published currently in the *Federal register* (CK212).

Kept up-to-date by pocket supplements, cumulating annually.

———— Title 3, The president. Compilation containing the full text of presidential documents. With ancillaries and index, 1943/48–1971/75. v.1–9. **CK211**

United States. Federal register, March 14, 1936– . Wash., Govt. Prt. Off., 1936– . Daily, except Sun., Mon., and day following a legal holiday. **CK212**

Contains all presidential proclamations and executive orders; rules and regulations of the various bureaus and departments of the

government; and decisions of fact-finding bodies. Has monthly, quarterly, and annual indexes. J1.A2

United States code Congressional and administrative news. Acts of 76th Congress, Jan. 3, 1939– . St. Paul, Minn., West Pub. Co.; Brooklyn, N.Y., Edward Thompson Co., 1942– . **CK213**

Published semimonthly during the session of Congress, and monthly when Congress is not in session, with annual bound cumulations. Coverage varies somewhat; recent volumes include all public laws (full text), legislative history, executive orders, presidential proclamations, administrative regulations, messages of the president, popular names of laws, etc. Current issues contain an index-digest of bills enacted.

Great Britain

Gt.Brit. Laws, Statutes, etc. The laws of the earliest English kings, ed. and tr. by F. L. Attenborough . . . Cambridge, Univ. Pr., 1922. 256p. (Repr.: N.Y., Russell, 1963) **CK214**

Anglo-Saxon and modern English versions, with Latin when the original Anglo-Saxon is lost.

———— Statutes in force. . . . Official rev. ed. London, [H.M.S.O.], 1972– . Looseleaf. (In progress) **CK215**

Contains all acts in force, of a public nature, in chronological order with extensive notes. Each volume has subject and chronological indexes. Nearest equivalent to an official codification. Acts are published in separate pamphlets, alphabetically arranged.

Kept up-to-date by the annual volumes of *Public general acts* and the *Church assembly measures*; similar to the United States *Statutes at large.*

Earlier editions: *Statutes of the realm* (London, Record Commission, 1810–28. 1v.); *The statutes,* 2d rev. ed. . . . 1235–1920 (London, Stat. Off., 1888–1929. 24v.); *The statutes . . . 1235–1948,* 3d rev. ed. (London, Stat. Off., 1950. 32v.). KD132.1972

———— Acts and ordinances of the Interregnum, 1642–1660. Ed. by C. H. Firth and R. S. Rait. London, Stat. Off., 1911. 3v. **CK216**

v.3, Chronological table of acts and ordinances; Index to subjects; Index of names, places, and things.

———— Halsbury's statutes of England. 4th ed. Managing ed., Paul Brown. London, Butterworth, 1985. v.1–4. (In progress) **CK217**

3d ed. 1968–81. 52v.

Contains all public general acts in force, including amendments and corrections of the text; annotations inlcude brief descriptions of cases citing an Act and other explanatory data. Comparable to the *United States code* or the *United States code service.* Arranged alphabetically by broad subjects.

Kept up-to-date by annual continuation volumes and annual cumulative supplements.

Latin America

U.S. Library of Congress. Hispanic Law Division. Index to Latin American legislation, 1950–1960. Boston, G. K. Hall, [1961]. 2v. **CK218**

Contents: v.1, Argentina–Cuba; v.2, Dominican Republic–Venezuela.

Covers national legislation appearing in the official gazettes of the 20 Latin American republics. Arranged alphabetically by subject under each country.

———— ———— Supplement 1–3. Boston, 1970–78. 6v.

Contents: Suppl. 1, 1961–65 (2v.); Suppl. 2, 1966–70 (2v.); Suppl. 3, 1971–75 (2v.).

CRIMINOLOGY

Guides

Wright, Martin. Use of criminology literature. [Hamden, Conn.], Archon Books; [London, Butterworth, 1974]. 242p. **CK219**

A guide to the major literature and reference tools, with chapters by specialists on: search methodology; sociological aspects; criminological aspects of psychology; alcoholism and crime; drug dependence; treatment of offenders; criminal law and the administration of criminal justice; police; statistics; prisons and penal practices; illustrations; and official publications. Subject index.

Z5118.C9W74

Bibliography

Beyleveld, Deryck. A bibliography on general deterrence. [Westmead, Farnborough, Hants., Eng.], Saxon House, [1980]. 452p. **CK220**

"The aims of this bibliography are to display, summarise and assess empirical research which attempts to elaborate or test 'deterrence theory', to evaluate the deterrent effectiveness of crime control measures, or to provide a rational basis for crime control policies." —*Introd.* The work combines abstracts of items, a review of the literature, and monographic treatment of the methodology of deterrent research. Includes nearly 600 studies. Author and subject indexes. HV7431.B43

Brantley, James R. and **Kravitz, Marjorie.** Alternatives to institutionalization: a definitive bibliography. [Rockville, Md.], Dept. of Justice, Law Enforcement Assistance Administration, National Institute of Law Enforcement and Criminal Justice. [Wash., for sale by Supt. of Docs.], 1979. 240p. **CK221**

A title listing of more than 2,200 entries on such alternatives to institutionalization as juvenile training centers, prerelease centers, halfway houses, work-release programs, community service orders, group and foster homes, and probation and parole. Brief annotations are provided. Author and subject indexes. Z5703.4.C65B7

Cabot, Phillippe Sidney de Q. Juvenile delinquency; a critical annotated bibliography. N.Y., Wilson, 1946. 166p. **CK222**

972 numbered entries of books and periodical articles covering the period 1914–44. Arranged alphabetically with subject index. Z5118.C9C3

Chambliss, William J. and **Seidman, Robert B.** Sociology of the law; a research bibliography. Berkeley, Calif., Glendessary, [1970]. 113p. **CK223**

A selective, classed bibliography of book and periodical materials. Author index. KF1.C45

Christianson, Scott. Index to minorities & criminal justice: an index to periodicals and books relating to minorities and criminal justice in the United States. 1981 cumulative ed. Albany, N.Y., Center on Minorities and Criminal Justice, School of Criminal Justice, State Univ. of New York at Albany, [1981]. 247p. **CK224**

Includes about 3,000 references from some 400 periodicals, books, government reports, dissertations, selected court cases, Keyword subject index; author index with abstracts; index to court cases. HV6197.U5C48

Cordasco, Francesco and **Alloway, David N.** Crime in America: historical patterns and contemporary realities; an anno-

tated bibliography. N.Y., Garland, 1985. (Garland reference library of social science, v.264) **CK225**

A topically-arranged bibliography focusing on publications since the mid-1960s. Includes chapters on "basic" sources, periodicals, and major organizations. 1,879 entries; author index.

Z5703.C67

Crime and punishment in America: a historical bibliography. Santa Barbara, Calif., ABC-Clio, [1984]. 346p. **CK226**

A collection of 1,396 abstracts published 1973–82, drawn from the database which produces *America: history and life*; broad subject arrangement, with subject and author indexes. Z5703.5.U5C7

Cumming, *Sir* **John Ghest.** A contribution towards a bibliography dealing with crime and cognate subjects. 3d ed. London, pr. by the Receiver for the Metropolitan Police District, New Scotland Yard, 1935. 107p. (Repr.: Montclair, N.J., Patterson Smith, 1970) **CK227**

A classified bibliography of books and some periodical articles, covering approximately 50 years. International in scope, but from the British viewpoint. Author index. Z5118.C9C9

Ende, Rudolf vom. Criminology and forensic sciences: an international bibliography, 1950–1980. München, K. G. Saur, [1981–82]. 3v. (2389p.) **CK228**

Title and introductory material also in German.

Cites books, periodical articles, collected works, research reports, conference papers, symposia, and *Festschriften*. The introduction reviews other bibliographies in the field. Author arrangement; use is severely limited by lack of a subject index. Z5703.E52

Felkenes, George T. and **Becker, Harold K.** Law enforcement: a selected bibliography. 2d ed. N.Y., Scarecrow Pr., 1977. 329p. **CK229**

1st ed. 1968.

A classed list of more than 6,900 books and periodical articles arranged in five main groups, with appropriate subdivisions: (1) police personnel administration; (2) police functions and practices; (3) criminal law; (4) criminal evidence; (5) administration of justice. Brief annotations for most entries. Detailed table of contents; author index. KF9201.F44

Hawkins, Keith. Parole: a select bibliography with especial reference to American experience. 2d ed., rev. and enl. Cambridge, Eng., Univ. of Cambridge, Inst. of Criminology, 1971. 57p. (Cambridge. Univ. Inst. of Criminology. Bibliographical ser., no.3) **CK230**

1st ed. 1969.

Includes books, periodical articles, dissertations, and some reports of research organizations. Author and subject indexes.

Hewitt, William H. A bibliography of police administration, public safety, and criminology to July 1, 1965. Springfield, Ill., Thomas, [1967]. 242p. **CK231**

A topical bibliography with chapters in alphabetical order by function; subheadings are alphabetical within chapters. More than 11,000 entries. No index. Z7164.P76H4

Hopkins, Isabella, Maxwell, John K. and **Mattson, Charyl.** Organized crime: a selected bibliography. [Austin], Univ. of Texas School of Law, Criminal Justice Reference Lib., 1973. 99p. **CK232**

A classed bibliography of more than 900 items. Name index.

Z5703.4.O7H66

Jerath, Bal K., Larson, Paul E. and **Lewis, Jesse F.** Homicide: a bibliography of over 4,500 items. Augusta, Ga., Pine Tree Pubns., 1982. 599p. **CK233**

An international bibliography of books, articles, and dissertations. Broad subject classification (e.g., the murderer, the victim, assassination), with more detailed subsections (murders, male; genocide; assassination of presidents and heads of state). Subject and author indexes. Z5703.4.M87J47

—— —— Supplement 1984. Augusta, Ga., Pine Tree Pubns., [1984]. 43p.

Adds 485 citations.

Kemmer, Elizabeth Jane. Violence in the family: an annotated bibliography. N.Y., Garland, 1984. 192p. (Garland reference library of social science, v.182)   **CK234**

Comprises 1,055 citations to English-language publications, 1960–82. Main-entry arrangement; subject and author indexes.
                                                    Z7164.C5K46

McDade, Thomas M. The annals of murder: a bibliography of books and pamphlets on American murders from colonial times to 1900. Norman, Univ. of Oklahoma Pr., 1961. 360p. il.   **CK235**

Lists "separate publications devoted primarily to a single murder case which took place in what is now the United States and which occurred prior to 1900. . . . It includes trials, confessions, lives of murderers (but generally not of victims), speeches of counsel, etc."—*Pref.* Arranged by murderer when known, otherwise by victim. Name index.   KF219.M3

Prostano, Emanuel T. and **Piccirillo, Martin L.** Law enforcement: a selective bibliography. Littleton, Colo., Libraries Unlimited, 1974. 203p.   **CK236**

Covers English-language books, pamphlets and audiovisual materials published between 1967 and 1972, with a section listing serial titles. Subject arrangement using such headings as alcoholism, behavioral and social science, civil rights, etc. 250 starred titles are highly recommended. Author and title indexes.   Z7164.P76P74

Radzinowicz, Leon and **Hood, Roger.** Criminology and the administration of criminal justice: a bibliography. Westport, Conn., Greenwood Pr., [1976]. 400p.   **CK237**

Nineteen chapters list books, periodical articles, and government reports chronologically within subject area. "Focus on criminology has been predominantly sociological rather than psychiatric and . . . in criminal justice and penology more concerned with issues of policy and the results of research than with day-to-day practical matters."—*Introd.* Primarily literature of the period 1954–74, with a supplement updating to Feb. 1976. Author index.   Z5118.C9R3

Radzinowicz Library. The library catalogue of the Radzinowicz Library, Institute of Criminology, University of Cambridge, England. Boston, G. K. Hall, 1979. 6v.   **CK238**

Contents: v.1–3, Author catalogue. Periodicals; v.4–6, Classified catalogue. Alphabetical subject index.

Represents holdings of the library of the Institute of Criminology, established in 1959. The library contains more than 19,000 monographs, about 9,500 pamphlets and offprints, 192 current periodicals and other inactive periodical titles. Excludes statistical and annual reports, microforms, and ephemera. The classified catalog uses the 1st ed. of the Bliss Bibliographic Classification.
                                                    Z5119.R32

Rank, Richard. The criminal justice systems of the Latin-American nations: a bibliography of the primary and secondary literature. South Hackensack, N.J., Rothman, 1974. 540p. (New York Univ. Criminal Law Education and Research Center. Pubn., 11)   **CK239**

A classed list of about 9,000 items covering Central and South America, Cuba, the Dominican Republic, Haiti, and Puerto Rico. Arranged by country, with subsections on general works, criminal law, criminal procedure, criminology, and military criminal law. For some countries, state or provincial material is also included. No index.

Simpson, Antony E. and **Duchaine, Nina.** The literature of police corruption. N.Y., John Jay Pr., [1977–79]. 2v.
                                                    CK240

Contents: v.1, A guide to bibliography and theory (214p.); v.2, A selected annotated bibliography (192p.).

v.1 presents a review of the literature, followed by a bibliography of about 600 titles and an author/subject index. v.2 is a more selective bibliography of about 400 titles, which include disserta-

tions and textbooks (excluded from v.1). Broad subject chapters parallel those of the first volume, though there are subdivisions for a more specific approach; author index.   HV7936.C85S55

Social Science Research Council. Committee on Survey of Research on Crime and Criminal Justice. A guide to material on crime and criminal justice . . . prep. by Augustus Frederick Kuhlman. . . . N.Y., Wilson, 1929. 633p.   **CK241**

"A descriptive, classified, union catalog of books, monographs, and pamphlets in thirteen selected libraries, and of articles listed in the leading periodical indexes relating to all phases of crime and criminal justice in the United States."—*Pref.*

Arranged by class with a subject index.

—— —— Author index, prep. by D. C. Culver. N. Y., Wilson, 1934. 32p.

The work is continued by: Z5118.C9S6

California. University. Institute of Governmental Studies. Bibliography of crime and criminal justice, 1927–1931, 1932–1937, comp. by Dorothy Campbell Culver [Tompkins]. N.Y., Wilson, 1934–39. 2v. (413p., 391p.)   **CK242**

Issued under the Bureau's earlier name: Bureau of Public Administration.

A comprehensive, classified bibliography of books and periodical articles. Includes works in various languages.   KF9223.A1C25

—— Sources for the study of the administration of criminal justice, comp. by Dorothy Campbell Tompkins. Sacramento, California State Board of Corrections, 1949. 294p.   **CK243**

Includes items published since 1938. Emphasizes material pertinent to conditions in California.

—— Administration of criminal justice, 1949–1956; a selected bibliography, comp. by Dorothy Campbell Tompkins. Sacramento, California Board of Corrections, 1956. 351p.   **CK244**

                                                    KF9223.A1C2

Suvak, Daniel. Memoirs of American prisons: an annotated bibliography. Metuchen, N.J., Scarecrow Pr., 1979. 227p.
                                                    CK245

In three main sections: (1) civil prisoners, both criminals and prisoners of conscience; (2) voluntary prisoners committed for the purpose of studying and reporting on the institutions and prisoners; (3) military prisoners, from the Revolution to World War II internment camps. About 770 entries. Indexed by name, title, and prison.
                                                    Z5703.5.U5S9

Teng, Ssu-yu. Protest and crime in China: a bibliography of secret associations, popular uprisings, peasant rebellions. N.Y., Garland, 1981. 455p. (Garland reference library of social science, v.86)   **CK246**

3,854 citations. In two parts: authors, books and articles in Occidental languages (p.1–147), and a similar section for materials in Oriental languages (p.148–415), plus an addenda. Author arrangement; subject index. Emphasis is on crime prevention and control in ancient and modern times.   Z7164.S36T46

Tompkins, Dorothy Campbell. The offender; a bibliography. Berkeley, Univ. of California Inst. of Governmental Studies, 1963. 268p.   **CK247**

"Covers the years since 1937, and in a measure supplements the Culver *Bibliography of crime and criminal justice, 1932–1937* [CK242]. It draws on the fields of psychiatry, psychology, medicine, education, sociology, social welfare, and criminology."—*Pref.*

Classified, with author-subject index.   Z5118.C9T6

—— The prison and the prisoner. Berkeley, Inst. of Governmental Studies, Univ. of California, 1972. 156p. (Public policy bibliographies, 1)   **CK248**

A classed bibliography concerned with publications 1967–71 on the prison and the adult prisoner. Indexed.   Z5118.C9T62

—— Probation since World War II; a bibliography. Berkeley, Inst. of Governmental Studies, Univ. of California, 1964. 311p.   **CK249**

An annotated bibliography of works in English, published since World War II, on probation and parole. Supplements the author's other bibliographies on criminal justice.   Z5118.C9T63

—— Sentencing the offender; a bibliography. Berkeley, Inst. of Governmental Studies, Univ. of California, 1971. 102p.   **CK250**

A classified bibliography which supplements, in part, the compiler's *Administration of criminal justice* (CK244).   KF9685.A1T6

—— White collar crime: a bibliography. Berkeley, Inst. of Governmental Studies, Univ. of California, 1967. 85p.   **CK251**

Classed bibliography with author and subject index. Includes a section on "Protection of the consumer against sharp and illegal practices."   KF9350.T64

Triche, Charles W. The capital punishment dilemma, 1950–1977: a subject bibliography. Troy, N.Y., Whitston, 1979. 278p.   **CK252**

In three sections: (1) books, essays, pamphlets, and government publications listed by author or article title, if anonymous; (2) journal and newspaper articles, listed by subject; (3) author index to the first and second sections.   Z5703.4.C36T74

Trott, Lloyd. Mafia: a select annotated bibliography. Cambridge, Eng., Institute of Criminology [Cambridge Univ.], 1977. 141p. (*Its* Bibliographical ser., 7)   **CK253**

Focuses on monographic, periodical, and newspaper literature written before 1975, and excludes law reports, trial texts, and local government and citizens' investigations materials. Classified by broad subject; author/title and subject indexes.   Z5118.C9C37 no. 7

Whitehouse, Jack E. A police bibliography. N.Y., AMS Pr., [1980]. 525p. (AMS studies in criminal justice, no.3)   **CK254**

Subtitle: Published and unpublished sources through 1976, with an addendum.

Presents about 17,400 entries in a detailed subject classification of 1,100 headings, grouped under broad chapters and parts. Emphasizes material published since 1960. Topics include law enforcement agencies, field operations, police personnel management, education and training, relations with the community, comparative police administration, crime and criminal justice. Indexed.   Z7164.P76W45

Wolfgang, Marvin E., Figlio, Robert M. and **Thornberry, Terence P.** Criminology index: research and theory in criminology in the United States, 1945–1972. N.Y., Elsevier, 1975. 2v.   **CK255**

Sponsored by the Center for Studies in Criminology and Criminal Law, University of Pennsylvania.

A bibliography and citation source on theoretical and empirical work in criminology, composed of three main sections: (1) the "Source document index," or bibliography, divided into two sections, (a) articles, and (b) books, dissertations, and reports; (2) the "Subject index," a paired keyword-in-title listing; (3) the "Criminology citation index," a list of all works cited by authors appearing in the "Source document index," divided into anonymous works, general works, and legal documents. Does not include works on the administration of justice, police, courts, and corrections, or doctoral dissertations done before 1968. There is an addendum to the "Source document index."   Z5118.C9W64

Zorin, Libushe. Soviet prisons and concentration camps: an annotated bibliography, 1917–1980. Newtonville, Mass., Oriental Research Partners, 1980. 118p. il. (Russian bibliography ser., no.3)   **CK256**

An international bibliography of more than 500 entries, including material on Soviet psychiatric prisons. Title and author indexes.   HV9712.Z67

Bibliography of bibliography

Davis, Bruce L. Criminological bibliographies: uniform citations to bibliographies, indexes, and review articles of the literature of crime study in the United States. Westport, Conn., Greenwood Pr., [1978]. 182p.   **CK257**

A cumulation of more than 1,400 citations to bibliographies, indexes, catalogs, and review articles arranged chronologically within seven broad categories; each category has a detailed subject index, and the compiler and source agency indexes are comprehensive. Stresses literature on criminal behavior and criminal justice administration; legal literature (statutes, court decisions, reporters, etc.) is excluded.   Z5703.A1D38

Klein, Carol and **Horton, David M.** Bibliographies in criminal justice: a selected bibliography. [Wash.], U.S. Dept. of Justice, National Institute of Justice (for sale by Supt. of Docs.), [1980]. 47p.   **CK258**

Prep. for the National Institute of Justice, U.S. Dept. of Justice, by Aspen Systems Corp.

An annotated bibliography of more than 200 publications in monographic, article, and document form. Author arrangement, with subject and title indexes.   Z5703.A1K58

Current

Criminal justice abstracts. v.9, no.1– , Mar. 1977– . Hackensack, N.J., Nat. Council on Crime and Delinquency, 1977– . Quarterly.   **CK259**

Supersedes *Crime and delinquency literature* and continues its numbering. Coverage and format remain the same as in the earlier publication, the name having been changed "to reflect more accurately the nature of the contents."—*v.9,no.1,p.1.*   HV6001.C67

Criminal justice periodical index, 1975– . Ann Arbor, Indexing Services, University Microfilms, 1975– . 3 issues per yr., the 3d issue being the annual cumulation.   **CK260**

Offers separate author and subject indexes to the contents of about seventy English-language periodicals, with special attention to those issued by professional or research organizations active in the areas of police administration, corrections, juvenile delinquency, criminal law, and security. Entries are repeated in both indexes.   Z5118.C9C74●

Criminology & penology abstracts. v.1– , Jan./Feb. 1961– . Amsterdam, Kugler Pubns. 1961– . Bimonthly.   **CK261**

Title varies: v.1–8, *Excerpta criminologica*; v.9–19, *Abstracts on criminology and penology.*

An abstract journal of periodical articles and books on subjects relating to criminology. International in scope.   HV6001.E9

Dictionaries and encyclopedias

Branham, Vernon Carnegie and **Kutash, Samuel B.** Encyclopedia of criminology. N.Y., Philosophical Lib., [1949]. 527p.   **CK262**

Includes some 100 fairly long articles signed by specialists. Bibliographies are appended. Uneven in quality.   HV6017.B7

De Sola, Ralph. Crime dictionary. N.Y., Facts on File, [1982]. 219p.   **CK263**

Briefly defines and identifies legal and law enforcement terms, medical and psychiatric terms relating to crime and drug addiction, abbreviations, weapons, nicknames and slang, and individual figures, gangs and terrorist groups. Appendixes provide definitions of selected foreign-language terms, place-name nicknames, and selected bibliography.   HV6025.D43

Dizionario di criminologia, per opera di numerosi autori ed a cura di Eugenio Florian, Alfredo Niceforo [e] Nicola Pende. Milano, Vallardi, 1943. 2v. il. **CK264**

Long, signed articles with bibliographies; titles primarily in Italian and French. HV6017.D5

Elsevier's Dictionary of criminal science, in eight languages: English/American, French, Italian, Spanish, Portuguese, Dutch, Swedish, and German; comp. . . . by Johann Anton Adler. Amsterdam, Elsevier, 1960. 1460p. **CK265**

English base with indexes from the other languages. HV6017.E4

Encyclopedia of crime and justice. Sanford H. Kadish, ed. in chief. N.Y., Free Pr., [1983]. 4v. (1790p.) **CK266**

An impressive interdisciplinary survey of "the nature and causes of criminal behavior . . . the prevention of crime, the punishment and treatment of offenders, the functioning of the institutions of criminal justice, and the bodies of law that define criminal behavior and govern the processes through which the criminal law is applied."—*Foreword.* American in emphasis, with international comparisons. Alphabetically arranged articles vary in length from 1,000 to 10,000 words. Glossary; legal and general indexes. HV6017.E52

Gaute, J. H. H. and **Odell, Robin.** The murderers' who's who: outstanding international cases from the literature of murder in the last 150 years. N.Y., Methuen, 1979. 269p. il. **CK267**

Provides brief summaries of about 500 murder cases, arranged by surname of the perpetrator or by popular name of the case. Each case refers by code number to a relevant source in the bibliography of 711 English-language books. HV6499.G38

International handbook of contemporary developments in criminology. Ed. by Elmer H. Johnson, Westport, Conn., Greenwood Pr., [1983]. 2v. il. **CK268**

Contents: v.1, General issues and the Americas; v.2, Europe, Africa, the Middle East, and Asia.

Presents state-of-the-art reviews of criminology in specific countries; surveys are written by specialists. Bibliographic references and bibliographies; indexed. HV6028.I57

Nash, Jay Robert. Almanac of world crime. Garden City, N.Y., Anchor Pr./Doubleday, 1981. 452p. il. **CK269**

Offers brief biographies and narratives arranged by broad subject categories, e.g., assassination, bombings, female criminals, organized crime, prostitution, terrorism, etc. Bibliography; index. HV6025.N33

Rush, George Eugene. Dictionary of criminal justice. Boston, Holbrook Pr., [1977]. 374p. **CK270**

Covers terms, cases, names, and places in the areas of law enforcement, courts, probation, parole, and corrections. Many definitions have been reprinted from 25 sources, and are identified by an abbreviated reference to the source. HV6017.R87

Sifakis, Carl. The encyclopedia of American crime. N.Y., Facts on File, [1982]. 802p. il. **CK271**

Includes entries for criminals, victims of crime, gangs, and terms relating to crime. Subject index. HV6789.S54

Williams, Vergil L. Dictionary of American penology: an introductory guide. Westport, Conn., Greenwood Pr., [1979]. 530p. **CK272**

About one-half of the entries discuss issues, administrative methods, recent historical events, and therapeutic and rehabilitative approaches toward the offender; most of the remaining entries describe federal and individual state prison systems and a few individual prisons. Some biographies are also included. Articles vary in length from one to two pages. Appendixes present addresses of organizations, agencies, and correctional systems, as well as statistical data. Bibliography of about 400 titles. Indexed. HV9304.W54

Directories

Directory of criminal justice information sources. Ed.[1]– , 1976– . [Wash.], Nat. Inst. of Law Enforcement and Criminal Justice, Law Enforcement Assistance Admin., 1976– . Biennial. **CK273**

"The organizations included in this directory were chosen because of their particular information resources, such as computerized literature search services, interlibrary loan programs, reference services, or technical assistance provisions that are available to criminal justice professionals."—*Introd.* An alphabetical arrangement of more than 250 organizations; information on each includes notes on information services and resources, user restrictions, cost, and publications. Subject and geographical indexes. HV8138.D5

Juvenile and adult correctional departments, institutions, agencies and paroling authorities, United States and Canada. [Ed.42]– . College Park, Md., American Correctional Assoc., [1982]– . Annual. **CK274**

Title has varied (with catalog entry usually under name of the association): 1933–58, *State and national correctional institutions* . . . ; 1959–65, *State and federal correctional institutions* . . . , etc.; in some recent issues the word *Directory* has preceded the title as given above.

A directory of institutions and personnel involved in correctional service in the United States and Canada; some statistical data is provided; name index. The association also publishes the *National jail and adult detention directory* and the *Probation and parole directory.* HV9463.D57

National prison directory; a prison reform organizational and resource directory, with a special section on public library service to prisoners. 3d ed. Ed. by Mary Lee Bundy and Alice Bell. College Park, Md., Urban Information Interpreters, [1984]. 205p. **CK275**

1st ed. 1975.

Offers profiles of citizen groups and programs, legal organizations, and professional correctional associations in the United States whose principal concern is reform of the penal system. Organized by state, with subject and name access. HV8987.N37

Newton, Anne, Perl, Kathleen Yaskiw and **Doleschal, Eugene.** Information sources in criminal justice; an annotated guide to directories, journals, newsletters. [Hackensack, N.J.], Information Center, Nat. Council on Crime and Delinquency, 1976. 164p. **CK276**

Includes 57 directories, 185 criminal justice journals, and 254 newsletters; each of these three types of publication is organized by subject, then alphabetically by organization and title. No index. HV8665.N46

Statistics

Sourcebook of criminal justice statistics, 1973– . [Wash., Nat. Criminal Justice Information and Statistics Service; for sale by U.S. Govt. Prt. Off., 1974–] il. Annual. **CK276a**

"The primary goal . . . is to bring together into a single, comprehensive, reference volume existing nationwide statistical data of interest to the broad criminal justice community."—*Pref.* Main sections include: criminal justice system; public opinion; illegal activities; persons arrested; judicial proceedings; persons under correctional supervision. Annotated bibliography of sources; appendixes; index. HV7245.N37b

CANON LAW

Canon law abstracts: a half-yearly review of periodical literature in canon law. v.1– . Melrose, Scotland, Canon Law Society of Great Britain, 1958– . Semiannual. **CK277**

Each issue comprises a bibliography of articles and case reports published during a given period; international in coverage. A section on "General and historical subjects" surveys material pertinent to medieval canon law.

Catholic Church. Codex Juris Canonici. Code of canon law; Latin-English edition. Wash., D.C., Canon Law Society of America, 1983. 668p.   **CK278**

Title page also in Latin.

"Translation prep. under the auspices of the Canon Law Society of America."—*t.p.*

A complete revision of the norms which govern the Church as a society; effective for the entire Latin Catholic Church Nov. 23, 1983. Official Latin text and English translation on facing pages. Glossary of Latin terms; index.

Cunningham, Richard G. An annotated bibliography of the work of the Canon Law Society of America, 1965–1980. Wash., CLSA, [1982]. 121p.   **CK279**

More than 500 citations are interfiled in an author/subject arrangement, with main entry and annotation under author.

Dictionnaire de droit canonique, contenant tous les termes du droit canonique, avec un sommaire de l'histoire et des institutions et de l'état actuel de la discipline; publié sous la direction de R. Naz, avec le concours d'un grand nombre de collaborateurs. Paris, Letouzey, 1935–65. 7v.   **CK280**

Published in parts, 1924–65.

Signed articles by specialists, with bibliographies. Contains many biographies. Forms part of the *Encyclopedie des sciences religieuses* (*see* note under Encyclopedias and Dictionaries, p.361).

                 BX1936.D5

U.S. Library of Congress. The canon law collection of the Library of Congress: a general bibliography with selective annotations. Comp. by Darío C. Ferreira-Ibarra, Hispanic Law Division, Law Library. Wash., Lib. of Congress, 1981. 210p. il.   **CK281**

A topically arranged bibliography of 2,444 citations; an additional 63 entries in the appendix update the bibliography through mid-1979. Author and subject indexes.

INTERNATIONAL LAW

Guides

Williams, John W. Research tips in international law. [Wash.], Nat. Law Center, George Washington Univ., [1981]. 321p.   **CK282**

A brief introductory essay on international legal research is followed by a guide to the major primary and secondary sources; no index. (Publ. as v.15, no.1 of the *Journal of international law and economics.*)

Bibliography

A collection of bibliographic and research resources. Dobbs Ferry, N.Y., Oceana, 1984– . Looseleaf. (In progress)   **CK283**

Contents: [1] Public international law and international organization bibliography, by S. V. Kleckner; [2] International trade law bibliography, by B. Kudej; [3] New law of the sea bibliography, by B. Kudej; [4] Global communication and information bibliography, by E. Reiter.

A collection of individual bibliographies of primary and secondary materials, arranged by subject or by type (treaties, reference works, etc.). Only the fourth title includes periodical articles.

                 Z6461.C65

The consolidated index to the I.L.O. legislative series, 1919–1970. Ed. by Mina Pease. N.Y., UNIFO Pub.; Oxford, Oxford Microform Pub., 1975. 264p.   **CK284**

Covers the legislation published in the International Labor Office's *Legislative series* which is still in force, excluding international treaties and agreements. Chronological and subject indexes. Also serves as an index to the microfiche collection, *The ILO legislative series (1919–1970),* covering translated texts of labor and social security legislation from 140 countries.

Doimi di Delupis, Ingrid. Bibliography of international law. London & N.Y., Bowker, [1975]. 670p.   **CK285**

Concentrates on books published between 1920 and 1974, but includes many journal articles as well. "Important" sections begin with an introduction which mentions particularly significant works in that section. The detailed classification scheme is outlined in the table of contents. Author index. Typography does not meet the usual Bowker standard, and a highly critical review appeared in the *International journal of law libraries* 4:160–62; however, the work includes a broad range of materials.   Z6461.D63

Glassner, Martin Ira. Bibliography on land-locked states. Alphen aan den Rijn, Neth.; Rockville, Md., Sijthoff & Noordhoff, 1980. 50p.   **CK286**

A selective bibliography of post-1945 materials, arranged by type: books, periodicals, reports, unpublished materials, and United Nations documents, subdivided by agency. Treaties are excluded. Indexed.

Gould, Wesley L. and **Barkun, Michael.** Social science literature; a bibliography for international law. Princeton, N.J., publ. for the Amer. Soc. of Internat. Law by Princeton Univ. Pr., [1972]. 641p.   **CK287**

More than 2,800 annotated entries for books, periodical articles, and research reports of social science literature relevant to international law. Classed arrangement with author index. Publications are mainly of the 1955–65 period.

An earlier, complementary volume, *International law and the social sciences* by the same authors (Princeton, N.J., 1970), surveys selected topics demonstrating interrelationships of the two fields; it includes many bibliographic notes.   Z6461.G68

Grieves, Forest L. International law, organization, and the environment; a bibliography and research guide. Tucson, Univ. of Arizona Pr., [1974]. 131p. (Institute of Government Research. International studies, 4)   **CK288**

Selects, classes by broad topic, and briefly annotates English-language books, periodical articles, and documentary materials "not so much [to serve] as recommended reading, but rather as a vehicle for surveying the range of materials available."—*Introd.* Includes lists of relevant periodical titles and international organizations. Covers general materials, the seas and other waters, polar areas, air space and outer space, nuclear and thermal issues, resources and land uses, overpopulation.

Harvard University. Law School. Library. Catalog of international law and relations. Ed. by Margaret Moody. Cambridge, Mass., 1965–67. 20v.   **CK289**

This book catalog, reproduced from some 360,000 cards, represents the international law materials in the Harvard Law School Library, based on the famous collection of the Marquis de Olivart, acquired by Harvard in 1911.

Dictionary arrangement; full bibliographic information is given on main entry. Subject and added entries in shortened form.

Hasse, Adelaide Rosalie. Index to United States documents relating to foreign affairs, 1828–1861. Wash., Carnegie Inst., 1914–21. 3v. (Carnegie Inst. Pubn. 185) (Repr.: N.Y., Kraus, 1965)   **CK290**

Indexes (1) the reports of Congress, (2) the Senate executive journal for diplomatic and consular appointments and treaty ratifications, (3) the opinions of the attorney-general for decisions of questions of international controversy, (4) the statutes-at-large, and (5) the *Congressional globe.*   Z1223.Z7H22

Heere, Wybo P. International bibliography of air law, 1900–1971. Leiden, Sijthoff; Dobbs Ferry, Oceana, 1972. 569p.   **CK291**

Table of contents and subject index in English, French, and Spanish.

Book and periodical materials in classed arrangement with author and subject indexes. Covers publications from about 1910 to early 1972 on a worldwide basis.

—— —— Supplement 1972–1976. Leyden, Sijthoff, 1976. 169p.

—— —— Supplement 1977–1980. The Hague, Nijhoff, 1981. 356p.

Z6464.A4H43

Human rights: a topical bibliography. Boulder, Colo., Westview Pr., [1983]. 299p.   **CK292**

Prep. by the Staff of the Center for the Study of Human Rights, Columbia University. J. Paul Martin, Project Director and Ed.

More than 7,000 citations to English-language books and articles are arranged according to a detailed subject classification. Includes reference sources and directories of selected periodicals and organizations. Author index.   Z7164.L6H84

Human rights in Latin America, 1964–1980: a selective annotated bibliography. Comp. and ed. by the Hispanic Division. Wash., Lib. of Congress, 1983. 257p.   **CK293**

1,827 citations are arranged by country or by issuing agencies—churches, private groups, international agencies, U.S. government. Also includes reference titles and a directory of organizations. Author index.   Z7164.L6H85

Kavass, Igor I. and **Blake, Michael J.** United States legislation on foreign relations and international commerce: a chronological and subject index of public laws and joint resolutions of the Congress of the United States. Buffalo, N.Y., W. S. Hein, 1977–84. v.1–5. (In progress)   **CK294**

Contents: v.1, 1789–1899; v.2, 1900–1929; v.3, 1920–1949; v.4, 1950–1969; v.5, 1970–1979.

Based on texts published in the *Statutes at large,* and thus includes repealed and superseded legal provisions, as well as those in effect as presented in the *Revised statutes* and the *United States code.* The main text of each volume consists of a chronological index, with short summaries of each statute or joint resolution, followed by a subject index.

Kozicki, Richard J. International relations of South Asia, 1947–1980: a guide to information sources. Detroit, Gale, [1981]. 166p. (International relations information guide ser., v.10)   **CK295**

An annotated, selected bibliography of English-language publications on the post-1947 international relations of India, Pakistan, Bangladesh, Sri Lanka, Nepal, Sikkim, Bhutan, and Afghanistan. Includes sections on reference sources and basic books. Organized by country, with subheadings for major bilateral relationships. Author and subject indexes.   Z3185.K69

Kurdiukov, Gennadii Irinarkhovich. Mezhdunarodnoe pravo. Bibliografiia 1917–1972gg. Moskva, IUridicheskaia Literatura, 1976. 598p.   **CK296**

A selective bibliography of about 8,000 entries for books and periodical articles written by Soviet scholars on international law; updates V. N. Durdenevskii's *Sovetskaia literatura po mezhdunarodnomu pravu, 1917–1957* (Moscow, 1959). Arranged in 19 broad subject sections, with author index. Reviews of the most important works are noted.   Z6461.K87

Lewis, John Rodney. Uncertain judgment: a bibliography of war crimes trials. Santa Barbara, Calif., ABC-Clio, [1979]. 251p. (War/peace bibliography ser., 8)   **CK297**

In four parts: general reference tools useful to the new researcher in law, history, and political science; background issues of philosophical concepts and international law of war crimes; historical works (about 2,000 entries on war crimes trials from 1474 to 1976,

with particularly detailed coverage of World War II trials); and subsidiary issues, such as group criminality and civil-military relations. Lists about 3,300 original documents and secondary sources. Detailed table of contents; author index.   Z6464.W33L48

Li, Kuo Lee. World wide space law bibliography. Toronto, Carswell Co., distr. by ICASL, McGill University, Montreal, 1978. 700p.   **CK298**

At head of title: Institute and Center of Air and Space Law, Institut et Centre de Droit Aérien et Spatiel.

Organizes a wide variety of materials in a detailed subject classification, including works on astronautics, astropolitics, space telecommunications, and socio-economic aspects of space. Makes a special effort to identify United Nations documents and international agreements. Author and subject indexes.   Z6464.S62L48

McDorman, Ted L., Beauchamp, Kenneth P. and **Johnston, Douglas M.** Maritime boundary delimitation: an annotated bibliography. Lexington, Mass., Lexington Books, [1983]. 207p.   **CK299**

Includes primarily materials written since 1960, with emphasis on legal periodicals. Appendix of all bilateral ocean boundary agreements; indexed by country and author.   Z6464.M2M37

Merrills, J. G. A current bibliography of international law. London & Boston, Butterworths, 1978. 277p.   **CK300**

An annotated bibliography of English-language literature, with emphasis on titles published since 1960. Detailed classed arrangement; author index.   Z6461.M47

O'Connor, Barry. International human rights: a bibliography, 1970–1975. Rev. ed. Notre Dame, Ind., Center for Civil and Human Rights, Univ. of Notre Dame Law School, 1980. 172p.   **CK301**

1976 ed. by William Miller carried dates 1970–76.

Covers English-language materials. Publications are grouped by type (i.e., periodical articles listed by author; anonymous articles; monographs; documents), with subject, country, and area indexes.   K3236.O25

Papadakis, Nikos. International law of the sea: a bibliography. Alphen aan den Rijn & Germantown, Md., Sijthoff & Noordhoff, 1980. 457p.   **CK302**

A subject classified bibliography of more than 4,500 English- and French-language books, periodical articles, and documents, with author and subject indexes.   Z6464.M2P36

—— and **Glassner, Martin.** International law of the sea and marine affairs: a bibliography. Supplement to the 1980 ed. The Hague, Nijhoff; Hingham, Mass., Kluwer (distr.), 1984. 579p.   **CK302a**

Adds more than 10,100 citations; multilingual and international. Appendixes list reference works and journal titles. Author index.   Z6464.M2P36 Suppl.

Robinson, Jacob. International law and organization: general sources of information. Leyden, Sijthoff, 1967. 560p.   **CK303**

Lists sources wholly concerned with international law and international organization. Includes sections for encyclopedias and dictionaries, treatises, bibliographies, biobibliographies, periodicals and yearbooks, plus a chapter on study and research in this field.   Z6466.R6

Schutter, Bart de and **Eliaerts, Christian.** Bibliography on international criminal law. Leiden, Sijthoff, 1972. 423p.   **CK304**

A classed bibliography listing more than 5,000 books, essays in collective works, periodical and newspaper articles, and official documents of international organizations. Treats such topics as extraterritorial jurisdiction, extradition, war crimes, genocide, piracy, slavery, humanitarian law, etc. Author and subject indexes.   Z6464.C8S38

United Nations Library (Geneva, Switzerland). League of Nations & United Nations monthly list of selected articles;

cumulative, 1920–1970: political questions. Ed. by Norman S. Field. Dobbs Ferry, N.Y., Oceana, 1971–73. 6v.

CK305

Contents: v.1, 1920–28; v.2, 1929–45; v.3, 1946–60; v.4, 1961–70; v.5, Special problems, 1920–70; v.6, Security and international peace, 1920–70.

A compilation arranged by subject and country in chronological order. Based on the card file used to issue the Library's *Liste mensuelle d'articles sélectionnés.*   Z6461.U46

Vogel, Robert. A breviate of British diplomatic blue books, 1919–1939. Montreal, McGill Univ. Pr., 1963. 475p.

CK306

A continuation of Harold W. V. Temperley and Lillian M. Penson, *A century of diplomatic blue books, 1814–1914* (Cambridge, Univ. Pr., 1938. 600p.).

Attempts to list the titles of all parliamentary papers, published between 1919 and 1939, directly related to British foreign policy. Arranged in chronological order. Includes subject index.

Z2009.V6

Wiktor, Christian L. Canadian bibliography of international law. Toronto, Univ. of Toronto Pr., [1984]. 767p.   **CK307**

A detailed classed bibliography of about 8,700 citations, principally to Canadian writings on public international law and legal implications of international relations; some brief annotations, with reviews noted. Indexed by author, corporate name, conference, and series.   Z6464.W3W54

Worldwide bibliography for the year 1964–73 of space law and related matters. no.1–10, Aug. 1965–July 1974. Paris, International Institute of Space Law, 1965–74. Annual.

CK308

Title and explanatory matter also in French.

A classified bibliography with author index. Titles are given in the original language, but those in languages other than French or English are also translated into one or the other of those languages. References to papers presented at international meetings are included, and there are separate listings for United Nations documents, international agreements, and reviews of previously published books.   JX5810.W65

Current

Checklist of human rights documents. v.1, no.1/5– . Austin, Tex., Tarlton Law Library, Univ. of Texas School of Law, 1976– . Monthly.   **CK309**

Publ. in cooperation with the United States Institute of Human Rights, New York.

Continues in part a journal with the same title published by the United States Institute of Human Rights and the Charles B. Sears Law Library of the State University of New York at Buffalo, but with an expanded scope. Current issues list documents of: (1) international and regional organizations, national governments, and nongovernmental organizations; and (2) commercial publications, subdivided as yearbooks, monographs, journals, and journal articles. Separate sections for ratifications and accessions, and for current announcements. No index.   K3226.C54

Public international law, a current bibliography of articles. v.1, no.1– , 1975– . Berlin [etc.], Springer-Verlag, 1976– . Semiannual.   **CK310**

A classed listing of periodical articles and essays from collected works, selected from some 1,000 journals and collective volumes. Case notes and book reviews are selectively included. International in scope. Author and subject index in each issue, cumulating annually.   Z6461.P83

Refugee abstracts. v.1, no.1– , [Mar. 1982]– . Geneva, Internat. Refugee Integration Resource Centre, 1982– . Quarterly.   **CK311**

Provides abstracts of a wide variety of international publications,

as well as book reviews. Broad subject arrangement; author and subject indexes.

Wiktor, Christian L. and **Foster, Leslie A.** Marine affairs bibliography. v.1, [no.1]– . Halifax, Dalhousie Law School, [1980]– . Quarterly, with annual cumulations.   **CK312**

Subtitle: A comprehensive index to marine law and policy literature.

Prep. under the auspices of Dalhousie Ocean Studies Programme.

A detailed classed index to international literature in a wide variety of formats, indexed by author, corporate names, conferences, and series, and by geographical area. Book reviews are noted.

Z6464.M2W54

Digests and collections

A British digest of international law, comp. principally from the Archives of the Foreign Office. Clive Parry, ed. London, Stevens, 1965–67. (In progress)   **CK313**

Contents: Phase I: v.2b, pt.iii, Territory. Chap.7, International waterways. Chap.8, Rights in foreign territory; v.5, pt.vi, The individual in international law. Chap.15, Nationality and protection; v.6, pt.vi, The individual in international law. Chap.16, Aliens. Chap. 17, Extradition; v.7, pt.vii, Organs of states. Chap.18, Central organs. Chap.19, Diplomatic agents; v.8, pt.vii, Organs of states. Chap.20, Consular officers. Chap.21, Functions of diplomatic envoys and consular officers, etc., in relation to foreign marriages.

Published under the auspices of the International Law Fund.

The material offered here is almost exclusively British, but it is "something more than a collection of documents, since it has been sought to reproduce every document selected for printing in its context."—*General pref., v.5.*

To cover the period 1860–1914 in 10v., and 1914–60 in 5v.

Volumes dealing with materials belonging to the period prior to the outbreak of the first World War are designated as Phase I; later materials as Phase II.   JX3225.B76

Brownlie, Ian. African boundaries: a legal and diplomatic encyclopaedia. London, C. Hurst; Berkeley, Univ. of Calif. Pr. for the Royal Inst. of Internat. Affairs, [1979]. 1355p. maps.   **CK314**

For each boundary there is provided a map, historico-political background, geographical description and demarcation, text of relevant treaties and documents, references to relevant map sheets, current issues, and bibliography. Geographical arrangement; index.

DT31.B776

—— Basic documents on human rights. 2d ed. Oxford, Clarendon Pr., 1981. 505p.   **CK315**

1st ed. 1971.

A collection of representative sources, with introductory notes and bibliographical references. The section on individual documents on human rights in national legal systems has been omitted to make room for recent material such as the Final Act of the Helsinki Conference.   K3228.A1B76

Déak, Francis and **Jessup, Philip C.** Collection of neutrality laws, regulations and treaties of various countries. Wash., Carnegie Endowment for Internat. Peace, 1939. 2v. (Repr.: Westport, Conn., Greenwood Pr., 1974)   **CK316**

Includes laws, regulations, and treaties from 1800 to Oct. 1, 1938.

JX5355.D4

Digest of commercial laws of the world. George Kohlik, ed. Rev. ed. Dobbs Ferry, N.Y., Oceana, [1975–]. 6v., looseleaf.

CK317

Published for the National Association of Credit Management.

A country-by-country summary, each section by a specialist. Uniform presentation within sections.

Kept up-to-date by supplements or by complete revision of sections as necessary.

Digest of United States practice in international law, 1973– . [Wash., U.S. Govt. Prt. Off.], 1974– . Annual. (U.S. Dept. of State. Publ. 8756 [etc.]) **CK318**

Continues M. M. Whiteman's *Digest of international law* (below) and is updated by the section "Contemporary practice of the United States relating to international law" in each quarterly issue of the *American journal of international law.* JX21.R68

Whiteman, Marjorie Millace. Digest of international law. Wash., Govt. Prt. Off., 1963–73. 15v. (U.S. Dept. of State. Pubn.) **CK319**

Contents: v.1, Ch.1, International law; Ch.2, States, territories, and governments; v.2, Ch.3, Recognition; Ch.4, State succession; Ch.5, Territory and sovereignty of states; v.3, Ch.6, Boundaries and related matters; Ch.7, International rivers and river basins; Ch.8, Inter-oceanic canals; v.4, Ch.9, Territorial sea and contiguous zones; Ch.10, High seas; Ch.11, Continental shelf; Ch.12, Fisheries; v.5, Ch.13, Rights and duties of states; v.6, Ch.14, National jurisdiction; Ch.15, Exemptions from territorial jurisdiction; Ch. 16, Extradition; v.7, Ch.17, Diplomatic missions and embassy property; Ch.18, Consular officers and consulates; Ch.19, International copyright; Ch.30, Industrial property; v.8, Ch.21, Nationality. Ch.22, Passports and other travel documents; Ch.23, Aliens; Ch.24, State responsibility for injuries to aliens;

v.9, Ch.25, Maritime navigation and transportation; Ch.26, Aviation; Ch.27, Communications, transportation, and travel; Ch.28, Aspects of meteorology; v.10, Ch.29, Armed conflict; Ch.30, Armed conflict at sea; Ch.31, Belligerent interference with neutral commerce; v.11, Ch.32, Prize; Ch.33, Neutrality in a changing world; Ch.34, Arms control and disarmament; Ch.35, International criminal law; v.12, Ch. 36, Legal regulation of use of force; Ch.37, The International Court of Justice; v.13, Ch.38, Certain legal problems common to international organizations; Ch.39, The United Nations; Ch.40, The United Nations Secretariat; Ch.41, Freedom of information; v.14, Ch.42, Treaties and other international agreements; Ch.43, Developing international economic law; v.15, General index; List of cases.

A compilation of official and unofficial materials. It is a "successor digest to Hackworth's *Digest of international law* . . . [but] does not incorporate the Hackworth volumes."—*Pref.*

Hackworth, Green Haywood. Digest of international law. Wash., Govt. Prt. Off., 1940–44. 8v. (*In* U.S. Dept. of State. Pubn.) **CK320**

Includes the documents and files accumulated in the Dept. of State since 1906. Supplements and does not duplicate Moore's *Digest* (below). v.8 is a general index and list of cases. JX237.H3

Moore, John Bassett. Digest of international law. Wash., Govt. Prt. Off., 1906. 8v. (U.S. 56th Cong., 2d sess. House doc.551) **CK321**

Full title: A digest of international law as embodied in diplomatic discussions, treaties and other international agreements, international awards, the decisions of municipal courts, and writings of jurists, and especially in documents, published and unpublished, issued by presidents and secretaries of state of the United States, the opinions of the attorneys-general, and the decisions of courts, federal and state.

v.1–7, Digest; v.8, Index. Table of cases. List of documents.
JX237.M7

Human rights: a compilation of international instruments. [4th ed.] N.Y., United Nations, 1983. 147p. ([Document] United Nations; ST/HR/1/Rev. 2) **CK322**

Prep. by the Division of Human Rights of the United Nations Secretariat.

1st ed. 1968.

Includes the texts of conventions, declarations, and recommendations on human rights adopted by the United Nations. Arranged by broad topic, with a chronological listing. K3238.H8

United Nations. Legal Dept. Laws concerning nationality. [Prep. by the Division for the Development and Codification of International Law] N.Y., United Nations, 1954. 594p. (United Nations legislative ser., no.4) **CK323**

———— ———— Supplement. 1959. 179p. (United Nations legislative ser., no.9)

Contains the texts of the basic current laws of various states concerning nationality. In English except for those originally published in French. JX1977.A2

Annuals and current surveys

American foreign policy current documents, 1950/55– . Wash., Dept. of State [for sale by U.S. Govt. Prt. Off.], 1956– . Annual. **CK324**

Issued by U.S. Dept. of State. Office of the Historian.

Years 1968–80 covered by *American foreign policy basic documents, 1977–1980,* and two other monographs scheduled for future publication.

Vols. for 1981– have an annual supplement on microfiche.

Continues a series begun in 1950 with publication of *A decade of American foreign policy: basic documents, 1941–1949* (Senate document 123, 81st Cong., 1st Session). Presents the principal public foreign policy messages and congressional testimony by the executive branch of the U.S. government. Organization is chronological within topical and geographical areas. Longer documents are often printed in part; their full texts and those of many other documents are found in the microfiche supplement. Indexed. JX1417.A33

American foreign relations; a documentary record, 1971–78. N.Y., New York Univ. Pr., 1976–79. Annual. **CK325**

Ed. by Richard P. Stebbins and Elaine P. Adam.

"Continuing the series of foreign policy surveys initiated by the Council of Foreign Relations in 1931 under the title *The United States in World Affairs,* the volume also maintains the service provided for more than three decades by the separate *Documents on American Foreign Relations* series [below]" (*Pref.,* 1975), thus combining narrative with documentation. Appendix lists principal sources. Indexed. Ceased publication. JX231.D6

Documents on American foreign relations, [v.1]–31, Jan. 1938/39–70. N.Y., Council on Foreign Relations, 1939–73. Annual. **CK325a**

v.8 covers July 1, 1945–Dec. 31, 1946, instead of the 12-month period July–June of previous volumes. Beginning with v.9, each volume covers a calendar year.

Published by World Peace Foundation, 1938/39–52.

Includes presidential messages, speeches, reports, letters, communiqués, news conference comments, official statements, resolutions, etc. Continued by *American foreign relations* (above). JX231.D6

Documents on international affairs. 1928–63. London, Oxford Univ. Pr., 1929–73. Annual. **CK326**

Issued under the auspices of the Royal Institute of International Affairs.

"Prepared to accompany and supplement the annual *Survey of international affairs.*"—*Introd., 1928.*

Coverage is several years behind dates of publication, e.g., 1963 documents appear in volume published 1973. Ceased publication.
D442.S82

Freedom in the world: political rights and civil liberties, 1978– . N.Y., Freedom House, [1978]– . Annual. **CK327**

"Publ. by Freedom House in cooperation with G. K. Hall and Co."—*t.p.*

In three parts: (1) a comparative survey of political rights and civil liberties throughout the world; (2) essays on particular countries or problems; (3) individual country summaries, outlining political rights (especially for minorities), civil liberties, and a comparative ranking in terms of the status of freedom. Indexed. JC571.G336

Hague. International Court of Justice. Yearbook. 1946/ 47– . [The Hague], 1947– . Annual. **CK328**

Published also in French: *Annuaire.*

Gives information on the composition of the Court, biographies of the judges, lists of the states entitled to appear before the Court, matters dealt with, summary of judgments, bibliography of works published on the Court, etc.   JX1971.6.A25

Dictionaries and handbooks

See also CK482.

Becker, Carol A. International relations dictionary. Rev. 1980. [Wash.], Dept. of State Lib. [for sale by Supt. of Docs.], 1980. 80p.   **CK329**

An extremely useful dictionary which is not intended to be comprehensive, but to supplement other dictionaries and reference works for terms which are too current or specialized, or which are not indexed or cross-referenced in other sources. Each entry consists of the term and its definition; a "Notes" section which contains documentation for the term; and a "See also" section referring to related terms.   JX1226.B42

Border and territorial disputes. Alan J. Day, ed. [Harlow, Essex], Longman, [1982]. 406p. maps.   **CK330**

"The aim . . . is to present concise accounts of [approximately 70] currently unresolved border and territorial issues between states . . . , arranged alphabetically in five sections covering broad geographical areas."—*Introd.* Selected bibliography; subject index.
     D843.B623

Dictionnaire de la terminologie du droit international: tables en anglais, italien, espagnol, allemand. Publié sous le patronage de l'Union Académique Internationale. [Paris], Sirey, 1960. 755p.   **CK331**

Provides fairly lengthy definitions, many with bibliographic references to legal sources, citations, etc. Indexes from the other four languages to the French word or phrase equivalent. Begun in 1938, but interrupted by World War II.

Encyclopedia of public international law. Publ. under the auspices of the Max Planck Institute for Comparative Public Law and International Law, under the direction of Rudolf Bernhardt. Amsterdam & N.Y., North-Holland, [1981–84]. v.1–7. (In progress)   **CK332**

Contents: v.1, Settlement of disputes; v.2, Decisions of international courts and tribunals and international arbitrations; v.3–4, Use of force, war, neutrality and peace treaties; v.5, International organizations in general, universal international organizations and cooperation; v.6, Regional cooperation, organizations and problems; v.7, History of international law, sources of international law, treaties.

Provides lengthy articles, signed by specialists and with bibliographies. Articles are in English; follows the plan of Karl Strupp's *Wörterbuch des Völkerrechts* (2. Aufl. hrsg. von Hans-Jürgen Schlochauer. Berlin, W. de Gruyter, 1960–62. 4v.).

A French-language encyclopedia of international law is the *Répertoire du droit international* (Paris, Jurisprudence Générale, Dalloz, 1968– . v.1– ; kept up-to-date by supplements).   JX1226.E5

Fawq al-'Adah, Samūhi. A dictionary of diplomacy and international affairs, English-French-Arabic. Beirut, Librairie du Liban, [1974]. 550p.   **CK333**

Arranged by English word or phrase, followed by French and Arabic equivalents; French and Arabic indexes.   JX1226.F3

Gamboa, Melquiades Jereos. A dictionary of international law and diplomacy. Quezon City, Philippines, Central Lawbook Pub. Co.; Dobbs Ferry, N.Y., Oceana, [1973]. 351p.
     CK334

"The contents of the writer's previous book, *Elements of diplomatic and consular practice, a glossary* (1966) after having been revised and updated, are incorporated in this present work."—*Pref.*

Includes terms relevant to international law in general and to the United Nations, as well as those concerned strictly with diplomatic and consular practice.   JX1226.G29

Humana, Charles. World human rights guide. N.Y., Pica Pr., [1984]. 224p. maps.   **CK335**

Provides evaluative comparisons of the human rights situation in 117 countries, according to 50 criteria drawn from United Nations and other human rights standards. Criteria are grouped under: freedom/rights; state power (censorship, police, corporal and capital punishment); maximum punishments in penal code for selected offenses; compulsory documents for citizens. Regional, then country arrangement.

Paenson, Isaac. English-French-Spanish-Russian manual of the terminology of public international law (law of peace) and international organizations. Brussels, Bruylant; Deventer, Neth., Kluwer, [1983]. xlviii, 846p.   **CK336**

"Publ. for the Graduate Institute of International Studies, Geneva, and 'INTERCENTRE'."—*t.p.*

A polyglot dictionary arranged by subject, with parallel texts in English, French, Spanish, and Russian; alphabetical indexes in the four languages.   JX1226.P26

Plano, Jack C. and **Olton, Roy.** The international relations dictionary. 3d ed. Santa Barbara, Calif., ABC-Clio, [1982]. 488p.   **CK337**

1st ed. 1969.

Offers definitions of terms relating to international relations and foreign policy, together with comments on the significance of each term. Entries are grouped within topical sections rather than being in a single alphabetical sequence. Index of terms.   JX1226.P55

Satow, *Sir* **Ernest Mason.** Satow's Guide to diplomatic practice. 5th ed. Ed. by Lord Gore-Booth. London, Longman, [1979]. 544p. il.   **CK338**

1st ed. 1917.

A scholarly history and description of diplomatic practice, originally written by a British civil servant. In five main sections: (1) diplomacy in general; (2) diplomatic agents in general; (3) consular matters; (4) international transactions, i.e., congresses, conferences, treaties and other international instruments; (5) international organizations. Appendixes give short glossary of terms, description of important conferences, membership of international organizations, etc. Lengthy notes and bibliography. Indexed.   JX1635.S3

Sen, Biswanath. A diplomat's handbook of international law and practice. 2d rev. and enl. ed. The Hague, Nijhoff, 1979. 529p.   **CK339**

1st ed. 1965.

A handbook of practical information on diplomatic relations, functions, and privileges. Also considers selected topics of international law of special interest to those in foreign service (e.g., diplomatic protection of citizens abroad, passports, and visas).
     JX1662.S44

Vincent, Jack Ernest. A handbook of international relations; a guide to terms, theory and practice. Woodbury, N.Y., Barron's Educational Series, [1969]. 456p.   **CK340**

Includes terms, doctrines, conferences, etc., important in the field. Much space is devoted to various international organizations and their subsidiary agencies. Bibliography, p.437–56.   JX1395.V53

Directories

Garling, Marguerite. The human rights handbook: a guide to British and American international human rights organizations. N.Y., Facts on File, 1979. 299p.   **CK341**

Comp. for the Writers and Scholars Educational Trust.

Concentrates on British voluntary and professional organizations; briefer sections for American and international non-governmental organizations are to be expanded in the next edition. Organizations are classed by type, with a name index. Introductory sections, particularly that on refugee admission, tend to be lengthy. Narrative descriptions focus on organizational work and finance.
     JC571.G32

Human rights organizations & periodicals directory, 1973– . Berkeley, Calif., Meiklejohn Civil Liberties Inst., 1973– .
     CK342

3d ed., 1977, ed. by David Christiano.

Intended as "a referral list for people seeking information or assistance in human rights cases; as a guide for teachers, students, and researchers seeking hard-to-find sources of information; and as a resource for attorneys concerned with human rights cases."—*Introd., 2d ed.* In two parts: (1) Alphabetical guide and (2) Subject index.   KF4741.H84

North American human rights directory. Comp. by Laurie S. Wiseberg and Hazel Sirett. Wash., Human Rights Internet, 1984. 264p.   **CK343**

A project of Human Rights Internet.

The previous edition (1980) was a revised and enlarged edition of the *Human rights directory 1979* (Wash., Human Rights Internet and MCPL Education Fund, 1980). Offers directory information, as well as information on the purpose, program, structure, and publications of nearly 500 U.S. or Canadian organizations, governmental, and intergovernmental bodies. A supplementary chapter on human rights resources surveys the research collections of about 54 libraries and documentation centers in the United States.

Human Rights Internet has also issued *Human rights directory: Latin America, Africa, Asia* (1981) and *Human rights directory: Western Europe* (1982).

TREATIES

Bibliography

United Nations. Office of Legal Affairs. List of treaty collections. [Comp. by the Codification Division] N.Y., United Nations, 1956. 174p. (United Nations. [Document] ST/LEG/5) (Repr.: Holmes Beach, Fla., Wm. W. Gaunt, 1981)   **CK344**

Title and prefatory matter in English, French and Spanish.

An annotated bibliography of treaty collections published since the late 18th century. In three parts: general collections; subject collections; collections by states (further subdivided by collections, indexes and chronologies, special topics, and treaties with separate states). Notes and comments in English or French. Indexed.

    JX1977.A2ST

Collections and indexes

Bowman, M. J. and **Harris, D. J.** Multilateral treaties: index and current status. Comp. and annotated within the Univ. of Nottingham Treaty Centre. London, Butterworths, 1984. 516p.   **CK345**

Presents data on status, signatories, and locations of texts for more than 900 multilateral treaties. Chronological arrangement, with broad subject, keyword, and treaty title indexes. To be kept up-to-date by supplements.

The consolidated treaty series. Ed. and annotated by Clive Parry. Dobbs Ferry, N.Y., Oceana, [1969–81]. 231v.   **CK346**

The series covers the period 1648 through 1919, i.e., to the beginning of the League of Nations *Treaty series* (CK352). Reproduces "such prints of treaties in their original languages as can be found in whatsoever collection along with such translations into English or French as again, which is very often the case, can be found. If no such translation is discoverable it is proposed wherever possible and desirable to supply instead a species of calendaring or summary in one of those languages. It is proposed also to annotate in some measure the texts reproduced."—*Pref.*   JX120.P35

Index-guide to treaties: based on The consolidated treaty series, ed. and annotated by Clive Parry, LL.D., and all other series therein utilised. Dobbs Ferry, N.Y., Oceana, 1979–85. v.1–5. (In progress)   **CK347**

Serves as an index to *The consolidated treaty series* (above), and to

the original sources used in its compilation. In chronological arrangement, each entry providing treaty title, date, signatories, and references to textual sources.

The final volume will be a party/country index to the series. A *Special chronological list* forms a second part of the *Index-guide,* covering colonial treaties, postal and telegraph agreements. v.5 has title: Major peace treaties of modern history, 1967–1979.

    JX120.P352

Current international treaties. Ed. by T. B. Millar with Robin Ward. [N.Y.], New York Univ. Pr., [1984]. 558p.   **CK348**

A collection of important bilateral and multilateral treaties, grouped by subject, principal party, and chronology. Most are excerpted, with references to major treaty series for the full text.

    JX171.C87

Grenville, John Ashley Soames. The major international treaties, 1914–1973; a history and guide with texts. N.Y., Stein and Day, [1974]. 575p. maps.   **CK349**

Each section begins with a brief history and analysis of circumstances leading up to the treaties, and concludes with versions of the treaties edited to remove formal legal materials and focus on the important articles. Arrangement is chronological through World War II, then regional. Source references are given for the full texts of treaties included. Indexed.   JX171.G74

Harvard University. Law School. Library. Index to multilateral treaties; a chronological list of multi-party international agreements from the sixteenth century through 1963, with citations to their text. Vaclav Mostecky, ed.; Francis R. Doyle, asst. ed. Cambridge, Mass., 1965. 301p.   **CK350**

Deals with "those international agreements which have been signed by three or more international persons."—*Pref.* Includes 3,859 items from 1596 through 1963 in chronological arrangement, with subject and regional index. Entry includes date of signature; brief descriptive title or key words (in English); list of sources carrying full text of the treaty; and the language or languages of the text. Kept up-to-date by occasional supplements.

Israel, Fred L., ed. Major peace treaties of modern history, 1648–1967. With an introductory essay by Arnold Toynbee. Commentaries by Emanuel Chill. N.Y., Chelsea House, 1967–80. 5v.   **CK351**

Provides texts of the treaties in English, plus brief commentary.

    JX121.I8

League of Nations. Treaty series; publication of treaties and international engagements registered with the Secretariat of the League. v.1–205 (Treaty no.1–4834). Sept. 1920–1944/46. London, Harrison, 1920–46. 205v.   **CK352**

———— ———— General index, 1920–1946. no.1–9 (v.1–205). Geneva, 1927–46. 9v.

Index issued at end of every 500 treaties.

Continued by United Nations *Treaty series* (CK358).

    JX170.L4

Rohn, Peter H. Treaty profiles. Santa Barbara, Calif., ABC-Clio, [1976]. 256p.   **CK353**

A quantitative inventory and survey of national, regional, and global treaty patterns from 1946 to 1965. Offers a standard, one-page profile of the treaty pattern of every country and treaty-making international organization. Tabular format lists treaty partners in descending order, with total number of treaties and mutual treaties between the two countries; for the latter category, presents information on number signed within specific time periods, topics, international organizations referred to in the text, etc. Covers more than 12,000 treaties.

A companion series is: JX171.R62

———— World treaty index. 2d ed. Santa Barbara, Calif., ABC-Clio, [1983–84]. 5v.   **CK354**

Contents: v.1, Reference volume; v.2–3, Main entry section, pts.1–2, 1900–59, 1960–80; v.4, Party index; v.5, Keyword index.

1st ed. 1974.

An inventory and index to more than 44,500 bilateral and multilateral treaties appearing in *LTS, UNTS,* and the national treaty collections of 120 countries. Full bibliographic citations appear in the main entry section and provide: name of instrument and whether uni- , bi- , or multilateral; series or source citation; date of signature and entry into force; registrant; number of articles; languages; title keywords; topics; reference to international government organizations; reference to other treaties; procedural references; names of parties; annex information from *LTS/UNTS.* Index sections in v.4–5 refer to date, parties, topical subjects and classed subjects. The set is a product of the database maintained by the Treaty Research Center at the University of Washington, which offers individual research consultations and computer print-outs.

JX171.R63

Rönnefarth, Helmuth K. G. Konferenzen und Verträge; Vertrags-Ploetz, ein Handbuch geschichtlich bedeutsamer Zusammenkünfte und Vereinbarungen. 2. erw. und veränd. Aufl. Würzburg, A. G. Ploetz, 1958–63. T.II, Bd.3–4^A–B^. (In progress?) **CK355**

Contents: T.II, Bd.3, Neuere Zeit, 1492–1914; Bd.4^A^, Neueste Zeit, 1914–1959; Bd.4^B^, Neueste Zeit, 1959–63.

1st ed. 1952.

Provides brief background information, list of parties involved, and a summary of the provisions of historically significant conferences and agreements. Bibliography in each volume.   JX173.R62

The Third World without superpowers: the collected documents of the non-aligned countries. [Comp. by] Odette Jankowitsch and Karl P. Sauvant. Dobbs Ferry, N.Y., Oceana, 1978–[84]. [v.1–5] (In progress) **CK356**

Assembles documents adopted by the non-aligned countries at the Conferences of Heads of State or Government, mid-term conferences of ministers of foreign affairs, by the Coordinating Bureau at the Ministerial Level, etc.; excludes drafts, papers not formally adopted, and most speeches. Subject index; bibliography.

See also Group of 77, *The third world without superpowers* (CH134)   JX68.T48

Treaties and alliances of the world. Comp. and written by Henry W. Degenhardt. 3d ed. Detroit, Gale, [1981]. 409p. maps.   **CK357**

1st ed. 1968.

Provides concise summaries of the most important treaties in force from 1945 to the present, with many excerpts from the treaties themselves. Most of the information is derived from *Keesing's Contemporary archives.* Includes maps, tables, and an index of countries and international organizations.   JX4005.T72

United Nations. Treaty series; treaties and international agreements registered or filed and recorded with the Secretariat of the United Nations. v.1– , 1946/47– . N.Y., 1947– .   **CK358**

Continues the *Treaty series* issued by the League of Nations (CK352).

Includes bilingual text, English and French, plus original language texts. Chronological index issued at end of every 50 to 100 treaties. A privately published index for the 1969–74 period is:

JX170.U35

Vambery, Joseph T. and **Vambery, Rose V.** Cumulative list and index of treaties and international agreements registered or filed and recorded with the Secretariat of the United Nations, December 1969–December 1974. Dobbs Ferry, N.Y., Oceana, 1977. 2v.   **CK359**

Lists some 4,000 international agreements registered or filed and recorded with the Secretariat for the period 1969–74, as well as ratifications, accessions, prorogations, corrections and additions made during these years to agreements registered or filed and recorded before Dec. 1, 1969. The chronologically arranged entries note date and method of entry into force of the agreement, date of registration, and language of text. Subject and parties indexes.

JX171.V35

United Nations. Secretariat. A survey of treaty provisions for the pacific settlement of international disputes, 1949–1962. N.Y., United Nations, 1966. 901p.   **CK360**

Like the United Nations's *Systematic survey of treaties . . . 1928–48* (below), this volume serves to update the study made in 1927 by the Secretariat of the League of Nations, *Arbitration and security; systematic survey of the arbitration conventions and treaties of mutual security deposited with the League of Nations,* which covered the period 1919–27. Both give texts of treaties in English, and include treaties not registered with either the League of Nations or the United Nations. While the *Systematic survey . . . 1928–48* is more or less limited to the treaties on settlement of disputes, the *Survey . . . 1949–62* includes other related categories and presents them according to subject matter. Introductory material is limited; no general chronological table and no index.   JX1985.U44

United Nations. Secretariat. Systematic survey of treaties for the pacific settlement of international disputes, 1928–1948. Lake Success, N.Y., [1949]. 1201p.   **CK361**

Pt.1 Analyses of treaties; pt.2, Texts of treaties; pt.3, Tables of treaties: chronological, alphabetical, multipartite.   JX1985.U45

U.S. Dept. of State. Catalogue of treaties, 1814–1918. Wash., Govt. Prt. Off., 1919. 716p. (Repr.: Dobbs Ferry, N.Y., Oceana, 1964)   **CK362**

A general chronological catalog of treaties with an index by countries. Gives information as to place and date signed and ratified, with references to printed text and indication of the languages involved.   JX171.A4

United States

Davenport, Frances Gardiner, ed. European treaties bearing on the history of the United States and its dependencies. Wash., Carnegie Inst., 1917–37. 4v. (Carnegie Inst., Pubn. 254) (Repr.: Gloucester, Mass., P. Smith, 1967)   **CK363**

v.4 ed. by Charles Oscar Paullin.

Covers 1455–1815.   E173.D24

U.S. Dept. of State. Foreign relations of the United States. Diplomatic papers, 1861– . Wash., Govt. Prt. Off., 1862– . Annual.   **CK364**

Title varies: 1861–1931, *Papers relating to the foreign relations of the United States.* Usually cited by binder's title: *Foreign relations.*

Annual volumes of diplomatic correspondence between the United States and foreign countries. Includes correspondence, text of treaties, the president's annual message to Congress (in volumes after 1865), and special messages on foreign subjects, etc. Several volumes are published each year, the date of publication being much later than the year covered, e.g., volumes on 1942 published 1960. Many volumes have subtitles designating the country or area treated, e.g., *The Soviet Union, The Near East and Africa.*

———— ———— General index, 1861–99, 1900–1918. Wash., Govt. Prt. Off., 1902–41. 2v.

JX233.A3

———— The cumulated index to the U.S. Department of State papers relating to the foreign relations of the United States, 1939–1945. Millwood, N.Y., Kraus Internat., [1980]. 2v. (cxcix, 1031p.)

A cumulation of the indexes from the 57v. of the *Foreign relations* series for the period indicated, including the regular annual volumes, the special volumes on China (1942–49), and the special volumes on the heads-of-government conferences attended by Presidents Roosevelt and Truman (Dec. 1941–Aug. 1945). Tables of contents from all volumes indexed are reproduced in the first volume of this index.

———— List of treaties submitted to the Senate, 1789–1934. Wash., Govt. Prt. Off., 1935. 138p. (*Its* Pubn. 765)   **CK365**

The "List of treaties submitted" gives for each treaty its date, subject, and status, e.g., whether accepted without change, accepted with amendment, withdrawn, etc.; the "Numerical list of the Treaty series" gives for each treaty its date, country with which negotiated, subject, and a reference to the volume of the *Statutes at large* (CK206) containing the text. JX236 1934b

—— Treaties submitted to the Senate, 1935–1944. Wash., 1945. 28p. (*Its* Pubn. 2311) **CK366**

Supersedes annual supplements.
Continued by the Department's *United States treaty developments,* 1947–50.

—— Treaties in force; a list of treaties and other international agreements of the United States in force. Wash., Govt. Prt. Off., [1929?–]. Irregular (annual since 1958). (*Its* Pubn. ser.) **CK367**

Subtitle varies slightly.

U.S. Treaties. Treaties and other international agreements of the United States of America, 1776–1949. Comp. under the direction of Charles I. Bevans. Wash., Govt. Prt. Off., 1968–76. 13v. (U.S. Dept. of State. Pubn. ser.) **CK368**

Contents: v.1, Multilateral, 1776–1917; v.2, Multilateral, 1918–1930; v.3, Multilateral, 1931–1945; v.4, Multilateral, 1946–1949; v.5, Afghanistan–Burma; v.6, Canada–Czechoslovakia; v.7, Denmark–France; v.8, Germany–Iran; v.9, Iraq–Muscat; v.10, Nepal–Peru; v.11, Philippines–United Arab Republic; v.12, United Kingdom–Zanzibar; v.13, General index.
Designed to complement *United States treaties and other international agreements* (CK370) with respect to the earlier period. It provides easier access to treaties entered into by the United States between 1937 and 1950, heretofore available only in the *United States statutes at large.* Arrangement is chronological in the multilateral treaties volumes, with brief index in each volume. Only English texts (or official English translations) are included. Some headnotes and annotations are given. JX236 1968.A5

—— Treaties and other international acts, as of Dec. 27, 1945, no.1501– . Wash., Govt. Prt. Off., 1946– . **CK369**

Cited as *TIAS.*
Issued singly in pamphlets. Continues the "Treaty series" ([18–?]–1946), and the "Executive agreement series" (1929–45). The combined numbers in these two series having reached 1500, the new series begins with 1501.
Contains authentic texts of treaties, declarations, constitutions and charters of international organizations, etc.

—— United States treaties and other international agreements, v.1– , 1950– . Wash., Govt. Prt. Off., 1952– . Annual. **CK370**

Suggested form of citation: *UST.*
From the calendar year 1950, this becomes the official place of publication and legal evidence for treaties and international agreements to which the United States is a party. Prior to this they were included in the *Statutes at large* (CK206). Arranged in numerical order as originally published in pamphlet form in *Treaties and other international acts* series, no.1501– (above). Subject and country index.
Indexed by: JX231.A34

Kavass, Igor I. and **Michael, Mark A.** United States treaties and other international agreements cumulative index 1776–1949. Buffalo, N.Y., W. S. Hein, 1975. 4v. **CK371**

Subtitle: Cumulative index to United States treaties and other international agreements 1776–1949 as published in Statutes at large, Malloy, Miller, Bevans, and other relevant sources.
Contents: v.1, In numerical order of TS, EAS, TIAS and AD numbers . . . (and a list of United States postal agreements 1844–1949); v.2, Chronological index; v.3, Country index; v.4, Subject index.
Lists about 2,600 treaties and international executive agreements, either bilateral or multilateral, entered into by the United States with foreign countries and international organizations; excludes treaties with American Indians.
Continued by: JX231.K4

Kavass, Igor I. and **Sprudzs, Adolf.** UST cumulative index 1950–1970; cumulative index to United States treaties and other international agreements. 1950–1970: 1 UST–21, UST, TIAS nos. 2010–7034. Buffalo, N.Y., W. S. Hein, 1973. 4v. **CK372**

Contents: v.1, In numerical order of TIAS numbers, 2010–7034; v.2, Chronological index; v.3, Country index; v.4, Subject index.
Indexes and arranges in appropriate lists some 5,000 treaties and agreements included in *UST* for this period.
Continued by: JX231.K38

—— UST cumulative index 1971–1975: a cumulative index to United States treaties and other international agreements 1971–1975: 22 UST–26 UST, TIAS nos. 7035–8224. Buffalo, N.Y., W. S. Hein, 1977. 593p. **CK373**

Divided into sections corresponding to the volumes of the previously mentioned sets: (1) Numerical list of documents, arranged by TIAS number; (2) Chronological index; (3) Country index, subdivided by bilateral and multilateral treaties and agreements; (4) Subject index.

—— UST cumulative indexing service, 1976–[79]: cumulative index to United States treaties and other international agreements, 1976–[79]: 27 UST–[31] UST, TIAS nos.8225–[9697]. Buffalo, N.Y., W. S. Hein, 1978–83. Looseleaf. **CK374**

A cumulative index covering 1976–79 of *UST,* with the same indexing arrangement as its predecessor volumes (above). Updated by *Current treaty index* (CK375) which indexes slip treaties and agreements in *TIAS* prior to their inclusion in *UST.*

Current treaty index, 1982– . Buffalo, N.Y., W. S. Hein, 1982– . Annual. **CK375**

Comp. by Igor I. Kavass and Adolf Sprudzs.
Cumulative index to the *United States slip treaties and agreements.* Volume for 1982 includes information on *TIAS* 9605– . Updates *UST cumulative indexing service* (above) and follows its indexing arrangement. JX236.5.C87

Unperfected treaties of the United States of America, 1776–1976. Dobbs Ferry, N.Y., Oceana, 1976–84. v.1–6. (In progress) **CK376**

Ed. and annotated by Christian L. Wiktor.
Contents: v.1, 1776–1855; v.2, 1856–1882; v.3, 1883–1904; v.4, 1905–18; v.5, 1919.
Presents, in chronological order, the texts of all international agreements concluded by the United States which have failed to go into force (excluding Indian treaties and postal agreements). Each text is preceded by a note giving: the name of the party or parties, short title, place and date of signature, Senate action, location in the treaty file of the National Archives, source of printed text, and history. Each volume is provided with a list of works cited, a table of contents listing the treaties, and an index; there will be a cumulative index in the final volume. JX236 1776.U56

China

Johnston, Douglas M. and **Chiu, Hungdah.** Agreements of the People's Republic of China, 1949–1967, a calendar. Cambridge, Harvard Univ. Pr., 1968. 286p. (Harvard studies in East Asian law, 3) **CK377**

A chronological calendar of treaties, with textual sources indicated. Indexed by treaty partner and subject.
Updated by: Z6464.T8J63

Chiu, Hungdah. Agreements of the People's Republic of China, 1966–80: a calendar. N.Y., Praeger, [1981]. 329p. **CK378**

JX926 1981.C48

Rhode, Grant F. and **Whitlock, Reid E.** Treaties of the People's Republic of China, 1949–1978: an annotated compilation. Boulder, Colo., Westview, [1980]. 207p. maps. **CK379**

Provides English-language translations of texts, with numerous footnotes to primary and secondary sources. Arranged by type of treaty (friendship, boundary, commercial, etc.), with chapter introductions. JX926 1980.C47

Great Britain

Gt.Brit. Foreign Office. Treaty series, 1892– . London, Stat. Off., 1892– . **CK380**

Issued as command papers, but numbered and indexed so that they can be bound as a separate set. General indexes are issued every few years as one of the numbers in the middle of a volume. JX636 1892

———— British and foreign state papers, 1812–1967/68, with which is incorporated Hertslet's Commercial treaties. London, Stat. Off., 1841–1978. v.1–170. **CK381**

Incorporates *Hertslet's Commercial treaties* (below) from v.116, 1922.

Contains treaties, correspondence about foreign affairs, and many documents of historical interest and importance, especially texts of the constitutions of foreign countries and similar organic laws. Each volume has a good index, and there are six general indexes: (1) v.64 indexes v.1–63; (2) v.93 indexes v.65–92; (3) v.115 indexes v.94–114; (4) v.138 indexes v.116–37; (5) v.165 indexes v.139–64; (6) v.170 indexes v.166–69. Material included is mainly that of the 19th and 20th centuries, but some papers are of an earlier date. JX103.A3

Hertslet's Commercial treaties; a collection of treaties and conventions between Great Britain and foreign powers, and of the laws, decrees, orders in council, etc., concerning the same, so far as they relate to commerce and navigation, slavery, extradition, nationality, copyright, postal matters, etc. London, Stat. Off., 1827–1925. 31v. **CK382**

Title varies.

v.22 is general index to v.1–21; v.31 is index to v.23–30.

Continued in *British and foreign state papers,* beginning with v.116, 1922 (above). JX636 1827

Parry, Clive and **Hopkins, Charity.** An index of British treaties, 1101–1968. London, Stat. Off., 1970. 4 pts. in 3v. (1816p.) **CK383**

Comp. under the auspices of the International Law Fund and the British Institute of International and Comparative Law.

Contents: v.1, pt.1, Index of multilateral treaties by subject; pt.2, Index of bilateral treaties by country; pt.3, Index of bilateral treaties by subject; v.2, Chronological list of treaties, 1101–1925; v.3, Chronological list of treaties, 1926–1968. (v.2–3 comprise pt.4.)

"The aim has been to exhaust the Treaty series, and in addition not only the international treaty series—those of the League of Nations and the United Nations—but also other British (in the sense of United Kingdom) sources of an official or semi-official character. For a subsidiary purpose of the work is to refer the user to the place or places where the text of a treaty listed is to be found."—*Pref.*

"A complete consolidated index to the Treaty series of the United Kingdom, which began in 1892, is still continued." JX636 1970.P37

Korea, North

Ginsburgs, George and **Kim, Roy U. T.** Calendar of diplomatic affairs, Democratic People's Republic of Korea, 1945–1975. [Moorestown, N.J.], Symposia Pr., 1977. 275p. **CK384**

"Sponsored by the Social Science Research Council."—*t.p.*

Entries are arranged chronologically and identified as to nature of the item (unilateral, bilateral, etc.), agents, place signed, and subject. Identifies source where text of each document can be located, and

secondary information thereon. Indexes by country and plurilateral treaties. Appendix provides a list of Korean ambassadors. DS935.5.G56

Latin America

Organization of American States. General Secretariat. Inter-American treaties and conventions. Rev. 1980. Wash., 1980. 306p. il. (Treaty ser., no.9) **CK385**

1st ed. 1954.

Lists treaties and conventions signed at the various conferences of the American states, giving "signatures, ratifications, and deposits with explanatory notes."

Kept up-to-date by:

———— Status of Inter-American treaties and conventions. Wash., 1936– . Annual. **CK386**

Title varies: 1940–58, *Status of the Pan American treaties and conventions.*

In Spanish, English, Portuguese, French.

Gives current information in tabular form. Originally formed pt.5 of the Organization of American States *Treaty series.*

Union of Soviet Socialist Republics

Slusser, Robert M. and **Triska, Jan F.** A calendar of Soviet treaties, 1917–1957. Stanford, Stanford Univ. Pr., 1959. 530p. **CK387**

A chronological listing of all verified agreements to which the U.S.S.R. was a party; each entry provides a brief synopsis of the document, source of the text, and bibliographical references from Soviet publications or United Nations and national treaties series. Indexed by country.

Continued by: JX756 1917

Ginsburgs, George and **Slusser, Robert M.** A calendar of Soviet treaties, 1958–1973. Alphen aan den Rijn, Neth. & Rockville, Md., Sijthoff & Noordhoff, 1981. 908p. **CK388**

JX757.5.G56

CONSTITUTIONS

Collections

Blaustein, Albert P. and **Flanz, G. H.** Constitutions of the countries of the world; a series of updated texts, constitutional chronologies and annotated bibliographies. Permanent ed. Dobbs Ferry, N.Y., Oceana, [1971–]. 17v. Looseleaf. **CK389**

Kept up-to-date by looseleaf supplements.

Separate pamphlets for each country (edited by one or more scholars) were issued for insertion alphabetically into looseleaf binders. Covers more than 160 countries, with supplements and replacement parts for many of them. For each country gives a chronology of national development, text of the constitution in English, and a bibliography.

Blaustein, Albert P. and **Blaustein, Eric B.** Constitutions of dependencies and special sovereignties. Dobbs Ferry, N.Y., Oceana, [1975–]. 6v. Looseleaf. **CK390**

Contents: v.1, United States [and] United Kingdom; v.2, British dependent territories; v.3, British associated states; v.4, In association with the British crown, Australian overseas territories, New Zealand territories; v.5, French overseas departments, French overseas territories, Scandinavian territories, Soviet territories with recognized sovereignty, Democratic Arab Republic of the Sahara, Macao, Netherlands Antilles, Palestine, Turkish Federated State of

Cyprus, Vatican City State; v.6, Republic of South Africa, homelands.

Serves as a companion to Blaustein and Flanz's *Constitutions of the countries of the world* (above). For each associated state, dependent territory, and area of special sovereignty, a pamphlet provides an outline of constitutional status, a copy of the constitution in English, and a briefly annotated bibliography.

The constitutions of the communist world. Ed. by William B. Simons. Alphen aan den Rijn & Germantown, Md., Sijthoff & Noordhoff, 1980. 644p. **CK391**

"A publication issued by the Documentation Office for East European Law, University of Leyden."

Presents English-language translations of constitutions in force in 1979. Revisions or new constitutions will be published in the quarterly *Review of socialist law.* Includes constitutions for the 14 states represented in J. F. Triska's *The constitutions of the communist-party states* (CK396), as well as the 1975 Kampuchean constitution. A systematic index provides a comparative reference to the contents of all the constitutions. K3157.E5C66

Dareste de la Chavanne, François Rodolphe and **Dareste de la Chavanne, Pierre.** Les constitutions modernes . . . traductions accompagnées de notices historiques et de notes explicatives. 4.éd., entièrement refondue par Joseph Delpech et Julien Laferrière. Paris, Recueil Sirey, 1928–34. 6v. in 7. maps. **CK392**

Contents: v.1–3, Europe; v.4, Amérique Latine; v.5, Empire Britannique, Afrique, Asie, Territoires sous mandat A; v.6, États-Unis d'Amérique du Nord. Les États de l'Union de l'Amérique du Nord; Extra volume, unnumbered, Espagne: Constitution du 9 déc. 1931 (59p.).

A comprehensive standard collection; for each country gives: (1) Historical notes, (2) Bibliographical references, and (3) Text, in French, of the constitutions in force, with explanatory notes.
JF12.D22

Hawgood, John Arkas. Modern constitutions since 1787. London, Macmillan, 1939. 539p. **CK393**

A textbook with a useful annotated bibliography (p.467–525), which includes collections, texts, commentaries, histories, etc.

al-Marayati, Abid A., comp. Middle Eastern constitutions and electoral laws. N.Y., Praeger, [1968]. 483p. **CK394**

Offers English translations of the constitutions and electoral laws of Iran, Iraq, Israel, Jordan, Kuwait, Lebanon, Saudi Arabia, Syria, Turkey, United Arab Republic, and Yemen, with brief historical introductions.

Peaslee, Amos Jenkins, ed. Constitutions of nations. Rev. 4th ed. Prep. by Dorothy Peaslee Xydis. The Hague, Nijhoff, 1974. v.1. (In progress) **CK395**

1st ed. 1950; 3d ed. 1965–70, 4v. in 7.
Contents: v.1, Africa.

Offers texts of the constitutions in English. Instead of the single alphabetical sequence of the previous editions, constitutions are now grouped by continent. Introductory notes are provided for each country, giving a summary of international status, information on the executive, legislative, and judicial departments, etc.

Triska, Jan F., ed. Constitutions of the communist party-states. Stanford, Calif., Hoover Inst. on War, Revolution and Peace, [1968]. 541p. (Hoover Inst. pubn. 70) **CK396**

Texts of the constitutions, with amendments, are presented in English. Updated by *Constitutions of the communist world* (CK391).

United States

❖The text of the Constitution of the United States is given in many general reference books, e.g., *World almanac* (AC87), and is also included in the *United States code* (CK207a), the *United States code annotated* (CK208), the

United States code service (CK209), the House and Senate *Manuals* (CJ146, CJ147), and the various state or legislative manuals. A good edition to keep on hand for reference purposes is that of the *House manual,* which is indexed and contains full notes of all ratifications. State constitutions are given in the various state manuals.

United States. Constitution. The Constitution of the United States of America: analysis and interpretation. Annotations of cases decided by the Supreme Court of the United States to June 29, 1972. [Rev. ed.] Wash., Govt. Prt. Off., 1973. 1961p. (92d Cong., 2d Sess. Senate doc. no. 92–82) **CK397**

Prep. by the Congressional Research Service, Library of Congress; Lester S. Jayson, supervising ed.
First issued 1923.

The "Historical note" reprints PL91-589, which calls for cumulative pocket supplements to be issued every two years (also as Senate documents) until the next edition. KF4527.J39

Browne, Cynthia E. State constitutional conventions, from Independence to the completion of the present Union, 1776–1959: a bibliography. Westport, Conn., Greenwood Pr., [1973]. 250p. **CK398**

A bibliography of the "publications of state constitutional conventions, commissions, and legislative or executive committees, and all publications for or relating to these conventions and commissions issued by other agencies of state government."—*Pref.* Entries are arranged chronologically within each state.
Continued by: KF4501.B76

Yarger, Susan Rice. State constitutional conventions, 1959–1975; a bibliography. Westport, Conn., Greenwood Pr., [1976]. 50p. **CK399**

"Included in this collection are [citations for] all publications of state constitutional conventions, commissions, and legislative or executive committees, and all special studies prepared for the convention or commission bodies. The documents selected . . . were generally of an official, noninterpretive nature, such as, enabling legislation, proceedings, journals, resolutions and rules, public hearings, the proposed constitution, and the constitution as revised and implemented by the electorate. Exception to 'noninterpretive' materials was made for the many special studies commissioned by the various conventions."—*Pref.* Includes Arkansas, Connecticut, Florida, Hawaii, Illinois, Louisiana, Maryland, Michigan, Montana, New Hampshire, New Jersey, New Mexico, New York, North Dakota, Pennsylvania, Rhode Island, Tennessee, and Texas.
Supplemented in part by: KF4501.Y37

Canning, Bonnie. State constitutional conventions, revisions, and amendments, 1959–1976; a bibliography. Westport, Conn., Greenwood Pr., [1977]. 47p. **CK400**

Subtitle: A supplement to State constitutional conventions, from Independence to the present Union, 1776–1959, comp. by Cynthia E. Browne, and State constitutional conventions, 1959–1975, comp. by Susan Rice Yarger.

Cites official published and unpublished materials for states holding constitutional conventions and those revising their constitution through other procedures. Includes California, Delaware, Florida, Kentucky, Louisiana, New Jersey, Texas, Washington, and Wisconsin, and supplements Yarger (above) for Louisiana, Texas, Florida, and New Jersey. Subject index. KF4501.B76 Suppl.

Chandler, Ralph C., Enslen, Richard A. and **Renstrom, Peter G.** The constitutional law dictionary. Santa Barbara, Calif., ABC-Clio, [1985]– . v.1– . (In progress) **CK401**

Contents: v.1, Individual rights. 507p. (Clio dictionaries in political science, 8)

v.1 focuses on constitutional concepts, words and phrases, and leading court cases of the U.S. Supreme Court. Chapters 1 and 8, constitutionalism and legal words and phrases, follow a dictionary arrangement. Chapters 2–7 follow a topical-issue arrangement—the first, fourth, fifth, sixth and eighth constitutional amendments, and equal protection and privacy; significant court cases are outlined. Several appendixes; index.

A second volume is to deal with governmental powers (and will appear as no.13 of the Clio series).   KF4548.5.C47

Columbia University. Legislative Drafting Research Fund. Constitutions of the United States, national and state. 2d ed. Dobbs Ferry, N.Y., Oceana, 1974–78. 6v. Looseleaf.
CK402

1st ed. 1962.
Current texts and amendments of the United States Constitution, the state constitutions, the constitution of Puerto Rico, and the constitutions and acts of possessions and territories of the United States are all included.   KF4530.C6

———— ———— Index. N.Y., Oceana, 1980– . 1v., looseleaf.

Designed to replace the *Index digest of state constitutions* (2d ed. 1959 and suppls.) as a topical index.   KF4530.C642

Hall, Kermit. A comprehensive bibliography of American constitutional and legal history, 1896–1979. Millwood, N.Y., Kraus Internat., [1983]. 5v.   **CK403**

A topically arranged bibliography in seven main sections: general surveys; institutions; constitutional doctrine; legal doctrine; biographical; chronological; geographical. Focuses on scholarly historical materials, not theoretical or contemporary studies. About 70,000 citations. Author and subject indexes in v.5.   KF4541.H34

McCarrick, Earlean M. U.S. Constitution: a guide to information sources. Detroit, Gale, [1980]. 390p. (American government and history information guide ser., v.4)
CK404

An annotated bibliography of primary and secondary sources arranged in 12 chapters: the first five deal with general materials, the historical background, and basic principles of the Constitution; the remaining chapters treat specific articles, amendments, and the Bill of Rights. Author, title, and subject indexes.   KF4546.A1M26

Mason, Alpheus Thomas and **Stephenson, D. Grier.** American constitutional development. Arlington Heights, Ill., AHM Publ. Co., [1977]. 166p.   **CK405**

A select bibliography of more than 2,900 English-language sources, arranged in five subject sections, with numerous specific subsections: (1) general sources; (2) origins; (3) political, social, economic, and intellectual context, subdivided by chronological period; (4) political institutions; (5) doctrines and powers. Emphasizes theoretical works. Author index.   KF4546.M38

Millett, Stephen M. A selected bibliography of American constitutional history. Santa Barbara, Calif., ABC-Clio, [1975]. 116p.   **CK406**

A brief discussion of primary sources is followed by a list of more than 1,000 secondary works topically arranged: surveys; historical origins of the Constitution; particular articles and sections; the Bill of Rights and Amendments; case histories; judicial biographies; and extrajudicial events which have affected constitutional history. List of pertinent journals and addenda. Author index.   KF4546.M54

Swindler, William Finley, ed. Sources and documents of United States constitutions. Dobbs Ferry, N.Y., Oceana, 1973–79. 10v.   **CK407**

". . . an annotated collection of the fundamental instruments recording the historical development of constitutional government in each state in the Union. It thus complements the collection of current state constitutions prepared by the Legislative Drafting Research Fund of Columbia University and published under the title, *Constitutions of the United States, National and State* [CK402], as well as the Fund's *Index-Digest of State Constitutions.*"—*v.1, p.iii.* Documents are arranged by state in alphabetical sequence. Analytical index for each state.
Complemented by: KF4530.S94

Sources and documents of United States constitutions. Second series. Ed. and annotated by William F. Swindler. Dobbs Ferry, N.Y., Oceana, 1982– . [v.1]– . (In progress)
CK408

Contents: [v.1] National documents, 1492–1800.
This series will reprint documents on the national American constitutional development, as opposed to documents relating to individual states included in the original set (above). It will also integrate the chronological order of both state and national documents, and cumulate the indexes for both series. The first volume provides a table, "American constitutional chronology," correlating documents from both series in chronological order. A second volume is to provide comparative analyses of state constitutions, and the texts of selected 19th-century national constitutional documents. The third and final volume is to cumulate the indexes to all volumes in both series, and provide selected 20th-century national constitutional documents.   KF4530.S68

Union of Soviet Socialist Republics

The constitutions of the USSR and the Union republics: analysis, texts, reports. Alphen aan den Rijn & Germantown, Md., Sijthoff & Noordhoff, 1979. 366p. il.   **CK409**

F. J. M. Feldbrugge.
A publication issued by the Documentation Office for East European Law, University of Leyden. Provides the text of the 1977 USSR constitution in Russian and in English, with a parallel text of the 1936 constitution; also provides comparative texts of the constitutions of the 15 Union republics. State arms and flags of the USSR and the Union republics are illustrated. Indexed.

TERRORISM

Mickolus, Edward F. The literature of terrorism: a selectively annotated bibliography. Westport, Conn., Greenwood Pr., [1980]. 553p.   **CK410**

3,869 annotated citations to books, articles, government documents, and documents of international organizations are grouped by subject, e.g., tactics, philosophies, linkages, responses to terrorism, guerrilla warfare, the media, and terrorism in geographic regions and countries. Author and title indexes.   Z7164.T3M53

———— Transnational terrorism: a chronology of events, 1968–1979. Westport, Conn., Greenwood Pr., [1980]. 967p.
CK411

"This chronology attempts to centralize all unclassified reporting on transnational terrorism that occurred from 1968 through 1979" (*p. [xxxvii]*), and begins with examples throughout history (most incidents having occurred in the 20th century). All aerial highjackings, regardless of motivation or geographical location, are included; incidents occurring between different ethnic groups within a disputed area (e.g., Palestinian attacks in Israeli territory) are excluded. Indexed by location, date, and groups involved.
HV6431.M5

Norton, Augustus R. and **Greenberg, Martin H.** International terrorism: an annotated bibliography and research guide. Boulder, Colo., Westview Pr., 1980. 218p.   **CK412**

Some 1,000 titles are classed by topic or geographic area, with about one-third of them annotated. Author index.   Z7164.T3N67

Schmid, Alex P. Political terrorism: a research guide to concepts, theories, data bases and literature. Amsterdam, North Holland; New Brunswick, N.J., Transaction Books, [1983]. 585p. il.   **CK413**

"With a bibliography by the author and a world directory of 'Terrorist' organizations by A. J. Jongman."—*t.p.*
At head of title: SWIDOC: Royal Netherlands Academy of Arts and Sciences, Social Science Information- and Documentation Centre; Centre for the Study of Social Conflicts (C.O.M.T.), State University of Leiden.
Particularly valuable for its comprehensiveness and its survey of numerical/chronological databases.

Terrorism: an annual survey. [By] John L. Scherer. [Minneapolis], Scherer, 1982– . v.1– . il. Annual. **CK414**

In four sections: (1) Chronology (v.1 covers 1981), with index by countries and groups; (2) news of national liberation and terrorist organizations by country; (3) statistics by country; (4) general information and statistics. HV6431.T458

INTERNATIONAL ORGANIZATIONS

Bibliography

Atherton, Alexine L. International organizations: a guide to information sources. Detroit, Gale, [1976]. 350p. **CK415**

Classed listing, primarily of 20th-century English-language books, with a few articles, doctoral dissertations, and U.S. government reports. Pt.I is a guide to reference sources in the field; pt.II is a bibliography, with annotations for the more significant titles. A guide primarily for the beginner. Author, title, and subject indexes. Z6464.I6A74

Baer, George W. International organizations, 1918–1945: a guide to research and research materials. Wilmington, Scholarly Resources, [1981]. 260p. **CK416**

Approximately 50 pages are devoted to discussion of the archives of selected international organizations, national archives and documents, and other collections; the remainder of the volume lists primary and secondary sources, arranged topically within a broadly chronological framework, with some brief annotations. Name index. Z6464.A1B33

Dimitrov, Théodore Delchev. World bibliography of international documentation. Pleasantville, N.Y., UNIFO, 1981. 2v. **CK417**

Contents: v.1, International organizations; v.2, Politics and world affairs.

First publ. under title *Documents of international organisations* (London, Internat. Univ. Pubns.; Chicago, Amer. Lib. Assoc., 1973).

v.1 provides a bibliography of secondary literature on the principal international organizations, as well as a list of their basic primary documents; references to collection development, cataloging, indexing, and other aspects of bibliographic control are also included. v.2 provides bibliographic references on world politics, arms issues, and relevant journal titles. Appendixes list major United Nations conferences and holidays. Indexed by author, corporate body, and subject. Z6481.D57

Haas, Michael, comp. International organization; an interdisciplinary bibliography. Stanford, Hoover Inst. Pr., [1973]. 944p. (Hoover Inst. bibliographical ser., 41) **CK418**

A classed bibliography of more than 7,900 items; author and subject indexes. Some brief annotations. Z6464.I6H3

Johnson, Harold S. and **Singh, Baljit.** International organization; a classified bibliography. East Lansing, Michigan State Univ., Asian Studies Center, 1969. 261p. (Mich. State Univ. Asian Studies Center. Occasional paper no.11) **CK419**

About 4,000 entries for book and periodical materials from the period 1945–66. Classed arrangement; no index. Z6461.J63

Speeckaert, Georges Patrick. Bibliographie sélective sur l'organisation internationale, 1885–1964. Select bibliography on international organization. Bruxelles, Union des Associations Internationales, 1965. 150p. **CK420**

A revision and reworking of the author's *International institutions and international organization* (1956), dropping numerous citations from the earlier work and adding many new ones. In two parts, the first listing references on international organization in general; the second devoted to materials on individual organizations. More than 1,000 entries; author index. Z6464.I6S68

Yearbook of international congress proceedings. Ed. 1–2. Brussels, Union of International Associations, [1969–70]. 2v. **CK421**

Contents: Ed.1, Bibliography of reports arising out of meetings held by international organizations during the years 1960–67; Ed.2, Bibliography of reports arising out of meetings held by international organizations during the years 1962–69.

Continues the listings in the *Bibliography of the proceedings of international meetings* published by the Union in 1963–66 and covering the years 1957–59. The new publication includes some supplementary listings for the earlier period. Reports and proceedings are listed by congress, and indexed by authors and subjects. No more published?

Current

International bibliography. v.1– , Mar. 1973– . N.Y., Bowker and Unipub, 1973– . Quarterly. **CK422**

Title varies; 1973–Wint. 1982, *International bibliography, information, documentation;* also referred to as *IBID.*

A publication of the United Nations system. Harry N. M. Winton, ed.

Concerned with the publications and publishing programs of the United Nations system of intergovernmental organizations. Each issue has three principal sections: (1) Information and news; (2) Bibliographic record (which lists books, pamphlets, etc., under about 40 subject categories, with bibliographic description and brief subject analysis); (3) Periodicals record (which gives tables of contents for current issues of most of the periodicals listed). The fourth quarterly issue includes a subject index to the volume. Information on ordering the publications is given in each issue. Z6482.I55

Directories and handbooks

Annuaire de la vie internationale: unions, associations, instituts, commissions, bureaux, offices, conférences, congrès, expositions, publications; publié pour l'Union des Associations Internationales avec le concours de la Fondation Carnegie pour la Paix Internationale et de l'Institut International de la Paix. 2. sér., 1908/09–1910/11. Bruxelles, Off. Central des Inst. Internat., [1909–12]. 2v. **CK423**

Earlier series called 1.–3. année, 1905–1907.

Contains a great deal of information about the history, organization, membership, purposes, meetings, etc., of all types of international organizations, governmental and private, but not so much about their publications. Each volume includes: (1) Public (i.e., governmental) unions, conferences, etc., arranged by subject according to the Universal Decimal Classification; (2) Private organizations, similarly arranged; (3) Chronological list of international meetings, giving name, date, and place; and (4) Index of persons, Index of subjects. While the second volume contains the later information, it does not entirely displace the first and refers to it for earlier material. JX1904.A4

Council on Foreign Relations. American agencies interested in international affairs, comp. by Donald Wasson. 5th ed. N.Y., Praeger, [1964]. 200p. **CK424**

1st ed. 1931. First four editions comp. by Ruth Savord.

A directory listing 293 private organizations "which conduct serious programs of research in international affairs."—*Pref.* A few international organizations with strong American interest are included. Information given includes name, address, founding date, activities, publications, personnel, etc. Contains a subject and personnel index. JX27.C62

International organization and integration: annotated basic documents and descriptive directory of international organizations and arrangements. Board of eds., P. J. G. Kapteyn [and others]. 2d, completely rev. ed. The Hague, Nijhoff, [1981–84]. v.1–2 in 6v. (In progress) **CK425**

1st ed. 1969.

Contents: v.I.A, The United Nations organization; v.I.B, Organizations related to the United Nations; v.II.A, European Communities; v.II.B–II.D, Organizations and arrangements of the northern hemisphere; v.II.E–II.J, Organizations and arrangements outside the northern hemisphere; v.II.K, Functional organizations and arrangements.

Provides brief histories and texts of important documents.

JX171.I54

Peaslee, Amos Jenkins. International governmental organizations: constitutional documents. Rev. 3d ed., prep. by Dorothy Peaslee Xydis. The Hague, Nijhoff, 1974–[79]. pts.1–5 in 5v.   **CK426**

1st ed. 1956.

Contents: pt.1, General and regional, political, economic, social, legal, defense (2v.); pt.2, Agriculture, commodities, fisheries, food, plants (1v.); pts.3–4, Education, culture, copyright, science, health (1v.); pt.5, Communications, transport, travel (1v.).

Within each volume arranged alphabetically by organization; contains the basic constitutional documents of more than 200 "international organizations created by governments, and themselves of a governmental nature."—*Foreword.* Unofficial private organizations are not included.

Brief summaries of the history and constitutional development, membership, functions, organs, headquarters, etc., are given for each organization, with selective bibliographies.

Political and Economic Planning. A handbook of European organizations, by Michael Palmer [and others]. N.Y., Praeger, [1968]. 519p.   **CK427**

British ed. (London, Allen & Unwin, 1968) has title *European unity.*

A revised and updated edition of *European organisations* (London, 1959). Each of the major western European international organizations (Organization for European Economic Cooperation, European Economic Community, Council of Europe, North Atlantic Treaty Organization, etc.) is considered in a separate chapter, with information on its history, structure, and achievements.

JN94.P6

Unesco handbook of international exchanges. Échanges internationaux; répertoire de l'Unesco. [Paris], UNESCO, 1965–67. v.1–2.   **CK428**

Title and limited amount of text also in Spanish and Russian.

Intended to provide "information on the aims, programmes and activities of national and international organizations, and on agreements concluded between States, concerning international relations and exchanges in the fields of education, science, culture and mass communication."—*Introd.* Supersedes Unesco's *Directory of cultural relations services* (1959) and *Index of cultural agreements* (1962). Also includes some information previously published in *Study abroad* (CB298) and *Travel abroad.* Separate section for international organizations; national organizations are entered by country, then grouped by field. Country and organizational index. No more published.   AS8.U35

Abbreviations

Buttress, F. A. World guide to abbreviations of organizations. 7th ed. Detroit, Grand River Books, [1984], 731p.   **CK429**

1st–2d ed. (1954, 1960) had title: *World list of abbreviations of scientific, technological and commercial organizations.* 3d ed. (1966) published under title: *World list of abbreviations.*

More than 27,500 abbreviations of organizations from Western Europe, the Americas, Africa, and international agencies. Russian and Eastern European abbreviations are not included.   AS8.B8

Spillner, Paul. World guide to abbreviations. Internationales Wörterbuch der Abkürzungen von Organisationen. 2d ed. N.Y., Bowker; München-Pullach, Verlag Dokumentation, 1970–72. 3v.   **CK430**

1st ed. (1967) had title: *Ullstein-Abkürzungslexikon.*

Subtitle: A list of more than 50,000 abbreviations with an international bibliography of dictionaries of abbreviations.

P365.S6

Yearbooks

Yearbook of international organizations. Annuaire des organisations internationales. 1948– . 1st ed– . Brussels, Union of Internat. Assoc., 1948– . Irregular.   **CK431**

In English and French, varying with editions.

A comprehensive work, giving a general survey and detailed information about international organizations and associations currently active. Includes dates of conferences and meetings, and lists of publications. Arrangement varies; beginning 1983, published in 3v.: v.1, Organization descriptions and index; v.2, Geographic volume; v.3, Subject volume, Global action networks, with publications index.

The following are spin-offs from the 1984/85 edition (publ. 1984): *African international organization directory and African participation in other international organizations; Arab and Islamic international organization directory and Arab/Islamic participation in other international organizations; International organization abbreviations and addresses;* and *Intergovernmental organization directory.*

JX1904.A42

Year book of world affairs. v.1–38, 1947–84. Publ. under the auspices of the London Institute of World Affairs. London, Stevens, 1947–84.   **CK432**

Includes survey articles, book reviews, etc.   JX21.Y4

Congresses and meetings

Bibliographic guide to conference publications: 1975– . Boston, G. K. Hall, [1976]– . Annual.   **CK433**

Each volume is a bibliography in the form of a dictionary catalog (i.e., main entries plus added entries as applicable for editors, titles, series, and subject headings). Covers publications cataloged by the Research Libraries of the New York Public Library together with additional entries from Library of Congress MARC tapes. "Included are works in all languages and all forms—non-book materials as well as books and serials."—*Pref.* (Coverage is of works *cataloged* during the year in question, so that each volume includes many publications of earlier date.)

A volume from the same publisher, *Conference publications guide: 1974,* Gerald L. Swanson, ed., is derived solely from MARC data and lists main entries, subject entries, "area studies entries," series, and titles in separate sections. Although announced as an annual, this title is evidently superseded by the *Bibliographic guide* series.

Z5051.B5

International congress calendar, 1960/61– . Brussels, Union of Internat. Assoc., 1961– . Annual.   **CK434**

Some issues have title also in French: *Calendrier des congrès internationaux.* Introductory notes in English and French.

Lists projected meetings of international congresses over a period of about five years. Geographical and chronological sections are indexed by organization and subject keyword. The 13th ed. covers a 13-year period, 1973/1985.

Kept up-to-date by monthly supplements published in the periodical *Transnational associations.*   AS8.I63

International congresses and conferences, 1840–1937; a union list of their publications available in libraries of the United States and Canada, ed. by Winifred Gregory under the auspices of the Bibliographical Society of America. . . . N.Y., Wilson, 1938. 229p. (Repr.: Millwood, N.Y., Kraus, 1980)   **CK435**

Running title: Union list of international congresses.

Arranged alphabetically by name of congress or conference. Includes subject index. Excludes diplomatic congresses and conferences, and those held under the auspices of the League of Nations. Lists holdings in more than 100 libraries. Z5051.I58

Staatsbibliothek der Stiftung Preussischer Kulturbesitz. Abteilung Gesamtkataloge und Dokumentation. Gesamtverzeichnis der Kongress-Schriften in Bibliotheken der Bundesrepublik Deutschland einschliesslich Berlin (West). Schriften von und zu Kongressen, Konferenzen, Kolloquien, Symposien, Tagungen, Versammlungen und dergleichen vor 1971 mit Besitznachweisen Stand: 1976. München, Verlag Dokumentation, 1976. 2v. **CK436**

Added title page in English: *Union list of conference proceedings in libraries of the Federal Republic of Germany including Berlin (West).*

A companion publication to the *Gesamtverzeichnis ausländischer Zeitschriften und Serien (GAZS)* and its supplements (AE195), listing conference proceedings not already registered in *GAZS*. Most foreign proceedings are listed after 1959, and international conference proceedings after 1967. Listing is by name of conference or sponsoring body; v.2 is a keyword index of the names of conferences and corporate bodies. Supplements were published 1978, 1980, 1982.

Union of International Associations. Les congrès internationaux de 1681 à 1899, liste complète. International congresses, 1681 to 1899, full list. Bruxelles, 1960. 76p. (Documents, no.8; Pubn. no.164) **CK437**

Chronological arrangement of more than 1,400 congresses, giving name, place of meeting, and dates, with keyword indexes in French and in English.
Continued by: AS5.U5 no.8

—— Les congrès internationaux de 1900 à 1919, liste complète. International congresses 1900 to 1919, full list. Bruxelles, 1964. 143p. (Documents, no.14; Pubn. no.188) **CK438**

Treats 2,528 international congresses. Includes cumulative subject index in English and French for this and the preceding volume. AS5.U5 no.14

—— The 1,978 international organizations founded since the Congress of Vienna: chronological list, with an introduction by G. P. Speeckaert. Brussels, 1957. 204p. (Documents, no.7) **CK439**

A chronological list for the period 1815–1956 (with two earlier listings for 1693 and 1783). AS5.U5 no.7

World list of future international meetings ... June 1959/May 1962–Sept.1969/Aug.1972, prep. by the International Organizations Section. Wash., Reference Dept., Lib. of Congress, 1959–69. 16v. **CK440**

Ceased publication, but useful as a historical record.

Each issue in two parts: (1) Science, technology, agriculture, medicine; (2) Social, cultural, commercial, humanistic.

Listed future meetings which were internationally organized, financed, or sponsored. Through June 1962, each monthly issue covered projected meetings for three years; thereafter, only the quarterly issues (Sept., Dec., March, June) contained a record of all meetings for the 3-year span, and the interim monthly issues included only the new meetings and changes in previously listed meetings. Indexed by subject, by sponsor, and by place of meeting. AS8.W73

European communities

Guides

The European Community: bibliographical excursions. Ed. by Juliet Lodge. Phoenix, Oryx Pr., [1983]. 259p. **CK441**

22 chapters by specialists are grouped in three main sections: integration theory, decision-making, and institutions in the Community; Community internal policies; Community external relations. Each chapter serves as a bibliographic review essay on the relevant English-language primary and secondary literature. HC241.2.E83415

Sources of information on the European Communities. Ed. by Doris M. Palmer. London, Mansell, 1979. 230p. il. **CK442**

Chapters by specialists discuss printed sources, library collections, and government agencies as information sources on European Communities—institutions, legislation, companies, trade, statistics, environment, etc. Bibliographic references and select bibliography; index. Z7165.E8S684

Bibliography

Bildungswerk Europäische Politik. Bibliographie zur europäischen Integration. 3., rev. und erw. Aufl. [Köln, Europa-Union Verlag, 1970] 299p. **CK443**

1st ed. 1962.

An annotated bibliography of books in various languages on the federation of Europe. Author index. Z2000.B5

Böttcher, Winfried. Britische Europaideen, 1940–1970: eine Bibliographie. Düsseldorf, Droste, [1971–73]. 2v. **CK444**

Contents: Bd.1, Bücher und Broschüren; Bd.2, Zeitschriften.

Title also in English and French: *Great Britain and Europe; La Grand Bretagne et l'Europe.* Text in German, English, and French.

Bd.1 is a chronological list of books and brochures published in Britain on European integration; within each year, titles are arranged alphabetically by author. Person and subject index. Bd.2 follows a similar arrangement, but includes more material from British periodicals on conditions within individual European countries. Indexed by author, and by subject (Europe, individual country, and person). Z2000.B64

Collester, J. Bryan. European communities: a guide to information sources. Detroit, Gale, [1979]. 265p. (International relations information guide ser., v.9) **CK445**

An annotated, classed bibliography of more than 1,400 sources on the political aspects of European integration and the European Community. Excludes foreign-language material, most periodical articles, and documentation and official reports. Indexed. Z7165.E8C58

Hopkins, Michael. Policy formation in the European Communities; a bibliographical guide to Community documentation, 1958–1978. [London], Mansell, [1981]. 339p. **CK446**

An annotated bibliography of primary documents, grouped into 13 chapters dealing with individual areas of policy; each chapter begins with a descriptive essay making supplementary references to serial and statistical Community publications, and concludes with a bibliographical record of documents in chronological order. Indexed. Z7165.E8H65

Jeffries, John. A guide to the official publications of the European Communities. 2d ed. [London], Mansell; N.Y., H. W. Wilson, 1981. 131p. **CK447**

A descriptive guide to the public papers of various bodies of the Communities. Organization is according to institution, except for publications of the Commission of the European Communities, which are arranged by topic. Includes sections on bibliographic aids, documentation centers and depository libraries, distribution and sales offices. Z7165.E8J44

Kujath, Karl. Bibliographie zur Europäischen Integration: mit Anmerkungen. Bonn, Europa Union, [1977]. 777p. **CK448**

Title and prefatory matter also in French and English.

A major international bibliography, concentrating on monographs and periodical titles, arranged within a detailed subject classification. Covers international organizations, European unification and integration in general, and each of the intergovernmental and supranational European organizations. Personal name index.

Z7165.E8K84

Regional problems and policies in the European Community: a bibliography. Gen. ed., Kevin Allen. [Farnborough, Eng.], Saxon House (distr. by Unipub), 1978. 2v.   **CK449**

Contents: v.1, Federal Republic of Germany, Italy, United Kingdom; v.2, Belgium, Denmark, France, Ireland, the Netherlands.

A selected bibliography of monographs, articles, reports and documents, most of them produced in the 1970s. The section for each country follows a standard format: (1) survey materials—bibliographical sources and major historical surveys; (2) aspects of the regional problem—economic and social indicators and factors, area industries, area studies and plans, industrial and services location requirements and experiences; (3) regional policy; each section is produced by a different set of editors and is indexed by author.

Z7164.R33R34

Siemers, J. P. and **Siemers-Hidma, E. H.** European integration: select international bibliography of theses and dissertations, 1957–1980. 2d rev. and enl. ed. The Hague, Nijhoff, 1981. 412p.   **CK450**

Title, prefatory matter, and headings in English, German and French.

1st ed. 1979.

A classed bibliography of materials from more than 200 universities and other institutions of higher learning, principally in the United States and Western Europe. Author and subject indexes.

Z7165.E8S56

EC index. v.1, no.1– , Jan. 1985– . Maastricht, Neth., Europe Data, [1985]– . Monthly, with quarterly and annual cumulations.   **CK451**

Subtitle: European Communities index: an abstracting and indexing guide to publications and documents of the European Communities.

Preceded by an issued designated v.0, no.0 (Oct. 1984).

Each issue is in two sections, and each cumulation in two parts: Bibliographic/abstracts section, abstracting official journals, legislation, monographs, periodicals, annuals, and series (arranged by issuing body); Index section, with approaches by name, subject, title, title keyword, and publication number.

Dictionaries

See also CK482.

Paxton, John. A dictionary of the European Communities. 2d ed. N.Y., St. Martin's, 1982. 282p.   **CK452**

1st ed. (1977) had title *A dictionary of the European Economic Community.*

Brief entries for acronyms and abbreviations, persons, places, and topics relevant to the EEC. Longer articles on treaties and other important documents summarize rather than quote. Entries for countries belonging to the EEC give brief data on area, population density, vital statistics, labor force, international and EEC trade, and standard of living. Select bibliography of books, p.279–82.

JN12.P29

Directories and handbooks

Cook, Chris and **Francis, Mary.** The first European elections: a handbook and guide. [London, Macmillan (distr. in U.S.A. by Humanities Pr.), 1979] 193p. il.   **CK453**

Provides background information on British accession into the European Community and data on the Community. The main section of the book offers an analysis of the political parties, electoral systems and representation, current issues and controversies, and voting behavior predicted for the first European Parliament to be directly elected. A similar handbook is planned for the 1984 elections.   JN36.C66

Craig, Fred W. S. and **Mackie, T. T.** Europe votes 1: European parliamentary election results 1979. [Chichester, Eng.], Parliamentary Research Services, [1980]. 152p.   **CK454**

A companion to Craig's *British parliamentary election results* (CJ346), this is the first volume of a new series designed "to provide a record of elections of the European Parliament from the first elections held on June 7 to 10, 1979."—*Pref.* An alphabetical listing of the members of the European Parliament and a list of changes which occurred between June 1979 and April 1980 precede the country-by-country record of election returns.   JN36.C7

Morris, Brian, Crane, Peggy and **Boehm, Klaus.** The European Community; a guide for business and government. Bloomington, Indiana Univ. Pr., [1981]. 303p.   **CK455**

A handbook in which entries are arranged alphabetically, providing brief descriptions of the subject matter, relevant tables, references to European Community publications, and contact points at national and Community level. Provides directory data for the European Parliament, national government departments, and representative organizations. Indexed. A new edition was scheduled for 1985 publication.   HC241.2.M64

Wood, G. David and **Wood, Alan.** The Times guide to the European Parliament. London, Times Books, [1979]. 267p. il.   **CK456**

Provides voting figures for elections in the nine participating countries, with photographs and biographical details for all members of the first European Parliament. Also provides background information, chronology, manifestoes, etc. A 1984 compilation was edited by Alan Wood (London, Times Books, 1984. 287p.).

JN33 1979.T55

Yearbooks

European Parliament. Directorate General for Research and Documentation. Europe today: state of European integration, 1975– . [Luxembourg], The Parliament, 1975– . Annual.   **CK457**

Presents a collection of politically relevant and important legislative acts from the European Community. In six main sections: (1) Constitution; (2) The Common Market; (3) Common agricultural policy; (4) Economic and social policy; (5) External relations; (6) Relations with particular countries and regions. Provides references to treaties, official documents, parliamentary reports and opinions, with publication source. Subject index.

Biography

European Communities' Who's who and other European organizations. Who's who des Communautés Européennes et d'autres organisations européennes. Réd. en chef, Georges-Francis Seingry. 2d ed. Bruxelles, Editions Delta, 1981. 240p.   **CK458**

1st ed. 1978.

Prefatory material in English and French.

Presents biographical sketches of senior officials working within the European Communities and other European organizations, members of the Permanent Representations of the member states, and the diplomatic missions of the states which have submitted application for membership. Entries are in the language chosen by the biographee. When biographical data are lacking, the official position, address, and telephone number are given.

League of Nations

Aufricht, Hans. Guide to League of Nations publications; a bibliographical survey of the work of the League, 1920–1947. N.Y., Columbia Univ. Pr., 1951. 682p.   **CK459**

Selective, but includes some items that were confidential and some that were never on public sale. Emphasis is on the inclusion of important publications. Also lists publications of affiliated organizations, such as the International Labor Office and the Permanent Court of International Justice.

Appendixes include texts of documents relating to the League of Nations, the transfer of the League of Nations assets to the United Nations, and the Statutes of the International Labor Office and the Permanent Court of International Justice.

Arrangement is by broad subject with index.   Z6473.A85

Birchfield, Mary Eva. Consolidated catalog of League of Nations publications offered for sale. Dobbs Ferry, N.Y., Oceana, 1976. 477p.   **CK460**

Consolidates the entries from the League's *Catalog of publications, 1930–35* and its supplements, and includes additional material from M. J. Carroll's *Key to League of Nations documents* (1920–29, with supplements through 1947). Arrangement is by category (e.g., Assembly, Council, Library, Health, Social Questions, Legal, etc.), then chronologically unless some other arrangement is dictated for ease of use. Indexes by official number, sales number, and subject/title.   Z6479.Z9B57

Ghebali, Victor Yves and **Ghebali, Catherine.** A repertoire of League of Nations serial documents, 1919–1947. Dobbs Ferry, N.Y., Oceana, 1973. 2v.   **CK461**

At head of title: Carnegie Endowment for International Peace.

Title and explanatory matter also in French.

Not an inventory of individual documents, "but rather a survey of all the known *series* of documents."—*Foreword.* An explanation of the numbering systems of League documents is followed by four main sections: (1) League institutional structure; (2) League activities in connection with the implementation of peace treaties; (3) League activities in connection with the maintenance of international peace and security; (4) League activities in connection with the promotion of functional cooperation. Within each section, series are systematically grouped in further subdivisions. Indicates which numbers were issued in a given series, dates, etc. Indexed.   Z6473.G45

Reno, Edward A., ed. League of Nations documents, 1919–1946; a descriptive guide and key to the microfilm collection. New Haven, Conn., Research Pubns., 1973–75. 3v.   **CK462**

Contents: v.1, Subject categories IA through IV; v.2, Subject categories V through VII; C.P.M. documents; Minutes and reports of the Permanent Mandates Commission; and 19/F/– , 19/6/– , 20/6/– , 21/6/– , Documents; v.3, Subject categories VIII through General, serial publications reel index, Minutes of the Directors' meetings reel index.

A guide prepared for use with the microfilm edition of League of Nations documents published by Research Publications, Inc. (This microfilm set is presumably as complete as any that is likely to be assembled.) The guide should, however, be independently useful.

Documents have been grouped in 18 categories for the microfilm edition: IA, Administrative Commissions; IB, Minorities; IIA, Financial questions; IIB, Economic questions; III, Health; IV, Social questions; V, Legal questions; VIA, Mandates; VIB, Slavery; VII, Political questions; VIII, Communications and transit; IX, Disarmament; X, Financial administration of the League of Nations; XI, Traffic in opium and other dangerous drugs; XIIA, Intellectual cooperation; XIIB, International Bureaux; XIII, Refugees; G, General. v.3 includes a consolidated index for subject categories IA through G, "followed by separate listings for the Permanent Mandates Commission (C.P.M.) Documents, the Minutes and Reports

of the Permanent Mandates Commission, and the collection of Secretariat communications known as the 19/F/– , 19/6/– , 20/6/– , and 21/6/– Series."—*p.v.*

For each item is given: the document number, place of issue if other than Geneva, subject title of the document, and a descriptive abstract. Listings in the guide follow the filming sequence, and reel indicators are provided at appropriate intervals.   Z6473.R45

United Nations system

Guides and handbooks

Brimmer, Brenda [and others]. A guide to the use of United Nations documents. Dobbs Ferry, N.Y., Oceana, 1962. 272p.   **CK463**

An excellent guide for the research worker in using United Nations materials and for the librarian in organizing a UN collection regardless of size. A new edition would be welcome.   Z674.B7

A chronology and fact book of the United Nations, 1941/61– . Dobbs Ferry, N.Y., Oceana, 1962– . (6th ed. 1979)   **CK464**

An earlier publication (1959) had title *A chronology of the United Nations, 1941–1958* (comp. by Waldo Chamberlin and others).

New editions with extended period of coverage issued at irregular intervals.

A chronological listing of the important acts, events, meetings, membership, etc., of the UN, many with brief identifying statement. Subject index.

A comprehensive handbook of the United Nations: a documentary presentation in two volumes. Comp. and ed. by Min-chuan Ku. [N.Y.], Monarch Pr., [1978]. 2v. il.   **CK465**

v.1 covers background material, organizational documents and procedural rules of the principal organs of the United Nations; v.2 treats the specialized agencies, nongovernmental organizations having relations with the United Nations, trusteeship agreements, regional agencies, and General Assembly resolutions. Bibliography; indexed.   JX1977.C6123

Everyone's United Nations. Ed. 9– . N.Y., United Nations, 1979– . Irregular.   **CK466**

Continues *Everyman's United Nations* (1948–68).

"This volume . . . describes the structure and activities of the United Nations and the 17 intergovernmental agencies related to it, concentrating on their work during the 12 years up to 1977/1978. It forms a companion volume to the eighth volume of *Everyman's United Nations,* published in March 1968."—*t.p.*   JX1977.A37E9

Hajnal, Peter I. Guide to Unesco. London [etc.], Oceana, 1983. 578p. il.   **CK467**

In three main parts: background, structure, activities and financing; modes of action; annotated bibliography of selected works by and about Unesco. Appendixes; index.   AS4.U83H33

——— Guide to United Nations organization, documentation & publishing for students, researchers, librarians. Dobbs Ferry, N.Y., Oceana, 1978. 450p.   **CK468**

In five parts: (1) structure, functions and evolution of the United Nations, and its relations to other organizations within and outside the United Nations system; (2) publishing and documentation patterns; (3) use, acquisition, and organization of United Nations publications; (4) a select, annotated bibliography of works by and about the United Nations; (5) a selection of important documents. Concludes with an appendix describing intergovernmental organizations related to the United Nations.   JX1977.H22

Bibliography

Hüfner, Klaus, and **Naumann, Jens.** The United Nations system, international bibliography. Das System der Vereinten Nationen, internationale Bibliographie. München, Verlag Dokumentation, 1976–79. 3v. in 5.   **CK469**

A publication of the Research Unit of the German United Nations Association, Bonn/Berlin.

Prefatory matter and headings in English and German.

Contents: v.1, The United Nations system; an international bibliography . . . 1945–65; v.2A, Learned journals, 1965–70; v.2B, Learned journals, 1971–75; v.3A, Monographs and articles in collected volumes, 1965–1970; v.3B, Monographs and articles in collective volumes, 1971–1975.

A bibliography of secondary literature published in English, German, and French on the United Nations and its specialized agencies. v.1 is a reprint of Hüfner's *Zwanzig Jahre Vereinte Nationen . . . 1945–1965.* v.2–3 cover articles produced between 1965 and 1975 in about 360 journals and 13,300 books and essays. The classification scheme is in four sections: (1) The United Nations as part of the empirical solutions for four main functional problems of world society [polity, adaptation, normative integration, cultural problems]; (2) The United Nations system and its internal structures and processes; (3) The United Nations system—institutional and organizational arrangements; (4) The United Nations system—actual and potential areas of activity. Detailed table of contents; author index.   Z6481.H83

United Nations. Dag Hammarskjöld Library. Current bibliographical information. Renseignements bibliographiques d'actualité. v.1– , Jan. 1971– . N.Y., United Nations, 1971– . Monthly.   **CK470**

Frequency varies.

Formed by the merger of the Library's *Current issues* (1965–70) and *New publications* (1949–63).

Serves as the Library's acquisitions list and current awareness tool. Classed list of non-U.N. publications, selected publications of the United Nations specialized agencies, and selective listing of articles from about 900 periodicals. In two sections: computer-produced section for roman alphabet materials (monthly author and subject indexes available); section for non-roman alphabet materials (no index). No cumulative features.

Publications

Guides

Winton, Harry N. M., comp. Publications of the United Nations system: a reference guide. N.Y., Bowker, 1972. 202p.   **CK471**

"The primary purposes of this reference guide are to present a brief overview of the organizations of the United Nations and their publications, to call attention to a number of valuable reference works published by these organizations, and to provide a comprehensive list of their periodicals and selected other recurrent publications."—*Pref.* The lists of reference publications and periodicals are annotated and supplementary sources are often indicated. Indexed.   Z6481.W55

Indexes and catalogs

Register of United Nations serial publications. [Geneva, Inter-Organization Board for Information System, 1982] 261p.   **CK472**

An alphabetical title list of about 1,800 serial titles produced by 34 United Nations organizations. Publication details include ISSN, language of publication, keyword subject scope, and Universal Decimal Classification number. Indexed by organization name and keyword subject.   Z6482.R43

United Nations. The complete reference guide to United Nations sales publications, 1946–1978. Pleasantville, N.Y., Unifo, 1982. 2v.   **CK473**

Contents: v.1, The catalogue, comp. and ed. by Mary Eva Birchfield; v.2, Indexes: sales number index, title index, comp. by Mary Eva Birchfield; key word in context index, comp. by Jacqueline Coolman.

"The body of the Catalogue text is a listing of publications arranged alphabetically from A/- (Assembly) to WFC/- (World Food Council). . . . Information for each publication includes titles, dates . . . , languages of publication, pagination, and sales number."—*Introd.* Title index includes complete and shortened version, and subtitles. Subject approach is through key-word-in-context index.   Z6485.Z9B57

United Nations. Dag Hammarskjöld Library. Checklist of United Nations documents, 1946–49. N.Y., 1949–53. (ST/LIB/SER.F)   **CK474**

Originally intended to be "a complete list of the documents issued by the organs of the United Nations" (*Pref.*), printed and mimeographed. Issued in parts, each one devoted to the documents of a particular unit. Every part issued in consecutive numbers, the initial numbers covering 1946–49.

Very detailed indexing, with information as to original publication and where documents were republished, if any. Detailed subject index.

Continued in part by: JX1977.A2

——— United Nations documents index. v.1–24, Jan. 1950–Dec. 1973. [N.Y.], 1950–73. Monthly. (ST/LIB/SER.E)   **CK475**

Often referred to as *UNDI.*

Indexes to v.23–24 not published.

Each volume includes an annual cumulative index which supersedes indexes of the monthly issues; beginning with v.14 (1963) the monthly issues were superseded at the end of the year by the index and the annual *United Nations documents index: cumulative checklist* (CK477).   JX1977.A2

United Nations documents index. United Nations and specialized agencies documents and publications. Cumulated index, volumes 1–13, 1950–1962. N.Y., Kraus-Thomson, 1974. 4v.   **CK476**

Cumulates in a single alphabetical sequence the author and subject indexes for the first 13v. of the series.

United Nations. Dag Hammarskjöld Library. United Nations documents index: cumulative checklist. v.14–24, 1963–73. N.Y., United Nations, 1964–75. Annual. (ST/LIB/SER.E/CUM.)   **CK477**

Ceased with v.24, 1973.

Supersedes the monthly issues of *United Nations documents index* (CK475); also indexed by that publication's annual cumulative index.

Contains consolidated lists, by symbol, of all documents and publications issued by the United Nations and the International Court of Justice during the year.

Beginning 1974, the *United Nations documents index* was superseded by:

United Nations. UNDEX; United Nations documents index. Series A: Subject index. v.1–9, Jan. 1970–78. N.Y., 1970–80. Monthly (except July and Aug.). (ST/LIB/SER.1/A.)   **CK478**

Provides the information needed for locating a document on a given topic through its United Nations document symbol. Includes "references to the subject matter of documents and publications issued by the United Nations for which analytical annotations have been stored in computer-based files."—*Introd. note.* Information "has been selected, extracted and compiled mechanically in four languages (English, French, Russian and Spanish) from annotations prepared in English only and stored in a computer together with quadrilingual lists of terms used in the preparation of the annotations." The index entry contains the subject (given in fairly precise terminology), type of document (e.g., Decisions, Meeting records, Voting), and document symbol.

——— ——— Series B: Country index. v.1–9, Jan. 1970–Dec. 1978. N.Y., 1970–78. Monthly (except July and Aug.). (ST/LIB/ SER.1/B.)

An alphabetical listing by member states, indicating participation in United Nations activities. Name of country is followed by type of action or participation (voting, statements in debates, documents submitted, etc.), subject on which action was taken, and document symbol. JX1977.A2

——— ——— Series C: List of documents issued. v.1–6, Jan. 1974–Jan. 1979. N.Y., 1974–79. Monthly (except July and Aug.). (ST/LIB/ SER.1/C.)

Prepared by conventional methods rather than computer techniques used for Series A and B (above). The three series supersede the *United Nations documents index, 1950–73* (CK475).

Series C "contains a listing and the bibliographical description of all documents and publications of the United Nations, except restricted material and internal papers, and all printed publications of the International Court of Justice."—*Introd. note.* Coverage of each issue is limited to specific series of documents, following a set pattern outlined in the prefatory note. Entry is by series symbol; gives full information on language versions, etc.

A partial cumulation was published as:

UNDEX Series "C": cumulative edition, 1974–77. White Plains, N.Y. UNIFO Publ., [1979–80]. 4v.

Contents: v.1, General Assembly; v.2, ECOSOC, Secretariat, and Regional Economic Commissions; v.3, Security Council, Trusteeship Council, International Court of Justice, and miscellaneous; v.4, [Supplement] 1978.

Comp. and ed. by Milton Mittelman and Mina Pease.

Cumulates 40 issues of *UNDEX series C* published between 1974 and 1978. Listings are by agency and document series number, with microfiche availability indicated. JX1976.A95Un2

UNDOC: current index; United Nations documents index. v.1, no.1– , Jan./Feb. 1979– . N.Y., United Nations, 1979– . 10 nos. per yr.; annual cumulation. **CK479**

Successor to *UNDEX* (CK478).

Each monthly issue is composed of: (1) checklist of documents and publications, with full bibliographic description, arranged by series symbol and session; (2) list of official records; (3) list of sales publications; (4) list of documents republished in the official records or elsewhere; (5) language table of materials indexed; (6–8) subject, author, and title indexes. The annual cumulation is in three parts: (1) checklist of documents, official records, and sales publications; (2) subject index; (3) author and title indexes, documents republished, new document series symbols, and United Nations maps reproduced in documents. JX1977.A2

United Nations. Dag Hammarskjöld Library. List of United Nations document series symbols. Sept. 1952– . N.Y., United Nations, 1952– . Irregular. **CK480**

Title varies: 1952, *Consolidated list of United Nations document series symbols;* 1955, *United Nations document series symbols.*

The 1978 edition is entitled *United Nations document series symbols, 1946–1977: cumulative list with indexes* and is in two parts: (1) an alphanumeric list of series symbols which identifies issuing body, subsidiary organization, and title of conference or meeting, with date that series symbol was first used; (2) a subject/series title index followed by the series symbols. This is the third revision of the cumulative list and supersedes that published in 1970.
JX1977.A24

United Nations Educational, Scientific and Cultural Organization. Bibliography of publications issued by Unesco or under its auspices; the first twenty-five years, 1946 to 1971. Paris, 1973. 385p. **CK481**

Title page also in French; introductory matter and captions in French and English.

More than 5,000 books and journals are arranged according to the Universal Decimal Classification and indexed by author and title.

Official records and publications are grouped separately at the beginning of the classification, and are not repeated in the bibliography.

Continued by: Z6483.U5U47

——— Unesco list of documents and publications, 1972–1976. [Paris], Unesco, [1979]. 2v.

Contents: v.1, Annotated list of documents and publications, personal name index, conference index; v.2, Subject index.

Includes all publications, documents, and periodical articles issued by Unesco during this period; a list of Unesco-sponsored publications is to be issued separately at a later date. Brief descriptive annotations. Arranged by title or corporate entry; indexed by personal name, geographic location of conference, and subject.

Dictionaries and encyclopedias

Osmańczyk, Edmund Jan. The encyclopedia of the United Nations and international agreements. Philadelphia & London, Taylor and Francis, 1985. 1059p. **CK482**

A dictionary of: the United Nations system, intergovernmental and nongovernmental organizations; terms used in international law, diplomacy, policy, economics, military science, and political geography; agreements, conventions, or treaties entered into since the late 19th century, quoted in part or in their entirety. Bibliographical references for most entries. Indexed by topic and by treaty.
JX1977.O8213

Biography

Who's who in the United Nations and related agencies. 1st ed. N.Y., Arno Pr., 1975. 785p. **CK483**

Table of contents in English, French, Spanish, Russian, Chinese and Arabic.

A biographical directory of delegates and senior personnel, past presidents of the General Assembly, and principal officials of the UN media correspondents' association, the World Federation of UN Associations, and non-governmental organizations accredited to the United Nations. An organizational roster lists office-holders by their posts, and other material includes a directory of UN agencies in each country, a list of member states as of the end of 1974, addresses of the permanent missions in New York and Geneva, a list of General Assembly Presidents 1946–74, names of the principal office-holders from 1946–74, a directory of the World Federation of United Nations Associations, and a list of United Nations depository libraries. Index by nationality.
JX1977.W467

Yearbooks

United Nations. Yearbook of the United Nations, 1946/47– . N.Y., United Nations, Dept. of Public Information, 1947– . Annual. **CK484**

The third yearbook covered Sept. 21, 1948 to Dec. 31, 1949. Each succeeding volume covers a calendar year.

Summarizes the activities, proceedings, and decisions of the United Nations. v.1, 1946/47, covers the origin and the evolution of the United Nations, the 1st General Assembly, and the organization and work of subsidiary and allied organizations. Includes documentary bibliography, subject index, and an index of names.
JX1977.A37Y4

——— United Nations juridical yearbook. 1962– . N.Y., United Nations, 1963– . Annual. **CK485**

Presents documentary materials of a legal character concerning the United Nations and related intergovernmental organizations. Each volume includes a legal bibliography of books and articles on the United Nations and related organizations published during the year. The 1962 yearbook was issued in a "provisional edition" in mimeographed form.

C L

Geography

❖For answering questions in geography four principal types of reference books are useful:

1. Bibliographies and indexes to the material published in books, periodicals, and the publications of learned societies.
2. Gazetteers, both general and special, which serve to tell where a given place is and furnish descriptive information about it.
3. Dictionaries of place-names, which indicate the origin and meaning of such names, and the different forms which have been in use at different times.
4. Atlases, which supply maps and, through their indexes, aid in the location of places.

Guidebooks, which supply a different kind of descriptive material from that given in the gazetteers, and contain many maps, especially local maps and town plans, not given in the general atlases, are treated in section BJ.

Wright and Platt's *Aids to geographical research* (CL6), although now out-of-date, remains a useful guide to geographical reference materials. A more recent reference guide is Brewer's *The literature of geography* (CL1). These and similar guides should be consulted for aid in selecting books for the library and for discovering what books to use to answer particular reference questions.

The average library will need a comprehensive gazetteer, such as the *Columbia Lippincott gazetteer* (CL111) or *Webster's New Geographical dictionary* (CL121), and a general atlas, such as Rand McNally's *Cosmopolitan world atlas* (CL325) or the *Times atlas of the world* (CL336). It should also be remembered that most of the general encyclopedias include maps, either gathered together in an atlas volume or scattered throughout the volumes with the articles on the regions covered.

Automobile road maps, available from gasoline dealers, are also useful for certain types of questions.

GENERAL WORKS

Guides

Brewer, James Gordon. The literature of geography: a guide to its organisation and use. 2d ed. London, Bingley; Hamden, Conn., Linnet Books, [1978]. 264p. il.   **CL1**

1st ed. 1973.
Retains the subject chapter arrangement of the original edition (i.e., information on scope and use of geographical literature followed by bibliographic essays on types of material), and adds more than 400 references published since 1972; a new chapter on cartobibliography has been added.   Z6001.B74

Durrenberger, Robert W. Geographical research and writing. N.Y., Crowell, [1971]. 246p.   **CL2**

A guide for the student, with a bibliography of guides, bibliographies and sources of geographical information.   G73.D97

A guide to information sources in the geographical sciences. Ed. by Stephen Goddard. London, Croom Helm; Totowa, N.J., Barnes & Noble, [1983]. 273p. maps.   **CL3**

Thirteen chapters by academics and librarians provide bibliographical reviews of the literature and reference works of thematic fields of geography (e.g., agricultural), regional areas (Africa, South Asia, the United States, the Soviet Union), and tools (maps, aerial photographs and satellite data, statistical analysis and computers, and archival materials). Some British emphasis; no index.   Z6001.G84

Harris, Chauncy Dennison. Bibliography of geography. Chicago, 1976–84. pt.1–2. (Chicago. Univ. Dept. of Geography. Research paper no. 179, 206) (In progress)   **CL4**

Contents: pt.1, Introduction to general aids. 276p.; pt.2. Regional: v.1, United States of America. 178p.

Does not intend to fully supersede Wright and Platt (CL6) for, although "many items in Wright and Platt are out of date or superseded by later or better works, yet the essential core of older works of enduring value published up to 1946, carefully selected and expertly annotated, remains recorded there and does not need to be repeated."—*Pref.* Chapters on bibliographies of bibliographies (guides, comprehensive retrospective and current bibliographies of geography, specialized bibliographies) are followed by sections for bibliographies of books, serials, government documents, dissertations, photographs, maps and atlases, gazetteers, place name dictionaries, dictionaries, encyclopedias, statistics, and methodology.

In each chapter, introductory remarks are followed by carefully annotated lists of bibliographies. The sections on the comprehensive current and retrospective bibliographies are particularly precise and detailed. Appendix 1 lists "Gazetteers of the U.S. Board on Geographic Names"; Appendix 2 is an annotated list comprising "A small geographical reference collection." Indexed.

Pt.2, Regional geography, will consist of five segments: the United States, the Soviet Union, the Americas, Europe, and Africa, Asia, Australia, and the Pacific. The United States volume emphasizes bibliographies, reference works, and data sources in four main areas: general aids; physical geography, earth science and environment; human geography; and individual regions, states, and cities. 1,257 entries, mostly annotated, for English-language sources published since 1969. Indexed.   H31.C514 no.179, 206

—— Guide to geographical bibliographies and reference works in Russian or on the Soviet Union. Chicago, Univ. of Chicago, Dept. of Geography, 1975. 478p. maps. (Chicago. Univ. Dept. of Geography. Research paper, no.164)   **CL5**

"Annotated list of 2660 bibliographies or reference aids."—*t.p.*
Intended as an aid to individuals outside the Soviet Union who wish to become informed on "the corpus of serious scientific work in geography and related disciplines published in Russian or in other languages of the Soviet Union or dealing with the geography of the Soviet Union."—*Pref.* Classed arrangement with author-title-subject index. Primarily non-Western language materials; entries are given in transliteration, with an English translation of the title.   H31.C514 no.164

Wright, John Kirtland and **Platt, Elizabeth T.** Aids to geographical research; bibliographies, periodicals, atlases, gazetteers, and other reference books. 2d ed. compl. rev. N.Y., publ. for the American Geographical Society by Columbia Univ. Pr., 1947. 331p. (American Geographical Soc. Research ser., no.22)   **CL6**

1st ed. 1923.
A valuable manual, though now much out-of-date. In three main sections: (1) General aids; (2) Topical aids; (3) Regional aids and general geographical periodicals from each country. The coverage is comprehensive and includes materials in many languages. Annotations are descriptive and evaluative. Author, subject, and title index.
Includes, as an appendix, a "Classified index of American profes-

sional geographers, libraries of geographical utility, and institutions engaged in geographical research," p.276–94.   Z6001.A1W9

Bibliography

Aiyepeku, Wilson O. Geographical literature on Nigeria, 1901–1970: an annotated bibliography. Boston, G. K. Hall, 1974. 214p. map.   **CL7**

Includes 1,441 English-language books, journal articles, essays, conference papers, master's theses and doctoral dissertations classified by subject categories developed by the Association of American Geographers. Lists of core authors, periodical titles, and bibliographies consulted. Author, place, and subject indexes.   Z3597.A657

American Geographical Society of New York. Research catalogue. Boston, G. K. Hall, 1962. 15v. and map suppl.   **CL8**

A photographic reproduction of the cards in the Research Catalogue of the Society's library, arranged by a systematic classification and a regional classification. Includes books, periodical articles, pamphlets, and government documents.   Z6009.A48

———— ———— Supplement 1–2. Boston, G. K. Hall, 1972–78. 6v.

Contents: Suppl.1, 1962–71: [pt.1] Regional (2v.); [pt.2] Topical (2v.); Suppl.2, 1972–76: v.1, Topical; v.2, Regional.

Cumulates the citations first published in *Current geographical publications* (CL56), v.25–39.

Arnim, Helmuth. Bibliographie der geographischen Literatur in deutscher Sprache. Baden-Baden, Librairie Heitz, 1970. 177p. (Bibliotheca bibliographica Aureliana, 21)   **CL9**

A classed bibliography of more than 1,500 items; author index.   Z6001.A74

Bederman, Sanford Harold. Africa, a bibliography of geography and related disciplines: a selected listing of recent literature published in the English language. 3d ed. Atlanta, Publ. Serv. Div., Sch. of Bus. Admin., Georgia State Univ., 1974. 334p.   **CL10**

1st–2d eds. (1970–72) published under title: *A bibliographic aid to the study of the geography of Africa.*

A geographically classified list of over 3,600 English-language citations (principally periodical articles). The general and regional sections each have a topical index, and there is also a country index subdivided into topics. Author index.   Z3501.B4

Bibliotheca geographica; Jahresbibliographie der geographischen Literatur. Hrsg. von der Gesellschaft für Erdkunde zu Berlin, 1891/92–1911/12. Berlin, Kuhl, 1895–1917. 19v.   **CL11**

Subtitle varies.

An important annual bibliography of books and periodical articles, listing more titles than the *Bibliographie géographique internationale* (CL55), but without annotations. Classified, with author index. No more published.   Z6001.B582

Blotevogel, Hans H. and **Heineberg, Heinz.** Bibliographie zum Geographiestudium. Paderborn, Schöningh, [1976]. 2v.   **CL12**

Contents: Teil 1, Fachtheorie. Didaktik der Geographie. Arbeitsmethoden. Physische Geographie/Geoökologie; Teil 2, Kulturgeographie. Sozialgeographie. Raumplanung. Entwicklungsländerforschung. Statistische Quellen.

A classed, annotated bibliography of books, articles, and essays, mainly in German and English. Important introductory works have been noted typographically. Both volumes have personal name indexes; v.2 has a regional index covering both volumes.   Z5814.G34B56

Cox, Edward Godfrey. A reference guide to the literature of travel, including voyages, geographical descriptions, adven-

tures, shipwrecks and expeditions. Seattle, Univ. of Washington, 1935–49. 3v. (Univ. of Washington. Pubn. in language and literature, v.9–10, 12) (Repr.: N.Y., Greenwood Pr., 1969)   **CL13**

Contents: v.1, The Old World. 401p.; v.2, The New World. 591p.; v.3, Great Britain. 732p.

Classified with author index. Lists "in chronological order, from the earliest date ascertainable down to and including the year 1800, all the books on foreign travels, voyages and descriptions printed in Great Britain, together with translations from foreign tongues and continental renderings of English works."—*Pref.*   Z6011.C87

Documentatio geographica. Geographische Zeitschriften- und Serien-Literatur. 1966–73. Bearb. und hrsg. vom Institut für Landeskunde, Bad Godesberg; E. Meynen, Direktor. Bad Godesberg, Bundesanstalt für Landeskunde und Raumforschung, 1967–73.   **CL14**

Frequency varies: originally bimonthly with annual cumulation; 1971/72 combined; 1973, quarterly with annual cumulation.

Subtitle also in English (Papers of geographical periodicals and serials), French, Spanish, and Russian.

An international bibliography of geographical literature appearing in periodicals and monographic series. Arranged by Universal Decimal Classification; the annual cumulation includes a separate *Register* volume which provides indexes by author, subject, and region, plus a UDC index offering references to related subject areas for each article.

Continued by: Z6001.D63

Dokumentation zur Raumentwicklung. Jahrg. 1974/75–78. Bonn-Bad Godesberg, Bundesforschungsanstalt für Landeskunde und Raumordnung, 1975–79. Quarterly, with annual index.   **CL15**

Subtitle: Vierteljahreshefte zur Literaturdokumentation aus Raumforschung, Raumordnung, Regionalforschung, Landeskunde und Sozialgeographie/A current and annotated bibliography of regional science, regional planning and social geography.

Published in 2v. per year: T.1, Titelband (comprising 4 quarterly issues); T.2, Registerband (issued annually in publisher's binding).

A classed bibliography, with author, subject, and regional indexes.   Z7164.R33D64

Dumont, Maurice E. and **Smet, L. de.** Aardrijkskundige bibliographie van België; Bibliographie géographique de la Belgique. Gent, Seminarie voor Menselijke Aardrijkskunde der Rijksuniversiteit, 1954–56. 450p. (Bibliographia belgica, 14–17)   **CL16**

Issued in parts.

A classed bibliography of the geography of Belgium, interpreted to include physical, human, economic geography, etc. Author index. Covers to 1954.   Z2407.B5 no.14, etc.

———— ———— Aanvulling. Supplément, 1–3. Bruxelles, 1960–70. (Bibliographia belgica, 48, 82, 113)

The supplements carry the work forward to 1968.

Dunbar, Gary S. The history of modern geography: an annotated bibliography of selected works. N.Y., Garland, 1985. 386p. (Bibliographies of the history of science and technology, v.9; Garland reference library of the humanities, v.445)   **CL17**

An international bibliography of works in western and central European languages on the history of geography from the mid-18th century to the present. 1,717 citations are classed within 22 chapters in three main parts: general and topical; geography in various countries; biographical works. Author and keyword subject indexes.   Z6001.D86

Encyclopedia of geographic information sources. Paul Wasserman, managing ed. 3d ed. Detroit, Gale, 1978. 167p.   **CL18**

Subtitle: A detailed listing of publications and agencies of interest to managerial personnel, with a record of sourcebooks, periodicals, guides to doing business, government and trade offices, directories, handbooks, bibliographies, and other sources of information on each location; a companion volume to *Encyclopedia of business information sources,* 3d ed. [CH184].

Originally issued as v.2 of the *Encyclopedia of business information sources.*

A guide to information sources, principally English-language, on 390 geographic locations and regions. "The emphasis . . . has been on sources of economic and financial materials . . . with greater coverage of analytical reports, trade directories, and newsletters, as well as economic planning documents and domestic trade directories."—*Introd.* A supplement is to be published 1985.

HF5353.E54

Engelmann, Wilhelm. Bibliotheca geographica. Verzeichniss der seit der Mitte des vorigen Jahrhunderts bis zu Ende des Jahres 1856 in Deutschland erschienenen Werke über Geographie und Reisen, mit Einschluss der Landkarten, Pläne und Ansichten. Leipzig, Engelmann, 1858. 1225p. **CL19**

A comprehensive list of 18th- and 19th-century German works on geography and travels in various parts of the world, arranged for the most part by geographical location. Subject index. Z6001.E57

Food and Agriculture Organization of the United Nations. Bibliography on land settlement. Rome, 1976. 146p. **CL20**

Introductory material in English, French, and Spanish.

Defines land settlement as "the planned movement of populations to areas of under-utilized agricultural potential. The Bibliography also contains references on projects for the settlement of nomads, refugees, youth, pensioners, and for persons displaced by the construction of dams and by natural disasters, as well as literature on settlement policy, land administration, land consolidation, village modernization and the improvement of rural infrastructure . . . and various types of farms."—*Pref.* Literature is from 1958 to 1975. Geographical arrangement; author index. Z7164.L3F64

Freedman, Robert L. Human food uses: a cross-cultural, comprehensive annotated bibliography. Westport, Conn., Greenwood Pr., [1981]. 552p. **CL21**

For full information *see* EK227a.

A geographical bibliography for American libraries. Ed. by Chauncy D. Harris [and others]. [Wash.], Assoc. of American Geographers, 1985. 437p. **CL22**

"A joint project of the Association of American Geographers and the National Geographic Society."—*t.p.*

"Since the predecessor volume, *A geographical bibliography for American college libraries* (1970 [below]), still provides an excellent guide to works published before 1970, the current bibliography focuses on publications for the period 1970–1984."—*Introd.* Entries and brief annotations for many new sections, including publications suitable for school libraries, were prepared by more than 70 contributors. 2,903 citations to monographs, bibliographies, serials, and atlases in detailed classed/regional arrangement. Brief, critical annotations; indexed. A major and indispensable work. Z6001.G44

Lewthwaite, Gordon Rowland, Price, Edward T. and Winters, Harold A. A geographical bibliography for American college libraries. Rev. ed. Wash., Assoc. of Amer. Geographers, Commission on College Geography, [1970]. 214p. (Assoc. of Amer. Geographers. Comm. on College Geography. Pubn. 9) **CL23**

"A revision of *A basic geographical library; a selected and annotated book list for American colleges.* Original ed. compiled and edited by Martha Church, Robert E. Huke [and] Harold A. Winters [1966]."—*title page.*

A list of 1,760 items "selected as a core for the geography collection of an American undergraduate college library."—*Introd.* Emphasis is on recent books in English, but "many books in foreign languages and older books, even though not currently available, have been included where their subject or quality seemed needed." Classed arrangement; brief annotations; author index.

Z6001.L48

Giraldo Jaramillo, Gabriel. Bibliografía colombiana de viajes. Bogotá, Ed. ABC, 1957. 224p. (Biblioteca de bibliografía colombiana, 2) **CL24**

A bibliography of books and articles in various languages on travels in Colombia. In two parts: (1) Viajeros colombianos; (2) Viajeros extranjeros en Colombia. Titles are mainly from the 19th and 20th centuries. Z7146.G5

Goodman, Edward J. The exploration of South America: an annotated bibliography. N.Y., Garland, 1983. 174p. (Garland reference library of social science, v.148; Themes in European expansion, v.4) **CL25**

General sections on bibliographies, documents collections, and contemporary accounts are followed by chapters arranged by historical period, then by geographic area. 915 entries. Author and subject indexes. Z1212.G66

Grim, Ronald E. Historical geography of the United States; a guide to information sources. Detroit, Gale, [1982]. 291p. (Geography and travel guide information ser., v.5) **CL26**

An annotated bibliography in three parts: cartographic sources, archival and historical materials, and secondary topical literature produced or reprinted since 1965. Intended to complement D. R. McManis's *Historical geography of the United States* (below).

Z1247.G74

McManis, Douglas R. Historical geography of the United States: a bibliography, excluding Alaska and Hawaii. [Ypsilanti? Div. of Field Services, Eastern Michigan Univ., 1965] 249p. **CL27**

Includes citations to monographs and scholarly periodical articles, especially state and local historical society publications. Arranged by region, state, and topic (such as exploration and settlement, population, agriculture, urban developments). Covers through the 19th century. No index. Z1236.M3

Harvard University. Library. Geography and anthropology: classification schedules; classified listing by call number; chronological listing; author and title listing. Cambridge, Publ. by the Harvard University Library; distr. by Harvard Univ. Pr., 1979. 270p. (Widener Library Shelflist, 60) **CL28**

For a note on the series *see* AA145.

Includes some "9000 shelflist entries comprising the Widener *Geog* and *An* classes."—*Foreword.* It should be kept in mind that "Harvard's major research collection in anthropology is in the Tozzer Library, whose holdings are represented by the *Catalogue of the Library of the Peabody Museum of Archaeology and Ethnology* . . . [CE12]." Z6009.H37

Hopkins, Stephen T. and **Jones, Douglas E.** Research guide to the arid lands of the world. [Phoenix, Ariz.], Oryx Pr., 1983. 391p. maps. **CL29**

An annotated guide to reference sources on the physical and human geography of the world's drylands. Emphasizes current information sources such as databases. In two parts: geographic regions, and broad subjects. Author and subject indexes.

Z6004.A7H66

International Geographical Union. Commission on Humid Tropics. A select annotated bibliography of the humid tropics, comp. by Theo L. Hills. Montreal, Geography Dept., McGill Univ., 1960. 238p. **CL30**

Comprises several thousand items, arranged by continent, then by country or other smaller area. Within each section is given a classed list of books, articles, and reports, including general and social materials as well as geographical. Annotations generally very brief. No indexes. Z6004.T7I5

Kinauer, Rudolf. Lexikon geographischer Bildbände. Wien, Hollinek, [1966]. 463p. **CL31**

A bibliography designed to enable the user easily to find pictures and photographs illustrating various aspects of geography.

Z6001.K5

Kish, George. Bibliography of International Geographic Congresses, 1871–1976. Boston, G. K. Hall, [1979]. 540p. (Ser. of studies of the history of geography, v.1) **CL32**

Publ. under the auspices of the Commission on the History of Geographical Thought, International Geographical Union.

Lists almost 7,000 papers presented at the 23 International Geographical Congresses held between 1871 and 1976. Arranged chronologically by congress, and within congress by group presentation, with complete bibliographical references to the published proceedings. Classed subject and author indexes. Z6001.K55

Land use planning abstracts. N.Y., Environment Information Center, 1974–79. Annual. **CL33**

Subtitle, 1974: A select guide to land and water resources information since 1970.

1975 ed. covers publications of 1974–75; 1977 (called "3d ed.") covers 1976–77.

The volume covering 1976–77 offers abstracts of about 1,800 journal articles, conference papers, government hearings, and special studies grouped under 21 main headings (e.g., air pollution, chemical and biological contamination, energy). Subject index. A "Review" section at the beginning of each volume presents essays on the state of land use planning and policy. HD171.A1L35

Lautensach, Hermann and **Feio, Mariano.** Bibliografia geográfica de Portugal. Lisboa, Inst. para a Alta Cultura, Centro de Estudos Geográficos, 1948. 256p. **CL34**

Based on bibliographies covering 1915–43, prepared for the *Geographisches Jahrbuch*, v.45 and 59, and for *Portugal auf Grund eigener Reisen und der Literatur* (1937).

Lists Portuguese geographical works from early times. Geography is broadly interpreted to include climate, anthropology, ethnography, agriculture, fishing, commerce, etc. Z2726.L38

Leng, Gunter. Desertification: a bibliography with regional emphasis on Africa. [Bremen, Universität Bremen, Presseund Informationsamt], 1982. 177p. map. (Bremen Beiträge zur Geographie und Raumplanung, Hft.4) **CL35**

In two parts—desertification worldwide, and desertification in Africa—further subdivided by topic and region. Separate section for United Nations documents. Author index. Z6004.D4L46

Martínez Ríos, Jorge. Tenencia de la tierra y desarrollo agrario en México: bibliografía selectiva y comentada, 1522–1968. México, [Ediciones Preliminares, Dirección General de Publicaciones, Universidad Nacional Autónoma de México], 1970. 1x, 305p. **CL36**

An international bibliography of more than 1,550 citations to a wide variety of materials, arranged by historical period, then by subject. Mexican library locations noted. Indexed. Z7165.M45M33

Mexico. Dirección General de Geografía y Meteorología. Bibliografía geográfica de México, recopilación y ordenamiento de Angel Bassols Batalla. México, [1955]. 652p. **CL37**

A comprehensive bibliography dealing with the geography of Mexico: historical, physical, economic, etc. Classed arrangement with geographical and author indexes. Z1425.A52

Morrison, Denton E., Hornback, Kenneth E. and **Warner, W. Keith.** Environment: an annotated bibliography of social science and related literature. Prep. for Office of Research and Monitoring, U.S. Environmental Protection Agency. Wash., Govt. Prt. Off., 1974. 860p. (Socioeconomic environmental studies series, EPA-600/5-74-011) **CL38**

A comprehensive, unannotated bibliography of "nearly 5,000 items covering literature in and related to the fields of anthropology, communications, economics, education, design, geography, history, human ecology, landscape architecture, management, planning, politics and government, population, psychology, public administration, recreation, social psychology and sociology. The emphasis is on literature that is substantively, methodologically or theoretically relevant to man and his activities in relationship to natural environ-

ments."—*Abstract.* Author listing with a "subject-title index" which lists the titles within 42 subject categories. Z7161.M56

Muñoz Reyes, Jorge. Bibliografía geográfica de Bolivia. La Paz, Academia Nacional de Ciencias de Bolivia, 1967. 170p. (Academia Nacional de Ciencias de Bolivia. Pubn. no.16) **CL39**

An author listing without subject index. Z1656.M8

Ofori, Patrick E. Land in Africa: its administration, law, tenure and use; a select bibliography. Nendeln, [Liechtenstein], KTO Pr., 1978. 200p. **CL40**

Citations to 1,789 books, articles, theses, legislative documents, and other materials are arranged geographically—the continent as a whole, by region, then by country—with other sections on bibliographies and general works. Author and subject indexes.

Z7164.L3O34

Owens, Peter L. and **House, Richard.** Radical geography, an annotated bibliography. Norwich, [Eng.], Geo Books, 1984. 260p. (Geo abstracts bibliography, no.13) **CL41**

1,314 citations drawn from the database of *Geo abstracts* (CL57), which illustrate the left-oriented approach to social and economic geography. Topical arrangement with author and keyword subject indexes. Z6001.O9

Owings, Loren C. Environmental values, 1860–1972; a guide to information sources. Detroit, Gale, 1976. 324p. (Man and the environment information guide ser., v.4) **CL42**

"The theme of this bibliography is the historical development of attitudes toward, and concern for, nature in the United States."—*Introd.* Chapters cover general works, travel reports, landscape painting, national parks, conservation and the idea of wilderness, conservation and the ecological ethic, nature study, camping, "Back to Nature" movement, and general reference works. Annotated. Author-title-subject index. Z5861.O93

Paylore, Patricia. Desertification: a world bibliography. Tucson, Univ. of Arizona, Office of Arid Lands Studies, [1976]. 644p. **CL43**

1st ed., 1973, had title: *World desertification: cause and effect.*

A computer-produced, annotated bibliography on desertification rather than simply arid lands. Includes books, chapters of books, articles, reports, proceedings, and government documents. Geographical arrangement, with introduction and author-keyword indexes for each region (except for the Soviet Union, which has a more detailed subject breakdown within its section). Primarily literature of the past decade. An update covering 1976–80 was published 1980. Z6004.D4P35

Pelzer, Karl Josef. Selected bibliography on the geography of Southeast Asia. New Haven, Conn., Southeast Asia Studies, Yale Univ., by arrangement with Human Relations Area Files, 1949–56. v.1–3. (Behavior science bibliographies) **CL44**

Contents: v.1, Southeast Asia—general; v.2, The Philippines; v.3, Malaya. No more published.

"A companion to the bibliography of *Peoples and cultures of mainland southeast Asia* by Professor John F. Embree" (*Pref.*) for which *see* DE109.

Entries, which include monographs and periodical articles on physical, cultural, economic, and political geography, are arranged under broad subject headings, with no index. Z3221.P4

Rey Balmaceda, Raul C. Bibliografía geográfica referida a la República Argentina. Buenos Aires, Gaea, Sociedad Argentina de Estudios Geográficos, 1975– . v.1– . (Serie especial —Gaea, Sociedad Argentina de Estudios Geográficos, no.2) (In progress) **CL45**

A classified, international bibliography of about 9,200 citations produced from 1955 to 1969. Some titles have brief annotations clarifying content, noting appearance in other sources, reviews, etc. Indexed by author, personal names, geographic and topical subjects.

Royal Geographical Society, London. New geographical literature and maps. London, 1951–80. n.s.v.1–9. Semiannual (irregular). **CL46**

Issued 1918–41 as *Recent geographical literature, maps, and photographs* . . . as a supplement to *Geographical journal*. No more publ.

Lists books and articles in leading British and foreign geographical journals, and new maps and atlases. Also contains annual lists of completed theses in geography from British universities.

Z6009.R882

Sanguin, André Louis. Géographie politique: bibliographie internationale. Montréal, Presses de l'Université du Québec, 1976. 232p. **CL47**

An attempt to distinguish political geography from geopolitics. Subject-classed list of works on cultural geography; the nation and the state; the frontier; territorial conflicts; oceans and international rivers; space; military, administrative, and electoral geography; international affairs and regionalism; and colonialism. Within each topic, citations are usually arranged by general or regional content, with subdivisions by book or article format. Author index.

Z6004.P7S3

Sukhwal, B. L. South Asia: a systematic geographic bibliography. Metuchen, N.J., Scarecrow Pr., 1974. 827p. **CL48**

More than 10,300 entries. Within geographic divisions (South Asia, India, Pakistan, Bangladesh, Sri Lanka, Tibet, Kingdom of Nepal, Kingdoms of Bhutan and Sikkim, Indian Ocean and islands), materials are listed in classed arrangement. Author index.

Z3185.S94

Thompson, Edgar T. The plantation: an international bibliography. Boston, G. K. Hall, [1983]. 194p. il. **CL49**

Presents 1,362 annotated citations to books and periodical articles on plantation society in the American South, West Indies, South America, the Pacific, and South and Southeast Asia. Includes belles lettres materials. Subject arrangement; author index.

Z5071.T48

U.S. Library of Congress. Reference Dept. Soviet geography: a bibliography. Nicholas R. Rodionoff, ed. Wash., 1951. 668p. (Repr.: N.Y., Greenwood, 1969) **CL50**

Pt.1, U.S.S.R. geography by subject; pt.2, Administrative, natural and economic regions.

Geography "is construed herein as the science describing the land, sea, air and the distribution of plant and animal life, excluding man but not his industries."—*Pref.* Material is largely in Russian. Locates copies.

Z2506.U58

West, Henry W. and **Sawyer, Olive Hilda Matthew.** Land administration: a bibliography for developing countries. Cambridge, Cambridge Univ. Pr., 1975. 292p. **CL51**

English-language books, periodical articles, papers and conference proceedings (published 1960–73) on land ownership, policy, tenure and law are grouped first by continent, then by country. Author index.

Z7164.L3W47

Wisconsin. University-Madison. Land Tenure Center. Library. Agrarian reform in Latin America: an annotated bibliography. Madison, The Center, 1974. 2v. in 1. (Land economics monographs, 5) **CL52**

"Published . . . under the sponsorship of *Land Economics*."—*t.p.*

A guide to book, journal, pamphlet, and unpublished material on land tenure, land reform, and problems of the small farmers. Entries are grouped by region (Latin America, Central America, the Caribbean), then by individual country. Items of particular interest or importance are specially coded. Personal and corporate author indexes, classified subject index.

Z7164.L3W56

———— Land tenure and agrarian reform in Africa and the Near East: an annotated bibliography. Boston, G. K. Hall, [1976]. 423p. **CL53**

Entries for books, articles, pamphlets, and unpublished materials

are grouped by region (Africa, Near East and North Africa) and then by country. Author, corporate author, and classified subject index.

Z7164.L3W56

———— Land tenure and agrarian reform in East and Southeast Asia: an annotated bibliography. Boston, G. K. Hall, [1980]. 557p. **CL54**

Comp. by the staff of the Land Tenure Center Library under the direction of Teresa J. Anderson, Librarian.

Follows the pattern established by similar volumes (above). Entries are grouped by geographic region, then by individual country. Based on the holdings of the Library. Indexed by personal and corporate name, and by classified subject. Z7165.A743W57

Current

Bibliographie géographique internationale, 1891– . Paris, Centre National de la Recherche Scientifique, 1894– . v.1– . Quarterly. **CL55**

Title varies slightly; v.1–24 issued with *Annales de géographie.* Publisher varies. Frequency varies.

A most important international bibliography. Classed arrangement with author index and detailed table of contents. Some annotations. Indexed by subject, place, and author. Z6001.B57●

Current geographical publications; additions to the Research catalogue of the American Geographical Society. v.1– , 1938– . N.Y., The Society, 1938– . v.1– . Monthly, except July and Aug. **CL56**

Publisher varies; now issued by the Library, Univ. of Wisconsin, Milwaukee.

A classified index to current books, pamphlets, government publications, and periodical articles in the field of geography. v.1 has no index; v.2– have indexes by subject, author, and regions.

From Oct. 1940 through Dec. 1952, each issue contained a supplement listing photographs in publications received in the library of the American Geographical Society. Since Nov. 1964 selected maps are listed in a separate section. Z6009.A47

Geo abstracts, 1972– . [Norwich, Eng., Univ. of East Anglia], 1972– . Each section publ. 6 times a year, with annual indexes. **CL57**

Supersedes *Geographical abstracts, A-D* (1966–71).

Issued in seven parts, each part available on separate subscription: A, Landforms and the quaternary; B, Climatology and hydrology; C, Economic geography; D, Social and historical geography; E, Sedimentology; F, Regional and community planning; G, Remote sensing, photogrammetry and cartography. Subject arrangement within sections. The annual index is in two parts: pt.1 covers A, B, E, and G; pt.2 covers C, D, and F.

Geographisches Jahrbuch, 1866– . Gotha, Perthes, 1866– . v.1– . Irregular. **CL58**

———— Index, 1866–1925, in v.40, p.ix–xix.

A comprehensive and extensive series originally published annually. Each volume includes surveys of the published work in special fields of geography, the fields varying from volume to volume. For a convenient key to the reports in this series, *see* Wright and Platt, *Aids to geographical research*, p.52–57 (CL6).

Book reviews

Van Balen, John. Geography and earth sciences publications: an author, title and subject guide to books reviewed, and an index to the reviews. [Ann Arbor, Mich.], Pierian Pr., 1978. 2v. **CL59**

Contents: v.1, 1968–1972; v.2, 1973–1975.

v.1 contains about 3,400 entries and 4,900 book review citations from 21 geographical journals; v.2, about 2,500 entries and 3,700 book review citations from 38 geographical journals. Author listing, with broad subject, geographical area, and title indexes.

Z6001.V33

Periodicals

Harris, Chauncy D. Annotated world list of selected current geographical serials. 4th ed. Chicago, Dept. of Geography, Univ. of Chicago, 1980. 165p. (Chicago. Univ. Dept. of Geography. Research paper, 194) **CL60**

1st ed. 1960.
"443 current geographical serials from 72 countries, with a study of serials most cited in geographical bibliographies."—*t.p.*
HC31.C514 no.194

———— and **Fellmann, Jerome D.** International list of geographical serials. 3d ed., rev., expanded, & updated. Chicago, Univ. of Chicago, Dept. of Geography, 1980. 457p. (Chicago. Univ. Dept. of Geography. Research paper, 193) **CL61**

1st ed. 1960. An earlier version had title: *Union list of geographical serials* (2d. ed. 1950).
"A comprehensive retrospective inventory of 3,445 geographical serials from 107 countries in 55 languages with locations in union lists."—*t.p.* HC31.C514 no.193

Dissertations

Browning, Clyde Eugene. Bibliography of dissertations in geography, 1901 to 1969: American and Canadian universities. Chapel Hill, Univ. of North Carolina, Dept. of Geography, 1970. 96p. (Studies in geography, no.1) **CL62**

The compilation is based mainly on the dissertation lists published in the periodical *The professional geographer.* Z6001.B89

———— A bibliography of dissertations in geography: 1969 to 1982, American and Canadian universities. Chapel Hill, Univ. of North Carolina, Dept. of Geography, [1983]. 145p. (Studies in geography, no.18)

Forms a supplement to the above, listing 2,270 dissertations from the 1969–82 period. Based on the listings appearing in *The professional geographer* and the *Guide to departments of geography in the United States and Canada* (CL102). Classed arrangement with author index. Z6001.B76

Stuart, Merrill M. A bibliography of master's theses in geography: American and Canadian universities. Tualatin, Ore., Geographic and Area Study Publs., [1973]. 275p. **CL63**

More than 5,000 entries in classified arrangement, with author and regional indexes. Includes items from the lists appearing in *The professional geographer,* plus other titles reported by various degree-granting institutions. Z6001.S78

Dictionaries and encyclopedias

British Association for the Advancement of Science. Research Committee. A glossary of geographical terms. Ed. by Dudley Stamp and Audrey N. Clark. 3d ed. London & N.Y., Longman, [1979]. 571p. **CL64**

1st ed. 1961.
Provides comparative definitions of geographical terms from various reference sources and texts. Many foreign-language terms are included. This edition has added new entries in the areas of human geography, cartography, biogeography, and climatology.
G107.9.B74

Clark, Audrey N. Longman dictionary of geography. [London], Longman, [1985]. 724p. map. **CL65**

Definitions for the geographical terms are based on the fuller information in the *Glossary of geographical terms* (above), and are complemented by Chisholm's *Handbook of commercial geography* by L. Dudley Stamp (20th ed., rev. by G. Noel Blake and Audrey N. Clark. London, Longman, 1980). G63.C56

Day, Alan Edwin. Discovery and exploration: a reference handbook. München, K. G. Saur; London, Clive Bingley, [1980]– . v.1– . (In progress) **CL66**

Contents: [v.1] The old world (295p.).
The first volume presents 455 alphabetically arranged entries for persons, institutions, and published sources relevant to the exploration of Europe, Asia, and the Arctic. Indexed by region and authors/titles of published sources.
A second volume is to cover the new world. G80.D36

DeSola, Ralph. Worldwide what & where: geographic glossary & traveller's guide. Santa Barbara, Calif., ABC-Clio, [1975]. 720p. **CL67**

A miscellany of geographical facts, abbreviations, places, names, etc., in dictionary arrangement. For many localities lists "scenic spectacles," cities ranked by population (without figures), unusual place names. Addenda include list of capital cities, ferry routes, festivals, museums, and abbreviations. G63.D47

A dictionary of basic geography, by Allen A. Schmieder [and others]. Boston, Allyn & Bacon, [1970]. 299p. il. **CL68**

For the beginning student and the geography teacher. Includes terms from cultural, political, and economic geography as well as from physical geography. G108.A2D5

Dictionary of human geography. Ed. by R. J. Johnston. N.Y., Free Pr., [1981]. 411p. il. **CL69**

Provides about 500 signed definitions of basic concepts, major topics, subfields of human geography (urban, cultural, economic, Marxist, etc.), and organizations; definitions are followed by references and bibliography. Indexed. GF4.D52

Dictionnaire de la géographie. Sous la direction de Pierre George. 3e éd. rev. et augm. [Paris], Presses Universitaires de France, [1984]. 485p. il. **CL70**

1st ed. 1970.
Provides variant terms in different languages, definitions organized by subfields (meteorology, human geography, geomorphology, etc.), and bibliographic references for some entries.
G108.F7D52

The discoverers: an encyclopedia of explorers and exploration. Ed. by Helen Delpar. N.Y., McGraw-Hill, [1980]. 471p. il. **CL71**

Emphasizes the age of discovery that began in 15th-century Europe and continued up to the 20th century, with main stress on explorers of Western European origin. Articles are of three types: (1) biographical; (2) geographical, on continents or regions, reviewing the history of their exploration; (3) topical, on themes such as ancient or medieval exploration. Articles are signed; most have bibliographies. Cross references; index. G200.D53

Fischer, Eric and **Elliott, Francis E.** A German and English glossary of geographical terms. N.Y., Amer. Geographical Soc., 1950. 111p. (Amer. Geog. Soc., Library Ser., no.5) (Repr.: Westport, Conn., Greenwood Pr., 1976) **CL72**

German-English, English-German. G108.A2F5

Groom, Nigel. A dictionary of Arabic topography and place-names; a transliterated Arabic-English dictionary with an Arabic glossary of topographical words and placenames. [Beirut], Librarie du Liban; [London], Longman, [1983]. 369p. **CL73**

A ready reference source on the meaning of Arabic place names and words for topographic features as transliterated into Roman script. Arranged alphabetically by transliterated version with Arabic index. DS36.55.G76

International geographic encyclopedia and atlas. Boston, Houghton Mifflin, [1979]. 1300p. il., maps. **CL74**

"Houghton Mifflin Company adapted, revised, and supplemented the encyclopedic text entries that originally appeared as geographic entries in *The New Columbia Encyclopedia* [AC9], published by Columbia University Press."—[p.iv].
Provides entries for about 25,000 geographic names and terms,

and a 64-page atlas of 4-color maps produced by Rand McNally, plus an index to these maps. More than 200 black-and-white maps are distributed throughout the text.   G105.I57

Kratkaia geograficheskaia entsiklopediia. Glav. redaktor, A. A. Grigor'ev. Moskva, Sovetskaia Entsiklopediia, 1960–66. 5v. il., maps.   **CL75**

A geographical encyclopedia covering various phases of economic and physical geography. Section of tables and a supplement in v.5.
                    G103.K76

Larkin, Robert P. and **Peters, Gary L.** Dictionary of concepts in human geography. Westport, Conn., Greenwood Pr., [1983]. 286p. (Reference sources for the social sciences and humanities, 2)   **CL76**

For some 100 English-language terms, brief essays provide definitions, historical development, bibliographic references, and sources of additional information. Indexed.   GF4.L37

Lock, Clara Beatrice Muriel. Geography and cartography; a reference handbook. 3d ed. rev. and enl. London, Bingley; Hamden, Conn., Linnet Books, [1976]. 762p.   **CL77**

A combined and revised edition of *Geography: a reference handbook*, first published 1968 (2d ed. 1972), and of *Modern maps and atlases*, first published 1969 (CL256). It constitutes an enlarged edition of the *Geography* handbook with "additional extended articles" and includes "some of the updated cartographical material that would otherwise appear in a revised *Modern maps. . . ."—Foreword*.

The review in *RQ*, 16:259 (Spr. 1977) concludes that "for libraries having the second edition [of *Geography: a reference handbook*], the purchase of *Geography and Cartography* is not recommended due to the large amount of duplicate information present and to the high price."   G63.L6

Logie, Gordon. Glossary of land resources: English-French-Italian-Dutch-German-Swedish. Amsterdam & N.Y., Elsevier, 1984. 303p. (International planning glossaries, 4)
                    CL78

Deals with land resources, landed property, land forms, climate, agriculture, forestry, recreation, urbanization and pollution. Divided into sections as just noted, with further topical subdivisions. Base language is English, with equivalents given in the other five languages; indexes in each language.   HD107.7.L63

Monkhouse, Francis John. A dictionary of geography. 2d ed. [London], Arnold, [1970]. 378p. il.   **CL79**

1st ed. 1965.
In addition to the words used to describe the various features of the earth's surface, the work includes those terms that have been used "in a specific geographical context, or in a specialist sense which differs from general practice or popular usage."—*Pref.* Nearly 4,000 entries.   G108.E5M6

—— and **Small, Ronald John.** A dictionary of the natural environment. N.Y., Wiley, [1978]. 320p. il.   **CL80**

Based in part on the revisions prepared for a new edition of *A dictionary of geography* (above), with 465 new definitions, line diagrams, and photographs. Emphasizes terms used by physical geographers and environmental scientists.   GB10.M64

Moore, Wilfred George. A dictionary of geography; definitions and explanations of terms used in physical geography. 5th ed. Harmondsworth, Penguin, 1974. 246p. il., maps.
                    CL81

1st ed. 1949.
Less extensive than either the dictionary by Clark (CL65) or that by Monkhouse (CL79).   GB10.M66

Pötke, Evasusanne and **Pötke, Peter Michael.** Deutsch-englisches/englisch-deutsches Wörterbuch der Geographie. German and English glossary of geographical terms. Meinersen, Gesellschaft für Raumplanung und Raumordnung, 1982. 380p. (Veröffentlichungen der Gesellschaft für Raumplanung und Raumordnung. Sonderhefte, 1)   **CL82**

Provides equivalent terms in both languages, abbreviations, and measures and weights.

U.S. Defense Mapping Agency. Topographic Center. Glossary of mapping, charting, and geodetic terms. 4th ed. Wash., 1981. 264p.   **CL83**

1st ed. 1967.
"For the most part, only those terms considered germane to some specific aspect of mapping, charting, and geodesy were included."—*Introd.*   GA102.D43

Westermann Lexikon der Geographie. Hrsg. im Auftrag des Georg Westermann Verlages von Wolf Tietze. [Braunschweig], G. Westermann, [1968–72]. 5v. il.   **CL84**

About 20,000 entries, mainly for place-names and geographical areas, but including numerous personal names and terms relating to geography. Extensive bibliographies for many of the longer articles; numerous maps, charts, tables, and line drawings. v.5 is an index.
                    G103.W47

Whittow, J. B. The Penguin dictionary of physical geography. London, A. Lane, 1984. 591p. il.   **CL85**

Designed for the British undergraduate. A companion volume dealing with human geography is planned.   GB10.W48

Bibliography

Meynen, Emil. Bibliography of mono- and multilingual dictionaries and glossaries of technical terms used in geography as well as in related natural and social sciences. Wiesbaden, Steiner, 1974. 246p.   **CL86**

Title page and all explanatory material in English and French.
Comp. and ed. by the International Geographical Union Commission, "International Geographical Terminology."
A selective, classed list of dictionaries and glossaries published 1920 and later in monographic and periodical article format. Excludes gazetteers of geographical names and dictionaries of regional data, with the more comprehensive treatment given to multilingual, rather than monolingual works. Includes bibliographical references and a supplement. Author index includes titles if they are the main entry. Each citation indicates languages used in the work.   Z6004.D5M48

Handbooks

Boyer, Richard and **Savageau, David.** Places rated almanac; your guide to finding the best places to live in America. [Completely rev. updated 2d ed.] N.Y., Rand McNally, 1985. 448p. il.   **CL87**

Ranks metropolitan areas according to nine factors: climate, housing, health care and environment, crime, transportation, education, recreation, the arts, and economics. Each chapter on a particular factor lists cities in rank order, then alphabetically, and presents capsule descriptions of metropolitan area features. Many tables and lists of related statistical data, with sources indicated. List of tables, maps, and diagrams, but no index.   HN60.B69

Cities of the world. Detroit, Gale, [1982]. 4v.   **CL88**

Subtitle: A compilation of current information on cultural, geographical, and political conditions in the countries and cities of six continents, based on the Department of State's "Post reports."
Contents: v.1, Africa; v.2, The Western hemisphere (exclusive of the United States); v.3, Europe and the Mediterranean Middle East; v.4, Asia, the Pacific, and the Asiatic Middle East.
Provides guidebook-type information for more than 2,000 cities in 131 countries, excluding those with which the United States does not maintain diplomatic relations. A library which owns the *Post reports* will not need this set (which has not reproduced the valuable city maps included in the *Reports*).   G153.4.C57

—— Supplement. Ed. by Margaret Walsh Young, with the assistance of Susan L. Stetler. Detroit, Gale, [1983]. 466p.

Based on 30 *Post reports* issued by the State Department since publication of the basic set. Covers 92 cities, 47 of which are new in this volume (including Geneva and Ugandan cities). New features include local holidays, schools for foreigners, and recommended readings.

Cleare, John. The world guide to mountains and mountaineering. N.Y., Mayflower Books, [1979]. 208p. il., maps. **CL89**

A guidebook for the individual climber, focusing on interesting and accessible mountain ranges. Excludes British Columbia's interior and coast ranges, the Chilean and Argentinian Andes, the Japanese Alps, and the Taurus, Pontine, and Elburz ranges of Turkey and Iran. Arranged by continent, then by mountain range. Each range is described in terms of its geography and history of climbing expeditions; major peaks, passes, glaciers, nearby towns, huts, methods of access, maps, and guidebooks are listed adjacent to a map of the area. Many black-and-white and color photographs, including illustrations of equipment. Brief glossary; bibliography; index. GV200.C58

Deserts of the world. Ed. by William G. McGinnies, Bram J. Goldman [and] Patricia Paylore. [Tucson], Univ. of Arizona Pr., [1968]. 788p. il. **CL90**

For full citation and annotation *see* EE14.

Gresswell, R. Kay and **Huxley, Anthony Julian.** Standard encyclopedia of the world's rivers and lakes. London, Weidenfeld & Nicolson; N.Y., Putnam, [1966]. 384p. il. **CL91**

For full information *see* EE7.

Huxley, Anthony Julian. Standard encyclopedia of the world's mountains. N.Y., Putnam, [1962]. 383p. il., maps. **CL92**

For full information *see* EE8.

—— Standard encyclopedia of the world's oceans and islands. N.Y., Putnam, [1962]. 383p. il., maps. **CL93**

For full information *see* EE9.

Julyan, Robert Hixson. Mountain names. Seattle, Mountaineers, [1984]. 233p. il. **CL94**

For about 300 mountain peaks and ranges throughout the world, gives: elevation in feet and meters; date of first ascent and name of climber; descriptive history of derivation of name, important events, importance of the site, etc. Pronunciation not indicated. GB501.2.J85

Mirot, Léon. Manuel de géographie historique de la France. 2. éd. Ouvrage posthume revue et publié par Albert Mirot. Paris, Picard, 1947–50. 2v. maps, genealogical tables. **CL95**

Contents: v.1, L'unité française; v.2, Les divisions religieuses et administratives de la France.

1st ed. 1929.

A manual, with maps, of the historical geography of France from the Gallo-Roman period to the 20th century. The first volume deals with France as a whole, the second with its ecclesiastical and administrative divisions. Extensive indexes to persons, places, and subjects. DC20.5.M513

Rand McNally encyclopedia of world rivers. Chicago, Rand McNally & Co., [1980]. 350p. il., maps. **CL96**

First published in the United Kingdom (London, Bison Books, 1980).

"The major considerations in selecting the rivers were length, natural beauty and geographic importance. However, a myriad of smaller rivers were also included because their banks provided sites for important towns, they were once significant trade routes or they were the scenes where historic events—battles, conferences and the like—occurred."—*Introd.* Arrangement is by continent, then alphabetically by name of river. Inset maps locate principal rivers, and these are treated in depth. Handsomely illustrated. Unfortunately, no index nor bibliography. GB1201.4.R36

Reference handbook on the deserts of North America. Gordon L. Bender, ed. Westport, Conn., Greenwood Pr., [1982]. 594p. il., maps. **CL97**

Offers lengthy chapters by specialists on the geology and biology of seven major deserts of the Arctic, the southwestern United States and Mexico, and briefer chapters on various aspects of desert life, the process of desertification, and research facilities. Extensive bibliographies and use of photographs, maps, and tables. Indexed. GB612.R43

Rolling rivers: an encyclopedia of America's rivers. Richard A. Bartlett, ed. N.Y., McGraw-Hill, [1984]. 398p. il. **CL98**

Consists of essays written by professional historians, emphasizing historical developments along each of 117 North American rivers. Introductory "profile" provides geographical data (source, mouth, length, cities, agriculture, etc.), and further readings are suggested. Indexed; no maps. GB1215.R64

The world factbook. 1981– . Wash., Central Intelligence Agency, 1981– . maps. Annual. **CL99**

Produced by National Foreign Assessment Center; continues *National basic intelligence factbook.*

For each country of the world, provides brief data on geography, population, government, membership in international intergovernmental organizations, economy, communications, and defense. Small maps of each country; regional maps in color.

Handbook of the nations (2d ed. Detroit, Gale, 1981) is a reprint of *World factbook* in a smaller format, without the regional maps. G122.U56a

Directories

Association of American Geographers. AAG directory, 1956– . Wash., The Assoc., 1956– . Irregular. **CL100**

Title varies: 1956–66, *Handbook-directory;* 1967–78, *Directory of the Association of American Geographers.*

Includes geographers and geography students, indicating their specialties or areas of interest. G64.A8

Geographisches Taschenbuch und Jahrweiser für Landeskunde. Wiesbaden, Steiner, 1949– . il. Biennial. **CL101**

Title varies.

A biennial handbook including regional reports and papers, research and expeditions, etc., and a directory of authorities, institutes and organizations in specified countries, etc. G1.G43

Guide to departments of geography in the United States and Canada, 1968/69– . Wash., Assoc. of American Geographers, [1968]– . Annual. **CL102**

Title varies: 1968/69–83/84, *Guide to graduate departments of geography in the United States and Canada.*

Entries include requirements, programs, facilities, financial aid, and faculty. Personal name index. G76.5.U5G8

Orbis geographicus. World directory of geography. Adressar géographique du monde. Geographisches Weltadressbuch, 1952– . Wiesbaden, Steiner, 1952– . **CL103**

1952 edition had title *World directory of geographers,* prep. with the financial assistance of Unesco.

1960 comp. and ed. on behalf of the International Geographic Union in cooperation with the national committees by E. Meynen, and issued as Sonderheft of *Geographisches Taschenbuch* for 1960/61. 1980/84 ed. publ. 1980.

Lists geographical societies, congresses, institutes, medals, etc., and includes a directory of geographers by country. G64.O7

Paylore, Patricia. Arid lands research institutions; a world directory. Rev. and updated ed. Tucson, Univ. of Arizona Pr., 1977. 317p. **CL104**

1st ed. 1967.

Format and geographical arrangement follow that of the 1st ed., which expanded and updated Unesco's *Directory of institutions engaged in arid zone research* (1953). Information is derived from direct correspondence with the institutions, and several institutions have been dropped. Name and subject indexes.　　　GB841.P38

Biography

See also CL71.

Bonacker, Wilhelm. Kartenmacher aller Länder und Zeiten. Stuttgart, A. Hiersemann, 1966. 243p.　　　**CL105**

Lists mapmakers from all countries and periods, giving dates, place, and special field of activity. Reference is provided to standard biographical sources where possible.　　　Z6021.B69

Geographers: biobibliographical studies. v.1– . Ed. by T. W. Freeman, Marguerita Oughton and Philippe Pinchemel. [London], Mansell, 1977– . il. Annual.　　　**CL106**

Published on behalf of the International Geographical Union Commission on the History of Geographical Thought.

Presents studies on deceased figures important in the history of geography. The biographical section of each study deals with personal background, career development, and contribution to the field; the bibliographies are selective, usually including primary, secondary, and archival sources. International in scope. Indexed.

Z6001.G42

Henze, Dietmar. Enzyklopädie der Entdecker und Erforscher der Erde. Graz, Akademische Druck u. Verlags-anstalt, 1975–80. Lfg.1–7. (In progress)　　　**CL107**

Contents: Lfg.1–7, A–Fouc.

Offers biographical articles on explorers and discoverers. Entries include bibliographies of primary and secondary writings. Scope encompasses persons from ancient to modern times.　　　G200.H37

Tooley, Ronald Vere. Tooley's Dictionary of mapmakers. N.Y., Alan R. Liss; Amsterdam, Meridian Publ. Co., [1979]. 684p. il.　　　**CL108**

"Originally, the first half of the work appeared in parts in *Map Collectors' Circle*, which has now been discontinued."—*Foreword.*

Gives brief information on persons concerned with production of maps from earliest times to 1900. Aims to give for each: "name, dates of birth and death (whenever known), titles of honour (if any), working addresses and changes of addresses, . . . main output of maps or atlases, with dates wherever known."—*Foreword.* Many entries provide only title and date of a published work. A supplement was published 1985.　　　GA198.T66

GAZETTEERS

❖The gazetteer, or dictionary of places, is an interesting type of reference book in which the most recently revised work and the old work are of almost equal value, although for different purposes. If the question calls for current information about a place—its present population, importance, industries, its political affiliations, i.e., the county, state, province, nation, within which it is located—only the most recent works in the field will serve, and the older works may be almost worthless or even misleading.

On the other hand, the old gazetteer is often very useful for historical information, for place-names that have since changed, or for bits of local history that are difficult to find elsewhere. An old gazetteer which indicates the industries that flourished in a town a century ago may be a source for the economic or social history of the place, and, if the relative importance of the place has declined, may treat it at greater length than the more modern work can afford to do. For countries for which no good older gazetteer is available, an old encyclopedia will sometimes serve this same purpose.

Bibliography

Meynen, Emil. Gazetteers and glossaries of geographical names of the member-countries of the United Nations and the agencies in relationship with the United Nations: bibliography 1946–1976. Wiesbaden, Steiner, 1984. 518p.　　　**CL109**

Title and prefatory matter also in French.

A bibliography, including atlases which have place-name indexes. In five parts: lists of country and territory names; world gazetteers and indexes; gazetteers by continent, regions and oceans; gazetteers and indexes by countries; glossaries of generic, oceanographic, and foreign terms; gazetteers being published 1977–82.

Z6004.D5M49

General

Chambers's World gazetteer and geographical dictionary, ed. by T. C. Collocott and J. O. Thorne. Rev. ed. [repr. with rev. suppl.] Edinburgh, London, Chambers, 1965. 806p.

CL110

Issued in the United States as *Macmillan world gazetteer and geographical dictionary* (N.Y., Macmillan, 1955).

A useful, small, general gazetteer with emphasis on Great Britain. Indicates pronunciation.　　　G103.C47

Columbia Lippincott gazetteer of the world, ed. by Leon E. Seltzer with the Geographical Research Staff of Columbia University Press and with the cooperation of the American Geographical Society, with 1961 suppl. N.Y., Columbia Univ. Pr., [1962]. 2148p., 22p.　　　**CL111**

1st ed. 1952.

A successor to *Lippincott's New gazetteer* (published in various editions, 1855–1931) but essentially a completely new work. Lists, in one alphabet, the places of the world, both political subdivisions and geographic features, giving variant spellings, pronunciation, population (with date), geographical and political location, altitude, trade, industry, agriculture, natural resources, communications, history, cultural institutions, and other pertinent facts. Comprises some 130,000 names with more than 30,000 cross references. The supplement includes the major politico-geographical changes since 1952, with identification of new nations. Contains 1960 United States census figures.

A useful and important work.　　　G103.L7

Fisher, Morris. Provinces and provincial capitals of the world. 2d ed. Metuchen, N.J., Scarecrow Pr., 1985. 248p.

CL112

1st ed. 1967.

For each of 224 countries, gives number, type, and name of major administrative units or provinces and their capitals. Country arrangement; name index.　　　G103.5.F57

Geograficheskii entsiklopedicheskii slovar': geograficheskie nazvaniia. Glav. red. A. F. Treshnikov. Moskva, Sovetskaia Entsiklopediia, 1983. 527p. il., maps.　　　**CL113**

A geographic dictionary of places, international in scope. Numerous maps, and some illustrations.

Kurian, George Thomas. Geo-data; the World almanac gazetteer. Detroit, Gale, [1983]. 623p.　　　**CL114**

Publ. in cooperation with World Almanac Pubns.

In four main sections: (1) detailed data about towns and cities in the United States with population of over 10,000, and information on counties, states, and territories; (2) a variety of geographic, demographic, and political information about foreign countries; (3) geographic information on natural features such as continents, oceans, rivers, mountains, etc.; (4) rankings. United States population data based on 1970 census. Indexed.　　　G103.5.K87

Lana, Gabriella, Iasbez, Liliana and **Meak, Linda.** Glossary of geographical names in six languages: English, French,

Italian, Spanish, German & Dutch. Amsterdam and N.Y., Elsevier, 1967. 184p. **CL115**

Lists geographical proper names which vary from language to language. The basic table employs the English form followed by variants in other languages. Consolidated index. G104.5.L3

Paxton, John. The statesman's year-book world gazetteer. 2d ed. N.Y., St. Martin's Pr.; [London, Macmillan, 1979]. 653p., 24p. maps. **CL116**

1st ed. 1975.

Intended as a companion to *The statesman's year-book* (CG62). Gives brief information on places of size and importance. Some statistical tables and a glossary of about 800 statistical terms are supplied. G103.5.P38

Room, Adrian. Place-name changes since 1900: a world gazetteer. Metuchen, N.J., Scarecrow Pr., 1979. 202p. **CL117**

Each entry provides present name, identification, location, former name or names, and year or years of renaming; cross references are provided from earlier names. The majority of name changes are Russian or Chinese. Bibliography. G103.5.R66

Times, London. Index-gazetteer of the world. London, Times Pub. Co., 1965; Boston, Houghton, 1966. 964p. **CL118**

Lists about 345,000 geographical features with latitude and longitude. The approximately 198,000 locations shown in the Mid-Century edition of the *Times atlas* (CL335) formed the basis of this work, and map references are given for locations in that series of atlases. Longitude and latitude coordinates, however, make the volume useful with any map marked with lines of parallels and meridians. G103.T5

U.S. Board on Geographic Names. Gazetteer. no.1–129. Wash., Govt. Prt. Off., 1955–84. Irregular. **CL119**

Prepared in the Office of Geography, Dept. of the Interior.

Each number is on a special country, listing places and geographical features, with approved names and cross references from variant names, latitude and longitude, and location on specified official maps. Numbered through 130 (Surinam, 1974), then without numbers since 1974. The contents note below provides geographical area, number, edition, and date of publication. Since 1976 the issuing body is the U.S. Defense Mapping Agency.

Contents: Afghanistan (119, 1971); Africa and Southwest Asia, Gazetteer suppl. (126, 1972); Africa, British East (1, 1955); Albania (8, 2d ed., 1961); Algeria (127, 1972); Americas, Gazetteer suppl. (120, 1971); Andorra (51, 1961); Angola (20, 1956); Antarctica (14, 3d ed., 1969); Arabian Peninsula (54, 1961); Argentina (103, 1968); Asia, Gazetteer suppl. (124, 1972); Asia, Southwest, Gazetteer suppl. (126, 1972); Australia (40, 1957); Australia, New Zealand, and Oceania, Gazetteer suppl. (125, 1972); Austria (66, 1962); Bahrain, Kuwait, Qatar, and United Arab Emirates (1976); Bangladesh (1976); Belgium (73, 1963); Berlin, East (43, 1959); Berlin, West (47, 1960); Bermuda (7, 1955); Bolivia (4, 1955); Borneo, British (10, 2d ed., 1970); Brazil (71, 1963); Brunei (10, 2d ed., 1970); Bulgaria (44, 1959); Burma (9, 1955; 96, 1966); Burundi (84, 1964); Cambodia (74, 2d ed., 1971); Cameroon (60, 1962); Canal Zone (110, 1969); Cape Verde Islands (50, 1961); Central African Republic (64, 1962); Ceylon (49, 1960); Chad (65, 1962); Chile (6, 2d ed. 1967); China, People's Republic (22, 2d ed., 1968; 1979); China, Republic of (5, 1955; 1974); Colombia (86, 1964); Comoro Islands (2, 1955); Congo (Brazzaville) (61, 1962); Congo (Léopoldville) (80, 1964); Costa Rica (18, 1956; 2d ed. 1983); Cuba (30, 2d ed., 1963); Czechoslovakia (1955);

Dahomey (91, 1965); Denmark (53, 1961); Djibouti (1983); Dominican Republic (33, 2d ed., 1972); Ecuador (36, 1957); Egypt (45, 1959); El Salvador (26, 1956); Ethiopia (1982); Europe, Gazetteer suppl. (118, 1971); Faeroe Islands (53, 1961); Fiji (1974); Finland (62, 1962); France (83, 2v., 1964); French West Indies (34, 1957); Gabon (59, 1962); Gambia (107, 1968); Gaza Strip (45, 1959); Germany, East (43, 1959); Germany, West (47, 1960); Ghana (102, 1967); Greece (11, 1955); Greenland (2d ed., 1983); Guatemala (94, 1965; 2d ed. 1984); Guinea (90, 1965); Guinea, Portuguese (105, 1968); Guyana (1976); Haiti (28, 2d ed., 1973); Hawaiian

Islands (24, 1956); Honduras (27, 1956; 2d ed., 1983); Honduras, British (16, 1956); Hong Kong (5, 1955; 128, 1972); Hungary (52, 1961); Iceland (57, 1961); Indian Ocean (32, 1957); Indonesia (13, 2d ed., 1968; 3d ed., 1982, 2v.); Iran (19, 1956; 2d ed., 1982, 2v.); Iraq (37, 1957); Israel (114, 1970; 2d ed., 1983); Italy (23, 1956); Ivory Coast (89, 1965); Japan (12, 1955); Jordan (3, 2d ed., 1971); Kenya (78, 1964); Korea, North (75, 1963; 2d ed., 1982); Korea, South (95, 1965); Kuwait (1976); Laos (69, 2d ed., 1973); Lebanon (115, 1970); Liberia (106, 1968; 2d ed., 1976); Libya (41, 2d ed., 1973);

Macao (5, 1955; 128, 1972); Madagascar (2, 1955); Malawi (113, 1970); Malaya (10, 2d ed., 1970); Mali (93, 1965); Malta (121, 1971); Mauritania (100, 1966); Mexico (15, 1956); Mongolia (116, 1970); Morocco (112, 1970); Mozambique (109, 1969); Nauru (1974); New Caledonia (1974); New Guinea (13, 2d ed., 1968); New Hebrides (1974); Nicaragua (25, 2d ed., 1956; 1976); Niger (99, 1966); Nigeria (117, 1971); Norway (77, 1963); Nyasaland (17, 1956); Oman (1976); Pakistan (67, 1962; 3d ed. 1983); Panama and the Canal Zone (110, 1969); Paraguay (35, 1957); Poland (1955, 2v.); Portugal (50, 1961); Puerto Rico (38, 1958); Qatar (1976); Réunion (2, 1955); Rhodesia (17, 1956); Rumania (48, 1960); Rwanda (85, 1964);

São Tomé e Principe (63, 1962); Senegal (88, 1965); Sierra Leone (101, 1966); Singapore (10, 2d ed., 1970); Solomon Islands (1974); Somalia (1982); South Atlantic (31, 1957); South Pacific (39, 1957); Southern Rhodesia (129, 1973); Southwest Pacific (29, 1956); Spain (51, 1961); Spanish Sahara (108, 1969); Sudan (68, 1962); Surinam (130, 1974); Sweden (72, 1963); Syria (104, 1967; 2d ed. 1983); Taiwan (5, 1955; 22, 1956; 1974); Tanzania (92, 1965); Thailand (97, 1966); Tibet (5, 1955); Togo (98, 1966); Tonga (1974); Tunisia (81, 1964); Turkey (46, 1960; 2d ed., 1984, 2v.); Uganda (82, 1964); United Arab Emirates (1976); Underseas features (111, 2d ed., 1971; 3d ed. 1981); Upper Volta (87, 1965); Uruguay (21, 1956); U.S.S.R. (42, 2d ed., 1970, 7v.; 118, 1971); Venezuela (56, 1961); Vietnam, Northern (79, 1964); Vietnam, Southern (58, 2d ed., 1971); Virgin Islands (38, 1958); West Indies, British (7, 1955); Yemen, People's Democratic Republic of (1976); Yemen Arab Republic (1976); Yugoslavia (55, 1961; 2d ed. 1983); Zambia (123, 1972); Zanzibar (76, 1964); Gazetteer of conventional names (1977).

Vivien de Saint Martin, Louis and **Rousselet, Louis.** Nouveau dictionnaire de géographie universelle. Paris, Hachette, 1879– 95. 7v. **CL120**

————— ————— Supplément. Paris, Hachette, 1895–1900. 2v.

The most complete of the general gazetteers, covering physical, political, economic, and historical geography, ethnography, etc. The longer articles are by specialists and are of a high grade; information is much fuller than that given in the *Columbia Lippincott* (CL111); and many names are included, especially minor European or Asian names which are not given in works in English. Out-of-date and less useful for ordinary questions than the *Columbia Lippincott,* but more useful than that work when very detailed or out-of-the-way information is needed. Includes names of tribes and races, as well as place-names. G101.V86

Webster's New geographical dictionary. Springfield, Mass., Merriam-Webster, [1984]. 1376p. maps. **CL121**

Represents a thorough revision of *Webster's Geographical dictionary* which was first published 1949 and reprinted from time to time with limited revisions.

A pronouncing dictionary of more than 47,000 geographical names, including not only current but also historical names from biblical times, ancient Greece and Rome, medieval Europe, World Wars I and II, etc. Some 15,000 cross references are provided for equivalent and alternate spellings of foreign language names and former names. Gives the usual gazetteer information, e.g., location, area, population, altitudes of mountains, etc.; for the largest cities, important countries, and each of the United States, also gives geographical features, points of interest, and a concise history. Includes full-page and smaller, inset maps by C. S. Hammond Co. Introductory material includes a list of geographical terms with language of origin and English equivalents. G103.5.W42

Wilcocks, Julie. Countries and islands of the world; a guide to nomenclature. 2d ed. [London, Clive Bingley, 1985] 122p.   **CL122**

An alphabetical dictionary of the changes in name and government that have occurred since the 15th century in independent countries, islands, states and provinces of federations, and former kingdoms and principalities which have been important in modern history.   G103.5.W54

Ancient and medieval

Besnier, Maurice. Lexique de géographie ancienne. Paris, Klincksieck, 1914. 893p.   **CL123**

A compact handbook; gives only brief information about each place, but is full in its references to ancient writers in whose works the place is mentioned. Useful on account of these many references.   DE25.B4

Deschamps, Pierre. Dictionnaire de géographie ancienne et moderne. Paris, Firmin-Didot, 1870. 1592col. (Repr.: Hildesheim, G. Olms, 1965)   **CL124**

Also issued as v.9 of Brunet's *Manuel du libraire* (AA111).

Arranged alphabetically by the medieval name (Latin or Greek); gives, under each, an indication of the modern name and brief information about the place with special emphasis on the history of printing in that place, establishment of presses, etc. Index of modern names.   Z1011.B9M5

Grässe, Johann Georg Theodor. Orbis latinus; Lexikon lateinischer geographischer Namen des Mittelalters und der Neuzeit. Grossausgabe, bearb. und hrsg. von Helmut Plechl . . . unter Mitarbeit von . . . Sophie-Charlotte Plechl. Braunschweig, Klinkhardt & Biermann, [1972]. 3v.   **CL125**

At head of title: Graesse, Benedict, Plechl.

1st ed. 1866.

A listing of medieval Latin place-names with their modern equivalents.   G107.G8

Smith, *Sir* William. Dictionary of Greek and Roman geography. London, Murray; Boston, Little, 1873–78. 2v. il., maps. (Repr.: N.Y., AMS Pr., 1966)   **CL126**

A standard work of the 19th century, still useful for its detailed articles on places of the ancient world. Includes many references to classical authors.   DE25.S67

United States

❖A national gazetteer of the United States is in progress (CL128). Useful complements are the *IMS Ayer directory of publications* (AE32), which gives brief, up-to-date gazetteer information about each city or town for which a newspaper is listed, and the *Rand McNally commercial atlas and marketing guide* (CL344).

Gannett, Henry. Dictionary of altitudes in the United States. 4th ed. Wash., Govt. Prt. Off., 1906. 1072p. (U.S. Geological Survey. Bull. 274) (Repr.: Detroit, Gale, 1967)   **CL127**

Arranged alphabetically by state, and under state by city; gives altitude and refers to authority.   QE75.B9 no.274

The national gazetteer of the United States of America. Prep. by the U.S. Geological Survey in cooperation with the U.S. Board on Geographic Names. [Wash.], Govt. Prt. Off., 1982–85. il., maps. (Geological Survey professional papers, 1200) (In progress)   **CL128**

Derived from the Geographic Names Data Base of the Geological Survey which presently contains information for about two million names. Separate volumes for states or territories will provide for each geographic name: type of feature, official status, variant names,

county location, geographic coordinates, elevation, and location on the Geological Survey's topographic maps. Volumes for New Jersey, Delaware, and Kansas have been published thus far. Also available in microfiche from the National Cartographic Information Center, Reston, Virginia.

Van Zandt, Franklin K. Boundaries of the United States and the several states, with miscellaneous geographic information concerning areas, altitudes, and geographic centers. Wash., Govt. Prt. Off., 1976. 191p. il. (U.S. Geological Survey Bull. 909)   **CL129**

Original ed. prep. by Henry Gannett and issued 1885 as *Bulletin* 13. A 1930 revision by Edward M. Douglas appeared as *Bulletin* 817; the 1966 revision by Van Zandt as *Bulletin* 1212.

A useful compilation, giving the histories and changes of the boundaries of the United States and of the individual states and territories, with references to sources. "The revisions include clarification and modification of descriptions of certain boundaries, some of which are based on court decisions or international agreements; they also include more accurate figures for certain statistical data and numerous minor additions and deletions as appropriate."—*Pref.*   E179.5.V34

Afghanistan

India. Army. General Staff Branch. Historical and political gazetteer of Afghanistan. Ed. by Ludwig W. Adamec. Graz, Akadem. Druck- u. Verlagsanst., 1972–80. v.1–5. (In progress?)   **CL130**

Contents: v.1, Badakhshan Province and Northeastern Afghanistan; v.2, Farah and Southwestern Afghanistan; v.3, Herat and Northwestern Afghanistan; v.4, Mazar-i-Sharif and North-Central Afghanistan; v.5, Kandahar and South-Central Afghanistan.

The present edition includes the formerly secret *Gazetteer of Afghanistan* (1st ed. 1871, with revisions at intervals through 1914), "with corrections and additions of maps and considerable new material to take into account developments up to 1970."—*Pref., v.1.*   DS351.I5

Albania

Permanent Committee on Geographical Names for British Official Use. A Gazetteer of Albania. Prep. . . . at the house of the Royal Geographical Society. London, pr. by Williams, Lea & Co., 1946. 210p.   **CL131**

    DR701.S495P4

Argentina

Argentine Republic. Instituto Geográfico Militar. Diccionario geográfico argentino. [Buenos Aires], 1954– . v.1–2.   **CL132**

Contents: t.1, Entre Rios, Corrientes, Misiones; t.2, Neuquén, Río Negro, Chubut, Comodoro Rivadavia, Santa Cruz, Tierra del Fuego, Malvinas. No more publ.   F2804.A675

Latzina, Francisco. Diccionario geográfico argentino, con ampliaciones enciclopédicas rioplatenses. 3. ed. Buenos Aires, Peuser, 1899. 814p.   **CL133**

1st ed. 1891.

Long historical and statistical articles on places in the Argentine.

———— ———— Suplemento, que contiene las adiciones, correcciones y ampliaciones aplicables á la 3ª. edición de dicha obra . . . Buenos Aires, Compañia Sud-americana de Billetes de Banco, 1908. 762p.

Toponimia de la República Argentina. Ejército Argentino, Instituto Geográfico Militar. Buenos Aires, El Instituto, 1982– . v.1, pt.1– . maps. (In progress) **CL134**

Contents: v.1, Territorio Nacional de la Tierra del Fuego, Antártida e Islas del Atlántico Sur: pt.1, Tierra del Fuego.

An official gazetteer of place names, with notes on historical derivation, references to map series, and bibliographical references.
F2804.T66

Belgium

Seyn, Eugène de. Dictionnaire historique et géographique des communes belges. 3. éd., augm. et mise à jour. Turnhout, Brepols, [194?]. 2v. (1562p.) il., maps. **CL135**

1st ed. 1924–26. 2v.

Gives detailed information on each place with historical notes, coats of arms, population to 1938, etc. DH414.S42

Bolivia

Diccionario geográfico de la República de Bolivia. La Paz, Impr. "El Nacional" de I. V. Vila, 1890–1904. 4v. il. **CL136**

v.2 and v.4 publ. by the Oficina Nacional de Inmigración, Estadística y Propaganda Geográfica.

Contents: v.1, M. V. Ballivián y E. Idiaquez. Departamento de La Paz (1890); v.2, F. Blanco. Departamento de Cochabamba (1901); v.3, Sociedad Geográfica Sucre. Departamento de Chuquisaca (1903); v.4, P. A. Blanco. Departamento de Oruro (1904).

No more published. F3304.D54

Gonzales Moscoso, René. Diccionario geográfico boliviano. La Paz, Editorial Los Amigos del Libro, 1984. 257p. il., maps. **CL137**

A basic dictionary of brief entries. A more detailed version, to be entitled *Diccionario geográfico general de Bolivia,* is in preparation.

Brazil

Dicionário de geografia do Brasil, com terminologia geográfica. Organização geral, Departamento Editorial das Edições Melhoramentos; redação de temas e verbetes, Erasmo d'Almeida Magalhaes [et al.]. [2. ed. São Paulo], Edições Melhoramentos, [1976]. 544p. **CL138**

Combines gazetteer information on major cities and states, and definitions of geographical terms and concepts, with emphasis on Brazilian aspects. Supplementary list of cities with more than 20,000 people is based on 1970 census figures. Bibliography.
F2504.D48

Dicionário geográfico brasileiro, com numerosas ilustrações, inclusive mapas dos estados e territórios. 2. ed. Pôrto Alegre, Editôra Globo, [1972]. [621p.] il., maps. **CL139**

1st ed. 1966.

Offers far more detailed gazetteer information on a greater number of geographical features, cities, towns, states, and territories in Brazil than does the *Dicionário de geografia do Brasil* (above). Provides population figures based on 1970 census estimates. Bibliography. F2504.D5

Moreira Pinto, Alfredo. Apontamentos para o Diccionario geographico do Brazil. Rio de Janeiro, Impr. Nacional, 1894–99. 3v. **CL140**

F2504.M86

Canada

See also CL362.

Canada. Board on Geographical Names. 18th–19th reports containing all decisions to July 31, 1927. Ottawa, 1924–27. 2v. **CL141**

18th report, Decisions to March 1924; 19th report, Decisions, April 1924–July 1927.

Alphabetical lists of place-names, with index by provinces, counties, etc. The main alphabet in each report gives form of name decided on, location of place, and origin of name when known, with cross references from superseded names. Supersedes the earlier reports of the Board except for certain appendixes which are still useful for the fuller or special information they contain. These appendixes (also issued as separates) are:

9th report, 1910: pt.2, Place-names in Quebec, by James White, p.153–219; pt.3, Place-names, Thousand Islands, St. Lawrence River, by James White, p.221–29; pt.4, Place-names in Northern Canada, by James White, p.229–455.

17th report, 1922: Meaning of Canadian city names, by R. Douglas, p.34–52; Place-names on Anticosti Island, by W. P. Anderson, p.53–65; Place-names on Magdalen Islands, by R. Douglas, p.66–74.

Additional lists issued by the Geographic Board include: Place-names of Prince Edward Island, with meanings, by R. Douglas (1925. 55p.); Place-names of Alberta (1928. 138p.); Place-names of Manitoba (1933. 95p.). G104.C2

Canada. Permanent Committee on Geographical Names. Gazetteer of Canada. Répertoire géographique du Canada. Ottawa, 1952– . (In progress) **CL142**

The following volumes have been published: Alberta (2d ed. 1974); British Columbia (2d ed. 1966); Manitoba (3d ed. 1981); New Brunswick (2d ed. 1972); Newfoundland and Labrador (1968); Northwest Territories (1980); Yukon (4th ed. 1981); Ontario (2d ed. 1974); Prince Edward Island (1973); Saskatchewan (2d ed. 1969); Southwestern Ontario (1952); Nova Scotia (2d ed. 1977).
F1004.A2

———— ———— Special supplement. Ottawa, 1964– .

Contents: no.1, A list of named glaciological features in Canada, by C. F. Stevenson (1964); no.2, Geographical features in Canada named for surveyors, by T. Jolicoeur (1966).

White, James. Dictionary of altitudes in the Dominion of Canada. (2d ed.) Ottawa, Mortimer, 1916. 251p. **CL143**

Published by the Conservation Commission.

Arranged by province, then alphabetically by place-name. Supplementary to *Altitudes in Canada* (2d ed. 1915), by the same author, which gives altitudes arranged by railroad routes. GB498.15.W5

Chile

Risopatrón Sánchez, Luis. Diccionario jeográfico de Chile. Santiago, Impr. Univ., 1924. 958p. **CL144**

Gazetteer information on places in Chile. F3054.R58

China

Playfair, George M. H. The cities and towns of China; a geographical dictionary. 2d ed. Shanghai, Kelly and Walsh, 1910. 582p., lxxvip. **CL145**

1st ed. 1879.

Brief information on towns. Names are given in transliteration and in Chinese characters. DS705.P7

Tien, H. C., Hsia, Ronald and **Penn, Peter.** Gazetteer of China. Hong Kong, Oriental Book Co., 1961. 237p.
CL146

Gives name of locality, pronunciation, name in Chinese characters, province, longitude and latitude.

U.S. Defense Mapping Agency. Gazetteer of the People's Republic of China. Wash., The Agency, 1979. 919p. **CL147**

Contains the names of approximately 22,000 populated places and physical features. In three parts: (1) Pinyin names cross-referenced to Wade-Giles names; (2) Wade-Giles names with the corresponding Pinyin names; (3) conventional names with the corresponding Pinyin names.   DS705.D43

Colombia

Colombia. Instituto Geográfico Agustín Codazzi. Diccionario geográfico de Colombia. [Bogotá, Editorial Andes, 1971] 2v. (1447p.) il., maps. 32cm.   **CL148**

A gazetteer of about 60,000 names, with many longer articles. A 2d ed. was published 1980 (2v., 1813p.).   F2254.A55

Gómez, Eugenio J. Diccionario geográfico de Colombia. Bogotá, Banco de la República, 1953. 359p. maps.   **CL149**

Brief gazetteer information with some longer articles.
F2254.G6

Czechoslovakia

Chromec, Brĕtislav. Místopisný slovník Československé republiky. 2. doplnené a rozmnozené vyd. V Praze, Československého Kompasu, 1935. 778p.   **CL150**

1st ed. 1929.
A detailed gazetteer with accompanying postal information.
DB194.C5

Denmark

Trap, Jens Peter. Danmark. 5. Udg. red. af Niels Nielsen, Peter Skautrup [og] Povl Engelstoft. København, Gad, 1953–72. Bd.1–15 in 32v. il., maps.   **CL151**

Originally publ. as *Statistik-topographisk beskrivelse af Kongeriget Danmark* (1872–79. 6v. in 5). 4th ed. 1919–32 (11v.).
Gives historical and descriptive notes about places in Denmark. A detailed and exhaustive work.   DL109.T74

Ecuador

Instituto Geográfico Militar (Ecuador). Indice toponímico de la República del Ecuador. [Quito], El Instituto, [1978?]– 82. v.1–8. (In progress)   **CL152**

Contents: v.1–8, A–Q.
A gazetteer of place-names, indicating type of feature, location, administrative division, and coordinates of latitude and longitude. To be in 10v.   F3704.E28

France

Joanne, Paul Bénigne. Dictionnaire géographique et administratif de la France. Paris, Hachette, 1890–1905. 7v. il.
CL153

1st and 2d ed. (1865, 1869) included Alsace-Lorraine.
The standard geographical dictionary of France, containing much historical information, with detailed articles on early place-names, as well as later ones, and various geographical features. Long articles, many illustrations, but no bibliographies. Adequate for

most questions, but for special work needs to be supplemented by the many regional dictionaries of the provinces, *départements,* etc.
DC14.J63

Germany

Meyers Orts- und Verkehrs-Lexikon des Deutschen Reichs. 5. vollständig neubearb. und verm. Aufl. Auf grund amtlicher Unterlagen von Reichs- , Landes- und Gemeindebehörden hrsg. von E. Uetrecht. Mit 51 Stadtplänen, 19 Umgebungs- und Übersichtskarten, einer Verkehrs-Karte und vielen statistischen Beilagen. Leipzig, Bibliographisches Inst., 1912–13. 2v. maps, plans.   **CL154**

The 5th ed. is a gazetteer of Germany before World War I. The 6th ed. (Leipzig, 1935. 867p.) was also issued, much reduced in size, as Ergänz. Bd.1 of *Meyers Lexikon,* 7. Aufl.   DD14.M5

Müller, Friedrich. Müllers Grosses deutsches Ortsbuch, Bundesrepublik Deutschland: vollständiges Gemeindelexikon. 21., überarbeitete und erweiterte Auflage, bearb. von Joachim Müller. Wuppertal, Post- und Ortsbuchverlag, 1982–83. 1194p.   **CL155**

A frequently updated gazetteer of West German place names, originally produced by a postmaster. More than 109,000 names in this edition.   DD14.M8

Great Britain

Bartholomew (John) and Son, Ltd. Bartholomew gazetteer of Britain. [Edinburgh], Bartholomew, [1977]. xlviii, 271p., 128 pl. maps. 30cm.   **CL156**

Oliver Mason, comp.
An earlier work by John G. Bartholomew was first published 1904 as *Survey gazetteer of the British Isles* and in 1966 as *Gazetteer of the British Isles.* This edition updates statistical sections in accordance with the 1971 census, with provisional figures for 1975. Area covered is England, Scotland, Wales, and the Isle of Man.
DA640.B24

Geographia, Ltd., London. Commercial gazetteer of Great Britain [including full-colour reference atlas], ed. by E. Hudson. London, "Geographic, Ltd.," [1957?]. 364p., 48p. of maps, 64p.   **CL157**

Contents: pt.1, Gazetteer of England and Wales: towns, villages, counties, urban and rural areas, etc., in alphabetic order; map section: 48p. of maps in full color, by counties; pt.2, Gazetteer of Scotland: Scottish towns, villages, counties, urban and rural areas.
Gives very brief gazetteer information, including 1951 population, "early closing" and market days, National Grid reference, etc.
DA640.G43

Gt.Brit. General Register Office. Census 1971, England and Wales; index of place names. London, H. M. Stationery Off., 1977. 2v. (1087p.)   **CL158**

A similar index was published 1965 in connection with the 1961 census, and 1955 for the 1951 census; prior to that, the latest index of this kind was the 1924 publication in the 1921 census series.
An alphabetical listing of names of counties, boroughs, urban and rural districts, civil parishes, and many "localities" having a name but no legally defined boundaries. Location (i.e., within county, parish, etc.) is given, as is population at the time of the 1971 census.
DA640.A25

Lewis, Samuel. Topographical dictionary of England. 5th ed. London, Lewis, 1845. 4v. il. and atlas, 55 maps.   **CL159**

Subtitle: Comprising the several counties, cities, boroughs, corporate and market towns, parishes, and townships, and the islands of Guernsey, Jersey, and Man, with historical and statistical descriptions: and embellished with engravings of the arms of the cities, bishoprics, universities, colleges, corporate towns, and boroughs; and of the seals of the various municipal corporations.

Still useful for the historical information to be found in the long, detailed articles about places of all sizes.   DA625.L676

Mason, Oliver. The gazetteer of England; England's cities, towns, villages and hamlets: a comprehensive list with basic details on each. [Totowa, N.J.], Rowman and Littlefield, [1972]. 2v.   **CL160**

Aims to provide "a comprehensive list of English places, from the largest cities down to all but the smallest hamlets, with certain essential information about each."—*Expl. notes.* Each place-name is followed by the name of the county in which it is situated, map reference to the Ordnance Survey National Grid System, and distance and direction from another place. Indication of administrative status and population is also given; additional notes and descriptive matter appear with many entries.   DA640.M35

Greece

Permanent Committee on Geographical Names for British Official Use. A gazetteer of Greece. Prep. at the house of the Royal Geographical Society. London, pr. by W. Clowes, 1942. 161p. incl. maps.   **CL161**
DF714.P4

Guatemala

Diccionario geográfico de Guatemala. Compilación crítica, Francis Gall. 2a ed. Guatemala, Instituto Geográfico Nacional, 1976–83. 4v. maps.   **CL162**

1st ed. 1961–62.
A geographical dictionary listing the place-names, cities, towns, villages, rivers, mountains, etc. For the larger places gives considerable detail on history, demography, ethnography, geology, archaeology, etc.   F1462.D53

Honduras

Bonilla, Marcelina. Diccionario histórico-geográfico de las poblaciones de Honduras. [2. ed. Tegucigalpa,] Impr. Calderón, [1952]. 310p. il.   **CL163**

1st ed. 1945.   F1502.B6

Instituto Geográfico National (Honduras). Diccionario geográfico de Honduras. [Tegucigalpa], Ministerio de Comunicaciones, Obras Públicas y Transporte, Instituto Geográfico Nacional, 1976–80. v.1–2. il., maps. (In progress)   **CL164**

Contents: t.1, Departamento de Atlántida; t.2, Departamento de Cortés; t.3, Departamento de Copán.
Each volume serves as a gazetteer for one of the 18 departments in Honduras. Volumes will be published in alphabetical order according to department name and, upon completion, will be consolidated alphabetically in a single-volume, official geographical dictionary.   F1502.I57

India

Gazetteer of India: Indian Union. [Comp. by] Central Gazetteers Unit, Govt. of India. [Delhi], Publications Division, Ministry of Information and Broadcasting, [1965–78]. 4v.   **CL165**

Contents: v.1, Country and people; v.2, History and culture; v.3, Economic structure and activities; v.[4] Administration and public welfare.
Plans for updating the *Imperial gazetter* (below) call for revision or compilation of district gazetteers by the state governments, and for simultaneous work by the central government on revision, rewriting, and amplification of the Indian volumes. Chapters are contributed by one or more experts; a bibliography is provided at the end of each chapter.
District gazetteers published by the individual states have been appearing in parts since 1957 for Arunachal Pradesh, Assam, Bihar, Goa, Daman and Diu, Gujarat, Haryana, Himachal Pradesh, Karnataka, Kerala, Madhya Pradesh, Madras, Maharashtra, Mysore, Nagaland, Orissa, Pondicherry, Punjab, Rajasthan, Tripura, Uttar Pradesh, West Bengal.   DS407.G37

Imperial gazetteer of India. New ed., publ. under the authority of His Majesty's Secretary of State for India in Council. Oxford, Clarendon Pr., 1907–31. 26v. maps.   **CL166**

1st ed., 9v., 1881, and 2d ed., 14v., 1885–87, ed. by Sir William Wilson Hunter. The present work may be considered as a new work, rather than a new edition.—cf. *General pref.*
Editor for India: 1902–1904, William Stevenson Meyer; 1905–1909, Richard Burn. Editor in England: James Sutherland Cotton.
Contents: v.1–4, Indian Empire (v.1, Descriptive; v.2, Historical; v.3, Economic; v.4, Administrative); v.5–24, Gazetteer; v.25, General index; v.26, Atlas (new rev. ed., 1931).
Includes historical, topographical, ethnic, agricultural, industrial, administrative, and medical aspects of the various districts of British India. For updating of v.1–4, *see* the *Gazetteer of India* (above).   DS405.H95

Iran

Adamec, Ludwig W. Historical gazetteer of Iran. Graz, Austria, Akademische Druck- und Verlagsanstalt, 1976–81. v.1–2. maps. (In progress)   **CL167**

Contents: v.1, Tehran and northwestern Iran; v.2, Meshed and northeastern Iran.
This work adds to and updates material originally presented in the General Staff of British India's *Gazetteer of Persia* (1914; republished 1918); the text has been reprinted, with new entries and passages added. Includes geographical features, villages and towns, ethnographic groups, etc., arranged alphabetically, plus a glossary, index of subtribes, and a map section. Statistics are based on the 1966 census.   DS253.A54

Ireland

Lewis, Samuel. Topographical dictionary of Ireland . . . 2d ed. London, Lewis, 1846. 2v. and atlas, 32 maps. il. (Repr.: Baltimore, Genealogical Pub. Co., 1984)   **CL168**

Subtitle: Comprising the several counties, cities, boroughs, corporate, market, and post towns, parishes and villages with historical and statistical descriptions, embellished with engravings of the arms of the cities, bishoprics, corporate towns, and boroughs; and the seals of the several municipal corporations.
1st ed. 1837.
Still useful for the historical information to be found in the long, detailed articles about places of all sizes.   DA979.L48

Italy

Amati, Amato. Dizionario corografico dell' Italia. Opera illustrata da circa 1000 armi comunali colorate e da parecchie centinaia di incisioni intercalate nel testo rappresentanti i principali monumenti d'Italia. Milano, Vallardi, [1875?–86?]. 8v. il. (coats of arms)   **CL169**

Long articles, some with extensive bibliographies. Colored coats of arms. Includes many more names than *La nuova Italia* (below).   DG415.A48

La nuova Italia; dizionario amministrativo, statistico, industriale, commerciale dei comuni del regno e dei principali paesi d'Italia oltre confine e colonie. Milano, Vallardi, [1908?–10?]. 3v. il. and atlas of 26 col. pl. (coats of arms). **CL170**

A successor to, but not a substitute for, the preceding work.
Compiled to show the development of industrial, commercial, and agricultural Italy during the first 40 years of its life as a nation, with detailed articles by place-name.   DG415.N8

Japan

Gerr, Stanley. A gazetteer of Japanese place names in characters and in Rōmaji script giving latitudes and longitudes. Cambridge, Harvard Univ. Pr., 1942. 269p. 225p. **CL171**

Two lists dealing with the same places, one in Rōmaji script (Latin alphabet), the other in Sino-Japanese character. Besides the names of cities, towns, etc., includes the names of mountains, rivers, islands, etc.
"Based on the map of the Japanese Empire published in 1937 by the Japanese Kokusai Bunka Shinkōkai (Society for International Cultural Relations). It contains about 4500 place names covering Japan proper, Korea, Formosa, Kwangtung leased territory, Saghalien, and the Japanese mandated islands, but does not include Manchuria or other territory recently occupied by Japan. . . ."— *Pref. note.*   DS805.G4

U.S. Hydrographic Office. Gazetteer of the Japanese Empire, containing place names from the Japanese hydrographic charts and sailing directions on issue in 1936. Wash., 1943. 378p. (H.O. Pubn. no.880. Repr. Aug. 1944 as H.O. miscellaneous no.10,947)   **CL172**

A listing of some 15,000 place-names, arranged alphabetically by Rōmaji transcription, giving the Japanese form and the latitude and longitude.   DS805.U45

Netherlands

Laan, Kornelis ter. Van Goor's aardrijkskundig woordenboek van Nederland. 3ᵉ druk geheel opnieuw bewerkt door A. G. C. Baert. Den Haag, van Goor, [1968]. 528p. il.   **CL173**

1st ed. 1942.
Includes names of cities, villages, minor places, church groups, and geographical terms. Lists fewer names than the *Lijst der aardrijkskundige namen* (below), but gives more information about each item and more up-to-date figures.   DJ14.L2

Nederlandsch Aardrijkskundig Genootschap, Amsterdam. Lijst der aardrijkskundige namen van Nederland. Leiden, Brill, 1936. 494p.   **CL174**

An extensive list which includes many names but gives very brief information about each, usually merely the location.   DJ15.N35

New Zealand

New Zealand guide: a comprehensive gazetteer, geographical reference and travel guide. Dunedin, H. Wise, 1952– . Irregular.   **CL175**

Title varies: *Wise's New Zealand guide.*
Supersedes *Wise's New Zealand index to every place in New Zealand* (10th ed. 1948).
Arranged alphabetically by place-name and geographical location.

Frequently gives history, legends, origin of name, etc., as well as the usual gazetteer information.   DU405.N55

Peru

Catálogo de nombres geográficos del Perú. [Lima], Instituto Geográfico Militar, 1979– . v.1– . (In progress)   **CL176**

Contents: v.1, IGM-001-1979.
A gazetteer of place names, providing latitude, longitude, altitude, and administrative location. Arranged by department and province; indexed by geographic name.   F3404.C37

Stiglich, Germán. Diccionario geográfico del Perú. 2. y última parte. Lima, Torres-Aguirre, 1922. 3v.   **CL177**

An older work, still occasionally useful, is Mariano Felipe Paz Soldan's *Diccionario geográfico estadístico del Perú* (Lima, 1877. 1077p.).   F3404.S85

Philippines

U.S. Bureau of Insular Affairs. Pronouncing gazetteer and geographical dictionary of the Philippine Islands. Wash., Govt. Prt. Off., 1902. 933p. il., maps.   **CL178**

Detailed information on all aspects of life in the Philippines at turn of the century.   DS654.U56

Poland

Słownik geograficzny Królestwa polskiego i innych krajów słowiańskich; wydany pod redakcyą Filipa Sulimierskiego [and others]. Warszawa, Druk "Wieku," 1880–1902. 15v. in 16. (Repr.: Warszawa, Wydawn. Artsytyczne i Filmowe, 1975–77)   **CL179**

v.15 is a supplement in 2v.
Long articles, many of them signed.   DJK7.S46

Puerto Rico

Arana Soto, Salvador. Diccionario geográfico de Puerto Rico. San Juan de Puerto Rico, 1978. 228p. il.   **CL180**

Presents brief gazetteer information on about 8,000 place names. Some longer entries, and numerous lists of rivers, sugar plantations, forests, etc. Bibliography.

El Salvador

Salvador. Instituto Geográfico Nacional. Diccionario geográfico de El Salvador/Ministerio de OO.PP.[Obras Públicas], Instituto Geográfico Nacional. [San Salvador], El Instituto, 1970 [i.e., 1971–76]. 4v. il.   **CL181**

A gazetteer, with detailed historical, geographical, and statistical information on 24,519 names. Each volume contains data on a number of "departamentos": v.1, Ahuachapán, Santa Ana and Sonsonata; v.2, La Libertad, Chalatenango, San Salvador, and Cuscatlán; v.3, La Paz, Cabañas and San Vicente; v.4, Usulután, San Miguel, Morazán, and La Unión. An index was published 1978 in 2v.   F1482.S35

Scotland

Johnston & Bacon. Johnston's Gazetteer of Scotland, including a glossary of the most common Gaelic names. [3d ed.] Rev. by R. W. Munro. Edinburgh, Johnston & Bacon, [1973]. 353p. **CL182**

1st ed. 1937.

This edition revised and expanded, with population figures from official 1969 estimates. DA869.J74

Lewis, Samuel. Topographical dictionary of Scotland . . . London, Lewis, 1846. 2v. and atlas. il. **CL183**

Subtitle: Comprising the several counties, islands, cities, burgh and market towns, parishes, and principal villages with historical and statistical descriptions, . . . a large map of Scotland and engravings of the seals and arms of the different burghs and universities.

Still useful for the historical information to be found in the long, detailed articles about places of all sizes. DA865.L67

South Africa

South Africa. Place Names Committee. Amptelike plekname in die Republiek van Suid-Afrika en in Suidwes-Afrika: goedgekeur tot 1 April 1977. Official place names in the Republic of South Africa and in South-west Africa: approved to 1 April 1977. Pretoria, Die Staatsdrukker, 1978. 329p. **CL184**

Prefatory matter in Afrikaans and English.

A revised and supplemented edition of a 1952 list of official place names of townships, agricultural holdings, post offices, railway stations, etc.; does not cover names of geographical features. Includes some names from Transkei, Swaziland, Lesotho, Botswana, and Zimbabwe. DT752.A63

Spain

Diccionario geográfico de España. Madrid, Ed. del Movimento, 1956–61. 17v. **CL185**

Publisher varies.

A detailed gazetteer of Spanish places. Some long, signed articles with quite extensive information on physical characteristics, climate, vegetation, agriculture, industries, cultural opportunities, history, etc. Some articles much shorter, with gazetteer information only. DP12.D5

Switzerland

Knapp, Charles, Borel, Maurice and **Attinger, V.** Dictionnaire géographique de la Suisse; publié sous les auspices de la Société Neuchâteloise de Géographie. . . . Neuchâtel, Attinger, 1902–10. 6v. il., maps. **CL186**

One of the finest regional dictionaries, with authoritative articles and excellent illustrations. Articles contain more scientific geographical and geological information than is usual in local gazetteers. v.6 includes a supplement, p.685–1136. DQ14.D5

Union of Soviet Socialist Republics

Slovar' geograficheskikh nazvanii SSSR. [Sost. N. P. Aniskevich et al.] Izd. 2-e, perer. i dop. Moskva, Nedra, 1983. 296p. **CL187**

At head of title: Glavnoe Upravlenie Geodezii i Kartografii pri Sovete Ministrov SSSR. TSentralnyi Ordena "Znak Pocheta" Nauchno-issledovatel'skii Institut Geodezii, Aerosemki i Kartografii im F. N. Krasovskogo.

A dictionary of geographical names, identifying them as to type of feature, and providing general location. DK14.S53

Volostnova, M. B. Slovar' russkoi transkriptsii geograficheskikh nazvanii. Moskva, Uchpedgiz, 1955–59. 2v. **CL188**

Pt.1, Geograficheskie nazvaniia na territorii SSSR; pt.2, Geograficheskie nazvaniia na territorii zarubezhnykh stran.

A dictionary of transciption into Russian of geographic names, designed to stabilize usage for school maps and geography texts. Pt.1 lists the names of cities, towns, lakes, mountains, etc., in non-Russian territories of the USSR in one alphabet (Russian), with latitude and longitude; cross references are given from variants. Pt.2 lists the same type of information for countries outside the USSR.

An English edition of pt.1 appeared as: G103.V93

—— Dictionary of Russian geographical names. Transliterated and translated by T. Deruguine. N.Y., Telberg Book Co., [1958]. 82p. **CL189**

G103.V933

Uruguay

Araújo, Orestes. Diccionario geográfico del Uruguay. 2. ed., completamente reform. y aum. con más de 1,000 voces nuevas. Montevideo, Tipo-litografía Moderna, 1912. 528p. il. **CL190**

1st ed. 1900. F2704.A665

Venezuela

Sivoli G, Alberto. Diccionario geográfico de Venezuela. Caracas, Eneva, [1976?]. 196p. il., maps. **CL191**

Offers very brief gazetteer information.

Wales

See also CL158.

Lewis, Samuel. Topographical dictionary of Wales . . . 3d ed. London, Lewis, 1844. 2v. and atlas. il. **CL192**

Subtitle: Comprising the several counties, cities, boroughs, corporate and market towns, parishes, chapelries, and townships, with historical and statistical descriptions: embellished with engravings of the arms of the bishoprics, and of the arms and seals of the various cities and municipal corporations, and illustrated by maps of the different counties.

Still useful for the historical information to be found in the long, detailed articles about places of all sizes.

Zimbabwe

Smith, Robert C. Avondale to Zimbabwe: a collection of cameos of Rhodesian towns and villages. Borrowdale [Zimbabwe], Smith, [197-]. 314p. il., map. **CL193**

Contains a concise history of 130 cities and villages, along with their latitude, longitude, altitude, and rainfall. DT962.5.S44

GEOGRAPHICAL NAMES AND TERMS

General works

See also CL84, CL115.

Egli, Johann Jacob. Geschichte der geographischen Namen-kunde. Leipzig, Brandstetter, 1886. 430p. (Repr.: N.Y., B. Franklin, 1963. 2v.)   **CL194**

Surveys the literature of the historical study of place-names.
G106.E35

——— Nomina geographica. Sprach- und Sacherklärung von 42,000 geographischen Namen aller Erdräume. 2. verm. und verb. Aufl. Leipzig, Brandstetter, 1893. 1035p. (Repr.: N.Y., B. Franklin, 1971)   **CL195**

Gives the origin of place-names in various countries of the world, with references to sources.
G105.E3

Permanent Committee on Geographical Names for British Official Use. Glossaries. London, 1942–54. v.1–8.   **CL196**

Contents: v.1, Modern Greek (1942); v.2, Russian (1942); v.3, Albanian (1943); v.4, Serbo-Croat and Slovene (1943); v.5, Romanian (1944); v.6, Thai (Siamese) (1944); v.7, Turkish (1945); v.8, Japanese (1954).

Glossaries not of place-names but of words, abbreviations, and contractions found on official maps, charts, and geographical texts of the country concerned, with transliteration (if from a non-Roman alphabet), meaning, and application.

More countries were covered, but much more briefly, in a series of *Short glossaries* published by the General Staff, Geographical Section, War Office, 1943–45 in 23 numbers.   G108.A1P4

——— [Lists of names]. London, Royal Geographical Soc., 1921–38.   **CL197**

An unnumbered series of pamphlets, in two main groups: (1) general lists (by continents); and (2) national or regional lists, each giving the names of a country, dominion, protectorate, etc. A special pamphlet was issued 1932, *Rules for the spelling of geographical names.*

Contents: (1) General lists: African names, 1st list, 1921, corr. 1926; Asiatic names, 1st–2d lists, 1921–25, rev. 1930; European names, 1st–2d lists, [1921]–23, corr. and rev. 1929; Oceanic names, 1st–4th lists, 1922–35; (2) National lists: Abyssinia, 1st list, 1925; Albania, 1st list, 1938; Anglo-Egyptian Sudan, 1st list., 1927; Arabia, 1st list, 1931, 2d list, 1937; Belgium and Luxemburg, 1st list, 1938; Czechoslovakia, 1st–3d lists, 1924–30; Egypt (Upper), 1st list, 1929; Fiji, 1st list, 1925; Gold Coast and British Togo, 1st list, 1923; India, 1st list, 1924; Iraq (Mesopotamia), 1st list, 1922, rev. 1932; Nigeria and British Cameroons, 1st list, 1928; Palestine, 1st list, 1925, rev. 1937; Persia (South), 1st list, 1928; Persia (North), 2d list, 1929, 1947 suppl. to North and South; Poland (West) and Danzig, 1st list, 1928; Poland (East), 2d list, 1930; Romania, 1st–2d lists, 1926–28; Somaliland Protectorate, 1st list, 1928; Sudan, 1st list, 1927; Syria, 1st list, 1927; Tanganyika territory, 1st list, 1926; Tonga, 1st list, 1927; Trans-Jordan, 1st list, 1927; Turkey (West), 1st list, 1935; Yugoslavia, 1st and 2d lists, 1928–31.

Gives brief information, including correct spelling and pronunciation of name, rejected forms of name, and location of place.

——— Lists of names (New series). London, 1954– . no.1– . (In progress)   **CL198**

Contents: [1], Poland (1954; supersedes 1st and 2d lists, 1928–30); [2], Persia (1955; supersedes 1st and 2d lists, 1928–29); 3, Czechoslovakia (1958; supersedes 1st–3d lists, 1924–30); 4, Bulgaria (1959); 5, [Not yet publ.?]; 6, Bahrain (1962); 7, Kuwait and the Neutral Zone (1962); 8–10 [Not yet publ.?]; 11, Armenian S.S.R. (1966); 12, Moldavian S.S.R. (1966); 13, Tsinghai (1970).

Sharp, Harold S. Handbook of geographical nicknames. Metuchen, N.J., Scarecrow Pr., 1980. 153p.   **CL199**

Both generally accepted names and nicknames appear in one alphabetical list. Nicknames are cross-referenced to the accepted names or main entries; the latter are followed by a brief notation

giving locations and description, and a list of applicable nicknames. American nicknames are excluded since they are covered by Kane and Alexander's *Nicknames and sobriquets of U.S. cities, states and counties* (CL205).   G105.S5

U.S. Geographic Board. Sixth report, 1890–1932. Wash., Govt. Prt. Off., 1933. 834p.   **CL200**

Includes: (1) Geographic names, discussion of characteristics, problems, etc.; (2) The U.S. Geographic Board, its method of work, history, etc.; (3) Decisions, arranged alphabetically by approved form of name, with cross references from other forms, p.76–834.

The *Decisions* form a dictionary of many thousand place-names throughout the world, incorporating in one alphabetical list: the material of the *Fifth report* (1921); subsequent decisions; the 2,500 foreign place-names included in the *First report on foreign geographic names* (1932); and the Philippine and Hawaiian names given in separate lists in the *Fifth report.* For each name gives approved form, locates the place, indicates rejected forms, and, in some cases, marks pronunciation.

"This report contains, with the exception of a comparatively small number, all the decisions rendered by the Board from its organization in 1890 through June, 1932, and supersedes all previous reports. Not included . . . are such decisions as have either been vacated, or being revised, have been replaced by new decisions listed under the revised name or spelling."—*Foreword.*

Kept up-to-date by: G105.U5

U.S. Board on Geographic Names. Decisions. 1934/35– . Wash., 1936– . Irregular.   **CL201**

Issued at irregular intervals in leaflet form. Contains general lists of decisions; some lists were issued for special locations (e.g., National parks) or on specific foreign countries (e.g., Tibet, Mongolia, Italy).

Title varies: *Decision lists.*

United States

❖Because of the very full *Bibliography of place-name literature,* by Sealock, Sealock and Powell, listed below, works on place-names of the United States, its individual states, Canada and its individual provinces are not listed here in any detail.

Sealock, Richard B., Sealock, Margaret M. and **Powell, Margaret S.** Bibliography of place-name literature: United States and Canada. 3d ed. Chicago, Amer. Lib. Assoc., 1982. 435p.   **CL202**

1st ed. 1948 by R. B. Sealock and P. A. Seely.
More than 4,800 items, both books and periodical articles. Separate sections for the United States and Canada; each begins with listings of general studies and gazetteers, followed by sections for individual states and provinces. Many brief annotations; index.
Z6824.S4

Harder, Kelsie B. Illustrated dictionary of place names, United States and Canada. N.Y., Van Nostrand Reinhold, [1976]. 631p. il.   **CL203**

"The names of all provinces, states, provincial and state capitals, counties and county seats are listed. An attempt is also made to include a comprehensive selection of the most viable and interesting United States cities and towns, based on current census reports and ZIP code directories."—*Introd.* Major geographical features are also covered. Illustrations depict persons for whom places were named, the site named, or a historical event related to the site. Bibliography.
E155.H37

Kane, Joseph Nathan. The American counties. 4th ed. Metuchen, N.J., Scarecrow Pr., 1983. 546p.   **CL204**

1st ed. 1960.
Subtitle: Origins of county names, dates of creation and organization, area, population including 1980 census figures, historical data, and published sources.
E180.K3

—— and **Alexander, Gerard L.** Nicknames and sobriquets of U.S. cities, states, and counties. 3d ed. Metuchen, N.J., Scarecrow Pr., 1979. 429p. **CL205**

The 1st ed., 1965, had title *Nicknames of cities and states of the U.S.* and combined and expanded the lists in Kane's *1,000 facts worth knowing* (1938) and Alexander's *Nicknames of American cities, towns, and villages* (1951). The new edition is a further expansion. Explanatory notes are frequently given, but source of the information is not indicated. E155.K24

Stewart, George Rippey. American place names; a concise and selective dictionary for the continental United States of America. N.Y., Oxford Univ. Pr., 1970. 550p. **CL206**

About 12,000 entries. The principal categories of names treated are: (1) names of well-known places; (2) repeated names, i.e., those which appear on several or many places; and (3) unusual names, i.e., those which attract attention and arouse curiosity or controversy. Good introduction on the general background and classification of place names; bibliography. E155.S79

Australia

Martin, Archibald Edward. One thousand and more place names in New South Wales. Sydney, Australia, N.S.W. Bookstall Co., 1943. 108p. **CL207**

The same author and publisher have produced a number of similar works on the place names of Australia and the adjacent areas under the series title "The romance of nomenclature"; these include: *Place names in Queensland, New Zealand and the Pacific* (Sydney, 1944. 109p.); *Place names in Victoria and Tasmania* (Sydney, 1944. 107p.); and *Twelve hundred and more place names in South Australia, Western Australia and the Northern Territory* (Sydney, 1943. 109p.). DU155.M3

Reed, Alexander Wyclif, comp. Aboriginal place names and their meanings. Sydney, Australia, [etc.], Reed, [1967]. 144p. **CL208**

The list of Australian place names with their meanings is followed by a word list which offers a subject approach to the Aboriginal names. DU91.R4

Austria

Schiffmann, Konrad. Historisches Ortsnamen-Lexikon des Landes Oberösterreich. München, Oldenbourg, 1935. 2v. map. **CL209**

—— —— Ergänzungsband; Nachträge, Erklärung der Namen und Verweisungen. München, Oldenbourg, [1940]. 556p.

Zwanziger, Ronald. Bibliographie der Namenforschung in Österreich. Wien, Österreichische Gesellschaft für Namenforschung, 1980– . v.1– . (Österreichische Namenforschung. Sonderreihe, 3–) (In progress) **CL210**

1,172 citations to books, articles, and dissertations are grouped according to geographic region in v.1. International in scope. Author index. Z6824.Z93

Belgium

Carnoy, Albert Joseph. Dictionnaire étymologique du nom des communes de Belgique, y compris l'étymologie des principaux noms de hameaux et de rivières. Louvain, Éd. Universitas, 1939–40. 2v. **CL211**

Brazil

Souza, Bernardino José de. Dicionário da terra e da gente do Brasil. São Paulo, Companhia Ed. Nacional, [1961]. 346p. (Brasiliana. Série grande formato, v.19) **CL212**

5. ed. da *Onomástica geral da geografia brasileira* (1927). Explanations of Brazilian place-names. F2504.S73

Canada

See also CL202, CL203.

Armstrong, George Henry. Origin and meaning of place names in Canada. Toronto, Macmillan, 1930. 312p. **CL213**

F1004.A25

Hamilton, William B. The Macmillan book of Canadian place names. Toronto, Macmillan of Canada, [1978]. 340p. **CL214**

Begun as a revision of G. H. Armstrong's *Origin and meaning of place names in Canada* (above), but in effect a new work. Selection criteria included: (1) size (i.e., "major centres of population and the most important physical features."—*Pref.*); (2) historical significance; and (3) human interest. Bibliography, p.333–40.

F1004.H35

Egypt

Gauthier, Henri. Dictionnaire des noms géographiques contenus dans les textes hiéroglyphiques. Caire, L'Impr. de l'Inst. Français d'Archéologie Orientale pour la Société Royale de Géographie d'Égypte, 1925–31. 7v. **CL215**

v.7 includes indexes and maps. PJ1435.G3

France

Dauzat, Albert and **Rostaing, Charles.** Dictionnaire étymologique des noms de lieux en France. 2. éd. rev. et complétée par Ch. Rostaing. Paris, Guénégaud, 1978. 738, xxiii p. **CL216**

1st ed. 1963.
A reprinting of the earlier edition with a list of "corrections typographiques" and a supplement (p.I–[XXIV]) of some 800 names, either new to this edition or with additional or corrected information. DC14.D28

Dauzat, Albert and **Deslandes, Gaston.** Dictionnaire étymologique des noms de rivières et de montagnes en France. Revu et corrigé par Charles Rostaing. Paris, Klincksieck, 1978. 233p. (Études linguistiques, 21) **CL217**

In two parts, "Noms de rivières" and "Noms de montagnes." Each entry provides etymological derivation, as well as any name variants, with accompanying dates; numerous cross references.

GB1293.D37

France. Comité des Travaux Historiques et Scientifiques. Dictionnaire topographique de la France comprenant les noms de lieu anciens et modernes, publié par ordre du Ministère de l'Instruction Publique et sous la direction du Comité des Travaux Historiques et Scientifiques. Paris, Impr. Nationale, 1861–1984. v.[1–32]. (In progress) **CL218**

A monumental work, still in process of publication, 1v. for each *département.* Each volume lists all place-names of its *département,* even names of farms, giving for each: location; derivation; variations in form from the earliest period to the present, with date when each form was used and exact references to manuscripts or printed authorities; and, in the case of important names, a brief history and description of the place. Entry in the dictionary proper is under the modern form of name; cross references from old forms are given in a table at the end of the volume.

Volumes thus far published are: Ain, by E. Philipon, 1911; Aisne, by A. Matton, 1871; Alpes (Hautes), by J. Roman, 1884; Aube, by Th. Boutiot and E. Socard, 1874; Aude, by the Abbé Sabarthès, 1912; Calvados, by C. Hippeau, 1883; Cantal, by E. Amé, 1897; Cher, by H. Boyer and R. Latouche, 1926; Côte d'Or, by A. Roserot, 1924; Deux-Sèvres, by B. Ledain, 1902; Dordogne, by A. J. D. de Gourgues, 1873; Drôme, by J. Brun-Durand, 1891; Eure, by B. E. P. de Blosseville, 1878; Eure-et-Loir, by L. Merlet, 1861; Gard, by E. Germer-Durand, 1868; Hérault, by E. Thomas, 1865; Loire (Haute), by A. Chassaing and A. Jacotin, 1907; Marne, by A. Longnon, 1891; Marne (Haute), by A. Roserot, 1903; Mayenne, by L. Maitre, 1878; Meurthe, by H. Lepage, 1862; Meuse, by F. Lienard, 1872; Morbihan, by L. Rosenzweig, 1870; Moselle, by E. de Bouteiller, 1874; Nièvre, by J. H. G. R. de Soultrait, 1865; Pas-de-Calais, by A. C. H. Menche de Loisne, 1908; Pyrénées (Basses), by P. R. L. Raymond, 1863; Rhin (Haut), by G. Stoffel, 1868; Sarthe, by E. Vallée, rev. et pub. by R. Latouche, 1950–52; Seine et Marne, by H. Stein and J. Hubert, 1954; Vienne, by L. Rédet, 1881; Vosges, by P. Marichal, 1941; Yonne, by M. Quantin, 1862; Seine-Maritime, by C. de Beaurepaire, revu, complété, entièrement refondu et publié par J. Laporte, 1982–84 (2v.)

Longnon, Auguste Honoré. Les noms de lieu de la France; leur origine, leur signification, leurs transformations; résumé des conférences de toponomastique générale faites à l'École Pratique de Hautes Études. . . . Pub. par Paul Marichal et Léon Mirot. Paris, Champion, 1920–29. 831p. (Repr.: N.Y., B. Franklin, 1973) **CL219**

DC14.L6

Bibliography

Mulon, Marianne. L'onomastique française: bibliographie des travaux publiés jusqu'en 1960. Paris, La Documentation Française, 1977. 454p. **CL220**

At head of title: Archives Nationales.

Aims to present an exhaustive, non-critical bibliography of works on French personal and place names. In three main sections: (1) Études générales: (2) Études régionales; (3) Études locales par départements. About 6,900 items. Indexed. Z2181.G37M84

Germany

Bach, Adolf. Deutsche Namenkunde. Heidelberg, Winter, 1952–56. 3v. in 5. il. **CL221**

For Bd.1, which is devoted to personal names, *see* AK186.

Bd.2, Die deutschen Ortsnamen: Hlbbd.1, Einleitung. Zur Laut- und Formenlehre, zur Satzfügung, Wortbildung und bedeutung der deutschen Ortsnamen; Hlbbd. 2, Die deutschen Ortsnamen in geschichtlicher, geographischer, soziologischer und psychologischer Betrachtung. Ortsnamenforschung im Dienste anderer Wissenschaften; Bd. 3, Registerband, bearb. von Dieter Berger. A 2d ed. of Bd.2, Hlbbd.2 was published 1981.

A detailed treatment of German names; the first volume dealing with personal names, the second with place-names. The third provides indexes to the other two. PF3576.B33

Bahlow, Hans. Deutschlands geographische Namenwelt; etymologisches Lexikon der Fluss- und Ortsnamen alteuropäischer Herkunft. Frankfurt am Main, V. Klostermann, 1965. 554p. **CL222**

Abundant cross references from variant forms are provided.

PF3576.B34

Historisches Ortsnamenbuch von Bayern. München, Kommission für Bayerische Landesgeschichte, 1951–77. il. (In progress) **CL223**

"In Verbindung mit dem Institut für Fränkische Landesforschung herausgegeben von der Kommission für Bayerische Landesgeschichte bei der Bayerischen Akademie der Wissenschaften."—*title page.*

Contents: *Mittelfranken:* Bd.1, Stadt- und Landkreis Fürth, von W. Wiessner; Bd.2, Land- und Stadtkreis Weissenburg i. Bay., von E. Strassner; Bd.3, Landkreis Scheinfeld, von W. D. Ortmann; Bd. 4, Land- und Stadtkreis, Schwabach, von E. Wagner.

Oberbayern: Bd.1, Landkreis Ebersberg, von K. Puchner.

Oberfranken: Bd.1, Land- und Stadtkreis Kulmbach, von Erich *Freiherr* von Guttenburg; Bd.2, Landkreis Pegnitz, von J. Pfanner. Bd.3, Rehau-Selb, von R. Höllerich.

Oberpfalz: Bd.1, Stadt- und Landkreis Amberg, von H. Frank.

Schwaben: Bd.1, Landkreis Marktoberdorf, von R. Dertsch; Bd.2, Landkreis Krumbach, von F. Hilble; Bd. 3, Stadt- und Landkreis Kaufbeuren, von R. Dertsch; Bd.4, Land- und Stadtkreis Dillingen a.d. Donau, von R. H. Seitz; Bd.5, Stadt- und Landkreis Kempten, von R. Dertsch; Bd.6, Stadt- und Landkreis Lindau, von H. Löffler; Bd.7, Landkreis Sonthofen, von R. Dertsch. DD801.B33H5

Oesterley, Hermann. Historisch-geographisches Wörterbuch des deutschen Mittelalters. Gotha, Perthes, 1883. 806p. **CL224**

A history of medieval German place-names. DD14.O29

Great Britain

Cameron, Kenneth. English place-names. 3d ed. London, Batsford, [1977]. 258p. il. **CL225**

A discussion of the elements of English place-names. Indexes of place-names, street-names, and field-names. DA645.C3

Ekwall, Eilert. Concise Oxford dictionary of English place-names. 4th ed. Oxford, Clarendon Pr., 1960. 546p. **CL226**

1st ed. 1936.

The 4th ed. has been reset, incorporating corrections and addenda from the earlier editions; many articles were rewritten. Lists about 15,000 names.

"Embraces names of the country, of the counties, and other important divisions, towns (except those of late origin), parishes, villages, some names of estates and hamlets, or even farms whose names are old and etymologically interesting, rivers, lakes—also names of capes, hills, bays for which early material is available. Names of hundreds, as being no longer in use, have been omitted." —*Introd.*

While the concise information given is considerably less full than that in the various volumes of the English Place-Name Society, it includes in general: modern form, location (in county), derivation of meaning, older forms with dates, and some references to sources. Pronunciation is given in some cases. DA645.E38

———— English river names. Oxford, Clarendon Pr., 1928. 488p. **CL227**

Gives detailed etymology for river names, with references to sources of information. DA645.E5

English Place-Name Society. [Survey of English place-names]. Cambridge, Univ. Pr., 1924– . v.1– . maps. (In progress) **CL228**

v.1, pt.1, Introduction to the survey of English place-names, by A. Mawer and F. M. Stenton (1924. 201p.); v.1, pt.2, Chief elements used in English place-names, by A. Mawer (1924. 67p; for rev. ed. *see* CL233); v.2, Place-names of *Buckinghamshire,* by A. Mawer and F. M. Stenton (1925. 274p.); v.3, Place-names of *Bedfordshire* and

Huntingdonshire, by A. Mawer and F. M. Stenton (1926. 316p.); v.4, Place-names of *Worcestershire,* by A. Mawer and F. M. Stenton (1927. 420p.); v.5, Place-names of the *North Riding of Yorkshire,* by A. H. Smith (1928. 352p.); v.6–7, Place-names of *Sussex,* by A. Mawer and F. M. Stenton (1929–30. 2v.); v.8–9, Place-names of *Devon,* by J. E. B. Gover, A. Mawer and F. M. Stenton (1931–32. 2v. and case of maps); v.10, Place-names of *Northamptonshire,* by J. E. B. Gover, A. Mawer and F. M. Stenton (1933. 311p.); v.11, Place-names of *Surrey,* by J. E. B. Gover, A. Mawer and F. M. Stenton (1934. 445p.); v.12, Place-names of *Essex,* by P. H. Reaney (1935. 698p.); v.13, Place-names of *Warwickshire,* by J. E. B. Gover, A. Mawer and F. M. Stenton (1936. 409p.); v.14, Place-names of the *East Riding of Yorkshire and York,* by A. H. Smith (1937. 351p.); v.15, Place-names of *Hertfordshire,* by J. E. B. Gover, A. Mawer and F. M. Stenton (1938. 342p.); v.16, Place-names of *Wiltshire,* by J. E. B. Gover, A. Mawer and F. M. Stenton (1939. 547p.); v.17, Place-names of *Nottinghamshire,* by J. E. B. Gover, A. Mawer and F. M. Stenton (1940. 348p.); v.18, Place-names of *Middlesex,* apart from the city of London, by J. E. B. Gover, A. Mawer and F. M. Stenton (1942. 235p.); v.19, Place-names of *Cambridgeshire* and the *Isle of Ely,* by P. H. Reaney (1943. 396p.); v.20–22, Place-names of *Cumberland,* by A. M. Armstrong, A. Mawer, F. M. Stenton and Bruce Dickins (1950–52. 3pts. 565p.); v.23–24, Place-names of *Oxfordshire,* by Margaret Gelling, based on material collected by Doris Mary Stenton (1953–54. 2v.); v.25–26, English place-name elements, *see* CL233; v.27–29, Place-names of *Derbyshire,* by Kenneth Cameron (1959. 3v.); v.30–37, Place-names of the *West Riding of Yorkshire,* by A. H. Smith (1961–63. 8v.); v.38–41, The place-names of *Gloucestershire,* by A. H. Smith (1964–65. 4v.); v.42–43, The place-names of *Westmorland,* by A. H. Smith (1967. 2v.); v.44–48, 54, The place-names of *Cheshire,* by J. McN. Dodgson (1970–81. 6v.; pt.5 still in prep.); v.49–51, The place-names of *Berkshire,* by Margaret Gelling (1973–76. 3v.); v.52–53, Place-names of *Dorset,* pts. 1–2, by A. D. Mills (1977–80); v.55, Place-names of *Staffordshire,* pt.1, by J.P. Oakden (1984). DA645.A4

Field, John. Place-names of Great Britain and Ireland. London, David & Charles; Totowa, N.J., Barnes and Noble, [1980]. 208p. maps. **CL229**

A selective alphabetical dictionary of place names in England, Scotland, Wales, the Isle of Man, and the Irish island, intended for the general reader. Early forms of less common names are provided, with dates of usage. Includes glossary of common elements of place names and brief bibliography. No guide to pronunciation. DA645.F53

Gelling, Margaret, Nicolaisen, Wilhelm F. H. and **Richards, Melville.** The names of towns and cities in Britain. London, Batsford, [1970]. 215p. **CL230**

Treats town and city names of England, Scotland, and Wales in a single alphabet. The names included "have been chosen for one reason only: they are the names of those places—towns and cities—in which most people in Great Britain live to-day"—*Introd.* (i.e., names were not chosen merely for intrinsic interest or because they illustrate some linguistic peculiarity). Separate section for Greater London names. DA645.G44

Rivet, Albert Lionel Frederick and **Smith, Colin.** The place-names of Roman Britain. Princeton, N.J., Princeton Univ. Pr., [1979]. 526p. **CL231**

Chapters entitled "The literary authorities," "Ptolemy's geography," "Itineraries," "The Ravenna cosmography," and "Inscriptions" precede the "Alphabetic list of names" (about half of the book) which gives derivations and identifications. Index of modern names in Britain. DA645.R58

Room, Adrian. A concise dictionary of modern place-names in Great Britain and Ireland. Oxford & N.Y., Oxford Univ. Pr., 1983. xliii, 148p. **CL232**

Explains derivations of more than 1,000 names that have arisen since 1500. Bibliography. DA645.R66

Smith, Albert Hugh. English place-name elements. Cambridge, Univ. Pr., 1956. 2v. (English Place-Name Society. [Survey of English place-names] v.25–26) **CL233**

Contents: pt.1, Introduction, bibliography, the elements A–Iw, maps; pt.2, The elements Jafn–Ytri, index and maps.

A detailed study of the derivation of the elements found in English place-names, with bibliographical references to sources. Expands and revises A. Mawer, *Chief elements used in English place-names (see* CL228, v.1, pt.2). DA645.A4 v.25–26

❖In addition to the publications of the English Place-Name Society listed above, there is a wealth of publications relating to the place-names of Britain. These publications include: Place-names of *Aberdeenshire,* by W. M. Alexander (Aberdeen, Third Spalding Club, 1952. 419p.); Place-names of *Bedfordshire,* by W. W. Skeat (Cambridge, Antiquarian Soc., 1906. 74p.; *its* Pubn. no.42); Place-names of *Berkshire,* by W. W. Skeat (Oxford, Clarendon Pr., 1911. 118p.); Place-names of *Cambridgeshire,* by W. W. Skeat (2d ed. Cambridge, Antiquarian Soc., 1911. 82p.); *Cornish* names, an attempt to explain over 1600 Cornish names, by T. F. G. Dexter (London, Longmans, 1926. 89p.); Place-names of *Cumberland* and *Westmorland,* by W. J. Sedgefield (Manchester, Univ. Pr., 1915. 208p.); Place-names of *Derbyshire,* by B. Walker (Derbyshire, Archaeological Soc., 1915. 310p.); Place-names of *North Devonshire,* by Bertil Blomé (Uppsala, Appelberg, 1929. 189p.); Place-names of *Dorset,* by A. Fägersten (Uppsala, Appelberg, 1933. 334p.); Place-names of *Durham,* by Charles E. Jackson (London, Allen & Unwin, 1916. 114p.); Place-names of *Gloucestershire,* by W. St. C. Baddeley (Gloucester, Bellows, 1913. 185p.); Place-names of *Herefordshire,* by A. T. Bannister (Cambridge, Author, 1916. 231p.);

Place-names of *Hertfordshire,* by W. W. Skeat (Hertford, Austin, 1904. 75p.); Place-names of *Kent,* by J. K. Wallenberg (Uppsala, Appelberg, 1934. 626p.); Place-names of *Lancashire,* by Eilert Ekwall (Manchester, Chetham Soc., 1922. 280p.; *its* Remains . . . , n.s.v.81); Handbook of *Lancashire* place-names, by J. Sephton (Liverpool, Young, 1913. 256p.); Place-names of *Lancashire,* by Henry C. Wyld and T. O. Hirst (London, Constable, 1911. 400p.); Place and river names of the West Riding of Lindsey, *Lincolnshire,* by T. B. F. Eminson (Lincoln, Ruddock, 1934. 288p.); Place-names of the *Liverpool* district, by Henry Harrison (London, Stock, 1898. 104p.); Place-names of the *Isle of Man,* by J. J. Kneen (Douglas, Manx Soc., 1925–29. 6 pts., 645p.); An attempt to ascertain the true derivation of the names of towns and villages and of rivers, and other great natural features . . . of *Norfolk,* by George Munford (London, Simpkin, 1870. 239p.); Place-names of *Northumberland* and *Durham,* by A. Mawer (Cambridge, Univ. Pr., 1920. 271p.); Place-names of *Nottinghamshire,* by H. Mutschmann (Cambridge, Univ. Pr., 1913. 179p.);

Place-names of *Oxfordshire,* by Henry Alexander (Oxford, Clarendon Pr., 1912. 251p.); *Shropshire* place-names, by E. W. Bowcock (Shrewsbury, Wilding, 1923. 271p.); The place-names of *Somerset,* by J. S. Hill (Bristol, St. Stephen's Pr., 1914. 373p.); Notes on *Staffordshire* place-names, by William H. Duignan (London, Frowde, 1902. 178p.); Place-names of *Suffolk,* by W. W. Skeat (Cambridge, Antiquarian Soc., 1913. 132p.); Place-names of the County of *Surrey,* including London in Surrey, by D. Hopwood (Capetown, 1926. 101p.; Annals of the Univ. of Stellenbosch, v.4, sec.B, no.2); Place-names of *Sussex,* by Richard G. Roberts (Cambridge, Univ. Pr., 1914. 210p.); A catalogue of place-names in *Teesdale,* by D. Embleton (London, Williams and Norgate, 1887. 223p.); Non-Celtic place-names in *Wales,* by Bertie G. Charles (London, Univ. College, 1938. 326p.); Place-names of *Wales,* by Thomas Morgan (2d rev. ed. Newport, Mon., Southall, 1912. 262p.); Rhestr o enwau lleoedd (Gazetteer of *Welsh* place-names), ed. by Elwyn Davies for the Language and Literature Committee, Board of Celtic Studies, University of Wales (3d ed. Cardiff, Univ. of Wales Pr., 1967. 119p.); *Warwickshire* place-names, by W. H. Duignan (London, Frowde, 1912. 130p.); The place-names of the *Isle of Wight,* by H. Kökeritz (Uppsala, Appelberg, 1940. 306p.); Place-names of *Wiltshire,* their origin and history, by Einar L. Ekblom (Uppsala, Appelberg, 1917. 187p.); *Worcestershire* place-names, by W. H. Duignan (London, Frowde, 1905. 185p.); Place-names of south-west *Yorkshire,* by Armitage Goodall (Rev. ed. Cambridge, Univ. Pr., 1914. 313p.); Place-names and surnames, their origin and meaning, with special reference to the West Riding of *Yorkshire,* by Taylor Dyson (Huddersfield, Alfred Jubb, 1944. 216p.); Place-names of the West Riding of *Yorkshire,* by Frederic Moorman (Leeds, Thoresby Soc., 1910. 218p.; *its* Pubn. v.18).

Hungary

Kiss, Lajos. Földrajzi nevek etimológiai szótára. Budapest, Akadémiai Kiadó, 1978. 728p.　　　　**CL234**

An etymological dictionary of place names, with extensive references to some 4,000 geographical sources of reference for further data. Not limited to Hungarian place names, but fullest treatment is offered to them.　　　　PH2576.K5

Ireland

See also CL229, CL232.

Hogan, Edmund. Onomasticon goedelicum locorum et tribuum Hiberniae et Scotiae. Dublin, Hodges, 1910. 695p. map.　　　　**CL235**

Subtitle: An index, with identifications to the Gaelic names of places and tribes.　　　　DA979.H6

Joyce, Patrick W. Origin and history of Irish names of places. 7th ed. London, N.Y., Longmans, 1901–02. 2v. (Repr.: Wakefield, E. P. Publishing, 1972)　　　　**CL236**

The best dictionary of Irish place-names, giving for each name its location, derivation, meaning, and an explanation of the meaning where necessary. v.1–2, originally published 1869–71, are treatises, arranged in chapters with alphabetical indexes, but v.3 is a regular dictionary list. As v.3 does not duplicate many of the names in v.1–2, use must still be made of those earlier volumes.

DA920.J893

Mexico

Peñafiel, Antonio. Nomenclatura geográfica de México. Etimologías de los nombres de lugar correspondientes a los principales idiomas que se hablan en la república. México, Oficina Tipografía de la Secretaría de Fomento, 1897. 2v. and atlas of 709 plates.　　　　**CL237**

F1204.P39

Mozambique

Cabral, António Carlos Pereira. Dicionário de nomes geográficos de Moçambique, sua origem. Lourenço Marques, 1975. 180p. il.　　　　**CL238**

Discusses the background of some 850 names. Bibliography.

DT452.C3

Netherlands

Flou, Karel de. Woordenboek der toponymie van Westelijk Vlaanderen, Vlaamsch Artesië, het Land van den Hoek, de graafschappen Guines en Boulogne, en een gedeelte van het graafschap Ponthieu. Brugge, Poelvoorde, 1914–38. 18v.

CL239

Sponsored by the Vlaamsche Academie voor Taal en Letterkunde. An extensive listing, in dictionary arrangement, of Flemish place-names with explanations and references to original usages, etc.

Wijer, H. J. van de. Bibliographie van de Vlaamsche plaatsnaamkunde (begin XIXe eeuw tot en met 1927). Den Haag, Nijhoff, 1928. 156p. (Nomina geographica flandrica, I)　　　　**CL240**

New Zealand

See also CL207n.

Andersen, Johannes Carl. Maori place-names, also personal names and names of colours, weapons, and natural objects. Wellington, Polynesian Soc. of New Zealand, 1942. 494p. [Polynesian Society memoir, no.20]　　　　**CL241**

Legends and histories of Maori names.　　　　DU405.A7

——— Place-names in New Zealand; rules of nomenclature and lists of names approved or changed or expunged. Wellington, 1934. 47p. (N.Z. Geographic Board. Bulletin, no.1; Polynesian Society, Wellington. Repr. no.4)　　**CL242**

Poland

Taszycki, Witold. Bibliografia onomastyki polskiej. Opracował Witold Taszycki przy współudziale Mieczysława Karasia i Adama Turasiewicza. Kraków, [Nakł. Uniwersytetu Jagielleńskiego], 1960–83. 3v. (Varia, t.5, 76)　　**CL243**

Editor varies; publisher varies.
At head of title, v.3: Polska Akademia Nauk. Instytut Języka Polskiego.
Contents: [t.1] Do roku 1958 włacznie; t.2, Od roku 1959 do roku 1970 włacznie; t.3, Od roku 1971 do roku 1980 włacznie.
A classed bibliography of Polish place-name literature, international in scope. Indexed by methodology, geographic names, and authors.　　　　Z6824.T3

Scotland

See also CL235.

Johnston, James B. The place-names of Scotland. [3d ed. enl.] London, Murray, 1934. 335p. (Repr.: Wakefield, S. R. Publishers, 1970)　　　　**CL244**

Gives the origin and meaning of place-names in Scotland.

DA869.J72

Mackenzie, William Cook. Scottish place-names. London, K. Paul, 1931. 319p.　　　　**CL245**

Discusses the elements in, and the types of, a selected list of Scottish place-names, in such chapters as "The rivers and their burns," "The nesses and the lochs," "The bogs and the marshes," etc.　　　　DA869.M14

Nicolaisen, Wilhelm Fritz Hermann. Scottish place-names: their study and significance. London, Batsford, [1976]. 210p. maps.　　　　**CL246**

Aims to provide "a cohesive and systematic, although not a comprehensive, account of the study of Scottish place names."— *Pref.* Indexed.　　　　DA869.N53

Watson, William John. History of the Celtic place-names of Scotland, being the Rhind lecture on archaeology (expanded) delivered in 1916. Publ. under the auspices of the Royal Celtic Society. Edinburgh, Blackwood, 1926. 558p. (Repr.: Shannon, Irish Univ. Pr., 1973) **CL247**

DA869.W3

❖Place-names of specific regions of Scotland are treated in: The place-names of *Aberdeenshire,* by W. McC. Alexander (Aberdeen, pr. for the Third Spalding Club, 1952. 419p.); Place-names of *West Aberdeenshire,* by James Macdonald (Aberdeen, pr. for the University, 1900. 347p.); Place-names around *Alyth,* by James Meikle (Paisley, Gardner, 1925. 203p.); Place-names of *Argyll,* by Hugh Gillies (London, Nutt, 1906. 273p.); Place-names of *Birsay,* by Hugh Marwick (Aberdeen, Aberdeen Univ. Pr., 1970. 135p.); Place-names of *Cowal,* by Angus McLean (Dunoon, Dunoon Observer, 1982? 137p.); Place-names of upper *Deeside,* by Adam Watson (Aberdeen, Aberdeen Univ. Pr., 1984. 192p.); Place-names of *Dumbartonshire,* by J. Irving (Dumbarton, Bennett and Thomson, 1928. 61p.); Place-names of *Dumfriesshire,* by Sir Edward Johnson-Ferguson (Dumfries, Courier Pr., 1935. 140p.); Place-names of *Elginshire,* by D. Matheson (Stirling, Mackay, 1905. 208p.); Place-names of *Galloway,* their origin and meaning considered, by Sir Herbert E. Maxwell (Glasgow, Jackson, 1930. 278p.); Place-names in *Glengarry* and *Glenquoich* and their associations, by Edward Ellice (2d ed. rev. London, Routledge, 1931. 163p.); *Hawick* place-names, by W. S. Robson (Hawick, Hood, 1947. 82p.); Place-names of *Lewis* and *Harris,* by Donald Maciver (Stornoway, "Gazette" Off., 1934. 102p.); Gaelic place-names of the *Lothians,* by John Milne (London, McDougall's Educ. Co., 1912. 51p., 44p., 30p.); Place-names of *Mull,* by Duncan M. MacQuarrie (Inverness, MacQuarrie, 1982. 102p.); Place-names of *Ross* and *Cromarty,* by William John Watson (Inverness, Northern Counties Pr. and Pub. Co., 1904. 302p.); Place-names of *Shetland,* by Jacob Jakobsen (London, Nutt, 1936. 273p.); Place-names of *Skye* and adjacent islands, with lore mythical, traditional and historical, by Alexander R. Forbes (Paisley, Gardner, 1923. 495p.); Place-names in *Strathbogie,* by James MacDonald (Aberdeen, Wyllie, 1891. 300p.); The place-names of *West Lothian,* by Angus Macdonald (Edinburgh, Oliver and Boyd, 1941. 179p.).

South Africa

Nienaber, G. S. and **Raper, P. E.** Hottentot (Khoekhoen) place names. Tr. by P. S. Rabie. Durban, Publ. for the Onomastic Research Centre, Human Sciences Research Council, by Butterworth, [1983]. 243p. il., maps. (Southern African place names, 1) **CL248**

Based on the authors' *Toponymica hottentotica* (Pretoria, 1977–80. 3v.). Bibliography p.227–42. DT752.5.N48

Pettman, Charles. South African place-names, past and present. Queenstown, Daily Representative, 1931. 194p. **CL249**

DT752.5.P4

Raper, P. E. Bronnegids vir toponimie en topologie. Source guide for toponymy and topology. Pretoria, S. A. Naamkundesentrum, Raad vir Geesteswetenskaplike Navorsing, 1975. 478p. (Naamkundereeks, 5) **CL250**

A bibliography for "the study of places and place names."—*Pref.* Includes books, pamphlets, periodical and newspaper articles, and theses. In two sections, the first arranged by subject or place name; the second by author. Full information is given in both sections.

Z3608.A5R36

Switzerland

Hubschmid, Johannes. Bibliographia onomastica helvetica. Bernae, Bibliotheca Nationalis, 1954. 50p. map. **CL251**

Some 750 citations are arranged by topical geographical region. Indexed by author and detailed subject. Z6824.H8

Jaccard, Henri. Essai de toponymie; origine des noms de lieux habités et des lieux dits de la Suisse romande. Lausanne, Bridel, 1906. 558p. (Société d'Histoire de la Suisse Romande. Mémoires et documents, 2. sér., t.7) (Repr.: Genève, Slatkine, 1978) **CL252**

An extensive listing showing the development of Swiss place-names with references to sources. DQ15.J32

Studer, Julius. Schweizer Ortsnamen; ein historisch-etymologischer Versuch. . . . Zürich, Schulthess, 1896. 288p. **CL253**

A listing of German-Swiss names, giving early usages and etymologies.

Union of Soviet Socialist Republics

Onomastika; ukazatel' literatury izdannoi v SSSR. 1963/70– . Moskva, Akademiia Nauk SSSR, Institut Nauchnoi Informatsii po Obshchestvennym Naukam, 1976– . [v.1]– . Irregular. **CL254**

Arranged by author, with indexing by subject, personal and geographical names, etymological endings, etc. The second volume, covering 1970/75, includes a section of data for 1918/62. A third volume, covering 1976/80, was published 1984. Z6824.O56

ATLASES

❖Atlases are important and necessary reference books in any library. As they are expensive and vary greatly in quality, they should be chosen with care, after a check of critical estimates by experts and an examination of the books themselves to note their suitability for the particular library in question. Atlases which are general in scope (i.e., cover the whole world) differ considerably in their contents according to the country in which they are published. An American atlas, for example, will include more or larger maps of American regions and cities than will be found in an English or French atlas. An English atlas will include more maps of British territory. Generally, the workmanship of the best foreign atlases is better than that of American atlases, and an American library should take that fact into account in forming its collection, including some British, French, and German atlases for the quality of their maps, and some American atlases for their more numerous maps of American regions. A useful survey of atlases is given in Wright and Platt, *Aids to geographical research,* p.83–99 (CL6), and a more recent and more extensive survey is Lock's *Modern maps and atlases* (CL256); English-language in-print atlases are evaluated in Kister's guide (CL255). Ena L. Yonge's articles in *Geographical review* are also useful: "World and thematic atlases: a summary survey," 52:583–96, Oct. 1962; "Regional atlases: a summary survey," 52:407–32, July 1962; and "National atlases: a summary," 47:570–78, Oct. 1957.

See also the "Reference books bulletin" section of *Booklist* (AA502n) and the *Bulletin* of Special Libraries Association's Geography and Map Division for detailed reviews of atlases. A recent comprehensive atlas review appeared in *Booklist* 80: 40–50 (Sept. 1, 1983).

In studying atlases, in addition to following the general directions for examining reference books, the librarian should note the following special points:

I. Atlas as a whole
  A. Scope
    1. Does the atlas include all types of maps: political, physical, historical, economic, etc.?
  B. Country of origin, as indication of both quality of maps and emphasis of atlas
  C. Date: publication, copyright, preface, revision
  D. Index
    1. Is there a general index for the whole atlas, or are there separate indexes for each country or map?
    2. If there is a general index, is it in a separate volume or bound with the atlas?
    3. Does the index include population figures or other additional information, e.g., pronunciation, latitude and longitude, etc.?
    4. Does the index list only names printed on the maps, or are other places included?
    5. How does the index refer to the location of a place on a given map?
      a) By locational squares indicated by marginal letters and figures?
      b) By latitude and longitude?
  E. Supplementary material
    1. Does the atlas contain any material in addition to maps and index, e.g., bibliographies; general descriptive, statistical, commercial, or ethnographic information; lists of commercial products; gazetteer lists of places; illustrations, etc.?
II. Maps
  A. Name and nationality of the maker, as indication of the quality of the work
  B. Date (If map is undated, the name and address of the maker may show this approximately, or the date may be indicated by some kind of internal evidence, such as: inclusion or omission of new places, changed names, boundaries and explorations which were established or made at certain dates.)
  C. Method of indicating relief
    1. By hachuring?
    2. By layer method of altitude tints?
    3. By contour lines with altitude figures?
    4. By shading?
  D. Color
    1. Is the color definite and varied enough to be clear, and at the same time not so dark as to obscure lettering?
    2. Does each map have a key, showing the meaning of the colors used?
  E. Scale
    1. Is the scale plainly indicated?
  F. Lettering and other details
    1. Is the lettering distinct and easily read?
    2. Are other details, e.g., rivers, railroads, boundaries, canals, etc., plain and well differentiated?
  G. Form of names
    1. Are geographical names in the vernacular or translated?
  H. Authority
    1. Are there bibliographical or other references to indicate the source and authority of the maps?
  I. Accuracy
    1. Are the maps accurate in detail? (The librarian who is not a specialist naturally cannot judge the whole atlas on this point, but he can examine some one map of a small region with which he is familiar and judge its accuracy and completeness on points known to him.)

Atlases on specific themes (e.g., history or economics) will be found in relevant sections of the *Guide*.

Guides

Kister, Kenneth F. Kister's Atlas buying guide: general English-language world atlases available in North America. [Phoenix, Ariz.], Oryx Pr., 1984. 236p.   **CL255**

For 105 atlases, provides complete bibliographic data and critical evaluations, including review citations. Also features general guide to atlas evaluation (p.5–29), comparative charts, annotated bibliography, and directory of dealers for out-of-print materials. Indexed.
     Z6021.K5

Lock, Clara Beatrice Muriel. Modern maps and atlases; an outline guide to twentieth century production. [London], Bingley; [Hamden, Conn.], Archon Books, [1969]. 619p.
  CL256

A survey of map sources and production, and the bibliographical control of maps on an international basis. Sections on (1) Techniques of modern cartography; (2) International maps and atlases; (3) National and regional maps and atlases; (4) Thematic maps and atlases; and (5) Map librarianship. Many bibliographical references; detailed index. Valuable historical and critical notes on national and international cartographic agencies and their publications.
     GA246.L6

Walsh, James Patrick, comp. General world atlases in print, 1972–1973; a comparative analysis. [4th ed.] N.Y., Bowker, [1973]. 211p.   **CL257**

1st ed. 1966.

Intended as a practical guide for the non-specialist in the choice of a general reference world atlas. Treats 40 major atlases and about 100 smaller ones, all of which were published in the United States or the United Kingdom, or are translations or adaptations for the English-speaking user of foreign atlases. Gives information on publisher; publishing history and revision program; editors, cartographers, and contributors; home sale and retail prices; purpose and age suitability; size and number of pages; total map pages and types of maps; scale; balance; indexing; scope; contents, and arrangement; a summary of features, strengths and weaknesses; and references to critical reviews and sources of information on the atlas. Indicates overall quality and gives graded recommendations.   Z6028.W27

Bibliography and indexes

Alexander, Gerard L. Guide to atlases: world, regional, national, thematic; an international listing of atlases published since 1950. Metuchen, N.J., Scarecrow Pr., 1971. 671p.   **CL258**

Atlases are listed by date, then alphabetically within four main groups: (1) world, (2) regional, (3) national, and (4) thematic. Publisher, pagination, and size in centimeters are indicated. Indexed.   Z6021.A43

————Guide to atlases supplement: world, regional, national, thematic. Metuchen, N.J., Scarecrow Pr., 1977. 362p.

"An international listing of atlases published 1971 through 1975 with comprehensive indexes."—*t.p.*

Includes some entries from the 1950–70 period overlooked in the basic volume (above). Indexed by publisher and by author/cartographer/editor.

American Geographical Society of New York. Map Dept. Index to maps in books and periodicals. Boston, G. K. Hall, 1968. 10v.   **CL259**

Photoreproduction of a card catalog maintained by the Society's Map Department. Entries are alphabetical by subject and geographical-political division. Z6028.A5

—— —— First supplement. Boston, G. K. Hall, 1971. 603p.

—— —— Second supplement. Boston, G. K. Hall, 1976. 568p.

This supplement covers the period 1972–75; format remains the same.

British Museum. Dept. of Printed Books. Map Room. Catalogue of printed maps, charts and plans. Photolithographic ed. complete to 1964. London, Trustees of the British Museum, 1967. 15v. **CL260**

An earlier catalog was published in 1885 in 2v. and was kept up-to-date by a series of accessions lists. This new set lists pertinent materials acquired by the British Museum through 1964, whether part of the Map Room collection or of other parts of the library.

—— —— Corrections and additions. London, Trustees, 1968. 55p. (Alternate pages blank)

The additions consist mainly in cross references; post-1964 imprints are not included. Z6028.B863

British Library. Map Library. Catalogue of printed maps, charts and plans. Ten-year supplement, 1965–1974. [London], British Museum Publications, [1978]. 1380 cols. **CL261**

For the main set *see* above.

Contains entries for "(a) maps, atlases, globes and related materials, including literature on them, acquired by the Map Library during 1965–1974, and (b) the more important cartographic materials in other collections of the Department of Printed Books and of the Department of Oriental Manuscripts and Printed Books of the British Library Reference Division catalogued during the same period."—*Pref.* The first in a projected series of ten-year supplements. Z6028.B855

California. University, Berkeley. Bancroft Library. Index to printed maps. Boston, G. K. Hall, 1964. 521p. **CL262**

Photographic reproductions of the catalog cards of the map collection. A supplement with about 12,000 additional entries was published 1975. For catalog of the Bancroft Library, *see* DB130. Z6028.C17

Chubb, Thomas. Printed maps in the atlases of Great Britain and Ireland; a bibliography, 1579–1850 . . . with an introd. by F. P. Sprent and biographical notes on the map makers, engravers and publishers by T. Chubb assisted by J. W. Skells and H. Beharrell. . . . London, Homeland Assoc., [1927]. 479p. il., maps. **CL263**

Contents: (1) Atlases of England and Wales; (2) of Scotland; (3) of Ireland; (4) biographical notes on the map makers, engravers, and publishers. Index.

Partially superseded by Skelton (CL276) and Hodson (CL277). Z6027.G7C5

Claussen, Martin Paul and **Friis, Herman R.** Descriptive catalog of maps published by Congress, 1817–1843. Wash., 1941. 104p. **CL264**

"This is a catalog of the 503 maps that are scattered throughout v.1–429 of the 'Congressional series' . . . 15th through the 27th Congress, between 1817 and 1843."—*Introd.*

Arranged chronologically by Congress with index to area, place-names that appear in title, names of persons, government agencies, and institutions involved in compiling the maps. Z6027.U5C6

Gt. Brit. Public Record Office. Maps and plans in the Public Record Office. London, H.M.S.O., 1967–[82]. v.1–3. (In progress) **CL265**

Contents: [v.1] British Isles, c.1410–1860; [v.2] America and the West Indies; [v.3] Africa.

A catalog of maps listed or indexed in records of the Colonial and Foreign Offices and in other classes of records retained by the Public Record Office. v.2 covers North and South America and the Caribbean. Geographical arrangement; descriptive notes for each map. Personal name index. Z6028.G767

International maps and atlases in print. Ed. by Kenneth L. Winch. 2d ed. N.Y. & London, Bowker, [1976]. 866p. il., maps. **CL266**

1st ed. 1974.

Classed arrangement by the world, region, and country notation of the Universal Decimal System. Within each area, the publications are divided into maps and atlases, and each of these types is subdivided by subject (general, town plans, official surveys, political and administrative, etc.); arrangement within the subject groups is by scale. Index diagrams of multi-sheet series have been reproduced to show publication status. Full bibliographic details for each publication. Index of countries, regions, and islands. Very useful. Z6021.I596

Koeman, Cornelis. Atlantes Neerlandici; bibliography of terrestrial, maritime and celestial atlases and pilot books, published in the Netherlands up to 1880. Amsterdam, Theatrum Orbis Terrarum, [1967–71]. 5v. il. **CL267**

Contents: v.1–3, Terrestrial atlases, A–Z; v.4, Celestial and maritime atlases; v.5, Indexes.

A comprehensive listing of early Dutch atlases. Full bibliographical descriptions and notes on variant editions. Library locations of copies are indicated. Z6028.K6

Kosack, Hans-Peter and **Meine, Karl-Heinz.** Die Kartographie 1943–1954, eine bibliographische Übersicht. Lahr-Schwarzwald, Astra Verlag, 1955. 216p. (Kartographische Schriftenreihe, Bd.4) **CL268**

Includes material in many languages, although German titles predominate. Lists books, periodical articles, and serial publications of societies and governments, on all phases of cartography. Classed arrangement with author index.

Continued by *Bibliotheca Cartographica* (CL296).

Lowery, Woodbury. The Lowery collection. A descriptive list of maps of the Spanish possessions within the present limits of the United States, 1502–1820. Ed. with notes by P. L. Phillips. Wash., Govt. Prt. Off., 1912. 567p. **CL269**

Detailed descriptions of maps with references to sources. Chronological arrangement with author index. The collection was left to the Library of Congress. Z881.U5

Mickwitz, Ann-Mari and **Miekkavaara, Leena.** The A. E. Nordenskiöld collection in the Helsinki University Library: annotated catalogue of maps made up to 1800. [Helsinki], Publ. by Helsinki Univ. Lib.; distr. by Almqvist & Wiksell, Stockholm, [and] Humanities Pr., Atlantic Highlands, N.J., [1979]– . v.1– . il., maps. (In progress; to be in 5v.) **CL270**

Contents: v.1, Atlases A–J.

The Nordenskiöld Collection is one of the world's outstanding collections of geographical and cartographic literature. "The catalogue lists all the pre-nineteenth-century maps in the . . . Collection, contained in atlases, books, or as loose sheets. The facsimiles are also catalogued. . . . In addition to the area depicted on each map, all the important information concerning their preparation and identification has been taken into account for cataloguing purposes."—*p.xxix.* Arranged by author or publisher, with anonymous works entered by title (or, if lacking a title, under "Collection"). Z6028.M52

Modelski, Andrew M. Railroad maps of North America: the first hundred years. Wash., Lib. of Congress, 1984. 186p. il., maps. 29 x 36 cm. **CL271**

Illustrates and describes 92 of the 5,000 railroad maps in the Library's Geography and Map Division. Under each country (United States, Canada, Mexico), maps are grouped by type—surveys, general or regional maps, travelers' maps, railroad lines, and terminals. Indexed. G1106.P3M6

New York. Public Library. Map Division. Dictionary catalog of the Map Division. Boston, G. K. Hall, 1971. 10v.

CL272

Lists about 280,000 sheet maps, 11,000 volumes on cartography, periodical articles, and bibliographies, and some 6,000 atlases (with many analytics for atlases published before 1800). Also includes manuscript maps in the Manuscript Division, early printed maps in the Rare Book Division, and the Phelps Stokes American Historical Views in the Prints Division. Updated by the *Bibliographic guide to maps and atlases* (CL294).   Z6028.N58

Ristow, Walter William. Guide to the history of cartography; an annotated list of references on the history of maps and mapmaking. Wash., Lib. of Congress, 1973. 96p.   **CL273**

Revised version of a work originally entitled *A guide to historical cartography* (1st ed. 1954; 2d ed., 1960, repr. 1962), comp. by W. W. Ristow and Clara E. LeGear, issued by the Map Division, Library of Congress.

This is a greatly expanded edition, listing nearly 400 items on the history of maps and mapmaking (not specifically historical maps). Includes 19th- and early 20th-century references (almost entirely monographs) as well as earlier periods. Alphabetical main entry listing with index of subjects, geographical areas, and secondary authors.   Z6021.R57

Shibanov, F. A. Ukazatel' kartograficheskoi literatury, vyshedshei v Rossii s 1800–1917 god. [Leningrad], Izd-vo Leningradskogo Universiteta, 1961. 222p.   **CL274**

The literature on cartography published in Russia from 1800 to 1917, in a bibliography arranged by topics such as: applied astronomy, geodesy, topography, marine surveying, and the history of these subjects. Lists reviews and announcements of maps and atlases. Author index.   Z6021.S45

Shirley, Rodney W. The mapping of the world: early printed maps, 1472–1700. London, Holland Pr., 1983. xlvi, 669p. il., maps. 35cm. (Holland Pr. cartographica, 9)   **CL275**

Lists, annotates, and illustrates 639 pre-18th century printed world maps, excluding Oriental works and globes, with references to about 90 lost or apochryphal titles. Chronological arrangement, with locations in major map collections and bibliographic references. Chronological charts; appendixes; index.   Z6028.S48

Skelton, Raleigh Ashlin, comp. County atlases of the British Isles, 1579–1850; a bibliography. London, Carta Pr., 1970. 262p. 40 pl.   **CL276**

Contents: 1579–1703 (sometimes designated as v.1).

Based on Thomas Chubb's *Printed maps in the atlases of Great Britain and Ireland* (CL263), but more than a mere revision of that work; "it has been rewritten throughout and is entirely new both in substance and in form. The text of the descriptive notices, on a more systematic plan, is new, and it includes bibliographical collations, besides a general discussion of each atlas and its history."—*Pref.* Indexed.

Continued by: Z6027.G7S55

Hodson, Donald. County atlases of the British Isles published after 1703: a bibliography. [Tewin, Welwyn, Hertfordshire], Tewin Pr., [1984]– . v.1– . il., maps. (In progress)   **CL277**

Contents: v.1, Atlases published 1704 to 1742 and their subsequent editions.

All editions of an atlas are arranged under the first, with titles listed in chronological order; a strict chronological list of all editions is presented in an appendix. Facsimiles are excluded. Contents, descriptive notes, publication history, and locations are noted. Numbers begin with 125 to continue Skelton (above). Appendixes; index.

Spain. Ejército. Servicio Geográfico. Sección de Documentación. Cartoteca historica: índice de atlas universales y mapas y planos históricos de España. Madrid, 1974. 268p.   **CL278**

In two main parts: atlases, in chronological order from the 16th

through 20th centuries (p.1–18); maps and plans of Spain printed prior to the 20th century, listed by region and city (p.19–268).

Z6027.S72S72

Thiele, Walter. Official map publications; a historical sketch, and a bibliographical handbook of current maps and mapping services in the United States, Canada, Latin America, France, Great Britain, Germany, and certain other countries. Chicago, Amer. Lib. Assoc., 1938. 356p.   **CL279**

"The primary purpose of this handbook is to serve as a guide to the map publications which are currently made available by national government mapping services."—*Pref.* Pt.1, Historical sketch; pt.2, Current government maps and mapping services, including reference lists of map publications issued by the various governments. Care of maps. Appendixes: (1) State governments of the United States as map sources; (4) Public planning organizations in the United States and their map publications; (5) List of international maps.   Z6021.T43

U. S. Library of Congress. Library of Congress catalog: a cumulative list of works represented by Library of Congress printed cards: Maps and atlases. Wash., 1953–55. 3v. Semiannual, with annual cumulations.   **CL280**

Ceased publication.

Contains entries for maps, relief models, globes, and geographical atlases, received by the Library of Congress and other American libraries participating in the cooperative cataloging program, insofar as these works are represented by Library of Congress printed cards. Arrangement is alphabetical by geographical area, with name and subject indexes.

Before 1953 and after 1955, entries are included in the *National union catalog* (AA128) and its predecessors. Currently issued on microfiche as *NUC Cartographic materials.*   Z881.A1C327

—— Maps and charts of North America and the West Indies, 1750–1789: a guide to the collections in the Library of Congress. Comp. by John R. Sellers and Patricia Molen Van Ee. Wash., Lib. of Congress, for sale by U.S. Govt. Prt. Off., 1981. 495p. il.   **CL281**

An annotated bibliography of 2,146 items, arranged by geographic area. Bibliography; index.   Z6027.N68U54

—— Geography and Map Division. The bibliography of cartography. Boston, G. K. Hall, 1973. 5v.   **CL282**

Reproduces the cards from a file maintained in the Geography and Map Division, containing some 90,000 entries relating to maps, mapmakers, and the history of cartography.

—— —— First supplement. Boston, G. K. Hall, 1980. 2v. (1028p.)

Adds about 21,500 entries, including new articles from 275 periodicals in cartography, geography, and library science, as well as a collection of approximately 4,000 pamphlets, offprints and reprints.

—— Panoramic maps of cities in the United States and Canada; a checklist of maps in the collections of the Library of Congress, Geography and Map Division. Comp. by John R. Hébert; rev. by Patrick E. Dempsey. 2d ed. Wash., Lib. of Congress, 1984. 181p. il.   **CL283**

1st ed. 1974 had title *Panoramic maps of Anglo-American cities.*

Lists 1,726 panoramic maps of cities in 47 states, the District of Columbia, and Canada. Arranged by state, then by city. Indicates artist, publisher, lithographer or printer, and map size. Indexed.

Z6027.U5L5

—— Railroad maps of the United States: a selective annotated bibliography of original 19th-century maps in the Geography and Map Division of the Library of Congress. Comp. by Andrew M. Modelski. Wash., The Library; for sale by Govt. Prt. Off., 1975. 112p. maps.   **CL284**

"Described are 622 maps chosen from more than 3,000 railroad maps and about 2,000 regional, state, and county maps, and other maps ... includes only separate printed and manuscript maps preserved in the Geography and Map Division."—*Pref.* Arranged by nation as a whole, region, state, and individual railroad lines. Descriptive notes; index. Z6026.R3U54

—— **Reference and Bibliography Section.** Fire insurance maps in the Library of Congress: plans of North American cities and towns produced by the Sanborn Map Company: a checklist. Wash., Lib. of Congress, for sale by U.S. Govt. Prt. Off., 1981. 773p. il., maps. **CL285**

A checklist of some 700,000 items in a "uniform series of large-scale maps, dating from 1867 to the present and depicting the commercial, industrial, and residential sections of some twelve thousand cities and towns in the United States, Canada, and Mexico ... an unrivaled source of information about the structure and use of buildings in American cities."—*Pref.* Arranged by country, state and town; indexed by county, city and town. Z6026.I7U54

U.S. Library of Congress. Map Division. A list of geographical atlases in the Library of Congress, with bibliographical notes. Wash., Govt. Prt. Off., 1909–74. 8v. **CL286**

v.1–4, comp. by Philip Lee Phillips; v.5–7, by Clara Egli LeGear.

Contents: v.1, Titles 1–3265 (1909); v.2, Author list and index (1909); v.3, Titles 3266–4087 (acquired 1909–14) (1914); v.4, Titles 4088–5324 (acquired 1914–20) (1920); v.5, Titles 5325–7623 (acquired 1920–55) (1958); v.6, Titles 7624–10254 (acquired 1920–60) (1963); v.7, Titles 10255–18435 (acquired 1920–69) (1973); v.8, Index to v.7 (1974).

An important catalog of an outstanding collection which includes many rare and early atlases. v.1–4 form the record of 5,324 atlases in the Library of Congress in 1920, giving for each full description and contents. v.2 is an index volume containing an author list and a detailed analytical index referring to all maps listed in the contents notes. v.3–4 are supplements to the main work, listing new acquisitions, each containing an author list and an analytical index. The author list in v.4 cumulates, combining the author lists to v.1–4, and is also published separately (1920. clxiiip.).

v.5–6, published in continuation of the Phillips catalog, bring forward the record with the same minute detail: v.5 lists world atlases acquired 1920–55; v.6 describes atlases of Europe, Asia, Africa and Oceania, the polar regions and the oceans, and includes some 800 Oriental atlases, mainly Chinese, Japanese, and Korean. Each includes full tables of contents for atlases published before 1820 and for some miscellaneous volumes published later; an author list; and a detailed analytical index to areas, subjects, maps, engravers, publishers, etc.

v.7 describes atlases of the Western hemisphere received in the Library of Congress between 1920 and 1969 (excluding atlases published after 1967). v.8 is an index to v.7. Z6028.U56

—— List of maps of America in the Library ... preceded by a list of works relating to cartography by P. Lee Phillips. Wash., Govt. Prt. Off., 1901. 1137p. (Repr.: N.Y., B. Franklin, 1967) **CL287**

Lists maps to be found in books and atlases as well as those separately issued. Describes many old state and county maps and city plans. Z663.35.L55

—— United States atlases; a list of national, state, county, city, and regional atlases in the Library of Congress, comp. by Clara Egli LeGear. Wash., Govt. Prt. Off., 1950–53. 2v. (Repr.: N.Y., Arno, 1971) **CL288**

v.2 adds "and cooperating libraries" to title.

The two volumes list almost 6,700 atlases. v.2 lists not only atlases received by the Library of Congress between 1949 and 1953, but also those held by some 180 other libraries. Location of copies is shown. Z881.U5

U.S. National Archives. Guide to cartographic records in the National Archives. [By Charlotte M. Ashby and others.] Wash., U.S. Govt. Prt. Off., 1971. 444p. **CL289**

Offers descriptive notes on the maps and aerial photographs in the Cartographic Branch of the National Archives as of July 1, 1966. Arrangement is according to the order in which the agency generating the records are listed in the *U.S. Government manual.* Detailed index. Z6028.U575

Vatican. Biblioteca Vaticana. Monumenta cartographica. Vaticana iussu Pii XII P.M. Ed., Roberto Almagia. Città del Vaticana, 1944–55. 4v. maps. 43cm. **CL290**

An extensive catalog depicting the history of cartography from the 14th to the 17th centuries. Excellent descriptions and reproductions of maps with references to sources. GA195.V3V38

Wheat, Carl Irving. Mapping the Transmississippi West, 1540–1861. San Francisco, Inst. of Historical Cartography, 1957–63. 5v. in 6. maps. 37cm. **CL291**

Contents: v.1, The Spanish *Entrada* to the Louisiana Purchase, 1540–1804; v.2, From Lewis and Clark to Frémont, 1804–1845; v.3, From the Mexican War to the Boundary Surveys, 1846–1854; v.4, From the Pacific Railroad surveys to the onset of the Civil War, 1855–1860; v.5, From the Civil War to the Geological Survey, 1861–1870's. 2v.

A beautifully produced work with detailed textual descriptions, facsimile maps, "biblio-cartographies," and references to sources. Discusses many hundreds of maps. GA405.W5

Wheat, James Clements and **Brun, Christian F.** Maps and charts published in America before 1800; a bibliography. Rev. ed. [London], Holland Pr.; [N.Y., R. B. Arkway, etc., 1978]. 215p. (Holland Pr. cartographica, 3) **CL292**

1st ed. 1969.

The "rev. ed." is merely a reprint of the 1969 ed. with the addition of a new preface followed by four additional entries.

A bibliography "which attempts to describe the entire known cartographical contribution of the American press prior to 1800."—*Pref.* Includes maps and charts appearing in books, pamphlets, almanacs, and magazines, as well as those published separately. Z6027.U5W47

Yonge, Ena L. A catalogue of early globes made prior to 1850 and conserved in the United States; a preliminary listing. N.Y., Amer. Geographical Soc., 1968. 118p. (American Geographical Soc. Library ser., 6) **CL293**

The first published work in a series proposed by the Committee on Ancient Cartography of the International Geographical Congress to provide a worldwide inventory of the present locations of early globes. GA193.U5Y6

Current

Bibliographic guide to maps and atlases, 1979– . Boston, G. K. Hall, [1980]– . Annual. **CL294**

Lists selected publications cataloged during the year of coverage by the Research Libraries of the New York Public Library and the Library of Congress. Includes individual and set maps, atlases, globes, books about maps, history and study of mapmaking, techniques, computer cartography, and cartobibliographies. Journal articles and analytics covered by the New York Public Library, as well as selected articles in non-map sources, are also included. Serves as a supplement to the New York Public Library's *Dictionary catalog of the Map Division* (CL272).

Bibliographia cartographica. no.1– , 1974– . Pullach bei München, Verlag Dokumentation, [1974–]. Semiannual. **CL295**

Issued by Staatsbibliothek Preussischer Kulturbesitz in cooperation with the Deutsche Gesellschaft für Kartographie.

Except for structural publishing changes and a new section on school cartography, this is a continuation of *Bibliotheca cartographica* (below). Author index. Z6021.B48

Bibliotheca cartographica. Bibliographie des kartographischen Schrifttums ... 1957–72. Remagen, 1957–72. Hft. 1/2–30. Semiannual. **CL296**

Continues Kosack's *Die Kartographie,* 1943–54 (CL268). Continued by *Bibliographia cartographica* (above). Issued by the Bundesanstalt für Landeskunde und Raumforschung, in cooperation with the Deutsche Gesellschaft für Kartographie.

Lists books and periodical articles on cartography in classified arrangement, including materials from several countries of Europe, South Africa, South America, and the United States. Tables of contents and subject headings in German, English, and French.

Z6021.B55

Bibliographie cartographique internationale, 1936– . Paris, Colin, 1938– . Annual (irregular).   **CL297**

Title varies: 1936–45, *Bibliographie cartographique française.*

1936 and 1937 published as *Suppléments au Bulletin du Comité National Français de Géographie,* 1938–39. 1938/45, 1946/47 each published in 1v.

1948– , published annually under the auspices of the Comité National Français de Géographie and the Union Géographique Internationale by M. Foncin and P. Sommer, with the aid of Unesco.

Lists general, political, and topographical maps and atlases; road maps; maps of cities, etc., from all parts of the world.   Z6021.B5

Guide to U.S. government maps: geologic and hydrologic maps. 1975– . McLean, Va., Documents Index, [1976–]. Annual.   **CL298**

Covers maps published by the U.S. Geological Survey since 1879; entries and annotations were taken from the Survey's *Publications* lists. Arrangement is by series, with area, subject, and coordinate indexes. Brief descriptive annotations for some entries. A list is included following each section showing maps currently available and their prices.   Z6034.U49A53

Kartograficheskaia letopis'; organ gosudarstvennoi bibliografii SSSR. 1931–1940, 1946– . Moskva, Vsesoiuznaia Knizhnaia Palata, 1932?– . Annual since 1947.   **CL299**

A section of the Soviet national bibliography which lists the year's output of maps and atlases (scientific, school, tourist, etc.) with full bibliographic description and annotation.

1931–40 and 1946, quarterly. Publication suspended 1941–45. Title for 1939 and 1940: *Bibliografiia kartograficheskoi literatury i kart.* Index, *Svodny ukazatel',* 1941–50, published 1953.

Z6021.K3

Handbooks

Lister, Raymond. How to identify old maps and globes, with a list of cartographers, engravers, publishers, and printers concerned with printed maps and globes from *c.*1500 to *c.*1850. Hamden, Conn., Archon Books, [1965]. 256p.

CL300

Gives attention to methods of map production, decorations and conventional signs, etc.   GA201.L56

Directories

Feild, Lance. Map user's sourcebook. London & N.Y., Oceana, [1981]. 194p. il.   **CL301**

A directory of organizations providing maps, with descriptive notes on major map series, especially those produced by the federal government. In four main sections: private sector, public (state) sector, federal, and international map sources. Tables; bibliography; glossary. A subject index would have increased the volume's utility.

GA105.3.F44

Map collections in the United States and Canada: a directory. 4th ed. David K. Carrington and Richard W. Stephenson, eds. N.Y., Special Libraries Assoc., 1985. 178p.

CL302

A project of the Geography and Map Division, Special Libraries Association.

1st ed. 1954.

Describes 804 map collections in the United States and Canada. Arranged alphabetically by city within a state or province. For each collection gives: name, staffing level, size of collection and annual accessions, area and subject specialization, dates, special collec-

tions, depository status, clientele, service facilities, and publications. Indexed.   GA193.U5M36

World directory of map collections. Comp. by the Geography and Map Libraries Sub-Section; ed. by Walter W. Ristow. München, Verlag Dokumentation, 1976. 326p. (IFLA pubns., 8)   **CL303**

Lists by country some 285 map and chart collections in 46 countries, with information on size and type of collection, reference services, reproduction facilities, and publications. Only selected entries for countries with existing directories of map collections (Canada, German Federal Republic, France, the United States).

GA192.W67

General

Aguilar, José. Atlas universal/Aguilar. Madrid, Aguilar, [1985]. 213p., maps. 21cm.   **CL304**

First publ. 1954. Frequently reprinted.

A general world atlas, incorporating a considerable amount of text, illustration, charts, and statistics. Includes topical world maps, maps of individual continents and countries, and a separate section on Spain and its provinces. Place-names are in language of country treated. A vocabulary of geographical terms is followed by an index of place-names.   G1019.A289

Andree, Richard. Andrees allgemeiner Handatlas in 231 Haupt- und 211 Nebenkarten. 8. neubearb. u. verm. Aufl., 5. verb. u. verm. Abdruck. Hrsg. von Ernst Ambrosius. Bielefeld, Velhagen, 1930. 2v. 45cm., 29cm.   **CL305**

Contents: v.1, Atlas; v.2, Namenverzeichnis, 644p.

One of the outstanding German atlases preceding World War II. Includes largely political maps, with some physical and economic. Still useful when up-to-date material is not needed.   G1019.A6

The atlas of the earth. Tony Loftas, ed. [London], Mitchell Beazley Ltd., [1972]. 144p., 303p. il., maps. 38cm.

CL306

Preceding the section of world maps in color is a 143-page section of illustrations and text "dealing with the formation of the Earth and its oceans, the environment they provide for the vast and varied assemblage of their animal and plant inhabitants; the origin of life, and its history during the huge span of evolutionary time."—*p.6.*

Following the world maps are sections for Europe, Asia, Africa, Australasia, and the Americas. There are also sections for climatic graphs and for national parks of the world. Map index, p.193–303. Cartography is clear and attractive and, in addition to physical and political maps, the work includes maps showing population density, vegetation, rainfall, etc., for many areas.   G1019.A873

Goode, John Paul. Goode's World atlas. 16th ed., ed. by Edward B. Espenshade, Jr. Chicago, Rand McNally, [1983]. 368p. il., maps. 29cm.   **CL307**

Formerly *Goode's School atlas,* first publ. 1923. Frequently revised.

Emphasizes physical and political maps, and maps showing resources and products. The United States is given by sections but not by individual states. Maps of city environs. An index of more than 30,000 names indicate pronunciation. An excellent, small atlas for student use.   G1021.G6

Der grosse Brockhaus Atlas; Erdkunde, Wirtschaft, Geschichte. Wiesbaden, Brockhaus, 1960. 664p. il., maps. 25cm.   **CL308**

Not numbered in the set, but designed in format and size to serve as an additional volume of *Der grosse Brockhaus* (AC42). Offers excellent small maps: political, physical, and economic. Includes sections of photographs illustrating land formations, industry, agriculture, etc., in various parts of the world. Extensive index of place-names.

Hammond Inc. [Hammond world atlases.] Maplewood, N.J., Hammond, [1982, etc.].   **CL309**

Over the years the Hammond Company has published a number of series of reputable atlases of varying size and content, and using some of the same titles to distinguish the different versions (e.g., an *Ambassador world atlas* first appeared in 1954). In 1982 the Hammond series included *Medallion, Ambassador, International,* and *Citation* volumes.

In addition to general updating of information, several innovations of the 1970s distinguish the atlases from their predecessors: a smaller page size (recommending the volumes for more convenient home and office use), the inclusion of postal zip code numbers for United States communities, and (in the larger volumes) three new sections of historical maps representing biblical, world, and United States history. There is also a section entitled "Environment and life." As in the earlier editions, an index with population figures (incorporating 1980 census data for the United States, as well as for Mexico, the Soviet Union, and the Democratic Republic of the Congo) accompanies each political map. There is also an index of more than 100,000 names for the world map section; U.S. zip codes appear in both indexes. Small topographical maps, reproductions of flags, and tables of salient facts about each country are provided with the political maps. Despite the smaller page size, maps of all but the largest and most populous political units are fairly uncluttered, legible, and generally attractive.

For a comparison of the various volumes in the "Hammond atlas family," *see Booklist* 80: 40–42 (Sept.1, 1983).

An extensive review in the *Bulletin* of the Special Libraries Association Geography and Map Division (no. 137, Sept. 1984, p.71–3) compares the *Citation, Ambassador,* and *Medallion* volumes and recommends the *Ambassador* (1982. 484p. il., maps, 32cm.).

Herder Verlag. Herders grosser Weltatlas. 7.Völlig neu bearb. u. ergänz. Aufl. Freiburg, Herder, [1976]. 464p. col.maps. 40cm. **CL310**

Frequently reprinted with minor updating.

"268 Seiten Kartenteil mit plastischer Geländedarstellung und 100,000 Namen . . . Geographische und statistische Angaben über die Länder der Erde."—*title page.* G1021.H6

Kartographishes Institut Bertelsmann. Der grosse Bertelsmann Weltatlas. Leitung, W. Bormann. [Gütersloh], Bertelsmann, [1965]. 188p., 52p., 120p. col.maps. 33cm. **CL311**

Previous edition 1961. This edition offers minor changes and updating.

Excellent maps, with good color and shading, and a wealth of detail. In two sections: (1) the major part, including maps for all parts of the world with its own extensive index, is followed by (2) a special section of maps on Central Europe with its own index. G1019.K375

Kidron, Michael and **Segal, Ronald G.** The state of the world atlas. N.Y., Simon & Schuster, [1981]. il., maps. 26cm. **CL312**

A graphic presentation of major topics of popular concern—the proliferation of nations and their claims on resources, the military situation, natural resources, government, business, labor, societal problems, the environment, protest movements and crises. Information sources and notes are provided for each of the 65 colored, double-page maps. Subject index.

A 2d, rev. ed. was published 1984 as *The new state of the world atlas.* G1021.K46

Kremling, Ernst and **Kremling, Helmut.** Der grosse JRO Weltatlas: Luxusausgabe. [1. Aufl. d. neubearb. 26. Aufl. d. Grossen JRO-Weltatlas] München, JRO Verlag, [1970]. 1v., various pagings. 44cm. **CL313**

1st ed. 1949.

In three sections: (1) Allgemeiner Teil: Die Erde in Zahlen. Die Welt von heute. Der Weltraum. Die Länder der Erde. Die Welt im Bild; (2) Kartenteil I: Physische und politische Karten der Welt, der Kontinente und der europäischen Länder mit Register; (3) Kartenteil II: Spezialkarten von Mitteleuropa. Register. G1019.K7

Larousse, *firm, publishers, Paris.* Atlas international Larousse politique et économique. [Nouvelle éd.] Publié sous la direction de Ivan du Jonchay [et] Sándor Radó. Paris,

Larousse, [1966]. Maps in portfolio, with index and statistical tables. 51cm. **CL314**

1st ed. 1950.

Title and descriptive matter also in English and Spanish.

Stresses the unifying physical and economic factors of world geography. Continents and groups of countries are given emphasis rather than the political boundaries of individual states. Includes about 75 maps (most of them folded) showing physical, political, economic, and some historical aspects of world geography, together with economic and statistical tables. While the maps are generally attractive and readable, some are too dark in color to be easily legible; others have a cluttered appearance. Includes statistical data to about 1964. G1019.L37

Maps on file. Ed. by Lester A. Sobel. N.Y., Facts on File, 1981. 1v., looseleaf. maps. 30cm. **CL315**

A looseleaf collection of approximately 350 maps designed for easy photocopying. In fourteen sections arranged by continent, theme (demography, resources, economic, social, etc.), historical period, or type (e.g., outline maps). Indexed; annual supplements.

A related title is: G1046.A1M16

Martin Greenwald Associates. Historical maps on file. N.Y., Facts on File, [1983]. 1v., looseleaf. maps. **CL316**

More than 300 maps suitable for photocopying are grouped in nine main sections: ancient civilizations; Europe to 1500 A.D.; Europe, 1500–1815; Europe, 1815 to the present; United States; Western hemisphere; Africa and the Middle East; Asia; Australia. Indexed. G1033.M128

Meyers grosser Weltatlas. Hrsg. vom Geographisch-Kartographischen Institut Meyer unter Leitung von Adolf Hanle. 3., verb. u. erw. Aufl. Mannheim, etc., Bibliographisches Institut, [1979]. 458, 140p. maps. 38cm. **CL317**

A new work designed to accompany the Meyers encyclopedia (AC46) and designated as Bd.27 of that work. Includes both political and physical maps in color (many of them folded) and an extensive index. The maps offer a wealth of detail, but unfortunately the numerous double-page spreads do not lie flat and a great deal is lost at the inner margin.

A 4th ed. is to be published 1985. G1021.M26

National Geographic Society, Washington, D.C. Cartographic Division. National Geographic atlas of the world. 5th ed. Wash., 1981, 383p. il., maps. 47cm. **CL318**

1st ed. 1963.

Well-drawn maps based on those produced for the *National geographic magazine.* Well balanced in coverage between the United States and the rest of the world, with maps by area rather than by state or country. While some maps have a crowded appearance, they are legible and generally up-to-date. Index of more than 125,000 names.

A review appears in *Booklist* 80:44 (Sept. 1, 1983); also reviewed in *Wilson library bulletin,* Feb. 1982, p.462. G1019.N38

Der neue Herder Handatlas. Hrsg. von Carl Troll. Freiburg, Herder, [1966]. 200p. maps. 55cm. **CL319**

Constitutes Bd.7–8 of *Der neue Herder* (AC45). A good general atlas.

The New York Times atlas of the world. Rev. ed. N.Y., Times Books, [1980]. 40p., 143p., 84p. maps. 38cm. **CL320**

1st ed. 1972.

A version of *The Times atlas,* "Comprehensive edition," reduced both in size and content. Reviewed in *Booklist* 78:515 (Dec. 1, 1981). G1019.N498

Odyssey world atlas. N.Y., [Odyssey, 1966]. 317p. maps. 42cm. **CL321**

Cartography by General Drafting Co., Inc.

Maps for each region are presented in parallel sequence: (1) physical features, (2) political maps, and (3) thematic maps depicting selected topics such as population, climate, vegetation, natural resources. The separation of political and relief maps, the use of relief insets on political pages, the limiting of names of physical features to those of major significance, and the decision to omit highway and rail routes have all contributed to a clear and generally uncluttered appearance. The index includes about 105,000 entries. Unfortunately there seem to be no plans for a new and updated edition. G1019.O3

Oxford University Press. The new Oxford atlas. Prep. by the Cartographic Dept. of the Oxford Univ. Pr. Rev. ed. [Oxford], Oxford Univ. Pr., [1978]. 202p. il., maps. 39cm. **CL322**

1st ed., 1951 (frequently reprinted with revisions), entitled *The Oxford atlas.*

Termed "a development rather than a straightforward second edition" (*Pref.*), the work "retains the scales, projections, sheet lines, and general colouring of its topographic maps, whilst incorporating complete revision of all information liable to change and a re-styling of certain elements of map design in the interests of greater clarity. Its thematic or special subject maps, which are particularly concerned with the basic aspects of physical geography and demography, incorporate the results of modern research and latest available information and are presented by newly-evolved cartographic techniques." Index of towns and topographical features shown on the maps (plus, in italics, some historical place-names not shown but located by reference to places shown on the maps). G1021.O9

Poland. Wojsko Polskie. Służba Topograficzna. Pergamon world atlas. Oxford and N.Y., Pergamon, 1968. 525p. 42cm. **CL323**

"Prepared and printed by the Polish Army Topographical Service."—*p.iii.* Teodor Naumienko, ed. in chief.

An English edition of *Atlas swiata,* prepared by the Topographical Service and published 1962–65. In addition to general updating (the political maps represent the world as of Jan. 1967), additional maps have been added for the United Kingdom and Canada. Scale bars in miles and altitudes in feet have been added for convenience in countries not using the metric system. Most map pages fold out, allowing presentation of large-scale maps while avoiding the problems presented by conventionally bound double-page layouts. Index of some 140,000 names. G1019.P6752

Prentice-Hall's Great international atlas. [Trade ed.] Englewood Cliffs, N.J., Prentice-Hall, [1981]. various pagings. il., maps. 37cm. **CL324**

An introductory section on the use of maps and atlases is followed by 96 pages of historical and thematic maps and illustrations. The 160 colored maps and the index were produced and copyrighted by George Philip and Son, Ltd., London; most are double-spread, 6-color physical maps of excellent clarity and detail. An "Economic section" provides basic economic statistical data for each country. Pinyin is used for Chinese names, with cross references from Wade-Giles variations. Index-gazetteer of about 55,000 entries. An extensive review appeared in *Booklist* 80:46 (Sept. 1, 1983); also reviewed in *Wilson library bulletin* (Feb. 1982, p.462).

A smaller work, the *Prentice-Hall illustrated atlas of the world* (Englewood Cliffs, N.J., Prentice-Hall, 1982. 208p. 29cm.), also includes photographs and statistical information along with the maps and index-gazetteer, but a review in *Library journal* 108:577 (Mar. 15, 1983) terms the maps "too small for serious atlas users" and concludes that "Libraries seeking an inexpensive or moderately priced general world atlas would do better to select . . . *Goode's World Atlas,* the *Rand McNally Cosmopolitan World Atlas,* or the *Hammond Ambassador World Atlas.*"

Also derived from Philip's maps are the *Prentice-Hall new world atlas* (Englewood Cliffs, N.J., Prentice-Hall, 1984. 48, 128, 96p. 29cm.) and the *Prentice-Hall world atlas* (Englewood Cliffs, N.J., Prentice-Hall, 1984. 80, 61p. 29cm.). A review in *Choice* (Feb. 1985, p.797) describes them as appropriate for the undergraduate library and the home collection, respectively. The *Prentice-Hall American world atlas* (Englewood Cliffs, N.J., Prentice-Hall, 1984. various pagings. 31cm.) focuses on the United States and North America; *Booklist* 82:322 (Oct. 15, 1985) described it as a "good, inexpensive atlas for home and school use" although a *Choice* review (July–Aug. 1985, p.1620) noted inconsistencies. G1021.P7

Rand McNally and Co. Rand McNally cosmopolitan world atlas. Census ed. Chicago, [1981]. 1xip., 142p., 159p. il., col.maps. 38cm. **CL325**

1st ed. 1949; 1965, 1966, and 1967 editions had title *Rand McNally new cosmopolitan world atlas.*

In this atlas the world has been mapped on a regional basis, centered around a major country or group of countries, with a special preliminary section on the world's environment. Maps are clear and up-to-date. Includes maps for individual states of the United States and the Canadian provinces, with small insets for areas of large cities. There is also a special section of "World metropolitan area maps." Special tables include world political information by country, tables of distances, list of principal lakes, rivers, islands, etc. Economic and historical maps appearing in some earlier editions of the *Cosmopolitan* atlas are omitted here.

Like the Hammond company (*see* above), Rand McNally publishes a series of atlases of varying size, content, and price range. These include the Rand McNally *Family world* edition, its *Premier,* and *Worldmaster* atlases, all of which derive largely from the *Cosmopolitan.* A review offering comparative information on the atlases of this series appears in *Booklist* 80:42–3 (Sept. 1, 1983), 81:1320 (May 15, 1985) and 81:1649–50 (Aug. 1985). G1021.R35

———— The new international atlas. Chicago, Rand McNally, [1980]. 320, 232p. col. il., col. maps. 39cm. **CL326**

Editorial and cartographic direction, Russell L. Voisin, Jon M. Leverenz.

Title and prefatory matter in English, German, Spanish, French, and Portuguese.

1969 ed. had title: *The international atlas.*

In the interest of wide international usage, the metric system is employed, and there is strong emphasis on the local language for geographic names throughout, with English used only for names of major features extending across international borders. Maps were designed as components of five series: (1) continents portrayed in natural colors at 1:24,000,000; (2) political maps of major regions of the world, at 1:12,000,000; (3) inhabited areas of the earth at 1:6,000,000 or 1:3,000,000, depending on population density; (4) key regions of the world at 1:1,000,000; and (5) major urban areas at 1:300,000. Map sequences follow from world to metropolitan maps; individual map layouts depict geographic and economic regions rather than individual countries. Concluding portion of the atlas offers a series of thematic maps, glossary, tables of geographic changes, population of cities and towns, and an index of 160,000 names. Maps are exceptionally clear and easy to interpret.

A very positive review appeared in Special Libraries Association Geography and Map Division's *Bulletin* (no.141, Sept. 1985, p.69–70); also reviewed favorably in *Wilson library bulletin* (Feb. 1982, p.462), and in *Booklist* (78:560–61, Dec. 15, 1981).

———— Our magnificent earth: a Rand McNally atlas of earth resources. N.Y., Rand McNally in assoc. with Mitchell Beazley, London, [1979]. 208p. il., maps. 37cm. **CL327**

Originally publ. under title: *Atlas of earth resources* (London, M. Beazley, 1979).

An attempt to describe in textual and graphic form the status of natural resources such as minerals, the various forms of energy, water, land, forests, fish, etc. It has been "planned and organized on the basis of self-contained, two-page spreads" (*p.9*) with "connections" boxes on each spread suggesting related readings on other pages. Section on planning for tomorrow features useful statistics and predictions in graphic form. Glossary, bibliography, and index. G1046.G3R34

Russia (1923– U.S.S.R.) Glavnoe Upravlenie Geodezii i Kartografii. Atlas mira. 2. izd. [Redaktsionnaia kollegiia: A. N. Baranov i dr.] Moskva, 1967. 250p. maps. 51cm. **CL328**

———— Ukazatel' geograficheskikh nazvanii. 2.izd. Moskva, 1968. 533p.

1st ed. 1954; English translation of text and legends by V. G. Telberg published in New York, 1956.

A general world atlas, prepared by the Chief Administration of Geodesy and Cartography of the Ministry of Internal Affairs. Maps are primarily locational, emphasizing centers of population, communication routes, hydrography, relief, and political-administrative boundaries. Maps of the USSR make up something less than 20% of the total (somewhat less than in the first edition). Plans of the world's large cities are included. Non-Russian names are phonetically transcribed into Cyrillic characters. The index volume (*Ukazatel' geograficheskikh nazvanii*) includes more than 190,000 names.

G1019.R96

—— The world atlas. 2d ed. Moscow, 1967. 250p. maps. 51cm. **CL329**

An English-language edition of *Atlas mira* (above).

G1019.R9602

—— Fiziko-geograficheskii atlas mira. Red. koll. IU. V. Filippov i dr. Moskva, 1964. 289p., 249 col.maps. 32x50cm. **CL330**

249 colored plates are supplemented by explanatory text. Includes relief and physical maps: geology, meteorology, hydrology, soil, vegetation, zoology, etc. Plates 2–76 contain maps of the world, the Arctic, and the Antarctic; 78–190, the continents; 192–249, SSSR.

Legends and explanatory text have been published as:

Soviet geography: review and translation. Physical-geographic atlas of the world. Moscow, 1964. N.Y., American Geographical Society, [1965]. 403p. (*Its* Special issue of May–June 1965) **CL331**

"A translation of the legend matter and explanatory text of the *Fiziko-Geograficheskiy Atlas Mira.* . . ."—*p.1.*

Russia (1923– U.S.S.R.) Glavnoe Upravlenie Geodezii i Kartografii. Geograficheskii atlas; dlia uchitelei srednei shkoly. 4-e izd. Moskva, 1980. 238p. maps. 38cm. **CL332**

A world atlas of which 60 plates are devoted to the USSR, and 95 plates to other world areas. Although designed as a teaching aid for secondary schools in the Soviet Union, it is useful for its economic maps and other special features not included in map form in the *Atlas mira* (above).

An *English guide,* by John P. Cole and Dennis R. Mills, was published in 1956 by the Dept. of Geography, Univ. of Nottingham. 73p. G1019.S.57

Snead, Rodman E. Atlas of world physical features. N.Y., Wiley, [1972]. 158p. maps. 29cm. **CL333**

103 maps depict landforms such as fault zones, volcanoes, rivers and drainage basins, and glaciation; many other related natural physical aspects such as mangrove vegetation, coral reefs, and tidal vegetation are also depicted on world and regional maps. Explanatory text; bibliography; index. G1046.C1S6

Stieler, Adolf. Stieler's Atlas of modern geography; 263 maps on 114 sheets, engraved on copper. 10th ed. International ed., publ. by Dr. Hermann Haack, with the cooperation of Dr. Berthold Carlberg and Rudolf Schleifer. Gotha, Perthes, 1934–38. Pts.1–34. maps. 41cm. **CL334**

No more published.

One of the best of the prewar German atlases. This edition appeared in parts and was to have been completed in some 114 sheets. It was a thorough revision—with addition of various, entirely new sheets—of the 10. Aufl. of *Stieler's Handatlas* (Gotha, Perthes, 1931/32. 40cm.).

In the International edition, the maps are in the language of the country mapped; explanatory notes, etc., are in English, French, German, Italian, Portuguese, and Spanish. Also published with French title.

The 1931/32 edition included 108 sheets of maps, most of them double spreads, and an index of 337 pages.

The Times, London. The Times atlas of the world: mid-century edition, ed. by John Bartholomew. London, Times Pub. Co., 1955–59. 5v. (chiefly col. maps) 50cm. **CL335**

Earlier ed. 1920.

A thoroughly revised edition of a famous atlas designed for general, official, and library use. Gives as many place-names as possible, preferably in the form of spelling officially used by the inhabitants of a given country. "In the case of important places

where English practice has familiarized an alternative form of the name" (*Pref., v.3*), this is also shown, in brackets, both forms appearing in the index. Elevation is shown by color tints. Main roads, airports, etc., are indicated.

Each volume covers a different section of the world, and each has its own index-gazetteer: v.1, World, Australasia and East Asia (1958); v.2, Southwest Asia and Russia (1959); v.3, Northern Europe (1955); v.4, Southern Europe and Africa (1956); v.5, The Americas (1957). G1019.T52

The Times atlas of the world. Comprehensive ed. [6th ed.] [N.Y.], Times Books, [1980]. 123 plates, 227p. maps. 46cm. **CL336**

Maps prep. by John Bartholomew & Son, Ltd., Edinburgh, based on those in the 1955–59 ed. (above). A publication of *The Times,* London.

1st ed. 1967.

In addition to general updating, Mainland China names are given in Pinyin spelling in this edition. An extremely fine atlas. Reviewed in *Booklist* 78:1273–74 (May 15, 1982). G1021.T55

Touring Club Italiano. Atlante internazionale . . . 8. ed. Milano, [Touring Club Italiano], 1968. 173 col.maps (partly folded). 49cm. **CL337**

"Opera redatta . . . sotto la direzione di Luigi V. Bertarelli, Olinto Marinelli, Pietro Corbellini. Nuova edizione interamente rielaborata a cura di Manilio Castiglioni e Sandro Toniolo."—*verso of title page.*

1st ed. 1927.

One of the finest of the European atlases, devoted to physical and political geography. Most of the maps are double-page spreads, hinged so that they lie flat and nothing is lost at the inner margin; some have an additional fold-out section. Maps are beautifully produced, include great detail, and have insets for major metropolitan areas. Place-names are in the spelling of the country concerned, and are indexed in the separate index of some 250,000 names.

—— Indice dei nomi. Milano, 1968. 1032p.

G1019.T6

Vidal de la Blache, Paul Marie Joseph. Atlas historique et géographique Vidal-Lablache. 385 cartes et cartons; index de 32,000 noms. Paris, Colin, 1951. 130 [i.e., 134]p., 30p., incl. 98 col.maps. 40cm. **CL338**

1st ed. 1894: *Atlas général Vidal-Lablache.* Frequently reprinted before World War II with revisions.

Includes historical, physical, political, economic maps, etc., with an index-gazetteer. This edition reduced in size from the pre-World War II editions. G1019.V53

The world book atlas. Chicago, World Book, [1981]. 446p. il., col. maps. 29cm. **CL339**

First published 1964; frequently reprinted with minor updating.

Designed as a complement to the *World book encyclopedia* (AC22), and planned for student use. Arranged by large groupings; under each has physical, political, and historical maps. Individual maps for states of the United States. Population tables are followed by a general index, which includes place-names, islands, rivers, mountains, etc. Maps and index are essentially the same as *Goode's World Atlas* (CL307). G1019.R5285

National and regional

United States

Adams, John S. A comparative atlas of America's great cities: twenty metropolitan regions. [Minneapolis], Univ. of Minnesota Pr., [1976]. 503p. il., maps. 34cm. **CL340**

Editor, Ronald Abler; text, John S. Adams and Ronald Abler; chief cartographer, Ki-Suk Lee.

A product of the Comparative Metropolitan Analysis Project of the Association of American Geographers, Cambridge, Mass., which published two companion volumes: *Contemporary metropolitan*

America: twenty geographical vignettes and *Urban policymaking and metropolitan dynamics: a comparative geographical analysis* (1976).

The atlas is in four parts: (1) Introduction; (2) Current patterns in American cities (with comparative maps for housing, the people, socio-economic characteristics, and topics of special interest for each city or Standard Metropolitan Statistical Area); (3) Metropolitan problems (offering maps showing aspects of metropolitan physical environment, open space for metropolitan leisure-time use, housing, transportation and communication, metropolitan growth, education, public health, socio-economic segregation, employment and poverty, urban renewal); and (4) Policy requisites for American metropolitan regions. Glossary; index/gazetteer.   G1201.A1A3

Andriot, John L. Township atlas of the United States; named townships. [2d ed.] McLean, Va., Andriot Associates, 1979. 1184p. maps. 29cm.   **CL341**

1st ed. 1977.

"The purpose of this volume is to provide a handy atlas showing the named townships which exist today, their relative size and location within the county, and a detailed index to the 46,900 townships. . . ."—*Foreword.* Each section on a particular state contains a state map showing all counties with a county location index, and a state name index of all incorporated places and unincorporated places of 1,000 or more population, giving the name of the county where each is located; within each state section, county maps are alphabetically arranged. The township index concludes the volume.

Coverage has been expanded for all minor civil divisions from 22 states in the 1st ed. to the entire 50 states. Reproduces census maps from the 1970 Census of Population, with comparable maps taken from the 1950 or 1940 censuses for states having census county divisions. Maps for each state show counties, census county divisions, election precincts, urbanized areas, and other minor civil divisions. A companion volume is Andriot's *Population abstract* (CG86).   G1201.F7A5

Historical atlas and chronology of county boundaries, 1788–1980. John H. Long, ed. Boston, G. K. Hall, 1984. 5v. maps. 29cm.   **CL342**

Produced in cooperation with the Hermon Dunlap Smith Center for the History of Cartography, the Newberry Library.

Contents: v.1, Delaware, Maryland, New Jersey, Pennsylvania; v.2, Illinois, Indiana, Ohio; v.3, Michigan, Wisconsin; v.4, Iowa, Missouri; v.5, Minnesota, North Dakota, South Dakota.

Scale ca.1:625,000. For each state provides a chronology of county boundary developments, followed by maps of individual counties and chronology of that county's boundary changes; bibliographies. Regional history maps show development of county boundaries every ten years.   G1201.F7H47

Martin Greenwald Associates. State maps on file. N.Y., Facts on File, [1984]. 1 atlas in 7v. maps. 30cm.   **CL343**

Contents: [v.1] New England; [v.2] Mid-Atlantic; [v.3] Southeast; [v.4] Midwest; [v.5] Mountain and prairie; [v.6] Southwest; [v.7] West.

Scales vary widely. For each state maps generally illustrate county and legislative district boundaries, topographic areas, rivers and waterways, precipitation, agricultural and mineral products, population density, historical Indian tribes, early exploration and settlement. There is great variation in the historical maps. Volumes are sold separately or as a set.   G1200.F3

Rand McNally and Co. Rand McNally commercial atlas and marketing guide. N.Y., Rand McNally, 1876– . 53cm. Annual.   **CL344**

Primarily an atlas of America, as most of the maps included are of that region, but includes a section of maps of foreign countries with its own index. United States maps are indexed individually by state. Includes many statistical tables of population, business and manufacturers, agriculture, and other commercial features.

An airline map of the United States and a road atlas of the United States, Canada, and Mexico are issued as supplements.

U.S. Geological Survey. The national atlas of the United States of America. Wash., 1970. 417p. maps. 49cm.
                CL345

An impressive work "designed to be of practical use to decision makers in government and business, planners, research scholars, and others needing to visualize countrywide distributional patterns and relationships between environmental phenomena and human activities."—*Introd.* In plan and progress for more than 20 years, the work was produced with the cooperation and assistance of 84 federal agencies and bureaus.

Includes 765 maps, many of them double-page spreads, presenting in cartographic format "the principal characteristics of the country, including its physical features, historical evolution, economic activities, socio-cultural conditions, administrative subdivisions, and place in world affairs."—*Introd.* Sources of information represented on the special subject maps are indicated either on the map itself or in an introductory note. Index of 41,000 entries for names of political entities, populated places, and physical and cultural features appearing on the maps.   G1200.U57

Handbooks

Thompson, Morris Mordecai. Maps for America; cartographic products of the U.S. Geological Survey and others. 2d ed. [Reston, Va., U.S. Dept. of the Interior, Geological Survey Nat. Ctr.; Wash., for sale by Govt. Prt. Off., 1981] 265p. il., maps.   **CL346**

1st ed. 1979.

Offers detailed descriptions of kinds of maps and map data, as well as various sources of maps and related information, which are available from United States government agencies. Glossary and bibliographic references; index.   GA405.T46

Africa

Africana Publishing Company, New York. Liberia in maps. Stefan Gnielinski. N.Y., 1972. 111p. maps. 29 cm.
                CL347

Offers a series of black-and-white line maps on physical geography, history, social conditions, agriculture, rural and urban life, economic conditions, communications, transport, etc. Explanatory text; bibliography; glossary.

The same publisher has issued *Malawi in maps,* by Swanzie Agnew and Michael Stubbs (N.Y., 1972. 143p.); *Nigeria in maps,* by K. Michael Barbour [and others] (N.Y., 1982. 148p.); *Sierra Leone in maps,* by John I. Clarke (2d ed. N.Y., 1972. 120p.); *Tanzania in maps,* by L. Berry (N.Y., 1972. 172p.); and *Zambia in maps,* by D. Hywel Davies (N.Y., 1972. 128p.).

Les Atlas Jeune Afrique. Paris, Jeune Afrique.   **CL348**

This publisher's series includes several good atlases of francophone sub-Saharan Africa; they offer color thematic maps and accompanying text, with glossary and index, in a 29 to 30cm. format. The list includes:

Atlas de la République Unie du *Cameroun.* Georges Laclavère. 1979. 72p.

Atlas de la République *Centrafricaine.* Pierre Vennetier. 1984. 64p.

Atlas de la République Populaire du *Congo.* Pierre Vennetier. 1977. 64p.

Atlas de la *Côte d'Ivoire.* Pierre Vennetier [and others]. 2e. éd., rev. et mise à jour. 1983. 72p.

Atlas de la *Haute-Volta.* Yves Péron. 1975. 47p.

Atlas du *Mali.* Mamadou Traoré [and others]. 1980. 64p.

Atlas de la République Islamique du *Mauritanie.* Charles Toupet and Georges Laclavère. 1977. 64p.

Atlas du *Niger.* Edmond Bernus and Sidikou A. Hamidou. 1980. 64p.

Atlas du *Sénégal.* Paul Pélissier. 1980. 72p.

Atlas du *Togo.* Yema E. Gu-Konu. 1981. 64p.

Institut Géographique National (France). The atlas of Africa. Régine van Chi-Bonnardel, ed. N.Y., Free Pr., [1974]. 335p. il., col. maps. 42 cm.   **CL349**

Also published in French as *Grand atlas du continent africain* by Éditions Jeune Afrique.

General physical and thematic maps are followed by maps for individual countries. Each country section has accompanying text.
G2445.F72

West African international atlas. Atlas international de l' Ouest Africain. [Dakar, Univ. de Dakar, Inst. Fondamental d'Afrique Noire, 1968–71] 1v. Looseleaf. maps. 55cm. **CL350**

Running title: *International atlas of West Africa.*
Folded plates with explanatory matter issued in installments.
On cover: Under the auspices of the Organisation of African Unity, Scientific, Technical and Research Commission, and with the assistance of the Ford Foundation.
Explanatory text in French and English. Detailed physical and relief maps, plus maps of geology, climate, zoogeography, sources of energy, administrative and political boundaries, etc.   G2640.W4

Antarctica

American Geographical Society of New York. Antarctic map folio series. [Vivian C. Bushnell, ed. N.Y.], Amer. Geographical Soc., 1964–75. 19v. maps. 44cm.   **CL351**

"The objective of the . . . Series is to summarize in a succinct manner the present knowledge of the Antarctic . . . [with each folio] devoted to one subject or scientific discipline."—*Ed.note.* Each folio consists of introductory text and bibliographic references, and numerous plate maps. Topics covered include hydrographic data, birds, fishes, morphology, marine sediments, mammals, and the history of Antarctic exploration and scientific investigation.
G3100.A4

Sovetskaia antarkticheskaia ekspeditsiia, 1955– . Atlas Antarktiki. [Glav. red. E. I. Tolstikov] Moskva, Glavnoe Upravlenie Geodezii i Kartografii MG SSSR, 1966–69. 2v. il., maps. 60cm.   **CL352**

A major atlas with sections on history, physical geography, geology, climate, morphology, oceanography, biology, etc.
G3100.S6

Arab countries

Dempsey, Michael W. Atlas of the Arab world. N.Y., Facts on File, [1983]. ca.118p. il., maps. 25cm.   **CL353**

38 double-page four-color maps provide graphic presentation of geographic and socioeconomic aspects of the Arab world. Brief gazetteer entries are made for each country. Statistical sources are indicated for each map in a descriptive notes section.
DS63.7.D45

Argentina

Randle, Patricio H. Atlas del desarrollo territorial de la Argentina. Buenos Aires, OIKOS, [1981]. 1v., 313*l.* of col. maps. 55cm.   **CL354**

Accompanied by two *anexos:* "Memoria" and "Serie de estadísticas históricas" (37cm.).
Contents: El territorio se configura; La producción y la población; El equipamiento territorial; El proceso de urbanización.
A major national atlas illustrating both historical and contemporary geography. Scale ca. 1:10,000,000. The "Memoria" provides explicative text for the atlas maps; "Statistics" includes figures presented graphically in the socio-economic maps.   G1755.R3

Asia, Southeast

Djambatan Uitgeversbedrijf, N.V., Amsterdam. Atlas of south-east Asia, with an introduction by D. G. E. Hall. London, Macmillan; N.Y., St. Martin's, 1964. 84p. il., maps. 35cm.   **CL355**

60 colored maps of the countries and islands of southeast Asia,

usually showing climate, agriculture, population, minerals and industries, communications, etc. Includes plans of the larger cities.
G2360.D5

Australia

Australia. Dept. of National Development. Geographic Section. Atlas of Australian resources. 2d ser. Canberra, 1962–75. 30 col. maps. 75x72cm. folded to 37x19cm.   **CL356**

Issued in sheets, each accompanied by a commentary.
1st ser. publ. 1952–60 by Dept. of National Development, Regional Development Div.
Contents: Landforms; Geology; Mineral deposits; Climate; Temperature; Rainfall; Surface water resources; Groundwater; Water use; Soils; Natural vegetation; Land use; Croplands; Crop production; Fish and fisheries; Mineral industry; Electricity; Manufacturing industries; Population distribution; Immigration; Railways; Roads and aerodromes; Ports and shipping; Government; Major urban areas; Livestock; Sheep and wool; Grasslands; Forest resources; Locational index.
Maps range in scale from 1:36,000,000 to 1:250,000. Each map is accompanied by an illustrated booklet written by specialists especially for this series. The series designation indicates a process of continuous revision; a third series was begun in 1977, with a single map for "Roads and aerodromes" issued to date. A 3d ser. began publication 1980.   G2751.G3A3

Reader's Digest atlas of Australia. Produced in conjunction with the Div. of Nat. Mapping, Dept. of Nat. Resources, who prepared the maps. Ed. and designed by Readers Digest Services Pty. Sydney, Readers Digest Services, 1978. 287p. il., maps. 40cm.   **CL357**

The 148 topographical maps were originally prepared for the *International map of the world* (a topographical map series published by each national survey department for its own territory, at a uniform scale and in a uniform style) and were revised in 1976–77; scale is 1:1,000,000. Pages 161–216 consist of text, diagrams, graphs, and thematic maps illustrating history, population, government, and economic conditions. Index-gazetteer of about 40,000 names.   G2750.R4

Austria

Akademie der Wissenschaften, Vienna. Kommission für Raumforschung und Wiederaufbau. Atlas der Republik Österreich. Hrsg. unter der Gesamtleitung [von] Hans Bobek und unter redaktioneller Mitarbeit von Erik Arnberger [et al.]. Vienna, Freytag-Berndt & Artaria, 1961–80. Looseleaf. 47x73cm. (In progress)   **CL358**

A detailed national atlas covering a wide range of topics.
G1935.A3

Belgium

Comité National de Géographie, Belgium. Atlas de Belgique. Atlas van België. Bruxelles, Inst. Géographique Militaire, 1950–72. Looseleaf. col. maps. 62cm.   **CL359**
G1865.C6

Bolivia

Instituto Nacional de Estadística (Bolivia). Atlas censal de Bolivia. [La Paz], 1982. 294p. maps.   **CL360**

Data is based on the 1976 census; includes statistics on population, housing, language, etc.   G1746.E1I5

Brazil

Ira, Rudolf and **Klettner, Edgar.** Atlas do Brasil globo, com os mapas político e físico do Brasil e os mapas dos seus estados e territórios . . . Índice remissivo e descritivo dos topônimos pelo Lourenço Mario Prunes. Rio de Janeiro, Ed. Globo, [1960]. 98p. maps. 45cm. **CL361**

33 plates of colored maps, physical and regional. Index-gazetteer.
G1775.I7

Canada

Canada gazetteer atlas. [Toronto], Publ. by Macmillan of Canada in co-operation with Energy, Mines and Resources Canada and the Canadian Government Publishing Centre, Supply and Services Canada, 1980. 164p. maps. 46cm.
CL362

Also published in French under title *Canada atlas toponymique.*
". . . a completely new reference work, consisting of 48 [double-page] maps and an index giving the name, status, population, and position of the populated places recorded in the 1976 Census of Canada. Selections of physical features, roads, railways, and important national and provincial parks are also included. . . ."—*Introd.*
Names are given "in the language actually approved by the respective name authorities for the provinces and territories." Serves as a complement to the *National atlas of Canada* (below).
G1115.C6313

Canada. Surveys and Mapping Branch. Geography Division. The national atlas of Canada. 4th ed. (rev.). Toronto, Macmillan, 1974. 254p. maps. 38cm. **CL363**

1st ed. 1906. 1st–3d eds. publ. under title *Atlas of Canada;* 1st– 2d eds. issued by the Dept. of the Interior; 3d ed. issued by the Geographical Branch.
The 4th ed. (1970–73) was first issued in a small press run of loose sheets. The bound volume supersedes those sheets.
A 5th ed. began publication 1980. G1115.C55

Handbooks

Nicholson, Norman Leon and **Sebert, L. M.** The maps of Canada: a guide to official Canadian maps, charts, atlases and gazetteers. [Folkestone, Kent, Eng., Dawson; Hamden, Conn., Archon, 1981] 251p. il., maps. **CL364**

A survey of official publications and their uses. Appendixes; bibliographic notes and references; index. GA471.N52

Caribbean region

Atlas regional del Caribe. [Havana], Editorial Academia [y] Editorial Científico-Técnica, [1979]. 69p. il., maps. 33x53cm. **CL365**

"Departamento de Geografía Económica del Instituto de Geografía de la Academia de Ciencias de Cuba."—*t.p.*
Table of contents in Spanish and English.
Maps, with text, are topically arranged within categories such as general political and economic structures, agriculture, population, industry, transport, foreign trade, national income.

Central America

Atlas of Central America. Stanley A. Arbingast [and others]. [Austin], Bureau of Business Research, Univ. of Texas at Austin, [1979]. 62p. maps. 28x37cm. **CL366**

Presents relief, thematic, and geological maps for the area and for Guatemala, Belize, Honduras, El Salvador, Nicaragua, Costa Rica, and Panama. Statistical sources are noted. G1550.A8

China

Chang, Chi-yun, ed. National atlas of China. 1st–2d ed. Taiwan, National War College, 1960–67. 5v. **CL367**

v.2–3 (1st ed.) have title *Atlas of the Republic of China.*
Contents: v.1, Taiwan (2d ed., 1967); v.2, Hsitsang (Tibet), Sinkiang and Mongolia (1st ed. 1960); v.3, North China (1st ed., 1961); v.4, South China; v.5, General maps of China.
Place-names appear both in Chinese characters and in romanization; indexes from both forms.
The general maps illustrate communications, climate, soils, vegetation and forestry, agriculture, fishing, livestock, minerals, population, and major languages. No more published?

Hsieh, Chiao-min. Atlas of China, ed. by Christopher L. Salter. [N.Y., McGraw-Hill, 1973] 282p. il., maps. 31cm.
CL368

Maps are grouped in four main sections: (1) Physical; (2) Cultural; (3) Regional; and (4) Historical. Background text and explanatory text accompany the maps. Indexed (separate index for the historical section). G2305.H83

The Times atlas of China. [London], Times Books; [N.Y.], Quadrangle/New York Times Book, [1974]. xlp., 145p., 27p. il., maps. 39cm. **CL369**

Editors and chief contributors: P. J. M. Geelan, D. C. Twitchett; Cartographic consultant, John C. Bartholomew & Son, Ltd.
Offers maps and explanatory text representing a variety of historical, economic, and physical topics, maps of the provinces of China, and a section of city plans. Wade-Giles system of transcription of Chinese names is used on the maps. In the index names are arranged alphabetically by Wade-Giles transcription with the Pinyin transcription following; cross references are provided from the old Post Office spellings. It is clearly stated in the Introduction that some of the information is fairly tentative since "detailed geographical and particularly statistical information at the time of writing is, by Western standards, hard to come by." G2305.T47

U.S. Central Intelligence Agency. People's Republic of China—atlas. Wash., Govt. Prt. Off., 1971. 82p. il., maps. 44cm. **CL370**

"This volume goes beyond the scope of a conventional atlas. It presents a wider variety of information, including geographic, economic, historical, and cultural data. . . . To make so much information . . . as meaningful as possible, a great deal of it is placed in a familiar context—that is, by drawing comparisons between China and the United States."—*Pref.*
Issued commercially as *Rand McNally illustrated atlas of China* (Chicago, Rand McNally, 1972. 80p. 39cm.). G2305.U55

Colombia

Instituto Geográfico "Agustín Codazzi." Atlas de Colombia. 3. ed., rev. y aumentada. Bogotá, Instituto, 1977. 283p. il., maps. 49cm. **CL371**

1st ed. 1967.
A national atlas with historical, physical, and thematic maps; also includes maps of smaller administrative divisions such as *departamentos* and cities.
The Instituto has also published regional atlases of Colombia: *Atlas regional andino* (1982. 168p. 49x40cm.) and *Atlas regional pacífico* (1983. 96p. 49cm.). G1730.C65

Costa Rica

Sánchez Chinchilla, Luis Angel and **Flores Silva, Eusebio.** Atlas estadístico de Costa Rica, no.2. [Prep. en la Sección de Cartografía Censal] 2a ed. San José, Costa Rica, Dirección General de Estadística y Censos, Oficina de Planificación Nacional y Política Económica, 1981. [184p.] il., maps. 30x45cm. **CL372**

A revised edition of *Atlas estadístico de Costa Rica* (1953).
Presents maps, city plans, diagrams and graphs based on the censuses of 1950, 1963 and 1973. G1580.S2

Cuba

Instituto Cubano de Geodésia y Cartografía. Atlas de Cuba: XX aniversario del triunfo de la revolución cubana. La Habana, El Instituto, 1978. 143,[25]p. il., maps. 26x36cm. **CL373**

Presents thematic and relief maps, most on a 1:300,000 scale, with a place-name index. More thematic maps are available in the *Atlas demográfico de Cuba,* prepared by the Comité Estatal de Estadísticas (La Habana, Instituto Cubano de Geodésia y Cartografía, 1979. 99p.). G1605.I5

Czechoslovakia

Česká Akademie Věd a Umění, Prague. Atlas Republiky Československé. Atlas de la République Techécoslovaque. [Praze, Nákl. Akc. Spol. Orbis, 1935–36] 2v. maps. 44cm. **CL374**

"Publié par l'Académie Tchèque sous les auspices du Ministère des Affaires Étrangères de la République Tchécoslovaque."—*verso of title page.*
In two parts: (1) atlas of 55 double plates of maps (442 maps); and (2) accompanying text. 43p.
A good, detailed atlas, covering economic and physical geography, demography, political and cultural aspects, etc.

Kartografie *(firm).* Atlas ČSSR. [Spracovala Kartografie; zodpovědny redaktor Jindřich Svoboda; zodpovědny redaktor slovenského vydania Josef Ščipák] 6. vyd. Bratislava, Slovenská Kartografia, 1982. 1v. (14p., 42p. of plates). maps. 33cm. **CL375**

A small, up-to-date atlas with some city maps. G1945.K3

Denmark

Nielsen, Niels. Atlas over Danmark, Tekst og Fotografier. København, H. Hagerup, 1949–61. v.1–2. 29cm. and atlas 55cm. **CL376**

Contents: v.1, Landskabsformerne, forfatter Axel Schou. Text and atlas; v.2, Befolkningen, forfatter Aage Aageson. Text and atlas. No more published? G2055.N5

Europe

Bartholomew/Scribner atlas of Europe: a profile of Western Europe. Edinburgh, Bartholomew; N.Y., Scribner, [1974]. 128p. il., maps. 31cm. **CL377**

Presents economic and social information on 18 countries through maps, graphs, diagrams, and tabulations. Data presented is for the 1960–70 period. Most illustrations show data for all 18 countries; individual country maps and statistical profiles are also included. Glossary, list of sources, and subject and individual country map indexes.

Collins (William) Sons and Company, Ltd. Collins road atlas: Europe. London, Collins, 1965. 232p., 70p. maps. 24cm. **CL378**

Intended as a guide for the "planning stage" of a European motor trip, giving essential information for outlining a trip. Includes mileage-distance tables. G1796.P2C6

Göttinger Arbeitskreis. Staats- und Verwaltungsgrenzen in Ostmitteleuropa: historisches Kartenwerk ... München, Oldenbourg, 1954–55. v.1–3. maps. 31cm. (Der Göttinger Arbeitskreis. Veröffentlichungen, 114–116) **CL379**

Maps in portfolios. No more published.

Contents: I, Die baltischen Lande, bearb. von H. Laakmen; II, Das Preussenland, bearb. von Erich Keyser; III, Pommern, bearb. von Franz Engel. G2081.F7G6

Hammond Incorporated. Hammond atlas of European cities. Maplewood, N.J., Hammond, [1967]. 95p. maps. 20cm. **CL380**

For the tourist. Main thoroughfares are clearly marked on small maps of the heart of each city. G1799.A1H3

Finland

Finland. Maanmittaushallitus. Fennia: suuri Suomi-kartasto: kartverk över Finland. Finland in maps. Finnischer Atlas. Kartat ja paikannimihakemiston laatinut, Maanmittaushallitus. [Espoo], Weilin & Göös, [1979]. 224p. maps. 30cm. **CL381**

Title and prefatory matter also in Swedish, English and German.
Colored topographic maps with road and highway information, on a 1:250,000 scale. Based on information and maps derived from the National Board of Survey's *Road map of Finland* (1:200,000) and its *Basic map of Finland* (1:20,000) of about 1977. Includes maps of major city centers. Index of about 9,000 place names.
G2075.F44

Geografiska Sällskapet i Finland, Helsingfors. Suomen kartasto, 1960. Atlas of Finland. Atlas över Finland. Helsinki, Otava, [1961] 12p. 39 maps. 46cm. **CL382**

———— ———— Teksti. [1961] 123p.

1st ed. 1899; 3d ed. 1925.
Explanatory text in Finnish, English, and Swedish. Covers physical, economic, and social geography. G2075.G42

France

Atlas départemental. Cartes conçues et réalisées par la Société Française d'Études et de Réalisations Cartographiques. Documentation rassemblée par Jean Barbier et Nicole Boubounelle. ... Paris, Larousse, [1983]. 313p. maps. 18cm. **CL383**

Small maps in color of each département are accompanied by statistical notes based on censuses from 1975–82. Place-names index. G1844.20.A78

Centre d'Études de Géographie Tropicale. Atlas des départements français d'outre-mer. Réalisé par le Centre de Géographie Tropicale du C.N.R.S., Bordeaux-Talence.... Paris, Institut Géographique National, [1975–82]. 4v. il., maps. 49x59cm. **CL384**

Contents: v.1, La Réunion; v.2, La Martinique; v.3, La Guadeloupe; v.4, La Guyane.
Comprehensive atlases of French overseas departments.
G1835.C4

Comité National Français de Géographie. Atlas de France. 2.éd. ... Paris, Éd. Géographiques de France, 1951–59. 2v. fold., col. maps in portfolio. 50cm. **CL385**

1st ed. 1933–45.
A regional atlas of the highest grade, covering geomorphology, climatology, hydrography, biogeography, agriculture, industry, commerce, and human and political geography. G1840.C6

Sélection du Reader's Digest. Service Artistique. Grand atlas de la France. [Paris], Sélection du Reader's Digest, [1969]. 244p. il., maps. 41cm. **CL386**

An atlas devoted exclusively to France, with 48 physical maps on the scale of 1:500,000. There is also a section of small thematic maps, a pictorial section, and an index. G1840.S4

Great Britain

Gt. Brit. Ordnance Survey. The Ordnance Survey atlas of Great Britain. Ordnance Survey [and] Country Life Books. [London], Country Life Books, [1982]. 224p. maps. 31cm. **CL387**

Pages 18–143 present Ordnance Survey maps on a 1:250,000 scale (basically regional physical maps with highway information). Thematic maps with accompanying text illustrate the historical geography of Britain from prehistoric times through the late 19th century (p.144–57) and modern Britain (p.158–79). Index map key to the Ordnance Survey maps on front and back endpapers.

G1812.2.G7

Oxford University Press. Atlas of Britain and Northern Ireland, planned and directed by D. P. Bickmore and M.A. Shaw . . . Oxford, Clarendon Pr., 1963. 200p. maps. 53cm. **CL388**

Index unpaged.

A beautifully reproduced atlas intended to do for the United Kingdom what national atlases have done for other countries, although this work was not issued as a state publication. The Editorial Committee was composed of a group of outstanding geographers and economists who were assisted by numerous scholars and official bodies.

Covers England, Scotland, Wales, and Northern Ireland with major emphasis on physical and economic maps, representing mainly conditions in the mid-20th century. Maps are clear, with good color and design. Comparative statistics are printed on the maps, and authorities, notes, and sources given. Includes a gazetteer index of some 16,000 names.

G1810.O85

Reader's Digest Association, Ltd. The Reader's Digest complete atlas of the British Isles. London, [1965]. 229p. il., maps. 40cm. **CL389**

Subtitle: Including Great Britain, England, Wales, and Scotland, with the Orkney and Shetland Islands, Northern Ireland, the Channel Islands, Jersey, Guernsey and associated islands, Isle of Man, and the Republic of Ireland.

In addition to detailed regional maps, there are smaller maps illustrating various aspects of political and natural history, economics, climate, population, etc.

G1810.R4

Ireland

Irish National Committee for Geography. Atlas of Ireland. Dublin, Royal Irish Academy, 1979. 104p. il., maps. 42cm. **CL390**

A thematic atlas for the whole of Ireland, with some 250 maps grouped in 13 sections: general reference; geology and geophysics; geomorphology and hydrology; soils; climate; flora and fauna; settlement, population; primary production; manufacturing; tertiary activities; society and culture; the Irish landscape (air photographs). There is an additional section of ordnance survey maps. (For historical maps the user is referred to v.9 of *A new history of Ireland,* [DC386], still in preparation.) A high percentage of maps are at a scale of 1:1,250,000, although there are several double-page spreads at a larger scale, and numerous smaller maps. Indexed.

G1830.I7

Israel

Israel. Mahleket ha-Medidot. Atlas of Israel; cartography, physical geography, history, demography, economics, education. Jerusalem, 1956–64. 1v., looseleaf. maps. 50cm. **CL391**

Title page and text in Hebrew; above title from added title page.

Includes about 100 double sheets of maps grouped in sections for Cartography, Geomorphology, Geology, Climate, Hydrology, Zoology, Botany, History, Population, Agriculture, Industry, etc. Maps are handsomely printed in as many as 15 colors, with explanatory

texts overleaf. While some maps are restricted to Israel, Palestine is represented wherever reliable information is available.   G2235.I8

———— Atlas of Israel; cartography, physical geography, human and economic geography, history. [2d ed.] Amsterdam, publ. by Survey of Israel, Ministry of Labour, Jerusalem, and Elsevier, 1970. 1v., various pagings. maps. 49cm. **CL392**

Represents a 2d, English-language, edition of the looseleaf edition published in Hebrew (above). The work has been revised, slightly condensed, and brought up-to-date for this edition.   G2235.I82

Italy

Dainelli, Giotto. Atlante fisico-economico d'Italia; 82 tavole, 508 carte. Milan, Consociazione Turistica Italiana, 1940. xviip., 82 maps. 49cm. **CL393**

———— ———— Note illustrative, a cura del Aldo Sestini. 1940. 147p.

Shows physical features, geology, volcanoes, climatology, vegetation, population, labor, agriculture, industries, communication, education, etc.

Jamaica

Clarke, Colin G. Jamaica in maps: graphic perspectives of a developing country. Cartography by Alan G. Hodgkiss. N.Y., Africana Publ. Co., [1974]. 104p. il., maps. 23x29cm. **CL394**

Contains 42 black-and-white sheet maps, each accompanied by a brief essay. Bibliography.   G1625.C5

Japan

Kokudo Chiriin. The national atlas of Japan / Geographical Survey Institute. [Tokyo, Japan Map Center, 1977] 366p. il., maps. 61cm. **CL395**

In English.

Consists of approximately 85 thematic maps over double-facing pages, with explanatory text, seven regional maps, and a list of administrative areas. Scales of principal maps are 1:2,500,000 and 1:4,000,000. Socio-economic thematic maps are based on figures from the 1970 census; sources are indicated. Detailed introduction; index of place names.   G2355.K57

Kokusai Kyōiku Jōhō Sentā. Atlas of Japan: physical, economic, and social. 2d [rev.] ed. Tokyo, Internat. Soc. for Educational Information, 1974. 64p., 64p. maps. 37cm. **CL396**

Prep. under the joint guidance of Akira Ebato and Kazuo Watanabe.

1st ed. 1970.

Text in English, French, and Spanish.

64 map plates illustrating land forms, weather, cities, population, agriculture and land use, mineral resources, manufacturing industries, cultural elements, and transportation, are followed by 64 pages of explanatory notes. Figures have been updated for the 1970–73 period. Map of Japan in pocket.   G2355.K65

Kenya

Kenya. Survey of Kenya. National atlas of Kenya. 3d ed. [Nairobi], The Survey, 1970. 103p. il., maps. 41cm. **CL397**

1st ed. 1959.

About 40 full-page maps with descriptive text and illustrations on facing pages; some historical maps and city plans. Gazetteer-index.   G2530.K42

Luxembourg

Luxembourg. Ministère de l'Education Nationale. Atlas du Luxembourg. [Luxembourg, 1971–76] Looseleaf. il., maps. 50cm.   **CL398**

In six main sections: historical, physical, administrative, demographic, economic, and social.   G1870.L8

Mexico

Atlas of Mexico. [2d ed.] Stanley A. Arbingast [and others], eds. [Austin], Bureau of Business Research, Univ. of Texas at Austin, [1975]. 164p. il., maps. 28x37cm.   **CL399**

1st ed. 1970.
A section of physical maps is followed by groups of topical maps showing population distribution, agricultural production, transportation, commerce, and industry.   G1545.A9

El territorio mexicano. Víctor M. Ruiz Naufal, Ernesto Lemoine, Arturo Gálvez Medrano. México, Instituto Mexicano del Seguro Social, 1982. 2v. il., maps. 39cm. plus 1 portfolio (176 sheets of col. maps, 46x48cm).   **CL400**

Contents: t.1, La nación; t.2, Los estados.
A monumental work of historical geography focusing on the mid-sixteenth century until about 1930. Both volumes are heavily illustrated with facsimile plans and maps which include descriptive contents notes. The portfolio contains facsimile plates of about 36 maps dating from the mid-sixteenth century to 1980. There are both general and cartographic bibliographies. A beautiful work.
F1226.T47

Namibia

National atlas of South West Africa (Namibia). Ed., J. H. van der Merwe. Goodwood, Cape [Town], Nat. Book Printers, 1983. [184]p. il., maps. 31cm.   **CL401**

In English and Afrikaans.
Presents 92 maps, mostly thematic, in seven sections: orientation; natural environment; settlement structure; population structure; economic structure; infrastructure; urban structure. No index.

New Zealand

McLintock, Alexander H. A descriptive atlas of New Zealand. Wellington, R. E. Owen, Govt. Printer, 1960. 109p. maps. 31cm.   **CL402**

Textual material on New Zealand geography and related topics is followed by an extensive map section. Index.   G2795.M3

New Zealand atlas. Ed. by Ian Wards. Wellington, A. R. Shearer, Govt. Printer, 1976. 291p. il., maps. 32cm.
CL403

Although undertaken as a revised edition of *A descriptive atlas of New Zealand* ed. by A. H. McLintock (above), only two maps are carried over from that work; the rest of the compilation, cartographic and textual, is new.
"The aim has been an even balance between cartographic exposition, textual explanation and photographic illustration, each complementary to the other."—*Introd.* In addition to topographic maps (including numerous maps of urban areas), there are maps showing discovery and settlement, population distribution, climate, geology, forests, fauna, fishing, mineral resources, etc. Index gazetteer. Beautifully illustrated.   G2795.N4

New Zealand in maps. Ed. by A. Grant Anderson; cartography by Don Branch, Denis Kelsall, Jacqueline Malcolm. London, Hodder and Stoughton, [1977]. 141p. il., maps. 34cm.   **CL404**

Black-and-white line maps with accompanying text, prepared by the faculty of the Dept. of Geography, Univ. of Auckland. In five main parts: physical environment; biological environment; population and settlement; economic organization; economic and social infrastructure. Bibliography.   G2796.G1N4

Pacific Islands

Atlas of the South Pacific. [Wellington, Publ. for the External Intelligence Bureau, Prime Minister's Dept. by the Dept. of Lands and Survey, 1979] 46p. maps. 45x33cm.   **CL405**

About 20 maps of South Pacific countries with text on facing pages giving facts on land area, geology, soil types, vegetation, climate, population, ethnic groups, language, land use, and the economy. Scales vary. Relief maps, with index map and gazetteer index.   G2862.S6A8

Kennedy, Thomas Fillans. A descriptive atlas of the Pacific islands: New Zealand, Australia, Polynesia, Melanesia, Micronesia, Philippines. 3d ed., rev. and extended. Wellington, N. Z., Reed, [1974]. 79p. il., maps. 24cm.   **CL406**

Black-and-white maps with descriptive text. Intended for school use in the Pacific Islands and surrounding countries but of value for bringing together maps of the main island groups and the more important individual islands.   G2860.K4

Philippines

Fund for Assistance to Private Education. Philippine atlas. Manila, The Fund, 1975. 2v. (304p., 125p.) il., maps. 39cm.
CL407

Contents: v.1, A historical, economic and educational profile of the Philippines; v.2, Directory of schools, assistance groupings, and index.
v.1 surveys the situation of the Philippines in the world in terms of land area, population and education; describes, through text, maps, and illustrations, the physical geography, history, culture, population, and economy; and describes the educational structure. v.2 gives descriptive data on 695 higher education institutions, identifies public and private sources of educational funding, and includes name/place and general index.   G2391.G1F8

Hendry, Robert S. Atlas of the Philippines. [Manila, Phil-Asian Pub., 1959] 228p. il., col.maps. 49cm.   **CL408**

Political and economic maps of the islands, with separate maps for each province, and historical sketch. Gives area and population, roads, etc.   G2390.H4

Portugal

See also CL414.

Girão, Aristides de Amorim. Atlas de Portugal. Atlas of Portugal. 2. ed. . . . Coimbra, Inst. de Estudos Geográficos, Faculdade de Letras, 1957–59. [177] p., incl. 43 maps (part col.). 43cm.   **CL409**

1st ed. 1941.
Issued in parts, in portfolio. In Portuguese and English.
Maps cover geology, topography, climate, vegetation, population, agriculture, industries, etc.   G1976.G1G5

Portugal. Ministerio das Corporações e Segurança Social. Gabinete de Planeamento. Atlas sócio-económico. Lisboa, Centro de Informacão e Documentacão, [1971?]. 131p. maps. 43cm.   **CL410**

Presents a variety of social and economic facts based on the 1960 and 1970 censuses.   G1976.E1P6

Rwanda

Atlas du Rwanda. Réalisateurs Christian Prioul [et] Pierre Sirven. [Réalisé avec le concours du Ministère de la Coopération de la République Française pour le compte de Univ. de Kigali, i.e., Univ. Nationale du Rwanda] [Nantes], Assoc. pour l'Atlas des Pays de Loire, 1981. 75p. il., maps. 32x45cm.   **CL411**

22 full-page maps with descriptive text on facing pages. Bibliography.   G2539.5.A8

South Africa

Reader's Digest Association South Africa. Reader's Digest atlas of Southern Africa. Produced in conjunction with the Directorate of Surveys and Mapping, Dept. of Community Development. [Cape Town, Reader's Digest Assoc. of S.A., 1984] 256p. il., maps. 44cm.   **CL412**

Thematic maps of South Africa begin the volume (p.1–75) and are followed by six-color relief maps based on the official topographic maps prepared by the South African Directorate of Surveys and Mapping (p.76–213). Scales range from 1:50,000 to 1:1,000,000. An index map is included in pocket. Gazetteer index of about 30,000 place names (some both in English and Afrikaans); subject index to thematic maps. A handsome volume.   G2565.R4

Talbot, A. M. and **Talbot, William John.** Atlas of the Union of South Africa; prep. in collaboration with the Trigonometrical Survey Office, and under the aegis of the National Council for Social Research. Pretoria, Govt. Printer, 1960. 178p. maps (part col.). 45x58cm.   **CL413**

English and Afrikaans; added title page in Afrikaans.

Maps, in black-and-white, cover: relief, geology, vegetation, fisheries, etc.; climate and water resources; population; agriculture; industries and occupations; transportation; external trade.

G2566.J1T3

Spain

Atlas de España y Portugal. Realización, Victoria Zalacain, con la colaboración de B. Blanc [et al.]. [Paris, Zalacain, 1982] 144p. il., maps. 22x29cm.   **CL414**

Presents maps illustrating physical geography, climate, soils, migration, economic situation, social conditions, and population (based on the 1970 censuses). Particularly strong on economic themes. Place name index.   G1960.A8

Spain. Instituto Geográfico y Catastral. Atlas nacional de España. Madrid, 1965. 2v. and 100 folded maps in portfolio. 56cm.   **CL415**

An impressive national atlas with detailed physical and thematic

maps. Includes geology, climate, hydrology, population, energy, industry, agriculture, commerce, communications, culture, etc. The two bound volumes comprise *Reseña geográfica de España* and *Indice toponímico.*   G1965.S65

Sweden

Svenska Sällskapet för Antropologi och Geografi. Atlas över Sverige. Stockholm, Generalstabens Litografiska Anstalts Förlag, [1953–71]. il., maps. Looseleaf. 44cm.   **CL416**

Issued in fascicles.

A regional atlas of Sweden on some 150 folio-size sheets (including 520 maps in all) with descriptive text. Arranged in sections, with material on geophysics and geology, meteorology and hydrography, pasturage and animal husbandry, population, agriculture, forestry, industry, communications, trade, economic conditions, social conditions, cultural development, political geography, and history. Extensive English summaries of the Swedish textual material in each folio section, and parallel English headings for all maps and tables.

G2070.S8

Union of Soviet Socialist Republics

Dewdney, John C. The U.S.S.R. in maps. N.Y., Holmes & Meier, [1982]. 117p. maps. 27x24 cm.   **CL417**

"This volume contains 49 [full-page] maps and diagrams, each with a page (or more) of supporting text, designed to illustrate the present-day geography—physical, human and economic—of the Union of Soviet Socialist Republics. . . . "—*Introd.* Black-and-white maps. Classed bibliography; index.   G2110.D5

Venezuela

Venezuela. Dirección de Cartografía Nacional. Atlas de Venezuela. 2.ed. [Caracas], Ministerio del Ambiente y de los Recursos Naturales Renovables, Dirección de Información e Investigación del Ambiente, Dirección de Cartografía Nacional, 1979. 331p. il., maps. 46cm.   **CL418**

1st ed. 1969.

A national atlas with many thematic maps for demography, economic conditions, communications, etc., as well as physical and political maps.   G1725.V4

D

History and Area Studies

❖Many approaches are possible to the study of history, ranging from the school child's concentration on his text-book to the scholar's search for original sources. Furthermore, the term "history" no longer concerns itself mainly with the political and military history of individual countries, but is often interpreted to include all the various aspects of life in a country or in a larger area. Therefore, "area studies" have become more and more important. These may treat the topography, ethnology, natural resources, religion, sociology, economy, law, government, history, culture (or any combination of these) for an area, large or small. Such area studies are listed in this section, as well as the more conventional historical guides, bibliographies, handbooks, dictionaries, and encyclopedias. In addition to more traditional tools, the librarian and researcher should keep in mind newer approaches such as the various numerical databases now available. But, while bibliographic databases offer new methods of access to citations, the online sources do not replace the printed works for easy scanning and browsing.

A few of the large general histories which contain detailed bibliographies and indexes are listed, but, for the most part, history texts are not included here even though in actual reference work they will sometimes be very useful.

It should be remembered, also, that for many historical questions, materials in other parts of this *Guide* will be needed: encyclopedias, biographical dictionaries, atlases, gazetteers and guidebooks, statistical compilations, national and special library collections, indexes to periodicals and government publications, and many others. Materials in the social sciences sections in particular often have special relevance for students of history and area studies, and placement of individual items was not always easy. Generally speaking, the following guidelines governed placement of reference works in certain inter-related areas: (1) most materials on ethnic groups and women, whether general, historical, or sociological in nature, are listed in section CC, "Sociology"; (2) popular culture titles are in CF, "Mythology, Folklore, and Popular Culture"; (3) works on the conduct of diplomacy and military affairs are cited in sections CJ, "Political Science" and CK, "Law," while the foreign relations and military history of a country are in the relevant "History and Area Studies" subsection; (4) compilations of historical statistics are to be found in section CG, "Statistics and Demography." Although selected items have

been entered in more than one section, users of the *Guide* are urged to follow up the *see also* references to other item numbers and to consult the general index for additional references.

The first section (DA) contains the general works and the chronological periods of history: Archaeology and ancient history (with Classical antiquities as a subsection thereunder), Medieval and Renaissance, and Modern.

The succeeding sections (DB–DH) are arranged by continent and subdivided as follows: (1) General works on the continent; (2) Sections of the continent; (3) Countries arranged alphabetically—with the exception that under "The Americas," the United States and Canada are followed by the countries of Latin America.

D A

General History

GENERAL WORKS

Guides

American Historical Association. Guide to historical literature. George Frederick Howe, Chairman, Board of Editors. N.Y., Macmillan, 1961. 962p. **DA1**

A successor to the *Guide to historical literature,* ed. by George M. Dutcher [and others] (N.Y., Macmillan, 1931). The new *Guide,* generally similar in plan, is a selective, annotated bibliography of treatises and source materials, arranged in broad subject and country groups, each group selected and described by specialists. Within each section, materials are arranged as practicable by form, e.g., bibliographies, encyclopedias and dictionaries, general and specialized histories, biographies, government documents, printed collections of sources, etc.

Although somewhat dated, it remains an important first aid for students and librarians. Z6201.A55

Poulton, Helen J. The historian's handbook; a descriptive guide to reference works. Norman, Univ. of Oklahoma Pr., [1972]. 304p. **DA2**

A bibliographic guide to major reference sources for the student and beginning researcher. Includes library catalogs, statistical guides, almanacs, newspaper indexes, quotation dictionaries, etc. Many of the illustrative examples are drawn from American history. General index and index of titles. Z6201.P65

Walford, Albert John. Walford's Guide to reference material. 4th ed. [London], Lib. Assoc., 1982. v.2. **DA3**

For full information *see* AA507.

v.2 is devoted to the social and historical sciences, philosophy and religion.

Historical method

Barzun, Jacques and **Graff, Henry F.** The modern researcher. 4th ed. San Diego & N.Y., Harcourt Brace Jovanovich, [1985]. 450p. **DA4**

1st ed. 1957.

The 4th ed. is a thorough revision of the text, with much new illustrative material. The authors have skillfully combined a manual of research methods, an essay on the evaluation and interpretations of facts, and a textbook on the writing of acceptable expository English. Designed for "anyone who is or will be engaged in research and report writing . . ." *(Foreword)*, it is probably most useful to graduate students in the humanities and the social sciences since examples and bibliographical citations emphasize research in the field of history. New material on the use of computers, word processors, and data banks and "the place and function in the contemporary mind of psycho-history, quantified history, and the vast literature of retrospective sociology."—*Note.* DB13.B334

Shafer, Robert Jones, ed. A guide to historical method. 3d ed. Homewood, Ill., Dorsey, 1980. 272p. **DA5**

1st ed. 1969.

Intended for the student of history at the college level, particularly for use "in a tutorial situation in which the beginning researcher receives aid from an experienced scholar."—*Pref.* Supplies additional information on concepts and methodologies of the social and behavioral sciences, the function of inference in historical reasoning, problems of exposition, etc. This edition includes a section on quantitative method and expands the material on writing.
D16.S47

Bibliography

C.R.I.S: the combined retrospective index set to journals in history, 1838–1974. Annadel N. Wile, exec. ed., . . . introduction and user's guide by Evan I. Farber. Wash., Carrollton Pr., 1977–78. 11v. **DA6**

Contents: v.1–4, World history; v.5–9, United States history; v.10–11, Author index.

Offers selective indexing of more than 900 journals in history, political science, and sociology under four or five keyword or subject headings. Topical arrangement within geographical areas. Author index. Similar to the same publisher's combined indexes for political science (CJ15) and sociology (CC5).

Inasmuch as indexing was done by computer, and because entries are not duplicated and cross referencing is skimpy, care should be taken to check all relevant sections. Z6205.C18

Czarra, Fred R. and **Irwin, Leonard Bertram.** A guide to historical reading: non-fiction; for schools, libraries, and the general reader. 11th rev. ed. Wash., Heldref Publ., [1983]. 312p. (McKinley bibliographies, v.2) **DA7**

1st–6th eds. made up part of Hannah Logasa's *Historical fiction;* 7th–8th eds., by Logasa, had title *Historical non-fiction,* as did the 9th rev. ed. (1970) by L. B. Irwin; 10th ed. (1976) had present title.

An annotated list of books of history, most of them published since 1950. Arranged by geographical area, with period divisions for Europe and the United States. Each section subdivided for books for adult readers and those for young adults (junior and senior high school students). In this edition there is a "new category added on the Middle East and Near East and the categories on Asia and Africa have been expanded."—*Introd.* Author/title index. Z6201.I7

Gilmore, William J. Psychohistorical inquiry: a comprehensive research bibliography. N.Y., Garland, 1984. (Garland reference library of social science, v.156) 317p. **DA8**

A bibliography of the literature of psychohistory; coverage aims to be comprehensive for English-language materials, with a selection of citations in other languages. Sections on bibliography and methodology are followed by geographical sections listing psychohistorical studies; the sections for European and United States civilization are further subdivided topically and by time period. Author index; lack of a subject index lessens the work's usefulness. Z6208.P78G54

Harvard University. Library. General European and world history; classification schedule, classified listing by call number, chronological listing, author and title listing. Cambridge, Mass., Harvard Univ. Lib.; distr. by Harvard Univ. Pr., 1970. 959p. (Widener Library shelflist, 32) **DA9**

For a note on the series *see* AA145.

Encompasses the H, HB, HP, and "Crus" classes from the Widener shelflist—some 37,000 titles. The H and HB classes provide for world history and the history of Europe in general, though it should be noted "that most European wars before World War I are in the various classes for a particular country or region."—*p.3.* "The HP class includes scholarly journals devoted to European or world history and covering the whole field of history of the medieval and modern periods."—*p.36.* The "Crus" class is devoted to the Crusades, and this section updates and supersedes v.1 of the shelflist series. Z6209.H34

Holtzmann, Walther and **Ritter, Gerhard.** Die deutsche Geschichtswissenschaft im zweiten Weltkrieg; Bibliographie des historischen Schrifttums deutscher Autoren 1939–1945, hrsg. im Auftrag des Verbandes der Historiker Deutschlands und der Monumenta Germaniae Historica. Marburg/Lahn, Simons Verlag, 1951. 149p., 512p. **DA10**

In two parts: pt.1, Pre-history and ancient history; pt.2, Medieval and modern history. Author index.

Covers German historical writings of the war years and thus helps to supplement the *International bibliography of historical sciences* (DA22) and the *Jahresberichte für deutsche Geschichte* (DC183a), which were suspended during this period. Z6201.H6

International Committee of Historical Sciences. Bibliographie internationale des travaux historiques publiés dans les volumes de "Mélanges," 1880/1939–1940/50. . . . International bibliography of historical articles in Festschriften and miscellanies. Établie avec le concours des comités nationaux sous la direction de Hans Nabholz par Margarethe Rothbarth et U. Helfenstein. Éd. par le Comité International des Sciences Historiques. Paris, Armand Colin, 1955–65. 2v. **DA11**

Contents: v.1, 1880–1939; v.2, 1940–1950, avec compléments au Tome 1.

Mélanges are grouped by country, with a classified index and a name index. v.2 has two additional indexes which combine references to both Tome 1 and Tome 2 for the complete 1880–1950 period: one of persons treated in the studies, the other of geographical subjects dealt with. Z6201.I5

Jahresberichte der Geschichtswissenschaft; im Auftrage der Historischen Gesellschaft zu Berlin. 1.–36. Jahrg., 1878–1913. Berlin, Mittler, 1880–1916. 36v. Annual. **DA12**

Publisher varies.

International in scope, listing the historical works published in each year. A valuable record for the period covered. The section for

Germany is continued by *Jahresberichte für deutsche Geschichte* (DC183a) and its continuation (DC184). Z6201.J25

Kaplan, Jonathan. International bibliography of Jewish history and thought. München, K. G. Saur; Jerusalem, Magnes Pr., 1984. 483p. **DA13**

At head of title: Rothberg School for Overseas Students, The Hebrew University; Dor Hemschech Institutes, The World Zionist Organisation.

Text in English and Hebrew.

A selective bibliography designed "to furnish the educator, the student and the librarian with a basic list of books that are of major importance for the study of Jewish History and the History of Jewish Thought, and to assist them in the selection of books best suited to their respective needs and interests."—*Introd.* More than 2,000 items (briefly annotated) in Hebrew, English, German, Spanish, Portuguese and French; selection criteria are spelled out in the introduction. A section on general works is followed by four chronological sections (topically subdivided) and one on Jewish communities throughout the world. Index of names.

The final chapter is supplemented by Morris Fine's *Israel-Diaspora relations; a selected annotated bibliography 1973-1983* (N.Y., Inst. on American Jewish–Israeli Relations, Amer. Jewish Committee, 1983. 45p.). Z6366.K34

Koner, Wilhelm. Repertorium über die vom Jahre 1800 bis zum Jahre 1850 in Akademischen Abhandlungen, Gesellschaftsschriften und wissenschaftlichen Journalen auf dem Gebiete der Geschichte und ihrer Hülfswissenschaften erschienenen Aufsätze. Berlin, Nicolai, 1852–56. 2v. (Repr.: Graz, Akademische Druck- und Verlagsanstalt, 1968) **DA14**

A closely classified bibliography with subject index of articles on historical subjects appearing in some 500 periodicals and society publications in various languages. Includes some American publications. v.2, p.76–169, lists biographical articles arranged alphabetically by subject. The names of these biographees do not appear in the index. Z6205.K82

Palumbo, Pier Fausto. Bibliografia storica internazionale, 1940–1947; con una introduzione sullo stato degli studi storici durante e dopo la seconda guerra mondiale. Roma, Ed. del Lavoro, 1950. 1xiii p., 241p. **DA15**

Partially fills the period still not covered by the *International bibliography of historical sciences* (DA22). A long introductory section outlines the course of historical studies in various countries during and after World War II; the bibliographical listings are by broad period, subdivided by subject. Periodical articles are included, and there are indexes by author and by subject. Z6201.P3

Reuss, Jeremias David. Repertorium commentationum a societatibus litterariis editarum. Secundum disciplinarum ordinem . . . T.8, Historia. . . . Gottingae, Dieterich, 1810. 674p. (Repr.: N.Y., B. Franklin, 1961.) **DA16**

Contents: Historia—subsidia historica (geographia, chronologia, monumenta veterum populorum, inscriptiones, numi et res numaria, ars diplomatica, heraldica); Historia universalis; Historia generis humani; Historia mythica; Historia specialis—Asiae, Africae, Americae, Europae; Historia ecclesiastica; Historia litteraria.

A valuable index to the publications of the learned societies of various countries up to 1800. Classed arrangement with author index.

For description of complete set *see* EA22. Z5051.R442

Revue d'histoire ecclésiastique: bibliographie. v.1– . Louvain, Université Catholique de Louvain, 1900– . Quarterly. **DA17**

v.1-55, "Bibliographie" issued as pt.II of the *Revue;* v.56– , "Bibliographie" issued as a separately paged section in each issue.

An extensive bibliography of books, articles, and reviews published throughout the world on the history of the church. In four main sections, subdivided by topic: (1) Sciences auxiliaires; (2) Publications de sources et critique des sources; (3) Travaux historiques proprement dits; (4) Compte rendus d'ouvrage précédement annoncés. Name index. BX940.R5

Current

Bibliography of historical works issued in the United Kingdom, 1940/45–1971/75. London, Univ. of London, Inst. of Historical Research, 1947–77. 6v. **DA18**

Publisher varies.

Editor varies: 1940/45 (publ. 1947), by Louis B. Frewer; 1946/56 (publ. 1957), by Joan C. Lancaster; 1957/60 (publ. 1962), 1961/65 (publ. 1967), 1966/70 (publ. 1972), by William Kellaway; 1971/75 (publ. 1977), by Rosemary Taylor.

Volume for 1940/45 edited for the British National Committee of the International Committee of Historical Sciences, with title: *Bibliography of historical writings published in Great Britain and the Empire.* Later volumes compiled for the Anglo-American Conference of Historians.

The 1940/45 volume followed the pattern of the *International bibliography of historical sciences* (DA22) and was a record of the books and periodical articles published in Great Britain and the Commonwealth during the period of coverage, on all aspects of history. Later volumes do not include periodical articles or publications of Commonwealth countries. Works inadvertently omitted from a given volume are included in the next.

Historical abstracts, 1775–1945; bibliography of the world's periodical literature . . . Erich H. Boehm, ed. v.1–16, 1955–70. Santa Barbara, Calif., Clio Pr. with the Internat. Social Science Inst., 1955–70. v.1–16. Quarterly. **DA19**

Publisher varies. Subtitle varies.

An abstract journal, with signed abstracts contributed by scholars, mainly from the United States. To 1964 covers the world's periodical literature on history from 1775 to 1945, in a classified arrangement with annual author, biographical, geographical, and subject indexes (these vary). After 1964 the United States and Canada are excluded (*see America: history and life,* DB47). D299.H5

—— Five year index. v.1–5. 1963; v.6–10. 1965; v.11–15. 1970; 16–20, 1979.

Includes subject and author indexes.

—— v.17, no.1– , Spr. 1971– . Santa Barbara, Calif., Amer. Bibliographical Center, 1971– . Quarterly. **DA20**

Contents: Pt.A, Modern history abstracts, 1450–1914; pt.B, Twentieth century abstracts. (Each pt. issued quarterly; no.4 of each pt. is a cumulative index.)

Now selectively indexes some 2,200 journals, articles in *Festschriften* and homage volumes, and, with v.31 (1980), includes citations for books and dissertations. Dissertation citations are drawn from *Dissertation abstracts international* (and therefore the list is not exhaustive); book citations are selected from reviews in *Choice, Library journal,* and eleven English-language history journals. D299.H5●

—— [Retrospective index], v.26–30. Santa Barbara, Calif., Amer. Bibliographical Center, 1980– . (In progress) **DA21**

When completed, these volumes will offer retrospective indexing of journal articles omitted from the series prior to 1971 (when scope was expanded to include the period 1450 to the present). In addition, they provide indexing of earlier volumes of numerous journals added to *Historical abstracts* at various periods over the years.

The "List of periodicals surveyed for *America: history and life* and *Historical abstracts*" (rev. 1980) appears in v.26A, p.707–32; it gives the years of coverage for each journal indexed. D299.H5●

International bibliography of historical sciences, ed. for the International Committee of Historical Sciences . . . 1926– . Oxford, Univ. Pr.; N.Y., Wilson, 1930– . v.1– . Annual; occasionally biennial. (Repr.: N.Y., Kraus, 1963. v.1–14, 16–41) **DA22**

Subtitle: Internationale Bibliographie der Geschichtswissenschaften; Bibliografía internacional de ciencias históricas; Bibliographie internationale des sciences historiques; Bibliografia internazionale delle scienze storiche.

Imprint varies: Paris, Colin; Rome, P. Maglione; Berlin, W. de Gruyter; Madrid, Ed. Hernando; beginning 1980, publ. by K. G. Saur, München.

A very useful selected, classified list of historical publications, interpreted in a wide sense to include political, constitutional, religious, cultural, economic, and social aspects; international relations; etc. Includes references to critical reviews.

Interrupted during World War II; v.15, to cover 1940–46, has not been published; v.49 (covering 1980) published 1984 latest received.

Z6205.I61

Recently published articles. v.1, no.1– , Feb. 1976– . Wash., Amer. Historical Assoc., 1976– . 3 issues per yr.   **DA23**

The classified, current bibliography formerly published as part of the regular issues of the *American historical review.* Arranged by country, subdivided by period as warranted. Includes articles in collections as well as periodicals. The United States section cumulates into the annual volumes of *Writings on American history.*

Z6205.A49a

Dissertations

See also DC286.

Canada. Public Archives. Register of post-graduate dissertations in progress in history and related subjects. Répertoire des thèses en cours portant sur des sujets d'historie et autres sujets connexes. no.1– , 1966– . [Ottawa], Canadian Historical Assoc., 1966– . Annual.   **DA24**

For full information *see* DB192.

Jacobs, Phyllis M. History theses 1901–70: historical research for higher degrees in the universities of the United Kingdom. [London], Univ. of London, Inst. of Historical Research, 1976. 456p.   **DA25**

An attempt to provide a comprehensive list of theses "completed and approved for the degree of B.Litt. and for doctor's and master's degrees in universities of the United Kingdom."—*Introd.* More than 7,600 entries; classed arrangement with author and subject indexes. Unfortunately, it is "not a list of theses which are necessarily available for consultation, since in nearly all British universities it is only in relatively recent years that students have been required to place a copy of their work on deposit." A supplement covering 1971–80, comp. by J. M. Horn, was published 1984 (294p).

Although regularly published lists of research for university degrees have been issued by the Institute of Historical Research from 1920 to date (DC286), the compiler went beyond a mere cumulation of the printed lists, attempting to verify citations, correct errors, and winnow out theses which may have been listed as completed but which were, in fact, never approved.

For annual lists issued by the Institute *see* DC286.   Z6201.J23

Kuehl, Warren F. Dissertations in history; an index to dissertations completed in history departments of United States and Canadian universities. [Lexington], Univ. of Kentucky Pr., 1965–[72]. 2v.   **DA26**

Contents: [v.1], 1873–1960; v.2, 1961–June 1970.

Intends to include "only those doctoral dissertations which have been written under formally organized departments of history and for which the degree of doctor of philosophy has been conferred."—*Introd., v.1.* It does not, therefore, include dissertations of a historical nature completed in a related discipline. The first volume lists more than 7,600 dissertations; the second, about 5,900, including some from the 1873–1960 period omitted from the earlier volume. Arrangement is alphabetical by author, with detailed subject index. (Indexing of v.2 was done largely from abstracts rather than title alone, and is therefore more complete.) No attempt has been made to indicate publication information.

A volume covering dissertations of 1970–80 was published in 1985 by ABC-Clio, Santa Barbara (466p.).   Z6201.K8

List of doctoral dissertations in history in progress or recently completed in the United States, 1909–1970/73. Wash., Amer. Historical Assoc., 1909–74. 50v.   **DA27**

Title varies; publisher varies.

Frequency varies: annual, 1909–41; irregular, 1947–73.

Series originally ed. by J. F. Jameson (1901–35) and publ. by Carnegie Institution of Washington; 1939–73 publ. by A.H.A. 1942–46 not publ. Projects for Canadian universities included 1939–42.

v. for 1970 supplemented by *Titles of dissertations in progress registered between . . . and completed dissertations reported during that period* (issued 1971–75).

A very useful list arranged by historical field, with author and university indexes.

Continued by: Z5055.U49L7

Doctoral dissertations in history. v.1– , Jan./June 1976– . [Wash.], Amer. Historical Assoc., Institutional Services Program, 1976– . v.1– . Semiannual.   **DA28**

v.1, no.1 preceded by an unnumbered issue dated July/Dec. 1975. With the July–Dec.1976 issue the issue number is included in the numbering (i.e., v.1, no.2–).

Each issue follows a chronological (Ancient, Medieval, Modern)/geographical arrangement, with the United States section broken down by subject. Within each section "in progress" listings precede the completed dissertations. Author index. A précis supplied by the author is included with the listing.   Z6205.D6

Sims, Michael. United States doctoral dissertations in Third World studies, 1869–1978. Comp. with the assistance of Mitsue Frey and Dale Seecof. [Waltham, Mass.], Crossroads Pr., [1980]. 436p.   **DA29**

"For the purposes of this book, the Third World will be considered to consist of those countries located in the following geographic areas: Africa, Latin America (including the Caribbean), the Middle East, and Asia. Because of cultural similarities, North Africa is being considered as a part of the Middle East."—*Introd.* Dissertations are listed by region, then by country studied. Indexes of subjects, place names, personal names, languages, and ethnic groups. "Dissertations pertaining to the ancient history of the regions are included, as are those regarding the languages of Third World countries." About 18,900 entries.   Z7164.U5S54

Manuscript sources

See also AK39.

Hale, Richard Walden. Guide to photocopied historical materials in the United States and Canada. Publ. for the American Historical Association. Ithaca, N.Y., Cornell Univ. Pr., 1961. 241p.   **DA30**

"Designed to supply basic bibliographical information on the photocopied manuscripts of interest to historians which are available in depositories in the United States and Canada."—*Pref.*

Arranged by geographical area, listing government records, personal papers, church records, educational records, ships' logs, etc. Index of names.   Z6209.H3

Periodicals

Historical periodicals directory. Eric H. Boehm, Barbara H. Pope and Marie S. Ensign, eds. Santa Barbara, Calif., ABC-Clio, [1981–85]. v.1–4. (In progress)   **DA31**

Contents: v.1, USA and Canada; v.2, Europe: West, North, Central and South; v.3, Europe: East and Southeast; USSR; v.4, Latin America and the West Indies.

Intended as a "comprehensive, authoritative source of accurate, up-to-date information on journals and selected serial publications in the field of history . . . for all current publications, both scholarly and popular, and those that have ceased publication since 1960."—*Introd.* Information is presented in a standard format and includes a statement of scope or purpose for each journal. "Interdisciplinary journals and those devoted to disciplines other than history are included if at least thirty percent of the articles are historical in content." The fifth and final volume is to treat periodicals of

Australia, New Zealand, and the international organizations, and is to include cumulated subject and title indexes to the full set.

Intended to replace Eric Boehm and Lalit Adolphus' *Historical periodicals* (Santa Barbara, 1961) which may still be useful for information on discontinued publications. Z6205.H654

Kramm, Heinrich. Bibliographie historischer Zeitschriften, 1939–1951 . . . Marburg, Otto Rasch, 1952–54. 366p. **DA32**

Published in 3 Lfg.

At head of title: Westdeutsche Bibliothek.

Contents: 1.Lfg., Deutschland, Österreich, Schweiz; 2.Lfg., Groszbritannien, Irland, Niederlande, Belgien, Luxemburg, Frankreich, Portugal, Spanien, Italien; 3.Lfg., Norwegen, Schweden, Dänemark, Finnland, Tschechoslowakei, Ungarn, Jugoslawien, Rumänien, Bulgarien, Griechenland, Polen, Baltische Länder, Sowjetunion.

For each country there is a list of general historical periodicals subdivided by subject; subdivisions by geographical or political areas, as appropriate. Index in each Lieferung. Z6205.K87

Steiner, Dale R. Historical journals: a handbook for writers and reviewers. Santa Barbara, Calif., ABC–Clio, [1981]. 213p. **DA33**

A guide for the writer interested in placing works for publication in historical journals. Brief sections offering advice on articles and book reviewing are followed by an alphabetical listing of historical journals, with directory information about each journal and its policies regarding acceptance of manuscripts and book reviews. Z6205.S73

Historiography

Berding, Helmut. Bibliographie zur Geschichtstheorie. Göttingen, Vandenhoeck & Ruprecht, 1977. 331p. (Arbeitsbücher zur modernen Geschichte, Bd.4) **DA34**

A classed bibliography of book and periodical materials on the theory and writing of history. Includes sections for interdisciplinary materials (e.g., history and sociology; history and psychology). Lacks an index. Z6201.A2B47

Birkos, Alexander S. and **Tambs, Lewis A.** Historiography, method, history teaching; a bibliography of books and articles in English, 1965–1973. [Hamden, Conn.], Linnet Books, 1975. 130p. **DA35**

In four main sections: (1) Research methods in history; (2) Teaching of history; (3) Historiography and philosophy of history; (4) Historiographical studies by area. Author index. The bibliography "is designed not only to aid university, college and high school historians in their teaching, research and publication, but also to facilitate their awareness of new and often conflicting trends in current historiography."—*Pref.* Z6208.H5B57

Comité Français des Sciences Historiques. La recherche historique en France de 1940 à 1965. Paris, Éditions du Centre National de la Recherche Scientifique, 1965. 518p. **DA36**

Presents a survey of contemporary French historiography and historical research, together with a bibliography of historical writings by French scholars 1940–64. Includes a valuable list of the principal organizations and centers for historical research in France, and another of the leading French historical journals. Name index to the bibliography section. D13.C62

Fueter, Eduard. Geschichte der neueren Historiographie. 3., um einen Nachtrag verm. Aufl., besorgt von Dietrich Gerhard und Paul Sattler. München, Oldenbourg, 1936. 670p. (Handbuch der mittelalterlichen und neueren Geschichte. Abt.1, Allgemeines) (Repr.: N.Y., Johnson, 1968) **DA37**

Originally published 1911. Translated into French by É. Jeanmaire as *Historie de l'historiographie moderne* (Paris, Alcan, 1914. 785p.), with some corrections and additions. The 3d ed. includes only minor changes in the text and marginal cross references.

A basic work on historical writing from the time of the Renaissance to about 1870, giving biographical sketches of European and American historians with brief critical estimates of their work. D13.F77

International handbook of historical studies: contemporary research and theory. Ed. by George G. Iggers and Harold T. Parker. Westport, Conn., Greenwood Pr., [1979]. 452p. **DA38**

Complements and extends the similar survey, *Historical studies today,* ed. by Felix Gilbert and Stephen Graubard (N.Y., 1971). Essays by contributing scholars seek "to assess the present state of the discipline, to examine innovations in historical method and perspective as well as continuities with older patterns of scholarship."—*Pref.* Bibliographic notes; index. D13.I62

Stephens, Lester D. Historiography: a bibliography. Metuchen, N.J., Scarecrow Pr., 1975. 271p. **DA39**

In four main sections: (1) Theories of history; (2) Historiography; (3) Historical methods; (4) Reference works. Nearly 2,300 items; many brief annotations; index. Z6208.H5S73

Fellowships, grants, etc.

Grants and fellowships of interest to historians. 1976/77– . [Wash.], Amer. Historical Assoc., Institutional Services Program, [1977]– . Annual (irregular). **DA40**

Title varies.

Listing is by name of the fund or the grant-giving agency. Indicates requirements for eligibility, amount and term of the grant, application deadline, etc.

Dictionaries

Cook, Chris. Dictionary of historical terms; a guide to the main themes, events, cliques & innuendoes of over 1000 years of world history. London, Macmillan, 1983. 304p. **DA41**

American ed. (N.Y., Peter Bedrick Books, 1983) has title: *Dictionary of historical terms; a guide to the main themes and events of over 1000 years of world history.*

Aims to cover "as many as possible of the historical terms that are frequently encountered by both undergraduates and research students."—*Pref.* Included are foreign words, very new terms, technical terms, etc. Users should follow up on *see also* references since many terms given a one-sentence definition receive fuller treatment in another, related entry. D9.C67

Cornell, James. The great international disaster book. 3d ed. N.Y., Scribner's, [1982]. 472p. il. **DA42**

1st ed. 1976.

An encyclopedia of natural and man-made disasters, classified by category. "Each category begins with a list of the worst disasters of that particular type, as measured by loss of life. This is followed by a short introductory definition of the disaster phenomenon itself . . . followed by an extensive summary of all major disasters in that category, in chronological order."—*Introd.* Excludes war, mass murders, massacres, and pogroms. Indexed. D24.C65

Dupuy, Richard Ernest and **Dupuy, Trevor N.** The encyclopedia of military history; from 3500 B.C. to the present. Rev. ed. N.Y., Harper & Row, [1977]. 1464p. il. **DA43**

1st ed. 1970.

Wars, warfare, and military affairs are treated in a series of chronologically and geographically arranged chapters. Detailed general index and a separate index of battles and sieges. Covers through 1975. D25.A2D8

Eggenberger, David. A dictionary of battles. N.Y., Crowell, [1967]. 526p. maps.   **DA44**

"Attempts to provide the essential details of all the major battles in recorded history."—*Pref.* Covers more than 1,500 separate engagements, "from the first battle of Megiddo in 1479 B.C. to the fighting in Vietnam in the 1960s." Includes approximately 100 battle maps. Index of names and places.   D25.E35

Haberkern, Eugen and **Wallach, Joseph Friedrich.** Hilfswörterbuch für Historiker. Mittelalter und Neuzeit. 3. Aufl. Bern, München, Francke Verlag, 1972. 2v.   **DA45**

1st ed. 1935.
Medieval and modern historical terms in various languages, listed in alphabetical order with the equivalent and definition in German. Minimal changes from earlier eds.   D9.H2

Harbottle, Thomas Benfield. Dictionary of battles. 3d rev. ed. by George Bruce. N.Y., Van Nostrand; London, Granada, 1981. 303p.   **DA46**

1st ed. 1904.
Battles, sieges, raids, etc., are listed alphabetically by place-names, with indication of the war or campaign, dates, and a brief description of the fighting and outcome. In the 2d ed. (1971) errors were corrected, sequences standardized, and 20th-century battles added (often in some detail); for the 3d ed., Vietnam and the Sino-Vietnamese War have been updated to early 1979, otherwise there are few changes.   D25.A2H2

Larned, Josephus Nelson. New Larned history for ready reference, reading and research; the actual words of the world's best historians, biographers and specialists . . . completely rev., enl., and brought up to date . . . by D. E. Smith . . . ed. in chief; Charles Seymour, A. H. Shearer, D. C. Knowlton, assoc. eds. Springfield, Mass., Nichols, 1922–24. 12v. il.   **DA47**

1st ed., with title *History for ready reference,* 1893–95 in 5v.; rev. ed., with supplementary volume covering 1894–1900, 1901 in 6v.; 2d supplement, covering 1901–10, 1910 (v.7).
An alphabetical dictionary of universal history, with many cross references. Under each subject is given, not an original article, but one or more quoted articles or extracts from recognized authorities; as extracts are given with exact references, the work serves the double purpose of encyclopedia and index. Interspersed with the extracts are brief biographical sketches, definitions, etc.   D9.L32

Sanderson, Michael W. B. Sea battles: a reference guide. Middletown, Conn., Wesleyan Univ. Pr., [1975]. 199p. maps. il.   **DA48**

Offers concise accounts of more than 250 battles "fought between considerable forces in the open sea . . . [but] naval bombardments, combined operations, inland-water engagements and single-ship actions have been excluded."—*Foreword.* Covers 494 B.C. to 1944 A.D. Chronology precedes the text.   D27.S34

Wetterau, Bruce, comp & ed. Macmillan concise dictionary of world history. N.Y., Macmillan, [1983]. 867p.   **DA49**

An alphabetical arrangement of entries for persons, places, terms, and events relating to world history of all periods. Entries for individual countries, major wars, etc., usually consist mainly of a chronology. Uneven in coverage (e.g., a surprising number of entries for mythological figures; emphasis on American persons and events).   D9.W47

Young, Peter and **Calvert, Michael.** Dictionary of battles. [London], New English Library; N.Y., Mayflower Books, [1977–78]. v.3–4. maps. (In progress; to be in 4v.)   **DA50**

Contents: v.3, 1715–1815; v.4, 1816–1976.
Published in reverse order, these are the first volumes to appear. Within each volume battles are arranged by region of the world or by specific conflict, then alphabetically. Each entry provides location, date, aim of the respective commanders, size of the forces, description of the action, casualties, and effect. Both volumes have brief, select bibliographies; v.4 is indexed.   D25.A2Y68

Pictorial works

Parmentier, André Émile Emmanuel. Album historique, publié sous la direction de Ernest Lavisse. Paris, Colin, 1907–10. 4v. il.   **DA51**

Contents: t.1, Le moyen âge (du 4ᵉ au 13ᵉ siècle). 4.éd., 1910; t.2, La fin du moyen âge (14ᵉ et 15ᵉ siècles). 3d.éd., 1907; t.3, Le 16ᵉ et le 17ᵉ siècles. 4.éd., 1910; t.4, Le 18ᵉ et le 19ᵉ siècles. 1907.
Contains a large number of excellent illustrations of costume, furniture, civil and military life, manners and customs, dwellings, industries, etc.   D101.5.P25

Chronologies, outlines, tables

Collison, Robert Lewis. Newnes dictionary of dates. [2d rev. ed.] London, Newnes, [1966]. 428p.   **DA52**

1st ed. 1962.
In two sections: (1) an alphabetical listing of personal and place-names, events, etc., with their dates; and (2) a listing by month and day of significant happenings on that day down through the years. No index or cross references.   D11.5.C6

Cronologia universale: dalla preistoria all'età contemporanea. [Coordinamento di Giuliano Martignetti] [Torino], Unione Tipografico-Editrice Torinese, [1979]. 1273p.
                                                DA53

On spine: *Grande dizionario enciclopedico.*
Issued in uniform binding with the *Grande dizionario enciclopedico* (*see* AC59) but not numbered as part of that set. An extensive chronology with detailed index. Includes events in social, religious, and cultural history as well as political and military affairs and technological advances.   D11.C79

Delorme, Jean. Chronologie des civilisations. [3d ed. rev. and enl.] Paris, Presses Universitaires de France, 1969. 509p.   **DA54**

1st ed. 1949.
Chronological tables from 3000 B.C. to A.D. 1969, with alphabetical index. Sources of information are indicated.   D11.D38

Freeman-Grenville, Greville Stewart Parker. Chronology of world history; a calendar of principal events from 3000 BC to AD 1976. 2d ed. London, Collings; distr. [Totowa, N.J.], Rowman & Littlefield, 1978. 746p.   **DA55**

1st ed. 1975.
Events and developments are presented in tabular form, six columns on facing pages. The first five columns are devoted to politico-historical matters arranged under geographical headings (with variations in the headings to reflect shifting emphasis); the sixth column is headed "Religion & culture" and chronicles developments in all geographical areas. Index of persons, places, events, etc.
The 2d ed. is updated to 1976, with added entries mainly in the "Religion & culture" column.   D11.F75

Grun, Bernard. The timetables of history: a horizontal linkage of people and events. New, updated ed. N.Y., Simon & Schuster, [1979]. 676p.   **DA56**

"Based on Werner Stein's *Kulturfahrplan.*"—*t.p.*
1st ed. 1975.
Contemporary names and events in various fields are presented in parallel columns: (A) History, politics; (B) Literature, theater; (C) Religion, philosophy, learning; (D) Visual arts; (E) Music; (F) Science, technology, growth; (G) Daily life. Much of the material is directly translated from Werner Stein's *Kulturfahrplan,* first published 1946. This edition covers events through 1978.   D11.G78

Haydn, Joseph Timothy. Dictionary of dates and universal information relating to all ages and nations, by the late Benjamin Vincent. Rev. and brought up to date by eminent authorities. 25th ed. . . . London, Ward, Locke, 1910; N.Y., Putnam, 1911. 1614p. (Repr.: N.Y., Dover, 1969)   **DA57**

1st ed. 1841.

A dictionary of history and general information alphabetically arranged, with information under each heading given mainly in chronological lists. Convenient for specific facts of history and for its various lists, e.g., Lord Mayors of London, famous fires, inundations, etc. Addenda list includes events to Oct. 1910.   D9.H45

Langer, William Leonard. The new illustrated encyclopedia of world history. N.Y., H. N. Abrams, [1975]. 2v. (1368p.) il.   **DA58**

1st ed. 1940.

The first edition constituted a new version of Ploetz's useful *Manual of universal history* (Boston, Houghton, 1925), giving concise, accurate outlines, not tables. Devoted primarily to political, military, and diplomatic history. Includes outline maps and genealogical tables. A 3d ed. (1952) added new sections on the Second World War and the postwar world. The 4th ed. was fully revised and reset, with much new material added and numerous corrections made. This latest edition includes world developments through 1970 and adds a chapter on "The recent period" with sections devoted to "The exploration of space" and "Scientific and technological advances."

A Subscription Books Committee review in the *Booklist* (73:276) indicates that the text is the same as that of the 1972 edition except for correction of a few errors in the index; the illustrations are new.   D21.L276

Peters, Arno. Synchronoptische Weltgeschichte. [Überarb. und wesentlich erw. Aufl.] München, Hamburg, Universum-Verlag, 1965–70. 2v. 33cm.   **DA59**

Contents: v.1, Tables; v.2, Topical lists.

Chronological columns indicating world political, religious, economic, technical, literary, and artistic developments.   D11.P42

Steinberg, Sigfrid Henry. Historical tables, 58 B.C.–A.D. 1978. 10th ed. N.Y., St. Martin's Pr.; London, Macmillan, [1979]. 269p.   **DA60**

1st ed. 1939.

A tabular chronology of world history, arranged in six parallel columns by period. Political history is subdivided by geographical areas, with additional headings for constitutional and economic history, ecclesiastical history, and cultural life (these vary slightly according to period). The tables for 1914–78 are by geographical areas, with special subdivisions for the two World Wars. The 9th edition was brought up to date by Christine Steinberg and John Paxton; tables from 1945 have been rearranged.   D11.S83

Tapsell, R. F. Monarchs, rulers, dynasties and kingdoms of the world. [London], Thames and Hudson; N.Y., Facts on File, [1983]. 511p.   **DA61**

In two sections: (1) an alphabetically arranged series of brief articles on individual dynasties and states, including various genealogical charts, and (2) about 1,000 dynastic lists arranged geographically, then chronologically. For individuals, gives only name, years ruled, and relationships.   D107.T36

Trager, James. The people's chronology; a year-by-year record of human events from prehistory to the present. N.Y., Holt, Rinehart & Winston, [1979]. 1206p.   **DA62**

More than 30,000 entries for major events in a broad range of topics—political affairs, technology, art and photography, environment, consumer protection, food and drink—designated by symbols. Although much is found here that is not readily located in similar chronologies, the shortcoming is in the indexing (*see* review in *Library journal*, Sept. 1, 1979, p.1685).   D11.T83

Atlases

Banks, Arthur. A world atlas of military history. N.Y., Hippocrene Books, [1973–84]. v.1, [3–4]. il., maps. 26cm. (In progress)   **DA63**

First publ. in London by Seeley Service and Co.; v.4 publ. in London by Leo Cooper in assoc. with Secker and Warburg.

Contents: v.1, To 1500 [reissued 1982 as *Atlas of ancient and medieval warfare*]; [v.3] 1861–1945 (publ. 1978); [v.4] 1945–1984, by Tom Hartman.

Black-and-white maps with notes printed on the maps. Some general maps in addition to those for wars, particular battles, defense systems, etc. Indexes of battles, individuals, groups of peoples, and places.   G1030.B27

Bayerischer Schulbuch-Verlag, Munich. Grosser historischer Weltatlas. München, 1978–81. 33cm.   **DA64**

Various editions.

Contents: pt.1, Vorgeschichte und Altertum (6. Aufl., 1978); pt.2, Mittelalter (2. Aufl., 1980?); pt.3, Neuzeit (4. Aufl., 1981).

An excellent example of German map-making. Clear, comprehensive maps with detailed table of contents and place-name index for each part. Pt.1 covers prehistory of approximately 1200; pt.3, from late 15th century to the present.   G1030.B38

Gilbert, Martin. Jewish history atlas. 2d ed. London, Weidenfeld & Nicolson, [1976]; N.Y., Macmillan, [1977]. 121p. maps. 26cm.   **DA65**

1st ed. 1969.

Mainly single-page maps in black-and-white tracing "the worldwide Jewish migrations from ancient Mesopotamia to modern Israel."—*Pref.* Some maps have been revised and expanded, and the number of maps in this edition increased to 121 (from 112). The index of the earlier edition was dropped, but the bibliography has been retained and enlarged.

A recent compilation with more text and illustrations is N. R. M. DeLange's *Atlas of the Jewish world* (Oxford, Phaidon; N.Y., Facts on File, 1984. 240p.).

Lloyd, Christopher. Atlas of maritime history. [Feltham, Middlesex, Eng.], Country Life; N.Y., Arco Publ. Co., [1975]. 144p. il., maps. 34cm.   **DA66**

Maps and explanatory text "aim at displaying the entire maritime history [i.e., economic and political as well as naval aspects] of the western nations from the time of the Greeks and the Phoenicians to that of the Americans and the Russians of the present day."—*Pref.* Index to the maps and diagrams.   G1060.L65

Meer, Frederic van der. Atlas of Western civilization. English version by T. A. Birrell. 2d rev. ed. Princeton, N.J., Van Nostrand, 1960. 240p. 36cm.   **DA67**

First published 1954 (Amsterdam, Elsevier).

Concerned with the development of Western culture and civilization rather than with political and military history. Photographs (of works of art and architecture as well as of historic and geographic sites) outnumber the maps.   G1030.M42

Muir, Ramsay. Muir's Historical atlas: ancient, medieval, and modern, ed. by R. F. Treharne and Harold Fullard. 10th ed. N.Y., Barnes & Noble, 1964. various pagings. 116p. of col. maps. 29cm.   **DA68**

First published in this form in 1938 as *Philips' Atlas of ancient, medieval, and modern history.*

Consists of two sections which are also published separately: (1) *Atlas of ancient and classical history.* 6th ed. 1963; (2) *Historical atlas: Medieval and modern.* 11th ed. [1969]. Each section has its own index. Covers from about 15th century B.C. to 1965. A good, serviceable, reasonably priced atlas for schools and colleges.   G1030.M838

Rand McNally and Company. Atlas of world history, ed. by R. R. Palmer. Chicago, Rand McNally, [1965]. 216p. maps (part col.) 27cm.   **DA69**

First published 1957 (216p.).

Well-made maps, about 75 in color and almost 50 in black-and-white. Most detailed treatment is of North American and European history (particularly for 19th and 20th centuries), but with maps also of Asia, Africa, and Latin America. Textual comment. Name index.   G1030.R3

Shepherd, William Robert. Historical atlas. 9th ed. N.Y., Barnes & Noble, 1964. 226p. of col. maps (part folded), 115p. 27cm.   **DA70**

1st ed. 1911; 7th ed. 1929, the last published under Shepherd's direction.

For many years the standard and most used historical atlas. Covers from 1450 B.C. to 1964. The 9th ed. contains all the maps of the 7th ed. and a special supplement (plates 218–26) of maps for the period since 1929, prepared by C. S. Hammond & Company.

The Index is in three parts: (1) Original index; (2) Index-Supplement, which includes names contained in the maps for the period 1911–29, as well as some earlier ones, but does not include the new section, 1930–64; (3) Additional changes.

Sections have also been published separately, e.g., *Atlas of ancient history; Atlas of medieval and modern history.* G1030.S4

The Times atlas of world history, ed. by Geoffrey Barraclough. Rev. ed. London, Times Books; Maplewood, N.J., Hammond, 1984. 360p. il., maps. 37cm. **DA71**

Aims "to present a view of history which is world-wide in conception and presentation and which does justice, without prejudice or favour, to the achievements of all peoples in all ages and in all quarters of the globe."—*Introd.* Plates, with accompanying text by contributing scholars, are grouped in seven main sections: (1) The world of early man; (2) The first civilisations; (3) The classical civilisations of Eurasia; (4) The world of divided regions; (5) The world of the emerging West; (6) The age of European dominance; (7) The age of global civilisation. Glossary, p.297–334; index, p.335–60.

The revised edition is updated to the early 1980s and there are minor revisions and corrections. G1030.T54

Vries, Sjoerd de, Luykx, Theo and **Henderson, William O.** An atlas of world history. [London], Nelson, 1965. 183p. 28cm. **DA72**

Based on Vries's *Elseviers historische atlas* (Amsterdam, 1963).

A brief introduction to the history of the Western world with many illustrations, followed by 64 maps in color and a number of black-and-white sketch maps. Index. G1030.V75

Westermann, Georg, *firm, publishers, Brunswick.* Grosser Atlas zur Weltgeschichte. Hrsg. von Hans-Erich Stier [et al.]. Bearb. von Hans-Erich Stier [et al.]. Unter Mitarbeit von Ekkehard Aner . . . [Aufl. 1981/82] Braunschweig, Westermann, [1983?]. 170p. of col. maps, 78p. 30cm. **DA73**

1st ed. 1956.

A good modern atlas primarily of Europe and western Asia. Covers from ancient times to about 1960, with occasional later data. Includes many detailed maps of cities and other special areas. Index of place-names. G1030.W448

Directories

Duffy, James, Hevelin, John and **Osterreicher, Suzanne.** International directory of scholars and specialists in third world studies. [Waltham, Mass.], Crossroads Pr., [1981]. 563p. **DA74**

Provides biographical sketches of some 3,300 persons specializing in third world studies. HC59.7.D783

ARCHAEOLOGY AND ANCIENT HISTORY

❖For archaeology of a particular country, *see* under that country. Archaeology of the Holy Land is entered in the Religion section. *See also* CE12.

Guides

Bengtson, Hermann. Introduction to ancient history. Berkeley, Univ. of California, Pr., 1970. 213p. **DA75**

Translated by R. I. Frank and Frank D. Gilliard from the 6th ed. of *Einführung in die alte Geschichte.*

Pt.1 is a series of essays followed by bibliography on broad areas of historiography (e.g., "The scope of ancient history," "The sources," "The monuments," "The history of the study of antiquity from Renaissance to the present"). Pt.2 is a bibliography of studies, organized to follow the *Cambridge ancient history* (1924–39); many of the titles cited are in English. Z6202.B413

Bibliography

Allen, Peter S. and **Lazio, Carole.** Archaeology on film; a comprehensive guide to audio-visual materials. [Boston], Archaeological Inst. of Amer., [1983]. 240p. **DA76**

A title listing of films and videotapes currently available in the United States which "deal explicitly with archaeology or artifacts recovered from scientific excavation."—*Introd.* Gives production information, distributor, audience level, references to reviews, and brief description. Broad subject and geographic area index.

Banner, János. A Közép-Dunamedence régészeti bibliográfiája a legrégibb időktől a XI. századig. [Irták] Banner János [és] Jakabffy Imre. Budapest, Akadémiai Kiadó, 1954. 581p. **DA77**

A bibliography of books dealing with the archaeology of the Middle-Danubian Basin up to the 11th century. Z2142.B3

—— A Közép-Dunamedence régészeti bibliográfiája, 1954/1959, 1960/1966. Összeállította Jakabffy Imre. Budapest, Akadémiai Kiadó, 1961–68. 2v. (250p., 242p.)

Supplements to the above work. Z2142.B32

Déchelette, Joseph. Manuel d'archéologie préhistorique celtique et gallo-romaine. Paris, Picard, 1908–27. v.1–4, and appendix to v.2 in 2v. il. (v.1–2 repr.: Westmead, Farnborough, Hants., Gregg Intl., 1971. 2v. in 5) **DA79**

Contents: v.1, Archéologie préhistorique. 1908; v.2, Archéologie celtique ou protohistorique: Âge du bronze. 1910; appendix to v.2, 1910–12 (in 2v.); v.3, Premier âge du fer, ou Époque de Hallstatt. 1927; v.4, Second âge du fer, ou Époque de la Tène. 1927.

For v.5–6 *see* Grenier (DA99). DC63.D35

Deutsches Archäologisches Institut. Römische Abteilung. Bibliothek. Kataloge der Bibliothek . . .; Autoren- und Periodica Kataloge; Systematischer Katalog; Zeitschriften-Autorenkatalog. Boston, G. K. Hall, 1969. 13v. **DA80**

The three sections of the catalog are available separately: the author and periodical catalogs in 7v.; the classified catalog in 3v.; and the author catalog of periodical references in 3v.

Reproduces the catalog cards of one of the world's strongest archaeological libraries, representing some 91,000 volumes in all areas of European and Near Eastern archaeology and philology, from the prehistoric to the Byzantine period. Coverage of the *Zeitschriften-Autorenkatalog* begins with articles published in 1956 in periodicals, *Festschriften,* and other special publications; articles indexed are limited to classical archaeology and epigraphy.

An earlier edition of the catalog is still useful for its references to journal articles of the pre-1956 period and the more complete book citations: *Katalog der Bibliothek des Kaiserlich Deutschen Archäologischer Instituts in Rom . . .* (Berlin, W. de Gruyter, 1913–32. 2v. in 4) and supplement (1930. 516p.).

The Institut has also issued a useful list of journals received in the library: *Zeitschriftenverzeichnis* (Wiesbaden, Steiner, 1964. 327p.). It gives publication history and indicates title changes.

Z5134.R764

Ellis, Linda. Laboratory techniques in archaeology; a guide to the literature, 1920–1980. N.Y., Garland, 1982. 419p. (Garland reference library of social science, v.110) **DA81**

A thorough bibliography of some 3,755 items (in English, German, French, Italian, Spanish, or Russian) dealing with the application of any of the sciences to archaeology. Arranged by problem areas (remote sensing, chronometry, environmental reconstruction, materials analysis, data management) plus a general section, each appropriately subdivided. Indexed by author, geographic area, method of analysis, type of material analyzed.

Z5131.E43

Gaudel, Paul. Bibliographie der archäologischen Konservierungstechnik. [2. verb. Aufl.] Berlin, Hessling, 1969. 374p. (Berliner Jahrbuch für Vor- und Fruhgeschichte. Ergänzungsbande, 2)   **DA82**

1st ed. 1960.

About 1,800 books and periodicals are listed in classed arrangement, with name and subject indexes. Extensive annotations.

Z5131.G38

Hachmann, Rolf. Ausgewählte Bibliographie zur Vorgeschichte von Mitteleuropa. Wiesbaden, Stuttgart, Steiner, 1984. lxiii, 390p.   **DA83**

Sponsored by Römisch-Germanische Kommission des Deutschen Archäologischen Instituts.

Offers some 10,821 entries for books and articles in classed arrangement, with author index. Covers all of Europe (except Greece and Albania) through the Iron Age. Good section on cultural life. List of serial abbreviations, p.xxxiii–lxiii.

Harvard University. Library. Ancient history. Classification schedule, classified listing by call number, chronological listing, author and title listing. Cambridge, Mass., publ. by Harvard Univ. Lib.; distr. by Harvard Univ. Pr., 1975. 363p. (Widener Library shelflist, 55)   **DA84**

For a note on the series see AA145.

"This volume . . . lists more than 11,000 titles concerning the history, civilization, government, economic and social conditions, and geography of the Mediterranean region and Western Asia down to the Barbarian invasions in Europe and the Arab conquest in Asia and Africa. Also included are works on Egyptian and Assyro-Babylonian literatures and on the archaeology of Assyria and Babylonia. In general, archaeological works and works on prehistoric times are excluded."—*Pref.*   Z6202.H37

———— Archaeology: classification schedules; classified listing by call number; chronological listing; author and title listing. Cambridge, Publ. by Harvard Univ. Lib.; distr. by Harvard Univ. Pr., 1979. 442p. (Widener Library shelflist, 56)   **DA85**

For a note on the series see AA145.

Includes about 14,300 shelflist entries for the Widener *Arc* class which "provides for archaeology and the related disciplines of palaeography and diplomatics, sigillography, and numismatics."—*p.3.*   Z5131.H37

Heizer, Robert Fleming, Hester, Thomas R. and **Graves, Carol.** Archaeology; a bibliographical guide to the basic literature. N.Y., Garland, 1980. 434p. (Garland reference library of social science, v.54)   **DA86**

A compilation of over 4,800 English-language references published up to 1979 and grouped as: Nature and purpose of archaeology; History of archaeology; The work of the archaeologist; Archaeology as a profession; Sources of primary data. Sections are subdivided as appropriate. Intends to identify "those publications which are important reference and research aids" (*Pref.*); emphasis is on New World archaeology, although an effort was made "to include reasonable coverage of the Old World, Africa, and Asia." Author index only.   Z5131.H44

Jerusalem. École Biblique et Archéologique Française. Bibliothèque. Catalogue . . . (Catalog of the Library of the French Biblical and Archeological School, Jerusalem). Boston, G. K. Hall, 1975. 13v.   **DA87**

For full information see BB98.

Rounds, Dorothy. Articles on antiquity in Festschriften: the ancient Near East, the Old Testament, Greece, Rome, Roman law, Byzantium; an index. Cambridge, Harvard Univ. Pr., 1962. 560p.   **DA88**

An index of *Festschriften,* including in one alphabet: names of scholars and institutions honored, names of authors of articles, and all significant words in the titles of the articles.   Z6202.R6

Vogt, Joseph and **Bellen, Heinz.** Bibliographie zur antiken Sklaverei. Neu bearb. von Elisabeth Herrmann in Verbindung mit Norbert Brockmeyer. Bochum, Brockmeyer, 1983. 2v. (391p.)   **DA89**

1st ed. 1971.

A classed bibliography of slavery in antiquity (5,162 entries). A high percentage of citations relates to Greece and Rome, but there are references to slavery in other parts of Europe, Egypt, the Middle East, East Asia, etc. Indexed.   Z7164.S6V64

Current

Archäologische Bibliographie, 1913– . Berlin, W. deGruyter, 1914– . Annual.   **DA90**

Title varies; publisher varies. Issued by the Deutsches Archäologisches Institut.

Continues the bibliographies previously included in the "Archäologischer Anzeiger" section of the Institut's *Jahrbuch,* 1889–1912; vols. for 1913–72 issued as "Beilage" to the *Jahrbuch.* Frequency varies: annual except 1916/17–1923/24 and 1944/48.

A useful, topically arranged bibliography of books, periodical articles, and book reviews; broad in scope, international in coverage. Originally indexed by name (personal and place); beginning 1976, has name index, reviewer index, and a topical index (which includes names of periodicals devoted to a given topic).

For its brief period of coverage, 1952–1959/60, the *Annuario bibliografico di archaeologia* (Modena, Soc. Tipografica, 1954–66) is a useful complement.   Z5132.A67

Art and archaeology technical abstracts. v.1– , 1955– . N.Y., 1955– .   **DA91**

For full information *see* BE53.

Sovetskaia arkheologicheskaia literatura; bibliografiia, 1918/40–1973/75. Sost. N. A. Vinberg i dr. Leningrad, Nauka, 1959–83. 6v.   **DA92**

At head of title: Akademiia Nauk SSSR. Biblioteka . . . Institut Arkheologii.

Issued as follows: 1918–40, ed. by N.A. Vinberg (1965. 376p.); 1941–57, ed. by N.A. Vinberg (Moscow, 1959. 773p.); 1958–62, ed. by T. N. Zadnieprovskaia (1969. 414p.); 1963–67, ed. by T. N. Zadnieprovskaia (1975. 471p.); 1968–72, ed. by T. N. Zadnieprovskaia (1980. 557p.); 1973–75, ed. by T. N. Zadnieprovskaia (1983. 376p.).

A classified bibliography of Soviet publications in archaeology, covering paleolithic times to the 17th century. In addition to books and periodical articles, there are citations to dissertations and parts of books, as well as reviews of major publications. Indexes for authors, archaeological monuments, and related subjects such as numismatics, sphragistics, and history of technology.

Z2517.A8S6

Swedish archaeological bibliography, 1939/48–1966/75. Uppsala, Almqvist & Wiksell, 1951–78. Quinquennial.

DA93

A survey, in English, sponsored by the Svenska Arkeologiska Samfundet and listing Swedish archaeological literature. Since the initial publication, volumes cover a 5- or 6-year period as follows: 1939–48, ed. by Sverker Janson and Olof Vessberg (1951. 360p.); 1949–53, ed. by Christian Callmer and Wilhelm Holmqvist (1956. 294p.); 1954–59, ed. by Wilhelm Odelberg and Hilding Thylander (1965. 259p.); 1960–65, ed. by Marten Stenberger and Anders Hedvall (1968. 289p.); 1966–70, ed. by Marten Stenberger and Anders Hedvall (1972. 331p.); 1971–75, ed. by Sverker Janson and Hilding Thylander (1978. 338p.).   Z5111.S86

Dissertations

Drexhage, Hans-Joachim. Deutschsprachige Dissertationen zur alten Geschichte, 1844–1978. Wiesbaden, Franz Steiner Verlag, 1980. 142p.　　　**DA94**

An author listing of about 2,700 German-language dissertations (including those from Austrian and Swiss universities) on ancient history. Three indexes: Personen- und Völkernamen, Orts- und Ländernamen, Sachregister.　　　Z6207.G7D73

Encyclopedias, dictionaries, and handbooks

Bray, Warwick and **Trump, David.** The American Heritage guide to archaeology. N.Y., American Heritage, [1970]. 269p. il.　　　**DA95**

Includes terms, personal and place names, etc., in dictionary arrangement. No attempt was made to cover classical, medieval, or industrial archaeology.　　　CC70.B7

The Cambridge encyclopedia of archaeology. Ed., Andrew Sherratt. N.Y., Crown/Cambridge Univ. Pr., [1980]. 495p. il., maps.　　　**DA96**

A topically arranged encyclopedia, each of its 64 chapters contributed by a specialist. A work for the educated general reader rather than for the scholar. In three main sections, the first treating the development of modern archaeology; the second (and most extensive) treating the various archaeological periods, regions, empires, etc., of archaeological study; and the third devoted to "Frameworks: dating and distribution." Chapter-by-chapter bibliography, p.453–67. Indexed.

A review by Stuart Piggott appears in *TLS*, Aug. 15, 1980, p. 919.　　　CC165.C3

Champion, Sara. A dictionary of terms and techniques in archaeology. Oxford, Phaidon; N.Y., Facts on File, 1980. 144p. il.　　　**DA97**

A well-written dictionary "for the non-professional archaeologist" (*Introd.*), covering terms used in the scientific and technical aspects of archaeology; thus, considerable attention is given to matters such as dating techniques, but there are no definitions for cultures or artifacts. For major articles on techniques (e.g., aerial photography) a single, carefully chosen bibliographical reference is provided, and there is a general bibliography. Additional cross references would have been welcome.

The review in *Booklist* 77:1310 (June 1, 1981) points out that despite the "decided British emphasis in the examples and illustrations used," the dictionary "covers American work and usage quite adequately."　　　CC70.C48

Cottrell, Leonard, ed. Concise encyclopedia of archaeology. 3d ed. London, Hutchinson, [1974]. 430p.　　　**DA98**

1st ed. 1960.

A dictionary for the "intelligent amateur." Entries for archaeological discoveries and techniques, as well as for archaeologists. Emphasis is on archaeology outside Greece and Rome and medieval Europe. Useful, although depth of treatment is uneven.

A similar work, *The illustrated encyclopedia of archaeology,* ed. by Glyn Daniel (N.Y., Crowell, 1977. 244p.), offers short articles and surveys; it is especially strong in Egyptian archaeology.　　　CC70.C6

Grenier, Albert. Manuel d'archéologie gallo-romaine. Paris, Picard, 1931–60. 4v.　　　**DA99**

v.1–2 also published as v.5–6 of Déchelette (DA79).

Contents: t.1, Généralités. Travaux militaires. 1931; t.2, Archéologie du sol. 1934; t.3, L'architecture: (a) L'urbanisme, les monuments (capitole, forum, temple, basilique); (b) Ludi et circenses (théâtres, amphithéâtres, cirques). 1958; t.4, Les monuments des eaux. 2v. 1960.

Handbuch der Archaeologie, im Rahmen des Handbuchs der Altertumswissenschaft . . . hrsg. von Walter Otto. Munich,

Beck, 1939–54. v.1–2, 3^1, 4^1. il. (I. P. E. Müller, Handbuch der Altertumswissenschaft. 6. Abt.)　　　**DA100**

A heavily documented history, each volume accompanied by a section of plates. A new edition has begun to appear as:　　　CC65.H3

——— Neu hrsg. von Ulrich Hausmann. München, Beck, 1969–83. v.1–4. (In progress)　　　**DA101**

Contents: [v.1] Allgemeine Grundlagen der Archäologie, mit Beiträgen von Hellmut Brunner [et al.]; [v.2] Vorderasien I. Mesopotamien, Babylonien, Iran, und Anatolien von Barthel Hrouda; [v.3] Die antiken Gemmen von Peter Zazoff; [v.4] Römische Sarkophage von Guntran Koch und Hellmut Sichtermann.

Lexikon der alten Welt. [Hrsg. von Carl Andresen *et al.*] Zürich, Stuttgart, Artemis Verlag, 1965. 3524 col.　　　**DA102**

Signed articles on various aspects of ancient civilization (including references to Oriental and early Christian cultures), embracing literature, philosophy, political and cultural history, religion, law, economics, and technology.　　　D54.L48

The Macmillan dictionary of archaeology. Ed., Ruth D. Whitehouse. London, Macmillan, [1983]. 597p. il.　　　**DA103**

Publ. in the United States as *The Facts on File dictionary of archaeology* (N.Y., Facts on File, 1984).

As far as possible, uses non-technical language. Entries for terms, sites, persons, etc. Cross references; subject index (including a geographical approach); select bibliography.

Müller-Karpe, Hermann. Handbuch der Vorgeschichte. München, Beck, 1966–80. v.1–4 in 10v. il., maps, plates. (In progress)　　　**DA104**

Contents: v.1, Altsteinzeit (1. Aufl., 1966; 2. Aufl., 1977. 2v.); v.2, Jungsteinzeit (1968. 2v.); v.3, Kupferzeit (1974. 3v.); v.4, Bronzerzeit (1980. 3v.); v.5, Frühe Eisenzeit (not yet publ.).

Discussions of the state of knowledge of each period (covering chronology, art, religion, social life, etc.) are followed by surveys of relevant sites arranged by country and giving for each a brief description and bibliography. Heavily illustrated with plates showing tools and art works; well indexed.

Max Ebert's *Reallexikon der Vorgeschichte* . . . (Berlin, W. de Gruyter, 1924–32. 15v.) may still prove useful, particularly in view of its dictionary arrangement.　　　GN739.M8

Reallexikon der Assyriologie, unter Mitwirkung zahlreicher Fachgelehrter, hrsg. von Erich Ebeling . . . und Bruno Meissner. Berlin, W. de Gruyter, 1928–83. v.1–6^{7-8}. il. (In progress)　　　**DA105**

Issued in fascicles.

Contents: v.1–6^{7-8}, A–Libanon.

A scholarly encyclopedia on Assyriology, with signed articles and extensive bibliographies.　　　DS69.1.R4

❖In addition to the works listed above, the research worker in classical antiquities will often need to refer to Iwan Müller's *Handbuch der Altertumswissenschaft* (München, Beck, 1923–), a series of scholarly treatises on subjects in classical literature, antiquities, etc., the various volumes of which have appeared in many different editions. Some of the volumes are the most comprehensive and definitive works in their fields; others are much briefer. For a partial list of contents *see* Malclès, v.2, pt.1, p.105–06 (AA487).

Atlases

Baines, John and **Málek, Jaromír.** Atlas of ancient Egypt. N.Y., Facts on File; Oxford, Phaidon, [1980]. 240p. il., maps.　　　**DA106**

A historical atlas with maps, plans and illustrations (mainly in color) presented in conjunction with the text. In three sections: (1) The cultural setting; (2) A journey down the Nile; (3) Aspects of

Egyptian society. Includes a list of museums with Egyptian collections, a glossary, bibliography, gazetteer, and index.   DT56.9.B34

Beek, Martinus Adrianus. Atlas of Mesopotamia. [N.Y. & London], Nelson, 1962. 164p. il., maps. 36cm.   **DA107**

For full information *see* DE73.

Whitehouse, David and **Whitehouse, Ruth.** Archaeological atlas of the world, with 103 maps drawn by John Woodcock and Shalom Schotten. London, Thames and Hudson; San Francisco, W. H. Freeman, [1975]. 272p.   **DA108**

Small maps, with explanatory notes, "pinpointing some 5,000 pre- and proto-historic sites."—*Introd.* Suggestions for further reading accompany the notes. Index with map grid references.

For maps and drawings of specific sites *see* Jacquetta Hawkes' *Atlas of ancient archaeology* (N.Y., McGraw–Hill, 1974. 272p.). Hawkes has also compiled the *Atlas of early man* (N.Y., St. Martin's Pr., 1976. 255p.), covering 35,000 B.C. to A.D. 500; eight time frames are compared across the world.   G1046.E15W5

Directories

Åström, Paul, comp. Who's who in Cypriote archaeology; biographical and bibliographical notes. Göteborg, Paul Aströms Förlag, 1971. 88p. (Studies in Mediterranean archaeology, v.23)   **DA109**

Includes only scholars active in the field in 1970.   CC110.A87

Dawson, Warren Royal and **Uphill, Eric Parrington.** Who was who in Egyptology. 2d rev. ed. London, Egypt Exploration Soc., [1972]. 315p.   **DA110**

1st ed. 1951.
Subtitle: A biographical index of Egyptologists; of travellers, explorers, and excavators in Egypt; of collectors of and dealers in Egyptian antiquities; of consuls, officials, authors, benefactors, and others whose names occur in the literature of Egyptology, from the year 1500 to the present day, but excluding persons now living.
This edition considerably revised and enlarged.   PJ1063.D3

General histories

Cambridge ancient history. . . . Cambridge, Univ. Pr.; N.Y., Macmillan, 1923–39. 12v. and 5v. plates. maps.   **DA111**

Contents: v.1, Egypt and Babylonia to 1580 B.C. (2d ed. 1928); v.2, Egyptian and Hittite empires to ca. 1000 B.C.; v.3, Assyrian Empire; v.4, Persian Empire and the West; v.5, Athens; v.6, Macedon; v.7, The Hellenistic monarchies and the rise of Rome; v.8, Rome and the Mediterranean, 218–133 B.C.; v.9, Roman Republic, 133–44 B.C.; v.10, Augustan Empire, 44 B.C.–A.D. 70; v.11, Imperial peace, A.D. 70–192; v.12, Imperial crisis and recovery, A.D. 193–324.

Excellent reference history; each chapter written by a specialist, with full bibliographies at the end of each volume. The volumes of plates contain illustrations without comment.   D57.C25

Cambridge ancient history. 2d–3d ed. London, Cambridge Univ. Pr., 1970–84. v.1–3, 7, pt.1. (In progress)   **DA112**

Contents: v.1, pt.1, Prolegomena and prehistory, ed. by I. E. S. Edwards, C. J. Gadd, and N. G. L. Hammond (3d ed. 1970); v.1, pt.2, Early history of the Middle East, ed. by I. E. S. Edwards, C. J. Gadd, and N. G. L. Hammond (3d ed. 1971); v.2, pt.1, History of the Middle East and the Aegean region, ca. 1800–1380 B.C., ed. by I. E. S. Edwards, C. J. Gadd, N. G. L. Hammond, and E. Sollberger (3d ed. 1973); v.2, pt.2, History of the Middle East and the Aegean region c1380–1000 B.C., ed. by I. E. S. Edwards [and others] (3d ed. 1975); plates to v.1–2, ed. by I. E. S. Edwards [and others] (2d ed. 1977); v.3, pt.1–3, The history of the Balkans; and the Middle East and the Aegean world, tenth to sixth centuries B.C., ed. by J. Boardman [and others] (2d ed. 1982. 2v.) and Plates, ed. by J. Boardman (1984); v.7, pt.1, The Hellenistic world, ed. by F. W.

Walbank [and others] (2d ed. 1984) and Plates, ed. by R. Ling (1984).

Individual chapters, each written by a specialist, began to appear in 1961 as fascicles of the revised edition. These fascicles are not published in chronological sequence, and pages are renumbered for the completed, bound volumes. Footnotes, extensive bibliographies, index.   D57.C252

Classical antiquities
Guides

Petit, Paul. Guide de l'étudiant en histoire ancienne (antiquité classique). [3e éd.] Paris, Presses Universitaires de France, 1969. 239p.   **DA113**

1st ed. 1959.
A bibliographical guide for the student. Considers auxiliary sciences, such as archaeology and numismatics, as well as the history of antiquity and the study of classical texts. Indexed.

Another introductory guide, *Introduction to classical scholarship; a syllabus and bibliographical guide* (Wash., 1971) by Martin R. P. McGuire, is also very helpful.   Z6202.P45

Bibliography

See also BD1382 and BE18.

Christ, Karl. Römische Geschichte, eine Bibliographie. Darmstadt, Wissenschaftliche Buchgesellschaft, 1976. 544p.   **DA114**

A guide to recent (i.e., 20th-century) books, articles, and some dissertations on the history of the Roman world through the 5th century A.D. Topical arrangement with subject index.
Z2340.C49

Fasti archeologici; annual bulletin of classical archaeology. v.1– , 1946– . Firenzi, Sansoni, 1948– . Annual.   **DA115**

At head of title: International Association for Classical Archaeology.

An extensive bibliography of books, catalogs, reports, and periodical articles, topically arranged in six sections: General; Prehistoric and classical Greece; Italy before the Roman Empire; The Hellenistic world and the Eastern provinces of the Roman Empire; The Roman West; Christianity and late antiquity. Most sections are subdivided for regions and sites; many brief annotations; fully indexed.

Publication runs late (e.g., v.30/31, covering 1975/76, was published 1982).   GN700.I552

Fifty years (and twelve) of classical scholarship: being Fifty years of classical scholarship, revised with appendices. [2d ed.] Oxford, Blackwell; N.Y., Barnes & Noble, 1968. 523p.   **DA116**

For full information *see* BD1375.

Harvard University. Library. Classical studies: classification schedules; classified listing by call number; chronological listing; author and title listing. Cambridge, Publ. by Harvard Univ. Lib.; distr. by Harvard Univ. Pr., 1979. 215p. (Widener Library shelflist, 57)   **DA117**

For full information *see* BD1377.

Sociedad Española de Estudios Clasicos. Bibliografia de los estudios clasicos en España (1939–1955). Madrid, 1956. 453p. (*Its* Publicaciones, 1)   **DA118**

——— ——— (1956–1965). Madrid, 1968. 486p. (*Its* Publicaciones, 8)

Lists books and articles in all areas of classical studies published in Spain. Arranged by broad topic, with author index.
James K. Demetrius' *Greek scholarship in Spain and Latin America* (Chicago, Argonaut, 1965. 144p.) is useful for its listing of studies

on specific Greek authors and also for its non-Spanish language entries.   Z7016.S6

Dissertations

Thompson, Lawrence Sidney. A bibliography of American doctoral dissertations in classical studies and related fields. [Hamden, Conn.], Shoe String Pr., 1968. 250p.   **DA119**

"All aspects of the culture of Greece and Rome, from the prehistory of Greece and Italy through the arbitrary terminal date of 500 A.D., are included . . ."—*Pref.* Author listing with detailed subject and title index. Cutoff date is generally 1964, with some 1965 dissertations included.   Z7016.T48

———— A bibliography of dissertations in classical studies: American, 1964–1972; British, 1950–1972; with a cumulative index, 1861–1972. [Hamden, Conn.], Shoe String Pr., 1976. 296p.   **DA120**

This is "somewhat more than a supplement to *A Bibliography of American Doctoral Dissertations in Classical Studies . . .* [above]" (*Pref.*) since, in addition to listing American doctoral studies of the 1964–72 period (as well as some earlier ones omitted from the previous compilation), it lists British master's theses and doctoral dissertations for 1950–72. The cumulative index serves both volumes.   Z7016.T482

Manuals, dictionaries, and handbooks

Daremberg, Charles Victor and **Saglio, Edmond.** Dictionnaire des antiquités grecques et romaines d'après les textes et les monuments. Paris, Hachette, 1873–1919. 5v. and index. il. (Repr.: Graz, Akad. Druck- und Verlagsanstalt, 1962–63. 5v. in 10)   **DA121**

A work of the highest authority, with long, signed articles by specialists and very detailed bibliographical references. Covers public and private life, manners and customs, institutions, arts, sciences, industries, religion, costume, furniture, military affairs, money, weights and measures, etc. Does not include biography and literature. Indexes of authors, Greek words, Latin words, and subjects.   DE5.D21

Illustrated encyclopaedia of the classical world [by] Michael Avi-Yonah and Israel Shatzman. N.Y., Harper & Row, [1975]; Maidenhead, Sampson Low, 1976. 509p. il.   **DA122**

Intended "to satisfy the requirements of those who have no direct training in the classical disciplines."—*Foreword.* Comprises about 2,300 articles "comprehending the main themes, persons and places of Greek and Roman history, classical mythology and religion, philosophy and thought, together with the most important writers, artists and statesmen, the chief sites, the topography and the social background of the ancient world." Some brief bibliographical citations. Index of names, terms and subjects which are not entries in the main body of the encyclopedia.   DE5.I44

Laurand, Louis. Manuel des études grecques et latines. Ed. entièrement ref. par A. Lauras. Paris, Picard, 1956–57. 3v.   **DA123**

Issued in fascicles. Edition numbers for fascicles vary.

Contents: t.1, *Grèce:* fasc.1, Géographie, histoire, institutions grecques; fasc.2, Littérature grecque; fasc.3, Grammaire historique grecque; t.2, *Rome:* fasc.4, Géographie, histoire, institutions romaines; fasc.5, Littérature latine; fasc.6, Grammaire historique latine; fasc.7, Métrique, sciences complémentaires, t.3, Compléments, atlas, tables.

The work is published in many editions. This printing incorporates the material in the original 7 fasc. and the appendixes, and includes indexes with each fascicle instead of a cumulated index. *Supplément, pour mieux comprendre l'antiquité,* was not updated.

A manual for the study of the classics, with interspersed bibliographies.   DA93.L3

Nash, Ernest. Pictorial dictionary of ancient Rome. Rev. ed. London, Thames & Hudson; N.Y., Praeger, 1968. 2v. (544p.) il. (Repr.: N.Y., Hacker, 1981)   **DA124**

Prep. in collaboration with the Deutsches Archaeologisches Institut.

1st ed. 1961.

An authoritative dictionary presenting each surviving monument of ancient Rome through photographs and drawings, with exhaustive bibliography for each. Index of names of places (including categories such as streets, squares, churches).   NA310.N28

Oxford classical dictionary. 2d ed., ed. by N. G. L. Hammond and H. H. Scullard. Oxford, Clarendon Pr., 1970. 1176p.   **DA125**

1st ed. 1949.

A scholarly dictionary, with signed articles, covering biography, literature, mythology, philosophy, religion, science, geography, etc. Most of the articles are brief, but there are some longer survey articles, e.g., Rome, music, scholarship, etc. Bibliographies are appended to most articles, and are usually limited to a few of the best works on the subject, in English and foreign languages. Bibliographies for the articles on the great classical writers usually include texts, commentaries, translations, lexicons, style, life, criticism, etc.

For the second edition all articles were reviewed for revision or replacement; bibliographies were updated to about 1967–68; and new material on the archaeological background was added. The number of entries for persons and places was increased, and an "Index of names etc. which are not titles of entries" makes a useful addition.   DE5.O9

Pauly, August Friedrich von. Paulys Real-Encyclopädie der classischen Altertumswissenschaft; neue Bearb. begonnen von Georg Wissowa, unter Mitwirkung zahlreicher Fachgenossen hrsg. von Wilhelm Kroll und Karl Mittelhaus. Stuttgart, Metzler, 1894–1978. v.1–24^1; 2. Reihe, v.1–10A; Suppl. v.1–15. maps. (Repr.: Munich, Artemis, 1981)   **DA126**

Contents: Bd.1–24^1, A–Quosenus; 2. Reihe (R–Z), Bd.1–10A, R–Zythos; Suppl., Bd.1–15. (Volumes were not published in straight alphabetical sequence, but in two series with a supplement).

The standard scholarly German work covering the whole field of classical literature, history, antiquities, biography, etc. Long, signed articles by specialists, with extensive bibliographies. Generally cited as *Pauly-Wissowa;* in German references sometimes cited as *RE.* Indispensable for scholarly work in classical antiquities.

The arrangement and the alphabeting are sometimes complicated. Many volumes include *"Nachträge und Berichtigungen,"* which in the later volumes are quite extensive. The volumes of the Supplement are geared to the volumes of the main set, each supplementary volume starting with A and continuing to a later part of the alphabet.   DE5.P33

Gärtner, Hans and **Wünsch, Albert.** Paulys Realencyclopädie der classischen Altertumswissenschaft; Register der Nachträge und Supplemente. München, Druckenmüller, 1980. 250p.   **DA127**

Indexes articles, corrections, and addenda in the supplementary volumes and the *Nachträge,* but not the main alphabet. Each entry consists of a short summary (with corrections, as pertinent) of the article as well as index reference.

Murphy, John P. Index to the supplements and suppl. [*sic*] volumes of Pauly-Wissowa's R.E. Chicago, Ares, 1980. 144p.   **DA128**

Subtitle: Index to the *Nachträge* and *Berichtigungen* in vols. I–XXIV of the first series. Vols. I–X of the second series. And supplementary vols. of Pauly-Wissowa Kroll's *Realenzyklopädie.* With an appendix to suppl. vol. XV.

Because significant additions to articles in the main set may appear in several supplementary volumes, because some subjects treated in the supplements may not appear in the basic set, and because some articles in the supplements replace those in earlier volumes, this index is especially welcome. In a single alphabet it lists all the articles in the supplements, giving the volume number and a symbol for the type of article: replacement, new entry, major addition, minor addition.

Pauly, August Friedrich von. Der kleine Pauly; Lexikon der Antike. Auf der Grundlage von Pauly's Real-Encyclopädie der classischen Altertumswissenschaft unter Mitwirkung zahlreicher Fachgelehrter, bearb. und hrsg. von Konrad Ziegler und Walther Sontheimer. Stuttgart, Alfred Druckenmüller Verlag, 1964–75. 5v. il.   **DA129**

An abridgment of *Pauly-Wissowa* (DA126), including a high percentage of its articles in concise form. Articles are signed with initials. New advances in scholarship, where relevant, are reflected, and bibliographic references have been updated as necessary.

Reference to the longer article in the parent work is often given (cited as *RE*). Note should also be taken of the *Nachträge* in v.1 and v.3 of the abridgment. Corrigenda and addenda in v.5.   DE5.K5

Pfeiffer, Rudolf. History of classical scholarship from the beginnings to the end of the Hellenistic age. Oxford, Clarendon Pr., 1968. 311p.   **DA130**

Following a brief survey of the nature of historical writing in the pre-Hellenic periods and the oriental backgrounds, the work concentrates on "the foundation laid by Greek poets and scholars in the last three centuries B.C. for the whole future of classical scholarship."—*Pref.* Extensive footnotes and references to original sources; brief selection of modern secondary literature.   AZ301.P4

——— History of classical scholarship from 1300 to 1850. Oxford, Clarendon Pr., 1976. 214p.   **DA131**

A survey of classical studies, editions, commentaries, transmission and effect of major scholarship from pre-humanism to German neohellenism. Extensive notes and bibliographies.   AZ201.P43

The Princeton encyclopedia of classical sites. Richard Stillwell, ed. Princeton, Princeton Univ. Pr., 1976. 1019p. plates, maps.   **DA132**

Aims "to provide a one-volume source of information on sites that show remains from the Classical period."—*Pref.* (The "Classical period" is understood to cover from about 750 B.C. to the 6th century A.D.) In general, entry is under the form of the name of the site as it was known in classical times, with the modern name, when it differs, following. Location and historical notes are given, together with dates of excavation expeditions and a general summary of the extent of the work done. Bibliographical references are provided and indication is made of those works which include site maps, plans, or illustrations. Some corrections and additions are included in Charles Delvoye's review in *L'antiquité classique*, XLVI (1977), p.345–47.   DE59.P7

Sandys, Sir John Edwin. Companion to Latin studies. 3d ed. Cambridge, Univ. Pr.; N.Y., Macmillan, 1925. 891p. il. (Repr.: N.Y., Hafner, 1963)   **DA133**

1st ed. 1910; 2d ed. 1913.

A handbook covering such subjects as the geography and ethnology of Italy, fauna and flora, history, religion and mythology, private and public antiquities, art, literature, epigraphy, paleography, etc. Includes bibliographies.   DG77.S3

Traulos, Ioannes N. Pictorial dictionary of ancient Athens [translated from the Greek]. London, Thames & Hudson; N.Y., Praeger, 1971. 590p. il., maps, plans.   **DA134**

Prep. in collaboration with the Deutsches Archäologisches Institut.

Similar in intent to Nash's work (DA124), and is a dictionary of monuments, temples, and other extant structures from prehistoric through classical times in Athens. Includes photographs, plans, and extensive bibliographies. Topical index.   NA280.T68

Whibley, Leonard. Companion to Greek studies. 4th ed., rev. Cambridge, Univ. Pr., 1931. 790p. il. (Repr.: N.Y., Hafner, 1968)   **DA135**

1st ed. 1905; 3d ed. 1916.

The work by Sandys (DA133) and this by Whibley are prepared on the same plan and similarly arranged. Each consists of a series of articles, by specialists, on topics of importance such as geography,

ethnology, flora, science, chronology, coins, ships, buildings, population, slavery, etc. Articles are well written, with useful bibliographies, and each volume has four indexes: (1) persons, deities, and races; (2) places, rivers, and mountains; (3) scholars and modern writers; (4) Greek (or Latin) words and phrases. Very useful as supplementing the various classical dictionaries.   DF77.W5

Who was who in the Greek world, 776 BC–30 BC. Ed. by Diana Bowder. Oxford, Phaidon; Ithaca, Cornell Univ. Pr., [1982]. 227p. il.   **DA136**

Similar in design and purpose to the same editor's biographical dictionary for the Roman world (below). Bibliographic references; illustrations drawn from works of art, coins, portrait busts, etc. Index of persons mentioned but not accorded an entry in the text.   DF208.W48

Who was who in the Roman world, 753 BC–AD 476. Ed. by Diana Bowder. Ithaca, Cornell Univ. Pr.; Oxford, Phaidon, [1980]. 256p. il.   **DA137**

Aims "to provide a biographical reference work of scholarly accuracy and reliability that is easily accessible to the student and general reader of Roman history, and . . . to unite with it an important collection of pictorial documentation. . . . "—*Introd.* One or more bibliographic citations follows each entry.   DG203.W46

Chronologies

Bickerman, Elias Joseph. Chronology of the ancient world. Rev. ed. [London], Thames & Hudson; Ithaca, N.Y., Cornell Univ. Pr., [1980]. 223p. il.   **DA138**

1st ed. 1968.

This English edition is based on the author's *Chronologie* (2. Aufl., Leipzig, 1963), with much supplementary material added. "The plan of the book is therefore to explain the structure of the ancient calendar, the principles followed in antiquity in computing the years, and the rules which we can derive from those principles in relating ancient dates to our own time reckoning."—*Introd.* Tables include the astronomical canon, rising and setting of stars, Olympic years, lists of rulers, etc., and chronological tables of Greek and Roman history.   D54.5.B5

Samuel, Alan Edouard. Greek and Roman chronology; calendars and years in classical antiquity. München, Beck, [1972]. 307p. (Handbuch der Altertumswissenschaft, Abt.I, t.7)   **DA139**

A scholarly and carefully documented work. A discussion of the astronomical background is followed by chapters on Greek astronomical calendars, Greek civil calendars, calendars of the Hellenistic kingdoms, the Roman calendar, calendars of the Eastern Roman provinces, Greek chronography, and Roman chronography.   PA25.H24

Atlases

Atlas of classical archaeology. Ed. by M. I. Finley; maps and plans by John Flower. London, Chatto and Windus; N.Y., McGraw-Hill, 1977. 256p. il. 29cm.   **DA140**

Intended for students "and other 'stay-at-home' readers" but primarily for travelers. "We have omitted cities and districts regardless of their importance in antiquity, if, for one reason or another, the visible *classical* remains are scanty or uninteresting to the specialist."—*Introd.* Arranged by country, moving from west to east; each chapter presents an overview of a particular site, with a map of the region, plan of the site, photographs of representative art and of the site, and a short bibliography. Appendixes: chronological table; Roman emperors; Greek vase types; Greek architectural orders; glossary. Indexed.   G1046.E15A8

Cornell, Tim and **Matthews, John.** Atlas of the Roman world. N.Y., Facts on File; Oxford, Phaidon, [1982]. 240p. il., maps.   **DA141**

A survey of "the Roman world in its physical and cultural setting" (*Introd.*) presented through a combination of text, maps, photographs and drawings. Covers from the founding of Rome to the Byzantine reconquest of Italy in 540 A.D. Selected bibliography; gazetteer; index.　　　DG77.C597

Heyden, A. A. M. van der and **Scullard, Howard Hayes.** Atlas of the classical world. London, Nelson, 1959. 221p.
　　　　　　　　　　　　　　　　　　　　　　DA142

Originally published as *Atlas van de antieke wereld* (Amsterdam, Elsevier, 1958).

An excellent atlas depicting the life and cultures of the classical world in maps and pictures, with textual comment. The photographs of art and archaeological subjects are outstanding.

The *Shorter atlas of the classical world* (London, Nelson, 1963. 239p.) is the work of the same compilers and includes good illustrations.　　　DE29.H463

MEDIEVAL AND RENAISSANCE

Guides

See also AA250–AA262.

Caenegem, R. C. van. Guide to the sources of medieval history. With the collaboration of F. L. Ganshof. Amsterdam, etc., North-Holland Publ. Co., 1978. 428p. (Europe in the Middle Ages. Selected studies, v.2)　　　**DA143**

Earlier versions appeared in Dutch (*Encyclopedie van de Geschiedenis der Middeleeuwen.* Ghent, 1962) and German (*Kurze Quellenkunde des west-europäischen Mittelalters.* Göttingen, 1964); this is a revised and expanded edition, not merely a translation.

In five main sections: (1) Typology of the sources of medieval history; (2) Libraries and archives (i.e., repositories of medieval manuscripts); (3) Great collections and repertories of sources; (4) Reference works for the study of medieval texts; (5) Bibliographical introduction to the auxiliary sciences of history. Each section consists of a number of explanatory or bibliographic chapters citing and describing a wide range of sources for the many aspects of medieval studies. Detailed table of contents; index of names and anonymous titles.　　　Z6203.C25

Medieval studies; an introduction. Ed. by James M. M. Powell. [Syracuse], Syracuse Univ. Pr., 1976. 389p.
　　　　　　　　　　　　　　　　　　　　　　DA144

Designed to offer the student "a convenient orientation in the field."—*Introd.* Essays by various authors on all aspects of medieval studies. Bibliographical footnotes and/or substantial bibliographies at the end of each chapter. Includes paleography, diplomatics, chronology, literature, music, etc., as well as history.　　　D116.M4

Pacaut, Marcel. Guide de l'étudiant en histoire médiévale. 2.éd. Paris, Presses Universitaires de France, 1973. 179p.
　　　　　　　　　　　　　　　　　　　　　　DA145

1st ed. 1968.

A basic guide to bibliographies, dictionaries, atlases, journals, large collections of texts and primary sources, etc., useful to the beginning student. L. Halphen's *Initiation aux études d'histoire du Moyen Âge* (3.éd. 1952) is still useful as an introduction to methodology.　　　Z6203.P22

Bibliography

Chevalier, Cyr Ulysse Joseph. Répertoire des sources historiques du Moyen Âge. Nouv. éd. refondue, corr. et augm. Paris, Picard, 1894–1907. 2v. in 4. (Repr.: N.Y., Kraus, 1959–60. 4v.)　　　**DA146**

Publisher varies.

Contents: Bio-bibliographie, nouv. éd.; refondue, corr. et consi-

dérablement augm. 1903–07. 2v.; Topobibliographie, 1894–1903. 2v.

Of first importance for the literature of medieval history. The first part is arranged alphabetically by personal name (in the French form), the second by place and topic. Under each name, references are given to sources. An immense mass of material is indexed, but with no critical indication of value. For further information on the bio-bibliographical section, *see* AJ11.　　　Z6203.C52

Crosby, Everett U., Bishko, C. Julian and **Kellogg, Robert L.** Medieval studies: a bibliographical guide. N.Y., Garland, 1983. 1131p.　　　**DA147**

About 9,000 items (books and monographs) in classed arrangement; nearly all entries are briefly annotated. Lists "the major collections of sources and the secondary literature considered to be of basic importance for the history and the culture of the western European Middle Ages, Byzantium, and medieval Islamic civilization."—*Introd.* Detailed table of contents; indexes of authors and topics.　　　Z5579.5.C76

North Carolina. University. Library. Humanities Division. Medieval and Renaissance studies; a location guide to selected works and source collections in the libraries of the University of North Carolina at Chapel Hill and Duke University. Prep. by the Reference Staff of the Humanities Division, University of North Carolina Library, under the supervision of Louise McG. Hall. Chapel Hill, Univ. of North Carolina, 1974. 325p., 15p.　　　**DA148**

A bibliographical guide for the whole range of medieval and Renaissance studies. Although prepared as a finding aid for scholars using the Duke University and University of North Carolina libraries, the lists will prove useful in other situations.

This edition updated from the previous one (1967) by the addition of "Addenda II" (15p.).　　　Z733.A52.N862

Paetow, Louis John. A guide to the study of medieval history. Rev. and corr. ed. with errata comp. by Gray C. Boyce and an addendum by Lynn Thorndike. Millwood, N.Y., Kraus Reprint, [1980]. cxii, 643p.　　　**DA149**

"Prep. under the auspices of the Medieval Academy of America." —*t.p.*

A reprinting of the 1931 ed. (repr. 1959) with the addition of an errata section, p.xxi–li, and an addendum section, p.liii–cxii, of titles of books and articles not cited in previous editions. Items in this latter section are keyed to appropriate sections of the main work; only works published through 1930 are included.

Supplemented by:　　　Z6203.P25

Boyce, Gray Cowan. Literature of medieval history. 1930–1975; a supplement to Louis John Paetow's A guide to the study of medieval history. Millwood, N.Y., Kraus Internat. Pubns., [1981]. 5v.　　　**DA150**

Sponsored by the Medieval Academy of America.

Follows much the same arrangement as the earlier work (above), with an "accent on the needs of advanced students and scholars."— *Pref.* Also like the earlier work, this supplement concentrates on medieval studies of Western Europe with "restricted attention to Eastern and Northern Europe" and excludes material specifically on English history. Coverage of medieval culture has been expanded to the year 1500. The index (v.5) is only of personal names as either author or subject.　　　Z6203.P25

Potthast, August. Bibliotheca historica medii aevi. Wegweiser durch die Geschichtswerke des europäischen Mittelalters bis 1500. 2.verb. und verm. Aufl. Berlin, Weber, 1896. 2v. (Repr.: Graz, Akademische Druck- u. Verlagsanstalt, 1954)　　　**DA151**

Subtitle: Vollständiges Inhaltsverzeichnis zu Acta Sanctorum Boll., Bouquet, Migne, Monum. Germ. Hist., Muratori, Rerum Britann. Scriptores, etc. Anhang: Quellenkunde für die Geschichte der europäischen Staaten während des Mittelalters.

An indispensable work, though incomplete and sometimes inaccurate, listing medieval chronicles and analyzing many of the large source collections as indicated in the subtitle. The second part is an alphabetical list of medieval writers with, when possible, characterizing phrase and dates, indicating manuscripts, editions, and commentaries.

A new edition is in progress: Z6203.P87

Repertorium fontium historiae medii aevi, primum ab Augusto Potthast digestum, nunc cura collegii historicorum e pluribus nationibus emendatum et auctum. Romae, Istit. Storico Italiano per il Medio Evo, 1962–84. v.1–5. (In progress) **DA152**

At head of title: Istituto Storico Italiano per il Medio Evo. Unione Internazionale degli Istituti di Archeologia, Storia e Storia dell' Arte in Roma.

Contents: v.1, Series collectionum; v.2–5, Fontes, A–H.

The first volume of the "new Potthast" corresponds generally to the first major section of the old work, i.e., an alphabetical listing of sets of chronicles, miscellanies, and other collections of medieval sources, together with their contents. It contains some sets omitted by Potthast and many published since that work appeared, including Byzantine, Arabic, Jewish, and Turkish sets, not covered in Potthast. Bibliographic treatment is good. Introductory and explanatory material is in Latin.

The "Fontes" section offers a repertory of medieval writings arranged by individual author's name or anonymous title of the chronicle or document treated. Whereas the listings in Potthast were limited to works relating to historical studies in the strict sense, the new work extends coverage to works of theology, philosophy, law, economics, art, and literature. As in the earlier work entries include, as far as possible, an identifying note together with references to manuscripts, translations, facsimiles, editions, and commentaries.
Z6203.R427

——— Additamenta. Rome, Istituto Storico Italiano per il Medio Evo, 1977– . v.1– . (In progress)

Contents: v.1, Series collectionum continuata et aucta (1962–1972). (181p.)

Cites new collections and additions to those listed in v.1; corrections to listings in v.1, p.175–81.

Quirin, Karl Heinz. Einführung in das Studium der mittelalterlichen Geschichte. Mit einem Geleitwort von Hermann Heimpel. 3. verm. Aufl. Braunschweig, Westermann, 1964. 363p. **DA153**

1st ed. 1950.

A useful handbook supplementing Paetow (DA149). Gives much information on location and use of source materials. Bibliography, p.292–363. D116.Q82

Rouse, Richard H. Serial bibliographies for medieval studies. Berkeley, Univ. of California Pr., 1969. 150p. (Univ. of Calif., Los Angeles. Center for Medieval and Renaissance Studies, Pubn. 3) **DA154**

An annotated listing of 283 serial publications (national and regional bibliographies and archival publications as well as periodicals and bibliographical annuals), useful to the research worker in medieval studies. Items are grouped by field of interest, with numerous cross references. Title index. Z6203.R66

Simon, Konstantin Romanovich and **Nersesova, E. A.** Istoriia srednikh vekov. Bibliograficheskii ukazatel'; literatura, izd. v SSSR. [Moskva], Izd. Mosk. Un-ta, 1968–84. v.1–2³. (In progress) **DA155**

Contents: v.1, 1918–1957; v.2, pt.1–3, 1958–68.

A bibliography of historical works on the Middle Ages published in the USSR. Classed arrangement with personal and geographical name indexes. More than 7,300 items in v.1. Z6203.S44

Toronto medieval bibliographies. Toronto, Univ. of Toronto Pr., 1967– . no.1– . (In progress) **DA156**

Contents: no.1, Old Norse-Icelandic studies, H. Bekker-Nielsen (1967. 94p.); no.2, Old English language, F. C. Robinson (1970. 68p.); no.3, Medieval rhetoric, J. J. Murphy (1971. 100p.); no.4, Medieval music, A. Hughes (rev. ed., 1980. 360p.); no.5, Medieval Celtic literature, R. Bromwich (1974. 109p.); no.6, Medieval monasticism, G. Constable (1976. 171p.); no.7, La littérature occitane du moyen âge, R. A. Taylor (1977. 166p.); no.8, Medieval Latin

palaeography, L. Boyle (1984. 399p.); no.9, Medieval Latin liturgy, R. W. Pfaff (1982. 129p.).

A series of authoritative, annotated bibliographies.

Williams, Harry Franklin. An index of mediaeval studies published in Festschriften, 1865–1946, with special reference to Romanic material. Berkeley, Univ. of California Pr., 1951. 165p. **DA157**

An index of the contributions concerning medieval art, customs, history, philosophy, literature, language, and science of Western Europe found in anniversary or homage volumes published in honor of scholars, occasions, or institutions, covering more than 5,000 items from about 500 volumes of such studies. Not all volumes are fully indexed, since material not pertinent to medieval studies is omitted. The emphasis is on Romanic material. Includes a list of the *Festschriften,* a list of reviews of some 170 *Festschriften,* an index of authors, and one of subject matter. Z6203.W5

Current

Bibliographie internationale de l'humanisme et de la Renaissance. Travaux parus en 1965– . Genève, Droz, 1966– . v.1– . Annual. **DA158**

At head of title: Fédération Internationale des Sociétés et Instituts pour l'Étude de la Renaissance.

Lists books and articles in all areas—literature, philosophy, history, religion, the arts, economics, political science, law, science —of study on the 15th and 16th centuries in Europe. Arrangement is alphabetical by author, with subject index. Z6207.R4B5

Cahiers de civilisation médiévale X^e–XIIe siècles: bibliographie. 1958– . Poitiers, Centre d'Études Supérieures de Civilisation Médiévale, Université de Poitiers, 1958– . Annual. **DA159**

The bibliography was issued as part of the journal 1958–68; beginning 1969 the bibliography is issued separately.

An extensive listing of articles and books, primarily on European history and civilization of the 10th–12th centuries; to a lesser extent includes materials relating to Byzantine, Islamic, Slavic, and Middle Eastern civilizations. Annual author index; index for v.1–5 of names, places, texts, etc. CB3.C3

Deutsches Archiv für Erforschung des Mittelalters (Monumenta Germania Historica). Köln, Graz, 1937– . Semiannual. **DA160**

1937–44 called *Deutsches Archiv für Geschichte des Mittelalters.*

A bibliography of articles and books concerning medieval studies. Topical arrangement; descriptive annotations. DD126.A1D4

International medieval bibliography, 1967– . Leeds, Eng.; Minneapolis, Dept. of History, Univ. of Minnesota, [1968–]. [v.1–] Semiannual. **DA161**

Originally issued in card form. The first volume reproduces (in reduced size) the cards issued during 1967; beginning with 1968, the bound volumes appear semiannually. Covers the whole range of medieval studies. Articles indexed are drawn from journals and from *Festschriften;* critical reviews are noted. Arrangement is by subject, with indexes of authors and of personal and place names mentioned in the titles. Z6203.I63

Medioevo latino: bollettino bibliografico della cultura europea dal secolo VI al XIII. Spoleto, Centro Italiano di Studi Sull'Alto Medioevo, 1980– . v.1– . Annual. (Appendice bibliografica a "Studi medievali," v.20–) **DA162**

Claudio Leonardi, ed.

v.2– called 1979– .

Although a high percentage of items in v.1 were published in 1978, numerous publications from 1977 and earlier are included.

An extensive bibliography of primary and secondary sources. Classed arrangement, with indexes of authors and manuscripts. Includes citations to critical reviews.

Dissertations

Monumenta Germaniae Historica. Hochschulschriften zur Geschichte und Kultur des Mittelalters 1939 bis 1972/74 (Deutschland, Österreich, Schweiz), zusammengestellt von Mitarbeiten der Monumenta Germaniae Historica. München, 1975. 3v. (1051p.) (*Its* Hilfsmittel, 1)   **DA163**

A classed listing of some 8,400 dissertations, both published and unpublished. Author and subject indexes in v.3.   Z5579.M66

Dictionaries and compendiums

Dictionary of the Middle Ages. N.Y., Scribner's, [1982–85]. v.1–5. il., maps. (In progress)   **DA164**

Joseph R. Strayer, ed. in chief.

Contents: v.1–5, Aachen-Groote, Gurt.

The completed set is to comprise some 5,000 signed articles ranging in length from about 100 to 10,000 words dealing with various aspects of the many disciplines and interests of medieval scholarship, and intended to be useful at all levels, from high school student to specialist scholar. Chronological limits are roughly A.D. 500 to 1500, with geographic scope "limited to the Latin West, the Slavic world, Asia Minor, the lands of the caliphate in the East, and the Muslim-Christian areas of North Africa."—*Pref.* Among the contributors, U.S. and Canadian scholars predominate; as far as possible, bibliographies emphasize English-language works. *See* and *see also* references; numerous black-and-white maps; illustrations relate mainly to art history.

Two useful one-volume dictionaries of the Middle Ages are the *Dictionary of medieval civilization* by Joseph Dahmus (N.Y., Macmillan, 1984. 700p.) and *The illustrated encyclopedia of medieval civilization* by Arveh Grabois (London, Octopus; N.Y., Mayflower; Jerusalem, Jerusalem Publ. House, 1980. 751p.). Both are meant for the general public and both treat all countries. Because Dahmus offers short definitions, identifications, etc., his work appears to cover more topics (but includes no bibliographies and has no index); Grabois has longer articles (often surveys) with illustrations, provides short bibliographies, and includes a chronology and an index.   D114.D5

Lexikon des Mittelalters. Redaktion: Liselotte Lutz [et al.]. München, Artemis Verlag, [1977–84]. Bd.1, Lfg.1–3⁴. (In progress)   **DA165**

Contents: Bd.1–3, Lfg.1–4, Aachen–Deutschland.

To be in 5v. plus index.

A new work with signed contributions by an international roster of scholars. Entries for persons, places, terms, etc. Bibliographies. Covers the period 300–1500 A.D., concentrating on Europe.   D101.5.L49

Mas-Latrie, Louis, *Comte de.* Trésor de chronologie d'histoire et de géographie pour l'étude et l'emploi des documents du moyen âge. Paris, Palme, 1889. 2300col. (Repr.: Torino, Bottego d'Erasmo, 1962)   **DA166**

An extremely useful compilation (though at times unreliable), including perpetual calendars; historical chronologies; lists of saints and Fathers of the church, popes, cardinals, bishops, and archbishops; rulers of many countries in Europe, Asia, and Africa, etc.   D114.M139

Meyer, Otto and **Klauser, Renate.** Clavis mediaevalis; kleines Wörterbuch der Mittelalterforschung. Wiesbaden, Harrassowitz, 1962. 311p. il.   **DA167**

A small handbook giving encyclopedic articles on terms used in medieval studies, with bibliographical references.   D114.M4

Storey, R. L. Chronology of the medieval world, 800 to 1491. Gen. ed., Neville Williams. N.Y., David McKay; London, Barrie & Jenkins, 1973. 705p.   **DA168**

Political events are shown chronologically on the left-hand pages, with contributions to religious, intellectual and artistic developments appearing on the corresponding right-hand pages. Index of persons, places, subjects, titles of works of literature and art, occupations by nationality.   D118.S855

General histories

Cambridge mediaeval history, planned by J. B. Bury. . . . Cambridge, Univ. Pr.; N.Y., Macmillan, 1911–36. 8v. maps.   **DA169**

Contents: v.1, The Christian Roman Empire and the foundation of the Teutonic kingdoms. 2d ed. 1924; v.2, Rise of the Saracens and the foundation of the Western Empire; v.3, Germany and the Western Empire; v.4, Eastern Roman Empire; v.5, Contest of empire and papacy; v.6, Victory of the papacy; v.7, Decline of empire and papacy; v.8, Close of the Middle Ages.

An excellent reference history, written by specialists, with full bibliographies at the end of each volume.   D117.C3

——— [2d ed.] Cambridge, Univ. Pr., 1966–67. v.4 in 2v.   **DA170**

Contents: v.4, ed. by J. M. Hussey, pt. 1, Byzantium and its neighbors; pt.2, The Byzantine empire: government, church and civilisation.

These first published parts of the new edition represent a complete reworking of the earlier volume for the Byzantine Empire. The limiting dates, 717–1453, of the first edition have been retained, but two new introductory chapters have been added to sketch the background from the time of Constantine to 717. Fully indexed; extensive bibliography.   D117.C32

Previté-Orton, Charles William. The shorter Cambridge medieval history. Cambridge, Univ. Pr., 1952. 2v.   **DA171**

Issued in paperback 1975.

Contents: v.1, The later Roman Empire to the twelfth century; v.2, The twelfth century to the Renaissance.

A concise version by one of the editors of the original *Cambridge medieval history.*   D117.P75

Byzantine studies

Bibliography

Allen, Jelisaveta S. and **Ševčenko, Ihor.** Literature in various Byzantine disciplines, 1892–1977. London, Publ. for the Dumbarton Oaks Ctr. for Byzantine Studies, Wash. [by] Mansell, 1981– . v.1– . (Dumbarton Oaks bibliographies, ser.2) (In progress)   **DA172**

Contents: v.1, Epigraphy (386p.).

A cumulation of the entries from the bibliographies, articles, and book reviews appearing in *Byzantinische Zeitschrift* III Abt. (DA175). Arranged topically, then chronologically; good indexes.

v.1 includes some 2,473 items and adds a dated inscription index. A useful "Key to periodicals and abbreviated titles" includes full name, place of publication, and date the periodical began. v.2 is to cover numismatics and sigillography.   Z6207.B9A44

Dölger, Franz and **Schneider, Alfons Maria.** Byzanz. Bern; Francke, 1952. 328p. (Wissenschaftliche Forschungsberichte. Geisteswissenschaftliche Reihe. Bd.5)   **DA173**

A survey of Byzantine studies published 1938–50, with bibliographical footnotes. The first section covers history, literature, and language; the second, early Christian and Byzantine art. Author index for each section.

Charles Diehl's bibliography in *Byzantium; greatness and decline* (New Brunswick, N.J., Rutgers Univ. Pr., 1957, p.301–57) emphasizes English language works.   Z6207.B9D6

Dumbarton Oaks. Dictionary catalogue of the Byzantine collection of the Dumbarton Oaks Research Library, Washington, D.C. Boston, G. K. Hall, 1975. 12v.   **DA174**

At head of title: Harvard Uniiversity.

Provides photographic reproductions of catalog cards of one of the richest libraries on Byzantine civilization, including strong collections relating to "antecedent cultures which exerted an important influence on the development of Byzantium as well as contemporary cultures which influenced or were influenced by Byzantium [i.e., late Graeco-Roman world, early and medieval Islam, and the world of the Orthodox Slavs]. . . . "—Introd. Dictionary arrangement of main and added entries and subject entries for books, journals, documents, etc. Z6207.B9D85

Current

Byzantinische Zeitschrift: III. Abteilung. München, C. H. Beck, 1892– . Bd.1– . Semiannual. **DA175**

Bd.1–41 (1892–1941) reprinted by Johnson Reprint, N.Y., 1964.

An important current listing of books, articles, and essays published in Europe and North America in all European languages on the Byzantine period (325–1453). Subject arrangement with some annotations and references to reviews; annual author index.

A cumulation of the entries on Byzantine art from 1892–1967 (*see* BE6) and one for entries on epigraphy from 1892–1977 (*see* DA172) have been published in the "Dumbarton Oaks bibliographies" series.

For coverage of the writings during the World War II years see the compilation sponsored by the Association Internationale des Études Byzantines, *Dix années d'études byzantines . . . 1939–1948* (Paris, 1949. 170p.).

Byzantinoslavica: revue internationale des études byzantines. Prague, Ceskoslovenska Akademie Ved, 1929– . v.1– . Semiannual. **DA176**

Beginning 1931, each issue includes a lengthy bibliography of recent books and articles on Byzantine history to 1461. Topical arrangement; frequent annotations; references to reviews; author index. CB231.B9

Crusades

See also DA9.

Atiya, Aziz Suryal. The crusade; historiography and bibliography. Bloomington, Indiana Univ. Pr., 1962. 170p. **DA177**

A companion volume to the author's *Crusade, commerce and culture* (1962).

Includes chapters on historiography with descriptions of the great historical collections and a bibliography of books and periodical articles in various languages on the Crusades. Z6207.C97A8

Mayer, Hans Eberhard. Bibliographie zur Geschichte der Kreuzzüge. Hannover, Hahnsche Buchhandlung, 1960. 270p. **DA178**

Lists almost 5,400 numbered entries on the age of the Crusades up to about 1453 in a classified arrangement. Includes both books and periodical articles published before 1957/58 in Western languages and also in Arabic, Hebrew, and Chinese. The field is interpreted broadly to include the church, legal, economic, social, and intellectual history of the time.

MODERN

Bibliography

Bibliographie internationale d'histoire militaire. t.2– , 1975/77– . [Berne, Comité de Bibliographie de la CIHMC], 1979– . Annual. **DA179**

At head of title: Comité International des Sciences Historiques, Commission Internationale d'Histoire Militaire Comparée, Comité de Bibliographie.

Introduction and annotations in French and English; German is to be added with v.3.

A first volume covering selected publications of 1974/76 was published 1978 as *Bulletin de bibliographie* of the Comité.

Provides an international survey of monographic publications on military history. Main entry listing with chronological, geographic, name, and subject indexes. Z6724.H6B84

Bibliographie zur Zeitgeschichte, 1953–1980. Im Auftrag des Instituts für Zeitgeschichte München, hrsg. von Thilo Vogelsang und Hellmuth Auerbach. München, K. G. Saur, 1982–83. 3v. **DA180**

Contents: Bd.1, Allgemeiner Teil; Bd.2, Geschichte des 20. Jahrhunderts bis 1945; Bd.3, Geschichte des 20. Jahrhunderts seit 1945.

Represents a cumulation of the citations in the quarterly "Bibliographie zur Zeitgeschichte" published as a *Beilage* to the *Vierteljahrshefte für Zeitgeschichte,* Jahrg. 1–28 (1953–80). Classed arrangement. Includes monographs, periodical articles, and dissertations. Z6204.B59

Floyd, Dale E. The world bibliography of armed land conflict from Waterloo to World War I: wars, campaigns, battles, revolutions, revolts, coups d'état, insurrections, riots, armed confrontations. Wilmington, Del., Michael Glazier, Inc., [1979]. 2v. **DA181**

In three main sections, each with numerous subdivisions: (1) General military history; (2) Continents, smaller land areas and countries; (3) Armed confrontations. Nearly 4,000 entries, including books, periodical articles, pamphlets, and doctoral dissertations. Lacks an index. Z6724.H6F56

Foreign affairs bibliography; a selected and annotated list of books on international relations, 1919/32–1962/72. N.Y. and London, publ. by Harper [etc.] for the Council on Foreign Relations, 1933–76. 5v. **DA182**

Useful bibliographies with critical annotations, based on bibliographies appearing quarterly in *Foreign affairs,* revised and enlarged, with some titles dropped, many added, and many annotations rewritten. Includes numerous foreign-language titles. Z6463.F73

Foreign affairs 50-year bibliography; new evaluations of significant books on international relations, 1920–1970. Byron Dexter, ed. N.Y., Bowker, 1972. 936p. **DA183**

Not a cumulation of reviews from earlier *Foreign affairs* bibliographies, but rather a selective bibliography (with new appraisals) of more than 2,100 outstanding books on international relations published 1920–70. Selection and reappraisal was the work of 400 advisers and reviewers. Z6461.F62

Foreign Relations Library. Catalog of the Foreign Relations Library, Council on Foreign Relations, Inc., New York. Boston, G. K. Hall, 1969. 9v. **DA184**

An author, subject, and selective title catalog of a collection which aims to "cover all phases of international relations since 1918, but reference and source material necessary to an understanding of pre-World War I diplomatic and economic relations are also included." —*Pref.* Includes books, pamphlets, government publications (especially those of the United States) and publications of international organizations (except League of Nations).

———— ———— First supplement. Boston, G. K. Hall, 1979. 3v.

Reflects cataloging of the 1968–78 period.

The catalog is complemented by the Royal Institute of International Affairs Library's *Index to periodical articles,* 1950/64, 1965/72, and 1973/78 (Boston, G. K. Hall, 1964–79. 4v.); it follows a classified arrangement and is based on that Library's collection. Z6209.F656

Great Britain. Foreign Office. Catalogue of the Foreign Office Library, 1926–1968. Boston, G. K. Hall, 1972. 8v. **DA184a**

Lists works relating to politics, government, economic development, and international relations between Britain and countries outside the Commonwealth. Author, title, subject, and classified indexes. Builds on an earlier compilation, *Catalogue of the printed books in the Library of the Foreign Office, London* (London, HMSO, 1926).

The Foreign Office merged with the Colonial Office in 1968 to form the Foreign and Commonwealth Office; for supplements to this catalog *see* DC318 which represents holdings of the combined library of the two offices. Z921.G682

Novaia istoriia. Ukazatel' literatury; izdannoi v SSSR na russkom iazyke, 1917–1940. [Moskva], Izd. Moskovskogo Universiteta, 1980– . chast 1– . (In progress) **DA185**

At head of title: Moskovskii Gosudarstvennyi Universitet imeni M. V. Lomonsova. Nauchnaia Biblioteka imeni A. M. Gor'kogo.

Contents: chast 1, Obshchii otdel pervyi period novoi istorii 1640–1870gg. Pod red. A.V. Ado i M. S. Meiera.

A classed bibliography of Russian writings on modern history published during the 1917–40 period. Includes books, parts of books, and periodical articles.

Roach, John Peter Charles, ed. A bibliography of modern history. Cambridge, Univ. Pr., 1968. 388p. **DA186**

Bibliographies were omitted from the *New Cambridge modern history* (DA197); this volume is intended to compensate for that omission and to serve as a bibliographical tool in its own right. The lists, however, are highly selective in comparison with the detailed bibliographies appearing in the older edition of the *Cambridge modern history*. "The great majority of the lists have been provided by the authors of the various chapters of the *History*."—*Introd.* Cutoff date is generally 1961. Subject index. Z6204.R62

Stanford University. Hoover Institution on War, Revolution and Peace. The library catalogs of the Hoover Institution . . . ; catalog of the Western language collections. Boston, G. K. Hall, 1969. 63v. **DA187**

Reproduces the catalog cards for the Western-language books, pamphlets, and special collections of one of the major libraries of late 19th and 20th century economic, social and political history of Europe and Asia. The same publisher has issued a separate catalog of Western-language periodicals and newspapers (3v.), and catalogs of materials in the Chinese- (13v.), Japanese- (7v.), Arabic- (1v.), and Turkish and Persian- (1v.) language collections.

An extensive guide to the library's archival and manuscript holdings acquired to 1978 is: *Guide to the Hoover Institution Archives,* comp. by Charles G. Palm and Dale Reed (Stanford, Hoover Inst. Pr., 1980. 418p. Hoover bibliographical ser., 59). Z881.S785

———— ———— 1st–2d supplement. Boston, G. K. Hall, 1972–77.

Contents: Suppl. 1, Catalog of the Western language collection (5v.), Chinese collection (2v.), Japanese collection (1v.); Suppl. 2, Western language collections (6v.), Chinese collection (2v.), Japanese collection (1v.).

Covers materials cataloged July 1969–June 1973. Unlike the main set, the supplements do not include government documents, society publications, Western-language serials and newspapers, and archives and manuscripts.

Dictionaries and compendiums

Harper encyclopedia of the modern world; a concise reference history from 1760 to the present. Ed. by Richard B. Morris and Graham W. Irwin. N.Y., Harper, [1970]. 1271p. **DA188**

In two parts: "a 'Basic Chronology,' which deals with political, military, and diplomatic history by state, region, and area; and a 'Topical Chronology,' in which are handled, on a world-wide basis, economic, social, and constitutional history, and the history of science, thought, and culture."—*Pref.* Despite this division and the later beginning date of coverage, the overall concept of the work is similar to Langer's *Encyclopedia of world history* (DA58). As in the latter work, the detailed index is essential. D205.H35

Palmer, Alan. The Facts on File dictionary of 20th century history, 1900–1978. N.Y., Facts on File, [1979]. [403]p. **DA189**

Based on the 20th-century entries in Palmer's *Penguin dictionary of modern history, 1789–1945,* but extensively revised and expanded to cover through early 1979. Focuses on "political, diplomatic, military, economic, social and religious affairs, but not on the arts, music, sport, literature, pure science or abstract thought."—*Author's note.* Short entries with many cross references. No bibliography. D419.P27

Chronologies

Williams, Neville. Chronology of the expanding world, 1492–1762. N.Y., McKay; London, Barrie & Rockliff, 1969. 700p. **DA190**

D11.5.W48

———— Chronology of the modern world, 1793–1965. Rev. ed. Harmondsworth, Eng., Penguin, 1975. 1020p. **DA191**

1st ed. 1967.

The two chronologies include events in the fields of arts and sciences as well as political and international events of historical interest. Extensive indexes.

The text of the latter has been revised for errors and omissions, and entries have been updated to take account of deaths, changes of title, etc. D11.5.W5

Annuals and current surveys

Annual register; a record of world events, 1758– . London, Longmans; N.Y., St. Martin's Pr., 1761– . Annual. **DA192**

Title varies: Annual register, 1758–1953; Annual register of world events, a review of the year, 1954–63; Annual register: world events, in 1964–74. Publisher varies.

v.1–205 (1758–1963) available on microfilm from Research Publications, Woodbridge, Conn., in its "Early English newspapers" series.

For a brief publishing history *see* Lowndes (AA792), v.1, p. 48.

Contents vary. 19th- and early-20th-century volumes are strong in biographical information in the obituary sections. Recent volumes have very few obituary notices. Includes survey articles on the year's developments in the United Kingdom, the Commonwealth, and other countries of the world; international organizations; and chapters on religion, science, law, the arts, economics, etc.

Includes some public documents, and many abstracts of political speeches. Gives English affairs with more fullness than those of other countries.

———— General index to Dodsley's Annual register, 1758 to 1819. London, Baldwin, 1826. 938p.

D2.A7

Facts on file; world news digest with index. v.1– , Oct./Nov. 1940– . N.Y., Facts on File, 1940– . v.1– . Looseleaf. maps, tables. Weekly, with annual bound volumes available. **DA193**

Subtitle varies.

A weekly classified digest of news arranged under such headings as: World affairs, National affairs, Foreign affairs, Latin America, Finance, Economy, Arts, Science, Education, Religion, Sports, Obituaries, Miscellaneous, etc. Indexes are published twice monthly and are cumulative throughout the year. The annual bound volume is called *Facts on file yearbook.* Spinoffs include *News dictionary* (annual, 1964–80) and *Latin America* (annual, 1972–78).

———— Five-year index: the index to world events. 1957– .

Contents: 1946–50 (publ. 1958); 1951–55 (publ. 1957); 1956–60 (publ. 1961); 1961–65 (publ. 1966); 1966–70 (publ. 1971); 1971–75 (publ. 1976); 1976–80 (publ. 1981). D410.F3●

Keesing's Contemporary archives; weekly diary of world events with index continually kept up-to-date. v.1–28, July 1, 1931–82. London, Keesing's, 1931–83. Looseleaf. Weekly. **DA194**

Subtitle varies.

A weekly diary of important events in all countries, including texts of speeches and documents, obituaries, statistics, etc., with source of report cited. Detailed indexes cumulate fortnightly, quarterly, annually, and biennially, two years completing a volume. (Until 1954, three years made up a volume.) Beginning in 1959/60, an index of names was added, published quarterly, cumulating annually and biennially.

v.1 preceded by a supplement, "Synopsis of important events," 1918 (end of World War)–1931 (June). 35p.

Also published in French, German and Dutch.

Continued by: D410.K4

Keesing's Contemporary archives; record of world events. v.29, no.1– , Jan. 1983– . London, Longman, 1983– . Monthly. **DA195**

Now presents wider coverage, with contents reorganized into chronological, geographical, and topical sections. A cumulative outline index in each issue supplements the quarterly and annual indexes.

Atlases

New Cambridge modern history atlas, ed. by H. C. Darby and Harold Fullard. Cambridge, Univ. Pr., 1970. 319p. col. maps. **DA196**

Comprises 288 pages of colored maps, plus a subject index, p.289–319. Covers the period 1459–1950. Published as v.14 of the *New Cambridge modern history* (below).

General histories

New Cambridge modern history. Cambridge, Univ. Pr., 1957–79. 14v. **DA197**

Contents: v.1, Renaissance; v.2, Reformation; v.3, Counterrevolution and price revolution; v.4, Decline of Spain and Thirty Years War; v.5, Ascendancy of France; v.6, Rise of Great Britain and Russia; v.7, Old regime; v.8, American and French Revolutions; v.9, War and peace in an age of upheaval; v.10, Zenith of European power; v.11, Material progress and world-wide problems; v.12, Shifting balance of world forces. 2d ed. (1st ed. called: Era of violence); v.13, Companion volume; v.14, Atlas.

Originally publ. as *Cambridge modern history* (1902–26. 13v. and atlas).

The most important general modern history, useful for reference purposes because of its high authority. Unfortunately the bibliographies and indexes were not included in this edition, but a very selective bibliography was separately published as a companion work: J. P. C. Roach's *Bibliography of modern history* (DA186).

v.13, "Companion volume," is a collection of essays on continuity and change. The "Geneaological tables and lists" which made up v.13 of the earlier set (1902) is still useful because the information is not cumulated in the new edition. D208.N4

The World Wars
Guides

Bayliss, Gwyn M. Bibliographic guide to the two World Wars; an annotated survey of English-language reference materials. London & N.Y., Bowker, [1977]. 578p. **DA198**

Undertakes "to describe the most important published aids available" *(Introd.)* for the study of the two World Wars. Arranged by form or type of reference work: general guides, bibliographies, periodical directories and library catalogs, dictionaries and encyclopedias, periodicals, biographies, etc. Author, title, regional/country, and subject indexes. Z6207.E8B39

Bibliography

Bloomberg, Marty and **Weber, Hans H.** World War II and its origins: a select annotated bibliography of books in English. Littleton, Colo., Libraries Unlimited, 1975. 311p. **DA199**

Aims "to help provide a selected body of literature on the origins of World War II and on the military, political, social, cultural, and technological events of the war years, from 1939 to 1945."—*Introd.* Limited to books originally published in English or translated into English. About 1,600 items in classed arrangement, with "Author-title-biographee" index. Z6207.W8B58

Enser, Alfred George Sidney. A subject bibliography of the First World War: books in English 1914–1978. [London], André Deutsch, [1979]. 485p. **DA200**

Subject headings appear in alphabetical order, with citations arranged by author thereunder; author index. In general, "works of less than forty pages, as well as poetry, fiction, juvenile books, humour, rolls of honour and the publications of the War Graves Commission" (*Pref.*) are omitted. Z6207.E8E58

———— A subject bibliography of the Second World War: books in English 1939–1974. Boulder, Colo., Westview Pr.; London, Deutsch, [1977]. 592p. **DA201**

Intended as a guide for "both the general reader and the researcher."—*Pref.* Lists, by subject, items appearing in the British Museum subject catalog, the *Cumulative book index,* the *British national bibliography* and *Whitaker.* Author index. Z6207.W8E57

New York. Public Library. Reference Dept. Subject catalog of the World War I collection. Boston, G. K. Hall, 1961. 4v. **DA202**

During World War I and its reconstruction period the New York Public Library attempted to obtain everything relevant to the war and its aftermath published in the United States and Europe—about 35,000 items. Relevant subject cards from the catalog in the Reference Department are reproduced here; material from the Slavonic, Oriental and Jewish Divisions are not included. Entries for books, pamphlets, and important periodical articles. Z6207.E8N48

New York. Public Library. Research Libraries. Subject catalog of the World War II collection. Boston, G. K. Hall, 1977. 3v. **DA203**

Reproduction of the subject cards from the Research Libraries' catalog, but including only materials in Roman alphabet. Includes related headings as well as World War II subdivisions; in addition to the expected strengths for military and diplomatic history, prisoners, and concentration camps, other areas of special note are communications, propaganda (with many examples of clandestine publications), economic aspects of the war and post-war planning, the effect of the war on art, literature and philosophy, and more than 3,000 personal accounts. Z6207.W8N48

Parrish, Michael. The U.S.S.R. in World War II, an annotated bibliography of books published in the Soviet Union, 1945–1975; with an addenda for the years 1975–1980. N.Y., Garland, 1981. 2v. (Garland reference lib. of social sci., v.75) **DA204**

A classed listing of more than 7,500 items. Brief descriptive annotations; author index.

For a Russian counterpart *see* t.3, vyp.4 of *Istoriia SSR* (DC520): *SSSR v gody Velikoi Otechestvennoi voiny (Iun 1941–Sentiabr 1945g); ukazatel' sovetskoi literatury za 1941–1967gg.* Z6207.W8P37

Schaffer, Ronald. The United States in World War I: a selected bibliography. Santa Barbara, Calif., Clio Books, [1978]. 224p. (War/peace bibliography ser., no.7) **DA205**

A selective bibliography of some 2,900 English-language books, journal articles, and government documents arranged topically. Range of publications is broad: "they include biographies, novels, narrative histories, diaries, letters . . . , joke books, photograph collections, lists of persons who fought."—*Introd.* Author index.

Z6207.E8S3

Smith, Myron J. World War II: the European and Mediterranean theaters; an annotated bibliography. N.Y., Garland, 1984. 450p. (Wars of the United States, 2; Garland reference library of social science, 217) **DA206**

Sections on reference works and special studies are followed by sections for "The war in the air," "The war on land," and "The war at sea," each topically subdivided. About 2,800 items; concise annotations; author and subject indexes. Includes a "Documentary film guide" and a list of journals consulted. Z6207.W8S573

—— World War II at sea: a bibliography of sources in English. Metuchen, N.J., Scarecrow Pr., 1976. 3v.

DA207

Contents: v.1, The European theater; v.2, The Pacific theater; v.3, pt.1, General works, naval hardware, and the All hands chronology (1941–45), pt.2, Home fronts and special studies.

Nearly 10,500 items (books and periodical articles) in classed arrangement. Some annotations. Volumes 1 and 2 each have their own author and name indexes; v.3 has comprehensive author and name indexes to all volumes. Z6207.W8S57

World War II from an American perspective: an annotated bibliography. Santa Barbara, ABC–Clio, [1983]. 277p.

DA208

Aims to cover "all aspects of World War II as it relates to North America."—*Introd.* Author arrangement with detailed subject index. Entries and abstracts are derived from *America: history and life.* Z6207.W8W67

Manuscripts and archives

Gt.Brit. Public Record Office. The Second World War; a guide to documents in the Public Record Office. London, H.M.S.O., 1972. 303p. (Public Record Office handbooks, 15) **DA209**

"This *Guide* has been prepared to accompany the general release of papers early in 1972 and the information it contains has been assembled while the records of the war were still being processed. It is not confined to the 'most significant' records and it must not be assumed that all the classes of records described in the *Guide* can be made available to the public at the beginning of 1972. Where it was known that classes have a longer period of closure than the thirty years prescribed for them this is noted in the *Guide*."—*Introd.* Includes useful historical notes on the ministries, offices, etc. Appendixes of code names, abbreviations, War Cabinet committees, and a list of the "Official histories of the Second World War."

CD1043.A58

Mayer, Sydney L. and **Koenig, William J.** The two World Wars: a guide to manuscript collections in the United Kingdom. London & N.Y., Bowker, [1976]. 317p.

DA210

"The primary material covered . . . concentrates on military and naval records in the public domain as well as the diplomatic and political records which impinge directly on the course of the wars themselves. With one or two exceptions, material still in private ownership has not been included."—*Introd.* Intended as an introductory tool to identify repositories and the nature of their contents rather than as a comprehensive guide. Arranged by place, then by repository. Subject index. Z6611.H5M38

Dictionaries and encyclopedias

Goralski, Robert. World War II almanac: 1931–1945; a political and military record. N.Y., Putnam, [1981]. 486p. il. **DA211**

A chronology of events leading up to the war, and virtually day-by-day summaries of developments during the war years themselves. Statistical tables; bibliography; index. D743.5.G64

The historical encyclopedia of World War II. Ed. by Marcel Baudot [and others]. Tr. from the French by Jesse Dilson, with additional material by Alvin D. Coox, Thomas R. H. Havens. N.Y., Facts on File, [1980]. 548p. maps, charts.

DA212

Original French ed. (Paris, 1977) had title: *Encyclopédie de la guerre 1939–1945.*

A brief introduction to the origins of the war is followed by a dictionary arrangement of entries for persons, places, events, battles, terms, etc. There is a concluding chapter on "Immediate and long-range consequences of the war" and a chronology. Most of the longer articles are signed. Cross references; very little bibliography.

On the whole, the Simon & Schuster work (below) is to be preferred as more comprehensive. D740.E5213

The Simon and Schuster encyclopedia of World War II. Ed. by Thomas Parrish. N.Y., Simon & Schuster, [1978]. 767p. il. **DA213**

An attempt to present an accurate and balanced account of World War II through a series of alphabetically arranged, mainly short articles dealing with the events, persons, places, equipment, terms, etc., that figured prominently in the war. A list of contributing writers, with credentials, is given, but most articles are unsigned. "See" references are provided, and "See also" references are signaled by use of small capitals within the text; there is also a detailed index. Chronology, p.708–15; selected bibliography, p.716–21.

D740.S57

Snyder, Louis L. Louis L. Snyder's Historical guide to World War II. Westport, Conn., Greenwood Pr., [1982]. 838p.

DA214

A dictionary arrangement of entries for causes, developments, results, individuals, weapons, code names, Allied war conferences, catastrophes, social and cultural aspects, spies, counterspies, etc.; emphasis is on non-military aspects of the war. Some brief bibliographies; cross references; index. D740.S65

10 eventful years; a record of events of the years preceding, including and following World War II, 1937 through 1946; prep. under the editorial direction of Walter Yust, ed. of Encyclopaedia Britannica. Chicago, Encyclopaedia Britannica, [1947] 4v. il. **DA215**

An alphabetically arranged encyclopedia covering events, personalities, and developments in science, technology, literature, etc., of a crucial period. Does not supersede the annual *Britannica book of the year* (AC15) for the period, as many articles in the annuals are not included, but it cumulates, summarizes, and surveys the events of the era. Includes useful chronologies, tables, and summaries. Many articles are signed, bibliographies are included, and illustrations are clear, as is the typography. Comprehensive index. AG5.T35

U.S. Office of Naval Operations. United States naval chronology, World War II. Wash., Govt. Prt. Off., 1955. 214p.

DA216

Prep. in the Naval History Division, Office of the Chief of Naval Operations, Navy Dept.

Covers Sept. 1, 1939–Sept. 1945. "A brief factual chronological record of significant events . . . includes, also, a record of the loss or damage of every U.S. naval vessel of any size, as well as every ship sinking by U.S. forces."—*Foreword.* D743.5.U62

Atlases

Banks, Arthur. A military atlas of the First World War, with commentary by Alan Palmer. N.Y., Taplinger; London, Heinemann Educational, [1975]. 338p. maps. 26cm.

DA217

Black-and-white maps, together with diagrams and brief notes. General index of names and topics; "Armed forces index" by country and unit. G1037.B3

Goodenough, Simon. War maps: World War II, from September 1939 to August 1945, air, sea and land, battle by battle. N.Y., St. Martin's Pr.; London, Macdonald, [1982]. 192p. il., maps. 30cm. **DA218**

Maps of the main military and naval events (with explanatory text and illustrations) are grouped by theater of operation (Europe, North Africa, Italy, Russian front, Allied invasion of Northwest Europe, the Orient). Indexed. G1038.G65

Biography

Herwig, Holger H. and **Heyman, Neil M.** Biographical dictionary of World War I. Westport, Conn., Greenwood Pr., [1982]. 424p. **DA219**

Offers biographical sketches of about 325 key World War I figures with emphasis on their roles in the war. Bibliographical references; historical introduction; chronology; select bibliography; index. A table (p.377–93) lists the biographees by country, with indication of their prewar, wartime, and postwar occupations. D507.H47

D B

The Americas

GENERAL WORKS

Bibliography

Brown, John Carter. Bibliotheca americana. A catalogue of books relating to North and South America in the library of John Carter Brown of Providence, R.I. Providence, 1865–71. 3pts. in 4v. (Available in microform from Readex Microprint; Pt.3 repr.: N.Y., Kraus, 1963. 2v.) **DB1**

Contents: pt.1, 1482–1600; pt.2, 1601–1700; pt.3, 1701–1800. 2v. 2d ed. 1875–82, pts.1–2 only.

The catalog of a very rich collection now in the Brown University Library. Pts. 1–2 are largely superseded by the 1919–31 edition (below). The set lists 4,173 numbered, annotated items, arranged chronologically with alphabetical index of authors. Detailed bibliographic information.

The Kraus reprint includes additions and corrections made by Wilberforce Eames in the New York Public Library copy.

Z1203.B87

Brown University. John Carter Brown Library. Bibliotheca americana. Catalogue of the John Carter Brown Library in Brown University. Providence, Lib., 1919–31. 3v. in 5. (Repr.: N.Y., Kraus, 1961–75) **DB2**

Contents: v.1, pt.1, to 1569; v.1, pt.2, 1570–99; v.2, pt.1, 1600–34; v.2, pt.2, 1634–58; v.3, 1659–74.

Still said to be the most complete chronological list available for this period. Lists 3,737 items.

An additional catalog covering books printed 1675–1700 (Providence, 1973. 484p.) was followed by a short-title list of additions, 1471–1700 (Providence, 1973. 167p.), thus completing the record of books printed before 1701 that were in the Library on July 1, 1971.

Z881.P9665

Church, Elihu Dwight. Catalogue of books relating to the discovery and early history of North and South America,

forming a part of the library of E. D. Church, comp. and annotated by George Watson Cole. N.Y., Dodd, 1907. 5v. il. (Repr.: Gloucester, Mass., P. Smith, 1951) **DB3**

A monumental work which includes 1,385 entries of books about America, arranged chronologically by date of publication from the earliest period to 1884, with author and title index. Gives for each book: full title, collation, and important historical and bibliographical annotations, with notes of differences in copies and location of copies in some 50 public and private libraries. Gives many facsimile reproductions of title pages, colophons, etc. The Church collection is now part of the Huntington Library, Huntington, Calif.

Z1203.C55

European Americana: a chronological guide to works printed in Europe relating to the Americas, 1493–1776. N.Y., Readex Books, 1980–82. v.1–2. (In progress) **DB4**

For full information see AA556.

Genoa. Biblioteca Civica Berio. Catalogo della raccolta Colombiano. Catalog of the Columbus collection. [2d ed.] Boston, G. K. Hall, 1963. 151p. **DB5**

1st ed. Genoa, 1906: *Catalogo delle opere componenti la raccolta Colombiana.* 126p.

A photographic reproduction of the author card catalog of the Berio Civic Library, Genoa, comprising 3,156 cards of books, pamphlets, and analytics.

A complementary work is *Contributi alla bibliografia colombiano,* by Gabriela De Paoli and others (Genova, Tilgher, 1980. 140p.)

Z8187.G45

Harrisse, Henry. Bibliotheca americana vetustissima. A description of works relating to America published between the years 1492 and 1551. N.Y., Philes, 1866. 519p. **DB6**

———— ———— Additions. Paris, Librairie Tross, 1872. 199p. (Repr. of both parts: Paris, Maisonneuve, 1922; Madrid, V. Suarez, 1958; Amsterdam, Schippers, 1967)

A standard early work listing, with great bibliographical detail, 304 works relating to America, published anywhere, 1492–1551. Copious footnotes; references to sources.

The "Additions" volume is "not a continuation of the *Bibliotheca americana vetustissima,* but a series of notes and additions intended to aid towards forming a complete list of works relating to America, printed previous to the year 1551."—*Introd.* H1202.H3

Sanz López, Carlos. Bibliotheca americana vetustissima; últimas adiciones. Madrid, Librería General V. Suárez, 1960. 2v. il. **DB7**

Contents: v.1, Hasta 1507; v.2, Hasta 1551. Z1202.H3152

———— Comentario crítico e índice general cronológico. Madrid, Librería General V. Suárez, 1960. 79p. **DB8**

The first two volumes of the above items are "final" supplements to the Harrisse bibliography of the same title (DB6); the other is an index to the Harrisse volumes, the two new volumes, and two other works by Sanz López, *Henry Harrisse . . .* (1958) and *El gran secreto de la carta de Colón* (1959). In 1958 Suárez reprinted the original Harrisse volumes and issued all these titles under the series title, *Bibliotheca americana vetustissima.*

James Ford Bell Library. The James Ford Bell Library: an annotated catalog of original source materials relating to the history of European expansion 1400–1800, University of Minnesota. Boston, G. K. Hall, 1981. 493p. **DB9**

A main entry listing of the Bell Library's holdings as of Dec. 31, 1980. The collection is strong in accounts of the discoveries and explorations of America; includes books, maps, and manuscripts. This volume incorporates the listings in the Library's earlier published catalogs: *Jesuit relations and other Americana in the Library of James Ford Bell* (1950) and the lists of additions to the collection published 1955, 1961, 1967, 1970 and 1975. (Those catalogs remain useful for their chronological approach and for the fuller descriptions, collations, and facsimiles found in the basic volume.) Supplements are to appear in *The merchant explorer,* an annual publication of the Library. Z1212.J35

New York. Public Library. Reference Dept. Dictionary catalog of the history of the Americas. Boston, G. K. Hall, 1961. 28v.   **DB10**

Reproduction of nearly 600,000 author, subject, and other catalog cards of an outstanding collection in North and South American history and related topics. Many subject cards are included for periodical articles indexed by the Library.   Z1201.N4

———— ———— First supplement. Boston, G. K. Hall, 1974. 9v.

Reproduces cards for all materials added to the collection through Dec. 31, 1971. After that date additions appear in the *Dictionary catalog of the Research Libraries* (AA147) and the *Bibliographic guide to North American history* (DB49).

Newberry Library, Chicago. Edward E. Ayer Collection. Dictionary catalog of the Edward E. Ayer collection of Americana and American Indians in the Newberry Library. Boston, G. K. Hall, 1961. 16v.   **DB11**

This collection of some 90,000 pieces is particularly strong in early discoveries and explorations of America, the American Indian, missionary activities, western exploration and travel, cartography, the history of Latin America, the Philippines, and the Hawaiian Islands. The volumes are a reproduction of the entire Ayer dictionary catalog, but do not include the Greenlee and Graff collections.

———— ———— 1st–2d supplement. Boston, G. K. Hall, 1970–80. 7v.

The first supplement adds 9,500 books, pamphlets and serials cataloged for the Ayer Collection and 285 titles added to the Everett D. Graff Collection of Western Americana. The second supplement adds another 9,500 titles for the Ayer Collection (including selected materials from its holdings on Indian linguistics and dissertations on the American Indian). In addition, the Graff Collection is now fully represented here, including additions thereto not included in the first supplement. The latter collection was formerly accessible only through its *Catalogue of the Everett D. Graff Collection of Western Americana,* comp. by Colton Storm (Chicago, Univ. of Chicago Pr., 1968. 854p.).

UNITED STATES

Guides to research

Brooks, Phillip Coolidge. Research in archives; the use of unpublished primary sources. Chicago, Univ. of Chicago Pr., [1969]. 127p.   **DB12**

A manual for the beginning research worker rather than for the archivist. Includes a good section on "Limitations on access and use." Concerned almost wholly with American sources, with special attention to the Library of Congress and the National Archives. Selected bibliography; index.   D16.B87

Burnette, O. Lawrence. Beneath the footnote; a guide to the use and preservation of American historical sources. Madison, State Historical Soc. of Wisconsin, 1969. 450p.   **DB13**

A study of historiography and methodology "offered as a contribution to the care and use of the primary sources for American history, as a guide for neophyte, fledgling, and amateur historians. ... It is not a finding aid. Rather, it is concerned with the origins and evolution of those institutions and practices involved in the care and use of the primary forms of American historical evidence."— *Pref.*   CD3021.B93

Hockett, Homer Carey. The critical method in historical research and writing. N.Y., Macmillan, 1955. 330p. (Repr.: Westport, Conn., Greenwood Pr., 1977)   **DB14**

"A rewritten and expanded edition of the author's *Introduction to research in American history* [2d ed. 1948]."—*title page.*

Treats the principles of historical criticism, and the preparation of the master's essay and the doctoral dissertation. Bibliography, p.265–95.

Although the discussion is somewhat general, the point of view and the bibliography are primarily concerned with American history.   E175.7.H6446

Bibliography

See also DB136.

American foreign relations; a historiographical review. Gerald K. Haines and J. Samuel Walker, eds. Westport, Conn., Greenwood Pr., [1981]. 369p. (Contributions in American history, 90)   **DB15**

A series of essays by scholars surveying the "most significant literature in American diplomatic history . . . through the 1940s" (*Introd.*) and placing them in their historical framework. Essays cover specific periods, the concluding one dealing with "Some sources and problems for diplomatic historians in the next two decades." Author index.   E183.7.A56

American studies: topics and sources. Robert H. Walker, ed. Westport, Conn., Greenwood Pr., [1976]. 393p. (Contributions in American studies, no.24)   **DB16**

Offers bibliographical articles by various scholars, with the opportunity to update the articles since their first appearance in *American studies international.* The 21 essays cover both the traditional disciplines of history—religious history, the presidency, cartography, etc.—and interdisciplinary studies such as popular culture, women's studies, and urban history (these last dealing with books, archives, journals). A bibliography of all works cited serves as an author index; additional title index.

Continued by: E175.8.A582

Sources for American studies. Ed. by Jefferson B. Kellogg and Robert H. Walker. Westport, Conn., Greenwood Pr., [1983]. 766p. il. (Contributions in American studies, 64)   **DB17**

A series of bibliographic essays by contributing scholars, followed by a combined bibliography (arranged by author or other main entry) giving full citations to the works discussed. Serves as a companion to *American studies: topics and sources* (above), adding essays on new topics and updating those that appeared in the earlier volume. New topics include Afro-American studies, architectural history, detective fiction, economic history, folklore, foreign policy, historiography, immigration, journalism, linguistics, military history, music, national character, philosophy, poetry, and the Supreme Court.   E175.S58

Arksey, Laura, Pries, Nancy and **Reed, Marcia.** American diaries, an annotated bibliography of published American diaries and journals. Detroit, Gale, [1983]. v.1. (In progress)   **DB18**

For full information *see* BD473.

Beers, Henry Putney. Bibliographies in American history; guide to materials for research. N.Y., Wilson, 1942. 487p. (Repr.: N.Y., Octagon, 1975)   **DB19**

"Published January 1938. Revised edition March 1942."—*verso of title page.*

A classified list of more than 11,000 bibliographies including separate works, analytics, compilations in progress, and manuscript bibliographies, with author and subject index.

Covers many aspects of American history, including political, diplomatic, economic, military, religious, cultural, local, etc.

Continued by: Z1236.A1B4

———— Bibliographies in American history, 1942–1978: guide to materials for research. Woodbridge, Conn., Research Pubns., 1982. 2v. (946p.)   **DB20**

Forms a supplement to the above, listing nearly 11,800 works which are primarily bibliographic in nature or which include relevant lists of publications, descriptions and inventories of archival and manuscript collections, and similar research aids. Index of main entries and subjects. Z1236.B39

Bryson, Thomas A. United States/Middle East diplomatic relations, 1784–1978; an annotated bibliography. Metuchen, N.J., Scarecrow Pr., 1979. 205p. **DB21**

About 1,350 English-language items—books, periodical articles, documents, and dissertations. Arrangement is mainly chronological, with separate sections for general materials and for dissertations. Author index. Z3014.R44B79

Cole, Garold. Travels in America from the voyages of discovery to the present: an annotated bibliography of travel articles in periodicals, 1955–1980. Norman, Univ. of Oklahoma Pr., [1984]. 291p. **DB22**

Brings together citations to travel narratives (mostly from the 18th and 19th centuries) which have appeared as articles in some 220 periodicals. 1,028 entries are grouped by region, state, and date of content. Indexed by traveler, place, subject, author, editor, and translator. Z1236.C64

Coletta, Paolo Enrico. A bibliography of American naval history. Annapolis, Naval Inst. Pr., [1981]. 453p. **DB23**

Nearly 4,900 items are grouped within chronological sections (preceded by chapters on "Selected bibliographic aids and reference works" and "The European heritage"). Within period divisions there are separate sections for books, documents, dissertations and theses, periodical articles and essays in books, oral history interviews, and fiction. In addition to purely naval matters, attention is given to relevant publications concerning "diplomatic, maritime, Marine Corps, military, aviation, geographical, political, economic, social, intellectual, scientific, technological, organizational, administrative, and personal history, and to the U.S. Coast Guard when it operated as part of the U.S. Navy."—*p.vii.* Includes publications through 1979. Indexed. Z1249.N3C64

The craft of public history; an annotated select bibliography. David F. Trask and Robert W. Pomeroy III, gen. eds. Westport, Conn., Greenwood Pr., [1983]. 481p. **DB24**

"Prep. under the auspices of the National Council on Public History."—*t.p.*

Intended as a basic guide to the literature of "public history"—a term denoting "the practice of history and history-related disciplines in settings elsewhere than in educational institutions."—*Pref.* Some 1,700 items (books and periodical articles) are topically arranged and annotated within eleven chapters edited and introduced by contributing scholars. Chapters include research and writing, training, and business management in the field of public history; archives and records management; genealogy and family history; historical editing; historical resource management; library science; media; oral history; and policy history. Emphasis is on "how-to-do-it" aspects. Author index. Z6208.H5C73

Freidel, Frank, ed. Harvard guide to American history. Rev. ed. . . . with the assistance of Richard K. Showman. Cambridge, Belknap Pr. of Harvard Univ. Pr., 1974. 2v. (1290p.) **DB25**

The 1st ed., 1954, was the successor to and a revision of Channing, Hart, and Turner's *Guide to the study and reading of American history* (Boston, Ginn, 1912). This is a new, greatly revised, and expanded edition citing publications through June 1970 (with occasional later listings). About a third of the entries are new to this edition.

The basic reference bibliography for American history. A selective listing covering the whole range of American history, and including citations to both book and periodical materials. Entries in v.1 are arranged by topic; the arrangement of v.2 is chronological, then by topic within historical period. The first chapters are again devoted to "Research methods and materials," and successive parts are: (2) Biographies and personal records; (3) Comprehensive and area histories; (4) Histories of special subjects. The major chronological divisions in v.2 are: America to 1789; United States, 1789–1860; Civil War and reconstruction; Rise of industry and empire; Twentieth century. There are numerous subdivisions within each major section of both volumes; a detailed table of contents; a list of serial

abbreviations; and separate name and subject indexes (the former including entries for authors of specific books and articles cited). An indispensable first source for this field. Z1236.F77

Grim, Ronald E. Historical geography of the United States: a guide to information sources. Detroit, Gale, [1982]. 291p. (Geography and travel information guide ser., 5) **DB26**

In three main sections: (1) Cartographic sources; (2) Archival and other historical sources; (3) Selected literature in historical geography; each section is subdivided by topic or type of source material. Author, title, and subject indexes. Z1247.G74

Guide to American foreign relations since 1700. Ed. by Richard Dean Burns. Santa Barbara, ABC-Clio, [1983]. 1311p. maps. **DB27**

Sponsored by the Society for Historians of American Foreign Relations.

A successor to the *Guide to the diplomatic history of the United States, 1775–1921* by Samuel Flagg Bemis and Grace Gardner Griffin (Wash., 1935; repr. Gloucester, Mass., Peter Smith, 1959. 979p.), but emphasizing foreign relations rather than the more narrowly defined "diplomatic history" of that work. Bemis and Griffin remains useful for references to earlier materials, and particularly for references to manuscript collections. The new work follows a chronological/topical plan and provides "a ready introduction to basic printed (and occasionally microfilmed) books, monographs, essays, documents, and reference works related to the topics that make up America's diplomatic record."—*Introd.* Descriptive annotations, with some critical comment; the great bulk of materials is in English. A cooperative effort; contributing editors and scholars are listed for each chronological/topical chapter. The introduction to each chapter briefly surveys the scholarship of the field and points out areas for further research; sections for "Resources and overviews" and "Personalities" precede the further topical subdivisions. Separate author and subject indexes (the latter subdivided for topics and for individuals). Z6465.U5G84

Guide to the sources of United States military history, ed. by Robin Higham. Hamden, Conn., Archon Books, 1975. 559p. **DB28**

Offers bibliographical essays by historians; surveys the field of U.S. military history, with sections on specific wars, periods, or topics (e.g., military and naval medicine). Each chapter indicates important general references or histories, documents, journals, primary sources, specialized articles and books, and suggests areas for further research; full bibliographic citations appear at the end of each chapter. Materials are judiciously selected with no intention of being comprehensive. No index. Z1249.M5G83

——— Supplement 1. Ed. by Robin Higham and Donald J. Mrozek. [Hamden, Conn.], Archon Books, 1981. 300p.

Extends coverage for areas treated in the basic volume through 1978 and adds new chapters for the U.S. Marine Corps; nuclear war and arms control; military law, martial law, and military government; and U.S. government documentation. Sections are again the work of contributing scholars. Not indexed. Z1249.M5G83

A guide to the study and use of military history. [By] John E. Jessup, Jr. and Robert W. Coakley. [Wash.], Center of Military History, U.S. Army, [1979]. 507p. **DB29**

Chapters by specialists, describing and evaluating works on a given aspect of military history, are followed by bibliographies. In four main sections: (1) Military history, its nature and use; (2) Bibliographical guide; (3) Army programs, activities, and uses; (4) History outside the U.S. Army. Index of names and titles.

The U.S. Army Military History Institute, Carlisle Barracks, Penn., issues a "Special bibliography" series based on the holdings of their very extensive library. Examples are: *U.S. Army and domestic disturbances* (1970); *The U.S. Army and the Indian wars in the Trans-Mississippi West, 1860–1898* (1978); *The War in the Pacific* (1978). E181.G85

Harvard University. Library. American history. Cambridge, Harvard Univ. Lib.; distr. by Harvard Univ. Pr., 1967. 5v. (Widener Library shelflist, 9–13) **DB30**

Contents: v.1–2, Classified listing; v.3–4, Alphabetical listing; v.5, Chronological listing.

For a note on the series *see* AA145.

Lists the nearly 125,600 volumes and pamphlets in this distinguished collection. Z1236.H28

Herstein, Sheila R. and **Robbins, Naomi C.** United States of America. Santa Barbara, Calif., Clio Pr., [1982]. 307p. (World bibliographical ser., v.16) **DB31**

An attempt to "compile a basic core collection for the serious non-specialist reader who wishes to learn more about the United States."—*Pref.* The annotated listing of books and a few documents is arranged by broad subjects from "The country and its people" to "Broadcasting." Index of authors, titles and subjects.

Z1215.H47

Hoy, Suellen M. and **Robinson, Michael C.** Public works history in the United States: a guide to the literature. By the Public Works Historical Society. Nashville, Tenn., Amer. Assoc. for State and Local History, [1982]. 477p. **DB32**

An annotated bibliography in 14 sections (Waterways, Flood control and drainage, Sewers and wastewater treatment, Urban mass transportation, Energy, etc.) with name and title index. The main criterion for inclusion was that a work be written as history; primary sources and technical literature are generally excluded.

Z7164.P97H68

Kaplan, Louis. A bibliography of American autobiographies. . . . Madison, Univ. of Wisconsin Pr., 1961. 372p. **DB33**

For full information *see* AJ96.

Lane, Jack C. America's military past: a guide to information sources. Detroit, Gale, [1980]. 280p. (American government and history information guide ser., v.7) **DB34**

An annotated guide to the major "works dealing with American land and air forces without including any naval sources" (*Introd.*) in view of the comprehensiveness of Myron Smith's *The American Navy* (CJ553–CJ558). Books, government publications, and periodical articles are cited in topical sections within a chronological framework. Author and subject indexes. Z1249.M5L36

Mitterling, Philip I. U.S. cultural history: a guide to information sources. Detroit, Gale, [1980]. 581p. (American government and history information guide ser., v.5) **DB35**

An annotated bibliography of book and periodical materials in the broad field of cultural history. Chapters on reference materials and general works are followed by sections on architecture and the arts; biography; economic, political, and social thought; education; historiography; literature; popular culture; religion; science and medicine. Author, title, and subject indexes. Emphasis is on materials published since 1950. Z1361.C6M57

Monaghan, Frank. French travellers in the United States, 1765–1932: a bibliography, with supplement by Samuel J. Marino. N.Y., Antiquarian Pr., 1961. 130p. il. **DB36**

First published in the *Bulletin* of the New York Public Library, 1933.

An annotated bibliography of 1,583 numbered items, including variant editions and translations. Locates copies. The supplement (p.115–30) adds about 70 more items, with its own index.

Z1236.M

Okinshevich, Leo. United States history & historiography in postwar Soviet writings, 1945–1970. Santa Barbara, Calif., [Clio Pr., 1976]. 431p. **DB37**

A bibliography of nearly 3,700 items. Arrangement is mainly by historical period (with topical subdivisions), but there are additional sections for United States cultural history; church and religion; history of particular regions and dependencies; and Soviet evaluation and criticism of American studies. Separate indexes for Soviet authors, non-Soviet authors, and subjects. Titles are given in transliteration, with an English translation supplied. Occasional explanatory notes. List of periodicals cited, p.377–88.

The semiannual *Soedinennye Shtaty Ameriki*, 1971/72– (Mos-

kva, Akad. Nauk SSSR, Institut Nauchnoi Informatsii po Obshchestvennym Naukam, 1971–) lists books and articles about the United States published in the U.S.S.R.; it includes citations to reviews of American books appearing in Russian journals.

Z1236.O44

Pamphlets in American history. Henry Barnard, ed. Sanford, N.C., Microfilming Corp. of Amer., 1979– . Group 1– . Microfiche. (In progress) **DB38**

Contents: Group 1, Biography (general), Indians, Revolutionary War, Revolutionary War biography, women; Group 2, Civil liberties, labor, tariffs and free trade; Group 3, Cooperative societies, finance, Mexican War 1846–1848, socialism, War of 1812.

A microform series based on the pamphlet collection at the State Historical Society of Wisconsin, augmented by other special collections. Z1236.P27

Pamphlets in American history, Group I– ; a bibliographic guide to the microform collection. Henry Barnard, ed. Sanford, N.C., Microfilming Corp. of Amer., 1979– . (In progress) **DB38a**

Serves as a bibliography of selected pamphlet literature as well as a guide to the microform collection (*see* above). A "numerical index" for each category of pamphlets lists the items in the order in which they appear on the microfiches; author, title, and subject indexes are provided. Z1236.P27E178

Religion and society in North America; an annotated bibliography. Robert deV. Brunkow, ed. Santa Barbara, Calif., ABC-Clio, [1983]. 515p. **DB39**

Cites some 4,300 articles published 1973–80, drawn from the database for *America: history and life,* relating to religion and religious experience in the United States and Canada since the 17th century. Topical arrangement, with index.

The same publisher's *The Jewish experience in America; a historical bibliography* (Santa Barbara, 1983. 190p.) gives some 827 citations to works on Jews and Jewish life in the United States and Canada. Another specialized bibliography for religious/historical studies is *American Puritan studies: an annotated bibliography of dissertations, 1882–1981,* compiled by Michael S. Montgomery (Westport, Conn., Greenwood Pr., 1984. 419p.). Z7831.R44

Smet, Antoine de. Voyageurs belges aux États-Unis du XVIIᵉ siècle à 1900; notices bio-bibliographiques. Bruxelles, 1959. 201p. il. **DB40**

"Publié par le Patrimoine de la Bibliothèque Royale de Belgique." —*verso of title page.*

Bio-bibliographical notes on Belgian voyagers to the United States, with references to manuscripts and documents, and bibliographies of sources. Z1236.S56

Snow, Peter. The United States: a guide to library holdings in the UK. [Wetherby, Eng.], The British Library, Lending Division; Westport, Conn., Meckler Publ., [1982]. 717p. **DB41**

Publ. in assoc. with the Standing Conference of National and University Libraries.

"Printed, microform and audio-visual holdings on all subjects pertaining to United States studies are the subject of coverage."— *Pref.* (Manuscripts are omitted, having been treated in Raimo's guide, DB60.) In addition to describing relevant holdings of more than 350 libraries, provides general directory information (including terms of access, etc.) for the libraries. Includes an appendix of some 1,800 microforms and multi-volume works, with library locations.

A *Guide to the study of United States history outside the U.S., 1945–1980* under the general editorship of Lewis Hanke has been announced for 1985 publication (Millwood, N.Y., Kraus Internat. 3v.); it is to cover research, archives, and the teaching of U.S. history in 55 countries outside the United States. Z1215.S64

Trask, David F., Meyer, Michael C. and **Trask, Roger R.** A bibliography of United States-Latin American relations since 1810; a selected list of eleven thousand published references. Lincoln, Univ. of Nebraska Pr., [1968]. 441p. **DB42**

In two main sections: (1) a chronological survey, and (2) a country-by-country survey. Author index.

Continued by: Z1609.R4T7

Meyer, Michael C. Supplement to A bibliography of United States-Latin American relations since 1810. Lincoln, Univ. of Nebraska Pr., [1979]. 193p.   **DB43**

Lists new publications and some earlier works not included in the basic volume. Follows the plan of the earlier work, adding a few new subsections. 3,568 entries. Cross references, including references to the basic volume. Author index.   Z6465.L29T7 Suppl.

U.S. Library of Congress. General Reference and Bibliography Division. A guide to the study of the United States of America; representative books reflecting the development of American life and thought. Prep. under the direction of Roy P. Basler, by Donald H. Mugridge and Blanche P. McCrum. Wash., Govt. Prt. Off., 1960. 1193p.   **DB44**

Basically a compilation of works on various aspects of American civilization. The 32 chapters include such headings as: literature; geography; general, diplomatic, military, intellectual, and local history; science and technology; education; religion; economic life, etc. Nearly 6,500 numbered entries, most of them annotated, plus citations and evaluative notes for many related works not listed as numbered entries. Terminal date for some sections is 1955; others include publications through 1958.   Z1215.U53

———— ———— Supplement, 1956–65; prep. under the direction of Roy P. Basler by Oliver H. Orr, Jr., and the staff of the Bibliography and Reference Correspondence Section. Wash., 1976. 526p.

A few pre-1956 titles are included, but most works cited were published 1956–65.

Wisconsin. State Historical Society. Library. Subject catalog . . . including the Pamphlet subject catalog beginning in volume 22. Westport, Conn., Greenwood Pr., [1971]. 23v.   **DB45**

Photographic reproduction of subject catalog cards for books, pamphlets, some federal and state documents, Wisconsin obituaries since 1846, selected periodical articles on Wisconsin history, and name entries for biographical sketches in Wisconsin county histories published prior to 1955. The library also has strong collections on "the American Indian, the Revolutionary War, the Civil War, the trans-Mississippi West, the old Northwest, denominational and church history, state and local history, radical social movements, the Negro, and genealogy."—*Introd.* The labor movement and Mormonism are also well represented. Pamphlets are included in the main subject catalog if acquired before 1967; thereafter subject cards for pamphlets appear in v.22–23. The pamphlet collection is being reproduced on microfiche with a finding aid (DB38–DB38a).

The author-title catalog of the library was issued on microfiche (Westport, Conn., Greenwood, 1974. 600 fiches); it includes separate sections for city directories, atlases (by publisher and by geographic area), United States and Canadian newspapers, and labor newspapers.   Z1236.W57

Witherell, Julian W. The United States and Africa: guide to U.S. official documents and government-sponsored publications on Africa, 1785–1975. Wash., Lib. of Congress, 1978. 949p.   **DB46**

For full information *see* DD20–DD21.

Current

America: history and life. A guide to periodical literature. v.1, no.1– , July 1964– . Santa Barbara, Calif., Clio Pr., 1964– . v.1– . Quarterly.   **DB47**

Abstracts "articles on the history of the United States and Canada published throughout the world, and . . . articles dealing with current American life and times."—*Note.* Some 2,200 serial publications are now surveyed (including annuals and *Festschriften*). No.1–3 of each volume contain abstracts; the 4th quarterly issue is the annual index.

Beginning 1974, issued in four parts: A, Article abstracts and citations (Spr., Sum., Fall); B, Book reviews (Spr., Fall); C, American history bibliography (i.e., articles cited in pt.A, books cited in pt.B, and dissertations; annual); D, Annual index (title index added with v.16, 1979).   ●

———— Five year index 1964/69–1979/83. Santa Barbara, 1970–85.

The index covering v.11–15 (1974–78) also includes indexing for the supplement to v.1–10 (below).

———— Supplement to volumes 1–10 (1964–1973). Santa Barbara, Calif., Amer. Bibliographical Center of ABC-Clio, Inc., [1980]. 2v. (759p.)

Contents: pt.I, Article abstracts and citations; pt.II, Index.

Provides abstracts and indexing of some 8,744 articles "originally omitted from *America: History and Life* because either the journals were not received or there were not enough abstracters and editors to complete them."—*Introd.* Also includes some coverage for the 1954–62 period.   ●

American studies bibliography, 1974– . [London], Univ. of London, Inst. of United States Studies, 1975– . Microfiche. Monthly with annual cumulation.   **DB48**

The bibliography for 1974 was issued only as an annual cumulation; beginning Jan. 1975, issued monthly with annual cumulation. Each section of the bibliography can be purchased separately.

In four sections: (1) Author; (2) Title; (3) Subject; (4) Dewey classified. Each entry in all sections provides full bibliographic information for any book, pamphlet, government document, or conference proceedings relevant to the study of the United States. For a full description *see Microform review* 5:194–95 (July 1976).

Bibliographic guide to North American history. v.1– , 1978– . Boston, G. K. Hall, 1979– . Annual.   **DB49**

A dictionary catalog of the monographs and serials cataloged by the Research Libraries of the New York Public Library and by the Library of Congress during the year of coverage. North America is defined as including the United States and Canada, although a few general works on the Americas are included, as is material on the American Indian. Full bibliographic information appears only under the main entry, with briefer information under other entries.

According to the introduction, this is to be the annual supplement to the "United States local history catalog," the two-volume supplement to the New York Public Library Local History and Genealogy Division's *Dictionary catalog* (AK31), but it would seem to supplement the Library's *Dictionary catalog of the History of the Americas Collection* (DB10) as well.   Z1236.B47

Writings on American history, 1902–61. Wash., Amer. Historical Assoc.; Millwood, N.Y., Kraus-Thomson, 1904–1978. 49v.   **DB50**

No bibliographies issued for 1904–05, 1941–47.

Subtitle varies: 1906–35, A bibliography of books and articles on United States and Canadian history . . . with some memoranda on other portions of America.

Imprint varies: 1902, Princeton, N.J., Library Book Store; 1903, Wash., Carnegie Inst., Publ. no.38; 1906–08, N.Y., Macmillan; 1909–11, repr. from the *Annual report* of the A.H.A.; 1912–17, New Haven, Yale Univ. Pr.; 1918–20, issued as suppl. to the *Annual report* of the A.H.A.; 1932, v.3 of the *Annual report;* 1933–34, the *Annual report;* 1930–31, 1935–60, v.2 of the *Annual report.* From 1948 some volumes issued as House documents in the "U.S. serial set."

Index: 1902–40 (publ. 1956).

An excellent annual bibliography and index employing a classified arrangement, with author, title, and subject index. Includes many contents and descriptive notes and, through 1940, critical reviews are cited.

Through 1935 included all books and articles, wherever published, which contained anything of value on the history of the United States and British Canada, and all books published in the United States or Europe on Latin America and the Pacific Islands. Beginning with 1936, the scope was changed to include only writings on the history of the United States and its outlying possessions. The index volume covering 1902–40 expanded the indexing of the annual volumes and "contains references and subject classifications which will not be found in the separate indexes."—*Foreword.*

When the series resumed with coverage for 1948, scope, arrangement, and indexing were again somewhat changed: e.g., (1) only books and articles having any research value for the history of the United States are included; (2) reviews are not cited; (3) titles are cited chronologically according to the beginning date of the subject matter rather than alphabetically by author; (4) indexing is much expanded. Other changes are noted in the preface to the volumes. The list of "Periodicals cited" is a valuable serials record.

For a new series of the same title *see* below.   Z1236.L331

Writings on American history, 1962–73; a subject bibliography of articles. James J. Dougherty, comp.-ed. Wash., Amer. Historical Assoc.; Millwood, N.Y., KTO Pr., 1976. 4v.
DB51

Contents: v.1, Chronological; v.2, Geographical; v.3, Subjects; v.4, Subjects [cont.]; Author index.

Designed to fill the gap between the National Historical Publications Commission's final volume of the same series title and the first volume of a further series edited by Dougherty beginning with coverage of 1973/74 (*see* below). Only periodical articles are included: some 33,000 citations from 510 journals. Each volume is appropriately subdivided (though categories tend to be very broad) to facilitate searching, but there is no detailed subject index. The Library of Congress enters this set and the new series beginning 1973/74 under the compiler-editor's name.

Writings on American history 1962–73, a subject bibliography of books and monographs based on a compilation by James R. Masterson (White Plains, N.Y., Kraus Internat., 1985. 10v.) covers books of that period. Created from Library of Congress catalog cards, the entries follow the same arrangement as the journal bibliography; there are author and name indexes.

—— 1973/74– ; a subject bibliography of articles. James J. Dougherty, comp.-ed. Millwood, N.Y., Kraus-Thomson [for] Amer. Historical Assoc., 1974– . Annual.   **DB52**

The first volume of this new series covers the period June 1973–June 1974, and subsequent annual volumes follow that pattern. Listings are derived from the "Recently published articles" section of the *American historical review* (now separately published), with the addition of supplementary material. Topical subject arrangement with author index. Lacks a detailed subject index.

Dissertations

Christman, Calvin L. Doctoral dissertations in U.S. foreign affairs. *In* Diplomatic history, v.3, no.2– , 1979– . Annual.
DB53

An annual list appearing in each Spring issue of *Diplomatic history.* Titles are drawn from *Dissertation abstracts international;* topical arrangement.

Manuscripts and archives

See also DB140.

Allard, Dean C., Crawley, Martha L. and **Edmison, Mary W.** U.S. naval history sources in the United States. Wash., Naval History Div., Dept. of the Navy, 1979. 235p. il.
DB54

Updates and expands the coverage of the Naval History Division's 1970 publication *U.S. naval history sources in the Washington area.* Aims "to aid students of naval history by identifying manuscript, archival, and other special collections deposited in more than 250 American archives and libraries. Most of these materials are the private papers of officers, men, and civilian officials

of the U.S. Navy."—*Introd.* Arranged by state, then by repository. Index of names of persons, institutions, ships, etc.
Z1249.N3A48

Beers, Henry Putney. The French in North America; a bibliographical guide to French archives, reproductions, and research missions. Baton Rouge, Louisiana State Univ. Pr., 1957. 413p.   **DB55**

A textual account of the bibliographic activities of institutions and individuals in obtaining reproductions of French documents relevant to American (primarily United States) history. Extensive bibliography of archival materials and detailed index.
Z1361.F8B4

—— The French and British in the Old Northwest; a bibliographical guide to archive and manuscript sources. Detroit, Mich., Wayne State Univ. Pr., 1964. 297p.
DB56

"Presents an historical account of the acquisition, preservation and publication . . . of the original records . . . in the Old Northwest (the region south of the Great Lakes) chiefly during the 18th century, and of officials and governing bodies of Canada relating to that region."—*Pref.* Bibliographical sources, p.195–255.   F478.2.B4

—— Spanish & Mexican records of the American Southwest: a bibliographical guide to archive and manuscript sources. Tucson, Univ. of Arizona Pr., [1979]. 493p. maps.
DB57

Offers "a historical account of the acquisition, preservation, and publication, by American institutions and individuals, of the original records created by Spanish and Mexican officials in what became the American Southwest, from the beginning of settlement in the early 1600s to the mid-nineteenth century. The historical treatment primarily concerns public records that have been preserved in official custody. . . . Descriptive information regarding the records, derived from a wide variety of finding aids and other publications, is included, and records of the Franciscan and Jesuit missions are also described."—*Pref.* Records of New Mexico, Texas, California, and Arizona are treated in separate chapters. Bibliography, p.385–454. Detailed index.   Z1251.S8B4

Carnegie Institution, Washington. [Guides to manuscript materials for the history of the United States]. Wash., Inst., 1906–43. 23v. (Repr.: Millwood, N.Y., Kraus Reprint, 1965)   **DB58**

Contents: *American:* Guide to the archives of the government of the United States in Washington, by C. H. Van Tyne and W. G. Leland. Rev. ed. 1907. 327p.; Diplomatic archives of the Department of State, 1789–1840, by A. C. McLaughlin. Rev. ed. 1906. 73p.; Inventory of unpublished material for American religious history in Protestant church archives and other repositories, by W. H. Allison. 1910. 254p.; Calendar of papers in Washington archives relating to the territories of the United States (to 1873), by D. W. Parker. 1911. 476p.

British and British American: Guide to the manuscript materials for the history of the United States to 1783 in the British Museum, in minor London archives and in the libraries of Oxford and Cambridge, by C. M. Andrews and F. G. Davenport. 1908. 499p.; Guide to the materials for American history, to 1783, in the Public Record Office of Great Britain, by C. M. Andrews: v.1, State papers. v.2, Departmental and miscellaneous papers, 1912–14. 2v.; Guide to materials in London archives for the history of the United States since 1783, by C. O. Paullin and F. L. Paxon. 1914. 642p.; Guide to British West Indian archive materials in London and in the Islands, for the history of the United States, by H. C. Bell and D. W. Parker. 1926. 435p.; Guide to materials in Canadian archives, by D. W. Parker. 1913. 339p.

European (except Spanish): List of manuscripts concerning American history preserved in European libraries and noted in their published catalogues and similar printed lists, by D. M. Matteson. 1925. 203p.; Guide to the manuscript materials relating to American history in German state archives, by M. D. Learned. 1912. 352p.; Guide to materials for American history in the libraries and archives of Paris, by W. G. Leland. 1932–43. v.1–2; Guide to the materials for American history in Roman and other Italian archives, by C. R. Fish. 1911. 289p.; Guide to materials for American history in Russian archives, by F. A. Golder. 1917–37. 2v.; Guide to the materials for American history in Swiss and Austrian archives, by A. B. Faust. 1916. 299p.

Spanish and Spanish American: Guide to the materials for American history in Cuban archives, by L. M. Pérez. 1907. 142p.; Descriptive catalogue of the documents relating to the history of the United States in the Papeles Procedentes de Cuba, deposited in the Archivo General de Indias at Seville, by R. R. Hill. 1916. 594p.; Guide to materials for the history of the United States in the principal archives of Mexico, by H. E. Bolton. 1913. 553p.; List of documents in Spanish archives . . . which have been printed or of which transcripts are preserved in American libraries, by J. A. Robertson. 1910. 368p.; Guide to materials . . . in Spanish archives, by W. R. Shepherd. 1907. 107p.

A series of volumes compiled to help the research worker find the materials for the history of the United States located in foreign archives and libraries. Still useful, although in some cases more recent inventories have been made.

A very useful article placing the Carnegie guides in context of more recently published guides for American historians (and also pointing out lacunae) is John J. McCusker's "New guides to primary sources on the history of early British America" in *William and Mary quarterly,* 3d ser., v.41 (Apr. 1984), p.277–95.

Guide des sources de l'histoire des États-Unis dans les archives françaises. Madeline Astorquia [et al.], comp. Paris, France Expansion, 1976. 390p. **DB59**

A survey of documents in the Archives Nationales, Services d'Archives de la Guerre et de la Marine through 1940, and through 1929 for the Ministère des Affaires Étrangères relating to American history. Includes: 16th–17th centuries, America in general; 18th century–1815, North America and the Caribbean; after 1815, only the United States. For the most part, the papers in the municipal libraries are pre-20th century. No indexes.

French consuls in the United States: a calendar of their correspondence in the Archives Nationales by A. P. Nasatir and G. E. Monell (Wash., Lib. of Congress, 1967. 605p.) is a guide to the microfilm copy on deposit at the Library of Congress of early consular records relating to the United States to about 1834; appendixes include lists of French ministers and diplomatic agents, and biographical sketches of French consular agents. CD1192.A2G84

A guide to manuscripts relating to America in Great Britain and Ireland. A revision of the guide ed. in 1961 by B. R. Crick and Miriam Alman. Ed. by John W. Raimo. Westport, Conn., Meckler Books; London, Mansell, [1979]. 467p. **DB60**

Publ. for the British Association for American Studies.

A revised and expanded edition of this important guide which "seeks to draw attention to the location and to give a brief description of all manuscripts in Great Britain and Ireland relating to the history and literature of the American colonies and the United States which did not fall within the scope of the . . . volumes published by the Carnegie Institution [DB58]."—*Introd.* (Descriptions are of collections of papers, not of individual manuscripts.) Arranged by county, then by repository. Detailed index of personal and geographical names, subjects, and repositories.

Many of the collections are available in microform (particularly in the series "British records relating to America" published by Microform Ltd., East Ardsley, Eng.) but such availability is not indicated in this guide.

Grace Gardner Griffin's *Guide to manuscripts relating to American history in British depositories reproduced for the Division of Manuscripts of the Library of Congress* (Wash., 1946. 313p.) remains useful. Z1236.C74

Hebrew Union College—Jewish Institute of Religion. American Jewish Archives. Guide to the holdings of the American Jewish Archives, by James W. Clasper and M. Carolyn Dellenbach. [Cincinnati], American Jewish Archives, [1979]. 211p. (American Jewish Archives. Pubns., no.11) **DB61**

For full information *see* BB547.

Jewish immigrants of the Nazi period in the USA. Herbert A. Strauss, ed. N.Y., K. G. Saur (distr. by Gale, Detroit), [1978–82]. v.1–3. (In progress; to be in 6v.) **DB62**

"Sponsored by the Research Foundation for Jewish Immigration, New York."—*t.p.*

Contents: v.1, Archival resources, comp. by Steven W. Siegel; v.2, Classified and annotated bibliography of books and articles on the immigration and acculturation of Jews from Central Europe to the USA since 1933, comp. by Henry Friedlander [and others]; v.3, pt.1, Guide to the oral history collection of the Research Foundation for Jewish Immigration, New York, comp. by Joan C. Lessing; v.3, pt.2, Classified list of articles concerning emigration in Germany. Jewish periodicals, Jan. 30, 1933 to Nov. 9, 1938, comp. by David R. Schwartz.

A major research project which documents "the immigration, resettlement, and acculturation in the USA of Jews from Germany and Austria who were uprooted by Nazi persecution."—*Pref.,v.1.* Volumes published to date deal with archival sources, published materials, and oral history interviews. Indexed. E184.J5J558

Meckler, Alan M. and McMullin, Ruth. Oral history collections. N.Y., Bowker, 1975. 344p. **DB63**

In two main sections: (1) name and subject index, and (2) directory of oral history centers (subdivided as United States and foreign centers). The index includes both the names of persons interviewed and those prominently mentioned in the interviews. The compilers plan future editions with the hope of achieving a "comprehensive annotated listing of oral history collections located in libraries, oral history centers, and archives. The names of those whose memoirs are included comprise a list of the people most active in recent and contemporary history."—*Foreword.* AI3.M4

National union catalog of manuscript collections. 1959/61– . Hamden, Conn., Shoe String, 1962– . Annual. **DB64**

At head of title: The Library of Congress catalogs.

"Based on reports from American repositories of manuscripts." —*title page, 1959–61.*

Comp. and ed. by the Descriptive Cataloging Division of the Library of Congress. Publisher varies.

Each volume includes reproductions of catalog cards for collections reported by repositories throughout the United States during the period covered. Each entry gives number of items, physical description, scope and content, location, restrictions on access, finding tools, availability of microfilm copies, etc.

The collections consist largely of personal papers: "manuscripts or typescripts, originals or copies, of letters, memoranda, diaries, accounts, log books, drafts, and the like. . . ."—*Introd.* Volumes for 1965– indicate holders of duplicates and holders of original materials as reported by repositories holding reproductions. Beginning 1970, lists oral history interview transcripts and collections containing sound recordings.

Indexes: [v.3], 1959–62 (732p.); 1963–66 in volume for 1966; 1967–69 in volume for 1969; 1970–74 in volume for 1974; 1975– 79. Beginning 1975, indexes are issued in separate volumes which cumulate annually, then quinquennially. In alphabetical arrangement, listing names, places, subjects, and named historical periods. Z6620.U5N3

Philippine-American relations: a guide to manuscript sources in the United States. Comp. and ed. by Shiro Saito. Westport, Conn., Greenwood Pr., [1982]. 256p. **DB65**

For full annotation *see* DG24.

Spalek, John M. Guide to the archival materials of the German-speaking emigration to the United States after 1933. Verzeichnis der Quellen und Materialien der deutschsprachigen Emigration in den U.S.A. seit 1933. Charlottesville, Publ. for the Bibliographical Soc. of the Univ. of Virginia by the Univ. Pr. of Virginia, [1978]. 1133p. **DB66**

A guide to the location of manuscripts and archival materials of German-speaking intellectuals who came to the United States from Europe after 1933. Arranged by personal name. Brief descriptions of collections; index of names (including names cited in the descriptive notes). Includes materials in private hands. Appendixes of names of individuals for whom only a very small amount of material was located and of names of individuals for whom no material was found. Z6611.G46S62

U.S. Library of Congress. A guide to the microfilm collection of early state records. Collected and comp. under the direction of William Sumner Jenkins; ed. by Lillian A. Hamrick. Wash., Lib. of Congress, 1950. various pagings. **DB67**

Begun in 1941 as a joint project of the Library of Congress and the University of North Carolina to locate and reproduce early state legislative proceedings. When the project was resumed after World War II, the coverage was expanded to include also statutory laws; constitutional, administrative, executive, and court records; some local records; records of American Indian nations; and a miscellaneous group.

The *Guide* is an index to more than 2,500,000 pages of records represented on 160,000 feet of microfilm. General arrangement is by the classifications noted above for each state. Items within these classifications are arranged chronologically. Library locations and reel numbers are given for each item.

————— ————— Supplement . . . Collected, comp. and ed. by William Sumner Jenkins. Wash., Lib. of Congress, 1951. xxiii p., 130p., xviii p.

A guide to some 170 reels of microfilm remaining after the regular project had been completed, under five special classes: (1) local records, (2) records of American Indian nations, (3) newspapers, (4) records of rudimentary states, and (5) miscellany.
Z1223.5.A1U47

————— **Manuscript Division.** Members of Congress: a checklist of their papers in the Manuscript Division, Library of Congress. Comp. by John J. McDonough. Wash., Lib. of Congress, 1980. 217p. il. **DB68**

A checklist of the collections of personal papers of "894 Senators, Representatives, and Delegates to the Continental Congress" *(Introd.)* to be found in the Manuscript Division of the Library. "All discrete collections . . . are included . . . , regardless of size or quality." Gives name of the Congressman, birth and death dates as applicable, state represented, term(s) of congressional service, an indication of size of the collection, and indication of any restrictions and of microfilm availability. Z1236.U613

U.S. National Archives and Records Service. Catalog of National Archives microfilm publications. Wash., National Archives and Records Service, 1974. 184p. **DB69**

Supersedes the agency's *List of National Archives microfilm publications,* 1947–68; like that publication it will, presumably, appear periodically, each new edition superseding the previous one.

Lists the source materials and unpublished documents housed in the National Archives which are now available for purchase on positive microfilm—more than 2,100 microfilm publications. Arrangement is by department of the government, with index by keyword and geographical names.

The first volume of this new series contains "roll-by-roll lists of the records of the Continental Congress and the Department of State. Future editions will expand this listing to include other series" until every roll is listed individually.—cf. *Introd.*

"Supplementary list of National Archives microfilm publications, 1974–80," appeared in *Prologue* 13:60–72 (Spr. 1981). Special lists of microfilmed records relating to the American Indian and to Afro-Americans were issued by the National Archives in 1972 and 1973, respectively. CD3027.M514

————— Guide to the National Archives of the United States. Wash., for sale by Supt. of Docs., 1974. 884p. **DB70**

Previous ed., 1948, had title *Guide to the records in the National Archives.*

Lists and briefly describes the various collections of official records accessioned as of June 30, 1970, regardless of where the records are located. "Collectively, these records document the history of the Government from its establishment through the mid-20th century."—*Introd.* Arranged by branch of government, then by bureau or agency; subject index.

The National Archives has also published guides for special topics, e.g., Latin America (DB267) and Cartographic records (CL289). CD3023.U54

Prologue; journal of the National Archives. v.1– , Spring 1969– . Wash., 1969– . 3 times a yr. **DB71**

Contains articles describing activities of the National Archives and various special collections in the Archives. CD3023.P7

U. S. National Historical Publications and Records Commission. Directory of archives and manuscript repositories. Wash., Nat. Archives and Records Service, 1978. 905p. **DB72**

The first published result of what is intended to be an ongoing and expanded revision of the Hamer *Guide* (1961; below), this directory derives from an automated data base which is to be regularly updated and which will be capable of producing further publications of varying specifications and detail.

As it now stands, the *Directory* serves as a companion rather than a successor to Hamer's *Guide:* it aims to give current (i.e., mid-1977) information regarding name of institution, address, telephone number, hours of opening, terms of access, availability of copying facilities, acquisitions policy, volume of holdings of historical source material (with brief description thereof), and bibliographic references to the Hamer *Guide, National union catalog of manuscript collections,* and other printed finding aids. Gives "full entries for 2,675 repositories in all states, District of Columbia, Puerto Rico, the Canal Zone, the Virgin Islands, and the Northern Marianas Trust Territory. "In addition, 575 institutions listed in either the Hamer *Guide* or *NUCMC* which did not return a repository form . . . have been entered as abbreviated listings with minimal identifying information."—*Introd.* Arranged by state or other political unit, then by city and repository. Listing of repositories by type. Index of subjects and repositories. CD3020.U54

U.S. National Historical Publications Commission. A guide to archives and manuscripts in the United States. Philip M. Hamer, ed. New Haven, Yale Univ. Pr., 1961. 775p. **DB73**

"Source materials for the study of the history of the United States and its relations with other nations and peoples."—*Pref.*

Designed not as a union catalog of manuscripts, but as a guide to direct the searcher to the most useful source for his need. Arrangement is by depository, alphabetically by state and then by city. Description of holdings is in textual form, the materials in each depository being grouped by category or type, with individual names—when relevant—then listed alphabetically. Whenever possible, nature and extent of each collection are indicated. References are given to any published guides to an individual collection. Detailed index. CD3022.A45

17th and 18th centuries

Greene, Evarts Boutell and **Morris, Richard B.** A guide to the principal sources for early American history (1600–1800) in the city of New York. 2d ed. rev. by Richard B. Morris. N.Y., Columbia Univ. Pr., 1953. 400p. **DB74**

1st ed. 1929.

A guide to manuscript and printed sources for the study of early American history to be found in the libraries and other depositories in the city of New York. Classed arrangement with general index.
Z1236.G82

Leonard, Eugenie Andruss, Drinker, Sophie Hutchinson and **Holden, Miriam Young.** The American woman in colonial and revolutionary times, 1565–1800; a syllabus with bibliography. Philadelphia, Univ. of Pennsylvania Pr., 1962. 169p. (Repr.: Westport, Conn., Greenwood Pr., 1975) **DB75**

For full information *see* CC543. Z7964.U49L4

Smith, Dwight La Vern. The War of 1812; an annotated bibliography. N.Y., Garland, 1985. 340p. (Wars of the

United States, v.3; Garland reference library of social science, v.250) **DB76**

A well organized bibliography of some 1,400 entries for books, essays, articles, diaries, memoirs, speeches, satires, pamphlets, poems, songs, novels, juvenile literature, dissertations, and sermons. Excludes broadsides and government documents. The war is presented from Canadian, American, and British perspectives; political, social, and economic aspects are included along with the military. Arranged topically; author and subject indexes. Cut-off date is 1981. Z1240.S65

American Revolution

Bibliography

Adams, Thomas Randolph. The American controversy: a bibliographical study of the British pamphlets about the American disputes, 1764–1783. Providence, Brown Univ. Pr.; N.Y., Bibliographical Soc. of Amer., 1980. 2v. (1102p.) **DB77**

A census of some 1,400 titles in about 2,350 editions or issues. For each, gives transcription of title page, collation, and notes which "include bibliographical information, information concerning the circumstances surrounding the printing and publication, the extent of its publication in America, and the appearance of the text or some part of it in London newspapers and magazines" *(p.xx)*, original price, and number of copies printed. Title index and general index of names, places, and subjects. Z1238.A39

—— American independence: the growth of an idea; a bibliographical study of the American political pamphlets printed between 1764 and 1776 dealing with the dispute between Great Britain and her colonies. Austin, Jenkins and Reese, 1980. 264p. (Contributions to bibliography, 5) **DB78**

"First appeared in the Publications of the Colonial Society of Massachusetts, Transactions, v.43."—*verso of t.p.* Subsequently publ. by Brown Univ. Pr., 1965.

Pamphlets are listed chronologically by first imprint date with indication of later editions. Gives brief transcription of title page, census of copies and, in many cases, information about circumstances leading to publication. Also includes a short-title list of some 19 pamphlet exchanges. This edition includes additions and corrections (p.183–86) and a study, "The British pamphlet press and the American controversy, 1764–1783," reprinted from the *Proceedings of the American Antiquarian Society*, v.89 (Apr. 1979). Z1238.A4

Blanco, Richard L. The War of the American Revolution; a selected annotated bibliography of published sources. N.Y., Garland, 1984. 654p. (Wars of the United States, v.1; Garland reference library of social science, v.154) **DB79**

Lists more than 3,700 books, journals, articles and essays, government publications, and dissertations published to 1980 in topical arrangement with author and subject indexes. The compiler has "blended items about traditional military, naval and diplomatic subjects with topics representative of the newer 'social' history, such as crowd behavior, prisoners of war, and women in the Revolution." —*Pref.* Little emphasis on primary source material since the work is meant for students and the interested public. Z1238.B55

Clark, David Sanders. Index to maps of the American Revolution in books and periodicals illustrating the Revolutionary War and other events of the period 1763–1789. Westport, Conn., Greenwood Pr., [1974]. 301p. **DB80**

An index to maps in monographs, journals, general histories, textbooks and standard reference books which portray any part of the United States, Canada, the Caribbean and West Indies of the period 1763–89. Although the maps are largely military and naval, many show population, roads and boundaries, towns, etc. Geographical arrangement; extensive subject and name index. Z6027.U5C57

Gephart, Ronald M. Revolutionary America, 1763–1789: a bibliography. Wash., Lib. of Congress, 1984. 2v. (1671p.) **DB81**

Designed as "a guide to the more important printed primary and secondary works" in the Library of Congress, "the bibliography represents a comprehensive review of monographs, doctoral dissertations, collected works, festschriften, pamphlets, and serial publications in both general and special collections."—*Pref.* Arranged in 12 topico-chronological chapters, with numerous subsections, it intends to encompass a broad range of interests, needs, and approaches to the study of the Revolution and its historical, social and cultural setting. Extensive section of biographies and personal primary sources, and a chapter on the preservation and publication of documentary sources on the American Revolution. Selectively annotated. Cut-off date is Dec. 31, 1972. "The index is limited, for the most part, to proper names (authors, editors, compilers, historical figures, corporate bodies, geographic locations, etc.) with descriptive subdivisions." Detailed table of contents. Z1238.G43

White, J. Todd and **Lesser, Charles H.** Fighters for independence; a guide to sources of biographical information on soldiers and sailors of the American Revolution. Chicago, Univ. of Chicago Pr., 1977. 112p. **DB83**

A discussion of the types of records deemed useful for research in this area, followed by an annotated bibliography of published and unpublished lists of soldiers and sailors. Also includes a bibliography of diaries, journals, memoirs, and autobiographies, and a bibliography of more general works. Subject index. Z1238.W45

❖Several earlier bibliographies are still useful: *The era of the American Revolution,* ed. by Dwight L. Smith (Santa Barbara, Calif., ABC-Clio, 1975. 381p.), is a classified listing of 1,400 entries from *America: history and life*; Robert W. Coakley and Stetson Conn's *The War of the American Revolution* (Wash., U.S. Army, Ctr. of Military History, 1975. 257p.) includes a brief narrative, a chronology, and a select bibliography; and John Shy's *The American Revolution* (Northbrook, Ill., AHM Publ. Corp., 1973. 134p.) lists books, articles, and dissertations for the period 1763–1783.

Manuscripts and archives

Documentos relativos a la independencia de Norteamérica existentes en archivos españoles. Madrid, Ministerio de Asuntos Exteriores, Dirección General de Relaciones Culturales, 1976–80. v.1–7. (In progress; to be in 11v.) **DB84**

Contents: v.1, Medina Encina, P. Archivo General de Indias, Sección de Gobierno (años 1752–1822) (2v.); v.2, Siles Saturnino, R. Archivo General de Indias, Sección Papeles de Cuba, Correspondencia y documentación oficial de los Gobernadores de Luisiana (1777–1803); v.3, León Tello, P. Archivo histórico nacional, correspondencia diplomatica (años 1801–1820) (3v.); v.4, León Tello, P. Archivo histórico nacional, expedientes (años 1801–1820); v.5, Represa Fernández, M.F. [et al.] Archivo General de Simancas, Secretaría de Estado: Inglaterra (años 1750–1820) (2v.); v.6, Archivo general de Simancas secretaría de estado: Francia (años 1774–1786); v.7, Archivo general de Indias, sección papeles de Cuba: correspondencia y documentación oficial de varias autoridades de Luisiana y de las dos Floridas (años 1778–1817).

Provides a calendar for the papers of each archive. Z1238.D62

Koenig, William J. and **Mayer, Sydney L.** European manuscript sources of the American Revolution. London & N.Y., Bowker, [1974]. 328p. **DB85**

"It is not our intention to provide a comprehensive guide to the documentary material [on the American Revolution] in Europe, but rather to offer the scholar, particularly the graduate student, an introduction to the source material in Europe so that research can be more effectively planned. This volume is really a *point d'appui* and time saver, a tool which the scholar can use to identify repositories, with summaries of their contents and notices of relevant bibliography."—*Gen.Introd.* Arranged by country, then by city and repository; general index. Provides references to published descriptions of the collections, of individual manuscripts, etc.   CD1002.K63

U.S.Library of Congress. American Revolution Bicentennial Office. Manuscript sources in the Library of Congress for research on the American Revolution. Wash., Lib. of Congress, 1975. 372p.   **DB86**

Comp. by John R. Sellers, Gerald W. Gawalt, Paul H. Smith, and Patricia Molen van Ee.

"In the preparation of this guide virtually every collection in the Library's Manuscript Division, Rare Book Division, and Law Library was surveyed for documents from the Revolutionary era [1763 to 1789]."—*Introd.* Includes photostats, transcripts, and microfilms as well as original manuscripts. In two main sections: (1) Domestic collections, and (2) Foreign reproductions. Descriptive notes vary according to the specific item or collection in question: "Collections that are extremely large and uniform in content may receive more cursory treatment than smaller collections containing a variety of documents." Index to repositories and a detailed subject index.

Z1238.U57

Dictionaries, handbooks, source books

Boatner, Mark Mayo. Encyclopedia of the American Revolution. N.Y., McKay, [1966]. 1287p. maps.   **DB87**

As in the same author's *Civil War dictionary* (DB103), biographical sketches predominate; there are entries for battles, issues, etc., plus "covering" articles for background and related aspects of the war. Some articles include bibliographic references. There is a general bibliography and an index to the maps.

A "Bicentennial edition" (N.Y., McKay, 1974. 1290p.) is a reprinting, with minimal changes and emendations, of the 1966 edition. A few new bibliographic references have been supplied in the text, but the general bibliography has not been updated apart from a brief "Addendum," p.1273.   E208.B68

Dupuy, Trevor Nevitt and **Hammerman, Gay M.** People & events of the American Revolution. N.Y., Bowker; Dunn Loring, Va., Dupuy Associates, 1974. 473p.   **DB88**

In two main sections: a chronology of events 1733–83, and an alphabetical section of names with short biographies. Index covers events listed in the chronology.   E209.D86

Morison, Samuel Eliot. Sources and documents illustrating the American Revolution, 1764–1788, and the formation of the federal constitution. 2d ed. Oxford, Clarendon Pr., 1929. 378p. (Repr.: N.Y., Oxford Univ. Pr., 1965)   **DB89**

1st ed. 1923.

Includes "more important acts, resolves, state constitutions, royal instructions, etc.," as well as samples of "debates, letters, pamphlets, Indian relations and frontier petitions, which illustrate and often influenced public opinion."—*Pref.*   E203.M86

Stember, Sol. The bicentennial guide to the American Revolution. N.Y., Saturday Review Pr. [distr. by Dutton], 1974. 3v. maps.   **DB90**

Contents: v.1, The war in the North; v.2, The Middle Colonies; v.3, The war in the South.

On cover: Touring guide to Revolutionary War sites.

Sites are considered area by area, and as much in chronological sequence of the war as is feasible without constant back-tracking over the same region.   E230.S74

Atlases

Atlas of early American history: the Revolutionary era, 1760–1790. Lester J. Cappon, ed. in chief. [Princeton, N.J.], publ. for the Newberry Lib. and the Inst. of Early American History and Culture by Princeton Univ. Pr., 1976. 157p. 47cm.   **DB91**

An impressive new historical atlas containing 74 pages of colored maps of varying size, followed by extensive explanatory text and a detailed index. "The basic framework . . . is chronological, con-

ceived as a work of history rather than one of historical geography. Three periods are easily recognized in the table of contents: (1) the colonial years before 1776; (2) the War of the American Revolution; and (3) the postwar years of Confederation period."—*Introd.*

G1201.S3A8

Nebenzahl, Kenneth. Atlas of the American Revolution; map selection and commentary by Kenneth Nebenzahl; narrative text by Don Higginbotham. Chicago, Rand McNally, [1974]. 218p. il. maps. 39cm.   **DB92**

Reproductions of 18th-century maps with commentary and narrative text. Indexed.   G1201.S3N4

19th century

Carman, Harry James and **Thompson, Arthur W.** A guide to the principal sources for American civilization, 1800–1900, in the city of New York. N.Y., Columbia Univ. Pr., 1962. 2v.   **DB93**

Contents: v.1, Manuscripts; v.2, Printed materials.

Chronological successor to the Greene and Morris guide for the period 1600–1800 (DB74). Basic arrangement of each volume is topical; within chapters materials for the country are presented first, then for each state. Name index in each volume.   Z1236.C25

Civil War

Bibliography

Aimone, Alan Conrad. The official records of the American Civil War: a researcher's guide. [2d ed.] [West Point, N.Y.], U.S. Military Academy, [1978?]. 50p. (U.S.M.A. Library bulletin no.11A)   **DB94**

1st ed. 1972.

Offers information on the background, content, accuracy, and omissions in the compilations of official records of the Army and Navy. Appendix A is a "Diagram, map, picture, and sketch index to the N[aval] O[fficial] R[ecords] and the O[fficial] R[ecords]."

Arnold, Louise. The era of the Civil War, 1820–1876. Carlisle Barracks, Penn., U.S. Army Military History Inst., 1982. 704p. (Special bibliography, 11; available from U.S. Govt. Prt. Off.)   **DB95**

An earlier bibliography of the same title, by B. Frankling Cooling, was published 1974.

An extensive bibliography based on the holdings of the Army Military History Institute. Topical arrangement of published books, pamphlets, and government documents, together with brief essays on the Institute's manuscript holdings and museum collections. Not indexed.   Z1242.U588

Coulter, Ellis Merton. Travels in the Confederate states; a bibliography. Norman, Univ. of Oklahoma Pr., 1948. 289p. (American exploration and travel ser., [no.11])   **DB96**

Lists more than 500 accounts of travels in the South during the Civil War, written either at the time or at a later date. Fills in, for 1861–65, the *Travels* series edited by T. D. Clark (DB122–DB123).

Text of titles listed are available on microcard from Lost Cause Press, Louisville, Ky.   Z1251.S7C68

Crandall, Marjorie Lyle. Confederate imprints; a check list based principally on the collection of the Boston Athenaeum. [Boston], Boston Athenaeum, 1955. 2v. (Robert Charles Billings Fund pubn. no.11)   **DB97**

Contents: v.1, Official publications (408p.); v.2, Unofficial publications (p.409–910). v.2, pt.3, Sheet music, comp. by Richard B. Harwell.

Lists more than 5,300 titles in classed arrangement. Locates copies.

Volumes listed are being reproduced in microform by Research Publications, Inc.

Continued by: Z1242.5.C7

Harwell, Richard Barksdale. More Confederate imprints. Richmond, Virginia State Lib., 1957. 2v. (Virginia State Lib. pubn., no.4–5) **DB98**

Contents: v.1, Official publications (158p.); v.2, Unofficial publications (p.159–345).

A supplement to Crandall's *Confederate imprints* (above), recording 1,773 additions.

These may be supplemented by *Confederate imprints in the University of Alabama Library,* comp. by Sara Elizabeth Mason [and others] (University, Ala., 1961. 156p.), which lists some 700 additional titles, and by Harwell's *Confederate imprints in the University of Georgia Libraries* (Athens, Ga., 1964. 49p.), which includes 100 new items. Z1242.5.H33

Dornbusch, Charles Emil. Military bibliography of the Civil War. N.Y., New York Pub. Lib., [1962–72]. 3v. **DB99**

Contents: v.1, Northern states (originally issued in 7 pts.): pt.1, Illinois; pt.2, New York; pt.3, New England states; pt.4, New Jersey and Pennsylvania; pt.5, Indiana and Ohio; pt.6, Iowa, Kansas, Michigan, Minnesota, and Wisconsin; pt.7, Index of names; v.2, Regimental publications and personal narratives: Southern, Border, and Western states and territories; Federal troops; Union and Confederate biographies; v.3, General references; armed forces; and campaigns and battles.

The first volume appeared under the title: *Regimental publications and personal narratives of the Civil War.* The new title was introduced to signal the broadened scope of the second and third volumes which include more general references to the military aspects of the war. Z71242.D612

Nevins, Allan, Robertson, James I. and **Wiley, Bell I.** Civil War books; a critical bibliography. Baton Rouge, publ. for the U.S. Civil War Centennial Commission by Louisiana State Univ. Pr., [1967–69]. 2v. **DB100**

Contents: v.1, Military aspects; Prisons and prisoners of war; The Negro; The navies; Diplomacy; v.2, General works; Biographies, memoirs, and collected works; The Union; The Confederacy; Cumulative index.

A selective bibliography intended for both the scholar and the general reader and restricted to literature in book and pamphlet form bearing solely on the war years, not on causes and results of the war. Citations are reproduced from Library of Congress catalog cards, with the addition of a critical note for each. Each section compiled by a specialist scholar. General index in v.2. Z1242.N35

Manuscripts and archives

Beers, Henry Putney. Guide to the archives of the government of the Confederate States of America. Wash., Nat. Archives, Nat. Archives and Records Service, 1968. 536p. (National Archives pubn. no.68–15) **DB101**

Describes, as far as possible, "all the records of the Confederacy in the National Archives, the Library of Congress, and in other custody."—*Pref.* Arrangement is by agency with a subject index. CD3047.B4

Munden, Kenneth White and **Beers, Henry Putney.** Guide to federal archives relating to the Civil War. Wash., Nat. Archives, Nat. Archives and Records Service, 1962. 721p. (National Archives pubn. no.63-1) **DB102**

Describes the records, relating to the Civil War, of the various agencies of the federal government, arranged by agency with a subject index. CD3047.M8

Dictionaries and handbooks

Boatner, Mark Mayo. The Civil War dictionary. N.Y., McKay, 1959. 974p. il. maps. **DB103**

Maps and diagrams by Allen C. Northrop and Lowell I. Miller.
Includes articles on campaigns, battles, and laws, but biographical articles predominate. E468.B7

Dyer, Frederick Henry. Compendium of the war of the rebellion, comp. and arranged from official records of the Federal and Confederate armies, reports of the adjutant generals of the several states, the army registers, and other reliable documents and sources. Des Moines, Iowa, Dyer, 1908. 1796p. (Repr., with a new introd. by Bell Irwin Wiley: N.Y., Yoseloff, 1959. 3v.) **DB104**

Contents: pt.1, Number and organization of the armies of the United States; pt.2, Chronological record of the campaigns, battles, engagements, actions, combats, sieges, skirmishes, etc., in the United States, 1861 to 1865; pt.3, Regimental histories. E491.D99

Warner, Ezra J. and **Yearns, W. Buck.** Biographical register of the Confederate Congress. Baton Rouge, Louisiana State Univ. Pr., [1975]. 319p. il. **DB105**

Biographical sketches of the 267 members of the Confederate Congress. Includes some bibliographical notes. Appendixes: (1) Sessions of the Confederate Congress: (2) Standing committees of the Confederate Congresses; (3) Membership of the Congresses [by state]; (4) Maps of occupied Confederate territory. JK9663.W3

Atlases

U.S. Military Academy, West Point. Dept. of Military Art and Engineering. West Point atlas of the Civil War. Chief ed., Vincent J. Esposito. N.Y., Praeger, 1962. lv., various pagings. 154 col. maps. **DB106**

Adapted from the *West Point atlas of American wars* (DB164). G1201.S5U58

U.S. War Dept. The official atlas of the Civil War. Introd. by Henry Steele Commager. N.Y., Yoseloff, 1958. 29p., 175pl. **DB107**

Reproduction of the *Atlas to accompany the official records of the Union and Confederate armies . . .* Wash., Govt. Prt. Off., 1891–95.

Includes 171 plates, often with several maps to a plate, covering military operations: battles, engagements, campaigns, defenses, etc.; topographical maps; military divisions and departments; and four additional plates showing uniforms, ordnance, transportation of sick or wounded, and corps flags, badges, etc.

A battlefield atlas of the Civil War by Craig L. Symonds (Annapolis, Md., Nautical and Aviation Pub. Co., 1983. 106p.) is well adapted to student use. G1201.S5U6

20th century

❖For works on the First and Second World Wars *see* DA198–DA219; for the Korean and Vietnamese wars *see* under those countries.

Bibliography

Bloxom, Marguerite D. Pickaxe and pencil; references for the study of the WPA. Wash., Lib. of Congress, 1982. 87p. il. **DB108**

A selective bibliography of books and periodical articles on various aspects of the WPA—what it was, what it did, and what became of many of the projects. Nearly 400 entries, both contemporary with the WPA and retrospective; numerous annotations. Separate list of doctoral dissertations. Author index. Z7164.P97B58

Buenker, John D. and **Burckel, Nicholas C.** Progressive reform: a guide to information sources. Detroit, Gale, [1980]. 366p. (American government and history information guide ser., v.8) **DB109**

An annotated bibliography of more than 1,600 books, periodical articles, and doctoral dissertations on the progressive reform period in the United States from the depression of the 1890s to the end of World War I. Broad topical arrangement, with author and subject indexes. Z1242.8.B84

Burke, Robert E. and **Lowitt, Richard.** The new era and the New Deal, 1920–1940. Arlington Heights, Ill., Harlan Davidson, [1981]. 215p. (Goldentree bibliographies in American history) **DB110**

A selective bibliography of more than 4,200 items; doctoral dissertations and unpublished materials are omitted. Classed arrangement with author index. Z1244.B87

Filler, Louis. Progressivism and muckraking. N.Y., Bowker, 1976. 200p. (Bibliographic guides for contemporary collections) **DB111**

Comprises a series of brief bibliographic essays grouped in four main sections: (1) A meaning for modern times; (2) Progressivism; (3) Progressivism: second phase; (4) Search for values. A bibliography, p.121–68, lists the books cited in the essays. Subject and title index. Z7164.S66F54

The Great Depression: a historical bibliography. Santa Barbara, Calif., ABC-Clio, [1984]. 260p. (ABC-Clio research guides, 4) **DB112**

A classed bibliography of 959 citations, with abstracts, primarily to periodical literature. Derived from the ABC-Clio database (which generates *America: history and life*). Author and subject indexes. Z7165.U5G73

Killen, Linda and **Lael, Richard L.** Versailles and after: an annotated bibliography of American foreign relations, 1919–1933. N.Y., Garland, 1983. 469p. (Garland reference library of social science, v.135; American diplomatic history, v.2) **DB113**

Cites "English-language books, articles, dissertations, indexes, guides, bibliographies, and manuscript collections which provide insight into the diverse diplomatic issues facing the nation" *(Introd.)* during the period indicated. Classed arrangement; subject and author indexes. Omits citations to articles in *Foreign affairs, Current history, Annals* of the American Academy of Political and Social Sciences, and the *Proceedings* of the Academy of Political Science. Z6465.U5K4

Dictionaries

The Harlem Renaissance, an historical dictionary for the era. Bruce Kellner, ed. Westport, Conn., Greenwood Pr., [1984]. 476p. il. **DB114**

Covers significant figures, events, and locales relating to the "rich surge of black arts and letters" *(Introd.)* during the period 1917–35, with entries for politicians, educators, poets, clergymen, musicians, churches, journals, theaters, and including plots and notes on the critical reception of representative literary and theatrical works. Bibliographies at the end of each article cite both primary and secondary sources. Appendixes offer chronologies (including literary and dramatic events), a list of newspapers and other serial publications, and a glossary of Harlem slang. Indexed. NX511.N4H37

Regional and local

Jones, Houston Gwynne. Local government records: an introduction to their management, preservation and use. Nashville, Amer. Assoc. for State and Local History, 1980. 208p. **DB115**

Aims to be an introduction to the topic rather than a guide or how-to-do-it manual. Pt.1, "Management and preservation," discusses general principles and is directed to local officials, encouraging them to develop and/or evaluate a records management program. Pt.2, "Use of local records," is intended for the researcher and explains the various government divisions that produce records, the types of records (e.g., records of orphans, apprentices, and the disadvantaged; tax records), and briefly discusses how to approach those records. Appendixes describe records management services

for each state and give names and addresses of sources of information.

A favorable review appears in *Journal of American history* 67:647–48 (Dec. 1980). CD3024.J66

New York. Public Library. Local History and Genealogy Division. Dictionary catalog of the Local History and Genealogy Division. Boston, G. K. Hall, 1974. 20v. **DB116**

For full information *see* AK31.

Shearer, Barbara Smith and **Shearer, Benjamin F.** Periodical literature on United States cities: a bibliography and subject guide. Westport, Conn., Greenwood Pr., [1983]. 574p. **DB117**

Lists selected periodical articles published 1970–81 on 170 United States cities with a population of 100,000 or more. Arrangement is alphabetical by name of city, with subsections for general articles, arts and architecture, education and media, environment, government and politics, housing and urban development, social and economic conditions, and transportation. Author and subject indexes.

A complementary work is *Urban America; a historical bibliography,* ed. by Neil L. Shumsky and Timothy Crimmins (Santa Barbara, Calif., ABC-Clio, 1983. 422p.); it is a topical arrangement of over 4,000 abstracts of periodical articles drawn from v.11–17 of *America: history and life.* Z5942.S464

U.S. Library of Congress. United States local histories in the Library of Congress: a bibliography. Ed. by Marion J. Kaminkow. Baltimore, Magna Carta Book Co., 1975–[76]. 5v. **DB118**

Contents: v.1–2, Atlantic States; v.3, Middle West, Alaska, Hawaii; v.4, The West; v.5, Supplement and index.

". . . includes all the books cataloged and classified under the local history portion of the Library of Congress classification schedule (F1–975) for which cards had been filed in the Library's shelflist by mid-1972."—*Pref.* Arrangement is by classification number (which provides a state-by-state listing). For each state a classification schedule is given, as is a "Supplementary index of places." The supplement adds citations from cards filed mid-1972 to beginning of 1976. General index of personal names in all volumes; corrections to v.1–4 in v.5, p.567–69. Z1250.U59

West Virginia. University. Library. Appalachian bibliography. Morgantown, The Library, 1972. 2v. **DB119**

A topically arranged bibliography, with subject headings in alphabetical sequence. Includes books and periodical articles on social, economic, and historical aspects of the region. More than 7,600 entries; numerous annotations.

Periodicals

Crouch, Milton and **Raum, Hans.** Directory of state and local history periodicals. Chicago, Amer. Lib. Assoc., 1977. 124p. **DB120**

A state-by-state listing of "state and local history periodicals currently being published in the United States" *(Introd.),* with title index. Information on published or unpublished indexes is included with the citation. Z1250.C76

New England

Bibliographies of New England history. Boston, G. K. Hall, 1976–83. v.1–5. (In progress) **DB121**

Contents: v.1, Massachusetts, ed. by John Haskell. 583p.; v.2, Maine, ed. by John D. Haskell. 279p.; v.3, New Hampshire, ed. by John D. Haskell and T. D. Seymour Bassett. 330p.; v.4, Vermont, ed. by T. D. Seymour Bassett. 391p.; v.5, Rhode Island, ed. by R. Parks. 229p.

Under the auspices of the Committee for a New England Bibliography.

For a description of the project and guidelines for compilation *see* the *New England quarterly* 43:523–26 (Sept. 1970).

Books, collected series, journal articles are arranged alphabetically within a geographical framework. Cutoff date for Massachusetts is generally Dec. 1972; for the Maine volume, 1975; for New Hampshire, 1977; for Vermont, 1979; and for Rhode Island, 1981, with a few later publications cited. If no location is indicated in the *National union catalog* or the printed catalog of the Library of Congress, a location symbol is given. Indexes cite authors, editors, subjects, and geographical places (including variant names and extinct places).

Besides volumes for other states, future plans include publication of guides to manuscripts and official publications as well as a final volume on New England as a whole.

The South

Clark, Thomas Dionysius. Travels in the old South; a bibliography. Norman, Univ. of Oklahoma Pr., 1956–59. 3v. (American exploration and travel ser., no.19)   **DB122**

Contents: v.1, The formative years, 1527–1783. From the Spanish explorations through the American Revolution; v.2, The expanding South, 1750–1825. The Ohio Valley and the cotton frontier; v.3, The ante-bellum South, 1825–1860. Cotton, slavery and conflict.

Each volume is divided into sections, each compiled by a specialist. Annotations are descriptive and often include critical comments; location of copies is indicated. Each volume has an index of authors, subjects, and names of persons and places.

Text of titles listed are available on microcard from Lost Cause Press, Louisville, Ky.

For 1861–65, *see* E. M. Coulter (DB96).   Z1251.S7C4

———— Travels in the new South; a bibliography. Norman, Univ. of Oklahoma Pr., 1962. 2v. il. (American exploration and travel ser., no.36)   **DB123**

Contents: v.1, The postwar South, 1865–1900. An era of reconstruction and readjustment; v.2, The twentieth-century South, 1900–1955. An era of change, depression and emergence.

Companion volumes to DB96 and DB122, completing the series. These materials also available on microcard from Lost Cause Press.   Z1251.S7C38

The encyclopedia of Southern history. Ed. by David C. Roller and Robert W. Twyman. Baton Rouge, Louisiana State Univ. Pr., [1979]. 1421p.   **DB124**

Designed "to answer those questions about the South most frequently asked by scholars, teachers, students, and laymen."— *Pref.* Features signed articles (most of them with select bibliographies) on events, terms, persons, places, etc., relevant to southern history from earliest times to the present. "The South" is defined "as encompassing the District of Columbia and those states that accepted the practice of slavery in 1860." Articles on the region's 16 states are an important feature of the work. Indexed.   F207.7.E52

Green, Fletcher M. and **Copeland, J. Isaac.** The old South. Arlington Heights, Ill., AHM Publ. Corp., [1980]. 173p. (Goldentree bibliographies in American history)   **DB125**

A selective bibliography of major books and periodical articles, topically arranged. Designed for advanced undergraduates and entering graduating students. Emphasis on the economic, cultural, and social history of the South since the Civil War. Author index.   Z1251.57G69

Ross, Charlotte T. Bibliography of Southern Appalachia; a publication of the Appalachian Consortium, Inc. Boone, N.C., Appalachian Consortium Pr., [1976]. 235p., 16p.   **DB126**

A union list of the books, monographs and films relating to Southern Appalachia held by the thirteen libraries of the Appalachian Consortium. Author/main entry listing with subject index; separate section for films.   Z1251.A7B53

The Midwest

Hubach, Robert Rogers. Early midwestern travel narratives: an annotated bibliography, 1634–1850. Detroit, Mich., Wayne State Univ. Pr., 1961. 149p.   **DB127**

Lists books and periodical articles in chronological order by period, with full descriptive annotations. Includes journals and diaries, published and unpublished. Author and place-name index. "Midwest" is here understood to include the western border of Pennsylvania and all territory north of the Ohio River and north of the present states of Arkansas and Oklahoma to the Canadian border.   Z1251.W5H8

The West

Adams, Ramon Frederick. Six-guns and saddle leather: a bibliography of books and pamphlets on western outlaws and gunmen. New ed., rev. and greatly enl. [Norman, Univ. of Oklahoma Pr., 1969] 808p.   **DB128**

1st ed. 1954.

2,491 numbered items, arranged alphabetically, dealing with western outlaws. Detailed index; annotations.

Similar bibliographies by the same compiler are: *Burs under the saddle; a second look at books and histories of the West* (Norman, Okla., 1964), *More burs under the saddle; books and histories of the West* (Norman, Okla., 1978), and *The rampaging herd; a bibliography of books and pamphlets on men and events in the cattle industry* (Norman, Okla., 1959).   Z1251.W5A3

Borderlands sourcebook; a guide to the literature on northern Mexico and the American Southwest. Ed., Ellwyn R. Stoddard, Richard L. Nostrand and Jonathan P. West. Norman, Univ. of Okla. Pr., publ. under sponsorship of the Assoc. of Borderlands Scholars, [1983]. 445p. maps.   **DB129**

Sixty bibliographic essays survey all areas of research on this region. In three main sections: (1) Delineating the U.S.-Mexican borderlands; (2) Specific border phenomena (e.g., Society and culture, History and archaeology, Economics); (3) Borderlands information resources. A "Composite bibliography" gives full citations to all works mentioned in the essays and includes sections for documents and theses (topically arranged). Enhanced by maps, time scales, tables and charts.   Z1251.S8B67

California. University, Berkeley. Bancroft Library. Catalog of printed books. Boston, G. K. Hall, 1964. 22v.   **DB130**

Photographic reproduction of the cards of the dictionary catalog representing some 150,000 printed books, pamphlets, scrapbooks, government documents, broadsides, magazines, special issues of modern newspapers, as well as extensive files of early western papers.

The scope of the library is broad, but generally covers historical materials for the study of the western half of North America, including all of Mexico and Central America. Particularly strong in the history, religion, politics, economics, and social conditions of the region, with special collections on the Mormons, the Catholic church in Mexico, early California printing, voyages and travels, maps from the 16th–20th centuries, etc.

Manuscripts are described in *A guide to the manuscript collections of the Bancroft Library,* ed. by Dale L. Morgan and George P. Hammond (Berkeley, Univ. of Calif. Pr., 1963–72. 2v.).   Z881.C1523

———— ———— Supplements 1–3. Boston, G. K. Hall, 1969–79. 13v.

These supplements cover materials added 1964–68, 1969–73 and 1974–78, dealing with western North America from Alaska through Panama. Of special interest is the acquisition of a collection of Mexican political pamphlets from the 1880s to the 1960s.

The frontier experience; a reader's guide to the life and literature of the American West. Ed. by Jon Tuska and Vicki Piekarski. Jefferson, N.C., McFarland, [1984]. 434p.

DB131

A critically annotated bibliography of books on "the entire American frontier experience but with special emphasis on the American West."—*Introd.* In two sections ("The life" and "The literature"), each consisting of numerous chapters (e.g., "Frontier professionals," "Transportation and communication," "Western films"). An introductory survey of each topic is followed by the annotated bibliography, then a list of suggested fiction and suggested films. Name and title indexes only.

A useful annotated bibliography of periodical articles is Dwight L. Smith's *The American and Canadian West* (Santa Barbara, ABC-Clio, 1979. 558p.) which is a collection of some 4,157 abstracts drawn from *America: history and life,* 1964–73. Z1251.W5F76

The reader's encyclopedia of the American West. Ed. by Howard R. Lamar. N.Y., T. Y. Crowell, [1977]. 1306p. il.

DB132

"Historically the term *American West* has meant either any part of the continental United States in its formative or frontier period or the entire trans-Mississippi West from the time of first exploration to the present. The editor has employed both these approaches. Thematically the *Encyclopedia* embraces the story of Indian-white relations; the diplomacy of American expansion; the overland trails experience; the era of the fur trader, the miner, the cowboy, and the settler; and those western subcultures we call Texas and Mormon."—*Pref.* Includes entries for persons, places, organizations, events, terms, etc. About 2,400 entries by some 200 contributors. Articles are signed with initials; many include bibliographic references.

F591.R38

Smith, Charles Wesley. Pacific Northwest Americana: a check list of books and pamphlets relating to the history of the Pacific Northwest. 3d ed., rev. and extended by Isabel Mayhew. Portland, Oregon Historical Soc., Binfords and Mort, 1950. 381p.

DB133

1st ed. 1909; 2d ed. 1921. This edition has been thoroughly revised and enlarged, and includes the holdings of 38 libraries in the area served by the Pacific Northwest Bibliographic Center.

A union list, not a comprehensive bibliography of imprints, listing books and pamphlets on the history of the Pacific Northwest.

Continued by: Z1251.N7S62

Pacific Northwest Americana 1949–1974: a supplement to Charles W. Smith's third edition, 1950. Comp. by the Pacific Northwest Library Committee on the Smith Bibliography Supplement, Richard E. Moore, chairman. . . . Portland, Ore., Binford & Mort, 1981. 365p.

DB134

Extends the Smith bibliography (above) through 1974, listing books, government publications, and pamphlets by geographical areas. Location information is not included. Author index to the basic volume and the supplement.

Thomas Gilcrease Institute of American History and Art, Tulsa, Okla. Library. The Gilcrease-Hargrett catalogue of imprints. Lester Hargrett, comp. [Norman, Univ. of Oklahoma Pr., 1972] 400p.

DB135

". . . an annotated bibliography of printed materials pertaining to the American Indian. Most of the items deal with the Five Civilized Tribes of Oklahoma, but there is also a broad range of western Americana, both Indian and white, most of it published in the nineteenth century."—*Introd.* Listing is chronological within an alphabetical topical arrangement. Indexed.

A guidebook to manuscripts in the Library, comp. by Mrs. H. H. Keene, was issued 1969 (101p.). Z1209.2.U5T48

Vail, Robert William Glenroie. The voice of the old frontier. Philadelphia, Univ. of Pennsylvania, 1949. 492p. (Rosenbach fellowship in bibliography, 10) (Repr.: N.Y., Octagon, 1970)

DB136

Comprises three lectures delivered at the University of Pennsylvania in 1945, supplemented by a bibliographical appendix. The bibliography of North American frontier literature, 1542–1800

(p.84–466), is "a selection of works written by those living on the frontier of what is now the United States, stories of Indian captivity within this area and promotion tracts by agents for the sale of frontier lands, the first editions of which appeared not later than 1800."—*Introd.* Locates copies in American and European libraries.

Z1249.F9V3

Wagner, Henry R. and **Camp, Charles L.** The plains & the Rockies: a critical bibliography of exploration, adventure and travel in the American West, 1800–1865. 4th ed. rev., enl. and ed. by Robert H. Becker. San Francisco, John Howell Books, 1982. 745p. il.

DB137

1st ed. 1920 (corrected reissue 1921).

A descriptive bibliography of some 1,800 issues and editions of about 690 individual works, arranged by year, then by author. This is a complete reworking of the 3d ed. (1961), aiming to provide a "standard bibliographical form," and with notes edited and usually shortened; it retains the numbering scheme of the earlier editions. Locates copies. Indexed.

A series based on the 3d ed. and issued by the Lost Cause Press, Louisville, Ky., makes most of the items available on microcard.

Z1251.W5W2

Winther, Oscar Osburn. A classified bibliography of the periodical literature of the trans-Mississippi West (1811–1957). Bloomington, Indiana Univ. Pr., 1961. 626p. (Indiana Univ. social science ser., no.19)

DB138

Lists 9,244 items in classified arrangement with author index. Supersedes the author's *The trans-Mississippi West (1811–1938).*

Supplemented by: Z1251.W5W53

—— and **Van Orman, Richard A.** A classified bibliography of the periodical literature of the trans-Mississippi West; a supplement (1957–67). Bloomington, Indiana Univ. Pr., 1970. 340p. (Indiana Univ. social science ser., no.26)

Adds more than 4,500 entries.

Yale University. Library. Yale Collection of Western Americana. Catalog . . . Boston, G. K. Hall, [1961]. 4v. **DB139**

Contents: v.1–3, A–Z; v.4, Shelf list.

A photographic reproduction of the card catalog of the Western Americana collection, which consists of a number of special collections in the field, mostly of a rare-book nature, including early imprints of books, pamphlets, and periodicals. Authors, titles, and subjects are in one alphabet. The shelflist serves as a classed guide.

The catalog includes only those books cataloged for the collection at time of publication; this means that some notable collections are omitted, and materials in the general library are not included.

Z1251.W5Y35

—— A catalogue of the Frederick W. and Carrie S. Beinecke collection of Western Americana: manuscripts. Comp. by Jeanne M. Goddard and Charles Kritzler; ed. by Archibald Hanna. New Haven, Yale Univ. Pr., 1965. 114p.

DB140

Lists and describes 285 items in the collection, which emphasizes materials "on the Spanish Southwest and California, from the period of discovery and exploration by the Spanish down through the Mexican War and the gold rush."—*Introd.*

It should be noted that almost all of the Beinecke collection is omitted from the *Catalog of the Yale collection of Western Americana* (above). Z1251.W5Y37

Societies

Directory of historical societies and agencies in the United States and Canada. 1956– . Madison, Wis., Amer. Assoc. for State and Local History, 1956– . Irregular. **DB141**

Lists the names and addresses of the societies, with the title of the officer of each to whom correspondence should be addressed. Indicates libraries and museums, with hours of opening, publications, etc. E172.A538

Dunlap, Leslie Whittaker. American historical societies, 1790–1860. ... Madison, Wis., priv. pr., 1944. 238p. (Repr.: Philadelphia, Porcupine Pr., 1974) **DB142**

Pt.1 is a history of American historical societies before the Civil War, with many bibliographical footnotes. Pt.2 includes sketches describing the 65 societies organized within this period.

E172.A1D86

Griffin, Appleton Prentiss Clark. Bibliography of American historical societies (the United States and the Dominion of Canada). 2d ed. rev. and enl. Wash., Govt. Prt. Off., 1907. 1374p. (*In* American Historical Assoc. Annual report, 1905. v.2) (Repr.: Detroit, Gale, 1966) **DB143**

A useful index to material in the various publications of the American historical societies, general and local, to 1905. Arranged by societies, with full contents of each volume and with two alphabetical indexes to the contents: (1) Author and subject index; (2) Biographical index. Continued, informally, in the *Annual magazine subject index* (AE243), and for material published 1906 on, by the analytical indexing in *Writings on American history* (DB50).

Z1236.G86

Encyclopedias, dictionaries, handbooks

The almanac of American history. Arthur M. Schlesinger, Jr., gen. ed. N.Y., Putnam, [1983]. 623p. il. **DB144**

Basically a chronology with summaries of important events. In five chronological sections, each with an introductory essay by a contributing scholar. Biographical sketches and extended notes on specific events and developments are interspersed with the chronologies. Index is not sufficiently detailed. E174.5.A45

Carruth, Gorton and Associates. The encyclopedia of American facts and dates. 7th ed., with a supplement of the 70s. N.Y., Crowell, [1979]. 1015p. **DB145**

1st ed. 1956
Chronologically arranged in columnar form, covering: (1) Politics and government, war, disasters, vital statistics; (2) Books, painting, drama, architecture, sculpture; (3) Science, industry, economics, education, religion, philosophy; and (4) Sports, fashions, popular entertainment, folklore, society.

Information through 1971 (p.1–915) is reprinted from the previous edition. Entries through 1977 have been added in the supplement, and there is a new index to the supplement (making it necessary to consult two indexes).

A review by the Reference and Subscription Books Review Committee concludes that "Libraries owning the sixth edition . . . and such standards as *Facts on File* and *The New York Times Index* could wait for the eighth edition of *Carruth* in the hope that the 1970s will not continue to be handled as a supplement."—*Booklist* 76:1627 (July 1, 1980). E174.5.C3

Dictionary of American history. Rev. ed. N.Y., Scribner, [1976]. 8v. **DB146**

Louise Bilebof Ketz, managing ed.
1st ed. 1940.
In general, consists of clear, compact articles each dealing with a separate and definite aspect of American history and each signed with full name of contributor. Also contains a number of articles on broader subjects, which include cross references to related articles on specific aspects. Covers political, economic, social, industrial, and cultural history, but omits biography as this is considered the province of the *Dictionary of American biography* (AJ63). However, the activities of prominent persons may frequently be traced through the references under their names in the analytical index.

Includes many catchwords and popular names of bills and laws, etc., e.g., Hawley-Smoot act, Wade-Davis bill. The bibliographies are usually very brief, in most cases consisting of two or three items chosen "so far as possible, with a view to accessibility in the average library."

This is a thorough revision. All entries were reviewed and articles revised, updated, or completely rewritten as necessary; some entries were deleted, and some 500 new articles were added. (There are 7,200 entries in the revised edition, with revisions and new entries representing the work of some 800 contributors.) In addition to general revision and updating, special attention was given to strengthening coverage of science and technology, history of the arts, Native Americans, and Afro-Americans. An analytical index constitutes v.8. E174.D52

———— Concise dictionary of American history. [New ed.] N.Y., Scribner, [1983]. 1140p. **DB147**

1st ed. 1962.
David William Voorhees, managing ed.
An abridgment of the 8v. work (above), offering condensed versions of more than 6,000 articles found in the parent set.

A desk dictionary based on the "Bicentennial Edition" of the *Dictionary of American history* and intended for school, home, or office is the *Scribner desk dictionary of American history* (N.Y., Scribner, 1984. 631p.). E174.D522

Encyclopedia of American economic history: studies of the principal movements and ideas. Glenn Porter, ed. N.Y., Scribner, [1980]. 3v. (1286p.) **DB148**

For full information *see* CH50.

Encyclopedia of American foreign policy; studies of the principal movements and ideas. Ed., Alexander De Conde. N.Y., Scribner, 1978. 3v. (1201p.) **DB149**

Offers some 95 well-written and researched "essays of original scholarship . . . [which] explore concepts, themes, large ideas, theories, and distinctive policies in the history of American foreign relations."—*Pref.* Conventional accounts of major episodes are excluded. Brief, but judiciously selected bibliographies are appended; cross references to related essays are provided. A biographical dictionary, p.995–1138, is based on information from the *Concise dictionary of American biography* (AJ64) and the 5th suppl. to the *Dictionary of American biography* (AJ63). Extensive name and subject index. JX1407.E53

Encyclopedia of American history. 6th ed., ed. by Richard B. Morris. N.Y., Harper & Row, [1982]. 1285p. maps. **DB150**

1st ed. 1953.
A standard work, frequently revised. This ed. in four main parts: (1) basic chronology, which lists the major political and military events of American history from aboriginal times to Dec. 1981; (2) topical chronology, which lists events under such headings as the expansion of the nation, population and immigration, leading Supreme Court decisions, the American economy, science and technology, thought and culture, and mass media; (3) 500 notable Americans, with biographical sketches; (4) structure of the federal government, giving lists of Presidents and their cabinets, tables of party strength in Congress, list of Supreme Court Justices, and texts of the Declaration of Independence and the Constitution.

A chronological manual with index rather than an encyclopedia as usually understood. No bibliography and no references to sources.

E174.5.E52

Encyclopedia of American political history: studies of the principal movements and ideas. Jack P. Greene, ed. N.Y., Scribner, [1984]. 3v. (1420p.) **DB151**

An authoritative, scholarly encyclopedia of some 90 articles on "major issues, themes, institutions, processes and developments as they have been manifest throughout the whole of United States history from before the decision for independence to the present." —*Pref.* Each article is by a contributing scholar and gives a detailed account of the topic (e.g., "Agricultural policy," "Historiography of American political history," "Women's rights"); each has a good bibliography. Well indexed. E183.E5

Johnson, Thomas Herbert. The Oxford companion to American history. N.Y., Oxford Univ. Pr., 1966. 906p. **DB152**

A good single-volume reference work in the "Oxford companion" tradition. E174.J6

Noël Hume, Ivor. Historical archaeology. N.Y., Knopf, 1969. 355p.   **DB153**

For the amateur, the student of archaeology, or the professional. Describes methods of excavation based on the author's extensive experience; emphasis is on work in the United States. Includes a substantial bibliography. Does not include a section on the identification of artifacts, a topic the author has treated in a separate volume: CC73.N6

―――― A guide to artifacts of colonial America. N.Y., Knopf, 1970. 323p. il.   **DB154**

Presents information to help identify objects which have been or could be dug up on British American sites inhabited during the 17th and 18th centuries. Arranged alphabetically by name of artifact (e.g., bayonet, buckles), with a bibliography for each entry. The author was director of the Department of Archaeology at Colonial Williamsburg.   E159.5.N6

Sweetman, Jack. American naval history, an illustrated chronology of the U.S. Navy and Marine Corps, 1775–present. Annapolis, Md., Naval Inst. Pr., 1984. 331p. il., maps.   **DB155**

Covers Apr. 19, 1775–Apr. 28, 1984, listing significant events (battles, technological firsts, etc.) along with some typical, though relatively minor, ones. Entries include indication of effect as well as description of the event. Calendar index by month and day; indexes of American naval vessels, of other vessels, and general index.   VA58.4.S94

The timetables of American history. Laurence Urdang, ed. N.Y., Simon and Schuster, [1981]. 470p. il.   **DB156**

Information is presented chronologically in tabular form. Each double-page spread has columns for history and politics, the arts, science and technology, and miscellaneous, with separate columns thereunder for events and developments in America and elsewhere. Covers through 1980. Indexed.   E18.5.U75

Webster's Guide to American history; a chronological, geographical, and biographical survey and compendium. Springfield, Mass., G. & C. Merriam, [1971]. 1428p. il.   **DB157**

Charles Van Doren and Robert McHenry, eds.
In three parts plus an index. Pt.I comprises a chronology of events (1492–1969), with excerpts from contemporary documents, speeches, letters, etc., appearing in parallel columns. (Unfortunately these excerpts are not always precisely identified.) Pt.II offers a section of tables and maps; and pt.III presents biographical sketches of more than 1,000 notable Americans.   E174.5.W4

Wilson, Josleen. The passionate amateur's guide to archaeology in the United States. N.Y., Collier Books, [1980]. 464p. il.   **DB158**

A geographical listing of "every prehistoric site in the country open to the public and museums that have prehistoric holdings."—*p.33.* For each museum or site is given address, phone number, a note on points of interest, directions for reaching the site, hours, admission fees. For each state information is given on organizations to join, opportunities for amateurs, and address of the state preservation or historical office. Brief bibliography of recommended readings; brief directory of national organizations; index.   E159.5.W55

Atlases

American Heritage. The American Heritage pictorial atlas of United States history, by the editors of American Heritage. N.Y., American Heritage, [1966]. 424p. il. 29cm.   **DB159**

Attractive maps (in color) with accompanying text. Chapter texts are unsigned, but the title page credits them to a list of distinguished contributors. Although the atlas includes material not found in either Paullin (DB162) or Lord (DB161), it does not truly supersede either of those standard works. There is a particularly good section

on United States operations in World War II. Elaborate color spreads, or "pictorial maps," of major battles of the Revolutionary and Civil wars, and of the National parks are unusual features.   G1201.S1A4

Atlas of American history. Rev. ed. Kenneth T. Jackson, ed.; James Truslow Adams, ed. in chief, original ed. N.Y., Scribner, [1978]. 294p. maps. 22x28cm.   **DB160**

1st ed. 1943.
Retains all the maps from the earlier edition and adds 51 new maps to the original 147. "Most of the new maps deal with twentieth-century developments or with other subjects [e.g., major Utopian experiments, universal male suffrage, woman's suffrage, abolition of slavery, various general economic developments] that were considered only slightly or not at all by Adams and his coworkers. . . . A third of the new maps are essentially demographic in nature."—*Introd.* New table of contents and revised index.   G1201.S1J3

Lord, Clifford L. and **Lord, Elizabeth H.** Historical atlas of the United States. Rev. ed. N.Y., Holt, 1953. 238p. maps. 28cm. (Repr.: N.Y., Johnson, 1972)   **DB161**

A useful, inexpensive, historical atlas with 312 outline maps, mostly in black-and-white. Supplements, but does not replace, Paullin (below). Divided into four sections: (1) General maps; (2) Colonial period; (3) 1775–1865; (4) 1865–1950. Maps cover political and economic history including military campaigns, population, transportation, suffrage, education, slavery and abolition, agriculture, forests, labor, manufacturing, natural resources, etc.

Appendixes contain statistical tables of population, presidential elections, immigration, railroad mileage, etc. Index of place-names and subjects.   G1201.S1L6

Paullin, Charles Oscar. Atlas of the historical geography of the United States, ed. by John K. Wright. [Wash., N.Y.], publ. jointly by Carnegie Inst. of Washington and the Amer. Geographical Soc., 1932. 162p. 688 maps. 36cm. [Carnegie Inst. pubn. 401] (Repr.: Westport, Conn., Greenwood Pr., 1975)   **DB162**

The first adequate atlas of American history, with good maps, including reproductions of early maps, and descriptive text for each with lists of sources; indispensable in any library doing much work in United States history. Indexed.   G1201.S1P3

This remarkable continent, an atlas of United States and Canadian society and culture. College Station, [Tex.], Publ. for the Society for the North American Cultural Survey by Texas A & M Univ. Pr., [1982]. 316p. il., maps. 24x32cm.   **DB163**

Gen. eds., John F. Rooney, Jr., Wilbur Zelinsky and Dean R. Louder; cartographic ed., John D. Vitek.
Offers 390 black-and-white maps chosen to show "how the inhabitants of this continent, past and present, differ from place to place in terms of origins, traditions, beliefs, patterns of thought and behavior, and ways of organizing themselves upon the land."—*Introd.* Maps are grouped in 13 chapters introduced by scholars; sources of the maps are given at the end of the volume. Indexed.   G1201.E1T5

U.S. Military Academy, West Point. Dept. of Military Art and Engineering. The West Point atlas of American wars. Chief ed., Vincent J. Esposito. N.Y., Praeger, [1959]. 2v. maps. 27x37cm.   **DB164**

Contents: v.1, 1689–1900; v.2, 1900–1953.
Includes maps of campaigns, battles, etc. Text and maps on facing pages.
The Civil War material is also available separately, *see* DB106.   G1201.S1U5

General histories

Morison, Samuel Eliot, Commager, Henry Steele and **Leuchtenburg, William E.** The growth of the American Republic. 7th ed. N.Y., Oxford Univ. Pr., 1980. 2v. il.   **DB165**

1st ed. 1930.

A good general history, well-written and frequently revised. This edition adds material on developments of the 1970s. A one-volume edition, abridged and revised has been published as *A concise history of the American Republic* (N.Y., Oxford Univ. Pr., 1983. 2d ed. 765p.).

A complementary single-volume general history is Howard Zinn's *A people's history of the United States* (N.Y., Harper & Row, 1980. 614p.).   E178.M85

Pageant of America; a pictorial history of the United States. Ralph Henry Gabriel, ed. New Haven, Yale Univ. Pr., 1925–29. 15v. il.   **DB166**

Contents: v.1 Adventures in the wilderness, by Clark Wissler, C. L. Skinner, William Wood; v.2, Lure of the frontier, by R. H. Gabriel; v.3, Toilers of land and sea, by R. H. Gabriel; v.4, March of commerce, by Malcolm Keir; v.5, Epic of industry, by Malcolm Keir; v.6, Winning of freedom, by William Wood and R. H. Gabriel; v.7, In defense of liberty, by William Wood and R. H. Gabriel; v.8, Builders of the Republic, by F. A. Ogg; v.9, Makers of a new nation, by J. S. Basset; v.10, American idealism, by L.A. Weigle; v.11, American spirit in letters, by S. T. Williams; v.12, American spirit in art, by F. J. Mather, Jr., C. R. Morey, William Henderson; v.13, American spirit in architecture, by T. F. Hamlin; v.14, American stage, by O. S. Coad and Edwin Mims, Jr.; v.15, Annals of American sport, by J. A. Krout.   E169.1.P145

Source books

Commager, Henry Steele, ed. Documents of American history. 9th ed. N.Y., Appleton, [1973]. 634p., 815p.   **DB167**

8th ed. 1968.

Includes significant documents from 1492 through mid-1973. As in previous revisions, a few earlier documents were dropped and new ones added from the period since 1966. Index by topic and personal name.   E173.C66

Historic documents, 1972– . Wash., Congressional Quarterly, 1973– . Annual.   **DB168**

A chronological arrangement of "statements, court decisions, reports, special studies, speeches" *(Foreword)*, with a brief introduction for each giving background, source (not always published), frequently a short summary, and indication of subsequent events. Well indexed, each index cumulating over a 5-year period (e.g., the 1983 index covers 1979–83).   E839.5.H57

MacDonald, William. Select charters and other documents illustrative of American history, 1606–1775, ed. with notes. N.Y., London, Macmillan, 1899. 401p.   **DB169**

E173.M131

——— Select documents illustrative of the history of the United States, 1776–1861, ed. with notes. N.Y., London, Macmillan, 1898. 465p. (Repr.: N.Y., B. Franklin, 1968)   **DB170**

Frequently reprinted.   E173.M13

——— Select statutes and other documents illustrative of the history of the United States, 1861–1898, ed. with notes. N.Y., London, Macmillan, 1903. 442p.   **DB171**

A series of documentary source books designed for student use.   E173.M132

——— Documentary source book of American history, 1606–1926. 3d ed. rev. and enl. N.Y., Macmillan, 1926. 713p.   **DB172**

A selection of documents from the three collections noted above, with some later additions; designed for one-year courses in American history.   E173.M129

New American world: a documentary history of North America to 1612. Ed., with a commentary by David B. Quinn. N.Y., Arno Pr. and Hector Bye, Inc., 1979. 5v. (2602p.) maps.   **DB173**

Contents: v.1, America from concept to discovery; Early exploration of North America; v.2, Major Spanish searches in Eastern North America; The Franco-Spanish clashes in Florida; The beginnings of Spanish Florida; v.3, English plans for North America; The Roanoke voyages; New England ventures; v.4, Newfoundland from fishery to colony; Northwest passage searches; v.5, The extension of settlement in Florida, Virginia, and the Spanish Southwest; Index.

Brings together a vast collection of documents (translated, if not originally in English), drawn from printed sources and from archive and manuscript collections throughout Europe and North America. Designed to portray the discovery and settlement of North America up to 1612, the documents chosen include narrative accounts, administrative records, diplomatic correspondence, business records, broadsides, 147 contemporary maps, etc. Almost all are printed in full. Headnotes provide reference to original sources, other translations available, problems with the texts, etc. Each of the principal sections has an introduction which "attempts to point to the major characteristics of the selection in that volume and to bring out major comparative points of relationship."—*Introd.* v.5 includes a general index to the set and a bibliography of all manuscript and printed sources used.   E101.N47

Schlesinger, Arthur Meier, comp. The dynamics of world power; a documentary history of United States foreign policy, 1945–1973. N.Y., Chelsea House, 1973. 5v.   **DB174**

Contents: v.1, Western Europe, ed. by R. Dallek; v.2, Eastern Europe and the Soviet Union, ed. by W. La Feber; v.3, Latin America, ed. by R. Burr; v.4, The Far East, ed. by R. Buhite; v.5, The United Nations, ed. by R. C. Hottelet; Subsaharan Africa, ed. by J. Herskovits.

Brings together in convenient form, on a region-by-region basis, the essential documents in the history of American foreign policy for the period 1945–73.   E744.S395

U.S. President. A compilation of the messages and papers of the Presidents . . . (with additions and encyclopedic index by private enterprise). N.Y., Bureau of Nat. Literature, [1917?] 20v.   **DB175**

For full information on this and related series, *see* AG73–AG75.

The United States and Russia: the beginnings of relations, 1765–1815. Ed. by Nina N. Bashkina [and others]. [Wash., Govt. Prt. Off., 1980] 1184p. il., maps.   **DB176**

Prep. under the direction of a Joint Soviet-American Editorial Board.

A collection of some 560 documents selected by Russian and American archivists and historians; documents were drawn from repositories in both countries.

A review article by David M. Griffiths appears in *William & Mary quarterly,* 3d ser., 38:725–30 (Oct. 1981).   E183.8.R9U59

Biography

American historians 1607–1865. Ed. by Clyde N. Wilson. Detroit, Gale, [1984]. 382p. (Dictionary of literary biography, v.30)   **DB177**

Offers long, signed essays on 46 writers on American history whose careers fall within the 1607–1865 period. Bibliographies.   E175.45.A48

Twentieth-century American historians. Clyde N. Wilson, ed. Detroit, Gale, 1983. 519p. (Dictionary of literary biography, v.17)   **DB178**

Offers lengthy, signed essays on 59 American historians whose careers belong to the 20th century. Includes bibliographies of primary and secondary works as well as career assessments.   E175.45.T85

CANADA

Guides

Beaulieu, André, Hamelin, Jean and **Bernier, Benoit.** Guide d'histoire du Canada. Québec, Presses de l'Université Laval, 1969. 540p. (Québec. Université Laval. Institut d'Histoire. Cahiers, 13)   **DB179**

Based on an earlier (1965) work, *Guide de l'étudiant en histoire du Canada*. This edition is greatly revised, augmented, and provided with an index. Includes sections for reference works, bibliographies, published and manuscript sources, periodicals, and related fields.
    Z1382.B4

Bibliography

Aubin, Paul. Bibliographie de l'histoire du Québec et du Canada, 1966–1975. [Québec, Québeçois de Recherche sur la Culture, 1981] 2v.   **DB180**

More than 20,000 citations to books, articles, and dissertations drawn from standard bibliographies and some 400 journals. In three sections: (1) classed order; (2) analytic (i.e., names of persons, places, organizations, and subject terms in alphabetical order); (3) authors.   Z1382.A88

Bibliographic guide to North American history. v.1– , 1978– . Boston, G. K. Hall, 1979– . Annual.   **DB181**

For full information *see* DB49.

Dick, Trevor J. O. Economic history of Canada; a guide to information sources. Detroit, Gale, [1978]. 174p.   **DB182**

For full information *see* CH90.

Gagnon, Philéas. Essai de bibliographie canadienne. Inventaire d'une bibliothèque comprenant imprimés, manuscrits, estampes, etc., relatifs à l'histoire du Canada et des pays adjacents. . . . Québec, Auteur, 1895–1913. 2v. il. **DB183**

Contents: v.1, Books, pamphlets, periodicals, no.1–3747. Autographs and manuscripts, no.3748–4406. Prints, etc., no.4407–4745. Ex-libris, no.4746–5018; v.2, Additions to the collection, 1895–1909.

Contains both English and French material. Information given for each book includes: author, full title, place, publisher, date, paging, size, with occasional bibliographical notes, facsimiles of title pages, etc. The Gagnon collection was acquired in 1909 by the city of Montreal as a nucleus for the Public Library.   Z1365.G2

Harvard University. Library. Canadian history and literature; classification schedule, classified listing by call number, alphabetical listing by author or title, chronological listing. Cambridge, Harvard Univ. Lib.; distr. by Harvard Univ. Pr., 1968. 411p. (Widener Library shelflist, 20)   **DB184**

For a note on the series *see* AA145.
More than 10,000 titles.   Z1365.H3

Matthews, William. Canadian diaries and autobiographies. Berkeley, Univ. of California Pr., 1950. 130p.   **DB185**

Lists 1,276 published and unpublished diaries and autobiographies of Canadians of both British and French origin. Arrangement is alphabetical with topical index.   Z5305.C3M3

Page, Donald M. Bibliography of works on Canadian foreign relations, 1945–1970. [Toronto], Canadian Inst. of Internat. Affairs, [1973]. 441p.   **DB186**

More than 6,000 books, pamphlets, documents, periodical articles, and dissertations appearing since 1945 are listed by broad topics and geographical areas, with detailed subject and author indexes. Sec. VI is a "Chronological list of statements and speeches issued by the Department of External Affairs," followed by an "Index to the Monthly report on Canadian external relations and International Canada, 1962–1970."   Z6465.C2P33

———— ———— Supplement 1971–1975. [Toronto, 1976] 300p.

Follows the arrangement of the basic volume and adds materials issued 1971–75.

Public Archives of Canada. Library. Catalogue of the Public Archives Library. Boston, G. K. Hall, 1979. 12v.   **DB187**

Added title page in French: *Catalogue de la Bibliothèque des Archives Publiques.*

An author/title catalog of both primary and secondary materials in the library: government records, private papers, pamphlets, reference materials, and "books relevant to the writing of Canadian history."—*Introd.* Also includes a chronological catalog of pamphlets published up to 1950.

A reader's guide to Canadian history. Toronto, Univ. of Toronto Pr., [1982]. 2v.   **DB188**

On cover: An authoritative critical bibliographical guide to Canadian historical writing . . . what is good and why.

Contents: v.1, Beginnings to confederation, ed. by D. A. Muise; v.2, Confederation to the present, ed. by J. L. Granatstein and P. Stevens.

v.2 was previously publ. as *Canada since 1867: a bibliographical guide* (2d ed. 1977).

Offers bibliographic essays by contributing scholars assessing the best and most useful publications for the study of Canadian history. Emphasis is on recent materials; book citations predominate, but some periodical articles are discussed. Follows a thematic arrangement within a regional context. Index of subjects, but not of authors.

The history of Canada, ed. by Dwight L. Smith (Santa Barbara, Calif., ABC-Clio, 1983. 327p.), lists some 3,362 articles, with abstracts, drawn from the *America: history and life* database, 1973–78.   Z1382.R4

Ryder, Dorothy E. Checklist of Canadian directories, 1790–1950; répertoire des annuaires canadiens. Ottawa, National Library of Canada, 1979. 288p.   **DB189**

National, provincial, county, and city directories are listed geographically, then chronologically. 1790 marks publication of the first directory; 1950 the beginning of *Canadiana*. Locates copies.
    Z5771.4.C2R92

Thibault, Claude. Bibliographia Canadiana. [Don Mills, Ont.], Longmans Canada, [1973]. 795p.   **DB190**

Preface, chapter headings, index, etc., in English and French.

A comprehensive bibliography of writings on Canadian history, topically arranged within chronological divisions. Includes both books and periodical articles. Subject index.   Z1382.T47

Toronto. Public Library. Bibliography of Canadiana; being items in the Public Library . . . relating to the early history and development of Canada; ed. by Frances M. Staton and Marie Tremaine, with an introd. by George H. Locke. Toronto, Lib., 1934. 828p. il.   **DB191**

An author catalog of 4,646 numbered items from the reference department of the library, described with full titles, collations, many contents notes, and references to bibliographical sources. Covers the period 1534–1867.   Z1365.T64

———— ———— First supplement . . . ed. by Gertrude M. Boyle, assisted by Marjorie Colbeck. Toronto, Lib., 1959. 333p.

Continues the item numbering of the main volume, adding 1,640 entries.

Dissertations

Register of post-graduate dissertations in progress in history and related subjects. Répertoire des thèses en cours portant sur des sujets d'histoire et autres sujets connexes. no.1– , 1966– . [Ottawa], Canadian Historical Assoc., 1966– . Annual.   **DB192**

Under the auspices of the Public Archives of Canada.

Continues the list published in the *Canadian historical review,* 1927–65. Concerned with theses in progress at Canadian universities at both the master's and the doctoral level. Also lists theses dealing with topics in Canadian history, government, and politics in progress at non-Canadian universities.

Manuscripts and archives

See also DB55, DB183.

National Library of Canada. Research collections in Canadian libraries. [Ottawa, Information Canada, 1972–76]
DB193

For full information *see* AB131; portions having particular relevance for history and area studies include: [pt.] I: 1, Prairie provinces; 2, Atlantic provinces; 3, British Columbia; 4, Ontario; 5, Quebec; 6, Canada.   Z735.A1N37

Public Archives of Canada. General inventory: manuscripts. Inventaire général: manuscrits. Ottawa, 1971–77. v.1–5, 7–8.   **DB194**

Contents: v.1, MG1–MG10: Archives des colonies, Archives de la marine, Archives nationales, Archives de la guerre; Ministère des affaires étrangères, Archives départementales, municipales, maritimes, et de bibliothèques, Paris; Bibliothèques de Paris; Documents relatifs à la Nouvelle-France et au Québec (XVIIᵉ–XXᵉ siècles); Provincial, local, territorial records; Records of foreign governments; v.2, MG11–16: Public Record Office, London: Colonial Office, Admiralty, War Office, Audit Office, Treasury, Foreign Office; v.3, MG17–21: Archives religieuses, Documents antérieurs à la cession, Fur trade and Indians, Hudson's Bay Company archives, Transcripts from papers in the British Museum; v.4, MG22–MG25: Autographs; Late 18th century papers; 19th century pre-Confederation papers; Genealogy; v.5, MG26–MG27: Papers of the prime ministers; Political figures, 1867–1950; v.7, MG29: Nineteenth century post-Confederation manuscripts; v.8, MG80: Manuscripts of the first half of the twentieth century ("accessions completed before 1 April 1976").

"Intended to provide researchers with a complete guide to all documents kept in the Manuscript Division of the Public Archives of Canada . . . [the series] will cover about 100 groups of public records (RGs) and 30 groups of manuscripts (MGs)."—*Introd.*

Preliminary inventories for both groups were published between 1951 and 1967. Entries have been revised for the *General inventory,* descriptions completed, and a more systematic arrangement devised. Covers accessions prior to Jan. 1, 1972. Includes descriptions of microfilm copies of documents from archives outside Canada as well as the Canadian documents in the Public Archives. Detailed index in each volume.

The Archives' "General inventory series" describes specific record groups as to content and availability (no.1–9 publ. 1975–77, plus unnumbered issues publ. 1979–81).   DC3626

―――― Guide to the reports of the Public Archives of Canada, 1872–1972. [By] Françoise Caron-Houle. Ottawa, [The Archives; available from Information Canada], 1975. 97p. il.   **DB195**

Provides an index to the calendars and inventories of private and public papers, documents, maps, plans, and photographs to be found in the *Annual reports* of the Public Archives.   Z5140.P82

―――― **Federal Records Division.** Historical records of the government of Canada. [Comp. by] Terry Cook and Glenn T. Wright. [2d ed.] Ottawa, Public Archives, 1981. 84p., 88p.   **DB196**

1st ed. 1978.

The Federal Archives Division houses and provides access to all permanently retained records of the departments and agencies of the government of Canada since 1867. Listing is by "Record group," giving years covered and amount of material in each of the subfiles; indexed by broad subject and by agency. In this edition a brief paragraph describes the administrative function or background of each department or agency.

The Public Archives' bimonthly journal *Archivist* provides updated information.   CD3627.P8P82

Union list of manuscripts in Canadian repositories. Rev. ed. Ottawa, Public Archives, 1975. 2v. (1578p.)   **DB197**

"Joint project of the Public Archives of Canada and the Humanities Research Council of Canada."—*t.p.*

Title also in French; text in English or French.

1st ed. 1968.

Represents about 27,000 collections in 171 repositories. Arranged by name of the collection with an index of names, subjects, and cross references. An added feature is a "Catalogue-by-repositories" which brings together the names of all collections in a given repository.   CD3622.A2U54

―――― Supplement 1976–79/80. Ottawa, Public Archives, 1976–82. 3v.

The 1976 supplement adds some 5,000 new entries for materials received by repositories Jan. 31, 1974–Mar. 31, 1976, plus about 1,000 entries inadvertently omitted from the 1975 edition; the 1977/78 volume lists an additional 3,000 entries from 66 archives. The 1979/80 supplement describes 3,300 archives at 78 institutions.

Regional and local

See also DB130.

Artibise, Alan F. J. Western Canada since 1870; a select bibliography and guide. Vancouver, Univ. of British Columbia Pr., [1978]. 294p. il.   **DB198**

A selective bibliography of books, pamphlets, periodical articles, theses and dissertations on any area of Western Canadian studies (i.e., Manitoba, Saskatchewan, Alberta, British Columbia). Topical arrangement; author index. Select subject index for ethnic groups and political parties and politicians.   Z1392.N7A77

―――― and **Stelter, Gilbert A.** Canada's urban past: a bibliography to 1980 and guide to Canadian urban studies. Vancouver, Univ. of British Columbia Pr., [1981]. 396p.
DB199

A major reference compilation of some 7,000 entries (books, articles, and theses) topically arranged within a general section and sections for each province. Author, geographical, and subject indexes. Supplements appear in *Urban history review* (1981–84, Oct. issue).

A similar publication, *Bibliography of Canadian urban history,* comp. by F. H. Armstrong, A. F. J. Artibise, and Melvin Baker (Monticello, Ill., Vance Bibliographies, 1980. 6v.) follows much the same arrangement.   Z7165.C2A77

Atlantic provinces checklist: a guide to current information in books, pamphlets, government publications, magazine articles and documentary films relating to the four Atlantic provinces. v.1–9, 16, 1957–72. [Halifax, N.S.], Maritime Lib. Assoc., in cooperation with Atlantic Provinces Economic Council, 1958–74.   **DB200**

v.10–15 not published?

Covers New Brunswick, Newfoundland, Nova Scotia, Prince Edward Island.   Z1392.M37A8

Bishop, Olga B. Bibliography of Ontario history, 1867–1976; cultural, economic, political, social. Toronto, Univ. of Toronto Pr., 1980. 2v. (1760p.)   **DB200a**

1st ed. (1978) had title: *Ontario since 1867.*

An extensive bibliography covering all periods. Topically organized; includes books, periodicals, and government reports. Updated by the *Annual bibliography of Ontario history* (Sudbury, Ont., Laurentian Univ. Pr., 1980–) sponsored by the Ontario Historical Society.   Z1392.O6O67

Canadian local histories to 1950: a bibliography. W. F. E. Morley, ed. [Toronto], Univ. of Toronto Pr., [1967–78]. 3v.
DB201

Contents: v.1, The Atlantic provinces, by W. F. E. Morley (137p.);

v.2, Quebec, by André Beaulieu (328p.); v.3, Ontario and the Canadian North, by W. F. E. Morley (322p.).

Extensive bibliographies with locations of copies. The Prairie provinces are dealt with in B. B. Peel's bibliography (DB205).

Dekin, Albert A. Arctic archaeology: a bibliography and history. N.Y., Garland, 1978. 279p. (Garland reference library of science and technology, v.1)   **DB202**

For the most part, the Arctic is here defined as Alaska, the present Tundra regions of Canada and Greenland, and parts of the coasts of Quebec, Labrador, and Newfoundland. The bulk of the volume is a history of the research and publications on Arctic archaeology; the bibliography is an author listing of books, articles and book reviews, essays, dissertations and conference papers, and technical reports. Includes a short directory of museums with extensive Arctic archaeological materials, and a list of serial publications with significant content on the subject. No index.   E99.E7D36

Glenbow-Alberta Institute. Library. Catalogue of the Glenbow Historical Library. Boston, G. K. Hall, 1973. 4v.   **DB203**

Reproduces the author, title, and subject cards for a collection of books, pamphlets, government publications, and some periodical articles concentrating on material relating to the Prairie region of Canada; much material on bordering states is also included.   Z1392.N7G57

Messier, Jean-Jacques. Bibliographie relative à la Nouvelle-France. Montréal, L'Aurore, [1979]. 198p.   **DB204**

A classed bibliography of books, theses and periodical articles. Includes agriculture, archaeology, art, cartography, commerce, costume, exploration, economy, folklore, religious history, military affairs, money, population, etc. About 2,300 entries; author index. Mainly French-language materials.   Z1383.M47

Peel, Bruce Braden, comp. A bibliography of the Prairie Provinces to 1953, with biographical index. 2d ed. Toronto, Univ. of Toronto Pr., 1973. 780p.   **DB205**

1st ed. 1956; suppl., 1963.

Lists books and pamphlets on the region defined by the compiler as "that agricultural arc resting on the international boundary." Chronological arrangement with author and subject indexes. The new edition was expanded to include a selection of post-1953 publications, as well as earlier books and documents not previously noted.   Z1365.P4

Current surveys

Canadian news facts. v.1, no.1– , Jan. 16, 1967– . Toronto, Marpep, 1967– . Biweekly with monthly indexes cumulating quarterly and annually.   **DB206**

Subtitle: The indexed digest of Canadian current events.

A looseleaf service for Canadian news events, similar to *Facts on file.*

Dictionaries and encyclopedias

Burpee, Lawrence Johnstone. Oxford encyclopaedia of Canadian history. Oxford, Univ. Pr., 1926. 699p. il. (Makers of Canada, anniversary ed., v.12)   **DB207**

Compact articles, in alphabetical arrangement, include biographical sketches and historical events in the political, economic, social, and cultural life of Canada, with brief bibliographies.

A revised and enlarged edition of the author's *Index and dictionary of Canadian history* (Toronto, 1911; *Makers of Canada,* v.21), which served as an index to the *Makers of Canada* series as well as providing encyclopedic articles on topics not treated in the volumes indexed. The newer work omits the indexing feature.

Encyclopedia Canadiana. Toronto, Grolier, 1977. 10v. il.   **DB208**

Kenneth H. Pearson, ed. in chief.

Follows a continuous revision policy.

Based on the *Encyclopedia of Canada* published 1935–37, 1948–49, under the editorship of W. Stewart Wallace.

A good, popularly written encyclopedia on all aspects of Canadian life, past and present. For major topics there are long, signed articles, many with bibliographies, with excellent coverage in short articles of personal and place-names. Illustrations are well chosen and plentiful, and v.10 contains an extensive atlas of Canada with a detailed index and a brief section of contemporary biographies. No general analytical index for the set.   F1006.E62

LeJeune, Louis Marie. Dictionnaire général de biographie, histoire, littérature, agriculture, commerce, industrie et des arts, sciences, moeurs, coutumes, institutions politiques et religieuses du Canada. Ouvrage orné de 187 photographies et de 56 gravures hors-texte. [Ottawa], Université d'Ottawa, 1931. 2v. il.   **DB209**

A general encyclopedia, with many fairly long articles, particularly strong in matters dealing with French Canada. Bibliography at the end of most articles.   F1006.L52

Story, Norah. The Oxford companion to Canadian history and literature. Toronto, [etc.], Oxford Univ. Pr., 1967. 935p.   **DB210**

Broader in scope than other volumes in the *Oxford companion* series, this work intends "to provide a single source in which anyone reading a Canadian book in English or French can find an explanation of references that would otherwise be obscure."—*Introd.* Includes biographies, general articles, and bibliographies. Unusual features are the provision of cross references from the names of authors mentioned in the bibliographies, and an alphabetical list of titles referred to in the text. A valuable addition to this handbook series.   PR9106.S7

———— ———— Supplement to the Oxford companion to Canadian history and literature. Gen. ed. William Toye. Toronto, Oxford Univ. Pr., 1973. 318p.

Includes articles by 37 contributors on books that appeared between 1967 and 1972; survey articles on forms of literature (anthologies, drama, historical studies, etc.) and on writers (novelists, poets, playwrights, historians). A new "companion" for literature alone was published 1983 (*see* BD770).   PR9180.2.T6

Atlases

Kerr, Donald Gordon Grady. A historical atlas of Canada. 3d rev. ed. [Don Mills, Ont.,] Nelson, [1975]. 100p. il., maps. 32cm.   **DB211**

1st ed. 1960. 3d ed. updated to the early 1970s for most charts, maps, and bibliography.

Prep. in cooperation with the Canadian Historical Association's Committee on a Historical Atlas of Canada. In addition to historical maps, includes a section of charts and graphs illustrating main economic and political trends.

Much revision is evident, especially in pt.6, "Main economic and political trends since 1867." A few maps from the earlier edition were dropped or combined.   G1116.S1K4

Trudel, Marcel. Atlas de la Nouvelle-France. An atlas of New France. [Québec], Presses de l'Université Laval, 1968. 219p. 30cm.   **DB212**

A further revision and expansion of the author's 1948 work, *Collection de cartes anciennes et modernes pour servir à l'étude de l'histoire de l'Amérique et du Canada* which was published in a revised edition in 1961 under the title *Atlas historique du Canada français des origines à 1867.*

General maps, grouped by century, are presented first, followed by special maps of settlements, population, and cities.   G1116.S1T7

General histories

The Canadian centenary series. A history of Canada. Ed. by W. L. Morton and D. G. Creighton. Toronto, McClelland & Stewart; N.Y., Oxford Univ. Pr., 1963–79. 18v.   **DB213**

Contents: v.1, Early voyages and northern approaches, 1000–1632, by T. J. Oleson; v.2, The beginnings of New France, 1524–1663, by Margaret Trudel; v.3, Canada under Louis XIV, 1663–1701, by W. J. Eccles; v.5, New France: the last phase, 1744–1760, by G. F. G. Stanley; v.6, Quebec: the revolutionary age, 1760–1791, by H. M. Neatby; v.7, Upper Canada: the formative years, 1784–1841, by G. M. Craig; v.8, Lower Canada, 1791–1840, by F. Quellet; v.9, The Atlantic provinces: the emergence of colonial society, 1712–1857, by W. S. MacNutt; v.10, The union of the Canadas: the growth of Canadian institutions, 1841–1857, by J. M. S. Careless; v.11, The fur trade and the Northwest to 1857, by E. E. Rich; v.12, The critical years: the union of British North America, 1857–1873, by W. L. Morton; v.13, Canada 1874–1896: arduous destiny, by P. B. Waite; v.14, Canada, 1896–1921; a nation transformed, by Robert Craig Brown and Ramsey Cook; v.16, The opening of the Canadian North, 1870–1914, by M. Zaslow; v.18, The forked road: Canada 1939–1957, by D. Creighton.

v.4, 15, 17 not published.

Each period is treated by a specialist, and the series (originally intended to be in 17v.) forms the definitive history of Canada. Copious notes, lengthy bibliographies, index.

v.2 is mainly a condensation of v.1–3 of Trudel's *Histoire de la Nouvelle-France* (Montreal, 1963–75). v.8 is a translation and bridgement of Quellet's *Le bas Canada* (Ottawa, 1976).

Source books

Canadian historical documents series. Scarborough, Ontario, Prentice-Hall of Canada, [1965–66]. 3v.   **DB214**

Contents: v.1, The French régime, ed. and trans. by C. Nish; v.2, Pre-Confederation, ed. by P. B. Waite; v.3, Confederation to 1949, ed. by R. C. Brown and M. E. Prang.

Offers collections of important Canadian historical documents, indicating original sources, and with introductory notes. Bibliography of primary and secondary sources in each volume.

Public Archives of Canada. Documents relating to constitutional history of Canada, 1759–1791, selected and ed. by Adam Shortt and A. G. Doughty. 2d and rev. ed. by the Historical Documents Publication Board. Ottawa, J. de L. Taché, 1918. 2v. (1084p.). maps.   **DB215**

———— ———— 1791–1818, selected and ed. by A. G. Doughty and D. A. McArthur. Ottawa, C. H. Parmelee, 1914. 576p. maps.

———— ———— 1819–1828, selected and ed. with notes by A. G. Doughty and Norah Story. Ottawa, Patenaude, 1935, 538p.

Collections of documents, arranged chronologically, with citations to sources. Index in each volume.   JL11.A2

LATIN AMERICA

General works

Bibliography

See also EH6.

Alcina Franch, José and **Palop Martínez, Josefina.** América en la época de Carlos V; aportación a la bibliografía de este período desde 1900. Madrid, Gráficas Orbe, 1958. 236p. (Asociación Hispanoamericana de Historia)   **DB216**

A classified bibliography of material (1,653 entries), written in the 20th century, about America during the first half of the 16th century.

Continued by: Z1201.A48

Alcina Franch, José. América en la época de los Austrias. Aportación a la bibliografía de este período desde 1900. Madrid, Asociación Hispanoamericana de Historia, 1962. 295p.   **DB217**

A continuation of the above. Covers publications (2,061 entries) between 1900 and 1958/59. Classed arrangement with subject and author indexes.   Z1201.A49

Central America, a bibliography. 2d ed., rev. Los Angeles, Latin American Studies, California State Univ., [1981]. 146p. (Latin America bibliography ser., 2)   **DB218**

Based on collections in the libraries at California State University and Consejo Superior Universitário Centroamericano, San José, Costa Rica. Covers history, politics, economics, geography, anthropology, and some literary works. Lists works in Spanish and English published 1960–81; arrangement is alphabetical by country, with separate listings for books and articles. No index.   Z1437.C44

Chilcote, Ronald H. Revolution and structural change in Latin America; a bibliography on ideology, development, and the radical left (1930–1965). Stanford, Calif., Hoover Institution on War, Revolution and Peace, 1970. 2v. (Hoover Inst. bibliographical ser., 40)   **DB219**

A country-by-country listing of books, pamphlets, and periodical articles. Emphasis is on the period 1930–65, with some earlier materials noted. Most references are in English, French, Portuguese, or Spanish, but some Russian and German materials are listed. v.2 includes an author index and a subject approach by broad topical categories.   Z1601.C496

Dahlin, Therrin C., Gillum, Gary P. and **Grover, Mark L.** The Catholic left in Latin America; a comprehensive bibliography. Boston, G. K. Hall, [1981]. 410p.   **DB220**

A bibliography of materials published 1960–78, in any language, which the compilers felt could be located in the United States. Concerned with the Catholic Left movement in any area of Latin America, including the Caribbean and any dependencies. Topical arrangement within geographical areas; author and title indexes. Since there is no subject index, items dealing with several topics or geographic areas are listed more than once.   Z7165.L3D33

Delorme, Robert. Latin America: social science information sources, 1967–1979. Santa Barbara, Calif., ABC-Clio, [1980]. 262p.   **DB221**

A listing of some 5,600 books and journal articles published 1967–79 on all areas of Latin America. Geographical arrangement, with entry repeated for items which deal with as many as three countries. Most citations are to English-language materials, but many Spanish, French or Portuguese items are included. Author and subject indexes, the latter somewhat lacking in detail.

Z7165.L3D44

———— Latin America, 1979–1983; a social science bibliography. Santa Barbara, Calif., ABC-Clio, [1984]. 224p.   **DB222**

Adds 3,728 citations in English, Spanish, and Portuguese for books, parts of books, and periodical articles published mid-1978 through Sept. 1983. Arranged by country, then subdivided by form of publication. Author index; subject index of fairly broad terms with geographic subdivisions.

Latin American politics; a historical bibliography (Santa Barbara, Calif., ABC-Clio, 1984. 290p.) lists articles with abstracts drawn from *America: history and life,* 1973–82.   Z7165.L3D439

Dorn, Georgette Magassay. Latin America, Spain and Portugal, an annotated bibliography of paperback books. 2d rev. ed. Wash., Lib. of Congress, 1976. 322p. (Hispanic Foundation bibliography ser., no.14)   **DB223**

1964 ed. by D. H. Andrews had title: *Latin America, a bibliography of paperback books.*

Lists 2,200 titles in three sections: Latin America; Spain and Portugal; dictionaries, grammars, readers, and textbooks. Subject index.　　　　　　　　　　　　　　　　　　　Z1601.D

Finan, John J. and **Child, John.** Latin America, international relations; a guide to information sources. Detroit, Gale, [1981]. 236p. (International relations information guide series, v.11)　　　　　　　　　　　　　　　　**DB224**

Intended for a general audience, with emphasis on the more basic and readily available English-language books and articles (although a few Spanish and Portuguese materials are included). A general section is followed by topical chapters on economic and developmental aspects, the O.A.S., security, etc. A country section covers all of the Americas, including the Caribbean, as well as Canada and the United States as they relate to "an inter-American system." Annotated; author and subject indexes.　　　　Z6465.L29F56

Griffin, Charles Carroll, ed. Latin America: a guide to the historical literature. Austin, publ. for the Conference on Latin American History by Univ. of Texas Pr., [1971]. 700p. (Conference on Latin American History. Pubn., 4)　　　　　　　　　　　　　　　　　　　　**DB225**

A cooperative effort sponsored jointly by the Conference on Latin American History and the Hispanic Foundation, Library of Congress. It attempts "to provide a selective scholarly bibliography, accompanied by critical annotations, covering the whole field of Latin American history."—*Introd.* Sections have been compiled by scholar specialists who have also contributed introductory notes and annotations. More than 7,000 items; cutoff date for publications included is 1966. Sections on reference works and general materials are followed by period sections, each with numerous subdivisions. There is an author index, but the detailed table of contents provides the only subject approach.

Other older bibliographies which may still prove useful because of extensive coverage, valuable annotations, or good indexing include: S. A. Bayitch, *Latin America and the Caribbean; a bibliographical guide to works in English* (Coral Gables, Univ. of Miami Pr., 1967. 943p.); R. A. Humphreys, *Latin American history; a guide to the literature in English* (London, Oxford Univ. Pr., 1958. 197p.); M. H. Sable, *A guide to Latin American studies* (Los Angeles, Latin American Center, Univ. of Calif., 1967. 2v.); and A. C. Wilgus, *Latin America, Spain and Portugal: a selected and annotated bibliographical guide to books published in the United States, 1954–1974* (Metuchen, N.J., Scarecrow Pr., 1977. 910p.).　　　Z1601.G75

Gropp, Arthur Eric. A bibliography of Latin American bibliographies. Metuchen, N.J., Scarecrow Pr., 1968. 515p.　　　　　　　　　　　　　　　　　　　**DB226**

For full information, related and supplementary works *see* AA77–AA80.

Latin America, a guide to economic history, 1830–1930. Berkeley, 1977. 685p.　　　　　　　　　　　**DB227**

For full information *see* CH109.

Latin American bibliography; a guide to sources of information & research. By Julia Garlant [and others]; ed. by Laurence Hallewell. [London, Publ. for the SCONUL Latin American Group by the Inst. of Latin American Studies, 1978] 227p.　　　　　　　　　　　　　　**DB228**

An "initial guide" to reference materials and resources for the study of "all the Americas south of the Rio Grande (including the adjacent islands . . .), plus the Spanish speaking areas and minority groups within the U.S."—*p.xi.* Assembled by 11 librarians, the materials are arranged by form or according to the library problem: library facilities, interlibrary loan, official publications.　　　　　　　　　　　　　　　　　　Z1601.L324

Markman, Sidney David. Colonial Central America; a bibliography, including materials on art and architecture, cultural, economic, and social history, ethnohistory, geography, government, indigenous writings, maps and plans, urbanization, bibliographic and archival documentary sources.

Tempe, Arizona State Univ., Center for Latin Amer. Studies, [1977]. 345p.　　　　　　　　　　　　**DB229**

2,250 items in classed arrangement, with an "Index of authors, people, places and subjects." Brief annotations.　　Z1437.M37

Okinshevich, Leo. Latin America in Soviet writings: a bibliography. Robert G. Carlton, ed. Baltimore, publ. for the Library of Congress by the Johns Hopkins Pr., [1966]. 2v.　　　　　　　　　　　　　　　　　　　　**DB230**

Contents: v.1, 1917–1958; v.2, 1959–1964.

Supersedes and extends the coverage of the bibliography of the same title by Okinshevich and C. J. Gorokhoff (Wash., Lib. of Congress, 1959. 257p.). Now includes 8,688 entries, topically arranged.　　　　　　　　　　　　　　　　　Z1601.O55

Sable, Martin Howard. A guide to nonprint materials for Latin American studies. Detroit, Blaine Ethridge-Books, [1979]. 141p.　　　　　　　　　　　　　　　**DB231**

An annotated bibliography of films, filmstrips, slides, photographs, posters, videotapes, recordings, cassettes, arts and crafts, games, maps, museum collections dealing in some way with Latin America and useful to teachers of primary grades through graduate school. Indexes: author, title, subject by genre.　F1409.9.Z9S22

———— Latin-American studies in the non-Western world and Eastern Europe; a bibliography on Latin America in the languages of Africa, Asia, the Middle East, and Eastern Europe, with transliterations and translations in English. Metuchen, N.J., Scarecrow Pr., 1970. 701p.　　**DB232**

Books, articles, etc., are arranged by country of publication, then according to the area treated. More than 2,900 items. Author and subject indexes.　　　　　　　　　　　　　　Z1601.S26

Sánchez Alonso, Benito. Fuentes de la historia española e hispanoamericana. 3. ed., corr y puesta al día. Madrid, Consejo Superior de Investigaciones Científicas, 1952. 3v.　　　　　　　　　　　　　　　　　　　　**DB233**

For full information *see* DC485.

Tropical Science Center, San José, Costa Rica. Occasional paper. Estudio ocasional. no.2–7. San José, 1965–67.　　　　　　　　　　　　　　　　　　　　**DB234**

Contents: no.2, Anthropological bibliography of aboriginal Panama, by E. W. Shook (1965); no.3, Anthropological bibliography of aboriginal Nicaragua, by J. A. Lines (1965); no.4, Anthropological bibliography of aboriginal El Salvador, by J. A. Lines (1965); no.5, Anthropological bibliography of aboriginal Honduras, by J. A. Lines (1966); no.6, Anthropological bibliography of aboriginal Guatemala, British Honduras, by J. A. Lines (1967); no.7, Anthropological bibliography of aboriginal Costa Rica, by J. A. Lines (1967).

Bibliographies of the principal studies from colonial times up to the recent present (i.e., citations and references up to the end of 1965) for each Central American country. Author listing; no index.

Welch, Thomas L. and **Figueras, Myriam.** Travel accounts and descriptions of Latin America and the Caribbean, 1800–1920; a selected bibliography. Wash., Columbus Memorial Lib., 1982. 293p.　　　　　　　　　　**DB235**

A geographically arranged bibliography of "impressions and observations" recorded between 1800 and 1920 by a "writer who was not a native of the area," and including "such items as prospectuses for would-be investors and railroad and commercial guides . . . since they provide information that may not be available elsewhere."—*Introd.* Excludes archeological reports, manuscript materials, technical treatises on development programs. No index.

Werlich, David P. Research tools for Latin American historians: a select, annotated bibliography. N.Y., Garland, 1980. 269p. (Garland reference library of social science, v.60)　　　　　　　　　　　　　　　　　　　　**DB236**

A classified, annotated bibliography of some 1,400 English, Spanish, Portuguese, French, and German reference works, collections of source materials, and periodicals useful for Latin American historians. Materials specifically dealing with Puerto Rico or non-Hispanic Caribbean are excluded. Pt.I lists reference materials concerned with specific types of publications, e.g., newspapers, official publications, current event sources, etc. Pt.II concentrates on 20 individual countries, listing the basic reference materials for each. Index of main entries and of selected topics.   Z1601.W47

Wilgus, A. Curtis. Latin America; a guide to illustrations. Metuchen, N.J., Scarecrow Pr., 1981. 250p.   **DB237**

Pictures are indexed by country (subdivided by period and by individuals), the index being keyed to a bibliography of books and magazines where the illustrations appear. Limited to English-language sources, with emphasis on readily available materials.
                                                          F1408.W667

——— Latin America in the nineteenth century; a selected bibliography of books of travel and description published in English. Metuchen, N.J., Scarecrow Pr., 1973. 174p.
                                                              DB238

Lists 1,182 titles of travelers' accounts of all areas south of the United States (as well as Bermuda and the Bahamas). Also includes guide books, geographies, some histories, diaries, letters, memoirs and reminiscences, autobiographies, selected collections of private and public documents and papers, and occasional fiction. Select list of references, p.158–74. Author and geographical indexes.
                                                          Z1601.W686

Woods, Richard Donovon. Reference materials on Latin America in English: the humanities. Metuchen, N.J., Scarecrow Pr., 1980. 639p.   **DB239**

An annotated main-entry listing of about 1,250 English-language reference works on Latin America. Title and subject indexes.
                                                          Z1601.W75

Current

See also AA518.

Bibliographic guide to Latin American studies. v.1– , 1978– . Boston, G. K. Hall, 1979– . Annual.   **DB240**

Added title page in Spanish; prefatory matter in English and Spanish.

A continuation of the *Catalog of the Latin-American Collection* of the Library of the University of Texas at Austin and its supplements (*see* DB246).

Reflects cataloging done for the University of Texas Latin American Collection from OCLC tapes during the year indicated, supplemented by relevant material from Library of Congress MARC tapes for that year. Full bibliographical information is given under main entry, with briefer information under added entries.

The University of Texas Library continues its policy of acquiring all materials written by Latin American authors or concerning Latin America in any language, including Indian dialects of Latin America.   Z1610.B52

Handbook of Latin American studies, 1935– . Gainesville, Univ. of Florida Pr.; Austin, Univ. of Texas Pr., 1936– . v.1– . Annual.   **DB241**

Publisher varies.

Of first importance, this is an extensive, annotated bibliography of material relating to Latin America, prepared by a group of scholars. Coverage varies; e.g., v.25 (publ. 1963) covers anthropology, art, economics, education, geography, government, history, international relations, language and literature, law, music and philosophy, sociology, and travel. Each volume also contains special articles on particular phases of life and culture or inter-American relations.

With 1964 issue, divided into two sections—social sciences and humanities—now published in alternate years; i.e., v.26, *Humanities,* covers art, history, language, literature, music, and philosophy; v.27, *Social sciences,* includes anthropology, economics, education, geography, government and international relations, law, and sociology.

——— Author index to . . . no.1–28, 1936–1966. Comp. by Francisco José and Maria Elena Cardona. Gainesville, Univ. of Florida Pr., 1968. 421p.

                                                          Z1605.H23

Historiografía y bibliografía americanistas, 1954– . Sevilla, Escuela de Estudios Hispano-Americanos, 1955– . Annual.
                                                              DB242

Issues for 1954–68 published as a section of the *Anuario de estudios americanos.*

Each issue contains articles, bibliographical essays, surveys of archives, reprinted documents, and an extensive annotated bibliography, topically arranged, covering all areas of Latin America.
                                                          F1401.H68

Library catalogs

Florida. University. Libraries. Catalog of the Latin-American collection. Boston, G. K. Hall, 1973. 13v.   **DB243**

Reproduction of the cards from this author/subject catalog representing 120,000 books, pamphlets, periodicals and government documents in original form and 9,000 units of microform, dealing with Latin America including the Caribbean. The collection is especially strong in materials relating to Brazil and the Caribbean, and in official documents and periodicals.

The *Catalog* of the Latin American Library of Tulane University Library (Boston, G. K. Hall, 1970. 9v. and suppls. 1–3, 1973–78, 6v.) is particularly strong in Central American materials.

                                                          Z1610.F6

——— ——— First supplement. Boston, G. K. Hall, 1979. 7v.

Reproduces an additional 99,000 cards representing cataloging May 1973–1978.

Harvard University. Library. Latin America and Latin American periodicals. Cambridge, publ. by the Harvard Univ. Library; distr. by the Harvard Univ. Pr., 1966. 2v. (Widener Library shelflist no.5–6)   **DB244**

Contents: v.1, Classification schedule; Classified listing by call number; v.2, Alphabetical listing by author or title; Chronological listing.

For a note on the series, *see* AA145.

27,292 titles, "primarily works on history, civilization, government, general geography and travel, general economic and social conditions . . . , religious affairs, and the various races" (*Note on the classification*) of the West Indies, Mexico, Central and South America.   Z1610.H35

Madrid. Biblioteca Nacional. Catálogo de obras iberoamericanas y filipinas de la Biblioteca Nacional de Madrid . . . por Luisa Cuesta [y] Modesta Cuesta. Madrid, Dirección General de Archivos y Bibliotecas, Servicio de Publicaciones del Ministério de Educación Nacional, 1953. v.1. (Catálogos de archivos y bibliotecas)   **DB245**

On cover: Obra núm. 15 de Publicaciones de Educación Nacional.

Some 3,364 items on Latin America and the Philippines are listed in this volume, which is devoted to general works. Other volumes were planned for individual countries but only v.1 (322p.) was published.   Z945.M22

Texas. University at Austin. Library. Latin American Collection. Catalog of the Latin American collection. Boston, G. K. Hall, 1969. 31v.   **DB246**

Reproduction in book form of the dictionary catalog of this outstanding collection. Includes cards for about 175,000 books, pamphlets, serials, and microforms.   Z1610.T48

——— ——— Supplement 1–4. Boston, G. K. Hall, 1971– 77. 19v.

The supplements cover materials processed for the collection 1969–74. Suppl. 1 includes cards for "Hilea–Hispanidad A" which were omitted from the 1969 catalog. Suppl.3–4 include a number of pre-1970 imprints from the cataloging backlog.

Continued by DB240.

Dissertations

Deal, Carl W. Latin America and the Caribbean, a dissertation bibliography. [Ann Arbor, Mich.], University Microfilms Internat., [1978]. 164p. **DB247**

More than 7,200 dissertation titles accepted through 1977 are arranged by broad subject areas, subdivided by country. Includes only those dissertations available from University Microfilms. Author index. Z1610.D4

Walters, Marian C. Latin America and the Caribbean II; a dissertation bibliography. [Ann Arbor], University Microfilms Internat., [1980]. 78p. **DB247a**

Forms a supplement to the above, adding dissertations from the period 1977–June 1980 which are available for purchase from University Microfilms; it is therefore not a complete listing. Subject arrangement with country subdivisions; author index. Supplements appear irregularly.

Hanson, Carl A. Dissertations on Iberian and Latin American history. Troy, N.Y., Whitston, 1975. 400p. **DB248**

In addition to United States and Canadian dissertations on Latin America completed in history departments, the bibliography includes studies on: "Iberia and its non-Latin American holdings; other European possessions, past and present, on the perimeter of Latin America; dissertations completed in British and Irish universities and colleges; and titles from disciplines other than history."— *Introd.* Geographical/chronological arrangement. Author index. More than 3,500 entries. Z1601.H32

Theses in Latin American studies at British universities in progress and recently completed. no.1– . London, Institute of Latin American Studies, Univ. of London, 1967– . Annual. **DB249**

Title varies slightly: no.1–13 issued as *Theses in Latin American studies at British universities in progress and completed.*

Listing is by university, with indexes by author and broad subject field.

The same institute also publishes *Latin American studies in the universities of the United Kingdom: staff reports in progress or recently completed in the humanities and the social sciences,* 1968/69– (London, [1969]– . Annual). Z1601.L66

Serial publications

See also AA518.

Birkos, Alexander S. and **Tambs, Lewis A.** Latin American studies. [Kent, Ohio], Kent State Univ. Pr., [1971]. 359p. (Academic writer's guide to periodicals, 1) **DB250**

For a note on the series *see* AE18.

Covington, Paula Hattox. Indexed journals; a guide to Latin American serials. Madison, Wis., Secretariat, Seminar on the Acquisition of Latin American Library Materials, Memorial Lib., Univ. of Wisconsin, [1983]. 458p. (SALALM bibliography ser., 8) **DB251**

For full information *see* AE216.

Latin American newspapers in United States libraries, a union list. Comp. in the Serial Div., Lib. of Congress, by Steven M. Charno. Austin, Univ. of Texas Pr., [1969]. 619p. (Conference on Latin American History. Pubn. no.2) **DB252**

For full record *see* AF51.

Latin American serial documents; a holdings list. Comp. by Rosa Quintero Mesa. Ann Arbor, Mich., University Microfilms, 1968–73. 11v. **DB253**

For full information *see* AG157.

Guides to records

Bartley, Russell H. and **Wagner, Stuart L.** Latin America in basic historical collections: a working guide. Stanford, Calif., Hoover Inst. Pr., [1972]. 217p. (Hoover Institution bibliographical ser., 51) **DB254**

Attempts "to provide researchers with concise descriptive statements and bibliography on major archives, libraries and special collections germane to the study of Latin American history."— *Introd.* Includes notes on repositories throughout the world, though emphasis is on resources in the United States. Extensive bibliography, p.139–211. Indexed.

For descriptions of specific United States libraries *see* W. V. Jackson's *Latin American collections* (Nashville, Vanderbilt Univ. Bookstore, 1974. 142p.). Z1601.B32

Documentos relativos a la independencia de Norteamérica existentes en archivos españoles. Madrid, Ministerio de Asuntos Exteriores, Dirección General de Relaciones Culturales, 1976–80. **DB255**

For full information *see* DB84.

Gómez Canedo, Lino. Los archivos de la historia de América. Período colonial español. México, Inst. Panamericano de Geografía e Historia, 1961. 2v. (Pan American Inst. of Geography and History. Commission on History. Pubn. 87; Pan American Institute of Geography and History, Pubn. 225) **DB256**

Presents historical and descriptive notes on the pertinent archives in Spanish America, Europe, and North America which have important collections of materials on colonial Spanish America. CD3681.G6

Grow, Michael. Scholars' guide to Washington, D.C. for Latin American and Caribbean studies. Wash., Smithsonian Inst. Pr., 1979. 346p. (Scholars' guide to Washington, D.C., 2) **DB257**

Publ. for the Latin American Program of the Woodrow Wilson International Center for Scholars.

Intended as "a descriptive and evaluative survey of research resources" (*Introd.,*) primarily for the serious scholar. In two main sections: (1) Collections (which lists, briefly describes and evaluates pertinent libraries, archives, museums and art collections, music and sound recording collections, map collections, film collections, and data banks); (2) Organizations (both public and private, "which deal with Latin America and are potential sources of information or assistance to researchers"). Indexed. Z1601.G867

Guide to manuscript sources for the history of Latin America and the Caribbean in the British Isles; ed. by Peter Walne. Oxford, Univ. Pr. in collaboration with the Inst. of Latin American Studies, Univ. of London, 1973. 580p. **DB258**

Sponsored by the International Council on Archives.

This is the first comprehensive survey of archival and manuscript materials for this area. Also includes the Philippine Islands. Entries are arranged alphabetically by English counties, followed by listings for Scotland, Wales, and Ireland; within geographical area, arrangement is alphabetical by name of repository or owner of the papers described. References to any published descriptions or guides to particular collections are noted. Includes archives of business firms preserved in public and private hands. Subject index includes names of collections, owners and holders of records. CD1048.L35G84

Guide to the sources of the history of the nations. A. Latin America. The Hague, Govt. Pub. Office, [1966–69]. v.3–4. (In progress?) **DB259**

At head of title: Conseil International des Archives. International Council on Archives. Consejo Internacional des Archivos.

Contents: v.3, fasc.2, Guides to the sources in the Netherlands for the history of Latin America, by M. P. H. Roessingh (1968. 232p.); v.4, Guía de fuentes para la historia de Ibero-Americo conservadas en España, ed. for Direccion General de Archivos y Bibliotecas, Spain (1966–69. 2v.).

A microfiche series assembled by Inter Documentation, Zug, Switz., reproduces inventories available on paper from other publishers: *Guide des sources de l'histoire d'Amérique Latine conservées en Belgique* by L. Liagre (Brussels, 1967. 132p.); *Übersicht über die Quellen zur Geschichte Lateinamerikas in Archiven der D.D.R.* comp. at the Staatliche Archivverwaltung of the German Democratic Republic (Potsdam, 1971. 122p.); *Führer durch die Quellen zur Geschichte Lateinamerikas in der Bundesrepublik Deutschland,* v.2,pt.1, by R. Hauschild-Thiessen (Bremen, 1972. 437p.); *A guide to the manuscript sources for the history of Latin America and the Caribbean in the British Isles* by P. A. Walne (DB258); *Guida delle fonti per la storia dell'America latina esistenti in Italia* by E. Lodolini (Rome, 1976. 403p.); *Fuentes para la historia de Ibero-América: Escandinavia* by M. Mörner (Stockholm, 1968. 105p.); *Guide to materials on Latin America in the National Archives* comp. at the U.S. National Archives (*see* DB267); *Guida delle fonti per la storia dell'America Latina negli archivi della Santa Sede e negli archivi ecclesiastici d'Italia* by L. Pásztor (Vatican, 1970. 665p.).

All are surveys of materials in archives and libraries important for research in Latin American studies.   CD941.G83

Hanke, Lewis. Guía de las fuentes en hispanoamérica para el estudio de la administración virreinal española en México y en el Perú, 1535–1700. Wash., Secretaría General, OAS, 1980. 523p.   **DB260**

A survey of materials dealing with the colonial period (1535–1700) in Mexico and Peru as found in the archives of individual South American nations. For some countries (e.g., Bolivia) the information is quite full.

Hanke has also compiled *Guía de las fuentes en el Archivo General de Indias para el estudio de la administración virreinal española en México y en el Perú, 1535–1700* (Köln, Böhlau, 1977. 3v.), of which v.1 is particularly useful since, besides providing an overview of viceregal sources, it gives short biographies and bibliographies of the viceroys of Mexico and Peru.   Z1426.H36

Hill, Roscoe R. The national archives of Latin America; ed. for the Joint Committee on Latin American Studies of the National Research Council, the American Council of Learned Societies, and the Social Science Research Council. Cambridge, Harvard Univ. Pr., 1945. 169p. il. (Joint Committee on Latin American Studies. Misc. pubn. no.3)   **DB261**

Survey of the history, housing, personnel, and contents of the national archives of each of the 20 Latin-American republics. Still useful for its historical material and for references to published portions of various archives.   CD3683 1945.H5

Marchant, Alexander Nelson de Armand. Boundaries of the Latin American republics; an annotated list of documents, 1493–1943. (Tentative version) Wash., Govt. Prt. Off., 1944. 386p. (U.S. Dept. of State Pubn. 2082; Inter-American ser. 24)   **DB262**

A guide to documents; introduction in English, Spanish, and Portuguese.

Contents: pt.1, Documents arranged in chronological order, p.21–214; pt.2, Documents arranged according to boundary, p.215–351; Bibliography, p.355–86.   Z1609.B7U52

Misiones americanas en los archivos europeos. México, Inst. Panamericano de Geografía e Historia, 1949–57. (Comisión de Historia. Pubn. 8, 22, 28, 32, 33, 47, 65, 73, 80, 85) (No more publ.?)   **DB263**

Contents: no.1, Mexican, by Manuel Carrera Stampa (1949); no.2, American, by Roscoe R. Hill (1951); no.3, Cuban, by Manuel Moreno Fraginals (1951); no.4, Brazilian, by Virgilio Correa Filho (1952); no.5, Colombian, by Enrique Ortega Ricaurte (1951); no.6, Chilean, by Alejandro Soto Cárdenas (1953); no.7, Argentinian, by Raúl A. Molina (1955); no.8, Venezuelan, by Joaquín Gabaldón Márquez (1954); no.9, Ecuadorian, by José María Vargas (1956); no.10–11, not published; no.12, Nicaraguan, by Carlos Molina Argüello (1957).

The series offers calendars of copies of documents in European archives relating to the individual Latin American countries; the copies were acquired by various "missions" sent out by the Latin American countries.

Nauman, Ann Keith. A handbook of Latin American and Caribbean national archives. Guía de los archivos nacionales de América Latina y el Caribe. Detroit, Blaine Ethridge-Books, [1983]. 127p.   **DB264**

In English and Spanish.

Presents information gathered by questionnaires sent to archivists and scholars in an effort to determine the scope of the national archives in Central and South America, including the Caribbean islands. Most entries give name, address, director, hours, history, description of the collection, type of catalog, services available (including copying), admission requirements. Bibliography, p.118–27, lists other descriptions of the various national archives.   CD3680.N38

Naylor, Bernard, Hallewell, Laurence and **Steele, Colin.** Directory of libraries and special collections on Latin America and the West Indies. [London], Athlone Pr., 1975. 161p. (London. Univ. Inst. of Latin Amer. Studies. Monographs, no.5)   **DB265**

Concentrates on collections of printed materials in British repositories and is therefore complementary to the *Guide to manuscript sources for the history of Latin America and the Caribbean in the British Isles* (DB258).   Z1601.N37

Research guide to Andean history: Bolivia, Chile, Ecuador, and Peru. John J. TePaske, coordinating ed. Durham, N.C., Duke Univ. Pr., 1981. 346p.   **DB266**

A collection of contributed articles (a few of them in Spanish), each describing a particular archive or a group of repositories having materials relating to a specific historical period or topic. Articles are grouped by country, with an introductory note for each country section. Includes directory information for many of the individual archives, as well as references to published guides and descriptions. The index is limited to a listing of the archives and libraries by country, including references to repositories outside the four countries under consideration.   Z1656.R47

U.S. National Archives & Records Service. Guide to materials on Latin America in the National Archives of the United States. By George S. Ulibarri and John P. Harrison. Wash., Nat. Archives & Records Serv., 1974. 489p.   **DB267**

"This guide supersedes the *Guide to Materials on Latin America in the National Archives* (vol. I, 1961), compiled by Dr. John P. Harrison, and includes the records descriptions contained in that guide. In addition, it includes descriptions of pertinent records of the executive, legislative, and judicial branches of the Government that were not included in the earlier guide."—*Introd.* The 1961 guide was intended to be in 2v.; the present work results from a decision to present the earlier material in revised form together with much new information.   CD3023.U54

Historiography

Esquenazi-Mayo, Roberto and **Meyer, Michael C.** Latin American scholarship since World War II; trends in history, political science, literature, geography, and economics. Lincoln, Univ. of Nebraska Pr., [1971]. 335p.   **DB268**

A series of essays by scholars surveying research on various eras and countries of Latin America during the 25-year period since World War II. Each essay concludes with a bibliography of titles cited. Includes 7 essays on historical scholarship; 4 on political research.   F1409.9.E8

Wilgus, Alva Curtis. Histories and historians of Hispanic America. [2d ed.] N.Y., Wilson, 1942. 144p. (Repr.: N.Y., Cooper Sq., 1965)   **DB269**

Chronologically arranged by centuries, then grouped geographically by countries. Discusses the principal writings of more than 1,000 historians.   Z1601.W66

—— The historiography of Latin America: a guide to historical writing, 1500–1800. Metuchen, N.J., Scarecrow Pr., 1975. 333p.   **DB270**

Provides an account of the principal individual historians and their works. Separate sections for the 16th, 17th, and 18th centuries. Within each section a "Historical note" and several pages of "Lifecharts" (indicating birth and death dates of the historians and their relative periods of activity) precede the "Authors" section, which is subdivided by country; a supplementary list of writers is given for each century. "Selected references," p.280–311. Index of names.   F1409.7.W54

Current surveys

ISLA: information services on Latin America. July 1970– . Oakland, Calif., ISLA, [1970]– . [v.1, no.1]– . Monthly. il. (Looseleaf)   **DB271**

Reproduces articles from ten English-language newspapers (7 of them American, 3 European); articles deal primarily with political, social, and economic news of all areas of Latin America (including Central America and the Caribbean). Arrangement is geographical, then chronological within country sections; each issue ranges from 300 to 450 pages.

An index covering Jan.–June 1982 was published 1984; it provides indexing by country (subdivided by topic), international organizations, personal names, and bylines.

Latin American and Caribbean contemporary record. v.1– , 1981/82– . London & N.Y., Holmes & Meier, [1983]– . Annual.   **DB272**

Jack W. Hopkins, ed.

Offers current, authoritative, analytical surveys in five major sections: Current issues; Country-by-country review; Documents; Economic, social, and political data; Book abstracts. Names and subjects index. Similar to *Africa contemporary record* (DD51) and *Middle East contemporary record* (DE69).

Encyclopedias, dictionaries, and handbooks

Encyclopedia of Latin America. Ed. by Helen Delpar. N.Y., McGraw-Hill, [1974]. 651p. il.   **DB273**

Intended as a "comprehensive yet concise reference book offering authoritative information on the history, economy, politics, arts, and other aspects of Latin America."—*Introd.* Treats "the eighteen Spanish-speaking republics plus Brazil, Haiti, and Puerto Rico," with a survey article included for each of these countries. Emphasis is on the national period, but attention is given to important colonial figures and institutions. Employs an alphabetical arrangement, with numerous *see* and *see also* references. Articles are signed; the longer ones include bibliographical citations. Statistical appendix, p.644–47; select bibliography of bibliographies, p.649–51.
F1406.E52

Latin American historical dictionaries. General ed., A. Curtis Wilgus. Metuchen, N.J., Scarecrow Pr., 1970–81. 21v.
DB274

Contents: v.1, Guatemala, ed. by Richard E. Moore (rev. ed., 1973); v.2, Panama, ed. by Basil C. and Anne K. Hedrick (1970); v.3, Venezuela, ed. by Donna Keyse and G. A. Rudolph (1971); v.4, Bolivia, ed. by Dwight B. Heath (1972); v.5, El Salvador, ed. by Philip F. Flemion (1972); v.6, Nicaragua, ed. by Harvey K. Meyer (1972); v.7, Chile, ed. by Salvatore Bizzarro (1972); v.8, Paraguay, ed. by Charles J. Kolinski (1973); v.9, Puerto Rico and the U.S. Virgin Islands, by Kenneth R. Farr (1973); v.10, Ecuador, by Albert Bork and Georg Maier (1973); v.11, Uruguay, by Jean Willis (1974); v.12, British Caribbean, by William R. Lux (1975); v.13, Honduras, by Harvey K. Meyer (1976); v.14, Colombia, by Robert H. Davis (1977); v.15, Haiti, by Roland I. Perusse (1977); v.16, Costa Rica, by Theodore S. Creedman (1977); no.17, Argentina, by Ione S. Wright and Lisa M. Nikhom (1977); no.18, French and Netherlands Antil-

les, by Albert Gastmann (1978); no.19, Brazil, by Robert M. Levine (1979); no.20, Peru, by Marvin Alisky (1979); no.21, Mexico, by Donald C. Briggs and Marvin Alisky (1981).

A series of historical dictionaries with brief entries for personal names, places, and events of individual Latin-American nations. Quality of the individual volumes is somewhat uneven.

Véliz, Claudio. Latin America and the Caribbean; a handbook. N.Y., Praeger; [London], A. Blond, [1968]. 840p. il.
DB275

Similar to the handbook for Asia (DE24), with each section contributed by an area specialist.   F1408.V43

Atlases

Lombardi, Cathryn L. and **Lombardi, John V.** Latin American history, a teaching atlas. Madison, Wis., Publ. for the Conference on Latin American History by the Univ. of Wisconsin Pr., [1983]. 104p., 40p. maps. 29cm.   **DB276**

Offers more than 100 black-and-white maps covering all areas of Latin America and the Caribbean from discovery and conquest until about 1976; there is a 1982 map of the Falklands. Basic presentation is chronological, with many maps depicting economics, culture, the environment, etc. Index of names and topics.   G1541.S1L6

Directories

Latin America data catalog. Williamstown, Mass., Roper Research Center, [1976?]. 268p.   **DB277**

A catalog of machine-readable data on Latin America located at the Roper Public Opinion Research Center; the International Data Library and Reference Service, Univ. of Calif., Berkeley; the Institute for Social Research, Univ. of Mich.; the Latin American Data Bank, Univ. of Fla.; or held by individual researchers. Arrangement is by country; each sample survey is described, followed by descriptions of census enumerations. A final section deals with cross-national data sets.   Z7164.S667L37

Mesoamérica: directorio y bibliografía 1950–1980. Alfredo Méndez-Domínguez, ed. Guatemala, Universidad del Valle de Guatemala, 1982. 313p.   **DB278**

Each entry gives information (based on replies to questionnaires received from 700 professionals in Europe, North and South America) concerning education, present position, address, special interests, languages, and, in many cases, an extensive bibliography. Indexed by country of interest, subdivided by broad topic (e.g., anthropology, archeology, ethnohistory and history, folklore, geology, geography, linguistics).   Z1209.2.C45M47

Sable, Martin H. The Latin American studies directory. Detroit, Blaine Ethridge-Books, [1981]. 124p.   **DB279**

A listing of colleges and universities offering courses in Latin American studies in the United States and elsewhere is followed by select lists of relevant research centers; professional associations, government agencies; fellowships and grants; libraries, information centers and data banks; book, map, and globe publishers; periodicals subscription agents; and Latin American specialists in the United States. Indexed.

The review in *Library journal* (Jan. 15, 1982, p.166) notes "some very arbitrary selections as well as . . . some rather glaring omissions."   F1409.9.S2

Thomas, Jack Ray. Biographical dictionary of Latin American historians and historiography. Westport, Conn., Greenwood Pr., [1984]. 420p.   **DB280**

Provides biographical sketches, with notes on their work, of Latin American historians from the colonial period to the present (i.e., includes 20th century writers who died prior to 1983). "The major considerations for inclusion were that the writer either produced a significant amount of historical writing or that a portion of his scholarly production was so important to the discipline of history that he could not be excluded."—*Pref.* Bibliography at the end of each article, and a general bibliography p.403–11. Extensive introductory essay; index.

The *National directory of Latin Americanists* (2d ed. Wash., Hispanic Foundation, Lib. of Congress, 1972. 684p.) is still occasionally useful.　　　　　　　　　　　　　　　F1409.8.A2T48

Histories and source books

Cambridge history of Latin America. Leslie Bethell, ed. Cambridge & N.Y., Cambridge Univ. Pr., 1985– . [v.1]– . (In progress)　　　　　　　　　　　　　　　**DB281**

Contents: [v.1] Colonial Latin America, 2v.

To be in 7v. Similar in plan to other Cambridge histories, this aims to be the "first large-scale authoritative survey of Latin America's unique historical experience during almost five centuries from the first contacts between the Native American Indians and Europeans (and the beginnings of the African slave trade) in the late fifteenth and early sixteenth centuries to the present day."—*Pref.* Each chapter is by a specialist, and each is accompanied by an extremely useful bibliographic essay.

The first two volumes published cover Spanish and Portuguese rule from the end of the 15th century up to the end of the 18th.　　　　　　　　　　　　　　　　　　　　F1410.C1834

New Iberian world: a documentary history of the discovery and settlement of Latin America to the early 17th century. Ed. with commentaries by John H. Parry and Robert G. Keith, with the assistance of Michael Jimenez. N.Y., Times Books, Hector & Rose, [1984]. 5v. il.　　　　**DB282**

Contents: v.1, The conquerors and the conquered; v.2, The Caribbean; v.3, Central America and Mexico; v.4, Andes; v.5, Coastlines, rivers, and forests.

Offers translations of travel narratives, government accounts, chronicles and descriptions of Latin America. Many of the documents are newly translated for this work, though most are "ruthlessly excerpted"—*Introd.* General introduction for each section; headnotes for individual documents indicate source. Glossary of terms (especially nautical and legal ones) common in the 16th century documents. Contemporary or near-contemporary maps in each volume; bibliography (v.5, p.497–506) lists works mentioned or quoted in the text. Indexed.

Argentina

Bibliography

Feigen de Roca, Elisabeth and **Gaer de Sabulsky, Alicia.** Historiografía Argentina, 1930–1970. Buenos Aires, Servicio de Documentación Librería Piloto, 1972. 2v. (674*l*)　　　　　　　　　　　　　　　　　　　　　**DB282a**

Nearly 5,100 books and articles are cited in topical arrangement (including names of biographees). Author index.　　Z1626.F44

Ferre, Dominique. Le Péronisme: bibliographie. Rennes, Univ. de Haute Bretagne, Centre d'Études Hispaniques et Hispano-Américaines, [1977?]. 79*l*.　　　　　　**DB283**

A classed bibliography of books and periodical articles relating to Peron and contemporary Argentine history. Author and subject indexes.　　　　　　　　　　　　　　　　　Z1620.F47

Fúrlong Cárdiff, Guillermo and **Geoghegan, Abel Rodolfo.** Bibliografía de la Revolución de Mayo, 1810–1828. Ed. especial con motivo del Sesquicentenario de la Revolución de Mayo de 1810. Buenos Aires, Biblioteca del Congreso de la Nación, 1960. 704p.　　　　　　　　**DB284**

A detailed, classified listing of materials on the period of the Argentine revolt from Spain. Nearly 10,000 items—monographs, periodical articles, and documents—are included, with annotations and often tables of contents for the more significant works. Author index.　　　　　　　　　　　　　　　　　Z1629.F8

Matijevic, Nicolás and **Matijevic, Olga H. de.** Bibliografía patagónica y de las tierras australes. Bahía Blanca, Centro de Documentación Patagónica, Univ. Nacional del Sur, 1973–78. v.1–2. (In progress)　　　　　　　**DB285**

Contents: v.1, Historia; v.2, Geografía.

Each volume is a topically arranged bibliography of more than 2,000 entries, with indexes of names and of geographic areas.

Further volumes are to cover: (3) Indígenas; (4) Botánica y zoología; (5) Geología y paleontología; (6) Recursos naturales y desarrollo.　　　　　　　　　　　　　　　　Z1634.P58M38

Universidad de Buenos Aires. Bibliografía argentina: catálogo de materiales argentinos en las bibliotecas de la Universidad de Buenos Aires. Boston, G. K. Hall, 1980. 7v.　　　　　　　　　　　　　　　　　　　　　**DB286**

For full information *see* AA612.

Historiography

Bohdziewicz, Jorge C. Bibliografía de bibliografías individuales: historia y antropología. Buenos Aires, Instituto Bibliográfico "Antonio Zinny," 1979. 56p.　　**DB287**

An annotated bibliography arranged by name of Argentine scholar; includes lengthy bibliographies published in books and periodical articles.

Carbia, Rómulo D. Historia crítica de la historiografía argentina (desde sus orígenes en siglo XVI). La Plata, República Argentina, [Buenos Aires, Impr. López], 1939. 483p. (Biblioteca humanidades, ed. por la Facultad de Humanidades y Ciencias de la Educación de la Universidad de La Plata, t.22)　　　　　　　　　　**DB288**

A considerably enlarged and revised version of a book by the same author with almost the same title, published in 1925 as v.2 of *Biblioteca humanidades.* It is a survey of Argentine historiography, including historical works by foreigners on the Plata region. "Indice bibliográfico," p.383–477.　　　　　　　　　F2829.C24

Etchepareborda, Roberto. Historiografía militar argentina. Buenos Aires, Círculo Militar, 1984. 205p. (Biblioteca del oficial, v.717)　　　　　　　　　　　　　　**DB289**

A comprehensive bibliography of writings on military actions up to 1943, including wars of revolution, coup d'états, civil wars, border wars, and the "conquest of the Indians."

Tanzi, Hector José. Historiografía argentina contemporânea. Caracas, 1976. 167p. (Institutos Panamericano de Geografía e Historia. Comision de Historia. Historiografías IX)　　　　　　　　　　　　　　　　　**DB290**

A survey of Argentinian historiography since 1940.

　　　　　　　　　　　　　　　　　　　　　F2829.T36

Dictionaries and encyclopedias

Diccionario histórico argentino, publ. bajo la dirección de Ricardo Piccirilli, Francisco L. Romay [y] Leoncio Gianello. Buenos Aires, Ed. Históricas Argentinas, 1953–54. 6v.　　　　　　　　　　　　　　　　　　　　　**DB291**

Covers all phases of Argentine history; especially strong in biography.　　　　　　　　　　　　　　　　　F2804.D5

Gran enciclopedia argentina, [por] Diego A. de Santillán. Buenos Aires, Ediar, 1956–63. 8v. il., maps.　　**DB292**

Subtitle: Todo lo argentino ordenado alfabeticamente; geografía e historia, toponimias, biografías, ciencias, artes, letras, derecho, economía, industria y comercio, instituciones, flora y fauna, folklore, léxico regional.

A national rather than a general encyclopedia, providing a large body of reference material not easily available otherwise. Biographical entries are numerous, including living persons.

———— ———— Apendice 1964. Buenos Aires, Ediar, 1964. 460p. il.

F2804.G82

Belize

Woodward, Ralph Lee. Belize. Oxford, Eng., & Santa Barbara, Calif., Clio Pr., [1980]. 229p. map. (World bibliographical ser., v.21)   **DB293**

Offers an "annotated compilation of the most significant and useful publications on Belize" *(Introd.)*—books, periodical articles, documents, and theses. Topical arrangement with author/title/subject index.   Z1441.W59

Bolivia

Abecia Baldivieso, Valentín. Historiografía boliviano. 2. ed. La Paz, Editorial "Letras," 1973. 588p.   **DB294**

1st ed. 1965.
An extensive discussion of the writing of the history of Bolivia as presented by Bolivian scholars. Covers all periods; name index.
F3320.4.A2

Uribe, Maruja and **Hernández, Margarita.** Bibliografía selectiva sobre desarrollo rural en Bolivia. Bogotá, Biblioteca IICA, 1980. 134p. (Documentación e Información agrícola, no.92)   **DB295**

An extensive bibliography of more than 1,000 books, articles, and documents (mainly published 1960–80) arranged by broad topics (e.g., historical aspects, planning, legislation), with an author index. Includes a directory of organizations and a listing of 86 relevant periodical publications.   Z7164.C842U74

Brazil

Bibliography

Amazônia; bibliografia. Rio de Janeiro, Instituto Brasileiro de Bibliografia e Documentaçao, 1963–77. 4v.   **DB296**

Contents: v.1, 1614–1962; v.2, 1601–1970; v.3, 1971–72; v.4, 1973–74. No more publ.?
Includes references to books, periodical articles, and other documents arranged by Universal Decimal Classification. Author index.
Documentaçao Amazônica: catalogo colectivo (Belém, SUDAM, 1974–75. 3v.) reproduces catalog cards for books, journals, monographic serials and documents dealing with the Amazon added by cooperating libraries 1960–74. Author, subject and geographic indexes.   Z1694.A55R5

Chilcote, Ronald H. Brazil and its radical left; an annotated bibliography on the Communist movement and the rise of Marxism, 1922–1972. Millwood, N.Y., Kraus Internat., [1980]. 455p.   **DB297**

For full information *see* CJ461.

Dutra, Francis A. A guide to the history of Brazil, 1500–1822: the literature in English. Santa Barbara, Calif., ABC-Clio, [1980]. 625p.   **DB298**

For the student of Brazilian and Latin American history who knows only English. "History has been taken in its broadest sense and every effort has been made to include books, articles, and dissertations on art, literature, geography, sociology, anthropology and archaeology when they were of interest and value to the historian."—*Pref.* More than 900 items with descriptive and evaluative annotations. Topical/chronological arrangement, with material presented in such a way as to provide a historical survey of colonial Brazil. Chronology, glossary, indexes.   Z1686.D87

Garraux, Anatole Louis. Bibliographie brésilienne; catalogue des ouvrages français et latins relatifs au Brésil (1500–1898). 2. ed. Rio de Janeiro, J. Olympio, 1962. 519p. (Coleção documentos brasileiros, 100)   **DB299**

An author listing with subject index. Some few periodicals are indexed; occasional annotations.   Z1671.G23

Lacombe, Américo Jacobina. Introduçao ao estudo da história do Brasil. São Paulo, Companhia Editora Nacional, [1974]. 208p. (Brasiliana, v.349)   **DB300**

A useful manual. Chapters on sources include archives, periods of history, regional history, academies and associations.
F2520.7.L32

Levine, Robert M. Brazil, 1822–1930; an annotated bibliography for social historians. N.Y., Garland, 1983. 487p. (Garland reference library of social science, v.132)   **DB301**

An annotated bibliography of books, collections of essays, articles, and dissertations on Brazilian society and culture, as well as its historical and political evolution from independence to 1830. About half the entries are in English, the others in Portuguese, Spanish, French, and German; cut-off date for publications is 1981. Author and subject indexes.
Continued by: Z1671.L478

———— Brazil since 1930: an annotated bibliography for social historians. N.Y., Garland, 1980. 336p. (Garland reference library of social science, 59)   **DB302**

Books, periodical articles, theses and dissertations, government publications, and unpublished papers which deal "not only with [Brazil's] political evolution but with its society and culture as well" *(Pref.)* are arranged in nine broad sections with appropriate subdivisions. More than half the works cited are in English. Informative annotations; author and subject indexes.
Os remanejamentos do poder na ordem burguesa . . . by J. L. F. W. da Silva, M. E. Brits and R. L. A. da Silva (Rio de Janeiro, 1984. 41p.) deals with political life in Brazil, 1922–84; it is the first of a planned series of introductory bibliographies by the compilers.
Z1671.L48

Moraes, Rubens Borba de. Bibliographia brasiliana: rare books about Brazil published from 1504 to 1900 and works by Brazilian authors of the colonial period. Rev. and enl. ed. Los Angeles, UCLA Latin American Ctr. Pubns., Univ. of Calif.; Rio de Janeiro, Livraria Kosmos Editôra, [1983]. 2v. (xxvii, 1074p.) il. (UCLA Latin American Ctr. pubns., Ref. ser., v.10)   **DB303**

1st ed. 1958.
Introduction and annotations in English.
The purpose is "to describe and comment upon rare books about various aspects of Brazil and upon books by Brazilian authors which were printed outside the borders of Brazil before or shortly after Independence in 1822. I have incorporated the entries from my *Bibliografia brasileira do periodo colonial . . .* [1969] and shortened the commentaries. In this revised edition, there is more emphasis on entries for books of the sixteenth, seventeenth, and eighteenth centuries than on books published in the nineteenth century when production increased. . . ."—*Pref.*
Commentaries emphasize the importance of the book in relation to Brazil; short biographies of the author or printer are supplied in some cases. Subject index; works cited in the commentaries are indexed by subject as well as by author and title.   Z1671.M6

———— and **Berrien, William.** Manual bibliográfico de estudos brasileiros. Rio de Janeiro, Souza, 1949. 895p.
DB304

An annotated bibliography of works in various languages on the origins and development of Brazilian culture, divided broadly by subject, and covering mainly material published prior to 1942 in the humanities and social sciences. Periodical articles are included. Author index. Each section was compiled under the direction of a specialist who also provided a historical outline of Brazilian achievement in his field, which precedes the actual bibliography.
Z1686.M6

Porter, Dorothy Burnett. Afro-Brasiliana; a working bibliography. Boston, G. K. Hall, [1978]. 294p.   **DB305**

For full information *see* CC391

Rodrigues, José Honório. A pesquisa histórica do Brasil. 4. ed., rev. e atualizada. São Paulo, Companhia Editora Nacional, [1982]. 314p. (Brasiliana, serie grande formato, v.20)   **DB306**

1st ed. 1952.

A guide for the student of Brazilian history. Includes discussions of archives, sources, historiography, etc. This edition includes notes, additions, revisions to the 2d ed. (1968), p.294–302, and an appendix of new editions with emphasis on those relating to archives, p.273–93.   F2520.4.R6

U.S. Library of Congress. Library of Congress Office, Brazil. Accessions list, Brazil. Rio de Janeiro, Lib. of Congress Off., Brazil, 1975– . Bimonthly.   **DB307**

For full information *see* AA644.

Library resources

Jackson, William Vernon. Library guide for Brazilian studies. Pittsburgh, 1964. 197p.   **DB308**

A survey describing the holdings in 1963–64 of resources for Brazilian studies in the major research collections of the United States. Includes chapters on general materials, humanities, social sciences, science, and technology, with indications of strengths and weaknesses in specific subject areas. Contains a bibliography of published guides, catalogs, and descriptions of specific collections; useful appendixes include a "Union list of selected Brazilian periodicals in the humanities and social sciences," and indexes to the Library of Congress classification schemes for Brazilian history and literature. The index of libraries, plus a number of maps and tables, add to the value of the guide.   Z1671.J3

Historiography

Burns, E. Bradford. Perspectives on Brazilian history; ed. with an introd. and bibliographical essay. N.Y., Columbia Univ. Pr., 1967. 235p.   **DB309**

Offers translations of nine essays by Brazilian scholars on Brazilian historiography, plus "A bibliographical essay on Brazilian historiography" by Burns, p.197–206.   F2520.4.B8

Rodrigues, José Honório. História da história do Brasil. São Paulo, Companhia Editora Nacional, 1979– . v.1– . (Brasiliana, v.21–) (In progress)   **DB310**

Contents: v.1, Historiografía colonial.

To be in 3v. An extensive, authoritative discussion of writings on colonial Brazil constitutes v.1, replacing the compiler's *Historiografía del Brasil* (México, 1957–63. 2v.).   F2520.4.R615

Skidmore, Thomas E. The historiography of Brazil, 1889–1964. *In:* Hispanic American historical review, LV (Nov. 1975), p.716–48; LVI (Feb. 1976), p.81–109.   **DB311**

A survey of scholarship on the political and economic aspects of Brazilian history between the fall of the Empire in 1889 and the military-civilian coup of 1964. Emphasis is on recent publications.

Dictionaries and encyclopedias

See also DC487–DC488.

Dicionário de história do Brasil, moral e civismo. Organização geral, Departamento Editorial das Edições Melhoramentos redação de temas e biografias, Brasil Bandecchi [et al.], colaboração Hélio Vianna [et al.]. 4. ed. São Paulo, Melhoramentos, 1976 [c.1973]. 618p.   **DB312**

1st ed. (1970) entitled: *Novo dicionário de história do Brasil.*
Offers brief unsigned articles on persons and events. This edition omits illustrations, but adds supplementary sections of national dates, description of the organization of the federal government, and sections on moral and civic education (including a summary of the laws and a description of the commission of that name).

Another useful one-volume dictionary of similar vintage is the *Dicionário de história do Brasil* by Antônia da Rocha Almeida (Pôrto Alegre, Editôra Globo, 1969. 533p.). Although strongly biographical, it has articles on events, wars, movements, etc., as well as tables of presidents, viceroys, and title-holders.   F2504.D49

Diccionário histórico-biográfico brasileiro 1930–1983. Coordenação de Israel Biloch e Alzira Alves de Abreu. [Rio de Janeiro], Forense-Universitária, [1984]. v.1–3. il. (In progress)   **DB313**

At head of title: Fundação Getúlio Vargas. Centro de Pesquisa e Documentação de História Contemporânea do Brasil.

Contents: v.1–3, Abbink–Pereira Júnior. (To be in 4v.)

An authoritative historical dictionary. Articles are mainly biographical, but there are entries for parties, governmental bodies, and other organizations. Brief list of sources at the end of each article.

Grande enciclopédia portuguesa e brasileira. 2. parte: Brasil. Lisboa, Rio de Janeiro, Editorial Enciclopédia, [1964?–74]. v.1–3². (In progress)   **DB314**

Issued in fascicles.

Contents: 2.pt., v.1–3, no.2, A–Guaranésia.

For the first part of this dictionary-encyclopedia, *see* DC465.

This part is devoted to Brazilian topics.   AE37.G73

Verbo; enciclopédia luso-brasileira de cultura. Lisboa, Ed. Verbo, 1963–76. 18v. and suppl. (1979).   **DB315**

For full information *see* DC466.

Chile

Bibliography

See also DB285.

Aranguiz Donoso, Horacio. Bibliografía histórica (1959–1967). Santiago, Universidad Católica de Chile, Instituto de Historia, 1970. 84p.   **DB316**

A broad topical listing of 1,291 citations drawn from the history section of *Fichero* (AA933); works deal with the history of Chile or are historical works published in Chile.   Z1716.A7

Oppenheimer, Robert. Chile. Los Angeles, Latin American Studies Center, [1977?]. 91p. il. (Latin America bibliography ser., 6)   **DB317**

A selective bibliography of books, articles, and some government publications on Chile up to about 1976. Arranged by broad periods following an initial general section. No index.   Z1701.O66

Portales, Carlos. Bibliografía sobre relaciones internacionales y política exterior de Chile, 1964–1980. Santiago de Chile, Facultad Latinoamericana de Ciencias Sociales, [1981]. 19p. (Documento de trabajo, Programa FLACSO, 108)   **DB318**

An author listing of books, articles, essays and documents in Spanish and English. Subject index.

Williams, Lee H. The Allende years; a union list of Chilean imprints, 1970–1973, in selected North American libraries, with a supplemental holdings list of books published elsewhere for the same period by Chileans or about Chile or Chileans. Boston, G. K. Hall, 1977. 339p.   **DB319**

The Chilean holdings of fourteen United States libraries are cited in three main sections: (1) Chilean monographs published 1970–73; (2) Books published outside Chile, 1970–73, about Chile or by Chileans; (3) Serial publications issued in Chile, 1970–73. The first two sections are subdivided by topic. Personal and corporate name index.   Z1701.W55

Historiography

Feliú Cruz, Guillermo. Historia de las fuentes de la bibliografía chilena: ensayo crítico. Santiago, 1966–69. 4v.
DB320

On cover: "Obra realizada por la Biblioteca Nacional bajo los auspicios de la comisión Nacional de conmemoración del Centenario de Muerte de Andrés Bello."

A collection of critical essays on historians, bibliographers, and chroniclers of Chile. Coverage is continued by "A survey of recent Chilean historiography, 1965–1976" in *Latin American research review* XIV, no.2 (1979), p.55–88.   Z1702.5.F44

Archives and libraries

Sehlinger, Peter J. A select guide to Chilean libraries and archives. Bloomington, Latin American Studies Program, Indiana Univ., 1979. 35p. (Latin American studies working papers, 9)   **DB321**

For each library or archive is given: name, address, person in charge, and description of relevant collections, together with references to any published guides or finding aids.   Z771.A1S43

Dictionaries

Diccionario histórico de Chile. Jordi Fuentes [et al.]. 8. ed. puesta al día. Santiago de Chile, Zig-Zag, 1984. 663p.
DB322

1st ed. 1963.
Runs heavily to biographical entries, but includes articles on battles, political events, institutions, place-names, etc. Covers the history of Chile to 1973 with an appendix for new and updated material.
The *Diccionario político de Chile, 1810–1966* (Santiago, Editorial Orbe, 1967. 532p.) by Jordi Fuentes and Lía Cortés remains useful.   F3054.F8

Colombia

Bibliography

Banco de la República, Bogotá. Biblioteca Luis-Angel Arango. Catálogo de la Biblioteca Luis-Angel Arango: Fondo Colombia. [Bogotá], Tall. Gráf. del Banco de la República, [1972–75?]. 4v.   **DB323**

————— Suplemento I. Bogotá, [1977–78]. 3v.

A classified (U.D.C.) catalog of books, pamphlets, government publications dealing with Colombia; works in Spanish from all periods are included. Author index in each volume.
The same organization has issued *Papeletas bibliograficas para el estudio de la historia de Colombia* compiled by Mario German Romero *et al.* (1961. 115p.).   Z907.B22

Bernal Villa, Segunda. Guía bibliográfica de Colombia de interés para el antropólogo. Bogotá, Ediciones Universidad de los Andes, 1969. 782p.   **DB324**

For full information *see* CE57.

Giraldo Jaramillo, Gabriel. Bibliografía colombiana de viajes. Bogotá, Editorial ABC, 1957. 224p. (Biblioteca de bibliografía colombiana, 2)   **DB325**

An alphabetical listing of travelers accounts by Colombians or by non-Colombians journeying to Colombia. Brief annotations; no index.   Z1746.G5

Martinson, Tom L. Research guide to Colombia. Prep. . . . with the assistance of Gerald R. Showalter. [Mexico], Pan American Inst. of Geography and History, 1975. 58p. maps. (Pubn. no.341)   **DB326**

"The objective of this manual is to present, in index maps, accompanying text, and bibliography, a guide to contemporary basic source materials for development studies in Colombia."—*Introd.* The bibliography, p.36–58, is arranged by form: government publications, articles, books, pamphlets and monographs.

Ocampo Lopez, Javier. Historiografía y bibliografía de la emancipación del Nuevo Reino de Granada. Tunja, Universidad Pedagogica y Tecnologica de Colombia, 1969. 555p.   **DB327**

A brief historiographical section is followed by a lengthy bibliography of the emancipation of Colombia, covering mainly the years 1810–19. In addition to the listing of archives, documents, and contemporary sources, there is a broad subject arrangement of secondary materials. Author, biographical, and subject indexes.   Z1749.O23

Dictionaries

Gomez Aristizábal, Horacio. Diccionario de la historia de Colombia. Bogotá, Plaza & Janes, [1984]. 269p. il.
DB328

Offers brief entries (about 1 or 1-1/2 columns) for topics, biographies, and some historical events. Appendix includes a short bibliography, chronological lists of governors and vice-regents (1550–1810) and presidents and other rulers (1810–1986).

Costa Rica

Araya Incera, Manuel E. Materiales para la historia de las relaciones internacionales de Costa Rica, bibliografía fuentes impresas. [San Pedro, Costa Rica], Univ. de Costa Rica, Centro Investigaciones Históricas, 1980. 91p.   **DB329**

Lists some 533 books, articles, theses, and government publications (including United Nations materials) in topical arrangement. Cross references, but no index.   Z6465.C8A7

Elizondo, Carlos L., González, Juan B. and **Martínez, Luis F.** Research guide to Costa Rica. [Mexico], Pan American Inst. of Geography and History, 1977. 138p. maps.   **DB330**

Tr. of *Guía para investigadores de Costa Rica* (1977).
An inventory of published and unpublished maps in Costa Rica (listed by type) is followed by a topically arranged bibliography of books, pamphlets, and articles, mainly in Spanish (with occasional English entries) and mainly published 1960–74. Intended as a "guide to contemporary resources of information for studies on the development of Costa Rica, and the planning of resources, both physical and human, by means of index maps, descriptive texts, and bibliography."—*Introd.*
A supplementary bibliography by Manuel J. Carvajal, *Bibliography of poverty and related topics in Costa Rica* ([Wash.?], Rural Development Division, Agency for Internat. Development, 1979. 329p.), cites books, articles and government documents published since about 1960; it is well indexed.   Z6027.C83E4313

Proceso de estructuración territorial en Costa Rica, bibliografía sobre la problemática urbana y regional, 1945–81. Allan M. Lavell, Miguel Morales, Jorge Arriaga. San José, Instituto Geográfico Nacional, [1981]. 410p.   **DB331**

Lists books, essays, and some articles and theses in broad subject sections with author index at end of each section.

Ecuador

Bibliography

Ecuador. Junta Nacional de Planificación y Coordinación Económica. Sección de Investigaciones Sociales. Bibliografía social, económica y política del Ecuador. [Quito, 1973?] 2v. (708p.)   **DB332**

Preliminary ed. (1972?) had title: *Listado parcial de la bibliografía social, socio-económica y política del Ecuador.*

Cites some 4,000 books, articles, and dissertations in Spanish or English published approximately 1890–1969 in all areas of the social sciences; includes a long section for history, subdivided by period and region. Most citations are annotated; topical arrangement; no index.

A more recent bibliography covering some of the same subjects is *Ecuador, aspectos socio-económicos, bibliografía* by Lucia Alzamora C. (2.ed., Quito, Junapla, 1977. 212p.); it lists approximately half the number of books, documents and articles in Spanish, English, French, and German in topical arrangement, but without annotations; no index.   Z7165.E28E26

Larrea, Carlos Manuel. Bibliografía científica del Ecuador; antropología, etnografía, arquelogía, prehistoria, lingüística. 3. ed. Quito, Corporación de Estudios y Publicaciones, 1968. 289p.   **DB333**

For annotation *see* CE62.

Norris, Robert E. Guía bibliográfica para el estudio de la historia ecuatoriana. Austin, Inst. of Latin American Studies, Univ. of Texas, [1978]. 295p. (Guides and bibliographies ser., 11)   **DB334**

A classed bibliography of books and periodical articles; author and subject indexes. 3,577 entries.   Z1776.N67

Uribe, Maruja, Salazar, Blanca Cecilia and **Hernández, Margarita.** Bibliografía selectiva sobre desarrollo rural en el Ecuador. Bogotá, Instituto Interamericano de Ciencias Agrícolas-OEA, 1979. 203p. (Documentación e Información Agrícola, no.75)   **DB335**

An extensive bibliography of 1,549 references, published mainly 1960–79, on broad topics such as planning, cooperatives, legislation, and historical aspects. Includes a directory of 121 organizations and 139 periodicals. Author index.

Historiography

Barrera, Isaac J. Historiografía del Ecuador. México, 1956. 124p. (Inst. Panamericana de Geografía e Historia. Comisión de Historia. Pubn. 81. Historiografías, 3)   **DB336**

Instituto Panamericano de Geografía e Historia. Pubn. 189. A discussion of historians and their work; no bibliography.

Archives

Archivo Nacional de Historia (Ecuador). Guía del Archivo Nacional de Historia. Quito, Edit. Casa de la Cultura Ecuatoriana, 1981. 219p.   **DB337**

Describes collections available in the Archivo Nacional; most files of government departments end in the 19th century; files of personal papers close prior to World War II.   CD4126 1981

French Guiana

Abonnenc, Émile, Hurault, J. and **Saban, R.** Bibliographie de la Guyane Française. Paris, Éd. Larose, 1957. v.1.   **DB338**

Contents: t.1, Ouvrages et articles de langue française concernant la Guyane et les territoires avoisinants (278p.). No more publ.

A comprehensive bibliography of books and periodical articles which appeared from the end of the 16th century to 1955. Listing is alphabetical by author with subject index. A second volume was planned to cover non-French materials.   Z1811.A2

Guatemala

Franklin, Woodman B. Guatemala. Oxford, Eng. & Santa Barbara, Calif., Clio Pr., [1981]. 109p. map. (World bibliographical ser., v.9)   **DB339**

"Books and articles in this bibliography are meant to constitute a core collection for the interested, but not specialized, reader."—*Introd.* Annotated entries (mainly English-language materials) are arranged by topic. Indexed.

Does not include Eric S. Graber's *An annotated bibliography of rural development and levels of living in Guatemala* (Wash., Rural Development Div., Bureau for Latin Amer., AID, 1979. 81p.).   Z1461.F73

Lamadrid, Lázaro. A survey of the historiography of Guatemala since 1821. *In* The Americas; a quarterly review of inter-American cultural history, v.8, no.2 (Oct. 1951), p.189–202; no.3 (Jan. 1952), p.305–20.   **DB340**

A survey of the sources and writings on Guatemalan history from 1821 to about 1947.

Laporte Molina, Juan Pedro. Bibliografía de la arqueología guatemalteca. Guatemala, Ediciones de la Dirección General de Antropología e Historia, 1981– . v.1– . (In progress)   **DB341**

Contents: v.1, A–I.

An extensive bibliography arranged by topic (but including sections for individual authors). Sections include general works on Mayan archeology; physical characteristics of the area (including geological analysis, soil condition, flora and fauna); specific archeological areas; epigraphy, the calendar, and religion; ethnohistory and historical sources.   Z1209.2.G9L36

Honduras

Arqueta, Mario. Investigación y tendencias recientes de la historiografía hondureña; un ensayo bibliográfico. Tegucigalpa, Ed. Universitaria, 1981. 28p. (Colección cuadernos universitarios, 3)   **DB342**

A good bibliographical essay covering scholarship since the early 1970s.

Oqueli, Ramón. Bibliografía sociopolítica de Honduras. Tegucigalpa, Editorial Universitaria, 1981. 106p. (Colección cuadernos universitarios, no.15)   **DB343**

An author listing of books, documents, dissertations, and monographic series; no index.   Z1471.O68

Mexico

Bibliography

Bernal, Ignacio. Bibliografía de arqueología y etnografía Mesoamérica y norte de México, 1514–1960. México, Inst. Nacional de Antropología e Historia, 1962. 634p. maps.   **DB344**

For full information *see* CE56.

Bibliografía general del desarrollo económico de México 1500–1976. [Comp. by] Jorge Ceballos [and others]. México, SEP, Inst. Nacional de Antropología e Historia, Departamento de Investigaciones Historicas, [1980]. 3v. (1177p.) (Colección científica, 76. Bibliografías)   **DB345**

An extensive, annotated bibliography, topically arranged, but with no period divisions. Especially strong for 19th century material. Particularly useful for 20th century study is a description of the content of each census taken since 1895. Author index; locates copies in 34 Mexican and U.S. libraries.   Z7165.M45B525

Bibliografía histórica mexicana. [no.]1– , 1967– . [México], El Colegio de México, [1967–]. Annual. **DB346**

A classed list of books, periodical articles, and theses, with author index. Brief annotations for many items. Z1411.B5

Borderlands sourcebook; a guide to the literature on northern Mexico and the American Southwest. Ed. by Ellwyn R. Stoddard, Richard L. Nostrand and Jonathan P. West. Norman, Univ. of Oklahoma Pr., [1983]. 445p. **DB347**

For full information *see* DB129.

Bustamante, Jorge A. México—Estados Unidos, bibliografía general sobre estudios fronterizos. [México], El Colegio de México, [1980]. 251p. **DB348**

Following a lengthy introduction (which includes statistical tables), 2,290 books, articles, theses, and films are listed under fourteen broad topics such as "Mexican—U.S. relations," "Sociopolitical movements," "Chicanos." Author index. Z1361.R4B87

California. State Library, Sacramento. Sutro Branch, San Francisco. Catalogue of Mexican pamphlets in the Sutro collection (1623–[1888]). Prep. by the personnel of the Works Progress Administration . . . A. Yedidia, supervisor. P. Radin, ed. Sponsored by the California State Library. San Francisco, 1939–40. 10 pts. (963p.) (Repr.: N.Y., Kraus, 1971) **DB349**

————— ————— Supplement (1605–1887). San Francisco, 1941. 3 pts. (290p.)

————— ————— Author index. . . . San Francisco, 1941. 65p.

A chronological listing of a large collection of pamphlets, in the Spanish language, on Mexico or printed in Mexico. The author index covers both the main work and the supplement.

Z1431.C15

Cole, Garold. American travelers to Mexico, 1821–1972: a descriptive bibliography. Troy, N.Y., Whitston, 1978. 139p. **DB350**

An annotated author bibliography of some 477 accounts (excluding guidebooks, promotional literature, etc.) in books or parts of books. Lacks an index. Z1425.C64

Cosío Villegas, Daniel. Cuestiones internacionales de México; una bibliografía. México, Secretaría de Relaciones Exteriores, 1966. 588p. (Archivo Histórico Diplomático Mexicano. Guías para la historia diplomática de México, 4) **DB351**

10,776 items in classed arrangement on all aspects of Mexican international relations and diplomatic affairs. Indexed.

————— Última bibliografía política de la historia moderna de México. *In:* Memoria de El Colegio Nacional, v.7, no.1 (1970), p.41–222. **DB352**

A bibliography of some 1,858 secondary sources for Mexican political history, 1867–1911, arranged alphabetically within five main sections: reference materials, general history, local history, biographical studies, and problems of the period.

Gerhard, Peter. A guide to the historical geography of New Spain. N.Y., Cambridge Univ. Pr., 1972. 476p. (Cambridge Latin American studies, 14) **DB353**

Offers a "regional listing of contemporary source material descriptive of central and southern Mexico throughout the three centuries of Spanish rule, and a synthesis of certain data gleaned from these documents."—*Pref.* Includes bibliographical references to governors, agriculture, church, population, and settlements.

F1231.G37

González y González, Luis. Fuentes de la historia contemporánea de México: libros y folletos. Estudio preliminar . . . con la colaboración de Guadelupe Monroy y Susana Uribe. México, El Colegio de México, 1961–62. 3v. **DB354**

Contents: v.1, Generalidades. Territorio. Sociedad; v.2, Econo-

mía. Política. Religión; v.3, Educación. Filosofía y ciencias. Letras y artes.

An extensive bibliography on the whole range of Mexican culture for the period 1910–40. v.3 contains general and title indexes.

Z1426.5.G6

Greenleaf, Richard E. and **Meyer, Michael C.** Research in Mexican history: topics, methodology, sources and a practical guide to field research. Lincoln, Univ. of Nebraska Pr., [1973]. 226p. **DB355**

"Comp. for the Committee on Mexican Studies, Conference on Latin American History."—*t.p.*

An extremely useful guide to doing research in Mexican archives. Offers chapters by contributing scholars on specific archives, periods, or topics. Includes practical information and suggestions for topics needing research. F1225.5.G73

Johnson, Charles W. México en el siglo XX; una bibliografía social y politica de publicaciones extranjeras, 1900–1969. Ed. prelim. México, Instituto de Investigaciones Sociales, 1969. 435p. **DB356**

Classed bibliography with author index. More than 2,600 items, including books, theses, and periodical articles. Z7165.M45J6

López Rosado, Diego H. Bibliografía de historia económica y social de México. México, Univ. Nacional Autónoma de México, 1979–82. 13v. (UNAM. Instituto de Investigaciones Bibliográfias. Serie: Bibliografías, 8) **DB357**

Contents: v.1, Fuentes para el estudio de la agricultura, la ganadería y la silvicultura de México; v.2, . . . Propiedad de la tierra y colonización; v.3, . . . Minería y el petróleo; v.4, . . . Industría y la promoción industrial; v.5, . . . Comunicaciones y transportes; v.6, . . . Relaciones de trabajo; v.7, . . . Comercio interior y exterior; v.8, . . . Sistemas monetario y del crédito; v.9, . . . Finanzas publicas; v.10, . . . Obras publicas; v.11, . . . Clases sociales; v.12, . . . Organización politica y los partidos políticos; v.13, Indice general; bibliografía general; indice de materias.

A bibliography of Spanish-language books, articles, government documents, etc., covering economic and social history of Mexico from pre-Hispanic times through 1925. Classified arrangement within period divisions; works are closely analyzed.

Z7165.M45L66

México. Comisión de Estudios Militares. Biblioteca del Ejército. Apuntes para una bibliografía militar de México, 1536–1936 . . . M. C. Nestor Herrera Gómez [y] Silvino M. González. México, Talleres Graficos de la Nación, 1937. 469p. **DB358**

A bibliography of more than 1,800 titles on Mexican military history, 1536–1936. Z6725.M6M6

Orozco, Edna María and **Platas, Alma Rosa.** Bibliografía general de historia de México. México, SEP, Instituto Nacional de Antropología e Historia, Dirección de Estudios Históricos, 1979. 142p. (Collección científica, 69) **DB359**

An annotated bibliography of some 700 Spanish-language items, mostly books. The first part is arranged by topic within broad subject areas (e.g., politics, social history); the second is topical by broad time periods. Author index. Could be a useful starting point for research. Z1425.O76

Raat, W. Dirk. The Mexican Revolution: an annotated guide to recent scholarship. Boston, G. K. Hall, [1982]. 275p. **DB360**

Nearly 1,250 items (both books and periodical articles) are listed in classed arrangement, with subject and name indexes. Does not replace Ramos (DB362) for older materials. Z1426.5.R15

Ramos, Roberto. Bibliografía de la historia de México. 2. ed., corr. y aum. México, Instituto Mexicano de Investigaciones Económicas, 1965. 688p. **DB361**

1st ed. 1956.

Includes 5,164 items in alphabetical sequence by author; no index. Mainly book materials, with a few periodical articles and monographic series. Z1425.R3

—— Bibliografía de la revolución mexicana. 2. ed. México, 1959–60. 3v. (Biblioteca del Inst. Nacional de Estudios Históricos de la Revolución Mexicana. [15]) **DB362**

More than 5,000 items on the Mexican revolution, 1910–22. v.1–2 are reprints of the edition published 1931–35. v.3, originally published in 1940, has been considerably expanded, listing nearly 2,000 items published since 1935. Z1426.5.R2

Robbins, Naomi C. and **Herstein, Sheila R.** Mexico. Oxford, Eng., & Santa Barbara, Calif., Clio Pr., [1984]. 165p. map. (World bibliographical ser., 48) **DB363**

640 annotated entries arranged in 48 subject categories. Highly selective, with all but a few items in English. Author/title/subject index.

Ross, Stanley Robert. Fuentes de la historia contemporánea de México: periódicos y revistas. [México], Colegio de México, [1965–78]. 5v. **DB364**

A classed bibliography of articles from Spanish-language magazines, newspapers, and journals published in Mexico and the southwestern United States between 1908 and 1968. Brief annotations; indexes of authors, names, and places in v.2 and 5. Z1426.5.R6

Tutorow, Norman E. The Mexican-American war: an annotated bibliography. Westport, Conn., Greenwood Pr., [1981]. 427p. maps. **DB365**

About 4,500 items in eight main sections: (1) Reference works; (2) Manuscript collections; (3) Government documents; (4) National archives of the U.S.; (5) Periodical literature; (6) Books; (7) Theses and dissertations; (8) Miscellaneous works: graphics, cartography, and addenda. Sections are topically or geographically subdivided as appropriate. Indexed. Z1241.T87

Valle, Rafael Heliodoro. Bibliografía maya. . . . México, [1937–41]. 404p. **DB366**

For full information *see* CE73.

Historiography

Parcero, María de la Luz. Introducción bibliográfica a la historiografía política de México, siglos XIX y XX. México, Univ. Nacional Autónoma de México, Faculdad de Filosofía y Letras, 1982. 347p. **DB367**

Concerned with historical writings of the 19th and 20th centuries dealing with all periods of Mexican history. Analytical chapters are grouped in three sections: El proceso histórico-político de México, Los regímenes políticos y las grandes crisis del sistema, El proceso histórico regional; the bibliography is similarly arranged. No index. F1231.5.P37

Guides to records

Mexico (City). Universidad Nacional. Instituto de Investigaciones Bibliográficas. Serie guías. México, Univ. Nacional Autónoma de México, Inst. de Invest. Bibliograficas, 1969–78. 6v. **DB368**

Contents: v.1, Grajales Ramos, G. Guía de documentos para la historia de México en archivos ingleses (siglo XIX) (1969. 455p.); v.2, Moreno Valle, L. Catálogo de la Colección Lafragua de la Biblioteca Nacional de México, 1821–1853 (1975. 1203p.); v.3, Río, I. Guía del Archivo Franciscano de la Biblioteca Nacional de México (1975. 499p.); v.4, Yhmhoff Cabrera, J. Catálogo de obras manuscritas en Latin de la Biblioteca Nacional de México (1975. 459p.); v.5, Fernández de Zamora, R. M. Las publicaciones oficiales de México, guía de publicaciones periódicas y seriadas, 1937–1970 (1977. 238p.); v.6, Quiñones Melgoza, J. Catálogo de obras de autores latinos en servicio en la Biblioteca Nacional de México (1978. 133p.).

Millares Carlo, Agustín. Repertorio bibliográfico de los archivos mexicanos y de los europeos y norteamericanos de interés para la historia de México. México, 1959. 366p. (Biblioteca Nacional de México. Inst. Bibliográfico Mexicano. [Pubn.] 1) **DB369**

Lists more than 1,000 published bibliographies, catalogs, and guides to archives and special collections in Europe and America relating to Mexican history, with numerous annotations; subject index.

A much enlarged revision of the first section of the author's *Repertorio bibliográfico de los archivos mexicanos y de las colecciones diplomáticas fundamentales para la historia de México* (México, 1948). The second section of that work, which lists collections of documents for the history of Mexico, is not carried over. Z1411.A1M53

Dictionaries and encyclopedias

Diccionario Porrúa de historia, biografía y geografía de México. 4. ed. corr. y aum., con un suplemento. México, D. F., Editorial Porrúa, [1976]. 2v. (2761p.) **DB370**

1st ed. 1964.

An encyclopedia of Mexican affairs running heavily to entries for personal and place names. The third edition incorporates articles from the supplement to the second edition into the main body of the work and adds some new material. The 4th ed. is a reprinting of the 3d, with new material added in the supplement (p.2357–2746); statistics are updated to 1975. F1204.D56

Enciclopedia de México. [4. ed.] Ciudad de México, Enciclopedia de México, 1978. 12v. il. **DB371**

José Rogelio Alvarez, director.

"Todo lo Mexicano ordenado alfabéticamente: antropología, arqueología, arte, bibliografía, biografías, ciencias, derecho, economía, estadística, etimología, etnografía, fauna y flora, folclore, geografía, historia, instituciones, léxico regional, literatura, mitología, música, paremiología, semántica, sociología, toponimia, turismo, etc."—*title page.*

1st ed. 1966–71.

v.5–12 are 3d ed.

Some articles are signed; some carry bibliographies. Heavily illustrated. F1204.E5

Enciclopedia yucatanense. 2. ed. Patrocinada por el Gobierno del Estado de Yucatán a cargo del Dr. Francisco Luna Kan; publicada bajo la dirección de la Comisión Reeditora de la Enciclopedia Yucatanense, integrada por Luis H. Hoyos Villanueva [et al.]. México, Gobierno de Yucatán, 1977–80. 11v. il. **DB372**

1st ed. 1944–47, ed. C. A. Echánove Trujillo.

This ed. is a reprinting of the 8v. 1st ed. with an additional 3v. of new material. v.8 of the earlier ed., "Bibliografía general yucatanense," is now divided between v.8 and 9, with indexes of subjects, names, and illustrations added, together with a "Suplemento a la bibliografía general yucatanense (hasta 1947)." v.10–11 are supplements, "Actualization y amplicación."

A classed encyclopedia aiming to cover all aspects of Yucatan history and life. Each section is written by an authority, and most have bibliographies. v.7, *Biografías,* deals with only 14 individuals, but more biographical material is included in an extensive alphabetical list of works published in and on Yucatan. F1376.E55

Nicaragua

Barquero, Sara Luisa. Gobernantes de Nicaragua, 1825–1947. 2. ed. [Managua], Ministerio de Instrucción Pública e. f., [1945]. 248p. **DB373**

Biographical sketches, three to four pages in length, of the heads of Nicaraguan government. F1522.7.B36

Nicaragua revolucionaria; bibliografía 1979–1984. Managua, Nicaragua, INIES, Instituto de Investigaciones Económicas y Sociales; CRIES, Coordinadoro Regional de

Investigaciones Económicas y Sociales, [1984]. 140p. (Cuadernos de pensamiento propio. Serie bibliografía, 1) **DB374**

A topically arranged bibliography of more than 1,000 entries in English and Spanish. Author index.

Woodward, Ralph Lee. Nicaragua. Oxford, Eng. & Santa Barbara, Calif., Clio Pr., [1983]. 254p. (World bibliographical ser., v.44) **DB375**

A "guide to the most significant publications in each field" (*Introd.*) of Nicaraguan studies, emphasizing English-language materials when available. Books, articles, and theses are arranged by subject, with brief annotations. Indexed.

Omits the *Bibliografía socioeconómica de Nicaragua* by G. Gutiérrez (Managua, Univ. Nac. Autónoma de Nicaragua, 1977. 45p.) which is based on the collection of the Biblioteca del Banco Central de Nicaragua.

Panama

Alba C, Manuel María. Cronología de los gobernantes de Panamá 1510–1967. Panamá, 1967. 399p. **DB376**

Offers biographical sketches of heads of state, including juntas, in chronological order. Brief bibliography, p.389–92. F1566.A317

Bray, Wayne D. Controversy over a new canal treaty between the United States and Panama; a selective annotated bibliography of United States, Panamanian, Colombian, French, and international organization sources. Wash., Library of Congress, 1976. 70p. **DB377**

An annotated bibliography of books, articles, manuscripts, documents, etc. Includes travel books, histories, biographies, and articles from legal and general periodicals. Each citation is graded as to whether it is indispensable, supportive or expansive, or marginal. Z6465.P3B72

Canal Zone. Library-Museum, Balboa Heights. Subject catalog of the special Panama Collection of the Canal Zone Library-Museum: the history of the Isthmus of Panama as it applies to interoceanic transportation. Boston, G. K. Hall, 1964. 341p. il., maps. **DB378**

7,000 cards representing nearly 500 subject headings have been reproduced. Although the strength of the collection lies in materials on the planning and construction of the Canal, there is much on exploration, travelers' accounts, and political and social life. Works cited are in English and Spanish. Z1500.C35

Garst, Rachel. Bibliografía anotada de obras de referencia sobre Centroamérica y Panamá en el camp de las ciencias sociales. San José, Costa Rica, Inst. de Investigaciones Sociales, Univ. de Costa Rica; Friends World College, Latin American Ctr., 1983. 2v. (662p.) **DB379**

Lists some 1,445 reference works in Spanish and English—bibliographies and catalogs, directories, indexes, document collections, maps. Broad subject arrangement. Annotations; library locations. Indexes of authors, titles, subjects. Z7165.C4G37

Langstaff, Eleanor De Selms. Panama. Oxford, Eng. & Santa Barbara, Calif., Clio Pr., [1982]. 184p. (World bibliographical ser., v.14) **DB380**

Books, articles, documents of international organizations, and a few dissertations are arranged by topic, with brief annotations. Spanish-language materials are included on topics for which English sources were not available. Z1500.L36

Lucena Salmoral, Manuel. Historiografía de Panamá. Panamá, Universidad Santa María la Antigua, 1967. 76p. **DB381**

Books and articles (mainly from the 20th century, with some late 19th century entries) are arranged alphabetically by author; most works are in Spanish, but there are some English titles. No index. Z1500.L83

Paraguay

Cardozo, Efraím. Historiografía paraguaya. México, 1959. v.1. (Inst. Panamericano de Geografía e Historia. Comisión de Historia. Pubn. 83. Historiografías, 5) **DB382**

Inst. Panamericano de Geografía e Historia. Pubn. 221.
Contents: v.1, Paraguay indígena, español y jesuíta. Bibliografía, p.461–524.
Detailed bio-bibliographies of historians with a comprehensive bibliography of material about them.
No more published?

Jones, David Lewis. Paraguay: a bibliography. N.Y., Garland, 1979. 499p. (Garland reference library of social sciences, v.51) **DB383**

Aims "to present a fairly comprehensive list of works relating to Paraguay for the use of students in other countries."—*Introd.* Includes books in European languages and Guarani, and articles from Paraguayan periodicals deemed "reasonably accessible in British, United States and Canadian libraries." Classed arrangement with author/subject index. More than 4,400 entries.
Z1821.J66

Peru

Bibliography

Basadre, Jorge. Introducción a las bases documentales para la historia de la República del Perú, con algunas reflexiones. [Lima], Ediciones P.L.V., [1971]. 3v. **DB384**

An extensive bibliography of Peruvian history from independence in 1822 to 1933, including diplomatic and military history, legal and legislative affairs, statistics, material on the theater, literature, memoirs, etc. Arranged by topic within period divisions; good introductory chapters on archival and library guides, bibliographies, collections of documents. Indexes of personal names, geographical names, serial publications, and topics by chapter. Z1851.B35

Herbold, Carl and **Stein, Steve.** Guía bibliográfica para la historia social y política del Perú en el siglo XX (1895–1960). [Lima], Instituto de Estudios Peruanos, [1971]. 165p. **DB385**

102 important works—books and articles—are listed in alphabetical order with lengthy annotations. That section is followed by essays and/or lists dealing with bibliographies of bibliography, periodicals, documents, biographical sources, Lima libraries, and 33 topics for research. Subject index. Z7165.P4H47

Martínez, Héctor, Cameo C, Miguel and **Ramirez S, Jésus.** Bibliografía indígena andina peruana (1900–1968). [Lima, Centro de Estudios de Población y Desarrollo, 1969] 157p. **DB386**

For annotation *see* CE65.

Moreyra y Paz Soldán, Carlos. Bibliografía regional peruana (Colección particular). Lima, Libreria Internacional de Peru, 1967. 518p. **DB387**

A listing of books on geography, history, literature, and social problems of the provinces and districts of Peru. Arranged by region, with name and title indexes. Some extensive annotations. Z1879.M65

Muñoz de Linares, Elba and **Céspedes de Reynaga, Alicia.** Bibliografía de tesis peruanos sobre indigenismo y ciencias sociales. Lima, Instituto Indigenista Peruano, 1983. 2v. (733p.) (Serie bibliográfica, 4) **DB388**

Topical arrangement; chapter headings are given for each work cited. Indexed by author, subject, ethnic group, place name, and institution.

Among the other useful bibliographies in the Institute's series is the *Bibliografía sobre identidad cultural en el Perú* (1982. 126p.).

Peru. Biblioteca Nacional, Lima. Catalogo de autores de la colección peruana. . . . Boston, G. K. Hall, 1979. 6v. **DB389**

For full information *see* AA1012.

Tauro, Alberto. Bibliografía peruana de historia, 1940–1953. Lima, Talleres Gráficos, 1953. 196p. **DB390**

Books and monographs printed in Peru, or in other countries, relating to Peru, 1940–53.

Supplement in *Revista historica* (v.22, 1955–56, p.361–461) adds materials published 1954–57 and 1935–39, as well as titles omitted from the original list. Includes citations to book reviews. Z1866.T35

———— Guía de estudios históricos. Lima, 1955. 109p. (Separata del Boletín bibliográfico, v.25, no.1–4) **DB391**

Serves as a companion to the work above, listing periodical articles.

Vargas Ugarte, Ruben. Manual de estudios peruanistas. 4. ed. Lima, Librería e Imprenta Gil, 1959. 455p. **DB392**

1st ed., 1939, had title *Historia del Perú; Fuentes.*

A bibliographical survey of materials on the history, bibliography, religion, literature and language, social sciences, etc., of Peru. Additions appeared in *Boletín bibliográfico de la Universidad Nacional Mayor de San Marcos*, año 33, dic. 1960, p.3–49.

Dictionaries and encyclopedias

Mendiburu, Manuel de. Diccionario histórico-biográfico del Perú. 3. ed. adiciones y notas bibliográficas. Lima, Editorial Arica, [1976]– . v.1– . **DB393**

For full description *see* AJ331.

Pease García, Henry and **Verme Insúa, Olga.** Perú, 1968–1973: chronología política. Lima, Centro de Estudios y Promoción del Desarrollo, Area de Estudios Políticos, 1974– . Annual (beginning with v.3) **DB394**

Contents: v.1, 1968–71; v.2, 1972–73; v.3–9, 1974–80.

Beginning with v.2 there are indexes by personal name, organization, and broad topic. F3448.P36

Tauro, Alberto. Diccionario enciclopédico del Perú. Lima, Editorial Mejía Baca, [1967]. 3v. il. **DB395**

Brief articles relating to Peruvian life, culture, and history, but without bibliographies or lists of sources. Includes biographical sketches and entries for place-names, educational and cultural institutions, and the flora and fauna of Peru.

———— ———— Apendice. Lima, [1975]. [338]p. il.

Adds 360 biographical sketches and a glossary of terms peculiar to Peru. F3404.D5

History

Basadre, Jorge. Historia de la Republica del Perú, 1822–1933. 6. ed. aumentada y corr. Lima, Editorial Universitaria, [1968–70]. 17v. il. **DB396**

1st ed. 1939.

Contents: v.1–2, La determinación de la nacionalidad; v.3–5, La prosperidad falaz; v.6–8, La crisis económica y hacendaria y la guerra con Chile; v.9–10, La reconstrucción; v.11–12, La república aristocrática; v.13, El oncenio y sus consecuencias inmediatas; v.14, Notas sobre la crisis política, económica y social de 1930 a 1933; v.15, Notas para una historica educacional y cultural, 1895–1933; v.16, La prosperidad falaz; v.17, Bibliografía general [superseded by DB384, above]. F3446.5.B342

El Salvador

García, Miguel Angel. Diccionario histórico-enciclopédico de la República de El Salvador. San Salvador, Tipografía "La Luz," 1927–51. v.1–13. **DB397**

Contents: v.1–13, A–Col. No more published?

Historical and biographical articles in one alphabet, often including reproduction of documentary sources. F1483.G21

Krusé, David Samuel and **Swedberg, Richard.** El Salvador bibliography and research guide. [Cambridge, Mass.], Central America Information Office, 1982. 233p. **DB398**

Books, magazine and newspaper articles, and government documents are included in this topically arranged listing "that contains (a) important new information, (b) tracks the works of key authors and policy actors, and (c) provides a data base for analyzing key institutions and organizations."—*p.40.* Focus is on the Civil War, with good sections on background. Z1491.K78

Suriname

Encyclopedie van Suriname. Hoofdredactie, C. F. A. Bruijning, J. Voorhoeve; Samensteller, W. Gordijn. Amsterdam, Elsevier, 1977. 716p. il. **DB399**

A national encyclopedia with articles relating to the immediate area (natural and political history, physical features, flora, fauna, places, personalities, etc.).

Nagelkerke, Gerard A. Suriname; a bibliography, 1940–80. Leiden, Dept. of Caribbean Studies, R. Institute of Linguistics & Anthropology; The Hague, Smits Drukkers-Uitgevers, [1980]. 316p. **DB400**

In Dutch and English.

A revision of the compiler's 1972 work, *Literatuur-overzicht van Suriname 1940 tot 1970.*

Citations to over 2,600 monographs and articles are arranged by author, with subject and author index. The topic of Surinamers in the Netherlands is selectively treated. Based on the collection in the Library of the Royal Institute of Linguistics and Anthropology. Z1806.N33

Uruguay

Araújo, Orestes. Diccionario popular de historia de la República o. del Uruguay, desde la época del descubrimiento de su territorio, hasta la de su independencia. Montevideo, Dornaleche y Reyes, 1901–03. 3v. **DB401**

A dictionary of persons, places, and events; includes documentary sources. F2704.A67

Centro Latino-Americano de Pesquisas em Ciências Sociais. Estratificación y movilidad social en el Uruguay; fuentes bibliograficas, 1880–1958. Rio de Janeiro, 1959. 60p. (*Its* Publicación, 5) **DB402**

An annotated bibliography of some 327 books, plus a few articles and essays. Works are grouped as (1) Theory, (2) Before 1930, (3) Contemporary, and (4) Documentation (which includes statistical studies, biography, autobiography, and legislation). Entries are graded for importance on a scale of 1 to 4.

Venezuela

Bibliography

Carrera Damas, Germán. Historia de la historiografia venezolana, textos para su estudio. Caracas, Univ. Central de Venezuela, Ed. de la Biblioteca, 1961. 650p. **DB403**

Reprints some 48 historiographical essays covering archives, specific periods, etc. Index of persons, topics, and works cited.
F2320.C3

Lombardi, John V., Carrera Damas, Germán and **Adams, Roberta E.** Venezuelan history; a comprehensive working bibliography. Boston, G. K. Hall, [1977]. 530p. **DB404**

Intended as "a starting place for the study of Venezuelan history." —*Pref.* More than 4,600 entries arranged under the following main headings: (1) General reference; (2) History; (3) Bolivar; (4) Church; (5) Civilization; (6) Education; (7) Geography; (8) Petroleum; (9) Population; (10) Urbanization. There is an author index, but none of detailed subjects.

Another guide is R. J. Lovera DeSola's *Guía para el estudio de la historia de Venezuela* (Caracas, 1982. 217p.). Z1911.L64

Sánchez, Manuel Segundo. Obras. Caracas, [Banco Central de Venezuela], 1964. 2v. **DB405**

v.1 is a reprint of the author's *Bibliografía venezolanista . . .* (Caracas, Empresa el Cojo, 1914. 494p.), which lists 1,438 works, annotated, on Venezuela published in foreign countries. v.2 contains a biographical sketch of the author and a bibliography of his works. v.3 is an index. Z1926.S26

Dictionaries

Arellano Moreno, Antonio. Guía de historia de Venezuela. 3a. ed. [Caracas, Ediciones Centauro, 1977] 262p.
DB406

1st ed. 1955.
A chronology of Venezuelan history, 1498–1977, with tables and lists of presidents, coups, buccaneers and pirates, constitutions, etc.
F2319.5.A8

Calvo Baca, Emilio. Diccionario venezolano de político y el parlamentario: contiene catálogo de términos, conceptos, principios, síntesis biográficas, instituciones y usos parlamentarios. Caracas, Ediciones Calvin, 1983. 202p.
DB407

Offers brief entries for terms, issues, movements, and major figures. JL3805.C34

ISLANDS OF THE CARIBBEAN AND WEST ATLANTIC

General works

Bibliography

Comitas, Lambros. The complete Caribbeana, 1900–1975; a bibliographic guide to the scholarly literature. Millwood, N.Y., KTO Pr., [1978]. 4v. **DB408**

Prep. under the auspices of the Research Institute for the Study of Man.

Contents: v.1, People; v.2, Institutions; v.3, Resources; v.4, Indexes.

Based on the same author's *Caribbeana 1900–1965* (1968), but representing a thorough revision thereof, expanding the geographical coverage to include Bermuda and the Bahamas along with the other non-Hispanic areas, and extending the period of coverage through 1975. Now lists "over seventeen thousand complete references to authored publications such as monographs, readers, conference proceedings, doctoral dissertations, master's theses, journal articles, reports, pamphlets, and other miscellaneous works."—*Pref.* v.1–3 are each divided into three main sections with numerous subdivisions: v.1, Introduction to the Caribbean; The past; The people; v.2, Elements of culture; Health, education and welfare; Political issues; v.3, Socio-economic activities and institutions; The environment and human geography; Soils, crops and livestock.

Separate author and geographical indexes. Library location indicated for most items.

Updated by *Bibliography of the English-speaking Caribbean: books, articles and reviews in English from the arts, humanities and the social sciences,* 1978– (Parkersburg, Ia., R. J. Neymeyer, 1979–); by the *CARICOM bibliography,* 1977– (*see* AA666); and by *CARINDEX: social sciences,* 1977– (St. Augustine, Trinidad, ACURIL, Indexing Committee, 1977– . Semiannual).
Z1595.C63

Jordan, Alma and **Comissiong, Barbara.** The English-speaking Caribbean; a bibliography of bibliographies. Boston, G. K. Hall, [1984]. 411p. **DB409**

For full information *see* AA48.

Miami, University of, Coral Gables, Fla. Cuban and Caribbean Library. Catalog. . . . Boston, G. K. Hall, 1977. 6v.
DB410

"Books chosen for inclusion are those whose subject headings or titles indicate content specifically within the scope of the Catalog; books by known authors important to the Caribbean, Cuban, Dominican, Puerto Rican literature, history, art, music, etc., as could be determined by classification in our shelf list."—*Introd.* Government publications and periodicals are not included. Geographic areas covered are Cuba, the Antilles, Guyanas, Venezuela, Mexico, Colombia, and all of Central America except San Salvador.
Z1595.M5

Oltheten, Theo M. P. Inventory of Caribbean studies; an overview of social scientific publications on the Caribbean by Antillean, Dutch and Surinamese authors in the period 1945–1978/79. Leiden, Dept. of Caribbean Studies, R. Institute of Linguistics & Anthropology, 1979. 280p.
DB411

More than 2,000 listings are arranged by topic within four categories: Netherlands Antilles, Surinam, Antilleans and Surinamers in the Netherlands, Caribbean general. Aims to be as complete as possible for sociology, anthropology, social geography, political science, education, psychology, and includes some entries for law, economics, and literature. List of journals indexed. Z1595.O44

Ragatz, Lowell Joseph. A guide for the study of British Caribbean history, 1763–1834, including the abolition and emancipation movements. Wash., Govt. Prt. Off., 1932. 725p. (American Historical Assoc., Annual report, 1930, v.3) **DB412**

An extensive, classified, annotated list of books, manuscripts, documents, and periodical articles, with author, title, subject, and proper-name index. Z1502.B5R22

Royal Commonwealth Society, London. Library. Subject catalogue. v.3, Dominion of Canada . . . the West Indies, and colonial America. London, 1932. **DB413**

For full description *see* DC320.

Dissertations

Baa, Enid M. Theses on Caribbean topics, 1778–1968. San Juan, P.R., Inst. of Caribbean Studies, Univ. of Puerto Rico, 1970. 146p. (Caribbean bibliographic ser., 1) **DB414**

A preliminary edition, computer-produced, appeared in 1969. Doctoral dissertations and master's theses appear in separate listings, alphabetical by author. Indexes by university at which the work was done, by country studied, by subject, and by date of completion.
Z1501.C33

Commonwealth Caribbean Resource Centre. Theses on the Commonwealth Caribbean, 1891–1973. London, Ont., Office of Internat. Education, Univ. of Western Ontario, [1974?]. 136p. **DB415**

An author listing of dissertations accepted mainly in British, United States, and Canadian universities. "Geographical index of countries studied," but no topical index. Useful for supplementing and updating the Baa compilation (above), though not as complete nor as accurate. Z1502.B5C65

Hills, Theo L. Caribbean topics; theses in Canadian university libraries. [4th ed. Montreal, McGill Univ., Centre for Developing-Area Studies], 1973. 25*l*. **DB416**

23 universities are represented by 250 master's and doctoral theses. Arranged by university, then topically.
Supplemented by *Caribbean topics; theses from McGill University, 1972–75 . . .*, by Robyn Bryant [et al.] (Montreal, 1977. 35*l*.).
Z1595.H54

Manuscripts

Ingram, Kenneth E. Sources for West Indian studies, a supplementary listing, with particular reference to manuscript sources. Zug, Inter Documentation Co., [1983]. 412p. **DB417**

Describes collections in archives of Great Britain, Ireland, Holland, Denmark, Australia, Barbados, Jamaica, St. Kitts, Trinidad & Tobago dealing with the Commonwealth Caribbean, especially Jamaica. Very comprehensive. Name and broad subject index.
Z1502.B5I47

Tyson, George F. A guide to manuscript sources in United States and West Indian depositories relating to the British West Indies during the era of the American Revolution. Wilmington, Del., Scholarly Resources, [1978]. 96p. **DB418**

United States repositories are listed by state, then by library or institution; for the West Indies, listing is by island, then by library. Individual collections are briefly described. Indexed.
Z1238.T954

Historiography

Goveia, Elsa V. A study on the historiography of the British West Indies to the end of the nineteenth century. México, 1956. 183p. (Inst. Panamericano de Geografía e Historia. Comisión de Historia. Pubn. 78. Historiografías, 2) **DB419**

Inst. Panamericano de Geografía e Historia. Pubn. 186.
A discussion of the histories of the British West Indies and their writers. Brief bibliography, p.179–81. F2131.G6

Barbados

Chandler, Michael John. A guide to records in Barbados. Oxford, B. Blackwell for the Univ. of the West Indies, 1965. 204p. **DB420**

First of a series surveying the records of the English-speaking territories of the West Indies. Records are grouped according to class—central government, local government, semipublic, ecclesiastical, private—and listed by repository as they existed in 1961. Historical notes on government departments are given. Subject index. CD3985.B3C5

Handler, Jerome S. A guide to source materials for the study of Barbados history, 1627–1834. Carbondale, Southern Illinois Univ. Pr., [1971]. 205p. **DB421**

Lists books, pamphlets, parliamentary papers, newspapers, and manuscript collections relevant to the early history of Barbados. Detailed index. Z1561.B3H34

Bermuda

Rowe, Helen. A guide to the records of Bermuda. Hamilton, Bermuda Archives, 1980. [132]p. (looseleaf) il. **DB422**

A guide to the records kept in the Bermuda Archives, the Maritime Museum, and the historical societies, schools, and churches of Bermuda, together with material in archives in Great Britain, the United States, Canada, Ireland, Spain, and the West Indies. Also includes a list of records on microfilm in the Bermuda Archives. Indexed. CD3985.B47R68

Cuba

Cuba en la mano; enciclopedia popular ilustrada. La Habana, [Ucar, Gardía], 1940. 1302p. il. **DB423**

Esteban Roldan Oliarte, ed.
Includes sections on geographical names, natural history, history, printing, biography, education and culture, communications, politics, statistics, etc. F1754.C8

Havana. Biblioteca Nacional "José Martí." Impresos relativos a Cuba editados en las Estados Unidos de Norteamérica. Comp. bajo la dirección de Lilia Castro de Morales . . . Habana, 1956. 370p. **DB424**

At head of title: Ministerio de Educación.
Lists 2,014 books and pamphlets by Cubans, or about Cuba, published from 1762 to 1956. Arranged chronologically with author index. Z1511.H3

Pérez Cabrera, José Manuel. Historiografía de Cuba. México, 1962. 394p. (Inst. Panamericano de Geografía e Historia. Comisión de Historia. Pubn. 106. Historiografías, 7) **DB425**

Inst. Panamericano de Geografía Historia. Pubn. 262.
A résumé of historical writings, 15th century to about 1900, with annotated bibliographies throughout.

Cuban Revolution

Fort, Gilberto V., comp. The Cuban revolution of Fidel Castro viewed from abroad; an annotated bibliography. [Lawrence], Univ. of Kansas Libraries, 1969. 140p. (Kansas. Univ. Pubns. Library ser., 34) **DB426**

Lists books and pamphlets in a classed arrangement, then chronologically within classes. Author index. Z1525.F63

Perez, Louis A. The Cuban revolutionary war, 1953–1958: a bibliography. Metuchen, N.J., Scarecrow Pr., 1976. 225p. **DB427**

A classed bibliography of nearly 2,500 items. Author index.
Z1525.P43

―――― Historiography in the Revolution: a bibliography of Cuban scholarship, 1959–1979. N.Y., Garland, 1982. 318p. (Garland reference library of social science, v.90) **DB428**

In three parts: (1) a general section followed by sections on specific historical periods; (2) topical sections (e.g., women, communism in Cuba, labor, peasantry); (3) biography. Nearly 3,800 entries; author and subject indexes. Z1511.P44

Suchlicki, Jaime. The Cuban revolution: a documentary bibliography, 1952–1968. Coral Gables, Fla., Univ. of Miami, Research Inst. for Cuba and the Caribbean, 1968. 83p. **DB429**

A chronological listing of speeches, editorials, manifestos, communiqués, etc., relating to the Cuban revolution. Index of names.
Z1525.S93

Valdés, Nelson P. and **Lieuwen, Edwin.** The Cuban revolution; a research-study guide (1959–1969). Albuquerque, Univ. of New Mexico Pr., [1971]. 230p. **DB430**

A classed bibliography of more than 3,800 items (books, documents, pamphlets, periodical articles). Author index. Z1525.V33

Dominican Republic

Enciclopedia dominicana. 2. ed., ampl., corr. y actualizada. Santo Domingo, Enciclopédica Dominicana, S.A., [1978]. 8v. il. **DB431**

1st ed. 1976 in 8v.
Contents: v.1–7, A–Z; v.8, Antología poética.
An encyclopedia of Dominican affairs, with many biographical and historical articles, statistical tables, maps, etc. F1932.E52

Hitt, Deborah S. and **Wilson, Larman C.** A selected bibliography of the Dominican Republic; a century after the restoration of independence. Wash., American Univ., Center for Research in Social Systems, 1968. 142p. **DB432**

A selective, unclassified bibliography of books, articles, and some public documents on the Dominican Republic of the 20th century. Most references are in English or Spanish. Z1536.H56

Martínez, Rufino. Diccionario biográfico-histórico dominicano, 1821–1930. Santo Domingo, Ediciones de la Universidad Autónoma de Santo Domingo, 1971. 541p. (Publicaciones de la Univ. Autónoma de Santo Domingo, CLII; Colección historia y sociedad, 5) **DB433**

Offers extensive coverage of historical figures up to the time of the rise of Trujillo. No bibliography. F1933.M37

Wiarda, Howard J. Materials for the study of politics and government in the Dominican Republic 1930–1966. [Santiago de los Caballeros], UCMM, [1968]. 142p. (Univ. Católica Madre y Maestra. Colección estudios, 5) **DB434**

In English and Spanish.
A listing of books, articles, and manuscripts arranged in sections for the Trujillo and post-Trujillo periods; each entry has a one-line annotation. Includes lists of relevant libraries and of journals and newspapers. No index.
Wolf Grabendorff's *Bibliographie zu Politik und Gesellschaft der Dominikanischen Republik, neuere Studien, 1961–1971* (München, Weltforum Verlag, 1973. 103p.) is useful for extending the coverage of the Hitt and Wiarda works (above). Z7165.D6W5

Falkland Islands

Laver, Margaret Patricia Henwood. An annotated bibliography of the Falkland Islands and the Falkland Islands dependencies (as delimited on 3rd March, 1962). Cape Town, Univ. of Cape Town Libraries, 1977. 239p. **DB435**

Comp. for the diploma in librarianship, Univ. of Cape Town, 1974.
Some 1,539 books, articles, periodicals, manuscripts, mimeographed materials, and government documents are listed in 63 subject categories, plus a supplement. Annotated; author and selected titles index.
A more recent listing of book materials is *The Falkland/Malvinas Islands . . . (1619–1982)* by Sara de Mundo Lo (Urbana, Ill., Albatross, 1983. 65p.). Z1945.L38

U.S. Library of Congress. Hispanic Division. A selective listing of monographs and government documents on the Falkland/Malvinas Islands in the Library of Congress. Comp. by Everette E. Larson. Wash., Lib. of Congress, [1982]. 26p. (Hispanic focus, no.1) **DB436**

An alphabetical listing; includes command papers.
Books, parts of books, and periodical articles from the Jan.1955–June 1982 period are listed in *Islas Malvinas, geografía—bibliografía* by Raúl C. Rey Balmaceda (Buenos Aires, OIKOS, Asociación para la promoción de los Estudios Territoriales y Ambientales, 1982. 242p.). Z1945.L5

Torre Revello, José. Bibliografía de las Islas Malvinas; obras, mapas y documentos; contribución. Buenos Aires, Impr. de la Universidad, 1953. 260p. maps, facsims. (Univ. de Buenos Aires. Facultad de Filosofía y Letras. Pubn. del Inst. de Investigaciones Históricas, no.99) **DB437**

A bibliography of more than 800 items on the history and geography of the Falkland Islands, with a section listing unpublished documents, 1534–1953. Many of the works listed are in Spanish, but some titles in other languages are included. Z1945.T6

Haiti

Chambers, Frances. Haiti. Oxford, Eng. & Santa Barbara, Calif., Clio Pr., [1983]. 177p. (World bibliographical ser., v.39) **DB438**

550 citations (primarily English language) to books and periodical articles arranged in 37 categories. Brief annotations. Aims to meet the "needs of the general reader, undergraduate college student, and the librarian interested in building a library collection."—*Introd.* Indexed. Z1531.C47

Laguerre, Michel S. The complete Haitiana: a bibliographic guide to the scholarly literature, 1900–1980. Millwood, N.Y., Kraus Internat. Pubns., [1982]. 2v. **DB439**

Prep. under the auspices of the Research Institute for the Study of Man.
A classed bibliography of books, parts of books, periodical articles, and government publications. Detailed table of contents; author index. Includes writings on the ecological setting as well as Haitian history, population, social and cultural affairs, politics, education, etc. Complements *The complete Caribbeana* by L. Comitas (DB408) which omits Haiti. Z1531.L33

Pressoir, Catts, Touillot, Ernst and **Touillot, Henock.** Historiographie d'Haïti. México, 1953. 298p. (Inst. Panamericano de Geografía e Historia. Comisión de Historia. Pubn. 66. Historiografías, 1) **DB440**

Inst. Panamericano de Geografía e Historia. Pubn. 168.
Treats historical writers and their works from 1492 to the 20th century; includes travel accounts. Few of the works deal with the 20th century, but many were published in this century. Bibliography, p.287–98.

Jamaica

Ingram, K. E. Jamaica. Santa Barbara, Calif., Clio Pr., [1984]. 369p. (World bibliographical ser., 45) **DB441**

Lists more than 1,180 books, periodical articles, dissertations, government publications, and technical reports on all aspects of Jamaican life and culture. Topically arranged; good annotations. Index of authors, titles, and subjects.
The *Jamaica national bibliography* (AA914) can be used for continuous updating since it lists books about Jamaica or by Jamaicans regardless of place of publication. Z1541.I52

—— Sources of Jamaican history, 1655–1838; a bibliographical survey with particular reference to manuscript sources. Zug, Switz., Inter Documentation Co., [1976]. 2v. (1310p.) **DB442**

Revision of the author's thesis, University of London, 1970.
A survey of manuscript collections in British and Jamaican repositories, with some attention to European and North American archives. The only printed sources included are newspapers, almanacs, legislative documents, etc., and these are listed chronologically with library locations. A supplement, p.1124–93, adds materials discovered since 1970 when the survey was originally made. Extensive index of names and subjects. Z1541.I53

Leeward Islands

Baker, E. C. A guide to records in the Leeward Islands. Oxford, B. Blackwell for the Univ. of the West Indies, 1965. 102p. **DB443**

A companion to Chandler's guide for Barbados records (DB420). Comprises a section on federal records, followed by sections on the records of Antigua, Montserrat, Nevis, St. Christopher, and the British Virgin Islands, each arranged by repository and including historical and descriptive notes. CD3985.W5B3

Martinique

Archives de la Martinique. Guide des Archives de la Martinique. Liliane Chauleau, comp. Fort-de-France, Archives Départementales, 1978. 68p. **DB444**

Offers a description of the arrangement and contents of each file in the Archives, plus a chapter on copies of items from the Archives Nationales in Paris which are also available for use. CD3985.M47A7

Jardel, Jean Pierre, Nicolas, Maurice and **Relouzat, Claude.** Bibliographie de la Martinique. [Fort-de-France, Centre d'Études Régionales Antilles-Guyane, 1969] v.1. (Les cahiers de CERAG, 1969, no.3) **DB445**

A classified bibliography of books and periodical articles on Martinique and the Antilles in general. v.2 was to be a subject and author index. Z1561.M3J37

Netherlands Antilles

Nagelkerke, Gerard A. Netherlands Antilles; a bibliography, 17th century–1980. Leiden, Dept. Caribbean Studies, R. Institute of Linguistics & Anthropology; The Hague, Smits Drukkers-Uitgevers, 1982. 422p. **DB446**

Offers "a survey of the collection of books, articles, manuscripts, etc., relating to the Netherland Antilles kept in the library of the Royal Institute of Linguistics and Anthropology (KITLV) in Leiden."—*Introd.* The library has tried to collect everything available in the humanities and social sciences dealing with this area. Listing is by author/title, with indexes for names and title "catchwords/subjects." Z1502.D7N33

Encyclopedie van de Nederlandse Antillen. Hoofdredacteur H. Hoetink. Amsterdam, Elsevier, 1969. 708p. il. **DB447**

Entries relate to the history, culture, natural history, etc., of the islands of Aruba, Bonaire, Curaçao, Saba, Saint Eustatius, and Saint Martin. F2141.E5

Encyclopaedie van Nederlandsch West-Indië. H. D. Benjamins [and] J. F. Snelleman [eds.]. 'sGravenhage, Nijhoff, 1914–17. 782p. maps. (Repr.: Amsterdam, Nijhoff, 1981) **DB448**

An encyclopedia on all aspects of the region; includes biographies. Scholarly, signed articles; good bibliographies. Useful for historical purposes. F2141.E53

Puerto Rico

Bibliography

Bird, Augusto. Bibliografía puertorriqueña de fuentes para investigaciones sociales, 1930–1945. Ed. provisional. [Rio Piedras], Centro de Investigaciones Sociales, Univ. Puerto Rico, 1946–47. 2v. (547p.) **DB449**

An extensive classified bibliography of books and periodical articles, covering the natural history, anthropology, health, econom-

ics, history, political science, and culture of Puerto Rico. No author index. Z1551.B5

Cardona, Luis A. An annotated bibliography on Puerto Rican materials and other sundry matters. Bethesda, Md., Carreta Pr., [1983]. 156p. il. **DB450**

Works are grouped by type of material: books; government reports and documents; conferences/reports/studies; journals; oral history; plus a section on materials relating to Puerto Rico in the U.S. National Archives. Indexed.

See also Elena E. Cevallos and Sheila R. Herstein's *Puerto Rico* (Santa Barbara, Clio Pr., 1985. 193p. World bibliographical series, 52). Z1551.C37

Pedreira, Antonio Salvador. Bibliografía puertorriqueña (1493–1930). Madrid, Impr. de la Librería y Casa Ed. Hernando, 1932. 707p. (Monografías de la Universidad de Puerto Rico. Ser.A. Estudios hispánicos, núm.1) (Repr.: N.Y., B. Franklin, 1974) **DB451**

Includes works by natives and foreigners about Puerto Rico, the artistic literary works of Puerto Ricans, and a selected list of works by Puerto Ricans on various subjects—cf. *Introd., p.xvii.* Classified, with author and subject indexes. Z1551.P37

Puerto Rico. University. Social Science Research Center. Bibliografía puertorriqueña de ciencias sociales. Rio Piedras, Editorial Universitaria, Univ. de Puerto Rico, 1977. 2v. in 1 (600p.) **DB452**

An extensive bibliography treating social science very broadly (e.g., including "Society and culture," "Media and communication," "Art"). Topical arrangement within separate sections for publications of 1931–54 and 1954–60. No index. Z7165.P94P85

Dissertations

Dossick, Jesse John. Doctoral research on Puerto Rico and Puerto Ricans. [N.Y., School of Education, New York Univ., 1967] 34p. **DB453**

More than 300 items in classed arrangement with author index. Z1551.D67

Encyclopedias

La gran enciclopedia de Puerto Rico. Madrid, [Ed. R, 1976]. 14v. il. **DB454**

Vincente Baez, ed.

Contents: v.1, Historia; v.2, Politica; v.3, Poesia; v.4, Cuento; v.5, Novela; v.6, Teatro; v.7, Musica; v.8, Artes plasticas; v.9, Arquitectura leyes; v.10, Educacion, flora, fauna, economia; v.11, Deportes; v.12, Folklore; v.13, Municipios; v.14, Diccionario historico-biografico.

A heavily illustrated general encyclopedia. Each volume is made up of essays by specialists on the topics covered; v.14 is a biographical dictionary. Name index and brief bibliography in each volume. F1954.G72

Hostos, Adolfo de. Diccionario histórico bibliografico comentado de Puerto Rico. [Barcelona, Industrias Gráficas Manuel Pareja], 1976. 952p. **DB455**

"Publicacion de la Academia Puertorriqueña de la Historia."— *t.p.*

Includes entries for names, events, terms, etc., in Puerto Rican history. Articles are usually quite brief; bibliographic references are cited in many entries. F1954.H67

Ribes Tovar, Federico, ed. Enciclopedia puertorriqueña ilustrada. The Puerto Rican heritage enciclopedia. San Juan and N.Y., Plus Ultra Educational Pubs., [1970]. 3v. il. **DB456**

Spanish and English text in parallel columns.
A topical encyclopedia dealing with Puerto Rican history and culture. v.2 is concerned with the Puerto Rican in New York.

Selected general bibliography in v.3. Lack of an index seriously limits use as a reference tool. F1958.R5

Histories

Puerto Rico, a political and cultural history. [Ed. by] Arturo Morales Carrión. N.Y., Norton; Nashville, Tenn., Amer. Assoc. for State and Local History, [1983]. 384p. **DB457**

A well-written history of Puerto Rico in English. Contributors are Puerto Rican scholars whose aim was to bring out "a more balanced perspective of what Puerto Rico constitutes as a people, a cultural nationality, or a distinctive Caribbean entity."—*Introd.*

F1973.P83

Virgin Islands

Reid, Charles Frederick. Bibliography of the Virgin Islands of the United States. Nathan Habib, assoc. ed.; Florence D. Clark and Caroline Simonini, asst. eds. N.Y., Wilson, 1941. 225p. **DB458**

"Prepared with the assistance of the Federal Works Agency, Works Projects Administration for the City of New York, Division of Community Service Programs, 'Bibliographies of the territories and outlying possessions of the United States.' "—*verso of title page.*

Lists books, manuscripts, documents, and periodical articles in an annotated, classified bibliography with alphabetical index. Still useful for materials on piracy and slavery. Z1561.V8R4

Windward Islands

Baker, Edward Cecil. A guide to records in the Windward Islands. Oxford, B. Blackwell for the Univ. of the West Indies, 1968. 95p. **DB459**

A companion to Baker's records guide for the Leeward Islands (DB443) and M. J. Chandler's volume for Barbados (DB420). Surveys the records of Grenada, Saint Vincent, Saint Lucia, and Dominica. Indexed. CD3985.W5B3

D C

Europe

GENERAL WORKS

Bibliography

Aldcroft, Derek Howard and **Rodger, Richard.** Bibliography of European economic and social history. Manchester, Eng., Manchester Univ. Pr., [1984]. 243p. **DC1**

Covers the period 1700–1939 and relates to all of continental Europe (including Turkey in Europe); cites more than 6,000 books, journal articles and a few government reports, mainly 20th century publications. Arranged by area or country within about a dozen topical headings. Author index.

The European bibliography, ed. by Hjalmar Pehrsson and Hanna Wulf (Leyden, Sijthoff, 1965. 472p.) lists works on European problems and efforts at unification published 1945–63.

Z7165.E8A4

Bainton, Roland Herbert and **Gritsch, Eric W.** Bibliography of the continental Reformation; materials available in English. 2d ed., rev. and enl. [Hamden, Conn.], Archon Books, 1972. 220p. **DC2**

1st ed. 1935 by R. H. Bainton.

A topically arranged bibliography without author index.

Z7830.B16

Europe. Préparé . . . sous la direction de Philippe Wolff. Paris, Klincksieck, 1977. 544p. (Guide international d'histoire urbaine, v.1) **DC3**

At head of title: Commission Internationale pour l'Histoire des Villes.

Brief sections on "La ville antique" and "La ville byzantine" are followed by entries for the individual countries of Europe in alphabetical sequence. Each country section begins with a brief historical introduction, followed by a review of the principal sources, published and unpublished, for urban history research (with attention to archives and their organization), a list of institutes and periodicals concerned with urban history, and a selected bibliography.

Frey, Linda, Frey, Marsha and **Schneider, Jeanne.** Women in Western European history: a select chronological, geographical, and topical bibliography from antiquity to the French Revolution. Westport, Conn., Greenwood Pr., [1982–84]. 2v. **DC4**

For full information *see* CC561.

Halstead, John P. and **Pocari, Serafino.** Modern European imperialism: a bibliography of books and articles, 1815–1972. Boston, G. K. Hall, 1974. 2v. **DC5**

Contents: v.1, General and British Empire; v.2, French and other empires, regions.

A classed bibliography of more than 33,000 entries. Historical treatments of imperialism are given emphasis, but "the searcher will find a wide selection of materials ranging from primary sources to fiction."—*Pref.* Although "designed as a guide to secondary works for the serious scholar or student," most sections include a selection of documents and papers as an indication of the kinds of primary sources available. Detailed table of contents for each volume, but no index. Z6204.H35

Harvard University. Library. General European and world history; classification schedule, classified listing by call number, chronological listing, author and title listing. Cambridge, Harvard Univ. Lib.; distr. by Harvard Univ. Pr., 1970. 959p. (Widener Library shelflist, 32) **DC6**

For full information *see* DA9.

International Committee of Historical Sciences. Commission Internationale d'Histoire Ecclésiastique Comparée. Bibliographie de la réforme, 1450–1648. Leiden, Brill, 1958–82. Fasc.1–8. (In progress) **DC7**

Contents: fasc.1, Allemagne, Pays-Bas; fasc.2, Belgique, Suède, Norvège, Danemark, Irlande, États-Unis d'Amérique; fasc.3, Italie, Espagne, Portugal; fasc.4, France, Angleterre, Suisse; fasc.5, Pologne, Hongrie, Tchécoslovaquie, Finlande; fasc.6, Autriche; fasc.7, Écosse; fasc.8, Benelux.

Subtitle varies to reflect period of coverage.

Lists books, dissertations, and periodical articles on the Reformation published in the countries indicated. Z7830.I5

—— **British Sub-Commission.** The bibliography of the Reform, 1450–1648, relating to the United Kingdom and Ireland for the years 1955–70. Ed. by Derek Baker. Oxford, Blackwell, 1975. 242p. **DC8**

Serves as a companion to the *Bibliographie de la réforme* (above).

In three main sections: (1) England and Wales; (2) Scotland; and

(3) Ireland. Within each section, items are grouped as books, periodical articles, reviews, and theses. Author listing within subsections. No subject index. Z7830.I522

Reformation Europe: a guide to research. Ed. by Steven Ozment. St. Louis, Center for Reformation Research, [1982]. 390p. **DC9**

Offers 16 surveys by American and English scholars on as many subjects in Reformation history (e.g., Martin Luther; pamphlet literature of the German Reformation; social history). Designed to assess the present state of research on a topic, to indicate key issues requiring scholarly investigation, and to identify research collections for a given subject. Bibliography for each essay.
BR305.2.R39

Current

Archiv für Reformationsgeschichte. Beiheft: Literaturbericht, v.1– . Gütersloh, G. Mohn, 1972– . Annual.
DC10

Added title page: Archive for Reformation history, an international journal concerned with the history of the Reformation and its significance in world affairs. Supplement: Literature review.

Published under the auspices of the Verein für Reformationsgeschichte and the American Society for Reformation Research.

A selective bibliography of books, collections of essays, and periodical articles arranged topically or by geographic area. Brief abstracts; no index. Z7830.A7

Guides to records

Carter, Charles Howard. The Western European powers, 1500–1700. Ithaca, N.Y., Cornell Univ. Pr.; London, Hodder & Stoughton, 1971. 347p. (The sources of history: studies in the uses of historical evidence) **DC11**

Discusses "sources of diplomatic origin and the sources of diplomatic history" in collections and repositories, their nature and use. Four countries are principally used as examples: Spain, France, England, Spanish Netherlands. Z6204.C34

Guide international des archives: Europe. Rome, Annales Institutorum, 1934. 3v. facsims. (Bibliothèque des "Annales Institutorum," v.4) (Repr.: Zug, Switz., I.D.C. 1975. 10 microfiches) **DC12**

At head of title: v.1, Société des Nations. Institut International de Coopération Intellectuelle; v.2–3, Comité des Annales Institutorum Urbis Romae.

Contents: v.1, Guide; v.2, Tables et documents; v.3, Supplément: S. Pistolese, Les archives européennes du onzième siècle a nos jours, essai historique et juridique.

v.1, the *Guide,* is arranged alphabetically by country, describing the nature and extent of its archives, facilities of use, etc., and sometimes including bibliographies of inventories, catalogs, etc.

A supplement by Robert Henri Bautier appeared in *Journal of documentation,* v.9, Mar. 1953. CD1001.G8

Thomas, Daniel H. and **Case, Lynn M.** The new guide to the diplomatic archives of Western Europe. [Philadelphia], Univ. of Pennsylvania Pr., [1975]. 441p. **DC13**

1st ed. 1959.

21 chapters, each by a specialist, describe the diplomatic archives of 18 countries and 3 international collections. For each, gives an account of the history, content, administration, and conditions of use of the collections, and usually a bibliography. Subject index. Chapters on Finland, Greece, and Luxembourg have been added in this revised and updated edition, and there are new subsections for the International Labour Organisation and the International Telecommunication Union. CD1001.T4

Library resources

Dillon, Kenneth J. Scholars' guide to Washington, D.C. for Central and East European studies: Albania, Austria, Bulgaria, Czechoslovakia, Germany (FRG & GDR), Greece (Ancient & Modern), Hungary, Poland, Romania, Switzerland, Yugoslavia. Wash., Smithsonian Inst. Pr., 1980. 329p. (Scholars' guide to Washington, D.C., no.5) **DC14**

Publ. for the Woodrow Wilson International Center for Scholars. Like other volumes in the series this is intended as a "descriptive and evaluative survey of research resources" (*Introd.*) and is presented in two parts: (1) collections (offering information on libraries, archives, databanks, etc.) and (2) organizations which deal with Central and Eastern Europe and are potential sources of information or assistance to researchers. Indexed. Z2483.D54

Pitschmann, Louis A. Scholar's guide to Washington, D.C. for northwest European studies. Wash., Smithsonian Inst. Pr., 1984. 436p. (Scholar's guide to Washington, D.C., no.10) **DC15**

Concerned with Belgium, Denmark, Finland, Great Britain, Greenland, Iceland, Ireland, Luxembourg, The Netherlands, Norway, Sweden. Like the other guides in the series sponsored by the Woodrow Wilson International Center for Scholars, it lists and describes collections (libraries, archives, museums, etc.) and organizations (research centers, academic programs, government agencies, associations, etc.) which have resources or provide services to scholars. Z2551.P57

Handbooks and histories

Cambridge economic history of Europe; general editors, J. H. Clapham and Eileen Power. Cambridge, Cambridge Univ. Pr., 1941–78. 7v. **DC16**

Edition note varies. Some volumes have title *Cambridge economic history.*

Contents: v.1, The agrarian life of the Middle Ages, ed. by M. M. Postan (2d ed. 1966); v.2, Trade and industry in the Middle Ages, ed. by M. M. Postan and E. E. Rich (1952); v.3, Economic organization and policies in the Middle Ages, ed. by M. M. Postan, E. E. Rich, and E. Miller (1965); v.4, The economy of expanding Europe in the 16th and 17th centuries, ed. by E. E. Rich and C. H. Wilson (1967); v.5, The economic organization of early modern Europe, ed. by E. E. Rich and C. H. Wilson (1977); v.6, The industrial revolutions and after: incomes, population and technological change, ed. by H. H. Habakkuk and M. M. Postan (1965. 2v.); v.7, The industrial economies: capital, labour and enterprise, ed. by Peter Mathias and M. M. Postan: pt.1, Britain, France, Germany and Scandinavia; pt.2, The United States, Japan and Russia (1977–78. 2v.). HC240.C312

Chandler, David G. Dictionary of the Napoleonic Wars. N.Y., Macmillan, [1979]. 570p. il., maps. **DC17**

A dictionary arrangement of articles on the battles, persons, places, and events relating to the Napoleonic Wars. Chronologies of the various campaigns are appended. Bibliography, p.558–70.
DC147.C47

Palmer, Alan. An encyclopedia of Napoleon's Europe. London, Weidenfeld and Nicolson; N.Y., St. Martin's, [1984]. 300p. il., maps. **DC18**

Offers entries for leading political, military, and literary institutions, events, and people in all countries of Europe during the 1797–1815 period. General headings for social, economic and religious themes. Brief bibliography (p.299–300). DC147.P34

Williams, E. Neville. The Facts on File dictionary of European history, 1485–1789. N.Y., Facts on File, [1980]. 509p.
DC19

Also published as *The Penguin dictionary of English and European history.*

Offers entries on important personalities and topics (but not themes). Aims to "follow the mainstream of political history without diverging too far into economic history, cultural history, and so on."—*Pref.* Cross references; general subject index; no bibliographies.   D231.W54

Zophy, Jonathan W. The Holy Roman Empire: a dictionary handbook. Westport, Conn., Greenwood Pr., [1980]. 551p.
                                                                              DC20

Offers signed articles with bibliographies on persons, places, terms, documents, etc., relating to the Holy Roman Empire "from the time of Charlemagne to the Napoleonic dissolution in 1806."—*Introd.* Emphasis is on biographical entries. Cross references; index.
                                                                     DD84.Z66

EASTERN AND SOUTHEASTERN EUROPE

See also names of individual countries.

Bibliography

Akademiia Nauk SSSR. Fundamental'naia Biblioteka Obshchestvennykh Nauk. Sovetskoe slavianovedenie; literatura o zarubeshnykh slavianskikh stranakh na russkom iazyke, 1918–1960. Sost. I. A. Kaloeva. Moskva, 1963. 401p.
                                                                              DC21

A bibliography of Soviet publications in the Russian language in the field of Slavic studies in general and for countries outside the USSR. In addition to history and philology, it includes economics, law and state, and social structure, giving special attention to documentary materials and archival publications.   Z6207.S6A45

Byrnes, Robert Francis. Bibliography of American publications on East Central Europe, 1945–1957. Bloomington, Ind., 1958. 213p. (Indiana Univ. pubn. Slavic and East European ser., v.12; incorrectly numbered v.11)   **DC22**

Attempts to be a complete list of books and articles published in the United States from 1945 to 1957, with some from Canada, and also a few articles published by Americans in German, Dutch, and English journals.

Classified arrangement under country, with author index. "East Central Europe . . . in this book refers to Albania, Bulgaria, Czechoslovakia, Finland, Hungary, Poland, Rumania, Yugoslavia and the Baltic States . . . Estonia, Latvia and Lithuania; East Germany and Greece are not included. . . ."—*Pref.*

Continued by *American bibliography of Russian and East European studies* (DC39).   Z2483.B9

Horak, Stephan M. Russia, the USSR, and Eastern Europe; a bibliographic guide to English language publications, 1964–1974. Littleton, Colo., Libraries Unlimited, 1978. 488p.   **DC23**

"Although initially intended as a revision of the compiler's *Junior Slavica* [N.Y., 1968], a bibliography of basic English-language publications in the social sciences . . . , coverage has been broadened to include titles in literature, linguistics, and the fine arts."—*Introd.* Classed arrangement with author/title and subject indexes. Entries are annotated, with most of the annotations excerpted from reviews appearing in leading American and British journals of Slavic studies.   Z2483.H54

—— Russia, the USSR, and Eastern Europe: a bibliographic guide to English language publications, 1975–1980. Littleton, Colo., Libraries Unlimited, 1982. 279p.   **DC24**

Adds about 1,000 items, including a few 1974 publications not listed in the basic volume.

Horak is also the compiler of *The Soviet Union and Eastern Europe; a bibliographic guide to recommended books for small and medium-sized libraries and school media centers* (Littleton, Colo., Libraries Unlimited, 1985. 373p.).   Z2483.H54 Suppl.

Horecky, Paul Louis, ed. East Central Europe; a guide to basic publications. Chicago, Univ. of Chicago Pr., [1969]. 956p.   **DC25**

Intended as "a highly selective and judiciously evaluated inventory of the most important publications" (*Pref.*) relating to the area. The bibliography is presented in six main sections: (1) a bibliographical overview of the area; (2) Czechoslovakia; (3) East Germany; (4) Hungary; (5) Poland; and (6) Sorbians (Lusatians) and Polabians. For each of the four countries represented there are sections for general reference aids and bibliographies, the land, the people, history, the state, the economy, the society, and intellectual and cultural life. Entries are annotated; each subsection is the work of one or more area specialists.   Z2483.H56

—— Southeastern Europe; a guide to basic publications. Chicago, Univ. of Chicago Pr., [1969]. 755p.   **DC26**

Together with its companion volume for East Central Europe (above), the bibliography was prepared by a Subcommittee on East Central and Southeast European Studies appointed by the Joint Committee on Slavic Studies of the American Council of Learned Societies and the Social Science Research Council.

A bibliographical overview of the area is followed by separate sections for Albania, Bulgaria, Greece, Romania, and Yugoslavia. Each section is further subdivided as: general reference aids and bibliographies; general and descriptive works; the land; the people; history; the state; the economy; the society; intellectual and cultural life. Subsections comprise annotated bibliographies contributed by area specialists. More than 3,000 items. Detailed index.
                                                                     Z2831.H67

Hundert, Gershon David and **Bacon, Gershon C.** The Jews in Poland and Russia; bibliographical essays. Bloomington, Indiana Univ. Pr., [1984]. 276p.   **DC27**

Offers two bibliographical essays, "The Jews in Poland-Lithuania from the twelfth century to the first partition," and "East European Jewry from the first partition of Poland to the present"; each essay ends with a bibliography of books, articles, and published documents cited in the text.   Z6373.P7H86

Hunter, Brian. Soviet-Yugoslav relations, 1948–1972; a bibliography of Soviet, Western and Yugoslav comment and analysis. N.Y., Garland, 1976. 223p. (Garland reference library in social science, v.18)   **DC28**

In three sections: (1) The Soviet view; (2) The Western view; (3) The Yugoslav view. Arrangement is chronological within sections. Author, subject, and periodical indexes. Many brief descriptive notes.   Z2517.R4H85

Kanet, Roger E. Soviet & East European foreign policy; a bibliography of English- & Russian-language publications 1967–1971. Santa Barbara, Calif., ABC-Clio, [1974]. 208p.
                                                                              DC29

An author listing of more than 3,200 items (books and periodical articles), with subject index. "The selection of items for this bibliography is as inclusive as possible and all non-Soviet items published in English noted by the editor are included. All of the Russian-language and Soviet-published English materials that concern Soviet or East European foreign policy directly have been included. In addition, there is a selection of Soviet books and articles which deal primarily with such general topics as developing countries and imperialism and also concern Soviet or East European foreign policy."—*Pref.* Russian-language titles are given in transliteration, with a translation supplied in brackets. Not annotated.
                                                                     Z2510.K3

Magocsi, Paul Robert. Galicia: a historical survey and bibliographic guide. Toronto, Publ. in assoc. with the Canadian Inst. of Ukrainian Studies and the Harvard Ukrainian Research Inst. by Univ. of Toronto Pr., [1983]. 299p. maps.
                                                                              DC30

" . . . intended to serve as an introduction to the basic historical problems of Galicia and to direct the reader to the major published primary and secondary sources dealing with those problems."—*Introd.* Bibliographic essays (arranged by period) treat some 3,000 items on political, socioeconomic, and literary matters.

DK511.G14M34

Meyer, Klaus. Bibliographie zur osteuropäischen Geschichte. Verzeichnis der zwischen 1939 und 1964 veröffentlichten Literatur in westeuropäischen Sprachen zur osteuropäischen Geschichte bis 1945. Berlin, Wiesbaden, O. Harrassowitz, 1972. 434p. (Bibliographische Mitteilungen des Osteuropa-Instituts an der Freien Universität Berlin, Heft 10) **DC31**

More than 12,000 entries (books, periodical articles, monographs) arranged by topic, with name index. Lists publications in many languages on Eastern Europe, including Baltic Republics, Finland, and Poland.

Continued by: Z2483.M43

Schmidt, Christian D. Bibliographie zur osteuropäischen Geschichte: Verzeichnis der zwischen 1965 und 1974 veröffentlichten Literatur in westeuropäischen Sprachen zur osteuropäischen Geschichte bis 1945. Wiesbaden, Harrassowitz, 1983. 1059p. (Bibliographische Mitteilungen des Osteuropa-Instituts an der Freien Universität Berlin, 22) **DC32**

Added title page in English: Bibliography of Russian and East European history: list of books published between 1965 and 1974 in Western European languages on Russian and East European history to 1945.

An extensive bibliography of almost 18,000 books, essays, articles relating to Russia and the Soviet Union, Poland, Finland, and the Baltic States. Geographical arrangement with many subdivisions. Author index. Z2483.S34

Nowak, Chester Michael. Czechoslovak-Polish relations, 1918–1939: a selected and annotated bibliography. Stanford, Hoover Inst. Pr., 1976. 219p. (Hoover Inst. bibliographical ser., 55) **DC33**

Based on the author's thesis, Boston Univ., 1971.

Offers an "annotated selection of books, pamphlets, articles, and press reports necessary, or useful, for the study of Czechoslovak-Polish relations during 1918–1939 . . . [including] some basic materials showing Polish-Czech contacts during the years 1914–1918."
—*Introd.* Name index. Z2138.R4N68

Remington, Robin Alison. The international relations of Eastern Europe; a guide to information sources. Detroit, Gale, [1978]. 273p. **DC34**

An annotated bibliography for students, listing books, essays and articles published through about 1975. A general chapter on the region is followed by sections on Albania, Bulgaria, Czechoslovakia, East Germany, Hungary, Poland, Romania, and Yugoslavia. Title and subject indexes. Z6465.E853R45

Südosteuropa-Bibliographie . . . München, Oldenbourg, 1956–76. v.1–5. (In progress?) **DC35**

Contents: Bd.1, 1945–50: T.1, Slowakei, Rumänien, Bulgarien. T.2, Jugoslawien, Ungarn, Albanien, Südosteuropa und grössere Räume; Bd.2, 1951–55: T.1, Südosteuropa und grössere Teilräume, Jugoslawien, Ungarn. T.2, Albanien, Bulgarien, Rumänien, Slowakei; Bd.3, 1956–60: T.1, Slowakei, Ungarn, Rumänien. T.2, Albanien, Bulgarien, Jugoslawien, Südosteuropa allgemeine; Bd.4, 1961–65: T.1, Südosteuropa und grössere Teilräume, Ungarn, Rumänien, Slowakei; T.2, Albanien, Bulgarien, Jugoslawien; Bd.5, 1966–70: T.1, Südosteuropa und grössere Teilräume, Rumänien, Ungarn, Slowakei; T.2, Albanien, Bulgarien, Jugoslawien.

Arranged by country, then divided by topic. Includes periodical articles as well as books. Z2831.S8

Thomson, Erik. Baltische Bibliographie, 1945–1956. Würzburg, Holzner-Verlag, 1957. 218p. (Ostdeutsche Beiträge aus dem Göttinger Arbeitskreis. Bd.5) (Der Göttinger Arbeitskreis: Veröffentlichung Nr. 173) **DC35a**

In two principal sections, one listing books and society publications by authors of the German Baltic region; the other, works about the area. Each list classified by subject.

Supplemented by: Z2531.T5

Baltische Bibliographie 1957–1961 und Nachträge 1945–1956. Würzburg, Holzner-Verlag, 1962. 115p. (Ostdeutsche Beiträge aus dem Göttinger Arbeitskreis, Bd. 23; Der Göttinger Arbeitskreis: Veröffentlichung 269) **DC35b**

Zeps, Valdis J. Baltica in microform. Madison, Wis., Assoc. for the Advancement of Baltic Studies, 1981. 36*l*. **DC36**

A main-entry listing of 950 titles of interest to scholars concerned with the Baltic countries and available on microfilm. One location is indicated for each title.

The Association has also issued Zeps's *Lettica in microform; a subject guide* (1982. 33p.).

Current

ABSEES; Soviet and East European abstract series. v.1, no.1– , July 1970– . Glasgow, Scot., Univ. of Glasgow, Inst. of Soviet and East European Studies, 1970– . 3 issues per yr. **DC37**

Publisher varies; frequency varies.

v.1–7 ed. and publ. on behalf of the National Association for Soviet and East European Studies; v.8– sponsored by the National Association for Soviet and East European Studies in collaboration with the Centre for Russian and East European Studies, University of Birmingham.

Replaces the former "Information supplement" to the journal *Soviet studies.* 1971–74 included "Soviet, East European, and Slavonic Studies in Britain," now covered in DC42. Covers the USSR, Albania, Bulgaria, Czechoslovakia, East Germany, Hungary, Poland, Romania, and Yugoslavia, providing abstracts of periodical and newspaper articles and books on these areas. Classed arrangement within country divisions. Each issue includes a select bibliography on a specific topic (e.g., April 1974 contains "Government policy and the economic system of East Germany, 1967–1973; a selected bibliography").

Beginning with v.8 each number is issued as a printed pamphlet which includes microfiche in pockets interleaved with printed pages. Arrangement and coverage are much the same in the new format, i.e., classed listing within country divisions for citations to periodical and newspaper articles. Each citation is followed by a very brief abstract; for most citations a longer abstract appears on the accompanying microfiche. The latter abstracts are very full, even reproducing statistical tables from the articles; occasionally the entire text is reproduced. Topical index for each issue.

Abstracts of Soviet and East European émigré periodical literature. [v.1, no.] 1– . [Pacific Grove, Calif.], Abst. of Soviet and E. Eur. Émigré Periodical Lit., [1981]– . Quarterly. **DC38**

Also called *ASEEPL.*

Provides abstracts of articles originating in 50 to 75 Russian- and East European-language newspapers and periodicals published in the United States, Western Europe, and Israel, including such titles as *Novaia zhizn', Novoe russkoe slovo,* and *Russkaia mysl'.* Broad subject arrangement, with subject and author indexes.

American bibliography of Russian and East European studies, 1956–66. Bloomington, Indiana Univ., 1957–67. Annual. (Indiana Univ. pubn. Russian and East European ser., v.9–10, 18, 21, 26, 27, 29, 32, 34, 37, 40) **DC39**

Title varies: 1956, *The American bibliography of Slavic and East European studies in language, literature, folklore and pedagogy;* 1957–59, *The American bibliography of Slavic and East European studies.*

An interdisciplinary annual bibliography of books and articles, mainly of American authorship.

Superseded by: Z2483.A65

American bibliography of Slavic and East European studies, 1967– . [Columbus], Ohio State Univ. Pr., 1972– . Annual. **DC39a**

Continues the above.
Includes book reviews.   Z2483.A65

Bibliographic guide to Soviet and East European studies.
1978– . Boston, G. K. Hall, 1979– . Annual.   **DC40**

Represents materials cataloged by the New York Public Library
and the Library of Congress from Sept. of the previous year through
Aug. of the year of coverage. Includes all book and non-book
materials published in or dealing with any East European country or
the Soviet Union, together with any materials written in an East
European, Baltic, or Slavonic language. A dictionary catalog with
full information only under main entry.   Z2483.B48

**Canadian publications on the Soviet Union and Eastern
Europe,** 1975– . (*In* Canadian Slavonic papers, v.19– ,
1977– ; Dec. issue) Annual.   **DC41**

**European bibliography of Soviet, East European and Slavonic
studies.** v.1– , 1975– . Birmingham, Eng., Univ. of Birmingham, 1977– . Annual.   **DC42**

Title and prefatory matter also in French and German.
Incorporates "Travaux et publications parus en français . . . sur la
Russie et l'URSS" (publ. in *Cahiers du monde russe et soviétique*)
and "Soviet, East European and Slavonic studies in Britain" (publ.
in *ABSEES: Soviet and East European abstracts series*; DC37).
A comprehensive annual bibliography of books, essays, and periodical articles, together with references to major articles in British
newspapers on Russia and the eight countries of Eastern Europe.
Strong coverage in the social sciences and humanities; "materials
relating to science and technology included only where relevant to
political, economic and social life."—*Introd.* A topically arranged
general section is followed by geographical sections also subdivided
by topic. Name index.

Reference books of 1972/73– . Stanford, Calif., 1974– .
Annual. (*In* Slavic review, Sept. or Fall issue)   **DC43**

An annual listing of 20 to 30 major new reference works dealing
with Russia or Eastern Europe, with signed, evaluative annotations
written by librarians at the Slavic and East European Library,
University of Illinois at Urbana-Champaign.

Sovetskoe slavianovedenie . . . 1961/62–78/82. Sost. I. A.
Kaloeva. Moskva, Akad. Nauk SSSR, Obshchestvennykh
Nauk, Institut Nauchnoi Informatsii, 1973–83. (In progress)
                                                        DC44

Continues *Sovetskoe slavianovedenie* (DC21).
Volumes covering 1961–62 through 1978–82 have been issued in
seven parts per volume.   Z6207.S6A45

Zalewski, Wojciech. Reference materials in Russian-Soviet
area studies, 1973– . Stanford, Calif., 1975– . Annual. (*In*
Russian review, Apr. issue)   **DC45**

Each annual article is a bibliographic essay on major new reference works published in any Western language or in Russian dealing
with the Soviet Union or pre-Revolutionary Russia.

Library catalogs

Harvard University. Library. Slavic history and literatures.
Cambridge, Mass., publ. by Harvard Univ. Lib.; distr. by
Harvard Univ. Pr., 1971. 4v. (Widener Library shelflist,
28–31)   **DC46**

Contents: v.1, Classification schedule; Classified listing by call
number; v.2, Chronological listing; v.3–4, Author and title listing.
Includes "the classes *Slav, PSlav,* and *Slav Doc,* which treat the
history and literatures of the U.S.S.R. and its component states
(except the history of the Baltic states and Armenia, and related
literatures) and of Poland, Czechoslovakia, Yugoslavia and Bulgaria.
In all, approximately 120,000 titles are represented."—*Pref.*
For a note on the series *see* AA145.   Z5118.S6H35

Johann Gottfried Herder-Institut, Marburg. Bibliothek. Alphabetischer Katalog. Boston, G. K. Hall, 1964. 5v.
                                                        DC47

The Library's holdings "cover East Central Europe, the territory
itself; the inhabitants and all their activities through the course of
history, from prehistoric times to the present; and all aspects of
cultural life—law, government, economics, religion and church, art
and literature."—*Foreword.* Photoreproduction from catalog cards.
Chiefly main entries, with some subject cards.   Z2483.J6

——— ——— First–second supplement. Boston, G. K.
Hall, 1971–81. 5v.

Suppl.1 covers new material cataloged through 1970, including a
gift of a specialized library on Polish and Baltic history. The second
supplement adds acquisitions from 1971–77.

New York. Public Library. Slavonic Division. Dictionary
catalog of the Slavonic collection. . . . 2d ed., rev. and enl.
Boston, G. K. Hall, 1974. 44v.   **DC48**

1st ed. 1959.
A photographic reproduction of the catalog cards for Slavic and
Baltic materials, and for materials in other languages on these areas
published through 1971. The basic collection in literature and social
science was augmented later by science and technology titles. The
724,000-entry catalog is notable for analytics and references to
periodical articles. Transliteration differs from the Library of Congress system.
Supplemented by *Bibliographic guide to Soviet and East European
studies* (DC40).   Z881.N59

Dissertations

Scherer, Anton. Südosteuropa-Dissertationen, 1918–1960.
Eine Bibliographie deutscher, österreichischer und schweizerischer Hochschulschriften. Graz, Hermann Böhlau,
1968. 221p.   **DC49**

Dissertations on the political, social, and cultural history of
southeastern European countries are listed in topical groups within
country sections. Author index.   Z2831.S3

Periodicals

Birkos, Alexander S. and **Tambs, Lewis A.** East European
and Slavic studies. [Kent, Ohio], Kent State Univ. Pr.,
[1973] 572p. (Academic writer's guide to periodicals, 2)
                                                        DC50

For a note on the series *see* AE18.   Z2483.B56

Hoskins, Janina W. The USSR and East Central and
Southeastern Europe: periodicals in Western languages. 4th
ed. rev. Wash., Library of Congress, 1979. 87p.   **DC51**

1st ed. 1958.
This edition includes currently published Western-language journals in the social sciences and humanities, grouped by area or by
country of Eastern Europe. Annotations; subscription information
is given as available. Also includes a very selective list of journals
which have ceased publication but which are of continuing research
value. Title and sponsoring body index.   Z2483.H63

Library resources

See also DC14.

Budurowycz, Bohdan. Slavic and East European resources in
Canadian academic and research libraries. Ottawa, Collec-
tions Development Branch, Resources Survey Division,
Nat. Lib. of Canada, 1976. 595p. (Research collections in
Canadian libraries, II: Special studies, no.4)   **DC52**

A survey of 67 Canadian libraries, reporting for each the extent
and nature of the collections of printed materials, microforms, and
manuscripts in whatever language originating in or dealing with the
following countries: Albania, Bulgaria, Czechoslovakia, Hungary,
Poland, Romania, the USSR (including Estonia, Latvia and Lithuania), and Yugoslavia. Extensive index.

East Central and Southeast Europe, a handbook of library and archival resources in North America. Paul L. Horecky, chief ed. Santa Barbara, Calif., Clio Pr., 1976. 466p. (Joint Committee on Eastern Europe. Pubn. ser., no.3)   **DC53**

A survey of "the essential collections available in major libraries, archives, and research institutions in the U.S. and Canada, . . . outlining the profiles of these collections and offering broad guidance to their subject and area contents. The focus is on the humanities and the socioeconomic and political sciences."— *Foreword.* Forty-three institutions are described; there is a geographical breakdown within each entry. Area and subject index.

A careful review by Patricia Grimsted appears in *Slavic review* 37:146–48 (Mar. 1978).   Z2483.E2

Hoover Institution on War, Revolution, and Peace. Russia, the Soviet Union, and Eastern Europe; a survey of holdings at the Hoover Institution. . . . Ed. by Joseph D. Dwyer. Stanford, Hoover Inst. Pr., 1980. 233p. (Hoover Press survey, 6)   **DC54**

A survey of Hoover holdings, published and unpublished, on each of the Central (including the Balkan states and Greece) and East European countries. Not indexed.   Z2491.R57

Lewanski, Richard C. Eastern Europe and Russia/Soviet Union: a handbook of West European archival and library resources. N.Y., [etc.], K. G. Saur, 1980. 317p.   **DC55**

For full information *see* AB113.

Resources for Soviet, East European and Slavonic studies in British libraries. Ed. by Gregory Walker. Birmingham, 1981. 240p.   **DC56**

At head of title: University of Birmingham, Centre for Russian and East European Studies.

Intended as a replacement for Crosby Lockwood's *Directory of libraries and special collections on Eastern Europe and the USSR* (1971). Aims "to record library collections in the United Kingdom to be of use for advanced study or research, and to describe their contents in sufficient detail for the enquirer to make an informed choice among the resources available."—*Introd.* Arranged by city, then by repository; indexed. Treats 104 libraries.   Z2483.R47

Dictionaries and handbooks

Istoriki-slavisty SSSR: biobibliograficheskii slovar—spravochnik. Moskva, Izd-vo "Nauka," 1981. 205p.   **DC57**

At head of title: Akademiia Nauk SSSR. Nauchnyi Sovet po Kompleksym Problemam Slavianovedeniia i Balkanistiki. Institut Slavianovedeniia i Balkanistiki.

Comp. by S. I. Sidelnikov and others.

A dictionary of 20th century Russian scholars (living or deceased) whose specialty was any Slavic country. Gives academic or other affiliation, dissertation subject, and most important publications. Indexes of names and of organizations/institutions. Includes a survey of the development of Slavic studies in Russia.   Z2483.I84

Language and area studies: East central and southeastern Europe; a survey. Ed. by Charles Jelavich. Chicago, Univ. of Chicago Pr., [1969]. 483p.   **DC58**

Prep. by a Subcommittee on East Central and Southeast European Studies appointed by the Joint Committee on Slavic Studies of the American Council of Learned Societies and the Social Science Research Council.

Two chapters devoted to graduate training and undergraduate instruction in the pertinent areas are followed by 15 essays on as many social science and humanities disciplines (history, political science, literature, linguistics, etc.); each examines the state of American scholarship and gives a brief account of its development, its recent achievements and present needs, suggestions for new areas of research, and an evaluation of graduate training, and recommendations for its improvement and expansion.

Serves as a companion to Horecky's bibliographical guides to the two areas (DC25–DC26).   DR34.8.L33

Slavianovedenie v dorevoliutsionnoi Rossii: biobibliograficheskii slovar'. [Otv. red. V. A. Diakov] Moskva, Nauka, 1979. 426p.   **DC59**

At head of title: Akademiia Nauk SSSR. Institut Slavianovedeniia i Balkanistiki.

A biobibliography of pre-Revolutionary Russian scholars in the fields of history, archaeology, ethnography, literature, linguistics, paleography, and art of Slavic countries. Indexed.   Z2483.S55

Soviet Union and Eastern Europe; a handbook. Ed. by George Schöpflin. N.Y., Praeger, [1970]. 714p.   **DC60**

Specialists have contributed chapters on the political, economic, social, and cultural conditions of the Soviet Union and the Communist-ruled countries of Europe. Similar to John Calmann's *Western Europe* (N.Y., Praeger, 1967. 697p.); now considerably out of date.   DK17.S64

Südosteuropa-Handbuch. Hrsg. Klaus-Detlev Grothusen in Verbindung mit dem Südosteuropa-Arbeitskreis der Deutschen Forschungsgemeinschaft. Göttingen, Vandenhoeck u. Ruprecht, 1975–80. v.1–3. (In progress)   **DC61**

Contents: Bd.1, Jugoslawien; Bd.2, Rumänien; BD.3, Griechenland.

Title also in English: *Handbook on South Eastern Europe.*

Articles contributed by authorities from Germany, the United States, Yugoslavia, etc., survey the political and legal structure, the economic system, social and cultural life. Each volume includes an extensive bibliography and a brief biographical dictionary of contemporary politicians of the country.

Atlases

Adams, Arthur E., Matley, Ian M. and **McCagg, William O.** An atlas of Russian and East European history. N.Y., Praeger, [1967]. 204p. 21cm.   **DC62**

Small black-and-white maps with accompanying text.   G2111.S1A2

The Balkans
Bibliography

Bengescu, George. Essai d'une notice bibliographique sur la question d'Orient: Orient européen, 1821–1897. Paris, Le Soudier, 1897. 327p.   **DC63**

Lists more than 2,100 separate works—historical, political, and military—on the Balkans, published in France and Belgium from 1821 to 1897. Arranged chronologically, with author index and index to anonymous works.   Z6464.E1B4

Nationalism in the Balkans; an annotated bibliography. [Ed. by] Gale Stokes. N.Y., Garland, 1984. 243p. (Canadian review of studies in nationalism, v.3; Garland reference library of social science, v.160)   **DC64**

A reissue, with some updating, of bibliographies originally published as research aids for scholars in the *Canadian review of studies in nationalism.* Covers post-World War II literature relating to the nationalism of a country or a national group (with countries defined according to present-day political boundaries). There are annotated bibliographies for Greece, Romania, Bulgaria, and Yugoslavia (plus seven additional chapters for ethnic groups within Yugoslavia). Books, articles, and theses in all languages are listed; author index.   Z2846.N37

Répertoire d'études balkaniques, 1966–1975 [sous la direction de N. Todorov et al.]. Sofia, Éditions de l'Académie Bulgare des Sciences, 1983–84. v.1–2. (In progress)   **DC65**

Contents: v.1, Histoire des peuples balkaniques (XVᵉ s.–1945); v.2, Histoire de la culture des peuples balkaniques.

Derived from issues of the *Bibliographie d'études balkaniques, 1966–75* (DC68), this is a topical listing of books and articles in any language on all countries of the Balkans, including Greece and Turkey in Europe. Personal and geographic name indexes in Roman letters are followed by indexes in the Cyrillic alphabet.

v.1 concentrates on economic and political history, including social aspects; v.2 covers culture and ideas—literature, art, education, printing, ethnography and folklore. **Z2846.R46**

Savadjian, Léon. Bibliographie balkanique, 1920–38. Paris, Revue des Balkans, 1931; Soc. Générale d'Impr. et d'Édit., 1933–39. **DC66**

[v.1], 1920–30 (publ. 1931. 270p); [v.2], 1931–32 (publ. 1933. 151p.); [v.3], 1933–38, annual.

1920–30 issued as *Revue des Balkans*, n.s., v.2–3, av.– sept. 1931.

Contains material concerning Albania, Bulgaria, Greece, Romania, Turkey, and Yugoslavia in French, German, Italian, and English. **Z2831.S26**

Terry, Garth M. A bibliography of Macedonian studies. Nottingham, Nottingham Univ. Lib., 1975. 121p. **DC67**

A classed bibliography of more than 1,600 items. Name index. Macedonia is considered to be "historic Macedonia (i.e., the pre-1912 area), Yugoslav or Vardar Macedonia (1913–1944), or the Socialist People's Republic of Macedonia."—*Introd.* Includes a brief section on Pirin and Aegean Macedonia (post-1912).
Z2957.M3T47

Current

Bibliographie d'études balkaniques. v.1– , 1966– . Sofia, Bulgarska Akademiia na Naukite, Institut za Balkanistika, 1968– . Annual. **DC68**

At head of title: Académie bulgare des sciences. Institut d'études balkaniques "Ludmila Jivkova." Centre d'information et de documentation balkaniques.

An extensive bibliography, international in scope, covering the history, culture, language, folklore, and ethnography of the people and countries of the Balkans (including Cyprus, Greece and Western Turkey). Originally in classified arrangement with personal name, geographic name, and subject indexes; beginning with v.8 (1973) arranged alphabetically by topic with personal name and geographic name indexes. Historical period covered was originally from the mid-14th century; with v.13 (1978) the beginning point is the 7th century. **Z2831.B5**

Valkanikē vivliographia. v.1– , 1973– . Thessalonike, Hidryma Meletōn Chersonēsou tou Haimou, 1973– . Annual. **DC69**

Added title page in English: Balkan bibliography.

A bibliography of books, articles, and reviews in any of the Balkan languages, Russian, or any of the "main" western languages concerning the Balkans from the fall of the Byzantine Empire to the end of World War II. Arranged under eight major headings, with various subdivisions; name index. With v.6 the coverage of Greek periodicals is increased, and English translations of titles are added to the entries.

With each volume is issued a separately published supplement of studies (primarily bibliographical) and translations by the Institute's associates. **Z2831.V34**

ALBANIA

Hetzer, Armin and **Roman, Viorel S.** Albanien, ein bibliographischer Forschungsbericht mit Titelübersetzungen und Standortnachweisen. Albania, a bibliographic research survey with location codes. München, K. G. Saur, 1983. 653p. (Bibliographien zur regionalen Geographie und Landeskunde, 3) **DC70**

Introductory matter, chapter notes, and headings in German and English.

A classed bibliography with sections for general works, history (including politics), law, and business and economics. International coverage; includes books, periodical articles, pamphlets, official documents. Cutoff date is mainly 1980. Author index; detailed table of contents, but no subject index.

Parts of a supplementary bibliography by Hetzer were published 1980 as *Arbeitsmaterialien zu einer Landesbibliographie, Albanien; Geschichte, Politik, Recht, Wirtschaft, in sechs Heften* (Bremen, Univ. Bremen, Bibliothek, Abteilung Jura. 4 Heft, Recht; 5 Heft, Wirtschaft). **Z2854.A5H47**

Jubani, Bep. Bibliografi e arkeologjisë dhe historisë së lashtë të shqipërisë (1945–1971). Tiranë, 1972. 222p. **DC71**

At head of title: Universiteti i Tiranës. Instituti i Historisë. Sektori i Arkeologjisë e Historisë Lashtë të Shqipërisë.

Added title page in French: Bibliographie de l'archéologie et de l'histoire antique de l'Albanie.

Introduction in Albanian and French.

An annotated author listing of about 700 items. Entries are first given in the original language, with annotations in Albanian, then repeated in a second section with titles translated into French and with annotations in French.

ARMENIA

Avakian, Anne M. Armenia and the Armenians in academic dissertations. Berkeley, Calif., Professional Pr., [1974]. 38p. **DC72**

An author listing of some 260 dissertations and master's essays completed through 1972 at foreign as well as American universities. Topical index. **Z3461.A85**

Nersessian, V. An index of articles on Armenian studies in Western journals. London, Luzac, [1976]. 95p. **DC73**

A classed bibliography without index. Includes religion and theology, history, numismatics, mythology and folklore, palaeography, philology and linguistics, and the arts. **Z3461.N5**

Salmaslian, Armenag. Bibliographie de l'Arménie. Nouv. éd. entièrement rev. et considérablement augm. Erévan, Éditions de l'Académie des Sciences de la R.S.S. de l'Arménie, 1969. 468p. **DC74**

At head of title: Académie des Sciences de la R.S.S. de l'Arménie. Bibliothèque Fondamentale.

1st ed. 1946.

A classed list, with author index, of works published on Armenia from the 16th century to 1959. Includes material in French, German, English, and some other European languages. Periodical articles are included in this edition. **Z3461.S2**

AUSTRIA

See also Germany.

Bibliography

Alfoldi, Laszlo M. The armies of Austria-Hungary and Germany, 1740–1914. Carlisle Barracks, Pa., U.S. Army Military History Research Collection, 1975. 277p. (Special bibliography, 12, v.1) **DC75**

A subject arrangement of "all works in English, German, Russian, Hungarian, and French on file in the Military Research Collection" (*Introd.*) which includes field manuals, contemporary accounts, histories, biographies, etc. Many brief annotations. Author index.
Z6725.G4A57

Behrmann, Lilly-Ralou, Proché, Peter and **Strasser, Wolfgang.** Bibliographie zur Aussenpolitik der Republik Österreich seit 1945. (Stand: 31. Dez. 1971). Wien, W. Braunmüller, 1974. 505p. (Schriftenreihe der österreichischen Gesellschaft für Aussenpolitik und internationale Beziehungen, Bd. 7)   **DC76**

Lists books, pamphlets, periodical articles, and essays in a chronological/topical arrangement with author index; country breakdown within chronological sections.

Bridge, F. R. The Hapsburg monarchy, 1804–1918; books and pamphlets published in the United Kingdom between 1918–1967; a critical bibliography. London, Univ. of London (School of Slavonic and East European Studies), [1967]. 82p.   **DC77**

An annotated bibliography of 649 books and pamphlets; broadly divided by period under "General history" and "Diplomatic and military history"; concluding section of biography and memoirs. Indexes of authors, persons, subjects.   Z2119.B7

Low, Alfred D. The Anschluss movement, 1918–1938: background and aftermath; an annotated bibliography of German and Austrian nationalism. N.Y., Garland, 1984. 186p. (Canadian review of studies in nationalism, v.4; Garland reference library of social science, v.151)   **DC78**

An annotated bibliography of books, pamphlets, Austrian and American academic theses, essays, and articles, together with a representative listing of Nazi propaganda materials. In three chronological sections: (1) Roots of the Anschluss movement 1848–1918; (2) The Anschluss movement, 1918–1938; (3) Allied occupation and the rebirth of the Austrian state and nation, 1945 to the present. In many copies the number eight must be added to the index number in order to find the correct page.   Z2120.L68

Malina, Peter and **Spann, Gustav.** Bibliographie zur osterreichischen Zeitgeschichte 1918–1978, eine Auswahl. Wien, Verlag für Geschichte und Politik, 1978. 70p. (Politische Bildung, 28–30)   **DC79**

A very selective, annotated bibliography of German-language books and a few periodical articles, most of them published after 1970. Sections for general bibliographies and handbooks on Austria, general histories of Austria for the period, histories of Austria for more specific periods, and specialized topics (e.g., foreign relations, neofascism, minorities). Author index.   Z2120.3.M34

Strassmayr, Eduard. Bibliographie zur oberösterreichischen Geschichte. Linz a. Donau, Winkler, 1929–57. v.1–4. (Bibliographie zur Geschichte, Landes- und Volkskunde Oesterreichs. 1.Abt.: Oberösterreich, Bd.1–4)   **DC80**

Contents: Bd.1, 1891–1926; Bd.2, 1927–1934; Bd.3, 1935–1948; Bd.4, 1949–1953.

Publisher varies. Bd.3–4 hrsg. vom Oberösterreichischen Landesarchiv.

Continued by: Z2124.A9S83

Bibliographie zur oberösterreichischen Geschichte, 1954/ 65– . Linz, Oberösterreichisches Landesarchiv, 1972– . [v.1–] (In progress)   **DC81**

Contents: [v.1] 1954/65, comp. by Alfred Marks (Wien, Bohlaus, 1972. 429p.); [v.2] 1966/75, comp. by Johannes Wunschheim (1980. 518p.); [v.3] 1976/80, comp. by Johannes Wunschheim (1982. 308p.).

Each volume is a topical listing of books, articles, and essays; includes a good biographical section. Name and subject indexes.

Uhlirz, Karl. Handbuch der Geschichte Österreichs und seiner Nachbarländer Böhmen und Ungarn. Bearb. von Mathilde Uhlirz. Graz, Leuschner und Lubensky, 1927–44. 4v.   **DC82**

A guide to research on the history of Austria, Bohemia, and Hungary, with extensive bibliographies.

A new edition has begun publication as: DB38.U4

—— Handbuch der Geschichte Österreich-Ungarns [von] Karl und Mathilde Uhlirz. 2. neubearb. Aufl. von Mathilde Uhlirz. Hrsg. von der Südostdeutschen Historischen Kom-

mission. Graz, In Kommission bei H. Böhlaus Nachf., 1963– . v.1– . (In progress)   **DC83**

Bd.1 covers to 1526.

Current

Österreichische historische Bibliographie. Austrian historical bibliography. [v.1–], 1965– . Santa Barbara, Calif., Clio Pr., [1968–]. Annual.   **DC84**

A classed bibliography of historical literature published in Austrian periodicals or by Austrian publishing houses, the bulk of the material relating to Austria. Author index.   Z2116.O48

—— Fünf-Jahres-Register . . . 1965/69–1975/79. Bearb. von Günther Hödl [et al.]. Salzburg, W. Neugebauer; Santa Barbara, Clio Pr., [1974–83]. 3v.

Z2116.O48

Paulhart, Herbert and **Paulhart, Hermine.** Österreichische historische Bibliographie: Liste der Zeitschriften 1945– 1979. . . . Salzburg, W. Neugebauer; Santa Barbara, Calif., Clio Pr., [1980]. 32p. (Osterreichische historische Bibliographie. Beiheft, 1)   **DC85**

Title also in English: *Austrian historical bibliography: list of periodicals 1945–1979.*

Gives title, place, issuing body, and volumes/years covered in the bibliography. 300 titles.   Z2120.3.P38

Dictionaries

Österreich-Lexikon. Hrsg. Richard Bamberger und Franz Maier-Bruck. Wien, Österreichischer Bundesverlag, [1966– 67]. 2v. (1320p.) il., maps.   **DC86**

Offers extensive coverage of topics relating to Austria during all periods. Short articles predominate, with about 100 long entries (e.g., Beethoven, Biedermeier, Kaffeehaus). Most entries include bibliographies.   DB14.O48

BELGIUM

Bibliography

Belder, J. de and **Hannes, J.** Bibliografie van de geschiedenis van België. Bibliographie de l'histoire de Belgique. 1865– 1914. Louvain, Nauwelaerts, 1965. 301p. (Centre Interuniversitaire d'Histoire Contemporaine. Cahiers, 38)   **DC87**

Continues the sequence begun with P. Gérin's bibliography for the period 1789–1831 (DC89) and that of S. Vervaeck (DC91) for 1831–65. Covers all aspects of Belgian history and follows the classed arrangement of the Gérin work.

Cosemans, A. and **Heyse, Th.** Contribution à la bibliographie dynastique et nationale. Bruxelles, van Campenhout, 1954–61. Pts.1–4. (Cahiers belges et congolais no.23–25, 27–30, 32–33, 35–36)   **DC88**

Title also in Flemish.

Contents: pt.1, Partie générale; pt.2, Règne de Léopold Ier (1831– 1865); pt.3, Règne de Léopold II (1865–1909); pt.4, Règne d'Albert (1909–1934).

A detailed classified bibliography of books and periodical articles covering Belgian history from the beginning of the present dynasty in 1831, through the reign of Albert I.   Z2416.C67

Gérin, Paul. Bibliographie de l'histoire de Belgique, 1789– 21 juillet 1831. Louvain, Éd. Nauwelaerts, 1960. 429p. (Centre Interuniversitaire d'Histoire Contemporaine. Cahiers, 15)   **DC89**

The first of a series of bibliographies on the history of Belgium since 1789 (*see* DC87 and DC91). Covers all phases of history: political, military, social, economic, religious, cultural, etc., with indexes by author and subject.

Complementary to D. Weerdt's *Bibliographie rétrospective des publications officielles de la Belgique, 1794–1914* (Louvain, 1963).

Pirenne, Henri. Bibliographie de l'histoire de Belgique; catalogue méthodique et chronologique des sources et des ouvrages principaux relatifs à l'histoire de tous les Pays-Bas jusqu'en 1598 et à l'histoire de Belgique jusqu'en 1914. 3. éd., rev. et compl. avec la collaboration de Henri Nowé et Henri Obreen. Bruxelles, Lamertin, 1931. 440p. (Repr.: Hildesheim, G. Olms, 1979) **DC90**

A revised and much enlarged edition of the standard bibliography of Belgian history, now listing 4,151 titles. Classed arrangement within two parts: Recueils et ouvrages généraux; Histoire par époques. Author index. Z2416.P67

Vervaeck, Solange. Bibliografie van de geschiedenis van België. Bibliographie de l'histoire de Belgique. 1831–1865. Louvain, Nauwelaerts, 1965. 303p. (Centre Interuniversitaire d'Histoire Contemporaine. Cahiers, 37) **DC91**

Continues the work begun by Paul Gérin (DC89) for the period 1789–1831, and follows the classed arrangement of that work. Continued by J. de Belder's volume (DC87) for the 1865–1914 period.

Wachter, Leo de. Repertorium van de Vlaamse gouwen en gemeenten. Heemkundige dokumentatie. Antwerpen, De Sikkel, 1942–57. 6v. **DC92**

Contents: v.1, Algemeen gedeelte en gewesten; v.2–4, Gemeenten, A–Z. Register; v.5–6, 1940–1950, Algemeen gedeelte en gewesten. Gemeenten A–Z. Register.

A bibliography of book and periodical material on Flemish local history. Indexes some 500 periodicals in various languages. Z2423.W3

Current

Bibliographie de l'histoire de Belgique. Bibliografie van de geschiedenis van Belgie, 1952– . (*In* Revue belge de philologie et d'histoire. v.31– , 1953–) Annual. **DC93**

Continues the series published in *Revue du nord*, 1947–49 in v.32; 1950 in v.33; 1951 in v.34 (publ. 1950–52). Item numbers run consecutively through both series.

Classified arrangement. No indexes to date.

Archives

Nicodème, Jacques. Répertoire des inventaires des archives conservées en Belgique, parus avant le 1ᵉʳ Janvier 1969. Bruxelles, [Commission Belge de Bibliographie], 1970. 121p. (Bibliographia belgica, 107; Archives et bibliothèques de Belgique. Numéro spécial, 2) **DC94**

A bibliography of inventories and descriptions of documents presented as (1) general inventories; (2) published inventories of the Archives Générales du Royaume and the Archives de l'État in the provinces and in other central governmental archives; and (3) inventories of archives of towns, parishes, and public and private institutions arranged by place. Indexes of topics, authors, and places.

Rijksarchief in de provinciën: overzicht van de fondsen en verzamelingen. Brussel, [Algemeen Rijksarchief], 1975. 2v. maps. **DC94a**

Contents: v.1, De Vlaamse provinciën; v.2, Les provinces wallonnes.

An extensive listing of government archives, giving brief histories, descriptions of collections, including church records, legal records, and special collections (e.g., genealogical lists, parish registers). Arranged by province, then by city. Index of people and places cited in the text.

Encyclopedias

Flandria nostra; ons land en ons volk, zijn standen en beroepen door de tijden heen, onder redactie van J. L. Broeckx [et al.]. Antwerpen, Standaard-Boekhandel, 1957–60. 5v. il. **DC95**

A non-alphabetical encyclopedia with long, signed articles and extensive bibliographies. Emphasis is on "the land and the people" rather than on political or historical events. DH71.F55

Grande encyclopédie de la Belgique et du Congo. Bruxelles, Wauthoz-Legrand, 1938–52. 2v. il. **DC96**

Non-alphabetical. Signed articles with some bibliography. Maps. v.1 deals with the Royal family, the geology, geography, demography, and history of Belgium to the end of the war in 1918; v.2, with the fine arts and the sciences. DH418.G7

Historische W. P. encyclopedie. Hoofredactie: Ph. de Vries [en] Th. Luykx. [Uitg. onder auspiciën van de Winkler Prins Stichting] Amsterdam, Elsevier, 1957–59. 3v. il. **DC96a**

Covers the political history of the world from earliest times to the present. Longer articles are signed and include brief bibliographies. Illustrations, while not numerous, are pertinent and well-reproduced, and there are good historical maps. An introductory section in the first volume includes chapters on chronology, archaeology, numismatics, epigraphy, etc., and the historiography of several countries. D9.H54

Winkler Prins encyclopedie van Vlaanderen. [Brussels], Elsevier Sequoia, [1972–74]. 5v. il. **DC97**

A new regional encyclopedia concentrating on political, cultural, economic, and historical aspects of the Flemish area of Belgium and closely related matters. An introductory section on the physical and economic milieu of the area precedes the alphabetical sequence of articles. v.4 begins with introductory essays on Flemish art; v.5 with essays on Flemish literature, language, music, and science. v.5 also includes supplementary articles updating introductory essays throughout the set. DH801.F4W562

BULGARIA

Bibliography

Búlgarskata Akademiia na Naukite, Sofia. Institut za Istoriia. Bulgarskata istoricheska nauka. Bibliografiia, t.1–4, 1960/64–75/79. Sofia, 1965–81. (In progress?) **DC98**

Contents: t.1, La science historique Bulgare 1960–1964 . . . Lilija Kirkova, Emilija Kostova-Jankova (1965); t.2, La science historique Bulgare 1965–1969 . . . Lilija Kirkova (1970); t.3, 1970–1974 . . . Emiliia Kostova (1975); t.4, 1975–1979 . . . Emiliia Kostova (1981).

Each volume was published on the occasion of a meeting of the International Congress of Historical Sciences, and each is a topical listing of books and articles written in Bulgaria on Bulgarian history. With the 1965/69 volume a section of theses is added, and to the author index is added indexes for personal names, geographic names, and topics.

Diabina, N. I., Kaloeva, I. A. and Rozhnova, L. A. Sovetskaia bolgaristika: ukazatel literatury, 1945–1980. Moskva, Akademiia Nauk SSSR, Inst. Nauch. Informatsii po Obshchestvennym Nauka, 1981. 3v. **DC99**

Topical arrangement of citations to almost 5,000 books, articles, and parts of books published in Russia on Bulgaria. Indexed. Z2896.D44

Lazarov, Mikhail. Bulgariia na balkanite, 1944–1974: bibliografiia. Sofiia, 1975. 371p. **DC100**

At head of title: Bulgarska Akademiia na Naukite. Institut za Balkanistika.

Title also in English: *Bulgaria in the Balkans.*

A classified listing of books, essays, articles, and reviews published in Bulgaria "which directly refer to the Balkans, individual Balkan countries and the relations of the People's Republic of Bulgaria with them and such as treat problems of the Danube, the Black Sea, etc."—*Notes.* In addition to historical, economic, and political studies, materials on art, the cinema, the press, religion and atheism, linguistics, etc., are also cited.

Lazarov's *Development and achievements of bibliography on the history of Bulgaria* (Sofia, CIBAL, Centre International d'Information sur les Sources de l'Histoire Balkanique, 1977. 98p.) is a bibliographical essay concerning about 250 bibliographies published over the last century relating to Bulgaria and the Balkans.
Z2831.L39

Pundeff, Marin V. Bulgaria, a bibliographic guide. Wash., Slavic and Central European Div., Library of Congress, 1965. 98p. (Repr.: N.Y., Arno Pr., 1968) **DC101**

Offers bibliographic essays on reference works and sources for the study of Bulgaria presented in seven broad categories, followed by an alphabetically arranged list of all items discussed in the essays. No index.
Z2896.P8

Spasov, Emil and **Draganov, Gancho Ganchev.** Trinadeset veka Bulgariia, istoricheskaia bibliografiia. Sofiia, Narodna Biblioteka 'Kiril i Metodii', 1980. 401p. **DC102**

A classified listing of Bulgarian books, dissertations, essays, and journal articles published 1944–78 on the history of Bulgaria. Based on the Bulgarian national bibliography and the catalog of the Bulgarian national library. Indexes of authors, personal names, and geographic names.
See also 1300 godini Bulgariia: tematichna prepor'chitelna bibliografiia, comp. by G. G. Draganov *et al.* (Sofiia, Narodna Biblioteka, 1973. 363p.).
Z2896.S72

Archives

Bulgarski Istoricheski Arkhiv. Obzor na arkhivnite fondove, kolektsii i edinichni postupleniia, sukhraiavani v Bulgarski istoricheski arkhiv. [Elisaveta Miladinova et al.] Sofiia, Narodna Biblioteka "Kiril i Metodii," [1963–83]. v.1–6. (In progress) **DC103**

Title also in English: Guide to the archive groups, collections, and single documents preserved in the Archives of Bulgarian History at the Cyril and Methodius National Library.

An inventory with notes on finding aids and detailed descriptions of the scope and character of each collection. Index of compilers, geographical areas, and subjects in each volume. CD1954. 1981

Encyclopedias and dictionaries

Cholov, Petur. Bulgarski istoritsi: biografichno- bibliografski spravochnik. Sofiia, Nauka i Izkustvo, 1981. 527p. **DC104**

Offers about 750 biobibliographies of 20th century Bulgarian historians, giving education, career, and publications. Includes all Bulgarian historians, but the great majority are concerned with Bulgarian history. Subject and geographic indexes. Z2896.C49

Entsiklopediia Bulgariia. Sofiia, Izd. na Bulgarskata Akademiia na Naukite, 1978–82. v.1–3. il., maps. (In progress) **DC105**

At head of title: Bulgarska Akademiia na Naukite. Bulgarska Entsiklopediia.
Contents: v.1–3, A–L.
An encyclopedia of Bulgarian history, cultural affairs, etc. Numerous biographical sketches; bibliographies appended to some articles.
DR53.E57

Information Bulgaria; a short encyclopedia of the People's Republic of Bulgaria. Ed. by [the Editorial Committee of] the Bulgarian Academy of Sci-

ence, tr. by Sofia Press Agency. Oxford & N.Y., Pergamon, [1985]. 976p. il., maps. **DC106**

A comprehensive one-volume encyclopedia written and translated by a team of Bulgarian experts. Covers "all major aspects of the physical, political, social, economic, and cultural life of the country."—*Introd.* Topical arrangement, each section concluding with a brief bibliography of which most citations are to Bulgarian works. Lavishly illustrated. Appendix: "Bulgaria in figures" (p.919–63). Topical index (excluding the appendix). DR53.I54

CYPRUS

Coufoudakis, Evangelos. A bibliography on Cyprus. *In* Modern Greek society, v.12, no.1 (Dec. 1984), p.4–92. **DC107**

A broad topical listing of books, articles, government documents and dissertations (primarily in English, but with some Greek, Turkish, and French citations) focusing on the relationship between Cyprus and Greece/Turkey. Not indexed.

Kitromilides, Paschalis and **Evriviades, Marios L.** Cyprus. Oxford, Eng. & Santa Barbara, Calif., Clio Pr., [1982]. 193p. map. (World bibliographical ser., 28) **DC108**

An annotated bibliography, mainly of recent or easily accessible works in English. Topical arrangement with author, title, and subject index. Z3496.K57

CZECHOSLOVAKIA

Bibliography

Bibliografie české historie za rok 1904–41. Praha, Nákl. Klubu Historického, 1905–51. Annual. **DC109**

Very comprehensive, annual record of material in Czech and other languages on the history of Czechoslovakia.
Volumes for 1904–14, 1930–36 published in—and later as a supplement to—*Český časopis historický* (Prague). Other volumes published separately.
Continued by: Z2136.B58

Bibliografie československé historie za rok 1955–65. Praha, Nákl. Československa Akademie Věd, 1957–68. Annual. **DC110**

Annual volumes covering 1955–58 were published 1957–62; 1959–60 published in 1v., 1964; 1961 published in 1v., 1965; 1962–63 published in 1v., 1967; 1964 published in 1v., 1968.
The subject classification was revised with the 1961 volume.
Continued by:

Bibliografie déjin Československa, 1971– . Praha, Academia, 1979– . Annual. **DC111**

Vols. for 1971–73 publ. 1979–84.
An annual bibliography covering the "history of nations and ethnical groups living on Czechoslovakia's territory, published in Czech or abroad and written by our or foreign scholars."—*Pref.* Also includes publications by Czech historians on other, non-Czech areas. Cites books, essays, and articles in a classified arrangement. Indexed by author and by title of collection. Z2136.B58

Hejzlar, Zdeněk and **Kusin, Vladimir.** Czechoslovakia, 1968–1969: chronology, bibliography, annotation. N.Y., Garland, 1975. 316p. **DC112**

Includes a bibliography of publications of 1968–74 on the "Prague spring," a bibliography of Czech and Slovak articles relating to 1968–70, major documents in English translation, etc.
DB215.6.H44

Historiografie v Československu 1970–1980; v ýběrová bibljografie. [Sestavili Bohumila Houbová, et al.] Praha, Ústav Československých a Světových Déjin CSAV, 1980. 385p. **DC113**

Lists more than 6,300 monographs, essays, documents, biographies, articles, etc., published in Czechoslovakia or elsewhere on Czech or Slovak history, together with Czech publications on world history. Author and title indexes. Z6201.H578

Prpíc, George J. Croatia and the Croatians; a selected and annotated bibliography in English. Scottsdale, Ariz., Associated Book Publishers, [1982]. 315p. maps. **DC114**

An annotated listing by broad topics within sections for books and pamphlets, articles, theses and dissertations. Includes a section on Croatian emigrants. Appendixes; author and title indexes. Z2957.C7P75

Sturm, Rudolf. Czechoslovakia; a bibliographic guide. Wash., Lib. of Congress, 1967. 157p. **DC115**

Prep. under the sponsorship of the Slavic and Central European Division, Library of Congress.

In two parts: (1) a bibliographical survey, followed by (2) an alphabetical listing of the more than 1,500 items discussed. Z2136.S7

Wildová Tosi, Alena. Bibliografia degli studi italiani sulla Cecoslovacchia (1918–1978). [Roma], Bulzoni, [1980]. 318p. (Il bibliotecario, 4) **DC116**

A topically arranged bibliography of Italian works on the social sciences, literature, and arts of Czechoslovakia. Name index. Z2136.W54

Zeman, Jarold K. The Hussite movement and the reformation in Bohemia, Moravia and Slovakia (1350–1650); a bibliographical study guide (with particular reference to resources in North America). Ann Arbor, publ. under auspices of the Center for Reformation Research by Michigan Slavic Pubns., [1977]. 390p. (Reformation in Central Europe, no.1) **DC117**

An inventory of some fifty research libraries in the United States and Canada, designed to identify "manuscripts, microfilms of manuscripts, rare books, unpublished theses and a few important modern critical works, both sources and literature."—*Purpose.* Includes a bibliography of books, essays, articles, and *Festschriften.* Topically arranged, with indexes by name and format. Z7845.H85Z45

Encyclopedias

Encyklopédia slovenska. Bratislava, Slovenskej Akadémia Vied, 1977–83. 6v. il. **DC118**

A regional encyclopedia emphasizing Czech and Slovak topics, personalities, and events after 1968. DB2707.E5

DENMARK

See also Scandinavia.

Bjerg, Hans Christian. Dansk marinehistorisk bibliografi, 1500–1975. København, Marinehistorisk Selskab, Akademisk Forlag, 1975. 166p. (Marinehistorisk selskabs skrift, 12) **DC119**

A topical listing of more than 2,000 books and articles. Includes a section for biographies of individual officers. Author index. Z2581.N3B64

Erichsen, Balder and **Krarup, Alfred.** Dansk historisk Bibliografi; systematisk Fortegnelse over Bidrag til Danmarks Historie til Udgangen af 1912 (i Tilslutning til Bibliotheca

danica). Udg. paa Carlsbergfondets Bekostning. København, Gad, 1917–27. 3v. **DC120**

A very full list, including books, pamphlets, and many analytical references to articles in periodicals and other composite works.

v.1–2 are a classified list of more than 20,000 references on history, topography, etc., with detailed indexes of authors and titles. v.3 is a list of published biographies of persons living between 1830 and 1912, in continuation of a similar section in v.3 of Bruun, *Bibliotheca danica* (AA718), and including some names of the earlier period omitted from Bruun. Z2576.E68

Bruun, Henry. Dansk historisk bibliografi, 1913–1942. Udg. af den Danske Historiske Forening. København, Rosenkilde og Bagger, 1966–77. 6v. **DC121**

Contents: v.1, Indledning. Politisk Historie samt Stats- og Kulturforhold til og med Erhvervsliv; v.2, Stats- og Kulturforhold fra Aandsliv og ud.; v.3, Danmarks Topografi. Sønderjyllands (Hertugdømmernes) Historie, indre Forhold og Topografi; v.4, Personalhistorie, almindelig Del og speciel Del, A–J; v.5, Personalhistorie, almindelig Del og speciel Del, K–AA; v.6, Registre.

Designed to fill the gap between Erichsen and Krarup's work of the same title (above), which covers through 1912, and Bruun's earlier volume (below) for the 1943–47 period. Classed arrangement. The final volume includes a list of corrections and additions, indexes of authors, titles, *Festschriften,* periodicals indexed, and topical headings used. Z2576.B7

Danske Historiske Forening. Dansk historisk bibliografi, 1943–1947. Udg. af den Dansk Historiske Forening, ved Henry Bruun. København, Hagerup, 1956. 594p. **DC122**

The first volume of a new series to cover 5-year periods, designed to provide a comprehensive record of writings on Danish history. Similar in scope and arrangement to Erichsen and Krarup (DC120). Z2576.D3

Jansen, Henrik M. A select bibliography of Danish works on the history of towns published 1960–1976. Odense, [Odense Universitet, Institut for Historie og Samfundsvidenskab], 1977. 85p. (Byhistoriske hjlpemidler 2; Skrifter fra Institut for Historie og Samfundsvidenskab, Odense Univ.: Historie, 21) **DC123**

Extends the coverage of the *International bibliography of urban history* . . . (DC3) for Danish towns and for towns outside Denmark if the work was written by a Dane. Includes books, articles, essays, and archival lists. Z7165.D4J35

ESTONIA

British Library. Reference Division. Catalogue of books and periodicals on Estonia in the British Library Reference Division. Comp. by Salme Pruuden. London, British Lib.; N.Y., Garland, 1981. 309p. (Garland reference library of social science, v.71) **DC124**

A comprehensive, topical listing of books and journals with materials relating to Estonia. Includes all areas except fiction and poetry; encompasses materials in any language. Index of authors, editors, and compilers. Z2533.B75

FINLAND

See also Scandinavia.

Harvard University. Library. Finnish and Baltic history and literatures: classification schedule; classified listing by call number; chronological listing; author and title listing. Cambridge, publ. by Harvard Univ. Lib., distr. by Harvard Univ. Pr., 1972. 250p. (Widener Library shelflist, 40) **DC125**

About 8,600 titles representing "the classes *Balt* and *Balt Doc* which provide for works on the history and literatures of Finland,

Estonia, Latvia, and Lithuania, and for writings in other Finno-Ugrian languages except Hungarian."—*Pref.*

For a note on the series *see* AA145. Z2520.H37

Screen, J. E. O. Finland. Oxford, Eng. & Santa Barbara, Calif., Clio, [1981]. 212p. map. (World bibliographical ser., 31) **DC126**

A brief introductory survey of Finnish history and life is followed by an annotated bibliography of 768 books, periodical titles (not articles), and documents, mainly in English. Arranged by broad topic; author, title, subject index. Z2520.S24

Suomen historiallinen bibliografia. Finsk historisk bibliografi. Bibliographie historique finlandaise, 1544–1970. Helsinki, 1940–83. (Suomen historiallinen Seura. Käsikirjoja, 2,4–6,9) **DC127**

Contents: v.[1], 1544–1900, by J. Vallinkoski and H. Schauman (1961); v.[2], 1901–1925, by A. H. Maliniemi and E. Kivikoski (1940); v.[3], 1926–1950, by J. Vallinkoski and H. Schauman (1955–56); v.[4], 1951–1960, by P. Laminén (1968); v.[5], 1961–1970, by T. Rantanen and L. Pärssinen (1983).

A series of comprehensive bibliographies of Finnish historical works, including both books and periodical articles. Classed arrangement with author indexes. Headings are given in Finnish, Swedish, and French. Most of the material is in Finnish, though some titles are in Swedish, German, and other languages.

History is interpreted in its broad sense to include not only political and economic history of all periods, but also allied interests, e.g., history of the church, education, literature, folklore, etc., and local history.

FRANCE

Bibliography

Bibliographie critique des principaux travaux parus sur l'histoire de 1600 à 1914, en 1932 et 1933–35. Paris, Maison du Livre Français, 1935–37. 5v. (Publications de la Société d'Histoire Moderne. Série des instruments de travail) **DC128**

"Publiée par le Comité de Direction de la Revue d'Histoire Moderne."—*title page.*

Ed. by Georges Pagès, Léon Cahen, and Marc Jaryc.

1932/33, General; 1934–35, with subtitle, Travaux de langue française ou relatifs à l'histoire de France.

1934 issue includes, in four sections, works in the French, English, and German languages on the history of France, and works in the French language on foreign countries.

1935 issue adds works in Italian, Polish, and Russian languages on the history of France. Z6204.B58

Chambers, Frances. France. Oxford, Eng. & Santa Barbara, Calif., Clio Pr., [1980]. 175p. (World bibliographical ser., 13) **DC129**

Lists 542 books and articles selected as "a 'core' collection of books about France for an English-speaking reader who has a serious interest in the country and its culture, but who is not a specialist."—*Introd.* Indexed. Z2161.C5

France. Armée. Service Historique. Guide bibliographique sommaire d'histoire militaire et coloniale française. Paris, Impr. Nationale, 1969. 522p. **DC130**

A section of general works is followed by sections dealing with the military history of specific periods. Brief descriptive notes are sometimes included. Indexed. Z6725.F8A5

Franklin, Alfred. Les sources de l'histoire de France. Notices bibliographiques et analytiques des inventaires et des recueils de documents relatifs à l'histoire de France. Paris, Firmin-Didot, 1877. 681p. (Repr.: Nendeln, Kraus Reprint, 1967) **DC131**

Lists the contents of many of the great French historical collec-

tions, e.g., *Catalogue de l'histoire de France, Collection des documents inédits relatifs à l'histoire de France, Bibliothèque de l'École des Chartes,* and many others, and for this purpose is still useful. Z2176.F83

Heggoy, Alf Andrew and **Haar, John M.** The military in imperial history: the French connection. N.Y., Garland, 1984. 302p. (Military history bibliographies, v.4; Garland reference library of social science, v.192) **DC132**

Introductory chapters on topics such as "Organization of the French military," "French Foreign Legion," and "Colonialism" are followed by chapters for each country or area in the French empire. A brief survey of the role of the French army in a given area precedes the bibliographic listings for that area. Covers books and articles; name index. Z2181.C7H43

Lepointe, Gabriel. Éléments de bibliographie sur l'histoire des institutions et des faits sociaux, 987–1875. Paris, Montchrestien, 1958. 232p. **DC133**

"Avec le concours de André Vandenbossche."

Arranged alphabetically, with an index by subject. Includes books and periodical articles on the history of social conditions in France, prepared to accompany the author's *Histoire des institutions et des faits sociaux de la France* (1956).

Continued by: Z2161.L57

―――― Bibliographie en langue français d'histoire du droit. 1957/59–1974. Paris, Montchrestien, 1961–78. 19v. **DC134**

1957–59 issued in 1v.; 1960–69, annual. 1957/59–62 issued without volume numbering; 1963–69 called v.6–12.

Despite the title, the coverage is much the same as that in the preceding work. Lists books and articles in French on the social history of France from 987 to 1875. A few articles on other countries are included.

No more published? Z2161.L572

Paris. Bibliothèque Nationale. Dépt. des Imprimés. Catalogue de l'histoire de France. Paris, Didot, 1855–95. 11v., index, and 6 suppl. (Repr.: Paris, Bibliothèque Nationale, 1968–69. 16v.) **DC135**

A very comprehensive catalog of books, pamphlets, etc., printed before 1875 on the history of France prior to 1875. Classed (15 main and 904 subclasses), with author index.

Contents: t.1, Préliminaires et généralités. Histoire par époques. Histoire par règnes [à Louis XIII]; t.2, Louis XIV–Louis XVI; t.3, 1792–1848; t.4, 1848–1856. Journaux et publications périodiques; t.5, Histoire religieuse; t.6, Histoire constitutionnelle; t.7, Histoire constitutionnelle [suite]. Histoire administrative, diplomatique, militaire. Moeurs et coutumes. Archéologie; t.8, Histoire locale; t.9, Histoire locale [suite]. Biographie; t.10, Biographie [suite]. [Six additional supplements to special classes of the main work.]

―――― ―――― Biographies individuelles 1879–1943. Carnets d'inventaire. 1973. 1v. unpaged.

―――― ―――― Table des auteurs. 1895. 798p.

―――― ―――― Tables des divisions. 1966. 65p.

An outline of v.1–10 only.

―――― ―――― Table générale alphabétique des ouvrages anonymes. 1905–32. 15v.

Contents: Table des noms de personnes, v.1–4; Table des noms de lieux, v.5–15. Z2176.P23

Répertoire bibliographique de l'histoire de France, par Pierre Caron et Henri Stein. Publication de la Société Française de Bibliographie, subventionnée par la Confédération des Sociétés Scientifiques Françaises, à l'aide des fonds alloués par le Parlement. Paris, Picard, 1923–38. v.1–6. Biennial. **DC136**

Covers publications of the period 1920/21–1930/31.

The standard current bibliography for France to 1914, listing historical writings in various languages, both books and periodical articles. Classified, with name and place indexes.

Continued by DC155. Z2179.R43

Ross, Steven T. French military history, 1661–1799: a guide to the literature. N.Y., Garland, 1984. 305p. (Military history bibliographies, v.6; Garland reference bibliography of social science, v.190) **DC137**

A comprehensive bibliography of books, articles, and manuals relating to the army in the foreign and domestic affairs of France; includes works on the evolution of the French army, campaigns, and leaders. In three main sections: General works; The old régime; The French Revolution. Author index. Z2181.M5R67

Les sources de l'histoire de France depuis les origines jusqu'en 1815, par A. Molinier [and others]. Paris, Picard, 1901–35. 1.–3.pt. (in 18v.). (Repr.: 1.pt., N.Y., B. Franklin, 1964; 2.pt., Nendeln, Kraus, 1966) **DC138**

A valuable bibliography listing printed sources. The volumes to cover the period 1715–1815 were never published.

An expanded version of 1.pt., t.1 was published as *La Gaule jusqu'au milieu de Ve siècle*, by Paul-Marie Duval (Paris, Picard, 1971. 2v.). Z2176.S75

Early

Montandon, Raoul. Bibliographie générale des travaux palethnologiques et archéologiques (époques préhistorique, protohistorique et gallo-romaine). France. . . . Genève, George, 1917–38. v.1–5. **DC139**

A comprehensive bibliography of books and periodical articles, arranged by geographical division.

—— —— Supplément du t.1–3. 1921–29. v.1–3.

—— —— Supplément. Le Mans, Monnoyer, 1952. (Société préhistorique française. Bullétin, v.49, no.9, Sept. 1952)

Includes "2^{ieme} suppl. du t.3; 2^{ieme} suppl. du t.1; 1^{ier} suppl. du t.4." Z5117.M75

Répertoire archéologique de la France, pub. par ordre du Ministre de l'Instruction Publique et sous la direction du Comité des Travaux Historiques et des Sociétés Savantes. Paris, Impr. Nationale, 1861–88. 8v. (Collection de documents inédits sur l'histoire de France, ser. vii, 7) **DC140**

Contents: *Alpes (Hautes)*, by Joseph Roman (1888); *Aube*, by Henri d'Arbois de Jubainville (1861); *Morbihan*, by Louis Rosensweig (1863); *Nièvre*, by J. H. G. R. de Soultrait (1875); *Oise*, by Emmanuel Woilez (1862); *Seine-Inférieure*, by J. B. D. Cochet (1872); *Tarn*, by Hippolyte Crozes (1865); *Yonne*, by Maximilien Quantin (1868).

Stein, Henri. Bibliographie générale des cartulaires français ou relatifs à l'histoire de France. Paris, Picard, 1907. 627p. (Manuels de bibliographie historique, 4) (Repr.: Nendeln, Kraus, 1967) **DC141**

Lists and describes 4,522 cartulaires arranged alphabetically by place-name. Z2178.S85

To 1789

Du Peloux, Charles. Répertoire général des ouvrages modernes relatifs au dix-huitième siècle française (1715–1789). Paris, Grund, 1926. 306p. **DC142**

—— —— Supplément, table méthodique. 1927. 62p.

Lists books published since 1789 in French, English, German, and Italian. Includes an alphabetical list of those persons of the 18th century who have been the subjects of biographies, with the names of the authors of such works. Z2178.D93

Lindsay, Robert O. and **Neu, John.** French political pamphlets, 1547–1648: a catalog of major collections in American libraries. Madison, Univ. of Wisconsin Pr., 1969. 510p. **DC143**

More than 6,700 items; chronological arrangement, with author-title index. Locates copies.

Most of the items listed are available on microfilm from Research Publications, New Haven, Conn (86 reels; publ. 1978). That company has also issued *French political pamphlets 1547–1648; a supplement listing the microform additions to the original edition*, comp. by R. O. Lindsay and J. Neu (Woodbridge, Conn., 1981. 40p.). Z2177.5.L54

Newberry Library, Chicago. A checklist of French political pamphlets 1560–1644 in the Newberry Library, comp. by Doris Varner Welsh. Chicago, Lib., 1950. 204p. **DC144**

About 1,200 items, mostly unavailable elsewhere in the United States, arranged alphabetically under year of publication, with an index by author and title.

Although primarily political, this collection is valuable also for social and economic data of the period.

—— A second checklist . . . 1560–1653. 1955. 190p.

Adds 1,340 titles and includes a cumulated index to both volumes.

Items cited in the two bibliographies above are available on microfilm from Bell & Howell, Micro Photo Div., Wooster, Ohio (28 reels). Z2174.P2N4

Saulnier, Eugène and **Martin, A.** Bibliographie des travaux publiés de 1866 à 1897 sur l'histoire de la France de 1500 à 1789. Paris, Presses Universitaires, 1932–38. v.1–2, fasc.2. (Publication de la Société d'Histoire Moderne) **DC145**

No more published.

Contents: v.1, Histoire intérieure, Histoire des institutions, Histoire diplomatique, Histoire militaire, Histoire de la marine militaire, Histoire religieuse; v.2, fasc.1–2, Histoire économique et sociale, Histoire coloniale, Histoire des familles, Biographies.

A comprehensive listing of books and periodical articles, with references to reviews. Classified arrangement. Not completed, and lacks indexes.

French Revolution

Caron, Pierre. Manuel pratique pour l'étude de la Révolution française. Nouv. éd. mise à jour. Paris, Picard, 1947. 324p. **DC146**

1st ed. 1912. This edition revised and reorganized. An indispensable guide to the archival and manuscript sources, collections, bibliographical aids, etc., for the study of the French Revolution. Z2179.C29

Monglond, André. La France révolutionnaire et impériale; annales de bibliographie méthodique et description des livres illustrés. Paris, Impr. Nationale, 1930–78. 10v. il. **DC147**

Imprint varies.

A very detailed bibliography, including books, pamphlets, and articles dealing with all phases of life and literature in France, 1789–1812. Additions and corrections in each volume.

v.10 is an "Index général. 2 éd., revue et corrigée." (Repr.: Genève, Slatkine, 1978) Z2171.M74

Paris. Bibliothèque Nationale. Dépt. des Imprimés. Catalogue de l'histoire de la Révolution française, par André Martin et Gérard Walter. Paris, Éd. des Bibliothèques Nationales, 1936–[69]. 6v. in 7. **DC148**

Contents: v.1–4¹, Écrits de la période révolutionnaire—Auteurs; v.4², Anonymes; v.5, Journaux et almanachs; v.6, Table analytique, par G. Walter.

A very comprehensive bibliography of works published during the French Revolution. Z2179.P27

Roberts, John Morris and **Cobb, Richard Charles,** eds. French revolution documents. Oxford, Blackwell, 1966–73. 2v. **DC149**

> Contents: v.1, 1787–1792; v.2, 1792–1795.
> Official documents, memoirs, letters, etc., are presented in chronological arrangement. Headnotes and detailed indexes add to the usefulness of the work. DC141.R6

Walter, Gérard. Répertoire de l'histoire de la Révolution française: Travaux publiés de 1800 à 1940. Paris, Bibliothèque Nationale, 1941–51. 2v. (Repr. 1968) **DC150**

> Contents: t.1, Personnes; t.2, Lieux.
> Works on persons and places, including books and periodical articles. Z2178.W34

Since 1789

Caron, Pierre. Bibliographie des travaux publiés de 1866 à 1897 sur l'histoire de la France depuis 1789. Paris, Cornély, 1912. 831p. (Repr.: Genève, Slatkine, 1974) **DC151**

> A valuable bibliography including 13,496 titles of books, pamphlets, and articles in periodicals, society publications, and other composite works. Indicates book reviews and abstracts of important items. Indexes the historical articles in some 394 French and 260 foreign periodicals. Classified arrangement with two indexes: (1) authors and persons, (2) places. Forms the main volume in Caron's series of indexes of the history of France since 1789.
> Continued by: Z2179.C25

Répertoire méthodique de l'histoire moderne et contemporaine de la France, pour les années 1898–1913. Paris, Rieder, 1899–1932. v.1–7, 9–11; Paris, Éditions du Centre National de la Recherche Scientifique, 1965. v.8 **DC152**

> v.1–6, 1898–1903, ed. by G. Brière and P. Caron; v.7, 1904–1906, ed. by G. Brière, P. Caron, and J. Lépine; v.8, 1907–1909, ed. from the manuscript notes of P. Caron *et al.,* and published 1965; v.9, 1910/11, ed. by P. Caron and R. Burnaud; v. 10–11, 1911/12–1912/13, ed. by M. Bouteron, R. Burnaud, and P. Caron; v.12, 1913–19, not published.
> v.1–3, 1894–96 reprinted from *Le moyen age,* v.8–10 (1895–97). Z2179.R42

Menyesch, Dieter and **Manach, Bérénice.** France-Allemagne, relations internationes et interdépendances bilatérales; une bibliographie 1963–1982. München, Saur, 1984. 793p. **DC153**

> Title also in German.
> An extensive bibliography of books, articles, essays, theses, and some archival materials arranged under five broad headings (general, political relations, government relations, economic relations, and cultural relations) with some subdivision. Topical and name indexes. Z6465.F7M46

Young, Robert J. French foreign policy, 1918–1945; a guide to research and research material. Wilmington, Scholarly Resources, [1981]. 242p. **DC154**

> Introductory chapters describe the conduct of foreign policy in France and the relevant contents of archives, libraries, research institutions, etc. The remainder of the volume is a bibliography of more than 1,500 entries for reference sources, documentary series, memoirs, and secondary sources. Appendices provide registers and brief biographical data on ministers and administrators. Partial subject and name indexes. Z6465.F7Y68

Current

Bibliographie annuelle de l'histoire de France du cinquième siècle à 1939. Année 1955– . Paris, Éd. du Centre National de la Recherche Scientifique, 1956– . Annual. (Comité Français de Sciences Historiques) **DC155**

> Date in title varies according to period of coverage.

A detailed, classified bibliography with author and subject indexes. Z2176.B5

Local

Dollinger, Philippe, Wolff, Philippe and **Guenée, Simonne.** Bibliographie d'histoire des villes de France. Paris, Klincksieck, 1967. 752p. **DC156**

> At head of title: Commission Internationale pour l'Histoire des Villes.
> Nearly 10,000 references (book and periodical materials) on more than 300 cities. Z2176.D6

Lasteyrie du Saillant, Robert Charles, *Comte de.* Bibliographie générale des travaux historiques et archéologiques publiés par les sociétés savantes de la France, dressée sous les auspices du Ministère de l'Instruction Publique. Paris, Impr. Nationale, 1888–1918. 6v. (Repr.: N.Y., B. Franklin, 1972) **DC157**

> Publication of the Comité des Travaux Historiques et Scientifiques. Issued in parts, 1885–1918.
> v.1–4 cover the literature published to the year 1885; v.5–6 deal with publications of 1886–1900.
> A monumental undertaking, the most important work on French societies. Arranged alphabetically first by *département,* then by town, and under each by society. For each society gives: brief history, changes of name, suspensions, mergers, etc.; full titles, dates, etc., of all of its publications; full contents of each volume. An index of societies (arranged by *département*) at the end of v.6 links together references to the same society in the main part and the supplement. Includes also societies in the French colonies and French societies abroad. Most useful at present for the historical matter about the societies and for the titles, collation, and contents of the sets of their publications, but cannot be used rapidly for the analytical material. An alphabetical author and subject index was projected but never published. Continued on the same plan and scale by the following: Z2183.L34

Bibliographie annuelle des travaux historiques et archéologiques publiés par les sociétés savantes de la France . . . 1901/02–1909/10. Paris, Impr. Nationale, 1906–14. 3v. in 9 pts. **DC158**

> Each volume consists of three annual issues.
> Contents: v.1, 1901/02–1903/04; v.2, 1904/05–1906/07; v.3, 1907/08–1909/10.
> An annual continuation of the Lasteyrie work, listing in the nine annuals 42,612 analyticals. Indexes to be noted: v.3, no.3, 1909/10, has general index of societies (but not of analytics) in v.1–3; v.1, no.1, 1901/02, has both an author and a subject index to the analytical material in that issue.
> Continued by: Z2183.L34

Gandilhon, René. Bibliographie générale des travaux historiques et archéologiques publiés par les sociétés savantes de la France; dressée sous les auspices du Ministère de l'Éducation Nationale . . . Période 1910–1940. Paris, Impr. Nationale, 1944–61. 5v. **DC159**

> Follows the plan of the original work with slightly increased coverage, adding to history and archaeology such related materials as geography, folklore, prehistoric studies, obituaries, etc. Z2183.G3

Dissertations

Bowditch, John and **Grew, Raymond.** A selected bibliography on modern French history, 1600 to the present. Ann Arbor, Mich., Xerox University Microfilms, 1974. 126p. **DC160**

> Pages 57–112 list some 1,200 dissertations completed in American universities; topical arrangement with author index. The first part of the volume is merely a list of those works on French history which are available from Xerox University Microfilms.

Archives and manuscripts

France. Archives Nationales. État général des fonds. Jean Favier, éd. Paris, Archives Nationales, 1978–80. t.1–4. (In progress) **DC161**

Contents: t.1, L'ancien régime; t.2, 1789–1940; t.3, Marine et outre-mer; t.4, Fonds divers et additions et corrections aux tomes I, II, et III.

Offers a detailed inventory of the contents of each file in the Archives Nationales, including materials added up to July 1, 1976. Each section begins with a headnote giving a brief description and an indication of any registers or published guides to the collections. v.4 also includes a list of microfilms of collections in other archives, p.328–93. CD1196

France. Direction des Archives. État des inventaires des archives nationales, départementales, communales et hospitalières au 1. janvier 1937. [Par Henri Courteault]. Paris, Didier, 1938. 703p. **DC162**

———— ———— Supplément (1937–1954). [Par Robert H. Boutier]. Paris, Impr. Nationale, 1955. 344p.

A description and listing of the inventories of French archives. Includes bibliographies. CD1192.A5

Langlois, Charles Victor and **Stein, Henri.** Les archives de l'histoire de France. Paris, Picard, 1891–93. 1000p. (Manuels de bibliographie historique) (Repr.: Nendeln, Kraus, 1966) **DC163**

Contents: Les archives de l'histoire de France en France; Les archives de l'histoire de France à l'étranger; Les archives de l'histoire de France dans les bibliothèques de manuscrits.

Guide to source materials in French and foreign archives. CD1191.L28

Welsch, Erwin K. Libraries and archives in France: a handbook. Rev. ed. N.Y., Council for European Studies, 1979. 147p. **DC164**

For full information *see* AB133.

Historiography

See also DA36.

La recherche historique en France depuis 1965. Paris, Éditions du C.N.R.S., 1980. 154p. **DC165**

At head of title: Comité Français des Sciences Historiques.

In two parts, the first being an assessment of trends and developments in historical research in France during the 15 years since 1965; the second, a survey of institutions and centers for historical research, followed by a list of French historical journals and a bibliography of relevant French theses for the doctorate submitted 1965–79. D13.R365

Dictionaries and handbooks

See also DC17–DC18.

Anderson, Frank Maloy. The constitutions and other select documents illustrative of the history of France, 1789–1907. 2d ed. rev. and enl. Minneapolis, Wilson, 1908. 693p. (Repr.: N.Y., Russell & Russell, [1967]) **DC166**

A useful collection of translations from the original texts. Sources are indicated, and brief annotations with additional references included. DC58.A2A52

Cabourdin, Guy and **Viard, Georges.** Lexique historique de la France d'ancien régime. Paris, Armand Colin, [1978]. [325]p. **DC167**

Not intended as an encyclopedia, but as an introductory dictiona-

ry for the period. Covers all areas from institutions to art and science; bibliographical citations conclude most articles. Liberal use of cross references. DC35.C3

Charlton, D. G. France; a companion to French studies. 2d ed. London, Methuen, 1979. 690p. **DC168**

1st ed. 1972.

Offered "as a detailed introduction and guide to the history and culture of France from the time of the Renaissance to the present day."—*Pref.* Chapters by contributing scholars each deal with a facet of French life and provide a bibliography. In this edition various sections have been revised to take account of new scholarship, new interpretations, and recent events; bibliographies have been expanded into brief essays. Indexed. DC33.C478

Dictionnaire d'histoire de France Perrin. Sous la direction de Alain Decaux et André Castelot. [Paris], Perrin, [1981]. 1076p. il. **DC169**

Includes entries for persons, places, terms, and events important to the understanding of French history from earliest times to the recent past. Certain events of unusual significance (Diên Biên Phu, the Resistance) are given extended treatment and appear on pages with colored borders. Heavily illustrated; occasional *see* references; no bibliography. DC35.D53

Faugères, Arlette and **Ferré, Régine.** Répertoire des historiens français pour la période moderne et contemporaine. Paris, Éditions du Centre National de la Recherche Scientifique, 1983. 358p. **DC170**

At head of title: Centre National de la Recherche Scientifique. Institut d'Historie Moderne et Contemporaine.

A directory of French historians with information derived from questionnaires distributed to affiliates of CNRS, universities, archives, libraries, and museums in France. In addition to address and institutional affiliation, aims to include titles of theses, specialties, works in progress or published 1979–81. Topical, period, geographic area, and specialty indexes. Directory of organizations.

France. Commission de la Topographie des Gaules. Dictionnaire archéologique de la Gaule, époque celtique. Pub. par la Commission instituée au Ministère de l'Instruction Publique et des Beaux-Arts. Paris, Impr. Nationale, 1875–1923. 2v., volume of plates. il. (Collection de documents inédits sur l'histoire de France. sér. 6, t.20) **DC171**

Contents: v.1, A–G (1875); v.2, H–Z (1878–1923).

Continué, après la lettre L, par les soins de Émile Cartailhac.

An alphabetical arrangement by place-name of the archaeological remains of France. DC63.A3A3

Historical dictionary of the French Revolution, 1789–1799. Ed. by Samuel F. Scott and Barry Rothaus. Westport, Conn., Greenwood Pr., [1984]. 2v. (1143p.) **DC172**

About 525 articles by 96 contributing scholars cover various aspects of the French Revolution—personalities, events, constitutional developments, etc. Short bibliography with each entry; numerous cross references; chronology of principal events. Indexed.

An older work is *Dictionnaire historique et biographique de la Révolution et de l'Empire, 1789–1815,* by J. F. E. Robinet *et al.* (Paris, Librairie Historique de la Révolution et de l'Empire, 1899. 2v.). DC147.H57

Lalanne, Ludovic. Dictionnaire historique de la France. 2. éd. Paris, Hachette, 1877. 2v. (Repr.: N.Y., B. Franklin, 1968) **DC173**

A handbook for ready reference including brief articles on persons, places, and institutions connected with the history of France through 1876. DC35.L19

Pierrard, Pierre. Dictionnaire de la IIIᵉ République. Paris, Larousse, [1968]. 255p. il. **DC174**

Brief entries for individuals, events, institutions, etc., of historical significance for the period 1870–1940 in French history. DC337.P5

Atlases

Atlas historique: Provence, Comtat Venaissin, Principauté d'Orange, Comté de Nice, Principauté de Monaco [par] Édouard Baratier, Georges Duby et Ernest Hildesheimer. [Paris], Librairie Armand Colin, [1969]. 208p., 326 maps. 35cm. (Atlas Belfram) **DC175**

Historical, geographical, and linguistic maps of southern France. The volume of commentary gives sources for the information depicted on the maps, plus lists of cardinals, bishops, genealogical charts, county officials, and a gazetteer. G1843.P7A3

Boussard, Jacques. Atlas historique et culturel de la France. Paris, Elsevier, 1957. 214p. il. **DC176**

A combination of maps, text, and illustrations, the last particularly numerous and effective. DC35.5.B65

GERMANY

Bibliography

Bibliographie zur deutschen Geschichte ... 1889–1927. Leipzig, Teubner, 1889–1918; Dresden, Baensch, 1920–31. Annual. **DC177**

No more published.

Issued as a supplement to the *Historische Vierteljahrschrift.*

A useful annual bibliography, arranged by subject with author index. Each issue lists books, pamphlets, and periodical articles, with references to reviews of items listed.

Bird, Keith W. German naval history; a guide to the literature. N.Y., Garland, 1985. 1121p. (Military history bibliographies, v.7; Garland reference library of social science, v.215) **DC178**

In two sections: (1) overview and discussion of research, with chapters on "The writing of German naval history," "Sources of German naval history," and on the German navy in various historical periods up to 1945–83; and (2) a bibliography of the works discussed—some 4,871 items (books, essays, articles)—listed by author, with reference to page or section where cited. Z2241.N3B57

Buse, Dieter K. and **Doerr, Juergen C.** German nationalism; a bibliographic approach. N.Y., Garland, 1985. 230p. (Canadian review of studies in nationalism, 5; Garland reference library of social science, v.161) **DC179**

An annotated bibliography of English and German language books, articles, and essays dealing with nationalism, national consciousness, and national identity in Germany. Arranged by period (each spanning about 30 to 50 years), with lengthy introduction to each period. Author and subject indexes. Z2241.N28B88

Dahlmann, Friedrich Christoph and **Waitz, Georg.** Dahlmann-Waitz. Quellenkunde der deutschen Geschichte. 9. Aufl. hrsg. von Hermann Haering. Leipzig, Koehler, 1931–32. 2v. (1292p.) **DC180**

Contents: v.1, Bibliography, 992p.; v.2, Index, p.993–1292. The standard bibliography of German history in all its phases, covering through World War I. Indispensable in any library where research work in that subject is done. The 9th ed. contains 16,337 entries in classified arrangement.

A new edition has begun to appear as: Z2236.D14

—— Dahlmann-Waitz. Quellenkunde der deutschen Geschichte; Bibliographie der Quellen und der Literatur zur deutschen Geschichte. 10. Aufl. Hrsg. im Max-Planck-Institut für Geschichte von Hermann Heimpel und Herbert Geuss. Stuttgart, A. Hiersemann, 1965–85. Lfg.1–50. (In progress) **DC181**

Contents: A, Allgemeiner Teil, v.1–4; B, Die einzelnen Zeitalter, v.5–7. Publication has proceeded as follows: v.1, Abschnitt 1–38,

Lfg.1,4–11 (complete); v.2, Abschnitt 39–57, Lfg.12–20 (complete); v.3, Abschnitt 58–120, Lfg.21–23/24,48 (complete); v.4, Abschnitt 108–124, Lfg.43–47,49–50 (in progress); v.5, Abschnitt 158–236, Lfg.25–34/35 (complete); v.6, Abschnitt 237–274, Lfg.36–42 (in progress); v.7, Abschnitt 393–402, Lfg.2–3 (in progress).

To be in 7v., with publication spread over the next several years. Coverage is extended to the end of World War II, and includes works published through 1960. The general plan of the work remains the same, but a greater number of non-German writings is to be included throughout.

Examination of the parts thus far received and of the outline for the new edition indicates substantial reworking of the various sections. The publisher estimates three times as many entries as for the 9th ed., but since numerous citations are evidently being dropped, most libraries will want to retain the 9th ed. in the reference collection.

—— —— Register zu Band 1 und 2. Stuttgart, Hiersemann, 1985. 496p.

Provides indexes of authors and of personal and geographic names as subjects.

Grundriss der Geschichtswissenschaft, zur Einführung in das Studium der deutschen Geschichte des Mittelalters und der Neuzeit, hrsg. von Aloys Meister. Leipzig, Teubner, 1908–23. 1. Reihe, Abt.1–4a, 6–7; 2. Reihe, Abt. 1–6, 8. (Repr. in part: Hildesheim, Olms, 1974) **DC182**

Contents: 1. Reihe, Historische Hilfswissenschaften u. Propädeutik; 2. Reihe, Historische Sonderwissenschaften.

—— Ergänzungsband. Bd.1, Die antiken Grundlagen der frühmittelalterlichen Privatkunde, 1927.

A monographic series in which each volume is written by an expert. The first series deals with the technique of historical method; the second, with the interpretation of various phases of medieval and modern German history. For the advanced student. DD86.G8

Jahresberichte der deutschen Geschichte. Jahrg. 1–7, 1918–1924. Breslau, Priebatsch, 1920–26. 7v. **DC183**

A valuable annual survey preceded by the *Jahresberichte der Geschichtswissenschaft,* 1878–1913 (DA22), and continued by: Z2236.J25

Jahresberichte für deutsche Geschichte. 1.–15/16. Jahrg., 1925–39/40. ... hrsg. von Albert Brackmann u. Fritz, Hartung. Leipzig, Koehler, 1927–42. v.1–15/16. Annual. **DC183a**

Each volume in two parts: (1) Bibliographie; (2) Forschungsberichte, with author and subject indexes. Continued by: Z2236.J26

—— n.F. 1.– , Jahrg., 1949– , im Auftrage der Deutschen Akademie der Wissenschaften zu Berlin. Berlin, Akademie-Verlag, 1952– . v.1– . (v.1–2, Annual; v.3– , Biennial) **DC184**

Sponsoring body varies.

A revival of this important series, now devoted entirely to bibliography, listing writings on German history from early times through World War II. 1941–48 not yet covered.

Jahrbuch der historischen Forschung in der Bundesrepublik Deutschland, 1974– . Stuttgart, Klett-Cotta; München, Saur, 1975– . Annual. **DC185**

Hrsg. von der Arbeitsgemeinschaft Ausseruniversitärer Historischer Forschungseinrichtungen in der Bundesrepublik Deutschland.

A topically arranged listing of in-progress, in-press, or recently published historical research (including dissertations) in Germany; includes all geographical areas and all periods. Indexed by author, persons, place names, and institutions.

Two ten-year cumulative records of research in East Germany are provided by Gerhard Becker's *Historische Forschungen in der DDR 1960-1970* and *Historische Forschungen in der DDR 1970-1980,*

Analysen und Berichte (Berlin, Deutscher Verlag der Wissenschaften, 1980. 2v.). **DD86.J255**

Showalter, Dennis E. German military history, 1648–1982; a critical bibliography. N.Y., Garland, 1984. 331p. (Military history bibliographies, v.3; Garland reference library of social science, v.113) **DC186**

A section of general works is followed by chapters on nine historical periods, each with an introductory essay discussing the bibliographic listings which follow. Author index. **Z2241.M5S5**

To 1600

Lorenz, Ottokar. Deutschlands Geschichtsquellen im Mittelalter seit der Mitte des dreizehnten Jahrhunderts. 3. in Verbindung mit Arthur Goldmann umgearb. Aufl. Berlin, Hertz, 1886–87. 2v. (Repr.: Graz, Akademische Druck- und Verlagsanstalt, 1966) **DC187**

This work and that of Wattenbach (DC189–DC190) furnish comprehensive and critical guides to the historiography of medieval Germany. Continues from the middle of the 13th century, where the 6th ed. of Wattenbach ceases. **DD86.L86**

Schottenloher, Karl. Bibliographie zur deutschen Geschichte im Zeitalter der Glaubensspaltung 1517–1585. . . . Leipzig, Hiersemann, 1933–66. 7v. **DC188**

Im Auftrag der Kommission zur Erforschung der Geschichte der Reformation und Gegenreformation.
Contents: Bd.1–2, Personnen, A–Z. Orte u. Landschaften; Bd.3, Reich u. Kaiser. Territorien u. Landesherren; Bd.4, Gesamtdarstellungen der Reformationszeit. Stoffe; Bd.5, Nachträge und Ergänzungen. Zeittafel; Bd.6, Verfasser und Titelverzeichnis; Bd.7, Das Schrifttum von 1938–1960, hrsg. Ulrich Thürauf.
A very comprehensive bibliography of books and periodical articles, including those published during the period as well as later works about the period. **Z2237.S37**

Wattenbach, Wilhelm. Deutschlands Geschichtsquellen im Mittelalter bis zur mitte des dreizehnten Jahrhunderts. 6. Aufl. Berlin, W. Hertz, 1893–94. 2v. (Repr.: Darmstadt, Wissenschaftliche Buchgesellschaft, 1976) **DC189**

An important guide to the printed sources of German history. v.1, *Vorzeit und Karolinger,* covers from early times through the Carolingians to the treaty of Verdun in 843; v.2, *Deutsche Kaiserzeit,* covers through the Ottos, 900–1050.
Newly revised parts have begun to appear as:

———————— Vorzeit und Karolinger. Bearb. von Wilhelm Levison und Heinz Löwe. Weimar, Böhlaus, 1952–73. v.1–5, Beiheft. (In progress?) **DC190**

Contents: Heft 1, Die Vorzeit von der Anfängen bis zur Herrschaft der Karolinger; Heft 2, Die Karolinger von Anfang des 8. Jahrhunderts bis zum Tode Karls des Grossen; Heft 3, Die Karolinger vom Tode Karl des Grossen bis zum Vertrag von Verdun; Heft 4, Die Karolinger vom Vertrag von Verdun bis zum Herrschaftsantritt der Herrscher aus dem sächsischen Hause Italien und Papsttum; Heft 5, Die Karolinger vom Vertrag von Verdun bis zum Herrschaftsantritt der Herrscher aus dem sächsischen Hause des westfränkische Reich; Beiheft: Rechtsquellen von Rudolf Buchner.

Holtzmann, Robert. Deutschlands Geschichtsquellen im Mittelalter; die Zeit der Sachsen und Salier. Neuausgabe, besorgt von Franz-Josef Schmale. Köln, Böhlau Verlag, 1967–71. Teil 1–3. (In progress) **DC191**

Contents: Teil 1 (Heft 1–2), Das Zeitalter des Ottonischen Staates (900–1050); Teil 2 (Heft 3–4), Das Zeitalter des Investiturstreits (1050–1125); Teil 3, Italien (1050–1125), England (900–1135), Nachträge zum ersten und zweiten Teil. **DD86.H573**

Wattenbach, Wilhelm and **Schmale, Franz-Josef.** Deutschlands Geschichtsquellen im Mittelalter vom Tode Kaiser Heinrichs V. bis zum Ende des Interregnum. Darmstadt, Wissenschaftliche Buchgesellschaft, 1976– . v.1– . (In progress) **DC192**

Contents: v.1, Vom Tode Kaiser Heinrichs V. bis zum Ende des Interregnum.
The first volume of this new series supersedes the second half of the second volume of the 6th ed. of Wattenbach's *Deutschlands Geschichtsquellen im Mittelalter* (publ. 1894). **DD125.S38**

20th century

Deutsche Gesellschaft für Auswärtige Politik Forschungsinstitut, Frankfurt am Main. Schrifttum über Deutschland, 1918–1963, ausgewählte Bibliographie zur Politik und Zeitgeschichte. 2. erw. Aufl. Bearb. in Gemeinschaft mit dem Forschungsinstitut der Deutschen Gesellschaft fur Auswärtige Politik durch Inter Nationes, Bonn. Wiesbaden, Franz Steiner, [1964]. 292p. **DC193**

1st ed. 1962.
An annotated, classified bibliography of writings about Germany, 1918–62. Includes a section of works in languages other than German. **Z2221.D48**

Goguel, Rudi. Antifaschistischer Widerstand und Klassenkampf; die faschistische Diktatur 1933 bis 1945 und ihre Gegner. Bibliographie deutschsprachiger Literatur aus den Jahren 1945 bis 1973. Unter bibliographischer Mitarbeit von Jutta Grimann, Manfred Püschner, Ingrid Volz. [Berlin], Militärverlag der Deutschen Demokratischen Republik, [1976]. 567p. **DC194**

A classed listing of some 4,700 items, with author and subject indexes. **Z2241.A53G63**

Hersch, Gisela. A bibliography of German studies, 1945–1971: Germany under Allied occupation, Federal Republic of Germany, German Democratic Republic. Bloomington, Indiana Univ. Pr., [1972]. 603p. **DC195**

An interdisciplinary bibliography in classed arrangement. Author, title, subject index. **Z2221.H48**

Kehr, Helen and **Langmaid, Janet.** The Nazi era, 1919–1945; a select bibliography of published works from the early roots to 1980. [London], Mansell, [1982]. 621p. **DC196**

A selective, classified bibliography of about 6,500 items, almost exclusively works published in book form. Selectivity for the World War II period was particularly stringent, the primary aim being "to represent the German outlook of the time, while including a number of bibliographies and basic works which can point the way for further research."—*Introd.* Intended for the interested layman as well as the serious student. Indexed. **Z2240.K44**

Kimmich, Christoph M. German foreign policy, 1918–1945: a guide to research and research materials. Wilmington, Scholarly Resources, [1981]. 293p. **DC197**

The conduct of German foreign policy and the materials held in libraries, archives, and research institutes in Germany, Europe and the United States are described in the first two chapters. The largely annotated bibliography of reference sources, documentary series, memoirs, and secondary literature is arranged in broadly chronological order, and indexed by author, documentary series title, and subject. **Z6465.G4K54**

Merritt, Anna J. and **Merritt, Richard L.** Politics, economics, and society in the two Germanies, 1945–75; a bibliography of English-language works. Urbana, Univ. of Illinois Pr., [1978]. 268p. **DC198**

A computer printout listing more than 8,500 titles of books and periodical articles published before mid-1976 and relating to the post-war Germanies. Arrangement is by subject within six major divisions: (1) general (including the historical and demographic background); (2) the Occupation; (3) political systems; (4) economic systems; (5) social systems; and (6) foreign policy issues. Each item is cited only once in the bibliography. Author index. **Z7165.G3M47**

Price, Arnold Hereward, comp. East Germany; a selected bibliography. Wash., Lib. of Congress, 1967. 133p. **DC199**

Comp. in the Slavic and East European Division, Reference Dept., Library of Congress. An earlier bibliography with the same title was prepared by Fritz T. Epstein in 1959.

A selective, classified bibliography concerned with conditions within the Soviet Zone of Germany and the Soviet sector of Berlin. Emphasis is on works published since 1958. Z2244.E38P7

—— The Federal Republic of Germany; a selected bibliography of English-language publications. 2d rev. ed. Wash., Lib. of Congress, 1978. 116p. **DC200**

1st ed. 1972.

A very selective bibliography intended as a guide to American scholarship in contemporary German politics, economics, and social problems. Emphasis is on developments since 1949. Includes books, pamphlets, periodical articles, and government publications. Subject arrangement, with index by author or issuing agency. The 2d ed. "reflects developments that have occurred over the last ten years."—*Pref.* Z2240.3.P75

Stachura, Peter D. The Weimar era and Hitler, 1917–1933. Oxford, Clio Pr., [1977]. 276p. **DC201**

A topically arranged bibliography of Western-language books, pamphlets, *Festschriften,* theses, and other secondary materials published mainly between May 1945 and early 1975. Aims to be comprehensive, but critical annotations distinguish the more useful from the slighter studies. Author and subject indexes.

The Weimar Republic; a historical bibliography (Santa Barbara, Calif., ABC-Clio, 1984. 285p.) serves to update. Z2240.S74

The Third Reich, 1933–1939: a historical bibliography. Santa Barbara, Calif., ABC-Clio, [1984]. 239p. (ABC-Clio research guides, 10) **DC202**

932 periodical references, with abstracts, from the 1973–82 period. Entries were derived from the ABC-Clio database (on which *Historical abstracts* [DA20] is based). Citations are grouped in broad topical sections; author and detailed subject indexes.

Continued by *The Third Reich at war; a historical bibliography* (Santa Barbara, Calif., ABC-Clio, 1984. 270p.). Z2240.T47

Wiener Library, London. After Hitler: Germany, 1945–1963. London, publ. for the Wiener Library by Vallentine, Mitchell, 1963. 265p. (*Its* Catalogue ser., no.4) **DC203**

A classified listing of some 2,700 books and pamphlets on "Germany now." Includes such sections as: Wartime plans for Germany, Germany under occupation, The problem of Berlin, The new Germany, The Federal Republic, East Germany, Jews in postwar Germany, etc. Z2240.3.W5

—— From Weimar to Hitler: Germany, 1918–1933. 2d, rev. and enl. ed. London, publ. for the Wiener Library by Vallentine, Mitchell, 1964. 268p. (*Its* Catalogue ser., no.2) **DC204**

A list of monographs and essays held by the Library. Arranged by topic, with detailed index. Z2240.W53

—— Persecution and resistance under the Nazis. London, Inst. of Contemporary History, 1978. 500p. (*Its* Catalogue ser., no.7) **DC205**

Pt.1 originally publ. 1949 under title *Books on persecution, terror and resistance in Nazi Germany;* rev. 2d ed. 1959.

Topical arrangement of citations to more than 4,700 books, pamphlets, documents, and a few periodical articles. Pt.1 is a reprinting of the 2d ed. which expanded coverage to Jews in any Nazi-occupied territory and added new sections for individual cities or regions and on the after-effects on the health of the persecuted. Pt.2, also topically arranged, lists publications added to the Wiener Library from about 1959–74. Appendixes list unpublished eyewitness reports, unpublished Nuremberg documents, periodicals of Germans in exile, illegal pamphlets and periodicals. Full index to both parts. Z2240.W5

Local

Keyser, Erich. Bibliographie zur Städtegeschichte Deutschlands. Köln, Böhlau, 1969. 404p. (Bisherige Veröffentlichungen der Internationalen Kommission fur Städtegeschichte. Bibliographien) **DC206**

At head of title: Acta collegii historiae urbanae societatis historicorum internationalis.

Similar to (and published in the same series with) Dollinger's bibliography for the history of French cities (DC156). More than 4,700 items in geographical arrangement, with indexes of place-names and of authors. Z2243.K48

Dissertations

Gabel, Gernot U. and **Gabel, Gisela R.** Theses on Germany accepted for higher degrees by the universities of Great Britain and Ireland, 1900–1975: a bibliography. Hamburg, Gemini, 1979. 89p. **DC207**

A bibliography of theses at both the master's and doctoral level, arranged by broad subject classes (e.g., philosophy, religion, history/politics, science), with author and subject indexes. Language and literature are excluded as having been covered in *Theses in Germanic studies* (BD835). Z2221.G25

Milatz, Alfred and **Vogelsang, Thilo.** Hochschulschriften zur neueren deutschen Geschichte; eine Bibliographie. 1. Ausg., 1945–1955. Im Auftrage der Kommission fur Geschichte des Parlamentarismus und der Politischen Parteien sowie des Instituts fur Zeitgeschichte. Bonn, Kommission für Geschichte des Parlamentarismus und der Politischen Parteien, 1956. 142p. **DC208**

Lists 1,925 completed dissertations and 400 in progress on modern German history. Includes master's and doctoral theses from universities in West and East Germany, Austria, Switzerland, France, England, Holland, and the United States. Z2240.M5

Guides to records

See also AB134, AB136.

American Historical Association. Committee for the Study of War Documents. A catalogue of files and microfilms of the German Foreign Ministry archives, 1867–1920. Oxford, Univ. Pr., 1959. 1290col. (Repr.: N.Y., Kraus, 1970) **DC209**

Designed to present a complete record of the files of the Political Dept. of the German Foreign Ministry for the period 1867–1920, and at the same time to give details of the filming programs which have been carried out on these files. Indicates holders of negative copy. Serves as an index to U.S. National Archives Record Group 242. CD1261.A52

—— Guides to German records microfilmed at Alexandria, Va. Wash., Nat. Archives, Nat. Archives and Records Service, General Services Admin., 1958–1985. Pts.1–83. (In progress) **DC210**

Each part describes the filmed records of one of the Reich ministries or other record groups. The microfilms have been deposited in the National Archives, Record Group 242. D735.A58

—— A list of archival references and data of documents from the archives of the German Foreign Ministry, 1867–1920, microfilmed at Whaddon Hall for the American Committee for the Study of War Documents. Buckinghamshire, Whaddon Hall, 1957. 179p. **DC211**

The microfilms have been deposited in the National Archives in Washington (National Archives Record Group 242), and in the Public Record Office in London.

Haase, Carl. The records of German history in German and certain other record offices, with short notes on libraries and other collections. Boppard (am Rhein), Boldt, 1975. 194p.
DC212

Title also in German.

A guide for historians, treating archives and libraries in both East and West Germany, and giving for each the address, hours of opening, and a statement of collection size. Name index.
CD1220.H37

Schwändt, Ernst. Index of microfilmed records of the German Foreign Ministry and the Reich's Chancellery covering the Weimar period, deposited at the National Archives. Wash., Nat. Archives, 1958. 95p.
DC213

One of a series of indexes of microfilms of German documents which make up National Archives Record Group 242.

Covers the period of the Weimar Republic, 1919–33.
Z2240.S3

U.S. Dept. of State. Historical Office. A catalog of files and microfilms of the German Foreign Ministry archives, 1920–1945, comp. and ed. by George O. Kent. Stanford, Calif., Hoover Inst., Stanford Univ., 1962–72. 4v.
DC214

v.4 issued as Hoover Institution *Pubn.* 120.

"Continues and completes the work of the *Catalogue of German Foreign Ministry files and microfilms, 1867-1920* [DC209]."—Pref.

Published as a joint project of the U.S. Dept. of State and the Hoover Institution on War, Revolution, and Peace.

Lists all files from the *Politisches Archiv* of the German Foreign Ministry, 1920–1945, which were seized by the American and British armies at the end of World War II, and indicates which have been microfilmed. The films make up National Archives Record Group 242.

"The availability of new materials, specifically the files from various German missions and consulates in Europe as well as from some of the overseas offices, necessitated publication" (*Pref.*) of this final volume of the series.
CD1261.A65

Verzeichnis der schriftlichen Nachlässe im deutschen Archiven und Bibliotheken. Boppard am Rhein, H. Boldt, [1971–83]. 3v.
DC215

Contents: v.1, Die Nachlässe in den deutschen Archiven, bearb. W. A. Mommsen (2v.); v.2, Die Nachlässe in den Bibliotheken der Bundesrepublik Deutschland, bearb. Ludwig Denecke (2. Aufl. völlig neu bearb. Tilo Brandis. 538p.).

A survey of collections of papers; listing is by personal name, with dates, profession, and brief description of the papers and their location. Fully indexed.

Weinberg, Gerhard L. Guide to captured German documents, prep. by Gerhard L. Weinberg and the WDP staff under the direction of Fritz T. Epstein. [Maxwell Air Force Base, Ala., Human Resources Research Inst., 1952] 90p. (U.S. Human Resources Research Inst. Research memorandum, no.2, v.1)
DC216

At head of title: War Documentation Project. Study no.1.

Pts.1–2 list books and periodical articles which include German documentary material; pt.3 lists, by location, files of captured documents in various depositories, including the Library of Congress, the National Archives, the Hoover Institution, etc. Annotated; indexed.

—— —— Supplement. Wash., Nat. Archives, 1959. 69p.

Lists additional holdings in the various depositories.
Z2240.W4

Dictionaries and handbooks

Fest, Wilfried. Dictionary of German history, 1806–1945. N.Y., St. Martin's Pr.; London, Prior, [1978]. 189p.
DC217

Attempts to provide "salient facts and dates of Germany's politi-

cal, social and economic history . . . from the dissolution of the Holy Roman Empire of the German nation in 1806 to the collapse of the German Reich in 1945."—*Pref.* Most of the approximately 700 articles include at least one bibliographic reference. Chronological table; cross references. No index.
DD203.F47

Gebhardt, Bruno. Handbuch der deutschen Geschichte. 9. neu bearb. Aufl. hrsg. von Herbert Grundmann. Stuttgart, Union, 1970–76. 4v. in 5.
DC218

Contents: v.1, Frühzeit und Mittelalter; v.2, Von der Reformation bis zum Ende des Absolutismus; v.3, Von der Französischen Revolution bis zum Ersten Weltkrieg; v.4, Der Zeit der Weltkriege (2v.).

A very useful compendium, arranged chronologically, covering up to 1946–50. The work of several scholars, it originally appeared 1891–92 and has been issued in several revised editions under various editors. Each volume has name and subject indexes. v.4, pt.2 includes an appendix of lists and tables for 20th century statistics, political memberships of cabinets, parties, and government departments.
DD90.G32

Germany: a companion to German studies. Malcolm Pasley, ed. 2d ed. London & N.Y., Methuen, [1982]. 690p.
DC219

1st ed. 1972. An earlier work of the same title was edited by Jethro Bithell (1st–5th eds., 1932–55).

A handbook with bibliographies, covering German history, politics and the law; chapters contributed by specialists. Topical index.
DD61.G42

Grotefend, Hermann. Zeitrechnung des deutschen Mittelalters und der Neuzeit. Hannover, Hahn, 1891–98. 3 pts. in 2v.
DC220

Contents: Bd.1, Glossar und Tafeln (1891); Bd.2, Abt.1, Kalender der diöcesen Deutschlands, der Schweiz und Skandinaviens (1892); Abt.2, Ordenskalender. Heiligenverzeichniss. Nachträge zum Glossar (1898).

Glossaries, calendars, and tables showing the chronology of German history in the Middle Ages.

Published in various abridged editions, the latest of which is:
CE61.G3G83

—— Taschenbuch der Zeitrechnung des deutschen Mittelalters und der Neuzeit. 10. erw. Aufl. hrsg. von Th. Ulrich. Hannover, Hahn, 1960. 222p.
DC221

See also Gerhard Hellwig's *Daten zu deutschen Geschichte* (Berlin, Golmann, 1977. 384p.).
CE61.G3G8

Handwörterbuch des Grenz- und Auslanddeutschtums, unter Mitwirkung von etwa 800 Mitarbeitern und in verbindung mit u. prof. dr. H. Aubin . . . u. prof. dr. M. Bierbaum . . . [u.a.] heraus. von u.-prof. dr. Carl Petersen und u.-prof. d. dr. Otto Scheel. Breslau, Ferdinand Hirt, 1933–40. v.1–3. maps.
DC222

Contents: v.1–3, A–Massachusetts. Nachtrag.

No more published.

A comprehensive encyclopedia with long, signed articles, and bibliographies, on the life and culture of Germans in countries outside of Germany. Includes biography.
DD68.A2H3

Jung, Kurt Michael. Weltgeschichte in einem Griff. [Berlin, Safari-Verlag, 1968] 1200p. il.
DC223

Represents a 2d ed. of *Weltgeschichte in Stichworten* (Berlin, 1965), extending coverage to early 1967.

A chronology of events from earliest times, set forth in parallel columns for German, European, world, social, economic, and cultural history. Name and subject index. Emphasis is on European history, especially German history. Illustrated with photographs and maps.
D11.J8

Lexikon der deutschen Geschichte: Personen, Ereignisse, Institutionen, von der Zeitwende bis zum Ausgang des 2. Weltkrieges. Unter Mitarbeit von Historiken und Archivaren hrsg. von Gerhard Taddey. Stuttgart, Alfred Kröner Verlag, [1977]. 1352p.
DC224

Brief, signed articles on persons, events, institutions important in German history. Bibliographic references accompany many entries. A 2. überarbeitete Aufl. was published 1983 by Kröner in Stuttgart (1391p.). DD84.L48

Overesch, Manfred and **Saal, Friedrich Wilhelm.** Chronik deutscher Zeitgeschichte: Politik, Wirtschaft, Kultur. Düsseldorf, Droste Verlag, [1982–83]. Bd.1–2$^{1-2}$. (In progress) **DC225**

At head of title: Droste Geschichts-Kalendarium.

Contents: Bd.1, Die Weimarer Republik; Bd.2^1, Das Dritte Reich, 1933–1939; Bd.2^2, Das Dritte Reich, 1939–1945.

To be complete in 4v. Each volume offers a day-by-day summary of events and includes an index of names. DD232.O9

Reallexikon der germanischen Altertumskundes. Begründet von Johannes Hoops. 2. völlig neu bearb. und stark erw. Aufl. Hrsg. Herbert Jankuhn [et al.]. Berlin, W. de Gruyter, 1968–85. Lfg.1–6$^{1/2}$. (In progress) **DC226**

Contents: Bd.1–6, Lfg. 1/2, Aachen-Dubra.

1st ed. 1911–19 in 4v.

Virtually a new work, articles having been wholly rewritten and updated, with many new entries added. Signed articles; bibliographies. Promises to be a valuable reference source for archaeology, Germanic philology, and related fields. DD51.R42

Rössler, Hellmuth and **Franz, Günther.** Sachwörterbuch zur deutschen Geschichte. München, Oldenbourg, 1956–58. 1472p. (Repr.: Nendeln, Kraus, 1978. 2v.) **DC227**

A companion volume to the authors' *Biographisches Wörterbuch zur deutschen Geschichte* (AJ208). Dictionary arrangement, dealing with "events, institutions, countries, peoples and ideas," including the cultural, political, and economic aspects, of all periods. Includes bibliographies. DD84.R6

Sachwörterbuch der Geschichte Deutschlands und der deutschen Arbeiterbewegung. Berlin, Dietz, 1969–70. 2v. il. **DC228**

A dictionary of modern German history presented in terms of the working-class movement from the time of the French Revolution to the present, and emphasizing socialist and communist theories and developments, organizations, congresses, party publications, etc. DD84.S2

Snyder, Louis Leo. Encyclopedia of the Third Reich. N.Y., McGraw-Hill, [1976]. 410p. il. **DC229**

Entries for persons, places, terms, events, etc. "The major area covered is the period from the rise of National Socialism to the fall of the Third Reich in 1945. There are selected entries from the time of the Weimar Republic, which preceded Hitler, and from the Bonn Republic, which succeeded him. . . . The names of the biographees selected are those that would be recognized by most historians of the Third Reich as of some significance."—*Pref.* Brief bibliographies appended to many articles (English translations are cited in preference to the German originals); general bibliography, p.389–410. Terms are entered under the German form with cross references from the English equivalent. DD256.5.S57

GIBRALTER

Green, Muriel M. A Gibraltar bibliography. [London], Univ. of London, Inst. of Commonwealth Studies, 1980. 108p. **DC230**

Lists 984 books, periodical articles, government publications, and unpublished materials under ten broad subject headings. Author index. Locates copies in English and Gibraltar libraries.

——— ——— Supplement. 1981. p.109–36.

Z2704.G44G74

GREAT BRITAIN

Bibliography

Bibliography of British history. Issued under the direction of the American Historical Association and the Royal Historical Society of Great Britain. [1st–2d ed.] Oxford, Clarendon Pr., 1928–77. 6v. **DC231**

Contents: To 1485, ed. by Edgar B. Graves. 1975; Tudor period, 1485–1603, ed. by Conyers Read. 2d ed. 1959. (1st ed. 1933); Stuart period, 1603–1714, ed. by Mary Frear Keeler. 2d ed. 1970. (1st ed. 1928 by Godfrey Davies); The eighteenth century, 1714–1789, ed. by Stanley Pargellis and D. J. Medley. 1951; 1789–1851, ed. by Lucy M. Brown and Ian R. Christie. 1977; 1851–1914, ed. by Harold J. Hanham. 1976.

Covers all aspects of history: political, constitutional, legal, ecclesiastical, economic, military, cultural, and social, including discovery and exploration, colonization, etc. Each volume is a selected, classified-subject list—with author index—of book, pamphlet, and document material, with a liberal inclusion of articles in periodicals and society transactions.

Indispensable for the student of history, and useful also for literature and social studies.

Bruce, A. P. C. A bibliography of British military history, from the Roman invasions to the Restoration, 1660. München, K. G. Saur, 1981. 349p. **DC232**

A classed bibliography of books and periodical articles. Author index; many brief annotations. Nearly 3,300 items.

Continued chronologically by: Z2021.M5B78

——— A bibliography of the British Army, 1660–1914. London, K. G. Saur, 1985. 422p. **DC233**

Books, periodical articles, government documents, and unpublished official and personal papers are grouped in four broad subject chapters: (1) Bibliographies, guides, indexes and general works; (2) Organization, management and personnel; (3) Military theory, tactics, drill and equipment; (4) Military operations and overseas garrisons. Each chapter is subdivided by type of material, subjects, or chronological period. Indexed. Z6725.G7B78

Chaloner, W. H. and **Richardson, R. C.** Bibliography of British economic and social history. Manchester, Eng., Manchester Univ. Pr., [1983]. 208p. **DC234**

1st ed. 1976 had title: *British economic and social history.*

Some 5,800 entries are arranged by broad subjects within four chronological periods: 1066–1300, 1300–1500, 1500–1700, 1700–1970. Sections for Scotland and Ireland have been considerably expanded in this edition, as have those for family history, leisure and recreation, and crime. Author index. Z7165.G8C46

Gt. Brit. Foreign Office. Library. Catalogue of the Foreign Office Library, 1926–1968. Boston, G. K. Hall, 1972. 8v. **DC235**

For full information *see* DA184a.

Harvard University. Library. British history. Classification schedule, classified listing by call number, chronological listing. Cambridge, Mass., publ. by Harvard Univ. Lib., distr. by Harvard Univ. Pr., 1975. 2v. (Widener Library shelflist, 53–54) **DC236**

For a note on the series *see* AA145.

Lists "more than 45,000 titles of works on the history of the British Isles."—*Pref.* Z2016.H37

Higham, Robin. A guide to the sources of British military history. Berkeley, Univ. of California Pr., 1971. 630p. **DC237**

"Sponsored by the Conference on British Studies."—*title page.*

Scholar specialists have contributed bibliographic essays on the whole range of British military history from earliest times to the present. Attention is given to the general histories, bibliographies, selected special studies, and sources. Each chapter includes a section on research opportunities, pointing out areas where initial research is needed or where reappraisals are in order. Mention is also made of archives and special collections of papers and documents, with suggestions on how to obtain access to them. No general index.

Z2021.M5H54

Matthews, William. British diaries; an annotated bibliography of British diaries written between 1442 and 1942. Berkeley, Univ. of California Pr., 1950. 339p.　**DC238**

For full information *see* BD672.

Mullins, Edward Lindsay Carson. Texts and calendars: an analytical guide to serial publications. London, Offices of the Royal Historical Soc., 1958. 674p. (Royal Historical Soc. Guides and handbooks, no.7; repr. with corrections 1978 as no.12)　**DC239**

"An analytical guide to printed texts and calendars relating to English and Welsh history" (*Pref.*) issued in general collections such as the Rolls series, the Historical Manuscripts Commission reports, etc., and in the publications of societies such as the Hakluyt Society, the English Historical Society, the Camden Society, and numerous others. Lists publications 1802–1957.

Continued by:　Z2016.M8

—— Texts and calendars II: an analytical guide to serial publications, 1957–1982. London, Offices of the Royal Historical Soc., Univ. College London, 1983. 323p. (Royal Historical Soc. guides and handbooks, no.12)　**DC240**

Continues coverage of the above for publications issued between Mar. 1957 and Oct. 1982. Some organizations founded after 1957 are included. Notes on scope of the introductory material are now included. Corrections to the 1958 and 1978 volumes, p.317–20.

Z2016.M82

Smith, Harold. The British labour movement to 1970: a bibliography. [London], Mansell, [1981]. 250p.　**DC241**

A topically arranged listing of books, pamphlets, and periodical articles in English published 1945–70. Index of authors and subjects (though closer subject indexing would have been helpful). Decennial supplements are planned.　Z7164.L1S47

Current

Annual bibliography of British and Irish history. Publications of 1975– . [Hassocks, Eng.], Harvester Pr. for the Royal Historical Soc., [1976–]. Annual.　**DC242**

Designed to provide interim coverage in view of the long delays in publishing *Writings on British history* (DC247).

"Auxiliary" and "General" sections are followed by chronological sections for England/Britain, Medieval Wales, Scotland before the Union, and Ireland, each with appropriate subdivisions (e.g., Politics, External affairs, Religion, Social structure and population). Separate author and subject indexes. Items covering more than one category are entered only once, with cross references from the other sections.　Z2016.A55

Bindoff, Stanley Thomas and **Boulton, James T.** Research in progress in English and history in Britain, Ireland, Canada, Australia, and New Zealand. London, St. James Pr.; N.Y., St. Martin's Pr., [1976]. 284p.　**DC243**

Represents a new edition of the same editors' *Research in progress in English and historical studies in the universities of the British Isles* (1971). Now includes listings of work of scholars being carried on privately or under other than university auspices, and also work in progress in the other Commonwealth nations mentioned in the title.

Z6201.B59

Current research in British studies by North American scholars. [8th ed.] Manhattan, Kans., Military Affairs, 1980. 78p.　**DC244**

Earlier editions published 1953, 1955, 1957, 1960, 1964, 1969, 1975; now published for the Conference on British Studies. Some issues have title *Bibliography of current research in British history in the U.S. and Canada.*

Robert K. Donovan, ed.

A listing of research in progress, including doctoral research, based on information from questionnaires. Arranged mainly by period. Author index.　Z2016.C86

Historical Association, London. Annual bulletin of historical literature. v.1– , 1911– . London, 1912– . Annual.

DC245

—— —— General index. v.1–12, 1911–22. London, 1923. 68p.

Survey articles by specialists on the annual production of historical works. Chiefly British, though other countries are included, particularly Western Europe. Author index.

None issued 1914; 1940–41, 1942–45 issued in 2v.

Z6205.H65

Writings on British history, 1901–1933. London, Jonathan Cape, 1968–70. 5v.　**DC246**

Subtitle: A bibliography of books and articles on the history of Great Britain from about 400 A.D. to 1914, published during the years 1901–1933 inclusive, with an appendix containing a select list of publications in these years on British history since 1914.

Contents: v.1, Auxiliary sciences and general works; v.2, The Middle Ages, 450–1485; v.3, The Tudor and Stuart periods, 1485–1714; v.4, The eighteenth century, 1714–1815; v.5, 1815–1914 and Appendix.

A retrospective bibliography for 20th-century writings published prior to the beginning of the annual series of the same title (below). Purpose and scope are the same as for the volumes covering the later period, except that publications of societies are generally excluded, those materials being listed in E. L. C. Mullins's *Guide to the historical and archaeological publications . . .* (DC257), C. S. Terry's *Catalogue . . . 1780–1908* (DC336), and C. Matheson's *Catalogue . . . 1908–27* (DC337).　Z2016.W74

—— 1934– . . . . comp. by Alexander Taylor Milne. London, J. Cape, 1937– . [v.1–] Annual (irregular).

DC247

Contents: 1940–45 publ. 1960 in 2v.; 1946/48, ed. by D. J. Munro; 1949/51, ed. by D. J. Munro; 1952/54, ed. by J. M. Sims; 1955/57, ed. by J. M. Sims and P. M. Jacobs; 1958/59, ed. by H. J. Creaton; 1960/61, ed. by C. H. E. Philpin and H. J. Creaton; 1962/64–1971/72, ed. by H. J. Creaton.

Previously sponsored by the Institute of Historical Research; now published under the auspices of the Royal Historical Society.

A bibliography of books and articles on the history of Great Britain from about A.D. 400 to 1914, published during the years 1934– , with an appendix containing a select list of publications in these years on British history since 1914.

A comprehensive, classified bibliography with detailed indexes. Prior to the issue covering 1946–48, book reviews were noted; review articles continue to be included.　Z2016.R88

Early (including archaeology)

Altschul, Michael. Anglo-Norman England, 1066–1154. [London], Univ. Pr., 1969. 83p. (Conference on British Studies. Bibliographical handbooks)　**DC248**

Similar to Levine's bibliography for Tudor England (DC264) in the same series. Slightly more than 1,800 items in subject sections, with author index.　Z2017.A43

Archaeological bibliography for Great Britain and Ireland, 1940/46– . London, Council for British Archaeology, 1949– . Annual.　**DC249**

Frequency varies: biennial, 1948/49–1952/53.

1948/49 entitled *Archaeological bulletin.*

Intended to cover the period from the earliest times to A.D. 1600. Offers a complete list of articles published in British and Irish periodicals on archaeology of Great Britain and Ireland during the year under review. The Council publishes abstracts of periodical articles, monographs, *Festschriften,* and government publications important to researchers in this field in *British archaeological abstracts* (London, 1967–). Z2027.A8C59

A bibliography of English history to 1485, based on The sources and literature of English history from the earliest times to about 1485 by Charles Gross. Ed. by Edgar B. Graves. Oxford & N.Y., Clarendon Pr., 1975. 1103p. (Bibliography of British history) **DC250**

For a note on the series *see* DC231.

"Issued under the sponsorship of the Royal Historical Society, the American Historical Association and the Mediaeval Academy of America."—*t.p.*

Like Charles Gross's *Sources and literature of English history . . .* (2d ed. rev. and enl. London, Longmans, 1915. 820p.), which is largely superseded, this edition is planned as "a systematic survey of the printed materials relating to the political, constitutional, legal, social, and economic history of England, Wales and Ireland down to 1485."—*Pref.* Older standard or seminal works have been retained and recent writings added, "especially those which set forth new or controversial interpretations or include modern specialized bibliographies." Includes works published through Dec. 1969 for the pre-1066 period; through Dec. 1970 for the period 1066–1485. The sections for economic and cultural and social history are considerably expanded. Extensive index. Z2017.B5

Bonser, Wilfrid. A prehistoric bibliography; extended and ed. by June Troy. Oxford, Blackwell, 1976. 425p. **DC251**

About 9,000 items in classed arrangement with an author/subject index. In five main sections: (1) Men and methods in archaeology; (2) Field archaeology; (3) Specific sites; (4) Material finds; (5) Culture.
Continued by: Z2007.A67B65

—— A Romano-British bibliography, 55 B.C.–A.D. 449. Oxford, B. Blackwell, 1964 [i.e. 1965]. 2v. **DC252**

Includes materials published in books and journals to the end of 1959, relating to the period from Julius Caesar's first arrival in Britain through 449. v.2 is an index.
Continued by: Z2017.B62

—— An Anglo-Saxon and Celtic bibliography (450–1087). Berkeley, Los Angeles, Univ. of California. Pr., 1957. 2v. (Repr.: Philadelphia, R. West, 1977) **DC253**

v.1 is an extensive listing of books and articles on all historical aspects of the period, including geography, archaeology, general culture, art, etc. v.2 provides an author index and a subject and topographical index. Z2017.B6

Gomme, George Laurence. Index of archaeological papers, 1665–1890. London, Constable, 1907. 910p. (Repr.: N.Y., B. Franklin, 1965) **DC254**

A useful author index to some 94 sets of English archaeological periodicals and transactions of local antiquarian societies. Principally British archaeology, but includes also material on classical and other non-British antiquities. Continued by: Z2027.A8I6

Index of archaeological papers published in 1891–1910. London, Constable, 1892–1914. v.1–20. **DC255**

An annual continuation of Gomme above, indexing the same type of material and following the same plan as far as the author index is concerned, but differing from the main work in that each annual volume has a subject index to the author list. While each volume nominally covers one year, many cover a longer period since whenever a new periodical is added to the list, it is indexed back to 1891.

Publication suspended after 1914. Most of the periodicals indexed are now included in the *Subject index to periodicals* (AE237) and the *British humanities index* (AE238). Archaeological articles are also included, 1929–1942/46, in *Guide to the historical publications of the societies of England and Wales* (DC256). The period 1903–33 is covered by Mullins (DC257), and currently in the *Archaeological bibliography . . .* (DC249). Z2027.A8I7

Guide to the historical publications of the societies of England and Wales; Suppl. 1–13, 1929–1942/46. London,

Longmans, 1930–48. 13v. (Bulletin of the Inst. of Historical Research, Suppl., Nov. 1930–48) **DC256**

Ceased publication.

Prepared by a committee of the Institute and of the Congress of Archaeological Societies, the supplements appearing before the basic work which has not yet appeared. Planned to do for the societies of England and Wales what Terry (DC336) and Matheson (DC337) do for those of Scotland, and also to take the place of the discontinued *Index of archaeological papers* (DC255). The supplements merely record issues for the years covered, leaving the historical information about the societies and the records of publication, index, etc., to be given in the basic volume.

Mullins's *Guide* (below) provides a list of contents of the series.

Mullins, Edward Lindsay Carson. A guide to the historical and archaeological publications of societies in England and Wales, 1903–1933; comp. for the Institute of Historical Research. London, Athlone Pr., 1968. 850p. **DC257**

Lists and indexes the books and articles issued by more than 400 local and national societies of England, Wales, Isle of Man, and the Channel Islands during the period in question. Listing is under name of the society, with an author index and a detailed subject index. Serves as a complement to *Writings on British history* (DC246). Z5055.G6M8

Medieval

See also DC250.

Davis, Godfrey Rupert Carless. Medieval cartularies of Great Britain: a short catalogue. London, Longmans, 1958. 182p. **DC258**

"Cartularies are registers of . . . the title deeds (*carte*), charters of privilege (*privilegia*) and other documents kept by landowners as evidence of their personal or corporate rights. . . . This book is an attempt to provide a brief survey of the present state of knowledge [of existing cartularies]."—*Introd.*

Guth, DeLloyd J. Late-medieval England, 1377–1485. Cambridge & N.Y., Univ. Pr., for the Conference on British Studies, [1976]. 143p. (Conference on British Studies. Bibliographical handbooks) **DC259**

Classified arrangement listing some 2,500 printed materials published through Dec. 1974 and dealing with England and Wales (plus a few references to Scotland and Ireland), 1377–1485. Some annotations. Index of editors, authors, and translators. Z2017.G87

Wilkinson, Bertie. The high Middle Ages in England, 1154–1377. Cambridge, Univ. Pr. for the Conference on British Studies, [1978]. 130p. (Conference on British Studies. Bibliographical handbooks) **DC260**

A select bibliography for the student and scholar. Classed arrangement, with author index. Includes books and periodical articles. 2,259 items. Z2017.W54

16th and 17th centuries

Abbott, Wilbur Cortez. A bibliography of Oliver Cromwell; a list of printed materials relating to Oliver Cromwell, together with a list of portraits and caricatures. Cambridge, Harvard Univ. Pr., 1929. 551p. **DC261**

Material on the Cromwell period published from 1597 to 1928. Z8200.A14

Davies, Godfrey. Stuart period, 1603–1714. 2d ed. [ed. by] Mary Frear Keeler. Oxford, Clarendon Pr., 1970. 734p. (Bibliography of British history) **DC262**

For information on the series *see* DC231.

A complete revision, expansion, and updating of the first edition (1928) by Godfrey Davies. Cutoff date for books is mainly 1962 and for periodical articles 1958, although selected items of later date appear in both categories. 4,350 numbered items, plus additional references in the notes and annotations. Indexed.

A list of corrigenda appears in *Irish historical studies* 18:123–26 (March 1972).

The first edition should be retained because it is much stronger in legal and ecclesiastical history than the new edition. The Keeler edition, on the other hand, has better coverage in economic history. For a comparison of the two editions *see* the review in *English historical review* 89:118–22 (Jan. 1974). Z2018.D25

Grose, Clyde Leclare. A select bibliography of British history, 1660–1760. Chicago, Univ. of Chicago Pr., 1939. 507p. (Repr.: N.Y., Octagon Books, 1967) **DC263**

Divided by periods: General, 1660–1760; 1660–88; 1689–1714; 1715–60. Classified arrangement, the detailed table of contents showing the scheme. Includes some major collections of manuscripts as well as printed works. Annotated. Works considered exceptionally useful are starred. Z2016.G86

Levine, Mortimer. Tudor England, 1485–1603. Cambridge, Univ. Pr., [1968]. 115p. (Conference on British Studies. Bibliographical handbooks) **DC264**

A selective, classified bibliography intended for the scholar and advanced student. Much more selective than Conyers Read's bibliography for the same period (DC267), but has a later closing date. Z2017.5.L4

Morrill, John Stephen. Seventeenth-century Britain, 1603–1714. [Folkestone, Eng.], Dawson; [Hamden, Conn.], Archon, [1980]. 189p. (Critical bibliographies in modern history, v.2) **DC265**

A selective bibliography "limited in its scope to a study of the recent secondary literature. . . . It is assumed that all the books included are of value to those studying history at school, college or university (although 'difficult' and 'technical' works are included with appropriate warning)."—*Introd.* Classed arrangement, with author index. Appendix of key periodical articles published 1958–79. Z2018.M63

New York. Union Theological Seminary. Library. Catalogue of the McAlpin collection of British history and theology; comp. and ed. by C. R. Gillett. N.Y., 1927–30. 5v. **DC266**

Valuable for historical material published from 1500 to 1700. Arranged chronologically with alphabetical index.
For full record *see* BB224. Z7757.E5N5

Read, Conyers. Tudor period, 1485–1603. 2d ed. Oxford, 1959. 624p. (Bibliography of British history) **DC267**

For information on the series *see* DC231.
1st ed. 1933.
A major scholarly bibliography of books, articles, documents and pamphlets covering the period between the Graves (DC250) and Keeler (DC262) bibliographies. Topical listing; each subsection has an introductory note emphasizing the more important works. This edition is exhaustive to Jan. 1, 1957, with some later works included. A few items from the earlier edition were dropped, and about 2,500 added. Z2018.R28

Sachse, William Lewis. Restoration England, 1660–1689. Cambridge, Univ. Pr. for the Conference on British Studies, [1971]. 114p. (Conference on British Studies. Bibliographical handbooks) **DC268**

A selected, classified bibliography similar to the Altschul and Altholz volumes (DC248, DC269). Index of authors and editors. Z2018.S3

18th and 19th centuries

Altholz, Josef Lewis. Victorian England, 1837–1901. Cambridge, [Eng.], publ. for the Conference on British Studies at the Univ. Pr., 1970. 100p. (Conference on British Studies. Bibliographical handbooks) **DC269**

A selective bibliography, "the chief criterion being that of poten-

tial scholarly utility."—*Pref.* Similar to Altschul's *Anglo-Norman England* (DC248) and Levine's *Tudor England* (DC264) in the same series. Z2019.A56

Batts, John Stuart. British manuscript diaries of the nineteenth century: an annotated listing. Fontwell, Centaur Pr.; Totowa, N.J., Rowman and Littlefield, 1976. 345p. **DC270**

For full information *see* BD671.

Brown, Lucy M. and **Christie, Ian R.** Bibliography of British history, 1789–1851. Oxford, Clarendon Pr., 1977. 759p. (Bibliography of British history) **DC271**

For a note on the series *see* DC231.
"Issued under the direction of the American Historical Association and the Royal Historical Society of Great Britain."—*t.p.*
Very selective in its inclusiveness. "The various sections and subsections have been prepared with the object of providing, first, a representative sample of the more prolific forms of contemporary imprints, such as pamphlets and essays; secondly, an outline of each field as treated in the literature concerned with it, drawing attention to leading features and/or personalities; thirdly, reference, where this is possible, to up-to-date authoritative treatment; and fourthly, an indication of further immediate guidance to be found, for instance, in specialist bibliographies, in reading lists of books, or by reference to specialist journals or series."—*Pref.* Cutoff date appears to have been approximately 1973, with some items as late as 1975 noted. Z2019.B76

Gipson, Lawrence Henry. A bibliographical guide to the history of the British Empire, 1748–1776. N.Y., Knopf, [1968]. 478p. (The British Empire before the American Revolution, v.14) **DC272**

A classified listing of books, pamphlets, and periodical articles. Detailed index. A companion volume dealing with manuscripts is:

————— A guide to manuscripts relating to the history of the British Empire, 1748–1776. N.Y., Knopf, 1970. 490p. (The British Empire before the American Revolution, v.15) **DC273**

Forms a companion to Gipson's *Bibliographical guide* for printed materials (above) and completes the series. Arrangement is by depository, with notes on the manuscript holdings in general, and descriptions of special collections of papers. Indexed.

Hanham, Harold John. Bibliography of British history, 1851–1914. Oxford, Clarendon Pr., 1976. 1606p. **DC274**

For a note on the series *see* DC231.
"Issued under the direction of the American Historical Association and the Royal Historical Society of Great Britain."—*t.p.*
Aims "to list the major works which a student is likely to wish to consult, a selection of other works which makes clear the scope of contemporary printed materials, and a selection of biographies and autobiographies."—*Pref.* Cutoff date was generally 1970, but some publications as late as 1973 have been included. Author and subject index, p.1239–1606. Z2019.H35

Harrison, John Fletcher Clews and **Thompson, Dorothy.** Bibliography of the Chartist movement, 1837–1976. Hassocks, Sussex, Eng., Harvester Pr.; Atlantic Highlands, N.J., Humanities Pr, [1978]. 214p. **DC275**

". . . intended as a modest tool for working scholars and as a survey of the state of Chartist scholarship to date."—*Introd.* Aims to include known Chartist items in local and national archives of Britain, together with materials in important Chartist collections abroad. In five main sections: (1) Bibliographies; (2) Manuscript sources; (3) Contemporary printed sources; (4) Unpublished secondary material; (5) Published secondary material. Manuscript materials are listed by repository; library locations are given for the less usual printed items. Indexed. Z7164.L1H36

Morgan, William Thomas and **Morgan, Chloe Siner.** Bibliography of British history (1700–1715) with special reference to the reign of Queen Anne. Bloomington, Ind., 1934–42. 5v. (Indiana Univ. studies, no.18–19, 23–26, 94–95, 114–24) (Repr.: N.Y., B. Franklin, 1973) **DC276**

Contents: v.1–2, Pamphlets and memoirs, 1700–1715; v.3, Source materials published in 1717 and later. Correspondence, autobiographies, diaries, and journals. Periodicals, including newspapers and annuals (1700–1715). Plays and other dramatic works. Secondary materials (to about June 1938); v.4, Unpublished manuscripts with index; v.5, Addenda and corrigenda. Supplements to v.1–3. Appendixes. Comprehensive index to v.1, 2, 3, and 5.

Z2018.M6

Nicholls, David. Nineteenth-century Britain, 1815–1914. [Folkestone, Kent], Dawson; [Hamden, Conn.], Archon Books, [1978]. 170p. **DC277**

More than 950 items, most of them briefly annotated. Classed arrangement with author index. Z2019.N5

Pargellis, Stanley and **Medley, D. J.** The eighteenth century, 1714–1789. Oxford, Clarendon Pr., 1951. 642p. (Bibliography of British history) (Repr.: Totowa, N.J., Rowman and Littlefield, 1977) **DC278**

For information on the series *see* DC231.

A major scholarly bibliography for this period. Concentrates heavily on source material, attempting "to provide some sort of guide through the mass of contemporary literature, much of which is yet undiscovered by students."—*Pref.* Within each topical section entries are arranged by date of publication or date of coverage, earliest first. Includes sections for the American colonies and India, as well as local history, Scotland, Ireland, and Wales. Brief commentary; indexed by main entry and subject. Fits chronologically between Keeler (DC262) and Brown (DC271) in the series.

Smith, Robert A. Late Georgian and Regency England. Cambridge, Eng., Univ. Pr. for the Conference on British Studies, [1984]. 114p. (Conference on British studies. Bibliographical handbooks) **DC279**

A topically arranged bibliography of "the best of the voluminous literature on later eighteenth and early nineteenth century England."—*Pref.* 2,514 entries; author index. With a few exceptions, publications are pre-1981. Z2041.S64

Williams, Judith Blow. A guide to the printed materials for English social and economic history, 1750–1850. N.Y., Columbia Univ. Pr., 1926. 2v. (Records of civilization: sources and studies, ed. by J. T. Shotwell) (Repr.: N.Y., Octagon Books, 1966) **DC280**

An annotated bibliography, in classified arrangement, covering all phases of economic and social life in England during the Industrial Revolution, including sections on biography and local history. Still useful for the many citations to materials contemporary to the period. Z7165.G8W7

20th century

Aster, Sydney. British foreign policy 1918–1945; a guide to research and research materials. Wilmington, Del., Scholarly Resources, 1984. 324p. **DC281**

A survey of archives and libraries is followed by a bibliography of printed primary and secondary literature grouped as Parliament and the government, memoirs, and period divisions. Includes a discussion of the Foreign Office and how policy is made; appendix of names of secretaries and undersecretaries of state, ambassadors and consuls. Name index to the archives and bibliography section.

Havighurst, Alfred F. Modern England, 1901–1970. Cambridge & N.Y., Univ. Pr. for the Conference on British Studies, [1976]. 109p. (Conference on British Studies. Bibliographical handbooks) **DC282**

". . . a bibliographical handbook designed as a ready book of reference for the scholar, for the teacher, for the student, and for the general reader."—*Pref.* Classified arrangement; index of authors, editors, translators. Z2020.H38

Mowat, Charles Loch. Great Britain since 1914. Ithaca, N.Y., Cornell Univ. Pr.; London, Hodder & Stoughton,

1971. 224p. (Sources of history: studies in the uses of historical evidence) **DC283**

A discussion of materials and approaches to research in British history since 1914. Z2020.M63

Dissertations

See also DA25.

Bell, S. Peter. Dissertations on British history, 1815–1914; an index to British and American theses. Metuchen, N.J., Scarecrow Pr., 1974. 232p. **DC284**

In five main sections: (1) political history; (2) economic history; (3) social history; (4) ecclesiastical history; (5) history of education. Sections are subdivided as necessary. Indexes of authors, persons, places and subjects. About 2,300 entries. British master's essays are included, but not American; also, theses submitted prior to 1914 are omitted. Z2016.B43

Gilbert, Victor Francis. Labour and social history theses: American, British, and Irish university theses and dissertations in the field of British and Irish labour history, presented between 1900 and 1978. [London], Mansell, [1982]. 194p. **DC285**

A classified bibliography of theses on political and trade union movements, together with social history topics such as housing, public health, income, which affected working-class life. Indexes of persons, places, subjects, and authors.

Updated by an annual list published in the Autumn issue of the *Bulletin* of the Society for the Study of Labour History.

Z7164.L1G3

London. University. Institute of Historical Research. Historical research for university degrees in the United Kingdom, 1931/32–1952. (Bulletin . . . Theses supplement, no.1–14) London, Longmans, 1933–53. **DC286**

Ceased publication.

Each number is in two parts: (1) Theses completed during the year; (2) Theses in progress. "The former follows on the lists published annually in *History* from 1920 to 1929 [covering 1911/19–1927/28], and in the *Bulletin* from 1930 to 1932; the latter is an innovation suggested by the Anglo-American Historical Committee."—*Pref. note to no.1.*

Superseded by: Z5055.G695

——— ——— Theses completed. 1953– . London, 1954– . Annual.

——— ——— Theses in progress. 1954– . London, 1954– . Annual.

Issues for 1954–66 published as *Theses supplement* no.15–27 to the *Bulletin.* Beginning 1967 (list no.28) the lists appear as separate publications of the Institute.

Each section, 1953–59, was arranged by university with author index (for completed theses there were also subject indexes). Beginning with 1960, each section is arranged under "broad chronological and topographical headings" with indexes of authors. Again, for completed theses, there are also subject indexes.

Guides to records

Cook, Chris. Sources in British political history, 1900–1951. Comp. for the British Library of Political and Economic Science. London, Macmillan; N.Y., St. Martin's Pr., 1975–85. 6v. **DC287**

Contents: v.1, A guide to the archives of selected organisations and societies; v.2, A guide to the private papers of selected public servants; v.3–4, A guide to the private papers of Members of Parliament; v.5, A guide to the private papers of selected writers, intellectuals and publicists; v.6, First consolidated supplement.

A report on "the results of a survey of twentieth-century British political archives."—*Foreword.* The project was "intended to locate the papers of all persons and organisations influential in British politics between 1900 and 1951, encourage their preservation, and publish a guide," but certain priorities have necessarily been established: "Whilst a comprehensive search is being made for the papers of all members of the House of Commons, the papers of individual members of other categories are being sought more selectively, on the basis either of their rank or of their known political activity."

In v.1, entry is alphabetical by name of organization, society, or political movement. A historical note is followed by notes on the papers, indication of their location, and availability. v.2 "is concerned with the private papers of some 1,500 senior public servants who were active and influential in British public life between 1900 and 1951" (*Introd.*), including diplomats, civil servants, colonial administrators, and the armed forces.

v.3–4 "are concerned with the surviving private papers of all Members of Parliament from the General Election of September 1900 to the fall of the Atlee Government in the election of October 1951 . . . [and] attempt to include every M.P. elected during this period, together with every holder of a ministerial appointment."—*Introd.*

v.5 includes journalists, Fabians, businessmen, religious leaders, trade unionists, etc. v.6 records changes in location of materials, new deposits, and reorganization or new information gathered between 1977 and July 1, 1984.   Z2020.C66

Foster, Janet and **Sheppard, Julia.** British archives; a guide to archive resources in the United Kingdom. Detroit, Gale, [1982]. 533p.   **DC288**

For full information *see* AB141.

The pamphlet *British national archives* issued annually by the Stationery Office, London, as no.24 in the series "Government publications sectional list," provides a listing of all Record Office publications whether in print or not.

Galbraith, Vivian Hunter. Introduction to the use of the public records. London, Oxford Univ. Pr., 1952. 112p. il.   **DC289**

"Reprinted . . . from . . . first ed. (1934) with corrections in 1952, 1963, and 1971."—*verso of title page.*

A practical handbook for the beginner to the main types of records and how to procure them. Bibliography.   CD1043.G3

Gt.Brit. Historical Manuscripts Commission. A guide to the reports on collections of manuscripts of private families, corporations and institutions in Great Britain and Ireland issued by the Royal Commissioners for Historical Manuscripts. London, Stat. Off., 1914–38. 2v. in 3.   **DC290**

Pt.1, Topographical index. 1914. 233p.; pt.2, v.1–2, Index of persons. 1938. 859p.

Pt.2 has title *Guide to the reports of the Royal Commission on Historical Manuscripts, 1870–1911,* and is an alphabetical index of names, with reference under each to the report or reports in which some letter or document connected with the person is listed or calendared. Continued by: DA25.M25

—— Guide to the reports of the Royal Commission on Historical Manuscripts, 1911–1957. London, Stat. Off., 1966–73. 2pts. in 4v.   **DC291**

Contents: pt.1, Index of places; pt.2, Index of persons, 3v.

A continuation of the Commission's *Guide to reports . . . 1870–1911* (above).   DA25.M1G73

Gt.Brit. Public Record Office. Guide to the contents of the Public Record Office . . . rev. (to 1960) from the *Guide* by the late M. S. Giuseppi. London, Stat. Off., 1963–68. 3v.   **DC292**

Contents: v.1, Legal records, etc.; v.2, State papers and departmental records; v.3, Documents transferred 1960–1966.

v.1–2 are based on, and in large measure a revision and updating of the Giuseppi *Guide to the manuscripts preserved in the Public Record Office* (London, 1923–24. 2v.), adding the records transferred to the Public Record Office, 1923–60, many of which fall into new classes. v.3 "takes account of transfers of new classes of records and of changes in existing classes" (*Introd.*) effected during the period indicated.

A cumulation and updating of the *Guide* is being issued on microfiche as *Current guide to the contents of the Public Record Office* (Kew, P.R.O., 1983–). Only v.2–3 have been issued thus far, covering material in the paper edition of v.2 and the relevant portion of v.3; the microform v.3 is an index. The earlier set will continue to be useful for its introductory materials, brief histories of the departments, notes on finding aids, etc.

The "Handbook" series issued by the Public Record Office includes various items of interest, including: no.3, The records of the Colonial and Dominions Offices (1964); no.8, List of Colonial Office confidential prints (1965); no.13, Records of the Foreign Office, 1782–1939 (1969); no.15, The Second World War (DA209); no.17, The Cabinet Office to 1945 (1975).   CD1043.A553

—— PRO microfilm catalogue, May 1983. [London, P.R.O., 1983] 75*l.* microfiche.   **DC293**

1st ed. (1970) entitled *Public Record Office film catalogue.*

". . . lists all of the items on film amongst the records held by the PRO at Kew."—*Introd.* " Arranged by group (e.g., Foreign Office); references to more extensive descriptions which appeared in earlier editions are omitted.

Guides to sources for British history based on the National Register of Archives. London, H.M.S.O., [1982]–85. no.1–4. (In progress)   **DC294**

At head of title: The Royal Commission on Historical Manuscripts.

Contents: no.1, Papers of British cabinet ministers, 1782–1900; no.2, The manuscript papers of British scientists, 1600–1940; no.3, Guide to the locations of collections described in the Reports and calendars series, 1870–1980; no.4, Private papers of British diplomats, 1782–1900.

The series aims to publish systematically revised digests of selected segments of the unpublished information accumulated by the Commission in the National Register of Archives, concentrating "on the areas of historical study for which the information itself is most comprehensive and most obviously in scholarly demand."—*Pref., v.1.*

MacFarlane, Alan. A guide to English historical records. Cambridge, Cambridge Univ. Pr., [1983]. 134p.   **DC295**

Offers brief descriptions of types of records (for property, church, courts, etc.) and discussions of their use.   DA32.5.M33

Storey, Richard and **Madden, Lionel.** Primary sources for Victorian studies: a guide to the location and use of unpublished materials. [London], Phillimore, [1977]. 81p.   **DC296**

For full information *see* BD547.

Historiography

Elton, Geoffrey Rudolph. Modern historians on British history, 1485–1945; a critical bibliography, 1945–1969. London, Methuen; Ithaca, N.Y., Cornell Univ. Pr., [1970]. 239p.   **DC297**

Essentially a bibliographic essay on British historical writings of the period indicated. Author and subject indexes.   Z2016.E44

Recent views on British history: essays on historical writing since 1966, ed. for the Conference on British Studies by Richard Schlatter. New Brunswick, Rutgers Univ. Pr., [1984]. 525p.   **DC298**

Offers essays by American scholars detailing the most significant developments in the field of British historiography from 1966–78 (although some contributions finished after the original deadline include later publications). Updates *Changing views of British history,* ed. by Elizabeth C. Furber (Cambridge, Harvard Univ. Pr., 1966).

Each essay covers writings on a particular period, with separate essays for Scotland, Ireland, and the British Empire/Commonwealth.   DA1.R4

Watson, Charles A. The writing of history in Britain: a bibliography of post-1945 writings about British historians and biographers. N.Y., Garland, 1982. 726p. (Garland reference library of social science, v.91) **DC299**

Not a bibliography of writings on historiography, but of writings about the historians and biographers. Arranged by period, with author and subject indexes. Z6208.H5W37

Dictionaries and handbooks

Adkins, Lesley and **Adkins, Roy A.** A thesaurus of British archaeology. Newton Abbott, Eng., David & Charles; Totowa, N.J., Barnes & Noble, [1982]. 319p. il. **DC300**

Also publ. as *The handbook of British archaeology* (London, Macmillan, 1983).

Concerned with the archaeology of England, Scotland and Wales, from the palaeolithic to the medieval periods. Arranged by period, then topically within chapters. Select bibliography and detailed index. DA90.A6

Butler, David and **Sloman, Ann.** British political facts, 1900–1979. 5th ed. [London, Macmillan, 1980] 492p. **DC301**

For full information *see* CJ331.
A new edition was published 1985.

Cheney, Christopher Robert. Handbook of dates for students of English history. London, Offices of the Royal Historical Soc., 1945. 164p. (Royal Historical Soc. Guides and handbooks, no.4) (Repr. with corrections 1978) **DC302**

Combines some of the useful features of various other handbooks. Four sections are reprinted, with some revision, from Powicke, *Handbook of British chronology* (DC308), viz., Reckonings of time, Rulers of England, Saints' days and festivals, and Legal chronology. The 36 tables of calendars for all possible dates of Easter are based on Grotefend, *Zeitrechnung* (DC220), and Edward Alexander Fry, *Almanacks for students of English history* (1915). DA34.C5

Cook, Chris and **Wroughton, John.** English historical facts, 1603–1688. [London, Macmillan]; Totowa, N.J., Rowman and Littlefield, [1980]. 231p. **DC303**

Similar in choice of topics and arrangement to the volume for 1485–1603 (DC307), this volume covering the Stuart and Cromwell periods, with tables, lists, chronologies, etc., in chapters on the monarchy, selected holders of public office, central government, Parliament, local government, the church, armed forces, overseas trade and the colonies, education, population, and towns. Selected biographies; select bibliography. No index.

Continued by *British historical facts* (below). DA375.C7

Cook, Chris and **Stevenson, John.** British historical facts, 1760–1830. [London, Macmillan]; Hamden, Conn., Archon Books, 1980. 197p. **DC304**

Presents various lists, tables, chronologies, etc., within sections such as: The monarchy; Ministries and administrations; Selected holders of public office; Parliament and elections; Foreign affairs; Armed forces; Law and order; The press; Religion; The economy.

Continued by: DA505.C57

Cook, Chris and **Keith, Brendan.** British historical facts, 1830–1900. [London, Macmillan, 1975] 279p. (Repr.: N.Y., St. Martin's, 1984) **DC305**

A compilation of lists, tables, etc., bringing together a great deal of political information from many sources. Emphasis is on people, listing "almost all those who held high political, judicial, military or administrative office in Britain between 1830 and 1900."—*Pref.* JN216.C65

Cook, Chris and **Stevenson, John.** The Longman handbook of modern British history, 1714–1980. London, Longman, [1983]. 380p. **DC306**

Offers a variety of chronologies, statistical tables, lists of principal ministers, biographical sketches, etc., relating to British political, social, religious, and economic history. Indexed. DA470.C65

Powell, Ken and **Cook, Chris.** English historical facts, 1485–1603. [London, Macmillan]; Totowa, N.J., Rowman & Littlefield, [1977]. 228p. **DC307**

Offers a variety of lists, chronologies, and background information on historical events and developments of the Tudor period, presented in chapters on: The crown and central government; Parliament; The judicature and the courts; Local government; The church; Education; War, rebellion and diplomacy; Scotland and Ireland; Tudor economic legislation; Population and growth of towns. "Selected Tudor biographies," p. 206–20; brief bibliography, p. 221–28. Lacks an index which would have greatly enhanced the ready reference value. Continued by DC303. DA315.P68

Powicke, Frederick Maurice and **Fryde, E. B.** Handbook of British chronology. 2d ed. London, Royal Historical Soc., 1961. 565p. (Royal Historical Soc. Guides and handbooks, no.2) **DC308**

1st ed. 1939.
Partial contents: Bibliographical guide to the lists of English office-holders; Chronological lists of rulers of England, Wales, Scotland and the Isle of Man; Officers of State of England, Ireland and Scotland; Bishops of England, Wales, Scotland, Ireland; Dukes, Marquesses, and Earls (England), 1066–1714, (Ireland) (Scotland); English parliaments to 1832; Provincial and national councils of the Church in England to 1536.

This edition omits the section, "Reckonings of time," which has been reprinted in revised form in Cheney, *Handbook of dates for students of English history* (DC302). It includes several new lists, with some extensions and revisions of others. No index.

DA34.P6

Saul, Nigel. The Batsford companion to medieval England. London, Batsford; Totowa, N.J., Barnes & Noble, [1983]. 283p. il. **DC309**

A dictionary arrangement of relatively short articles on people, institutions, events, and various aspects of life and culture in medieval England. Aims to provide "a reference work to which a non-specialist, though not just a non-specialist, may turn with profit and with pleasure."—*Pref.* Bibliographies are generally limited to one or two citations. DA175.S38

Steinberg, Sigfrid Heinrich and **Evans, I. H.** Steinberg's Dictionary of British history. 2d ed. London, Arnold, 1970; N.Y., St. Martin's, [1971]. 421p. **DC310**

Previous ed., 1963, had title *A new dictionary of British history.*
A successor to *A dictionary of British history* by J. A. Brendon (London, E. Arnold, 1937). A dictionary of brief articles written by a group of scholars, covering England and her overseas possessions so long as they maintained their British connection. Biographies are omitted; no bibliographical references.

Also see *The Cambridge historical encyclopedia of Great Britain and Ireland*, ed. Christopher Haigh (Cambridge, Univ. Pr., [1985], 392p.), for lavishly illustrated essays grouped by period.
DA34.S7

General histories

Oxford history of England. 2d ed. Ed. by *Sir* George Clark. Oxford, Clarendon Pr., 1937–62. v.1–4, 8–11, 13. (In progress) **DC311**

1st ed. 1934–65, 15v. The 2d ed. began publication before the 1st ed. was completed. The above volumes are available in the 2d ed. v.2 has also appeared in a 3d ed. 1971.

Contents: v.1, R. G. Collingwood and J. N. L. Myers. Roman Britain and the English settlements (being replaced by v.1A, Roman Britain, by P. Salway, publ. 1981, and v.1B, The English settlements, by J. N. L. Myres, in press); v.2, F. M. Stenton. Anglo-Saxon England; v.3, Austin L. Poole. From Domesday Book to Magna Carta, 1087–1216; v.4, *Sir* M. Powicke. The thirteenth century, 1216–1307; v.5, M. McKisack. The fourteenth century, 1307–1399;

v.6, E. F. Jacob. The fifteenth century, 1399–1485; v.7, J. D. Mackie. The earlier Tudors, 1485–1558; v.8, J. B. Black. The reign of Elizabeth, 1558–1603; v.9, G. Davies. Early Stuarts, 1603–1660; v.10, *Sir* G. Clark. The later Stuarts, 1660–1714; v.11, B. Williams. Whig supremacy, 1714–1760, rev. by C. H. Stuart; v.12, J. S. Watson. The reign of George III, 1760–1815; v.13, E. L. Woodward. Age of reform, 1815–1870; v.14, R. C. K. Ensor. England, 1870–1914; v.15, A. J. P. Taylor. English history, 1914–1945.

Traill, Henry Duff and **Mann, J. S.** Social England, a record of the progress of the people in religion, laws, learning, arts, industry, commerce, science, literature and manners from the earliest times to the present day. [New illus. ed.] London, Cassell; N.Y., Putnam, 1909. 6v. il. (Repr.: N.Y., Greenwood, 1969) **DC312**

A valuable illustrated record of England's cultural history to 1909.
DA30.T77

Source books

English historical documents. Gen. ed., David C. Douglas. London, Eyre and Spottiswoode, 1953–77. 12v. il.
DC313

Contents: v.1, English historical documents, *ca.* 500–1042, ed. by Dorothy Whitelock (1955); v.2, 1042–1189, ed. by David C. Douglas and George W. Greenaway (1953); v.3, 1189–1327, ed. by Henry Rothwell (1975); v.4, 1327–1485, ed. by A. R. Myers (1969); v.5, 1485–1558, ed. by C. H. Williams (1967); v.8, 1660–1714, ed. by Andrew Browning (1953); v.9, American colonial documents to 1776, ed. by Merrill Jensen (1955); v.10, English historical documents, 1714–1783, ed. by D. B. Horn and Mary Ransome (1957); v.11, 1783–1832, ed. by A. Aspinall and E. Anthony Smith (1959); v.12, pt.1, 1833–1874, ed. by G. M. Young and W. D. Handcock (1956); v.12, pt.2, 1874–1914, ed. by W. D. Handcock (1977).

Covers the complete span of English history from A.D. 500 to 1914. The early documents are given in English translation from the original Latin, French, or Anglo-Saxon. A valuable collection, with extensive introductions and bibliographies. DA26.E56

—— General ed., David C. Douglas. 2d ed. London, Eyre Methuen; N.Y., Oxford Univ. Pr., 1979–81. v.1–2. (In progress) **DC314**

For the 1st ed. *see* above.
Contents: v.1, c. 500–1042, ed. by Dorothy Whitelock; v.2, 1042–1189, ed. by D. C. Douglas and G. W. Greenaway.

v.1 of the new edition includes 240 of the most significant documents, chronicles, charters, histories, guild statutes, law codes, and letters—translated, if necessary—which offer an introduction to English history from the Anglo-Saxon period to the accession of Edward the Confessor. The introductions and notes have been extensively revised, the bibliographies updated, several new texts added, the *Historia Brittonum* retranslated, and new genealogical charts supplied.

v.2 has substantially the same contents as the earlier edition, but offers improved translations and updated bibliography.
DA26.E55

Atlases

Freeman-Grenville, G. S. P. Atlas of British history. Cartography, Lorraine Kessel. London, Rex Collings, 1979. unpaged. 25cm. **DC315**

Comprises 140 maps of various sizes which aim to portray "the principal themes and events in the history of the British Isles from prehistoric times until 1978."—*Pref.* Chronological arrangement. Indexed.

Hill, David. An atlas of Anglo-Saxon England. Toronto, Univ. of Toronto Pr.; Oxford, B. Blackwell, [1981]. 180p. maps. 29cm. **DC316**

Attempts "to display all the evidence on Anglo-Saxon England

that can be placed in a topographic or chronological framework."—*Pref.* Black-and-white maps with accompanying text and a number of tables and charts are grouped in five main sections: (1) the background; (2) the events; (3) administration; (4) the economy; (5) the church. Bibliography; index. G1812.21.S2H5

Historical atlas of Britain. Malcolm Falkus, John Gillingham, eds. N.Y., Continuum, [1981]. 223p. il., maps. 29cm.
DC317

Aims to present in text, maps, and pictures a comprehensive view of British history—political, economic, and social—from earliest times to the present. Gives attention to overseas possessions. Indexed. G1812.21.S1H5

British Empire and Commonwealth

Gt.Brit. Colonial Office. Library. Catalogue of the Colonial Office Library, London. Boston, G. K. Hall, 1964. 15v.
DC318

Lists works relating to all aspects of the organization and development of any country that has been a member of the British Commonwealth at any time during the last 300 years. For former members, the collection is complete through the date on which the country left the Commonwealth; thereafter, the collection is selective, devoted to administration, external relations, and economic and social development of the nation. Material acquired before 1950 is in a subject catalog and an author index; post-1950 acquisitions are arranged by authors and titles, by subjects, and in classified order by the LC system. In 1968 the Library was merged with the Foreign Office Library, now Foreign and Commonwealth Office Library; supplements 2–3 reflect the merger. Z921.L388

—— —— 1st–3d supplements. Boston, G. K. Hall, 1967–79. 7v.

Contents: 1st suppl., 1963–67 (1967. 894p.); 2d suppl., 1968–71 (1972. 2v.); 3d suppl., May 1971–June 1977 (1979. 4v.).

Hewitt, Arthur R. Guide to resources for Commonwealth studies in London, Oxford and Cambridge, with bibliographical and other information. London, Univ. of London, publ. for the Institute of Commonwealth Studies, [by] Athlone Pr., 1957. 219p. **DC319**

"The purpose of this *Guide* is to assist advanced research workers, particularly those who have come to Great Britain from overseas, to locate material for the study of the British Commonwealth."—*Foreword.* Deals mainly with materials in history and the social sciences. Describes the resources of libraries and other institutions in London, Oxford, and Cambridge, with bibliographical references.
Z2001.H4

Royal Commonwealth Society, London. Library. Subject catalogue of the Library of the Royal Empire Society, formerly Royal Colonial Institute, by Evans Lewin. [London, Soc.], 1930–37. 4v. (Repr.: London, Dawsons, 1967) **DC320**

Contents: v.1, British Empire generally, and Africa; v.2, Commonwealth of Australia, Dominion of New Zealand, South Pacific, general voyages and travels, and Arctic and Antarctic regions; v.3, Dominion of Canada and its provinces, Dominion of Newfoundland, the West Indies, and Colonial America; v.4, Mediterranean colonies, Middle East, Indian Empire, Burma, Ceylon, British Malaya, East Indian Islands, and the Far East.

A fine catalog, particularly for the history, description, etc., of certain regions for which no separate bibliographies exist. Arranged geographically and by subject under each country. Entries are chronological under subject. Includes books, pamphlets, periodical articles, etc. Author index in each volume.

Continued by: Z7164.C7R82

—— Subject catalogue of the Royal Commonwealth Society. Boston, G. K. Hall, 1971. 7v. (4477p.) **DC320a**

Contents: v.1, British Commonwealth and Europe, Asia in general, Mideast, India; v.2, Other Asian areas, Africa in general, North Africa; v.3, West Africa, East Africa; v.4, Noncommonwealth Africa including former foreign colonies, Republic of South Africa, other southern African countries; v.5, The Americas; v.6, Australia, New Zealand, Pacific; v.7, Biography, voyages and travels, World War I and II.

Supplements the 1930–37 edition of the *Subject catalogue* (above) and the *Biography catalogue* (AJ240) "by reproducing all the cards between their publication and March 1971."—*Pref.*

The manuscript catalogue of the Library . . . (London, Mansell, 1975. 199p.) lists some 600 items. Supplements were published in the Society's *Library notes* Jan./Mar. 1976 and Jan./Mar. 1978.

Z7164.C7R83

—— —— First supplement. Boston, G. K. Hall, 1977. 2v.

Covers additions to the Library for Mar. 1971–Dec. 1976 and adds a list of periodical holdings, as well as indexing of certain albums and collections of photographs and volumes of engravings.

Winks, Robin W., ed. The historiography of the British Empire–Commonwealth; trends, interpretations and resources. Durham, N.C., Duke Univ. Pr., 1966. 596p. **DC321**

A collection of 21 critical assessments by specialists of the writings on the history of the Empire; Canada; Australia; New Zealand; British Territories in the Pacific; South Africa; British Central Africa; British East Africa; Egypt and the Sudan; Gibralter, Malta, and Cyprus; British West Indies; India; Pakistan; Ceylon; Burma; Malaysia; Ireland 1922–49; American colonies. Treats publications through 1963. DA1.W55

Cambridge history of the British Empire. Gen. eds.: J. Holland Rose, A. P. Newton, E. A. Benians. N.Y., Macmillan; Cambridge, Univ. Pr., 1929–63. 8v. in 9. **DC322**

Editors vary.

Contents: v.1, The old empire from the beginnings to 1783; v.2, Growth of the new empire, 1783–1870; v.3, The Empire-Commonwealth, 1870–1919; v.4, British India, 1497–1858; v.5, Indian Empire, 1858–1918, with chapters on the development of administration, 1818–58; v.6, Canada and Newfoundland; v.7, pt.1, Australia. pt.2, New Zealand; v.8, South Africa, Rhodesia, and the High Commission Territories (2d ed., 1963).

v.4–5 published also as v.5–6 of the *Cambridge history of India* (DE207), and furnished in binding to match either set.

Bibliographies at end of each volume. DA30.C3

Regional and local

Anderson, John Parker. The book of British topography; a classified catalogue of the topographical works in the library of the British Museum relating to Great Britain and Ireland. London, Satchell, 1881. 472p. (Repr.: Baltimore, Genealogical Pub., 1970) **DC323**

Lists historical works about the places of England, Wales, Scotland, and Ireland, arranged by county and then by place.

Z2023.A54

Gross, Charles. A bibliography of British municipal history. 2d ed. Leicester, Leicester Univ. Pr., 1966. 461p. **DC324**

1st ed. 1897. The "2d ed." is a photographic reprint of the 1897 ed., with only a preface by G. H. Martin added.

A comprehensive bibliography, giving general authorities, including public records, followed by histories of particular towns, p.150–430.

Continued by: Z7164.L8G8

Martin, Geoffrey Haward and **McIntyre, Sylvia.** A bibliography of British and Irish municipal history. [Leicester], Leicester Univ. Pr., 1972– . v.1– . (In progress) **DC325**

Contents: v.1, General works.

A continuation of Charles Gross's *Bibliography of British municipal history* (above). Limited to materials published before 1967 which were not included in Gross. Items on particular towns will appear in later volumes.

Topical arrangement with a good general index. Z2023.M26

Humphreys, Arthur Lee. Handbook to county bibliography, being a bibliography of bibliographies relating to the counties and towns of Great Britain and Ireland. London, Strangeways, 1917. 501p. (Repr.: London, Dawsons, 1974) **DC326**

An indispensable record of bibliographies relating to the topography of Great Britain and Ireland, including those published in periodicals and society publications. Z2023.A1H9

Stephens, W. B. Sources for English local history. [Rev. & exp. ed.] Cambridge, Cambridge Univ. Pr., 1981. 342p. **DC327**

First published 1973; reprinted with minor amendments 1975.

A fairly detailed guide (to both published and unpublished source materials) intended to be of use "to undergraduates reading history, to college of education students, to postgraduate students training for teaching or archive work, to those beginning research for higher degrees, to members of adult education classes, and to teachers at various levels, as well as to the many interested amateurs who wish to pursue seriously the study of their neighbourhood."—*Pref.* An introductory section is followed by chapters on population and social structure; local government and politics; poor relief, charities, prices and wages; industry, trade and communications; agriculture; education; religion. Indexed.

Besides correcting and augmenting various sections, the revised edition adds new information on the use of sources and new material on family history, oral history, and housing. Z2023.S8

Victoria history of the counties of England. London, Oxford Univ. Pr., 1901– . il. (In progress) **DC328**

First published by Constable, then by the St. Catherine Press, and later by the Oxford University Press for the University of London, Institute of Historical Research. Many volumes reprinted by Dawsons of Pall Mall.

Of first importance for its large amount of detailed information on the natural history, archaeology, industries, religious houses, political and social history, manorial history, topography, biography, and genealogy of each county. Contains numerous excellent illustrations and maps and many references to sources of information. Indispensable in any library doing much research in English local history.

Contents:

The Victoria history of the counties of England: general introduction, by Ralph B. Pugh. 1970.
Bedford, ed. by H. A. Doubleday and William Page. 1904–14. 3v. and index.
Berkshire, ed. by P. H. Ditchfield and William Page. 1906–27. 4v. and index.
Buckingham, ed. by William Page. 1905–28. 4v. and index.
Cambridge and the Isle of Ely: v.1–2, ed. by L. F. Salzman. 1938–48; v.3, ed. by J. P. C. Roach. 1959; v.4, ed. by R. B. Pugh. 1953; v.5, ed. by C. R. Elrington. 1973; v.6, ed. by A. P. M. Wright. 1978; v.7, Roman Cambridgeshire, ed. by J. J. Wilkes and C. R. Elrington. 1978; v.8, ed. by A. P. M. Wright. 1982; Index to v.1–4.
Chester: v.2–3, ed. by E. B. Harris. 1979–80.
Cornwall, ed. by William Page. 1906. v.1; v.2, pts. 5 and 8 bound with v.1.
Cumberland, ed. by James Wilson. 1901–1905. v.1–2.
Derby, ed. by William Page. 1905–1907. v.1–2.
Devon, ed. by William Page. 1906. v.1.
Dorset: v.2, ed. by William Page. 1908; v.3, ed. by R. B. Pugh. 1968 (includes index to v.2).
Durham, ed. by William Page. 1905–28. v.1–3.
Essex: v.1, ed. by H. A. Doubleday and William Page. 1903; v.2, ed. by William Page and J. H. Round. 1907; v.3, with index to v.1–3, ed. by W. R. Powell. 1963; v.4–8, ed. by W. R. Powell. 1956–83; Bibliography, ed. by W. R. Powell. 1959.

Gloucester: v.2, ed. by William Page. 1907; v.6, ed. by G. R. Elrington. 1965; v.7, ed. by N. M. Herbert. 1981; v.8, ed. by G. R. Elrington. 1968; v.10, ed. by G. R. Elrington and N. M. Herbert. 1972; v.11, ed. by N. M. Herbert. 1976.

Hampshire and the Isle of Wight: v.1-2, ed. by H. A. Doubleday. 1900-1903; v.3-5, ed. by William Page. 1908-12; Index. 1914. 5v. and index.

Hereford, ed. by William Page. 1908. v.1.

Hertford, ed. by William Page. 1902-23. 4v. and index.

Hertfordshire families, ed. by Duncan Warrand. 1907.

Hungtindon, ed. by William Page. 1926-38. 3v. and index.

Kent, ed. by William Page. 1908-32. v.1-3.

Lancaster: v.1-2, ed. by William Page. 1906-1908; v.3-8, ed. by William Farrar and J. Brownbill. 1907-14.

Leicester: v.1, ed. by William Page. 1907; v.2-3, ed. by W. G. Hoskins. 1954-55; v.4, ed. by R. A. McKinley. 1958; v.5, ed. by J. M. Lee and R. A. McKinley. 1964.

Lincoln, ed. by William Page. 1906. v.2.

London, ed. by William Page. 1909. v.1.

Middlesex: v.1, ed. by J. S. Cockburn, H. P. F. King and K. G. T. McDonnell. 1969; v.2, ed. by William Page. 1911; v.3, with index, v.2-3, ed. by Susan Reynolds. 1962; v.4, ed. by J. S. Cockburn and T. F. T. Baker. 1971; v.5-8, ed. by T. F. T. Baker. 1976-85.

Norfolk: v.1, ed. by H. A. Doubleday. 1901; v.2, ed. by William Page. 1906.

Northampton: v.1-2, ed. by W. Ryland, D. Adkins and R. M. Serjeantson. 1902-1906; v.3, ed. by William Page. 1930; v.4, ed. by L. F. Salzman. 1937.

Northamptonshire families, ed. by Oswald Barron. 1906.

Nottingham, ed. by William Page. 1906-10. v.1-2.

Oxford: v.1, ed. by L. F. Salzman. 1939; v.2, ed. by William Page. 1907; v.3 (The University of Oxford), ed. by H. E. Salter and M. D. Lobel. 1957-64; v.4, The City of Oxford, ed. by Alan Crossley. 1979; v.5-8, ed. by M. D. Lobel. 1957-64; v.9 (Bloxham Hundred), ed. by M. D. Lobel. 1969; v.10-11, ed. by Alan Crossley. 1972-83.

Rutland, ed. by William Page. 1908-36. 2v. and index.

Shropshire, v.1, ed. by William Page. 1908; v.2 and index to v.1-2, ed. by A. T. Gaydon. 1973; v.3, ed. by G. C. Baugh. 1979; v.8, ed. by A. T. Gaydon. 1968; v.11, ed. by G. C. Baugh. 1985.

Somerset, v.1-2, ed. by William Page. 1906-11; v.3-5, ed. by R. N. Dunning. 1974-85.

Stafford: v.1, ed. by William Page. 1908; v.2 and index to v.1-2, ed. by M. W. Greenslade and J. G. Jenkins. 1967; v.3, ed. by M. W. Greenslade. 1970; v.4-5, ed. by L. M. Midgley. 1958-59; v.6, ed. by M. W. Greenslade and D. A. Johnson, 1979; v.8, ed. by J. G. Jenkins. 1963; v.17, ed. by M. W. Greenslade. 1976; v.20, ed. by M. W. Greenslade. 1984.

Suffolk, ed. by William Page. v.1, 1911; v.2, 1907.

Surrey, ed. by H. E. Malden. 1902-14. 4v. and index.

Sussex: v.1-2, ed. by William Page. 1905-1907; v.3-4, ed. by L. F. Salzman. 1935-53; v.6, pt.1, ed. by T. P. Hudson. 1980; v.7, ed. by L. F. Salzman. 1940; v.9, ed. by L. F. Salzman. 1937; Index v.1-4, 7, 9, ed. by S. M. Keeling and C. P. Lewis. 1984.

Warwick: v.1, ed. by L. F. Salzman. 1904; v.2, ed. by William Page. 1908; v.3-6, ed. by L. F. Salzman. 1945-51; v.7 (The City of Birmingham), ed. by W. B. Stephens. 1964; Index, v.1-6. 1955; v.8 (The City of Coventry and Borough of Warwick), ed. by W. B. Stephens. 1969.

Wiltshire: v.1, pt.1, ed. by R. B. Pugh and Elizabeth Crittall. 1955; v.1, pt.2, ed. by Elizabeth Crittall. 1973; v.2-5, ed. by R. B. Pugh and Elizabeth Crittall. 1955-57; v.6, ed. by Elizabeth Crittall. 1962; v.7, ed. by R. B. Pugh and Elizabeth Crittall. 1953; v.8-10, ed. by Elizabeth Crittall. 1965-75; v.11-12, ed. by D. A. Crowley. 1980-83.

Worcester: v.1, ed. by J. W. Willis-Bund and H. A. Doubleday. 1901; v.2-4, ed. by J. W. Willis-Bund and William Page. 1906-24; Index. 1926. 4v. and index.

York, ed. by William Page. 1907-25. 3v. and index.

York, East Riding: v.1 (The City of Kingston upon Hull), ed. by K. J. Allison. 1969; v.2-5, ed. by K. J. Allison. 1974-84.

York, North Riding, ed. by William Page. 1914-25. 2v. and index.

Yorkshire (The City of York), ed. by P. M. Tillott. 1961.

West, John. Village records. London, N.Y., St. Martin's, 1962. 208p. il. **DC329**

A handbook of documentary study for English local history, with descriptions of types of documents, and bibliographical references.

Several pamphlets in the Historical Association's *Helps for students of history* series supplement this work: no.69, *English local history handlist* (4th ed., 1969); no.85, *Local record sources in print and in progress, 1971-72* (1972). DA1.W45

Atlases

Historic towns; maps and plans of towns and cities in the British Isles, with historical commentaries from earliest times to 1800. Gen. ed., M. D. Lobel. Oxford & London, Lovell Johns; Baltimore, Johns Hopkins Pr., 1969-75. v.1-2. 41cm. (In progress) **DC330**

Contents: v.1, Banbury, Caernarvon, Glasgow, Gloucester, Hereford, Nottingham, Reading, Salisbury. 151p.; v.2, Bristol, Cambridge, Coventry, Norwich. various pagings. (Each town also published separately.)

Publisher varies.

"Not facsimiles of early maps, but modern scientific plans which should incorporate data derived from early maps, documents, and material remains."—*Introd.* The base map is "a large-scale plan (1:5000 scale) of each selected town as it was in the first quarter of the 19th century before it had been much affected by the Industrial Revolution and the accompanying rise in population." On this map are imposed features of the medieval town, including medieval street names; it is preceded by maps showing the site within the region, with principal roads. The historical introduction for each town presents "the relevant factors in the story of the town's origin, physical growth or contraction." No indexes. G1814.A1H5

Northern Ireland

A social science bibliography of Northern Ireland, 1945-1983: material published since 1945 relating to Northern Ireland since 1921. Comp. by Bill Rolston [and others]. Belfast, Queen's Univ., 1983. 270p. **DC331**

A bibliography of books, periodical articles, essays, pamphlets, government publications, and academic theses. "Social sciences" is broadly interpreted to include history, psychology, and medicosocial material. Classed arrangement; author, subject, and geographic indexes. Z7165.G82N676

Scotland

Bibliography

See also AA1070.

Grant, Eric G. Scotland. Oxford, Eng. & Santa Barbara, Calif., Clio, [1982]. 408p. map. (World bibliographical ser., 34) **DC332**

An annotated bibliography of more than 1,400 books and pamphlets, most published since 1960, on Scottish history and culture. Topically arranged; author/title/subject index. Z2051.G7

Hancock, Philip David. A bibliography of works relating to Scotland, 1916-1950. Edinburgh, Univ. Pr., [1959-60]. 2v. (Edinburgh Univ. pubn.) **DC333**

Intended as a supplement to *A contribution to the bibliography of Scottish topography,* by Mitchell and Cash (below). Follows the arrangement of the original work, with a somewhat more detailed subject classification in the second part. Z2061.H3

Mitchell, *Sir* **Arthur** and **Cash, C. G.** A contribution to the bibliography of Scottish topography. Edinburgh, Univ. Pr., 1917. 2v. (Pubn. of the Scottish Historical Soc. 2d ser., v.14-15) **DC334**

A detailed record of books and periodical articles on Scottish history, life, and culture. v.1 indexes material by place; v.2, by subject.

Scotland. General Registry Office of Births, Deaths and Marriages. Guide to the public records of Scotland deposited in H. M. General Register House, Edinburgh, by M. Livingstone. Edinburgh, General Register House, 1905. 233p. **DC335**

Contents: (1) Crown, parliament, revenue, and administration; (2) Judicial records; (3) Titles to land, dignities, and offices; (4) Ecclesiastical and miscellaneous. CD1072.A3

Terry, Charles Sanford. Catalogue of the publications of Scottish historical and kindred clubs and societies, and of the volumes relative to Scottish history issued by His Majesty's Stationery Office, 1780–1908. Glasgow, Maclehose, 1909. 253p. **DC336**

Contents: (1) Catalog of the publications of over 50 Scottish historical and kindred clubs and societies arranged alphabetically by name of society, giving for each its corporate name, date of founding, purpose, list of its publications, and contents of each volume if several papers are included; (2) Author and subject index to the publications and contents notes. The index is often useful for analytic references on minute or localized facts in Scottish history.
Continued by: Z2061.T32

Matheson, Cyril. Catalogue of the publications of Scottish historical and kindred clubs and societies, and of the papers relative to Scottish history issued by H. M. Stationery Office, including the reports of the Royal Commission on Historical MSS., 1908–27, with a subject index. Aberdeen, Milne and Hutchison, 1928. 232p. **DC337**

A continuation of two works by C. S. Terry: (1) his *Catalogue* (above), and (2) his *Index to the papers relating to Scotland . . . in the Historical MSS. Commission's reports* (Glasgow, Maclehose, 1908).
Contents: (1) Catalog of the publications of societies, arranged alphabetically, continuing Terry's *Catalogue* from 1908 and referring to pages in Terry for earlier titles; (2) Author and subject index; (3) Index to Terry's *Catalogue;* (4) Index to papers relating to Scotland in Historical MSS. Commission's reports. Z2061.T34

Dictionaries and source books

A companion to Scottish culture. Ed., David Daiches. London, Arnold; N.Y., Holmes & Meier, [1981]. 441p. il., maps. **DC338**

Offers a "compendium of information about all significant aspects of Scottish culture . . . throughout history with articles on both movements, institutions and individuals."—*Pref.* Articles, some quite lengthy, are alphabetically arranged. "Further reading," p.408–18, lists books and periodical articles in topical arrangement. Indexed. DA772.C63

Dickinson, William Crofts, Donaldson, Gordon and **Milne, Isabel A.** A source book of Scottish history. 2d ed., rev. and enl. London, Nelson, [1958–61]. 3v. **DC339**

Contents: v.1, From earliest time to 1424; v.2, 1424 to 1567; v.3, 1567–1707.
A collection of documents and extracts with commentaries. DA755.D52

Donaldson, Gordon and **Morpeth, Robert S.** A dictionary of Scottish history. Edinburgh, John Donald Publ. [1977]. 234p. **DC340**

A short-entry dictionary stressing events, institutions, titles, and offices, with some biographical and geographical entries. Brief chronology. DA757.9.D66

Atlas

An historical atlas of Scotland, c.400–c.1600; ed. Peter McNeill and Ranald Nicolson; cartographer W. J. Davie. St. Andrews, Atlas Committee of Scottish Medievalists, 1975. 213p. 29cm. **DC341**

Offers very clear, black-and-white maps with accompanying text (signed by contributors) and selected bibliography. No index. G1826.S1H5

Wales

Wales. University. Board of Celtic Studies. History and Law Committee. A bibliography of the history of Wales. 2d ed. Cardiff, Univ. of Wales Pr., 1962. 330p. **DC342**

1st ed. 1931.
A classified bibliography of some 3,500 items covering political, ecclesiastical, social, and economic history, etc. Supplements have appeared in the *Bulletin* of the Board of Celtic Studies. Z2081.W229

GREECE

See also Classical antiquities, DA113–DA142.

Argenti, Philip Pandely. Bibliography of Chios, from classical times to 1936 . . . with a pref. by J. L. Myres. Oxford, Clarendon Pr., 1940. 836p. **DC343**

Contents: pt.1, Classified catalog, p.1–567; pt.2, Author's catalog, p.571–801; pt.3, List of maps, 1422–1937, p.805–32. Alphabetical index of classifications, p.833–36.
A comprehensive bibliography of works in many languages. Z3490.C5A7

Basilikon Hidryma Ereunōn. Kentron Neoellēnikōn Ereunōn. Quinze ans de bibliographie historique en Grèce (1950–1964), avec une annexe pour 1965. Athènes, Centre de Recherche Neo-hellénique de la Fondation Royale de la Recherche Scientifique, 1966. 293p. **DC344**

A listing by year of all books and articles dealing with any period of Greek history in any language. Indexes of subjects, personal and place names, and authors. Includes a list of journals indexed.
Continued by: Z2281.B37

Cinq ans de bibliographie historique en Grèce (1965–1969) avec un supplément pour les années 1950–1964. Athènes, 1970. 133p. **DC345**

Continued by: Z2296.C5

Quatre ans de bibliographie historique en Grèce, 1970–1973; avec un supplément pour les années 1965–1969. Ahtènes, 1974. 151p. **DC346**

Z2281.Q38

Cincinnati. University. Libraries. Catalog of the Modern Greek collection. Boston, G. K. Hall, 1978. 5v. **DC347**

Reproduction of the catalog cards (in dictionary arrangement) for this outstanding collection. Lists both monographic and serial holdings. The collection was originally devoted to "works of Greek scholars on Ancient Greek authors, history and archaeology" (*Introd.*), but collecting policy was soon extended to encompass works "on Byzantium, Modern Greek literature, linguistics, history, folklore, religion, philosophy, economics and sociology."
An earlier catalog was published 1960. Z2281.C55

Clogg, Mary Jo and **Clogg, Richard.** Greece. Santa Barbara, Calif., Clio Pr., [1980]. 224p. (World bibliographical ser., 17) **DC348**

An annotated bibliography of books, essays, and articles on medieval and modern Greece; primarily English-language materials. It is not intended for the specialist, but rather for those "who wish to acquire an informed understanding of the present state of Greece and of the forces that have helped to shape her present society."—*Introd.* Annotations; index of names and subjects. Z2281.C58

Davaras, Costis. Guide to Cretan antiquities. Park Ridge, N.J., Noyes, [1976]. 370p. il., maps. **DC349**

A dictionary of brief articles on "all important cultural, natural, social and technological elements, artistic tendencies, individual works of art and historic happenings in Crete" *(Pref.)* up to the 20th century. Does not include biographies. Appendix of maps showing sites by period; index to sites; chronology. DF901.C82D38

Fleischer, Hagen and **Bowman, Steven.** Greece in the 1940s; a bibliographic companion. Hanover & London, Univ. Pr. of New England, 1981. 94p. (Modern Greek Studies Assoc. ser., 5) **DC350**

In two parts: Greece under the Axis occupation, a bibliographical survey, by Fleischer; Jews in wartime Greece, select annotated bibliography, by Bowman. Both bibliographies cover published and unpublished material in all languages, although most entries are in Greek. There are separate listings for unpublished primary sources, published primary sources, and secondary literature; the latter entries are coded to indicate specific subject matter or source. Most entries are annotated; no index. Z2296.F56

Gennadius Library. Catalogue. Boston, G. K. Hall, 1968. 7v. **DC351**

Photoreproduction of the catalog cards for this collection of more than 50,000 volumes concerning "the history and achievement of Greece in its entirety, from earliest antiquity to the present."—*Introd.*

The library is affiliated with the American School of Classical Studies in Athens. Z2309.A46

—— —— Supplement I–II. Boston, G. K. Hall, 1973–81. 2v.

The first supplement adds acquisitions of Dec. 1968–Feb. 1973, plus revised cataloging of many items appearing in the original catalog. The second supplement reflects cataloging of Mar. 1973–Mar. 1979, together with titles recataloged under the heading "Newspapers and periodicals—Gennadeion Collection" (which constitutes an alphabetical title listing of all the library's serials).

HUNGARY

Bibliography

Apponyi, Sándor. Hungarica. Ungarn betreffende im Auslande gedruckte Bücher und Flugschriften. München, Rosenthal, 1903–27. 4v. (Repr.: Nendeln, Liechtenstein, Kraus, 1969) **DC352**

Contents: Bd.1, 15. und 16. Jahrhundert; Bd.2, 17. und 18. Jahrhundert (bis 1720); Bd.3, Neue Sammlung. I, 15. und 16. Jahrhundert besorgt von L. Dézsi; Bd.4, 17. und 18. Jahrhundert besorgt von L. Dézsi.

Includes works on Hungary in languages other than Hungarian published both in and outside of Hungary from 1470 to 1798. Each volume has its own index. For non-Hungarian books on Hungary, *see also* Károly Szabó, *Régi magyar Könyvtár* (AA864). Z2141.A65

Bako, Elemer. Guide to Hungarian studies. Stanford, Hoover Inst. Pr., [1973]. 2v. (1218p.) il. (Hoover Inst. Bibliographical ser., 52) **DC353**

An extensive guide to the history, cultural life, fine arts, education, science, etc. Includes books, articles, reference works, journals, monographic series. Lists publications through 1965 only. Z2146.B3

Banner, János. Bibliographia archaeologica hungarica, 1793–1943. Szeged, Ed. Inst. Archaeologicum Universitatis de Nicolao Horthy, 1944. 558p. (Fontes rerum archaeologicarum hungaricarum, t.1) **DC354**

Bibliographia Hungariae. Verzeichnis der 1861–1921 erschienenen, Ungarn betreffenden Schriften in nichtungarischer Sprache. Zusammengestellt vom Ungarischen Institut an der Universität Berlin. Berlin, de Gruyter, 1923–29. 4v.

(Ungarische Bibliothek für das Ungarische Institut an der Universität Berlin. 3. Reihe) **DC355**

Contents: (1) Historica; (2) Geographica. Politico-oeconomica; (3) Philologica. Periodica; (4) Register.

The above bibliographies offer retrospective coverage for Hungarian archaeology; a classified list of current Hungarian literature on archaeology appears annually in the periodical *Archaeológiai ertesitö, 1949– . See also* DA77. Z2141.B58

Halász de Beky, I. L. A bibliography of the Hungarian Revolution, 1956. Toronto, Univ. of Toronto Pr., 1963. 179p. **DC356**

"Pub. under the auspices of the Canadian Institute of International Affairs."—*title page.*

A listing of 2,136 items: books and pamphlets, periodical articles, monitored broadcasts, and motion pictures, covering the period Oct. 1956–Dec. 1960. Arranged by language (15 languages). Z2148.A5H3

—— —— Supplement, 1956–1965. Wash., 1967. (*In* Wagner, Francis S., The Hungarian Revolution in perspective, p.256–350)

A second supplement appeared in the *Canadian review of Hungarian studies,* v.3, pt.2 (1976), p.195–202.

Harvard University. Library. Hungarian history and literature: classification schedule, classified listing by call number, chronological listing, author and title listing. Cambridge, publ. by Harvard Univ. Lib., distr. by Harvard Univ. Pr., 1974. 186p. (Widener Library shelflist, 44) **DC357**

For a note on the series *see* AA145.

"This volume . . . lists 6,550 titles concerning the history and literature of Hungary. The present boundaries of the country define the scope of local history coverage."—*Pref.* Z2146.H37

Kabdebó, Thomas. Hungary. Oxford, Eng. & Santa Barbara, Calif., Clio Pr., [1980]. 280p. (World bibliographical series, 15) **DC358**

Lists 1,094 items, almost all in English, providing an introductory survey of Hungarian life. Topical arrangement with author, title, and subject index. Z2146.K32

Kertbeny, Károly Mária. Bibliografie der ungarischen nationalen und internationalen Literatur. 1. Bd. Ungarn betreffende deutsche Erstlingsdrucke, 1454–1600. Budapest, Kön. Ung. Univ.-Buchdr., 1880. clxxxivp., 760p., 14p. **DC359**

No more published.

Supplements Apponyi (DC352) for German books on Hungary for the period 1454–70. Z2142.K42

—— Ungarns deutsche Bibliographie, 1801–1860. Verzeichniss der in Ungarn und Ungarn betreffend im Auslande erschienenen deutschen Drucke. Im Auftrage des K. Ung. Ministerium für Cultus und Unterricht. Fortgesetzt und mit einer wissenschlaftlichen Uebersicht versehen von Géza Petrik. Budapest, Kön. Ung. Univ.-Buchdr., 1886. 2v. **DC360**

Contents: v.1, 1801–30; v.2, 1831–60.

Added title page in Hungarian.

Lists German books printed in and about Hungary. Z2141.K42

Kosáry, Domokos G. Bevezetés a magyar történelem forrásaiba és irodalmába. Budapest, 1951–58. 3v. **DC361**

At head of title: A Magyar Tudományos Akadémia Történettudományi Intézete.

Publisher varies.

Contents: v.1, [to 1711]. 1951; v.2, 1711–1824. 1954; v.3, Supplement and index. 1958.

A bibliographical guide to Hungarian history. Includes chapters on general materials, and guides to archives, with specific chapters by locality and by period. International in scope; textual annotations.

A new edition is in progress as: DB921.5.K6

—— Bevezetés magyarország történetének forrásaiba és irodalmába. [2. kiad.] Budapest, Tankönyvkiadó, 1970– . v.1– . (In progress) **DC362**

Contents: v.1, Átalános rész. I–II.
A fully revised and expanded edition. Z2146.K67

Magyar Tudományos Akadémia. Történettudományi Intézet. Magyar történeti bibliográfia, 1825–1867. . . . I. Tóth Zoltán vezetésével. Budapest, Akadémiai Kiadó, 1950–59. 4v. **DC363**

Contents: v.1, General works. 118p. (1950); v.2, Economics. 260p. (1952); v.3, Politics and ideology. 407p. (1950); v.4, History of non-Hungarian people. 675p. (1959).
Classified arrangement. Imprints as late as 1948 are included; monographs and periodical and newspaper articles, in various languages, are covered. A second series, for the years 1867–1945 was planned. As yet, no author index. Z2146.M3

—— A magyar történettudomány válogatott bibliográfiája, 1945–1968. Budapest, Akadémiai Kiadó, 1971. 855p. **DC364**

Classed arrangement, with index by personal and place names. Lists books and articles published in Hungary for the period indicated, plus some articles about countries outside Hungary. Annotated. Z2146.M33

Telek, J. History of Hungary and the Hungarians, a select bibliography. Toronto, [Pannonia Books, 1972–78]. 2v. (Hungarian historical studies, 1, 3) (Repr. with corrections 1980–81) **DC365**

Based on the collections of the University of Toronto Library, the Library of Congress, and the British Library. Topical arrangement; index of names and serials. Z2148.A5T44

Historiography

Vardy, Steven Bela. Modern Hungarian historiography. Boulder, Colo., East European Quarterly (distr. by Columbia Univ. Pr.), 1976. 333p. (East European monographs, 17) **DC366**

A survey "of the development of Hungarian historical sciences from the eleventh to the middle of the twentieth century" (*Pref.*), with special emphasis on the 20th century. Appendix, p.299–309: "Significant source publication series since 1857." Detailed name and subject index. DB923.V372

Handbooks

Erdei, Ferenc, ed. Information Hungary. Budapest, Akadémiai Kiadó, 1968. 1144p. il. (Countries of the world information series, v.2) **DC367**

"The organization and compilation of this work was undertaken . . . by an editorial committee appointed by the Hungarian Academy of Sciences. . . . This is the Hungarian view of Hungary."—*Pref.* DB906.E7

ICELAND

Horton, John J. Iceland. Oxford, Eng. and Santa Barbara, Calif., Clio Pr., [1983]. 346p. map. (World bibliographical ser., 37) **DC368**

A classified, annotated bibliography of English-language materials relating to Iceland. 960 items, plus references to many additional titles in the annotations. Index of authors, titles and subjects.

Leeds, Eng. University. Library. Icelandic Collection. A catalogue of the Icelandic collection. Leeds, The Library, 1978. 166p. **DC369**

For full information *see* BD911.

IRELAND

Bibliography

Asplin, P. W. A. Medieval Ireland c.1170–1495; a bibliography of secondary works. Dublin, Royal Irish Academy, 1971. 139p. **DC370**

First in a projected series of publications ancillary to *A new history of Ireland* being prepared under the auspices of the Royal Irish Academy. This is a classed bibliography of more than 700 items. Many annotations; index. Z2041.A85

Dublin. National Library of Ireland. Bibliography of Irish history, 1870–1911, 1912–1921, by James Carty. Dublin, Stat. Off., 1936–40. 2v. **DC371**

1870–1911, publ. 1940, 319p.; 1912–1921, publ. 1936, 177p.
Lists books and periodical articles on the history of Ireland during these periods. Classified arrangement; author index. Z2041.D8

Ireland. Public Record Office. A guide to the records deposited in the Public Record Office of Ireland, by Herbert Wood. Dublin, Stat. Off., 1919. 334p. **DC372**

CD1103.A3

Kenney, James Francis. Sources for the early history of Ireland; an introduction and guide. v.1, Ecclesiastical. N.Y., Columbia Univ. Pr., 1929. 807p. (Records of civilization: sources and studies, v.11) (Repr.: Dublin, P. O'Tailluir, 1979) **DC373**

An introduction and guide to the manuscript and printed sources for the ecclesiastical history of Ireland up to the 12th century. No more published.
Gives detailed analysis of 659 manuscript sources with bibliographic references for each. Z2041.K362

Maguire, Maria. A bibliography of published works on Irish foreign relations, 1921–1978. Dublin, Royal Irish Academy, 1981. 136p. **DC374**

About 1,300 items—books, articles, pamphlets, government publications, and doctoral dissertations—in classed arrangement with author index. Z6465.I73M33

National Library of Ireland. Manuscript sources for the history of Irish civilisation. Richard J. Hayes, ed. Boston, G. K. Hall, 1965. 11v. **DC375**

Contents: v.1–4, Persons; v.5–6, Subjects; v.7–8, Places; v.9–10, Dates; v.11, Lists of manuscripts.
An inventory of manuscript materials relating to Irish civilization and history from the 5th to the 20th centuries as found in 678 libraries and archives in thirty countries and in more than 600 private collections. Gives brief description, location (if not in the National Library of Ireland), and source if printed. Separate list of Gaelic manuscripts in v.11.

—— —— First supplement, 1965–1975. Boston, G. K. Hall, 1979. 3v.

Covers materials "newly added to the collections of the National Library . . . and other repositories, or newly noted, in the period

1965–1975; the volumes also include itemised treatment of some materials dealt with in summary form in 1965 and make good some earlier omissions."—*Introd.*

The Irish Manuscript Commission's *Catalogue of publications issued and in preparation 1928–1966* (Dublin, 1966. 79p.) offers an annotated list of the Commission's publications, some of which describe manuscript publications or, in some cases, publishes them.   Z2041.D85

Shannon, Michael Owen. Modern Ireland: a bibliography on politics, planning, research, and development. Westport, Conn., Greenwood Pr.; London, Library Assoc., [1981]. 733p.   **DC376**

A classed bibliography of more than 5,400 items covering "the fields of history, politics, geography and natural resources, business, economics, regional development, the social sciences, and public and social services."—*Introd.* Some annotations; name and subject indexes.   Z2041.S5

Writings on Irish history, 1936–78. (*In* Irish historical studies, v.1–42, 1938–79) Annual.   **DC377**

Compiled in cooperation with the Bibliographical Subcommittee of the Irish Committee on Historical Sciences.
Continued by:

Writings on Irish history, 1979/80– . Dublin, Irish Committee of Historical Sciences, 1982– . Microfiche. (In progress?)   **DC378**

Title page for 1979/80 reads: Writings on Irish history 1979 and 1980, incorporating addenda from 1975 to 1978; comp. by Clara Cullen and Monica Henchy, ed. by R. V. Comerford.

The listing in *Irish historical studies* is an alphabetical one; the microfiche list is classified by chronological period according to the arrangement of the *New history of Ireland* (DC386). Includes books, essays, and periodical articles; if a work relates to two periods, it is cited twice, etc. Excludes works of reference, newspaper articles, and parliamentary publications. No index.

A "Select bibliography of writings on Irish economic and social history" appears annually in *Irish economic and social history* (v.1– , 1974–); coverage begins with 1973 publications.

Historiography

Moody, T. W. Irish historiography, 1936–70. Dublin, Irish Committee of Historical Sciences, 1971. 155p.   **DC379**

A revision and updating of a series entitled "Thirty years' work in Irish history" which appeared in *Irish historical studies,* 1967–69. Offers surveys by various scholars of work done in any English-speaking country on Irish history during the period indicated.
Continued by: Z2041.M65

Irish historiography, 1970–79. Ed. by Joseph Lee. [Cork], Cork Univ. Pr., 1981. 238p.   **DC380**

Publ. under the auspices of the Irish Committee of Historical Sciences.

Bibliographic essays by contributing scholars cover chronological periods, economic history, and ecclesiastical history. Not indexed.
                                                          DA908.I74

Dictionaries, handbooks, and source books

Curtis, Edmund and **McDowell, Robert Brendon.** Irish historical documents, 1172–1922. London, Methuen, 1943. 331p. (Repr.: N.Y., Barnes & Noble, 1968)   **DC381**

A source book of the "principal Irish constitutional and political

documents." Documents in Latin or French have been translated into English.   DA905.C8

Encyclopaedia of Ireland. Dublin, Allen Figgis, 1968. 463p. il.   **DC382**

Victor Meally, principal ed.

A topical encyclopedia covering all aspects of Irish life and culture, government, economics, natural history and physical geography of the island, etc. Emphasis is on the Republic of Ireland, with less detailed treatment of Northern Ireland. Brief bibliographies follow most sections of the work. Indexed.   DA979.E5

Hickey, D. J. and **Doherty, J. E.** A dictionary of Irish history since 1800. [Dublin], Gill and Macmillan; Totowa, N.J., Barnes & Noble, [1980]. 615p.   **DC383**

A dictionary of brief articles covering both Irelands since 1800 (the year of the Act of Union), with history broadly interpreted to include articles on the arts, literature, folk customs, religion, and economics as well as political and military affairs. Cross references, but no index; no bibliographies.   DA949.7.H53

Ireland: a cultural encyclopaedia. Gen. ed., Brian de Breffny. [London], Thames and Hudson; N.Y., Facts on File, [1983]. 256p. il.   **DC384**

"Culture" is here broadly interpreted "to mean the aesthetic endeavor of a people and the manifestation of their intellectual, artistic and even social development."—*Introd.* Offers brief, signed articles on persons, places, terms and objects relating to language, literature, fine arts, architecture, decorative arts, music, theater, applied arts, etc. Some bibliographic references.   NX546.A1I73

A new history of Ireland. Ancillary publications. Dublin, Royal Irish Academy, 1971–78. no.1–4. (In progress?)
                                                            DC385

Contents: no.1, Medieval Ireland c.1170–1495, P. W. A. Asplin (1971); no.2, Irish historical statistics: population, 1821–1971, W. E. Vaughan and A. J. Fitzpatrick (1978); no.3, Giraldus Cambrensis. Expugnatis hibernica/The conquest of Ireland, ed. A. B. Scott and F. X. Martin (1978); no.4, Parliamentary election results in Ireland, 1801–1922, Brian M. Walker (1978).

General histories

A new history of Ireland. T. W. Moody, F. X. Martin, F. J. Byrne, eds. Oxford, Clarendon Pr., 1976–84. v.3–4, 8–9. maps. il. (In progress; to be in 10v.)   **DC386**

Contents: v.3, Early modern Ireland, 1534–1691; v.4, Eighteenth century Ireland, 1691–1800; v.8, A chronology of Irish history to 1976 (A companion to Irish history, v.1); v.9, Maps, genealogies, lists (A companion to Irish history, v.2).

Comp. under the auspices of the Royal Irish Academy.

Planned to be the authoritative history of Ireland, with "history" broadly interpreted to include sections on literature, the arts, the church, etc. Each section contributed by a specialist.

Other volumes are to cover: v.1, Prehistoric and early medieval Ireland; v.2, Medieval Ireland (1169–1534); v.5, Ireland under the union, I (1801–1870); v.6, Ireland under the union, II (1870–1921); v.7, Ireland since 1921; v.10, Illustrations, statistics, bibliography, documents.   DA912.N48

Atlases

Edwards, Ruth Dudley. An atlas of Irish history. 2d ed. London, Methuen, [1981]. 286p.   **DC387**

1st ed. 1973.

Primarily concerned with social and political developments and characteristics of the Irish people. Includes a section on the Irish abroad.   G1831.S1E3

ITALY

See also Classical antiquities, DA113–DA142.

Bibliography

Cassels, Alan. Italian foreign policy, 1918–1945; a guide to research and research materials. Wilmington, Del., Scholarly Resources, [1981]. 271p.   **DC388**

Two chapters which discuss how foreign policy was made in Italy, and international archives, libraries, research institutes, and newspaper collections, are followed by an annotated bibliography, topically arranged. The bibliography is indexed by authors and serial titles.   Z6465.I8C37

D'Andrea, Anna. Il secondo dopoguerra in Italia, 1945–1960; proposte per una bibliografia ragionata. [Cosenza, Edizioni Pellegrini, 1977] 229p. (Collana interventi, 2)   **DC389**

A classed bibliography of the socioeconomic and political history of the post–World War II period in Italy. In two main sections: (1) Gli anni 1945–1950: ricostruzione democratica o restaurazione capitalistica? (2) Gli anni cinquanta: espansione economica e sue contraddizioni. Items are listed chronologically within subsections; index of names.   Z7165.I8D35

Devoto, Andrea. Bibliografia dell'oppressione nazista fino al 1962. Firenze, Olschki, 1964. 149p.   **DC390**

An international bibliography of about 1,500 books in many languages arranged by topic, subdivided by geographical area. Author index.

Continued by:

———— L'oppressione nazista: considerazioni e bibliografia, 1963–1981. [Firenze], Olschki, 1983. 207p.   **DC390a**

A lengthy introductory essay is followed by an "Appendice bibliografica" (p.81–201), an international bibliography of some 1,701 items on the Holocaust and concentration camps, topically arranged. Name index.   Z6374.H6D48

Evola, Niccoló Domenico. Origini e dottrina del fascismo. Firenze, Sansoni, 1935. 166p. (Guide bibliografiche dell' Istit. Nazionale Fascista di Cultura. I) (Repr.: N.Y., AMS, 1975)   **DC391**

A bibliography of books and periodical articles on the origin and development of fascism in its political, legal, economic, and social aspects. Still useful for materials contemporary to the period.   Z2361.F2E8

Fay, George Emory. A bibliography of Etruscan culture and archaeology, 1498–1981. Greeley, Colo., Univ. of Northern Colo., 1981. 2v. (OPCS occasional pubns. in classical studies, monograph no.1)   **DC392**

An author listing of books, articles, and parts of books on archeological and linguistic studies of Etruscan culture.

Fossati Bellani, Luigi Vittorio. I libri di viaggio e le guide della raccolta Luigi Vittorio Fossati Bellani: catalogo descrittivo a cura di Antonio Pescarzoli. Roma, Ed. di Storia e Letteratura, 1957. 3v. (Sussidi eruditi, 9–11)   **DC393**

The catalog of a private collection of Italian travel literature containing more than 5,000 books and pamphlets from earliest times to the 1950s. With the exception of some 300 rare items on general travel, the works deal with Italy. Most of the works are in Italian, though other western European languages are represented. Detailed bibliographic descriptions. Arranged by place name; author index.   Z997.F75

Harvard University. Library. Italian history and literature: classification schedule, classified listing by call number, chronological listing, author and title listing. Cambridge, publ. by Harvard Univ. Lib., distr. by Harvard Univ. Pr., 1974. 2v. (Widener Library shelflist, 51–52)   **DC394**

For a note on the series *see* AA145.

These volumes "cover Italian history and literature, a collection comprising more than 72,000 titles. Historical topics include the government and administration, religious affairs, civilization, social life and customs, and geography and description of peninsular Italy, Sicily, and Sardinia, as well as Malta, Monaco, and San Marino. Literary histories, anthologies, and works by and about authors writing in Italian from the Duecento to the present are included in the sections for literature."—*Pref.*   Z2341.H37

Lemmi, Francesco. Il risorgimento. Roma, Fondazione Leonardo, 1926. 320p. (Guide bibliografiche [23–24])
                                                          DC395

Contents: pt.1, Periodo del principi riformatori (1748–1789); pt.2, Periodo della rivoluzione e dell' impero napoleonico (1789–1815); pt.3, Periodo delle rivoluzioni e delle guerre per l'indipendenza e l'unità politica (1815–1870).

Lists some 3,000 items covering the period 1748–1870.
                                                          Z2359.L55

Lovett, Clara M. Contemporary Italy. Wash., Lib. of Congress, 1985. 106p.   **DC396**

About 1,300 Italian books and monographs concerning Italy since 1945 are listed in topical arrangement; a few English-language titles are listed in a separate section. Most items were published 1978–83, older works being included to fill certain gaps. Subject and author indexes.   Z2360.3.L68

Pine-Coffin, R. S. Bibliography of British and American travel in Italy to 1860. Firenze, Olschki, 1974. 371p. (Biblioteca di bibliografia italiana, 76)   **DC397**

British and American works are listed in separate chronological sections. Brief annotations. Indexes of (1) persons; (2) anonymous titles; (3) places; (4) publishers, printers and booksellers.
                                                          Z2356.P55

Current

Bibliografia storica nazionale. Anno 1– , 1939– . Giunto Centrale per gli Studi Storici. Bari, Laterza, 1942– . Annual.
                                                          DC398

Publisher varies; some years combined.

A classified record of books and periodical articles, published in Italy about Italy. Name index. In many cases indicates location of reviews. Follows the general form of the *International bibliography of historical sciences* (DA23).   Z6201.B54

Periodicals

Istituto Nazionale per la Storia del Movimento di Liberazione in Italia. Catalogo della stampa periodica della Biblioteche dell' Istituto Nazionale per la Storia del Movimento di Liberazione in Italia e degli Istituti associati, 1900/1975, a cura di Francesca Ferratini Tosi [et al.]. Milano, 1977. 374p.
                                                          DC399

A catalog of periodicals relating to antifascism and the Italian resistance. Locates files in some 23 Italian libraries.

Archives

Dolci, Fabrizio. L'associazionismo operaio in Italia (1870–1900) nelle raccolte della Biblioteca Nazionale Centrale di Firenze, catalogo. Firenze, Giunta Regionale Toscana, La Nuova Italia, 1980. 506p. facsims., plates. (Inventari e cataloghi toscani, 5)   **DC400**

An extensive catalog of the papers of labor organizations (unions, clubs, societies, etc.) held by the Biblioteca Nazionale in Florence, with very brief annotations. Arranged by geographic area; indexed by subject (e.g., decorative arts, metals) and by province; list of printers by city.   Z7164.T7D64

Guida generale degli archivi di Stato italiani. Direttori Piero D'Angiolini, Claudio Pavone. Roma, Ministerio per i Beni Culturali e Ambientali, Ufficio Centrale per i Beni Archivistici, 1981–83. v.1–2. (In progress)   **DC401**

Contents: v.1–2, A–M.
An extensive inventory of government archives, both federal and local, with long descriptions, notes on finding aids, and lists of contents. Each archive has its own table of contents and index of "fondi."   CD1424.G84

Encyclopedias and handbooks

A concise encyclopaedia of the Italian Renaissance. Ed. by J. R. Hale. N.Y., Oxford Univ. Pr.; London, Thames and Hudson, 1981. 360p. il.   **DC402**

Offers brief signed articles on the people, institutions, events, etc., of Renaissance Italy. "It is designed to answer questions about what went on but also to suggest what it might have been like to have lived then."—*[p.5]* A "subject index" lists the entries topically. Bibliographies.   DG445.C66

Dictionary of modern Italian history. Frank J. Coppa, ed. in chief. Westport, Conn., Greenwood Pr., [1983]. 496p.   **DC403**

A dictionary arrangement of brief articles covering Italian political, economic, cultural, social, and religious life from the 18th century to the present. Many entries include at least one bibliographic reference; an appendix gives chronologies and lists of political and religious leaders. Indexed.   DG545.D53

Enciclopedia dell' antifascismo e della Resistenza. [Milano], La Pietra, [1968–84]. v.1–4. il. (In progress)   **DC404**

Contents: v.1–4, A–Q.
Concerned primarily with people and events important to Italian history of the period 1919–45, but including many articles on a wide range of related figures and topics.   DG571.A2E5

―――― Appendice. [Milano] La Pietra, 1971. v.1.

Gardner, Edmund Garratt. Italy: a companion to Italian studies. London, Methuen, 1934. 274p.   **DC405**

Survey articles by specialists on the history and culture of Italy, with bibliographies at the end of each chapter.   DG441.G3

Historical dictionary of fascist Italy. Philip V. Cannistraro, ed. in chief. Westport, Conn., Greenwood Pr., [1982]. 657p. maps.   **DC406**

Concentrates on "the Italian variety of fascism" (*Pref.*), offering signed articles—some of considerable length—on individuals, organizations, events and movements, terms, etc. Sources of further information are cited; useful appendixes; index.   DG571.A1H57

New Century Italian Renaissance encyclopedia. Ed. by Catherine B. Avery. [N.Y., Appleton-Century-Crofts, 1972] 978p. il.   **DC407**

A handbook to the culture and civilization of the Renaissance. More than 3,700 entries for terms, events, literary works and characters, and heavy emphasis on biographical sketches.
                                                    DG537.8.A1N48

LATVIA

Caune, Andris and **Caune, C.** Latvijas PSR arheologija, 1940–1974; literatūras rādītājs. Rīgā, Viļa Lāča Latvijas PSR Valsts Bibliotēka, 1976. 290p.   **DC408**

Added title page, table of contents, introduction and chapter/section headings in Russian and German.
Topical arrangement of books and articles published mainly in

Latvia and Russia (with a few German titles) during the 1940-Jan. 1975 period and concerned with archaeology in Latvia. Person, place, and subject indexes.   Z2535.C36

Latvijas PSR mazā enciklopēdija. [Glavenais redaktors V. Samsons] Riga, Izdevnieciba "Zinātne," 1967–72. 3v. and index.   **DC409**

Concerned with Latvian culture and affairs. Many biographical sketches. Most articles are signed; some carry bibliographies. An index entitled *Personu un prieksmetu alfabetiskais rādītājs* was published 1972.   AE57.L34

Latvijas padomju enciklopēdija. Rīga, Galvenā Enciklopēdiju Redakcija, 1981–83. v.1–3. il. (In progress)   **DC410**

Contents: v.1–3, A–Hain. (To be in 10v.)
A general encyclopedia, but with strong national and East European emphasis (e.g., biographical sketches run heavily to Latvian personalities). Some bibliographies.   AE35.5.L37

Latvju enciklopēdija. Redaktors Arveds Švābe. Stokholmā, Trīs Zvaigznes, 1950–55. 3v.   **DC411**

A national encyclopedia of things Latvian or related to Latvia. Most articles are short, unsigned, and without bibliographies; a few are considerably more extensive and include some bibliographic references. Illustrations are numerous and generally good.
A complementary work is in progress as *Latvju enciklopēdija, 1962–1982,* comp. by Edgar Anderson (Lincoln, Nebr., Augustums Prtg. Serv., 1983– . v.1, A–I); it offers much information on Latvians outside Latvia.   DK511.L157L3

―――― Papildinājumi. Redaktore Arveds Švābe. Stokholmā, Trīs Zvaigznes, 1962. 214p.

Ozols, Selma Aleksandra. Latvia; a selected bibliography. Wash., K. Karusa, 1963. 144p.   **DC412**

Classed arrangement with author-title index. Includes publications to 1957 only. Locates copies.   Z2535.O9

LIECHTENSTEIN

Fürstentum Liechtenstein. The Principality of Liechtenstein, a documentary handbook, ed. by Walter Kranz. [Tr. from the German by J. A. Nicholls] 5th rev. & enl. ed. [Vaduz], Press and Information Office of the Govt. . . . of Liechtenstein, 1981. 302p. il.   **DC413**

Brief essays by various authors survey "the history of the Principality and the Princely House, the State with its legal, social and fiscal institutions, culture and folklore, . . . economy and the educational system."—*Foreword.*   DB540.5.P7

Roeckle, Heidi. Liechtensteinische Bibliographie 1960– 1973. Vaduz, Liechtensteinische Landesbibliothek, 1979. 278p.   **DC414**

Classed arrangement of some 1,840 citations to books, maps and plans, articles, and new journals dealing with any subject area relating to Liechtenstein; materials are primarily those published in Liechtenstein. Name and keyword indexes.
Continued by *Liechtensteinische Bibliographie* (AA939).
                                                    Z2820.R63

LITHUANIA

Encyclopedia Lituanica. Boston, [Juozas Kapočius], 1970– 78. 6v. il.   **DC415**

Attempts to provide information in English "about Lithuania and the Lithuanian nation from the earliest times until the most recent events."—*Pref.* Many articles are signed with the initials of the contributor; many include bibliographies; most were written in

Lithuanian and translated into English. v.6 includes a supplement (p.365–486), a list of contributors, and a general index to the set.
DK511.L2E5

Kantautas, Adam and **Kantautas, Filomena.** A Lithuanian bibliography: a check-list of books and articles held by the major libraries of Canada and the United States. [Edmonton], Univ. of Alberta Pr., 1975. 725p. **DC416**

A classed bibliography with author and title indexes. More than 10,000 items. Locates copies. Includes sections for Lithuanians abroad. Z2537.K33

——— Supplement to A Lithuanian bibliography; a further check-list of books and articles held by major libraries of Canada and the United States. [Edmonton], Univ. of Alberta Pr., 1979. 316p.

Lists materials cataloged 1972–77. Z2537.K33

Lietuviškoji tarybine enciklopedija. [Vyriausiasis redaktorius J. Zinkus] Vilnius, Mokslas, 1976–84. 12v. il. **DC417**

A general encyclopedia with strong national and regional emphasis. Occasional brief bibliographies. AE35.55.L53

LUXEMBOURG

Bibliographie zur Geschichte Luxemburgs für das Jahr 1964– . (Mit Nachträgen für früheren Jahren) Luxemburg, National Bibliothek, 1965– . Annual. **DC418**

Added title page in French: Bibliographie de l'histoire Luxembourgeoise.
Topical listing of books and periodical articles significant for the study of Luxembourg history. Author index.

Hury, Carlo and **Christophory, Jules.** Luxembourg. Oxford, Eng. & Santa Barbara, Calif., Clio Pr., [1981]. 184p. (World bibliographical ser., 23) **DC419**

Lists about 480 books and articles in topical arrangement; many items are in English, but French and German titles are included. Name and subject index. Z2461.H87

MONACO

Handley-Taylor, Geoffrey. Bibliography of Monaco. 2d ed. Chicago, St. James Pr., 1968. 62p. il. **DC420**

1st ed. 1961.
"Represents a selection of publications (wholly or in part) relating to some aspect of the Principality or the family. . . ."—Pref.
Most articles and manuscripts cited in the first edition have been omitted; some newer items have been added, as has a subject index. Z2191.H3

NETHERLANDS

Bibliography

See also DE216–DE218.

Bibliographia neerlandica. The Hague, Nijhoff, 1962. 598p. **DC421**

Contents: Pt.1, Books on the Netherlands in foreign languages, 1940–57, comp. by A. M. P. Mollema, p. 1–384; pt. 2, Translations of Dutch literature, 1900–1957, comp. by P. M. Morel, p.385–491. Indexes, p.493–598.
Title, introductory material, and captions in English, French, German, and Spanish.
Continued in part by: Z2446.M64

Bibliografie van vertalingen van Noord- en Zuidnederlandse werken [uitgeg. door de K. Bibliotheek te 'sGravenhage en de K. Bibliotheek te Brussels]; sammegesteld door E. van Raan. 'sGravenhage, Staatuitgervij, 1974. 233p. **DC422**

Continues the Morel section of the above.

Buck, Hendrik de. Bibliografie der geschiedenis van Nederland. Leiden, Brill, 1968. 712p. (Repr.: Utrecht, HES, 1979) **DC423**

Comp. under the auspices of the Nederlands Comité voor Geschiedkundige Wetenschappen.
Modeled on Pirenne's bibliography for Belgian history (DC90). A classed bibliography of more than 8,600 items covering the whole range of Netherlands history through 1945. Indexes of authors, personal names, and place-names. Z2446.B8

Carasso-Kok, Marijke. Repertorium van verhalende historische bronnen uit de Middeleeuwen: Heiligenlevens, annalen, kronieken en andere in Nederland geschreven verhalende bronnen. The Hague, Nijhoff, 1982. 498p. (Bibliografische reeks van het Nederlands Historisch Genootschap, 2) **DC424**

A bibliography of sources arranged in two parts: (1) saints lives, giving for Dutch saints a brief biography and lists of manuscripts, editions, and secondary works; (2) other writings, including legends, chronicles, etc., and giving for each a brief description, lists of manuscripts, editions, and secondary works. Index of incipits, of abbreviations, of libraries, and of editors and places. Z2417.C37

Coolhaas, Willem Philippus. A critical survey of studies on Dutch colonial history. 2d ed., rev. by G. J. Schutte. The Hague, Nijhoff, 1980. 264p. (Bibliographical ser. K. Instituut voor Taal-, Land- en Volkenkunde, 4) **DC425**

1st ed. 1960.
Offers bibliographical essays describing and evaluating published works on the colonial empire of the Netherlands. Presentation is mainly chronological, but there are separate chapters on archives; journals, institutes and university chairs; bibliographies; travel accounts. This edition adds post-1960 material and earlier important items inadvertently omitted previously. Includes a list of titles discussed; indexes of personal and geographic names.

Herwijnen, G. van. Bibliografie van de stedengeschiedenis van Nederland. Leiden, Brill, 1978. 355p. **DC426**

At head of title: Acta collegii historiae urbanae societatis historicorum internationalis.
A general section on the history of towns in the Netherlands is followed by sections for individual provinces, each further subdivided by specific cities and towns, and thereunder by topic. 3,331 items. Indexes of place names and of authors. Z2423.H47

Repertorium der verhandelingen en bijdragen betreffende de geschiedenis des vaderlands, in tijdschriften en mengelwerken tot op 1900 verschenen. In opdracht van de Commissie voor Geschied- en Oudheidkunde van de Maatschappij der Nederlandsche Letterkunde te Leiden bewerkt door L. D. Petit. Leiden, Brill, 1907. 1638col. **DC427**

A revision of the first edition (1863) and its supplements. Lists publications through 1900.

——— 2.–5. deel. Leiden, Brill, 1913–53.

Contents: 2.deel, 1901–10. 884col.; 3.deel, 1911–20, 904col.; 4.deel, 1921–29. 1132col.; 5.deel, 1930–39. 764col.
A comprehensive, classified bibliography of analytical material on all aspects of Dutch history, indexing articles on the subject in more than 1,000 periodicals, society transactions, composite books, etc., principally Dutch publications but including some in other languages. List of titles indexed varies in the different volumes.
Z2416.R46

Repertorium van boeken en tijdschriftartikelen betreffende de geschiedenis van Nederland. 1940– . Leiden, Brill, 1943– . v.1– . Triennial since 1942. **DC428**

Title varies.
Continues the preceding entry, but on a smaller scale.

A bibliography of books and periodical articles on the history of the Netherlands. Index for 1940/50 separately published; index for 1975/80 in volume for 1980.   Z2416.R48

Archives

De Rijksarchieven in Nederland; eindred. L. P. L. Pirenne, . . . met medew. van P. van Iterson en P. G. J. M. Wagenaar. 'sGravenhage, Staatsdrukkerij- en Uitgeverijbedrijf, 1973. 2v. maps.   **DC429**

A listing of government archives, giving for each: name, address, hours, and lengthy descriptions of contents, together with lists of published catalogs. Indexed.

Overzichten van de archieven en verzamelingen in de openbare archiefbewaarplaatsen in Nederland (Alphen aan den Rijn, Samson, 1979–85. v.1–11; in progress) provides an extensive listing of archives; each volume is devoted to one province.   CD1692.A2R54

Dictionaries and handbooks

Strubbe, Egied I. and **Voet, Leon.** De chronologie van de middeleeuwen en de moderne tijden in de Nederlanden. Antwerp, Standaard-Boekhandel, 1960. 551p.   **DC430**

Chiefly tables, including a calendar for the years 396–2000, and chronological lists of popes, bishops of Dutch sees, selected European dynasties, and early Dutch rulers and landholders.   DH101.S7

Volmuller, H. W. J. Nijhoffs Geschiedenis-lexicon: Nederland en België. Samengesteld . . . in samenwerking met de redactie van De Grote Oosthoek. 'sGravenhage, Nijhoff, 1981. 655p. il.   **DC431**

Offers brief entries for personal and place names, events, etc., relating to the history of the Low Countries. Bibliographical references are appended to many articles.   DH101.V64

Atlases

Geschiedkundige atlas van Nederland . . . Uitg. door de Commissie voor den Geschiedkundigen Atlas van Nederland en geteekend door het lid der Commissie. 'sGravenhage, Nijhoff, 1913–38 (incompl.). 37v. text, 25cm.; 19v. maps in 16v., 51cm.   **DC432**

Historical maps of the various sections of the Netherlands, with detailed textual comment.

—— Verbeteringen en aanvullingen. 'sGravenhage, Nijhoff, 1932–35. 2v. 25cm.

NORWAY

See also Scandinavia.

Bibliografi til norges historie, 1916–1925, 1926–1935, 1936–74/75. . . . Utgitt av den Norske Historiske Forening. Oslo, Grøndahl, 1972–77. Annual; biennial from 1956/57.   **DC433**

Issued as supplements to *Historisk tidsskrift* (Oslo).

Full bibliography, including books, pamphlets, and analytical material in periodicals, etc. General title pages and general author

indexes are issued for 10-year periods, 1916–25, 1926–35, 1936–45, 1946–55, 1956–65, 1966–75. Items are numbered consecutively throughout the 10-year period.

Continued by: Z2606.N83

—— 1976/77– ; utarbei det ved Universitetsbibliotheket i Oslo av Cecilie Wiborg Bonafede. Utgitt av Den Norske Historiskie Forening. Oslo, [1981?]– . Microfiche. Biennial?

Coverage and arrangement are similar to the above. Fully indexed. Now produced from a database at the Universitetsbibliothek in Oslo and based on the collection at that institution.

Johnsen, Arne Odd and **Wasberg, Gunnar C.** Norsk militarhistorisk bibliografi. Utg. av Forsvarets krigshistoriske avdeling. Oslo, Gyldendal, 1969. 373p.   **DC434**

A topical listing of materials, mainly in Norwegian, on Norwegian military history of all periods. Author, place, and subject indexes.

Supplemented by Harald Sandvik's *Norsk militaerhistorisk bibliografi; tillegg* (Oslo, Gyldendal, 1977. 59p.).   Z2611.M5J64

Nysæter, Egil. Norske arkivkatalogar: oversikt over katalogar, register, mikrofilm, kjeldeutgåver m.m. i offentlege norske arkiv. 2. opplag. Oslo, Noregs Allmennvitskaplege Forskingeråd, 1983. 333p.   **DC435**

1st ed. 1982.

Covers government archives in all parts of Norway. For each archive gives brief history, list of catalogs and finding aids, address, microfilming projects (if any), and descriptive notes on major portions of the collection. Indexed.   CD1812.A2N95

Ørvik, Nils. Norwegian foreign policy; a bibliography, 1905–1965. [Oslo], Universitetsforlaget, 1968. 91p. (Norsk bibliografisk bibliotek, 34)   **DC436**

Topical listing within sections for books, articles, and government publications. Author index.

Continued by: Z2617.R4O382

—— —— 1965–1970. Oslo, [1973]. 74p. (Norsk bibliografisk bibliotek, 49)

Schiötz, Eiler H. Utlendingers reiser i Norgi, en bibliografi. Oslo, Universitetsforlaget, [1970]. 589p. (Norsk bibliografisk bibliotek, 44)   **DC437**

Added title page in English: Itineraria Norvegica, a bibliography on foreigners' travels in Norway until 1900.

Lists more than 1,278 accounts, in any language, of travels to any area of Norway, with indication of every place mentioned in each. Personal name index; topographic and chronological register; index of books relating to the Lapps.   Z2606.S32

Schweigaard, Johan Elias. Norges topografi; bibliografisk fortegnelse over topografisk og lokal-historisk literatur. Kristiania, Grøndahl, 1918. 291p.   **DC438**

—— —— Tillegg, 1917–1927, 1928–1945, ved W. P. Sommerfeldt. Oslo, Brøgger, 1930–55. 2v. (1928/45 issued as Norsk bibliografisk bibliotek, 14)

Detailed bibliographies on the topography and local history of Norway.

Updated by *Norsk localhistorie, en bibliografi,* by Harald Andresen (Oslo, Universitetsforlag, 1969; Norsk bibliografisk bibliotek, Bd.38), and *Lokalhistorisk litteratur 1969–1979,* by Rolf Fladby and E. Arnesen (Oslo, Norsk Lokalhistorisk Institutt, 1981).   Z2591.S38

Universitetsbiblioteket i Oslo. Norsk lokalhistorisk litteratur, 1946–1970. Oslo, Universitetsbiblioteket i Oslo, 1976–81. v.1–19. maps. (In progress)   **DC439**

Devotes a volume to each province or major city; in each there is a general section followed by subdivisions for local areas. Lists books, pamphlets, etc., many of them published locally. Indexed by author and by Universal Decimal Classification.   Z2606.O7

POLAND

Bibliography

Bibliografia historii Polski, 1815–1914. Warszawa, Państwowe Wydawnictwo Naukowe, 1954. 235p. **DC440**

Tom wstepny, introductory volume, comp. by Halina Bachulska and others. No more published.

1st ed. 1939 (of which v.1, pt.1, only, was published), had title *Bibliografia historii polskiej, 1815–1914.*

Continues Ludwik Finkel's *Bibliografia historyi polskiej* (DC444). Contains general bibliographies, encyclopedias, works on general and Polish history, historiography, archives, museums, and libraries. Limited primarily to works published up to 1939.

For bibliography of specific periods of 19th-century Polish history, *see Bibliografia historii Polski XIX wieku* (below). Z2526.B56

Bibliografia historii Polski XIX wieku. Wrocław, Zakład Narodowy im. Ossolińskich, 1958–83. v.1–2⁴². (In progress) **DC441**

At head of title: Polska Akademia Nauk. Instytut Historii.

Contents: v.1, 1815–1831; v.2¹⁻⁴², 1832–1864.

Comp. by Halina Bachulska and others. Ed. by Stanisław Płoski.

Continues Ludwik Finkel's *Bibliografia historyi polskiej* (DC444).

For general historical aids for the 19th century, *see Bibliografia historii Polski, 1815–1914* (above). Z2528.A4B5

Bibliografia historii polskiej, 1944/47– . Oprac. Jan Baumgart. Wrocław, Ossolińskich, 1952– . Annual. **DC442**

Began publication with volume for 1948; 1944/47 published 1962.

At head of title, 1961– : Instytut Historii-Zakład Dokumentacij Polskiej Akademii Nauk.

An extensive classified list, usually issued annually, of books and articles in various languages on Polish history and related fields. Author indexes. Z2526.B53

Davies, Norman. Poland, past and present; a select bibliography of works in English. Newtonville, Mass., Oriental Research Partners, 1977. 187p. **DC443**

English-language books and articles (plus a few items in French, German or Italian) relating to any period of Polish history are listed in topical arrangement with an author index. Addenda of materials published Dec. 1975–Autumn 1976. Appendixes include a glossary of Polish terms most likely to be encountered, a gazetteer, and an international list of periodicals most relevant to the study of Polish history. For the beginning researcher or general reader.

Z2526.A1

Finkel, Ludwik. Bibliografia historyi polskiej. Wspólnie z dr. Henrykiem Sawczyńskim i członkami Kółka historycznego uczniów Uniwersytetu lwowskiego zebrał i ułożył dr. Ludwik Finkel. W Krakowie, Nakł. Komisyi Historycznej Akademii Umiejętności w Krakowie, 1891–1906. 2150p. **DC444**

Issued in 7 parts.

2d ed., v.1, pts.1–4 (Lwów, Nakł. Polskiego Towarzystwa Historycznego, 1931–37).

———— ———— Dodatek 1–2¹. Kraków, 1906–14.

An excellent bibliography listing works published down to 1900 on Polish history to 1815. The 2d supplement lists original sources published 1901–10. The 2d ed. remains incomplete and with no index. Z2526.F48

Lewanski, Richard Casimir. Poland. Oxford, Eng. & Santa Barbara, Calif., Clio Pr., [1984]. 267p. (World bibliographical ser., 32) **DC445**

A selective, annotated bibliography of books, journals, articles, maps, etc., dealing with all areas of Polish civilization. Arranged by broad topic; most entries are for English-language titles, with a few Polish materials cited (mainly for their illustrative matter). Index of authors, titles, subjects. Z2526.L47

Polska Akademia Nauk. Instytut Historii. Bibliografia historii Polski. Pod red. Heleny Madurowicz-Urbańskiej oprocowali Wiesław Bieńkowski [et al.]. Warszawa, Państwowe Wydawnictwo Naukowe, 1965–78. 3v. **DC446**

Contents: v.1, pt.1, Do roku 1454; pt.2, 1454–1795; pt.3, Do roku 1795, indeksy; v.2, pt.1, 1795–1918; pt.2, Indeksy; v.3, pt.1, 1918–45; pt.2, Indeksy.

Explanatory notes in English, French, and Russian.

A bibliography of Polish history from earliest times to 1945. The first section of pt.1 is a general guide to bibliographic and reference aids, methodology, historiography, archives and libraries, and auxiliary studies; it is followed by a bibliography of Polish history arranged by periods to 1454, with appropriate subdivisions. The second part continues the period sections to 1795, and the third part provides indexes to the nearly 20,000 items listed. v.2 deals with Polish history to 1918, and v.3 covers the years following. Although coverage extends to such subjects as statistics, economics, and sociology, the bibliography is meant to be selective rather than exhaustive. Both books and periodical articles are included; there are some brief annotations.

While this work extends the period of coverage, as well as updates, the listings in Finkel's *Bibliografia historyi polskiej* (DC444), the older bibliography will still be found useful.

Publications of 1935–39 are listed in Wiesław Bieńkowski's *Bibliografia polskiej* (Wrocław, Zakł. Narrod. im. Ossolińskich, 1976–81. 2v.). Z2526.P64

Polska Akademia Nauk. Komitet Nauk Historycznych. La Pologne au XIIIᵉ Congrès International des Sciences Historiques à Moscou. Warsaw, Éditions Scientifiques de Pologne, 1970. 2v. **DC447**

Added title page in Polish.

Contents: v.1, La recherche historique en Pologne, 1945–1968, rédigé par Andrzej Wyczański; v.2, Bibliographie sélective des travaux des historiens polonais parus dans les années 1945–1968, rédigé par Janusz Tazbir.

v.1 offers essays on historical research and training in Poland, followed by directories of Polish archives, libraries, etc. v.2 is a topically arranged bibliography of Polish works on history published during the period indicated. Not indexed.

Rister, Herbert. Schrifttum über Polen, 1943–1951: mit besonderer Berücksichtigung des Posener Landes (Auswahl). Im Auftrage der Historisch- Landeskundlichen Kommission für Posen und das Deutschtum in Polen bearb. Marburg/ Lahn, Johann Gottfried Herder Inst., 1953. 147p. (Wissenschaftliche Beiträge zur Geschichte und Landeskunde Ost-Mitteleuropas. Nr.10) **DC448**

Continued by:

———— ———— 1952–1953 und Nachträge (Auswahl). 1955. 207p.; 1954–55 und Nachträge (Auswahl). 1958. 315p.; 1956–58 und Nachträge (Auswahl). 1960. 2v.; 1959–60. 1966. 444p. (Johann Gottfried Herder Institut. Wissenschaftliche Beiträge, 75)

Continued by:

Schrifttum über Polen (ohne Posener Land). Bearb. von Johanna Stiller. Marburg/Lahn, J. G. Herder-Instituts, 1971– . (Wissenschaftliche Beiträge zur Geschichte und Landeskunde Ost-Mitteleuropas, 90, 95–) **DC449**

"Im Auftrage der Historisch-Landeskundlichen Kommission für Posen und das Deutschtum in Polen."—*t.p.*

Contents: 1961–1962 und Nachträge (Auswahl); 1963–1965 und Nachträge (Auswahl); 1966–1970 und Nachträge (Auswahl); 1971–1973 (Auswahl).

Represents a continuation of Rister's *Schrifttum über Polen* (above). Because the literature for the Poznań region has become so extensive, a separate bibliography is being published for that area: *Schrifttum über das Posener Land 1961–1970,* ed. by Herbert Rister (Marburg/Lahn, 1976–).

Skwirowska, Stefania. Bibliographie des travaux des historiens polonais en langues étrangères parus dans les années

1945–1968. Wrocław, Zakład Narodowy im Ossolińskich, 1971. 91p. **DC450**

A bibliography of works in French, Spanish, English, German, Russian, or Italian on Polish history. Includes books, articles in journals and proceedings, together with translations published in Poland. Fully indexed.

Archives

Płaza, Stanisław. Zródła rekopismienne do dziejów wsi w Polsce feudalnej, studium archiewoznawcze. Warszawa, Państ. Wydaw. Naukowe, 1976. 440p. **DC451**

A guide to church and national archives containing material on medieval history. Indexed by topics, localities, and persons.
CD1742.P55

Encyclopedias and handbooks

Encyclopédie polonaise . . . publiée par le Comité des Publications Encyclopédiques sur la Pologne. Lausanne, 1916–20. il. v.1–4, pt.1. **DC452**

Contents: v.1, Géographie et ethnographie; v.2, Territoire et population; v.3, Vie économique; v.4, pt.1, Régime politique et administratif dans la Pologne prussienne. DK404.E45

———— Atlas. Fribourg, 1920– .

Contents: fasc.1, Vie économique de la Pologne; fasc.2, Territoire et population (Pologne historique).

Unfinished, but an authoritative work as far as it goes. Partially published in an English edition as: G1950.E5

Polish encyclopaedia. . . . Publ. by the Committee for the Polish Encyclopaedic Publications at Fribourg and Geneva. Geneva, Atar, 1922–26. (v.1, 1926) 3v. maps. (Pubn. of the Polish National Committee of America) (Repr.: N.Y., Arno, 1972) **DC453**

Contents: v.1, The Polish language. History of literature. History of Poland; v.2, Territory and population of Poland; v.3, Economic life of Poland.

Poland, a handbook. Warsaw, Interpress Publ., 1974. 573p. il., maps. **DC454**

A collection of English-language articles by Polish writers on all aspects of life in Poland: history; social, economic, political policy; sports; tourism; art (including cinema); foreign relations, etc. No bibliography, but many statistical tables and other illustrative material. DK404.P625613

Polska. Zarys encyklopedyczny. Wyd. 2. Warszawa, Państwowe Wydawnictwo Naukowe, 1979. 807p. il., maps. **DC455**

1st ed. 1974.
A topical encyclopedia treating Polish history, economy, industry, art, culture, etc. Detailed table of contents, but no general index.
DK403.P65

General histories

Cambridge history of Poland. Ed. by W. F. Reddaway [and others]. Cambridge, Cambridge Univ. Pr., 1941–50. 2v. (Repr.: N.Y., Octagon, 1971) **DC456**

Contents: v.1, From the origins to Sobieski (to 1696) (publ. 1950); v.2, From Augustus II to Pilsudski (1697–1935) (publ. 1941).

Chapters by specialists. A third volume was to have been a bibliography. DK414.C32

PORTUGAL

See also Spain.

Bibliography

See also DB248.

Academia Portuguesa da História. Guia da bibliografia histórica portuguêsa. Lisboa, 1959. v.1, fasc.1. (No more publ.) **DC457**

Planned to constitute, when complete, a comprehensive bibliography of Portuguese history from the 9th century to 1910. This fascicle lists collections of sources (documents, diplomatic records, etc.); no index.

Coutinho, Bernard Xavier da Costa. Bibliographie franco-portugaise; essai d'une bibliographie chronologique de livres français sur le Portugal. Pôrto, Lopes da Silva, 1939. 409p. **DC458**

On cover: Publiée sous les auspices de l'Institut Français au Portugal et de l'Instituto para a Alta Cultura, avec le concours du Secrétariado da Propaganda Nacional.

Arranged chronologically from the 16th to the 20th centuries; lists almost 3,000 items. Z2737.R4C6

Kettenring, N. Ernest. A bibliography of theses and dissertations on Portuguese topics completed in the United States and Canada, 1861–1983. [Durham, N.H.], Internat. Conference on Modern Portugal, Dept. of History, Univ. of New Hampshire, [1984]. 87p. **DC459**

An author listing with index by country and broad topic. Includes a small number of South African theses and research papers; thorough coverage for the U.S. and Canada.

Lisbon. Biblioteca Nacional. Subsidios para a bibliografia da história local portuguêsa. Lisboa, Biblioteca Nacional, 1933. 425p. **DC460**

Ed. by Antonio Mesquita de Figueiredo.
A bibliography of local history. Z2733.L77

Marques, António Henrique R. de Oliveira. Guia de história de la República Portuguesa. Lisboa, Estampa, 1981. 662p. **DC461**

A bibliography in essay form covering the Portugal of 1910–32, and indicating bibliographies, sources, studies, and periodicals. Broad topical arrangement with subdivisions. Includes all forms of history—cultural, demographic, etc.—and "auxiliary sciences of history," extending to cinematography and chronology. Indexed.

———— Guia do estudante de história medieval portuguesa. 2. ed. Lisbôa, Editorial Estampa, 1979. 265p. (Imprensa universitaria, 15) **DC462**

1st ed. 1964.
Intended as a researcher's manual or guide to principal sources and published studies in the field. Includes special sections for archives and manuscript repositories. This edition includes publications as late as 1979. Indexed.

Newberry Library, Chicago. A catalog of the Greenlee collection. Boston, G. K. Hall, 1970. 2v. (1465p.) **DC463**

An outstanding, comprehensive collection of Portuguese history and literature. Dictionary arrangement.

The earlier catalog edited by Doris Varner Welsh (Chicago, 1953) should still be used since it includes additional materials at the Newberry Library which are not in the Greenlee collection.
Z2739.N483

Dictionaries and encyclopedias

Dicionário de história de Portugal. Dirigido por Joel Serrão. [2d ed.] Porto, Livraria Figueirinhas, 1981. 6v.   **DC464**

1st ed. 1963–71.

Covers political, cultural, religious, and economic history of Portugal. Includes entries for political parties, wars, battles, treaties, cultural and religious movements, etc., as well as general articles on Portuguese art and archaeology, literature, language, science, and philosophy. Many biographical articles. Longer entries are signed and carry bibliographies.

Grande enciclopédia portuguesa e brasileira. Lisboa, Rio de Janeiro, Ed. Enciclopédia, [1935–58]. 37v. il.   **DC465**

A dictionary-encyclopedia treating in one alphabet: Portuguese words, including technical terms and modern slang; biographies, including living persons; and encyclopedic articles on the history and culture of Portugal, national institutions, flora, fauna, geography, etc. Articles are not signed, and bibliographies are inconsistently furnished.

———— Apêndice. 1958–60. 4v. il.

v.1 bound with main work; v.2–4 called v.38–40.   AE37.G7

———— Actualização. Lisboa, Editorial Enciclopédia, [1981–82]. v.1–3. (In progress)

Contents: v.1–3, A–Czestochowa.

Articles have been updated, and there is much new material on technology. Double asterisks refer to articles in the earlier set. To be in 10v.

———— 2.parte: Brasil. [1964?–75]. v.1–3. il. (In progress)

Contents: v.1–3, A–Guaranésia.

This second part, devoted to Brazilian subjects, is projected to be in 4v. Biographical sketches include living persons.   AE37.G73

[Machado, Herlânder Alves] Dicionário de história de Portugal ilustrado. [Lisboa], Formar, [1982]. 2v. il.   **DC465a**

A heavily illustrated, quick reference dictionary of Portuguese history. Strong in biography, but includes many survey articles. Chronologies; no bibliography.   DP535.M33

Verbo; enciclopédia luso-brasileira de cultura. Lisboa, Ed. Verbo, 1963–84. 20v. il.   **DC466**

A Portuguese-Brazilian encyclopedia with signed articles and many bibliographies listing works in various languages. Treats mainly the culture and history of Portugal and Brazil, but includes articles of some length on the continents and other countries. Many well-produced, small colored illustrations. v.19–20 are supplements.   AE37.V4

ROMANIA

Bibliografia istorica a României. Bucureşti, Editura Academiei Republicii Socialiste România, 1970–80. v.1–5. (In progress?)   **DC467**

Contents: v.1, 1944–1969: Bibliografii selectiva; v.2,t.1, Secolul XIX: Cadrul general. Tara si locuitorii; v.3,t.5, Secolul XIX: Biografi; v.4, 1969–1974: Bibliografii selectiva; v.5, 1974–1979: Bibliografii selectiva.

An extensive bibliography of books and articles on history published in Romania. Emphasis is on Romanian history, with brief sections on world history in v.1, 4–5. Each volume has its own author index.   Z2926.B5

Enciclopedia României. [Bucharest?, Asociatia Stiintificà Pentru Enciclopedia României], 1938–43. v.1–4. il.   **DC468**

Contents: A. Organizarea politica-administrativa: v.1, Statul; v.2, Tara romaneasca. B. Economia; v.3, Economia nationala. Cadre si productie; v.4, Economia nationala. Circúlatie, distributie si con-

sum. (Two projected volumes have not been published: C. Cultura: v.5, Cultura nationala; v.6, Institutii si personalitati culturale.

Scholarly, monographic articles arranged by large classes, with detailed tables of contents and indexes in each volume. Articles are signed by authorities and include bibliographies except in v.2, which presents gazetteer information and includes an index to all places in Rumania.

Rally, Alexandre and **Rally, Getta Hélène.** Bibliographie franco-roumaine. Paris, Leroux, 1930. 1. pt., t.1–2.   **DC469**

Contents: (1¹), Les oeuvres françaises des auteurs roumains; (1²), Les oeuvres françaises relatives à la Roumanie.

t.1, arranged alphabetically by author; t.2, arranged by class with alphabetical index to names and places.

To a large extent supersedes the earlier work by Georges Bengescu, *Bibliographie franco-roumaine depuis le commencement du XIX siècle jusqu'à nos jours* (Paris, 1907), of which only v.1 was published (2d ed. with suppl., 1895–1906). The bibliographical descriptions in Bengescu are longer, but the coverage is less complete.   Z2928.R4R2

U.S. Library of Congress. Slavic and Central European Division. Rumania, a bibliographic guide, by Stephen A. Fischer-Galati. Wash., Govt. Prt. Off., 1963. 75p.   **DC470**

A concise, descriptive, bibliographic survey, totaling 748 items, arranged by subject and covering all areas of knowledge except medicine and the natural sciences. Includes monographs and periodicals, mostly in Romanian, though publications in other languages are represented. Locates copies.   Z2291.U5

SCANDINAVIA

See also Denmark, Finland, Norway, Sweden.

Kulturhistorisk Leksikon for nordisk Middelalder fra Vikingetid til Reformationstid. Dansk redaktør, John Danstrup. København, Rosenkilde og Bagger, 1956–78. 22v. il.   **DC471**

Editors vary.

Written by the leading medievalists in Denmark, Norway, Sweden, and Finland. Each article signed, and most include bibliography; v.21 includes a supplement; v.22 is an index.   DL30.K8

Kvamme, Janet. Index nordicus: a cumulative index to English-language periodicals on Scandinavian studies. Boston, G. K. Hall, 1980. 601p.   **DC472**

Prep. under the auspices of the American Scandinavian Foundation.

A computer-produced index of the six leading English-language journals for Scandinavian studies from the founding date of each through 1976; three of the six are not currently indexed in the standard periodical indexes. Articles are indexed by author, joint authors, and subjects; only signed book reviews are indexed, and listing is under author of the book reviewed.   Z2551.K87

Meyen, Fritz. The North European nations as presented in German university publications, 1885–1957, a bibliography. Bonn, H. Bouvier; Charlottesville, Bibliographical Soc. of the Univ. of Virginia, 1959. 124p. (Bonner Beiträge zur Bibliotheks- und Bücherkunde. 4)   **DC473**

Added title page in German.

Contents, preface, and headings in English and German.

Lists 1,099 dissertations and habilitation theses "that exclusively or preponderatingly, treat a theme relative to Denmark, Sweden, Norway, Iceland, or Finland."—*Pref.* Includes both published and unpublished works. Topical arrangement; author and subject indexes.   Z2000.M4

Oakley, Stewart P. Scandinavian history, 1520–1970: list of books and articles in English. London, Historical Assoc., [1984]. 232p. (Helps for students of history, 91)   **DC474**

Lists some 2,478 items by century, subdivided by country and by topic. Introductory notes for each chapter point up significant publications and provide cross references. Aims to "include all secondary material published in English between 1880 and 1980 on all aspects of the history of Scandinavia as well as some items of special interest which appeared earlier and accounts by travellers in the region before the middle of the nineteenth century."—*Pref.* Author index.

Svenska Stadshistoriska Institut. International bibliography of urban history: Denmark, Finland, Norway, Sweden. Stockholm, Swedish Inst. for Urban History, Univ. of Stockholm, 1960. 73p. **DC475**

The first of a projected series of bibliographies dealing with the history of cities. The plan is to present each country separately. In this volume the Scandinavian countries are treated individually; in each case, general bibliographies and other materials are followed by histories of individual cities.

SPAIN

Bibliography

Bardi, Ubaldo. La guerra civile di Spagna; saggio per una bibliografia italiana. Urbino, Argalìa Editore, [1974]. 134p. **DC476**

A classed list of Italian writings on the Spanish Civil War of 1936–39. Lacks an index. Z2700.B37

Bibliografía general sobre la Guerra de España (1936–1939) y sus antecedentes históricos; fuentes para la historia contemporánea de España. Introd. general y dirección y revisión de Ricardo de la Cierva. Madrid, Ministerio de Información y Turismo, 1968. 729p. **DC477**

An alphabetical main-entry listing, but with entries under each letter of the alphabet subdivided as "Antecedentes" and "Guerra." Indexes of names, places, and topical subjects. Z2700.B52

Burgo, Jaime del. Bibliografía del siglo XIX: guerras carlistas, luchas políticas. 2. ed. rev. y puesta al día. Pamplona, [Diputación Foral de Navarra], 1978. 1072p. **DC478**

1st ed. 1953–66 had title *Bibliografía de las guerras carlistas.* . . . An extensive bibliography of books and pamphlets (with a few periodical articles) dealing with political strife in Spain in the 19th century. This edition incorporates the earlier supplement and adds references to 1975. Z2699.B87

Cortada, James W. A bibliographic guide to Spanish diplomatic history, 1460–1977. Westport, Conn., Greenwood Pr., [1977]. 390p. **DC479**

Organized by reign, then by country (with occasional topical subdivisions). Author index, but none of subjects. Only published books, pamphlets, government documents, and periodical articles are included. Z2696.C67

Foulché-Delbosc, Raymond and **Barrau-Dihigo, Louis.** Manuel de l'hispanisant. N.Y., Putnam; Hispanic Soc. of America, 1925. v.1–2. **DC480**

For full description *see* AA96. Z2681.A1F7

González Ollé, Fernando. Manual bibliográfico de estudios españoles. Pamplona, Ediciones Universidad de Navarra, 1976. 1375p. **DC481**

A classed bibliography covering the whole range of Spanish studies. Arranged in 22 main categories, each closely subdivided, with chronological and geographical sub-sections where appropriate. Author and subject indexes in addition to a very detailed table of contents. Z2681.G58

Harvard University. Library. Spanish history and literature. Classification schedule; classified listing by call number; chronological listing; author and title listing. Cambridge,

publ. by Harvard Univ. Lib., distr. by Harvard Univ. Pr., 1972. 771p. (Widener Library shelflist, 41) **DC482**

". . .lists more than 30,000 titles comprising the classes *Span, PSpan,* and *Span Doc* which contain most of the Library's books and periodicals on Spain, but not her present or former colonies. Historical topics covered include civilization, religious affairs, government and administration, foreign relations, social life and customs, and geography and travel. Works on economic and financial affairs and on certain aspects of social conditions are classed elsewhere, as are Catalan and Valencian literature."—*Pref.*

For a note on the series *see* AA145. Z2709.H35

Kinder, A. Gordon. Spanish protestants and reformers in the sixteenth century; a bibliography. London, Grant & Cutler, 1983. 108p. (Research bibliographies and checklists, 39) **DC483**

Covers "the reform-minded heterodox antecedents of Spanish Protestantism, its brief flourishing in its homeland, and its dying echoes abroad" (*Introd.*)—i.e., mainly 1500–1600. Listing is divided as (1) Manuscripts and (2) Editions and studies. Cut-off date is 1979. Indexed.

Ruhl, Klaus-Jörg. Der spanische Bürgerkrieg; Literatur und Bibliographie. München, Bernard & Graefe, [1982]– . Bd.1– . (Schriften der Bibliothek für Zeitgeschichte. N.F.Bd.22) **DC484**

Contents: Bd.1, Der politische Konflikt. A topically arranged bibliography of documents, books, and articles in any language relating to the Spanish Civil War; includes much contemporary writing. Name index. A second volume is promised. Z2700.R83

Sánchez Alonso, Benito. Fuentes de la historia española e hispanoaméricana. . . . 3. ed. corr. y puesta al día. Madrid, Consejo Superior de Investigaciones Científicas, 1952. 3v. (Pubn. de la Revista de filología española, 8) **DC485**

Subtitle: Ensayo de bibliografía sistemática de impresos y manuscritos que ilustran la historia política de España y sus antiguas provincias de ultramar.

A comprehensive bibliography of books and periodical articles covering Spanish history from early times through the 19th century. An author index and three subject indexes: (1) biographical, (2) geographical, and (3) miscellaneous. Z2696.S21

Simón Díaz, José. Bibliografía regional y local de España. Madrid, CSIC, 1976– . v.1– . (Cuadernos bibliográficos, 33) (In progress?) **DC486**

Contents: v.1, Impresos localizados (siglos XV–XVII). For each local area (city, bishopric, etc.), v.1 lists all publications from the 15th–17th centuries relating to that area—books, documents, histories, etc. Arranged by area, then by date of publication. Locates copies in libraries of Western Europe and the United States. Index of personal names and topics. Z2703

Utrecht. Rijksuniversiteit. Bibliotheek. España e Hispanoamérica: catálogo de libros españoles y publicaciones extranjeras sobre España e Hispanoamérica. Utrecht, 1948. 360p. **DC487**

————— Suplemento, 1–10, 1949–68.

A classified catalog of Spanish and foreign books on Spain and Spanish America. The main volume lists publications acquired by the Library up to 1944; the supplements list later acquisitions. Z2709.U8

Current

Índice histórico español. v.1– . Barcelona, Ed. Teide, 1953– . v.1– . Quarterly. **DC488**

An extensive bibliography which aims to list books and articles on Spanish history published in Western Europe and the Americas, with a section on the history of Latin America. Titles are annotated and evaluated by experts, and references to critical reviews are often given. Annual author and subject indexes.

v.1, fasc.1–8, also issued in bound form (859p.) with title *Bibliografía histórica de España e Hispanoamérica*.   Z2696.I6

Dissertations

Hanson, Carl A. Dissertations on Iberian and Latin American history. Troy, N.Y., Whitston, 1975. 400p.   **DC489**

For full information *see* DB248.   Z1601.H32

Historiography

Sánchez Alonso, Benito. Historia de la historiografía española, ensayo de un examen de conjunto. . . . Madrid, Sánchez de Ocaña, 1944–47. v.1–2. (Pubn. de la Revista de filología española) (In progress?)   **DC490**

At head of title: Consejo Superior de Investigaciones Científicas. Contents: v.1, Hasta la publicación de la crónica de Ocampo (. . . 1943), 2. ed. rev. y añadida, 1947; v.2, De Ocampo a Solís (1543–1684), 1944.   DP63.S3

Dictionaries

Diccionario de historia de España. Dirigido por Germán Bleiberg. 2. ed., corr. y aum. Madrid, Ediciones de la Revista de Occidente, [1968–69]. 3v.   **DC491**

1st ed. 1952.
An alphabetical dictionary of persons, events, and subjects in the history of Spain, compiled by a group of scholars. Articles are generally brief, though some of the more important entries cover several pages; all are signed. The earlier edition included events only to 1931. Although this edition has been revised and reset (with some updating and additional articles), treatment of the 1931–68 period is confined largely to the chronology and the bibliographical section appended to v.3 (p.1083–1113).

Historical dictionary of the Spanish Civil War, 1936–1939. Ed. by James W. Cortada. Westport, Conn., Greenwood Pr., [1982]. 571p. maps.   **DC492**

Offers signed articles on persons, places, organizations, events, etc., relating to the Spanish Civil War. A high percentage of the short articles was contributed by the editor. Bibliographies accompany many articles. Numerous appendixes, including a detailed chronology and a concise military history of the war. Indexed.
DP269.H54

Muñoz y Romero, Tomás. Diccionario bibliográfico-histórico de los antiguos reinos, provincias, ciudades, villas, iglesias y santuarios de España. Madrid, Rivadeneyra, 1858. 329p.   **DC493**

An older work still useful for local history.   Z2703.M96

Russell, Peter Edward, ed. Spain, a companion to Spanish studies. [New ed.] London, Methuen, 1973. 592p.   **DC494**

"An entirely new version of the work of the same title, edited by the late Prof. E. Allison Peers, which was first published in 1929."— *Pref.* Each area of Spanish studies (literature, music, history, Spanish-American literature, etc.) was contributed by a specialist and is designed to be a complete survey of the field. Bibliography (emphasizing English-language works when possible) at the end of each chapter.   DP48.R87

General histories

Menéndez Pidal, Ramón. Historia de España. Madrid, Espasa-Calpe, 1935–71. v.1–6, 15, 17–19, 26. (In progress)   **DC495**

Edition note varies. 1st ed. 1935–50.

Contents: v.1, España prehistórica, por. Eduardo Hernandez-Pacheco [et al.]. 3d ed., 1963; v.2, España romana (218A.de J.C.–414 de J.C.), por. Pedro Bosch Gimpera [et al.]. 3d ed., 1962; v.3, España visigoda (414–711 de J.C.), por Manuel Torres Lopez [et al.]. 2d ed. corr. y ampliada, 1963; v.4, España musulmana hasta la caída del Califato de Córdoba (711-1031 de J.C.), por E. Levi-Provençal. 2d ed., 1957; v.5, España musulmana, . . . : Instituciones y vida social e intelectual, por E. Levi-Provençal. 1957; v.6, España cristiana, comienzo de la reconquista (711–1038), por Fray Justo Pérez de Urbel y Ricardo del Arco y Garay. 3d ed., 1971; v.7, España Christiana de los siglos VIII al XI, por C. Sanchez-Albornoz. 1980; v.14, La crisis de la Reconquisto (ca. 1350–ca. 1410), por L. Suarez Fernandez. 3d ed., 1966; v.15, Los trastámaras de Castilla y Aragón en el siglo XV: Juan II y Enrique IV de Castilla (1407–1474); El compromiso de Caspe, Fernando I, Alfonso V y Juan II de Aragón (1410–1479), por L. Suarez Fernandez [et al.]. 1965; v.17, La España de los reyes católicos (1474–1516), por Luis Suárez Fernandez y Juan Mata Carriazo Arroquia. 1968. 2v.; v.18, La España del emperador Carlos V (1500–1558; 1517–1556), por Manuel Fernández Alvarez. 1966; v.19, España en tiempo de Felipe II (1556–1598), por P. Luis Fernández y Fernández de Retana. 2d ed., 1966. 2v.; v.26, La España de Fernando VII, por Miguel Artola Gallego. 1969; v.24, España de Felipe III, por C. Pérez Bustamente. 1982; v.25, España de Felipe IV, por F. Tomás y Valiente [et al.]. 3d ed., 1982; v.32, España de Fernando VII, por M. Artola Gallego. 2d ed., 1978; v.34, Era Isabella y el sexanio democrático (1834–1874), por T. Villarrova. 1981; v.37, Comienzos del siglo XX: la población/la economía/la sociedad (1898–1931), por J. L. García Delgado. 3d ed., 1984.

A collaborative work by outstanding Spanish historians, to cover from prehistoric times. Illustrated in black-and-white and in color.
DP66.M35

SWEDEN

See also Scandinavia.

Bring, Samuel Ebbe. Itineraria svecana; bibliografisk förteckning över resor i Sverige fram till 1950. Stockholm, Almqvist & Wiksell, [1954]. 586p. il. (Svenska bibliotekariesamfundets skriftserie, 3)   **DC496**

A bibliography of almost 3,250 works of travel in Sweden, in various languages. Arranged chronologically, 944–1950, with author index.   Z2636.B83

Svensk historisk bibliografi; systematisk förteckning över skrifter och uppsatser som röra Sveriges historia, 1880– . Stockholm, Norstelt; Uppsala, Almqvist & Wiksell, 1881– . Annual. (v.1–3 repr.: Nendeln, Kraus, 1975)   **DC497**

An annual bibliography of books and periodical articles; issued as a supplement to *Historisk tidskrift* (Stockholm 1880–1949). Cumulated as follows:
1875–1900 (publ. 1907) and 1901–20 (publ. 1923) ed. by Kristian Setterwall; 1921–35 (publ. 1956), ed. by Paul Sjögren; 1936–50 (publ. 1964), ed. by Harald Bohn and Percy Elfstrand; 1951–60 (publ. 1968), ed. by Jan Rydbeck; 1961–70 (publ. 1984), ed. by M. L. Bachman. Cumulations form part of the series *Svenska historiska föreningen. Skrifter*, 2–3, 5–8.
See also Kristian Setterwall's *Svensk historisk bibliografi 1771–1874* (Uppsala, 1937. 911p.).   Z2636.S9

SWITZERLAND

Guides

Santschy, Jean-Louis. Manuel analytique et critique de bibliographie générale de l'histoire suisse. Berne, Herbert Lang, 1961. 250p.   **DC498**

A guide to sources—general, archival, periodical, and monographic—rather than a bibliography as such. Chapter arrangement, according to type and date of material. Annotations are full; author and subject indexes. Z2786.S3

Bibliography

Barth, Hans. Bibliographie der schweizer Geschichte enthaltend die selbständig erschienenen Druckwerke zur Geschichte der Schweiz bis Ende 1912. Basel, Basler Buch- und Antiquariatshandlung, 1914–15. 3v. (Quellen zur schweizer Geschichte hrsg. von der Allgemeinen Geschichtforschenden Gesellschaft der Schweiz. n.F. 4. Abt. Handbücher) **DC499**

v.1, General history, by periods; v.2–3, Special subjects, e.g., biography, religious history, etc. Author and title index.

A very comprehensive bibliography, including more than 32,000 entries. May be supplemented by the following: (1) for material after 1912 by the annual *Bibliographie der Schweizergeschichte* (below); (2) for analytical material before 1900 by the two volumes of the *Repertorium* (DC501). Z2786.B28

Bibliographie der Schweizergeschichte. Bibliographie de l'histoire suisse. Jahrg. 1913– . Zurich, Leemann, 1914– . v.1– . Annual (some years combined). **DC500**

Publisher varies.

Volumes for 1913–19 published as supplements to the *Anzeiger für schweizerische Geschichte;* those for 1920–34, as supplements to the *Zeitschrift für schweizerische Geschichte.*

Classed arrangement. Later volumes have author and subject indexes. Includes material on history, bibliography, biography, church, art, literature, music, customs, etc.

Continues Hans Barth's *Bibliographie der schweizer Geschichte* (above). Z2786.B58

Brandstetter, Josef Leopold. Repertorium über die in Zeit- und Sammelschriften der Jahre 1812–1890, 1891–1900, enthaltenen Aufsätze und Mitteilungen schweizergeschichtlichen Inhaltes. Hrsg. von der Allgemeinen Geschichtforschenden Gesellschaft der Schweiz. Basel, Basler Buch- und Antiquariatshandlung, 1892–1906. 2v. **DC501**

1812–90, comp. by J. L. Brandstetter; 1891–1900, by Hans Barth.

Classed lists—arranged by small subject, with alphabetical index of authors—to articles on Swiss history, biography, etc., in more than 300 periodicals and society transactions. The sections on biography in each volume give, in addition to the references to the articles, the dates of birth and death and a brief characterizing phrase, and so supply some direct biographical information. Z2786.B81

Guyer, Paul. Bibliographie der Städtegeschichte der Schweiz. Zürich, Verlag Leemann, 1960. 70p. (Schweizerische Zeitschrift für Geschichte. Beiheft, 11) **DC502**

763 entries for books and periodical articles in geographical arrangement. Name index. Gives population of each town in 1850 and in 1950. Z2793.G8

Dictionaries and encyclopedias

Dictionnaire historique et biographique de la Suisse, publié avec la recommandation de la Société Générale Suisse d'Histoire. . . . Neuchâtel, Admin. du Dictionnaire, 1921–34. 7v. and suppl. il. **DC503**

Issued also in an edition in German, *Historisch-biographisches Lexikon der Schweiz.*

Contents: v.1–7, A–Z; suppl., A–Z, p.1–184; 2d suppl., A–Z, p. 185–208. Table systématique.

May be considered a companion work to the *Dictionnaire géographique de la Suisse* (CL186), published by Attinger. Covers the fields of general, political, local, economic, and social history; topography; genealogy; and biography of the country. Signed articles, bibliographies, and many good illustrations. Many bio-

graphical articles, including some on persons still living at time of compilation. DQ51.D5

Schweizer Lexikon. Zurich, Encyclios-Verlag, [1945–48]. 7v. il. **DC504**

A general encyclopedia with short articles, usually with brief bibliographies. Illustrations are clear and well chosen. AE69.S35

TURKEY

Bibliography

Battersby, Harold R. Anatolian archaeology: a bibliography. New Haven, Human Relations Area Files, 1976. 2v. (Anatolian studies, 1) **DC505**

5,169 articles, essays, books, and periodical titles are listed in two alphabetical author sequences, with index by topic or excavation site. Z2857.A67B38

Bodurgil, Abraham. Kemal Atatürk; a centennial bibliography (1881–1981). Wash., Near East Section, African and Middle Eastern Div., Lib. of Congress, 1984. 214p. **DC506**

1st ed. 1974 had title: *Atatürk and Turkey.*

A topically arranged bibliography of about 2,000 books, articles, dissertations, conference papers, and motion pictures. Author index and a very full subject index.

For Turkish-language materials *see* Muzaffer Gökman's *Atatürk ve devrimleri tarihi bibliyografyasi* (3. bas. Ankara, Kültür Bakanliq, 1981–82. 2v.). Z2850.A85B6

—— Turkey—politics and government: a bibliography, 1938–1975. Wash., Lib. of Congress, 1978. 156p. **DC507**

Continues coverage of the period following the author's *Kemal Atatürk* (above), listing 2,020 books, journal articles, Turkish and U.S. government publications on politics, government, social and economic conditions, religion, geography, international relations of Turkey. More than half the citations are to Turkish sources, with Turkish titles also given in English; about two-thirds of the remaining citations are in English, with the balance in French, Russian, German, Italian, and Spanish. Subject and author indexes. Z2850.B64

Güçlü, Meral. Turkey. London, Eng. & Santa Barbara, Calif., Clio Pr., [1981]. 331p. (World bibliographical ser., 27) **DC508**

Citations to books and a few periodical articles are arranged topically; good annotations. All are English-language materials except for a few recent Turkish titles chosen arbitrarily as examples. Author, title, subject index. Z2831.G83

Koray, Enver. Türkiye tarih yayinlari bibliyografyasi, 1729/1955– . Istanbul, Maarif Basimevi, 1959– . [v.1–2] (In progress) **DC509**

Contents: [v.1, 2. basim] 1729–1955. 680p. (1959); [v.2, 1. basim] 1955–1968. 510p. (1970).

[v.1] supersedes an earlier edition covering 1729–1950 (publ. 1952).

A bibliography of Turkish historical writings. Lists general works, collections, encyclopedias, etc., followed by books on the history of individual countries, and then works in related fields such as archaeology, biography, and ethnology. Author and title indexes. Z2846.K62

Kornrumpf, Hans-Jürgen and **Kornrumpf, Jutta.** Osmanische Bibliographie mit Besonderer Berücksichtigung der Turkei in Europa. Leiden, Brill, 1973. 1378p. (Handbuch der Orientalistik. 1 Abt. Der Nahe und der Mittlere Osten. Ergänzungsband, 8) **DC510**

Pages 1–726 comprise an alphabetical author listing of books (including book reviews), essays, and articles in all languages. A second section, p.729–1378, provides a listing in classed arrangement of the items in the first section. A useful feature is the indication at the end of each entry in the author part of the classification used for that item in the subject section.

Z2831.K67

Mikhov, Nikola V. Bibliographie des articles de périodiques allemands, anglais, français et italiens sur la Turquie et la Bulgarie, [par] Nicholas V. Michoff. Sofia, Impr. de la Cour, 1938. 686p. **DC511**

At head of title: Académie Bulgare des Sciences.

A comprehensive compilation of more than 10,000 titles of articles appearing in the periodicals of Western Europe from 1715 to 1880 (with some additional entries to 1891), arranged chronologically by year, with indexes by author and personal name and by subject and place-name. "Liste de abréviations des titres de périodiques," p.1–58. Z2846.M63

———— Naselenieto na Turtsiia i Bulgariia priezu XVIII i XIX v; bibliografsko-statistichni izsludvaniia . . . La population de la Turquie et de la Bulgarie au XVIIIe et XIXe siècles. Recherches bibliographico-statistiques . . . Sofia, Impr. de la Cour Royale, 1915–67. 5v. **DC512**

v.1 has added title page: Bulgarska Akademiia na Naukite. Sbornik. Kniga 4. Klon Istoriko-filologichen i filosofsko-obshtestven, 3.

Lists more than 3,000 books and periodical articles in Western languages on demographic statistics, etc. Each volume is arranged alphabetically by author or other main entry, with two indexes: (1) Index géographique et ethnographique; (2) Index alphabétique des noms de personnes. Z7554.T9M6

———— Bibliografskii iztochnitsa za istoriiata na Turtsiia i Bulgariia . . . Sources bibliographiques sur l'histoire de la Turquie et de la Bulgarie. Sofia, 1914–34. 4v. **DC513**

A bibliography of works of the 19th and 20th centuries, in various languages, on the history of Turkey. Cumulated author and subject indexes to all four volumes in v.4. Z6464.E1M6

Sverchevskaia, A. K. and **Cherman, T. P.** Bibliografiia Turtsii, 1917–1958. Moskva, Izd-vo Vostochnoi Lit-ry, 1959. 189p. **DC514**

At head of title: Akademiia Nauk SSSR. Institut Vostokovedeniia.

Bibliography of scientific and popular Soviet writings on Turkey and Turkology, and of Turkish authors translated into Russian. Z2846.S9

———— ———— 1713–1917. Moskva, Izd-vo Vostochnoi Lit-ry, 1961. 266p. **DC515**

Z2846.S89

Tamkoç, Metin. A bibliography on the foreign relations of the Republic of Turkey, 1919–1967, and brief biographies of Turkish statesmen. Ankara, Orta Dogu Teknik Universitesi, Idari Ilimler Facultesi, 1968. 248p. (Ankara. Orta Dogu Teknik Universitesi. Yayinlar, 11) **DC516**

A classed bibliography of about 1,800 entries. Turkish and foreign sources are listed in separate sections. English translations of the Turkish titles are added. Index of names. Z2857.R4T3

Dissertations

Suzuki, Peter T. French, German, and Swiss university dissertations on twentieth century Turkey; a bibliography of 593 titles, with English translations. Wiesbaden, WDS-Schnelldruck, 1970. 138p. (Newsletter for European researchers on modern Turkey. Suppl. no.1, rev.) **DC517**

An author listing with broad subject index. Covers French dissertations accepted 1900–67; German dissertations, 1900–65; Swiss dissertations, 1900–68. Includes some works completed at the universities of Graz and Vienna.

Encyclopedias and histories

Shaw, Stanford J. History of the Ottoman Empire and modern Turkey. Cambridge, Cambridge Univ. Pr., 1976–77. 2v. **DC518**

Contents: v.1, Empire of the Gazis: the rise of the Ottoman Empire, 1280–1808; v.2, Reform, revolution, and republic: the rise of modern Turkey, 1808–1975.

Based on both Ottoman and European sources, the work attempts to present a balanced history from the foundations of the Ottoman Empire through the beginning of the Republic of Turkey. Bibliography at the end of each volume.

For contrasting scholarly opinions of the work *see* reviews in the *English historical review* 93:393–95 (Apr. 1978), in the *Bulletin* of the School of Oriental and African Studies 41:160–62 (1978), and in the *Slavic review* 37:162–63 (Mar. 1978). DR440.S5

Yurt ansiklopedisi: Turkiye, il dünü bügünü, yarini. Istanbul, Anadolu Yayincilik, 1981–83. 10v. il. **DC519**

Arranged by place name, giving extensive information in all subject areas—historical, political, cultural, literary, etc.

UNION OF SOVIET SOCIALIST REPUBLICS

See also Eastern and Southeastern Europe.

Bibliography

Akademiia Nauk SSSR. Fundamental'naia Biblioteka Obshchestvennykh Nauk. Istoriia SSSR; ukazatel' sovetskoi literatury za 1917–1952 gg. Moskva, 1956–81. v.1–2,3^{2,4}. (In progress) **DC520**

Contents: v.1, Istoriia SSSR s drevneishikh vremën do vstupleniia Rossii v period kapitalizma; v.2, Istoriia SSSR v period kapitalizma 1861–1917; v.3, Istoriia sovetskogo obshchestva: výp.2, Velikaia oktiabrskaia sotsialisticheskaia revoliutsita i Grazhdanskaia voina (mart 1917–1920gg.); vyp.4, SSSR v gody Velikoi Otechestvennoi voiny (iiun 1941–Sent. 1945g.).

———— ———— Prilozhenie. Skhema klassifikatsii. Vspomogatel'nye ukazateli. Moskva, 1956–81. v.1–2,3^{2,4}. (In progress)

A major bibliography of Soviet historical writing, published between 1917 and 1952, on Russian history. Separate appendix volumes contain an outline of the classification, and name, subject, and other indexes. Planned in three main chronological divisions. Z2506.A4

Bibliografiia trudov po otechestvennomu istochnikovedeniiu i spetsial'nym istoricheskim distsiplinam izdannykh v XVIII v. [Sost. A. I. Aksenov et al.] Moskva, Akademiia Nauk SSSR, 1981. 209p. **DC521**

An annotated bibliography of 18th century publications useful to students of history. Includes materials on sources, genealogy, heraldry, numismatics, and reports of archaeological commissions. Name index.

British Museum. Dept. of Oriental Printed Books and Manuscripts. Catalogue of Georgian and other Caucasian printed books in the British Museum, comp. by David Marshall Lang. London, 1962. 430p. **DC522**

A carefully made catalog of the Georgian collection in the British Museum, rich in early printed books but including later ones as well. The catalog also contains "a selection of reference books compiled by European specialists, as well as a wide range of books and periodical articles in Western languages relating to Caucasian languages and literatures."—*Pref.* Z7049.C3B74

Christensen, Johnny. International relations and foreign policy—by countries and subjects: a bibliography of Soviet publications 1960–1978; 1500 titles. Aarhus, Arkona, 1979. 198p. **DC523**

Continues V. N. Egorov's *Mezhdunarodnye otnoseniia; bibliograficheskii spravochnik 1945–1960* (Moskva, 1961. 405p.). The two works list books published in Russia on diplomacy and foreign relations during the periods indicated. Not indexed. Z6204.C48

Clendenning, Philip and **Bartlett, Roger.** Eighteenth century Russia: a select bibliography of works published since 1955. Newtonville, Mass., Oriental Research Partners, 1981. 262p. (Russian bibliography ser., 2) **DC524**

Intended for the undergraduate and beginning graduate student. Aims "to provide up-to-date and representative coverage of recent writing on Russia in the eighteenth century."—*Pref.* Includes books and periodical articles in English, French and German, as well as Russian materials. Classed arrangement with index of names. Detailed table of contents, but no alphabetical subject approach. Z2508.C58

Crowther, Peter A. A bibliography of works in English on early Russian history to 1800. Oxford, Blackwell; N.Y., Barnes & Noble, 1969. 236p. **DC525**

Intended as a companion to D. M. Shapiro's *Select bibliography of works in English on Russian history, 1801–1917* (DC540). More than 2,000 items in classed arrangement, with name and subject index. Z2506.C75

Dmitrieva, Rufina Petrovna. Bibliografiia russkogo letopisaniia. Leningrad, Izd-vo Akademii Nauk SSSR, 1962. 352p. **DC526**

Comprehensive bibliography of editions of the early Russian chronicles and of the historical and literary commentary and research concerning them. Russian, Ukrainian, and Belorussian publications of the years 1674–1917; Soviet work for the period 1918–1959; and selected foreign publications are included. Chronologically arranged, with various indexes. Z2506.D5

Dvizhenie dekabristov: ukazatel' literatury 1960–1976; otvetstvennyi redaktor M. V. Nechkina. Moskva, Izd-vo "Nauka," 1983. 301p. **DC527**

At head of title: Akademiia Nauk SSSR. Institut Istorii SSSR. Gosudarstvennaia Publichnaia Istoricheskaia Biblioteka RSFSR.

Continues the coverage of R. G. Eimontova's *Dvizhenie dekabristov: ukazatel' literatury 1928–1959* (Moskva, 1960. 434p.), listing some 3,800 Soviet books, articles (including articles in provincial newspapers), and chapters in textbooks on the Decembrists. Topical arrangement with name and title index. Z2509.D88

Glavatskikh, G. A., Kadushkina, N. V. and **Maslova, L. M.** Istoriia SSSR; annotirovannyi ukazatel' bibliograficheskikh posobii, opublikovannykh na russkom iazyke s nachala XIX v. p. 1982 g.; v dvukh chastiiakh. 3-e izd., dop. i perer. Moskva, Gos. Biblioteka SSSR imeni V. I. Lenina, 1983–84. 2v. **DC528**

1st ed., 1957, had title: Bibliografiia russkoi bibliografii po istorii SSSR. Compilers vary.

At head of title: Gosudarstvennaia Publichnaia Istoricheskaia Biblioteka RSFSR.

An annotated bibliography of bibliographies of historical works, topically arranged. This edition includes materials published up to 1982. Z2506.G53

Harvard University. Library. Russian history since 1917: classification schedule, classified listing by call number, alphabetical listing by author or title, chronological listing. Cambridge, publ. by the Harvard Univ. Library; distr. by the Harvard Univ. Pr., 1966. 698p. (Widener Library shelflist, no.4) **DC529**

For a note on the series *see* AA145.

13,772 titles encompassing general histories and descriptive works on the Soviet Union since 1917, including works on all aspects of the political, economic, and social life of the period. Local

histories and geographies of the individual autonomous republics, cities, etc., are not found in this segment of the shelflist. Z2510.H35

Horecky, Paul L. Basic Russian publications; an annotated bibliography on Russia and the Soviet Union. Chicago, Univ. of Chicago, Pr., 1962. 313p. **DC530**

Z2491.H6

—— Russia and the Soviet Union; a bibliographic guide to Western-language publications. Chicago, Univ. of Chicago Pr., 1965. 473p. **DC531**

Companion volumes of selective bibliography representing the judgments of numerous area-study specialists and providing a "rigorously pruned inventory of Russian and Western publications."—*Introd.* Major sections are: General reference aids and bibliographies; The land; The people: ethnic and demographic features; The nations; Civilizations and politics; History; The state; The economic and social structure; The intellectual and cultural life. Works relevant to the organizational, research, and socio-economic aspects of science and technology are represented. Z2491.H64

Istoriia dorevoliutsionnoi rossii v dnevnikakh i vospominaniiakh; annotirovann'yi ukazatel' knig i publikatsii v zhurnalakh. Sost. G. A. Glavatskikh [et al.]. Moskva, Izd. "Kniga," 1976–84. v.1–4². (In progress) **DC532**

At head of title: Nauchnaia Biblioteka imeni A. M. Gor'kogo, Moskovskogo Gosudarstvennogo Universiteta imeni M. V. Lomonosova, Gosudarstvennaia Biblioteka SSR imeni V. I. Lenina.

Contents: t.1, XV–XVIII veka; t.2, 1801–1856 (2pts.); t.3, 1857–1894 (4pts.), t.4, 1895–1917 (2pts.)

An annotated bibliography of pre-revolutionary Russian diaries, memoirs, travel accounts, etc., published in books, journals and collections. Foreign-language accounts are cited if published in Russia. Topically arranged within historical period. To be in 4v. Indexes in v.1; Names and titles cited; Geographic and ethnic names; Collections used for v.1; Periodicals and other serials used for v.1–4. Z2506.I87

Jones, David Lewis. Books in English on the Soviet Union, 1917–73: a bibliography. N.Y., Garland, 1975. 331p. (Garland reference library of social science, v.3) **DC533**

Limited to "books written in the English language . . . which are wholly concerned with the Soviet Union."—*Foreword.* Pamphlets are excluded, as are books which deal with both the Tsarist and Soviet periods. Classed arrangement, with name index. Nearly 4,600 items. Z2491.J65

Korduba, Myron. La littérature historique soviétique-ukrainienne; compte-rendu 1917–1931. Munich, Fink, [1972]. 365p. (Harvard series in Ukrainian studies, v.10) **DC534**

Reprint of the Warsaw, 1938, edition, with an editor's preface, a bibliography of Korduba's works, three additional surveys, and new indexes. Z2514.U5K636

Mezhov, Vladimir Izmailovich. Russkaia istoricheskaia bibliografiia, 1800–54. St. Petersburg, Sibiriakov, 1892–93. 2v. **DC535**

Added title page in French: Bibliographie des livres et articles russes d'histoire et sciences auxiliaires de 1800–1854 incl.

Contents: v.1, Documents historiques et histoire politique de la Russie; v.2, Biographies. Sciences auxiliaires: généalogie, la science héraldique, chronologie, archéologie, paléographie, numismatique, sphragistique, mythologie; v.3, Géographie, hydrographie, orographie, cartographie, voyages, statistique, éthnographie, histoire des cultes et de l'église, agiologie, histoire de l'instruction publique.

34,994 entries. No index.

Continued by:

Lambin, Petr Petrovich. Russkaia istoricheskaia bibliografiia, 1855–64. St. Petersburg, Akademii Nauk, 1861–84. 10v. Annual. **DC536**

Continued by: Z2506.R89

Mezhov, Vladimir Izmailovich. Russkaia istoricheskaia bibliografiia, 1865–76. St. Petersburg, Akademii Nauk, 1882–90. 8v. **DC537**

Classified, with subject indexes. Z2506.R9

Moscow. Gosudarstvennaia Publichnaia Istoricheskaia Biblioteka. Istoriia istoricheskoi nauki v SSSR. Bibliografiia. [Otv. red. M. V. Nechkina] Moskva, Nauka, 1965–80. 2v. **DC538**

Contents: v.1, Do oktiabr'skii period; v.2, Sovetskii period, oktiabr' 1917–1967g.
A bibliography of historiographical literature published in the USSR and dealing with pre-revolutionary and Soviet history. Includes writings on the activities of historical societies and institutions. Classed arrangement with index. Z2511.H5I84

Nerhood, Harry W. To Russia and return; an annotated bibliography of travelers' English-language accounts of Russia from the ninth century to the present. [Columbus], Ohio State Univ. Pr., [1968]. 367p. **DC539**

More than 1,400 items. Arrangement is chronological by date of the visit to Russia; author and title indexes. Z2491.N435

Shapiro, David. Select bibliography of works in English on Russian history, 1801–1917. Oxford, Blackwell, 1962. 106p. **DC540**

Lists books and articles, primarily in English, published up to Dec. 1961. Topical arrangement. Mainly secondary works; reviews are frequently noted. Name index. Z2509.S5

Simmons, John S. G. Russian bibliography, libraries and archives. Oxford, [A. C. Hall], 1973. 76p. **DC541**

Comprises bibliographical lists compiled in connection with Russian studies at Oxford University. Includes books and articles on libraries and archives, general bibliographies and reference works, and bibliography in the fields of Russian history, literature, politics and social thought, philosophy, theology, and linguistics.
Z2491.A1S54

The Sino-Soviet conflict; a historical bibliography. Santa Barbara, Calif., ABC-Clio, [1985]. 190p. (ABC-Clio research guides, 13) **DC542**

Cites 842 journal articles with abstracts taken from *Historical abstracts* database, 1965–82. Covers Chinese- Russian relations from 1917 to the present. Z6465.C6S56

Sovetskaia strana v period vosstanovleniia narodnogo khoziaistva (1921–1925gg.): bibliograficheskii ukazatel' dokumental'nykh publikatsii. Sost. L. A. Kotel'nikova [et al.]. Moskva, Kniga, 1975. 629p. **DC543**

At head of title: Gosudarstvennaia Publichnaia Istoricheskaia Biblioteka RSFSR.
Offers citations to 9,611 documents published 1921–25, arranged topically and with a geographical index. Published in series with *Velikaia oktiabr'skaia sotsialisticheskaia revoliutsiia (see* BD1340) and *Sovetskaia strana v period grazhdanskoi voiny (1918–1922gg.)* (Moscow, 1961). Z2510.S67

Spravochnik po istorii dorevoliutsionnoi Rossii. Bibliograficheskii ukazatel'. Nauchnoe rukovodstvo, redakiia i vstupilelnaia statia professora P. A. Zaionchkovskogo. [Sost. G. A. Glavatskikh et al.] Izd. 2-e, red. u dop. Moskva, Kniga, 1978. [639]p. **DC544**

1st ed. 1971.
A bibliography of materials on pre-revolutionary Russia, topically arranged. Cites many statistical works and directories.

Thompson, Anthony. Russia/U.S.S.R.; a selective, annotated bibliography of books in English. Oxford, Eng. & Santa Barbara, Calif., Clio Pr., [1979]. 287p. map. (World bibliographical ser., 6) **DC545**

Lists 1,247 books selected for the undergraduate or general reader "which will serve to stimulate interest in, and to illuminate the geography, history, social and economic system, and other aspects

of the Soviet Union and its peoples."—*Introd.* Author, title, subject index. Z2491.T45

Dissertations

Bruhn, Peter. Russika und Sowjetika unter den deutschsprachigen Hochschulschriften, 1961–1973: bibliographisches Verzeichnis. Wiesbaden, Harrassowitz; Berlin, Osteuropa-Inst. an d. Freien Univ., 1975. 166p. (Bibliographische Mitteilungen des Osteuropas-Instituts an der Freien Universität Berlin, 11) **DC546**

Serves as a continuation of Gerhard Hanusch's list of "Osteuropa-Dissertationen" covering the period 1945–60, which appeared as supplements in the *Jahrbücher für Geschichte Osteuropas,* 1953–60.
Continued by: Z2491.B88

——— Russika and Sowjetika unter den deutschsprachigen Hochschulschriften (1973–1975), mit Nachträgen für 1963 bis 1972. Wiesbaden, Harrassowitz, 1981. 420p. (Bibliographische Mitteilungen des Osteuropas-Instituts an der Freien Universität Berlin, 21) **DC547**

Z2491.B883

Dossick, Jesse John. Doctoral research on Russia and the Soviet Union. N.Y., New York Univ. Pr., 1960. 248p. **DC548**

Arranged by subject field; in each section lists American and Canadian dissertations followed by "Aids to further research." Separate sections on British dissertations, and bibliography of bibliographies of doctoral dissertations. No index.
Continued by: Z2491.D6

——— Doctoral research on Russia and the Soviet Union, 1960–1975; a classified list of 3,150 American, Canadian, and British dissertations, with some critical and statistical analysis. N.Y., Garland, 1976. 345p. (Garland reference library of social science, v.7) **DC549**

Supersedes the annual supplements appearing in the *Slavic review* 1964–1974, and adds some items missed in the earlier volume.
Arranged by subject (agriculture to sports), with American and Canadian works in one scheme and the British in a second, similar scheme. Indexes of Russian/Soviet names, American and Canadian authors, and British authors. Annual supplementary lists continue to appear in the *Slavic review,* Dec. 1976– . A list of corrections and some suggestions for improving the next edition appear in *Slavonic and East European review* 40:134–35 (Jan. 1977). Z2491.D62

Seydoux, Marianne and **Biesiekierski, Mieczysław.** Répertoire des thèses concernant les études slaves, l'U.R.S.S. et les pays de l'Est européen et soutenues en France de 1824 à 1969. Paris, Institut d'Études Slaves, 1970. 157p. (Travaux publiés par l'Institut d'Études Slaves, 30) **DC550**

Listing is by country, then classified. More than 1,300 items. Author index.
Reprinted in the Institut's *Guide du slaviste* as issued in looseleaf form in 1971. Looseleaf supplements adding some new theses as late as 1972 (together with some from the pre-1969 period) were issued in 1972. Z2483.S49

Archives and manuscripts

Grant, Steven A. and **Brown, John H.** The Russian Empire and the Soviet Union: a guide to manuscripts and archival materials in the United States. Boston, G. K. Hall, 1981. 632p. **DC551**

For full information *see* AB118a.

Grant, Steven A. Scholars' guide to Washington, D.C. for Russian/Soviet studies. Wash., Smithsonian Inst. Pr. for

Kennan Inst. for Advanced Russian Studies of the Woodrow Wilson Internat. Center for Scholars, 1977. 403p.   **DC552**

Intended as the first of a series of scholars' guides to the Washington, D.C. area. In two main sections: (1) Collections (i.e., libraries, archives, museums, data banks, etc.); (2) Organizations (i.e., associations, government agencies, research centers, etc.). Indexed.
Z2491.G67

Grimsted, Patricia Kennedy. Archives and manuscript repositories in the USSR: Estonia, Latvia, Lithuania, and Belorussia. Princeton, Princeton Univ. Pr., 1981. 929p.
DC553

For full information *see* AB155.

——— Archives and manuscript repositories in the USSR: Moscow and Leningrad. Princeton, N.J., Princeton Univ. Pr., [1972]. 436p.   **DC554**

For full information *see* AB156.

Grossman, IU. M. and Kutik, Vitalii N. Spravochnik nauchnogo rabotnika—archivy, dokumenty, issledovatel'. Izd. 2-e, perer. i dop. L'vov, Izd-vo pri Lvovskogo un-ta, 1983. 499p.   **DC555**

1st ed. 1979.
Discussions of general history and organization of the Soviet archives, and methods of research are followed by an extensive directory of Soviet manuscript and archival repositories, detailing holdings and listing finding aids. Bibliography, p.354–453.
CD965.R8G76

Moscow. Publichnaia Biblioteka. Otdel Rukopisei. Vospominaniia i dnevniki XVIII-XX vv.: ukazatel' rukopisei. Red. S. V. Zhitomirskaia. Moskva, "Kniga," 1976. 619p.
DC556

A catalog of manuscripts of personal memoirs and diaries in the Lenin State Library. Many of the manuscripts are described at some length, and the contents notes are fully indexed. Continues *Ukazatel' vospominanii, drevnikov i puterykh zapisok XVIII–XIX vv.* (Moskva, 1951).
Z6611.B6M76

Soviet Union. Glavnoe Arkhivnoe Upravlenie. Gosudarstvennye arkhivy Soiuza SSSR; kratkii spravochnik. Pod red. G. A. Belova [i dr.]. Moskva, 1956. 507p.   **DC557**

A general guide to government archives, federal and regional, in the USSR. Name, address, and brief historical note on each archive are followed by a general description of the type and extent of documentary material, its chronological limits, and the names of some individuals whose papers or collections are included. Contains a list of archives omitted from the Guide, a bibliography of publications between 1941 and 1956, and a name index.
CD1711.A54

——— Katalog arkhivovedcheskoi literatury i sbornikov dokumentov, 1960–1963 gg. Pod red. I. N. Firsova. Sost. S. V. Nefedova i dr. Moskva, 1964. 140p.   **DC558**

A bibliographic index to archival publications and to the literature pertaining to archival affairs in the Soviet Union. Combines and continues chronologically: Z6208.A7R82

——— Katalog arkhivovedcheskoi literatury 1917–1959 gg. Pod red. A. I. Loginovoi i dr. Moskva, 1961. 191p.
DC559

Z6208.A7R8

——— Katalog sbornikov dokumentov, izdannykh arkhivnymi uchrezhdeniiami SSSR, 1917–1960 gg. Pod red. A. I. Loginovoi i dr. Moskva, 1961. 110p.   **DC560**

Z2506.A25

——— Katalog arkhivovedcheskoi literatury i sbornikov dokumentov, 1964–1967gg. Pod red. G. P. Lebedeva. Moskva, 1970. 181p.   **DC561**

For volumes covering earlier periods *see* above.

Extends the coverage of this bibliography of archival publications and articles and books relating to archives.
Continued by:

——— Katalog arkhivovedcheskoi literatury i sbornikov dokumentov, 1968–1970; vsesoiuznyi nauchno-issledovatelskii. [Pod red.] L. I. Panina; sost. M. G. Artsruni [et al.]. Moskva, Glavnoe Arkhivnoe Upravlenie pri Sovete Ministrov SSSR, 1977. 171p.   **DC562**

——— Lichnye arkhivnye fondy v gosudarstvennykh kranilishchakh SSSR: ukazatel'. [Sost. E. V. Kolosova et al.] Moskva, [1963–80]. 3v.   **DC563**

At head of title: Gosudarstvennaia Biblioteka SSSR imeni V. I. Lenina. Arkhiv Akademiia Nauk SSSR.
Editor varies; publisher varies.
A directory of personal and family papers in the Soviet Union. v.1–2 concerned mainly with the pre-Revolutionary period; v.3 concentrates on figures active during the Soviet period and adds collections not previously covered.   CD1734.R87

Historiography

Mazour, Anatole Gregory. Modern Russian historiography. Rev. ed. Westport, Conn., Greenwood Pr., 1975. 224p.
DC564

First published 1939 as *An outline of modern Russian historiography.*
Surveys the "historiographic development in Russia prior to 1917."—*Pref.* The same author has treated developments after 1917 in *The writing of history in the Soviet Union* (Stanford, Hoover Inst. Pr., 1971).   DK38.M3

Encyclopedias and handbooks

The Cambridge encyclopedia of Russia and the Soviet Union. Gen. eds., Archie Brown [and others]. Cambridge, [Eng.], Cambridge Univ. Pr., [1982]. 492p. il.   **DC565**

A topically arranged encyclopedia with signed articles on fairly specific subjects. Principal sections include: Territory and peoples; History; Religion; Art and architecture; Language and literature; Music, theatre, dance and film; The sciences; The Soviet political system; The economy; Soviet society; Military power and policy; The world role. Index at front; brief bibliography; no prefatory statement regarding aim or scope.   DK14.C35

Grazhdanskaia voina i voennaia interventsiia v SSSR: entsiklopediia. [Sost.] S. S. Khromov. Moskva, "Sov. entsiklopediia," 1983. 702p. il., maps.   **DC566**

An encyclopedia relating to Allied intervention in Russia, 1918–1920. Articles cover biography, cities, battles, weaponry, etc. Bibliography, p.683–97.   DK265.4.G7

Guide to the study of the Soviet nationalities: non-Russian peoples of the USSR. Stephan M. Horak, ed. Littleton, Colo., Libraries Unlimited, 1982. 265p.   **DC567**

A bibliography of 1,346 items arranged by nationality.
Z2517.E85G84

Handbook of major Soviet nationalities. Zev Katz, ed. N.Y., Free Pr.; London, Collier Macmillan, [1975]. 481p.
DC568

For full information *see* CC352.

An introduction to Russian history, ed. by Robert Auty and Dimitri Obolensky. Cambridge, London & N.Y., Cambridge Univ. Pr., [1976]. 403p. (Companion to Russian studies, 1)   **DC569**

Offered as a "first orientation" for students beginning work in

Russian studies. Each of the ten sections was contributed by a specialist; a "Guide to further reading" concludes each section. Index. DK40.I57

McLane, Charles B. Soviet-Third world relations. London, Central Asian Research Centre; distr. by Columbia Univ. Pr., 1973-74. 3v. **DC570**

For volume on the Middle East *see* DE68; on Asia, *see* DE22; on Africa, *see* DD99.

The modern encyclopedia of Russian and Soviet history. Ed. by Joseph L. Wieczynski. [Gulf Breeze, Fla.], Academic Internat. Pr., 1976-85. v.1-39. (In progress) **DC571**

Contents: v.1-39, Aachen-Trubetskoi.

To be in about 50v. Aims "to become the most comprehensive aid to the study of the Russian past ever created in the English language" (*v.1,p.vi*), with information encompassing "all major facts, events, personalities and institutions important to the history of the Russian Empire and the Soviet Union." While the editor's note states that the work "will reproduce in English information contained in the many standard Russian reference series," the sources of specific articles are not given (nor is there an indication whether the information is a direct translation from a single source). Additional information is derived from monographs and research studies, and new articles have been contributed by an international roster of contemporary scholars. Longer articles are signed, and include bibliographies of both Russian- and English-language materials. Intended to be useful "to undergraduate students, government and private researchers and even high school students as well as to professional historians and scholars," but highly specialized information of narrow interest is omitted on the assumption that the specialist can obtain it from Russian-language sources. Supplements are anticipated to cover material inadvertently omitted from volumes already published. DK14.M6

Paxton, John. Companion to Russian history. London, Batsford; N.Y., Facts on File, [1983]. 503p. maps. **DC572**

A dictionary of some 2,500 brief entries covering Russian history from the 10th century to the fall of Khrushchev. Entries include places, movements, arts, foreign influences, people, often with brief bibliographies. Statistics used are meant to be current as of 1981. Chronology, p.453-68; select bibliography, p.469-75; historical maps, p.476-503. DK36.P39

Pushkarev, Sergei Germanovich. Dictionary of Russian historical terms from the eleventh century to 1917. New Haven, Yale Univ. Pr., 1970. 199p. **DC573**

". . . designed to assist English-speaking readers to understand the specialized terms they encounter in Russian historical sources and in English-language works on Russia, terms explained very briefly if at all in an ordinary Russian-English dictionary."—*Pref.* DK36.P78

Roy, A. India and the Soviet Union; a chronology of political and diplomatic cooperation. Calcutta, Firma KLM, 1982. 194p. **DC574**

For full information *see* DE202.

SSSR. Entsiklopedicheskii spravochnik; glavnyi redaktor A. M. Prokhorov [et al.]. Moskva, "Sovetskaia Entsiklopediia," 1982. 607p. il., maps. **DC575**

Reprints the second part of v.24 of the *Bol'shaia sovetskaia entsiklopediia* (AC70), which is devoted to the Soviet Union, with updating to 1981.

An English translation from the encyclopedia section appears as v.31 of the *Great Soviet encyclopedia* (AC71), updated by the editors of the translation. DK14.S18

Sovetskaia istoricheskaia entsiklopediia; glavny red. E. M. Zhukov. Moskva, Sovetskaia Entsiklopediia, 1961-80. 16v. il., maps, facsims. **DC576**

Offers some 25,000 articles (often with chronologies, maps, tables, bibliographies) on biographical, historical, political and similar subjects. Universal in coverage; strongest on Russian topics, but much attention is given to history, etc., of Third World countries. D9.S64

Velikaia Oktiabr'skaia sotsialisticheskaia revoliutsiia. Entsiklopediia. Pod red. G. N. Golikova, M. I. Kuznetsova. Moskva, Izd. "Sovetskaia Entsiklopediia," 1977. 712p. il. **DC577**

Brief articles, in dictionary arrangement, concerning persons, places, events, etc., of the 1917 Russian revolution. Selected bibliography, p.700-9. Based on a 1968 work of the same title.

Current surveys

Current digest of the Soviet press. v.1- , Feb. 1, 1949- . N.Y., Joint Committee on Slavic Studies, 1949- . Weekly. **DC578**

For full information *see* AF100.

The Soviet Union: domestic policy, the economy, foreign policy, 1973- . N.Y., Holmes & Meier, 1975- . Annual. **DC579**

Translation of: Sowjetunion: Innenpolitik, Wirtschaft, Aussenpolitik, Analyse und Bilanz, edited at the Bundesinstitut für Ostwissenschaftliche und Internationale Studien, Cologne.

A yearly survey of the Soviet Union arranged by the three topics mentioned in the subtitle. Each chapter offers conclusions and adds a short bibliography. Many tables; appendixes of general statistics, names of party members, etc. Name index.

USSR and the third world. v.1- , Dec. 7, 1970/Jan. 10, 1971- . [London, Central Asian Research Centre], 1971- . Bimonthly. **DC580**

Attempts to "compile the most complete information available in the West and provide an up-to-date, critical balance sheet" (*Introd.*) on both domestic developments and foreign policy. Arranged by region and country. Summary tables; charts; name index. DK266.A2U16

Atlases

Chew, Allen F. An atlas of Russian history; eleven centuries of changing borders. Rev. ed. New Haven, Yale Univ. Pr., 1970. 127p. **DC581**

1st ed. 1967.

Maps depict important changes in Russia's boundaries and possessions from the ninth century to recent changes resulting from World War II. G2111.S1C5

Gilbert, Martin. Russian history atlas. N.Y., Macmillan; London, Weidenfeld & Nicolson, [1972]. unpaged; 146 numbered maps. **DC582**

Small black-and-white maps relating to Russian history from earliest times to the present. G2111.S1G5

VATICAN CITY

Walsh, Michael J. Vatican City State. Oxford, Eng. & Santa Barbara, Calif., Clio Pr., [1983]. 105p. (World bibliographical series, 41) **DC583**

Cites 368 items (mainly English-language publications) in a topical arrangement. Author, title, subject index. Z2372.W34

YUGOSLAVIA

Bibliography

Horton, John J. Yugoslavia. Oxford, Clio Pr., [1977]. 195p. (World bibliographical ser., 1) **DC584**

Primarily a listing of English-language materials, with a few titles in French, German, and Serbo-Croatian. The books and articles cited are those considered most useful for the general reader, for specialists in related areas, the beginning researcher, and the librarian building a collection. Critical annotations. Topical arrangement with author, title, subject index. Z2951.H67

Jovanovič, Slobodan and **Rojnič, Matko.** A guide to Yugoslav libraries and archives. [Columbus, Ohio, Am. Assoc. for the Advancement of Slavic Studies, 1975] 113p. **DC585**

For full information *see* AB157.

Petrovich, Michael B. Yugoslavia, a bibliographic guide. Wash., Lib. of Congress, Slavic and Central European Div., 1974. 270p. **DC586**

A survey of more than 2,500 titles of basic materials, mainly books published before 1968. 13 chapters, each devoted to a specific subject, are followed by an author listing of all works discussed.

See also Rusko Matulić's *Bibliography of sources on Yugoslavia* (Palo Alto, Calif., Ragusan Pr., 1981. 252p.) which lists materials in English and in other European languages not spoken in Yugoslavia. Z2956.P48

Terry, Garth M. Yugoslav studies: an annotated list of basic bibliographies and reference works. [Twickenham, Eng.], Anthony C. Hall, 1977. 89p. **DC587**

In three sections: (1) General reference works (including handbooks, statistical compilations, encyclopedias, dictionaries, library catalogs, atlases, etc.); (2) General bibliographies (subdivided by geographical area); (3) Subject bibliographies and reference works. About 550 items; indexes of authors and of titles as main entries.

A review by Richard Kindersley in *TLS*, Mar. 24, 1978, p.340, suggests additional language and biographical dictionaries for inclusion, as well as sources for maps.

Titova reč u publikacijama JNA 1941–1980, anotirana bibliografija. [Glavni urednik Rula Dragon . . . materijal istražili i bibliografski obradili Kujovič Obrad et al.] Beograd, Centar za Vojnonaučnu Dokumentaciju i Informacije, 1982. 682p. **DC588**

A chronologically arranged bibliography of books, journals, articles and chapters, government and communist party publications concerning the career of Tito. About 2,700 items. Topical and name indexes. Z2958.A5T57

Encyclopedias

Enciklopedija jugoslavije. Zagreb, Leksikografski Zavod, 1955–71. 8v. il. **DC589**

A well-produced encyclopedia dealing with the life and culture of the Yugoslav peoples. Articles, many of considerable length, are signed and include bibliographies. Illustrations and maps are excellent. A new edition is in progress: DR304.E5

—— [Glavni urednik Miroslav Krleza. 2. izd.] Zagreb, Jugoslavenski Leksikografski Zavod, 1980–84. v.1–3. il., maps. (In progress) **DC590**

1st ed. 1955–71 in 8v. (above).
Contents: v.1–3, A–D.
Although there are some general articles, they often show a strong national orientation (e.g., country articles emphasize relations with Jugoslavia); biographical sketches are almost exclusively on Yugoslav figures. Signed articles; bibliographies.

D D

Africa

GENERAL WORKS

Hartwig, Gerald W. and **O'Barr, William M.** The student Africanist's handbook; a guide to resources. [Cambridge, Mass.], Schenkman, [1974]. 152p. **DD1**

Includes chapters on the nature of African studies; a brief overview of the societies, cultures and modern nations of Africa; general references and disciplinary sources; bibliography of African regions and countries; aids for intensive research; and special topics. Lacks an index. Z3501.H27

Panofsky, Hans E. A bibliography of Africana. Westport, Conn., Greenwood Pr., [1975]. 350p. (Contributions in librarianship and information science, no.11) **DD2**

". . . a handbook for students of Africa (particularly those with bibliographic needs beyond their own discipline or geographic area of specialization), librarians other than those fully specialized in African bibliography, and, not least, laymen who want to gain more depth on some aspects of Africa."—*Introd.* Sections for: (1) The study of Africa; (2) Bibliographies and serials; (3) Guide to resources by subject and discipline; (4) Guide to resources in non-African areas; (5) Guide to resources in African nations; and (6) On collecting and disseminating Africana. Subject index (with a few titles included), but no author/title index to the great bulk of citations in the text. Z3501.P15

Bibliography

Africa since 1914; a historical bibliography. Santa Barbara, Calif., ABC-Clio, [1985]. 402p. (Clio bibliographical ser., 17) **DD3**

Presents a geographical arrangement of the abstracts published 1973–82 in *Historical abstracts* (DA19) which relate to Africa since 1914. Indexing was derived from the same source, with additional cross references added. Z3501.A44

Akademiia Nauk SSSR. Biblioteka. Spravochnaia literatura po stranam Azii i Afriki. Svodnyi katalog inostrannykh fondov B-ki AN SSSR i Gos. publichnoi b-ki im. M. E. Saltykova-Shchedrina, 1945–1968. Pod red. T. A. Vaganovoi i S. S. Bulatova. Leningrad, 1972. 534p. **DD4**

More than 3,500 items in classed arrangement, with index of authors and other main entries. *See also* Mary Holdsworth's *Soviet African studies, 1918–1959* (Oxford, Oxford Univ. Pr., 1961) and DD18. Z3009.A63

Asamani, J. O. Index Africanus. Stanford, Calif., Hoover Inst. Pr., [1975]. 659p. (Hoover Inst. bibliographies, 53) **DD5**

". . . a catalogue of articles in Western languages dealing with Africa and published from 1885 to 1965 in periodicals, Festschriften or memorial volumes, symposia, and proceedings of congresses and conferences."—*Pref.*

A general section is followed by regional sections, each subdivided by country, then by subject. More than 24,600 entries; author index. A more detailed table of contents or a subject index would have greatly facilitated use of the volume. Z3501.A73

Bibliografía afroasiática en español. Coordinadora Graciela de la Lama; compiladores Arturo Guadian y Enrique Guadian. [México], Colegio de México, [1981]. 238p.   **DD6**

Intended as a state-of-the-art survey of scholarship in Latin America. Lists some 3,000 books (most published since 1945) in a classified arrangement and covering the 16th century to 1979. Author index.   Z3501.B49

Chicago. Center for Research Libraries. Cooperative Africana Microform Project. CAMP catalog, 1977 cumulative edition. Chicago, publ. by the Cooperative Africana Microform Project and the Center for Research Libraries, 1977. 203p.   **DD7**

"The Cooperative Africana Microform Project (CAMP) was created in 1963 to bring together in microform a collection of research materials [books, pamphlets, government documents, journals] related to Africa for the cooperative use of the members."—*Introd.* These materials are acquired, housed, and cataloged by the Center for Research Libraries. In this volume all materials cataloged as of Sept. 1976 are listed alphabetically by main entry, with a name and topic index.

—— —— 1981 cumulative supplement. Chicago, [1981]. 151p.

Includes, in addition to cataloging of CAMP materials Sept.1976–Dec.1981, "a number of titles related to Africa that were purchased in microfilm by The Center . . . with funds other than CAMP's and several newspaper titles that are the property of the Foreign Newspaper Microfilm Project."—*Introd.*
Biennial supplements list recent acquisitions and "on order" items.

DeLancey, Mark W. African international relations; an annotated bibliography. Boulder, Colo., Westview Pr., [1981]. 365p.   **DD8**

Lists 2,840 items from the 1960–78 period in broad subject arrangement. Subject index.   Z6465.A36D44

Fontán Lobé, Juan. Bibliografía colonial; contribución a un índice de publicaciones africanas. Madrid, "Selecciones Gráficas," 1946. 669p. (Ediciones de la Dirección General de Marruecos y Colonias)   **DD9**

An alphabetical catalog of nearly 17,000 titles of books and periodical articles in various languages. Particularly rich in Spanish and Portuguese materials. Geographical and subject indexes.
For the period since 1945 *see* the two excellent bibliographic essays in *The transfer of power in Africa,* ed. by Prosser Gifford and W. R. Louis (New Haven, Yale Univ. Pr., 1982).   Z3501.F6

Harvard University. Library. African history and literatures; classification schedule, classified listing by call number, chronological listing, author and title listing. Cambridge, distr. by Harvard Univ. Pr., 1971. 600p. (Widener Library shelflist, 34)   **DD10**

For a note on the series *see* AA145.
Supersedes no.2 of the series (*Africa.* 1965).
Lists "works on all the countries of the African continent and some of the neighboring islands" and includes "primarily works on history, civilization and government, general geography and travel, general social and economic conditions . . . , religious affairs, and the various races of these countries."—*Note on the classification.* Almost 20,300 titles listed by class, by date of publication, and by author and title.
About 1960 an addition was made at the end of the classification scheme for literature of Africa in both European and indigenous languages (although it does not provide for Afrikaans literature or literatures in the Semitic and Hamitic languages of northern Africa). Generally speaking, only current materials are put into this new part of the "Afr" class.   Z3509.H37

Hogg, Peter C. The African slave trade and its suppression; a classified and annotated bibliography of books, pamphlets and periodical articles. London, Cass, [1973]. 409p.   **DD11**

4,675 entries, most of them with brief annotations. Indexes of

authors, personal names, geographical names, and anonymous titles. Includes some government documents and academic theses.   Z7164.S6H63

International African Institute. Cumulative bibliography of African studies; . . . classified catalogue. Boston, G. K. Hall, 1973. 3v.   **DD12**

—— Cumulative bibliography of African studies; . . . author catalogue. Boston, G. K. Hall, 1973. 2v.

Reproduction of cards from a file maintained at the Institute, containing entries for all books and periodical articles listed in the quarterly bibliography appearing in the journal *Africa,* 1929–70, and in that journal's supplementary publication, *International African bibliography,* 1971–72. Also includes some items not appearing in the published bibliographies.   Z3509.I57

International African bibliography, 1973–1978: books, articles and papers in African affairs. J. D. Pearson, ed. [London], Mansell, [1982]. 343p.   **DD13**

A cumulation of the quarterly issues (DD25) for v.3–8 (about 20,000 citations), plus an additional 3,000 entries not appearing in the quarterlies. Arranged geographically, then topically; index of authors, editors, and translators. Covers all of Africa except Egypt.
Current bibliographic listings now appear in *International African bibliography* (DD25) which became an independent publication beginning with v.3, no.1.   Z3501.P3

London. University. School of Oriental and African Studies. Library. Library catalogue. Boston, G. K. Hall, 1963. 28v.   **DD14**

Reproduces the catalog cards for this outstanding collection, covering intensively all aspects of Africa, Asia, and Oceania, except science, medicine and technology which are treated less thoroughly. All types of materials are cited, including manuscripts, maps, and sound recordings.
Continued by:

—— —— Library catalogue supplement 1–3. Boston, G. K. Hall, 1968–79. (Suppl. 1, 16v.; Suppl. 2, 16v.; Suppl. 3, 19v.)

The three supplements reflect cataloging from 1963 through summer 1978, following the earlier arrangement.   Z3009.L63

Martin, Michel L. L'armée et la société en Afrique, essai de synthèse et d'investigation bibliographique. Bordeaux, Centre d'Étude d'Afrique Noire, 1975. 241p.   **DD15**

A topical arrangement of about 1,700 books and articles relating to themes such as civil-military relations, military intervention and regimes, and the process of modernization; emphasis is on the period since 1945. Author and geographical indexes.
Updated in part by Joseph P. Smaldone's "Bibliographic sources for African military studies" in *Current bibliography on African studies,* v.11, no.2 (1978/79), p.101–09.   Z6725.A4M37

Melville J. Herskovits Library of African Studies. The Africana conference paper index. Boston, G. K. Hall, 1982. 2v.   **DD16**

Based on the collection of papers from 562 conferences held by the Herskovits Library at Northwestern University. Includes both published and mimeographed materials. Most conferences date from the 1960s and '70s, though some are of earlier date; about half the papers are in English. Conferences are listed alphabetically by main entry, with resulting papers; keyword-in-context index.   DT1.5.M45

—— Catalog of the Melville J. Herskovits Library of African Studies, Northwestern University Library and Africana in selected libraries, Evanston, Ill. Boston, G. K. Hall, 1972. 8v.   **DD17**

1962 ed. publ. as *Catalog of the African collection,* Northwestern Univ. Lib.
Author, title, and added entries for some 60,000 volumes of books, periodicals, newspapers, manuscripts, maps, photographs, phonograph records, microforms, etc. Emphasis is on sub-Saharan Africa, especially West Africa. The catalog includes cards from

libraries which contribute to the *Joint acquisitions list of Africana* (*JALA*) (DD26).

Continued by: Z3509.M45

———— Catalog . . . 1st supplement. Boston, G. K. Hall, 1978. 6v.

v.1–4 reproduce catalog cards for materials added to the Herskovits Library during the 1972–77 period, together with revised records for some materials cited in the basic set.

v.5–6 offer a cumulation of reports of African materials cataloged at selected libraries in the United States which were included in *JALA* (Joint acquisition list of Africana), 1962–77 (DD26).

        Z3509.M45

Miliavskaia, S. L. Bibliografiia stran Afriki i Arabskogo Vostoka: ukazatel' literatury na russkom iazike, opublikovannoi v SSSR v 1917–1967 gg. Moskva, Glavnaia Redaktsiia Vostochnoi Literatury Izdatel'stvo Nauka, 1979–80. 2v.   **DD18**

Contents: v.1, Obshchie raboty; Afrika (tropicheskaia i iuzhnaia); v.2, Arabskie strany.

A classed bibliography of Russian-language publications on Africa and the Middle East. v.1 offers a section of general works followed by sections for Africa as a whole, specific regions, and individual countries of Africa. Detailed table of contents; index. v.2 follows the same plan, covering Northern Africa and the Middle East.

        Z3551.M54

Wiley, David S. [and others]. Africa on film and videotape, 1960–1981: a compendium of reviews. East Lansing, African Studies Center, Michigan State Univ., 1982. 551p.   **DD19**

Considers almost 7,500 films selected on the basis of "accuracy, balance, organization, and objectivity."—*Introd.* Gives basic information about each film (including suggestions for use and appropriate age or grade level), and "overview critique," citations to other reviews, and overall quality rating. Index of titles and topics.

A supplementary publication is *Films on Africa,* comp. by Paul Lazar, based on the collection at Indiana University (Bloomington, African Studies Program, 1982. 50p.).   DT19.8.Z9W54

Witherell, Julian W. The United States and Africa: guide to U.S. official documents and government-sponsored publications on Africa, 1785–1975. Wash., Lib. of Congress, 1978. 949p.   **DD20**

A partially annotated bibliography of selected publications issued by or for the United States government relating to any part of Africa, including the southeast Atlantic and the Western Indian Ocean islands; Egypt is excluded. Sections covering the periods 1820 through 1951 are "limited primarily to congressional and presidential documents, commercial reports, diplomatic papers and treaties" (*Pref.*), whereas the 1952–75 period also includes "translations issued by JPRS and printed and mimeographed studies concerning American assistance programs prepared by or for federal government agencies." Arranged by geographic area, subdivided by topic in the 1952–75 section. Index by topic, issuing body, main entry.

Continued by: Z3501.W57

———— The United States and sub-Saharan Africa; a guide to U.S. official documents and government-sponsored publications, 1976–1980. Wash., Lib. of Congress, 1984. 721p.   **DD21**

Continues that portion of the above which covers sub-Saharan Africa; includes some publications of 1973–75 inadvertently omitted therefrom. A geographical/topical listing of 5,047 publications issued by or for the U.S. government (including ERIC, JPRS, and NTIS reports), but omitting classified documents, congressional bills and resolutions, and reports prepared by the Congressional Research Service. Author, subject, title index.   Z3501.W58

Current

ASA news, v.1– , 1968– . [Los Angeles], African Studies Assoc., 1968– . Quarterly.   **DD22**

v.1–13 (1968–80) had title *African studies newsletter.*

The official journal of the Association, offering annual lists of recent doctoral dissertations on Africa, African reference books, and occasional lists of research in progress, grants and awards, etc., together with news of the Association, conferences, etc.

The British equivalent is *African research & documentation* (Birmingham, Eng., SCOLMA, 1973– . 3 nos. per yr.), which offers similar information to scholars.   DT19.9.U5A65

Africa bibliography, 1984– . Hector Blackhurst, ed. Manchester, Manchester Univ. Pr., [1985]– . Annual.   **DD23**

Sponsored by the International African Institute.

"Having lost all connection with the *International African bibliography,* the Institute felt it was time to resuscitate such a service;" to that end this publication is offered as "a reasonably priced bibliography which would enable [scholars] to have access to information on the latest publications relating to Africa."—*Foreword.* The first issue covers books, essays, and articles published 1983–84, mainly in the social sciences and humanities. Topical arrangement; covers the entire continent and associated islands.

A current bibliography of African affairs, v.1, no.1– , Apr. 1962– . [Farmingdale, N.Y.], Baywood Publ. Co., 1962– . Quarterly. (v.1–6 repr.: Westport, Conn., Greenwood Pr., 1971)   **DD24**

Publ. for the African Bibliographic Center.

Each issue is in three parts: (1) original studies, bibliographies or bibliographic essays; (2) book reviews; (3) bibliography of newly published books, articles, government documents, and visual aids arranged by general subject or geographical area. Author index.

The Center also issued a *Special bibliographic series* (v.1–8, 1963–73; n.s.v.1–6, 1975–78) devoted to longer bibliographies.

        Z3501.C87

International African bibliography. Bibliographie internationale africaine, 1971– . London, Mansell, 1971– . v.1– . Quarterly.   **DD25**

Publisher varies. 1971–72 issued by International African Institute; 1973– sponsored by the University of London's School of Oriental and African Studies.

Subtitle: Current books, articles and papers in African studies.

Serves as a continuation of the bibliography of current publications which appeared in the journal *Africa,* 1929–70.

Each issue has a section for the whole of Africa, followed by geographical subdivisions. Entries for each region are grouped by subject. For cumulations *see* DD12–DD13.

JALA, joint acquisitions list of Africana, 1962– . Comp. by the Melville J. Herskovits Library of African Studies. Evanston, Ill., Northwestern Univ. Lib., 1962– . 6 nos. per yr.   **DD26**

Lists, without indexes, based on cataloging at about ten contributing institutions in the United States as reported to the Herskovits Library. Issues for 1972–77, with re-editing and further authority work, were cumulated in an author/title arrangement and published in v.5–6 of the first supplement of the Herskovits catalog (DD17). A cumulation of the 1978–83 issues, arranged by main entry with a geographical index, was issued on microfiche (with accompanying leaflet) by the Herskovits Library in 1984. G. K. Hall, Boston, has also issued a cumulation covering 1973–78, with supplements for 1979 and 1980.   Z3509.J64

Book reviews

Easterbrook, David L. Africana book reviews, 1885–1945: an index to books reviewed in selected English-language publications. Boston, G. K. Hall, [1979]. 247p.   **DD27**

Lists reviews of Africana items appearing in 44 English-language journals during the period indicated. Listing is by main entry of the work under review. Title index.   Z3501.E35

Henige, David. Works in African history: an index to reviews, 1960–1974. Waltham, Mass., African Studies Assoc., Brandeis Univ., [1976]. 54p.   **DD28**

Some 75 journals were searched for book reviews and review essays (marked with an asterisk) on 442 books dealing with Africa south of the Sahara. Arranged by author of book; no index.

Supplemented by: Z3508.H5H46

—— —— 1974–1978. [Waltham, Mass.?], Crossroads Pr., [1978]. 58p. **DD29**

—— —— 1978–1982. Los Angeles, Crossroads Pr., [1984]. 127p. **DD30**

Lists an additional 1,000 titles; about 500 journals are now covered.

Dissertations

Köhler, Jochen. Deutsche Dissertationen über Afrika; ein Verzeichnis für die Jahre 1918–1959. Zusammengestellt von Jochen Köhler. Hrsg. vom Wissenschaftlichen Ausschluss durch H. Abel, E. Ackermann, [und] W. Fröhlich. Bonn, Kurt Schroeder, 1962. unpaged. **DD31**

A classified list of nearly 800 items. Catchword and author indexes. Prepared under the auspices of the Deutsche Afrika Gesellschaft, Bonn. Z3501.K6

Répertoire des thèses africanistes françaises, 1977–1980/81. Paris, CARDAN, 1980–84. v.1–4. (In progress) **DD32**

Sponsored by the Centre d'Études Africaines, École des Hautes Études en Sciences Sociales.

Represents a merger of the *Inventaire de thèses africainistes de langue française en cours* (1970–76) and *Inventaire de thèses et mémoires africainistes de langue française soutenus* (1970–76).

Lists theses in the humanities and social sciences concerning any part of Africa. In two sections: Thèses soutenues, and Thèses inscrites. Geographical arrangement with topical subdivisions; author and subject indexes. Z3501.R44

Sims, Michael and **Kagan, Alfred.** American & Canadian doctoral dissertations & master's theses on Africa, 1886–1974. Waltham, Mass., African Studies Assoc., Brandeis Univ., [1976]. 365p. **DD33**

Based on *American doctoral dissertations on Africa 1886–1972* by Anne Schneller and Michael Bratton (1973).

Arranged by country or geographic area, then by broad subject field. Subject and author indexes. More than 6,000 items. Z3501.S5

Standing Conference on Library Materials on Africa. Theses on Africa accepted by universities in the United Kingdom and Ireland. Cambridge, Heffer, 1964. 74p. **DD34**

Arranged by region and country, with subject subdivisions. Author index. 1,142 items covering the period 1920–62.

Continued by: Z3501.S83

—— Theses on Africa, 1963–1975, accepted by universities in the United Kingdom and Ireland. Comp. by J. H. St.J. McIlwaine. London, Mansell, 1978. 123p.

This volume "contains 2,231 items accepted between 1963 and 1975. . . . In addition, 124 theses submitted *before* 1962 but omitted from the original volume have been included in an Appendix."—*Introd.* A classed list with author index. Z3501.S8

Periodicals

Michigan. State University, East Lansing. Library. Research sources for African studies; a checklist of relevant serial publications based on library collections at Michigan State University, by Eugene de Benko and Patricia L. Butts. [East Lansing, Mich.], African Studies Center, 1969. 384p. **DD35**

Lists more than 2,000 serial publications relevant to African studies in the Michigan State University Library. Z3503.M52

Mullan, Anthony Páez. Africana serials in microform in the Library of Congress. Wash., Lib. of Congress, 1978. 36p. **DD36**

". . . prepared as an operational document in an edition of 250 copies for internal use in the Library of Congress and limited outside distribution."—[*p.ii*]

Lists "a selection of serials in microform relating to Africa. . . . Most of the serials are in European and African languages that use the Roman alphabet. However, since the scope of the list covers all of Africa, a number of Arabic publications are also listed."—*Pref.*

Travis, Carole and **Alman, Miriam.** Periodicals from Africa; a bibliography and union list of periodicals published in Africa. Boston, G. K. Hall, [1977]. 619p. **DD37**

For full information *see* AE199.

U.S. Library of Congress. Serial & Government Publications Division. African newspapers in the Library of Congress. Comp., John Pluge, Jr. 2d ed. Wash., Lib. of Congress, 1984. 144p. **DD38**

1st ed. 1977.

Lists more than 930 African newspapers from 52 countries held by the Library. Geographical arrangement; title index.

Z6959.Z9L53

Library resources (including archives)

Bhatt, Purnima Mehta. Scholars' guide to Washington, D.C. for African studies. Wash., Smithsonian Inst. Pr., 1980. 347p. (Scholars' guide to Washington, D.C., no.4) **DD39**

Publ. for the Woodrow Wilson International Center for Scholars.

In two parts: the first dealing with "the resource *collections* in the Washington area which include libraries; archives; museums; music, film, and map collections; and data banks. The second part focuses on Washington-based *organizations,* both public and private, which have Africa-related interests and are potential sources of information for researchers."—*p.xiii.* Concerned primarily with African studies and does not generally include materials for the study of Afro-Americans. Indexed. Z3501.B48

Collins, Robert O. and **Duignan, Peter.** Americans in Africa; a preliminary guide to American missionary archives and library manuscript collections on Africa. Stanford, Calif., Hoover Inst., 1963. 96p. (Hoover Inst. bibliographical ser., 12) **DD40**

A listing, by institution, of missionary archives and library collections, giving descriptions of their holdings. DT1.C57

Directory of documentation, libraries and archives services in Africa. Répertoire des services de documentation, de bibliothèque et d'archives d'Afrique. 2d ed. by Dominique Zidouemba, rev. & enl. by Eric de Grolier. Paris, Unesco, 1977. 311p. (Documentation, libraries and archives. Bibliographies and reference books, 5) **DD41**

1st ed. 1965 entitled *Directory of archives, libraries, and schools of librarianship in Africa*

Information is based on responses to questionnaires sent to national, university, and special libraries and documentation centers in the 40 Unesco member nations in Africa. Country arrangement with topical index. Z857.A1D57

Duignan, Peter. Handbook of American resources for African studies. [Stanford, Calif.], Hoover Institution on War, Revolution, and Peace, Stanford Univ., 1967. 218p. (Hoover Inst. bibliographical ser., 29) **DD42**

Describes library and manuscript collections, church and missionary archives, art and ethnographic collections, and some business archives relating to Africa in American institutions and museums. Z3501.D8

Études africaines en Europe. Paris, A.C.C.T., Karthala, [1981]. 2v. **DD43**

Contents: v.1, Bilan et inventaire; v.2, Inventaire/France.

A survey of the state of African studies in Western European countries; essays based on information derived from questionnaires, point out relevant bibliographies, research institutes, libraries, etc. Country arrangement; directory information for universities, libraries, research associations, etc., follow the individual essays. Inasmuch as the essays for France are included with the others in the first volume, v.2 is a directory only. Indexed.　　　　DT19.8.E83

Guide to federal archives relating to Africa. Comp. by Aloha South. [Waltham, Mass., African Studies Assoc., 1977] 556p.　　　　　**DD44**

Comp. and ed. by the National Archives and Records Service for the African Studies Association.

Describes the "known Africa-related records in the National Archives of the United States. The records, which include textual material, maps, sound recordings, motion and still pictures, are located in the National Archives Building, the General Archives Division in the Washington National Records Center, Presidential libraries, and the regional archives branches that are part of the Federal Archives and Records Centers."—*Introd.* Arranged alphabetically by name of agency, with subordinate agencies thereunder. Indexes of subjects, of places, of proper names, of ships, and of ethnic groups.

A second volume is to cover Africa-related material in nongovernmental archives and libraries.

Although published separately, this is part of the series "Guides to the sources of the history of nations: Africa" (DD95).　　Z3509.S67

The SCOLMA directory of libraries and special collections on Africa in the United Kingdom and Western Europe. Ed., Harry Hannam. 4th rev. and exp. ed. [Oxford], Zell; München, K. G. Saur, 1983. 183p.　　　　**DD45**

1st ed. 1963 had title *The SCOLMA directory of libraries and special collections on Africa.*

This edition expanded to include 133 libraries in Western Europe along with 142 in the United Kingdom. Directory information (based on responses to a questionnaire) includes reference to finding aids and brief description of resources for African study. Geographical arrangement. Fully indexed.　　　　Z3501.S8

Dictionaries and handbooks

African historical dictionaries. no.1– . Metuchen, N.J., Scarecrow Pr., 1974– . no.1– . (In progress)　　**DD46**

Contents: no.1, Historical dictionary of Cameroon, by Victor T. LeVine (1974. 198p.); no.2, People's Republic of the Congo, by V. McL. Thompson and R. Adloff (2d ed. 1984. 139p.); no.3, Swaziland, by John J. Grotpeter (1975. 251p.); no.4, Gambia, by Harry A. Gailey (1975. 172p.); no.5, Republic of Botswana, by R. P. Stevens (1975. 189p.); no.6, Somalia, by Margaret Castagno (1975. 213p.); no.7, Dahomey (People's Republic of Benin), by Samuel Decalo (1976. 201p.); no.8, Burundi, by Warren Weinstein (1976. 368p.); no.9, Togo, by Samuel Decalo (1976. 243p.); no.10, Lesotho, by Gordon Haliburton (1977. 223p.); no.11, Mali, by Pascal J. Imperato (1977. 204p.); no.12, Sierra Leone, by C. P. Foray (1977. 279p.); no.13, Chad, by Samuel Decalo (1977. 413p.); no.14, Upper Volta, by D. M. McFarland (1978. 239p.); no.15, Tanzania, by L. S. Kurtz (1978. 363p.); no.16, Guinea, by T. E. O'Toole (1978. 183p.); no.17, Sudan, by J. O. Voll (1978. 193p.); no.18, Rhodesia/Zimbabwe, by R. K. Rasmussen (1979. 445p.); no.19, Zambia, by J. J. Grotpeter (1979. 410p.); no.20, Niger, by S. Decalo (1979. 376p.); no. 21, Equatorial Guinea, by M. Liniger-Goumaz (1979. 222p.); no.22, Republics of Guinea Bissau and Cape Verde, by R. A. Lobban (1979. 193p.); no.23, Senegal, by L. G. Colvin (1980. 355p.); no.24, Morocco, by W. Spencer (1980. 152p.); no.25, Malawi, by C. A. Crosby (1980. 280p.); no.26, Angola, by P. Martin (1980. 196p.); no.27, Central African Republic, by P. Kalck (1980. 194p.); no.28, Algeria, by A. Heggoy (1981. 247p.). no.29, Kenya, by B. A. Ogot (1981. 279p.); no.30, Gabon, by D. E. Gardinier (1981. 254p.); no.31, Mauritania, by A. G. Gerteiny (1981. 98p.); no.32, Ethiopia, by C. P. Rosenfeld (1981. 436p.); no.33, Libya, by L. Hahn (1981.

116p.); no.34, Mauritius, by L. Rivière (1982. 172p.); no.35, Western Sahara, by T. Hodges (1982. 431p.); no.36, Egypt, by J. Wucher King (1984. 719p.); no.37, South Africa, by C. C. Saunders (1983. 241p.); no.38, Liberia, by D. Elwood Dunn and Svend E. Holsoe (1985. 274p.); no.39, Ghana, by D. M. McFarland (1985. 296p.).

Following a brief survey of the history and economics of the country, each dictionary is an alphabetical arrangement of entries for people and topics. Most volumes end with a selective bibliography.

For a description of one of the better volumes in the series *see* the Subscription Books Committee review of the Togo dictionary in the *Booklist* 74: 1758–59 (July 15, 1978).

Cultural atlas of Africa. Ed. by Jocelyn Murray. N.Y., Facts on File; Oxford, Phaidon, [1981]. 240p. il. 31cm.　　**DD47**

Intends to "provide an introduction to the continent as a whole" *(Introd.)* by means of maps, illustrations and text. Articles by contributing scholars are grouped in three main sections: The physical background; The cultural background; The nations of Africa. Information appears to be current as of about 1977. Brief bibliography (p.227–29); gazetteer; subject index.

Although not presented as an atlas, *The Cambridge encyclopedia of Africa*, ed. by Roland Oliver and Michael Crowder (Cambridge & N.Y., Cambridge Univ. Pr., 1981. 492p.) offers similar information for the whole of Africa during all periods, with copious illustrations.　　　　DT14.C83

Lystad, Robert A., ed. The African world; a survey of social research. Ed. for the African Studies Association. N.Y., Praeger, [1965]. 575p.　　　　　**DD48**

A review of social studies and techniques in the African field, intended for students and as an aid to scholars who are not subject specialists in this area. 18 social scientists contributed chapters on the state of research in their specific fields (e.g., law, history, education, linguistics), reporting on achievements, theories, and trends in research, and indicating areas for future work. A good bibliography is included.　　　　DT19.8.L9

Chronologies

Diggs, Ellen Irene. Black chronology, from 4000 B.C. to the abolition of the slave trade. Boston, G. K. Hall, [1983]. 312p.　　　　　　**DD49**

For full information *see* CC420.

Freeman-Grenville, Greville Stewart Parker. Chronology of African history. [London & N.Y.], Oxford Univ. Pr., 1973. 312p.　　　　　**DD50**

"These historical tables display, in a calendrical fashion, the whole course, so far as it is known, of the principal events and dates in the whole continent of Africa from c.1000 BC until the end of 1971."—*Introd.* Indexed.　　　　DT17.F73

Current surveys

Africa contemporary record: annual survey and documents, 1968/69– . London, Africa Research Ltd., 1969– . Annual.　　　　　　　**DD51**

Colin Legum and John Drysdale, eds.

Intended as a "survey of major economic, social and political developments."—*Pref.* In three main sections, the first presenting essays by specialists on current issues and developments; the second offering a country-by-country review of events (with statistics on production, lists of top government officials, etc.); and the third reprinting documents relating to international relations, political issues, and social, economic, and cultural developments. An index was added in the 1969/70 volume.　　　　DT1.L43

Africa diary. v.1– , July 1–7, 1961– . New Delhi, Africa Publ., 1961– . Weekly, with quarterly and annual indexes. Looseleaf. **DD52**

Hara Sharan Chhabra, ed.

Subtitle on cover: Weekly record of events in Africa, with index.

Countries are arranged alphabetically, followed by a general section for the continent as a whole. DT1.A213

Africa research bulletin. v.1– , Jan. 1964– . Exeter, Eng., Africa Research Ltd., 1964– . Monthly. Looseleaf. **DD53**

In two parts: (1) Political series (formerly Political and cultural series, 1964–Jan.14, 1985); (2) Economic series (formerly Economic, financial, and technical series, 1964–Jan.14, 1985).

Offers summaries of major events, decisions, movements, surveys, etc., drawn mainly from newspaper coverage; source is indicated. An annual index for each part is arranged geographically with topical subdivisions.

African recorder: a fortnightly record of African events with index. v.1– , Jan. 1–14, 1962– . New Delhi, 1962– . Fortnightly, with semiannual and annual indexes. Looseleaf. **DD54**

Summaries of events are entered under country (the countries arranged alphabetically), with an added section for events relating to "Africa outside Africa." DT1.A228

Directories

AF: Log I–II. Wash., African Bibliographic Ctr., 1975–81. v.1–2. (Current reading list 11, no.2; 12, no.2) (In progress?) **DD55**

Contents: v.1, African interests of American organizations; v.2, African affairs in Washington.

v.1 covers American organizations, universities, and institutions having African programs; v.2, non-governmental agencies in the Washington metropolitan area. Gives name, address, publications, and a descriptive paragraph for each.

Bradbury, R. E. Directory of African studies in United Kingdom universities. Comp. for the African Studies Association of the United Kingdom. [Birmingham, Eng., 1969?] 73p. **DD56**

Describes the relevant programs at 38 universities and colleges. DT19.9.G7B7

Directory of African & Afro-American studies in the United States, 1971/72–79. Waltham, Mass., African Studies Assoc., 1972–79. 6v. **DD57**

Title varies; 1971/72–74/75 entitled *Directory of African studies in the United States.*

The 1979 ed. lists some 900 colleges and universities offering relevant courses, with names of courses, faculty members, etc. DT19.9.U5D56

Duffy, James, Frey, Mitsue and **Sims, Michael.** International directory of scholars and specialists in African studies. [Waltham, Mass.], Crossroads Pr., [1978]. 355p. **DD58**

About 2,700 biographical sketches of Africanists throughout the world. Information is based on questionnaires "distributed to individuals, universities, and international research organizations." —*Pref.* DT19.5.D83

International African Institute. Research Information Liaison Unit. International guide to African research studies. Enl. & rev. ed. London, 1975. 185p. (Current Africanist research, 4) **DD59**

1st ed. 1971 had title *International register of organisations undertaking Africanist research.*

Offers information (address, staff, research disciplines, regional focus, publications) of research organizations, centers, institutes, museums, and university departments throughout the world. Geographical arrangement; information based on responses to questionnaires.

Kept up-to-date by listings in *Current Africanist research; international bulletin,* Nov. 1971– . DT19.8I58

General history

Cambridge history of Africa. J.D. Fage and Roland Oliver, gen. eds. Cambridge, University Pr., 1975–84. v.1–6,8. (In progress; to be in 8v.) **DD60**

Contents: v.1, From the earliest times to c.500 B.C., ed. J. Desmond Clark. 1981. 1157p.; v.2, From c.500 BC to AD 1050, ed. J. D. Fage. 1978. 840p.; v.3, From c.1050 to c.1600, ed. Roland Oliver. 1977. 803p.; v.4, The sixteenth and seventeenth centuries, ed. Richard Gray. 1975. 738p.; v.5, From c.1790 to c. 1870, ed. John E. Flint. 1977. 617p.; v.6, From 1870 to 1905, ed. Roland Oliver and G. N. Sanderson. 1985. 956p.; v.8, c.1940–c.1975, ed. Michael Crowder. 1984. 1011p.

Chapters written by specialists include full bibliographies; there is also a bibliographical essay at the end of each volume. Detailed index; maps. Of the same high caliber as other Cambridge histories.

Various chapters have been republished in separate volumes: e.g., David Birmingham's *Central Africa to 1870: Zambezia, Zaire, and the South Atlantic* (Cambridge, 1981) is drawn from chapters in v.3–5; and *Ancient Egypt, a social history,* ed. by B. G. Trigger (Cambridge, 1983) is a reprinting of three chapters from v.1.

Another authoritative history still in progress is the *General history of Africa* (Berkeley, Univ. of California Pr., 1981–), sponsored by Unesco; each volume is edited by a native specialist and emphasizes oral tradition. Volumes published to date are: v.1, Methodology and African prehistory, ed. J. Ki-Zerbo (1981); v.2, Ancient civilizations of Africa, ed. G. Mokhtar (1981); v.4, Africa from the twelfth to the sixteenth century, ed. D. T. Niane (1984); v.7, Africa under colonial domination, 1880–1935, ed. A. Adu Boahen (1985). DT20.C28

Atlases

Clark, John Desmond. Atlas of African prehistory. Chicago, Univ. of Chicago Pr., [1967]. 62p., 50 maps. 52cm. **DD61**

Designed to meet the "need for maps to show the distribution of prehistoric industries in Africa and their relations to ecological data," concentrating on the Stone Age. Base maps show ecological data (e.g., topography, soils, hypothetical rainfall, vegetative zones); transparent overlays indicate "industrial and other significant distributions" such as fossil pollen sites, fossil man sites. A supplement provides a gazetteer of important prehistoric sites. G2446.E1C5

Historical atlas of Africa. Gen. eds., J. F. Ade Ajayi and Michael Crowder. Cambridge & N.Y., Cambridge Univ. Pr.; Essex, Longman, 1985. 167p. maps. 40cm. **DD62**

An excellent work reflecting the editors' desire to "bring together experts on different periods of African history to produce an atlas in full colour that made use of the latest cartographic techniques."— *Pref.* Maps and text (by contributing scholars) on facing pages; photographs are also employed. Maps are of three kinds: (1) event oriented; (2) historical process oriented (e.g., "before and after"); (3) quantitative (especially for economic topics); sources are sometimes indicated. Index of personal and place names appearing on maps and in text; many cross references. List of contributors.

Worthwhile atlases intended for student or school use include John D. Fage's *An atlas of African history* (2d ed. London, E. Arnold, 1978. unpaged); G. S. P. Freeman-Grenville's *Modern atlas of African history* (London, R. Collings, 1976. 63p.); Colin McEvedy's *Penguin atlas of African history* (London, A. Lane, 1980. 142p.); and

African history in maps, comp. by Michael Kwamena-Poh (London, Longman, 1982. 76p.). G2446.S1H5

AFRICA, NORTHERN

See also Asia—Near and Middle East.

Bibliography

Bibliographie analytique de l'Afrique antique. v.1–11, 1961/62–75. Paris, E. de Boccard, 1969–79. **DD63**

Frequency has varied; annual beginning 1967. Ceased publ.?
Jehan Desanges and Serge Lancel, comps.
Continues a bibliography published annually in *Libyca,* 1953–61.
Covers North Africa, although many issues are offprints from *Bulletin d'archéologie algérienne.* Arranged by period; lists books, articles, and essays wherever published.
The journals indexed are listed in *Bibliographie de l'Afrique du nord antique: périodiques et séries,* by René Rebuffat, Isabelle Gabard, Yahn Le Bohec (Paris, Presses de l'École Normale Supérieure, 1980. 94p.). Z3511.B5

Blaudin de Thé, Bernard. Essai de bibliographie du Sahara français et des régions avoisinantes, éd. avec le concours de l'Organisation Communes des Régions Sahariennes. 2.éd. Paris, Arts et Métiers Graphiques, Librairie C. Klincksieck, 1960. 258p. **DD64**

1st ed. 1959. This edition enlarged and somewhat rearranged.
In two parts: pt.1 is a partial reprint of *Les territoires du sud de l'Algérie,* 3.pt. (Alger, 1930), with titles arranged chronologically under classification headings; pt.2, also classified but with titles arranged alphabetically by author, lists books and articles published through 1958. Materials are preponderantly in French, totaling some 9,300 items. Author index. Z3709.B55

France. Armée. Etat-major. Service Historique. L'Afrique française du nord. Bibliographie militaire des ouvrages français ou traduits en français et des articles des principales revues françaises relatifs à l'Algérie, à la Tunisie et au Maroc de 1830 à 1926. Paris, Impr. Nationale, 1930–35. 4v. (Repr.: N.Y., AMS Pr., 1975. 2v.) **DD65**

A comprehensive bibliography, annotated and classified. In v.1–2, *L'Algérie,* the arrangement in each class is alphabetical by author; in v.3–4, *La Tunisie,* it is chronological by date of publication.
v.1–2 contain works published from 1830 to 1926; v.3–4, publications issued up to 1927, and those published prior to 1830, as well. Z3515.F81

McClintock, Marsha Hamilton. The Middle East and North Africa on film; an annotated filmography. N.Y., Garland, 1982. 542p. **DD66**

For full information *see* DE45.

Shinar, Pessah. Essai de bibliographie sélective et annotée sur l'Islam maghrébin contemporain: Maroc, Algérie, Tunisie, Libye (1830–1978). Paris, Éditions du CNRS, 1983. 506p. **DD67**

Offers more than 2,000 annotated entries for books and articles concerning life—political, ethnographic, and cultural as well as religious—in North Africa since about 1830. Topical arrangement with author, subject, and word indexes. Z7835.M6S5

Dissertations

Sluglett, Peter. Theses on Islam, the Middle East and North-West Africa, 1880–1978. London, Mansell, 1983. 147p. **DD68**

For full information *see* DE63.

Library resources

Collison, Robert Lewis. Directory of libraries and special collections on Asia and North Africa. Hamden, Conn., Archon, [1970]. 123p. **DD69**

For full information *see* DE15. Z3001.C583

Guides to the sources for the history of the nations. 3d ser.: North Africa, Asia and Oceania. Detroit, Gale, 1980– . **DD70**

For full information *see* DE16.

Dictionaries and surveys

Annuaire de l'Afrique du Nord. 1– , 1962– . Paris, Centre Nationale de la Recherche Scientifique, 1963– . Annual. **DD71**

For full information *see* CJ233.

Ronart, Stephan and **Ronart, Nandy.** Concise encyclopaedia of Arabic civilization: the Arab West. N.Y., Praeger, [1966]. 410p. **DD72**

A companion to the authors' concise encyclopedia for the Arab East (DE70). This volume provides similar coverage for Morocco, Algeria, Tunisia, and Libya, plus some consideration of the Arab era in the Iberian peninsula. DT173.R6

AFRICA, SOUTHERN

Bibliography

American-Southern African relations: bibliographic essays. Ed. by Mohamed A. El-Khawas and Francis A. Kornegay, Jr. Westport, Conn., Greenwood Pr., [1975]. 188p. (African Bibliographic Center. Special bibliographic ser., n.s., no.1) **DD73**

Contents: American involvement in Angola and Mozambique by M. A. El-Khawas; A short bibliographic essay on U.S. policy toward Southern Rhodesia (Zimbabwe), by S. Nyang; Namibia, by B. Rogers; United States investments in Southern Africa, by T. Hultman and R. Kramer; Black America and U.S.-Southern African relations, by F. A. Kornegay, Jr.
Each essay is followed by full citations to works cited in the text. Not indexed.

Bridgman, Jon and **Clarke, David E.** German Africa, a select annotated bibliography. Stanford, Hoover Inst. on War, Revolution and Peace, Stanford Univ., 1965. 120p. (Hoover Inst. bibliographical ser., 19) **DD74**

Lists holdings of the Hoover Institution on German activity in Africa from 1870 to the present, "concentrating on German government, politics, foreign relations, military activity and territorial expansion." The collection includes much material published in Germany after World War I when the "recovery of the colonies became a domestic political issue."—*Pref.* Z3751.B7

Cape Town. University of Cape Town. Library. Preliminary finding-list of southern African pamphlets in the University of Cape Town libraries, comp. by Ellen S. Roberts. Cape Town, 1959. 203p. (*Its* Varia ser. I) **DD75**

A classified listing of the rather elusive pamphlet material on sub-Saharan Africa, not limited by language or period. No index. Z965.C22

Duignan, Peter and **Gann, Lewis H.,** eds. A bibliographical guide to colonialism in sub-Saharan Africa. Cambridge, Cambridge Univ. Pr., 1973. v.5. (Hoover Institution publications) **DD76**

Content of v.5, Colonialism in Africa, 1870–1960, by Lewis H. Gann (552p.).

Covers publications on the historical, political, societal, and related problems from 1870 to 1960. Stress is on historical material, but works in anthropology, law, economics, and geography are also cited. Includes publications to early 1972. Provides a guide to reference sources, libraries, archives, etc., as well as a subject guide to the literature.

Duignan, Peter and **Conover, Helen F.** Guide to research and reference works on sub-Saharan Africa. Stanford, Calif., Hoover Institution Pr., [1972?]. 1102p. (Hoover Inst. bibliographical ser., 46) **DD77**

A preliminary version. For the librarian and the student; useful as a guide to collection-building for African studies as well as a reference bibliography. More than 3,100 entries, with annotations. Because conventional reference works do not exist for various areas of African studies, scholarly specialized books and articles have been substituted to fill the gaps. Indexed. Z3501.D78

Gowan, Susan Jean. Portuguese-speaking Africa 1900–1979, a select bibliography. Braamfontein, S.Afr., South African Inst. of Internat. Affairs, [1982–83]. 4v. in 3. (Bibliographical ser., no.9–11) **DD78**

Contents: v.1, Angola; v.2, Mozambique; v.3, Portuguese Guinea/Guinea Bissau, Cape Verde, São Tomé e Principe, Portuguese-speaking Africa as a whole; v.4, United Nations documentation on Portuguese-speaking Africa, by Elna Schoeman.

Lists selected books, essays, periodical articles, and government publications, mainly in Portuguese or English, covering the period 1900 to 1979. v.1–2 arranged by broad topics within two larger sections, Pre-Independence and Post-Independence, with author and subject indexes. v.3 lists works on the whole of Portuguese-speaking Africa, on Angola and Mozambique together, and on any of the former Portuguese colonies in topical or geographical arrangement, with author and subject indexes. v.4 is exclusively a listing of 197 United Nations documents "on the decolonization process of the Portuguese colonies and their subsequent attainment of independence."—*Pref.* It includes annotations and author and subject indexes. Z3871.P67

Hategekimana, Grégoire. Sources bibliographiques des états de l'ancien domaine colonial belge d'Afrique Centrale: Rwanda, Burundi, Zaire. Éd. abrégée. Kigali, Author, 1983 [c.1979]. 204p. (Contribution á la recherche bibliographique sur les états de la Communauté économique des pays des Grands Lacs, 1) **DD79**

A topically arranged bibliography of bibliographies, the first part dealing with the countries mentioned in the title, the second with Africa in general. Cites some 1,017 books, pamphlets, and articles in various Western languages; some annotations; no index.

Hess, Robert L. and **Coger, Dalvan M.** Semper ex Africa. A bibliography of primary source[s] for nineteenth-century tropical Africa as recorded by explorers, missionaries, traders, travelers, administrators, military men, adventurers, and others. [Stanford, Calif., Hoover Institution, 1972] 800p. (Hoover bibliographical ser., 47) **DD80**

Lists more than 7,700 items concerned with "that area of the continent exclusive of the Muslim Arab North and of the Afrikaner-controlled Republic of South Africa"—*Introd.* Geographical arrangement with author index. Includes both books and periodical articles. Z3501.H47

Obdeijn, Herman. The political role of Catholic and Protestant missions in the colonial partition of Black Africa; a bibliographical essay. Leiden, [Leiden Center for the History of European Expansion], 1983. 95p. (Intercontinenta, no.3) **DD80a**

Offers "a survey of recent [post-1950] studies on the political role of missionary work in Africa south of the Sahara at the time this continent was divided among European powers."—*Introd.* Each essay covers a different geographical area; publications discussed are in English, French, German, or Dutch. Not indexed.

BV3520.O23

Pélissier, René. Africana. Bibliographies sur l'Afrique luso-hispanophone (1800–1980). Orgeval, Ed. Pélissier, 1980. 205p. **DD81**

Reprints review essays and bibliographies published 1965–79 in the *Revue française d'études politiques africaines* and in *Genève-Afrique.* Concentrates on the areas which were formerly Spanish and Portuguese colonies; includes publications of all countries. Index by geographical area. Z3871.P44

Sahel bibliographic bulletin. East Lansing, Sahel Documentation Ctr., Michigan State Univ., 1977–85. v.1–9, no.2. Quarterly. **DD81a**

Text in English or French. Ceased publication.

Books, articles, papers and documents dealing with agricultural and economic development in the Sahel (Cape Verde, Chad, Gambia, Mali, Mauritania, Niger, Senegal, and Upper Volta) are listed by country, with a subject index. Also includes notes on research projects, information centers and services and bibliographies on special subjects.

More than 900 documents from the Center's collection, plus about 100 American doctoral dissertations have been reproduced on microfiche by University Microfilms International; the fiches are accompanied by a printed pamphlet, *Sahel, a guide to the microfiche collection . . .* (Ann Arbor, Mich., 1981). Z7165.S23S23

Scheven, Yvette. Bibliographies for African studies, 1970–1975. Waltham, Mass., African Studies Assoc., 1977. 135p. **DD82**

Cites about 1,000 bibliographies issued as books, articles, parts of edited volumes, etc., relating to sub-Saharan Africa. Topical/geographical arrangement, with continuing bibliographies cited at the end of each section. Index of names, titles, and subjects.

Continued by: Z3501.A1S32

———— ———— 1976–1979. [Waltham, Mass.], Crossroads Pr., [1980]. 142p. **DD83**

More than 800 bibliographies in the humanities and social sciences relating to Africa south of the Sahara are listed under broad topics or by geographical area. Bibliographies in Western European languages (excluding Slavic and Scandinavian languages) are included, whether appearing as books, articles, or parts of edited volumes. Indexed by subject and author.

Continued by: Z3501.A1S33

———— ———— 1980–1983. München, Hans Zell/K. G. Saur, 1984. 300p. **DD84**

Cites nearly 1,200 bibliographies from the 1980–83 period.

Skurnik, W. A. E. Sub-Saharan Africa; a guide to information sources. Detroit, Gale, 1977. 130p. **DD85**

A useful, but somewhat dated, guide for the undergraduate or beginning researcher. Broad topical arrangement, each chapter beginning with a "substantive introduction" which describes methodological problems, gives definitions, and provides a survey of research; an annotated bibliography follows. Z3501.S55

U.S. Library of Congress. African Section. Africa south of the Sahara: index to periodical literature, 1900–1970. Boston, G. K. Hall, 1971. 4v. **DD86**

An important bibliography compiled from the bibliographic card services of three European research institutes, from various publications of the International African Institute in London, and from a number of journals not adequately covered by existing indexes. Files of more than 1,500 periodical titles have been gleaned; a high percentage of articles is from the last decade of the period covered. (Unfortunately there is no indication as to which years of a given periodical are indexed.) French and English are the predominant languages, though practically every other European language is represented. Arrangement is by country or area, then by subject. Emphasis is on the social sciences; citations to about 3,000 African literary works are given in an appendix. Entries vary widely in form and amount of bibliographic information, depending on the source from which taken; some are annotated. Z3503.U47

—— —— 1st–3d supplement. Boston, G. K. Hall, 1973–85. 3v.

Includes entries for materials added during the period Jan. 1971–Dec. 1977. Author indexes.

U.S. Library of Congress. Library of Congress Office, Nairobi, Kenya. Accessions list, Eastern Africa, v.1, no.1– , Jan. 1968– . Bimonthly. **DD87**

Frequency varies.

Covers book, serial, and government publications of Angola, Burundi, Comoros, Ethiopia, Kenya, Madagascar, Malawi, Mauritius, Réunion, Rwanda, Seychelles, Sudan, Tanzania, Uganda, Zambia, and Zimbabwe. Monographs are listed by geographical area, then by language; annual index of main and added entries. Includes occasional lists of non-book materials and of significant United Nations publications. The July issue is a serials supplement, and an "Annual publishers' directory, monographs and serials" is issued at the end of the year. Z3516.U52

Wilding, Richard. A bibliography of the history and peoples of the Swahili-speaking world, from earliest times to the beginning of the 20th century. Nairobi, Lamu Soc., 1976. 98p. **DD87a**

Cover title: Swahili culture.

A geographically arranged listing of books and articles selected "to introduce the reader of the major West European languages to the history and cultures of the area in which the Swahilis now live, and those areas in which they have lived in the past or with which they have at some time maintained close cultural links."—*Pref.* No index. Z3516.W54

Zoghby, Samir M. Arab-African relations, 1973–1975; a guide. Wash., General Reference and Bibliography Div., Reader Services Dept., Lib. of Congress, 1976. 26p. (Maktaba-African relations, no.1) **DD88**

"Books and periodical articles on contemporary relations between Arab states and Sub-Saharan Africa" (*Pref.*) published during the 1973–75 period are arranged by author, with a subject index. Brief annotations. Z3013.Z63

—— Islam in sub-Saharan Africa, a partially annotated guide. Wash., Lib. of Congress, 1978. 318p. **DD89**

A partially annotated bibliography of selected books and periodical articles pertaining to the social, religious, and political structure of the Muslim populations, the Islamization of sub-Saharan Africa, "the resistance of Muslim leaders and reformers to European imperial designs, and the role of Islam as a major variable in political relations between Muslim states in the twentieth century." —*Pref.* Chronological arrangement subdivided by geographical area, then by topic. Indexed. Z7835.M6Z63

Current

Africa index to continental periodical literature. v.3– , 1978– . Oxford, Hans Zell (Publ. for the African Bibliographical Centre), 1981– . Annual (slightly irregular). **DD90**

Continues *Africa index,* v.1–2 (1976–78).

Intends to index "selected scholarly and semi-scholarly journals published but not necessarily printed within the African continent excluding South Africa. . . . Report literature, conference papers, and papers presented to seminars in African countries are also included."—*Introd.* Popular magazines are selectively indexed; book reviews are excluded, but review articles are indexed. Arranged by broad topic; code letters by each entry indicate geographical area treated. Z3501.A43

Bibliographie de l'Afrique sud-saharienne: science humaines et sociales, 1925/30–80. Tervuren, Belg., K. Museum voor Midden-Afrika, 1932–84. Annual. **DD91**

Title varies: *Bibliographie ethnographique du Congo Belge . . . ,* 1925–59; *Bibliographie ethnographique de l'Afrique sud-saharienne,* 1960–77.

Books, essays, and periodical articles are listed by author, with subject index. Includes all Western languages. Earlier volumes included annotations whereas now only subject descriptors are given. Z5113.T33

Bibliographie des travaux en langue francaise sur l'Afrique au Sud du Sahara. Sciences humaines et sociales, 1977– . Paris, CNRS [for] École des Hautes Études en Sciences Sociales, Centre d'Études Africaines, 1979– . Annual. **DD92**

Formed by the union of: Centre d'Analyse et de Recherche Documentaires pour l'Afrique Noir, Paris. *Fiches d'ouvrages,* 1968– 1975/76, and *Bibliographie française sur l'Afrique au Sud du Sahara,* 1968–76.

Lists books (including new editions and translations), periodical articles, essays, some mimeographed publications, but not literary texts, unpublished dissertations, or scientific works. A general section is topically arranged, but the main body of the work is by geographical area without further subdivision. Author and subject indexes. Z3501.B527

Dissertations

Maurer, Barbara and **Schwarz, Klaus.** Hochschulschriften zu Schwarz-Afrika, 1960–1978: Deutschland—Österreich —Schweiz. Freiburg, Klaus Schwarz Verlag, 1979. 226p. (Materialien zur Afrikakunde, 1) **DD93**

Serves as a continuation of Köhler's *Deutsche Dissertationen über Afrika* (DD31), with coverage extended to include Austrian and Swiss dissertations (including Swiss dissertations written in French). Classed arrangement; author and subject indexes. Z3501.M29

Pollak, Oliver B. and **Pollak, Karen.** Theses and dissertations on Southern Africa: an international bibliography. Boston, G. K. Hall, [1976]. 236p. **DD94**

Arranged by broad subject headings, each subdivided by country or other geographical area. Author index, but no detailed subject approach. Lists some 2,400 academic theses (including B.Litt. and B.Ed., as well as M.A. and Ph.D. papers) accepted for advanced degrees between 1884 and 1974. Represents work at more than 200 institutions in 30 countries. Z3518.P55

Manuscripts and archives

Guide to the sources of the history of the nations. B. Africa . . . Zug, Inter Documentation, [1970–83]. v.1–9. (In progress) **DD95**

Publisher varies.

At head of title: Conseil International des Archives. International Council on Archives. Consejo Internacional des Archivos.

Contents: v.1, Quellen zur Geschichte Afrikas südlich der Sahara in dem Archiven der Bundesrepublik Deutschland (1970); v.2, España. Guía de fuentes para la historia de Africa Subsahariana (1971); v.3-4, Africa: sources de l'histoire de l'Afrique au Sud du Sahara dans les archives et bibliothèques françaises, 4v. (1971-76); v.5-6, Guida delle fonti per la storia dell'Africa a Sud del Sahara esistenti in Italia, 2v. (1972-74); v.7, Guida delle fonti per la storia dell'Africa a Sud del Sahara negli Archivi Santa Sede e negli Archivi Ecclesiastici d'Italia (1983; Collectana archivi vaticana, 3); v.8, Scandinavia. Sources in Denmark, Norway and Sweden (1971); v.9, Guide to the sources of the history of Africa south of the Sahara in the Netherlands (1978).

The volumes for Belgian, British, and American archives have been or are to be published outside this series (*see* DD44, DD96).

Surveys of library and archival materials important for research in African studies. Some volumes lack indexes. CD941.G84

Matthews, Noel and **Wainwright, M. Doreen.** A guide to manuscripts and documents in the British Isles relating to Africa. Ed. by J. D. Pearson. London, Oxford Univ. Pr., 1971. 321p. **DD96**

"The area covered . . . is the African continent south of the Sahara, including the islands off the coast of the continent, and embraces, together with Ethiopia, most of the African territories formerly colonized by Britain, France, Belgium, Portugal, Spain, Italy, Germany, and the Netherlands."—*Pref.* Listing is by repository with an index of names and subjects. CD1048.A3M36

Dictionaries and handbooks

Africa south of the Sahara. Ed.1– . London, Europa Pubns., 1971– . Annual. **DD97**

A handbook and directory of information. Originally duplicated much material found in *World of learning* (CB205), but this was dropped with the 1974 edition.

In three main parts: (1) Background to the continent; (2) Regional organizations; (3) Country surveys. The third part includes information for each country on physical and social geography, recent history, economy, statistics. The directory section gives names of political parties, members of government, media, banks, trade unions, shipping companies, periodicals, etc. Country surveys include select bibliographies. Organization index added with 11th ed. (1981); more economic and political articles included in the opening section beginning with 13th ed. (1983). DT351.A37

Black Africa; a comparative handbook [by] Donald G. Morrison [and others]. N.Y., Free Pr., [1972]. 483p. **DD98**

Aims to present "in a clear and readily accessible form the latest comparable information available (up to publication time) for 32 independent black African nations."—*Pref.* Pt.1 presents comparative profiles under such headings as: (1) Demography, ecology, and pluralism; (2) Social and economic development; (3) Political development; (4) Security systems and stability; (5) International linkages; (6) Urban and ethnic patterns. Pt.2 offers individual country profiles. Much of the information is presented in tabular form. Detailed table of contents, but no index. DT352.8.B56

McLane, Charles B. Soviet-African relations. London, Central Asian Research Centre; distr. by Columbia Univ. Pr., 1974. 190p. (Soviet–Third world relations, v.3) **DD99**

Surveys "Soviet relations with 36 sovereign African nations south of the Sahara" (*Pref.*), excluding those countries which were still colonies or dependencies in 1972 as well as South Africa and Rhodesia. Soviet relationship with each country is presented in tabular form—political, economic, cultural—chronologically arranged. List of references for each country section. A "Regional perspective" section offers a "discussion of the broad tendencies of Soviet interest in Africa from the late 1950s to the end of 1972, as measured by the substance of Soviet press commentaries, the volume of aid and trade and the diplomatic response to competition from other non-African powers, notably China. . . ."—*Pref.*

For companion volumes on Asian and Middle East relations *see* DE22, DE68. DT38.9.R8M27

Rosenthal, Eric. Encyclopaedia of Southern Africa. 7th ed. Cape Town, Juta, [1978]. 577p, il. **DD100**

1st ed. 1961. Frequently revised and updated.

An alphabetical encyclopedia treating the history, biography, literature, geography, geology, natural history, social life and customs, etc., of southern Africa, originally comprising South Africa, Rhodesia, Zambia, Malawi, South West Africa, Mozambique, Lesotho, Swaziland, and Botswana. This edition updated, and with many new entries added. Mozambique and the territories north of the Zambezi have been omitted from this edition. DT29.R65

AFRICA, WEST

Cardinall, Allan Wolsey. Bibliography of the Gold Coast. Accra, Govt. Pr., [1932]. 384p. (Repr.: Westport, Conn., Negro Univ. Pr., 1970) **DD100a**

Issued as a companion volume to the census report of 1931.
Lists more than 5,000 items in many languages on the Gold Coast

(now Ghana), Togoland, Dahomey, Upper Volta, and the Ivory Coast. Z3785.C3

Darch, Colin. A Soviet view of Africa: an annotated bibliography on Ethiopia, Somalia and Djibouti. Boston, G. K. Hall, [1980]. 200p. **DD101**

A classified bibliography of Russian writings on the Horn of Africa. About 1,200 items, including "printed monographs, collections, periodical articles and book reviews in Russian which deal wholly or in part with the history, linguistics, social sciences, natural science and medicine of the Horn of Africa. Newspaper articles have generally been relegated to an appendix; maps are omitted."—*Introd.* Publication dates range from the 19th century to about 1975. Titles are given in transliteration, with English translation. Indexes of names and subjects.

Darch is also the compiler of *Russian writings on Tanganyika, Zanzibar, and Tanzania* (Dar es Salaam, Bureau of Resource Assessment, Univ. of Dar es Salaam, 1976. 68p.; Research report, n.s., 19). Z3521.D37

Guides to materials for West African history in European archives. no.1–5. London, Univ. of London, Athlone Pr., 1962–73. **DD102**

Contents: no.1, Materials for West African history in the archives of Belgium and Holland, by Patricia Carson (1962); no.2, . . . Portuguese archives, by A. F. C. Ryder (1965); no.3, . . . Italian archives, by Richard Gray and D. S. Chambers (1965); no.4, . . . French archives, by Patricia Carson (1968); no.5, . . . archives of the United Kingdom, by Noel Matthews (1973). CD1000.G8

Joucla, Edmond A. Bibliographie de l'Afrique occidentale française. . . . Paris, Soc. d'Éditions Géographiques, Maritimes et Coloniales, 1937. 704p. (Bibliographie générale des colonies françaises par G. Grandidier et E. A. Joucla) **DD103**

An extensive bibliography of books and articles, primarily in French, arranged alphabetically by author. Z3711.J68

ALGERIA

Lawless, Richard I. Algeria. Oxford, Eng. & Santa Barbara, Calif., Clio Pr., [1980]. 215p. map. (World bibliographical ser., 19) **DD104**

Lists 742 books and articles in an effort "to provide a range of basic references to all key aspects of the country and its people" (*Pref.*); mainly English-language materials, but with standard works in French included in all sections, and all considered to be readily available in the United Kingdom and the U.S. Annotations; author/title/subject index. Z3681.L378

——— Algerian bibliography: English language publications, 1830–1973. London & N.Y., Bowker, in assoc. with the Centre for Middle Eastern and Islamic Studies of the Univ. of Durham, [1976]. 114p. (Centre for Middle East and Islamic Studies pubns., 4) **DD105**

Some 1,490 books and periodical articles are listed under 12 topics, subdivided as appropriate. The first section, "Bibliography," includes titles in all languages; the other sections cite only English-language materials. Author index. Z3683.A4L38

ANGOLA

See also DD78.

Greenwood, Margaret Joan. Angola; a bibliography. Cape Town, Univ. of Cape Town, School of Librarianship, 1967. 52p. **DD106**

A broad subject listing of books, pamphlets, and a few periodical articles, with author and subject indexes.

Updated in part by the *Boletim bibliográfico* of the Instituto de Angola, Luanda ([1964?]–75), which lists books, pamphlets, and serials. Z3891.G7

BOTSWANA

Henderson, Francine I. and **Modisakeng, Tiny.** A guide to periodical articles about Botswana 1965–80. Gaborone, Nat. Inst. of Development and Cultural Research, Documentation Unit, Univ. College of Botswana, 1982. 147p. (Working bibliography, 9) **DD107**

A broad subject listing of some 1,232 English-language entries compiled from bibliographies and indexes. Includes any area of study on Botswana. Author index.

Botswana's environment by Francine Henderson and Johannes Opschoor (Gaborone, 1981. 83p.) covers socioeconomic development and environmental impact since 1966. Z3559.H46

Kerven, Carol and **Simmons, Pamela.** Bibliography on the society, culture, and political economy of post-independence Botswana. Gaborone, Nat. Migration Study, Central Statistics Off., 1981. 131p. **DD108**

Offers a "selection of works representing research and data collection on the society, culture, economics and politics of Botswana during the post-independence (1966) period."—*Introd.* Main entry listing with subject index and brief author index. Locates items in four Gaborone libraries.

A bibliography of Bechuanaland, by Paulus Mohome and John B. Webster (Syracuse, N.Y., Syracuse Univ. Program of Eastern African Studies, 1966; Supplement, 1968), lists publications prior to independence. Z7165.B65K47

Parsons, Q. N. A consolidated checklist of theses and dissertations on Botswana. Gaborone, Univ. of Botswana, Nat. Inst. of Development Research & Documentation, [1982]. 75p. (N.I.R. working bibliography, no.8) **DD109**

Supersedes an earlier (1971) list published in *Botswana notes and records,* adding new entries and extending coverage to all academic disciplines; also includes undergraduate theses. International coverage. Classed arrangement with author index. Z3559.P36

BURKINA FASO

Izard, Françoise. Bibliographie générale de la Haute-Volta, 1956–1965. Paris, CNRS-CVRS, 1967. 300p. (Recherches voltaïques, 7) **DD110**

A topical listing of over 1,500 articles, books, seminar papers, and government documents. Some annotations. Well indexed.

Supplemented in part by *French-speaking West Africa: Upper Volta today, 1960–1967; a selected and introductory bibliographical guide* (Wash., African Bibliographic Ctr., 1969. 37p.).

BURUNDI

Rodegem, F. M. Documentation bibliographique sur le Burundi. Bologna, EMI, 1978. 346p. **DD111**

About 5,800 books, articles, government reports, films, discs, and maps are cited within broad topics; author and subject indexes. Covers pre-1976 publications; includes a list of periodicals published in Burundi.

CAMEROON

DeLancey, Mark W. and **DeLancey, Virginia H.** A bibliography of Cameroon. N.Y., Africana Publ. Co., [1975]. 673p. (African bibliography ser., 4) **DD112**

Covers "from the onset of German colonization (1884) through the beginning of 1972," with some later publications. Books, articles, some documents and recordings are listed; book reviews and abstract references are noted. Z3761.D44

CHAD

Bibliographie du Tchad (sciences humaines). 2. éd. rev., corr. et suivi d'un supplément par Jacqueline Moreau et Danielle Stordeur. Fort-Lamy, Inst. Nat. Tchadien pour les Sciences Humaines, 1970. 353p. (Études et documents tchadiens, sér. A, 5) **DD113**

1st ed. 1968.

Lists almost 2,450 books, articles, films, and theses published to Dec. 31, 1969. Indexed.

Continued by: Z3695.B5

Bériel, Marie-Magdeleine. Complément à la Bibliographie du Tchad. ... N'Djaména, Inst. Nat. des Sciences Humaines, 1974. 103p. (Études et documents tchadiens, sér. A, 6) **DD113a**

Adds about 500 items published 1970–73.

A concise bibliography of Northern Chad and Fezzan in Southern Libya. Mohamed A. Alawar, gen. ed. Outwell, Cambridgeshire, Arab Crescent Pr. (distr. in U.S. by Westview Pr., Boulder, Colo.), [1983]. 229p. **DD114**

Aims to include "all major items that concern the border issue in the Chad-Libya dispute; documents concerned with Libyan-Chad relations in general; and materials relating to the geography, history, economics and political backgrounds to Northern Chad and Fezzan in southern Libya."—*Introd.* Books, essays, and articles are topically arranged, with author index. Z3695.C66

CONGO

See Zaire.

EGYPT

Bibliography

Annual Egyptological bibliography. Bibliographie égyptologique annuelle. 1947– . Comp. by Jozef M. A. Janssen. Leiden, Brill, 1948– . Annual. (International Association of Egyptologists) **DD115**

Publisher varies.

An alphabetical, annotated list, begun to fill the need of an annual bibliography caused by the cessation of the "Bibliografia metodica degli studi de egittologia e di papirologia," published in *Aegyptus,* 1920–43.

Annotations are in either French or English.

——— Indexes, 1947–1956, by Jozef M. A. Janssen. Leiden, Brill, 1960. 475p.

Includes an alphabetical index by authors, giving titles and full information; followed by many specialized indexes, e.g., topography, pharaohs, hieroglyphs, divinities, biblical references and Hebrew words, classical authors, subject index. Z3656.A2A6

Blake, Gerald Henry and **Swearingen, William Davis.** The Suez Canal; a commemorative bibliography, 1975. [Durham], Univ. of Durham, Ctr. for Middle Eastern and Islamic Studies, [1975]. 49p. (Occasional papers, 4)
DD116

Lists about 600 books and articles which trace "the changing role of the Canal in relation to Western Europe."—*Pref.* Chronological arrangement.

See also Munir D. Ahmed's *Suezkanal-Bibliographie; Bibliography on the Suez Canal* (Hamburg, Deutsche Orient Institut, 1974. 70p.).
Z3657.S93B55

Ibrahim-Hilmy, *Prince.* The literature of Egypt and the Soudan from the earliest times to the year 1885 [i.e., 1887] inclusive. A bibliography: comprising printed books, periodical writings and papers of learned societies; maps and charts; ancient papyri, manuscripts, drawings, etc. London, Trübner, 1886–88. 2v. (Repr.: Nendeln, Kraus, 1966)
DD117

An author list of some 20,000 titles, with some subject and form headings. Appendix of additional works to May 1887 in v.2, p.371–459.
Z3651.I14

Maunier, René. Bibliographie économique, juridique et sociale de l'Égypte moderne (1798–1916). . . . Le Caire, Impr. de l'Inst. Français d'Archéologie Orientale, 1918. 372p. (Soc. Sultanieh d'Économie Politique, de Statistique et de Législation. Travaux spéciaux . . . no.1)
DD118

A classified bibliography of almost 6,700 titles of books and periodical articles primarily in French, but with some in other European languages, on the economic, legal, and social activities of early modern Egypt. Author and subject indexes. Includes a "Liste chronologique des revues publiées (en langues européennes) en Égypte de 1798 à 1916," p.xxiii–xxxi.
Z3651.M45

Sinai Peninsula; informative abstracts of researches, studies and news (1960–1980). Cairo, Prep. and publ. by the Nat. Information & Documentation Ctr. (NIDOC), 1982. 310p. maps.
DD119

Offers 472 abstracts on the Sinai in topical arrangement; author and subject index. Most items were published 1960–80 and deal with the life and physical sciences, but there are sections for history, language, etc.
DS110.5.S49

Weeks, Kent R. An historical bibliography of Egyptian prehistory. Winona Lakes, Ind., Publ. for American Research Center in Egypt by Eisenbrauns, [1985]. 138p. (Amer.Res.Ctr. in Egypt. Catalogs, v.6)
DD120

Lists more than 2,500 books, articles and essays in any language on the archaeology of Egypt to the end of the Old Kingdom. Author arrangement; no index.

Ida A. Pratt's two bibliographies, *Ancient Egypt* (N.Y., 1925; Supplement, 1942; both repr.: N.Y., Kraus, 1969) and *Modern Egypt* (N.Y., 1929) are concerned only with materials available in the New York Public Library.
Z5113.W43

Dictionaries

Lexikon der Ägyptologie. Hrsg. Wolfgang Helck und Eberhard Otto. Wiesbaden, O. Harrassowitz, 1972–85. v.1–6³. il. maps. (In progress)
DD121

Contents: v.1–6³, A–Thinis. Separate indexes have been published for v.1 and v.2.

An authoritative encyclopedia of Egyptian civilization intended for both the specialist and the student. Signed articles with lengthy bibliographies; a few articles are in English or French. Focus is on Egypt of the Pharoahs to the Hellenistic period, with sketchy treatment given to later periods, prehistory, and countries of conquest (the user being referred to more comprehensive encyclopedias such as the *Reallexikon für Assyriologie*). Excellent indexes for each completed volume.
DT58.L49

Posener, Georges. Dictionnaire de la civilisation égyptienne . . . , en collaboration avec Serge Sauneron et Jean Yoyotte. Paris, Fernand Hazan, 1959. 323p. il.
DD122

A small, popular dictionary with copious illustrations in color and in black-and-white. Articles are signed. No bibliography.

Translated into English as *Dictionary of Egyptian civilization* (London, Methuen; N.Y., Tudor, 1962. 323p.)
DT58.P653

Atlases

Baines, John and **Málek, Jaromír.** Atlas of ancient Egypt. Oxford, Phaidon; N.Y., Facts on File, [1980]. 240p.
DD123

For full information *see* DA106.

EQUATORIAL GUINEA

Liniger-Goumaz, Max. Guinea Ecuatorial, bibliografía general. Berne, Commission Nationale Suisse pour l'Unesco, 1974–80. v.1–4. (In progress)
DD124

A bibliography of books, articles, and government publications issued since 1705. Author listing with geographical and topical indexes. About 1,700 to 2,000 entries per volume. A final volume, announced for 1985, is to have cumulative indexes to the full set.
Z3937.L56

ETHIOPIA

See also DD101.

Brown, Clifton F. Ethiopian perspectives, a bibliographical guide to the history of Ethiopa. Westport, Conn., Greenwood Pr., [1978]. 264p. (African Bibliographic Center. Special bibliographic ser., n.s., no.5)
DD125

"Ethiopian history" is interpreted in the broadest sense, so that ethnology, health, religion, etc., are included. Books and periodical articles in all languages are listed in topical sections alphabetically arranged; index of authors and anonymous titles.

A short guide to the study of Ethiopia, by Alula Hidaru and D. Rahmato (Westport, Conn., Greenwood Pr., 1976. Spec. bibliographic ser., n.s., 2) emphasizes archival sources and government publications.

Fumagalli, Giuseppe. Bibliografia etiopica. . . . Milano, Hoepli, 1893. 288p. (Repr.: Farnsborough, Gregg, 1971)
DD126

Subtitle: Catalogo descrittivo e ragionato degli scritti pubblicati dalla invenzione della stampa fino a tutto il 1891, intorno alla Etiopia e regioni limitrofe.

A classified bibliography, with author index, of writings on Ethiopia, published from the 15th century to 1891.
Continued by:
Z3521.F97

Zanutto, Silvio. Bibliografia etiopica, in continuazione alla "Bibliografia etiopica" di G. Fumagalli. Roma, Sindicato Italiano Arti Grafiche, 1932–36. 2v. il.
DD127

Contents: Pt.1, Bibliografia. 2d ed., 1936. 54p.; pt.2, Manoscritti etiopici. 1932. 178p.

Pt.1 continues the listing of materials on Ethiopia from 1891 to 1936; pt.2 lists Ethiopian manuscripts to be found in the various libraries of the world.
Z3521.F97Z3

Lockot, Hans Wilhelm. Bibliographia Aethiopica, die äthiopienkundliche Literatur des deutschsprachigen Raums. Wiesbaden, Franz Steiner, 1982. 441p. (Äthiopistische Forschungen, 9)
DD128

A bibliography of about 7,770 citations to German-language

books, articles, book reviews, and serials; covers to about 1976, with a few listings as late as 1979. Covers all areas of study; topical listing with author/editor index.   Z3521.L62

Marcus, Harold G. The modern history of Ethiopia and the horn of Africa, a select and annotated bibliography. Stanford, Hoover Inst. Pr., [1972]. 641p. (Hoover Inst. bibliographical ser., 56)   **DD129**

2,042 annotated entries for articles appearing in 19th-century geographical journals; includes materials on history, economics, political science, anthropology, geology, climatology. Entries are grouped mainly by language; author, geographical, and subject indexes.   Z3521.M35

Research and Information Centre on Eritrea. Bibliography on Eritrea. Rome, The Centre, 1982. 235p.   **DD130**

Cites some 3,376 publications on Eritrean society, past and present, under twenty main headings. Gives Italian library locations.   Z3523.E74B52

GABON

Darkowska-Nidzgorska, Olenka. Connaissance du Gabon; guide bibliographique. Libreville, Univ. Nationale el Hadj Omar Bongo, 1978. 151p. (Projet documentaire; pubn. no.1)   **DD131**

A classed bibliography of some 1,025 items relating to all aspects of Gabon—geography, demography, politics, education, history, etc. Index of names.   Z3697.D37

GAMBIA

See also AA766.

Gamble, David P. A general bibliography of the Gambia (up to 31 December 1977). Boston, G. K. Hall, [1979]. 266p.   **DD132**

The compiler's earlier (1973) bibliography, which had very limited distribution, formed the basis of this work. Classed arrangement with detailed table of contents and indexes of personal names, organizations, place names, etc. Nearly 4,500 items.   Z3735.G33

GHANA

Bibliography

Afre, S. A. Ashanti region of Ghana: an annotated bibliography, from earliest times to 1973. Boston, G. K. Hall, [1975]. 494p.   **DD133**

A revised and updated edition of the author's 1967 thesis for Fellowship of the British Library Association.

Attempts "to list all books, pamphlets and periodical articles; academic theses, dissertations, and project reports; maps and atlases; and unpublished seminar and conference papers relating or containing important references to Ashanti published or produced up to and including the year 1973."—*Introd.* Broad subject listing with author and subject indexes. 2,781 items.   Z3785.A64

Aguolu, Christian Chukwunedu. Ghana in the humanities and social sciences 1900–1971; a bibliography. Metuchen, N.J., Scarecrow Pr., 1973. 469p.   **DD134**

A classed bibliography of more than 4,200 items; author index; some annotations.   Z3785.A65

Johnson, Albert Frederick. A bibliography of Ghana, 1930–1961. Accra, publ. for the Ghana Library Board by Longmans, 1964. 210p.   **DD135**

In some respects a continuation of A. W. Cardinall's *A bibliography of the Gold Coast* (DD100a). Aims to be a comprehensive listing of publications on the Gold Coast and Ghana during the formative years 1930–61, with selected periodical articles. A classified listing of more than 2,600 items.

Supplemented by: Z3785.J63

Kotei, S. I. A. Selected annotated bibliography of Ghana. Accra, 1965. 46p. (Ghana Library Board. Padmore Research Library on African Affairs. Bibliographical ser. Special subject bibliography, no.5)   **DD136**

Continues the listings in the Johnson bibliography (above).

Dissertations

Kafe, Joseph Kofi. Ghana: an annotated bibliography of academic theses, 1920–1970 in the Commonwealth, the Republic of Ireland and the United States of America. Boston, G. K. Hall, 1973. 219p.   **DD137**

Pt.1 is an annotated bibliography in classed arrangement; annotations are meant to be descriptive rather than evaluative. Pt.2 lists the dissertations by country, then by degree-granting institution. Author index.   Z3785.K33

Archives

Dumett, Raymond E. Survey of research materials in the National Archives of Ghana. Basel, Afrika-Verlag der Kreis, 1974. 48p. (Mitteilungen der Basler Afrika Bibliographien, 11)   **DD138**

Archives are grouped by type—government, missionary societies, family and business papers—with brief descriptions. No index.   CD2353.D85

GUINEA-BISSAU

McCarthy, Joseph M. Guinea-Bissau and Cape Verde Islands, a comprehensive bibliography. N.Y., Garland, 1977. 196p. (Garland reference library of social science, v.27)   **DD139**

A topically arranged bibliography of books, periodical articles, and government publications in English and Portuguese. Author index.

See also Joyce L. Bowman's "Guinea-Bissau" in *Current bibliography of African affairs*, 7:219–42 (1984/85).   Z3873.G8M3

IVORY COAST

Janvier, Geneviève. Bibliographie de la Côte d'Ivoire. [Abidjan], Université d'Abidjan, 1972–78. 4v.   **DD140**

Contents: [v.1] Sciences de la vie; [v.2] Sciences de l'homme; [v.3], Sciences physiques et de la terre; [v.4] Sciences de la terre; Sciences de la vie, 1970–76.

A topical listing of books and essays, mainly in French and English. Author index.   Z3689.N34

KENYA

Collison, Robert L. Kenya. Oxford, Eng., & Santa Barbara, Calif., Clio Pr., [1982]. 157p. (World bibliographical ser., 25)   **DD141**

A topical arrangement of citations to more than 500 English-language books and periodical articles. Annotations; chronology. Indexed. Z3586.C64

Gregory, Robert G., Maxon, Robert M. and **Spencer, Leon P.** A guide to the Kenya National Archives: to the microfilms and district annual reports, record books, and handing-over reports, miscellaneous correspondence and intelligence reports. Syracuse, N.Y., Program of Eastern African Studies, Syracuse Univ., 1968. 452p. (Eastern African bibliographical ser., no.3) **DD142**

An annotated index to the microfilm collection which includes some documents as recent as 1963. Includes notes on content of the documents; index of names and organizations; subject index to the miscellaneous correspondence. CD2364

Ng'ang'a, James Mwangi. Theses and dissertations on Kenya: an international bibliography. Nairobi, Africa Book Service, [1983]. 272p. **DD143**

A topical listing of almost 1,400 dissertations and theses accepted between 1937 and 1980 on any subject relating to Kenya. Intends to be exhaustive for works accepted at American, British, and East African universities, but many other countries are represented. Author, subject, and university indexes. Z3587.N45

Norgaard, Ole. Kenya in the social sciences, an annotated bibliography 1967–1979. [Nairobi], Kenya Literature Bureau, [1980]. 372p. **DD144**

A topically arranged bibliography of books, articles, dissertations and working papers on Kenyan population, language, government, education, and economic development and planning. Author and keyword indexes.

LESOTHO

Lesothana: an annotated bibliography of new and newly located Lesotho materials. no.1– , Aug. 1982– . Roma, Lesotho, Documentation Centre, Inst. of Southern African Studies, Nat. Univ. of Lesotho, 1982– . Irregular.

DD145

Intended as an ongoing supplement to the Lesotho bibliography of Willet and Ambrose (below). Each issue is a classed listing of publications in a limited number of subject fields, without index. (Plans call for keyword indexing at a later date.) Includes book and periodical references, most of them works published outside Lesotho. Early issues are devoted mainly to control of a backlog of older materials.

Willet, Shelagh M. and **Ambrose, David P.** Lesotho; a comprehensive bibliography. Oxford, Eng. & Santa Barbara, Calif., Clio Pr., [1980]. 496p. (World bibliographical ser., 3) **DD146**

An extensive bibliography with "the needs of the research worker kept in mind."—*Introd.* Cites books and articles in many languages, together with mimeographed reports and theses. Topical arrangement; author, title, subject index. Z3558.W55

LIBERIA

Gray, Beverly Ann and **Batiste, Angel.** Liberia during the Tolbert era: a guide. Wash., Lib. of Congress, 1983. 79p. **DD147**

A selection of about 450 items (books, pamphlets, periodical articles, dissertations, and Liberian government documents) concerning Liberia during the presidency of W. R. Tolbert, 1971–80. Classed arrangement with author/subject index. Z3821.G7

Solomon, Marvin David and **d'Azevedo, Warren L.** A general bibliography of the Republic of Liberia. Evanston, Ill., Northwestern Univ., 1962. 68p. (Northwestern Univ. Working papers in social science, no.1) **DD148**

". . . a working draft . . . prior to the publication of a revised and amplified version."—*Introd.*

Photographic reproduction of cards listing books and periodical articles on Liberia, its territory, and its peoples.

LIBYA

See also DD114.

Hill, Roy Wells. A bibliography of Libya. [Durham, Eng.], Durham Colleges in the Univ. of Durham, Dept. of Geography, 1959. 100p. (Research papers, ser. no.1, 1959)

DD149

A classified bibliography dealing primarily with the geography and economy of Libya. No index. Z3971.H5

Schlüter, Hans. Index Libycus; bibliography of Libya 1957–1969, with supplementary material 1915–1956. Boston, G. K. Hall, 1972. 305p. **DD150**

Designed to extend and supplement Hill's *Bibliography of Libya* (above). Classed arrangement with author index. Covers Western-language materials in all areas of study.

Continued by: Z3971.S36

—— —— 1970–1975, with supplementary material. Boston, G. K. Hall, [1979]. 2v. **DD151**

Added title page in Arabic.

Contents: v.1, Titles; v.2, Cumulative index.

Continues the item numbering of the earlier volume, adding another 4,000 titles. A cumulative index covers the Hill volume as well as the two by Schlüter. Z3971.S37

MALAGASY REPUBLIC (MADAGASCAR)

Duignan, Peter. Madagascar (The Malagasy Republic): a list of materials in the African collections of Stanford University and the Hoover Institution on War, Revolution, and Peace. Stanford, Calif., Hoover Inst., 1962. 25p. (Hoover Inst. bibliographic ser., 9) **DD152**

A listing of documents, books, and monographs on Madagascar.

A short, comprehensive list of English-language materials is "Basic bibliography of Madagascar" in *Journal of modern African studies*, 7:337–42 (1981). Z3701.D8

Grandidier, Guillaume. Bibliographie de Madagascar. Paris, Comité de Madagascar, 1905/06–57. 3v. **DD153**

Contents: [v.1], 1500–1904 (publ. 1905–1906. 905p.); [v.2], 1904–1933 (Paris, Soc. d'Édit. Géographiques, Maritimes et Coloniales, 1935. p.759–1350); v.3, 1934–1955 (Tananarive, Inst. de Recherche Scientifique de Madagascar, 1957. p.1351–1910). Volumes are paged continuously, disregarding the supplement in v.1.

A comprehensive bibliography of manuscripts, books, pamphlets, and periodical articles published on Madagascar from its discovery in 1500 to 1955.

For materials published since 1955 *see* J. R. Fontvieille's *Bibliographie nationale de Madagascar* (AA941). Z3701.G85

MALAWI

Boeder, Robert B. Malawi. Oxford, Eng., Santa Barbara, Calif., Clio Pr., [1979]. 165p. (World bibliographical ser., 8) **DD154**

An annotated bibliography of about 550 items (plus an unannotated, unnumbered listing of theses and dissertations). Classed arrangement with author/subject index. Z3577.B63

MALI

Brasseur, Paule Marion. Bibliographie générale du Mali (anciens Soudan Français et Haut-Sénégal-Niger). Dakar, IFAN, 1964. 461p. map. (Inst. Français d'Afrique Noire. Catalogues et documents, XVI) **DD155**

A classified listing of 4,873 numbered items—books and periodical articles—almost entirely in French, on all phases of life, culture, and history of the Sudan. Many titles are annotated.
Continued by: Z3711.B7

——— Bibliographie générale du Mali (1961–1970). Dakar, Nouvelles Éditions Africaines, 1976. 284p. (Institut Fondamental d'Afrique Noire. Catalogues et documents, no.16–2) **DD156**

Adds almost 3,000 documents, books, periodical articles, mimeographed reports. Entries are mainly in French; brief annotations. Topical arrangement; author and subject index. Z3716.B7

MAURITIUS

Mauritius. Archives Dept. Bibliography of Mauritius (1502–1954), covering the printed record, manuscripts, archivalia and cartographic material, by A. Toussaint and H. Adolphe. Port Louis, Esclapon, 1956. 884p. **DD157**

A comprehensive bibliography of 8,865 items, in six sections: (1) Early imprints issued in Mauritius, 1768–1954; (2) Periodicals, newspapers and serials, 1773–1954; (3) Government and semi-official publications issued in Mauritius and Great Britain, 1810–1954; (4) Publications relative to Mauritius issued abroad in English, French, Dutch, and other languages, 1600–1954; (5) Manuscripts and archivalia, 1598–1954; (6) Cartographic material, 1502–1954. Z3703.M3A5

MOROCCO

Cenival, Pierre de. Bibliographie marocaine, 1923–1933. Paris, Larose, 1937. 606p. (Repr. from Hesperis) **DD158**

Continued in *Hesperis* as follows: 1934/35 in v.26, 1939; 1936/39 in v.30, 1943; 1940/43 in v.34, 1947; 1944/47 in v.38, 1951; 1948/51 in v.42, 1955; and in *Hesperis Tamuda*, 1952/53 in v.3, 1962.
A comprehensive bibliography of books and periodical articles on all phases of life in Morocco. Works are primarily in French. Z3836.C38

Findlay, Anne M., Findlay, Allan M. and **Lawless, Richard I.** Morocco. Oxford, Eng. & Santa Barbara, Calif., Clio Pr., [1984]. 311p. map. (World bibliographical ser., 47) **DD159**

A listing of some 927 books, articles, essays, and a few dissertations and documents arranged by broad topics. Items are primarily in English. Good annotations; index. Z3836.F56

MOZAMBIQUE

See also DD78.

Chonchol, Maria Edy. Guide bibliographique du Mozambique: environnement naturel, développement et organisation villageoise. Paris, L'Harmattan, [1979]. 135p. maps. **DD160**

Emphasis is on development and natural resources, but includes material on colonization and village life. Some annotations. Z3881.C45

NAMIBIA

Schoeman, Elna. The Namibian issue, 1920–1980; a select and annotated bibliography. Boston, G. K. Hall, [1982]. 247p. **DD161**

An expanded edition of *South West Africa/Namibia* (Johannesburg, 1978).
Books, articles from scholarly journals, conference papers, theses, and documents of governments and international organizations are listed in broad subject categories, with author and subject indexes. Chronology, 1884–1980. Z3774.A5S36

Schoeman, Stanley and **Schoeman, Elna.** Namibia. Oxford, Eng. & Santa Barbara, Calif., Clio Pr., [1984]. 186p. map. (World bibliographical ser., 53) **DD162**

Lists books and articles, mainly English-language, in 33 categories. Annotations; author, title, subject index. Intends "to guide the reader towards an understanding of the country, its people, their aspirations and problems as well as an appreciation of the region's natural assets."—*Pref.* Z3771.S37

Strohmeyer, Eckhard. NNB: Namibische National-Bibliographie, 1971/75– . Basel, Basler Afrika Bibliographien, 1978– . (Mitteilungen der Basler Afrika Bibliographien, v.20,24) **DD163**

For full information *see* AA965. Z3771.S77

NIGERIA

Červenka, Zdenek. The Nigerian War, 1967–1970: history of the war, selected bibliography and documents. Frankfurt am Main, Bernard u. Graefe Verlag für Wehrwesen, 1971. 459p. (Schriften der Bibliothek für Zeitgeschichte, n.F., Heft 10) **DD164**

Offers "a selection of what was written about the Nigerian crisis and the war in Great Britain, the United States, France, the Soviet Union, the Federal Republic of Germany, and other European countries."—*Introd.* "History of the war," p.1-213; "Selected documents [reprinted]," p.217-380; bibliography, p.382-451. Author index. DT515.9.E3C4

DeLancey, Mark and **Normandy, Elizabeth L.** Nigeria: a bibliography of politics, government, administration, and international relations. [Los Angeles], Crossroads Pr., [1983]. 188p. **DD165**

Covers the period from Nigerian independence in 1960 to the end of 1980, listing books, articles, dissertations, and some government publications. About half the entries are annotated; many give reference to book reviews. Personal name and subject indexes. Z3597.D45

Eitner, Kurt. Nigeria: Auswahlbibliographie. Hamburg, Institut für Afrika-Kunde in Verbund der Stiftung Deutsches Übersee-Institut, Dokumentations-Leitstelle Afrika, 1983. 2v. maps, tables. (Dokumentationsdienst Afrika. Reihe A, 20) **DD166**

Contents: v.1, Country studies, politics, law; v.2, Economics, society.
Prefatory matter, explanatory notes, topical headings, and index of subject headings in German and English.
Lists 1,883 books, pamphlets, serials, and articles in topical arrangement; except for serials, only publications of 1975–82 are

included. Indexes of subject headings and corporate authors in each volume cover both volumes.   Z3597.E34

RHODESIA

See Zimbabwe.

RWANDA

Trincaz, Pierre Xavier. Essai d'une bibliographie sur Rwanda. Kigali, O.C.A.M., Institut Africain et Mauricien de Statistique et d'Économie Appliquée, 1980. 64*l*.   **DD167**

An author listing without index. Citations are mainly to works in the humanities; some references to periodical articles are included.   Z3721.T75

Walraet, Marcel. Les sciences au Rwanda, bibliographie 1894–1965. Brussels, Bibliothèque Royale de Belgique, 1966. [213]p. (Institut Nationale de Recherche Scientifique, Butare. Pubn. 3)   **DD168**

More than 1,900 citations in all disciplines are arranged by subject, with geographical and personal name indexes.

Joseph Clement's *Essai de bibliographie du Ruanda-Urundi* (Usumbura, Service des A.I.M.O., 1959. 201p.) remains useful.

SENEGAL

Porgès, Laurence. Bibliographie des régions du Sénégal, Dakar, 1967. 705p. fold. maps.   **DD169**

At head of title: République du Sénégal. Ministère du Plan et du Développement.

A general bibliography of works on the region from early times through 1965, with emphasis on publications since 1945. Arranged by geographical area, with author and subject indexes.

SIERRA LEONE

Luke, Harry Charles Joseph. A bibliography of Sierra Leone, preceded by an essay on the origin, character and peoples of the colony and protectorate. 2d enl. ed. London, Oxford Univ. Pr., 1925. 230p. il. (Repr.: N.Y., Negro Univ. Pr., 1969)   **DD170**

A classified bibliography, now somewhat out-of-date, but still useful for the large amount of material collected. Includes 1,103 entries arranged under the headings: (1) General literature; (2) Native languages; (3) Colonial law and ordinances of Sierra Leone; (4) Articles in journals of societies, etc.; (5) Periodical publications; (6) State and parliamentary papers; (7) Maps. Appendix of "Chartered companies and governors of Sierra Leone, 1592–1925," p.218–20.   Z3553.S5L8

Williams, Geoffrey J. A bibliography of Sierra Leone, 1925–1967. N.Y., Africana Publ. Corp., [1971]. 209p.   **DD171**

A classified listing of more than 3,000 items (both book materials and periodical articles) concerned with Sierra Leone. Author and geographical indexes. Intended to supplement Harry Luke's *Bibliography of Sierra Leone* (above) which covered up to 1925.

See also Hans M. Zell's *Bibliography of non-periodical literature on Sierra Leone 1925–1966* . . . (Freetown, Fourah Bay College Bookshop, Univ. Sierra Leone, 1966. 44p.).   Z3553.S5W55

SOMALI

Salad, Mohamed Khalief. Somalia, a bibliographical survey. Westport, Conn., Greenwood Pr., 1977. 468p. (African Bibliographic Center. Special bibliographic ser., n.s., no.4)   **DD172**

A bibliography of books, journal and newspaper articles, and maps. Concentrates on the present-day Somali Democratic Republic but includes some material relating to "other Somali territories and their constituent populations still under foreign administrations." —*Introd.* Covers all disciplines. No index.

Somaliland, Italian. Camera di Commercio, Industria ed Agricoltura. Bibliografia somala. Mogadiscio, Scuola Tipografia Missione Cattolica, 1958. 128p. il.   **DD173**

A classified bibliography of 19th- and 20th-century materials on Italian Somaliland, primarily in Italian but with a few titles in other languages.   Z3796.S6

SOUTH AFRICA

Bibliography

Bibliografie van buitelandse publikasies oor Suid-Afrika, 1969/71–78/80. Pretoria, Die Staatsbiblioteek, 1973–81. Irregular.   **DD174**

Added title page in English: Bibliography of overseas publications about South Africa, including publications by South Africans and translations of South African works published abroad.

Ceased publication?

Arranged by Dewey Decimal Classification, with index of authors, titles, editors, etc. Also includes Bantu language materials and special issues of periodicals.

Bibliographies on South African political history. Boston, G. K. Hall, [1979–82]. 3v.   **DD175**

For full information *see* CJ414.

Mendelssohn, Sidney. A South African bibliography to the year 1925, being a revision and continuation of Sidney Mendelssohn's South African bibliography (1910), ed. at the South African Library, Cape Town. London, Mansell, 1979. 4v.   **DD176**

"With the financial assistance of the Human Sciences Research Council."—*t.p.*

Added title page in Afrikaans; prefatory matter in English and Afrikaans.

A revision and continuation to 1925 of the Mendelssohn bibliography (London, 1910. 2v.), giving library locations in South African libraries for books, articles, etc. Adds items published up to 1909 not recorded in the 1910 work, as well as variant editions and new materials published up to 1925 (chosen as the cut-off year because of the existence of other bibliographies for later periods). "Annotation is confined to bibliographical information, the identification of the author and relationship with other works and, of course, the location of each item."—*Introd.* A main entry listing, with subject entries provided only "for biographies where additional entries have been made under the names of biographees."

Leonard M. Thompson's *South African history before 1900, a select bibliography of articles* (Stanford, Hoover Inst. Pr. 1971) is also useful.   Z3609.M45

Musiker, Naomi. South African history: a bibliographical guide with special reference to territorial expansion and colonization. With the assistance of Reuben Musiker. N.Y., Garland, 1984. 297p. (Themes in European expansion, 5; Garland reference library of social science, 153)   **DD177**

An annotated bibliography of about 1,000 books. Arrangement is basically | chronological, but there are special sections for political parties, Prime Ministers, race relations, missionaries, and population. Author/title index.   Z3606.M84

Musiker, Reuben. South Africa. Santa Barbara, Calif., Clio Pr., [1979]. 194p. (World bibliographical ser., 7)   **DD178**

"The work is largely limited to books published in the Republic of South Africa. Exceptions to this criterion have been made where an overseas publication fills a gap in the local literature or where it is considered to be of some importance."—*Introd.* 577 items in classed arrangement, with annotations. Author/subject index.

This volume is meant to replace Musiker's *Guide to South African reference books* (5th ed., 1971; AA488).

Rogaly, Gail Lynda. South Africa's foreign relations, 1961–1979; a select and partially annotated bibliography. [Braamfontein, South African Inst. of Internat. Affairs, 1980] 462p. (Bibliographical ser.,7)   **DD179**

Includes books, government publications, journal articles, and conference papers concerning "bilateral relations with other states, Southern African questions, relations with international organizations and such specific questions as the involvement of multinational corporations in the Republic."—*Pref.* Arranged by main entry with author author and subject indexes.

Continued by: Z6465.S6R63

Kalley, Jacqueline Audrey. South Africa's foreign relations, 1980–1984. Braamfontein, South African Inst. of Internat. Affairs, [1984]. 283p. (Bibliographical ser., no.12)   **DD179a**

South African history and historians; a bibliography. Ed. by C. F. J. Muller and others. Pretoria, Univ. of South Africa, [1979]. 411p. (Documenta-Unisa, 21)   **DD180**

An updating of R. Musiker's *A select bibliography of South African history* (Pretoria, 1966; *Suppl.*, 1974).

Aims to "include most of the more important items appearing before August 1978, together with certain new editions and published theses which came to our attention while the book was in its final stages."—*Introd.* "History" is intrepreted broadly to include language, arts and crafts, armed forces, etc.   Z3606.S67

Encyclopedias and source books

Eybers, George von Welfling. Select constitutional documents illustrating South African history, 1795–1910. London, Routledge, 1918. 582p.   **DD181**

Selections with citations to sources.   JQ1911.E8

Standard encyclopaedia of Southern Africa. [Cape Town], NASOU [Nasionale Opvoedkundige Uitgewery Bpk.] Ltd., [1970–76]. 12v.   **DD182**

A regional encyclopedia for which preparation began in 1957. Main emphasis of the work is on the Republic of South Africa and its immediate neighbors, but special sections have been devoted to countries such as Angola, the Democratic Republic of the Congo, and the East African states of Kenya, Uganda, and Tanzania. Most articles are signed; many include bibliographies. The final volume is a supplement and an index to the full work.   DT729.S7

SUDAN

Daly, M. W. Sudan. Oxford, Eng. & Santa Barbara, Calif., Clio Pr., [1983]. 175p. (World bibliographical ser., 40)   **DD183**

A classed bibliography with brief annotations. 559 numbered entries. Index of authors, titles, and subjects.   Z3665.D36

Hill, Richard Leslie. A bibliography of the Anglo-Egyptian Sudan, from the earliest times to 1937. . . . London, Oxford Univ. Pr., 1939. 213p.   **DD184**

Classified, with indexes of persons and subjects. Includes books and periodical articles in various European languages.

Continued by: Z3711.H64

el Nasri, Abdel Rahman. A bibliography of the Sudan, 1938–1958. London, publ. on behalf of the University of Khartoum by the Oxford Univ. Pr., 1962. 171p.   **DD185**

A classed bibliography of 2,763 books and periodical articles.   Z3711.N3

Khartum, Jāmi'at al-Khartūm. al-Maktabah. [al-Fihris al-muṣannaf li-majmū'at al-Sūdān] The classified catalogue of the Sudan collection in the University of Khartoum Library. Khartum, 1971. 1v., unpaged.   **DD186**

More than 5,000 entries for books, periodicals, pamphlets, government publications, and newspapers arranged by classification number, with author index. Reputed to be the most comprehensive collection anywhere of printed material about the Sudan.   Z3665.K48

SWAZILAND

Nyeko, Balam. Swaziland. Oxford, Eng. & Santa Barbara, Calif., Clio Pr., [1982]. 135p. map. (World bibliographical ser., 24)   **DD187**

478 entries, with annotations, for English-language books and articles. Topical arrangement; author/title/subject index. Separate list of theses and dissertations.   Z3560.N93

University College of Swaziland. Library. Swaziana: an annotated bibliography of materials relating to Swaziland in the libraries of the University College of Swaziland. Comp. by Thokozile Nkabinde. Kwaluseni, Univ. Coll. of Swaziland, 1978. 45*l.* (Swaziland libs. pubns., no.4)   **DD188**

A classed listing with author/title index.   Z3560.U54

TANZANIA

Darch, Colin. Tanzania. Oxford, Eng. & Santa Barbara, Calif., Clio Pr., [1985]. 316p. map. (World bibliographical ser., 54)   **DD189**

A selective bibliography intended "as an entry point, through the use of which an English-speaking reader can approach the various aspects of national life and culture."—*Pref.* Topical listing, with author, title, subject index. All items—mainly books plus a few articles—are in English; good annotations.

Tanzania annual bibliography, 1965– . (*In* Tanzania notes and records, no.65– , Mar. 1966–) Irregular.   **DD190**

Comp. by B. W. Langlands.

A bibliography of books, articles, government publications, and (since 1974) dissertations. Covers a broad range of materials, including archaeology, botany, demography, etc. Topically arranged without index.

Tanzania notes and records occasionally includes bibliographies such as "A bibliography of Tanganyika, 1959–64: local and tribal studies," by A. Roberts (no.65,1967); "A bibliography of primary sources for Tanzania, 1799–1899 (books only)," by A. Roberts (no.73, 1974); "Islam in Tanzania," by A. H. Nimitz (no.72, 1973).

TUNISIA

Findlay, Allan M., Findlay, Anne M. and **Lawless, Richard I.** Tunisia. Oxford, Eng. & Santa Barbara, Calif., Clio Pr., [1982]. 251p. map. (World bibliographical ser., 33)   **DD191**

"The aim is to provide a range of basic references on all key aspects of that country and its people . . . readily available to readers in the United Kingdom and the USA."—*Pref.* Lists some 895 annotated entries for books and articles, mainly in English. Author, title, and subject indexes. Z3685.2.F55

Tunisia. Maktabah al-Qawmiyah. Bibliographie historique sur la Tunisie 1881–1955; livres se trouvant à la Bibliothèque Nationale, Tunis. Tunis, La Bibliothèque, [197?]. 98*l.* **DD192**

Books, journal and newspaper articles are cited by historical period. Z3685.M35

UGANDA

Collison, Robert Lewis. Uganda. Oxford, Eng. & Santa Barbara, Calif., Clio Pr., [1981]. 159p. (World bibliographical ser., 11) **DD193**

Offers a topical arrangement of citations to some 500 English-language books and articles, with annotations. Brief chronology. Indexed. Z3586.C64

Kleinschmidt, Harald. Amin collection: bibliographical catalogue of materials relevant to the history of Uganda under the military government of Idi Amin Dada. Heidelberg, P. Kivouvou, Ed. Bantoues, [1983]. 107p. **DD194**

Aims to "function as a step into the historical research in the social and political aspects of Uganda under the Amin government and to provide materials apt to connect the 'Amin' period with earlier periods of Ugandan history."—*Pref.* About 1,500 entries arranged by date of publication, 1900–80, with author and subject indexes.

Also useful is M. O. Afolabi's "President Idi Amin Dada of Uganda, a bibliography" in *Current bibliography on African affairs,* v.10, no.4 (1977/78), p.309–27, a partially annotated list of 256 items. Z3586.K57

UPPER VOLTA

See Burkina Faso.

WESTERN SAHARA

Sipe, Lynn F. Western Sahara; a comprehensive bibliography. N.Y., Garland, 1984. 418p. (Garland reference library of social science, 178) **DD195**

"Western Sahara" designates the former Spanish colony of Rio de Oro or Spanish Sahara. A comprehensive bibliography of books and articles in Western European languages published 1884 to early 1983. Topical arrangement. Indexed. Z3933.S57

ZAÏRE

Bibliographies analytiques sur l'Afrique Centrale, no.1– . Bruxelles, CEDAF [Centre d'Étude et de Documentations Africaines], 1978– . Irregular. **DD196**

Contents: no.1, Les périodiques Zaïrois 1970–77; no.2, Les périodiques Congolais 1960–69; no.3, Les périodiques Zaïrois 1970–77, supplément; no.4, L'education en République du Zaïre 1960–1979; no.5, L'économie de la République du Zaïre 1960–1er semestre 1980; no.6, La politique en République du Zaïre 1955–1er semestre 1981.

Nos.1–3 list periodicals published in Zaïre, with tables of contents for each, and with author and subject indexes. Z3517.B5

Heyse, Théodore. Bibliographie du Congo Belge et du Ruanda-Urundi. . . . Bruxelles, van Campenhout, 1946–53. (Cahiers belges et congolais, no.4–7, 9–12, 16–22) **DD197**

Contents: no.4, Géologie et mines (1939–45); no.5, Régime foncier; no.6, Littérature, arts oraux indigènes (1939–47); no.7, Agriculture, élevage, produits et industries agricoles, forêts, chasse, pêche, parcs, flore, et faune (1939–47); no.9, Transports, travaux publics, P.T.T. et radio-diffusion, forces hydro-electriques (1939–48); no.10, Économie générale, industrie et commerce, effort de guerre, banques et finances, matières économiques spéciales, main d'oeuvre (partie non-legislative) (1939–48); no.11, Beaux-arts, urbanisme, arts-indigènes, cinéma (1939–49); no.12, Documentation générale, histoire et expansion belge, biographies, Stanley, articles et ouvrages généraux (1939–49); no.16, Politique générale, politique indigène, enseignement, cultes et missions (1939–50); no.17, Hygiène et assistance sociale, service médical, éthnographie, langues et linguistique, suivi d'un complément à la "Politique indigène" (période antérieure à 1940) (1939–50); no.18, Sciences coloniales: répertoire suivi d'un complément à la "Politique indigène," période antérieure à 1940 (1939–51); no.19, Documentation générale: bibliographies et centres d'études, expositions, presse et propagande; répertoire suivi d'un complément à la "Politique indigène" . . . (1939–51); no.20, Documentation générale: folklore, philatélie, sports, tourisme; répertoire suivi d'un complément à la "Politique indigène" . . . (1939–51); no.21–22, L'Afrique centrale dans le conflit mondiale (1939–51), 2v. (For related volumes in the "Cahiers" series, *see* DC88.)
Continued by: Z3631.H

—— Documentation générale sur le Congo et le Ruanda-Urundi, 1953–60, . . . Bruxelles, van Campenhout, 1956–60. (Cahiers belges et congolais, no.26, 31, 34) **DD198**

Contents: no.26, 1953–55 (also publ. as Bibliographia belgica, no.18); no.31, 1955–58 (also publ. as Bibliographia belgica, no.39); no.34, 1958–60 (also publ. as Bibliographia belgica, no.56).

Bibliographies of documentation on the Congo and Ruanda-Urundi. Z3631.H43

Vellut, Jean Luc. Guide de l'étudiant en histoire du Zaïre. Kinshasa, Éditions du Mont Noir, [1974]. 207p. ([Collection "Objectif 80"], Série "Essais," no.8; Collection cours universitaires, no.1) **DD199**

Chapters surveying archival and printed sources and discussing research methods, etc., are followed by a classed bibliography. Index to the bibliography. Z3631.V4

ZAMBIA

Bliss, Anne M. and **Rigg, J. A.** Zambia. Oxford, Eng., & Santa Barbara, Calif., Clio Pr. [1984]. 233p. (World bibliographical ser., 51) **DD200**

"As well as selecting material that will help the reader to gain a balanced picture of the country, the compilers had another objective—to endeavour to emphasize those subject areas in which potential visitors or travellers are primarily interested [i.e., wildlife, history, and archaeology]."—*Introd.* Topical listing of about 800 annotated entries; subject, author, and title indexes. Z3579.B55

Graham, Ivor M. and **Halwindi, B. C.** Guide to the public archives of Zambia. Lusaka, Nat. Archives of Zambia, 1970. v.1. **DD201**

Contents: v.1, 1895–1940. (No more publ.)

A listing of official records, personal and family documents, etc., giving for each the name of the collection and the dates covered. (v.1 covers from the beginning of colonial rule to 1940, with a few later years included.) Arranged by provenance under regional sections. A promised supplement and index have not appeared.

CD2491.Z3G7

Rau, William E. A bibliography of pre-independence Zambia: the social sciences. Boston, G. K. Hall, [1978]. 357p.
DD202

Books, articles, dissertations, and government publications are listed within the following categories: General reference, Archaeology, Anthropology, Linguistics, Geography, Description and travel, History, Economics, Government and politics, Sociology, Health and medicine, Religion, Education, Wildlife, and Biography. Ethnographic/linguistic groups index, personal and place names in titles index, and author index. Most citations are to English-language materials. Z3579.R38

Williams, Geoffrey J. Independent Zambia; a bibliography of the social sciences, 1964–1979. Boston, G. K. Hall, [1984]. 538p. il., maps. **DD203**

An extensive listing of books, government publications, dissertations, conference proceedings, and book reviews in classified arrangement. "Social sciences" is here interpreted to include art, history, and linguistics as well as more traditional fields. Indexes by author, geographic area, and ethnographic/linguistic groups. Z3579.W54

ZANZIBAR

Bennett, Norman Robert. The Arab state of Zanzibar; a bibliography. Boston, G. K. Hall, [1984]. 231p. **DD204**

The "primary emphasis is on the period from the late eighteenth century through the revolution of January 1964" *(Pref.)*, but the 2,500 publications cited were issued from the 18th century to mid-1984 in Britain, France, Germany, Belgium, Portugal and the United States. Topical arrangement with indexes of persons, places, and subjects. Z3589.B46

ZIMBABWE

Doro, Marion E. Rhodesia/Zimbabwe; a bibliographic guide to the nationalist period. Boston, G. K. Hall, [1984]. 247p. **DD205**

Period of coverage is 1960–80. Lists books, articles, and government publications issued through 1981. Subject index; author index for books only. Z3578.D67

Encyclopaedia Rhodesia. Gen. ed., Mary Akers. [Salisbury, Rhodesia, College Pr., 1973] 445p. il. **DD206**

Offers brief articles "on Rhodesian history, geography, flora and fauna, the way of life of its peoples, law, central Government and various other aspects of Rhodesia." A short bibliography precedes the main text, but bibliographical references are not provided with the articles themselves. DT962.2.E53

National Archives of Rhodesia. Guide to the public archives of Rhodesia. T. W. Baxter, Ed. [Salisbury], Nat. Archives of Rhodesia, 1969– . v.1– . (In progress?) **DD207**

Contents: v.1, 1890–1923 (rev. ed.; 1st ed. 1956).
Arranged by issuing agency, with brief history and general indication of contents and dates of coverage. Indexed.
Guide to the historical manuscripts in the National Archives of Rhodesia, comp. by T. W. Baxter and E. E. Burke (Salisbury, Nat. Archives, 1970. 527p.) lists "diaries, letters, notebooks, reminiscences, maps, and memoranda created by the travellers, the missionaries, the administrators . . . also groups of private archives from family, society or business sources."—*Introd.* CD2432.A45

Pollak, Oliver B. and **Pollak, Karen.** Rhodesia/Zimbabwe: an international bibliography. Boston, G. K. Hall, [1977]. 621p. **DD208**

A comprehensive bibliography "based on searches in over 230 bibliographies which produced over 11,300 citations including monographs, academic theses, essays within books as well as period-

ical literature in over 1,100 journals."—*Introd.* Classed arrangement with author index. Covers anthropology, ethnology, religion, sociology, communications, economics, education, fine arts, geography, history, natural science, political science and international relations. Z3578.P64

D E

Asia

GENERAL WORKS

Guides

Nunn, Godfrey Raymond. Asia: reference works; a select annotated guide. London, Mansell, 1980. 365p. **DE1**

Although based on Nunn's *Asia, a selected and annotated guide* (Cambridge, Mass., 1971), this is virtually a new work, less than a third of the 1,567 titles in the present edition having been retained without change from the earlier publication. Employs a regional/country arrangement, providing annotated listings of encyclopedias, handbooks, yearbooks, dictionaries, directories, atlases, gazetteers, chronologies, statistical sources, and bibliographies within each geographical section. Oriental and Western-language (mainly English) materials are cited. Author/title index. Does not include the Middle East or Central Asia. Z3001.N79

Pearson, James Douglas. Oriental and Asian bibliography; an introduction, with some reference to Africa. London, Lockwood; N.Y., Shoe String, 1966. 261p. **DE2**

A useful guide, developed from notes for courses of lectures in librarianship; intended not as a bibliography of bibliographies in the field, but as "a statement of the position reached in the provision of bibliographical aids up to the Spring of 1965."—*Pref.* In three main parts: (1) the institutions, organizations, etc., producing the literature; (2) bibliographical control of the literature; and (3) the libraries and archives serving as storehouses of the literature, and special problems affecting them. An appendix of booksellers in Asia, and another comprising a bibliography of works referred to in the text. Indexed. Z7046.P4

Bibliography

See also BJ103, DD14.

American Oriental Society. Library. Catalog of the library; ed. by Elizabeth Strout. New Haven, Yale Univ. Pr., 1930. 308p. **DE3**

A list of about 5,500 works. Includes writings, primarily in the western European languages, on all of Asia. Z7050.A51

New York. Public Library. Oriental Division. Dictionary catalog of the Oriental collection. Boston, G. K. Hall, 1960. 16v. (Also available on microfilm) **DE4**

A catalog of books, serials, and some periodical articles in Eastern languages (including Arabic) and materials in Western languages concerning any part of Asia.

—— —— First supplement. Boston, G. K. Hall, 1976. 8v.

Adds materials cataloged 1961–71, after which time Oriental materials are included in the *Dictionary catalog of the Research Libraries* (AA147).

Orientalische Bibliographie, 1887–1911, 1926, pt.1. Berlin, Reuther, 1888–1922, 1928. v.1–26. (Repr.: München, Kraus, 1980) **DE5**

No more published.

An important annual bibliography, including books, pamphlets, periodical articles, and reviews in the whole field of Oriental studies: language, literature, geography, ethnology, folklore, history, etc.

For material before 1887, the following should be consulted: Julius Theodor Zenker's *Bibliotheca orientalis,* 1846–61; *Wissenschaftlicher Jahresbericht über die morgenländischen Studien,* 1859–81; Karl Friederici's *Bibliotheca orientalis,* 1876–83; and *Litteraturblatt für orientalische Philologie,* 1883–86. Z7046.O7

Union catalogue of Asian publications, 1965–1970. Ed. by David E. Hall. London, Mansell, 1971. 4v. **DE6**

"Compiled under the auspices of the Orientalists' Group, Standing Conference of National and University Libraries; sponsored by and edited at the School of Oriental and African Studies, University of London."—*t. p.*

Records Asian publications acquired by British libraries (except the Bodleian Library and the library of the School of Oriental and African Studies which publishes its own catalog) since the beginning of 1965. Thus it includes numerous early imprints as well as recent publications. "The term 'Asian Publications' refers to works published in all languages in Asia outside the Soviet Union, and to those published in non-European scripts in North and North-East Africa."—*Pref.* Periodicals are not included, nor are works in pure science. Annual supplements were planned, but only one appeared: Z3009.U53

—— Supplement, 1971. London, Mansell, 1973. 704p.

Records new accessions in the libraries previously reporting, and also "includes for the first time many entries from the School of Oriental and African Studies and the first entries from the Bodleian Library." The editors suggest that the user begin his search with the supplementary volume, because errors and omissions are rectified therein and entries are repeated for items showing additional locations.

For older materials the *Catalogue of printed books published before 1932 in the library* of the Royal Asiatic Society of Great Britain and Ireland (London, 1940. 541p.) is occasionally useful.

Current

Asien-Bibliographie. Jahrg.1– , Sept./Dez. 1949– . Frankenau/Hessen, Asien-Bücherei, 1949– . Quarterly. **DE7**

Lists new publications in the German language on all parts of Asia, plus some materials on North Africa, and Oceania. Some entries are annotated. Includes periodical articles. *Bibliographia asiatica,* published by Asien-Bücherei in Frankenau, Hesse, 1953–77, has now merged into *Asien-Bibliographie.* Z3001.A84

Bibliography of Asian studies. 1956– . (*In* Journal of Asian studies, Sept. 1957–) Annual. **DE8**

Formerly entitled "Far Eastern bibliography," appearing in the *Far Eastern quarterly,* 1936–55 (title varies slightly).

An extensive, classified listing of books, pamphlets, and periodical articles on all phases of life and culture in Asia, in the English language. Coverage varies. Earlier volumes treated East and Southeast Asia, but, beginning with 1956, coverage was extended to include also South and Central Asia, the Philippines, etc. Z3001.B49

Cumulative bibliography of Asian studies, 1941–1965. Author bibliography. Boston, G. K. Hall, [1969]. 4v. **DE9**

—— Subject bibliography. Boston, G. K. Hall, [1970]. 4v.

These two catalogs cumulate the entries from the *Bibliography of Asian studies* and its predecessors. The subject part follows the same general arrangement as the original bibliographies.

—— [Supplement] 1966–1970. Author bibliography; Subject bibliography. Boston, G. K. Hall, 1972–73. 6v.

Z3001.C93

Dissertations

Bloomfield, Barry Cambray. Theses on Asia; accepted by universities in the United Kingdom and Ireland, 1877–1964. London, Cass, 1967. 127p. **DE10**

2,571 theses. The main listing is geographical, with appropriate subdivisions. Author index. Z3001.B56

Grunendahl, Reinhold. Hochschulschriften zu Süd- und Südostasien: Deutschland, Österreich, Schweiz (1959–1979). Wiesbaden, Harrassowitz, 1981. 254p. **DE11**

A bibliography of some 1,352 dissertations and *Habilitationsgeschichte.* Topical arrangement within country divisions. Name and subject indexes. Z3185.G78

Stucki, Curtis W. American doctoral dissertations on Asia, 1933–June 1966; including appendix of master's theses at Cornell University, 1933–June 1968. Ithaca, N.Y., Cornell Univ., Dept. of Asian Studies, Southeast Asia Program, 1968. 304p. (Cornell Southeast Asia Program. Data paper no.71) **DE12**

An earlier list covering 1933–62 was published 1963.

Includes the Far East, the Philippines, South Asia, and the Pacific Islands. Classified by region, by country, and by academic discipline; attempts to cover all doctoral studies in the fields of social sciences and humanities. Author index.

Partially updated by listings in the Association for Asian Studies *Newsletter,* 1969 and 1971, the *Asian studies professional review,* Fall 1971–Spr. 1974, and Frank J. Shulman's *Doctoral dissertations on Asia, 1975–1976/77* (Ann Arbor, Mich., UMI for the Assoc. for Asian Studies, 1975–77). Z3001.S72

Historiography

London. University. School of Oriental and African Studies. Historical writing on the peoples of Asia. London, Oxford Univ. Pr., 1961–62. 4v. **DE13**

Contents: D. G. E. Hall. Historians of South East Asia; W. G. Beasley and E. G. Pulleyblank. Historians of China and Japan; C. H. Philips. Historians of India, Pakistan and Ceylon; Bernard Lewis and P. M. Holt. Historians of the Middle East. DS32.5.L6

Library resources (including archives)

Asia and Oceania, a guide to archival & manuscript sources in the United States. G. Raymond Nunn, ed. London, Mansell, 1985. 5v. **DE14**

A major finding aid for manuscripts and archival collections in the United States. Covers from Afghanistan to the Pacific (including Turkey and Persia, but not the rest of the Middle East), the Pacific Islands (excluding Hawaii and Australia, and material relating to overseas Asians and Pacific Islanders). Excludes major manuscript collections in East Asian, Turkish, and Persian languages. Arrangement is by state and city, then by name of repository (with address, hours, restrictions, etc.). Descriptions of collections (some given in much detail) include type, size, dates, guides or finding aids, NUCMC listing if any, and content. Extensive index in v.5. Might be considered the United States volume in the *Guides to the sources for the history of nations* series (DE16).   Z3001.A78

Collison, Robert Lewis. Directory of libraries and special collections on Asia and North Africa. Hamden, Conn., Archon Books, [1970]. 123p.   **DE15**

At head of title: SCONUL [Standing Conference of National and University Libraries] Sub-Committee of Orientalist Libraries.

Briefly describes pertinent collections in the libraries of Britain.

Z3001.C583

Guides to the sources for the history of the nations: 3d series, North Africa, Asia and Oceania. München, Saur; Detroit, Gale, 1972–84. v.1–6. (In progress)   **DE16**

Publisher varies; [v.1] publ. Brussels, Archives Générales.

Contents: [v.1] Guide des sources de l'histoire . . . conservées en Belgique, comp. E. Vandewoude et A. Vanrie; v.2, Sources . . . dans les archives et bibliothèques françaises (2v.); v.3, Sources . . . in Finland, Norway and Sweden (2v.); [v.4–5] Guide to the sources in the Netherlands concerning the history of Asia and Oceania 1796–1949 (2v.; also available on microfiche); v.6, Quellen zur Geschichte Nordafrikas, Asiens und Ozeaniens in der Bundesrepublik Deutschland bis 1945, ed. Ernst Ritter.

Offers inventories of archive and manuscript collections dealing with North Africa, Asia (including the Middle East), and Oceania. For the United States volume in the series *see* DE14.

Wainwright, M. D. and **Matthews, Noel.** A guide to Western manuscripts and documents in the British Isles relating to South and South East Asia. London, Oxford Univ. Pr., 1965. 532p.   **DE17**

Lists, by depository, collections of manuscripts in all subject groups: history, literature, sciences, social sciences, and humanities. Includes some private collections, but collections of the India Office Library are excluded. Index of names and subjects.

CD1048.A8W3

Yang, Winston L. Y. and **Yang, Teresa S.,** eds. Asian resources in American libraries; essays and bibliographies. N.Y., [Foreign Area Materials Center, Univ. of the State of New York], 1968. 122p. (Univ. of the State of N.Y., Foreign Area Materials Center. Occasional pubn., 9)   **DE18**

A bibliographical guide to published information on library resources and a directory of Asian library resources and area study programs in the United States make up more than half the volume.

Dictionaries, encyclopedias, and handbooks

Association for Asian Studies, Mid-Atlantic Region. Committee on Academic Resources. Mid-Atlantic directory to resources for Asian studies. Archie R. Crouch, ed. [Wash.], The Assoc., 1980. 145p.   **DE19**

An aid to locating "background information concerning peoples and nations of Asia."—*Introd.* Lists organizations (including ethnic organizations); colleges, universities, and academic associations; embassies, missions, consulates, etc.; libraries and information services; museums, galleries and places to visit; sources for curriculum development; bookstores and book publishers. Directory-type information; name and title indexes. (The Mid-Atlantic region covers Delaware, District of Columbia, Maryland, New Jersey, Pennsylvania, and New York south of Poughkeepsie.)

DS32.9.U5A87

Historical and cultural dictionaries of Asia. Metuchen, N.J., Scarecrow Pr., 1972–76. no.1–9. (In progress)   **DE20**

Contents: no.1, Saudi Arabia, by Carroll L. Riley (1972. 139p.);

no.2, Nepal, by Basil C. Hedrick and Anne K. Hedrick (1972. 205p.); no.3, Philippines, by Ester G. Maring and Joel M. Maring (1973. 240p.); no.4, Burma, by Joel M. Maring and Ester G. Maring (1973. 296p.); no.5, Afghanistan, by M. Jamil Hanifi (1976. 149p.); no.6, Thailand, by Harold E. Smith (1976. 219p.); no.7, Vietnam, by Danny J. Whitfield (1976. 377p.); no.8, India, by George T. Kurian (1976. 329p.); no.9, Sultanate of Oman and the Emirates of Eastern Arabia, by J. D. Anthony [et al.] (1976. 144p.).

Following a brief survey of the history and economics of the country, each dictionary is an alphabetical arrangement of entries for personal names and topical subjects. Most volumes end with a selective bibliography.

Louis-Frédéric. Encyclopaedia of Asian civilizations. [Villecresnes, France], Louis-Frédéric, [1977–84]. 10v. (distr. in U.S. by Cheng & Tsui Co., Cambridge, Mass.)   **DE21**

Introductory matter in English and French.

Intended as "a practical and multidisciplinary reference work" (*Introd.*) on the various civilizations of Asia. Oriental names, terms, etc., have been romanized and are entered in a single alphabet. Includes entries for personal and place names; terms in literature, art and religion; titles of written works; historical events, etc. Each entry is identified according to the culture from which it derives. Numerous cross references. v.10 includes corrigenda and presumably completes the set.   DS4.L68

McLane, Charles B. Soviet-Asian relations. London, Central Asian Research Centre; distr. by Columbia Univ. Pr., 1973. 150p. (Soviet–Third world relations, v.2)   **DE22**

"The present volume deals with Soviet relations with 14 developing nations in Asia stretching from Afghanistan to the Philippines." —*Pref.* The data, presented in three columns—political, economic, cultural—are drawn primarily from Soviet sources and are arranged chronologically. List of references for each country section.

For companion volumes on African and Middle East relations *see* DD99, DE68.   DK68.M15

Miliband, Sofiia Davidovna. Biobibliograficheskii slovar' sovetskikh vostokovedov. Moskva, Nauka, 1975. 732p.   **DE23**

A biographical dictionary of more than 1,450 Soviet orientalists alive at time of publication. Brief biographical information with emphasis on career; extensive bibliography of works by and about the scholar. Geographic index.

Wint, Guy. Asia; a handbook. N.Y., Praeger, [1966]. 856p.   **DE24**

A revised and abridged edition was published (Harmondsworth, Penguin, 1969. 735p.).

Contains chapters by specialists on a wide range of topics relative to the political, economic, social, and cultural affairs of this vast region in general, and of the individual countries in particular. Includes brief bibliographies, a detailed index, and an appendix of texts of postwar treaties and agreements.

A similar work is *The nations of Asia* by Donald N. Wilbur (N.Y., Hart, 1966).   DS5.W5

Current surveys

Asian recorder; a weekly digest of outstanding Asian events. v.1– , Jan.1/7, 1955– . New Delhi, K. K. Thomas at Recorder Pr., 1955– . Weekly.   **DE25**

Publisher varies.

A specimen copy entitled *Asian archives* was issued Sept.26/Oct. 3, 1954.

Arranged by country, each issue giving a summary of events occurring during the previous week. Source of information (newspaper, periodical, radio broadcast, etc.) is given. Quarterly indexes cumulate annually; indexing is under 33 broad subject headings.

DS1.A4747

NEAR AND MIDDLE EAST

See also Africa, Northern.

Guides

Arab Islamic bibliography; the Middle East Library Committee guide. Ed. by Diana Grimwood-Jones, Derek Hopwood, J. D. Pearson. [Hassocks, Eng.], Harvester Pr.; [Atlantic Highlands, N.J.], Humanities Pr., [1977]. 292p.
DE26

"Based on Giuseppe Gabrieli's *Manuale di bibliografia musulmana* [1916]."—*t.p.*
Offered as a "new guide to reference materials for Islamic studies along the same lines as Gabrieli's work, retaining or referring to all that remains useful in the original publication and supplementing this with information on what has been contributed by scholars, librarians, bibliographers and others since the publication of the *Manuale.*" —*Foreword.* Sections contributed by scholars and librarians on bibliographies, encyclopedias and reference works, Arabic grammars, genealogy and biographical dictionaries, press and periodicals, maps and atlases, geographical names, *Festschriften,* scientific expeditions, institutions, manuscripts, archives, epigraphy, numismatics, printing and book production, libraries. Index of authors and anonymous titles. Does not include Persia or Iran.
Z3013.A66

Middle East and Islam: a bibliographical introduction. Rev. & enl. ed., ed. by Diana Grimwood-Jones. Zug, Switz., Inter Documentation, [1979]. 429p. (Bibliotheca asiatica, 15)
DE27

At head of title: Middle East Libraries Committee.
1st ed. 1972.
A cooperative effort, with sections on individual topics (e.g., Islamic history, Islamic law, Anthropology, Political science) contributed by scholars and librarians.
"The pattern of the volume is substantially the same as the first edition, though the range of subjects has been broadened considerably, and thus some papers, e.g. Islamic Philosophy, Islamic Theology, Oil, Berber Studies are completely new."—*Introd.*
Z3013.M48

Sauvaget, Jean. Introduction to the history of the Muslim East: a bibliographical guide. Based on the 2d ed. as recast by Claude Cahen. Berkeley, Univ. of California Pr., 1965. 252p. (Repr.: Westport, Conn., Greenwood Pr., 1982)
DE28

Not merely an English translation of Cahen's 1961 revision of the French text, but actually a new edition incorporating changes, corrections, and new materials. A scholarly and useful bibliographic survey.
Z3013.S314

Simon, Reeva S. The modern Middle East; a guide to research tools in the social sciences. Boulder, Colo., Westview Pr., [1978]. 283p.
DE29

Intended as a working, selective handbook for students, scholars, librarians, specialists and non-specialists doing research on the Middle East of the 19th and 20th centuries. Arrangement is by type of reference material (e.g., bibliography of bibliography, printed library catalogs, current bibliography) within five main divisions: (1) Bibliography, (2) Periodicals, (3) Primary source material, (4) Reference sources, (5) Report literature. Annotated. Author, title, subject index.
Z3013.S55

The study of the Middle East: research and scholarship in the humanities and the social sciences. Ed. by Leonard Binder. N.Y., Wiley, [1976]. 648p.
DE30

"A project of the Research and Training Committee of the Middle East Studies Association."—*t.p.*
Each chapter is a bibliographic survey and assessment of research and scholarship on an aspect of Middle Eastern studies. Each essay by a different scholar or team of scholars. Chapters on: Area studies;

Islamic religious tradition; History; Anthropology; Islamic art and archaeology; Political science; Philosophy; Linguistics; Literature; Sociology; and Economics. Separate author and subject indexes.
DS61.8.S78

Bibliography

Anderson, Margaret. Arabic materials in English translation: a bibliography of works from the pre-Islamic period to 1977. Boston, G. K. Hall, [1980]. 249p.
DE31

A classed listing with sections for Islamic studies, philosophy, music, history of science, history, geography, social sciences, and Arabic literature. Brief descriptive annotations for many items. Indexed.
Z3014.L56A52

Articles on the Middle East, 1947–1971: a cumulation of the bibliographies from the *Middle East journal.* Peter N. Rossi and Wayne E. White, eds. Ann Arbor, Mich., Pierian Pr., 1980. 4v. (1646p.)
DE32

"Reproduced from original bibliographies and items appear as they did in the pages of the journal."—*Foreword.*
Covers the Muslim world from Morocco to Pakistan (with Palestine and Israel added since 1964). Emphasis is on modern history, politics, social conditions, language and literature from the late 18th century to the present. Broad topical arrangement; separate section for book reviews. Includes materials in all European and Middle Eastern languages. Annotations. Indexes in v.4.
Z3013.A76

Atiyeh, George Nicholas. The contemporary Middle East, 1948–1973; a selective and annotated bibliography. Boston, G. K. Hall, [1975]. 664p.
DE33

A classed bibliography with author and subject indexes. Emphasis is on the social sciences. Materials are mainly in English, French, German, Italian and Spanish, with some works in Arabic, Turkish and Persian included "either because they represent new trends in their fields or because they complete the coverage of topics that otherwise would not be well represented."—*Introd.* Nearly 6,500 items. Intended for the student and beginning researcher.
Z3013.A85

Banuazizi, Ali. Social stratification in the Middle East and North Africa; a bibliographic survey. London, Mansell, [1984]. 248p.
DE34

Goes beyond social stratification and inequality to include related areas of social history, geography, and anthropology. Covers Afghanistan to Morocco. Includes 19th century to contemporary times in order to demonstrate social continuities. About 2,000 books, essays, dissertations, research reports and periodical articles in English and French, published 1946–82. Geographical arrangement; author and subject indexes.
Z7165.N35B36

Beirut. Université Saint-Joseph. Centre d'Études pour le Monde Arabe Moderne. Arab culture and society in change, a partially annotated bibliography of books and articles in English, French, German and Italian, comp. by the staff of CEMAM ("Centre d'Études pour le Monde Arabe Moderne"). . . . Beirut, Dar el-Mashreq Publ., [1973]. 318p.
DE35

Lists books and articles dealing with the Arab countries of the Middle East and North Africa in their contacts with "Western" culture from the period of the First World War to the present. Topical arrangement with indexes by authors, persons, regions, and broad subjects.
Z3013.B43

Bevis, Richard W. Bibliotheca cisorientalia; an annotated checklist of early English travel books on the Near and Middle East. Boston, G. K. Hall, 1973. 317p.
DE36

Provides " a reasonably complete checklist of books reporting at first hand on the Mideast after the Moslem conquest, published in English before 1915."—*Introd.* Author listing within five sections: English language travel books; Translations into English; Collections; Biography, criticism and scholarship; Bibliography. Most entries are briefly annotated; library locations are indicated.

Z3013.B47

Bibliographie de la culture arabe contemporaine. Sous la direction de Jacques Berque. [Paris], Sindbad/Presses de l'Unesco, [1981]. 483p. **DE37**

A classified, partially annotated bibliography on various aspects of contemporary Arabic culture, including the social, political, historical and religious background. Arabic titles are given in transliteration in the body of the work, but there are author and title indexes in Arabic as well as a general index of names. Annotations in French or English. Z3013.B49

Bolton, Alexander Rollo Colin. Soviet Middle East studies: an analysis and bibliography. Oxford, distr. for the Royal Institute of International Affairs by the Oxford Univ. Pr., 1959. 8 pts. in 1v. (Chatham House memoranda) **DE38**

Contents: 1, Introduction and general indexes; 2, Arabs and the Arab world; 3, The Arabian peninsula; 4, Egypt; 5, Iraq; 6, Palestine (Israel) and Jordan; 7, The Sudan; 8, Syria and Lebanon.

Annotated listings of both book and periodical materials.

Z3013.B6

Bryson, Thomas A. United States/Middle East diplomatic relations, 1784–1978; an annotated bibliography. Metuchen, N.J., Scarecrow Pr., 1979. 205p. **DE39**

About 1,350 English-language items—books, periodical articles, documents, and dissertations. Arrangement is mainly chronological, with separate sections for general materials and for dissertations. Author index. Z3014.R44B79

Cairo. Dar al-Katub al-Misriyah. Bibliographical lists of the Arab world. Cairo, Nat. Lib. Pr., 1960–65. no.1–10.
DE40

Contents: 1, Algeria (2d ed. 1963); 2, Palestine and Jordan (2d ed. 1964); 3, Syria (2d ed. 1965); 4, Lebanon (1960); 5, Iraq (1960); 6, Sudan (1961); 7, al-Maghrib (1961); 8, Tunisia (1961); 9, Libya (1961); 10, Arabian peninsula (1963).

Each number lists 19th and 20th-century works in various languages. Title, headings, etc., in English and Arabic.

Clements, Frank, comp. The emergence of Arab nationalism from the nineteenth century to 1921. [London], Diploma Pr., [1976]; Wilmington, Del., Scholarly Resources Inc., 1977. 289p. **DE41**

An annotated bibliography of books, periodical articles, and pamphlets. In three main sections: (1) The struggle between the Arabs and Turks; (2) The peace settlement and its consequences; (3) The fertile crescent under the mandate system. Extensive annotations; index.

Ellis, Richard S. A bibliography of Mesopotamian archaeological sites. Wiesbaden, Harrassowitz, 1972. 113p.
DE42

Limited to pre-Islamic sites in Iraq "and those sites in Syria and Turkey that show typically Mesopotamian culture."—*Introd.* Lists publications relating to each site. Z3039.A8E5

Groot, Alexander H. de. A bibliography of Dutch publications on the Middle East and Islam 1945–1981. Nijmegen, Nederlandse Vereniging voor de Studie van het Midden-Osten en de Islam, 1981. 80p. **DE42a**

1st ed. 1976.

Aims to provide "a representative listing of all the various currents of research undertaken in the Netherlands at the present time" (*Pref.*) on the Arab world, including studies on the European parts of Turkey, the Ottoman Empire, and Afghanistan. Broad topical arrangement; author index.

Hussain, Asaf. Islamic movements in Egypt, Pakistan and Iran; an annotated bibliography. [London], Mansell, [1983]. 168p. **DE43**

Designed to examine the political role of Islamic movements in

the countries mentioned by providing an annotated listing of books and journal articles (mainly in English). Country arrangement; annotations intend to "bring out the essential points of the article or book and in many cases the viewpoint of the authors."—*Introd.* Author index. Z7835.M6H9

Littlefield, David W. The Islamic Near East and North Africa; an annotated guide to books in English for non-specialists. Littleton, Colo., Libraries Unlimited, 1977. 375p. **DE44**

A guide for the general reader and the librarian. Some 1,166 numbered items are fully annotated as a basic collection for the field. Additional, supplementary items are noted in the annotations. Separate author, title, and subject indexes. Z3013.L653

McClintock, Marsha Hamilton. The Middle East and North Africa on film; an annotated filmography. N.Y., Garland, 1982. 542p. (Garland reference library of the humanities, v.159) **DE45**

A listing of films and videotapes produced between 1903 and Jan. 1980; limited to "English, English sub-titled and silent films in 8, super 8, 16 and 33mm and tapes in ½, ¾ and 2 inch formats."—*Introd.* Geographical arrangement, with country divisions subdivided topically. Title/series index and distributor/location index. Gives full information for each film, together with brief annotation and location. DS44.M43

Meiseles, Gustav. Reference literature to Arabic studies; a bibliographical guide. Tel-Aviv, University Publishing Project, [1978]. 251p. **DE46**

A classed listing of reference sources for Arabic studies (in the broad sense), and making a special point of including both Western-language and Arabic materials. Z3013.M4313

The Middle East in conflict; a historical bibliography. Santa Barbara, Calif., ABC-Clio, [1985]. 302p. (Clio bibliography ser., 19) **DE47**

A topical/geographical arrangement of entries drawn from *Historical abstracts* (DA19), 1973–82. Covers Pakistan to Morocco and the Western Sahara in the 20th century. Subject and author indexes.

DS62.4.M53

Olson, William J. Britain's elusive empire in the Middle East, 1900–1921; an annotated bibliography. N.Y., Garland, 1982. 404p. (Themes in European expansion, exploration and the impact of empire, v.2; Garland reference library of social science, v.109) **DE48**

Covers "British policy in the Middle East from 1900 to 1921, beginning roughly with the Baghdad Railway Concession to the Germans, and ending with the Cairo Conference which set out the main features of Britain's post-war policy in the area."—*Pref.* Cites monographs, articles, and book reviews (mainly post-1950 publications) in topical arrangement. Annotations; cross references; index.

Z3014.R44O47

Patai, Raphael. Jordan, Lebanon and Syria: an annotated bibliography. New Haven, Conn., Human Relations Area Files, 1957. 289p. (Behavior science bibliographies)
DE49

Includes books and articles, with (1) a section on the area generally, followed by (2) a section on each of the three countries.

Z3013.P3

Weber, Shirley Howard. Voyages and travels in the Near East made during the XIX century; being a part of a larger catalogue of works on geography, cartography, voyages, and travels, in the Gennadius Library in Athens. Princeton, N.J., Amer. School of Classical Studies at Athens, 1952. 252p. (Catalogues of the Gennadius Library, I) **DE50**

The Gennadius Library is a rich and unique collection of more than 55,000 books, pictures, and maps relating to Greece, the Balkans, and the Near East from medieval to modern times. Contains 1,206 annotated titles, representing only a portion of the material on geography and travel in the Library. The titles are entered by date of publication; a general index and a name index of travelers and authors are given at the end of the volume.

Z3013.W4

────── Voyages and travels in Greece, the Near East and adjacent regions made previous to the year 1801. Princeton, Amer. School of Classical Studies at Athens, 1953. 208p. (Catalogues of the Gennadius Library, II) **DE51**

Subtitle: Being a part of a larger catalogue of works on geography, cartography, voyages and travels, in the Gennadius Library in Athens.

A companion to the above, covering from the first century to 1801. Lists travel accounts, voyages, descriptive and topographic works, and guide books of Greek Orthodox pilgrims; appendix of works which are mainly pictorial. Indexed. Z6016.L6W4

The world of Islam, images and echoes: a critical guide to films and recordings. Ellen-Fairbanks Bodman, gen. ed. N.Y., Amer. Council of Learned Societies, [1980]. 208p. **DE52**

Lists about 500 16mm. films and audio recordings concerning "those countries and areas whose history and culture, and daily life were and are influenced by Islam . . . [which] stretches from West Africa to the Philippines."—*Foreword.* Recordings and films are listed by title in separate sections; geographical index for each section. DS35.6.W67

Zoghby, Samir M. Arab-African relations, 1973–1975; a guide. Wash., 1976. 26p. **DE53**

For full citation and annotation *see* DD88.

Current

The Middle East: abstracts and index. v.1, no.1– , Mar. 1978– . Pittsburgh, Library Information and Research Service, 1978– . Quarterly. **DE54**

Amy C. Lowenstein, ed.

Offers citations, with abstracts, of English-language materials in the humanities and social sciences relating to countries of the Middle East. A section of general materials applicable to the entire area is followed by one on the Arab-Israeli conflict and another on the "Arab World"; then follow sections on individual countries. Within sections the materials are grouped by type: journal articles (drawn from a wide range of periodicals), editorials, government documents, interviews, NTIS documents, speeches and statements, doctoral dissertations, reprints, statistics, books and reviews. Each issue has author and subject indexes which cumulate annually in the December issue.

Mideast file. v.1, no.1– , Mar. 1982– . Oxford, Eng. & [Medford], N.J., Learned Information, 1982– . Quarterly. **DE55**

Issued by the Shiloah Center, Dept. of Middle Eastern and African History, Tel-Aviv University.

An index to books, book reviews, scholarly periodical articles, important newspaper articles, government publications, and research reports from institutions and corporations. Covers the Mideast between Iran and Libya, Turkey and Sudan; regional or country arrangement; emphasis on social sciences and religion. Author and subject indexes. DS42.4.M53

Library catalogs

Chicago. University. Library. Catalog of the Middle Eastern Collection [formerly the Oriental Institute Library]. Boston, G. K. Hall, 1970–77. 16v. and Suppl. 1. **DE56**

The library aims "to collect all useful printed material on every aspect of the Near East" (*Pref.*) and is especially strong in materials on the ancient Near East and medieval Islam. Dictionary arrangement. Includes books, periodical articles, periodicals and series, pamphlets, and book reviews. The supplement is a main entry catalog of recently added materials relating to all aspects of the

Middle East, plus works written in the Arabic, Persian, and Turkish languages regardless of subject. (The library has been integrated into the Regenstein Library, although the catalog remains separate.)

Z3013.C43

Harvard University. Library. Catalog of the Arabic collection. Fawzi Abdulrazak, ed. [2d ed.] Boston, G. K. Hall, 1983. 6v. **DE57**

1st ed. 1968 comprised v.1–3 of the Library's *Catalogue of Arabic, Persian, and Ottoman Turkish books.*

Photoreproduction of 90,000 catalog cards for books and journals in Arabic from the 17th century to the present. Z3015.H37

Middle East Institute, Washington, D.C. Library. Catalog. . . . Boston, G. K. Hall, 1984. 4v. **DE58**

Contents: v.1–2, Author/title; v.3–4, Subject.

Reproduction of the catalog cards of the George Camp Keiser Library at the Middle East Institute. "The strength of the collection at present lies mainly in Western language works emphasizing history and politics of the Middle East, Islamic studies, economics and nineteenth century travel accounts."—*Introd.* In addition to the cataloged books and journals, in-process material to the end of 1983 is included without subject entries. Separate author/title lists for Arabic, Turkish, Farsi, and Hebrew at the end of v.2.

U.S. Library of Congress Office, Cairo. Accessions list, Middle East. v.1– , Jan. 1963– . Cairo, The Office, 1963– . Bimonthly. **DE59**

Frequency varies; issuing agency varies. v.1–12,no.5/6 (Jan. 1963–May/June 1974) available on microfiche from the Library of Congress Office, New Delhi.

Lists publications, both commercial and government, acquired by the Office from any of the Arab world countries (except Djibouti, Somalia and Sudan which are covered in the East Africa list, DD87), for distribution to participants in the PL480 program. Alphabetical arrangement until 1983; now a country listing with separate lists of monographs and serials. Annual author/title index published as a supplement to the Nov./Dec. issue; cumulative serials list issued annually in the July/Aug. number. Beginning Sept. 1982, availability of selected items on microfiche through Library of Congress is noted. Z3013.U54

Utah. University. Middle East Library. Arabic collection, Aziz S. Atiya Library for Middle East Studies. Salt Lake City, Univ. of Utah Pr., 1968. 841p. (Catalog ser., v.1) **DE60**

────── ────── Supplement 1–2. Salt Lake City, 1971–79. 2v.

Catalog of a collection acquired since 1959 by judicious purchase of books, periodicals, and microfilms. Particularly useful for the librarian who does not know Arabic, because the work includes transliterated author and title indexes. The supplements include materials cataloged through 1976. Z3013.U76

Dissertations

Dix ans de recherche universitaire française sur le monde arabe et islamique, de 1968–69 à 1979. Paris, publié avec le concours du ministère [sic] de l'Education Nationale et du ministère [sic] des Relations Extérieures [par] Editions Recherche sur les Civilisations, 1982. 438p. **DE60a**

Almost 6,000 dissertations accepted by French universities concerning the Islamic world are topically arranged within broad geographic divisions: e.g., Monde arabe contemporain, Maghreb contemporain, Monde turc. Index of thesis advisors only. Brief bibliography and directory of major sources in France.

Z3013.D59

Selim, George Dimitri. American doctoral dissertations on the Arab world, 1883–1974. 2d ed. Wash., Lib. of Congress, 1976. 173p. **DE61**

1st ed. 1970.
Lists 1,825 dissertations. Z3013.S43

—— —— Supplement, 1975–1981. Wash., Lib. of Congress, 1983. 200p. **DE62**

Lists United States and Canadian dissertations accepted 1975–81, together with some pre-1975 items not previously reported.

Sluglett, Peter. Theses on Islam, the Middle East and North-West Africa, 1880–1978, accepted by universities in the United Kingdom and Ireland. [London], Mansell, [1983]. 147p. **DE63**

A classed listing of more than 3,000 theses at both the master's and doctoral level. Sections on Islamic studies, Islam outside the Middle East and Northwest Africa, Arabic studies, and Christianity in the Middle East and North Africa precede the geographical sections (including Cyprus and Malta) with their topical subdivisions. Author index. Z3013.S57

Historiography

Rosenthal, Franz. History of Muslim historiography. 2d rev. ed. Leiden, Brill, 1968. 656p. **DE63a**

1st ed. 1952.
A comprehensive history and discussion of historical writing among the Muslim peoples. Includes translations of Muslim texts on historiography (al-Kafiyaji, as-Sahawi, Tasköprüzadeh).
D198.2.R67

Library resources (including archives)

See also DE16.

Dorr, Steven R. Scholars' guide to Washington, D.C. for Middle Eastern studies: Egypt, Sudan, Jordan, Lebanon, Syria, Iraq, the Arabian peninsula, Israel, Turkey, Iran. Wash., Smithsonian Inst. Pr., 1981. 540p. (Scholars' guide to Wash., D.C., no.7) **DE64**

Another in the series of guides sponsored by the Woodrow Wilson International Center for Scholars. Lists and describes collections, research facilities, services, etc., available in libraries, archives, museums, research centers, and organizations concerned with the Middle East in the Washington, D.C. area. Z3013.6.D67

Matthews, Noel and **Wainwright, M. Doreen.** A guide to manuscripts and documents in the British Isles relating to the Middle East and North Africa. Ed. by J. D. Pearson. Oxford, Oxford Univ. Pr., 1980. 482p. **DE65**

A guide to collections of Western-language manuscripts and documents in United Kingdom repositories. "The area covered here encompasses the Arab countries of the Middle East and North Africa, Israel, Cyprus, Turkey, Iran and certain regions of the Caucasus, Central Asia and the Crimea."—*Pref.* Briefly describes the collections and lists important documents in each. Detailed index.

A companion to the volumes surveying British manuscript collections relating to South and South East Asia (DE17), Africa (DD96) and the Far East (DE129). CD1048.N4M37

Netton, Ian Richard. Middle East materials in United Kingdom and Irish libraries: a directory. London, Lib. Assoc., publ. in assoc. with the Centre for Arab Gulf Studies, Univ. of Exeter, [1983]. 136p. **DE66**

"A MELCOM [Middle East Libraries Committee] guide to libraries and other institutions in Britain and Ireland with Islamic and Middle Eastern books and materials."—*t.p.*

Indicates hours of opening, terms of access, etc., as well as providing brief descriptions of holdings. Bibliography of catalogs and directories cited in the text; index. Z3013.6.N47

Dictionaries, handbooks, and surveys

Bacharach, Jere L. A Middle East studies handbook. Seattle, Univ. of Washington Pr., [1984]. 160p. il., maps. **DE67**

1st ed. 1974 (rev. 1976) entitled *A Near East studies handbook.*
A useful handbook which aims to bring together pertinent information for the beginner. Includes discussion of problems of converting dates and of transliteration, lists of standard abbreviations for periodicals and reference works, tables of dynasties, rulers, etc. Lengthy chronology; historical atlas. Indexed. DS61.B3

McLane, Charles B. Soviet-Middle East relations. London, Central Asian Research Centre; distr. by Columbia Univ. Pr., 1973. 126p. (Soviet-Third world relations, v.1) **DE68**

Provides an overview of Soviet relations with 16 countries in the Middle East and North Africa (including Cyprus, but not Afghanistan and Sudan) by giving for each country an introductory account followed by a chronology. Each chronology lists in parallel columns political, economic, and cultural events (e.g., diplomatic agreements and exchanges, major credit and technical assistance agreements, exchange of economic and cultural delegations and, to a lesser extent, trade union and professional exchanges) through 1970. Bibliography, p.123–26. No index.

For companion volumes on Asian and African relations *see* DD99, DE22. DS63.2.R9M3

Middle East contemporary survey, 1976/77– . N.Y., Holmes & Meier, 1978– . Annual. **DE69**

Colin Legum, ed.
Each annual volume comprises a series of essays by scholars from the United States, Great Britain, and Israel "which study developments relating to internal and external issues, both regionally and internationally," (e.g., "The Red Sea in the Arab/African context," "The Soviet bloc and the Middle East") followed by "a country-by-country survey of each of the Middle East entities excluding the three North African states of Tunisia, Algeria and Morocco."—*Pref.* Maps, tables, charts. Indexed. DS62.8.M53

Ronart, Stephan and **Ronart, Nandy.** Concise encyclopaedia of Arabic civilization; the Arab East. Amsterdam, Djambatan, 1959; N.Y., Praeger, 1960. 589p. **DE70**

Concise information on individual aspects of Arabic civilization, including persons, places, and specific terms. A second volume on the Arab West appeared in 1965 (DD72). DS215.R6

Shimoni, Yaacov and **Levine, Evyatar.** Political dictionary of the Middle East in the twentieth century. Rev. & updated ed. N.Y., Quadrangle, 1974. 510p. il. **DE71**

1st ed. 1972.
Presents concise, signed articles in dictionary arrangement "on countries and peoples, on national and political movements, parties and leaders, on ideas and ideologies, on disputes and wars, alliances and treaties" (*Foreword*) of the Middle East of the present and recent past. Includes a supplement for the years 1971–74, edited by Itamar Rabinovich and Haim Shaked, p.[435]–510. An asterisk before the entry in the main section of the work indicates that there is updated information in the supplement. DS61.S52

Source books

Hurewitz, Jacob Coleman. The Middle East and North Africa in world politics, a documentary record. 2d ed., rev. & enl. New Haven, Yale Univ. Pr., 1975–79. 2v. **DE72**

1st ed. (1956) had title: *Diplomacy in the Near and Middle East.*
Contents: v.1, European expansion, 1535–1914; v.2, British-French supremacy, 1914–1945.
A collection of English translations of important documents relating to Western European and American contacts with countries of the Middle East—Afghanistan to non-Soviet southwest Asia—

and North Africa. Each document is preceded by a short essay indicating its importance. Lengthy bibliography at the end of v.1.
DS42.H87

The Middle East, 1914–1979. T. G. Fraser, comp. [London], Edward Arnold; N.Y., St. Martin's Pr., [1980]. 205p. maps. **DE72a**

A selection of documents (most of them previously unpublished) on three major areas: the conflict between Arab nationalism and Zionism; the role of the "Great Powers" and the United States; the growth of the oil industry. Section notes place documents in context. Indexed.
DS119.7.M4717

Atlases

Beek, Martinus Adrianus. Atlas of Mesopotamia; a survey of the history and civilisation of Mesopotamia from the Stone Age to the fall of Babylon. Tr. by D. R. Welsh; ed. by H. H. Rowley. London, Nelson, 1962. 164p. il., 22 col. maps. 36cm. **DE73**

Published also in German and in Dutch.
A historical survey with many plates showing the art and archaeology of the country, and historical maps.
G2251.E6B42

An historical atlas of Islam. Ed. by William C. Brice under the patronage of the Encyclopaedia of Islam. Leiden, Brill, 1981. 71p. maps. **DE74**

Maps are arranged chronologically within broad regional divisions (e.g., Near and Middle East; Anatolia and the Balkans). Covers down to the time of World War I. Index of place-names and ethnics (including alternate forms of the names); astronomical index; economic index.
A review by Robert Irwin in the *TLS*, Sept. 10, 1982, p.970, asserts that "its patchy coverage reflects work in progress rather than a balanced survey of Islamic history" and points out numerous inconsistencies and shortcomings.
G1786.S1H6

Robinson, Francis. Atlas of the Islamic world since 1500. N.Y., Facts on File; Oxford, Phaidon, [1982]. 238p. il., maps. 31cm. **DE75**

Using a combination of text, maps, and illustrations, aims "to demonstrate how Islamic society has been maintained, how it has been transmitted from generation to generation, and how it has been spread throughout the world."—*Pref.* Illustrations tend to outnumber the maps. Bibliography; gazetteer; index.
DS35.6.R6

Arab-Israeli conflict

Bibliography

The Arab-Israeli conflict 1945–1971; a bibliography. John Sherman, gen. ed. N.Y., Garland, 1978. 419p. (Garland reference library of social science, v.52) **DE76**

Lists books, pamphlets, government documents, and articles in English chronologically by date of publication. Some annotations; translations into other languages are noted. Author and subject indexes.
Z3479.R4A7

DeVore, Ronald M. The Arab-Israeli conflict; a historical, political, social, and military bibliography. Santa Barbara, Calif., Clio Books, [1976]. 273p. **DE77**

Directed toward the undergraduate student, the bibliography concentrates almost exclusively on important English-language books and articles published before 1974. "An attempt was made to include works which present a diversity of views on a given subject in order to give the user a broad perspective on the evolution of the conflict."—*Note.* Detailed subject arrangement with name index.
Z3479.R4D48

Khalidi, Walid and **Khadduri, Jill.** Palestine and the Arab-Israeli conflict, an annotated bibliography. Beirut, Inst. for Palestine Studies; Kuwait, Univ. of Kuwait, 1974. 736p. **DE78**

"The focus of the bibliography is on Palestine as a political problem during, roughly, the past century (1880–1971)."—*Pref.* Books, articles, easily accessible academic theses, government documents, and private papers are included in a classified arrangement based on time periods. Materials are mainly in English, Arabic and Hebrew; most entries are annotated. Index of authors, titles, and persons. Supplements are planned.
Z3479.R4K45

Source books

The Arab-Israeli conflict, ed. by John Norton Moore, sponsored by the American Society of International Law. Princeton, Princeton Univ. Pr., 1974. 3v. **DE79**

Contents: v.1–2, Readings; v.3, Documents.
In v.1–2 is assembled a selection of scholarly readings from the international legal literature on the principal issues and alternatives for their settlement; v.3 reprints the principal documents regarding the international legal aspects of the conflict. "Selected bibliography on the Arab-Israeli conflict and international law," v.3, p.1200–23.
A revised and abridged edition was published 1977 (1283p.).
DS119.7.A6718

Atlases

Gilbert, Martin. The Arab-Israeli conflict: its history in maps. 4th ed. London, Weidenfeld & Nicolson, 1984. 126p. 26cm. **DE80**

1st ed. 1974.
Some 126 maps in black-and-white trace "the history of the Arab-Jewish conflict from the turn of the century to the present day [i.e., Sept. 3, 1983]."—*Pref.*
G2206.S1G5

ASIA, NORTHEAST
(including Soviet Central Asia)

Allworth, Edward. Soviet Asia, bibliographies; a compilation of social science and humanities sources on the Iranian, Mongolian and Turkic nationalities. N.Y., Praeger, 1975. 686p. **DE81**

For full information *see* CC303.

Kerner, Robert Joseph. Northeastern Asia, a selected bibliography; contributions to the bibliography of the relations of China, Russia and Japan, with special reference to Korea, Manchuria, Mongolia, and eastern Siberia, in oriental and European languages. . . . Berkeley, Univ. of California Pr., 1939. 2v. (Pubn. of the Northeastern Asia Seminar of the Univ. of Calif.; ed. by R. J. Kerner) (Repr.: N.Y., B. Franklin, 1968) **DE82**

Classified, with full tables of contents and subject indexes. 14,000 titles, of which 10,000 are in Chinese, Japanese, Korean, and Russian. Uneven. Covers material, published through 1937, on all phases of life in northeastern Asia: geographic, political, economic, social, historical, cultural, international, etc.
Contents: v.1, pt.1, Asia, The Far East, The Pacific; pt.2, China, including Manchuria, Manchukuo, Mongolia, Northwestern China, Tibet; v.2, pt.1, The Japanese Empire, including Korea; pt.2, The Russian Empire and the Soviet Union in Asia and on the Pacific.
Z3001.K38

Lee, Don Y. An annotated bibliography on inner Asia: premodern. Bloomington, Ind., Eastern Pr., 1983. 183p. **DE83**

In two parts: (1) Northern Asia; (2) Inner Asia and Tibet; each section is subdivided for prehistorical and historical eras. Lists books and articles in any language. Useful despite the lack of a subject approach.　　　Z3126.L44

Pierce, Richard A. Soviet Central Asia: a bibliography. Berkeley, Center for Slavic and East European Studies, Univ. of California, [1966]. 3 pts.　　**DE84**

Contents: pt.1, 1558–1866; pt.2, 1867–1917; pt.3, 1917–1966. A classed bibliography. Separate author index for each part.
　　Z3411.P53

Sinor, Denis. Introduction à l'étude de l'Eurasie centrale. Wiesbaden, Harrassowitz, 1963. 371p.　　**DE85**

In effect, a series of bibliographic essays serving as a guide to the literature on the history, languages, and people of the area.

ASIA, SOUTH

Bibliography

See also BJ105.

Case, Margaret H. South Asian history, 1750–1950; a guide to periodicals, dissertations and newspapers. Princeton, N.J., Princeton Univ. Pr., 1968. 561p.　　**DE86**

A selective, annotated bibliography of periodical articles, together with a list of about 650 doctoral dissertations accepted through 1965 and a list of newspapers (with locations) published in South Asia since 1800. Well indexed.　　Z3185.C3

Chicago. Center for Research Libraries. South Asia Microform Project. SAMP catalog. 1980 cumulative ed. Chicago, [1980]. 246p.　　**DE87**

1st ed. 1974; suppl. 1976–78.
"The South Asia Microform Project (SAMP) exists to make available in microform [to member libraries] research materials related to the study of South Asia. This catalog represents all titles acquired by SAMP through the early part of 1979."—Introd. Items are listed alphabetically by main entry; index is mainly geographic. Includes revelant holdings from the ARL Foreign Newspaper Microform Project.　　Z3499.C45

Harvard University. Library. Southern Asia: Afghanistan, Bhutan, Burma, Cambodia, Ceylon, India, Laos, Malaya, Nepal, Pakistan, Sikkim, Singapore, Thailand, Vietnam; classification schedule, classified listing by call number, alphabetical listing by author or title, chronological listing. Cambridge, Harvard Univ. Lib.; distr. by Harvard Univ. Pr., 1968. 543p. (Widener Library shelflist, 19)　　**DE88**

For a note on the series see AA145.
Approximately 10,292 titles, including "primarily works on the history, civilization, government, geography and travel, religious affairs, and the races of these countries."—Pref.　　Z3185.H3

Kozicki, Richard J. International relations of South Asia, 1947–1980. Detroit, Gale, [1981]. 166p. (International relations information guide ser., v.10)　　**DE89**

A selective, annotated bibliography of English-language books, pamphlets, essays, articles, and government publications on India, Pakistan, Bangladesh, Sri Lanka, Nepal, Sikkim, Bhutan, Afghanistan, but excluding Burma. Topical arrangement; author index.
　　Z3185.K69

Minnesota. University. Ames Library of South Asia. Catalog. Boston, G. K. Hall, 1980. 16v.　　**DE90**

Reproduction of the catalog cards for more than 90,000 books, pamphlets, government documents, periodicals, maps and district gazetteers, and manuscripts in the humanities and social sciences. Includes materials relating to India, Pakistan, Nepal, Bhutan, Sikkim, Sri Lanka, Bangladesh, Afghanistan, and Burma. Though the collection encompasses materials from the 18th to the 20th centuries, its special strength is the 19th century.　　Z3185.A5

Patterson, Maureen L. P. South Asian civilisations; a bibliographic synthesis. Chicago, Univ. of Chicago Pr., [1981]. 853p.　　**DE91**

Lists books, theses, and long review articles on South Asia "between the Himalayas and the Indian Ocean, and adjacent islands" (Introd.) in a finely classified arrangement. About 28,000 entries; based on the collection at the University of Chicago. Outline of headings used; author and keyword indexes.　　Z3185.P37

Pearson, James D. South Asian bibliography. [Hassocks], Sussex, Harvester; [Atlantic Highlands], N.J., Humanities Pr., [1979]. 381p.　　**DE92**

An important guide which is the "product of a series of seminars organized by the South Asia Library Group and held over a period of several years with the aim of compiling a guide to works of reference . . . ."—Pref. Offers essays describing archives and manuscript collections of South Asian materials in various countries, together with bibliographies of theses. A second section deals with reference works for published sources, including maps, periodicals and newspapers. Indexed.　　Z3185.S65

Roda, Jean Claude. Ocean indien. Saint-Denis, Bibliothèque Universitaire de la Réunion, 1976. 91p. (Bibliographie de l'histoire des grandes routes maritimes, 1932–74, v.5)
　　DE93

A subject listing of books and periodical articles, mainly 1932–74 publications, on travel in the Indian Ocean area during all periods. Includes economic, religious, political, and scientific aspects. Author index.

U.S. Library of Congress Office, New Delhi. Accessions list, South Asia. v.1, no.1– , Jan. 1981– . New Delhi, The Office, 1981– . Monthly.　　**DE94**

Represents a merger of the accessions lists for India (1962–79), Pakistan (1962–79), Bangladesh (1972–79), Sri Lanka (1973–79), Nepal (1966–79), and Afghanistan (1978–79); those lists, in turn, might be considered a continuation of the Southern Asia accessions list (1952–60) issued by the Orientalia Division of the Library of Congress.
Lists government and commercial publications of the countries noted above and adds coverage for Bhutan and Maldives. Country listing subdivided for monographs, serials, and special materials. Cumulative author, title, and subject indexes; a serials supplement is published irregularly, cumulating new titles and changes. Beginning Jan. 1982, availability of selected items on microfiche through Library of Congress is noted.　　Z3185.L52

Dissertations

Krishan Gopal. Theses on Indian sub-continent, 1877–1971: an annotated bibliography of dissertations in social sciences and humanities accepted with the universities of Australia, Canada, Great Britain and Ireland, and United States of America. Ed. by Dhanpat Rai. Delhi, Hindustan Publ. Corp., [1977]. 462p. (Bibliographical research ser., 1)
　　DE95

Intended as "a comprehensive and interdisciplinary guide to all dissertations, published during 1877–1971, that deal in whole or in parts with Bangladesh, India, Nepal-Sikkim-Bhutan, Pakistan and Sri Lanka."—Pref. Topical arrangement within geographical divisions; author and subject indexes.　　Z3185.K74

Shulman, Frank J. Doctoral dissertations on South Asia, 1966–1970; an annotated bibliography covering North America, Europe, and Australia. Ann Arbor, Center for South and Southeast Asian Studies, Univ. of Michigan, 1971. 228p. (Michigan papers on South and Southeast Asia, 4)　　**DE96**

A listing of 1,305 dissertations in classed arrangement, with author, institutional, and subject indexes. Entries are mainly from North American and Western European institutions, and exclude theses from universities of South Asia itself.　　Z3185.S58

Library resources (including archives)

Cambridge. University. Centre for South Asian Studies. Cambridge South Asian archive: records of the British period in South Asia relating to India, Pakistan, Ceylon, Burma, Nepal and Afghanistan held in the Centre. Mary Thatcher, comp. and ed. [London], Mansell, 1973. 346p.
DE97

Describes "primary source material [such] as papers, letters, and photographs, written or collected by those who had served and lived in South Asia, which were capable of throwing light on economic, social and political conditions during the period of British rule in the former Indian Empire and Ceylon."—*Introd.* Also includes tapes, records, etc. Arranged by name of collection, with chronological, subject, and donor indexes. Z6616.A2C35

India Office. Library. Guide to the India Office Library, with a note on the India Office records. Comp. by S. C. Sutton. 2d ed. London, H.M.S.O., 1967. 122p. il. **DE98**

1st ed. 1952.
A description of each of the major sections of the Library (now under the Commonwealth Office): printed books, manuscripts, drawings and prints, photographs, and India Office records. Indicates scope and arrangement, catalogs, and publications.
Z792.I6

Low, Donald Anthony, Iltis, J. C. and **Wainwright, M. D.** Government archives in South Asia: a guide to national and state archives in Ceylon, India and Pakistan. [London], Cambridge Univ. Pr., 1969. 355p. **DE99**

Information on each archive generally includes name, address, and officer in charge, followed by "a note about the latest available information on rules of access; a short historical account of the territory whose archives are described; a short account of the history of its archival administration; a note about the nature and extent of the holdings the archives possess; and a brief guide to any published aids to reference."—*Pref.* CD2081.L6

Rahim, Enayetur. Scholars' guide to Washington, D.C. for South Asian studies: Afghanistan, Bangladesh, Bhutan, India, Maldives, Nepal, Pakistan, Sri Lanka. Wash., Smithsonian Inst. Pr., 1981. 438p. (Scholars' guide to Washington, D.C., no.8) **DE100**

"Woodrow Wilson International Center for Scholars."—*t.p.*
Describes relevant scholarly resources available in libraries, archives and manuscript repositories, museums, galleries, map collections, film collections and data banks, together with information on organizations, associations, and agencies which may be helpful to the scholar. Indexed. Z3185.R34

South Asian library resources in North America; a survey prep. for the Boston Conference, 1974. Maureen L. P. Patterson, ed. Zug, Switz., Inter Documentation, [1975]. 223p. (Bibliotheca Asiatica, 11) **DE100a**

Sponsored by the Committee on South Asian Libraries and Documentation of the Association for Asian Studies.
An inventory based on responses to questionnaires. For each institution indicates teaching and research interests, description of relevant library holdings, access, and cooperative arrangements.
Z3185.B67

Atlases

A historical atlas of South Asia. Ed. by Joseph E. Schwartzberg. Chicago, Univ. of Chicago Pr., 1978. 352p. maps. 41cm. (Assoc. for Asian Studies. Reference ser., no.2)
DE101

"This atlas seeks to provide a comprehensive cartographic record of the history of South Asia from the Old Stone Age to the present day. South Asia we normally take to include the present areas of India, Pakistan, Bangladesh, Afghanistan, Nepal, Bhutan, Sri Lanka, and the Maldives. Burma is included for the period from the

mid-18th century until the granting of its independence in 1948."— *Introd.* For some topics coverage extends to broader areas. "More than half the atlas . . . relates to historical events and processes at work during the period since 1857 and to the patterns of human geography by which those events and processes are spatially expressed." Map and photographic plates occupy the first 149 pages, with text, bibliography (p. 267–304), and index following. Maps and text follow a chronological arrangement. G2261.S1H5

ASIA, SOUTHEAST

Guides

Johnson, Donald Clay, comp. A guide to reference materials on Southeast Asia, based on the collections in the Yale and Cornell University Libraries. New Haven, Conn., Yale Univ. Pr., 1970. 160p. (Yale Southeast Asia studies, 6) **DE102**

A classed bibliography of reference sources for all aspects of Southeast Asia studies. Author index. No annotations.
Z3221.J63

Southeast Asian research tools. [Honolulu], Southeast Asian Studies, Asian Studies Program, Univ. of Hawaii, 1979. 9v. (Southeast Asia papers, 16) **DE103**

Contents: v.1, Summary and needs, by Shiro Saito; v.2, Indonesia, by Lan Hiang Char; v.3, Burma, by Michael Aung Thwin; v.4, Malaysia, Singapore, Brunei, by William R. Roff; v.5, The Philippines, by Edita R. Baradi; v.6, Thailand, by Charles F. Keyes; v.7, Laos, by Charles F. Keyes; v.8, Cambodia, by Charles F. Keyes; v.9, Vietnam, by Michael G. Cotter.
Constitutes a revised and expanded version of Donald C. Johnson's *A guide to reference materials on Southeast Asia* (above). Each volume provides a survey of the reference tools available for the particular country or countries treated, followed by an annotated bibliography of relevant bibliographies, archival guides, etc., in whatever language. Author index in each volume. Z3221.S68

Bibliography

Akademiia Nauk SSSR. Institut Narodov Azii. Bibliografiia IUgo-Vostochnoi Azii; dorevoliutsionnaia i sovetskaia literatura na russkom iazyke, original'naia i perevodnaia. Moskva, Izd-vo Vostochnoi Lit-ry, 1960. 255p. **DE104**

Comp. by A. M. Grishina and others.
A bibliography of publications in the Russian language from the pre-Revolutionary and Soviet period through 1958, pertaining to Southeast Asia, and of translations into Russian from the literature of the area. Chapters include Burma, British North Borneo, Vietnam, Indonesia, Cambodia, Laos, Malaya and Singapore, Sarawak, Thailand, and the Philippines.
Continued by: Z3221.A4

Larionova, O. S. Bibliografiia stran IUgo-Vostochnoi Azii, 1959–1970: Sovetskaia literatura na russkom iazyke, originalnaia i perevodnaia. Moskva, Izd-vo Nauka, 1980. 433p.
DE105

Z3221.L37

Attar Chand. Southeast Asia and the Pacific: a select bibliography, 1947–1977. New Delhi, Sterling, [1979]. 378p.
DE106

Books and periodical articles published 1947–77 are listed topically with geographical subdivisions. The introduction, p.1–54, surveys developments in each country. Author index.
Z3221.A88

Burns, Richard Dean and **Leitenberg, Milton.** The wars in Vietnam, Cambodia and Laos, 1945–1982: a bibliographic guide. Santa Barbara, Calif., ABC-Clio, [1984]. 290p. (War/peace bibliography ser., 18) **DE107**

Updates the same compilers' *Vietnam conflict* (Santa Barbara, ABC-Clio, 1973), but does not include every item listed in that work. Aims to provide a selected guide to the "important contemporary and retrospective books, dissertations, research papers and essays" (*p.3*), including periodical articles and some government documents. Topical arrangement, with introductory notes for each chapter. Author index; detailed table of contents, but no subject index. Z3228.V5B87

Cornell University. Libraries. Southeast Asia catalog. Boston, G. K. Hall, 1976. 7v. **DE108**

Contents: v.1–3, Western language monographs; v.4–5, Vernacular monographs; v.6, Vernacular monographs (cont'd); Other language monographs; Serials; v.7, Serials (cont'd.); Newspapers; Maps.

Photographic reproduction of catalog cards for all monographs, serials, newspapers, maps, and microfilms relating to Burma, Cambodia, Indonesia, Laos, Malaysia, Singapore, Brunei, the Philippines, Portuguese Timor, Thailand, and Vietnam. Includes many subjects of wider interest, e.g., Buddhism, Islam, ethnic minorities, and languages of bordering regions. Z3221.C86

—— —— First supplement. Boston, G. K. Hall, 1983. 3v.

Follows the arrangement of the basic set, adding catalog records up to Dec. 31, 1980.

Embree, John Fee and **Dotson, Lillian Ota.** Bibliography of the peoples and cultures of mainland Southeast Asia. New Haven, Yale Univ., 1950. 821p. (Yale Univ. Southeast Asia studies) **DE109**

An extensive bibliography which includes books and periodical articles in Western languages ranging in date from the 17th century to the present. Material is grouped under broad areas with references on race, racial history, migration, ethnology, cultural history, social organization and law, religion, folklore, language, and writing. Some titles are annotated. A detailed table of contents but no author index.

A companion to K. J. Pelzer's *Selected bibliography on the geography of Southeast Asia* (New Haven, HRAF, 1949–56. 3v.). Z3001.E5

Irikura, James K. Southeast Asia: selected annotated bibliography of Japanese publications. New Haven, Conn., Southeast Asia Studies, Yale Univ., in association with Human Relations Area Files, 1956. 544p. (Behavior science bibliographies) **DE110**

Titles listed are from the libraries of Congress, Yale, Harvard, and Columbia. Areas covered include Burma, Indochina, Indonesia, Malaya, the Philippines, Thailand, and "general southeast Asia." Authors and titles are listed first in the roman alphabet and then in Japanese characters. Annotations are generally quite full. Classed arrangement with author index. Z3221.I7

Johnson, Donald Clay. Index to Southeast Asian journals, 1960–1974; a guide to articles, book reviews, and composite works. Boston, G. K. Hall, [1977]. 811p. **DE111**

Indexes articles and book reviews in 44 journals published 1960–74 which are "internationally oriented" and deal with several countries for a single discipline. The reviews were used to identify collections of essays, and some 120 of these "composite works" are indexed by subject. Author index. Z3221.J64

Shu, Austin C. W. and **Wan, William W. L.** Twentieth century Chinese works on Southeast Asia: a bibliography. [Honolulu], East-West Center, 1968. 201p. (Hawaii. Univ. East-West Center. Inst. of Advanced Projects. Annotated bibliography ser., 3) **DE112**

757 items grouped by country: Borneo, Burma, Indochina, Indonesia, Malaya-Singapore, the Philippines, Thailand. Names and titles are given in romanization and in Chinese characters; titles also in English translation. Author and subject indexes. Z3221.S48

Smith, Myron J. Air war, Southeast Asia, 1961–1973; an annotated bibliography and 16mm film guide. Metuchen, N.J., Scarecrow Pr., 1979. 298p. **DE113**

A main-entry listing of more than 3,100 English-language printed sources (including government documents, doctoral dissertations, and master's theses), research studies done at Air University of the United States Air Force, 16mm films, and photographic sources. Subject index. Z3228.V5S63

Those who were there: eyewitness accounts of the war in Southeast Asia, 1956–1975 & aftermath; annotated bibliography of books, articles & topic-related magazines, covering writings both factual & imaginative. [Paradise, Calif., Dust-Books, 1984] 297p. **DE114**

Merritt Clifton, coordinating ed.

Includes "veterans of all military and guerilla forces active or stationed in Vietnam, Laos, Cambodia, and Thailand; civilians of these nations; journalists who actually witnessed combat or traveled with military units; & any others . . . whose writings describe or reflect their first-hand experience."—*Introd.* Arranged by genre; not indexed. Z3228.V5T46

Tregonning, Kennedy G. Southeast Asia; a critical bibliography. Tucson, Univ. of Arizona Pr., [1969]. 103p. **DE115**

" . . . a selected, graded, annotated list of works, mainly in English, that contribute to the academic study of traditional and modern Southeast Asia."—*Foreword.* Classed arrangement within country divisions. More than 2,000 items (books and periodical articles), nearly all of them published since 1945. Indexed. Z3221.T7

U.S. Library of Congress. Orientalia Division. Southeast Asia subject catalog. Boston, G. K. Hall, 1972. 6v. **DE116**

Contents: v.1, Brunei, Burma, Cambodia; v.2, Indonesia; v.3, Laos, Malaysia; v.4, Philippines; v.5, Sabah, Sarawak, Singapore, Thailand, South Vietnam; v.6, North Vietnam, Southeast Asia—General.

Reproduction of cards from a catalog maintained some 25 years in the Southern Asia Section of the Orientalia Division of the Library of Congress. Z3221.U525

U.S. Library of Congress Office, Jakarta. Accessions list, Southeast Asia. v.1, no.1– , Jan./Mar. 1975– . Djakarta, The Office, 1975– . Bimonthly. **DE117**

Frequency varies.

Supersedes *Accessions list, Indonesia, Malaysia, Singapore and Brunei,* 1964–74.

Lists commercial and government publications in country arrangement subdivided for monographs and serials. Annual author/title index; cumulative lists of serials (superseding earlier issues) are issued irregularly. Beginning Sept. 1979, coverage includes Burma, Laos, and Thailand as well as Indonesia, Malaysia, Singapore and Brunei. From Apr. 1978 availability of selected items on microfiche through the Library of Congress is noted. Z3221.U54

Dissertations

Sardesai, D. R. and **Sardesai, Bhanu D.** Theses and dissertations on Southeast Asia; an international bibliography in social sciences, education, and fine arts. Zug, Inter Documentation Co., [1970]. 176p. (Bibliotheca Asiatica, 6) **DE118**

More than 2,800 master's and doctoral theses are grouped in broad subject classes, then by geographic area; author index. Includes "titles of most of the work submitted for the doctorate in the United States, Soviet Union, British Isles, Malaysia, Singapore, Australia, New Zealand, the Philippines, the Netherlands, Czechoslovakia, and Japan. The coverage of research in France, Germany, Thailand, India and Canada is not as extensive."—*Pref.*
Z3221.S26

The, Lian and **Van der Veur, Paul W.** Treasures and trivia; doctoral dissertations on Southeast Asia accepted by universities in the United States. [Athens, Ohio], 1968. 141p. (Ohio. Univ. Center for International Studies. Papers on international studies. Southeast Asia ser., no.1) **DE119**

More than 900 dissertations in classed arrangement. Includes items through mid-1968. No author index.   Z3221.T5

Library resources

Mayerchak, Patrick M. Scholars' guide to Washington, D.C. for Southeast Asian studies: Brunei, Burma, Cambodia, Indonesia, Laos, Malaysia, Philippines, Singapore, Thailand, Vietnam. Wash., Smithsonian Inst. Pr., 1983. 411p. (Scholar's guide to Washington, D.C., no.9)   **DE120**

Sponsored by the Woodrow Wilson International Center for Scholars.

More than 400 collections, organizations, and agencies and their services are described, giving name, address, hours of opening, collection strengths, unique features. Appendixes list Vietnam War archives, bookstores, libraries by size of collection. Indexes by subject strength, subject, and name.   Z3221.M37

ASIA, EAST

Bibliography

Bayerische Staatsbibliothek. Ostasiensammlung. Katalog der Ostasiensammlung. Wiesbaden, L. Reichert, 1984–85. v.1–3. (In progress)   **DE121**

Contents: v.1–3, Chinese: A–Li Sheng.

The completed catalog will include the Chinese, Japanese, and Korean materials in the Bavarian State Library. Includes books, serials, and manuscripts. Author and title listings; manuscripts are included in both the main list and in a separate listing. In the Chinese part entries are given in Chinese characters and in transcription according to the Wades-Giles transliteration.   Z3009.B39

California. University. Library. East Asiatic Library. Author-title catalog; Subject catalog. Boston, G. K. Hall, 1968. 19v.   **DE122**

Photoreproduction in book form of the catalog cards for this outstanding collection.   Z3009.C33

———— ———— 1st supplement. Boston, G. K. Hall, 1973. 4v.

Covers materials added 1968–72. Cross references and added entries are not included in the supplement.

Chicago. University. Library. Far Eastern Library. Catalogs of the Far Eastern Library. Boston, G. K. Hall, 1973. 18v.   **DE123**

Contents: Author-title Chinese catalog, 8v.; Author-title Japanese catalog, 4v.; Classified catalog and subject index, 6v.

The Chinese collection was established in 1936 with emphasis on selecting research materials on "Chinese literature, history and institutions, especially of the ancient period."—*Pref., v.1.* Added to this strength are the collections in archaeology and the fine arts, the pre-modern period, and local gazetteers. Arranged in romanized order with romanization based on the Wade-Giles system and subjects divided according to the Harvard-Yenching classification.

The Japanese collection was established in 1958 and is especially strong in the humanities and history; there is also a notable collection of Japanese works in Chinese studies. Entries are arranged in romanized order according to the modified Hepburn system and use of the Harvard-Yenching classification.   Z881.C5365

———— ———— First supplement. Boston, G. K. Hall, 1981. 12v.

Contents: [pt.1] Author-title catalog of the Japanese collection (4v.); [pt.2] Author-title catalog of the Chinese collection (4v.); [pt.3] Classified catalog of the subject index to the Chinese/Japanese collections (4v.).

The Library has issued a list of its East Asian serials (Chicago, Univ. of Chicago Lib., 1977. 370p.).

Harvard University. Library. China, Japan and Korea; classification schedule, classified listing by call number, alphabetical listing by author or title, chronological listing. Cambridge, Harvard Univ. Lib., distr. by Harvard Univ. Pr., 1968. 494p. (Widener Library shelflist, 14)   **DE124**

For a note on the series *see* AA145.

"Briefly, this volume lists works in western languages dealing with the history, civilization, government, geography and description, economic and social life and conditions, religions, and races of Japan, Korea, and China including Outer Mongolia, Eastern Turkestan, and Tibet."—*Pref.* Literary and philosophical works are also included. Holdings of the Harvard Yenching Library are not included.   Z3109.H3

Harvard-Yenching Library. Chinese and Japanese catalogues of the Harvard-Yenching Library. N.Y., Garland, 1985– . v.1–22. (In progress)   **DE125**

Materials are listed by language, with the Japanese portion being published first. Each portion will be in three parts: author/title, subject, serials. Includes analytics for works in collections and series.

Harvard-Yenching is the "largest university library for East Asian research in the Western world . . . with comprehensive coverage of history, language and literature, philosophy and religion, fine arts, and primary sources for the study of modern and contemporary periods."—*Introd.*

The Library has previously issued a *Classified catalogue of Korean books* (DE273) and a *Classified catalogue of Chinese books in the Chinese-Japanese Library* (Cambridge, 1938–40. 3v.).   Z3301.H34

Michigan. University. Library. Asia Library. Catalogs of the Asia Library. . . . Boston, G. K. Hall, 1978. 25v.   **DE126**

Contents: v.1–13, Chinese catalog; v.14–25, Japanese catalog.

Photographic reproduction of the dictionary card catalog of this extensive collection of materials from China, Japan and Korea (the Japanese section includes Korean materials). Comprehensive coverage in the humanities and social sciences, with special strengths for modern and contemporary China, local histories, the theater, and legislation and statistical publications of Japan.

U.S. Library of Congress. Orientalia Division. Far Eastern languages catalog. Boston, G. K. Hall, 1972. 22v.   **DE127**

Photographic reproduction of the catalog cards for Chinese, Japanese, and Korean works processed at the Library of Congress since 1958. Special strengths are in the humanities, social sciences, and law; relatively strong in science and technology, although the collection does not try to duplicate holdings of the National Library of Medicine and the National Agricultural Library. Dictionary arrangement.   Z3009.U56

Library resources

Kim, Hong N. Scholars' guide to Washington, D.C. for East Asian studies (China, Japan, Korea, and Mongolia). Wash., Smithsonian Inst. Pr., 1979. 413p.   **DE128**

Third in the series of guides to scholarly resources in Washington, D.C., prepared under the auspices of the Woodrow Wilson International Center for Scholars. Describes collections of East Asian materials in libraries, archives, museums, etc., and gives information regarding governmental and non-governmental organizations of interest to researchers in this field. Indexed.   Z3001.K49

Matthews, Noel and **Wainwright, M. Doreen.** A guide to manuscripts and documents in the British Isles relating to the Far East. [London], Oxford Univ. Pr. for the School of Oriental and African Studies, 1977. 182p.   **DE129**

A survey of English, Welsh, Scots, and Irish (both Northern Ireland and the Republic) depositories, including some papers in private custody.   CD1048.A77M37

Yang, Teresa S., Kuo, Thomas C. and **Shulman, Frank Joseph.** East Asian resources in American libraries. N.Y., Paragon Book Gallery, 1977. 143p. **DE130**

An outgrowth of Yang and Yang's *Asian resources in American libraries* (DE18), but concentrating on East Asia rather than sources relating to the whole of Asia.

Contains two essays, "American library resources on East Asia," by T. S. Yang, and "East Asian collections in American libraries," by T. C. Kuo; a bibliographical guide to East Asian resources by F. J. Shulman; and a directory of East Asian collections in American libraries by T. S. Yang. The bibliographic guide concentrates on publications of the 1968–76 period—i.e., works appearing since publication of the earlier guide mentioned above. Index of authors and other main entries. Z3001.Y35

AFGHANISTAN

Ball, Warwick. Catalogue des sites archéologiques d'Afghanistan. Archaeological gazetteer of Afghanistan. Paris, Éd. Recherches sur les Civilisations, 1982. 2v. il., maps. (Synthèse 8) **DE131**

An extensive catalog and bibliography of all known sites and monuments within the modern day borders of Afghanistan, from the lower palaeolithic period to the Timurids. Includes published and unpublished materials. Main listing is by site name, giving location, date, description, field work, collections of artifacts, and sources. The bibliography is arranged by broad topic and is fairly comprehensive. Atlas of site plans and of regional and period maps. Appendixes include listing of sites by date and by date of field work; listing of study collections; glossary. Subject index. DS353.B35

Hanifi, M. Jamil. Annotated bibliography of Afghanistan. 4th ed. rev. New Haven, Conn., Human Relations Area Files, 1982. 545p. **DE132**

1st ed. 1956. Previous ed. by D. N. Wilber.

A classified list of book and periodical items on physical, social, and humanistic aspects of the country. Author-title index. Includes material in Western languages and in Russian, Arabic, Persian, and Pushtu, published both within and outside Afghanistan. This edition revised and enlarged; cut-off date is Jan. 1982. Z3016.H36

Kukhtina, Tat'iana Ivanovna. Bibliografiia Afganistana. Moskva, Izd. Nauka, 1965. 271p. **DE133**

Sponsored by Akademiia Nauk SSSR, Institut Narodov Azii. Z3016.K8

McLachlan, Keith Stanley and **Whittaker, William.** A bibliography of Afghanistan: a working bibliography of materials on Afghanistan with special reference to economic and social change in the twentieth century. Wisbech, Cambridgeshire, Middle East & North African Studies Pr., [1983]. 671p. **DE134**

Aims to present an "up-to-date classified list of western language materials . . . for use by social scientists and other researchers with interests in the development of Afghanistan."—*Introd.* Includes books, government publications, dissertations, periodical articles, and maps. Indexes for personal names, organization names, and authors of dissertations. Cut-off date is 1979; brief addendum of 1979–81 (and a few 1982) publications. Z3016.M4

BAHRAIN

Unwin, P. T. H. Bahrain. Santa Barbara, Calif., Clio Pr., [1984]. 265p. (World bibliographical ser., 49) **DE135**

Books and some government documents in Western European languages (but primarily English) are arranged by broad topics. About 900 annotated entries; author, title, subject index. Z3028.B34U58

BANGLADESH

See also Pakistan.

Satyaprakash. Bangla Desh: a select bibliography. Gurgaon, Indian Documentation Service, 1976. 218p. (International bibliography ser., 3) **DE136**

Lists some 2,500 titles (3,699 entries) of books, book reviews, journal articles and articles from the *Times of India* dealing with Bangladesh and published 1962–76. Arranged by author and topic. Z3186.S27

Zafarullah, Habib Mohammad. Government and politics in Bangladesh; a bibliographical guide. Dacca, Bangladesh, Ctr. for Administrative Studies, [1981]. 140p. **DE137**

About 1,000 books, articles, official publications, and newspapers are listed by topic in three chronological sections: 1947–71, 1971, 1971–80. Author index. Z3186.Z34

BURMA

Bernot, Denise. Bibliographie birmane, années 1950–1960. Paris, Éditions du Centre National de la Recherche Scientifique, 1968. 228p. (Atlas ethno-linguistique. 3.série: Bibliographies) **DE138**

Intended to supplement the Burma sections of Cordier's *Bibliotheca Indosinica* (DE212) and Embree and Dotson's *Bibliography of the peoples and cultures of mainland Southeast Asia* (DE109). Items are listed both in classed arrangement and alphabetically by author. Z3216.B4

———— ———— années 1960–1970. Paris, Éditions du Centre National de la Recherche Scientifique, 1982–85. Fasc.1–4. (In progress; to be in 8 fasc.) **DE139**

Contents: v.1, Partie méthodique (2 fasc.); v.2, Partie alphabétique, fasc.1–2, A–L.

A continuation of the above, following the arrangement of that work. Z3216.B43

Maretin, IU. V. Birma, rekomendatelnyi bibliograficheskii spravochnik. Moskva, Kniga, 1983. 63p. **DE140**

At head of title: Gosudarstvennaia Ordena Trudovogo Krasnogo Znameni Publichnaia Biblioteka Imeni M. E. Saltykova-Shchedrina. Geograficheskoe Obshchestvo SSSR. Sovetskoe Obshchestvo Druzhby i Kulturnykh Sviazei c Birmae.

A highly selective list of books and articles in Russian on Burma since 1948. Lengthy annotations; author index. Z3216.M37

New York University. Burma Research Project. Japanese and Chinese language sources on Burma, an annotated bibliography. New Haven, Conn., HRAF, 1957. 122p. (Behavior science bibliographies) **DE141**

Prep. by Burma Research Project at New York University, Frank N. Trager, director and editor; Japanese sources, Hyman Koblin; Chinese sources, Lu-yu Kiang.

A companion volume to the following: Z3216.N44

Trager, Frank N. Burma; a selected and annotated bibliography. New Haven, Human Relations Area Files Pr., 1973. 356p. **DE142**

Undertaken as a revised and updated edition of the New York University Burma Research Project's *Annotated bibliography of Burma* (New Haven, 1956), this is, in effect, a new work.

Main listing is by form, i.e., monographs, periodical articles, documents, dissertations, and lists of serials important to the study of Burma. Mainly English-language materials, with sections of Burmese-language sources and Russian- and Eastern-language sources. Author and topical indexes. More than 2,000 entries. Users should familiarize themselves with the Preface which notes significant types of materials omitted. Z3216.T7

CAMBODIA

Aschmoneit, Walter. Kampuchea: sozialhistorische Bibliographie zu Kampuchea von der Vorgeschichte bis 1954. Münster, SZD-Verlag, 1981. 184p.   **DE143**

Books, essays and articles in French, German, and English are arranged by period, then by broad subject categories. A complementary volume covering 1954–80 was announced for 1984 publication, but seems not yet to have appeared.

Mary L. Fisher's *Cambodia; an annotated bibliography of its history, geography and politics since 1954* (Cambridge, MIT Center for Internat. Studies, 1967. 66p.) offers partial updating.
                                                      Z3228.C3A82

Zaleha Tamby. Cambodia; a bibliography. Singapore, Inst. of Southeast Asian Studies, 1982. 61p. (Inst. of Southeast Asian Studies. Library bulletin, 12)   **DE144**

A topical listing of about 700 books, serials, official publications, and articles from books and newspapers; mainly in English. Based on the collection of the Institute. Emphasis is on political life and international relations. Author, personal and corporate name indexes.   Z3228.C3Z34

CHINA

Guides

Nathan, Andrew J. Modern China, 1840–1972: an introduction to sources and resource aids. Ann Arbor, Univ. of Mich., Center for Chinese Studies, [1973]. 95p. (Michigan papers in Chinese studies, 14)   **DE145**

Describes major primary sources and research aids in all languages for historical and social science research. Discusses important libraries and archives of research materials for this field.
                                                      Z3108.A4N37

Teng, Ssu-yü and **Biggerstaff, Knight.** An annotated bibliography of selected Chinese reference works. 3d ed. Cambridge, Harvard Univ. Pr., 1971. 250p. (Harvard-Yenching Institute studies, 2)   **DE146**

1st ed. 1936; 2d ed. 1950.

This edition includes some 200 new titles (mostly indexes) of which 25 are in Japanese. About 100 works from the 2d ed. were dropped. Lists very few works devoted entirely to events since 1949 since this period is well covered by Berton and Wu's *Contemporary China* (DE149). Arranged by form (bibliographies, encyclopedias, dictionaries, geographical works, tables, yearbooks, Sinological indexes); lengthy annotations. Index of titles, authors and compilers.
                                                      Z1035.T32

Wilkinson, Endymion. The history of imperial China, a research guide. Cambridge, East Asian Research Center, Harvard Univ.; distr. by Harvard Univ. Pr., 1973. 213p. (Harvard East Asian monographs, 49)   **DE147**

A survey of "primary sources and the reference aids to them in Chinese, Japanese, and Western languages."—*Pref.* Concentrates on the period from the third century B.C. to the 18th century. An introductory section, "Research hints" discusses the main problems (i.e., converting dates, locating places, finding biographical information, etc.) encountered in using primary materials. Subject and author/title indexes.   DS734.7.W5

Wolff, Ernest. Chinese studies; a bibliographic manual. San Francisco, Chinese Materials Ctr., 1981. 152p. (Bibliographical ser., 1)   **DE148**

A manual of basic reference tools for "the topics and problems of Chinese bibliography or Chinese research methodology."—*Pref.* Works are described and their usefulness discussed in chapters presented in a mainly topical arrangement. No index.

A similar guide for students preparing for thesis research is

Chinese studies research methodology, by P. A. Herbert and T. Chiang (Hong Kong, Chinese Materials Ctr., 1982. 269p.).
                                                      Z3106.W64

Bibliography

See also DC542.

Berton, Peter Alexander Menquez and **Wu, Eugene.** Contemporary China; a research guide. Stanford, Calif., Hoover Institution on War, Revolution, and Peace, 1967. 695p. (Hoover Inst. bibliographical ser., 31)   **DE149**

This "is essentially a reference work keyed to those materials providing *access* to sources on contemporary China and, to a lesser extent, to the sources themselves."—*Pref.* Limited largely to materials on post-1949 Mainland China and post-1945 Taiwan; in general, the cutoff date for publications is 1963. Chinese, Japanese, English, and Russian materials are listed but not Korean. Oriented toward humanities and social sciences, with very limited coverage of natural sciences and technology. Classed arrangement; good annotations; index. Includes a list of dissertations and master's essays, p.560–84, and another of monographs, pamphlets, reports, etc. issued in series, p.482–515.   Z3106.B39

Cheng, Peter. China. Oxford, Eng. & Santa Barbara, Calif., Clio Pr., [1983]. 390p. map. (World bibliographical ser., 35)
                                                      DE150

"The goal is to present a selection of over 1450 works in English which will provide basic information on China, including its culture, its place in the world and the qualities which make it unique."—*Introd.* Most citations are to works published 1970–82. Topical arrangement; only books are included. Indexed.
                                                      Z3106.C465

Cordier, Henri. Bibliotheca sinica. Dictionnaire bibliographique des ouvrages relatifs à l'Empire Chinois. 2d éd., rev., corr. et considérablement augm. Paris, Guilmoto, 1904–08. 4v. (Repr. with suppl.: Taipei, Ch'eng-wen Publ. Co., 1966. 5v.)   **DE151**

—— —— Supplément. Paris, Geuthner, 1922–24. 4v. in 1.

An exhaustive listing of books and periodical articles in many languages, primarily of the 19th century, on all aspects of life in China. The lack of an author index, which previously seriously hampered the use of this work, has been at least temporarily filled by the issue in multigraphed form of: Z3101.C8

—— —— Author index to the Bibliotheca sinica. Comp., issued, and distr. by the East Asiatic Library, Columbia Univ. Libraries. N.Y., 1953. 84p.

Cornell University. Libraries. The catalog of the Wason Collection on China and the Chinese. Paul P. W. Cheng, comp. and ed. Wash., Ctr. for Chinese Research Materials, Assoc. of Research Libs., [1978–80]. 8v. (Bibliographical ser., no.17a–b)   **DE152**

Contents: pt.1, Serials catalog; pt.2, Catalog of monographs.

Covers Western language, Chinese, Japanese, and Korean materials in the Wason Collection. Listing is by language, then by main entry. Includes analytics and holdings for serials. No subject approach.

—— —— Supplement. Wash., [1985]. 708p. (Bibliographical ser., no.17c)

Adds cataloging for the 1978–80 period; catalog records are to appear in RLIN thereafter.   Z3109.C67

Esser, Alfons. Bibliographie zu den deutsch-chinesischen Beziehungen, 1860–1945. [München], Minerva, [1984]. 120p. (Berliner China-Studien 6)   **DE153**

Lists books, dissertations, articles, government documents, and archival and manuscript material concerning relations between Germany and China during 1860–1945—diplomatic, cultural, economic, etc. International coverage; broad topical arrangement. Indexes of topics and of names as subjects. Z2247.R4E86

Fairbank, John King and **Banno, Masataka.** Japanese studies of modern China; a bibliographical guide to historical and social-science research on the 19th and 20th centuries. Rutland, Vt., publ. for the Harvard-Yenching Inst. by Tuttle, 1955. 331p. (Repr.: Harvard Univ. Pr., 1971) **DE154**

"Describes more than 100 Japanese books and articles, which constitute the main body of Japanese research on modern China." —*Introd.* Annotations are in English.
Supplemented by: Z3106.F3

Kamachi, Noriko, Fairbank, John K. and **Ichiko, Chūzō.** Japanese studies of modern China since 1953; a bibliographical guide to historical and social science research on the nineteenth and twentieth centuries. Supplementary volume for 1953–1969. Cambridge, Mass., East Asian Research Center, Harvard Univ.; distr. by Harvard Univ. Pr., 1975. 603p. (Harvard East Asian monographs, 60) **DE155**

Z3106.K28

Fairbank, John King and **Liu, Kwang-Ching.** Modern China; a bibliographical guide to Chinese works, 1898–1937. Cambridge, Harvard Univ. Pr., 1950. 608p. (Harvard-Yenching Inst. studies, v.1) **DE156**

An annotated bibliography of Chinese works published 1898–1937, covering works of general reference; history, government, and law; foreign affairs; economics; social problems; cultural movements; education; intellectual and literary history; selected newspapers and learned journals.
Author and title are given in both Chinese characters and in the Wade-Giles romanization, with English translation. Annotations are in English.
The *Union catalog of Chinese literature on modern China* (Tokyo, Inst. of Asian Economic Affairs, 1967–70. 10v.) covers works on modern China since 1912. Z3108.A5F3

Franke, Wolfgang. An introduction to the sources of Ming history. Kuala Lumpur, Univ. of Malaya Pr.; distr. by Oxford Univ. Pr., 1968. 347p. **DE157**

An enlarged and revised edition of the author's *Preliminary notes on the important Chinese literary sources for the history of the Ming dynasty* (Chengtu, 1948). Z3106.F7

Hsieh, Winston. Chinese historiography on the Revolution of 1911, a critical survey and a select bibliography. Stanford, Calif., Hoover Inst. Pr., 1975. 165p. (Hoover Institution studies, 34) **DE157a**

A bibliographical essay (p.3–103) is followed by "A selected bibliography on the 1911 Revolution, with addenda," p.104–42, giving citations to Chinese works with English translation of titles, and notes on any English translation or summary of the complete work. Subject index. DS773.H7

Hsüeh, Chün-Tu. The Chinese communist movement, an annotated bibliography of selected materials in the Chinese Collection of the Hoover Institution on War, Revolution and Peace. [Palo Alto], Hoover, Inst., 1960–62. 2v. (Hoover Inst. bibliographical ser., 8, 11) **DE158**

Contents: v.1, 1921–37; v.2, 1937–49.
A survey of primary and secondary Chinese materials on the history of Chinese communism available at the Hoover Institution. Lists books, pamphlets, periodicals, newspapers, and manuscripts in the East Asian Library; topical arrangement. Excludes translations into Chinese. Name index. Z3108.A5H8

Liu, Kwang-Ching. Americans and Chinese; a historical essay and a bibliography. Cambridge, Harvard Univ. Pr., 1963. 211p. **DE159**

The bibliography lists and locates manuscripts and archives; bibliographies; memoirs and published letters; newspapers and periodicals; and reference works. Treats traders and entrepreneurs; missionaries; and Chinese who emigrated to the United States.

J. M. McCutcheon's *China and America* (Honolulu, Univ. of Hawaii Pr., 1972. 75p.) concentrates on secondary works.
Z1361.R4L5

Lust, John. Index sinicus: a catalogue of articles relating to China in periodicals and other collective publications, 1920–1955. Comp. with the assistance of Werner Eichhorn. Cambridge, Heffer, [1964]. 663p. **DE160**

A classified listing of almost 20,000 articles in Western languages, dealing with China, in periodicals, memorial volumes, proceedings of conferences and congresses, etc. Supplements Cordier (DE151), which lists works to 1924 and T. L. Yüan's *China in Western literature* (DE170) covering 1921–57. Author and subject indexes.
Z3101.L8

Modern Chinese society, an analytical bibliography. Stanford, Stanford Univ. Pr., 1973. 3v. **DE161**

Contents: v.1, Publications in Western languages 1644–1972, G. W. Skinner, ed. (802p.); v.2, Publications in Chinese 1644–1969, G. W. Skinner and W. Hsieh, eds. (801p.); v.3, Publications in Japanese 1644–1971, G. W. Skinner and S. Tomita, eds. (531p.).
Cites published secondary works and unpublished dissertations. Includes periodical articles, but not newspaper articles. Classified arrangement, with each entry coded as to library location, "type-of-place" (urban, rural, etc.), geographic location, historical period, and subject.
Indexes: (1) Historical index (a subject index to entries arranged by historical period and showing nature of the source); (2) Geographical index (a subject index to entries, arranged by geographic location and indicating historical era and type of place); (3) Author index; (4) Institutional author index; (5) General index (an alphabetical index of selected topics, terms, events, and proper names, with references to coding categories and to the analytical indexes as well as to particular entries). Z7165.C6M62

Morton, Andrew. Union list of Chinese local histories in British libraries. Oxford, China Library Group, 1979. 140p. **DE162**

Based on a survey of seven British libraries. Identifies and locates 1,100 original and 1,700 reprinted titles of official gazetteers, including 64 analyzed collections. Arranged by province with indexes of place-names in Pinyin transliteration and in Chinese characters.
Chinese local histories (Chicago, 1969. 139p.) is a finding aid for relevant materials in the University of Chicago's Far Eastern Library. Fang-hua Chang's *Checklist of Chinese local histories* (Berkeley, Stanford-Berkeley Joint East Asia Ctr., 1980. 470p.) offers similar coverage for the libraries at Stanford and the University of California, Berkeley. Z3109.M66

Posner, Arlene and **Keijzer, Anne J. de.** China; a resource and curriculum guide. 2d ed., rev. Chicago, Univ. of Chicago Pr., [1976]. 317p. **DE163**

1st ed. 1972.
Aims to list "a wide range of materials currently available to the public and offering representative views of the social, economic, political and cultural aspects of China's society and international relations, both past and present."—*Pref.* Offers essays on teaching about China; lists of audiovisual materials, books, and periodicals with evaluative annotations; resource materials from the People's Republic of China; and lists of resource centers, publishers and distributors.
Mary Robinson Sive's *China: a multimedia guide* (N.Y., Neal Schuman, 1982. 245p.) offers partial updating. Z3106.P67

Revue bibliographique de Sinologie. Paris, Mouton, 1957– . Année 1–14; n.s.1– , 1955–68/70, 1983– . Annual.
DE164

Sponsored by the École Pratique des Hautes Études (later the École Pratique des Hautes Études en Sciences Sociales).
Lists books and articles (not necessarily in Chinese) on China in topical arrangement with a brief review in English or French. Long delays in publication. Z7059.R4

Skachkov, Petr Emel'ianovich. Bibliografiia kitaia. Moskva, Izd-vo Vostochnoi Lit-ry, 1960. 690p. **DE165**

1st ed. 1932.

A bibliography of Russian-language publications from 1730 to 1957 on all phases of Chinese history and culture. This edition is extensively revised, almost doubling the number of entries. Some newspaper articles and many reviews are included, but journal articles are omitted in some sections (e.g., Art). A single alphabetical index for authors, compilers, editors, translators, commentators, reviewers, and titles of anonymous works. Z3106.S62

A Sung bibliography. Bibliographie des Sung. Initiated by Etienne Balazs, ed. by Yves Hervouet. [Hong Kong], Chinese Univ. Pr., [1978]. 598p. **DE166**

Introduction and instructions to the reader in English and French; notices in English or French.

A bibliography with extensive descriptive notes for texts issued during the Sung dynasty, with references to the most important later editions. Topical arrangement, e.g., official records, encyclopedias, works on bureaucracy, *The classic of filial purity.* Indexes of names, titles, and subjects. Z3102.S77

Teng, Ssu-Yü. Protest & crime in China; a bibliography of secret associations, popular uprisings, peasant rebellions. N.Y., Garland, 1981. 455p. (Garland reference library of social science, v.86) **DE167**

Lists about 4,000 articles, books, reviews, dissertations, etc., in any language covering all periods to 1981. Separate sections for occidental and oriental language materials, plus an addenda section in all languages. Subject index. Z7164.S36T46

Wang, James C. F. The cultural revolution in China: an annotated bibliography. N.Y., Garland, 1976. 246p. (Garland reference library of social science, v.16) **DE168**

A topical listing of 364 English-language books and periodical articles widely available in American libraries. Annotations; author and subject index. Z3108.A5W35

Yu, Ping-Kuen. Chung-Kuo shih hsüeh lun wên yin tê. Chinese history: index to learned articles. Hong Kong, East Asia Inst., Univ. of Hong Kong; Cambridge, Mass., Harvard-Yenching Lib., 1963–[70]. 2v. **DE169**

Text in Chinese; prefatory matter in English and Chinese.

Contents: v.1, 1902–1962, comp. in the Fung Ping Shan Library, Univ. of Hong Kong; v.2, 1905–1964, based on the collections in American and European libraries.

An author listing of articles published in Chinese periodicals. v.1 indexes articles on Chinese history to the end of the Ch'ing dynasty in 335 periodicals, and includes a subject index. v.2 lists articles on Chinese history, philosophy, language and literature in 599 periodicals. Z3106.Y79

Yüan, T'ung-li. China in Western literature: a continuation of Cordier's Bibliotheca sinica. New Haven, Conn., Far Eastern Publ., Yale Univ., 1958. 802p. **DE170**

For Cordier's *Bibliotheca sinica see* DE151.

This supplementary list covers books and monographs published from 1921 to 1957 in English, French, German, and Portuguese but does not include periodical articles. The classed arrangement differs somewhat from that used by Cordier, and there is an author index.

"The bibliography represents a comprehensive survey of all types of writings on China, with no attempt to select or reject, but rather to record and describe."—*Pref.*

Supplemented by J. Lust's *Index sinicus* (DE160). Z3101.Y8

——— Russian works on China, 1918–1960, in American libraries. New Haven, Conn., Far Eastern Publ., Yale Univ., 1961. 162p. **DE171**

Within subject groupings under China Proper, Northeastern Provinces, Mongolia, Sinkiang, Tibet, and Taiwan are listed 1,348 Russian books and periodical titles, but not articles, on all phases of the life of these areas. Available translations are noted. No specific library locational symbols are given, but entries are in Library of Congress cataloging form and transliteration. Name index. Z3106.Y83

Dissertations

Gordon, Leonard H. D. and **Shulman, Frank J.** Doctoral dissertations on China; a bibliography of studies in Western languages, 1945–1970. Seattle, Univ. of Washington Pr., for the Assoc. of Asian Studies, [1972]. 317p. (Reference ser., no.1) **DE172**

Lists 2,217 dissertations submitted between 1945 and 1970. Works are mainly from the United States, the USSR, France, Germany, and Great Britain, since "it is there that the major centers of Western scholarship on China are to be found" (*Introd.*), but dissertations from other countries are included. Arrangement is topical or chronological according to subject area; subject, author, and institutional indexes. Z3106.G65

Shulman, Frank Joseph. Doctoral dissertations on China, 1971–1975; a bibliography of studies in Western languages. Seattle, Univ. of Wash. Pr., [1978]. 329p. **DE173**

Forms a supplement to Gordon and Shulman's earlier bibliography (above). 1,573 entries for the 1971–75 period, with an appendix of 228 pre-1971 theses not listed in the earlier compilation.

Z3106.G65

Dictionaries and handbooks

The Cambridge encyclopedia of China. Gen. ed., Brian Hook. Cambridge, Cambridge Univ. Pr., [1982]. 492p. il., maps. **DE174**

A topically arranged encyclopedia offering signed articles on fairly specific subjects. Index at front; brief bibliography. No prefatory statement regarding scope or aim. DS705.C35

Couling, Samuel. Encyclopaedia sinica. Shanghai, Kelly and Walsh; London, N.Y., Oxford Univ. Pr., 1917. 633p. (Repr. 1983) **DE175**

A useful encyclopedia of information about China: its history, geography, literature, art, religions, institutions, flora, fauna, biography, etc. Most of the articles are by the editor, but there are articles by other authorities, some signed. Some bibliographies.

DS733.C7

Dillon, Michael. Dictionary of Chinese history. London, Frank Cass, 1979. 239p. **DE176**

A short-entry dictionary covering Chinese history from the prehistoric period to 1977; useful for quick identification or definition. Terms included are those which "occur most frequently in English-language works on China and which can usefully be explained in a few hundred words."—*Pref.* The transliterated form of a word is that most frequently encountered in English-language books. No bibliography. DS733.D54

Encyclopedia of China today. Ed. by Frederic M. Kaplan, Julian M. Sobin, Stephen Andors. 3d. ed. rev. & exp. N.Y., Eurasia Pr. (distr. by Harper & Row), [1981]. 446p. il. **DE177**

1st ed. 1979.

A handsome and readable one-volume encyclopedia on the People's Republic of China, concentrating on the last 30 years. The information is given in nine broad subject divisions, and presentation is enhanced by photographs, maps, charts, glossaries, and a large number of statistical tables. Other interesting features: travel information for both private and commercial travelers; an overview of information sources (including translation services); and a bibliography (p. 301–20). This edition adds a new section for pre-1949 matter and expands coverage of art, culture, and health.

DS705.E54

Lieberthal, Kenneth. A research guide to Central Party and government meetings in China, 1949–1975, with a foreword by Michael Oksenberg. White Plains, N.Y., Internat. Arts and Sciences Pr., [1976]. 322p. (Michigan studies on China, special no.) **DE178**

A chronological listing of the meetings, giving topic, dates, place, major agenda items, attendance, summaries of speeches and reports, indication of documents passed, reference to published accounts of the meeting and to any important secondary works. Index to meeting summaries.

Source books

The People's Republic of China, 1949–1979; a documentary survey. Harold C. Hinton, ed. Wash., Scholarly Books, 1980. 5v. **DE179**

A careful selection of Chinese government publications, newspaper articles, speeches, press releases, radio broadcasts, etc., which aims to provide an overview of the period. Full text is given in English in a basically chronological arrangement; source of the translation of each document is given; headnotes indicate importance of the document. (Title of the document is the only indication of its original source.) Brief index in each volume.

DS777.55.P4243

General histories

Cambridge history of China. General eds., Denis Twitchett and John K. Fairbank. Cambridge, Cambridge Univ. Pr., 1978–83. v.3,10,11², 12¹. (In progress) **DE180**

Contents: v.3, pt.1, Sui and T'ang China, 589–906, ed. by Denis Twitchett; v.10, Late Ch'ing, 1800–1870, ed. by J. K. Fairbank; v.11, pt.2, Late Ch'ing, 1800–1911, ed. by J. K. Fairbank and Kwang-Ching Liu; v.12, pt.1, Republican China, ed. by J. K. Fairbank.

Similar to the other "Cambridge histories," and with sections written by specialists, the series will offer a survey of the "current state of knowledge" of the history of China, excluding the predynastic period. To be in 14v. DS735.C3I45

Atlases

Blunden, Caroline and **Elvin, Mark.** Cultural atlas of China. Oxford, Phaidon; N.Y., Facts on File, [1983]. 237p. **DE181**

Offers topically arranged essays on all periods of Chinese life; aims to show the continuity of Chinese history, but points up distinct breaks therein. Heavily illustrated. Gazetteer; brief bibliography; index. DS721.B56

Herrmann, Albert. An historical atlas of China. New ed. Norton Ginsburg, gen. ed. Chicago, Aldine, [1966]. xxxii p., 88p. 30cm. **DE182**

Based on Herrmann's *Historical and commercial atlas of China* (Cambridge, Harvard Univ. Pr., 1935). New economic and cultural maps of modern and contemporary China replace those in the earlier work, and the historical maps have been redrafted, with some changes in the sequence of presentation. G2306.S1H4

HONG KONG

Rydings, H. Anthony. A Hong Kong union catalogue: works relating to Hong Kong in Hong Kong libraries. [Hong Kong], Centre of Asian Studies, Univ. of Hong Kong, 1976. 2v. (967p.) (Centre of Asian Studies bibliographies and guides, no.10) **DE183**

Attempts to list by subject all books, essays and parts of books, periodical articles, periodicals published in Hong Kong, maps, theses, and mimeographed materials dealing mainly with Hong Kong which are located in Hong Kong libraries. Author/title index. Supplements are planned. Z3107.H7R93

INDIA

Bibliography

See also AE284.

Akademiia Nauk SSSR. Institut Narodov Azii. Bibliografiia Indii; dorevoliutsionnaia i sovetskaia literatura na russkom iazyke i iazykakh narodov SSSR, original'naia i perevodnaia. Moskva, Nauka, 1965. 607p. **DE184**

Lists more than 9,000 books, articles, monographs published in Russian in the Soviet Union. Subject arrangement, with detailed table of contents and name index.

Continued by: Z3206.A72

Sosina, N. N. and **Tansykbaeva, S. I.** Bibliografiia Indii, 1968–1975: sovetskaia i perevodnaia literatura. Moskva, Izd-vo "Nauka," 1982. 164p. **DE185**

Adds 2,108 entries, following the same arrangement.

Z3206.S67

Annotated bibliography on the economic history of India 1500 A.D. to 1947 A.D. V. D. Divekar, Chief ed. New Delhi, Indian Council of Social Science Research, 1977–80. 4v. in 5. **DE186**

For full information *see* CH82.

Annual bibliography of Indian archaeology, publ. with the aid of the Government of Netherlands India with the support of the Imperial Government of India, 1926– . Leyden, Brill, 1928– . v.1– . Annual (irregular). (1970/72 publ. 1984) **DE187**

An extensive, annotated bibliography, including books and periodical articles in various languages, and sometimes reviews of books. Z5133.I4I6

Chambard, Jean-Luc. Bibliographie de civilisation de l'Inde contemporaine. [Paris], Publications Orientalistes de France, [1977]. 340p. **DE188**

A classed bibliography covering Indian geography, history, sociology/ethnography, demography, economics, agricultural economy, politics, and foreign relations. Predominantly English-language materials. Detailed table of contents, but no author or subject index. Z3206.C44

Early writings on India: a union catalogue of books on India in English language published upto [*sic*] 1900 and available in Delhi libraries. Ed. by H. K. Kaul. New Delhi, Arnold-Heinemann, [1975]. 324p. **DE189**

A classified catalog of 3,277 items with author/title index.

Z3209.E22

Gupta, Brijen K. and **Kharbas, Datta S.** India. Oxford, Eng. & Santa Barbara, Calif., Clio Pr., [1984]. 264p. map. (World bibliographical ser., 26) **DE190**

A selective and annotated bibliography intended to express India's "unique culture and its importance in the family of nations." —*Introd.* Topical arrangement; only English-language materials were chosen. Indexed. Z2306.G86

India Office Library. Catalogue of European printed books, India Office Library, Commonwealth Relations Office (London). Boston, G. K. Hall, 1964. 10v. **DE191**

The collection covers all aspects of "Indology." Accessions until 1936 are listed only by author; after 1936 there are both author and subject entries. Z3209.I53

———— Index of post-1937 European manuscript accessions, India Office Library, Commonwealth Relations Office (London). Boston, G. K. Hall, 1964. 156p. **DE192**

Indexes private papers of many secretaries of state for India, viceroys and governors of India and Indian provinces, and prominent Indian citizens from 1801. To a lesser extent, the collection also deals with Burma and Ceylon.   Z6621.G78E92

Scholberg, Henry. Bibliographie des français dans l'Inde. [Pondicherry, Historical Soc. of Pondicherry, 1973] 216p.   **DE193**

Brief survey chapters of "Historical writing on the French in India" and "Bibliographic resources for a study of the French in India" are followed by a bibliography of books, government publications, and a few theses in topical arrangement. Lists of maps and atlases and of titles of periodicals (including government serials) most relevant to the French presence in India are also included. Index of authors, subjects and anonymous titles.   Z3208.A39S36

———— Bibliography of Goa and the Portuguese in India. New Delhi, Promilla; Atlantic Highlands, N.J., Humanities Pr., 1982. 413p.   **DE194**

An extensive bibliography of books and pamphlets focusing on the period between 1497 and 1961. Topical arrangement with author and subject index. Locates copies. A supplement discusses archival materials in India, Portugal, and Great Britain and offers bibliographical essays on Goan independence.   Z3207.G6S36

Sharma, Jagdish Saran. Indian National Congress; a descriptive bibliography of India's struggle for freedom. 2d ed. Delhi, S. Chand, 1971. 816p., 131p. (National bibliographies, no.3)   **DE195**

1st ed. 1959.
A classified bibliography of materials largely in English and with many annotations, followed by an extensive "Chronology of selected events 1885–1958." A separately paged supplement lists publications from Jan. 1959–Aug. 1969.   Z3208.A5S47

———— Mahatma Gandhi; a descriptive bibliography. [2d ed.] Delhi, S. Chand, [1968]. 650p. (National bibliography, no.1)   **DE196**

1st ed. 1955.
A comprehensive bibliography of materials by and about Gandhi. A supplement, p.569–650 adds materials published 1954–68, bringing the total number of items to more than 4,500. Each section has its own index.
M. K. Gandhi; a bibliography, sponsored by the Indian Council of Social Science Research (New Delhi, Orient Longman, 1974. 379p.) indexes monographs in English published before 1973. *Gandhiana, 1962–1976,* by Satyaprakash (Gurgaon, Indian Documentation Service, 1977. 184p.) lists relevant articles, book reviews, news stories, etc., from 100 English-language Indian journals and the *Times of India.*   Z8322.7.S48

———— Sources of Indian civilization; a bibliography of works by world orientalists other than Indian. Delhi, Vikas, [1974]. 360p.   **DE197**

A bibliography of more than 3,500 books in classed arrangement according to broad Dewey classes. Brief subject index; some annotations. A high percentage of the works listed is in English, but Indologists from 15 countries are represented.   Z3206.S49

Up-to-date encyclopaedia of all Indological publications published in India and other countries relating to ancient Indian learning. Classified and arranged subjectwise in alphabetical order. Delhi, Mehar Chand Lachman Das, [1962]. 385p., 39p.   **DE198**

A bibliography attempting to list "all publications, ancient and modern, whether printed in India or abroad, in Sanskrit, Hindi, English, German, French, etc., dealing with ancient Indian learning."—[*p.iii*].   Z3201.A6

Wilson, Patrick. Government and politics of India and Pakistan, 1885–1955; a bibliography of works in Western languages. Berkeley, Univ. of California, Inst. of East Asiatic Studies, South Asia Studies, 1956. 356p. (Modern India project. Bibliographical study, no.2)   **DE199**

Includes books, pamphlets, and government documents, arranged by broad subject division with an index of authors and other names.   Z3208.A5W5

Chronologies

Rickmers, C. Mabel Duff. The chronology of India, from the earliest times to the beginning of the sixteenth century. Westminster, Constable, 1889. 409p.   **DE200**

DS433.R5

Burgess, James. The chronology of modern India for four hundred years from the close of the fifteenth century, A.D. 1494–1894. Edinburgh, Grant, 1913. 483p. (Repr.: Shannon, Irish Univ. Pr.; N.Y., Barnes & Noble, 1972)   **DE201**

Reprinted (Delhi, Cosmo Pubns., 1972) with title *The chronology of Indian history: medieval and modern.*
A list of historical events, in chronological order, with a minute alphabetical index; on the same general plan as Rickmers (above), the two together forming a continuous chronology of India from the earliest times to 1894.   DS433.B8

Roy, A. India and the Soviet Union; a chronology of political and diplomatic cooperation. Calcutta, Firm KLM, 1982. 194p.   **DE202**

The chronology covers Apr.1945–Sept. 1982; an appendix reprints important documents.   DB450.R8R63

Sharma, Jagdish Saran. India since the advent of the British, a descriptive chronology from 1600 to Oct. 2, 1969. Delhi, S. Chand, 1970. 817p. (National bibliography, 7)   **DE203**

A chronology with comprehensive index of names of places, events, subjects, newspapers, important books, etc.   DS433.S47

Encyclopedias and handbooks

Balfour, Edward Green. Cyclopaedia of India and of eastern and southern Asia, commercial, industrial, and scientific; products of the mineral, vegetable and animal kingdoms, useful arts and manufactures. 3d ed. London, Quaritch, 1885. 3v. (Repr.: Graz, Akad. Druck– u. Verlagsanstalt, 1967–78)   **DE204**

A comprehensive, alphabetically arranged encyclopedia still valuable for its geographical, historical, and ethnographical material.   DS405.B18

Saletore, Rajaram Naravan. Encyclopaedia of Indian culture. New Delhi, Sterling Pr. (distr. in U.S. by Humanities Pr., Atlantic Highlands, N.J.), 1981–84. v.1–4. (In progress)   **DE205**

Contents: v.1–4, A–U.
A dictionary arrangement of articles examining all elements of Indian culture (including science, folklore, numismatics) in their Brahman, Buddhist and Jaina aspects, but excluding Muslim views. Covers from earliest times to 19th century. Each entry includes at least one bibliographic reference; an extensive bibliography is to appear in the final volume.   DS423.S218

Sharma, Jagdish Saran. Encyclopaedia Indica. 2d rev. ed. New Delhi, S. Chand, 1981. 2v.   **DE206**

1st ed. 1975.
A dictionary arrangement of about 10,000 brief entries, with cross references, covering all aspects of India. This edition updated to include 1981 census information. Broad topical index.

DS405.S52

General histories

Cambridge history of India. Cambridge, Univ. Pr.; N.Y., Macmillan, 1922–37. v.1, 3–6. il. (Repr.: Delhi, S. Chand, 1958–64)   **DE207**

Contents: v.1, Ancient India, by E. J. Rapson; v.3, Turks and

Afghans, by Sir Wolseley Haig; v.4, The Mughal period, by Sir Wolseley Haig; v.5, British India, 1497–1858, by H. H. Dodwell; v.6, Indian Empire, 1858–1918, by H. H. Dodwell, with chapters on the development of administration, 1818–1858; additional chapters on the last phase, 1919–1947 by R. R. Sethi. No more published?

Written by authorities; extensive bibliographies, chronologies, etc.

————— Suppl. volume: The Indus civilization, by Sir Mortimer Wheeler. 3d ed. 1968. 143p. il., maps.

In effect, an additional chapter to v.1 of the set, summarizing new evidence available since that volume was published.

The Cambridge economic history of India, edited by T. Raychaudhura and I. Habib (Cambridge, Cambridge Univ. Pr., 1981–83. 2v.) is designed to accompany the *Cambridge history of India,* expanding on the few economic chapters therein, summarizing existing knowledge, and pointing up fruitful areas for research.

A useful one-volume history is Vincent A. Smith's *Oxford history of India* (4th ed., ed. by Percival Spear; Delhi & N.Y., Oxford Univ. Pr., 1981. 945p.). **DS436.C22**

Atlases

Davies, Cuthbert Collin. An historical atlas of the Indian peninsula. 2d ed. [Madras], Oxford Univ. Pr., 1959. 94p. 47 maps. 24cm. **DE208**

1st ed. 1949.
Black-and-white outline maps. **G2281.S1D38**

Habib, Irfan. Atlas of the Mughal Empire, political & economic maps with detailed notes, bibliography and index. [Aligarh], Ctr. of Advanced Study in History, Aligarh Muslim Univ.; Delhi, Oxford Univ. Pr., 1982. 105p. maps. 44cm. **DE209**

An outstanding atlas of political and economic maps of the Indian subcontinent, 1550–1750. Black-and-white maps; extensive notes; bibliography of 250 items; detailed index. **G2282.M6H3**

INDOCHINA

See also names of individual countries.

Auvade, Robert. Bibliographie critique des oeuvres parues sur l'Indochine française: un siècle d'histoire et d'enseignement. Paris, Maisonneuve & Larose, 1965. 153p. **DE210**

Classed arrangement; extensive annotations. **Z3226.A85**

Boudet, Paul and **Bourgeois, Remy.** Bibliographie de l'Indochine française, 1913–1926. Hanoi, Impr. d'Extrême-Orient, 1929. 75p. **DE211**

————— ————— 1927–1929. 240p.; 1930. 196p.; 1931–1935. 496p.

Lists books and periodical articles, on all phases of life in French Indochina. **Z3226.B68**

Cordier, Henri. Bibliotheca indosinica; dictionnaire bibliographique des ouvrages relatifs à la péninsule indochinoise. . . . Paris, Impr. Nationale, Leroux, 1912–32. 4v. and index (309p.). (Pubn. de l'École Française d'Extrême-Orient. v.15–18) (Repr.: N.Y., B. Franklin, 1967) **DE212**

An extensive, classified bibliography of materials in Western languages on the peninsula formerly called Indochina. The index volume contains both author and subject indexes. **Z3221.C78**

Désiré, Michel. La campagne d'Indochine, 1945–1954: bibliographie. Vincennes, État-Major de l'Armée de Terre, Service Historique, 1971–77. 4v. in 5. **DE213**

An extensive bibliography concerning French involvement in Indochina from pre-World War II times to the arrival of the Americans. Books, articles, theses, and manuscript sources (mainly in French, with some English-language materials) are listed in topical/chronological arrangement. Chronology in v.1; no index.

Pretzell, Klaus-Albrecht and **Bode, Jutta.** Indochina. Hamburg, Dokumentations Leitstelle Asien, 1980. 2v. (Dokumentationsdienst Asien. Reihe A, 14) **DE214**

Contents: v.1, Indochina, Laos, Kambodscha/Cambodia; v.2, Vietnam.

"The main purpose of this bibliography is to provide literature on the Indochina problem, its various aspects, its background and its origins."—*Foreword.* Arranged by geographical area, subdivided by topic; each country section begins with a brief description of the history, geography, and political, economic and social conditions. Indexed by geographic area, author, personal and corporate names. Locates copies. **Z3226.P73**

INDONESIA

Bibliography

See also DC425.

Chijs, Jacobus Anne van der. Proeve eener Ned. Indische bibliographie (1659–1870). . . . [Batavia, Bruining & Wijt, 1875–1903] 325p. and 2 suppl.: 93p., 64p. (Verhandelingen van het Bataviaasch Genootschap van Kunsten en Wetenschappen, deel 37, 55) **DE215**

Basic list, 1659–1870; the two supplements give additions and corrections for the years 1720–1870.

A chronological listing of works on the Netherlands East Indies, primarily in Dutch but with some works in other languages. **AS522.L418**

Hague. Koloniale Bibliotheek. Catalogus der Koloniale Bibliotheek van het Kon. Instituut voor de Taal-, Land- en Volkenkunde van Ned. Indië en het Indisch Genootschap, door G. P. Rouffaer en W. C. Muller. 'sGravenhage, Nijhoff, 1908–75. 1053p. and 6 suppl. **DE216**

Suppl. 1, 1915. 426p.; 2, 1927. 458p.; 3, 1937. 438p.; 4, 1966. 801p.; 5, 1972. 728p.; 6, 1975. 323p. (Titles vary)

A classified catalog of a very extensive collection on colonial affairs, not only of the Netherlands East Indies, but of other colonies of other countries in various parts of the world. Author/title and subject indexes. **Z3279.H31**

Hooykaas, J. C. Repertorium op de koloniale litteratuur, of, Systematische inhoudsopgaaf van hetgeen voorkomt over de koloniën (beoosten de Kaap) in mengelwerken en tijdschriften van 1595–1865 uitg. in Nederland en zijne overzeesche bezittingen. . . . Amsterdam, van Kampen, 1874–80. 2v. **DE217**

Contents: 1. deel; I, Het land. II, Het volk; 2. deel: III, Het bestuur. IV. de Wetenschap.

An extensive bibliography—listing more than 21,000 items—of Dutch materials on Dutch colonies throughout the world.
Continued by: **Z2451.C7H75**

Repertorium op de literatuur betreffende de Nederlandsche koloniën, voor zoover zij verspreid is in tijdschriften en mengelwerken . . . Samengesteld door A. Hartmann. 'sGravenhage, Nijhoff, 1895–1935. 454p. and suppl. 1–8. **DE218**

Basic volume: East Indies, 1866–93; West Indies, 1840–93. Supplements 1–8: v.1, 1894–1900 (1901. 224p.); v.2, 1901–1905 (1906. 233p.); v.3, 1906–10 (1912. 271p.); v.4, 1911–15 (1917. 378p.); v.5, 1916–20 (1923. 508p.); v.6, 1921–25 (1928. 522p.); v.7, 1926–30 (1935. 712p.); v.8, 1931–32 (1934. 189p.).

Treats Dutch colonies in the East Indies and the West Indies, including a large amount of indexing of periodical and other analytical material, much of which is not easily available in other forms. Z2451.C7H76

Kennedy, Raymond. Bibliography of Indonesian peoples and cultures. 2d rev. ed. Rev. and ed. by Thomas W. Maretzki and H. Th. Fischer. New Haven, Conn., Human Relations Area Files, 1962. 207p. maps. (Behavior science bibliographies. Southeast Asia Studies, Yale Univ.) **DE219**

1st ed. 1945; rev. 1955. This edition "substantially the same. No new titles have been added" (*p.vi*), but format has been changed.

Concentrates on the peoples and cultures of the area and is mainly anthropological—including ethnography, archaeology, and linguistics—and sociological, including geography, education, economics, history, colonial administration, etc. Lists both books and periodical articles. Z5115.K4

Current

Excerpta Indonesia, no.1– , Jan. 1970– . [Leyden, Centre for Documentation of Modern Indonesia, Royal Inst. of Linguistics & Anthropology], 1970– . Semiannual. **DE220**

Offers "abstracts of selected periodical articles . . . and annotations of selected books on Indonesia in the field of the social sciences and humanities" (*t.p.*) in many languages. About 200 citations per issue; indexed by author and subject. Cumulative indexes for every ten issues (i.e., nos.1–10 publ. 1975; nos. 11–20 publ. 1981).

The Institute also publishes periodic surveys of research: *Current Indonesian studies in the Netherlands, 1978/79* was published 1979; earlier surveys for 1970, 1973 and 1976 were published in *Excerpta Indonesia,* nos.2, 7 and 11, respectively. Z3273.E83

Encyclopedias

Encyclopaedie van Nederlandsch-Indië. 2. druk. met medewerking van verschillende geleerden ambtenaren en officieren. 'sGravenhage, Nijhoff, 1917–40. v.1–8, 9 (incompl.). **DE221**

Contents: v.1–4, A–Z; v.5–8, Suppl.1–4; [v.9], Suppl.5, Afl.61–62.

An encyclopedia of the region: its geography, inhabitants, products, etc., as well as its history; includes biography. An excellent work, with authoritative articles by specialists and good bibliographies. Still useful for the Dutch period.

An abridged edition based upon v.1–4 is: *Beknopte encyclopaedie van Nederlandsch-Indië . . . bewerkt door T. J. Bezemer* (Nijhoff, 1921. 632p.). DS633.E512

IRAN

Bibliography

Berghe, Louis van den. Bibliographie analytique de l'archéologie de l'Iran ancien. Leiden, Brill, 1979. 329p. **DE222**

"Avec la collaboration de B. Wulf et E. Haerinck."—*t.p.*

Citations to publications issued from the end of the 19th century to the end of 1977 are arranged by topic within three broad categories: general, region or site, and period. Index of authors and places.

———— ———— Supplement I: 1978–1980. Leiden, Brill, 1981. 109p.

Adds publications of 1978–80, plus some items omitted from the main volume. Z3369.A8B47

Bibliographic guide to Iran: the Middle East Library Committee guide. L. P. Elwell-Sutton, ed. Brighton, Sussex, Harvester Pr.; Totowa, N.J., Barnes & Noble, [1983]. 462p. **DE223**

A companion to *Arabic Islamic bibliography* (DE26).

A topically arranged bibliography of "the most useful and significant books and articles in each of the fields . . . and as far as possible [indicates] the scope and usefulness of each."—*Foreword.* A joint effort of some 30 scholars, covering from pre-Islamic times to the departure of the Shah. International coverage, but English-language materials predominate. Topical arrangement; brief annotations; author index. Z3366.B5

Ehlers, Eckart. Iran; a bibliographic research survey, with comments and annotations. Munich, Saur, 1980. 441p. **DE224**

Title also in German.

A comprehensive bibliography of all aspects of Iranian studies; topically arranged, with author index. Includes materials in all Western languages, but a high percentage of publications is in English. Chapter introductions in English and German.

Gitisetan, Dariush. Iran, politics and government under the Pahlavis: an annotated bibliography. Metuchen, N.J., Scarecrow Pr., 1985. 201p. **DE225**

Lists books, articles, government publications, and dissertations (mainly in English, but including French, German, Italian and Spanish publications) in topical arrangement with name index. Includes social and economic conditions as well as politics and government. Descriptive annotations. Thorough for the period of coverage. Z3366.G58

Iran media index. Comp. by Hamid Naficy. Westport, Conn., Greenwood Pr., [1984]. 264p. (Bibliographies and indexes in world history, 1) **DE226**

A topically arranged listing of "all non-fiction films, filmstrips and television news and public affairs programs produced by major English-speaking countries regarding Iran with emphasis on the United States."—*Introd.* Also includes "Iranian produced films and videotapes distributed or shown in the United States and samples of important films and television programs made by film makers of other countries. Covers to Jan. 1984. Table of addresses of producers, holders, and distributors. DS254.5.N34

Iranian opposition to the Shah: 701 selected dissident publications; a documentary history on microfiche: Guide, ed. by Wolfgang H. Behn. Zug, Switz., Inter Documentation, [1984]. 110p. **DE227**

A topically arranged finding aid for the microfiche collection. Publications were selected from three bibliographies compiled by Behn: *The Iranian opposition in exile . . . publications from 1341/ 1962 to 1357/1979* (Wiesbaden, Harrassowitz, 1979); *Islamic revolution or revolutionary Islam in Iran . . . from the overthrow of the Shah until his death* (Berlin, Adiyok, 1980); *Power and reaction in Iran, a supplement . . .* (Berlin, Adiyok, 1981). A fourth bibliography by Behn has appeared as *The end of a revolution, a bibliographical postscript to the Islamic revolution in Iran* (Berlin, Adiyok, 1984).

Nawābī, Y. M. A bibliography of Iran: a catalogue of books and articles on Iranian subjects, mainly in European languages. Tehran, Iranian Culture Foundation, [1969–84]. 6v. (Iranian Culture Foundation, v.53, 106, 261, 271, 275, 531) (In progress) **DE228**

Added t.p. in Persian.

Contents: v.1, Studies on Avesta, Mani & Manichaeism, Old Persian, Pahlavi (Parsik & Parthian), Parsis of India and Zoroaster & Zoroastrianism; v.2, Persian language and literature; v.3, Archaeology, architecture and art; v.4, Travel and description; v.5, History, mythology & foreign relations; v.6, Religion, philosophy & science.

A bibliography of book and periodical materials; author listing within broad subject classes; no index. A further volume is to cover linguistics. Z3366.N38

Pearson, James Douglas. A bibliography of pre-Islamic Persia. [London], Mansell, 1975. 288p. (Persian studies ser., 2)   **DE229**

About 7,300 items in classed arrangement, with author index. The principal sections are: (A) Languages and literatures; (B) History; (C) Religion; and (D) Art and archaeology; each is appropriately subdivided. Full table of contents but no detailed subject index. International in coverage (but omitting Russian materials); generally speaking, the cutoff date is 1970.   Z3366.P36

Sabā, Mohsen. Bibliographie française de l'Īrān. Bibliographie méthodique et raisonnée des ouvrages français parus depuis 1560 jusqu'à nos jours. 3 éd. rev. et augm. Téhran, Impr. de l'Université de Téhran, [1966]. 297p. (Tehran. Univ. Pubn. 1077)   **DE230**

1st ed. 1936.
A comprehensive, classed list of books and periodical articles, with author index.   Z3366.S2

Encyclopedias and general histories

Cambridge history of Iran. Cambridge, Univ. Pr., 1985. v.1–5. (In progress)   **DE231**

A. J. Arberry [and others], eds.
Contents: v.1, The land of Iran, ed. by W. B. Fisher; v.2, The Median and Achaemenian periods, by I. Gershevitch; v.3, The Seleucid, Parthian, and Sasanian period, ed. by E. Yarshater (2v.); v.4, The period from the Arab invasion to the Saljugs, ed. by R. N. Frye; v.5, The Saljuq and Mongol periods, ed. by J. A. Boyle.
To be in 8v. Chapters are contributed by scholar specialists. Each volume has its own bibliography and index, and the final volume will be devoted to bibliography, a survey of research, and indexes.
                                                    DS272.C34

Encyclopaedia Iranica. Ed. by Ehsan Yarshater. London, Routledge & Kegan Paul, [1983]–85. v.1, fasc.1–9; v.2, fasc.1. il. (In progress)   **DE232**

Contents: v.1, fasc.1–9, Āb-Anāhīd. (complete); v.2, fasc.1, anāmaka-anthropology.
Aims "to provide accurate and up-to-date presentations on topics of archeological, geographic, ethnographic, historical, artistic, literary, religious, linguistic, philosophical, scientific, and folkloric interest" (*Introd.*) for scholars, specialists and students in Iranian studies and related fields. Covers from prehistoric times to the present, but biographies of living persons are not included. Gives careful attention to reciprocal cultural influences between Iran and its neighbors. Signed articles (in English) by specialists; bibliographic references. Entry is usually under the transliterated Persian or Arabic form of a term or name, with adequate cross referencing promised. Includes entries for individual book titles. Figures and plates are generally limited to maps, plans of architectural monuments, sketches of archeological artifacts, or representative works by an artist or calligrapher.   DS253.E53

IRAQ

'Abd al-Rahmān, 'Abd al-Jabbār. Iraq. Oxford, Eng. & Santa Barbara, Calif., Clio Pr., [1984]. 162p. (World bibliographical ser., 42)   **DE233**

"The aim has been to list material which will provide the general reader, researcher, and librarian with a reasonably comprehensive picture of Iraq . . . focussing his attention on books while referring to a wide range of periodicals rather than citing articles."—*Introd.*
Primarily English-language materials. Topically arranged; annotated; well indexed. Separate list of theses and dissertations.
                                                   Z3036.A653

ISRAEL

See also Palestine.

Bibliography

See also BB571.

Alexander, Yonah, Alexander, Miriam and **Chertoff, Mordecai.** A bibliography of Israel. N.Y., Herzl Pr., 1981. 263p.
                                                        DE234

A topically arranged, annotated listing of English-language books, including biographies, autobiographies, fiction and poetry. Emphasis is on social and political life in contemporary Israel, but there is some treatment of Palestine and biblical Israel. Author and title indexes.   Z3476.A66

Fine, Morris. Israel-Diaspora relations; a selected, annotated bibliography 1973–1983. N.Y., Inst. on Amer. Jewish-Israeli Relations, Amer. Jewish Committee, [1983]. 45p.
                                                        DE235

Lists 216 books, pamphlets and articles in topical arrangement. Emphasis is on areas of agreement and disagreement between Jews of America and Israel.   Z3476.F55

Wallach, Jehuda L. Israeli military history; a guide to sources. N.Y., Garland, 1984. 291p. (Military history bibliographies, v.1; Garland reference library of social science, v.191)   **DE236**

Offers bibliographic essays, followed by bibliography of the works discussed. Period arrangement. Lists books in Western languages and Hebrew, with Arabic materials included only if available in translation.   Z3479.M5W34

Library resources (including archives)

Guide to America-Holy Land studies, 1620–1848. Nathan M. Kaganoff, ed. N.Y., Arno Pr., 1980–84. v.1–4. (In progress)   **DE237**

Publisher varies.
Contents: v.1, American presence; v.2, Political relations and American Zionism; v.3, Economic relations and philanthropy; v.4, Resource material in British, Israeli and Turkish repositories; v.5 [to be publ.], Culture and science.
Based on on-site surveys of libraries and archives in the United States, Israel, London, and Turkey that are likely to house primary source material "reflecting the relationship of the United States and the Holy Land from the earliest nineteenth century until 1948." Arranged alphabetically by point of contact—agency, society, person—with descriptions of the archives. Name index.
                                                   Z3479.A43G84

Guide to the archives of Israel. P. A. Alsberg, ed. Jerusalem, Israel Archives Assoc., 1973. 257p.   **DE238**

Hebrew ed., 1966, entitled *Madrikh la-arkhivonim ha-historiyim be-Yisrael.*
Twenty-one short surveys treat the organization, access, and governance of individual archives, together with an inventory prepared by the library or documentation center concerned. Index of organizations and personal names.   CD2012.G84

Atlases

Gilbert, Martin. Jewish history atlas. Cartography by Arthur Banks and T. A. Bicknell. 3d ed. London, Weidenfeld & Nicolson, [1985]. [128]p. maps.   **DE239**

1st ed. 1969.
Small black-and-white maps designed to portray "worldwide

Jewish migrations from ancient Mesopotamia to modern Israel."—*Pref.* Lacks an index. G1030.G5

Vilnay, Zev. The new Israel atlas; Bible to present day. Maps prep. by Carta Jerusalem. Jerusalem, Israel Universities Pr., 1968; N.Y., McGraw-Hill, 1969. 112p. il., maps. **DE240**

Tr. by Moshe Aumann from the Hebrew original, *Atlai tav shin Kaf het* (Jerusalem, 1968).
A historical atlas offering numerous maps with explanatory text. Indexed. G2235.V52

JAPAN

Guides

Bibliography of reference works for Japanese studies. Ed. by Naomi Fukuda. Ann Arbor, Center for Japanese Studies, Univ. of Michigan, 1979. 210p. **DE241**

Title also in Japanese on cover: *Nihon no sankē toshe.*
A selective, annotated bibliography of Japanese-language reference materials in the humanities and social sciences (excluding law and education). Arranged by detailed subject with a title index. Includes books published through 1977. Z3306.B48

Hall, John Whitney. Japanese history: a guide to Japanese reference and research materials. Ann Arbor, Univ. of Michigan Pr., 1954. 165p. (Center for Japanese studies. Bibliographical ser., 4) (Repr.: Westport, Conn., Greenwood Pr., 1973) **DE242**

A bibliographic guide to Japanese history. Emphasis is on reference and research materials dealing with the period before 1868. In five major sections: (1) Bibliographies, (2) Reference works, (3) Historical sources, (4) Periodicals, and (5) Survey histories. Approximately 1,550 entries.

——— ——— Index. Prep. by the School of Oriental Studies, Univ. College, Canberra, Australia. [195?] 33p.

Z3306.H27

Webb, Herschel. Research in Japanese sources: a guide. N.Y., Columbia Univ. Pr., 1965. 170p. **DE243**

Published for the East Asian Institute, Columbia University.
A handbook designed as a beginner's guide to Japanese bibliography, particularly in the fields of the humanities and social sciences. Discusses: bibliography and general reference materials; problems of dates, chronology, weights, and measures; statistics; people's names, place-names; words and their meanings; source materials; laws and official sources, etc. Bibliography, p.143–60. Z3306.W4

Bibliography

Akademiia Nauk SSSR. Institut Narodov Azii. Bibliografiia IAponii; literatura, izdannaia v Sovetskom Soiuze na russkom iazyke s 1917 po 1958 g. Moskva, Izd-vo Vostochnoi Lit-ry, 1960. 327p. **DE244**

Comp. by V. A. Vlasov and others.
Based on materials about Japan in the Lenin Library; lists documents, monographs, and articles in collections and journals published in Russian in the Soviet Union between 1917 and 1958. Arranged in 18 major subject categories. Name index to the 6,000 entries.
Continued by: Z3306.A73

Bibliografiia IAponii: literatura, izdannaia v Sovetskom Soiuze na russkom iazyke s 1959 po 1973 g. [Sost. N. F. Leshchenko i dr.] Moskva, Izd-vo Nauka, Glav. red. Vostochnoi Lit-ry, 1984. 335p. **DE245**

At head of title: Akademiia Nauk SSSR. Ordena Trudovogo Krasnogo Znameni Institut Vostokovedeniia.
Lists an additional 5,172 books and articles in topical arrangement with author index. Z3306.B47

Akademiia Nauk SSSR. Institut Narodov Azii. Bibliografiia IAponii; literatura, izdannaia v Rossii s 1734 po 1917 g. Moskva, Nauka, 1965. 378p. **DE246**

Lists documents, monographs, periodical articles and notes on Japan appearing in the Russian and Soviet press 1734–1917, but excluding newspaper articles. Z3301.A73

Berlin. Japan-Institut. Bibliographischer Alt-Japan-Katalog, 1542–1853; bearb. und hrsg. vom Japan-Institut in Berlin und vom Deutschen Forschungsinstitut in Kyoto. Kyoto, Deutsches Forschungsinstitut, 1940. 415p. (Repr.: München, Verlag Dokumentation, 1977) **DE247**

An excellent bibliography of older Western materials on Japan, giving complete bibliographical information and also location (in 1940) of copies in German and Japanese libraries. Complements Cordier (DE249). Z3306.B4

Borton, Hugh [and others]. A selected list of books and articles on Japan in English, French and German. Rev. and enl. Cambridge, Harvard Univ. Pr. for the Harvard-Yenching Institute, 1954. 272p. **DE248**

1st ed. 1940.
An annotated listing of almost 1,800 items including, in classified groupings: bibliographies, reference works, periodicals, geography, history, World War II and the Occupation (1941–52), economics, government and politics, sociology and ethnology, education and journalism, mythology, religion, philosophy, language, literature, and art. Title and subject index. Z3306.B67

Cordier, Henri. Bibliotheca japonica; dictionnaire bibliographique des ouvrages relatifs à l'Empire Japonais rangés par ordre chronologique jusqu'à 1870, suivi d'un appendice renfermant la liste alphabétique des principaux ouvrages parus de 1870 à 1912. Paris, Leroux, 1912. 762col. (Pubn. de l'École des Langues Orientales Vivantes. 5. sér., v.8) **DE249**

A chronological, annotated listing of materials in Western languages from pre-Marco Polo times to 1870. The appendix lists, alphabetically, the principal works published from 1870 to 1912. Z3301.C7

Domon, Shuhei. Japanese military history; a guide to the literature. N.Y., Garland, 1984. 88p. (Military history bibliographies, v.5; Garland reference library of social science, v.195) **DE250**

Intended as a starting point for the beginning student with a knowledge of Japanese, a high percentage of references being in that language (although titles are given in translation rather than in Japanese characters). Presented as five bibliographical essays in chronological sequence, followed by a list of works cited. Indexed. Z3308.M5D65

Fukuda, Naomi. Union catalog of books on Japan in Western languages. Reprint ed. [Tokyo], International House Library, 1968. 543p. **DE251**

Reprint of a work first published 1967. A main entry listing of books on Japan in a number of Japanese libraries. Z3301.F8

Hoover Institution on War, Revolution and Peace. East Asian Collection. A checklist of monographs and periodicals on the Japanese colonial empire in the East Asian collection. . . . Michiko Kiyohara, comp. Stanford, Hoover Inst. Pr., [1981]. 334p. **DE252**

All relevant monographs, newspapers, and periodicals listed in the Japanese card catalog at Hoover are here arranged by colony and then by topic: colonial empire, Korea, Taiwan, Kwantung, leased territories, Micronesia, Sakhakin, Kuril Islands. Lists materials on each area from the time it became a colony. Author and title indexes. Z3308.C7H65

Iwasaki, Ikuo. Japan and Southeast Asia; a bibliography of historical, economic and political relations. [Tokyo], Library Institute of Developing Economies, 1983. 176p.
DE253

Covers relations between Japan and southeast Asian countries, Burma to Thailand, from the 16th century to 1983. Arranged by country, then topically, with separate sections for Western language and Chinese/Japanese materials. Author index. DS525.9.J3I93

Kokusai Bunka Shinkokai, Tokyo. K.B.S. bibliography of standard reference books for Japanese studies with descriptive notes. Tokyo, 1959–73. v.1–4, 5^{A-B}, 6^{A-B}, 7^{A-B}, 8, 9^{B1}, 10.
DE254

Contents: v.1, Generalia (rev. ed. 1971); v.2, Geography and travel (rev. ed. 1973); v.3$^{1-3}$, History and biography (1963–64); v.4, Religion (1963); v.5A$^{1-2}$, History of thought (1964–65); v.5B, Education (1966); v.6A, Language (rev. ed. 1972); v.6B$^{1-5}$, Literature (1962–68); v.7A, Arts and crafts (rev. ed. 1971); v.7B, Theatre, dance and music (1960); v.8, Manners and customs, and folklore (1961); v.9B^1, Law (1968–70); v.10$^{1-2}$, Economics (1969).
Intended to be complete in 10v. A classed, annotated bibliography of standard works and source materials in the vernacular. Titles are romanized, and annotations are in English. Some volumes revised and updated.
Continued by: Z3306.K794

Introductory bibliography for Japanese studies. Tokyo, Univ. of Tokyo Pr.; distr. by Internat. Scholarly Book Services, Portland, Ore., 1974– . v.1– . (In progress) **DE255**
Prep. for the Japanese Foundation.
A continuation of *K.B.S. bibliography of standard reference books* (above), with emphasis on materials published since 1970.
Each volume is published in two parts (pt.1, Social sciences; pt.2, Humanities), the parts appearing in alternate years and listing important books and periodical articles of the two years following the previous period of coverage for that part. Publication is delayed; v.4, pt.2, covering 1978–79 (publ. 1984) is the latest to appear. Education has been added to the social sciences coverage; art history to the scope of the humanities volumes. Subject indexes were added beginning with v.2. Z3306.I57

Nachod, Oskar. Bibliographie von Japan, 1906–1937: Enthaltend ein ausführliches Verzeichnis der Bücher und Aufsätze über Japan, die seit der Ausgabe des zweiten Bändes von Wenckstern "Bibliography of the Japanese Empire" bis 1926 in europäischen Sprachen erschienen sind. . . . Leipzig, Hiersemann, 1928–70. v.1–7. **DE256**
v.1–2 also published with English title: *Bibliography of the Japanese Empire, 1906–26* (London, Goldston, 1928).
Contents: v.1–2, Books and articles, 1906–26 (1928); v.3, 1927–29 (1931); v.4, 1930–32, von Hans Praesent (1935); v.5, 1933–35, von Hans Praesent und Wolf Haenisch (1937); v.6, 1936–37, von Wolf Haenisch und Hans Praesent (1940); v.7, 1938–43, von Hans Praesent (1970).
A comprehensive, classified list, including books, pamphlets, and periodical articles. Each volume includes some titles of earlier dates omitted from previous volumes. Continues Friedrich von Wenckstein's *Bibliography of the Japanese Empire* (Leiden, Brill, 1895. 2v.; Repr.: Stuttgart, Hiersemann & Nendeln, Kraus, 1970) covering 1859–1906. Z3301.W472

Têng, Ssǔ-Yü. Japanese studies on Japan and the Far East; a short biographical and bibliographical introduction. . . . With the collaboration of Masuda Kenji and Kaneda Hiromitsu. Hong Kong, Hong Kong Univ. Pr., 1961. 485p.
DE257

Includes nearly 5,000 books and articles by 760 Japanese scholars, arranged by subject (Humanities, Social science, Fine arts). Within each group, listing is alphabetical by author, for each of whom brief biographical information is noted. Titles are given in: (1) transliteration, (2) Japanese characters, and (3) English translation. Index of authors, subjects, and many titles. Z3306.T4

Ward, Robert Edward and **Shulman, Frank Joseph.** Allied occupation of Japan, 1945–1952; an annotated bibliography of Western-language materials. Chicago, Amer. Lib. Assoc., 1974. 867p. **DE258**

Comp. and ed. for the Joint Committee on Japanese Studies of the Social Science Research Council-American Council on Learned Societies and the Center for Japanese Studies of the University of Michigan.
More than 3,000 annotated entries, including books, articles, doctoral dissertations, government publications, and archival materials. Topical arrangement, covering areas such as war crimes trials, land and educational reforms, Allied plans for postwar Japan, revisions of the Japanese constitution. Author and periodical indexes. Appendix: List of occupational personnel, p.835–67.
Intended as a companion to *Nihon senryō bunken mokuroku* (Tokyo, Gakujutsu Shinkōkai, 1972. 349p.), which includes some 3,000 entries in the Japanese language on the Allied occupation of Japan. Z3308.A5W35

Dissertations

Shulman, Frank J. Japan and Korea; an annotated bibliography of doctoral dissertations in Western languages, 1877–1969. Chicago, Amer. Lib. Assoc., 1970. 340p. **DE259**
Updates and expands Peter Cornwall's *Unpublished doctoral dissertations relating to Japan . . . 1946–63* (Ann Arbor, Univ. of Mich., Center for Japanese Studies, 1965). It "attempts to be a comprehensive, interdisciplinary guide to all Western-language dissertations, 1877–1969."—*Introd.* 2,586 titles in classed arrangement with author and institutional indexes.
Continued by: Z3306.S54

——— Doctoral dissertations on Japan and on Korea, 1969–1979; an annotated bibliography of studies in Western languages. Seattle, Univ. of Wash. Pr., [1982]. 473p.
DE260

Forms a supplement to the above, adding 3,508 entries for the 1969–79 period. Z3306.S54

Library resources (including archives)

Fukuda, Naomi. Survey of Japanese collections in the United States. Ann Arbor, Ctr. for Japanese Studies, Univ. of Michigan, 1980. 180p. (Michigan papers in Japanese studies, 4) **DE261**
Presents profiles of the Japanese collections at each of 28 universities and the Library of Congress. Gives background, organization, strengths, size, etc. Appendix of statistics from all the libraries presented in tabular form. Z3306.F84

Uyehara, Cecil H. Checklist of archives in the Japanese Ministry of Foreign Affairs, Tokyo, Japan, 1868–1945; microfilmed for the Library of Congress 1949–1951. Wash., Photoduplication Service, Lib. of Congress, 1954. 262p.
DE262

The documents are arranged in categories, the main series being from the Meiji-Taishō periods, 1868–1912, 1912–1926, and the Shōwa period, 1926–1945, with some additional archives. Analytical index. CD2175.U9

Chronologies

Kai, Miwa and **Yampolsky, Philip B.** Political chronology of Japan, 1885–1957. N.Y., East Asian Inst. of Columbia Univ., 1957. 63p. (Columbia Univ. East Asian Inst. Studies, no.5) **DE263**
Lists of cabinets, Diet sessions, and other political data. JQ1611.K26

Encyclopedias and handbooks

Chamberlain, Basil Hall. Things Japanese; being notes on various subjects connected with Japan, for the use of travellers and others. 6th ed. rev. London, Kegan Paul, 1939. 584p. il. **DE264**

An alphabetical dictionary by large subjects, with index of smaller subjects; bibliographical references. The 6th ed. contains revisions, additions, and supplementary material.

Some copies of this edition were censored by officials of the Imperial Japanese government, and p.11–12, 79–94, 247–52, and 345–46 were deleted. DS821.C445

Dictionnaire historique du Japon. Sous la direction de Iwao Seiichi. Tokyo, Librairie Kinokuniya, [1963–84]. Fasc.1–10. (In progress) **DE265**

Contents: Fasc.1–10, A–J.

An extensive dictionary of Japanese history and culture; articles cover a broad range of topics—divinities, biographies, animism, places, titles, etc. Bibliography of one to five items accompanies each article. DS833.D5

Hunter, Janet. Concise dictionary of Japanese history. Berkeley, Univ. of Calif. Pr., [1984]. 347p. **DE265a**

Aims to be a "handy source of information on the individuals, events, and organizations that have played a significant role in Japan's modern history" (*Pref.*) during the 1853–1980 period. Material covering earlier periods is included when important to the understanding of modern developments. Brief entries in alphabetical arrangement; most include at least one bibliographic reference. Glossary; appendixes of tables, charts, and lists of names. DS881.9.H86

Kodansha encyclopedia of Japan. [Tokyo], Kodansha, [1983]. 9v. il., maps. **DE266**

A comprehensive survey of Japanese life and culture offering "9,417 entries covering 37 categories of information, from such standard ones as history, literature, art, religion, economy, and geography to less obvious fields, such as science, technology, law, women, folklore, plant and animal life, food, clothing, sports, and leisure."—*Introd.* Represents extensive international scholarly cooperation, with articles contributed by some 680 Japanese and 524 non-Japanese scholars from 27 nations. Bibliographies appended to many articles. v.9 is an index. DS805.K633

JORDAN

Seccombe, Ian J. Jordan. Oxford, Eng. & Santa Barbara, Calif., Clio Pr., [1984]. 278p. (World bibliographical ser., 55) **DE267**

Aims to "provide a range of basic references on all key aspects of the country."—*Pref.* Except for a very few important works in French and German, coverage is limited to English-language books, articles, and government publications. Topical arrangement; annotations; author/title/subject index. Z3471.S43

KOREA

Guides

Studies on Korea: a scholar's guide. Ed. by Han-Kyo Kim with the assistance of Hong-Kyu Park. Honolulu, Univ. Pr. of Hawaii, [1980]. 438p. **DE268**

A guide to materials in 14 academic disciplines intended for "the college-level readers and others in the United States and elsewhere who may not have much background knowledge in Korean studies but who wish to read materials available in English or other Western languages on Korea."—*Pref.* Each chapter has an introductory essay

giving an overview of research, followed by an annotated bibliography subdivided by period, form, or topic. Chapter 15 deals with North Korea; chapter 16 with Russian-language materials on Korea. Author index. Z3316.S78

Bibliography

California. University. Institute of East Asiatic Studies. Korean studies guide, comp. by B. H. Hazard, Jr. [and others]. Ed. by Richard Marcus. Berkeley, Los Angeles, Univ. of California Pr., 1954. 220p. maps. **DE269**

Lists works in Korean and Western languages with annotations. Classified arrangement, covering many phases of Korean life. Author and title indexes. Z3316.C3

California. University. East Asia Studies. Russian supplement to the Korean studies guide, comp. by Robert L. Backus. Berkeley, 1958. 211p. **DE270**

Attempts to cover, with some comprehensiveness, "books, monographs, periodical literature, bibliographies and indexes relative to Korea . . . published in Russia from mid-19th century to early 1956."—*Pref.* Lists 893 items with annotations in English. Z3316.C32

Courant, Maurice. Bibliographie coréenne; tableau littéraire de la Corée, contenant la nomenclature des ouvrages publiés dans ce pays jusqu'en 1890 ainsi que la description et l'analyse détaillées des principaux d'entre ces ouvrages. Paris, Leroux, 1894–96. 3v. il. (Pubn. de l'École des Langues Orientales Vivantes. 3.sér., v.18–20) (Repr.: N.Y., B. Franklin, 1966) **DE271**

Contents: v.1, Enseignement, Étude des langues, Confucianisme, Littérature; v.2, Moeurs et coutumes, Histoire et géographie; v.3, Sciences et arts, religions, relations extérieures. Index.

————— ————— Supplément (jusqu'en 1899). Paris, 1901. 122p. (Pubn. de l'École des Langues Orientales Vivantes. 3.sér., v.21)

With the supplement, lists 3,821 titles, many with critical and bibliographical annotations. Z7101.K8C8

Ginsburgs, George. Soviet works on Korea 1945–1970. Los Angeles, Univ. of Southern Calif. Pr., 1973. 179p. (Univ. of Southern Calif. School of Internat. Relations. Far Eastern and Russian research ser., 4) **DE272**

Prep. for the Joint Committee on Korean Studies of the American Council of Learned Societies and the Social Science Research Council.

An extensive listing of books and pamphlets, articles, and dissertations written in the Soviet Union concerning Korea. Titles are given in Russian, followed by an English translation in parentheses. Topical arrangement with author index. Essays on the history of Soviet research on Korea and the state-of-the-art, p.17–62. Z3316.G55

Harvard-Yenching Library. A classified catalogue of Korean books in the Harvard-Yenching Institute Library at Harvard University. Cambridge, 1962–80. 3v. **DE273**

Lists books and serials in classed arrangement with name index. Z3316.H38

Koh, Hesung Chun. Social science resources on Korea; a preliminary computerized bibliography. New Haven, Human Relations Area Files, 1968. 2v. **DE274**

About 2,000 citations arranged by topic in all areas of the social sciences. Keyword, subject, geographical, and author indexes.

A listing of some 500 bibliographies discovered during the compilation of this work has been published as: Z3319.S6K6

————— Korea: analytical guide to bibliographies. New Haven, HRAF, 1971. 334p. **DE275**

"An attempt has been made to be as comprehensive as possible and approximately 500 bibliographies are included here. These are in eight languages and cover publications issued over a 70-year period beginning with 1896 and extending to 1970. This bibliography contains not only sources of book length but also journal articles, serials and dissertations. . . . Various other materials—such as catalogs of libraries, private collections, book exhibits and indexes to journals and newspapers— . . . have also been processed in this publication."—*Introd.* Topical arrangement with analytical indexes.

Z3316.A1K64

Dissertations

Shulman, Frank J. Japan and Korea; an annotated bibliography of doctoral dissertations in Western languages, 1877–1969. Chicago, Amer. Lib. Assoc., 1970. 340p.
DE276

For full information *see* DE259.   Z3306.S54

———— Doctoral dissertations on Japan and on Korea, 1969–1979. . . . Seattle, Univ. of Wash. Pr., [1982]. 473p.
DE277

For full information *see* DE260.

Handbooks

Handbook of Korea. 5th ed. Seoul, Korean Overseas Information Service, Ministry of Culture & Information, [1983]. 867p. il.   **DE278**

1st ed. 1978.
A heavily illustrated handbook on South Korea and its people. Topical arrangement; name and subject indexes. Statistical tables have been updated to about 1982. Bibliography, p.810–16.

DS902.H2864

KUWAIT

Clements, Frank. Kuwait. Oxford, Eng. & Santa Barbara, Calif., Clio Pr., [1985]. 195p. map. (World bibliographical ser., 56)   **DE279**

Aims to present a "comprehensive picture of Kuwait for the general reader, the librarian, or researcher."—*Introd.* 799 annotated entries for English-language materials. Publications on the Gulf are "deliberately excluded" except in the fields of language and literature where there is little material in English. Indexed.

D247.K82Z992

LAOS

Lafont, Pierre-Bernard. Bibliographie du Laos. Paris, École Française d'Éxtrême-Orient, 1964–80. 2v. (Pubn. de l'École Française d'Extrême-Orient, v.50)   **DE280**

Contents: v.1, 1666–1962; v.2, 1962–75.
A classified listing of books and periodical articles on all phases of history, life, and culture of Laos. Titles are largely in French, but some material in English and other languages is included; v.2 extends coverage of English and German materials. Separate indexes for publications in Lao, Thai, Vietnamese, and Russian; author indexes include corporate bodies such as national governments and political parties.
Continued by: Z3228.L3L3

Mogenet, Luc. Bibliographie complémentaire du Laos 1962–1973; suivi de références à quelques archives françaises concernant le Laos. Vientiane, Bibliothèque Nationale, 1973. 85p.   **DE281**

An author listing of books and articles published 1962–73, plus an inventory of French official archives relating to Laos, mainly of the 1893–1954 period.

LEBANON

Khairallah, Shereen. Lebanon. Oxford, Eng. & Santa Barbara, Calif., Clio Pr., [1979]. 154p. map. (World bibliographical ser., 2)   **DE282**

A classed, annotated bibliography with author/title/subject index. 650 English and French items.   Z3483.L4K48

Saliba, Maurice. Index Libanicus. Antílias, Saliba; Beirut, Nat. Archives Ctr., 1979–82. 2v.   **DE283**

Contents: v.1, Analytical survey of publications in European languages on Lebanon; v.2, Theses submitted at universities in Lebanon, 1906–1980.
v.1 is an author listing of 5,350 publications issued 1515–1979 in any European country, relating to the history of Lebanon, its people, etc.; topical index. v.2 lists theses at both the master's and doctoral level at any Lebanon university; author listing within language sections, with topical and geographic indexes.   Z3466.S24

MALAYSIA

Ding, Choo Ming. A bibliography of bibliographies on Malaysia. [Petaling Jaya], Hexagon Elite Pubns., [1981]. 184p.   **DE284**

An annotated listing of more than 650 bibliographies, indexes, catalogs, checklists, etc., "containing bibliographic data wholly or partially pertinent to Malaysia."—*Introd.* Author and title indexes.   Z3246.A1D56

Heussler, Robert. British Malaya; a bibliographical and biographical compendium. N.Y., Garland, 1981. 193p. (Themes in European expansion, v.1; Garland reference library of social science, v.79)   **DE284a**

Designed to supersede Harold A. R. Cheeseman's *Bibliography of Malaya* (London, 1959). In two parts: (1) a bibliography covering the British years in Malaya, 1867–1942, in topical arrangement; (2) biographical sketches of personnel of the Malayan civil service (both British and Malayan). Author index.   Z3246.H48

Karni, Rahadi S. Bibliography of Malaysia & Singapore. Kuala Lumpur, Penerbit Universiti Malaya, 1980. 649p.   **DE285**

Books, government publications, periodical articles in all Western languages are listed in topical arrangement. Coverage ends with 1966; not indexed. Useful because of depth of coverage.   Z3236.K37

Pelzer, Karl Josef. West Malaysia and Singapore: a selected bibliography. New Haven, Human Relations Area Files Pr., 1971. 394p.   **DE286**

A revised and greatly expanded edition of the compiler's *Selected bibliography on the geography of Southeast Asia: pt.III, Malaya* (New Haven, 1956). Includes materials relative to anthropology, economics, geography, political science, history, and the natural sciences of West Malaysia. Classed arrangement with author index.   Z3246.P4

Shulman, Frank Joseph. Doctoral research on Malaya and Malaysia, 1895–1977: a comprehensive bibliography and statistical overview. (*In* Malaysian studies: present knowledge and research trends, ed. John A. Lent. DeKalb, Ctr. for Southeast Asian Studies, Northern Illinois Univ., 1979. *Its* Occasional paper, no.7, p.250–436)   **DE287**

Lists 689 dissertations in chronological order by date of completion, with author, institution, and subject indexes. International coverage; occasional annotations referring to later publications based on the dissertations.   DS595.9.M34

Tregonning, K. G. Malaysian historical sources; a series of essays on historical material mainly in Malaysia on Malaysia. Singapore, Dept. of History, Univ. of Singapore, 1962. 130p. il. **DE288**

A guide to sources in Chinese, Arab-Persian, English, and Malay, with descriptions of newspapers, archives, etc. DS596.T7

NEPAL

Bibliographie du Népal. Paris, Éditions C.N.R.S., 1969–84. v.1, 3¹⁻³. (Cahiers Népalais) (In progress) **DE289**

Contents: v.1, Sciences humaines: Références en langues européennes, par L. Boulnois et H. Millot; v.3, Sciences naturelles: t.1, Cartes du Népal dans les bibliothèques de Paris et de Londres, par L. Boulnois; Supplément, 1967–1973, par L. Boulnois; t.2, Botanique, par J.-F. Dobremez, F. Vigny, L. H. J. Williams; t.3, Géologie de l'Himalaya Central, par I. Cloitre-Trincano.

An attempt to provide a comprehensive, though selective, international bibliography of works relating to Nepal in classed arrangement. There are occasional descriptive notes and references to reviews. Author index for each volume. v.2 is to provide references in Oriental languages to the humanistic sciences. Z3210.B5

Bibliography of Nepal. Comp. and ed. by Khadga Man Malla. Kathmandu, Royal Nepal Academy, 1975. 529p. **DE290**

Title and introductory matter in English and Nepali.
A classified bibliography of some 8,300 books and periodical articles on various aspects of Nepalese history, life and culture published up to 1972. Annotations in Nepali. Indexed. Z3207.N4B52

Birman, D. A. and **Kafitina, M. N.** Bibliografiia Nepala, 1917–1967. Moskva, Nauka, 1973. 22p. **DE291**

At head of title: Akademiia Nauk SSSR. Institut Vostokovedeniia.
Lists 254 books, articles, and essays (including translations into Russian) in topical arrangement. Author index. Z3207.N4B57

NETHERLANDS EAST INDIES

See Indonesia.

NORTH KOREA

See also CJ391.

An, Tai Sung. North Korea: a political handbook. Wilmington, Del., Scholarly Resources, [1983]. 294p. **DE292**

Aims to offer "an objective, compact description and analysis of North Korea's present political system and the kinds of possible or probable changes that might be expected in the future . . . compiled from information available in openly published materials."—*Pref.* Broad topical arrangement; includes directory and biographical information. DS932.A76

OMAN

Shannon, Michael Owen. Oman and southeastern Arabia: a bibliographic survey. Boston, G. K. Hall, [1978]. 165p. **DE293**

Aims "to record to the fullest extent possible all the major works which have appeared in the West on this Sultanate and surrounding Arab territories."—*Introd.* Main entry listing with subject/author/title index. Includes books and periodical articles; 988 items. Intends to be reasonably complete through 1976, with some 1977 items listed. Z3028.O5S52

PAKISTAN

Aziz, K. K. The historical background of Pakistan, 1857–1947; an annotated digest of source material. Karachi, Pakistan Inst. of Internat. Affairs, [1970]. 626p. **DE294**

Concentrates on the history of modern Muslim India and the creation of Pakistan. Mainly English-language materials; books are topically arranged, periodical articles by date of publication. Annotations; author and subject indexes. Z3201.A9

Jones, Garth N. and **Ali, Shaukat.** A comprehensive bibliography: Pakistan government and administration. [Lahore], All Pakistan Public Admin. Ctr., 1970–83. 4v. **DE295**

Broad topical arrangement (including sections for fiction and autobiography). v.1 lists books, articles, government publications, theses and dissertations on Pakistan from independence to 1968; v.2 covers 1968–70 publications, excluding government documents; v.3 lists 1970 materials (adding agriculture); v.4 covers 1970–81. Only English-language materials are included.
Pakistan; a comprehensive bibliography of books and government publications with annotations, 1947–1980 (Islamabad, Inst. of Islamic History, Culture and Civilization, Islamic Univ., 1981. 515p.) lists more than 8,300 books, pamphlets, government publications, and theses. Z7165.P3J65

Pakistan and Bangladesh; bibliographical essays in social science. Ed. by W. Eric Gustafson. [Islamabad], Univ. of Islamabad Pr., 1976. 364p. **DE296**

"This collection of bibliographical essays is a product of the National Seminar on Pakistan and Bangladesh which has met at the Southern Asian Institute, Columbia University, since Nov. 1970." —*Pref.* Seven essays survey scholarship in the areas of foreign policy, economics, social science, anthropology, political science, and Muslim separatism. Z3196.P34

Dissertations

Anwar, Mumtaz A. Doctoral research on Pakistan; a bibliography of dissertations accepted by foreign universities up to 1971. Lahore, Pak Book Corp., 1976. 72p. **DE297**

A classed bibliography with author index. More than 600 entries. "Research done prior to 1947 and relating to areas constituting Pakistan or to subjects directly relating to Pakistan have also been included."—*Pref.* Z3196.A64

Muhammad Anwar. Doctoral dissertations on Pakistan. Islamabad, Nat. Commission on Historical and Cultural Research, 1976. 124p. **DE298**

Attempts to list "all the theses accepted for doctoral degrees by universities abroad up to the academic year 1975, which in some way or other deal with Pakistan."—*Pref.* Cites 877 dissertations in classed arrangement, with author index. Z3196.M84

PALESTINE

See also Israel.

Jones, Philip. Britain and Palestine 1914–1948, archival sources for the history of the British mandate. [Oxford], Publ. for the British Academy by Oxford Univ. Pr., [1979]. 246p. **DE299**

Presents the findings of a survey conducted by the Anglo-Palestinian Archives Committee "to locate and list briefly the unpublished papers and records of those individuals and organisations, whose base was in Britain, that had involvement or interest in events in Palestine during the first half of this century."—*Introd.* Most of the collections described are in England. Divisions include: Personal papers, Records of selected organisations, Official archives in Britain, Archives outside Britain. Not indexed. Z6374.Z5J65

Thomsen, Peter. Die Palästina-Literatur; eine internationale Bibliographie in systematischer Ordnung mit Autoren- und Sachregister. ... Leipzig, Hinrich, 1911–72. v.1–7. (In progress) **DE300**

Contents: v.1 (2.Ausg.), 1895–1904; v.2, 1905–1909; v.3, 1910–14; v.4, 1915–25; v.5, 1925–34; v.6, 1935–39; v.7, Lfg.1–3, 1940–45.

v.6–7, ed. by Fritz Maass and Leonhard Rost.

1st ed. of v.1 (1908) had title *Systematische Bibliographie der Palästina-Literatur.*

A very comprehensive index to book and periodical literature in many languages. Z3476.T42

—— —— Bd.A, Die Literatur der Jahre 1878–1894. Leipzig, 1957–60. 905p.

Issued in 3 Lfg. Ed. by Otto Eissfeldt and Leonhard Rost.

Encyclopedias

Press, Jesaias. Erez-Yiśrael. Topographical-historical encyclopaedia of Palestine. Jerusalem, Rubin Mass, 1948–55. 4v. il. **DE301**

v.1 issued in a 2d ed., 1951.

In Hebrew with added title page and introduction in English. An encyclopedia, treating the history of Palestine from ancient times to modern Israel and Arabic Palestine. DS107.3.P76

QATAR

Unwin, P. T. H. Qatar. Oxford, Eng. & Santa Barbara, Calif., Clio Pr., [1982]. 162p. (World bibliographical ser., 36) **DE302**

Intends to present a "wide spectrum of basic texts on all major aspects of the country . . . in English."—*Pref.* Topical listing, with annotations, of 574 books, government publications, articles, and essays. Well indexed. Z3828.Q3U58

SAUDI ARABIA

Clements, Frank A. Saudi Arabia. Oxford, Eng. & Santa Barbara, Calif., Clio Pr., [1979]. 197p. map. (World bibliographical ser., 5) **DE303**

Lists 789 English-language books and periodical articles in topical arrangement. Annotations; author/title/subject index.

Z3026.C57

Philipp, Hans-Jürgen. Saudi Arabia: bibliography on society, politics, economics. München, Saur, 1984. 405p. (Bibliographies on regional geography and area studies, 4) **DE304**

Title page, table of contents, introduction, and index also in German.

A topically arranged bibliography of nearly 3,700 books, periodical articles, government publications, corporation reports, and reports from international organizations and research institutions, etc., covering from 1745 to the present. Limited to Western language materials with a high percentage in English. Index of subjects, authors, and corporate authors. Locates copies in German libraries.

Z3026.P48

SINGAPORE

See also Malaysia.

Books about Singapore 1984. Singapore, Reference Services Division, National Library, 1984. 98p. **DE305**

Subtitle: Special issue commemorating Singapore's twenty-fifth year of nationhood.

1st ed. 1970. Frequently revised; title varies.

An annotated bibliography of some 364 English-language books on Singapore acquired by the National Library to Mar. 1984. Topical arrangement; indexed by author and title. Z3248.S5L56

University of Singapore. Library. Catalogue of the Singapore/Malaysia collection. Boston, G. K. Hall, 1968. 757p. **DE306**

Bibliographic information on books, government publications, serials, newspapers, microfilms of manuscripts and archives, dissertations and theses is presented in the form of catalog cards. Mainly English-language materials.

—— —— Supplement, 1968–1972. Prep. by the Cataloguing Dept. [Singapore], Singapore Univ. Pr., 1974. 324p.

Adds about 3,100 cataloged items. Includes analytics for collective works, special issues of journals, and conference papers.

Z3250.S56

SRI LANKA

de Silva, Daya and **de Silva, Chandra Richard.** Sri Lanka (Ceylon) since independence (1948–1976), a bibliographical survey of the literature of Sri Lanka in the field of the social sciences. Hamburg, Asia Documentation Center, [1978]. 172p. **DE307**

Intended as a "guide to the literature on society, economy, religion and politics in contemporary Sri Lanka."—*Introd.* Lists Western-language publications—books, government publications, dissertations, annual reports, journal articles—under broad subject headings. Author index. Z7165.S77D4

Goonetileke, H. A. I. A bibliography of Ceylon. Zug, Inter Documentation, [1970–83]. 5v. (Bibliotheca asiatica, 5) **DE308**

Subtitle: A systematic guide to the literature on the land, people, history and culture published in Western languages from the sixteenth century to the present day.

A classed bibliography of more than 11,600 items. Books, parts of books, pamphlets, periodical articles, and government publications are included. Some brief annotations. v.3–5 are supplements adding materials to Dec. 1978. Author index in v.5. Z3211.G65

SYRIA

Bleaney, C. H. Modern Syria, an introduction to the literature. [Durham], Univ. of Durham, Ctr. for Middle Eastern and Islamic Studies, [1979]. 91p. (Occasional papers ser., no.6) **DE309**

Offered as "an introductory reading-list on modern Syria for a newcomer to the subject [providing] good background knowledge on the country since World War I."—*Pref.* About 950 books, articles, and government publications in topical arrangement with author index. Emphasizes political, social and economic development.

Z3481.B55

Masson, Paul. Éléments d'une bibliographie française de la Syrie. Marseille, Barlatier, 1919. 528p. (Chambre de Commerce de Marseille, Congrès Français de la Syrie) **DE310**

Subtitle: Géographie, ethnographie, histoire, archéologie, langues, littératures, religions.

A chronological listing of more than 4,500 French works on Syria from the 13th century to 1919, with author and class indexes.

Z3480.M42

THAILAND

Bibliography of material about Thailand in Western languages. Comp., Central Lib. of Chulalongkorn Univ. Bangkok, 1960. 325p. **DE311**

"The first comprehensive subject bibliography of material about Thailand in Western languages ever to be compiled by Thai nationals. . . ."—*Pref.*

Included are books, periodical articles, pamphlets, mimeographed documents, microfilms, and films concerning all phases of life in Thailand. Classed arrangement. No index.

A supplement covering 1960–73 was prepared by Suthilak Ambhanwong (Bangkok, Dept. of Lib. Sci., Chulalongkorn Univ., 1981. 780p.).

G. A. Nagelkerke's *Bibliographical survey of Thailand* (Leyden, 1974. 63p.) is based on the holdings of the Library of the Koninklijk Instituut voor Taal– , Land– en Volkenkunde; it includes an index to the *Journal* of the Siam Society. Z3236.B54

TIBET

Attar Chand. Tibet, past and present; a select bibliography and chronology of historical events 1660–1981. New Delhi, Sterling Pubns., [1982]. 257p. **DE312**

A bibliography of English-language books and articles published on Tibet since 1650. Topical arrangement with name index. Detailed chronology beginning 1650. Z3107.T5A88

UNITED ARAB EMIRATES

Clements, Frank A. United Arab Emirates. Oxford, Eng. & Santa Barbara, Calif., Clio Pr., [1983]. 162p. (World bibliographical ser., 43) **DE313**

Covers the Federation of Abu Dhabi, Dubai, Sharjah, Ajman, Umm al-Qaiwain, Ras al-Khaimah and Fujairah, listing books, articles, and a few government documents in English or translated into English. Topical arrangement; annotations; good index.

Z3028.U54C57

VIETNAM

See also Southeast Asia.

Cotter, Michael. Vietnam: a guide to reference sources. Boston, G. K. Hall, [1977]. 272p. **DE314**

Presented as the "first known compilation of reference works about Vietnam. It lists about 1400 books, periodical articles, serials, government publications, and other materials in the human and natural sciences, primarily in romanized Vietnamese (quôc-ngữ), French, and English from 1651 (the date of the first dictionary using romanized Vietnamese . . .) until 1976."—*Introd.* Classified arrangement; annotations; name/title index. Z3228.V5C68

Descours-Gatin, Chantal and **Villiers, Hugues.** Guide de recherches sur le Vietnam; bibliographies, archives et bibliothèques de France. Paris, L'Harmattan, [1983]. 259p. **DE315**

In two parts, the first listing bibliographies and other works of reference (library catalogs, periodical indexes, maps and atlases, yearbooks, chronologies, biographical dictionaries, language dictionaries, official documents, etc.); the second providing a guide to French libraries and archives, with descriptions of holdings related to Vietnam. Covers materials from early times to the recent past. Detailed table of contents, but no index. Z3228.V5D47

Jumper, Roy. Bibliography on the political and administrative history of Vietnam, 1802–1962 . . . [Saigon?] Michigan State Univ., Vietnam Advisory Group, 1962. 179p. **DE316**

An annotated bibliography of more than 950 entries, including books and periodical articles. Almost half the work is devoted to historical materials, but special attention is given to economic and social conditions. Developments in the Democratic Republic of Vietnam since 1954 largely excluded. Z3228.V5J8

Legler, Anton and **Bauer, Frieda.** Der Krieg in Vietnam; Bericht und Bibliographie. Frankfurt am Main, Bernard und Graefe, 1969–76. 4v. (Schriften der Bibliothek für Zeitgeschichte, n.F., Heft 8, 11, 13, 16) **DE317**

Contents: [v.1] Bis 30.9.1968; [v.2] Oktober 1968–September 1969; v.3, Oktober 1969–September 1971; v.4, Oktober 1971–Januar 1973.

An extensive bibliography of periodical articles, government publications, and books in Western languages. Topical arrangement with author index. Each volume has an introductory survey of Vietnam, Laos, and conduct of the war during the period covered.

DS557.7.L43

Leitenberg, Milton and **Burns, Richard Dean.** The Vietnam conflict; its geographical dimensions, political traumas, and military developments. Santa Barbara, Calif., Clio Books, 1973. 163p. **DE318**

Presents a "working" bibliography of books, articles, and government publications dealing with background and ongoing aspects of the war. Primarily English-language materials, with some French titles. Index. Z3228.V5L44

Sugnet, Christopher L. and **Hickey, John T.** Vietnam War bibliography: selected from Cornell University's Echols Collection. Lexington, Mass., Lexington Books, 1983. 572p. **DE319**

Lists more than 3,000 books, pamphlets, government publications, manuscripts, and maps, plus notes on the content of journals, newspapers and press releases relating to "U.S. involvement (1945–1975) including the War's international context and its interaction with U.S. domestic politics."—*Introd.* Title listing with topical index; some annotations. Z3226.S9

U.S. Library of Congress. Vietnamese holdings in the Library of Congress; a bibliography. Wash., The Library, 1982. 236p. **DE320**

Comp. by A. Kohar Rony, Southern Asia Section, Asian Division.

Offers separate listings of monographs, serials, and newspapers in Vietnamese acquired by the Library to June 1979. Index of titles, subjects, and issuing bodies. Z3228.V5L52

Vietnam; the definitive documentation of human decision. Gareth Porter, comp. Stanfordville, N.Y., Coleman Enterprises, 1979. 2v. **DE321**

A chronological presentation of documents from 1941 to May 1975 which the compiler feels "will illuminate the ideology, assumptions, strategy, and tactics of the two sides, as well as the interaction between decisions made by both sides" (*Introd.*) during the Vietnam conflict. Documents are derived from both U.S. and Vietnamese sources; Vietnamese documents are given in English translation. Each document has a headnote giving source and a summary. Public figure index; broad subject index.

DS556.8.V53

YEMEN

Smith, Gerald Rex. The Yemens: the Yemen Arab Republic and the People's Democratic Republic of Yemen. Oxford, Eng. & Santa Barbara, Calif., Clio Pr., [1984]. 161p. map. (World bibliographical ser., 50)   **DE322**

A topical arrangement of 130 entries for materials "reasonably accessible" in the United Kingdom—mainly English and French materials, with a few Italian and German items. Annotations; separate list of theses; author/title/subject index.   Z3028.Y39S65

D F

Australia and New Zealand

GENERAL WORKS

See also CE107–CE117.

Bibliography

Burton, Robert E. Travel in Oceania, Australia, and New Zealand: a guide to information sources. Detroit, Gale, [1980]. 123p. (Geography and travel information guide ser., v.2)   **DF1**

For full information *see* DG3.   Z4001.B87

Robert, Willem Carel Hendrik. Contributions to a bibliography of Australia and the South Sea Islands. 2d ed., rev. and enl. Amsterdam, Philo Pr., 1968–72. 4v.   **DF2**

Contents: v.1, Printed material relating to discovery, exploration and travel issued in the Netherlands to 1921; v.2, Index and bibliography of Dutch manuscripts and manuscript-charts relating to the discovery; v.3, Printed material relating to discovery, exploration and travel issued in Europe, excepting the Netherlands, to 1853, with a geographical index and an index of ships cited; v.4, Printed material relating to discovery, exploration and travel issued in Europe, except the Netherlands, 1836–1921, with a geographical index.

An earlier edition in 3v. appeared in 1964.   Z4001.R562

Manuscripts and archives

Mander-Jones, Phyllis. Manuscripts in the British Isles relating to Australia, New Zealand, and the Pacific. Honolulu, Univ. of Hawaii Pr., 1972. 697p.   **DF3**

Sponsored by the National Library of Australia and the Australian National University.

Lists "manuscript material in Great Britain and Ireland relating to Australia and New Zealand, New Guinea, Melanesia, Micronesia, Polynesia, Antarctica, the sub-Antarctic islands in southern Pacific

and Indian Oceans."—*Pref.* Arranged by county, with London holdings described first. Detailed index.   CD1048.A85M35

Handbooks

Osborne, Charles, ed. Australia, New Zealand and the South Pacific; a handbook. N.Y., Praeger; London, Blond, [1970]. 580p. il.   **DF4**

Chapters by specialists on a wide range of topics relating to the governmental, economic, industrial, social, and cultural affairs of the areas concerned. Includes numerous statistical tables and bibliographical references. Indexed.   DU15.O8

AUSTRALIA

Bibliography

See also AA39.

Crowley, Francis Keble. South Australian history; a survey for research students. Adelaide, Libraries Board of South Australia, 1966. 200p.   **DF5**

Basically a bibliography of published writings on South Australian history (including economic and business history, social history, religion, and education), but with some references to archival and source materials. Indexed.   Z4251.C7

Ferguson, John Alexander. Bibliography of Australia. Sydney, London, Angus & Robertson, 1941–69. 7v.   **DF6**

Contents: v.1, 1784–1830; v.2, 1831–1838; v.3, 1839–1845; v.4, 1846–1850; v.5–7, 1851–1900.

Arranged chronologically. Indexes are not cumulative. v.2–4 include lists of Addenda. A promised index and further addenda were not published.

The standard bibliography of Australia, which aims to include all books, pamphlets, broadsides, newspapers, magazines, and government papers printed from 1784 to 1900. Does not include manuscripts. Extensive annotations. Locates copies in ten Australian libraries and the British Museum.   Z4011.F47

Kepars, I. Australia. Oxford, Eng. and Santa Barbara, Calif., Clio Pr., [1984]. 289p. (World bibliographical ser., 46)   **DF7**

An annotated bibliography of recent books in English, arranged by topic (e.g., environment, Australian aborigines, food and drink). Intended for the "informed general reader as well as the scholar who wishes to obtain background information in a field other than his own."—*Foreword.* Author, title, subject index.   Z4011.K46

Politzer, Ludwig Louis. Bibliography of Dutch literature on Australia. Melbourne, priv. pr., 1953. 13p. map.   **DF8**

Arranged chronologically; no author index. Some brief annotations. *See also* DF2.   Z4011.P62

———— Bibliography of French literature on Australia, 1595–1946. Melbourne, priv. pr., 1952. 44p.   **DF9**

A chronological index is followed by an alphabetical list by author. Brief annotations are given for many items, and locations in Australian libraries and private collections are also included in most cases.   Z4001.P63

———— Bibliography of German literature on Australia, 1770–1947. Melbourne, Pan Pr., 1952. 47p.   **DF10**

A chronological index is followed by an alphabetical bibliography. Some annotations; a few locations.   Z4011.P63

Dissertations

Fry, E. C. Theses on Australian history accepted for higher degrees of universities in the United Kingdom, 1901–1976: a bibliography. Canberra, Nat. Lib. of Australia, 1980. 55p. **DF11**

An author listing with subject and period indexes.

Encyclopedias and dictionaries

The Australian encyclopaedia. Richard Appleton, ed. in chief. 4th ed. Sydney, Grolier Soc. of Australia, 1983. 12v. il., maps. **DF12**

1st ed. 1925–26.

An authoritative reference encyclopedia aiming to present "a comprehensive picture of Australia and its people, both past and present."—*Pref.* Covers all aspects of the country; most articles include a list for "Further reading." More than 2,000 photographs, line drawings, prints, maps, charts, etc. v.12 is an index, with appendix of statistics, historical dates, etc.

This edition thoroughly revised, with new treatment of notable Australians, women, music, towns, and public institutions; particular attention was given to revision of articles discussing the country's original inhabitants. DU90.A82

Collins Australian encyclopedia. Sydney, Collins in assoc. with D. Bateman, [1984]. 848p. il., maps. **DF13**

John Shaw, ed.

A well illustrated dictionary arrangement of articles relating to all aspects of Australian life and culture. Bibliographic references at the end of most articles; cross references; topical index. Appendixes include a chronology, lists of awards, disasters, sports championships, and a glossary of scientific terms. Most statistics as recent as 1980–81. DU90.C64

Murphy, Brian. A dictionary of Australian history. Sydney & N.Y., McGraw-Hill, [1982]. 304p. il., maps. **DF14**

Covers "events, issues, personalities in Australian history" (*Pref.*) for the student and the general reader. Cross references; subject index. DU90.M87

NEW ZEALAND

Guides

Wood, G. A. A guide for students of New Zealand history. Dunedin, Univ. of Otago Pr., 1973. 63p. **DF15**

Offers a guide to the primary and secondary sources of New Zealand history. For the student. Z4116.W66

Bibliography

Bagnall, Austin Graham. New Zealand national bibliography to the year 1960. Wellington, A. R. Shearer, Govt. Printer, 1969–80. v.1–4. (In progress) **DF16**

For full information *see* AA979. Z4101.B28

Chapple, Leonard James Bancroft. Bibliographical brochure containing addenda and corrigenda to extant bibliographies of New Zealand literature. Dunedin, Reed, 1938. 47p. **DF17**

Lists 116 items, published in 1909 or earlier, not found in Hocken or Johnstone (DF19). Z4101.C46

Grover, Ray. New Zealand. Oxford, Eng. & Santa Barbara, Calif., Clio Pr., [1980]. 254p. map. (World bibliographical ser., 18) **DF18**

Lists 878 books and some periodical articles selected for the "intelligent general audience."—*Introd.* Annotations. Author/title/subject index. Z4101.G76

Hocken, Thomas Morland. Bibliography of the literature relating to New Zealand. Wellington, Mackay, 1909. 619p. **DF19**

The standard bibliography, arranged chronologically with author and subject index, listing some 4,000 items, most of them annotated. Newspapers are included only for the early years of the colony. Supersedes earlier works by J. D. Davis and J. Collier.

—— —— Supplement, comp. by A. H. Johnstone. Auckland, Whitcombe & Tombs, 1927. 73p.

Lists some 500 works, without annotations, published before 1900 and not given in Hocken, and some published 1909 to 1926. Z4101.H7

Writings in New Zealand history. (*In* Historical studies, Australia and New Zealand. Melbourne, Univ., 1940– . Annual) **DF20**

An annual record of monographic and periodical publications.

Dissertations

Rodger, Margaret Diana, comp. Theses on the history of New Zealand. [Palmerston North], Massey Univ., 1968–72. 4v. (Massey Univ. Library ser., no.1–4). **DF21**

Contents: v.1, Biographical studies (27p. 1968); v.2, Political history (53p. 1969); v.3, Social history (138p. 1970); v.4, Economic, agricultural and industrial history (95p. 1972).

—— —— Additions and corrections, pts.1, 2, and 3. [Palmerston North, Massey Univ., 1970] unpaged.

Z4116.R6

Archives

New Zealand. National Archives. A guide to Dominion archives. Wellington, Dept. of Internal Affairs, 1953. 27p. **DF22**

Includes a section on government publications and bibliography, p.25–27. (Earlier name of issuing body: Dominion Archives.) CD2563.A52

—— Preliminary inventory, no.1–9. Wellington, Dept. of Internal Affairs, 1953–60. **DF23**

Contents: Archives of: no.1, The Governor-General. 12p.; no.2, The New Zealand Company. 16p.; no.3, The Army Dept. 16p.; no.4, The provinces of New Ulster and New Munster and of the Civil Secretary's Office. 15p.; no.5, The provinces of Otago and Southland. 16p.; no.6, The provinces of Wellington and Hawke's Bay. 15p.; no.7, The provinces of Auckland and Taranaki. 15p.; no.8, The provinces of Nelson and Marlborough and of the Nelson Trust Funds Board. 27p.; no.9, The old land claims commission. 42p.

Ceased publication. The *National register of archives and manuscripts in New Zealand* has been announced as a looseleaf service beginning 1985.

Encyclopedias and dictionaries

Bateman New Zealand encyclopedia. Gordon McLauchlan, ed. in chief. Auckland, David Bateman Ltd., [1984]. 656p. il., maps. **DF24**

Aims to present a popular and comprehensive view of New Zealand history, politics, society, the environment, literature, people, etc. Appendixes include a chronology of New Zealand history, population statistics, agricultural statistics, overseas trade statistics. Subject index.

Encyclopaedia of New Zealand. A. H. McLintock, ed. Wellington, R. E. Owen, Govt. Printer, 1966. 3v. il. **DF25**

Prepared under government auspices, and more than six years in preparation, this is the first really comprehensive encyclopedia for New Zealand. An alphabetical arrangement is employed, but, where practicable, closely related topics are grouped under broad subject headings (e.g., "Universities" are treated under "Education"; "Army" under "Defense") with appropriate subdivisions and cross references. There are, of course, lengthy articles on New Zealand history, literature, etc., and an extensive series on aspects of Maori life and culture. Biographies given separate entries are largely confined to deceased persons; a section on "Expatriates" offers biographical sketches of a considerable number of New Zealanders who are more or less permanently living or working abroad. Most articles (particularly the longer ones) are signed with the initials of the contributors, and many carry bibliographies. Numerous line drawings, maps, and statistical tables (1961 census figures are used) are scattered throughout the text, and there are plates of black-and-white photographs. Good general index in v.3. **DU405.E5**

D G

Oceania

GENERAL WORKS

Bibliography

See also CE107–CE117.

Bernice P. Bishop Museum. Library. Dictionary catalog of the library, Bernice P. Bishop Museum, Honolulu, Hawaii. Boston, G. K. Hall, 1964. 9v. **DG1**

Photoreproduction of the author, subject, and title cards from the Library's catalog. The Museum "confines its efforts entirely to study of the peoples and natural areas of the Pacific," and concentration of interest is in "cultural anthropology, archaeology, marine zoology, malacology, entomology, music, further recording of linguistic material, astronomy, bibliography."—*Pref.*

————— ————— 1st-2d supplement. Boston, G. K. Hall, 1967–69. 2v.

Z881.H785

Bibliography of periodical articles relating to the South Pacific. v.1–5, 1974–78. Suva, Fiji, Univ. of the South Pacific Lib., 1976–82. Annual. **DG2**

Esther Dam, comp. and ed.

A classed listing within geographical sections for Oceania, Melanesia, Micronesia, Polynesia. Author index. References are drawn from about 200 periodicals received in the University of the South Pacific Library. Continued by *South Pacific periodicals index,* v.6–8 (1979–81), publ. 1984.

Burton, Robert E. Travel in Oceania, Australia, and New Zealand: a guide to information sources. Detroit, Gale, [1980]. 123p. (Geography and travel information guide ser., v.2) **DG3**

An annotated bibliography of 360 periodicals and books, with preference given to available titles published in the last ten years and older books of significant historical or anthropological value. In-

cludes Pitcairn and Easter Island, but not Hawaii, the Philippines, or Indonesia. Provides general information on government, capital, languages, currency, ethnic groups, tourist offices, airline and steamship offices. Z4001.B87

California. University, Santa Cruz. Library. Catalog of the South Pacific collection. Santa Cruz, The Library, 1978. 722p. **DG4**

Contents: Pt.1, Author, title, series; pt.2, Subject entries.

Lists more than 8,500 titles cataloged for this special collection through Spring 1978.

Cammack, Floyd M. and **Saito, Shiro.** Pacific island bibliography. N.Y., Scarecrow Pr., 1962. 421p. **DG5**

"Based on a selection of materials in the Pacific collection at the University of Hawaii's Gregg M. Sinclair Library."—*Introd.*

Includes more than 1,730 items in various languages, published since 1948, in the social sciences, including education and languages. Arranged by island group: Oceania, Melanesia, Micronesia, and Polynesia. Supplements the 2d ed. (1965) of C. R. H. Taylor's *Pacific bibliography* (DG9). Z4001.C3

Du Rietz, Rolf. Bibliotheca Polynesiana; a catalogue of some of the books in the Polynesiana collection formed by the late Bjarne Krospelien and now in the Oslo University Library. Oslo, priv. pub., 1969. 455p. **DG6**

More than 1,350 items representing a selection from an outstanding collection of Oceanic books. Author listing; annotations.

Z4501.D8

Sachet, Marie-Hélène and **Fosberg, Frances Raymond.** Island bibliographies. [Wash.], Nat. Academy of Sciences–Nat. Research Council, 1955. 577p. (N.R.C. Pubn., no.335) **DG7**

————— ————— Supplement. Wash., Nat. Academy of Sciences, 1971. 427p.

For full record *see* EC83. Z5358.O3S3

Snow, Philip A. A bibliography of Fiji, Tonga, and Rotuma. Prelim. working ed. Coral Gables, Fla., Univ. of Miami Pr., 1969. 418p. **DG8**

More than 10,000 items. Classified arrangement within geographical sections; author index. Includes books, periodical articles, government publications, vernacular language items, and references to pertinent material in selected British newspapers. Z4651.S65

Taylor, Clyde Romer Hughes. A Pacific bibliography; printed matter relating to the native peoples of Polynesia, Melanesia and Micronesia. 2d ed. Oxford, Clarendon Pr., 1965. 692p. **DG9**

1st ed. 1951.

A bibliography of books and periodical articles in various languages dealing with Pacific Island groups. Arrangement is by island group, subdivided by such headings as: bibliography, ethnology, physical and mental characteristics, origins and migrations, culture contacts, tribal and family organizations, religion, medicine, language, folklore, music, arts, archaeology, dress, houses, handicrafts. In this edition listings are as complete as possible up to 1960.

The New Zealand and Maori section was revised, updated, and issued separately as item CE115. Z4501.T3

Dissertations

Coppell, William G. and **Stratigos, Susan.** A bibliography of Pacific Island theses and dissertations. [Honolulu], Research School of Pacific Studies, Australian National Univ. in conjunction with the Inst. for Polynesian Studies, Brigham Young Univ.—Hawaii Campus, [1983]. 520p. **DG10**

Aims to present "a comprehensive listing on a world-wide basis from the earliest relevant dissertation to a cut-off point at the end of 1980."—*Introd.* Omits New Zealand and Hawaii in anticipation of separate lists for those areas. Includes theses at the bachelor's and diploma levels through the doctoral level. Author listing with detailed subject index. Z4651.C66

GUAM

Nieves M. Flores Memorial Library. Union catalog of the Guam Public Library: Guam and the Pacific area materials; collections of the Guam Public Library and the Micronesian Area Research Center. [Agana, Guam], 1974. 464p. **DG11**

A main-entry listing of books, government publications, serials, and some periodical articles. In view of the lack of subject approach, Charles F. Reid's *Bibliography of the island of Guam* (N.Y., Wilson, 1939. 102p.) remains useful for earlier materials. Z4741.N54

NEW CALEDONIA

O'Reilly, Patrick. Bibliographie méthodique, analytique et critique de la Nouvelle-Calédonie. Paris, Musée de l'Homme, 1955. 361p. (Société des Océanistes. Pubn. no.4) **DG12**

A comprehensive, annotated bibliography of some 4,100 entries, covering the voyages, geology, botany, zoology, geography, ethnology, history, economy, medicine, and literature of the area. Texts in the native language are grouped with the ethnology section.
Continued by: Z4805.O7

Pisier, George. Bibliographie méthodique, analytique et critique de la Nouvelle-Calédonie, 1955–1982. Noumía, Société d'Études Historiques de la Nouvelle-Calédonie, 1983. 350p. il. (Pubn. no. 34) **DG13**

A topical listing of 3,338 books, articles, theses, and book reviews. Non-evaluative. Name index. Z4805.P57

NEW GUINEA

See Papua New Guinea.

NEW HEBRIDES

O'Reilly, Patrick. Bibliographie méthodique, analytique et critique des Nouvelles-Hébrides. Paris, Musée de l'Homme, 1958. 304p. (Société des Océanistes. Pubn., no.8) **DG14**

A comprehensive, annotated bibliography of books and periodical articles which refer to many aspects of life in the islands of the New Hebrides. For biographical material on this region, *see* the author's *Hébridais: répertoire bio-bibliographique* (AJ351). Z4820.O7

PAPUA NEW GUINEA

Faircloth, Susan, Holzknecht, Hartmut and **May, R. J.** Politics and government in Papua New Guinea. Boroko, Papua New Guinea, Inst. of Applied Social and Economic Research, 1978. 253p. (IASER bibliography, 4) **DG15**

A topical listing of books, dissertations, and scholarly articles on "social organization and control, dispute settlement, ceremonial exchange, warfare" (*Introd.*), as well as public administration, parties, interest groups, etc. More extensive than the Jones work (DG17), but does not cover history and legal materials as that does. Z7165.P33F34

Galis, Klaas Wilhelm. Bibliography of West New Guinea. [New Haven], Yale Univ., 1956. 135p. (Yale Univ. Southeast Asia Studies. Bibliography ser.) **DG16**

American edition of the author's *Bibliographie van Nederlands-Nieuw Guinea* (Hollandia, 1955).
Issued as a companion volume to the new edition of Kennedy's *Bibliography of Indonesian peoples and cultures* (DE219). Lists alphabetically by author (no subject index) 3,760 titles of books and articles in various languages, mostly Dutch. Z4813.W4G3

Jones, Gregory. Papua New Guinean history & politics; an annotated bibliography, 1950–1974. [Canberra], Canberra College of Advanced Education Lib., 1975. 133*l*. (Library bibliography ser., no.2) **DG17**

A classified arrangement of books and government publications, with author, subject and series indexes. Z4811.J64

Encyclopedias

Encyclopaedia of Papua and New Guinea. [Melbourne], Melbourne Univ. Pr. in assoc with the Univ. of Papua and New Guinea, [1972]. 3v. il., maps. **DG18**

Peter Ryan, gen. ed.
A regional encyclopedia intended for the intelligent layman, but including a number of articles of restricted interest addressed more or less to the specialist. Articles (signed, and usually including bibliographic references) deal with persons, places, terms, and with topics bearing on the historical, social, political, and economic aspects of the area. Emphasis is on Papua New Guinea (the unified name for the former Territory of Papua and the former Trust Territory of New Guinea), but covers much of what is now West Irian as well. v.3 includes both a gazetteer and an index.
DU740.E5

PHILIPPINES

Blair, Emma Helen and **Robertson, James Alexander.** The Philippine Islands, 1493–1898. v.53, Bibliography. Cleveland, Ohio, Arthur H. Clark Co., 1908. 433p. (Repr.: N.Y., Kraus, 1970) **DG19**

The 55v. set is a collection of English translations of original source materials from the time of discovery to the end of Spanish rule.
v.53 is an extensive annotated bibliography: (1) a bibliography of bibliographies published in various countries concerning the Philippines, p.55–99; (2) other printed books, pamphlets, etc., mostly published in whole or in part in *The Philippine Islands, 1493–1898;* (3) Philippine manuscripts, arranged chronologically by authors, p.143–419. DS653.B63

Chicago. University. Philippine Studies Program. Selected bibliography of the Philippines, topically arranged and annotated. Preliminary ed. New Haven, Conn., Human Relations Area Files, 1956. 138p. (Behavior science bibliographies) (Repr.: Westport, Conn., Greenwood Pr., 1973) **DG20**

Prepared by Philippine Studies Program: Fred Eggan, director; E. D. Hester, associate director.
Classed list of books and articles, mainly in English. Author index. Z3291.C45

Ferrer, Maxima M. Union catalog of Philippine materials. Quezon City, Univ. of the Philippines Pr., 1970–76. 2v. **DG21**

An enlarged ed. of *Union catalog of Philippine materials in sixty-four government agency libraries of the Philippines* (1962).
Lists materials in all subject areas and languages. Z3299.F47

Lietz, Paul S. Calendar of Philippine documents in the Ayer collection of the Newberry Library. Chicago, Newberry Lib., 1956. 259p.   **DG22**

A detailed, annotated bibliography of 370 manuscript items, *ca.* 1557–1903, "letters, journals, diaries, *testimonios* and *expedientes,* official and unofficial reports, histories and public records."—*Introd.*

Much of this material is included in the Newberry Library's *Dictionary catalog of the Edward E. Ayer collection of Americana and American Indians* (DB11).   CD3209.C5N4

Netzorg, Morton J. The Philippines in World War II and to independence (December 8, 1941–July 4, 1946); an annotated bibliography. Ithaca, N.Y., Southeast Asia Program, Dept. of Asian Studies, Cornell Univ., 1977. 232p. (Data paper, 105)   **DG23**

Lists books, essays, theses, government documents, journal articles, files of newspapers and periodicals published to 1974, covering the Japanese occupation. Author listing; no index. Annotations.   Z3298.A5N48

Philippine-American relations: a guide to manuscript sources in the United States. Comp. and ed. by Shiro Saito. Westport, Conn., Greenwood Pr., [1982]. 256p.   **DG24**

A guide to the location and general content of collections of "unpublished materials, manuscripts, and official records providing contemporary descriptions or records of the various phases of the Philippine-American encounter."—*Pref.* Includes relevant official, diplomatic, business, shipping, missionary records, etc. Information was collected through literature search, questionnaires, and visits to repositories. Listing is alphabetical by personal or institutional name of collection; general index, repository index, and chronological index.   Z1361.R4P47

Philippine studies: history, sociology, mass media, and bibliography. [De Kalb], Northern Illinois Univ. Ctr. for Southeast Asian Studies, [1978]. 402p. (Occasional paper, 6)   **DG25**

Based on papers presented at the 26th Midwest Conference on Asian Affairs, De Kalb, Oct. 1977.

For each subject area gives current information on the state of that discipline in Philippines studies, suggested research topics, and an annotated bibliography of most important sources.   DS667.28.P485

Philippines. National Library. Filipiniana materials in the National Library. Isagani R. Medina, comp. and ed. Quezon, Nat. Lib., 1972. 353p.   **DG26**

A topical listing of major holdings in whatever language, but predominantly Spanish and Philippine publications. Author index.   Z3299.M36

Saito, Shiro. The Philippines; a review of bibliographies. [Honolulu], East-West Center Lib., East-West Center, 1966. 80p. (Hawaii, Univ. East-West Center. Library. Occasional papers, 5)   **DG27**

A bibliographical essay with an author-title-subject index. Discusses Philippine bibliographies in all fields. D. V. Hart's *Annotated bibliography of Philippine bibliographies* (AA89) provides updating through 1974.   Z3291.A1S3

RYUKYU ISLANDS

King, Norman D. Ryukyu Islands; a bibliography. Wash., Govt. Prt. Off., 1967. 105p. (DA pamphlet 550-4)   **DG28**

Lists about 2,100 English-language publications arranged by broad subject areas. Includes books, articles, government publications. Some annotations; name index.   Z3307.R9K55

Thomas Hale Hamilton Library, Manoa. Ryukyu; an annotated bibliography. Comp. by Masato Matsui, Tomoyoshi

Kurokawa, Minako I. Song. Honolulu, Ctr. for Asian and Pacific Studies, Univ. of Hawaii, [1981]. 345p.   **DG29**

The Library's collection concerning Okinawa is one of the most extensive outside Japan. In three parts: (1) bibliographical essays on "Okinawan studies in the United States during the 70s" and "Ryukyuan resources at the University of Hawaii"; (2) a partially annotated listing of the collection (books, newspapers, manuscripts, maps, etc.) in topical arrangement with author index; (3) a topical listing of other materials at the University of Hawaii useful for Ryukyuan studies, with author and title indexes.   Z3307.R9T48

SAMOA

Holmes, Lowell Don. Samoan Islands bibliography. Wichita, Poly Concepts, 1984. 329p.   **DG30**

Books, chapters and page references in books, essays, periodical articles, newspaper articles (from the *New York times* and the *Samoan reporter*), theses, films, archives and manuscript collections, and documents are cited within broad subject sections. All periods of history and many languages are represented. No index.   Z4891.H65

TAHITI

O'Reilly, Patrick and **Reitman, Édouard.** Bibliographie de Tahiti et de la Polynésie française. Paris, Musée de l'Homme, 1967. 1046p. (Société des Océanistes. Pubn., 14)   **DG31**

A classified, annotated bibliography of 10,501 items.   Z4501.O72

D H

Arctic and Antarctic

BIBLIOGRAPHY

Antarctic bibliography. v.1– , 1965– . Wash., Lib. of Congress, 1965– .   **DH1**

Sponsored by the Office of Antarctic Programs, National Science Foundation. George A. Doumani, ed.

An ongoing series which, with items DH9 and DH10, now offers continuous coverage for Antarctic materials. (The first volume provided references, with abstracts, of items published between 1962 and 1964.) Arrangement is by broad subject category (biological sciences; expeditions; geological sciences; ice and snow; political geography, etc.) with subject, author, geographic, and grantee indexes. International coverage. Locates copies.

New volumes appear at irregular intervals (i.e., whenever 2,000 abstracts have been compiled, they are assembled for publication in form of a bound volume).   Z6005.P7A55

——— Indexes. [v.1–2] Wash., 1977–84. 2v.

Contents: [v.1] v.1–7; [v.2] v.8–12.

Cumulates the volume indexes according to the same categories mentioned above. Anonymous journal articles are indexed under journal title.

Arctic Institute of North America. Arctic bibliography, prep. for and in cooperation with the Dept. of Defense. Wash., Govt. Prt. Off., 1953–75. v.1–16. maps. Annual. **DH2**

Publisher varies.

Prepared under the general direction of Marie Tremaine. v.1–3 form the basic bibliography, and list some 20,000 publications in many languages representing all phases of the subject: geographical, scientific, and sociological. Emphasis is on the 19th and 20th centuries. In two parts: (1) Alphabetical author list with full title in the original language, imprint, and collation. Russian titles are given in LC transliteration. Translations into English are added for foreign titles. Entries include books, government documents, and periodical articles. There are brief annotations or abstracts, and location is given for the copy used; (2) A comprehensive subject-geographic index of some 100,000 entries, arranged under 18,000 subject and geographic headings.

v.4 emphasizes material published 1950–52; v.5 covers material published 1950–53, but in both volumes earlier material is included.

v.6–16 published annually, each volume lists as many current or recent items as possible, as well as older materials not previously included. Emphasis is on scientific, technical, and medical materials, and the number of items in foreign languages, particularly in Russian, is increased. Ceased publication. Z6005.P7A7

Arctic Institute of North America, Montreal. Library. Catalogue of the Library. Boston, G. K. Hall, 1968. 4v. **DH3**

The institute was founded in 1945 "to promote objective study of arctic and cold weather conditions, principally by the encouragement of both applied and basic research in the physical, biological and social sciences, as well as technology."—*Pref.* Its Library, the catalog cards for which are here reproduced, is one of the world's largest polar collections.

Continued by:

———— ———— 1st–3d Supplement. Boston, G. K. Hall, 1971–80. 1v., 2v., 3v.

The supplements cover additions to the library from 1968 through early 1978. No further supplements are to be published by G. K. Hall. In 1979 the Arctic Institute and Library became part of the University of Calgary; its collection policy now stresses materials pertaining to the Canadian north. Z6005.P7A73

Chavanne, Josef, Karpf, Alois and **LeMonnier, Franz.** Die Literatur über die Polar-Regionen der Erde. Wien, E. Hölzel, 1878. 335p. (Repr.: Amsterdam, Meridian Publ. Co., 1962) **DH4**

Added title page and preface in English: The literature on the polar regions of the earth.

6,617 items—books and periodical articles—in various languages. Classified under geographical area, with author index. Z6005.P7C5

Dekin, Albert A. Arctic archaeology: a bibliography and history. N.Y., Garland, 1978. 279p. **DH5**

For full information *see* DB202.

Hayton, Robert D. National interests in Antarctica, an annotated bibliography. Comp. for the U.S. Antarctic proj-

ects officer, 1959. Wash., Govt. Prt. Off., 1960. 137p. folded map. **DH6**

An "area" bibliography which "associates together the relevant material on international law, foreign policy, economic exploitation, strategic significance, world politics, explorations, and expeditions affecting national claims (potential and declared), and analogous rivalries and considerations in the Arctic."—*Introd.*

Lists books, articles, and documents under 27 countries and the United Nations. Detailed author, title, and subject index. Z6005.P7H35

Scott Polar Research Institute. Library. The library catalogue of the Scott Polar Research Institute, Cambridge, Eng. Boston, G. K. Hall, 1976. 19v. **DH7**

Contents: v.1–7, Author catalog; v.8–14, Subject catalog; v.15–19, Regional catalog.

———— ———— First supplement. Boston, 1981. 5v.

Lists books, pamphlets, conference proceedings, articles, and files of periodicals on all areas of study relating to the Arctic and Antarctic. Z6005.P7S22

Stefansson Collection. Dictionary catalog of the Stefansson collection on the polar regions in the Dartmouth College Library. Boston, G. K. Hall, 1967. 8v. **DH8**

Photoreproduction of the catalog cards representing the Collection as of 1962. Z6005.P7S8

U.S. Naval Photographic Interpretation Center. Antarctic bibliography. Wash., Govt. Prt. Off., 1951. 147p. maps. (Repr.: N.Y., Greenwood Pr., 1968) **DH9**

5,500 items, arranged in classified form, with author index. The five main divisions, each with detailed subdivisions, are: (1) biological sciences; (2) geo-physical sciences; (3) geographical sciences; (4) geographical exploration; and (5) other subjects.

Continued chronologically by: Z6005.P7U57

U.S. Library of Congress. Antarctic bibliography, 1951–1961. Wash., Lib. of Congress, 1970. 349p. **DH10**

"Prep. by the Library of Congress and sponsored by the Office of Polar Programs, National Science Foundation."—*title page.*

Fills the gap between the Naval Photographic Interpretation Center's *Antarctic bibliography* (above) and the continuing series of the same title (DH1). Z6005.P7U563

ATLASES

Thorén, Ragnar. Picture atlas of the Arctic. Amsterdam and N.Y., Elsevier, 1969. 449p. il. **DH11**

Photographs, text, and small maps are combined to provide a survey of Arctic regions, including such matters as water and ice conditions, mineral resources, transportation, etc. Chapters are devoted to the Arctic Ocean, drifting ice stations, the Arctic regions of Alaska, the Canadian Arctic, Greenland, Iceland, Norwegian Islands in the Arctic, Arctic Scandinavia, and the Soviet Arctic. Bibliographical references; index. G610.T45

E

Science, Technology, and Medicine

❖The need for up-to-date, factual information in science, technology, and medicine was the guiding concern in the compilation of this section. As a result, there is an emphasis on current publications such as handbooks and directories which supply data, and the abstract and index journals which are the access tools for the primary literature. Older publications, especially bibliographies, which continue to have validity are included here; however, outdated publications, even if unique, are not included in most instances. There is, for example, a noticeable lack of recent directory publications comparable to the works published two decades ago dealing with Soviet science; but since the older works no longer provide accurate information, they are excluded.

The needs of specialized or large, comprehensive science, technical, and medical libraries determined the selection of works for inclusion in this section. While most of the works are of interest to the research institution, many of the same works will serve the needs of any library or individual seeking information in the disciplines included in this section.

The works in Section E, while frequently highly specialized, represent a selection of published materials and not necessarily the most specialized. In each subsection there are listings of guides which allow the reader to gain access to even more specialized or detailed publications.

In the medical subsection (EK) particular attention has been given to the concepts of "self-help" and the "consumer's right to know." Works have been selected according to criteria which emphasize authority and accuracy.

It is the practice in this section to include the comprehensive, discipline-wide indexes and abstract journals and to exclude those with narrow or specific coverage; however, many of the latter exist. Both types of works may be judged on the basis of authority, coverage, promptness, and indexes. Questions considered in evaluating works include the following:

I. Authority
   A. Is it sponsored by a recognized society or group?
   B. Is the abstracting done by a competent office force with the help and advice of experts? By scholars who are specialists in the field?
II. Completeness of coverage and adequacy of abstracting and listing

A. Is the coverage comprehensive, including all articles in the field published in the periodicals of all countries?
B. Are the abstracts adequate, including precise and detailed data, formulas, measurements, etc.?
C. Are the titles of articles given in the original language or in translation?
D. Is there a complete and up-to-date list of abbreviations for the periodicals abstracted?
III. Promptness
   A. How soon after the publication of the original article does the abstract appear?
   B. Is the nature of the material such that promptness is essential?
IV. Comprehensiveness and kind of index
   A. Are there author, subject, formula, and patent indexes?
   B. Are they detailed and well organized?
   C. How frequently are they published? Do they cumulate?

E A

General Works

GUIDES

See also EA55.

Aluri, Rao and **Robinson, Judith Schiek.** A guide to U.S. government scientific and technical resources. Littleton, Colo., Libraries Unlimited, 1983. 259p.   **EA1**

"This guide is organized to reflect the normal patterns of scientific communications where the information goes through a number of successive stages. . . . [It] is a guide to the literature and *not* a current bibliography."—*Introd.* Emphasizes the type of information available and the means of gaining access to it. Indexed.

Q224.3.U6A43

Chen, Ching-Chih. Scientific and technical information sources. Cambridge, Mass., M.I.T. Pr., [1977]. 519p. **EA2**

This guide organizes the literature into 23 categories according to format or subject (e.g., Guides to the literature, Handbooks, History). Entries include brief annotations and references to reviews. Compiled for library school students as well as professionals, the guide includes an extensive bibliography of references arranged by topic. Indexed. Z7401.C48

Grogan, Denis Joseph. Science and technology: an introduction to the literature. 4th ed. London, Clive Bingley, distr. in U.S.A. by Shoe String Pr., 1982. 400p. **EA3**

1st ed. 1970.
This textbook introduces the student to the forms of the literature of science and technology both in print and online. Examples are used as illustrations in describing the uses of reference sources; however, there is neither a subject emphasis nor an attempt to provide a defined level of listing for any form. Subject index, but none of titles. Q223.G76

Herner, Saul. A brief guide to sources of scientific and technical information. 2d ed. Arlington, Va., Information Resources Pr., 1980. 160p. **EA4**

1st ed. 1969.
An annotated guide to basic information sources intended for the engineer and the scientist. Includes a listing of principal science libraries in the United States, with information about collections and services. Indexed. Q225.5.H47

Malinowsky, Harold Robert and **Richardson, Jeanne M.** Science and engineering literature: a guide to reference sources. 3d ed. Littleton, Colo., Libraries Unlimited, 1980. 342p. **EA5**

1st ed. (1967) had title: *Science and engineering reference sources.*
A guide for the student and special librarian. The text has been rewritten, restructured, and reduced, and the number of reference sources expanded from 1,096 to 1,273. Annotated entries are arranged by form and by subject. Indexed. Z7401.M28

Primack, Alice Lefler. Finding answers in science and technology. N.Y., Van Nostrand Reinhold, [1984]. 364p. il. **EA6**

"This book is intended for use by 'hobby' scientists, advanced high school, junior college, and undergraduate college students, and the teachers and librarians helping these users."—*Pref.* A subject arranged narrative guide to using printed and online science resources. Indexed. Z7401.P86

Smith, Robert V. Graduate research: a guide for students in the sciences. Philadelphia, ISI Pr., [1984]. 182p. il. **EA7**

"This book addresses the problems of developing and improving research skills and preparing for professional careers."—*Pref.* In 11 chapters from "Getting started" to "Getting a job," the guide discusses concerns such as time management, ethics, and library and literature work. Bibliography; index. Q180.55.M4S58

Walford, Albert John. Walford's Guide to reference material. 4th ed., with the assistance of Anthony P. Harvey and H. Drubba. [London], Library Assoc. [distr. in North America by Amer. Lib. Assoc.], [1980]- . v.1- . (In progress) **EA8**

3d ed., 1973-77 had title: *Guide to reference material (see AA506).*
Contents: v.1, Science & technology (697p.).
v.1 covers UDC classes 5/6 and includes about 4,000 titles with references to 1,000 more "subsumed entries" within the annotations. Compilation ended in Mar. 1979. Coverage is comprehensive, although there is emphasis on recent and British publications. Many

annotations include a reference to a review. Indexed by main entry and subject; "subsumed entries" are not indexed. Z1035.1.W33

BIBLIOGRAPHY

Bibliographie der deutschen naturwissenschaftlichen Literatur, hrsg. im Auftrage des Reichsamtes des Innern vom Deutschen Bureau der Internationalen Bibliographie in Berlin. Jena, Fischer; Berlin, Neymanns, 1902-14. 18v. **EA9**

The German titles as furnished in the *International catalogue of scientific literature* (EA17). Z7403.B55

Blackwell, Richard J., comp. A bibliography of the philosophy of science, 1945-1981. Westport, Conn., Greenwood Pr., [1983]. 585p. **EA10**

"Our purpose is to provide assistance to both the neophyte and the expert in finding one's way around within the vast contemporary literature on the philosophy of science."—*Introd.* Citations to books and articles are arranged in seven major categories with subdivisions. Entries within subdivisions are by author. Appendixes include lists of major series and periodicals cited. Index of personal names.
Z7405.P74B57

British Museum (Natural History). Library. Catalogue of the books, manuscripts, maps and drawings in the British Museum (Natural History). London, Trustees, 1903-40. 8v. **EA11**

Contents: v.1-5, A-Z; v.6-8, Supplement, A-Z.
An author catalog of one of the world's finest collections on natural history. Includes many analytics and occasional descriptive notes. A subject approach is provided for atlases, dictionaries, encyclopedias, and gazetteers. Titles of words in non-roman alphabets are transliterated, then translated. Z7409.B85

British scientific and technical books. 1935/52-1953/57. London, publ. for Aslib by J. Clarke; [N.Y.] Hafner, 1956-60. 2v. **EA12**

Supplements the *Catalogue of British scientific and technical books* (3d ed. British Science Guild, 1930).
A listing of the "most important and useful books on science and technology published in the United Kingdom and the Dominions . . ." —*Introd.* Reappraises the books listed in the *Aslib book list* (EA25), omitting some and adding others, in order to present a comprehensive bibliography of books published by commercial publishers during the period. "Books in all the divisions of pure and applied science are represented together with those publications in such fields as psychology, documentation, architecture and photography which are of interest to technical readers." Notes presence of illustrations or bibliographies, date of previous edition, and level of difficulty. Arranged by Universal Decimal Classification with author and subject indexes. Z7407.G7B85

Clark, Alan J. Book catalogue of the Library of the Royal Society. [Frederick, Md.], Univ. Pubns. of America, 1982. 5v. **EA13**

Photographic copies of catalog cards for 62,500 books and pamphlets cataloged through November 30, 1981. Entries are in alphabetical order by personal or corporate name; personal name is preferred. A valuable source for historians of science since the Library of the Royal Society was established in 1667.
Z792.R69C53

Deniker, Joseph and **Descharmes, René.** Bibliographie des travaux scientifiques (sciences mathématiques, physiques et naturelles) pub. par les sociétés savantes de la France depuis l'origine jusqu'en 1888; dressée sous les auspices du Ministère de l'Instruction Publique. Paris, Impr. Nationale, 1922. v.1-2. **EA14**

Publ. in parts, 1895-1922; v.1, ed. by Joseph Deniker; v.2, by René Descharmes.
Contents: v.1-2, pt.1, Ain-Sarthe.
A companion work to Lasteyrie's *Bibliographie générale des*

travaux historiques . . .; on the same scale and intended to do for scientific societies what Lasteyrie has done for historical. Unfortunately not finished.

Arranged by *département* and then by city. Complete contents are given for each volume of the publications of the societies included. No index. For plan and general arrangement, *see* Lasteyrie (DC157). Z7403.D39

A guide to the culture of science, technology, and medicine. Paul T. Durbin, gen. ed. N.Y., Free Pr., [1980]. 723p. **EA15**

Specialists have contributed nine survey articles, with extensive bibliographies, on the state-of-the-art of the history, philosophy, and sociology of science, technology, and medicine. Focus of the work is on value issues in the sciences and the place of science, technology, and medicine in contemporary culture. There is only incidental coverage of environmental issues. Bibliographic introductions to the individual essays vary in content, some discussing major reference sources, others citing classic or standard works. Indexed. Q175.5.G84

Index bibliographicus. 4th ed. La Haye, Fédération Internat. de Documentation, 1959–64. 2v. **EA16**

Contents: v.1, Science and technology; v.2, Social sciences.

Each volume is a classified directory of abstracting and bibliographical services which were published on a current basis at time of compilation of the lists. Z1002.I38

International catalogue of scientific literature, 1st–14th annual issues. Publ. for the International Council by the Royal Society of London. London, Harrison, 1902–21. 14v. **EA17**

An annual bibliography covering books and articles in a large number of important scientific journals.

Each annual issue consists of 17 sections: A, Mathematics; B, Mechanics; C, Physics; D, Chemistry; E, Astronomy; F, Meteorology; G, Mineralogy; H, Geology; J, Geography, mathematical and physical; K, Paleontology; L, General biology; M, Botany; N, Zoology; O, Human anatomy; P, Anthropology; Q, Physiology; R, Bacteriology.

Each part includes: (1) schedules and indexes in four languages; (2) an author catalog; and (3) a subject catalog. The purpose is to record the titles of all original contributions since Jan. 1, 1901, in certain branches of science.

While issued, this was the most important current bibliography covering all the sciences. Publication was suspended after the issue of the volumes for 1914.

———— List of journals with abbreviations used in the Catalogue as references. London, 1903. 312p. Suppl., 1904. 68p.

Z7403.I61

John Crerar Library, Chicago. Author-title catalog. Boston, G. K. Hall, 1967. 35v. **EA18**

Photoreproduction of the catalog of about 563,000 cards. The classified subject catalog is also available (Boston, 1967. 42v. plus index). Z881.C5212

———— Industrial technical library, a bibliography. Wash., Technical Aids Branch, Off. of Industrial Resources, Internat. Cooperation Admin., [1960]. 264p. **EA19**

"Annotated listings of approximately 3000 books and periodicals, representing a sound guide for the selection of a balanced industrial technical library."—*Foreword.* Classified arrangement; no author index. Z7911.J63

Mitcham, Carl and **Mackey, Robert.** Bibliography of the philosophy of technology. Chicago, Univ. of Chicago Pr., [1973]. 205p. **EA20**

Originally published as v.14, no.2, pt.2 (April 1973) of *Technology and culture.*

In four main sections: (1) Comprehensive philosophical works; (2) Ethical and political critiques; (3) Religious critiques; (4) Metaphysical and epistemological studies.

Lists works showing an "awareness of the philosophical significance of modern technology."—*Introd.* Concentrates on works of the period 1925–72. Where it seemed advisable, foreign-language titles have been translated and placed in brackets. Important and/or hard-to-secure sources are annotated more extensively than others. Only articles worthy of special notice are cited independently of general collections. There is an appendix of "Classical documents" and "Background materials." No index.

Pure & applied science books: 1876–1982. N.Y., Bowker, [1982]. 6v. **EA21**

Subtitle: Subject index, author index, title index.

This listing "of over 220,000 titles in science and technology published and distributed in the United States and spanning publication dates from before 1800 [*sic*] through 1982 covers all aspects of the physical and biological sciences and their applications . . . as well as every type of technology, engineering, agriculture, domestic arts and science and manufactures."—*Pref.* Entries are arranged by LC subject heading and include full LC cataloging data. Indexed by author (personal and corporate) and by title. Z7401.P89

Reuss, Jeremias David. Repertorium commentationum a societatibus litterariis editarum. Secundum disciplinarum ordinem digessit I. D. Reuss. . . . Gottingae, apud Henricum Dieterich, 1801–21. 16v. (Repr.: N.Y., B. Franklin, 1961) **EA22**

Contents: (1) Historia naturalis, generalis et zoologia; (2) Botanica et mineralogia; (3) Chemia et res metallica; (4) Physica; (5) Astronomia; (6) Oeconomia; (7) Mathesis, mechanica, hydrostatica, hydraulica, hydrotechnia, aerostatica, pnevmatica, technologia, architectura civilis, scientia navalis, scientia militaris; (8) Historia; (9) Philologia, linguae, scriptores graeci, scriptores latini, litterae elegantiores, poesis, rhetorica, ars antiqua, pictura, musica; (10–16) Scientia et ars medica et chirurgica.

A very valuable index to the publications of the learned societies of various countries from the time of the founding of each society to 1800, thus preceding the Royal Society's *Catalogue of scientific papers* (below). Z5051.R44

Royal Society of London. Catalogue of scientific papers, 1800–1900. London, Clay, 1867–1902; Cambridge, Univ. Pr., 1914–25. 19v. (Repr.: Metuchen, N.J., Scarecrow Pr., 1968) **EA23**

v.1–6, 1st ser., 1800–63; v.7–8, 2d ser., 1864–73; v.9–11, 3d ser., 1874–83; v.12, Supplementary volume, 1800–83; v.13–19, 4th ser., 1884–1900.

A monumental index of the first importance in scientific or large reference libraries. Papers of a purely literary, technical, or professional nature are excluded; medicine is excluded unless the material relates to anatomy or physiology. An author index, for the whole of the 19th century, to 1,555 periodicals in various languages including the transactions of the European academies and other learned societies. Gives, for each article entered: author's name in full when it can be found, full title, title of periodical, volume, date, and inclusive paging. For Russian articles the original title is given followed by French, German, or English translation in brackets. A listing of abbreviations and sources consulted precedes each series, giving considerable bibliographic information and noting instances when particular volumes were not available for review.

Z7403.R88

———— ———— Subject index. Cambridge, Univ. Pr., 1908–14. v.1–3 in 4. **EA24**

Contents: v.1, Pure mathematics; v.2, Mechanics; v.3, Physics: pt.1, Generalities, heat, light, sound; pt.2, Electricity and magnetism.

A subject index to the same material as covered by the above author catalog, classified according to the schedules of the *International catalogue of scientific literature* (EA17). The original plan was to publish separate index volumes for each of the 17 sciences of the schedules of the *International catalogue,* but only the first three were issued. These index 116,687 articles from 1,555 periodicals. The *Subject index* gives sufficiently full information to be used independently of the author volumes, i.e., author's name, brief title, periodical, volume date, and paging; though, for full title, reference must be made to the author index.

Continued, for material after 1900, by the *International catalogue of scientific literature.* Z7403.R881

Current

Aslib book list: a monthly list of recommended scientific and technical books with annotations. v.1– , Oct. 1935– . London, Aslib, 1935– . **EA25**

Frequency varies: 1936–47, quarterly; March 1948– , monthly. Subtitle varies.

A classed list intended as a selection guide for public, university, and special librarians. Brief annotations often indicate the reason for a book being recommended. Annual index.

For cumulations *see* EA12. Z7403.A84

Bibliographia scientiae naturalis Helvetica. v.1– , 1925– . Bern, Apud Bibliothecam Nationalem, 1927– . Annual. **EA26**

Title varies: 1925–47, *Bibliographie der schweizerischen naturwissenschaftlichen und geographischen Literatur* (varies slightly).

Records books and articles in the exact, geological, and biological sciences which concern Switzerland. Titles appear in the language of publication. Classed arrangement with subject and author indexes. Z7401.B5

Kyed, James M. and **Matarazzo, James M.** Scientific, engineering, and medical societies publications in print, 1980–1981. N.Y., Bowker, 1981. 626p. **EA27**

1974 ed. publ. under title: *Scientific, technical and engineering societies publications in print, 1974–75.*

Contains in-print lists of 303 societies. Arrangement of lists is alphabetical by society. Information includes: society address, order or sales office address, and publications with prices. Author index; periodical title index. Z7911.K92

New York. Public Library. New technical books; a selective list with descriptive annotations. 1915– . N.Y., Lib., 1915– . v.1– . 10 nos. a yr. **EA28**

Subtitle varies. Frequency varies.

A selective list of current noteworthy American imprints, with occasional notice of foreign imprints of importance. Annotations usually consist of full tables of contents followed by short descriptive notes. "Subject emphasis is on the pure and applied physical sciences, mathematics, engineering, industrial technology, and related disciplines," but titles in the natural and physical sciences sometimes appear. Level of content ranges from introductory to advanced. Arranged by broad Dewey classification with annual classified, author, and subject indexes. Z5854.N542

Scientific and technical books and serials in print. 1972– . N.Y., Bowker, 1972– . Annual. **EA29**

Title varies.

An author, title, and subject index to scientific and technical books available from United States publishers. Derived from *Books in print* (AA590).

General and juvenile

Appraisal; children's science books. v.1, no.1– , Winter 1967– . Cambridge, Mass., Children's Science Book Review Committee, 1967– . 3 times a yr. **EA30**

Sponsored by the Harvard Graduate School of Education and the New England Round Table of Children's Librarians.

Succinct criticisms by a scientist and a librarian for each title covered, with ratings by each reviewer. Intended for children's librarians, teachers, and other buyers and users of children's books. Z7401.A63

Deason, Hilary J. The AAAS science book list; a selected and annotated list of science and mathematics books for secondary school students, college undergraduates and non-

specialists. 3d ed. Wash., Amer. Assoc. for the Advancement of Science, 1970. 439p. **EA31**

1st ed. 1959.

An annotated list of 1,530 titles, arranged according to Dewey classification, in the biological, physical, behavioral, medical, engineering, agricultural, and mathematical sciences. Contains evaluative annotations and designation of level of difficulty. Indexed by author, subject and title.

Science books & films. v.11, no.1– . [Wash.], Amer. Assoc. for the Advancement of Science, 1975– . 5 nos. per yr. **EA32**

Title varies: *AAAS science books & films.*

Continues *Science books; a quarterly review* (v.1–10, 1965–75).

An annotated, classified listing of new books, films, filmstrips, and videocassettes in the pure and applied sciences. Provides a useful selection guide for libraries serving students from the elementary grades through the first two years of college. Symbols indicate reading level, recommendation, etc.

Three selective compilations of evaluations appearing in *Science books & films* have been published: *The best books for children: a selected and annotated list of science books for children ages five through twelve,* comp. and ed. by Kathryn Wolff and others (Wash., Amer. Assoc. for the Advancement of Science, 1983. 271p.; AAAS pubn. 83–5); *Films in the sciences: reviews and recommendations; selected science and mathematics films for students, teachers, professional, and general audiences,* comp. and ed. by Michele M. Newman and Madelyn A. McRae (Wash., Amer. Assoc. for the Advancement of Science, 1980. 172p.; AAAS pubn. 80–9); and Kathryn Wolff's *The best science films, filmstrips, and videocassettes for children* (Wash., Amer. Assoc. for the Advancement of Science, 1982. 140p.; AAAS pubn. 82–6). Z7403.S83

Wolff, Kathryn and **Storey, Jill.** AAAS book list supplement. Wash., Amer. Assoc. for the Advancement of Science, 1978. 457p. **EA33**

"A selected and annotated list of science and mathematics books which supplements the *AAAS science book list* [EA31] for secondary school students, undergraduates, teachers and nonspecialist readers."—*t.p.* Arranged by Dewey Decimal Classification. Author index; title and subject index. Z7401.W64

Yearbooks

See also EA97.

Science year; the World book science annual, 1965– . Chicago, Field Enterprises, 1965– . il. Annual. **EA34**

Offers a series of clear and detailed articles by specialists on specific topics, plus a "Science file" which provides (in alphabetical arrangement) reports on the recent developments in various areas of science. Also includes a biographical section on recent science award winners, a list of the year's awards and prizes, and a necrology. Good color illustrations. Indexed. Useful beyond the juvenile level. Q9.S33

Yearbook of science and the future, 1975– . Chicago, Encyclopaedia Britannica, [1976–]. il. Annual. **EA35**

Continues *Britannica yearbook of science and the future,* 1969–74.

Designed to provide those who have little or no background in science with authoritative, up-to-date information about current scientific and technological efforts and advances. A useful reference source for the general reader. Q9.B78

Translations

Gt. Brit. Dept. of Scientific and Industrial Research. Translated contents lists of Russian periodicals. . . . London, 1949–58. no.1–117. Monthly. **EA36**

Subtitle: With list of recent accessions of Russian scientific and technical books and parts of serial publications available in the British Museum.

Each issue contains a list of periodicals whose contents are included, the translated contents pages, translations of periodical articles available from the Science Museum Library, and a list of accessions of Russian scientific and technical books and individual periodical issues received by the British Museum in the weeks preceding publication.

Ceased publication Dec. 1958. Continued by: Z7403.G65

NLL translations bulletin. v.1–12, 1959–70. London, Stat. Off., 1959–70. v.1–12. Monthly.   **EA37**

Title varies: v.1–2, *LLU translations bulletin,* issued by Gt. Brit. Dept. of Scientific and Industrial Research, Lending Library Unit.

Issues contain listings of new books received from the USSR with introduction or author's preface given in translation, new cover-to-cover translations available from the National Lending Library or from other sources, and translations of articles available from the Library, but giving only citation and shelf number. Ceased publication.   Q4.N12

National Translations Center. Consolidated index of translations into English. N.Y., Special Libraries Assoc., 1969. 948p.   **EA38**

Brings together "information on the availability of translations which have appeared in a number of different lists issued by different agencies at different times. . . . Included are translation bibliographies, selective translation journals and collections of translations. Cover-to-cover translations of journals are not listed article by article. . . . Items included . . . are restricted to translations (in English) of serially published originals such as journals, patents, standards, etc."—*Introd.* In two sections: (1) Serial citation index; and (2) Patent citation index. In the serial section, listing is alphabetical by title of the journal, followed by indication of year of publication, volume, issue, pages, and source from which the translation is available. Patents are listed under the name of the country issuing the patent.

Supplemented by: Z7403.N273

Translations register-index. v.1, no.1– . [Chicago], National Translations Center, John Crerar Library, 1967– . Monthly, with semiannual and annual cumulated indexes.   **EA39**

Frequency varies.

The National Translations Center is a depository and information source for unpublished translations into English in the whole range of natural, physical, medical, and social sciences. The *Translations register-index* lists (in classed arrangement) new accessions to the Center, together with references to translations available from the National Technical Information Service (formerly the Clearinghouse for Federal Scientific and Technical Information) and from commercial sources.

The *Register-index* is the direct successor to *Technical translations* (Wash., U.S. Dept. of Commerce, Office of Technical Services, 1959–67), which in turn superseded *Translation monthly* (Chicago, Special Libraries Assoc., 1955–58). Holdings of the National Translations Center are listed in those earlier publications, as well as in the *S.L.A. list of translations* (N.Y., 1953) and its 1954 supplement (both published by the Special Libraries Association's Translations Activities Committee), and in the *Bibliography of translations from Russian scientific and technical literature* prepared by the Scientific Translations Center of the Library of Congress (List 1-39, Oct. 1953–Dec. 1956).

World index of scientific translations and list of translations notified to ETC. v.6–10, 1972–76. Delft, European Translations Centre, 1972–76. Monthly.   **EA40**

Supersedes *World index of scientific translations* (v.1–5, 1967–71) and assumes its numbering.

In two sections, the first listing the monthly acquisitions of the Centre in broad subject categories, and giving full citations. The second part is the "World index." Listing here is by name of the periodical in which the material originally appeared, with indication of year, volume, and page numbers of the article translated (but not the author and title of the article) and of the source from which the translation is available.

Continued by:

World index of scientific translations and list of translations notified to the International Translations Centre. v.11. Delft, International Translations Centre, 1977. Monthly.   **EA41**

Continued by:

World transindex. v.1– , 1978– . Delft, International Translations Centre, 1978– . Monthly.   **EA42**

Subtitle: Announcing translations in all fields of science and technology.

"A joint publication of International Translations Centre, Commission of the European Communities, Centre National de la Recherche Scientifique."—*t.p.*

Text in English, French, and German.

Dissertations

Masters theses in the pure and applied sciences, accepted by colleges and universities of the United States and Canada, 1955/56– . N.Y., Plenum, 1957– . v.1– . Annual.   **EA43**

Title varies: v.1–2, *Master's theses accepted by U.S. colleges and universities in the fields of chemical engineering, chemistry, mechanical engineering . . .* v.3, *Master's theses and doctoral dissertations in the pure and applied sciences. . . .*

Publisher varies: The first 12v. were produced, published, and distributed by the Thermophysical Properties Research Center, School of Mechanical Engineering, Purdue University, Lafayette, Ind.; v.13–17 (1969–73) were produced by the Center and printed and distributed by Xerox University Microfilms; v.18– , 1974– published and distributed by Plenum Press.

An annual list of master's theses completed at accredited colleges and universities. Arrangement is alphabetical by discipline, subdivided by university, then alphabetically by author. "Mathematical and most life sciences have been excluded from this publication, on a purely arbitrary basis. . . . Biochemistry, biophysics, and bioengineering are included in the coverage when titles in these areas are reported together with chemistry, physics and engineering and not as a separate discipline."—*Contents page.* Covers theses completed since 1955. Subject indexing discontinued after 1960. Canadian theses are listed beginning with v.18, 1974.   Z7401.M35

Maire, Albert. Catalogue des thèses de sciences soutenues en France de 1810 à 1890 inclusivement. Paris, Welter, 1892. 224p.   **EA44**

Lists over 2,100 theses, giving publication information, format, and pagination, date, and brief biographical information for each author. Arranged by university, then chronologically. Author and subject indexes.   Z7403.M22

Lavaud, Suzanne. Catalogue des thèses de doctorat ès sciences naturelles, soutenues à Paris de 1891 à 1954. Paris, Person, 1955. 257p.   **EA45**

A partial continuation of Maire, above. Arranged chronologically with author and subject indexes.

Periodicals

Bibliography

BioSciences Information Service of Biological Abstracts. Bibliographic guide for editors and authors. [By] Biosciences Information Service of Biological Abstracts, Chemical Abstracts Service, Division of the American Chemical Society [and] Engineering Index, Inc. Wash., Amer. Chemical Soc., 1974. 362p.   **EA46**

Prepared through the combined efforts of BIOSIS, CAS, and EI, Inc. to aid in improving the reliability and usefulness of bibliographic information found in scientific and technical publications. Contents divided into three sections: (1) *Guideline for use of the coded bibliographic strip;* (2) *Bibliographic standards,* an annotated list of international standards especially relevant for editors and authors; (3) *Serial titles, abbreviations and codes,* giving the complete titles with the standardized abbreviations and ASTM CODEN for some 27,700 serial publications.

Superseded in part by *International serials catalogue* (EA51).

Z6945.A2B55

Bolton, Henry Carrington. Catalogue of scientific and technical periodicals, 1665–1895 . . . together with chronological tables and a library check-list. 2d ed. Wash., Smithsonian Inst., 1897. 1247p. (Smithsonian miscellaneous collections, v.40) (Repr.: N.Y., Johnson, 1965) **EA47**

8,603 titles. Pt.1 (4,954 titles) is a reprint of the 1st ed., 1885, with changes to date; pt.2 includes additions to titles in pt.1, and titles 5001–8477; addenda, titles 8478–8603.

"Intended to contain the principal independent periodicals of every branch of pure and applied science, published in all countries from the rise of this literature to the present time."—*Pref.* Excludes medicine but includes anatomy, physiology, and veterinary science. Usually omits publications of learned societies. Gives full titles, names of editors, changes of titles, dates, etc. The chronological tables permit the finding of volume numbers for specific years.

Z7403.B69

British Museum (Natural History). Library. List of serial publications in the British Museum (Natural History) Library. [London, Trustees of the British Museum], 1980. 3v. **EA48**

1st ed. 1968.
An alphabetical listing of about 20,000 serials held by the library. Emphasis is on the life sciences, geology, mineralogy, general science, and natural history.

Continued by: Z7403.B844

———— Serial publications in the British Museum (Natural History) Library. 1984– . London, [The Museum], 1985– . Microfiche. Semiannual. **EA49**

The first microfiche edition (January 1985) contains approximately 24,000 entries.

Chicago. Center for Research Libraries. Rarely held scientific serials in the Midwest Inter-Library Center. Publ. under a grant from the National Science Foundation. Chicago, 1963. 197p. **EA50**

Issued under the Center's earlier name, Midwest Inter-Library Center.

An alphabetical listing of those titles abstracted in *Chemical abstracts* and *Biological abstracts* which were not received by member libraries of the Center. Many cross references for alternate forms of title, including those used by the two abstracting services. The Center undertook to subscribe to all of these periodicals beginning with 1957, and its holdings are included with each entry.

———— ———— Supplement 1–5. Chicago, 1964–68.

Z7403.M615

International Council of Scientific Unions. Abstracting Board. International serials catalogue. [Paris], Internat. Council of Scientific Unions, Abstracting Board; distr. by Biosciences Information Service, Philadelphia [1978]. 2v. **EA51**

Contents: Pt. I, Catalogue; Pt. II, Index/Concordance.
The *Catalogue* lists in alphabetical order the serial publications abstracted and indexed by the member services of the ICSUAB, and includes journal abbreviation, CODEN, ISSN, and the initials of the services indexing the journal. The *Index/Concordance* includes an ISSN to CODEN list in numerical order and a CODEN to ISSN list in alphabetical order; each is associated with corresponding page numbers in the *Catalogue.*

United Nations Educational, Scientific and Cultural Organization. List of annual reviews of progress in science and technology. Liste de "mises au point" annuelles sur les progrès de la science et de la technique. 3d ed. [Paris, UNESCO, 1981] 43p. **EA52**

1st ed. 1965.
Introduction in English and French.
A classed listing of "annual series containing papers which review fairly narrow topics within the broader subject designated by the serial title."—*Introd.*

World list of scientific periodicals published in the years 1900–1960. 4th ed., ed. by Peter Brown and George Burder Stratton. London, Butterworth, 1963–65. 3v. **EA53**

1st ed. 1925–27.
More than 60,000 titles of periodicals concerned with the natural sciences, of which issues were published during the period 1900–60. Periodicals first published at any time before 1900 are listed so long as they continued publication into the 20th century. Because of the growth in scientific publication in the years 1951–60, titles appearing during this period account for about a quarter of the present edition. Some 10,000 titles which appeared in the 3d ed. have been omitted as being of social or commercial rather than of scientific interest. Arrangement is alphabetical by title with standard abbreviation, location, dates of publication, and coverage given where known. Holdings of British participating libraries are given. "Titles in the Cyrillic and Greek alphabets are arranged according to their transliterated form, but the transliteration and original alphabet are both given in the entries; titles in other non-Roman alphabets are given only in transliteration."—*Editors' note.*

Now continued in *British union-catalogue of periodicals, incorporating World list of scientific periodicals* (AE197). Z7403.W923

Japanese

Directory of Japanese scientific periodicals. Tokyo, Nat. Diet Lib., 1974. 1000p. **EA54**

Published irregularly. Previous ed. 1967. A classified list.

Z6958.J3D5

Gibson, Robert W. and **Kunkel, Barbara K.** Japanese scientific and technical literature: a subject guide. Westport, Conn., Greenwood Pr., [1981]. 560p. **EA55**

A preliminary section entitled "Analysis of information activities and bibliographic control in Japan: scientific and technical literature," is followed by a "Subject guide to Japanese scientific and technical journals." The latter lists some 9,116 science and technology journals published in Japan. Arrangement is by modified Universal Decimal Classification, with a title index. Titles are given in romanized Japanese with English translation. Sources in which a journal is indexed or abstracted are indicated by symbols.

Z699.5.S3G5

Russian

Mezhenko, IU. A. Russkaia tekhnicheskaia periodika, 1800–1916; bibliograficheskii ukazatel'. Moskva, Izd-vo Akademii Nauk SSSR, 1955. 299p. **EA56**

An annotated, descriptive bibliography, with subject and other indexes, of 415 Russian periodicals in technological fields, published between 1800 and 1916. Z7403.M57

U.S. Library of Congress. Science and Technology Division. Scientific and technical serial publications of the Soviet Union, 1945–1960. Prep. by Nikolay T. Zikeev. Wash., 1963. 347p. **EA57**

Alphabetical arrangement of Soviet journals, annuals, monographic series, etc. Titles are given in transliteration, with bracketed English translation, followed by beginning date, frequency, and LC classification number. Z7403.U5368

Abbreviations

Akademiia Nauk SSSR. Institut Nauchnoi Informatsii. Ukazatel' sokrashchennykh i polnykh nazvanii nauchnoi i tekhnicheskoi literatury. Moskva, 1957. 236p. **EA58**

Key to the abbreviations of some 12,000 world periodical titles in the series of Russian abstract journals, *Referativnyi zhurnal* (EA81), for various fields of science and technology. Lists full title and country of origin for each abbreviation. Z6945.A2A4

American Chemical Society. Chemical Abstracts Service. Chemical Abstracts Service source index; 1907–1984 cumulative. [Columbus, Ohio], Amer. Chemical Soc., [1985]. 2v. **EA59**

For full description *see* ED17.
The principal source for titles and abbreviations in the physical sciences, the life sciences, and engineering.

Dictionary of report series codes, ed. by Lois E. Godfrey and Helen F. Redman. 2d ed. N.Y., Special Libraries Assoc., 1973. 645p. **EA60**

1st ed., 1962, issued by Report Series Dictionary Committee of the SLA Rio Grande Chapter; 2d ed., a project of SLA Rio Grande Chapter members and friends.
It is the purpose of this dictionary to identify as many report series codes as possible with agencies originating the reports or assigning the numbers. Only codes used for two or more reports are included. In addition to pairing codes with related agencies and agencies with codes, notes are given on the identification of widely varying types of codes, including ambiguous numerical codes, ambiguous alphabetical codes, and codes of specific agencies. Also included is a bibliography on the report code literature.
Z6945.A2D5

International CODEN directory. 1980– . Columbus, Ohio, Chemical Abstracts Service, 1980– . Annual, with annual suppl. Microfiche. **EA61**

1st ed. 1963. Previously entitled: *Coden for periodical titles (including) non-periodical titles and deleted coden;* publisher varies.
A directory of all CODEN (unique six character codes which identify serial publications) assigned since 1950—approximately 150,000. In three parts: an index in CODEN order, an alphabetical index by full title, and a KWOC title index.

Audiovisual materials

See also EA32.

AAAS science film catalog. Wash., Amer. Assoc. for the Advancement of Science; N.Y., Bowker, 1975. 398p. **EA62**

Ann Seltz-Petrash, project ed. and comp.; Kathryn Wolff, managing ed.
Provides selection and ordering information for about 5,600 science films (pure sciences, technology, and social sciences) for elementary grades through adult level that can be bought, borrowed, or rented from United States producers and/or distributors. Arranged by subject; indexed by title. Q192.A17

INDEXES AND ABSTRACT JOURNALS

Bibliography

Abstracting and indexing services directory. Ed.1, issue no.1– , July 1982– . Detroit, Gale, 1982– . Irregular. **EA63**

For full information *see* AE215.
Provides information on about 2,250 titles in all subject areas.

International Federation for Documentation. Abstracting services. 2d ed. The Hague, Internat. Federation for Documentation, 1969. 2v. (FID pubn. 455) **EA64**

1st ed. 1965.
Contents: v.1, Science, technology, medicine, agriculture; v.2, Social sciences, humanities.
Approximately 1,500 abstracting services arranged by title—1,300 in v.1; 200 in v.2. The descriptions of the services include

editorial body, publisher, publishing history and availability, number of journals covered, language and subject. A second section gives titles arranged by UDC number and alphabetical lists of subject headings in English, French, Russian, and Spanish. Z695.I62

Owen, Dolores B. Abstracts and indexes in science and technology; a descriptive guide. 2d ed. Metuchen, N.J., Scarecrow Pr., 1985. 235p. **EA65**

1st ed. 1974.
Gives descriptions of 223 abstracts and indexes arranged in 11 subject categories, with information on arrangement, coverage, scope, a description of the abstracts, characteristics of the indexes, and existence of online databases. Title index. Z7403.O95

Indexes

Applied science and technology index (formerly Industrial arts index). N.Y., Wilson, 1913– . v.1– . Monthly (except July), with quarterly and annual cumulations. **EA66**

From 1913 to 1957, entitled *Industrial arts index.* With v.46, 1958, this was divided into two indexes: (1) *Applied science and technology index,* which carried on the old volume numbering, and (2) the *Business periodicals index* (CH203).
A cumulative subject index to about 335 English-language periodicals in the fields of aeronautics and space science, automation, chemistry, construction, earth sciences, electricity and electronics, engineering, industrial and mechanical arts, materials, mathematics, metallurgy, physics, telecommunication, transportation, and related subjects. No author entries except for a separate listing, by author, of book reviews. Z7913.I7●

Current contents . . . Philadelphia, Inst. for Scientific Information, 1961– . Weekly. **EA67**

The *Current contents* series of "current awareness" publications has appeared in various sections since 1961, continuing in part *Current contents of pharmacomedical publications.* Each weekly number reproduces the tables of contents from the most recent issues of journals in the relevant fields; a list of first authors with addresses is provided. The series is presently published in seven sections, each of them available separately: (1) *Current contents: physical, chemical & earth sciences* (formerly in separate sections for physical sciences and chemical sciences); (2) *Current contents: engineering, technology & applied sciences;* (3) *Current contents: social & behavioral sciences* (formerly in separate sections for education and for the behavioral, social, and management sciences); (4) *Current contents: life sciences;* (5) *Current contents: agriculture, biology & enviromental sciences;* (6) *Current contents: clinical practice;* (7) *Current contents: arts & humanities.*

General science index. v.1– , July 1978– . N.Y., Wilson, 1978– . Monthly (except June and December), with annual bound cumulation. **EA68**

A cumulative subject index to more than 100 English-language general science periodicals not completely covered by other abstracts and indexes. In addition, an author listing of citations to book reviews follows the main body of the index. No other author entries are included. ●

Repertorium der technischen Journal-Literatur, 1823–1908. Berlin, Heymann, 1856–1909. 40v. **EA69**

Title varies; publisher varies.
Contents: 1823–53, publ. 1856 (1049p.); 1854–68, publ. 1871–73 (2v.); 1869–73, publ. 1876–78 (2v.); 1874–1908, publ. 1875–1909 (35v.).
1823–76, hrsg. im Auftrage des Königlich Preussischen Ministeriums für Handel, Gewerbe und öffentliche Arbeiten; 1877–1908, hrsg. im Auftrage des Kaiserlichen Patentamts.
A subject index to more than 400 periodicals in various languages, arranged alphabetically by the German subject word followed, in volumes from 1892 on, by the French and English equivalents. Each volume has a detailed subject index to this subject list which, in volumes before 1892, is an index of German words only, but from

1892 includes French and English words in the same alphabet; volumes from 1897 on have an author index also. Still useful for older and foreign material.

Continued by the *Fortschritte der Technik* (1.–2. Jahrg., 1909–11. Berlin, Bibliographisch Zentralverlag, 1910–11. 9v.).

Z7913.R42

Repertorium technicum. v.1–12⁴, 1931–Apr. 1943. 'sGravenhage, Nijhoff, 1931–43. Bimonthly. **EA70**

At head of title: Nederlandsch Instituut voor Documentatie en Registratur.

An international, bimonthly bibliography, listing some 25,000–30,000 titles annually, of books and articles appearing in periodicals on technical and allied subjects. Arranged by the Universal Decimal Classification. Besides the citation to the location of the article, reference is also given, when possible, to a journal in which an abstract may be found.

Reuss, Jeremias David. Repertorium commentationum a societatibus litterariis editarum . . . T.7. Gottingae, Dieterich, 1808. 514p. (Repr.: N.Y., B. Franklin, 1961) **EA71**

Contents: Mathesis, mechanica, hydrostatica, hydraulica, hydrotechnica, aerostatica, pnevmatica, technologia, architectura civilis, scientia navalis, scientia militaris.

For complete set *see* EA22.

Science citation index. 1961– . Philadelphia, Inst. for Scientific Information, 1961– . Bimonthly with annual cumulation. **EA72**

Subtitle (varies): An international interdisciplinary index to the literature of science, medicine, agriculture, technology, and the behavioral sciences.

In three sections: Citation index, Source index, and Permuterm index. Based on the concept of citation indexing which links current and past publications, *SCI* indexes current publications (over 3,800 journals and monographic series) and lists current works in the Source index by first author. Works cited in the current publications are listed by the original (first) author in the Citation index. The Permuterm index provides subject access, based on the words in titles of articles, to the current publications listed in the Source index. Instructions for use are included inside the front cover of each volume. The annual cumulation includes "SCI journal citation reports: a bibliometric analysis of science journals in the ISI data base."

Five year cumulations issued for 1966/69–1975/79. 1955/64, also published in cumulation, includes six years not originally published in annual format. Z7401.S34●

—— **Abridged ed.,** 1984– . Philadelphia, Inst. for Scientific Information, 1984– . Monthly (except June and December) with semiannual cumulations. **EA73**

Based on the same indexing principles as *Science citation index* (above) but intended for college and public libraries not having or needing the larger work. "Nearly 550 journals are covered [including] the most important English language journals covered in the *SCI* as well as some new journals considered particularly relevant to undergraduate studies."—*Pref.* Each issue is organized into three sections: Source index, Citation index, and Subject index. The latter is the equivalent of the Permuterm index.

Technical book review index, issued by the Technology Dept. of the Carnegie Library of Pittsburgh, 1917–28. Pittsburgh, Carnegie Lib., 1917–29. 12v. Quarterly. **EA74**

An index listing much material not found in the *Book review digest* (AA513). Gives title of book and bibliographical data, references to periodicals, and brief quotations.

Continued informally, though with a gap of seven years, by:

—— Comp. and ed. in the Technology Dept., Carnegie Library of Pittsburgh. N.Y., Special Libraries Assoc., 1935– . v.1– . Monthly (except July and Aug.). **EA75**

A very useful guide to reviews in scientific, technical, and trade journals, with brief quotations from the reviews cited. Classed arrangement; an annual author index only.

Beginning Jan. 1973 (v.39, no.1) coverage was expanded to include "all scientific, technical and medical (except clinical) subjects, including life sciences and mathematics. Management and behavioral sciences will be included in the cases where they interface with science or technology." Z7913.T36

Abstract journals

France. Centre National de la Recherche Scientifique. Bulletin signalétique. Paris, Centre de Documentation du C.N.R.S., 1948–60. v.9–21. Monthly. **EA76**

Title varies: v.1–8 had title *Bulletin analytique;* v.9–16, in a new pattern of organization, also were called *Bulletin analytique.* Changes since 1960 are detailed below.

An international abstract journal, exhaustive in coverage, surveying more than 5,000 periodicals from many countries. Titles are translated into French; abstracts are in French.

v.9–21 in two parts: pt.1, Mathématiques, astronomie, physique, chimie, sciences de l'ingénieur, sciences de la terre; pt.2, Sciences biologiques, sciences pharmacologiques, industries alimentaires, agriculture.

Superseded by the following sections which continued the volume numbering of the earlier series:

Sec.1, Mathématiques pures et appliquées; Sec.2, Astronomie et astrophysique; Physique du globe; Sec.3, Physique I, Généralités—physique mathématique, mécanique, acoustique, optique, chaleur, thermodynamique; Sec.4, Physique II, Électricité; Sec.5, Physique nucléaire; Sec.6, Structure de la matière; Sec.7, Chimie I, Chimie générale, chimie physique, chimie minérale, chimie analytique, chimie organique; Sec.8, Chimie II, Chimie appliquée, métallurgie; Sec.9, Sciences de l'ingénieur; Sec.10, Sciences de la terre I, Minéralogie, géochimie, pétrographie; Sec. 11, Sciences de la terre II, Physique du globe, géologie, paléontologie; Sec.12, Biophysique. Biochimie. Chimie analytique biologique; Sec.13, Sciences pharmacologiques, toxicologie; Sec.14, Microbiologie. Virus. Bactériophages. Immunologie; Sec.15, Pathologie générale et experimentale; Sec.16, Biologie et physiologie animales; Sec.17, Biologie et physiologie végétales; Sec.18, Sciences agricoles, zootechnie, phytiatrie et phytopharmacie, aliments et industries alimentaires; Sec.19, Sciences humaines, philosophie (*see* BA34); Sec.20, Psychologie. Pédagogie; Sec.21, Sociologie. Sciences du langage; Sec.22, Histoire des sciences et des techniques.

After v.29, 1968, the organization of the series was again changed, the sections were renumbered, and many of the previous subsections were issued as separate abstract journals. Several new sections devoted to areas not previously covered in depth have also been added. Library of Congress cataloging practice now enters each section under title, *Bulletin signalétique,* with numerical designation of the section. These include:

101. Information scientifique et technique; 110, Mathématiques pures et appliquées; 120, Astronomie, physique spatiale, géophysique; 130. Physique I, Généralités, physique mathématique, mécanique, acoustique, optique, chaleur, thermodynamique; 140, Physique II, Électricité; 145, Électronique; 150, Physique, chimie et technologie nucléaires; 160, Structure de la matière I, Physique de l'état condensé, physique atomique et moléculaire; spectroscopie; 161, Structure de la matière II, Crystallographie; 170, Chimie—chimie générale et chimie physique, chimie minérale, chimie analytique, chimie organique; 210, Sciences de la terre I, Minéralogie, géochimie, géologie extraterrestre, pétrographie; 214, Sciences de la terre II, Géologie appliquée; 216, Sciences de la terre III, Géologie, paléontologie; 320, Biochimie. Biophysique. Génie biologique et médical; 330, Sciences pharmacologiques, toxicologie; 340, Microbiologie, virologie, immunologie; 346, Ophtalmologie; 347, Otorhinolaryngologie; 348, Dermatologie; 350, Pathologie générale et experimentale; 360, Biologie et physiologie animales; 361, Endocrinologie et reproduction. Génétique; 370, Biologie et physiologie végétales; 380, Sciences agricoles, zootechnie, phytiatrie et phytopharmacie, aliments et industries alimentaires; 390, Psychologie, psychopathologie; 522, Histoire des sciences et des techniques; 730, Combustibles, énergie thermique; 740, Métaux, métallurgie; 761, Microscopie électronique, diffraction électronique; 780, Polymères,

chimie et technologie; 880, Chimie appliquée, génie chimique, céramique, eaux, corps gras, papier, pollution atmosphérique; 890, Sciences de l'ingénieur.

Beginning in 1984 the sections were renumbered and many were renamed. A few sections were subdivided. The current organization follows; the numbers in parentheses refer to the pre-1984 organization.

T205(101), Sciences de l'information, documentation; E26(110), Sciences économiques, problèmes de gestion; E33(110), Informatique; E34(110), Robotique, automatique et automatisation des processus industriels; E48(120), Environnement cosmique terrestre, astronomie et géologie extraterrestre; E49(120), Météorologie; F10(130), Mécanique et acoustique; E27(130), Méthodes de formation et traitement des images; E32(130), Métrologie et appareillage en physique et physiochimie; F21(140), Électrotechnique; F20(145), Électronique et télécommunications; E12(160), État condensé; E13(161), Structure des liquides et des solides, cristallographie; E11(165), Physique atomique et moléculaire, plasmas; D01(166), Base de données "GAPHYOR"; F17(171,173), Chimie générale, minérale et organique; F16(172), Chimie analytique minérale et organique; T210(210), Industries agroalimentaires; T215(215), Biotechnologies (édition française); T216(215), Biotechnology (English edition); T022(22), Sciences de la terre; F40(220), Minéralogie, géochimie, géologie extraterrestre; F41(221), Gisements métalliques et non-métalliques, économie minière; F42(222), Roches cristallines; F43(223), Roches sédimentaires, géologie marine; F44(224), Stratigraphie, géologie régionale, géologie générale; F45(225), Tectonique, géophysique interne; F46(226), Hydrologie, géologie de l'ingénieur, formations superficielles; F47(227), Paléontologie; T235(233), Médecine tropicale; T251(251), Cancérologie (Cancernet); E84(310), Génie biomédical, informatique biomédicale; F52(320), Biochimie, biophysique moléculaire, biologie moléculaire et cellulaire; E63(330), Toxicologie; F70(330), Pharmacologie, traitements médicamenteux; E61(340), Microbiologie: bactériologie, virologie, mycologie, protozoaires pathogènes; E62(340), Immunologie; E71(346), Ophtalmologie; E72(347), Otorhinolaryngologie, stomatologie, pathologie cervicofaciale; E73(348), Dermatologie, maladies sexuellement transmissibles; E83(349), Anesthésie et réanimation; E74(352), Pneumologie; E75(352), Cardiologie et appareil circulatoire; E76(354), Gastroentérologie, foie, pancreas, abdomen; E77(355), Néphrologie, voies urinaires; E78(356), Neurologie; E79(357), Pathologie et physiologie ostéoarticulaires; E80(359), Hématologie; F54(361), Reproduction des vertébrés, embryologie des vertébrés et des invertébrés; E64(361), Endocrinologie humaine et expérimentale, endocrinopathies; E82(361), Gynécologie, obstétrique, andrologie; E81(362), Maladies métaboliques; E60(363), Génétique; T260(364), Zoologie fondamentale et appliquée des invertébrés (milieu terrestre, eaux douces); F53(365), Anatomie et physiologie des vertébrés; F56(365), Écologie animale et végétale; F55(370), Biologie végétale; F56(370), Écologie animale et végétale; E65(390), Psychologie, psychopathologie, psychiatrie; E99(401), Congrès, rapports, thèses; T230(730), Énergie; T240(740), Métaux, métallurgie; T245(745), Soudage, brasage et techniques connexes; E30(761), Microscopie électronique et diffraction électronique; F24(780), Polymères, peintures, bois; F23(880), Génie chimique, industries chimique et parachimique; E36(885), Pollution de l'eau, de l'air et du sol; F10(891), Mécanique et acoustique; T295(892), Bâtiment, travaux publics; F25(892), Transports terrestres et maritimes.   •

Government reports announcements. v.1–75, no.6, 1946–Mar. 21, 1975. [Springfield, Va.], National Technical Information Service, 1946–75. Semimonthly.   **EA77**

Title varies: Jan. 1946–June 1949, *Bibliography of scientific and industrial reports*; July 1949–Sept. 1954, *Bibliography of technical reports* (varies slightly); Oct. 1954–1964, *U.S. government research reports*; 1965–Mar. 1971, *U.S. government research and development reports*; Mar. 1971–Mar. 1975, *Government reports announcements*.

Frequency varies; issuing agency varies.

"The National Technical Information Service (NTIS) is the central source for the public sale of Government-sponsored research and development reports, and other Government analyses prepared by Federal agencies, their contractors or grantees. Federally sponsored translations and some reports written in foreign languages are also available. . . . The *Government Reports Announcements* (GRA)

is published . . . to simplify and improve public access to new report literature as it becomes available."—*Introd.*

Includes English abstracts of reports arranged by 22 subject fields with appropriate subdivisions.

Government reports announcements & index. v.75, no.7– . Apr. 4, 1975– . [Springfield, Va.], Nat. Technical Information Service, 1975– . Biweekly.   **EA78**

Formed by the union of *Government reports index* (EA80) and *Government reports announcements* (above).

Maintains the organization of *GRA*. Indexes in five sections: keyword, personal author, corporate author, contract/grant number, and NTIS order/report number.   •

Government reports annual index. v.75– . 1975– . [Springfield, Va.], Nat. Technical Information Service, 1976– . Annual.   **EA79**

Continues the cumulative indexing of *Government reports index* (below).

In five sections: keyword, personal author, corporate author, contract/grant number, and NTIS order/report number.

Government reports index. v.1–74, Feb. 15, 1965–74. [Springfield, Va.], Nat. Technical Information Service, 1965–75. Semimonthly with quarterly and annual cumulations.   **EA80**

Frequency varies. Title varies: 1965–67, *Government-wide index;* 1968–71, *U.S. government research and development reports.*

Issuing agency varies; coverage varies.

Issued concurrently with, and indexing all reports announced in *Government reports announcements* (EA77) by corporate author, subject, personal author, contract number, and accession/report number.

Referativnyi zhurnal: . . . Moskva, 1953– . Issued by: Akademiia Nauk SSSR. Institut Nauchnoi Informatsii. Frequency varies.   **EA81**

A major abstract journal for the world's literature in most branches of science and technology. Bibliographic information is listed in original languages following the Russian entry.

Titles and coverage of series have varied greatly since establishment of the journal. As of 1985 it is in 69 subject series covering the whole range of science and technology (mathematics and agriculture are included, but not clinical medicine). A current title listing is found in the "Abstracts and indexing services" section of *Ulrich's International periodicals directory* (AE10). For a good description of the series, a list of its subject sections, and a key to the distribution of specific subjects, *see:*

Copley, Eric James. A guide to Referativnyi zhurnal. 3d ed. rev. London, National Reference Library of Science and Invention, 1975. 20p. (British Library. Science Reference Library. Occasional pubn.)   **EA82**

1st ed. 1970.

"The objects of this booklet are to give a brief description of [*Referativnyi zhurnal*] and to explain how it can be used as a means of identifying literature on a wide range of subjects, even though the reader has only very limited knowledge of Russian."—*p.1.* Includes information on the scope, form, and use of *Referativnyi zhurnal.*

U.S. Defense Documentation Center. Defense Supply Agency. Technical abstract bulletin, 1953–67. Alexandria, Va., 1953–67. Semimonthly.   **EA83**

Ceased publication.

"This bulletin is provided for the users of the D.D.C." (*v.1, no.1*) and was distributed only to qualified users.

"TAB announces the availability of research, development, test and evaluation documents acquired by the . . . center."

——— Technical abstract bulletin indexes. Semimonthly.   **EA84**

Ceased publication.

Publisher and frequency vary; title varies: Mar. 1953–Aug. 1957, *Title announcement bulletin.*

Includes four indexes: (1) Corporate author—Monitoring agency; (2) Subject; (3) Personal author; and (4) Contract.

Correlation indexes

Special Libraries Council of Philadelphia and Vicinity. Correlation index: document series and PB reports, comp. by the Science-Technology Group, Special Libraries Council of Philadelphia and Vicinity, with the cooperation of Office of Technical Services, U.S. Dept. of Commerce, Wash., D.C. Ed. by Gretchen E. Runge. N.Y., Special Libraries Assoc., 1953. 271p. **EA85**

"Many of the unclassified and declassified documents listed as PB Reports in the *Bibliography of Technical Reports* have also appeared under other series designations. . . . This correlation has been compiled to show the relationship of these miscellaneous document series to the PB Report numbers. . . ."—*Pref.*

For the *Bibliography of technical reports,* see EA77.   Z7916.S65

U.S. Defense Documentation Center. Correlation index of technical reports (AD-PB reports). Wash., U.S. Dept of Commerce, Off. of Technical Services, 1958. 184p. (PB 151567S) **EA86**

A cross index from ASTIA document numbers (AD) to the ones assigned by the Office of Technical Services (PB) in making the reports available for sale to the public.

ENCYCLOPEDIAS AND HANDBOOKS

Ballentyne, Denis William George and **Lovett, D. R.** A dictionary of named effects and laws in chemistry, physics, and mathematics. 4th ed. London, Chapman & Hall; N.Y., Methuen, 1980. 346p. il. **EA87**

1st ed. 1958.
A dictionary of terms known by the names of the scientists who discovered them or worked in the fields with which their names have become connected, e.g., Curie's law, Einstein's principle of relativity, Fourier's series, etc. Gives brief definitions of the law or theory, but no indication as to who the scientist was or when he lived.
Q123.B32

Concise encyclopedia of the sciences. John-David Yule, ed. N.Y., Facts on File, [1978]. 590p. il. **EA88**

Intended to be "both a dictionary of the most commonly encountered words of science and an encyclopedia of the background material necessary for understanding their use in a wider context." —*Pref.*

Darmstaedter, Ludwig. Handbuch zur Geschichte der Naturwissenschaften und der Technik . . . 2. umgearb. und verm. Aufl. unter Mitwirkung von R. du Bois-Reymond und C. Schaefer, hrsg. von L. Darmstaedter. Berlin, Springer, 1908. 1262p. (Repr.: N.Y., Kraus, 1960) **EA89**

Chronological list of about 12,000 important scientific discoveries and inventions, dating from 3500 B.C. to 1908 A.D., giving for each its date, name of discoverer or inventor, and other brief data. Alphabetical indexes of names and of subjects. Q125.D24

Diagram Group. Comparisons: of distance, size, area, volume, mass, weight, density, energy, temperature, time, speed and number throughout the universe. N.Y., St. Martin's Pr., [1980]. 240p. il. **EA90**

Provides graphic representations of measurable phenomena. "By making comparisons between like and like and between like and unlike we can evaluate the different properties of the known world."—*Foreword.* Indexed. QC39.D5

Gardner, Martin. Fads and fallacies in the name of science. Rev. ed. N.Y., Dover, [1957]. 363p. **EA91**

A revised and expanded edition of the work first published in 1952 under the title *In the name of science.*

A collection of essays giving information about modern pseudo scientists and their theories, e.g., Voliva's flat earth, Velikovsky's worlds in collision, Bates's perfect sight without glasses, etc. New bibliographic information is included in the appendix. Index of names. Q173.G35

Geigy scientific tables. Ed. by C. Lentner. 8th rev. & enl. ed. [Basel & West Caldwell, N.J.], Ciba-Geigy, (distr. in U.S.A. by Geigy Pharmaceuticals, Ardsley, N.Y.), [1981–82]. v.1– 2. (In progress) **EA92**

Contents: v.1, Units of measurement, body fluids, composition of the body, nutrition; v.2, Introduction to statistics, statistical tables, mathematical formulae.

The tables aim to "provide scientists and, in particular, doctors with a concise compendium of scientific data backed by literature references."—*By way of explanation.* Indexed. QP33.5.G45

Greenstein, Carol Horn. Dictionary of logical terms and symbols. N.Y., Van Nostrand Reinhold, [1978]. 188p. **EA93**

"The primary objective of the *Dictionary of Logical Terms and Symbols* is to present compactly, concisely, and side by side a variety of alternative notational systems currently used by logicians, computer scientists, and engineers."—*Pref.* Notations are arranged by function, e.g., logical gate notation, truth tables, etc. Includes list of abbreviations, glossary, and bibliography. QA9.G698

Handwörterbuch der Naturwissenschaften. 2. Aufl. hrsg. von R. Dittler, G. Joos, [and others]. Jena, Fischer, 1931–35. 10v. il. **EA94**

——— Sachregister und systematische Inhaltsübersicht. Jena, Fischer, 1935. 242p. 16p.

An authoritative encyclopedia for scholars and specialists, covering botany, zoology, paleontology, physiology, mineralogy, geology, physics, and chemistry. Long, signed articles with bibliographic references; biographies of scientists no longer living. Does not include separate entries on species. Q121.H3

Harper encyclopedia of science. Ed. by James R. Newman. Rev. ed. N.Y., Harper, 1967. 1379p. il. **EA95**

1st ed. 1963 in 4v. This is not a major revision—pagination remains the same, but there is some updating.

Nearly 4,000 articles covering astronomy, biochemistry and biophysics, biology, chemistry, geology, history and philosophy of science (and logic), mathematics, meteorology, physics, and technology. Articles have been contributed by some 450 specialists and are signed. For the most part they are concise and are written for the scientist or the intelligent, educated layman. Bibliographies are not affixed to the articles, but there is a classified bibliography which lists reference works, general discussions, survey texts, and works on special topics. All material is in English. Comprehensive index.
Q123.H26

McGraw-Hill encyclopedia of science & technology. 5th ed. N.Y., McGraw-Hill, [1982]. 15v. il. **EA96**

Subtitle: An international reference work. . . .
1st ed. 1960.
A comprehensive encyclopedia covering all branches of science and technology. This edition "is the most ambitious revision since this reference work was first published in 1960. . . . The articles are written by leading authorities each writing about his or her particular areas of expertise in clear, readable language that is useful to students and nonprofessionals as well as to professionals."—*Pref.*

An introductory article generally provides a broad survey of each branch of science, and separate articles cover the main subdivisions and more specific aspects. Cross references lead to related topics. Biographical and historical articles are excluded. Bibliographies follow most of the longer articles. Articles are signed. v.15 includes a list of contributors, scientific notation used in the encyclopedia, a detailed analytical index, and a "Topical index" which groups the articles under 75 major subject areas of science and technology.

Kept up-to-date between editions by the *McGraw-Hill yearbook of science and technology* (1962–).

The publisher has derived a number of other encyclopedias from this edition, including: *McGraw-Hill concise encyclopedia of science and technology* (1984. 2200p.); *McGraw-Hill encyclopedia of astronomy* (1983. 450p.); *McGraw-Hill encyclopedia of chemistry* (1983. 1195p.); *McGraw-Hill encyclopedia of electronics and computers* (1983. 964p.); *McGraw-Hill encyclopedia of engineering* (1983. 1264p.); *McGraw-Hill encyclopedia of physics* (1983. 1343p.).

Q121.M3

Powell, Russell H., ed. Handbooks and tables in science and technology. 2d ed. [Phoenix, Ariz.], Oryx Pr., [1983]. 297p.   **EA97**

1st ed. 1979.

A guide to approximately 4,000 publications. Entries provide full bibliographic information, LC number, ISBN, document or report access number, price, and series. Entries are annotated. Subject index; author/editor index. Publisher's directory.   Z7405.T3P68

Special Libraries Association. Science-Technology Division. Handbook of scientific and technical awards in the United States and Canada, 1900–1952, ed. by Margaret A. Firth. N.Y., Assoc., [1956]. 491p.   **EA98**

"A selected listing of the most important awards presented by certain of the scientific and technical societies in the United States and Canada to individuals in recognition of their meritorious achievements in scientific fields."—*Introd.*

Arranged alphabetically by name of society with the awards listed chronologically under society, giving names of the recipients and, from 1929 to 1952, citations of published references concerning the awards. Also describes the award, the criteria for selecting the recipient, and whether there is a monetary reward, a citation, or a medal. Provides biographical facts about recipients and specific accomplishments for which award was granted. Canadian awards appear as a separate listing following American awards. An index of recipients and award titles, and a separate subject index.

Q141.S63

——— ——— Supplement 1. N.Y., Assoc., 1981. 1v., various paging.

Van Nostrand's Scientific encyclopedia. 6th ed. N.Y., Van Nostrand Reinhold, [1983]. 3067p. (Publ. in 2 eds.: 1v.; 2v.) il.   **EA99**

Subtitle: Animal life; biosciences; chemistry; earth and atmospheric sciences; energy source and power technology; mathematics and information sciences; materials and engineering sciences, medicine, anatomy, and physiology; physics; plant science; space and planetary sciences.

Douglas M. Considine, ed.; Glenn D. Considine, managing ed. 1st ed. 1968.

A single, alphabetical arrangement of terms used in science and technology. Entries vary in length from a few lines to several pages. Selected references are added to longer entries. A useful work for the scientist and the layman.   Q121.V3

The way things work; an illustrated encyclopedia of modern technology. N.Y., Simon & Schuster, [1967]–1971. 2v. il.   **EA100**

Translated and adapted from *Wie funktioniert das?* by "an English-American team," using English terminology with footnotes giving American equivalents. ". . . not a reference book in the ordinary sense. It has been designed to give the layman an understanding of *how things work,* from the simplest mechanical functions of modern life to the most basic scientific principles and complex industrial processes that affect our well-being."—*Foreword.*

T47.W3913

Style manuals and report writing

Booth, Vernon. Communicating in science: writing and speaking. Cambridge, Cambridge Univ. Pr., [1985]. 68p.   **EA101**

The successor to an essay first written in 1970.

A succinct guide to the elements of style. Bibliography; index.   Q223.B665

Day, Robert A. How to write and publish a scientific paper. 2d ed. Philadelphia, ISI Pr., [1983]. 181p.   **EA102**

1st ed. 1979.

"The purpose of this book is to help scientists and students of the sciences in all disciplines to prepare manuscripts that will have a high probability of being accepted for publication and of being completely understood when they are published."—*Pref.* Indexed.

T11.D33

Freedman, George and **Freedman, Deborah A.** The technical editor's and secretary's desk guide. N.Y., McGraw-Hill, [1985]. 1v., various pagings.   **EA103**

In two parts: (1) Technical narration and notation; (2) Reference section. "This book is addressed to those who transcribe or type scientific or technical material."—*Pref.* Provides descriptive, contextual assistance rather than being a prescriptive style manual. Includes a 147-page dictionary of technical terms. Indexed.

T11.4.F74

O'Connor, Maeve and **Woodford, F. Peter.** Writing scientific papers in English; an ELSE-Ciba Foundation guide for authors. N.Y. & Amsterdam, Elsevier, 1976. 108p.   **EA104**

"Sponsored by the International Union of Biological Sciences, the International Union of Geological Sciences, and EDITERRA [European Association of Earth-Science Editors]."—*t.p.*

"This guide is for scientists of any nationality who want to submit papers to journals published in English. . . . Our guidelines are in general agreement with the recommendations to authors contained in the (American) *CBE Style Manual,* but they take both British and American English usage into account as well as certain European printing practices that differ from those in the USA."—*Introd.*

T11.O25

Weisman, Herman M. Basic technical writing. 5th ed. Columbus, Ohio, Merrill, [1985]. 479p. il.   **EA105**

1st ed. 1960.

A detailed style manual to assist writers to convey technical and scientific information and ideas. Emphasizes expository techniques, technical report writing, and short forms of technical writing such as correspondence and proposals. Contains examples. Bibliography; index.   T11.W43

Bibliography

Society of Technical Writers and Publishers. An annotated bibliography on technical writing, editing, graphics, and publishing, 1950–1965. Eds.: Theresa Ammannito PhiFor, Ruth K. Hersch and Helen V. Carlson. [Wash., 1966]. 1v., unpaged.   **EA106**

Published jointly by the Society of Technical Writers and Publishers and the Carnegie Library of Pittsburgh.

A computer-produced bibliography of 2,000 entries. Permuted title index and author index.

Continued by: Z7405.T4S6

An annotated bibliography on technical writing, editing, graphics, and publishing, 1966–1980. Eds. Helen V. Carlson, *et al.* [Wash., Soc. for Technical Communications, 1983] 1v., unpaged.   **EA107**

DICTIONARIES

Bibliography

International bibliography of specialized dictionaries. Fachwörterbücher und Lexika, ein internationales Verzeichnis. 6th rev. ed. [Editorial direction: Helga Lengenfelder] München & N.Y., K.G. Saur, 1979. 470p. (Handbook of international documentation and information, v.4)   **EA108**

1st ed. 1960 published as *Technik und Wirtschaft in fremden Sprachen; internationale Bibliographie der Fachwörterbücher*, by Karl Otto Saur.

This edition employs a classified subject arrangement, with indexes of authors and editors, publishers and distributors, and subject fields. About 5,000 entries. Emphasis is on works published since 1960, but includes older works which are still in print.

Z7004.D5I55

Marton, Tibor W. Foreign-language and English dictionaries in the physical sciences and engineering; a selected bibliography 1952 to 1963. Wash., 1964. 189p. (U.S. National Bureau of Standards. Miscellaneous pubn. 258) **EA109**

"Lists over 2800 unilingual, bilingual, and polyglot dictionaries, glossaries and encyclopedias . . . arranged in 49 subject classes. . . . Forty-seven foreign languages are represented."—*Abstract.* The principal selection criterion was usefulness of the cited work to the English-speaking scientific community. For the majority of titles English is either the source language, target language, or the language in which the definitions are written. Entries consist of author, original title, abbreviated translation of foreign title, LC card number, and approximate number of terms. QC100.U57

Rechenbach, Charles William and **Garnett, Eugene R.** A bibliography of scientific, technical, and specialized dictionaries: polyglot, bilingual, unilingual. Wash., Catholic Univ. of America Pr., 1969. 158p. **EA110**

More than 1,200 items in subject arrangement, with language, subject, and compiler indexes. Z7405.D5R42

United Nations Educational, Scientific and Cultural Organization. Bibliography of interlingual scientific and technical dictionaries. Bibliographie de dictionnaires scientifiques et techniques multilingues. Bibliografía de diccionarios científicos y técnicos plurilingües. 5th ed. [Paris], UNESCO, [1969]. 250p. **EA111**

1st ed. 1951.
Introductory matter in English, French and Spanish.
Arranged by Universal Decimal Classification; lists some 2,500 dictionaries in about 75 languages. An index by languages, an index by authors, and subject indexes in English, French, and Spanish are provided.

Wüster, Eugen. Bibliography of monolingual scientific and technical glossaries . . . Bibliographie de vocabulaires scientifiques et techniques monolingues . . . [Paris], UNESCO, [1955–59]. 2v. **EA112**

Contents: v.1, National standards; v.2, Miscellaneous sources.
v.1 lists only the standardized technical glossaries as approved by the national associations of standardization; v.2 lists 1,043 privately published glossaries in 26 languages. Arranged by Universal Decimal Classification, and then by language.
"A 'monolingual technical glossary (or vocabulary, or dictionary)' is taken here to include any publication which lists the stock of terms ('vocabulary') appertaining to any given field of knowledge in any one language, whether with or without explanations other than translations"—*Introd.* Gives full bibliographic information for each entry, arrangement, and whether explanation of terms is by definition or illustration. Author, subject, and language indexes.

Z7913.W8

General

Cailleux, André and **Komorn, Jean.** Dictionnaire des racines scientifiques. 3ème éd., rev. et augm. Paris, Société d'Éditions d'Enseignement Supérieur, [1981]. 263p. **EA113**

1st ed. 1961.
A dictionary of word roots in the pure and applied sciences. About 1,200 entries added in this edition. Q123.C3

Concise science dictionary. Oxford & N.Y., Oxford Univ. Pr., 1984. 758p. il. **EA114**

"Aims to provide school and first-year university students with

explanations of unfamiliar words they might come across in the course of their studies, in their own or adjacent disciplines."—*Pref.*
Q123.C68

Crispin, Frederic Swing. Dictionary of technical terms. 11th ed. rev. N.Y., Bruce, [1970]. 455p. il. **EA115**

1st ed. 1929.
"This Dictionary has been prepared for the use of students, draftsmen, mechanics, builders, electricians, and for workmen generally to assist them in understanding the technical terms which are in use in all sections of the United States."—*Pref.* Includes definitions of commonly used terms and expressions from a large number of fields (e.g., aeronautics, architecture, woodworking and building trades, printing, plastics, chemistry, televison). T9.C885

Daintith, John. A dictionary of physical sciences. N.Y., Pica; distr. by Universe Books, 1977 [c.1976]. 333p. il. **EA116**

A companion to *A dictionary of earth sciences* (EE4) and *A dictionary of life sciences* (EC21). A handy, easy-to-use, concise dictionary for the physical sciences. Q123.D22

Dictionary of science and technology. Eds.: T. C. Collocott and A. B. Dobson. Rev. ed. [London], Chambers, 1975. 2v. **EA117**

1st ed. 1971.
On spine: Chambers's Dictionary of science and technology.
A direct successor to *Chambers's Technical dictionary* (1st–3d eds. 1940–58). Consists primarily of an alphabetical listing of terms with short definitions whose purpose is "to set on record the basic language of communication between those engaged or interested in the numerous branches of scientific activity today."—*Pref.* Appendixes contain a table of chemical elements with such handbook data as specific gravity, melting point, discoverer, and date of discovery; the periodic table; taxonomies of igneous and sedimentary rocks and of plant and animal kingdoms; physical concepts, physical constants, and standard values. Physical concepts and physical constants are also expressed in SI (Système International) units.
Q123.D53

Graham, Elsie Challand, ed. The Basic dictionary of science. Edited in Basic English for the Orthological Institute. N.Y., Macmillan, [1966]. 568p. **EA118**

First published London, Evans Bros., 1965.
Lists some 25,000 terms in the fields of chemistry, physics, biology, medicine, psychology, astronomy, geology, anthropology, engineering, aeronautics, and metallurgy, with definitions given in Basic English, a selection of 850 English words chiefly representative of those key ideas into which more complex ones may be broken down. "The general level of selection and detail is about that of first-year university work."—*Pref.* Entries give part of speech and discipline to which terms pertain. Appended are lists of technical abbreviations, the chemical elements, homologous series of organic chain compounds, geological timetable, plant and animal kingdom classifications, weights and measures, and conversion factors.
Q123.G7

Hough, John Newbold. Scientific terminology. N.Y., Rinehart, 1953. 231p. **EA119**

This small handbook, intended for the student, aims to help those who have little or no knowledge of Latin or Greek to understand the meaning and formation of scientific terms. Most of the chapters have brief, annotated bibliographies. Q179.H68

McGraw-Hill dictionary of scientific and technical terms. Syvil P. Parker, ed. in chief. 3d ed. N.Y., McGraw-Hill, [1984]. 1781p. il. **EA120**

1st ed. 1974.
The standard dictionary for science and technology. This edition includes 98,500 terms with 115,000 definitions. Definitions are brief; each term is identified according to the field of science or technology. Pronunciation is not indicated. Uses SI (International System) units. An appendix includes data such as the periodical table, symbols, etc.
The publisher has derived several specialized dictionaries from

this lexical base; titles available include: *McGraw-Hill dictionary of chemistry* (1984. 665p. il.; *see* ED41); *McGraw-Hill dictionary of earth sciences* (1984. 850p. il.); *McGraw-Hill dictionary of electronics and computer technology* (1984. 522p. il.); *McGraw-Hill dictionary of engineering* (1984. 659p. il.); *McGraw-Hill dictionary of science and engineering* (1984. 942p. il.).   Q123.M15

Nybakken, Oscar Edward. Greek and Latin in scientific terminology. Ames, Iowa State College Pr., [1959]. 321p.
EA121

Deals with the "construction of the technical terms, names, and specific epithets used in the medical and biological sciences."—*Pref.* Includes discussion on language in general and the Latin and Greek languages in particular, especially in regard to scientific terminology. Includes alphabetical lists of Latin and Greek root words with the English scientific terms which are derived from them.
Q179.N9

Speck, George Eugene and **Jaffe, Bernard,** eds. A dictionary of science terms. N.Y., Hawthorn, [1965]. 272p. il.
EA122

Published in London (1954) under title *The science reader's companion.*
A useful work for the layman.   Q123.S6

Abbreviations

Ocran, Emanuel Benjamin. Ocran's Acronyms: a dictionary of abbreviations and acronyms used in scientific and technical writing. London, Routledge & Kegan Paul, [1978]. 262p.
EA123

A collection of abbreviations and acronyms found in journal articles and technical reports. Excludes foreign abbreviations and acronyms and those for associations, institutions, and governmental bodies. Entries in the main alphabetical section are subdivided and listed by 47 subject fields.   Q179.O24

Wennrich, Peter. Anglo-American and German abbreviations in science and technology. 1st ed. N.Y. Bowker; München, Verlag Dokumentation, 1976–77. 3v.   **EA124**

Subtitle: *Anglo-amerikanische und deutsche Abkürzungen in Wissenschaft und Technik.*
A compilation of more than 150,000 German and Anglo-American abbreviations taken from some 800 international journals. "More than 60% [of the abbreviations] are found in the Anglo-American sphere. . . ."—*Foreword.* German and English words are interfiled in a single alphabetical sequence.   Q179.W44

—— —— Supplement. N.Y., Bowker; München, Verlag Dokumentation, 1980. 618p.

Zimmerman, Oswald Theodore and **Lavine, Irwin.** Scientific and technical abbreviations, signs and symbols. 2d ed. Dover, N.H., Industrial Research Service, 1949. 541p. il.
EA125

1st ed. 1948. Arranged by groups including: General list of abbreviations and symbols, Chemistry, Mechanics, Shop terms, Electricity, Mapping, etc. Brief subject index, but no general index to abbreviations. The chief purpose is to answer the question "What is the standard abbreviation for . . .?" rather than "What does this abbreviation stand for?"   Q179.Z5

Juvenile

Compton's Illustrated science dictionary. Ed. in chief, Charles A. Ford. Indianapolis, David-Stewart, [1969]. 632p. il.
EA126

"Prepared to help young people and adults understand and use correctly the exacting language of today's science and technology." —*Pref.*
Gives pronunciation, definition, and a sentence illustrating the

use of each word. Indicates differing meanings of words in the different sciences. The words have been chosen from 14 sciences taught in the schools: aeronautics, anatomy, astronautics, astronomy, biology, botany, chemistry, earth science, engineering, mathematics, medicine, physics, physiology, and zoology. The vocabulary of the definitions is at the lowest reading level possible. Simple illustrations are provided. Appendix material includes the periodic table, scientific symbols and abbreviations, plant and animal kingdom classifications, and prefixes and affixes of scientific terms.
Q123.C65

Foreign terms

Czech

Kapesní anglicko-český a česko-anglický technický slovník. Sest. Josef Novák. 2. vyd. Praha, Státni Nakl. Technické Literatury, 1959. 495p.   **EA127**

Added title page: A concise English-Czech and Czech-English technical dictionary.   T9.K15

French

Cusset, Francis. Technical dictionary; electricity, mechanics, mining, metallurgy, sciences. English-French, French-English. 7th ed. rev. and enl. N.Y., Chemical Publ. Co., 1967. 434p.   **EA128**

1st ed. 1946 had title *English-French and French-English technical dictionary.*
A simple glossary without explanatory or introductory remarks of any kind. A brief appendix provides conversion data from and to metric measure.

DeVries, Louis. French-English science and technology dictionary. 4th ed. N.Y., McGraw-Hill, 1976. 683p.   **EA129**

1st–3d ed. (1940–62) publ. under title: *French-English science dictionary for students in agricultural, biological, and physical sciences.* This ed. rev. and enl. by Stanley Hochman.
"This new edition has been revised to include some 4,500 terms. . . . The new entries have been incorporated into the Supplement which follows the main body of the dictionary."—*Introd.*
Q123.D37

Dorian, Angelo Francis. Dictionary of science and technology: English-French. N.Y. & Amsterdam, Elsevier, 1979. 1586p.   **EA130**

A massive dictionary with over 150,000 terms from over 100 fields. Entries indicate the field to which the term belongs and the French equivalent. Definitions are given only when necessary to obviate ambiguity.   Q123.D672

—— Dictionary of science and technology: French-English. N.Y. & Amsterdam, Elsevier, 1980. 1086p.   **EA131**

A companion to the compiler's English-French volume (above).

German

DeVries, Louis and **Herrmann, Theo M.** German-English technical and engineering dictionary. 2d ed., rev. and enl. N.Y., McGraw-Hill; Wiesbaden, Brandstetter Verlag, [1966]. 1178p.   **EA132**

1st ed. 1950; supplement, 1959, by Louis De Vries.
Gives English equivalents of German words and expressions. This edition "has been completely revised, antiquated terms removed and the valid material of the supplement incorporated. In addition, the vocabulary has been considerably enhanced and brought up to date by the valuable and generous contributions from various branches of industry which supplied the newly-coined terminology from recent development and research."—*Pref.*   T9.D48

—— English-German technical and engineering dictionary. 2d ed., rev. and enl. N.Y., McGraw-Hill, [1967]. 1154p.   **EA133**

1st ed., 1954, and supplement, 1959, by Louis De Vries.
A companion to the German-English volume, above.   T9.D47

DeVries, Louis. German-English science dictionary. 4th ed. N.Y., McGraw-Hill, [1978]. 628p.   **EA134**

"Updated and expanded by Leon Jacolev with the assistance of Phyllis L. Bolton."—*t.p.*

1st ed. 1954.

"The Fourth Edition introduces the newly specialized terminologies of nuclear science and engineering, computer science and data processing, solid state physics, molecular biology, genetics, automation, soil and environmental sciences, electronics, etc. . . . For the sake of expediency . . . the new terms have again been . . . incorporated into the Addendum."—*Pref.*   Q123.D42

Dorian, Angelo Francis. Dictionary of science and technology. English-German. 2d rev. ed. N.Y. & Amsterdam, Elsevier, 1978, 1401p.   **EA135**

Added title page: *Handwörterbuch der Naturwissenschaft und Technik. Englisch-Deutsch.*

1st ed. 1967.

"A large number of terms which could rightly be regarded as ballast has been eliminated and about 16,000 new lemmata inserted, mainly relating to those branches of science and technology which are being constantly developed in our times."—*Pref.*   Q123.D67

—— Dictionary of science and technology. German-English. 2d rev. ed. N.Y. & Amsterdam, Elsevier, 1981. 1119p.   **EA136**

Added title page: *Handwörterbuch der Naturwissenschaft und Technik.*

1st ed. 1970.

A companion to the compiler's English-German volume (above).

Leibiger, O. W. and **Leibiger, I. S.** German-English and English-German dictionary for scientists, comprising chemistry, physics, mathematics, engineering, aeronautics, dynamics, biology, physiology, medicine, and other sciences. 1st ed. Ann Arbor, Mich., J. W. Edwards, 1950. 381p., 360p.   **EA137**

Compiled over a period of 30 years from scientific writings in both languages. Comprises a glossary of "scientific words of special interest which could not be found in existing dictionaries."—*Pref.*   Q123.L4

Leidecker, Kurt Friedrich. German-English technical dictionary. Based on data comp. by the U.S. Air Force. N.Y., Vanni, 1951. 2v. (968p.)   **EA138**

Subtitle: Of aeronautics, rocketry, space-navigation, atomic physics, higher mathematics, jet-engines, turbines, hydraulics, petroleum industry, civil and mechanical engineering, ballistics, electronics, radio, radar, aerophotography, television, infrared research, communication, meteorology, topography, aeromedicine.

A glossary of 100,000 terms related to aeronautics, compiled at the end of World War II to assist in the clarification of new concepts, phenomena, and devices revealed by the capture of German documents.

Lueger, Otto, ed. Lueger Lexikon der Technik. 4. vollst. neubearb. und erw. Aufl. Hrsg. von Alfred Ehrhardt und Hermann Franke. Stuttgart, Deutsche Verlags-Anstalt, [1960–72]. 17v. il.   **EA139**

Contents: Bd.1, Grundlagen des Maschinenbaues; Bd.2, Grundlagen der Elektrotechnik und Kerntechnik; Bd.3, Werkstoffe und Werkstoffprüfung; Bd.4, Lexikon der Bergbaues; Bd.5, Lexikon der Hüttentechnik; Bd.6–7, Lexikon der Energietechnik und Kraftmaschinen; Bd.8–9, Lexikon der Fertigungstechnik und Arbeitsmaschinen; Bd.10–11, Lexikon der Bautechnik; Bd.12, Lexikon der Fahrzeugtechnik; Bd.13–14, Lexikon der Feinwerktechnik; Bd.15, Lexikon der Fabrikorganisation und Fördertechnik; Bd.16, Verfahr-

enstechnik, Nahrungsmitteltechnik, Haushalttechnik; Bd.17, Registerband.

Each volume is an alphabetically arranged dictionary, with frequent cross references and with definitions varying in length from a few lines to several columns, many with bibliographies. Definitions are enhanced by generous use of plates, diagrams, figures, and tables. Contributors are identified by means of numerical codes.   T9.L953

Webel, A. A German-English dictionary of technical, scientific, and general terms. 3d ed. London, Routledge, 1953. 939p. (Repr. 1974)   **EA140**

Subtitle: Including a list of atomic weights, specific gravities, melting and boiling points of elements, abbreviations, signs and symbols, botanical section, and an appendix of new words.

1st ed., 1930, entitled *A German-English technical and scientific dictionary.*   T10.W4

Greek

Charalampēs, Iōnnēs B. Technikon Anglohellēnikon lexikon. Athēnai, 1958. 486p.   **EA141**

Hungarian

Magyar-angol müszaki szótár. [Szerk: Nagy Ernö, Klár János és Katona Lóránt vezetésével az Akadémiai Kiadó müszaki szótárszerkesztöi munkaközössége] 5. változatlan kiad. Budapest, Akadémiai Kiadó, 1983. 752p.   **EA142**

1st ed. 1957.

Added title page: Hungarian-English technical dictionary.

The first Hungarian-English dictionary of scientific and technical words and terms. Lists about 120,000 Hungarian technical terms with English equivalents.   T9M14

Angol-magyar müszaki szótár. Szerk: Nagy Ernö [és] Klár János. 5. változatlan kiad. Budapest, Akadémiai Kiadó, 1980 [c.1959]. 791p.   **EA143**

Added title page: English-Hungarian technical dictionary. Compl. rev. and enl. ed.

1st ed. 1951. A companion volume to the entry above.   T10.A575

Italian

Denti, Renzo. Dizionario tecnico italiano-inglese, inglese-italiano . . . Abbreviazioni techniche anglo-americane aggiornate, tabelle di conversione e riduzione, ecc. 10. ed. riv., ampliata ed aggiornata. Milano, Hoepli, [1981]. 1643p.   **EA144**

Added title page: Italian-English, English-Italian technical dictionary.

1st ed. 1946.   T10.D45

Gatto, Simon. Dizionario tecnico scientifico illustrato: italiano-inglese, inglese-italiano. A dictionary of technical and scientific terms: English-Italian, Italian-English. Milan, Ceschina, [1960]. 1381p. il.   **EA145**

A collection of some 60,000 terms covering both engineering and other scientific fields, including many new terms culled from scientific literature.   T9.G35

Marolli, Giorgio. Dizionario tecnico: inglese-italiano, italiano-inglese. Technical dictionary: English-Italian, Italian-English. 11. ed. interamente riv. ed ampl. Firenze, Le Monnier, 1980. 2215p.   **EA146**

A comprehensive bilingual dictionary.   T9.M18

Norwegian

Ansteinsson, John. English-Norwegian technical dictionary. Engelsk-norsk teknisk ordbok. 3d rev. ed. Trondheim, Brun, 1984. 541p.   **EA147**

1st ed. 1948.

——— Norwegian-English technical dictionary. Norsk-engelsk teknisk ordbok. Trondheim, F. Brun; N.Y., Kraus, 1954. 327p.   **EA148**

At head of title: Norwegian Council for Technical Terminology.
A glossary of Norwegian technical terms and their English equivalents. Entries grouped by root words with related expressions.

Polyglot

See also EA157.

Medeiros, Manuel Francisco da Silva de. Dicionário técnico poliglota: português, espanhol, francês, italiano, inglês, alemão. Lisboa, Gomes & Rodrigues, [1949–53]. 8v.   **EA149**

Contents: pt.1, Lexicon. 3v.; pt.2, Indexes. 5v.
Covers pure and applied sciences, medicine and pharmacy, engineering and architecture, military science, transport and communications, industry and commerce. The Lexicon lists, in alphabetical order, some 131,000 Portuguese terms and expressions, each followed by its synonym in Portuguese, and by its translation into five languages: Spanish, French, Italian, English, German. The indexes cover each language and are numerically keyed to the Lexicon. Each index volume includes one language, plus Latin.   T10.M43

Technologisches Wörterbuch . . . 6. vollkommen neubearb. Aufl., hrsg. von Alfred Schlomann. Berlin, Springer, 1932. 3v.   **EA150**

English subtitle: Crafts and industries, engineering and engineering science, mining and metallurgy; raw and finished materials . . .; electrical and communication engineering; metrology; . . . optical, medical, and sanitary engineering; safety engineering; civil engineering and chemical technology; agriculture and forestry; foodstuffs, textile and clothing industries; trade, banking, and fair practice; traffic, . . . motor engineering; shipbuilding and navigation; patents, law, and customs [etc.].
Contents: v.1, German-English-French; v.2, English-German-French; v.3, French-German-English.
A general technical dictionary that attempts to cover the entire field of technology and its allied subjects. There is a preface to each volume in the first-named language of the volume. Includes 100,000 terms in each of the languages covered. "Expressions which are preferred, or are used almost exclusively, in the United States, are marked (A)."—*Pref., v.2.*   T10.T27

Tekniikan sanasto, saksa-englanti-suomi-ruotsi. Teknisk ordbok, tysk-engelsk-finsk-svensk. Technisches Wörterbuch, deutsch-englisch-finnisch-schwedisch. Technical vocabulary, German-English-Finnish-Swedish. Toimituskunta: Väinö Airas . . . Väinö Valkola . . . Lauri Hendell-Auterinen. . . . Helsinki, Kustannusosakeyhtiö Otava, [1940]. 1232col.   **EA151**

T10.T35

Portuguese

See also EA149.

Furstenau, Eugênio E. Dicionário de têrmos técnicos, inglês-português. 5. ed. Porto Alegre, Ed. Globo, 1974. 2v. il.   **EA152**

1st ed. 1947.   T9.F89

Russian

Alford, Mark Hugh Tankerville and **Alford, V. L.** Russian-English scientific and technical dictionary. Rev. ed. Oxford, Pergamon, 1981. 2v.   **EA153**

1st ed. 1970.
About 100,000 entries, drawing on terminology from 94 specialized fields. Stresses are shown for all terms; irregular verb forms included. Does not cover belles-lettres or popular science. Also includes instructions for learning large vocabularies; instructions for use of dictionary; reference sources; supplementary dictionary of Russian word endings.   Q123.A4

Chernukhin, Adol'f Efimovich. Anglo-russkii politekhnicheskii slovar': 80000 terminov. Izd. 3. Moskva, Russkii Iazyk, 1976. 647p.   **EA154**

Added title page: *English-Russian polytechnical dictionary.*
About 80,000 terms.   T10.C52

Kratkii politekhnicheskii slovar'. Moskva, Gos. Izd-vo Tekhniko-Teoreticheskoi Lit-ry, 1955. 1136p.   **EA155**

An encyclopedic dictionary with short articles on terms in technology and general science, and numerous drawings. Names of contributing authors are listed at the beginning, but individual articles are unsigned.   T9.K82

TSimmerman, Moisei Genrikhovich. Russian-English translators dictionary; a guide to scientific and technical usage [by] Mikhail G. Zimmerman. N.Y., Plenum, 1967. 293p.   **EA156**

". . . not a dictionary of terms or idioms, but a collection of typical examples from scientific and technical sources."—*Introd.* Rather than merely giving equivalent English terms for the Russian words and idioms, this work gives a number of examples of English usage of the equivalent term drawn from scientific and technical literature.   Q123.T83

Załucki, Henryk. Dictionary of Russian technical and scientific abbreviations with their full meaning in Russian, English, and German. Comp. and arr. on a Russian alphabetical basis. Amsterdam, N.Y., Elsevier, 1968. 387p.   **EA157**

About 7,300 entries. Except in the largest collections where there may be call for the German equivalents, most libraries will not need this, but will find the more comprehensive *Glossary of Russian abbreviations and acronyms* (AD675), issued by the Library of Congress Aerospace Technology Division, fully adequate.   PG2693.Z3

Spanish

Castilla's Spanish and English technical dictionary. London, Routledge and Paul; N.Y., Philosophical Lib., 1958. 2v.   **EA158**

Contents: v.1, English-Spanish. 1611p.; v.2, Spanish-English. 1137p.
A comprehensive, modern dictionary. "Only the fields of engineering technology are included, and the physical, chemical and biological sciences are excluded, except for those words which are of importance to engineers."—*Introd.* Abbreviations are given at the beginning of each letter of the alphabet. Important commercial and legal terms are included, as well as some words of significance in everyday language. The words selected are in current usage, not obsolete terms, and "the language used is that of Spain and Latin America in the Spanish language and of England and the United States in the English language." The field to which a term belongs is indicated only in cases of ambiguity.   T9.C34

Chambers Diccionario tecnológico, español-inglés: inglés-español . . . dir. por C. F. Tweney y L. E. C. Hughes; la traducción española . . . dir. por Carlos Botet. Barcelona, Ed. Omega, [1952]. 1227p., 289p.   **EA159**

Based on *Chambers's Technical dictionary (see* EA117*n).*

The Spanish-English section gives English equivalents for terms and full explanations in Spanish; the second part gives, briefly, Spanish equivalents for English terms. Covers pure and applied science, medicine, industry, engineering, etc.

Collazo, Javier L. Encyclopedic dictionary of technical terms, English-Spanish, Spanish-English. N.Y., McGraw-Hill, 1980. 3v. **EA160**

Added title page in Spanish.

Pt.I, in two volumes, is an English-Spanish lexicon with nearly 100,000 entries, many of which have extended definitions including subentries and synonyms. Pt.II, is a Spanish-English lexicon of 43,000 entries providing English equivalents of Spanish words but not definitions. T10.C593

Diccionario de términos científicos y técnicos. Daniel N. Lapedes, redactor jefe. Barcelona, Marcombo, 1981. 5v. il. **EA161**

Translation of *McGraw-Hill dictionary of scientific and technical terms,* 2d ed. 1978 (*see* EA120 for 3d ed. 1984).

Entries in v.1–4 give the Spanish term, the English term, the field of science or technology, and a brief definition. v.5 is an alphabetical list of English terms with the Spanish equivalent.

Diccionario politécnico de las lenguas española e inglesa. 3ª ed. aum. y actualizada. Madrid, Ediciones Castilla, 1965. 2v. **EA162**

1st ed. 1958.

Contents: v.1, Inglés-Español. 1755p.; v.2, Español-Inglés. 1464p.
An extensive dictionary of scientific and technical terms.

Guinle, R.L. A modern Spanish-English & English-Spanish technical & engineering dictionary, suitable for Spain and all the Spanish-speaking countries of Central America and South America. Mexico, Continental, 1980 [c1969]. 311p. **EA163**

1st ed. 1938.

Title also in Spanish: Nuevo diccionario técnico y de ingenieria Español-Inglés e Inglés-Español aplicable a todos los países de lengua española tanto de Europa como de Centro y Sud America. T10.G83

Swedish

Engström, Einar. Svensk-engelsk teknisk ordbok. 10. uppl. Stockholm, Svensk Trävaru-Tidning Förlaget, 1977. 973p. **EA164**

T9.E5

——— Engelsk-svensk teknisk ordbok. 13. uppl. Stockholm, Svensk Trävaru-Tidning Förlaget, 1978. 1026p. **EA165**

T9.E48

TABLES

Landolt, Hans Heinrich. Zahlenwerte und Funktionen aus Physik, Chemie, Astronomie, Geophysik und Technik. 6. Aufl. Berlin, Springer, 1950–80. v.1–4 (in various pts.). (In progress) **EA166**

This edition aims to present "the compilation of all the certain results of physical, chemical, and technological research, characterized by both the greatest possible completeness and a critical attitude."—*Pref., New series.* Uniformity of presentation is achieved by dividing the work into major units on atomic and molecular physics, macrophysics and chemistry, astronomy and geophysics, and technology, each consisting of several subdivisions. Data are presented largely in tabular and graphic form. Extensive references to primary sources. QC61.L33

——— Landolt-Börnstein Zahlenwerte und Funktionen aus Naturwissenschaften und Technik. Neue Serie. Gesamtherausgabe: K. H. Hellwege. Berlin, Springer, 1961–84. Gruppe 1–6 (in various pts.). (In progress) **EA167**

Added title page in English: Landolt-Börnstein. Numerical data and functional relationships in science and technology. New series.

Contents: Gruppe I, Kern- und Teilchenphysik. Nuclear and particle physics; Gruppe II, Atom- und Molekularphysik. Atomic and molecular physics; Gruppe III, Kristall- und Festkörperphysik. Crystal and solid state physics; Gruppe IV, Makroskopische und technische Eigenschaften der Materie. Macroscopic and technical properties of matter; Gruppe V, Geophysik und Weltraumforschung. Geophysics and space research; Gruppe VI, Astronomie, Astrophysik und Weltraumforschung. Astronomy, astrophysics and space research.

Not a 7th ed., but new series having "as principal feature, that the inflexible division into a few subdivided volumes, i.e., the principle of planned subdivision, is given up. In the future volumes will be published in simple succession: closed fields will be supplemented by new volumes, whereas new treatments will appear with greater frequency for fields which are being newly opened up or are evolving rapidly."—*Pref., New series.* Much material appears in English; later volumes have text in both German and English, with some in English only. QC61.L332

National Research Council. International critical tables of numerical data, physics, chemistry and technology, prep. under the auspices of the International Research Council and the National Academy of Sciences by the National Research Council of the United States of America; ed. in chief, Edward W. Washburn. . . . N.Y., publ. for the National al Research Council by McGraw-Hill, 1926–33. 7v. and index. diagrams. **EA168**

Data based on the material in the *Tables annuelles de constantes* . . . (Paris, Gauthier-Villars; Chicago, Univ. of Chicago Pr., 1912–).

Covers chemistry, physics, and technology. Represents the efforts of a large number of specialists, each of whom was charged with the critical compilation of the quantitative information available on his topic. "Critical" means the "best" value which the expert could derive with an estimate of its probable reliability. Derived from the literature published up to 1924, data are presented in the form of text, equations, tables, graphs, and charts. Citations given to publications from which information was obtained. In 300 sections, such as laboratory technique, physical properties of chemical substances, and astronomic and geodetic data. Detailed index. Q199.N32

DIRECTORIES

Commission of the European Communities. Directorate-General for Research, Science, and Education. Inventory of major research facilities in the European Community. München, Verlag Dokumentation, 1977. 2v. **EA169**

Prefatory matter in English, Danish, Dutch, French, German, and Italian.

An alphabetically arranged directory of about 656 research facilities. Gives address, telephone and telex numbers, administrative personnel, legal status and affiliation, budget, staffing, fields of activity, main subjects of research, and special research equipment. Language of the description is usually that of the country where the facility is located. Indexed by country. Q180.E9C67

Current contents address directory: science & technology. 1984– . Philadelphia, Inst. for Scientific Information, 1985– . Annual. 1984 ed. in 4v. **EA170**

Subtitle: An international directory of scientists and scholars.

Supersedes in part *Current bibliographic directory of the arts & sciences* 1978–83 (CA76), which in turn superseded *Who is publishing in science,* 1971–78. Companion publication entitled: *Current contents address directory: social sciences/arts & humanities* (1985–).

"Contains the names and addresses of authors who published during 1984."—*Introd.* Information is derived from other current awareness and indexing sources published by ISI. In three sections: author, organization, and geographic. The author section is the principal section, containing 840,484 addresses in the 1984 ed.; it also lists the source(s) of the author's publication(s). The organization section (corporate and governmental) refers to country and city. The geographic section is arranged first by states of the United States and then by foreign countries. For each state and country there is a subdivision according to the place name in the author's address and within the place name subdivision entries are again subdivided by organization name. Under the organization name are listed authors listing that affiliation. v.1 contains intriguing statistical summaries based on the geographic data.

European research centres: a directory of organizations in science, technology, agriculture, and medicine. 5th ed. London, [Longman, distr. in U.S.A. by Gale, 1982]. 2v. (1920p.) **EA171**

Continues *European research index* (4th ed. 1977) and *East European research index* (1977).

A listing of research centers in 30 European countries. Includes international organizations as well as universities, government agencies, and industrial research centers. Arranged by country, then by organization name. Name is also given in English, except for industrial firms. For countries using non-roman alphabets name is translated into English. Gives address, name of director and scope of research. Names of other principal personnel, e.g., university department chairmen, sometimes appear.   Q180.E9E9

European sources of scientific information. Anthony P. Harvey and Ann Pernet, eds. 5th ed. Harlow, [Eng.], Longman, [distr. in U.S.A. by Gale], 1981. 504p.   **EA172**

1st–4th eds. 1964–76 entitled: *Guide to European sources of technical information*. Publisher varies.

A directory of about 2,000 European information centers. Arranged by three general fields and 26 subject fields; each field is subdivided by country. Provides the following information: official name of organization/English translation, postal address, telephone number and telex and cable addresses, affiliation, contact person, subject coverage, and publications.   T10.65.E8E84

Guide to American scientific and technical directories. Barry T. Klein, ed. 2d ed. Rye, N.Y., Todd Pubns., [1975]. 271p.   **EA173**

1st ed. 1972.

A listing of some 2,500 directories under such headings as: Advertising and marketing, Agriculture, Audio-visual and communications, Biography, Chemical, Dentistry, Education, Engineering, Forestry, Industrial development, Manufacturers (subdivided by state), Marine, Nuclear science, Textile industry, etc. Indexed.   Z7914.M3K53

Research centers directory. Ed.1– , 1960– . Detroit, Gale, 1960– . (10th ed. 1985)   **EA174**

1st ed., 1960, had title *Directory of university research bureaus and institutes*.

Subtitle: A guide to approximately 8,300 university-related and other nonprofit research organizations established on a permanent basis and carrying on continuing research programs in agriculture, astronomy and space sciences, behavioral and social sciences, biological sciences and ecology, business and economics, computers and mathematics, education, engineering and technology, government and public affairs, humanities and religion, labor and industrial relations, law, medical sciences, physical and earth sciences, and regional and area studies.

Arranged by broad subject field. Entries may consist of the following elements: sequential entry number, institution name, research center name, acronym, address, telephone number, year founded, head of organization, governance/former names, sources of support, staff, volume of research, fields of research, specialized equipment, publications and services, publications, recurring seminars, and library.

Index in 5 parts: Alphabetical index of research centers and projects, Acronyms index of research centers, Institutional index, Special capabilities index, and Subject index.

Supplemented between editions by: AS25.R47

New research centers. [2d ed.] no.1– , May 1965– . Detroit, Gale, 1965– . Irregular.   **EA175**

Renumbers with each edition of *Research centers directory.*
Cumulative indexes in each issue.   AS25.D52

Research in British universities, polytechnics and colleges. Ed.1– , 1979/80– . Boston Spa, [Eng.], British Lib., 1979– . Annual.   **EA176**

Supersedes *Scientific research in British universities and colleges* (1951/52–74/75).

Each edition is in 3v.: v.1, Physical sciences; v.2, Biological sciences; v.3, Social sciences.

A guide to research in progress. Arranged by broad subject, then by institution and researcher. Includes a short statement regarding research interest. Name and keyword indexes.   Q180.G7S4

Scientific and technical organizations and agencies directory. Margaret Labash Young, ed. Detroit, Gale, [1985]. 2v.   **EA177**

A directory of over 12,000 scientific and technical organizations in the United States which are sources of information in the physical and applied sciences. Arranged by type of institution in eleven chapters: Scientific, engineering, and technical organizations; Research and development centers; Federal government agencies—research and programs; Federal grants and domestic assistance; State agencies; Computer information service organizations; Engineering consulting firms; Standards organizations; Patent organizations; Technical libraries and information centers; and Educational institutions. Information provided varies according to chapter. Indexed.   Q145.S36

Swannack-Nunn, Susan. Directory of scientific research institutes in the People's Republic of China. Wash., Nat. Council for U.S.-China Trade, 1977–78. 3v.   **EA178**

Contents: v.1, Agriculture, fisheries, forestry; v.2, Chemicals, construction; v.3 (in 2 pts.), Electrical and electronics; energy; light industry; machinery, including metals and mining; transportation.

Contains introductory material on the organization and state of scientific research in the People's Republic of China, followed by listings of research organizations by subject area. Includes institutional names both in English and in Chinese characters, address, organizational structure, journals in which the institution has recently published, areas of research activity, staff when known; sometimes includes abstracts of recent publications. "The institutions in the directory do not represent a definitive listing. . . . We are limited to institutions mentioned in PRC publications and those visited by foreign delegations. . . . Universities and social science institutions are not included."—[*Note*]   Q180.C5S92

SOCIETIES AND CONGRESSES

Directories

Akademiia Nauk SSSR. Fundamental'naia Biblioteka Obshchestvennykh Nauk. Nauchnye s'ezdy, konferentsii i soveshchaniia v SSSR. Bibliograficheskii ukazatel'. 1946/53–1954/60. Moskva, "Nauka," 1958–66. 3v.   **EA179**

Lists Russian-language publications of and about scholarly congresses, conferences, and meetings in the Soviet Union. Includes both natural and social sciences.   AS258.A55

Bates, Ralph Samuel. Scientific societies in the United States. 3d ed. Cambridge, Mass., M.I.T. Pr., [1965]. 326p.   **EA180**

1st ed. 1945.

A history of the growth of American scientific societies from 1727. Covers the main national societies and the specialized and technical societies of the various states. Bibliography, p.245–93. Indexed.   Q11.A1B3

Scientific and learned societies of Great Britain: a handbook, comp. from official sources. London, Allen & Unwin, 1884– . v.1– . Irregular. **EA181**

Title on title page, 1884–1929, *Year-book of the scientific and learned societies of Great Britain and Ireland;* 1930/31–38/39, *Official yearbook.* . . . Publication suspended 1940–50. Publisher varies.

Coverage varies, but usually includes: (1) government and public bodies (excluding university departments and technical colleges) conducting scientific research in Great Britain, research in industry and medicine, and the public health laboratory service; (2) general science; (3) subject groups (e.g., chemistry, geography, literature, etc.); (4) index of society names.

A useful list, giving for each society: corporate name, address, date of founding, object, officers, meetings, membership, titles of publications, and (in some cases) contents of publications for the period covered. The first volume, 1884, was a basic volume, containing considerable historical information not reprinted in later issues. Ed. 61 (1964) last published.

World guide to scientific associations and learned societies. 4th ed. München & N.Y., Saur, 1982. 619p. **EA182**

For full information *see* CA122.

Meetings

MInd, the meetings index. Series SEMT, science, engineering, medicine, technology. v.1– , Feb. 1984– . Harrison, N.Y., InterDok, 1984– . Bimonthly. **EA183**

"Lists forthcoming meetings (congresses, conferences, courses, symposia, seminars, summer schools & similar meetings) which will be held worldwide."—*Pref.* Meetings are arranged by topical keyword. There is a sponsor index and a location index.

Scientific meetings. v.1– , Spring 1957– . N.Y., Special Libraries Assoc., 1957– . v.1– . Quarterly. **EA184**

Subtitle (varies): Describing future meetings of technical, scientific, medical, and management organizations and universities.

Publisher varies. Frequency varies.

"An alphabetical listing of organizations . . . sponsoring future national, international, and regional meetings, symposia, colloquia, and institutes."—*inside front cover.* Includes a chronological listing and a subject index.

World meetings: United States and Canada. v.1, no.1– , Sept. 1963– . N.Y., Macmillan Information, 1963– . Quarterly. **EA185**

Subtitle: A two-year registry of future medical, scientific, and technical meetings; completely revised and updated quarterly.

Issues for Sept. 1963–Jan. 1967 had title *Technical meetings index.*

Publisher varies.

Full information on the meetings is given in the "Data Section" which is divided into eight parts, one for each calendar quarter of the 2-year period following the publication date of a particular issue. Gives sponsors, source of general information, technical sections or brief meeting description, number of papers to be presented, languages and translation facilities, projected attendance, availability of abstracts or papers, and information regarding exhibits. Indexes by date of meeting, keyword, location, deadline for abstracts or papers, and by sponsor.

A companion publication for other countries is:

World meetings outside U.S.A. and Canada. v.1, no.1– , Jan. 1968– . N.Y., Macmillan Information, 1968– . Quarterly. **EA186**

Subtitle: A two-year registry of future medical, scientific, and technical meetings.

Publisher varies.

A companion to *World meetings: United States and Canada* (above), following the arrangement of that publication.

Publications

Bibliographic guide to conference publications, 1975– . Boston, G. K. Hall, 1976– . Annual. **EA187**

For full information *see* CK433.

British Library. Lending Division. BLL conference index, 1964–1973. Boston Spa, [Eng.], British Library, Lending Division, 1974. 1220p. **EA188**

"Cumulated publication containing details of all conferences . . . listed, up to the end of 1973 in the *Index of conference proceedings received by NLL* [National Lending Library], Numbers 1–75 inclusive."—*Pref.* Coverage from inception tried to be comprehensive for subject fields of science and technology, then extended to the social sciences in 1966. Contains 46,500 conferences cross-indexed under 27,500 keyword headings. Entries are arranged in four columns: (1) date of conference; (2) title in language of document and sponsoring organization, truncated to fit one line; (3) place of conference; (4) location within BLLD. In 1973 coverage was extended to all subject fields; for annual cumulation (no. 69–) *see* below. Z7403.B8

——— Index of conference proceedings received. Boston Spa, [Eng.], British Library, Lending Division, 1973– . no. 69– . Annual. **EA189**

Continues a publication started in 1965 with same title and issued by the National Lending Library. Coverage from 1973 forward "includes all subject fields."—*Pref.* Each entry consists of the title (in the language of the document, with English preferred when multilingual), sponsoring organization, date and place of conference, and location within BLLD. Entries are arranged under subject keywords.

Three cumulations have been published: *BLL conference index, 1964–73* (EA188); *Index of conference proceedings received, 1974–1978* (Boston Spa, Eng., British Library, Lending Div., 1980. Microfiche); and *Index of conference proceedings received, 1964–1981* (Boston Spa, Eng., British Library, Lending Div., 1982. Microfiche). Z7403.B768

Cambridge. University. Library. Union catalogue of scientific libraries in the University of Cambridge; scientific conference proceedings 1644–1974. London, Mansell, 1975. 2v. 1221p. **EA190**

"Compiled at the Scientific Periodicals Library, University of Cambridge."—*t.p.*

A computer-produced catalog of "about 25,000 entries for approximately 6,000 conferences and symposia" (*Pref.*) of the period 1644–1972. A name and keyword catalog with entries for each conference under several headings—official name of conference, title of published proceedings, corporate bodies involved, and venues. Z7409.C35

Conference papers index. Louisville, Ky., Data Courier, 1978– . v.6– . Monthly, with cumulated annual index available separately. **EA191**

Continues *Current programs,* v.1–5, 1973–77, and assumes its numbering. Frequency of indexing varies.

Monthly issues have programs of scientific and technological conferences grouped by subject. Information includes the full title of the meeting, inclusive dates, location, names of sponsoring organizations, ordering information for publications, and a list of papers presented. This list includes the name and mailing address for the first author, complete title of paper, and any order number assigned to the paper in the printed program. Since *Conference papers index* is derived from the final program of the meeting rather than from subsequently published conference proceedings, it is timelier than other conference indexes; on the other hand, order information for the published proceedings may not be available. Beginning with v.7 (1979) each monthly issue includes both author and keyword indexes which cumulate into the separate annual index volume.

●

Directory of published proceedings. Series SEMT—science, engineering, medicine, technology. v.1– , Sept. 1965– .

White Plains, N.Y., InterDok Corp., 1965– . Monthly, except July–Aug., with annual cumulation.   **EA192**

At head of title: InterDok.

v.1–2 lacked the series designation, and included proceedings for the social sciences and humanities. Beginning 1968, the latter disciplines are covered in a separate (*SSH*) series (*see* CA118).

"A bibliographic directory of preprints and published proceedings of congresses, conferences, symposia, meetings, seminars, and summer schools which have been held world-wide from 1964 to date."—*verso of title page.* Arranged chronologically by date of conference, and indexed by keywords in the name of the conference, the sponsors, and the titles. 5-year cumulated indexes were published for v.1–5, Sept. 1965–June 1970; v.6–10, Sept. 1970–June 1975; v.11–15, Sept. 1975–June 1980.   Z7409.D56

Index to scientific and technical proceedings. Philadelphia, Inst. for Scientific Information, Jan., 1978– , v.1– . Monthly with semiannual cumulations.   **EA193**

Indexes published conference proceedings at the individual paper level with Permuterm indexing of keywords from titles of papers, an author/editor index, and an index of authors' corporate affiliation. Also indexes conferences by category (i.e., subject), sponsor, and meeting location, but does not index by date of conference. Publishes full information about published proceedings including title, date, and place held, sponsor, editors, how published, price, and order information. Includes tables of contents of papers presented, giving title of paper, authors' names and corporate affiliation, and page number. Does not attempt to give comprehensive coverage of published proceedings; it attempts to select the more important proceedings. The publisher estimates that the 3,000 proceedings covered in 1978 are about half of the proceedings published that year and make up about 75%–90% of the significant conference literature.

Proceedings in print. v.1, no.1/2– , Oct. 1964– . [Arlington, Mass., Proceedings in Print, Inc.], 1964– . v.1– . Bimonthly.   **EA194**

v.1, no.1/2–v.3, no.2, published by the Aerospace Division, Special Libraries Association.

Originally meant as an index to "all conference proceedings pertinent to aerospace technology"(*v.1, no.1*), coverage was soon expanded to "the various fields of science, technology and medicine" (*v.2, no.1*) and, beginning with v.3, no.3, to all published conference proceedings regardless of subject. Currently covers proceedings of a broad range of meetings, e.g., hearings, seminars, institutes, colloquia, in all languages. Each issue in two parts, one containing entries for publications appearing within the last two years, and one for those published previously. Entries include place and date of conference, sponsoring agencies, publisher, order information, and price. A single index includes corporate authors, agencies, editors, and keyword or subject headings. Cumulative index for each volume.   Z5063.A2P7

LABORATORIES

American Society for Testing and Materials. Directory of testing laboratories, commercial-institutional. 6th ed. Philadelphia, 1982. 194p. (Special technical publications, 333E)   **EA195**

1st ed. 1955.

A geographically arranged directory of approximately 3,000 laboratories in the United States prepared to undertake testing related to materials, products, systems, and services.

Industrial research laboratories of the United States. 19th ed. Ed. by Jaques Cattell Pr. N.Y., Bowker, 1985. 742p.   **EA196**

1st ed. 1920; 18th ed. 1983.

"A compilation of the research and/or development capabilities of the industrial organizations in the United States."—*Pref.* Contains 10,977 entries consisting of 5,996 parent organizations and 4,981 subsidiaries. Entries are listed alphabetically by the name of

the parent organization with subsidiaries following the parent. Information includes address, telephone number, officers, number of professional staff, and fields of research and development. Geographic index, personnel index, and classification (field) index.   T176.I51

MUSEUMS

Murray, David. Museums, their history and their use, with a bibliography and list of museums in the United Kingdom. Glasgow, Maclehose, 1904. 3v.   **EA197**

Contents: v.1, History. List of museums in the United Kingdom; v.2–3, Bibliography.

International in scope. Still valuable for its extensive bibliography, which lists (1) works about museums and museum work, and (2) catalogs and other works relating to particular museums.   AM5.M9

The official museum directory. 1971– . N.Y., Amer. Assoc. of Museums, [1971]– .   **EA198**

For full information *see* BE140.

SCIENTIFIC EXPEDITIONS

Terek, Eugenie. Scientific expeditions. Jamaica, N.Y., Queens Borough Pub. Lib., 1952. 176p.   **EA199**

A list of scientific expeditions compiled primarily to assist the cataloger in establishing correct forms of entry. Expeditions are listed alphabetically with many cross references. Under each expedition is given, insofar as possible, the source, purpose, members, equipment, and sponsors. Contains supplementary lists showing geographical distribution, subject classification, bibliography of sources, and indexes of members and sponsors.   Q115.T35

HISTORY OF SCIENCE

Bibliography

American Philosophical Society. Library. Catalog of books in the American Philosophical Society Library, Philadelphia, Pennsylvania. Westport, Conn., Greenwood Pr., [1970]. 28v.   **EA200**

Reproduction of the catalog cards for this important collection "concentrating on particular aspects of the history of science and related fields."—*Introd.* Includes extensive holdings of publications of scientific academies. In addition, there are strong collections on Franklin, evolution, and American Indian linguistics. Mainly an author and subject catalog, but with some title entries as well as many entries for journal articles in the areas of the Society's special interests.   Z881.P5318

—— Catalog of manuscripts . . . including the archival shelflist. Westport, Conn., Greenwood Pr., [1970]. 10v.   **EA201**

Reproduction of the catalog cards for this collection which contains "much of great value for scholars interested in the general history of America before 1800 and the history of science since about 1700."—*Introd.* (The Franklin papers, for which a separate catalog was published in 1908, are not included.)   Z881.P5319

Ferguson, Eugene S. Bibliography of the history of technology. Cambridge, Mass., Soc. for the History of Technology and M.I.T. Pr., [1968]. 347p.   **EA202**

"The purpose of this book is to provide a reasonably comprehensive introduction to primary and secondary sources on the history of technology."—*Pref.* "Technology" is defined as those "activities of man that result in artifacts." Intended for the serious student. Includes many general guides and reference sources as well as an extensive chapter listing monographs, articles, and bibliographies in specific subject fields. Entries are annotated, often at some length. Indexed. An important work for this field.

Earlier versions of parts of the book appeared in *Technology and culture*, v.3–6 (1962–65).

Supplemented by the *Current bibliography in the history of technology* (EA216). Z7914.H5F4

Forbes, Robert James. Bibliographia antiqua. Philosophia naturalis. . . . Leiden, Nederlandsch Inst. van het Nabije Osten, 1940–50. 10 pts. in 1v. **EA203**

A listing of nearly 11,000 books and periodical articles in various languages published through 1939. Each of the ten parts treats an area of ancient science and technology, such as mining and geology, building materials, and pottery, faience, glass, glazes, beads. No index.

────── ────── Supplement 1, 1940–50. 1952; Supplement 2, 1950–60. 1963.

The supplements give greater attention to ancient mathematics, physics, and astronomy. Z7401.F6

Horblit, Harrison D. One hundred books famous in science; based on an exhibition held at the Grolier Club. N.Y., Grolier Club, 1964. 449p. il., facsims. **EA204**

Examples of early scientific works in theoretical, experimental, and applied science, including technology. Full bibliographical descriptions with facsimiles of title pages, and with brief notes on the importance of these books in the history of science. Entries are sometimes accompanied by references to other books or papers which introduce, amplify, or complete their meaning. Alphabetical author arrangement. Z7401.H6

Information sources in the history of science and medicine. Pietro Crosi and Paul Weindling, eds. London, Butterworths, [1983]. 531p. **EA205**

Consists of 23 topical chapters (e.g., The history of technology, Scientific instruments, Medicine since 1500) written by authorities. Each chapter includes background and history, a discussion of the literature, and an extensive list of references. Indexed.

R118.2.I53

Isis cumulative bibliography; a bibliography of the history of science formed from Isis critical bibliographies 1–90, 1913–65. Ed. by Magda Whitrow. [London], Mansell in conjunction with the History of Science Society, 1971–84. 6v. **EA206**

Contents: v.1, Personalities, A–J; v.2, Personalities, K–Z and Institutions A–Z; v.3, Subjects; v.4, Civilizations and periods, prehistory to Middle Ages; v.5, Civilizations and periods, 15th to 19th centuries, Addenda to v.1–3; v.6, Author index.

A classed arrangement of the listings appearing in the *Isis* critical bibliographies. Serves as a "guide to the literature of the history of science during fifty most significant years [and] an analytical guide to *ISIS* itself [since] throughout most of its history *ISIS* has been fully analyzed in the Critical Bibliographies."—*Foreword,* v.1. The bibliography, while massive, is selective in keeping with George Sarton's intentions for the critical bibliographies.

Entries without reference to period or civilization, those that refer to two centuries in the modern period, those that deal with two or more civilizations but are not restricted to a particular period, and those dealing with the 20th century or the 19th and 20th centuries together are included in v.3. v.5 includes a subject index to v.4 and v.5. v.6 is an author index for v.1–5. Z7405.H612

Isis cumulative bibliography, 1966–1975; a bibliography of the history of science formed from Isis critical bibliographies 91–100 indexing literature published from 1965 through 1974. Ed. by John Neu. [London], Mansell in conjunction with History of Science Soc., 1980–85. v.1–2. (In progress) **EA207**

Contents: v.1, Personalities and institutions. 483p.; v.2, Subjects, periods and civilizations. 711p.

Continues the earlier series (above), cumulating the references as they appeared in the annual bibliography published in *Isis*.

Z7405.H612

Jayawardene, S.A. Reference books for the historian of science; a handlist. London, Science Museum, 1982. 229p. (Science Museum Library, Occasional pubn., 2) **EA208**

A classified list of 1,034 titles. Major works are annotated. Author/title index; subject index. Z7405.H6J38

John Crerar Library. A list of books on the history of science. Jan. 1911. Prep. by A. G. S. Josephson. Chicago, 1911. 297p. **EA209**

"Includes the social, physical, natural and medical sciences, but omits the applied sciences. . . . Publications on the history of learned institutions have not been included . . . and only such biographies as have a direct bearing on the position of their subjects in the history of science."—*Pref.* Includes monographs printed in serials, contents of proceedings and congresses, and *Festschriften*. Entries occasionally give scope notes and tables of contents. Arranged by large class, then by period, then by author. Author index.

────── ────── Supplement, Dec. 1916. Chicago, 1917. 139p.

────── ────── 2d Supplement, prep. by R. B. Gordon. Chicago, 1942–46. Pts.1–6.

Z7405.H6J7

The manuscript papers of British scientists, 1600–1940. London, H.M.S.O., [1982]. 109p. (Guides to sources for British history, 2) **EA210**

Initiated by the Royal Commission on Historical Manuscripts and the Royal Society. Lists 635 scientists with the location of manuscript materials both in Great Britain and other countries. Excludes living scientists; however, scientists who died up to 1980 are included if their substantive work was completed by 1940. Index of locations. Z7407.G7M35

Rink, Evald. Technical Americana: a checklist of technical publications printed before 1831. Millwood, N.Y., Kraus Internat., [1981]. 776p. **EA211**

For full information *see* EJ7.

Rothenberg, Marc. The history of science and technology in the United States: a critical and selective bibliography. N.Y., Garland, 1982. 242p. (Bibliographies of the history of science and technology, v.2; Garland reference library of the humanities, v.308) **EA212**

A guide to secondary literature on the history of American science and technology (excluding medicine) published between 1940 and 1980. The 832 annotated entries are arranged by subject within six chapters—Bibliographies and general studies, Special themes, The physical sciences, The biological sciences, The social sciences, and Technology and agriculture. Author index; subject index.

Z7405.H6R67

Sarton, George. A guide to the history of science; a first guide for the study of the history of science with introductory essays on science and tradition. Waltham, Mass., Chronica Botanica Co., 1952. 316p. il. **EA213**

At head of title: Horus.

In two parts: the first and shorter explains the purpose and meaning of the history of science through a series of three lectures; the second part is a bibliographic survey prepared for students and scholars. The bibliography is in four parts, each consisting of six to eight chapters: (1) history; (2) science (dealing with method, philosophy, periodicals, and national academies and societies); (3) history of science; (4) organization of the study and teaching of the history of science. The entries are not annotated, but many contain detailed notes. Evaluative remarks often appear at the beginning or end of chapters. Q125.S24

Thornton, John Leonard and **Tully, R. I. J.** Scientific books, libraries and collectors; a study of bibliography and the book trade in relation to science. 3d rev. ed. London, Lib. Assoc., 1971. 508p. il.   **EA214**

1st ed. 1954.

12 chapters present "an introductory history of the production, distribution and storage of scientific literature from the earliest times."—*Pref., 1st ed.* Includes material on the rise of scientific societies, the growth of the scientific periodical literature, scientific bibliographies and bibliographers, scientific publishing, and scientific libraries. Records the writings of prominent scientific authors and lists the more important printed editions of their work. Bibliography; index.   Z7401.T45

———— ———— Supplement, 1969–75. London, Lib. Assoc., 1978. 172p.

Current

Critical bibliography of the history of science and its cultural influences. (*In* Isis, v.46– , June 1955–) Annual.   **EA215**

A continuation, with a reorganized classification, of the 79 lists, with slightly different title—compiled by George Sarton and covering 1912–52—which appeared in *Isis*, v.13–44, 1913–53. None published 1954.

Issues usually include: A, History of science. General references and tools; B, Science and its history from special points of view; C, Histories of the special sciences; D, Chronological classification. Each of the foregoing is subdivided into more specific categories. Lists books and articles. Many entries are annotated, often with references to reviews. Contains an index of all personal names appearing in the bibliography.

Cumulated in two series: 1–90, 1913–65 (EA206) and 91–100, 1966–75 (EA207).

Current bibliography in the history of technology, 1962– . (*In* Technology and culture, v.5– , 1964–) Annual.   **EA216**

Comp. by Jack Goodwin, 1962–81; 1982 comp. by Stephen H. Cutliffe and others.

A classified bibliography of current materials intended to survey the literature of a given year. There is a gap of about two years between the date of publication and the year of focus. Items omitted from one year's compilation may appear in following years. Many brief annotations. Author and subject indexes.

Encyclopedias and dictionaries

Bynum, W. F., Browne, E. J., and **Porter, Roy,** eds. Dictionary of the history of science. Princeton, N.J., Princeton Univ. Pr., [1981]. 494p.   **EA217**

"We have planned this *Dictionary* in the hope of explaining—to lay people as well as the scientifically trained—core features of recent Western science within the context of its development."—*Introd.* In alphabetical order, signed entries consist of one or more paragraphs which discuss terms. There are extensive cross references from specific terms to the more general articles. Some entries include bibliographical references. The biographical index gives dates, field of interest, and subject reference in the dictionary.   Q125.B98

Lexikon der Geschichte der Naturwissenschaften: Biographien, Sachwörter und Bibliographien. Mit einer Einführung "Die Zeitalter der Naturforschung" und einer Übersichtstabelle von Josef Mayerhöfer . . . Wien, Hollinek, [1959–76]. Lfg.1–8.   **EA218**

Contents: Bd.1 (Lfg.1–6)–2 (Lfg.7–8), Aachen–Edelsteinkunde.

Deals with the history of science from ancient times to the end of the 19th century, with much biography as well as articles on scientific subjects and geographical areas. Includes quite extensive bibliographies at the end of articles; in the case of biographical articles, bibliographies include works both by and about the person.

Continued by: Q141.L49

Archiv der Geschichte der Naturwissenschaften: Biographien, Sachwörter und Bibliographien. Wien, Hollinek, 1980–83. Heft 1–8/9. (In progress)   **EA219**

Supersedes *Lexikon der Geschichte der Naturwissenschaften* (above) and continues its contents. The article on "Edelsteinkunde" left incomplete in Bd.2, Lfg.8 is reprinted in full. Now published in looseleaf format; articles are not in progressive alphabetical sequence. Issues include notices and occasional original articles.   Q141.A2

History

Sarton, George. Introduction to the history of science. Baltimore, publ. for Carnegie Institution by Williams and Wilkins, 1927–48. v.1–3 in 4. (Carnegie Inst. pubn. 376)   **EA220**

Contents: v.1, Homer to Omar Khayyam; v.2, Rabbi Ben Ezra to Roger Bacon; v.3, Science and learning in the 14th century.

An important reference history, rich in biography and bibliography, covering European and Asian countries. With the exception of the first four chapters, which cover longer periods, treatment is by periods of one-half century. Each period is introduced with a simplified survey, followed by detailed analyses. A general index in v.3 is relatively complete for v.3, but for v.1–2 it lists only the main personalities treated, giving the page of the main article and the page of the index in v.1 or 2 where other references may be found.

Addenda and errata are included in the *Critical bibliography of the history and philosophy of science . . .* appearing in *Isis (see* EA215).   Q125.S32

BIOGRAPHY

American men and women of science: physical and biological sciences. 15th ed. Ed. by Jaques Cattell Pr. N.Y., Bowker, 1982. 7v.   **EA221**

1st–11th eds., 1906–68, entitled *American men of science*. Earlier eds. publ. at irregular intervals (14th ed. 1979); content has varied.

The 15th edition contains biographical data for 130,000 living physical scientists, biological scientists, public health scientists, engineers, mathematicians, statisticians, and computer scientists. 7,500 appear for the first time. Criteria for inclusion are achievement or research activity of high quality or attainment of a position of substantial responsibility. "Full entries are repeated for former listees who do not return forms but whose current location can be verified in secondary sources. References to the previous edition are given for those who do not return forms and cannot be located, but who are presumed to be still active in science or engineering. A notation is made when an entrant from the previous edition is known to be deceased."—*Pref.*

Entries provide minimal personal information such as date of birth and emphasize education, professional career, memberships, honors, and research interests. The geographic and discipline indexes included in earlier editions have been discontinued in printed form.   Q141.A5●

———— Cumulative index, editions 1–14. Comp. by Jaques Cattell Pr. N.Y., Bowker, 1983. 847p.   **EA222**

An index to over 270,000 scientists included in editions 1–14 and supplements. Indicates sections, if appropriate, and editions in which scientists were listed.

Asimov, Isaac. Asimov's Biographical encyclopedia of science and technology. 2d rev. ed. Garden City, N.Y., Doubleday, 1982. 941p. il.   **EA223**

Subtitle: The lives and achievements of 1510 great scientists from ancient times to the present chronologically arranged.

1st ed. 1972.

Biographies ranging in time from Imhotep (fl. 2980–2950 B.C.) to Stephen W. Hawking (b. 1942), of varying length, and written in an informal, nontechnical style. Index of subjects and names not included as biographees. Q141.A74

A biographical dictionary of scientists. 3d ed. N.Y., Wiley, [1982]. 674p. **EA224**

1st ed. 1969.

Ed. by Trevor I. Williams; asst. ed. Sonia Withers.

Brief sketches of deceased scientists are signed with the initials of the contributor; a limited number of bibliographical references are usually appended. International in scope with broad coverage from science, technology, and medicine. Biographies added since the 2d ed. are listed separately as "Additional Biographies". There is a chronological list of anniversaries, an appendix listing names occurring in the book but for whom there is not a full biography, and a subject index. Q141.B528

A biographical encyclopedia of scientists. N.Y., Facts on File, [1981]. 2v. **EA225**

Ed. by John Daintith, Sarah Mitchell, and Elizabeth Tootill.

Includes living and deceased scientists with some biographies drawn from medicine and technology. Entries provide limited biographical data and a discussion of the importance of the biographee. There is a chronology, book list, index of names, and index of subjects. Q141.B53

Concise dictionary of scientific biography. N.Y., Scribner, 1981. 773p. **EA226**

Based on the *Dictionary of scientific biography* (below).

All entries from the main work including the supplement have been retained; however, the text is substantially reduced. Q141.C55

Dictionary of scientific biography. Charles Coulston Gillispie, ed. in chief. N.Y., Scribner, [1970–80]. 16v. **EA227**

Contents: v.1–14, Abailard–Zwelfer; v.15, Suppl.I, Biographies and topical essays; v.16, Index.

". . . published under the sponsorship of the American Council of Learned Societies with the endorsement of the History of Science Society."—*Pref.*

A completely new work, international in coverage, including scientists from all periods of history (though excluding living persons), and encompassing the fields of astronomy, biology, chemistry, the earth sciences, mathematics, and physics. "Technology, medicine, the behavioral sciences, and philosophy are included only in the instances of persons whose work was intrinsically related to the sciences of nature or to mathematics."—*Pref.* An important selection criterion was whether or not a person's contributions to science "were sufficiently distinctive to make an identifiable difference to the profession or community of knowledge." The Editorial Board notes a certain imbalance in coverage of 20th-century figures and of ancient Indian, Chinese, Japanese, and Near Eastern scientists owing mainly to the shortage of technically qualified contributors for these areas.

Articles are signed by the contributing scholars (in some cases different scholars have treated specific aspects of an individual scientist's work); include bibliographies of original and secondary works; and emphasize the scientific accomplishments and careers of the biographees. In some cases the article is the first or the most comprehensive study of a figure's total contribution to science.

v.15 is in two parts: the first part consists of biographical articles on scientists not included in the main work, either because they only recently died, or because the article was planned for the *Dictionary* but not included in the main work (in which case there is a reference to the Supplement under the scientist's name in the main work) or simply because the scientist was previously overlooked. The second part offers topical essays "on the scientific outlook and accomplishments of certain ancient civilizations."—*Pref.*

v.16 includes the following sections: Index, Contributors, Societies indexed, Periodicals indexed, Lists of scientists by field, Errata.

An 8v. edition (N.Y., Scribner's, 1981) is a reprinting, in fewer physical volumes, of the original set. Q141.D5

Elliott, Clark A. Biographical dictionary of American science: the seventeenth through the nineteenth centuries. Westport, Conn., Greenwood Pr., [1979]. 360p. **EA228**

"This *Dictionary* is deliberately designed as a retrospective companion to *American men of science.* . . . The *Dictionary* includes major entries, averaging between 300 to 400 words, for nearly 600 scientists never included in AMS."—*Pref.* Also includes about 300 important 19th-century scientists in *American men of science.* Appendixes list biographees by year of birth, place of birth, education, occupation, and fields of science. Indexed. Q141.E37

Gascoigne, Robert Mortimer. A historical catalogue of scientists and scientific books from the earliest times to the close of the nineteenth century. N.Y., Garland, 1984. 1177p. **EA228a**

Contents: pt.1, Ancient and medieval periods; pt.2, Early modern period (ca. 1450–1700); pt.3, Eighteenth and nineteenth centuries.

"This catalogue is designed to serve both as a general reference work and as a research tool for historians of science. It is . . . a chronological list of 13,300 persons who were of some degree of significance in the development of science . . . for whom biographical information is available in reference books."—*Introd.* Consists of 15,918 entries; most include reference to major sources of biographical data. There are four indexes—a main index which includes persons, institutions, and ships, an index of selected titles, an index of dictionaries and encyclopedias, and an index of bibliographies and book catalogs. Q141.G38

Liudi russkoi nauki; ocherki o vydaiushchikhsia deiateliakh estestvoznaniia i tekhniki. Pod red. I. V. Kuznetsova. Moskva, Gos. Izd-vo Fiziko-Matematicheskoi Lit-ry, 1961–65. 4v. il. **EA229**

Contents: [v.1], Matematika, mekhanika, astronomiia, fizika, khimiia (1961); [v.2], Geologiia, geografiia (1962); [v.3], Biologiia, meditsina, sel'skokhosiaistvennie (1963); [v.4], Tekhnika (1965).

A biographical dictionary of major Russian scientists of the 19th and 20th centuries. No living persons are included. Articles are signed, and include bibliographies of principal works and additional biographical and scientific references.

McGraw-Hill modern scientists and engineers. [N.Y., McGraw-Hill, 1980] 3v. il. **EA230**

1st ed. 1966–68 had title: *McGraw-Hill modern men of science.*

Intended to be a biographical supplement to the 4th ed. (1977) of the *McGraw-Hill encyclopedia of science and technology.* A revised and expanded edition of the earlier work; 300 of the 1,140 biographies are new. "The individuals were selected by the editors from recipients of major awards and prizes given by the leading societies, organizations, and institutions of the world. The scope is international and extends in time from the leaders of the 1920s to the 1978 Nobel Prize winners."—*Pref.* Discusses research achievements and provides sketchy biographical data for each biographee. Gives references to background articles in the encyclopedia. Field index and analytical (name and subject) index. Q141.M15

Poggendorff, Johann Christian. Biographisch-literarisches Handwörterbuch zur Geschichte der exakten Wissenschaften. Leipzig, Barth, 1863–1904; Verlag Chemie, 1925–40. Bd.1–6 in 11v. (Repr.: Ann Arbor, Mich., Edwards, 1945) **EA231**

Title varies.

Bd.1–2, to 1857; Bd.3, 1858–83; Bd.4, 1883–1904; Bd.5, 1904–22 (2v.); Bd.6, 1923–31 (4v.).

The standard and indispensable work for information about the life and works of mathematicians, astronomers, physicists, chemists, mineralogists, geologists, and other scientists of all countries. For each scientist gives brief biographical sketch, followed by a detailed bibliography of his writings, including periodical articles. Z7404.P74

—— Biographisch-literarisches Handwörterbuch der exakten Naturwissenschaften, unter Mitwirkung der Akademien der Wissenschaften zu Berlin, Göttingen, Heidelberg, München und Wien, hrsg. von der Sächsischen Akademie der Wissenschaften zu Leipzig. Red. von Rudolph Zaunick und Hans Salié. Berlin, Akademie-Verlag, 1955–85. v.7a–7b$^{1-8:1}$. (In progress) **EA232**

Contents: Bd.7a, T.1–4, A–Z, Anhang und Schlusswort; 7a, Supplement, A–Z; Bd.7b, 1932 bis 1962, T.1–8, Lfg.1, A–St.

This series includes supplementary material for names mentioned in earlier volumes as well as new biographical sketches. Bd.7a contains bio-bibliographies of scientists, technologists, and doctors from Germany, Austria, and Switzerland from 1932 to 1953. Bd.7b covers scientists of other countries from the period 1932–62.

The *Anhang* includes "Zeitschriftenliste," T.4, p.7–134; and "Totenliste," p.135–55.

Royal Society of London. Obituary notices of Fellows of the Royal Society, v.1–9, 1932/35–Nov. 1954. London, Soc., 1932–54. il. Annual. **EA233**

Ceased publication.

Long, biographical articles with excellent autographed portraits of deceased Fellows of the Royal Society, including foreign members. Usually includes bibliographies, some quite extensive.

Previous obituary notices were published in the *Proceedings*. In 1905, v.75 of the *Proceedings* was published "containing obituaries of deceased Fellows chiefly for the period 1898–1904 with a general index to previous obituary notices." This general index covers 1860–99.

Continued by: Q171.R8

———— Biographical memoirs of Fellows of the Royal Society, 1955– . London, Soc., 1955– . v.1– . Annual. **EA234**

Follows the same general pattern as the earlier series.

Who was who in American history—science and technology. Chicago, Marquis, [1976]. 688p. **EA235**

"A component of *Who's who in American history.*"—*t.p.*

A compilation of biographical information for "some 90,000 deceased American notables within the covers of the [*Who was who in America*] volumes . . . from the early days of the colonies to mid-1973."—*Pref.* Q141.W43

Who's who in frontier science and technology. 1st ed. 1984–1985. Chicago, Marquis Who's Who, [1984]. 846p. **EA236**

"This volume includes approximately 16,500 scientists and technologists who are currently working in North America in the frontier areas of their respective specialties."—*Pref.* Gives standard who's who information. Indexed by fields and subspecialties. Q141.W446

Who's who in science in Europe: a biographical guide to science, technology, agriculture, and medicine. 4th ed. Harlow, [Eng.], Longman, distr. in U.S.A. by Gale, 1984. 3v. **EA237**

1st ed. 1967; 3d ed. 1978 in 4v.

Provides current biographical and professional information for approximately 30,000 senior scientists active in 30 European countries (excluding the USSR). Includes a list of European national academies of science and names of members. The country index is a listing of biographees by subject specialty for each country. Q141.W5

Who's who of British scientists, 1980/81. 3d ed. [Dorking, Surrey], Simon Books (distr. in U.S.A. by St. Martin's Pr.), [1980]. 589p. **EA238**

1st ed. 1969.

An alphabetical listing of scientists in British universities and polytechnics, research establishments, and industry. Entries include recent publications. Biographical section is followed by two organizational directories: "Scientific research establishments" and "Scientific societies and professional institutions." Q145.W46

Indexes

Ireland, Norma Olin. Index to scientists of the world from ancient to modern times: biographies and portraits. Boston, Faxon, 1962. 662p. (Useful reference ser., no.90) **EA239**

Indexes 338 collections in the English language, covering all phases of science, with listings for 7,475 world scientists from ancient to modern times. Emphasizes the indexing of portraits. Gives full name, years of birth and death, and distinguishing identification. Intended as an aid for group assignments. General non-reference books as well as many basic juvenile books have formed the core of works indexed; encyclopedias generally excluded. Z7404.I7

Pelletier, Paul A. Prominent scientists: an index to collective biographies. [N.Y.], Neal-Schuman, [1980]. 311p. **EA240**

Lists 10,122 scientists, living and dead, for whom biographies have appeared in 163 books, published primarily between 1960 and 1979. Principal list is by surname; additional lists by field. Q141.P398

PATENTS

Burge, David A. Patent and trademark tactics and practice. 2d ed. N.Y., Wiley, [1984]. 213p. il. **EA241**

1st ed. 1980.

"My intention is to outline fundamental principles that should be understood by inventors and businesspersons engaged in the development, protection, and management of intellectual property."—*Pref.* In narrative form, concentrating on patents and trademarks but also dealing with other forms of intellectual property and other issues such as design patents, plant protection, copyrights, computerware, and biotechnology. Glossary; index. KF3120.B87

Calvert, Robert Peyton, ed. The encyclopedia of patent practice and invention management. N.Y., Reinhold, [1964]. 860p. il. (Repr.: Palm Bay, Fla., Krieger, 1974) **EA242**

Subtitle: A comprehensive statement of the principles and procedures in solicitation, enforcement and licencing of patents and recognition and utilization of inventions, written by an eminent staff of contributing authors.

Over 125 chapters on patent practice arranged alphabetically by title. Covers all phases of patent preparation, prosecution, enforcement, and profit realization, as well as U.S. patent history. Makes frequent reference to court decisions as bases for opinions. Case and author index, and subject index.

Fenner, Terrence W. and **Everett, James L.** Inventor's handbook. N.Y., Chemical Pub., 1969. 309p. il. **EA243**

Offers practical information for the inventor on how to proceed from idea through model building, patenting, marketing, etc. T212.F44

Houghton, Bernard. Technical information sources; a guide to patent specifications, standards and technical reports literature. 2d ed. [London], Clive Bingley; [Hamden, Conn.], Linnet Books, [1972]. 119p. **EA244**

1st ed. 1967.

A brief survey which attempts to explain "the nature and evolution of patents, standards and technical report literature to those who have never before encountered these documents but who will be confronted by them when they take up professional posts in technical libraries, information services and industry."—*Introd.* The ten chapters cover the structure of the patent system, with emphasis on British and, to a lesser extent, the U.S. systems; the use of patents as a source of technical information, and their bibliographic control; the uses of standards and specifications and their bibliographic control; the technical report literature, and problems in its handling. T10.7.H6

Jones, Stacy V. The inventor's patent handbook. N.Y., Dial, 1966. 229p. **EA245**

An earlier (1962), similar work had title *You ought to patent that.*

Practical information on how to obtain a patent, use of the Copyright Office, selling patents, contract agreements, compensation for inventions in various industrial and research situations, etc. T339.J74

Maynard, John T. Understanding chemical patents: a guide for the inventor. Wash., Amer. Chemical Soc., 1978. 146p. **EA246**

"This is in no sense a book about patent law or about patent licensing and management. . . . This book tries to answer immediate practical questions of chemists and engineers about how to read and to understand patents, how to use patents as a source of information, how to recognize that an invention has been made, how to work with attorneys or agents in seeking patent protection for inventions, how to keep adequate notebook records, how to watch for infringement of patents, and so on."—*Pref.* QD39.2.M38

Muncheryan, Hrand M. Techniques for preparing and obtaining your own patent. Indianapolis, Sams, [1973]. 96p. il. **EA247**

Intended for the layman, "to explain the procedures involved in filing for a patent" (*Pref.*) and to guide the individual in filing his own patent application.

Severance, Belknap. Manual of foreign patents. Wash., Patent Off. Soc., 1935. 161p. **EA248**

Arranged by country, describing the patent publications—periodicals, specifications, abridgments, indexes, etc.—as they apply to each. Z7914.P3S5

U.S. Patent Office. Official gazette, 1872– . Wash., Govt. Prt. Off., 1872– . v.1– . il. Weekly; annual index. **EA249**

Contains brief advance descriptions and simple drawings of the patents, trademarks, designs, and labels issued each week; and decisions of the Commissioner of Patents and of United States courts in patent cases.

Beginning Feb. 2, 1971, issued in two separate weekly sections: (1) *Official gazette: patents,* and (2) *Official gazette: trademarks.* T223.A

—— —— General index, 1872–75. Wash., Govt. Prt. Off., 1872–76. 4v.

Continued by the following:

—— Annual report of the Commissioner of Patents, 1876–1925. Wash., Govt. Prt. Off., 1877–1926. il. **EA250**

Forms an annual index to the *Official gazette* (EA249) and to the *Specifications and drawings of patents* (1871–1912). Continued by: T223.H2

—— Index of patents issued from the United States Patent Office, 1920– . Wash., Govt. Prt. Off., 1921– . v.1– . Annual. **EA251**

The indexes for 1920–25 are included also in the *Annual report* of the Commissioner of Patents; 1926 on, they are issued only in this separate form.

Contents vary somewhat but include an alphabetical list of patentees and one of inventions. T223.D3

—— Index of trade-marks issued from the United States Patent Office, 1927– . Wash., Govt. Prt. Off., 1928– . v.1– . Annual. **EA252**

STANDARDS

American National Standards Institute. Catalog. 1969– . N.Y., 1969– . Annual? **EA253**

Earlier catalogs of standards issued under the Institute's earlier names, American Standards Association, and United States of America Standards Institute.

American Society for Testing and Materials. Annual book of ASTM standards. 1939– . Philadelphia, Soc., 1939– . il. Annual. **EA254**

Frequency varies; formerly issued triennially with annual supple-

ments. Number of parts varies; the 1985 ed. consists of 16 sections in 66v.

Supersedes *ASTM standards, ASTM tentative standards,* and *Book of A.S.T.M. standards,* with related material.

The American Society for Testing and Materials is a scientific and technical organization formed for "the development of standards on characteristics and performance of materials, products, systems, and services; and the promotion of related knowledge." Included are "all current formally approved ASTM standard and tentative test methods, definitions, recommended practices, classifications, and specifications, and other related material, such as proposed methods."—*Introd., 1973 rev.* Parts appear at various times throughout the year, each part devoted to a particular topical area. Length may range from a few hundred to over a thousand pages, and numbers of standards from less than 50 to 300. About 30 percent of each part is new or revised annually. Each part contains its own index; there is also a general index. TA401.A653

BSI catalogue. 1984– . London, British Standards Inst., 1983– . Annual. **EA256**

Continues the *Yearbook* 1937–83 (title varies).

Contains lists of British standards in numerical order, with date of standard, description, amendments, and number of pages. Also lists work in progress, revised standards, withdrawn standards, location of depository sets of standards, and membership of committees. Subject index. Kept up-to-date by *BSI news* (issued monthly). QC100.B7

Chumas, Sophie J., ed. Directory of United States standardization activities. Wash., Nat. Bureau of Standards, 1975. 223p. (Nat. Bureau of Standards. Special pubn. 417) **EA257**

Supersedes *Miscellaneous publication* 288 (dated 1967), which superseded *Miscellaneous publication* 230, *Standardization activities in the United States* (1960).

—— Index of international standards. Wash., Nat. Bureau of Standards. 1974. 206p. (Nat. Bureau of Standards. Special pubn. 390) **EA258**

A KWIC index to over 2,700 titles of the International Organization for Standardization, the International Electrotechnical Commission, the International Commission on Rules for the Approval of Electrical Equipment, the International Special Committee on Radio Interference, and the International Organization of Legal Metrology.

Struglia, Erasmus J. Standards and specifications information sources; a guide to literature and to public and private agencies concerned with technological uniformities. Detroit, Gale, [1965]. 187p. (Management information guide, 6) **EA259**

A bibliographic guide to agencies and organizations concerned with the formulation of standards and specifications, primarily in the United States. Includes sections for: (1) General sources and directories; (2) Bibliographies and indexes to periodicals; (3) Catalogs and indexes of standards and specifications; (4) Government sources; (5) Associations and societies; (6) International standardization; and (7) Periodicals. Some annotations. Author-title and subject indexes. Z7914.A22S87

U.S. National Bureau of Standards. Publications of the Bureau of Standards complete from the establishment of the Bureau (1901) to June 30, 1947. Wash., Govt. Prt. Off., 1948. 375p. (*Its* Circular 460) **EA260**

Includes brief abstracts.

Supplemented by cumulative lists: July 1, 1947–June 30, 1957; July 1, 1957–June 30, 1960; July 1960–June 1966.

Lists for 1957–60 and 1960–66 include titles of papers published in outside journals, 1950–65 (with subject and author indexes).

—— Publications of the National Bureau of Standards, catalog; a compilation of abstracts and key word and author indexes. 1966–67; 1968–69; 1970– . Wash., Govt. Prt. Off., 1969– . Annual. (National Bureau of Standards. Special pubn. 305, and suppls.) **EA261**

Betty L. Hurdle, ed.
Supplements NBS Circular 460, *Publications of the Bureau of Standards complete from the establishment of the Bureau (1901) to June 30, 1947,* and its supplements: 1947–57; 1957–60; 1960–66 (above).

FORMULAS AND RECIPES

Chemical formulary; a collection of valuable, timely, practical commercial formulae and recipes for making thousands of products in many fields of industry. H. Bennett, ed. Brooklyn, N.Y., Chemical Pub. Co., 1933– . v.1– . Irregular.
EA262

——— Cumulative index for v.1–15. N.Y., Chemical Publ. Co., 1972. 396p.

These volumes may be useful both to the layman and the chemist requiring information on chemical compounding and treatment in areas foreign to him. Formulas have been provided and reviewed by chemists and engineers engaged in many industries. Each volume presents a collection of new, up-to-date formulas not appearing in previous volumes. Grouping is under broad headings such as: Adhesives, Cosmetics and drugs, Foods and beverages, Paints and lacquers, Soaps and cleaners. Includes lists of chemicals and suppliers. Indexed.   TP151.C53

Hiscox, Gardner Dexter. Henley's Twentieth century book of formulas, processes and trade secrets. Rev. 1956 by Harry E. Eisenson; new rev. and enl. ed. by T. O'Conor Sloane. N.Y., Books, 1957. 867p. il.   **EA263**

Subtitle: A valuable reference book for the home, factory, office, laboratory and the workshop, containing ten thousand selected household, workshop and scientific formulas, trade secrets, chemical recipes, processes and money-saving ideas for both the amateur and professional worker.
First issued 1907 as *Henley's twentieth century book of recipes, formulas and processes.* A standard work which has gone through many editions and was frequently reissued with slight changes. Includes a glossary of technical terms and their corresponding common names, information on materials needed for compounding formulas, and a section on workshop and laboratory methods. Indexed.   T49.H6

Swezey, Kenneth M. Formulas, methods, tips, and data for home and workshop. N.Y., Popular Science, [1969]. 691p.
EA264

Offers a wide range of practical information for the do-it-yourself enthusiast. Among the topics treated are: wood selection, finishing, and preservation; paints and paint removers; finishing, plating, and working metals; working with concrete, brick, and plaster; adhesives and sealing compounds; laundering, stain removing, and dyeing; photography; calculations and conversions.   TT153.S88

E B

Astronomy

❖In addition to the highly technical works on astronomy, many popularly written works useful to the amateur have been published, and a number of these have been included

in the listings below. Volumes in the series of *Harvard books on astronomy* (EB40) treat various aspects of astronomy at an intermediate level. *Sky and telescope* (EB20) is a convenient source of current information for readers at all levels.

GENERAL WORKS

Guides

New and revised astronomy education materials resource guide. Dennis W. Sunal, ed. Morgantown, W.Va., West Virginia University, distr. by West Virginia Bookstore, [1982]. 102p.   **EB1**

A project "supported by V.M. Slipher Fund of the National Academy of Sciences."—*t.p.*
Attempts to facilitate dissemination of "non-published astronomy educational material used with pre-school through college and adult students."—*Introd.* Intended as an aid to astronomy teachers, the work is also useful to museum staffs, recreation personnel, and adults interested in astronomy. The 67 entries are arranged in the broad sections: Computer software, media, and instructional program aids; Classroom activities; Laboratory lessons and modules; Lab manuals and curriculum guides; and Astronomy education resource materials and teacher guides. Subheadings include topics such as planets, planetariums, astronomy reports and analemma. The table of contents lists these with the intended age groups. Each entry includes title, cost, education goal, general description, and the address for obtaining course outlines, material, or enrolling. The majority of entries is for secondary schools, universities, or planetariums.   QB62.N4

Seal, Robert A. A guide to the literature of astronomy. Littleton, Colo., Libraries Unlimited, 1977. 306p.   **EB2**

Serves as an introduction to the literature of astronomy. "Full bibliographic data, annotations, and a brief evaluation are provided for each work. The guide is intended mainly for those individuals who are totally unfamiliar with astronomical information, or who wish to gain better knowledge of the literature than they currently possess."—*Introd.* Indexed.   Z5151.S4

Bibliography

Baranowski, Henryk. Bibliografia kopernikowska, 1509–1955. Warszawa, Państwowe Wydawnictwo Naukowe, 1958. 448p.   **EB3**

At head of title: Polska Akademia Nauk. Komitet Historii Nauki.
Listing of some 3,750 works by and about Copernicus; supersedes earlier bibliographies. Aims to be universal in scope, although a high percentage of titles is in Polish. Includes books, periodical articles, and parts of books.   Z8192.5.B3

Collard, Auguste. L'astronomie et les astronomes. Bruxelles, Van Oest, 1921. 119p.   **EB4**

A classed catalog with author index, of works published after 1880; supplements Houzeau and Lancaster (EB9).   Z5151.C69

Collea, Beth A. and **Aveni, Anthony F.** A selected bibliography of native American astronomy. Hamilton, N.Y., Colgate Univ., Dept. of Physics and Astronomy, 1978. 148p.
EB5

A bibliography compiled from the literature of "archaeology, ethnology, geography and architecture as well as astronomy to examine the evidence of the practice of astronomy . . . [among] the aboriginal inhabitants of the two New World continents. Information included deals with astronomy before European contact as well as post-contact survivals of these practices."—*Pref.* The 1,480 citations from books and journals are arranged by author. Subject index. Z5151.C65

Collins, Mike. Astronomical catalogues 1951–75. [Old Working, Eng.], Inst. of Electrical Engineers, [1977]. 325p. (INSPEC bibliography series no.2) **EB6**

"Presents a collection of nearly 2500 catalogues . . . covering . . . 1951 to 1975 inclusive. Some catalogues published in 1976 and 1977 are also included. The bibliography contains lists of celestial objects, phenomena and equipment as well as books and slides. Each entry contains full bibliographic details and most have an abstract and a summary. . . ."—*Abstract.* Author, corporate author, and designation indexes. Z5154.S8C64

DeVorkin, David H. The history of modern astronomy and astrophysics: a selected, annotated bibliography. N.Y., Garland, 1982. 434p. (Bibliographies of history of science and technology, v.1; Garland reference library of the humanities, 304) **EB7**

An expansion of the historical listings in D.A. Kemp's *Astronomy and astrophysics: a bibliographic guide* (EB13). The period covered "begins with the invention and application of the telescope to astronomy . . . emphasis is placed upon the literature of recent astronomy, dating from the middle of the 19th to the middle of the 20th century."—*Introd.* Contains popular and scholarly works which are reasonably accessible in major public and university libraries. The annotated citations are grouped as: Bibliographies; General histories; Instrumentation; Descriptive astronomy; Theoretical astronomy; Positional astronomy; Astrophysics; Biographical, autobiographical and collected works; and Textbooks and popular works. The index merges author, institution, and subject entries. Z5154.H57D48

Drake, Milton. Almanacs of the United States. N.Y., Scarecrow Pr., 1962. 2v. **EB8**

A listing of more than 14,000 almanacs published from 1639 to 1850, arranged by state and then chronologically. Locates copies. Bibliography, v.2, p.1374–97. No index. Z1231.A6D7

Houzeau, Jean Charles and **Lancaster, Albert.** Bibliographie générale de l'astronomie jusqu'en 1880. Nouvelle éd. avec introd. et table des auteurs par D. W. Dewhirst. London, Holland Pr., 1964. 2v. in 3. **EB9**

Added title page in English: *General bibliography of astronomy to the year 1880.*

A major bibliographic source for historical references, first published 1880–89, 2v. in 3. This edition is largely a reprint of the original work (which was issued in 5 pts.), retaining the original page numbering of the bibliography proper, with some additional material—chiefly a new "Editorial introduction" and a name index to v.1, pts.1–2, by D. W. Dewhirst. A third volume intended to cover astronomical observations was never published.

Contents: v.1, pt.1–2, Ouvrages séparés, tant imprimés que manuscrits; v.2, Mémoires et notices insérés dans les collections académiques et les revues. Z5151.H84

International Astronomical Union. Bibliography of astronomy 1881–1898. Tylers Green, High Wycombe, Buckingham, England, Univ. Microfilms Ltd., 1970. 18 reels, 35mm. microfilm. **EB10**

Prepared by P. Stroobant, 1932–1936, and by the Belgian National Committee for Astronomy, 1938–1965.

The literature of this period, over 52,000 items, was recorded by the Observatoire Royal de Belgique. The purpose "is to fill the gap which previously existed between two great works of astronomical bibliography: the *Bibliographie générale de l'astronomie* by J.C. Houzeau and A. Lancaster [EB9], which dealt with publications up to 1880 and the *Astronomischer Jahresbericht* [EB18]."—*Its Guide, p. 15.* Arrangement is by subject within nine two-year periods. Eight subjects were deleted because of the existence of special bibliographies. These subjects are: Determination of elements of orbits of minor planets; Perturbations; Determination of elements of orbits of comets; Radiants and orbits of meteors and fire balls; Positions of comparison stars published only in connection with observations of

celestial objects; Observations of double stars; Determination of elements of orbits of visual double stars; Variable stars, including novae, cluster variables and stars suspected of variability; and Geodesy.

——— Guide to the bibliography of astronomy 1881–1898 on microfilm, by J.B. Sykes. Tylers Green, High Wycombe, Buckingham, England, Univ. Microfilms Ltd., 1970. 16 frames of microfilm. **EB11**

Includes the arrangement, scope, nature, and history of the bibliography. Gives a detailed listing of the subject classification and the publication information for the eight subjects which were not included because of existing special bibliographies.

International catalogue of scientific literature: E, Astronomy. 1st–14th annual issues. London, 1902–18. 14v. **EB12**

For full description *see* EA17.

Kemp, D. Alasdair. Astronomy and astrophysics: a bibliographical guide. London, Macdonald Technical and Scientific; Hamden, Conn., Archon Books, 1970. xxiii, 584p. **EB13**

A standard reference source for contemporary astronomy. Most of the 3,642 annotated entries are for materials published post–World War II to 1969. Arrangement is chronological within a unique classification system of 75 sections which begins with reference media, star catalogs and ephemerides and ends with sections on stellar evolution, cosmology, abundance and origin of the elements, and cosmo-, gamma-, and x-ray astronomy. Author and subject indexes.

For an expansion of the historical section *see* DeVorkin's *The history of modern astronomy and astrophysics* (EB7). Seal's *A bibliography of astronomy* (EB16) provides an update. Z5151.K45

Lalande, Joseph Jérôme le Français de. Bibliographie astronomique, avec l'histoire de l'astronomie depuis 1781 jusqu'à 1802. Paris, Impr. de la République, 1803. 966p. (Repr.: Amsterdam, Gieben, 1970) **EB14**

Covers the period 480 B.C. through 1802 A.D. Approximately 5,000 titles are arranged chronologically. Coverage precedes that of the *Bibliography of astronomy* (EB10). Z5151.L19

Reuss, Jeremias David. Repertorium commentationum a societatibus litterariis editarum. T.5, Astronomia. Gottingae, Dieterich, 1804. 548p. (Repr.: N.Y., B. Franklin, 1961) **EB15**

A valuable index to the publications of learned societies up to 1800. For description of the complete set *see* EA22.

Seal, Robert A. and **Martin, Sarah A.** A bibliography of astronomy, 1970–1979. Littleton, Colo., Libraries Unlimited, 1982. 407p. **EB16**

This is an updating of Kemp's *Astronomy and astrophysics: a bibliographic guide* (EB13). The arrangement of the text is by the classification system of *Astronomy and astrophysics abstracts* (EB19). The list of 2,119 items "is fairly comprehensive in its coverage of review and bibliographic sources . . . Exclusions [include] primarily those items only indirectly related to astronomy, such as general optics, plasma physics, time astronautics, etc."—*Introd.* History is covered only by bibliographic materials. The appendix includes listings of the International Astronomical Union Symposia 1969–1979, and the abbreviations used. Indexes for monographic title/conference proceedings, author and subject. Z5151.S38

Zinner, Ernst. Geschichte und Bibliographie der astronomischen Literatur in Deutschland zur Zeit der Renaissance. Stuttgart, Anton Hiersemann, 1964. 480p. **EB17**

1st ed. 1941.

An unaltered reprint of the 1941 ed., together with a new supplement. Covers 1448–1630 in chronological arrangement, with author index. Includes astronomical works and works in related fields if they affected the development of astronomy as a science. Z5152.Z5

Abstract journals, etc.

See also EG10, EJ200–EJ201, EJ365.

Astronomischer Jahresbericht. Bd.1–68, 1899–1968. Berlin, W. de Gruyter, 1900–69. Bd.1–68. Annual.   **EB18**

A comprehensive, classed bibliography covering the literature from all countries appearing in the year preceding publication. Titles are given in the language of publication, with transliteration provided for Russian-language entries. Abstracts, appearing more frequently in the earlier volumes, are in German. Classed arrangement, e.g., Instrumente; Sonne; Erde; Interplanetare Objekte; Sterne; Doppelsterne; Mehrfachsterne. Author and subject indexes.   QB1.A797

Astronomy and astrophysics abstracts. v.1– , 1969– . Berlin and N.Y., Springer-Verlag, 1969– . Semiannual.   **EB19**

Supersedes *Astronomischer Jahresbericht* (above).

"A publication of the Astronomisches Rechen-Institut Heidelberg, member of the International Council for Scientific and Technical Information, Astronomy and Astrophysics Absracts is prepared under the Auspices of the International Astronomical Union."—*t.p., v.37, 1984.*

"Aims to present a comprehensive documentation of the literature concerning all aspects of astronomy, astrophysics, and their border fields."—*Pref., v.37.* The text of the abstracts is primarily in English with some in French or German. Popular articles are not abstracted. Abstracts are arranged in an unique classification system. There is a "Concordance Relation" between ICSU-AB (International Classification System for Physics) and its system. Each volume includes: list of abbreviations; periodicals, proceedings, books, and activities abstracted; author and subject indexes.

Author and subject indexes are issued periodically as numbered volumes of the set: i.e., v.15/16 provides indexing to v.1–10, covering the literature of 1969–73; v.23/24 indexes v.17–22, covering 1974–78; and v.35/36 indexes v.25–34, covering literature of 1979–83.   Z5153.A862

Sky and telescope. Cambridge, Mass., Sky Pub. Corp., Harvard College Observatory, 1941– . v.1– . Monthly.   **EB20**

An excellent source for general current information and articles on popular topics. Illustrated, with fine color photography. Contains review articles, articles on current events, monthly star maps and calendars, reviews of important professional and amateur meetings, book reviews, etc. Good for all levels of interest. Indexed by author, title, departments and features, and selected topics and celestial objects.   QB1.S536

Dictionaries and encyclopedias

The Cambridge encyclopedia of astronomy. Ed. in chief, Simon Mitton. N.Y., Crown, 1977. 481p. il.   **EB21**

Prepared by astronomers, the encyclopedia presents a broad-based survey of astronomy with emphasis on firmly established new results. The 23 major topics, which have "been gathered into cohesive themes in order to present a more accurate and understandable guide to the new Universe" (*Introd.*), are intended for amateur and professional. The index is specific and extensive with references to the main text, photographs, and diagrams. A 14-page "Star atlas" of stars visible to the naked eye in the Northern and Southern hemispheres, and "An outline of physics" are provided in the appendixes.   QB43.2.C35

Encyklopädie der mathematischen Wissenschaften, ... Leipzig, Teubner, 1898–1935.   **EB22**

v.6, pt.2 is *Astronomie.*
For full record *see* EF23.   QA36.E56

Handbuch der Astrophysik, hrsg. von G. Eberhard, A. Kohlschütter, H. Ludendorff . . . Berlin, Springer, 1928–36. 7v. in 10. il.   **EB23**

Contents: v.1–3, W. E. Bernheimer [and others], Grundlagen der Astrophysik; v.4, Georgio Abetti, Das Sonnensystem; v.5–6, Friedrich Becker [and others], Das Sternsystem; v.7, Ergänzungsband, Berücksichtigend die Literatur bis ende 1934. Generalregister.

Chapters by specialists; some in German, some in English.   QB461.H3

❖*See also Handbuch der Physik,* v.50–54 (EG19), for authoritative articles with extensive bibliographies.

Hopkins, Jeanne. Glossary of astronomy and astrophysics. 2d ed. Chicago, Univ. of Chicago Pr., [1980]. 224p.   **EB24**

1st ed. 1976.

"This volume is published under the auspices of *Astrophysical journal.*"—*verso of t.p.*

Offers brief definitions of the most commonly used terms in astronomy and astrophysics. An expanded and updated revision.   QB14.H69

The Macmillan dictionary of astronomy. Ed. by Valerie Illingworth. London, Macmillan, [1979]. 378p. il.   **EB25**

Also published as *The Facts on File dictionary of astronomy* (N.Y., Facts on File, 1979) and *The Anchor dictionary of astronomy* (Garden City, N.Y., Anchor/Doubleday, 1980).

"The set of entries for each field [within the broad subject of astronomy] has been written by one scientist or by a group of scientists working together."—*Pref.* Cross references; tables at the back contain general information.   QB14.M25

Murdin, Paul and **Allen, David.** Catalogue of the universe. N.Y., Crown; London, Cambridge Univ. Pr., [1979]. 256p. il.   **EB26**

"With original photographs by David Malin."—*t.p.*

Arranged in descending order of distance from galaxies to objects in our solar system, with photographs and descriptive articles about "a comprehensive selection of objects in the Universe."—*Pref.* Includes a brief glossary. Indexed.   QB44.2.M869

The new space encyclopaedia: a guide to astronomy and space exploration. [2d ed. Gen. ed., M. T. Bizony] Horsham, Artemis; N.Y., Dutton, 1973. 326p. il.   **EB27**

First published 1957 under title *The space encyclopedia.*

An alphabetical dictionary and encyclopedia, giving definitions of terms and brief articles on astronomy, missiles, and aspects of space exploration. An appendix includes brief summaries of the orbital details of Apollo space flights 11 through 17, information on the comet Kohoutek, conjectures on Mars and Skylab. Popular in tone.   QB14.S66

Satterthwaite, Gilbert Elliott. Encyclopedia of astronomy. London, Hamlyn Group, 1970; N.Y., St. Martin's, [1971]. 537p. il.   **EB28**

About 2,200 entries in A–Z arrangement, covering all aspects of astronomy and including biographical sketches of outstanding astronomers of the past. For serious amateurs and lay people. Cross references.   QB14.S28

Weigert, Alfred and **Zimmermann, Helmut.** Concise encyclopedia of astronomy. 2d English ed. London, Adam Hilger; dist. by Crane, Russak, N.Y., [1976]. 532p. il., maps.   **EB29**

Translation of *ABC der Astronomie,* 3d ed. 1971, rev. by H. Zimmermann. Tr. by J. Home Dickson.

1st English ed. (1967) had title: *ABC of astronomy.*

A publication in dictionary format combining concise definitions with more extended articles, intended for a general audience. Up-to-date and comprehensive.   QB14.W4513

Foreign terms

Anglo-russkii astronomicheskii slovar'. Sost. . . . O. A. Mel'nikov. Moskva, "Sov. Entsiklopediia," 1971. 504p.   **EB30**

Added title page: English-Russian astronomical dictionary.

About 20,000 terms. English words and phrases are given with Russian equivalents. Separate listing for abbreviations and acronyms; specific names of galaxies, asteroids, etc., are grouped in another list. Observatory names, societies, and astronomical publications make up a fourth alphabetical arrangement. An index under Russian terms refers only to the word and phrase section.

QB14.A54

Chiu, Hong-yee, ed. Chinese-English, English-Chinese astronomical dictionary. N.Y., Consultants Bureau, 1966. 173p. **EB31**

The Chinese-English part is taken, in slightly modified form, from a Chinese-Russian-English astronomical nomenclature published by the Scientific Publishing House, Peking, in 1959; the English-Chinese section is new. QB14.C5

Kleczek, Josip. Astronomical dictionary. Astronomicheskii slovar' . . . N.Y., London, Academic Pr., [1961]. 972p. **EB32**

A polyglot astronomical dictionary containing terms in English, Russian, German, French, Italian, and Czech. Includes some of the more important phrases used by astronomers in mathematics, atomic physics, spectroscopy, etc. The first part of the dictionary is arranged in 34 subject categories. The second part is an alphabetical index for each of the six languages. QB14.K55

Kramer, Alex A. Russko-angliiskii slovar' po astronomii. Russian-English dictionary on astronomy. [Trenton, N.J., Scientific Russian Translating Service, 1962] 191p. **EB33**

In addition to astronomical terms there are entries for chemical elements, abbreviations, astronomical journals, and names of astronomers and astronauts. QB14.K7

Trifonova, Nina Fedorovna and **Chekulaeva, Zoia Danilovna.** Anglo-russkii astrogeofizicheskii slovar'. Moskva, Glav. red. Inostrannykh Nauchno-Tekhn. Slovarei Fizmatgiza, 1962. 512p. **EB34**

Added title page: English-Russian astronomical and geophysical dictionary. QC801.9.T7

Directories

Directory of physics and astronomy staff members. 1959/60– . N.Y., Amer. Inst. of Physics, [1959–]. Annual. **EB35**

For full information *see* EG35.

Kirby-Smith, H. T. U.S. observatories: directory and travel guide. N.Y., Van Nostrand Reinhold, [1976]. 173p. il. **EB36**

A compilation of information about United States observatories and some important museums and planetariums. Gives descriptions of facilities, equipment, and the kind of work done, as well as histories and information on the availability of public tours. Indexed. QB81.K57

Handbooks

Allen, Clabon Walter. Astrophysical quantities. 3d ed. London, Athlone Pr.; Atlantic Highlands, N.J., Humanities Pr., 1973. 310p. **EB37**

1st ed. 1955; 2d ed. 1963.

"The intention of this book is to present the essential information of astrophysics in a form that can be readily used. . . . The information is as up to date as possible."—*Pref.* "The book should contain all experimental and theoretical values, constants, and conversion factors that are fundamental to astrophysical arguments."—*Introd.*

See also The astronomical almanac (EB60).

Burnham, Robert. Burnham's Celestial handbook. Rev. & enl. ed. N.Y., Dover, [1978]. 3v. il. **EB38**

Subtitle: An observer's guide to the universe beyond the solar system.

1st ed. 1966 publ. by Celestial Handbook Publications.

Covers celestial objects outside our solar system that are within the range of 2- to 12-inch telescopes. Entries (arranged by constellations in which the objects appear) give names, celestial coordinates, classification, and descriptive notes. Includes an extensive introduction to fundamental observational astronomy. Indexed.

QB64.B85

Flammarion, Camille. Flammarion book of astronomy. N.Y., Simon & Schuster, 1964. 670p. il. **EB39**

Based on the author's *Astronomie populaire,* but "an entirely new ed. of the original work of Camille Flammarion prepared under the direction of Gabrielle Camille Flammarion and of André Danjou in collaboration with a group of astronomers. Tr. into English by Anabel and Bernard Pagel."—*verso of half title.*

A popularly written review of the astronomical sciences. Major sections include: The earth; The moon; The sun; The planets; Comets, meteors and meteorites; The sidereal universe; Instruments of astronomy; Artificial satellites and space vehicles. Brief section of astronomical data; planisphere of the heavens for the Northern and Southern hemispheres. Indexed. QB44.F5913

Harvard books on astronomy. Cambridge, Mass., Harvard Univ. Pr. **EB40**

A series, edited by Harlow Shapley and Cecilia Payne-Gaposchkin, of individual works by specialists covering astronomy at an intermediate level. Includes such titles as: *Between the planets; Earth, moon, and planets; Galaxies; The Milky Way; Our sun; Stars in the making; Tools of the astronomer;* and *The x-ray universe.*

Howard, Neale E. The telescope handbook and star atlas. Updated ed. N.Y., Crowell, [1975]. 226p. il. **EB41**

First published 1967.

An introduction and guide to telescopes and to observing the heavens, for students and other beginning astronomers. The "Star atlas" section includes the atlas, a gazetteer to 234 named stars, numerous tables of data for the observer, and the Messier Catalog with 104 familiar astronomical objects listed on a day-to-day basis. Appendixes are mainly conversion tables. Glossary; index.

QB63.H68

Jackson, Joseph Hollister and **Baumert, John H.** Pictorial guide to the planets. 3d ed. N.Y., Harper & Row, 1981. 246p. il. **EB42**

1st ed. 1965.

This book has "tried to compress and integrate the most significant features of the vast solar and planetary knowledge" *(Acknowledgement),* from 1965 to 1980. More than an atlas, it includes a great deal of information on space hardware and engineering developments in addition to discussions about the moon, interplanetary space, asteroids, meteors, and comets. Nine tables of various data; indexed. QB601.J3

Robinson, J. Hedley. Astronomy data book. N.Y., Wiley, [1972]. 271p. **EB43**

"This book is intended as a reference tool for the student and amateur astronomer and for those interested in the earth sciences. . . . It is intended that the observer shall use this book in conjunction with a Star Atlas."—*Introd.* Brings together basic data and information on such topics as the sun, the moon, planets, comets, etc. Includes a glossary and important historical dates.

QB64.R58

Roth, Günther Dietmar, ed. Astronomy; a handbook. Tr. and rev. by Arthur Beer. N.Y. & Berlin, Springer, 1975. 567p. il. **EB44**

Based on 2d ed. of *Handbuch für Sternfreunde,* 1967.

Consists of 21 signed chapters on astronomical topics, including chapters on astronomical literature and nomenclature, and on astronomical instruments. Indexed; contains bibliographies.

QB64.R59

Royal Astronomical Society of Canada. The observer's handbook. Toronto, 1907– . Annual (slightly irregular).   **EB45**

Continues *Canadian astronomical book.*

Narrative information and tabular data to assist amateur astronomers in their observations. Emphasizes the sky over Canada.
     QB9.R7

Shapley, Harlow and **Howarth, Helen E.** A source book in astronomy. N.Y., McGraw-Hill, 1929. 412p. il. (Source books in the history of the sciences)   **EB46**

Intended to be "a fairly comprehensive synopsis of the great contributions to astronomy of the past four hundred years (1500–1900)"—*Author's pref.* Consists of extracts from the classic works in the astronomical sciences, avoiding very technical and mathematical explanations. Indexed.   QB3.S5

Shapley, Harlow. Source book in astronomy, 1900–1950. Cambridge, Mass., Harvard Univ. Pr., 1960. 423p. il., tables. (Source books in the history of the sciences)
     EB47

A continuation of the preceding, covering 1900–50, the period when Shapley, himself, was most active.   QB3.S52

A source book in astronomy and astrophysics, 1900–1975. Ed. by Kenneth R. Lang and Owen Gingerich. Cambridge, Mass., Harvard Univ. Pr., 1979. 922p. il. (Source books in the history of the sciences)   **EB48**

A continuation of *A source book in astronomy,* ed. by Harlow Shapley and Helen E. Howarth (EB46). To some extent supersedes Shapley's *Source book in astronomy, 1900–1950* (EB47) but differs from it in selection of articles. "We have resisted the temptation to document the progress of . . . astronomy through review articles. . . . our articles present the fundamental ideas in their original statements, rather than in more polished or popularized forms."—*Pref.*
     QB51.S67

History

Native American astronomy. Ed. by Anthony F. Aveni. Austin, Tex., Univ. of Texas Pr., 1977. 286p.   **EB49**

"Edited version of papers presented at a symposium held . . . 1975."—*verso of t.p.*

Consists of contributed papers by specialists in both astronomy and astrophysics and on American Indians. The subject coverage includes the records of astronomical events, use of solar observatories and calendars, and religious astronomical rites as evidenced by archaeological findings. Notes on contributors, references, and subject index.   E59.A8N37

Pannekoek, Antonie. A history of astronomy. N.Y., Interscience, 1961. 521p. il.   **EB50**

Translation of *De groei van ons wereldbeeld* (Amsterdam, 1951).

A comprehensive and scholarly history. Appendix A: Aristarchus' derivation of the sun's distance; Appendix B: Apollonius' derivation of the planets' stations; Appendix C: Newton's demonstration of the law of areas; Appendix D: Newton's derivation of the force of attraction. Indexed.   QB15.P283

Atlases

Briggs, Geoffrey and **Taylor, Fredric.** The Cambridge photographic atlas of the planets. Cambridge, Cambridge Univ. Pr., 1982. 255p. il., maps. 31cm.   **EB51**

A compilation of 200 illustrations and maps with detailed description and information about Mercury, Venus, Earth and moon, Mars, the Jovian system, and the Saturnian system.   QB605.B74

Ernst, Br. and **De Vries, Tj. E.** Atlas of the universe, tr. by D. R. Welsh, ed. by H. E. Butler. [London], Nelson, 1961. 226p. il. 27cm.   **EB52**

A section of 94 plates is followed by an alphabetical encyclopedia

written for non-specialists. Many short entries; line drawings and data tables are prevalent.   QB65.E713

Kopal, Zdeněk. A new photographic atlas of the moon. London, Hale; N.Y., Taplinger, [1971]. 311p. il. 31cm.
     EB53

An earlier work (1965) had title *Photographic atlas of the moon.*

Consists of photographs with explanatory text. Includes pictures taken from earth-based apparatus and from cameras on space vehicles near the moon. Tables of data on lunar spacecraft; glossary of terms; indexed.   QB595.K59

Moore, Patrick. The atlas of the universe. N.Y., Chicago, Rand McNally, [1970]. 272p. il. 38cm.   **EB54**

Maps, charts, photographs, and diagrams present a history and explanation of man's exploration and knowledge of space. Brief, popular-level articles on many topics within the five main sections: (1) Observation and exploration of space; (2) Atlas of the earth from space; (3) Atlas of the moon; (4) Atlas of the solar system; and (5) Atlas of the stars. Includes a catalog of stellar objects, a glossary of terms used in astronomy, and a "Beginner's guide to the heavens." Indexed.   QB44.M5425

The Times, London. The Times atlas of the moon. Ed. by H. A. G. Lewis. London, [1969]. 110p. il. 35cm.   **EB55**

A brief introductory section covers: The moon, The far side; Mapping the moon; The lunar landscape; and Techniques of lunar flight. The atlas consists of 110 pages of maps at a scale of approximately 20 miles to 1 inch. Based on the work of the U.S. Air Force Aeronautical Chart and Information Center. Index and key to the maps.

STARS

Norton, Arthur P. Norton's Star atlas and reference handbook (epoch 1950.0). 17th ed. Cambridge, Mass., Sky Pub. Corp.; Edinburgh, Gall and Inglis, 1978. 116p. charts, maps, & tables. 29cm.   **EB56**

Subtitle: The reference handbook and lists of interesting objects.

Ed. by Gilbert E. Satterthwaite in consultation with Patrick Moore & Robert G. Inglis.

1st ed. 1919, had title *A star atlas and telescopic handbook (epoch 1920).*

All the features of the original maps are retained with appropriate additions and changes in the notations to include new techniques and information. "The intention of the original edition has been maintained—to provide the amateur observer and the general reader with a reference book to which he can turn for an explanation of unfamiliar terms—especially the terminology of observational astronomy which is inadequately dealt with in many textbooks . . . the Editors decided not to include an annotated bibliography here, in view of the rate at which lists of available astronomical works go out of date, compared with the longevity enjoyed by previous editions."—*Pref.* Includes hints on observing, care and use of the telescope, definitions of terms, star charts showing constellations and objects down to the sixth or seventh magnitude. Indexed.
     QB65.N7

Smithsonian Institution. Astrophysical Observatory. Smithsonian Astrophysical Observatory star atlas of reference stars and nonstellar objects, prep. by the staff. Cambridge, Mass., M.I.T. Pr., [1969]. Plates and charts in case. 38cm.
     EB57

A companion to the SAO *Star catalog* (below), which serves as gazetteer to this atlas. Shows about 260,000 stars and "is nearly complete to visual magnitude 9 but contains many fainter stars to 11 and occasionally beyond."—*Foreword.*   QB65.S65

———— Star catalog. Wash., Smithsonian Inst., 1966. 4v. il. (Smithsonian publ. 4652)   **EB58**

Subtitle: Positions and proper motions of 258,997 stars for the epoch and equinox of 1950.0.

"Sources for the catalog," v.1, p.xx–xxiv. QB6.S57

nac, prep. jointly by the Nautical Almanac Offices of the United Kingdom and the United States of America. London, Stat. Off., 1961. 505p.

NAVIGATION

American practical navigator, 1802– . [Wash., U.S. Dept. of Defense, Defense Mapping Agency, Hydrographic Center; distr. by Govt. Prt. Off.], 1802– . il. Irregular. **EB59**

"An epitome of navigation, originally by Nathaniel Bowditch."—*t.p.*

First published under title *The new American practical navigator.* Imprint varies; issuing agency varies; now issued by Defense Mapping Agency, Hydrographic Center as *Pubn.* no.9 (v.1, 1977 ed., 1316p.; v.2, 1975 ed., 716p.).

The purpose is to provide a compendium of navigational material understandable to the mariner. "Emphasis has been given to the fact that the aids provided by *science* can be used effectively to improve the *art* of navigation only if a well-informed person of mature judgment and experience is on hand to interpret information as it becomes available. Thus, the facts needed to perform the mechanics of navigation have been supplemented with additional material intended to help the navigator acquire the perspective in meeting the various needs that arise."—*Pref.*

v.1 gives the necessary in-depth background or historical information needed to use the tables in v.2; it contains sections on: Fundamentals, piloting and dead reckoning, Celestial navigation, Practice of navigation, Navigation safety, Oceanography, Weather, and Electronics and navigation, together with 26 appendixes with headings such as Greek alphabet, Navigation coordination, Constellations, Hand-held digital calculators, Sea state, and Geodesy for the navigator. v.2 is an "extensively revised edition providing tables, formulas, data, and instructions needed by the navigator to perform many of the computations associated with dead reckoning, piloting, and celestial navigation."—*Pref.* Each volume is indexed.

VK555.A48

The astronomical almanac. For the year 1981– . Wash., Govt. Prt. Off.; London, H.M.S.O., 1980– . Annual. **EB60**

Subtitle: Data for astronomy, space sciences, geodesy, surveying, navigation and other applications.

Supersedes *The American ephemeris and nautical almanac* (EB62) and the *Astronomical ephemeris* (EB63), which, beginning with the editions for 1960, have been virtually identical, only some introductory pages differing.

"The principal ephemerides . . . have been computed from fundamental ephemerides of the planets and the Moon prepared at the Jet Propulsion Laboratory, California in cooperation with the U.S. Naval Observatory."—*Pref.* Includes lists of related publications and their publishers' addresses (e.g., *Nautical almanac* and *Air almanac*). QB8.U6A77

Gt.Brit. Board of Trade. The 1931 international code of signals, American ed. Wash., Govt. Prt. Off., 1952. v.1–2. (U.S. Hydrographic Office. Pubn. no.103, 88) **EB61**

Contents: v.1, For visual and sound signaling. Corrected repr. 1962. 367p. il. (H.O. no.103); v.2, For radio signaling. Repr. 1952. 418p. (H.O. no.88)

Methods, general instructions, and systematic treatment for specific types of signals.

U.S. Nautical Almanac Office. American ephemeris and nautical almanac, 1855–1979. Wash., Govt. Prt. Off., 1852–1980. Annual. **EB62**

See note for *The astronomical almanac* (EB60). QB8.U1

Astronomical ephemeris, 1767–1979. London, Stat. Off., 1767–1980. Annual. **EB63**

See note for *The astronomical almanac* (EB60). QB8.G6

———— Explanatory supplement to the Astronomical ephemeris and the American ephemeris and nautical alma-

Dictionaries

Harbord, John Bradley. Glossary of navigation; a vade mecum for practical navigators. 4th ed., rev. and enl. by C. W. T. Layton. Glasgow, Brown & Ferguson, [1938]. 451p. il. **EB64**

First published 1862.

Definitions and practical explanations of terms. Retains numerous terms of historical interest. V23.H3

U.S. Naval Oceanographic Office. Navigation dictionary. 2d ed. Wash., Govt. Prt. Off., 1969. 292p. (*Its* H.O. pubn. no. 220) **EB65**

1st ed. 1956 published by the U.S. Hydrographic Office.

Alphabetical listing of terms. Includes parts of speech, synonyms and antonyms. V23.U557

CHRONOLOGY

Bond, John James. Handy-book of rules and tables for verifying dates with the Christian Era. London, Bell, 1875. 465p. (Repr.: N.Y., Russell & Russell, 1966) **EB66**

Subtitle: Giving an account of the chief eras, and systems used by various nations, with easy methods for determining the corresponding dates; with regnal years of English sovereigns from the Norman Conquest to the present time, 1066–1874. CE11.B7

Cappelli, Adriano. Cronologia, cronografia e calendario perpetuo. Dal principio dell' èra cristiana ai giorni nostri. Tavole cronologico-sincrone e quadri sinottici per verificare le date storiche. 3. ed. aggiornata ed ampliata. Milano, Hoepli, 1969. 602p. **EB67**

1st ed. 1906.

Forty year English-Jewish calendar with corresponding English dates from 1960 till 2000; to be used also as a Yarzeit calendar. [n.p.], Greenfield, 1963. 1v., unpaged. **EB68**

Half-title: Hebrew-English calendar.

Freeman-Grenville, Greville Stewart Parker. The Muslim and Christian calendars, being tables for the conversion of Muslim and Christian dates from the Hijra to the year A.D. 2000. London, Oxford Univ. Pr., 1963. 87p. **EB69**

Includes examples to illustrate how the tables are to be used. CE59.F7

Ginzel, Friedrich Karl. Handbuch der mathematischen und technischen Chronologie, das Zeitrechnungswesen der Völker. Leipzig, J. C. Hinrichs, 1906–14. 3v. **EB70**

Contents: Bd.1, Zeitrechnung der Babylonier, Ägypter, Mohammedaner, Perser, Inder, Südostasiaten, Chinesen, Japaner und Zentralamerikaner; Bd.2, Zeitrechnung der Juden, der Naturvölker, der Römer und Griechen, sowie Nachträge zum 1. Bande; Bd.3, Zeitrechnung der Makedonier, Kleinasier und Syrer, der Germanen und Kelten, des Mittelalters, der Byzantiner (und Russen), Armenier, Kopten, Abessinier, Zeitrechnung der neueren Zeit, sowie Nachträge zu den drei Bänden. Each volume has its own index.

CE11.G5

Master Reporting Company. A 200-year series of calendars, 1828–2028. N.Y., Master Reporting Co., [1932?] [16p.] **EB71**

A convenient, small handbook to keep at an information desk. Fixes the day of the week for every date, 1828–2028.

Welch, Windon Chandler. Chinese-American calendar for the 102 Chinese years commencing Jan. 24, 1849, and ending Feb. 5, 1951. Wash., Govt. Prt. Off., 1928. 102p. (U.S. Dept. of Labor. Bureau of Immigration)   **EB72**

One page for each year: figures in black represent the Chinese day; red figures are used for the corresponding English day.

———— Chinese-American calendar for the 40th through the 89th year of the Chinese Republic, Feb. 6, 1951 to Jan. 23, 2001. [Supplement] Rev. 1957. Wash., Admin. Division, Immigration and Naturalization Service, [1957]. 50p.
EB73
CE37.W4

E C

Biological Sciences

❖This section includes publications of interest to the student, the researcher and the lay person. Particular attention has been given to identifying and including reference sources suitable for the collection at the level of the college library. However, the sources for the field are typified by a relatively small number of basic works such as dictionaries and a relatively large number of highly specialized publications. Directories have been screened with particular attention to currency; consequently, some titles from earlier editions of the *Guide*, while still unique, have been deleted.

The research collection will include both *Biological abstracts* (EC10) and *The zoological record* (EC183), major index journals in the field. All libraries needing access to journal literature will find *Biological & agricultural index* (EC7) useful.

Popular works, especially field guides, are included selectively with the purpose of identifying typical publications. Many more titles exist than are listed; field guides in particular are a burgeoning form of publication.

The guides to the literature listed below will provide more detailed information. In addition, the *Guide to sources for agricultural and biological research* (EH1), although emphasizing agriculture, supplements this section through its lists of specialized sources.

GENERAL WORKS

Guides

Bottle, Robert Thomas and **Wyatt, H. V.** The use of biological literature. [2d ed. Hamden, Conn.], Archon Books, [1971]. 379p.   **EC1**

1st ed. 1966.
20 articles describing primary sources of biological information and the indexing and abstracting services providing access to them. In this edition chapters have been added on ecology, genetics, and experimental aspects of botany, and there is a new section on machine-searchable tapes and services. British sources are empha-

sized. Includes a list of important abbreviations, special UK collections, and exercises in the use of cited tools. Subject and title index.
QH303.B6

Davis, Elizabeth B. Using the biological literature. N.Y. & Basel, Marcel Dekker, [1981]. 286p.   **EC2**

An expansion of handouts intended to familiarize undergraduate and graduate students with biological literature. Divides the literature into broad categories (e.g., botany, ecology, physiology), then into subcategories. Lists important primary journals for each category, with scope of coverage. Indexed.   QH303.D39

Smith, Roger C., Reid, W. Malcolm and **Luchsinger, Arlene E.** Smith's Guide to the literature of the life sciences. 9th ed. Minneapolis, Burgess, [1980]. 223p.   **EC3**

1st–7th eds. (1943–67) had title *Guide to the literature of the zoological sciences*; 8th ed. (1972) had title *Guide to the literature of the life sciences.*
"The aim . . . is to present (1) an introduction to the most useful materials for the library phase of biological research, and (2) suggestions for the reporting of research to the scientific community."—*Pref.* Arranged by topics such as "Abstracts and abstracting journals"; "Searching the literature"; and "Preparation for scientific writing." Includes library assignments. Indexed.   QH303.S6

Bibliography

International catalogue of scientific literature: L, General biology. 1st–14th annual issues, 1901–14. London, 1901–19. 14v.   **EC4**

For full description *see* EA17.

Murray, Margaret Ransome and **Kopech, Gertrude.** A bibliography of the research in tissue culture, 1884–1950; an index to the literature of the living cell cultivated in vitro. N.Y., Academic Pr., 1953. 2v. (1741p.)   **EC5**

"Tissue culture has been defined as the maintenance of isolated portions of multicellular organisms in artificial containers outside the individual for considerable periods of time."—*Introd.* Represents 15,000 original articles from serials and books, expanded to 86,000 entries by cross-indexing, using a comprehensive subject classification scheme. Authors and subjects arranged in one alphabet. Entries include references to abstracts in *Biological abstracts.*

———— ———— Supplementary author list, 1950. (Incomplete and unverified, Oct. 1953) N.Y., Academic Pr., 1953. 11p.

Z6663.T5M7

Smit, Pieter. History of the life sciences; an annotated bibliography. N.Y., Hafner Pr., [1974]. 1074p.   **EC6**

Contents: Chap. I, General references and tools; Chap. II, Historiography of the life and medical sciences; Selected list of biographies, bibliographies, etc., of famous biologists, medical men, etc., including some modern reissues of their publications; Index of personal names.
" . . . originated as a plan to produce an extension of the parts of Sarton's 'Guide to the History of Science' [EA213] that deal with the life sciences."—*Introd.* More than 4,000 entries with full bibliographical information and short summary review (about 90 words).
Z5320.S55

Indexes

Biological & agricultural index, a cumulative subject index to periodicals in the fields of biology, agriculture, and related sciences, 1964– . N.Y., Wilson, 1964– . v.19– . Monthly (except Aug.) with annual cumulation.   **EC7**

Continues the *Agricultural index* (EH29).
An alphabetic subject index to approximately 200 English-language periodicals in the agricultural and biological sciences. Publi-

cations of U.S. and state government agencies and of university service and research facilities are not included. The list of periodicals indexed (decided by subscriber vote) gives subscription information. Book reviews are listed by author in a separate section; no other author entries. Z5073.A46●

Biological abstracts/RRM. v.18– , Jan. 1980– . Philadelphia, BioSciences Information Service, 1980– . Monthly. **EC8**

"Reporting worldwide research in life science."—*t.p.*
v.1–17 (1967–79) had title: *Bioresearch index.*
A supplement to *Biological abstracts* (EC10), concentrating on reports, reviews, meetings, and books. Entries do not include abstracts; however, concepts (key words) are listed after the bibliographic information. Author, biosystematic, generic, and subject indexes. Semiannual cumulative indexes. Z5321.B672

Current awareness in biological sciences. v.100– , 1983– . Oxford & N.Y., Pergamon, 1983– . v.100– . Monthly. **EC9**

Continues in part *International abstracts of biological sciences* (EC13).
A computer-generated, subject-arranged listing of periodical articles. Coverage: biochemistry, cell and developmental biology, ecological sciences, genetics, microbiology, plant science, physiology, pharmacology, toxicology, and immunology. Abstracts as found in the earlier title were discontinued. Author index. QH301.I475

Abstract journals

Biological abstracts. v.1– , Dec. 1926– . Philadelphia, BioSciences Information Service, 1926– . Semimonthly. **EC10**

"Reporting worldwide research in life science."—*t.p.*
Subtitle varies. Frequency varies; now published semimonthly, with semiannual (formerly annual) cumulative indexes.
The principal abstracting journal for the subject of biology. Preceded by *Abstracts of bacteriology,* v.1–9, 1917–25 (Baltimore, Williams & Wilkins), and *Botanical abstracts,* v.1–15, 1918–26 (Baltimore, Williams & Wilkins), which merged to form *Biological abstracts.*
Each issue consists of five sections: Abstracts, Author index, Biosystematic index, Generic index, and Subject index. Entries are arranged within the abstracts section according to 84 major concept headings. All titles are given in English; the language of the original, when not English, is noted. Gives affiliation of the first author. Abstracts are detailed. The Author index includes both personal and corporate names; up to ten co-authors are indexed. The Biosystematic index gives access by taxonomic categories. The Generic index gives access according to genus or genus-species names. The Subject index gives access on the basis of all significant words in the author's title or text, or words added by BIOSIS; it is a keyword-in-context index. QH301.B37●

—— Indexes on microfilm. Philadelphia, BioSciences Information Service, 1959/64– . **EC11**

Quinquennial cumulations of volume indexes to *Biological abstracts* (above). Available: v.34–45, 1959–64; v.46–50, 1965–69; v.51–58, 1970–74; v.59–68, 1975–79; v.69–78, 1980–84. The last three are also available on microfiche.

Serial sources for the BIOSIS data base. Philadelphia, BioSciences Information Service. 1971– . Annual. **EC12**

The 1984 list includes 16,520 serials contributing to *Biological abstracts* (EC10) and *Biological abstracts/RRM* (EC8). Full titles are entered but the list is arranged by the standard BIOSIS abbreviated title. Entries include CODEN, frequency, and a number keyed to the list of 6,404 publishers at the back.

International abstracts of biological sciences. v.1–99, 1954– 82. London, Pergamon, for Biological and Medical Abstracts, 1954–82. v.1–99. Monthly. **EC13**

Title varies: v.1–3, *British abstracts of medical sciences.*

Attempted to cover "the important papers in experimental biology, approaching the subject from the fundamental point of view, with emphasis on anatomy, oral biology, biochemistry, immunology and experimental pathology, microbiology, pharmacology, physiology, animal behavior, cytology, genetics and experimental zoology."—*Aims and scope.* Titles of foreign-language articles are translated into English; language of article is indicated if other than English. Abstracts are signed; not all entries carry abstracts. Author and subject indexes. Continued (without abstracts) by *Current awareness in biological sciences* (EC9). QH301.I475

Encyclopedias

Clark, George Lindenberg. The encyclopedia of microscopy. N.Y., Reinhold, [1961]. 693p. il. **EC14**

Alphabetical arrangement of signed articles covering instruments, uses, techniques and theories of microscopy, techniques of preparation, and the structures and substances which can be studied using microscopy. Bibliographies follow most articles. No index. QH211.C54

Gray, Peter. The encyclopedia of microscopy and microtechnique. N.Y., Van Nostrand, [1973]. 638p. il. **EC15**

Comprises signed articles, in alphabetic sequence, on instruments in theory or practice, techniques of microscopy and preparation, disciplines, individual subjects and materials intended for examination, and reagents. A list of references follows each article. Indexed. QH203.G8

—— ed. The encyclopedia of the biological sciences. 2d ed. N.Y., Van Nostrand Reinhold, [1970]. 1027p. il. **EC16**

1st ed. 1961.
An alphabetically arranged encyclopedia of signed articles with bibliographies, covering all aspects of the broad field of the biological sciences, including biographies, but excluding the applied biological sciences and the behavioral sciences except as they apply to animals. Prepared for the non-specialist, the teacher, the librarian, and the student, although some highly technical articles on the more specialized subjects are included. Black-and-white drawings and photographs. Indexed. QH13.G7

General taxonomy

Synopsis and classification of living organisms. Sybil P. Parker, ed. in chief. N.Y., McGraw-Hill, [1982]. 2v. il. **EC17**

"In these volumes, the systematic positions and affinities of all living organisms are presented in synoptic articles for all taxa down to the family level."—*Pref.* Organized into four kingdoms—virus, monera, plantae, and animalia. Consists of 8,200 signed synoptic articles with literature references. Indexed. QH83.S89

Dictionaries

Abercrombie, M., Hickman, C. J. and **Johnson, M. L.** The Penguin dictionary of biology. [New ed.] [London], Allen Lane; [N.Y.], Viking, [1977]. 311p. **EC18**

1st ed. 1951.
"This hardback edition, based on sixth paperback edition, 1977"—*verso of t.p.*
For the student and layman. QH203.A2

The biographical dictionary of scientists, biologists. David Abbott, general ed. N.Y., Peter Bedrick Bks., [1983]. 182p. **EC19**

Includes a selection of significant biologists from ancient times through the present day. The dictionary emphasizes the nature and significance of the subjects' work. Biographees are clustered under one name in cases of collaboration, with *see* references in the text. Glossary. Subject and name index.   QH26.B54

Cowan, Samuel Tertius. A dictionary of microbial taxonomy. Cambridge, Cambridge Univ. Pr., [1978]. 285p.
EC20

Ed. by L.R. Hill.
1968 ed. had title: *A dictionary of microbial taxonomic usage.*
Intended "for those whose work brings them to taxonomy, often reluctantly."—*Pref.* Modeled on Fowler's *Dictionary of modern English usage,* so that comparisons of terms and discussions of broader subjects generally accompany the definitions.   QR9.C66

Dictionary of life sciences. Ed. by Elizabeth A. Martin. 2d ed. rev. N.Y., Pica; distr. by Universe Books, [1983]. 396p. il.   **EC21**

1st ed. 1977.
A handy, easy-to-use, concise dictionary for the life sciences.
QH302.5.D52

Dumbleton, C. W. Russian-English biological dictionary. Edinburgh, Oliver & Boyd, 1964. 512p.   **EC22**

Gives equivalent English terms for Russian terms in the biological sciences, excluding pathology. Includes the scientific names of species. Assumes a knowledge of Russian grammar and syntax.
QH13.D78

Gray, Peter. The dictionary of the biological sciences. N.Y., Reinhold, [1967]. 602p. il.   **EC23**

A work by the author of the *Encyclopedia of the biological sciences* (EC16), made up largely of brief definitions for terms which did not warrant entries in the *Encyclopedia.* Users should note that all words from a given root are listed under that root, usually without cross reference.   QH13.G68

Henderson, Isabella Ferguson. Henderson's Dictionary of biological terms. 9th ed. N.Y., Van Nostrand Reinhold, [1979]. 510p.   **EC24**

Ed. by Sandra Holmes.
1st ed. 1920. Title varies.
An extensive revision of a standard work, now listing about 22,500 terms. Taxonomic terms are included down to the order level. Three appendixes: Classification of the plant kingdom, Classification of the animal kingdom, and Common chemical elements.
QH13.H4

Herbert, W. J. and **Wilkinson, P. C.,** eds. A dictionary of immunology. 2d ed. Oxford, Blackwell Scientific; distr. by J. B. Lippincott, Philadelphia, 1977. 197p. il.   **EC25**

"Compiled by members of [*sic*] staff of the Department of Bacteriology and Immunology, Department of Pathology, and Institute of Virology, University of Glasgow."—*t.p.*
1st ed. 1971.
The purpose is to provide a glossary for use in undergraduate teaching and "to include a range of terms wide enough to satisfy the needs of any biologist, clinician or biochemist who requires easy reference to current immunological usage . . . the definitions given are not intended to reflect our personal views as to how the terms *should* be used but, rather, to tell the reader how they *have been* used in the literature."—*Pref.*   QR180.4.H47

Jacobs, Morris B., Gerstein, Maurice J. and **Walter, William G.** Dictionary of microbiology. Princeton, N.J., Van Nostrand, [1957]. 276p. il.   **EC26**

Provides definitions only for "terms commonly used in microbiology and the related fields of bacteriology, mycology, virology, cytology, immunology and immunochemistry, serology and microscopy."—*Pref.* Includes names of families, genera, etc., of organisms. Few illustrations.   QR9.J18

Jaeger, Edmund Carroll. The biologist's handbook of pronunciations. Springfield, Ill., Thomas, [1960]. 317p. il.
EC27

Gives pronunciation of some 9,000 scientific terms used in the biological sciences. "Many commonly used terms and generic names

of obvious sound and accentuation have been omittted."—*Pref.* In some cases, lists less acceptable alternatives following the preferred pronunciation.   QH13.J3

——— A source-book of biological names and terms. 3d ed. Illus. by Merle Gish and the author. Springfield, Ill., Thomas, [1955]. 317p. il. (Rev. 2d printing, 1959)   **EC28**

1st ed. 1944; 2d ed. 1950.
An alphabetical list of some 12,000 elements from which scientific biological names and terms are made, with their Greek, Latin, or other origins and their concise meanings, with examples of usage. This edition includes some corrections in the main text and adds a supplement of more than 1,000 entries, which include "a limited number of much used geographical place-name stems employed in forming adjectival trivial and varietal names of plants and animals and . . . more than 280 short biographies of persons commemorated in botanical and zoological generic names."—*Pref.*   QH83.J3

Jeffrey, Charles. Biological nomenclature. 2d ed. N.Y., Crane, Russak, [1977]. 72p.   **EC29**

1st ed. 1973.
"The purpose of this handbook is to provide a practical guide to the use of the nomenclatural parts of taxonomic literature, to promote understanding of the problems, principles and practice of biological nomenclature and to act as an introduction to the Codes of Nomenclature themselves."—*Pref.*   QH83.J43

Roe, Keith E. and **Frederick, Richard G.** Dictionary of theoretical concepts in biology. Metuchen, N.J., Scarecrow Pr., 1981. 267p.   **EC30**

Lists 1,166 named concepts and cites "original sources and reviews in which these concepts are elucidated."—*Introd.*
QH302.5.R63

Singleton, Paul and **Sainsbury, Diana.** Dictionary of microbiology. Chichester, [Eng.] & N.Y., Wiley, [1978]. 481p.
EC31

Combines dictionary entries and longer articles. Includes over 1,000 microbial taxa. The taxonomic scheme is based on *Bergey's Manual (see* EC243). Appendix of metabolic pathways.
QR9.S56

Steen, Edwin B. Dictionary of biology. N.Y., Barnes & Noble, [1971]. 630p.   **EC32**

Provides brief definitions of about 12,000 terms. "Taxonomic names, except for some of the major groups, are not included as entries with definitions; however, under their common names, representatives of the principal groups are listed and the groups are characterized."—*Pref.*   QH13.S74

Tootill, Elizabeth, ed. The Facts on File dictionary of biology. [2d ed.] N.Y., Facts on File, [1981]. 282p. il.
EC33

"First edition published in the United Kingdom in 1981 by Intercontinental Book Productions Limited. . . . "—*verso of t.p.*
About 3,100 entries defining the most important and commonly used biological terms.   QH13.T66

Woods, Robert S. An English-classical dictionary for the use of taxonomists. [Claremont, Calif.], Pomona College, [1966]. 331p.   **EC34**

"The purpose . . . is to present in the most adaptable form all words found in unabridged classical Greek and Latin lexicons which could conceivably be used in scientific nomenclature . . ."—*Pref.*
QH83.W58

——— The naturalist's lexicon, a list of classical Greek and Latin words used, or suitable for use, in biological nomenclature, with abridged English-classical supplement. Pasadena, Calif., Abbey Garden Pr., 1944. 282p.   **EC35**

Includes more than 15,000 words; designed to facilitate the use by naturalists of Latin and Greek terms in naming species. Latin terms and their Greek equivalents and transliterated Greek terms are listed in one alphabet, with brief definitions in English. Includes a brief introductory article on the Latin and Greek languages. The

English-classical supplement consists of alphabetical lists of English nouns and Latin and Greek equivalents, arranged by subject, and similar lists of adjectives and verbs.

—— —— Addenda . . . Comprehensive classified English-classical key to descriptive terms. Additions and emendations to the classical-English lexicon. Pasadena, Calif., Abbey Garden Pr., 1947. 47p.

QH83.W6

Handbooks

Altman, Philip L. and **Dittmer, Dorothy S.**, eds. Biology data book. 2d ed. Bethesda, Md., Federation of American Societies for Experimental Biology, [1972–74]. 3v. **EC36**

1st ed. 1964.

". . . a three-volume compilation of evaluated reference data in the life sciences" (*Foreword, v.3.*) in tabular form. Consists largely of quantitative data but also includes some descriptive data, such as experimental results, interrelationships of organisms and of biochemical processes, and characteristics of organisms and conditions. v.1 covers genetics, cytology, reproduction, development, and growth; v.2, biological regulators and toxins; and v.3, nutrition, digestion, and excretion; metabolism; respiration and circulation; and blood and other fluids. Each volume is indexed separately, but there is no index to the entire set. QH3110.A392

—— eds. Environmental biology. Prep. under the auspices of the Committee on Biological Handbooks. Bethesda, Md., Federation of American Societies for Experimental Biology, [1966]. 694p. il. **EC37**

A compilation, mainly tabular, of qualitative and quantitative data on the effects on living entities of various natural and synthetic external factors, including chemical constituents of the surrounding media, radiations, and temperature. The index includes all species covered in the tables, as well as the environmental conditions and constituents considered and the physiological characteristics measured. QH310.A395

—— Respiration and circulation. Bethesda, Md., Federation of Amer. Societies for Experimental Biology, [1971]. 930p. (Biological handbooks) **EC38**

Constitutes a complete revision and combination of *Handbook of respiration* (1958) and *Handbook of circulation* (1959).

A collection of authoritative data, quantitative and descriptive, on respiration and circulation. For the most part concerned with man and other vertebrates but includes sections on invertebrates and on plants. QP101.R47

Altman, Philip L. and **Katz, Dorothy Dittmer.** eds. Cell biology. Bethesda, Md., Federation of Amer. Societies for Experimental Biology, [1976]. 454p. (Biological handbooks, n.s., v.1) **EC39**

A detailed tabulation of data on the cell, with emphasis on vertebrate cells. 102 tables are arranged in seven sections: (1) General cell characteristics; (2) Cell environment; (3) Cell periphery; (4) Mitochondria: (5) Endoplasmic reticulum, microsomes, ribosomes, and Golgi; (6) Lysosomes, peroxisomes, granules, and microbodies; (7) Nuclei. Includes appendixes of animal and plant names. QH581.2.C34

CRC handbook of microbiology. 2d ed. Cleveland & Boca Raton, Fla., CRC Pr., 1977–84. v.1–7. il. (In progress) **EC40**

1st ed. 1973.

Allen I. Laskin and Hubert A. Lechevalier, eds.

Contents: v.1, Bacteria; v.2, Fungi, algae, protozoa, and viruses; v.3, Microbial composition: amino acids, proteins, and nucleic acids; v.4, Microbial composition: carbohydrates, lipids, and minerals; v.5, Microbial products; v.6, Growth and metabolism; v.7, Microbial transformation.

A comprehensive source of current information in microbiology. Each volume consists of signed articles; many have tabular data,

illustrations, and lists of references. Some of the latter are extensive. Each volume contains a taxonomic index and a topical index.

QR6.C2

Fisher, *Sir* **Ronald A.** and **Yates, Frank.** Statistical tables for biological, agricultural and medical research. 6th ed. rev. and enl. N.Y., Hafner; Edinburgh, London, Oliver and Boyd, [1963]. 146p. **EC41**

1st ed. 1938.

34 tables, with introductions, providing solutions to statistical problems with direct application to biological, agricultural, and medical research. QH324.F52

Style manuals

CBE Style Manual Committee. CBE style manual. 5th ed., rev. and expanded. Bethesda, Md., Council of Biology Editors, Inc., [1983]. 324p. **EC42**

Subtitle: A guide for authors, editors, and publishers in the biological sciences.

1st–4th eds. 1960–78; title varies.

Intended primarily as a guide for authors preparing articles for publication in biological journals. New chapters deal with ethical conduct, copyright, and illustrative material. There is an annotated list of other, similar works. Subject index. Z250.6.B5C65

Zweifel, Frances W. A handbook of biological illustration. [Chicago,] Univ. of Chicago Pr., [1961]. 131p. il. **EC43**

"Intended primarily for the guidance of the student or professional biologist who is unfamiliar with materials and techniques of illustrating. . . ."—*Pref.* A succinct how-to book, emphasizing black-and-white drawing, but including some discussion of color illustration. Does not include photography but does cover graphs, maps, and lettering. QH318.Z97

History

Dawes, Benjamin. A hundred years of biology. London, Duckworth, [1952]. 429p. il. **EC44**

Bibliography, p.385–418. QH305.D3

ECOLOGY

Burke, John Gordon and **Reddig, Jill Swanson.** Guide to ecology information and organizations. N.Y., Wilson, 1976. 292p. **EC45**

Intended primarily for public libraries and their patrons. Includes "both print and nonprint materials, as well as names of persons who are willing to share their expertise."—*Introd.*

In various sections: Citizen action guides, Indexes, Reference books, Histories, Monographs, Government publications, Nonprint media, Periodicals, Organizations, Government officials. Includes a directory of publishers and distributors, and a detailed index.

Z5861.B87

Grzimek's Encyclopedia of ecology. Ed. in chief, Bernhard Grzimek. English ed. N.Y., Van Nostrand Reinhold, [1976]. 705p. il. **EC46**

Ed. by Bernhard Grzimek, Joachim Illies, Wolfgang Klausewitz. Translation of the 1973 German ed.

" . . . a supplement to the thirteen-volume Grzimek's Animal Life Encyclopedia [EC187]."—*Foreword.*

Over 40 experts have made contributions to the 33 essays in this one-volume encyclopedia. In pt. 1, "The environment of animals," the 22 essays are arranged under four headings: (1) Adaptations to the abiotic environment; (2) Adaptations to the biotic environment;

(3) Habitats and their fauna; (4) Man as a factor in the environment of animals. Pt. 2 entitled "The environment of man." Index.
QL45.G7913 Suppl.

Lincoln, R.J., Boxshall, G.A. and **Clark, P.F.** A dictionary of ecology, evolution and systematics. Cambridge, Cambridge Univ. Pr., [1982]. 298p.   **EC47**

Brief definitions of terms in the broad field of evolutionary biology. There are 21 brief appendixes with useful information.
QH540.4.L56

NATURAL HISTORY

Bibliography

American Museum of Natural History, New York. Library. Research catalog of the Library of the American Museum of Natural History; authors. Boston, G. K. Hall, 1977. 13v.
EC48

"Provides access by personal, corporate, and joint authors, compilers, editors, and illustrators of note, as well as biographical and critical materials. . . . Of particular value are author entries for journal articles and chapters in books."—*Pref.*   Z7409.A43

Freeman, Richard Broke. British natural history books, 1495–1900, a handlist. [Folkestone, Eng.], Dawson; [Hamden, Conn.], Archon Books, [1980]. 437p.   **EC49**

Lists "all books about the fauna and flora of the British Islands, including all Ireland, the Channel Islands. . . . all general natural history books written by inhabitants of these islands, and . . . translations into English of relevant books by foreign authors and a few American books which have appeared in British editions."—*Introd.* Lists 4,206 publications by main entry, giving full bibliographic information. Includes a list by imprint date and a subject index.
Z7408.G7F73

———— The works of Charles Darwin: an annotated bibliographical handlist. 2d ed. Rev. & enl. Folkestone, [Eng.], Dawson; [Hamden, Conn.], Archon Books, [1977]. 235p.
EC50

1st ed. 1965.
Contents: pt.1, Books and pamphlets; pt.2, Publications in serials.
"The first part of the . . . list contains all the editions and issues of books, pamphlets and circulars, both British and foreign, which I have seen, or seen reliably recorded, from the first in 1835 up to the end of 1975. . . . The second part contains a list of papers, notes and letters which were originally published in serials."—*Pref.* A listing of 1,805 items. Includes a review of the publication history for each title listed in the books and pamphlets section. Indexed.
A complementary work is: Z8217.F7

A concordance to Darwin's *Origin of species,* **first edition.** Ed. by Paul H. Barrett, Donald J. Weinshank, and Timothy T. Gottleber. Ithaca, N.Y., Cornell Univ. Pr., [1981]. 834p.
EC51

A keyword-in-context concordance based on the 1964 Harvard Univ. Pr. reprint of the 1st ed. There is a list of stop words and their frequency.   QH365.O8B37

Meisel, Max. Bibliography of American natural history; the pioneer century, 1769–1865. . . . Brooklyn, N.Y., Premier Pub. Co., 1924–29. 3v.   **EC52**

Subtitle: The role played by the scientific societies; scientific journals; natural history museums and botanic gardens; state geological and natural history surveys; federal exploring expeditions in the rise and progress of American botany, geology, mineralogy, paleontology and zoology.
v.1, Annotated bibliography of the publications relating to the history, biography and bibliography of American natural history and its institutions during colonial times and the pioneer century, which have been published up to 1924; with a classified subject and geographical index and a bibliography of biographies; v.2 and 3,

Chronological bibliography of the publications of institutions which have contributed to the rise and progress of American natural history which were founded or organized between 1769 and 1865, with short histories of the institutions. Bibliography of books, articles, and miscellaneous publications not published in the proceedings and transactions of scientific societies, etc. Chronological tables; index of authors and institutions; addenda.   Z7408.U5M5

Indexes

Munz, Lucile Thompson and **Slauson, Nedra G.** Index to illustrations of living things outside North America: where to find pictures of flora and fauna. [Hamden, Conn.], Archon Books, 1981. 441p.   **EC53**

"A companion volume to John W. Thompson's *Index to illustrations of the natural world: where to find pictures of the living things of North America* [EC54]."—*t.p.*
An index to illustrations of more than 9,000 species of animals and plants to be found in 209 books published since 1963. Subject entries are by common name; a scientific name index supplies the latter.   Z7998.N67M85

Thompson, John W., comp. Index to illustrations of the natural world. Nedra Slauson, ed. Syracuse, N.Y., Gaylord Professional Publ., 1977. 265p.   **EC54**

Subtitle: Where to find pictures of the living things of North America.
Approximately 6,200 entries for plants, birds, and animals. For each item is listed the common name, scientific name, and citations to three to ten illustrations. The pictures cited are found in a total of 178 books which "have been published since 1960, but some classic works published earlier have been included. . . . The availability of the books in most medium-size and large libraries was an important criterion in selection."—*Introd.* Includes a 77-page index from the scientific name to the common name.   Z7998.N67T45

Encyclopedias

Grzimek's Encyclopedia of evolution. Ed. in chief, Bernhard Grzimek. English ed. N.Y., Van Nostrand Reinhold, [1976]. 560p. il.   **EC55**

Ed. by Gerhard Heberer and Herbert Wendt.
Translation of the 1972 German ed.
Over 200 contributors from all over the world have prepared the 23 essays in this one-volume encyclopedia. The many general aspects of evolutionary theory, phylogeny, genetics effect, paleontology, paleobotany, paleogeology, and the evolution of man are covered, as well as such subjects as the origin of life, early history of the earth, the path to warm-bloodedness, origin of mammals, the conquest of the air, etc. Includes supplementary readings and index.
QE711.2.G79

Dictionaries

Compton's Dictionary of the natural sciences. Chicago, Compton, [1966]. 2v. il.   **EC56**

Ed. in chief, Charles A. Ford.
Written in simple, easily understandable language, this work is useful not only to young people, but to the non-specialist at all educational levels. Entries run heavily to plants, animals, birds, fishes, insects, and the like, but there are entries for terms in geology, astronomy, etc. Genus and scientific names are given for plants, etc., as applicable. An "Illustrated index and glossary of terms" offers definitions of numerous terms (with pronunciation) not included in the main text, together with references (mainly from variant forms) to articles in the text.   QH13.C65

Fitter, Richard Sidney Richmond and **Fitter, Maisie.** The Penguin dictionary of British natural history. [Harmondsworth, Eng.], Penguin, [1967]. 348p. **EC57**

"In this dictionary of the natural history of the British Isles the term 'natural history' is interpreted in the broadest sense to include all living things and natural phenomena of the earth and its atmosphere."—*Scope*. QH137.F539

Directories

Conservation directory. 30th ed. Wash., Nat. Wildlife Federation, [1985]. 302p. **EC58**

Subtitle: A list of organizations, agencies and officials concerned with natural resource use and management.

1st ed. 1900; title varies. Now published annually.

A classified directory which emphasizes United States, international, and Canadian organizations and agencies. Includes national, state, and provincial governments. For most entries gives address, scope of work or concern, personnel information, subagencies or subprograms, and publications. Includes miscellaneous information such as U.S. national wildlife refuges, forests, parks, and seashores. Personal name index. S920.C64

The naturalists' directory and almanac (international). 43d ed. Baltimore, World Natural History Pubns., [1978]. 310p. **EC59**

100th anniversary ed.

42d ed. (1975) had title: *The naturalists' directory international*.

The directory section is an alphabetical listing of naturalists with addresses. The almanac section includes indexes to the naturalists by country, city, and reference number, a geographical list of museums and zoological and botanical gardens, and miscellaneous information. Q145.N3

Handbooks

Audubon Society field guide series. N.Y., Knopf, 1977– . **EC60**

Each guide in the series is written by an authority. Virtually limited to the contiguous United States; illustrated with colored photographs. Generic and English name index in each volume.

The series includes *A field guide to North American:* birds, Eastern region edition; birds, Western region edition; butterflies; fishes; fossils; insects; mammals; reptiles and amphibians; rocks and minerals; seashells; seashore creatures; trees, Eastern edition; trees, Western edition; wildflowers, Eastern region; wildflowers, Western region; natural places of the mid-Atlantic states (v.1, coastal; v.2, inland).

Collins, Henry Hill. Harper & Row's Complete field guide to North American wildlife, Eastern edition. N.Y., Harper & Row, [1981]. 714p. il. **EC61**

Subtitle: Covering 1500 species of birds, mammals, reptiles, amphibians, food and game fishes of both fresh and salt waters, mollusks, and the principal marine invertebrates occuring in North America east of the 100th meridian from the 55th parallel to Florida north of the Keys.

A substantial revision of *Complete field guide to American wildlife: east, central and north* (1959). Indexed. QL151.C62

Jaques, Harry Edwin. Pictured-key nature series. Dubuque, Ia., Wm. C. Brown, 1946– . **EC62**

A series of popular, illustrated handbooks for identifying plants, animals, etc., suitable for the beginner but scientifically reliable. Titles begin *How to know . . .*, and include such topics as beetles, economic plants, insects, land birds, living things, plant families, protozoa, trees, water birds, weeds.

Peterson, Roger Tory. The Peterson field guide series. Boston, Houghton Mifflin, 1947– . **EC63**

Designed as basic guides for the nature student, beginner, or expert, each volume by a specialist in the subject.

The series includes *A field guide to*: birds; Western birds; shells of the Atlantic and Gulf coasts and the West Indies; butterflies; mammals; Pacific coast shells (including shells of Hawaii and the Gulf of California); rocks and minerals; birds of Britain and Europe; animal tracks; ferns and their related families of Northeastern and Central North America; trees and shrubs; reptiles and amphibians of Eastern and Central North America; birds of Texas and adjacent states; Rocky Mountain wildflowers; stars and planets; Western reptiles and amphibians; wildflowers of Northeastern and North-Central North America; mammals of Britain and Europe; insects of America north of Mexico; Mexican birds; birds' nests (found east of Mississippi River); Pacific states wildflowers; edible wild plants of Eastern and Central North America; Atlantic seashore; Western birds' nests; atmosphere; coral reefs of the Caribbean and Florida; Pacific coast fishes; beetles; moths; Southwestern and Texas wildflowers; Atlantic coast fishes.

Ransom, Jay Ellis. Harper & Row's Complete field guide to North American wildlife, Western edition. N.Y., Harper & Row, [1981]. 809p. il. **EC64**

Subtitle: Covering 1800 species of birds, mammals, reptiles, amphibians, food and game fishes of both fresh and salt waters, mollusks, and the principal marine invertebrates occurring in North America west of the 100th meridian from the 55th parallel to the border of Mexico.

Indexed. QL151.R36

BOTANY

General works

Bibliography

Bay, Jens Christian. Bibliographies of botany; a contribution toward a bibliotheca bibliographica. (*In* Progressus rei botanicae 3, pt.2:331–456. Jena, Fischer, 1909) **EC65**

A valuable, annotated historical bibliography of bibliographies including detailed records of periodicals; general, local, and subject bibliographies; library catalogs; auction and sales catalogs, etc.

Beale, Helen Purdy. Bibliography of plant viruses and index to research. N.Y., Columbia Univ. Pr., 1976. 1495p. **EC66**

This international bibliography of plant virus articles covers a span of 78 years, from 1892 to 1970. Over 29,000 entries arranged alphabetically by author. The virus diseases included are chiefly those of higher plants. Extensive subject indexes. Z5185.V5B42

Frodin, D.G. Guide to standard floras of the world. Cambridge, Cambridge Univ. Pr., [1984]. 619p. **EC67**

Subtitle: An annotated, geographically arranged systematic bibliography of the principal floras, enumerations, checklists and chorological atlases of different areas.

Geographical index; author index. Z5351.F76

Nissen, Claus. Die botanische Buchillustration, ihre Geschichte und Bibliographie. 2. Aufl. Stuttgart, A. Hiersemann, 1966. 3v. in 1. **EC68**

1st ed. in 2v., 1951–52.

Consists of a reproduction of the two volumes of the 1st ed. together with a 94p. supplement as v.3.

v.1 offers a succinct presentation of the history of botanical book illustration, emphasizing German artists but including brief discussions on the art and artists of other countries. v.2 contains an alphabetical listing of authors and their works, with references to the artists of the illustrations therein; an alphabetical list of anonymous works and serial publications, with references to artists; an index to artists, with codes designating the mediums in which they worked; subject and geographical indexes; an author index for both volumes; and addenda. Z5351.N49

Stafleu, Frans Anthonie and **Cowan, Richard S.** Taxonomic literature. 2d ed. Utrecht, Bohn, Scheltema & Holkema, 1976–85. v.1–5. (In progress) (Regnum vegetabile, v.94, 98, 105, 110, 112)   **EC69**

Subtitle: A selective guide to botanical publications and collections with dates, commentaries and types.

Previous ed. 1967.

Contents: v.1–5, A–Ste.

This bibliography attempts to give extensive information on the authors of botanical works "by going into more detail with respect to their collections, the biographical and bibliographical literature about them (one aspect of the book now is that it has become a 'bibliography of bibliographies'), and possibly further information of use for the systematist or for the historian of botany. We also provide information on outstanding botanical explorers and collectors."—*Introd.* Each volume includes a title index and a name index.

QK96.R4

Swift, Lloyd H. Botanical bibliographies; a guide to bibliographic materials applicable to botany. Minneapolis, Burgess, [1970]. 804p.   **EC70**

This is the first part of a projected "Guide to literature useful in botany" designed primarily for the beginning graduate student. Arranged in 65 numbered sections, the first seven of which are concerned with general bibliography and the remainder with bibliographies of particular subject areas. Introductory notes for each section indicate scope or special features of the more important bibliographies, and suggested subject headings for use in searching the general bibliographies are noted in each section. Index of authors, subjects, and titles.   Z5551.A1S8

Early

Hunt, Rachel McMasters Miller. Catalogue of botanical books in the collection of Rachel McMasters Miller Hunt. Pittsburgh, Hunt Botanical Lib., 1958–61. v.1–2 in 3. il., facsims.   **EC71**

Contents: v.1, Printed books, 1477–1700, with several manuscripts of the 12th, 15th, 16th & 17th centuries, comp. by Jane Quinby; v.2, pt.1, Introduction to printed books 1701–1800, comp. by Allan Stevenson; pt.2, Printed books, 1701–1800, comp. by Allan Stevenson.

A catalog of the collection, which is now the property of Carnegie Institute of Technology, arranged chronologically by date of imprint. Each entry consists of a detailed bibliographic description, collation, physical description, and annotation, with a list of references. Each volume contains its own detailed index; in addition, v.2, pt.2, has an index to scientific names. v.2, pt.1, includes a comprehensive article on a bibliographical method for the description of botanical books, a list of bibliographic sources, and lists of symbols and abbreviations.   Z5360.H83

Jackson, Benjamin Daydon. Guide to the literature of botany. Being a classified selection of botanical works, including nearly 6000 titles not given in Pritzel's "Thesaurus." London, publ. for the Index Society by Longmans, 1881. 626p. (Index Society. Pubn. 8)   **EC72**

A selective listing of approximately 9,000 works in the form of a short-title catalog, classified by type of publication (for general works), or by subject. Individual articles from serials are not included, but serial publications are cited in a separate section. The addenda contains citations which were found too late for inclusion in the main text. The index covers all sections of the book.

Z5351.J12

Pritzel, Georg August. Thesaurus literaturae botanicae omnium gentium, inde a rerum botanicarum initiis ad nostra usque tempora, quindecim millia operum recensens. Ed. novam reformatam. Lipsiae, Brockhaus, 1872–[77]. 576p. (Repr.: Milan, Görlizh, 1950)   **EC73**

A bibliography attempting to include all separately published books which appeared through the third quarter of the 19th century. Arranged alphabetically by author, with some brief biographical information and references to the *Catalogue of scientific papers.*

"Anonyma et periodica" cited in a separate section. Systematic, topical and geographical, author, and anonymous titles indexes.

Z5351.P96

Reuss, Jeremias David. Repertorium commentationum a societatibus litterariis editarum . . . T.2, Botanica et mineralogia; T.6, Oeconomia. Gottingae, Dieterich, 1802–06. 604p., 476p.   **EC74**

A valuable index to the publications of learned societies up to 1800. Classed arrangement with author index. For description of complete set *see* EA22.

Modern

Barton, Lela Viola. Bibliography of seeds. N.Y., Columbia Univ. Pr., 1967. 858p.   **EC75**

More than 20,000 citations in author arrangement, with a plant index for both scientific and common names and a subject index. Based on a file of literature references maintained at the Boyce Thompson Institute for Plant Research. Coverage includes seed research, seed technology, and agricultural practices worldwide, to June 1, 1964.   Z5354.S4B3

Blake, Sidney Fay. Geographical guide to floras of the world, an annotated list with special reference to useful plants and common plant names. Pts.1–2. Wash., Govt. Prt. Off., 1942–61. v.1–2. (U.S. Dept. of Agriculture. Misc. pubn. no.401, 797) (In progress?)   **EC76**

Joint contribution from the U.S. Bureau of Plant Industry and the U.S. Dept. of Agriculture Library.

Pt.1, Africa, Australia, North America, South America, and Islands of the Atlantic, Pacific, and Indian Oceans; pt.2, Finland, Sweden, Norway, Denmark, Iceland, Great Britain with Ireland, Netherlands, Belgium, Luxembourg, France, Spain, Portugal, Andorra, Monaco, Italy, San Marino, and Switzerland.

An annotated list of floras and floristic works, including those in periodical literature. Author index in each volume includes birth and death dates.   Z5358.A12B5

Boureau, Édouard. Rapport sur la paléobotanique dans le monde. World report on palaeobotany. Utrecht, 1956–71. v.1–8. (Regnum vegetabile, 7, 11, 19, 24, 35, 42, 57, 78)   **EC77**

Edited by the International Organization of Palaeobotany and published by the International Bureau for Plant Taxonomy and Nomenclature.

An international bibliography of paleobotany. Covers 1950–65, each volume including additional entries for all previous volumes. Includes 16,186 consecutively numbered entries in the eight issues published to date.

Beginning with the second issue (1958) each bibliography (except no.4) has been preceded by a directory of paleobotanists, "Paléobotanistes du monde."

British Museum. Dept. of Printed Books. A catalogue of the works of Linnaeus (and publications more immediately relating thereto) preserved in the libraries of the British Museum (Bloomsbury) and the British Museum (Natural History) (South Kensington). 2d ed. London, Museum, 1933. 246p., 68p. il.   **EC78**

———— An index to the authors (other than Linnaeus) mentioned in the Catalogue. . . . London, Museum, 1936. 59p.

Z8508.B86

Index londinensis to illustrations of flowering plants, ferns and fern allies, being an emended and enlarged edition continued up to the end of the year 1920 of Pritzel's Alphabetical register of representations of flowering plants and ferns comp. from botanical and horticultural publications of the XVIIIth and XIXth centuries; prep. under the auspices of the Royal Horticultural Society of London at the Royal Botanic Gardens, Kew, by O. Stapf. Oxford, Clarendon Pr., 1929–31. 6v.   **EC79**

Added title page: Iconum botanicarum index londinensis.

Includes almost all references found in Pritzel (2. ausg. Berlin, 1861–66) plus later material. Arrangement is alphabetic by genera. No list of references from abbreviations to full titles.

—————— Supplement for the years 1921–35 . . . Prep. under the auspices of the Royal Horticultural Society of London at the Royal Botanic Gardens, Kew, by W. C. Worsdell under the direction of Arthur W. Hill. Oxford, Clarendon Pr., 1941. 2v.

"This supplement to the six volumes of the *Index londinensis* . . . now concludes that work. . . . Although no further supplements are to be issued, it has been arranged that references to new illustrations shall be given in the entries of new names included in future supplements of the *Index kewensis* [EC101] from 1936 onwards. Such entries will be prefixed by an asterisk."—*Pref., v.1.*

Includes references to illustrations from periodicals and independent works published during the years 1921–35, inclusive, and also some references from books prior to 1921 not included in the main work. QK11.P95

International catalogue of scientific literature: M, Botany. 1st–14th annual issues, 1901–14. London, Harrison, 1902–19. 14v. **EC80**

For full description *see* EA17.

Merrill, Elmer Drew and **Walker, Egbert Hamilton.** A bibliography of eastern Asiatic botany. . . . Sponsored by the Smithsonian Institution, Arnold Arboretum of Harvard University, New York Botanical Garden, Harvard-Yenching Institute. Jamaica Plain, Mass., Arnold Arboretum of Harvard Univ., 1938. 719p. **EC81**

A comprehensive, briefly annotated bibliography of books and articles on the taxonomic botany of China, Japan, Formosa, Korea, Manchuria, Mongolia, Tibet, and eastern and southern Siberia, through 1936; where pertinent, papers pertaining to adjacent geographical areas and peripheral subject areas are included. Authors and titles are included in one alphabetic list. Appendixes: Older Oriental works; Reference lists of Oriental serials; Reference lists of Oriental authors. Subject, geographic, and systematic indexes.

—————— —————— Supplement 1– , by Egbert H. Walker. Wash., Amer. Inst. of Biological Sciences, 1960– . v.1– .

Suppl. 1 covers through the year 1958 and includes pre-1936 references noted too late for inclusion in the original *Bibliography.*

Nissen, Claus. Die botanische Buchillustration, ihre Geschichte und Bibliographie. 2 Aufl. Stuttgart, Hiersemann, 1966. 3v. in 1. **EC82**

For full information *see* EC68.

Sachet, Marie-Hélène and **Fosberg, Frances Raymond.** Island bibliographies: Micronesian botany; Land environment and ecology of coral atolls; Vegetation of tropical Pacific islands. Comp. under the auspices of the Pacific Science Board. [Wash.], Nat. Academy of Sciences–Nat. Research Council, 1955. 577p. (N.R.C. Pubn., no.335) **EC83**

In three separate sections, as indicated in the title, arranged alphabetically by author, and each with its own index to geographical locations and subjects.

Includes books, periodical articles, and some unpublished works, with no limitations on date or source, to Nov. 1954. List of serial abbreviations and addenda.

—————— —————— Supplement. Wash., Nat. Acad. of Sciences, 1971. 427p.

Follows the plan of the main volume. Lists new publications, some older items not included in the main work, and incorporates the addenda from that work. Z5358.O3S3

Sandbergs Bokhandel, Stockholm. A catalogue of the works of Linnaeus, issued in commemoration of the 250th anniversary of the birthday of Carolus Linnaeus, 1707–1778. Stockholm, [1957]. 179p. il. **EC84**

Based on the collection of Axel Liljedahl.

892 entries, giving short bibliographic, historic, and descriptive notes on most items. In sections according to form or topic. Includes biographies and bibliographies. Indexes to Linnaeus's works, to authors prior to 1850, and to selected subjects.

Simon, James E., Chadwick, Alena F. and **Craker, Lyle E.** Herbs: an indexed bibliography, 1971–1980. [Hamden, Conn.], Archon Books, 1984. 770p. **EC85**

Subtitle: The scientific literature on selected herbs, and aromatic and medicinal plants of the temperate zone.

Includes 64 commercially significant herbs. Arranged in two sections: (1) herbs, and (2) subject classifications. The first section gives cultural, commercial, or medicinal information and bibliographic references coded to the broad subject classifications of the second section. Author index; subject index. Z5996.H37S56

U.S. National Agricultural Library. Plant science catalog: botany subject index. Boston, Microphotography Co., 1958. 15v. **EC86**

A photographic reproduction of the subject card catalog section of the *Plant science catalog* of the U.S. Dept. of Agriculture Library, compiled from 1903 to July 18, 1952, when work on it ceased because of lack of funds. Worldwide in scope; contains references to botanical literature from earliest times, as published in books and periodicals.

Periodicals

Hunt Botanical Library. B-P-H; Botanico-Periodicum-Huntianum. George H. M. Lawrence [and others], eds. Pittsburgh, Pa., 1968. 1063p. **EC87**

A list of abbreviations for more than 12,000 titles of serial publications "that regularly contain (or, in some period of their history, included) articles dealing with the plant sciences and botanical literature, and with persons who have contributed to botany and its literature."—*Pref.* An attempt to provide a set of standardized abbreviations for *Bibliographia huntiana* (*see* the yearbook *Huntia* 1:17–24). Arranged alphabetically, entries include full title, bibliographic information, title history, and a reference to the citation in *Union list of serials.* Includes 12,000 references from alternate abbreviations. Z5353.H85

Abstract journals and indexes

Botanisches Zentralblatt; referierendes Organ für das Gesamtgebiet der Botanik. Im Auftrage der Deutschen Botanischen Gesellschaft . . . 1.–40. Jahr. (Bd.1–142), 1880–1919; Bd.143–79 (Neue Folge, Bd. 1–37, no.8), 1922–45. Cassell, T. Fischer, etc., 1880–1905; Jena, G. Fischer, 1906–45. il. **EC88**

Frequency varies: weekly, 1880–1919; publication suspended, 1920–21; irregular, 1922–45. Ceased publication.

Title varies: *Botanisches Centralblatt.*

International coverage of the botanical literature. Provides lengthy signed abstracts for books and somewhat shorter abstracts for articles, in a classed arrangement. The "Neue Literatur" is a current awareness section (published separately, 1902–19, v.91, 94, 97, etc. each vol. of "Neue Folge" has two sections: "Referate" and Literatur"). Most volumes include some kind of alphabetical author list.

"Generalregister," v.1–60, 1880–94. "Generalregister" appears in the Neue Folge at 5-year intervals.

—————— General register zu den Bänden 1 bis 30 [Neue Folge] (Bd.143–72), bearb. von Wilhelm Dörries. . . . Jena, Fischer, 1927–38. 3v.

QK1.B6

Index to Australasian taxonomic literature. 1968– . Utrecht, Internat. Bureau for Plant Taxonomy and Nomenclature, 1970– . Annual. (Regnum vegetabile, 66, 75, 83, etc.) **EC89**

An index to "current literature and names of new taxa relevant to the study of the systematics of vascular plants of Australasia and Polynesia." Modelled on the *Index to European taxonomic literature* (below).

Index to European taxonomic literature. 1965– . Utrecht, Internat. Bureau for Plant Taxonomy and Nomenclature, 1966– . Annual. (Regnum vegetabile, 45, 53, 61, 70, 80, etc.)   **EC90**

An index to "current literature relevant to the study of the systematics of vascular plants of Europe and adjacent regions."—*Introd., 1965.* A general section is followed by listings of books and periodical articles arranged in taxonomic groups. New names are listed alphabetically under the relevant genus or family, following the references to papers.   QK96.R4

Torrey Botanical Club. Index to American botanical literature. . . . (*In* Torrey Botanical Club. Bull. v.15– , 1888– . Bimonthly)   **EC91**

Appears in each issue of the *Bulletin*. Alphabetical author arrangement of citations under general subject headings. Aims to include all literature on botany in the Western hemisphere.

Beginning with v.21, 1894, the index has also been reprinted on cards for which annual subscriptions may be placed. From 1959, author cards are printed annually by G. K. Hall, Boston. Cards covering the period 1886–1966 have been cumulated as:

────── Index to American botanical literature, 1886–1966. Boston, G. K. Hall, 1969. 4v.   **EC92**

Photoreproduction of the card file cumulating the entries from the "Index" feature which appeared serially in the *Bulletin* of the Torrey Botanical Club (above). Includes works relating to "taxonomy, phylogeny, and floristics of the fungi, bryophytes, pteridophytes, and spermatophytes; morphology, anatomy, cytology, genetics, physiology, and pathology of the same groups; plant ecology; and general botany, including biography and bibliography."—*Pref.*   Z5358.A4T6

────── Index to American botanical literature; first supplement. 1967–76. Boston, G. K. Hall, 1977. 740p.   **EC93**

A supplement to the above.   Z5358.A4T6

Dictionaries

American Joint Committee on Horticultural Nomenclature. Standardized plant names. 2d ed. A revised and enlarged listing of approved scientific and common names of plants and plant products in American commerce or use, prep. by Harlan P. Kelsey and William A. Dayton. Harrisburg, Pa., J. Horace McFarland Co., 1942. 675p.   **EC94**

1st ed. 1923.

Purpose is to establish a standardized "scientific" name and a standardized "common name" for every tree, shrub, and plant in American commerce. Alphabetic arrangement includes genera, subdivided by species, and general common name, subdivided by the specific common name of each plant. Also has entries for commercial names and plant patents issued from Aug. 18, 1931, to July 1, 1941. Many entries for hobby and commercial plants include names of originators or introducers, with date. Glossary.   QK11.A5

Britten, James and **Holland, Robert.** Dictionary of English plant-names. London, publ. for the English Dialect Society by Trübner, 1886. 618p.   **EC95**

Originally issued in three parts, 1878–84, as no.22, 26, and 45 (forming v.10) of *Publications* of the English Dialect Society.

Arranged by common name followed by scientific name with explanation of origin and references to uses in literature, frequently with quotations.

Carleton, R. Milton. Index to common names of herbaceous plants. Boston, G. K. Hall, 1959. 129p.   **EC96**

Lists the common or vernacular names of plants as used in the United States, or in English and American literature, with Latin equivalents.   QK13.C33

Carnoy, Albert Joseph. Dictionnaire étymologique des noms grecs de plantes. Louvain, Publ. Universitaires, Inst. Orientaliste, 1959. 277p. (Bibliothèque du Muséon, v.46)   **EC97**

The romanized form of the Greek name is followed by the word in the Greek alphabet together with an explanation of its meaning and derivation in French. Many references to the literature.   QK9.C3

Carpenter, John Richard. An ecological glossary. Norman, Univ. of Oklahoma Pr., 1938. 306p. il. (Repr.: N.Y., Hafner, 1956)   **EC98**

Defines nearly 3,000 terms, in many cases with references to the works in which the terms were originally used or discussed. Includes a discussion of the development of ecological nomenclature and several appendixes of charts and maps.   QH541.C3

Featherly, Henry Ira. Taxonomic terminology of the higher plants. Ames, Iowa State College Pr., 1954. 166p.   **EC99**

Intended "for students in taxonomy, plant distribution, and speciation."—*Pref.* Omits obsolete and seldom-used words. In four sections, each of which deals with a particular area of terminology: (1) Glossary of botanical technical terms; (2) Subject classification; (3) Some specific epithets with their meanings; (4) Some Greek and Latin components of scientific words.   QK9.F4

Gerth van Wijk, H. L. Dictionary of plant names. Publ. by the Dutch Society of Sciences at Haarlem. The Hague, Nijhoff, 1911–16. 2v.   **EC100**

Contents: v.1, Latin names, A–Z; v.2, Index of English, French, Dutch, and German names.

A dictionary of names and terms only; arranged alphabetically by the Latin name and giving under each Latin name the equivalent popular and literary names in the English, Dutch, French, and German languages. Aims to include names of all wild and cultivated plants, flowers and fruits, varieties and subvarieties, and parts of plants now or formerly used in medicine or industry. The only work of its kind; accurate.

Index kewensis plantarum phanerogamarum nomina et synonyma omnium generum et specierum a Linnaeo usque ad annum MDCCCLXXXV complectens nomine recepto auctore patria unicuique plantae subjectis. Sumptibus beati Caroli Roberti Darwin ductu et consilio Josephi D. Hooker confecit B. Daydon Jackson. . . . Oxford, Clarendon Pr., 1893–95. 2v.   **EC101**

Added title page in English: Index kewensis, an enumeration of the genera and species of flowering plants from the time of Linneaus to the year 1885 inclusive together with their authors' names, the works in which they were first published, their native countries and their synonyms.

Arrangement is alphabetical by names of genera, with species listed under their particular genera. No listing of references from serial abbreviation to full title is given.

────── Supplementum . . . nomina et synonyma omnium generum et specierum ab initio anni MDCCCLXXXVI usque ad finem anni MDCCCCLV nonulla etiam antea edita complectens. . . . Oxford, Clarendon Pr., 1901–74. v.1–15. (In progress)

v.1, 1886–95, with quinquennial supplements to Suppl. 15, 1966/70 (publ. 1974).

Arrangement is the same as for original *Index*. From 1936 on, in order to further supplement *Index londinensis* (EC79), includes references to illustrations of new plants.   QK11.I4

Index nominum genericorum (plantarum). Utrecht, Bohn, Scheltema & Holkema; The Hague, Junk, 1979. 3v. (Regnum vegetabile, v.100–102)   **EC102**

Ellen R. Farr, Jan A. Leussink, and Frans A. Stafleu, eds.

Intended as an aid in stabilizing nomenclature, the index consists of an alphabetical list of validly published scientific names of all plant genera. Entries include citations to the authors to whom the names are attributed; citations to the first valid publication of names; a record of existing homonymy; an indication of taxonomic placement.   QK96.R4 v.100–102

International code of botanical nomenclature. Adopted by the 13th International Botanical Congress, Sydney, August, 1981. Prep. and ed. by E.G. Voss [and others]. Utrecht, Bohn, Sheltema & Holkema, 1983. 472p. (Regnum vegetabile, v.111) **EC103**

"This Code aims at the provision of a stable method of naming taxonomic groups. This edition of the Code supersedes all previous editions."—*Preamble*. Text and index published in English, French, and German. The Code consists of 75 articles governing nomenclature and substantial appendixes—names of hybrids, names of families to be retained, and generic names retained and rejected.
QK96.R4

Jackson, Benjamin Daydon. Glossary of botanic terms with their derivation and accent. 4th ed. rev. and enl. Philadelphia, Lippincott, [1928]. 481p. (Repr.: London, Duckworth, 1949) **EC104**

1st ed. 1900.
Does not include technical terms not relating to botany and gives only the botany-related definition of terms having meaning in other fields. The "Supplement of additional terms" from the 3d ed. has not been incorporated into the main glossary but has again been appended. QK9.J1

Kartesz, John T. and **Kartesz, Rosemarie.** A synonymized checklist of the vascular flora of the United States, Canada, and Greenland. Chapel Hill, Univ. of North Carolina Pr., [1980]. 498p. (The Flora of North America, v.2) **EC105**

"In confederation with Anne H. Lindsey and C. Ritchie Bell."—*t.p.*
A computer-generated list of 56,941 names in three sections: pteridophyta, gymnospermae, and angiospermae. "Within each section all names of taxa are arranged sequentially and alphabetically by family, genus, species, subspecies, and variety."—*Introd.* This volume is intended to be the first of three. Indexed. QK110.K37

Keysers Lexikon der Pflanzen, von A. Schindlmayr. Heidelberg, Keyser, [1956]. 439p. il. **EC106**

Alphabetically arranged by scientific name with cross references from German common name; includes descriptions. QK9.K3

Little, R. John and **Jones, C. Eugene.** A dictionary of botany. N.Y., Van Nostrand Reinhold, [1980]. 400p. il. **EC107**

Provides brief definitions of about 5,500 terms, excluding taxonomic and common plant names. Bibliography. QK9.L735

Marshall, William Taylor and **Woods, Robert S.** Glossary of succulent plant terms. [Pasadena, Calif., Abbey Garden Pr.], 1945. 112p. il. **EC108**

1st printing 1938.
Subtitle: A glossary of botanical terms and pronouncing vocabulary of generic and specific names used in connection with xerophytic plants.
Illustrated with photographs and line drawings. Includes etymology as part of entries for terms whose derivative elements are not defined elsewhere in the text. QK10.M37

National list of scientific plant names. Rev. ed. Wash., Soil Conservation Service, [1982]. 2v. **EC109**

1st ed. 1971.
"The revision . . . contains symbols for scientific names; accepted names for genera, species, subspecies, and varieties; authors of plant names; symbols for source manuals; family names; symbols for plant habits; and symbols for regions of distribution."—*Pref.*
QK96.U57

A provisional checklist of species for flora North America (revised). [St. Louis], Missouri Botanical Garden, 1978. 199p. (Flora North America report, 84) **EC110**

Ed. by Stanwyn G. Shetler and Lawrence E. Skog.
"This *Checklist* is being published in its highly provisional state to satisfy a growing need for a simple working list of the species of vascular plants in North America. It covers . . . the United States (including Alaska), Canada, and Greenland—stopping at the Mexi-

can boundary."—*Introd.* A computer-generated checklist in taxonomic order—family, genus, species. Gives name of author first identifying species, plant characteristics (in code), geographic regions, and primary source of species entry. QK110.P76

Snell, Walter Henry and **Dick, Esther A.** A glossary of mycology. Rev. ed. Cambridge, Harvard Univ. Pr., 1971. 181p. il. **EC111**

1st ed. 1957.
Based on Walter H. Snell's *Three thousand mycological terms* (Providence, R.I., 1936).
Defines about 7,000 terms in mycology. Includes color, obsolete, and non-technical terms. Gives Latin and Greek derivations and references to the literature. QK603.S53

Usher, George. A dictionary of botany, including terms used in biochemistry, soil science and statistics. London, Constable, 1966. 404p. **EC112**

Brief definitions. Intended for high school and college students. "Definitions of all the phyla, classes, orders and families have been given, but descriptions of genera and species have been omitted."—*Pref.* QK9.U8

Foreign terms

Bedevian, Armenag K. Illustrated polyglottic dictionary of plant names in Latin, Arabic, Armenian, English, French, German, Italian and Turkish languages; including economic, medicinal, poisonous and ornamental plants and common weeds. . . . Cairo, Argus and Papazian Presses, 1936. 2 pts. in 1v. (644p., 455p.) il. **EC113**

Davydov, Nikolai Nikolaevich. Botanicheskii slovar': russko-angliisko-nemetsko-frantsuzsko-latinskii. Izd. 2. Moskva, Fizmatgiz, 1962. 335p. **EC114**

1st ed. 1960.
Compiled on a Russian base. Some 6,000 terms, including common names of plants. Gives equivalent terms in English, German, French, and Latin; for plant names, the Latin term given is the scientific name and family. For each of the four non-Russian languages, there is an index with references to the number of the equivalent Russian term. Preface in Russian, English, German, and French. QK9.D3

Elsevier's Lexicon of plant pests and diseases: Latin, English, French, Italian, Spanish, and German. Comp. and arr. by Manuel Merino-Rodríguez. Amsterdam & N.Y., Elsevier, 1966. 351p. **EC115**

Lists terms in current usage. A companion to the compiler's *Lexicon of parasites and diseases in livestock* (1964). SB600.E4

Stearn, William T. Botanical Latin; history, grammar, syntax, terminology and vocabulary. 3d ed. rev. Newton Abbot, [Eng.], London, David & Charles, [1983]. 566p. il. **EC116**

1st ed. 1966.
"Aims to provide a working guide to the special kind of Latin internationally used by botanists for the description and naming of plants."—*Apologia.* Valuable both as a combination style manual and grammar and as a conventional dictionary (i.e., the vocabulary section). Indexed. QK10.S74

Steinmetz, E. F. Vocabularium botanicum. Planten-terminologie. Woordenlijst in zes talen (Latijn, Grieks, Nederlands, Duits, Engels en Frans) van de voornaamste wetenschappelijke woorden, die in de plantkunde gebruikt worden. 2. druk. Amsterdam, Steinmetz, [1953]. 149p. **EC117**

1st ed. 1947.
Title page also in German, English, and French.
Arranged alphabetically by Latin and/or Greek term. Lists equivalent terms in Dutch, German, English, and French, in tabular form.
QK9.S8

Directories

Ayensu, Edward S. and **DeFilipps, Robert A.** Endangered and threatened plants of the United States. Wash., Smithsonian Inst. and World Wildlife Fund, 1978. 403p. **EC118**

Contains diverse information about endangered plants, with sections arranged by species; by family, genus, and species; and by state. Includes extensive bibliographies.   QK86.U6A93

Henderson, D. M. and **Prentice, H. T.** International directory of botanical gardens. 3d ed. Utrecht, Bohn, Scheltema & Holkema, 1977. 270p. (Regnum vegetabile, v.95)   **EC119**

1st ed. 1963.
Arranged by country, then by city. Gives full directory information, including personnel. Index to personal names; index to towns and gardens.   QK96.R4

Hyams, Edward. Great botanical gardens of the world. Photography by William MacQuilty. [N.Y.], Macmillan, [1969]. 288p. il.   **EC120**

A geographical arrangement of descriptions and histories of 42 of the largest botanical gardens in the world, plus a special section on gardens in Japan. More than half of the contents are black-and-white and color plates and other illustrations of garden scenes, buildings, grounds plans, and particular plants. Includes an index and a comprehensive list, with map, of the botanical gardens of the world.   QK71.H9

International Union for Conservation of Nature and Natural Resources. The IUCN plant red data book. Morges, Switz., IUCN, 1978. 540p.   **EC121**

Subtitle: Comprising Red Data Sheets on 250 selected plants threatened on a world scale.
Compiled by Gren Lucas and Hugh Synge for the Threatened Plants Committee of IUCN with the help and advice of experts throughout the world.
For each entry gives status, distribution, habitat and ecology, conservation measures taken, conservation measures proposed, biology and potential value, description, and references. Species index.   QK86A1.I58

Lanjouw, Joseph and **Stafleu, F. A.** Index herbariorum: a guide to the location and contents of the world's public herbaria. Utrecht, 1954–76. (In progress) (Regnum vegetabile)   **EC122**

Contents: pt.1, The herbaria of the world. 5th ed. 1964; pt.2, Collectors. pt.1–4, A–M. 1954–76.
Arranged alphabetically by city, pt.1 lists address, dates, affiliation, amount, and type of material collected and research specializations, staff, publications, and loan and exchange information. Index to personal and scientific names. Pt.2 is a coded alphabetical listing of collectors and their dates, types of plants and localities where specimens were collected, with dates, and final dispositions of their collections.

Handbooks

Gray, Asa. Gray's Manual of botany. A handbook of the flowering plants and ferns of the central and northeastern United States and adjacent Canada. 8th (centennial) ed. Largely rewritten and expanded by Merritt Lyndon Fernald with assistance of specialists in some groups. . . . N.Y., Amer. Book Co., [1950]. 1632p. il.   **EC123**

1st ed., 1848, had title *A manual of the botany of the United States.*
A descriptive flora of 8,340 vascular plants arranged systematically. For each species, gives description, habitat, range, and sometimes an illustration, with further specifics on varieties and forms. Aids to locating information on a particular plant include a synopsis of orders and families, an artificial analytical key to the families, and

indexes to Latin and colloquial names. Includes a glossary and a table showing the numbers of genera, species, varieties, and forms of the families of plants included.   QK117.G75

Hortus third; a concise dictionary of plants cultivated in the United States and Canada. N.Y., Macmillan, [1976]. 1290p. il.   **EC124**

"Initially compiled by Liberty Hyde Bailey and Ethel Zoe Bailey. Revised and expanded by the Staff of the Liberty Hyde Bailey Hortorium."—*t.p.*
1941 ed. had title: *Hortus second.*
"Provides a contemporary assessment of the kinds and the names of plants cultivated in the continental United States and Canada, Puerto Rico, and Hawaii. Initially planned as a simple revision of *Hortus second, Hortus third* evolved . . . into an essentially new work. . . . Innovations included are: author or authors for each botanical name, illustrations of representative members of most families, a separate glossary of botanical terms, an index to common names, and a list of authors cited."—*Pref.*   SB45.H67

Kingsbury, John Merriam. Poisonous plants of the United States and Canada. Englewood Cliffs, N.J., Prentice-Hall, 1964. 626p. il. (part col.)   **EC125**

Intended as a reference for physicians, veterinarians, and medical and veterinary students. Provides descriptions of the plants and their habitats and ranges, of poisonous principles, and of the symptoms and conditions of poisoning for each plant. Introductory material includes discussions of the chemistry of toxic compounds. Bibliographies; index.   SB617.K5

Klein, Richard M. and **Klein, Deana T.** Research methods in plant science. Garden City, N.Y., publ. for the American Museum of Natural History by the Natural History Pr., 1970. 756p. il.   **EC126**

A book of methods, covering such areas as acquisition and maintenance of plant collections; environmental control of plant growth; measurements; general procedures for the cultivation of plants; separation and analysis of plant components; reproduction; plant diseases; and preparation of manuscripts reporting research findings. Indexed.   QK51.K53

Lampe, Kenneth F. and **McCann, Mary Ann.** AMA handbook of poisonous and injurious plants. Chicago, Amer. Medical Assoc., distr. by Chicago Review Pr., [1985]. 432p. il.   **EC127**

Contents: (I) Systemic plant poisoning; (II) Plant dermatitis; (III) Mushroom poisoning.
"The purpose . . . is to provide physicians and other health care professionals with an easily used reference for the management of plant intoxications. The format also makes it useful as a field guide."—*Pref.*
Entries for plants include information on symptoms and management, and references. Color illustrations. Indexed.   RA1250.L27

Martin, Alexander Campbell and **Barkley, William D.** Seed identification manual. Berkeley, Los Angeles, Univ. of California Pr., 1961. 221p. il.   **EC128**

Black-and-white photographs and nontechnical descriptions of 600 seeds and seed-like dry fruits intended "to help agriculturists, foresters, wildlife biologists and others interested in land-use programs to identify the seeds in their particular ecological fields of interest."—*Introd.* Photographs are arranged by habitat and family; "Identification clues," including textual descriptions and graphic illustrations, are arranged by family. Index to common and scientific names.   QK661.M37

Uphof, Johannes Cornelis. Dictionary of economic plants. Weinheim, Ger., H. R. Engelmann; N.Y., Hafner, 1959. 400p.   **EC129**

Presents brief descriptions of economic plants, with their geographical distribution, products, and principal uses. Includes plants not only of commercial value but of any practical use to humanity. Entries under scientific names of plants, with references from common names and products. Brief classed bibliography.

Biography

Desmond, Ray. Dictionary of British and Irish botanists and horticulturists: including plant collectors and botanical artists. London, Taylor & Francis, 1977. 747p.   **EC131**

1st ed. 1893; 2d ed. (1931) had title: *A biographical index of deceased British and Irish botanists.*

"In this revision of the 1931 edition the number of entries has been almost quadrupled. This has been achieved not only by scanning books and periodicals published up to 1975, but also by substantially enlarging the scope of the work."—*Pref.* This edition adds horticulturalists but continues to be limited to deceased subjects. Entries include dates, education, qualifications, honors, biographical references in books and periodicals, location of plant collections, herbaria, etc., and any plant commemorating the individual. Subject index.   Z5358.G7B7

Ferns

See also EC146.

Tryon, Rolla M. and **Tryon, Alice F.** Ferns and allied plants with special reference to tropical America. N.Y., Springer, [1982]. 857p. il.   **EC132**

"This systematic treatment of the ferns and allied plants provides a modern classification of the Pteridophyta based on an assessment of the wealth of new data published during the last few decades."—*Pref.* Includes about 9,000 species arranged by family and genus. Gives citations to naming authors. Includes references. Scientific name index.   QK524.4.T78

Flora

Bailey, Liberty Hyde. Manual of cultivated plants most commonly grown in the continental United States and Canada. Rev. ed., compl. restudied. N.Y., Macmillan, 1949. 1116p. il.   **EC133**

1st ed. 1924.

Completely revised and greatly enlarged edition of an important handbook for the identification of the most common species of plants for food, ornament, utility, etc. Arranged by scientific name, with indexes to scientific and common name.   QK110.B3

Clapham, Arthur R., Tutin, T. G. and **Warburg, E. F.** Flora of the British Isles. 2d ed. Cambridge, Univ. Pr., 1962. 1269p. il.   **EC134**

A 4-volume work by the same authors and with the same title was published 1957–65.

An excellent handbook, intended primarily for the student and the amateur botanist.   QK306.C57

Gleason, Henry Allan. The new Britton and Brown illustrated flora of the northeastern United States and adjacent Canada. [N.Y., New York. Botanical Garden, 1952] 3v. il.   **EC135**

Original work by N. L. Britton and Addison Brown. 1st ed. 1896–98; 2d ed. 1913 (frequently repr.); 3d ed. 1952 (repr. 1963 with slight revisions).

The 3d ed. has been entirely rewritten, and new material added. Attempts to describe all known species of native and successfully introduced seed plants, ferns, and fern allies. Intended "for the interested laity rather than the professional botanist."—*Pref.* A glossary defines the more technical terms used in the text.

For each species gives description, variant names, common name, habitat and range, and illustration. v.1–2 have their own indexes. v.3 contains the general index to all divisions, classes, subclasses, orders, families, genera and species, and English names.

QK117.G5

Graf, Alfred Byrd. Tropica: color cyclopedia of exotic plants and trees from the tropics and subtropics for warm-region horticulture—in cool climate the sheltered indoors. 2d ed., rev. and enl. East Rutherford, N.J., Roehrs Co., [1981]. 1136p.   **EC136**

1st ed. 1978.

Contents: The tropics and subtropics; Warm area horticulture; Plants indoors; Colorama of plants and trees [main section]; Plant descriptions.

Includes 7,000 photographs representing 1,630 genera. "Most species in this book, except such as Fruit trees, Conifers, Ferns, and Carnivorous plants, are classified within their natural systemic families."—*Prelude.* Includes bibliography and literature references. Common names index of exotic plants; generic botanical index.   SB407.G73

Hay, Roy and **Synge, Patrick M.** The color dictionary of flowers and plants for home and garden. American consultant, George Kalmbacher. London, Joseph; N.Y., Crown, [1969]. 373p. il.   **EC137**

A section of color illustrations of more than 2,000 plants is followed by a dictionary section giving brief descriptions which are intended as useful notes to the pictures.   SB407.H292

Newcomb, Lawrence. Newcomb's Wildflower guide. Boston & Toronto, Little, Brown, [1977]. 490p. il.   **EC138**

Il. by Gordon Morrison.

"An ingenious new key system for quick, positive field identification of the wildflowers, flowering shrubs and vines of Northeastern and North-central North America."—*t.p.*

"This guide provides a new and eminently workable key system, which is based on the most easily seen features that make each species unique."—*Introd.* Identification is based on examining a specimen for flower type, plant type, and leaf type and referring to the locator key with the information derived. The locator key refers the user to the page on which the wildflower is identified.

QK118.N38

Polunin, Oleg. Flowers of Europe: a field guide. London and N.Y., Oxford Univ. Pr., 1969. 662p. il.   **EC139**

A work for the student and the serious amateur. Attempts to describe and illustrate "the commoner and most attractive seed-bearing plants to be found throughout Europe."—*Pref.* Includes about 2,600 species. Arrangement is adapted from *Flora Europaea,* v.1, 1964 (EC143). Indexes of popular names, of English names, and of Latin names. Bibliography, p.586–91.   QK281.P65

Popular encyclopedia of plants. Vernon H. Heywood, chief ed.; Stuart R. Chant, assoc. ed. Cambridge, Cambridge Univ. Pr., [1982]. 368p. il.   **EC140**

"An illustrated guide to the main species of plants used by man."—*Introd.* This work consists of short entries arranged both by genus and by common name. Includes plant products and principal crop species. Provides information about distribution and uses of plants. Does not include cultural information. Generous number of color photographs. 31 special feature articles one or two pages in length. Indexed by scientific names and by common names.

SB107.P67

Rickett, Harold William, gen. ed. Wild flowers of the United States. N.Y., McGraw-Hill, [1966–73]. 6v. in 14. il.   **EC141**

Contents: v.1, The Northeastern states. 2v.; v.2, The Southeastern states. 2v.; v.3, Texas. 2v.; v.4, The Southwestern states. 3v.; v.5, The Northwestern states. 2v.; v.6, The Central mountains and plains. 3v.

A publication of the New York Botanical Garden.

A flora for laymen which attempts to include all wildflowers of the areas covered. Arranged in groups according to characteristics recognizable to the layman. Gives concise descriptions of plants, habitats, seasons, etc., with color photographs of most species. Each volume has an illustrated general explanation and glossary, and its own index.   QK115.R5

—— —— Complete index for the six volumes. N.Y., McGraw-Hill, [1975]. 152p.   **EC142**

Index comp. by Lee Pennington from the separate indexes in the six individual volumes.

Lists artists, photographers, common and botanical names. The latter gives families, genera, and species.   QK115.R5

Tutin, Thomas Gaskell [and others], eds. Flora Europaea. Cambridge, Cambridge Univ. Pr., 1964–80. 5v.   **EC143**

Contents: v.1, Lycopodiaceae to Plantanaceae; v.2, Rosaceae to Umbelliferae; v.3, Diapensiaceae to Myoporaceae; v.4, Plantaginaceae to Compositae (and Rubiaceae); v.5, Alismataceae to Orchidaceae.

A cooperative effort of many European scholars. Comprehensive to the level of subspecies. Gives synonyms, brief descriptions of structure, habitat, and European distribution, with references to the article where first identified, and diploid chromosome number, where possible. Each volume includes keys to abbreviations, a glossary, Vocabularium Anglo-Latinum, an index to scientific names, and a section of maps.   QK281.T8

Halliday, G. and **Beadle, M.** Consolidated index to *Flora Europaea*. Cambridge, Cambridge Univ. Pr., [1983]. 210p.   **EC144**

"Compiled from the separate indices of Volumes 1 to 5."—*t.p.*

U.S. Agricultural Research Service. Selected weeds of the United States. [By Clyde F. Reed] Wash., Govt. Prt. Off., 1970. 463p. il.   **EC145**

Reprint ed. (N.Y., Dover, 1971) has title *Common weeds of the United States.*

"The 224 species of weeds included in this handbook were selected by weed scientists largely from the composite list of 1,775 weeds published in *WEEDS* 14:347–386, 1966. Those selected are some of the prevalent weeds in croplands, grazing lands, noncroplands, and aquatic sites."—*Introd.* Illustrates and describes the weeds and indicates their geographical distribution in the United States. Arranged by family, then alphabetically by genera and species according to scientific name. Glossary of terms. Index includes popular as well as scientific names.   SB612.A2A46

Willis, John Christopher. Dictionary of the flowering plants and ferns. 8th ed., rev. by H. K. Airy Shaw. Cambridge, Univ. Pr., 1973. 1245p.   **EC146**

1st ed. 1897; 7th ed. 1966.

A corrected and enlarged edition of the 7th ed., which differs from earlier editions by being confined to generic and family names and excluding botanical terms, common and vernacular names, and economic products. Consists largely of short coded entries showing equivalents and taxonomic relationships; entries for families are more lengthy.   QK11.W53

Wit, H. C. D. de. Plants of the world. Tr. by A. J. Pomerans. N.Y., Dutton, 1966–69. 3v. il.   **EC147**

Contents: v.1, The higher plants I; v.2, The higher plants, II (tr. of *Hogere planten I–II*. The Hague, 1963–65); v.3, The lower plants (tr. of *Lagere planten*. The Hague, 1965).

Plants are grouped by family. In addition to physical descriptions (and illustrations) of the individual plants there are notes on uses, historical notes, etc. Indexed.   QK98.W7213

Fungi

Ainsworth, Geoffrey Clough and **Bisby, Guy Richard.** Ainsworth & Bisby's Dictionary of the fungi. 6th ed. Farnham Royal, Commonwealth Mycological Inst., 1971. 663p. il.   **EC148**

1st ed. 1943.

The main body of the work lists systematic position, distribution, and number of species for every genus of fungi, excluding bacteria and lichens; definitions and explanations of terms and concepts related to mycology; common and scientific names of important fungi, and explanations of the chief families, orders, and classes of fungi and of bacteria and lichens. Supplemented by a table showing the systematic arrangement of the genera of fungi; a key to the families of fungi, which lists major characteristics of the families within the various orders of fungi; and a section of figures which illustrate the forms and phases of some of the genera.   QK603.A5

Ainsworth, Geoffrey Clough, ed. The fungi; an advanced treatise. N.Y., Academic Pr., 1965–73. 4v. il.   **EC149**

Contents: v.1, The fungal cell; v.2, The fungal organism; v.3, The fungal population; v.4 (in 2 pts.), A taxonomic review with keys.

"The object of this work is . . . to summarize what is known about fungi as fungi. . . . The work, as the subtitle implies, is also intended as a reference book."—*Pref.*   QK603.A33

Lange, Morten and **Hora, F. Bayard.** Collins guide to mushrooms and toadstools. London, Collins, 1963. 257p. il.   **EC150**

"With 96 colour plates from *Flora Agaricina Danica* by Jakob E. Lange with additions by Ebbe Sunesen and P. Dahlstrøm."—*title page.*

Lindau, Gustav and **Sydow, P.** Thesaurus litteraturae mycologicae et lichenologicae ratione habita praecipue omnium quae adhuc scripta sunt de mycologia applicata quem congesserunt. Leipzig, Borntraeger, 1908–17. 5v. (Repr.: N.Y., Johnson, 1954)   **EC151**

—— —— Supplementum, 1911–1930, by Raffaele Ciferri. Papia, Cortina, 1957–60. 4v.

Smith, Alexander Hanchett. A field guide to western mushrooms. Ann Arbor, Univ. of Michigan Pr., [1975]. 280p. il.   **EC152**

Seeks to provide information on 201 species of western mushrooms. "Seventy of the species included here were known only from the western area or were described from it originally but have since been found elsewhere. Over twenty-five poisonous or very undesirable species for the table from the areas are illustrated and described. Many species are in the 'edible' column meaning that as far as it is known they are not poisonous. About fifteen of these are considered to be of 'gourmet' calibre. Finally there is the residuum of species of which the edibility is still apparently unrecorded. These have for the most part been listed as 'not recommended'."—*Introd.* Glossary; bibliography; index.   QK617.S55

—— and **Weber, Nancy Smith.** The mushroom hunter's field guide. Ann Arbor, Univ. of Michigan Pr., [1980]. 316p. il.   **EC153**

1st ed. 1958.

Intended for use in identifying fleshy fungi throughout the United States and Canada. Includes most edible species as well as most dangerous ones. Glossary; index.   QK617.S56

Watling, Roy and **Watling, Ann Elizabeth.** A literature guide for identifying mushrooms. [Eureka, Calif, Mad River Pr., 1980] 121p.   **EC154**

An annotated bibliographic guide to articles and books on fungi. In two principal sections: taxonomic and geographic. Includes a list of general works and mycological journals. Indexed.

    Z5356.F97W35

Mosses

Grout, Abel Joel. Mosses with a hand lens: 4th ed. A popular guide to the common or conspicuous mosses and liverworts of the United States and Canada. Liverworts by M. A. Howe, etc. Newfane, Vt., Author, [1947]. 344p. il.   **EC155**

1st ed. 1900.   QK541.G8

Trees

Elias, Thomas. The complete trees of North America: field guide and natural history. N.Y., Outdoor Life/Nature Book, Van Nostrand Reinhold, [1980]. 948p. il., maps. **EC156**

A guide by family to over 652 native trees north of Mexico and 100 common introduced trees. Species are illustrated by drawings of branchlets, many showing spring and summer or fall characteristics. Ranges shown on maps. Indexed. QK481.E38

Hough, Romeyn Beck. Handbook of the trees of the northern states and Canada east of the Rocky Mountains. Photodescriptive. N.Y., Macmillan, 1947. 470p. il. **EC157**

First published 1907. This is a reprint of that edition.

Descriptions of "the native and naturalized trees of the region of North America lying north of the northern boundaries of North Carolina, Tennessee, Arkansas and Oklahoma and east of the Rocky Mountains, and extending southward in the Appalachian region to northern Alabama and Georgia."—*p.1.* Basic arrangement is by genus. Includes photographs of the leaves, fruit, and bark of each species but not of the overall appearance of the trees. Maps show the range of each species. QK481.H8

Krüssmann, Gerd. Manual of cultivated broad-leaved trees & shrubs. Beaverton, Ore., Timber Pr., 1984– . v.1– . (In progress) **EC158**

Translation of *Handbuch der Laugehölze.* Ed. by Gilbert S. Daniels; tr. by Michael E. Epp.

Published in cooperation with the American Horticultural Society.

Contents: v.1, A–D.

To be in three volumes, the manual is an extensive guide to trees, shrubs, subshrubs, vines, and some herbaceous plants. In alphabetical order by genera with more than 5,000 species and over 6,000 cultivars. Emphasizes descriptive information and contains notes of interest to gardeners. SB435.K94

Little, Elbert Luther. Check list of native and naturalized trees of the United States (including Alaska). Wash., U.S. Forest Service, 1953. 472p. (Agriculture handbook, no.41) **EC159**

Listed by accepted scientific name with approved common names, giving current synonyms, arranged chronologically with citations to the literature. Used as the official standard for tree names in the U.S. Forest Service. QK481.L5

Oxford encyclopedia of trees of the world. Oxford & N.Y., Oxford Univ. Pr., 1981. 288p. il., maps. **EC160**

Consultant editor: Bayard Hora.

A compilation of illustrations and descriptions of the principal trees of the world. Includes 149 genera and over 500 species. Illustrated with drawings and color photographs. Identification key, bibliography, glossary. Index of common names; index of Latin names. QK475.O8

Preston, Richard J. North American trees (exclusive of Mexico and tropical United States). [2d ed.] Ames, Iowa State Univ. Pr., [1961]. 395p. il. **EC161**

1st ed. 1948.

Subtitle: A handbook designed for field use, with plates and distribution maps.

Briefly describes for the non-technical reader, 568 native, naturalized, and commonly planted exotic species. Systematic arrangement with "Key to the genera" outlining general characteristics; "Keys to the species" are included with the material on each genus. All illustrations are line drawings. Brief introduction to trees; glossary; index to scientific and common names. QK481.P68

Rehder, Alfred. Manual of cultivated trees and shrubs hardy in North America, exclusive of the subtropical and warmer temperate regions. 2d ed. rev. and enl. N.Y., Macmillan, 1940. 996p. **EC162**

1st ed. 1927.

A systematically arranged manual describing 2,685 varieties in full and briefly describing 1,400 other species and hybrids. Rarely cultivated genera, varieties, and garden forms are not included. Intended for the horticulturist, entries give concise descriptions of plants and indication of the origin and date of cultivation, plus the climatic zone in which each plant thrives. Glossary; key to authors' names; index to scientific and common names.

Supplemented by the author's *Bibliography of cultivated trees and shrubs hardy in the cooler temperate regions of the Northern Hemisphere* (EC165). QK481.R4

Sargent, Charles Sprague. The silva of North America; a description of the trees which grow naturally in North America exclusive of Mexico . . . il. with figures and analyses drawn from nature by Charles Edward Faxon. Boston, Houghton, 1891–1902. 14v. 740pl. (Repr. 1947. 14v. in 7) **EC163**

Systematic arrangement of descriptions of "all woody plants which grow up from the ground with a single stem."—*Pref.* Includes complete descriptions of characteristics, habitats, and economic and medicinal uses of all genera included; not all species are completely described. Large, detailed engravings of leaves, flowers, and fruit. Extensive footnotes; no bibliography. General index in v.14 includes scientific and common names, authors' names and subjects. QK481.S24

U.S. Division of Timber Management Research. Silvics of forest trees of the United States, comp. and rev. by H. A. Fowells. Wash., U.S. Dept of Agriculture, Forest Service, 1965. 762p. il. (U.S. Dept of Agriculture. Agriculture handbook no.271) **EC164**

". . . an edited compendium of nearly 125 silvical leaflets prepared by specialists at the Forest Service experiment stations."— *Foreword.* Gives habitat conditions (climate, soils and topography, associated trees and shrubs), life history, and races and hybrids of the individual species. Includes bibliographic references. Indexes of common names and scientific names. SD395.U5

Bibliography

Rehder, Alfred. Bibliography of cultivated trees and shrubs hardy in the cooler temperate regions of the Northern Hemisphere. Jamaica Plain, Mass., Arnold Arboretum of Harvard Univ., 1949. 825p. **EC165**

Designed to "give references to sources of the botanical names, valid names and synonyms, of the woody plants" (*Introd.*) arranged approximately the same as in the author's *Manual of cultivated trees and shrubs* (EC162), to which it is a companion volume. Index to scientific names. Z5356.T8R42

ZOOLOGY

General works

Bibliography

Animal identification: a reference guide. London, British Museum (Natural History); Chichester, [Eng.] & N.Y., Wiley, [1980]. 3v. **EC166**

Ed. by R. W. Sims.

Contents: v.1, Marine and brackish water animals; v.2, Land and freshwater animals (*not* insects); v.3, Insects (ed. by D. Hollis).

"It is the intention in these volumes to provide . . . help by listing primary reference sources so that the non-specialist by himself will be able to set about identifying any animal from any part of the world."—*Introd.* Citations to articles and books are arranged by phylum. Within each phylum entries are subdivided into general, systematic, and geographical sections. v.3 has a group name index; no other indexes.   Z7994.I34A54

Blacker-Wood Library of Zoology and Ornithology. A dictionary catalogue of the Blacker-Wood library. . . . Boston, G. K. Hall, 1966. 9v.   **EC167**

At head of title: McGill University, Montreal.
Reproduction of the catalog cards for this collection of about 60,000 volumes.   Z7991.B67

Blackwelder, Richard Eliot. Guide to the taxonomic literature of vertebrates. Ames, Iowa State Univ. Pr., [1972]. 259p.   **EC168**

Intended for student use and based on material appearing in the *Zoological record,* this is a bibliography of items "published during the past 50 years or more which may be taxonomically useful themselves or may lead the student to the older literature."—*Pref.* Under each class of vertebrates, citations are grouped by type of work, i.e., bibliographies, faunas, glossaries, etc. Revisionary works are listed alphabetically by family name, with references to alphabetical author lists with complete citations. In general, works on fossils are not included. No indexes.

Engelmann, Wilhelm. Bibliotheca historico-naturalis. Verzeichniss der Bücher über Naturgeschichte, welche in Deutschland, Scandinavien, Holland, England, Frankreich, Italien und Spanien 1700–1846 erscheinen sind. . . . Mit einem Namen- und Sach-Register. Leipzig, Engelmann, 1846. 786p.   **EC169**

Citations are arranged in groups according to the types and topics of the works included. Each section is divided into subsections of German and "foreign" works. Covers anatomy and physiology, zoology, and paleontology.
Continued, for zoology, by: Z7401.E56

Bibliotheca zoologica [I]. Verzeichnis der Schriften über Zoologie welche in den periodischen Werken enthalten und vom Jahre 1846–1860 selbständig erscheinen sind. Mit Einschluss der allgemein-naturgeschichtlichen, periodischen und palaeontologischen Schriften. Bearb. von J. Victor Carus und Wilhelm Engelmann. Leipzig, Engelmann, 1861. 2v. (Bibliotheca historico-naturalis, hrsg. von Wilhelm Engelmann. Supplement Bd.)   **EC170**

Autoren- und Sach-Register.
Continued by: Z7991.B58

Bibliotheca zoologica II. Verzeichnis der Schriften über Zoologie welche in den periodischen Werken enthalten und vom Jahre 1861–1880 selbständig erscheinen sind. . . . Bearb. von O. Taschenberg. Leipzig, Engelmann, 1887–1923. 8v.   **EC171**

No indexes.
The three works comprise an international, classed bibliography covering the literature on zoology from 1700 to 1880.   Z7991.B58

Harvard University. Museum of Comparative Zoology. Library. Catalogue. Boston, G. K. Hall, 1968. 8v.   **EC172**

A main-entry catalog, but with many useful analytics under the author entries. The collection contains nearly 250,000 volumes.   Z7999.H32

————— ————— First supplement. Boston, G. K. Hall, 1976. 770p.   **EC173**

"The First supplement . . . includes new titles added to the Library since 1966 as well as cataloging information for many older titles revised according to the Anglo-American cataloging rules."—*Pref.*   Z7999.H32

International catalogue of scientific literature: N, Zoology. 1st–14th annual issues, 1901–14. London, 1902–16. 14v.   **EC174**

For description of the full set *see* EA17.
Of this section, v.6–14, 1906–14, were issued jointly with the *Zoological record,* v.43–51.

Nissen, Claus. Die zoologische Buchillustration, ihre Bibliographie und Geschichte. Stuttgart, A. Hiersemann, 1966–78. 2v.   **EC175**

Contents: v.1, Bibliographie; v.2, Geschichte der zoologischen Buchillustration.
Issued serially in 16 pts. v.1 is a bibliography of illustrated works listed alphabetically by first author and by illustrator, with indexes to subject, geographic area, animal, and author (including co-authors and editors). v.2 is a history of zoological illustration and is indexed by author, illustrator, geographic area, subject and animal; it also includes a supplement to v.1 which has a closing date of Sept. 1975.   Z7991.N5

Reuss, Jeremias David. Repertorium commentationum a societatibus litterariis editarum . . . T. 1, Historia naturalis, generalis et zoologia. Gottingae, Dieterich, 1801. 574p. (Repr.: N.Y., B. Franklin, 1961)   **EC176**

A valuable index to the publications of the learned societies up to 1800. Classed arrangement with author index. Index to v.1 is combined with that for v.2. For record of complete set *see* EA22.

Ruch, Theodore Cedric. Bibliographia primatologica; a classified bibliography of primates other than man . . . v.1. Springfield, Ill., Baltimore, Thomas, 1941. 241p. (Yale Univ. School of Medicine. Yale Medical Library. Historical Library. Pubn. no.4)   **EC177**

Contents: pt.1, Anatomy, embryology and quantitative morphology; Physiology, pharmacology and psychobiology; Primate phylogeny and miscellanea.
Covers material published through 1938. Classed arrangement; author index. 4,630 entries.   Z7996.P85R8

Wood, Casey Albert. An introduction to the literature of vertebrate zoology; based chiefly on the titles in the Blacker Library of Zoology, the Emma Shearer Wood Library of Ornithology, the Bibliotheca Osleriana and other libraries of McGill University, Montreal. London, Oxford Univ. Pr., 1931. 643p.   **EC178**

Issued also as *McGill University publications, ser. XI (Zoology),* no.24.
Contents: Introduction to the literature of vertebrate zoology, p.1–146; Students' and librarians' ready index to short author-titles on vertebrate zoology arranged geographically and in chronological order, p.147–72; A partially annotated catalog of the titles on vertebrate zoology in the libraries of McGill University, p.173–643.   Z7996.V4W8

Abstract journals and indexes

Bibliographia zoologica . . . v.1–43, 1896–1934. Zurich, Sumptibus Concilii Bibliographici, 1896–1934. 43v.   **EC179**

Publisher varies.
v.1–22 published as v.19–35 of *Zoologischer Anzeiger,* continuing *Literatur* published in that periodical, v.1–18.
An international classed bibliography of the periodical literature of zoology, similar in format to the earlier works of the related title (EC170–EC171), but with updated classification schemes. Includes paleozoology. Comprehensive coverage starts approximately with the literature for 1895. The individual volumes have no indexes, but the *Bibliographia zoologica* is indexed in the *Register* of the *Zoologischer Anzeiger,* Jahrg. 16–40, 1899–1922 (5v.).   Z7991.B6

Wildlife review. no.1– , Sept. 1935– . [Ft. Collins, Colo.] 1935– . Quarterly.   **EC180**

Place of publication, issuing body, frequency, and format vary. Issued currently by U.S. Dept. of the Interior, Fish and Wildlife Service.
A subject-arranged index to serial and report literature on wildlife management. Entries are not annotated. Issues include author, geographical, and subject indexes. Indexes cumulated annually starting with no.180, 1981.   S590.W55

U.S. Fish and Wildlife Service. Wildlife abstracts; a bibliography and index of the abstracts in Wildlife review. no.1/66– , 1935/51– . Wash., 1954– .   **EC181**

Subtitle varies; imprint varies.

Later volumes cover 1952/55, 1956/60, 1961/70, 1971/75, 1976/80.

Cumulations of the citations and indexing appearing in *Wildlife review.*   SK351.U52

Zentralblatt für Zoologie, allgemeine und experimentelle Biologie. Bd.1–6. Leipzig, Teubner, 1912–18. 6v.   **EC182**

Formed by the union of the *Zoologisches Zentralblatt,* 1894–1911, and the *Zentralblatt für allgemeine und experimentelle Biologie.* Includes surveys of the literature with abstracts for the most important papers.

The zoological record. v.1– , 1864– . Philadelphia, BioSciences Information Service; London, Zoological Soc. of London, 1865– . v.1– . Annual.   **EC183**

v.1–6 entitled *Record of zoological literature.*

v.43–52, 1906–15, issued also as Sec. N of the *International catalogue* (EC174).

Jointly published by BIOSIS and the Zoological Society beginning with v.115.

A comprehensive index to worldwide serials literature in systematic zoology. Now published in 20 sections. As applicable, each section consists of five indexes: author, subject, geographical, palaeontological, and systematic. Full bibliographical information is given in the author index; the remaining indexes refer to the numbers assigned to the author entries. The previous long delay between publication of the cited articles and their indexing is now substantially eliminated.   Z7991.Z87●

Zoologischer Bericht; im Auftrage der Deutschen Zoologischen Gesellschaft . . . Bd.1–55. Jena, G. Fischer, 1922–1943/44. 55v.   **EC184**

Ceased publication.

—— General-Autoren Register. Bd.1–25, 1922–31; Bd. 26–50, 1931–40.

Contains abstracts of books and periodical material in various languages.

Zoologischer Jahresbericht. Hrsg. von der Zoologischen Station zu Neapel. 1879–1913. Leipzig, 1880–1924. v.1–35. Annual.   **EC185**

—— Autoren- und Sachregister, 1886–90, 1891–1900, 1901–10.

A bibliographical and review journal covering the whole field of zoology through 1884. Subsequently, systematic zoology was omitted, as it was covered by the *Zoological record* (EC183). Systematic arrangement, with various indexes in each volume.   Z7991.Z89

Dictionaries and encyclopedias

George, J. David and **George, Jennifer J.** Marine life: an illustrated encyclopedia of invertebrates in the sea. N.Y., Wiley, [1979]. 288p. il.   **EC186**

Includes only living species, arranged systematically by 27 invertebrate phyla with marine representatives. Entries are keyed to 128 pages of photographs, virtually all in color. Indexed.   QL121.G4

Grzimek, Bernhard, ed. Grzimek's Animal life encyclopedia. N.Y., Van Nostrand Reinhold, [1972–75]. 13v. il.   **EC187**

Translation of *Grzimeks Tierleben; Enzyklopädie des Tierreiches* (Zürich, 1968. 13v.).

Contents: v.1, Lower animals; v.2, Insects; v.3, Mollusks and echinoderms; v.4, Fishes I; v.5, Fishes II and amphibia; v.6, Reptiles; v.7–9, Birds I–III; v.10–13, Mammals I–IV.

Each volume is made up of chapters by an international group of scholars treating the various classes, orders, families, etc., according to modern zoological classification and names. Profusely illustrated. Each volume includes an outline of systematic classification; an

"Animal dictionary" giving corresponding names in English, German, French, and Russian; a list of supplementary readings; and an index to the volume in question.   QL3.G7813

International code of zoological nomenclature. Ed. by W.D.L. Ride [and others]. 3d ed. [London], International Trust for Zoological Nomenclature, Berkeley, Univ. of California Pr., 1985. 338p.   **EC188**

Adopted by the XX General Assembly of the International Union of Biological Sciences.

1st ed. 1961.

This edition "has one fundamental aim, which is to provide the maximum universality and continuity in the scientific names of animals compatible with the freedom of scientists to classify animals according to taxonomic judgments."—*Introd.* The text is in French and English on facing pages. There is a glossary and an index in each language and an index of scientific names.   QL353.I67

Leftwich, A. W. A dictionary of zoology. [3d ed.] London, Constable, [1973]. 478p.   **EC189**

1st ed. 1963.

Offers concise definitions of about 6,700 technical terms relating to zoology and related branches of biology including taxonomy, comparative anatomy, physiology, histology, genetics, ecology, etc. There is a separate section with short entries and/or references for 800 English names of animals; a section on classification and nomenclature; and a bibliography.   QL9.L4

Pennak, Robert William. Collegiate dictionary of zoology. N.Y., Ronald, [1964]. 583p.   **EC190**

Intended for specialists as well as students. Gives succinct definitions of 19,000 terms in the zoological disciplines; includes paleontological terms, scientific and common names, and biographical entries. Appendix: Condensed taxonomic outline of the animal kingdom.   QL9.P4

Handbooks

Handbuch der Zoologie; eine Naturgeschichte der Stämme des Tierreiches. Gegründet von Willy Kükenthal. Hrsg. von J. G. Helmcke [et al.]. 2. Aufl. Berlin, W. de Gruyter, 1968– . il. (In progress)   **EC191**

The 1st ed. of this work, which began publication in 1923, is still in progress. The 2d ed. begins with v.4 (Arthropoda: Insecta). A comprehensive descriptive work covering all animals of the world. Includes discussions of paleontology and of all aspects of the biology of the various orders, classes, genera, etc. Basic arrangement is systematic. Mainly in German; some of the more recently published sections include occasional articles in English. Each of the major bibliographic sections has its own index. No general index.

The IUCN invertebrate red data book. Gland, Switz., IUCN, 1983. 632p.   **EC192**

"Compiled jointly by Susan M. Wells, Robert M. Pyle and N. Mark Collins of the IUCN [International Union for Conservation of Nature and Natural Resources] Conservation Monitoring Centre with the help and advice of the Species Survival Commission of IUCN and other experts throughout the world."—*t.p.*

For each entry gives summary, description, distribution, population, habitat and ecology, scientific interest and potential value, conservation measures taken, conservation measures proposed, captive breeding, and references. Indexed.   QL362.I82

International zoo yearbook. 1959– . Ed. by P.J.S. Olney. London, Zoological Soc., 1959– . v.1– . Annual. (v.23, 1984)   **EC193**

Contents vary from year to year with each edition including feature topics. A recurrent feature is "Zoos & aquaria of the world; new buildings and exhibits." Each volume includes a reference section listing species bred in captivity and multiple generation births, and a census of rare animals in captivity. Indexed.

QL76.A1I5

Melby, Edward C. and **Altman, Norman H.** CRC handbook of laboratory animal sciences. Cleveland, CRC Pr., 1974–76. 3v.   **EC194**

v.1 deals with legislative regulations pertaining to laboratory animals for the United States and for Canada, and includes general and specific information for the management and control of various types of animals, e.g., fish, dogs. v.2 discusses neoplasias, zoonoses, and diseases of laboratory animals. v.3 covers new and additional information about laboratory animals, such as: nutrition, physiological data, effect of drugs on nervous system, spontaneous viral infections, hematology, immunology, virology. Cumulated index in v.3.   QL55.M45

Whiteley, Derek and **Nixon, Marion.** The Oxford book of vertebrates: cyclostomes, fish, amphibians, reptiles and mammals. London, Oxford Univ. Pr., 1972. 216p. il.   **EC195**

Illustrates and describes "the wide variety [about 340 species] of vertebrates found in and around the British Isles."—*Introd.* The book is one of the publisher's series of similar works such as *The Oxford book of birds,* by Bruce Campbell (London, 1964); *The Oxford book of insects,* by John Burton (London, 1968), and *The Oxford book of invertebrates,* by David Nichols and John Cooke (London, 1971).   QL255.W48

Treatises

Hyman, Libbie Henrietta. The invertebrates. N.Y., McGraw-Hill, 1940–67. v.1–6[1]. il. (In progress?)   **EC196**

Contents: [v.1], Protozoa through Ctenophora; v.2, Platyhelminthes and Rhynchocoela, the acoelomate Bilateria; v.3, Acanthocephala, Aschelminthes, and Entroprocta, the pseudocoelomate Bilateria; v.4, Echinodermata; v.5, Smaller coelomate groups; v.6[1], Mollusca.

A comprehensive treatise, arranged by phylum, on all aspects of the biology of the invertebrates. Describes all phyla included, but does not discuss separate species in detail. Serves as a reference manual for students and researchers in zoology and for workers in allied fields. Includes a bibliography for each phylum and an index to each volume.   QL362.H9

Traité de zoologie; anatomie, systématique, biologie. Pub. sous la direction de Pierre-P. Grassé. Paris, Masson, 1948– . v.1– . (In progress)   **EC197**

An exhaustive, multivolume treatise, arranged systemically and including extinct and fossil forms. Volumes are published in parts and out of sequence. Many detailed black-and-white drawings; black-and-white and color photographs. Bibliography for each topical section. Each physical volume has its own index.   QL45.T7

Generic indexes

Neave, Sheffield Airey. Nomenclator zoologicus; a list of the names of genera and subgenera in zoology from the tenth edition of Linnaeus 1758 to the end of [1945]. London, Zoological Soc. of London, 1939–50. 5v.   **EC198**

Contents; v.1–4, A–Z and suppl.; v.5, 1936–45.

Lists in alphabetical order, by name of genus or subgenus, the original reference for each name; in cases of doubt of validity or scarcity of the original work, additional references may be given. Does not include unapproved or hypothetical names.

Continued by: QL354.N4

Nomenclator zoologicus. . . . London, Zoological Soc. of London, 1966–75. v.6–7.   **EC199**

Contents: v.6, 1946–55, ed. by Marcia A. Edwards and A. Tindell Hopwood; v.7, 1956–65, ed. by Marcia A. Edwards and H. Gwynne Vevers.

Amphibians and reptiles

Cochran, Doris Mabel and **Goin, Coleman J.** The new field book of reptiles and amphibians; more than 200 photographs and diagrams. N.Y., Putnam, [1970]. 359p. il.   **EC200**

For the beginner. Intended as "an introduction to the salamanders, frogs and toads, turtles, crocodilians, lizards, and snakes now known to occur in the United States, including Alaska and Hawaii."—*Pref.*   QL644.C6

Ditmars, Raymond Lee. The reptiles of North America: a review of the crocodilians, lizards, snakes, turtles and tortoises inhabiting the United States and Northern Mexico. N.Y., Doubleday, 1936. 476p. il. 135pl. (part col.)   **EC201**

A revision of the author's *Reptile book* (N.Y., 1907).

Comprehensive in scope and inclusion of species. Popular in approach, using common names of species and non-technical descriptions and narrative style in discussion of coloration, distribution, habits, etc., of better-known species. Large section of photographic plates; index to scientific and common names.   QL651.D6

Frost, Darrel R., ed. Amphibian species of the world. Lawrence, Kan., Allen Pr. and the Assoc. of Systematics Collections, [1985]. 732p.   **EC202**

Subtitle: A taxonomic and geographical reference.

"Compiled for the Parties to the Convention on International Trade in Endangered Species of Wild Fauna and Flora to serve as a standard reference to amphibian nomenclature under the auspices of the World Congress of Herpetology and its Checklist Committee, William E. Duellman, Chairman."—*verso of half t.p.*

An annotated checklist of 4,014 nominal species. Organization: higher taxonomy; scientific name, authority, year of publication, and citation; type species; type specimen(s); type locality; distribution; comments; attribution; and protected status. Taxonomic index.   QL645.F76

Groombridge, Brian, comp. The IUCN amphibia-reptilia red data book. Pt.1: Testudines, Crocodylia, Rhynchocephalia. Gland, Switz., IUCN, 1982. 426p.   **EC203**

Comp. by Brian Groombridge assisted by Lissie Wright of the IUCN Conservation Monitoring Centre with the help and advice of the Species Survival Commission of IUCN and other experts throughout the world.

Earlier versions (1968–79), comp. by R. E. Honegger, appeared in looseleaf format as v.3 of the *Red data book* published by the International Union for Conservation of Nature and Natural Resources.

For each entry gives summary, distribution, population, habitat and ecology, threats to survival, conservation measures taken, conservation measures proposed, captive breeding, remarks, and references. Indexed.   QL641.G76

Harding, Keith A. and **Welch, Kenneth R. G.** Venomous snakes of the world: a checklist. Oxford & N.Y., Pergamon Pr., [1980]. 188p.   **EC204**

Publ. as suppl. 1 to the journal *Toxicon.*

Main section arranged taxonomically. Gives original description for genera, original description reference, type locality, and distribution for species and subspecies. Geographical distribution section lists genera by country. Author and subject indexes.   QL666.O6H34

Leviton, Alan E. Reptiles and amphibians of North America. N.Y., Doubleday, [1971]. 250p. il. (Animal life of North America ser.)   **EC205**

Offers popular descriptions of appearance, habits, habitat, etc., of families of amphibians and reptiles found north of Mexico. Includes short comments on specific species. Arranged by order, with an index to amphibians and an index to reptiles. Includes short general section on keeping reptiles, and a brief bibliography.   QL651.L42

Birds

A dictionary of birds. Ed. by Bruce Campbell and Elizabeth Lack. Vermillion, [S. Dak.], Buteo Books, [1985]. 670p. il. **EC206**

"Published for the British Ornithologists' Union."—*t.p.*

A revised and rewritten edition of *A new dictionary of birds* (1964) which was a successor to Alfred Newton's *Dictionary of birds* (1896). "The Dictionary consists of articles on general subjects relating to birds, and on different kinds of birds mainly treated by family."— *Introd.* With contributions by more than 280 specialists, the work combines elements of a dictionary and an encyclopedia. Longer entries include references. QL677.D53

The encyclopedia of birds. Ed. by Christopher M. Perrins and Alex L. A. Middleton. N.Y., Facts on File, [1985]. 447p. il. **EC207**

"We have tried to provide the reader with an encapsulated but up-to-date account of the world's birds."—*Pref.* Consists of articles dealing with single families or several families; recognizes 8,805 species. Gives information on distribution, habitat, dimension, plumage, voice, nests, eggs, and diet. Colored illustrations and maps. Indexed. QL673.E53

Gruson, Edward S. Checklist of the world's birds; a complete list of the species, with names, authorities and areas of distribution. N.Y., Times Books, [1976]. 212p. **EC208**

"It is the purpose of this book to provide as complete a listing of the species of birds of the world as possible, to give the scientific name and an English common name for each of the species, to provide a source to which the reader is referred if more information about the species is wanted and to give a gross idea of its range."— *Introd.* QL677.G76

Howard, Richard and **Moore, Alick.** A complete checklist of the birds of the world. Oxford & N.Y., Oxford Univ. Pr., 1980. 701p. **EC209**

A taxonomically arranged checklist. For each species gives geographic distribution and English name. There is a 40-page list of literature references arranged by family and subfamily. Indexed by species. QL677.H75

Kress, Stephen W. The Audubon Society handbook for birders. N.Y., Scribner's, [1981]. 322p. il. **EC210**

"An introductory technique manual and source book."—*Pref.* Contents: Field trip techniques; Binoculars and spotting scopes; Observing birds; Photographing and recording birds; Educational programs; Research programs welcoming amateurs; Periodicals and organizations; Building a bird-watcher's library. Indexed. QL677.5.K73

Palmer, Ralph S., ed. Handbook of North American birds. New Haven, Conn., Yale Univ. Pr., [1962]–76. 3v. il., maps. **EC211**

"Sponsored by American Ornithologists' Union and New York State Museum and Science Service."—*p.[i]*.

Contents: v.1, Loons through flamingos; v.2, Waterfowl (first part); v.3, Waterfowl (concluded).

An encyclopedic treatment. Entries are arranged taxonomically, mainly according to the Wetmore classification; indexed. QL681.P3

Peterson, Roger Tory. A field guide to the birds: a completely new guide to all the birds of eastern and central North America. 4th ed. Boston, Houghton Mifflin, 1980. 384p. il., maps. **EC212**

For list of other titles in the Peterson "Field guide" series *see* EC63.

1st ed. 1934.

"This edition of *A Field Guide to the Birds,* the flagship book of the Peterson Field Guide Series, is more than a revision; it is completely new, with 136 plates, as against 60 in the previous edition. Every illustration is new or redrawn. All species are now shown in color; some are repeated in monochrome, but only when

flight patterns are more clearly diagnosed in that way."—*Introd.* A classic updated. Indexed. QL681.P45

Rickert, Jon E. A guide to North American bird clubs. 1st ed. Elizabethtown, Ky., Avian Publ., 1978. 565p. **EC213**

Lists over 835 bird clubs in North America. In six sections: National organizations (U.S.A. and Canada); State and local clubs in the U.S.A. (by state); Puerto Rico; Virgin Islands; Provincial and local clubs in Canada (by province); and other North American nations (by nation). Entries give person(s) to contact, birding report, publications, field trips, and meetings. No index. QL681.R52

Robbins, Chandler S., Bruun, Bertel and **Zim, Herbert S.** Birds of North America. N.Y., Golden Pr., [1966]. 340p. il. **EC214**

At head of title: A guide to field identification

A comprehensive, but inexpensive guide. Arranged by family, giving popular and scientific names, brief description, range, habitat, and verbal descriptions and "Sonograms" of songs or calls. Indexed. QL681.R59

Strong, Reuben Myron. A bibliography of birds: with special reference to anatomy, behavior, biochemistry, embryology, pathology, physiology, genetics, ecology, aviculture, economic ornithology, poultry culture, evolution, and related subjects. Chicago, Natural History Museum, 1939–59. v.1–4. (Museum. Pubn. 442, 457, 581, 870. Zoological ser., v.25, pts.1–4) **EC215**

Compiled for the research worker in ornithology, pts.1–2 are an author catalog of about 20,000 articles and books. Means to be comprehensive in coverage from earliest times through 1926, but includes additional titles through 1938. Authors' dates and references to biographies are included when known. Also gives library locations.

Pt.3 is an extensive subject index. The "Finding index," pt.4, helps the reader to find all entries for topics and names which occur in more than one place in the subject index. Z5331.S92

Terres, John K. The Audubon Society encyclopedia of North American birds. N.Y., Knopf, 1980. 1109p. il. **EC216**

"The encyclopedia is arranged alphabetically and includes the following categories: biographies of North American birds (and foreign visitors); major articles about bird life and bird biology and its study; definitions of ornithological terms; short biographies of some of the great ornithologists, naturalists and explorers whose names are associated with North American birds; and about 4,000 cross-references that link related articles and function as an index."—*Pref.* QL681.T43

World Association of Veterinary Anatomists. Nomina anatomica avium: an annotated anatomical dictionary of birds. London & N.Y., Academic Pr., 1979. 637p. il. **EC217**

Prepared by the International Committee on Avian Anatomical Nomenclature, a committee of the World Association of Veterinary Anatomists.

Ed. by Julian J. Baumel, Anthony S. King, Alfred M. Lucas, James E. Breazile, and Howard E. Evans. Consultant for taxonomy: Richard L. Zusi; consultant for classical languages: Lubomir Malinovsky.

"An inescapable commitment of the NAA [Nomina anatomica avium] has been to produce Latin names for major structures which have been described but not named, or named only in the vernacular by the author. . . . These broad objectives connected with usage can be summarized as follows: (1) To select one term where two or more are in general use for the same structure; (2) to replace terms which are grossly defective; (3) to produce new terms in Latin where none is available; and (4) within the limitations of the above, to codify prevailing usage."—*General introd.* Organized anatomically, e.g., osteology, digestive system, etc. Taxonomic list (scientific and common names); references; subject index. QL697.W79

Wynne, Owen E. Biographical key—names of birds of the world—to authors and those commemorated. Fordingbridge, Hants., Eng., Author, [1969]. 246p. **EC218**

An alphabetical list of names of persons commemorated in bird names, with birth and death dates if known, genus of bird in which the name is commemorated, a biographical note or identifying phrase, and a reference to a biographical source.

Fishes

American Fisheries Society. Committee on Names of Fishes. A list of common and scientific names of fishes from the United States and Canada. 4th ed. Bethesda, Md., Amer. Fisheries Soc., 1980. 174p. (Special pubn. no.12)   **EC219**

By C. Richard Robins and others.

1st ed. 1948; 3d ed. 1970.

"The present list purports to include all species of fishes known from the fresh waters of the continental United States and Canada, and those marine species inhabiting contiguous shore waters on or above the continental shelf, to a depth of 200 meters (656 feet)."—*Introd.* Lists 2,268 species in family order giving occurrence and accepted common name. Appendixes list changes from 1970 list and comments, established exotic fishes, exotic fishes formerly established or of local occurrence, and fishes known or suspected to be extinct. Indexed.   QL618.A48

The aquarium encyclopedia. By Gunther Sterba. Cambridge, Mass., M.I.T. Pr., [1983]. 605p. il.   **EC220**

Translation of *Lexikon der Aquaristik und Ichthyologie* (Leipzig, 1978). Also publ. as *The aquarist's encyclopedia* (Poole, Dorset, Blandford Pr., 1983). Dick Mills, English ed.; Susan Simpson, tr.

Compiled as "a reference work for freshwater and sea-water aquarium-keeping [and to provide] basic information about general and specialist ichthyology, hydrology, fish economy, the biology of freshwater animals and marine biology."—*Foreword.* Emphasis on genera.   SF456.5.L4913

Aquatic sciences & fisheries abstracts. v.1– . London, Information Retrieval Ltd., 1971– . v.1– . Monthly with annual index.   **EC221**

Comp. by the Food and Agricultural Organization of the United Nations with the collaboration of Institut für Dokumentationswesen, Frankfurt, Bundesforschungsanstalt für Fischerei, Hamburg, [etc.].

An amalgamation and continuation of the *Current bibliography for aquatic sciences and fisheries,* produced by the FAO.

International coverage; abstracts in English.

Axelrod, Herbert R. and **Vorderwinkler, William.** Encyclopedia of tropical fishes; with special emphasis on techniques of breeding. 27th ed. Jersey City, T. F. H. Publs., [1983]. 631p. il.   **EC222**

1st ed. 1957. Frequently reissued.   QL78.A86

Axelrod, Herbert R. and **Schultz, Leonard P.** Handbook of tropical aquarium fishes. Rev. ed. Neptune City, N.J., T.F.H. Publs., 1983. 718p. il. (part col.)   **EC223**

1st ed. 1955.

Designed for the hobbyist as well as the scientist.

The introductory chapters give a brief survey of ichthyology, the aquarium and its management, aquarium plants, and the diseases of fishes. The main part of the work illustrates and describes some 500 fishes, giving identification, range, size, temperament, sex differences, breeding, temperature requirements, food, color patterns, etc. Glossary; brief bibliography; index.   QL78.A87

Dean, Bashford. A bibliography of fishes; enl. and ed. by C. R. Eastman. N.Y., Amer. Museum of Natural History, 1916–23. 3v.   **EC224**

The most comprehensive bibliography on fishes, "their habits, structure, development, physiology, pathology, distribution and kinds."—*Pref.* v.1–2 are the author list; v.3 offers a subject index, a list of general bibliographies, voyages, periodicals, etc.

Z5971.D35

Herald, Earl Stannard. Living fishes of the world. Garden City, N.Y., Doubleday, [1961]. 303p. il.   **EC225**

Arranged by systematic classification, with excellent underwater photographs, some in color.   QL615.H45

Wheeler, Alwyne C. Fishes of the world; an illustrated dictionary. N.Y., Macmillan, [1975]. 366p. il.   **EC226**

"The dictionary entries are arranged in alphabetical order, separate entries being made for families (cross-referenced to genera included), and under the scientific name of the species of fish. . . . Widely used vernacular names mostly in the English language are also given and cross-indexed. The [500 color] plates are arranged in systematic order of families, thus bringing the closest related groups together."—*Introd.* Over 2,000 entries, which include some 700 line drawings. "Common names are fully cross-referred in the dictionary section."—*Contents.*   QL614.7.W47

Mammals

Burton, Maurice. Systematic dictionary of mammals of the world. Illus. by David Pratt. 2d ed. London, Museum Pr., [1965]. 307p. il.   **EC227**

1st ed. 1962. 307p.

General descriptions are given of the various subclasses, orders, suborders and families. For certain species, detailed descriptions are given, including general characters, habits, habitat, food, breeding, present status, range, and longevity. Species included are those "about which most information is available, adding where possible more shortened notes on related forms."—*Introd.*   QL708.B85

Corbet, Gordon B. and **Hill, J. E.** A world list of mammalian species. London, British Museum (Natural History); Ithaca, N.Y., Comstock Publ. Assoc., a division of Cornell Univ. Pr., [1980]. 226p.   **EC228**

"This book is an attempt to present a comprehensive list of all living species of mammals as far as current knowledge allows. Recently extinct species are noted. Endangered species are also included."—*Introd.* Arranged by order, family, and species. For each species gives Latin name, English name, and brief description of range; occasionally habitat is given. Includes a classed bibliography; indexed by species and English name.   QL708.C67

Current primate references. Feb. 1965– . Seattle, Regional Primate Research Center, Univ. of Washington, 1966– . Weekly.   **EC229**

A current awareness bibliography for publications dealing with all aspects of primate study. No cumulations to date.

The encyclopedia of mammals. Ed. by David Macdonald. N.Y., Facts on File, [1984]. 895p. il.   **EC230**

Contents: The carnivores; Sea mammals; The primates; Large herbivores—the ungulates; Small herbivores; Insect-eaters; Marsupials.

"The bulk of this encyclopedia is devoted to individual species, groups of closely related species or families of species. The text on these pages covers details of physical features, distribution, evolutionary history, diet and feeding behavior, social dynamics and spatial organization, classification, conservation and relationships with man."—*Pref.* Indexed.   QL703.E53

Hall, Eugene Raymond. The mammals of North America. 2d ed. N.Y., Wiley, [1981]. 2v. il., maps.   **EC231**

1st ed. 1959.

A summary of taxonomic studies of North American native mammals from 1492 to June 1977 arranged systematically by order and family. "Genera and species are arranged in order of inferred geologic age, oldest to youngest. Subspecies are arranged alphabetically."—*Pref.* For subspecies includes reference to the original description and, when necessary, reference to the first use of the current name. Includes descriptive information, marginal records, and keys to identification. Each volume contains a cumulative "Index to vernacular names" and a cumulative "Index to technical names."   QL715.H15

The IUCN mammal red data book. Part 1: Threatened mammalian taxa of the Americas and the Australasian zoogeographic region (excluding Cetacea). Gland, Switz., IUCN, 1982. 516p. **EC232**

Comp. by Jane Thornback and Martin Jenkins of the IUCN Conservation Monitoring Centre with the help and advice of the Species Survival Commission of IUCN and other experts throughout the world.

Earlier eds. (1966–78) published in looseleaf format as v.1 of the *Red data book* of the International Union for Conservation of Nature and Natural Resources.

For each entry gives summary, distribution, population, habitat and ecology, threats to survival, conservation measures taken, conservation measures proposed, captive breeding, remarks, and references. Indexed. QL703.I86

Macmillan illustrated animal encyclopedia. Ed. by Philip Whitfield. N.Y., Macmillan, [1984]. 600p. il. **EC233**

Arranged in 5 sections: mammals, birds, reptiles, amphibians, and fishes. Seeks to be a comprehensive catalog of vertebrates at the family level, except for the fish section which is treated at the order level. A representative selection of species is included. Profusely illustrated with colored drawings. Indexed. QL7.M33

Mammal species of the world. Ed. by James H. Honacki, Kenneth E. Minman, and James W. Koeppl. Lawrence, Kan., Allen Pr. and the Assoc. of Systematics Collections, [1982]. 694p. **EC234**

Subtitle: A taxonomic and geographic reference.

"Compiled for the Parties to the Convention on International Trade in Endangered Species of Wild Fauna and Flora to serve as a standard reference to mammalian nomenclature with scientific advice from members of the American Society of Mammalogists and its Checklist Committee, Robert S. Hoffmann, Coordinator."—*verso of half t.p.*

A checklist of about 4,170 species. Organization: taxonomic arrangement; scientific name and authority; type locality; distribution; comments; protected status; and ISIS numbers. Includes a bibliography of cited literature and a taxonomic index.

QL708.M35

Morris, Desmond. The mammals: a guide to the living species. London, Hodder and Stoughton; N.Y., Harper, [1965]. 448p. il. **EC235**

Provides notes on each of the mammalian orders, and lists the species within each order. Both scientific and popular names are included; geographical distribution of the order is indicated; and abbreviations are used to denote references to each species in standard technical writings. 300 representative animals (at least one from each order) have been selected for brief description and illustration. Though the text is popularly written, the lists of species have real reference value. Indexes of popular and scientific names.

QL703.M68

Napier, John Russell and **Napier, Prue H.** A handbook of living primates: morphology, ecology and behaviour of nonhuman primates. London & N.Y., Academic Pr., 1967. 456p. il. **EC236**

Major sections include a lengthy general presentation on the functional morphology of primates; alphabetically arranged, concise profiles of primate genera; and supplementary sections dealing with systematics, names, taxonomy, habitats, limbs and locomotion, data on macaques, and vital statistics. Lengthy bibliography. Index of animals. QL737.P9

The new Larousse encyclopedia of animal life. N.Y., Larousse, 1980. 640p. il. **EC237**

1st ed. 1967 was based largely on Léon Bertin's *La vie des animaux* (Paris, 1949–50), revised, updated, and with new material added.

A systematic arrangement of popular-level articles giving general discussions of each class followed by more detailed descriptions of orders and species. Includes a classification list for orders and families, a glossary, and an index. QL50.N48

Simpson, George Gaylord. The principles of classification and a classification of mammals. N.Y., American Museum

of Natural History, 1945. 350p. (Amer. Mus. of Nat. Hist. Bulletin, 85) **EC238**

In three parts: (1) Principles of taxonomy; (2) Formal classification of mammalia; (3) Review of mammalian classification.

Based both on the published literature and on new, original research. Pt. 1 is an introductory essay; pt.2 is intended as a working classification and includes literature references. Includes a bibliography arranged alphabetically by author. Indexes of technical and vernacular names.

Walker, Ernest Pillsbury. Walker's Mammals of the world. By Ronald M. Nowak and John L. Paradiso. 4th ed. Baltimore, Johns Hopkins Univ. Pr., 1983. 2v. (1362p.) il. **EC239**

1st ed. 1964.

A substantially revised edition of a standard work. In family order, seeks to include every known genus with information on distribution, appearance, and habits. Endangered or threatened status is noted. Most genera are illustrated with a photograph of a living animal. Bibliography of literature cited in v.2. Indexed.

QL703.W3

Shells

Abbott, Robert Tucker. American seashells: the marine mollusca of the Atlantic and Pacific coasts of North America. 2d ed. N.Y., Van Nostrand Reinhold, [1974]. 663p. il. **EC240**

1st ed. 1954.

For the advanced amateur and professional. Describes in detail about 2,000 species and lists another 4,500. Basically a taxonomic survey of marine species found along the shores and continental shelf of North America. QL411.A19

Rogers, Julia Ellen. The shell book; a popular guide to a knowledge of the families of living mollusks, and an aid to the identification of shells, native and foreign. [Rev. ed.] Boston, C. T. Branford, [1951. c.1936]. 503p. il. (part col.) **EC241**

1st ed. 1908. Preface to revised edition dated 1951. The text has not been changed, but a "List of modern names" has been appended to update the book.

Systematic arrangement of descriptions of the shells, animal behavior, and habitat of each species included. Index to scientific and common names. QL405.R72

BACTERIOLOGY

Approved lists of bacterial names. Wash., Amer. Soc. for Microbiology, 1980. 420p. **EC242**

A listing by genera and species of names valid as of Jan. 1, 1980. For each species or subspecies gives citation to the initial primary literature reference, type strain or species, and citation to descriptive literature reference. QR81.A66

Bergey's Manual of systematic bacteriology. John G. Holt, ed. in chief. Baltimore, William & Wilkins, [1984]– . v.1– . il. (In progress) **EC243**

Noel R. Krieg, ed. v.1.

Replaces *Bergey's Manual of determinative bacteriology.* (1st ed. 1923; 8th ed. 1974.)

To be published in four subvolumes "divided roughly as follows: (a) the Gram-negatives of general, medical or industrial importance; (b) the Gram-positives other than actinomycetes; (c) the archaebacterial, cyanobacterial and remaining Gram-negatives; and (d) the actinomycetes."—*Pref.*

The manual, consisting of individually written articles, is to assist in the identification of bacteria and to show the relationships between bacteria. v.1 (964p.) includes an extensive bibliography and an index of scientific names of bacteria. QR81.B46

Grainger, Thomas H. A guide to the history of bacteriology. N.Y., Ronald, [1958]. 210p. (Chronica botanica, no.18)
EC244

An annotated, bibliographical guide to the literature and history of bacteriology. Originally compiled for use in a course in the history of microbiology at Lehigh University.

International catalogue of scientific literature: R, Bacteriology. 1st–14th annual issues. London, 1901–20. 14v.
EC245

For full description of the set *see* EA17.

Paris. Institut Pasteur. Bulletin de l'Institut Pasteur; revues et analyses des travaux de bactériologie et de médicine, biologie générale, physiologie, chimie biologique dans leurs rapports avec la microbiologie. Paris, Masson, 1903–70.
EC246

Through 1970, contains abstracts in French from world literature on bacteriology. Beginning 1971, the *Bulletin* continues as a journal publishing original articles, but no longer includes abstracts.

Zentralblatt für Bakteriologie, Parasitenkunde, Infektions-Krankheiten und Hygiene. Abt. 1, Medizinisch-hygienische Bakteriologie, Virusforschung und Parasitologie. Referate. Jena, 1902– . v.31– .
EC247

Title varies: *Centralblatt für Bakteriologie, Parasitenkunde und Infektionskrankheiten.*

Provides lengthy abstracts of articles and books in a classified arrangement. International in scope, but includes mostly German publications. "Neue Literatur" section meant for current awareness purposes. Author and subject indexes in each volume.

BIOCHEMISTRY

Barman, Thomas E. Enzyme handbook. N.Y., Springer, 1969. 2v.
EC248

Provides data on the physical and chemical characteristics and specificities of approximately 800 enzymes included in the Enzyme Commission's list. Arrangement follows the Enzyme Commission classification system in which the enzymes are grouped according to their activities and specificities. Indexed.   QP601.B26

———— ———— Supplement 1. N.Y., Springer, 1974. 517p.
EC249

"In the five years since the appearance of the *Enzyme Handbook* several hundred new enzymes have been described. The *Supplement* includes molecular and kinetic data on about half of these and also on several enzymes omitted from the *Handbook.*"—*Pref.*
QP601.B26

Concise encyclopedia of biochemistry. Berlin & N.Y., W. DeGruyter, 1983. 509p. il.
EC250

Translation of *Brockhaus ABC Biochemie,* 2d ed. 1981. Tr., rev., and enl. by Thomas Scott and Mary Brewer.

A compact encyclopedia with entries ranging from a single sentence to several pages. Includes numerous tables, molecular structures, and metabolic pathways. Abundant *see* references. Not indexed.   QD415.B713

Croft, L. R. Handbook of protein sequence analysis. 2d ed. Chichester, [Eng.] & N.Y., Wiley, [1980]. 628p.   **EC251**

Subtitle: A compilation of amino acid sequences of proteins with an introduction to the methodology.

1st ed. (1973) had title: *Handbook of protein sequences.*

Contains new sequences and complete reappraisal of sequence data published to the end of 1978. In two sections: an introduction containing 8 chapters covering enzymic and chemical cleavage, purification of peptides, sequenator, etc.; and a reference section arranged under 20 headings from "protein sequences," "enzymes,"

through "milk proteins," "miscellaneous proteins." Appendixes: human haemoglobins, amino acid replacements, etc. Author index and index of protein sources, protein names, and general methodology section.   QP551.C77

Data for biochemical research. Ed. by R. M. C. Dawson [and others]. 2d ed. Oxford, Clarendon Pr., 1969. 654p. il.
EC252

1st ed. 1959.

A compilation of chemical and physical data in tabular form. Includes references to sources of information. Arranged by type of compound, each section has named contributors and a general bibliography. In addition, there are sections on reagents and their preparation, and on analytical methods. The index covers chemical names.   QH324.D28

Fruton, Joseph S. A bio-bibliography for the history of the biochemical sciences since 1800. Philadelphia, Amer. Philosophical Soc., 1982. 885p.   **EC253**

A revision of a work first published in 1974 and revised in 1977.

Arranged in alphabetical order by author, each entry gives biographical references, if found, and bibliographical references to books and articles. Living persons born before 1911 are included in this edition.   Z5524.B54F78

Handbook of biochemistry and molecular biology. Gerald D. Fasman, ed. 3d ed. Cleveland, CRC Pr., [1976–77]. 9v.
EC255

Herbert A. Sober, consulting ed.

1st–2d eds., 1968–70, had title: *Handbook of biochemistry.*

Contents: Proteins—amino acids, peptides, polypeptides, proteins (3v.); Nucleic acids—purines, pyrimidines, nucleotides, oligonucleotides, tRNA, DNA, RNA (2v.); Lipids, carbohydrates, steroids (1v.); Physical and chemical data, miscellaneous—ion exchange, chromatography, buffers, miscellaneous [e.g. vitamins] (2v.); Cumulative series index.   QP514.H34

International Union of Biochemistry. Nomenclature Committee. Enzyme nomenclature 1984. Orlando, Fla., Academic Pr., 1984. 646p.   **EC256**

Subtitle: Recommendations of Nomenclature Committee of the International Union of Biochemistry on the nomenclature and classification of enzyme-catalysed reactions.

Copy prepared for publication by Edwin C. Webb.

1st ed. 1961; previous ed. 1974.

A classified list of 2,477 enzymes. Entries are arranged by Enzyme Classification number and give recommended name, reaction, other names, basis for classification (systematic name), comments, and references. Includes 4,478 published references. Name index.
QP601.I54

Long, Cyril [and others]. Biochemists' handbook, comp. by 171 contributors. London, Spon; Princeton, N.J., Van Nostrand, 1961. 1192p.   **EC257**

Tabular data and short articles on specific biochemicals, reagents and analytic methods, and on topical areas: metabolic pathways; chemical composition of animal tissue and related data; chemical composition of plant tissues and related data; and physiological and nutritional data. Bibliographies; general index.   QD245.L6

National Research Council. Committee on Specifications and Criteria for Biochemical Compounds. Specifications and criteria for biochemical compounds. 3d ed. Wash., Nat. Academy of Sciences, 1972. 216p.   **EC258**

1st ed. 1960.

"This publication is the result of a program to improve the quality of chemicals available for biochemical research by establishing criteria, standards, or specifications useful for describing such chemicals, particularly with regard to purity."—*Pref.* Lists 521 compounds by type of compound and specific name. Gives standard handbook data such as formula, structure, weight, sources, and methods of purification and assaying for purity. Many entries include references. Compound index.   QD415.7.N37

—— —— Supplement: biogenic amines and related compounds. Wash., Nat. Academy of Sciences, 1977. 20p.

Stenesh, J. Dictionary of biochemistry. N.Y., Wiley, [1975]. 344p. **EC259**

" . . . contains approximately 12,000 entries drawn from . . . textbooks and reference books . . . and from the research literature . . . ; all the source material consulted has been published since 1962. The recommendations of the Commission on Biological Nomenclature of the International Union of Pure and Applied Chemistry and the International Union of Biochemistry were among the sources used."—*Pref.* QP512.S73

Williams, Roger John and **Lansford, Edwin M.** The encyclopedia of biochemistry. N.Y., Reinhold, [1967]. 876p. il. **EC260**

For the non-specialist. Articles on broader topics presuppose only general scientific background; specialized topics are more technical. The alphabetically arranged articles cover general and specific topics in chemistry, physics, methodology, metabolism, nutrition, diseases, and disorders as related to biochemistry, as well as short biographies and more peripheral topics. Longer articles have appended references. Indexed. QP512.W5

ENTOMOLOGY

Arnett, Ross H. American insects: a handbook of the insects of America north of Mexico. N.Y., Van Nostrand Reinhold, [1985]. 850p. il. **EC261**

Intended to provide the nonspecialist with both identification and access to the source literature. "I have attempted to compile in a single reference book a tool that will be useful to those working without a major collection and library."—*Pref.* Arranged taxonomically; extensively illustrated with photographs and drawings. Indexed. QL474.A76

Chamberlin, Willard Joseph. Entomological nomenclature and literature. 3d ed. rev. and enl. Dubuque, Iowa, W. C. Brown, [1952]. 141p. **EC262**

Includes general discussions of the development and status of the nomenclature, instructions on bibliographic methods, bibliographies of principal entomological literature, and aids to preparing scientific articles. Z5856.C5

De La Torre-Bueno, José Rollin. A glossary of entomology; Smith's "An explanation of terms used in entomology," compl. rev. and rewritten. Lancaster, Pa., Science Pr., 1937. 336p. il. **EC263**

Published by Brooklyn Entomological Society, Brooklyn, N.Y.

Sets forth definitions for a comprehensive list of terms in entomology and other life sciences fields as they relate to entomology. Citations to authoritative works are referred to in many of the entries. Appended plates illustrate anatomical terms.

Supplemented by: QL462.3.D4

Tulloch, George S. Torre-Bueno's glossary of entomology. Suppl. A. Lancaster, Pa., Business Pr., 1960. 36p. **EC264**

Derksen, Walther and **Scheiding, Ursula.** Index litteraturae entomologicae. Serie II: Die Welt-Literatur über die gesamte Entomologie von 1864 bis 1900. Berlin, Deutsche Akad. der Landwirtschaftswissenschaften zu Berlin, 1963–75. 5v. **EC265**

Contents: Bd.1–4, A–Z; Bd.5, Register. Z5856.I53

Gilbert, Pamela. A compendium of biographical literature on deceased entomologists. London, British Museum (Natural History), 1977. 455p. **EC266**

Contains references to biographical information and bibliographical listings published before the end of 1975 for some 7,500 deceased entomologists. Z5856.G55

—— and **Hamilton, Chris J.** Entomology: a guide to information sources. [London], Mansell, distr. in U.S.A. by H.W. Wilson Co., [1983]. 237p. **EC267**

"The work is intended to be an introduction and source book for entomology by subject instead of systematic groups."—*Pref.* A guide to literature, libraries, and organizations. Annotated; indexed. QL468.2.G55

Horn, Walther and **Schenkling, Sigmund.** Index litteraturae entomologicae. Ser.I, Die Welt-Literatur über die gesamte Entomologie bis inklusive 1863. Berlin-Dahlem, 1928–29. 4v. **EC268**

A revision of H. A. Hagen's *Bibliotheca entomologica* (Leipzig, 1862–63. 2v.), with the addition of some 8,000 titles, covering the field up to the beginning of the *Zoological record* (EC183). Arranged alphabetically by author. No index, although Hagen included an author-subject index which may be used with either work for the material he covered. Z5856.H81

Howe, William H. The butterflies of North America. Garden City, N.Y., Doubleday, 1975. 633p. il. **EC269**

"*The Butterflies of North America* is a comprehensive volume on the butterflies and skippers of Canada and the United States, including Alaska and Hawaii."—*Pref.* QL548.H68

Johnson, Warren T. and **Lyon, Howard H.** Insects that feed on trees and shrubs: an illustrated practical guide. Ithaca, N.Y., Cornell Univ. Pr., [1976]. 464p. il. **EC270**

"With the collaboration of C. S. Loehler, N. E. Johnson, and J. A. Weidhaas."—*t.p.*

Contents: Insects that feed on conifers; Insects that feed on broad-leaved evergreens, and deciduous plants; Sources of information on pest control; Selected references; Glossary; Index of insects, mites and animals; Index to insects by host plants.

"This book is a reference manual. It covers essential information about many of the important insects, mites, and other animals associated with woody ornamental plants. Its audience is intended to be agricultural advisor, teacher, student, nurseryman, arborist, forester, gardener, scientist, as well as any person having direct or peripheral responsibility for the maintenance of trees and shrubs. It deals in a pragmatic way with the science of entomology, and provides assistance in the identification of insects and related animals often considered pests."—*Introd.* More than 700 insects and mites are discussed, listed, or illustrated. Over 1,000 photographs of the pests and their damage to the host tree or shrub, including some 200 color plates. SB931.J64

Mallis, Arnold. American entomologists. New Brunswick, N.J., Rutgers Univ. Pr., [1971]. 549p. il. **EC271**

Biographical essays on some 200 American entomologists from the 18th century to the present. Arrangement is according to area of interest. Portraits; index of names. QL26.M24

Osborn, Herbert. A brief history of entomology, including time of Demosthenes and Aristotle to modern times, with over five hundred portraits. Columbus, Ohio, Spahr and Glenn, 1952. 303p. il. **EC272**

Intended mainly for the layman. General outlines of the history of entomology, followed by an alphabetical list of "founders and leaders of entomological science," giving brief biographical data for each. The portraits, 12 on each plate, are taken from photographs or contemporary paintings. QL462.5.O7

Review of applied entomology. Ser. A: Agricultural. London, Commonwealth Inst. of Entomology, 1913– . v.1– . Monthly. **EC273**

SB599.R38

—— Ser. B: Medical and veterinary. London, Commonwealth Inst. of Entomology, 1913– . v.1– . Monthly. **EC274**

Both sections are international abstract journals in classed arrangement. Each issue contains an author index; each volume a cumulative author and subject index. SF601.R4

GENETICS

King, Robert C. and **Stansfield, William D.** A dictionary of genetics. 3d ed. N.Y., Oxford Univ. Pr., 1985. 480p.
EC275

1st ed. 1968.
"The scope . . . has been expanded to reflect the broadly interdisciplinary nature of modern genetics."—*Pref.* Intended for the non-specialist. Includes 5,920 entries. Appendix C is a detailed chronology.   QH431.K48

Knight, Robert L. Dictionary of genetics, including terms used in cytology, animal breeding and evolution. 1st ed. Waltham, Mass., Chronica Botanica, 1948. 183p. il. (Lotsya, a biological miscellany. v.2)   **EC276**

An attempt at standardizing terminology. Briefly defines about 2,500 older and modern terms. Nine appendixes consist mostly of standard genetics and statistical data.   QH13.K5

Rieger, Rigomar, Michaelis, Arnd and **Green, Melvin M.** A glossary of genetics and cytogenetics, classical and molecular. 3d ed., compl. rev. N.Y., Springer-Verlag, 1968. 506p. il.
EC277

1st (1954) and 2d (1958) eds. were published in German under the title *Genetisches und Cytogenetisches Wörterbuch.*
This is a new English-language edition, not a translation from German. Approximately 2,500 entries, lengthly definitions. Where possible, includes references to the specific paper in which the term or concept was introduced. Bibliography.   QH431.R4913

VIROLOGY

Nicholas, Robin and **Nicholas, David.** Virology: an information profile. [London], Mansell, distr. in U.S.A. by H.W. Wilson, [1983]. 236p.   **EC278**

Contents: History and scope of virology; Organizations and their role in virology; Conferences; The literature of virology; Searching the literature; Culture collections; Legislation and laboratory safety; Bibliography; Directory; and Index.
"A one-place reference to all sources of information on virology."—*Pref.*   Z5185.V5N53

E D

Chemistry

❖A number of guides to the literature of chemistry are available: Mellon's guide (ED5) is relatively recent; that by Crane, Patterson, and Marr (ED3) is an older standard work. These should be consulted for information about how to use the indexes and compendiums as well as how to ascertain titles in the field. *Chemical abstracts* (ED22) is one of the oldest and best-known abstract journals, and now has computer-produced indexes and the facility for machine searches. Its list of periodicals, *CASSI* (ED17), is one of the most useful bibliographies of scientific periodicals.

GENERAL WORKS

Guides

Antony, Arthur. Guide to basic information sources in chemistry. N.Y. Wiley, [1979]. 219p.   **ED1**

"This guide . . . is primarily intended for the student of chemistry from college freshmen through graduate level."—*Pref.* Chapters treat types of sources—nomenclature, guides to techniques, access to primary publications other than journals, major reference tools. Author/title and subject indexes.   QD8.5.A57

Bottle, Robert Thomas, ed. The use of chemical literature. 3d ed. London & Boston, Butterworths, [1979]. 306p. il.
ED2

1st ed. 1962.
18 chapters by various authorities provide a guide to the use of the literature: primary sources, abstracting and information retrieval services, nomenclature, tables, specialized references and the literature of particular fields, etc. Appendixes provide exercises and answers for practical literature questions. Indexed.   QD8.5.B6

Crane, Evan Jay, Patterson, Austin M. and **Marr, Eleanor B.** A guide to the literature of chemistry. 2d ed. N.Y., Wiley, [1957]. 397p.   **ED3**

1st ed. 1927.
Treatment and discussion of the procedures of literature searching, with listings and descriptions of the standard reference books, periodicals, and organizations. General subject index, but no index to the books treated.   Z5521.C89

Maizell, Robert E. How to find chemical information. N.Y., Wiley, [1979]. 261p. il.   **ED4**

Subtitle: A guide for practicing scientists, teachers, and students.
". . . this book presents the most important and enduring of the classical tools of chemical information; the more significant newer books; and, most importantly, the underlying methods, principles, and keys the chemist and engineer need to cope with the constantly changing array of chemical information sources and tooks."—*Pref.* A new edition was announced for 1986 publication.   QD8.5.M34

Mellon, Melvin Guy. Chemical publications, their nature and use. 5th ed. N.Y., McGraw-Hill, [1982]. 419p. il.
ED5

1st ed. 1928.
The first part, Publications: kinds and nature, describes the principal sources for reference and research, including primary sources (periodicals, technical reports, patents, etc.), secondary sources (abstracts, reference compilations of various sorts, treatises, textbooks, etc.), and tertiary sources (guides and directories). The second part, Publications: storage and use, describes libraries and information centers and how to search manually and with on-line databases; it also includes, as Chapter 16, examples of library problems. Indexed.   QD8.5.M44

Skolnik, Herman. The literature matrix of chemistry. N.Y., Wiley, [1982]. 297p.   **ED6**

Intended to "delineate the scope and content of the literature matrix so that the reader can interact with and gain access to it effectively."—*Pref.* The author is a distinguished chemical information scientist. Indexed.   QD5.S58

Wolman, Yecheskel. Chemical information, a practical guide to utilization. N.Y., Wiley, [1983]. 191p. il.   **ED7**

Based on a course presented to undergraduate chemistry students, this book emphasizes real search problems and their solutions using current information sources. Accordingly, its organization is by sections on current awareness, obtaining numerical data, synthetic reaction search, etc., unlike the organization of most other guides to chemical literature, which it complements. Indexed.

QD8.5.W64

Woodburn, Henry M. Using the chemical literature; a practical guide. N.Y., Marcel Dekker, [1974]. 302p.   **ED8**

Intended for instruction in the use of the chemical literature, "the book is a practical guide and not a bibliography of sources."—*Pref.*

QD8.5.W66

Bibliography

Bibliography of chemical kinetics and collision processes; an annotated bibliography of gas-phase reaction rates and low-energy cross sections of atoms, ions, and small molecules. Prep. under the direction of Adolf R. Hochstim, ed. N.Y., IFI/Plenum, 1969. 953p. **ED9**

"An annotated world bibliography (1900–1966) of about 20,000 entries from about 7000 selected references."—*verso of half-title.* Two computer-produced tables comprise the major portion of the book. Table I gives an alphabetical listing by reactant; the complete reaction is included as well as the author's name and citation using a journal coden. Table II classes reactions according to nine category types, with author and journal coden citation. The complete literature references are found in the author index. An alphabetical list of journal coden provides the full titles of the journals.

Z5524.R5B52

Bolton, Henry Carrington. A select bibliography of chemistry 1492–[1902]. Wash., Smithsonian Inst., 1893–1904. 4v. **ED10**

Basic list, 1492–1892 (repr.: N.Y., Kraus, 1973); 1st suppl., 1492–1897 (publ. 1899); 2d suppl., 1492–1902 (publ. 1904); Academic dissertations (publ. 1901). Issued as *Smithsonian miscellaneous collections,* v.36, 39, 44, and 41.

Eight sections: (1) Bibliography; (2) Dictionaries; (3) History; (4) Biography; (5) Chemistry, pure and applied; (6) Alchemy; (7) Periodicals; (8) Academic dissertations.

Includes some 18,000 independent works but does not list analytics. Sec.8, Academic dissertations, is particularly strong in dissertations from the universities of France, Germany, Russia and the United States. Z5521.B69

Duveen, Denis I. Bibliotheca alchemica et chemica; an annotated catalogue of printed books on alchemy, chemistry and cognate subjects in the library of Denis I. Duveen. London, Weil, 1949. 669p. il. (Repr.: Rijwijk, Utrecht, Krips/ Oosthoek, 1965; London, Dawsons, 1965) **ED11**

Includes works, with full bibligraphical description, from the 16th to the 19th centuries. Collection now housed at the University of Wisconsin Libraries (*see* ED16). Z5526.D8

Glasgow. Royal College of Science and Technology. Andersonian Library. Bibliotheca chemica: A catalogue of the alchemical, chemical and pharmaceutical books in the collection of the late James Young of Kelly and Durris. By John Ferguson. Glasgow, Maclehose, 1906. 2v. **ED12**

A rich collection of early works useful for the history of chemistry, particularly in alchemy. Detailed bibliographical descriptions. Frequently mentioned are other editions, translations, and additional works of an author which are not included in the Young collection. Biographical information and an evaluation of an author's work are added features.

Collection bequeathed to the chair of technical chemistry of Anderson's College, now incorporated in the Royal Technical College, Glasgow. Z5524.A35G42

International catalogue of scientific literature: D, Chemistry. 1st–14th annual issues, 1901–14. London, Harrison, 1902–19. **ED13**

For full description *see* EA17.

Pritchard, Alan. Alchemy: a bibliography of English-language writings. London, Routledge & Kegan Paul jointly with the Library Assoc., [1980]. 439p. **ED14**

A scholarly and "purposeful attempt to draw together into one document all writings in the English language on and about alchemy—texts and secondary works respectively. It adds to these,

works which mention alchemy *en passant,* and works on some of the byways which seem . . . to be imbued with Hermetic thinking, or which throw light on those works which are directly concerned with alchemy."—*Pref.* In three main sections: (1) Alchemical texts; (2) Works about alchemy: countries; (3) Works about alchemy: subjects. Indexed. Z5524.A35P75

Reuss, Jeremias David. Repertorium commentationum a societatibus litterariis editarum . . . T.3, Chemia et res metallica. Gottingae, Dieterich, 1803. 221p. (Repr., N.Y., B. Franklin, 1961) **ED15**

A valuable index to the publications of learned societies up to 1800. Classed arrangement with author index. For description of complete set *see* EA22.

Wisconsin. University. Libraries. Chemical, medical, and pharmaceutical books printed before 1800, in the collections of the University of Wisconsin Libraries. Ed. by John Neu. Madison, Univ. of Wisconsin Pr., 1965. 280p. **ED16**

Full bibliographical listings of 4,442 items, including the D. I. Duveen collection in chemistry and alchemy (*see* ED11). No annotations. Z5526.W5

Periodicals

American Chemical Society. Chemical Abstracts Service. Chemical Abstracts Service source index; 1907–1984 cumulative. [Columbus, Ohio], Amer. Chemical Soc., [1985]. 2v. **ED17**

Cited as *CAS source index;* also cited as *CASSI.*

The cumulative version of *Chemical Abstracts Service source index* was first published in 1975 and has appeared every 5 years since. It supersedes the publication of the same title that first appeared in 1971, superseding *Access* (1969), which in turn superseded the *List of periodicals . . .* issued irregularly in connection with *Chemical abstracts.*

This most important publication is broad in scope since *Chemical abstracts* covers not only the chemical sciences but also related biological, engineering, and physical sciences (*see* ED22); moreover, to the publications indexed there *CASSI* has added publications indexed by *BIOSIS* (EC12), *Engineering index* (EJ9), and the Institute for Scientific Information, as well as those publications covered by *Chemische Zentralblatt* (ED25) and its predecessors from 1830–1969, and those cited by *Beilstein* (ED90) prior to 1907. It includes both periodicals and non-serial publications such as proceedings of nonrecurring meetings and other compilations of articles.

Each entry includes the full title, with the abbreviated parts of the title printed in bold face; the entries are alphabetized letter-by-letter according to this abbreviated title. All titles are printed in the Roman alphabet; for titles not in western European languages a translation is included. Entries also include CODEN, ISSN, ISBN; reference to previous and successor titles; information on language(s) of publication, summaries and table of contents; history and frequency of publication; current volume/year correlation; address of publisher or source (or abbreviation if a standard source); indication of year of publication, date and place of meeting, for non-serial titles; cross references, including references to title-to-title translations journals if they exist (e.g., for Slavic titles); abbreviated entry as cataloged under *Anglo-American cataloging rules* (2d ed.); and information on location in libraries throughout the world, with library holdings. Also includes a list of the 1,000 journals most frequently cited in *Chemical abstracts* volumes 99–100 (July 1983–June 1984), i.e., the journals which have had the most articles abstracted during that period.

Invaluable for determining full titles from abbreviations, for determining publication history including changes of titles and discontinuations, for finding title-to-title translation journals for Slavic and Oriental publications, for locating suppliers of obscure publications, for verification of bibliographic information, etc.

Kept up-to-date by:

———— Chemical Abstracts Service source index; quarterly supplement. [Columbus, Ohio], Amer. Chemical Soc., 1985– . Quarterly.   **ED18**

> Cited as *CAS source index, quarterly supplement*.
> Supersedes *Access quarterly* (1970).
> The 4th issue of each year is a cumulation for the year.
> Both of the above are indexed by: Z5523.A52

———— CASSI keyword-out-of-context index. 1907–1984. [Columbus, Ohio], Amer. Chemical Soc., 1985– . Microfiche (48x). Annual.   **ED19**

> Accompanied by *User's guide* both in fiche and as 9p. pamphlet. Also cited as *CASSI KWOC*.
> Each annual ed. cumulates the entries from *CASSI 1907–1984* (53 fiches) and the suppls. that have appeared.
> An index to all words from the title/reference data fields in each *CASSI* record, omitting stopwords (a list of which is included) and nonindex terms (words beginning with lower case letters, e.g., prepositions and articles; words of more than 30 characters). About 50 titles consisting only of stopwords and nonindex terms are listed separately.
> This index permits identification of titles for which only title fragments are known. Entries give keyword at the left, followed by title or reference entry from *CASSI*, and the item's CODEN.

Pflücke, Maximilian and **Hawelek, Alice.** Periodica chemica: Verzeichnis der im Chemischen Zentralblatt referierten Zeitschriften mit den entsprechenden genormten Titelabkürzungen. 2. neubearb. Aufl. Berlin, Akademie-Verlag; Weinheim/Bergstr., Verlag Chemie, 1952. 411p.   **ED20**

> 1st ed. 1940.
> An international list of chemical periodicals indicating all changes of title which have taken place since 1930, with abbreviations as used in *Chemisches Zentralblatt* (ED25). Arrangement is alphabetical by title, with separate listings of Russian periodicals in Cyrillic and in non-Cyrillic alphabets.   Z5523.P45

Indexes and abstract journals

❖*See* Bottle, *The use of the chemical literature* (ED2) for description of *Chemical abstracts* and other abstracting services.

British abstracts, issued by the Bureau of Abstracts. A, Pure chemistry; B, Applied chemistry; C, Analysis and apparatus. London, Bureau of Abstracts, 1926–53. A and B, monthly; C, quarterly.   **ED21**

> Title varies: 1926–37, British chemical abstracts; 1938–44, British chemical and physiological abstracts. Continues the abstract volumes previously published in the *Journal* of the Chemical Society and the *Journal* of the Society of Chemical Industry.
> The list of periodicals abstracted duplicates, to a considerable extent, the list for *Chemical abstracts* (ED22), but does include some not covered there.
> 1937–53, pt.A in three sections: (1) General physical and inorganic chemistry and geochemistry; (2) Organic chemistry; (3) Physiology, biochemistry, and anatomy. 1945–53, pt.B in three sections: (1) Chemical engineering and industrial inorganic chemistry including metallurgy; (2) Industrial organic chemistry; (3) Agriculture, foods, sanitation. 1944–53, pt.C, Analysis and apparatus.
> Ceased publication in 1953. Superseded by several publications, as follows:
> Pt.A, Sec. 3, replaced by *International abstracts of biological sciences,* v.1, 1954– . Monthly (irregular). v.1–3 had title *British abstracts of medical sciences,* 1954–56 (EC13).
> Pt.B (Applied chemistry), Sec.1–2, continued in a supplement to the *Journal of applied chemistry* (later *Journal of applied chemistry and biotechnology*), 1951– . Monthly.
> Pt.B, Sec.3, continued in the *Journal of the science of food and agriculture,* 1954– . Monthly.

Pt.C (Analysis and apparatus), replaced by *Analytical abstracts,* 1954– . Monthly.   QD1.B68

Chemical abstracts, publ. by the American Chemical Society, 1907– . Columbus, Ohio, 1907– . v.1– . Weekly.   **ED22**

> Imprint varies.
> Now the most comprehensive of the abstract journals, with an international reputation for comprehensive coverage of the literature. Over 14,000 serials and conferences included in the *Chemical Abstracts Service source index* (*see* ED17). Abstracts are prepared from publications in more than 50 languages. Initially issued biweekly, publication is now weekly. Indexes in current issues: keyword index, author index, numerical patent index, patent concordance. The keyword indexes should not be confused with the subject indexes.
> Subject indexing is done in a thorough manner for each volume. Beginning with v.76 (1972), the subject index was divided into two separate parts: the chemical substance index and the general subject index. Within the past few years a variety of indexes and aids have been introduced. The Index Guide first appeared as pt.1 of the subject index to v.69. Annual revisions are issued with the subject indexes for the odd-numbered volumes of *Chemical abstracts*. A Registry Number Index began in 1969; the Index of Ring Systems with v.66 (1967; *see also* the *Ring systems handbook,* ED24). The HAIC (hetero atom in context) index was initiated prior to 1970 but it was discontinued.
> *Chemical abstracts* is also on machine-readable magnetic tape. In addition, special subject areas of the abstracts are now being packaged for six separate topics; these six information services are available for computer searching.   QD1.A51●

———— Decennial author and subject indexes, 1907/16–1947/56.

———— Collective index, 1957/61; 1962/66; 1967/71; 1972/76; 1977/81.

> Each quinquennial "Collective index" has separate author, subject, and patent sections. The 1967/71 index introduces the "Index guide." Beginning with the 1972/76 index, separate chemical substances and general subject indexes replaced the former subject index.

———— Formula index, v.14–40, 1920–46; v.41–50, 1947–56; v.51–55, 1957–61; v.56–65, 1962–66; v.66–75, 1967–71; v.76–85, 1972–76; v.86–95, 1977–81.

———— Patent index to *Chemical abstracts,* 1907–1936, comp. by the Science-Technology Group of Special Libraries Association. . . . Ann Arbor, Mich., Edwards, 1944. 479p.

> Numerical lists, by country, of all patents included in the first 30v. of *Chemical abstracts*.

———— Collective numerical patent index to *Chemical abstracts,* v.31–40, 1937–46; v.41–50, 1947–56; v.51–55, 1957–61; v.56–65, 1962–66; v.66–75, 1967–71; 76–85, 1972–76; v.86–95, 1977–81.

> The patent concordance appeared with the 1962–66 index. It "correlates patents issued by different countries for the same basic invention."—*Introd.*

Chemical titles: current author and keyword indexes from selected chemical journals. A publication of the Chemical Abstracts Service. Columbus, Ohio, Amer. Chemical Soc., 1960– . no.1– . Biweekly.   **ED23**

> A computer-produced index to titles of chemical research papers. Each issue in three parts: (1) keywords arranged alphabetically down the center of the column; (2) a bibliographic listing of titles of current papers from selected journals, arranged as tables of contents of the journals; and (3) an index of authors. Titles are selected from over 700 journals in pure and applied chemistry and chemical engineering.
> Serves as a current awareness listing and as a means of locating recent articles on a topic before they appear in *Chemical abstracts* (ED22).   Z5523.C44

Ring systems handbook. A publication of Chemical Abstracts Service. [Wash.], Amer. Chemical Soc., 1984– . il. Irregular. **ED24**

Supersedes *Parent compound handbook* (1976–83), which in turn superseded *The ring index* (1st ed. 1940, 2d ed. 1960 with suppls. 1–3, 1963–65).

"The *Ring systems handbook* is intended to be a major reference work for chemists and others who use *Chemical Abstracts (CA)*. . . . The first part of the Handbook, the Ring Systems File (RSF), contains structural diagrams and related data for nearly 60,000 unique, representative *CA* index ring systems. The RSF also includes data on cage systems (polyboranes, metallocenes, etc.). Information accompanying each ring system includes a Ring File (RF) number, the CAS Registry Number, a structural diagram illustrating the numbering system, the current *CA* index name, the molecular formula, and the Wiswesser Line Notation. The ring systems are arranged by their ring analysis, which is given before each group of ring systems having a common ring analysis, except for cage systems. The Handbook also includes the Ring Formula Index (RFI) and the Ring Name Index (RNI) which are designed to provide access to the contents of the RSF by molecular formula and by ring name . . . Supplements to the RSF, RFI, and RNI are cumulative and are issued semiannually in one volume."—*Introd.*

1984 issued in four parts: Ring formula file I; Ring systems file II; Ring formula index, Ring name index; and Ring WLN index. QD390.R56●

Chemisches Zentralblatt. . . . Jahrg. 1–140. Berlin, Verlag Chemie, 1830–1969. v.1–140. il. Weekly. **ED25**

Title and imprint vary. 1897–1945, published by the Deutsche Chemische Gesellschaft. v.112–16, pt.1, reprinted by J. W. Edwards, Ann Arbor, Mich. 1946–69, hrsg. im Auftrage der Deutschen Akademie der Wissenschaften zu Berlin, der Chemischen Gesellschaft in der DDR, der Akademie der Wissenschaften zu Göttingen, und der Gesellschaft Deutscher Chemiker.

Author index in each issue; annual and cumulated author, subject, patent, and organic formula indexes (vary somewhat).

An abstracting journal for pure and applied chemistry, particularly valuable because of the length of the period covered. Many of the abstracts are more detailed than those in *Chemical abstracts*. Before 1919, did not include abstracts on applied chemistry, as these appeared in *Angewandte Chemie*.

Ceased publication. QD1.C7

Encyclopedias

See also EJ91, EJ94.

Brockhaus ABC Chemie. Etwa 12,000 Stichwörter und 800 Abbildungen . . . Leipzig, Brockhaus, 1965. 2v. il. **ED26**

An encyclopedia of chemical terms. Some of the longer articles carry bibliographies. QD5.B8

The encyclopedia of chemical process equipment. Ed. by William J. Mead. N.Y., Reinhold; London, Chapman & Hall, [1964]. 1065p. il. **ED27**

Intends to "correlate, describe, and illustrate the many classes of machinery and equipment used in the various branches of the chemical industry."—*Pref.* Contributions, by specialists, are signed and include bibliographies. TP9.E65

Encyclopedia of industrial chemical analysis. Ed. by Foster Dee Snell and Clifford L. Hilton. N.Y., Interscience, 1966–74. 20v. il. **ED28**

General techniques of analysis, especially instrumental methods, are discussed in v.1–3. The remaining 17v. contain articles on chemicals of industrial importance, emphasizing methods and techniques for identification and analysis.

Subject index for v.1–3 in v.3; v.20 has a subject index for v.4–19, plus lists of contents and contributors for the whole encyclopedia. QD131.E5

Encyclopédie des gaz. Gas encyclopaedia. [Comp. by Société] L'Air Liquide, Division Scientifique. N.Y. & Amsterdam, Elsevier, [1976]. 1150p. il. **ED29**

Text in French and English.

Offers articles on 138 gases from air to xenon, with an "enormous scope of the subjects covered: chemical and physical properties, operating conditions, flammability limits, toxicity, biological properties, materials of construction, uses, etc. . . . [with] short but effective bibliography."—*Pref.* TP247.E52

Hampel, Clifford A., ed. Encyclopedia of the chemical elements. N.Y., Reinhold, [1968]. 849p. il. **ED30**

Each of 103 elements is discussed in relation to its history, prevalence, sources, physical and chemical properties, applications, importance of the elements and its compounds, and biological and biochemical aspects (including toxicology). Data tables are used frequently. Articles are signed; subject index. QD466.H295

International encyclopedia of chemical science. Princeton, N.J., Van Nostrand, [1964]. 1331p. il. **ED31**

Prepared for chemists, chemical engineers, teachers, and students. Alphabetically arranged definitions and explanations of theory and practice, processes and operations, tests and testing methods. At the back of the book are glossaries in French, German, Russian, and Spanish into English, devised for use in reading the foreign literature, and in finding the corresponding English entry in the book. QD5.I5

Kingzett, Charles Thomas. Kingzett's Chemical encyclopaedia; a digest of chemistry and its industrial applications. Gen. ed., D. H. Hey. 9th ed. London, Baillière; Princeton, N.J., Van Nostrand, [1966]. 1092p. il. **ED32**

1st ed. 1919; 8th ed. 1952.

Entries for trade names, prefixes, methods, names of reactions, etc. Inorganic compounds usually are listed under a discussion of the parent element and its compounds. Very few tables; British spelling predominates. Index consists only of alternate names for entries appearing in the main portion of the book. QD5.K4

Römpps Chemie-Lexikon. Völlig neubearb. und erw. 8. Aufl., fortgeführt von Erhard Ühlein, neubearb. von Otto-Albrecht Neumüller. Stuttgart, Franckh, [1979–83]. v.1–3. (In progress). **ED33**

1st–6th eds. had title: *Chemie Lexikon.* 7th ed. 1972–77 in 6v.

Contents: v.1–3, A–L.

An alphabetically arranged, comprehensive encyclopedia, revised, updated, and enlarged. Contains information on chemical compound types, trade-name products, statistics, industrial chemicals, etc., as well as biographical sketches. Includes bibliographies. To be complete in 6v. QD5.R62

Van Nostrand Reinhold encyclopedia of chemistry. 4th ed. Douglas M. Considine, ed. in chief. N.Y., Van Nostrand Reinhold, [1984]. 1082p. il. **ED34**

1st ed. 1957. Earlier eds. had title *Encyclopedia of chemistry.*

A very much revised edition containing over 85% new text. The roughly 1,300 entries range from brief definitions to articles, some of them signed, which may include tabular data and references. Includes topics from fields related to chemistry, such as materials science, energy sources and conversion, biochemistry and biotechnology, wastes and pollution. Cross references; index. QD5.V37

Dictionaries

Bennett, Harry. Concise chemical and technical dictionary. 3d ed. enl. N.Y., Chemical Publ. Co., 1974. 1175p. **ED35**

1st ed. 1947.

Over 50,000 definitions of scientific terms, chemicals, trademark products (with manufacturer for American products) and drugs. "Brevity rather than extended definition has been the rule."—*Pref.* QD5.B45

The condensed chemical dictionary. 10th ed. Rev. by Gessner G. Hawley. N.Y., Van Nostrand Reinhold, [1981]. 1135p. il. **ED36**

1st ed. 1919.

Concise definitions for terms relating to chemistry and the chemical industry. Includes short retrospective biographies of outstanding scientists and brief information about some American technical societies. Many *see* references. Entries for compounds give other commonly accepted names, molecular formula, properties, source or occurrence, commercial grades available, hazards, uses in large scale applications, and shipping regulations. Proprietary names in the alphabetical listings are set within quotation marks. A superscript number denotes the manufacturer's name listed at the end of the book; manufacturers' addresses are also given. An appendix gives the origins of some chemical terms. QD5.C5

Daintith, John, ed. The Facts on File dictionary of chemistry. [2d ed.] N.Y., Facts on File, [1981]. 233p. il. **ED37**

"First edition published in the United Kingdom in 1981 by Intercontinental Book Productions Limited. . . ."—*verso of t.p.*

About 2,200 entries defining the most important and commonly used chemical terms. QD5.D26

Eklund, Jon. The incompleat chymist: being an essay on the eighteenth-century chemist in his laboratory, with a dictionary of obsolete chemical terms of the period. Wash., Smithsonian Institution Pr., 1975. 49p. (Smithsonian studies in history and technology, no. 33). il. **ED38**

The essay on 18th-century chemical practices, with bibliographic references, is followed by a 30-page "Dictionary of British eighteenth-century chemical terms" which gives brief explanations or modern equivalents for the terms. Includes Latin and French phrases that were common in British journals and treatises. Cross references. QD14.E38

Flood, Walter Edgar. The dictionary of chemical names. N.Y., Philosophical Lib., [1963]. 238p. **ED39**

Published in London as *The origins of chemical names*.

In two parts: (1) names of chemical elements; (2) compounds, minerals and other substances. Some entries include a number of related compounds. The date of the earliest use of the name is added when known. QD5.F55

Hackh, Ingo Waldemar Dagobert. Chemical dictionary, American and British usage; containing the words generally used in chemistry, and many of the terms used in the related sciences of physics, astrophysics, mineralogy, pharmacy, agriculture, biology, medicine, engineering, etc., based on recent chemical literature. 4th ed., completely rev. and ed. by Julius Grant. N.Y., McGraw-Hill, [1969]. 738p. **ED40**

1st ed. 1929.

Definitions are given in simple language. Includes trade names (capitalized for quick identification), symbols, prefixes, abbreviations, etc. Both American and British usage are noted; entries are listed under the American spelling. About 55,000 entries. QD5.H3

McGraw-Hill dictionary of chemistry. Sybil P. Packer, ed. in chief. N.Y., McGraw-Hill, [1984]. 665p. **ED41**

" . . . focuses on the vocabulary of theoretical and applied chemistry rather than on chemicals and materials. . . . Terms and definitions . . . were selected from the McGraw-Hill Dictionary of Scientific and Technical Terms (3d ed., 1984 [EA120]). Synonyms, acronyms, and abbreviations are given with the definitions and are also listed in the alphabetical sequence as cross-references. . . ."—*Pref.* QD5.M357

Miall's Dictionary of chemistry. 5th ed. Ed. by D. W. A. Sharp. [Harlow, Essex], Longman, [1981]. 501p. **ED42**

1st ed. 1940 by Stephen Miall; 4th ed. 1968 by L. M. Miall and D. W. A. Sharp. Previous eds. had title *A new dictionary of chemistry*.

Intended for university teaching where chemical terms may be encountered, and for professionals outside their own specialty. Industrial processes, manufacture, and use are given particular attention in this edition; some data on annual production is includ-

ed. Brief biographical information is given for prominent chemists, past and contemporary. Trade names are kept to a minimum; abbreviations are omitted. British spelling is used. QD5.M52

Snell, Foster Dee and **Snell, Cornelia T.** Dictionary of commercial chemicals. 3d ed. Princeton, N.J., Van Nostrand, [1962]. 714p. **ED43**

1st ed. 1939.

"Designed to furnish information on the composition of actual commercial products as sold in commerce rather than the pure chemicals of a textbook."—*Pref.* TP200.S55

Thorpe, Jocelyn Field and **Whiteley, M. A.** Thorpe's Dictionary of applied chemistry . . . 4th ed. rev. and enl. N.Y., London, Longmans, 1937–56. 12v. **ED44**

Consists primarily of short entries, with some long articles. General index in v.12. TP8.T72

Foreign terms

French

Patterson, Austin McDowell. French-English dictionary for chemists. 2d ed. N.Y., Wiley, [1954]. 476p. **ED45**

1st ed. 1921.

Phrases and abbreviations are included among the 42,000 entries. Common forms of various irregular verbs are entered separately rather than being grouped under the parent verb. The introduction discusses some of the common French chemical suffixes and their English equivalents. QD5.P25

German

De Vries, Louis. Dictionary of chemistry and chemical engineering. 2d ed., rev. and enl. Weinheim & N.Y., Verlag Chemie, 1978–79. 2v. **ED46**

1st ed. 1970–72.

Added title page: Wörterbuch der Chemie . . . .

Contents: v.1, German-English; v.2, English-German.

Intended to be comprehensive for students, practicing scientists, and engineers. Brief entries. Includes trivial names of chemical substances. QD5.D47

Ernst, Richard and **Ernst von Morgenstern, Ingeborg.** Dictionary of chemistry, including chemical engineering and fundamentals of allied sciences. [3. Aufl.] Wiesbaden, Brandstetter, [1967–68]. 2v. **ED47**

1st ed. 1961–63.

Added title page: Fachwörterbuch der Chemie. . . . QD5.E732

Patterson, Austin McDowell. A German-English dictionary for chemists. 3d ed. N.Y., Wiley, [1950]. 541p. **ED48**

Designed primarily for chemists and chemical engineers but contains terms from related fields of science. Includes abbreviations, prefixes, suffixes, and obsolete chemical terms used in the early literature. Some non-scientific words have been included. About 59,000 terms. QD5.P3

Wohlauer, Gabriele E. M. and **Gholston, H. D.** German chemical abbreviations. N.Y., Special Libraries Assoc., 1965. 63p. **ED49**

A project of the Chemistry Section of the Science-Technology Division of Special Libraries Association.

In addition to technical abbreviations some non-technical and Latin entries are given. Information presented in parallel columns: the abbreviation in German (or Latin), the corresponding word or phrase written in full, and the English equivalent. About 2,500 entries. QD7.W6

Polyglot

Dictionary of chemistry and chemical technology in six languages: English, German, Spanish, French, Polish, Russian. Ed. by Z. Sobecka, W. Choiński, and P. Majorek. [Rev. ed.] Oxford, N.Y., Pergamon, [1966]. 1325p. **ED50**

1st ed. 1962 in four languages.

An alphabetical listing of English words or phrases, with equivalent terms in the other five languages; separate index for each language. Arrangement is in six parallel columns on facing pages. Where the word or term has several different meanings there are consecutive entries. Spelling is according to British usage. Approximately 12,000 terms are included. QD5.D5

Fouchier, Jean and **Billet, Fernand**. Chemical dictionary. Dictionnaire de chimie. Fachwörterbuch für Chemie. 3d ed. rev. and enl. [Amsterdam], Netherlands Univ. Pr., 1970. 566p., 421p., 477p. **ED51**

1st ed. 1953.

Compound names and terms for pure and applied chemistry. In three trilingual parts: English-French-German; French-German-English; German-English-French. Preceding each part is an alphabetical listing of abbreviations and the full expression in the first language of the part. Tables of equivalent weights and measures are included for the three languages. Structural formulas appear only in pt.1, English section. About 20,000 entries for each language. QD5.F6

Russian

Callaham, Ludmilla Ignatiev. Russian-English chemical and polytechnical dictionary. 3d ed. N.Y., Wiley, [1975]. 852p. **ED52**

1st ed., 1947, had title *Russian-English technical and chemical dictionary*.

Both technical and non-technical terms are included, together with abbreviations, prefixes, frequently used suffixes, and terms occurring in the older literature. There is a listing of common Russian technical word endings and a review of declensions. QD5.C33

Carpovich, Eugene A. and **Carpovich, Vera V.** Russian-English chemical dictionary; chemistry, physical chemistry, chemical engineering, materials, minerals, fuels, petroleum, food industry, pharmacology. 2d improved ed. N.Y., Technical Dictionaries, 1963. 352p. **ED53**

1st ed. 1961.

Includes some 29,000 Russian entries and is strong in new terms. Prepared for the English-speaking worker. TP9.C33

Directories

American Chemical Society. Committee on Professional Training. Directory of graduate research. Wash., 1953– . Biennial. **ED54**

Subtitle (varies): Faculties, publications, and doctoral and master's theses in departments or divisions of chemistry, chemical engineering, biochemistry, pharmaceutical/medicinal chemistry, clinical chemistry, and polymer science at universities in the United States and Canada.

In each subject field the institutions are listed alphabetically. For each department is given: degrees offered; fields of specialization; faculty members, with academic rank, year of birth, education, field of research, specific current research interests, and telephone number, followed by a list of research publications for the biennium covered and master's and doctoral candidates completing their degrees in the period covered, with the theses titles. Statistical summaries for the subject areas list the institutions alphabetically to show the numbers of full- and part-time faculty, postdoctoral appointments, graduate enrollments, and graduate degrees granted for the two years. Index of instructional staff. Z5525.U5A6

American Chemical Society. Dept. of Education Activities. College chemistry faculties. [Wash., 1965–] Irregular. **ED55**

". . . a directory of all chemistry teachers in universities, colleges, and junior colleges in the United States and Canada. They are listed first by department and subsequently in alphabetical order by name."—*Introd.*

Chem sources—Europe. Ormond Beach, Fla., Directories Publ. Co., 1973– . v.1– . Annual (slightly irregular). **ED56**

A companion to *Chem sources—USA* (below).

Lists alphabetically by chemical name over 50,000 chemicals and chemical products, giving suppliers in Western Europe.

Chem sources—USA. Ormond Beach, Fla., Directories Publ. Co., 1958– . v.1– . Annual. **ED57**

Title varies: 1958–72, *Chem sources*.

An alphabetical listing by chemical name; producers are identified by a 3-letter code. More than 65,000 organic and inorganic chemicals are included. Indexes: applications; companies by code; companies, alphabetical. TP12.C44

Chemical industry directory & who's who. 1923– . London, Chemical Age, Benn Brothers, 1923– . Annual. **ED58**

Title varies: 1923–58, *The chemical age year book;* 1959–63, *Chemical age directory and who's who*.

Primarily a directory for the United Kingdom. Buyer's guide follows classed subject arrangement. Also contains lists of chemical manufacturers, trade and professional groups, independent consultants, trade names, and "who's who" in the chemical industry. TP1.C34

Chemical research faculties, an international directory. Gisella Linder Pollock, project ed. Wash., Amer. Chemical Soc., 1984. 1v., various pagings. **ED59**

Provides, for departments of chemistry, chemical engineering, biochemistry, and pharmaceutical/medicinal chemistry outside of the United States and Canada the same sort of information as the *Directory of graduate research* (ED54) does for departments within the United States and Canada. In each subject field countries are listed alphabetically, and under each country institutions are listed alphabetically. For each department is given: address and telephone number (if different from main address of the university); advanced degrees offered; fields of specialization; faculty members, with academic rank, year of birth, education, field of research, areas of current research interest, and a listing of one or two recent research publications. Statistical summaries for the subject areas list the institutions alphabetically under their countries to show numbers of full-time faculty, postdoctoral appointments, graduate enrollments, and graduate degrees granted for 1980–81 and for 1981–82. Also included is a directory of chemical societies with current addresses, principal officer, major publications, organizational structure, and number of members. Faculty are indexed by name and by research subjects. A merged alphabetical listing of all institutions gives the country under which the user will find the department listing. QD40.C4317

Noyes Data Corporation. Chemical guide to the United States. [Ed.1–] 1963/64– . Park Ridge, N.J., 1963– . Irregular. **ED60**

Earlier volumes were issued by the Corporation under its previous name, Noyes Development Corporation.

Now describes some 400 of the largest chemical firms of the United States.

The same publisher also issues similar guides for Canada, Europe, Latin America, etc., and guides for specific types of firms (cosmetics, pharmaceuticals, etc.) in the United States and elsewhere. TP12.N615

Handbooks

Akademiia Nauk URSR, Kiev. Instytut Problem Materialoznavstva. Handbook of the physicochemical properties of the elements. G. V. Samsonov, ed. Tr. from the Russian. N.Y., IFI/Plenum, 1968. 941p. **ED61**

A translation, with revisions and updating, of Samsonov's *Fizikokhimicheskie svoistva elementov* (Kiev, 1965). Offers "concise information in tabular form on physical properties of the elements and on their chemical characteristics."—*Pref.* Numerous references to the literature. Indexed. QD466.A3413

American Chemical Society. Committee on Analytical Reagents. Reagent chemicals; American Chemical Society specifications. 6th ed. Wash., Amer. Chemical Soc., 1981. 659p. **ED62**

1st ed. 1950.

"Intended to serve for reagents to be used in precise analytical work."—*Pref.* ACS specifications given for 333 reagent chemicals. Definitions, tests, and reagent solutions are considered also.
QD77.A54

American Public Health Association. Standard methods for the examination of water and wastewater. 16th ed. Wash., Amer. Public Health Assoc., [1985]. 1268p. il. **ED63**

1st ed. 1905.

"Prepared and published jointly by American Public Health Association, American Water Works Association, Water Pollution Control Federation."—*t.p.*

The major divisions of the text are: General introduction, Physical examination, Determination of metals, Determination of inorganic nonmetallic constituents, Determination of organic constituents, Examination of water and wastewater for radioactivity, Toxicity test methods for aquatic organisms, Microbiological examination of water, and Biological examination of water. Each section has a bibliography and/or references. The table of contents includes listings of the tables, figures, and plates in the text. Indexed.
QD142.A5

Association of Official Analytical Chemists. Official methods of analysis of the Association of Official Analytical Chemists. 14th ed. Arlington, Va., Assoc. of Official Analytical Chemists, 1984. 1141p. **ED64**

Sidney Williams, ed.

Eds. 1–10, 1920–65, publ. by Association of Official Agricultural Chemists; ed. 11– , 1970– , by Association of Official Analytical Chemists.

Gives qualitative and quantitative methods for analysis of foods, fertilizers, pesticides, hazardous substances, drugs, cosmetics, color additives, poisons, and other materials. Has a section on preparation of standard solutions. Includes reference tables. Indexed.
S587.A8

Chemical technicians' ready reference handbook. Ed. by Gershon J. Shugar [and others]. 2d ed. N.Y., McGraw-Hill, [1981]. 867p. il. **ED65**

1st ed. 1973.

". . . this Handbook is designed to provide anyone with *every single step* to be followed when performing normal laboratory procedures. . . . The book details what equipment is needed, what each piece of equipment looks like (with photographs or drawings), how the pieces are used in a procedure, the sequential steps to be taken in performing the function or acquiring the experimental data, the cautions which must be observed, and finally the raw data, observations, and calculations which may be needed to utilize the experimental data."—*Pref.* Indexed. QD61.S58

CRC handbook of chemistry and physics: a ready-reference book of chemical and physical data. Ed. in chief, Robert C. Weast. Ed.1– . Boca Raton, Fla., CRC Press, 1913– . il. Annual. (66th ed. publ. 1985) **ED66**

1st–57th eds. had title: *Handbook of chemistry and physics.* Publisher formerly called Chemical Rubber Co.

"In collaboration with a large number of professional chemists

and physicists whose assistance is acknowledged in the list of general collaborators and in connection with the particular tables or sections involved."—*t.p.*

An indispensable tool for engineers and scientists. Each new ed. is revised, incorporating new material, additional tables. Indexed.
For supplementary volumes *see* ED97, ED112. QD65.H5

Dow Chemical Company. Thermal Research Laboratory. JANAF thermochemical tables. D. R. Stull and H. Prophet, project directors. 2d ed. Wash., Nat. Bureau of Standards, 1971. 1v., various pagings. (National standard reference data series. NSRDS-NBS-37) **ED67**

1st ed. 1964.

Provides, for elements, inorganic compounds, and simple organic compounds, "thermodynamic reference data of the highest quality and timeliness."—*Pref.* Filing order of tables is according to the modified Hill indexing system. An index to the filing order is given before the tables. QC100.U573

Gardner, William. Chemical synonyms and trade names; a dictionary and commercial handbook containing over 35,000 definitions. 8th ed. rev. and enl. by Edward I. Cooke and Richard W. I. Cooke. West Palm Beach, Fla., CRC Pr.; Oxford, Technical Pr., 1978. 769p. **ED68**

1st ed. 1924.

Brief definitions; British spelling; cross references. TP9.G28

Gordon, Arnold J. and **Ford, Richard A.** The chemist's companion: a handbook of practical data, techniques, and references. N.Y., Wiley, [1972]. 537p. il. **ED69**

Information is presented in sections for: (1) Properties of molecular systems; (2) Properties of atoms and bonds; (3) Kinetics and energetics; (4) Spectroscopy; (5) Photochemistry; (6) Chromatography; (7) Experimental techniques; (8) Mathematical and numerical information; (9) Miscellaneous. Indexed. QD65.G64

Haynes, Williams. Chemical trade names and commercial synonyms: a dictionary of American usage. 2d ed. rev. and enl. Princeton, N.J., Van Nostrand, 1955. 466p. **ED70**

1st ed. 1951.

Not a dictionary of chemical terms, but of trade names, with explanation of usage. TP9.H3

Hazards in the chemical laboratory. [3d ed.]. Ed. by L. Bretherick. London, Royal Soc. of Chemistry, [1981]. 567p. il. **ED71**

1st ed. 1971. Supersedes *Laboratory handbook of toxic agents,* 1st ed. 1960.

Publisher formerly called Chemical Soc.

Includes chapters on Safety planning and management, Fire protection, Reactive chemical hazards, Chemical hazards and toxicology, Health care and first aid, Precautions against radiation. The principal chapter, Hazardous chemicals, is a listing in alphabetical order of over 480 flammable, explosive, corrosive and/or toxic substances or groups of substances commonly used in chemical laboratories; entries include description of the substance, solubility, toxic and hazardous effects, first aid recommendations, fire-fighting procedures, and spillage disposal methods. Cross references. Includes an index to topics in the narrative chapters. QD51.H35

Keller, Roy A., ed. Basic tables in chemistry. N.Y., McGraw-Hill, [1967]. 400p. il. **ED72**

Limited to data tables, except for the introduction to the section on general mathematical information. Other sections: four place tables for quick reference; miscellaneous numerical tables; general information; chemical nomenclature (including a short glossary of organic nomenclature); analytical chemistry; thermal and electrochemical data. Some tables are reprinted from *Lange's Handbook of chemistry* (below). QD65.K34

Lange, Norbert Adolph. Lange's Handbook of chemistry. Ed.: John A. Dean. 13th ed. N.Y., McGraw-Hill, [1985]. 1v., various pagings. il. **ED73**

1st ed. 1934; 1st–10th eds. had title *Handbook of chemistry.*

A standard reference source for both the student and the professional chemist. Sections for mathematics, general information and conversion tables, atomic and molecular structure, inorganic chemistry, analytical chemistry, electrochemistry, organic chemistry, spectroscopy, thermodynamic properties, physical properties, and miscellaneous. Indexed.   QD65.L36

Linke, William F. Solubilities, inorganic and metal organic compounds; a compilation of solubility data from the periodical literature. 4th ed. Wash., Amer. Chemical Soc., 1958–65. 2v.   **ED74**

Publisher varies.

"A revision and continuation of the compilation originated by Atherton Seidell."—*title page.* 3d ed. 1940–41; suppl., 1952.

Arranged in the form of short data tables; each table is preceded by a brief evaluation of the data taken from the original literature. All of the numerical values were taken from publications covered by *Chemical abstracts.*

"Elements are listed alphabetically by their chemical symbol, and their compounds are listed alphabetically according to the chemical symbols of their anions or radicals."—*Pref.* Subject and author indexes for both volumes in v.2.

Often cited as "Seidell's Solubilities."   QD66.L5

Manufacturing Chemists' Association. Guide for safety in the chemical laboratory. 2d ed. N.Y., Van Nostrand, [1972]. 505p.   **ED75**

Intends "to offer only a starting point in the solution of laboratory safety problems. However, it will be found of considerable assistance in setting up safety programs for schools and industrial or institutional laboratories."—*Foreword.* Appendix contains numerous tables; subject index.   QD51.M349

Meites, Louis, ed. Handbook of analytical chemistry. N.Y., McGraw-Hill, [1963]. lv., various pagings. il.   **ED76**

In 15 sections, each with a detailed table of contents. Descriptive material readily available elsewhere has been omitted. Three sections are "primarily intended to aid in selecting an analytical procedure to meet the requirements of a specific problem." The remainder of the book "presents the fundamental data that characterize the behaviors of different substances toward the techniques of separation and measurement most widely used in chemical analysis, and also outlines the most important and most reliable of the analytical methods and procedures based on them."—*Pref.*
                                                        QD71.M37

Merck index; an encyclopedia of chemicals, drugs, and biologicals. 10th ed. Martha Windholz, ed. Rahway, N.J., Merck, 1983. 1v., various pagings. il.   **ED77**

1st ed. 1889. Subtitle varies.

For this edition, "without abandoning the original purpose of covering organic and inorganic chemicals, and drugs marketed worldwide, The Merck Index has been broadened in scope to incorporate more information on biochemistry, pharmacology, toxicology and metabolism and to treat a range of topics related to agriculture and the environment."—*Pref.* The number of substances treated remains approximately 10,000; a table lists the 500 or so substances deleted from this edition to make room for new entries, referring the reader to the 9th ed. (1976). Entries give formulas, alternate names, physical properties, uses, toxicity data, journal and patent references. A separate table gives Chemical Abstracts Service names and Registry Numbers. There are miscellaneous tables of abbreviations, isotopes, standard solutions, conversion factors, prescription notation, alchemical symbols used in biology and botany, etc. Includes a formula index and a detailed cross index of alternate names.   RS356.M4

Moscow. Vsesoiuznyi Institut Nauchnoi i Tekhnicheskoi Informatsii. Solubilities of inorganic and organic compounds. Ed. by Henry Stephen and T. Stephen. London, N.Y., Pergamon, 1963–[79]. 3v. in 7. il.   **ED78**

Added title page in Russian. Translation of *Spravochnik po rastrorimosti.*

Contents: v.1, pts.1–2, Binary systems; v.2, pt.1, Ternary systems; v.2, pt.2, Ternary and multicomponent systems; v.3 in 3v., Ternary and multicomponent systems of inorganic substances.

Contains tables of data without critical evaluation.
                                                        QD543.M7213

The NBS tables of chemical thermodynamic properties. Selected values for inorganic and C_1 and C_2 organic substances in SI units. [By] Donald D. Wagman [and others]. [N.Y.], [Amer. Institute of Physics], [1982]. 392p. (Journal of physical and chemical reference data, v.11, 1982, suppl. 2)
                                                        ED79

"Published by the American Chemical Society and the American Institute of Physics for the National Bureau of Standards."—*t.p.*

A new ed. of NBS Technical Note 270, *Selected values of chemical thermodynamic properties,* issued in 8 pts., 1965–81; that publication in turn superseded NBS Circular 500, 1952, of the same title.

Provides recommended values of chemical thermodynamic properties. Includes careful discussion of the process used to evaluate the data.

Sax, Newton Irving. Dangerous properties of industrial materials. 6th ed. N.Y., Van Nostrand Reinhold, [1984]. 3124p. il.   **ED80**

1st ed. 1957.

Five signed chapters on various aspects of hazardous materials, including references, are followed by an alphabetical list of nearly 20,000 materials. Entries give synonyms, molecular formula and molecular weight, toxicity information including bibliographic references by CODEN, hazard information, reference to review articles by CODEN, status with various government agencies if applicable, Chemical Abstracts Service Registry Number, and NIOSH (National Institute for Occupational Safety and Health) Number. Most entries are brief paragraphs; a few, such as D.D.T., run to several pages. Includes an index to the nearly 50,000 synonyms listed in the main section, and a listing of the references corresponding to the CODENs cited.   T55.3.H3S3

Steere, Norman V., comp. CRC handbook of laboratory safety. 2d ed. Cleveland, Ohio, Chemical Rubber Co., [1971]. 854p. il.   **ED81**

Intends "to provide convenient information for hazard recognition and control."—*Pref.* Specialists have contributed sections dealing with particular classes of hazards. Attention is given to such relatively recent hazards as those from radioactive sources, high-energy materials, plasma torches, lasers, and cryogenics.
                                                        QD51.S88

Szymanski, Herman A. and **Erickson, Ronald E.** Infrared band handbook. 2d ed. rev. and enl. N.Y., IFI/Plenum, 1970. 2v. il.   **ED82**

1st ed. and supplements, 1963–66.

Includes all the data in the 1st ed. and its supplements, plus much additional material. Entries are arranged in the order of ascending wave number and subarranged according to decreasing band strength. Each page contains data for 20 compounds, usually with structural formulas. No infrared spectra are given. Index for both parts in last volume; entries refer to wave numbers, not pages.
                                                        QC457.S983

Table of molecular weights; a companion volume to the Merck index, 9th edition. Rahway, N.J., Merck, 1978. 257p.
                                                        ED83

Martha Windholz, Susan Budavari, Margaret Noether Fertig and Georg Albers-Schönberg, eds.

"The book contains high-resolution molecular weights, arranged in ascending order associated with empirical formulae, compound names, and monograph numbers under which the specific compounds are listed in *The Merck Index.* We hope that this volume used with the *The Merck Index* will serve as an important tool in making the identification of chemical compounds easier."—*Pref.*
                                                        RS57.T2

Welcher, Frank Johnson. Chemical solutions; reagents useful to the chemist, biologist, and bacteriologist. N.Y., Van Nostrand, 1942. 404p. (Reissued 1966)   **ED84**

"The purpose . . . is to collect in one place for convenient reference the methods for preparing those solutions most frequently required by the chemist."—*Pref.* Usually gives for each solution: the use, procedure for use, substances which interfere, sensitivity of the reagents, remarks, and literature reference. Alphabetical arrangement according to the most commonly known name. Cross references. The index classifies the solutions according to their use.

QD77.W4

Style manuals

American Chemical Society. Handbook for authors of papers in American Chemical Society publications. 3d ed. Wash., Amer. Chemical Soc., 1978. 122p. il.   **ED85**

1st ed. (1965) entitled: *Handbook for authors of papers in the research journals of the American Chemical Society;* 2d ed. (1967) entitled: *Handbook for authors of papers in the journals of the American Chemical Society.*

A manual on manuscript preparation, giving information on preferred use of terms, illustrations, presentation of data, and typing of final copy. Includes a section on the editorial process.   T11.A4

INORGANIC

Comprehensive inorganic chemistry. Editorial board: J. C. Bailar, Jr. [and others]. [Oxford], Pergamon Pr., [1973]. 5v. il.   **ED86**

Designed to fill the gap between single-volume works and the multivolume sets found only in larger libraries. "It was envisaged that the treatise would be of service to a wide range of readers many of whom would not be professional chemists. Convenience for all classes of reader was of paramount importance so that if a conflict arose between brevity and ease of use, the latter was preferred."—*Pref.* Each chapter by a specialist. Bibliographic footnotes. v.1–4 are indexed individually, and there is a master index to the set in v.5. All indexes cover subjects only.   QD151.2.C64

Gmelins Handbuch der anorganischen Chemie. 8. Aufl. Hrsg. von der Deutschen Chemischen Gesellschaft, bearb. von R. J. Meyer, unter beratender Mitwirkung von Franz Peters. Berlin, Springer Verlag, 1924– . v.1– . (In progress)   **ED87**

Publisher varies.

Earlier editions by Leopold Gmelin.

Volumes published since 1981 have title *Gmelin handbook of inorganic chemistry.*

A monumental work which attempts to include all inorganic compounds ever described, with references to the original articles. The material is critically evaluated according to current knowledge. Volumes are not published in numerical sequence. Tables of contents and paragraph headings in English have been used for a number of years. From 1981 most articles have appeared in English.   QD151.G522

—— Alphabetische Folge zur Systematik der Sachverhalte. Weinheim, Verlag Chemie, 1959. 109p.

—— Ergänzungswerk. Berlin, Springer Verlag, 1970– . v.1– . (In progress)

Publisher varies.

This supplementary series is being compiled on a selective basis; some articles appear in English.

—— Index. Formula index. Berlin, N.Y. Springer Verlag, 1975–80. 12v.

Covers all volumes of the main series that had appeared up to the end of 1974, and of the suppl. that had appeared up to the end of 1973.

—— —— 1st Supplement. Berlin, N.Y. Springer Verlag, 1983–85. v.1–4. (In progress)

Continues indexing from the period covered by the *Formula index* up to the end of 1979. Will consist of 8v.; now being prepared with extensive use of computers to allow speedier publication of cumulations in the future.

International Union of Pure and Applied Chemistry. Commission on the Nomenclature of Inorganic Chemistry. Nomenclature of inorganic chemistry. 2d ed. N.Y., Pergamon, [1971]. 110p.   **ED88**

1st ed. 1959.

Also published as v.28, no.1 of *Pure and applied chemistry.*

"Definitive rules 1970."—*t.p.*

Contains a preamble and 11 chapters, each with numbered rules; tables of prefixes or affixes, ion and radical names are included in an appendix. Indexed.   QD7.I58

Mellor, Joseph William. A comprehensive treatise on inorganic and theoretical chemistry. London, N.Y., Longmans, 1922–37. 16v. il.   **ED89**

Detailed treatment of the elements and their compounds. Extensive bibliographies. Sequence of elements discussed follows the periodic table. Indexes in each volume; complete index in v.16.

—— —— v.II, Supplement I–III. London, N.Y., Longmans, [1956–63]. 3v.

—— —— v.V, Supplement I, pt.A– . London, N.Y., Longmans, [1980]– . (In progress)

—— —— v.VIII, Supplement I–III. [London], Longmans, [1964–71]. 3v.

The supplements purposely omit theoretical aspects. Recent developments in the literature are presented, together with an evaluation of the work.   QD31.M52

ORGANIC

Beilstein, Friedrich. Handbuch der organischen Chemie. 4. Aufl. Die Literatur bis 1. Januar 1910 umfassend, hrsg. von der Deutschen Chemischen Gesellschaft, bearb. von Bernhard Prager und Paul Jacobson, unter ständiger Mitwirkung von Paul Schmidt und Dora Stern. . . . Berlin, Springer, 1918–40. v.1–31. tables.   **ED90**

Editors vary.

This monumental compilation, the most important reference work in organic chemistry, provides a thorough summary of published data on organic compounds. The fourth supplement for 1950–59 (*see* below) is still in progress. Subject and formula indexes for the main work and the first two supplements are in v.28–29 of suppl. 2.

The 3d ed. (1893–99) is frequently referred to in Richter's *Lexikon* (ED113). The 4th ed. has been much enlarged, and its content modified. The general plan of arrangement is given in the *System der organischen Verbindungen* (ED92) and in Huntress (ED91). Another description may be found in Mellon's *Chemical publications* (ED5).   QD251.B4

—— —— I. Ergänzungswerk, die Literatur von 1910–1919 umfassend, hrsg. von der Deutschen Chemischen Gesellschaft, bearb. von Friedrich Richter. Berlin, Springer, 1928–38. 27v.

—— —— II. Ergänzungswerk, die Literatur von 1920–1929 umfassend. . . . Berlin, Springer, 1941–57. v.1–29$^{1–3}$.

—— —— III. Ergänzungswerk, die Literatur von 1930–1949 umfassend, hrsg. vom Beilstein-Institut für Literatur der Organischen Chemie. Berlin, Springer, 1958–74. v.1–16.

—— —— III und IV. Ergänzungswerk, die Literatur von 1930–1959 umfassend, hrsg. vom Beilstein-Institut für Literatur der Organischen Chemie. Berlin, N.Y., Springer, 1974–85. Bd.17–27.

Beginning with v.17, the 3d and 4th suppls. are combined in order to relieve some of the delay in coverage of the literature.

———— ———— IV. Ergänzungswerk, die Literatur von 1950 bis 1959 umfassend, hrsg. vom Beilstein-Institut für Literatur der Organischen Chemie. Bearb. von Hans G. Boit. Berlin, Springer, 1972– . Bd.1– . (In progress)

———— ———— V. Supplementary series, covering the literature from 1960–79, comp. by the Beilstein-Institut für Literatur der Organischen Chemie . . . Executive ed., Reiner Luckenbach. Berlin, N.Y., Springer, 1984– . v.17– . (In progress)

Title appears as *Beilstein handbook of organic chemistry*.

Volumes of the 5th suppl. are in English. Publication began with v.17–27 (heterocyclic compounds) because "an extensive survey . . . indicated a clear preference amongst users for information about these compounds. Publication of v.1–16 . . . will be undertaken as soon as possible."—*Foreword*.

———— ———— Gesamtregister für das Hauptwerk und die Ergänzungswerke I, II, III und IV. Die Literatur bis 1959 umfassend . . . Sachregister. Berlin, N.Y., Springer, 1975– . Bd.1– . (In progress)

Subject indexes, volume-by-volume for the main work and first 4 suppls.

———— ———— Gesamtregister für das Hauptwerk und die Ergänzungswerke I, II, III und IV. Die Literatur bis 1959 umfassend . . . Formelregister. Berlin, N.Y., Springer, 1975– . Bd.1– . (In progress)

Formula indexes, volume-by-volume for the main work and first 4 suppls.

Huntress, Ernest Hamlin. A brief introduction to the use of Beilstein's Handbuch der organischen Chemie. 2d ed. rev. N.Y., Wiley, 1938. 44p. **ED91**

A systematic presentation using rules and examples to explain the method of classification used in the 4th ed. of Beilstein (above). No index. QD251.B43

Deutsche Chemische Gesellschaft. System der organischen Verbindungen; ein Leitfaden für die Benutzung von Beilsteins Handbuch der organischen Chemie. . . . Berlin, Springer, 1929. 246p. **ED92**

An explanation of the arrangement used in Beilstein (ED90). Includes a detailed listing of system numbers.

Weissbach, Oskar. The Beilstein guide, a manual for the use of Beilstein's Handbuch der Organischen Chemie. Berlin, N.Y., Springer Verlag, 1976. 95p. il. **ED93**

Gives the system of rules for the arrangement of compounds in Beilstein (ED90). QD251.B43

Comprehensive heterocyclic chemistry. The structure, reactions, synthesis and uses of heterocyclic compounds. Editorial board: Alan R. Katritzky, chairman; Charles W. Rees, co-chairman. Oxford & N.Y., Pergamon, [1984]. 8v. il. **ED94**

Contents: v.1, Introduction, nomenclature, review literature, biological aspects, industrial uses, less-common heteroatoms; v.2, Six-membered rings with one nitrogen atom; v.3, Six-membered rings with oxygen, sulfur or two or more nitrogen atoms; v.4, Five-membered rings with one oxygen, sulfur or nitrogen atom; v.5, Five-membered rings with two or more nitrogen atoms; v.6, Five-membered rings with two or more oxygen, sulfur or nitrogen atoms; v.7, Small and large rings; v.8, Author, subject, ring and data indexes.

Signed, authoritative articles include literature references. QD400.C65

Comprehensive organic chemistry. The synthesis and reactions of organic compounds. Editorial board: Sir Derek Barton, Chairman; W. David Ollis, deputy chairman. Oxford & N.Y., Pergamon, 1979. 6v. il. **ED95**

Contents: v.1, Stereochemistry, hydrocarbons, halo compounds,

oxygen compounds; v.2, Nitrogen compounds, carboxylic acids, phosphorus compounds; v.3, Sulphur selenium, silicon, boron, organometallic compounds; v.4. Heterocyclic compounds; v.5, Biological compounds; v.6, Author, formula, subject, reagent, reaction indexes.

Signed, authoritative articles include literature references. ZD245.C65

Comprehensive organometallic chemistry. The synthesis, reactions and structures of organometallic compounds. Ed., Sir Geoffrey Wilkinson; deputy ed., F. Gordon A. Stone. Oxford & N.Y., Pergamon, [1982]. 9v. il. **ED96**

Each of the first 7v. contains signed, authoritative articles, including tabular data and literature references, on the organic compounds of specific metals. v.8 contains articles on special topics such as the use of various organometallics in organic synthesis, polymer supported catalysts, etc. v.9 contains subject, author, and formula indexes, an index of structures determined by diffraction methods, and an index of review articles and books. QD411.C65

CRC handbook of data on organic compounds. Robert C. Weast and Melvin J. Astle, eds. Boca Raton, Fla., CRC Press, [1985]. 2v. il. **ED97**

The main body of this work is an alphabetical listing of 24,700 compounds, each of which is assigned a reference number (HODOC number). Entries include synonyms, Beilstein number, Chemical Abstracts Service Registry Number, refractive index, molecular weight, molecular formula, melting and boiling points, density, crystalline form, color, specific rotation, and solvents. This listing is followed by a table arranged by HODOC number giving references for IR, UV, NMR, and mass spectra found in standard compilations, another table arranged by HODOC number giving structural formulas, and tables giving melting points and boiling points in one degree increments with corresponding HODOC numbers. Includes formula index. QD257.7.C73

Dictionary of organic compounds. 5th ed. N.Y. & London, Chapman & Hall, [1982]. 7v. il. **ED98**

1st ed. 1934.

This edition is the most radical and comprehensive revision of the publication ever undertaken. Entries are included for fundamental organic compounds of simple structures, compounds of widespread industrial or commercial value, important natural products, compounds frequently encountered as solvents, reagents or starting materials, and other compounds of particular interest because of their chemical, structural, or biological properties. Arranged alphabetically by "DOC Name" (the name which, in the opinion of the editors, is most likely to be known by most readers), entries also include synonyms considered useful or important. Names used by Chemical Abstracts Service during the 8th and 9th Collective Index periods are labeled with suffixes 8CI and 9CI; names recommended by various national or international organizations are also labeled. Information on derivatives is frequently included under the entry for the parent compound.

Entries include constitution, physical and chemical properties, use, and bibliographic references; this new edition also includes hazard and toxicity information and Chemical Abstracts Service Registry Numbers. A name index, listing in alphabetical order all "DOC Names" and synonyms contained in the main work makes up v.6.; v.7 consists of a molecular formula index, a heteroatom index to the formulae of compounds containing atoms other than C, H, O, N, or halogens, and a CAS Registry Number index.

Kept up-to-date by:

———— Supplement, 1st– . N.Y. & London, Chapman & Hall, [1983]– . Annual.

Contains new and updated entries derived from the primary literature of the preceding year. The second and subsequent supplements have cumulative indexes derived from the entries in all the supplements. QD246.D5

Dictionary of organometallic compounds. N.Y. & London, Chapman & Hall, [1984]. 3v. il. **ED99**

Complements the *Dictionary of organic compounds* (above) by providing, for organometallics, the same types of information as that work supplies for organic compounds.

This work "is divided into element sections; within each section the arrangement of entries is in order of molecular formula according to the Hill convention (i.e., C, then H, then other elements in alphabetical sequence of element symbol . . .). There is a section for every element except for the halogens, the noble gases, unstable radioactive elements for which no organometallic compounds have been well characterised, and the following: H, C, N, O, P, S, Se, and Te. (Entries for organic compounds containing only these elements are included in the companion . . . *Dictionary of organic compounds.*) The entries for compounds which contain more than one type of metal atom are printed in full in all relevant sections, thus obviating the need for cross-references."—*Introd.*

Each element section begins with a brief description of physical properties, availability, analysis, handling, and toxicity of the element, with the name of the element in French, German, Spanish, Italian, Russian, and Japanese, plus references. Longer element sections also include a structure index with molecular structures displayed for rapid location. Each entry is numbered. Entries include names of compounds as reported in the literature, and *Chemical abstracts* names; the latter are identified by suffixes 8CI, 9CI, or 10CI depending on which collective index period they correspond to. Chemical Abstracts Service Registry Numbers are also given. American spelling is used for all chemical names. Entries include structural formulae and stereochemical description as appropriate, physical and chemical information, use, hazard and toxicity information, and bibliographic references.

v.3 contains a name index listing every compound name or synonym; a molecular formula index of all molecular formulas including derivatives, in Hill convention order; and a Chemical Abstracts Service Registry Number index. All indexes refer to the entry number.

To be kept up to date by an annual supplement.   QD411.D53

Dub, Michael, ed. Organometallic compounds: methods of synthesis, physical constants and chemical reactions. [2d ed.] N.Y., Springer Verlag, 1966–68. 3v.   **ED100**

1st ed. 1961.

Contents: v.1, Compounds of transition metals; v.2, Compounds of germanium, tin and lead, including biological activity and commercial application; v.3, Compounds of arsenic, antimony, and bismuth.

Presented as a "comprehensive, non-critical source of information concerning organometallic compounds. The scope is limited to the compounds containing at least one carbon-metal bond. The information includes methods of preparation, properties, chemical reactions and applications."—*Pref.*   QD411.D82

————— ————— Formula index; covering the literature from 1937 to 1964. N.Y., Springer Verlag, 1969. 343p.

————— ————— First supplement, covering the literature from 1965 to 1968. N.Y., Springer Verlag, 1973–75. 3v.

Elsevier's Encyclopaedia of organic chemistry, ed. by E. Josephy and F. Radt. Berlin, Springer Verlag, 1940–69. 3v. in 12; 1 suppl. in 8v. il.   **ED101**

Publisher varies.

Attempts to present all known facts on the chemical, physical, and physiological properties of organic compounds. Covers the literature up to and including 1936 or 1946, and, in certain cases, the literature up to the date a particular volume went to press. Originally planned to be in 20v., with general subject and formula indexes. However, v.1–11 (Series I and II) were never published. Series III began with v.12 (publ. in 12 pts.), followed by v.13–14 and 8 supplements to v.14.   QD251.E4

Fieser, Louis Frederick and **Fieser, Mary.** Fieser and Fieser's Reagents for organic synthesis. N.Y., Wiley, [1967–84]. 11v. il.   **ED102**

v.1–7 had title *Reagents for organic synthesis,* some with order of authors reversed. v.7 is the last with Louis Fieser as co-author.

Published approximately annually since v.7.

v.1 describes more than 1,000 reagents of use to organic chemists.

Reagents are listed alphabetically, with structural formula, molecular weight, physical constants, and preferred methods of preparation given for each. Bibliographic references are included. Subsequent volumes describe additional reagents and add new information and references for reagents previously described. Each volume has author and subject indexes.   QD262.F5

Handbook of organometallic compounds. Ed.: Nobue Hagihara [and others]. N.Y., Benjamin, 1968. 1044p. il.   **ED103**

"The principal part of this book consists of data and includes the organic compounds of both nontransition and transition metals. Preceding each section of tables is a short descriptive section on general properties of the group of metals under discussion."—*Pref.* Pt.II is a glossary of terms.   QD411.Y8313

Index of reviews in organic chemistry. London, Royal Soc. of Chemistry (distr. in U.S. by American Chem. Soc.), 1971– . Annual.   **ED104**

Publisher formerly named Chemical Soc.

Originally prepared for internal use at Imperial Chemical Industries in 1959, this publication has developed into a continuing series. Cumulation issued in 1971 supersedes all previous issues; a second cumulation issued in 1977 covers the literature 1971–May 1976. The 1979 suppl. (publ. 1980) covers May 1976–1978; 1981 suppl. covers 1979–November 1980. A volume covering 1981–82 was issued in 1983; from 1984 the publication has been annual, covering the literature of the previous year.

Through the 1981 suppl., arranged in three sections: articles on individual compounds or classes of compounds; articles on "name reactions"; articles on specific chemical processes or phenomena. Subsequent issues have omitted the section on "name reactions." Covers journals, books, monographs, technical reports, and conference proceedings.   QD291.I523

Index to reviews, symposia volumes and monographs in organic chemistry. 1940/60–1963/64. N.Y., Pergamon, 1962–65. 3v.   **ED105**

Ed. by Norman Kharasch and others.

Contents: v.1, 1940–60. 345p.; v.2, 1961–62. 260p.; v.3, 1963–64. 326p.

Each volume in three divisions: (1) Reviews in journals and periodic publications; (2) Reviews in symposia, collective volumes and non-periodical publications; (3) Monographs on organic chemistry. In the first two divisions the arrangement is by periodical or monograph, giving complete contents for each volume. The third section omits contents but includes full bibliographic information. Entries limited to French, German, English, and Russian (if an English translation is readily available). Author and subject indexes.   Z5524.O8.I5

International Union of Pure and Applied Chemistry. Commission on the Nomenclature of Organic Chemistry. Nomenclature of organic chemistry. 4th ed. Oxford & N.Y., Pergamon, 1979. 559p. il.   **ED106**

Prep. for publ. by J. Rigaudy and S. P. Klesney.

1st ed. 1958; 3d ed. 1971.

Contains 4th ed. of Sections A and B, 3d ed. of Section C, 1st ed. of Sections D, E, F, H.

Contents: Section A, Hydrocarbons; Section B, Fundamental heterocyclic systems; Section C, Characteristic groups containing carbon, hydrogen, oxygen, nitrogen, halogen, sulfur, selenium and/or tellurium; Section D, Organic compounds containing elements that are not exclusively carbon, hydrogen, oxygen, nitrogen, halogen, sulfur, selenium and tellurium; Section E, stereochemistry; Section F, General principles for the naming of natural products and related compounds; Section H, Isotopically modified compounds.   QD291.I57

Krauch, Helmut and **Kunz, Werner.** Organic name reactions: a contribution to the terminology of organic chemistry, biochemistry and theoretical organic chemistry. Tr. from the 2d rev. German ed. (with addendum) by John M. Harkin. N.Y., Wiley, 1964. 620p.   **ED107**

Translation of the authors' *Namenreaktionen der organischen Chemie*.

Contains more than 500 reactions named for the discoverers and 15 reactions given title entry. Each reaction is explained in words, together with an equation, reaction conditions, and several literature citations. Entry length varies from one-half page to three pages. Author index includes persons identified with name reactions as well as authors mentioned in literature references. Subject index.
QD291.K713

Methoden der organischen Chemie (Houben-Weyl). 4. völlig neu gestaltete Aufl. Hrsg. von Eugen Müller. Stuttgart, Thieme Verlag, 1952–85. 15v. in 64 (incomplete); Suppl. to v.1–5 in 6v. il. (In progress)   **ED108**

1st ed. 1908–10.
The work of many specialists and a standard reference in the field. Discusses methods of preparation in terms of classes of compounds. The first 4v. treat techniques and methods. Each volume has its own index; a comprehensive index is promised.   QD258.M44

Molecular structures and dimensions. Utrecht, Bohn, Scheltema & Holkema; distr. in U.S.A. by Polycrystal Book Service, Pittsburgh, 1970– , v.1– . Annual.   **ED109**

"Published for the Crystallographic Data Centre Cambridge and the International Union of Crystallography."—*t.p.*
Ed. by Olga Kennard, David G. Watson, Frank H. Allen and Stella M. Weeds.
A classified bibliography of organic and organometallic crystal structures, with author, formula, and transition metal indexes. Indexing both by standard formula and permuted formula; beginning with v.8 includes a KWIC index of compound names. v.1 and v.2 cover the literature from 1935–69; v.3, 1969–71; v.4, 1971–72; subsequent volumes cover the literature of a 12-month period beginning in mid-year, after the pattern of v.4.   Z5524.C8M6

———— Guide to the literature 1935–1976; organic and organometallic crystal structures. Ed. by Olga Kennard, Frank H. Allen and David G. Watson. Utrecht, Bohn, Scheltema & Holkema, [1977]. 1v., various pagings.

Includes KWIC indexes of compound names for organic and organometallic compounds, molecular formula index, permuted formula index, and author index citing entries in *Molecular structures and dimensions,* v.1–8; also an index arranged by those entry numbers and giving the journal citation from which the entry was taken.

Pouchert, Charles J. The Aldrich library of infrared spectra. 3d ed. [Milwaukee], Aldrich Chemical Co., [1981]. 1867p. il.   **ED110**

1st ed. 1970.
". . . it is . . . the intention of this book to present a large number of spectra on each of the important organic functional groups along with a short written description and graphic representation of their spectral features for the purpose of review by the average chemist who is not a specialist in infrared spectroscopy."—*Pref.* Compounds are grouped by category. Includes compound name and molecular formula indexes.   QD96.I5P67

———— The Aldrich library of NMR spectra. 2d ed. [Milwaukee], Aldrich Chemical Co., [1983]. 2v. il.   **ED111**

1st ed. 1974.
A compilation of spectra arranged by chemical class of compounds, "to assist the average chemist who is not a specialist in nmr spectroscopy."—*Pref.* Includes indexes of compound names and molecular formulas.   QD96.N8P68

Rappoport, Zvi. CRC handbook of tables for organic compound identification. 3d ed. Cleveland, Ohio, Chemical Rubber Co., [1967]. 564p.   **ED112**

1st ed. (1960) and 2d ed. (1964) comp. by Max Frankel and others and published under title *Tables for identification of organic compounds.*
Compounds are arranged according to functional group, with subarrangement in order of increasing melting point, boiling point, etc. Includes more than 8,100 parent compounds. Indexed.
QD291.R28

Richter, Max Moritz. Lexikon der Kohlenstoff-Verbindungen. 3. Aufl. Leipzig, Voss, 1910–12. 4v. il.   **ED113**

A formula index to all compounds known to Dec. 31, 1909. Includes more than 144,000 compounds, with references to the literature which describes preparation and properties, but not to purely theoretical papers. References to Beilstein refer to the 3d ed. of the *Handbuch* rather than to the 4th ed. listed above (ED90).
Continued by:

Deutsche Chemische Gesellschaft. Literatur Register der organischen Chemie, geordnet nach M. M. Richters Formelsystem, redigiert von Robert Stelzner. Bd.1–5, 1910/11–1919/21. Leipzig, Verlag Chemie, 1913–26. 5v. (Repr.: Ann Arbor, Mich., Edwards, 1948)   **ED114**

Cited as Stelzner. Publisher varies.
Arranged by formulas in continuation of Richter (above). Each volume covers the literature of from two to three years.
Merged with Index to *Chemisches Zentralblatt* (ED25).
Z5524.O8D47

Sittig, Marshall. Organic chemical process encyclopedia. 2d ed. Park Ridge, N.J., Noyes Development Corp., [1969]. 712p. il.   **ED115**

1st ed. 1967.
Consists of 711 flow sheets showing the manufacture of the major organic chemicals, as of 1969. Petroleum chemicals are emphasized. Included in the standard format for each entry are reaction utilized, a labeled drawing showing feed materials and conditions (catalyst, solvent, temperature, pressure, etc.), major product and uses, co-products where known, and references to one or more patents. No index.   TP690.S56

Sugasawa, Shigehiko and **Nakai, Seijiro.** Reaction index of organic syntheses. [Rev. ed.] Tokyo, Hirokawa; N.Y., Wiley, [1967]. 251p.   **ED116**

All reactions listed in the annual volumes of *Organic syntheses* have been classified into 31 types. No index.   QD262.S87

Synthetic Organic Chemical Manufacturers Association. SOCMA handbook: commercial organic chemical names. [Wash.], Amer. Chemical Soc., 1965. 666p.   **ED117**

"Provides a means by which the chemical composition or structure of 6300 industrial organic compounds can be identified from any of the many names by which they go."—*Introd.*   QD291.S9

University of Cincinnati. Department of Chemistry. Organic Division. The vocabulary of organic chemistry, [by] Milton Orchin [and others]. N.Y., Wiley, [1980]. 609p. il.   **ED118**

"The purpose of this book is to identify the fundamental vocabulary of organic chemistry and then to present concise, accurate definitions, with examples where appropriate, for the words and concepts. . . ."—*Pref.* Arranged in topical chapters; numbered paragraphs within chapters present words and concepts placed in a sequence that makes pedagogical sense to the authors. Where possible, the authors adhere to recognized definitions such as those prescribed in various publications of the International Union of Pure and Applied Chemistry. Includes bibliographic citations. Some cross references. Indexed.   QD291.C55

Utermark, Walther and **Schicke, Walter.** Melting point tables of organic compounds. 2d rev. and supplemented ed. N.Y., Interscience, 1963. 715p.   **ED119**

Original German edition, 1951.
Added title page in German, French, and Russian.
Compounds are arranged in ascending order of melting point. Included with each entry are molecular and structural formulas, Beilstein (ED90) citation, solubility, etc. Column headings are in German. The preface, list of abbreviations, and index of special

terms appear in English, French, German, and Russian. The formula index refers only to the German name.   QD518.U7

HISTORY

Haynes, Williams. American chemical industry: a history. N.Y., Van Nostrand, 1945–54. 6v. il.   **ED120**

Contents: v.1, Background and beginning, 1608–1911; v.2–3, The World War I period, 1912–1922; v.4, The merger era, 1923–1929; v.5, Decade of new products, 1930–1939; v.6, The chemical companies.
Subject and name indexes in each volume.   TP23.H37

Partington, James Riddick. A history of chemistry. London, Macmillan; N.Y., St. Martin's, 1961–70. v.1[1], 2–4. il.   **ED121**

A heavily documented history. v.1, pt.1, covers the theoretical background; v.2–3, the 16th–18th centuries; v.4, the 19th and early 20th centuries. v.1, pt.2, unfinished at the author's death, was to cover the earliest period.   QD11.P28

BIOGRAPHY

American chemists and chemical engineers. Ed. by Wyndham D. Miles. Wash., Amer. Chemical Soc., 1976. 544p.   **ED122**

Contains bibliographical sketches, ranging from a few paragraphs to several pages, of over 500 deceased American chemists and chemical engineers. Biographies cover the period from colonial times to the present; bibliographies of biographical information are included. Index of names mentioned in the biographies.   QD21.A43

The biographical dictionary of scientists, chemists. General ed., David Abbott. N.Y., Peter Redrick, [1983]. 203p. il.   **ED123**

A historical introduction is followed by brief narrative biographies, alphabetically arranged, of living and deceased chemists; no references are included. Brief glossary and an index to topics studied by the biographees.   QD21.B48

Chemical who's who. Ed.1–4, 1928–56. N.Y., Lewis Historical Co., 1928–56. 4v.   **ED124**

Subtitle: Biography in dictionary form of the leaders in chemical industry, research, and education.
Contains a geographical index including some names from countries other than the United States.   TP139.W4

Farber, Eduard. Great chemists. N.Y., Interscience, 1961. 1642p. il.   **ED125**

A collection of more than 100 biographies of famous chemists from ancient times to the 20th century, not including living persons. The essays were written by scholars of the last two centuries, and some have been translated from other languages for this work. Includes bibliographies.   QD21.F35

—— Nobel prize winners in chemistry, 1901–1961. Rev. ed. London & N.Y., Abelard-Schuman, 1963. 341p. il.   **ED126**

1st ed. 1953.
For each person gives a biographical sketch, a description of the prize-winning work, and an estimate of its consequences in theory and practice.   QD21.F37

Nobelstiftelsen, Stockholm. Chemistry. Amsterdam, Elsevier, 1964–73. 4v. il.   **ED127**

Contents: v.1, 1901–21; v.2, 1922–41; v.3, 1942–62; v.4, 1963–70.
Nobel lectures, including presentation speeches and laureates'

biographies. Each volume has a name index, subject index, and an index of biographies.   QD39.N735

Smith, Henry Monmouth. Torchbearers of chemistry; portraits and brief biographies of scientists who have contributed to the making of modern chemistry. N.Y., Academic Pr., [1949]. 270p. il.   **ED128**

A collection of portraits of 223 chemists who have been influential in the history of chemistry, including some contemporary chemists. A short biographical sketch accompanies each portrait. The "Bibliography of biographies" by Ralph E. Oesper, p.263–70, gives further references for each person.   QD21.S55

E E

Earth Sciences

❖This section lists a selection of reference materials in geology, crystallography, hydrology, meteorology, mineralogy, oceanography, paleontology, petrology, seismology, and volcanology. As in the biological sciences section, both scientific and popular works are included, as there is demand in many libraries for popularly written manuals or handbooks on rocks, fossils, etc. Many specialized abstract journals are available in these fields, but only a few of them can be listed here.

GENERAL WORKS

Guides

Hopkins, Stephen T. and **Jones, Douglas E.** Research guide to the arid lands of the world. Phoenix, Ariz., Oryx Pr., 1983. 391p. maps.   **EE1**

A comprehensive 3,199-entry bibliography for interdisciplinary research on countries and geographic areas which contain arid lands. Arrangement is geographical with subject and author indexes. The broad subject coverage includes geology, climatology, hydrology, biology, botany, agriculture, anthropology, urban geography, transportation and other fields.   Z6004.A7H66

Wood, David Norris, ed. Use of earth sciences literature. [Hamden, Conn.], Archon Books, 1973. 459p.   **EE2**

A useful guide covering materials published through 1970, plus selected items through 1972. In addition to discussion of broadly pertinent periodicals, report literature, theses, conference proceedings, reference and review publications, bibliographies, abstracts and indexes, the work treats translation sources, non-Western publications, guides to geological maps, and the literature of specific areas of the geological sciences.   Z6031.W67

Dictionaries and encyclopedias

The Cambridge encyclopedia of earth sciences. Cambridge, Cambridge Univ. Pr., [1982]. 496p. il., maps.   **EE3**

Ed. by David G. Smith.

A collection of long, signed articles written by specialists as surveys of different earth sciences. "Designed to be used as a work of reference . . . but it is also a book that is designed to be picked up and read."—*Introd.* Includes glossary, index, and bibliography.

QE26.2.C35

A dictionary of earth sciences. Ed. by Stella E. Stiegeler. N.Y., Pica; distr. by Universe Books, 1977 [c.1976]. 301p. il. **EE4**

A companion to *A dictionary of life sciences* (EC21) and *A dictionary of physical sciences* (EA116). A handy, easy-to-use, concise dictionary for the earth sciences. QE5.D54

Fairbridge, Rhodes Whitmore, series ed. Encyclopedia of earth sciences. N.Y., Van Nostrand Reinhold, 1966– . il. (In progress) **EE5**

A series of autonomous, single-volume encyclopedias with subject focus. Signed articles with bibliographic references appear in alphabetical arrangement. Numerous cross references, including references to other volumes of the series. Detailed subject indexes.

Volumes published through 1984: v.I, *The encyclopedia of oceanography* (see EE217); v.II, *The encyclopedia of atmospheric sciences and astrogeology* (see EE137); v.III, *The encyclopedia of geomorphology* (see EE6); v.IVA, *The encyclopedia of geochemistry and environmental sciences* (see EE70); v.IVB, *The encyclopedia of mineralogy* (see EE178); v.VI, *The encyclopedia of sedimentology* (see EE71); v.VII, *The encyclopedia of paleontology* (see EE238); v.VIII, *The encyclopedia of world regional geology, part 1, Western Hemisphere (including Antarctica and Australia)* (see EE72); v.XII, *The encyclopedia of soil science, part.1: physics, chemistry, biology, fertility, and technology* (see EH38); v.XIII, *The encyclopedia of applied geology* (see EE73); v.XV, *The encyclopedia of beaches and coastal environments* (see EE13).

Volumes to be published: *The encyclopedia of world regional geology, part 2, Europe and Asia*; *The encyclopedia of structural geology*; *The encyclopedia of field and general geology*; *The encyclopedia of igneous and metamorphic petrology, volcanology, and geothermal resources*; *The encyclopedia of soil science, part 2: morphology, genesis, classification, and geography*; *The encyclopedia of world regional geology, part 3: Africa and the Middle East*; *The encyclopedia of geo-archeology*; *The encyclopedia of snow, ice, and glaciology*; *The encyclopedia of climatology*; *The encyclopedia of geophysics*; *The encyclopedia of stratigraphy*.

—— The encyclopedia of geomorphology. N.Y., Reinhold, [1968]. 1295p. il. (Encyclopedia of earth sciences, ser., v.3) **EE6**

Signed articles, with bibliographies, on the analytic physiography of the earth's surface and closely related topics. The editor notes that in presenting the series, many overlaps have purposely been allowed "because expressed in different language or in a different context the overlap may present an interesting or new viewpoint."—*Pref.* GB10.F3

Gresswell, R. Kay and **Huxley, Anthony Julian.** Standard encyclopedia of the world's rivers and lakes. N.Y., Putnam, [1965]. 384p. il. **EE7**

A companion to Huxley's volumes on mountains (EE8) and on oceans and islands (EE9), with a similar format. GB1203.G73

Huxley, Anthony Julian. Standard encyclopedia of the world's mountains. N.Y., Putnam, [1962]. 383p. il., maps. **EE8**

A popularly written work, arranged alphabetically by name of mountain; gives location, height, dates, and names of first climbers, etc., and a brief description and history. Illustrated with black-and-white and color photographs. Includes a gazetteer and an index.

GB501.H8

—— Standard encyclopedia of the world's oceans and islands. N.Y., Putnam, [1962]. 383p. il., maps. **EE9**

A popularly written work arranged alphabetically by name of ocean or island, giving location; dimensions; etc. (in case of oceans the maximum depth); and a brief description and history. Format is similar to that of the two preceding items. Includes a gazetteer and an index. GB471.H9

International dictionary of geophysics; seismology, geomagnetism, aeronomy, oceanography, geodesy, gravity, marine geophysics, meteorology, the earth as a planet and its evolution. Ed., S. K. Runcorn [and others]. Oxford and N.Y., Pergamon, [1967]. 2v. and map portfolio. il. **EE10**

Includes more than 700 articles contributed by an international roster of some 300 contributors. With the exception of certain brief definitions, entries consist of lengthy articles including bibliographies which refer to both standard and specialized works. An index supplements the dictionary arrangement. QC801.9.I5

McGraw-Hill encyclopedia of the geological sciences. N.Y., McGraw-Hill, 1978. 915p. il. **EE11**

Daniel N. Lapedes, ed. in chief.

Some articles have been taken from the *McGraw-Hill encyclopedia of science and technology* (4th ed. 1977). Covers the broad scope of the geological sciences. An appendix lists the properties of 1,500 mineral species. Subject index. QE5.M29

The planet we live on; illustrated encyclopedia of the earth sciences, ed. by Cornelius S. Hurlbut, Jr. N.Y., Abrams, [1976]. 527p. il. **EE12**

A reference book for the general reader, having short articles in nontechnical language, arranged alphabetically and with cross references. No bibliographies are given. QE5.P55

Schwartz, Maurice L., ed. The encyclopedia of beaches and coastal environments. Stroudsburg, Pa., Hutchinson Ross; distr. by Van Nostrand Reinhold, [1982]. 940p. il., maps. (Encyclopedia of earth sciences, v.15) **EE13**

A survey of the field of coastal studies including the geomorphic, biologic, engineering, and human aspects of the world's coast. Signed articles, with cross references and bibliographies, are arranged alphabetically. Indexed. GB450.4.E53

Handbooks

Deserts of the world; an appraisal of research into their physical and biological environments. Ed. by William G. McGinnies, Bram J. Goldman, [and] Patricia Paylore. [Tucson], Univ. of Arizona Pr., [1968]. 788p. il. **EE14**

A summary and evaluation of the state of knowledge of the characteristics of all deserts of the world, "based upon critical reviews of the published literature augmented by consultations with specialists."—*Foreword.* Discusses climate, geomorphology, surface materials, vegetation, fauna, and groundwater hydrology. Includes extensive bibliographies. GB612.D4

Reeves, Robert G., ed. Manual of remote sensing. Falls Church, Va., Amer. Soc. of Photogrammetry, [1975]. 2v. il. **EE15**

Contents: v.1, Theory, principles and techniques; v.2, Photographic interpretation and applications.

A substantial revision and expansion of the American Society of Photogrammetry's *Manual of photographic interpretation* (1960), also using material from its *Manual of photogrammetry* (3d ed., 1966), *Manual of color aerial photography* (1968), and the periodical *Photogrammetric engineering.* "The two volumes of this manual contain comprehensive treatments of remote-sensing theory, instruments, and techniques and their applications to agricultural, earth, and environmental sciences, natural resources, and engineering."—*Pref.* G70.4.M36

Wedepohl, Karl Hans, ed. Handbook of geochemistry. Berlin, Springer, 1969–72. 2v. in 4. il. **EE16**

v.1 (442p.) is concerned with the "fundamental facts of geochemistry, geophysics and cosmochemistry, together with definitions, methods of evaluation, etc."—*Pref.* v.2 was issued in looseleaf installments, each chapter dealing with a separate element, and giving tables, graphs, text, and references on abundance and various aspects of the chemical and physical properties.   QE515.W42

Atlases

Atlas of landforms. Ed. by H. Allen Curran [and others]. 3d ed. N.Y., Wiley, 1984. 165p. il., maps. 32x38cm.   **EE17**

1st ed. 1966.

An instructional aid illustrating various geomorphic principles and features for introductory courses in earth sciences. Consists of maps and photographs of various land forms, with some explanatory text, in a topical arrangement; includes the lunar surface and submarine topography. Subject index.   G1046.C2A8

Derry, Duncan R. World atlas of geology and mineral deposits. London, Mining Journal Books, 1980. 110p. maps. 25x33cm.   **EE18**

A whole world approach "intended for use of students, travelling amateurs and professional earth scientists."—*Introd.* The first part consists of ten maps intelligible to those with relatively little background in geology. The second part consists of ten land maps of the world with a geological history. Includes suggested readings, sources of additional information, and glossary.   G1046.C5D8

Rand McNally and Co. Our magnificent earth. N.Y., Rand McNally, [1979]. 208p. il., maps. 38cm.   **EE19**

For full information *see* CL327.   G1046.G3R34

GEOLOGY

Guides

Mackay, John Watson. Sources of information for the literature of geology; an introductory guide. [2d ed.] London, Geological Society of London, [1974]. 59p.   **EE20**

1st ed. 1973; the 2d ed. corrects errors in the 1st ed.

"Intended to be a comprehensive listing of all companies and individuals directly connected with, or engaged in, the geophysical exploration for petroleum."—*Foreword.*   QE40.M32

Ward, Dederick C., Wheeler, Marjorie W. and **Bier, Robert A.** Geologic reference sources. Metuchen, N.J., Scarecrow Pr., 1981. 560p.   **EE21**

Subtitle: A subject and regional bibliography of publications and maps in the geological sciences.

1st ed. 1972 by D.C. Ward and M.W. Wheeler. Earlier ed. 1967 by D.C. Ward.

This edition is "completely revised, being over 25 per cent larger . . . with only one-third of the citations carried over."—*Pref.* The general section (with subdivisions for general information sources, current awareness services, bibliography and abstracting services, indexes, encyclopedias, dictionaries, etc.) is followed by a subject section (subdivided as earth science, meteorology, oceanography, mineralogy, petrology, etc.), and a regional section (including maps). Items listed range from introductory works to highly technical ones, and from standard reference works to texts, treatises, and serials. Some brief annotations. Subject and geographic indexes.   Z6031.W35

Bibliography

Annotated bibliography of economic geology. 1928–65. [Urbana, Ill.], Economic Geology Pub. Co., 1929–66. v.1–38. Semiannual.   **EE22**

Compiled by the Bibliographic Staff of the Geological Society of America and prep. under the auspices of GSA and the Society of Economic Geologists. A bibliography, with signed annotations of both book and periodical material in various languages. Covers about 150 periodicals.

Ceased publication.

―――― General index, v.1–25, 1928–54. Urbana, Ill., 1961. 1493p.

Z6033.E4A2

Avnimelech, Moshe A. Bibliography of Levant geology, including Cyprus, Hatay, Israel, Jordania, Lebanon, Sinai and Syria. Jerusalem, Israel Program for Scientific Translations, 1965–69. 2v. map.   **EE23**

v.1 includes about 4,500 items in an author listing, covering the literature from about the years 1250 to 1963, with chronological and subject indexes. v.2 adds another 200 items, largely from the years 1950 to 1968, with some earlier items.   Z6034.N35A9

Belikov, Evgenii Fedorovich. Bibliograficheskii ukazatel' geodezicheskoi literatury za 40 let 1917–1956. Sost., E. F. Belikov. Red., L. S. Khrenov. Moskva, Izd-vo Geodezicheskoi Lit-ry, 1961. 535p.   **EE24**

Books and articles, published in the USSR from 1917 through 1956, on geodesy and related sciences. Some 8,800 items are arranged in 20 topical chapters and further subdivisions. Brief bibliographical identification. Author index.

The period to 1917 is covered by: Z6000.B4

―――― and **Solov'ev, Leonid P.** Bibliograficheskii ukazatel' geodezicheskoi literatury do 1917 g. Moskva, "Nedra," 1971. 272p.   **EE25**

Z6000.B42

Bibliographie des sciences de la terre. Cahiers A–H. Feb. 1968–71. Orléans, Département Documentation, Bureau de Recherches Géologiques et Minières, 1968–71. Monthly.   **EE26**

Supersedes the bibliographical card service of the Bureau de Recherches Géologiques et Minières.

A computer-produced bibliography, international in coverage. Issued in eight monthly sections (*cahiers*): A, Minéralogie, géochimie et géologie extraterrestre; B, Gitologie et économie minière; C, Roches cristallines; D, Roches sédimentaires et géologie marine; E, Stratigraphie, géologie régionale et géologie générale; F, Tectonique et géophysique; G, Hydrogéologie, géologie de l'ingénieur et formations superficielles; H, Paléontologie. Most of these include two or more subsections. There is a separate, annual cumulated index for each section.

Each *cahier* or subsection thereof is in four parts: (1) Index des auteurs (an alphabetical list of authors with reference to entry number in the "Liste des références"); (2) Index-matières (a keyword-in-title index, again with reference to entry number); (3) Index géographique; and (4) Liste des références, which gives the complete citation. Entries in the latter section are numbered consecutively and appear in the order in which they were fed into the computer; periodical titles are given in abbreviated form; language of the article is indicated; French library locations are given.

Ceased publication. Merged in 1972 with parts of the *Bulletin signalétique* (EE28) to form new sections of that publication.

Bibliographie des sciences géologiques, publiée par la Société Géologique de France avec le concours de la Société Française de Minéralogie. 1.–7. année, juil. 1923–29; 2. sér. t.1–26, 1930–55. Paris, Société Géologique de France, 1923–55. Annual.   **EE27**

Ceased publication.

1948–55 published as: Extrait du *Bulletin analytique* du Centre National de la Recherche Scientifique.

A classed bibliography of worldwide coverage, with annual (irregular) author indexes covering materials in various languages.

Continued by: Z6032.B58

France. Centre National de la Recherche Scientifique. Bulletin signalétique. Paris, Centre de Documentation du C.N.R.S., 1956–83. v.17–44.   **EE28**

Continues the Centre's *Bulletin analytique.*

Earth sciences coverage is included in the following sections: 1.pt.: *Mathématiques, astronomie, physique, chimie, sciences de l'ingénieur, sciences de la terre* (1956–60. v.17–21). Subsequently subdivided into sections: Sec.10, Sciences de la terre, I. Minéralogie, géochimie, pétrographie (1961–68. v.22–29); Sec.11, Sciences de la terre, II. Physique du globe, géologie, paléontologie (1961–68. v.22–29). Later subdivided as: Sec.210, Sciences de la terre, I. Minéralogie, géochimie, géologie extraterrestre, pétrographie (1969–70. v.30–31); Sec.214, Sciences de la terre, II. Géologie appliquée (1969–70. v.30–31); Sec.216, Sciences de la terre, III. Géologie, paléontologie (1969–70. v.30–31). Further subdivided as Sec.220–227, then merged into Sec.22, Sciences de la terre (1971–83. v.32–44).

A classed bibliography of worldwide coverage, with brief abstracts in French. Annual author index, but no subject index.

Continued by:

PASCAL thema. T022, Sciences de la terre. Paris, Centre de Documentation Scientifique et Technique dur C.N.R.S., 1984– . v.1– . 10 nos. per yr. **EE29**

●

Bibliography and index of geology exclusive of North America. v.1–32, 1933–1968. Boulder, Colo., Amer. Geological Inst., 1934–69. **EE30**

Imprint varies. Compilers vary.

Frequency varies: v.1–8, annual; v.9–11, biennial; v.12–30, annual; v.31–32, monthly with annual index.

A comprehensive bibliography of articles from the periodicals of many countries dealing with the geology of all parts of the world except North America, thus complementing the *Bibliography of North American geology* (EE32).

Beginning with v.31 (1967), issued as a monthly citation journal with an annual cumulative bibliography and index. No separate volume was published for 1966.

Superseded by: Z6031.G4

Bibliography and index of geology, v.33, no.1– , Jan. 1969– . [Boulder, Colo.], publ. by the Geological Soc. of America in cooperation with the American Geological Inst., 1970– . Monthly with annual cumulation. **EE31**

Represents a change of title for the *Bibliography and index of geology exclusive of North America* (above), and continues its numbering. Coverage includes North American geology. The bibliography is now produced with the use of data-processing equipment. Follows the classed arrangement of the preceding volumes (i.e., v.31–32 of the earlier title); a series of descriptors or keywords is sometimes provided in place of the abstracts which were a feature of v.31–32. Each monthly issue includes author and subject indexes. The annual index is in four parts: pts.1–2 cumulate the bibliography in author arrangement, giving the full bibliographical citation, but omitting the descriptors supplied in the monthly issues; pts.3–4 cumulate the monthly subject indexes, giving authors' names and references to item numbers in the monthly issues.

"Photocomposed from citations in GeoRef, a database produced at the American Geological Institute."—*verso of 1985 t.p.*

Z6081.B57●

Bibliography of North American geology. 1919/28–70. Wash., Govt. Prt. Off., 1931–73. (U.S. Geological Survey. Bull.) Annual. **EE32**

Cumulations issued as follows: 1919–1928, comp. by John M. Nickles; 1929–39, comp. by Emma M. Thom; 1940–49, comp. by Ruth Reece King [and others]. Ceased with volume for 1970.

Represents cumulations of, and since 1950, annual (formerly biennial) supplements published with the same title in the *Bulletin* series.

Each volume consists of a comprehensive bibliography with detailed index, covering the geology of the North American continent, including Greenland, the West Indies and other adjacent islands, Hawaii, Guam, and other island possessions of the United States. *See* above for continuation.

Canada. Geological Survey. Annotated catalogue of and guide to the publications of the Geological Survey, Canada,

1845–1917, by W. F. Ferrier, assisted by Dorothy J. Ferrier. Ottawa, Taché, 1920. 544p. **EE33**

Lists of publications are arranged according to subject, giving citations and some short explanatory notes. Index maps accompany "Finding lists" arranged by province and series. Author arrangement in separate section. Index of publication numbers.

Z6034.C19F3

——— Publications of the Geological Survey of Canada (1917–1952), comp. by Lorne B. Leafloor. Ottawa, Cloutier, 1952. 82p. **EE34**

——— Index of publications of the Geological Survey of Canada (1845–1958), by A. G. Johnston. Ottawa, Dept. of Mines and Technical Surveys, [1961]. 378p. **EE35**

Pt. I lists all publications of the Geological Survey of Canada to the end of 1958, arranged according to series. Pt. II is classified by area. Includes National Topographic System index map.

——— Index of publications, Geological Survey of Canada (1959–1969). [Comp. by Leona R. Mahoney and others] Ottawa, [Information Canada], 1970. 123p. **EE36**

Kept up-to-date by supplements in the Survey's *Papers* series.

——— Index to reports of Geological Survey of Canada from 1927–50, comp. by W. E. Cockfield, E. Hall and J. F. Wright. Ottawa, Dept. of Mines and Technical Surveys, [1962]. 723p. **EE37**

This is the 6th in a series: no.1 covers 1863–84; no.2, 1884–1904; no.3, Separate reports, 1906–10. Summary reports, 1905–16; no.4, Palaeontology reports, 1847–1916; no.5, Memoirs, 1910–26. Bulletins, 1913–26. Summary reports, 1917–26.

Provides in one alphabet an author and subject index to Annual reports, Economic geology series, Geological bulletins, Maps without reports, and Museum bulletins, 1927–50; Geological papers, 1935–50; and Summary reports, 1927–33.

Challinor, John. The history of British geology: a bibliographical study. Newton Abbott, David & Charles; N.Y., Barnes & Noble, [1971]. 224p. **EE38**

In two main sections, the first listing works chronologically by date of publication; the second being a treatment of publications in a thematic context.   QE13.G7C3

Clapp, Jane. Museum publications: a classified list and index of books, pamphlets and other monographs, and of serial reprints. N.Y., Scarecrow Pr., 1962. 2v. **EE39**

Contents: pt.1, Publications in anthropology, archaeology, and art (4,416 publications); pt.2, Publications in biological and earth sciences (9,231 publications).

"A classified bibliography of the publications available from 276 museums in the United States and Canada."—*Foreword.*

Z5051.C5

Corbin, John Boyd, comp. An index of state geological survey publications issued in series. N.Y., Scarecrow Pr., 1965. 667p. **EE40**

Intended as a companion to Clapp's *Museum publications* (above). Includes monographic publications issued in numbered series by the state geological surveys through 1962. Listing is by state, with author and subject indexes.

Continued by: Z6031.C6

——— ——— Supplement, 1963–1980. Metuchen, N.J., Scarecrow Pr., 1982. 449p. **EE41**

Includes Alaska, Hawaii, and South Carolina, as well as older series which were omitted from the initial volume.

Darton, Nelson Horatio. Catalogue and index of contributions to North American geology, 1732–1891. Wash., Govt. Prt. Off., 1896. 1045p. (U.S. Geological Survey. Bull. no.127) **EE42**

An author-subject index in one alphabet. "All composite works are segregated into the separate contributions of individual authors as far as practicable."—*Introd.* Geographic and stratigraphic subject entries are used. Includes both monographs and periodicals.

Deutsche Geologische Gesellschaft, Berlin. Bibliothek. Katalog der Bibliothek, im Auftrage der Gesellschaft bearb. von P. Dienst. Stuttgart, Enke, [1930]. 1161p.   **EE43**

The classified subject catalog, with author index, of an outstanding collection.   Z6035.B51

Faessler, Carl. Cross-index to the geological illustration of Canada. [Quebec, 1947–58] 4 v. in 3. (Université Laval. [Faculté des Sciences] Géologie et Minéralogie. Contribution no. 75, 117, 127)   **EE44**

v.1–2 issued in 1v. without general title.

Contents: v.1–2, Cross-index to the maps and illustrations of the Geological Survey and the Mines Branch (Bureau of Mines) of Canada, 1843–1946 (incl.); v.3, Geological illustrations published by Ontario Department of Mines 1891–1955; v.4, Geological illustrations published by Quebec Department of Mines, 1898–1957.

Publications containing geological illustrations are listed by series, with author and subject indexes.

—————— ——————Supplement, 1946–1956. Cross-index to the geological illustration of Canada. Québec, 1956. 193p. (Contribution no.118)

Supplements v.1–2 of the *Cross-index.*

Geological Society of London. Library. List of geological literature added to the Geological Society's library, [no.1]–37, July, 1894–1934. . . . London, Soc., 1895–1935. Annual.   **EE45**

Title varies.

Not published 1913–19; ceased with issue covering 1934.
      Z6035.G34

Geotitles weekly. v.1, no.1– , July 14, 1969– . London, Geosystems Publications, 1969– .   **EE46**

Publisher varies.

Subtitle (varies): The current awareness service for geoscience.

A classified listing of new publications, international in scope. Author index and serial source index in each issue.   Z6032.G37

Hazen, Robert M. and **Hazen, Margaret H.** American geological literature, 1669 to 1850. Stroudsburg, Pa., Dowden, Hutchinson & Ross, 1980. 431p.   **EE47**

"Conceived as a reference tool for historians of American geology, it includes geology related books, reviews, maps, broadsides, pamphlets, journal articles, and other nonnewspaper sources . . . in the United States."—*Pref.* Lists secondary references used to compile the 11,129 entries which are arranged alphabetically by author, then chronologically. Index includes minerals, places, and broad concepts.   Z6034.U49H39

International catalogue of scientific literature, sec. H, Geology. 1st–14th annual issues, 1901–14. London, 1903–20. 14v.   **EE48**

For full set *see* EA17.

Margerie, Emmanuel de. Catalogue des bibliographies géologiques; rédigé avec le concours des membres de la Commission Bibliographique du Congrès. Paris, Gauthier-Villars, 1896. 733p. (Congrès Géologique International. 5ᵉ session, Wash., 1891; 6ᵉ session, Zürich, 1894)   **EE49**

Covers monographs and serial publications containing bibliographies, published approximately 1726–1895. The first section covers general bibliographies; the rest of the work is arranged by country or region. Author index, but not complete subject indexes.
      Z6031.M32

Mathews, Edward Bennett. Catalogue of published bibliographies in geology, 1896–1920. . . . Wash., Nat. Research Council, 1923. 228p. (Bull. of the Council, v.6, no.5; whole no.36)   **EE50**

Continues, in a somewhat simplified form, the bibliography by

Margerie (above). Arranged by subject with author index. Separate section for personal bibliographies.

Nickles, John Milton. Geologic literature on North America, 1785–1918. Wash., Govt. Prt. Off., 1923–24. 2v. (U.S. Geological Survey. Bull. no. 746, 747)   **EE51**

An author list, with subject index, covering the geology, paleontology, petrology, and mineralogy of the continent of North America and the adjacent islands, Panama, and the Hawaiian Islands. Lists both books and periodical articles; indexes all articles on American geology in more than 500 periodicals, including some foreign journals. A cumulation of the annual bibliographies issued by the Geological Survey.

Continued in part by:

Pestana, Harold R. Bibliography of congressional geology. N.Y., Hafner, 1972. 285p.   **EE52**

Gives full citation to, and indexes all of the geologic documents published from 1818 to 1907 in the "Serial set."   Z6034.U49P47

Richards, Horace Gardiner and **Fairbridge, Rhodes W.** Annotated bibliography of quaternary shorelines, 1945–1964. Philadelphia, Academy of Natural Sciences, 1965. 280p. (Academy of Natural Sciences special pubn. 6)   **EE53**

Prepared for the VII International Congress of the International Association for Quaternary Research (INQUA) meeting at Boulder, Colo., 1965.

About 2,400 articles in geographical groupings with author index. International in coverage; annotations in English.   Z6033.S8R5

—————— —————— Supplement 1965–1969. Philadelphia, Academy, 1970. 240p. (Spec. pubn. 10)

Squire, Jeannette W. and **Eustus, Amber.** Catalogue of translations of Russian papers in geology, solid-earth geophysics and related sciences, [1953]/1961. Wash., 1962. 89p. (Special supplement. International geology review, v.4, no.10, pt.2, Oct. 1962)   **EE54**

"Lists all the publicly available translations . . . of which the American Geological Institute Translations Office has record, covering the period from approximately 1953 through December 1961." —*Pref.* Consists of two mutually exclusive lists: (1) Soviet periodicals translated cover-to-cover; and (2) separate Soviet papers in English translation, arranged by author and with references to sources. Includes "Major-subject index of translations" and "Index of sources."

U.S. Geological Survey. Publications of the Geological Survey, 1879–1961. Wash., Govt. Prt. Off., 1964. 457p.   **EE55**

"A permanent catalog of books, maps, and charts issued by the Geological Survey through December 1961."—*title page.* Supersedes all earlier lists. Citations are arranged by series, with subject, geographic, and author indexes.

Supplemented by an annual listing, 1962– , which cumulates the monthly *New publications of the Geological Survey.*
      Z6034.U49U53

—————— —————— 1962/70– . [Supplement] Wash., 1972– .

The 1962/70 volume is a permanent supplement superseding the annual issues for that period.

—————— **Library.** Catalog of the United States Geological Survey Library. Boston, G. K. Hall, 1964. 25v.   **EE56**

Reproduces the cards from the Library's catalog. Scope of the collection—the largest of its kind—makes this a valuable tool for bibliographic verification.   Z881.U597

U.S. Library of Congress. Science and Technology Division. United States IGY bibliography, 1953–1960, comp. by Frank M. Marson and Janet R. Terner. (NAS/NRC Pubn. 1087) Wash., Nat. Academy of Sciences–Nat. Research Council, 1963. 391p. (World Data Center A. IGY General Report, no.18)   **EE57**

Subtitle: An annotated bibliography of United States contributions to the IGY and IGC (1957–1959).

Abstract bibliography of works covering United States participation in the International Geophysical Year and International Geophysical Cooperation–1959, from the formation of the IGY program to its scientific results. Topical arrangement, with author and subject indexes.

Dissertations

Chronic, John and **Chronic, Halka.** Bibliography of theses written for advanced degrees in geology and related sciences at universities and colleges in the United States and Canada through 1957, by John Chronic and Halka Chronic and Petroleum Research Corp. Boulder, Colo., Pruett Pr., 1958. 1v., unpaged.   **EE58**

An alphabetical author listing of 11,091 graduate theses written in 131 universities in the United States and Canada. Includes geology theses and those in such closely allied fields as geophysics, geochemistry, geological engineering, and petroleum engineering, as well as mining and meteorology when there is a geological connection. Index by geologic names, and general index arranged primarily by geographic area and secondarily by geologic time and subject matter.

————— Bibliography of theses in geology, 1958–63. Wash., Amer. Geological Inst., [1965]. 1v., unpaged.   **EE59**

Continues the same authors' earlier bibliography covering through 1957 (above). Lists an additional 5,886 theses. Extends subject coverage to space science, hydrology, and biological and meteorological subjects completed in earth science, geophysics, or geology departments.

Ward, Dederick C. Bibliography of theses in geology, 1964. (*In* Geoscience abstracts, v.7, no.12, pt.1, Dec. 1965, p.101–37)   **EE60**

Continues the Chronic bibliography (above), listing an additional 682 theses.

————— and **O'Callaghan, T. C.** Bibliography of theses in geology, 1965–66. [Wash.], Amer. Geological Inst., [1969]. 255p.   **EE61**

"Published by the American Geological Institute in cooperation with the Geoscience Information Society."—*title page.*

Ward, Dederick C. Bibliography of theses in geology, 1967–1970. [Boulder, Colo., Geological Soc. of Amer., 1973] 160p., 274p. (Geological Society of America. Special paper, 143)   **EE62**

A classed subject arrangement with subject, author, and geologic name indexes, and a directory of colleges and universities.

The continuations for 1965–66 and 1967–70 were prepared with automatic data-processing equipment, and the contents are stored on magnetic tape as part of the larger GEO-REF permanent data file.

Citations to master's and doctoral theses in geology for 1971– appear in the monthly issues of the GSA *Bibliography and index of geology,* and no further separate bibliographies of geology theses are planned.   Z6034.U49W32

Periodicals

Lomský, Josef. Soupis periodik geologických věd: periodica geologica, palaeontologica et mineralogica. Příruční seznam s citačními zkratkami názvovými. Praha, Nakl. Československé Akademie Věd, 1959. 499p.   **EE63**

An alphabetical listing by first word of title of the geological periodicals of the world, past and present. Classified index. Gives title, publishing body, place, dates, and abbreviation.   Z6032.L6

Abstract journals

Geologisches Zentralblatt. Anzeiger für Geologie, Petrographie, Palaeontologie und verwandte Wissenschaften . . . Leipzig, Borntraeger, 1901–42. Bd.1–70. Semimonthly.   **EE64**

Frequency varies.
Ceased publication.
1932–42 in two parts: Abt. A, Geologie (no more published). Abt. B, Palaeontologisches Zentralblatt (continued in *Neues Jahrbuch für Mineralogie, Geologie und Paläontologie,* EE66).
Signed abstracts of book and periodical material in various languages in a subject arrangement, with author, geographical, and subject indexes in each volume. Cumulative indexes to Bd.1–15, 16–30, 31–50.   QE1.G494

GeoScience abstracts. v.1–8. Wash., Amer. Geological Inst., 1959–66. Monthly.   **EE65**

Ceased publication.
Superseded *Geological abstracts* (1953–58).
A classed abstract journal of publications on the geology, solid-earth geophysics, and related areas of science published in North America, or, if published elsewhere, dealing with North America. Also includes abstracts of Soviet literature which has been translated and published in North America. Subject and author index published annually.
Superseded by *Abstracts of North American geology,* which was published 1966–71.

Neues Jahrbuch für Mineralogie, Geologie und Paläontologie, 1830–1949. Stuttgart, Schweizerbart'sche Verlagsbuchhandlung, 1830–1949. 192v.(?)   **EE66**

Title varies.
This bibliographical periodical has had a long and complicated history with varying coverage, but has usually included "Neues Literatur" and, from 1925 to 1942, "Referate." Abstracts generally presented in a subject arrangement, with yearly indexes. Some cumulated indexes were also published.
"Referate" became *Zentralblatt für Mineralogie, Geologie und Paläontologie,* 1943–49; superseded by EE68 and EE174.

U.S. Geological Survey. Geophysical abstracts. 1929–71.Wash., 1929–73. Monthly.   **EE67**

Frequency varies. Ceased publication with issue for Dec. 1971.
Abstracts 1–86 were issued in mimeographed form by the Bureau of Mines. On July 1, 1936, the geophysical section was transferred to the Geological Survey, which issued abstracts 87–111. By Departmental Order of Oct. 5, 1942, the geophysical section was again placed with the Bureau of Mines, and abstracts 112–27 were issued by that bureau. Beginning July 1, 1947, it was transferred again to the Geological Survey.
Offers worldwide coverage of literature pertaining to the physics of the solid earth and to geophysical exploration. Abstracts in English. Annual author and subject indexes. (Index for 1971 published 1973.)   QE500.U5

Zentralblatt für Geologie und Paläontologie. Stuttgart, Schweizerbart'sche Verlagsbuchhandlung, 1950– . v.1– .   **EE68**

In two sections (titles vary): T.1, Allgemeine, angewandte, regionale und historische Geologie (13 nos. per yr.); T.2, Paläontologie (7 nos. per yr.).
International in scope. Topical arrangement of signed abstracts, mainly in German. Annual author, subject, and topographic indexes.
Supersedes in part the *Zentralblatt für Mineralogie, Geologie und Paläontologie,* 1943–49 (*see* EE66).   QE1.Z45

Encyclopedias and handbooks

American Geological Institute. Conference, Duluth, 1959. Geology and earth sciences sourcebook for elementary and secondary schools. Robert L. Heller, ed. Prep. under the guidance of the American Geological Institute, National Academy of Sciences–National Research Council. N.Y., Holt, [1962]. 496p. il. **EE69**

A textbook and practical handbook presenting various areas of the earth sciences, with introductions, suggestions for methods and activities, problems, teaching aids, and references. Geologic topics for biology, chemistry, and physics courses are discussed. The appendix lists sources of information in geology and earth science as well as suppliers of teaching aids. Indexed. QE41.A55

Fairbridge, Rhodes Whitmore, ed. The encyclopedia of geochemistry and environmental sciences. N.Y., Van Nostrand Reinhold, [1972]. 1321p. il. (Encyclopedia of earth sciences, v.4A) **EE70**

"Geochemistry is coupled with Environmental Science in this volume because it is the chemical pollution of our planet's air and water that is claiming the attention of many geologists and chemists today."—*Pref.* Signed articles with bibliographical references appear in alphabetical arrangement. Numerous cross references, including references to articles in other volumes of the *Encyclopedia of earth sciences* series. Detailed subject index. QE515.F24

———— and **Bourgeois, Joanne,** eds. The encyclopedia of sedimentology. Stroudsburg, Pa., Dowden, Hutchinson & Ross; distr. by Academic Pr., N.Y., [1978]. 901p. il., maps. (Encyclopedia of earth sciences, v.6) **EE71**

"The *Encyclopedia of sedimentology* is a comprehensive, alphabetical treatment of the discipline of sedimentology. It is intended to be a reference book for sedimentologists, geologists, and others who come in contact with sediments. . . . Some attempt has been made to define terms and to adhere to definitions in this volume, but an encyclopedia is *not* a dictionary."—*Pref.* Signed articles have bibliographies and cross references. Index. QE471.E49

Fairbridge, Rhodes Whitmore. The encyclopedia of world regional geology. Stroudsburg, Pa., Dowden, Hutchinson & Ross; distr. by Academic Pr., N.Y., 1975– . pt.1– . il., maps. (Encyclopedia of earth sciences, v.8, pt.1) **EE72**

Contents: pt.1, Western hemisphere (including Antarctica and Australia); pt.2, Eastern hemisphere, to be published.

Provides geologic and geomorphic data by continent, region, country, and island group. Signed articles, with cross references and bibliographies, are arranged alphabetically. Indexed. QE5.F33

Finkl, Charles W., Jr. The encyclopedia of applied geology. N.Y., Van Nostrand Reinhold, [1984]. il. (Encyclopedia of earth sciences, v.13) **EE73**

"Topics in this volume largely center around the field of engineering geology and deal with landscapes, earth materials, or the management of geological processes."—*Pref.* Signed articles with bibliographic references appear in alphabetical arrangement. Numerous cross references. Indexed. QE5.E5

International Union of Geological Sciences. International Subcommission on Stratigraphic Classification. International stratigraphic guide: a guide to stratigraphic classification, terminology, and procedure. N.Y., Wiley, [1976]. 200p. il. **EE74**

Hollis D. Hedberg, ed.

An international standard to replace national and regional codes and unify stratigraphic usage; an essential reference. Has an extensive bibliography. Indexed. QE651.I57

Lexique stratigraphique international. Paris, Centre National de la Recherche Scientifique, 1956–77. v.1–8. il. 31cm. (In progress?) **EE75**

Contents: v.1, Europe; v.2, U.R.S.S.; v.3, Asie; v.4, Afrique; v.5, Amérique Latine; v.6, Océanie; v.7, Amérique du Nord; v.8, Termes stratigraphiques majeurs.

A lexicon of stratigraphic nomenclature in all continents and countries of the world, which is published in various parts, each covering a particular country. Gives a description of the formation, the type of locality, age, and reference wherein described.

A "Nouvelle série" began publication 1983.

National Research Council. Handbook of physical constants. Ed. by Sydney P. Clark, Jr. Rev. ed. [N.Y.], Geological Soc. of America, 1966. 587p. il. (Geological Society of America. Memoir 97) **EE76**

Contains an impressive amount of physical data needed for geological and geophysical calculations. The compilations of data are grouped by topic. Index to properties. This edition revised and greatly expanded from the 1942 edition. Q199.N25

Dictionaries

American Geological Institute. Dictionary of geological terms, prepared under the direction of the American Geological Institute. Garden City, N.Y., Anchor/Doubleday, 1976. 472p. **EE77**

Ed. by William H. Matthews III and Robert E. Boyer.

1st ed. 1957.

An abridgment of the *Glossary of geology*, 1972.

"Intended for use by students of geology; elementary and secondary school science teachers; hobbyists . . . and others who have occasion to use but are unfamiliar with geological terminology."—*Pref.* A 3d ed. was publ. 1984 (Garden City, N.Y., Anchor Pr. 571p.) QE5.A48

Bates, Robert L. and **Jackson, Julia A.,** eds. Glossary of geology. 2d ed. Falls Church, Va., Amer. Geological Inst., 1980. 749p. **EE78**

1st ed. 1972.

"The terms listed in the Glossary have appeared in English-language publications, and reflect North American usage unless otherwise noted. Foreign language terms are included if they have been used by writers in English. Many obsolete terms are retained, as they remain valuable for readers using older literature. Besides giving current or preferred meaning of a term, some definitions include information on original usage or historical development."—*Introd.* This edition has 36,000 terms including 4,400 mineral names. Definitions may include references to the literature, comparable terms, synonyms, and etymology. Bibliography. QE5.G37

Beringer, Carl Christoph. Geologisches Wörterbuch, begründet von Carl Christian Beringer. 5. erg. und erw. Aufl. bearb. von Hans Murawski. Stuttgart, Enke, 1963. 243p. il. **EE79**

"Erklärung der geologischen Fachausdrücke der deutschen Literatur für Geologen, Paläontologen, Mineralogen, Geographen, Geophysiker, Bodenkundler, Bau- und Bergingenieure, Studierende und alle Freunde der Geologie."—*title page.*

1st ed. 1937. QE5.B4

Challinor, John. A dictionary of geology. 5th ed. N.Y., Oxford Univ. Pr., 1978. 368p. **EE80**

1st ed. 1961.

Defines geological terms and gives quotations from the literature (mainly from British works) to show usage. "This edition is again thoroughly revised and considerably enlarged."—*Pref.* A 6th ed. was publ. 1986. QE5.C45

Nelson, Archibald and **Nelson, Kenneth Davies.** Dictionary of applied geology; mining and civil engineering. N.Y., Philosophical Lib.; London, Newnes, [1967]. 421p. il. **EE81**

Intended mainly "for school and college students, and engineers in the mining and civil engineering professions."—*Pref.* A work of British origin. QE5.N44

Rice, Clara Mabel. Dictionary of geological terms (exclusive of stratigraphic formations and paleontologic genera and species). [Ann Arbor, Mich., Edwards Bros.], 1961. 465p. **EE82**

Reprint of the 1940 edition with addenda, p.463–65.

Aims to include the definitions of terms used in general geology, structural geology, economic geology, physiography, glacial geology, petrology, mineralogy, evolution, invertebrate and vertebrate paleontology, and stratigraphy. QE5.R5

Wilmarth, Mary Grace. Lexicon of geologic names of the United States (including Alaska). (Also includes the names and ages, but not the definitions, of the named geologic units of Canada, Mexico, the West Indies, Central America, and Hawaii) Wash., Govt. Prt. Off., 1938. 2v. (U.S. Geological Survey. Bull. 896) **EE83**

Name is followed by a definition, usually giving lithology, thickness, age, underlying and overlying formations, and type locality, with bibliographical references.

Some updating is provided by: QE5.W5

Wilson, Druid [and others]. Geologic names of North America. Wash., Govt. Prt. Off., 1959. 622p. (U.S. Geological Survey. Bull. 1056) **EE84**

Contents: A, Geologic names of North America introduced in 1936–1955: a compilation of new geologic names of North America, including Greenland, the West Indies, the Pacific Island possessions of the United States, and the Trust Territory of the Pacific Islands. 1957; B, Index to the geologic names of North America: geologic names arranged by age and by area containing type locality.

Prepared to bring up to date the *Lexicon of geologic names* by Wilmarth (above), and to serve as the first step in the preparation of a new edition.

Keroher, Grace C. [and others]. Lexicon of geologic names of the United States for 1936–1960. Wash., Govt. Prt. Off., 1966. 3v. (4341p.) (U.S. Geological Survey. Bull. 1200) **EE85**

"A compilation of the geologic names of the United States, its possessions, the Trust Territory of the Pacific Islands, and the Panama Canal Zone."—*title page.*

Continues and brings further up to date the *Lexicon* of Mary Grace Wilmarth (EE83), but covers a smaller geographic area. Includes 14,634 names, of which 9,128 appeared in the Wilmarth work and 5,506 are post-1935 or pre-1935 names not included by Wilmarth.

Continued by: QE7.K4

———— Lexicon of geologic names of the United States for 1961–1967. Wash., Govt. Prt. Off., 1970. 848p. (U.S. Geol. Survey. Bulletin 1350) **EE86**

"A compilation of the new geologic names introduced into the literature from 1961–1967 in the United States, its possessions, the Trust Territory of the Pacific Islands, and the Panama Canal Zone."—*title page.*

Includes 2,860 names, including cross references.

Foreign language and multilingual

Czech

Prague. Ústřední Ústav Geologický. Naučný geologický slovník. Sestavil autorský kolektiv pot vedením J. F. Svobody. 1. vyd. Praha, Nakl. Československé Akademie Věd, 1960–1961. 2v. and suppl. il. **EE87**

Bibliography, v.1, p.10–13.

———— ———— Příloha: Stratigrafické tabulky. [Praha, 1959] 37 fold. charts.

QE5.P7

Zeman, Otakar and **Beneš, Karel.** English-Czech geological dictionary. Praha, Nakl. Československé Akad. Věd, 1963. 367p. **EE88**

"With index of Czech terms with elementary terms of geomorphology, economic geology, engineering, geology, mineralogy, paleontology, petrography."—*title page.* QE5.Z4

French

Davies, George MacDonald. French-English vocabulary in geology and physical geography. London, Murby; N.Y., Van Nostrand, [1932]. 140p. (Repr.: London, J. Mann, 1960) **EE89**

Lists English equivalents of French words used in a semitechnical sense in the geological literature. Words whose English equivalents are obvious are omitted. QE5.D3

German

Watznauer, Adolf, ed. Dictionary of geosciences. Amsterdam, Elsevier, 1982. 2v. charts. **EE90**

Translation of: *Wörterbuch Geowissenschaften.*

Contents: [v.1] German-English; [v.2] English-German.

Contains approximately 38,000 terms used in the earth sciences, but limits inclusion from allied fields. Charts of geologic time scale, scale of seismic intensity, and Beaufort scale. QE5.W6513

Russian

Burgunker, Mark E. Russian-English dictionary of earth sciences. N.Y., Telberg Book Co., 1961. 94p. **EE91**

Gives English terms for Russian words, sometimes with explanations and definitions. Not comprehensive, but constitutes "the 'hard core' of the nomenclature of tectonics, geomorphology, hydrology, paleogeography and geophysics."—*Pref.* Includes personal names

QE5.B8

English-Russian dictionary of applied geophysics. Oxford, Pergamon, 1983. 487p. **EE92**

Ed. by B.V. Gusev *et al.*

Gives Russian terms for English words. Contains about 30,000 terms based on seismic, gravity, magnetic, and electrical exploration. TN269.A5413

Sofiano, Tat'iana Alekseevna. Anglo-russkii geologicheskii slovar'. Moskva, Gos. Izd-vo Tekhniko-Teoretich. Lit-ry, 1957. 523p. **EE93**

Added title page in English.

(2d ed., repr. from the 1st, 1961. 525p.) QE5.S58

———— Russko-angliiskii geologicheskii slovar'. Moskva, Glavnaia red. Inostrannykh Nauchno-Tekhnicheskikh Slovarei Fizmatgiza, 1960. 559p. **EE94**

Lists English equivalents of 35,000 Russian terms in the geological sciences.

———— ———— American supplement, comp. by V. G. Telberg. N.Y., Telberg Book Co., 1961. 49p.

QE5.S59

Telberg, V. G. Russian-English dictionary of geological terms. N.Y., Telberg Book Co., [1964]. 149p. **EE95**

Equivalent terms only—no definitions. QE5.T45

Spanish

Diccionario de geología y ciencias afines. Dirigido por Pedro de Novo y Fernández-Chicarro. Barcelona, Ed. Labor, 1957. 2v. il. **EE96**

Contents: t.1, Geografía física, cristalografía, mineralogía, petrografía; t.2, Paleontología, estratigrafía, orogenía y tectónica.

Terms are arranged alphabetically under each subject, with a general alphabetical index at the end of v.2. QE5.D5

Multilingual

Nederlands Geologisch Mijnbouwkundig Genootschap. Geological nomenclature. Ed. by A. A. G. Schieferdecker. Gorinchem, J. Noorduijn, 1959. 523p. (Royal Geological and Mining Society of the Netherlands)   **EE97**

Classed arrangement of definitions of English terms, giving Dutch, French, and German equivalents. Combined index of terms in all languages.   QE5.N413

Zylka, Romauld. Geological dictionary: English-Polish-Russian-French-German. Warsaw, Wydawnictwa Geologiczne, 1970. 1439p.   **EE98**

Arranged alphabetically by English terms. Approximately 25,000 terms followed by Polish, Russian, French, and German renderings and important synonyms. Indexes from the other languages.   QE5.Z95

Directories

Directory of geoscience departments: United States and Canada. Ed.1– , March 1952– . Wash., Amer. Geological Inst., 1952– . Annual.   **EE99**

Ed. 1–7 issued as *Reports* of the Institute.
Title varies: 1952–1956/57, *Departments of geological science in educational institutions of the United States and Canada;* 1958–69, *Directory of geoscience departments in the colleges and universities of the United States and Canada.*
Alphabetical listing of colleges and universities granting undergraduate and graduate degrees in earth sciences and engineering, and geography. Provides address, phone number, faculty, specialties, and degrees offered. Separate chart of summer field courses. Degree program index; specialty index; faculty index.

Geophysical directory. Houston, Tex., 1946– . v.1– . Annual.   **EE100**

"Intended to be a comprehensive listing of all companies and individuals directly connected with, or engaged in the geophysical exploration for petroleum."—*Foreword.*   TN867.G46

Howell, Jesse V. and **Levorsen, Arville Irving.** Directory of geological material in North America; 2d ed. rev. and enl., with the assistance of Robert H. Dott and Jane Weaver Wilds. Wash., Amer. Geological Inst., 1957. 208p.   **EE101**

1st ed. 1946.
Includes information on maps, aerial photography, geological publications, microfilms, and other materials and services of interest to geologists, with a record of the firms, libraries, museums, book dealers, etc., from which the material may be obtained. In two parts: (1) "Sources national and continental in scope," subarranged by type of organization and type of material; and (2) "Sources provincial in scope."   QE23.H6

Worldwide directory of mineral industries education and research. Ed. by Herbert Wöhlbier [and others]. Houston, Gulf Pub., 1968. 451p.   **EE102**

An international directory of geoscience departments in universities and institutes, with notes on research activities. Country arrangement.   TN165.W66

Worldwide directory of national earth-science agencies and related international organizations. [Reston, Va.], U.S. Geological Survey, 1981. 87p. maps. (Geological Survey circular 834)   **EE103**

"A listing of governmental earth-science agencies and selected major international organizations whose functions are similar to those of the U.S. Geological Survey."—*t.p.*

History and biography

Brush, Stephen G. and **Landsberg, Helmut E.** The history of geophysics and meteorology: an annotated bibliography.

N.Y., Garland, 1985. 450p. (Bibliographies of the history of science and technology, 7)   **EE104**

Includes general histories, biography, institutional history, and various subdivisions of geophysics and meteorology. Name and subject indexes.   Z6041.B78

Geikie, *Sir* **Archibald.** The founders of geology. 2d ed. London, Macmillan, 1905. 486p. (Repr.: N.Y., Dover, 1962)   **EE105**

A standard history of geology based on the lives and works of outstanding geologists. The major portion of the book emphasizes "the history and development of geology during the period between the middle of the eighteenth and the close of the second decade of the nineteenth century."—*Pref.*   QE11.G3

La Rocque, Aurèle. Contributions to the history of geology. Columbus, Ohio State Univ., Dept. of Geology, 1964. 3v.   **EE106**

Contents: v.1, Biographies of geologists, 1961. Suppl. 1, [1962?]. Suppl. 2, 1964; v.2, Bibliography of the history of geology, 1964. Suppl. 1, 1960. Suppl. 2, 1962; v.3, Biographic index, 1964.
Preliminary paper presented at the Conference on the History of Geology supported by the National Science Foundation and held at the University of Nevada, Reno, Aug. 1964.
Biographies of geologists of all periods and countries from ancient times to the present. Length of article varies from one to several columns. The index gives full name, years of birth and death, nationality, field of interest, and references to the literature.

Merrill, George Perkins. First 100 years of American geology. New Haven, Conn., Yale Univ. Pr.; London, Milford, 1924. 773p. il. (Repr.: N.Y., Hafner, 1964)   **EE107**

A survey history including biographies of geologists but no bibliographical references. A revised version of the author's *Contributions to the history of American geology* (1904).   QE13.U6M6

Sarjeant, William A. S. Geologists and the history of geology: an international bibliography from the origins to 1978. N.Y., Arno, 1980. 5v.   **EE108**

Contents: v.1, Introduction, general histories of science, of geology and its subdivisions, and allied sciences. Historical accounts of institutions concerned with geology. Histories of the petroleum industry. Accounts of geological events; v.2–3, Individual geologists; v.4, Geologists index by country and speciality; v.5, Index of authors, editors and translators. Appendix.
A short biography is included with the bibliography of each geologist.   Z6031.S28

Zittel, Karl Alfred von. Geschichte der Geologie und Paläontologie bis Ende des 19. Jahrhunderts. München, Oldenbourg, 1899. 868p. il.   **EE109**

English translation by Maria M. Ogilvie-Gordon, *History of geology and palaeontology to the end of the nineteenth century* (London, Walter Scott, 1901; repr.: N.Y., Hafner, 1962).
A standard history; treatment is by general subject area. Author and subject indexes.   QE11.Z7

Surveys of research

New Hampshire Inter-disciplinary Conference on the History of Geology, Rye Beach, 1967. Toward a history of geology; proceedings. Cecil J. Schneer, ed. Cambridge, M.I.T. Pr., [1969]. 450p. il.   **EE110**

Sponsored by the History of Science Society, and the Council on Education in the Geological Sciences of the American Geological Institute.
25 papers with an interdisciplinary focus concerning the origins of geology, and offering "a new composite view of the development of geology up to the time of Darwin."—*Introd.* Includes bibliographic references, biographical sketches of contributors, and an index.   QE11.N47

Atlases

Owen, H.G. Atlas of continental displacement: 200 million years to the present. Cambridge, Cambridge Univ. Pr., [1983]. 159p. maps. 31cm. (Cambridge earth science series)   **EE111**

The atlas is the "first of a two-part work designed to provide maps of the distribution of continental and oceanic crust during the last 700 million years of the Earth's history."—*Pref.* 76 maps in seven sections.   G1046.C55

Shell Oil Company. Exploration Department. Stratigraphic atlas of North America and Central America. Prepared by the Exploration Department of Shell Oil Company, Houston, Texas. Princeton, N.J., Princeton Univ. Pr., [1975]. 272p. il., maps. 43cm.   **EE112**

Ed. by T. D. Cook and A. W. Balley.
A collection of black-and-white maps, on a scale of 1:25,000,000, and stratigraphic sections, together with extensive bibliographies.   G1106.C57S54

Snead, Rodman E. World atlas of geomorphic features. Huntington, N.Y., Krieger, 1980. 301p. maps. 29cm.   **EE113**

103 maps grouped in six sections. Brief text defines the landforms and describes the major characteristics of the features. Bibliography and index.   G1046.C256

Ziegler, Peter A. Geological atlas of Western and Central Europe. The Hague, Shell Internationale Petroleum Maatschappij B.V.; distr. by Elsevier, 1982. 130p. il., maps in portfolio. 31cm.   **EE114**

This work presents "an overview of the tectonic and stratigraphic framework of Western and Central Europe and with a summary of its evolution."—*Pref.* Portfolio contains 38 maps (tectonic, geological, paleogeographic, isopach, and stratigraphic) plus separate charts of legends and abbreviations. Bibliography.   QE260.Z53

CRYSTALLOGRAPHY

See also Mineralogy.

France. Centre National de la Recherche Scientifique. Bulletin signalétique. Sec. 6, Structure de la matière: crystallographie, solides, fluides, atomes, ions, molécules. Paris, Centre de Documentation du C.N.R.S., 1961–68. v.22–29. Monthly.   **EE115**

Supersedes in part the Centre's *Bulletin signalétique*, ptie. 1.
A classed bibliography of worldwide coverage, with brief abstracts in French. Monthly subject and author indexes.
Superseded by the Centre's *Bulletin signalétique: 160, Structure de la matière I; physique de l'état condensé, physique atomique et moléculaire, spectroscopies*, v.30–44, 1969–83, and *Bulletin signalétique: 161, Structure de la matière II; cristallographie*, v.30–44, 1969–83.
Continued by:

PASCAL explore. E12, État condensé. Paris, Centre de Documentation Scientifique et Technique du C.N.R.S., 1984– . v.1– . 10 nos. per yr.   **EE116**

—— E13, Structure des liquides et des solides. Cristallographie. Paris, Centre de Documentation Scientifique et Technique du C.N.R.S., 1984– . v.1– . 10 nos. per yr.   **EE117**

International Union of Crystallography. International tables for crystallography. Dordrecht, Holland; Boston, D. Reidel, 1983. v.A. (In progress)   **EE118**

Contents: v.A, Space–group symmetry, ed. by Theo Hahn. 834p.
Corresponds to v.1 of the *International tables for x-ray crystallography* (below), but of a more general nature. "The aim of the present work is to provide data and text which are useful for all aspects of crystallography."—*Pref.*

—— International tables for X-ray crystallography. Birmingham, Eng., Kynoch Pr., 1952–74. 4v.   **EE119**

Contents: v.1, Symmetry groups, ed. by N. F. M. Henry and K. Lonsdale; v.2, Mathematical tables, ed. by J. S. Kasper and K. Lonsdale; v.3, Physical and chemical tables, ed. by C. H. MacGillavry and G. D. Rieck; v.4, Revised and supplementary tables, ed. by J. A. Ibers and W. C. Hamilton.
Intended for "those who are actually engaged in the determination of crystal structures, those who are using x-ray methods in the study of crystals in general, and students of crystallography."—*General Pref.* Each volume includes a list of crystallographic terms, with the French, German, Russian, and Spanish equivalents of the English word or phrase. Subject index in v.3.   QD945.I55

Wyckoff, Ralph W. G. Crystal structures. 2d ed. N.Y., Interscience, 1963–71. v.1–6$^{1-2}$. il.   **EE120**

A revision of the compilation previously published in loose-leaf form (1948–53), written for crystallographers, physicists, biochemists, geologists, and mineralogists. Gives detailed descriptions of structures with illustrations. Following the text of each chapter is a bibliography in tabular form. Individual volumes have name and formula indexes.   QD951.W82

GEODESY

Bibliographia geodaetica; Internationale geodaetische Dokumentation. Jahrg.1, no.1– , Jan. 1963– . Berlin, Akademie Verlag, 1963– . Monthly.   **EE121**

Hrsg. vom Nationalkomitee für Geodäsie und Geophysik der Deutschen Demokratischen Republik bei der Deutschen Akademie der Wissenschaften zu Berlin.
Subtitle also in French, English (International geodetic documentation), and Russian.
A classed bibliography with annual author and subject indexes. Each issue includes sections in German, French, English, and Russian, the same citations appearing in each section but with brief abstracts in the different languages.

Mueller, Ivan Istvan and **Rockie, John D.** Gravimetric and celestial geodesy; a glossary of terms. N.Y., Ungar, [1966]. 129p. il.   **EE122**

Supplements and updates *Definitions of surveying, mapping, and related terms* (1954) prepared by the Committee on Definitions of Surveying Terms of the American Society of Civil Engineers, and H. C. Mitchell's *Definitions of terms used in geodetic and other surveys* (1949).
Intends to analyze and define "as accurately as possible, terminology in the fields of gravimetric (physical) geodesy, geodetic astronomy, and satellite geodesy."—*Pref.*   QB279.M8

HYDROLOGY

Bibliography

Bibliography of hydrology, United States of America . . . 1935/36– 40. Wash., Amer. Geophysical Union, Section of Hydrology, 1937–41.   **EE123**

Ceased publication.
"The United States cahier . . . of the International Bibliography of Hydrology established by the International Association of Scientific Hydrology."
Continued by:

American Geophysical Union. Annotated bibliography on hydrology, 1941–1950 (United States and Canada). Wash., Govt. Prt. Off., 1952. 408p. (U.S. Federal Inter-Agency

River Basin Committee. Notes on hydrologic activities bull. no.5)   **EE124**

——— Annotated bibliography on hydrology (1951–54) and sedimentation (1950–54), United States and Canada. Wash., Govt. Prt. Off., 1956. 207p. (U.S. Inter-Agency Committee on Water Resources. Joint hydrology-sedimentation bull. no.7)

Arranged by author, with a list of organizations and their publications.

Continued by:

U.S. Geological Survey. Annotated bibliography on hydrology and sedimentation: United States and Canada, 1955–1958. Wash., U.S. Govt. Prt. Off., 1962. 236p. (Water supply paper no.1546)   **EE125**

Includes papers, articles, books, data compilations, and data reports that are not part of a series. "Listings are arranged alphabetically by author, followed by a combined subject and geographic location or river basin index. Each article is indexed by primary subject, and by geographic area if applicable."—*Introd.*

Continued by a series of bibliographies with the same title prepared for the U.S. Interagency Committee on Water Resources and published as issues of the *Joint hydrology-sedimentation bulletin:* 1959/62, publ. 1964 (Bull. no.8); 1963/65, publ. 1969 (Bull. no.9); 1966/68, publ. 1970 (Bull. no.10).   TC801.U2

Hydata. v.1–14, Jan. 1965–Dec. 1978. Urbana, Ill., American Water Resources Assoc., 1965–78. Monthly.   **EE126**

Contains tables of contents pages from current periodicals in the field of water resources and hydrology. In addition there are other lists: Selected article titles from other periodicals; Tables of contents of non-periodical literature (primarily conferences); Selected titles of non-periodical literature (reports).

Continued by *Hydro-index* (July 1980–), a monthly index of titles of the world's literature on water.

Selected water resources abstracts. v.1, no.1– , Jan. 1968– . [Springfield, Va., Clearinghouse for Federal Scientific and Technical Information], 1968– . Semimonthly with annual index.   **EE127**

For full information *see* EJ155.

Van der Leeden, Frits. Ground water: a selected bibliography. Port Washington, N.Y., Water Information Center, [1971]. 116p.   **EE128**

Topical arrangement of about 1,500 citations to important papers, reports, theses, and monographs on various aspects of hydrogeology. Has no chronological or geographical limitations, but omits most papers on local hydrogeologic conditions. No author index.
                                                    Z7935.V35

Handbooks and dictionaries

Chow, Ven Te. Handbook of applied hydrology; a compendium of water-resources technology. N.Y., McGraw-Hill, [1964]. 1v., various pagings. il.   **EE129**

Contains 25 sections written by various specialists. Designed for scientists, engineers, and consultants. Interdisciplinary aspects are stressed. Includes bibliographies.   GB661.C56

Pfannkuch, Hans-Olaf. Elsevier's Dictionary of hydrogeology in three languages: English-French-German. N.Y., American Elsevier, 1969. 168p.   **EE130**

Arranged on an English base with indexes from the other languages.   GB1003.P46

Singer, Lothar. Russian-English-German-French hydrological dictionary. London, Scientific Information Consultants, [1967]. 151p.   **EE131**

About 1,500 terms arranged on a Russian base with indexes from the other languages.   GB655.S5

METEOROLOGY

Bibliography

See also EE104.

International catalogue of scientific literature: F, Meteorology. 1st–14th annual issues. London, Harrison, 1902–19. v.1–14.   **EE132**

For full description *see* EA17.

Meteorological and Geoastrophysical Abstracts. Bibliography on meteorological satellites (1952–1962). Prep. by Elemer Kiss. Wash., Govt. Prt. Off., 1963. 380p. (U.S. Weather Bureau)   **EE133**

Lists 988 titles—books and articles—arranged under year, then alphabetically by author (from 1 article in 1951 to 230 in 1962).
                                                    Z6683.A7M4

Meteorological and geoastrophysical abstracts. v.1– , Jan. 1950– . Boston, Amer. Meteorological Soc., 1950– . v.1– . Monthly.   **EE134**

Title varies: v.1–10, *Meteorological abstracts and bibliography.*
Beginning with v.11, 1960, supported by U.S. Dept. of the Army, National Aeronautics and Space Administration, National Oceanographic Data Center, U.S. Weather Bureau, U.S. National Science Foundation.

A classified arrangement of abstracts in English on important meteorological and geoastrophysical literature in all languages. Includes various lists of serial publications, and occasional selective annotated bibliographies on subjects of immediate or special interest to meteorologists, geophysicists, and astrophysicists. Each issue has author, subject, and geographical indexes. Most yearly volumes have cumulated indexes.

A cumulated index has been published as: ●

American Meteorological Society. Cumulated bibliography and index to Meteorological and geoastrophysical abstracts, 1950–1969; classified subject and author arrangements. Boston, G. K. Hall, 1972. 9v.   **EE135**

Contents: Author sequence, 5v.; Universal Decimal Classification cumulation, 4v.
A cumulation of the entries without the abstracts.
                                                    QC851.A6314

U.S. Army. Signal Corps. Bibliography of meteorology. . . . Wash., Signal Off., 1889–91. 4v.   **EE136**

Subtitle: A classed catalogue of the printed literature of meteorology from the origin of printing to the close of 1881; with a supplement to the close of 1887, and an author index. Prepared under the direction of Brigadier General A. W. Greely . . . ed. by Oliver L. Fassig.
Contents: v.1, Temperature; v.2, Moisture; v.3, Winds; v.4, Storms.
Includes some 60,000 titles by 13,000 authors. v.3–4 include literature to 1889.   Z6681.U58

Dictionaries and encyclopedias

Fairbridge, Rhodes Whitmore, ed. The encyclopedia of atmospheric sciences and astrogeology. N.Y., Reinhold, [1967]. 1200p. il. (Encyclopedia of earth sciences, 2)
                                                    EE137

Intended "for all scientists, from those still in high school to the emeritus professor who would like to check on a few items."—*Pref.* A dictionary arrangement is followed; articles are signed; an index complements the dictionary arrangement; bibliographies are included.   QC854.F34

Glossary of meteorology. Ed. by Ralph E. Huschke. Boston, Amer. Meteorological Soc., 1959. 638p. (Repr. 1970, 1980)
                                                    EE138

"Sponsored by U.S. Dept of Commerce, Weather Bureau [and others]."—*title page.*

"Purports to define every important meteorological term likely to be found in the literature today."—*Pref.*

A dictionary compiled and written by specialists with definitions "understandable to an undergraduate in a technical college yet [with] sufficient detail to satisfy the working specialist."—*Pref.* Primarily United States usage, but with some terms used in other countries.   QC854.G55

Gt.Brit. Meteorological Office. Meteorological glossary; comp. by D. H. McIntosh. [5th ed.] London, Stat. Off., 1972. 318p. il.   **EE139**

Also published as "First American ed." by Chemical Publishing Co., New York, 1972.

1st ed. 1916.

Provides definitions and discussions of about 2,000 terms as used in meteorology. Length of entries ranges from a single phrase to several short paragraphs. Includes photographs, maps, charts, and graphs.   QC854.G7

World Meteorological Organization. International meteorological vocabulary. Geneva, Secretariat of the World Meteorological Organization, 1966. 276p. (*Its* Publication 182, TP.91)   **EE140**

Title also in French, Spanish, and Russian.

Includes nomenclature in English, French, Russian, and Spanish; definitions of these terms in English and French are given in separate sections. A comprehensive reference work.

Foreign terms

French

Proulx, Gerard-J. Standard dictionary of meteorological sciences: English-French/French-English. Montreal, McGill-Queen's Univ. Pr., 1971. 307p.   **EE141**

QC854.P76

Russian

Ainbinder, M. I. Anglo-russkii meteorologicheskii slovar'. Moskva, Gos. Izd-vo Fiziko-Matematicheskoi Lit-ry, 1959. 244p.   **EE142**

Added title page: English-Russian meteorological dictionary.

QC854.A35

Mamontova, Lidiia Ivanovna and **Khromov, S. I.** Anglo-russkii meteorologicheskii slovar'. [Okolo 6000 meteorologicheskikh terminov] Leningrad, Gidrometeorologicheskoe Izd-vo, 1959. 172p.   **EE143**

QC854.M3

Noveck, Sonia. Russian-English glossary of physics of fluids and meteorology. N.Y., Interlanguage Dictionaries Publ. Corp., 1959. 93p.   **EE144**

Subtitle: . . . contains the most up-to-date Russian-English vocabulary in the fields of physics of fluids and meteorology. There are over 4,000 terms comp. from the latest Russian and English sources in the field.   QC145.N6

Spanish

Brazol, Demetrio. Dictionary of meteorological and related terms. Buenos Aires, Hachette, 1955. 557p.   **EE145**

Contents: English-Spanish, Spanish-English.   QC854.B75

Handbooks

American Meteorological Society. Committee on the Compendium of Meteorology. Compendium of meteorology . . . ed. by Thomas F. Malone. Boston, Soc., 1951. 1334p. il.   **EE146**

Topical arrangement of 108 survey articles, each by a different author and including a list of references. Subject index.

QC852.A5

Berry, Frederick Aroyce, Bollay, E. and **Beers, Norman R.** Handbook of meteorology. N.Y., McGraw-Hill, 1945. 1068p. il.   **EE147**

"Designed to furnish the student and the professional meteorologist a convenient text reference for data, fundamental theory, and weather analysis and forecasting. The emphasis has been conscientiously placed on the scientific and engineering aspects of meteorology, rather than on current techniques."—*Pref.* Information is presented in a topical arrangement in the form of text, tables, and maps. Subject index.   QC861.B43

Houghton, David D., ed. Handbook of applied meteorology. N.Y., Wiley, [1985]. 1461p. il., maps.   **EE148**

The handbook "presents, for the first time, an authoritative, concise, and comprehensive reference for meteorological knowledge and technology, designed for professionals and technicians outside the meteorological profession."—*Pref.* A chapter on resources includes bibliographic references, as well as directories to data, university departments, research centers, and societies. Glossary and index.   TA197.H36

U.S. Air Force. Cambridge Research Laboratories. Handbook of geophysics and space environments. N.Y., Mc-Graw-Hill, [1965]. 1v., various pagings.   **EE149**

A handbook of text, tables, and charts dealing with the atmosphere, gravity, geomagnetism, solar phenomena, planetary environments, astrophysics, and astronomy. Meant for use in the design of aerospace systems.   QC806.U55

World Meteorological Organization. Guide to hydrological practices. 3d ed. Geneva, World Meteorological Organization (available from Unipub, N.Y.), 1974. 1v., looseleaf, various pagings. (*Its* WMO [pubn.] no. 168)   **EE150**

1st ed. (1965) entitled: *Guide to hydrometeorological practices.*

A revised and improved edition, the new title indicating the broader scope of its contents.   QC925.W667

———— Guide to meteorological instrument and observing practices. 4th ed. Geneva, World Meteorological Organization (available from Unipub, N.Y.), 1971. 1v., looseleaf, various pagings. (*Its* WMO [pubn.] no.8-TP-3)   **EE151**

1st ed. 1954.

Climatology

Clayton, Henry Helm. World weather records, collected from official sources by Dr. Felix Exner [and others]. Assembled and arranged for publication by H. Helm Clayton. Publ. under grant from John A. Roebling. Wash., Smithsonian Inst., 1927. 1199p. maps. (Smithsonian miscellaneous collections, v.79) (Repr. 1944)   **EE152**

———— ———— Errata. Wash., Smithsonian Inst., 1929. 28p.

Geographical arrangement of tables showing monthly and annual means of pressure and temperature, and totals of rainfall for weather stations all over the world. Beginning years vary; latest years listed are usually 1920–25. The appendix is a list of monthly sun-spot numbers. Index by country, station, etc.; index by latitude.

Continued by: QC982.C5

—— World weather records . . . 1921–1930, 1931–1940. Wash., Smithsonian Inst., 1934–37. 2v. (Smithsonian miscellaneous collections, v.90, 105)

Type of data and arrangement conform to the earlier volume, with the following exceptions: 1921–30 volume includes atmospheric pressures over the northern oceans and sea-level pressures at selected land stations, late reports and additional data not published in v.79, and solar radiation; 1931–40 volume includes lake and river levels.
Continued by:

U.S. Weather Bureau. World weather records, 1941–50. Wash., 1959. 1361p.   **EE153**

Statistical tables giving pressure at station level, temperature, and precipitation, by month. Arranged by continent, subdivided by station. Index.
Continued by:

—— —— 1951–60. Wash., Govt. Prt. Off., 1965–68. 6v.

Contents: v.1, North America. 535p.; v.2, Europe. 547p.; v.3, South America, Central America, West Indies, the Caribbean and Bermuda. 355p.; v.4, Asia. 576p.; v.5, Africa. 545p.; v.6, Antarctica, Australia, Oceanic Islands, and Ocean weather stations. 605p.

Tables give the same type of data as the three works cited above.
Continued by:

World weather records, 1961–1970. Asheville, N.C., Dept. of Commerce, National Oceanic and Atmospheric Admin., Environmental Data and Information Service, National Climatic Center (for sale by Govt. Prt. Off.), 1979. v.1–2. maps, tables.   **EE154**

Contents: v.1, North America; v.2, Europe.   QC982.W6

Climate normals for the U.S. (Base: 1951–80). Detroit, Gale, [1983]. 712p.   **EE155**

"Data elements compiled by National Climatic Center, Environmental Data and Information Service, National Oceanic and Atmospheric Administration."—*t.p.*
Gives average temperature and precipitation data by state and station.   QC983.C53

The climates of the states. 2d ed. Detroit, Gale, [1980]. 2v. maps.   **EE156**

Subtitle: National Oceanic and Atmospheric Administration narrative summaries, tables, and maps for each state, with overview of state climatologist programs.
1st ed. 1974.
Includes new material by James A. Ruffner.   QC983.C56

Grayson, Donald K. A bibliography of the literature on North American climates of the past 13,000 years. N.Y., Garland, 1975. 206p. (Garland reference library of natural science, v.2)   **EE157**

Not an exhaustive bibliography of its subject area, nor a critical compilation of the literature, although it includes "much, perhaps even most, of the pertinent literature."—*Introd.* Publications are listed by author and numbered; an index gives access to the literature by seven broad geographic subdivisions of North America.
                                                        Z6683.C5G66

Rudloff, Willy. World climates: with tables of climate data and practical suggestions. Stuttgart, Wissenschaftliche Verlagsgesellschaft, 1981. 632p.   **EE158**

For 1,474 weather stations throughout the world, gives tables presenting a general climatic description and monthly mean temperatures, precipitation, sunshine, recommended clothing, and scale of heat stress. For 116 select stations, hygrothermal diagrams show mean daily values of air temperature and humidity for every month, indicating conditions at about dawn and in the early afternoon.
                                                        QC982.R83

Ruffner, James A. and **Bair, Frank E.** The weather almanac. 4th ed. Detroit, Gale, [1984]. 812p. il., maps.   **EE159**

1st ed. 1974.

"A reference guide to weather, climate, and air quality in the United States and its key cities, comprising statistics, principles, and terminology. Provides weather/health information and safety rules for environmental hazards associated with storms, weather extremes, earthquakes and volcanoes. Also includes world climatological highlights and special features."—*t.p.*   QC983.R83

Storm data for the United States, 1970–1974. Detroit, Gale, 1982. 884p.   **EE160**

Subtitle: A quinquennial compilation of the U.S. Environmental Data Service's official monthly reports of storm activity logged by the National Weather Service with damage extent estimates, and counts of injuries and deaths.
Reprints of monthly, *Storm data,* issued by the U.S. Environmental Data Service. Listed alphabetically by state within month. Not indexed.
Continued by: QC943.5.U6S83

Storm data for the United States, 1975–1979. Detroit, Gale, 1982. 946p.

A second quinquennial compilation following the pattern of the earlier volume.   QC943.5.U6S84

U.S. Environmental Data Service. Climatological data [issued in sections, representing states, possessions, and groups of states]. v.1–, Jan. 1914– . Wash., Bureau, 1914– . il. Monthly (with annual summaries).   **EE161**

Title varies: *Climatological data . . . by sections.*
Previously issued by U.S. Weather Bureau and U.S. Environmental Science Services Administration.
Contains weather statistics from 47 separate areas, most sections corresponding to a state. Printed in the various section centers and assembled and bound in Washington.   QC983.A5

—— Climatological data; national summary. Asheville, N.C., 1950– . v.1– . Monthly and annual.   **EE162**

Previously issued by U.S. Weather Bureau and U.S. Environmental Science Services Administration.
Provides tables and maps containing data from every state.

—— Daily weather maps; weekly series. Wash., 1968– . Weekly.   **EE163**

A continuation of the principal charts of the former U.S. Weather Bureau publication, *Daily weather map,* which was discontinued April 14, 1968.
For each day of the week, provides maps of the 48 adjacent states and southern Canada, showing surface weather and station weather, 500-millibar height contours, precipitation amounts, and high and low temperatures.

—— Selective guide to climatic data sources. Prep. by Staff, National Weather Records Center, Asheville, N.C. Wash., Govt. Prt. Off., 1969. 90p. (*Its* Key to meteorological records documentation, no.4.11)   **EE164**

Previous ed. (1963) had title: *Selective guide to published climatic data sources.*
Arranged alphabetically by title within four groups: (1) Current publications; (2) Publications carrying additional time-sequential tables; (3) Special climatological publications; (4) Collateral climatological publications.

World survey of climatology. H.E. Landsberg, ed. in chief. Amsterdam, Elsevier, 1969–84. 15v.   **EE165**

Contents: v.1–3, General climatology; v.4, Climate of the free atmosphere; v.5, Climates of northern and western Europe; v.6, Climates of central and southern Europe; v.7, Climates of the Soviet Union; v.8, Climates of northern and eastern Asia; v.9, Climates of southern and western Asia; v.10, Climates of Africa; v.11, Climates of North America; v.12, Climates of Central and South America; v.13, Climates of Australia and New Zealand; v.14, Climates of polar regions; v.15, Climates of the oceans.
Each volume represents the contributions of a group of specialists, and the complete set is intended to provide a systematic appraisal of the state of knowledge in the field of climatology throughout the

world. In each volume there is an index of bibliographical references, a geographic index, and a subject index. QC981.W67

Atlases

Visher, Stephen Sargent. Climatic atlas of the United States. Cambridge, Harvard Univ. Pr., 1954. 403p. 1031 maps. 30cm. **EE166**

"The 1031 maps and diagrams are presented in 34 chapters grouped in seven parts. Five parts embrace the major elements of climate: temperature, wind, sunshine, humidity, and precipitation, and the other two, some consequences of climate and weather, and climatic regions and climatic changes. The consequences include those to agriculture, health, soil erosion, soil moisture, soil freezing, lakes, streams, and topography."—*Foreword.* Includes bibliographic references and sources of maps. Indexed. G1201.C8V5

MINERALOGY

Guides

Kaplan, Stuart R., ed. A guide to information sources in mining, minerals, and geosciences. N.Y., Interscience, [1965]. 599p. (Guides to information sources in science and technology, v.2) **EE167**

Covers "the fields of metallic and nonmetallic mining, metals, fuels, minerals, geology, geophysics, beneficiation and processing, geography and the broad area of pure and applied earth sciences."—*Introd.* Emphasis is on current and continuing sources of information. In two parts: (1) organizations (arranged by geographical areas, with address, purpose, functions, publications, etc.); and (2) literature (arranged by subject field and listing bibliographies, handbooks, dictionaries, abstracts, journals, yearbooks). Separate indexes to the literature and to the organizations. Z7401.G83

Bibliography

International catalogue of scientific literature: G, Mineralogy. 1st–14th annual issues, 1901–14. London, 1902–17. 14v. **EE168**

For full description *see* EA17.

Mineralogical abstracts, issued by the Mineralogical Society, v.1– , 1920– . London, Simpkin, Marshall, 1922– . v.1– . **EE169**

Frequency varies. v.1–13 (1920–58) issued only with *Mineralogical magazine;* v.14– , published jointly by the Mineralogical Society of Great Britain and the Mineralogical Society of America.

A classified list of signed abstracts of current literature—books, pamphlets, reports, periodical articles, etc. International in coverage. Annual author and subject indexes. Supplements the record in the *International catalogue of scientific literature* (above), by summarizing the mineralogical literature from 1915. QE351.M35

Repertorium der mineralogischen und krystallographischen Literatur, 1876–[1902]; und Generalregister der Zeitschrift für Krystallographie und Mineralogie . . . Bd.1–40. Leipzig, Engelmann, 1886–1910. 4v. **EE170**

Each volume is in two parts: (1) a bibliography of material published during the period covered, and (2) an index to the *Zeitschrift.* The *Repertorium* covers 1876–85, 1885–91, 1891–97, 1897–1902. Z6033.M6R5

Reuss, Jeremias David. Repertorium commentationum a societatibus litterariis editarum . . . T.2, Botanica et mineralogia. Gottingae, Dieterich, 1802. 604p. **EE171**

A valuable index to the publications of learned societies up to 1800. Classed arrangement with author index. For description of the complete set *see* EA22.

Ridge, John Drew. Annotated bibliographies of mineral deposits in the Western hemisphere. Boulder, Colo., Geological Soc. of America, 1972. 681p. maps. (Geological Soc. of America, Memoir 131) **EE172**

Together with *Annotated bibliographies of mineral deposits in Africa, Asia (exclusive of the USSR) and Australasia* (below) and that for Europe (EE173a), this will form a revised and expanded version of *Selected bibliographies of hydrothermal and magmatic mineral deposits,* 1958.

"I have included in these bibliographies all deposits that have, in my opinion, been formed in whole or in part by magmatic or hydrothermal processes, including those produced by volcanic exhalations reaching the sea floor, for which I believe a worthwhile literature exists."—*Introd.* Thoroughly annotated. Arranged geographically; indexed by author, by deposit, by age of mineralization, by metals or minerals produced, and by Lindgren Classification Index. Z6738.075.R5

——— Annotated bibliographies of mineral deposits in Africa, Asia (exclusive of the USSR) and Australasia. Oxford & N.Y., Pergamon, [1976]. 545p. maps. **EE173**

For annotation *see* previous entry. Z6739.A3R53

——— Annotated bibliographies of mineral deposits in Europe. Oxford & N.Y., Pergamon, 1984. v.1. (In progress) **EE173a**

Contents: v.1, Northern Europe including examples from the USSR in both Europe and Asia. Z6738.O75R49

Zentralblatt für Mineralogie. 1950– . Stuttgart, Schweizerbart, 1950– . v.1– . **EE174**

Supersedes in part *Neues Jahrbuch für Mineralogie, Geologie und Paläontologie* (EE66).

In two sections: T.1, Kristallographie und Mineralogie (7 issues per yr.); T.2, Petrographie, technische Mineralogie, Geochemie und Lagerstättenkunde (title varies slightly; 13 issues per yr.).

Signed abstracts in German, arranged by subject; international coverage of serial and monographic literature. Author and subject indexes published two to three years after each volume is complete. QE351.Z45

Dictionaries and encyclopedias

Bailey, Dorothy and **Bailey, Kenneth C.** An etymological dictionary of chemistry and mineralogy. London, Edward Arnold, 1929. 307p. **EE175**

Gives the "derivation of chemical and mineralogical names which have been current in the literaure . . . at any period later than the middle of the 19th century."—*Pref.*

Bradley, J. E. S. and **Barnes, A. C.** Chinese-English glossary of mineral names. N.Y., Consultants Bureau, 1963. 120p. **EE176**

Basically a table of English equivalents of Chinese terms of minerals, based on the sounds of the Chinese characters, in an arrangement similar to Hey's *Index* (EE192). Includes an English index. QE355.B75

Chambers's Mineralogical dictionary, with 40 plates of coloured illustrations. [New ed.] London, Chambers; N.Y., Chemical Pub. Co., 1948. 47p. il. 40pl. **EE177**

Various printings.

Concise definitions of mineralogical terms, with brief descriptions of the more important minerals. QE355.C46

Frye, Keith, ed. The encyclopedia of mineralogy. Stroudsburg, Pa., Hutchinson Ross, [1981]. 794p. il. (Encyclopedia of earth sciences, v.4B) **EE178**

Consists of "articles by practicing mineralogists about the many aspects of their science."—*Pref.* Signed articles, with cross references and bibliographies, are arranged alphabetically. Contains a mineral glossary of nearly 3,000 entries, defined with chemical composition, structural group, and crystal system, plus cross references to articles. Indexed.   QE355.E49

A manual of new mineral names, 1892–1978. N.Y., Oxford Univ. Pr., 1980. 467p.   **EE179**

Ed. by Peter G. Embrey and John P. Fuller.

"A collection of the thirty Lists of New Mineral Names that have been published in the *Mineralogical Magazine.*"—*Foreword.* Offers an alphabetical listing of mineral names with complete bibliographic citation for first article which names and chemically identifies the mineral. Author index. Minerals which do not conform to the nomenclature of the new minerals and mineral names of the International Commission on Mineralogical Association have been included until new investigation can authenticate or relegate them to synonymy. Incorporates lists 1–21 by L. J. Spencer and 22–30 by M. H. Hey.   QE357.M36

Shipley, Robert Morrill [and others]. Dictionary of gems and gemology, including ornamental, decorative and curio stones. . . . 6th ed. Santa Monica, Calif., Gemological Inst. of America, 1974. 230p.   **EE180**

1st ed. 1945.

"A glossary of over 4,000 English and foreign words, terms and abbreviations which may be encountered in English literature or in the gem, jewelry or art trades."—*title page.*

Includes names of some persons, societies, museums, journals, etc. Entries within quotation marks identify misnomers. Pronunciation included for difficult words.   TN980.S5

Thrush, Paul W. A dictionary of mining, mineral, and related terms. [Wash., U.S. Bureau of Mines], 1968. 1269p.   **EE181**

For full citation and annotation *see* EJ336.   TN9.T5

Webster, Robert. Gems, their sources, descriptions, and identification. 4th ed. London & Boston, Butterworths, 1983. 1006p. il.   **EE182**

Rev. by B.W. Anderson.
1st ed. 1962.
A useful, comprehensive work.   QE392.W37

Directories

International Mineralogical Association. World directory of mineralogists. Ed. by Fabien Cesbron; comp. with the help of the representatives of the national mineralogical societies. Orleans, France, Bureau de Recherches Géologiques et Minières; Marburg, West Germany, Internat. Mineralogical Assoc., 1985. 361p. il.   **EE183**

1st ed. 1962.   QE361.A115

Handbooks

Bögel, Hellmuth. A collector's guide to minerals and gemstones. [Tr. from the German by Eva Fejer and Patricia Walter] Ed. and rev. by John Sinkankas. London, Thames & Hudson, 1971. 304p. il.   **EE184**

German edition, 1968, had title *Knaurs Mineralienbuch.* English translation also published with title *The studio handbook of minerals* (N.Y., Viking, 1972).

An illustrated handbook for the amateur. Includes a section of "Determinative tables" for identification of minerals.   QE363.2.B6413

Börner, Rudolf. Minerals, rocks, and gemstones. Tr. and ed. by W. Mykura. [English ed. repr. with additional plates and references] Edinburgh, London, Oliver & Boyd, [1966]. 250p. il.   **EE185**

"A translation of *Welcher Stein ist das?* by Rudolf Börner first

published in 1938 by Franckh'sche Verlagshandlung W. Keller & Co., Stuttgart." 1st English edition, 1962.

Adapted for use in Great Britain with rock classifications conforming to current English usage.

Designed as an aid to identification of specimens in the field with only minimal equipment. In three parts: the first gives properties, uses, and localities of 200 important minerals; the second provides an introduction to rocks, their uses and properties, and includes a short glossary of important rocks; the third, an introduction to the study of gemstones. Much information in tabular form. Bibliography; index.   QE365.B613

Dana, James Dwight and **Dana, Edward S.** The system of mineralogy. 7th ed. entirely rewritten and greatly enl. by Charles Palache, Harry Berman and Clifford Frondel. N.Y., Wiley, 1944–62. 3v.   **EE186**

1st ed. 1837.

Contents: v.1, Elements, sulfides, sulfosalts, oxides; v.2, Halides, nitrates, borates, carbonates, sulfates, phosphates, arsenates, tungstates, molybdates, etc.; v.3, Silica minerals.

Essentially a new work because of the accumulation of new data, and the development of analytical techniques and new classificatory systems since the 6th ed. (1892). An exhaustive treatment for the professional geologist, in classed arrangement, with information on each mineral, usually including sections on classification, morphological crystallography, X-ray crystallography, habit, physical properties, optical properties, chemistry, occurrences, alteration, synthesis, name, nomenclature, synonymy, bibliography, and abbreviation. Each volume individually indexed. The format of v.3 varies slightly in coverage of properties.   QE372.D23

Deer, William Alexander, Howie, R. A. and **Zussman, J.** Rock-forming minerals. London, Longmans, [1962–63]. 5v. il.   **EE187**

Contents: v.1, Ortho- and ring silicates; v.2, Chain silicates; v.3, Sheet silicates; v.4, Framework silicates; v.5, Nonsilicates.

Covers the common minerals of igneous, metamorphic, and sedimentary rocks. Within each volume information on each mineral or mineral group is divided into five subsections: Structure, giving brief description of atomic structure and the use of X-rays to determine chemical composition; Chemistry, giving principal variations in chemical composition, structural formula, and synthesis and breakdown of the minerals; Optical and physical properties, relating them to structure and chemistry; Distinguishing features, giving means or tests by which minerals may be recognized; and Paragenesis, giving principal rock types and typical mineral assemblages. Condensed tables and references accompany each entry. Each volume individually indexed.

A new edition has begun publication:

—————— —————— 2d ed. London, Longmans; N.Y., Halsted, [1978–82]. v.1A–2A. (In progress)   **EE188**

Contents: v.1A, Orthosilicates; v.2A, Single-chain silicates.

". . . completely new edition maintains the general principles and organization adopted for the first edition."—*Pref.*   QE364.2.R6

Dixon, Colin J. Atlas of economic mineral deposits. Ithaca, Cornell Univ. Pr., 1979. 143p. maps.   **EE189**

"Forty-eight mineral deposits or groups of deposits are described with world distribution maps of five selected groups of commodities."—*Introd.* The five sections cover the geological environment of the earth's surface, sedimentary rock, felsic magmatic environments, basic and ultrabasic magmatic rocks, and mineral deposits. Each diagram or map has text giving location, history, mining, and geology of deposits. Excludes deposits in USSR, China, and Eastern Europe. Indexed.   TN263.D57

Fay, Gordon S. The rockhound's manual. N.Y., Harper & Row, [1972]. 290p. il.   **EE190**

A handbook for the hobbyist. "Determinative tables and how to use them," p.223–71.   QE365.F22

Fisher, Peter Jack. The science of gems. New York, Scribner, [1966]. 189p. il.   **EE191**

English edition (1965) had title *Jewels*.

Presents information on the history of gems, their nature, methods of testing, characteristics, mining, synthesizing, and use and on the cutting of diamonds and other important gems. Contains a glossary and a bibliography. QE392.F53

Hey, Max Hutchinson. An index of mineral species & varieties arranged chemically, with an alphabetical index of accepted mineral names and synonyms. 2d, rev. ed., repr. with corrections. London, pr. by order of the Trustees of the British Museum, 1962. 728p. **EE192**

On cover: Chemical index of minerals.

A chemically classified list of minerals, followed by an alphabetical index. QE386.B8417

——— ———Appendix. London, Museum, 1963. 135p.

Johnstone, Sydney J. and **Johnstone, Margery G.** Minerals for the chemical and allied industries. 2d ed. London, Chapman & Hall, 1961. 788p. **EE193**

1st ed. 1954.

Alphabetically arranged chapters on various minerals giving as pertinent: description, world production, uses, bibliography, etc. Appendixes give names of organizations and firms which have assisted in supplying information incorporated in the volume, and a list of international and overseas standards organizations. The new edition contains information on synthetic minerals and the composition of some products marketed by commercial firms. Indexed. TN260.J6

Lefond, Stanley J. Handbook of world salt resources. N.Y., Plenum, 1969. 384p. **EE194**

Concise accounts of salt resources and deposits in individual countries (and the individual states of the United States) are presented, together with tables of chemical analysis, statistics on production, and bibliographical references. Indexed. TN900.L44

Nicolay, H. H. and **Stone, A. V.** Rocks and minerals: a guide for collectors of the eastern United States. South Brunswick, N.J., Barnes, [1967]. 255p. il. **EE195**

A state-by-state, county-by-county guide indicating the types of rocks and minerals to be found in each area. For the amateur and hobbyist. QE364.N49

Picot, Paul and **Johan, Zdenek.** Atlas of ore minerals. Orleans, France, Bureau de Recherches Géologiques et Minières; Amsterdam, Elsevier, 1982. 458p. il. **EE196**

Detailed criteria for determination and identification of more than 350 ore minerals. Critera include color, reflectance, anisotopy, and structure; there is a color photograph for most entries. QE390.P52

Pough, Frederick H. A field guide to rocks and minerals. 4th ed. Boston, Houghton Mifflin, 1976. 317p. il. **EE197**

1st ed. 1953.

A practical handbook for mineral identification. In two parts, the first describing matters pertaining to care and maintenance of a collection, geographical distribution of minerals, physical properties, crystal classifications, chemical classification, and testing techniques. In the second and major part, properties of individual minerals are described, each mineral appearing with related minerals in a classed arrangement by type. Gives details of environment, where found, description, composition, distinguishing characteristics, occurrence, etc. Numerous plates, some in color. Glossary, bibliography, and index. QE367.P6

Ransom, Jay Ellis. A range guide to mines and minerals; how and where to find valuable ores and minerals in the United States. [1st ed.] N.Y., Harper, [1964]. 305p. il. **EE198**

Introductory chapters on mineral collection are followed by a range guide arranged by state, county, township, and range. Short glossary and bibliography. TN23.R25

Roberts, Willard Lincoln, Rapp, George Robert and **Weber, Julius.** Encyclopedia of minerals. N.Y., Van Nostrand Reinhold, [1974]. 693p. il. **EE199**

Alphabetically arranged descriptions of 2,200 minerals, giving chemical composition, crystallographic data, physical properties and description, mode of occurrence, best reference in English, and a color photograph. Includes a brief glossary. QE355.R63

Scalisi, Philip and **Cook, David.** Classic mineral localities of the world: Asia and Australia. N.Y., Van Nostrand Reinhold, 1983. 226p. il., maps. **EE200**

Describes sites that are "generally acknowledged to have produced some of the finest examples of mineral species."—*Pref.* Includes descriptions of individual specimens, as well as photographs and crystal drawings. TN99.S28

Sinkankas, John. Van Nostrand's Standard catalog of gems. Princeton, N.J., Van Nostrand, [1968]. 286p. il. **EE201**

A guide to values rather than a guide for identification of gems. TS752.S53

U.S. Bureau of Mines. Minerals yearbook, 1932/33– . Wash., Govt. Prt. Off., 1933– . il. Annual. **EE202**

Supersedes the Bureau's *Mineral resources of the United States,* 1882–1931, as well as various interim summaries.

The volumes dated 1932/33 through 1940 contain reviews of 1932 through 1939. In 1941, designation was changed to use the date of period covered. Therefore, two volumes bear the date 1940: (1) 1940 (review of 1939), and (2) the actual review of 1940.

Beginning 1952, issued in 3 to 4 volumes per year. The 1983 yearbook is in 3v.: v.1, Metals and minerals; v.2, Area reports: domestic; v.3, Area reports: international.

Provides information on worldwide industrial performance for the year covered. The material is largely tabular in format, but background information is provided to permit interpretation of the year's developments. Contents of volumes in recent years have included chapters on metallic, non-metallic, and mineral fuel commodities and their relationship to the domestic economy, a review of the mineral industries, technological trends, and area reports, which cover mineral production and economic indicators for states within the United States and for foreign countries. Arrangement of v.1 is alphabetical by mineral, and by state or country in the area reports. No index. TN23.U642

——— ——— Statistical appendix. 1932/33–1935. Wash., Govt. Prt. Off., 1934–36. 3v. il.

No more published.

Later statistical figures included in the *Yearbook.*

Meteorites

British Museum (Natural History). Dept. of Mineralogy. Catalogue of meteorites, with special reference to those represented in the collection of the British Museum (Natural History). 3d rev. and enl. ed. by Max H. Hey. London, Trustees of the British Museum, 1966. 637p. **EE203**

1st ed. 1923; 2d ed. 1953.

The new edition attempts to include "the names of all well-authenticated meteorites known up to December 1965."—*Introd.* QE395.B88

Brown, Harrison Scott. A bibliography on meteorites. Assoc. eds.: Gunnar Kullerud, Walter Nichiporuk. Chicago, Univ. of Chicago Pr., 1953. 686p. (An international catalogue of meteorites) **EE204**

The first of a projected 3v. catalog of meteorites. This covers, in chronological order, literature published from 1491 to 1950, with an author index. Cites papers and books, giving references to abstracts where possible. Z6033.M5B7

Directory of meteorite collections and meteorite research. Paris, UNESCO, [1968]. 50p. **EE205**

By country, this directory lists collections, catalogs, research institutions, researchers, and topics of research.   QE395.U54

OCEANOGRAPHY

Bibliography

Collected bibliographies on physical oceanography (1953–1964). Wash., Amer. Meteorological Soc., 1965. 807p. (Special bibliographies on oceanography. Contribution no.1)
EE206

"This compilation consists of 13 Special Bibliographies comprising over 3600 abstracts of literature pertinent to various aspects of Physical Oceanography, selected from 170 special bibliographies originally published in the monthly issues of *Meteorological Abstracts and Bibliography (MAB)* and *Meteorological and Geoastrophysical Abstracts (M&GA)* during the period 1950–1964."—*Introd.*

Deep sea research, part B: Oceanic literature review. v.26– , Jan. 1979– . Oxford, Pergamon, 1979– . Monthly.
EE207

Issued as a part of *Deep sea research;* subtitle, frequency, and format vary. v.1–13, entitled "Oceanographic abstracts" and "Oceanographic bibliography," were published within issues of *Deep sea research*; v.14–23 were published separately as "Oceanographic abstracts and oceanographic bibliography section"; v.24–25 were published separately as "Oceanographic abstracts and bibliography."
"A monthly selection of references from recent literature on oceanography and related disciplines."—*Pref.* Classified abstracts with quarterly subject and author indexes; annual cumulative index.

Library of the Marine Biological Laboratory and the Woods Hole Oceanographic Institution. Catalog. Boston, G. K. Hall, 1971. 12v.
EE208

Reproduction of the catalog cards for a collection of some 12,000 books and monographs, reports of 138 expeditions, and nearly 300,000 journal articles. Arranged alphabetically, except that periodicals (about 4,000 titles) are separately listed in v.12, the "Journal catalog."   Z881.L72

Sears, Mary. Oceanographic index; author cumulation, 1946–1970. Boston, G. K. Hall, 1971. 3v.   **EE209**

Z6004.P6S43

────── Oceanographic index; subject cumulation, 1946–1971. Boston, G. K. Hall, 1972. 4v.   **EE210**

Z6004.P6S44

────── Oceanographic index; regional cumulation, 1946–1970. Boston, G. K. Hall, 1971. 706p.   **EE211**

Reproduction of a card file maintained by the compiler and based on the collection of books and journals held in the library of the Marine Biological Laboratory, Woods Hole, Mass. Emphasis is on biological oceanography, physical oceanography, marine chemistry, geology, and meteorology.   Z6004.P6S436

U.S. Defense Documentation Center, Arlington, Va. Oceanography, a report bibliography, comp. by Esther E. Thompson. Arlington, Va., 1963. 355p.   **EE212**

An abstract bibliography on oceanography including biological, chemical, economic, physical and practical, and applied oceanography as well as marine geology and scientific research in these areas.
Z6004.P6U37

U.S. Environmental Science Services Administration. ESSA libraries holdings in oceanography and marine meteorology, 1710–1967. Rockville, Md., The Administration, Scientific Information and Documentation Division, 1969. 4v.
EE213

Contents: v.1, Bibliography; v.2, Author and subject indexes; v.3, Systematic indexes; v.4, Keyword (KWIC) index.
A computer-produced catalog of about 3,000 references.

Current

Oceanic index. v.1–4, 1964–67. La Jolla, Calif., Oceanic Research Inst., 1964–68.   **EE214**

Frequency varies.
Title varies: v.1–2 entitled *Oceanic coordinate index.*
A computerized index of the literature of the ocean sciences, including physics, chemistry, biology, geology, meteorology, and other related areas.
Superseded in part by:

Oceanic citation journal, with abstracts. v.5–8, 1968–71. La Jolla, Calif., Oceanic Research Inst., 1968–72.   **EE215**

Supersedes the citation section of *Oceanic index* and continues its numbering.
Superseded by: Z6004.P6O25

Oceanic abstracts with indexes. v.9– , Feb. 1972– . [La Jolla, Calif., Pollution Abstracts, Inc.], 1972– . 6 nos. a yr.
EE216

A classified abstracts section is followed by a "keytalpha" subject index and an author index. Covers aspects of biology, geology, oceanography, pollution, engineering, ships, and other marine-related subjects. Includes citations to foreign-language materials, with abstracts in English. Annual cumulated indexes.   GC1.O24

Dictionaries and encyclopedias

Fairbridge, Rhodes Whitmore. The encyclopedia of oceanography. N.Y., Reinhold, [1966]. 1021p. il. (Encyclopedia of earth sciences, v.1)   **EE217**

Signed articles (with bibliographies) ranging from the general to the highly technical, and including closely allied topics such as navigation. Numerous charts, illustrations, and tables; cross references and index.   GC9.F3

Firth, Frank E., ed. The encyclopedia of marine resources. N.Y., Van Nostrand Reinhold, [1969]. 740p. il.   **EE218**

Signed articles by specialists on the most significant aspects of the ocean's resources and closely related topics. Oceanography and marine engineering are given only brief treatment. Many entries include bibliographical references. Cross references; index.
SH201.F56

Groves, Donald G. and **Hunt, Lee M.** Ocean world encyclopedia. N.Y., McGraw-Hill, [1980]. 443p. il.   **EE219**

Intended for the non-specialist. Includes articles on physical, geological, chemical, and biological oceanography, oceanographic instrumentation, hurricanes, international marine science organizations, and biographies of famous oceanographers. Indexed.
GC9.G76

Hunt, Lee M. and **Groves, Donald G.,** eds. A glossary of ocean science and undersea technology terms. Arlington, Va., Compass Pubns., 1965. 173p.   **EE220**

Subtitle: An authoritative compilation of over 3,500 engineering and scientific terms used in the field of underwater sound, oceanography, marine sciences, underwater physiology and ocean engineering.
Many of the definitions are quoted from other sources, and reference to the quoted work is indicated. Appendix of useful charts and tables.   GC9.H85

U.S. Naval Oceanographic Office. Glossary of oceanographic terms. Ed. by B. B. Baker, Jr., W. R. Deebel, and R. D. Geisenderfer. 2d ed. Wash., U.S. Nat. Oceanographic Office, 1966. 204p. il. (*Its* Special publication, SP-35)   **EE221**

Provides definitions of technical terms which "represent current and, in some places, past usage in the marine aspects of physics, chemistry, biology, geology, geophysics, geography, mathematics, and meteorology, particularly in the manner that these terms are used in the U.S. Naval Oceanographic Office research, operations, and publications."—*Pref.* Appendixes list sources of definitions; abbreviations and acronyms; and oceanographic institutions, agencies, activities, and groups.   GC9.U5

Directories

International directory of marine scientists. 3d ed. Paris, UNESCO, 1983. 1v., various pagings.   **EE222**

1st ed. 1970.
"A product of the joint FAO/IOC/UN(EOTC) Aquatic Sciences and Fisheries Information System (ASFIS) with support from Unesco."—*t.p.*
Identifies approximately 2,500 institutions and 18,000 specialists in marine sciences. Scientists are grouped by institution within country. Name and subject indexes.   GC10.I57

Ocean research index; a guide to ocean and freshwater research, including fisheries research. Guernsey, [Channel Isls.], F. Hodgson, [1970]. 507p.   **EE223**

Attempts to bring together "information on organisations throughout the world which conduct, promote or encourage research in marine and freshwater science and related fields."—*Introd.* Arrangement is by country, then alphabetically by name of the unit; helpful cross references are provided to direct the user to appropriate government departments, etc. In most entries the address, name of the director, and scope of interests are indicated.   GC10.O26

U.S. directory of marine scientists, 1982. Wash., Nat. Academy Pr., 1982. 214p.   **EE224**

Provides information on 4,192 individuals based on a 1980 questionnaire. Scientists are listed alphabetically by field of expertise; organizations alphabetically and regionally (by zip code).   GC10.U17

Handbooks

Handbook of marine science. Boca Raton, Fla., CRC Pr., 1974–76. [Sec. I] 2v.; [Sec.II] 2v.   **EE225**

Contents: [Sec.I] Oceanography—v.1, Physical (F. G. Walton Smith, ed.); v.2, Biological (Frederick A. Kalber and F. G. Walton Smith, eds.); [Sec.II] Marine products—v.1, Compounds from marine organisms (Joseph T. Baker and Vreni Murphy, eds.).
Sec.I consists of tables assembled from many sources to provide a convenient source of information for oceanographers; each volume is separately indexed. Sec.II is a compilation of information about organic compounds derived from marine organisms.

Atlases

Couper, Alastair, ed. The Times atlas of the oceans. N.Y., Van Nostrand Reinhold, [1983]. 372p. il., maps. 37cm.   **EE226**

Coverage of physical and biological oceanography, ocean resources, ocean use, ocean management, and the law of the sea. Appendixes, glossary, bibliography, and index.   G2800.T5

Rand McNally atlas of the oceans. N.Y., Rand McNally, [1977]. 208p. il., maps. 38cm.   **EE227**

A clearly written, profusely illustrated, and well-indexed encyclopedic guide for the non-specialist. Includes information on physical and biological oceanography and on man's interactions with the ocean. The final chapter is a brief encyclopedia of marine life, arranged taxonomically.   GC11.2.R35

World ocean atlas. Sergei Georgievich Gorshkov, editor in chief. Oxford & Elmsford, N.Y., Pergamon, 1976–78. 2v. maps. 46cm.   **EE228**

Contents: v.1, Pacific ocean; v.2, Atlantic ocean.
Includes charts on ocean bed, climate, hydrology, hydrochemistry, biogeography, navigation, and many other topics, presented with great care on beautifully colored plates. Text, keys, and captions to figures are in Russian. A translation (poorly done) is provided only for the brief introductory text and index.

PALEONTOLOGY

Bibliography

Bibliography and index of micropaleontology. v.1– , Jan. 1972– . N.Y., Micropaleontology Pr. of the American Museum of Natural History, 1972– . Monthly.   **EE229**

"This specialized bibliography and index is produced in cooperation with the American Geological Institute's (AGI) bibliographic staff. . . . These records are added to the Geological Reference File (GEO-REF) of the AGI, which is a computerized indexed reference file supported by the National Science Foundation."—*Pref., v.1, no.1.*   QE719.B5●

Bibliography of vertebrate paleontology and related subjects. 1945/46– . [Chicago?], Soc. of Vertebrate Paleontology, 1947– . Annual.   **EE230**

No.1–20 prepared from periodicals received by the Library of the American Museum of Natural History in New York. Previously included in the *News bulletin* of the Society of Vertebrate Paleontology. No.20– (1965/66–) prepared from working files for forthcoming volumes of the *Bibliography of fossil vertebrates* (see EE232).
Arranged alphabetically by author. Through 1964/65, each issue in two parts: (1) the preceding year and earlier, and (2) the year covered.   Z6033.P2B5

Hay, Oliver Perry. Bibliography and catalogue of the fossil vertebrata of North America. [v.1] Wash., Govt. Prt. Off., 1902. (U.S. Geological Survey Bull. no.179)   **EE231**

——— Second bibliography and catalogue . . . Wash., Carnegie Inst., 1929–30. 2v. (Carnegie Inst. Pubn. no.390)

Comprehensive author bibliographies covering North America to 1927, with subject and systematic indexes. The second compilation extends the coverage to include Greenland, Mexico, and Central America.
Supplemented by: Z6033.P2H4

Camp, Charles Lewis [and others]. Bibliography of fossil vertebrates. 1928–72. N.Y., Geological Soc. of America, 1940–73. 9v. Quinquennial. (G.S.A. Special papers, no.27, 42; G.S.A. Memoir, no.37, 57, 84, 92, 117, 134, 141)   **EE232**

Contents: 1928–33; 1934–38; 1939–43; 1944–48; 1949–53; 1954–58; 1959–63; 1964–68; 1969–72.
Consists of author catalogs, international in scope, of serial and separate publications. Subject and systematic indexes.
Continued by: Z6033.P2C32

Green, Morton [and others]. Bibliography of fossil vertebrates, 1973–1977. Rapid City, S.D., South Dakota School of Mines and Technology, 1979. 1v., various pagings. (Dakoterra, no.1)   **EE233**

Continued by:

Gregory, Joseph T. [and others]. Bibliography of fossil vertebrates. 1978– . Falls Church, Va., Amer. Geological Inst., 1981– . Annual.   **EE234**

A subset of citations from the GeoRef database, selected, edited, and indexed by editors at the University of California, Berkeley. Subject and systematic indexes.   Z6033.P2B48●

Hiltermann, Heinrich [and others]. Bibliographie stratigraphisch wichtiger mikropaläontologischer Publikationen von etwa 1830 bis 1958 mit Kurzreferaten. Stuttgart, E. Schweizerbart'sche Verlagsbuchhandlung, 1961. 403p.   **EE235**

A bibliography of microfossils in connection with stratigraphic problems. International scope. Classed arrangement, with author and subject/place indexes.   Z6033.P2H5

International catalogue of scientific literature: K. Paleontology. London, 1902–19. 14v.   **EE236**

For full description *see* EA17.

Romer, Alfred Sherwood [and others]. Bibliography of fossil vertebrates exclusive of North America, 1509–1927. N.Y., Geological Soc. of America, 1962. 2v. (1544p.) (G.S.A. Memoir 87)   **EE237**

A comprehensive international bibliography of serial literature, separately published volumes, and pamphlets, through the year 1927, arranged alphabetically by author. No subject index. Complements Hay (EE231).   Z6033.P2R6

Encyclopedias

The encyclopedia of paleontology. Stroudsburg, Pa., Dowden, Hutchinson & Ross, 1979. 886p. (Encyclopedia of earth sciences, v.7)   **EE238**

Rhodes W. Fairbridge and David Jablonski, eds.

"Coverage is an attempt to provide a survey of many of the objects and concepts encompassed by this multifaceted field within the limits of a single volume. The entries are written at several conceptual levels from the most basic [to] inclusive articles . . . the extensive reference lists and cross-references at the end of each [entry] are designed to lead the reader deeper into the subject."—*Pref.*   QE703.E52

Fossil indexes

Andrews, Henry Nathaniel. Index of generic names of fossil plants, 1820–1965. Based on the Compendium index of paleobotany of the U.S. Geological Survey. Wash., 1970. 354p. (U.S. Geological Survey. Bull. 1300)   **EE239**

Arranged alphabetically according to genus, then by species. Gives names of authors and an abbreviated citation. Complete references are given in the bibliography.   QE906.A7

Ellis, Brooks Fleming and **Messina, Angelina R.** Catalogue of Foraminifera. . . . Special publication. N.Y., Amer. Museum of Natural History, 1940. 30v. and supplements (looseleaf). il.   **EE240**

v.30 is "Index to taxonomic changes and Bibliography."

For each species, arranged alphabetically by genus, gives synonymy, type reference, type figure, type description, type level, type locality, and type specimen. In many cases, includes illustrations. Supplements (1945–) have similar arrangement.   QL368.F6E5

—— Catalogue of index Foraminifera. Special publication. N.Y., Amer. Museum of Natural History, 1965–67. 3v. il.   **EE241**

Records the geologic and geographic distribution of Foraminifera. Bibliographic references.   QE772.E4

—— Catalogue of Ostracoda. N.Y., Amer. Museum of Natural History, 1952–64. 20v. and supplements.   **EE242**

Provides the same type of information as the author's *Catalogue of Foraminifera,* but is arranged stratigraphically. Beginning 1964, about two supplements per year have been issued, containing units on new species, plus some units which update previous entries. Entire set is in looseleaf format.   QL444.08.E38

Fossilium catalogus. I, Animalia. Pars. 1– . 1913– . Amsterdam, Kugler, Publ. by W. Junk, 1913–83. Pars.1–127. (In progress)   **EE243**

—— II, Plantae. Pars. 1– . 1913– . Amsterdam, Kugler, Publ. by W. Junk, 1913–85. Pars.1–91. (In progress)   **EE244**

The two sections make up an important, comprehensive series, each published part on a separate subject by a specialist. The Animalia section has proceeded through pt.127 in 1983; the Plantae section through pt.91 in 1985.

Each part consists of a catalog of known species and an index and bibliography pertaining to the class covered.

Purnell, Louis R. Catalog of the type specimens of invertebrate fossils. Wash., Smithsonian Institution Pr., 1968– . pt.1– . il. (U.S. National Museum. Bull. 262) (In progress?)   **EE245**

Contents: pt.1, Paleozoic cephalopoda.

First in a proposed series listing invertebrate fossil-type specimens in the collection of the Division of Invertebrate Paleontology of the Smithsonian Institution.

Arranged by subclass and then alphabetically by species. Gives author and brief reference, type, catalog number, rock unit, and geographic source of the specimen. Complete citations in bibliography.   Q11.U6

Shimer, Hervey Woodburn and **Shrock, Robert R.** Index fossils of North America. A publication of the Technology Press, Massachusetts Institute of Technology. N.Y., Wiley, [1944]. 837p. il.   **EE246**

Subtitle: Based on the complete revision and reillustration of Grabau and Shimer's *North American index fossils.*

"An index fossil is one which identifies and dates the strata or succession of strata in which it lies."—*p.1.* This work is a systematic arrangement of descriptions of index fossil animals, with brief inclusion of fossil plants. Index of genera; index of species.   QE745.S48

Treatise on invertebrate paleontology. Directed and ed. by Raymond C. Moore. [N.Y.], Geological Soc. of America, 1953–83. Pt.[A–W]. il. (In progress)   **EE247**

Parts are assigned letters, A to W, with a view to indicating their systematic sequence, but are published at whatever time each is ready. Parts published include: A, C–I, K–L, N$^{1–2}$, O–W.

The parts are divided according to phylum, and the orders, classes, genera, species, etc., in each phylum are described: their growth and development, general features, characteristics, etc., with references to the literature.

New editions of some parts have begun to appear as: QE770.T7

—— 2d editions directed and ed. by Curt Teichert. 2d ed., rev. and enl. Boulder, Colo., Geological Soc. of America, 1970– . Pt. E^1, G, V.   **EE248**

QE770.T72

Directories

Cleevely, R. J. World palaeontological collections. London, British Museum, Mansell, [1983]. 365p.   **EE249**

Includes list of published catalogs, alphabetical index of collectors, geographic index of institutions, and collection holdings.   QE716.G72

International Paleontological Union. Directory of palaeontologists of the world (excl. Soviet Union & continental China). 2d ed. Comp. by G. E. G. Westermann. Hamilton, Ont., McMaster Univ., 1968. 250p.   **EE250**

Includes listings by selected disciplines, regional specializations, systematic specializations, and institutions.

Handbooks

Fenton, Carroll Lane and **Fenton, Mildred Adams.** The fossil book; a record of prehistoric life. Garden City, N.Y., Doubleday, [1958]. 482p. il.   **EE251**

"This book surveys the realm of fossils from the earliest plantlike organisms to beasts and birds that lived a few centuries ago. Only man is omitted."—*Acknowledgments.*   QE711.F38

Kummel, Bernhard and **Raup, David,** eds. Handbook of paleontological techniques. San Francisco, Freeman, [1965]. 852p. il.   **EE252**

Prep. under the auspices of the Paleontological Society.

A series of essays on various techniques, followed by a section of bibliographies on paleontological techniques and other bibliographies of use to workers in this area. Indexed.   QE718.K8

Piveteau, Jean, ed. Traité de paléontologie. Paris, Masson, [1952–69]. 7v. in 10. il.   **EE253**

An excellent series, with bibliographies, glossaries, index, etc.   QE711.P62

Ransom, Jay Ellis. Fossils in America: their nature, origin, identification and classification, and a range guide to collecting sites. N.Y., Harper, [1964]. 402p. il.   **EE254**

A popularly written work with detailed information on the origin, nature, and collecting of fossils. Fossil localities are arranged by state, with subdivisions.   QE746.R3

Rhodes, Frank Harold Trevor, Zim, Herbert S. and **Shaffer, Paul R.** Fossils, a guide to prehistoric life. N.Y., Golden Pr., [1962]. 160p. il.   **EE255**

A good guide for the beginning fossil collector. Illustrations are excellent.   QE714.3.R5

Thompson, Ida. The Audubon Society field guide to North American fossils. N.Y., Knopf, [1982]. 846p. il., maps.   **EE256**

A detailed guide for the collector, with more than 500 color plates. Appendixes; index.   QE718.T5

Biography

Lambrecht, Kalman and **Quenstedt, W.** Palaeontologi. Catalogus bio-bibliographicus. 'sGravenhage, W. Junk, 1938. 495p. (*In* Fossilium catalogus. I, Animalia, ed. by W. Quenstedt, pars 72)   **EE257**

An alphabetical list of paleontologists of many countries and periods, giving full name, places and dates of birth and death, identification data, and references to biographical data.

PETROLOGY

See also Natural history.

Fenton, Carroll Lane and **Fenton, Mildred Ames.** The rock book. N.Y., Doubleday, 1940. 357p. il.   **EE258**

A popularly written handbook on rocks and minerals. Offers text, black-and-white drawings, and black-and-white and color photographs, in a topical arrangement. Indexed.   QE431.F4

Holmes, Arthur. Nomenclature of petrology, with references to selected literature. London, Murby, [1928]. 284p.   **EE259**

1st ed. 1920; this edition incorporates a few corrections and modifications.   QE425.H6

Johannsen, Albert. A descriptive petrography of the igneous rocks. Chicago, Univ. of Chicago Pr., 1931–38. 4v. il. (v.1, 2d ed. 1939)   **EE260**

Contents: v.1, Introduction, textures, classifications, and glossary; v.2, The quartz-bearing rocks; v.3, The intermediate rocks; v.4: pt.1, The feldspathoid rocks; pt.2, The peridotites and perknites. Index of authors, of localities, of rock names.

A standard, basic work, with bibliographical footnotes. v.1 includes appendixes: Miscellaneous definitions; Definitions of textural terms.   QE461.J6

Telberg, Vladimir George. Russian-English petrographic dictionary. N.Y., Telberg, [1967]. 250p.   **EE261**

Russian terms with English equivalents. Names and abbreviations are omitted.   QE425.T4

Tomkeieff, S.I. Dictionary of petrology. Chichester; N.Y., Wiley, 1983. 680p.   **EE262**

Ed. by E.K. Walton and others.

Approximately 10,000 terms, with bibliographic references to early usage. Synoptic classification tables provide a subject grouping of terms and serve as a thesaurus.   QE425.T65

SEISMOLOGY

Ganse, Robert A. and **Nelson, John B.** Catalog of significant earthquakes, 2000 B.C.–1979, including quantitative casualties and damage. Boulder, Colo., World Data Center A for Solid Earth Geophysics, 1981. 154p. (Report SE-27)   **EE263**

Includes 2,484 events meeting the following criteria: damage greater than $1 million, or more than 10 deaths, or magnitude greater than 7.5. Listed chronologically and by longitude and latitude. References.

Montessus de Ballore, Fernand, *Comte* de. Bibliografía general de temblores y terremotos. Publicada por la Sociedad Chilena de Historia y Geografía. Chile, Impr. Universitaria, 1915–19. 7 pts. (1515p.)   **EE264**

Contents: 1. pt., Teorías sismológicas. Efectos geológicos de los terremotos. Catálogos sísmicos mundiales; 2. pt., Europa septentrional y central; 3. pt., Países circunmediterráneos; 4. pt., Asia, África, y Oceanía; 5. pt., América, Tierras antárticas y océanos; 6. pt., Fenómenos accesorios. El movimiento sísmico . . . Literatura sísmica. Historia de la sismología. Misceláneas; 7. pt., Prólogo. Suplemento. Apéndice. Addenda. (Indexes not published?)

Also published in *Revista chilena de historia y geografía,* 1915–19.

Covers books and periodicals from all countries, with no chronological limitations.   Z6033.E1M7

U.S. Coast and Geodetic Survey. Earthquake history of the United States. Rev. ed. (through 1963). Wash., Govt. Prt. Off., 1965–66. 2v. (*Its* [Pubn.] 41-1, rev.)   **EE265**

Contents: pt.1, Stronger earthquakes of the United States (exclusive of California and Western Nevada), by R. A. Eppley; pt.2, Stronger earthquakes of California and Western Nevada, by H. O. Wood and N. H. Heck. Rev. ed. (through 1963) by R. A. Eppley.

Consists of chronological listings, with descriptions, of major, intermediate and minor earthquakes, arranged by region. Pt.1 has a state-by-state listing of dates of quakes.   QE535.U622

United States earthquakes, 1928– . Wash., Govt. Prt. Off., 1930– . Annual.   **EE266**

Issuing body varies: 1928-68, U.S. Coast and Geodetic Survey; 1969-72, National Oceanic and Atmospheric Administration; 1973– , NOAA in cooperation with the U.S. Geological Survey.

An annual report of earthquakes felt in the United States. Includes some general discussions and information, earthquake descriptions arranged by region, descriptions and charts on miscellaneous activities, and strong-motions seismograph data.

VOLCANOLOGY

International Volcanological Association. Catalogue of the active volcanoes of the world including solfatara fields. Naples, 1951–67. 21 pts. il. **EE267**

Each part treats a different area of the world.

Usually gives for each volcano: name and location, with information on type, geographical position, and height; form and structure, with a short description of the volcano; volcanic activity, with dates of eruptions and details of occurring events or phenomena; petrography, giving kind and analysis of rocks; and a bibliography, listing principal literature. Also included are maps of craters, and information on volcanoes which had eruptions in historic time but are now extinct. QE522.I6

Simkin, Tom [and others]. Volcanoes of the world. Stroudsburg, Pa., Hutchinson Ross, 1981. 232p. **EE268**

Subtitle: A regional directory, gazetteer, and chronology of volcanism during the last 10,000 years.

Includes a gazetteer of 5,345 volcanic names, synonyms, and feature names; a chronology of 5,564 eruptions; a regional directory of 1,343 volcanoes; and a bibliography of 709 references. QE522.V92

E F

Mathematics

❖Parke's *Guide to the literature of mathematics and physics* (EF4) although dated, should be consulted for additional titles in these fields. A general reference collection will need a mathematics dictionary such as James's *Mathematics dictionary* (EF26) or Karush's *The crescent dictionary of mathematics* (EF27), and perhaps the *Universal encyclopedia of mathematics* (EF33); possibly one of the handbooks, e.g., Merritt's *Mathematics manual* (EF48) or Korn's *Mathematical handbook for scientists and engineers* (EF46); and, according to circumstances, one or more of the compendiums of statistics.

GENERAL WORKS

Guides

Dick, Elie M. Current information sources in mathematics; an annotated guide to books and periodicals, 1960–1972. Littleton, Colo., Libraries Unlimited, 1973. 281p. **EF1**

Intended "to provide students, instructors, and research workers with an up-to-date bibliography of recent sources in mathematics,

with an emphasis on monographic materials."—*Pref.* Limited to books in English and English translations, published 1960 to mid-1972. Classed arrangement with author and subject indexes. Includes a section listing the most prominent mathematics periodicals, with bibliographic and subscription information. Z6651.D53

Dorling, Alison Rosemary, ed. Use of mathematical literature. Woburn, Mass., Butterworths, 1977. 260p. (Information sources for research and development) **EF2**

Chapters on mathematical literature, organizations, reference materials, mathematics education, and the history of mathematics are followed by nine chapters on topical areas in mathematics, with bibliographies. Includes author and subject indexes. QA41.7.U83

Loria, Gino. Guida allo studio della storia delle matematiche; generalità, didattica, bibliografia. Appendice: Questioni storiche concernenti le scienze esatte. 2. ed. rif. e aum. Milano, Hoepli, 1946. 385p. **EF3**

A comprehensive guide to the literature of the history of mathematics, covering all periods and all countries. Includes material on the history, manuscripts, biographical sources, reviews, periodicals, etc. Unfortunately, many typographical errors.

Parke, Nathan Grier. Guide to the literature of mathematics and physics including related works on engineering science. 2d rev. ed. N.Y., Dover, [1958]. 436p. **EF4**

1st ed. 1947.

A useful handbook comprising chapters on principles of reading and study, searching the literature, types of materials, library use, etc., and a bibliography of some 5,000 titles published up to 1956, arranged by subject, with notes for each section. Author and subject indexes. Stresses the applied mathematical point of view. Z6651.P3

Schaefer, Barbara Kirsch. Using the mathematical literature: a practical guide. N.Y., Dekker, [1979]. 141p. **EF5**

Addressed to students, teachers, and practitioners of mathematics, scientists in other fields, and students and practitioners of library science. Not intended to be comprehensive, but a guide to different types of mathematical literature. QA41.7.S3

Bibliography

See also EF31.

Dauben, Joseph W. The history of mathematics from antiquity to the present. A selective bibliography. N.Y., Garland, 1985. 467p. (Bibliographies of the history of science and technology, no. 6). **EF6**

The 2,384 entries in this bibliography are divided into six main sections: (I) General reference works; (II) Source materials; (III) General histories of mathematics; (IV) The history of mathematics: chronological periods; (V) The history of mathematics: sub-disciplines; (VI) The history of mathematics: selected topics. All entries have been read critically and annotated by members of an international group of 49 expert contributors. A nineteen-page introduction by the author on the historiography of mathematics includes references. This book and May's *Bibliography and research manual of the history of mathematics* (EF12) are indispensable tools for the historian of mathematics. Indexed. Z6651.D38

Forsythe, George Elmer. Bibliography of Russian mathematics books. N.Y., Chelsea, 1956. 106p. **EF7**

Lists alphabetically by author more than 600 book titles in pure and applied mathematics, published (or reprinted) in Russian or Ukrainian since 1930, excluding works translated into Russian. Some entries include a reference to the *Mathematical reviews* entry for that title. Classified "subject index." Table showing transliteration systems used in various bibliographic sources. Z6651.F6

International catalogue of scientific literature: A, Mathematics. 1st–14th annual issues, 1901–14. London, Harrison, 1902–17. v.1–14. **EF8**

For full description *see* EA17.

International Statistical Institute. Bibliography of basic texts and monographs on statistical methods, 1945–1960. [2d ed. by William R. Buckland and Ronald A. Fox] Edinburgh, Oliver & Boyd; N.Y., Hafner, [1963]. 297p. **EF9**

For full information *see* CG12.

Karpinski, Louis Charles. Bibliography of mathematical works printed in America through 1850 . . . with the cooperation for Washington libraries of Walter F. Shenton. Ann Arbor, Univ. of Michigan Pr.; London, Milford, Oxford Univ. Pr., 1940. 697p. il. (incl. facsim.) **EF10**

A chronological record of mathematical works in various languages printed in America. Later editions and issues of each title are listed under the 1st edition. Includes more than 1,000 titles and some 3,000 editions. Locates copies in more than 100 libraries.

Indexes: General index of authors' names and anonymous titles; Topical indexes; Index of non-English and Canadian works; Index of printers and publishers.

—— —— Supplements, 1–2. (*In* Scripta mathematica 8:233–36, Dec. 1941; 11:173–77, June 1945)

Z6651.K18

Mathematical Association of America. Committee on the Undergraduate Program in Mathematics. A basic library list for four-year colleges. 2d ed. Wash., Mathematical Assoc. of America, 1976. 106p. **EF11**

1st ed. 1966.
Lists approximately 700 books and journals arranged by broad subject areas. Author index.

May, Kenneth Ownsworth. Bibliography and research manual of the history of mathematics. [Toronto], Univ. of Toronto Pr., [1973]. 818p. **EF12**

Pt. I, Research Manual, consists of brief comments on information retrieval and storage, and historical analysis and writing. Pt. II, Bibliography, is a classified listing of about 31,000 entries in five main sections: (1) Biography; (2) Mathematical topics; (3) Epimathematical topics; (4) Historical classifications; (5) Information retrieval. Extensive list of serials in which articles on mathematics and its history have appeared, p.707–818. No index. Z6651.M38

Royal Society of London. Catalogue of scientific papers, 1800–1900; Subject, v.1, Pure mathematics. Cambridge, Univ. Pr., 1908. 666p. **EF13**

For full description *see* EA23.

Smith, David Eugene. Rara arithmetica; a catalogue of the arithmetics written before the year MDCI, with a description of those in the library of George Arthur Plimpton, of New York. Boston, London, Ginn, 1908. 507p. il. **EF14**

—— —— Addenda. . . . Boston, London, Ginn, 1939. 52p. il.

Chronological arrangement. Gives brief identification of authors, full bibliographic entries, other editions printed before 1601, and other descriptive and historical notes. Includes many facsimiles of title pages. Index of dates. Index of names, places, and subjects. This extensive collection was presented to the Columbia University Libraries in 1936. Z6654.A7S7

Current

American Mathematical Society. Index to translations selected by the American Mathematical Society. 1949/65–1966/73. Providence, R.I., 1966–73. 2v. **EF15**

Indexes all translations published in the Society's *Translations,*

and in *Selected translations in mathematical statistics and probability* for the years indicated. Author and subject indexes.

Z6651.A55

Current index to statistics: applications, methods and theory. v.1– , 1975– . Washington, Amer. Statistical Assoc., [1976]– . Annual. **EF16**

Sponsored by American Statistical Association and Institute of Mathematical Statistics.

A comprehensive index to journal and monographic literature, covering statistics in a very broad sense. The author index giving bibliographic citations is followed by a permuted-term subject index; it may be necessary to refer back to the author index to obtain a complete title for a monograph. Some entries are taken from published abstracts, in which case reference is made to the abstract source and number. QA276.A1

Index of mathematical papers. v.1–9, July/Dec. 1970–77. Providence, R.I., Amer. Mathematical Soc., 1972–[79]. **EF17**

v.1–4 semiannual; v.5–9 annual.
An author and subject index of all papers and books reviewed in *Mathematical reviews.* The subject index is arranged according to the AMS (MOS) Subject Classification Scheme (1970). Superseded by *Mathematical reviews* annual indexes (*see* EF19). Z6653.I5

Abstract journals

Jahrbuch über die Fortschritte der Mathematik, begr. von Carl Ohrtmann. Bd.1–68¹, 1868–1942. Berlin, W. de Gruyter, 1871–1942. 68v. **EF18**

Editor and publisher vary. Ceased publication. (The *Revue semestrielle des publications mathématiques,* t.1–39, 1893–1934, was a bibliography of mathematical material in various languages, with a very few abstracts. With its v.37, it joined with the *Jahrbuch,* and ceased separate publication after v.39.)

Brief, signed abstracts. Classed arrangement with author index.

Mathematical reviews. v.1– , 1940– . Providence, R.I., Amer. Mathematical Soc., 1940– . v.1– . Monthly. **EF19**

Offers comprehensive coverage of the pure and applied mathematics literature, through critical, signed abstracts arranged according to the AMS (MOS) Subject Classification Scheme. Monthly and cumulated semiannual author indexes. Starting with v.45 (Jan.–June 1973) also has semiannual classified subject indexes. Most reviews are in English; in some cases, only the author's summary is provided.

Sponsored by the American Mathematical Society in cooperation with mathematical societies and institutes throughout the world. ●

—— Indexes: Author index, v.1–20 (1940–59); v.21–28 (1960–64); v.29–44 (1965–72); v.45–58 (1973–79). Providence, 1961–[81]. 15v.

Gives author, full title, and full citation.

—— Indexes: Cumulative subject index, v.1–19 (1940–58). Providence, [1983]. 413p.

Combines annual subject indexes, with original cross references augmented by cross references from each major word in any main heading or subheading. Index for v.20–44 (1959–72) planned for 1985 publication.

—— Indexes: Subject index, v.45–58 (1973–79). Providence, [1981]. 5v.

Arranged by AMS (MOS) Subject Classification Scheme (1970). Refers to *Mathematical reviews* abstract number for full citation.

—— Indexes: Annual indexes. 1978– . Providence, [1979]– .

Annual author and subject indexes. Subject index arranged by AMS (MOS) Subject Classification Scheme (1970) through 1979; beginning with 1980 subjects are arranged by 1980 Mathematics

Subject Classification. Supersedes *Index of mathematical papers* (EF17).

Statistical theory and method abstracts. v.1– . Edinburgh, Longman Group, for the International Statistical Institute, 1959– . v.1– . 4 issues a yr., plus index supplement. **EF20**

Publisher varies.

Title varies: v.1–4, *International journal of abstracts. Statistical theory and method. Index and review supplement.*

An international abstract journal in classified arrangement, with author index. Titles are translated into English, and abstracts are in English. Annual index supplement includes a cumulated author index and a section on "New statistical tables" designed to keep up to date the *Guide to tables in mathematical statistics*, by Greenwood and Hartley (EF55).

Zentralblatt für Mathematik und ihre Grenzgebiete; Mathematics abstracts. Berlin, Springer, 1931– . Bd.1– .   **EF21**

Subtitle varies.

Suspended Nov. 1944–June 1948.

A classified arrangement of signed abstracts of books and papers, stressing coverage of eastern European, American, and Japanese publications, but including some publications of other countries. Most abstracts and titles in German or English. Author and subject indexes. Some cumulative indexes.   QA1.Z4

Dictionaries and encyclopedias

Encyclopedia of statistical sciences. Samuel Kotz and Norman L. Johnson, eds. in chief. N.Y., Wiley, [1982–85]. v.1–5. (In progress)   **EF22**

Contents: v.1–5, A–Multitrait.

Planned to be in 8v. plus an index/supplement volume. Provides information on an extensive selection of topics in statistical theory and applications of statistical methods. Signed articles, many with bibliographies; cross references. "This information is intended primarily to be of value to readers who do not have detailed information about the topics but have encountered references . . . that they wish to understand."—*Pref.* Includes biographical articles.   QA276.14.E5

Encyklopädie der mathematischen Wissenschaften mit Einschluss ihrer Anwendungen. Hrsg. im Auftrage der Akademien der Wissenschaften zu Göttingen, Leipzig, München und Wien, sowie unter Mitwirkung zahlreicher Fachgenossen. Leipzig, Teubner, 1898/1904–1935. 6v. in 23.   **EF23**

Contents: (1) Arithmetik; (2) Analysis; (3) Geometrie; (4) Mechanik; (5) Physik; (6¹) Geodäsie und Geophysik; (6²) Astronomie.

Parts of a 2d ed. have appeared as: QA36.E56

Enzyklopädie der mathematischen Wissenschaften. . . . 2. völlig neubearb. Aufl. hrsg. von H. Hasse und E. Hecke. Leipzig, Teubner, 1939–58. v.1– . (In progress)   **EF24**

Contents: Bd.1, Algebra und Zahlentheorie: 1. Teil: A, Grundlagen. B, Algebra; 2. Teil: C, Reine Zahlentheorie. D, Analytische Zahlentheorie.

An important encyclopedia of the subject, containing long articles by specialists, with full bibliographic notes, though in some cases articles are now out of date. For the advanced student and specialist. A French edition of the original set (Paris, Gauthier-Villars, 1904–16. 7v.) was never completed, but included some revision.

International dictionary of applied mathematics. W. F. Freiberger, ed. in chief. Princeton, N.J., Van Nostrand, [1960]. 1173p. il.   **EF25**

"Defines the terms and describes the methods in the application of mathematics to thirty-one fields of physical science and engineering" in order to provide the means "to obtain the necessary mathematical results by the best available methods."—*Pref.* Indexes in French, German, Spanish, and Russian.   QA5.I5

James, Glenn and **James, Robert C.** Mathematics dictionary. 4th ed., N.Y., Van Nostrand Reinhold, [1976]. 509p. il.   **EF26**

1st ed. 1942.

Gives definitions of terms and phrases in the various fields of pure and applied mathematics. Includes tables, formulas, mathematical symbols, and vocabularies giving English equivalents of mathematical terms in French, German, Russian, and Spanish.   QA5.J32

Karush, William. The crescent dictionary of mathematics. Oscar Tarov, gen. ed. N.Y., Macmillan, 1962. 313p.   **EF27**

Intended to meet the educational needs of high school and college students and teachers, and for non-specialists. Covers standard high school and college mathematics material as well as a variety of terms in advanced and applied mathematics. Appended material includes some brief tables of functions, symbols, etc., plus notes on the work of famous mathematicians.   QA5.K26

Mathematical Society of Japan (Nihon Sūgakkai). Encyclopedic dictionary of mathematics. Cambridge, Mass., M.I.T. Pr., [1977]. 2v. il.   **EF28**

Ed. by Shôkichi Iyanaga and Yukiyosi Kawada. Tr. by the Mathematical Society of Japan with the cooperation of the American Mathematical Society. Translation reviewed by Kenneth O. May.

A translation of *Iwanami sūgaku jiten* (Tokyo, 1954; 2d ed. 1968).

A scholarly, comprehensive, and up-to-date encyclopedia consisting of 436 medium-length articles arranged alphabetically, and thoroughly indexed. Technical terms are set in boldface and defined where they initially appear; subsequent appearances are marked with a dagger, indicating that they appear in the subject index. Articles contain references to the technical literature. Cross references.   QA5.N513

Millington, T. Alaric and **Millington, William.** Dictionary of mathematics. London, Cassell, 1966. 259p.   **EF29**

Intended for the student.   QA5.M495

Naas, Josef and **Schmid, Hermann Ludwig.** Mathematisches Wörterbuch mit Einbeziehung der theoretischen Physik. 2. unveränderte Aufl. Berlin, Akademie Verlag; Stuttgart, Teubner, 1962. 2v. il.   **EF30**

"Im Auftrage des Instituts für Reine Mathematik an der Deutschen Akademie der Wissenschaften zu Berlin."—*title page.*

An encyclopedia and dictionary containing definitions and current terminology in mathematics and physics, including principles, formulas, some biographical sketches of outstanding mathematicians, and (in many cases) bibliographies at the end of the articles. Alphabetical arrangement. No indexes.   QA5.N25

Patil, Ganapati Parashuram and **Joshi, Sharadchandra W.** A dictionary and bibliography of discrete distributions. Edinburgh, Oliver & Boyd, for the International Statistical Inst., 1968. 268p. il.   **EF31**

A classified section of definitions, with index, is followed by a bibliography—arranged alphabetically by author—of more than 2,900 items. A classified section, with references to item numbers in the author listing, serves as a subject index to the bibliography.   Z6654.P7P3

Sneddon, Ian Naismith, ed. Encyclopaedic dictionary of mathematics for engineers and applied scientists. N.Y., Pergamon Pr., [1976]. 800p.   **EF32**

"The aim has been to select those mathematical concepts and techniques which are most widely and frequently used in engineering, and by an extensive cross-reference system to bind together a vast amount of information giving easy access to the fundamental definitions and main results of each of the major branches of mathematics. While the mathematics is always sound, it is the applications rather than the theory which is emphasized."—*Foreword.* Indexed.   TA330.S66

Universal encyclopedia of mathematics. Foreword by James R. Newman. N.Y., Simon & Schuster, 1964. 715p.   **EF33**

Designed for the high school and college student; covers topics in arithmetic through calculus. Pt.1 is an alphabetically arranged encyclopedia by subject; pt.2 contains mathematical formulae; pt.3, mathematical tables.   QA5.U5413

Foreign terms

German

Herland, Leo Joseph. Dictionary of mathematical sciences. 2d ed., rev. and enl. N.Y., Ungar, [1965]. 2v.   **EF34**

1st ed. 1951–55.
Added title page in German.
Contents: v.1, German-English; v.2, English-German with a supplement of new words.
Statistical entries by Gregor Sebba; commercial entries by Robert Grossbard.   QA5.H42

MacIntyre, Sheila and **Witte, Edith.** German-English mathematical vocabulary. With a grammatical sketch by Lilias W. Brebner. 2d ed. Edinburgh, Oliver & Boyd; N.Y., Interscience, 1966. 95p.   **EF35**

1st ed. 1956.
Lists German terms and their English equivalents, in the field of pure mathematics, excluding applied mathematics, statistics, and mathematical logic.   QA5.M36

Polyglot

Eisenreich, Günther. Dictionary of mathematics. In four languages: English, German, French, Russian. Amsterdam & N.Y., Elsevier Scientific; Berlin, VEB Verlag Technik, 1982. 2v.   **EF36**

Volume 1, alphabetized by English-language terms, gives the corresponding terms in the other three languages; volume 2 has sections alphabetized by each of the other languages, with references to the entry number of volume 1. Because of the complexity of synonyms and homonyms, each term is assigned one or more subject categories; many terms are followed by brief explanatory notes. The emphasis is on pure mathematics.   QA5.E35

Russian

Milne-Thompson, Louis Melville. Russian-English mathematical dictionary; words and phrases in pure and applied mathematics with roots and accents, arranged for easy reference. Madison, Univ. of Wisconsin Pr., 1962. 191p. (U.S. Army. Mathematical Research Center, Univ. of Wisconsin, pubn. no.7)   **EF37**

Lists Russian terms in pure mathematics with their English equivalents. Brief outline of Russian grammar included.
                                                     QA3.U45 no.7

Russian-English dictionary of the mathematical sciences. By A. J. Lohwater with the collaboration of S. H. Gould, under the joint auspices of the National Academy of Sciences of the USA, the Academy of Sciences of the USSR, [and] the American Mathematical Society. Providence, R.I., Amer. Mathematical Soc., 1961. 267p.   **EF38**

"The present volume is intended for use . . . at any level in mathematics and theoretical physics and a short grammar of mathematical Russian precedes the vocabulary." In preparing the dictionary the guiding principle was that a person "would be able to read virtually any publication reviewed either in *Referativnyi zhurnal: Matematika* or in *Mathematical reviews* without the aid of any other dictionary."—*Foreword.*   QA5.R8

Akademiia Nauk SSSR. Matematicheskii Institut. Anglorusskii slovar' matematicheskikh terminov. Moskva, Izd. Inostrannoi Literatury, 1962. 369p.   **EF39**

Serves as an English-Russian companion to the above.
                                                     QA5.A493

Spanish

García Rodríguez, Mariano. Diccionario matemático; español-inglés, inglés-español. Mathematics dictionary; Spanish-English, English-Spanish. N.Y., Hobbs, Dorman, [1965]. 78p.   **EF40**

Limited to presentation of equivalent words and phrases in Spanish and English.   QA5.G36

Directories

World directory of mathematicians. Ed.1– . Bombay, Tata Institute, [1959?]– . (7th ed. 1982)   **EF41**

Publisher varies.
Published quadrennially (slightly irregular) under the auspices of the International Mathematical Union.
An alphabetically arranged listing of mathematicians and addresses, with a geographical index.

Handbooks

Bartsch, Hans-Jochen. Handbook of mathematical formulas. N.Y., Academic Pr., [1974]. 528p.   **EF42**

"Translation of the 9th ed. of *Mathematische Formeln* by Herbert Liebscher, Leipzig."—*verso of t.p.*
"The scope of this collection of formulas covers the whole field from the fundamental rules of arithmetic, via analytic geometry and infinitesimal calculus through to Fourier's series and fundamentals of probability calculus."—*Pref.*   QA41.B313

Burington, Richard Stevens and **May, Donald Curtis.** Handbook of probability and statistics, with tables. 2d ed. N.Y., McGraw-Hill, [1970]. 462p.   **EF43**

1st ed. 1953.
"The book is intended to provide a convenient summary of theory, working rules, and tabular material useful in the study and solution of practical problems involving probability and statistics."—*Pref.* Designed to complement Burington's *Handbook of mathematical tables and formulas* (EF67).
Topical arrangement, with indexes to names, Greek symbols, numerical tables, and subjects.   QA273.B925

Grazda, Edward E., ed. Handbook of applied mathematics. Morris Brenner and William R. Minrath, assoc. eds. 4th ed. Princeton, N.J., Van Nostrand, [1966]. 1119p. il.   **EF44**

Based on the original work of the same title by Martin E. Jansson, Herbert D. Harper, and Peter L. Agnew (3d ed. 1955). This edition is revised and updated, with new tables added.   TA330.G7

Korn, Granino Arthur and **Korn, Theresa M.** Manual of mathematics. N.Y., McGraw-Hill, [1967]. 391p. il.   **EF45**

Each chapter provides an outline of an entire mathematical subject. Based largely on the pertinent sections of the authors' *Mathematical handbook for scientists and engineers* (below). Indexed.   QA40.K596

—— Mathematical handbook for scientists and engineers; definitions, theorems, and formulas for reference and review. 2d enl. and rev. ed. N.Y., McGraw-Hill, [1968]. 1130p.   **EF46**

1st ed. 1961.
A comprehensive reference collection of mathematical definitions, theorems, and formulas for scientists, engineers, and undergraduate and graduate students. Topically arranged chapters attempt to survey entire mathematical subjects but exclude proofs. Includes numerical tables and a glossary of symbols and notations. Cross references; index.   QA40.K598

Kuipers, Lauwerens and **Timman, Reinier,** eds. Handbook of mathematics. English translation ed. by I. N. Sneddon. Oxford, etc., Pergamon, [1969]. 782p.   **EF47**

A translation of *Handboek der Wiskunde* (Amsterdam, 1963).

Scholars have contributed chapters on the whole range of mathematical topics: history of mathematics, number systems, linear algebra, analytical geometry, analysis, sequences and series, theory of functions, ordinary differential equations, special functions, vector analysis, partial differential equations, numerical analysis, the Laplace transform, probability, and statistics.   QA37.K8513

Merritt, Frederick S. Mathematics manual; methods and principles of the various branches of mathematics for reference, problem solving, and review. N.Y., McGraw-Hill, 1962. 378p.   **EF48**

"The scope . . . ranges from simple arithmetic through higher mathematics, including matrices, tensors, probabilities and statistics." Gives "the important definitions, principles, theorems, corollaries, relationships, and methods of the most commonly used branches of mathematics."—*Pref.*   QA40.M42

Moritz, Robert Edouard. On mathematics and mathematicians. Dover, [1958, c1942]. 410p.   **EF49**

Unabridged and unaltered republication of *Memorabilia mathematica; or, The philomath's quotation-book* (N.Y., Macmillan, 1914).

A book of more than 2,100 quotations about mathematics, its nature, value, philosophy, application, etc., grouped by class with an extensive index. Quotations from foreign authors are given only in English, but references to original sources are cited.   QA3.M7

Pearson, Carl E., ed. Handbook of applied mathematics: selected results and methods. 2d ed. N.Y., Van Nostrand Reinhold, [1983]. 307p.   **EF50**

1st ed. 1974.

"Most of the topics in applied mathematics dealt with in this handbook can be grouped rather loosely under the term *analysis*. They involve results and techniques which experience has shown to be of utility in a very broad variety of applications."—*Pref.* The emphasis is on technique. The 21 chapters, contributed by 20 mathematicians, include bibliographic references and have been extensively indexed.   QA40.H34

Rektorys, Karel, ed. Survey of applicable mathematics. Tr. from the Czech by Rudolf Výborný [et al.]. English translation ed. by the staff of the Mathematics Dept., Univ. of Surrey. Cambridge, Mass., M.I.T. Pr., [1969]. 1369p.   **EF51**

A translation of *Přehled užité matematiky* (2d ed., 1968).

Offers a comprehensive survey for engineers and research workers in related fields. "The book omits proofs of the theorems and derivation of the results, but theorems and formulae are complemented with explanatory remarks and appropriate examples."—*Pref.* Fully indexed.   QA37.R4313

Style manuals

Chaundy, Theodore W., Barrett, P. R. and **Batey, Charles.** The printing of mathematics: aids for authors and editors and rules for compositors and readers at the University Press, Oxford. London, Oxford Univ. Pr., 1954. 105p. il.   **EF52**

Includes sections on: (1) The mechanics of mathematical printing; (2) Recommendations to mathematical authors; (3) Rules for the composition of mathematics at the University Press, Oxford. Discusses the preparation of manuscripts and how they can best be set in type.   Z250.6.M3C5

Swanson, Ellen. Mathematics into type; copyediting and proofreading of mathematics for editorial assistants and authors. Rev. ed. Providence, R.I., Amer. Mathematical Soc., [1979]. 90p.   **EF53**

1st ed. 1971.

Covers the publication of mathematics from manuscript to the printed book or journal article, with emphasis on preparation of

copy for the compositor, and proofreading and makeup of the publication. Includes bibliography. Indexed.

Tables

Bibliography

Fletcher, Alan [and others]. An index of mathematical tables. 2d ed. Reading, Mass., publ. for Scientific Computing Service, by Addison-Wesley, 1962. 2v. (994p.)   **EF54**

1st ed. 1946.

Contents: v.1, Introduction. pt.1, Index according to functions; v.2: pt.2, Bibliography (p.609–780); pt.3, Errors; pt.4, Index to Introduction and pt.1.

An important index to well-known tables of functions and to other lesser known tables appearing in books and periodicals, which are of current value and have not been superseded.   QA47.F55

Greenwood, Joseph Arthur and **Hartley, H. O.** Guide to tables in mathematical statistics. Princeton, N.J., Princeton Univ. Pr., 1962. 1014p.   **EF55**

Sponsored by the Committee on Statistics of the Division of Mathematics of the National Academy of Sciences–National Research Council.

"A sequel to the guides to mathematical tables produced by and for the Committee on Mathematical Tables and Aids to Computation of the National Academy of Sciences–National Research Council"—*Pref.*: Derrick H. Lehmer, *Guide to tables in the theory of numbers* (National Research Council *Bulletin*, no.105, Feb. 1941; EF57); Harry Bateman and R. C. Archibald, "Guide to tables of Bessel functions," *Mathematical tables and other aids to computation* 1:205–63 (July 1944); and A. Fletcher, "Guide to tables of elliptic functions," *ibid.*, 3:229–81 (Jan. 1948).

Classified arrangement of explanatory text and references to specific tables which have been published separately or in the periodical literature. Includes a section listing contents of books of tables. Author index gives full citations. Subject index.   Z6654.T3G7

Lebedev, Aleksandr Vasil'evich and **Fedorova, R. M.** A guide to mathematical tables. English ed. prep. from the Russian by D. G. Fry. Oxford, N.Y., Pergamon, 1960. 586p.   **EF56**

———— ———— Supplement, no.1– , by N. M. Burunova. 1960– .

"This book has been prepared from the original Russian edition by a photographic process. The Russian text has been replaced by English, but the tabular matter has been reproduced direct from the original."—*Translator's pref.*

The main volume gives references, in topical arrangement, to tables published in separate editions through 1952; some published in 1953 and 1954; and those included in periodicals through 1953. The supplement gives tables published up to about 1959.

Excludes theory of numbers, mathematical statistics, astronomy, and geodesy. Number of decimal places supplied by each table is specified.   Z6654.T3L42

Lehmer, Derrick Henry. Guide to tables in the theory of numbers. Wash., Nat. Research Council, Nat. Academy of Sciences, 1941. 177p. incl. tables. (Bull. of the National Research Council, no.105, Feb. 1941).   **EF57**

Contents: pt.1, Descriptive account of existing tables; pt.2, Bibliography, arranged alphabetically by author, giving exact references to the sources of the tables referred to in pt.1; pt.3, Lists of errata in the tables.

Bibliography, with location of copies in libraries of the United States and Canada, p.85–125.   QA241.L53

Schütte, Karl. Index mathematischer Tafelwerke und Tabellen aus allen Gebieten der Naturwissenschaften. 2., verb. u. erhebl. erw. Aufl. München, Oldenbourg, 1966. 239p.   **EF58**

Added title page (*Index of mathematical tables from all branches of sciences*) and preface in English; section headings in German and English.

1st ed. 1955.

Lists some 2,800 tables in a classified arrangement. Not so extensive as Fletcher's *Index of mathematical tables* (EF54), but provides a different approach since Fletcher's work is alphabetical. Indexes of authors and institutes. Z6654.T3S34

Compendiums

Abramowitz, Milton and **Stegun, Irene A.** Handbook of mathematical functions with formulas, graphs, and mathematical tables. Wash., Govt. Prt. Off., 1964. 1046p. (U.S. National Bureau of Standards. Applied mathematics ser. 55) **EF59**

The work has been through numerous printings with corrections, e.g., "6th printing, Nov. 1967, with corrections" and a "7th corr. Dover printing" (N.Y., Dover, 1970).

Attempts to cover the entire field of special functions, and to satisfy the needs of scientists in all fields. Subject index; index of notations. QA47.A34

Apelblat, Alexander. Table of definite and indefinite integrals. Amsterdam & N.Y., Elsevier Scientific, 1983. 457p. (Physical sciences data, v.13) **EF60**

" . . . in this collection, special attention is directed to integrals that are not included in previous publications. . . . For convenience, equivalent reducible forms . . . and particular cases of existing integrals of special interest, are also presented. This volume should be considered supplementary to the existing literature."—*Pref.* Includes references. QA310.A63

Barlow, Peter. Barlow's Tables of squares, cubes, square roots, cube roots and reciprocals of all integers up to 12,500, ed. by L. J. Comrie . . . 4th ed., new impression. London, Spon; N.Y., Chemical Pub. Co., 1960. 258p. **EF61**

1st ed. 1814; 4th ed. 1941.

Also provides the values for n to the fourth power up to $n = 1000$, for the factorial $n!$ up to $n = 100$, for the reciprocal of the square root up to $n = 1000$, and for the square root of $10n$ for $n = 1000$ through $n = 12,500$. Additional tables provide values for n to fourth through tenth powers up to $n = 100$, and the 11th through 20th powers of the integers 1–10. QA47.B4

Bateman Manuscript Project, California Institute of Technology. Tables of integral transforms. Based, in part, on notes left by Harry Bateman, and compiled by the staff of the Bateman Manuscript Project. A. Erdélyi, ed. N.Y., McGraw-Hill, 1954. 2v. **EF62**

A very extensive compilation of integral transforms of great practical use in finding solutions to integrals that are encountered in many fields. Includes Fourier transforms, Laplace transforms, and many less common integral transforms. A portion of v.2 contains miscellaneous integrals involving higher transcendental functions, many of which cannot be written as transforms. Each volume has an index of notations. QA351.B22

Bauschinger, Julius and **Peters, Jean.** Logarithmisch-trigonometrische Tafeln mit acht Dezimalstellen . . . 3. Aufl. Weinheim/Bergstrasse, H. R. Engelmann, 1958. 2v. **EF63**

Added title page in English (*Logarithmic trigonometrical tables to eight decimal places*); preface in English and German.

Contents: v.1, Table of the logarithms to eight decimal places of all numbers from 1–200,000; v.2, Table of logarithms to eight decimal places of the trigonometrical functions for every sexagesimal second of the quadrant. QA55.B313

Beyer, William H., ed. CRC handbook of tables for probability and statistics. 2d ed. Cleveland, Chemical Rubber Co., [1968]. 642p. **EF64**

1st ed. 1966.

The 2d ed. incorporates corrections of errors detected in the 1st ed., and includes expanded and additional tables and graphs.

Offers a brief textual survey on important theorems and functions, extensive sections of statistical tables and graphs, and a section of commonly used mathematical tables. Indexed. QA276.B44

Bierens de Haan, David. Nouvelles tables d'intégrales définies. Ed. of 1867, corr.; with an English translation of the introd. by J. F. Ritt. N.Y., Stechert, 1939. 716p. (Reissued: N.Y., Hafner, 1957) **EF65**

Classified arrangement of 8,339 functions of definite integrals. Includes references to discussions of the functions in earlier works of the author.

British Association for the Advancement of Science. Mathematical tables. . . . London, Assoc., 1931–52. v.1–10. (v.1, 3d ed., 1951) **EF66**

Contents: v.1, 3d ed., Circular and hyperbolic functions, exponential and sine and cosine integrals, factorial function and allied functions, hermitian probability functions; v.2, Emden functions, being solutions of Emden's equation together with certain associated functions; v.3, Minimum decompositions into fifth powers, prep. by L. E. Dickson; v.4, Cycles of reduced ideals in quadratic fields, prep. by E. L. Ince; v.5, Factor table, giving the complete decomposition of all numbers less than 100,000, prep. by J. Peters, A. Lodge, E. J. Ternouth, E. Gifford; v.6, Bessel functions: pt.1, Functions of orders zero and unity; v.7, The probability integral, by W. F. Shepard; v.8, Number-divisor tables, designed and in part prep. by J. W. L. Glaisher; v.9, Table of powers, giving integral powers of integers, initiated by J. W. L. Glaisher; v.10, Bessel functions: pt.2, Functions of positive integer order 2–20, by W. G. Bickley [and others].

Continued as the *Royal Society mathematical tables* (EF76). QA47.B7

Burington, Richard Stevens. Handbook of mathematical tables and formulas. 5th ed. N.Y., McGraw-Hill, [1973]. 500p. **EF67**

1st ed. 1933; 4th ed. 1965.

Intended "to meet the needs of students and workers in mathematics, engineering, physics, chemistry, science, and other fields in which mathematical reasoning, processes, and computations are required."—*Pref.* Pt.1 offers summaries of the more important formulas and theorems of algebra, trigonometry, analytical geometry, calculus, and vector analysis; pt.2 contains tables of logarithms, trigonometric functions, etc. Index of tables and subject index.

Serves as a companion to the *Handbook of probability and statistics, with tables* by R. S. Burington and D. C. May (EF43). QA47.B8

CRC handbook of mathematical sciences. Ed. by William H. Beyer. 5th ed. West Palm Beach, Fla., CRC Pr., [1978]. 982p. il. **EF68**

Title varies; 1st ed. 1962 had title: *Handbook of mathematical tables.*

Extensive compilation of tables of values for mathematical functions and lists of formulas and constants in pure and applied mathematics. QA47.H324

Camm, Frederick James. Mathematical tables and formulae. 6th ed. London, Newnes, 1957. 144p. (Repr.: N.Y., Philosophical Lib., 1958) **EF69**

1st ed. 1943. TA151.C313

Dwight, Herbert Bristol. Tables of integrals and other mathematical data. 4th ed. N.Y., Macmillan, [1961]. 336p. il. **EF70**

1st ed. 1934.

Lists various formulas, series, integrals, and derivatives, arranged by type of function. The appendix contains tables of numerical values for several different functions. QA310.D8

Gradshtein, Izrail Solomonovich and **Ryzhik, Iosif Moisevich.** Table of integrals, series, and products. Corr. & enl. ed.

prep. by Alan Jeffrey; incorporating the 4th ed. prep. by Yu. V. Geronimus and M. Yu. Tseytlin. N.Y., Academic, 1980. 1160p.   **EF71**

Translated from the Russian by Scripta Technica, Inc.

Incorporates the 4th ed. (N.Y., 1965). Russian edition (Moscow, 1963) had title: *Tablitsy integralov, summ, riadov i proizvedenii.*

Gives comprehensive coverage of elementary functions and special functions and their definite and indefinite integrals. This enlarged edition includes basic Fourier and Laplace transforms, and material on inequalities that allow the estimation of solutions using computers. Also includes bibliography from the Russian edition and a classified supplementary bibliography by Alan Jeffrey.

QA55.G6613

Hansen, Eldon R. A table of series and products. Englewood Cliffs, N.J., Prentice-Hall, [1975]. 523p.   **EF72**

A systematic table of series and products, including about 1,200 new entries. Provides systematic access not only to series involving elementary and special functions, but also to numerical power series, which are written "in a canonical form so that a given numerical power series can be found . . . about as easily as one finds a given numbered page in a book. . . . The 'average' reader finding a series in the literature will almost certainly also find his series in this table." —*Pref.*   QA295.H25

Mathematical Tables Project. [Mathematical tables], prep. by the Mathematical Tables Project, Work Projects Administration of the Federal Works Agency. Conducted under the sponsorship of the National Bureau of Standards. . . . N.Y., Columbia Univ. Pr., 1939–44. 40v.   **EF73**

Originally published by the Work Projects Administration for the City of New York under the sponsorship of the National Bureau of Standards. After 1942, when the WPA was discontinued, the work was taken over by the sponsoring agency, and the later volumes were published by Columbia University Press. Many of the tables have been reissued by the U.S. Bureau of Standards Computation Laboratory.

For complete contents *see* Parke, *Guide to the literature of mathematics,* p.135–37 (EF4).

Owen, Donald Bruce. Handbook of statistical tables. Reading, Mass., Addison-Wesley, 1962. 580p. il.   **EF74**

Consists of tables, with brief introductory notes, intended for statistics students, practicing statisticians, quality control workers and industrial engineers, and research workers. Subject and name index.   HA48.O9

Pearson, Egon Sharpe and **Hartley, H. O.,** eds. Biometrika tables for statisticians. [Reprinted with corrections] London, Biometrika Trust (available from Charles Griffin & Co., Buckinghamshire, Eng.), 1976. 2v.   **EF75**

v.1 is a corrected reprint of the 3d ed., 1976 (originally publ. 1954; 2d ed. 1958); v.2 is a corrected reprint of the 1st ed. of that volume published 1972. The work represents a revision and expansion of *Tables for statisticians and biometricians,* ed. by Karl Pearson (1st ed. 1924; 3d ed. 1948).

Taken together, these two volumes of tables cover the vast majority of situations encountered by statisticians. v.1 contains all of the more commonly used tables; more specialized tables are in v.2. Each volume has an extensive introduction defining the functions covered and describing their use; illustrative examples are given.   QA276.P431

Royal Society of London. Royal Society mathematical tables. Cambridge, Univ. Pr., 1950–68. v.1–11. (In progress?)
                                                                    EF76

Continues the series of *Mathematical tables* issued by the British Association for the Advancement of Science (1931–52; EF66).

Contents: v.1, E. H. Neville. Farey series of order 1025 (1950); v.2, E. H. Neville. Rectangular-polar conversion tables (1956); v.3, J. C. P. Miller. Table of binomial coefficients (1954); v.4, H. Gupta [and others]. Tables of partitions (1958); v.5, H. Gupta [and others]. Representations of primes by quadratic forms (1960); v.6, C. B. Haselgrove and J. C. P. Miller. Tables of Riemann Zeta function

(1960); v.7, F. W. J. Olver. Bessel functions, pt.3: Zeros and associated values (1960); v.8, W. E. Mansell. Tables of natural and common logarithms to 110 decimals (1964); v.9, A. E. Western and J. C. P. Miller. Tables of indices and primitive roots (1968); v.10, A. Young and A. Kirk. Bessel functions, pt.4: Kelvin functions (1964); v.11, A. R. Curtis. Coulomb wave functions (1964).

Selected tables in mathematical statistics. Ed. by the Institute of Mathematical Statistics. Providence, R.I., Amer. Mathematical Soc., [1970–85]. v.1–8. (In progress)   **EF77**

v.1 originally publ. by Markham, Chicago.

Each volume contains one or more sections of tables on specific topics, with introductory notes and references for each. Further volumes are planned.   QA276.25.S43

Thompson, Alexander John. Logarithmetica Britannica, being a standard table of logarithms to 20 decimal places. Cambridge, Univ. Pr., 1924–52. 9v. (Tracts for computers, no. 11, etc.) (Repr. 1952 in 2v.)   **EF78**

Contents: pt.1, no.10,000–20,000 (1934); pt.2, no.20,000–30,000 (1952); pt.3, no.30,000–40,000 (1937); pt.4, no.40,000–50,000 (1928); pt.5, no.50,000–60,000 (1931); pt.6, no.60,000–70,000 (1933); pt.7, no.70,000–80,000 (1935); pt.8, no.80,000–90,000 (1927); pt.9, no. 90,000–100,000 (1924).   QA55.T4

U.S. National Bureau of Standards. Applied mathematics series, no.1– . Wash., Govt. Prt. Off., 1948– .   **EF79**

"The Applied Mathematics Series contains mathematical tables, manuals and studies of special interest to physicists, engineers, chemists, biologists, mathematicians, computers, and others engaged in scientific and technical work. Some of the volumes are reissues of the mathematical tables prepared by the Project for the Computation of Mathematical Tables conducted by the Federal Works Agency, Works Project Administration for the City of New York. . . ."—*U.S.N.B.S. Publications of the National Bureau of Standards, 1966-67, p.35.*   QA3.U5

Biography

Taylor, Eva Germaine Rimington. The mathematical practitioners of Tudor and Stuart England. Cambridge, [Eng.], publ. for the Institute of Navigation at the University Pr., 1954. 442p. il. (Reissued 1967)   **EF80**

In three parts: (1) a narrative account of mathematical practice and the work of outstanding mathematicians of the period 1485–1715; (2) biographies of 582 practitioners; and (3) a list of "Works on mathematical arts and practices, with descriptive notes," plus a "Bibliography of secondary works consulted." Indexed.

QA27.G7T3

——— The mathematical practitioners of Hanoverian England, 1714–1840. London, Cambridge Univ. Pr. for the Institute of Navigation, 1966. 503p.   **EF81**

"A sequel to *The mathematical practitioners of Tudor and Stuart England* by the same author."—*title page.* With that work, an important reference source for the history of science.

A narrative of the scientific and technical advances of the period is followed by 2,282 biographical sketches of mathematicians, including teachers, philosophers, and makers of mathematical, optical, and nautical instruments. Indexed.   QA27.G7T28

——— An index to The mathematical practitioners of Hanoverian England, 1714–1840 by E. G. R. Taylor. Compiled by Kate Bostock, Susan Hurt, Michael Hurt from the 1966 edition, published by Cambridge University Press. London, H. Wynter, 1980. 23p.

A listing in one alphabetical sequence of all of the practitioners in the biographical section of Taylor's book; in that work the biographies are divided into fourteen groups by dated period, and only those accorded six lines or more are indexed.

E G

Physics

❖Parke's *Guide to the literature of mathematics and physics* (EG2) and Whitford's *Physics literature* (EG3) are particularly useful guides to materials in physics. Although somewhat out of date, both volumes list many of the basic works in this field. For more recent listings, *see Information sources in physics* (EG1), the current bibliographies noted under Science, Technology, and Medicine, p.1135, and the *Technical book review index* (EA75).
See also Nuclear Engineering, p.1268.

GENERAL WORKS

Guides

Information sources in physics. [2d ed.] Dennis F. Shaw, ed. London & Boston, Butterworths, [1985]. 456p.　　**EG1**

1st ed. 1975, ed. by Herbert Coblans, had title: *The use of physics literature.*
Most of the twenty chapters by physicists and specialist librarians deal with the literature in specific fields of physics; there are also chapters on "The scope and control of physics and its literature," "Science libraries, reference material and general treatises," "Abstracting, indexing and on-line services," "Grey literature," and "Patent literature." Indexed.　　Z7141.I54

Parke, Nathan Grier. Guide to the literature of mathematics and physics including related works on engineering science. 2d rev. ed. N.Y., Dover, [1958]. 436p.　　**EG2**

1st ed. 1947.
For full description *see* EF4.　　Z6651.P3

Whitford, Robert Henry. Physics literature; a reference manual. 2d ed. Metuchen, N.J., Scarecrow Pr., 1968. 272p.　　**EG3**

1st ed. 1954.
A bibliographical manual for the college student, describing available materials and outlining library methods. Arrangement is by "usual lines of inquiry," termed "approaches" (e.g., bibliographical, historical, experimental, topical), with subdivisions for form of literature or by nature of subject. Commentaries, annotations, and excerpts from the literature accompany the bibliographical entries. Author and subject indexes.　　Z7141.W47

Bibliography

Datensammlungen in der Physik; data compilations in physics. Karlsruhe, Fachinformationszentrum, 1976–79. v.1–4. (In progress) (Physik Daten. Physics data. nos. 3-1, 3-2, 3-3, 3-4)　　**EG4**

A main volume and three supplements which together index about 2,800 data compilations published through Sept. 1979. "The aim of this bibliogrpahy is to inform about existing data compilations in the field of physics and to facilitate the search for data. . . . We have endeavored to make this survey as complete as possible for

physics."—*Introd.* Compilations are arranged under topical headings in German and English; subject index in English.　　QC52.P49

International catalogue of scientific literature: C, Physics. 1st–14th annual issues, 1901–14. London, 1902–17. 14v.　　**EG5**

For full description *see* EA17.

Reuss, Jeremias David. Repertorium commentationum a societatibus litterariis editarum . . . T. 4, Physica. Gottingae, Dieterich, 1805. 416p. (Repr.: N.Y., B. Franklin, 1961)　　**EG6**

A valuable index to the publications of learned societies up to 1800. Classed arrangement with author index.
For full description *see* EA22.

Royal Society of London. Catalogue of scientific papers, 1800–1900: Subject index, v.3, Physics. Cambridge, Univ. Pr., 1912–14. 2v.　　**EG7**

Contents: Pt.1, Generalities, heat, light, sound; pt.2, Electricity and magnetism.
For full description *see* EA23.

Dissertations

Marckworth, M. Lois. Dissertations in physics: an indexed bibliography of all doctoral theses accepted by American universities, 1861–1959. Stanford, Calif., Stanford Univ. Pr., 1961. 803p.　　**EG8**

Compiled with the assistance of the staff of the Advanced Systems Development Division and Research Laboratories, International Business Machines Corporation, San Jose, California.
In two sections: pt.1, an alphabetical list of 8,216 dissertations; pt.2, a permutation subject index coded by important words in the titles. Although the entries are primarily for physics subjects, some dissertations written under the auspices of a physics department are oriented toward astronomy, bio- and geophysics, electrical and mechanical engineering, and chemical, mathematical, or agricultural physics.　　Z7141.M3

Abstract journals and indexes

See also Energy research abstracts (EJ274), *Nuclear science abstracts* (EJ366).

Physics briefs. Physikalische Berichte. Weinheim, Physik Verlag, 1979– . v.1– . Semimonthly.　　**EG9**

A comprehensive abstract journal edited by the Deutsche Physikalische Gesellschaft and Fachinformationszentrum: Energie, Physik, Mathematik, in cooperation with the American Institute of Physics. Continues *Physikalische Berichte* (Braunschweig, 1920–78; publication suspended 1945–June 1947) which, in turn, continued the abstracting service of the *Fortschritte der Physik*, 1845–1918 (Braunschweig, 1847–1919. 74v. in 141).
Abstracts, in English, are arranged by *Physics briefs* classification scheme, with references from other classes as appropriate. Each issue contains a subject guide with terms from the subject classification in keyword form, and an index to authors and editors. Semiannual author and subject indexes. Currently publishes about 120,000 abstract entries per year.　　QC1.P6535

Science abstracts . . . Sec. A, Physics abstracts. London, Inst. of Electrical Engineers, 1898– . v.1– . Semimonthly, with semiannual author and subject indexes.　　**EG10**

Publisher varies. Frequency varies.
1898–1902 title reads: *Science abstracts, physics and electrical engineering;* 1903– , issued in two sections: A, *Physics;* B, *Electrical engineering.* Beginning with 1941, titles changed to A, *Physics abstracts,* and B, *Electrical engineering abstracts.*
Entries are arranged according to a subject classification listed on the back cover of each issue. Coverage is international and includes periodicals, reports, books, dissertations, patents, and conference

papers. A complete list of periodicals is issued as a part of the semiannual author indexes. Author and subject indexes, plus several "small indexes"—bibliography index, book index, patent and report index, conference index. Now has about 130,000 abstract entries per year.

Available on magnetic tape for computer searching. Microfiche edition also issued by publisher. Q1.83●

——— ——— Cumulative author index, 1955–1959, 1960–1964, 1965–1968, 1969–1972, 1973–1976, 1977–1980. London, [1960–81]. 1v., 4v., 2v., 3v., 4v., 4v.

——— ——— Cumulative subject index, 1955–1959, 1960–1964, 1965–1968, 1969–1972, 1973–1976, 1977–1980. London, [1960–81]. 1v., 2v., 3v., 4v., 8v., 6v.

Dictionaries and encyclopedias

Besancon, Robert Martin, ed. The encyclopedia of physics. 3d ed. N.Y., Van Nostrand Reinhold [1985]. 1378p. il. **EG11**

1st ed. 1966.
Concise, signed articles—most of them including bibliographic references—on physics in general, its major areas, divisions, and subdivisions as well as related topics such as astrophysics, geophysics, and biophysics. Intended for physicists who need information outside their special field of interest, librarians, teachers, engineers, and other scientists "who encounter physical concepts in pursuit of their professions."—*Pref.* As a rule, the technical level of the writing is higher for the more specialized areas than for the general topics. Useful cross references. Indexed. QC5.B44

Clark, George Lindenberg. Encyclopedia of X-rays and gamma rays. N.Y., Reinhold, [1963]. 1149p. il. **EG12**

350 articles by more than 300 authors offer a "compendium of widely scattered information on every facet of all the diversified branches of X-ray and Gamma ray science."—*Pref.* In addition to coverage of spectrometry and diffractometry, topics of public concern such as chemical and biological effects of radiation, shielding, and recent advances in X-ray microscopy, flash radiography, and cineradiography are included. Articles are arranged alphabetically by title keyword, and many contain references. Cross references and index. QC481.C475

Encyclopedia of physics. Reading, Mass., Addison-Wesley, [1981]. 1157p. il. **EG13**

Ed. by Rita G. Lerner and George L. Trigg.
"This Encyclopedia is intended as a comprehensive introductory reference source in a single volume. Our aim has been to make the broad range of ideas of modern physics readily accessible to physicists seeking information about fields outside their own, as well as to serve other scientists, students, and non-scientists interested in the subject."—*Pref.* Brief, signed articles by authorities in their fields include bibliographies and cross references. Indexed. QC5.E545

The encyclopedia of spectroscopy. Ed. by George L. Clark. N.Y., Reinhold, [1960]. 787p. il. **EG14**

An encyclopedia "with topics arranged alphabetically, first according to principal kinds of . . . spectroscopy, and then under each of the various aspects of history, theory, instrumentation, techniques, interpretations and applications of each method, which taken together cover the topic as completely as possible."—*Pref.* Articles are signed. Cross references; some extensive bibliographies. QC451.E5

Encyclopaedic dictionary of physics: general, nuclear, solid state, molecular, chemical, metal and vacuum physics, astronomy, geophysics, biophysics and related subjects. Ed. in chief, J. Thewlis. London, N.Y., Pergamon, 1961–64. 9v. **EG15**

Contents: v.1–7, A–Z; v.8, Subject and author indexes; v.9, Multilingual glossary: English, French, German, Spanish, Russian, Japanese.
Edited in England, with an international list of some 2,000

contributors. Not a modern version of Sir Richard Glazebrook's *Dictionary of applied physics* (London, Macmillan, 1922–23. 5v.), but largely replaces that standard work.

Articles are signed and range in length from a few lines to approximately 3,000 words. Each is self-contained, but cross references are provided to related articles, and bibliographies refer the reader to more detailed works.

——— Supplement 1–5. N.Y., Pergamon, [1966–75]. 5v.

Volumes in the supplementary series "are designed to deal with new topics in physics and related subjects, new developments in topics previously covered and topics which have been left out of earlier volumes for various reasons. They will also contain survey articles covering particularly important fields."—*Foreword, Suppl.1.* Bibliographies are included, as are sections of addenda and errata for the *Dictionary* and its supplements. Each volume has its own index. QC5.E52

The Facts on File dictionary of physics. [2d ed.] John Daintith, ed. N.Y., Facts on File, [1981]. 217p. il. **EG16**

First publ. in the United Kingdom in 1981.
About 2,000 entries defining the most important and commonly used terms related to physics. QC5.F34

Fizicheskii entsiklopedicheskii slovar'. B. A. Alekseevich, glav. red. Moskva, Sovetskaia Entsiklopediia, 1960–66. 5v. il. **EG17**

The longer articles are signed; many include bibliographies. QC5.F48

Gray, Harold James and **Isaacs, Alan,** eds. A new dictionary of physics. N.Y., Longman, 1975. 619p. **EG18**

1958 ed. had title: *Dictionary of physics.*
Most entries are brief, but a few are longer; includes a number of biographical sketches. Quantitative data are in SI units. A number of tables are appended, including brief data on elementary particles, the chemical elements, and nuclides. QC5.G7

Handbuch der Physik, hrsg. von S. Flugge. Berlin, Springer, 1955–84. v.1–54 (incomplete). (In progress) **EG19**

Earlier edition 1926–29. 24v. and index.
Added title page in English: Encyclopedia of physics.
Contents: v.1, Mathematical methods, I (1956); v.2, Mathematical methods, II (1955); v.3, pt.1, Principles of classical mechanics and field theory (1960); v.3, pt.2, Principles of thermodynamics and statistics (1959); v.3, pt.3, Non-linear field theories of mechanics (1965); v.4, Principles of electrodynamics and relativity (1962); v.5, pt.1, Principles of quantum theory, I (1958); v.6, Elasticity and plasticity (1958); v.6a$^{1-4}$, Mechanics of solids (1972–74); v.7, pt. 1, Crystal physics, I (1955); v.7, pt.2, Crystal physics, II (1958); v.8, pt.1, Fluid dynamics, I (1959); v.8, pt.2, Fluid dynamics, II (1963); v.9, Fluid dynamics, III (1960); v.10, Structure of liquids (1960); v.11, pt.1, Acoustics, I (1961); v.11, pt.2, Acoustics, II (1962); v.12, Thermodynamics of gases (1958); v.13, Thermodynamics of liquids and solids (1962); v.14, Low temperature physics, I (1956); v.15, Low temperature physics, II (1956); v.16, Electric fields and waves (1958); v.17, Dielectrics (1956); v.18, pt.1, Magnetism (1968); v.18, pt.2, Ferromagnetism (1966); v.19, Electrical conductivity, I (1956); v.20, Electrical conductivity, II (1957);

v.21, Electron emission. Gas discharges, I (1956); v.22, Gas discharges, II (1956); v.23, Electrical instruments (1967); v.24, Fundamentals of optics (1956); v.25, pt.1, Crystal optics. Diffraction (1961); v.25, pt.2a, Light and matter, Ia (1967); v.25, pt.2b, Light and matter, Ib (1974); v.25, pt.2c, Light and matter, Ic (1970); v.25, pt.2d, Light and matter, Id (1984); v.26, Light and matter, II (1958); v.27, Spectroscopy, I (1964); v.28, Spectroscopy, II (1957); v.29, Optical instruments (1967); v.30, X-rays (1957); v.31, Corpuscles and radiation in matter, I (1982); v.32, Structural research (1957); v.33, Corpuscular optics (1956); v.34, Corpuscles and radiation in matter, II (1958); v.35, Atoms, I (1957); v.36, Atoms, II (1956); v.37, pt.1, Atoms, III. Molecules, I (1959); v.37, pt.2, Molecules, II (1961); v.38, pt.1, External properties of atomic nuclei (1958); v.38, pt.2, Neutrons and related Gamma ray problems (1959); v.39, Structure of atomic nuclei (1957); v.40, Nuclear reactions, I (1957);

v.41, pt.1, Nuclear reactions, II (1959); v.41, pt.2, Beta decay (1962); v.42, Nuclear reactions, III (1957); v.44, Nuclear instrumentation, I (1959); v.45, Nuclear instrumentation, II (1958); v.46, pt.1, Cosmic rays, I (1961); v.46, pt.2, Cosmic rays, II (1967); v.47, Geophysics, I: The earth's body (1956); v.48, Geophysics, II (1957); v.49, pts.1–7, Geophysics III (1966–84); v.50, Astrophysics, I (Stellar surface-binaries) (1958); v.51, Astrophysics, II (Stellar structure) (1958); v.52, Astrophysics, III (The solar system) (1959); v.53, Astrophysics, IV (Stellar systems) (1959); v.54, Astrophysics, V (Miscellaneous) (1962).

An encyclopedic treatment of all areas of physics. Articles contributed by various authors in German, English, and French. 54 is the last numbered volume, but parts within volumes continue to appear. Articles are extremely comprehensive and contain extensive bibliographic references. Each volume is fully indexed in English and German; both listings include equivalent terms in the other languages. A French index is included only in those volumes containing articles written in French. QC21.H327

International dictionary of physics and electronics. Walter C. Michels, ed. in chief. 2d ed. Princeton, N.J., Van Nostrand, 1961. 1355p. il. **EG20**

1st ed. 1956.
Designed for those whose primary activities lie in a different field of science (e.g., chemistry, engineering, biology). An introductory essay indicates relationship between classical and modern physics by reviewing significant accomplishments in the development of the discipline. The 2d ed. is substantially revised and rearranged, with an increased number of entries dealing with atomic and nuclear physics, relativistic mechanics, quantum theory, etc. The complexity of presentation varies from entry to entry according to the probable need of the user. Cross references; new indexes in French, German, Spanish, and Russian. QC5.I5

Jerrard, Harold George and **McNeill, D. B.** A dictionary of scientific units; including dimensionless numbers and scales. 4th ed. London, Chapman & Hall; N.Y., Methuen, 1980. 212p. **EG21**

1st ed. 1963.
400 entries supplemented by about 500 references to sources. Gives definition, relevant historical facts, and, usually, some indication of the magnitude of the unit. Arrangement is alphabetical by name of unit. Appendixes give table of fundamental physical constants, details of standardization committees and conferences, a table of British and American weights and measures, and conversion tables. In the latest edition "particular attention has been given to SI units and tables are provided which give the factors needed to convert CGS to SI values and vice-versa."—*Pref.* Indexed. QC82.J4

Lexikon der Physik, hrsg. von Hermann Franke. 3d ed. Stuttgart, Franckh, [1959]. 3v. il. **EG22**

1st ed. 1950–52.
A dictionary-encyclopedia defining the words and concepts of modern physics, illustrated with line drawings, diagrams, tables and plates. Biographical articles are included, and references are given at the end of many articles. QC5.L42

McGraw-Hill dictionary of physics and mathematics. Daniel N. Lapedes, ed. in chief. N.Y., McGraw-Hill, [1978]. 1074p. il. **EG23**

Definitions were either written especially for this work or drawn from the *McGraw-Hill dictionary of science and technology* (2d ed., 1978). Definitions are preceded by abbreviations indicating the fields in which they are primarily used. Includes appendixes on constants, symbols, notations. Cross references. QC5.M23

Thewlis, James. Concise dictionary of physics and related subjects. 2d ed. Oxford & N.Y., Pergamon, [1979]. 370p. **EG24**

1st ed. 1973.
". . . covers not only Physics proper, but to a greater or lesser extent, such related subjects as Astronomy, Astrophysics, Aerodynamics; Biophysics, Crystallography, Geophysics, Hydraulics, Mathematics, Medical Physics, Meteorology, Metrology, Photogra-

phy, Physical Chemistry, Physical Metallurgy and so on."—*Foreword.* Brief definitions of terms restricted to one concept. Many cross references. Appendixes include the periodic table, conversion tables from CGS and Imperial units to SI units, and values of the general physical constants. QC5.T5

Abbreviations

Dictionary of physics and mathematics abbreviations, signs and symbols. David D. Polon, ed. N.Y., Odyssey, [1966]. 333p. **EG25**

Includes separate sections on abbreviations for use in text, letter symbols, abbreviations for scientific and learned societies, abbreviations for government and military agencies (each giving the terms alphabetically by abbreviation, then alphabetically by definition or name), and a list of mathematical signs and symbols. QC5.D55

Foreign terms

German

De Vries, Louis and **Clason, W. E.** Dictionary of pure and applied physics. Amsterdam, Elsevier, 1963–64. 2v. **EG26**

Contents: v.1, German-English; v.2, English-German.
More than 25,000 terms. Intended for students in science and technology in the United States. QC5.D4

Dictionary of physics and allied sciences. N.Y., Ungar, [1978]. 2v. **EG27**

Added title page in German: *Wörterbuch der Physik und verwandter Wissenschaften.*
Covers terms in theoretical physics and related sciences and their applications in technology and engineering. v.1, German-English, ed. by Charles J. Hyman with suppl. by R. Idlin; v.2, English-German with suppl., ed. by R. Idlin. QC5.D52

Polyglot

Béné, Georges J. [and others]. Nuclear physics and atomic energy. Amsterdam, Elsevier, 1960. 213p. (Glossarium interpretum, 2) **EG28**

Subtitle: Terms of nuclear physics and nuclear technology in English, French, German, Russian.
"This volume is a compilation of terms and expressions peculiar to nuclear physics and atomic energy; it also contains the terms relating to general physics and technology which are most commonly met with in publications on nuclear physics."—*Pref.* 2,117 entries arranged alphabetically by English term with French, German, and Russian equivalents. Indexes from each of the other languages. QC772.B4

Elsevier's Dictionary of general physics, in six languages . . . Comp. and arr. on an English alphabetical base by W. E. Clason. Amsterdam, Elsevier, 1962. 859p. **EG29**

The languages are: English/American, French, Spanish, Italian, Dutch, and German. Confined to the principal terms in the various branches of physics. Each term in English is followed by notation of area of use, a short definition in English, and then by equivalent terms in each of the other languages. Indexes in each of the other languages. Appropriate designation is made when British and American usage differs. QC5.E46

Lettenmeyer, Lore. Atomterminologie, Atomic terminology, Terminologie atomique, Terminologia atomica. München, Isar Verlag, [1958]. 298p. **EG30**

1,814 scientific and technical terms used in atomic and nuclear physics and associated fields, arranged on an English base with indexes from the other languages (German, French, Italian). QC772.L4

Russian

Emin, Irving. Russian-English physics dictionary, by Irving Emin and the Consultants Bureau staff of physicist translators. N.Y., Wiley, [1963]. 554p.   **EG31**

Compiled by specialists. Includes the terminology of all important branches of physics and the vocabulary of astronomy, astrophysics, chemistry, geophysics, and general technology. Russian abbreviations for scientific units, journal titles, institutions, and transliterations of the names of many scientists are also included.   QC5.E48

Voskoboinik, David I. and **TSimmerman, M. G.** Anglorusskii iadernyi slovar'. Moskva, Glav. red. Inostr. Nauchno-Tekhn. Slovarei Fizmat., 1960. 400p.   **EG32**

Added title page in English: English-Russian nuclear dictionary. 20,000 English terms and their Russian equivalents.   QC5.V6

———— Russko-angliiskii iadernyi slovar' Moskva, Glav. red. Inostr. Nauchno-Tekhn. Slovarei Fizmat., 1960. 334p.   **EG33**

Added title page in English: Russian-English nuclear dictionary. 20,000 Russian terms and their English equivalents.   QC772.V6

Directories

American Institute of Physics. Graduate programs in physics, astronomy, and related fields. 1976/77– . N.Y., Amer. Inst. of Physics, 1976– . Annual.   **EG34**

Supersedes *Graduate programs in physics and astronomy,* 1968.

". . . designed to provide easily accessible, comparative information on the graduate programs and research in physics and in fields based upon the principles of physics. . . . Each entry in the book describes the graduate programs offered by an academic department at an institution of higher learning in North America . . . with separate parts for . . . the United States and Canada. Within these parts, entries are organized . . . by state or province."—*Introd.*

Information for each department includes address and telephone number, admissions information, information on degree programs, size and budget of department, and lists of faculty (including fields of specialization); recent publications are included for some departments.   QC30.A48

Directory of physics and astronomy staff members. 1959/60– . N.Y., Amer. Inst. of Physics, [1959]– . Annual.   **EG35**

Subtitle varies.

Latest issue (1984/85) publ. as pt.II of v.29, no.10, of the *Bulletin of the American Physical Society* (Dec. 1984).

Lists staff members of North American physics faculties, research centers, and government laboratories, giving address and telephone number, academic or other rank if supplied by institution. Currently lists about 30,000 staff members at 2,700 institutions.   QC30.D57

Handbooks

AIP 50th anniversary physics vade mecum. Herbert L. Anderson, ed. in chief. N.Y., Amer. Inst. of Physics, [1981]. 330p.   **EG36**

The 22 chapters include tables, references, and formula compilations for subjects broadly representative of the fields of physics. A general section contains fundamental constants, units, conversion factors, magnitudes, basic mathematical and physical formulae, and a list of physics data centers; in the following sections the contributing editors provide ten pages each of the most useful formulas, numerical data, and references in their fields. Indexed.   QC61.A37

American Institute of Physics. American Institute of Physics handbook. Section eds.: Bruce H. Billings [and others].

Coordinating ed.: Dwight E. Gray [and others]. 3d ed. N.Y., McGraw-Hill, [1972]. 1v., various pagings. il.   **EG37**

1st ed. 1957.

Each section edited by a specialist. Provides authoritative, up-to-date information on various aspects of physics. Treats mathematical aids to computation, mechanics, acoustics, heat, electricity and magnetism, optics, atomic and molecular physics, nuclear physics, and solid-state physics. Includes definitions, tables, formulas, bibliographic references, etc. Indexed.   QC61.A5

CRC handbook of laser science and technology. Ed., Marvin J. Weber. Boca Raton, Fla., CRC Pr., [1982]. v.1–2. il. (In progress)   **EG38**

Contents: v.1, Lasers and masers; v.2, Gas lasers.

Updates and considerably extends the *CRC handbook of lasers* ed. by Robert J. Pressley (1971).

"The object of this series is to provide a readily accessible and concise source of data in tabular and graphical form for workers in the areas of laser research and development."—*Pref.* Signed articles include tabular data and references. Indexed.   TA1675.L38 (v.1)
          TA1695.G34 (v.2)

Condon, Edward Uhler and **Odishaw, Hugh.** Handbook of physics. 2d ed. N.Y., McGraw-Hill, 1967. 1v., various pagings. il.   **EG39**

1st ed. 1958.

A standard handbook with chapters by specialists; encyclopedic in nature. In nine main sections: (1) mathematics; (2) mechanics of particles and rigid bodies; (3) mechanics of deformable bodies; (4) electricity and magnetism; (5) heat and thermodynamics; (6) optics; (7) atomic physics; (8) solid state; (9) nuclear physics. Includes bibliographies; indexed.   QC21.C7

Handbook of optics, ed. by Walter G. Driscoll and William Vaughan. N.Y., McGraw-Hill, [1978]. 1v., various pagings. il.   **EG40**

"Sponsored by the Optical Society of America."—*t.p.*

Intended to fill "a need for a convenient compilation of optical information [as expressed by members of the Society, including] not only those engaged in optical physics, lens design, vision, color and other specializations traditionally associated with optics but also chemists, engineering scientists, and medical scientists. . . ."—*Pref.*   QC369.H35

Hix, C. F. and **Alley, R. P.** Physical laws and effects. N.Y., Wiley; London, Chapman & Hall, [1958]. 291p. il.   **EG41**

Arranged alphabetically by the name of the law. Each entry provides a brief description and explanation of the law, an indication of expected magnitude, references to sources of additional information, and a brief inventory of quantities. Indexed alphabetically by name of law, by physical quantities involved, and by fields of science.   QC28.H53

Martin, Brian Robert Charles. Statistics for physicists. London, N.Y., Academic Pr., 1971. 209p.   **EG42**

Intended as "a brief, but fairly systematic, guide to the more commonly used statistical ideas and techniques, together with enough theoretical background to relate one idea to another."—*Introd.* For the working physicist and advanced student.   QC175.M247

Streeter, Victor Lyle. Handbook of fluid dynamics. N.Y., McGraw-Hill, 1961. 1v., various pagings. il.   **EG43**

Chapters written by specialists; the first half of the book "deals with fundamental concepts and principles, while the second half is devoted to applied fields."—*Pref.* Bibliography at the end of each chapter.   QA911.S85

Tuma, Jan J. Handbook of physical calculations. 2d ed. N.Y., McGraw-Hill, [1983]. 478p. il.   **EG44**

1st ed. 1976.

"Definitions — formulas — technical applications — physical tables — conversion tables — graphs — dictionary of physical terms."—*t.p.*

Presents a concise summary of major definitions, formulas,

tables, and examples of elementary and intermediate technical physics, arranged by field. Intended to "serve as a desk-top reference book for practicing engineers, architects, and technologists. . . ." —*Pref.* Emphasizes practical applications; uses no mathematics beyond elementary calculus. Appendixes include tables of data and conversion factors. Includes references; brief bibliography. Indexed.

QC61.T85

Tables

See also Mathematics—Tables, p.1220.

Ardenne, Manfred, *Baron von.* Tabellen zur angewandten Physik: Elektronenphysik, Ionenphysik, Vakuumphysik, Kernphysik, medizinische Elektronik, Hilfsgebiete. 2. umgearb. und stark erw. Aufl. der Tabellen. Berlin, Deutscher Verlag der Wissenschaften, 1962–64. 2v. il. **EG45**

1st ed., 1956, had title *Elekronenphysik, Ionenphysik und Übermikroskopie.*

Contents: Bd.1, Elektronenphysik, Übermikroskopie, Ionenphysik; Bd.2, Physik und Technik des Vakuums, Plasmaphysik.

This work presents, with short commentaries, the most important formulas, fundamentals, methods, groupings, conclusions, technical physical data, and characteristics of matter in tabular form, with references to the principal literature sources. Related fields of high-vacuum technology, optics, heat, magnetism, nuclear physics, and mathematics are included. Subject index and index to the literature cited. QC61.A72

Kaye, George William Clarkson and **Laby, Thomas Howell.** Tables of physical and chemical constants and some mathematical functions. Originally comp. by G. W. C. Kaye and T. H. Laby. 14th ed. London & N.Y., Longman, [1973]. 386p. **EG46**

First published 1911.

Includes sections of tables for general physics, chemistry, atomic physics, and mathematical tables. References; index. QC61.K3

Lang, Kenneth R. Astrophysical formulae; a compendium for the physicist and astrophysicist. N.Y. & Berlin, Springer, 1974. 735p. il. **EG47**

"This book is meant to be a reference source for the fundamental formulae of astrophysics. Wherever possible, the original source . . . is referenced, together with references to more recent modifications and applications."—*Pref.* Uses centimeter-gram-second units. Indexed by subject and author; includes extensive bibliographies.

QB461.L35

Lederer, Charles Michael, and **Shirley, Virginia S.,** eds. Table of isotopes. 7th ed. N.Y., Wiley, 1978. 1523p. il. **EG48**

Edgardo Browne, Janis M. Dairiki, and Raymond E. Doebler, principal authors.

Early editions appeared as articles by G. T. Seaborg and others in *Reviews of modern physics,* 1940–58; 6th ed. 1967.

"An Isotope Index, ordered by atomic number (Z) and suborder-ed by mass number (A), precedes the main table. It contains all stable muclei, radioisotopes, and isomers that appear in the *Table of isotopes.* . . . The main table is ordered by mass number and subordered by atomic number. For each mass number there is an abbreviated mass-chain decay scheme. . . . Following the mass-chain decay scheme, tabulated data and detailed nuclear level schemes are given for individual isotopes. . . . As in the 6th edition, each tabulated entry consists of a critical selection of reported data."—*Introd.* QD466.L37

Menzel, Donald Howard, ed. Fundamental formulas of physics. N.Y., Dover, [1960]. 2v. **EG49**

First published 1955 by Prentice-Hall.

"Each chapter stands as a brief summary of the field represented" (*Pref.*) and is written by a specialist. Some chapters consist primarily of basic formulas, while others have considerable explanatory text. Includes bibliographies; indexed. QA401.M492

Smithsonian Institution. Smithsonian physical tables. 9th rev. ed., prep. by William E. Forsythe. Wash., Inst., 1954. 827p. il. (Smithsonian miscellaneous collections, v.120) **EG50**

1st ed. 1896.

". . . consists of 901 tables giving data of general interest to scientists and engineers, and of particular interest to those concerned with physics in the broader sense."—*Pref.* Indexed.

QC61.S6

Zimmerman, Oswald Theodore and **Lavine, Irvin.** Industrial Research Service's Conversion factors and tables. 3d ed. Dover, N.H., Industrial Research Service, 1961. 680p. **EG51**

1st ed. 1944; 2d ed. 1955.

Designed to provide "an accurate source of fundamental physical relationships and thousands of useful constants for the conversion of units."—*Pref.* This is a completely revised edition with new material added. "Every conversion factor . . . was recalculated on the basis of the latest and most accurate fundamental data available." QC61.Z5

Biography

The biographical dictionary of scientists: physicists. Gen. ed., David Abbott. N.Y., Peter Redrick, [1984]. 212p. il. **EG52**

A six-page historical introduction is followed by brief narrative biographies, alphabetically arranged, of living and deceased physicists; no bibliographical references are included. Brief glossary; index to topics studied by the biographees. QC15.B56

Nobelstiftelsen, Stockholm. Physics. Amsterdam, Elsevier, 1964–72. 4v. il. **EG53**

Contents: v.1, 1901–21; v.2, 1922–41; v.3, 1942–62; v.4, 1963–70.

Text of Nobel lectures, together with presentation speeches and laureates' biographies. Texts have been translated into English when not originally in that language. Name and subject indexes.

QC71.N64

COLORS

British Colour Council. The British Colour Council dictionary of colour standards. 2d ed. A list of colour names referring to the colours shown in the companion volume. London, Council, 1951. 57p. and atlas of mounted samples. **EG54**

"The purpose . . . is to simplify work in connection with colour throughout all colour-using industries so that the standard name or standard number will always signify the colour so designated in this Dictionary."—*Note.*

Kelly, Kenneth L. and **Judd, Dean B.** Color: universal language and dictionary of names. [Wash.], U.S. Dept. of Commerce, National Bureau of Standards [for sale by Govt. Prt. Off.], [1976]. 158p. il. (Nat. Bureau of Standards. NBS special pubn. 440) **EG55**

Supersedes and combines *The ISCC-NBS method of designating colors and a dictionary of color names* by Kelly and Judd (1955; NBS Circular 553) and *A universal color language* by K. L. Kelly (1965).

"The purpose of this dictionary is to assist the scientist, businessman, and layman to understand the different color vocabularies used in the many fields of art, science, and industry. . . . The dictionary will serve not only as a record of the 7,500 individual color names listed but it will also enable anyone to translate from one color vocabulary to another."—*Pref.* QC100.U57 no.440

Maerz, Aloys John and **Paul, Morris Rea.** Dictionary of color. 2d ed. N.Y., McGraw-Hill, 1950. 208p. 56pl.(col.)   **EG56**

Partial contents: Introduction; Table of terms found in literature; Table of principal color names; Polyglot table of principal color names; Bibliography; Color plates; Brief history of color standardization; Notes on color names; Index of color names.

"This work is primarily intended as a reference for the individual who seeks to relate colors with the names by which they are commonly identified."—*Pref.* Contains "the most extensive range of colors as yet published, together with a list of practically all recorded color names in use up to this time in the English language."   QC495.M25

Smithe, Frank B. Naturalist's color guide. N.Y., Amer. Museum of Natural History, [1975]. 2pts. pt.I, looseleaf, 24p.; pt.II, 229p.   **EG57**

Pt.I, *Naturalist's color guide,* consists of 86 swatches, named and numbered. Pt.II, *Naturalist's color guide supplement,* retains much of the terminology from Robert Ridgway's *Color standards and color nomenclature* (Wash., 1912), analyzes each color, correlates each color with many similar colors, and mentions numerous others.   QL767.S63

Society of Dyers and Colourists, Bradford, Eng. Colour index. 3d ed. Bradford, Eng., Soc. of Dyers and Colourists; Lowell, Mass., Amer. Assoc. of Textile Chemists and Colorists, [1971–76]. 6v.   **EG58**

1st ed. 1924–28.

The standard work in the field. 7,898 C.I. generic names. "Volumes 1–3 contain in tabular form the technical information for each C.I. Generic Name and Volume 4 gives structural formulae, where known, together with an outline of the method of preparation and literature references. The entries in Volumes 1–3 and Volume 4 are cross-referenced. Volume 5 contains lists of manufacturers and the code letters allocated to them, the C.I. Generic Names Index and the Commercial Names Index."--*Introd.* A revised and expanded v.5 was issued in 1976; v.6 (1975) is a first supplement to v.1–4.

Wyszecki, Günter and **Stiles, W. S.** Color science: concepts and methods, quantitative data and formulas. 2d ed. N.Y., Wiley, [1982]. 950p. il.   **EG59**

1st ed. 1967.

A compilation of the quantitative tools for work on color, including working concepts, formulas, and tables, intended for those concerned with color problems in industry and for the research worker in color, whether physicist, physiologist, or psychologist. In eight major sections: (1) Physical data; (2) The eye; (3) Colorimetry; (4) Photometry; (5) Visual equivalence and visual matching; (6) Uniform color scales; (7) Visual thresholds; (8) Theories and models of color vision. "For the most part, descriptive and qualitative material on color phenomena which would properly find a place in a textbook or introductory treatise on color has not been included."—*Pref.* List of references; author and subject indexes.   QC495.W88

E H

Agricultural Sciences

❖Blanchard and Farrell's *Guide to sources for agricultural and biological research* (EH1) provides an excellent, detailed presentation of sources of information. The principal index-

es in this field are the *Bibliography of agriculture* (EH30) and *Biological & agricultural index* (EC7, EH32). The publications of the U.S. Department of Agriculture provide a vast amount of information. In addition, a large amount of statistical data will be found in the publications of the Food and Agriculture Organization of the United Nations. Most public libraries will want a considerable range of reference works on gardening, on pet care, and on wines and cookery, only a few examples of which are included here.

AGRICULTURE

Guides

Guide to sources for agricultural and biological research. Ed. by J. Richard Blanchard and Lois Farrell. Berkeley & Los Angeles, Univ. of California Pr., [1981]. 735p.   **EH1**

"Sponsored by the United States Agricultural Library, United States Department of Agriculture, Beltsville, Maryland."—*t.p.*

An updating of Blanchard and Ostvold's *Literature of agricultural research,* 1958.

Contents: (A) Agriculture and biology: general; (B) Plant sciences; (C) Crop protection; (D) Animal sciences; (E) Physical sciences; (F) Food science and nutrition; (G) Environmental sciences; (H) Social sciences; (I) Computerized data bases for bibliographic research.

"The purpose of this work is to describe and evaluate important sources of information for the fields of agriculture and biology with the major emphasis on agriculture with related subjects."—*Pref.*

This extensive guide to 5,700 sources is organized by subject with subheadings by form. Almost all entries are annotated. An exceptional, indispensable guide.   Z5071.G83

Bibliography

Brown, Mary Ruth, Moss, Eugenie Lair and **Bright, Karin Drudge.** Agriculture education in a technical society: an annotated bibliography of resources. Chicago, Amer. Lib. Assoc., 1973. 228p.   **EH2**

Aims to present annotated lists of books, periodicals, government documents, sources of pamphlets, audiovisual aids, information on societies, industries, and organizations concerned with agriculture and related fields. Listings are according to the various categories just noted. Includes only English-language materials believed to be in print at the end of 1970, and suitable for use in junior colleges and technical schools.   Z5071.B78

Lauche, Rudolf. Internationales Handbuch der Bibliographien des Landbaues. World bibliography of agricultural bibliographies. Hrsg. im Auftrag des land- und forstwirtschaftlichen Forschungsrates mit Unterstützung der deutschen Forschungsgemeinschaft. München, Bayerische Landwirtschaftsverlag, 1957. 411p.   **EH3**

In classified arrangement; lists more than 4,100 agricultural bibliographical sources published between 1596 and 1957. Gives full bibliographical information, concise annotations, and (in many cases) locations in German and Austrian libraries. Author-title index and subject indexes in German and English.   Z5071.L3

Niklas, Hans and **Hock, A.** [and others]. Literatursammlung aus dem Gesamtgebiet der Agrikulturchemie. . . . Leipzig, Helingsche Verlagsanstalt, 1931–39. 5v.   **EH4**

Publisher varies.

Title pages, introductory matter, subtitles, and subject headings in German and English. Added title page, v.1–3: *A bibliographical list of the entire domain of agricultural chemistry.*

Contents: v.1, Soil science; v.2, Soil analysis; v.3, Plant nutrition; v.4, Manuring and fertilizers; v.5, Supplementary volume to v.4.

Classed arrangement, with each topical section alphabetical by author.

Perkins, Walter Frank. British and Irish writers on agriculture. 2d ed. Lymington, Eng., King, 1932. 142p.   **EH5**

1st ed. 1929.

"A bibliography of some 1300 British and Irish writers on the agriculture of the United Kingdom from the earliest printed books until, and including 1900. . . . Included are books on Agricultural Chemistry, Botany, Grasses, Weeds, Drainage, Improvements, Weights and Measures."—*Introd.*

Sable, Martin Howard. Latin American agriculture: a bibliography on pioneer settlement, agricultural history and economics, rural sociology and population (including immigration and foreign minorities), agricultural cooperatives and credit, from the holdings of the Widener Library, Harvard University. Milwaukee, [1970]. 74p. (Wisconsin. Univ. Latin American Center. Special pubn. no.1)   **EH6**

About 1,000 items in classed arrangement, subdivided by country. Author index.

Tolsado Picazo, Francisco. Bibliografía española de agricultura, 1495–1900. Madrid, 1953. 122p., 51pl.   **EH7**

At head of title: Instituto Nacional del Libro Español.
Classed arrangement with alphabetical index.   Z5071.T6

U.S. National Agricultural Library. Dictionary catalog of the National Agricultural Library, 1862–1965. N.Y., Rowman & Littlefield, 1967–70. 73v.   **EH8**

Reproduces the main entry and subject listings for monographs, serials, and analytics for the works cataloged for the main collection of the National Agricultural Library and for its Bee Culture and Beltsville branches. More than 1,500,000 entries. v.73 lists translations of articles, A–Z.

Kept up-to-date by:

———— National Agricultural Library catalog. v.1– , Jan. 1966– . Totowa, N.J., Rowman & Littlefield, 1966– . Monthly with annual and quinquennial cumulations.   **EH9**

Published as a supplement to the *Dictionary catalog of the National Agricultural Library* (above), to keep specialists and librarians informed of new additions to the collection. Monthly issues now contain: (1) a list of main entries by broad subject categories; (2) indexes by specific subject headings, personal authors, corporate authors, and titles (Indexes cumulate in June and Dec.); and (3) an alphabetical list of translations added to the collection during the previous month (these are also listed by category in the main entry section). A quinquennial cumulation, 1966/70, appeared in 1973 in 4v. It is a names and subjects catalog like the work it supplements, and v.4 includes a cumulation of the "Translations" sections. A cumulative index for 1971/75 appeared in 1978.

Current

Historia agriculturae: jaarboek uitgegeven door het Nederlands Agronomisch-Historisch Instituut. (Yearbook issued by Institute for Agricultural History) Groningen, J. B. Wolters, 1953– . Annual (irregular).   **EH10**

Includes annual bibliographies of European countries, with lesser coverage for other continents. Also contains articles.   S11.H55

U.S. Dept. of Agriculture

Lists and indexes

❖The U.S. Dept. of Agriculture has been a prolific publisher of material on all phases of agriculture, and much valuable information may be found in its various publications. Some of the lists and indexes which help to make the material available are:

Bimonthly list of publications and visuals. U.S. Dept. of Agriculture, Office of Governmental and Public Affairs. July/Aug. 1973– . Wash., 1973– . Bimonthly.   **EH11**

Title, frequency, and issuing body vary. Began as *Monthly list of publications and motion pictures,* Nov. 1944–Feb. 1964; continued as *Bimonthly list of publications and motion pictures,* Mar./Apr. 1964–May/June 1973.

U.S. Dept. of Agriculture. List by titles of publications of the U.S. Dept. of Agriculture from 1840 to June, 1901, inclusive. Comp. and compared with the originals by R. B. Handy and Minna A. Cannon. Wash., Govt. Prt. Off., 1902. 216p. (Division of Pubns. Bull. no.6)   **EH12**

———— List of publications of the U.S. Dept. of Agriculture from January, 1901, to December, 1925, inclusive; comp. by comparison with the originals by Mabel G. Hunt. Wash., Govt. Prt. Off., 1927. 182p. (Miscellaneous pubn. 9)   **EH13**

The two lists cited above are title lists of the serial publications and unnumbered publications of the USDA and its various divisions.
Continued by 5-year supplements: 1926/30–1941/46.

———— Index to authors with titles of their publications appearing in the documents of the U.S. Dept. of Agriculture, 1841–1897, by George F. Thompson. Wash., Govt. Prt. Off., 1898. 303p. (Division of Pubns. Bull. no.4)   **EH14**

———— Index to publications of the U.S. Dept. of Agriculture, 1901–40, ed. by Mary A. Bradley. Wash., Govt. Prt. Off., 1932–43. 4v.   **EH15**

1901–25. 2689p.; 1926–30. 694p.; 1931–35. 518p.; 1936–40. 763p.
Author and subject indexes to all of the publications of the USDA for the period, except for the periodicals issued by USDA bureaus, but including *Journal of agricultural research* and the *Official record.*

———— **Publications Division.** List of available publications of the United States Department of Agriculture. Wash., U.S. Dept. of Agriculture, Publications Div., Office of Governmental and Public Affairs, (for sale by Govt. Prt. Off.), 1978– . Annual. (List: no.11)   **EH16**

Continues an established series of the same title, with variations in the name of the issuing agency.
Includes subject and title indexes.

U.S. Superintendent of Documents. List of publications of the Agricultural Department, 1862–1902, with analytical index. Wash., Govt. Prt. Off., 1904. 623p. (Bibliography of United States public documents. Dept. list no.1)   **EH17**

Z1223.A12

Zimmerman, Fred Lyon and **Read, Phyllis Rogers.** Numerical list of current publications of the U.S. Dept. of Agriculture, comp. by comparison with the originals. . . . Wash., Govt. Prt. Off., 1941. 929p. (U.S. Dept. of Agriculture. Miscellaneous pubn. 450)   **EH18**

Under each number are listed the titles of the various USDA serial publications bearing that number.

Annual reports

U.S. Dept. of Agriculture. Index to the annual reports of the U.S. Dept. of Agriculture for the years 1837 to 1893 inclusive. Wash., Govt. Prt. Off., 1896. 252p. (Division of Pubns. Bull. no.1)   **EH19**

A subject index.

Bulletins

U.S. Dept. of Agriculture. Index to department bulletins, no.1–1500; by Mabel G. Hunt. Wash., Govt. Prt. Off., 1936. 384p.   **EH20**

An author and subject index.

Department bulletins ceased publication and were continued by *Technical bulletin.*

———— Index to technical bulletins, no.1–750; by Mabel G. Hunt. Wash., Govt. Prt. Off., 1937–41. 2v.   **EH21**

No.1–500 (1937. 249p.); no.501–750 (1941. 169p.).
An author and subject index.   S21.A72

———— Index to farmers' bulletins, no.1–1750. . . . Wash., Govt. Prt. Off., 1920–41. 3v.   **EH22**

An author and subject index.   S21.A6

Reports of the statistician

U.S. Dept. of Agriculture. Division of Publications. Synoptical index of the reports of the statistician, 1863 to 1894, by George F. Thompson. Wash., Govt. Prt. Off., 1897. 258p. (*Its* Bull. no.2)   **EH23**

S21.P9

Agricultural experiment stations

U.S. Dept. of Agriculture. List of bulletins of the agricultural experiment stations in the United States from their establishment to the end of 1920. Wash., Govt. Prt. Off., 1924. 186p. (*Its* Department bull. 1199)   **EH24**

"A list of approximately 12,500 of the 17,500 or more publications of the State experiment stations (including those of Alaska and the insular possessions) from 1875 to 1920, inclusive."—*Pref.*

Continued by biennial supplements: Bulletin 1199, suppl. 1, 2, 3; Miscellaneous publications 65, 128, 181, 232, 294, 362, 459; Bibliographical bulletin no.4, covers 1941/42 (publ. 1944).

Periodicals

Agricultural journal titles and abbreviations. 2d ed. Phoenix, Ariz., Oryx Pr., 1983. 136p.   **EH25**

1st ed. 1982.

Lists journals indexed in the *Bibliography of agriculture* (EH30) from January 1979 to March 1981. In two sections: journal titles and journal title abbreviations. Each section gives both full title and abbreviations, ISSN, and number of citations to the journal during the period of coverage.   Z5073.A47

Boalch, Donald Howard, ed. Current agricultural serials; a world list of serials in agriculture and related subjects (excluding forestry and fisheries) current in 1964. Oxford, International Assoc. of Agricultural Librarians and Documentalists, 1965–67. 2v.   **EH26**

Contents: v.1, Alphabetical list; v.2, Indexes.

A list of more than 12,400 serials, current at time of compilation, in agriculture and a broad range of related subjects. New or changed titles are reported in the *Quarterly bulletin* of the International Association of Agricultural Librarians and Documentalists.

Z5073.B68

Cáceres Ramos, Hugo. Guía de publicaciones periódicas agrícolas de América Latina. Turrialba, Costa Rica, Instituto Interamericano de Ciencias Agrícolas, Centro de Enseñanza e Investigación, 1966. 148p. (IICA. Bibliotecología y documentación, no.9)   **EH27**

Title listing with indexes by country and by subject.

Stuntz, Stephen Conrad. List of the agricultural periodicals of the United States and Canada published during the century July 1810 to July 1910, ed. by Emma B. Hawks.

Wash., Govt. Prt. Off., 1941. 190p. (U.S. Dept. of Agriculture. Miscellaneous pubn. no. 398)   **EH28**

Alphabetical title list, giving place of publication, frequency, volumes, inclusive dates, change of title, consolidations, etc. Lists 3,753 journals.

Indexes

Agricultural index, subject index to a selected list of agricultural periodicals and bulletins, 1916–64. N.Y., Wilson, 1919–64. v.1–18.   **EH29**

No more published.

Detailed, alphabetical subject index to agricultural and related periodicals and to many reports, bulletins, and circulars of agricultural departments, experiment stations, etc. Most of the periodicals are in English, including American, British, and colonial publications, but a few journals in foreign languages are included.

Continued as *Biological & agricultural index,* with v.50, no.1, Oct. 1964 (EC7, EH32). (Issues are numbered differently from cumulated volumes.)   Z5073.A46

Bibliography of agriculture. v.1– , 1942– . Phoenix, Ariz., Oryx Pr., 1942– . Monthly with cumulated annual indexes.   **EH30**

Subtitle: Data provided by National Agricultural Library, U.S. Department of Agriculture.

Publisher, title, and format vary.

This work is a major index to agriculture and allied sciences. In the current format issues are divided into nine sections. The principal main-entry section consists of classified indexing of journal articles and selected reports published throughout the world. Main-entry subsections list publications of the following: U.S. Department of Agriculture, state agricultural experiment stations, state agricultural extension services, and FAO; the last subsection lists translations. Entries in the subsections are also included in the main section and are indexed from that section. There are three indexes: corporate author, personal author, and subject.

Two supplements index literature not previously indexed:

Z5073.U55

———— 1983 supplement. Phoenix, Ariz., Oryx Pr., [1984]. 2v. (3603p.)

———— Transitional supplement 1985. Phoenix, Ariz., Oryx Pr., [1985]. 2v. (4625p.).

———— Retrospective cumulation on microfiche, 1970– 1978. Phoenix, Ariz., Oryx Pr., [1980].   **EH31**

A full cumulation of citations and indexing on 458 microfiche (48x).

Biological & agricultural index, a cumulative subject index to periodicals in the fields of biology, agriculture, and related sciences, 1964– . N.Y., Wilson, 1964– . v.19– .   **EH32**

Supersedes the *Agricultural index* (above). For complete record *see* EC7.   Z5073.A46●

FAO documentation. Current bibliography. 1972– . Rome, Food and Agriculture Organization of the United Nations. 1972– . Monthly with annual indexes.   **EH33**

Continues: *FAO documentation. Current index,* 1967–71.

Title and explanatory text in English, French, and Spanish; citations in English. Monthly indexes and annual cumulative author and subject indexes in English.   Z5073.F2

U.S. Dept. of Agriculture. Office of Experiment Stations. Experiment station record. Sept. 1889–1946. Wash., Govt. Prt. Off., 1890–1948. 95v. Monthly.   **EH34**

Discontinued.

———— ———— General index, v.1–80, 1889–1939. Wash., Govt. Prt. Off., 1903–49. 7v.

Contents: 1889–1901, v.1–12 (671p.); 1901–11, v.13–25 (1159p.); 1912–19, v.26–40 (640p.); 1919–24, v.41–50 (709p.); 1924–29, v.51–60 (677p.); 1929–34, v.61–70 (752p.); 1934–39, v.71–80 (832p.).

Consists largely of abstracts of publications of the experiment stations of the USDA and of its various divisions. Earlier volumes are arranged by station and division; later volumes are arranged by subject. Author and subject index to each volume. S21.E75

Abstract journals

Commonwealth Agricultural Bureaux. [Abstract journals]. **EH35**

The Commonwealth Agricultural Bureaux, Farnham Royal, England, publish 24 main abstract journals which are listed below. As noted, some of the titles are treated in other parts of the *Guide*. All are available for online searching; "*abstracts*" is the final word in most of the following titles. Imprints vary.

Agricultural engineering, 1976– ; *Animal breeding*, 1933– (EH74); *Arid lands (Development)*, 1980–82; *Dairy science*, 1939– ; *Field crop*, 1948– ; *Forest products*, 1978– ; *Forestry* 1939– (EH97); *Helminthological*, 1939– ; *Herbage*, 1931– ; *Horticultural*, 1931– ; *Index veterinarius*, 1933– (EH76); *Leisure, recreation and tourism*, 1976– ; *Nutrition*, 1931– (EK228); *Plant breeding*, 1930– ; *Protozoological*, 1977– ; *Review of applied entomology*, 1913– ; *Review of medical and veterinary mycology*, 1943– ; *Review of plant pathology*, 1922– ; *Rural development*, 1978– ; *Rural extension, education and training*, 1978– ; *Soils and fertilizers*, 1937– ; *Veterinary bulletin*, 1931– (EH78); *Weed*, 1952– ; *World agricultural economics and rural sociology*, 1959– .

CAB also publishes a number of specialist abstract journals; examples of subjects include faba bean, potato, and triticale. ●

Encyclopedias

Bailey, Liberty Hyde. Cyclopedia of American agriculture; a popular survey of agricultural conditions, practices, and ideals in the United States and Canada. N.Y., Macmillan, 1907–09. 4v. il. **EH36**

Contents: v.1, Farms; v.2, Crops; v.3, Animals; v.4, Farm and community; Biographies.

Contains signed articles by specialists, with bibliographies. Topical arrangement, with an index for each volume. Excellent when first issued, but now much out-of-date.

Various reprints, termed "editions" (1909–17), have no change in text. In 1922, v.2, Crops, and v.3, Animals, were reissued, with no change in text, but with new title pages and prefaces, as separate books, under the titles *Cyclopedia of farm crops* and *Cyclopedia of farm animals*. S493.B2

———— Standard cyclopedia of horticulture. N.Y., Macmillan, 1914–17. 6v. il. (Reissue, 1947, in 3v.; 20th printing 1963) **EH37**

Subtitle: A discussion, for the amateur, and the professional and commercial grower, of the kinds, characteristics, and methods of cultivation of the species of plants grown in the regions of the United States and Canada for ornament, for fancy, for fruit and for vegetables; with keys to the natural families and genera, descriptions of the horticultural capabilities of the states and provinces and dependent islands, and sketches of eminent horticulturists.

Founded upon the author's *Cyclopedia of American horticulture* (1902–1904. 4v.), but so revised and enlarged as to be practically a new work. Aims to cover completely the horticultural flora of the continental United States and Canada and to include the more outstanding species grown in a horticultural way in Puerto Rico, Hawaii, and the other islands. The last volume includes supplementary articles, a finding list of binomials, and a general index.

Special features to be noted are: (1) the very comprehensive inclusion of American native plants, trees, and shrubs, which makes the work useful for questions in botany; (2) the full indexing of

illustrations, both black-and-white and colored, included in many other works (e.g., in periodicals and collections). SB45.B17

The encyclopedia of soil science. Ed. by Rhodes W. Fairbridge and Charles W. Finkl, Jr. Stroudsburg, Pa., Dowden, Hutchinson & Ross, 1979. Pt.I. (In progress) (Encyclopedia of earth sciences, v.12) **EH38**

Contents: Pt.1, Physics, chemistry, biology, fertility, and technology (646p.).

Fairly lengthy articles on general subjects. Includes references to other volumes of the series. Bibliographies. Subject and author indexes. S592.E52

Everett, Thomas H. The New York Botanical Garden illustrated encyclopedia of horticulture. N.Y. & London, Garland, [1980–82]. 10v. il. **EH39**

"A comprehensive description and evaluation of horticulture as it is known and practiced in the United States and Canada by amateurs and by professionals."—*Pref.* Attempts to describe the majority of genera known to be in cultivation. Follows the nomenclature adopted in *Hortus third* (EC124). Genera and families are entered under Latin name with references from familiar name; vegetables, fruits, herbs, and ornamentals are entered under familiar name. The encyclopedia also includes definitions and subject articles. Numerous black-and-white photographs and some in color.

The New York Botanical Garden has sponsored a revision of James and Louise Bush-Brown's *America's garden book* (N.Y., Scribner, 1980. 819p.), a topically arranged work for the family gardener. SB317.58.E94

Hortus third; a concise dictionary of plants cultivated in the United States and Canada. N.Y., Macmillan, [1976]. 1290p. il. **EH40**

For full record *see* EC124.

Wyman, Donald. Wyman's Gardening encyclopedia. Revised and expanded. N.Y., Macmillan, [1977]. 1221p. il. **EH41**

1st ed. 1971.

"This Revised Edition contains many plant name changes that have been recorded in the recently published *Hortus III*."—*Foreword.* A table of contents has been added. Authoritative; geared to United States conditions. SB45.W97

Dictionaries

Dalal-Clayton, D. B. Black's Agricultural dictionary. London, Adam & Charles Black, [1981]. 499p. il. **EH42**

"This book is intended as a reference source for farmers, students of agriculture and all those involved in or associated with the agricultural industry in whatever capacity."—*Pref.* The pronounced emphasis on British terms and economic concerns limits the utility of this dictionary. S411.D245

Elsevier's Dictionary of soil mechanics in four languages: English/American, French, Dutch, and German. Comp. and arr. by A. D. Visser. Amsterdam, Elsevier, 1965. 359p. **EH43**

English base with indexes from the other languages. More than 4,100 entries. TA710.E45

Haensch, Günther and **Haberkamp, Gisela.** Dictionary of agriculture: German, English, French, Spanish. 3d ed. Amsterdam and N.Y., Elsevier, 1966. 746p. **EH44**

1st ed., 1959, had title *Wörterbuch der Landwirtschaft*.

The main part of the work lists terms in a classified order, on a German base, with consecutive numbering throughout. Alphabetical indexes in each language refer by number to the classified section. An "Index latinus" is included in the new edition. S411.H2613

Nijdam, J. Tuinbouwkundig woordenboek in acht talen. Horticultural dictionary in eight languages. Rev. and expanded ed. of the Horticultural word list in seven languages. N.Y., Interscience, [1961]. 504p. **EH45**

First published in 1961 by Ministry of Agriculture and Fisheries, Horticultural Division, The Hague, The Netherlands.

Includes some 400 words and expressions in Dutch, English, French, German, Danish, Swedish, Spanish, and Latin. Arranged on a Dutch base with indexes from the other languages. SB45.N673

Usovskii, B. N. [and others]. Comprehensive Russian-English agricultural dictionary. 2d ed. rev. and enl. Oxford & N.Y., Pergamon, [1967]. 470p. **EH46**

Added title page in Russian: *Russko-angliiskii sel'skokhoziaistvennyi slovar'*.

Based on the 1960 Russian edition (Moskva, Fizmatgiz. 504p.). About 40,000 Russian terms with English equivalents.
S411.U7513

Agricultural terms. 2d ed. Phoenix, Ariz., Oryx Pr., 1978. 122p. **EH47**

Subtitle: As used in the *Bibliography of agriculture,* from data provided by the National Agricultural Library, U.S. Department of Agriculture.

Lists about 37,000 terms. Z695.1.A4T54

Organizational and biographical directories

Agricultural research centres: a world directory of organizations and programmes. 7th ed. Harlow, Eng., Longman (distr. in U.S.A. by Gale), 1983. 2v. (1276p.) **EH48**

Ed. by Nigel Harvey.

1st–4th eds. (1944/45–50) entitled *Farming and mechanised agriculture;* 5th–6th eds. (1970–78) entitled *Agricultural research index.*

Contents: v.1, International, Albania to Libya; v.2, Madagascar to Zimbabwe.

Directory information for over 9,000 entities within more than 2,500 organizations. Indexed. S530.5.A33

North American horticulture, a reference guide. Comp. by the American Horticultural Society. N.Y., Scribner's, [1982]. 367p. **EH49**

A directory of U.S. and Canadian horticultural societies, organizations, and associations. Also includes other categories of information such as pesticide and herbicide regulations, libraries, gardens, awards, and flower shows, etc. Indexed. SB317.56.U6N67

Who's who in world agriculture. 2d ed. Harlow, Eng., Longman (distr. in U.S.A. by Gale), 1985. 2v. (1300p.) **EH50**

Subtitle: A biographical guide in the agricultural and veterinary sciences.

In two sections: the first contains about 12,000 biographies; the second lists experts by country and specific subject areas.
S415.W47

Handbooks

Bienz, D. R. The why and how of home horticulture. San Francisco, W.H. Freeman, [1980]. 513p. il. **EH51**

Written as a textbook, this work is also intended for the serious gardener. A useful source of information. Indexed. SB453.B49

A geographical atlas of world weeds. N.Y., Wiley-Interscience, [1979]. 391p. **EH52**

Comp. by Leroy Holm [and others].

A checklist, rather than an atlas, in alphabetical order by genus of over 7,000 weed species. Current nomenclature is used, but up to three common synonyms are given. The entry for each species includes a matrix of two elements—ranking of importance of the species as a weed and country in which the weed is found. The rankings are categorized as serious weed, principal weed, common

weed, present as a weed, and flora (present, but unconfirmed as a weed). Rankings are provided by a weed specialist in the country in which the weed appears. Introduction and table of country names (symbols) in ten languages. SB611.G38

Kingsbury, John Merriam. Poisonous plants of the United States and Canada. Englewood Cliffs, N.J., Prentice-Hall, 1964. 626p. il. **EH53**

For full record *see* EC125.

Pesticide handbook—Entoma. 1965– . College Park, Md., Entomological Soc. of America, 1965– . Ed.17– . Biennial. (30th ed. 1983) **EH54**

Formed by the union of *Pesticide handbook* (1st ed. 1949) and *Entoma* (1935–61/62) and continues the volume numbering of the *Handbook.*

A directory to such information as poison control centers, laboratories, commercial products, and manufacturers. SB951.P415

Pesticide index. 5th ed. College Park, Md., Entomological Soc. of America, 1976. 328p. **EH55**

Comp. and ed. by William J. Wiswesser.

1st ed. 1961.

Contents: Pesticide index—Alphabetic listings, numeric listings; Chemical Abstracts Service nomenclature index; Molecular formulas; Wiswesser line notations; Appendix I, A selected list of some basic chemical manufacturers owning registered trademarks; Appendix II, A selected list of some recent publications dealing with pesticide names.

The alphabetic listings contain all the available information for the pesticide, i.e., CAS nomenclature, CAS registry number, molecular formula, use, physical appearance. SB951.P42

The pesticide manual: a world compendium. 7th ed. [Croydon, Eng.], British Crop Protection Council, [1983]. 695p. **EH56**

Charles R. Worthing, ed.; S. Barrie Walker, asst. ed.

"The intention has been to include all chemical and microbial agents used as active components of products to control crop pests and diseases, animal ectoparasites, and pests in public health."—*Pref.* An alphabetically arranged listing of agents giving nomenclature and development, properties, uses, toxicology, formulations, and analysis (for many agents this category gives one or more literature references). Four indexes: Wiswesser line-formulation notation; molecular formulae; code numbers; chemical, common and trivial names, and trademarks. SB951.P434

Richey, C. B. [and others]. Agricultural engineers' handbook. N.Y., McGraw-Hill, 1961. 880p. il. **EH57**

Contents: I, Crop-production equipment; II, Soil and water conservation; III, Farmstead structures and equipment; IV, Basic agricultural data. S675.R5

U.S. Dept. of Agriculture. Yearbook of agriculture, 1894– . Wash., Govt. Prt. Off., 1895– . Annual. **EH58**

Title varies.

Prior to 1936 the *Yearbook* contained articles and statistics. Beginning with 1936, statistics are published in a separate volume entitled *Agricultural statistics* (EH64); and the *Yearbook,* instead of containing brief summaries of miscellaneous developments, devotes itself to particular subjects, as follows: 1936, Better plants and animals, I; 1937, Better plants and animals, II; 1938, Soils and men; 1939, Food and life; 1940, Farmers in a changing world; 1941, Climate and man; 1942, Keeping livestock healthy; 1943–47, Science in farming; 1948, Grass; 1949, Trees; 1950–51, Crops in peace and war; 1952, Insects; 1953, Plant diseases; 1954, Marketing; 1955, Water; 1956, Animal diseases; 1957, Soil; 1958, Land; 1959, Food; 1960, Power to produce; 1961, Seeds; 1962, After a hundred years; 1963, A place to live; 1964, Farmer's world; 1965, Consumers all; 1966, Protecting our food; 1967, Outdoors USA; 1968, Science for better living; 1969, Food for us all; 1970, Contours of change; 1971, A good life for more; 1972, Landscape for living; 1973, Handbook for the home; 1974, Shopper's guide; 1975, That we may eat; 1976, The face of rural America; 1977, Gardening for food and fun; 1978, Living on a few acres; 1979, What's to eat?; 1980, Cutting energy costs; 1981, Will there be enough food?; 1982, Food—from farm to table; 1983, Using our natural resources; 1984, Animal health; 1985, U.S. agriculture in a global economy.

———— ———— Indexes, 1894–1900, 1901–1905, 1906–1910, 1911–1915.

S21.A35

U.S. Forest Service. Seeds of woody plants in the United States. Wash., Forest Service, 1974. 883p. il. (Agricultural handbook no.450) **EH59**

Completely rewritten and greatly expanded edition of *Woodyplant seed manual*, 1948 (U.S. Dept. of Agriculture. Misc. pubn. no.654).

"Part 1 includes chapters on the principles and general methods of producing and handling seeds. Part 2 is a compilation of seed data on 188 genera of woody plants including flowering and fruiting dates, seed processing methods, storage conditions, seed yields and weights, methods of breaking seed dormancy, germination tests, and a large collection of fruit and seed photographs."—*verso of t.p.*

S501.U53

The world's worst weeds: distribution and biology. LeRoy G. Holm [and others]. Honolulu, publ. for the East-West Center by Univ. Pr. of Hawaii, [1977]. 609p. il., maps. **EH60**

"This is an inventory of the [about 300] principal weeds of the world's [16] major crops, with particular emphasis on their distribution, seriousness, and their known biology."—*Pref.*

The arrangement is by weeds (pt.I) and by crops (pt.II). Appendix A lists useful publications on weed distribution, identification, biology and control. Appendix B lists books and special publications on poisonous plants. The index is comprehensive and is international in the choice of common names. SB611.W67

Statistics

FAO production yearbook. v.30– , 1976– . Rome, Food and Agriculture Organization of the United Nations, 1977– . Annual. (FAO statistics series) **EH61**

Continues: *Production yearbook* (1958–75) and assumes its numbering.

Title and text in English, French, and Spanish.

A yearbook of statistical tables for political and geographical entities. Categories include crops, livestock, food supply, pesticides, and prices. HD1421.F585

FAO trade yearbook. v.30– , 1976– . Rome, Food and Agriculture Organization of the United Nations, 1977– . Annual. (FAO statistics series) **EH62**

Continues: *Trade yearbook,* 1958–75.

Title and text in English, French, and Spanish.

In four parts: I, FAO regional index numbers of agricultural trade; II, Trade in agricultural products; III, Trade in agricultural requisites; IV, Value of agricultural trade, by countries.

HD9000.4.F66

The state of food and agriculture. 1947– . Rome, Food and Agriculture Organization of the United Nations, 1947– . Annual. (FAO agricultural series) **EH63**

Title varies.

Each volume includes special chapters with narrative and statistical information (e.g., the 1983 edition treats two topics: "World review: the situation in sub-Saharan Africa" and "Women in developing agriculture"). A consistent feature of each volume is the "Annex tables" which give statistics on agricultural, fishery, and forest products. Categories include volume of production, indexes of food production and agricultural production, volume of exports and imports. Tables giving data by country include importance of agriculture in the economy, resources and their use in agriculture, and measures of output and productivity in agriculture.

S401.U6A317

U.S. Dept. of Agriculture. Agricultural statistics, 1936– . Wash., Govt. Prt. Off., 1936– . Annual. **EH64**

Covers "agricultural production, supplies, consumption, facilities, costs, and returns."—*Introd., 1974.* Each volume contains hundreds of tables of data on the quantity and value of agricultural products of the United States and, in some cases, of foreign countries. Most of the tables contain the annual statistics for the past 3–10 years; some include references to earlier tables. Indexed.

History

Bidwell, Percy Wells and **Falconer, John I.** History of agriculture in the northern United States, 1620–1860. Wash., Carnegie Inst., 1925. 512p. il. (Carnegie Inst. of Washington. Pubn. no.358) (Repr.: N.Y., Peter Smith, 1941) **EH65**

A scholarly, well-documented work covering the field of agriculture and agricultural economics in the northern states to the time of the Civil War. Includes a classified and critical bibliography with discussions of source materials, public and private records, books, periodicals, society publications, etc. S441.B5

Gray, Lewis Cecil and **Thompson, Esther Katherine.** History of agriculture in the southern United States to 1860. Wash., Carnegie Inst., 1933. 2v. il. (Carnegie Inst. of Washington. Pubn. no.430) (Repr.: N.Y., Peter Smith, 1941 and 1958) **EH66**

A companion work to Bidwell (above), covering all phases of agriculture and its economics in the southern states up to the time of the Civil War. Well documented. Extensive bibliography, including references to books, periodicals, newspapers, and manuscripts.

S445.G8

Schapsmeier, Edward L. and **Schapsmeier, Frederick H.** Encyclopedia of American agricultural history. Westport, Conn., Greenwood Pr., [1975]. 467p. **EH67**

Aims "to provide information on all areas bearing on agricultural history" (*Pref.*) for the beginning student as well as the scholar. Includes entries for terms, persons, events, organizations, publications, legislative acts, etc. Some bibliographic references. Includes a general index and a number of special indexes which group references topically. S441.S36

Bibliography

Edwards, Everett Eugene. A bibliography of the history of agriculture in the United States. Wash., Govt. Prt. Off., 1930. 307p. (U.S. Dept. of Agriculture. Misc. pubn. no.84) (Repr.: Detroit, Gale, 1967) **EH68**

An older, but still useful work. Classed arrangement of references to book and periodical literature, covering the publications of the years 1900–29 almost exclusively. Author/subject index.

Work toward a new and updated edition has been going forward in sections, and preliminary lists of a number of parts have been issued. These are enumerated in the preface to Douglas Bowers's *A list of references for the history of agriculture in the United States, 1790–1840* (Davis, Agricultural History Center, Univ. of California, 1969. 141p.).

Schlebecker, John T. Bibliography of books and pamphlets on the history of agriculture in the United States, 1607–1967. Santa Barbara, Calif., Clio Pr., 1969. 183p. **EH69**

More than 2,000 items listed alphabetically by author, with index of subjects and titles. Some entries have brief annotations, some of which are critical. Z5075.U5S28

U.S. National Agricultural Library. Historic books and manuscripts concerning general agriculture in the collection of the National Agricultural Library, comp. by Mortimer L. Naftalin. Wash., 1967. 94p. (*Its* Library list, no.86) **EH70**

An alphabetical author listing with full citations. Includes books published in Europe prior to 1800 and in the United States prior to 1830.

——— Historic books and manuscripts concerning horticulture and forestry in the collection of the National Agricultural Library, comp. by Mortimer L. Naftalin. Wash., 1968. 106p. (*Its* Library list, no.90)   **EH71**

Alphabetical author list, with full citations, of pre-1800 European imprints and pre-1830 American imprints. Some selected later publications also included.

Atlases

Van Royen, William. Atlas of the world's resources. N.Y., Prentice-Hall for the Univ. of Maryland, Dept. of Geography, 1952–54. v.1–2. il., maps. 32x40cm.   **EH72**

Contents: v.1, The agricultural resources of the world (1954. 258p.); v.2, The mineral resources of the world (1952. 181p.).

Each volume is arranged according to commodity or resource. Consists of text, tabular data, and maps providing information on cultivation and mining in all countries, with emphasis on the United States.

A third volume, on forest and fishery resources, was not published.   HC55.V3

World atlas of agriculture; under the aegis of the International Association of Agricultural Economists. Monographs ed. by the Committee for the World Atlas of Agriculture. Novara, Italy, Istituto Geografico de Agostini, 1969–76. 4v. and portfolio.   **EH73**

Contents: v.1, Europe, U.S.S.R., Asia Minor; v.2, South and East Asia, Oceania; v.3, Americas; v.4, Africa.

An attempt to provide comparable data and cartographic illustration of agricultural and forestry resources, land utilization, etc., of countries throughout the world. Country-by-country arrangement, with each country section contributed by one or more specialists and presented in five sections: (1) Physical environment and communications; (2) Population; (3) Exploitation of resources, ownership, and land tenure; (4) Land utilization, crops, and animal husbandry; (5) Agricultural economy. A bibliography is included for each country.

There is a separate, looseleaf volume of "Land utilization and relief maps" (60cm.) with plates, following the arrangement of the text volumes.   G1046.J1W6

ANIMAL SCIENCE

Bibliography and abstract journals

Animal breeding abstracts. v.1– , Apr. 1933– . Edinburgh, Oliver & Boyd, 1934– . Quarterly.   **EH74**

Imprint varies.
Prepared by the Commonwealth Bureau of Animal Breeding and Genetics, Edinburgh.
Cumulative annual author, subject, and geographical indexes.
SF1.A63●

Index-catalogue of medical and veterinary zoology. 1932/ 52– . Wash., Govt. Prt. Off., 1932– . v.1– .   **EH75**

At head of title: U.S. Dept. of Agriculture.
Issued by the Zoological Division, Bureau of Animal Industry.
A basic catalog (Authors, A–Zyukov), published in 18v., 1932–52, and kept up-to-date by supplements. An international bibliography.
Incorporates, and is a revision and continuation of, the *Index-catalogue of medical and veterinary zoology—authors,* published 1902–12 as Bureau of Animal Industry bulletin 39.

Index veterinarius. v.1– , Apr. 1933– . Weybridge, Eng., Commonwealth Bureau of Animal Health, 1933– . v.1– . Monthly.   **EH76**

Imprint varies. Frequency varies; quarterly through 1971.
Prepared by the Commonwealth Bureau of Animal Health.
A subject and author index to articles in various languages dealing with the literature of veterinary and related sciences.
SF601.I52●

Kerker, Ann E. and **Murphy, Henry T.** Comparative & veterinary medicine; a guide to the resource literature. [Madison], Univ. of Wisconsin Pr., [1973]. 308p.   **EH77**

Intended as "a selective guide to the recent literature for research workers and practitioners in comparative and veterinary medicine and in related biomedical disciplines which utilize animals as subjects."—*Pref.* In four sections: (1) Materials of general interest, including indexes and abstracting journals, reference works, handbooks, etc.; (2) Specific disciplines; (3) Veterinary medicine, subdivided by the various species of animals normally encountered in practice; and (4) Laboratory animals. Includes introductory notes to the sections and occasional annotations. Author index and list of conferences, congresses, symposia, and other meetings cited. Detailed subject index.

The veterinary bulletin. v.1– , Apr. 1931– . Weybridge, [Eng.], Commonwealth Agricultural Bureaux, 1932– . Monthly.   **EH78**

Prepared by the Commonwealth Bureau of Animal Health.
Absorbed *Veterinary reviews* in 1962.
An international abstracting service in classed arrangement. Each issue includes a review of a specific topic. Monthly and annual author and subject indexes.   SF601.V52●

Dictionaries and encyclopedias

Veterinarians' blue book and therapeutic index. Ed.1– , 1953– . [N.Y., R. H. Donnelly], 1953– . Annual.   **EH79**

Title varies: 1953–65, *Veterinary drug encyclopedia and therapeutic index.*
"Each product description includes current information on its ingredients, actions, uses, administration, cautions, applications and supply."—*Pref.*   SF915.V47

West, Geoffrey P., ed. Black's Veterinary dictionary. 15th ed. [London], Adam & Charles Black (distr. in U.S.A. by Barnes & Noble), 1985. 896p.   **EH80**

1st ed. 1928; 4th–12th eds., 1957–77, published by Williams & Wilkins under title *Encyclopedia of animal care.*
Gives comprehensive coverage of terms in veterinary medicine and animal husbandry, as well as the anatomy and physiology of domesticated animals. Some inclusion of public health matters and techniques of interest to farmers. Dictionary arrangement; cross references.   SF609.M5

Directories

American Veterinary Medical Association. AVMA directory. [Chicago], Amer. Veterinary Medical Assoc., [1984–]. Biennial.   **EH81**

Cover title for 1984: *Caring for animals.*
1st ed. 1956; frequency irregular until 1974.
Description based on 33d ed., 1984. Lists "AVMA members in the United States, Canada, and other countries and those nonmember veterinarians for whom data is available in AVMA records. The listings and statistics contained in the AVMA directory do not reflect the total veterinary population in the United States or any other country."—*Foreword.* In three sections: alphabetical, by veterinarian's name giving city, state, province, or country; geographic, listing state, town (or country), veterinarian's name, spouse's name, full address, school and year of graduation, professional specialty,

type of employment, and employment function; and a reference section containing information on the AVMA.   SF611.A53

Simmons, M. L. Career guide to the animal health field. 2d ed. Media, Pa., Harwal Publ., [1984]. 84p. il.   **EH82**

1st ed. 1980.

Provides basic information about career opportunities in veterinary medicine, science, animal health technology, and laboratory technology. Gives admission information for participating colleges and universities from the United States, Canada, and South America.   SF756.28.S55

Handbooks

The complete desk reference of veterinary pharmaceuticals & biologicals. 1978/79– . Media, Pa., Harwal Publ., 1978– . Biennial?   **EH83**

Continues *Comprehensive desk reference of veterinary pharmaceuticals and biologicals* (1976). Also called *Veterinary pharmaceuticals & biologicals.*

Gives product information for biologicals, pharmaceuticals, diet and nutritional supplements, parasiticides, diagnostic aids, equipment, and supplies. Each product entry gives manufacturer's name, trade name, composition, indications of use, dose administration warnings, caution, and how supplied. Various lists and indexes.   SF917.C56

Current veterinary therapy: small animal practice. Ed. by Robert W. Kirk. Philadelphia, Saunders, [1983]. 1267p. il.   **EH84**

A series of essays arranged by disease, then by animal group. Bibliography; index.   SF745.C87

Kirk, Robert W. and **Bistner, Stephen I.** Handbook of veterinary procedures & emergency treatment. 4th ed. Philadelphia, Saunders, 1985. 1000p. il.   **EH85**

1st ed. 1969.

Contents: sect.1, Emergency care; sect.2, Interpreting signs of disease; sect.3, Medical records and special systems examination; sect.4, Clinical procedures; sect.5, Interpretation of laboratory tests; sect.6, Charts and tables.

Deals with domestic animals—almost exclusively the cat and the dog. Indexed.   SF748.K57

Merck veterinary manual; a handbook of diagnosis and therapy for veterinarians. 5th ed. Rahway, N.J., Merck, 1979. 1672p.   **EH86**

1st ed. 1955.

Emphasis is on treatment of animals of North America. Includes sections on diseases of large and small animals; toxicology of pesticides, etc.; diseases of poultry; management and disease problems of fur, 'aboratory, and zoo animals; animal nutrition; laboratory routines and procedures; prescriptions. Indexed.   SF745.M4

Universities Federation for Animal Welfare. The UFAW handbook on the care and management of laboratory animals. 5th ed. Edinburgh, Churchill Livingstone, 1976. 635p.   **EH87**

1st ed. 1949.

A detailed and practical approach to the care and management of laboratory animals. Chapters 1–15 give general information on such topics as: genetic aspects of breeding methods, the animal house and its equipment, transportation of laboratory animals, anaesthesia, euthanasia, and post-mortem techniques for laboratory animals. Chapters 16–51 give information for specific animals or groups of animals. Includes the more common animals such as: anura, cats, dogs, guinea pigs, hamsters, mice, rabbits, rats, primates; and the less common such as: gerbils, ferrets, fowl, reptiles, freshwater fish, land freshwater molluscs, blowflies, beetles, wild rats, etc. Information given for specific animals or animal groups includes: standard biological data, husbandry, feeding, disease control and treatment, uses, and a list of references for additional and/or more specific information. Indexed.   SF406.U54

Domestic animals

The book of the cat. Ed. by Michael Wright and Sally Walters. N.Y., Summit Books, [1980]. 256p. il.   **EH88**

Contents: (1) The evolution of the cat; (2) The breeds of cats; (3) Understanding your cat; (4) Keeping a cat; (5) Your cat's health; (6) Breeding and showing cats.

An extensive array of information about cats. Many colorful illustrations. Indexed.   SF442.B66

Carlson, Delbert G. and **Giffin, James M.** Cat owner's home veterinary handbook. N.Y., Howell Book House. [1983]. 391p. il.   **EH89**

A companion to the authors' earlier work (below).   SF985.C29

———— Dog owner's home veterinary handbook. N.Y., Howell Book House. 1980. 364p. il.   **EH90**

"Attempts to describe in the dog, signs and symptoms which will help the owner arrive at a preliminary diagnosis—so he can weigh the severity of the problem."—*Introd.* First chapters cover emergencies, worms/intestinal parasites, and infectious diseases; the remaining 15 chapters are physiological, i.e., skin, ears, lungs, etc. Index of signs and symptoms on inside cover. Appendix: Normal physiology. Indexed.   SF991.C25

The complete dog book; the photograph, history, and official standard of every breed admitted to AKC registration, and the selection, training, breeding, care, and feeding of purebred dogs. 17th ed. N.Y., Howell Book House, 1985. 768p. il.   **EH91**

1st ed. 1929. Sponsored by the American Kennel Club.

Dogs are treated by group (e.g., sporting dogs, hounds, terriers), then alphabetically by breed. Includes a section on "Caring for your dog." Glossary; index.   SF426.C66

Ensminger, M. Eugene. The complete encyclopedia of horses. South Brunswick, N.J., A.S. Barnes, [1977]. 487p. il.   **EH92**

Aims to present "in concise, quick, and easy-to-find form, scientific—yet practical, information about the whole gamut of the horse business—from vitamins to saddlery, from breeding to showing or racing."—*Pref.* Numerous tables and line drawings as well as photographs. Lists of breed magazines and "horse books."   SF278.E57

FORESTRY

Bibliography

Davis, Richard C. North American forest history: a guide to archives and manuscripts in the United States and Canada. Santa Barbara, Calif., ABC-Clio, 1977. 367p.   **EH93**

Sponsored by Forest History Society, Inc. Companion to the Fahl volume (below).

A guide to the 108 repositories in forest archives which were identified in 1956. Each of the 3,830 groups or collections of documents is numbered and arranged by state. Subject index is to entry number.   Z5991.D33

Fahl, Ronald J. North American forest and conservation history: a bibliography. Santa Barbara, Calif., ABC-Clio, 1977. 408p.   **EH94**

Sponsored by Forest History Society, Inc. Companion to the Davis volume (above).

A historical bibliography listing primary and secondary sources covering the exploitation, utilization, and appreciation of the forest and its resources. Over 8,000 annotated references, listed alphabetically, and indexed by subject.   Z5991.F33

Munns, Edward Norfolk. A selected bibliography of North American forestry. Wash., Govt. Prt. Off., 1940. 2v. (U.S. Dept. of Agriculture. Miscellaneous pubn. 364)   **EH95**

Classified, with author index. Includes references to materials in books, periodicals, government bulletins, etc., published in the United States, Canada, and Mexico prior to 1930.   Z5991.M91

Periodicals

Grünwoldt, Franz. Répertoire international des périodiques forestiers; sylviculture, économie du bois, protection de la nature et chasse d'après leur état au 1er janvier, 1940. Berlin-Wannsee, Centre Internationale de Sylviculture, 1940. 204p. (Sylvae orbis . . . no.1)   **EH96**

A geographical listing of 1,254 forestry serials, with alphabetical title and place indexes. Information given includes date of first issue, publisher, frequency, price, editor, address, etc. Preliminary matter and half titles in French, German, English, Spanish, Italian.   Z5991.G73

Abstract journals

Forestry abstracts, comp. from world literature. Farnham Royal, Eng., Commonwealth Agricultural Bureaux, 1939– . v.1– . Monthly.   **EH97**

Imprint varies. Frequency varies: 1939–72, quarterly.
Foreign titles are translated into English; abstracts in English. Annual indexes.   SD1.F66●

Dictionaries and encyclopedias

Encyclopedia of American forest and conservation history. Richard C. Davis, ed. N.Y., Macmillan, [1983]. 2v. (871p.) il.   **EH98**

"The goal . . . has been to produce the standard, authoritative guide and reference to the history of forestry, conservation, forest industries, and other forest-related subjects in the United States."—*Pref.* Most articles are signed by one of the 203 contributors. Many articles include bibliographies. Appendixes include the national forests and parks of the U.S., a chronology of relevant federal legislation, a chronology of administrations, and an atlas. Indexed.   SD143.E53

McCulloch, Walter F. Woods words: a comprehensive dictionary of loggers terms. [Portland], Oregon Historical Soc. and the Champoeg Pr., 1958. 219p.   **EH99**

A glossary, with some longer explanations of some 4,000 words and phrases, used in the logging camps of the old Northwest.   PE3727.L8M3

Society of American Foresters. Committee on Forestry Terminology. Forestry terminology; a glossary of technical terms used in forestry. 3d ed. Wash., Soc., 1958. 97p.   **EH100**

1st ed. 1944.
Scope limited to: "(1) terms used in a special sense by foresters and (2) terms from other sciences and industry the meaning of which a forester should know and which may not be defined in other glossaries or texts that are readily available under average working conditions."—*Pref.*   SD126.S6

Weck, Johannes. Dictionary of forestry in five languages: German, English, French, Spanish, Russian. Amsterdam, N.Y., Elsevier, 1966. 573p.   **EH101**

Arranged on a German base, with indexes from the other languages. Includes appendixes of tree species, and of animals and plants causing forest pests and diseases.   SD126.W35

Handbooks

Forestry handbook. Ed. for the Society of American Foresters by Karl F. Wegner. 2d ed. N.Y., Wiley, [1984]. 1335p. il.   **EH102**

1st ed. 1955.
This edition provides "a reference book of data and methods in all phases of forestry and allied fields [for] the practicing field forester."—*Pref.* Sections such as forest ecology, silviculture, and logging were written by specialists. Bibliographies. Indexed.   SD373.F58

The international book of wood. Martyn Bramwell and Janette Place, eds. N.Y., Simon and Schuster, 1976. 276p. il.   **EH103**

Major sections of text: anatomy of wood, renewable resources, architecture in wood, sacred buildings, living with wood, ships and shipwrights, artistry in wood, lore and legend and belief, and survey of wood timbers. In the last section 144 hard and soft woods are described in detail, giving their use, treatment, and properties that make them commercially important. Index.   TS820.I56

Mohlenbrock, Robert H. The field guide to U.S. national forests. N.Y., Congdon & Weed, (distr. by St. Martin's), 1984. 324p. maps.   **EH104**

A guide by region to 153 national forests. Entries include information on location, facilities and services, special attractions, activities, and wildlife. Indexed.   SD426.M64

Record, Samuel James and **Hess, Robert W.** Timbers of the new world. New Haven, Yale Univ. Pr., 1943. 640p. il. (Repr.: N.Y., Arno, 1972)   **EH105**

A successor to *Timbers of tropical America* (1924), containing more than twice the amount of material. Covers "the trees and larger shrubs of the entire Western Hemisphere, exclusive of the islands of the Pacific. Contains descriptions of the trees, tells where they grow and the sizes they attain, and attempts to evaluate their present and potential economic importance."—*Pref.* Arranged alphabetically by families and genera within two principal groups: gymnosperms and angiosperms. Includes lists of families classified with reference to special properties and uses of their bark, leaves, and timber. Index to scientific and common names.   SD434.R4

Rendle, Bernard John. World timbers. London, E. Benn; Toronto, Univ. of Toronto Pr., 1969–70. 3v.   **EH106**

Contents: v.1, Europe and Africa; v.2, North and South America, including Central America and the West Indies; v.3, Asia and Australia and New Zealand.
During the period 1936–60 the journal *Wood* published a series on wood specimens and world timbers. Plates illustrating the grain of each type of wood have been selected from the series and reissued here in a more systematic arrangement, with revised and updated technical information (including notes on distribution and supply) to accompany each plate. Timbers were selected for economic importance or interest on the world market.   SD536.R4

Statistics

Yearbook of forest products. 1967– . Rome, Food and Agriculture Organization of the United Nations, 1968– . Annual. (FAO forestry series) (37th yearbook, 1982–83, publ. 1985)   **EH107**

Continues: *Yearbook of forest products statistics,* 1947–66.
Title and text in English, French, and Spanish.
Tables on the quantity and value of the imported and exported forest products for most of the world's countries, with totals for the world and for various regions.   HD9750.4.Y4

Atlases

Atlas of United States trees. By Elbert L. Little, Jr. Wash., Govt. Prt. Off., 1971–81. 6v. maps. 31cm. (U.S. Dept. of Agriculture Miscellaneous pubn. no. 1146, 1293, 1314, 1342, 1361, 1410) **EH108**

Contents: v.1, Conifers and important hardwoods; v.2, Alaska trees and common shrubs, by Leslie A. Viereck and Elbert L. Little, Jr.; v.3, Minor western hardwoods; v.4, Minor eastern hardwoods; v.5, Florida; v.6, Supplement.

Each volume consists of maps with political boundaries to the county level showing the distribution of individual species. Index of common names and index of scientific names in each volume.

S21.A46

HOME ECONOMICS

East, Marjorie. Home economics: past, present, and future. Boston, Allyn & Bacon, [1980]. 292p. il. **EH109**

"A book about home economics which examines its historical roots, its several definitions, its students and professionals, its potentials, and which asks many questions and answers a few."—*verso of t.p.* Offers a comprehensive survey of the field. Bibliography, p.270–86; index. TX145.E27

Bibliography

Feret, Barbara L. Gastronomical and culinary literature: a survey and analysis of historically oriented collections in the U.S.A. Metuchen, N.J., Scarecrow Pr., 1979. 124p. **EH110**

Aims "to survey, identify, and analyze important U.S. collections of printed materials on the culinary arts."—*Introd.* An introductory section reviews the nature and development of the literature of cookery and gastronomy in the Western world by country and by period, citing significant works. The section on collections offers information on the strengths and specialties of some 56 libraries and private collections, often citing specific early and rare works held. Bibliography of culinary bibliographies, and one of secondary historical texts and references. Indexed. Z5776.G2F47

U.S. Dept. of Agriculture. Home economics research report. no.1– , April 1957– . Wash., Govt. Prt. Off., 1957– . il. Irregular. **EH111**

Subjects covered: clothing, fabrics, child development, nutrition, cooking, food storage, and family finance. Includes semitechnical and technical publications formerly issued as the Department's *Agricultural handbooks, Agriculture information bulletins, Miscellaneous publications,* and *Circulars.* A321.9.Ag8

Dissertations

American Home Economics Association. Titles of dissertations and theses completed in home economics, 1968/69– . Wash., Assoc., 1970– . Annual. **EH112**

At head of title: Home economics research.

A classified listing with author index. Similar listings appeared in the *Journal of home economics,* 1964–69. Z5775.A63

Home economics research abstracts. 1966– . Wash., Amer. Home Economics Assoc., 1967– . **EH113**

Issued in 5 to 7 sections per year.

Contents (varies): 1, Family economics—home management; 2, Institution administration; 3, Textiles and clothing; 4, Art and housing, furnishings, and equipment; 5, Home economics communication and home economics education; 6, Family relations—child

development; 7, Food and nutrition. (Some sections combined in recent issues.)

Each issue in the series is a compilation of abstracts of doctoral dissertations and master's theses from schools offering graduate programs in home economics.

U.S. Agricultural Research Service. Titles of completed theses in home economics and related fields in colleges and universities of the United States. 1942/46–1961/62. Wash., [1947?]–63. 17v. in 6. **EH114**

"Intended to supplement the list *'Research in foods, human nutrition and home economics at the landgrant institutions'* comp. annually by the Office of Experiment Stations . . . 1935/36–1955/56 and the list of *'Notes on research in home economics education'* comp. in the Office of Education, 1934/36–1945. 6v."—*Pref.*

Title varies: 1942/46, *Completed theses in home economics and related fields in colleges and universities of the United States.*

Issued 1942/46–1951/52 by the Bureau of Human Nutrition and Home Economics; 1952/53–1961/62 by the Agricultural Research Service. Issued as U.S. Dept. of Agriculture, PA [Program aid], 1944/49–1961/62. Continued in the *Journal of home economics,* 1964–69; currently continued by American Home Economics Association, *Titles of dissertations and theses . . .* (EH112).

A listing of master's and doctoral theses, arranged by subject with author index.

The series of "Abstracts of doctoral theses related to home economics" formerly appearing in the *Journal of home economics* has been discontinued, but the *Journal* continues to carry abstracts of selected articles of interest to home economists, together with notes on new books and audio-visual materials.

Handbooks

American Home Economics Association. Home Economics in Business Section. Housing, Furnishings, and Equipment Committee. Handbook of household equipment terminology. 3d ed. Wash., Assoc., [1970]. 50p. **EH115**

1st ed. 1959; 2d ed. 1965.

Aims "to promote uniformity of descriptive terms and to provide a handy reference for all who deal either directly or indirectly with household equipment and the consumer."—*Pref.* Terms are grouped according to type of equipment and there is a general index.

TX298.A6

McGowan, John and **DuBern, Roger.** The Good Housekeeping illustrated book of home maintenance. N.Y., Hearst, [1985]. 240p. il. **EH116**

A comprehensive manual addressed to "anyone with a home to maintain and the desire to improve it," offering clear, well-illustrated instructions for the "willing but inexperienced handy person."—*Introd.* Three chapters on procedures in home decorating (painting, tiling, carpeting, etc.); maintenance (electricity, plumbing, heating, insulation, etc.), the cleaning, care and repair of home furnishings, and two "photographic reference" sections on the materials needed and on the tools for the home workshop. Excellent illustrations throughout. Indexed.

Management for modern families, by Irma H. Gross, Elizabeth W. Crandall and Marjorie M. Knoll (4th ed. Englewood Cliffs, N.J., Prentice-Hall, 1980. 466p.) is a basic text for college home management courses.

Food and cookery

See also EH110 and Nutrition, EK227–EK243.

Bibliography

Axford, Lavonne B. English language cookbooks, 1600–1973. Detroit, Gale, 1976. 675p. **EH117**

Title-ordered list of over 11,000 cookbooks. No annotations. Author index; subject index.

Bitting, Katherine Golden. Gastronomic bibliography. San Francisco, Calif., priv. pr., 1939. 718p. il.   **EH118**

A comprehensive bibliography of some 6,000 works in several languages—mainly English, French, and German—covering the 15th to the 20th centuries. Includes many American cookbooks produced by societies, lodges, churches, etc. In three parts: (1) by author; (2) by title, if anonymous; (3) by short title and selected subjects. Detailed bibliographic information for each entry, with some annotations. Government and other official publications are usually not listed.   Z5776.G2B6

Lowenstein, Eleanor. Bibliography of American cookery books, 1742–1860. Worcester, Mass., Amer. Antiquarian Soc., 1972. 132p.   **EH119**

"Based on Waldo Lincoln's *American Cookery Books, 1742–1860*."—*title page.*

The Lincoln work on which this is based first appeared in 1929 and was revised and enlarged by Lowenstein in 1954. Some titles from the earlier work have been dropped as "ghosts" or as outside the scope of a bibliography of cookery books as such.

About 835 titles with full bibliographic information and occasional descriptive or explanatory notes. Chronological arrangement with author and title indexes. Locates copies in 51 American libraries on a selective basis.

Patten, Marguerite. Books for cooks: a bibliography of cookery. N.Y., Bowker, 1975. 526p.   **EH120**

An annotated bibliography of more than 1,700 cookery books of relatively recent publication date, mainly in print at time of compilation. Aims "to cover every available type of cuisine and cookery." —*Introd.* Author listing with subject and title indexes.

Rudolph, G. A. Kansas State University receipt book and household manual. Manhattan, Kansas State Univ. Lib., 1968. 230p. (Kansas State Univ. Lib. Bibliography ser., 4)   **EH121**

A bibliography of pre-20th-century cookery books and household manuals in the Kansas State University Library. 803 numbered entries are arranged by year of publication from 1541 to 1899. Indexed by author and by title.   Z5777.R93

Simon, André Louis. Bibliotheca gastronomica, a catalogue of books and documents on gastronomy, comp. and annotated with an introd. . . . London, Wine and Food Soc., 1953. 196p. il.   **EH122**

"The production, taxation, distribution and consumption of food and drink, their use and abuse in all times and among all peoples." —*title page.*

An annotated listing of 1,644 items, arranged alphabetically by author, with indexes by short title and by subject.   Z5776.G2S5

Vicaire, Georges. Bibliographie gastronomique. Introd. by André L. Simon. [2d ed.] London, Derek Verschoyle Academic and Bibliographical Publ., 1954. 972col.   **EH123**

Subtitle: A bibliography of books pertaining to food and drink and related subjects, from the beginning of printing to 1890.

Originally published: Paris, Rouquette, 1890.

An annotated bibliography of some 2,500 works pertaining to gastronomy. Titles are largely in French, but some are in other western European languages. Annotations provide detailed bibliographic information and notes on content. Arranged alphabetically by author or by title when the work is anonymous. Title index.   Z5776.G2V5

Dictionaries and encyclopedias

Coyle, L. Patrick. The world encyclopedia of food. N.Y., Facts on File, [1982]. 790p. il.   **EH124**

Includes about 4,000 entries ranging from aardvark to zwirn. "Priority has been given to identification (including the scientific

name), description, and discussions of where and how an item is eaten or drunk and what it tastes like."—*Introd.* Most items in the book are individual items of food but such prepared foods as sausage, cheese, wine, bread, and sauces are included. While most entries are brief, there are some lengthy ones, e.g., "Nutritive values of the edible part of foods" and "Wine and liquor terms". Bibliography; index.   TX349.C69

Foods and food production encyclopedia. Douglas M. Considine, ed. in chief; Glenn D. Considine, managing ed. N.Y., Van Nostrand Reinhold, [1982]. 2305p. il.   **EH125**

Food production covers three states: "1. The *start* or *initiation* of the natural food-growth cycle—the seed, rootstocks, . . . 2. The nurture of growing plants and animals through harvest roundup. . . . 3. The processing of 'raw' food materials into more refined and complex products for the marketplace."—*A glance at this encyclopedia.* The 1,201 separate entries with 2,950 cross-reference headings, 1,006 illustrations, and 587 tables attempt to address all three stages. Though a country-by-country approach is not used, methods and technology from less advanced or less sophisticated areas are included when the practices are widespread. Entries range from two or three lines to the essays of four or more pages with bibliographies on such topics as alfalfa, almonds, amino acids, feedstuffs, and swine. The appendixes include a 78-page table of "Additives and other food chemicals—principally characteristics," which gives common names, formula, general characteristics, usual sources, and solubility. Indexed.   TX349.F58

Montagné, Prosper. Larousse gastronomique; the encyclopedia of food, wine and cookery. Introd. by A. Escoffier and Ph. Gilbert; ed. by Charlotte Turgeon and Nina Froud . . . [Text tr. from the French by Nina Froud and others] N.Y., Crown, [1961]. 1101p. il., maps.   **EH126**

First published 1938 in France.

An alphabetically arranged encyclopedia of foods and wines, with methods of preparation, notes on the origins of raw materials, notes on the culinary specialties of the various regions of France, etc. Includes more than 8,500 recipes and nearly 1,000 illustrations. Includes comprehensive measurement tables and line drawings showing the principal cuts of meat in France, England, and America. Index and bibliographies in French. Extensive cross references.   TX349.M613

Simon, André Louis and **Howe, Robin.** Dictionary of gastronomy. N.Y., McGraw-Hill, [1970]. 400p. il.   **EH127**

An earlier volume by Simon, with the same title, appeared in 1949.

Entries for foods, utensils, terms used in cookery, etc. Includes 64 color plates and numerous illustrations. Selected bibliography of nearly 200 items.   TX349.S53

Handbooks

American Home Economics Association. Food and Nutrition Section. Terminology Committee. Handbook of food preparation. 8th ed. Wash., Assoc., [1980]. 152p.   **EH128**

1st ed. 1946.

A useful compilation of facts and figures (much of it in tabular form) for all who work with foods. Intends to promote uniform terminology in regard to ingredients, units of measure, processes, times and temperatures, etc. Includes useful buying guides and information for the shopper. Indexed.   TX355.A54

McGee, Harold. On food and cooking. N.Y., Scribner, [1984]. 684p. il.   **EH129**

Subtitle: The science and lore of the kitchen.

Contents: pt.1, Foods; pt.2, Food and the body; pt.3, The principles of cooking: a summary.

Explains the nature of foods, their composition and origin, and why the techniques employed in cooking work. Indexed.   TX651.M37

Cookbooks

The Fannie Farmer cookbook. 12th ed. Rev. by Marian Cunningham with Jeri Laber. N.Y., Knopf, 1979. 811p. il. **EH130**

1st ed. 1896. Frequently revised. Various editions published under title *The Boston Cooking-School cook book.*
A standard American cookbook. TX715.F234

Rombauer, Irma S. and **Becker, Marion.** Joy of cooking. Indianapolis & N.Y., Bobbs-Merrill, [1975]. 915p. il. **EH131**

First published 1931. Frequently revised.
A greatly revised and expanded edition of this standard cookbook, now including more than 4,500 recipes. TX715.R75

Wines

Johnson, Hugh. The world atlas of wine; a complete guide to the wines and spirits of the world. 3d. ed. N.Y., Simon and Schuster, [1985]. 320p. il., maps. **EH132**

1st ed. 1971.
Contents: Introduction, Choosing and serving wine, France, Germany, Southern and eastern Europe and the Mediterranean, The new world, Spirits.
Describes the wines of specific parts of the world. Each area is accompanied by a map, generally detailed. Index; gazetteer. TP548.J66

Lichine, Alexis. New encyclopedia of wines and spirits. In collaboration with William Fifield. 4th ed. N.Y., Knopf, 1985. 733p. il., maps. **EH133**

1st ed. 1967. Title varies slightly.
Brief chapters on the history, making, serving, etc., of wine precede the alphabetical section. Appendixes include directories of Bordeaux and German wines, and a vintage chart. Indexed. TP546.L5

E J

Engineering

❖This section includes a selected list of reference works in the various branches of engineering. For libraries specializing in these fields, much more material will be needed, and the various guides to the literature of the subjects should be consulted. Current literature is of prime importance, and the indexes and abstract journals are essential as guides to this material. (For a discussion of abstract journals, *see* Science, Technology, and Medicine, p.1132.) Most of the branches of engineering have handbooks and manuals which include data, charts, statistics, etc., useful to the practicing engineer. These handbooks are usually revised frequently to include new developments and practices. Dictionaries of technical terms, bilingual as well as those giving definitions in English, are much used in many libraries. For bibliographies of foreign language-English language dictionaries, *see* EA108–EA112.

GENERAL WORKS

Guides

American Society for Engineering Education. Engineering School Libraries Division. [Guides to literature] Wash., The Society, 1970–71. **EJ1**

This series of brief, useful guides for the engineering student includes: *Guide to literature on aerospace engineering,* by Jane C. Rowe; *Guide to literature on agricultural engineering,* by Elizabeth P. Roberts; *Guide to literature on chemical engineering,* by Virginia E. Yagello; *Guide to literature on computers,* by Karen T. Quinn; *Guide to literature on electrical and electronics engineering,* by Richard L. Funkhouser, William L. Corya, and Jean M. Lucas; *Guide to literature on environmental sciences,* by Rita McDonald; *Guide to literature on industrial engineering,* by Elsie Finley and Marcia Parsons; *Guide to literature on mechanical engineering,* by James K. K. Ho; *Guide to literature on metals and metallurgical engineering,* by Virginia L. Wilcox; and *Guide to literature on transportation engineering,* by Beverly Hickok.

Mount, Ellis. Guide to basic information sources in engineering. N.Y., Wiley, [1976]. 196p. **EJ2**

Not a comprehensive list of sources, but rather a book designed to orient an engineering student unfamiliar with library research. T10.7.M68

Parsons, Stanley Alfred James. How to find out about engineering. Oxford, Pergamon, [1972]. 271p. **EJ3**

A guide to various sources of information in engineering and its many branches. Contains chapters on careers, education and training programs, use of libraries, standard reference sources, and organizations, as well as information on specific engineering fields. Chapters are divided into brief sections, each of which deals with a particular type of information source, e.g., bibliographies, encyclopedias, dictionaries. Name and subject indexes. TA10.P37

Use of engineering literature. K. W. Mildren, ed. London & Boston, Butterworths, [1976]. 621p. (Information sources for research and development) **EJ4**

"... this book has been produced in an attempt to assist engineers, librarians and information officers in their awareness and use of published literature. ... Material included in the chapters has been chosen on a selective rather than comprehensive basis and the items mentioned are those found to be of most use by the respective contributors."—*Pref.* Indexed. T10.7.U83

Bibliography

New York. Engineering Societies Library. Classed subject catalog. Boston, G. K. Hall, 1963. 12v. **EJ5**

—— —— Index. Boston, G. K. Hall, 1963. 356p.

—— —— Supplement 1–9. Boston, G. K. Hall, 1964–73.

Reproduction of the catalog cards for the largest engineering library in the United States. Arrangement is according to modified Universal Decimal Classification. Z5854.N47

New York. Public Library. Research Libraries. Bibliographic guide to technology. 1975– . Boston, G. K. Hall, 1976– . Annual. **EJ6**

Serves as a supplement to the Engineering Societies Library's *Classed subject catalog* (above) and its supplements 1–9; the same publisher's *Technology book guide,* 1974, may be considered the 10th suppl.
Includes relevant publications cataloged during the year by the New York Public Library, with additional entries from Library of Congress MARC tapes and conference publications cataloged by the Engineering Societies Library. Z5854.N48a

Rink, Evald. Technical Americana: a checklist of technical publications printed before 1831. Millwood, N.Y., Kraus International, [1981]. 776p.   **EJ7**

"Sponsored by the Eleutherian Mills Historical Library."—*t.p.*

A topically arranged checklist with chronological arrangement within topics. Only separately published works are included; articles in periodicals are omitted unless they were also issued separately. Entries include full bibliographic description, references to bibliographical sources, occasional annotations, and locations indicated by National Union Catalog abbreviations (a key to locations is provided). Section headings: I, General works; II, Technology; III, Agriculture; IV, Crafts and trades; V, Medical technology; VI, Military technology; VII, Civil engineering; VIII, Mechanical engineering; IX, Manufacturing; X, Mining and mineral production; XI, Sea transportation; XII, Inland transportation. Detailed index.

Z7912.R56

Indexes

Current technology index. London, Lib. Assoc.; Phoenix, Ariz., Oryx Pr., 1981– . v.1– . Monthly, with annual cumulation.   **EJ8**

Supersedes *British technology index,* 1962–80.

"The index covers all branches of engineering and chemical technology, including the various manufacturing processes based on them. It also includes material on the pure sciences of man-made objects and industrial processes; the chemistry of individual substances; and instruments, irrespective of whether their application is in pure or applied science. CTI does not cover industrial economics, but articles of a mixed technical-economic character are included. From the management sphere, only material on physical and statistical techniques, such as work study, operations research and ergonomics, is included. In general, agriculture and medicine are omitted, but some borderline subjects are included."—*Introd.* Surveys about 400 British technical journals. Arranged alphabetically by subject; cross references. Author index.   Z7913.B7

Engineering index, 1906– . N.Y., Engineering Magazine, 1907–19; Amer. Soc. of Mechanical Engineers, 1920–34; Engineering Index, Inc., 1934–81; Engineering Information, Inc., 1982– . Annual.   **EJ9**

An earlier series with the same title was published 1892–1906 in 4v., covering the period 1884–1905. (v.1, 1884–1891, had title *Descriptive index of current engineering literature.*) It indexed about 250 engineering and technical periodicals in English, French, German, Italian, Spanish, and Dutch—an alphabetical subject index with no author approach. Information given included author, title, brief digest or description of the article, length in number of words, periodical, and exact date but not volume or pages.

The present publication continues the earlier series, covering the same field but, for the years 1906–18, with a different arrangement, i.e., a classed subject index (rather than an alphabetical subject index) grouped in eight large classes: civil engineering, electrical engineering, industrial economy, marine and naval engineering, mechanical engineering, mining and metallurgy, railway engineering, street and electric railways.

Beginning 1919, the form was changed to an alphabetical subject index, giving for each article exact reference to title, date, volume and page of the periodical, and a brief digest. From 1928 on, an author index is included. International in scope, it now indexes and annotates selectively, on the basis of engineering significance, the literature appearing in over 2,700 serials, including regular professional and trade journals, and the publications of engineering societies, scientific and technical associations, universities, laboratories and research institutions, government departments and agencies, and international organizations. Papers of conferences, symposia, separate and non-serial publications of various kinds, and selected books are also covered. Most of the material indexed is available in the Engineering Societies Library. A new companion series, *Ei Engineering conference* index, will index individual conference papers not included in *Engineering index*; the first annual volume was published in late 1985.

Since Oct. 1962 monthly issues have appeared as *Engineering*

index monthly, following the plan and layout of the annual volumes, each issue having an author index. The monthly issues are superseded by the annual volume.

Cumulative indexing is provided by: Z5851.E62●

The Engineering index cumulative index, 1973/1977, 1978/1981, 1982/1984. N.Y., [1979–85]. 9v., 9v., 9v.   **EJ10**

Content of each set: v.1–3, Subject index; v.4–7, Author index; v.8, Monthly number translation index; v.9, Annual number translation index.

Each cumulation is an index to the contents of the *Engineering index annual* and *monthly* for the period covered. Commencing with the 1973 edition, abstracts in the *Annual* are numbered consecutively within each year, and this numbering differs from the numbering in the *Monthly;* thus the final volume in each set provides "translation" between the numbering schemes.

Access to the controlled vocabulary subject headings is found in:

SHE; subject headings for engineering. N.Y., [1983]. 167p.   **EJ10a**

1st ed. 1970.

This extensively cross-referenced source is very useful in finding the correct subject heading to use in looking up a topic in *Engineering index.*

Dictionaries

Encyclopedia of engineering signs and symbols. David D. Polon, ed. N.Y., Odyssey, [1965]. 412p.   **EJ11**

Like the volume for physics and mathematics (EG25), this work is part of the publisher's series of dictionaries of signs, symbols, and abbreviations. Other volumes include: *Dictionary of architectural signs and symbols* (1966); *Dictionary of computer and control systems abbreviations, signs, and symbols* (1966); *Dictionary of electrical abbreviations, signs, and symbols* (1966); *Dictionary of electronics abbreviations, signs, and symbols* (1966). While some of the information is repeated in the various volumes, one or more should prove useful in the science collection.   TA11.E5

Engineers Joint Council. Thesaurus of engineering and scientific terms. [Rev. ed.] N.Y., 1967. 690p.   **EJ12**

Subtitle: A list of engineering and related scientific terms and their relationships for use as a vocabulary reference in indexing and retrieving technical information.

1964 edition had title *Thesaurus of engineering terms.*

In four divisions, the principal one being a thesaurus of 23,364 main entries, with the other divisions serving as indexes to it and consisting of Permuted index, Subject category index, and Hierarchical index. In the thesaurus each descriptor is shown with its hierarchical structuring, cross references, and scope notes. The Permuted index is an alphabetical listing of each significant word making up thesaurus terms. The Subject category index groups descriptors according to the COSATI (Committee on Scientific and Technical Information) *Subject category list,* and the Hierarchical index, by families of related descriptors.   Z695.1.E5E5

Ernst, Richard. Comprehensive dictionary of engineering and technology, with extensive treatment of the most modern techniques and processes. Cambridge, Cambridge Univ. Pr.; Wiesbaden, Oscar Brandstetter Verlag, [1982–84]. 2v.   **EJ13**

Based on the author's bilingual dictionaries of engineering and technology which previously appeared in separate French and English editions.

Added title-page in French.

Contents: v.1, French-English; v.2, English-French.

"I have been careful to place each term strictly within its own specialized field. All branches of modern industry have been dealt with. . . . Also included are farming, chemistry, electrical engineering, electronics, transport and commerce, space travel, . . . telecommunication; and finally . . . data processing and microprocessors.

Though 'Franglais' expressions have been included, they are marked as to be phased out and the correct French word is given."—*Pref.*

T10.E747

———— Dictionary of engineering and technology: with extensive treatment of the most modern techniques and processes. N.Y., Oxford Univ. Pr., [1981–85]. 2v.   **EJ14**

Added title page in German: *Wörterbuch der industriellen Technik;* previous eds. under that title.

Contents: v.1, German-English (4th ed., 1981); v.2, English-German (5th ed., 1985).

An authoritative dictionary, covering major industrial, technical, and basic scientific disciplines.   T10.E76

Institutional and biographical directories

Directory of engineering education institutions. Africa, Arab states, Asia, Latin America. 2d ed. Paris, Unesco, [1981]. 488p.   **EJ15**

1st ed. 1976.

"... presents data on degree-awarding engineering institutions in developing countries in the African, Arab states, Asian and Latin American regions which were Member States of Unesco at the time of reviewing this edition. ... The information presented covers concisely such items as the structure, staff, students, research and specializations offered."—*Pref.*   T165.D57

Directory of engineering societies and related organizations. 1956– . N.Y., Amer. Assoc. of Engineering Societies, 1956– .   **EJ16**

Publisher's name varies.

Provides information on national, regional, state, and local organizations primarily concerned with engineering or having activities related thereto. Also includes Canadian engineering societies and international organizations. Entries give address; officers; general data, e.g., founding date, number of staff, library services; publications; special or unconventional publications media; membership requirements/qualifications; and statement of objectives. Indexed.

TA1.D48

Engineering research centres. A world directory of organizations and programmes. Consulting eds., T. Archbold, J. C. Laidlaw, and J. McKechnie. [Harlow, Essex], Longman (distr. in U.S.A. by Gale, Detroit), [1984]. 1031p.   **EJ17**

International centers are followed by national centers alphabetically by nation. Entries include information on chief officers and department heads, address and telephone number, size of staff, annual expenditure, activities. Includes corporations, university and government laboratories, research institutes. Indexed by title of establishment and by subject.   TA160.E54

Who's who in engineering. 5th ed. Ed., Jean Gregory. N.Y., Amer. Assoc. of Engineering Societies, [1982]. 889p.

EJ18

1st (1970) and 2d (1973) eds. had title *Engineers of distinction.* Publisher formerly named "Engineers Joint Council."

Gives biographical data on engineers in the United States who have met stated criteria for inclusion. Also has a section on American and Canadian engineering societies. Includes a geographic index and an index to specialization.   TA139.E37

Who's who in engineering; a biographical dictionary of the engineering profession, 1922/23–64. N.Y., Lewis Historical Pub. Co., 1922–64. v.1–9.   **EJ19**

Subtitle varies. Editions issued for 1922/23, 1925, 1931, 1937, 1941, 1948, 1954, 1959, 1964. Ceased publication.

Standards for inclusion varied, but for many years required ten years of active practice with at least five years of responsibility in important engineering work, or ten years of teaching in engineering with at least five years of responsibility for major courses. Typical "who's who" type of entries. Contains a list of engineering and

allied organizations, both national and regional; a list of professional fraternities and honor societies; and a list of professional publications, although inclusion of these, too, has varied. Geographical index.   TA139.W4

Who's who in technology today. 4th ed. Barbara A. Tinucci, senior ed.; Louann Chaudier, assoc. ed. Lake Bluff, Ill., J. Dick (division of Research Pubns.), [1984]. 5v.   **EJ20**

1st ed. 1980.

Contents: v.1, Electronics and computer science; v.2, Physics and optics; v.3, Chemistry and biotechnology; v.4, Mechanical, civil, energy and earth science; v.5, Index.

Entries are arranged alphabetically under subfields in each volume; each volume has its own combined index of names. v.5 indexes the entire set both by name and by keyword headings under areas of expertise. Most of the information is supplied by the biographees. An attempt is made to include important contributors to technology and science; coverage is limited to the United States.   T39.W48

Who's who of British engineers. 1980. [5th ed.]. London, Simon Books, 1980. 352p.   **EJ21**

1st ed. 1966.

Entries include date of birth, education, past appointments, professional interest, publications, and address. Entries received late are included in an addendum. Also has a section on professional institutions, and a list of abbreviations used.

Handbooks

Jones, Franklin Day and **Schubert, Paul B.,** eds. Engineering encyclopedia; a condensed encyclopedia and mechanical dictionary for engineers, mechanics, technical schools, industrial plants, and public libraries, giving the most essential facts about 4500 important engineering subjects. 3d ed. N.Y., Industrial Pr., [1963]. 1431p. il.   **EJ22**

1st ed. 1941.

Definitions of engineering terms and brief articles are in one alphabetical arrangement. Includes some historical and background material.   TA9.J65

Kempe's Engineer's year-book. London, Morgan, 1894– . Annual. (88th ed., 1983.)   **EJ23**

Subtitle varies. Editors vary. Beginning 1948, issued in 2v. per year.

A standard handbook of about 80 chapters, dealing with major aspects of engineering such as gearing, powder metallurgy, wire ropes, and railway steam locomotives, and containing short bibliographies. Chapters are subdivided into brief sections dealing with specific aspects. Detailed index in v.2.   TA151.A1E6

Perry, Robert H. Engineering manual: a practical reference of design methods and data in building systems, chemical, civil, electrical, mechanical, and environmental engineering and energy conversion. 3d ed. N.Y., McGraw-Hill, [1976]. 1v., various pagings. il.   **EJ24**

1st ed. 1959.

Signed sections by specialists present commonly used formulas, data, and methods in the principal engineering fields. Many tables, graphs, etc. Indexed.   TA151.P645

Potter, James Harry, ed. Handbook of the engineering sciences. Princeton, N.J., Van Nostrand, [1967]. 2v. il.

EJ25

Contents: v.1, The basic sciences; v.2, The applied sciences.

Intended to meet the engineer's needs for explanations, calculations, and examples. "The guiding philosophy ... has been to assemble, categorize, and digest the more or less enduring fundamental considerations of the principal engineering sciences on a level approximating that of the first-year graduate student in engineering."—*Pref.* v.1 contains seven major sections, e.g., chemistry, physics, graphics, presented as background for the applied engineer-

ing sciences. v.2 contains 18 major sections (e.g., thermal phenomena, turbomachinery) dealing with the sciences themselves.
TA151.P79

Souders, Mott. The engineer's companion: a concise handbook of engineering fundamentals. N.Y., Wiley, [1966]. 426p.   **EJ26**

Intended as a ready reference work for both student and practicing engineer. Includes sections on mathematics, mechanics, fluid mechanics, thermodynamics, heat transfer, electricity and magnetism, nuclear physics, engineering economy, and mathematical and physical tables. Indexed.   TA151.S57

———— Handbook of engineering fundamentals. 3d ed. N.Y., Wiley, [1975]. 1562p. il. (Wiley engineering handbook ser.)   **EJ27**

"Prepared by a staff of specialists under the editorship of the late Ovid W. Eshbach and Mott Souders."—*t.p.*

1st ed. 1956.

A thorough revision, including the complete rewriting of the sections on aeronautics and chemistry, and the inclusion of new sections on astronautics, heat transfer, electronics, automatic control, and engineering economy. The section on engineering law has been omitted. Includes many tables and graphs; each chapter has bibliographic references. Indexed.   TA151.E8

Standard handbook of engineering calculations. 2d ed. Tyler G. Hicks, ed.; S. David Hicks, coord. ed. N.Y., McGraw-Hill, [1985]. 1v., various pagings.   **EJ28**

1st ed. 1972.

Presents step-by-step calculation procedures for solving problems met in engineering practice; separate sections for each branch of engineering. Indexed.   TA332.S73

Tuma, Jan J. Engineering mathematics handbook. 2d ed., enl. & rev. N.Y., McGraw-Hill, [1979]. 394p.   **EJ29**

Subtitle: Definitions, theorems, formulas, tables.

1st ed. 1970.

"A concise summary of the major tools of engineering mathematics."—*Pref.* In five parts: algebra and trigonometry, calculus, differential equations, numerical methods, and integrals. Bibliography; index.   TA332.T85

Biography

See also EJ18–EJ21.

Great engineers and pioneers in technology. Roland Turner and Steven L. Goulden, eds. N.Y., St. Martin's Pr., [1984]– . v.1– . il. (In progress)   **EJ30**

Contents: v.1, From antiquity through the Industrial Revolution (488p.).

Entries are arranged alphabetically within topical sections; articles by experts include lists of further reading. Includes a glossary, a chronology of important engineering events, and a bibliographical essay. Indexed.   TA139.G7

Roysdon, Christine and **Khatri, Linda A.** American engineers of the nineteenth century. N.Y., Garland, 1978. 247p. (Garland reference library of social science, v.53)   **EJ31**

Entries include brief descriptions of the individuals with dates of birth and death, and references to biographical articles in engineering journals.   Z5851.R7

Materials

Brady, George Stuart and **Clauser, Henry R.** Materials handbook: an encyclopedia for managers, technical professionals, purchasing and production managers, technicians, supervisors, and foremen. 12th ed. N.Y., McGraw-Hill, [1986]. 1038p.   **EJ32**

1st ed. 1929.

Describes the important characteristics and economics of over 14,000 commercially available materials. Entries are alphabetical by general category of material. Also includes brief section on nature and properties of material, with tabular data. Detailed index.
TA403.B75

Clauss, Francis Jacob. Engineer's guide to high-temperature materials. Reading, Mass., Addison-Wesley, [1969]. 401p. il.   **EJ33**

In three sections: (1) General background, defining "gross mechanical behavior of metals and alloys at elevated temperatures . . .;" (2) Specific materials, in which "a number of specific materials are categorized according to their composition and structure;" (3) Special topics, which include "conditions of service that are more realistic than ideal laboratory conditions, as well as mathematical procedures for making the best use of limited laboratory tests."—*Pref.* Selected references; index.   TA418.26.C55

Lynch, Charles T., ed. CRC handbook of materials science. Cleveland, CRC Pr., [1974–80]. 4v.   **EJ34**

Contents: v.1, General properties; v.2, Metals, composites, and refractory materials; v.3, Nonmetallic materials and applications; v.4, Wood.

"It has been the goal of the CRC *Handbook of Materials Science* to provide a current and readily accessible guide to the physical properties of solid state and structural materials. . . . Most of the information is in tabular format. . . . This reference is particularly aimed at the nonexperts, or those who are experts in one field but seek information on materials in another."—*Pref.* Each volume indexed separately.   TA403.4.L94

Mann, John Yeates, comp. Bibliography on the fatigue of materials, components and structures. Oxford, Pergamon, [1970–83]. 3v.   **EJ35**

"Published for and on behalf of the Royal Aeronautical Society (Fatigue Committee)."—*title page.*

Contents: v.1, 1838–1950; v.2, 1951–60; v.3, 1961–65.

Entries give title of work in the language of publication, followed by translation into English. (In some cases—e.g., works written in Russian, Japanese, Chinese, or Polish—the title is given in English only, followed by a letter to indicate language of publication.) Arrangement is chronological by year of publication, then alphabetical by author. Author and subject indexes.   Z5853.M38M35

Materials handling handbook. 2d ed. Ed. in chief, Raymond A. Kulwiec. Sponsored by The American Society of Mechanical Engineers and the International Material Management Society. N.Y., Wiley, [1985]. 1458p. il.   **EJ36**

1st ed. 1958.

36 chapters by specialists include information under the topics of unit materials handling, bulk materials handling, transportation interface, and safety, environment, and human factors. Chapters include references. Indexed.   TS180.M315

O'Bannon, Loran S. Dictionary of ceramic science and engineering. N.Y., Plenum, [1984]. 303p.   **EJ37**

" . . . a reference book listing the words, terms, materials, processes, products, and some of the more prominent business terms that are important to the ceramic and related industries."—*Pref.* Brief definitions; listings for minerals and other compounds include some physical data (molecular weight, melting point, specific gravity). Cross references. Includes bibliography.   TP788.O2

Parker, Earl Randall. Materials data book for engineers and scientists. N.Y., McGraw-Hill, [1967]. 398p.   **EJ38**

"The present book is primarily a collection of up-to-date tabulated data and is similar in form to the *Handbook of Chemistry and Physics.* The descriptive matter . . . is minimal; only information considered essential for interpretation and use of the tables has been included. Data on all the generally useful metals, alloys, ceramics, plastics, woods, and concretes have been included. In addition, sections on corrosion, welding, and suppliers' addresses have been added to guide engineers in the selection and procurement of materials."—*Pref.*   TA403.4.P3

AERONAUTICAL AND SPACE ENGINEERING

Bibliography

Benton, Mildred Catherine. The literature of space science and exploration. Wash., U.S. Naval Research Laboratory, 1958. 264p. (U.S. Naval Research Laboratory, Bellevue, D.C., Bibliography no. 13)   **EJ39**

2,274 numbered entries of "books, periodical articles, and research reports on the more scientific aspects of space exploration, both theoretical and applied."—*Introd.* Covers 1903–June 1958.
    Z5064.S7B4

Boffito, Giuseppe. Biblioteca aeronautica italiana illustrata. Precede uno studio sull'aeronautica nella letteratura, nell'arte e nel folklore. Firenze, Olschki, 1929. cxv p., 544p. il.   **EJ40**

—— —— Primo supplemento decennale (1927–1936) con aggiunte all'intera "Biblioteca" e appendice sui manifesti aeronautici del Museo Caproni in Milano descritti da Paolo Arrigoni. Firenze, Olschki, 1937. 678p. il.

A comprehensive bibliography on the history of aeronautics. Arranged alphabetically, with analytical indexes to names and subjects. Contents are given for many periodicals. The supplement gives biographical notes about many of the authors.   Z5065.I8B6

Brockett, Paul. Bibliography of aeronautics. Wash., Smithsonian Inst., 1910. 940p. (Smithsonian miscellaneous collections, v.55)   **EJ41**

An important bibliography of almost 13,500 titles, arranged alphabetically by author or title, including books and pamphlets and indexing the articles in nearly 200 periodicals. Covers the period up to July 1909.
Continued by: U.S. National Advisory Committee for Aeronautics, *Bibliography of aeronautics* (EJ47).   A5063.B85

Catoe, Lynn E. UFOs and related subjects; an annotated bibliography. Prep. by the Library of Congress, Science and Technology Division for the Air Force Office of Scientific Research, Office of Aerospace Research, USAF; supplemented by Unidentified flying objects by Kay Rodgers. Detroit, Gale, 1978. 392p., 15p.   **EJ42**

First published 1969 by U.S. Govt. Prt. Off. without supplementary material.
A classed, annotated bibliography of books, journal articles, pamphlets, conference proceedings, tapes, and original manuscripts. Includes reports of sightings dating from the 19th century. Author index.   Z5064.F5C373

New York. Public Library. History of aeronautics; a selected list of references to material in the New York Public Library, comp. by William B. Gamble. N.Y., Lib., 1938. 325p. (Repr. from the New York Public Library Bull. Jan. 1936–Sept. 1937; reissued 1971)   **EJ43**

A classed list of more than 5,500 entries to books and periodical articles in many languages, with indexes of authors and subjects.
    Z5063.N56

Ordway, Frederick I. Annotated bibliography of space science and technology, with an astronomical supplement. A history of astronautical book literature—1931 through 1961. [3d ed.] Wash., Arfor Publ., [1962]. 77p.   **EJ44**

1st ed., 1955, had title: *Specialized books on space flight and related disciplines.*
Arranged chronologically by year of publication.   Z5064.A8O7

U.S. Library of Congress. Map Division. Aviation cartography; a historico-bibliographic study of aeronautical charts, by Walter W. Ristow. 2d ed. rev. and enl. Wash., 1960. 245p.   **EJ45**

A history and discussion of aeronautical charts, p.1–53; the bibliography, p.55–231, lists 774 items alphabetically by author, with subject index.   Z663.35.A8

U.S. Library of Congress. Science and Technology Division. Air Force scientific research bibliography, 1950/1956–1965. Wash., Govt. Prt. Off., 1961–70. v.1–8.   **EJ46**

Contents: v.1, 1950–56; v.2, 1957–58; v.3, 1959; v.4, 1960; v.5, 1961; v.6, 1962; v.7, 1963–64; v.8, 1965.
Includes "abstracts of all technical notes, technical reports, journal articles, books, symposium proceedings, and monographs produced and published by scientists supported in whole or in part by the Air Force Office of Scientific Research during the period. . . . v.1 also includes all earlier reports supported by AFOSR or its anlage found during this search back through 1950."—*Pref., v.1.* Includes research in physics, chemistry, engineering sciences, life sciences (except medical), mathematics, and the information sciences.
Entries include source of document, title, personal author (if any), date, pagination, report number, contract number, and accession number. Arrangement is by contractor, then department or laboratory, then chronologically under contract. Indexes by subject, contract, AFOSR control number, and personal author.
Ceased publication.   Z663.41.A36

U.S. National Advisory Committee for Aeronautics. Bibliography of aeronautics, 1909–1932. Wash., Govt. Prt. Off., 1921–36. v.1–14.   **EJ47**

Contents: v.1, 1909–16. 1493p.; v.2, 1917–19. 494p.; v.3, 1920–21. 448p.; v.4–14 (annual volumes), 1922–32.
A continuation, on the same plan, of the basic bibliography by Brockett noted above (EJ41). "Citations of the publications of all nations have been included in the languages in which these publications originally appeared."—*Introd.* Author and subject entries in one alphabetical arrangement.   Z5063.B86

Periodicals

U.S. Library of Congress. Science and Technology Division. Aeronautical and space serial publications: a world list. Wash., 1962. 255p.   **EJ48**

A bibliography of 4,551 serial publications originating in 76 countries, but principally in the United States, Germany, Great Britain, France, and Russia. Arrangement is alphabetical by country, then by title or issuing agency. Includes periodicals, documents, annuals, numbered monographic series, and other serial publications. Entries include title, issuing agency, place of publication, frequency, dates published, indication of title change or suspension, LC call number, and currency of publication. Alphabetical title index. Supersedes *A checklist of aeronautical periodicals and serials in the Library of Congress* (1948).   Z5063.A2U64

Abstract journals

International aerospace abstracts. v.1– . Phillipsburg, N.J., Technical Information Service, Amer. Inst. of Aeronautics and Astronautics, 1961– . v.1– . Semimonthly.   **EJ49**

Covers published literature in periodicals and books; meeting papers and conference proceedings issued by professional and academic organizations; and translations of journals and articles in the fields of aeronautics and space science and technology.
Reports ("unpublished literature") are abstracted in *Scientific and technical aerospace reports* (*STAR;* below). These two services use the same subject categories and indexes, and thus "provide comprehensive access to the national and international unclassified report and published literature of current significance to aerospace science and technology."—*Introd., STAR v.1, no.1.* Indexes by subject, personal author, contract number, meeting paper and report number, and accession number. Indexes now cumulate semiannually and annually.   TL500.I57●

U.S. National Aeronautics and Space Administration. Scientific and technical aerospace reports; a semimonthly abstract journal with indexes. v.1– , Jan. 8, 1963– . Wash.,

1963– . v.1– . Semimonthly, with cumulative semiannual and annual indexes.   **EJ50**

Supersedes *Technical publications announcements,* with the same scope and coverage.

STAR is a comprehensive abstracting and indexing journal covering current worldwide report literature on the science and technology of space and aeronautics. Publications abstracted include scientific and technical reports issued by NASA and its contractors, other U.S. Government agencies, corporations, universities, and research organizations throughout the world. Pertinent theses, translations, NASA-owned patents and patent applications, and other separates are also abstracted. Citations and abstracts are grouped in 75 subject categories, although accession numbers run in unbroken sequence through the *STAR* issues, without regard to category assignment. Indexes by subject, personal author, corporate source, contract number, and report/accession number. Availability, whether hard copy or microfiche, and source are also given.

——— Guide to the subject indexes for scientific and technical aerospace reports. no.1– , April 1964– . Wash., 1964– .

Revised at irregular intervals   Z695.1.A25U57●

Dictionaries and encyclopedias

Aviation/space dictionary. Ed. by Ernest J. Gentle and Lawrence W. Reithmaier. 6th ed. Los Angeles, Aero, 1980. 272p. il.   **EJ51**

1st ed. 1940. Title and editors vary.

This edition includes terms from such fields as computer technology, geophysics, nucleonics, aviation and space technology, radar, electronics, and astronomy as well as selected terms from the basic sciences and mathematics. Designed for the intelligent layman rather than the technical specialist. Some plates and diagrams. Appendix includes abbreviations, symbols, and acronyms.
                                                        TL509.A8

The encyclopedia of UFOs. Ed. by Ronald D. Story. Garden City, N.Y., Doubleday, 1980. 440p. il.   **EJ52**

J. Richard Greenwell, consulting ed.

A collection of brief, signed articles, in alphabetical order, on topics and individuals associated with UFOs. "A general overview rather than an exhaustive treatment, is the goal for this book."—*Pref.* Includes a bibliography and list of UFO-related acronyms.
                                                        TL789.E52

Gunston, Bill. Jane's Aerospace dictionary. London & N.Y., Jane's, [1980]. 493p.   **EJ53**

Up to date and comprehensive. Fairly brief entries. Includes acronyms; cross references.   TL509.G86

Jane's Encyclopedia of aviation. Comp. and ed. by Michael J. H. Taylor. London, Jane's; Danbury, Conn., Grolier, [1980]. 5v. il.   **EJ54**

Concise, alphabetically arranged entries for about 5,000 of the more significant types of air and spacecraft in history, including some types that had "slipped through the editorial net" and were not included in the various editions of *Jane's All the worlds aircraft* (EJ83). Also includes a chronology, world directories of airlines and of air forces, and a list of aerospace world records. Indexed.

McGraw-Hill encyclopedia of space. N.Y., McGraw-Hill, [1968]. 831p. il.   **EJ55**

Translation of *La grande aventure de l'espace* (Paris, 1967).

Topical sections deal with the rocket, artificial satellites, space navigation and electronics, man in space, life in the universe, astronomy-astrophysics, the conquest of the moon, and astronautics in the world today. Written in a non-technical style and without bibliographic references. Well illustrated; indexed.   TL791.G713

Marks, Robert W., ed. The new dictionary & handbook of aerospace, with special sections on the moon and lunar flight. N.Y., Praeger, [1969]. 531p. il.   **EJ56**

Intended as "a moderately-priced dictionary and handbook which introduces the general reader to the structure, topography, and vocabulary of aerospace science."—*Pref.* Most of the data were adapted from official U.S. government sources.   TL509.M35

Moser, Reta C. Space-age acronyms; abbreviations and designations. 2d ed., rev. and enl. N.Y., IFI/Plenum, 1969. 534p.   **EJ57**

1st ed. 1964.

More than 15,000 acronyms with the 25,000 expressions for which they stand. Short supplementary lists treat missile, rocket, probe, and drone designation system; ship designations; communication electronic equipment designation system.   TL788.M6

Ocran, E. B. Dictionary of air transport and traffic control. London, Granada, [1984]. 243p.   **EJ58**

"This dictionary has been designed for the benefit of the student of air transport and traffic control, the air traffic controller, the air pilot, the travel agent, the airline operator, the aviation writer, instructors, managers and aviation authorities, and the layman air passenger."—*Introd.* Brief definitions; includes some abbreviations. Has an index of terms under 16 broad subject headings.
                                                        TL509.O554

U.S. Aerospace Studies Institute. Aerospace glossary. Woodford Agee Heflin, ed. [Maxwell Air Force Base, Ala.], 1959. 111p.   **EJ59**

Issued by the Institute under its earlier designation: Research Studies Institute, Air University.

". . . a guide to the specialized vocabulary that deals with aerospace missiles and vehicles, their employment and the physical laws that govern them."—*Pref.* Quotations from the aerospace literature illustrate usage.

Supplements *The United States Air Force dictionary* (below) and does not repeat terms found therein.

——— The United States Air Force dictionary. Ed. by Woodford Agee Heflin. Princeton, N.J., Van Nostrand, 1956. 578p.   **EJ60**

Issued by the Institute under its earlier designation: Research Studies Institute, Air University.

Supplemented by the same editor's *Aerospace glossary* (above).

Wragg, David W. A dictionary of aviation. [Reading, Eng.], Osprey, [1973]. 286p.   **EJ61**

Intends "to provide a guide to the more important events and personalities in aviation history"(*Introd.*), as well entries for terms, concepts, airlines, aircraft, and manufacturers. Non-technical in approach.

Foreign terms

Konarski, Michael M. Russian-English dictionary of modern terms in aeronautics and rocketry. Oxford & N.Y., Pergamon, 1962. 515p.   **EJ62**

14,500 terms derived from the Soviet scientific literature, the press, and other dictionaries. Includes terms used in related fields, e.g., radio, electronics, meteorology, and aerial photography. Index of English terms; a listing of Russian abbreviations used in Soviet aviation; and a section of "indispensable data," containing such information as the Russian alphabet and Morse code, aerodynamic configurations of supersonic aircraft (Soviet classification), mathematical constants, and mathematical signs.

——— Russian-English space technology dictionary. Oxford, etc., Pergamon, [1970]. 416p. il.   **EJ63**

About 10,600 terms. Follows the same arrangement as the preceding item. Includes a short glossary of aerospace biomedical terms frequently appearing in Russian scientific and popular literature. The section of "indispensable data" includes information on physical characteristics of the planets and on planetary orbits, the sun, and the moon. A listing of personal names of scientists which occur frequently in the literature is included to "alleviate at least partly the vexing problem of reconstructing such names from their often ambiguous Russian transliterations."—*Foreword.* TL788.K58

Murashkevich, Anatolii Mikhailovich, ed. Russko-angliiskii aviatsionno-kosmicheskii slovar'. Moskva, Voen. Izd.-vo., 1971. 791p. **EJ64**

Added title page: Russian-English aviation & space dictionary, More than 42,000 terms including a wide range of related technologies and fields. TL509.M82

———— and **Vladimirov, O. N.** Anglo-russkii slovar' sokrashchenii po aviatsionni i raketno-kosmicheskoi tekhnike: okolo 30,000 sokrashchenii. Moskva, Voen. Izd.-vo., 1981. 621p. **EJ65**

Added title page: English-Russian aviation and space dictionary. Prev. ed. had title *Anglo-russkii aviatsionnyi slovar'* (1964). TL509.M813

Oppermann, Alfred. Aeronautical-English. Technisches Taschenwörter- und Handbuch der Luftfahrt. Technical pocket dictionary and manual of aviation. München, Oppermann, 1957. v.1 (1170p.). il. **EJ66**

———— ———— Ergänzungsnachtrag 1. zur ersten Aufl. Supplement 1 to 1st ed. München, Oppermann, 1957. xxivp.

———— ———— Nachtrag 1/1960– . Supplement 1/1960– , von Claus-Jurgen Brey. München, Oppermann, 1960– .

Beginning 1972, has title *Wörterbuch der modernen Technik.*
Includes technical fields, such as rocket construction, space travel, machine tools, automotive industry, plastics, lasers, and cybernetics. German-English and English-German. TL509.O6

U.S. Library of Congress. Reference Dept. Russian-English glossary of guided missile, rocket, and satellite terms, comp. by Alexander Rosenberg. Wash., 1958. 352p. **EJ67**

Lists more than 4,000 terms taken from books and periodicals published in the USSR from 1955 to 1958. TL782.U5

Directories

Aerospace research index. A guide to world research in aeronautics, meteorology, astronomy, and space science. Consulting eds., A. P. Willmore and S. R. Willmore. Harlow, Essex, F. Hodgson; Detroit, Gale, [1981]. 597p. **EJ68**

Indexes establishments engaged in, or promoting, research into aerospace studies. Entries, arranged by country, include size and range of activities, titles of publications issued, names of administrative personnel, address. Title and keyword index; subject index. TL565.A37

Who's who in aviation and aerospace. U.S. ed. Compiled with the assistance of Jane's Publishing Co., Ltd. Boston, National Aeronautical Inst., 1983. 1415p. **EJ69**

Includes about 15,000 individuals living in the United States, from the full range of aviation and aerospace activities, selected on the basis of professional achievement. Includes a geographic index with subheadings for type of professional activity, and an index by institutional employer. TL539.W57

Handbooks

Battelle Memorial Institute, Columbus, Ohio. Columbus Laboratories. Handbook of Soviet space-science research. Written by the staff and consultants of Battelle Memorial Institute, Columbus Laboratories. Ed. by George E. Wukelic. N.Y., Gordon and Breach, [1968]. 505p. **EJ70**

Designed "to acquaint the reader with Soviet space-science accomplishments over the past 10 years and to assist interested researchers in their use of the Soviet information which is available to us."—*Foreword.* In five sections containing 20 chapters, each with

bibliographic references. Sections cover Soviet rocket, satellite, and space probes, Soviet biomedical space research, artificial earth satellite applications, and related topics. Includes photographs, diagrams, and tables. An appendix lists major Soviet publications and their translation availability. Author and subject indexes. QB500.B33

Johnson, Francis S., ed. Satellite environment handbook. 2d ed. Stanford, Stanford Univ. Pr., 1965. 193p. il. **EJ71**

1st ed. 1961.
Chapters prepared by various authors present data in classed arrangement and include lists of references. "The major satellite-environment factors—the structure of the upper atmosphere and the ionosphere, penetrating-particle radiation, solar radiation, micrometeorites, radio noise, thermal radiation from Earth, and geomagnetism—are discussed, and existing data are evaluated."—*Pref., 1st ed.* This edition includes revisions and additions to the description of the satellite environment. Indexed. QC879.5.J6

Lockheed Aircraft Corporation. Lockheed Missiles and Space Company. Space materials handbook. 3d ed. by John B. Rittenhouse and John B. Singletary. Wash., Off. of Technology Utilization, Nat. Aeronautics & Space Admin., 1969. 734p. (NASA SP-3051) **EJ72**

Previous edition 1965, by C. G. Goetzel and others; suppl., 1966.
In four parts: (1) Space environment; (2) Effect of space environment on materials; (3) Materials in space; (4) Biological interaction with spacecraft materials.

Martin Marietta Corporation. Aerospace Division. Design guide to orbital flight, by Jorgen Jensen [and others]. N.Y., McGraw-Hill, 1962. il. **EJ73**

A ready-reference work for vehicle-design engineers concerned with satellite flight mechanics. Includes "formulas of elliptic motion and their variations, geophysical and astronomical constants, analyses of trajectory problems, and numerical tables and graphical representations showing quantitative relations between the various astronomical and astronautical parameters."—*Foreword.* Each chapter has lists of references and appendixes of technical information. Indexed. TL796.6.E2M35

The RAE table of earth satellites, 1957–1980. Comp. at the Royal Aircraft Establishment, Farnborough, Hants, England by D. G. King-Hele [and others]. [London, Macmillan; N.Y., Facts on File, 1981] 656p. **EJ74**

"The Table is a chronological list of the 2145 launches of satellites and space vehicles between 1957 and the end of 1980, giving the name and international designation of each satellite and its associated rocket(s), with the date of launch, lifetime (actual or estimated), mass, shape, dimensions and at least one set of orbital parameters. . . . Including fragments, more than 12,000 satellites appear. . . . "—*t.p.* Indexed. TL796.6.E2.R253

Turnill, Reginald. Jane's Spaceflight directory. [London], Jane's, [1984]. 311p. il. **EJ75**

A completely revised version of the author's *Observer's spaceflight directory,* 1978.
Most of the work is devoted to articles describing space programs by nation, with pictures, descriptions of vehicles and payloads, and orbit information for some satellites. Also includes articles on military uses of space, launchers, space centers, space contractors, etc. Indexed. TL790.T84

U.S. Air Force. Cambridge Research Laboratories. Handbook of geophysics and space environments. Scientific ed., Shea L. Valley. N.Y., McGraw-Hill, [1965?]. 1v., various pagings. il. **EJ76**

"The topics included are those which currently concern the scientists and engineers who are engaged in research, planning, design, development, and operation of aerospace systems."—*Introd.* Contains sections on geodesy and gravity, winds, atmospheric composition, atmospheric optics, the geomagnetic field, the lunar environment, etc., which present a comprehensive collection of data, formulas, definitions, and theories about the earth's environment. Lists of references are included at the end of sections. Index and detailed table of contents. Two appendixes, one devoted to units, constants, and conversion factors; the other to blackbody radiation.   QC806.U48

U.S. Federal Aviation Agency. FAA statistical handbook of aviation. 1944– . Wash., 1944– . Annual.   **EJ77**

Title varies; name of issuing body varies (from 1967, Federal Aviation Administration).

Designed "to serve as a convenient source for historical data, and to assist in evaluating progress, determining trends, and estimating future aeronautical activity."—*Pref.* Principally tables. Each volume contains data for the preceding 11 years. Gives information on airports, airport activity, civil air-carrier fleet, civil air-carrier operating data, airmen, civil aircraft, general aviation, aeronautical production and exports, and accidents.   TL521.A416

U.S. National Aeronautics and Space Administration. Aeronautics and astronautics; an American chronology of science and technology in the exploration of space, 1915–1960, by Eugene M. Emme . . . Wash., 1961. 240p.   **EJ78**

A listing, by year and day, of important events in aeronautics from the date of founding of the National Advisory Committee for Aeronautics (NACA) and emphasizing U.S. efforts. Appendixes chronicle earth satellites and space probes; world airplane records; select balloon flights, 1927–60; awards and honors; and NACA membership, 1915–59. Selected bibliography; subject and name index.   TL521.A54283

——— Astronautical and aeronautical events of 1961–62. Wash., 1962–63. 2v.   **EJ79**

Supplements the above.

——— Astronautics and aeronautics. Chronology on science, technology, and policy. Wash., 1963– . Annual. (NASA SP). (The NASA history series).   **EJ80**

Continues *Astronautical and aeronautical events* (above). Subtitle varies.

Wilding-White, T. M., ed. Jane's Pocket book of space exploration. N.Y., Collier Macmillan, 1977. 238p. il.   **EJ81**

Contains illustrations of over 200 manned and unmanned space craft and launch vehicles, along with concise technical and historical data.   TL796.W48

Yearbooks

Aerospace year book. 1919–70. Official publication of the Aerospace Industries Association of America, Inc. Wash., Amer. Aviation Publ., 1919–70. v.1–48. il. Annual.   **EJ82**

Title varies: 1919–59, *The aircraft yearbook.* Not published 1963–65. Ceased publication.

Format and emphasis vary. Essentially a chronicle of the year's events, with particular attention to types of air- and spacecraft and their specifications. Contents of latest volumes have included a pictorial record of the year's highlights, plus information on the aerospace industry, government research and development, civil aviation, and a reference section containing specifications, performance, and other data on aerospace industry products and systems. Indexed.   TL501.A563

Jane's All the world's aircraft, 1909– . London, S. Low, 1909– . v.1– . il. Annual.   **EJ83**

Title varies: [v.1–2], *All the world's airships;* [v.3]–19, *All the world's aircraft.*

Offers illustrations, descriptions, and specifications of aircraft of various countries of the world including: airplanes, drones, sailplanes, airships, military missiles, research rockets, space vehicles, aero-engines. Arranged in sections by type of craft, then alphabetically by country of manufacture. Separate indexes according to type of craft with entries for manufacturer and individual model name. Indexes include references to ten previous editions.   TL501.J3

World aviation directory. Wash., Ziff-Davis, 1940– . v.1– . Biennial.   **EJ84**

Title varies: 1940–51, *American aviation directory.* Publisher varies.

Subtitle varies: 1972/73, Listing aerospace companies and officials, covering the United States, Canada, and 160 countries in Europe, Central and South America, Africa and Middle East, Australasia and Asia.

Absorbed *World space directory,* 1966.

A directory of "executive, administrative and operating personnel of world-wide scheduled airlines, major aerospace manufacturers, component aerospace manufacturers and major subcontractors, distributors and aerospace equipment, U.S. airports—terminal and non-terminal, aviation repair stations and schools, aerospace publications, aerospace oriented organizations and government operations, etc."—*Publisher's description.* Includes a buyer's guide to products and services and information on aerospace operations in foreign countries. Personnel index.   TL512.A63

AUTOMOTIVE ENGINEERING

Jennings, Ralph Ernest, ed. The automotive dictionary. [N.Y., Wm. Dogan Annual Publ. Associates], 1969. 277p. il.   **EJ85**

Brief definitions of some 8,000 terms.   TL9.J44

The new encyclopedia of motorcars, 1885 to the present. Ed. by G. N. Georgano 3d ed. N.Y., Dutton, [1982]. 688p. il.   **EJ86**

1st–2d eds. 1968–73, had title: *The complete encyclopedia of motorcars, 1885 to the present.*

Entries in alphabetical sequence for all makes of automobiles from all periods and the world over. Attempts to include at least one illustration for every make of automobile.   TN15.N37

SAE handbook. 1926– . N.Y., Soc. of Automotive Engineers, 1926– . il. Annual (slightly irregular).   **EJ87**

Contents, 1985: v.1, Materials; v.2, Parts & components; v.3, Engines, fuels, lubricants, emissions, & noise; v.4, On-highway vehicles & off-highway machinery; Index.

A standard handbook presenting SAE standards, recommended practices, and information reports. Includes numerous charts and tables. Indexed.   TL151.S62

CHEMICAL ENGINEERING

Guides

Bourton, Kathleen. Chemical and process engineering unit operations; a bibliographical guide, by Kay Bourton. N.Y., IFI/Plenum, 1968. 534p.   **EJ88**

Presents "a selection from the chemical engineering literature which will be a guide to the available aids to searching and to those works which are likely to serve as the most productive sources for retrieval."—*Pref.* Nearly 4,600 entries in classed arrangement. Annotations; author and subject indexes.   Z7914.C4B6

Abstract journals

See also ED22.

Theoretical chemical engineering abstracts. v.1– , Jan./Feb. 1964– . [London], Technical Information Co., 1964– . v.1– . Bimonthly with annual index.   **EJ89**

Imprint varies.

A classified listing of abstracts of periodicals and report literature; books are listed in a separate section at the end of each issue. Each abstract shows the number of bibliographical references in the original article or report. TP1.T47

Encyclopedias

Chemical technology: an encyclopedic treatment. Gen. ed., T. J. W. van Thoor. N.Y., Barnes & Noble, [1968–75]. 8v. il. **EJ90**

"The economic application of modern technological developments, based upon a work originally devised by the late Dr. J. F. van Oss."—*t.p.*

Contents: v.1, Air, water, inorganic chemicals and nucleonics; v.2, Non-metallic ores, silicate industries, and solid mineral fuels; v.3, Metals and ores; v.4, Petroleum and organic chemicals; v.5, Natural organic materials and related synthetic products; v.6, Wood, paper, textiles, plastics and photographic materials; v.7, Vegetable food products and luxuries; v.8, Edible oils and fats, Animal products, Material resources, General index, Appendix—Recent developments in materials and technology.

Intended for the layman as well as for the technologist, the work describes "the sources, manufacture, processing, and uses of both natural and synthetic materials."—*Pref.* A select bibliography accompanies each chapter. TP200.M35

Encyclopedia of chemical technology. 3d ed. N.Y., Wiley, [1978–84]. 24v. il. **EJ91**

At head of title: Kirk-Othmer.

Editorial board: Herman F. Mark, Donald F. Othmer, Charles G. Overberger, and Glen T. Seaborg.

1st ed. (1947–56) ed. by Raymond E. Kirk and Donald F. Othmer; 2d ed. (1963–72) 22v. plus suppl. and index.

Articles in this standard reference are written by specialists, are signed, and include bibliographies. This edition uses SI (Système international d'unités) as well as English units, and includes Chemical Abstracts Service Registry Numbers.

———— Supplement volume: Alcohol fuels to toxicology. N.Y., Wiley, [1984]. 924p.

———— Index to volumes 1–24 and supplement. N.Y., Wiley, [1984]. 1274p.

A brief version of the 3d ed. is: TP9.E685●

Kirk-Othmer concise encyclopedia of chemical technology. Executive ed., Martin Grayson; assoc. ed., David Eckroth. N.Y., McGraw-Hill, [1985]. 1318p. il. **EJ92**

An abridged version of the 24-volume *Encyclopedia of chemical technology* (above). All of the original 1,100 articles have been rewritten, some with new material; each includes a short list of references. Cross references; index. Very valuable for libraries that do not have the multivolume edition. TP9.K54

Hampel, Clifford A. The encyclopedia of electrochemistry. N.Y., Reinhold; London, Chapman & Hall, [1964]. 1206p. il. **EJ93**

"Contains 412 individual articles or entries arranged in alphabetical sequence and especially prepared by 271 contributors."—*Introd.* Articles are signed and include bibliographies. QD553.H3

Ullmann, Fritz. Ullmann's Encyclopedia of industrial chemistry. 5th, completely revised ed. Executive ed., Wolfgang Gerhartz. [Weinheim & Deerfield Beach, Fla.], VCH, [1985]– . v.A1– . il. (In progress) **EJ94**

1st ed. (1914) through 4th ed. (1972–84) had title: *Ullmanns Enzyklopädie der technischen Chemie.* 4th ed. in 24v. and index.

A European counterpart to the *Encyclopedia of chemical technology* (EJ91), this standard reference work is now published for the first time in English. "The Encyclopedia is organized in two series. The 28 'A' volumes contain alphabetically arranged articles on chemicals, product groups, areas of application, processes, and technological concepts. Basic principles are treated in the eight volumes of the 'B' series, beginning with topics such as fluid dynamics or transport phenomena in the first volume, unit operations in the second and third, chemical reaction engineering and materials science in the

fourth, analytical methods in volumes five and six, and environmental protection and plant safety in seven and eight. The plan is to publish three or four volumes each year. An annual cumulative index will provide easy access. ... Chemical Abstract Service Registry Numbers are given for all important chemicals. Nomenclature is consistent with IUPAC rules, and SI units are used."—*Pref.* Signed, authoritative articles contain substantial tabular data, extensive bibliographic references. Cross references. TP9.U57

Handbooks

Cremer, Herbert W. and **Davies, Trefor,** eds. Chemical engineering practice. London, Butterworths Scientific Pub., 1956–65. 12v. il. **EJ95**

Contents: v.1, General; v.2, Solid state; v.3, Solid systems; v.4, Fluid state; v.5–6, Fluid systems; v.7, Heat transfer; v.8, Chemical kinetics; v.9, Design and construction; v.10, Ancillary services; v.11, Works design, layout, etc.; v.12, Indexes.

Sections by specialists. Bibliographies. TP155.C7

Industrial solvents handbook. 3d ed. Ed. by Ernest W. Flick. Park Ridge, N.J., Noyes Data, [1985]. 648p. **EJ96**

1st ed. 1970.

Contains extensive tables providing "basic data on the physical properties of most solvents and on the solubilities of a variety of materials in these solvents."—*Foreword.* Arranged by class of solvent, e.g., halogenated hydrocarbons, ethers, acids; contains phase diagrams for multicomponent systems. Sources of data are indicated. Includes references. TP247.5.I53

Perry's Chemical engineers' handbook. 6th ed., prepared by a staff of specialists under the editorial direction of late ed. Robert H. Perry, ed. Don W. Green, assist. ed. James O. Maloney. N.Y., McGraw-Hill, [1984]. 1v., various pagings. il. **EJ97**

1st–3d eds. (1934–50) by John H. Perry. Previous eds. had title *Chemical engineers' handbook.*

A standard handbook revised and updated; this ed. uses both SI and U.S. customary units as much as possible and also includes conversion factors. Has contributions by 125 authorities in various engineering and scientific disciplines; sections include many tables, graphs, line drawings, literature references. Indexed. TP151.P45

Riegel, Emil Raymond. Riegel's Handbook of industrial chemistry. 8th ed. Ed. by James A. Kent. N.Y., Van Nostrand Reinhold, [1983]. 979p. il. **EJ98**

1st–5th eds. (1933–49) had title *Industrial chemistry;* 6th ed. (1962) *Riegel's Industrial chemistry;* 7th ed. (1974) *Handbook of industrial chemistry.*

" ... the aim of this book is to present an up-to-date account of the many facets of as broad a cross section of the chemical process industry as is reasonable in a single volume of this size."—*Pref.* Contains 25 chapters by 34 specialist contributors; chapters include tabular data, process diagrams, bibliographic references. Indexed. TP145.R54

Plastics

American Society of Tool and Manufacturing Engineers. Plastics tooling and manufacturing handbook; a reference book on the use of plastics as engineering materials for tool and workpiece fabrication. Prep. under the policy supervision of ASTME Publications Committee. Frank W. Wilson, ed. in chief. Englewood Cliffs, N.J., Prentice-Hall, [1965]. 243p. il. **EJ99**

Deals with plastics materials used in tooling, tool design, and fabrication of tooling, and also with properties and characteristics of the plastics, basic processes employed, etc. Indexed. TJ1194.A5

Brandrup, Johannes and **Immergut, E. H.,** eds. Polymer handbook. 2d ed. N.Y., Wiley, [1975]. 1v., various pagings. **EJ100**

1st ed. 1966.

Brings together a vast amount of physical and chemical data on polymers. Consists of chapter-length data tabulations and extensive bibliographies. Brief subject index.   QD388.B7

Dorian, Angelo Francis. Six-language dictionary of plastics and rubber technology; a comprehensive dictionary in English, German, French, Italian, Spanish, and Dutch. London, Iliffe, [1965]. 808p. **EJ101**

The English part (p.1–633) includes a definition of each term as well as the equivalents in the other languages; the other parts are merely foreign-language indexes to the English section.   TP1110.D6

Encyclopedia of polymer science and engineering. Ed. board: Herman F. Mark [and others]; ed. in chief, Jacqueline I. Kroschwitz. 2d ed. N.Y., Wiley, [1985]. v.1–3. il. (In progress) **EJ102**

1st ed. (1964–77), in 16v. and 2 suppls., had title *Encyclopedia of polymer science and technology.*

Contents: v.1–3, A–Cold forming. Expected to be complete in 19v.

Signed articles by specialist authors contain equations, graphs, tabular data, and extensive bibliographical references. Each volume begins with tables of conversion factors, abbreviations, and unit symbols. Coverage includes all aspects of polymer science (physics, chemistry, biology) and engineering. Cross references.   TP1087.E46

Glanvill, Alan Birkett. The plastics engineer's data book. Brighton, Machinery Publ., 1971; N.Y., Industrial Pr., 1973. 216p. **EJ103**

Intended for those who design and process plastics, and for the student entering the field.   TP1130.G55

Handbook of plastics and elastomers. ed. by Charles A. Harper. N.Y., McGraw-Hill, [1975]. 1008p. in various paging. il. **EJ104**

"The *Handbook of Plastics and Elastomers* was prepared as a thorough sourcebook of practical data for all ranges of interest. It contains an extensive array of property and performance data."—*Pref.* Cross references. Indexed.   TP1130.H36

Modern plastics encyclopedia, 1941– . N.Y., McGraw-Hill, 1940– . il. Annual. **EJ105**

Publisher varies.

Title varies: 1941, *Modern plastics catalog;* 1942–45, *Plastics catalog.* Issued as part of the periodical *Modern plastics.*

Now organized in four main sections: (1) Textbook (with brief chapters under four subsections: Materials; Chemicals, additives, fillers, property enhancers, reinforcements; Primary processing, including auxiliary, tooling, testing; Fabricating and finishing); (2) Design guide; (3) Data bank (including specialized data tables); (4) Suppliers (including classified index of products and services). Alphabetical index of companies and addresses.   TP986.A1M62

Mohr, John Gilbert, ed. SPI handbook of technology and engineering of reinforced plastics/composites. 2d ed. N.Y., Van Nostrand, Reinhold, [1973]. 405p. il. **EJ106**

1st ed., 1964, by S. S. Oleesky and J. B. Mohr, had title: *Handbook of reinforced plastics. . . .*

Sections deal with materials required for processing, equipment and tooling needed, the processing method itself, and product properties and performance data. Practical emphasis. Many data tables; subject index.   TP1177.M63

Society of the Plastics Industry. Plastics engineering handbook of the Society of the Plastics Industry, Inc., ed. by Joel Frados. 4th ed. N.Y., Van Nostrand Reinhold, [1976]. 909p. il. **EJ107**

1st ed. (1947) had title *SPI handbook;* 2d–3d eds. called *SPI plastics engineering handbook.*

The first three chapters offer a glossary and basic guide to plastics materials; later chapters concern important methods of plastics processing, some special types of plastics, design, materials handling, and testing. Indexed.   TP1130.S58

Whittington, Lloyd R. Whittington's Dictionary of plastics. 2d ed. Westport, Conn., Technomic Pub. Co., [1978]. 344p. **EJ108**

1st ed. 1968.

"Sponsored by the Society of Plastics Engineers, Inc."—*t.p.*

Mainly terms in plastics technology. Includes abbreviations, with reference to the full form.   T1110.W46

Wittfoht, Annemarie. Plastics technical dictionary: English-German, German-English. N.Y., Macmillan, 1981. 3v. il. **EJ109**

Previous ed., 1961, in 2v.

Also published in Germany with title *Kunststofftechnisches Wörterbuch* (München, Hanser, 1978–1981. 3v). Both editions have title pages in the two languages.

Contents: v.1, Alphabetical dictionary, English-German. 4th completely rev. ed.; v.2, Alphabetical dictionary, German-English; v.3, Reference volume, illustrated systematic groups E-G/G-E.

Includes nomenclature used in processing, fabricating, and using plastics, in testing, and in mold construction.   TP1110.W534

CIVIL ENGINEERING

Handbooks

Civil engineer's reference book. ed. by Leslie Spencer Blake. 3d ed. London, Butterworths; Levittown, N.Y., Transatlantic Arts, 1975. 1v., various pagings. il. **EJ110**

1st–2d eds., 1951–61, had title: *Civil engineering reference book.*

Completely revised, with additional material. Specialists have contributed chapters on all aspects of civil engineering. Includes extensive bibliographies. Indexed.   TA151.C58

Standard handbook for civil engineers. Frederick S. Merritt, ed. 3d ed. N.Y., McGraw-Hill, [1983]. 1v., various pagings. il. **EJ111**

1st ed. 1968.

Seeks to "provide in a single volume a compendium of the best of current civil engineering practices. . . . Emphasis is on fundamental principles and their practical applications, with special attention to simplified procedures."—*Pref.* Signed contributions by specialists include tabular data, line drawings, references. Indexed.   TA151.S8

Biography

American Society of Civil Engineers. Committee on History and Heritage of American Civil Engineering. A biographical dictionary of American civil engineers. N.Y., Society, 1972. 163p. (ASCE historical pubn., no.2) **EJ112**

The first of a proposed series of biographical dictionaries based on information in the files of the Biographical Archive of American Civil Engineers of the Smithsonian Institution. In two parts, the first containing biographical sketches of some 170 prominent civil engineers born before the Civil War; pt.2, is a list of the names of civil engineers about whom the Archive has biographical information.   TA139.A53

Environment and environmental problems

General works

Bibliography

Anglemyer, Mary, comp. A search for environmental ethics; an initial bibliography. Wash., Smithsonian Inst. Pr., 1980. 119p. **EJ113**

"Comp. by Mary Anglemyer, Eleanor R. Seagraves, Catherine C. LeMaistre. Under the auspices of Rachel Carson Council, Inc. With an introduction by S. Dillon Ripley."—*t.p.*

An annotated alphabetical listing by author, editor, or title of 446 articles and books published since 1945, although principally in the 1970s. "The natural environment is the focal point of this bibliography. . . . Works in science, philosophy, religion, education, literature, politics, and economics (wherever it touches on conservation-environmental values) are described."—*Pref.* Subject and name index. Z7405.N38A53

————— and **Seagraves, Eleanor R.,** comps. The natural environment; an annotated bibliography on attitudes and values. Wash., Smithsonian Inst. Pr., 1984. 268p. **EJ114**

A companion volume to *A search for environmental ethics* (above), this work has entries for 857 books, articles, proceedings and reports, grouped by broad topics. Indexed. Z7405.N38A52

Clark, Brian D., Bisset, Ronald and **Wathern, Peter.** Environmental impact assessment: a bibliography with abstracts. N.Y., Bowker, 1980. 516p. **EJ115**

Contents: Aids to impact assessment; Critiques and reviews of environmental impact assessment; Environmental impact assessment and other aspects of planning; Environmental impact assessment in selected countries; Information sources.

Covers citations from a wide variety of sources, but not all are abstracted. Indexed. Z5863.I57C56

EIS. v.1, no.1– , Jan. 1977– . Wash., Information Resources Pr., 1977– . Monthly with annual cumulation. **EJ116**

Subtitle (varies): "Digests of environmental impact statements." Each monthly issue provides abstracts detailing the purpose, positive and negative aspects, legal mandates, and any prior references, for about 100 draft and final environmental impact statements. Arranged in 11 broad subject chapters; indexed by subject, legal instrument, geographical site, issuing agency, and EIS and EPA numbers.

EIS retrospective, covering the 1970–76 period, is available in a similar format (3v.). Microfiche copies of the statements are available from the publisher. Z5863.E56E35●

EPA cumulative bibliography. 1970–1976. Springfield, Va., NTIS, 1976. 2v. (PB-265920) **EJ117**

Provides a cumulative listing of all reports entered into the NTIS collection through 1976 by the U.S. Environmental Protection Agency (EPA) and its predecessor agencies. v.1 contains bibliographic citations and abstracts, and title index; v.2 contains the subject, corporate source, author, contract number, and access/report number indexes. Updated quarterly by *EPA publication bibliography: quarterly abstract bulletin* (EJ124). Z5861.E15

Man and the environment information guide series. Seymour M. Gold, series ed. Detroit, Gale, 1975–80. 9v. **EJ118**

Contents: v.1, Environmental education, by William B. Stapp and Mary Dawn Liston (1975. 225p.); v.2, Wastewater management, by George Tchobanoglous (1976. 202p.); v.3, Environmental planning, by Michael J. Meshenberg (1976. 492p.); v.4, Environmental values, 1860–1972, by Loren C. Owings (1976. 324p.); v.5, Noise pollution, by Clifford R. Bragdon (1979. 524p.); v.6, Environmental law, by Mortimer D. Schwartz (1977. 191p.); v.7, Environmental toxicology, by Robert L. Rudd (1977. 266p.); v.8, Environmental econom-ics, by Betty C. Field and Cleve E. Willis (1979. 243p.); v.9, Water pollution, by Mary Ann Simmons (1980. 278p.).

A monographic series of guides to information sources.

Oi Committee International. International development and the human environment; an annotated bibliography. N.Y., Macmillan Information, [1974]. 334p. **EJ119**

"Compiled to acquaint the reader with the various aspects of ecology and international development in greater depth than an ordinary annotated bibliography, it still functions as an instrument of quick and efficient references. Each annotation and citation is indexed by author, subject, and publisher. Each of these refers to the entry by number."—*Introd.* Most material listed was published between 1968 and 1972. Z5861.O4

Sourcebook on the environment: a guide to the literature. Chicago, Univ. of Chicago Pr., [1978]. 613p. **EJ120**

Ed. by Kenneth A. Hammond, George Macinko, Wilma B. Fairchild.

"The goal of this sourcebook is to provide a broad guide to selected aspects of the environmental literature. Toward this end critically annotated commentaries from twenty-six specialists introduce the reader to the basic literature in the field and give directions for examination of more advanced and more specialized works."—*Pref.* Author and subject indexes. Literature cited is not indexed. Z5861.S66

Winton, Harry N. M. Man and the environment: a bibliography of selected publications of the United Nations system, 1946–1971. N.Y., Unipub, 1972. 305p. **EJ121**

1,219 entries in classed arrangement, most of them briefly annotated. Entries include monographs, dictionaries and glossaries, bibliographies, directories, yearbooks and other periodicals, and filmstrips. Covers a wide range of topics (e.g., natural resources and the earth sciences, oceanography, meteorology and climatology, water resources, food production and supply, demography, population studies, environmental health, air pollution, noise). Indexes of authors, titles, subjects, and serials/series. Z5322.E2W56

Indexes and abstract journals

Environment abstracts. v.1– , Jan. 1971– . [N.Y., Environment Information Center, Inc.], 1971– . Monthly. **EJ122**

Title varies. v.1–3 were called *Environment information access* and published semimonthly.

An indexing and abstracting service covering both published and nonprint (e.g., radio and television programming, films and film-strips) materials. Significant books, periodical articles (from scientific, scholarly, technical, and general publications), major conference proceedings, newspaper stories, and significant environmental entries from the *Federal register* are included. A classified "main entry section" provides a complete citation with abstract; this is followed by subject, industry, and author indexes. A calendar of conferences is included in each issue. Items designated by an asterisk may be purchased on microfiche, either singly or by subscription to one or more "main entry" categories. Other services (e.g., literature searches through the computerized data base) are available on inquiry. *Environment index,* which serves as a cumulative index, must be purchased separately. Z7171.E59●

Environment index, 1971– ; a guide to the key environmental literature of the year. N.Y., Environment Information Center, 1972– . v.1– . Annual. **EJ123**

Cumulates the subject, industry, author, and accession indexes from *Environment abstracts* (above), but the subject index can be used independently of that publication. Includes an annual listing of environmental books and films; an overview of the year's events, legislation, and conferences; a directory of pollution control officials; and a list of environmental control patents.

EPA publications bibliography: quarterly abstract bulletin. Springfield, Va., NTIS, 1977– . Quarterly, with annual cumulative index. **EJ124**

Includes abstracts and bibliography, title index, subject index, sponsoring EPA Office index, corporate author index, personal author index, accession/report number index, order form, and list of EPA libraries. For previous EPA publications *see EPA cumulative bibliography, 1970–1976* (EJ117).

Pollution abstracts. v.1, no.1– , May 1970– . [La Jolla, Calif.], 1970– . Bimonthly.   **EJ125**

Provides international coverage of technical literature on the environment. Covers air and water pollution, solid wastes, noise, pesticides, radiation, and general environmental quality. Includes books, technical journals, conference proceedings, papers, government reports, and limited-circulation documents. A permuted subject ("keytalpha") index and an author index. An annual cumulative index is available, but is not included in the yearly subscription.
TD172.P65●

Dictionaries

Allaby, Michael. A dictionary of the environment. N.Y., Van Nostrand Reinhold, [1977]. 532p.   **EJ126**

Compiled by an interdisciplinary panel of specialists. Defines and explains 6,000 words and phrases used in all sciences that relate to the environment.   QH540.4.A44

Sarnoff, Paul. The New York times encyclopedic dictionary of the environment. N.Y., Quadrangle Books, [1971]. 352p. il.   **EJ127**

Offers definitions of over 2,000 general, specialized, and technical terms from all fields relating to environment and environmental problems. Includes cross references.   TD173.S27

Directories

Environmental protection directory. 2d ed., ed. by Thaddeus C. Trzyna, with the assistance of Sally R. Ogsberg. Chicago, Marquis Academic Media, [1975]. 526p.   **EJ128**

Publ. for the Center for California Public Affairs.

1st ed. publ. 1973 as part of the *Directory of consumer protection and environmental agencies* (Orange, N.J., Academic Media).

Subtitle: A comprehensive guide to environmental organizations in the United States and Canada.

A "User's guide" is arranged topically "to help readers identify organizations concerned with a specific area of interest, such as water quality or fish and wildlife."—*Introd.* Remainder of the text follows geographic arrangement. Subject, organization, personnel, and publication indexes.   TD171.E57

Institute of Ecology. Directory of environmental life scientists. Wash., Govt. Prt. Off., 1974. 9v. (EP1105-2-3)   **EJ129**

Prepared for the U.S. Army Corps of Engineers to provide a directory of environmental life scientists for engineers in environmental studies and activities. Each of the 9v. is for a major region of the continental United States. The arrangement of data in each volume is under the organization's or individual's name. There are 4 indexes to assist in the location of experts when a specialty or specific information is important for: (1) a specific ecosystem or pollutant; (2) environmental impact experiences; (3) geographical familiarity; and (4) species, projects, research topics, etc.
QH35.I48

Onyx Group, Inc. Environment U.S.A.: a guide to agencies, people, and resources. Glenn L. Paulson, advisory editor. N.Y., Bowker, [1974]. 451p.   **EJ130**

A directory arranged according to type of organization or information source. Includes sections for federal and state government agencies, citizens' environmental and conservation organizations, professional societies and trade associations, conferences and meetings, educational programs, libraries, etc. There are brief chapters on fund-raising and on environmental law, and a listing of films classified by subject. Also includes a classified bibliography, p.340–405 and a glossary, p.406–28. Indexed.   TD171.E58

Pollution research index. A guide to world research in environmental pollution. 2d ed. Guernsey, Francis Hodgson; Detroit, Gale, [1979]. 555p.   **EJ131**

1st ed. 1975.

Entries arranged by country, include address, affiliation, director, scope of activity. Indexed.   TD178.5.P64

Schildauer, Carole. Environmental information sources: engineering and industrial applications; a selected annotated bibliography. N.Y., Special Libraries Assoc., 1972. 72p.   **EJ132**

Contains some 150 entries arranged by type of information resource (abstracts, directories, journals, handbooks, etc.) with a brief description of each. An appendix lists associations, agencies, etc., which are sources of information and services, giving address and short description of each. No index.   Z5863.E57S34

World environment directory: standard environmental reference since 1974. 4th ed. Silver Springs, Md., Business Publ. (distr. by Ballinger), 1980. 966p. il.   **EJ133**

Ed. by Beverly E. Gough.

1st–3d eds. (1974–78) had title: *World environmental directory.*

In this edition about 20 percent of the entries are new and about half have been revised. New indexes aid access to specific information. Factual data include name, address, phone number, cable address, etc., of the organization and names of persons to contact or in positions of responsibility. Personnel index.   TD12.W67

Handbooks

Burchell, Robert W. and **Listokin, David.** The environmental impact handbook. [New Brunswick, N.J.], Center for Urban Policy Research, 1975. 234p. il.   **EJ134**

A guide for land-use planners when preparing environmental impact studies in accordance with the National Environment Policy Act of 1969. Gives detailed, comprehensive explanations of the content, format, responsibilities, recommended procedures, and review processes used in preparing environmental impact studies.
HC110.E5B87

CRC handbook of environmental control. Cleveland, CRC Pr., 1973–78. 5v. and series index.   **EJ135**

Coordinating ed., Richard Prober.

Contents: v.1, Air pollution. 1973. 576p. Ed. by Richard G. Bond and Conrad P. Straub. Section headings: The atmosphere and air pollutants; Effect of air pollution; Emission sources; Air pollution control measures. Index. v.2, Solid waste. 1973. 580p. Ed. by Richard G. Bond and Conrad P. Straub. Section headings: Solid wastes—sources and composition; Effects of solid wastes; Solid waste controls and management. Index. v.3, Water supply and treatment. 1973. 835p. Ed. by Richard G. Bond and Conrad P. Straub. Section headings: Sources and quality; Needs; Quality criteria; Water treatment; Water distribution; Biological control in water supply systems; Recreational waters; Analytical methods; Monitoring. Index. v.4, Waste water: treatment and disposal. 1974. 928p. Ed. by Richard G. Bond and Conrad P. Straub. Section headings: Domestic sewage; Industrial wastes; River waters: oxygen balance; Nutrients, lakes, eutrophication. Index. v.5, Hospital and health care facilities. 1975. 440p. Ed. by Conrad P. Straub. Section headings: Kinds and numbers of institutions; Microbial considerations; Environmental hygiene and environmental health; Safety; General sanitation; Nursing homes; Index. [v.6] Series index. 1978. 128p.

"The aim of this series is to bring together pertinent information in tabular form that will be useful in evaluating the environment, not only from the standpoint of effects on the ecosystem, aquatic and terrestrial, but also on man's relationship to the environment and the environment's relationship to man."—*Pref.*
TD176.4.H35

Environmental impact data book. By Jack Golden [and others]. Ann Arbor, Mich., Ann Arbor Science, [1979]. 864p. il.   **EJ136**

"This book will serve as a data reference, to supplement other sources used regularly in the preparation of environmental impact assessments and statements. It is assumed that the user is already involved in the environmental impact process and knows the format and data required by law."—*Pref.* TD194.6.E6

Verschueren, Karel. Handbook of environmental data on organic chemicals. 2d ed. N.Y., Van Nostrand Reinhold, [1983]. 1310p. **EJ137**

1st ed. 1977.

Presents information on physical and chemical properties, air pollution factors, water pollution factors, and biological effects, for organic compounds, mixtures, and preparations. Includes bibliographical references. Formula index. TD196.O73V47

Air pollution

Bibliography

Davenport, Sara Jeannette and **Morgis, G. G.** Air pollution; a bibliography. Wash., Govt. Prt. Off., 1954. 448p. (U.S. Bureau of Mines. Bull., no.537) **EJ138**

3,902 entries, with abstracts, from many sources arranged by subject. Covers nature and origin of air pollution, composition of air pollutants, effects of air pollution, control of air pollution, legal aspects, etc.

A complementary listing of research projects in air pollution was provided by the U.S. Division of Air Pollution's series, *Guide to research in air pollution* (1st–6th eds., 1953–66; title and issuing agency vary). Z6673.D36

U.S. Air Pollution Technical Information Center. Odors and air pollution; bibliography with abstracts. Wash., 1972. 257p. (Air Programs Office. Pubn. AP-113) **EJ139**

"The abstracted documents are thought to be representative of available literature. . . ."—*Introd.* Classed arrangement with author and detailed subject index. International coverage with English abstracts. Titles of foreign-language works are given in English followed by the original title. One of a number of annotated bibliographies in the issuing agency's publications series.

U.S. Division of Air Pollution. Air pollution publications; a selected bibliography, 1955/62– . Wash., U.S. Dept. of Health, Education, and Welfare, Public Health Service, Div. of Air Pollution, 1963– . (U.S. Public Health Service pubn. 979) **EJ140**

A revision and extension of the first issue was published 1964 (covering 1955/63). Later issues cover 1963/66 (publ. 1966); 1966/68 (publ. 1969).

Classed arrangement with author and subject or title indexes. Includes references, with abstracts, mainly to journal articles, but also to books, monographs, report literature, and conference papers. Covers mainly English-language publications. Z6673.U44

Abstract journals

APCA abstracts. Publ. by the Air Pollution Control Association in cooperation with the United States Public Health Service and the Library of Congress. Pittsburgh, Air Pollution Control Assoc., 1955–71. v.1–16. Monthly. **EJ141**

Subtitle: Summarizing the current literature of air pollution.

Cumulated author and subject indexes issued irregularly.

Ceased publication with v.16, no.8, Jan. 1971. TD883.A25

Air pollution abstracts. v.1–7, no.6, 1969–June 1976. Research Triangle Park, N.C., Air Pollution Technical Information Center, 1969–76. Monthly. **EJ142**

Imprint varies; issuing agency varies.

v.1–2[1], 1969–Jan. 1971, issued by the National Air Pollution Control Administration as *NAPCA abstracts bulletin.* Later issued by U.S. Environmental Protection Agency.

Classed arrangement with author and detailed subject indexes. International coverage. Titles of foreign-language items are given in

English followed by the original title. Abstracts are in English. Some 7,000 periodicals were regularly scanned for pertinent material.

Ceased publication. TD881.A44●

Handbooks

American Public Health Association. Program Area Committee on Air Pollution. Guide to the appraisal and control of air pollution. 2d ed. N.Y., The Assoc., 1969. 80p. **EJ143**

1962 ed. had title *Guide to air pollution control.*

"This guide . . . has been prepared to assist the staff of an official agency which has been assigned responsibility for this aspect of environmental hygiene."—*Introd.* A non-technical handbook which includes chapters on evaluating the effects of air pollution, the role of the local agency in the control of air pollution, detection and measurement of air pollution, community relations, etc. Most chapters include a bibliography. Appendixes provide tables, smoke inspection guides, and a supplementary bibliography.

TD883.A58

Handbook of air pollution technology. Ed. by Seymour Calvert and Harold M. Englund. N.Y., Wiley, [1984]. 1066p. il. **EJ144**

"This handbook is intended to present the best available practical information on air pollution and its control. Engineers and other professionals, in a self-study situation, should be able to use this book to learn how to do the work required to define, analyze, and control air pollution."—*Pref.* 38 chapters by specialists on aspects of air pollution control include tabular data and references. Final chapter is on information resources. Indexed. TD883.H356

Industrial air pollution handbook. Ed. by Albert Parker. London & N.Y., McGraw-Hill, [1978]. 658p. il. **EJ145**

"This book has been planned to provide information which will be of value to all who are concerned with surveys of general pollution of the air in urban and rural areas, and to those who are involved in reducing to a realistic minimum the emission of air pollutants from industrial processes."—*Pref.* Most of the book deals with methods for reduction of pollutants; also includes a chapter on the effects of pollutants. A chapter on legislative control is concerned with British law, reflecting the British origin of this book. References. Indexed. TD883.7.G7

Industrial pollution control handbook. Ed. by Herbert F. Lund. N.Y., McGraw-Hill, [1971]. 1v., various pagings. il. **EJ146**

26 chapters contributed by specialists on various aspects of pollution problems and control presented in three main sections: (1) evolution of industrial pollution control; (2) pollution control by industry; and (3) pollution control equipment and operation. Includes a glossary of industrial air and water pollution control terms and an index. TD897.I42

Sheehy, James P., Achinger, William C. and **Simon, Regina A.** Handbook of air pollution. Durham, N. C., Nat. Center for Air Pollution Control, [1968]. 1v., various pagings. il. (U.S. Public Health Service pubn., 999-AP-44) **EJ147**

Brings together "data concerning the characteristics and behavior of air, gases and particles, and the chemistry of atmospheric pollutants" (*Purpose*), plus information of a general nature useful to workers in the field of air pollution. TD883.S47

Stern, Arthur Cecil, ed. Air pollution. 3d ed. N.Y., Academic Pr., 1976–77. 5v. **EJ148**

1st ed. 1962.

Contents: v.1, Air pollutants, their transformation and transport; v.2, The effects of air pollution; v.3, Measuring, monitoring and surveillance of air pollution; v.4, Engineering control of air pollution; v.5, Air quality management.

Revised and greatly expanded, with many new contributors represented. Each volume has its own subject index. TD883.S83

Noise

See also EJ186.

A bibliography of noise. Troy, N.Y., Whitston, 1973–83. Irregular.　　　　　　　　　　　　　　**EJ149**

Published to date: 1965–1970, 1971, 1972, 1973, all by Mary K. Floyd; 1974, 1975, by Judith Kramer-Greene; 1976, 1977–1981, by Irving E. Stephens and Dorothy L. Barnes. Ceased publication.

An international bibliography of noise and "its physiological, psychological, sociological, and cultural effects."—*Pref.* Books (arranged alphabetically by main entry) and periodical articles (alphabetically by title) are listed in separate sections. Subject and author indexes.

Harris, Cyril M. Handbook of noise control. 2d ed. N.Y., McGraw-Hill, [1979]. 1v., various pagings. il.　　**EJ150**

1st ed. 1957.
Chapters by specialists include bibliographies. Indexed.

TD892.H37

Water resources and water pollution

Bibliography

California. University. Water Resources Center. Archives. Dictionary catalog of the Water Resources Center Archives, University of California, Berkeley. Boston, G. K. Hall, 1970. 5v.　　　　　　　　　　　　　　**EJ151**

An author-subject catalog reproducing the catalog cards for this collection of about 80,000 pieces, dealing with water as a natural resource, water utilization, municipal and industrial water-use problems, flood control, reclamation, waste disposal, water pollution, water law, etc. Emphasis is on report literature.　　Z7935.C32

Giefer, Gerald J. Sources of information in water resources; an annotated guide to printed materials. Port Washington, N.Y., Water Information Center, [1976]. 290p.　　**EJ152**

"This guide, compiled for the use of the student and researcher, cites and annotates over 1100 titles found useful for reference purposes in the water resources field. . . . The emphasis here has been upon the literature of the United States."—*Pref.*

Z7935.G53

―――― and **Todd, David K.,** eds. Water publications of state agencies. Port Washington, N.Y., Water Information Center, [1972]. 319p.　　　　　　　　　　　**EJ153**

With the assistance of Mary Louise Quinn.
Subtitle: *A bibliography of publications on water resources and their management published by the states of the United States.*

"A listing of water resources publications issued by 335 state agencies in 50 states of the United States. Information is listed by state with publications grouped under the issuing agencies of each state."—*Pref.* Information on how to obtain publications is included.

―――― ―――― First supplement, 1971–1974, with the assistance of Beverly Fish. 1976. 189p.

Ralston, Valerie Hunter. Water resources: a bibliographic guide to reference sources. Storrs, Univ. of Connecticut, 1975. 123p. (The Library. Bibliography series no.2) (Institute of Water Resources. Report no.23)　　**EJ154**

More than 400 entries arranged by type, e.g., guides, dictionaries, encyclopedias, handbooks, statistical sources, with author and keyword indexes. Many items are annotated.　　TD224.C8A3

Selected water resources abstracts. v.1, no.1– , Jan. 1968– . [Springfield, Va. National Technical Information Service], 1968– . Monthly with annual index.　　　　　　**EJ155**

v.1, no.1–9, were published by the Bureau of Reclamation, Denver, Colo. Frequency varies.

Published for the Water Resources Scientific Information Center, U.S. Geological Survey, U.S. Dept. of the Interior.

Includes "abstracts of current and earlier pertinent monographs, journal articles, reports, and other publication formats" that "cover water resources as treated in the life, physical, and social sciences and the related engineering and legal aspects of the characteristics, supply condition, conservation, control, use, or management of water resources."—*Pref.* Topical arrangement with detailed subject, author, organizational, and accession number indexes in each issue.

TC1.S45●

Summers, W. Kelly and **Spiegel, Zane.** Ground water pollution: a bibliography. Ann Arbor, Mich., Ann Arbor Science, 1974. 83p.　　　　　　　　　　　　　　**EJ156**

A partially annotated bibliography "of ground water contamination of nitrates, heavy metals, pesticides and herbicides. The impact of urbanization and the effects of solid waste disposal, animal wastes and petroleum products on ground water quality are covered in the more than 400 entries."—*Pref.*　　　Z5862.2.W3S9

Unger, Samuel G., Jordening, David L., and **Tihansky, Dennis.** Bibliography of water pollution control benefits and costs. Wash., Govt. Prt. Off., 1974. 181p. (EPA-600/5-74-028)　　　　　　　　　　　　　　　　**EJ157**

Prep. for the Office of Research and Development, U.S. Environmental Protection Agency.

The computerized "bibliography includes approximately 3000 relevant references, alphabetized by author. . . . The references listed have been screened and are considered relevant to the problems inherent in estimating water pollution control benefits and costs."—*Pref.*　　　　　　　　Z5862.2.W3U53

Dictionaries

Glossary: water and wastewater control engineering. 3d ed. Wash., Amer. Public Health Assoc., [1981]. 441p.　**EJ158**

"Prepared by joint editorial board representing American Public Health Association, American Society of Civil Engineers, American Water Works Association, American Pollution Control Federation." —*t.p.*

1st ed. (1949) had title *Glossary: water and sewage control engineering.*

Includes relevant terms from chemistry and chemical engineering, and terms related to regulatory agency involvement, in addition to the terms from water and wastewater engineering. Cross references.

TD9.G55

Directories

Organization for Economic Cooperation and Development. Directorate for Scientific Affairs. Directory of water pollution research laboratories. [Paris], Organization for Economic Cooperation and Development, Directorate for Scientific Affairs, Central Service for International Co-operation in Scientific Research, 1965. 519p.　　　　**EJ159**

A country-by-country listing of laboratories and institutions which regularly engage in research of general interest on the pollution of fresh water. Information includes address, name of director, notes on organization, personnel, special facilities and equipment, documentation service or publications issued, and research programs.

U.S. Library of Congress. National Referral Center for Science and Technology. A directory of information resources in the United States: water. [Wash., Govt. Prt. Off.], 1966. 248p.　　　　　　　　　　　　　　　**EJ160**

Lists over 600 United States organizations and institutions engaged in research or in collecting data on water and water-related subjects. Focus is on fresh water, with oceanography excluded. Commercial, profit-making organizations are omitted. Subject index. Similar to the Center's directories for the physical sciences (1971) and for the social sciences (CA72).　　TD211.U5

Handbooks

American Society for Testing and Materials. Committee D-19 on Water. Manual on water. 4th ed. Philadelphia, Amer. Soc. for Testing and Materials, [1978]. 472p. il. (ASTM special technical pubn., no.442A) **EJ161**

1st–2d eds. (1953–59) had title *Manual on industrial water and industrial waste water.*

"This manual is intended as a brief reference source of information on water. It will not replace an adequate library on the subject, but it does provide basic information for routine use and cites references to the technical literature, thus serving as a point of departure for more specific and detailed studies."—*Introd.* Provides general discussions of the nature, sources, treatment, analysis, and uses of water, particularly industrial water. Includes numerous tables and charts; reference tables and curves included in an appendix. Indexed.

——— Supplement to Manual on water, 4th ed. Philadelphia, Amer. Soc. for Testing and Materials, [1983]. 47p. (ASTM special technical pubn., no.442A-S1)

Includes new chapters on ion-selective electrodes and on membrane filtration. TD353.A6

American Water Works Association. Water quality and treatment; a handbook of public water supplies. 3d ed. N.Y., McGraw-Hill, [1971]. 654p. il. **EJ162**

1st ed., 1940, had title *Manual of water quality and treatment.*

"The purpose of this book is to present authoritative information on water quality and on water-treatment principles and practice."—*Pref.* Consists of 19 chapters contributed by specialists. Bibliographies; numerous tables and figures. TD430.A6

Todd, David Keith, ed. The water encyclopedia; a compendium of useful information on water resources. Port Washington, N.Y., Water Information Center, [1970]. 559p. il. **EJ163**

All information is presented in tabular form; explanatory notes are brief. Includes sections on climate and precipitation, hydrologic elements, surface and ground water, water use, water quality and pollution control, water resources management, agencies and organizations, and constants and conversion factors. Indexed. TD351.T63

Van der Leeden, Frits. Water resources of the world: selected statistics. Port Washington, N.Y., Water Information Center, [1975]. 568p. il. **EJ164**

A compilation and summary tabulation of world-wide water resources statistics. Presents data on the characteristics of major lakes, rivers, and reservoirs; desalination; hydrologic cycle, including glaciers and the oceans; water supplies in developing nations; and international water development and financing programs. The 578 tables and numerous maps and diagrams are arranged by continents. Detailed references. GB661.V34

Water and water pollution handbook. Ed. by Leonard L. Ciaccio. N.Y., Dekker, 1971–73. 4v. **EJ165**

Consists of 32 chapters contributed by specialists, offering an interdisciplinary approach to water analysis and treatment. Bibliographies. Author index and subject index in v.4. TD380.W32

Hydraulic engineering and hydrodynamics

Bibliography

Kolupaila, Steponas. Bibliography of hydrometry. Notre Dame, Ind., Univ. of Notre Dame Pr., 1961. 975p. **EJ166**

A comprehensive, annotated bibliography of hydrometry—the science of measurement of water—including some 7,370 titles in more than 30 languages and from all periods. Titles are given in the original language, followed by a translation into English. Indexed. Z5853.H9K6

Rowe, Robert Seaman. Bibliography of rivers and harbors and related fields in hydraulic engineering. Princeton, N.J., Rivers and Harbors Section, Dept. of Civil Engineering, Princeton Univ., 1953. 407p. **EJ167**

International in scope. Includes some 6,000 references to books and monographs. Omits periodical articles, abstracts, etc. Some entries annotated. Indexed. Z5853.H9R6

Handbooks

Blevins, Robert D. Applied fluid dynamics handbook. N.Y., Van Nostrand Reinhold, [1984]. 558p. il. **EJ168**

"The purpose of this book is to provide a summary of theoretical, experimental, and statistical data on fluid flows. This book has been designed to present a wide range of fluid dynamics in a clear, concise form with extensive use of tables and graphics so that students, engineers, and researchers can rapidly locate an accurate, up-to-date summary of data and methods."—*Pref.* Chapters include bibliographic references. Indexed. TA357.B57

Brater, Ernest Frederick and **King, Horace Williams.** Handbook of hydraulics for the solution of hydraulic engineering problems. 6th ed. N.Y., McGraw-Hill, [1976]. 1v., various pagings. il. **EJ169**

1st ed. 1918. 1st–3d eds. by H. W. King, 4th–5th eds. by H. W. King and E. F. Brater. Title varies slightly.

Designed to "set forth the fundamentals needed in the solution of hydraulics problems, together with appropriate tables and graphs which facilitate the solution."—*Pref.* Revised and updated. Indexed. TK160.K5

Davis, Calvin Victor and **Sorenson, Kenneth E.,** eds. Handbook of applied hydraulics. 3d ed. N.Y., McGraw-Hill, [1969]. 1v., various pagings. **EJ170**

1st ed. 1942.

Intends "(1) to present clearly and concisely the fundamental principles which are basic to each subdivision of hydraulic engineering, and (2) to demonstrate the practical application of these principles by examples which have been drawn largely from the actual practice of hydraulic engineering."—*Pref.* In this edition new sections have been added for basic hydraulics, reservoir hydraulics, natural channels, regime canals, river diversion, basic principles of concrete dam design, cored-gravity and massive buttress dams, prestressed dams, barrages and dams on soft foundations, fish-passing facilities, pumped storage, flood control, navigation, groundwater, drainage, and tidal energy development. Numerous tables and graphs. Indexed. TC145.D3

Handbook of ocean and underwater engineering. Prep. under the auspices of North American Rockwell Corp. Ed. in chief, John J. Myers. N.Y., McGraw-Hill, [1969]. 1v., various pagings. il. **EJ171**

Intended for "the nonspecialist engineer, scientist, or technician involved with designing equipment, systems, or structures for the ocean, or involved in their installation and operation."—*Pref.* Specialists have contributed sections on basic oceanography and hydrodynamics; underwater fields and instrumentation; tools, rigging, and machinery; underwater cables and power sources; materials and testing; fixed structures; vessels and floating platforms; diving; ocean operations; and wind and wave loads. Indexed. TC1645.H35

Hydraulic Pneumatic Power. Hydraulic handbook, comp. by the editors of Hydraulic pneumatic power. 7th ed. Morden, Eng., Trade & Technical Pr., [1981]. 900p. **EJ172**

1st ed. 1958.

Offers a wide range of information on industrial hydraulics for "designers and manufacturers of equipment incorporating hydraulics, to the users and buyers of hydraulically operated equipment and machinery, and also to consulting engineers and technical and research personnel."—*Pref.*   TJ840.H97

Structural engineering

American Institute of Steel Construction. Manual of steel construction. 8th ed. Chicago, [1980]. 1v., various pagings. il.   **EJ173**

First published 1926 with title *Steel construction.*
Includes sections on: (1) Dimensions and properties; (2) Beam and girder design; (3) Column design; (4) Connections; (5) Specifications and codes; (6) Miscellaneous data and mathematical tables. Information presented in tabular form. Indexed.   TA684.A47

Building design and construction handbook. 4th ed. Ed. by Frederick S. Merritt. N.Y., McGraw-Hill, [1982]. 1v., various pagings. il.   **EJ174**

1st ed. 1958. Previous eds. had title *Building construction handbook.*
Intended to offer information which would be most useful to those concerned with building design and construction, especially those who have to make decisions affecting building materials and construction methods. Sections by specialists; bibliographic references; index.   TH151.B825

Gaylord, Edwin Henry and **Gaylord, Charles N.** Structural engineering handbook. 2d ed. N.Y., McGraw-Hill, [1979]. 1v., various pagings. il.   **EJ175**

1st ed. 1968.
For the engineer, architect, and student of civil engineering and architecture. Chapters, contributed by specialists, cover a wide range of structures, design in various media, soil mechanics and foundations, etc. Index; bibliographical references.   TA635.G3

Godel, Jules B. Sources of construction information; an annotated guide to reports, books, periodicals, standards and colors. Metuchen, N.J., Scarecrow Pr., 1977– . v.1– . (In progress)   **EJ176**

Contents: v.1, Books. 673p.
Three additional volumes were originally announced.
                                                                TA145.G62

Handbook of concrete engineering. 2d ed. Ed. by Mark Fintel. N.Y., Van Nostrand Reinhold, [1985]. 892p. il.
                                                                EJ177

1st ed. 1974.
" . . . contains up-to-date information on planning, design, analysis, and construction of engineered concrete structures . . . to provide engineers, architects, contractors, and students of civil engineering and architecture with authoritative practical design information."—*Pref.* Design information based on the 1983 ACI (American Concrete Institute) Code. Chapters by specialists include equations, diagrams, bibliographic references. Indexed.
                                                                TA682.H36

Handbook of heavy construction. Ed. by John A. Havers and Frank W. Stubbs, Jr. 2d ed. N.Y., McGraw-Hill, [1971]. 1v., various pagings. il.   **EJ178**

1st ed. 1960, by F. W. Stubbs, Jr.
Information, by specialists, is presented in three main sections: (1) construction management; (2) equipment; (3) applications. Indexed.   TA151.H29

Handbook of structural concrete. Ed. by F. K. Kong [and others]. N.Y., McGraw-Hill, [1983]. 1v., various pagings. il.
                                                                EJ179

" . . . intended as an international reference work on the current state of the art and science of structural concrete . . . the *Handbook* has been designed to meet the needs of practicing civil and structural engineers, consulting engineering and contracting firms, concrete materials producers and users, research institutes, universities and colleges."—*Pref.* Has sections on materials; design and analysis;

construction; structures; practical considerations. Chapters by specialist authors include references. Indexed.   TA439.H275

Merritt, Frederick S., ed. Structural steel designers' handbook. N.Y., McGraw-Hill, [1972]. 1v., various pagings. il.
                                                                EJ180

Emphasis is on bridge design and construction, but there are extensive sections on properties of structural steels and general structural theory. Chapters by specialists. Indexed.   TA684.M579

National Fire Protection Association. Fire protection handbook. 15th ed. Quincy, Mass., Assoc., [1981]. 1v., various pagings. il.   **EJ181**

1st ed. 1896.
" . . . a single source reference book on good fire protection and fire protection practices."—*Foreword.* Articles by specialists include bibliographies. Indexed.   TH9150.F47

National Forest Products Association. Wood structural design data. A manual for architects, builders, engineers, and others concerned with wood construction. 4th ed. Wash., [1970]. 236p. il.   **EJ182**

1st ed. 1934. Prev. eds. by National Lumber Manufacturers Assoc.
Includes tables, brief text, bibliography.   TA666.N28

Stein, J. Stewart. Construction glossary. An encyclopedic reference and manual. N.Y., Wiley, [1980]. 1013p. (Wiley series of practical construction guides)   **EJ183**

The glossary is arranged in 16 subject divisions, each with several subdivisions, within which definitions are listed alphabetically. Includes appendixes giving abbreviations and weights and measures. Indexed.   TH9.S78

Timber Engineering Company. Timber design and construction handbook. N.Y., F. W. Dodge Corp., 1956. 622p. il.
                                                                EJ184

Sections on wood properties, commercial lumber standards, preliminary design considerations, post-and-beam construction, roof trusses, arches, special framing, exterior structures, plywood, fabrication. Includes sections of reference data and design standards. A list of abbreviations of terms and a glossary precede the index.
                                                                TA666.T5

U.S. Forest Products Laboratory, Madison. Wood handbook: wood as an engineering material. Rev. ed. [Wash., Govt. Prt. Off.], 1974. 1v., various pagings. il. (Agricultural handbook, no.72).   **EJ185**

1st ed. 1940. Subtitle varies.
"This handbook provides engineers, architects, and others with a source of information on the physical and mechanical properties of wood, and how those properties are affected by variations in the wood itself."—*Pref.* Includes bibliographies, numerous figures and tables, glossary. Indexed.   TA419.U63

Transportation engineering

See also Aeronautical and space engineering (p.1243), Automotive engineering (p.1246).

Bibliography

See also CH434–CH442.

King, Richard L. Airport noise pollution: a bibliography of its effects on people and property. Metuchen, N.J., Scarecrow Pr., 1973. 380p.   **EJ186**

More than 2,100 numbered items in six broad subject categories: environmental noise pollution; aircraft noise pollution; airport noise pollution; noise pollution and human health; noise pollution and property values; and control and abatement of noise pollution. Includes a directory of government, university and research, professional, civic, business, and international and foreign organizations concerned with noise pollution. Author and subject indexes.

Z5064.N6K55

Li, Shu-t'ien. Bibliography on airport engineering. [N.Y.], Amer. Soc. of Civil Engineers, 1960. 170p. **EJ187**

Subtitle: A compilation of free world literature numbering 2335 entries classified into 26 groups and arranged chronologically.

Each entry appears once; there are no cross references. Period covered: 1938–59. Z5064.A28L5

Sources of information in transportation. 3d ed. Monticello, Ill., Vance Bibliographies, [1985]. 9pts. (Public administration series—bibliography, P1599–P1607) **EJ188**

1st ed. 1964, publ. for the Transportation Center at Northwestern Univ. by Northwestern Univ. Pr.

"Prepared in cooperation with the Special Projects Committee, Transportation Division, Special Libraries Association."

Contents: pt.1, General transportation, by Mary Jo Burke, David Vespa, and Marty Lovelock (71p.); pt.2, Air Transportation, by Jane Janiak and Marty H. Lovelock (40p.); pt.3, Shipping, by George J. Billy, Marty Lovelock, and Judith Nogrady (49p.); pt.4, Railroads, by Gilda Martinello (20p.); pt.5, Trucking, by Linda Rothbart, Ann Poole, and Charles James (67p.); pt.6, Inland water transportation, by Mary L. Roy (39p.); pt.7, Pipelines, by Marie Tilson and Jane Law (34p.): pt.8, Highways, by Daniel C. Krummes, Ann L. Poole, and Edie Darknell (68p.); pt.9, Urban transportation, by Michael C. Kleiber and Sylvie Hetu (23p.).

Abstract journals

Road abstracts. v.1–35, Feb. 1934–Apr. 1968. London, Stat. Off., 1935–68. Monthly. **EJ189**

Compiled by Dept. of Scientific and Industrial Research, Road Research Laboratory, London.

v.1–16 were issued as supplements to the *Journal* of the Institution of Municipal Engineers.

Covers finance, planning, construction and materials, soil engineering, maintenance, traffic planning and theory, road users, accidents and safety measures, etc. Titles of foreign articles are translated into English with indication of original language. TE1.R55

Transportation research abstracts. no.1–142; v.17, no.7–v.45. Wash., 1931–75. Monthly. **EJ190**

Title varies: no.1–v.44, no.6 called *Highway research abstracts.*

Published by the Highway Research Board of the National Research Council, National Academy of Sciences.

Includes English-language abstracts of journal articles, research reports, etc. The majority of publications are in English although there are a few in other languages. Volume numbering began with v.17, no.7, July 1947; previously publication was irregular. Annual subject index, 1962–75. Beginning 1937 the December issue was a "Synopsis" issue, containing abstracts of papers and reports scheduled for presentation at the annual meeting of the Highway Research Board. Each issue includes a list of new publications of the Board.

Absorbed by *Transportation research news* (1976–82, bimonthly), later *TR news* (1983–), with an "Abstracts" section at the end of each issue. TE1.N462

——— Index, 1931–1961. Wash., 1963.

Handbooks

Baker, Robert Fulton, ed. Handbook of highway engineering. N.Y., Van Nostrand Reinhold, [1975]. 894p. il. **EJ191**

"The purpose of this handbook is to provide a reference book of principles, processes and data for those interested in the application of technology to highway transportation."—*Pref.* Topical chapters by specialist authors include references. Indexed. TE151.B24

Transportation and traffic engineering handbook. Institute of Transportation Engineers. Wolfgang S. Homburger, ed.; Louis E. Keefer and William R. McGrath, assoc. eds. 2d ed. Englewood Cliffs, N.J., Prentice-Hall, [1982]. 883p. il. **EJ192**

1st ed., 1976, was a revision and enlargement of *The traffic engineering handbook,* 1965.

Chapters by different authorities; charts, tabular data, bibliographical references included. Little material on mass transportation. Well indexed. HE333.T68

Statistics

U.S. Federal Highway Administration. Highway statistics. 1969– . Wash., Govt. Prt. Off., 1971– . Annual. **EJ193**

Supersedes the series of the same title published by the U.S. Bureau of Public Roads (previously U.S. Public Roads Administration), 1945–68.

Presents "statistical and analytical tables of general interest on motor fuel, motor vehicles, driver licensing, highway-user taxation, state highway finance, highway mileage, and Federal aid for highways."—*Pref., 1972.* Statistics for the Commonwealth of Puerto Rico are included in a separate section.

——— Highway statistics; summary to 1975. Wash., Govt. Prt. Off., 1977. 286p. **EJ194**

Provides a general historical summary of information dealing with highways, their use and financing, bringing together a comprehensive statistical review of highway development in the United States through 1975. Serves as background material for the annual publication (above). Information supplements and in some instances supersedes similar data presented in other summaries covering to 1945, 1955, and 1965. HE355.A3A535

Yearbooks

Jane's Urban transport systems. 1982– . London, Jane's, 1982– . v.1– . il. Annual (slightly irregular). (Jane's Yearbooks) **EJ195**

A listing, alphabetically by city, of urban transport systems. Includes address, telephone, administrators' names, statistical summaries of operations, and photographs. Also lists manufacturers of transport equipment, arranged by category, with data on models, contracts, etc., and illustrations. Indexed. HE4211.J33

ELECTRICAL AND ELECTRONIC ENGINEERING

Bibliography

Electronic properties of materials; a guide to the literature. Ed. by H. Thayne Johnson. N.Y., Plenum Pr., 1965–71. 3v. in 6. **EJ196**

An extensive bibliography with coordinate index derived from the indexing project at the Electronic Properties Information Center, Hughes Aircraft Company, Culver City, California.

Z5838.M34E4

Moore, Charles Kenneth and **Spencer, Kenneth John.** Electronics: a bibliographical guide. London, MacDonald; N.Y., Plenum Pr., 1961–73. 3v. **EJ197**

A bibliography of bibliographies, abstracting journals, translating services, etc., in the field of electronics, with a selection of books and papers. Annotations included. Z5836.M56

Mottelay, Paul Fleury. Bibliographical history of electricity and magnetism chronologically arranged. London, Griffin, 1922. 673p. il. **EJ198**

Subtitle: Researches into the domain of the early sciences, especially from the period of the revival of scholasticism, with biographical and other accounts of the most distinguished natural philosophers throughout the Middle Ages.

A chronological history with many bibliographical references. Indexed.   QC507.M6

Shiers, George. Bibliography of the history of electronics. Metuchen, N.J., Scarecrow Pr., 1972. 323p.   **EJ199**

A classed bibliography of more than 1,800 items on historical aspects of electronics and telecommunications. Period covered: 1860 to the present. Most entries are annotated. Indexed.

Z5836.S54

Abstract journals

Science abstracts: Sec. B, Electrical & electronics abstracts. London, Inst. of Electrical Engineers, 1898– . v.1– . Monthly, with semiannual author and subject indexes.   **EJ200**

1898–1902 title reads: *Science abstracts. Physics and electrical engineering.* 1903–66, issued in two sections: A, Physics; B, Electrical engineering. Beginning with 1941, titles of sections changed to *Physics abstracts* and *Electrical engineering abstracts.* Title of Sec. B changed to *Electrical and electronics abstracts* beginning 1966. In Jan. 1967 the publication *Control abstracts* (later, *Computer and control abstracts,* EJ201) was designated as Sec. C of *Science abstracts.*

Entries are arranged according to a subject classification listed on the back cover of each issue. Coverage is international and includes periodicals, reports, books, patents, dissertations, and conference papers. A complete list of periodicals is issued as a part of the semiannual author indexes. Author and subject indexes, plus several "small indexes"—bibliography index, book index, patent and report index, conference index. Now contains more than 40,000 abstracts a year.

Microfiche edition also issued.   Q1.S3●

———— ———— Cumulative author index, 1955–1959, 1960–1964, 1965–1969, 1969–1972, 1973–1976, 1977–1980. London, [1960–81]. 1v., 2v., 1v., 1v., 2v., 2v.

———— ———— Cumulative subject index, 1955–1959, 1960–1964, 1965–1969, 1969–1972, 1973–1976, 1977–1980. London, [1960–81]. 1v., 1v., 2v., 2v., 3v., 3v.

———— Sec. C, Computer & control abstracts. London, Inst. of Electrical Engineers, 1966– . v.1– . Monthly, with semiannual author and subject indexes.   **EJ201**

Imprint varies.

Title varies: v.1–3, *Control abstracts.* Beginning Jan. 1967, designated as *Science abstracts,* Sec. C.

Entries are arranged according to a subject classification listed on the back cover of each issue. Coverage is international and includes periodicals, reports, dissertations, books, patents, and conference papers. A complete list of periodicals is issued as a part of the semiannual author indexes. Author and subject indexes, plus several "small indexes"—book index, bibliography index, patent and report index, conference index. Now contains over 24,000 abstracts a year.   ●

———— ———— Cumulative author and subject index, 1966–1968, 1969–1972, 1973–1976, 1977–1980. London, 1972–81. 1v., 2v., 3v., 3v.

Dictionaries and encyclopedias

Encyclopedia of instrumentation and control. Ed. by Douglas M. Considine. N.Y., McGraw-Hill, [1971]. 788p. il.

EJ202

About 700 topical entries in dictionary arrangement covering various aspects of instrumentation and control technology. Many of the articles are signed; some include bibliographic references. The alphabetical arrangement is supplemented by cross references, a classified index to the entry terms, and a subject index.

Q185.E52

IEEE standard dictionary of electrical and electronics terms. 3d ed. Frank Jay, ed. in chief. N.Y. Inst. of Electrical and Electronics Engineers; distr. N.Y., Wiley, [1984]. 1173p.

EJ203

"ANSI/IEEE Std 100–1984"—*t.p.*

1st ed. 1972.

Definitions have been taken from IEEE standards, ANSI (American National Standards Institute) publications, and recommendations from the International Electrotechnical Commission (IEC). Code numbers in the entries are keyed to a listing of sources of definitions at the back of the volume. The final section of the volume lists abbreviations, acronyms, etc. Some illustrations. Cross references.   TK9.I35

Jackson, Kenneth George and **Feinberg, Raphael.** Dictionary of electrical engineering. 2d ed. London & Boston, Butterworths, [1981]. 350p. il.   **EJ204**

1st ed. 1965.

Brief entries. Cross references.   TK9.J8

Markus, John. Electronics dictionary. 4th ed. N.Y., McGraw-Hill, [1978]. 745p. il.   **EJ205**

1st ed. 1945; 3d ed. (1966) had title: *Electronics and nucleonics dictionary.*

"Accurate, easy-to-understand, and up-to-date definitions for 17,090 terms used in solid-state electronics, computers, television, radio, medical electronics, industrial electronics, satellite communication, and military electronics."—*t.p.*   TK7804.M35

Modern dictionary of electronics. [By] Rudolf F. Graf. [6th ed.] Indianapolis, Sams, [1984]. 1152p.   **EJ206**

1st ed. 1962.

Brief definitions of several thousand terms. Additional sections: pronunciation guide for commonly mispronounced words; list of semiconductor symbols and abbreviations; schematic symbols.

TK7804.H6

Traister, John E. and **Traister, Robert J.** Encyclopedic dictionary of electronic terms. N.Y., Prentice-Hall, [1984]. 604p. il.   **EJ207**

" . . . a quick reference source for serious comprehension of the basics involved in electronics."—*Pref.* Entries are relatively long and detailed.   TK7804.T7

Foreign terms

Freeman, Roger L. English-Spanish, Spanish-English dictionary of communications and electronic terms. [London], Cambridge Univ. Pr., 1972. 206p.   **EJ208**

Title also in Spanish.

Has sections for English terms with Spanish equivalents; Spanish terms with English equivalents; English-Spanish and Spanish-English abbreviations lists.   TK7804.F74

Geiler, Leonid Benediktovich and **Dozorov, N. J.** English-Russian electrotechnical dictionary. 2d ed., rev. and enl. Moscow, State Pub. Office for Technical and Theoretical Literature, 1957. 711p.   **EJ209**

Added title page in Russian.

1961 reprinting called 3d ed.   TK9.G37

Goedecke, Werner. Wörterbuch der Elektrotechnik, Fernmeldetechnik und Elektronik. Wiesbaden, Brandstetter, [1964–68]. 3v.   **EJ210**

Also published London, Pitman; N.Y., Ungar.

Added title pages in English (Dictionary of electrical engineering, telecommunications and electronics) and French.

Contents: v.1, Deutsch-Englisch-Französisch; v.2, Französisch-Englisch-Deutsch; v.3, Englisch-Deutsch-Französisch.   TK9.G6

Höhn, Eduard. Dictionary of electrotechnology; German-English. London, Chapman & Hall, 1966. 705p. **EJ211**

Covers commercial, financial, and legal aspects of the electrical industry, in addition to the technical aspects, and scientific terms from closely related fields. TK9.H66

U.S. Dept. of the Army. English-Russian, Russian-English electronics dictionary. Wash., 1956. 944p. (*Its* Technical manual, TM30-545) (Repr.: N.Y., McGraw-Hill, 1958) **EJ212**

Includes some 22,000 Russian terms and abbreviations and some 25,000 English terms. Designed for the English-speaking person needing to use Russian-language publications on electronics and telecommunication. U408.3.A13

Handbooks

American electricians' handbook; a reference book for the practical electrical man. 10th ed., ed. by Wilford I. Summers. N.Y., McGraw-Hill, [1981]. 1v., various pagings. **EJ213**

1st ed. 1913. Originally edited by T. W. Croft.
A standard handbook. "The entire work has been carefully checked and revised so that it will be in accordance with the 1978 edition of the National Electrical Code."—*Pref.* TK151.A47

Electronics engineers' handbook. Donald G. Fink, ed. in chief. 2d ed. N.Y., McGraw-Hill, [1982]. 1v., various pagings. il. **EJ214**

1st ed. 1975.
A companion volume to the *Standard handbook for electrical engineers,* 11th ed. (EJ225); that volume is devoted primarily to the techniques of electrical power engineering, while this book is addressed to the field of electronics engineering. Signed articles by specialists are oriented toward application rather than theory; they include references. Detailed index. TK7825.E34

Electronics engineer's reference book. 5th ed. Ed. by F. F. Mazda. London, Butterworths, [1983]. 1v., various pagings. il. **EJ215**

1st ed. 1958. 3d ed. (1967) also published in U.S. as *Handbook of electronic engineering* (CRC Press).
Emphasis is on the latest technologies. Signed chapters by specialists include tabular data and diagrams, bibliographies. Indexed.
TK7825.E35

Fundamentals handbook of electrical and computer engineering. Ed. by Sheldon S. L. Chang. N.Y., Wiley, 1982. 3v. il. **EJ216**

Contents: v.1, Circuits, fields, and electronics; v.2, Communication, control, devices, and systems; v.3, Computer hardware, software, and applications.
Chapters by experts give concise coverage of major areas in electrical and computer engineering, include bibliographic references. Volumes are separately indexed. TK151.F86

Electronics designers' handbook. 2d. ed. Rev. and ed. by L. J. Giacoletto. N.Y., McGraw-Hill, [1977]. 1v., various pagings. il. **EJ217**

1st ed. (1957) by Robert W. Landee, Donovan C. Davis, and Albert P. Albrecht.
"This Handbook has been organized with the basic developments first, followed by numerical tabulation of material properties. Next, components, circuit analysis, and circuit design are introduced, and one progresses from smaller to larger systems."—*Pref.*
TK7825.L3

Illuminating Engineering Society of North America. IES lighting handbook. John E. Kaufman, ed. [6th ed.] N.Y., 1981. 2v. il. **EJ218**

1st ed. 1947. Previous eds. in 1v.
Contents: Reference volume; Application volume. (Volumes unnumbered.)

Sections include tabular data and references. It is planned to revise each volume on its own cycle; thus these volumes are identified by year rather than by edition. Each volume has an index to both volumes. TK4161.I46

Instrument engineers' handbook. Béla G. Lipták, ed. in chief. Rev. ed. Radnor, Pa., Chilton, [1985]. 2v. il. **EJ219**

1st ed. 1969–70, with suppl. 1972.
Volumes (unnumbered) entitled: Process measurement; Process control.
" . . . between these two volumes the reader should find all the information that is needed to solve problems related either to process measurement or process control"—*Introd.* Chapters include references and bibliographies. Both volumes are indexed.
TS156.8.I56

McPartland, Joseph F. How to design electrical systems. N.Y., McGraw-Hill, [1968]. 208p. il. **EJ220**

Subtitle: A complete manual on practical design and layout of electrical systems for power, light, heat, signals, and communications in commercial, industrial, and residential buildings.
TK145.M234

Markus, John. Modern electronic circuits reference manual. N.Y., McGraw-Hill, [1980]. 1238p. il. **EJ221**

Subtitle: Over 3,630 modern electronic circuits, each complete with values of all parts and performance details, organized in 103 logical chapters for quick reference and convenient browsing.
Includes references. Indexed. TK7867.M345

The National electrical code handbook. 3d ed. Based on the 1984 ed. of the *National Electrical Code.* Peter J. Schram, ed. Quincy, Mass., National Fire Protection Assoc., [1983]. 1074p. **EJ222**

"This is the third edition of *The National electrical code handbook* published by the National Fire Protection Association. The National Fire Protection Association formerly sponsored a handbook which was published by the McGraw-Hill Book Company and based on the National Electrical Code. This publication, *The National electrical code handbook,* does not emanate from and is not in any way connected with the McGraw-Hill Book Company."—*verso of t.p.*
The McGraw-Hill publication was publ. as the *National electrical code handbook,* 1st–11th eds., 1932–63, and as the *NFPA Handbook of the National electrical code,* 1st–4th eds., 1966–75. Since the end of the association of the National Fire Protection Association with McGraw-Hill, that company has issued *McGraw-Hill's National electrical code handbook,* 16th–18th eds., 1979–84 (ed. numbering reverting to that of the earliest title).
1st ed. of this title, 1978; 2d ed. 1981.
"*The National electrical handbook* is published by the National Fire Protection Association in order to assist those concerned with electrical safety in understanding the intent of the 1984 edition of the *Code.* A verbatim reproduction of the 1984 National Electrical Code is included, and added where necessary are comments, diagrams, and illustrations that are intended to clarify further some of the intricate requirements of the National Electrical Code."—*Pref.*

Reference data for engineers: radio, electronics, computer, and communications. 7th ed. Edward C. Jordan, ed. in chief. Indianapolis, H. W. Sams, [1985]. 1v., various pagings. il. **EJ223**

1st–6th eds. 1943–75 had title: *Reference data for radio engineers.*
Originally a production of the International Telephone and Telegraph Corporation, this reference work has in recent editions obtained material from outside the ITT system. Includes a wide range of data, tables, definitions and descriptions in separate chapters, with some bibliographic references.

Sams, Howard W. and Co. Handbook of electronic tables and formulas, comp. and ed. by Donald Herrington and Stanley Meacham. 5th ed. Indianapolis, Sams, 1979. 288p. **EJ224**

1st ed. 1959.

Covers electronics formulas and laws, constants and standards, symbols and codes, service and installation data, design data, mathematical tables and formulas, miscellaneous data.

TK7825.S3

Standard handbook for electrical engineers. Donald G. Fink and H. Wayne Beaty, eds. 11th ed. N.Y., McGraw-Hill, [1978]. 1v., various pagings. il.　　　　**EJ225**

1st ed. 1907.

An extensively revised and reorganized edition. Intends to include "all pertinent data within its scope, to be accurate and comprehensive in technical treatment, to be of use in engineering practice (as well as in study in preparation for such practice), and above all, to be oriented toward practical application, including the impact of economic considerations."—*Pref.*　　　　TK151.S83

Computer science

See also EJ201.

Bibliography

ACM guide to computing literature. 1977– . [N.Y.], Assoc. for Computing Machinery, 1978– . Annual (slightly irregular).　　　　**EJ226**

Continues the index to *Computing reviews* which covered the period 1960–76 under various titles: *Permuted (KWIC) index to Computing reviews (1960–63); Permuted and subject index to Computing reviews 1964–65; Comprehensive bibliography of computing literature, 1966–67; Bibliography and subject index of current computing literature, 1968–76.*

Although this publication serves as an annual index to the monthly current awareness and review publication *Computer reviews,* the *ACM guide . . . ,* unlike its predecessors, provides full bibliographic citations and thus can also serve as a stand-alone index to the computer science literature. Books, journal articles, conference proceedings, technical reports, and theses are indexed, in all fields of computer science and its applications. Indexing is by author, keyword, proper noun subjects (descriptors which are specific names, such as a particular computer language, hardware model, procedure or person), and category (subject-structured). Also indexes reviewers for *Computing reviews* so that their reviews may be located.　　　　QA75.7.A75

Artificial intelligence: bibliographic summaries of the select literature. Henry M. Rylko, compiling ed. Lawrence, Kans., Report Store, [1984]– . v.1– . (In progress).　　　　**EJ227**

To be in 2v., v.2 announced for late 1985.

Capsule reviews of monographs, conference proceeding volumes, special issues of journals, series, etc., are arranged alphabetically by personal or corporate author. Entries include summary, listing of contents, bibliographical information including ISBN. Includes index to all authors and editors mentioned in the entries, and a subject index with cross references. v.2 "will focus on current research literature."—*t.p.*　　　　Z7405.A7A77

Computer abstracts. v.1– , Oct. 1957– . London, Technical Information Co., 1957– . Monthly.　　　　**EJ228**

Publisher varies.

Title varies: 1957–58, *Bibliographical series. Computers;* 1959, *Computer bibliography.*

Offers abstracts of books, periodical articles, conference proceedings, U.S. government reports, and patents, in classified arrangement, with monthly author and patent indexes. Annual author and subject indexes.　　　　Z6654.C17C64

Cortada, James W. An annotated bibliography on the history of data processing. Westport, Conn., Greenwood Pr., [1983]. 215p.　　　　**EJ229**

Entries are grouped in four categories, each with a number of subcategories; alphabetized within subcategories. A 34p. introduc-

tion with references discusses the historiography of the subject. Author index.　　　　Z5640.C67

Hildebrandt, Darlene Myers. Computing information directory: a comprehensive guide to the computing literature. 1985 ed. Federal Way, Wash., Pedaro, 1985. 557p.

EJ230

1981 ed. had title *Computer science resources: a guide to professional literature.*

Contains chapters on journals; university computer center newsletters; books; technical reports; indexing and abstracting services; reviews; software and hardware resources; computer languages; directories, dictionaries and handbooks; publishers; and a chapter giving a proposed expansion of Library of Congress classification schedules QA75 and QA76. Individual chapters are indexed, but the volume as a whole is indexed only for monograph titles.

Z5640.H54

The Scientific Datalink index to artificial intelligence research, 1954–1984, N.Y., Scientific Datalink, 1985. 4v.

EJ231

Contents: v.1, Abstracts I; v.2, Abstracts II; v.3, Author and title indices; v.4, Subject indices.

Provides abstracts to technical reports and dissertations from major artificial intelligence research laboratories at universities, industrial research laboratories and research institutes in the United States. Does not cover published articles. Detailed subject index includes cross references.

An annual supplement volume is planned.

Youden, W. W. Computer literature bibliography. Wash., U.S. Dept. of Commerce, National Bureau of Standards, 1965–68. 2v. (National Bureau of Standards. Miscellaneous pubn. 266, 309)　　　　**EJ232**

Contents: v.1, 1946–63. 463p.; v.2, 1964–67. 381p.

v.1 indexes by source, title word, and author, all articles (more than 6,100) "published in 9 journals, 21 books, and over 100 proceedings." v.2 does the same for 5,200 articles in 17 journals, 20 books, and 43 conference proceedings. Also includes all references to items that were reviewed in the IEEE *Transactions on electronic computers.*

The two volumes have been reprinted (1970) by Arno Press in a single-volume edition entitled *Computer literature bibliography, 1946–1967.*　　　　QC100.U57

Dictionaries and encyclopedias

American national dictionary for information processing systems. Developed by American National Standards Committee X3, Information Processing Systems. Homewood, Ill., Dow Jones—Irwin, [1984]. 430p. (Information processing systems technical report X3/TR-1-82)　　　　**EJ233**

" . . . based on the *American national dictionary for information processing* (X3/TR-1-77) and its predecessor, the *American national standard vocabulary for information processing,* X#.12-1970."— *Foreword.*

Cross references.　　　　QA76.15.A42

Bürger, Erich and **Schuppe, Wolfgang.** Technical dictionary of data processing, computers, office machines. Oxford, etc., Pergamon; Berlin, VEB Verlag Technik, [1970]. 1463p.

EJ234

Title also in German, French, and Russian.

Separate alphabetical section for each language. In each section corresponding equivalent terms in the other three languages appear in parallel columns.　　　　QA76.15.B46

Burton, Philip E. A dictionary of minicomputing and microcomputing. N.Y., Garland, 1982. 346p. il.　　　　**EJ235**

Supersedes the author's *Dictionary of microcomputing* (1976).

Includes appendixes on special topics.　　　　QA76.5.B854

Christie, Lina Gail and **Christie, John.** Encyclopedia of microcomputer terminology. A sourcebook for business and professional people. Englewood Cliffs, N.J., Prentice-Hall, [1984]. 1v., unpaged. **EJ236**

A collection "of more than 4000 microcomputer terms that focus on those topics of interest to both the hobbyist and professional microcomputer user."—*Pref.* QA76.15.C468

Dictionary of computing. Valerie Illingworth, general ed. Oxford, Oxford Univ. Pr., [1983]. 393p. **EJ237**

"This dictionary contains, in a single alphabetical listing, over 3750 terms used in computing and in the associated fields of electronics, mathematics and logic."—*Pref.* Cross references. QA76.15.D526

Edmunds, Robert A. The Prentice-Hall standard glossary of computer terminology. Englewood Cliffs, N.J., Prentice-Hall, [1984]. 489p. **EJ238**

"All terms are described in a way that will make them as comprehensible as possible to the nontechnical reader without, at the same time, rendering the explanations useless to the information processing professional."—*Pref.* Includes acronyms. Cross references. QA76.15.E185

Encyclopedia of computer science and engineering. Anthony Ralston, ed. 2d ed. N.Y., Van Nostrand Reinhold, [1983]. 1664p. il. **EJ239**

1st ed. (1976) had title *Encyclopedia of computer science.*

This extensively revised edition has 550 articles from 301 contributors. These signed articles for the non-specialist range in length from short paragraphs to a dozen pages; most include brief bibliographies. Cross references; excellent index. QA76.15.E48

Gordon, Michael, Singleton, A. and **Rickards, C.** Dictionary of new information technology acronyms. London, Kogan Page; Detroit, Gale, [1984]. 217p. **EJ240**

"The aim of the book is to give a single source which can be used to trace the meaning(s) of any given acronym or abbreviation relating to [information technology]."—*Introd.* Terms are expanded, and in some cases annotated, but not defined. QA76.15.G67

The handbook of artificial intelligence. Stanford, Calif., HeurisTech; Los Altos, Calif., William Kaufmann, [1981–82]. 3v. **EJ241**

v.1 and v.2 ed. by Avron Barr and Edward A. Feigenbaum; v.3 ed. by Paul R. Cohen and Edward A. Feigenbaum.

"One can view these *Handbook* volumes as an encyclopedia of AI programming techniques, their successful applications, some of their limitations, and the computational concepts that have been used to describe them. . . . The *Handbook* contains several different kinds of articles. Key AI concepts and techniques are described in core articles. . . . Important individual AI programs . . . are presented in separate articles. . . . The problems and approaches in each major area are discussed in overview articles. . . ."—*Pref.* Articles list references; each volume has its own bibliography. Volumes 1 and 2 have their own name and subject indexes; v.3 has cumulated name and subject indexes. Q335.H36

The McGraw-Hill computer handbook. Ed. in chief, Harry Helms. N.Y., McGraw-Hill, [1983]. 1v., various pagings. il. **EJ242**

30 sections by specialist contributors present material on hardware, software, and special topics such as robotics and voice recognition, written for the non-expert. Indexed. QA76.M37

Meadows, A. J., Gordon, M. and **Singleton, A.** Dictionary of new information technology. London, Kogan Page, 1982. 206p. il. **EJ243**

A work for the nonspecialist. Includes acronyms; cross references. QA76.15.M4

Rosenberg, Jerry M. Dictionary of computers, data processing, and telecommunications. N.Y., Wiley, [1984]. 614p. **EJ244**

Over 10,000 entries; includes abbreviations. Has an appendix of Spanish and French equivalents. QA76.15.R67

Schmalz, Larry C. and **Sippl, Charles J.** Computer glossary for students and teachers. N.Y., Funk & Wagnalls, [1973]. 245p. **EJ245**

One in a series of glossaries making up the publisher's "Library of computer science." Other volumes include *Beginning computer glossary for businessmen,* by L. C. Schmalz and others; *Computer glossary for accountants and bankers,* by N. McFie and C. J. Sippl; *Computer glossary for engineers and scientists,* by W. M. Chow and C. J. Sippl; and *Computer glossary for medical and health sciences,* by W. Blessum and C. J. Sippl. QA76.15.S354

Sippl, Charles J. and **Sippl, Charles P.** Computer dictionary and handbook. [3d ed]. Indianapolis, Sams, [1980]. 928p. **EJ246**

1st ed. 1966.
Includes over 22,000 definitions and concept explanations. About a third of the book is taken up by 14 appendixes which constitute the handbook. QA76.15.S512

Weik, Martin H. Standard dictionary of computers and information processing. 2d ed. N.Y., Hayden, [1983]. 400p. **EJ247**

Definitions are meant to "reflect the best popular usage consistent with professional standards and compatible with national and international standards. Appropriate additional explanations, illustrations, examples, and cross-references for further clarification of concepts and meanings were added to the basic defining phrases."—*Pref.* A bibliography lists vocabularies, glossaries, and dictionaries used in the compilation of this work. QA76.15.W4

Wrathall, Claude P. Computer acronyms, abbreviations, etc. N.Y., Petrocelli, [1981]. 483p. **EJ248**

"Listed here are the meanings of more than 10,000 terms including many commonly used acronyms, abbreviations and names from the computer and communications fields."—*Pref.* Includes registered service marks and trade marks. QA76.15.W7

Directories and yearbooks

See also AB269–AB272.

Computer programs directory. 1971. N.Y., CCM Information Corp., [1971]. **EJ249**

Published for the Joint User Group of the Association for Computer Machinery.

Intended "to facilitate the exchange of program documentation among user groups."—*Pref.* Lists and describes some 1,200 programs in all areas of computer application. Provides indication of data submitted to user group, machine-sensible material, documentation, revision level, price per copy for documentation, author and submitter's affiliation, and other specifications. Subject index. QA76.5.A776

Computer-readable databases: a directory and data sourcebook. Martha E. Williams, ed. in chief. Chicago, Amer. Lib. Assoc., 1985. 2v. **EJ250**

For full information *see* AB269.

Computer yearbook. [1972]–79/80. Detroit, Computer Yearbook Co., [1972–80]. Irregular. **EJ251**

Supersedes *Computer yearbook and directory,* first published 1966. Foreword to the 1972 issue indicates that this is a successor to *The punched card annual* (1952–59; later *Data processing yearbook*).

The 1972 volume is in five main sections: (1) State-of-the-art, reviewing the financial structure of the industry, the major manufacturers, and the areas of strongest development; (2) Computer application, reviewing uses of computers in specific areas, such as education, engineering, government, medicine, and transportation; (3) The computer and the associations, containing short articles by representatives of computer-oriented associations; (4) Computer people, describing employment opportunities in the industry; and (5) Computer language summary, describing major programming languages and techniques.

Ceased publication? A successor publication, *Computer reference guide*, was announced in 1981 but has yet to appear.

Directory of online databases. v.1, no.1– , Fall 1979– . Santa Monica, Calif., Cuadra, [1979]– . Quarterly.
EJ252

For full information *see* AB272.

Encyclopedia of information systems and services. 6th ed., 1985–86. Ed. by John Schmittroth, Jr. Detroit, Gale, [1985]. 2v.
EJ253

Subtitle: An international descriptive guide to approximately 3,300 organizations, systems, and services involved in the production and distribution of information in electronic form. Including database producers and their products, online host services and time-sharing companies, videotex/teletext information services, library and information networks, bibliographic utilities, library management systems, information retrieval software, fee-based information on demand services, document delivery services, data collection and analysis centers and firms, and related consultants, service companies, professional and trade associations, publishers, and research activities.

1st ed. 1971. Previous eds. had Anthony T. Kruzas as ed. or co-ed.

Contents: International volume; United States volume.

Each volume separately indexed for databases, publications, software, function/service classification, personal names, subject, and geographic location; a combined master index is in the United States volume.
Z674.3.E52

The software catalog: microcomputers. Produced from the International Software Database. N.Y., Elsevier, [1983]– . Semiannual.
EJ254

Information on software programs for microcomputers, defined as systems costing up to approximately $15,000. Programs are arranged by International Standard Program Number (ISPN), which groups them by the software houses which produce them, then lists them approximately alphabetically by name within the producer groups. Address and telephone number are given with the producer name. Software entries include a brief description of the program and what it does, date of release, vendor information, whether the program is part of an integrated package, source code availability, program update availability, special hardware and software requirements, systems compatibility, minimum memory requirement, distribution medium, price, subject category. Indexed by computer system, operating system, and microprocessor on which programs will run, by programming language in which they are written, by subject and application, and by keyword and program name.

A companion volume is:
QA76.6.S6169

The software catalog: minicomputers. Produced from the International Software Database. N.Y., Elsevier, [1983]– . Semiannual.
EJ255

Information on software programs for minicomputers, defined as systems costing from approximately $10,000 to $100,000. Entry format and indexing essentially the same as for the companion *Software catalog: microcomputers* (above).

Many libraries will prefer to purchase one or more of the subject-oriented volumes derived from the two *Software catalog* titles. These include *The software catalog: business software, The software catalog: health professions*, and *The software catalog: science and engineering*. Each of these includes programs for both microcomputers and minicomputers, and is revised approximately annually.

Who's who in computers and data processing. 1971. [Chicago], Quadrangle Books, [1971]. 3v.
EJ256

Supersedes *Who's who in the computer field* (1963/64), which had been preceded by three earlier versions appearing in the periodical *Computers and automation* (1953–57).

1971 (called 5th ed.) in 3v.: (1) Systems analysts and programmers; (2) Data processing managers and directors; (3) Other computer professionals. About 15,000 biographies giving date of birth, education, occupation, year entering computer field, affiliation and title, organizational address, publications, and home address. Each

volume contains a complete index of names appearing in the set. Now outdated, but useful for historical information.

A more recent publication is the *Marquis who's who directory of online professionals* (Chicago, Marquis, 1984. 829p.).

Radio and television

The ARRL handbook for the radio amateur. Ed.1– . Newington, Conn., Amer. Radio Relay League, 1926– . il. Annual. (62d ed., 1985)
EJ257

Eds. 1–61 (1926–84) had title: *Radio amateur's handbook*.

" . . . designed to cover every aspect of Amateur Radio in a logical and easy-to-follow manner."—*Foreword*. Chapters covering fundamentals and changing technology in the field, include many tables, circuit diagrams, photographs, and occasional references. Indexed.
TK6550.R18

Barton, David Knox and **Ward, Harold R.** Handbook of radar measurement. Englewood Cliffs, N.J., Prentice-Hall, [1969]. 426p. il.
EJ258

Intends to present the results of studies of radar measurement "and to relate these results to design parameters of practical equipment."—*Pref.*
TK6580.B33

Freeman, Roger L. Reference manual for telecommunications engineering. N.Y., Wiley, [1985]. 1504p. il.
EJ259

"The aim of this manual is to provide a central source of basic information that will have repeated application."—*Pref.* Divided into 26 subject areas; includes references and bibliographies. Indexed.
TK5102.5.F68

Middleton, Robert Gordon. Television service manual. 4th ed. Indianapolis, Audel, 1977. 501p. il.
EJ260

1st–2d eds. (1951–61) had title *Audels television service manual*. Previous eds. by E. P. Anderson.

Covers system and circuit theory, system standards, installation and maintenance procedures.
TK6642.A56

Skolnik, Merrill Ivan, ed. Radar handbook. N.Y., McGraw-Hill, [1970]. 1v., various pagings. il.
EJ261

Chapters by specialists on the major topics of interest in the field of radar. "In general, the subjects are covered in breadth rather than depth."—*Pref.* Includes bibliographies.
TK6575.S478

Weik, Martin H. Communications standard dictionary. N.Y., Van Nostrand Reinhold, [1983]. 1045p. il.
EJ262

A comprehensive compilation of terms and definitions in the science and technology of communications. Words or terms used in definitions are italicized if they are themselves entries. Cross references.
P87.5.W4

ENERGY

General works

Balachandran, Sarojini. Energy statistics: a guide to information sources. Detroit, Gale, 1980. 272p. (Natural world information guide series, v.1)
EJ263

An expansion of *Energy statistics: a guide to sources* and *Energy statistics: an update* (Council of Planning Librarians. Exchange bibliography, nos. 1065 and 1247).

"The guide is divided into three major sections. The first contains a detailed alphabetical subject/keyword analysis of all recurring statistical data contained in some forty most used national and international energy serials. . . . The second section . . . gives full bibliographic descriptions of the sources analyzed in the earlier section. The rest of the book is an annotated guide to additional

sources of statistical information on individual sources of energy."
—*Introd.* Z5853.P83B25

Center for California Public Affairs. Energy: a guide to organizations and information resources in the United States. 2d ed. Claremont, Calif., Public Affairs Clearinghouse, [1978]. maps. (Who's doing what series, 1) **EJ264**

1st ed. 1974.

A subject-organized directory of key organizations concerned with energy in the United States. "Emphasis is given to organizations that influence, formulate, or administer policies affecting energy production, distribution, and use, or that provide information of interest to the nonspecialist."—*Introd.* Entries give address, telephone number, description of organization, and chief officer. Indexed. HD9502.U52C46

Crowley, Maureen, ed. Energy: sources of print and nonprint materials. N.Y., Neal-Schuman, [1980]. 341p. (Neal- Schuman sourcebook series) **EJ265**

Offers descriptions of almost 800 organizations that are sources of information and publications on energy; arranged by category of organization. Indexed. HD9502.A2C76

The energy directory. 1983. Ed. by Joanne Terminello. N.Y., EIC/Intelligence, 1983. 392p. **EJ266**

First issued 1974; beginning in 1975, was published in looseleaf format, with title *The energy directory update service.*

A comprehensive guide to national energy organizations, decision-makers, and sources of information. Includes names, titles, addresses, phone numbers, mission statements, programs, projects, publications, etc. Indexed. HD9502.U5E54

Energy research programs. Ed. by Jaques Cattell Pr. N.Y., Bowker, 1980. 444p. **EJ267**

An alphabetical listing of organizations conducting research and development projects in energy, with information on types of programs being conducted and names and titles of administrators and key research personnel. Geographical, subject, and personnel indexes.

Energy technology handbook, prepared by 142 specialists. Douglas M. Considine, ed in chief. N.Y., McGraw-Hill, [1977]. 1v., various pagings. il. **EJ268**

"This Handbook concentrates on those fundamental technologies which relate to energy sources, energy reserves, energy conversion, energy transportation and transmission, and to an extent limited both by time and space in the preparation of this volume, energy distribution, utilization, and the energy/environmental interface." —*Pref.* TJ163.9.E54

Hunt, V. Daniel. Energy dictionary. N.Y., Van Nostrand Reinhold, [1979]. 518p. il. **EJ269**

"The *Energy dictionary* has been prepared to meet the need for an up-to-date, authoritative yet concise compilation of the salient terms associated with the broad field of energy. . . . All definitions have been expressed as clearly and simply as possible without altering their acknowledged definition."—*Pref.* Includes table of conversion factors and bibliography. TJ163.2.H87

Loftness, Robert L. Energy handbook. 2d ed. N.Y., Van Nostrand Reinhold, [1984]. 763p. il. **EJ270**

1st ed. 1978.

Offers tabular data, including sources, and narrative information on a wide range of energy topics. Includes 16 chapters on topics such as consumption trends and projections, resources, costs, futures. Glossary; conversion factors; index. TJ163.235.L64

McAninch, Sandra. Sun power; a bibliography of United States government documents on solar energy. Westport, Conn., Greenwood Pr., 1981. 944p. **EJ271**

An index to documents published through 1979, including documents on biomass, ocean, thermal, solar, and wind energy. Entries are arranged by broad subject area. Indexed by author, title, agency, accession number. Z5853.S63M28

Oak Ridge Associated Universities. Industrial energy use data book. Oak Ridge, Tenn.; dist. N.Y., Garland, 1980. 1v., various pagings. **EJ272**

". . . this document has been prepared for the U.S. Department of Energy to serve as a standard reference for government officials and other groups concerned with policy analysis. . . . This data book is divided into three functional parts: Section I . . . addresses facets of overall industrial energy use; Section II . . . details energy use in the 13 most energy-intensive industrial sectors; Section III . . . presents the important environmental, regional, and social parameters of industrial energy use."—*Introd.* Chapters by specialists contain extensive tabular data, references. Appendixes give conversion factors, price deflators, annotated bibliography, glossary. Indexed. HD9502.U52O24

Texas A & M University, College Station. Libraries. Energy bibliography & index. Comp. by the Texas A & M University Libraries; Susan Lytle, research assoc. [and others]. Houston, Gulf, 1978–82. v.1–5. (In progress) **EJ273**

An index to all energy-related materials in the Texas A & M Library, the work consists of entries from the turn of the century on, with bibliographic information and abstracts. Each volume has subject, keyword-in-title, author, and corporate author and report series indexes. A promised 6th volume will have a cumulative index. Z5853.P83T49●

U.S. Department of Energy. Energy research abstracts. 1976– . Oak Ridge, Tenn., Technical Information Center, v.1– , 1976– . Semimonthly, with semiannual and annual indexes. **EJ274**

Partially supersedes U.S. Atomic Energy Commission's *Nuclear science abstracts* (EJ366). Supersedes U.S. Energy Research and Development, *ERDA research abstracts* (1975), nos.1–4 of which were titled *ERDA reports abstracts.* v.1–v.2, no.21 (1977) issued by the U.S. Energy Research and Development Administration as *ERDA energy research abstracts.*

". . . provides abstracting and indexing coverage of all scientific and technical reports, journal articles, conference papers and proceedings, books, patents, theses, and monographs originated by the U.S. Department of Energy, its laboratories, energy centers, and contractors. . . . ERA also covers other U.S. Government sponsored energy information and the international literature on reactor technology, waste processing and storage, and fusion technology. In addition, nonnuclear information obtained from foreign governments under agreements for cooperation is covered."—*[Note], 1978.* Z5853.P83U533●

Warren, Betty, comp. The energy and environment checklist: an annotated bibliography of resources. San Francisco, Friends of the Earth, 1980. 228p. **EJ275**

An annotated guide to over 1,600 items covering topics of current interest in energy and related fields. The final chapter lists government agencies and private organizations involved in energy and environmental studies. Z5863.E54W37

Weber, R. David. Energy information guide. Santa Barbara, Calif., ABC-Clio, 1982–84. 3v. **EJ276**

Contents: v.1, General and alternative energy sources; v.2, Nuclear and electric power; v.3, Fossil fuels.

A guide to the reference literature of energy, with broad coverage including social, political, economic and historical aspects as well as scientific and technical. Entries are annotated. Cross references. Each volume has author, title, subject, and document number indexes. Z5853.P83W38

World energy directory. A guide to organizations and research activities in non-atomic energy. 2d ed. Ed. by J. A. Bauly and C. B. Bauly. Harlow, Essex, Longman; Detroit, Gale, [1985]. 570p. **EJ277**

1st ed. 1981.

A companion to *World nuclear directory* (EJ373). Entries, arranged alphabetically by country, include address, telephone number, director, section heads, total R&D staff, projects, publications. Indexed by subjects, names, and keywords. TJ163.165.W67

Atlases

Cuff, David J. and **Young, William J.** The United States energy atlas. N.Y., Free Pr.; London, Collier Macmillan, [1980]. 416p. il., maps. 32cm.   **EJ278**

"This atlas strives to present a complete review of both renewable and non-renewable energy resources. It will serve as a reference for those who need detailed information on a specific resource and for those who need an overview of the various possibilities."—*Introd.*

Arranged in three parts: pt. 1 "Nonrenewable resources," and pt. 2 "Renewable resources," are divided into chapters on various specific resources. Pt. 3 is an overview. Includes a glossary, a list of suggested readings, a list of references for the chapters, and a brief appendix with conversion factors. Indexed. A 2d ed. was published 1985.   TJ163.25.U6C83

The world energy book: an A–Z atlas and statistical source book. N.Y., Nichols Publ., [1978]. 259p. il., maps. 28cm.   **EJ279**

Consultant eds. and principal contributors, David Crabbe and Richard McBride.

Contents: Introduction, A–Z, Energy resource atlas, Statistical appendixes.

"Intended as a comprehensive reference guide to energy sources, energy related terminology, economics and all factors related to the search for, extraction of, production and utilization of the major and alternative sources of energy."—*Introd.* Not indexed. A paperback edition is published by MIT Pr.   HD9502.A2W669

HEATING AND REFRIGERATION

ASHRAE handbook. Atlanta, Ga., Amer. Soc. of Heating, Refrigerating and Air-Conditioning Engineers, 1981– . 4v., each vol. issued quadrennially.   **EJ280**

Continues in part the *ASHRAE handbook and product directory* (1973–80), which split into this title and the annual *ASHRAE product specification file.* The previous title had been formed by merger of the *ASHRAE guide and data book* (1961–72) and *ASHRAE handbook of fundamentals* (1972).

Contents of parts and date of most recent issue: Applications (1982); Equipment (1983); Systems (1984); Fundamentals (1985). The Fundamentals volume was issued in 1985 in two editions: an SI edition containing *Système International* (SI) units, and an I-P edition containing *inch-pound* units.

Gilpin, Alan. Dictionary of fuel technology. London, Butterworths, 1969. 275p.   **EJ281**

Includes terms relating to solid, liquid, and gaseous fuels and other sources of energy, such as nuclear reactors. Attention is also given to pertinent "scientific units of measurement, economic and commercial terms and organizations concerned with fuel and power."—*Pref.* British in origin.   TP316.G5

Handbook of air conditioning, heating, and ventilating. 3d ed. Eugene Stamper, ed., Richard L. Koral, consulting ed. N.Y., Industrial Pr., [1979]. 1v., various pagings. il.   **EJ282**

1st ed. (1959) by Clifford Strock.

A handbook for engineers, contractors, and other practitioners; presents tabular data, formulas, graphs, etc., for the solution of problems of design, installation, and operation. Includes bibliographic references. Detailed index.   TH7687.S76

Heat bibliography, 1948/52– . Edinburgh, Stat. Off., 1959– . Annual.   **EJ283**

Prep. by the Heat Division, National Engineering Laboratory, East Kilbride, Scotland.

The first 3v. of the series covered 1948–52, 1953–54, and 1955–56; beginning with the volume for 1957, issued annually. Each annual includes only material *noted* in the National Engineering Library during that year and therefore contains some references to earlier papers. Most of the entries were obtained from abstracting and bibliographic journals, in which case the source is given along with indication of the presence of an abstract. Classed arrangement with subject, but no author, index.   Z5853.H27H4

International Institute of Refrigeration, Paris. Bibliographic guide to refrigeration, 1953–1968. Oxford, Pergamon, [1962–69]. 3v.   **EJ284**

Publisher varies. Title also in French, *Guide bibliographique du froid.*

Lists all documents abstracted in the *Bulletin* of the Institute during the 1953–68 period and gives the number of the abstract. Also includes lists of books received at the library of the Institute during the period covered and of the serials from which the abstracts were drawn. Classed arrangement with author and detailed subject indexes. The series ceased with v.3, being supplanted from 1969 by an annual keyword index to the contents of the *Bulletin* and to the abstracts appearing therein.   Z7914.R33I5

INDUSTRIAL ENGINEERING

American Society of Tool and Manufacturing Engineers. Handbook of industrial metrology. Englewood Cliffs, N.J., Prentice-Hall, [1967]. 492p. il.   **EJ285**

Subtitle: A reference book on principles, techniques, and instrumentation design and application for physical measurements in the manufacturing industries.   T50.A4

Handbook of industrial engineering. Ed. by Gavriel Salvendy. N.Y., Wiley, 1982. 1v., various pagings. il.   **EJ286**

Contains 107 chapters organized into 14 sections, written by an international group of 133 specialist authors. Intended for practicing industrial engineers and other practitioners, as well as for educators and students. Includes bibliographic references. Detailed index.   T56.23.H36

Handbook of industrial robotics. Ed. by Shimon Y. Nef. N.Y., Wiley, [1985]. 1358p. il.   **EJ287**

Chapters by specialists include bibliographic references. Includes sections on robotic terms, organizations, manufacturers, and journals. Indexed.   TS191.8.H36

Industrial engineering terminology. A revision, consolidation, and redesignation of ANSI Z94 Index and ANSI Z94.1–12. [Norcross, Ga.], Inst. of Industrial Engineers (distr. in cooperation with Wiley-Interscience), [1983]. 389p.   **EJ288**

"ANSI Standard Z94.0–1982. An American National Standard. Approved Dec. 9, 1982."—*t.p.*

Divided into 17 subject sections, with alphabetical arrangement of entries within sections or subsections. The "Overall index," a keyword-in-context index, includes all terms used in definitions and refers to the section under which the term is defined.   T55.5.I52

Ireson, William Grant and **Grant, Eugene L.** Handbook of industrial engineering and management. 2d ed. Englewood Cliffs, N.J., Prentice-Hall, [1971]. 907p. il.   **EJ289**

1st ed. 1955.

Chapters by specialists on industrial systems and organization, managerial economics, capital budgeting, factory planning and materials handling, industrial climatology, industrial standardization, industrial safety, computers and data processing, inspection and quality control, linear programming and its applications, etc. Includes bibliographic references; indexed.   T56.I7

Maynard, Harold Bright. Industrial engineering handbook. 3d ed. N.Y., McGraw-Hill, [1971]. 1v., various pagings. il.   **EJ290**

1st ed. 1956.

Chapters by specialists on the industrial engineering function, methods, work measurement techniques, wage and salary administration, planning and control procedures, computers, equipment and facilities, industrial engineering tools, etc. Includes bibliographies; indexed. T56.M38

Tver, David R. and **Bolz, Roger W.** Robotics sourcebook and dictionary. N.Y., Industrial Pr., [1983]. 258p. il. **EJ291**

Contents: pt.1, Introduction and dictionary of types; pt.2, Robotics dictionary of applications; pt.3, Robotics glossary and computer-control terminology; pt.4, Robotics manufacturers and typical specifications.

Covers "most of the key aspects of current industrial robots."—*Pref.* HD9696.R622T83

Waldman, Harry. Dictionary of robotics. N.Y., Macmillan, [1985]. 303p. **EJ292**

More than 2,000 terms, including acronyms, names of some laboratories and manufacturers, and some individuals. Brief entries. TJ210.4.W35

Woodson, Wesley E. Human factors design handbook. Information and guidelines for the design of systems, facilities, equipment, and products for human use. N.Y., McGraw-Hill, [1981]. 1047p. il. **EJ293**

" . . . directed specifically toward the engineer or designer, as opposed to being directed primarily toward the human factors specialist . . . the handbook is divided into chapters that are more or less related to the steps according to which any design program usually progresses, i.e., conceptual development at the overall system level, specification at the subsystem level, and detailed design at the component level."—*Pref.* Chapter 4 consists of compilations of human factors data. References. Indexed. TA166.W57

MARINE ENGINEERING

American Association of Port Authorities. Committee on Standardization and Special Research. A port dictionary of technical terms. New Orleans, Amer. Assoc. of Port Authorities, 1940. 208p. **EJ294**

Based on the *Port glossary* compiled by R. S. McElwee for the Association's Committee on Technical Language, 1927.
Contains more than 1,000 definitions. V23.A48

Eddington, Walter J. Glossary of shipbuilding and outfitting terms. N.Y., Cornell Maritime, 1943. 435p. il. **EJ295**

A comprehensive dictionary of practical maritime terms by a member of the U.S. Maritime Commission. Includes appendixes giving lists of deck-department, engine-room, and machine tools; tables; and other data. V23.E4

Kerchove, René de. International maritime dictionary; an encyclopedic dictionary of useful maritime terms and phrases, together with equivalents in French and German. 2d ed. Princeton, N.J., Van Nostrand, 1961. 1018p. il. **EJ296**

1st ed. 1948.
A comprehensive dictionary including terms—with clear, concise definitions—relating to seamanship, commercial shipping, maritime law, ship construction, insurance, naval architecture, navigation, meteorology, commercial fisheries, nautical instruments, etc. Describes characteristics of native or local craft from all parts of the world. The 2d ed. adds new terms relating to more recent methods and devices, etc. Definitions relating to deep-sea vessels have given way to basic terms on welding, telecommunications, radio navigation, and other terms with applications in the shipping field. French and German equivalents are given for most terms, and there are French and German indexes. Occasional bibliographical references, diagrams, and foldouts. V23.K4

Osbourne, Alan A. and **Neild, A. B.** Modern marine engineer's manual. 2d ed. N.Y., Cornell Maritime, 1965. v.1. il. **EJ297**

1st ed. 1941–43. v.2 of 2d ed. not published.
Includes sections on safety and first aid; engineering materials;

pipe fittings and packing; lubrication; bearings and shafting; pumps; thermodynamics; combustion; marine gas turbines; boilers; condensers and evaporators; marine steam turbines; reciprocating engines; mathematics and mechanics. Indexed. VM600.O82

MECHANICAL ENGINEERING

Guides

Houghton, Bernard. Mechanical engineering: the sources of information. Hamden, Conn., Archon Books; London, Bingley, [1970]. 311p. **EJ298**

Contains 15 chapters whose purposes are "to describe briefly the situations in which research is conducted in the United States and then to describe the various categories of publication which are published to document this research, indicating for each form its role and value to the engineer."—*Introd.* Coverage extends to names and addresses of organizations sponsoring research, research institutions, societies and associations, as well as major periodicals and reference tools. TJ160.5.H68

Bibliography

International catalogue of scientific literature: B, Mechanics. 1st–14th annual issues, 1901–14. London, 1902–15. 14v. **EJ299**

For full description *see* EA17.

Dictionaries

Audels new mechanical dictionary for technical trades, containing 11,000 definitions of commonly used terms in mechanical trades, physics, chemistry, electricity, etc. N.Y., Audel, [1962]. 740p. **EJ300**

A general technical dictionary adequate for the layman, probably not for the specialist. TA9.A8

Horner, Joseph Gregory, comp. A dictionary of mechanical engineering . . . 9th ed. rev. and enl. by G. K. Grahame-White. London, Technical Pr., 1967. 142p., 430p. **EJ301**

1st ed. 1888.
Earlier editions had title *Dictionary of terms used in the theory and practice of mechanical engineering.*
In two parts: (1) Dictionary of modern terms, and (2) Basic terminology. Only pt.1 was revised for this edition. TJ9.H82

Nayler, Joseph Lawrence and **Nayler, G. H. F.** Dictionary of mechanical engineering. [2d ed.] London, Butterworths, [1975]. 410p. il. **EJ302**

1st ed. 1966.
Brief entries on mechanical engineering interpreted as the production of, the means for, and the utilization of, mechanical power in engines, transport and mechanisms. Cross references. TJ9.N3

Foreign terms

Illustrated dictionary of mechanical engineering: English, German, French, Dutch, Russian. [By V. V. Schwartz and others] The Hague & Boston, Nijhoff, 1984. 417p. il. **EJ303**

"This dictionary is designed for people who have just started studying mechanical engineering terms in a foreign language, particularly for those who have little or no knowledge of either the terms or their meaning. . . . The terms are grouped according to subject. This makes it possible to study the terminology pertaining to the subjects which interest the user most. . . . When translating texts from one language into another, one is helped by the alphabetical indexes given at the end of the dictionary."—*Introd.* All terms in the dictionary are keyed to illustrations, diagrams, charts, etc. Tables of contents at the back of the volume give the subject grouping in each of the five languages. TJ9.I37

Karpovich, Evgenii Antonovich. Russian-English metals & machines dictionary. N.Y., Technical Dictionaries Co., 1960. 112p. **EJ304**

Terms relate to metallurgy, metals, alloys, metalworking, machines, machine elements, tools, processes, ore beneficiation.
TN609.K3

Walther, Rudolf. Dictionary of mechanics, strength of materials, and materials. English-German, German-English. Oxford, N.Y., Pergamon, [1965]. 356p. **EJ305**

About 13,000 terms. TA349.5

Handbooks

American Society of Mechanical Engineers. Metals Engineering Handbook Board. ASME handbook, ed. by Oscar J. Horger. 1st ed. N.Y., McGraw-Hill, 1953–58. 4v. il. **EJ306**

v.1, Metals engineering-design, ed. by Oscar J. Horger (1953), "discusses the essential properties which need to be evaluated by the design engineer in his selection of one material over another" —*Pref.*; v.2, Metals properties, ed. by Samuel L. Hoyt (1954), "tabulates the properties of metals about which a design engineer needs information"; v.3, Engineering tables, ed. by James Huckert (1956), "collects in one place many engineering tables to supplement the designer's knowledge of standards for shape, dimension, gears, and the like"; v.4, Metals engineering processes, ed. by Roger W. Bolz (1958), "deals with the processes by which metals are converted to finished product."

One volume of a 2d ed. has appeared as: TJ233.A57

———— ———— 2d ed. N.Y., McGraw-Hill, [1965]. [v.1]

Contents: Metals engineering: design, ed. by O. J. Horger.

American Welding Society. Welding handbook. 7th ed. Miami, Fla., Society, [1976–84]. 5v. il. **EJ307**

1st ed. 1938; 6th ed. 1968–73 (5v. in 6).
v.1 ed. by Charlotte Weisman; v.2–5 ed. by W. H. Kearns.
Contents: v.1, Fundamentals of welding; v.2, Welding processes: arc and gas welding and cutting, brazing, and soldering; v.3, Welding processes: resistance and solid state welding and other joining processes; v.4, Engineering applications: materials; v.5, Engineering applications: design.
Chapters are subdivided into topical sections, each with a bibliography. Volumes are separately indexed. TS227.A449122

Camm, Frederick James. Newnes engineer's reference book. Rev. by A. T. Collins. [10th ed.] London, Newnes, [1965]. 2066p. il. **EJ308**

1st ed. 1946.
A standard handbook, British in origin. TJ151.C335

Davidson, A., ed. Handbook of precision engineering. London, Macmillan; N.Y., McGraw-Hill, [1971–74]. 10v. il. **EJ309**

Translation of *Handboek van de fijnmechanische techniek* (Eindhoven, Centrex, 1966–70).
Contents: v.1, Fundamentals; v.2, Materials; v.3, Fabrication of nonmetals; v.4, Physical and chemical fabrication techniques; v.5, Joining techniques; v.6, Mechanical design applications; v.7, Electrical design applications; v.8, Surface treatment; v.9, Production engineering; v.10, Forming processes.
Each volume includes bibliographic references and has its own index. TJ145.D33213

Flügge, Wilhelm. Handbook of engineering mechanics. N.Y., McGraw-Hill, 1962. 1v., various pagings. il. **EJ310**

A handbook in seven parts: (1) Mathematics, (2) Mechanics of rigid bodies, (3) Theory of structures, (4) Elasticity, (5) Plasticity and viscoelasticity, (6) Vibrations, (7) Fluid mechanics. Each part, with the exception of the first which treats mathematical foundations, deals with some field within engineering mechanics and begins with a "brief description of the essential lines of thought of its subject." References to more extensive works are also included. Indexed. TA350.F58

Harris, Cyril M. and **Crede, Charles E.,** eds. Shock and vibration handbook. 2d ed. N.Y., McGraw-Hill, [1976]. 1v. various pagings. il. **EJ311**

1st ed. 1961, in 3v.
This edition has major changes, including the deletion of archival material and chapters whose importance has diminished because of technical developments; the treatment of current engineering problems of major interest has been expanded. Now comprises 44 signed chapters with references. Indexed. TA355.H35

Kent, William. Mechanical engineer's handbook, prep. by a staff of specialists. 12th ed. N.Y., Wiley, 1950. 2v. il. **EJ312**

1st ed. 1895 entitled *Mechanical engineer's pocket-book.*
Contents: v.1, Design and production, ed. by Colin Carmichael; v.2, Power, ed. by J. Kenneth Salisbury. TJ151.K4

Le Grand, Rupert. The new American machinists' handbook. Based upon earlier editions of American machinists' handbook, ed. by Fred H. Colvin and Frank A. Stanley. N.Y., McGraw-Hill, 1955. 1v. il. **EJ313**

1st–8th ed. by Colvin and Stanley, 1908–45. Now completely revised and rewritten. "Like its predecessor, the guiding principle . . . has been practicality of subject matter."—*Pref.* Major sections treat such topics as machining, metal-forming and assembly methods, materials finishing, fastening, drafting, and power-transmission equipment, plus a section on mathematics and tables.
TJ1165.L4

Machinery's Handbook; a reference book for the mechanical engineer, designer, manufacturing engineer, draftsman, toolmaker, and machinist, by Erik Oberg, Franklin D. Jones, and Holbrook L. Horton. 22d ed. N.Y., Industrial Pr., [1984]. 2512p. il. **EJ314**

1st ed. 1914.
Subtitle varies.
A standard handbook, frequently revised. Numerous charts, tables, line drawings, etc. TJ151.M3

Mechanical components handbook. Robert O. Parmley, ed. in chief. N.Y., McGraw-Hill, [1985]. 1v., various pagings. il. **EJ315**

Intends "to categorize, define, and discuss basic mechanical components used in current mechanical technology."—*Pref.* Chapters by specialists on topics such as gears and gearing, belts and pulleys, bearings, springs, retaining rings, etc. Indexed.
TJ243.M43

Mechanical design and systems handbook. 2d ed. Harold A. Rothbart, ed. in chief. N.Y., McGraw-Hill, [1985] 1v., various pagings. il. **EJ316**

1st ed. 1964.
Chapters by specialist contributors include bibliographic references. This revised edition includes material on recent topics such as computer-aided design. Indexed. TJ230.M43

Neale, Michael John. Tribology handbook. London, Butterworths; N.Y., Wiley, [1973]. 1v., various pagings. il.
EJ317

A handbook for designers and engineers in industry. "Tribology is concerned with understanding the action of the many common engineering components which move when in contact with each other, or with other materials. To make the Handbook easy to use the contents are divided into short sections concerned with these components, or with various practical problems."—*Pref.*
TJ1075.N4

Standard handbook for mechanical engineers. 8th ed., rev. by a staff of specialists. N.Y., McGraw-Hill, [1978]. 1v., various pagings. il. **EJ318**

Theodore Baumeister, ed. in chief; Eugene A. Avallone and Theodore Baumeister II, assoc. eds.

1st–6th eds., 1916–58, had title *Mechanical engineers' handbook*. Lionel S. Marks, ed. 1916–51. Also known as *Marks' Standard handbook for mechanical engineers*.

This revised ed. incorporates dual units—International System (SI), and U.S. Customary System (USCS)—as much as possible. Each chapter by a specialist or team of specialists. Includes bibliographic references. Indexed. TJ151.S82

Tool and manufacturing engineers handbook; a reference book for manufacturing engineers, managers, and technicians. 4th ed. Dearborn, Mich., Society of Manufacturing Engineers, [1983–84]. v.1–2. il. (In progress) **EJ319**

1st–2d eds. (1949–59) had title *Tool engineers handbook;* Society previously called "American Society of Tool Engineers" (1st ed.), and "American Society of Tool and Manufacturing Engineers" (2d ed.).

"Revised under the supervision of the SME Publications Committee in cooperation with the SME Technical Divisions"—*t.p.* Thomas J. Drozda, ed. in chief, v.1; Charles Wick, ed. in chief, v.2.

Contents: v.1, Machining; v.2, Forming; v.3, Materials and finishing; v.4, Assembly, testing, and quality control; v.5, Manufacturing engineering management. (v.3–5 not yet publ.)

"The scope of this edition is multifaceted, offering a ready-reference source of authoritative manufacturing information for daily use by engineers, managers, and technicians, yet providing significant coverage of the fundamentals of manufacturing processes, equipment, and tooling for study by the novice engineer."—*Pref.* Chapters include tabular data, line drawings, references and bibliographies; many include a glossary of terms used in the subject covered. Each volume has its own index. TS176.T63

Biography

Mechanical engineers in America born prior to 1861: a biographical dictionary. Sponsored by the History and Heritage Committee. N.Y., Amer. Soc. of Mechanical Engineers, [1980]. 330p. il. **EJ320**

"The fundamental purpose of the *Dictionary* is to supply essential biographical data on a selected group of American mechanical engineers active from the late 18th to the early 20th century, both as a resource for scholars in the history of technology and to give mechanical engineers . . . a basis for their conviction that the foundation of the profession is . . . the engineers themselves."— *Pref.* Inspired by the *Biographical dictionary of American civil engineers* (EJ112), this work has a similar format. It is in two parts, the first being a list of 1,688 engineers identified in the biographical files of the Division of Mechanical & Civil Engineering, National Museum of History & Technology, Smithsonian Institution, with dates where known. The second part contains biographical sketches of 500 of these engineers; for 50 of the 500 a portrait is included. TJ139.A47

Plant engineering and maintenance

Maintenance engineering handbook. 3d ed. Lindley R. Higgins, ed. in chief, L. C. Morrow, ed. N.Y., McGraw-Hill, [1977]. 1v., various pagings. il. **EJ321**

1st ed. 1957.
Chapters by specialists. Indexed. TS192.M65

Standard handbook of plant engineering. Robert C. Rosaler, ed. in chief. N.Y., McGraw-Hill, [1983]. 1v., various pagings. il. **EJ322**

Chapters are grouped in four sections: Pt. A, The basic plant facility: construction, equipment, and maintenance; Pt. B, Plant operation equipment: selection and maintenance; Pt. C, The main-

tenance function: basic equipment and supplies; Pt. D, Supplementary technical data. Chapters by specialists include bibliographic references. Indexed. TS184.S7

MINING AND METALLURGICAL ENGINEERING

Guides

Special Libraries Association. Metals/Materials Division. Guide to metallurgical information, ed. by Eleanor B. Gibson and Elizabeth W. Tapia. 2d ed. [N.Y.], Special Libraries Assoc., 1965. 222p. (SLA bibliography no.3) **EJ323**

1st ed., 1961, was a project of the Metals Division of the Special Libraries Association, designed to update Richard Rimbach's *How to find metallurgical information* (1936), and was edited by Elizabeth W. Tapia.

Covers all types of published literature, agencies, and other sources of metallurgical information in the following sections: General continuing sources; Metallurgy: science and technology sources; Metals/materials information sources; Translations and microforms. Most entries are annotated. International in coverage; the emphasis was on in-print publications issued since 1945. About 1,100 items with personal author, organization, general title, serial title, and subject indexes. Z6678.S65

Bibliography

U.S. Bureau of Mines. List of Bureau of Mines publications and articles, with subject and author index, by Rita D. Sylvester. 1960–64; 1965–69; 1970–74. Wash., Govt. Prt. Off., [1966, 1970, 1975]. (*Its* Special pubn.) **EJ324**

Supplements the U.S. Bureau of Mines, *List of journal articles . . . July 1, 1910, to Jan. 1, 1960 . . .* (below) and the U.S. Bureau of Mines, *List of publications . . . July 1, 1910 to Jan. 1, 1960 . . .* (EJ326). Z6736.U759

—— List of journal articles by Bureau of Mines authors publ. July 1, 1910, to Jan. 1, 1960, with subject index, comp. by Mae W. Hardison and Opal V. Weaver. Wash., Govt. Prt. Off., 1960. 295p. (*Its* Special pubn.) **EJ325**

Lists some 9,000 articles on mineral resources and industries, mine safety, and allied fields, published during these 50 years by the personnel of the Bureau in scientific and technical journals, the trade press, and other non-Bureau publications. Z6736.U758

—— List of publications issued by the Bureau of Mines from July 1, 1910 to Jan. 1, 1960 with subject and author index, by Hazel J. Stratton. Wash., Govt. Prt. Off., 1960. 826p. (*Its* Special pubn.) **EJ326**

Lists more than 7,500 titles of "virtually all scientific and technical publications issued by the Bureau of Mines . . . superseding all previous indexes of the Bureau's own publications."—*Foreword.*

Continued by the annual *List of Bureau of Mines publications and articles . . . 1961–* .

Dissertations

Hartman, Howard L. Bibliography of theses on mining in U.S. institutions. Golden, Colo., 1956. 70p. (Repr. from Colorado School of Mines quarterly, v.51, no.2, Apr. 1956) **EJ327**

Lists theses—master's and doctor's—on mining engineering completed in 23 schools offering graduate degrees from 1876 to about 1955. Arrangement is by subject, followed by a chronological listing under each school, and an author index.

Indexes

Crane, Walter Richard. Index of mining engineering literature, comprising an index of mining, metallurgical, civil, mechanical, electrical and chemical engineering subjects as related to mining engineering. N.Y., Wiley, 1909–12. 2v.
EJ328

Covers American and English material with some Australian and Canadian works, including periodicals, society transactions, and some government reports. v.1 indexes 18 publications covering 30 years to the end of 1907; v.2 brings up to date the periodicals indexed in that volume and indexes several additional titles, giving complete indexing for 26 periodicals and incomplete indexing for 20 other serials and 20 books. Classified arrangement with alphabetical index by subjects. No author indexes.   Z6737.C89

Abstract journals

American Society for Metals. Documentation Service. ASM review of metal literature: abstracts of the world's scientific, engineering and technical literature concerned with the production, properties, fabrication and applications of metals, their alloys and compounds. v.1–24, 1944–67. Metals Park, Ohio, 1945–67. Monthly.   **EJ329**

Subtitle varies.
Through 1964, cumulated into annual volumes with separate indexes. Changed format and classification notation with 1965. "Based on the decision to make RML completely compatible with and parallel to two new monthly abstract journals to be published by *Engineering Index* . . . in the fields of plastics and electrical and electronics engineering . . . will use interchangeable computer programs for generation of subject and author indexes."—*v.22, no.1.*
Merged with *Metallurgical abstracts*, Jan. 1968, to form *Metals abstracts* (EJ332).   TN1.A58

Institution of Mining and Metallurgy, London. IMM abstracts; a survey of world literature on economic geology, mining, mineral dressing, extraction metallurgy [and] allied subjects. v.1– . London, Institution, 1950– . Bimonthly.
EJ330

Subtitle varies.
Abstracts (many of them supplied by the authors) appear in classed arrangement according to Universal Decimal Classification. No index.

Metallurgical abstracts (general and non-ferrous). Ser.2–3. London, Inst. of Metals, 1934–67. Monthly.   **EJ331**

1931–33, issued monthly as a supplement to the *Journal of the Institute of Metals*. A classified abstracting service of material in all languages. Titles of foreign articles are translated into English. Symbols denote papers describing results of original research and outstanding critical reviews. Also lists contents of symposia in book form, new journals, and book reviews. Monthly issues are without indexes, but name and subject indexes are published at the end of the year.
Merged with *ASM review of metal literature* in Jan. 1968 to form *Metals abstracts* (below).

Metals abstracts. v.1, no.1– , Jan. 1968– . London, Metals Abstracts Trust, 1968– . Monthly.   **EJ332**

Published jointly by the Institute of Metals and the American Society for Metals, a result of the merger of the *Metallurgical abstracts* (above) and the *ASM review of metal literature* (EJ329).
Covers all aspects of the science and practice of metallurgy and related fields. International coverage. Now provides abstracts from more than 1,400 journals. Classed arrangement with author index in each issue.
A companion publication, *Metals abstracts index* (v.1, no.1– , Jan. 1968–), is issued simultaneously but mailed separately. It provides complete, computer-produced author and subject indexes to the abstracts. Annual cumulations of both abstracts and indexes are published.

Another companion publication *Alloys index* (v.1, no.1– , Jan. 1974–), provides indexing by alloy composition to complement the general indexing in *Metals abstracts*; all papers found in *Alloys index* are also in *Metals abstracts*.   TN1.M5153●

Dictionaries

American Society for Metals. ASM thesaurus of metallurgical terms: a vocabulary listing for use in indexing, storage, and retrieval of technical information in metallurgy. 3d ed. Metals Park, Ohio, 1979. 176p.   **EJ333**

1st ed. 1968.
Revised by the ASM Metals Information Technical Advisory Committee.   Z695.1.M55A5

Osborne, Alice Katherine, comp. An encyclopaedia of the iron & steel industry. 2d ed. enl. by the addition of a 44-page supplement of new terms prep. by A. K. Osborne & M. J. Wolstenholme. London, Technical Pr., 1967. 558p. il.
EJ334

1st ed. 1956.
A dictionary of terms rather than an encyclopedia. Aims to "provide a concise description of the materials, plant, tools and processes used in the Iron and Steel Industry, and in those industries closely allied to it."—*Pref., 1st ed.* Authority for many entries is provided through a list of references and bibliography at the end of the volume.   TN609.O8

Simons, Eric N. A dictionary of alloys. London, Muller, [1969]. 191p. il.   **EJ335**

Aims to provide brief details of "at least the majority of the better-known British and American alloys, as well as some continental and others."—*Pref.*   TA483.S55

Thrush, Paul W. A dictionary of mining, mineral, and related terms. Comp. and ed. by Paul W. Thrush and the staff of the Bureau of Mines. [Wash., U.S. Bureau of Mines], 1968. 1269p.   **EJ336**

Begun as a revision of the U.S. Bureau of Mines Bulletin 95, *A glossary of the mining and mineral industry*, by A. H. Fay (Wash., 1920; repr. 1947. 754p.), the new work is greatly expanded and includes up-to-date terminology of new methods and technologies. It is a comprehensive and authoritative work of about 55,000 entries and 150,000 definitions. Foreign terms have been excluded, except where no satisfactory English equivalent was available and for those Spanish-American and Mexican terms still in use in the American Southwest. Authority for each entry is provided through a list of sources at the end of the volume.   TN9.T5

Tottle, Charles Ronald. An encyclopaedia of metallurgy and materials. London, Metals Soc.; Plymouth, Macdonald and Evans, [1984]. 380p. il.   **EJ337**

Previous versions by Arthur Douglas Merriman had title: *A dictionary of metallurgy* (1958); *A concise encyclopaedia of metallurgy* (1965).
"Definitions have . . . been tailored to the varying needs of potential readers, so that for the non-technical reader, the most likely terms of interest are tackled as simply as possible without causing confusion, but for the student, the more scientific aspects are given wider treatment, assuming prior understanding of physics, chemistry or engineering."—*Pref.* More a dictionary than an encyclopedia; a section of tables precedes the main part of the work, which consists mainly of brief definitions, though some are longer and some include tabular data. Cross references.   TN609.T677

Foreign terms

Deruguine, Tanya. Russian-English dictionary of metallurgy and allied sciences. N.Y., Ungar, [1962]. 470p.   **EJ338**
TN609.D4

MacAndrew, Andrew Robert. A glossary of Russian technical terms used in metallurgy. [N.Y., Varangian Pr.], 1953. 127p. **EJ339**

Compiled at Columbia University under contract with the National Science Foundation. TN9.M2

Seebach, Hans Jobst von. Fachwörterbuch für Bergbautechnik und Bergbauwirtschaft. Dictionary for mining engineering and economics. Essen, Glückauf, 1947. 311p. **EJ340**

Contents: pt.1, German-English; pt.2, English-German.

Singer, Tibor Eric Robert. German-English dictionary of metallurgy. N.Y., McGraw-Hill, 1945. 298p. **EJ341**

Subtitle: With related material on ores, mining and minerals, crystallography, welding, metal-working, tools, metal products, and metal chemistry.

"No attempt has been made to include all the terms used in these related fields, nor have simple German words of nontechnical interest been included. . . ."—*Pref.* TN10.S5

Directories

Directory of iron and steel works of the United States and Canada. Ed.1– . N.Y., American Iron and Steel Institute, 1873– . **EJ342**

Frequency varies. Title varies.
Lists the companies, addresses, administrative personnel, equipment, etc. TS301.A6

Financial times mining international year book. 1983– . Harlow, Essex, Longman, 1983– . Annual. **EJ343**

Continues *Mining international yearbook* (1972/73–82), which had superseded *Mining year book* (1887–1971).
Provides information on mining companies throughout the world. TN13.M7

World mines register. 1975/76– . San Francisco, Miller Freeman, 1976–82. Biennial. **EJ344**

Superseded *Mines register*, v.1–29, 1900–70/71. Title of that publication varied (*The copper handbook*, v.1–11, 1900–13; *Mines handbook*, v.12–18, 1916–31; *Mines register*, v.19–29, 1937–70/71). Frequency irregular; suspended 1957–61, 1971–76.
Provides information (names of officers, brief history, capitalization, property, production, etc.) on mines, mining operations, and mining companies in the Western hemisphere. TN12.W66

Handbooks

ASM metals reference book. 2d ed. Compiled by the editorial staff, Reference Publications, American Society for Metals. Metals Park, Ohio, [1983]. 560p. il. **EJ345**

1st ed. 1981.
" . . . brings together data from many sources, including major contributions from the Eighth and Ninth Editions of *Metals handbook*."—*Pref.* Intended as a first-stop source for metals data, presented largely in tabular form with some diagrams. Includes references. The first section is a glossary of metallurgical and metalworking terms. TA459.A78

American Foundrymen's Society. Cast metals handbook. 4th ed. Des Plaines, Ill., 1957. 316p. il. **EJ346**

1st ed. 1935.
In six sections, beginning with a general treatment of cast metals, their properties, uses, and treatment, and followed by detailed sections on gray and white cast irons, malleable cast iron, nodular cast iron, steel casting, and nonferrous alloys. Bibliographies range from less than ten items to several hundred. Indexed. TS230.A5

American Institute of Mining, Metallurgical, and Petroleum Engineers. Industrial minerals and rocks (nonmetallics other than fuels). Stanley J. Lefond, ed. in chief. 5th ed. N.Y., The Institute, 1983. 2v. (1446p.) il. **EJ347**

1st ed. 1937.
Contents: pt.1, Introduction; pt.2, Industrial minerals grouped by uses; pt.3, Sources of information for industrial minerals; pt.4, Commodities.
Pt.4 contains chapters on individual minerals. Chapters are by specialists, include tables, maps, bibliographies (often extensive). Detailed index in each volume. TN799.5.A43

Bunshah, Rointan Framroze, ed. Techniques of metals research. N.Y., Interscience, 1968–76. 7v. il. **EJ348**

Contents: v.1, Techniques of materials preparation and handling. 3v.; v.2, Techniques for the direct observation of structure and imperfections. 2v.; v.2A, The stereographic projection and its applications. 2v.; v.3, Modern analytic techniques for metals and alloys. 2v.; v.4, Physiochemical measurements in metals research. 2v.; v.5, Measurement of mechanical properties. 2v.; v.6, Measurement of physical properties: pt.1, Some special properties; pt.2, Magnetic properties and Mossbauer effect; v.7, Techniques involving extreme environment, nondestructive techniques, computer methods in metals research, and data analysis. 2v.
The series constitutes a compilation of review articles on the various techniques of metals research. Extensive bibliographical references; author and subject indexes for each volume. TN607.B78

Hampel, Clifford A. Rare metals handbook. 2d ed. N.Y., Reinhold, 1961. 715p. il. **EJ349**

1st ed. 1954.
Chapters (usually a separate chapter for each metal) contain information on the metallic or elemental form of 55 less common metals about which there is an expanding interest. Included are discussions of production, fabrication techniques, present and potential uses, and tables of chemical and physical properties. Selected bibliographical references are included at the end of each chapter. TA459.H28

Metal bulletin handbook. Ed.1– , 1968– . London, Metal Bulletin Ltd., 1968– . Annual. **EJ350**

Supersedes *Quin's Metal handbook* (1914–65).
Beginning with 1982 issued in two parts: v.1, Prices; v.2, Statistics and memoranda.
Offers comprehensive coverage of "prices and statistics of production, consumption and trade relating to non-ferrous metals, iron and steel and scrap."—*Pref.* HD9506.4.M4

Metals handbook. 9th ed. Metals Park, Ohio, Amer. Soc. for Metals, [1978–85]. v.1–8. (In progress). **EJ351**

Prepared under the direction of the ASM Handbook Committee.
1st ed. 1927; 8th ed. 1961–76 in 11v.
Contents: v.1, Properties and selection: irons and steels; v.2, Properties and selection: nonferrous alloys and pure metals; v.3, Properties and selection: stainless steels, tool materials and special-purpose metals; v.4, Heat treating; v.5, Surface cleaning, finishing, and coating; v.6, Welding, brazing, and soldering; v.7, Powder metallurgy; v.8, Mechanical testing.
An extremely comprehensive handbook, the work of a large number of contributors, each volume treating a different aspect of the subject in great detail. Contains bibliographical references, extensive tabular data, and illustrative material. Each volume is individually indexed. TA459.A5

SME mining engineering handbook. Arthur B. Cummins, Chairman, Editorial board; Ivan A. Given, ed. N.Y., Soc. of Mining Engineers, 1973. 2v. il. **EJ352**

Supersedes Robert Peele's *Mining engineer's handbook* (3d ed. 1941).
" . . . includes not only modern data on and treatment of traditional underground and surface mining practices, but also covers numerous methods that previously were unknown or underdeveloped, such as marine mining, solution mining, arctic mining, nuclear application and others. Rock mechanics, fragmentation techniques, systems engineering and the use of computers have become highly developed, and likewise receive appropriate treat-

ment."—*Foreword.* Emphasizes principles and up-to-date information for mining engineers and practical operators. Chapters include bibliographies. Includes a chapter on engineering tables and information sources. Index in v.2.   TN151.S18.

Ross, Robert Ballantyne. Metallic materials specification handbook. 3d ed. London, E. & F. N. Spon, [1980]. 793p.   **EJ353**

1st ed (1968) entitled *Metallic materials.*

An effort to provide a comprehensive list of all known metallic-material trade names, symbols, and specifications. Designed to enable the user "to find the ingredients and properties of a symbol representing a specification or trade name" or, "knowing the desired properties, to find the specification and trade names which fulfill these requirements."—*How to use this book.* Includes 50,000 trade names, specifications or symbols of metals, and covers 250 private firms and 15 national organizations. "Materials [are] classified according to chemical analysis with a short note at the start of each group for the use of technicians."—*Pref.* Appendixes give names and addresses, trade names, firm names, and conversion tables. Indexed.   TA459.R65

Simons, Eric N. Guide to uncommon metals. London, F. Muller, [1967]. 244p.   **EJ354**

Metals are considered in alphabetical order, with information given as to classification, origin of the name, early history, principal ores and sources of supply, methods of extraction and production, a list of properties, and information on forms in which the metal can be obtained and the manner in which it is marketed.   TN758.S52

Smithells metals reference book. Eric A. Brandes, ed. 6th ed. London & Boston, Butterworths, [1983]. 1v., various pagings. il.   **EJ355**

1st ed. 1949. Previous eds. ed. by Colin James Smithells.

"A convenient summary of data relating to metallurgy is presented with values mainly in the form of tables and with descriptive matter reduced to a minimum. Although SI units are used throughout, many tables also give traditional units where these are still current. Full unit conversion tables are included. The values or formulations given are selected by the contributors as the most reliable but for a particular critical review the reader should consult the references. In the case of mechanical properties data, the values are for guidance only; for design purposes it is essential to consult the relevant specifications."—*Pref.* Indexed.   TN671.S55

Steel Founders' Society of America. Steel castings handbook. 5th ed. Ed. by Peter F. Wieser. [Rocky River, Ohio. The Soc., 1980] 1v. various pagings. il.   **EJ356**

1st ed. 1941.

Includes technical data on design, properties, physical values, wear resistance, applications, heat treatment, machinability, manufacture, etc. Indexed.   TS320.S78

Uhlig, Herbert Henry. The corrosion handbook; . . . sponsored by the Electrochemical Society, Inc. N.Y., Wiley, 1948. 1188p. il.   **EJ357**

". . . concerned primarily with corrosion protection, and the behavior of metals and alloys in environments at ordinary and elevated temperatures."—*Pref.*   TA462.U4

Woldman, Norman Emme Woldman's Engineering alloys. 6th ed. Metals Park, Ohio., Amer. Soc. for Metals, [1979]. 1815p.   **EJ358**

Ed. by Robert C. Gibbons.

1st ed. 1936. Previous editions had title: *Engineering alloys.*

Lists proprietary commercial and technical alloys manufactured in the United States and many alloys made in foreign countries, including England, France, Germany, and Sweden; gives alloy trade names, composition, properties, uses, and key numbers designating the manufacturer. "To accommodate the estimated 9000 new alloys that have been developed since publication of the Fifth Edition without materially enlarging the book, many obsolete and discontinued alloys have been eliminated from Section I [Alloy Data]. For reference purposes, these alloys have been included in Section IV [Obsolete Alloys]."—*Pref.*   TA483.W64

Statistics

Metal statistics. N.Y., Amer. Metal Mart, 1908– . v.1– . Annual.   **EJ359**

Statistics of various metals in the countries of the world, including production, shipment, prices, etc. Information exclusively in tabular form. Tables are grouped in sections, beginning with general information, followed by metals treated in alphabetical order. Gives information on metals in various forms, such as drawn wire, steel castings, and on such non-metal commodities as coal, oil, and gas. Includes a "Buyer's guide" and "Where to sell it."

HD9506.U6A5

NUCLEAR ENGINEERING

Guides

Glasstone, Samuel. Sourcebook on atomic energy. 3d ed. Princeton, N.J., Van Nostrand, 1967. 883p. il.   **EJ360**

1st ed. 1950.

A good treatment of atomic and nuclear physics for the beginning college student and the layman. The author's object has been "to describe in simple language, with a minimum of mathematics, what appear to be the most important developments in those areas of science covered by the general term 'atomic energy.' "—*Pref.* Selective bibliographies for further reading have been added at the end of each chapter. Author and subject indexes.   QC776.G6

Bibliography

International Atomic Energy Agency. List of bibliographies on nuclear energy. Vienna, 1960–74. v.1–12. Irregular.   **EJ361**

Ceased publication.

Includes references to bibliographies published or in preparation in English, French, German, Russian, and other languages. Classified list with author indexes.   Z7144.N8I525

——— List of references on nuclear energy. Vienna, 1959–68. v.1–10. Semimonthly; annual indexes.   **EJ362**

Published in English, with titles in original languages. "It answers bibliographical details of . . . scientific and technical literature dealing with the peaceful aspect of nuclear energy and the nuclear sciences in general, covering in particular books, research reports and other documents purchased by the Agency or received as gifts from the Member States."—*Foreword.*   Z5160.I42

United Nations. Dept. of Security Council Affairs. Atomic Energy Commission Group. An international bibliography on atomic energy. N.Y., 1949–53. 2v. and suppls.   **EJ363**

Contents: v.1, Political, economic, and social aspects (1949); Suppl. no.1 (1950); Suppl. no.2 (1953); v.2, Scientific aspects (1951); Suppl. no.1 (1952); Suppl. no.2 (1953).

Classified arrangement, with subject and author indexes. Includes books, periodical articles, government publications and documents, films, recordings, radio scripts, etc. In v.2 each section is preceded by a brief outline of the subject, written by a specialist.   JX1977.A2

U.S. Atomic Energy Commission. Bibliographies of interest to the atomic energy program, [comp. by James M. Jacobs and others]. Rev. 2. Oak Ridge, Tenn., Commission, Division of Technical Information, 1962. 295p. (*Its* TID-3043, rev.2)   **EJ364**

Supersedes the Commission's 1958 bibliography and its two supplements, 1959 and 1961.

An annotated bibliography of bibliographies and literature surveys relating to the atomic energy program, arranged by issuing organization, with author, subject, and report number indexes.

Z5160.U487

Abstract journals

INIS atomindex: an international abstracting service. Vienna, Internat. Atomic Energy Agency; distr. by Unipub., N.Y., 1970– . v.1– . Semimonthly with semiannual indexes. **EJ365**

Partially supersedes U.S. Atomic Energy Commission, *Nuclear science abstracts* (below). Supersedes International Atomic Energy Agency, *List of references on nuclear energy,* 1959–68 (EJ362).

"INIS is a cooperative, decentralized information system set up by the International Atomic Energy Agency and its Member States. Its purpose is to construct a data base identifying publications relating to nuclear science and its peaceful applications."—*Introd.* Availability of the report literature is indicated; many of the reports are available on microfiche from INIS. Z7144.N8I15

U.S. Atomic Energy Commission. Nuclear science abstracts. Oak Ridge, Tenn., Technical Information Branch, 1948–June 1976. v.1–33. Semimonthly. **EJ366**

Title varies.

Superseded the Commission's *Abstracts of declassified documents* and *Guide to published research on atomic energy.*

Subject, personal author, corporate author, and cumulative report indexes are available: v.1–4, 1948–50; v.5–10, 1951–56; v.11–15, 1957–61; v.16–20, 1962–66; v.21–25, 1967–71.

Abstracts and indexes the nuclear science literature. "It covers scientific and technical reports of the U.S. Atomic Energy Commission and its contractors, other U.S. Government agencies, other governments, universities, and industrial and research organizations. In addition, books, conference proceedings, individual conference papers, patents, and journal literature on a worldwide basis are abstracted and indexed."—[*note*] 1975. In classed subject arrangement; the Jan. 15 issue includes additional information on scope and arrangement. Availability of all Commission reports is indicated. Titles of foreign-language articles are translated into English; abstracts are in English.

In governmental reorganization the U.S. Atomic Energy Commission was eliminated and its publication, *Nuclear science abstracts,* ceased. Some of the functions of the AEC were taken over by the new agency, U.S. Energy Research and Development Administration and, subsequently, by the U.S. Department of Energy. Much of the coverage of *NSA* was taken over by *Energy research abstracts* (EJ274). *NSA* is also partially superseded by *INIS Atomindex* (EJ365). QC770.U64

Dictionaries

American Nuclear Society. Standards Committee. Subcommittee ANS-9. American National Standard glossary of terms in nuclear science and technology. [3d ed.] Hinsdale, Ill., The Society, [1976]. 110p. **EJ367**

1st ed. (1957) by the National Research Council Conference on Glossary of Terms in Nuclear Science and Technology, had title *A glossary of terms in nuclear science and engineering;* 2d ed. (1967) by the United States of America Standards Institute, had title *USA standard glossary of terms in nuclear science and technology.*

"ANSI N1.1–1976, revision of N1.1–1967"—*t.p.* QC772.A43

Foreign terms

Consultants Bureau Enterprises, N.Y. Russian-English glossary of nuclear physics and engineering. N.Y., 1957. 195p. **EJ368**

"This glossary incorporates all terms of the *Russian-English Dictionary of Nuclear Physics and Engineering* by N. N. Ershov, Y. V. Semenov, and A. I. Cherny . . . pub. by the Institute of Scientific

Information of the Academy of Sciences of the USSR. More than 2000 additional terms have been added."—*t.p.* Russian terms and expressions used in nuclear physics, atomic energy, and related fields drawn from Soviet scientific journals. QC5.C58

Karpovich, Evgenii A. Russian-English atomic dictionary. 2d rev. and enriched ed. N.Y., Technical Dictionaries Co., 1959. 317p. **EJ369**

1st ed. 1957.

". . . prepared for the English-speaking scientists, researchers, engineers, students, editors, and professional translators who deal with Russian-language publications in the atomic field."—*Pref.* Contains more than 23,000 Russian terms, primarily in nuclear science and technology, physics, mathematics and allied fields.

QC772.K3

Handbooks

Etherington, Harold. Nuclear engineering handbook. 1st ed. N.Y., McGraw-Hill, 1958. 1v., various pagings. il. **EJ370**

Chapters by specialists. TK9151.E8

Hogerton, John F. [and others]. The atomic energy desk book. Prep. under the auspices of the Division of Technical Information, U.S. Atomic Energy Commission. N.Y., Reinhold; London, Chapman & Hall, 1963. 673p. il. **EJ371**

Treats the background and status of atomic energy development in "more than 1000 alphabetically arranged entries ranging from brief definitions of terms to journal-length articles on major topics. It deals mainly with work being done in the United States on peaceful uses of atomic energy, but information is also given on military applications and there are entries on foreign atomic energy programs."—*Pref.* QC772.H64

Reactor handbook. Prep. under contract with the United States Atomic Energy Commission. 2d ed. rev. and enl. N.Y., Interscience, 1960–64. 4v. il. **EJ372**

1st ed. 1955.

Contents: v.1, Materials, ed. by C. R. Tyston, Jr.; v.2, Fuel processing, ed. by S. M. Stoller and R. B. Richards; v.3A, Physics, ed. by H. Soodak; v.3B, Shielding, ed. by E. P. Blizard and L. S. Abbott; v.4, Engineering, ed. by Stuart McLain and J. H. Martens.

"Organized along the lines of the functional utilization of the materials within a reactor."—*Pref.* Chapters by specialists. Includes extensive bibliographies. Each volume individually indexed.

TK9202.R37

World nuclear directory: a guide to organizations and research activities in atomic energy. 7th ed. Consultant ed., C. W. J. Wilson. Detroit, Gale, 1985. 1000p. **EJ373**

1st ed. 1961. 5th ed. (1976) had title *Nuclear research index.*

Lists government agencies connected with atomic energy; privately sponsored research organizations; universities and colleges with nuclear departments; learned and professional societies; industrial firms; pertinent consortia, etc. Indexed. QC770.W65

PETROLEUM ENGINEERING

Bibliography

Agout, Marthe. Bibliographie des livres, thèses et conférences relatifs à l'industrie du pétrole. [Paris, Gauthier-Villars], 1949. 322p. il. **EJ374**

A comprehensive, classified bibliography of 6,408 numbered items, based on the holdings of about 15 libraries and covering approximately 100 years from the start of the commercial development of petroleum in the mid-19th century. Scope is international;

locations are given wherever possible; and sources of reference are indicated for items not seen. Subject and author indexes.

DeGolyer, Everette Lee and **Vance, Harold.** Bibliography on the petroleum industry. College Station, Tex., [1944]. 730p. il. (School of Engineering. Texas Engineering Experiment Station. Bull. no.83) **EJ375**

Combines a bibliography of some 12,000 items, compiled by DeGolyer, with the bibliography of the Petroleum Engineering Dept. at the A. & M. College of Texas, and a bibliography on the Air-Gas Lift prepared by S. F. Shaw. Arranged by a decimal classification devised by L. C. Uren of the University of California, with an alphabetical subject index. Z6972.D4

Giddens, Paul H. The beginnings of the petroleum industry: sources and bibliography. Harrisburg, Pa., Pennsylvania Historical Commission, 1941. 195p. **EJ376**

In two parts: the first contains letters concerning the organization of the Pennsylvania Rock Oil Company of New York, the first petroleum company in the world; the second is a "Bibliography on the beginnings of the petroleum industry in 1871" (p.87–172), arranged by form, e.g., atlases, books, bibliographies, pamphlets, periodical literature. Some annotations. TN872.P4G5

Swanson, Edward Benjamin. A century of oil and gas in books: a descriptive bibliography. N.Y., Appleton, [1960]. 214p. **EJ377**

An annotated bibliography of books and monographs published in English from the mid-19th century to Aug. 1959. Arranged by topics, e.g., drilling and production, oil shales and shale oil, with sections on history and biography, reference works, general works, serials and periodicals. Author index. Z6972.S9

Special Libraries Association. Petroleum Section. Committee on U.S. Sources of Petroleum and Natural Gas Statistics. U.S. sources of petroleum and natural gas statistics, comp. by Margaret M. Rocq. N.Y., 1961. 94p. **EJ378**

An updating and expansion of Bradford A. Osborne's *An index to American petroleum statistics* (1943).

Indexes 231 publications. In three parts: the first lists trade journals, professional society, trade association, and company organs that are indexed; the second, the index, is an alphabetical list of products, plants, and other facilities, such as pipelines, wells, and refineries, keyed by number to the publications listed in the first part; and the third is a brief bibliography of statistical compilations not indexed in the second part, which include data on petroleum and natural gas. Only publications issued in the United States are indexed, but statistics about other countries are included. Z6972.S65

Dictionaries

Boone, Lalia Phipps. The petroleum dictionary. Norman, Univ. of Oklahoma Pr., 1952. 338p. **EJ379**

Gives definitions and sources of about 6,000 terms used in the oil industry, especially its colorful language. Bibliography, p.333–38. TN865.B6

Porter, Hollis Paine. Petroleum dictionary for office, field and factory. 4th ed. Houston, Tex., Gulf Pub. Co., 1948. 326p. **EJ380**

1st ed. 1930.
An enlarged edition of a standard work, now giving definitions for some 4,600 terms dealing with the prospecting, producing, and refining of petroleum. Definitions are generally brief, but some range to more than a page in length. Includes popular as well as technical terms. TN865.P6

Tver, David F. and **Berry, Richard W.** The petroleum dictionary. N.Y., Van Nostrand Reinhold, 1980. 374p. **EJ381**

A combination dictionary-handbook that covers the petroleum industry and related fields (e.g., geology, geophysics, seismology,

drilling, gas processes), and a detailed analysis of various refining operations and processes. TN865.T83

Handbooks, yearbooks, etc.

American Petroleum Institute. Petroleum facts and figures. Ed.1–18. N.Y., Inst., 1928–71. v.1–18. Irregular. **EJ382**

The 1959 Centennial edition, which gives the statistical history of the petroleum industry from its beginnings, supersedes all earlier editions. The 1967 edition continues the statistical series in that volume, superseding interim editions and supplements. Data, primarily in tabular form, is arranged in sections on production, refining, transportation, marketing and utilization, prices and taxation, and general (finance, labor, fire and safety, world data). The two volumes provide a 107-year record of the industry's activities. Ceased publication. HD9561.A7

Basic petroleum data book: petroleum industry statistics. Wash., Amer. Petroleum Inst., 1975–80. Looseleaf. **EJ383**

Contents: Sect.1, Energy; Sect.2, Reserves, crude oil; Sect.3, Exploration and drilling; Sect.4, Production; Sect.5, Financial; Sect.6, Price; Sect.7, Demand; Sect.8, Refining; Sect.9, Imports; Sect.10, Exports; Sect.11, Offshore; Section12, Transportation; Sect.13, Natural gas; Sect.14, OPEC; Sect.15, Miscellaneous.

Published in looseleaf format 1975–80 for continuous updating. Offers statistical tables organized according to the sections noted above. Beginning 1981, published in three issues per year (designated v.1, no.1– , but retaining the same title. HD9560.1.B37

Financial times oil and gas international year book. 1978/ 79– . London, 1978– . Annual. **EJ384**

Supersedes *Oil and gas international year book* (also called *Skinner's Oil and gas international year book*, 1973–78) which superseded *Oil and petroleum international year book* (1972), which had in turn superseded *Oil and petroleum year book* (1910–71).

A worldwide directory of oil, gas, and kindred companies.

International petroleum encyclopedia. Tulsa, Okla., Petroleum Pub. Co., 1967– . il. Irregular. **EJ385**

Brings together a good deal of information on petroleum production, refining capacities, reserves, and a country-by-country analysis of the role played by petroleum and gas in each. Includes directories of refineries, petrochemical plants, oil companies, and pipeline companies; information on the major oil and gas fields of the world; and statistics relating to all phases of the industry. Lacks a good general index. HD9560.5.I59

Moody, Graham B. Petroleum exploration handbook. N.Y., McGraw-Hill, 1961. 1v., various pagings. il. **EJ386**

Subtitle: A practical manual summarizing the application of earth sciences to petroleum exploration.

Discusses "fundamental concepts of exploration; the diagnostic traits of the explorationist; the organization required to prosecute the hunt for oil; the risks involved; how and why oil is trapped in some places but not in others."—*Pref.* Includes illustrations, diagrams, tables, and bibliographic references. Appendixes cover geological material, mapping and surveying, mathematical tables, and estimates of U.S. and Canadian reserves. Indexed.

TN271.P4M66

Petroleum processing handbook. William F. Bland and Robert L. Davidson, eds. N.Y., McGraw-Hill, 1967. 1v., various pagings. il. **EJ387**

". . . a compilation of practical information related to the refining (processing) of crude oil (petroleum) to convert it to useful petroleum products—primarily fuels and lubricants."—*Pref.* Sections contributed by specialists in the field provide basic data on processes, their uses and applications, and on construction and safe operation of plants. In addition to the references following each topical section, a chapter deals with sources of information. Glossary of processing terms; index. TP690.P47

E K

Medical and Health Sciences

❖With the advent of the consumer's right to know, to control, and to assume responsibility for her or his own health care, the library reference collection must contain a variety of handbooks, manuals, directories, etc., that exceeds the scope of what might previously have been thought appropriate. Publications chosen to satisfy the goal of thus expanding the reference collection were selected on the basis of two criteria—that the reader can find information for herself or himself directly in printed sources or that the reader will be led to sources of professional help through printed sources. This section has been compiled in recognition of the current state of expectations, while continuing to include the traditional sources of information.

Although entries in this section are specialized, they represent a selection and may not include the most highly specialized works. Access to additional sources may be gained by consulting such publications as Bowker's *Health science books, 1976–1982* (EK17), *The consumer health information source book* (EK28), and *Handbook of medical library practice* (EK4). For periodical literature the reader should consult *Index medicus* (EK52) or a specialized service such as *Literature search/National Library of Medicine* (EK19).

MEDICINE

Guides

Blake, John Ballard and **Roos, Charles.** Medical reference works, 1679–1966; a selected bibliography. Chicago, Medical Lib. Assoc., 1967. 343p. (Medical Library Assoc. pubn., 3)   **EK1**

Supersedes the bibliographies published as part of the 2d ed. (1956) of the Medical Library Association's *Handbook of medical library practice.*

Lists more than 2,700 titles in classed arrangement within 3 main sections: medicine, general; history of medicine; and special subjects. Titles have been selected for their usefulness in answering questions in bioscience libraries; titles especially useful for smaller medical libraries are marked with an asterisk. " . . . handbooks and treatises in the basic sciences and clinical medicine have only rarely been included."—*Pref.* Brief annotations.   Z6658.B63

——— ——— Suppl. 1–3. Chicago, Medical Lib. Assoc., 1970–75. 3v.

The 1st supplement follows the pattern of the main work, but excludes references on the history of medicine "since material of this sort is listed in the annual *Bibliography of the history of medicine* [EK149]."—*Pref.* Includes over 300 references with the emphasis on publications from 1967–68. The 2d and 3d supplements are computer-produced from the NLM *Current catalog* (EK33); therefore, these citations are arranged by author and subject. "General historical works, pharmacopoeias, reviews, and popular works have been excluded."—*Pref. suppl. 2.* A total of about

750 citations are added for the periods 1969–72 and 1973–74. Most references in the supplements are annotated.

Coping with the biomedical literature: a primer for the scientist and the clinician. Ed. by Kenneth S. Warren. N.Y., Praeger, 1981. 233p. il.   **EK2**

Contents: The structure of the information system: the development and structure of the biomedical literature, the ecology of the biomedical and information retrieval; Producing biomedical information: "first, do no harm," journals, reviewing reviews; Utilizing biomedical information: how to read a paper; Evaluation, requirements for scientific proof; Evaluation, requirements for clinical application; Sources of biomedical information: the National Library of Medicine, the Institute for Scientific Information, libraries and how to use them. The chapters are written by authorities. Bibliography. Index.   R118.6.C65

Finding the source of medical information: a thesaurus-index to the reference collection. Comp. by Barbara Smith Shearer and Geneva L. Bush. Westport, Conn., Greenwood Pr., [1985]. 225p.   **EK3**

The first part of the book is a listing of 447 reference books and textbooks, covering a wide range of subjects, prepared by the authors with the assistance of librarians, physicians, pharmacists, and nurses. The second part is a detailed subject thesaurus/index for the core books using natural language terms. The subject terms range from the general to the specific. In addition, subject entries are cross-referenced to broader, narrower, and related terms when appropriate.   Z6658.S4

Handbook of medical library practice. 4th ed. Louise Darling, ed.; David Bishop, Lois Ann Colaianni, assoc. ed. Chicago, Medical Lib. Assoc., 1982–83. v.1–2. (In progress)   **EK4**

1st ed. 1943, 3d ed. 1970.

Contents: v.1, Public services in health science libraries; v.2, Technical services in health science libraries; v.3 (in preparation), Administration and health sciences librarianship.

The purpose is "to serve as a practical manual reflecting accepted current methods for organizing and providing service from information resources to users of health science libraries of all types."—*Pref.* An indispensable handbook written by medical library specialists. All chapters include references. Indexed.   Z675.M4H236

Information sources in the medical sciences. 3d ed. London, Butterworths, [1984]. 534p. (Butterworths guides to information sources)   **EK5**

Ed. by Leslie Thomas Morton and S. Godbolt.

1st ed. 1974 had title: *Use of medical literature.*

"Attempts to provide a comprehensive guide to the general and specialist literature covering medical sciences. It is intended for clinicians, medical scientists, librarians and information scientists." —*Pref.*

Written by authorities. Chapters include: libraries and their use; primary sources of information; indexes, abstracts, bibliographies, and reviews; standard reference sources; mechanized sources of information retrieval; anatomy and physiology; biochemistry, biophysics and molecular biology; public health; pharmacology and therapeutics; tropical medicine; dentistry; historical, biographical and bibliographical sources; audiovisual materials; and the organization of personal files. Indexed.   R118.6.I54

Korb, Ruth Holcomb and **Carden, Jerry A.** Sourcebook for continuing education units in healthcare. Chicago, Amer. Soc. for Healthcare and Training, Amer. Hospital Assoc., 1983. 144p.   **EK6**

"Lists associations that award CEU and explains their requirements for application."—*on cover.*

Appendixes: questionnaire, responding associations not awarding CEU; sample application forms, and job titles.   R847.K67

Morton, Leslie Thomas. How to use a medical library. 6th ed. London, Heinemann Medical, [1979]. 118p.   **EK8**

1st ed. 1934.

A practical, short survey. This is a revised and updated edition describing "the principal indexing and abstracting tools, including computerized systems, the catalogue, classification schemes, reference works, pharmaceutical, historical and biographical material, and the present position of medical library provision in Britain." —*Pref.* Includes a chapter on audiovisual aids as applied to medical education.   Z675.M4M8

Roper, Fred and **Boorkman, Jo Anne.** Introduction to reference sources in health sciences. 2d ed. Chicago, Medical Lib. Assoc., [1984]. 302p.   **EK9**

1st ed. 1980.

"The purpose . . . is to discuss various types of bibliographic and information sources and their use in reference work in the health sciences. Although written with library school students in mind, practicing librarians and health science library users should also find the book of value."—*Pref. 1980.* Arranged under broad headings such as reference collection, bibliographic sources, and information sources. Each of the chapters covers specialized topics such as bibliographic sources for monographs, bibliographic sources for periodicals, terminology, medical and health statistics, and history sources.   Z675.M4R66

Bibliography

Andrews, Theodora. A bibliography of the socioeconomic aspects of medicine. Littleton, Colo., Libraries Unlimited, 1975. 209p.   **EK10**

Guide to the literature concerning the socioeconomic aspects of health care. "It is hoped that the librarians who wish to build collections in fields of health care and related areas will find this bibliography valuable."—*Introd.* Author and title index.

Z6675.E2A53

Besterman, Theodore. Medicine: a bibliography of bibliographies. Totowa, N.J., Rowman and Littlefield, 1971. 409p. (The Besterman world bibliographies)   **EK11**

Taken from *A world bibliography of bibliographies* (AA16).

Rather than listing the citations alphabetically as they were in the parent publication, this source lists them topically as follows: medicine, anatomy, hygiene, pharmacology, pharmaceutics, psychiatry, and special subjects such as adrenal glands, balneology, and yaws. "Useful to those who seek primary signposts to information in varied fields of inquiry."—*Pref.* Wide subject and language coverage.   Z6658.A1B4

Brodman, Estelle. The development of medical bibliography. Baltimore, Medical Lib. Assoc., 1954 (1981 printing). 226p. il. (Medical Library Assoc., pubn. 1)   **EK12**

A comprehensive survey of medical bibliography since 1500, covering printed medical bibliographies in Western languages which pertain to medicine in general rather than to its subdivisions or specialties. Personal bibliographies and bibliographies which do not make up the main portion of a work have been excluded, as have catalogs (with the exception of the *Index-catalogue* of the Library of the Surgeon General's Office). No distinction is made between indexes and abstracts as bibliographies.

"For each bibliography discussed there is a biographical sketch of the compiler, a description of the work emphasizing advances in technique, and a discussion of the importance of the work in the history of medical bibliography."—*Introd.* Appendix I lists references; Appendix II lists medical bibliographies since 1500 which were not discussed in the body of the text, arranged by century. General and author indexes.   Z6658.B7

Cordasco, Francesco and **Alloway, David N.** Medical education in the United States: a guide to information sources. Detroit, Gale, [1980]. 393p. (Education information guide series, v.8)   **EK13**

A bibliography of 2,364 sources arranged as follows: (1) bibliographies, dictionaries, directories, and general information; (2) history of medicine; (3) medical school admissions; (4) medical education; (5) health policy; (6) women's medical education; (7) hospitals; (8) autobiographies, biographies, reminiscences and related materials; (9) miscellaneous. Author, title, and subject indexes.

Z5818.M43C67

Environmental health-related information. [Wash.], Interagency Education Program Liaison Group, Task Force on Environmental Cancer and Heart and Lung Disease, (distr. by Nat. Technical Information Service), [1984]. 251p.   **EK14**

Subtitle: A bibliographic guide to federal sources for the health professional.

"The information included . . . is intended to assist health professionals in identifying and selecting appropriate materials to update and expand their own knowledge and to aid in the education of their students and patients."—*Introd.* Arrangement is alphabetical by 37 topics from Agriculture, Air pollution, and Asbestos to Vibration and Workers' compensation. Annotated citations include sources and availability of material. Includes five appendixes.

Z6675.I5E56

Gilbert, Judson Bennett. Disease and destiny: a bibliography of medical references to the famous . . . with additions and an introd. by Gordon E. Mestler. London, Dawsons of Pall Mall, 1962. 535p.   **EK15**

A listing of medical and scientific writings drawn largely from the *Index-catalogue. . .of the Surgeon General's Office,* the *Index medicus,* and the *Quarterly cumulative index medicus,* about famous people in history, the humanities, and the arts and sciences from ancient to modern times. International in scope. Personalities are listed alphabetically and are identified by dates of birth and death and a brief descriptive phrase; books and papers written about them are listed in chronological order. The introduction contains an excellent bibliography of monographic literature in the field of medico-biographical writing.   Z6664.A1G5

Health affairs information series. Detroit, Gale, [1978–83]. v.1–10. (In progress?)   **EK16**

Contents: v.1, Health care administration. Dwight A. Morris and Lunne D. Morris, eds. (1978. 264p.); v.2, Cross-national study of health systems; concepts, methods, and data sources. Ray H. Elling, ed. (1980. 293p.); v.3, Cross-national study of health systems; countries, world regions, and special problems. Ray H. Elling, ed. (1980. 687p.); v.4, Health statistics. Frieda O. Weise, ed. (1980. 137p.; for fuller information *see* EK34); v.5, The professional and scientific literature on patient education. Lawrence W. Green, ed. (1980. 330p.); v.6, Health care costs and financing. Rita M. Keintz, ed. (1981. 258p.); v.7, Health maintenance through food and nutrition. Helen D. Ullrich, ed. (1981. 305p.); v.8, Bioethics. Doris Mueller Goldstein, ed. (1982. 366p.; for fuller information *see* EK182]; v.9, Emergency medical service systems. Carlos Fernandez-Cabellero and Marianne Fernandez-Cabellero, eds. (1981. 183p.); v.10, Human ecology. Frederick Sargent, ed. (1983. 293p.).

Each volume has subtitle "A guide to information sources."

Edited by authorities, each volume is designed to aid health care professionals, scientists, librarians, and students. Classified, annotated lists of books, articles, periodicals, audiovisual aids, organizations, and other types of information sources on specific topics make up each volume of the series.   Z6663.N9U44

Health science books, 1876–1982. N.Y., Bowker, [1982]. 4v.   **EK17**

"Prepared by the R.R. Bowker Company's Dept. of Bibliography."—*verso of t.p.*

Contents: v.1–3, Subject index; v.4, Author index.

Arranged by Library of Congress subject headings, the entries provide complete LC entry with tracings, call number, and ISBN. Includes a guide to MeSH/LC equivalents and a guide to LC/MeSh equivalents for the health sciences.   Z6658.H4

International bibliography on burns. 1959/69– . Ann Arbor, Mich., Nat. Inst. for Burn Medicine, [1969–]. Annual.   **EK18**

Subtitle: Thermal, electrical, chemical, radiation, cold injuries; for better patient care research and teaching.

Irving Feller, ed., 1959/60–83. Publisher varies.

Issues for 1970–83 consist of annual supplements to the 1959/69 ed.

A classed bibliography of books and articles published since 1950 which deal with etiology, prevention, treatment, and considerations in metabolism, physiology, legal problems, etc. All titles are given in English, but the language of the original work is noted if published in another language. The 1959/69 ed. includes over 9,000 citations collected from more than 4,000 publications published in 27 languages. Author index.   Z6667.W6F4

Literature search/National Library of Medicine. no.7–67– . [Bethesda, Md.], Nat. Library of Medicine, [1967–]. Irregular.   **EK19**

No.1–65/21–65, *New bibliographic series.* No.22–65/66–67, *National Library of Medicine literature search.*

Contains citations to articles indexed for the Library's computerized Medical Literature Analysis and Retrieval System (MEDLARS). Each citation is listed with descriptors selected from Medical Subject Headings (MeSH) by which the article was indexed. A few of the titles/subjects covered are: osteoporosis, hospices, Alzheimer's disease, recurrent mood disorders, acquired immunodeficiency syndrome (AIDS), fetal surgery, and adolescent alcoholism. A list of the currently available bibliographies appears each month in *Index medicus* (EK52).

Manning, Diana Helen. Disaster technology: an annotated bibliography. N.Y., Pergamon, 1976. 282p.   **EK20**

An earlier ed. appeared 1973.

Contents: (1) Annotated references—Relief organizations; Medical aspects: planning; Medical aspects: general; Medical aspects: nutrition; Sociological aspects; Physical aspects: general; Physical aspects: earthquakes; (2) Reviews; (3) Subject classification.

"The purpose of this bibliography is to supply relief agencies with information on published and unpublished literature available concerning technical aspects of disaster relief and prevention with special emphasis on developing countries. It is also intended to provide those involved in relevant research with information on disaster topics from other disciplines."—*Introd.*

Each review is a brief discussion of general points with indications of controversial issues. The subject classification includes broad subject headings with reference numbers that refer to the annotated references or reviews. Author index.   Z5776.M35

Medical and health care books and serials in print. N.Y., Bowker, [1985–]. Annual.   **EK21**

Continues *Medical books and serials in print: an index to literature in the health sciences* (1972–84).

A comprehensive and authoritative source for information on new titles. The available books in medicine, dentistry, nursing, and veterinary medicine are classified in over 5,800 subject categories. The 1985 edition includes over 60,500 books in print and 14,400 serials. Indexed by author and title.   Z6658.B65

New York Academy of Medicine. Library. Author catalog. Boston, G. K. Hall, 1969. 43v.   **EK22**

———— ———— 1st supplement. Boston, G. K. Hall, 1974. 4v.

———— Subject catalog. Boston, G. K. Hall, 1969. 34v.

———— 1st supplement. Boston, G. K. Hall, 1974. 4v.

The two catalogs comprise reproductions of the catalog cards for this important collection. Entries for more than 373,200 volumes and over 169,300 pamphlets are included in the basic set.

———— Illustration catalog. 3d ed., rev. & enl. Boston, G. K. Hall, 1976. 264p.   **EK23**

1st ed. 1960.

Photographic reproduction of an index to illustrative material in medical works, early as well as recent. Arranged by subject. Over 22,000 illustrations are cataloged.   Z6676.N54

———— Portrait catalog. Boston, G. K. Hall, 1960. 5v.   **EK24**

Reproduction of the catalog cards listing the 10,784 separate portraits—paintings, woodcuts, engravings, photographs—in the Academy and 151,792 entries for portraits appearing in books and journals. When a portrait is accompanied by biographical material or an obituary, this is so indicated.   R153.5.N4

———— First supplement, 1959–1965. Boston, G. K. Hall, 1965. 842p.

———— Second supplement, 1965–1971. Boston, G. K. Hall, 1971. 593p.

———— Third supplement, 1971–1975. Boston, G. K. Hall, 1976. 589p.

Pearsall, Marion. Medical behavioral science: a selected bibliography of cultural anthropology, social psychology, and sociology in medicine. Lexington, Univ. of Kentucky Pr., 1963. 134p.   **EK25**

Cites monographs and articles directly related to health and medical practice which, with few exceptions, have been written by social anthropologists, sociologists, and social psychologists. 3,064 numbered entries in classed arrangement within 8 major subject divisions: the place of behavioral science in health and medicine; studies of roles and role relations; studies of the structural and organizational context of therapy; studies of health levels, health practices, and attitudes toward scientific medicine; rural health studies; healing roles and medical systems in other cultures; selected studies related to clinical problems; and behavioral science studies in mental health. Almost entirely devoted to English-language titles. Author index.   Z6658.P4

Popenoe, Cris. Wellness. [Wash.], Yes! Inc., (distr. by Random), [1977]. 443p. il.   **EK26**

This bibliographic guide annotates over 1,500 books on the wide range of holistic health and healing. Most of the books were published in the early 1970s. Author index.   Z6673.P34

Reading, Eng. University. Library. The Cole Library of early medicine and zoology: catalogue of books and pamphlets. Nellie B. Eales, comp. Oxford, Alden Pr. for the Univ. of Reading Lib., 1969–75. 2v. (Reading Univ. Lib. pubns., 1–2)   **EK27**

Contents: v.1, 1472 to 1800; v.2, 1800 to present day and supplement to v.1.

A descriptive catalog of a distinguished collection. Chronological arrangement, with subject and author indexes.   Z6676.R35

Rees, Alan M. and **Janes, Jodith.** The consumer health information source book. 2d ed. N.Y., Bowker, 1984. 530p.   **EK28**

1st ed. 1981.

"The most complete guide to health information for the lay person, identifying the essential materials and information sources: books, pamphlets, periodicals, newsletters, professional literature, health information clearinghouses and hotlines, book publishers." —*Back cover.* As a general rule material prior to 1979 is not included. The selections reflect the high standards (i.e., significance and validity of content and quality of writing) that the authors imposed in their selection. Annotated entries are arranged under a wide range of subjects, e.g., aging, allergies, alternative medicine, dental care, health clubs and spas, and sexuality. Appendixes include a directory of pamphlet suppliers and a directory of publishers. Indexed by author, title, and subject.   Z6673.R3

U.S. National Library of Medicine. A catalogue of sixteenth century printed books in the National Library of Medicine. Comp. by Richard J. Durling. Bethesda, Md., U.S. Dept. of Health, Education, and Welfare, Public Health Service, Nat. Lib. of Medicine, 1967. 698p.   **EK29**

4,808 numbered entries with brief bibliographical notes. Geographical and name indexes of printers and publishers. For a supplement *see* EK40.   Z6659.U59

———— Early American medical imprints; a guide to works printed in the United States, 1668–1820, by Robert B.

Austin. Wash., U.S. Dept. of Health, Education, and Welfare, Public Health Service, 1961. 240p. **EK30**

An alphabetical author listing of more than 2,100 separately published items, including books, pamphlets, theses, broadsides, and selected periodicals, with full bibliographical information and many annotations. Library holdings are indicated for 67 libraries. Appendixes include a chronological index and a list of 74 Evans's *American bibliography* items (AA557) which are not included in the bibliography because copies could not be located or because they could not be verified as having been printed. Z6661.U5A44

————— Index-catalogue of the library of the Surgeon General's Office, United States Army (Army Medical Library), authors and subjects. Ser.1–4, v.1–11. Wash., Govt. Prt. Off., 1880–1955. 58v. **EK31**

Contents: ser.1, A–Z (1880–95. 16v.); ser.2, A–Z (1896–1916. 21v.); ser.3, A–Z (1918–32. 10v.); ser.4, v.1–11, A–Mn (1936–55).

A dictionary catalog, including not only books and pamphlets but also a large number of references to periodical articles and other analytics. The National Library of Medicine (formerly the Surgeon General's Library, and the Army Medical Library) is one of the largest medical libraries in the world, and this monumental catalog is, therefore, a very important bibliography of all aspects of the subject. One of its special uses is for medical biography, as it indexes a large number of biographical and obituary articles. Z6676.U6

————— ————— 5th ser., 1959–61. 3v.

Contents: v.1, Authors and titles (1959); v.2–3, Subjects (1961). No more published.

These are the final volumes of the *Index-catalogue,* and are published as a supplementary series to include selected monographic material from the unpublished files of the *Index-catalogue* covering the 19th and first half of the 20th centuries. After a screening of these files, some 83,000 entries were selected, consisting of monographic imprints for 1950 or earlier and including "theses, project reports, monographic and series analytics, equipment and supply catalogs, legislative issuances and bibliographical reference works." —*Pref.*

————— Catalog. 1948–1965. Wash., Lib. of Congress, 1949–66. Annual, with quinquennial cumulations beginning 1950/54. **EK32**

April/Dec. 1948 issue was published in the 1948 cumulative catalog of the Library of Congress as a continuously paged supplement but with separate title page. Also issued separately as v.1 of this catalog.

Title varies: 1948, *Catalog cards;* 1949–50, *Author catalog.*

Library name varies: 1948–51, U.S. Army Medical Library; 1952–55, U.S. Armed Forces Medical Library.

Includes reproductions of catalog cards prepared for the NLM card catalog for newly received materials and for titles recataloged during the period.

Quinquennial cumulations cover 1950/54, 1955/59, 1960/65.

————— National Library of Medicine current catalog. Jan.1/14, 1966– . Wash., Govt. Prt. Off., 1966– . Quarterly, with annual cumulations. **EK33**

Frequently varies.

Supersedes the National Library of Medicine *Catalog* (above).

A computer-produced catalog; now issued quarterly, with annual and quinquennial cumulations. In addition, proof sheets are published weekly. Cumulations give citations for all publications cataloged, regardless of date of imprint, excepting pre-1801 and Americana titles.

Beginning July 1968, the National Library of Medicine entered into cooperative cataloging agreements with the Francis A. Countway Library of Medicine at Harvard University and the Upstate Medical Center of the State University of New York, and from that date the catalog is a union catalog for works cooperatively cataloged by the three libraries.

Catalogs and cumulations have included a varying number of sections, including: Main subject; Name; Technical report subject; Technical report names. Z675.M4U578nc

Weise, Frieda O. Health statistics: a guide to information sources. Detroit, Gale, [1980]. 137p. (Health affairs information guide series, v.4) **EK34**

An annotated bibliography of "basic sources of vital and health statistics in the United States. Vital and health statistics are broadly defined here to include . . . natality and mortality, marriage and divorce, morbidity, health care facilities, health manpower, health services utilization, health care costs and expenditures, health profession education, [and] population characteristics."—*Pref.* Author, title, and subject indexes. Z7553.M43W444

Wellcome Historical Medical Museum, London. Library. A catalogue of printed books in the Wellcome Historical Medical Library. London, 1962–76. v.1–3. (Publications . . . catalogue ser. PB1-PB3) (In progress) **EK35**

Contents: v.1, Books printed before 1641; v.2–3, Books printed from 1641 to 1850: A–L.

The first volume includes almost 7,000 titles arranged by author, with indexes by place of publication and by printer and publisher, and a concordance for English books with STC numbers. v.2–3 continue the record to 1850. Z6676.W4

Audiovisual materials

See also EK285.

Education-for-health: the selective guide. Ed. by the Mental Health Materials Center for the National Center for Health Education. N.Y., Nat. Center for Health Education in association with the Mental Health Materials Center, 1983. 927p. **EK36**

Subtitle: Health promotion, family life, and mental health; audiovisuals and publications.

Separate parts for audiovisuals and publications; each part is arranged by topics. Entries include citation, synopsis, assessment (giving purpose and critical evaluation), and intended audiences and uses. Indexed. RA440.55.Z9E38

National Medical Audiovisual Center catalog. 1974– . Bethesda, Md., Nat. Lib. of Medicine, Nat. Medical Audiovisual Ctr. (for sale by Supt. of Docs.), 1974– . Annual. **EK37**

Subtitle (varies): Films for the health scientist.

Continues *National Medical Audiovisual Center motion picture and videotape catalog* (1973) and *National Medical Audiovisual Center catalog* (1968–72), which in turn continued the U.S. Public Health Service *Film catalog* (1960–67).

Arranged by subject and title, giving purchase, rental, and loan policies. Includes a price list. Sponsor and producer code indexes. R835.N28

Incunabula

See also EK27, EK35.

Klebs, Arnold Clark. Incunabula scientifica et medica; short title list. Bruges, Belgium, St. Catherine Pr., 1938 [i.e., 1937]. 359p. (History of medicine ser., issued under the auspices of the New York Academy of Medicine) **EK38**

Reprinted from *Osiris,* v.4. Z240.K62

U.S. National Library of Medicine. A catalogue of incunabula and manuscripts in the Army Medical Library, by Dorothy M. Schullian and Francis E. Sommer. N.Y., publ. for the honorary consultants to the Army Medical Library by Henry Schuman, [1948?]. 361p. il. **EK39**

Pt.1 lists 490 incunabula, with full bibliographical descriptions and citations to listings in other bibliographies, and about 35 early Western manuscripts; pt.2 describes some 137 Oriental manuscripts. Z6676.U6186

————— A catalogue of incunabula and sixteenth century printed books in the National Library of Medicine: first supplement. Comp. by Peter Krivatsy. Bethesda, Md., Nat. Library of Medicine, (for sale by Supt. of Docs.), 1971. 51p. **EK40**

Supplements *A catalog of incunabula and manuscripts in the Army Medical Library* (EK39) and *A catalog of sixteenth century printed books in the National Library of Medicine* (EK29). Indexed by place and printer.

Periodicals

Index medicus. List of journals indexed. (*In* Index medicus, January issue; reprinted *in* Cumulated index medicus, 1963–) Annual. **EK41**

For full information *see* EK53.

Also available separately as:

U.S. National Library of Medicine. List of journals indexed in Index medicus. [Bethesda, Md.], 1960– . Annual. **EK42**

1962 not separately published.

Lists the more than 2,000 journals indexed for MEDLARS and indicates those that are only selectively indexed. Includes abbreviations listing and title listing.

—— Biomedical serials, 1950–1960; a selective list of serials in the National Library of Medicine, comp. by Lela M. Spanier. Wash., 1962. 503p. (Public Health Service pubn. no.910) **EK43**

Lists 8,939 serials, including some monographic serials, review journals, and proceedings and transactions of societies and institutes. Information for each entry includes title, publishing or issuing body, place of publication. Serials which began after 1960 are excluded. Z6660.U52

—— Index of NLM serial titles. [Ed.1]– . Bethesda, Md., U.S. Dept. of Health, Education and Welfare, [1972–]. Annual. (DHEW pubn. no. (NIH) 72–314, etc.) **EK44**

Subtitle: A keyword listing of serial titles currently received by the National Library of Medicine.

Includes over 19,000 titles. Gives NLM call numbers.

Z6660.U66

Vital notes on medical periodicals. v.1–30. Chicago, etc., 1952–82. 3 times a year. **EK45**

Published by the Periodicals and Serial Publications Committee of the Medical Library Association.

The first issue (Oct. 1952) was arranged by births and deaths of periodicals under specific fields; subsequent issues are arranged alphabetically by title, giving address, birth or death date, frequency, and sometimes price. Z6660.M458

World medical periodicals. Les périodiques médicaux dans le monde. Periódicos médicos del mundo. Medizinische Zeitschriften aller Länder. 3d ed. N.Y., World Medical Assoc., 1961. 407p. **EK46**

1st ed. 1953; 2d ed. 1957.

The 3d ed. includes the titles of more than 5,800 periodicals relating to medicine, pharmacy, dentistry, and veterinary medicine, as well as to hospital buildings, administration, and equipment. Gives address, frequency, language, and the *World list* (EA53) abbreviation of the title. Z6660.W6

—— Supplement. N.Y., 1968. 68p.

Abbreviations

See also EK42, EK52.

Artelt, Walter, Heischkel, Edith and **Wehmer, Carl.** Periodica medica: Titelabkurzungen medizinischer Zeitschriften. 4. neubearb. und erweit. Aufl. Stuttgart, Georg Thieme Verlag, 1952. 280p. **EK47**

1st ed. 1928. 3d ed. by Max Kuntze.

Added title page in English: Periodica medica: abbreviated titles of medical periodicals.

A listing of world medical periodicals with recommended abbreviations. This edition includes only medical titles, omitting the general scientific periodicals included in earlier editions.

Z6660.A78

Indexes

Index medicus, a . . . classified index of the current medical literature of the world. v.1–21, Jan. 1879–April 1899; 2d ser. v.1–18, 1903–20; 3d ser. v.1–6, 1921–June 1927. N.Y., Boston, and Wash., 1879–1927. **EK48**

Publisher varies.

The 1st ser. ceased publication with April 1899; was revived by the Carnegie Institution of Washington in Jan. 1903. During the interval a similar index, *Bibliographia medica (Index medicus),* was published by the Institut de Bibliographie of Paris.

From 1879 to 1927 the *Index* was a standard current bibliography of medicine, covering publications in all principal languages and including periodical articles and other analytical entries as well as books, pamphlets, and theses. Ser.1–2, published monthly, consists of references in a classified listing with an author index, cumulated annually, and an annual subject index. Ser.3 was published quarterly in an alphabetical subject arrangement with an author index cumulated annually, but has no annual subject index. Contains material not found in the *Index-catalogue* of the Surgeon General's Office.

Discontinued June 1927, and merged into the *Quarterly cumulative index medicus* (EK50). Z6660.I4

Quarterly cumulative index to current medical literature, 1916–26. Chicago, Amer. Medical Assoc., 1917–27. 12v. **EK49**

An important author-subject index to "original articles in the better and more accessible medical journals."—*Note.* Each annual volume includes, in addition to the index to periodicals, a bibliography of the important new books of the year, exclusive of new editions, and a list of government documents of interest to physicians. Titles of articles in foreign languages have been translated into English. In 1926, two semiannual volumes were issued instead of one annual.

Should be used with the *Index medicus* for this period.

Continued by: Z6660.A5

Quarterly cumulative index medicus, 1927–1956. Chicago, Amer. Medical Assoc., 1927–56. 60v. Quarterly with semi-annual cumulations. **EK50**

"This volume represents the culmination of efforts whereby the *Index Medicus,* published since 1879 under various auspices, and the *Quarterly Cumulative Index,* published since 1916 by the American Medical Association, are combined as the *Quarterly Cumulative Index Medicus.*"—*Pref., 1927.*

An author-subject index to some 1,200 periodicals in many languages, forming a fairly comprehensive general index to the journal literature. Includes medical biography. Also includes a list of journals and publications indexed and a list of new books published during the period, arranged alphabetically by author and followed by a subject classification of the same material. All subject entries are in English and the title is frequently inverted, shortened, or expanded to indicate the contents of the article more clearly. Complete bibliographic information is found under the author entry (including the title of the article in the original language if English, French, German, Spanish, Italian, or Portuguese).

Continued by: Z6660.A51

Current list of medical literature, v.19–36. Wash., Army Medical Lib., 1950–59. Monthly. **EK51**

1941–49, issued weekly, consists of the copied contents pages of English and foreign journals in a classified arrangement. Foreign-language titles are not translated. Index to journals but no subject approach to individual papers and no author index.

Beginning with v.19, July–Dec. 1950, published in a greatly

expanded form, analyzing nearly 1,500 journals. The journals are listed alphabetically, and items are numbered. Author and subject index in each issue, with a cumulative index for each volume.

Superseded by: Z6660.C8

Index medicus. Wash., Nat. Lib. of Medicine, 1960– . v.1– . Monthly.   **EK52**

v.1–3 were originally designated as "new series."

Cumulates annually into the *Cumulated index medicus* (EK56).

Each issue is now in three sections: (1) subjects, (2) names, (3) bibliography of medical reviews (since 1967; *see* below). In the alphabetical "Subject" section are given: title of English-language article or translation of non-English-language title; author; journal-title abbreviation, with volume, inclusive paging, and date, and an abbreviation indicating the original language of a non-English article. In the "Name" section are given authors' names (up to three) and names of biographees. Under authors, titles are given in the vernacular except for some of the lesser-known languages. English-language articles appear first under each subject, followed by foreign-language articles, set off by brackets and arranged alphabetically by language and within each language by journal title.

A comprehensive index to the world's medical literature, since 1966 compiled by mechanized means and representing a partial printout of the MEDLARS (Medical Literature Analysis and Retrieval System) computer-based file.

Over 2,000 periodicals are indexed, either completely or selectively. In addition to journals in the medical and health sciences, there are representative journals in the fields of biometry, botany, chemistry, entomology, physics, psychology, sociology, veterinary medicine, and zoology.

Issues for 1960–65 include a separate section, "Recent United States publications," which reproduces National Library of Medicine catalog cards for current titles.

Beginning 1965, issues include current listings of NLM *Literature search* (EK19) citations.

From Jan. 1970, an *Abridged index medicus* (Bethesda, Md., National Library of Medicine) has been published monthly "to afford rapid access to selected biomedical journal literature of immediate interest to the practicing physician."—*Introd.* Each issue (arranged by authors and subjects as in the parent work) contains citations from 100 English-language journals selected on the basis of quality and usefulness of content.   Z6660.I42●

—— List of journals indexed. (*In* the Jan. issue of *Index medicus*, 1963–).   **EK53**

A list of several thousand journals (1) by abbreviation, and (2) by full title. Reprinted in *Cumulated index medicus*, annually.

—— Bibliography of medical reviews. (*In* monthly issues of *Index medicus*, 1967–)   **EK54**

For issues prior to 1967 *see* EK60.

Appears as a separate section of each monthly issue of *Index medicus* and cumulates as part of *Cumulated index medicus*.

Includes references to those "articles which are well documented surveys of the recent biomedical literature."—*Introd.*

—— Medical subject headings. Main headings and cross references used in Index medicus and National Library of Medicine catalog, 1963– . Annual. (Issued as pt.2 of the Jan. issue of *Index medicus;* reprinted as part of *Cumulated index medicus*)   **EK55**

Has three basic applications, serving as (1) the subject-heading authority list for the indexing of the biomedical periodical literature in *Index medicus* and the MEDLARS computer-based file; (2) the authority list for the catalog of the National Library of Medicine; and (3) the key to the use of *Index medicus* and the machine search of the citations in MEDLARS. New headings and the headings they replace appear in each issue.

All cross references appear in this list and not in the *Index medicus,* and therefore the two must be used in close conjunction. The "Categorized lists," which group related subject headings by broad subject areas, are also only here, and aid in determining the most appropriate headings for a particular need.

The user of the *Index* should become familiar with this list of subject headings and should consult the list for the year being searched, to determine what headings were used at that time. The list of new headings indicates the major headings under which material on a given subject formerly appeared.

Cumulated index medicus. 1960– . Chicago, Amer. Medical Assoc., 1961– . v.1– . Annual.   **EK56**

Imprint varies.

The cumulation of the *Index medicus* (EK52). Comprises separate cumulated author and subject indexes for each year. Also includes an annual cumulation of the *Bibliography of medical reviews* (EK54, EK60) and reprints the *List of journals indexed* and the *Medical subject headings.*   Z6660.I422●

Reuss, Jeremias David. Repertorium commentationum a societatibus litterariis editarum. Secundum disciplinarum ordinem . . . T.10–16, Scientia et ars medica et chirurgica. Gottingae, Dieterich, 1813–21. (Repr.: N.Y., B. Franklin, 1961)   **EK57**

Contents: T.10, Propaedeutica, anatomia et physiologia, hygiene, pathologia seu nosologia generalis, semeiotica; T.11, Materia medica, pharmacia; T.12–15, Therapia generalis et specialis, A–Z; Operationes chirurgicae, Medicina forensis, legalis et politica; T.16, Ars obstetricia, Ars veterinaria.

A very valuable index to the contents of the publications of the learned societies of various countries before 1800. Classed arrangement with author indexes for each section.

For description of complete set *see* EA22.   Z5051.R44

Specialized indexes

❖Following is a sampling of the many specialized indexes available in the biomedical fields. In addition to *Literature search* (EK19), the National Library of Medicine, through its computer-based MEDLARS (Medical Literature Analysis and Retrieval System) produces a number of "Recurring bibliographies," which provide citations to journal articles in specific fields. Only a few of these are separately listed and annotated below, by way of example; the full list includes: *Anesthesiology bibliography* (quarterly); *Annual bibliography of orthopaedic surgery; Bibliography of acute diarrhoeal diseases* (quarterly); *Bibliography on medical education* (monthly); *Bibliography of podiatric medicine and surgery* (monthly); *Cranio-facial—cleft palate bibliography* (quarterly); *Current bibliography of plastic and reconstructive surgery* (bimonthly); *Current citations on strabismus, amblyopia, and other diseases of ocular motility* (quarterly); *Family medical literature index* (quarterly); *Hospital literature index* (quarterly, EK59); *Index of rheumatology* (annual); *Index to dental literature* (quarterly, EK190); *International nursing index* (quarterly, EK215); *Neurosurgical biblio-index* (quarterly); *Physical fitness/sports medicine* (quarterly); *Psychopharmacology bibliography* (quarterly); *Quarterly bibliography of major tropical diseases; Recurring bibliography on education in the allied health professions* (annual); *Recurring bibliography of hypertension* (bimonthly); *Schisto update* (quarterly).

A current listing and information about distributors will be found inside the back cover of each issue of *Index medicus* (EK52).

Cumulative index of hospital literature, 1945–1949, 1950–1954, 1955–1959. Chicago, Amer. Hospital Assoc., 1950–61. 3v.   **EK58**

Prepared by the Library of the American Hospital Association, Asa S. Bacon Memorial.

5-year cumulations of the semiannual *Hospital literature index.* Authors and subjects in one alphabet. Indexes 300–400 journals in the hospital and related fields.

Continued by:

Hospital literature index. June 1955– . Chicago, Amer. Hospital Assoc., 1955– . Quarterly.   **EK59**

Title varies.

From 1945 to 1961, published semiannually with 5-year cumulations; 1962– , issued quarterly with annual and 5-year cumulations.

This is an author-subject index of literature about administration of hospitals and related health care institutions.

A list of "Recent acquisitions" of the American Hospital Association Library (books, monographs, and journals) is included as a separate section.   Z6675.H75H67

Reviews

Bibliography of medical reviews. 1955– . Bethesda, Md., Nat. Lib. of Medicine, [1955?]– . Annual 1957–67; quinquennial 1966/70– .   **EK60**

Issues for 1956–67 numbered as v.2–12. v.6 is a cumulation, 1955 through 1960, superseding the annual volumes previously published for that period.

Each volume includes references to review articles in thousands of journals in many languages. Review articles include "articles which are well-documented surveys of the recent biomedical journal literature."—*Introd.* Excluded are histories of a subject, case reports with reviews as adjuncts to the main presentation, statistical and epidemiological surveys, bibliographies comprising only a list of references, monthly summaries of subject areas published as regular features in journals, subject reviews which are more appropriately considered refresher courses, and theses. Although some journals not indexed in *Index medicus* were covered prior to April 1965, all journals included since that date are also included in the *Index medicus*. Subject arrangement with name index.

From March 1965, appears monthly in each issue of *Index medicus*. Cumulated annually as part of *Cumulated index medicus (EK56)*.

Abstract journals

Abstracts of health care management studies. v.15– , Sept. 1978– . [Ann Arbor, Mich.], Health Administration Pr., 1978– . Quarterly.   **EK61**

Subtitle: An international journal with abstracts of studies of management, planning and public policy related to the delivery of health care.

Published for the Cooperative Information Center for Hospital Management Studies, the School of Public Health, the University of Michigan.

v.1–14, 1964–77, had title: *Abstracts of hospital management studies*.

Aims to "find significant new studies in health care management, published or unpublished, by research groups in the field. . . . To assemble current information from journals—and other pertinent literature. . . . [and] to publish abstracts of studies to keep researchers and practitioners up to date on work in the field, along with sources from which documents may be ordered."—*Purpose and policies.* Arrangement is by a classified system with 45 headings such as: Administrator and board, Admitting and bed control, Areawide planning: hospitals and related facilities, and Infection control. Author and subject indexes.   Z6675.H75A27

Aerospace medicine and biology; a continuing bibliography with indexes. Jan./Mar. 1964– . Wash., Scientific and Technical Information Branch, Nat. Aeronautics and Space Administration, 1964– .   **EK62**

Supersedes an earlier publication of the same title, issued 1952–63 (1952–53 called *Aviation medicine*).

Subtitle varies. Frequency varies.

References describe the "biological, physiological, psychological, and environmental effects to which man [and biological organisms of lower orders] is subjected during and following simulated or actual flight in the earth's atmosphere or in interplanetary space."—*Introd.* Although emphasis is placed on applied research, references to fundamental studies are also included. International coverage; signed annotations in English. Subject and personal author indexes in each volume are cumulated annually. Corporate source index.   Z6664.3.A36

Excerpta medica; the international medical abstracting service. Amsterdam, Excerpta Medica, 1947– . Monthly.   **EK63**

An important abstracting service listing articles from medical journals in all countries. Article titles are given in English translation and sometimes in the original language. Monthly issues are published for each section, with annual author and subject indexes for each.

Section titles have varied over the years; new sections have been added; some sections have split into two or more sections for a period of years, and these subsections have later been assigned new section numbers (usually continuing the volume numbering of the original section). The current section designations are:

Sec.1, Anatomy, anthropology, embryology and histology; Sec.2, Physiology; Sec.3, Endocrinology; Sec.4, Microbiology; Sec.5, General pathology and pathological anatomy; Sec.6, Internal medicine; Sec.7, Pediatrics and pediatric surgery; Sec.8, Neurology and neurosurgery; Sec.9, Surgery; Sec.10, Obstetrics and gynecology; Sec.11, Oto-, rhino-, laryngology; Sec.12, Ophthalmology; Sec.13, Dermatology and venereology; Sec.14, Radiology; Sec.15, Chest diseases; Sec.16, Cancer; Sec.17, Public health, social medicine and hygiene; Sec.18, Cardiovascular diseases; Sec.19, Rehabilitation and physical medicine; Sec.20, Gerontology and geriatrics; Sec.21, Developmental biology and teratology; Sec.22, Human genetics; Sec.23, Nuclear medicine; Sec.24, Anesthesiology; Sec.25, Hematology; Sec.26, Immunology, serology and transplantation; Sec.27, Biophysics, bioengineering and medical instrumentation; Sec.28, Urology and nephrology; Sec.29, Clinical biochemistry; Sec.30, Pharmacology and toxicology; Sec.31, Arthritis and rheumatism; Sec.32, Psychiatry; Sec.33, Orthopaedic surgery; Sec.34, Plastic surgery; Sec.35, Occupational health and industrial surgery; Sec.36, Health economics and hospital management; Sec.37, Drug literature index; Sec.38, Adverse reaction titles; Sec.40, Drug dependence; Sec.46, Environmental health and pollution control; Sec.47, Virology; Sec.48, Gastroenterology; Sec.49, Forensic science; Sec.50, Epilepsy; Sec.51, Leprosy and related subjects.   ●

Hospital abstracts: a monthly survey of world literature. London, Stat. Off., 1961– . v.1– . Monthly.   **EK64**

Prepared by the Dept. of Health and Social Security.

"Aims to cover the whole field of hospitals and their administration, with the exception of strictly medical and related professional matters."—*Note.*

Offers abstracts of journal articles and monographic materials. Classified arrangement with author index and a list of addresses of publications referred to in each issue. Foreign-language titles are given in English and in the original language; all abstracts are in English. Annual author and subject indexes.   RA960.H54

Tropical diseases bulletin. London, Bureau of Hygiene and Tropical Diseases, 1912– . v.1– . Monthly.   **EK65**

Published in association with *Abstracts on hygiene.* An international abstracting journal in classified arrangement, dealing with the various aspects of tropical diseases. Most articles are summarized; all summaries are in English. Includes a detailed table of contents and a listing of authors or sources in each monthly issue. Annual general index of subjects and index of authors or sources.

Encyclopedias and handbooks

American Heart Association. Heartbook; a guide to prevention and treatment of cardiovascular diseases. N.Y., Dutton, 1980. 370p. il.   **EK66**

Consists of articles written by specialists. Subjects covered include cardiovascular surgery, hypertension, cardiac emergencies, strokes, nutrition, and smoking. Indexed.   RC672.A44

The American Medical Association family medical guide. Ed. in chief, Jeffrey R.M. Kunz. N.Y., Random House, [1982]. 831p. il. (The American Medical Association home health library)   **EK67**

Compiled for the medical consumer, this book "shows how the body is structured, how it functions and what you must do to keep it healthy. It answers. . .questions about all the most common diseases and their symptoms."—*Pref.* Includes self-diagnosis charts, instructions for caring for the sick at home, essays on dying and death, and special problems such as infancy, adolescence, and aging. Indexed.
        RC81.A543

Bennington, James L. Saunders dictionary & encyclopedia of laboratory medicine and technology. Philadelphia, Saunders, [1984]. 1674p. il.   **EK68**

This dictionary "was created to provide in a single source comprehensive and authoritative definitions of terms used in the field. . . . [The compilers have] attempted to provide comprehensive coverage of currently used methods and techniques for laboratory analysis in the areas of clinical chemistry, biochemistry, toxicology, hematology. . .and respiratory medicine. For each test, assay, or examination, the basic principles of the methods or instrumentation, or both, used for analysis are discussed, along with the conditions that affect the accuracy and precision of detection and measurement, fundamentals of quality control, reference values, pathophysiologic alterations that produce abnormal values, and the chemical use of some applications of the procedures."—*Pref.* Appendixes include: cancer chemotherapy drugs, bacteriologic specimen collections, and reference ranges and laboratory values of clinical importance.   RB37.B453

Child health encyclopedia: the complete guide for parents. The Boston Children's Medical Center and Richard I. Feinbloom. N.Y., Delacorte Pr., [1975]. 561p.   **EK69**

An encyclopedia with detailed information contributed by specialists about children's diseases and conditions from infancy to adolescence. For a Spanish edition *see* below.   RJ26.C45

Children's Medical Center (Boston, Mass.). Enciclopedia de la salud del niño: guía complete para padres de familia. Mexico City, Diana, 1979. 359p.   **EK70**

A Spanish edition of the above.

Clark, Randolph Lee and **Cumley, Russell W.** The book of health: a medical encyclopedia for everyone. 3d ed. N.Y., Van Nostrand Reinhold, 1973. 925p. il.   **EK71**

1st ed. 1953.

"There are many things about the body and about the various diseases that the doctor does not have time to explain—things the patient should know in order to hold up his end of the medical partnership between physician and patient. It is hoped that these necessary explanations, which the physician often has to omit, may be found here. . . . many of today's physicians and scientists destined for future renown have edited the accounts of their contributions to medicine. Further, the care in its preparation and the expertness of knowledge of those who assisted make *The Book of Health* an acceptable source of information for the student of physiology and hygiene and for those preparing themselves for the study of medicine, nursing, dentistry, and technology."—*Foreword.* Includes comprehensive index and glossary.
For a Spanish edition *see* EK85.   RC81.C59

Conn's Current therapy; latest approved methods of treatment for the practicing physician. 1949– . Philadelphia, Saunders, 1949– . Annual.   **EK72**

Ed. by Howard F. Conn.
Presents authoritative, current methods of therapy. Arranged in ten sections offering broad coverage, e.g., infectious diseases, respiratory system, cardiovascular system, and diseases of allergy. Each section contains articles by specialists on more specific topics.
        RM101.C87

Cosminsky, Sheila and **Harrison, Ira E.** Traditional medicine. v.II, 1976–1981. N.Y., Garland, 1984. 324p. (Garland reference library of social science, v.147)   **EK73**

Subtitle: Current research with the implications for ethnomedicine, ethnopharmacology, maternal and child health, and public health: an annotated bibliography of Africa, Latin America, and the Caribbean.
Updates the compilers' earlier volume covering 1950–75 (EK81).
        Z5118.M4C67

Current emergency therapy. . . . Rockville, Md., Aspen Publ., 1984– . Annual.   **EK74**

Richard F. Edlich and Daniel A. Spyker, eds.
Description based on 1985 ed. An annual textbook "organized to allow the reader to assimilate the facts in a logical fashion in the shortest possible time. The physiologic bases of illness and injuries are therefore emphasized and the manifestations and diagnostic studies are considered as reflections of the pathophysiology. Therapy then becomes logical in the schematic presentation of information."—*Pref.* Intended for students and physicians but clear, concise presentations make information available for those who need to know, as in the cases of chronic illnesses. Indexed.   RC86.C87

Current medical diagnosis and treatment. 1974– . Los Altos, Calif., Lange Medical Pubns., [1974]– . Annual.   **EK75**

Also issued in German, Italian, Portuguese, Romanian, Serbo-Croation, and Spanish editions.
Supersedes *Current diagnosis & treatment* (1962–73).
"Intended to serve the practicing physician as a useful desk reference on widely accepted methods currently available for diagnosis and treatment."—*Pref. 1985.* Coverage ranges from general symptoms, fluid and electrolyte disorders, and skin and appendages to malignant disorders and immunologic disorders. Indexed.
        RC71.A14

Dimensions in wholistic healing: new frontiers in the treatment of the whole person. Chicago, Nelson-Hall, [1979]. 543p.   **EK76**

Ed. by Herbert A. Otto and James W. Knight.
31 signed, authoritative articles with literature references. Arranged in four parts: (1) the basis of wholistic healing (historic base and short history, general theory of psychic healing, and emerging medicine; (2) the framework of wholistic healing (utilizing the psychic or natural healer, nutrition and wholistic healing, etc.); (3) Western approaches to wholistic healing (self-regulatory therapies, biofeedback, dreams, etc.); (4) non-Western approaches to wholistic healing (Chinese medicine, acupuncture, Kundalini yoga, Tibetan art of healing, and Ayurvedic medicine). Includes directory of organizations and bibliography. Indexed.   R733.D53

The encyclopedia of alternative medicine and self-help. Devised and ed. by Malcolm Hulke. N.Y., Schocken, [1979]. 243p.   **EK77**

"This book is neither a recommendation nor a critique. It is a platform from which people holding different views may address you. An orthodox doctor read every entry to see if, in his view, any discipline could prove harmful. He found none."—*Foreword.* Contains about 80 articles ranging from "absent healing" and "acupuncture" through "Weight Watchers," "wine," and "yoga." List of contributors; directories of associations, products, training and treatment centers, and health spas and resorts. Bibliography; index.
        R733.E5

Facts at your fingertips. Ed.3– . [Hyattsville, Md.], U.S. Dept. of Health and Human Services, [1981–]. Biennial. (DHHS pubn.; no.(PHS) 81–1264)   **EK78**

Subtitle: A guide to sources of statistical information on major health topics.
1st ed. 1977. Previous title: *Facts at your fingertips—almost.*
Description based on 5th ed. 1981 (180p.). Under each topic the National Center for Health Statistics publications or data are cited first followed by other DHHS sources, other federal agencies, and private organizations or associations.   RA407.3.F22

Handbook of clinical neurology. Ed. by P. J. Vinken and G. W. Bruyn. Amsterdam, North-Holland Pub. Co.; N.Y., Wiley-Interscience, [1968–85]. v.1–48. il. (In progress)
EK79

Contents: v.1, Disturbances of nervous function; v.2, Localization in clinical neurology; v.3, Disorders of higher nervous activity; v.4, Disorders of speech, perception, and symbolic behaviour; v.5, Headaches and cranial neuralgias; v.6, Diseases of the basal ganglia; v.7–8, Diseases of nerves; v.9, Multiple sclerosis and other demyelinating diseases; v.10, Leucodystrophies and poliodystrophies; v.11–12, Vascular diseases of the nervous system; v.13, Neuroretinal degenerations; v.14, The phakomatoses; v.15, The epilepsies; v.16–18, Tumours of the brain and skull; v.19–20, Tumours of the spine and spinal cord; v.21–22, System disorders and atrophies; v.23–24, Injuries of the brain and skull; v.25–26, Injuries of the spine and spinal cord; v.27–29, Metabolic and deficiency diseases of the nervous system; v.30–31, Congenital malformations of the brain and skull; v.32, Congenital malformations of the spine and spinal cord; v.33–35, Infections of the nervous system; v.36–37, Intoxications of the nervous system; v.38–39, Neurological manifestations of systematic diseases; v.40–41, Diseases of muscle; v.42–43, Neurogenetic directory; v.44, Cumulative subject index for v.1–43; v.45, Clinical neuropsychology; v.46, Neurobehavioral disorders; v.47, Demyelinating diseases; v.48, Headaches.

Intends to present critical, balanced, and comprehensive views written by acknowledged experts to provide the clinical neurologist "with full information about any particular aspect of his subject with which he may find himself confronted."—*Pref.*   RC332.H3

Handbook of neurochemistry. Ed. by Abel Lajha. 2d ed. N.Y., Plenum, [1982–85]. 10v. il.   **EK80**

1st ed. 1969.
Contents: v.1, Chemical and cellular architecture; v.2, Experimental neurochemistry; v.3, Metabolism in the nervous system; v.4, Enzymes in the nervous system; v.5, Metabolic turnover in the nervous system; v.6, Receptors in the nervous system; v.7, Structural elements of the nervous system; v.8, Neurochemical systems; v.9, Alterations of metabolites in the nervous system; v.10, Pathological neurochemistry.

Each chapter is a concise and critical summary written by one or more specialists, with a supportive bibliography. Each volume is indexed.   QP356.3.H36

Harrison, Ira E. and **Cosminsky, Sheila.** Traditional medicine. [v.1, 1950–1975]. N.Y., Garland, 1976. 229p. (Garland reference library of social science, v.19)   **EK81**

Subtitle: Implications for ethnomedicine, ethnopharmacology, maternal and child health, mental health, and public health: an annotated bibliography of Africa, Latin America, and the Caribbean.

Traditional medicine means "native medical systems (healers, therapies, and belief)."—*Introd.* Covers the years from 1950 to 1975. Information is arranged by medical topics under Africa, Latin America, and the Caribbean. Mostly English language books, articles, dissertations, and papers. Author and country or area index.

For a continuation covering 1976–81 *see* EK73.   Z5118.M4H3

Hillman, Sheilah and **Hillman, Robert S.** Traveling healthy. N.Y., Penguin Bks., [1980]. 559p. il.   **EK82**

Subtitle: A complete guide to medical services in 23 countries.
Provides instructions and information on travel preparations for healthy, handicapped, and chronically ill travelers. The gazetteer lists languages spoken, emergency services, general information on doctors and hospital procedures for each country. Offers lists of emergency phone numbers in major cities for hospitals, specialists, dentists, and ambulances. Includes a listing of emergency language dictionaries, essential first aid and self-help information, and a pharmacopeia. Indexed.   RA783.5.H54

Inglis, Brian and **West, Ruth.** The alternative health guide. N.Y., Knopf, [1983]. 352p. il.   **EK83**

Gives descriptions of many non-traditional therapies not covered in traditional medical books. The first part discusses history, theory, and practice, and gives short explanations of therapies (e.g., natu-

ropathy, herbal medicine, homeopathy, chiropractic, and Alexander technique); psychotherapies (e.g., dream therapy and Gestalt); and paranormal therapies (e.g., exorcism, Christian Science, and psychic therapy). The second part deals with specific ailments such as allergies, cancer, and mental illness. Each condition is summarized, indicating the traditional medical therapy and where it fails; the guide then gives alternative therapies which have been shown to be effective. Bibliography and index.   R733.I497

Jacobs, David S. [and others]. Laboratory test handbook with DRG index. St. Louis, Mosby/Lexi Co., 1984. 848p.
EK84

"The handbook is intended as a quick reference for practitioners, residents, medical students, technologists, nurses and medical records personnel."—*Foreword.* This is a presentation of current laboratory tests information with emphasis on consensus of interpretations and practical considerations. References are included for more detailed information. Detailed instructions are included for DRG (diagnosis related groups). An index indicates those used for diagnostic purposes and those used for the management of an illness.   RB37.L22

El libro de la salud: una enciclopedia médica para todos. Mexico City, Continental, 1981. 982p. il.   **EK85**

Recomp. and ed. by Randolph Lee Clark and Russell W. Cumley. Trans. by Arturo Carrasco Sandoval.
Spanish ed. of *The book of health* (EK71).

Medical risks: patterns of mortality and survival. Lexington, Mass., D. C. Heath, Lexington Books, [1976]. 1v., various pagings.   **EK86**

A reference volume sponsored by The Association of Life Insurance Medical Directors of America and The Society of Actuaries.—*t.p.*

Richard B. Singer and Louis Levinson, eds.
"This book is a compilation of mortality and survival statistics in relation to risk factors identified in groups of people under follow-up observation."—*Chap.1.* The data were "known to exist in many published articles scattered throughout the medical literature. If articles could be retrieved, critically evaluated, and useful data presented on a comparative basis within a uniform format, it was thought that the resulting tables would be of value not only to medical directors, underwriters, and actuaries in the life insurance industry but also to many workers in the health sciences."—*Pref.*

The broad topical arrangement in pt.I, The text, and in pt. II, The tables, is the same: Physical, toxic and other risks; Cancer; Neuropsychiatric disorders; Cardiovascular disorders; Respiratory disorders; Digestive system diseases; Genitourinary diseases; Systemic disorders; Endocrine and metabolic diseases. Includes author and subject indexes.   RA407.M4

Merck manual of diagnosis and therapy. Ed.1– . Rahway, N.J., Merck, 1899– . il. Irregular.   **EK87**

Periodically revised to provide up-to-date medical information which will facilitate accurate diagnosis and promote effective treatment. Most entries include a definition or description, etiology, symptoms and signs, diagnosis, prognosis and treatment. Surgical procedures are rarely described. Includes tables and illustrations. Indexed.   RC71.M4

Salmon, Michael A. and **Lindenbaum, Richard H.** Developmental defects and syndromes. [Aylsbury, Eng.], HM&M Publ.; [Boston, Little, Brown, 1978]. 432p. il.   **EK88**

Offers descriptions of more than 200 rare syndromes to assist physicians in naming them. "Informal classification of syndromes has been attempted based largely on morphological data."—*Pref.* Index; cross references of syndromes, malformation type, and deficiency.   QM691.S23

Shakman, Robert A. Where you live may be hazardous to your health: a health index to over 200 American communities. N.Y., Stein & Day, [1979]. 260p. il., maps.   **EK89**

Approximately one-fourth of the text is devoted to articles on possible hazards: air pollution, allergies, climate, altitude and topography, natural disasters, and misconceptions about a healthy place to live. The profiles of the cities are arranged by state and give data on air pollution, climate, crime rate, natural disasters, and major allergies. Indexed. **RA565.S5**

Sourcebook on death and dying. James A. Fruehling, consulting ed. Chicago, Marquis Professional Pubns., [1982]. 788p. il. **EK90**

For full information *see* CC175.

Standard medical almanac. 2d ed. Chicago, Marquis Academic Media, [1980]. 712p. **EK91**

1st ed. 1977.

Contents: pt.1, Expenditures; pt.2, Personnel; pt.3, Education and licensure; pt.4, Facilities and ancillary services; pt.5, Disease, disability and health status; pt.6, Government and health status; pt.7, Indexes—author, organization and geographic.

Data for the almanac were collected from a health insurer, professional organizations, and government sources.

RA407.3.S73

Dictionaries

American Medical Association. CMIT: current medical information and terminology. 5th ed. [Chicago, 1981] 801p. **EK92**

[1st–3d eds.] 1963–66 had title *Current medical terminology.*

On cover: . . . for the naming and description of diseases and conditions in practice and in areas related to medicine.

The main section consists of 3,262 "preferred terms and definitions," with a definition and description of the disease, cause, physical signs, complications, and laboratory data. There is a section of cross references from French, German, and Spanish names of diseases, and a systematic classification of diseases. A KWIC index covering genus names, infections, geographic distributions of disease, genetic abnormalities, and organ involvements is included.

Black's Medical dictionary, by William R. Thompson. 34th ed. London, Black, 1984. 997p. il. **EK93**

1st ed. 1906.

A standard dictionary of British terminology. Each edition includes some new terms and revisions. **R121.B598**

Blakiston's Gould medical dictionary. Chairman of the editorial board, Arthur Osol. 4th ed. N.Y., McGraw-Hill, [1979]. 1632p. **EK94**

1st ed. 1949 and 2d ed. 1956 had title *Blakiston's New Gould medical dictionary.*

Subtitle: A modern comprehensive dictionary of the terms used in all branches of medicine and allied sciences; with illustrations and tables.

Based on Gould's *Medical dictionary* (5 eds. 1926–41) and its predecessors, published with varying titles in 1890, 1894, and 1904. More than 75,000 words are defined. Includes tables of anatomic structure, chemical constituents of the blood, common radioactive pharmaceuticals, etc. **R121.B62**

Butterworths medical dictionary. Macdonald Critchley, ed. in chief. 2d ed. London & Boston, Butterworths, [1978]. 1942p. **EK95**

First published in 1961 as *The British medical dictionary,* ed. by Sir Arthur Salusbury MacNalty.

Includes an appendix on anatomical nomenclature, relating Nomina Anatomica nomenclature to English equivalent. **R121.B75**

Dorland's Illustrated medical dictionary. 26th ed. Philadelphia, Saunders, [1981]. 1485p. il. **EK96**

[1st] ed. 1900.

Japanese, Spanish, and Braille editions are also available.

Designed to satisfy the conventional use of a dictionary, that is, to discover spelling, meaning, and derivation of specific terms and to assist in the creation of words by defining prefixes, suffixes, and stems. Includes a chapter on the "Fundamentals of medical etymology." **R121.D73**

Dox, Ida, Melloni, Biagio John and **Eisner, Gilbert M.** Melloni's Illustrated medical dictionary. 2d ed. Baltimore, Williams & Wilkins, [1985]. 533p. il. **EK97**

1st ed. 1979.

This dictionary is a "compilation of approximately 26,000 terms that comprise the common core of information for all of the health sciences, as well as a large number of terms most frequently used in the distinctive language of particular subspecialties: [it] was developed especially for students of the health sciences. . . . It will also be useful as a reference book for the general public. . . . It is the first dictionary of its size and scope to incorporate approximately 2,500 illustrations as visual components of the textual definitions of its terms."—*Pref.* **R121.D76**

Lawrence Urdang Associates. Urdang dictionary of current medical terms for health science professionals. N.Y., Wiley, [1981]. 455p. il. **EK98**

A clear, concise dictionary of current terminology in the basic sciences of anatomy, physiology, biochemistry, and pharmacology, as well as clinical medicine and surgery. **R121.L33**

Lorenzini, Jean A., comp. Medical phrase index. Oradell, N.J., Medical Economics Co., [1978]. 909p. **EK99**

Subtitle: A one-step reference to the terminology of medicine.

"For medical transcribers, medical records librarians, medical assistants, legal secretaries, insurance claims examiners—for anyone who must capture medical terminology accurately and quickly." —*Publ. notes.* Includes both formal and informal phrases which are cross-indexed for each major word. Entries are arranged alphabetically. For words with more than one spelling gives directions to common usage; sound-alikes are indicated. **R121.L865**

Medical word finder. 3d ed. Englewood Cliffs, N.J., Prentice-Hall, [1983]. 432p. **EK100**

Comp. by George Willeford.

1st ed. 1967.

A compact, easy-to-use guide to spelling, syllabication, and accentuation of frequently used medical terms. Includes word and prescription abbreviations. **R123.W47**

Stedman, Thomas Lathrop. Illustrated Stedman's medical dictionary. 24th ed. Baltimore, Williams & Wilkins, [1982]. 1678p. il. **EK101**

1st ed. 1911 entitled: *A practical medical dictionary;* title of later editions varies slightly.

A standard work frequently revised. The 24th edition offers approximately 100,000 entries. Includes a section on medical etymology with a comprehensive "Root word list"; appendixes include blood groups, laboratory analyses and observation (reference values), comparative temperature scales, weights and measures, and common Latin terms used in prescription writing. **R121.S77**

Taber's Cyclopedic medical dictionary. Ed. by Clayton L. Thomas. 15th ed. Philadelphia, Davis, [1985]. 2170p. **EK102**

1st ed. 1940.

An updated edition of this standard work giving definitions of medical terms and words. Pronunciation is given for all but the very common terms and the etymology for 90% of the words is included. The 18 appendixes include such information as emergency treatment, dietetic charts, Latin and Greek nomenclature, and normal reference laboratory values. **R121.T144**

Thompson, Robert. The Grosset encyclopedia of natural medicine. N.Y., Grosset & Dunlap, 1980. 291p. **EK103**

This compilation defines over 600 terms covering topics concerned "with natural medicine—Chinese acupuncture, iridology, reflexology, and kinesiology—and many other rediscovered or revived therapies."—*Introd.* Indexed. **RZ433.T47**

Specialized dictionaries

Etter, Lewis E. Glossary of words and phrases used in radiology, nuclear medicine, and ultrasound. 2d ed. Springfield, Ill., C. C. Thomas, [1970]. 355p. **EK104**

1st ed. 1960.

"Prepared from various sources for medical secretaries, x-ray technicians, medical students and residents in radiology [etc.]."—*t.p.* Covers more than 5,000 terms, including eponyms, with definitions, abbreviations, cross references and footnotes. Includes a list of radiological symbols and semantics, words which may be phonetically or otherwise confusing, suggested terminology for radiological reports, information on writing radiological reports, and sample radiological and ultrasonic reports. RM849.E87

Gastaut, Henri. Dictionary of epilepsy. Geneva, World Health Organization, 1973– . v.1– . (In progress?) **EK105**

Contents: pt.1, Definitions.

Published simultaneously in French and Spanish; a Russian edition is to follow. Pt.2 is to be a multilingual index to all four versions.

"The dictionary covers mainly terms pertaining to the clinical aspects of epilepsy. Terms used in neurophysiology and electroencephalography and clinical terms for conditions related to epilepsy . . . have not been included, with the exception of a few terms considered important for understanding certain clinical aspects of epilepsy."—*Introd.* Includes synonyms. RC372.A1G37

Jablonski, Stanley. Illustrated dictionary of eponymic syndromes and diseases and their synonyms. Philadelphia, Saunders, [1969]. 335p. il. **EK106**

Includes about 10,000 "eponymic names of pathological conditions named after the discoverers, literary and mythological characters and patients. All available eponyms used in naming clinical entities, animal diseases, experimental diseases (including cancers), important diagnostic signs, and pathological conditions are entered, along with their non-eponymic synonyms (descriptive names)."—*Introd.* Gives bibliographic citations, including a reference to the original description if it could be found. Numerous photographs and cross references. A term must have appeared in the literature at least twice to be included.

A complementary work is: R121.J24

U.S. National Library of Medicine. Index Section. Eponymous syndromes; MEDLARS indexing instructions. [Wash.], 1970. 132p. (PB-212064) **EK107**

Indicates the MeSH terms used for indexing the syndromes. Useful as a guide for machine searching as well as an aid for the user of *Index medicus* (EK52).

Leider, Morris and **Rosenblum, Morris.** A dictionary of dermatological words, terms, and phrases. N.Y., McGraw-Hill, [1968]. 440p. **EK108**

Nearly 3,000 entries with "thumbnail sketches of common or important diseases, abbreviated concepts of some theories, contextual variations of meaning and important historical or linguistic subtleties in addition to commonly accepted meanings and etymologic data."—*Pref.* Pronunciation is indicated. Includes many vernacular terms. RL39.L44

Magalini, Sergio. Dictionary of medical syndromes. 2d ed. Philadelphia, Lippincott, 1981. 944p. **EK109**

Alphabetic arrangement by name of syndrome, giving for each: synonyms, symptoms and signs, etiology, pathology, diagnostic procedures, therapy, prognosis, and bibliography. Indexed. RC69.M33

Regal, Waldo A. The inverted medical dictionary: a method of finding medical terms quickly. Westport, Conn., Technomic Publ. Co., 1976. 261p. **EK110**

"When the correct term is known, it is a simple matter of looking for its meaning in a standard medical dictionary. Conversely, when the meaning or situation is apparent but the proper medical term must be identified, the same dictionary is of little help. This book is a medical dictionary in reverse. Each 'meaning' has been reduced to a brief key phrase. Alphabetically arranged, each phrase is followed by the appropriate medical term. In many cases synonymous terms are included to enable the reader to select the most applicable one."—*Pref.* R121.R54

Thornton, Spencer P. Ophthalmic eponyms; an encyclopedia of named signs, syndromes, and diseases in ophthalmology. Birmingham, Ala., Aesculapius Pub. Co., [1967]. 324p. **EK111**

In two sections: (1) signs, syndromes, and diseases in medical, pediatric, and neuro-ophthalmology; and (2) eponyms in ophthalmic surgery. Arrangement is alphabetical within each section. Bibliographic references are included with most entries. RE21.T54

The way things work book of the body. N.Y., Simon & Schuster, [1979]. 541p. il. **EK112**

Translation and adaptation of *Der Mensch und seine Krankheiten* (1977).

Intended for the non-scientific reader. Contains over 250 articles with explanatory diagrams on such subjects as structure and function of the heart, tetanus, slipped disc, muscles, and acne. Indexed. RC81.V29

Foreign terms

Bunjes, Werner Ernst. Medical and pharmaceutical dictionary: English-German. 4th ed., with a supplement comprising more than 17,000 new entries. Stuttgart, G. Thieme, 1981. various pagings. **EK113**

1st ed. 1953 and 2d ed. 1968–69 also formed v.2 of *German-English, English-German dictionary for physicians* (EK116). 2d ed. also issued as v.2 of *Deutsch-Englisches, Englisch-Deutsches Wörterbuch für Aerzte* by F. Lejeune.

A comprehensive dictionary which includes eponyms, abbreviations, and acronyms. An entry consists of the English term, pronunciation, and German equivalents. R121.B86

Elsevier's Medical dictionary in five languages: English/American, French, Italian, Spanish, and German. Comp. and arr. on an English base by A. Sliosberg. 2d ed. rev. Amsterdam, Elsevier, 1975. 1452p. **EK114**

Includes more than 20,000 numbered English-language entries, exclusive of associated and compound terms. ". . . the first part comprises the English terms with their equivalents in the other four languages. The second section consists of indexes in the other languages, each referring back to the numbered entries in the first part."—*Pref.* A list of English synonyms is provided. R121.E5

Finch, Bernard Ephraim. Multilingual guide for medical personnel. Flushing, N.Y., Medical Examination Pub. Co., [1967]. 159p. il. **EK115**

Originally published under title *Being ill* (London, 1963).

Contains expressions, questions, and directions in English, French, Italian, German, Spanish, and Russian for medical personnel. R121.F48

Lejeune, Fritz and **Bunjes, Werner E.** German-English, English-German dictionary for physicians. 2d ed. Stuttgart, Thieme Verlag; N.Y., Intercontinental Medical Book Corp., 1968–69. 2v. **EK116**

Added title page in German.

Contents: v.1, German-English (2d ed., compl. rev.); v.2, English-German (2d ed., unrevised; for 4th ed. 1981 *see* EK113).

1st ed. 1951.

Includes some 85,000 entries covering all fields of medicine, but with restrictive coverage of peripheral fields and anatomical terms. Quasi-medical words, although formerly included, are omitted from this edition. R121.L373

Lexicon medicum: Anglicum, Russicum, Gallicum, Germanicum, Latinum, Polonum. Warszawa, Państwowy Zakład Wydawnictw Lekarskich, 1971. 1603p.   **EK117**

Includes nearly 20,000 terms arranged on an English alphabetical base, with Russian, French, German, Latin, and Polish equivalent terms in parallel columns, and indexes from the other languages.
R121.L44

Veillon, E. Medical dictionary. Medizinisches Wörterbuch. Dictionnaire medical. 5th ed. N.Y., Springer; rev. and enl. by Albert Nobel. Bern, Verlag Hans Huber, [1969]. 1329p.   **EK118**

1st ed. 1950.
"The main section contains the respective English, German (along with the Latin terms) and French terms running parallel and with consecutive numeration."—*Introd.* The 40,944 numbered entries in the main section are followed by indexes in German and French.
R121.V4

Abbreviations

Hughes, Harold Kenneth. Dictionary of abbreviations in medicine and the health sciences. Lexington, Mass., Lexington Books, 1977. 313p.   **EK119**

Covers usage in the United States, Canada, Great Britain, Ireland, other parts of English-using Europe, Australasia, southern Africa, and the United Nations. Contains more than 12,000 entries with some 20,000 meanings. The abbreviations included are used in all areas of medicine and the health sciences, e.g., clinical, research, and production activities in all phases of professional care; food and energy resources; remedial education; veterinary science; and safety. The appendix provides conversion tables for weights, measures, and temperatures.   R121.H89

Roody, Peter, Forman, Robert E. and **Schweitzer, Howard B.** Medical abbreviations and acronyms. N.Y., McGraw-Hill, 1977. 255p.   **EK120**

Attempts to "set forth, in an orderly and easily accessible fashion, the most common medical and health-related abbreviations and their preferred forms . . . efforts were directed at standardization." —*Pref.* Over 14,000 entries with cross references.   R121.R77

Steen, Edwin Benzel. Baillière's Abbreviations in medicine. 5th ed. London, Philadelphia, Baillière Tindall, [1984]. 255p.   **EK121**

1st ed. 1960.
This pocket book lists more than 15,000 common medical and related abbreviations. Includes bibliography.   R123.S84

Style manuals

The medical and scientific authors' guide. N.Y., Le Jacq Publ., [1984]. 1082p.   **EK122**

Subtitle: An international reference guide for authors to more than 500 medical and scientific journals.
Comp. by Joan Banes.
An alphabetically arranged listing of instructions to authors. Includes a list of journals by subject.   R119.M4

U.S. National Cancer Institute. A compilation of journal instructions to authors. [Bethesda, Md.], Dept. of Health, Education and Welfare, Public Health Service, Nat. Institutes of Health, Nat. Cancer Inst., 1979. 440p. (DHEW pubn. no. (NIH) 80- 1991)   **EK123**

Information is taken from a group of 219 journals which represents the "majority of journals to which National Cancer Institute research investigators might submit manuscripts for publication." —*Introd.*

Directories

International

Medical research centres: a world directory of organizations and programmes. Consultant eds. Leslie T. Morton and Jean F. Hall. Ed.5- . Harlow, [Eng.], Longman (distr. in U.S.A. by Gale), [1983]- . Irregular.   **EK124**

1st–4th eds. 1945–71 entitled: *Medical research index.*
Description based on 6th ed. 1983 (2v., 1350p.). Aims "to provide a comprehensive world directory of establishments conducting research in the medical and biochemical fields."—*Foreword.* Research establishments in 109 countries are arranged alphabetically by country; includes address, scope of interest, and key personnel.
R850.M43

World directory of medical schools. [Ed.1]- . Geneva, World Health Organization, 1953- . Irregular.   **EK125**

Description based on 5th ed. 1979 (538p.). "Lists institutions of undergraduate medical education in 106 countries and areas and gives a few pertinent facts about each. The information presented reflects the situation in various countries during the academic year 1975/76."—*Introd.*

United States

Allied health education directory. Ed. 7- . 1978- . Chicago, [Amer. Medical Assoc.], Committee on Allied Health Education and Accreditation, 1978- . Annual.   **EK126**

Continues: *Allied medical education directory,* 1972–76.
Contents (13th ed. 1985): I, Allied health education and accreditation; II, Occupational and educational programs information; III, Institutional sponsors of accredited allied programs.
Four appendixes include statistical information; glossary of terms, acronyms and initials; organizational references to individuals on AMA Council on Medical Education etc.; comparative tables on sponsorship, fees, and review committees.   R847.D57

American Hospital Association. The AHA guide to the health care field. 1972- . Chicago, Amer. Hospital Assoc., 1972- . Annual.   **EK127**

Supersedes the "Guide issue" of *Hospitals* (1949–71) which in turn superseded the *American hospital directory* (1945–48).
Provides "a central reference source for information on health care institutions, on the American Hospital Association, on organizations and agencies in the health field, and on national hospital statistical data."—*Introd. (1985).* Beginning with the 1972 volume, the section on hospital statistics has been enlarged and published as a separate booklet, *Hospital statistics.*

American medical directory. Ed.1- . Chicago, Amer. Medical Assoc., 1906- . Biennial.   **EK128**

Subtitle (varies): Directory of physicians in the United States, Puerto Rico, Virgin Islands, certain Pacific Islands and U.S. physicians temporarily located in foreign countries.
Publisher varies; frequency varies; publication suspended after v.25, 1969; resumed publication with the 26th ed. in 1973. The 28th ed., 1982, is in 4v.: pt.1, Alphabetical index of physicians; pt.2–4, Geographical register of physicians.   R712.A1A6

American Osteopathic Association. Yearbook and directory of osteopathic physicians. Ed.1- . Chicago, Amer. Osteopathic Assoc., [1899]- . Annual.   **EK129**

1st ed. 1899; annual since 1904. Title varies.
Description based on 76th ed., 1984, which includes membership listing for 1983–84 fiscal year, accreditation information for the year July 1984–July 1985; also includes AOA information—officers, copies of official documents, licensing information, etc. Main entry is in geographic section with an alphabetical index of physicians.

Association of American Medical Colleges. Medical school admission requirements. United States and Canada.

Ed.27– , 1977/78– . Evanston, Ill., Assoc. of Amer. Medical Colleges, 1978– . Annual. **EK130**

Continues: *Admission requirements of American medical colleges* (1951–57); *Admission requirements of American medical colleges, including Canada* (1957/58–63/64); *Medical school admission requirements. U.S.A. and Canada* (1964/65–76/77).

Contents, 1986/87: Nature of medical education; premedical planning; deciding whether and where to apply to medical school; Medical College Admission Test and American Medical College Application Service; medical school application and selection process; financial information for medical students; information for minority group students; information for applicants not admitted to medical school; information for high school students; information about U.S. medical schools; and information about Canadian medical schools.

The Association also publishes the *AAMC curriculum directory* (1972/73–) which gives data on required courses, conferences, laboratory periods, electives, opportunities for early specialization, etc. The annual *AAMC directory of American medical education* (title varies) lists member institutions, with information on their facilities and administration. R745.A8

Directory for exceptional children. . . . Ed.1– . Boston, Sargent, 1954– . Biennial (irregular). **EK131**

For full information *see* CB247.

Directory of medical specialists. Ed.15– , 1973/74– . Chicago, Publ. for the Amer. Board of Medical Specialties by Marquis, [1973]– . Biennial. **EK132**

Continues the *Directory of medical specialists holding certification by American specialty boards,* first publ. 1940. Title varies slightly.

Description based on 22d ed., 1985/86 (publ. 1984 in 4v.). Gives a "listing of physicians certified by 23 Specialty Boards of the American Board of Medical Specialties."—*Introd.* For each physician includes: name, certification(s), type of practice, birth date and place, education, career history, teaching positions, military record, professional memberships, office address and phone number. Includes an outline of certification requirements for each specialty and a statement of its purpose and function. R712.A1D57

Directory of national information sources on handicapping conditions and related services. [3d ed.] Wash., U.S. Dept. of Education, Off. of Special Education and Rehabilitation Services, Clearinghouse on the Handicapped, 1982. 263p. (Pubn. no.E-82-22007) **EK133**

For full information *see* CC194.

Directory of nursing homes. [Ed.1]– . [Phoenix, Ariz.], Oryx Pr., 1982– . Biennial? **EK134**

Subtitle: A state-by-state listing of facilities and services.
Description based on 2d ed. 1984 (1301p.) ed. by Sam Mongeau.
Entries include name of home, administrators and medical personnel, licensure, ownership, admission requirements, facilities, activities, and description of specialties, i.e., language spoken, religious affiliation, patient transportation, recreation, etc. Index for religious/fraternal/maternal affiliation. Alphabetic listing of facilities. RA997.A2D49

Directory of residency training programs accredited by the Accreditation Council. 1981/82– . Chicago, Amer. Medical Assoc., 1981– . Annual. **EK135**

Continues: *Directory of approved internship and residences* (1952–73/74). Title varies slightly.
Contents: 1. Information about accreditation; 2. Requirements for accreditation of programs—covers general and 55 specialties; 3. Summary of statistics on graduate medical education in the U.S.; 4. Directory of accredited residency programs—giving name of institution, address, program director, length of program and number of positions; 5. A directory of accredited institutions. The five appendixes cover: Combined medicine/pediatric programs, Certification requirements, Medical licensure requirements, List of medical schools in the U.S., and Abbreviations used. R840.D522

Encyclopedia of medical organizations and agencies. Ed. by Anthony T. Kruzas. Detroit, Gale, 1983. 768p. **EK136**

Subtitle: A subject guide to medical societies, professional and voluntary associations, foundations, research institutes, federal and state agencies, medical and allied health schools, information centers, data base services, and related health care organizations.

Arrangement is by subject from the most general to the specific. Major divisions include national and international associations, state and federal agencies, research centers, and information and database services. Indexed. R15.E52

Kruzas, Anthony, comp. Health services directory. Detroit, Gale, [1981]. 620p. **EK137**

Subtitle: A topical guide to clinics, treatment centers, rehabilitation facilities, counseling/diagnostic services, and care programs, with descriptions of related human service institutions, agencies, associations and other sources of information for each topic.

Appendix A: Related medical and social service organizations. Appendix B: Community information and referral services. Index of organizations and keywords.

This directory is to form v.3 of the 3d ed. (to be publ. 1986) of *Medical and health information directory* (below).

Medical and health information directory. [Ed.1]– . Detroit, Gale, [1977]– . **EK138**

Subtitle: A guide to associations, agencies, companies, institutions, research centers, hospitals, clinics, treatment centers, educational programs, publications, audiovisuals, data banks, libraries and information services in clinical medicine, basic bio-medical sciences, and the technological and socio-economic aspects of health care.

Anthony Thomas Kruzas, ed.

Description based on 3d ed. 1985 (3v.). Contents: v.1, Organizations, agencies and institutions; v.2, Libraries, publications, audiovisuals, and data base services; v.3, [to be publ.] Clinics, treatment centers, rehabilitation facilities, care programs and counseling/diagnostic services (to replace *Health services directory,* EK137). Entries include name, address, membership, purpose, meetings, and publications. R118.4.V6M4

National health directory. [9th ed.]. Rockville, Md., Aspen System Publ., 1985. 650p. **EK139**

John T. Grupenhoff, ed.
1st ed. 1977.

In addition to previous federal coverage, this edition has been expanded to include name, title, address, and telephone number of the following: governors, state health officers and legislative committees, all county and city health officials, federal regional officers including officials of the Professional Standards Review Organization, health systems agencies, state health planning and development agencies, and Medicare/Medicaid fiscal intermediaries and agencies. RA7.5.N37

Research programs in the medical sciences. [Ed.1]– . Comp. and ed. by Jaques Cattell Pr. N.Y., Bowker, 1981– . Biennial. **EK140**

Intended to "complement the database already containing *Industrial Research Laboratories of the United States* [EA196] and *Energy Research Programs* [EJ267]."—*Pref.*

Subject fields covered are medicine, biomedical science and engineering, dentistry, mental health, medical technology, pharmaceuticals and pharmacology, instrumentation therapeutics, health care, environmental and occupational health, and veterinary science. Arranged alphabetically by organization. For corporations, headquarters listings are followed by central research and development center, if any, and then by a listing of divisions and subsidiaries. For academic institutions gives name of university or college, then departments and divisions. For government units gives the hierarchical listing of various sections, etc. Geographic, personnel, and subject indexes.

The Saunders health care directory 84/85. Philadelphia, Saunders, [1984]. 894p. **EK141**

"A general information source designed specifically for health care professionals and librarians."—*General introd.*

In forty chapters, covers a range of topics such as adoption, programs for the aged, ambulance manufacturers, architects, associations, organizations and societies, professional schools, and sex education and counseling. Each chapter is arranged by state then alphabetically by the name of the organization. Gives address and telephone number.   R712.A1S28

Who's who in health care: Ed.1– . N.Y., Hanover Publ., 1977– . Irregular.   **EK142**

Contains biographical sketches, detailing professional background and achievements. "Every effort was made to insure the inclusion of the Nation's leadership in every possible aspect of the health care field, including: schools, pharmaceutical and insurance industries, voluntary associations, researchers, consultants, hospital executives, etc."—*Pref.*   R712.A1W35

Canada

Canadian hospital directory. Annuaire des hôpitaux du Canada. [Ed.1]– . [Toronto, Canadian Hospital Assoc.], 1953– . Annual.   **EK143**

Includes: Buyers' guide and statistical compendium.
Text in English and French.
Description based on 33d ed. (1985). Lists provincial hospital/health associations, Canadian Hospital Association (personnel), Association of Canadian Teaching Hospitals, Canadian Association of Paediatric Hospitals/Canadian Institute of Child Health, and outpatient health service centres. Includes comparison of provincial hospital plans and of their medical/health plans and education programs for personnel.   RA983.A1C3

Canadian medical directory. 1955– . Toronto, Seccombe House, 1954– . Annual.   **EK144**

Imprint varies.
Provides a list of qualified Canadian physicians, alphabetically, giving name, address, school, etc. Also includes a geographic list of physicians, and general lists of medical schools, nursing schools, hospitals, medical journals, etc.   R713.01.C3

Great Britain

Directory of medical and health care libraries in the United Kingdom and Republic of Ireland. 5th ed. London, Library Assoc., 1982. 228p.   **EK145**

1st ed. 1957; 4th ed., 1976, entitled *Directory of medical libraries in the British Isles.*
For each library listed gives location, stack policy, hours, holdings, classifications, computer facilities and availability, and user accessibility. Indexed by personal name, establishment, country, special collection, and library type.   Z675.M4L5

The medical directory, 1845– . London, Churchill, 1845– . Annual.   **EK146**

Title varies.
Lists registered practitioners in London, the provinces, Wales, Scotland, Ireland, abroad, and in the armed forces, giving brief biographical information. Includes lists of universities, colleges, medical schools, hospitals, associations, etc., and geographical lists of physicians in London, England, Wales, and Monmouthshire, Scotland, and Ireland.   R713.29.M4

Medical register, printed and publ. under the direction of the General Medical Council . . . comprising the names and addresses of medical practitioners. . . . London, publ. for the General Medical Council by Constable, 1859– . Annual.   **EK147**

Subtitle varies.
Brief directory information only, consisting of address, date and place of registration, qualifications. Includes names from the Commonwealth and foreign lists.

History

Bibliography

Bibliography of the history of medicine of the United States and Canada, 1939–1960. Ed. by Genevieve Miller. Baltimore, Johns Hopkins Pr., [1964]. 428p.   **EK148**

A consolidation of the annual bibliographies reprinted from the *Bulletin of the history of medicine,* covering the years 1939 through 1960. Classified arrangement; author index. A section, "Biography," p.1–126, lists books and periodical articles about persons under the names of the biographees.

——— 1961–64. Annual.

Ceased publication.

Bibliography of the history of medicine. no.1– , 1965– . Bethesda, Md., U.S. Public Health Service, 1966– . Annual, with quinquennial cumulations.   **EK149**

"Focuses on the history of medicine and its related sciences, professions, and institutions."—*Introd.* Works on the general history and philosophy of science are largely excluded. Includes journal articles, monographs and analytic entries for symposia, congresses, etc., and chapters in general monographs. Attempts to avoid extensive duplication of topics regularly covered in the *Isis* "Critical bibliographies" (*see* EA206, EA215). There is, however, considerable duplication between this publication and the *Current work in the history of medicine* (below); thus the quarterly, noncumulative aspects of the latter must be weighed against the cumulative feature of this annual.
The 1965 volume includes some material from 1964, and older items not prior to 1964 continue to be added in successive volumes. Subject and author listings.
Cumulative volumes have appeared as: Z6660.B582

——— 1964/69, 1970/74, 1975/79. [Bethesda, Md.], Nat. Lib. of Medicine, 1972–[81]. 3v. (1475p., 1069p., 924p.)

Current work in the history of medicine: an international bibliography. London, Wellcome Historical Medical Lib., 1954– . v.1– . Quarterly.   **EK150**

A quarterly index of articles on the history of medicine, arranged by subject, with an author index in each issue. International coverage. A list of new books on the history of medicine and science is provided at the end of each issue. No cumulation of the references is published, but a retrospective cumulative index is maintained at the Wellcome Library.   R131.A1C8

Guerra, Francisco. American medical bibliography, 1639–1783. N.Y., Lathrop C. Harper, 1962. 885p. facsims. (Yale Univ. Dept. of the History of Science and Medicine. Pubn. 40)   **EK151**

Subtitle: A chronological catalogue, and critical and bibliographical study of books, pamphlets, broadsides, and articles in periodical publications relating to the medical sciences—medicine, surgery, pharmacy, dentistry, and veterinary medicine—printed in the present territory of the United States of America during British dominion and the Revolutionary War.
In three sections: (1) books, pamphlets, broadsides; (2) almanacs; and (3) periodical publications: magazines and newspapers. Gives detailed bibliographic information, with references to other historical sources.   Z6659.G8

Kelly, Emerson Crosby. Encyclopedia of medical sources. Baltimore, Williams & Wilkins, 1948. 476p.   **EK152**

The author "kept a list of references to medical eponyms and original works. . . . A search for the earliest *or* best article has been conducted and great care has been exercised in copying the correct title with exact reference."—*Pref.* This bibliography of first-to-publish articles is arranged alphabetically by investigator/author and gives the contribution with its citation in the literature. Includes an index to the specific condition, disease, medication, treatment, test, etc.   Z6658.K4

Morton, Leslie T. A medical bibliography (Garrison and Morton); an annotated check-list of texts illustrating the history of medicine. 4th ed. Hampshire, Gower, [1983]. 1000p. **EK153**

1st ed. 1943.

A classified bibliography of books and periodical articles in various languages and of all periods from early times to the present. Classed arrangement with brief annotations indicating the significance of the work in the history and development of the medical sciences. Indexed. Z6658.G243

Osler, *Sir* **William.** Bibliotheca Osleriana; a catalogue of books illustrating the history of medicine and science, collected, arranged and annotated by Sir William Osler . . . bequeathed to McGill University. Oxford, Clarendon Pr., 1929. 785p. **EK154**

7,787 numbered entries in classed arrangement. Particularly valuable for its annotations. Z6676.O86

Subject catalogue of the history of medicine and related sciences. [London, Wellcome Inst. for the History of Medicine]; München, Kraus Internat., [1980]. 18v. **EK155**

Contents: v.1–9, Subject section; v.10–13, Topographical section; v.14–18, Biographical section.

This subject card catalogue of the library "is not an index to the entire collection, but is probably one of the most comprehensive guides in existence to the modern secondary literature of the history of medicine and allied sciences."—*Pref.*

Coverage is from 1954 to 1977. Over 200 journals are regularly indexed; articles from journals not directly related to the field are retrieved from MEDLARS. This catalogue includes more than is covered in the Library's *Current work in the history of medicine* (EK150) and, since it includes all the entries listed in *Current work* . . . , it also serves as an index to the latter. Z6660.8.W44

Historical surveys

Bordley, James, and **McGehee, A. Harvey.** Two centuries of American medicine, 1776–1976. Philadelphia, Saunders, 1976. 844p. **EK156**

Contents: pt.1, The first century—1776–1876; pt.2, Period of scientific advance—1987–1946; pt.3, Period of explosive growth—1946–1976; Appendix A, Population figures; Appendix B, Chronological summary of major events in American medical history.

The purpose is "to relate in language that can be understood by interested laymen, as well as the physician, an account of the extraordinary advances in medical education and in the prevention and treatment of disease that have taken place during the two centuries of this nation's political independence."—*Pref.* Includes bibliography and index. R151.B58

Castiglioni, Arturo. A history of medicine, tr. from the Italian and ed. by E. B. Krumbhaar. 2d ed. rev. and enl. N.Y., Knopf, 1947. 1192p. il. **EK157**

Does not supersede Garrison (below), but serves to supplement it. Comprehensive and readable. Especially strong in coverage of Greek and Roman history of medicine. Includes a useful bibliography (p.1147–92) arranged by subject. Index of subjects and index of names. R131.C272

Garrison, Fielding Hudson. Introduction to the history of medicine, with medical chronology, suggestions for study and bibliographic data. 4th ed. rev. and enl. Philadelphia, Saunders, 1929. 996p. il. (Repr. 1960) **EK158**

The most valuable reference history in English, covering the whole history of medicine from the earliest times to the 1920s. Much biography and bibliography are included for every period. Appendixes include: a chronology of medicine and public hygiene; hints on the study of medical history; bibliographic notes for collateral reading including histories of medicine, medical biography, and histories of special subjects. Index of personal names and index of subjects. R131.G3

Packard, Francis Randolph. History of medicine in the United States. N.Y., Hoeber, 1931. 2v. (1323p.) il. (Repr.: N.Y., Hafner, 1963. 2v.) **EK159**

An enlargement of the author's earlier work (1901). Contains much useful reference material, in both text and illustrations, on American medical history, biography, and bibliography. Gives a bibliography of pre-Revolutionary medical publications, p.489–512, and a general bibliography, p.1241–66. R151.P12

Biography
Bibliography

Thornton, John Leonard. A select bibliography of medical biography: with an introductory essay on medical biography. 2d ed. London, Lib. Assoc., 1970. 170p. il. (Lib. Assoc. Bibliographies, no.3) **EK160**

1st ed. 1961, by Thornton, A. J. Monk and E. S. Brooke.

Contains citations to books in English published in the 19th and 20th centuries. Includes more than 400 biographees, with several entries for many of them. Nearly 100 collective biographies are listed in a separate section. Indexed. Z6660.5.T5

International

Bailey, Hamilton and **Bishop, W. J.** Notable names in medicine and surgery. 3d ed. London, H. K. Lewis, 1959. 216p. il. **EK161**

Includes 79 biographical sketches of men whose names are associated with particular diseases or other medical discoveries, e.g., Potter's disease, Thomas's splint. Includes a list of biographies for additional reading. Indexed. R134.B3

Biographisches Lexikon der hervorragenden Ärzte aller Zeiten und Völker, unter Mitwirkung [von] E. Albert . . . A. Anagnostakis [u. A.] und unter Special-Redaktion von E. Gurlt und A. Wernich, hrsg. von August Hirsch. 2. Aufl. durchgesehen und ergänzt von F. Hübotter und H. Vierordt. Berlin, Urban, 1929–35. 5v. and Ergänzungsband. ports. (Repr.: Berlin, Urban, 1962) **EK162**

A very valuable medical biographical dictionary, international in scope, covering physicians who had achieved prominence before 1880. Includes biographical facts, bibliography of works by, and sometimes bibliographical references for further information. The *Ergänzungsband* includes corrections and additions to the main set.

To a large extent replaces its own first edition published 1884–88, and the *Biographisches Lexikon hervorragender Ärzte des neunzehnten Jahrhunderts* by Julius Leopold Pagel (Berlin, 1901), though occasionally these are useful for material omitted in the 2d ed.

Continued by: Z6658.B61

Fischer, Isidor. Biographisches Lexikon der hervorragenden Ärzte der letzten 50 Jahre, . . . Zugleich Fortsetzung des Biographischen Lexikons der hervorragenden Ärzte aller Zeiten u. Völker. Berlin, Urban, 1932–33. 2v. ports. (Repr.: Berlin, Urban, 1962) **EK163**

Serves as a continuation of the preceding set, covering the period from 1880 to 1930. Similar in scope, though the articles are somewhat briefer. Z6658.B62

International medical who's who: a biographical guide in the biomedical sciences. 2d ed. Harlow, [Eng.], Longman (distr. in U.S.A. by Gale), [1985]. 2v. **EK164**

1st ed. 1980.

A biographical dictionary which provides professional and personal information for more than 16,000 individuals from about 100 countries working for research institutions and industrial firms. R134.I57

New York Academy of Medicine. Library. Catalog of biographies. Boston, G. K. Hall, 1960. 165p. **EK165**

A photographic reproduction of the Library's shelflist, containing "single biographies of physicians and scientists, with a few autobiographies, family histories and occasional biographies written by physicians."—*Introd.*   R134.N4

Nobelstiftelsen, Stockholm. Physiology or medicine. Amsterdam, N.Y., Elsevier, 1964–72. 4v. il.   **EK166**

Contents: [v.1] 1901–1921 (1967); [v.2] 1922–1941 (1965); [v.3] 1942–1962 (1964); [v.4] 1963–1970 (1972).

At head of title: Nobel lectures, including presentation speeches and laureates' biographies.

Text in English.   QH311.N6

Sourkes, Theodore L. Nobel prize winners in medicine and physiology, 1901–1965. [New and rev. ed.] London and N.Y., Abelard-Schuman, [1967]. 464p. il.   **EK167**

Previous ed. by Lloyd G. Stevenson, covering 1901–50, published 1953.

Contains short biographical sketch of each prize winner, followed by a description of his prize discovery and an explanation of its meaning and importance. In addition to new chapters for the 1951–65 period, earlier biographies have been brought up-to-date in this edition, and some explanatory matter in the earlier chapters has been changed. Entries are chronologically arranged; name and subject indexes.   R149.S6

Talbot, Charles H. and **Hammond, Eugene A.** The medical practitioners in medieval England; a biographical register. London, Wellcome Historical Medical Lib., 1965. 503p. (Pubns. of the Wellcome Historical Medical Lib., 8)   **EK168**

Inspired by Ernest Wickersheimer's *Dictionnaire biographique des médecins en France au Moyen Âge* (Paris, 1936), but entries are generally longer than in that work. The period covered is from Anglo-Saxon times to about 1518, and physicians of England, Scotland, and Wales are included. Bibliographical references follow the articles, and the general index offers geographical and a wide variety of topical subject approaches.   R489.A1T3

American

See also EK132.

Dictionary of American medical biography. Westport, Conn., Greenwood Pr., [1984]. 2v. (1027p.)   **EK169**

Martin Kaufman, Stuart Galishoff, and Todd L. Savitt, eds.

Includes over 1,000 persons from the 17th century to those of the 20th century who had died prior to Dec. 31, 1976. "The major contribution of [this] work is the inclusion of biographical sketches representing developments which ocurred after the publication of Kelly and Burrage [EK171]."—*Pref.* The coverage is determined from various perspectives—blacks and women; non-physicians such as biochemists, medical educators, administrators; and those "persons outside the mainstream of American medicine—health faddists, patent medicine manufacturers, unorthodox practitioners, and others whose major role was to provide alternatives to traditional medicine."

A typical entry gives full name, date and place of birth, date and place of death, occupation and area of specialization, parents' names and occupations, marital information, career information, contributions, and a maximum of five citations to important or representative works. The appendix gives a listing by date of birth, place of birth, state where prominent, occupation and specialty, medical college or graduate level college, and females. Indexed.   R153.D53

Jaques Cattell Press. Biographical directory of the American College of Physicians, 1979. Comp. for the College by Jaques Cattell Pr. N.Y., Bowker, 1979. 1905p.   **EK170**

Previous ed. 1973.

Contains information for over 28,000 members. Each profile includes complete educational background, professional and academic activities, etc. Arranged by state and city; index of names.   R712.A1J36

Kelly, Howard Atwood and **Burrage, Walter L.** Dictionary of American medical biography. N.Y., Appleton, 1928. 1364p. (Repr.: Boston, Milford House, 1971)   **EK171**

Published in 1912 as *Cyclopedia of American medical biography,* and in 1920 as *American medical biographies.*

Good biographies, with bibliographies, of 2,049 deceased American physicians and surgeons from colonial days to 1927. Although each edition includes new biographical sketches, some material is dropped from each, and therefore the earlier editions may still be useful.   R153.K3

Pekkanen, John. The best doctors in the U.S.: a guide to the finest specialists, hospitals and health centers. N.Y., Seaview Books, 1979. 290p.   **EK172**

About 2,500 physicians' names arranged by their specialties. Introduction explains method of research and selection for the book.   R712.A1P44

British

Royal College of Physicians of London. The roll of the Royal College of Physicians of London, comprising biographical sketches of all the eminent physicians whose names are recorded in the annals . . . by William Munk. 2d ed., rev. and enl. London, publ. by the College, 1878–1984. v.1–7. (In progress)   **EK173**

v.4–7 have title: *Lives of the fellows.* Often cited as "Munk's roll." Imprint varies.

Contents: v.1, 1518 to 1700; v.2, 1701 to 1800; v.3, 1801 to 1825; v.4, 1826–1925 (comp. by G. H. Brown); v.5, Continued to 1965 (ed. by R. R. Trail); v.6, Continued to 1975 (ed. by G. Wolstenholme); v.7, Continued to 1983 (ed. by G. Wolstenholme).

v.1–3 have subtitle: Comprising biographical sketches of all eminent physicians, whose names are recorded in the annals from the foundation of the College in 1518 to its removal in 1825 from Warwick Lane to Pall Mall East.

v.4 contains short biographies of 874 Fellows elected between 1826 and 1925, who died before Jan. 1, 1954.

v.5 contains biographies of 422 Fellows who died since the end of 1953 or who died earlier, but were not included in the previous volume because they were elected to the Fellowship after 1925. Arranged alphabetically. Also designated as "Munk's roll, v.5."

Plarr, Victor Gustave. Plarr's Lives of the fellows of the Royal College of Surgeons of England, rev. by Sir D'Arcy Power. Bristol, Royal College; London, Simpkin, Marshall, 1930. 2v.   **EK174**

Covers lives of the Fellows from 1843, founding date of the Fellowship, to those who died before 1930. Much of the information was obtained from obituary notices and from friends and relatives of the Fellows. Includes, for each Fellow, references to publications sufficient to indicate the subjects in which he was particularly interested.   R489.A1P5

Power, *Sir* D'Arcy and **Le Fanu, William Richard.** Lives of the fellows of the Royal College of Surgeons of England, 1930–1951. London, College, 1953. 889p.   **EK175**

Continues the record by listing the biographies of the Fellows who died from 1930 to the end of 1951, including some who died before 1930 but were not included in Plarr (above). Includes lists of publications.

Continued by: R489.A1P63

Robinson, R. H. O. B. and **LeFanu, W. R.** Lives of the fellows of the Royal College of Surgeons of England, 1952–1964. Edinburgh, E. & S. Livingstone, 1970. 470p.   **EK176**

Continues the record by listing the biographies of the Fellows who died from 1952 to the end of 1964.

Continued by: R489.A1R6

Ross, James Paterson and **LeFanu, W. R.** Lives of the fellows of the Royal College of Surgeons of England, 1965–1973. London, Pitman Medical, 1981. 405p.   **EK177**

Continues the record by listing the biographies of Fellows who died from 1965 to the end of 1973. R489.A1R67

BIOETHICS

❖The entries in this section deal explicitly with bioethical information; they include a small sampling of reference works for bioethical problems. The interest in and the scope of bioethics is so broad and amorphous that the word, as yet, is not clearly defined. Ambiguity in terminology is evident in the subject headings found in *Index medicus* (EK52); they include "bioethics," "ethics," "ethics, dental," and "ethics, medical" among others and refer to related headings such as "confidentiality" and "human rights." The Library of Congress subject headings follow a similar pattern. Most bibliographic abstracts or indexes that deal with the human condition may be consulted for bioethical topics.

See also Sourcebook on death and dying (CC175), *Sourcebook for research in law and medicine* (EK208), and *Law, medicine & health care: a bibliography* (EK210).

Ball, Nicole. World hunger: a guide to the economic and political dimensions. Santa Barbara, Calif., ABC-Clio, [1981]. 386p. (War/peace bibliography, 15) **EK178**

An international bibliography of more than 3,200 books, monographs, and periodical articles on the problems of underdevelopment in the economic and rural sector, and food supply. Pts. I through IV consider these general problems; pt.V lists studies about regions or countries; and pt. VI details relevant reference sources. Critical introductory bibliographic notes for most subsections. Glossary; author and subject indexes. Z7164.F7B34

Bibliography of society, ethics and the life sciences. Hastings-on-the-Hudson, N.Y., Inst. of Society, Ethics and the Life Sciences, 1973– . Annual. **EK179**

Less comprehensive and not as well indexed as the *Bibliography of bioethics* (EK185), but coverage is more up-to-date and some annotations are provided. Classified subject arrangement; author index. Z5322.B5B52

Dictionary of medical ethics. Rev. and enl. ed. London, Darton, Longman & Todd, [1981]. 459p. **EK180**

Ed. by A.S. Duncan, G.R. Dunstan, and R.B. Welbourn. 1st ed. 1977.

In addition to supplying a definition, gives "access to a brief but authoritative statement on this or that subject which has moral or ethical implications."—*Introd. 1st ed.* Some entries include a bibliography; all entries are signed. Although a few of the contributors are from the United States, most are British. R724.D52

Encyclopedia of bioethics. Warren T. Reich, ed. in chief. N.Y., Free Pr., [1978]. 4v. (xxxix, 1933p.) **EK181**

315 original, signed articles, with an average length of 3,400 words, focus on the six core areas of bioethics: (1) concrete ethical and legal problems; (2) basic concepts and principles such as pain and suffering, life, death in Eastern and Western thought; (3) ethical theories; (4) religious traditions; (5) historical perspectives; (6) disciplines bearing on bioethics, such as the philosophy of biology, and the anthropology of medicine. No biographies are included. Most articles have extensive bibliographies. Articles are arranged alphabetically, with numerous cross references; systematic classification of articles and index are also provided. Appendix gives the texts of codes and statements related to medical ethics. QH332.E52

Encyclopaedia of occupational health and safety. 3d (rev.) ed. Geneva, Internat. Labour Office, [1983]. 2v. il. **EK182**

Luigi Parmeggiani, technical ed. 1st ed. 1930.

Comprises more than 1,000 signed articles with recent bibliographic references, by international specialists. This latest edition has about 200 new articles on aspects of toxicology, occupational cancer, diseases of migrant workers, and institutions active in the field of occupational health. Most articles stress preventive safety and health measures. Appendixes; index. RC963.3.E53

Goldstein, Doris M. Bioethics: a guide to information sources. Detroit, Gale, [1982]. 366p. (Health affairs information guide ser., v.8) **EK183**

An annotated bibliography of about 1,000 documents published between 1973 and 1981, arranged topically. Organizations, programs, and library collections are described; there is a section on periodicals and reference sources. Indexed. Z6675.E8G64

Muldoon, Maureen. Abortion, an annotated indexed bibliography. N.Y., E. Mellen, [1980]. ca.150p. (Studies in women and religion, v.3) **EK184**

A main-entry listing of 3,397 international titles, with brief contents notes; subject index. Special journal issues and symposia proceedings are listed separately. Z6671.2.A2M84

Walters, LeRoy. Bibliography of bioethics. Detroit, Gale, [1975]– . v.1– . Annual. **EK185**

Issued by the Center for Bioethics, Kennedy Institute, Georgetown University.

A subject bibliography listing English-language books, essays in books, journal and newspaper articles, court decisions, bills or laws, films, and audio cassettes. Concerned with ethical aspects of health care, contraception, abortion, population, reproductive technologies, genetic intervention, mental health therapies, human experimentation, artificial and transplanted organs or tissues, death and dying, etc. v.11 (publ. 1985) indexes materials issued during the 1981–84 period. Title and author indexes. Z6675.E8W34

DENTISTRY

Guides

American Dental Association. Bureau of Library Services. Basic dental reference works. 5th ed. Chicago, Amer. Dental Assoc., 1983. 22p. **EK186**

Prepared by Aletha Kowitz.

Lists of basic dental reference works, with short annotations, are arranged under the headings: dictionaries, indexes, surveys, syndromes, directories, bibliographies, current practice, histories, sources, and miscellaneous. RK51.A54

Bibliography

New York Academy of Medicine. Library. Dental bibliography; index to the literature of dental science and art as found in the libraries of the New York Academy of Medicine, and Bernhard Wolf Weinberger, comp. by B. W. Weinberger. 2d ed. [N.Y.], First District Dental Soc., State of N.Y., [1929–32]. 2v. **EK187**

Contents: [pt.1] A reference index; pt.2, A subject index, with additional reference index. Z6668.N53

Periodicals

Schmidt, Hans Joachim. Index der zahnärztlichen Zeitschriften der Welt. Stuttgart-Degerloch, Verlag der Deutschen Dokumentenstelle für Zahnärztliches Schrifttum, 1962. 125p. **EK188**

Title and introductory material also in French, English, Spanish, Italian, and Polish.

"Covers 1255 dental periodicals from 58 countries showing the full title, publisher's address and the abbreviated title. Both current and lapsed periodicals are listed."—*[Engl. pref.]* Z6668.S3

Indexes and abstract journals

Black, Arthur Davenport. Index of the periodical dental literature published in the English language, 1839–1936/38. Buffalo, Dental Index Bureau; Chicago, Amer. Dental Assoc., 1921–39. 15v.   **EK189**

Volumes are unnumbered and were not issued in regular chronological sequence.

Contents: 1839–75 (1923); 1876–85 (1925); 1886–90 (1926); 1891–95 (1927); 1896–1900 (1930); 1901–05 (1931); 1906–10 (1934); 1911–15 (1921); 1916–20 (1922); 1921–23 (1928); 1924–26 (1929); 1927–29 (1932); 1930–32 (1936); 1933–35 (1938); 1936–38 (1939).

Each volume is in two parts: (1) a classified subject index arranged by an extension of the Dewey Decimal Classification, and (2) an author index.

Continued by: Z6668.B62

Index to dental literature. 1939– . Chicago, Amer. Dental Assoc., 1943– . v.1– . Quarterly, with annual cumulation.
                        EK190

Frequency varies. Title varies: 1939–61, *Index to dental literature in the English language.*

An author and subject index to dental periodical literature. Beginning with 1962, includes periodicals in foreign languages. Contains lists of dental books. Also lists academic theses.

Beginning 1965, the index consists of citations retrieved by computer from MEDLARS database of the National Library of Medicine, and coverage is expanded to include articles in non-dental journals. Now in two main sections: (1) subjects, and (2) name index. Page format follows that of *Index medicus.*
                        Z6668.I45

Dental abstracts. v.1–6, Jan. 1945–Sept./Dec. 1950. N.Y., Columbia Univ., School of Dental and Oral Surgery, Dental Abstracts Soc., 1945–1950.   **EK191**

A few numbers of an earlier series were issued Dec. 1941–March 1943.

Dental abstracts: a selection of world dental literature. Chicago, Amer. Dental Assoc., 1956– . v.1– . Monthly.
                        EK192

Place of publication varies.

Fairly long abstracts in English of articles from the periodicals of the world. Titles of foreign-language items are translated into English, and original title is given. Annual subject and author indexes.   RK1.A5416

Oral research abstracts. v.1, no.1– , April 1966– . Chicago, Amer. Dental Assoc., 1966– . Monthly.   **EK193**

Signed abstracts in English of articles pertinent to oral health research, whether in dental journals or others and regardless of language. Abstracts are written by professionals, but are confined to data and fact without critical comment. Classed arrangement, with annual author and subject indexes.   RK1.O75

Dictionaries

Boucher, Carl O., ed. Current clinical dental terminology, a glossary of accepted terms in all disciplines of dentistry. St. Louis, Mosby, 1974. 442p.   **EK194**

The work of specialist contributors, giving meanings of several thousand terms.   RK28.B68

International Dental Federation. A lexicon of English dental terms, with their equivalents in Español, Deutsch, Français, Italiano. Comp. by Fédération Dentaire Internationale. The Hague, Sijthoff, 1966. 424p.   **EK195**

Intended for research workers, students, practitioners, and interpreters at dental meetings. The main section of the lexicon includes more than 7,000 terms arranged on an English base with equivalent terms in the other languages. Spanish, German, French, and Italian

indexes refer to numbered entries in the main section. Includes some medical and technological terms.   RK27.I5

Jablonski, Stanley. Illustrated dictionary of dentistry. Philadelphia, Saunders, [1982]. 919p. il.   **EK196**

Entries consist of dictionary term, phonetic pronunciation, etymological source, a descriptive definition, synonyms, trademarks if applicable and cross references. Appendixes include information about the American Dental Association, accreditation of schools and dental programs in the U.S. and Canada, and laboratory reference values of clinical importance.   RK27.J3

Directories

Admission requirements of U.S. and Canadian dental schools, 1974/75– . Wash., Amer. Assoc. of Dental Schools, 1974– . Annual.   **EK197**

Continues *Admission requirements of American dental schools,* 1963–74.

Provides an extensive range of information for each school: general information, description of programs, admission requirements, applications processes, costs, etc.   RK91.A54

American dental directory. [Chicago], Amer. Dental Assoc., 1947– . v.1– . Annual.   **EK198**

American dentists are listed by state and city, with an alphabetical index. Gives address, and indicates specialization and dental school with year of graduation. There are separate sections for dentists of the armed forces and for specialists.   RK37.A25

Dental research in the United States and other countries. 1975/76– . [Bethesda, Md.], Nat. Inst. of Health, [1980?]– . Biennial?   **EK199**

Continues: *Dental research in the United States, Canada and Great Britain.*

"Attempts to present a comprehensive picture of ongoing dental research in terms of project titles and descriptions, investigators, subject areas, sponsors, performing institutions, and funds ... includes all dental research projects registered with Smithsonian Science Information Exchange, Inc."—*Introd.* Primarily U.S. coverage. Indexed.   RK80.D46

The dentists register. 1879– . London, General Dental Council, 1879– . Annual.   **EK200**

Publisher varies.

Gives the names and addresses of registered dental practitioners arranged in three alphabetical lists: (1) United Kingdom list, (2) Commonwealth list, and (3) foreign list. Recent issues reprint the Dentists Act, 1957.   RK37.D5

Handbooks

Accepted dental therapeutics. Ed.33– , 1969/70– . Chicago, Amer. Dental Assoc., [1968–]. il. Biennial.   **EK201**

Subtitle: Drugs used in dental practice, including a list of brands accepted by the Council on Dental Therapeutics of the American Dental Association.

Replaces *Accepted dental remedies* and continues the numbering thereof. The work is "designed to assist the dentist in selecting appropriate drugs and procedures for the prevention and treatment of oral diseases."—*Pref.*   RK701.A3

Dentist's desk reference: materials, instruments and equipment. 2d ed. Chicago, Amer. Dental Assoc., 1983. 501p. il.
                        EK202

1st ed. 1981 superseded the *Guide to dental materials and devices* (1962–76/78).

"Products appearing in boldface print throughout this book have been evaluated and classified under either the Certification Program or the Acceptance Program of the Council on Dental Materials,

Instruments and Equipment of the American Dental Association."
—*verso of t.p.*

An authoritative source for dental material specifications and instrument and equipment standards. Includes bibliography and indexes. RK652.5.D47

Wood, Norman. The complete book of dental care. N.Y., Hart, [1978]. 336p. il. **EK203**

As a professor of oral surgery the author's aim is to educate the consumer from a dentist's point of view. Topics include how to cope with emergencies such as toothaches and bleeding gums, a description of what a dentist can do for the consumer's teeth, how to choose a dentist, reasonable fees, and the use of dental specialists. RK61.W63

History

Asbell, M. B. A bibliography of dentistry in America, 1790–1840. [Cherry Hill, N.J.], Sussex House, 1973. 107p. **EK204**

Intends to list all books and articles on dentistry published during the period indicated. Separate chronological list of books and articles. Locates copies of the books. List of journals searched, p.80–84.

Guerini, Vincenzo. A history of dentistry from the most ancient times until the end of the eighteenth century. Philadelphia, Lea & Febiger, 1909. 355p. il. ports. **EK205**

Published under the auspices of the National Dental Association of the United States of America.

A classic work in this field, well documented by footnotes to sources. Includes name and subject index. RK29.G8

Weinberger, Bernhard Wolf. An introduction to the history of dentistry, with medical and dental chronology and bibliographic data. St. Louis, Mosby, 1948. 2v. il. **EK206**

v.2 has title *An introduction to the history of dentistry in America.* RK29.W39

MEDICAL JURISPRUDENCE

See also EK221, EK245, EK289, EK292.

Bander, Edward J. and **Wallach, Jeffrey J.** Medical legal dictionary. Dobbs Ferry, N.Y., Oceana, 1970. 114p. **EK207**

"The purpose . . . is to provide the reader with a selective list of terms that should be familiar to those of the legal and medical professions. The stress has been on practical rather than definitive definitions. In many instances, readers are referred to more extensive texts and cases."—*Introd.* Includes more than 400 definitions. Includes an appendix on the relationship of doctors and lawyers in medical legal matters. KF2905.A68B3

Fiscina, Salvatore F. [and others]. A sourcebook for research in law and medicine. Owings Mills, Md., Nat. Health Pubns., 1985. 348p. **EK208**

Contents: Problems analysis and research design, Medicolegal information sources, Medicolegal references, Law primer, Cases in law and medicine, and Medicolegal consultants.

"The purpose is to provide an outline of medical and legal issues currently being addressed as well as a survey of resources available." —*Introd.* Includes bibliographies. KF3821.A1S67

Stedman, Thomas Lathrop. Illustrated Stedman's medical dictionary. 5th unabr. lawyers' ed. Cincinnati, Anderson, [1982]. various pagings. il. **EK209**

For the standard edition *see* EK101.

In this edition the "Lawyers' section" has been added to the *Illustrated Stedman's medical dictionary.* The 67-page section covers such topics as use of a medical library, institution members of the Medical Library Association, standard abbreviations of medical terms used in medical records, and medicine from the lawyer's point of view. The latter section approaches jurisprudence and/or forensic medicine from the following viewpoints: nervous system, skeletal system, muscular system, mental illness, epilepsy and arthritis, introduction of hospital records as evidence, frequently recurring forensic problems, risk management, and codes and model statutes. R121.S8

Ziegenfuss, James T. Law, medicine & health care: a bibliography. N.Y., Facts on File, [1983]. 265p. **EK210**

On cover: With over 3500 citations on all aspects of law and medicine.

This is a classified bibliography of citations to articles dealing with various types of interactions in the fields of law, medicine, and health care. Four topics are emphasized: individual specialists and specialties, medical care organizations, medical services and process, and legal processes. While the work is not indexed, the topical organization permits relatively direct use. There is a substantial section on law firms practicing in law, medicine, and health care. KF3821.A1Z53

NURSING

Guides

Binger, Jane L. and **Jensen, Lydia M.** Lippincott's Guide to nursing literature: a handbook for students, writers, and researchers. Philadelphia, Lippincott, [1980]. 303p. **EK211**

"The purpose of this book is to provide a brief, quick-access guide to timely nursing journals and references for nurses unfamiliar with this literature in the United States."—*Pref.* A listing of specific sources for information about nursing and allied subjects. RT24.B56

Strauch, Katina P. and **Brundage, Dorothy J.** Guide to library resources for nursing. N.Y., Appleton-Century-Crofts, 1980. 509p. il. **EK212**

Section I is an annotated listing by topic of books and reports. Section II presents information on using the library, citations, parts of the card catalog, and the classification systems for the National Library of Medicine and the Library of Congress, etc. Includes annotations and instruction on the use of ten abstracting and indexing services. Author, title, and subject indexes. Z6675.N7S7

Bibliography and indexes

Cumulative index to nursing literature. Glendale, Calif., Seventh Day Adventist Hospital Assoc., 1961–76. v.1/5–21. Annual. **EK213**

Frequency varies: v.1/5, 1956/60, is a collection in 1v. of 5 previously unpublished annual volumes, indexing, by author and subject, 17 journals; v.6/8, 1961/63, v.9/11, 1964/66, and v.12/13, 1967/68 are also single volume cumulations; v.14–21, 1969–76, are annual cumulations. In 1964 book reviews, films, filmstrips and recordings, and pamphlets were accorded a separate section. In 1967 the combined author-subject arrangement was changed to separate alphabetical listings by author and by subject.

Indexed all major English-language nursing periodicals, plus selective indexing of various medical journals.

Continued by:

Cumulative index to nursing & allied health literature. v.22– . Glendale, Calif., Glendale Adventist Medical Center, 1977– . Bimonthly with annual cumulation. **EK214**

Supersedes *Cumulative index to nursing literature* (above) and continues its numbering.

The change of title reflects the expanded coverage; now indexes all major nursing periodicals published in English, as well as selected periodicals for the following allied health professions: cardiopulmonary technology, health education, laboratory technology, medical assistant, medical records, occupational therapy, physical therapy and rehabilitation, radiologic technology, respiratory therapy, social service in health care. ●

International nursing index. v.1, no.1– , 1966– . Philadelphia, American Journal of Nursing, 1966– . Quarterly, with annual cumulation. **EK215**

Published in cooperation with the National Library of Medicine. "Over 200 nursing journals received from all over the world are indexed, as well as nursing articles in more than 2200 nonnursing journals currently indexed in *Index Medicus*."—*Pref., 1974.*

A computer-produced index using MEDLARS (Medical Literature Analysis and Retrieval System) facilities. Because subject headings were originally chosen for a medical index, a "Nursing thesaurus" (which appears as pt.2 of the first issue of each year and is included in the annual cumulation) gives commonly used nursing terms as cross references to the subject headings used in the index. Includes additional, brief sections listing nursing publications of organizations and agencies and books published by or for nurses. A list of doctoral dissertations by nurses appears in the annual cumulative volume. Z6675.N7I5●

Nursing studies index. Prep. by Yale University School of Nursing Index Staff under the direction of Virginia Henderson. Philadelphia, Lippincott, 1963–72. 4v. **EK216**

Contents: v.1, 1900–1929 (publ. 1972); v.2, 1930–1949 (publ. 1970); v.3, 1950–1956 (publ. 1966); v.4, 1957–1959 (publ. 1963).

Subtitle: An annotated guide to reported studies, research in progress, research methods and historical materials, in periodicals, books, and pamphlets published in English.

Provides retrospective coverage for a wide range of materials not treated elsewhere. The number of journals covered varies from 110 in v.1 to 239 in v.4, according to availability at the time of publication. Annotations note study methods used, nature and scope of the investigation, and frequently indicate the author's qualifications and the auspices under which the work was done. Includes unpublished doctoral dissertations but not master's theses. Subject arrangement with author index.

Thompson, Alice M. C. A bibliography of nursing literature . . ., with an historical introduction. London, Library Assoc. for the Royal College of Nursing and National Council of Nurses of the United Kingdom in association with King Edward's Hospital Fund for London, 1968–76. 3v. **EK217**

Contents: v.1, 1856–1960; v.2, 1961–70; v.3, 1971–76.

A guide to the first 125 years of nursing literature, covering periodical and monographic literature from English-speaking countries. In five main sections: (1) History of nursing; (2) Biography; (3) Nursing as a profession; (4) Specialties of knowledge and practice; and (5) Hospitals. No index. Z6675.N7T5

Encyclopedias and handbooks

Facts about nursing. 1935– . N.Y., Amer. Nurses' Assoc., 1935– . Annual. **EK218**

A statistical summary and basic data source book including information on nurse distribution, nursing education, the economic status of registered nurses, allied health personnel, functions and purposes of nursing organizations, and related information. Indexed by subject.

The Lippincott manual of nursing practice. 3d ed. Philadelphia, Lippincott, [1982]. 1531p. il. **EK219**

Contents: pt.1, Medical-surgical nursing; pt.2, Psychiatric nursing; pt.3, Maternity nursing; pt.4, Pediatric nursing.

The text gives a step-by-step explanation of a total physical examination and diagnostic procedures. The normal and abnormal conditions are identified and appropriate observations, with illus-

trations, for procedures, clinical manifestations, management, and health education are discussed. Indexed. RT51.B72

Miller, Benjamin Frank and **Keane, Claire B.** Encyclopedia and dictionary of medicine, nursing and allied health. 3d ed. Philadelphia, Saunders, [1983.] 1270p. il. **EK220**

1st ed (1972) had title: *Encyclopedia and dictionary of medicine and nursing.*

A concise work intended for students and workers in the nursing and paramedical fields. Pronunciation is indicated for all but the most common words. The greater emphasis on patient care and patient education is reflected in the title change. R121.M65

Rowland, Howard S. The nurse's almanac. 2d ed. [Germantown, Md.], Aspen Systems, [1984]. 849p. il. **EK221**

1st ed. 1978.

A compendium of information for the practicing or prospective nurse covering a broad range of subjects, e.g., education, nursing and the law, personnel practices and hospital administration, patient needs and services, hospitals, etc. Indexed. RT41.R78

Dictionaries and directories

Mosby's Medical & nursing dictionary. Laurence Urdang, ed. in chief; Helen Harding Swallow, managing ed. St. Louis, Mosby, 1983. 1484p. il. **EK222**

"Illustrated. Thirty-two page full-color anatomy atlas."—*t.p.*

The definitions are given in encyclopedic style; standard abbreviations are included. The 14 appendixes include information such as units of measure, symbols, prefixes and suffixes, nutrition, health history: a subjective database, maternity and obstetrics information. R121.M89

The national nursing directory. Kenneth E. Lawrence and Howard S. Rowland, eds. Rockville, Md., Aspen Systems, [1982]. 424p. **EK223**

"This directory presents a comprehensive review of active public and private resources in the following key areas: Credentialing; Licensure and certification; Patient/clinic health problems; Organizations that can help; Preventive health; Outreach and counseling organizations: Recruitment and retention resources; Nurse education; Scholarships, grants, and student loans; Libraries, clearinghouses and multi-media resources; State and federal health offices; Nursing-related professional associations; Leaders in American nursing."—*Introd.* Each section gives appropriate specific information. Indexed. RT25.U5L38

Who's who in American nursing. 1984– . [Wash.], Soc. of Nursing Professionals, [1984–]. Biennial. **EK224**

Includes biographical and professional information for individuals in nursing, nursing education, and administration.

RT25.U5W48

History

Bullough, Bonnie [and others]. Nursing, a historical bibliography. N.Y., Garland, 1981. 408p. (Garland reference library of social sciences, v.66) **EK225**

A bibliography of some 3,500 references collected from major sources. The cutoff date is 1978. Z6675.N7B84

Stewart, Isabel Maitland and **Austin, Anne L.** A history of nursing from ancient to modern times. 5th ed. N.Y., Putnam, [1962]. 516p. il. **EK226**

1st ed., 1920, had title *A short history of nursing.*

Intended especially for the student nurse. Pt.1 consists of 8 chapters sketching the history of nursing from ancient to modern times; pt.2 consists of 11 chapters on nursing today in various countries throughout the world. Includes a general classified bibliography and selected bibliographies for each chapter. Subject and name index. RT31.S7

NUTRITION

Bibliography

See also EK16.

Food and Agriculture Organization of the United Nations.
Food composition tables: updated annotated bibliography.
Rome, FAO; distr. by Unipub, N.Y., 1975. 181p.   **EK227**

1965 ed. had title: *Review of food composition tables;* 1970 ed. had
title: *Food composition tables: annotated bibliography.*
Arranged (1) by continent, (2) by country. Includes information
on techniques of gathering data.

Freedman, Robert L. Human food uses; a cross-cultural,
comprehensive annotated bibliography. Westport, Conn.,
Greenwood Pr., [1981]. 552p.   **EK227a**

Offers more than 9,000 citations to a wide variety of materials,
including theses, dissertations, and manuscripts. International in
scope; author arrangement with keyword index.

————— ————— Supplement. Westport, Conn., Greenwood
Pr., [1983]. 387p.

Provides an additional 4,025 citations.   Z5118.F58F73

Abstract journals

Nutrition abstracts and reviews. Aberdeen, Scot., Commonwealth Bureau of Animal Nutrition, 1931–76. v.1–46. Quarterly, with annual combined table of contents and author
and subject indexes.   **EK228**

Imprint varies.
Issued under the direction of the Commonwealth Agricultural
Bureaux Council, the Medical Research Council, and the Rowett
Research Institute.
An international abstracting service in classed arrangement.
Titles are given in the original language and in English translation.
Signed abstracts in English.
Continued in part by: RM214.N8

Nutrition abstracts and reviews. Series A: Human and experimental. v.47, no.1– , Jan. 1977– . Aberdeen, Scot., Commonwealth Bureau of Animal Nutrition, 1977– . Monthly.
   EK229

Continues in part *Nutrition abstracts and reviews* (above) and
continues its numbering.
Offers international coverage of the field. Abstracts appear in
classed arrangement, with monthly subject index and annual cumulated subject and author indexes.
Series B of this publication is concerned with "livestock feeds and
feeding".   QP141.A1N86●

Dictionaries and handbooks

Adams, Catherine F. Nutritive value of American foods in
common units. Wash., Agricultural Research Service, U.S.
Dept. of Agriculture, 1975. 291p. (Agriculture handbook,
no.456)   **EK230**

Based on Agriculture handbook no. 8, *Composition of foods: raw,
processed, prepared* (EK242).
"This publication has been prepared to serve as a basic reference
for data on nutrients in frequently used household measures and
market units of food."—*Introd.* Two basic sections: Table 1, Nutritive values for household measures and market units of foods; Table
2, Fatty acid values for household measures and market units of
foods. Uses generic names of foods.   TX551.A35

Bender, Arnold E. Dictionary of nutrition and food technology. 5th ed. London, Butterworths, [1982]. 309p. il.
   EK231

1st ed. 1960.
This dictionary is designed to define the broad range of words
used by individuals involved in nutrition and food technology.
Includes a bibliography of 180 standard books arranged by subject.
   QP141.B45

CRC handbook of food additives. Ed.: Thomas E. Furia. 2d
ed. Cleveland, CRC Pr., [1972]. 998p.   **EK232**

1st ed. 1968.
Sections by specialists, often with extensive bibliographies. Major
sections on enzymes; vitamins and amino acids; antimicrobial food
additives; antioxidants as food stabilizers; acidulants in food processing; sequestrants in foods; gums; starch in the food industry;
surface active agents; polyhydric alcohols; natural and synthetic
flavorings; flavor potentiators; nonnutritive sweeteners; color additives in food; phosphates in food processing. There is also an
extensive section on "Regulatory status of direct food additives"
and an index.   TX553.A3C2

————— v.II. Cleveland, CRC Pr., [1980]. 412p.

Gives updates on progress concerning oil soluble polymeric antioxidants, some polymeric food dyes, and high intensity sweeteners.
Reviews the traditional categories of food additives and updates the
bibliography on saccharin and cyclamates. Indexed.

Fenaroli, Giovanni. Fenaroli's Handbook of flavor ingredients: adapted from [his] Italian language works. 2d ed.
Cleveland, CRC Pr., [1975]. 2v. (928p.) il.   **EK233**

At head of title: CRC.
Ed., trans., and rev. by Thomas E. Furia and Nicolo Bellanca.
1st ed. 1971.
Contents: v.1, pt.1, General considerations; pt.2, Natural flavor;
v.2, pt.3, Synthetic flavor; pt.4, Use of flavor ingredients.
The aim of these volumes is the same as for the 1st ed., "to present
a current, authoritative, first-source description of natural and
synthetic flavor ingredients, their detailed characteristics, and their
application in food. It is primarily intended for those using flavors
rather than for the accomplished *flavorist.*"—*Editorial foreword. 1st
ed.* "New material presented includes the following: (1) Data on new
synthetic flavor ingredients; (2) Updating of natural occurrence of
flavor ingredients; (3) Addition of references, augmenting many of
the topics . . . ; (4) Through the cooperation of CRC Press utilization
of new, comprehensive reviews on significant flavor topics."—*Pref.*
Indexed.   TP418.F4613

Food chemicals codex. Committee on Codex Specifications,
Food and Nutrition Board, Division of Biological Sciences,
Assembly of Life Sciences, National Research Council. 3d
ed. Wash., Nat. Academy Pr., 1981. 735p. il.   **EK234**

1st ed. 1966.
The main section is an alphabetical listing of entries about food-
grade chemicals. Entries include their description, requirements of
purity and quality, tests for determining if the requirements are
achieved, packaging and storage, labeling and functional use in
foods. Other sections cover general test procedures for chemicals
added directly to foods for some desired effect and substances which
are used in processing that come into contact with food (e.g.,
extraction solvents or filter media). This edition includes specifications for ingredients which are usually considered foods but are also
used as additives (e.g., dextrose and fructose).   TP455.F66

————— First supplement to the third edition. Wash., Nat.
Academy Pr., 1983. 34p. il.

Goodhart, Robert S. and **Shils, Maurice E.** Modern nutrition
in health and disease. 6th ed. Philadelphia, Lea & Febiger,
1980. 1370p. il.   **EK236**

1st ed. 1955.
Contents: pt.1, The foundations of nutrition; pt.2, Safety and
adequacy of the food supply; pt.3, Interrelations of nutrients and
metabolism; pt.4, Malnutrition; pt.5, Nutrition during "physiologic" stress; pt.6, Nutrition in the prevention and treatment of disease.
Index.
"Serves as a textbook on nutrition and as a ready reference book
for students and practitioners in the field of nutrition, medicine,

dentistry and public health."—*Pref.* 40 signed, authoritative articles with literature references.   QP141.G63

Heath, Henry B. Source book of flavors. Westport, Conn., Avi Publ., [1981]. 863p. il.   **EK237**

Updates Joseph Merory's *Food flavoring* (2d ed. 1968).

Pt. 1, the major part of the book, contains chapters about the flavor industry; chemistry and chemists; research; materials—natural occurring and synthetic; manufacturing—methods, test procedures, patents, classification, quality assurance, label regulations; chemistry of fragrances; food colorations; international regulations, and toxicology. Pt. 2 is an alphabetic bibliography of some 140 flavoring materials which occur naturally or as a result of processing. Includes references to research reports, articles, etc., dealing with the chemical composition of each. Pt. 3 covers flavoring formulations. Subject, bibliographical, and formulary indexes.

TP418.H43

Leveille, Gilbert A., Zabik, Mary Ellen and **Morgan, Karen J.** Nutrients in foods. Cambridge, Mass., Nutrition Guild, 1983. 291p.   **EK238**

The introduction covers general information on human nutritional requirements and how to use and interpret the tables in this work. The information is compiled from the Michigan State University Nutrient Data Bank which included data from the USDA *Agriculture handbook* no.8 (EK242). Additional information on processed foods was provided by 64 major food companies. The tables list the nutrient composition for over 2,700 naturally occurring and processed foods. Tables include information on amino acids, vitamins, carbohydrates, ash, fibers (dietary and crude), minerals, and the US RDA (recommended daily allowance). Appendixes list caffeine and alcohol content of selected foods.   TX551.N56

Machlin, Lawrence J., ed. Handbook of vitamins: nutritional, biochemical, and clinical aspects. N.Y., Dekker, [1984]. 614p. il.   **EK239**

The purpose of this book is "to provide a relatively brief but authoritative and comprehensive source of information on the vitamins for the human and animal nutritionist, the dietician, clinician, biochemist, and interested lay person. [Each entry includes information on the vitamin's] chemistry, availability and content in food, metabolism, function, and deficiency symptoms; methods for evaluating overt or marginal deficiencies; nutritional requirements; the interaction of vitamins with environmental and disease factors, and the efficacy and safety when used at high levels."—*Pref.* There are bibliographic references with each essay. Indexed.   QP771.H36

National Research Council. Food and Nutrition Board. Recommended dietary allowances. Ed.1– . Wash., Nat. Academy of Sciences, 1941– . Irregular. (10th ed., 1985)   **EK240**

Describes the physiological and biochemical bases for recommended dietary allowances of each specific nutrient. A table of recommended daily dietary allowances shows calories and nutrients tabulated by sex and by age categories. Includes lists of references.   TX551.N39

Sourcebook on food and nutrition. 3d ed. Chicago, Marquis Academic Media, [1982]. 549p. il.   **EK241**

1st ed. 1978.

Contents: Introduction, the nutrients; dietary allowances and labelling; nutrition and life cycle; dieting and weight control; special diets; nutrition and health problems; food additives, carcinogens and food drug interactions; perspectives on world food production; organizations and agencies interested in food and nutrition. Index.

"Carefully documented and reflecting the latest available information from a variety of government and private sources . . . credits each source at the end of the selection."—*Pref.*   QP141.S567

Watt, Bernice Kunerth and **Merrill, Annabel L.** Composition of foods: raw, processed, prepared. Rev. Dec. 1963. Wash., Consumer and Food Economics Research Division, Agricultural Research Service, U.S. Dept. of Agriculture, [1964]. 180p. il. (U.S. Dept. of Agriculture. Agriculture handbook, no.8)   **EK242**

1st ed. 1950.

Chiefly tables giving data on the nutritive value of foods.

Updated by: TX541.W28

Consumer and Food Economics Institute (U.S.). Composition of foods: raw, processed, prepared. Wash., Agricultural Research Service, U.S. Dept. of Agriculture (for sale by Govt. Prt. Off.), 1976–84. pts.1–12. looseleaf. (Agricultural handbook, no.8-1–12) (In progress?)   **EK243**

Contents: no.8-1, Dairy and egg products; no.8-2, Spices and herbs; no.8-3, Baby foods; no.8-4, Fats and oils; no.8-5, Poultry products; no.8-6, Soups, sauces, and gravies; no.8-7, Sausages and luncheon meats; no.8-8, Breakfast cereals; no.8-9, Fruits and fruit juices; no.8-10, Pork products; no.8-11, Vegetables and vegetable products; v.8-12, Nut and seed products.

"This publication is a major revision of the 1963 edition of USDA Agriculture Handbook No.8, 'Composition of Foods . . . Raw, Processed, Prepared,' currently a basic source of food composition data in this country."—*Foreword.* "This revision . . . is being issued in sections so as to expedite release of data to the public. Each section contains a table of nutrient data for a major food group. The entire series will cover a wide range of food products."—*Pref.*   TX556.M5C68

PHARMACOLOGY

Guides

Sewell, Winifred. Guide to drug information. Hamilton, Ill., Drug Intelligence Publ., [1976]. 218p. il.   **EK244**

Prepared by librarian-bibliographers; primarily oriented toward problem-solving. Arranged in four parts: (1) handbooks, drug compendia, and related works with tables of comparative information and data; (2) use of primary sources—periodicals, monographs, etc.; (3) searching patterns and secondary sources—abstracts, indexes, etc.; (4) methods and use of current awareness searching and technology—computers, etc.   RS56.2.S48

Bibliography

Abel, Ernest L., comp. A comprehensive guide to the cannabis literature. Westport, Conn., Greenwood Pr., [1979]. 699p.   **EK245**

An alphabetical listing by author of books and journal articles on *cannabis sativa L.* Includes 8,177 entries in the main section and addendum. Intended to be comprehensive, the bibliography "includes references to the literature dealing not only with the psychotomimetic properties of this plant but also with other topics such as industrial usage, cultivation, history, and legal status published prior to 1978."—*Pref.* Subject index.   Z7164.N17A23

Andrews, Theodora. A bibliography on herbs, herbal medicine, "natural" foods, and unconventional medical treatment. Littleton, Colo., Libraries Unlimited, 1982. 339p.   **EK246**

Coverage includes a wide range of scientific and popular books on how to grow and use herbal plants for medicines, cosmetics, and foods, and books which challenge various medical practices and quackery. Critical annotations are provided for each book with specific comments on their strengths and weaknesses. Author and title index; subject index.   Z6665.H47A5

Abstract journals

Adverse reaction titles. Amsterdam, Excerpta Medica Foundation, 1966– . v.1– . Monthly.   **EK247**

On cover: A monthly bibliography of titles from approximately 3400 biomedical journals published throughout the world.

Forms section 38 of *Excerpta medica* (EK63).

Annually lists 5,000 to 6,000 items covering the complications, undesirable reactions, and untoward effects produced by drugs or other biologically active substances. Classed listing with subject and author indexes cumulated annually. •

International pharmaceutical abstracts. v.1– , Jan. 15, 1964– . [Wash.], Amer. Soc. of Hospital Pharmacists, 1964– . Semimonthly. **EK248**

Now computer-produced. Signed abstracts in English. International in coverage. Author and subject index now issued semiannually and annually. List of journals indexed appears annually in the Jan. 15 issue. RS1.I63●

Encyclopedias and handbooks

Albanese, Joseph A. Nurses' drug reference. 2d ed. N.Y., McGraw-Hill, [1982]. 958p. **EK249**

1st ed. 1979.

The text is divided into four parts, each part "presenting a synopsis of basic information designed to meet the clinical needs of nurses and nursing students."—*Pref.* In addition to presenting the drug indexes, comprehensive drug monographs, drug-related reference section and an appendix which contains useful nursing and drug-related information, there is a new OTC list. RM300.A487

American Medical Association. Dept. of Drugs. AMA drug evaluations. 5th ed. Chicago, Amer. Medical Assoc., [1983]. 1884p. il. **EK250**

1st ed. 1971.

Updated, and expanded. Organized by therapeutic category, each chapter has a brief introduction followed by an evaluation for each drug with information on dosage, actions and uses, contraindication, adverse effects. Includes structural formula for most single-entry drugs; selected list of further reading for each chapter. Indexed by drug name (generic, trademarks), indications, and adverse reactions. RM300.A553

Berdy, Janos. CRC handbook of antibiotic compounds. Boca Raton, Fla., CRC Pr., [1979–85]. v.1–12. il. (In progress) **EK251**

Contents: v.1, Carbohydrate antibiotics; v.2, Macrocyclic lactone (lactam) antibiotics; v.3, Quinone and similar antibiotics; v.4, pt.1, Amino acid and peptide antibiotics; v.4, pt.2, Peptolide and macromolecular antibiotics; v.5, Heterocyclic antibodies.; v.6, Alicyclic, aromatic, and aliphatic antibiotics; v.7, Miscellaneous antibiotics with unknown chemical structure; v.8, pts.1–2, Antibiotics from higher forms of life: higher plants; v.9, Antibiotics from higher forms of life—lichens, algae, and animal organisms; v.10, General index; v.11, pts.1–2, Microbial metabolites; v.12, Antibiotics from higher forms of life.

Aims "to provide in a concise form ready access to information on important physical, chemical, and biological characteristics of the compounds."—*Pref.* RS431.A6B47

Briggs, Gerald [and others]. Drugs in pregnancy and lactation, a reference guide to fetal and neonatal risk. Baltimore, Williams and Wilkins, [1983]. 415p. **EK252**

"This book was written to be used by the clinician who deals with pregnant patients [and] allows the clinician to have at his or her fingertips an up-to-date summary of available data bearing on specific drugs."—*Foreword.* Each drug entry includes fetal risk summary, breast feeding summary, and bibliographic references. Indexed. RG626.6.D76D79

Cutting, Windsor Cooper. Handbook of pharmacology: the actions and uses of drugs. 7th ed. Norwalk, Conn., Appleton, [1984]. 786p. il. **EK253**

1st ed. 1962.

Contains sections dealing with chemotherapeutic agents, somatic agents, and nervous system agents. Includes bibliographies. RM301.C8

Drug interaction facts. [1983–]. St. Louis, Facts and Comparison Division, Lippincott, [1983–]. Looseleaf; quarterly update. **EK254**

Compiled from the MEDIPHOR (Monitoring and Evaluation of Drug Interactions by a Pharmacy Oriented Reporting System) databank system by the Editorial Group at Stanford University School of Medicine.

Attempts "to cover all drug-drug interactions that have been reasonably well documented to occur in human subjects."—*Introd.* Interactions that are reasonably well documented are marked "Substantiated" in boldface page numbers; those drugs which lack clear evidence are designated as "Unsubstantiated" in large gray letters across the page. Significant information is given for each drug, such as, onset, severity, documentation, effects, mechanisms, management, plus discussion.

Drugs of choice, 1958/59– . St. Louis, Mosby, 1958– . Biennial. **EK255**

Walter Modell, ed.

Intended as a practical guide to the selection of the best drug for a particular therapeutic problem. Chapters on various types of drugs have been contributed by specialists. Fully indexed. RM101.D75

Facts and comparisons: drug information updated monthly. [1979–]. St. Louis, Facts and Comparisons, Inc., [1979–]. Looseleaf; monthly update. **EK256**

The format "is designed to provide a wide scope of drug information, in a manner which facilitates comparisons between drugs. A comprehensive index, table of contents for each chapter and extensive cross referencing enables the reader to quickly locate needed information."—*Introd.* Chapters cover: nutritional products, blood modifiers, hormones, diuretics and cardiovasculars, respiratory drugs, central nervous system drugs, gastro-intestinal drugs, anti-infections, biologicals, topical products, antineoplastic agents, and miscellaneous products. A typical entry includes action, indications, contraindications, warnings, precautions, adverse reactions, administration, and dosage.

Griffin, J. P. and **D'Arcy, P. F.** A manual of adverse drug interactions. 3d ed. Bristol, [Eng.], Wright, 1984. 419p. **EK257**

1st ed. 1975.

"The object of this book is to present in a readily accessible and easily understandable form the major drug interactions that are likely to be encountered in practical therapeutics, and to draw attention to some theoretical interactions that could be serious or life threatening. The book is intended as a convenient desk reference book for the prescribing physician and the pharmacist."—*Pref. 1st ed.* Contents: pt.I, Basic mechanisms of drug interactions, pt.II, Drug interaction tables. Entries have combination, interaction, and management information. Bibliographic references are given at the end of each of the 33 chapters. Indexed. RM302.G74

Handbook of non-prescription drugs. 7th ed. Wash., Amer. Pharmaceutical Assoc., [1982]. 682p. **EK258**

1st ed. 1969.

Offered as a definitive compilation of facts on home remedies. There are 32 chapters with broad headings such as: Antacid products, Laxative products, Asthma products. Each chapter discusses the etiology of the condition; the anatomy, physiology, and pathophysiology of the affected systems; the signs and symptoms; the treatment and adjunctive measures; an evaluation of ingredients in over-the-counter products; and important patient and product considerations. Bibliography; index. RM671.A1H35

Harkness, Richard. Drug interactions handbook. Englewood Cliffs, N.J., Prentice-Hall, [1984]. 341p. **EK259**

Prepared by a pharmacist for the drug user, each of the 24 chapters is divided into three sections: discussion of the ailment or condition, brand, and drug interaction. Indexed by brand name, ailment, and drug action. RM302.H367

Leung, Albert Y. Encyclopedia of common natural ingredients used in food, drugs, and cosmetics. N.Y., Wiley [1980]. 409p. **EK260**

Provides data on 310 natural ingredients; excludes prescription drugs and medicinal herbs not readily available in commerce. Arrangement is by common name. Entries give Latin name, synonyms, general description, chemical composition, pharmacology or biological activities, uses, commercial preparations, and references. Indexed. QD415.L48

Long, James W. The essential guide to prescription drugs; what you need to know for safe drug use. 4th ed. N.Y., Harper & Row, 1985. 1025p. **EK261**

1st ed. 1977.

The purpose is "to provide knowledge and understanding needed to use medicinal drugs with maximal benefit and minimal risks."—*Author's note*. The data are arranged under the generic drug names, for which are given dosage, side effects, adverse reactions, etc. There is a cross-index from over 1,500 brand names to the generic names. RM302.5.L66

Modern drug encyclopedia and therapeutic index. Ed.1– . N.Y., Yorke Medical Group, 1934– . Irregular. **EK262**

Title varies: *Modern drug encyclopedia: a compendium and therapeutic index.*

Pharmaceuticals and biologicals are arranged alphabetically, and a number of descriptive monographs are provided under the generic names of individual drugs or of the primary ingredient of combination products. Therapeutic, manufacturers, and general indexes. RS153.M57

Physicians' desk reference: PDR. 1947– . Rutherford, N.J., Medical Economics, [1946–]. il. Annual. **EK263**

Title varies: 1947–73 entitled *Physicians' desk reference to pharmaceutical specialties and biologicals.*

"PDR's purpose is to make available essential prescription information on major pharmaceutical products"—*Foreword*. Principal sections include: (1) Alphabetical index by manufacturer's name and by brand name; (2) Drug classification index; (3) Generic and chemical name index; (4) Product identification section, including more than 1,000 tablets and capsules shown in color and actual size as an identification aid; (5) Product information section, with over 2,500 pharmaceuticals listed by name of manufacturer and fully described as to composition, action, use, dosage, side effects, etc.; and (6) Diagnostic products information section. Product descriptions have been provided and approved by the manufacturers. New and revised product information is issued in periodic supplements. RS75.P5

Physician's desk reference for nonprescription drugs. Ed. 1– . Oradell, N.J., Medical Economics, 1980– . il. Annual. **EK264**

A companion to *Physicians' desk reference* (above).

The "purpose is to make available essential information on nonprescription drugs."—*Foreword*. Has product identification and product information sections. Indexed by manufacturer, product name, product category, and active ingredients. RM671.A1P48

Remington's Pharmaceutical sciences. Ed. 1– . Easton, Pa., Mack Publ., 1885– . il. Irregular. (17th ed. 1985) **EK265**

Subtitle: A treatise on the theory and practice of the pharmaceutical sciences, with essential information about pharmaceutical and medicinal agents; also a guide to the professionsl responsibilities of the pharmacist as the drug-information specialist of the health team. . . . A textbook and reference work for pharmacists, physicians, and other practitioners of the pharmaceutical and medical sciences.

1st–6th eds. had title *The practice of pharmacy*; 7th–12th eds., *Remington's Practice of pharmacy.*

Over 100 chapters are arranged in nine parts: pt.1, Orientation; pt.2, Pharmaceutics; pt.3, Pharmaceutical chemistry; pt.4, Radioisotopes in pharmacy and medicine; pt.5, Testing and analysis; pt.6, Pharmaceutical and medicinal agents; pt.7, Biological products; pt.8, Pharmaceutical preparations and their manufacture; pt.9, Pharmaceutical practice; Index. RS91.R4

Zimmerman, David R. The essential guide to nonprescription drugs. N.Y., Harper & Row, [1983]. 886p. **EK266**

An extensive compilation based on the FDA's ten-year review of the medically active ingredients in nonprescription or over the counter (OTC) drugs. Arrangement is alphabetical by therapeutic categories such as cold and cough remedies, digestive aids, and aphrodisiacs. Each chapter describes the condition to be treated, the type of drugs available, and the therapeutic claims of the active ingredients in the OTC drugs and gives a brand name product rating chart. Indexed. RM671.A1Z55

Dictionaries

See also EK113.

Elsevier's Dictionary of pharmaceutical science and techniques in six languages: English-French-Italian-Spanish-German-Latin. Comp. and arr. on English base by A. Sliosberg. v.2, Materia medica. N.Y., Elsevier, 1980. 552p. **EK267**

v.1, *Pharmaceutical technology* published 1968.

Materia medica deals particularly with substances of vegetal and animal origin used in preparation of drugs for animals and man. RS51.E48

Jablonski, Stanley. Russian drug index. 2d ed. Bethesda, Md., Nat. Institutes of Health, 1967. 384p. **EK268**

1st ed. 1961.

Includes the names of drugs which were developed in the Soviet Union or developed elsewhere and renamed in the Soviet Union as well as a few non-Russian names which appear in Soviet scientific literature but which may not be known to American scientists. Includes main entries for some 1,800 compounds and cross references from 3,700 synonyms. Each main entry includes the anglicized name of the drug, the transliterated Russian name, synonyms, molecular formula, a brief description of the properties of the drug, a Russian reference source, and an American reference, if available. A "Pharmacological index" permits identification of preparations with similar properties. RS91.J3

Marler, E. E. J., comp. Pharmacological and chemical synonyms; a collection of names of drugs and other compounds drawn from the medical literature of the world. 7th ed. Amsterdam, Excerpta Medica, 1983. 514p. **EK269**

1st ed. 1956.

Entry is under accepted international term (if any), with cross references from alternate names, trade names, chemical names, etc. RS51.M3

Steinbichler, Eveline. Lexikon für die Apothekenpraxis in sieben Sprachen. Frankfurt/Main, Govi-Verlag GmbH-Pharmazeutischer Verlag, [1963]. 474p. **EK270**

A listing of pharmaceutical terms in seven languages: German, English, French, Spanish, Italian, Greek, and Russian. Arranged in five sections, one for each of the languages in the Roman alphabet, giving equivalent terms in the other six languages. Does not include definitions. RS51.S75

Dispensatories and pharmacopoeias

American drug index. [1956]– . Philadelphia, Lippincott, 1956– . Annual. **EK271**

A listing of pharmaceuticals by generic, brand, and chemical name in alphabetical arrangement with information as to manufacturer, forms, size, dosage, and use. Includes list of drug manufacturers. RS355.A48

American druggist blue book. Ed.1– . N.Y., Amer. Druggist, 1928– . il. Annual. **EK272**

Title varies.

Drug products with prices, listed alphabetically by trade name. Includes a manufacturers index. HD9666.4.A6

American hospital formulary service drug information. 84– .
[Bethesda, Md.], Amer. Hospital Pharmacists, Inc., 1984– .
il. Annual with quarterly supplements. **EK273**

First published 1959; title varies slightly.
Description based on 1985. Gives comprehensive monograph/essay for each drug including pertinent information such as administration, dosage, chemical stability, pharmacology, uses, and cautions. Indexed for trade names, synonyms, and acronyms of drugs.

British pharmacopoeia, 1980. [13th ed.] London, H.M.S.O.,
1980. 2v. **EK274**

"Published on the recommendation of the Medicines Commission pursuant to the Medicines Act 1968."—*t.p.*
A compilation of monographs, alphabetically arranged, on drugs, preparations, etc., giving the official standard, description, dose, etc. Includes appendixes and indexes. Updated annually by an addendum. RS141.3.B75

National drug code directory 1982. 7th ed. [Rockville, Md.],
U.S. Dept. of Health and Human Services, Public Health
Service, Food and Drug Administration, [1982]. 2v.
(1717p.). **EK275**

Prepared by: Drug Listing Branch, National Center for Drugs and Biologics.
1st ed. 1969. Title varies; agency name varies.
Contents: v.1, Alphabetical index by product name; v.2, Numeric index of products by drug class, numeric index of products by national drug code, alphabetical index by short name.
The 1982 edition is limited to prescription drugs and selected OTC products. RS74.N35

——— Suppl. 1–8. Apr. 1983–June 1985. Quarterly.

Listings of products that have been added, changed, or discontinued since the publication of the main work.

The national formulary. Ed.1–14, 1888–1975. Wash., Amer.
Pharmaceutical Assoc., 1888–1975. **EK276**

Title varies.
"The fundamental purpose . . . is to provide standards and specifications which can be used to evaluate the quality of pharmaceuticals so that the physician can prescribe drugs with assurance, the pharmacist can dispense drugs with reliability, and the patient can consume drugs with confidence."—*Pref.* The main section of monographs on drugs, chemicals, and preparations is arranged alphabetically by basic drug with specifications for preparation. This is followed by a section on general tests, processes, techniques, and apparatus; a section on reagents and test solutions; and a section of general information.
Continued by *The United States pharmacopeia. The national formulary* (EK282). RS141.2.N3

Pharmaceutical Society of Great Britain. The pharmaceutical codex. 11th ed. London, Pharmaceutical Pr., 1979.
1101p. **EK277**

1st ed. 1907.
Incorporates the *British pharmaceutical codex.*
"Intended to be an encyclopedia of drug information for pharmacists and others who are engaged in work involving the preparation and use of medicines and medical preparations."—*Introd.* Entries are arranged alphabetically and preparations of drugs are appended to the appropriate drug entry. Indexed. RS151.3.B75

The pharmacopoeia of the United States of America (The
United States Pharmacopeia). Ed.1–19, 1820–1975.
Easton, Pa., Mack Prt. Co., 1820–1975. **EK278**

Imprint varies. Revised at 5-year intervals.
An official compendium of drug information, giving standards of purity and strength for each compound included.
Continued by *The United States pharmacopeia. The national formulary* (EK282). RS141.2.P5

Unlisted drugs. v.1– , Jan. 1949– . [Chatham, N.J., Unlisted
Drugs], 1949– . v.1– . Monthly. **EK279**

Imprint varies.
Each monthly issue contains descriptions of 180 to 200 new drugs

which are not yet recorded in standard sources. Also includes reviews of new books on drugs and other data of drug-information interest. Name and number indexes published annually.
RS1.U55

USP DI. 1980– . [Rockville, Md., U.S. Pharmacopeial
Convention, 1980–] Annual. **EK280**

Title varies. Cover title 1980–81: *United States pharmacopoeia dispensing information.*
Description based on 1985 ed. (2v.). "In Volume I (*Drug Information for the Health Care Provider*), the prescriber, dispenser, or administrator of medicines will find categories of use (including unlabeled uses where USP's advisory panels consider them warranted); indications; pharmacology; pregnancy, breast-feeding, pediatric, geriatric, and medical warnings; drug and drug/food interactions; diagnostic interference; side/adverse effects listed by presenting symptoms and underlying cause with indications of significance and incidence of occurrence; and patient consultation guidelines on safe and effective use. Guidelines for drug preparation immediately prior to administration, dosing information, and packaging and storage requirements are also given.
"Volume II (*Advice for the patient*) contains drug information for the patient. *Advice for the patient* monographs correspond directly to monographs in the professional section, supplement patient consultation guidelines, and feature lay language, larger type, and a format suitable for photocopying."—*verso of front cover.*
Spanish translation available for v.2. RS141.2.U5U2

——— Update. v.1– . 1980– . [Rockville, Md., U.S. Pharmacopeial Convention, 1980–] Bimonthly. **EK281**

"USP DI is kept current by means of the bimonthly *USP DI Update,* which presents monographs on selected, newly marketed drugs as well as significant changes in the information base of previously marketed drugs."—*verso of front cover.*

The United States pharmacopeia. The national formulary.
USP 20th revision. July 1, 1980– . NF 15th ed. July 1,
1980– . Rockville, Md., U.S. Pharmacopeial Convention,
1979– . Quinquennial. **EK282**

Supersedes *The pharmacopoeia of the United States of America* (1820–1975; EK278) and *The national formulary* (1888–1975; EK276).
The United States Pharmacopeial Convention obtained *The national formulary* in 1975; with the 1979 issue both publications appear in one volume.
"In 1980 the scope of both the USP and NF changed, the Pharmacopeia being limited to drug substances and dosage forms, and the National Formulary being limited to pharmaceutic ingredients."—*Pref. to NF XVI.*
Description based on USP 21st revision (Jan. 1, 1985); NF 16th ed. (Jan. 1, 1985), 1984, (1683p.). This is an official compendium of drug information of the USPC which is responsible for setting drug standards and specifications. Kept up to date between revisions by: RS141.2.P5

——— ——— USP NF supplement. no.1– . 1980– .

The International pharmacopoeia. Pharmacopoea internationalis. 3d ed. Geneva, World Health Organization, 1979–
81. 2v. il. **EK283**

1st ed. 1951–59.
Constitutes "a collection of recommended specifications which, in accordance with the resolution of the Third World Health Assembly, are offered to serve as references so that national specifications can be established on a similar basis in any country."—*Pref.* The purpose is to give specifications for quality control of pharmaceutical preparations.

History

Wootton, A. C. Chronicles of pharmacy. London, Macmillan, 1910. 2v. il. **EK284**

In narrative form; describes the discovery and use of various drugs, medicines, and nostrums from ancient times through the

19th century. Includes some biographical material of famous apothecaries. Indexed.

PUBLIC HEALTH

Guides

See also EK14.

Pease, Elizabeth Sue. Occupational safety and health: a sourcebook. N.Y., Garland, [1985]. 279p. (Garland reference library of social science, v.208)   **EK285**

An annotated bibliographic guide to about 500 English-language publications including audiovisuals, periodicals, reporters, databases, statistical sources, and reference works published 1970–84. Also serves as a directory to government agencies, special interest groups, and private associations interested in this area. Provides text of the 1970 Occupational Safety and Health Act, as well as some relevant reprints. Indexed.   Z6675.I5P39

Bibliography

World Health Organization. Publications of the World Health Organization, 1947/1957; a bibliography. Geneva, 1958– . Quinquennial.   **EK286**

Title varies.

Subject bibliography in two parts: (1) technical articles and publications; and (2) administrative and general articles and publications. Includes an author index, a country index, and a list of WHO publications by series. "It is intended to issue further volumes every five years."—*Introd.*   Z6660.W57

Abstract journals

Abstracts on hygiene and communicable diseases. v.56– , Jan. 1981– . London, Bureau of Hygiene and Tropical Diseases, [1981–]. Monthly.   **EK287**

Continues *Abstracts of hygiene,* v.43–56, 1968–80, which in turn continued *Bulletin of hygiene,* v.1–42, 1926–67.

Selective and critical abstracts and reviews of world literature prepared by specialists on various aspects of community and environmental health, hygiene, and communicable diseases. Annual author and subject indexes.   RA421.L618

Dictionaries and handbooks

A dictionary of epidemiology. Ed. by John M. Last. N.Y., Oxford Univ. Pr., 1983. 114p. il.   **EK288**

Has a broad range of coverage including biostatistics, community and public health, demography, and microbiology. Definitions range from one word to short essays which incorporate tables, graphs, charts, mathematical formulas, and diagrams. The more common terms are defined with cross references from their synonyms.   RA651.D53

Grad, Frank P. Public health law manual; a handbook on the legal aspects of public health administration and enforcement. 7th printing. [N.Y., Amer. Public Health Assoc.], 1980. 243p.   **EK289**

Prepared under the joint sponsorship of the U.S. Public Health Service and the American Public Health Association.

An earlier edition appeared in 1965.

Intended for use by health officers and other public health administrators in planning, developing, and implementing public health programs. Deals with basic legal procedures in public health enforcement—restrictions of persons; permits, licenses, and regis-

tration; searches and inspections; embargo, seizure, etc.—and with legal administrative techniques of public health administration.   KF3775.Z9G7

Health information for international travel. [Atlanta, Ga., Center for Disease Control, Public Health Service, U.S. Dept. of Health and Human Services, 1976–] Annual. (DHEW pubn; no.(CDC) 76-8280; DHHS pubn.)   **EK290**

First published 1952. Title varies; issuing agency's name varies.

Provides up-to-date and comprehensive information on immunization requirements and recommendations for international travelers.   RA783.5.C45a

Ives, Jane H. International occupational safety and health resource catalogue. N.Y., Praeger, [1981]. 311p.   **EK291**

In two main sections: (1) a directory of public and private agencies, associations, unions, etc., including their publications, arranged by region and country; (2) several appendixes, with bibliographic guides to educational materials in occupational safety and health. Name and subject indexes.   RC967.I86

O'Brien, Robert and **Cohen, Sidney.** The encyclopedia of drug abuse. N.Y., Facts on File, [1984]. 454p.   **EK292**

Coverage is comprehensive for the pharmacological and sociological aspects of drug abuse and includes terms which deal with the legal, biological, and epidemiological aspects. Appendixes include a list of slang and street terminology, statistical data, and a compilation of agencies and organizations in the U.S. and abroad that are involved with the management of those who abuse drugs. Bibliography; index.   HV5804.O24

Directories

See also EK138.

American Public Health Association. Biographical directory of the American Public Health Association. Comp. for the Association by Jaques Cattell Pr. N.Y., Bowker, 1979. 1207p.   **EK293**

Provides alphabetically arranged profiles of over 19,300 members. Each profile includes education, present and past activities, past professional experience, honors and awards, memberships, and mailing address. Geographic index.   RA424.4.A47

National directory of drug abuse and alcoholism treatment and prevention programs, September 1982. Rockville, Md., U.S. Dept. of Health and Human Services, Public Health Service, Alcohol, Drug Abuse, and Mental Health Admin., Nat. Inst. on Drug Abuse, Nat. Inst. on Alcohol Abuse and Alcoholism, (for sale by the Supt. of Docs.), [1983]. 301p. (DHHS pubn. no. (ADM) 83–321)   **EK294**

The National "Institutes have jointly conducted the National Drug and Alcoholism Treatment Utilization Survey (NDATUS), in cooperation with State agencies since 1979. The inclusion of approximately 7,500 alcoholism and drug abuse service units in this directory . . . [indicates] the success of the survey."—*Foreword.*

The directory is a source of information for treatment and prevention services in alcoholism and drug abuse. Arrangement is by state and city. Each entry gives address and telephone number and indicates the nature of the service program. A separate section lists Veterans Administration facilities and services by state.   RC566.N28

History

Rosen, George. A history of public health. N.Y., M.D. Publ., [1958]. 551p.   **EK295**

An 8-part history of public health from earliest times to the present. Includes: bibliography; list of memorable figures with brief biographical sketches; list of public health periodicals, arranged by country; list of worldwide public health societies and schools. Subject and author indexes.   RA424.R65

TOXICOLOGY

Guides

Wexler, Philip. Information resources in toxicology. N.Y., Elsevier/North Holland, [1982]. 333p.   **EK296**

A basic, comprehensive guide to the major sources of information. 813 annotated entries are classified by subject and arranged by format, such as, books, special monographs, and journals. There is a section for governmental and nongovernmental organizations which gives address, director, and an annotation about the institution. Indexed.   RA1193.4.W49

Abstract journals

Pesticides abstracts. v.7, no.1– , Jan. 1974– . [Wash., U.S. Environmental Protection Agency, Off. of Pesticide Programs, Technical Service Div.], 1974– . Monthly, with annual index.   **EK297**

Supersedes *Health aspects of pesticides; abstract bulletin* (v.1–6, 1968–73).

Classed arrangement with author and subject indexes. Listings are drawn from a review of about 1,150 domestic and foreign journals.   RA1270.P4H4

Handbooks

See also EC127, ED80.

Dreisbach, Robert Hastings. Handbook of poisoning: prevention, diagnosis & treatment. 11th ed. Los Altos, Calif., Lange Medical Publ., 1983. 632p. il.   **EK298**

1st–10th eds. publ. 1955–80; 1st ed. had title: *Handbook of poisons.*

Contents: I, General considerations; II, Agricultural poisons; III, Industrial hazards; IV, Household hazards—cosmetics, food poisoning, miscellaneous chemicals; V, Medicinal poisons; VI, Animal and plant hazards—reptiles, arachnids & insects, marine animals, plants.

"The purpose of this Handbook is to provide a concise summary of the diagnosis and treatment of clinically important poisons. Many other potentially poisonous agents which have not been important clinically are included in tabular form."—*Pref.*   RA1211.D7

Duke, James A. CRC handbook of medicinal herbs. Boca Raton, Fla., CRC Pr., [1985]. 677p. il.   **EK299**

Provides well documented information for 365 species of plants having medicinal or folk medicinal uses. All entries include the scientific name and authority, the scientific name of the plant family, and one or two colloquial or common names. Most entries have four sections giving uses, folk medicinal applications, chemistry, and toxicity. Most plants are illustrated. Extensive tables, bibliography, and index.   QK99.A1D83

Clinical toxicology of commercial products: acute poisoning. 5th ed. Baltimore, Md., Williams & Wilkins, [1984]. 1v. various pagings. il.   **EK300**

1st ed. 1957.

"The purpose of this book is to assist the physician in dealing quickly and effectively with acute chemical poisonings, arising through misuse of commercial products. The book provides (a) a list of trade name products together with their ingredients, (b) addresses and telephone numbers of companies for use when descriptions are not available, (c) sample formulas of many types of products with an estimate of the toxicity of each formula, (d) toxicological information including an appraisal of toxicity of individual ingredients, (e) recommendations for treatment and supportive care. . . . Over the years a second purpose of this reference manual has received increasing emphasis, namely to acquaint therapists and others with the pathophysical mechanisms, induced by various poisons, insofar as they are understood." —*Pref.* Includes citations to sources of original toxicological information and references to medical and toxicological literature.   RA1211.G5

Kaye, Sidney. Handbook of emergency toxicology; a guide for the identification, diagnosis, and treatment of poisoning. 4th ed. Springfield, Ill., C. C. Thomas, [1980]. 576p. il.   **EK301**

1st ed. 1954.

Subtitle: A guide for the identification, diagnosis, and treatment of poisoning.

In two sections: (1) brief chapters on symptoms and signs, lethal doses, antidotes and treatment, and analyses; (2) an alphabetical listing of nearly 170 poisons including information on synonyms, derivatives, properties, uses, minimum lethal dosage, acute and/or chronic symptoms, identification, interpretations, and treatment. Indexed.   RA1211.K3

Methodology for analytical toxicology. Ed. by Irving Sunshine. Cleveland, CRC Pr., 1975–82. 2v. il. (In progress)   **EK302**

A revision of *Handbook of analytical toxicology* (1969 ed.).

Includes therapeutic drugs and drugs of abuse. v.1 features heavy metals and organic volatile substances; v.2 features volatiles, neutral and acidic drugs, antibiotics, anticonvulsants, and antidepressants. For each substance two or three procedures are described in detail giving such information as principle, apparatus, reagents, procedures, calculation, interpretation, accuracy and precision, stability, and interfering substances. v.3 is to include an index.

RA1221.H36

Plunkett, Edmond Robert. Handbook of industrial toxicology. 2d ed. N.Y., Chemical Publ. Co., 1976. 522p. graphs.   **EK303**

1st ed. 1966.

Intended as a quick reference source, with topics listed in alphabetical order of the names by which they are best known. Information for each entry includes synonyms, description, occupational exposure, threshold limit value, toxicity, and preventive measures. "Bibliographic footnotes have been added where they represent good general review articles or where they contain excellent bibliographies to which the reader may refer."—*Pref.*   RA1216.P55

Registry of toxic effects of chemical substances. Rockville, Md., U.S. Dept. of Health, Education, and Welfare, 1975– . Annual. (U.S. Dept. of Health, Education, and Welfare, NIOSH series)   **EK304**

Edward J. Fairchild, ed.

Continues National Institute for Occupational Safety and Health, *Toxic substances list*, 1971–75.

The 1977 ed. is in 2v.: v.1 is an index volume, containing an alphabetical index to all substances covered as well as separate indexes to subfiles of compounds that are (a) carcinogenic and neoplastic, (b) teratogenic, (c) mutagenic, and (d) toxic to humans; v.2 contains, when available, Chemical Abstracts Service compound name, CAS registry number, synonyms, common or trade names, molecular weight, molecular formula, toxic levels with literature references, standards and regulations, and references to review articles.   RA1215.N37

Sittig, Marshall. Handbook of toxic and hazardous chemicals and carcinogens. 2d ed. Park Ridge, N.J., Noyes Publ., 1985. 950p. il.   **EK305**

1st ed. 1981 entitled: *Handbook of toxic and hazardous chemicals.*

The purpose is to "present concise chemical and safety information on nearly 800 toxic and hazardous chemicals . . . so that responsible decisions can be made by [those] who have contact with or interest in these chemicals due to their own or third party exposure."—*Pref.* Data is presented, as available, for each item giving: description; code number; DOT designation; synonyms; potential exposure; incompatibilities; permissible exposure limits and determination in air; permissible concentration and determination in water; routes of entry, harmful effects, symptoms, points of attack, medical surveillance, first aid, personal protective methods, and respirator selection; disposal method suggested; and references for, about, and to sources of more information.   RA1193.S58

Index

❖*This is an index of authors, editors, compilers, and sponsoring bodies which appear as main entries, of titles, and of subjects. Many personal and corporate names appearing in bibliographic notes are also included. In cases where a subject entry for a single item corresponds directly to a title and would merely repeat the same information, no subject entry is made. The letter* n *following an item number indicates that the indexed item is referred to in the annotation for the work designated by the code number. When a dash appears as part of the entry, it represents a single element (unlike usage in the text where a single dash represents repetition of the full boldface entry).*

Adams, J. T. and Jackson, K. T. Atlas of American history, DB160
Adams, R. E., Lombardi, J. V. and Carrera Damas, G. Venezuelan history, DB404
Adams, R. F. Six-guns and saddle leather, DB128
—— Western words, AD112
Adams, R. L. National job bank, CH782
Adams, T. R. American controversy, DB77
—— American independence, DB78
Addis, P. K. Through a woman's I, CC529
Addis, W. E. and Arnold, T. Catholic dictionary, BB445
Additions à la Bibliographie cornélienne, P. Le Verdier and E. Pelay, BD1041
Ade Ajayi, J. F. and Crowder, M. Historical atlas of Africa, DD62
Adeline, J. Adeline art dictionary, BE110
Adelman, I. and Dworkin, R. Contemporary novel, BD450
—— —— Modern drama, BD219
Adiciones á la Biblioteca boliviana de Gabriel René-Moreno, V. Abecía, AA633
Adiciones y continuación de "La imprenta en Manila," A. Pérez and C. Güemes, AA1016
Adjustment to widowhood, C. Strugnell, CC172
Adkins, C. and Dickinson, A. Doctoral dissertations in musicology, BH48
Adkins, R. A. and Adkins, L. Thesaurus of British archaeology, DC300
Adler, A. G. Automation in libraries, AB262
Adler, J. A. Elsevier's Dictionary of criminal science, CK265
Adler, M. J. and Van Doren, C. Great treasury of Western thought, BD125
Administration of criminal justice, California. University. Institute of Governmental Studies, CK244
Administration of government documents collections, R. M. Harleston and C. J. Stoffle, AB168
Administration of justice in the courts, F. J. Klein, CK44
Administration, personnel, buildings and equipment, D. F. Kohl, AB198
Admission requirements of U.S. and Canadian dental schools, EK197
Admussen, R. L. Petites revues littéraires, BD967
Adolescent mental health abstracts, CC147
Adolphe, H. and Toussaint, A. Bibliography of Mauritius, DD157
Adoption bibliography and multi-ethnic sourcebook, E. W. van Why, CC159
Adressbuch für den deutschsprachigen Buchhandel, AA342
Adventuring with books, National Council of Teachers of English. Committee on the Elementary School Booklist, AA465
Adverse reaction titles, EK247
Advertising & press annual of Southern Africa, AE157
Advertising and public relations bibliography, CH159–CH162
biography, CH180
dictionaries and encyclopedias, CH163–CH167
directories, CH168–CH172
guides, CH158
handbooks, CH173–CH179
Advertising slogans of America, H. S. Sharp, CH166
Aeronautical and space engineering abstract journals, EJ49–EJ50
bibliography, EJ39–EJ47
biography, EJ69
dictionaries and encyclopedias, EJ51–EJ61; foreign terms, EJ62–EJ67
directories, EJ68–EJ69
handbooks, EJ70–EJ81

periodicals, EJ48
yearbooks, EJ82–EJ84
Aeronautical and space serial publications, U.S. Library of Congress. Science and Technology Division, EJ48
Aeronautical-English, A. Oppermann, EJ66
Aeronautics and astronautics, U.S. National Aeronautics and Space Administration, EJ78
Aerospace glossary, U.S. Aerospace Studies Institute, EJ59
Aerospace medicine and biology, EK62
Aerospace research index, EJ68
Aerospace year book, EJ82
Aeschlimann, E. and Ancona, P. d'. Dictionnaire des miniaturistes du Moyen Âge et de la Renaissance, BE332
Aeschylus: bibliography, BD1408; indexes, BD1407
Affirmative action, CH291
Affirmative action, H. A. Hood and K. L. Padgett, CK42
Affirmative action and preferential admissions in higher education, K. Swanson, CB45
Afghanistan
bibliography, DE94
biography, AJ98–AJ99
gazetteers, CL130
history: bibliography, DE131–DE134
Afre, S. A. Ashanti region of Ghana, DD133
Africa
armed forces, CJ591
atlases, CL347–CL350
bibliography, AA602–AA603; bibliography of bibliography, AA33–AA34
biography, AJ100–AJ106
economic conditions, CH72–CH75
foreign relations: bibliography, DB46, DD8, DD20–DD21, DD88, DE53
government publications, AG83–AG92
history: atlases, DD61–DD62; bibliography, DD3–DD21 (current, DD22–DD26); book reviews, DD27–DD30; chronologies, DD49–DD50; current surveys, DD51–DD54; dictionaries and handbooks, DD46–DD48; directories, DD55–DD59; dissertations, DD31–DD34; general histories, DD60; guides, DD1–DD2; library catalogs, DD7, DD10, DD12, DD14, DD16–DD17, DD26, DD130, DD145, DD148, DD152, DD186, DD188, DD192; library resources, DD39–DD45; serial publications, DD35–DD38; see also under region (e.g., Africa, Southern), and under names of individual countries
military history: bibliography, DD15, DD65
politics and government, CJ232–CJ244
statistics: bibliography, CG120–CG127; compendiums, CG118–CG119
Africa, Northern
history: bibliography, DD63–DD67, DE6–DE7, DE32, DE35, DE44; dictionaries and surveys, DD71–DD72; dissertations, DD68; library resources, DD69–DD70, DE64; see also Near and Middle East, and under names of individual countries
Africa, Southern
foreign relations, DD73
history: bibliography, DD73–DD89 (current, DD90–DD92); dictionaries and handbooks, DD97–DD100; dissertations, DD93–DD94; manuscripts and archives, DD95–DD96; see also under Africa, and under names of individual countries
Africa, West
history: archives, DD102; bibliography, DD100a–DD101, DD103; see also

under Africa, Southern, and under names of individual countries
Africa, a bibliography of geography and related disciplines, S. H. Bederman, CL10
Africa administration, W. Z. Duic, CJ240
Africa and the Middle East, R. A. Vineberg, CJ244
Africa bibliography, DD23
Africa contemporary record, DD51
Africa diary, DD52
Africa index to continental periodical literature, DD90
Africa on film and videotape, D. S. Wiley, DD19
Africa research bulletin, DD53
Africa since 1914, DD3
Africa south of the Sahara, DD97
Africa south of the Sahara, U.S. Library of Congress. African Section, DD86
Africa who's who, AJ100
African authors, D. E. Herdeck, BD1459
African book publishing record, AA602
African book world & press, AA343
African books in print, AA603
African boundaries, I. Brownlie, CK314
African education and development since 1960, J. W. Hanson and G. W. Gibson, CB86
African governmental systems in static and changing conditions, M. d' Hertefelt, CE84
African historical demography, J. W. Gregory, D. D. Cordell and R. Gervais, CG122
African historical dictionaries, DD46
African history and literatures, Harvard University. Library, DD10
African international relations, M. W. DeLancey, DD8
African language materials, A. M. Van Hoosen, BC181
African languages: atlases, BC183; bibliography, BC177–BC182; see also under names of individual languages
African law bibliography, J. Vanderlinden, CK58
African literature: bibliography, BD744–BD747, BD1450–BD1458; biography, BD1459–BD1460
African music and oral data, R. M. Stone and F. J. Gillis, BH317
African nationalist leaders in Rhodesia, R. Cary and D. Mitchell, CJ441
African newspapers currently received by American libraries, M. K. Cason, AF31n
African newspapers in selected American libraries, U.S. Library of Congress. Serial Division, AF31
African newspapers in the Library of Congress, U.S. Library of Congress. Serial & Government Publications Division, DD38
African oral narratives, proverbs, riddles, poetry, and song, H. Scheub, CF108
African political dictionary, C. S. Phillips, CJ242
African political facts since 1945, C. Cook and D. Killingray, CJ238
African population census reports, J. R. Pinfold, CG124
African recorder, DD54
African slave trade and its suppression, P. C. Hogg, DD11
African social psychology, M. Armer, CE81
African Studies Association. ASA news, DD22
African theatre, N. B. East, BD1451
African trade unionism, G. R. Martens, CH665
African women, L. Kratochvil and S. Shaw, CC564
African world, R. A. Lystad, DD48
African writers (French), BD936–BD940

American and British theatrical biography, J. P. Wearing, BG109

American & Canadian doctoral dissertations & master's theses on Africa, M. Sims and A. Kagan, DD33

American and Canadian immigrant and ethnic folklore, R. A. Georges and S. Stern, CF76

American and English popular entertainment, D. B. Wilmeth, BG2

American anthology, E. C. Stedman, BD467

American Antiquarian Society, Worcester, Mass. Library. Dictionary catalog of American books, AA555

American architects directory, BE292

American architects from the Civil War to the First World War, L. Wodehouse, BE250

American architects from the first World War to the present, L. Wodehouse, BE251

American architectural books, H. R. Hitchcock, BE239

American architecture and art, D. M. Sokol, BE249

American architecture since 1780, M. Whiffen, BE285

American armory, C. K. Bolton, AK117

American art auction catalogues, H. Lancour, BE143

American art directory, BE134

American Association for State and Local History. Directory of historical societies and agencies in the United States and Canada, DB141

American Association of Architectural Bibliographers. Papers, BE231

American Association of Homes for the Aging. Membership directory, CC125

American Association of Law Libraries. Committee on Foreign and International Law. Basic Latin American legal materials, CK86; Union list of basic Latin American legal materials, CK87

American Association of Port Authorities. Committee on Standardization and Special Research. Port dictionary of technical terms, EJ294

American authors, S. J. Kunitz and H. Haycraft, BD417

American authors and books, W. J. Burke and W. D. Howe, BD405

American autobiography, M. L. Briscoe, AJ97

American badges and insignia, E. E. Kerrigan, CJ575

American Banker. Directory of U.S. banking executives, CH600

American Baptist Churches in the U.S.A. Directory, BB352

American Baptist Churches in the U.S.A. Yearbook, BB351

American Bar Association. Directory, CK174

American Behavioral Scientist. ABS guide to recent publications in the social and behavioral sciences, CA10

American bench, CK191

American bibliography, C. Evans, AA557

American bibliography, R. R. Shaw and R. H. Shoemaker, AA567

American bibliography, Modern Language Association of America, BD22

American bibliography of Russian and East European studies, DC39

American bibliography of Slavic and East European studies, DC39a

American black women in the arts and social sciences, O. Williams, CC402

American book auction catalogues, G. L. McKay, AA333

American book illustrators, T. Bolton, AA436

American book of days, J. M. Hatch, CF124

American book-prices current, AA326

American book publishing record. BPR annual cumulative, AA580; BPR cumulative, AA581

American book publishing record, AA579

American book publishing record cumulative 1876–1949, AA574

American book publishing record cumulative 1950–1977, AA575

American book trade directory, AA344

American Bureau of Shipping. Record of the American Bureau of Shipping, CH475

American business directories, M. V. Davis, CH255

American catalogue, AA573

American catalogue of books, J. Kelly, AA571

American Catholic who's who, AJ89

American chemical industry, W. Haynes, ED120

American Chemical Society. Chemical research faculties, ED59; Handbook for authors of papers in American Chemical Society publications, ED85
—————— Chemical Abstracts Service. CASSI keyword-out-of-context index, ED19; Chemical Abstracts Service source index, EA59, ED17; Chemical Abstracts Service source index; quarterly supplement, ED18; Chemical titles, ED23; Ring systems handbook, ED24
—————— Committee on Analytical Reagents. Reagent chemicals, ED62
—————— Committee on Professional Training. Directory of graduate research, ED54
—————— Dept. of Education Activities. College chemistry faculties, ED55

American chemists and chemical engineers, ED122

American church history series, BB285

American Civil War navies, M. J. Smith, CJ555

American clipper ships, O. T. Howe and F. C. Matthews, CH467

American clock, W. H. Distin and R. Bishop, BF54

American clocks and clockmakers, C. W. Drepperd, BF55

American college dictionary, AD12

American College of Physicians. Biographical directory, EK170

American community, technical, and junior colleges, CB213

American composers, D. Ewen, BH194

American constitutional development, A. T. Mason and D. G. Stephenson, CK405

American controversy, T. R. Adams, DB77

American costume, S. M. O'Donnol, BG121

American Council on Education. Overseas Liaison Committee. International directory for educational liaison, CB189

American counties, J. N. Kane, CL204

American country furniture, R. M. Kovel and T. H. Kovel, BF110

American county government, J. C. Bollens, J. R. Bayes and K. L. Utter, CJ184

American decorations, U.S. Adjutant General's Office, CJ579

American Dental Association. Bureau of Library Services. Basic dental reference works, EK186

American dental directory, EK198

American dialect dictionary, H. Wentworth, AD116

American dialects, L. Herman and M. S. Herman, BG71

American diaries, L. Arksey, N. Pries and M. Reed, BD473

American diaries, W. Matthews, BD472

American diaries in manuscript, W. Matthews, BD474

American dictionary of economics, CH43

American directors, J.-P. Coursodon and P. Sauvage, BG269

American dissertations on foreign education, F. Parker, CB117

American dissertations on the drama and the theatre, F. M. Litto, BG43

American doctoral dissertations, AH18

American doctoral dissertations in foreign language education, D. Birdsong, BC51

American doctoral dissertations on Asia, C. W. Stucki, DE12

American doctoral dissertations on the Arab world, G. D. Selim, DE61–DE62

American drama
annuals, BD432–BD433
bibliography, BD367, BD422–BD429
criticism, BD430–BD431
history, BD434–BD436

American drama, T. Bogard, R. Moody and W. J. Meserve, BD434

American drama criticism, F. E. Eddleman, BD430

American drama to 1900, W. J. Meserve, BD426

American drug index, EK271

American druggist blue book, EK272

American Economic Association. Survey of members, CH66

American economic business history information sources, R. W. Lovett, CH279

American economic history, W. K. Hutchinson, CH117

American education, R. G. Durnin, CB11

American educational history, M. W. Sedlak and T. Walch, CB98

American educators' encyclopedia, E. L. Dejnozka and D. E. Kapel, CB139

American electorate, CJ158

American electricians' handbook, EJ213

American encyclopedia of soccer, Z. Hollander, BJ54

American engineers of the nineteenth century, C. Roysdon and L. A. Khatri, EJ31

American engravers upon copper and steel, D. M. Stauffer, BE367

American engravers upon copper and steel, M. Fielding, BE365

American entomologists, A. Mallis, EC271

American ephemeris and nautical almanac, U.S. Nautical Almanac Office, EB62

American ethnic groups, F. Cordasco and D. N. Alloway, CC344

American ethnic groups and the revival of cultural pluralism, J. F. Kinton, CC322

American export register, CH390

American family history, CC217

American Federation of Labor. American Federation of Labor; history, encyclopedia, reference book, CH695

American Federation of Labor and Congress of Industrial Organizations pamphlets, M. E. Woodbridge, CH683

American Federation of Teachers bibliography, Wayne State University, Detroit. Archives of Labor and Urban Affairs, CB70

American fiction
annuals, BD454
bibliography, BD437–BD449; historical, BD437–BD438, BD445
criticism, BD450–BD453
history, BD455

American fiction, A. H. Quinn, BD455

American fiction, J. L. Woodress, BD446

American fiction, L. H. Wright, BD447–BD449

American fiction to 1900, D. K. Kirby, BD442

American Lutheran Church. Yearbook, BB377

American Management Association. Index to AMA resources of the seventies, CH289; Ten-year index of AMA publications, CH288

American Marketing Association. Bibliography series, CH748

American Mathematical Society. Index to translations selected, EF15

American Medical Association. CMIT, EK92

————— Dept. of Drugs. AMA drug evaluations, EK250

American Medical Association family medical guide, EK67

American medical bibliography, F. Guerra, EK151

American medical directory, EK128

American men and women of science. Cumulative index, EA222

American men and women of science, EA221

American men and women of science: Social and behavioral sciences, CA75

American merchant ships, F. C. Matthews, CH468

American Meteorological Society. Cumulated bibliography and index to Meteorological and geoastrophysical abstracts, EE135

————— Committee on the Compendium of Meteorology. Compendium of meteorology, EE146

American Missionary Association Archives see Amistad Research Center

American movies reference book, P. Michael, BG278

American Museum of Natural History, New York. Library. Research catalog, EC48

American music before 1865 in print and on records, BH57

American music handbook, C. Pavlakis, BH161

American music studies, J. R. Heintze, BH50

American musical theatre, G. M. Bordman, BH247

American national dictionary for information processing systems, EJ233

American National Standard glossary of terms in nuclear science and technology, American Nuclear Society. Standards Committee. Subcommittee ANS-9, EJ367

American National Standards Institute. Catalog, EA253

American naval history, J. Sweetman, DB155

American Navy, 1789–1860, M. J. Smith, CJ554

American Navy, 1865–1918, M. J. Smith, CJ556

American Navy, 1918–1941, M. J. Smith, CJ557

American newspaper journalists, AF122–AF123

American newspapers, AF18

American nicknames, G. E. Shankle, BD93

American notes and queries, BD94

American novel, D. L. Gerstenberger and G. Hendrick, BD452

American Nuclear Society. Standards Committee. Subcommittee ANS-9. American National Standard glossary of terms in nuclear science and technology, EJ367

American Numismatic Society. Numismatic notes and monographs, AK137

————— Library. Dictionary catalogue, BF145

American Oriental Society. Library. Catalog, DE3

American origins, L. G. Pine, AK13

American Osteopathic Association. Yearbook and directory of osteopathic physicians, EK129

American painting, L. Doumato, BE310

American painting, S. S. Keaveney, BE311

American painting, V. Barker, E326

American paintings, New York. Metropolitan Museum of Art, BE317

American paintings in the Metropolitan Museum of Art, New York. Metropolitan Museum of Art, BE318

American paintings in the Museum of Fine Arts, Boston, Boston. Museum of Fine Arts, BE313

American Paper and Pulp Association. Dictionary of paper, AA364

American periodicals, 1741–1900, J. Hoornstra and T. Heath, AE26

American Petroleum Institute. Petroleum facts and figures, EJ382

American philatelic dictionary and Colonial and Revolutionary posts, H. M. Konwiser, BF185

American philatelic periodicals, C. M. Smith, BF183

American Philosophical Society. Library. Catalog of books, EA200; Catalog of manuscripts, EA201

American place names, G. R. Stewart, CL206

American plays printed 1714–1830, F. P. Hill, BD424

American poetry: bibliography and indexes, BD456–BD464; collections, BD466–BD470; handbooks, BD465

American poetry index, BD457

American political dictionary, J. C. Plano and M. Greenberg, CJ98

American political parties, L. R. Wynar, CJ177

American Political Science Association. Biographical directory, CJ75

American political terms, H. Sperber and T. Trittschuh, CJ101

American political women, E. Stineman, CJ181

American popular culture, CF66

American popular culture, L. Landrum, CF80

American popular illustration, J. J. Best, BE14

American popular music, M. W. Booth, BH291

American popular songs, D. Ewen, BH261

American practical navigator, EB59

American presidency, CJ117

American presidency, K. E. Davison, CJ118

American prints in the Library of Congress, U.S. Library of Congress. Prints and Photographs Division, BE350

American Psychiatric Association. Biographical directory of fellows and members, CD125

————— Joint Commission on Public Affairs. Psychiatric glossary, CD76

American Psychological Association. Biographical directory, CD124; Publication manual, CD131

American Public Health Association. Biographical directory, EK293; Standard methods for the examination of water and wastewater, ED63

————— Program Area Committee on Air Pollution. Guide to the appraisal and control of air pollution, EJ143

American Radio Relay League. ARRL handbook for the radio amateur, EJ257

American reference books annual, AA476

American regional theatre history, C. F. W. Larson, BG34

American religion and philosophy, E. R. Sandeen and F. Hale, BB30

American Revised Version (Bible), p.347

American School of Classical Studies see Gennadius Library

American sculpture, J. Ekdahl, BE368

American seashells, R. T. Abbott, EC240

American sheet music, D. B. Priest, BH173

American short-fiction criticism and scholarship, J. Weixlmann, BD453

American Society for Engineering Education. Engineering School Libraries Division. [Guides to literature], EJ1

American Society for Metals. ASM metals reference book, EJ345; ASM thesaurus of metallurgical terms, EJ333; Metals handbook, EJ351

————— Documentation Service. ASM review of metal literature, EJ329

American Society for Testing and Materials. Annual book of ASTM standards, EA254; Directory of testing laboratories, EA195

————— Committee D-19 on Water. Manual on water, EJ161

American Society of Civil Engineers. Committee on History and Heritage of American Civil Engineering. Biographical dictionary of American civil engineers, EJ112

American Society of Composers, Authors and Publishers. ASCAP biographical dictionary, BH184; ASCAP index of performed compositions, BH58; ASCAP symphonic catalog, BH214

American Society of Heating, Refrigerating and Air-Conditioning Engineers. ASHRAE handbook, EJ280

American Society of Mechanical Engineers. Metals Engineering Handbook Board. ASME handbook, EJ306

American Society of Tool and Manufacturing Engineers. Handbook of industrial metrology, EJ285; Plastics tooling and manufacturing handbook, EJ99

American-Southern African relations, DD73

American spirit in architecture, T. F. Hamlin, BE288

American stage to World War I, D. B. Wilmeth, BG41

American Standard Version (Bible), p.347

American state governors, J. E. Kallenbach and J. S. Kallenbach, CJ205

American Statistical Association. Directory of statisticians and others in allied professions, CG42

American statistics index, CG108

American students, P. G. Altbach and D. H. Kelly, CB25

American studies, DB16

American studies and translations of contemporary Italian poetry, J. A. Molinaro, BD1085

American studies bibliography, DB48

American Theatre Planning Board. Theatre check list, BG69

American theatrical arts, W. C. Young, BG10

American theatrical periodicals, C. J. Stratman, BG44

American thesaurus of slang, L. V. Berrey and M. Van den Bark, AD94

American third parties since the Civil War, D. S. Rockwood, CJ175

American travelers to Mexico, G. Cole, DB350

American universities and colleges, CB214

American universities and colleges, A. H. Songe, CB160

American University of Beirut. Economic Research Institute. Selected and annotated bibliography of economic literature, CH76

American usage and style, R. H. Copperud, AD55

reports of the Public Archives of Canada, DB196

Cookbooks, EH130–EH131; bibliography, EH117–EH123

Cooke, O. A. Canadian military experience, CJ593

Coole, A. B. Bibliography on Far Eastern numismatology, BF147

Cooley, C. E. and Doubleday, N. Encyclopedia of world travel, BJ107

Coolhaas, W. P. Critical survey of studies on Dutch colonial history, DC425

Cooling, B. F. and Millett, A. R. Doctoral dissertations in military affairs, CJ515

Cooper, A. M. and Heath, D. B. Alcohol use and world cultures, CC139

Cooper, B. E. and Somer, J. American & British literature, BD382

Cooper, D. E. International bibliography of discographies, BH346

Cooper, L. Concordance to the works of Horace, BD1441

Cooper, R. and Uden, G. Dictionary of British ships and seamen, CJ597

Cooper, S. ESL theses and dissertations, BC49

———— Graduate theses and dissertations in English as a second language, BC48

Cooperative Africana Microform Project see under Chicago. Center for Research Libraries

Coopman, T. and Broeckaert, J. Bibliographie van den Vlaamschen taalstrijd, AA627

Coordinate index reference guide to community mental health, S. E. Golann, CD22

Coover, J. Musical instrument collections, BH328

Coover, J. B. Music lexicography, BH15

Copeland, J. I. and Green, F. M. Old South, DB125

Copenhagen. Marinens Bibliothek. Katalog, CJ504

———— Universitet. Bibliotek. Danish theses for the doctorate and commemorative publications of the University of Copenhagen, AH36

Copernicus: bibliography, EB3

Coping with the biomedical literature, EK2

Copinger, W. A. Supplement to Hain's Repertorium bibliographicum, AA270

Copious and critical English-Latin dictionary, W. Smith and T. D. Hall, AD546

Copley, E. J. Guide to Referativnyi zhurnal, EA82

Coppa, F. J. Dictionary of modern Italian history, DC403

Coppe, P. and Pirsoul, L. Dictionnaire bio-bibliographique des littérateurs d'expression wallonne, BD942

Coppell, W. G. World catalogue of theses and dissertations about the Australian Aborigines and Torres Strait Islanders, CE109

———— and Stratigos, S. Bibliography of Pacific Island theses and dissertations, DG10

Copperud, R. H. American usage and style, AD55

Coptic bibliography, W. Kammerer, BD1481

Coptic dictionary, W. E. Crum, AD234

Coptic etymological dictionary, J. Cerny, AD233

Coptic language: dictionaries, AD233–AD234

Coptic literature, BD1480–BD1481

Copy-editing, J. Butcher, AA414

Copy preparation, AA414–AA426

Copying methods manual, W. R. Hawken, AB306

Copyright, AA406–AA413

Copyright, M. Roberts, AA411

Copyright book, W. S. Strong, AA412

Copyright handbook, D. F. Johnston, AA409

Copyright laws and treaties of the world, United Nations Educational, Scientific and Cultural Organization, AA413

Copyright publications, New Zealand. General Assembly. Library, AA980

Corbet, G. B. and Hill, J. E. World list of mammalian species, EC228

Corbin, J. B. Index of state geological survey publications issued in series, EE40–EE41

Corbin, S. Répertoire de manuscrits médiévaux contenant des notations musicales, BH69

Cordasco, F. Eighteenth century bibliographies, BD525

———— History of American education, CB14b

———— Italian Americans, CC311

———— and Alloway, D. N. American ethnic groups, CC344

———— ———— Crime in America, CK225

———— ———— Medical education in the United States, EK13

———— ———— Sociology of education, CB81

———— and Bernstein, G. Bilingual education in American schools, CB51

———— and Brickman, W. W. Bibliography of American educational history, CB77

———— Bucchioni, E. and Castellanos, D. Puerto Ricans on the United States mainland, CC478

———— and Covello, L. Educational sociology, CB111

Cordeiro, D. R. Bibliography of Latin American bibliographies, AA78

Cordell, D. D., Gervais, R. and Gregory, J. W. African historical demography, CG122

Cordier, H. Bibliotheca indosinica, DE212

———— Bibliotheca japonica, DE249

———— Bibliotheca sinica, DE151

———— Imprimerie sino-européenne en Chine, AA680

Cordingley, A. and Tod, D. D. Check list of Canadian imprints, AA660

Córdova, E. and Morris, J. O. Bibliography of industrial relations in Latin America, CH666

Core collection, Harvard University. Graduate School of Business Administration. Baker Library, CH191

Core media collection for secondary schools, L. G. Brown, AA529

Core readings in psychiatry, CD13

Corley, N. T. Travel in Canada, BJ102

Cormier, R. Sources des statistiques actuelles, CG5

Corneille, P.: bibliography, BD1040–BD1042; dictionaries, BD1043

Cornell, J. Great international disaster book, DA42

Cornell, T. and Matthews, J. Atlas of the Roman world, DA141

Cornell University. Graduate School of Business and Public Administration. Management, CH293

———— Libraries. Catalogue of Runic literature, AA873; Catalogue of the Dante collection, BD1087; Catalogue of the Icelandic collection, AA872; Catalog of the Wason Collection on China and the Chinese, DE152; Catalogue of the Witchcraft Collection, CD143; Islandica, AA874; Petrarch, BD1445; Southeast Asia catalog, DE108

———— New York State School of Industrial and Labor Relations. Library. Library catalog, CH652

Cornelson, D. Handbook of the economy of the German Democratic Republic, CH93

Corner, C. M. and Gunston, C. A. German-English glossary of financial and economic terms, CH566

Corning Museum of Glass, Corning, N.Y.. History and art of glass, BF35

Cornish language: dictionaries, AD235–AD238

Corns, A. R. and Sparke, A. Bibliography of unfinished books in the English language, AA794

Cornyn, S. Theatre magazine, BG47

Corominas, J. Diccionari etimològic i complementari de la llengua Catalana, AD213

———— Diccionario crítico etimológico de la lengua castellana, AD734

Corporate America, CH274

Corporate treasurer's and controller's encyclopedia, Prentice-Hall, Inc., CH555

Corporate 500, CA104

Corpus Christianorum, BB302

Corpus dictionary of Western churches, BB236

Corpus juris secundum, CK142

Correlation index, Special Libraries Council of Philadelphia and Vicinity, EA85

Correlation index of technical reports, U.S. Defense Documentation Center, EA86

Correspondence schools, CB231, CB233, CB235

Corrigan, B. Catalogue of Italian plays, BD1084

Corrosion handbook, H. H. Uhlig, EJ357

Corsini, R. J. Encyclopedia of psychology, CD83

Corson, R. Stage makeup, BG114

Corswant, W. Dictionnaire d'archéologie biblique, BB186

Cortada, J. W. Annotated bibliography on the history of data processing, EJ229

———— Bibliographic guide to Spanish diplomatic history, DC479

———— Historical dictionary of the Spanish Civil War, DC492

Cortelazzo, M. and Zolli, P. Dizionario etimologico della lingua italiana, AD506

Cortés Conde, R. and Stein, S. J. Latin America, CH109

Cosemans, A. and Heyse, T. Contribution à la bibliographie dynastique et nationale, DC88

Cosenza, M. E. Biographical and bibliographical dictionary of the Italian humanists, BD1077

Cosío Villegas, D. Cuestiones internacionales de México, DB351

———— Última bibliografía política de la historia moderna de México, DB352

Cosminsky, S. and Harrison, I. E. Traditional medicine, CE10–CE11, EK73, EK81

Cosmopolitan world atlas, Rand McNally and Co., CL325

Costa, A. Dicionário de sinônimos e locuções da língua portuguêsa, AD636

Costa, J. J. Abuse of the elderly, CC92

Costa de la Torre, A. Catálogo de la bibliografía boliviana, AA634

Costa Rica
  atlases, CL372
  bibliography, AA688–AA689; current, AA690–AA691
  biography, AJ174
  foreign relations, DB329
  history: bibliography, DB329–DB331
  statistics, CG187

Costa Rica. Dirección General de Estadística y Censos. Anuario estadístico, CG187

Coston, H. Dictionnaire de la politique française, CJ296

———— Dictionnaire des dynasties

history, DA9; Geography and anthropology, CL28; German literature, BD816; Government, CJ19; Hungarian history and literature, DC357; Italian history and literature, DC394; Judaica, BB546; Kilgour collection of Russian literature, BD1334; Latin America and Latin American periodicals, DB244; Latin American literature, BD1194; Latin literature, BD1422; Literature: general and comparative, BD8; Periodical classes, AE5; Philosophy and psychology, BA17, CD28; Reference collections, AA485; Russian history since 1917, DC529; Slavic history and literatures, DC46; Sociology, CC6; Southern Asia, DE88; Spanish history and literature, DC482; Twentieth century Russian literature, BD1335; Widener Library shelflist, AA145
────── Chinese-Japanese Library. Catalog of Protestant missionary works in Chinese, BB317
────── Museum of Comparative Zoology. Library. Catalogue, EC172
────── Peabody Museum of Archaeology and Ethnology. Library. Catalogue, CE12
────── Psycho-Acoustic Laboratory. Bibliography on hearing, CC182
Harvard-Yenching Library. Chinese and Japanese catalogues, DE125; Classified catalogue of Korean books, DE273
Harvey, A. E. New English Bible: companion to the New Testament, BB196
Harvey, A. P. and Pernet, A. European sources of scientific information, EA172
Harvey, J. H. English mediaeval architects, BE296
────── Sources for the history of houses, BE280
Harvey, J. M. Sources of statistics, CG69
────── Statistics Africa, CG123
────── Statistics America, CG82
────── Statistics Asia & Australasia, CG140
────── Statistics Europe, CG204
Harvey, M. G. J. Current accounting literature 1971, CH138
Harvey, N. Agricultural research centres, EH48
Harvey, P. Oxford companion to classical literature, BD1394
────── Oxford companion to English literature, BD556
────── and Heseltine, J. E. Oxford companion to French literature, BD999
Harvey, V. A. Handbook of theological terms, BB256
Harwell, R. B. More Confederate imprints, DB98
Haskell, D. C. Check list of cumulative indexes to individual periodicals in the New York Public Library, AE219
────── Provençal literature and language, BD1125
Haslam, M. Marks and monograms of the modern movement, BF4
Hassall, W. O. History through surnames, AK176
Hasse, A. R. Index of economic material in documents of the states of the United States, CH116
────── Index to United States documents relating to foreign affairs, CK290
Hassinger, E. Bibliographie zur Universitätsgeschichte, CB37
Hastings, J. Dictionary of Christ and the Gospels, BB164
────── Dictionary of the Apostolic church, BB165
────── Dictionary of the Bible, BB162–BB163

────── Encyclopaedia of religion and ethics, BB51
Haswell, H. A. and Eells, W. C. Academic degrees, CB306
Hatch, E. and Redpath, H. A. Concordance to the Septuagint and the other Greek versions of the Old Testament, BB140
Hatch, J. M. American book of days, CF124
Hatch, J. V. Black image on the American stage, BG32
────── and Abdullah, O. Black playwrights, BD482
Hategekimana, G. Sources bibliographiques des états de l'ancien domaine colonial belge d'Afrique Centrale, DD79
Hathorn, R. Y. Crowell's Handbook of classical drama, BD1395
Hatin, L. E. Bibliographie historique et critique de la presse périodique française, AE68
Hatje, G. Encyclopaedia of modern architecture, BE268
Hatten tojō koku no tōkei shiryō mokuroku, CG10
Hattori, S. and Wurm, S. A. Language atlas of the Pacific area, BC191
Hatzfeld, A. and Darmesteter, A. Dictionnaire général de la langue française, AD294
Hatzfeld, H. Bibliografía crítica de la nueva estilística, BD931
────── Critical bibliography of the new stylistics, BD931–BD932
────── and Le Hir, Y. Essai de bibliographie critique de stylistique française et romane, BD933
────── and Willging, E. P. Catholic serials of the nineteenth century in the United States, AE188
Hauff, N. S. Stikords-katalog over norsk literatur, AA991
Haugen, E. Bibliography of Scandinavian languages and linguistics, BC109
────── Norwegian English dictionary, AD588
Haugen, E. L. Bibliography of Scandinavian dictionaries, AD148
Haulman, C. A., Hosni, D. A. and Raffa, F. A. United States employment and training programs, CH673
Hausa language: dictionaries, AD427
Hausa people, F. A. Salamone and J. A. McCain, CE91
Hauser, A. Social history of art, BE152
Hausmann, U. Handbuch der Archäologie, DA101
Haussig, H. W. Wörterbuch der Mythologie, CF9
Hauswedell, M. H. and Golay, F. H. Annotated guide to Philippine serials, AE134
Havana. Biblioteca Nacional "José Martí." Impresos relativos a Cuba editados en las Estados Unidos de Norteamérica, DB424
Havers, J. A. and Stubbs, F. W. Handbook of heavy construction, EJ178
Havighurst, A. F. Modern England, DC282
Haviland, V. Best of children's books, AA461
────── Children's literature, AA462
Havlice, P. P. Index to artistic biography, BE167
────── Index to literary biography, BD117
────── Popular song index, BH270
Hawaiian dictionary, M. K. Pukui and S. H. Elbert, AD429
Hawaiian language: dictionaries, AD428–AD429
Hawaiian legends in English, A. P. Leib and A. G. Day, CF81
Hawelek, A. and Pflücke, M. Periodica chemica, ED20

Hawes, G. R. Encyclopedia of second careers, CH780
────── and Hawes, L. S. Concise dictionary of education, CB150
Hawgood, J. A. Modern constitutions since 1787, CK393
Hawken, W. R. Copying methods manual, AB306
Hawkins, D. T. Online information retrieval bibliography, AB266
Hawkins, K. Parole, CK230
Hawley, G. G. Condensed chemical dictionary, ED36
Hawley, W. D. and Svara, J. H. Study of community power, CJ20
Hawtrey, S. C. and Abraham, L. A. Parliamentary dictionary, CJ337
Hay, O. P. Bibliography and catalogue of the fossil vertebrata of North America, EE231
Hay, R. and Synge, P. M. Color dictionary of flowers and plants for home and garden, EC137
Hayakawa, S. I. Funk & Wagnalls modern guide to synonyms, AD105
Hayavadana Rao, C. Indian biographical dictionary, AJ255
Haycraft, F. W. Degrees and hoods of the world's universities and colleges, CB302
Haycraft, H. and Kunitz, S. J. American authors, BD417
────── British authors before 1800, BD576
────── British authors of the 19th century, BD577
────── Junior book of authors, BD194
────── Twentieth century authors, BD107
Haydn, H. and Fuller, E. Thesaurus of book digests, BD71
Haydn, J. T. Book of dignities, AK102
────── Dictionary of dates, DA57
Haydon, G. Introduction to musicology, BH4
Hayes, G. P., Andrews, J. A. C. and Dupuy, T. N. Almanac of world military power, CJ532
────── and Martell, P. World military leaders, CJ543
Hayes, R. J. Manuscript sources for the history of Irish civilisation, DC375
Haykin, D. J. Subject headings, AB246
Hayne, D. M. and Tirol, M. Bibliographie critique du roman canadien-français, BD950
Haynes, W. American chemical industry, ED120
────── Chemical trade names and commercial synonyms, ED70
Hays, T. A. Anthropology in the New Guinea highlands, CE111
Hayton, R. D. National interests in Antarctica, DH6
Haywood, C. Bibliography of North American folklore and folksong, CF77
Hayyīm, S. Larger English-Persian dictionary, AD596
────── New Persian-English dictionary, AD597
────── Shorter Persian-English dictionary, AD598
Hazard, B. H. Korean studies guide, DE269
Hazard, J. N., Butler, W. E. and Maggs, P. B. Soviet legal system, CK105
────── and Stern, W. B. Bibliography of the principal materials on Soviet law, CK104
Hazard, M. C. Complete concordance to the American Standard Version of the Holy Bible, BB127
Hazard, P. and Bédier, J. Littérature française, BD1014
Hazards in the chemical laboratory, ED71

English romantic poets and essayists, BD649

Houzeau, J. C. and Lancaster, A. Bibliographie générale de l'astronomie, EB9

Hove, J. van. Répertoire des périodiques paraissant en Belgique, AE47

Hovemeyer, G. A. and Owens, E. A. Bibliography on taxation of foreign operations and foreigners, CH606a, CH606b

How-to, W. A. Katz and L. S. Katz, BJ100

"How to" books, BJ100–BJ101

How to catalog a rare book, P. S. Dunkin, AB214

How to debate, H. B. Summers, F. L. Whan and T. A. Rousse, BD356

How to design electrical systems, J. F. McPartland, EJ220

How to distinguish the saints in art, A. de Bles, BE200

How to do library research, R. B. Downs and C. D. Keller, AB28

How to enter and win black & white photography contests, A. Gadney, BF208

How to enter and win color photography contests, A. Gadney, BF207

How to enter & win film contests, A. Gadney, BG264

How to find chemical information, R. E. Maizell, ED4

How to find information about companies, CH185

How to find out about engineering, S. A. J. Parsons, EJ3

How to find out about statistics, G. A. Burrington, CG1

How to find out in psychiatry, B. Greenberg, CD5

How to find out in psychology, D. H. Borchardt and R. D. Francis, CD2

How to find the law, M. L. Cohen and R. C. Berring, CK3

How to find your family roots, T. F. Beard and D. Demong, AK3

How to get government grants, P. H. Des Marais, CA86

How to identify old maps and globes, R. Lister, CL300

How to locate reviews of plays and films, G. Samples, BG50

How to pronounce it, A. S. C. Ross, AD84

How to register a copyright and protect your creative work, R. B. Chickering and S. Hartman, AA406

How to start an audiovisual collection, AB170

How to use a law library, J. Dane and P. A. Thomas, CK4

How to use a medical library, L. T. Morton, EK8

How to write and publish a scientific paper, R. A. Day, EA102

Howard, D. London theatres and music halls, BG77

Howard, J. T. Bibliography of theatre technology, BG118

Howard, N. E. Telescope handbook and star atlas, EB41

Howard, P. C. Theses in American literature, BD387

—— Theses in English literature, BD505

—— and Fox, M. J. Labor relations and collective bargaining, CH691

Howard, R. and Moore, A. Complete checklist of the birds of the world, EC209

Howard, W., Kurtz, N. R. and Googins, B. Occupational alcoholism, CC141

Howard-Hill, T. H. Index to British literary bibliography, BD494

—— Shakespearian bibliography and textual criticism, BD703

Howard University. Library. Dictionary catalog of the Arthur B. Spingarn collection, BD1453

—— —— Moorland Foundation. Dictionary catalog of the Jesse E. Moorland Collection, CC376

Howard University bibliography of African and Afro-American religious studies, E. L. Williams and C. F. Brown, BB232

Howarth, H. E. and Shapley, H. Source book in astronomy, EB46

Howe, G. F. Guide to historical literature, DA1

Howe, O. T. and Matthews, F. C. American clipper ships, CH467

Howe, R. and Simon, A. L. Dictionary of gastronomy, EH127

Howe, W. D. and Burke, W. J. American authors and books, BD405

Howe, W. H. Butterflies of North America, EC269

Howell, J. B. East African community, AG86

—— Kenya, AG156

—— Style manuals of the English-speaking world, AA426

Howell, J. V. and Levorsen, A. I. Directory of geological material in North America, EE101

Howell, M. A. Bibliography of bibliographies of legal material, CK24

Howell, S., Fildes, R. and Dews, D. Bibliography of business and economic forecasting, CH189

Howells, J. G. and Osborn, M. L. Reference companion to the history of abnormal psychology, CD94

Howes, D. American women, AJ60

Howes, W. U.S.iana, AA300

Howie, R. A., Zussman, J. and Deer, W. A. Rock-forming minerals, EE187–EE188

Howitt, D. and Weinberger, M. I. Inc. magazine's Databasics, CH214

Howley, G. C. D., Bruce, F. F. and Ellison, H. L. New layman's Bible commentary, BB204

Hoy, S. M. and Robinson, M. C. Public works history in the United States, DB32

Hoyt, J. K. New cyclopedia of practical quotations, BD126

Hrobak, P. A. English-Slovak dictionary, AD708

Hrvatsko ili srpsko engleski rječnik, M. Drvodelić, AD701

Hsia, R., Penn, P. and Tien, H. C. Gazetteer of China, CL146

Hsia, T. Guide to selected legal sources of Mainland China, CK62

Hsieh, C. and Salter, C. L. Atlas of China, CL368

Hsieh, W. Chinese historiography on the Revolution of 1911, DE157a

Hsu, K. and Fraser, S. E. Chinese education and society, CB83

Hsüeh, C.-T. Chinese communist movement, DE158

Huang, H. C. Chinese periodicals in the Library of Congress, AE57

Huang, P. Cantonese dictionary, AD224

Hubach, R. R. Early midwestern travel narratives, DB127

Hubbard, F. H. Encyclopedia of North American railroading, CH456

Hubbard, W. J. Stack management, AB190

Hubin, A. J. Crime fiction, BD261

Hubschmid, J. Bibliographia onomastica helvetica, CL251

Huckabay, C. John Milton, BD686

Hudson, E. Commercial gazetteer of Great Britain, CL157

Hudson, G. W. Paradise lost, BD690

Huenefeld, I. P. International directory of historical clothing, BF69

Huff, R. L. National directory of retirement facilities, CC130

Huffman, F. E. and Proum, I. English-Khmer dictionary, AD528

Hüfner, K. and Naumann, J. United Nations system, CK469

Hughes, A. Medieval music, BH23

Hughes, C. W. American hymns old and new, BH202

Hughes, D. G. and Bryden, J. R. Index of Gregorian chant, BH215

Hughes, H. K. Dictionary of abbreviations in medicine and the health sciences, EK119

Hughes, L. E. C. and Tweney, C. F. Chambers Diccionario tecnológico, EA159

Hughes, M. M. Sexual barrier, CC510

Hughes-Hughes, A. Catalogue of manuscript music in the British Museum, BH62

Hugoniot, R. D. Bibliographical index of the lesser known languages and dialects of India and Nepal, BC159

Huguet, E. E. A. Dictionnaire de la langue française, AD344

Hulbert, J. R. and Craigie, W. A. Dictionary of American English, AD113

Hull, J., Knight, S. and Partington, M. Welfare rights, CC243

Human factors design handbook, W. E. Woodson, EJ293

Human food uses, R. L. Freedman, EK227a

Human migration, J. J. Mangalam, CC324

Human nonverbal behavior, C. E. Obudho, CD43

Human Relations Area Files, p.735

Human Relations Area Files. Sixty cultures, CE44

Human resource development, J. L. Franklin, CH296

Human resources abstracts, CC246

Human resources management and development handbook, CH342

Human Resources Network. User's guide to funding resources, CA90

Human rights, CJ223, CK292–CK293, CK301, CK309, CK315, CK322, CK335, CK341–CK343

Human rights, CK292, CK322

Human rights handbook, M. Garling, CK341

Human rights in Latin America, CK293

Human rights organizations & periodicals directory, CK342

Human services in postrevolutionary Cuba, L. R. Oberg, CC53

Human words, R. Hendrickson, AD41

Humana, C. World human rights guide, CK335

Humanists, BD1077

Humanities index, AE235

Humby, M. Guide to the literature of education, CB3

Hume, D.: bibliography, BA116–BA117

Hume, M. and Harbottle, T. B. Dictionary of quotations (Spanish), BD170

Hume, R. E. Treasure house of the living religions, BB73

Hummel, A. W. Eminent Chinese of the Ch'ing period, AJ167

Hummel, D. Collector's guide to the American musical theatre, BH253

Humpert, M. Bibliographie der Kameralwissenschaften, CH194

Humphery-Smith, C. R. Genealogist's bibliography, AK84

—— General armory two, AK121

Humphrey, H. Bibliography for the Gospel of Mark, BB96

Humphreys, A. L. Handbook to county bibliography, DC326

Humphreys, C. Popular dictionary of Buddhism, BB503

Luykx, T., Henderson, W. O. and Vries, S. de. Atlas of world history, DA72
―――― and Vries, P. de. Historische W. P. encyclopedie, DC96a
Luzuriaga, G. Bibliografía del teatro ecuatoriano, BD1238
Lyday, L. F. and Woodyard, G. W. Bibliography of Latin American theater criticism, BD1211
Lydenberg, H. M. and Archer, J. Care and repair of books, AA433
Lyer, S. and Holub, J. Stručny etymologický slovník jazyka českého, AD246
Lyle, G. R. and Guinagh, K. I am happy to present, BD354
Lyle, K. C. and Segal, S. J. International family-planning programs, CC234
Lynch, C. T. CRC handbook of materials science, EJ34
Lynch, M. J. Library data collection handbook, AB176
Lynch, R. C. Musicals, BH252
Lyndon B. Johnson School of Public Affairs. Alternate care for the elderly, CC105
Lynn, N. B., Matasar, A. B. and Rosenberg, M. B. Research guide in women's studies, CC495
Lynn, R. J. Chinese literature, BD1475
Lyon, H. H. and Johnson, W. T. Insects that feed on trees and shrubs, EC270
Lyonnet, H. Dictionnaire des comédiens français, BG100
Lysle, A. de R. and Gualtieri, L. L. Nuovo dizionario moderno delle lingue italiana e inglese, AD500
Lystad, R. A. African world, DD48
Lytle, S. Energy bibliography & index, EJ273
Lytle, W. M. and Holdcamper, F. R. Merchant steam vessels of the United States, CH469

MARC formats for bibliographic data, U.S. Library of Congress. Automated Systems Office, AB211
MBA's dictionary, D. Oran and J. M. Shafritz, CH222
MdR, M. Schwarz, CJ304
MIMP. Magazine industry market place, AE34
MIT Science Fiction Society's Index to the S-F magazines, E. S. Strauss, BD288
MInd, the meetings index, EA183
MLA directory of periodicals, Modern Language Association of America, BD31
MLA handbook for writers of research papers, Modern Language Association of America, AH7
MLA international bibliography, Modern Language Association of America, BD22
MLR, monthly labor review, U.S. Bureau of Labor Statistics, CH719
Ma, W. Y. and Edgar, N. L. Travel in Asia, BJ103
Maas, L. Handbuch der deutschen Exilpresse, AE78
McAleese, R. and Unwin, D. Encyclopaedia of educational media communications and technology, CB144
McAlester, V. and McAlester, L. Field guide to American houses, BE281
McAllister, I. and Pollock, L. Bibliography of United Kingdom politics, CJ322
―――― and Rose, R. United Kingdom facts, CJ333
McAlpin collection of British history and theology see New York. Union Theological Seminary. Library
MacAndrew, A. R. Glossary of Russian

technical terms used in metallurgy, EJ339
McAninch, S. Sun power, EJ271
McBrearty, J. C. American labor history and comparative labor movements, CH664
MacBride, D. D. Bibliography of appraisal literature, CH791
McBurney, W. H. Check list of English prose fiction, BD618
―――― and Taylor, C. M. English prose fiction, BD621
McCabe, J. P. Critical guide to Catholic reference books, BB418
McCaffree, M. J. and Innis, P. B. Protocol, CF137
McCagg, W. O., Adams, A. E. and Matley, I. M. Atlas of Russian and East European history, DC62
McCaghy, M. D. Sexual harassment, CC544
McCain, J. A. and Salamone, F. A. Hausa people, CE91
MacCampbell, D. Writing business, AA417
McCandless, B. and Furlong, W. R. So proudly we hail, AK147
McCann, M. A. and Lampe, K. F. AMA handbook of poisonous and injurious plants, EC127
MacCann, R. D. and Perry, E. S. New film index, BG189
McCarren, V. P. Critical concordance to Catullus, BD1436
McCarrick, E. M. U.S. Constitution, CK404
McCarthy, J. Arab world, Turkey, and the Balkans, CG132
McCarthy, J. M. Guinea-Bissau and Cape Verde Islands, DD139
McCarty, C. Published screenplays, BG175
McCarus, E. N. Kurdish-English dictionary, AD536
McCavitt, W. E. Broadcasting around the world, CH517
―――― Radio and television, CH503
McClellan, E. History of American costume, BF83
McClendon, C. C. and Chatham, J. R. Dissertations in Hispanic languages and literatures, BD1145
McClintock, M. H. Middle East and North Africa on film, DE45
McClure, A. F. Research guide to film history, BG162
MacCorkle, L. Cubans in the United States, CC480
McCormick, J. O. Syllabus of comparative literature, BD14
McCormick, M., Efron, V. and Keller, M. Dictionary of words about alcohol, CC143
McCoy, G. Archives of American Art, BE91
McCoy, M. and Halstead, D. K. Higher education financing in the fifty states, CB261
McCoy, R. E. Freedom of the press, AA338
McCrea, B. P., Plano, J. C. and Klein, G. Soviet and East European political dictionary, CJ286
McCready, W. T. Bibliografía temática de estudios sobre el teatro español antiguo, BD1164
McCue, J. K., Mersky, R. M. and Berring, R. Author's guide to journals in law, CK36
McCulloch, A. Encyclopedia of Australian art, BE100
Macculloch, J. A., Moore, G. F. and Gray, L. H. Mythology of all races, CF14
McCulloch, J. R. Literature of political economy, CH16
McCulloch, W. F. Woods words, EH99
McCusker, J. J. Money and exchange in Europe and America, CH421

McCutchan, R. G. Hymn tune names, BB342
McDade, T. M. Annals of murder, CK235
McDarrah, F. W. Museums in New York, BE139
―――― Stock photo and assignment source book, BF212
McDavid, R. I. Linguistic atlas of the Middle and South Atlantic states, BC93
McDermott, B. S. and Coleman, F. A. Government regulation of business, CH196
McDonagh, D. Complete guide to modern dance, BG151
Macdonald, D. Encyclopedia of mammals, EC230
―――― Parodies, BD670
McDonald, D. R. Masters' theses in anthropology, CE34
―――― and Mail, P. D. Tulapai to Tokay, CC451
Macdonald, J., Weihs, J. R. and Lewis, S. Nonbook materials, AB218
Macdonald, T. Union catalogue of the serial publications of the Indian government, AG148
MacDonald, W. Documentary source book of American history, DB172
―――― Select charters and other documents illustrative of American history, DB169
―――― Select documents illustrative of the history of the United States, DB170
―――― Select statutes and other documents illustrative of the history of the United States, DB171
Macdonnell, A. A. and Keith, A. B. Vedic index of names and subjects, BB511
McDonough, J. J. Members of Congress, DB68
McDorman, T. L., Beauchamp, K. P. and Johnston, D. M. Maritime boundary delimitation, CK299
McDormand, T. B. and Crossman, F. S. Judson concordance to hymns, BB343
McDowell, R. B. and Curtis, E. Irish historical documents, DC381
Macedonia: history, DC67
McEvedy, C. and Jones, R. Atlas of world population history, CG47
McFarland, G. B. Thai-English dictionary, AD771
MacFarlane, A. Guide to English historical records, DC295
McFeely, M. D. Women's work in Britain and America, CC515
McGarry, D. D. and White, S. H. World historical fiction guide, BD239
McGee, H. On food and cooking, EH129
McGehee, A. H. and Bordley, J. Two centuries of American medicine, EK156
McGeough, C. S., Jungjohan, B. and Thomas, J. L. Directory of college facilities and services for the handicapped, CB248
McGilvray, J. W. and Kirwan, F. Irish economic statistics, CG260
McGinnies, W. G., Goldman, B. J. and Paylore, P. Deserts of the world, EE14
McGlynn, E. A. Middle American anthropology, CE63
McGowan, F. and Katz, S. M. Selected list of U.S. readings on development, CH125
McGowan, J. and DuBern, R. Good Housekeeping illustrated book of home maintenance, EH116
McGraw-Hill computer handbook, EJ242
McGraw-Hill construction business handbook, CH809
McGraw-Hill dictionary of art, BE101
McGraw-Hill dictionary of chemistry, ED41
McGraw-Hill dictionary of modern economics, CH55

Manual of American college fraternities, CB308

Manual of bibliography, A. J. K. Esdaile, AA3

Manual of botany, A. Gray, EC123

Manual of business library practice, AB177

Manual of Chinese quotations, Ch'êng yü k'ao, BD137

Manual of cultivated broad-leaved trees & shrubs, G. Krüssmann, EC158

Manual of cultivated plants, L. H. Bailey, EC133

Manual of cultivated trees and shrubs hardy in North America, A. Rehder, EC162

Manual of educational statistics, United Nations Educational, Scientific and Cultural Organization, CB263

Manual of European languages for librarians, C. G. Allen, BC53

Manual of foreign languages, G. F. Von Ostermann, BC56

Manual of foreign patents, B. Severance, EA248

Manual of form for theses and term reports, K. Dugdale, AH3

Manual of government publications, E. S. Brown, AG2

Manual of Hispanic bibliography, D. W. Foster and V. R. Foster, BD1130

Manual of law librarianship, AB178

Manual of mathematics, G. A. Korn and T. M. Korn, EF45

Manual of music librarianship, Music Library Association, AB181

Manual of new mineral names, EE179

Manual of remote sensing, R. G. Reeves, EE15

Manual of steel construction, American Institute of Steel Construction, EJ173

Manual of the writings in Middle English, BD517

Manual of the writings in Middle English, J. E. Wells, BD516

Manual on water, American Society for Testing and Materials. Committee D-19 on Water, EJ161

Manuale critico-bibliografico per lo studio della letteratura italiana, M. Puppo, BD1054

Manuale di bibliografia musulmana, G. Gabrieli, BB515

Manuel II, King of Portugal. Livros antigos portuguezes, AA1034

Manuel, E. A. Dictionary of Philippine biography, AJ333

Manuel, E. V. and Mojares, R. B. Philippine literature in English, BD1511

Manuel analytique et critique de bibliographie générale de l'histoire suisse, J.-L. Santschy, DC498

Manuel bibliographique de la littérature française du Moyen Âge, R. Bossuat, BD970

Manuel bibliographique de la littérature française moderne, G. Lanson, BD961

Manuel bibliographique des études littéraires, B. Beugnot and J. M. Moureaux, BD952

Manuel bibliographique des sciences psychiques ou occultes, A. L. Caillet, CD141

Manuel bibliographique des sciences sociales et économiques, R. Maunier, CA6

Manuel d'archéologie gallo-romaine, A. Grenier, DA99

Manuel d'archéologie préhistorique celtique et gallo-romaine, J. Déchelette, DA79

Manuel d'archivistique, Association des Archivistes Français, AB200

Manuel de bibliographie, L.-N. Malclès, AA7

Manuel de bibliographie biographique et d'iconographie des femmes célèbres, A. Ungherini, AJ28

Manuel de bibliographie générale, H. Stein, AA12

Manuel de bibliographie littéraire, J. Giraud, BD958

Manuel de bibliographie philosophique, G. Varet, BA29

Manuel de diplomatique française et pontificale, A. de Boüard, AA250

Manuel de géographie historique de la France, L. Mirot, CL95

Manuel de l'amateur d'estampes au XVIIIᵉ siècle, L. Delteil, BE357

Manuel de l'amateur d'estampes des XIXᵉ et XXᵉ siècles, L. Delteil, BE358–BE359

Manuel de l'amateur de livres du XIXᵉ siècle, G. Vicaire, AA757

Manuel de l'hispanisant, R. Foulché-Delbosc and L. Barrau-Dihigo, AA96, AJ354

Manuel des études grecques et latines, L. Laurand, DA123

Manuel du libraire et de l'amateur de livres, J. C. Brunet, AA111

Manuel pratique pour l'étude de la Révolution française, P. Caron, DC146

Manufacturing Chemists' Association. Guide for safety in the chemical laboratory, ED75

Manufacturing industries
  bibliography, CH733–CH735
  dictionaries and encyclopedias, CH736–CH739
  directories, CH740–CH741
  handbooks, CH742–CH745
  statistics, CH746–CH747

Manuscript inventories and the catalogs of manuscripts, books and pictures, Arthur and Elizabeth Schlesinger Library on the History of Women in America, CC530

Manuscript papers of British scientists, EA210

Manuscript sources for the history of Irish civilisation, National Library of Ireland, DC375

Manuscript sources in the Library of Congress for research on the American Revolution, U.S.Library of Congress. American Revolution Bicentennial Office, DB86

Manuscripts
  ancient, medieval, and Renaissance: bibliography, AA233–AA234, BD1426; catalogs, AA235 (bibliography, AA236–AA243); diplomatics, handwriting and scripts, AA250–AA262; facsimiles and reproductions, AA159, AA162, AA246–AA248 (bibliography, AA249); scribes and artists, AA264–AA265; union lists, AA244–AA245
  guides (by location): Barbados, DB420; Belgium, DB259, DE16; Bermuda, DB422; Canada, DB183, DB194, DB197, DB259, DB422; Caribbean, DB418; Denmark, DD95; Europe, DB85, DB259, DB369, DB417; Finland, DE16; France, DB55, DB59, DD95, DE16; Germany, DB259, DD95, DE16; Gt.Brit., DA209–DA210, DB60, DB210, DB258, DB369, DB417, DB422, DC270, DC273, DC287, DC290–DC291, DC296, DC375, DD96, DE17, DE64, DE192, DE237, DF3; Ireland, DC375; Israel, DE237–DE238; Italy, DD95; Leeward Islands, DB443; Mexico, DB368; Netherlands, DB259, DD95, DE16; Norway, DD95, DE16; Scandinavia, DB259; Spain, DB84, DB255, DB259, DD95; Sweden, DD95, DE16; Turkey, DE237; U.S.S.R., DC553–DC554, DC556; United States, DA187n, DB54, DB56–DB58, DB61–DB62, DB64–DB68, DB72–DB74, DB84, DB86, DB93, DB418, DB422, DC273, DC375, DC551, DD40, DE14, DE159, DE237, DG22, DG24; Vatican, DB259, DD95; West Indies, DB417–DB418; Windward Islands, DB459
  guides (by subject)
    economics, CH40–CH41
    forestry, EH93
    history: DA30; Africa, DD40, DD95, DD96; Africa, North, DE16, DE64; Asia, DE14, DE16–DE17, DE129; Asia, East, DE129; Asia, South, DE17, DE192; Asia, Southeast, DE17; Australia, DF3; Barbados, DB420; Bermuda, DB422; Canada, DB183, DB193–DB197; Caribbean, DB258–DB259, DB418; China, DE159; Gt.Brit., DC270, DC273, DC287, DC290–DC291, DC296; Ireland, DC375; Japan, DE261; Latin America, DB258–DB259; Leeward Islands, DB443; Mexico, DB368–DB369; Near and Middle East, DE64, DE237; New Zealand, DF3; Oceania, DE14, DE16, DF3; Philippines, DG22, DG24; U.S.S.R., DC551, DC553–DC554, DC556; United States, DB54–DB74, DB84–DB86, DB93, DB101–DB102; West Indies, DB417–DB418; Windward Islands, DB459
    literature: English and American, BD30, BD389, BD545–BD548, BD580; French, BD955; German, BD836
    naval history, CJ547
    psychology, CD65
    science and technology, EA201, EA210
    Syriac, BD1513
    World Wars, DA209–DA210

Manuscripts in Baker Library, Harvard University. Graduate School of Business Administration. Baker Library, CH40

Manuscripts in the British Isles relating to Australia, P. Mander-Jones, DF3

Manvell, R. International encyclopedia of film, BG244

Manzoni, C. Biografia italica, AJ275

Mao, N. K., Yang, W. L. Y. and Li, P. Classical Chinese fiction, BD1479

Maori language: dictionaries, AD577

Maori place-names, J. C. Andersen, CL241

Map collections in the United States and Canada, CL302

Map librarianship, M. Larsgaard, AB174

Map user's sourcebook, L. Feild, CL301

Mapbook of English literature, J. D. Briscoe, R. L. Sharp and M. E. Borish, BD567

Mapes, J. L., Anderton, R. L. and Kirschner, C. D. Doctoral research in educational media, CB115

Mapp, E. Books for occupational education programs, CB57

Mapping of the world, R. W. Shirley, CL275

Mapping the Transmississippi West, C. I. Wheat, CL291

Maps see Atlases

Maps and charts of North America and the West Indies, U. S. Library of Congress, CL281

Maps and charts published in America before 1800, J. C. Wheat and C. F. Brun, CL292

Maps and plans in the Public Record

———— Bibliography of 17th century
German imprints, AA719
———— and Ober, K. H. Bibliography of
modern Icelandic literature in
translation, BD912
Mitchell, R. C. and Turner, H. W.
Comprehensive bibliography of modern
African religious movements, BB18
Mitchell, S. P., Flaherty, D. H. and Hanis,
E. H. Privacy and access to government
data for research, CC40
Mitchenson, J. and Mander, R. Theatres of
London, BG81
Mitros, J. F. Religions, BB19
Mitry, J. Bibliographie internationale du
cinéma et de la télévision, BG175a
Mittelhochdeutsches Taschenwörterbuch,
M. von Lexer, AD364
Mittellateinisches Wörterbuch, AD559
Mitterand, H., Dauzat, A. and Dubois, J.
Nouveau dictionnaire étymologique et
historique, AD314
Mitterling, P. I. U.S. cultural history,
DB35
Mitton, S. Cambridge encyclopedia of
astronomy, EB21
Mitzel, H. E. Encyclopedia of educational
research, CB145
Mladenov, S. and Balan, A. T. Bulgarski
tulkoven rechnik, AD205
Mobil guides, p.636
Mocker, D. W. and Spear, G. E. Urban
education, CB101
Modell, W. Drugs of choice, EK255
Modelski, A. M. Railroad maps of North
America, CL271
———— Railroad maps of the United
States, CL284
Modern accountant's handbook, CH154
Modern American literature, D. N. Curley,
M. Kramer and E. F. Kramer, BD399
Modern American muse, W. R. Irish,
BD461
Modern American poetry, L. Untermeyer,
BD470
Modern American usage, W. Follett, AD57
Modern Arab woman, M. Raccagni, CC568
Modern Arabic literature, S. J. Altoma,
BD1466
Modern archives and manuscripts, F. B.
Evans, AB204
Modern Australian prose, A. G. Day,
BD752
Modern black writers, BD45
Modern British and American private
presses, British Library, AA295
Modern British drama, C. A. Carpenter,
BD582
Modern British literature, R. Z. Temple
and M. Tucker, BD553
Modern British society, J. H. Westergaard,
A. Weyman and P. Wiles, CC61
Modern business language and usage, J. H.
Janis, CH221
Modern cambist, W. Tate, CH424
Modern Catholic dictionary, J. A. Hardon,
BB449
Modern China, A. J. Nathan, DE145
Modern China, J. K. Fairbank and K.-C.
Liu, DE156
Modern Chinese authors, A. C. W. Shu,
AA189
Modern Chinese society, DE161
Modern Commonwealth literature, BD742
Modern concordance to the New
Testament, BB130
Modern constitutions since 1787, J. A.
Hawgood, CK393
Modern dictionary, Arabic-English, E. A.
Elias and E. E. Elias, AD173
Modern dictionary, English-Arabic, E. A.
Elias and E. E. Elias, AD172
Modern dictionary of electronics, EJ206
Modern dictionary of sociology, G. A.

Theodorson and A. G. Theodorson,
CC28
Modern drama, I. Adelman and R.
Dworkin, BD219
Modern drama in America and England,
R. H. Harris, BD423
Modern drug encyclopedia and therapeutic
index, EK262
Modern electronic circuits reference
manual, J. Markus, EJ221
Modern encyclopedia of Russian and
Soviet history, DC571
Modern encyclopedia of Russian and
Soviet literature, BD1358
Modern encyclopedia of tennis, B. Collins
and Z. Hollander, BJ59
Modern England, A. F. Havighurst, DC282
Modern English biography, F. Boase,
AJ222
Modern English-Gujarati dictionary, P. G.
Deshpande, AD426
Modern English-Yiddish, Yiddish-English
dictionary, U. Weinreich, AD811
Modern European imperialism, J. P.
Halstead and S. Pocari, DC5
Modern French literature, BD992
Modern French literature and language,
L. W. Griffin, J. A. Clarke and A. Y.
Kroff, BD959
Modern German literature, A. K.
Domandi, BD843
Modern Greek-English dictionary, A.
Kyriakidēs, AD420
Modern Greek studies in the West, D. C.
E. Swanson, BC156, CF96
Modern guide to symphonic music, A. V.
Frankenstein, BH221
Modern historians on British history, G. R.
Elton, DC297
Modern history of Ethiopia and the horn
of Africa, H. G. Marcus, DD129
Modern Humanities Research Association.
Anglo-Norman dictionary, AD134;
Annual bibliography of English
language and literature, BD503
Modern Hungarian historiography, S. B.
Vardy, DC366
Modern Iberian language and literature,
H. H. Golden and S. O. Simches,
BD1136
Modern Ireland, M. O. Shannon, DC376
Modern Italian language and literature,
H. H. Golden and S. O. Simches,
BD1058
Modern Japanese literature in translation,
Kokusai Bunka Kaikan, Tokyo.
Toshoshitsu, BD1500
Modern Language Association of America.
Bibliography of critical Arthurian
literature, BD323; MLA directory of
periodicals, BD31; MLA handbook for
writers of research papers, AH7; MLA
international bibliography, BD22;
Reproductions of manuscripts and rare
printed books, AA159
———— French VI Bibliography
Committee. French VI bibliography,
BD985
———— French III. Bibliography of French
seventeenth century studies, BD980
Modern Latin American art, J. A. Findlay,
BE23
Modern Latin American literature, D. W.
Foster and V. R. Foster, BD1203
Modern legal glossary, K. R. Redden and
E. L. Veron, CK119
Modern legal systems cyclopedia, CK149
Modern maps and atlases, C. B. M. Lock,
CL256
Modern marine engineer's manual, A. A.
Osbourne and A. B. Neild, EJ297
Modern Middle East, R. S. Simon, DE29
Modern nutrition in health and disease,
R. S. Goodhart and M. E. Shils, EK236

Modern parliamentary procedure, R. E.
Keesey, CJ444
Modern Persian dictionary, F. D. Razi,
AD600
Modern plastics encyclopedia, EJ105
Modern researcher, J. Barzun and H. F.
Graff, DA4
Modern Romance literatures, D. N. Curley
and A. Curley, BD935
Modern Russian dictionary for English
speakers, E. A. M. Wilson, AD671
Modern Russian historiography, A. G.
Mazour, DC564
Modern Slavic literatures, BD1270
Modern Spanish dictionary, M. H.
Raventós, AD727
Modern Spanish-English & English-Spanish
technical & engineering dictionary, R.
Guinle, EA163
Modern Syria, C. H. Bleaney, DE309
Modern theatre practice, H. C. Heffner,
BG117
Modern woordenboek, J. Verschueren,
AD259
Modern world drama, M. Matlaw, BD226
Modern world theater, S. Kienzle, BG72
Moderna svenska författare, Å. Runnquist,
BD923
Moderne Linguistik, W. Welte, BC71
Modisakeng, T. and Henderson, F. I.
Guide to periodical articles about
Botswana, DD107
Moffat, D. W. Concise desk book of
business finance, CH551
———— Economics dictionary, CH58
Moffat Bible, p.348
Moffat Bible concordance, W. J. Gant,
BB125
Moffatt New Testament commentary,
BB201
Moffett, J. P. Handbook of Tanganyika,
CG349
Mogenet, L. Bibliographie complémentaire
du Laos 1962–1973, DE281
Mohan, R. P. and Martindale, D.
Handbook of contemporary
developments in world sociology, CC31
Mohlenbrock, R. H. Field guide to U.S.
national forests, EH104
Möhlenbrock, S. and Ottervik, G. Bibliotek
i Sverige, AB153
Mohr, J. G. SPI handbook of technology
and engineering of reinforced
plastics/composites, EJ106
Mohraz, J. E., Carroll, B. A. and Fink,
C. F. Peace and war, CJ617
Mohrmann, C. and Meer, F. van der. Atlas
of the early Christian world, BH335
Moid, A. and Siddiqui, A. H. Guide to
periodical publications and newspapers
of Pakistan, AE133
Moisés, M. Bibliografia da literatura
portuguêsa, BD1105
———— and Paes, J. P. Pequeno dicionário
de literatura brasileira, BD1117
Mojares, R. B. and Manuel, E. V.
Philippine literature in English,
BD1511
Molas, J. and Massot i Muntaner, J.
Diccionari de la literatura catalana,
BD1148
Molde, B. Illustrerad svensk ordbok,
AD749
Moldon, D. Bibliography of Russian
composers, BH212
Molecular structures and dimensions,
ED109
Molette, C. Guide des sources de l'histoire
des congrégations féminines françaises
de vie active, BB477
Moley, R., Tandon, J. C. and Batra, S.
Non-alignment, CJ29
Molhuysen, P. C., Blok, P. J. and
Kossmann, F. K. H. Nieuw

Gálvez Medrano, A. Territorio mexicano, CL400

Rule book, BJ30

Rulers and governments of the world, M. Ross, CJ230

Rules for compiling the catalogues of printed books, maps and music, British Museum. Dept. of Printed Books, AB227

Rules of order, L. Deschler, CJ443

Rumania see Romania

Rumania, U.S. Library of Congress. Slavic and Central European Division, DC470

Rumball-Petre, E. A. R. America's first Bibles, BB107
—— Rare Bibles, BB108

Runcorn, S. K. International dictionary of geophysics, EE10

Runge, G. E. Correlation index, EA85

Runnquist, Å. Moderna svenska författare, BD923

Runyon, J. H., Verdini, J. and Runyon, S. S. Source book of American presidential campaign and election statistics, CJ167

Rupley, L., Finucane, B. and Killick, T. Economies of East Africa, CH74

Rural elderly, J. H. Krout, CC104

Rusch, F. L. and Natoli, J. P. Psychocriticism, BD15

Rush, G. E. Dictionary of criminal justice, CK270

Rush, T. G., Myers, C. F. and Arata, E. S. Black American writers, BD479

Rusk, R. L. Literature of the middle western frontier, BD381

Russ-Eft, D. F., Rubin, D. P. and Holmen, R. E. Issues in adult basic education and other adult education, CB96

Russell, J. Marx-Engels dictionary, CJ494

Russell, J. B. and Berkhout, C. T. Medieval heresies, BB286

Russell, J. C. Dictionary of writers of thirteenth century England, BD578

Russell, P. E. Spain, DC494

Russell, R. and Baines, A. Catalogue of musical instruments, BH336

Russell's Official national motor coach guide, BJ124

Russia (1923– U.S.S.R.) Glavnoe Upravlenie Geodezii i Kartografii. Atlas mira, CL328; Fiziko-geograficheskii atlas mira, CL330; Geograficheskii atlas, CL332; World atlas, CL329

Russia, U.S. Library of Congress. Reference Dept., AA1061

Russia and the Soviet Union, P. L. Horecky, DC531

Russia and the U.S.S.R.: bibliography, AA1049–AA1050; 16th–17th centuries, AA1051; 18th century, AA1052–AA1058; 19th–20th centuries, AA1059–AA1061; current, AA1062–AA1066; see also Union of Soviet Socialist Republics

Russia, the Soviet Union, and Eastern Europe, Hoover Institution on War, Revolution, and Peace, DC54

Russia, the USSR, and Eastern Europe, S. M. Horak, DC23–DC24

Russia/U.S.S.R., A. Thompson, DC545

Russian and East European publications in the libraries of the United States, M. J. Ruggles and V. Mostecky, AB122

Russian and Soviet law, W. E. Butler, CK101

Russian bibliography, libraries and archives, J. S. G. Simmons, DC541

Russian dictionaries, Y. Aav, AD684

Russian drug index, S. Jablonski, EK268

Russian economic history, D. R. Kazmer and V. Kazmer, CH114

Russian Empire and Soviet Union, S. A. Grant and J. H. Brown, AB118a

Russian-English atomic dictionary, E. A. Karpovich, EJ369

Russian-English biological dictionary, C. W. Dumbleton, EC22

Russian-English chemical and polytechnical dictionary, L. I. Callaham, ED52

Russian-English chemical dictionary, E. A. Carpovich and V. V. Carpovich, ED53

Russian-English dictionaries, W. Zalewski, AD687

Russian-English dictionary, A. I. Smirnitskii, AD667

Russian-English dictionary of earth sciences, M. E. Burgunker, EE91

Russian-English dictionary of geological terms, V. G. Telberg, EE95

Russian-English dictionary of metallurgy and allied sciences, T. Deruguine, EJ338

Russian-English dictionary of modern terms in aeronautics, M. M. Konarski, EJ62

Russian-English dictionary of musical terms, L. Katayen and V. Telberg, BH143

Russian-English dictionary of social science terms, R. E. F. Smith, CA55

Russian-English dictionary of the mathematical sciences, EF38

Russian-English dictionary on astronomy, A. A. Kramer, EB33

Russian-English-German-French hydrological dictionary, L. Singer, EE131

Russian-English glossary of guided missile, rocket, and satellite terms, U.S. Library of Congress. Reference Dept, EJ67

Russian-English glossary of nuclear physics and engineering, Consultants Bureau Enterprises, N.Y, EJ368

Russian-English glossary of physics of fluids and meteorology, S. Noveck, EE144

Russian-English law dictionary, N. P. Prischepenko, CK134

Russian-English mathematical dictionary, L. M. Milne-Thompson, EF37

Russian-English metals & machines dictionary, E. A. Karpovich, EJ304

Russian-English petrographic dictionary, V. G. Telberg, EE261

Russian-English physics dictionary, I. Emin, EG31

Russian-English scientific and technical dictionary, M. H. T. Alford and V. L. Alford, EA153

Russian-English space technology dictionary, M. M. Konarski, EJ63

Russian-English translators dictionary, M. G. TSimmerman, EA156

Russian history atlas, M. Gilbert, DC582

Russian history since 1917, Harvard University. Library, DC529

Russian language: dictionaries, AD654–AD661 (abbreviations, AD672–AD675; bibliography, AD684–AD687; bilingual, AD662–AD671; etymology, AD676–AD678; synonyms, AD679–AD681; usage, AD682–AD683)

Russian literature
bibliography, BD1325–BD1348; current, BD1349
dictionaries and encyclopedias, BD1355–BD1360
dissertations, BD1350–BD1351
guides, BD1322–BD1324
history, BD1361–BD1364
translations, BD1352–BD1354

Russian literature in the Hispanic world, G. O. Schanzer, BD1344

Russian literature under Lenin and Stalin, G. Struve, BD1364

Russian publications on Jews and Judaism in the Soviet Union, B. Pinkus and A. A. Greenbaum, BB538

Russian studies of American literature, V. A. Libman, BD375

Russian supplement to the Korean studies guide, California. University. East Asia Studies, DE270

Russian surnames, B. O. Unbegaun, AK197

Russian, Ukrainian, and Belorussian newspapers, U.S. Library of Congress. Slavic and Central European Division, AF67

Russian works on China, T. Yüan, DE171

Russika und Sowjetika unter den deutschsprachigen Hochschulschriften, P. Bruhn, DC546, DC547

Russisches etymologisches Wörterbuch, M. Vasmer, AD678

Russkaia istoricheskaia bibliografiia, P. P. Lambin, DC536

Russkaia istoricheskaia bibliografiia, V. I. Mezhov, DC535, DC537

Russkaia khudozhestvennaia literatura i literaturovedenie, B. L. Kandel', L. M. Fediushina and M. A. Benina, BD1336

Russkaia narodnaia pesnia, Akademiia Nauk SSSR. Institut Mirovoi Literatury, BH290

Russkaia periodicheskaia pechat', A. G. Dement'ev, AE143

Russkaia periodicheskaia pechat', M. S. Cherepakhov and E. M. Fingerit, AE144

Russkaia periodicheskaia pechat', N. M. Lisovskii, AE146

Russkaia tekhnicheskaia periodika, IU. A. Mezhenko, EA56

Russkie anonimnye i podpisannye psevdonimami proizvedenniia pechati, Leningrad. Publichnaia Biblioteka, AA213

Russkie biograficheskie i bio-bibliograficheskie slovari, I. M. Kaufman, AJ389

Russkie entsiklopedii, I. M. Kaufman, AC76

Russkie literaturnye al'manakhi i sborniki, N. P. Smirnov-Sokol'skii, BD1345

Russkie pisateli, BD1342

Russkie pisateli vtoroi poloviny XIX nachala XX vv, Moscow. Publichnaia Biblioteka, BD1339

Russkie sovetskie pisateli, BD1343

Russkie sovetskie pisateli-prozaiki, Leningrad. Publichnaia Biblioteka, BD1337

Russkii biograficheskii slovar', AJ381

Russkii fol'klor, CF95

Russko-angliiskii aviatsionno-kosmicheskii slovar', A. M. Murashkevich, EJ64

Russko-angliiskii geologicheskii slovar', T. A. Sofiano, EE94

Russko-angliiskii slovar', AD666

Russko-angliiskii slovar' knigovedcheskikh terminov, T. P. Elizarenkova, AA368

Russko-angliiskii slovar' po astronomii, A. A. Kramer, EB33

Rust, B. Guide to discography, BH347
—— London musical shows on record, BH254

Rust, W. Verzeichnis von unklaren Titelkürzungen deutscher und ausländischer Zeitschriften, AE15

Rutgers University, New Brunswick, N.J. Center for the American Woman and Politics. Women in public office, CC586

Rutherford, P. R. Bibliography of American doctoral dissertations in linguistics, BC50

Ruttkowski, W. V. Nomenclator litterarius, BD66

Ruvigny and Raineval, M. A. H. D. Titled nobility of Europe, AK70

Rwanda
atlases, CL411
bibliography, AA1067, DD87
history: bibliography, DD79, DD167–DD168, DD197
statistics, CG328

Eugene P. Sheehy is head of the Reference Department of the Columbia University Libraries and editor of the ninth edition of *Guide to Reference Books.* He has also edited the column "Selected Reference Books" in *College and Research Libraries* for the past 20 years. In 1981, ALA's Reference and Adult Services Division awarded Sheehy the Isadore Gilbert Mudge Citation for distinguished contributions to reference librarianship.